FILM REVIEW ANNUAL

1994
Films of 1993

FILM

REVIEW

ANNUAL

1994

Films of 1993

Film Review Publications
JEROME S. OZER, PUBLISHER

Editor: Jerome S. Ozer
Associate editor: Richard Zlotowitz
Assistant editor: Genant B. Sheridan

ISBN 0-89198-147-0
ISSN 0737-9080

Manufactured in the United States of America

Jerome S. Ozer, Publisher
340 Tenafly Road
Englewood, NJ 07631

..

TABLE OF CONTENTS

FILM REVIEWS

ADDENDUM   1677

AWARDS   1687

INDEX   1698

ACCOMPANIST, THE

A Sony Pictures Classics release of a Film Par Film/Les Films de la Boissiere/Orly Films/Sedif/France 3 Cinema production. *Executive Producer:* Jean-José Richer. *Producer:* Jean-Louis Livi. *Director:* Claude Miller. *Screenplay (French with English subtitles):* Claude Miller and Luc Béraud. *Based on the novel by:* Nina Berberova. *Director of Photography:* Yves Angelo. *Editor:* Albert Jurgenson. *Music:* Alain Jomy. *Sound:* Paul Lainé. *Sound Editor:* Reine Wekstein. *Production Designer:* Jean-Pierre Kohut Svelko. *Art Director:* Michael Howells. *Set Designer:* Bernadette Saint-Loubert. *Special Effects:* Gilbert Pieri and Georges Demetrau. *Costumes:* Jacqueline Bouchard and Lolita Lempicka. *Make-up:* Thi-Loan Nguyen. *Running time:* 110 minutes. *MPAA Rating:* PG.

CAST: Richard Bohringer (Charles Brice); Elena Safonova (Irène Brice); Romane Bohringer (Sophie Vasseur); Bernard Verley (Jacques Ceniat); Samuel Labarthe (Jacques Fabert); Nelly Borgeaud (Madame Vasseur); Julien Rassam (Benoit Weizman); Jean-Pierre Kohut Svelko (General Heller); Claude Rich (Minister); Gabriel Cattand (Parisian Impresario); Neils Dubost (Young Man on Train); Valérie Bettencourt (Juliette); Alain Jomy (Clarinet Player); Gilbert Bahon (Royal Coachman); Florence Rouge (Manicurist); Murray Gronwall (German); Yves Elliot (Butcher); Sacha Briquet (Dignitary).

LOS ANGELES TIMES, 12/23/93, Calendar/p. 3, Kenneth Turan

The winter of 1942 in German-occupied Paris is especially brutal, and an awkward young woman of 20, clumsy in her heavy, utilitarian shoes, can be forgiven for moving uncertainly up an ornate hall stairway: But then a door opens and, like an apparition, a brilliant singer appears in recital, elegant and sophisticated in a shimmering, floor-length white gown. The younger woman is transfixed, utterly. In fact, it is not too much to say that in that moment she falls in love.

The singer is Irene Brice (Elena Safonova), a celebrated, self-confident soprano who lives a life of privilege almost unimaginable in wartime Paris. The woman in the policeman's shoes is Sophie Vasseur (Romane Bohringer), a tentative pianist who has come to talk about a job playing for the diva, a situation that turns into a complex symbiotic relationship more intricate than either woman anticipates.

"The Accompanist" is an assured and psychologically acute piece of filmmaking, as carefully done and beautifully mounted as the operatic pieces from Berlioz, Massenet and Straus Irene sings. And, like "Tous Les Matins Du Monde" and "Un Coeur En Hiver" before it, it uses classical music as a most effective counter-melody to its story, a way to delicately emphasize the several kinds of fatalistic love stories director Claude Miller and his co-screenwriter Luc Beraud have fashioned from Nina Berberova's novel.

At first, for Sophie at least, there is no one in the world but Irene. A bit like Eve Harrington in "All About Eve," she throws herself completely into the singer's affairs, acting not only as accompanist but also companion, maid, even accomplice in her married mistress's complex love life.

Though not oblivious to them, Sophie wants more than the surface luxuries of Irene's life, she wants to become psychologically indispensable, to abandon her own drab existence and live her life through her more glamorous employer's. Irene, for her part, genuinely cares about Sophie but only up to a point. With charming and characteristic frankness, she tells the younger woman that she will take nothing less than her complete devotion.

Sophie is willing, but given her own tricky personality, difficulties arise. She comes to realize how little of even Irene's reflected glory comes her way, yet her growing irritation at her idol's power seems to perversely increase her desire for even more closeness. Simultaneously jealous, adoring and complicit, Sophie's relationship with Irene threatens to become a dangerous one, though it is much to "The Accompanist's" credit that the sense of who is in most danger from what changes from moment to moment.

Complicating things even more are the other forces in Irene's life. Besides her husband, Charles Brice (Richard Bohringer), a brash and secure businessman who many people feel has made his fortune collaborating with the Germans, there are Irene's many suitors, the most killingly handsome being Jacques Fabert (Samuel Labarthe), a Resistance sympathizer. And there is the real world of the war, which finally but inevitably impinges even on Irene's cloistered existence with unlooked-for results.

Director Miller, who apprenticed with almost every notable French director, most often with Francois Truffaut, has directed "The Accompanist" with a deft and classical hand, allowing nothing to stray out of place while not neglecting the measured but intense emotions that live under the film's polished surface.

Though it is soprano Laurence Monteyrol who does the actual singing, Safonova and Romane Bohringer are exceptionally convincing both on stage and off, as is Romane's father Richard (a veteran of everything from "Diva" and "Madame Bovary" to "The Cook, The Thief, His Wife and Her Lover") as Irene's husband.

The younger Bohringer won France's Cesar for most promising new actress for her much showier role in Cyril Collard's forthcoming "Savage Nights," but she is if anything more impressive and devastating here as a woman in the quiet grip of an unexpected passion. Believing that "life is elsewhere, outside of you, it rubs against others but passes you by," Sophie's attempt to change that becomes a visit to the wilder shores of devotion, a place no one leaves unchanged.

NEW YORK POST, 12/23/93, p. 35, Thelma Adams

Ever feel like a bit player in your own life?

That's the premise behind Claude Miller's "The Accompanist." This richly evocative French film tries to focus on Sophie (Romane Bohringer), the pianist hired to accompany a beautiful singer, Irene Brice (Elena Safonova).

Like Sophie and Charles (Richard Bohringer), Irene's good-natured but impotent husband, the camera is sucked into the diva's orbit, seduced by her charisma.

By pulling Sophie from the wings, "The Accompanist" addresses those people who cannot escape being minor characters, who cede power to those selfish or confident or talented enough to demand it.

The good life the diva enjoys tempts the 20-year-old, who has lived with her mother in relative poverty. Sophie's love for Irene grows, but her affection is hobbled by her jealousy for the ease with which Irene assumes center stage, professionally and personally.

Like Sophie, Charles becomes Irene's accessory, trapped by his own passion. In her own way, Irene loves her husband, and even cares for Sophie, but her own desires and ambitions are always foremost. Ever the devoted husband, Charles is willing to tolerate the singer's indiscretions—up to a point.

By setting this odd triangle in German-occupied Paris and London in the winter of 1942-43, Miller ("The Little Thief") and co-scenarist Luc Beraud go on to make a larger point. However compelling the interaction within the triangle, these three are bit players on the historical stage.

In the Paris scenes, Charles tries to avoid taking a political position. The success of Irene's career takes her into the circuit of the Vichy government and gains her the attention of the Nazis.

Charles' decision to emigrate is less a principled stand against Nazism (although that is part of it), than a realization that to further Irene's ambitions they must finally make a choice: Embrace the Nazi regime or flee.

While the strength of "The Accompanist" is in character and atmosphere, the plot often seems forced. A shipboard romance between Sophie and a young Jewish resister has so little time to develop that it fails to take root in the audience's sympathies.

When the young man abruptly proposes marriage, Sophie turns to Irene for advice. The singer nudges Sophie back into the fold—she needs an accompanist—and the girl's chance to play a romantic lead in her own life is quickly extinguished.

Similarly, the climax—in which Irene is reunited with her lover in London with disastrous results—is pure melodrama, a jarring thump that plays against the subtler rhythms that Miller has composed.

But it is these subtler rhythms that are so enjoyable. Miller's direction can be so gentle that he gets a laugh out of a cat's slight movements, or wrings pain from the way Irene ties a belt around a coat.

The cast is universally excellent. Elena Safonova has the beauty and charisma to make Irene completely believable, both attractive and devastatingly self-serving. Young Romane Bohringer, who received the 1992 Cesar (France's Oscar) for most promising new actress, infuses a character whose meekness masks a steely will with a wordless gravity and pathos.

The star here is Romane's real-life father, Richard ("Diva"). The actor commands center stage as the husband who takes a back seat to his wife. Richard Bohringer's eyes become a pool of despair while his pointed, Cupid's mouth retains a shred of dignity. It is a compassionate portrait of a man betrayed, nurtured by a director with a finger-tip sensitivity for the shifting tensions in his characters.

NEWSDAY, 12/20/93, Part II/p. 55, John Anderson

Like the melodic movements of a sonata, the main characters in "The Accompanist" orbit each other, influence each other, yet remain as ephemeral as music itself. Less so, actually. Their universe is so small, they practically don't exist at all.

Considering that their place and time is Paris, 1942, the self-absorption that infects these characters is a considerable thing. But the war is little more than an inconvenience for the Brices: collaborationist-businessman Charles (Richard Bohringer) has remained as wealthy as ever, and his wife, the celebrated concert singer Irene (Elena Safonova) is in splendid professional health. Cooly beautiful, with a brilliant voice (that of Laurence Monteyrol), she casts a spell over her audience, which on this particular night consists of Nazis, their associates and Sophie Vasseur (Romane Bohringer), a 20-year-old pianist looking to become Irene's accompanist.

As she watches Irene perform, Sophie is entranced—by the music, of course, but also by the glamor, the glory, and most of all by Irene, who is everything Sophie thinks she wants. The attraction is partly sexual—with Charles, and Irene's lover Jacques (Samuel Labarthe), they will form a kind of love quadrangle—but life with Irene also offers creature comforts. "Over there, I'm warm," the usually taciturn Sophie barks at her widowed mother (Nelly Borgeaud). "I never go hungry ... life is fun." Life, as Sophie's turns out, is actually a curious series of illusions, most of which director Claude Miller has the sense to explore without exploding.

One of these illusions is demolished right away, though. In their first concert together, Sophie realizes just how subordinate she is to Irene's talent; she's been hired for her musical insights, but also, perhaps, because Irene knows she'll have no trouble from her. "So this is it," Sophie tells herself as she watches Irene sing. "She doesn't look at you ... the glory is hers ... so is the happiness." Torn by love of Irene's style, and hate for her indifference, Sophie, played by Bohringer with quiet determination, loses critical bits of herself. And the vicarious titillation she finds in Irene's affair with Jacques, which she gluttonously romanticizes, becomes tainted with guilt as she slowly becomes a part of not only Irene's life, but Charles'.

And it's Charles who dominates the film, especially its second half. Rather than let him become an object of pity or contempt for his cuckold's status, both Miller—this is one of his better efforts—and the veteran actor Richard Bohringer (father of Romane) strive to let him grow, from a contemptible opportunist into a Nazi baiter and then into something resembling nobility.

He's not above self-serving artifice, however, and neither is Miller: During the trio's flight from France aboard a London-bound freighter, we're subjected to a strafing by German fighter plane, and Sophie's shipboard romance with Benoit (Julien Rassam), neither of which are at all believable. Charles, meanwhile, allows his motive for fleeing to be read as patriotism reborn, rather than the desire of a husband to separate his wife from her lover.

But Jacques will follow them to England, and their fates will not be happy. And Miller, who has fashioned a film of high aspirations, foreshadows this: His camera, his eye, alternates between casual observer, one who occasionally discovers his unhappy subjects and can't look away, or one who's trying with great difficulty to avoid them altogether.

SIGHT AND SOUND, 11/93, p. 36, Martin Bright

Occupied Paris, 1942. Sophie Vasseur, a working-class girl, shares an apartment with her mother, a piano teacher. When Sophie is offered a job as a piano accompanist to the singer Irène Brice, she seizes the opportunity to escape her dull and unrewarding life. Sophie is immediately impressed by the opulent lifestyle of Madame Brice and her husband Charles, a successful businessman.

Sophie is pleased when Irène takes her into her confidence. She agrees to become a go-between; taking letters to Irène's lover, Jacques Fabert, a member of the Resistance. As Irène prepares for an important concert she asks Sophie to move in with her to make practising easier. Sophie's mother warns her that the Brices are known collaborators, but she doesn't care.

Irène's concert is a great success and she is invited to perform at Vichy in front of France's puppet government. But Charles is becoming increasingly uncomfortable with the compromises he is being forced to make and refuses an invitation to dine with a German general. At Vichy, an old family friend warns Charles to be careful and urges him to flee the country.

When they return to Paris after Irène's concert at Vichy, the Brices' apartment has been ransacked by the authorities. Charles decides that he and Irène must leave immediately for London where he will join de Gaulle's Free French. Sophie agrees to go with them and they travel incognito through Spain and Portugal. In Lisbon Sophie meets a young Jewish boy, Benoit Weizman, who is also travelling to London. During the crossing Benoit declares his love for Sophie, but on arrival in England, Sophie says she cannot marry him because of her commitment to Irène. At immigration control the Brices are detained because of their connections with the Vichy regime. They are released only after the intervention of Jacques Fabert, who is now working in London.

In England, Charles tries to re-establish his business connections, while Irène starts to rebuild her singing career. She auditions for the BBC and the resulting concert is a triumph. There is talk of a series of concerts in the United States, but Irène prefers to stay in London so that she can be near Jacques. Charles becomes increasingly lonely and frustrated in London and, depressed by Irène's continued infidelity, eventually shoots himself. After the war, Irène and Jacques leave together for America and Sophie returns alone to Paris.

France's film-makers have never really got to grips with the German occupation of their country during the Second World War. Recent half-hearted attempts to do so, like Claude Berri's *Uranus* or Bertrand Blier's *Merci la vie* have merely reduced the period to *'Allo 'Allo*-type farce. And although Claude Miller's *L'Accompagnatrice* is not a comedy, its reference points are exactly the same: decadent collaborators, seedy black marketeers, clean-cut Resistance heroes, amoral bourgeois beauties and Nazis with a taste for classical music. Even the archive wartime footage, which Miller has added to give an air of moral seriousness to his film, serves to reinforce the feeling that you've seen it all before. Similarly, the muted brown tones in which Miller has chosen to shoot most scenes is presumably supposed to give the impression of an old photograph. But it is more sludge than sepia and fails even as a stylistic device.

However, the film's uniform visual and narrative dullness does act as a pretty effective anaesthetic. And it also fits a certain, rather unpleasant way of looking at French history in which these stories and images that we've seen a thousand times take on a mythical quality. Collaboration is no longer something that happened in France at a particular point in time, it is merely part of some great panoply of human fairy tales. The French experience is thus rendered universal.

Most of the characters in *L'Accompagnatrice* are easily recognisable from this grim, ahistorical dumb-show. Only Charles Brice and Sophie herself are given enough definition to move, decide and doubt like real human beings. But even they are granted this freedom so that they can later discover their true roles in the drama—he as the cuckold, she as the accompanist

In a crashingly dull piece of symbolism, the sea-crossing to England acts as the defining moment of the film. As German planes dive-bomb their ship, Charles can temporarily shrug off his sordid racketeer past and become a morally upright hero as Irène's protector and Sophie's surrogate father. Meanwhile, for the duration of the voyage, Sophie can step out of Irène's shadow to allow herself a brief love-affair. Back on dry land, however, they both revert to type.

L'Accompagnatrice would be entirely without interest if this lifeless tableau approach to French history didn't have such a vampire-like effect on present-day France. The character of Sophie is familiar not just because she is such a cliché. She is familiar, too, because she is so representative of France's notoriously conservative Mitterrand generation, the target audience of the film. Like them, Sophie is bored with politics, in awe of the bourgeoisie, blissfully unaware of the burden of history, She is happy to act as an accompanist and nothing more.

TIME, 1/10/94, p. 60, Richard Corliss

Sophie Vasseur (Romane Bohringer) has eyes made for adoration. They are large, dark, serious, so very intense; they might belong to a puppy just saved from the city pound. Sophie's eyes have found their love object in Irène Brice (Elena Safonova), a concert singer in occupied Paris during World War II. Talented and highly spirited, apparently gliding through life, Irène can juggle the affections of a businessman husband (Richard Bohringer) and a lover (Samuel Labarthe) who is in the Resistance. Sophie, a promising pianist, is pleased to be Irène's accompanist and maid; she serves tea, irons, watches, tries to keep secrets. Servant and mistress, darkness and light—why, the two women might be in different movies.

We all have supporting roles in the movies that are other people's lives. Sometimes we are so enthralled with someone else that we barely star in our own. Denial of self becomes a silent declaration of love—especially a first love like Sophie's. She could be a sister to Willa Cather's Lucy Gayheart or a daughter to Stevens the butler in *The Remains of the Day*. This implosive sort of devotion is found often enough in life but rarely in films. That *The Accompanist* exists at all is the first reason to cherish it.

The main reason is the performances; this film is a gift to his actors from director Claude Miller (who, with Luc Béraud, adapted Nina Berberova's novel) and from the actors to the receptive viewer. Safonova is a blond vision of grace under all kinds of pressure. But the fresh revelation is Romane Bohringer, daughter of co-star Richard Bohringer. A solemn beguiler, she perfectly embodies pent-up passivity as it longs for the golden chains of an enslaving passion.

VILLAGE VOICE, 12/28/93, p. 88, Manohla Dargis

Be wary of the quiet girls, they'll get you every time. Or so it would seem in Claude Miller's *The Accompanist*. When Sophie (Romane Bohringer), a sour young thing in sensible flats, becomes the pianist for the ethereal diva Irène Brice (Elena Safonova), she soon finds herself in a grandiloquent intrigue of master and slave, love and hate, forte and pianissimo. The time is Vichy France. As a few tight-lipped Germans mill about, the dashing collaborationist Monsieur Charles Brice (Richard Bohringer) agonizes about money and morals, while a heroic sort with permanent stubble, who may or may not be Irène's lover, lingers in the shadows. *Ce ne fait rien.* For the women, the world is but an aesthetic refuge, secured by the likes of Massenet and Berlioz, perfumed by the erotics of friendship. Until, that is, Sophie and company are driven into exile. The slave, forced to iron madame's gowns and witness her erotic goings-on, bites her lip, and rages. Service curdles into need.

Despite its wiff of noxious female heat, its no surprise Miller's bizarre ménage à trois is dominated by Charles. Sophie, so stolid she looks like she's taken root, isn't permitted to flourish enough; while Irène, one of those self-absorbed beauties who make everybody suffer, remains more annoying than enticing. Charles, his features tugged out of place by dissipation, has the kind of ruinous grace that is the very essence of drama. Great actors like the Bohringer *père*—the Bohringer *fille* is very good, someday she'll be great—have the sort of faces that demand attention, faces in which every pockmark, every nose hair, is an *accent acute*. In *The Accompanist*, the duct sings but Charles soars.

Also reviewed in:
CHICAGO TRIBUNE, 1/28/94, Friday/p. A, Michael Wilmington
NEW REPUBLIC, 12/13/93, p. 31, Stanley Kauffmann
NEW YORK TIMES, 12/23/93, p. C7, Janet Maslin
VARIETY, 12/21/92, p. 62, Lisa Nesselson
WASHINGTON POST, 3/11/94, p. G6, Hal Hinson
WASHINGTON POST, 3/11/94, Weekend/p. 44, Desson Howe

ACLÀ

A Cineuropa '92 and Nova Films production in collaboration with Pentafilm. *Director:* Aurelio Grimaldi. *Screenplay (Italian with English subtitles):* Aurelio Grimaldi. *Story:* Aurelio Grimaldi. *Director of Photography:* Maurizio Calvesi. *Editor:* Raimondo Crociani. *Music:* Dario Lucantoni. *Running time:* 86 minutes. *MPAA Rating:* Not Rated.

WITH: Francesco Cusimano; Tony Sperandeo; Luigi Maria Burruano; Lucia Sardo; Giovanni Alamia; Benedetto Ranelli; Giuseppe Cusimano; Rita Barbancra; Salvatore Scianna; Ignazio Donato; Luciano Venturino.

NEW YORK POST, 12/3/93, p. 44, Thelma Adams

When I left "Acla," I felt bruised and beaten.

Given the subject matter of Aurelio Grimaldi's directorial debut, it's no surprise. In the 1930s, an impoverished Sicilian family sell their 11-year-old son, Acla (Francesco Cusimano), into indentured servitude.

Acla joins his father (Luigi Burruano) and two brothers in the local sulfur pits. The Floristella mine is run like the galley of a slave ship: the boss preys on the workers, the workers prey on the boys, the boys prey on each other or, given the chance, on frogs.

In the underground heat, the men strip down to loin cloths. A tow-headed beauty among dark hairy men, Acla is under the constant threat of beatings and rape. Before long, he is plotting his escape to the ocean, a dream for which he pays bitterly.

"Acla" was featured in the New Italian Film Festival 1992; Grimaldi's second movie, "The Rebel," plays this year's festival.

Grimaldi is a frank, direct filmmaker working from his own spare screenplay. He elicits naturalistic performances from his actors, and the charismatic Cusimano has no trouble holding the screen's center.

But the ends towards which the director employs his abundant talents seem slight. What appears to intrigue Grimaldi is the unspoken homosexual subculture among the horny diggers. The fairness of Acla's butt is widely discussed by the veteran miners who have sex with the boys during the week and with their wives on weekends and holidays.

The director saves the caresses of his camera for sulfur-lit shots of the men who sleep together in a woven mat of human flesh like slaves in the hold of a ship. For those outside the male beating-and-buns set who aren't simply masochistic, the movie goes nowhere except down the mine shaft.

That mine work is hard, that men can be brutal, that the weak prey on the strong—none of this is news nor is it revealed in a new way. Strip away the artful gloss and what remains is highbrow kiddie porn.

I can't forget the image of the grizzled father brutalizing his golden son after a failed escape attempt, but that hardly makes "Acla" an unforgettable film.

NEWSDAY, 12/3/93, Part II/p. 103, John Anderson

The people and the poverty are equally bitter in the sun-dusted land surrounding the Floristella sulphur mines. It's Sicily in the '30s, in a region where male children are sold by their parents into years of hard labor below ground. There, they cart the valuable mineral to the surface—where it will be used to make Fascist bombs—and are subject to their bosses' corporal and sexual abuse.

The boys of "Acla," Aurelio Grimaldi's disturbing new film, dwell in a particular kind of hell. If they flee, they shame their parents, who have already collected the 500 lira "death warranty" from the digger who's hired their child. If they stay, they either acquiesce to their masters—it's a miner's right, one says, to "screw young boys during the week and their wives and girlfriends on the weekend"—or live in terror and debasement.

"You're a man now," his mother tells Acla (Francesco Cusimano), after his first week in the mines, but he's not, of course. Just 11, Acla has a child's mind, but an ageless ferocity, which makes him constitutionally incapable of acquiescing to anyone, or anything. He's not particularly attractive, although his unusual blondness catches the eye of the randier miners. Acla is hardnosed and blunt, and as portrayed by the precocious Cusimano, a force of nature. He will escape, be beaten, escape, be beaten, and refuse to accept his plight. His master, Caramazza (Tony Sperandeo) is sadistic and a constant sexual threat; his father (Luigi Maria Burrauno) delivers brutal retribution for Acla's flights. But neither Caramazza's anger, his family's shame, nor his bruises mean anything to the boy.

What he does want is the sea, across which an older married sister has sailed to Australia, and writes home of the opportunities there, and the plenty. "Acla" is a story of dream fulfillment, and if it's a small, attainable dream, compared to Acla's life in the mines—where sexual favors are often traded for olives and sardines—it's paradise.

Grimaldi takes everyone to task, including the village priest, whose evangelical mission doesn't go as far as disturbing the economic equilibrium of his parish, or its peculiar semal balance either. But we do see Acla's suffering change him, particularly in his locations with his siblings, whom he's always treated like dirt, in keeping with family tradition. The film ends quite abruptly, in a way that suggests a number of alternative endings to Acla's tale, including the possibility that Grimaldi simply ran out of money. But the film is unforgettable nonetheless, a trip into a childhood sprung from Dante's brow.

VILLAGE VOICE, 12/7/93, p. 68, Georgia Brown

It used to be something of a movie taboo—putting children in mortal danger. No longer. Now it's getting to be the rage. But before extending my two cents, I'd like to divide the subject into two categories: the dead child and the child's hard life.

The Dead Child. When Truffaut interviewed Hitchcock about *Sabotage*, they spoke of the child who unknowingly carries a bomb—a bomb that eventually, while in his possession, goes off. Hitch argued that the boy walks around with the bomb too long, thereby building up too much sympathy. Truffaut begged to differ: "Making a child die in a picture is a rather ticklish matter; it comes close to an abuse of cinematic power." Hitchcock quickly came around: "I agree with that; it was a grave error on my part." But maybe the child with the bomb was just ahead of his time. Years later, maybe this would've seemed an audacity on the order of Janet Leigh's being rudely eliminated in *Psycho*'s first half hour.

Obviously, there's a ticklish commercial matter here. It's a safe bet that a fair share of any after-dark audience will be parents who have left a child at home, and child vulnerability is the last thing they will want to be reminded of while unavailable to save and protect. (I myself have never forgiven Nicholas Roeg for that cheesy horror flick *Don't Look Now*.)

Maybe because my kids have reached their lifelong heights, recent dead-child movies—*Olivier, Olivier*, Kieślowski's films, *Short Cuts, Fearless, Lorenzo's Oil* (death in life), and *Jurassic Park* (dead/back to life)—actually are endurable. Except for Spielberg's creepy play on Truffaut's *Short Change* stunt, dead-child movies are chiefly focused on parents' grief. Since we're talking about an event that, in life, conceivably could not be borne, these movies seem designed to engage some portion of our concern while hardly demanding whole identification.

While graphic enough, a small boy's demise in Altman's movie is much less affecting than the Carver short story it's taken from (despite the hotter medium), partly because nothing in *Short Cuts* is dwelt on long enough to preserve an impact. Instead, Altman creates a teeming, Calcutta-style universe where humans come and go, the only constant being Altmanesque irony. In *Fearless*, the death of baby Bubble exists only in his mother's grief, which in turn exists as an excuse to make a "different" sort of movie. George Miller's weepy *Lorenzo's Oil* really was a bit different and obviously suffered at the box office for it.

Different entirely are the deaths in Kieslowski's ongoing philosophical melodrama, with its emphasis on the mysterious counterlife: One lives/the other lives elsewhere. From the opening of *The Decalogue* (the scientist sending his son out to skate on thin ice) to *The Double Life of Veronique* to *Blue*, the death of a child signifies beginning, at least of the special Kieslowski story. In *Blue*, the child dies/the (m)other lives, only to discover that she has a twin (her husband's mistress) with a new child in the womb. The view of a child's face through glass, or ice in the one instance (the transparent barrier between this and the other world), becomes one of the most resonant of images. True, Kieslowski *uses* child death, but to personal, eccentric purpose.

Two of the best films in the last few years—Terence Davies's *Distant Voices, Still Lives* and Kanevski's *Freeze—Die—Come to Life* have been personal records of unhappy childhoods. And this year, no doubt riding the culture's child abuse mania, Hollywood has discovered the subject; witness *This Boy's Life* and *King of the Hill*. Neither, however, is made by the person who lived the life, and this—as Spielberg's adaptation of J.G. Ballard's *Empire of the Sun* showed—makes all the difference. Steven Soderbergh makes deprivation look like a mild and slightly inconvenient business.

But just to show that no rule always holds, the Taviani brothers created a masterpiece from Gavino Ledda's autobiography, *Padre Padrone: The Education of a Shepherd*. It may be the *Pinocchio* factor, but Italians appear to have a special affinity for tales of difficult childhoods. Using an oblique approach to abuse, last year's *Il ladro di bambini* (directed by Gianni Amelio) succeeded in being utterly responsible. On the other hand, Carlo Carlei (director of the currently touted *Flight of the Innocent*) seems far more interested in showing he can imitate Hollywood-style violence than in any innocent's plight.

This brings me to Aurelio Grimaldi's stylized *Aclá*, which at first glance appears to be trying for *Padre Padrone's* tact and elegance. Set in Sicily in the '30s, the film opens with 11-year-old Aclá facing a cruel sentence: five years labor in the sulfur mines of Floristella. Essentially, his father is selling him into slavery for 500 lira. Not a difficult decision since mining is the family calling. Each week Papa and two elder brothers set off for six days underground. On Saturday nights, Papa takes his bath (dirty water left for the sons), gets drunk in the village, and screws Mama. Aclá watches this last through a hole in the wall. Like Antoine Doinel in *The 400 Blows*, he dreams of escape to the sea.

The blond, rugged-looking Aclá ("white as a goat like his grandmother," observes Mama) quickly finds out what working in the mines entails (emphasis on tails). Wearing only loincloths because of the sweltering heat, the men dig and the boys act as donkeys, lugging 25-kilo loads of rock to the surface. Not surprisingly, given the nudity and mass sleeping arrangements, lust raises its little head, though the film is a bit coy about consequences. For one, you'd think all the sex was consensual. Men approach the beautiful Aclá, request his ass, then sit back and wait for him to say si. Aclá discovers that one of his brothers and another pretty fellow are an item. (The two endure some teasing since they really *like* each other.) A clumsy filmmaker, Grimaldi favors filtered shots of naked bodies with dusty bottoms.

What's the aim here? Is Grimaldi chronicling a social tragedy or using abuse (as Carlei uses kidnapping) for a bit of sensationalism? Although this community's grim existence has a certain interest, I never felt more than a detached sympathy. Whether or not Grimaldi's essential focus is naked boy bottoms, his movie fails my Child's Hard Life test: It doesn't shatter the heart.

Also reviewed in:
NEW YORK TIMES, 12/3/93, p. C12, Stephen Holden

ADDAMS FAMILY VALUES

A Paramount Pictures release. *Executive Producer:* David Nicksay. *Producer:* Scott Rudin. *Director:* Barry Sonnenfeld. *Screenplay:* Paul Rudnick. *Based on the characters created by:* Charles Addams. *Director of Photography:* Donald Peterman. *Editor:* Arthur Schmidt and Jim Miller. *Music:* Marc Shaiman. *Music Editor:* Scott Stambler and Nancy Fogarty. *Tango Choreographer:* Peter Anastos. *Choreographer Camp Chippewa:* Adam Shankman. *Sound:* Peter Kurland and (music) Tim Boyle. *Sound Editor:* Joseph Ippolito and Elizabeth Sterner. *Casting:* David Rubin and Debra Zane. *Production Designer:* Ken Adam. *Art Director:* William J. Durrell, Jr. *Set Decorator:* Marvin March. *Set Dresser:* Tamara Clinard. *Special Effects:* Kenneth D. Pepiot. *Visual Effects:* Alan Munro. *Costumes:* Theoni V. Aldredge. *Make-up:* Kevin C. Haney. *Stunt Coordinator:* Gary Hymes. *Running time:* 93 minutes. *MPAA Rating:* PG-13.

CAST: Anjelica Huston (Morticia Addams); Raul Julia (Gomez Addams); Christopher Lloyd (Fester Addams); Joan Cusack (Debbie Jellinsky); Christina Ricci (Wednesday Addams); Carol Kane (Granny); Jimmy Workman (Pugsley Addams); Kaitlyn Hooper and Kristen Hooper (Pubert Addams); Carel Struycken (Lurch); David Krumholtz (Joel Glicker); Christopher Hart (Thing); Dana Ivey (Margaret); Peter MacNicol (Gary Granger); Christine Baranski (Becky Granger); Mercedes McNab (Amanda Buckman); Sam McMurray (Don Buckman); Harriet Sansom Harris (Ellen Buckman); Julie Halston (Mrs. Glicker); Barry Sonnenfeld (Mr. Glicker); Nathan Lane (Desk Sergeant); John Franklin (Cousin Itt); Charles Busch (Cousin Aphasia); Laura Esterman (Cousin Ophelia); Maureen Sue Levin (Flora Amor); Darlene Levin (Fauna Amor); Carol Hankins (Dementia); Steven M. Martin (Donald); Douglas Brian Martin (Dexter); Ryan Holihan (Lumpy Adams); Lois deBanzie (Delivery Nurse); Vickilyn Reynolds (Forceps Nurse); Cynthia Nixon (Heather); Edye Byrde (Mrs. Montgomery); David Hyde Pierce (Delivery Room Doctor); Andreana Weiner (Obnoxious Girl); Peter Graves (Host); Rick Scarry (Lawyer); Monet Mazur (Flirting Woman); Francis Coady (Flirting Man); Ian Abercrombie (Driver); Chris Ellis (Moving Man); Camille Saviola (Concetta); Zack Phifer (Passport Clerk); Tony Shalhoub (Jorge); Jeffrey Van Hoose (Irwin); Micah Winkelspecht (Mordecai); Matthew Beebe (Wheelchair Camper); Micah Hata (Yang); Joey Wilcots (Jamal); Jason Fife (Camper #1); Karl David-Djerf (Camper #2); Haley Peel (Young Debbie).

LOS ANGELES TIMES, 11/19/93, Calendar/p. 1, Peter Rainer

The kinetically nutty "Addams Family Values" starts out with a full bag of tricks and keeps lobbing them straight at the audience for all of its 93 minutes. It never lets up—director Barry Sonnenfeld and screenwriter Paul Rudnick turn its assaultiveness into a comic style.

With something this scattershot and relatively plotless, it's inevitable that tedium would eventually set in, and it does, about halfway into the spree. But there are still some good laughs—more than in "The Addams Family," where the tedium set in with the credits.

The film begins with Morticia's surprise announcement to Gomez (Raul Julia) that she is pregnant, and about to have a baby. (Things happen fast *chez* Addams.) Their new infant son, dubbed Pubert (and, fittingly, played alternately by twin sisters Kaitlyn and Kristen Hooper), comes complete with Gomez's Lothario mustache and jet black hair. His baby bottle is spiked with vodka. (W.C. Fields would approve of this family.)

The rest of the clan is introduced in pungent, nutball cameos. Fester Addams (Christopher Lloyd), looking as fetid as ever, goes in for a little bedtime reading: the self-help guide "Strange Men and the Women Who Avoid Them." The two Addams' children, Wednesday (Christina Ricci) and Pugsley (Jimmy Workman), resentful of Pubert, concoct garish ways of disposing of him via guillotine and pincers. Lurch (Carel Struycken) and Thing (Christopher Hart, or at least his hand) plod and scamper, respectively, through the Addams' cobwebby environs. Granny (Carol Kane, all too briefly) does her potion thing. It's a family in need of a little lightening up.

Joan Cusack's Debbie Jellinsky, a serial murderess with her eyes on Fester's fortune, wedges her way into the gloom by posing as a nanny to the two brats (whom she arranges to pack off to camp). She's the perfect mate for Fester: The more slobbery he gets, the more she coos. Debbie is the real maniac in the bunch, by contrast, the Addamses are almost functional. But her cooing has its limits. When she and Fester are hitched, she refuses to be seen with him in public until he gets a make-over (i.e., a wig). Then her attempts to do him in—which begin by throwing a radio into his honeymoon bubblebath—are routinely squelched by Fester's plain dumb luck. It's as if the Fates had decreed, Nobody this weird can die.

The movie's central joke is that the Addamses are a lot more stable— they have better "family values"—than the straight-arrows on the outside. The camp that Wednesday and Pugsley attend is a nightmare of enforced cheerfulness where the sunny blond apple-polishers are favored and the nerdy, the minorities and a Jewish boy (David Krumholtz) with a crush on Wednesday are squelched.

The film could use more interaction between the Addamses and the "real" world. (There's a funny bit between Gomez and Nathan Lane as an uncomprehending yet know-it-all police captain.) Without enough confrontations between the two worlds, the film (rated PG-13 for "macabre humor") often pumps itself full of overfamiliar Addams Family shtick—the air of self-celebration is a little gooey. And it's a shame that the filmmakers didn't try to fight the family-entertainment format: The Addamses are, by definition, subversive, and a few more scenes like the one where Debbie sends Thing into a swoon by sucking on one of his fingers would have worked wonders.

Sonnenfeld does somewhat better with "Addams Family Values" than he did with "Addams Family." But he still gooses the film with hyperactive slapstick whenever things get talky; he doesn't trust the performers enough, or the material, which seems designed for a less frenetic approach. Rudnick smuggles some real wit into the proceedings, but it's the kind of wit that needs to be directed funkier, more deadpan. The actors gorge on the quiet moments: The best bits in the film come when Anjelica Huston's Morticia, her bone-white pallor glowing, moans her breathy S&M endearments to Gomez; or when Wednesday, auditioning for a camp play, forces herself to smile. Her ear-to-ear grin, which slowly accumulates before our eyes, is the funniest/creepiest thing in the movie.

Uneven as it is, "Addams Family Values" is considerably more enjoyable than its predecessor. At this rate, if there's a third installment, it'll be a knockout. Or at least a TKO.

NEW YORK, 11/29/93, p. 65, David Denby

For a writer, it's almost painful to see a movie written by Paul Rudnick—or even to read movie journalism written by Paul Rudnick—because one knows that one could never be as funny as he. As "Libby Gelman-Waxner," *Premiere's* princess-in-residence, he devastated the art fraud *Orlando* in the November issue. *Addams Family Values* is a rare comedy sequel that actually improves on the original, and the reason, I suspect, is that Rudnick, who wrote the screenplay, has been allowed to run wild. Rudnick and director Barry Sonnenfeld have seized on a possible meaning in Charles Addams's creations: They have made the Addams Family a metaphor for outsiders, all outsiders. The morbid family of greasy dark monsters becomes a weapon against the straight world.

The movie, of course, is not quite a pious exercise in political correctness. Morticia and Gomez have a baby, a beautiful little boy with a pencil-line mustache and slick black hair. This precious poisoned weed soon runs loose in the house. The only thing wrong with *The Addams Family* was that we zipped down those dark, elegantly cobwebby corridors a few times too many. But if that movie was claustrophobic, this one is expansive. When the older children, Wednesday and Pugsley, try repeatedly to murder the new arrival, they are shipped off to summer camp, where they join forces with the Jews, the blacks, the misfits, and everyone else who cannot stand the relentless good cheer of the place. Joan Cusack, who has become amazingly fleshy, shows up as a luxury-minded hussy with designs on Uncle Fester. Cusack has all the accoutrements of a femme fatale, but her lips keep slipping around the words—she's part of the straight world, too, the non-Addamses. Wednesday Addams (Christina Ricci), playing Pocahontas in the camp Thanksgiving pageant, leads a revolt of the outsiders in which the docile Indians burn down the colonial village. Will *Addams Family Values*, with its mix of gay and Jewish sarcasm, seem as funny outside New York and Los Angeles? I hope so. Rudnick and Sonnenfeld may have created the first hip mass-market hit.

NEW YORK POST, 11/19/93, p. 39, Michael Medved

The first "Addams Family" movie offered so little in the way of plot that its makers have tried to compensate by infusing its sequel, "Addams Family Values," with an abundance of dramatic developments.

As the movie opens, Gomez and Morticia (Raul Julia and Anjelica Huston) welcome a new addition to the family: baby Pubert, who comes conveniently equipped with a pencil-thin moustache that resembles his father's.

To protect this child from the murderous designs of his senior siblings, the parents hire a blonde, sweetly smiling nanny (Joan Cusack) who turns out to have more in common with Rebecca DeMornay in "The Hand That Rocks the Cradle" than she does with Mary Poppins.

Cusack is actually a psychotic serial killer who hopes to marry, then murder, wealthy Uncle Fester (Christopher Lloyd). As part of her evil master plan, she dispatches the two older kids to a sleepaway summer camp where Wednesday (played by the superb 13-year-old actress Christina Ricci, who steals the movie) ends up meeting her first boyfriend.

All of these epochal events keep the picture moving along at an energetic clip, in contrast to its ploddingly paced predecessor. The performers seem to have settled comfortably into their roles, and this time manage to do more acting and less mugging.

Screenwriter Paul Rudnick (who contributed to the final shooting script for the first "Addams Family" movie but is best known for his Obie award winning play "Jeffrey") provides some sassy dialogue that's food for frequent chuckles.

There's also a show-stopping tango performed at a fancy restaurant by Gomez and Morticia; their actual dancing isn't particularly impressive but the editing is so showy and the music is turned up so loud that moviegoers are supposed to be goosed into applause.

The funniest sequence in the movie involves the sappy summer camp where Wednesday and Pugsley rebel against the tyranny of two insufferably upbeat counselors (perfectly played by the grinning Peter MacNicol and Christine Baranski) who call for regular "group hugs" and consign misfit campers to a "Harmony Hut" complete with Michael Jackson "Heal the World" posters.

The ultimate triumph of the outcasts, during a mid-summer "Thanksgiving Pageant" prepared for visiting parents, is reminiscent of both "Animal House" and "Revenge of the Nerds," but still satisfying to watch.

Much less pleasing are elements of violence and sadism outrageously inappropriate in a movie so obviously aimed at kids. Several scenes show Wednesday and Pugsley trying to murder their infant brother—by throwing him from the top of the family's mansion, slicing off his head with a well-sharpened guillotine, or dropping an anvil onto his tiny skull.

If Beavis and Butt-head can get into trouble through their general celebration of pyromania, what can one say about this very specific and very dangerous—depiction of handling hostility toward younger siblings?

Like the picture's other gratuitously gross references, these sequences turn out to be scary rather than funny.

Diehard fans will laugh anyway; all those people who found something to like in the flaccid first movie will come away well-satisfied with the superior sequel. Box-office success should not, however, obscure the fact that in the final analysis "Addams Family Values" isn't for families, and has little value.

NEWSDAY, 11/19/93, Part II/p. 72, Jack Mathews

If it weren't for the exorbitant cost, an estimated $50 million for "Addams Family Values," it seems clear that the movie life of "The Addams Family" could go on indefinitely.

It was the beast-within-us attitude of Charles Addams' marvelously macabre New Yorker cartoons that made the family a natural for the 1960s TV sitcom, and with its live-action characters having been firmly re-established on film with the 1991 Christmas hit, further episodes are limited only by the imagination of their writers.

The writing, in fact, is much sharper on the sequel than it was on the first film, and the laughs, for those so disposed, more frequent.

Liberated from the task of having to introduce new audiences to the family—hot-blooded Gomez (Raul Julia), seductive Morticia (Anjelica Huston), freakish Uncle Fester (Christopher Lloyd), and the destructive kids, Pugsley (Jimmy Workman) and Wednesday (Christina Ricci)—screenwriter Paul Rudnick and returning director Barry Sonnenfeld were able to devote more time to situations and subplots.

One of their choices, I think, was ill-conceived, if not dangerous. In the opening moments, after Morticia delivers a mustachioed baby who looks just like his father, morbidly jealous Pugsley and Wednesday make several attempts to kill him, including dropping him from the roof.

As we saw recently with incidents of high school football players re-enacting a scene from "The Program," movie stunts do occasionally inspire imitation, and with sibling rivalry a natural occurrence in growing families, the infanticide jokes in "Addams Family Values" don't seem worth the effort.

With that warning light lit, we welcome Pubert to the family. It is his presence, in a black bassinet with flames occasionally shooting from it, that sets the other elements of the story—Uncle

Fester's whirlwind romance with a gold-digging nanny (Joan Cusack), Pugsley's and Wednesday's dark adventures at a summer camp—in motion.

After Uncle Fester and the nanny marry, and she orders him to never see his family again, Pubert turns into a cherub with blond hair and a taste for pastel nursery decor. Only by reuniting the family, says Granny (Carol Kane), can the curse be lifted and Pubert returned to darkness. Lloyd's Uncle Fester is not my favorite member of the new Addams family. Lloyd overplays the character so badly, you ran barely understand what he's saying half the time. Still, the idea of the grotesque, bald-headed, black-eyed, blubbery bumpkin losing his virginity and his bankroll to Cusack's conniving black widow is often very funny.

Cusack, who would make a terrific Morticia if Huston were to surrender the role, is probably the best screen comedienne working now, and her psychopathic Debbie Jellinsky, a serial husband killer, is more than a match for the Addams clan.

About half the film is set in Camp Chippewa, the rich kids camp where, at Debbie's suggestion, Pugsley and Wednesday are sent for the summer. Pugsley, who spent much of the first film blowing up the Addams mansion, is almost nonexistent in this episode. It is the deathly morose Wednesday, played with wonderful dead-pan sincerity by Ricci, who drives the camp's giddy counselors and its slew of future cheerleaders crazy.

Most of the jokes are routine stuff, the inevitably twisted morality ("You'll meet someone very special," Gomez assures Uncle Fester, "someone who won't press charges"). But Rudnick, an uncredited collaborator on the first film, also peppers his script with hip gags taken from current events.

That can sometimes be a trap. There's an Amy Fisher joke that would, given the sentencing this week of Pal Joey, have worked better as a Buttufuoco joke, but the deliciously cheap shot taken at Michael Jackson is still good.

NEWSWEEK, 11/22/93, p. 57, Jack Kroll

Addams Family Values (superb title) continues the saga of those cool ghouls created by New York cartoonist Charles Addams. "The Addams Family" (1991) grossed $113.4 million; this sequel cost $50 million to make and will no doubt gross out—er, outgross the original. The constituency is huge: after all, inside every normal family there's a monster family straining to break out. Addams's inspiration was to spot that. The major event in any family is a blessed event (which in the reverse world of the Addamses is, of course, a damned event) and so the new movie opens with the birth of the baby announced by Morticia (Anjelica Huston) at the end of the last movie. Baby Pubert is the image of his papa, Gomez (Raul Julia)—including the mustache. Brother Pugsley (Jimmy Workman) and sister Wednesday (Christina Ricci) greet the newcomer like properly sinister siblings: they try to guillotine him, toss him out the window, drop an anvil on him.

It's togetherness Addams style, and Pubert just keeps gurgling happily. In the main story line, love comes to Gomez's doorknob-headed brother, Fester (Christopher Lloyd), in the sumptuous shape of Debbie Jellinsky (Joan Cusack), a nanny who's really a notorious husband-killer. The virginal Fester falls doorknob-over-heels, they marry and set off in their car, to which the celebrants have merrily tied a corpse. The chief conjugal event of the honeymoon is attempted spousicide, and events escalate to a showdown between Debbie and the Addams clan. The latter has no objection to Debbie's lethal instincts: "You have placed Fester under some strange sexual spell," says Morticia. "I can respect that." What offends them is Debbie's tacky taste—her pink furbelows, the blond wig she makes Fester wear.

Paul Rudnick's clever screenplay is deftly cartoonified by director Barry Sonnenfeld. There are nice bits for all the Addamses: Granny (Carol Kane), Lurch the butler (Carel Struycken) and Thing, the family's handyman without a man. If you put each Addams on a T shirt, I'd want the one with Huston, who makes Morticia a pure grande (guignol) dame, an aristocrat to the graveyard born.

SIGHT AND SOUND, 2/94, p. 44, Kim Newman

When Morticia and Gomez Addams bring home the new-born Pubert, their jealous children Wednesday and Pugsley try to murder the indestructible baby. Debbie Jellinsky, the latest nanny, seems to fit in with the odd Addams lifestyle and makes up to Uncle Fester, who is lonely in his bachelorhood. But Debbie is actually the Black Widow, a serial killer who specialises in marrying and murdering rich men. When Wednesday and Pugsley suspect her, Debbie persuades Gomez and Morticia to send the children off to Camp Chippewa, where they do not fit in with the wholesome blonde children and the sweetly tyrannical directors Gary and Becky Granger.

Fester is inveigled into marrying Debbie at an Addams family celebration and the couple depart for Hawaii, where Debbie's attempts to murder her husband fail. She is forced to consider living with him, making him over with a wig and polyester pastels and decreeing he never see his family again. At Camp Chippewa, Wednesday earns the enmity of privileged Amanda Buckman and the admiration of misfit Joel Glicker, but is forced to take part in a Thanksgiving Pageant, playing Pocahontas opposite Amanda's Sarah Miller. Gomez and Morticia try to visit Fester, but Debbie has made him her slave, still intending to kill him. At the Chippewa pageant, Wednesday, playing Pocahontas, departs from Gary's script by foretelling the suppression of the American Indians by the settlers and ordering her tribe to burn down the set and scalp Amanda. Debbie tries to blow up Fester in their home, but he is rescued by Thing, the family's disembodied hand. She decides to murder the entire Addams family by electrocution, only to be thwarted and fried by the innocent intervention of Pubert. Fester is reconciled to the family, and takes a shine to Cousin Itt's nanny Dementia.

As if in answer to criticism that *The Addams Family* was all one-off jokes with a negligible plot, the sequel calls upon the services of respected playwright Paul Rudnick and is weighted down by story contrivances. Though less strung up with the business of introducing its characters, *Addams Family Values* is even more indebted to the TV sitcom its makers try to distance themselves from. It resembles three half-hour episodes haphazardly spliced together, as it follows the stories of the new baby, the murderous nanny and Camp Chippewa. Raul Julia's Gomez and Anjelica Huston's Morticia take a relatively minor role in the stories, the plots serving as showcases for wholly wonderful performances by Joan Cusack, an insane pastel temptress who explains her path to madness with a slide show, and Christina Ricci, whose blank-faced strangeness is used to even better effect than in the first film. In the one moment that manages to be eerie and affecting as well as funny, Ricci's Wednesday is forced to contort her face into a mawkish smile, eliciting not the expected sentimental ahhs but a child onlooker's panicky cry of "she's scaring me".

While the Fester-Debbie plot is well introduced by Fester gloomily lying in bed reading *Strange Men and the Women Who Avoid Them*, Cusack's kooky malevolence is ill-served by a succession of repetitive failed murder gags—although her dropping of a ghetto blaster into Fester's bath pays off with a well-remembered classic TV image, as he holds a lit-up electric bulb in his mouth. The Camp Chippewa scenes offer far more meat for the film's skewed values. The misfit Addamses—whose kind are seen in a somewhat too-blunt equation to include racial minorities and the handicapped—are opposed with pampered moppets who indulge in 'group hugs' and whose equivalent of the chain-gang sweatbox is a Wendy house with videos of *The Brady Bunch* and Disney films. *Addams Family Values* doesn't really work as a film and is often over-obvious—the Pubert jokes are especially duff, with a notable bit of cleaning-up as Charles Addams' great gag-line "Congratulations, it's a baby" is amended to a feeble "it's an Addams". But the film at least has a consistent enough parade of one-liners and singleton gags to keep the laugh-per-minute ratio acceptably high. And Christina Ricci should get a film of her own.

TIME, 11/29/93, p. 74, Richard Schickel

As it happens, Morticia and Gomez Addams (Anjelica Huston and Raul Julia) are also in need of a nanny as *Addams Family Values* opens, since they are expecting Pubert—who is born mustachioed [The reference is to *Mrs. Doubtfire*; see Schickel's review of that film] It would have been salutary if Mrs. Doubtfire had been given the job, for it would have been a true test of her mettle. But the job goes to one Debbie Jellinsky (Joan Cusack), who sets about seducing Uncle Fester (Christopher Lloyd) in what proves to be one of the movie's less profitable conceits. Like the first of the Addams chronicles, this is an essentially lazy movie, too often settling for easy gags and special effects that don't come to any really funny point.

But as both its director (Barry Sonnenfeld) and its writer (Paul Rudnick) have been at pains to point out, the Addamses are a truly functioning, happily extended family, impervious to the discontents of middle-class civilization. Mom and Dad are passionately in love with each other, beamily indulgent of their children and entirely happy in their chosen life-style. "Is the pain unbearable?" Gomez inquires hopefully as Morticia is wheeled into the delivery room, and her enraptured smile is all the answer he requires.

They are, as well, ferocious defenders of their individuality. In the movie's most carefully pointed passage, the older children, Pugsley and Wednesday (Jimmy Workman and the divinely evil Christina Ricci), are shipped off to summer camp, where their resistance to huggy communitarianism and conventional good cheer is exemplary. They can't be brain-washed, even when they are locked into a cabin with tapes of *The Sound of Music* and other uplifting material. Dragooned into the camp pageant, they organize the other misfits and contrive to burn their blond, blue-eyed chief tormentor at the stake. Bless their twisted souls: they could teach Robin Williams a useful thing or two about what it really means to be "childlike."

VILLAGE VOICE, 11/30/93, Film Special/p. 30, Manohla Dargis

For those who missed the plot-what-plot? in *The Addams Family* a few years back—as well as some crucial *Simpsons* episodes since—Barry Sonnenfeld's *Addams Family Values* should satisfy the rerun jones. For starters there's a cute critter that pops out of Angelica Huston's Morticia like a dog from a bun ("Good news dear. I'm going to have a baby ... *right now*"), and with the addition of Joan Cusack, and so many gags, it's almost possible to forget the sequel's sluggish direction. *Almost.*

The spitting image of Gomez, Baby Pubert comes fully loaded with a shoe-polish coif, penciled mustache, and a burp as fiery as a domesticated dragon's. Less than thrilled, the existing brood of two, Wednesday (Christina Ricci) and Pugsley (Jimmy Workman), take their revenge by executing several weirdly comic, weirdly unsettling instances of baby abuse. Hoping to stem these murderous sibling rivalries—and give Morticia the time "to seek out the dark forces and join their hellish covenant"—the Addamses hire a nanny. What they get is Cusack.

A homicidal maniac with a weakness for pastel, Cusack's Debbie is soon on Uncle Fester (Christopher Lloyd) like a maggot on meat. The result is the family's descent into dysfunction: Fester becomes Debbie's love slave, the kids are sent to summer camp, and the baby sprouts blond curls and a hint of a dimple. Forced into the miseries of summer camp, the burbs, and custody of a Raphael cherub, the Addamses go into crisis, the joke being that one family's heaven is this family's hell.

Knowing nothing sells better than the familiar, screenwriter Paul Rudnick raids the pop-cultural storehouse, sampling everything from *The Brady Bunch* to *Carrie, Black Widow,* the Hannibal Lecter franchise, and Amy Fisher, molding yesterday's scraps into tonight's meat loaf. The result is that *Addams Family Values* is at once vaguely different (it's a sequel) and reassuringly conventional (a sequel with much of the same ingredients), just the formula for knowing *yuks*—as when Wednesday and Pugsley are banished to the happiness hut at Camp Chippewa and forced, à la *Clockwork Orange,* to listen to *Annie* and watch *Bambi.* Call it Camp Lite.

The mixed-aged audience I was with didn't always appreciate Rudnick's more burlesque badinage (Uncle Fester, craving carnal intelligence; "I've always dreamed there'd be someone for me." Gomez: "There's Thing."), and Sonnenfeld doesn't help. In spite of a winning cast, pricey F/X, and more than a few good lines, *Addams Family Values* is seriously undercooked. Clearly smitten with the Steadicam—which alternates as a Thingcam and a Pubertcam—Sonnenfeld keeps the camera moving but has trouble animating either it or his actors; the scenes are fast but so is a spinning Habitrail.

For the most part, the cast is either dead on arrival (Carol Kane as Granny) or missing in action (Lloyd and Huston). Nevertheless, there are four reasons to see *Addams Family Values*:

1. It's the queeniest PG-13 comedy since I don't know when. (Debbie greets Thing by popping his index finger into her mouth: "I'm good with hands"; the Camp Chippewa summer show begins with all dancing, all singing turkeys belting out "Eat Me.")

2. The divine Ricci.

3. The divine Cusack.

4. Paul Rudnick, who can be very funny, even when he's cannibalizing crap.

Also reviewed in:
CHICAGO TRIBUNE, 11/19/93, Friday/p. C, Michael Wilmington
NEW YORK TIMES, 11/19/93, p. C3, Janet Maslin
VARIETY, 11/29/93, p. 31, Leonard Klady
WASHINGTON POST, 11/19/93, p. D6, Hal Hinson
WASHINGTON POST, 11/19/93, Weekend/p. 50, Desson Howe

ADVENTURES OF HUCK FINN, THE

A Walt Disney Pictures release.   *Executive Producer:* Barry Bernardi and Steve White. *Producer:* Laurence Mark.   *Director:* Stephen Summers.   *Screenplay:* Stephen Sommers. *Based on the novel "The Adventures of Huckleberry Finn" by:* Mark Twain.   *Director of Photography:* Janusz Kaminski.   *Editor:* Bob Ducsay.   *Music:* Bill Conti.   *Music Editor:* Steve Livingston and Ken Johnson.   *Sound:* Steve Aaron and (music) Lee DeCarlo.   *Sound Editor:* Fred Judkins.   *Casting:* Mary Goldberg.   *Production Designer:* Richard Sherman.   *Art Director:* Randy Moore.   *Set Designer:* Keith Neely.   *Set Decorator:* Michael Warga. *Set Dresser:* Nicola Hewitt.   *Special Effects:* Roy H. Arbogast.   *Costumes:* Betsy Faith Heimann. *Make-up:* Coree Lear.   *Stunt Coordinator:* Ben R. Scott.   *Running time:* 106 minutes. *MPAA Rating:* PG.

CAST: Elijah Wood (Huck);   Courtney B. Vance (Jim);   Robbie Coltrane (The Duke);   Jason Robards (The King);   Ron Perlman (Pap Finn);   Dana Ivey (Widow Douglas);   Anne Heche (Mary Jane Wilks);   James Gammon (Deputy Hines);   Paxton Whitehead (Harvey Wilks);   Tom Aldredge (Dr. Robinson);   Laura Bundy (Susan Wilks);   Curtis Armstrong (Country Jake); Mary Louise Wilson (Miss Watson);   Frances Conroy (Scrawny Shanty Lady);   Daniel Tamberelli (Ben Rodgers);   Denman Anderson (Book Worm);   Mickey Cassidy (Bully);   Alex Zuckerman (Joe Rodgers);   Marian Zinser (Levi Bell);   Renee O'Connor (Julia Wilks);   Leon Russom (Shanty Lady's Husband);   Garette Ratliff Henson (Billy Grangerford);   Richard Anders (Colonel Grangerford);   Elaine Fjellman (Miss Sophie Grangerford);   Paul Kropfl (Campfire Man);   Janet Shea (Mother Grangerford);   Jay R. Unger (Sirus);   Dion Anderson (Sheriff); Mark Allen Branson (William Wilks);   John Henry Scott (Abe Turner);   Hoskins Deterly (Curmudgeon);   Mike Watson (Joe Turner);   Gary Lee Davis (Fighting Man #1);   Ben R. Scott (Fighting Man #2);   Russell Paul Parkerson (The Fishing Boy);   Kimberly Latrice Hall (Louise); Paul Dewees (Auctioneer);   Evelyn B. Bunch (Jingo Lady).

CHRISTIAN SCIENCE MONITOR, 4/8/93, p. 14, David Sterritt

Family films are making a comeback. There's growing evidence to support the con-clusion—from the success of a PG romp like "Groundhog Day" to the enthusiasm over "The Ad-ventures of Huck Finn," the most exciting release from Walt Disney Pictures in recent memory.

This said, it must be added that Hollywood is not returning to the age when most theatrical pictures were suitable—or at least not totally *un*suitable—for most members of a typical family.

Plenty of R-rated movies are still in the pipeline, and some widely hailed young filmmakers are escalating violence to new levels. Even movies that keep violence and action to a comparatively modest level—such as "The Crying Game" and "A Few Good Men," both contenders in this year's Academy Awards race—may include moments that would have been unthinkable 30 years ago.

Statistics reported by Variety, the show-business newspaper, demonstrate that the trend away from family-geared fare has been going on for years. Two decades ago, the combined total of G and PG films roughly equaled the number of R movies. By contrast, 1992 served up 305 pictures in the G or PG categories and a whopping 374 with R ratings. The number of PG releases has been dropping, moreover, even though PG films are almost three times as likely as R movies to hit $100 million in box-office earnings.

Despite the relative scarcity of G and PG pictures, older audiences have not given up on moviegoing, as some alarmist observers have claimed. Ticket sales to people over 40 have risen more than 80 percent in the past dozen years.

Still, Hollywood has much to gain by catering more carefully to this audience. Since the studios are driven by box-office statistics, the lack of varied fare is a self-correcting problem.

And a look at this summer's slate of releases indicates that the correction won't be long in coming. Variety notes that "The Last Action Hero" was specifically designed for a PG-13 tag instead of the R that Arnold Schwarzenegger's films often carry. "The Secret Garden," directed by the respected Agnieszka Holland, and "Dennis the Menace," based on the popular comic strip and television show, are due from Warner Bros. along with "Thumbelina" and "Free Willy," all aimed at younger audiences—and marking quite a switch from "Point of No Return" and "Falling Down," among that studio's current attractions.

Numerous other producers and distributors are following suit. And of course Disney remains a reliable source of family-oriented movies. Not all its releases are sure-fire smashes like its recent animated hits, "Aladdin" and "The Little Mermaid"—nor do they deserve to be. But it's good to know Disney is staying loyal to the family market even as it reaches out to older audiences with movies from its Touchstone and Hollywood Pictures divisions. And it's heartening to know Disney can still turn out a genuinely first-class production from time to time—as with "The Adventures of Huck Finn," a splendidly produced picture that recalls the studio's glory days in the 1950s, when live-action movies from "Treasure Island" and "The Story of Robin Hood" to "Rob Roy, the Highland Rogue" and "20,000 Leagues Under the Sea" helped give Disney a glowing reputation in the family-film field.

"The Adventures of Huck Finn" follows some of the oldest Disney formulas. It's based on a time-tested classic, features a young and likable protagonist, mixes action and comedy in about equal measure, and gallops along at a rapid pace.

Above all, it has a number of excellent performances, most notably from 11-year-old Elijah Wood, who plays the title role with steady wit and conviction. He gets expert support from Courtney B. Vance as Jim, the runaway slave, and from Jason Robards and Robbie Coltrane—two seasoned professionals clearly enjoying their ripely ridiculous characters—as the con artists who make Huck their apprentice.

The picture has shortcomings, as well. It's considerably longer than it should be, and some portions may be confusing for very young spectators. It's unfortunate that girls and women get little attention compared with the males of the story.

The picture also slides perilously close to racial insensitivity when it dresses Jim up as an African "native" in scenes that are meant to be funny but deprive the character (and the actor) of dignity in a way that doesn't happen to the white people on the screen.

These flaws aside, "The Adventures of Huck Finn" is exciting and entertaining almost every step of the way. Credit goes to Stephen Sommers, who directed it from his own screenplay, and to cinematographer Janusz Kaminski, whose rich images add much to the story's impact. Curmudgeon that he was, Mark Twain himself would probably have enjoyed the energy and style they've brought to the latest version of his enduring masterpiece.

FILMS IN REVIEW, 6/93, p. 190, James M. Welsh

Everyone knows *The Adventures of Huckleberry Finn*, published in 1884, is an American classic, but the temptation is to play it as a children's story for an audience of youngsters, to emphasize the story rather than its main purpose. Jackie Coogan played Huck Finn in 1931, Mickey Rooney in 1939. J. Lee Thompson directed a musical version in 1974; a television version was done in 1975, and now we've got the Disney version for the politically correct 1990s, minus Mark Twain's sharp satire, and minus the "N" word. Hence Disney does Twain, but never the Twain shall meet!

Huck is a feral version of Tom Sawyer, with whom he is sometimes confused, a roustabout wanderer seeking freedom from his sinister father, on the one hand, and those who want to civilize him, on the other, drifting down the Mississippi with his friend Jim, a runaway slave who also seeks freedom.

The Disney version tends to sanitize Huck, as played by Elijah Wood, a very successful eleven-year-old actor, and opts for cuteness whenever possible. This Huck is not ragged and skeptical enough, but Huck's father, played by Ron Perlman is sufficiently sinister in this illustrated classic approach marketed as family entertainment. Even so *Washington Times* critic Gary Arnold considered the movie an appropriate introduction to the novel and a "defensible diminution of the original," At least it avoids dragging in Tom Sawyer and Becky and becoming a crowd pleasing pastiche.

The Disney promoters describe the story as "based upon" Mark Twain's "novel about a mischievous boy, a runaway slave, and the mighty river that will carry them on an unforgettable adventure toward freedom," as being "in the great tradition of Disney family entertainment," which is not exactly the same as being in the greater tradition of American literature.

Mark Twain was a satirist and an awesome skeptic, but ordinarily satire is not in the great tradition of Disney family entertainment." Certainly *The Adventures of Tom Sawyer* (1876) fits that "tradition" more comfortably than *Huckleberry Finn* (1884) or *Pudd'nhead Wilson* (1894). Director-screenwriter Stephen Sommers, a relative newcomer, cannot maintain the satiric edge if he intends to work within that "great tradition of Disney family entertainment" and deliver "a spit'lickin' good time." Consequently, even Huck's moral decision to help Jim (played with dignity by Courtney B. Vance) escape to freedom is awkwardly played in this watered down yarn of friendship on the Mississippi.

The novel is episodic, so Sommers makes his choices and takes his chances: Huck's escape from his besotted "Pap," his joining forces with Jim on Jackson Island, and some of his adventures downriver, notably his encounter with the feuding Grangerfords and Shepherdsons, and one encounter with "The King" (Jason Robards) and "The Duke" (Robbie Coltrane) in a scam to separate the trusting Mary Jane Wilks (Anne Heche) from her rightful inheritance. Twain gives The King and The Duke higher definition and a wider context, but Robards and Coltrane catch the essence of these rascals. Robards is especially amusing as the ultimate ham, pretending to be the English brother of the dead Mr. Wilks.

The art direction approximating the antebellum South is quite good, placing the action in and around Natchez and the Twin Oaks Mississippi mansion built in 1812 and at Dunleith, built in 1856, which serves as the Grangerford mansion. Riverboats were located in Paducah and Louisville, Kentucky, and sent downriver. Scenes on the mighty Mississippi are mighty pretty and classically atmospheric. Working for family entertainment, Disney has probably fashioned a hit, and the movie may send some viewers back to the novel. One could do worse.

LOS ANGELES TIMES, 4/2/93, Calendar/p. 1, Kenneth Turan

In all the annals of boyhood, has there ever been a lad quite like Huckleberry Finn? Irreverent and intrepid, prone to doing whatever's handiest and not likely to let the truth get in his way, good-hearted Huck is the most engaging urchin in American literature, and in scamp-and-a-half Elijah Wood he comes to life more than he ever has before.

"The Adventures of Huck Finn" is in no way the first time Mark Twain's celebrated novel of a boy, a slave, a raft and a river has been made into a film. But not even Mickey Rooney and Jackie Coogan, who starred in two of the earlier versions, captured the spunk and the spirit of the boy who wouldn't be civilized in quite the way Wood has.

With a face lively even in repose and eyes like great dark saucers, Wood displays more of an irrepressible imp persona than he showed in "Avalon" and "Radio Flyer." Yet it is not just his wholehearted relish for pranksterism that sets this Huck apart, it is his air of capability and self-possession. This is one small boy whose survival on his own is not at all hard to believe.

Huck, of course, is not totally on his own. His companion is Jim, the commonsensical runaway slave he shares adventures and raft space with. Given how much racial sensitivities have changed since Twain wrote his novel in 1876, this part is in many ways even more difficult to cast than Huck, but in Courtney B. Vance the film once again has gotten it right.

An accomplished stage actor who was Tony-nominated for his roles in the original productions of "Fences" and "Six Degrees of Separation," Vance projects a natural dignity that is the more impressive for not seeming anachronistic. He and Wood have developed a genuine rapport, and their scenes together reflect the quirky sense of equal partnership that animated the book.

Though it is basically a PG-rated family film, boy's adventure division, with actors this capable "Huck Finn" can't help but interest unaccompanied adults as well. It does bog down seriously in the middle, when the plot pushes Huck and Jim to the background, and it also exhibits a tendency to be more preachy than grown-ups may find diverting, but overall this is a successful effort, a straightforward yarn that will probably remind parents of the kind of cheerful Disney films they themselves grew up with.

Aside from the stars, much of the credit for this should go to 32-year-old writer-director Stephen Sommers, who not only adapted Twain's book with a reasonable amount of faithfulness but also did a nicely self-effacing job of directing. Intent on telling the story, not showing off his virtuosity, Sommers demonstrates what you can accomplish by not imposing an intrusive personal style on material that is better off without it. Though Huck seems cheerful enough giving a boxing lesson to an unlucky local tyke in the film's opening sequence, he soon turns frightened when he sees a distinctive footprint on the shores of the Mississippi. It can mean nothing but the return of his dread father, Pap, and after consulting with Jim, who does a little conjuring on the side, Huck decides to leave town. But the evil-tempered, alcoholic Pap (played by Ron Perlman like Tom Waits with a mean hangover) is too quick for him, and Huck ends up having to fake his own death to escape him. But when he sneaks back into town disguised as a girl (a sequence of the purest hilarity), Huck finds out that Jim, who has since run away, is suspected of his murder.

Though Huck has been taught to believe slavery is the Lord's plan, he can't bring himself to turn his friend in for fleeing, and he agrees to accompany Jim down the river to Cairo and freedom. Aside from various tumultuous adventures, Huck and Jim ending up sharing more conversations of the "all men should be free" variety than is strictly necessary (or that the more subtle Twain would have been happy with), though parents seeking to instill good values in their offspring will not be likely to object.

Also not particularly inspired is the interlude Huck and Jim spend under the spell of those faux-aristocratic frauds, the King and the Duke. Jason Robards and Robbie Coltrane are solid enough in these roles, but the whole extended sequence feels overly familiar and clashes with the freshness that Wood and Vance bring to their parts. When those two are front and center and the film is concentrating on their more rambunctious antics, all feels right in this particular world.

NEW YORK POST, 4/2/93, p. 25, Jami Bernard

I don't know how Mark Twain would feel about it, but the latest adaptation of his Huck Finn book to film is a politically correct, spit-lickin' adventure that should appeal to plenty of boys, and maybe a couple of girls too.

Spit-lickin', by the way, isn't my phrase, but belongs to Huck Finn, as played by the endearing Elijah Wood. "Get ready for a spit-lickin' good time!" he promises the audience before Disney's "The Adventures of Huck Finn" gets under way. His intro manages to keep him at a certain remove from the story, so the scary parts won't seem as scary to kids.

Twain's Huckleberry Finn was a river varmint who hated wearing shoes or combing his hair, and spoke pretty much the same vernacular as the black slave Jim, with whom he rafts away down the mighty Mississippi. Whatever racist elements of Twain's day there are that would make the story offensive now have been softened into a politically correct haze; Huck catches on to the theory of equal rights much easier than he takes to a weekly bath.

The movie is helped by Courtney B. Vance giving a wise and dignified performance as the runaway slave.

This Disney version is big on humor and adventure, including an extended sequence in which Huck and Jim reluctantly team up with a couple of outrageous con artists, played by Robbie Coltrane and Jason Robards, involving a scheme to bilk some womenfolk of their rightful inheritance.

It makes an odd juxtaposition with an earlier sequence in which frightening themes of child abuse are raised. But the whitewash that Huck's famous contemporary, Tom Sawyer, once used, is now used in a cinematic way to avoid any lingering nightmares in young viewers. In another universe, finding out your father's throat is cut would be a crushing experience, but in a Disney film, sadness lasts only so long.

"Jess 'cause an idea is popular, like slavery, don't make it right," is the spit-lickin' moral of the story, presented in a moderately entertaining way by winning actors.

NEWSDAY, 4/2/93, Part II/p. 63, John Anderson

The standard line on "Huckleberry Finn" is that depending on what age you are when you read it, you'll see something different. And that's probably true. But it's also true that the book doesn't lead you by the hand: If you want to see racism, you will. If you want to affirm your prejudices, you can.

And that's why Hollywood, which would put an outboard and hot tub on Huck's raft if it could, has taken a dive every time it's had to deal with the nuances of Huck, Jim, their idyll on the Mississippi, and Mark Twain's subtle indictment of American hypocrisy.

We've had one version with Jackie Coogan, one with Mickey Rooney, 1960 and 1974 mishmashes (the last one musical), and never has a director dealt honestly with how a barefoot, ill-educated intellectual hostage to southern religion and racism comes to understand that almost everything he believed in is wrong. Which is why Disney's shiny new "The Adventures of Huck Finn" is such a delightful surprise.

Elijah Wood as Huck is a bit fresh-faced, but he's properly vulgar and young enough for his mind to still be malleable. He begins thinking he'll go to hell for helping the runaway slave Jim (Courtney B. Vance) and in the end understands that Jim is his equal, or better, because his nobility makes him so. Vance, who gracefully balances Jim's subservience and native intelligence, is not the pitiable Jim that Twain created, but neither is he some billboard for liberal bleating. He's impoverished, superstitious, and a victim of circumstances.

Together, they share adventures that take them down river toward freedom for Jim, escaping civilization, bounty hunters, and Huck's reprobate father Pap (Ron Perlman), who really is the stuff of a child's nightmare. One of the rather courageous things "Huck Finn" does, considering the young audience at which it's aimed, is treat Huck's abuse by his father realistically.

There are others, too: Huck's escape from Pap's cabin, which he smears with freshly killed pig's blood to simulate his own murder; the virulence of the racism Jim encounters; and the gunning down of young Billy Grangerford (Garette Ratliff Henson) by the Shepherdsons, albeit offscreen. Twain's Huck couldn't describe the killing, and director Stephen Sommers wisely doesn't show it. But he does show a willingness to include details that could offend, but which give his film a great deal of depth, and make the golden hue that saturates "Huck Finn" something other than cheap color.

There's a lot of compression of plotline here, and some episodes are cut—there's no Tom Sawyer at all, for instance. Huck's escapades with the Duke and the King (Robbie Coltrane and Jason Robards), the river rats who swindle the Wilks girls of their family fortune, provide the bulk of the story. Although they're on screen too long, Coltrane and Robards make for a comically miserable pair who use Jim as a pawn against Huck, and whose malevolence and come-uppance ring true.

And so does most of "The Adventures of Huck Finn." There are some maudlin moments between Jim and Huck, naturally, but even Huck protests when things get too mushy. And that doesn't happen often. All in all, no one is ever going to get the "real" Huck—whatever that is—on screen, but until they do this new Disney version is the best we've got.

NEWSWEEK, 4/5/93, p. 56, David Ansen

Every male American writer who ever grappled with the theme of adolescence owes a debt to "Huckleberry Finn." The vernacular poetry of Huck's voice is the source that flows through Salinger's "The Catcher in the Rye" and, consciously or not, must have informed Tobias Wolff when he sat down to record his own memoir of coming of age in the 1950s, "This Boy's Life." Written a hundred years apart, Wolff's and Twain's books are nonetheless haunted by similar demons: violent, abusive father figures, the search for identity, the push-pull American battle between respectability and wildness.

It's curious that a new Disney version of *The Adventures of Huck Finn* should appear simultaneously with three other films about the agonies of adolescence: Michael Caton-Jones's stunning adaptation of Wolff's book, Marshall Herskovitz's *Jack the Bear*, which recounts a 12-year-old's rite of passage in Oakland, circa 1972, and the French-Canadian *Léolo*, a wildly personal and daring journey into a tormented 12-year-old's psyche. Following Mark Twain's lead, all four rely on a first-person narrator to navigate the rapids of turbulent boyhood memory, the traumas of fractured family. It's as if the inchoate emotions of adolescence can be wrestled under control only in the relative safety of the past tense, In these movies, growing up is always absurd, and always hard to do.

The beauty of *This Boy's Life* is in the details: this meticulously observed story gets the look of the late '50s down pat and, more important, captures the dissonance between the era's ideals of nuclear-family life and the painfully deracinated reality of young Toby Wolff s life. We first see our teenage hero (the astonishingly talented Leonardo DiCaprio) heading for Utah with his giddily optimistic mother, Caroline (Ellen Barkin), who's fleeing an abusive boyfriend in Florida. But their fantasies of striking it rich in uranium prove a mirage; the boyfriend tracks them down, and once again they flee, catching a bus to Seattle only because it leaves before the one to Phoenix.

Reality catches up with them in the Northwest, when Caroline meets Dwight (Robert De Niro), a hearty, nattily dressed suitor who lives with his three children in the backwater burg of Concrete. Desperate for stability, Caroline marries him, hoping that family life will tame her rebellious son, who's exhibiting the classic signs of juvenile delinquency. But behind Dwight's awkward bonhomie lies an authoritarian, childish bully. He instinctively senses Toby as a rival for Caroline's affection and proceeds to make the boy's life hell. Dwight is a scary guy, pumped up with a particularly '50s style of know-nothing macho that turns violent with drink, but he's nearly as pathetic as he is hateful. De Niro, always at his best in volatile parts, finds a kind of monstrous comedy in the role.

Toby hates his stepfather, but nothing in this film is that simple: he can also see himself becoming Dwight. Smart and self-destructive, Toby is a boy divided against himself—he has dreams of a prep-school future like his long-separated Princetonian brother (in real life writer Geoffrey Wolff), but he can't stay out of trouble: he wants to be cool like the dead-end working-class kids he hangs out with, but he's terrified of getting trapped in Concrete. "This Boy's Life" isn't a polemic, but it offers a biting critique of the crippling codes of American masculinity, which honor false swagger and the rule of the fist. The only other boy who understands Toby is the town "sissy," Arthur (marvelously played by Jonah Blechman), his resilient soul mate in alienation. Scottish director Caton-Jones ("Scandal," "Doc Hollywood") and screenwriter Robert Getchell tell Wolff's story with something approaching perfect pitch. This is well-crafted Hollywood filmmaking in full bloom—moving, smart and made with passion.

The widowed father in "Jack the Bear," John Leary (Danny DeVito), has trouble with booze, too (a motif in all these movies), but he's basically a Swell Guy, if self-destructive. Leary is the "Monster of Ceremonies" on a late-night Oakland horror show, struggling to raise his children on his own. But as our 12-year-old narrator Jack (Robert Steinmiller, Jr.) tells us, that fateful summer he would discover "that monsters are real." The monster, it turns out, is an absurdly sinister neo-Nazi neighbor the boys call Norman the Zombie (Gary Sinise), who hates John and kidnaps his 3-year-old son. This outburst of arbitrary melodrama completely derails "Jack the Bear," which is essentially the simple story of a boy grappling with the death of his mother. Director Herskovitz ("thirtysomething") clearly wants to make something "sensitive," but he doesn't trust his material. He falls back on TV-style sentimentality, hoked-up drama and an overreliance on Jack's too precocious narration to explain The Meaning of It All. What pathos it achieves (and that's about all it has on its mind) is due to the good work of DeVito and Steinmiller. Written by Steven Zaillian from a Dan McCall novel, "Jack the Bear" is as fuzzy as "This Boy's Life" is clear-eyed. It seems more interested in pitying its characters than illuminating them.

"Léolo" is something richer, fiercer and more strange. Jean-Claude Lauzon's semi-autobiographical memory film is a work of scabrous poetry, a scathing depiction of a Montreal childhood in a working-class family that redefines dysfunctional. Defiantly non-mainstream, it dips in and out of fantasy (the 12-year-old French-Canadian hero, Leo, insists he's really an Italian named Léolo, the son of a sperm-laden imported tomato!), ignores conventional narrative and is filled with raunch, scatology, bestiality and adolescent sexuality. This is not a movie for those who like their art polite and easy to digest. But under its sometimes shocking and darkly funny surface runs a deep tide of feeling: there are scenes here that can break your heart, but you never see them coming.

"Léolo" is Lauzon's portrait of the artist as a young dreamer. To escape the literal insanity of his family, the squalor of his Montreal slum, Léolo (Maxime Collin) flees into his imagination. "Because I dream, I'm not crazy," he intones, his internalized version of Huck's lighting out for the territory. We're not always sure what's real and what's fantasy; does he really try to murder his grandfather with a noose? Lauzon is an emotional daredevil, but he's got the technique to carry off his riskiest flights of fancy: the grotesqueness of his images is matched by their beauty. Especially moving is the relationship between Léolo and his brother, who becomes a bodybuilder after he's beaten up by a local bully but can't expunge the fear that makes him put on mountains of muscle. Only at the end does "Léolo" falter: logic points to Léolo's survival, his eventual blossoming into a writer, but the cryptic conclusion leaves him literally suspended in madness (Lauzon reportedly didn't have the funds to shoot the ending he wanted). It's a shame, but hardly fatal: at its heady best, "Léolo" transforms the terrors and desires of childhood into exhilarating, dangerous images.

I wish I could report that "The Adventures of Huck Finn," written and directed by newcomer Stephen Sommers, did justice to its great source, but though it has some charming moments, an engaging performance by 12-year-old Elijah Wood as Huck and flashes of the Twain wit, it's a pale shadow of the original. While remaining reasonably faithful to the events of Twain's novel, Sommers has reconceived it as a slam-bang action movie with an antislavery message. (Courtney Vance plays runaway slave Jim.) Who is this movie for? The violence is much too intense for small children and the staging too archly theatrical for adults. Sommers never lets the story open up and breathe: he catches Huck's bravado but loses his soul. Ten-year-old boys may like it; the rest of us can find Huck's restless spirit alive and well (if radically transformed) in "This Boy's Life" and "Léolo." Or in the library.

SIGHT AND SOUND, 7/94, p. 34, Geoffrey Macnab

Mississippi, the mid-nineteenth century. Huck Finn learns his drunken, brutal father is back in town. He makes plans to run away from his guardians, the Widow Douglas and her sister Miss Watson, before Pap can find him, but delays his departure for too long. Pap breaks into the Widow's house and kidnaps him, taking him to a cabin deep in the woods.

Huck escapes through the chimney, feigns his own death and goes into hiding. Soon, he bumps into Jim, one of Miss Watson's slaves. Rather than be sold to a New Orleans slave trader and separated from his family, Jim has scarpered. He swears Huck to secrecy. Scouting for provisions, Huck learns that Jim is being blamed for his supposed murder. The two head down the river on a raft. Their plan is to travel to a 'free' state. After various adventures, they are waylaid by a pair of mountebanks, the Duke and the King, who recognise Jim from posters and threaten to turn him into the authorities unless he co-operates.

Hoping to swindle the Wilks family out of their inheritance, the Duke and the King pretend to be the long-lost brothers of the recently deceased Peter Wilks. They also double-cross Jim, turning him in for a $400 reward. But their schemes soon founder. Huck tells Mary Jane Wilks, the oldest daughter, that they are con artists. After the real Wilks brothers turn up, they end up being tarred and feathered. In the ensuing chaos, Huck manages to free Jim from the jail. Together, the two flee from the irate townsfolk. In sight on a paddle steamer which would take them to safety, Huck is shot. Jim stays behind to nurse him. He is recaptured and is about to be lynched by the posse, but Mary Jane comes to his rescue.

Huck is nursed back to health, and Jim is given his freedom. Rather than go back to living with Widow Douglas, Huck runs off into the wilds.

"All modern American literature comes from one book by Mark Twain called *Huckleberry Finn*," Ernest Hemingway once proclaimed, but the qualities which make the novel so important do not translate readily to film. *Huckleberry Finn*, above all, a masterpiece of the vernacular: its use of slang and dialect, and its choice of a raw country boy as hero and narrator, went a long way towards freeing American fiction from the constraints of English literary language. Its studied roughness is well-nigh impossible to match in cinematic terms.

Not that this has stopped the filmmakers trying. *Huckleberry Finn* was first adapted for the screen back in 1920, and has been a staple of American cinema and TV ever since. Twain's radical formal innovations have long since been taken for granted, and the book is nowadays regarded as the kids' adventure *par excellence*: natural territory, in other words, for Disney, the latest to exhume the story.

The Disney version may stick closer to the original narrative than most of its predecessors, but at times it risks embalming Twain's fable by treating it with the same fussy reverence as the BBC in their Jane Austen adaptations. Painstaking care is taken to make the costumes and settings historically accurate and to avoid anachronism. There are no bottles on display (in Twain's time, glass factories were thin on the ground) and characters smoke pipes, not cigarettes.

In its casting, at least, *The Adventures of Huck Finn* also errs on the sentimental side. Following in the footsteps of Jackie Coogan and Mickey Rooney as Huck comes the 11-year-old Elijah Wood. A curly headed waif who wouldn't look out of place in a Pears Soap advertisement, the young actor, like his more celebrated avatars, is simply too cute to make a convincing backwoods boy. His relationship with Jim, the runaway slave (played with appropriate dignity by Courtney B. Vance) is so coyly handled that the film's message about racial tolerance ends up seeming saccharine and condescending, more in the manner of Harriet Beecher Stowe than of Mark Twain.

Still, this is certainly a handsome-looking picture, bolstered by fine location photography. As if acknowledging the impossibility of emulating Twain's storytelling style, the script makes only sparing use of first-person voice-over, instead relying on the visuals to propel the narrative. These are frequently quite spectacular. Night-time storms, huge paddle steamers crashing into rafts, sunken ships, fog and fire all contribute to the atmospheric intensity. Director Stephen Sommers shows a deft hand in the action sequences (at one stage, he even wryly parodies *The Wild Bunch*, staging a rousing, slow-motion shoot-out between two feuding Southern families). The film may start in slightly pedestrian key, but once Jim and Huck's epic journey by raft gets under way, it soon picks up momentum, managing to remind us in the process that Twain's story can be read as a precursor of twentieth-century American 'road' fiction, with the Mississippi standing in for the great American freeway. Given the way that Jim and Huck are sentimentalised, it is scarcely surprising that the supporting cast end up stealing the film. Wizened doctors, acerbic widows, bullies, bookworms, curmudgeons and scrawny men and women are featured, all with striking physiognomies and quirks to match. Jason Robards and Robbie Coltrane, working in tandem like a well-oiled vaudeville act, offer a zestful, hugely enjoyable comic turn as the two mountebanks, King and Duke. Robards, an older statesman of stage and screen generally noted for his gravitas, is allowed to indulge his sense of the ridiculous for a change. Masquerading as an English gentleman, he adopts a cockney accent so exaggerated it would make Dick Van Dyke blanch. And Coltrane, pretending to be his deaf younger brother, shows Oliver Hardy-like dexterity as he develops his own flamboyant variety of sign language. After these two are tarred and feathered and kicked out of town, the film simply drifts to a mawkish, stilted conclusion. In the end, its greatest failing is the way it lapses into cosy moralising. Twain prefaced his novel with the following injunction: "Notice: Persons attempting to find a motive in this narrative will be prosecuted; persons attempting to find a moral in it will be banished; persons attempting to find a plot in it will be shot." It wasn't one that Disney were ever going to pay heed to.

TIME, 4/5/93, p. 60, Richard Corliss

America is the land of the perpetual teen. We want to stay young forever, to build longer-lasting bodies and minds nourished on fantasy. Let somebody else play grownup; we're all too busy being Aladdin, pledging for Animal House, romping in the backyard with a dog named Beethoven, living in Wayne's World.

In Europe kids grow up different—earlier and tougher. Parents still wield authority; Papa could be Yahweh with a toothache, and Mama could sell her daughter into child prostitution. Sad because Death hangs around the house like a spinster aunt, the kids must ever be packed off to relatives for whom child care is just the latest of life's dirty tricks. Sometimes the kids run away and never come back. No wonder children in European films often look like stunted adults. Since birth they've been in a dress rehearsal for distress.

The proof of these dour bromides is found in five new movies about kids. Two are from abroad: Gianni Amelio's Italian drama *Il Ladro di Bambini* (Stolen Children) and Jean-Claude Lauzon's *Léolo*, from Quebec. Three are from Disney: Duwayne Dunham's *Homeward Bound:*

The Incredible Journey, Mikael Salomon's *A Far Off Place* and Stephen Sommers' *The Adventures of Huck Finn*.

Blame it all on Mark Twain. His novels about Tom Sawyer and Huckleberry Finn established not only the quest theme for 20th century American literature but also the matter and manner of kids' movies. Sommers' brisk, pretty version of Huck's wayward youth gets most of Twain's words right, even if the music sounds like a TV jingle. Huck (plucky Elijah Wood) eludes his troglodyte father (Ron Perlman, doing an uncanny Tom Waits impression) for an eventful honeymoon on a raft with Nigger Jim (just plain Jim here, in a nicely balanced performance by Courtney B. Vance). Huck's runaway mouth gets them in trouble, and his wit gets them out.

The other two Disney films have similar plots. Indeed, add a female character and the two pictures have identical plots. In *A Far Off Place*, three kids in their early teens—a New York City boy (Ethan Randall), a white girl raised in Africa (Reese Witherspoon) and a Bushman (Sarel Bok)—find that poachers have massacred the white children's parents, so they resolve to cross 1,300 miles of the Kalahari Desert to alert the law. The cutesy *Homeward Bound* is the same story, with three variations: the family is missing, not dead; the hostile terrain is the Western U.S.; and the intrepid youngsters are two dogs and a cat (voiced by Michael J. Fox, Sally Field and Don Ameche). Only the species have been changed to protect the copyright.

These and other American films about children are like a progressive preschool. In them, youngsters learn social skills through fantasy war games. Most of the favorite American kids' films, from *The Wizard of Oz* to *E.T.* and *Home Alone*, are rites of self-reliance. Children face adult obstacles (or rather, superhero torture tests) and in surmounting them become adults (or rather, Hollywood's ideal of adults, as kids with weapons). Real parents are redundant in fables for latch-key kids; all authority figures are oafish, evil or, mostly, absent. The lost child finds his own way home.

The downside of independence is isolation, and it's in this psychological Kalahari that non-American kid movies dare to dwell. Some of 1992's most provocative and poignant European films *Toto le Héros, Olivier Olivier* and *The Long Day Closes*, to be released in the U.S. in May—are about children whom cruelty or circumstance forces to create a world of their own. *Il Ladro di Bambini* has this theme. The state has removed two children (Valentina Scalici and Giuseppe Ieracitano) from their mother's care, since for two years she has forced the girl, 11, to be a child prostitute. A native policeman (Enrico Lo Verso) is directed to take them to an orphanage, where Rosetta is refused. Thus begins a road movie in which the cop becomes a playmate, then a father to the street-battered kids, and the children learn to trust people a little. A little too much.

This much lauded movie has some of young Scalici's sullenly vixenish charm. But *Stolen Children* is also a little too pat in its direction and characterizations and in its dramatic arc from bondage to liberation to mute acceptance of fate's bureaucratic whims. For a movie that worms inside a child's hopes and fears, that understands how kids can be both shaped by their family and in righteous rebellion against it, you should see—immediately—*Léolo*.

Léo Lozeau (Maxime Collin) lives in a Montreal hovel with his surpassingly strange family. Father (Roland Blouin) is a brute laborer; "wrinkles line his face and reveal nothing but the age that dug them." Mother (Ginette Reno) loves the boy, but she is obsessed with bowel movements as nature's prophylactic—"Push, my love," she whispers urgently to the infant Léo, a captive princeling enthroned on a potty. His near mute sisters Nanette and Rita shuttle dully from fantasy to insanity, from home to the local asylum. His brother, muscle-bound Fernand (Yves Montmarquette), is so frail of spirit that he is prey for the scrawniest bully. His gross grandfather (Julien Guiomar) has tried to drown Léo, who can't wait to return the favor.

The rest of the family gets along well enough—"at times," Léo says, "their lunacies harmonized"—but he is an outsider, an orphan. These people think he is theirs. Léo knows better: "Because I dream, I'm not." He is half Italian: Léolo Lozone, conceived during his mother's fruitful collision with a sperm-soaked Sicilian tomato. A bright, lonely boy could not be the spawn of this horrid clan. Surely he is not destined to replicate their mean lives and dead-end careers or the madness to which they are all heir. And so, in this slum of bruised humanity that never seems quite human to him, where "the birds endlessly bitch about winter," Léo will scribble his thoughts about his family. He will erect a castle of words on the fertile ground of his imagination, on the fetid soil of his craving for love, revenge and escape.

Mostly love—or lust, since Léo is 12 and increasingly preoccupied with "the tail that swelled between my legs." The two scents, sweet and acrid, mingle whenever he sees his dream girl, Bianca (Giuditta Del Vecchio), a dark-haired waif who lives nearby. He has visions of Bianca standing in a Sicilian glade, singing Italian love songs in her thin, pure voice. Through the bathroom keyhole he has other views of Bianca. He watches her adjust her underclothes, then sees she is not alone. Grandfather is in the tub, naked, handing her money. "Sex," Léo writes, "I discovered between ignorance and horror."

Can any child, isolated inside his best instincts, survive for long, when family, school, class, the whole sordid world conspire to crush him? Léo can't. But Léolo can; his autobiography is saved by the one stranger who might have helped him. Certainly Lauzon, who testifies that this grotesque family portrait is based on fact, survived and thrived—to make a beautiful film. His story, in this boldly voluptuous telling, reminds us of two truths: no remembered childhood is so bizarre that it cannot have occurred; and the surest way to purge demons is to impale them on the page or screen—to turn ignorance into understanding and horror into art.

Léolo finally declares, "And I shall rest my head between two worlds, in the Valley of the Vanquished." That is where we all live, suspended between childhood and its haunting afterimage. Hollywood wants us to think of youth as a ripping yarn, where every adventure has a happy ending. Léolo sees childhood as the acid test for maturity.

Also reviewed in:
CHICAGO TRIBUNE, 4/2/93, Friday/p. C, Dave Kehr
NEW YORK TIMES, 4/2/93, p. C5, Janet Maslin
VARIETY, 4/5/93, p. 175, Emanuel Levy
WASHINGTON POST, 4/2/93, p. D1, Hal Hinson
WASHINGTON POST, 4/2/93, Weekend/p. 44, Desson Howe

AGE OF INNOCENCE, THE

A Columbia Pictures release of a Cappa/De Fina production.   *Producer:* Barbara De Fina. *Director:* Martin Scorsese.   *Screenplay:* Jay Cocks and Martin Scorsese.   *Based upon the novel by:* Edith Wharton.   *Director of Photography:* Michael Ballhaus.   *Editor:* Thelma Schoonmaker. *Music:* Elmer Bernstein.   *Music Editor:* Suzana Peric and Suki Buchman.   *Sound:* Tod Maitland. *Sound Editor:* Skip Lievsay.   *Casting:* Ellen Lewis.   *Production Designer:* Dante Ferretti.   *Art Director:* Speed Hopkins.   *Set Decorator:* Robert J. Franco and Amy Marshall.   *Set Dresser:* Dave Weinman.   *Special Effects:* John Ottesen.   *Special Visual Effects:* Bill Taylor and Syd Dutton.   *Mechanical Effects:* Lynn Ledgewood.   *Costumes:* Gabriella Pescucci.   *Make-up:* Allen Weisinger.   *Make-up (Michelle Pfeiffer):* Ronnie Specter. *Special Effects Make-up:* Manlio Rocchetti.   *Running time:* 133 minutes.   *MPAA Rating:* PG.

CAST: Daniel Day-Lewis (Newland Archer); Michelle Pfeiffer (Ellen Olenska); Winona Ryder (May Welland); Linda Faye Farkas (Female Opera Singer); Michael Rees Davis, Terry Cook, and Jon Garrison (Male Opera Singers); Richard E. Grant (Larry Lefferts); Alec McCowen (Sillerton Jackson); Geraldine Chaplin (Mrs. Welland); Mary Beth Hurt (Regina Beaufort); Stuart Wilson (Julius Beaufort); Howard Erskine (Beaufort Guest); John McLoughlin and Christopher Nilsson (Party Guests); Miriam Margolyes (Mrs. Mingott); Siân Phillips (Mrs. Archer); Carolyn Farina (Janey Archer); Michael Gough (Henry van der Luyden); Alexis Smith (Louisa van der Luyden); Kevin Sanders (The Duke); W.B. Brydon (Mr. Urban Dagonet); Tracey Ellis (Gertrude Lefferts); Cristina Pronzati (Countess Olenska's Maid); Clement Fowler (Florist); Norman Lloyd (Mr. Letterblair); Cindy Katz (Stage Actress); Thomas Gibson (Stage Actor); Zöe (Herself); Jonathan Pryce (Rivière); June Squibb (Mingott Maid); Domenica Scorsese (Katie Blenker); Mac Orange (Archer Maid); Brian Davies (Philip); Thomas Barbour (Archer Guest); Henry Fehren (Bishop); Patricia Dunnock (Mary Archer); Robert Sean Leonard (Ted Archer); Joanne Woodward (Narrator).

CHRISTIAN SCIENCE MONITOR, 9/17/93, p. 11, David Sterritt

For years now, it has been clear that Martin Scorsese is the foremost American filmmaker of his generation.

If this endorsement of his talent needs a qualification, it's that Scorsese's abilities have shown most powerfully in his most physically bruising films, from "Mean Streets" and "Taxi Driver" to "Raging Bull" and "GoodFellas. " Pictures with more introspective styles or themes, such as "The King of Comedy" and "The Last Temptation of Christ," have been less successful, critically and commercially.

So it's a pleasure to report that Scorsese's new movie, "The Age of Innocence," marks a stunning new advance in his already remarkable career. Thoughtful and reflective, it stands with the most exquisitely crafted films in recent memory, joining eloquently conceived images to an uncommonly literate screenplay.

This doesn't mean it's a perfect movie. At times its rhythms bog down in conventional patterns and its understatement crosses the line into languor.

But such flaws are few and scattered. Not often has an established filmmaker taken such a dramatic turn in mid-career, mastering a new set of challenges so quickly and thoroughly.

"The Age of Innocence" takes its story from Edith Wharton's finely wrought novel, which appeared in 1920 and made her the first woman to receive a Pulitzer Prize for literature. The book is a satire, aiming to expose and deflate the pretensions, inhibitions, and hypocrisies of New York society in the pre-World War I era.

It's a refined and sympathetic satire, however, making its points with such painstaking subtlety that one responds to its most energetic sallies with rueful smiles rather than derisive laughter. Its genuine, self-assured dignity throws into comic relief the forced, overtaxed dignity of the characters it portrays with a mixture of affection, approbation, and irony.

It is a work of deservedly high repute, in short, and only a filmmaker of unusual maturity would think of bringing it to the screen at a time when Hollywood embraces very different values in most of its undertakings.

The main characters of "The Age of Innocence" are Newland Archer, a young man of good family and progressive views; May Welland, his attractive fiancee; and Ellen Olenska, a cousin of May's who has returned to New York after an unhappy marriage with a European count.

Ellen's somewhat mysterious history has rendered her vaguely unacceptable to her New York neighbors, who—seeing her through the veil of their own proprieties, prejudices, and utter lack of imagination—feel there must be something wrong with a person who has wandered outside their gaze into such exotic territory.

Newland, self-styled liberal that he is, leaps to the lady's defense. Unfortunately, he leaps so hard that he falls in love with her. This rather complicates his feelings toward May and their wedding plans. It also raises the question of whether he will stand up for individual freedom by acknowledging Ellen as his beloved or cave in to society's expectations by disregarding mere passion and fulfilling his obligations to May like a well-bred fellow.

A great deal of this story takes place not in the observable world of action and incident, but in the invisible minds and hearts of the major characters. Scorsese brings it visually alive through two strategies.

One is to maximize the efforts of his fine cast by framing their all-important dialogues in immaculately arranged settings that support and enhance the emotions evoked by the carefully written screenplay.

The other is to bring key resources of motion-picture artistry into open and visible display, in a manner quite rare for a commercial film. Aside from adventure and fantasy pictures, most movies downplay their specifically cinematic qualities in order to absorb us in characters.

By contrast, Scorsese revels in the stuff of cinema, blending the realism of his settings and per-formances—which are superbly authentic throughout the film—with gorgeous displays of purely filmic virtuosity. The setting of a table, the lighting of a cigar, the view from a theater box may be shown through half-a-dozen different shots, edited into a quick sequence that's the visual equivalent of a musical trill or melisma.

Just as the true intelligence of Wharton's prose ironically sets off the rigid thinking of her characters, the expressive artifice of Scorsese's filmmaking contrasts richly with the stiff artificiality of the society he's studying.

Add the sumptuousness of his lighting, and the unfailing rightness of his camera placements, and you have a veritable feast for the eyes.

Scorsese did not make "The Age of Innocence" alone, of course, and his collaborators—beginning with Jay Cocks, who wrote the screenplay with him—deserve full praise.

Daniel Day-Lewis does his finest work in ages as Newland, suggesting more with an inflection of the voice or a turn of the eye than many actors can accomplish with their whole bodies. While the women are somewhat less impressive, Michelle Pfeiffer shows unexpected depth as the countess, and Winona Ryder rises touchingly to the occasion when the climax of the story allows her to break away from the earlier confines of her character. Also noteworthy is Miriam Margolyes, who almost steals the show as Mrs. Mingott, a feisty dowager.

Michael Ballhaus did the dazzling cinematography, which—like other elements of the picture—sometimes recalls "The Magnificent Ambersons" and is almost too lovely for its own good. Thelma Schoonmaker, a Scorsese regular, did the utterly astonishing film editing. Dante Ferretti designed the production. Elmer Bernstein, one of Hollywood's greatest composers, wrote the steadily effective score. Bravo to all.

FILMS IN REVIEW, 11-12/93, p. 411, Andy Pawelczak

Edith Wharton's 1923 Pulitzer Prize winning novel of manners, *The Age Of Innocence*, is about the world of nineteenth-century New York high society in which Wharton spent her youth. The novel has a complex tone, simultaneously elegiac and slashingly satiric, and Martin Scorsese's astonishingly faithful adaptation sustains this difficult, highly literary tone in remarkably beautiful visual images and contrapuntal words from beginning to end. We're far from the embalmer's art in this movie. Constructing the film like a formal dance with stately balletic camera movements and complex visual passages that are like Wharton's sentences with their imbricated clauses and hieratic rhythms, Scorsese gives the novel a second life in film. If anyone doubted that Scorsese is our master filmmaker, this movie should lay those doubts to rest.

Worshipful of visiting titled dignitaries and obsessed with family pedigrees, New York high society in the 1870s is as far from the democratic ideal as the court of the Sun King. Scorsese, following Wharton, satirically treats this small social enclave as the object of almost metaphysical reverence for its communicants, a kind of Potala Palace lamasery closed to all but the initiates of its sacred mysteries. Under cover of darkness all the usual moral delinquencies flourish with perhaps more than usual vigor, but in the drawing rooms and theaters the inflexible rule is good form and proper decorum. Newland Archer (Daniel Day-Lewis), a young lawyer and scion of an influential old family, is privately amused at the hypocrisies of his milieu, but publicly he's a standard bearer for the established social order. Engaged to May Welland (Winona Ryder), a pretty, seemingly vacant young thing, his future is a predictable and settled as that of an objet d'art with impeccable provenance enshrined in an eighteenth century breakfront. However, things change with the arrival of Ellen Olenska (Michelle Pfeiffer), May's prodigal cousin and the estranged wife of a dissolute Polish count.

Ellen is the opposite of all that society reveres. Though not beyond the occasional posturing of a beautiful woman, she's unconventional, spontaneous, and emotionally authentic, and her presence causes comment in the opera house and drawing room and then consternation in her family when she announces her intention of divorcing her husband. Archer defends her against the gossip and then falls desperately in love with her, only to be rebuffed on the grounds that if he were to betray his fiance and the moral code he believes in, he would be destroying the very thing she loves in him. He soon marries May, and the rest of the movie is suffused with a sense of absence and grief stricken longing as the lovers manque occasionally meet in their different trajectories and ultimately become the objects of a family conspiracy to keep them apart.

The literary critic Philip Rahv once distinguished two traditions in American literature: the palefaces, the tradition of the genteel domestic novel exemplified by Henry James, and the redskins, represented by such writers as Hemingway and Faulkner, insurgent explorers of social and emotional frontiers. Wharton, of course, is a whiter shade of pale, but Scorsese has always been one of the wildest redskins in American cinema (think of the Mohawk haircut in *Taxi Driver*), so it's somewhat surprising, though it shouldn't be given his talent and intelligence, that he's so sensitive to the subtlest ironic nuances and moral shadings of Wharton's novel. A few examples will have to suffice, though I could go on for pages. At one point, Archer pleads with

Ellen to become his mistress and run away to a country where such words as mistress don't even exist, and she gently but mockingly asks him where is that country. In the next scene, his wife asks him why he's looking at a book of Japanese prints and he doesn't answer, and we know without being told that he's dreaming of that impossible country of freedom and love. Scorsese uses a voice-over narration from the novel (spoken by Joanne Woodward) to fill in important information, and the device contributes to some of his best effects. In the same scene mentioned above, Archer smiles at his doll-like wife as the narrator tells us that he's longing for her death, and it's a complicated moment, simultaneously funny and chilling—a glimpse into the not so genteel desires lurking behind these civilized exteriors.

Scorsese's affinity for Wharton is less surprising when you consider the similarities between Wharton's world and such films as *Mean Streets* and *Goodfellas*. Scorsese has always been concerned with tight, tribal societies in which the sine qua non is keeping up an imperturbable facade, whether to outwit a mafia colleague or just to impress a girl or drinking buddy. In this film, he lavishes attention, as he does in *Mean Streets*, on tribal rituals—evenings at the theater to see the same play for the umpteenth time, endless dinner parties followed by cigars in the library, intimate tete-a-tetes-and compiles detailed inventories of all the forms of artifice in which high society swaddles itself. And at the center of the movie, as in so many of Scorsese's films, is a man trapped by the very social code he subscribes to.

Under the influence of his feelings for Ellen, Archer almost becomes a redskin, but he ultimately lacks the inner resources to light out for the territories. He has imagination, passion, and a vestigial instinct for rebellion, but he's also slightly fatuous and in a crisis his moral nerve is apt to fail. Daniel Day-Lewis has the right physical build and grace for the role, and an eager, charismatic smile reminiscent of Montgomery Clift's. In the bit romantic scenes he has ardor to spare—a scene in which he unbuttons Ellen's glove to kiss her wrist is more erotic than most things in film today. But he really excels in those scenes in which he has to register a variety of complicated emotions, none of which can be expressed openly in words.

Ellen, as played by Michelle Pfeiffer, is an obscure object of desire. The film is told from Archer's point of view, so we never really get fully inside the character, but Pfeiffer brings to the role both flirtatious vivacity and the passionate moral seriousness appropriate to this sensitive, extravagantly alive woman who is sacrificed to the imperatives of patriarchal codes. As May, Archer's fiancee and then his wife, Winona Ryder is a revelation, perfectly capturing the character's surface girlishness undergirded by a profound intuitive grasp of the real score and a determination to get what she wants by any means necessary. The supporting cast is uniformly superior, particularly Miriam Margolyes as Mrs. Mingott, the clan's bloated matriarch who sits in regal splendor swathed in lapdogs and is the final arbiter in everything that matters, and Alec McCowen as Sillerton Jackson, high society's suave, civilized equivalent of Walter Winchell.

The movie has a few flaws—the pace is a trifle too deliberate, for example—but they're hardly worth troubling over considering the embarrassment of riches. Fifty years ago, James Agee, writing about the ill-health of the Hollywood film industry, said: "When an art is sick unto death, only men of the most murderous creative passion can hope to save it. In either condition (of health or sickness) it is generally, if by no means always, this dangerous sort of man who does the great work." In our time, Martin Scorsese is that director. *The Age of Reason* is a great film, full of wit, passion, and solemn human grief.

LOS ANGELES TIMES, 9/17/93, Calendar/p. 1, Kenneth Turan

Imagine a society where any love at all is a love that dares not speak its name. Where proper form is everything, women are nothing, and emotions are so rigidly repressed that the unbuttoning of a glove can be a breathtakingly sensual moment. A world "balanced so precariously its harmony could be shattered by a whisper." And then imagine Martin Scorsese putting it all on film.

This was the problematic setup for "The Age of Innocence", based on Edith Wharton's Pulitzer Prize-winning novel of New York society in the 1870s. Skeptics said that the visceral director who made "Taxi Driver," "Raging Bull" and "Cape Fear," the man who specialized in characters who never suppressed an emotion in their lives, was not an ideal choice to take on one of the great romantic novels of the 20th Century, a love story of surpassing delicacy and almost agonizing restraint.

But just as the Wharton novel surprises by its velvet-gloved power, so Scorsese impresses by how masterfully he has come up to the challenge. His "Age of Innocence" (co-scripted by Jay Cocks) is a beautifully done adaptation of the novel, polished, elegant and completely cinematic. It is also a bit distant, a film that doesn't wear its feelings on its sleeve, but given the effects it's after, that would be counterproductive.

Looked at from another point of view, there is little to be surprised at about the director's success here. For a lesser-known Scorsese has always existed alongside the more celebrated one: the student of film history, the zealot for preservation the champion of pictorial directors like Michael Powell and Luchino Visconti, whose joint influence on this strikingly visual film is noticeable.

Aside from the expected potent support from cinematographer Michael Ballhaus and editor Thelma Schoonmaker, both Scorsese regulars, the director has the advantage here of a cast headlined by Daniel Day Lewis, Michelle Pfeiffer and Wiona Ryder and chosen from top to bottom with exceptional shrewdness.

Day-Lewis plays Newland Archer, lawyer, dilettante and a pillar of proper society in 1870s Manhattan. Engaged to May Welland (Ryder), the most eligible as well as the most giggly young woman around, Newland takes the nature of the social order he is a part of more or less for granted unless Ellen Olenska (Pfeiffer) entered his life.

Actually, re-enters is more like it, for Newland and Ellen were childhood friends. But Ellen's family moved to Europe, where she eventually married Count Olenska, an apparently dissolute type whose mistreatment has led Ellen to leave him behind and return to what she hopes will be the safety of the city she grew up in.

Ellen is also May Welland's cousin, and, as an unattached woman soon to be related by marriage, partly Newland's responsibility. So when he hears malicious gossips like Larry Lefferts (Richard E. Grant) starting to target her, he chivalrously moves, much to May's satisfaction, to act protectively toward his old friend.

But Ellen, spirited, independent and unbound by convention, is a woman unlike any Newland has known. When, for instance, with typical mock sophistication he archly tells her he loves his fiancée as much as one can, she replies with disturbing directness, "Do you think there's a limit?"

And, in fact, the more Newland sees Ellen, the more he starts to feel stifled by the society whose suppression of women he took for granted and the less he feels sure about his love for May. And when as an attorney and Ellen's friend he is called on by the family to talk her out of her plans for a scandal-provoking divorce from the count, the intensity of his feelings gradually comes into sharper focus.

But no more than gradually, for one of the ways Scorsese and Cocks' script is faithful to the novel's nuances is by demonstrating how imperceptibly society's strictures and his own qualms turn Newland into "a prisoner in the center of an armed camp." Essential in setting and keeping this tone is the decision to have Joanne Woodward contribute a letter-perfect voice-over narration that catches Wharton's witheringly ironic sensibility.

And it is not just the verbal tone that has been preserved, but also the visual one. Like the old master he's become, Scorsese (helped by production designer Dante Ferretti and all kinds of experts from a Table Decoration Consultant to a Chef, 19th Century Meals) has re-created a bygone New York with special, almost tactile attention paid to details like the way a cigar end was cut or how clothing was worn. For Newland Archer's world is a world of things, a place where creature comforts inhibit and suffocate life as much as ease it.

In finding actors to fill this world, Scorsese and casting director Ellen Lewis have been careful with even the smallest roles to select those, ranging from Miriam Margolyes' amusing Mrs. Manson Mingott to Stuart Wilson's audacious Julius Beaufort, who seem at ease in it. And he has enlivened the telling with an overall cinematic elan and a range of effects including a by-now trademark Steadicam sequence and expressive use of the old-fashioned iris close.

Finally, however, the story of "The Age of Innocence" (rated PG) is the story of Newland, Ellen and May. Winona Ryder captures May's genteel self-satisfaction exquisitely, and Pfeiffer, though readers of the book will wish she was rather more mysterious, is especially effective in the film's most emotional scenes.

It is Day-Lewis, who couldn't be more different here than he was in "The Last of the Mohicans," who appears to greatest effect. He is the ideal Newland, a young man whose sensitivity and poetic indecision are reflected in his bright, handsome face. Longing, loss and an almost indescribable poignancy cross that face as well, signposts of emotions that, both Wharton and Scorsese know, are all the more affecting for being inarticulate and unexpressed.

NEW LEADER, 12/13/93, p. 20, David Bromwich

"A magnificent story, beautifully told." "A fiction classic now a film classic." "The tale of an age different from ours, deeper and more wicked, rendered in its living tones by the wise artistry of Martin Scorsese." I adapt, transpose, economize, but the reviews of *The Age of Innocence* have been in this vein. It is the kind of film that makes reviewers want to use a word like "artistry." Indubitably art-classic, Scorsese's latest work is cautious enough to prompt the question: "What other classic does it remind you of?"

David Lean's *Dr. Zivago* (said a wit at the time) had a bravura moment when, literally, the Russian Revolution came around the corner. The favorite motif of *The Age of Innocence* is an ember glowing and burning cold—a piece of ash off the end of a cigar, a log shifting in the fire before it crumbles—and after several variations on the image I realized Victorian Repression had come round the corner. The most eligible excerpt for talk shows and museum lectures has proved to be a textbook-masterful shot in which a character, seated in an opera box, with a sweeping gesture of the arm takes in the audience below and seems to say to us in the movie theater: "Here are the New York aristocracy of 1880." In spite of the occasional grand touch (a missed rendezvous at an ocean pier; a romantic meeting in a cabin in the snow), the film is chiefly composed of smaller gestures—the snub or the artful aspersion, the pregnant change of subject that alludes to the enormous unmentionable fact of adultery.

What has happened to the maker of *Mean Streets, Raging Bull* and *The King of Comedy*? His career since the mid-'80s has been the swing of a pendulum whose poles are Religion and Hollywood. Religion was *The Last Temptation of Christ*, a *tour de force* of indigestible piety. Hollywood was the remake of *Cape Fear* that astonishing fantasy of the good citizen's revenge, originally starring Robert Mitchum at the top of his form, which Scorsese rendered more gruesome and less gripping with layers of extra violence and the sop of mystical redemption spelled out on the villain's tattoo. *The Last Temptation* was banned, *Cape Fear* netted millions. In interviews, Scorsese has said that he would have become a priest if he had not become a movie director. This seems to me an unhappy sign. It is bad for your art to want to get credit for your roads not taken.

Nevertheless, there was truth in his confession. He has always cared too much about the approval of both the neighborhood gang and the priests. But *The Age of Innocence* is perhaps best understood as a genuine attempt to win the esteem of the rather different priests who operate the high culture of movies. No one alive today carries the history of film in his head the way Scorsese does, scene by scene and cut by cut, camera-angle by camera-angle. It is the sort of knowledge painters have often had of their art, and, listening to him talk about other people's films or tracing the allusions in his own, one realizes that motion pictures now have a long enough history for such knowledge to be interesting. Martin Scorsese, however, is not equipped to reflect a similar intimacy with books, and in adapting a famous American novel his natural temptation would be to build a monumental tomb.

Edith Wharton's *Age of Innocence* uneasily honors the successful effort of a society to crush the rebels against it. A repressive moralist with a romantic conscience, Wharton draws her heroine, Ellen Olenska, from a curious blend of Jamesian elements. She is at once Isabel Archer of *The Portrait of a Lady*, and Isabel's nemesis Madame Merle.

Society is represented here by May Welland, the fiancée of Newland Archer and an apparent innocent. By stratagems we learn of but never quite see, she plots to defeat Archer's love for the Countess Olenska; as the circle of propriety closes around the lovers, Archer comes to understand that Ellen Olenska has mysteriously been withdrawn from his reach. How that happened is a revelation saved for the denouement. So the film like the novel gathers momentum slowly in its first half, for the sake of a slow climax in its final episodes. This form of suspense is the element of Scorsese's adaptation that most people will probably recall with pleasure.

May Welland is played by Winona Ryder, Ellen Olenska by Michelle Pfeiffer, and neither is a happy choice. They say their sentences well enough, with an air of discovery about talking in periods, yet there is no getting around the fact that these actors are new to this way of talking. It is 19th-century English spoken like a dead language. Lines Bette Davis would have wound herself into with a careless ferocity of unspent power are sidled up to by Michelle Pfeiffer with the elocution of a well-behaved artist who will not get things far wrong if only she keeps them sincere. In the romantic scenes, she is fine at pathos and on firm ground when she can draw out a whisper for minutes at a time, but her voice grows thin as it rises, and in her fragile dignity there is not a touch of secrecy or majesty, the quality of dangerous allure that Ellen Olenska ought to hold in reserve. Nor does she seem an American woman who has gone over to Europe, been tested in a corrupt marriage, and come back with perhaps a taint of that corruption. The healthy seductiveness of her deportment is in keeping with the lanky athletic tone of her gym-trained upper arms.

Daniel Day-Lewis, as Archer, seems a convincing observer of his own life, eager or chastened as the company of the moment requires; but he modulates his performance downward in tone as well as pace, to blend with the other actors. The director's treatment of all three characters suggests uncertainty disguising itself as diffidence, and diffidence hoping to be taken for sensibility. There is a minute choreography of gestures, without a particle of spontaneous emotion. As you chalk up the on-purpose effects that work as they were meant to, your sympathy passes from the characters to the cast and crew who are taking the exam together.

The worst default of invention is the choice to narrate big chunks of the film in the author's words (read by Joanne Woodward). Such bland omniscience is a second-rate way of gaining an impression of veracity. Narration, if it is done at all, ought to characterize the director's temperament—the way the speed of voice-over in Truffaut sometimes suggested an affinity with Stendhal—or else it should make a precise and necessary counterpoint to the images on the screen. Scorsese uses narration in *The Age of Innocence* to introduce secondary characters, to get over arid stretches of action here and there, to point out details he did not think worth dramatizing—in short, to convey information.

NEW STATESMAN & SOCIETY, 1/28/94, p. 33, Jonathan Romney

The parlour game of the year so far has been trying to explain the incongruity of Martin Scorsese adapting Edith Wharton's *The Age of Innocence*. Of course Scorsese was attracted to a novel of tender passions in 1870s New York, one theory goes: it's a story of male desire tightly corseted by a façade that can barely contain it, and the hero Newland Archer is at heart a soul brother to *Raging Bull*'s Jake La Motta. He simply wears fancier gloves.

Or, another version has it, the delicate construction of social hierarchy in Wharton's world runs parallel to the rigorously stratified underworld of *GoodFellas* and *Mean Streets*. The Mingotts and van der Luydens don't offer their victims cement overcoats, but they can inflict a social exclusion that sinks them no less definitively. I'm inclined to the idea that this project, with its spectacular opportunities for window dressing (the hats, the flowers, the alignment of the fish knives) is as close as Scorsese, cinema's most famous ex-altarboy, has yet come to indulging his nostalgia for liturgical impedimenta.

But at one moment we're granted a sudden, startling insight into what he is really doing. It comes when we see a house isolated against the New York skyline and, miracle of miracles, there *is* no New York—just a gaping desolation of earthworks, the foundations of what will be Central Park. And we realise exactly what *The Age of Innocence* is: Scorsese's first science-fiction movie.

In this extraordinary matte shot, the whole film crystallises and we know why we've felt so ill at ease until now: because Scorsese's film observes the laws of SF. However much we think we're in a known world, we always find ourselves adrift. This New York is effectively another planet, and its inhabitants aliens, however human they look. Like the famous revelation of the Statue of Liberty at the end of *Planet of the Apes*, this uncanny image brings the point home.

The SF perspective also makes sense of the film's voice—over, a transcription of Wharton's narrative voice. It's read in august tones by Joanne Woodward, who plays up the text's cooly ironic hauteur so that you can practically hear the arching of her eyebrow. But it has the made-to-be-skipped quality of the "Now read on ..." introduction to *Star Wars*; a mere genre formality. It doesn't guide us in our relation to the visuals; rather it seems like a piece of music added to accentuate the strangeness rather than domesticate it. The voice purportedly offers an entrée into Wharton's salon world and its habitues; really, it tells us nothing because the richness of the visuals effectively deafens us to it.

We don't want to hear; we want to see, and Scorsese's film is entirely about seeing. It is predicated on a fundamental misunderstanding—or a wilful misreading—of the book: the assumption that Wharton's world is exotic. It isn't. Wharton casts a critical eye on a world of opulence, true, but of *regimented* opulence. There, everything had to justify its existence by signifying in a strictly codified way: "a hieroglyphic world, where the real thing was never said, or done or even thought, but only represented by a set of arbitrary signs".

It is *not* the world of wonders, but that is how Scorsese treats it. Towards the beginning, Newland Archer (Daniel Day-Lewis) walks up a staircase leading to a ballroom. The camera seems alternately to give us his viewpoint and then to sweep aside so that we can pause and look in amazement at the paintings we pass. Are we looking, or is Archer? This dapper habitué probably would not pause to look. If he did, he would do so with a more coolly appraising eye than this energetic shot tends to suggest. There's a thrill in the verve of the camerawork that suggests the viewer's presence as Newland's shadow—or as agitated cousin from the sticks, agawp at this feast.

Likewise in the opening scene. We've already understood that this will be a singularly florid film by the luscious opening titles in which Elaine and Saul Bass create a rhapsody in explosive rosebuds. Now we're transported to the opera and as one character scans the hall through glasses, we're shown what he sees in a sort of optical *skid*: a slurred vision, created by a mixture of stop-motion and printing. It charges the visuals with a libidinal energy that belongs less to the character than to the film itself. We're given similar effects throughout: a blush of red over the whole screen, or the superimposition of a finely calligraphed manuscript on the image itself.

Only the fact that Scorsese is so respectful of the text inclines me to read the film's tone against Wharton's. The problem is that he loses out on the spareness and the banality of Wharton's universe, because he too is in love with its glamour. So he misses its fine distinctions, its irony.

Where the novel is rigorously no-nonsense about this small world and its stilted mores, the film swoons over its props: the frocks, the fabrics, the paintings, the rows of gentlemen's gloves neatly arranged in rows. Scorsese shows everything that the novel merely mentions. Things become lovingly deployed fetish objects, rather than functional signs as in the book.

But Scorsese is less interested in irony than in the "real thing" that Wharton's characters can't mention: emotional discharge. Everything in the film becomes eroticised. Emotions repressed in the drama are displaced into the seeing itself. Hence that plethora of visual swoons in the fabric of the film. Rarely did a supposedly naturalistic film have so much *body*, and so erotically charged at that.

It's as if the film itself were *perfumed*. From the flowers onwards, it is as much about scent as anything else; about catching a whiff of something—a historical period, an atmosphere redolent of certain costume films dear to Scorsese (*The Magnificent Ambersons, The Heiress*) or a womanly perfume more rarefied than any that Scorsese's films have yet contained. The scent subliminally evoked throughout is one of those fetish elements that attach to the story's women. The erotic charge of Michelle Pfeiffer's Countess Olenska is infused into the flowers that surround her and into the stronger, more exotic smoke that curls up from her rakishly tilted cigarette.

The perfume is just one of the ways in which the film objectifies women. Its visible counterpart is their transformation into paintings, immobile objects of Newland's "connoisseur" gaze. Two images stand out. First is the porcelain pink-and-white of Newland's fiancée May (Winona Ryder), less a woman than a conglomeration of rosebuds *à la* Tissot. Then there's a fancifully exotic matte shot of Countess Olenska by a quayside, blazing in Turner gold. Both are remarkable shots, as artificial as each other, but neither presents a real woman by any stretch of the imagination. Both are exercises in displaying desire yet at the same time containing it in manageable, ceremonial form. They are academic paintings. At heart, for all its fragrance, the film is an academic exercise, with all the uneasy repression that suggests.

NEW YORK, 9/21/93, p. 64, David Denby

In the titles sequence for *The Age of Innocence*, Martin Scorsese's painfully beautiful version of Edith Wharton's 1920 classic, one rose after another blossoms with ecstatic speed, the petals opening, the pistils and stamen rising like dancers breaking out of an enfolded crouch—all of this happening behind a transparent curtain of black lace. Opinions will differ as to the meaning of the sequence. Does the image (devised by Elaine and Saul Bass) suggest rebirth and endless fecundity? Or life encased in the vise of repetition?

In 1993, it's hard for many of us to understand that "society"—and formal conversation between formally dressed young men and women—was ever a reality in this country, a ground of moral action and choice. But it did exist, at least for a tiny minority, and even more fervently as an imaginative possibility in the fiction of Henry James and Edith Wharton. In the "Old New York" of the 1870s, Newland Archer (Daniel Day-Lewis), the scion of a prominent family, becomes engaged to a conventionally beautiful and accomplished girl from his own circle, May Welland (Winona Ryder), but longs for her older cousin, the Countess Olenska (Michelle Pfeiffer). The Countess, having made a disastrous marriage to a gambling and whoring European aristocrat, has retreated to the United States amid talk of scandal—a lover—at the time of her departure from the Continent. We can see, however, that she is guileless and good.

The pale Winona Ryder, flowers in her hair or at her breast, her figure corseted to the size of a slender birch, speaks in a whisper, as if normal tones would betray evil thoughts. For Newland, May is no more than a limited, unimaginative girl who will smother his soul in duty. He's right about May's conventionality, but he doesn't understand how hard she'll fight for what she wants. Winona Ryder has dark, glossy hair, darkly glittering eyes, and a certain suppressed feverishness, and we understand something about May from her whispering yet driven performance that Newland doesn't—that May is a lot less simple than he imagines.

For more vivid possibilities—sexuality, spontaneity, a wider intercourse with the world—Newland looks to the Countess. Michelle Pfeiffer, hair piled up in a spectacular mass of blonde ringlets, her body wrapped to her ankles in silk, conveys the slight strangeness of an American who has spent many years in Europe. She puts out her hand to be kissed, and Day-Lewis, with a grin, shakes it. At first the Countess is amused by the proprieties of Victorian New York; she doesn't see the nasty hypocrisy behind them and the danger of punishment if one goes one's own way. She's not exotic or regal—she can't suppress an American giggle on occasion—but she's bold enough to publicly invite Newland to come to see her. Pfeiffer is the most consistently beautiful actress in the movies since Greta Garbo, and as she gets older, her beauty, like Garbo's, has taken on an aura of melancholy spirituality. Not that Pfeiffer has developed a grand manner—her acting, as always, is precise and modest. When she is thwarted, her mouth turns down; her face becomes a mask. In *The Age of Innocence*, she is the classic, heartbreaking Wharton heroine, superior to her surroundings and to the men who never quite come through for her.

Scorsese has placed these three attractive people among rooms, furnishings, clothes, and social rituals of a density and specific gravity without parallel in American cinema. Why so much fetishistic detail? A word of explanation: Wharton's characters lack the pedigree of European aristocrats. In their past, there is no heroic service to the king, no land and titles, no *blood*. The Archers and Manson Mingotts, descendants of a commercial class, are what the Europeans would call an *haute bourgeoisie*. Hence their obsession with forks and spoons, and also their extreme distaste for divorce and female adultery; manners and "form" are all that stand between these wealthy Americans and the newly rich department-store owners.

Wharton satirized Old New York, and Scorsese and co-screenwriter Jay Cocks do, too; yet the tactile properties of Scorsese's style are so alluring that the social rituals take on a magnificence that defies satire. Everyone will have his favorite lavishly loony detail. Mine is the multiple pairs of initialed white gloves presented to a gentleman, from a silver tray, as he enters a ball (one pair per partner, apparently). As for the human furniture, the assorted lions and dragons fill out the corners with tremendous vigor, especially that wily actor Alec McCowen as Sillerton Jackson, a viciously dirty-minded society bachelor who enjoys other people's discomforts, and Miriam Margolyes as Mrs. Mingott, the shrewd old lady who sees through the society's phonier pretenses.

Wharton, I believe, never made up her mind about the value of this class—*her* class—but she was clear about the price that men and women paid for believing in it. The scenes of renunciation between Day-Lewis and Pfeiffer have the kind of taut, nervy delicacy, the high-flying tremulous emotionalism that no one in Hollywood has tried for years. Scorsese himself has never done anything with so much feeling *reined in* and the Elmer Bernstein score, saturated in middle-period-Brahmsian melancholy, adds to the mood of yearning. The question remains: Are Newland and the Countess doing the higher thing, the finer thing? Or is Newland a weakling—in the words of another American movie director, an "asparagus"? The dithering, overrefined male is both a plausible member of the leisure class and a character that Wharton inherited from her mentor, Henry James. Newland, convinced that he can fulfill his desires only by betraying everything he believes in, is thoroughly hemmed in. But are we meant to take him as entirely honorable? Or as feeble, even frightened, a man who lacks the saving streak of egotism (or whatever it takes) to grab the flower of life?

If you have a scrupulous hero, you have to dramatize every hesitation, every withdrawal. Scorsese, the poet of emotional excess, must have realized that repression could be as sensual a cinematic experience as violation, and in Day-Lewis he has the right actor for this conception. Day-Lewis has the height and figure, the generous nose and wide smile of a man of distinction, but his sensitive eyes could burn holes in satin. At one point, he looks at Ryder with such loathing that you fear for her neck. Newland is in a state of despair that his training as a gentleman gives him no way of expressing. The movie takes his point of view throughout. When he enters a grand ball, Michael Ballhaus's camera trails him up the steps, then becomes his eyes, glancing at other people, stopping a moment to look at the paintings. The camera flows along, but the editing is restless. Newland is a man, irresolute in his feelings, who can see the value of many ways of acting.

For all its plush fastidiousness, *The Age of Innocence* has a vibrant, go-ahead energy; it's highly composed and highly unsettled at the same time. And with so many barriers to free emotional expression, every glancing touch of the hand becomes momentous. The flowers are essential—giving them, wearing them, walking among them. They become a permissible sensual expression within the system of larger inhibition. Wharton ridiculed her society, but she believed there was something fine and necessary in it, too—a stay against personal excess. Newland is damned either way, but which kind of damnation—renunciation or fulfillment has a touch of the sacred in it? That's the unresolved question at the heart of *The Age of Innocence*, and it has been reproduced in the movie, which throbs with the passion of a moment unconsummated.

NEW YORK POST, 9/17/93, p. 39, Michael Medved

Everyone who cares about quality moviemaking wants Martin Scorsese to succeed with "The Age of Innocence," an enormously ambitious $35 million undertaking that represents a daring departure for the acclaimed director of "GoodFellas" and "Raging Bull."

The nearly universal sympathy for the audacious aims of this film means it will probably receive more glowing reviews than it actually deserves. Dr. Samuel Johnson once commented: "If a horse can count to 10, then that makes him a remarkable horse, but not necessarily a remarkable mathematician."

By the same token, "The Age of Innocence" may be a remarkable film for Martin Scorsese, but it is not necessarily a remarkable work of art.

For instance even though it is an undeniably gorgeous period piece, the lavish creations of 1870s New York often overwhelm the story and the characters.

The grace with which actors stride through the past in Merchant Ivory productions like "Howards End" is sorely missing here. Scorsese has gone to such lengths to give life to a vanished world that is light years away from his usual mean streets that he's established an unnecessary distance between the audience and the characters.

Another problem is the narration, superbly read by Joanne Woodward and taken directly from the great 1920 Edith Wharton novel that inspired the film. The voiceover serves as a constant reminder that what you're watch is a filmed book and thereby makes the people and problems on screen seem even more remote from the audience.

Nevertheless the story remains so compelling that most moviegoers will be captivated. The protagonist is Newland Archer (Daniel Day-Lewis), a socially prominent lawyer torn between the pretty, proper girl he is engaged to marry (Winona Ryder) and a fascination for her cousin, the scandalous Countess Ellen Olenska (Michelle Pfeiffer).

This free-spirited expatriate has just shocked all of New York society by returning to America after a disastrous marriage to a decadent nobleman.

It's refreshing to watch the gradual and guilty emergence of the attraction between Day-Lewis and Pfeiffer. They work well together.

But it's actually Winona Ryder who delivers the film's most outstanding performance, as the deceptively innocent child whose sweetness masks a clearly focused and indomitable will. Miriam Margolyes is also marvelous as Pfeiffer's corpulent, kindly aunt, an arbiter of manners and morals in New York society.

In Wharton's novel there is a nearly perfect balance in presenting the claims of passion and propriety; but in a visual medium (and in the presence of Michelle Pfeiffer), we get passion with little content.

Despite its noble ambitions and luminous surfaces, Scorsese's "Age of Innocence" can't make up for that tilt, or enable us to understand his characters' high-minded inhibitions. Their situation therefore seems more pathetic than tragic, and the film that dramatizes it is always stimulating, but ultimately unsatisfying.

NEWSDAY, 9/17/93, Part II/p. 68, Jack Mathews

We're on a stage in an opera house, looking out past the performers at a picture-perfect high-society audience in 1870s New York. The image is exquisitely textured, the ladies' gowns standing out in colorful relief against the muted backdrop, tuxedoed gentlemen in aisle seats cutting perfect black and white diagonal stripes across the screen.

Take a scene, any scene, from Martin Scorsese's adaptation of Edith Wharton's "The Age of Innocence," and you'll find this sort of lush visual composition, images that, as is often said of movies whose beauty overwhelms their content, are suitable for framing.

The master of contemporary New York's mean streets and mob life has mastered the past's Fifth Avenue and chowder society, and it may be the best view of the city we will ever get. It may, in fact, be the richest and most elegantly detailed look at any period locale since Stanley Kubrick showed off his painterly touch with the otherwise forgettable "Barry Lyndon."

"The Age of Innocence" is not otherwise forgettable. For one thing, it has Daniel Day-Lewis where "Barry Lyndon" had Ryan O'Neal, a talent gap that would have to be measured in light years. More to the point, it registers because its beauty cannot be separated from its content.

Wharton, writing her Pulitzer Prizewinning novel in the 1920s, was looking back on a period and at a social class where appearance—in dress, decor and behavior—was as rigidly prescribed as the crochet pattern of a Victorian doily. Get one knot wrong, and the whole thing could come apart.

"The Age of Innocence" is about that, just that, the possibility that one knot may come undone, that Day-Lewis' Newland Archer, a handsome young lawyer with impeccable breeding, may throw over sweet, uncomplicated May Welland (Wynona Ryder) for the Countess Olenska (Michelle Pfeiffer), a spirited beauty whose bad marriage and a rumored past affair have tongues wagging in old New York.

It is a story of requited but unconsummated love, and it is easier to relate to than it would seem. He wants her, she wants him, he's already committed, and she isn't willing to face the consequences of following her heart. Social pressure isn't what it once was, but it's still strong enough in some circles to thwart such romance.

Scorsese, who wrote the script with Jay Cocks, doesn't treat the love story as a particularly unique event. It is clear from the outset that such attractions occurred frequently enough to keep the scandal guards on their toes, and Newland, as well-versed in the rules of his class as anyone, understands exactly where each decision and each act could take him.

The potential reactions to him are dictated by the mores of his social world, and Scorsese sets that up with inspired perfection. That opera scene in the beginning, where we tour the audience as if at a cocktail party, is brilliant film seduction. Scorsese is telling us that the audience is the show, that the real opera is in their hands, and when that scene ends we know both the players and the rules of the game.

As befits a high-society parlor game, the fineries are laid out in meticulous detail. From the opening, images of sensuous, time-lapse roses bursting into bloom, Scorsese never stops laying it on. The food, the furnishings, the breathtaking street scenes are as unapologetically self-conscious as the period was itself. The will-they-or-won't-they? tension between Newland and Ellen dominates the story, of course, and though the romance is mostly one of restrained passion, it produces one of the most erotic, non-explicit moments in modern film.

Remember the graphic limo scene between Kevin Costner and Sean Young in "No Way Out"? Scorsese turns the heat up just as high in the backseat of a horseless carriage, where the fevered Newland fumbles to unsnap a button on Ellen's glove, just so he can pull it down far enough to get his lips on the bare flesh of her wrist.

Still, if the characters are a far cry from the goodfellas of Scorsese's past work, they are also the weakest elements. The dialogue is faithfully drawn from the novel, and we don't question their refined nature of the speech. But the actors read their lines as if the words were bubbles of blown glass they are afraid might break, and there is a daintiness to their movements that seems to be almost choreographed artifice.

Day-Lewis alone manages some authentic emotion. Newland is nearly paralyzed by desire and by the fear of its being found out, and the actor keeps those emotions in check just beneath the surface.

Pfeiffer seems to be more chipper than free-spirited as Ellen, and very little of the mystique and charisma of Wharton's Countess Olenska comes through. When she lights a cigarette in public, you have the gnawing feeling you're watching a Virginia Slims commercial.

As it turns out, Ryder's May is a much more interesting character, a woman bred to be the perfect society wife and hostess, and who, despite her demure manner and vacuous giggle, knows exactly how to use the power of class order to get, or keep, what she wants.

It should be noted that as the film's omnipresent narrator, Joanne Woodward probably has more lines than anyone. Scorsese apparently has Woodward reading from the novel to convey Wharton's ironic point of view, and with almost narcotic eloquence, Woodward does her job.

But being constantly told what we're seeing and what the characters are feeling finally works against the love story. and its setting, and denies us the joy of discovery. In adapting "The Age of Innocence," there was always the danger of making a museum piece. With a tour guide, it's a fait accompli.

NEWSWEEK, 9/20/93, p. 63, Jack Kroll

Martin Scorsese directing Edith Wharton? Are you talkin' to me? What's the laureate of mean streets, raging bulls and goodfellas doing among the Fifth Avenue patricians of 1870s New York? What he's doing is making *The Age of Innocence*, an enthralling movie version of Edith Wharton's great 1920 novel about love and honor among the old New York aristocracy. Honor—that's the key. Scorsese's films vibrate with the tensions of codes that are broken at the breaker's peril. Get out of line and the mob puts out a hit. That's what happens to Newland Archer (Daniel Day-Lewis) in "Age of Innocence." Archer imperils the stability of the social order by his attraction to the unconventional Countess Ellen Olenska (Michelle Pfeiffer), the cousin of his fiancée, May Welland (Winona Ryder). This highborn mob needs no bullets to eliminate the problem.

A superb screenplay by Jay Cocks and Scorsese is faithful to Wharton's Pulitzer Prize-winning novel. You can feel Scorsese's glee as he dives right into Wharton's world of moneyed leisure, 13-course dinners, nights at the opera, ball gowns, jewels and an ambience of respectability that can turn from incense to poison gas. Edmund Wilson dubbed Wharton the poet of interior decoration, and Scorsese (with cinematographer Michael Ballhaus and production designer Dante Ferretti) floods the screen with lush detail. An opera house simmers with white ties and black lies at the sight of Ellen, separated from her dissolute Polish husband. At a ball, an overhead camera captures the decorous dizziness of waltzers orbiting about the monogrammed parquet. Close-ups: long rows of gentleman's white gloves lined up on a table, plates of food like Dutch still lifes; silver cigar clippers that snap like pistol shots.

Newland Archer doesn't even know he's trapped in this stifling world until he meets Ellen. He fights his attraction, hastening his marriage to the conventionally perfect May. Scorsese knows all about the perverse sensuality of repression. In a carriage Archer unbuttons Ellen's glove and kisses the sliver of flesh, a scene so erotic that there won't be a glove left in any store in the country. This glove-strip is as close as Archer and Ellen get to fulfillment. A dinner for Ellen becomes a ritual of obliteration as the social arbiters, in a salvo of smiles, dispatch her back to Europe.

This farewell dinner makes the carnage in "GoodFellas" look superficial. In "Age of Innocence," it's not blood that's spilled but souls. Day-Lewis is the real fugitive of this season's movies, a man fleeing from his own heart. Pfeiffer radiates the sorrowful beauty of a woman imprisoned in her gorgeous gowns and gorgeous, empty life. Ryder, in perhaps the toughest role, makes May a poignant blend of sweetness and cunning.

Wharton, who died at 75 in 1937, would have been amazed at Scorsese, the guy from New York's Little Italy who has so perfectly portrayed her world—and herself. Trapped in a sexless marriage, Wharton found her womanhood at 46 in an adulterous affair with Morton Fullerton, a bisexual American journalist. When she wrote to him about "last autumn, when I held absolute freedom in my hand, and didn't take it because I saw that you thought I ought not to," we hear the voice of Ellen giving up Newland Archer. The velvet irony of Wharton's voice is caught in the film's narration by Joanne Woodward; Scorsese told her to be "like someone whispering in the ear of the audience."

Scorsese fell in love with Wharton's language after Jay Cocks brought him the book in 1980. Actually, it was six years after—when Scorsese finally felt ready to read it. "My parents were workers and never had books in the house," he says. "So I developed visual literacy." Once into the book, he recognized immediately the forces Wharton wrote about. "They're wearing different clothes, but their behavior isn't that different from traditional mob behavior. When I staged that farewell dinner for Ellen, the footmen around the table looked like sentries, muscle for the mob. It was like 'this guy Archer, he's not going anywhere'."

Since the upper crust aped English manners, Scorsese assembled a brilliant supporting cast of British actors like Miriam Margolyes as the dowager Mrs. Mingott, a female Falstaff, inundated by lap dogs, and Alec McCowen as Sillerton Jackson, a serpent-tongued Satan of gossip.

Scorsese and his actors became totally Whartonized. "I was struck by her understanding of men," says Day-Lewis. "It's as if she's seeing through their eyes." He'd often tell Scorsese, "God! She's right again." Twenty-one-year-old Ryder was fascinated by the characters' eloquent reticence. "Everything is said through a smile. You said 'Good morning' and you meant 'I want to kill myself.' But I've done that in this day and age." And Pfeiffer felt the dark power underneath the crystal surface. "Marty considers this his most violent movie," she says.

Scorsese recalls: "When I was 9 my father took me to see 'The Heiress,' the Henry James story with Olivia de Havilland and Ralph Richardson. It was a double bill with a Western—my dad figured he'd get to see the good movie and I'd enjoy the Western. I don't remember the Western, but I never forgot this incredible movie. I felt this emotional violence between father and daughter. My dad and I always talked about it. "His father died last month; "The Age of Innocence" is dedicated to him.

Scorsese has his own fix on Archer's sacrifice. "Maybe it's my Catholic viewpoint," he says. "Even if God says, 'OK, you don't have to give up anything, I love you anyway,' I still think we have to give up something. God may forgive you, but can you forgive yourself?" With this movie, he reaches another level as an American artist in touch with our sensibility and its history. There's a wonderful slow-motion shot of a street crowded with men, all wearing derbies which they hang on to in a buffeting wind. It's the anonymous urban crowd, but from the high godlike vantage point you can sense the person under each derby. They slog on to their destiny, heads down in an eternal age of innocence.

SIGHT AND SOUND, 2/94, p. 45, Pam Cook

New York City, the 1870s, Lawyer Newland Archer is engaged to May Welland of the powerful Mingott family. He is anxious to announce the engagement at the Beauforts' annual ball, partly to deflect the gossips' annual ball, partly to deflect the gossips' attention from May's cousin Ellen Olenska, who has returned from Europe after the failure of her scandalous marriage to Count Olenski. Archer wants an early wedding, but May is under pressure from her mother to observe the proprieties. Meanwhile, the rumours about Ellen's past proliferate, much to Archer's annoyance. After New York society snubs Ellen by refusing to attend a dinner given in her honour by May's grandmother Mrs. Mingott, Archer asks the influential Van der Luydens to intervene. Ellen is invited to dinner at the Van der Luydens', where she asks Archer to visit her at home. Ellen arrives late for their appointment and Archer is disconcerted to see her with Julius Beaufort, a notorious womaniser. Afterwards, Archer orders the usual bouquet of lilies of the valley for May and sends yellow roses anonymously to Ellen.

Archer's boss Mr Letterblair asks him on behalf of the Mingott family to dissuade Ellen from going ahead with her divorce. Ellen is upset, but accepts Archer's advice that the scandal would be too damaging. Archer is increasingly drawn to Ellen and, when May goes away on holiday with her family, responds to a letter Ellen sends him from the Van der Luydens' by visiting her there. Before he can declare his feelings, they are interrupted by Julius Beaufort and Archer leaves angrily. He goes to see May and pressurises her to bring forward the wedding. May is suspicious of his reasons, but Archer assures her there is no one else. When he hears that the count wants Ellen back, Archer visits Ellen to persuade her not to return to her husband. He finally tells her he loves her, but Ellen, who returns his love, refuses him on the grounds that she could never hurt May. A letter arrives from May telling Ellen that her mother has agreed to the wedding being brought forward.

Eighteen months after the wedding, Archer, still obsessed with Ellen, hears that she is visiting Boston and invents an excuse to go there. Ellen explains that she is meeting Rivière, the count's secretary, who is trying to persuade her to return to her husband. Archer begs her not to go back to Europe, and she agrees to refuse the count's offer of recompense. Meanwhile, Beaufort's business collapses and Ellen loses her investments. After Mrs Mingott has a stroke, the impoverished Ellen returns to New York to take care of her. Archer and Ellen decide to meet and make love, but before the rendezvous takes place, May breaks the news to Archer that Ellen is leaving for Europe. Archer is devastated, and realises that May's family and friends, believing that he and Ellen are lovers, have conspired to keep them apart. Feeling trapped, he tries to tell May about his feelings and wish to travel, but she forestalls him with the news that she is pregnant. She reveals that she told Ellen about her pregnancy two weeks earlier. Archer finally accepts his fate. Many years later, after May's death, the 57-year-old Archer accompanies his son Ted on a business trip to Paris. Ted has arranged a surprise visit to Countess Olenska, but Archer sends him on ahead, and turns and walks away.

Scorsese's *Age of Innocence* might have been subtitled *The Man Who Could Not Love Women*. The poet of impotence has translated Edith Wharton's acerbic scrutiny of the suffocating codes and customs of late nineteenth-century New York into melodrama, centred on a tragic hero incapable of breaking through the social ties that bind. On the face of it, the film is a faithful adaptation of Wharton's book, even allowing the writer herself a voice in Joanne Woodward's narration. The minutiae of the novel's descriptions of decor and fashion have been lovingly recreated, as the matching of image and voice-over testifies. This is a meeting not only of minds but of compulsions: the obsessional film-maker has found a fellow fetishist in Wharton, whose fascination with fine detail takes social realism to excess. And, of course, they are both artists who study their society with outsiders' eyes.

The shift that takes place in this adaptation is subtle—as delicate as Wharton's *découpage*. Newland Archer, with his cultural aspirations and dreams of leaving, is as much the centre of the novel as the film, and Wharton, who was herself an exile in Europe, was clearly in sympathy with her hero's longing to escape. Yet the secret of her success in depicting Archer's psyche is the distance she takes on his attitude to women. For Wharton, Archer is a flawed, contradictory character, as much at the mercy of his own condescending view of the society women who surround him as of society itself. Scorsese has softened the novel's satire of Archer, reserving it instead, through the use of voice-over, for the manners and morals of fashionable New York. For Scorsese, Archer is pure victim—of his background, the claustrophobic matriarchal culture he inhabits—whereas for Wharton, his incapacity plays a key role in the victimisation of Ellen, whose own tragedy as social outcast is given more weight in the novel.

Such distance as Scorsese does take on Archer is realised, characteristically, partly as a problem of vision. His film is literally an art movie in which characters are judged according to their taste and the audience is tested on how many paintings and objets d'art it can identify. The camera follows Archer's gaze as he travels from room to room examining acquisition after acquisition. But the connoisseur's eye that sets him apart from most of his peers is also his downfall. Archer's approach to life and love is that of an aesthete—he would rather look than act. To him, May's niceness is a curtain hiding her basic emptiness, but it is his own inability to see beyond surfaces that separates him from the woman he professes to love. His first sight of Ellen after his marriage is from afar as he watches her on the seashore gazing out over the ocean. He promises himself that if she turns round, he will go to meet her, but she does not move and the moment is lost. The scene of Ellen on the shore is reminiscent of an Impressionist painting, with sparkling sunlight and soft colours creating a highly romanticised vista in which the static figure of a woman acts as a kind of guarantee of order and harmony.

Ellen's immobility in this sequence is the mirror image of Archer's passivity and resistance to change. The seashore scene is poignantly replayed at the end of the movie, when Archer, now 57, sits outside Ellen's flat in Paris trying to decide whether to go in to see her. As her manservant closes the window, the image dissolves into a thousand particles of light and Ellen is safely locked away as a memory. But then, she was never real, nor did Archer want her to be, in spite of his token defence of women's rights. Archer's aestheticisation of Ellen is reflected in the portraits of women which figure prolifically in the film, as well as in the painterly poses which the characters take up from time to time. And it is there in Archer's fetishism, his fixation on Ellen's shoe, her pink parasol, the whisper of her skirts, revealing that the emptiness or lack he so despises in May is actually at the heart of masculinity. Once again, Scorsese creates a dark, pessimistic vision of male desire in which woman is never more than an alibi.

But what if the woman should move? In 1920, when Wharton wrote *The Age of Innocence*, women were certainly on the move, and the novel registers, in the outcast figure of Countess Olenska, the social anxieties attendant on their economic and sexual emancipation. This clearly struck a chord with Scorsese, whose Archer is both dismayed by Ellen's unconventional behaviour and panic-stricken by May's single-mindedness. In the crucial scene in which his wife tells him she is pregnant, dashing for good his hopes of following Ellen to Europe, she rises from her chair and towers over him, causing him to recoil. Scorsese films her gesture twice, the second time focusing on the bustle-encased lower half of her body and heightening the rustle of her skirt. It is a powerful image of male terror in the face of the maternal body.

Scorsese seems unexpectedly at home with period drama, taking more than one cue from that other saga of social change and doomed love, *The Magnificent Ambersons*. As in Welles' film, the tension between tradition and modernity is signalled by the use of irises and masking, which looks back to silent cinema while at the same time acting as harbinger of the new medium about to take the late nineteenth century by storm. *The Magnificent Ambersons* is melancholic, treating its characters swept up in the tide of history with sympathy and projecting a sense of loss at what is sacrificed in the name of progress. At first glance, Scorsese's movie is less nostalgic, ending on a hopeful note which recognises that Archer's children will achieve the happiness he denied himself. For Scorsese, as for Wharton, Archer's final decision to walk away from love is the last nail in the coffin of the past in which he is entombed. Yet it is clear that the film-maker, more than the novelist, identifies with Archer's desire to live in his memories rather than face reality. Scorsese's *Age of Innocence* is suffused with fear of loss, most notably in its striving for period authenticity (always a lost cause) and in its obsession with faithfully reproducing the novel.

This lends the film a static, stultified quality which is entirely appropriate to Daniel Day-Lewis' frozen stiffness as Archer, but does less justice to the freewheeling body language of more unconventional characters, such as Julius Beaufort, played with vulgar verve by Stuart Wilson, or Michelle Pfeiffer's Ellen, who strides out with an appealing mannish swagger. All the performances are excellent, and the production is a visual *tour de force*; but it really is time to lift the shroud of despair.

TIME, 9/20/93, p. 82, Richard Corliss

In the New York Society of the 1870s, Newland Archer (Daniel Day-Lewis) is a true romantic gentleman. He is romantic because he wants to shrug off the opera cape of domestic respectability and follow his heart to hell with the Countess Olenska (Michelle Pfeiffer). He is a gentleman because, having already declared his love to pretty May Welland (Winona Ryder), he is bound to behave honorably. He knows that when passion and propriety collide, only bitter defeat may rise from the wreckage.

Newland is the hero of Edith Wharton's 1920 novel *The Age of Innocence*, and in his emotional corset he may seem a supporting player in life's melodrama, as far from the noisy concerns of our day as Polonius. The drawing-room virtues of reticence and gentility are considered dead in the Age of Prurience. Yet they still govern our lives whenever we check an impulse to explode in love or anger—when we don't shout at a reckless motorist, or we keep quiet when we mean to proclaim our ardor. If Richard Kimble is a hero for our fugitive fantasy egos, Newland Archer is the patron saint of our everyday conscience, the coachman on our journey as the years dissolve into decades and the decades into decay.

Wharton was a poet of repression. Another New Yorker, Martin Scorsese, is the bard of belligerence, the ace depictor of raging bulls. What could Wharton mean to Scorsese? Everything, it turns out: his faithful adaptation of *The Age of Innocence* (written with Jay Cocks, a TIME contributor) is a gravely beautiful fairy tale of longing and loss.

The heroine is Ellen Olenska, May's cousin, now separated from her European aristocrat husband and thus the subject of purring rumor from the town's smooth hypocrites. As the radiantly giddy May seems a child to Newland, so he feels like a boy in Ellen's presence. The two fall in furtive love. But it is not falling so much as tiptoeing in the dark. Once he kisses her slipper; later he unbuttons her glove and kisses her wrist, then her mouth, which opens more in anguish than in lust. Guilt is the barrier between their lips. And both could be underestimating sweet May; the child has a will and means of her own.

Scorsese's style is still intelligently abustle: fast dissolves of an opera audience, a quiet riot of gold when the blond countess receives yellow roses from Newland, a slow-motion vignette of working men—the people whose labor subsidizes the idle class. Throughout, he shows he can be as attentive to the tiniest twinges of the heart as he has been to the gunfire of taxi drivers' and goodfellas. Here, instead of shouting, people speak softly and in code. The movie is 135 thrilling minutes waiting for someone to come to the point. And that is the point: a man is at risk in this society if he says what he thinks or does what he feels.

The three stars (Day-Lewis superbly stooped by rectitude, Pfeiffer so elegant and bruised, Ryder a young Audrey Hepburn in all her wide-eyed guile) are swathed in glamorous costumes and period decor. The congestion of old masters on a matron's wall suggests the confined space in which the story unfolds and the straitened notions to which Newland and Ellen must pay homage. The handsomely fussy design is meant to dazzle and deaden the viewer's senses—as Newland is seduced by Ellen and suffocated by May.

The story is finally May's triumph, Ellen's rue, Newland's muted ruin. For him it is a tragedy, because he has been made aware of joys anticipated, delayed, crushed. Frequently he rewrites the tryst in his mind: one moment when Ellen might have caressed him, another when she could have turned around, smiled and changed his life.

Why can't we love without hurting people, without being devoured? That is a child's question, of course, and so plaintive because it can't be answered. Listening to this urgent whisper against the constraints of civilization, you can hear an old Scorsese bull snort under its breath. This is the rage of innocence.

VILLAGE VOICE, 9/21/93, p. 55, Georgia Brown

Well, Scorsese's *The Age of Innocence* finally meets its public. A woman friend calls the film a male weepie. A male who wept says it's Marty's *Leopard*, his most Italian film yet. A fan who's seen it twice, and is poised to return, views the film as a Rorschach and predicts vast disagreements over who's worth weeping for. If you don't know Edith Wharton's 1920 novel, the inward-leaning figures on screen—reticent, opaque, suffering in such decorous, decorated silences—may be hard to *place*, much less surrender your heart to. If you do know the book, they're still difficult.

The film is sumptuous, layered, meticulously controlled, stringent, and enigmatic; it shifts under the gaze. It's not, like *GoodFellas*, a gripper, and isn't meant to be. Once more, Scorsese has swung to another pole, fastidiously groping in a fastidious world. It's easy to show passion. But to show passion's silences?

Scorsese and his collaborator Jay Cocks are almost religiously respectful of Wharton's novel. Like an archeologist, Scorsese goes to every length in recreating the 1870s to get the second and third of a 13-course dinner precisely, to recreate paintings mentioned in the novel and imagine unmentioned paintings. A couple of stunning recreations of New York streetscapes make you gape: Okay, how'd they do *that*? There's an awesome collection of period paraphernalia here. (Dante Ferretti, who worked for Pasolini and Fellini, is the production designer.)

The movie's strategy is to impress us with the vast sensuous layer over the hidden one. Wharton's story concerns people who live in a "hieroglyphic world." Paying so much attention to detail, to codes of correctness, they're almost wholly distracted from their inner lives. In returning to the 1870s in her late fifties, Wharton was revisiting her youth, recreating the aura seeping invisibly from brownstones along lower Fifth Avenue, the gases that nearly stifled her.

The story is simple. Just as Newland Archer (Daniel Day-Lewis) and May Welland (Winona Ryder) announce their engagement, an older cousin of May's, the Countess Ellen Olenska (Michelle Pfeiffer), retreats from Europe, a whiff of scandal following. According to rumors, she's seeking a divorce from a caddish husband. Immediately, however, the countess beckons Archer enticingly. Come on over. Call on me. Tomorrow at five, then? Help me, Obi-Wan Kenobi, you're my only hope.

It's not clear whether Wharton or Scorsese mean the countess to be an aggressor, a tease, but, given Archer and May's announcement, she is. Her demeanor is careless, blunt, her manners as frizzy as her hair. She's a version of *Cape Fear*'s Max Cady, come to shake up the cozy, if fetid nest.

The heroes of *Taxi Driver* and *The Last Temptation of Christ* conceive it their mission to lift up a fallen woman. Here again the male's protective instinct—along with the sexual—is aroused. He resents how she's snubbed by the local powers. Her tastes and irreverence seem fresh to him. Archer has pretensions to broader, more cosmopolitan sensibilities (though nothing in his inner monologue persuades me of his depth). He starts viewing the eternally virginal May—always associated with white—less as a blank slate (on which he intended to write) and more as an empty vessel.

Newland Archer (James's Christopher Newman, *The American*, and Isabel Archer?) is the novel's point of view. But is he reliable? The two women are seen entirely through his eyes. Exchanging one ideal (chastity, innocence) for another, he interprets May and Ellen through his own emotional needs—reducing, typing, and destroying. I see him as another version of Ethan Frome—on the surface sympathetic for his wound, but essentially a man who turns women into monsters out of fear.

Deceived or not, Archer suffers. So does the countess. The lover's vocation (renunciation) is like a priest's. Inside, Archer creates a little private chapel, a "sanctuary" says the novel, a shrine. At the end, middle-aged and gray, he's virtually absent, preferring fantasy to reality. Day-Lewis takes on a dreamy but desiccated stare, and when he exits, the effect is so much less than Lancaster's in *The Leopard*.

This is why I love how Scorsese, inadvertently or not, rescues May from Archer's—and Wharton's—disdain. Or perhaps Ryder is simply electrifying; every time she's on screen she's riveting. (Perhaps Scorsese is tipping his hand by inserting himself as her bridal photographer. Father of two daughters, he can't resist capturing the wedding.) May is always turning, surprised, smiling like a radiant sunbeam at the camera—that is, at the increasingly insentient Archer. Her studied speech patterns—meant to show how much a creature of artifice she is—are filled with nuance. She's wily and clever and, more often than not, right about Archer. She's fighting for her life and their children. The movie makes me feel a great pity for wives.

What I find most moving (perversely maybe) aren't the agonizingly chaste love scenes between Archer and the countess but the painful domestic awkwardnesses between him and May. How gingerly they treat each other—carefulness somehow masking genuine care. Bound by decorum, they can easily avoid intimacy for a whole lifetime. His longing for the countess comes to seem like another way to evade what's nearby.

Despite her desire to be identified with James, Wharton the writer really was closer to Sinclair Lewis (who dedicated *Babbitt* to her). Basically, a satirist, she's a literal, almost didactic writer, not delicate or subtle, as she's treated here. She hammers at her themes: How thoroughly people are trapped by the rigid customs of the country. How women especially are bullied into preferring imitation over imagination. (Not a lot has changed here.) As Edmund Wilson, back in 1926, made the distinction, "Henry James, except at very rare moments, was never a preacher or a bitter social satirist; but Mrs. Wharton was perhaps the first American to write with indignant passion *against* American values as they had come to present themselves by the end of the last century."

Despite her effective polemics, Wharton's main characters in *The Age of Innocence* remain shadowy and insubstantial. Since Scorsese seems increasingly to have trouble creating people we care deeply about, this elegy of manners may be a doubly distanced project. Both times I've seen it, the movie left me slightly stunned, but by what I'm still not sure. Desire for desire?

What do you say about a reviewer who can't make up her mind? This is such a strange, beautiful, difficult movie, it's almost surreal. It makes me wonder if I saw what I think I saw or if I've just invented everything.

Also reviewed in:
CHICAGO TRIBUNE, 9/17/93, Friday/p. A, Michael Wilmington
NATION, 10/4/93, p. 364, Stuart Klawans
NEW REPUBLIC, 10/18/93, p. 30, Stanley Kauffmann
NEW YORK TIMES, 9/17/93, p. C1, Vincent Canby
NEW YORKER, 9/13/93, p. 121, Anthony Lane
VARIETY, 9/13/93, p. 31, Todd McCarthy
WASHINGTON POST, 9/17/93, p. D1, Rita Kempley
WASHINGTON POST, 9/17/93, Weekend/p. 52, Desson Howe

AIRBORNE

A Warner Bros. release of an Icon production. *Producer:* Bruce Davey and Stephen McEveety. *Director:* Rob Bowman. *Screenplay:* Bill Apablasa. *Story:* Bill Apablasa and Stephen McEveety. *Director of Photography:* Daryn Okada. *Editor:* Harry B. Miller III. *Music:* Stewart Copeland. *Sound:* Christopher Sheldon and Dane A. Davis. *Casting:* Robert J. Ulrich and Eric Dawson. *Production Designer:* John Myhre. *Stunt Coordinator:* Pat Parnell. *Running time:* 90 minutes. *MPAA Rating:* PG.

CAST: Shane McDermott (Mitchell); Seth Green (Wiley); Brittney Powell (Nikki); Chris Conrad (Jack); Edie McClurg (Aunt Irene); Patrick O'Brien (Uncle Louis); Jack Black (Augie); Jacob Vargas (Snake).

LOS ANGELES TIMES, 9/20/93, Calendar/p. 6, Chris Willman

As the first major filmic celebration of in-line skating and holy Rollerbladers, "Airborne" is hell on wheels and itchy limbo off. The occasional action scenes are as appropriately tortuous as the tired teen-out-of-water plot is torturous. This is a kid-flick that's speed-skating on one leg.

In the last 10 minutes or so, the picture actually lives up to its name and achieves a kind of movie liftoff. This climax is an exhilaratingly filmed race down the winding streets of a long Cincinnati hill between two teams of serious street skaters—around deadly curves, over parked cars, under skidding trucks, down sets of stairways (!), smack into trees and lakes. Kids will cheer this expert mayhem, while brittler-boned viewers may react to the danger by unconsciously massaging their intact joints.

If it weren't for the obvious illegality of this final life-and limb-endangering competition, the otherwise benign "Airborne" would probably bear a G rating instead of a PG. (It's surprising that Warner Bros. didn't put it out under the company's new Family Films imprint.) Off the blades, it's at best mediocre Nickelodeon fare. You keep itching for director Rob Bowman to wind up the puppy-love drama and bring on the action climax, in much the way that at home you might keep the TV burning waiting for Nick at Night to kick in.

Shane McDermott (of the TV soap "Swan's Crossing") plays Mitchell Goosen, a SoCal high-schooler heavy into boards and blades whose traveling parents send him to stay with relatives in Cincinnati for six months. Our severely bummed transplant has trouble making friends in Ohio—as he well ought, uttering movie surf-speak like "Como esta, ladies" and "Chill, man, let it go."

Soon, in the tradition of all filmic pretty boys from James Dean on, he's inexplicably become the target of every jock in his new school while acting as a chick magnet for all their girlfriends. If you had to choose your poison, this might be it.

Even in this unpopularity, Mitchell tends toward an irritating cockiness, so you keep waiting for him to get some kind of transforming comeuppance before he finally gives the bullies theirs. But character development is beyond this script's scope. The jocks just happen to be hockey nuts, so all the hero has to do is wait for the chance to butt in on a Rollerblading practice session to prove his prowess and his worthiness of the chief bad guy's sister.

Most of the kids do have charisma, especially Seth Green, providing effective comic relief as McDermott's nerdy/hip cousin Wiley, and Brittney Powell, who has far less to do as the damsel. The main adversary is Chris Conrad, looking like a big, beefy, malevolent Michael J. Fox.

The technical credits are perhaps better than Bill Apablasa's slightish screenplay deserves. Cinematographer Daryn Okada has given the proceedings a surprising natural-light look, and Stewart Copeland contributes a well-above-average rock score redolent of "Rumble Fish" and better times.

But the biggest kudos might well be given to second-unit director Steve Boyum, stunt coordinator Pat Parnell and the remarkable skaters of Team Rollerblade, who prove against expectations that in-line skating is inherently cinematic and whose work on the finale keeps "Airborne" from being a total Earth-hugger.

NEW YORK POST, 9/18/93, p. 13, Lawrence Cohn

"Airborne" answers the question, what's worse than a Pauly Shore movie? An imitation Pauly Shore movie, of course.

This crass, inept attempt to cash in on the current teen craze of in-line skating doesn't even make an audience wake-up call until the final reel, when a team racing down the highways and busy streets of Cincinnati provides some OK stunts.

The main problem is the script by neophyte writer Bill Apablasa, whose day job is working as a high school speech teacher. That profession accounts for the complete absence of profanity in a movie about high schoolers, and hockey players to boot.

Hero Shane McDermott, who seems to have overdosed watching Peter Fonda's 1960s films for acting inspiration, plays an LA surfer who also likes to roller skate. His parents go to Australia for six months, sending him to live with relatives in Cincinnati. Since there's no philosophy of rollerblade skating, the film uses the zen mumblings of a surfer dude as its plot basis.

Our fish out-of-water hero is tiresome enough, but he's saddled with an unfunny cousin, played with imitation Pauly Shore-hipness by Seth Green. The filmmakers are so shameless they even use Right Said Fred's hit "I'm Too Sexy (for my shirt) " during a Green fashion show, identical to its use in Shore's "Encino Man." After intense hazing by the local hockey-obsessed kids, McDermott instantly wins them over with his rollerblade prowess (actually attributable to his skating double Chris Edwards). A romantic subplot with his nemesis Chris Conrad's pretty sister (Brittney Powell) kills time in this boring stinker.

NEWSDAY, 9/18/93, Part II/p. 21, John Anderson

Back in 1965, the Trade Winds recorded "New York's a Lonely Town," about the only surfer boy around. Now, at long last, someone's made a movie version, although the story's been moved to Cincinnati, the film is really about roller-blading, and the main character quotes Gandhi (or maybe it's Ben Kingsley) while sounding like a cross between Marianne Williamson and Sean Penn in "Fast Times at Ridgemont High."

Other than that, it's groovy. And it's also reassuring to know that someone, like Warner Bros., is acting as curator of pop culture. Skateboarding, after all, had a movie—the unforgettable "Gleaming the Cube" with Christian Slater—so why not roller-blading? As "Airborne" proves, you can be just as annoying and suffer equally serious groin injuries on one or the other.

The story? Mitchell (Shane McDermott), whom we shouldn't hate just because he's beautiful, resides in California and loves to surf and rollerblade. When his egg-head parents get a grant to study the Australian wombat, he has to go live with his aunt and uncle in Cincinnati, where it snows. His cousin Wiley (Seth Green), a wannabe hipster who tries too hard, tries to keep Mitchell from irritating every large guy at Central High, and fails miserably.

The sport of choice at this school is hockey, which they play on ice and, fortunately for Mitchell, on asphalt. And although "Airborne" makes it tough to sympathize with Mitchell—he's so focused, so self-aware, so zen—he eventually wins over the good guys, and the good girl, Nikki (Brittney Powell), through athletic prowess and a staunch pacifism.

There are several good performances, from Chris Conrad, who plays Nikki's brother; Jack Black, who's funny as Jack's friend Augie, and Jacob Vargas, as the lone Hispanic student, Snake. And Seth Green's sweetly insecure Wiley provides refreshing contrast with Mitchell's, well, *zen* qualities.

Also reviewed in:
NEW YORK TIMES, 9/18/93, p. 14, Stephen Holden
VARIETY, 10/4/93, p. 39, Greg Evans
WASHINGTON POST, 9/20/93, p. B7, Rita Kempley

ALIVE

A Touchstone Pictures and Paramount Pictures release of a Kennedy/Marshall production. *Producer:* Robert Watts and Kathleen Kennedy. *Director:* Frank Marshall. *Screenplay:* John Patrick Shanley. *Based on the book by:* Piers Paul Read. *Director of Photography:* Peter James. *Editor:* Michael Kahn and William Goldenberg. *Music:* James Newton Howard. *Music Editor:* Jim Weidman. *Sound:* Eric Batut and (music) Shawn Murphy. *Sound Editor:* Wylie Stateman and Gregg Baxter. *Casting:* Michael Fenton and Valorie Massalas. *Production Designer:* Norman Reynolds. *Art Director:* Frederick Hole. *Set Decorator:* Tedd Kuchera. *Set Dresser:* Gordon Brunner. *Special Effects:* John Thomas. *Costumes:* Jennifer Parsons. *Make-up:* Linda Gill. *Special Effects Make-up:* Gordon Smith. *Stunt Coordinator:* Gary Hymes and J.J. Makaro. *Running time:* 125 minutes. *MPAA Rating:* R.

CAST: Ethan Hawke (Nando Parrado); Vincent Spano (Antonio Balbi); Josh Hamilton (Roberto Canessa); Bruce Ramsay (Carlitos Paez); John Haymes Newton (Tintin); David Kriegel (Gustavo Zerbino); Kevin Breznahan (Roy Harley); Sam Behrens (Javier Methol); Illeana Douglas (Lilliana Methol); Jack Noseworthy (Bobby Francois); Christian Meoli (Frederico Aranda); Jake Carpenter (Alberto Antuna); Michael De Lorenzo (Rafael Cano); Jose Zuniga (Fraga); Danny Nucci (Hugo Diaz); David Cubitt (Fito Strauch); Gian Di Donna (Eduardo Strauch); John Cassini (Daniel Fernandez); Michael Woolson (Juan Martino); Chad Willett (Pablo Montero); Richard Ian Cox (Moncho Sabella); Gordon Currie (Coche Inciarte); Ele Keats (Susana Parrado); Joshua Lucas (Felipe Restano); Silvio Pollio (Alex Morales); Nuno Antunes (Alvaro Mangino); Michael Tayles (Pancho Delgado); Steven Shayler (Pedro Algorta); Jason Gaffney (Victor Bolarich); Jerry Wasserman (Co-Pilot); Michael Sicoly (Pilot); Diana Barrington (Sra. Alfonsin); Jan D'Arcy (Eugenia Parrado); Frank Pellegrino (Steward); Seth James Arnett (Tomas Alonso); Aurelio Dinunzio (Dr. Solana); Fiona Roeske (Sra. Solana); Tony Morelli (Martinez); Patrick Ramano (Jorge Armas).

CHRISTIAN SCIENCE MONITOR, 1/22/93, p. 11, David Sterritt

Movies about survival in the wilderness have a long history, and most members of the breed can be divided into two categories. Some put their characters through terror and torture merely to exploit fear about the dangers of untamed places. Others take a more responsible approach, using the lost-in-the-wilderness motif to illustrate the resourcefulness and resilience of the human spirit.

When two new pictures about survival turned up on my screening schedule this month, I wondered which of these directions they would choose. I'm pleased to report that both take the more positive pathway, although they each contain enough harrowing moments to mandate caution for sensitive moviegoers.

"Alive" is based on Piers Paul Read's best-selling book about an Uruguayan rugby team whose airplane crashed in the Andes Mountains, leaving several survivors who managed to exist for about ten weeks under appalling conditions until two of them managed to reach an isolated valley community and guide a mission to rescue the others. One of the group's survival strategies was to use the bodies of crash victims as food, and advance word on the film version of "Alive" suggests that some moviegoers think this is what the picture is all about.

In fact, the issue of cannibalism dominates only a couple of scenes and is handled quite thoughtfully. The group's decision is based on a reasoned discussion of two facts: that the frozen bodies are no more than earthly remains and have nothing to do with the true selfhood of the deceased individuals; and that the survivors would *want* their remains to be used in this way if it meant their comrades would survive and see their loved ones again. The choice is thus related to selflessness rather than greed, and once this is arrived at, the film moves on to other matters.

None of this means "Alive" is a particularly great or insightful movie. Although it's lively enough to stave off boredom, the screenplay has plenty of lifeless dialogue—an unusual failing from John Patrick Shanley, who wrote it—and the characters are poorly sketched out as individuals, except for a couple of heroic types who take over the story at key points.

Part of the problem lies with the performers, including Ethan Hawke and Vincent Spano (how like Hollywood to make a film about Uruguayans with a conspicuously American cast!) and part must be attributed to director Frank Marshall, who shows little inventiveness in guiding them.

What the movie does have in its favor is a refreshingly optimistic view of human fortitude, and an unusual willingness to suggest that higher powers may have a part to play in meeting human needs. It's also splendidly photographed by Peter James, whose crisp mountain images will have you shivering.

The other new survival movie, "A Captive in the Land," is more ambitious, using the story of two men stranded in the Arctic—an American meteorologist and a Russian pilot—as a metaphor for the cold-war tensions that beset much of the world between World War II and the Soviet Union's recent disintegration. The movie itself reflects growing Russian-American cooperation, since it's a joint venture by a US production company and the Gorky Film Studio in Moscow, where the interior scenes were filmed. American filmmaker John Berry directed it.

There are a few stirring moments as the two heroes struggle to understand each other as well as cope with the challenges of their situation, and the movie provides vivid views of the Arctic locations where its outdoor portions were shot. Sam Waterston and Alexander Potapov also turn in solid performances.

Still, it seems a little late to be exploring the cold war in such heavily symbolic terms, and the melodrama often seems stagy and contrived. It's a well-meaning picture, but it doesn't have enough imagination to become as involving as it would like.

FILMS IN REVIEW, 8/93, p. 272, Andy Pawelczak

Alive, an adventure film based on Piers Paul Read's book about a real life plane crash in the Andes, unerringly finds most of the cliches of the survival movie. In a picture like this we know exactly what to look for, and what interest there is comes from small variations in the formula and the accumulation of convincing detail. After the crash in the mountain fastness, we wait to see which of the thirty-odd survivors will emerge as distinct personalities and which will take on the heroic roles. The movie doesn't have any stars, so the problem isn't solved in advance for us; as the characters individualize, it's like watching a polaroid slowly develop before your eyes. Will Antonio (Vincent Spano), the captain of the rugby team that was en route to Chile, continue to be the group's leader, or will Roberto (Josh Hamilton), the level headed six-month medical student, take command? How will the group cope with the practical problems of survival in the frozen wilderness? Will the three men who trek off into the mountains in search of the sheared off tail section of the plane (which contains batteries essential to their rescue) ever return? Such is the stuff of which these movies are made.

To the usual recipe, *Alive* adds a dash of cannibalism, served up with a spiritual relish. Before deciding to eat the bodies of the passengers who perished in the crash, the starving men have a theological discussion about the relationship of body and soul, one man averring that after death the body is just meat and another asserting that God wants us to struggle to live and there must have been situations like this all the way back to the first people. With this we're ready for the primal scene right out of *Totem and Taboo*, Freud's epic fantasy about cannibalism and the origins of the sacred. But first, in case we've missed it, John Patrick Shanley's script underlines the religious motif once again by having Roberto point out, as he's about to eat, that cannibalism is like holy communion and "from their death we will live." (This mystical theme appears right at the beginning of the movie in a framing scene in which John Malkovich, in a very small role as one of the survivors twenty years later, says that in the Andes he found the god hidden behind civilization. As it turns out, this god proves to be somewhat savagely Darwinian, though the film makers obscure that implication with a whitewash of sentimentality.) The movie takes the religious effusions at face value; there's no attempt to explore the idea that people in extremis will work out rationalizations for what they're going to do anyway. The cannibalism scene itself is shot with a minimum of histrionics and gore; the men chewing on bits of raw flesh look like they're trying to get down some tough beef jerky.

At a running time of two hours, the movie is far too long, and I drifted off into speculations about how other directors might have handled the same material. To go from the ridiculous to the sublime, Bresson, for example, might have focused on each man's solitude within the group and the physics of grace made manifest in the survivors' struggle with the intractable environment. Bunuel (who made a version of *Robinson Crusoe*) might have transformed the cannibalism scene into a black joke, a blasphemous parody of communion, and New York's Living Theater might deck the whole thing out in primal dramaturgy and expressionistic ritual. Frank Marshall, *Alive*'s director, chooses to go for bland uplift, making what could have been an exercise in the cinema of cruelty into something very like a fraternity initiation rite. The shots of the crash itself are harrowing and convincing, but after that the film sinks into a strange lassitude, perhaps induced by the Andean altitude.

The uniformly young and pretty male cast doesn't help. Though caught up in the rigors of an existential limit situation, they're never able to shake the look of a Gap ad, and the only actor with name recognition, Vincent Spano, isn't called upon to do much more than look intense and commanding. Shanley's script tries to have it every which way, adding big dollops of putative seriousness to the formula diversions and not succeeding with either one. When the film ended with a heartfelt rendition of "Ave Maria," I found myself hoping that the savage god of the marketplace would exact a terrible revenge on the whole project. *Alive* simply isn't very alive.

LOS ANGELES TIMES, 1/15/93, Calendar/p. 6, Kenneth Turan

"Alive" is going to do wonders for in-flight safety. A solid straightforward re-creation of a terrifying 1972 plane crash in the Andes and its unsettling aftermath, "Alive's" careful You Are There qualities will have even chronic scofflaws buckling those seat belts like there is no tomorrow.

In truth, "Alive" does everything it ought to except the one thing you really want with a story like this, and that is transcend its material. A once-in-a-lifetime situation, filled with incidents that almost defy belief, calls for more of a once-in-a-lifetime movie, and that is beyond this film's powers.

Taken from Piers Paul Read's international best-selling account of what happened on that frigid, snow-covered mountaintop between Argentina and Chile, "Alive" has avoided the more obvious mistake of letting the audience off the hook by soft-pedaling the horrors the crash survivors faced.

Rather its shortfall is that none of the film's elements, from the acting to the script credited to John Patrick Shanley to Frank Marshall's direction, has managed to crank themselves up that one step beyond that separates inspired films from more conventional ones. While its not in the cards for a story like this to lose our interest, this version doesn't enhance it either.

Flying over the Andes in a chartered plane was nothing special for the Uruguayan rugby squad "Alive" focuses on. Traveling with family members and friends, the young team members horse around and make jokes, oblivious to the harsh terrain around them. "Are we supposed to fly that close to the mountains," someone idly asks, but no one thinks much about it.

Then comes the crash, and a very detailed and realistic one it is, as the wings shear off one by one, the fuselage cracks and passengers go flying out the back to oblivion. ("Alive" is in fact rated R for "crash scenes too intense for unaccompanied children.") The cigar-shaped center section finally comes to rest on a snowbank in the middle of a frozen nowhere and the real terror begins.

Initially there is chaos, as the survivors focus on determining who is dead, who is dying, and who is still alive and capable of helping the others. The injured, often crushed by the seats behind them, are moaning things like "I'm in pain, I'm in so much pain" as the reality of their cold, isolated situation sinks in.

Though optimistic souls think rescue is imminent, this turns out to be very much not the case and one of more interesting things about "Alive" is the way the mantle of leadership gradually shifts over time. The most obvious choice and the initial take-charge guy is team captain and medical student Antonio (Vincent Spano), but events soon overtake him and as the days without rescue lengthen into weeks, the more unconventional Nando (Ethan Hawke) becomes the de facto leader.

Hawke, a vital young actor best known for his role in "Dead Poets Society," is, along with Spano, the film's most recognizable face, and the strength of his performance points up one of "Alive's" weaknesses. Though overstuffing disaster movies with movie stars is a perennial Hollywood foible, this film goes too far in the opposite direction. With the great majority of the dozen or so primary crash victims being played by unfamiliar actors, it takes most of the film to figure out who is who, and time better spent worrying about a particular character's fate is instead expended trying to remember exactly who he is.

And, except for the intense discussions that develop when necessity forces the survivors to consider cannibalism if they are to have any hope of getting out alive, the script, which lacks the spirit of Shanley's most characteristic work, doesn't give these young men anything very interesting to say, a problem that the film's indifferent staging of conversations invariably compounds.

What "Alive" does best is place you on that mountain (the film was in fact shot on a remote glacier in British Columbia) and pile physical detail upon physical detail until the cumulative effect of this daunting story of indomitability and endurance can't help but involve you to a certain extent.

But even at this level, the lack of transcendence remains a problem. "Alive's" characters, particularly John Malkovich in a brief and confusing prologue, talk a lot about spirituality and the experience of higher states of mind, but saying it and conveying it are very different things, and that is one mountain "Alive" is never able to climb.

NEW YORK, 1/25/93, p. 55, David Denby

Not every good story needs to be made into a movie. In 1972, an airplane carrying a Uruguayan rugby team to Chile crashed in the Andes, and the survivors lived in the freezing mountains for ten weeks before they were finally rescued, an event Piers Paul Read later fashioned into an international best-seller. Given up for lost, the young men (plus a few older passengers) quickly faced the gruesome necessity of eating the remains of those who died in the crash or soon after. Frank Marshall, director of *Alive*, makes the crash itself terrifying; the first few days of hope and despair, the perilous treks through treacherous snows, keep us involved. But the monotony of survivorship rubs off on the movie, and once *Alive* turns to cannibalism, all hope for the movie is lost.

After all, how do you stage the act? As a pragmatic decision? A Dionysian ritual of taboo-breaking wildness? Marshall does mainly the former, but he never overcomes a queasy tone that is impossible to use dramatically. Cannibalism, even as a life-affirming act, may be impossible to reenact in a movie. Despite much fervent talk of the beauty of the mountains and the closeness of God, *Alive* peters out. Ethan Hawke, as the brave kid who realizes he can walk out and get help, speaks his inspirational lines like a suburban boy on a skiing holiday. With a few heroic young actors, the picture might have worked, but I doubt it.

NEW YORK POST, 1/15/93, p. 29, Jami Bernard

Not coming to an in-flight movie near you is "Alive," the Truth-Is-Stranger-Than-Fiction story about a real-life rugby team from Uruguay that survived 10 weeks in the snow-covered Andes after its plane went down en route to a game in Chile.

Although the unmistakable Hollywood accents and rosy-cheeked appearance of the young actors make some of the John Patrick Shanley dialogue sound a little laughable, "Alive" manages to be totally gripping—not least because of what must have been an amazingly harsh physical production. The plane gets de-winged on its way down in a blizzard, its barrel body tunneling into the middle of an eternity of snow and eerie isolation.

Because it's a true story, and because it probably occurred during your own memory—1972 wasn't all that long ago—I hope it doesn't spoil it for you that the way the lads survived was to cannibalize their already dead teammates, whose bodies were preserved in the snow. It's the Donner party of the Andes, and everyone's invited!

The screenplay gingerly reserves the menu for the dramatic turning point of the story, throwing in plenty of religious and moral anxiety to make the bitter pill easier to swallow. Airplane food has never been so bad.

Director Frank Marshall has had a long association with Steven Spielberg, and it shows. "Alive" plays like a boy's adventure, in which the high points are when the hardiest of the rugby team, led by Ethan Hawke, set out to walk over the mountains to Chile to get help. It is well-known that American-made movies have to be upbeat, so if the curiosity factor is what makes people buy tickets in the first place, it's the exhilarating man-against-nature element that will keep them from getting grossed out. Hawke even pauses atop yet another impossible mountain to marvel at the scenery.

In the final analysis, 29 died and 16 survived the crash. The movie, though seemingly long and claustrophobic and plagued by silly jokes about ordering pizzas, turns out to be quite engrossing, as well as full of survival tips for people afraid of plane crashes. On your next trip, pack lots of chocolate and dress warm, and don't forget your lucky sneakers.

NEWSDAY, 1/15/93, Part II/p. 67, John Anderson

It's no surprise that the filmmakers have injected a large basting needle full of religion into "Alive," the ostensibly true story of a Uruguayan rugby team's 1972 ordeal in the Andes.

Having survived a spectacular plane crash, extreme hunger, brutal weather and the sight of their friends dying off one by one, the survivors might be expected to seek divine intervention. Having them line up as if for communion after they decide to eat their dead comrades, however, is a bit much.

"Alive" is a spectacular-looking film, and is based on an incredible-but-true tale of survival: Most of the passengers, who were heading for a rugby game in Chile, lived through the crash, and those who ultimately survived spent 10 weeks stranded in the snow-covered mountains before two made their way out. Those who lived did so by cannibalizing those who died. Food for thought, but the themes that the situation generates in "Alive" are never explored with anything like clarity. The acting is uniformly lackluster and the script, by John Patrick Shanley ("Moonstruck"), is shallow, ringing a lot of noble-sounding notes without dealing seriously with the moral issues it raises.

The crash scene itself is the most effective part of the film, and could do for the air what "Jaws" did for the water. When the plane fails to clear the mountains, the first impact cuts it in two; we see the seats toward the rear of the fuselage tumble out the back along with their occupants, seat belts securely fastened. The roof is sheared off, snow and ice pouring in. The wingless plane now looks and moves like a torpedo and when it finally stops, the remaining seats break free from their mounts and slide forward, trapping passengers, crushing their legs. It's hard to believe anyone could have lived through it.

They did, however, nearly 30 of them, and the film chronicles how they contend, together and individually, with not only a lack of food and exposure to a merciless climate, but the crushing of their hope, and the dynamics of the small society they comprise.

The team's captain, Antonio (Vincent Spano), initially takes charge, helping the more gravely wounded, directing the construction of shelter and rationing food. But he cracks after hearing a radio report that the search for the team has been called off. New leadership, in the form of Nando (Ethan Hawke) and Roberto (Josh Hamilton) has to arise. These two will eventually make the trek through the mountains to bring back help; when Antonio dies, it feels like retribution.

When a plane flies by, the group thinks it's saved, and gorges itself on the remaining provisions. But the help doesn't come, and they're left with no food. It's then that the issue of cannibalism arises, with Nando campaigning vigorously for the new menu. When his sister Susanna (Ele Keats) succumbs to her injuries, of course, he doesn't want anyone making a meal out of her. Although several of the actual survivors acted as consultants to the film, what's lacking is a real sense of the moral, physical or spiritual upheaval that these people must have had to go through, choosing between life and the isolation of every tenet that defines them as "civilized." "What's going to become of our innocence if we survive as cannibals?" a character asks. Unfortunately, we're never given a clue.

NEWSWEEK, 1/18/93, p. 59, David Ansen

In 1972, a plane carrying a Uruguayan rugby team to Chile crashed high in the snowcapped Andes. Many passengers died upon impact; the survivors, after their meager rations of wine and chocolate ran out, realized their only hope of staying alive was to eat human flesh. It's taken Hollywood two decades to get this true story of survival on screen, but director Frank Marshall and screenwriter John Patrick Shanley finally got it made, probably by pitching it as an inspirational adventure tale with a young-guns cast that includes Ethan Hawke, Vincent Spano and Josh Hamilton.

Piers Paul Read's acclaimed 1974 book, upon which the movie is based, paid special attention to the social structure that evolved among the group: the emergence of a warrior class and the counterbalance of a civilian government that looked out for the welfare of the weak and wounded. Marshall ("Arachnophobia") downplays the fascinating sociological details—and the ambiguities of character—in favor of action, heroism and a vague religiosity that's sprinkled over the story like powdered sugar. "Alive" does best what Hollywood movies usually do well: a thrilling crash, a terrifying avalanche, heart-stopping cliffhangers. But as an examination of the mystery of character under pressure, it doesn't probe very deep. The young cast (awfully robust after 70 days of hell) is somewhat erratic; after two hours of close contact with these boys, one barely knows them. Hawke, however, has subtle authority as the heroic Nando Parrado: he's got a face for which close-ups were invented. Marshall is a good technician, but there's no sense of artistic adventure in his sometimes exciting, sometimes draggy movie. He's content to scratch the surface of a great and harrowing story.

SIGHT AND SOUND, 5/93, p. 46. Kim Newman

October 13, 1972. A plane from Uruguay to Chile, chartered by a rugby team, runs into bad weather and flies too low over the Andes. After losing a wing-tip, the plane breaks in two and the nose comes to rest on a mountainside. Some of the passengers and crew are killed in the crash, but many survive. Antonio, the captain of the team, reluctantly takes charge and oversees the rationing of the meagre supplies found in the wreck; the survivors fortify the remains of the plane against the cold of the night. Roberto, a medical student, ministers to the wounded and dying; Nando, comatose since the crash, revives and is determined to survive.

After eight days, they hear over a transistor radio that the search for them has been abandoned. Three survivors set out to search for the tail of the plane, which contains batteries they hope can be hooked up to a radio, but are too weak from hunger to get very far. Nando convinces Roberto that if they are to escape, they must feed off the bodies of the dead and survive through the winter, then walk over the Andes to get help.

The survivors overcome their disgust and force themselves to become cannibals. In a night blizzard, an avalanche sweeps away the nose of the plane and eight of the survivors, including Antonio, are killed. A rescue party discovers the tail of the plane but it proves impossible to make the radio work. Two months after the crash, Nando urges Roberto to set out for Chile. After their first effort fails, they try again, armoured with a homemade sleeping bag, and press on, finally reaching civilisation. Nando and Roberto return in helicopters and their comrades are rescued. Sixteen survive the ordeal, but 29 have died on the mountain.

The *MFB* review of *Survival!* *(Los Supervivientes de los Andes)* labelled the 1976 exploitation effort—whose synopsis is identical with the current film—as "a penny-dreadful competitor to *Alive!*, the authorised film of the Andes air disaster." In the event, Rene Cardona Jr's quickie put the kibosh on a further dramatisation of the story for 16 years. That may have less to do with the pre-empting of the subject than the problems of dealing with a story that would work best as a silent mountain film or a talky stage play, torn as it is between astonishing visual impact and thornily uncinematic drama.

Frank Marshall, turning stone-faced after his witty *Arachnophobia*, takes advantage of the perils, staging many incredibly nerve-wracking moments. The crash itself, with passengers strapped in their seats sucked out through the gaping hole, and the wingless nose of the plane ploughing across snowy mountainscapes, is the best sequence of its type ever filmed. There are further gruelling action scenes in the avalanche that sweeps away and buries the fuselage, whittling down the cast, and a literal cliffhanging moment as Roberto clings to a precipice during the heroic last-reel trek across the Andes.

Despite these highs, the true story contains more characters than can easily be personalised. They spend their time simply sitting around a mountainside like sunbathers, waiting to be rescued or running the emotional gamut from insanity through fortitude and practicality to religious transportation. Despite the efforts of an excellent cast, Marshall is unable to make much of the characters (we are even unsure which of the shaggily 70s haircuts will grow to be the unbilled John Malkovich, who narrates the story in smoky close-ups). This shortcoming recalls John Carpenter's difficulties with the similarly ice-bound and gradually decimated crew of *The Thing*. When the avalanche strikes, it kills off not only the most recognisable actor and natural leader of the team (Vincent Spano) but the sole woman with a substantial role (Illeana Douglas), leaving the rest of the film bereft, as its convincingly sulky and petulant group of traumatised cannibals gradually turn to God. Eventually, the story produces a pair (Ethan Hawke, Josh Hamilton) who are less conventional take-charge heroes (cf. Hardy Kruger and James Stewart in *The Flight of the Phoenix*) than bit-players singled out at random and never elevated above their comrades except by virtue of having higher billing and more lines.

While cannibalism is still transgressive enough a subject to prompt extremely tactful treatment (nothing here like the *Andes Plane Crash Cook Book* referred to in Ted Kotcheff's *Who is Killing the Great Chefs of Europe?*), Marshall and screenwriter John Patrick Shanley take pains to play down this theme and turn the thrust of the picture to religion. "If we do this, we'll never be the same again," one survivor remarks just before sawing into a frozen dead buttock with a piece of glass, only for a fellow to reply, "it's like communion—from their death, we live." The most embarrassing aspect of the film is not the rigorously suppressed black humour; even the group's pledge that the dead will allow their team-mates to eat them is convincing. But what rankles is the persistent use of clichés, and the redundant dialogue about God being all around in the mountains.

Finally, in a desperate attempt to make sense of a tragedy which stands as testament to the human spirit, Malkovich talks of the shrine to the dead erected atop the mountain and the final credits roll with sweeping views of natural beauty accompanied by Aaron Neville's 'Ave Maria'. This stirring rendition is far less moving that the earlier use, perfect in period and jarring in context, of 'The Look of Love' and 'Do You Know the Way to San Jose?'—one hummed by a feeble survivor during the first night on the mountain, the other tinnily emanating from the transistor radio as Antonio tries to find news of the rescue parties.

VILLAGE VOICE, 1/26/93, p. 58, James Hannaham

What happens when a rugby team made up of devoutly Catholic, vaguely "South American" youths survives a plane crash in a remote area of the Andes? Well, *obviously*, they reenact the Last Supper in order to justify their cannibalism. "If I die," team captain/Christ figure Antonio Balbi (Vincent Spano) suggests, "you can eat me." They eventually do devour their martyr, washing him down with capfuls of wine and crossing themselves. Despite (or perhaps due to) its iron-fisted religious message, Frank Marshall's *Alive* carefully dodges most of the pitfalls a gruesome true story might present and escapes with a film surprisingly greater than the sum of its, er ... parts. After the plane crash scene—destined for film history—the mangled fuselage becomes a horrific, ick-a-minute funhouse of frostbitten feet, bleeding orifices, gammy legs, and manic, suffering passengers. Only the manly, fine young cannibals survive. Their makeshift radio tells them the search has been called off, but to Nando Parrado (Ethan Hawke), that's *good* news. When he says, "now we can save ourselves," he could mean spiritually, corporeally, or both. Literally and figuratively close to God (played majestically by the mountains of British Columbia), the survivors pay little attention to matters of the flesh, aside from its taste. And though it takes a heaping tablespoon of belief suspension to think that 16 teenage guys could survive three months without mentioning sex, the real shocker is that they spend all that time in the same heap of wreckage without any interpersonal revelations. But who bonds with their supper anyway?

Also reviewed in:
CHICAGO TRIBUNE, 1/15/93, Friday/p. F, Dave Kehr
NATION, 2/15/93, p. 209, Stuart Klawans
NEW YORK TIMES, 1/15/93, p. C6, Janet Maslin
VARIETY, 1/18/93, p. 77, Brian Lowry
WASHINGTON POST, 1/15/93, p. B7, Rita Kempley
WASHINGTON POST, 1/15/93, Weekend/p. 38, Desson Howe

AMAZONIA: VOICES FROM THE RAIN FOREST

A Tara Releasing release. *Producer:* Monti Aguirre and Glenn Switkes. *Director:* Monti Aguirre and Glenn Switkes. *Screenplay:* Monti Aguirre, Glenn Switkes, and Michael Rudnick. *Director of Photography:* Eduardo Poiano. *Editor:* Michael Rudnick. *Running time:* 70 minutes. *MPAA Rating:* Not Rated.

NARRATOR: Monti Aguirre.

NEW YORK POST, 5/10/93, p. 26, Matthew Flamm

Not since "Powaqqatsi" followed "Koyaanisqatsi" has there been a nature film as poetic and predictable as "Anima Mundi," which is as it should be: all three documentaries were directed by Godfrey Reggio, the New Mexico-based former monk whose love of repetition makes him a perfect match for his collaborator, the minimalist composer Philip Glass.

The new, half-hour documentary opens today on a double bill with the full-length "Amazonia Voices from the Rainforest" for a one-week run at the Cinema Village.

Combining archival footage with original material shot by Reggio's other longtime collaborator, Graham Berry, "Anima Mundi" (Latin for "spirit of the world") features an all-natural cast, ranging from lions, gazelles and buffalos to termites, bacteria and a human embryo.

It isn't always a pretty sight. Though there are visually stunning moments galore—bat rays undulating underwater in a Busby Berkeleyish ballet, wild horses on a stampede—the microscopic subjects are plenty creepy. Which is Reggio's point: the remarkable, unrecognized diversity of nature and the importance of its preservation.

Whatever the intentions of the film. It's hard not to zone out on the visuals. With no text and no story, only variations in film speed and Glass' mildly interesting but never overpowering score, "Anima Mundi," puts one in an ecologically agreeable stupor.

Just the opposite occurs with "Amazonia" which explores the multiple conflicts tearing apart Brazil's Amazon basin. The work of Glenn Switkes and Monti Aguirre, the documentary begins with the sad, 500-year-old story of the savaging of Brazil's Indian tribes, by invading whites.

The war over the land grows even more complex, with the rubber tappers falling victim to development—and, led by their articulate, soon-to-be martyred leader Chico Mendes, forging an alliance with their old enemies, the Indians.

Impoverished landless farmers and river dwellers form the next layer of the exploited, as ranchers expanding their territory and mining interests move into previously pristine areas.

Threaded through the interviews are animated sequences of traditional Indian tales and black-and-white archival footage of the early days of the rubber tappers. It all adds up to a persuasive documentary, as informative as it is moving.

Also reviewed in:
NEW YORK TIMES, 5/7/93, p. C12, Stephen Holden
WASHINGTON POST, 4/16/93, Weekend/p. 40, Desson Howe
WASHINGTON POST, 4/17/93, p. C2, Richard Harrington

AMERICAN FRIENDS

A Castle Hill Productions release of a British Screen presentation in association with the BBC of a Millennium/Mayday/Prominent Features production. *Producer:* Patrick Cassavetti and Steve Abbott. *Director:* Tristram Powell. *Screenplay:* Michael Palin and Tristram Powell. *Story:* Michael Palin. *Director of Photography:* Philip Bonham-Carter. *Editor:* George Akers. *Music:* Georges Delerue. *Music Editor:* Dennis McTaggart. *Sound:* Tony Jackson and (music) Eric Tomlinson. *Sound Editor:* Peter Best. *Casting:* Irene Lamb. *Production Designer:* Andrew McAlpine. *Art Director:* Chris Townsend. *Set Dresser:* Barbara Drake. *Costumes:* Bob Ringwood. *Make-up:* Peter Owen and Peter King. *Running time:* 95 minutes. *MPAA Rating:* Not Rated.

CAST: Michael Palin (Reverend Francis Ashby);   Trini Alvarado (Miss Elinor Hartley); Connie Booth (Miss Caroline Hartley);   Bryan Pringle (Haskell);   Fred Pearson (Hapgood); Alfred Molina (Oliver Syme);   Susan Denaker (Mrs. Cantrell);   Jonathan Firth (Cable);   Ian Dunn (Gowers);   Robert Eddison (William Granger Rushden, College President);   David Calder (Pollitt);   Simon Jones (Anderson);   Charles McKeown (Maynard);   Roger Lloyd Pack (Dr. Butler);   John Nettleton (Groves);   Alun Armstrong (Dr. Victor Weeks);   Sheila Reid (Mrs. Weeks);   Edward Rawle-Hicks (John Weeks);   Markus Gehrig (Swiss Guide);   Jo Stone-Fewings (Undergraduate "King Lear");   Jimmy Jewel (Ashby Senior);   Wensley Pithey (Cave);   Arthur Howard (Voe);   Charles Simon (Canon Harper).

LOS ANGELES TIMES, 4/23/93, Calendar/p. 15, Kevin Thomas

Several years ago Monty Python alumnus Michael Palin came across the diaries of his great-grandfather, an Oxford don, and they inspired his charming and understated "American Friends." It probably shouldn't be taken as a factual account of his ancestor's life, yet leaves us wishing that it were—so stunning is the film's ending.

Palin takes us into the rarefied, masculine world of an Oxford college in the 1860s, and we feel quickly that we're in Merchant-Ivory territory where everyone's slightest inflection is fraught with implication. Palin casts himself as the Rev. Francis Ashby, a senior tutor and the strongest contender to succeed the college's ailing, ancient president.

Ashby is a trim, pleasant-looking man of 46 of such proprietary dedication to his college, where he has resided for 27 years, that, it is remarked that he would be upset if so much as a soup tureen were purchased during his absence. Indeed, as he prepares for a walking tour of Switzerland, he says, "Holidays are anathema to me, and I shall be taking a considerable amount of work with me."

On vacation however, he makes the acquaintance of a forthright Philadelphian, Miss Caroline Hartley (Connie Booth); clearly his intellectual equal, and her young, rather bored niece Elinor (Trini Alvarado). Upon his return to Oxford, Ashby is astonished when the two women arrive unannounced and unescorted, thus flouting Victorian convention twofold.

From here on "American Friends" reveals the vulnerability of the individual who has always observed strictly the rigid, often oppressive conventions of the society in which he was born. Innate decency and good looks undercut Ashby's stuffiness, but he does give the impression that in middle age he is almost certainly a virgin. He is about to experience a clash between reason and emotion for the first time, and discover just how messy life can really be.

Ideally, the two young women should have arrived in Oxford, where they decide to spend the summer in the nearby countryside, after Ashby had secured his promotion. Ashby would have been attracted to Caroline as much as she is to him, and the attraction between Elinor and Alfred Molina's Oliver Syme, Ashby's key rival for the presidency, a younger, more liberal—and, alas, less principled—man would have been less superficial. Yet in the eye of the growing storm Ashby proves that, when tested, he is not wanting in character or courage, although at last, in taking decisive action, he cannot do so without hurting another.

"American Friends," which was written by Palin and its director Tristram Powell, is so dry, its humor as brittle as old parchment, that in its first third you may find your attention wandering. But it's worth waiting for it to kick in. Typical of such British period pictures, its settings, costumes and acting are impeccable. Of all the Merchant-Ivory films it brings to mind, it most resembles their version of Henry James' "The Europeans" in that it shows the terrible gamble a Victorian woman had to take if she deviated from convention in the slightest in her pursuit of happiness and security.

With its magnificent Oxonian settings and its lush pastoral scenes, "American Friends" (rated PG for some mild language and sensuality) is a beautiful film but one that's utterly, refreshingly, devoid of sentimentality and nostalgia.

MONTHLY FILM BULLETIN, 4/91, p. 98, John Pym

The 1860s. While on a solo walking tour of the Swiss Alps, Francis Ashby, aged 46, the correct Senior Tutor of a monastic Oxford college, reluctantly offers to guide two Americans, Caroline Hartley and her ward Elinor, after the party to which they were attached, led by Dr. Weeks, coincidentally also from Oxford, is forced by the vaporous Mrs. Weeks to turn back. The failing health of Rushden, the aged college president, requires Ashby's abrupt return to England, but not before both ladies have allowed romantic notions to take root and Ashby has bestowed a kiss on Elinor. The coming presidential election (the president must, of course, be a bachelor) will be between Ashby, a Classicist and the heir apparent, and the unscrupulous Oliver Syme, a go-ahead Darwinist. The American ladies appear in Oxford, not entirely innocently, to the delight of Syme, but the dismay of Ashby who, in addition, has made an enemy of Weeks by denying his son John admission to the college. While Caroline pursues her quest over a candlelit dinner, Elinor is chased by beadles and forced to shelter on Ashby's stairs, Later, Ashby escorts the rebuffed Elinor to her lodgings. Next morning, Ashby's ally Pollitt extracts a promise from him that he will henceforth have nothing more to do with the ladies. At Syme's riverside cottage, where the ladies are now staying, Elinor discovers a draft letter from Caroline to Ashby; and later, partly abstracted by her loss, she allows Syme to have his way with her. Caroline discreetly asks Ashby if she may hope ... but is rejected. Time passes; Rushden dies; the college gathers for the presidential election. Weeks tells Ashby that Elinor is pregnant; and Ashby communicates the news to an indifferent Syme. As a vote is about to be taken, Ashby resigns from the college and is reconciled with Elinor.

Another handsome Oxford story, directed by an Oxford man, Tristram Powell (his first film after a distinguished television career), and written by another, Michael Palin, who was inspired by a diary note of his great-grandfather, Edward Palin, who in 1866 resigned from St. John's College, Oxford, to marry an Irish-American girl he had met with her guardian on a walking tour in the Alps five years before. Unlike the clergyman played by Palin in *The Missionary* (and the actor is, in a sense, never better than as a muscular, undaunted, pedagogic clergyman), the Reverend Francis Ashby is not an overtly knockabout character. He may be ribbed in somewhat modern vein by his fellow, somewhat modern dons for his punctilious attention to the minutiae of college administration, and he may have, in Bryan Pringle's encrusted scout Haskell, a delightfully caricatured, proprietorial college servant, but the story through which he moves is underpinned with genuine feeling and has at its centre, in Trini Alvarado's Elinor, a young woman of arresting sensibility.

The film is full to bursting with filmic Oxford: the quad; the darkened chapel; candlelight on dark polished wood; leather-bound volumes reverently turned over; sculls on the river; the founder's port—all photographed to perfection by Philip Bonham-Carter. Set a film in nineteenth-century Oxford, and there's no escaping this; Powell's achievement, however, is not to make too much of it, while of course making everything of it. It is, though, the scenes in Switzerland—and particularly the rustic, evening entertainment on the eve of Ashby's return to England, after which Elinor chides him for having failed to ask her to dance and he bestows the fateful kiss—that give the story an edge and provide Ashby with a sense of the opportunities he is about to cast aside. They, too, are as conventional as the Oxford prospects, more so perhaps; but they are there to a purpose and boldly presented, as if for the large screen.

The plot is a shade circumstantial: the figure of Dr. Weeks greasing its wheels a little too conveniently. But, on the other hand, one is inclined to overlook the manipulation for the incidentals; in the case of Weeks, for the delightful scene in which the luckless John comes before Ashby with an ill-prepared Latin recitation: Palin gives a marvelous display of a man who has heard a thousand stumbling students and knows exactly the tone of voice he is expected to adopt. At moments, the tone seems about to grow serious—everything about Connie Booth's philanthropic Caroline is serious, believably serious—this, however, sits a little uneasily with the prevailing lightness, best caught, perhaps, by the knowing look of Alfred Molina's lubricious Syme. Accomplished, entertaining, understated: much more than a television film, if not quite a full-fledged movie.

NEW YORK POST, 4/9/93, p. 29, Jerry Tallmer

When last we looked at Michael Palin he was killing off all the Shih Tzus of a little old lady in "A Fish Called Wanda" Well, here's that Shih Tzu-killer transformed into a diffident Oxford don in the year 1861—the Rev. Francis Ashby, senior tutor in Greek and Latin, vice president of his college, coming to love a bit late in life through a tumble in the Alps.

You will find this austere but awakening gentleman, Prince Albert whiskers and all, in "American Friends," a quite nice British cinema-potion of tenderness, smiles and barbed wit, written by Palin together with the director whose first large-screen feature this is, Tristram (son of novelist Anthony) Powell.

There's a considerable amount of Oxonian lore, ceremony, injoking and infighting to be got through, complete with a frail old president—the one everyone's burning to succeed—who likens himself to Lear and babbles on his deathbed: The Visigoths are at the gates of Rome!" Especially hungry to be elected incoming president is Ashby's chief rival, Oliver Syme, a cynical, hardbitten Darwinian rationalist and womanizer with an eye on the main chance and a cozy cottage down by the river for part-time extra-curricular accommodations. He is played, marvelously as always, by the Alfred Molina who was Joe Orton's murderous roommate Kenneth Halliwell in "Prick Up Your Ears."

Into this set-up—these cloistered walls (actually shot in New College, Oxford)—there now march two American ladies, the 18-year-old Miss Elinor (Trini Alvarado) and the considerably older but still very attractive Miss Caroline Hartley (Connie Booth), the do-gooding "aunt" who'd adopted Elinor as a starving 5-year-old off the boat from famine-stricken Ireland. Elinor, on a sort of African safari of a picnic in the Alps with Caroline and others, had first espied the Rev. Ashby through field glasses, skinny-dipping by a waterfall near the Matterhorn; then acting as their guide, he had fallen down a mountain; then with him in bandages they had kissed—just one little sweet kiss. At which point I leaned over to Jessica De Mayo in the next seat and whispered: "Let's have a little bet. Which one do you think he'll end up with?,' "Oh, I'd be so happy if it was the aunt," said Jessie.

I'm afraid you're going to have to see the movie to learn how that bet comes out, but it should occasion more pleasure than pain. Perhaps predictable is the move that Alfred Molina will make on the girl, and perhaps you'd surely know that she'd fall into the river trying to debark from his rowboat, and that he'd rush her to the cottage to start drying her off. That, of course would be after she'd have cause to say, bitterly, to the Rev. Ashby, in his rooms, over an-all-too-chaste glass of Founder's Port: "Have you forgotten Switzerland?"

Aunt Caroline gets her bitter licks in too. In fact the whole competitive situation is strangely evocative of another involving an adopted child whose name is Soon-Yi, though nothing could have been farther from author Palin's mind. What he had in mind was his own great-grandfather, who taught at Oxford in the 1860s and married a girl like Elinor and left a diary to tell about it. I don't know if Palin also had in mind James Hilton, who wrote "Goodbye, Mr. Chips," or E. M. Forster, who wrote "A Room With a View" and other novels, but I did.

NEWSDAY, 4/9/93, Part II/p. 52, John Anderson

Francis Ashby (Michael Palin), a senior tutor at Oxford, is a man so preoccupied with the state of that vereable institution that even his obsessively compulsive colleagues are embarrassed.

"Imagine returning," another don says of Ashby, watching him prepare fretfully for his annual vacation, "and finding that a new soup tureen had been purchased without a full meeting of the college council ..."

It's clear that when, and if, love finds Ashby, he's going to fall—not without a great deal of dignity, of course—but he's going to fall hard. Which is what happens in "American Friends," a small, gentle comedy that stars former Monty Pythonite Michael Palin playing his own great-grandfather.

The screenplay, by Palin and director Tristram Powell, is based on the Rev. Edward Palin's 1861 diary, which recounts his meeting with a pair of American women, one older, one younger, while on a tour of Switzerland; he wound up marrying the younger. Now Palin and Powell have taken this 132-year-old May-December romance and made a film that is thoughtful, charming and funny.

It's actually more of a May-September romance: 18-year-old Elinor Hartley (Trini Alvarado), survivor of the Irish potato famine and ward of Miss Catherine Hartley (Connie Booth), meets, cajoles and is kissed with uncharacteristic impulsiveness by Ashby after they all meet, in Switzerland. After Ashby leaves abruptly, she carries that kiss around Europe and back to Oxford, where Catherine becomes infatuated with Ashby, Ashby neglects Elinor out of a sense of propriety, and Elinor becomes lovesick and seduced by another.

The two women also find themselves at the center of academic politics: Ashby has rushed back because the college's President Rushden (a wonderful comic turn by Robert Eddison) has taken ill, and opened the possibility that Ashby will be elected his successor. The orthodox Ashby will be challenged, however, by the rakish Darwinist don Oliver Syme (Alfred Molina), with the outcome hinging largely on personal morality. And then the two single women appear.

Much of the humor in "American Friends" is derived from the abject stuffiness of its setting, as well as Ashby's discomfiture with unfamiliar emotions. Palin hasn't been seen here in such a largely dramatic role before, which is too bad. He makes Ashby, in his priestly way, a little cranky, a little distracted, a little short with intruders into his cloistered consciousness. He's also kind, and not because it comes easily to him. There's charm, but Palin makes us feel how Ashby's soul is trussed up and stuffed with a stifling mix of selflessness and self-importance.

The film is a delight to look at. Cinematographer Philip Bonham-Carter is as adept at rendering the cracked leather and burnished surfaces of Oxford as he is the majesty of the Alps. And Powell's direction is always very proper. Even when Ashby takes a header down a Swiss Alp early in the film, the camera looks discreetly away, as if to avoid embarrassing him. Very British indeed.

VILLAGE VOICE, 5/4/93, p. 58, David S. Kim

On holiday in Switzerland, Victorian gent and Oxford bigwig Francis Ashby (Michael Palin) meets Elinor (Trini Alvarado), an 18-year-old Irish American touring Europe. After a polite but significant flirtation, Ashby abruptly flees to Oxford, where women and wives aren't allowed. Alvarado, in the Helena Bonham-Carter role, follows and proceeds to yank the emotional stick from his anus horribilis. Objective: matrimony.

Based on the journals of Palin's great-grandfather, *Friends* starts out as a quiet, personal film, albeit one possessed by the teetotaling spirit of Merchant-Ivory. The pastoral Swiss scenery, the pale, misty colors of exquisitely understated costumes (many are Victorian originals)—all connote a world where everything is just so.

Amazingly, Palin plays it straight—no winks, no pratfalls, no nicknames like "Squidgy." Instead, a familiar assortment of crotchety fussbudgets and clog-stompin' foreign yokels create the necessary diversions. Throw in an oily competitor (Alfred Molina), who seduces and impregnates Elinor, and you've got a mad dash of intrigue. Narrative clarity inevitably suffers: Ashby and Elinor's romantic epiphany, for example, never fully materializes onscreen.

Then again it's 1861—what's a fiftyish professor and a nice, upper-class girl to do? That Ashby's choice comes down to love or academic prestige merely reinforces the lack of choice for

AMERICAN FRIENDS   55

Elinor. Fine performances by Palin and Connie Booth, as Elinor's beleaguered adoptive mother, almost make up for this predictability, although what *Friends* gains from well-acted restraint it loses in juice. Besides, we've already visited this Swiss chalet, and—Anglophobes, take heart—there ain't nothing goin' on but the view.

Also reviewed in:
CHICAGO TRIBUNE, 7/9/93, Friday/p. L, Steve Johnson
NEW YORK TIMES, 4/9/93, p. C8, Vincent Canby
VARIETY, 3/18/91, p. 82
WASHINGTON POST, 4/9/93, p. D6, Rita Kempley

AMERICAN HEART

A Triton Pictures release of an Avenue Entertainment presentation in association with World Films. *Executive Producer:* Cary Brokaw. *Producer:* Rosilyn Heller, Jeff Bridges, and Neil Koenigsberg. *Director:* Martin Bell. *Screenplay:* Peter Silverman. *Story:* Martin Bell, Mary Ellen Mark, and Peter Silverman. *Director of Photography:* James R. Bagdonas. *Editor:* Nancy Baker. *Music:* James Newton Howard. *Music Editor:* Sally Boldt. *Sound:* Robert Anderson Jr., Mark (Frito) Long, and (music) Robert Schaper. *Sound Editor:* Hamilton Sterling. *Casting:* Reuben Cannon and Cecily Adams. *Production Designer:* Joel Schiller. *Set Decorator:* Rondi Tucker. *Set Dresser:* Drew Pinninger. *Special Effects:* Bob Riggs, Ray Brown, Terry Shattuck, and Joel Youngerman. *Costumes:* Beatrix Aruna Pasztor. *Make-up:* Gina Monaci. *Stunt Coordinator:* Chris Howell and Gil Combs. *Running time:* 113 minutes. *MPAA Rating:* R.

CAST: Jeff Bridges (Jack Nelson); Edward Furlong (Nick Kelson); Lucinda Jenney (Charlotte); Don Harvey (Rainey); Tracey Tyla Kapisky (Molly); John Boylan (Janitor); Greg Sevigny (Young Jack); Jayne Entwistle (Monique); Willie Williams and Roosevelt Franklin (The Gospel Fireballs); Melvyn Hayward (Normandy); Kit McDonough (Landlady); Wren Walker (Lisa); Cristine McMurdo-Wallis (School Administrator); Charlotte London (Flo); Loyd Catlett (Vernon the Bartender); Richard Joffrey (Taxi Dispatcher Voice); Christian Frizzell (Rollie); Tracey Kapisky (Molly); Benjamin Hinkle and Jared Hinkle (Roy); Flapjack (Creamo); Shareen Mitchell (Diane); Francisco Arenas (Moose); Michelle Matlock (Bandit); Marcus Chong (Terry Cosmos); Maggie Welsh (Freddie); Sam Strange (Stony); Mark Namer (Pool Bar Guy); Barbara Irvin (Nicole); Burke Pearson (Jack's Bum); Apollo Dukakis (Steve); Laura Bobovski (Girl in Food Bank); John DeLay (Building Supervisor); Gary Lee Dansenburg (Suburban Son); Todd Jamieson (Suburban Father).

LOS ANGELES TIMES, 5/14/93, Calendar/p. 4, Kevin Thomas

Not since "Straight Time" (1978) with Dustin Hoffman has there been a film that more convincingly depicted the plight of the ex-con in his struggle to earn an honest living than the engaging "American Heart". Indeed, "Straight Time" was based on the novel "No Beast So Fierce," whose author Eddie Bunker served as "American Heart's" technical adviser.

Jeff Bridges surely gives one of the finest portrayals ever as Jack Kelson, who means to learn from his mistakes, a guy for whom the everyday grind of trying to make ends meet and accepting an unwanted parenthood instills dreams of heading to Alaska for a better life. Bridges' Jack, with his rueful self-knowledge and restless spirit, cunning and charm, embodies the ex-con at his most romantic—sexy, laid-back and bulging with jail-house muscles. As his 14-year-old son Nick, Edward Furlong holds his own with a performance of sweetness, intelligence and tender sobriety.

As the opening credits for the highly engaging "American Heart" unroll, we're shown a series of cheerful snapshots of a smiling (Bridges) playing with his young son. The happy faces come to an abrupt stop with a prison mug shot of the man, now looking suitably grim.

Having served five years for robbing a jewelry store, Jack prepares to leave state prison when Nick arrives to meet him. Not at all happy to see his son, he even tries to ditch the kid, who promptly outsmarts him, and they're soon bound for Seattle, settling in a seedy, once grand Beaux Arts apartment house.

Nick, whose mother apparently disappeared soon after he was born, is implacably determined to reclaim his father. Director Martin Bell and his writer Peter Silverman understand well that it's crucial that Nick's struggle to win his father's love must be steadfastly free of sentimentality to seem real, but that it can be told with spiky humor. Gradually, we're able to see Jack's resistance to Nick as part of a larger uncertainty as to whether he can actually take responsibility for his own life and stay out of trouble.

In the film's deftest sequence we watch Jack call a woman (Lucinda Jenney) from a pay phone and proceed to meet her in a bar. It's not until after they've made love does he reveal he's the former inmate she's been writing to, courtesy of the American Heart, a publication in which prisoners solicit correspondence.

In the meantime Nick, who's taken on a paper route, finds himself drawn to a tough but angelic-looking neighbor girl (Tracey Kapisky), who's already hustling while her mother (Shareen Mitchell) works as a peep show go-go dancer.

Not surprisingly, "American Heart," photographed with a gritty lyricism by James R. Bagdonas, owes much of its atmosphere and its insight to Bell's "Streetwise" (1984). That's the director's remarkable Oscar-nominated documentary on Seattle's street kids, inspired by a Life magazine photo essay shot by his wife, Mary Ellen Mark, the renowned photojournalist who is "American Heart's" associate producer. For all its impact, and Bridges' deep drawing upon his resources, "American Heart" ultimately doesn't have the sharp, unforgettable edge of "Streetwise."

Bell and his actors adroitly involve us in the lives of Jack and Nick, their fate becoming a matter of increasing uncertainty and concern. So far so good, but Bell and Silverman propel them toward a fate that may well seem far more inevitable to the filmmakers than to us, leaving us realizing that sad endings have to be earned just as fully as happier ones.

There are credible alternatives to "American Heart's" finish, and they might have effectively involved Jenney's attractive Charlotte, whom the filmmakers all but drop from their story just at the point when her presence cries to be greater, offering a valid recourse for the son as well as the father. At the very least Charlotte, nicely played by Jenney, deserves to have been given as much a chance to impact upon the Kelsons as Jack's wily onetime protégé (Don Harvey).

For many viewers "American Heart" (rated R for language and for sexual situations) may have enough going for it to sustain a finish that seems shamelessly heart-tugging and overly preordained, but it might have been a richer, more encompassing experience had its makers not so easily equated being downbeat with being realistic and honest.

NEW STATESMAN & SOCIETY, 12/10/93, p. 35, Jonathan Romney

American Heart is what you might call a minor film. That's not to say it's not a good one, although it's by no means a show-stopper. But it does something quite rare. It takes you somewhere—nowhere extraordinary, admittedly—and lets you live there for 114 minutes.

All this might sound like some extreme exercise in damning with faint praise, but there's nothing wrong with a film being minor in the way this one is—that is, resolutely in a minor key. It doesn't set out to win your affections. Like its characters, the waifs and strays of Seattle, it sort of hangs around and asserts a sullen presence. Despite its subject matter, which you might expect to lend itself to a rhetoric of tears and inflated pathos, it doesn't make any gestures; it just shrugs its way into your attention.

We're used to hearing about mainstream films that purportedly deal with the Dark Underbelly of America, but that usually means the Lynch approach of depicting glossy banality with a Gothic undertow—severed ears, weirdly coiffured fat people and weird sex behind the mall. What never gets talked about—except perhaps in documentaries, and *American Heart* is the work of a documentarist—is the real underbelly of poverty and inner-city inertia. There's nothing remotely glamorous about it, and you'd be hard pressed to pitch that topic to a studio in 25 words. So *American Heart* is really out there on its own.

As dispassionate accounts of life's downside go, *American Heart* isn't quite Bresson, more your bog-standard dirty realism. But it's admirable for taking such a low-pitched approach while still observing rather straitlaced narrative and stylistic conventions. It seems flat, both visually and in its pacing, but that's part of the technique by which director Martin Bell consistently desensationalises his material. Despite its subject matter—the slow tentative reconciliation of an ex-con and his young son—the film doesn't bother trying to tear-jerk you until the end, and that, one suspects, is purely as a sop to ensure the production dollar. There's a matter-of-fact feel about the film that matches its characters' attitudes, a scene-by-scene impression of aimlessness that matches their day by day living. This is *Shiftless in Seattle*.

Martin Bell, the director, is a BBC alumnus who a few years ago made *Streetwise*, a documentary about Seattle's street children: hustlers, prostitutes, junkies and feckless dreamers. Here, he and writer Peter Silverman pick up that story and widen its scope. The focus is on one boy who's going the way of the *Streetwise* kids, and his father Jack (Jeff Bridges), a just-released jailbird who's determined to go straight, more out of fatigue than any other reason. When Jack hits Seattle, his young son Nick (Edward Furlong) is there tailing him like an unshakable conscience, Jack's more concerned to meet up with Charlotte (Lucinda Jenney in one of those tender-tough roles that Ellen Barkin eats up) a taxi driver who's been sending him passionate letters c/o *American Heart*, a pen-pal magazine for prisoners. It's one of the film's merits that it brings Jack, Nick and Charlotte together without ever opting for the nuclear-family triangle that would wring dead-cert sobs. They may get together for an in-car barbecue, but this is real life (or a convincing impression), so don't expect happy endings. Nick, meanwhile, ends up hanging out with the teenage hustlers and hookers downtown. There might seem to be some determinism at work—Jack's bravado means he can't resist tipping Nick off about the criminal life, even when he's trying to deter him. But the film argues against such easy connections. Nick struggles all the way against his "inevitable" fate, even when it's clearly the only thing that's going to get him out of a dead end, and it'll leave him as washed out as his dad.

Bells avoids the easy option of milking one dramatic focus. As one of the film's producers, Jeff Bridges could have chosen to walk away with the meat of it, but he doesn't. Instead, he plays Jack weary and sluggish, amiable but terminally undignified. It's a superbly unfussy performance—is he the only Hollywood star who knows how to be self-effacing when the occasion demands? He's beautifully partnered by Furlong, from *Terminator 2*, whose abrasive edge, matched by an androgynous blankness, sets Nick up as a *tabula rasa* just waiting to have pragmatic cynicism etched all over it.

But beside the lead pair, other characters get their incidental look-in. There's a wonderful telling touch, when the kids go down to the stripjoint where one girl's mother gyrates day long in a peepshow box. One girl, who so far seems more asexual than butch, slips into a separate booth and watches the strippers with barely concealed desire as the teasing shutters descend slowly, craning her neck to catch every last second. Bell gives you the girl's whole story in a shot, We immediately know everything about her sexuality, maybe more than she quite knows yet; but we also know that the life she leads means that her sexuality is never going to be quite her own to enjoy. You can imagine how another film might have played the character as a cheap running joke, but just the fact that she's allowed to come into focus for this throwaway second is a too-rare gesture of generosity.

The fact that much of the film has the flat, matter-of-fact look of a TV movie is an advantage. The Kelsons' cheap room isn't hopelessly squalid—just dreary, empty, liveable—but not Home, whatever that is. The fact that it's so anonymous, so no-place-in-particular, immediately makes you at ease with the daily banality of the Kelsons' life. The horror of it isn't screaming degradation—just that it's nothing special and getting less special every day.

Bell goes for only one rhetorical touch, and it's not too obtrusive—the black-and-white inserts of Nick in a snowbound reform school. A brief freeze-frame near the end suggests overtones of *Les 400 Coups*, and maybe, in the style of Truffaut's hero Antoine Doinel, there's scope to follow up the next phase of Nick's chilly career; for once, a sequel might not be a bad thing.

American Heart is enough out of its time to demand attention. It reminds you of the 1970s, when independent American cinema managed to deal with unglamorous topics and still have sweep, and didn't have to sell its conceits quite as whimsically as it does now. It's an adventurous but completely marginal film, which is why you'd do well to see it. Like Jack, they're an endangered breed.

NEW YORK POST, 5/14/93, p. 31, Jami Bernard

Joining Hollywood's unofficial Hair Club for Men is Jeff Bridges, who with Daniel Day Lewis in "Last of the Mohicans" and Matt Dillon in "Singles" is going for the male equivalent of the Amy Fisher look—long, long locks that look very sexy, at least when they're not over-conditioned.

In the poster for "American Heart," Bridges is shirtless and muscular on a Good Hair Day, which will no doubt lure in the women. But the movie is about male bonding—more specifically, about father-son bonding after father has been letting his hair down in jail, and son has been waiting for him lo these many years. When dad gets out, son is there to greet him.

The movie opens with Bridges, as Jack Kelson, getting out of jail and trying to ditch the kid (Edward Furlong) so he can fend for himself and get to Alaska. Jack turns out to be the least loving father you can get without incurring physical abuse as he makes the kid sleep on the boxspring so he can hog the mattress, and even takes his sleeping son's pillow away.

Although the opening credit sequence showed a montage of loving scrapbook photos of baby Nick with his dad, Jack turns out to have more hair than nurturing instincts. To get closer to Jack you'd have to be a barrette.

The two make a go of life together by fits and starts with dad washing windows and trying to walk the straight and narrow, and son hanging out with prostitutes and lowlifes on street corners. Director Martin Bell uses his skills from making the documentary "Streetwise" to paint a vivid portrait of urban adolescent street life.

Bridges is very good at bringing Jack to life—you get the feeling it's a realistic portrait of a type of man you wouldn't really want to meet. Child-actor Furlong, first seen in "Terminator 2" next to a lot of molten metal, seems very practiced for his age.

The movie's title refers to a pen-pal magazine that Jack subscribed to in jail, and that allowed him to hook up (in the postal sense) with taxi driver Lucinda Jenney, another hard-bitten, not overbright type you'll recognize but not necessarily like.

Therein lies the problem with "American Heart"—it's a no-frills collection of characters you may have wondered about but who are never too compelling as individuals. Director Bell's documentary skills serve to distance the viewer just enough that you never fall in love with the characters the way American audiences like to do.

NEWSDAY, 5/14/93, Part II/p. 71, Gene Seymour

As with the very best screen actors, Jeff Bridges does the kind of things you don't realize are amazing until after you've left the theater. Bridges doesn't merely portray Jack Kelson, the ex-con protagonist in "American Heart." He *inhabits* Kelson.

It's a typical Bridges performance—which is to say, its power sneaks up on you in an accumulation of small details. Like the way his character rubs the sleep from his eyes. Or the way he saunters along the back streets of Seattle with his secondhand bike, hunches his shoulders, pokes and scratches himself as if constantly checking his body for any lingering traces of the small-time sleazeball persona he hopes he'd shed in prison.

The Al Pacinos and Dustin Hoffmans can have all the big bravura moments they want. Give me Bridges' subtle, seamless workmanship any day, any movie.

Bridges' performance would dominate the movie (which he co-produced) if it weren't for an equally potent turn by Edward Furlong as Kelson's son Nick. Furlong, best known as Arnold Schwarzenegger's right-hand kid in "Terminator 2," shows surprising assurance in evoking Nick's grimly worn mixture of hope and despair, awkwardness and courage as he struggles to get close to a father who wishes his kid were back on a farm far away.

Jack, you see, has his plans. He wants to head north to Alaska "to get clean, start fresh." He'd rather not be responsible for Nick, whom he barely knows. He can just barely take care of himself, what with him spending the rent on beer and holding off the Dark Hand of Recidivism in the form of his still-active former partner (Don Harvey).

A warm-hearted cabbie (Lucinda Jenney) tries to keep Jack focused on the straight and narrow while Nick, like many an earnest hick before him, falls hard for a tough, worldly street-walker (Tracey Kapisky) not much older than he is.

That this tale of a father and son's arduous rapprochement is set in a fringe environment like Seattle's red-light subculture doesn't make it any less conventional in the telling. In fact, director Martin Bell, best known for the documentary, "Streetwise," follows the curved path of Jack and Nick's relationship so rigidly that some of the other interesting characters—the women, especially—are relatively obscured.

Still, Bell and cinematographer James R. Bagdonas give a rich, flavorful sense of Seattle. Singer-songwriter Tom Waits tosses in a couple of his patented growls from the lower depths for added seasoning.

SIGHT AND SOUND, 1/94, p. 40, Lizzie Francke

Seattle. Jack Kelson, just released from jail, is met by his 15-year-old son Nick. With his mother now dead, Nick wants to live with his father rather than his aunt. Jack does not welcome the prospect, as he was planning to migrate to Alaska. Jack's old partner Rainey asks him to work on another job, but Jack says he is going straight. Later, he checks into some rooms. Much to his annoyance, Nick is still hanging around. Jack looks up his prison pen-pal Charlotte, a taxi driver. He goes to a bar where she hangs out and, not introducing himself, chats her up. They start to hang out together.

Meanwhile, Nick bunks off school and gets a job delivering newspapers. One evening, he meets a neighbour, Molly, a young girl who has been kicked out of home for the night. Nick invites her to stay at Jack's. The following morning, Jack finds Molly at the foot of his bed. The parole officer turns up and misreads the situation. Nick intercedes, but Jack is ungrateful for his help. Later, Jack sees Charlotte and reveals his identity. She is initially embarrassed, but subsequently drawn closer to him, and joins him and Nick on a day trip.

One night Rainey tries to interest Nick in helping him on a job; Nick refuses. Later Nick and some other kids go back to Molly's, where her mother arrives and creates a scene. Jack, worried that Nick is getting too involved with the street scene, cautions him about his friendship with Molly. He now includes Nick in his plans for Alaska. Later Nick, Molly and the other kids visit Molly's mother at the strip joint where she works. On the way back, Nick nearly gets caught after Molly dares him to steal a pair of shoes. When Jack finds Nick hiding the shoes and a couple of joints, he goes wild. Nick hands him money that he has earned for the Alaska trip, which Jack stashes away. Later the money is stolen. The unsympathetic landlady serves them an eviction notice for unpaid rent. Jack and Nick fight after Nick learns his mother was a prostitute.

Nick runs off and tries to survive on the streets; Jack, now living at Charlotte's, hunts for him. Nick accepts a burglary job from Rainey. Later Jack meets Nick; they row, and Jack loses his job cleaning windows. During the burglary, a friend of Nick's is shot. Nick returns to the warehouse he has been living in, and finds Jack there. Jack gives him the money for the ferry to Alaska and they arrange to meet on the boat. Jack confronts Rainey and they fight, with Rainey left unconscious; but Rainey catches up with him at the ferry and shoots him. Nick finds his father slowly dying as the ferry makes its way to Alaska.

American Heart is the first fiction feature by documentarist Martin Bell. It returns him to the grim, rain-swept streets of Seattle, where he and his wife, photo-journalist Mary Ellen Mark, shot the *vérité* piece *Streetwise* (1984). That film chronicled the lives of a bunch of kids living rough in the city, including DeWayne, a 14-year-old who dreamed of going to Alaska with his con of a dad. The boy committed suicide before the trip could ever happen. In *American Heart*, Bell rescues his memory, reuniting him with the parent that he never saw again.

DeWayne's real life story might be beyond pathos but if it were invented it might seem patly contrived. Meanwhile Nick and Jack's tale wouldn't seem out of place in one of Warner's Depression-era movies. *Bicycle Thieves* also springs to mind; Jack and Nick's dream of Alaska is unravelled when their money and Jack's bike are stolen from their digs.

But despite an ending that smacks of dramatic desperation, *American Heart* keeps sentimentality at bay. Bell has the same clear eye for his characters' environment as he did in *Streetwise*. The low-rent lifestyle is not invested with sleazy kitsch glamour. Here the white trash folk are exactly that—people who have been thrown out and abandoned by society, orphans of the state. There is nothing to fetishize in Nick and Jack's sparsely furnished, beige-coloured room with its stained divan mattress and thin blankets. The bump-and-grind joint where Molly's mother performs her weary routine is shot in a harsh light. Molly peeps through the glass window in awe, later recalling her mom's movements, remembering to keep the smile on her face when she go-go dances in a bikini at a stag night. The moment is dispassionately depicted; Bell does not care to moralise. But as Nick looks on, the audience knows from the expression on his face just how sad he is that his young friend's life has come to this.

American Heart draws its strength from Edward Furlong's and Jeff Bridges' performances (Bridges executive-produced it, and in many ways it is his film). Furlong, who showed such promise in *Terminator 2*, is a young actor to watch, following in the hard mould of Jodie Foster or the late River Phoenix. He holds his character in, speaking volumes with the blankest of looks on his elfin face. Meanwhile, a fat, long-haired Bridges gets under Jack's grubby, tattooed skin. Though the film has been scripted (by Seattle-based writer Peter Silverman, whose only other prominent credits are the TV series *Moonlighting* and *Hill Street Blues*), it feels as though these two have injected an improvisational touch or two. The result is an affecting account of a father who, though at first dismissive, attempts to do right by his son and be a dad in the most traditional of ways, imparting advice on girls and other buddysome banter ("you keep me straight, I'll keep you straight"). It's as if Jack is earnestly learning to do the dad thing from some old film or book, so estranged has he become from the son whose only other previous object of emotional attachment was a pet pig. Jack buys him a pair of binoculars for the Neverland of Alaska, and takes him on a day trip in which they end up having a B-B-Q in Charlotte's taxi. It's an attempt at the red-blooded all-American dad. But though Jack is shot only in the final scene, there is a sense that throughout the film he is trying to staunch the wounds.

VILLAGE VOICE, 5/18/93, p. 64, Amy Taubin

If you've seen *Streetwise*, Martin Bell's documentary about Seattle street kids, you'll remember Dewayne, the runty 14-year-old with bad tonsils who dreams of going to Alaska with his father, a con man doing hard time for burglary and arson. Dewayne committed suicide before his father was released. *American Heart*, Bell's first fiction feature, is built on the shards of that father-and-son relationship. It gives them the chance to get together that they never had.

Jack (Jeff Bridges), a "middleweight criminal" on parole and desperately trying to go straight, and his pubescent son, Nick (Edward Furlong), struggling to reconcile the father of his fantasy with a semi-alcoholic greaser who steals the mattress out from under him, bond with an intensity that neither expect.

The film has more than its share of nuances and affecting moments, though it's too conventionally shaped to accommodate such messy lives. On the other hand, the acting is extraordinary. Bridges, who is both the greatest and most underrated American screen actor, forgoes the big-cat grace and the emotional ease that've carried him through otherwise forgettable movies. Here he's bulked-up—muscle-bound, stiff in the joints, and short of breath. His face is puffy and grizzled, his voice hollowed-out and raspy, he's so clenched that his feelings are like squawks. There's a lot of risk in a performance this self-effacing.

The opalescent-skinned Furlong plays Nick with a diffidence that's edged with despair, and the smaller parts, both kids and adults, are subtly cast. In a film about fathers and sons, the moment I most cherish happens between mother and daughter. In a grimy girlie parlor, a five-year-old presses her face against the glass and looks adoringly at the body she knows best, glamorously sequined and doing the strip.

Also reviewed in:
CHICAGO TRIBUNE, 10/15/93, Friday/p. O, Michael Wilmington
NEW REPUBLIC, 6/14/93, p. 30, Stanley Kauffmann
NEW YORK TIMES, 5/14/93, p. C10, Janet Maslin
NEW YORKER, 6/14/93, p. 94, Terrence Rafferty
VARIETY, 6/1/92, p. 66, Todd McCarthy

AMONGST FRIENDS

A Fine Line Features release of a Last Outlaw Films/Island World production.   *Executive Producer:* Rob Weiss.   *Producer:* Matthew Blumberg and Mark Hirsch.   *Director:* Rob Weiss.   *Screenplay:* Rob Weiss.   *Director of Photography:* Michael Bonvillain.   *Editor:* Leo Trombetta.   *Music:* Mick Jones.   *Sound:* Mark Paperno, Thomas Szabolcs, and Buck Dior.   *Sound Editor:* Leo Trombetta.   *Casting:* Rob Weiss and Mira Sorvino.   *Production Designer:* Terrence Foster.   *Art Director:* Sharon Lomofsky and Cheryl Taylor.   *Set Dresser:* Bill Walsh and Kevin Whelan.   *Costumes:* Traci Digesu and Danielle Hollywood.   *Make-up:* Bridget Bernhart.   *Fight Coordinator:* Pete Traina.   *Running time:* 88 minutes.   *MPAA Rating:* R.

CAST: EARLY EIGHTIES: Chris Santos (Young Andy);   Michael Leb (Young Trevor);   Christian Thom (Young Billy);   Lou Cantelmo (Andy's Father);   Jerry Leonard (Andy's Grandfather);   David Stepkin (Jack Trattner);   Greg Bernardi, Lou Bernardi, and Charles Mattina (Poker Players);   Adam Montalbano and Michael Sorvino (Kids in Fight);   Jay Gordon (Billy's Father);   Michael Weiss (Drug Dealer);   LATE EIGHTIES: Joseph Lindsey (Billy);   Andy Weiss (Kid at Door);   Patrick McGaw (Trevor);   Steve Parlavecchio (Andy);   Hayley Guzman (Girl on Couch);   Mira Sorvino (Laura);   Richard Mangogna (Driver Narc);   James Biberi (Passenger Narc);   Joseph Sciarrotta (Judge);   Maddi Amato (Stenographer);   Mort Carr (Attorney);   Steve Kaplan (Beating Victim);   1992: Brett Lambson (Friend);   Julio Barrier (Bodega Owner);   Michael Artura (Michael);   Bob Graziano (Guy outside of Bakery);   Don Damico (Louis);   Michael Ringer (Sal);   Frank Medrano (Vic);   Louis Lombardi (Eddie);   Jimmy Natale, Howard Goodman, Richie "the Boxer", and Chris "the Mayor" McMahon (Billy's Crew);   Steve "Buddha" Rosenbluth (Nicky);   Danielle Givner (Girl on Beach);   Jaime Baron (Guy on Beach 1);   Shoshana Ami (Guy on Beach 2);   Linda Gerstman (Guy on Beach 3);   Michael Blak (Craig);   Jeff Sternhell (Ernie);   Rob Weiss (Bobby);   Shawn A. English (Monte);   James Rich (Ricky);   Tommy Colmer (Tommy);   Huey Friedman (U-Mel);   Steven Miller (Bouncer Shot);   Sammy Pugliese (Bartender);   Kim Carlucci (Crying Girl);   Paul Badome and Al Marrero (Abused Bouncers);   Tony Fatone and Martin Haber (Jack's Crew);   Ford Sorvino (Fish);   Lou Mastantuono (Rubber);   Matt Schultz (Biker Crew Member);   Howard Cotler (Laura's Father);   Amy Pierce (Counter);   Chris James (Mitch the Dealer);   Steve Proto (Dave);   Lora Zuckerman (Leslie);   Peter Papageorgiou (Young Wiseguy);   Vincent Bandille and Al Lopez (Wiseguys in Lot);   Robert Canaan (Tony, Young Wiseguy);   Bernard Jaffe (Philly Valicio);   Stan Schwartz (Arnie the Jeweler);   Sara Sloves (Andy's Girl);   Sybil Temtchine (Laura's Friend);   Pete Traina (Arson).

LOS ANGELES TIMES, 8/11/93, Calendar/p. 4, Peter Rainer

The young toughs in "Amongst Friends" are a new breed in the movies who act like the old breed. They come on like junior-league Mafiosi but they're actually the scions of wealthy Jewish Long Island suburbanites.

Unlike most of their friends who have gone on to college after high school, Andy (Steve Parlavecchio), Billy (Joseph Lindsay) and Trevor (Patrick McGaw) have taken up the life of the small-time hustle with big-time aspirations.

Rob Weiss, the 26-year-old writer-director making his feature film debut, has a strong affinity for this milieu but, at the same time, he doesn't really make it believable. There's high comedy in the image of affluent Jewish kids swaggering and prancing like inner-city toughs; they don't respect their parents, who gave them everything, but they revere their grandparents, who scrounged and cheated to give their children everything. It's a great Generation X story but Weiss chooses to play it out as a crime melodrama. The characters never emerge from their welter of grudges and double-crosses.

Weiss, like most independent filmmakers of his generation, has been deeply influenced by the films of Martin Scorsese, specifically "Mean Streets." There are far worse models for a new director than "Mean Streets," but Weiss misunderstands the nature of that film. It wasn't about punk gangsterism; it was about character, and Catholicism and guilt and self-immolation.

The Jewish background of the kids in "Amongst Friends" is barely visible, we don't see the tradition they came out of, even in rebellion. Most of the movie seems to be taken up with Andy, Trevor, Billy and their cronies and enemies trying to out-tough guy one another. Their jags are sometimes funny but they go on too long and they make the same point—that these boys are looking for a way to feel big.

Andy, who is the most levelheaded of the trio, also comes across as the least stereotyped. When a botched robbery places him under the control of an old gangster buddy (David Stepkin) of his late grandfather's, he comes alive. He feels as if he's acting out his grandfather's rags-to-riches success story (minus the rags, of course.) Trevor, who spent two years in prison for a bungled drug drop, is the film's moody loner who still pines for his high school sweetheart (Mira Sorvino). He acts tough but inside he's hurting—oy, is he hurting.

Weiss keeps his actors in high energy, and a few set pieces, like the recurring Tweedledee/Tweedledum act of two warm-up-suited drug dealers (Frank Medrano and Louis Lombardi), are ticklish. But "Amongst Friends" (rated R for violence, drug use, sexuality and pervasive strong language) reminds you of so many other movies that finally it's unmemorable.

NEW LEADER, 10/4-18/93, p. 20, David Bromwich

Young directors with art credentials worn face-up have begun to weigh in with shockingly violent debuts. The screaming kill pushed close to the camera, the slow torture, the bullet-riddled corpse with every hole punched out—all the tokens of murderous authenticity are apt to materialize almost without a preface. The reason, say the publicity kits, is that the young director knows the neighborhood, but suppose we forget that snow job. No director so excruciatingly close to the mayhem ever survived to complete his first take; and besides, for the aspiring filmmaker art imitates art much more than it imitates life. They make violent movies because they grew up watching violent movies.

Rob Weiss, who at 26 has released *Amongst Friends*, is firmly in the grip of *GoodFellas, My Beautiful Launderette* and lots of other good or seductive pictures about the brutal intimacy of youthful bands of outsiders. The genre commonly offers a portrait of the drug terrorist as a young man, the making of a grown-up nihilist from whom the director holds himself at an uncertain distance. The surprise of *Amongst Friends* is that the gang is composed of Jewish boys from Long Island: an ethnic group till now unsung in the genre, and odd to find so neatly filled with the usual types. A point of the treatment here—glossed over by the action format, which works against individual traits—is that they aren't noticeably Jewish. Trevor (Patrick McGaw), Billy (Joseph Lindsey) and Andy (Steve Parlavecchio) have all melted into the broad savagery of the American money hustle.

This is a story of betrayal. The boys have been friends since their early teens, and together go from mooching to pilfering to dealing. Trevor, the thoughtful one, gets busted on a drug delivery, but he doesn't rat. He returns from prison a new man—riding a motorcycle, wearing a head-bandanna, accompanied by a new friend and guru who preaches indifference to money. They babble of California while Billy and Andy look on with awe. But Trevor has a weakness. He wants his old girlfriend back, and in a moment whose triteness comes from very old movies indeed, he swallows the line his pals feed him—"She'll want to live in style." To make some money, he falls in with Andy and Billy again, and the rest of the film is his personal war with Billy, the most relentless of the group.

One forgets now and then that the film is narrated as a flashback by the timid and pliable Andy. The narration, however, is prominent in early and late montages: a voice over home movie shots of the young hoods at cards and basketball, their rich suburban precincts tinted a glaring sunset red. This element is extremely effective and comes out of *GoodFellas*, where the jolt and speed were the narrator's coke habit talking. For Weiss, the jumpy style has become a vague metaphor for disenchanted American coming-of-age. The screenplay, also by Weiss, has been impoverished by faithful imitation of the same model, several "f---s" a minute covering the range of shock, pity, loathing, wonder, and exasperation, as in: "Yez a bunch of f---ing moils, yez a bunch of f---ing nobodies" and "This is f---ing tuna, I said chicken salad, dick."

With his well-honed surface, how does this director fare when a thought or feeling is called for—when his cinematographer (Michael Bonvillain), editor (Leo Trombetta), composer (Mick Jones), and the soundtrack of songs from Dylan to Tony Bennett fall away and we look to see whether the life on the screen can matter? Trevor and his girlfriend are stock young lovers; Trevor and Billy are the sentimental and cynical poles of almost any teenage melodrama. And just inches wide of the twenty-third "f---" the dialogue quits or congeals to a gruel of I-really-love-you and Now-at-last-we'll-be-rich. Near the end the half-muttered half-quoted appeal "You kill me, you'll kill yourself," does lazy duty for a whole unwritten screenplay.

The acting is often unratable, buoyed as it is by the stutter of streetwise patter and the expert editing. Patrick McGaw seems not yet formed enough to get much footing in the soft-edged and difficult role of Trevor. Joseph Lindsey's Billy struts convincingly, and he has nerve power around the eyes and mouth, but not one shock wave passes through the mold of the character—the sort of intensity that came off Ray Liotta the moment he walked on screen at the high school reunion in *Something Wild*. A central ambiguity hangs on a doubt about the arrest of Trevor earlier. Did Billy set him up? The answer to that unspoken question should be in Lindsey's face, but isn't. On the other hand, Steve Parlavecchio's Andy has the retentive look of the man who will be telling the story some day, and he grows in conviction scene by scene.

Amongst Friends suggests a canny eye for effects that will resonate—an ingratiating quality, but not a particularly youthful one. The film shows off its Long Island roots, with advertised place names like Cedarhurst; but really, the sense of the place is never dramatized. The Jewish message is cashed out in one line by Jackie, an old black market jewelry runner whom the boys fall in with. "Who are these kids?" someone asks Jackie, and he answers with glib thematic aptitude: "They're us, all over again." The line echoes a pan of the friends in deck chairs on the boardwalk, looking unconsciously like their parents, passing a cigar and chattering. Action credit, ethnic credit, local-loyalty credit—every bet is so finely hedged there is no room for surprise.

NEW YORK, 8/9/93, p. 77, David Denby

Having spent as a child several summers in Atlantic Beach, Long *Guy*land I was intrigued by the idea of a gangster film set in the Five Towns—a film about three upper-middle-class Jewish boys becoming hoods. (*Gutmenschen?*) The trouble is that Rob Weiss, in his first film, *Amongst Friends*, exploits only about half the comic possibilities of his subject. Weiss's three young men—Billy (Joseph Lindsey), the tough-talking poseur and betrayer; Trevor (Patrick McGaw), the victim who wants only to escape; and Andy (Steve Parlavecchio), the narrator, a nice boy out of his depth—jump into crime without our understanding how they managed to escape the more common fate of college and law school. The boys' parents are nowhere present, yet Andy has access to a luxurious house in Cedarhurst. The boys don't talk like Jews, and if the point is (as it seems to be) that they are imitating Italian and black toughs, then Weiss doesn't have much fun with that. Weiss heads straight for the rough Scorsese stuff—the rivalries, the betrayals and violence. At times, the situations are so standard—movieish that one seeks, without finding it, a Godardian irony, the sense that the young men are consciously seeing themselves as characters in movies.

Partly removed from the social context that would have made it special, the movie seems like Weiss's fantasy of himself and his buddies magically thrown into a Scorsese film. Not that Weiss lacks talent. The exposition is messy, but some of the action and the Cedarhurst-at-dusk moodiness are quite effective. Once it gets going, *Amongst Friends* has a sincere kind of gangster-movie desperation and tension. Weiss needs to work with a writer, and also with a producer strong enough to point out the holes in his ideas. The movie does, however, have one touch of bizarre authenticity—an elderly bookie and hood (David Stepkin) who seems like any coarse and avuncular old guy but who turns out to mean what he says.

NEW YORK POST, 7/23/93, p. 32, Audrey Farolino

It might seem that the last thing the world needs is yet another movie about a group of hoods caught up in a web of crime and betrayal where nothing means anything except who has the "juice," or power.

The theme's been explored—often masterfully—in everything from "GoodFellas" to "Reservoir Dogs" to "Laws of Gravity." So all the more credit is due to first-time writer/director Rob Weiss for taking that well-trod terrain and making it seem fresh and powerful again in "Amongst Friends."

This is an impressive first feature, even if one has to regret that just about every young male filmmaker who comes along seems to have watched every Martin Scorsese movie ever made about 10 times too often.

Weiss, a 26-year-old Long Island native, has said that the script for "Amongst Friends" virtually poured out of him in a few weeks. Watching the film's opening minutes, you can almost feel that torrent of creative energy spilling on to the screen.

The friends amongst whom this tragedy unfolds are Billy (Joseph Lindsey), Trevor (Patrick Mc-Gaw) and Andy (Steve Parlavecchio).

They grow up as close as brothers in the affluent Five Towns area of Long Island—where gamblers, rabbis and dentists live side by side and 16-year-old Jewish kids go around "acting like they're Flavor Flav."

Most of their peers go off to law school or Wall Street. But Billy, Trevor and Andy are cut from different cloth—as kids, they pull off minor schoolyard hustles. By their late teens, they're routinely dealing dope.

One night, Trevor is busted by undercover cops. After two years in prison and a few more on the road, he returns to the neighborhood, but things will never be the same again: Billy is not only seeing Trevor's old flame Laura (Mira Sorvino), he has also become a serious, small-time hood.

Both Andy and Trevor are ultimately set on a fatal collision course with Billy because of jealousy over Laura, and because of their new ties to an old but still ruthless gangster (David Stepkin).

What gives depth to the story is the emotions and poses it uncovers; they come across clearly and resonantly thanks both to Weiss' direction and to strong performances across the board. The most striking thing about "Amongst Friends," however, is the realism of its narrow world. You'll never pass through this area of Long Island again without wondering about the people who live behind its neat lawns and respectable doorways.

NEWSDAY, 7/23/93, Part II/p. 63, Jack Mathews

Young filmmaker Rob Weiss uses his first feature to tell the story of three upper-middle-class Long Island friends who grow up enchanted by the underworld in their clean, well-lighted midst and who manage to destroy their lives trying to catch a piece of the action.

It is, in its innocent, ambitious way, the suburban version of "Mean Streets," and it's the sort of movie any one of Weiss' three main characters might have made if he decided to be a filmmaker when he grew up instead of a bag man.

That may be what happened. Weiss, 26, grew up in the affluent Five Towns section of Long Island, and the film is brimming with seemingly astute observations about the kids who grow up there. Kids whose grandparents may have made an illegitimate fortune so their own children could become doctors and lawyers.

The three youths portrayed in "Amongst Friends" are apparently one generation removed from the hard criminals; they're products of comfort who brawl, steal, con and connive for the sport of it, fresh-faced thugs so mired in the fraternal hustle that they get lapped by life and get so far behind they have no hope of catching up.

In the film's clumsiest and most pertinent scene, Andy (Steve Parlavecchio) runs into a smug, former high school friend who is visiting from law school, and he can't get over how few of their old classmates are still around:

To Andy, the encounter underscores his failures, reminds him he is flailing through his 20s, running in place. Weiss is stretching the point to make Andy, Billy (Joseph Lindsey) and Trevor (Patrick McGaw) symbols of his own disengaged generation, and the criminal world he places them in seems to have been lifted from an old Warner Bros. gangster movie.

Underworld boss Jack Trattner (David Stepkin), Andy's grandfather's best friend, is like a Borsht-Belt don, his heavily lidded eyes welling up with tears as he recalls the good old days in gusts of criminal nostalgia. It's all he can do to keep his mind on business, which apparently is fencing diamonds and keeping sociopathic bullies employed.

"Amongst Friends" is cluttered with this kind of rank movie cliché, and there is less acting on view than studied posturing. We not only have trouble caring about Weiss' three mugs, we have trouble believing they could exist.

Yet the movie has a force field all its own. It's like a student film, from a talented A-student. The dialogue is crisp, the action sequences are first rate, and at least two of Weiss' young stars—Lindsey and Parlavecchio—have the tremendous screen presence.

In the story, the trio's childhood friendship is interrupted when Trevor is sent to prison on a drug conviction. When he returns, Billy is a mean-spirited professional crook, and Andy is a desperate wannabe, trying to scrape up enough money to buy his way into other people's scams.

Since Billy has moved in on Trevor's girlfriend, Laura (Mira Sorvino, daughter of Paul), there is little chance for rekindling their friendship, and after an ill-fated robbery dreamed up by Andy goes bad, all three are set on a fatal collision course.

Weiss made some real casting errors, it seems to me. Lindsey is perfect as Billy, a baby-faced thug with the potential to become a real killer. But the pivotal role is that of Trevor, the ex-con eager to reclaim his girl and go straight, and McGaw is much too passive and self-conscious an actor to pull that off.

Parlavecchio, who bears a striking resemblance to Brad Pitt, has a lot more fire in his soul, and if he and McGaw had merely switched parts, their characters, and the movie, would have been much stronger.

Still, the R-rated "Amongst Friends" may be the antidote for those who have overdosed on sanguine family movies. This one is frothing at the mouth with profanity, and the violence will catch your breath in a couple of spots. It's not quite "Reservoir Dogs," but it's got teeth.

SIGHT AND SOUND, 12/93, p. 39, Christopher Bray

Andy, Billy and Trevor are middle-class kids from Five Towns, Long Island, who want for nothing. But their parents' staid professions fail to fire their dreams. Instead they are drawn to the shady world inhabited by Andy's bookie grandfather and his hard-drinking gangster friends. The boys start out small, hustling other kids for nickels and dimes, but as they grow older their scams become more elaborate. By their teens the boys are commuting to Manhattan to gamble and run small-time scores; unlike their classmates, the boys choose not to go to college but to make drug runs.

On one such drop Trevor is caught by the police and sent to prison for two years. When he returns, he finds that things have changed: the boys are wearing designer suits and driving sports cars. Billy has moved in on Laura, Trevor's former girlfriend, but Trevor soon wins her back. Approached by a couple of neighbourhood drug dealers, the three decide to go for the big time by putting up $20,000 for a stash of dope. In order to finance this, they plan to rob a nightclub run by Jack Trattner, a local Jewish gangster. Things go wrong, however, and the boys are forced to work their debt off to Trattner, who turns out to have been a best friend of Andy's grandfather. When Trevor discovers that Laura has continued seeing Billy, a fight between the two men ensues and Trevor is killed. Disgusted, Andy kills Billy and pays Trattner off.

With its soft sepia opening shots Weiss's first feature was a remake of Robert Mulligan's *Summer of '42*. But once the credits are out of the way, it quickly becomes clear that this is no film about troubled adolescent love. Rather, it is a story of troubled adolescents in which the adolescents make the trouble, and its influences are Martin Scorsese, Martin Scorsese and Martin Scorsese.

The major difference between Weiss's characters and Scorsese's is that the guys in this movie have had a decent education. Weiss is dealing with privileged children, who have been raised not in the city but in a small town. They're dead end kids by choice—they come from good homes but they want to be good fellas. It is *Mean Streets* that Weiss has most obviously stolen from. Scorsese himself, of course, is nothing if not well versed in cinema history, but until recently he also managed to get quite a lot of observation from life into his films. The same, alas, does not obtain for Weiss; one suspects he has done little with his 26 years but watch movies. Nor do his characters seem to have done much but watch gangster pictures. Would that they had been more observant: you'd think these guys would know that on a drug drop there's a good chance your client will turn out to be a cop in disguise.

Not much in *Amongst Friends* rings true. The performances are flat and undifferentiated, the characters' dialogue interchangeable, the repertoire of tics and grimaces all too familiar. The film boasts but one scene that could be described as keenly felt: Billy and Trevor's argument over Laura is badly shot and edited, but at least Joseph Lindsey and Patrick McGaw seem to be acting out something they've seen and understood in the real world. However, even here Weiss has to try and kick-start things. Fists are raised, guns are drawn and the camera begins to circle, and within seconds we are back with the pop promo world we momentarily thought we'd left behind.

VILLAGE VOICE, 7/27/93, p. 55, Georgia Brown

Rob Weiss is a young writer/director setting his movie in the old neighborhood. *Amongst Friends* takes place in and among the mock-Tudor mansions of Long Island's so-called Five Towns. Here, according to the movie's hype, crime is the new chic: Gangsters (the grandfathers) begat professionals (the fathers), who in turn begat a new generation of con artists and wannabe hoods (the sons).

A schoolyard threesome (see the boys horse around in grainy Super 8) grows up getting into minor troubles until one of the three (the wrong one) is caught in a drug drop and does time. He's Trevor (Patrick McGaw), the cutest and the one with the weakest anti-social inclinations. The other two are Billy the bully (Joseph Lindsey) and Andy the anxious (Steve Parlavecchio), whose grandfather palled around with godfathers. Trevor leaves behind a girl, the angelic Laura (Mira Sorvino), who (improbably) takes up with the beastly Billy. Girls are so rare in this milieu that you (filmmakers) can do with them what you will, even if it totally violates their character.

The movie proper begins with Trevor's return, under wraps at first but still nursing a fatal tendency to trust his childhood buddies. Billy is now a full-fledged viper and Andy (who looks like a slightly pudgy James Dean) is hatching grandiose, palpably destructive plans for a robbery in order to buy into a drug deal promoted by two fast-talking fat guys in jogging suits. Luckily, Andy's family connections to an elderly Jewish mafioso (David Stepkin) save most of the gang from wiseguy revenge. But he can't save them from themselves or one another.

At any rate, the movie is scored with *beaucoup* songs, the way Scorsese does it, though here the music isn't well integrated; instead, it competes with the action. Certain attempts at camera virtuosity are gratuitous and some are embarrassing. In one scene the camera swirls around, the actors like a heat-maddened fly begging to be swatted. Just as its characters are wannabe gangstas, *Amongst Friends* is a wannabe Scorsese picture, a *Mean Tree-lined Streets*.

Also reviewed in:
CHICAGO TRIBUNE, 8/13/93, Friday/p. B, Clifford Terry
NEW REPUBLIC, 8/23 & 30/93, p. 30, Stanley Kauffmann
NEW YORK TIMES, 7/23/93, p. C10, Janet Maslin
VARIETY, 2/15/93, p. 84, Todd McCarthy
WASHINGTON POST, 8/13/93, p. D6, Hal Hinson

AMOS & ANDREW

A Castle Rock Entertainment release in association with New Line Cinema. *Producer:* Gary Goetzman, Jack Cummins, and Marshal Persinger. *Director:* E. Max Frye. *Screenplay:* E. Max Frye. *Director of Photography:* Walt Lloyd. *Editor:* Jane Kurson. *Music:* Richard Gibbs. *Music Editor:* Carlton Kaller. *Sound:* John Pritchett and (music) Shawn Murphy. *Sound Editor:* John Morris. *Casting:* Christine Sheaks and Joanna Colbert. *Production Designer:* Patricia Norris. *Set Decorator:* Leslie Morales. *Set Dresser:* Matthew Sullivan. *Special Effects:* Joey Di Gaetano. *Costumes:* Patricia Norris. *Make-up:* Jean A. Black. *Stunt Coordinator:* Glenn Randall, Jr. *Running time:* 92 minutes. *MPAA Rating:* PG-13.

CAST: Nicolas Cage (Amos Odell); Samuel L. Jackson (Andrew Sterling); Michael Lerner (Phil Gillman); Margaret Colin (Judy Gillman); Dabney Coleman (Chief of Police Cecil Tolliver); Brad Dourif (Officer Donnie Donaldson); Chelcie Ross (Earl); I.M. Hobson (Waldo Lake); Jeff Blumenkrantz (Ernie); Todd Weeks (Stan); Jordan Lund (Riley); Jodi Long (Wendy Wong); Michael Burgess (Black Reporter); Leonor Anthony (Hispanic

Reporter); Walter Raymond (Anchorman); Giancarlo Esposito (The Reverend Fenton Brunch); Loretta Devine (Ula); Bob Balaban (Dr. R.A. "Roy" Fink); Ron Taylor (Sherman); Aimee Graham (Stacy); Ernie Garrett (State Police Captain); Tracey Walter (Bloodhound Bob); Allison Mackie (Anchorwoman); Eric Paisley (Mainland Gatekeeper); Kim Staunton (Mrs. Andrew Sterling).

LOS ANGELES TIMES, 3/5/93, Calendar/p. 10, Peter Rainer

The difference between a good comedy and a lousy one is often a matter of a few moments in the timing. "Amos & Andrew" starts out with a promising premise but everything in it is off—the timing, the tone, the performances. It's the kind of film that makes you wonder from moment to moment just what E. Max Frye, the writer-director, had in mind. Maybe nothing? Andrew Sterling (Samuel T. Jackson) is a Pulitzer Prize-winning playwright and black activist who buys a summer home on an exclusive all-white island off the coast of Massachusetts. Mistaken by his neighbors (Michael Lerner and Margaret Colin) for a burglar, Andrew soon finds himself the target of a police siege.

When the police chief, played by Dabney Coleman, realizes he's attacking a celebrity, he cooks up a scheme to bail himself out. Amos Odell (Nicolas Cage), a recently arrested car thief, is promised his freedom if he will pose as an intruder who attempts to take Andrew hostage. The scheme backfires, of course, but not before a ravenous gaggle of media hounds swoop down on the scene. Amos and Andrew, in between bouts of sniping at each other, learn a few lessons in racial harmony. It's "The Defiant Ones" done up in clown-face but the brotherhood-of-man sentiments are served up straight.

Frye, who wrote the extraordinary, madcap script for Jonathan Demme's "Something Wild," has a few good ideas in "Amos & Andrew," but he's not enough of a director—it's his first feature—to put them across. Andrew is meant to be a hypocrite activist: He preaches racial pride but chooses to live in lily-white land. Amos, a wised-up low-life scrounger, confronts him with his own hypocrisy. (Not too many of Amos' assumptions are challenged.) There could be a good comedy about the way working-class whites react to upper-middle-class blacks: there could be an even better one in the way moneyed, exclusive-neighborhood whites react to their black counterparts.

But the racial humor in "Amos & Andrew" is so broad and yet so unadventurous that it leaves you with a sour feeling in your stomach. How are we supposed to react to a scene like the one where a raucous, headline-grabbing black activist preacher (Giancarlo Esposito) leads a demonstration against the islanders? The preacher intentionally comes across as a dangerous fool but the scene also seems to be saying that Andrew deserves what he gets.

The neighbors played by Lerner and Colin are caricatured mercilessly as white liberal hypocrites: they call the police at the first sign of a black face but suddenly turn forgiving when the face turns out to belong to a celebrity. Racism this broadly played isn't satirical: it's just obnoxious. Lerner, in particular, is encouraged to play up his character's comic loathsomeness. (It's the kind of performance that actors should avoid—it uses up a lot of audience good will.)

Cage is pretty funny in his scenes with Jackson, who plays most of the movie in a grim funk. Coleman does his trademark smarmy smarty-pants routine; Brad Dourif, as the assistant police chief, does his wide-eyed wacko bit, and Bob Balaban, as a hostage situation expert, rescues the movie a few times. (He turns out to be a hostage to his own delusions.) You keep wanting for "Amos & Andrew" (rated PG-13 for some drug content and language) to work itself into an all-out frenzy and get into some dangerous areas. But for all its hue and cry the film is conventional. It makes a great fuss about knocking down the same old tired targets.

NEW YORK POST, 3/5/93, p. 33, Jerry Tallmer

There is one instant when the fatuous wife of the fatuous-ass caricature phony white liberal in "Amos & Andrew" boasts that "Phil"—her husband—"was one of the lawyers of the Chicago 7," he off-handedly correcting it to: "I was associate, actually."

This is the same couple outside whose big white house with its three-car garage on an island very much like Martha's Vineyard there stands a little darkie hitching post. The same couple who at the start of the film observe something that horrifies them through the window of a neighboring house and put in a panic call to the local law with lawyer Phil proclaiming. "Believe me, Chief Tolliver, I'm not a racist, but when you see a black man on this island with his arms full of stereos ..."

Well, it so happens I was at the trial of the Chicago 7 for a while—Abbie Hoffman & Co. vs. the Honorables Richard J. Daley and Julius J. Hoffman—and while the assistant defense counsel was indeed the kind of gauche young radical who marched headlong, nay, hurled himself into every trap, he was very far from any other sort of caricature, especially such easy targets as "Amos & Andrew" sets up all down the line.

The result is that what should be a bright and biting comedy, isn't. Which is all the more sorry, because it was written and is the first directing job by E. Max Frye, who had previously scripted that "Something Wild" movie with Melanie Griffith that I loved.

So here's what happens. The black man who breaks into the house with his arms full of stereos is Andrew Sterling (Samuel L. Jackson), Pulitzer-prize-winning playwright so controlled and civilized—his face is on the cover of Forbes magazine—you'd hardly know he thinks of himself as a thorn in the side of white society. Of course the play he won the Pulitzer for is "Yo, Brother, Where Art Thou" which might give a clue. Anyway, the house is Andrew's own because he's bought it, thinking that this island is perhaps the one place a black person can live with relative security.

It is the threat of this dangerous criminal-at-large that gets Chief Tolliver (Dabney Coleman), running for re-election, to summon half an army of cops to surround the place. "Body arms for everyone and I want them to wear it," the chief snarls at the fumbling, bumbling overeager deputy (Brad Dourif) who blows the whole thing sky-high with shots in the night and a conjured-up "hostage" situation that brings press and TV (caricature style) swarming in from near and far.

But the movie, remember, is called "Amos & Andrew," a deliberate—and risk-taking—caricature title. Amos is Amos Odell (Nicolas Cage), a charming louse of a petty-criminal drifter who happens to be inhabiting Chief Tolliver's jail precisely at the moment the Chief needs him. Because the Chief has found out who Andrew Sterling is, he makes a deal with Amos: You go into that house, bring him out, then you get out of town fast, okay?

What happens from there on is farce or would-be farce, with a few good laughs here and there. Still, I hate to see so much talent, so many ideas, go so astray. The worst thing about this movie is that its heart is on the right side.

NEWSDAY, 3/5/93, Part II/p. 55, Jack Mathews

In E. Max Frye's "Amos & Andrew," the famous playwright and black activist Andrew Sterling (Samuel L. Jackson) moves into his new summer home on an affluent resort island and, within minutes, is mistaken for a burglar. Soon, he is cowering under a bed while trigger-happy cops blast away at his beautiful two-story colonial, and what is intended as a slapstick comedy of errors is on.

The only thing worse than this idea is the execution of it, and with the lone exception of Nicolas Cage, as the dim-witted thief recruited by police to help cover up their mistake, "Amos and Andrew" will be a smudge on the resumes of everyone involved.

Frye, who wrote the freshly clever screenplay for Jonathan Demme's "Something Wild" a few years back, gave himself a tough task here—to make a good-natured comedy out of racism—and in his eagerness to clear himself of the charge, he made a movie that is often as offensive as its targets. As the racial references pile up, it's like listening to someone let slip a racist remark then compound it by noting how many of his best friends are black.

It is no small irony that Jackson, so brilliant as the jumpy crack addict in "Jungle Fever," is the most squandered talent in this field. It is up to his character, as the victim of racism, to provide the film's conscience, which he does with a mixture of civility and anger totally out of sync with the cartoonish tone of the rest of the movie. He's playing the straight man in a gang of fools, and as black roles go, that's only marginally better than playing the fool in a straight drama.

Still, Jackson comes out of this mess with some dignity. The same cannot be said for Michael Lerner and Margaret Colin, as Sterling's hypocritical neighbors (they smoke pot and have rough sex, we learn), and Dabney Coleman, typecast as the smugly devious, self-loving chief of police.

What few pleasures the film offers come from Cage, a bumbling thief used by police as a foil for a faked hostage crisis. Cage's Amos isn't much different from the loopy low-life characters he developed in "Raising Arizona" and "Wild at Heart," and though he edges closer to caricature with each performance, it is still a plus here.

In fact, it is the only plus here.

VILLAGE VOICE, 3/16/93, p. 56, David D. Kim

Imagine a Rodney King-type incident on a WASPy resort island. Imagine that, instead of using clubs and fists, cops assault the unarmed "suspect" with volleys of gunfire. Imagine all of this on 35mm film instead of on video, and you've got the opening scenes of *Amos & Andrew*—a comedy.

Of errors. In his directorial debut, Frye (who also wrote the screenplay for *Something Wild*), strands us on a claustrophobic island and compresses the narrative into a single, sleepless night. Andrew Sterling (Samuel Jackson), a successful playwright and all-around righteous brother; moves to Watauga Island, where he's immediately taken for a burglar and shot at by local patrol forces. When the police chief (Dabney Coleman) realizes the mistake, he sets up petty crook Amos (Nicolas Cage) as Andrew's captor and the media's scapegoat.

From here, Frye forces Amos and Andrew (get it?) along the bumpy road to color consciousness. Amos begins by accusing the black bard—whose Broadway hit is titled *Yo, Brother, Where Art Thou?*—of selling his "soul," and the ensuing drama hinges on one question: Is Andrew a true brother or a white man in black drag?

For added symbolic effect, both Amos and an overeager cop smear their faces with dark grease; later on, however, Frye fancies himself too down to explain who the original Amos 'n' Andy were. Such earnestness is touching, especially considering that everywhere else, the misguided race message is scrawled in large block letters. When Mrs. Sterling shows up, for instance, her "blackness" is never questioned. She merely signifies *black* in the same way that Andrew's BMW signifies *white*.

Jackson, perhaps embarrassed by this damned-if-you-do-or-don't plot line, comes off awkward and tight-lipped. More likable is Cage, in spite of his limited role as another bumbling ne'er-do-well. For Best Supporting Racial Cliché, the nominees include a posse of angry, gospel-singing black folk; a Connie-wannabe Asian reporter; and the ever hyper Giancarlo Esposito as a Sharpton manqué. Most of these actors, trapped in a *Bonfire of the Vanities Goes to Nantucket*, look hopelessly lost at sea. Yo, director, where art thou?

Also reviewed in:
CHICAGO TRIBUNE, 3/5/93, Friday/p. C, Dave Kehr
NEW YORK TIMES, 3/5/93, p. C14, Vincent Canby
NEW YORKER, 3/8/93, p. 99, Terrence Rafferty
VARIETY, 2/22/93, p. 64, Lawrence Cohn
WASHINGTON POST, 3/5/93, p. C1, Hal Hinson
WASHINGTON POST, 3/5/93, Weekend/p. 40, Desson Howe

ANIMA MUNDI

A World Wildlife Fund and Bulgari presentation. *Executive Producer:* Gianfilippo Pedote. *Producer:* Lawrence Taub. *Director:* Godfrey Reggio. *Director of Photography:* Graham Berry. *Editor:* Miroslav Janek. *Music:* Philip Glass. *Running time:* 28 minutes. *MPAA Rating:* Not Rated.

NEW YORK POST, 5/10/93, p. 26, Matthew Flamm

[*Anima Mundi* was reviewed jointly with *Amazonia: Voices from the Rain Forest*; see Flamm's review of that film.]

Also reviewed in:
NEW YORK TIMES, 5/7/93, p. C12, Stephen Holden
WASHINGTON POST, 4/16/93, Weekend/p. 40, Desson Howe
WASHINGTON POST, 4/17/93, p. C2, Richard Harrington

ANOTHER STAKEOUT

A Touchstone Pictures release. *Executive Producer:* John Badham. *Producer:* Jim Kouf, Cathleen Summers, and Lynn Bigelow. *Director:* John Badham. *Screenplay:* Jim Kouf. *Based on characters created by:* Jim Kouf. *Director of Photography:* Roy H. Wagner. *Editor:* Frank Morris. *Music:* Arthur B. Rubinstein. *Music Editor:* Abby Treloggen. *Sound:* Rick Patton and (music) John Richards. *Sound Editor:* William L. Manger. *Casting:* Carol Lewis. *Production Designer:* Lawrence G. Paull. *Art Director:* Richard Hudolin. *Set Designer:* Richard Harrison. *Set Decorator:* Rose Marie McSherry. *Set Dresser:* Brent Bennett. *Special Effects:* John Thomas. *Costumes:* Stephanie Nolin. *Make-up:* Sandy Cooper. *Make-up (Emilio Estevez):* Kim Carrillo. *Stunt Coordinator:* Conrad Palmisano and Tony Morelli. *Running time:* 109 minutes. *MPAA Rating:* PG-13.

CAST: Richard Dreyfuss (Chris Lecce);   Emilio Estevez (Bill Reimers);   Rosie O'Donnell (Gina Garrett);   Dennis Farina (Brian O'Hara);   Marcia Strassman (Pam O'Hara);   Cathy Moriarty (Lu Delano);   John Rubinstein (Thomas Hassrick);   Miguel Ferrer (Tony Castellano);   Sharon Maughan (Barbara Burnside);   Christopher Doyle (McNamara);   Sharon Schaffer (Tilghman);   Rick Seaman and Jan Speck (Van Agents);   Gene Ellison (Vegas Police Captain);   Frank DeAngelo and J.R. West (Vegas Investigators);   Frank C. Turner (Unlucky);   Steven Lambert (Killer);   Dan Lauria (Captain Coldshank);   Denalda Williams (Desk Sergeant);   Larry B. Scott (Garage Attendant);   Christi Brasher (Blonde Date);   Sammy Jackson (Gaetano);   Blu Mankuma (Seattle Detective Wills);   Thomas Mitchell (Seattle Detective Gilliam);   Scott Anderson (Reynaldo);   Michael DeLano (Michael);   Al Goto (Pizza Man);   Steve Bacic (Neighbor Frank);   Taylor Estevez (Ronnie Burnside);   Bruce Barbour and Rick Blackwell (Cops);   Michael Steve Jones (Paramedic);   Chris Shoemaker (Doctor);   Nancy Sosna and Cammie Ann Crier (Nurses);   Martin Rogers (Coroner).

CHRISTIAN SCIENCE MONITOR, 8/12/93, p. 11, Marilynne S. Mason

[*Another Stakeout* was reviewed jointly with *So I Married an Axe Murderer*; see Mason's review of that film.]

LOS ANGELES TIMES, 7/23/93, Calendar/p. 4, Michael Wilmington

"Another Stakeout," reintroduces us to "Stakeout's" Richard Dreyfuss and Emilio Estevez as flighty Chris Lecce and steady-Eddie Bill Reimers, the squabbling Seattle surveillance team from John Badham's 1987 Touchstone cop comedy.

The boys are breezy; their companions glib and glittery. This big studio mix of bang-bang and badinage isn't really a bad movie. But a lot of it suggests a fancy misfire: a super-powered evening at the town's most expensive eatery, where everybody starts out psyched up to have Big Fun, and things start to slide.

What happens? The food disappears. The music is too loud. The conversations are brittle, the jokes are pushed too hard, everyone laughs too much. And, at the end, in case your attention starts wandering, people start pulling out guns and killing each other.

Audiences may be getting wise to sequels—which may be why "Another Stakeout" isn't called "Stakeout 2." There's evidence of a of a commitment to novelty. The whole "Stakeout" team—producer-writer Jim Kouf, director Badham, stars Dreyfuss and Estevez—seem hot to prove they're not just going to shoot the first movie all over again, like everybody else.

Estevez and Dreyfuss shave off their "Stakeout" mustaches and a horde of women have been invited to break up the Boy's Club atmosphere of that original cop-buddy, damsel-in-distress thriller. The settings are more posh: Las Vegas and the re-created sylvan hide-away of Bainbridge Island, Seattle.

In this pricier caper, the bickering buddies are hunkered down with their boss, wise-cracking, accident-prone Assistant Dist. Atty. Gina Garrett (Rosie O'Donnell), waiting for the mob to find a fugitive witness (Cathy Moriarty), after nearly blowing up half of Las Vegas trying to whack her.

Since the team is now a trio that includes a woman instead of the rowdy testosterone duo, we can expect a new, quasi-feminist slant. That's what it is: Quasi. Women assert themselves in "Another Stakeout" by being imperious and insulting, throwing things, getting violent or making braying buffoons of themselves. At one point, Moriarty's Lu Delano strikes the apogee of macha: kicking Estevez downstairs while he's tied to a chair and gagged. Dreyfuss is bonked himself, earlier on, by his own girlfriend. If you didn't recognize the genre, you might suspect "Another Stakeout" of misogyny.

But why dig for deeper meanings in something like this? "Another Stakeout" is what might be called a "zap-and-zinger": It's full of fancy locations, explosions, gunfights, dogs, cats, maniacs, *double entendres* and a lot of charming actors practically ogling us from the screen. Everyone works hard; you can almost see the cast sweating over their jokes.

At the beginning, in their zest to jolt us from torpor, the filmmakers have Dreyfuss and Steven Lambert, as a homeless serial killer, hurl themselves into a loaded garbage truck and burrow around for several would-be hilarious minutes.

Even in the worst circumstances, an evening with Dreyfuss, Estevez, O'Donnell, Moriarty and Miguel Ferrer (the heavy) is not wasted especially with a slick host like Badham moving them around. But it's Dennis Farina and Marcia Strassman, as the O'Haras, targets of the surveillance, who wind up saving, or at least stealing, the evening.

A prime source of the movie's humor is the O'Haras' interactions with the disguised cops, their flabbergasted, polite expressions as the Seattle sleuths pull one idiotic *faux pas* after another.

At one point, Farina, madly shoveling down an improvised ice cream sandwich to get away from these next-door lunatics, generates the movie's only killer laughs.

Is it revelatory that the straight people are funnier than the clowns? Maybe not. "Another Stakeout" (MPAA rated PG-13, for two comic-action violence scenes) is neither the best nor worst of a bloated lot of unimaginative sequels. It's pretty much what it's title suggests: another stakeout, another sequel. Another day, another dollar.

NEW YORK POST, 7/23/93, p. 31, Michael Medved

Police surveillance can be miserable, tedious work, but it certainly helps if the person you're supposed to watch turns out to be a beautiful woman.

That was the profound message of the original "Stakeout" back in 1987, a likable action comedy with Richard Dreyfuss and Emilio Estevez as a pair of wise-cracking Seattle cops who draw the assignment of spying on the gorgeous Madeline Stowe. Inevitably, Dreyfuss, who plays a lonely guy on the edge of middle age, falls in love with the subject of his surveillance, and that unlikely attraction gave the story its arc, its edge and its energy.

Unfortunately, there's no such driving force in "Another Stakeout," so this silly sequel tries to make up for the lack of romance or emotion with an overdose of tired slapstick and hammy banter. By the time the picture offers up its sixth dumb gag about a big slobbery dog, you know that the filmmakers are visibly straining to fill up their allotted running time.

The drooling dog in question belongs to Rosie O'Donnell, who plays an officious assistant D. A. assigned to join the boys (much to their chagrin) on their latest stakeout. This time they're supposed to help find a key witness (Cathy Moriarty) in a big organized-crime trial. She's taken it on the lam after escaping a murderous assault on her "safe house" which is blown up in one of the biggest, noisiest, and most flamboyantly fiery explosions since they stopped nuclear testing.

The authorities believe that she'll ultimately join her best friends (Dennis Farina and Marcia Strassman), who live in a gorgeous home on an exclusive island in Puget Sound. In order to spy on this thoroughly boring couple, Dreyfuss, Estevez and O'Donnell rent the house next door, pretending to be members of the same family so as not to arouse suspicion.

The script (by Jim Kouf, who also wrote the original movie) milks the idea of Emilio posing as Richard's son for all it's worth, which isn't much. The action ultimately degenerates to the "I Love Lucy" level, when O'Donnell and Dreyfuss invite their neighbors to an ill-fated dinner party while Estevez sneaks into their house next door to plant a bug.

The capable cast makes the most of this relentlessly cute, ultimately annoying material; Dreyfuss in particular is such a marvel of intensity and comic timing in this utterly unworthy role that you get the idea that this guy could do a dramatic reading of the telephone directory and still hold us spellbound. He even brings a few moments of surprising feeling to his brief scenes with Madeline Stowe, who's back for an uncredited cameo as the long-suffering girlfriend who's now trying to terminate the relationship with Dreyfuss she began in the first film.

Director John Badham ("Saturday Night Fever," "WarGames") is also back from the original "Stakeout," and, as always, he fills the screen with slick, shiny images in bright colors. In this case however, the high-gloss surface only reinforces the smug, self-satisfied tone as the dull plot mechanically unfolds.

The most effective "action comedies" (the first "Lethal Weapon," say, or the original "Stakeout") strike an effective balance between laughs and thrills, but this picture tilts disastrously in the direction of cutup comedy. along the way it may deliver a few laughs, but the thrill is gone.

NEWSDAY, 7/23/93, Part II/p. 63, John Anderson

At first glance "Another Stakeout" has everything wrong with it. It's a sequel. The plot is fatuous and formulaic. And it stars two of the more erratic and potentially annoying actors in Hollywood.

That it works as well as it does is thanks to director John Badham—who did the first "Stakeout"—and his two returning stars. Emilio Estevez, who epitomized everything there was to hate about the Brat Pack way back when he was a young gun with buns, is growing into himself. He generated actual sympathy and charm last year in "The Mighty Ducks." And in "Another Stakeout," in which he plays Det. Bill Reimers, slightly puffy and paternal partner of the more domestically unstable Chris Lecce (Richard Dreyfuss), he finds salvation in goofy self-deprecation.

Dreyfuss, too, is an actor who shines much brighter when his humor is aimed at himself. Chris, who can't bring himself to propose to his girlfriend Maria (an uncredited Madeleine, Stowe, who was the object of his professional/romantic attentions in the first "Stakeout", and who's a bit old to be chasing hoods down alleyways and out windows, is holding on to his adolescence with white knuckles. If Dreyfuss didn't make him so harried and funny, he'd be an object of pity.

Together, the two are a live-action Ren & Stimpy, although their constant serve-and-volley of wisecracks never interferes with their crack police work. Which is why Assistant D.A. Gina Garrett (Rosie O'Donnell) has them assigned to another stakeout, this time in search of Lu Delano (Cathy Moriarty), whose testimony is the foundation of a federal case against a Las Vegas mob. Delano disappeared after her "safe house" was blown up by hitman Tony Castellano (Miguel Ferrer) in a explosion so spectacular and overdone you wonder if Badham was trying to re-create the Los Alamos A-bomb tests. To find her, Gina, Chris and Bill rent a house outside Seattle, next door to Lu's friends Brian and Pam O'Hara (Dennis Farina and Marcia Strassman), posing as a family of three, and waiting for Lu to show up.

Of course "Another Stakeout" is predictable. The relationship between the two detectives and Gina is a small war fought with sexist jokes and fueled by the natural hostility between male cops and female prosecutors. That the three totally botch their undercover roles—Dreyfuss as dad, Estevez as son and O'Donnell as stepmom—is a given. That the O'Haras find this family bizarre is no surprise. And the fact that their whole case is being undermined by a traitorous federal prosecutor (John Rubinstein) should be taken for granted.

The one peculiar thing in "Another Stakeout" is that the talented O'Donnell, currently appearing in "Sleepless in Seattle" and in the part-time role of "Madonna's best friend," would be given a role that relies so exclusively on the kinds of clichéd female characterizations that went out with June Cleaver. Gina treats the O'Haras' phonetapped conversations like her personal soap opera, cries to get her way with Bill and Chris and generally affirms all their sexist notions about professional women. The three are pretty funny together, though, so perhaps asking for enlightenment is asking too much.

SIGHT AND SOUND, 2/94, p. 46, Kim Newman

Nevada. Hitman Tony Castellano fails to murder Lu Delano, a witness against a syndicate boss, but the woman disappears from custody and DA Thomas Hassrick, who is himself in league with the mob, orders a nationwide search. Seattle cops Chris Lecce and Bill Reimers are assigned, along with Assistant DA Gina Garrett, to stake out the luxury island home of Brian and Pam O'Hara, friends whom Lu may contact. Posing as a family, with Bill pretending to be Chris's son, the team fail to fit into the quiet neighbourhood. Against the cops' advice, Gina cultivates an acquaintance with the O'Haras, while Chris is distracted from the stakeout by the deterioration of his relationship with Maria, the girlfriend he refuses to marry and who has just moved out of his apartment.

While Chris and Gina have Brian and Pam over for a disastrously embarrassing dinner party, Bill breaks into the O'Hara house to plant a bug and is captured by Lu, who has been hiding in the basement. Thinking Bill is the hitman, Lu drags him off to kill him, with Chris and Gina in pursuit. After confusion on the waterfront, Bill is rescued and Lu detained by the cops. Hassrick alerts Castellano, who arrives and is immediately recognised as the killer by Chris and Bill, who have to shoot their way past a couple of cops to save Lu. Castellano kills the DA and is himself shot. Returning to his apartment, Chris finds Maria has returned and he proposes to her.

Spectacular enough for a Joel Silver film, when the reliably perfidious Miguel Ferrer cannily pumps liquid explosive into the septic tank of a desert retreat, this inflated sequel mainly plays down the original's thrills in favour of mild comedy. The mafia plot lies around ignored for most of the film, and it is never even confirmed that Lu does take the stand against the mob. This leaves the ever-amiable Richard Dreyfuss, sidekick Emilio Estevez and the bumbling Rosie O'Donnell—not to mention her annoying 'Beethoven'-style dog—to conduct themselves as if they are in a sitcom, the sort where the mock family would be on stakeout for as many seasons as the ratings could stand before the series was cancelled. The comic highlight, a farcical dinner party at which Gina serves meatloaf shaped like an armadillo and hard-boiled-egg-and-olive miniature penguins, depends on the typical sitcom device, with the neighbours misinterpreting the central characters' eccentricities.

A lot less skilled in its blend of comedy and action than *The Hard Way*, Badham's last effort in this area, *Another Stakeout* plays to the fans by lamely recapping a few gags: when Bill has fish poured on him in the introductory chase sequence, Chris gloats at this payback for the original's finale and is promptly dropped into a spaghetti-filled garbage dumpster. Despite likeable players and competent individual scenes, the film is rendered redundant by a persistent refusal to make anything of any of the characters' potential relationships—Chris and Gina's 'marriage', Chris and Bill's transition from cop-movie buddies to sitcom father and son. An unbilled Madeleine Stowe pops up to cap off the love interest of the first movie, partitioned off in her own section of the current film and serving only to prevent any real interest being generated in a potential fulfilment of the faked marriage between Chris and Gina. As usual, a Hollywood movie is prepared to take seriously romance between a greying, middle-aged male goon and a drop-dead gorgeous fashion model type, but not to allow a dumpy, silly woman equal time, although O'Donnell does get briefly to flirt with a handyman. Given that it comes along six years after the first, not exactly memorable, *Stakeout*, it is hardly surprising that this expensive but unnecessary item failed even to do the expected sequel business in the States and now seems set to repeat its fast fade to oblivion in the international market.

VILLAGE VOICE, 8/3/93, p. 58, Chris Goffard

Any movie that features an exploding septic tank in its first five minutes leaves you hoping that what follows will be bad enough to warrant use of this image in a review. But *Another Stakeout* achieves only modest badness. At least it does no injustice to the original *Stakeout*: neither offers memorable characters, drama, or high comedy, though both excel at buddy-picture one-liners and slapstick that is not *too* offensively boneheaded.

Lecce (Richard Dreyfuss) and Reimers (Emilio Estevez) are Seattle cops who team up with Assistant D.A. Gina Garrett (Rosie O'Donnell) on an unusual surveillance mission: the three must pose as a family while they spy on the house next door in hopes of finding Lu Delano (Cathy Moriarty), a vanished witness whose testimony is needed to convict a Vegas mobster. For the sake of drama we have Miguel Ferrer as Tony Castellano, a stalking assassin in a black suit absolutely indistinguishable from any other papier-mâché assassin.

The film is best when it embraces its silliness (though it tries too hard for cheap laughs with extreme close-ups of various cute animals making various cute expressions). The premise allows for endless jousting between the film's incompatible personalities, and the three leads have good chemistry. The moment destined to remain in viewers' minds is when portly O'Donnell reclines in a bathtub with cucumber slices over her eyes, wailing "Come On Get Happy" while a dog wails back.

Also reviewed in:
CHICAGO TRIBUNE, 7/23/93, Friday/p. J, Mark Caro
NEW YORK TIMES, 7/23/93, p. C8, Vincent Canby
VARIETY, 8/2/93, p. 44, Emanuel Levy
WASHINGTON POST, 7/23/93, p. C7, Hal Hinson
WASHINGTON POST, 7/23/93, Weekend/p. 45, Desson Howe

ARCHITECTS, THE

A DEFA-Studio Babelsburg, Potsdam production. *Producer:* Herbert Ehler. *Director:* Peter Kahane. *Screenplay (German with English subtitles):* Thomas Knauf and Peter Kahane. *Director of Photography:* Andreas Köfer. *Editor:* Ilse Peters. *Music:* Tamás Kahane. *Sound:* Andreass Kaufmann. *Running time:* 95 minutes. *MPAA Rating:* Not Rated.

CAST: Kurt Naumann (Daniel Brenner); Rita Feldmeier (Wanda Brenner); Uta Eisold (Renate Reese); Jürgen Watzke (Martin Bulla); Ute Lobosch (Franziska Scarf); Catherine Stoyan (Elke Krug).

VILLAGE VOICE, 11/2/93, p. 66, Leslie Camhi

East German builders created a series of hopeless, loveless, uniform landscapes, an empire of drabness. *The Architects*, one of the last East German film productions, questions the human costs. With its endless boxy buildings, the state stifled individuality and made home the ultimate prefabricated space. And within a short time, the buildings began crumbling, making even newer cities look perpetually bombed.

Daniel (Kurt Naumann) is an architect whose talents are wasted on bus stops and transformer stations. Finally, when he's almost 40, he's asked to assemble a team of young architects to design a cultural center for the East Berlin suburb where his wife languishes in sensory deprivation. As his family life erodes, Daniel attends a photography show where portraits of his postwar generation, people who have spent their lives under Soviet occupation, have the pinched and weary look of those whose ideals were stillborn.

Watching *The Architects*, I realized how much our moviegoing pleasure depends upon the representation of a high standard of living. Kahane's style is as lean as the means Daniel is given, but out of the stuff of pure monotony—bureaucracy, domestic alienation, and prefabrication—he shapes a gripping drama. It may be a tribute to East German realism that toward the end, claustrophobia made me wish to leave the theater. Even so, *The Architects* is well worth seeing as a monument to the unbuilt dreams of an entire epoch and a record of an untenable culture on the brink of collapse.

Also reviewed in:
NEW YORK TIMES, 10/27/93, p. C14, Stephen Holden
VARIETY, 3/11/91, p. 66

ARMY OF DARKNESS

A Universal Pictures release of a Dino De Laurentiis Communications release of a Renaissance Pictures production. *Producer:* Robert Tapert and Bruce Campbell. *Director:* Sam Raimi. *Screenplay:* Sam Raimi and Ivan Raimi. *Director of Photography:* Bill Pope. *Editor:* Bob Murawski and R.O.C. Sandstorm. *Music:* Joseph LoDuca. *Music Editor:* Doug Lackey. *Sound:* Al Rizzo and (music) Dennis Sands. *Sound Editor:* Steve Williams and Alan Howarth. *Casting:* Ira Belgrade. *Production Designer:* Tony Tremblay. *Set Decorator:* Michele Poulik. *Set Dresser:* Jonathan Bruce and Julie Hermelin. *Visual Effects:* William Mesa. *Mechanical Effects:* Vern Hyde. *Costumes:* Ida Gearon. *Make-up:* Camille Calvet. *Make-up (Ash & Sheila):* Tony Gardner. *Stunt Coordinator:* Chris Doyle. *Running time:* 77 minutes. *MPAA Rating:* R.

CAST: Bruce Campbell (Ash); Embeth Davidtz (Sheila); Marcus Gilbert (Arthur); Ian Abercrombie (Wiseman); Richard Grove (Duke Henry); Michael Earl Ried (Gold Tooth); Timothy Patrick Quill (Blacksmith); Bridget Fonda (Linda); Patricia Tallman (Possessed Witch); Theodore Raimi (Cowardly Warrior); Deke Anderson (Tiny Ash #1); Bruce Thomas (Tiny Ash #2); Sara Shearer (Old Woman); Shiva Gordon (Pit Deadite #1); Billy Bryan (Pit Deadite #2); Nadine Grycan (Winged Deadite); Bill Moseley (Deadite Captain); Michael Kenney (Henry's Man); Andy Bale (Lieutenant #1); Robert Brent Lappin (Lieutenant #2); Rad Milo (Tower Guard); Brad Bradbury (Chief Archer); Sol Abrams, Lorraine Axeman, Josh Becker, Sheri Burke, Don Campbell, Charlie Campbell, Harley Cokeliss, Ken Jepson, William Lustig, David O'Malley, David Pollison, Ivan Raimi, Bernard Rose, Bill Vincent, Chris Webster, and Ron Zwang (Fake Shemps).

LOS ANGELES TIMES, 2/19/93, Calendar/p. 8, Peter Rainer

Ash (Bruce Campbell) is a straight-arrow, square-jawed department store employee—housewares division—who gets hurtled back into the Dark Ages in "Army of Darkness," the new Sam Raimi fantasy fest. It's the kind of concoction we've come to expect from Raimi ("Evil Dead," "Darkman"): Goofball riffs crossed with cheesy/sophisticated horror effects. He's a gifted knock-about movie maniac who works on his own pop comic wavelength.

The time-traveler scenario, by Raimi and his brother Ivan, has a built-in gag: Ash, is as fatuously, pompously handsome as Gaston in Disney's "Beauty and the Beast." (He barely registers his maidenly lady-in-waiting, played by Embeth Davidtz.) He also has a jumbo-sized attitude, 20th-Century style, which perplexes his 13th-Century attackers. Even more, he totes a 12-gauge shotgun and has a chain saw where his right hand used to be.

Ash might have stepped out of the pages of one of the wilder and weirder "dark" comic books but he's so stalwart he's lunky—he's a parody of heroism even as he performs such amazingly heroic feats as staving off an army of galloping skeletons or battling a gloppy fanged creature at the bottom of a well. Ash's dialogue keeps the movie just goofy enough that even audiences that don't go in for schlock-horror phantasmagorias will be tickled.

Or at least they will be until the special effects get too frenetic and take over the picture. Raimi wants to kid the genre but he also wants to demonstrate that he's able to do it straight. The film (rated R for violence and horror) loses its prickly, nervy humor toward the end, when the skeletons launch a full-scale attack on a castle under Ash's protection and wave upon wave of creatures clamber over the parapets. Even here, Raimi's imagery, which is processed through a high-tech matte system called Introvision, is a cut above the norm: It's like a riper, darker version of what Ray Harryhausen did in films like "The 7th Voyage of Sinbad." But the film doesn't surprise us in the ways that make us laugh anymore. It doesn't turn serious, exactly, but it loses its parodistic edge.

Raimi, when he's really cooking, knows how to make the techniques of fantasy-horror seem funny all by themselves. When Ash shoots an arrow we get to follow the arrow all the way into its target. When this was done in "Robin Hood: Prince of Thieves" it was just a piece of whiz-bang derring-do but here it's kind of kicky too. Raimi builds our awareness of movie technique into our response; he makes us laugh at our connoisseurship because, after all, it's really a connoisseurship of *schlock*. Campbell, who also starred in the two "Evil Dead" movies, is the perfect actor for Raimi because he's both joke and in-joke. He toys with his stalwartness.

"Army of Darkness" is mostly a terrific piece of mindlessness. That may not sound like such a great recommendation—until you drop in on some of this season's high-minded clunkers.

NEW YORK POST, 2/19/93, p. 23, Jami Bernard

"Darkman" was good, but "Army of Darkness" is the movie Sam Raimi has obviously been dying to make. His sheer delight in furthering his own "Evil Dead" series is evident as he transplants the hapless hero Ash (Bruce Campbell) to the Dark Ages for yet another round with re-awakened skeletons and the blood-dripping Book of the Dead.

In the two "Evil Dead" movies, Ash was trapped in a woodland cabin with friends who bite the dust after they inadvertently awaken dead spirits by reading aloud from the Necronomicon, the Book of the Dead. The evil dead were personified by a low-to-the-ground, point-of-view camera whooshing toward its victim.

Now Raimi has a bigger budget, and the special effects department has used all kinds of devices to create an army of skeletons and other assorted wonders. The special effects, while primary, never overwhelm the movie, because the script—co-authored by Raimi and his brother, Ivan—never loses its comic thread.

Raimi is one of those directors like Joe Dante who have absorbed the history of pop culture through their skin and right into their bloodstreams; that is why the joking references to every-thing from the Three Stooges to "The Wizard of Oz," from detective pulp fiction to "The Terminator," seem so unforced. "Army of Darkness" contains plenty of gore and carn-age—although its short running time suggests it has lost some of that—but it is really a wacky comedy, almost Monty Pythonesque.

After a setup consisting of scenes from "The Evil Dead 2," we find Ash transplanted by those ill winds from his routine job in the housewares department of a five-and-dime to the year 1300 AD. There he is treated first as a slave and then as a prophesied hero, and reacts to it all as any 20th-century person might—with modern phrases (*"Yo! She-bitch!"*) and a Tobe Hooper chainsaw.

There is a whole section of the movie set in an isolated windmill that updates the survival shenanigans Ash faced during the last two "Evil Deads"—prying his face off a sizzling stove with a spatula, breaking his mirror image into a thousand tiny shards of himself (listed as "fake Shemps" in the credits), having his nose picked by a pack of obnoxious skeletons risen from the dead "Darkman" was the first time Raimi had been given a major budget and major stars (Liam Neeson was a burned scientist who cloned himself a new face), and it had a weighty lugubrious feel. "Army of Darkness" is happy juvenilia, delivered in a carefree, confident style. It doesn't hurt when the movie borrows liberally from Raimi's favorite movies of the past (there's even a score by Danny Elfman the "Batman" composer), because "Army of Darkness" is clever all on its own.

In fact, if the young Raimi were to spend the rest of his career updating and refining his original low-budget "Evil Dead" he will not have misspent his time, nor ours.

NEWSDAY, 2/19/93, Part II/p. 56, John Anderson

Writer/Director Sam Raimi packs "Army of Darkness" with so may whacked-out movie references that it's like a hysterical "Finnegans Wake" for horror/action/post-apocalyptic/ninja/sci-fi buffs—although, considering the kind of mind that would pick up all the references, "The Wasteland" might be a better comparison.

"Raiders of the Lost Ark," "Monty Python and the Holy Grail," the Three Stooges, "Predator," "Mad Max," Raimi's own horror classic "Evil Dead" and a lot more are all here in a shamelessly comic mix that's ably abetted by star Bruce Campbell. As the suave and debonair (pronounced, in this case, "swave" and "deboaner") chainsaw-wielding, shotgun-toting, non sequitur-slinging hero, he invades the Dark Ages like a one-man plague, although plagues are generally classier.

"My name is Ash," he says, as we watch shackled feet slogging through sand; if such a thing is possible, the feet overact. "As far as I can tell, the year is 1300 AD and I'm being marched to my death ..." Ash, the character Campbell played in "Evil Dead" has become an S-Mart clerk ("Shop smart ... shop S-Mart"), been possessed, cut off his hand, lost his girlfriend, Linda (a very brief cameo by Bridget Fonda) and he and his '73 Delta 88 have been dropped out of the sky and into medieval Britain.

Raimi's gleefully stupid (and accomplished) special effects come fast and furious, although they're as much a bowl of mixed nuts as Raimi's shooting styles, or the Britons Ash meets after he hits the ground: Arthur (Marcus Gilbert), a nobleman who's at war with Duke Henry (Richard Grove), who has become, like Ash, a prisoner of Arthur's; Sheila (Embeth Davidtz), who'll become Ash's love interest ("Give me some sugar, babe," he tells her during one medieval embrace); and Wiseman (Ian Abercrombie), who instructs Ash how to retrieve the Book of the Dead and be sent back to his own time—a task he screws up, thereby unleashing the Undead who'll attack the castle in the film's overly long but frenetic finale.

A lot gets overdone in "Army of Darkness." Everything, in fact. But Campbell, who as Ash wears a chainsaw on the stump of his arm, his shotgun on his back and a smirk on his lips, ultimately saves the film, just as Ash saves the day. First, however, he'll have to defeat his malevolent doppelganger, a gang of small, evil Ashes who tie him up like Gulliver; scrape his face off a griddle and confront an army of skeletons which I believe we first saw in that 1963 epic "Jason and the Argonauts." Eventually, Ash will leave behind the "primitive screwheads" of the 14th Century for life back at S-Mart, where he'll be visited by the occasional leprous crone and blow her away with his "boomstick."

With these kind of high-brow aspirations, how could Raimi have failed to create another cult classic?

SIGHT AND SOUND, 6/93, p. 46, Kim Newman

England, c. 1300. Ash, a supermarket employee, is zapped into the past after a brush with demonic forces that congregate around a grimoire called the *Necronomicon*. Enslaved by Lord Arthur, he is cast into a pit inhabited by mutants; but Arthur's alchemist advisor returns Ash's chainsaw to him and he escapes from the pit, bests the Lord in combat and frees his fellow slave, Duke Henry the Red, to return to his own fiefdom.

The alchemist tells Ash that the *Necronomicon* contains a spell that will return him to the 20th century, and that he must quest for the book, which can be found in a haunted graveyard. On his way to the graveyard, Ash breaks a magic mirror which disgorges miniature replicas of himself. One of the tiny Ashes dives into his mouth and grows inside him, splitting off into a life-sized malevolent doppelganger. Ash defeats, dismembers and buries his evil twin and proceeds to the graveyard where he muffs the necessary incantation as he takes the *Necronomicon*. This causes the nearby dead to emerge from their graves and form an army under the leadership of the re-animated Evil Ash.

Although he could now return to his own time, Ash opts to stay and help Lord Arthur's men defend the castle. Sheila, a princess who has fallen for Ash, is kidnapped by the Deadites and transformed into Evil Ash's hoyden. Ash's forces stave off the Deadites' attack, using makeshift technological weapons. As the castle is about to fall, Duke Henry's men reinforce the living. Ash destroys Evil Ash and takes his leave, returning to the present where he recounts his adventures to disbelieving colleagues at the supermarket, before taking a shotgun to the lingering last of the Deadites.

This much delayed and hacked-about third entry in the *Evil Dead* series opens with an alternative recap of the story so far, rewriting the events of previous films, with Bridget Fonda in a silent cameo as Ash's doomed girlfriend. Only called *Evil Dead III* in some foreign-language territories, this has a much-mutating title. Judging by the opening sequence, it actually appears to be called *Bruce Campbell vs Army of Darkness*, while the British release adds the subtitle *The Medieval Dead* for the publicity material.

The film now also features a revised all-action finish in place of a previewed, downbeat ending reminiscent of *Planet of the Apes*, in which the blundering Ash again fails at his spell and over-shoots the centuries, arriving in a devastated post-nuclear landscape dominated by a derelict Big Ben. The current coda, like much which precedes it, is at once busy and unresonant, but it does contain the poignant notion of Ash walking away from a magical kingdom and the love of a princess to spend the rest of his life announcing special offers in a supermarket.

Army of Darkness is not so much a splatter roller-coaster on the model of the earlier installments, more a fantasy adventure in the Ray Harryhausen tradition, as signified by the presence of a horde of animated sword-wielding skeletons. In fact, in its incredibly unconvincing British setting and sometimes ropey effects, it is even more reminiscent of such imitation-Harryhausen quickies as *Jack the Giant Killer* and *The Magic Sword*. As usual with Sam Raimi, there are multiple echoes of obscure or noteworthy genre items, with every borrowing overlaid by Three Stooges eye-poking slapstick. For instance, the creation of Evil Ash, who first appears as an eye in the hero's neck, is copied exactly from the 1961 Japanese film *The Split* (aka *The Manster*). As co-producer, Bruce Campbell hogs all the good lines, eclipsing the perfunctory supporting characters. This leaves the spectacular shocks strung out on an attenuated plot which reruns moments from *A Connecticut Yankee at the Court of King Arthur* along with fondly-remembered riffs (like Ash's cry "Groovy!") from the earlier *Evil Dead* movies.

Preoccupied with repetitive and clumsy battle scenes and mild, bloodless effects, *Army of Darkness* falls off the knife-edge between humour and horror walked by *The Evil Dead* and danced along by *Evil Dead II*. Without serious horror content, the film becomes a simple succession of gags, most notably in the extended and scrappy finale, which wastes such surefire melodramatic devices as Ash's *Alamo*-esque gathering of the staunch defenders, or the Duke Henry charging to the aid of his former foe. Even medieval swashbucklers as makeshift as Rudolph Maté's *The Black Shield of Falworth* used to summon up some enthusiasm for individual heroism and collective stands against evil; but Raimi's mocking tone and Ash's lack of character development prevent any actual audience involvement in this would-be epic struggle.

VILLAGE VOICE, 3/2/93, p. 54, Colson Whitehead

Ash (Bruce Campbell) has come a long way in the 14 years since *The Evil Dead*, and so has director Sam Raimi. In the first film, Ash was a bumbling geek, hardly able to keep one step ahead of the cackling demons. By *Army of Darkness*, the third in the *Evil Dead* series, he's become the "Promised One," transported to the 14th century to deliver the "primitive screwheads" from a battalion of the walking dead. Armed with a chainsaw, a sawed-off, and a quiver of creaky one-liners, Ash is now Rambo as portrayed by Jerry Lewis, a bad-ass who slips on banana peels but always gets his ghoul.

What made previous *Evil Dead* movies so wonderfully goofy was their unpredictability—Raimi was able to riff on the Marx Brothers and switch to *The Exorcist* without missing a note. For the first half of *Army of Darkness*, the film obeys that principle of pure, manic invention, and Ash is slapped, punctured, stretched like taffy, and cut in half like never before. Unfortunately, *Army* has the idea that it needs to be a conventional film—you know, with a comprehensible narrative and all that stuff—and lumbers into predictability. Raimi plugs Ash into the hero myth, but twice removed, an interpretation of *The Road Warrior*'s interpretation of the hero. And the *Connecticut Yankee* angle isn't worked beyond the gag of mocking the serfs with modern profanity—what's more obvious than teaching the peasants how to make gunpowder and explosives?

But at least Raimi, now that Dino "the Man" De Laurentiis is bankrolling him, no longer has to rely on Play-Doh for special effects and Radio Shack for his sound and lighting equipment. In *Army*, when geysers of blood erupt into the air (an *Evil Dead* motif), they're the greatest, grandest geysers of blood that money can buy.

Also reviewed in:
CHICAGO TRIBUNE, 2/19/93, Friday/p. C, Dave Kehr
NEW YORK TIMES, 2/19/93, p. C10, Janet Maslin
VARIETY, 10/19/92, p. 60, Peter Besas
WASHINGTON POST, 2/19/93, p. C7, Richard Harrington
WASHINGTON POST, 2/19/93, Weekend/p. 38, Desson Howe

ASPEN EXTREME

A Hollywood Pictures release in association with Touchwood Pacific Partners I. *Executive Producer:* Fred T. Gallo. *Producer:* Leonard Goldberg. *Director:* Patrick Hasburgh. *Screenplay:* Patrick Hasburgh. *Director of Photography:* Steven Fierberg and Robert Primes. *Editor:* Steven Kemper. *Music:* Michael Convertino. *Music Editor:* Ken Wannberg. *Sound:* David Brownlow and (music) Dennis Sands. *Sound Editor:* Alan Robert Murray and Walter Newman. *Casting:* Gail Levin. *Production Designer:* Roger Cain. *Art Director:* Dan Self. *Set Designer:* Alan Keith Neely. *Set Decorator:* Nina Bradford. *Set Dresser:* Nicola Hewitt. *Special Effects:* Neil N. Trifunovich. *Aerial Coordinator:* James B. Dirker. *Costumes:* Karen Patch. *Make-up:* Felicity Bowring. *Stunt Coordinator:* Gary Jensen and Mike McGaughy. *Running time:* 115 minutes. *MPAA Rating:* PG-13.

CAST: Paul Gross (T.J. Burke);   Peter Berg (Dexter Rutecki);   Finola Hughes (Bryce Kellogg);   Teri Polo (Robin Hand);   William Russ (Dave Ritchie);   Trevor Eve (Karl Stall); Martin Kemp (Franz Hauser);   Stewart Finley-McLennan (Rudy Zucker);   Tony Griffin (Gary Eimiller);   Julie Royer (Michelle Proux);   Patrick T. Johnson (Bill Swanson);   William McNamara (Todd Pounds);   Gary Eimiller (Jinx Stone);   Andy Mill (Himself);   Bill Ferrell (Official);   Catherine Parks (Karen);   Karla Olivares (Kimberly);   Valerie Kingston (Kimberly's Mom);   Monica Olivares (Suzy);   Jeronimo Olivares (Little Boy);   Rod McCary (Mr. Hanson); Rae Norman (Mrs. Hanson);   Rudi Davis (Kevin Hanson);   Ami Reade (Sarah Hanson); Bradley Mott (Morton Hayward);   Roger Wilson (Jake Neil);   Nicolette Scorsese (Tina); Dennis Holahan (Henri);   Claudia Cron (Scarlett);   Owen O'Farrell (Bartender);   Brett Porter (Bartender #2);   Marisa Redanty (Tourist);   Steven Brill (Waiter);   Kevin Bourland (Roy); Morgan Metzger (Randy);   Will MacMillan (Beard);   Charles Boswell (Suit);   John W. Hardy (Assembly Line Worker);   Stan Ivar (Mr. Parker);   Reuben Yabuku (Attendant);   Ken Oakes (Ski School Supervisor);   Chris Hanson and John Goulet (Ski Instructors);   Katerina Veisbein (Woman at Party);   Todd R. Beveridge (Cop);   Lynn Bopeley (Robin's Friend);   Christopher Tufty (Man on Horse).

LOS ANGELES TIMES, 1/23/93, Calendar/p. 2, Peter Rainer

If you snipped the skiing footage from "Aspen Extreme" you might have enough for a pretty exciting 20-minute documentary. The shots of downhill racers skidding and slaloming down the steep slopes are diverting, and there's a beauty of a sequence involving an avalanche that should by all rights have won the cameramen Purple Hearts.

As for the non-skiing stuff, it's strictly sudsville. T. J. (Paul Gross) and Dexter (Peter Berg) are best buddies who ditch their boring, soul-grinding auto assembly-line jobs in Detroit and head for Aspen to work as ski instructors for the rich and famous. T. J., a great skier and great-looking, quickly becomes king of the hill; a wealthy socialite vamp with the soap-opera-ish name of Bryce Kellogg (Finola Hughes) picks him as her plaything. Dexter, goofier and troubled, has a more difficult time negotiating the slopes of life.

We're supposed to regard these two as a variation on George and Lenny from "Of Mice and Men." We're also supposed to recognize that T. J., despite his dalliance with Bryce, is really in love with the flaxen-haired Robin (Teri Polo), who sees him for the sensitive soul he really is. T. J., you see, wants to be a famous author but he never went to college. Bryce fills the young man's arms with volumes from the Aspen library: Proust, Camus—you know, the biggies. But Robin actually inspires him to write a short story about her. Dexter inspires T. J.'s muse as well. A story about him ends up as the cover story in Powder magazine. (It's a magazine about skiing, not snorting.)

The plot synopsis for this film, which was written and directed by TV writer-producer and former Aspen ski instructor Patrick Hasburgh, may sound like a jamming together of bad soaps as reimagined by the guys who created "Airplane!" If only it were so. Hasburgh sets a shaggy, amiable tone for the first half hour or so and then sinks into the melodrama with a heavy thud. The mind begins to wander, particularly when we are shown the dewy lovers intercut with shots of flowers poking up through the ice.

Given all the recent hoopla about a winter boycott in Aspen, this film (rated PG-13 for some language, drug content and nudity) might have had some curiosity value. Aspen and its denizens are a great subject for a film, and a ski-bum hustler is a great protagonist. But T. J.'s motives are always impeccable. He's boringly humane even when he's being seduced and abandoned. "Aspen Extreme" is a snow job in more ways than one.

NEWSDAY, 1/23/93, Part II/p. 23, Terry Kelleher

The formulaic film neatly establishes a familiar promise in the first, say, 15 minutes.

The *extremely* formulaic film does it during the opening credits.

Exhibit A: "Aspen Extreme." The first shot is of an automobile assembly line in Detroit, but by the time "Written and Directed by Patrick Hasburgh" appears on the screen, the blue-collar protagonists have junked their jobs, hit the road and arrived in Aspen, Colo., "winter playground of the rich and famous."

Quickly, all the elements are in place. Lifelong pals T.J. (Paul Gross) and Dexter (Peter Berg) both want to be ski instructors, but the boss (Trevor Eve) deems Dexter too uncouth—perhaps because his mouth constantly hangs open. Loyal T.J. insists he won't work without his friend at his side. The boss readily gives in, being in need of gorgeous young specimens like T.J. to please moneyed sybarites like Bryce (Finola Hughes).

Almost immediately after Bryce, a predatory brunette, seduces T.J., he falls in true love with Robin (Teri Polo), the wholesome blonde who pulls the all-night DJ shift on Aspen radio (she could have had her own TV show in L.A., only she refused to sleep with the station manager).

The route from here seems clear: T.J. will agonize awhile before making the right romantic choice. Dexter will provide comic relief through his game attempts to train misfit skiers. The much-discussed, incredibly challenging "Powder Eight" competition will give us the requisite big finish on the slopes.

If Hasburgh had stuck to this basic formula, his debut feature might have been a trite but watchable affair, partially redeemed by flying snow and fancy stunts. Instead he went to extremes.

When Hasburgh himself was an Aspen ski instructor, he launched a writing career in his spare time. So T.J. must be an aspiring writer, too, cranking out magazine stories about Robin and Dexter to show how much he really cares about them. Before he turns her all warm and quivery, Robin analyzes this aspect of T.J.'s character with appropriate sarcasm: "A writer—how romantic. It goes real well with being a ski instructor. Gives him a little credibility."

Bidding in vain for seriousness as well as credibility, Hasburgh unexpectedly leads Dexter into crime, despair and tragedy—all this after we've come to accept him in the simpler role of doltish sidekick. Sorry, but the character wasn't built to carry so much weight.

"Aspen Extreme" ends with T.J. vowing to become "a real writer." Too bad didn't reach his goal in time to work on this script.

Also reviewed in:
NEW YORK TIMES, 1/23/93, p. 16, Vincent Canby
VARIETY, 1/25/93, p. 133, Lawrence Cohen
WASHINGTON POST, 1/25/93, p. B7, Hal Hinson

ATLANTIS

A Milestone Pictures release of a Gaumont/Cecchi Gori Group production. *Executive Producer:* Claude Besson. *Director:* Luc Besson. *Director of Photography:* Christian Pétron. *Editor:* Luc Besson. *Music:* Eric Serra. *Sound:* William Flageollet and (music) Dominik Borde and Matt Howe. *Sound Editor:* Patrice Crisolet. *Artic Expert:* André Laperrière. *Scientific/Technical Consultant:* Pierre Laboute. *Running time:* 75 minutes. *MPAA Rating:* Not Rated.

NEW YORK POST, 12/29/93, p. 32, Thelma Adams

"Atlantis" is an undersea "Fantasia." I never thought a fish movie would make me feel like dancing. But there I was, swaying in my seat as a "striped sweater" snake undulated across the sea floor to the funky Arabic rhythms set by composer Eric Serra.

"The Little Mermaid" this isn't. Fifteen times as dangerous as a cobra, the bite of the "striped sweater" can kill a person in 30 seconds.

"Atlantis" is a departure for Luc Besson. The French director is best known in the U.S. for "La Femme Nikita," a stylish, playful and visually vibrant thriller that was immediately remade by Hollywood as "Point of No Return."

Besson's last movie, "The Big Blue," was a big dud starring Rosanna Arquette—but it featured amazing underwater photography. In "Atlantis," Besson drops the plot and weighs anchor, pursuing an entirely different kind of star.

From the spotted dolphins of the Bahamas to the marine iguana of the Galapagos, from manatees to sharks, there are plenty of characters. By segmenting the movie into movements defined by simple white titles (light, tenderness, rhythm, birth), "Atlantis" flows forward by creating a symphony of moods and emotions.

Besson's shooting schedule spanned two years and took his team of divers and cameramen to the Galapagos Islands, New Caledonia, Florida, the Red Sea, British Columbia, French Polynesia, the Seychelles Islands, Australia and all the way to the North Pole.

It wouldn't be a French movie without sex scenes: Penguins do it, turtles do it, even electric yellow slugs do it. But hate is in the air as much as love. "Atlantis" builds to the arrival of battle-scarred sharks of all sizes but similar temperaments—a ravenous hunger.

One of the most enchanting sequences is titled "soul." Through brilliant editing, three manta rays—among the world's largest fish—glide to an aria sung by Maria Callas. With their enormous white wings, the rays seemed to soar and embody the diva's soul.

In the end, Besson plucks the viewer from below the polar icecap and returns her to the world above the sea, the sky now seems wondrous and unfamiliar, and the sea glimmering below seems like home.

After viewing "Atlantis" I left the theater refreshed, oddly elated, and dancing to the sexy rhythms of the "striped sweater" sea snake.

NEWSDAY, 12/29/93, Part II/p. 57, Gene Seymour

Always be wary of a film that urges you at the outset to give in, let go, abandon something or other. For one thing, it's kind of a redundant request. The very act of walking into a movie theater is an act of surrender, a decision to give up, temporarily, on real life.

"Atlantis" wants more. It starts off by soothingly encouraging its audience to forget dry land and go "deeper, *deeeeeeper*" (yes, the narrator actually says it like that) beneath the ocean surface. It asks—no, demands—that you become as "mindless" as nature, as weightless as a sea creature, as buoyant as a scuttled submarine.

Despite the opening pomposity, director Luc Besson, whose, previous film was the glossy, kinetic thriller "La Femme Nikita," has pieced together a very pretty meditation on ocean life from hundreds of hours of deep sea images shot all over the globe.

At times, the film becomes more stunning than anything you've ever seen in an underwater documentary. The most striking sequence juxtaposes the grand gliding of a giant manta ray with Maria Callas' performance of Bellini's aria, "La Sonnambula." The dense, haunting music seems to drape itself over the ray's undulating wings. When the music's over, schools of grouper and parrot fish are shown swimming frenetically to the sounds of applause. At that moment, we don't know whether to clap along or run around in joyous frenzy ourselves.

That may well be the only place in the movie where Besson's sense of ecstasy connects fully with the audience. The set pieces with Galapagos penguins, iguana and sea lions, sharks from Australia and Tahiti, giant octopi from Vancouver and Florida manatee are energetic enough. But they don't draw you in like the manta-and-Maria segment.

Much of the fault lies with Eric Serra's score, a hodgepodge of electronically synthesized white noise and banal symphonic themes that, if anything, keep your imagination at a distance from the imagery.

Besson's adroit orchestration of images is far more advanced than Serra's orchestration of sound. At one point, he follows up a picture of a manatee hitting a camera lens with a picture of the same manatee looking as if it's hiding its head in embarrassment, Still, such scenes only reinforce the suspicion that Besson is one of those directors who prefers to look for humanity in things and in animals more than in people.

SIGHT AND SOUND, 11/93, p. 36, Robert Yates

Atlantis consists of a series of short episodes of underwater life, with a musical soundtrack but no commentary. The episodes are self-contained, each concentrating on a particular example of marine life, with their borders marked by changes in the accompanying music. An episode might tell a story—the search of sharks for food, for instance—or might simply capture the movements of its subject.

Filming over three years from late 1988, in seas across the world, Luc Besson intended to create an "underwater opera". The film is also an implicit polemic against human abuse of the planet, since Besson chose to concentrate on fauna and flora threatened with extinction. However, while recording imminent losses, *Atlantis* is also a celebration. By regularly changing subject matter—no episode lasts for more than ten or so minutes—its structure works towards presenting a collection of underwater riches. The soundtrack is composed or assembled, with music and natural sounds often nicely integrated, by Eric Serra who also worked with Besson on *The Big Blue*. Playing up its subjects' connotations, it is playful when dolphins are framed, menacing if sharks appear. More distinct are the Maria Callas aria that makes the majestic mantra ray recall nothing so much as the Wagner-borne helicopters from *Apocalypse Now*, and the cheap electro-disco number which wittily underscores a succession of kissing marine couples.

Music apart, Besson infuses drama into the documentary by shaping the footage around a goal (as in the shark episode) or by breaking up an episode with an arresting cameo (once, memorably, from a madcap crab). Or else he exploits the qualities of a location, as when the camera approaches a forbidding polar ice formation via a beautifully-textured narrow crevice. The cine-matography, by Christian Petron, is hugely impressive, partly thanks to the technology used which included specially designed underwater Cinemascope equipment. More importantly, Besson's team is busy, alert to the striking perspective, managing several times to disorientate by taking advantage of the floating camera's ability to reshape the surroundings in a way difficult to emulate above ground. A declared labour of love, ultimately *Atlantis* is 'only' a very good under-water documentary. For all its claims to be an exemplary exercise in integrating music and image, it is likely that the viewer's interest will largely depend upon how much he wants to watch marine life. Even the polemical element is lost on those of us unable to identify an endangered species or plant. However, it certainly compares favourably with *The Big Blue*, Besson's earlier homage to the sea, not least by its omissions: *Atlantis* is, happily, free of that film's lame story and characters.

Also reviewed in:
NEW YORK TIMES, 12/29/93, p. C19, Caryn James
VARIETY, 8/26/91, p. 88, Lisa Nesselson

BAD BEHAVIOUR

An October Films release of a Parallax Pictures production for Channel 4 in association with British Screen. *Executive Producer:* Sally Hibbin. *Producer:* Sarah Curtis. *Director:* Les Blair. *Director of Photography:* Witold Stok. *Editor:* Martin Walsh. *Music:* John Altman. *Sound:* Bruce White and Neil Kingsbury. *Sound Editor:* David Old and Peter Elliott. *Casting:* Gail Stevens. *Production Designer:* Jim Grant. *Art Director:* Rebecca M. Harvey. *Costumes:* Janty Yates. *Make-up:* Louise Fisher. *Running time:* 103 minutes. *MPAA Rating:* R.

CAST: Stephen Rea (Gerry McAllister); Sinead Cusack (Ellie McAllister); Philip Jackson (Howard Spink); Clare Higgins (Jessica Kennedy); Phil Daniels (The Nunn Brothers); Mary Jo Randle (Winifred Turner); Saira Todd (Sophie Bevan); Amanda Boxer (Linda Marks); Luke Blair (Joe McAllister); Joe Coles (Michael McAllister); Tamlin Howard (Jake Spink); Emily Hill (Rosie Kennedy); Philippe Lewinson (Jason); Ian Flintoff (Chairperson); Kenneth Hadley (Priest); Siempre Caliente (Band).

LOS ANGELES TIMES, 9/29/93, Calendar/p. 5, Kenneth Turan

Not much happens in "Bad Behaviour" but what does is very easy to take. A shambling comic look at a love relationship that is wearing thin around the edges, it makes few demands other than asking that we settle in for the duration and get comfortable with the lives of its characters.

Directed by BBC veteran Les Blair, "Bad Behaviour" is also a film without a credited writer. That's because Blair, a believer in improvisation as a means toward creating character, has a working method similar to that of fellow Brit Mike Leigh.

While this picture lacks the bite and intensity of things like "Life Is Sweet" and the forthcoming "Naked"—it's in effect the diet version of Leigh's rich and turbulent works—"Behaviour" shares with them an ability to put strongly drawn and alive folks on screen.

Beautifully acted by Stephen Rea and Sinead Cusack, Gerry and Ellie McAllister are an amusingly realistic married-with-two-children couple. Irish born and bred though now living in the North London borough of Kentish Town, they are to varying degrees burnt out and frustrated with the patterns their lives have settled into.

Gerry works as a city planner, a career he caricatures for one of his sons as being superhero Paddy Plan-It, "Trapped in a World Not of His Making." A man whose shaggy exterior masks a sharp and witty interior, Gerry, despite the fetching presence of co-worker Sophie (Saira Todd), feels at odds with a job that only allows small victories like the turning of a vacant lot into a permanent home for traveling Gypsies.

Ellie, for her part, works in a local bookstore and regrets how little time she has to spare after taking care of the kids and serving as the neighborhood shoulder everyone cries on, especially Jess (Claire Higgins), a divorced mom who focuses on incense and Buddhism while her teen-age daughter fumes.

While in another film all this would be the background against which a crisis would play itself out, in "Bad Behaviour" it is pretty much the whole ball of wax. The pleasure of this film is not following a plot but watching these people be themselves, interacting with each other and trying to get on with their lives.

The closest thing to a conventional plot element involves Howard Spink (Philip Jackson), a mobile phone-addicted scam artist who convinces Ellie she needs to have a bathroom remodeled and then brings in Roy and Ray, the identical twin Nunn brothers (Phil Daniels) to do the job.

Perhaps as a consequence of the way it was made, "Bad Behaviour" has more than its share of scenes where nothing much at all seems to be happening, and its sensibility, abetted by a too-cheerful soundtrack, sometimes veers more toward the world of situation comedy than one would like.

But whenever your patience starts to wear thin, either Rea ("The Crying Game") or Cusack ("Waterland") come up with a marvelous scene, often with each other. Don't expect "Bad Behaviour" (rated R for language) to offer tidy resolutions, or anything else tidy for that matter, but if you accept its limitations you will be pleasantly entertained for the duration.

NEW YORK POST, 9/3/93, p. 28, Jerry Tallmer

Near the beginning of a lovely movie called "Bad Behaviour," a little boy named Joey, drawing pictures at the kitchen table in Kentish Town, north London, looks over at his mother peeling potatoes. "Mum," he says, "I'm bored."

Joey speaks for the entire family, with the possible exception of teen-age brother Michael, who's about to play bank robber in a movie directed by another boy. But Ellie McAllister, the mother of Joey and Mike, is certainly, after 15 years, bored and trapped, half at home, half in the bookstore where she works. "When I was at university I had the silly notion I might be a writer," she tells her best woman friend. "So what happened?" asks the friend. "Gerry happened."

Gerry McAllister, architectural draughtsman for the Town Council, a Londoner transplanted from his native Belfast, is certainly as trapped and bored as his wife. The house itself is closing in on him, plus Ellie's desire—sparked by Howard Spink, a neighborhood con-man and moral louse "indirectly" in the building trade—for a new sink and a new loo. "What's eating you?" Gerry asks at the end of a day. "I had half the population of north London here this afternoon," she wearily answers, meaning kids, friends, workmen, neurotic neighbors. "It can't be the menopause," she says. "I'm too young."

Gerry keeps from his wife—but lets his kid giggle at—the sporadic "PADDY PLAN-IT, Trapped in a World Not His Making" comic strip that lets out some of the frustrations. Ellie keeps her sporadic attempts at writing from her husband. He can't keep from her his anxiety-stoked asthma. She can't keep from him her taste for a glass, or two or three. What the hell, he has a taste too. They quarrel a lot.

The little victories Gerry wins in the Town Council—replanning a permanent camp for "travelers," *i.e.* Gypsies, for instance—are pretty shabby ones. He manages to preserve a dry, quiet, Irish humor. "Say hello to Mrs. McCallister," says a tiresome colleague. "I usually do," Gerry replies.

There's Sophie, a charming, spunky girl who greatly helps in Gerry's victories. They have a scene in a coffee house together, when little Joey barges in, that has all the breath-held emotion of the one between Ralph Richardson and Michelle Morgan in "The Fallen Idol." Sophie wouldn't mind if Gerry took her to Salsa Night and beyond, but "Belfast men don't dance, it's a known fact," he tells her, and goes home to mind the boys so that Ellie and her chum can go off to the Salsa.

When Ellie returns in the middle of the night, she's left the car back there in Camden Town. Gerry drags himself to his feet and—over her protest—bikes off to Camden Town to get it. "Why do you keep calling me Nellie?" she irritably demands. "Because I luv her." "Yes, I suppose you do."

This picture has all the sweetly nourishing marital texture, like new bread, of dramas along the lines of "Joe Egg," "Two for the Road," "The Pumpkin Eater." It also has two superb players, Stephen Rea and Sinead Cusack, in the leads, with long-nosed, saturnine Philip Jackson heading a splendid cast as bad-news Howard, delicious Saira Todd as Sophie. The director is Lee Blair, who believes in improvisational filmmaking. Here, it works—brilliantly.

NEWSDAY, 9/3/93, Part II/p. 62, Jack Mathews

There is a Woody Allen quality to British director Les Blair's "Bad Behaviour,"and the title has nothing to do with it. In Blair's exquisitely romantic comedy about a middle-class Irish couple living in North London, the bad behavior is all done by a neighborhood hustler whose attempt to beat the couple out of a few quid shakes them up and helps revive their flagging marriage.

The movie, largely improvised during rehearsals, is a slice of life cut out of the middle years of a good marriage caught in a slump. Gerry McAllister ("The Crying Game's" Stephen Rea) is a town planner bored with his work and vaguely responsive to an infatuated co-worker. Ellie (Sinead Cusack) is an exhausted housewife and mother of two growing increasingly anxious over the lack of accomplishment and direction in her life.

The Woody Allen quality is the ambivalent mix of affection and resentment between Gerry and Ellie, the way they respond to the social pressures on them and the way their edgy playfulness reveals the tension creeping into their marriage. Blair's characters use language much as Allen's do, as weapons cloaked in humor.

"Bad Behaviour" takes its time warming up, but once it's there you understand why it was necessary. Blair's interest here isn't in telling a story about a marriage in trouble, but in exploring the subtle, ways marriages often *get* in trouble. To appreciate the process, we need to know the subjects.

And they are worth the effort. Gerry is a bright, witty, thoughtful father and husband who's numbing the monotony of his world with increasing drink. Ellie, feeling trapped in a life without emotional arias and intellectually deadened by the daily grind, is constantly having her own problems overridden by those of people who count on her for strength.

When Gerry and Ellie attempt to get at the root of her unrest, during a conversation in bed, you sense the frustration over their loss of communication, and the effect it is having on their passion. It is easy to imagine what grand lovers they once were, but now she can only say of him that "he makes me laugh," and he views her as a comfortable habit.

What stirs this marriage up, like a stick plunged into the silt-covered bottom of a quiet pond, is not the expected affair and some tragic aftermath, but the bold move by Ellie, over Gerry's objections, to have the downstairs bath remodeled.

More marriages have probably been done in by unilateral home-improvement decisions than by extramarital affairs, and Blair uses the bathroom as a perfect metaphor. When the Nunn brothers, twin handymen recommended by neighborhood scoundrel Howard Spink (Philip Jackson), start chiseling tiles off the wall, the McAllisters' nerves are the first things to be exposed.

"Bad Behaviour" is a magical little movie, full of surprises, big laughs and delightfully acted characters.

The Nunn brothers, Ray and Ron (both played by Phil Daniels), are impossible to tell apart, until they start to work (one does, one doesn't). Clare Higgins is both sad and funny as Ellie's melancholy friend, a divorcee paralyzed by resentment. And Jackson gives us one of the year's most enjoyably despicable villains, a smarmy, high-roller wannabe with every electronic toy on the market but not enough money to pay his own rent.

In attempting to collect a consultant's fee for recommending the bathroom job, Howard inadvertently pulls a marriage back from the brink. It's a small fee but a large outrage, and the mutual enmity they feel for Howard gives Gerry and Ellie a common cause.

Rea and Cusack both credit Blair's improvisational process for the way their characters relate. The two were only allowed to speak to each other as Gerry and Ellie, and the rich dialogue of their scenes reportedly came out of the rehearsal process.

However it all came together, "Bad Behaviour" is as effective as it is because of that relationship, and because of the performances of Rea, whose engaging personality takes the edge off of his often hostile jokes, and Cusack, who can express an amazing range of emotions without saying a word.

These are not easy characters to develop. They don't have big scenes that reveal themselves in obvious ways. Yet, we get to know them very well and, in the end, wish them the best.

SIGHT AND SOUND, 6/93, p. 47, Claire Monk

Gerry and Ellie McAllister, an Irish couple in their late 30s, live in Kentish Town, north London, with two pre-adolescent sons. Gerry is a planner for Camden Council involved in legalising a local travellers' site; Ellie works part-time in a bookshop but has unfulfilled ambitions to write and is increasingly restless in her domestic role, especially when contrasting herself with her old friend Winifred, who is single and a successful journalist. Another friend of hers, Jess, is bitter about her recent breakup with her partner and struggling to care alone for her teenage daughter Rosie.

Howard Spink, whose son Jake plays with the McAllister boys, shows Ellie some cracks in her bathroom wall, and recommends a pair of local builders, the Nunn Brothers, calling them on the spot on his mobile phone. What the McAllisters don't know is that Howard is an unprincipled landlord embroiled in numerous building scams. Relations worsen between Jess and Rosie when the latter shows concern about her mother neglecting herself and not eating. Ellie tells Gerry she can't bear staying in London for ever: she would like to work full-time in the bookshop, but doesn't believe Gerry's flexitime is sufficient to reduce her domestic burdens. Howard instructs Roy Nunn to make a maintenance visit to a tenant, who proves to be Jess, as a front for valuing the property. Roy reminds Howard that his twin brother Ray is getting impatient about £1,200 Howard owes him.

The legalisation of the travellers' site is passed by the planning committee, and Gerry and his younger colleague Sophie celebrate at a tapas bar while Ellie and Winifred have a drunken heart-to-heart at home. Gerry and Sophie, also drunk, become increasingly close, Sophie inviting Gerry to a forthcoming salsa evening at the bar. Gerry returns home, where he underplays the planning success and says nothing of his night out. Ellie accuses him of driving Winifred away and goes to bed. One of the Nunns starts work early next morning, causing complaints about noise from the hungover Gerry. Rosie confides in Ellie about her deteriorating relationship with Jess. Ellie visits Jess, who complains about Rosie; Ellie suggests that Rosie could stay with her, and Jess leaps at the idea. The McAllisters are outraged to be billed by Howard for a consultancy fee; but when Gerry complains, Howard threatens legal action.

Jess brings Ellie a gift to thank her in advance for looking after Rosie but reveals that she hasn't mentioned the arrangement to Rosie. Ellie tells Jess she is driving Rosie away and suggests she needs professional help; Jess calls Ellie a selfish bitch. Meeting accidentally in a pub, Howard and Jess trade their supposed grudges against the McAllisters; Howard reveals that he's her landlord and drives her to her flat for afternoon sex, but they are interrupted by Rosie's arrival. Returning home, Howard is confronted by Gerry and the Nunns with their respective grievances, but announces that his house is about to be repossessed, and the Spinks drive away, leaving the three men on the doorstep. At work, Sophie reminds Gerry about the salsa evening that night and is disappointed when he says he can't go. Jess is evicted, but Howard is evasive when she calls him for help. Ellie has changed her working hours and started writing. Child-minding while Ellie and Winifred go out to the same salsa evening as Sophie and her colleagues, Gerry finds a story of Ellie's and reads it. Ellie and Winifred return happy and drunk, and Gerry cycles out to retrieve the car, which Ellie has left near the tapas bar. In bed, he compliments her on her story; contented, they fall asleep.

With its downbeat London locations, focus on the upwardly mobile former working class and comically observant eye for clashing values and lifestyles, Les Blair's improvised domestic drama invites obvious comparisons with the films of Mike Leigh—whose *Bleak Moments* he edited and produced—particularly with Leigh alumni Rea, Daniels and Jackson among the cast. As with Leigh, the bulk of Blair's earlier improvised films—including the advertising industry satire *Honest Decent and True* and the 1990 BAFTA award-winner *Newshounds*—have been made for television, and *Bad Behaviour*'s fly-on-the-wall naturalism doesn't make a concerted leap onto the big screen. while the office and domestic settings come refreshingly close to recreating the chaos of real life, the blurry documentary-style camerawork is relentlessly uncinematic. But stylistic reservations aside, Blair's application of *cinéma vérité* techniques to fictional material makes for a relaxed comedy with a richer, fuller view of human relations and 1990s urban life than we're likely to glean from Leigh's more grotesque creations.

The snippet-of-life narrative structure draws us into the thick of already-unfolding situations. Early scenes showing Howard discussing a dodgy piece of work with Roy, and tippexing out the copywright stamp on a questionably acquired council plan, give us advance warning of the state of his scruples and his involvement with the long-suffering Nunn Brothers. A contrasting professional exchange between Gerry and Sophie depicts—with considerable wishful thinking about the sexual politics of planners—a working relationship marked by co-operative camaraderie rather than a sexualised hierarchy. 'Overheard' dialogue intensifies this sense of eavesdropping on real lives. When Rosie interrupts Jess in bed with Howard, the full measure of the situation—the mature, self-controlled daughter and the immature, out-of-control mother—is conveyed in a shot of Rosie's face, while in the background Jess exclaims "Shit!" and Howard is heard making a post-coital phone call.

In its depiction of Howard and Jess's bad behaviour; the film skates close to a condemnatory satire, in stark contrast to its sympathetic treatment of the dilemmas faced by the McAllisters: Howard's mobile phone is particularly overused as a signifier of his dubious values. New Age enthusiasms are given equally short shrift, serving as a metaphor for Jess's flakiness and inconsistency: when Rosie is blamed for preventing her mother from escaping to a Buddhist weekend, the real problem turns out to be that Jess hasn't booked.

However, the minutiae Blair reveals in his characters' lives more often undermine our expectations than reinforce them. Jackson's Howard has affinities with the same actor's memorably disgusting car salesman in Leigh's *High Hopes*, but he reads Christopher Lasch's *The Culture of Narcissism* in bed and boasts a North London therapy-belt wife who's an expert on identical twins; in one of the film's funniest scenes, an irritated Nunn Brother evades her professional probing. And Gerry is revealed to be an accomplished cartoonist, drawing himself as a character called Paddy Plan-It. Significantly, these details have almost no plot significance: in structure and pace, *Bad Behaviour* comes closer to the diffuse rhythms of daily life than the expected cinematic patterns of drama and resolution. Gerry stays home on the very night when his closeness to Sophie might have developed into an affair; Ellie's discontents are eased by practical steps and Gerry's support rather than erupting into a crisis.

The success of this study of good behaviour is due above all to the brilliantly credible screen partnership between Rea and Cusack, their relaxed intimacy and bantering humour suggesting a relationship as familiar and easy to underestimate as a favourite pair of socks. Rea's genial, laid-back disillusioned idealist engages in food preparation and parenting without a trace of New Man smugness; and Cusack not only acquits herself marvellously in her first improvised work but shows infinitely better taste in her choice of roles than her husband Jeremy Irons did with another recent domestic drama, the wretched *Damage*.

TIME, 9/6/93, p. 68, Richard Schickel

In lieu of renovating her life, Ellie McAllister (the luminous Sinead Cusack) decides to renovate her loo. Redecoration instead of redirection: it is probably the most pervasive of middle-class sublimations.

But fixing up the bathroom is never quite as easy as it seems. For one thing, all these strangers start trooping through your house, your life, dragging their tools and their problems behind them. This being Kentish Town, in the north of London, they all want a cup of tea (or something stronger) as part of the bargain. For another, all you have to show at the end is a diminished bank account and pretty much the same old life that you started out with.

For Ellie, this includes a husband, Gerry (Stephen Rea of *The Crying Game*), a town planner engaged in a flirtation with a co-worker but too vague, wry and discontented with life to do anything conclusive about it or anything else; one female friend who is enviably up and abustle, another who is distressingly down and out, rendered dysfunctional by divorce; a part-time job in a bookstore and a full-time dream of becoming a writer herself.

It is, perversely, the movie's only thoroughly bad person, one Howard Spink (Philip Jackson), who more or less mobilizes everyone. He purports to be a construction consultant, and it's he who arranges the contractors for the job on the bathroom. They are the Nunn Brothers, and since they are identical twins (both played by Phil Daniels), they add immeasurably to the confusion in the McAllister household. Along the way Spink seduces the more vulnerable of Ellie's friends (she even supplies him with the change he needs to buy the requisite condom), cheats the Nunns, presents an exorbitant bill for his nonexistent services. In the end he flees everyone's wrath as he gathers up his family in order to escape an eviction notice on his own house.

None of this is presented melodramatically. *Bad Behaviour* was improvised, under Les Blair's direction, by its actors. They were obviously looking for characters to play, not a plot to follow or pre-existent outlines to fill in. For a change, this dangerous technique works: the film's best quality is its life-like drift. Like real people, and unlike movie people, these figures will do anything to escape confrontation with their problems, with themselves.

By the end, Gerry seems a little more engaged in family life and Ellie is actually writing something. But we can be pretty certain that distraction will reassert itself, probably sooner rather than later. Anyway, it would betray the film's spirit if everyone suddenly started tidying things up for a thumping conclusion. The theaters are full of such endings anyway. What's always in short supply are movies that have something to do with life as most of us actually experience it, *Bad Behaviour* briefly, smartly fills that gap.

VILLAGE VOICE, 9/7/93, p. 55, Georgia Brown

Ah, the mysteries of marriage. It's interesting that in recent years practically the only American films on the subject are made by Woody Allen, and what does he know? While romantic comedies (*Shameless in Seattle*) lead up to the altar, then drop the subject of compatibility like a hot potato, thrillers (*The Fugitive, Manhattan Murder Mystery*) take up the consequences of a violent split. It's as if the only way to get rid of a spouse is murder.

From abroad come a few good films about domestic strife, like *The Best Intentions*, directed by Bille August from Bergman's screenplay. But it's the English, often in made-for-TV movies, who're focusing most productively on what happens to strong personalities trapped under the same roof. Stephen Frears's light but hilarious *The Snapper* (coming soon by way of the New York Film Festival) deals uncommonly with a common crisis. And for years Mike Leigh has been turning out his own eccentric explorations, mostly of working-class families. Though I can't speak for his earlier films (*Honest, Decent and True* and *News Hounds*), Les Blair appears to be another director firmly committed to creating deceptively modest dramas out of the mundane. If his new film, *Bad Behaviour*, is much less hysterical and explosive than Leigh's are, it may be because his milieu here is more bourgeois.

Note that there's no writer's credit on *Bad Behaviour*. Working in the method popularized by Leigh, Blair makes what's called improvised cinema. Starting with a rough outline or treatment, he and his actors, over a period of weeks, invent and research characters, and only finally, in group rehearsals, develop dialogue and a firm plot. This may be something like the way families work, too.

A prime advantage of the method is that characters are far more lively, nuanced, and unpredictable than those any screenwriter can write. You really can't anticipate what they'll do next because they aren't there in the service of some rigid story. The story comes *from them*, not vice versa. Narratives tend to be loose, episodic, and essentially open-ended. An illusion is built up that we're meeting real people who will be going on with their lives after we've gone on our way.

For his very likable *Bad Behaviour*, Blair has enlisted two superb and intelligent actors to play/develop the characters of wife and husband: Sinead Cusack (Jeremy Irons's wife, also his fictional wife in *Waterland*) and Stephen Rea (you do know who he is, right?). They've become the McAllisters, Ellie and Gerry, fortysomething transplanted Dubliners settled in a comfy, if somewhat rundown row house in Kentish Town (a sort of North London Park Slope). The couple has two sons (one in his early teens, the other around six), though the kids haven't much of a role except to bring disruptive outsiders into the house. The movie's main focus, to use the shorthand, is Ellie's, and perhaps Gerry's, midlife crisis.

Now that her youngest is in school, Ellie is in between and on edge, feeling a potentially destructive, or creative, energy welling up. Half-days she works in a bookstore while still doing most of the chores at home. On the one hand, she's thinking of increasing her hours at the store; on the other, she wants "to write." At times, she also wants desperately to return to Ireland. She finds Gerry's gentle, taciturn deflections grating and patronizing. Wary of her moods, he's using all his wits to quiet her.

A city planner, Gerry takes refuge in the office where he's appreciated as a funny guy and calming influence. Obviously, he's doted on by a young, single coworker, Sophie (Saira Todd), his partner on a current project. (A slovenly charmer, Rea is perversely appealing.) Gerry does lead her on, lets her think he might fall, but his real heart's desire is hidden under layers of wry, deadpan humor. The possibility dawns that he really might want just Ellie. In some ways, he's such a mensch, he's almost too good. While Ellie feels imprisoned, her friends envy her. Both of them like booze, a potentially dangerous ingredient.

How long-term relationships work, adjust to change, is the movie's subject. And to its credit, there are always the nagging questions: Are they settling for security? Might some violent upheaval achieve more? In other words, how much do they really want? Is inertia the strongest force?

One immediate source of drama, and humor, turns out to be Howard Spink (Philip Jackson), father of one of their sons' friends, who sends over two contractors (identical twins played by Phil Daniels) to renovate a small bathroom. A pompous duck who keeps *The Culture of Narcissism* by his bedside, Spink is a congenital con man, though one so clumsy that he poses more of a threat to himself and his own family. His wife, a classy-looking developmental psychologist, is an odd, funny minor character.

But the real focus isn't the Spinks, the twin builders, or the failed marriage of a bitter neighbor, it's the tension and bond between the McAllisters. Will Gerry seek outside gratification? Can Ellie draw sustenance from nights out with girlfriends? In an American version, she'd either break out dramatically or produce a runaway bestseller. The fact is that Blair's modest explorations in personality are really far more ambitious than all the surface bluster of Hollywood.

Also reviewed in:
CHICAGO TRIBUNE, 12/24/93, Friday/p. F, Michael Wilmington
NEW YORK TIMES, 9/3/93, p. C6, Janet Maslin
VARIETY, 3/1/93, p. 60, Derek Elley
WASHINGTON POST, 10/8/93, Weekend/p. 36, Desson Howe
WASHINGTON POST, 10/11/93, p. D8, Hal Hinson

BALLAD OF LITTLE JO, THE

A Fine Line Features and Polygram Filmed Entertainment release of a Fred Berner/JoCo production. *Executive Producer:* Ira Deutchman and John Sloss. *Producer:* Fred Berner and Brenda Goodman. *Director:* Maggie Greenwald. *Screenplay:* Maggie Greenwald. *Director of Photography:* Declan Quinn. *Editor:* Keith Reamer. *Music:* David Mansfield. *Music Editor:* James Flatto. *Sound:* Felipe Borrero. *Sound Editor:* Stuart Emanuel. *Casting:* Judy Claman and Jeffrey Passero. *Production Designer:* Mark Friedberg. *Art Director:* Ginger Toupas. *Set Decorator:* Stephanie Carroll. *Set Dresser:* James Dungan, Elizabeth "Betsy" Alton, and Chad Branham. *Special Effects:* J.C. Brotherhood. *Costumes:* Claudia Brown. *Make-up:* Lori Hicks. *Stunt Coordinator:* Buddy Joe Hooker. *Running time:* 120 minutes. *MPAA Rating:* R.

CAST: Suzy Amis (Little Jo); Bo Hopkins (Frank Badger); Ian McKellen (Percy Corcoran); David Chung (Tinman Wong); Carrie Snodgress (Ruth Badger); Rene Auberjonois (Streight Hollander); Heather Graham (Mary Addie); Sam Robards (Jasper Hill); Ruth Maleczech (Shop Keeper); Tom Bower (Lyle); Olinda Turturro (Evvira); Irina Pasmur (Russian Mother); Anthony Heald (Mr. Henry Grey); Melissa Leo (Mrs. Grey); Sean Murphy (Young Henry Grey); Jeffrey Andrews (Sam); Cathy Haase (Mrs. Addie); Peadair S. Addie, Sr. (Mr. Addie); Jenny Lynch (Helen Monaghan); Vince O'Neil (Amos Monaghan); Karen Johnson (Farmwife); Troy Smith (Soldier #1); Keith Kamppinen (Soldier #2); Rusty Pegar (Duke Billy); Robert Erickson (Wilkins); Michael Rudd (Russian Father); David Ruben Plowman (9 Year Old Nick); Sasha Pasmur (14 Year Old Nick); Renee Tafoya (Woman Photographer); Barbara Jean Marsh (Laundress); Richard Osterman (Travelling Judge); Dennis McNiven (Mortician); Jamie Crabtree (Jo's Baby); Tracy Mayfield (John); Julianne Kirst (Nora Monaghan); Deborah J. Richard (Mabel); Netta Goodrich (Lucy); Becca Busch (Little Sue); Jim Dunkin (Mr. Brown); Homer Simon (Fiddler); Eryn L. Bent (Russian Girl); Peter Plowman (Young Russian Boy); Joe Freed (Older Russian Boy); Anne Plowman (Young Russian Girl); Melissa Ladvala (Older Russian Girl); Yevgeniy Yasyriu (Russian Father); Duane Ebel (Nick, age 40).

CINEASTE, Vol. XX, No. 2, 1993, p. 45, Karen Dackstein

If many films these days make a point of questioning—or appearing to question—the truisms of the past, *The Ballad of Little Jo* belongs firmly to the moment. Inspired by a real woman who, in the late 1860s, went west to the frontier and successfully posed as a man until death revealed her secret to the community, the film is a meditation on what might have made her don her disguise, and how she could have avoided detection (the actual details of her life story remain unknown). This narrative, with its focus on woman-playing-man, and its look at the western landscape, plays with two of the more dominant contemporary practices: gender-bending and genre-bending.

From *The Crying Game* to *Orlando*, spectators have recently had to confront protagonists whose gender remains either masked or ambiguous, confounding their expectations and (presumably) jerking them out of their complacency regarding male and female images. Of course, whether these films actually force viewers to find fresh ways of looking at gender roles is debatable; for all their obvious differences, films like *The Crying Game* and *Orlando* depend on bravura performance to carry their surprises, their wonder, and the brunt of their narrative weight, at least partly transferring the emphasis on politics to an emphasis on playacting.

But *The Ballad of Little Jo* marries its feminist message to generic revisionism, and the two can't be pried apart. Classical Hollywood's clear-cut ideas of genre still provide the model against which revisionist narratives play. But the use of genre can cut two ways. Like *Unforgiven*, the revision can explore only the world of the spectacle, delving into the meaning of generic pleasure, and the audience's investment in familiar patterns: by making spectators long to see hero Eastwood in the traditional climactic gunfight—in spite of the fact that the character's peaceful life should seem more noble than the outlaw's—*Unforgiven* prodded viewers to question their investments in these conventions. And if the film suggested that the Western told a history built on lies, it never offered an alternative 'truth.'

Other generic revisions, including *Little Jo* (or *Dances with Wolves*), try to find the 'reality' that once existed before our society's dominant ideologies deformed and transformed it, coloring in the areas that Hollywood's canvas left blank (although of course Hollywood films never really were as monolithic in their historical view as some might suggest). Such films often replace the traditional white male star with a female equivalent or recount the suppressed narratives of overlooked ethnic groups to bring to the surface their contributions to American culture, but they retain the storytelling structures of commercial cinema. In this respect, although it might seem cynical to say so, in commercial films women have it all over Native Americans, who still 'need' a Caucasian star to plead their cause.

The Ballad of Little Jo aims to present a tapestry of women's lives on the frontier, with its unorthodox heroine the exception that sets other choices in relief. Little Jo, born to a rich eastern family that tosses her into the streets for having a baby out of wedlock, deposits her child with a married sister and heads westward unaware of the dangers that await her. Her first cruel lesson in the realities of being a homeless woman wandering the frontier is enough; Jo dons men's clothes (illegal at the time) and slashes her face with a knife to destroy the last vestiges of her beauty.

In order to keep her secret, Little Jo, ironically, must mold her character and her actions to the outlines of the traditional male hero: laconic and moral, a person apart from the everyday concerns of the farmers and ranchers who work to build a community, quasi-mythical in her actions and the last voice of solitude in a rapidly 'civilizing' land. The quintessential savior, she steps in during moments of crisis and then rides away silently. Jo lives her life alone, tending sheep, and helps only outsiders; when she does get involved in the town's affairs, fighting against wealthy eastern capitalists out to grab every available (and unavailable) inch of land, she does so partly to save her own property, her own piece of heaven.

But what is the effect of using as a feminist model a woman who gains her freedom by passing as a man! And, related to but not the same as Jo's literal passing, what is the effect of placing female protagonists in narrative forms developed to express traditionally masculine concerns! Ultimately, like other 'outlaw heroines' such as *Thelma & Louise*, Jo receives an *'education insentimentale'* inevitably figured as violence and rape that emerges specifically from women's history (and never mind that the real Little Jo's of the West—for she was not alone—might have made their choice not as the result of a direct act of aggression but as a means of escaping the more quiet violence of their restricted lives).

In both cases, however implicitly, the characters' strength is measured by how closely it approximates male standards of power. We see that women are 'equal' because they can behave exactly like men, even if they do so more 'morally,' as evidenced by Little Jo's rescue of the Chinese drifter Tinman, whom the menfolk happily set out to lynch.

While a woman in pants chucking wood and herding sheep might have automatically spelled maleness in a period when the social structure did not allow for the possibility of such a creature, for contemporary audiences Suzy Amis's Little Jo, in her loose-fitting pants, long coat, and close-cropped hair, might just look rather distinctively like a contemporary woman. And, unlike a classical Western, which sets up a recognizable community dynamic with which to contrast the lone hero's solitude, *The Ballad of Little Jo* doesn't establish a clear picture of the rules of the world she enters.

Nor does the film explore in detail what Jo's disguise might have meant for her: while her love affair with Tinman shows that the affectation of self-sufficiency needed to conceal her womanhood hid a thirst for companionship and a buried sexuality, it leaves unexamined the more philosophical ramifications of denying one's gender and living a constant lie. On a larger scale, director Maggie Greenwald's stated goal of revealing the difficult life experienced by all women in the west not only through Jo's adventures but through those of the other female protagonists falls by the wayside because of flimsy characterization and a lack of screen time.

The Ballad of Little Jo has a visual style that eschews the majesty typically associated with classical Westerns: the wide-scale vistas that suggested endless space and opportunity in the past bow here to cluttered half-built towns, dusty and dirty. The attempt at capturing a form of reality works uneasily with a heroine who, like any subject of a folk ballad, must necessarily become an iconic, 'more than real' figure.

One might compare Little Jo to the silent drifter of Agnes Varda's *Vagabond*. In that film, the heroine defiantly remains a narrative cipher, with no history or psychological motivations. As she wanders from place to place, the reactions of those who come into contact with her reveal the narrow range of behavior the French bourgeoisie consider acceptable for women. Thus, a full portrait of the society emerges, and we gradually understand the Vagabond's unwillingness to be a part of it.

Little Jo's own refusal of the ordinary could have made her such a character, and her ballad might have told more about the west, had the film not so crudely explained away her 'transformation.' As a stark contrast to both the men and women who surrounded her, she could have been a catalyst for revelation of fears, desires and violence.

At times, the film comes close to this, but potentially interesting points—such as the homoerotic implications of both servant-girl Mary's and outcast Percy Corcoran's attraction to Jo—never get developed. Mary's affection for Jo becomes nothing more than a passing hope for a sweet husband rather than an inkling on her part that somehow Jo is really different from other men. The film also negates the possibility that Jo's companionship, and the difficult emotions it inspires, are a cause of Percy's rage. Rather than exploring the long-repressed emotions Jo's presence inspires, *The Ballad of Little Jo* seems satisfied with presenting Jo as merely a viewer who silently takes in events that would have happened anyway.

LOS ANGELES TIMES, 9/10/93, Calendar/p. 1, Kevin Thomas

"The Ballad of Little Jo" is a severely de-romanticized view of the Old West and the women who labored—in more ways than one—on its frontiers. At two hours, "Little Jo" is a long slog of revisionism, and by the end it doesn't necessarily seem any closer to the truth than the standard Hollywood Westerns. It's just bleaker.

Revisionist Westerns, like, most recently, Eastwood's "Unforgiven," usually explore the consequences of violence in a male-dominated society. What sets "Little Jo" apart from those films is its focus on a woman—Suzy Amis' real-life Jo Monaghan, who is banished by her well-to-do family when she has an illegitimate child and who survives alone by impersonating a man in the rough mining town of Ruby City.

This is a potentially great, new-to-movies subject: Women in the Old West who successfully passed themselves off as men to avoid the harassments of femalehood. (Charlie Parkhurst, the legendary Gold Rush stagecoach driver, for example, was only discovered to be a woman upon her death.) Maggie Greenwald, who wrote and directed, doesn't take a leering approach to Little Jo's transformation; Jo's mysterious melancholy fills out the action without ever really explaining why she would seek to efface herself so completely. Her makeover has a self-punishing quality, as if she wanted to ravage any trace of maidenliness. (To complete her changeover, Jo not only shears her long tresses but slices a long gash into her cheek.)

Greenwald's distanced approach to Jo also has its share of self-abnegation. She doesn't bring out any psychosexual crosscurrents in Jo's identity change. She doesn't bring out any humor in it either, or willfulness. We don't see how Jo might have relished her male trappings. In dramatic terms, Jo's existence is so clamped down and super-subtle that, after awhile, Greenwald's tact begins to resemble evasiveness. Probably she was counting on Amis to radiate a core of sympathy that would be far more suggestive than the usual deep-dish psychologizing. But Amis keeps things cool and distant, too. She's an extraordinary and undervalued actress—some of her best work, in films like "Twister" and "Rich in Love," has gone virtually unseen—but most of the time she closes herself off in "The Ballad of Little Jo."

Her stillness can be very eloquent, though, and there are some fine sequences when Jo lets down her guard and gets romantic with a Chinese hired hand (David Chung). When she's hanging around rancher Frank Badger (Bo Hopkins) she tenses up with wariness, as if her femaleness would be betrayed by any outward show of emotion. In her scenes with the miner Percy Corcoran (well played by Ian McKellen), who takes Jo on as a kind of mascot, she lets a little softness out (with disastrous consequences),

Greenwald tries to capture the flat, unconsoling look of the photo portraits of the Westerners that have come back to us from the last century. In a sense, Jo is a living daguerreotype: Her muteness and two-dimensionality are intended as a mythic memento from a bitter past. Jo's humanity is compromised by this approach—the film (rated R for sexuality and some violence,) ends as more of a dirge than a ballad. But occasionally it casts a forlorn spell. The meaning of Jo Monaghan's life may not really emerge in this film but its mystery lingers.

NEW YORK POST, 8/20/93, p. 25, Michael Medved

During the Gold Rush period in California, a stagecoach driver named Charlie Parkhurst won special recognition as one of the fastest, most reliable drivers for the California Stage Co. On several occasions his courage helped to save his passengers from bandits or natural disasters.

Only years later, when he died of old age, did his friends and neighbors discover that old Charlie was really a woman who had spent most of her life in a totally convincing gender-bender disguise.

"The Ballad of Little Jo" tells a similar story, inspired by the intriguing historical figure Jo Monaghan—about whom we know almost nothing other than the fact that she worked as a rancher and for several decades passed herself off as a man.

This film attempts to fill in the missing details of her life, beginning in 1866, with the elegantly dressed, properly corseted Josephine Monaghan (Suzy Amis) making her way west. We find out in flashback that she has recently scandalized her well-to-do Eastern family by bearing a child out of wedlock, causing her unforgiving father to drive her out of the house.

No sooner does she arrive on the raw frontier than she is brutally assaulted by two randy cowboys, leading to a fateful decision: She cuts off her hair and mutilates her face with a straight razor to create a long, ugly scar that will help her pass herself off as a man.

Amis is perfectly cast in the title role. She is a charismatic leading lady (most recently seen in attention-getting parts in "Rich In Love" and "Watch It") who possesses the sort of square-jawed, raw-boned beauty that makes her masquerade believable.

In contrast to Barbra Streisand in "Yentl," or even Julie Andrews in "Victor/Victoria," her male impersonation is persuasive enough so that you don't have to assume that the people around her are total idiots for believing it. Amis delivers a performance of such subtlety and power that in the course of the film she even shows Little Jo growing gradually—and visibly—more comfortable in her/his male identity.

Aside from its star, the other great asset of this picture is the stunning visual sense and admirable attention to detail by writer-director Maggie Greenwald. Nothing in her two previous well-regarded but little-seen films ("Home Remedy" and "The Kill Off") hinted at the sweeping, lyrical vistas and haunting sensitivity to light and shadow so evident here—and so surprising in a limited-budget, independent picture like this one.

In the bleak hills of southern Montana, Greenwald has painstakingly re-created the mining camp of Ruby City and focused our attention with rare immediacy and authenticity on the coarse, grimy and heart-breakingly lonely day-to-day realities of life on the frontier.

Unfortunately, this care and commitment is eventually undone by Greenwald's unnecessary surrender to some of the dumbest cliches of the old-fashioned horse opera. For instance, Little Jo learns to become a crack shot and blasts away at baddies in a climactic scene.

There's even a silly subplot about courageous sheep herders battling vicious cattle ranchers—given the inevitable spin of political correctness by identifying the cow capitalists as the tools of Eastern "money interests." Worst of all, there's a sappy, thoroughly implausible romance thrown in toward the end of the film that cheapens the rough poetry of everything that's gone before.

Another lamentable feature of the traditional western was the heavy-handed division of all characters into either good guys or bad guys, and the fact that this movie arranges that division strictly along gender lines doesn't make it any easier to accept. Every single female character in the picture is heroic—hard-working, stoic, sensitive and sensible. All the males, on the other hand (including a philosophical Brit—played by Sir Ian McKellen—who at first befriends Little Jo) turn out to be violent, filthy, selfish, sadistic pigs.

The only exception to that rule is, naturally, the one non-white male in the picture—a well-muscled, noble-hearted Chinese "coolie" played by David Chung, who is rescued from lynching when Little Jo faces down a mob of drooling racists. The fact that this time it's men in general, and not "Injuns" who are the bloodthirsty savages may add a note of trendy social commentary, but it doesn't prevent this often intriguing film from slipping to the level of two-dimensional melodrama.

NEWSDAY, 8/20/93, Part II/p. 69, John Anderson

The Old West was brutal. Worse, the men who lived there were rude, sexist psychopaths who smelled, snored, ate like swine and treated women like trash.

Is this revelation? Well, we've got another one: They were congenitally stupid, judging by how many actually believe Suzy Amis is a man in "The Ballad of Little Jo."

In this third feature by filmmaker Maggie Greenwald, we see a well-bred, unwed young mother, banished from her family home and baby back East, who puts on pants to keep from getting raped and flourishes as a sheep farmer in Montana. Along the way, Greenwald treats us to the dismantling of myths that were long ago dismantled, and establishes a few of her own.

In a film that revels in impotent outrage, Josephine Monaghan (Amis) arrives in the West and is betrayed by the first man she meets, a peddler named Hollander (Rene Auberjonois), who immediately sells her to two soldiers. She escapes with her honor, muddied and bloodied (Amis has the kind of face that retains its beauty regardless), and reaches to a general store where the only ready-made clothing is men's. It's against the law to dress like the opposite sex, she's told, so she takes the whole package, cutting her long red hair with the same razor she then uses to slice her cheek, from eye to jaw.

Ruby City, Mont., little more than a mining camp, is where Jo settles and is subjected to the kind of mean-spirited scrutiny reserved for any newcomer. The scrutiny isn't thorough enough to figure out that this kid with the pretty face and padded shoulders, who walks funny, talks funny, and whose pistol hangs from her belt in such a way that the barrel points directly at her crotch, isn't going to be getting married any time soon.

But she does make the acquaintance of Frank (Bo Hopkins), with whom she'll form a lifelong friendship; Percy (Ian McKellen), a well-read sicko who takes a broken bottle to a whore one night (all this face-cutting must be an homage to "Unforgiven"), and eventually, Tinman (David Chung), a wryly hip and handsome Chinese immigrant in whose serene Eastern mind, and bed, Jo finds solace. He's also the only one to figure out Jo's secret. Must be that serene, Eastern mind.

Greenwald is on her high horse, no pun intended, and so is Amis, who plays Jo so humorlessly she can't possible elicit much sympathy. There is a lot of entertaining Celtic- and bluegrass-flavored music from string virtuoso David Mansfield, which tends to move things along. But there's also a lot of dead air, long sequences meant to establish mood but which don't progress the narrative or develop the characters to any great degree and become long-winded exercises in earnestness. Add to this a great deal of stylized dialogue that seems meant to evoke "Our American Cousin" and "Little Jo" makes you long for "Bonanza."

SIGHT AND SOUND, 4/94, p. 36, Claire Monk

1866. Josephine Monaghan, a young woman from a well-off New York family, has been thrown out by her father after becoming pregnant by a photographer; her baby son is in the care of her sister Helen. Josephine accepts a lift from a pedlar heading West, but two soldiers shoot him dead and drag her away. Escaping, she tries to replace her torn frock, but the shop she finds only has fabric and thread. Instead she buys men's clothes, cuts off her hair, carves a scar into her cheek and becomes 'Little Jo'. She rides into Ruby City, a remote mining outpost, where she passes as a man.

Percy Corcoran, the mine superintendent, suggests work at the stables, and offers a room in his shack. She accepts, but puzzles him by keeping her distance. On a night when the men take turns with a visiting prostitute, Jo is called to intervene when Percy attacks the woman. Terrified of Percy learning her true sex, Jo asks sheep-rancher Frank Badger to hire her as his winter herder. Jo soon learns to shoot predators and comes to love the peace and privacy of life in the wilderness. On her return to town, Percy hands her a letter from Helen. Having read it and learned that Jo is a woman, he tries to rape her, but she holds him off at gunpoint. Percy agrees to leave but blackmails Jo into financing his move.

Now a rancher, Jo prevents a crowd, led by Frank, from lynching a Chinese man seeking work. Frank agrees to set 'Tinman Wong' free only if Jo will hire him as a cook. Accepting resentfully, she treats Tinman badly, making him sleep outdoors. Eventually she relents and helps him build a shelter; he reveals that he knows she is a woman, and they become lovers.

Frank warns Jo that the Western Cattle Company, who have been buying up small ranches in the area, are using violence, but Jo won't sell. When Jo finds a Russian refugee family lying slaughtered by Cattle Company horsemen, she throws Tinman out. He reenters to find Jo wearing a dress. She says she will sell. Tinman becomes ill, About to sign over the ranch to the Cattle Company's owner, Henry Grey, she changes her mind when she sees Tinman has recovered. On the day when Frank is standing for Mayor, three Company horsemen lie in wait for Jo and Frank, but they shoot all three dead. The elections proceed and the Company's tactics are defeated.

Years later, after Tinman's death, Frank finds Jo dead in bed. Preparing for a grand funeral, the undertaker undresses the corpse and learns the truth about Jo, and the townsfolk gather round in amazement. Frank finds Jo's family portrait and Helen's letters, and her story is made public.

In her recent book *West of Everything: The Inner Life of Westerns*, Jane Tompkins argues that the Western arose as a male reaction to the nineteenth century novel—it represents the enclosure of a strictly men-only territory, defined by its exclusion of the spheres of civilisation, domesticity and language which the novel had mapped out as female. In that light, it is no surprise that Maggie Greenwald's much-touted 'woman's Western' should be so preoccupied with women's lack of freedom to storm the West themselves.

Although based on the life of a real Josephine Monaghan, who lived undetected as a 'man' until her death, Greenwald's second appropriation of a male genre (following her adaptation of Jim Thompson's *The Kill-Off*) is organised around the impossibility of being a lone woman in the West. The emphasis is more on oppression than transgression, on showing us the brutal, misogynist, racist reality of the bad old West rather than re-imagining it as an all-cowgirl heaven.

For some, *The Ballad of Little Jo* will look like the straightest cross-dressing movie ever made—Jo even tries to buy frocks before settling on trousers and shirts, ex-model Amis is more gamine than butch, and the lesbian potential of the Ruby City women's affection for the gentle loner is passed by. For others, it may not even qualify as a Western: it's short on shoot-outs, and a sheep-rancher isn't quite a cowgirl.

Within its chosen brief, though, *The Ballad of Little Jo* is an exemplary and often starkly beautiful tale—a mix of adventure and romance which succeeds in reinstating female experience into a genre which has by definition sidelined it. One nice touch is that Jo's empathy for and solidarity with other women are crucial to her success as a woman and as a 'man': her near-unique 'male' civility among the universal misogynist violence and abuse in Ruby City eventually wins her the respect of men as well as women.

Even male misreadings of Jo's actions—notably her insistence on keeping male camaraderie at bay—have the effect of confirming her 'maleness'. Before his taste for sexual violence is out in the open, Percy is happy to suggest to Jo that prostitutes are "cheaper and less trouble" than taking a wife. When Jo tells him she won't be courting Mary, a young woman who seems particularly fond of her, he takes this to mean that she too is a woman-hater.

The West's irrational prejudices against any form of difference are sent up more overtly when Jo first enters Ruby City's saloon. Hostile gamblers are quick to accuse the newcomer of being a 'dude', but Jo demonstrates that 'he' is not wearing the loud stockings dudes apparently favour. When Jo ripostes that dudes "have as much right to be here as anybody", it is clear that all exclusions of otherness are being questioned, not merely the exclusion of women. It is no surprise, then, that the relationship between the white male West's sexual and racial outsiders—Jo and Tinman—proves to be the film's most intriguing element.

Most crucially, the shifting balance of power between the pair raises provocative questions about the political implications of Jo's gender-swap masquerade. She plays the imperious white male to the hilt; he gets the raw-deal role of housewife-cum-slave. While this role reversal has its amusing side—the joke is on Jo when she complains that dinner isn't done, unaware that Tinman's stir-fry will be ready in seconds—the suggestion is that acting as a white male inevitably entails adopting white male racial and gender hierarchies too.

However, Greenwald rightly shifts the relationship onto a more egalitarian footing before the two can become lovers. The transgression of racial and gender boundaries is both moving and playful, and Amis and Chung's sinuously muscled bodies, her hair short and his long, look extraordinary together. But there is never any simplistic pretence that inequality has vanished. Tinman's 'female' domestic duties continue as before, and when Jo pines for her son, he replies briskly, "Yes, but you are a free white man now. And some day soon, you will even vote." *The Ballad of Little Jo* may not quite be a Western, but such moments of astuteness compensate for plenty.

VILLAGE VOICE, 8/24/93, p. 64, Ann Powers

Transvestism signifies like crazy these days; its aesthetic take on sexual excess makes it an ideal fascination for culture watchers who believe the sensual is political. But beyond the eternal question, *How* does *RuPaul tuck*?, the debate rarely addresses gender trouble's practical side.

Maggie Greenwald's *The Ballad of Little Jo* corrects this by uncovering the gritty details in the tale of a woman forced to turn masculine by circumstance. The real-life story of Jo Monaghan, a disowned debutante who survived by becoming a "male" sheep rancher, Greenwald's film follows the rules of revisionist westerns that aim to repair historical misconceptions, rather than critique the western genre. It's more *Heartland* than *Posse*, moving slowly and lingering on those gritty details—the rough textures of the food, homely tools, and clothes Jo must adopt. Gorgeous pans of sunburnt Montana hills alternate with darkly lit interiors borrowed from *McCabe and Mrs. Miller*, showing the contradictions of the pioneer life, its freedoms countered by smalltown repression.

Suzy Amis's laconic performance as Jo sneaks up through a series of glances and muttered asides; her initial awkwardness eventually proves to be the heart of her character. The other actors, especially western vet Bo Hopkins as an ornery neighbor, match Amis's graceful quietude. As her Chinese servant and lover, Tinman Wong, David Chung gently understates his performance to finesse a role that drifts toward stereotype. The romance between Jo and Tinman suggests complicated desires that Greenwald's script doesn't quite express; sometimes the pairing seems like mere political correctness. Yet Amis and Chung do throw a few soft sparks. *Little Jo*'s gentle ways slightly undermine its impact, detracting from the story's urgency. But as a realistic portrait of an unusual life, it enhances our sense of the West and the western both.

Also reviewed in:
CHICAGO TRIBUNE, 9/10/93, Friday/p. C, Clifford Terry
NEW YORK TIMES, 8/20/93, p. 40, Stephen Holden
VARIETY, 8/30/93, p. 26, Emanuel Levy
WASHINGTON POST, 9/10/93, Weekend/p. 45, Desson Howe
WASHINGTON POST, 9/11/93, p. D2, Rita Kempley

BANK ROBBER

An I.R.S. Media and Initial Groupe release. *Executive Producer:* Jean Cazes, Miles A. Copeland III, and Paul Colichman. *Producer:* Lila Cazes. *Director:* Nick Mead. *Screenplay:* Nick Mead. *Director of Photography:* Andrej Sekula. *Editor:* Richard E. Westover and Maysie Hoy. *Music:* Stewart Copeland. *Sound:* Chuck Buch. *Casting:* Donald Paul Pemrick. *Production Designer:* Scott Chambliss. *Art Director:* Bradley Wishan. *Set Decorator:* Karen Manthey. *Costumes:* Dana Allyson. *Running time:* 94 minutes. *MPAA Rating:* NC-17.

CAST: Patrick Dempsey (Billy); Lisa Bonet (Priscilla); Olivia D'Abo (Selina); James Garde (Chris); Forest Whitaker (Officer Battle); Judge Reinhold (Officer Gross); Mariska Hargitay (Marisa Benoit); Michael Jeter (Night Clerk #1); Joe Alaskey (Night Clerk #2); John Chappoulis (Pizza Deliveryman).

LOS ANGELES TIMES, 12/10/93, Calendar/p. 10, Chris Willman

"Bank Robber" is the moron bait that offers the promise of not one but two former wholesome-teen TV actresses in the buff, and an NC-17 rating earned on a thrust-action technicality, as the only lures into its interminable story. Let the robbers beware.

The ads misleadingly suggest a sex thriller, but the smug, wandering tone is all failed black comedy. Patrick Dempsey stares as a dopey slacker who pulls an off-the-cuff heist as a way to buy trinkets for the object of his obsession, Olivia D'Abo, a three-timing hussy undeserving of such a heartfelt show of affection as a bank robbery.

Our anti-hero gets away clean and holes up in a downtown flop-house, where—in the movie's idea of a highly repeatable comic conceit—he's recognized by and extorted by all who see his mug, from the bellboy to the pizza deliverer.

Only one kind soul doesn't take advantage of Dempsey's newfound cache: Lisa Bonet, a hooker with such a heart of guess-what she undercharges the kid. (Their NC-17 sex montage actually looks unprovocative enough to pass for an R, but at least it provides a short break from the satire.)

The bulk of the movie consists of Dempsey—who's described by a newscaster as "misguided and possibly retarded"—avoiding cons and going nutso in his dank hotel room; by the time the still-boyishly handsome actor starts smearing pizza sauce on his face and shooting at bugs, it's turned into something like a sophomore-class restaging of "Barton Fink."

To escape the claustrophobia, debuting writer-director Nick Mead cuts away inconsequential-ly—a la "A Perfect World"—to the lawmen looking for Dempsey, played in drive-by, paycheck-collecting cameos by Forrest Whitaker and Judge Reinhold. *Their* comic conceit is that they're feel-good cops who get misty-eyed at the thought of catching Dempsey so they can get him therapy for his unhappy childhood.

With no real narrative to wrap up, "Bank Robber" doesn't have a traditional final scene so much as it just sort of ends, packing up its drowsy misanthropy as the credits roll like a kid whose cap-gun just ran out of ammo. And not a blank too soon.

NEW YORK POST, 12/10/93, p. 48, Bill Hoffmann

It's got a no-nonsense title, a cast of talented young players and a titillating NC-17 rating. So why is "Bank Robber" such a drag?

Despite so much promise this striving-to-be-hip, black comedy is one big, aimless bore.

First-time director Nick Mead tries hard to pull off a David Lynch trick with a quirky mix of bizarre characters, off-beat comedy and jarring violence.

But since even Lynch hasn't been able to duplicate his own brilliant weirdness in recent years, you know "Bank Robber" doesn't have a prayer.

Too bad, because it begins with a promising plot line.

Patrick Dempsey is Billy, the handsome son of a legendary bank robber. He pulls his own heist so he and his sexy blonde girlfriend can retire to an idyllic tropical island.

The bank job nets Billy a nice chunk of change. I also makes him an instant celebrity when his photo is slashed across the TV news.

Billy hides out in a seedy place called the Heartbreak Hotel—but finds little peace when it turns out everyone from the hotel manager to the pizza delivery man recognizes him.

They're all willing to keep their mouths shut for a fistful of Billy's cash—a price the fledgling crook gladly forks over every time.

The only one who doesn't exploit him is Priscilla (Lisa Bonet), the proverbial hooker with a heart of gold.

It's here where the film takes a wrong turn, becoming an irritating mishmash of odd, ill-timed comedy, bizarre behavior and conventional drama.

Mead tries to show us how good can mask itself in evil and vice versa. The movie's two angels are a criminal and a prostitute, while the bad guys are cops, evangelists and reporters.

Sounds good on paper, but "Bank Robber" never knows where it's going. It's full of loose ends and can't settle into a comfortable center on which the audience can focus.

The cast seems lost, particularly Forest Whitaker as a dumb, dope-smoking cop on the lookout for Billy. It's a shame to see such a brilliant actor wasted.

The picture has an interesting claustrophobic feel, since most of the action occurs in Billy's darkened hotel room. But even that doesn't help.

Dempsey, who resembles a young Bruce Springsteen, is likable, but grows tiresome midway through.

Some folks might be tempted to see "Bank Robber" on the strength of its adults-only, NC-17 rating. Don't. Even here, the film fails to pay off.

Graphic sex scenes between Dempsey and Bonet are curiously unerotic (and I state this as an unashamed admirer of Bonet's wonderful bod).

Other bedroom antics involving Billy's girlfriend (Olivia D'Abo) and two energetic brothers also fall flat.

"Bank Robber" ultimately robs the audience—of entertainment.

NEWSDAY, 12/10/93, Part II/p. 107, Gene Seymour

The best news "Bank Robber" offers is that Lisa Bonet is shaking off her lethargy and seems to be evolving into a smart-and-sexy comic actor with more presence and assurance than one remembered from her days as daffy Denise Huxtable on "The Cosby Show."

Bonet plays Priscilla, a prostitute summoned to a seedy hotel room by Billy (Patrick Dempsey), a pretty-but-dim bank robber who's hiding from the law after getting himself photographed while fleeing the scene of his crime. Though armed, he's far from dangerous. He's just a guy with a dream. Something to do with a boat, the sea and his beautiful blond girlfriend (Olivia "Wonder Years" D'Abo) by his side.

The governing irony here is that everyone from the hotel clerks (Joe Alaskey and Michael "Evening Shade" Jeter) to the pizza delivery guy (John Chappoulis) has seen Billy's picture in the papers and on TV. And all of them drop by, wanting a little of his loot as hush money. Which is why Billy's pizza costs $300 and a new light bulb costs ... well, you get the picture.

The cops, of course, are clueless. Two patrolmen (Forest Whitaker and Judge Reinhold) ride around the streets of L.A. wondering what societal forces made Billy turn bad. They would reach out and help him on the path of righteousness, if they could find him.

Everyone else can find Billy easily, like a TV newswoman who drops by for an exclusive interview and a drug dealer who won't take no for an answer. The one person Billy wishes *would* find him is his girlfriend, but she's busy being "cared for" by Billy's best friend. Only Priscilla, the hooker-with-a-heart-of-you-know-what, has his best interests at heart.

Writer-director Nick Mead is aiming here for the kind of absurdist whimsy that made Jim Jarmusch a demigod. But he lacks Jarmusch's sure way with pace and timing. After a while, the irony acquires fumbling fingers and wobbly knees. Only the vitality of the performers—especially Dempsey, Whitaker, Reinhold and, as noted, Bonet—makes you care what happens.

VILLAGE VOICE, 12/14/93, p. 78, David D. Kim

Little or no advance hype for a film usually means one of two things: it's either (1) a prospective sleeper hit with a canny word-of-mouth campaign, or (2) an iffy-to-stinky film that's got one foot in the theater and the other in the video store. Nick Mead's *Bank Robber* can be found behind door number two.

Striving desperately to come off as cool, offbeat comedy. *Bank Robber*'s forced loopiness—oddball musings lumped with arch humor—strikes lead at every turn. Apparently, the film's about keeping dreams alive: after a bank heist, Billy (Patrick Dempsey) pines for girlfriend Selina (Olivia D'Abo), restlessly planning their escape to an oceanside paradise. Meanwhile, plagued by annoying intruders and drug-induced nightmares, he hides out solo in the Heartbreak Hotel, a retro '50s fleabag.

Director of photography Andrej Sekula conjures up slick, ersatz seediness much less successfully than moodmasters Jim Jarmusch or the Coen brothers, whose influence practically seeps from the hotel's wallpaper. And the pseudo-impressionist sequences not only ape Scorsese's farcical *After Hours* but betray Mead's music-vid background, poorly transferred here to film. Direction is jumbled, and *Bank Robber*'s images feel strung together—like one of those movies in which a key performer dies and everything has to be recut.

Dempsey's charming enough, yet, despite his breakthrough potential, memorable film roles continually elude him. The other leads are strictly B-list: both D'Abo and Lisa Bonet (as Billy's savior-whore) merely promote *Bank Robber*'s video look by strutting around in microwear or nothing at all, Bonet has improved somewhat since *Angel Heart*, but the vixen role wears thin (dresses). Her best line is, "Get your dick out," which Dempsey does, though he never flashes his freed willy to the camera. All things considered, it wouldn't matter if he did.

Also reviewed in:
CHICAGO TRIBUNE, 12/10/93, Friday/p. J, Michael Wilmington
NEW YORK TIMES, 12/10/93, p. C10, Stephen Holden
VARIETY, 10/11/93, p. 74, Daniel M. Kimmel
WASHINGTON POST, 12/8/93, p. C12, Rita Kempley

BARAKA

A Samuel Goldwyn Company release of a Magidson Films production.   *Producer:* Mark Magidson.   *Director:* Ron Fricke.   *Screenplay:* Ron Fricke, Mark Magidson, and Bob Green.   *Director of Photography:* Ron Fricke.   *Editor:* Ron Fricke, Mark Magidson, David Aubrey, and Alton Walpole.   *Music:* Michael Stearns.   *Music Editor:* Grant Wakefield.   *Sound:* Tom Sherlock, Robert Jansen, Jeffrey Payne, David Lomino, and Joe Piantadosi.   *Running time:* 96 minutes.   *MPAA Rating:* Not Rated.

LOS ANGELES TIMES, 9/24/93, Calendar/p. 19, Kevin Thomas

To a considerable extent the impact of Ron Fricke's visionary, shimmeringly beautiful "Baraka" will depend on whether or not you've seen Godfrey Reggio's "Koyannisqatsi" or its sequel "Powaqqatsi." Like those two films, "Baraka" is a dazzling, disturbing collage of images of life on this planet warning us of the dangers of our increasing detachment from nature and our pillaging of the Earth's resources. It is far too similar to those earlier films for its own good, yet such is its sheer gorgeousness in its Todd AO 70mm grandeur and its superb sense of structure and movement that it is nevertheless affecting. "Baraka" takes its title from an ancient Sufi word suggesting the essence of life from which the evolutionary process unfolds.

Fricke, who in fact was "Koyannisqatsi's" cinematographer, cowriter and co-editor, has said his favorite theme is "Humanity's relationship to the eternal," which is precisely what he and his colleagues explore in "Baraka." It begins with a majestic half-hour survey of individuals in the timeless act of religious worship in ancient, glorious settings the world over. This sequence gives way to scenes of tribal peoples participating in traditional dances, but as the film moves toward its middle the images grow increasingly ominous, with depictions of the Earth's desecration and the frenetic, congested, quality of modern urban existence. In this segment, Fricke uses the speeded-up cinematography techniques he first employed in "Koyannisqatsi" to suggest humans becoming like ants and robots—he has a passion for shots of dehumanizing assembly lines.

This portion of "Baraka" seems the most derivative of his earlier efforts. Therefore, it is its least-satisfying part, but gradually his film regains momentum as it completes its circle by returning to concerns of worship. Without so much as a single word uttered, Fricke makes it perfectly clear that humanity has a choice—our survival depends upon choosing the spiritual over the material and caring for others and for our planet as much as we care for ourselves. His key colleagues in this accomplishment are his producer and co-writer/editor Mark Magidson and inspired composer Michael Stearns, whose soaring score at all times reinforces the film's images.

"Baraka" (Times-rated Mature) was shot in 24 countries over 14 months, but none of its locations, many of which are unfamiliar, are ever identified. Technically, the film is as awesome as its images. Like the Reggio films, it does not hesitate to use the most advanced technology to deplore the impact of technology upon our lives. Fricke's cinematography is so consistently magnificent in the compositions of its images and in their clarity, in its use of natural light and delicacy of hue that Fricke creates a further parody: His film is consistently beautiful even in its most ominous moments.

NEW YORK POST, 9/25/93, p. 13, Lawrence Cohn

Not since the Cinerama travelogues of the 1950s has there been a film like "Baraka," a mystical survey of eye-popping locations in 24 countries. It's unconventional film fare, but a real treat for fans of pure aesthetics. It would be impractical and hopelessly expensive to try and personally visit the unusual sites on view.

The recent prototype for this undertaking was the cult hit "Koyaanisqatsi," (meaning "Earth out of balance") and its sequel "Powaqqatsi," in which director Godfrey Reggio gave the planet a wakeup call to the tune of Philip Glass' droning music.

Now Reggio's cameraman, Ron Fricke, has trumped Reggio by directing and photographing this less-militant follow-up in the TODD-AO 70 mm process, whose grandeur was used in the 50s for "Around the World in 80 Days" and "Oklahoma."

Adding to that clarity is Fricke's innovation of a new time-lapse camera adapted to the wide-screen process. For the location closest to home, he transforms Park Avenue, as seen from the Helmsley Building, into a microcosm of the urban rat race as speeded-up cars and pedestrians create a visual ballet.

In contrast, Fricke slows down the pace for a wide range of folkways, such as locals bathing in the Ganges River in India or tribes dancing in Africa or South America.

Obviously there is a spiritual message underlying "Baraka" (whose title means "life force"), but without any dialogue or narration the film can be interpreted as one chooses. In fact, the most stunning scenes visiting mosques, cathedrals and synagogues in places like Luxor and Reims create a sense of awe for both the religious and the agnostic alike.

Perhaps the strongest narrative sequence is a processing plant where baby chicks are sorted and burned on the beak by dutiful assembly-line workers in a display of casual cruelty that could turn even Frank Perdue's stomach. Its metaphorical impact for us poor human viewers raises "Baraka" from the level of pretty pictures to serious documentary.

This is what event filmmaking is all about—the creation of an experience that can't be duplicated on TV. Having seen the film in both 35 and 70 mm versions at the same West Side TODD-AO screening room, I can report the significantly edge in clarity of the 70 mm original, making it worth your while to rush out and see the picture in first run.

NEWSDAY, 9/24/93, Part II/p. 63, Joseph Gelmis

The makers of "Baraka," two documentarists who work on a colossal scale, have created a 70mm film of awesome imagery and sounds, shot it in 24 countries on six continents. It's an overwhelming sensory experience, without a story or spoken narrative. But whether it works as intended depends as much on what you bring to it as on what producer Mark Magidson and director-cinematographer Ron Fricke put into it.

"Baraka" is meant to give us a transcendent experience of being alive, to cleanse our perceptions and make us see with new eyes. It's a kaleidoscopic view of the planet's natural wonders and of human culture through the ages. Part travelogue, part spiritual journey, partly a defense of the environment, it was undertaken by Magidson and Fricke in hopes of breaking out of the intellectual ghetto in which their last film, the award-winning "Chronos," was shown.

"Baraka" covers some of the same ground as "Chronos"—and of "Koyaanisqatsi," which Fricke photographed, as well. Using speeded-up (time-lapse) photography and using a frame twice the size and clarity of ordinary 35mm film, "Baraka" transports us to the Himalayas, to a stupendous cataract, to the ruins of ancient civilizations, to astonishing and spellbinding tribal ceremonies in Africa and Indonesia and Australia, to high-rise slums in the making, to strip-mines and forests being clear-cut, to assembly lines at high-tech and primitive factories.

It's a magnificent spectacle. But "Baraka" runs 96 minutes, twice the length of "Chronos" and of the typical Imax movie, and the grandeur of the images and the hypnotic Michael Stearns score are more likely to put you to sleep than to put you in touch with the ineffable. If you do plan to see "Baraka," do it during the day, when you're wide awake and physically receptive to an inspirational experience.

SIGHT AND SOUND, 8/93, p. 40, Louise Gray

A montage of documentary footage from around the world begins with a group of monkeys splashing in steaming volcanic baths in the Himalayas. Shots of the night sky follow, giving way to a sequence of devotional images: Buddhist monks, a Japanese zen garden, Jerusalem's Wailing Wall and some whirling Dervishes. Volcanic landscapes are followed by a visit to Ayers Rock, African tribal dances are followed by scenes of deforestation, apparently watched by a Polynesian chieftain. The technological world is represented by images of dynamite, shanty towns, a factory farm where day-old chicks pour off conveyor belts. The doors of offices revolve in a fast-motion blur. Amid the bustle of a Tokyo street, a Zen monk moves with slow, heel-to-toe steps. Street children beg in Brazilian gutters, women labour in an Indonesian cigarette factory. Shots of burning oil wells in Kuwait are followed by the Basra road and the debris—human and otherwise—left by the retreating Iraqi army. In Auschwitz and in Cambodia, the faces of Nazi and Khmer Rouge victims stare out from sheets of photographs. The film visits the funeral pyres along the Ganges, looks upon ruined temples, a solar eclipse and the tiny tomb where Christ was reputedly buried. In Japan, a monk carefully floats a flower and a candle on a small pool of water.

Baraka follows in a long tradition of films that use pictures and music to make implicit, profound and sometimes portentous statements about how we live and die in the world. Notable recent examples of such narrationless narrative are *Koyaanisqatsi* and *Powaqqatsi*, the two extant films in Godfrey Reggio's planned trilogy of collaborations with composer Philip Glass. The third, as yet unmade, film, *Naqqoyqatsi*, similarly takes its title from a word in the Hopi language, meaning something like "life is a state of war". However, it now looks as though Ron Fricke, Reggio's cinematographer on *Koyaanisqatsi*, has pipped *Naqqoyqatsi* at the post.

Like Reggio's films, *Baraka* takes its theme from human diversity: the things we do to each other and to the world. Not to be outdone by Reggio's espousal of the Hopi language, Fricke has named his film with an ancient Sufi word which crams a meaning encompassing blessings, breath and the essence of life into three short syllables. Unsurprisingly, *Baraka* is a huge film, filmed in 24 countries and six continents; it took Fricke 14 months to assemble his footage. Specially adapted 70mm cameras make much of it breathtakingly beautiful. At times *Baraka* comes over as an animated *National Geographic*.

Baraka is a very green film. The modern world is represented as a violent place filled with alienated populations who ride subways and probably eat the factory-farmed chickens that we see in one of the film's longest, most shocking scenes. The implicit message is apparently that the raison d'etre of the technological age is one of systematic destruction. Urban man has neither the literal horizons of the Buddhist monks halfway up the Himalayas, nor the spiritual ones afforded by any transcendental strategy. The Tokyo commuters barely notice the monk who uses the same street for an exquisitely slow walking meditation. Fricke's images of whirling Dervishes have a stillness that is simply beautiful.

Of *Baraka*'s soundtrack there is less to say. Although sound and image are carefully edited, Fricke does not have his own composer scoring the entire film, and consequently loses *Koyaanisqatsi*'s high integration of sound and image. Michael Stearns has contributed some effective original material; the rest of the music is imported (the soundtrack design favours breathy overtone chants). Considering that comparisons with Reggio's films are inevitable, Fricke made an odd decision in allowing an extended shot of a donkey, cart and mountains to be accompanied by a long organ drone which, in both key and sonority, replicates part of Glass' *Koyaanisqatsi* score.

Despite this, *Baraka* is a film of considerable impact. Part of this is to do with photography and geography alone: if the locations are not spectacular, then you can rely on the technicians getting every shot in perfect frame. But the lasting effect is more melancholic. The ruined temples of the epilogue recall the boasts of Shelley's Ozymandias; there are no refuges from the processes of the world. It remains to be seen whether such a conclusion is just pessimistic or, in some small way, represents a transcendental strategy of its own.

VILLAGE VOICE, 10/5/93, p. 58, Marco Spino

Part Omnimax extravaganza, part *National Geographic* multiiultural smorgasbord, the 70mm *Baraka* uses images and sounds to comment upon civilizations and their discontents. Director and photographer Ron Fricke traveled to 24 countries and shot contemporary urban and rural scenes as well as ancient ruins to argue that everywhere humans slave over jobs, congregate in masses, battle one another, live in poverty, bow down to a cosmology, and ultimately perish. Rituals such as dances, chants, and funerals from various cultures are filmed in anthropological detail. Some of the places and cultures are recognizable; others, like the glittering interior of a mosque, seem straight out of a fairy tale.

With its pro-eco bent, *Baraka* is not above heavy-handedness in its depictions of mistreated animals and indigent people, though this seems forgivable considering the rapidity with which environments and cultures are deteriorating. The dark images of war are also effective. Aerial views of hundreds of car and tank carcasses and burning oil wells in Kuwait show the ongoing havoc of the Gulf War. Even more disturbing are historical photographs of children killed in various concentration camps, coordinated to the sound of piercing screams.

Dazzling scenes of nature and art show the world's beauty. Through time-lapse photography, sunrise turns to sunset against the surreal background of a pyramid. Not even if you visited all of these places could you experience them in this hypersensory way. *Baraka* is an impressive, if somewhat homogenizing, metafilm that could appeal to as many cultures as it presents, especially to the generatlon that grew up on MTV.

Also reviewed in:
CHICAGO TRIBUNE, 11/12/93, Friday/p. K, Michael Wilmington
NEW YORK TIMES, 9/24/93, p. C14, Stephen Holden
VARIETY, 9/7/92, p. 60
WASHINGTON POST, 10/27/93, p. C1, Hal Hinson

BARJO

A Myriad Pictures release of a PCC Prods./Aliceleo/FR-3 Films/Centre Européen Cinematographique Rhone-Alpes coproduction with the participation of Sofinergie 2/Invest-images 3/CNC/Canal +. *Executive Producer:* Françoise Galfré. *Producer:* Patrick Godeau. *Director:* Jérôme Boivin. *Screenplay (French with English subtitles):* Jacques Audiard and Jerome Boivin. *Based on "Confessions of a Crap Artist" by:* Philip K. Dick. *Director of Photography:* Jean-Claude Larrieu. *Editor:* Anne Lafarge. *Music:* Hugues Le Bars. *Sound:* François Waledisch. *Production Designer:* Dominique Maleret. *Costumes:* Caroline de Vivaise. *Running time:* 85 minutes. *MPAA Rating:* Not Rated.

CAST: Anne Brochet (Fanfan); Hippolyte Giradot (Barjo); Richard Bohringer (Charles); Consuelo de Haviland (Mme. Hermelin).

LOS ANGELES TIMES, 12/15/93, Calendar/p. 4, Kevin Thomas

Venturesome French writer-director Jerome Boivin and the late science fiction novelist Philip K. Dick would seem a sure-fire combination. Boivin made a distinctive debut with the provocative and disturbing 1990 "Baxter," about a dog with a human capacity for thought but not for love or fear; Dick provided the original stories for "Blade Runner" and "Total Recall." However, "Barjo", Boivin's film of Dick's "Confessions of a Crap Artist" is highly problematical—a film that a few people are likely to love madly and the rest of us will find a bore.

"Barjo" ("Nut Case") is weird without being involving. A young wife and mother, Fanfan (Anne Brochet), married to Charles (Richard Bohringer), the prosperous, middle-aged owner of an aluminum manufacturing company, seems merely headstrong and impressive until her exceedingly strange twin brother, Barjo (Hippolyte Girardot), a skinny, nerdy guy with thick glasses, comes to live in her attic.

Barjo, who predicted the death of the sun and the end of the world when he was 12, seems part idiot savant and part Peter Sellers in "Being There." He's loaded with facts but little comprehension and compulsively types up everything that he thinks about or experiences in the course of the day as a kind of preparation for the apocalypse he prophesies.

Very soon after Barjo moves into the couple's handsome contemporary country estate Fanfan develops an instant, obsessive attraction to a young couple who lives nearby. In short, Charles abruptly has to contend with a pair of crazies, not to mention all manner of hard-to-explain phenomena.

It would seem that there is no line between Fanfan and Barjo's inner and outer selves, which means that they're monsters, especially Fanfan, who's totally unpredictable and reckless, utterly dangerous. Eventually Charles is sucked up into Fanfan and Barjo's madness to the extent that in the grip of a jealous rage he shoots a horse, eventually leaving his front yard strewn with dead animals.

There's no difficulty in recognizing in ourselves the passions and compulsions that drive these people or our terrible capacity for selfishness and cruelty but such insights are not likely to have the cosmic impact of revelation for many people, though this is what Boivin seems to intend. His actors are admirable in their highly focused intensity, but they cannot prevent the characters they portray from seeming anything but tedious and repellent in the extreme. The effectiveness of "Baxter" makes "Barjo" seem all the more disappointing.

NEW YORK POST, 7/7/93, p. 26, Jerry Tallmer

I don't know what the women's movement is going to do about Fanfan, the heroine, if that's the word, of Jerome Boivin's "Barjo."

A mere slim slip of a thing and devilishly attractive into the bargain, she's a hell of a lot stronger in willpower than all the men she's ever met or is going to meet. These notably include her husband Charles—whom she stole away from her best girlfriend—and the oddball kid brother she's lorded over all their lives, and that good-looking young philosophy prof she'll soon half-seduce, half-bulldoze into becoming her lover.

"God, they're beautiful," she says, eyeing Michel and Gwen, the philosophy couple—"straight out of Nietzsche." "*Who?*" husband Charles demands, later asking Barjo, the idiot (like Prince Myshkin) kid brother, for further Nietzsche data "Nineteenth century. Very sexual writer. Lived on a mountain," the dreamy lad supplies.

When poor Charles brings Michel and Gwen around to the house for a drink—to repay them for smashing into their car—Fanfan dashes upstairs to throw on the sexiest orange frock and earrings you ever saw. Descending the stairs, she's just delicious. "Is my mascara all right?" she whispers to her husband, and then with a little kiss, "Merci"—thanks for the present.

Delicious and dangerous. Ira Gershwin and Kurt Weill told us about Jenny, bright as a penny, who always made her mind up, always got her way. Fanfan is Jenny incarnate, transferred to France—from an American cult novel, Philip K. Dick's "Confessions of a Crap Artist." When she keeps after poor Charles in a badminton game on their cozy lawn, he suffers his first heart attack and the whole movie turns round, whirling on its axis from sex comedy to something else, something a good deal darker, uglier. I won't tell you what. I'll only say: if you love animals, be prepared to flinch.

The Crap-Artist is the narrator and protagonist of book and film. This Barjo is one of God's innocents, a milk-cap freak (he inhales them), an initial-letter freak ("Carrots, chestnuts, chocolate, Mr. Clean ... Political, poetic, positive"), an end-of-the-world freak (Atlantis, Pompeii), a teaching-words-to-cats freak (that one gets a house burned down), and a "Star Trek" freak who, taking a cue from Buster Keaton and Woody Allen, steps up into the TV frame from time to time to solicit advice on his sister's sex life and other such problems from the commander of the space ship.

See, Barjo is also a sex innocent to whom the overheard cries of copulation are a mystery wrapped in a riddle wrapped in an enigma. Out in the garden at his typewriter he starts a whole new research file on this, a crow fluttering down to sit on his head, a nice horse sashaying over for a look-see. The film ends in hints of incest that have been lurking beneath the celluloid all along, with Fanfan far from off the ethical hook.

Hippolyte Girardot, who plays Barjo, may remind you of our own Austin Pendleton; he did me. Anne Brochet, the Fanfan of the movie, has something about her—may God forgive me—of a young (naughtier) Audrey Hepburn. The toughest role, of course, is that of Charles, very wryly and persuasively rendered by Richard Bohringer. The scene where he goes to his aluminum factory to spill his soul to the night watchman about having beat up Fanfan, and should he apologize?—"if I call and she's in the bath, she'll yell at me"—is nice insight and movie-making indeed.

VILLAGE VOICE, 7/13/93, p. 54, Joe Levy

Confessions of a Crap Artist is the only "serious" book Philip K. Dick published before his death 11 years ago. It's a stark, creepy tale in which the sci-fi Dick was known for oozes around the edges of a family drama in the form of Jack Isidore, an underdeveloped crackpot who can't tell the difference between his fantasy magazines and scientific journals. Rescued from the seedy side of San Francisco by his sister and brother-in-law, Jack tends their house in Northern California, quietly waiting with local UFO trackers for the end of the world and watching as his sister's marriage falls apart. Weaving the workings of the many minds he describes richly, Dick achieves a slow burn worthy of Graham Greene, but the violence that shadows every thought and action is distinctly American. The unhinged dissatisfaction, the obsession with control and dominance, the crackpot and all his crap come from the world that gave us Harry Crews, Sean and Madonna, and *People Magazine*.

Barjo, the screen version of *Confessions of a Crap Artist*, comes from a different world: France, where Philip K. Dick has long been the object of the serious attention he craved but has only posthumously received here at home. A thoroughly winning and thoroughly odd movie, it's at once rigorously faithful to Dick's novel and completely different from it. It tells the same story, moving the action from '50s California to the contemporary French countryside, but where Dick saw the madness hovering behind ordinary actions as frightful, *Barjo* sees it as slapstick—not mad, but *MAD*. (You can even sense—in the frantic pacing, the nerdy nuttiness of Barjo the crap artist, and the retro-fitted '50s-modernist house where Barjo comes to live—the lingering spirit of another American object of serious French attention: Jerry Lewis.) Director Jerome Boivin transforms Dick's dystopia into farce, and makes it seem a natural consequence of putting human flesh behind the words. For Boivin (who directed *Baxter*), beneath every smile there lurks a bit of insanity. The rest is just camera angles and editing.

As Barjo (French for "crap-head," according the subtitles; "a kind of Candide, a gentle loony unchained from reality," according to Boivin), Hippolyte Girardot looks eerily like John Zorn——that is, his geek chic carries a whiff of cool, his obsessiveness the air of genius, and his glasses are now and forever on the verge of coming into style. We encounter him first as a voice, narrating his own birth, his journey from darkness into light, even as he looks forward to the moment when the sun will burn out (he can prove this, it's scientifically inevitable) and everything will be as before: in darkness. Images and words whiz by, and this breathless pace—along with its mix of memory and forward motion—will carry the whole film. Even when lyrical, *Barjo* seems rushed; even when doing the work of exposition, it's a flashback.

The sun doesn't burn out (I hope I haven't given too much away), but Barjo's house does burn to the ground, scrapping years of experimental research (he's taught his cat, seen in headgear Buck Rogers would envy, 35 words). Barjo's sister, known here only by her childhood name Fanfan, takes him to live in the house her husband built her, a stone mass of jutting planes that seems to have been rescued from a Frank Tashlin set and deposited in the French hills. Its angles are full of the dreams of rocket science, its furniture pulses with a rich red, and its dining-room table is crowned by a lamp in the shape of a glowing bouquet of flowers. This, the mutant glow seems to say, is where Barjo belongs. And so he moves into the attic (where he constructs a shower stall from a suitcase), begins cooking for Fanfan, her husband, Charles, and their two children, and compulsively takes notes to add to his scientific studies. "What were those noises you were making last night," he asks one morning, referring to his notebook: "A rhythmic banging and two moans: one high and one low." "You mean you really don't know?" replies an exasperated Charles. A nudge and a wink send Barjo off to transfer his notes to a new file: "Sexual Relations for Mammalian Reproduction."

That sort of sweet-and-sour humor is nowhere to be found in Dick's book. It's Boivin's, along with the cat in the hat and the shower in a suitcase. But even when he shifts the tone, Boivin lifts whole chunks of dialogue from the novel and retains almost all of Dick's plot: the sister becomes obsessed with a young academic couple and tracks them like a hunter, bagging the boy by convincing him that he is tracking her; the husband becomes obsessed with his wife's domineering personality, his rage bringing on a coronary that she, somehow, is the cause of; the crap artist falls under the sway of a woman who believes Superior Evolved Beings will arrive any day now; the children remain mute. And most of what the director changes or adds just brings *Barjo* further into Dick's universe—he's particularly effective at crossing the line between fiction and reality that Dick always found so thin, as when Barjo joins the children on the couch to watch a TV space opera only to find himself inside the TV, talking to the starship captain about his sister's affair with the philosophy student. (Devoted Dickheads will also note that Boivin makes Barjo and Fanfan twins, echoing Dick's obsession with his twin sister, Jane, who died shortly after their premature birth.) In some ways, Boivin has made a *Confessions of a Crap Artist* even more Dicklike than Dick did. And strangely enough, twisting the novel's psychic demons into a grin turns out to be anything but a betrayal; Boivin invests the characters with a rich human irrationality that seems utterly believable.

It's a remarkable achievement, really, a screen treatment that expands on, rather than diminishes, the author's vision. Dick's SF novels have already generated two American films (directed by a Brit and a Dutchman), *Blade Runner* and *Total Recall*. But like most writers, in Hollywood, Dick is little more than a blank canvas for Ridley Scott to splash with his vision or Schwarzenegger to tear apart. For Boivin, though, he's a sacred text; not just a wellspring of ideas, but a master builder of bridges between the highbrow and the lowbrow whose example is to be followed.

Still, there are nuances Boivin can't hope to capture. In Jack Isidore, Dick created a revolting vision of the prototypical SF fan that spoke volumes about the author's discontent with his own audience and the limitations of his work—a deft trick Schwarzenegger has gotten little credit for lately. Dick's crap artist was a racist, a porn lover, a man who wore the same clothes until someone threw them away, and his confessions were disturbing and ugly. Boivin's *Barjo* is similarly a tale told by an idiot, but full of clowns and whimsy. Though Boivin's transmutation of sorrow, emptiness, and betrayal into laughter and redemption may be flawless, his sweet-not-sour finish can't help recalling the happy ending tacked onto the studio cut of *Blade Runner*. Dick, it would seem, is finally too dark, too damn convinced that the sun will burn out, for the screen.

Also reviewed in:
CHICAGO TRIBUNE, 11/26/93, Friday/p. B, Michael Wilmington
NEW YORK TIMES, 7/7/93, p. C14, Vincent Canby
VARIETY, 12/7/92, p. 74, Lisa Nesselson

BATMAN: MASK OF THE PHANTASM

A Warner Bros. release. *Executive Producer:* Tom Ruegger. *Producer:* Benjamin Melniker and Michael Uslan. *Director:* Eric Radomski and Bruce W. Timm. *Screenplay:* Alan Burnett, Paul Dini, Martin Pasko, and Michael Reaves. *Story:* Alan Burnett. *Batman created by:* Bob Kane. *Editor:* Al Breitenbach. *Music:* Shirley Walker. *Music Editor:* Thomas Milano. *Sound:* Robert Fernandez. *Sound Editor:* Julia Evershade. *Casting:* Andrea Romano. *Production Designer:* Haven Alexander. *Background Design:* Ted Blackman. *Animation Director:* Se-Won Kim, Young-Hwan Sang, Chung Ho Kim, and Sun Hee Lee. *Running time:* 90 minutes. *MPAA Rating:* PG.

VOICES: Kevin Conroy (Batman);   Dana Delany (Andrea Beaumont);   Hart Bochner (Arthur Reeves);   Stacy Keach, Jr. (Phantasm/Carl Beaumont);   Abe Vigoda (Salvatore Valestra);   Dick Miller (Chuckie Sol);   John P. Ryan (Buzz Bronski);   Efrem Zimbalist, Jr. (Alfred);   Bob Hastings (Commissioner Gordon);   Robert Costanzo (Detective Bullock);   Mark Hamill (The Joker).

LOS ANGELES TIMES, 12/27/93, Calendar/p. 4, Charles Solomon

Ironically, the animated feature "Batman: Mask of the Phantasm" looks its best when it isn't moving.

Background stylist/co-director Eric Radomski has created a terrific-looking world of film noir-influenced Art Deco skyscrapers, shadows, gargoyles and windows. Unfortunately, some of the worst-animated characters in any recent feature get in front of those stylish backgrounds.

"Phantasm" looks exactly like what it is: A television program that's been expanded to fill a big screen. But enlarging the characters only takes the flaws in the Saturday-morning-style animation (done in South Korea) more evident.

The screenplay by Alan Burnett, Paul Dini, Martin Pasko and Michael Reaves has a number of loose ends that not only remain untied but flap in the wind that blows through the film. A convoluted series of flashbacks reveals that Batman/Bruce Wayne (voice by Kevin Conroy) once loved Andrea Beaumont (Dana Delaney), the adored daughter of prominent businessman Carl Beaumont (Stacy Keach Jr.). But the elder Beaumont set up dummy businesses for underworld figures, so his daughter couldn't marry a crime-fighting vigilante.

Years later, Andrea returns to Gotham City on business; at the same time, a mysterious Phantom in a long cape appears and begins executing aging mobsters. Batman is blamed for the murders, which leads to a climactic confrontation with the Joker (Mark Hamill) amid the ruins of the Gotham World's Fair (modeled after the '39 New York Fair). Needless to say, the good guy wins and all ends semi-happily.

Like the popular syndicated program on which it's based, "Phantasm" (rated PG) offers viewers a very dark version of the Caped Crusader, modeled after the antihero of Frank Miller's graphic novel "The Dark Knight Returns." The film is obviously aimed at the adolescents who tune in regularly on weekday afternoons: The stiff animation and campy voice acting will quickly bore parents and older siblings: the fistfights, shootouts and car crashes may frighten smaller children.

Also reviewed in:
NEW YORK TIMES, 12/28/93, p. C21, Stephen Holden
VARIETY, 1/3-9/94, p. 54, Leonard Klady
WASHINGTON POST, 12/27/93, p. D7, Richard Harrington

BEEKEEPER, THE

An MK2 release of a Greek Film Centre/Thodorus Angelopoulos/ERT1/MK2 Productions film. *Executive Producer:* Nikos Angelopoulos. *Director:* Thodorus Angelopoulos. *Screenplay*

(Greek with English subtitles): Thodorus Angelopoulos, Dimitris Nollas, and Toonino Guerra. *Director of Photography:* Giorgos Arvanitis.   *Editor:* Takis Yannopoulos.   *Music:* Eleni Karaindrou.   *Art Director:* Mikes Karapiperis.   *Sound:* Nikos Achladis.   *Costumes:* Giorgos Ziakas.   *Running time:* 120 minutes.   *MPAA Rating:* Not Rated.

CAST: Marcello Mastroianni (Spyros);   Nadia Mourouzi (The Girl);   Serge Reggiani (Sick Man);   Jenny Roussea (Spyros' Wife);   Dinos Iliopoulos (Spyros' Friend).

MONTHLY FILM BULLETIN, 1/88, p. 17, Tim Pulleine

Spyros, an elderly schoolteacher who has suddenly chosen to retire, attends the wedding of his younger daughter, then takes leave of his wife and adult son to make his annual excursion round the various sites where he keeps the beehives to which he devotes his spare time. Despite his dejection, he allows a young girl hitch-hiker to travel with him, and subsequently shares his food and accommodation with her, though nothing occurs between them. One night, she displays her indifference towards him to the extent of bringing a casual pick-up back to their room and making love in Spyros' presence. The couple separate without farewell, and Spyros' travels take him to a meeting with a friend of many years, now successful in business; the two men visit the hospital bed of a mutual friend, a Frenchman long domiciled in Greece (where he has served a prison sentence on unspecified grounds), who is now terminally ill. Spyros also makes a brief and unsatisfactory return to see his wife, and subsequently visits his estranged elder daughter. She is now married to the boorish but well-off proprietor of a garage and cafe, and father and daughter effect a reconciliation of sorts. By this time, Spyros has again seen the girl, now travelling with a young man in a sports car. Impulsively, he drives his van into the window of the restaurant where they are eating, and the girl unprotestingly leaves with him. They journey together to the furthest of the beehive sites, and camp out in an old cinema run by an acquaintance of Spyros'. They begin a passionate affair, and Spyros seems liberated by it. But the next night, after they have dined together in an otherwise deserted restaurant, she makes it clear that their relationship has no future. Spyros goes next day to the beehive site and in impotent despair scatters his hives, then falls to the ground in a paroxysm of grief.

While the preceding *Voyage to Cythera* marked something of a transition, *The Beekeeper* represents a turning away from the overtly political preoccupations of Angelopoulos' *The Traveling Players* and *The Huntsmen* toward a drama of interior feelings. Not that the distinction is a hard and fast one: Angelopoulos has spoken (*Positif*) of his protagonist as someone who "carries with him the weight of the past". While this burden, which takes symbolic shape in the van-load of beehives, is never directly confronted, it remains the film's existential underpinning; in particular, through the age gap between Spyros and his temporary companion, who at one point satirically dubs him "Mr. I Remember".

What is more immediately surprising at the beginning of the film—the wedding party and its aftermath—is how involvingly Angelopoulos renders an ostensibly conventional dramatic situation. The direction effortlessly incorporates symbolist detail (the dropped drinks tray) while also conjuring up mood (the wavering shot which accompanies Spyros across the mist-shrouded bridge opposite his house). Imposing its own rhythm, this opening represents a masterly exercise in exposition, although it becomes evident as the film progresses that the situation sketched here is not to be resolved in any traditional way.

In fact, once Spyros has taken off on his journey to "the other side of the map", the film takes on the quality (almost by definition open-ended) of a road movie, and the chance meeting with the girl brilliantly puts generic convention to heightened use. In the ensuing sequence at the roadside cafe, where she gyrates raptly to the sound of a juke-box, there is something strenuous about Angelopoulos' attempts to confront youth culture. (A comparison with the later Bresson might come to mind, although Angelopoulos—born 1936—is of course far younger.) But such an emphasis becomes necessary in the movie's scheme of things: while Spyros, imbued by Marcello Mastroianni with close psychological detail, is alienated, his companion, played in more external terms by Nadia Mourouzi, is in his eyes someone alien. Where he is drawn in terms of lassitude, she is depicted as essentially a creature of appetites: the perfunctory discourse between them turns mostly on food, drink and cigarettes, while the nature of her sexual appetite is shown, in the episode with the young soldier she picks up, as wholly biological.

This lack of deeper sensibility both attracts and repels Spyros. Which makes it curiously appropriate that, in the film's most sentimental sequence, the visit to the dying Frenchman (a figure whose past political commitment remains significantly unexplained), the focus is on natural, non-ideologically determined responses—drinking wine, watching the waves break on the shore—as a manifestation of shared feeling. This sequence also sets up a subterranean echo of linguistic distancing: where Serge Reggiani's character speaks only in French, the pop record ("All by myself/I'm bound to make it") which the girl repeatedly plays on juke-boxes is heard in English. In a sense, therefore, the concluding movement of the film, subsequent to Spyros' second encounter with the girl, explicitly rhymes his need for a satisfactory relationship with her, and by extension with the future, with his wish to reach an accommodation with his past. The duality is compounded on a Freudian level by Spyros' implied desire for and guilt towards his elder daughter.

If the film falters occasionally in the middle reaches, in those sequences—notably Spyros' brief return to see his wife—which come closest to conventional dramatisation, these later episodes limpidly allow surface action and location to speak for themselves. Real settings are utilised in a way that quite transcends realism. The scene in which Spyros drives his truck into the window of the restaurant where the girl is eating not only adumbrates an *amour fou* (in which the theme of appetite is startlingly recapitulated in the image of the girl biting Spyros' hand and licking the blood), but also gives concrete expression to his urge to break through to a new realm of responsiveness. Similarly, the blank white screen in the shabby cinema building where the couple's brief passion is enacted suggests both the inexpressibility of emotion and the notion, illusory as it may be, of a new start in life. Angelopoulos' control of his resources is such that he can get away, in the scene of the couple's parting, with the device of a slow-moving train intervening between camera and participants.

The succeeding sequence, in which Spyros scatters his beehives and falls desolately to the ground, might be perceived as a symbolic, or even actual, suicide. But the director insists that this is not the case, and that "He is tapping on the ground the way prisoners tap. ... he's the prisoner of a situation and tries to communicate with bygone events". To say the least, such an ambiguity is appropriate to a film which, however cerebral in conception, is hauntingly visceral in effect.

NEW YORK POST, 5/7/93, p. 27, Jerry Tallmer

She is a girl, a waif, a hitch-hiker, a bad penny, a run-away, a will-o'-the-wisp. And when you see her as Mastroianni sees her, crouched on an embankment on the far side of the highway where he has stopped for gas and has now strolled away from his truck, the one he'd just given her a lift in, you will think about it for a longtime—one of the dozens of stunning shots in "The Beekeeper" that make you feel *I was there, I saw that, I remember*, even though you have never known this girl or that gas station or that embankment alongside a highway in Greece, or, in fact, may never have been in Greece in your whole life.

"You don't talk much, do you?" the girl will say to Spyros—the teacher who quit job and wife and family to go back to the bees—when something first hangs in the air between them, immediately dismissed by an "All right, Pops" when he merely sits there, brooding. And surely Mastroianni has never—with all the logorrhea of Charles Bronson—had fewer words in a movie than in this one, where everything is between the lines, implicit rather than explicit.

And yet not many movies are so packed with emotion: the emotions of lost wars, lost causes, lost lives, lost loves, lost comrades (Serge Reggiani, 40 years after "Casque d'Or," now a dying old revolutionary); even the lost art of cinema.

What remains for the silent Spyros is the road, the truck, the bees, the hills on which to plant those humming gray boxes like so many gravestones in a cemetery.

And there is the girl, the waif, Nadia Mourouzi, lost and found, found and lost, making love to her young soldier in the next cot as Mastroianni blots the sound out with a blanket over his head—bizarre moment, perhaps, but not impossible. Presently, the girl will bite Spyros on the palm until the blood gushes, and then in a cinematic moment of extraordinary passion, will lick the palm clean.

He will crash his truck, this silent man, through the plate-glass window of a cafe where the girl sits with her soldier, and she will go off with him, the beekeeper, old enough to be her father and then some, to make love, she naked, he not—something I never understand—under the screen of the dead and empty shell of what was once the Pantheon Movie House in the town where Spyros was born.

Where, on a hill he will return to the cemetery of the bees and find the answer, there among them, to all the questions that this beautiful film asks and does not answer. The answer is in the asking.

SIGHT & SOUND, Winter 1987/88, p. 64, David Wilson

'You have to begin to lose your memory ... to realise that memory is what makes our lives. Our memory is our coherence, our reason, our feeling, even our action. Without it, we are nothing.' The words are Buñuel's, but they would make a fitting epitaph for *The Beekeeper*. Thodoros Angelopoulos' new film charts a doomed encounter between two generations for whom the past means everything and nothing. For Spyros, in late middle age, the past is the meaning to his life, and ought to fashion the future. His personal history is also, and inextricably, the tormented history of his country and the ideals he had for it. The teenage girl he meets on a journey through this country represents a generation with collective amnesia, a generation for whom the past has no meaning and the future is a casual encounter with the next moment.

Spyros was also the name of the central character of Angelopoulos' previous film, *Voyage to Cythera*, which ended in an image of bleak silence, sustained almost beyond endurance. An image also of isolation, as the Spyros of that film, a returned exile, was left on a raft at sea to contemplate the land he knew no more. *The Beekeeper* begins with an image of isolation. Spyros, a schoolteacher, is at the winter wedding of his daughter somewhere in northern Greece. Somehow troubled by the event, a landmark in his family history which he is unable to confront, he drifts away from the ritual. In one of those extended sequence shots familiar from Angelopoulos' previous films (but here used sparingly) the camera follows him as he walks along a river bank and across a bridge. The very length of the shot, and its stillness in movement, invites contemplation. In suggesting memory, as yet undelineated, the sequence asks us to follow this man and look with him at a past which has brought him to such an impasse with the present. The rest of the film subverts those expectations: we learn little about this man's past, private or public. If in his previous films Angelopoulos has uniquely and idiosyncratically confronted the history of his country, it is the present that now concerns him. He sees in it, through the numbed eyes of his protagonist, a desolate landscape.

The present is naturally that of Greece, a Greece in which the phoenix (named Papandreou) which rose from the ashes of dictatorship has somehow failed to fly. But the land traversed by the film offers a familiar present: a soulless, homogenised, EEC-harmonised landscape of power stations, motorway stops, fast food and empty noise. The melancholy vista extends beyond national boundaries. As often in cinema, it is a journey that represents both the state of a nation and a state of mind. Spyros has inherited his father's beehives, and as the damp Greek winter begins to turn into spring and the promise of flowers he travels south to inspect the hives, weed out the defunct colonies, set up new ones. It is a journey into the past, punctuated on the soundtrack by extracts from the diary of a previous journey, and a hope for the future. Except that for Spyros there is no future, because the present makes no connections with the past he knows.

Signposts. At one point Spyros drives his truck, the camera following in a single distant perspective, along a hillside track which suddenly gives out; at another, he visits the house he once lived in, its paint now faded, the view from the broken windows no longer as he remembers it. Meanwhile he has encountered the present, in the casually insistent form of a teenage girl (Nadia Mourouzi) who asks him to take her along with him, wherever he is going. The girl has no history ('I don't remember anything') and is given no name. She drifts from one place to the next, as featureless and disconnected as the clothes she wears and the roadside stops she momentarily inhabits. At one of these stops Spyros finds her dancing to a jukebox record, mindless of the world and of his watching presence. Later he discovers her at a fast food canteen, an incongruous gleaming excrescence in an old town square (Angelopoulos' cameraman is again Giorgos Arvanitis, and again he works wonders with the cold colours of this landscape). Their encounters are frequent and fleeting, and for Spyros both an irritation and a lure. In spite of himself, he tries to make contact with this insubstantial present.

In this world the past can only be a memory for people of a fading generation. A central sequence hauntingly evokes this sense of forlorn memory. With a friend, Spyros visits an old comrade, a Frenchman (Serge Reggiani) who came to Greece in 1948 to fight in the civil war for the cause they all believed in. Now dying in hospital, the man wants to look at the sea for the last time, and his two friends smuggle him and a bottle of good wine out to a beach at dawn. Memory fuelled by the wine, the man recalls those better times when they dreamed of changing the world. It is a scene of profound melancholy, yet the cold dawn light denies the indulgence of nostalgia. Angelopoulos is not concerned merely to revisit the past, another country where mistakes were also made. When Spyros breaks his journey to visit his wife, he asks her to stand in the light for a moment, then abruptly leaves. Memory has meaning: Spyros' daughter explains her husband's hostility to him by saying that he comes from the Mani, an area in the far south of Greece which saw some ruthless acts of vengeance during the civil war—'And you know how it is, they don't forget.' But memory cannot in itself sustain a future. The beehives need periodically to be renewed, or moved to a better position.

Spyros comes to terms with this truth through his relationship with the girl who sporadically tags along with him. Her capriciousness provokes him into silence. When she unblinkingly brings back a young soldier to spend the night with her in the hotel room she shares with Spyros, he pulls his blanket over his head to shut out their aimless sex. He has already refused the girl's casual offer ('O.K., papa') to him. But now, as she goes through the motions, she is looking not at the soldier but at Spyros, bemused by his immobility as he is by her fickleness. For all their disconnection there is a tentative complicity between them, and for Spyros at least a wish for contact more than casual. A desire that can even bring him out of what seems at times an almost catatonic listlessness. Seeing the girl in a restaurant with a boy, he drives his truck through the plate-glass window. Later, as he clumsily tries to make love to her, on the deck of a deserted ferry, the girl is disturbed by his sudden impulsiveness.

It is in another empty space that they finally make a kind of contact. Spyros takes the girl to a cinema he used to frequent in his youth, abandoned now except for the old friend who lovingly tends the long since silent projector. On the stage, beneath the blank white screen, he attempts a sexual contact. But there can be no connection between these people from different worlds, either physical (Spyros remains fully dressed) or emotional. Angelopoulos' camera watches from the stalls, a desolate image for a desolate act: as in *The Travelling Players*, theatre intrudes on life. The scene ends with a shot of Spyros, now himself seated in the stalls, staring at the empty screen. For Spyros, the journey can only end in oblivion, from the stings of his bees. As he dies on the hillside overlooking the town which holds his memories, the camera closes on his fist, clenched in pain.

In the bleakness of its images, and in the way it uses landscape as a correlative of emotional narcosis, Angelopoulos' film at times recalls the Antonioni of the early 1960s, *La Notte* and *Red Desert* in particular. No surprise, then, to discover that Tonino Guerra collaborated on the script. And Spyros is played by Marcello Mastroianni—an extraordinary performance, hinging on silence and self-effacement. In the cinema at least, we can still make connections with the past.

VILLAGE VOICE, 5/11/93, p. 60, Georgia Brown

As a sidebar to MOMA's Greek cinema retrospective, the Public Theater is showing Theo Angelopoulos's *The Beekeeper* (1986), the middle film—between the exquisite *Voyage to Cythera* and *Landscape in the Mist*—in the director's impressive "Trilogy of Silence." This road movie's subject is the effects of 20th century history on the present.

A solemn Marcello Mastroianni plays Spyros, a retired schoolmaster who follows what his beekeeper father called the "road of flowers." He transports the hives from north to south, following the spring blossoms—a journey that also leads to his hometown and a deserted movie theater of his youth, the primal screen. In the opening scene we see Spyros's alienation at his youngest daughter's wedding as well as a good dose of paternal lust. His own marriage is spent, signifying that the breach between generations extends too between men and women. Although he clearly loves his wife and daughters, warmth and identification are reserved for two resistance friends from prison. (They communicate, as they did in jail, by Morse code. At the very end of the film, Spyros's hand taps out the same untranslated message.)

On the road Spyros conducts an on-again, off-again relationship with a nameless leggy hitchhiker (Nadia Mourouzi). Unlike his two well-groomed daughters, she's sort of a feral kid (at one point she bites his hand and it squirts blood). At first he resists her, until she humiliates him into coming after her, smashing through glass to snatch her away. It's a distasteful spectacle, his being reduced to crude, impotent rapes.

The Beekeeper is abrasive, punishing, resistant. But the marvel as always in Angelopoulos is the play of textures and weathers, time's layering, the wistful poetry of ruin, abandonment, dilapidation. Again, we observe; the director's private geography: rugged mountains, drab or once elegant towns, cruel highways that never lead to escape. Then there's the way these characters suddenly focus, spellbound, transfixed by (internal) visions or vistas outside the frame, as if an alternate universe has revealed itself. Sometimes we see what holds them, sometimes not. The camera (Angelopoulos's long-time cameraman is the great Giorgos Arvanitis) shows us that alertness is what counts. Often Angelopoulos's people are so still they're statues—people who were alive, or the dead coming to life. Meet the ancient new Greeks.

Also reviewed in:
NEW YORK TIMES, 5/7/93, p. C21, Janet Maslin
VARIETY, 9/3/86, p. 18

BEETHOVEN'S 2ND

A Universal Pictures release. *Executive Producer:* Ivan Reitman. *Producer:* Michael C. Gross and Joe Medjuck. *Director:* Rod Daniel. *Screenplay:* Len Blum. *Director of Photography:* Bill Butler. *Editor:* Sheldon Kahn and William D. Gordean. *Music:* Randy Edelman. *Music Editor:* Kathy Durning. *Sound:* Gene S. Cantamessa and (music) Dennis Sands. *Sound Editor:* Per Hallberg and Larry Kemp. *Casting:* Steven Jacobs. *Production Designer:* Lawrence Miller. *Art Director:* Charles Breen. *Set Designer:* Cosmas A. Demetriou and Daniel Maltese. *Set Decorator:* Cloudia. *Set Dresser:* Gary Brewer, Dale E. Anderson, and Lawrence C. Haney. *Special Effects:* David M. Blitstein. *Costumes:* April Ferry. *Make-up:* Ken Chase and Jim Scribner. *Stunt Coordinator:* Ronald Rondell. *Running time:* 86 minutes. *MPAA Rating:* PG.

CAST: Charles Grodin (George Newton);   Bonnie Hunt (Alice Newton);   Nicholle Tom (Ryce);   Christopher Castile (Ted);   Sarah Rose Karr (Emily);   Debi Mazar (Regina);   Chris Penn (Floyd);   Ashley Hamilton (Taylor);   Danny Masterson (Seth);   Catherine Reitman (Janie);   Maury Chaykin (Cliff Klamath);   Heather McComb (Michelle);   Scott Waara (Banker);   Jeff Corey (Janitor);   Virginia Capers (Chemistry Teacher);   Devon Gummersall and Jason Perkins (Baseball Captains);   Jordan Bond (Newspaper Boy);   Robert Cavanaugh and Randall Slavin (Party Guys);   Dion Zamora (Bully);   Damien Rapp and Todd Kolker (Teen Hecklers);   Adena Bjork (Heather);   Pat Jankiewicz (Arthur Lewis);   Tom Dugan (Hot Dog Vendor);   Holly Wortell (Window Dresser);   Don Lake (Window Display Manager); Beethoven (Owned and Trained by Karl Lewis Miller).

LOS ANGELES TIMES, 12/17/93, Calendar/p. 10, Kevin Thomas

"Beethoven's 2nd", it's gratifying to report, is just as funny and appealing as "Beethoven" the first. Amid the year-end deluge of adult fare, a family film that actually can be enjoyed by the whole family is always welcome.

As millions of moviegoers will recall, Beethoven is the name given to lovable but horrendously messy Saint Bernard who escapes dognapers to become adopted by the Newtons, much to the chagrin of the fussy head of the family, George Newton (Charles Grodin).

The entire trust of the first film was to show George's exceedingly reluctant but nonetheless growing affection for the super-smart Beethoven, whose alertness saves the Newtons from disasters large and small. (The picture is especially amusing for those of us who aren't dog lovers and who are just as persnickety as George).

Since George ended up loving Beethoven as much as his wife Alice (Bonnie Hunt) and kids Ryce (Nicholle Tom), Ted (Christopher Castile) and Emily (Sarah Rose Karr) do, the challenge facing the sequel's writer Len Blum was where to take George and Beethoven next.

Blum came up with an answer as simple as it is sure-fire: Have Beethoven fall in love. It's one thing for George to come to accept Beethoven but another for him to accept a second dog—and of course, the inevitability of puppies.

Propelling the plot is the hilarious sheer nastiness of the owner (Debi Mazar) of Beethoven's true love, Missy, whom he meets in a park, appropriately enough.

Mazar is a skilled scene-stealer as the statuesque, totally mercenary Regina, who doesn't give a damn for Missy but is holding onto her to force her estranged husband (Maury Chaykin), who adores the animal, into giving her a $50,000-divorce settlement in return for custody of Missy.

The prospect of pure-bred puppies intensifies the hateful Regina's greed. Adding to our dismay is Regina's oafish boyfriend, played expertly by Chris Penn.

What really makes both "Beethoven" films work is that the Newtons come across as real, if admittedly idealized, family. Hunt's Alice understands but does not indulge her husband's exacting qualities, and their children are tremendously likable.

A key subplot involves Tom's Ryce, who has become a young woman since the first film, attracting young men—first Ashley Hamilton's handsome, shameless playboy and then the steadier Danny Masterson.

One loose end: We never do learn whether the Newtons decide to put at risk their large and expensive home to expand George's auto freshener manufacturing business.

"Beethoven's 2nd" has been made with care. The sunny glow cinematographer Bill Butler brings to the film is precisely right for a family film, and director Rod Daniel, ever adroit with comedy, makes everything work beautifully.

"Beethoven's 2nd" gets away with its fantastic moments because its story has been painstakingly grounded in the realities of everyday family life. The film's several animal trainers have done an amazing job anthropomorphizing the Saint Bernards.

As irresistible as the animals are, "Beethoven's 2nd" really belongs to Charles Grodin, who holds the patent on prissy males, but in both instances gets to show George endearingly in the round.

NEW YORK POST, 12/17/93, p. 39, Michael Medved

The one missing element in Hollywood's year-end movie mix has been old-fashioned, glamorous, heart-tugging romance; fortunately, there's a dashing St. Bernard star who's ready to rush in and fill the gap.

Beethoven, the title character of last year's surprise family hit (with an amazing $140 million worldwide theatrical grosses) is a furry, drooling, 180-pound hunk who burns up the screen with his debonair charm and romantic intensity.

This film begins when he meets the luscious, pink-ribboned Missy one day in the park, and then pursues her with single-minded determination. Their shared moments of magic soon result in four adorable St. Bernard pups, but the head of the Newton household (nervous poppa Charles Grodin) is no more eager to accept these new dogs than he was to welcome Beethoven in the original film.

His three spunky kids (Nicholle Tom, Christopher Castile and Sarah Rose Karr), however, are ready to take matters into their own hands. They must also confront comical bad guys who want to use Missy for their own selfish purposes, separating her from her one true love, and even trying to kidnap the pups.

These villains are nicely portrayed by Debbi Mazar, as a sort of New York-accented Cruella De Vil, and Chris Penn as her lunkish boyfriend.

The plot chugs along, punctuated with lots of intense close-ups of adorable dogs: the filmmakers used some 100 different St. Bernard pups to show the new additions at various stages of development.

Grodin is a savvy old pro who milks every imaginable laugh out of his role as the long suffering schlimazel of a dad, who's splattered with a half-dozen different substances at various points in the picture.

This sequel actually delivers more chuckles than the original (thanks in part to tighter pacing by the new director, Rod Daniel), and the family relationships are once again wholesome and loving, but never cloying.

With all of this sweetness and fun, in fact, it's a crime that the filmmakers found it necessary to insert tasteless, inappropriate elements that will discourage some parents from taking young kids who might otherwise enjoy the movie.

For instance, what's the need for a disturbing sequence in which Ryce, the family's budding 15-year-old daughter, confronts an attempted date rape? And why include a song on the soundtrack in the middle of the film that declares: "come on downtown and stay with me tonight/I got a rocket full of kryptonite."

Meanwhile, dear old Dad launches into a lengthy and specific explanation of reproduction (complete with information about eggs and "tadpoles"), and he must learn to accept a boyfriend (Danny Masterson) for his daughter who rides a motorcycle, sports an earring, and wears black T-shirts covered with skulls.

None of this is outrageous or offensive in its own right, but it does feel out of place in a movie which seems otherwise designed to appeal most powerfully to 5-year-olds. By trying to broaden the sequel's audience and targeting teen-agers, the producers have, to some extent broken faith with the core fans of the first film.

Nonetheless, in a holiday marketplace where movies for youngsters are in surprisingly short supply (with no Disney animated gem for the first time in three years), this reasonably cuddly comedy will probably do solid buginess.

It may even give rise to further adventures of Beethoven, Missy and their brood: as producer Joe Medjuck declares, "Beethoven wrote nine symphonies. This may be only the beginning."

NEWSDAY, 12/17/93, Part II/p. 90, John Anderson

The original "Beethoven" worked as well as it did because the Newtons—the doughy suburban family headed by would-be air-freshener mogul Charles Grodin—were an amusing accessory to a harmlessly predictable story. Someone overestimated their charm, however: "Beethoven 2nd" occasionally makes you feel like you're bound, gagged, strapped to a couch and forced to watch the home movies of a doughy suburban family run by a would-be air-freshener mogul.

They're all back: George Newton (Grodin), who's still trying to get financing for his fresheners, and get out of the house without a stain on his suit; Alice Newton (Bonnie Hunt), a wellspring of good sense and unspoken sexual frustration; their children, Ryce, Ted and Emily (Nicholle Tom, Christopher Castile and Sarah Rose Karr), and, oh yes, that big dog.

It's spring and Beethoven, the salivating St. Bernard, finds romance with Missy, another of his breed who's caught in a custody dispute: In order to blackmail her incipient ex-husband, Regina (Debi Mazar) has gotten a court order giving her Missy until he pays her $50,000. A live-action Cruella De Vil, Regina first wants to drown Missy's puppies, and then wants to sell them, but Ted, Ryce and Emily save them, feed them and get George to let them stay. But you know that Regina and her oafish boyfriend aren't going to go away.

That's the plot, but the screen time is filled by the oh-so-fascinating problems of the Newton children—Ted, for instance, isn't picked last for baseball; he's not picked at all—and Ryce's crush on Taylor, an obscenely good-looking and well-spoken 17-year-old (right) played by Ashley Hamilton. He's a jerk, of course, and she really should like Seth (Danny Masterson), whom she meets on vacation, but Taylor's so good looking ... "Oh,God!!!"

None of the acting is objectionable; Grodin is his usual bemused self, Hunt is a warm presence. But Mazar and Penn, who seem perfect for these roles, are wasted by a bad script and lazy direction. The dogs, of course, are too cute for words. And a litter of this goes a long, long way.

SIGHT AND SOUND, 4/94, p. 37, Louise Gray

Family life with the Newtons is as ordinary as three kids, a St Bernard dog called Beethoven and a father in the air-freshener business would allow. It's spring and Beethoven, alongside the Newtons' teenage kids, Ryce and Ted, is looking for that very special companion. In the park, Beethoven sees a man, Cliff, feeding an ice-cream cone to Missy, a female St Bernard who wears a pink ribbon; it is instant love. Gina, Cliff's ex-wife, who is holding his dog in order to extract extra alimony, collects Missy; Cliff has limited visiting rights. Beethoven follows Gina's car home; he and Missy have a touching balcony scene. As Gina and her new man, Floyd, anticipate the size of Cliff's cheque, Missy jumps over the balcony for a date with Beethoven.

Ten weeks later, Ryce is being courted by a boy at school, Taylor. Ted and his younger sister Emily follow Beethoven to the storage room of Gina's building, where they find Missy and four puppies. Gina arrives and drags Missy away; Ted, Emily and Beethoven return home and the puppies are hidden in their basement. The three children feed the puppies, keeping them secret from their father. George, stressed out and under-financed because of a new air-freshener flavour he is planning, discovers the puppies, and reluctantly agrees to keep them.

To celebrate the Fourth of July holiday, the Newtons borrow a cottage in the mountains. Gina and Floyd are staying nearby, as is Taylor. Seth, a local boy, takes Ryce to Taylor's cottage. She sees Taylor playing with other girls and retreats. The next night, Ryce passes Taylor's cottage. He is throwing a party; most of the teenage guests are drunk. She tethers Beethoven to a strut supporting the lake-side house. Taylor locks Ryce in his bedroom and attempts a seduction. Beethoven, goaded by louts pouring beer on his head, breaks his tether and pulls the strut away; Taylor and most of his bedroom fall into the lake.

The next day, the Newtons visit the local country fair. George and Beethoven win a burger-eating contest. Beethoven finds Missy locked in Gina's car. He helps her escape and together they run up the mountain. Gina and Floyd, alerted to the value of pedigree puppies, snatch the dogs from the children. When they discover Missy's escape, they set the puppies on the trail. Gina, Floyd, the Newtons and the puppies all run up the mountain. Floyd threatens to throw a puppy into the ravine far below if the Newtons refuse to hand over ownership of the puppies, but before he can act, the ground gives way. The puppy falls safely to earth as Floyd and Gina tumble into space, to be carried away by the fast-flowing river. Back home, Seth picks up Ryce on a first date and Cliff and Missy visit Beethoven and their ever-growing puppies.

In a film so supportive of what Dame Edna Everage would call "niceness", what could any moral fundamentalist have to say against Beethoven's 2nd? This is a film where love equals marriage, where sex is about love, fidelity and devotion and happens off-screen. Bad sex—that is, Taylor and his slick chat-up lines—is spectacularly prevented. Beethoven and Missy may not get married as such, but they clearly have a surfeit of family values sloshing around their bloodstreams. Not only that—of all dogs in the park, Beethoven and Missy only have eyes for each other. If this film were really about forbidden love, there would at least be a hint of miscegenation around. If the film's scriptwriters ever felt the urge to be transgressive, all they would need was a story line that involved Beethoven, a dachshund and a bath of custard.

But no—discord and disharmony are symbolised by Gina and Floyd. He is a slob, she has a Brooklyn accent, a red Mercedes and a wardrobe comprised of Miss Whiplash couture. They both hate nature (that is, the mountains) and they both hate dogs. The Newtons, encountered in the first Beethoven film, are a suburban version of the Waltons. Daddy strives to reproduce the smell of evergreen pine in his air-freshener; Mom bakes all day long; the kids are in school; Ryce is good at chemistry. Chaos has a limited definition which is usually linked to Beethoven's typically doggy antics.

These provide an easy source of standard comic turns: Beethoven raiding the larder, going window-shopping with Missy, those little puppy puddles that keep appearing. Beyond this, the plot line is simplistic and its key lies in the film's emphasis on relationships: dog to dog and human to human. This is a point of departure from the first film, where it seemed that the presence of a mad vet intent on giving the dog a lethal injection created a more interesting source of anxiety than Gina's plans to sell the pups or even Ryce's first boyfriend. Gum-snapping Gina, on the face of it, is a low-rent caricature of Cruella de Vil, the eminently more elegant villainess of One Hundred and One Dalmations. But, with her vapid and self-obsessed life, she hardly measures up to the model provided by Dodie Smith's book and its Disney adaptation, and neither do the Newtons. *Beethoven's 2nd* has all the wit and spontaneity of a suet pudding.

TIME, 12/20/93, p. 63, Richard Corliss

[*Beethoven's 2nd* was reviewed jointly with *Sister Act 2*; see Corliss' review of that film.]

Also reviewed in:
CHICAGO TRIBUNE, 12/17/93, Friday/p. C, Johanna Steinmetz
NEW YORK TIMES, 12/17/93, p. C10, Caryn James
VARIETY, 12/27/93, p. 51, Brian Lowry
WASHINGTON POST, 12/17/93, p. C6, Rita Kempley
WASHINGTON POST, 12/17/93, Weekend/p. 56, Desson Howe

BEING AT HOME WITH CLAUDE

A Strand Releasing release of a Les Productions du Cerf in association with the National Film Board of Canada. *Producer:* Louise Gendron. *Director:* Jean Beaudin. *Screenplay (French with English subtitles):* Jean Beaudin. *Based on the play by:* René-Daniel DuBois. *Director of Photography:* Thomas Vamos. *Editor:* André Corriveau. *Music:* Richard Grégoire. *Sound:* Michel Charron. *Sound Editor:* Marcel Pothier. *Art Director:* François Séguin. *Costumes:* Louise Jobin. *Make-up:* Louise Mignault. *Running time:* 84 minutes. *MPAA Rating:* Not Rated.

CAST: Roy Dupuis (Yves); Jacques Godin (Inspector); Jean-François Pichette (Claude); Gaston Lepage (Stenographer); Hugo Dubé (Policeman); Johanne-Marie Trembley (Inspector's Wife); Nathalie Mallette (Yves' Sister).

LOS ANGELES TIMES, 10/20/93, Calendar/p. 6, Kevin Thomas

Jean Beaudin's "Being at Home With Claude" makes a harrowing exploration of the connection between love and death. In its black-and-white pre-credit sequence, the French-Canadian film comes across as a thriller but it's actually an especially adroit filming of what is virtually a two-character play (written by René-Daniel DuBois).

Beaudin is amazing in his ability to sustain such a high-pitched intensity throughout; in the process he gets a pair of tour de force portrayals from Roy Dupuis and Jacques Godin.

At 11:30 on a Saturday night Yves (Dupuis), a handsome, muscular young hustler, calls the Montreal police to report the fatal throat-slashing of a young man named Claude (Pichette). At 12:45 a.m., he calls back to turn himself in, insisting that the police meet him in the chambers of a judge and telling them that he has already notified the press.

For much of the first half of the film, the Inspector (Godin), a seasoned, middle-aged cop, browbeats Yves—who wishes to disclose nothing of his motives—in an attempt to reconstruct the crime. In the second half, Yves, finally broken down, takes us on a journey into a veritable heart of darkness. All the while we wonder what will be revealed by the time the film ends.

Why did Yves kill Claude? (We witness the murder—or think we do.) Will we ever learn how Yves came by the set of keys that allows him entrance to the judge's handsome, book-lined chamber?

Although the filmmakers surely are not opposed to keeping us guessing, they are primarily interested in probing the sometimes overpowering nature of love rather than in generating suspense.

Until Claude shyly picks up Yves in a park, the hustler has kept his cool, admitting to being attracted to some johns while being repelled by others, yet always maintaining a professional detachment. Living on the edge, by nature and profession a loner, Yves has never known love until crossing paths with Claude, whom he has met only a month earlier. Claude's love is apparently unconditional, as he is aware that Yves has a need to hustle beyond supporting himself. In any event, the filmmakers do not judge the way Yves makes a living.

"Being at Home With Claude's" long speeches are at times grueling, but their arduousness is integral to what the drama is expressing about the nature of emotion: Beaudin's energy and pacing never falter, and the performances that he draws from Dupuis and Godin are so complete that it comes as a surprise to learn that they did not create them on stage.

Yves may be gay, but the concerns of "Being at Home With Claude" (Times-rated Mature for a scene of lovemaking and adult themes) transcend sexual orientation.

NEW YORK POST, 8/6/93, p. 26, Jerry Tallmer

I wonder when the convention of going from color into black and white for flashbacks, and back into color again, is going to become outworn. I mean it isn't such an old cinematic convention, but it's been used so much these past few years, it's already worn me out.

"Being at Home With Claude," a French-Canadian import, is one such movie, with its love-making and murder and flight—*run, run, run, pant, pant, pant*, through the dark city—in black and white, its interrogation that retraces the ground in some rather watery "living color" of a judge's law library in, so to speak, present time.

The picture wore me out for another reason anyway. It's so damned overheated; a hothouse movie, sexually and artistically.

In Montreal in July, when the city is packed with tourists for what's supposed to be a jazz festival, but looks photographically more like a Mardi Gras, somebody calls the police one night to say that there's a dead body in the kitchen of a certain apartment on Cosgrain Street, near a homosexual district called The Mountain.

The somebody—having turned himself in by prearrangement in that law library of one of his johns—turns out to be a hustler who refuses to give his name or the name of the corpse.

It doesn't take an irate police inspector with 30 years on the vice beat more than a few hours to establish the identities of Yves the hustler and Claude the student with a slashed throat (Jean-Francois Pichette). But it takes what seems to be an eternity of the inspector (Jacques Godin) and the hustler (Roy Dupuis) shouting at the top of their lungs at one another in that library until—in a Dostoevskian monologue that must run to 30 minutes of screen time, even if the camera may have stopped for a break now and then—the hustler lays bare, with intensity, why he did it.

And a laying bare, if you'll forgive me, is where the answer lies, on the floor of that kitchen, in white-hot purity of passion, true love, etc., splashed with red. Jean Beaudin directed this movie. The only two women in it are seen for no more than a couple of seconds each, one of them, the inspector's wife, in *her* kitchen, from the back.

NEWSDAY, 8/6/93, Part II/p. 69, Gene Seymour

The virtuoso opener of "Being at Home With Claude" could be used in film schools as a model of how to start a crime story. It shows the streets of Montreal in full festive uproar during a jazz festival. Fast cuts of revelers and musicians interspersed with sharp, scattered noises. Sharp cries of what could be pain are heard through the celebratory din. Scenes flash by of two men making love.

The scenes cut back and forth from the lovers to the festival. A wine glass breaks. Drums and sax are playing. A knife falls. Revelers mug and laugh at the camera. A streak of blood becomes the only color that pierces the black-and-white sequence. One of the men flees into the streets away from the festival and into the subway. Great stuff.

Much of the rest of "Being at Home With Claude" can also be used in film schools as a model of how *not* to film an interrogation scene. It focuses on the runaway lover (Roy Dupuis), a hustler who is confessing the murder to a blustery police detective (Jacques Godin), who believes, some-what inexplicably, that the kid is up to something.

Director Jean Beaudin tries a little too hard to cinematically "open up" what had been a two-character play by Rene-Daniel DuBois. An outdoor sequence here, an evocative black-and-white flashback there. Ultimately, Beaudin leans heavily on the script's language as delivered by two very good actors. The problem, however, is that none of what they say is as compelling as the hustler's vivid and moving monologue at the end—by which time one wonders why all that other rhetorical frenzy was even necessary.

SIGHT AND SOUND, 6/93, p. 48, Tom Charity

Montreal. On a hot summer's night during the city's jazz festival, two men, Claude and Yves, make passionate love. As he climaxes, Yves grabs a steak knife and cuts Claude's throat. A couple of days later, Yves breaks into a judges chambers and calls the police to hear his confession. The inspector demands an explanation for the crime, but Yves is evasive at first. Gradually, the story unfolds: Claude, a sexually inexperienced intellectual from a wealthy background, timidly approached the young street hustler one night, but collapsed in an alcoholic stupor before the transaction was consummated, whereupon Yves returned his down payment. The pair fell in love, but the rebellious punk Yves soon became aware that he would never fit in with Claude's milieu. He killed Claude for love.

Jean Beaudin's film begins with a bang—a quick-fire black and white montage of downtown Montreal sleaze, its staccato rhythm scored with an ominous drum roll and smatterings of jazz, underlaid with the desperate pants and groans of frenzied intercourse as the camera homes in on Claude's apartment: the window, the bathroom, the passageway, the kitchen, two men making love on the floor. The impact is sustained by extreme close-ups and slow motion as first a wineglass and then a steak knife fall to the ground with the thud of destiny. When it comes, the murder is both the inevitable climax of this cinematic crescendo and a shocking release from it. The hustler runs off through the city to lose himself in the night. The titles roll. The movie is over and René-Daniel DuBois' stage play begins.

It is a two-hander. The scene is the judge's chambers (law books and stained glass window, the inner sanctum of the Establishment). Yves confronts the elderly, angry police inspector, who demands an explanation for the crime. The first act is busy and loud. So is the second. Mostly they feature the inspector hectoring and bullying the recalcitrant Yves while filling in background information for the audience's benefit. The conflict is between old age and youth, innocence (ironically found in the older man) and experience—(the streetwise punk), a guardian of society and an outsider. They reach an uneasy rapprochement via the boy's cathartic, searing 25-minute monologue.

"Why don't words work?" asks Yves, rhetorically. "They're worn out—you can't crank 'em up." Ironically, words are vitally important to DuBois' play, which is full of them (though hindered here by the propensity of the sometimes lazy subtitles to stumble over slang). Beaudin, who credits himself with 'cinematic adaptation' as well as direction, expends a good deal of energy trying to crank up the words. Unusually for an interrogation film, the actors spend little time seated. They are constantly on the move, pacing and posturing, and the camera is equally restless. Flashbacks break the tyranny of the single set, while sound effects deliberately flout narrative expectations (the mention of a war movie cues a barrage of artillery). Such relentless technique betrays a lack of confidence in the material; this, one feels, is a filmmaker all pumped up with nowhere to go. The play ends, after all, with a whimper.

VILLAGE VOICE, 8/17/93, p. 60, Robert Massa

From the first frame, *Being at Home With Claude* is marked by a relentless, breakneck energy—no small feat for a film version of one-set, two-character drama. French Canadian Jean Beaudin's screenplay, based on a play by René-Daniel DuBois, has a promisingly macabre premise: A baby-faced hustler who has abruptly slit his boyfriend's throat in the midst of lovemaking tells reporters to meet him at the home of a prominent judge, promising a scoop. He then calls the cops and confesses to the murder, but the police are reluctant to arrest him fearing he'll tell the press he has the judge's keys, implicating the judge as his client.

All of this unravels in a labyrinth of hard facts and philosophical musings; we keep thinking we're getting close to understanding the hustler's motives, but keep realizing he's leading us in circles—it's almost a sexual tease. Director Jean Beaudin squeezes every conceivable ounce of tension from this heady material, jumping from long, reeling takes in the judge's stained-glass-lined library to murky, nightmarish b-w flashbacks; the effect is all the more dizzying when you're trying to follow the dialogue in subtitles. Roy Dupuis as the hustler—the movie is nearly his monologue—might have conveyed more deviousness, but stays at a high pitch without becoming overbearing.

And yet there is something sort of academic about the entire enterprise. As abruptly as he committed the murder, the hustler gives up the game; the threat to the judge is almost a red herring. We're left with a sort of vague, ultra-aesthetic message about the links between love and death, or sex and death, a message that might resonate in the context of AIDS, but ultimately seems exploitative. I suspect it would seem less so in the more intellectual, word-centered world of a theater, where the murder likely would remain offstage. But in the film we see the bloody deed, so it's hard to gain enough sympathy for the hustler to care about his existential crisis. Especially—though of course this could not have been anticipated by the filmmakers—since *Claude* has opened the very week our local tabloids are screaming: GAY STALKER.

Also reviewed in:
CHICAGO TRIBUNE, 10/29/93, Friday/p. K, Michael Wilmington
NEW YORK TIMES, 8/6/93, p. C8, Stephen Holden
VARIETY, 3/2/92, p. 56, Susan Ayscough

BENEFIT OF THE DOUBT

A Miramax Films and CineVox Entertainment release of a Monument Pictures production. *Executive Producer:* Bob Weinstein and Harvey Weinstein. *Producer:* Michael Spielberg and Brad M. Gilbert. *Director:* Jonathan Heap. *Screenplay:* Jeffrey Polman and Christopher Keyser. *Story:* Michael Lieber. *Director of Photography:* Johnny Jensen. *Music:* Hummie Mann. *Music Editor:* Susan Mick. *Sound:* Reinhard Stergar and (music) Gary Denton. *Sound Editor:* Gregory King. *Casting:* Sunny Siebel. *Production Designer:* Marina Kieser. *Art Director:* David Seth Lazan. *Set Decorator:* Larry Dias. *Set Dresser:* Veronique Lievre. *Special Effects:* John Gray. *Costumes:* Diane Cornelius. *Make-up:* Patricia Ann Mackin. *Make-up (Donald Sutherland):* Ann Brodie. *Stunt Coordinator:* Rob King. *Running time:* 91 minutes. *MPAA Rating:* R.

CAST: Donald Sutherland (Frank Braswell); Amy Irving (Karen Braswell); Rider Strong (Pete Braswell); Christopher McDonald (Dan); Graham Greene (Calhoun); Theodore Bikel (Gideon Lee); Gisele Kovach (Susanna); Ferdinand Mayne (Mueller); Julie Hasel (Young Karen); Patricia Tallman (Karen's Mom); Ralph McTurk (Trooper); Shane McCabe (Wayland); Margaret Johnson (Waitress); Heinrich James (Marina Guard); Jean Fowler (Examiner); Steve Easterling (Coach); John Bachelder (Young Guy); Don Collier (Charlie); Douglas Deane (Turner); David Hammond (Jimmy); Dustin Leighton (Luke).

LOS ANGELES TIMES, 7/16/93, Calendar/p. 12, Michael Wilmington

Anyone can play a hero; all it takes is billing. But playing a really convincing villain? That's the acting job that separates the movie men from the boys.

In "Benefit of the Doubt", Donald Sutherland gets a chance at a classy, mean high-melodrama heavy: a killer-father, a Jekyll-Hyde good guy/maniac who alternates between menacingly restrained niceness and nicely unrestrained menace.

Sutherland makes the most of this juicy part: paroled wife-killer Frank Braswell, who returns to his hometown to woo his daughter and grandson, and insinuate himself back into their lives. And it's a good thing the star is cooking, because "Benefit" itself is erratic and mostly weak. Sutherland's Braswell is the sort of star turn that might redeem a movie, if it were capable of redemption. But, like killer Frank, this film isn't.

It's the sort of psychological thriller someone might dream up after a steady diet of made-for-TV movies and airline bestsellers. Except for Sutherland's performance, it has no resonance or depth. The movie is set in Sedona, Ariz., but the whole town seems generic anyway: chain-movie-mall Middle America. The characters themselves—feisty ma, adventurous kid, raffish boyfriend, *paterfamilias* sheriff, exotic jeweler, avuncular psychiatrist—are generic, too. After a while, it seems a little chilling that Frank is the only one with any personality or surprises. Do modern scriptwriters only exert themselves when trying to confront evil?

Fortunately, Sutherland has exactly the right equipment for his role. With his hulking, imposing frame, his pale, watery, yearning eyes, that twisting half-goofy smile and that peculiar almost sinister lisp, he makes Braswell a convincing monster, even an appealing one. He exudes a murderous friendliness. There's only one moment in "Benefit," where you feel the actor isn't giving enough: a late tantrum scene that seems too contained, impacted.

Around him, the rest of the cast seem stranded. As confused daughter Karen, befuddled perhaps by the movie's flashbacks, Amy Irving is brittle, rather than tough. As Sheriff Calhoun, a stick lawman, Graham Greene doesn't get to exploit the wonderful comic/sardonic vein he used in "Clearcut" or "Thunderheart."

Jonathan Heap, the young director making his feature debut with "Benefit of the Doubt" (MPAA-rated R for violence, sexuality and language), deserves full credit for helping Sutherland steal the show and for staging a slam-bang, picturesque Lake Powell chase climax. But, in the end, powerful villains need strong or likable antagonists. Evil has to feed on good—or, at least on the *illusion* of good. In "Benefit of the Doubt," Sutherland's Frank is a maniac without a country, a Devil trapped in the Purgatory of banality.

NEW YORK POST, 7/16/93, p. 33, Michael Medved

If actors had the right to sue directors and writers for artistic malpractice, then poor Donald Sutherland would have an airtight case for "Benefit of the Doubt."

In this painfully disappointing thriller, the veteran star gives an altogether remarkable performance in a movie that takes a promising premise and mishandles it completely.

Sutherland plays the soft-spoken Frank Braswell, who has served 22 years in prison for the murder of his wife. He has always maintained his innocence, insisting that she fell down the stairs accidentally in the midst of an argument, but the eyewitness testimony of his 12-year-old daughter convicted him.

When he's paroled from prison at the beginning of the film, Braswell returns to his Arizona home town and tries to reconnect with that daughter (Amy Irving), who's now a struggling single mom and a cocktail waitress at a local topless bar. At first, she's afraid that her father will seek violent revenge, but his soothing manner helps to convince her that he may have been innocent after all, and she's prepared to give him "the benefit of the doubt."

The problem is that the script makes it so obvious that he's a dangerous psychopath that we can't possibly accept her idiotic naivete. Sutherland does a splendid job balancing the sick, twisted aspects of his role with a kindly, grandfatherly exterior, but the clumsy script won't let him exploit these ambiguities. The picture quickly degenerates into a typical Hollywood tale of a monstrous murderer on an unstoppable rampage. Shouldn't it be possible to create a nasty villain without turning him into a bloodthirsty serial killer of superhuman cunning and strength?

Amy Irving fans will be pleased to see that this underused star looks absolutely sensational, with a sassy, savvy, intensely sexy edge that she's never displayed before. Unfortunately, this sizzling screen presence can't help her cope with the demands of her ridiculous role, and at moments of high emotion she demonstrates a distressing tendency to forget the twangy cowgirl accent she has employed in most of her role.

At key points in the movie, you find yourself ignoring the hardworking actors and concentrating instead on the gorgeous Arizona scenery, stunningly photographed by Danish cinematographer Johnny Jensen (who previously lensed the lovely "Rambling Rose"). Mr. Jensen, and that riveting performer Donald Sutherland, most definitely deserve better material to display their talents.

NEWSDAY, 7/16/93, Part II/p. 60, John Anderson

There's never been a doubt that Donald Sutherland can play the villain, and do it with palpable malevolence.

His heroes, after all, have worked because their goodness seems like a temporary affliction, an aberrant pause between acts of cunning. But he can't do the galoot, and he can't do a character that is less a character than an amorphous amalgamation of junked Freudian parts,

The supposed hook to "Benefit of the Doubt," one of the more hare-brained psychological thrillers to boast an actor of even Sutherland's now-wobbly stature, is whether his character, Frank Braswell, is a deranged wife-killer, or the wronged man he claims to be.

There never seems to be much doubt, actually, because the nervous music and nervous camera tell us we're supposed to be in a murder mystery. And Frank—with his leering grin and uncanny ability to ominously appear whenever and wherever it's most convenient—is the runaway favorite for bad guy.

But his psychological motivation keeps changing: It travels from psychosis to obsession to simple panic to sexual deviation, leaving the audience not only lost but uninterested.

Frank's daughter Karen (Amy Irving), who looks like she hasn't slept since Dad went off to the big house, is a mess. Since she was 5, and saw her mother take a lethal header down a flight of stairs, she's lived in fear of the day her father would get out of prison. The only evidence against him was her testimony, and when he left the courtroom for prison Karen heard him say, "Daddy won't forget this."

As a result, she's a single, chain-smoking mother, a waitress in a topless bar where she fights off greasy drunken men and where she lets her son Pete (Rider Strong) do his homework.

Somewhere, there was a germ of an idea about how crimes of violence can visit themselves on future generations. And the characters have a latent tragedy about them.

But neither Sutherland, Irving nor director Jonathan Heap let us worry too much about any of it.

Perhaps we should thank them.

SIGHT AND SOUND, 12/93, p. 41, Philip Kemp

After 22 years in jail for the murder of his wife, Frank Braswell is let out on parole and heads for Cottonwood, Arizona, where his daughter Karen lives. Karen, a single mother working as a waitress at a strip joint, is alarmed to hear of Frank's release since it was her testimony that got him convicted. She warns her 11-year-old son Pete to have nothing to do with him, but Pete has already met his grandfather and taken to him. Karen appeals to the sheriff, Bob Calhoun, but he can do nothing except warn Frank off. Frank gradually wins Pete's trust and that of Dan, Karen's boyfriend, explaining he simply wants to be accepted back into the family. Karen begins to wonder if she was mistaken about her mother's death, which Frank insists was a tragic accident, and her mistrust of him lessens.

Discovering that Dan plans to marry Karen, Frank visits the cement factory where he works and pushes him off the roof. Dan's death is taken for an accident by everyone except Calhoun, who starts to investigate. Meanwhile the grief-stricken Karen allows Frank to move in with her and Pete, despite the misgivings of her friend Susanna. One night Frank comes to Karen's room and gets into her bed. Waking in horror, she regains her memory of his earlier attempt at incest which led to her mother's death. She flees with Pete, pausing at a diner to phone Calhoun. Pursued by Frank, they make their way over the mountains to Lake Powell, where Susanna owns a houseboat. Calhoun follows and arrests Frank, but Frank kills him and shows up on the houseboat, where he shoots a security guard. Karen and Pete escape in a motorboat and climb a cliff, but Frank is waiting at the top. Karen shoots him with a gun Pete took from the guard's body, and Frank falls to his death.

Benefit of the Doubt crosses *Cape Fear* with *The Stepfather*, chucks in some modish child abuse and ends with a vertiginous canyon-edge finale borrowed from at least half a dozen recent films. What saves it from being no more than movie-making by numbers is the ingenuity of the script and an acutely gauged performance from Donald Sutherland, balancing affability and menace in a way that De Niro's mannered, overwrought Max Cady never managed. Like Mitchum in the original *Cape Fear*, Sutherland has no need to hang upside down to convince us he's psychotic.

Even before we see him we hear Frank Braswell's voice over the credits, preaching family togetherness to his parole board and deploring "the state this country's got itself into". "Don't you think you're part of that?" retorts one skeptical board member, but Frank's act evidently sways the majority. The dissident member is right, though. Frank is very much "part of that"—not because he's a plausible hypocrite, but precisely because he believes every word he says.

The specious opposition between the disruptions of present-day society and 'old-fashioned family values' gets short shrift in *Benefit of the Doubt*, where one derives only too inevitably from the other. The traditional close-knit family that Frank yearns to recreate—there's a telling shot of him leaving Dan's funeral with one arm round Karen, the other round Pete, every inch the protective paterfamilias—is exposed as the ideal locus for abuse and violence, the breeding ground for emotional alienation. Karen's reluctance to commit to a relationship traces straight back to the buried trauma of her childhood. None of these ideas is startlingly new, of course, but it's encouraging to see them so unequivocally taken on by a mainstream Hollywood thriller.

"Sometimes you're the only one that knows the truth," Frank tells Pete. "Doesn't make it any less true." The film plays with notions of subjective and relative truth: "I proved it, the jury convicted him—that makes it true," Karen is told by the DA who stage-managed her testimony. According to events, her memory of her mother's death shifts and mutates. In one flashback, swayed by Frank's account, she hears drunken recrimination; next time round, the newly-recalled incest utterly transforms the scene. One word makes a world of difference. "Daddy won't forget this," is what Karen remembers Frank saying after his trial. His version is the devoted father's "Daddy won't forget you."

The trouble with letting so much hinge on nuances of perception, and on the subtleties of Sutherland's performance, is that once the ambiguity is resolved most of our interest goes with it. Up to Dan's murder we're still guessing: maybe Frank's on the level, maybe someone else (Calhoun?) will be revealed as the villain. But from then on everything's out in the open, clearly demarcated, and it's still a long way to the final chase—which itself is far too drawn-out to maintain tension. *Benefit of the Doubt* is a halfway good film: had it contrived to keep us doubting until the end (or yet better, even after the end), it would have reaped the benefit.

VILLAGE VOICE, 6/22/93, p. 63, Mike Rubin

As a convict at upstate's Fishkill Correctional Facility observed to my colleague Mark Schone a few weeks ago, folks in prison watch television because there's "nothing else to do." With the American family wasting away each day in Oprah Winfreyville, all that unfree time watching the tube could turn a dull boy into *The Shining*'s Jack. Such a character might be *Benefit of the Doubt*'s Frank Braswell (Donald Sutherland), a convict who seems to have internalized the extremes of the family values debate during his 22 years in the hole. "I believe the strength of this nation lies in the strength of its families," he tells his parole board, pleading for (and receiving) his release in order to help his daughter Karen (Amy Irving), a single mother struggling to provide for her young son.

But the family he left behind is less nuclear than it is atomically charged. They want nothing to do with him; after all, he murdered his wife by throwing her down a flight of stairs, and it was Karen who testified against him. As the old man insists on a reconciliation, however, bearing gifts and patching symbolic cracks in the sidewalk while radiating sincerity in a measured, supremely rational, Volvo-commercial tone, the old fell-or-pushed question gives way to other issues. Was Karen right the first time, or was she coached by an overeager prosecutor? Is she still forgetting something? Is blood thicker than other bodily fluids? If Dad keeps everyone stocked with glasses of warm milk, does it really matter?

Fueled by Sutherland's creepy performance, *Benefit* flirts with being a decent psychological thriller, examining the way that memory gets fuzzy. But repressed-memory twists are on the predictable side—at least if you've been watching Oprah—and its recent influences too obvious: *The Stepfather*, *Max Dugan Returns*, and a climactic cliffside chase scene that seems cribbed from another Sutherland vehicle, *Eye of the Needle*. With its plausibility problems, flat dialogue, and characters who are only half-drawn (Graham Greene in particular is wasted as a county sheriff whose good police work but bad knowledge of plot devices get him into trouble), *Benefit* has that made-for-cable feeling; all the better to be fed back into the prison system, I guess.

Also reviewed in:
CHICAGO TRIBUNE, 7/16/93, Friday/p. B, Clifford Terry
NEW YORK TIMES, 7/16/93, p. C17, Vincent Canby
VARIETY, 7/19/93, p. 71, Emanuel Levy
WASHINGTON POST, 7/16/93, p. C1, Hal Hinson

BENNY & JOON

A Metro-Goldwyn-Mayer release. *Executive Producer:* Bill Badalato. *Producer:* Susan Arnold and Donna Roth. *Director:* Jeremiah Chechik. *Screenplay:* Barry Berman. *Story:* Barry Berman and Leslie McNeil. *Director of Photography:* John Schwartzman. *Editor:* Carol Littleton. *Music:* Rachel Portman. *Music Editor:* Bill Abbott. *Sound:* James Thornton and (music) John Richards. *Sound Editor:* J. Paul Huntsman and John Haeny. *Casting:* Risa Bramon Garcia and Heidi Levitt. *Production Designer:* Neil Spisak. *Art Director:* Pat Tagliaferro. *Set Decorator:* Barbara Munch. *Set Dresser:* J. Michael Davis and Peter Hoobyar. *Special Effects (Fire):* Alan Hall. *Special Effects:* J.D. Street IV. *Costumes:* Aggie Guerard Rodgers. *Make-up:* Patty York. *Stunt Coordinator:* Noon Orsatti. *Running time:* 98 minutes. *MPAA Rating:* PG.

CAST: Johnny Depp (Sam); Mary Stuart Masterson (Joon); Aidan Quinn (Benny); Julianne Moore (Ruthie); Oliver Platt (Eric); C.C.H. Pounder (Dr. Garvey); Dan Hedaya (Thomas); Joe Grifasi (Mike); William H. Macy (Randy Burch); Liane Alexandra Curtis (Claudia); Eileen Ryan (Mrs. Small); Don Hamilton (UPS Man); Waldo Larson (Walter); Irvin Johnson and Shane Nilsson (Orderlies); Leslie Laursen (Admitting Nurse); Faye Killebrew (Video Customer); Ramsin Amirkhas (Video Clerk); Lynette Walden (Female Customer); Amy Alizabeth Sanford (Young Joon); Brian Keevy (Young Benny); John Grant Phillips (Policeman); Tony Lincoln (Local); Noon Orsatti and Don Kamin (Patrons).

LOS ANGELES TIMES, 4/16/93, Calendar/p. 4, Peter Rainer

With "Benny & Joon" we're back in the fantasyland popularized by movies like "One Flew Over the Cuckoo's Nest" and, before that, "David and Lisa"—where being crazy is the only sane response to an insane world.

Joon (Mary Stuart Masterson) is the kookily unbalanced sister of Benny (Aidan Quinn), a soulful, overprotective auto mechanic. When Sam (Johnny Depp), a quirky, clownish spirit who idolizes Keaton and Chaplin, enters their lives, they learn the meaning of love and togetherness and all that jazz. It's the kind of scenario that might bring a tear to the eye of Al Franken's Stuart Smalley, the pseudo-pop therapist on "Saturday Night Live."

This sentimental stew is not without its flavors, and the cast tries hard to be winsome and adorably distraught. Benny plays poker with his buddies and scrupulously avoids female companionship because his life is so complicated by his homebody sister that he can't conceive of a life apart from her. He staggers about befogged by his responsibilities.

Joon, who wavers between rational alertness and hyper-anxious loopiness, spends much of her time painting goopy expressionist canvases. When Sam, a cousin of one of Benny's friends, becomes their housemate as the result of a poker bet, we're primed for a heartwarming communion. Sam and Joon are supposed to be soul mates two innocents who learn to groove on their own flightiness.

It's part of the film's game plan that we're never quite sure just how unbalanced Joon or Sam are supposed to be. Director Jeremiah Chechik and screenwriter Barry Berman, who used to be a circus clown, aren't geared up to alienate the audience with too many throes of misery; this is, after all, a movie where to be out of touch with reality is to be in touch with yourself.

"Benny & Joon" (rated PG for theme, sensuality and language) wants us to know that everybody is magical once you get past their hang-ups. Sam, who lopes around like one of his beloved silent film heroes and lives owl-like in a tree when he's temporarily without shelter, might ordinarily appear to be the object of fun in a film with less weighty matter on its mind. But if he's a fool, he's a holy fool—a redeemer. He transforms not only Joon's life, but Benny's as well.

These transformations are foregone conclusions—surprises aren't real big in fables. But at least a few of the performers bring something fresh to their roles. Quinn has a naturalness that ultimately makes his bemused reverence for Sam almost believable, we can see how Benny is closer to Joon's kind of magical thinking than he has allowed himself to admit. Depp performs some of his slapstick routines with grace, and his cracked yearning for Joon comes through without sappiness. Masterson has a more difficult time convincing us that she's elfin. Her malcontent is saddled with so many symbols that she doesn't quite make it as a "real" person. Or an unreal one either.

NEW YORK POST, 4/17/93, p. 15, Michael Medved

"Benny & Joon" is a maddening mix of psychosis and psychosis and sentimentality, an ill-considered attempt to present desperately disturbed characters as the focus of a manipulative romantic comedy. The tone wobbles wildly between gritty realism and fairy-tale fatuity, while the dark elements of the story keep undermining the picture's feeble efforts to generate gentle laughs or quirky charm.

Ironically, part of the problem stems from Mary Stuart Masterson's compelling and subtle performance in the movie's pivotal role. She plays Joon (short for Juniper) Pearl, a severely troubled recluse who lives alone with Benny (Aidan Quinn), her protective older brother. Masterson is too fine an actress to smooth over her character's schizophrenia as some adorable idiosyncrasy; instead, she infuses Joon's psychotic breaks with enough menace and pain to suggest that this woman is a real danger to herself and to others.

It's easy to understand why Benny, a hard-working auto mechanic in Spokane, Wash., insists that she needs to be supervised at all times, even though her rages make it impossible to retain the services of a housekeeper.

It turns out that the only calming influence on Joon (and her only hope of avoiding the hospitalization threatened by an officious psychiatrist) comes from Sam, a mysterious wanderer whom Benny is forced to welcome to his home after losing a hand in a poker game (don't ask).

We know instantly that Sam is supposed to be an angelic good guy because he's a functional illiterate, he boasts an encyclopedic knowledge of old movies, and he's played by teen heartthrob Johnny Depp. While sporting the dress and grooming of one of the "Droogs" from "A Clockwork Orange" Sam also displays the gentle mannerisms, sad eyes and slapstick routines he has learned from old Chaplin and Keaton movies.

Depp has begun to make a specialty of this sort of other-worldly misfit; his part in this film bears an uneasy resemblance to the mechanically assembled boy he played (with far greater effectiveness) in "Edward Scissorhands," and even recalls the weepy 1950s rebel he portrayed in John Waters' campy musical "Cry Baby."

But here, his moody stares and perpetual pouting tell us nothing whatever about the character, as if Depp himself never decided whether Sam is supposed to be severely delusional and withdrawn or merely a willful eccentric.

In any event, this childlike alien takes over as Joon's caretaker and companion and the resulting romance is both totally predictable and utterly unconvincing. The two lovebirds primarily share a passion for exotic eats: Joon likes to grind up Cap'n Crunch cereal (together with milk) in a blender, and Sam prepares grilled cheese sandwiches on an ironing board, his iron turned up to the rayon setting.

These culinary innovations should tickle some of the teen-aged moviegoers, who will doubtless comprise "Benny & Joon's" principal audience. It's true that we all feel like oddballs and lunatics at many points in our adolescence, and this movie advances the encouraging notion that even the most lavishly weird lost souls will ultimately find true romance with one another.

What's more, Sam and Joon end up teaching important life lessons to poor workaholic Benny and Spokane's other stuffy but well-intentioned defenders of convention. It's a variation on the all-too-familiar theme of kids-know-best (and crazies-know-best) that's prominently featured in numerous films of recent years.

Director Jeremiah Chechik presents this material (derived from a screenplay by first-timer Barry Berman) in a style so quaint, precious and bogus that one might have expected him to retitle the picture "Ye Olde Benny & Joon shoppe."

Countless scenes are festooned with distracting curios, and the charming riverside home of the two title characters is a prime example of distracting and inappropriate set design.

This is only Chechik's second film (after the forgettable "National Lampoon's Christmas Vacation") and, like many another veteran of TV commercials and music videos, he can't resist irrelevant montages. On two occasions when the picture seems to be working up some rare forward momentum, the energy is stopped cold by shimmering, smoky, flat-footed sequences used to back mediocre songs by the likes of John Hiatt and Temple of the Dog.

These interludes are especially annoying since Rachel Portman (who previously composed the impressive music for "Used People") created an inventive, haunting and poignant score that provides "Benny & Joon" with one of its few unmitigated assets.

It says volumes about the shortcomings of this stubbornly joyless motion picture that by far its most satisfying moments came in listening to Portman's full-blown themes while watching the end credits unroll over the black and empty screen.

For audiences in New York (or in other cities with significant populations of mentally ill homeless people) this picture's underlying message will leave a sour aftertaste even after those credits conclude.

The script's old-fashioned and simple-minded certainty that the best way to handle severely psychotic individuals is to respect them as they are and to send them on their independent way to "find themselves"—is mocked by the muttering and lost unfortunates that many of us encounter on the streets on our way home from the theater.

NEWSDAY, 4/16/93, Part II/p. 66, Jack Mathews

Edward Scissorhands is back, without the scissor-hands and doing Buster Keaton and Charlie Chaplin impressions instead of ice sculptures.

So it seems anyway. In "Benny & Joon," another romantic fable set in an American suburb, Johnny Depp plays a character named Sam instead of Edward, and his handicap is social rather than physical. But he is the same quiet, gentle soul who had such a salutary effect on his neighbors in "Edward Scissorhands."

Depp is very good at this character. He has a mime's ability to express himself physically, and there is a benign quality to his boyish face that translates to instant likability on screen.

"Edward Scissorhands" director Tim Burton used those qualities perfectly in convincing audiences a neighborhood could rally behind a kid who is simply a sweet version of Frankenstein's monster. And Canadian director Jeremiah Chechik put them to similar use in making Sam, a young man who wears a bowler hat and hangs out in trees, the sympathetic center of "Benny & Joon."

The parallels between the two Depp movies end there, unfortunately. Chechik, whose resumé includes many TV commercials and music videos but only one feature film (the slapstick "National Lampoon's Christmas Vacation"), has neither the confidence, nor vision of Burton, and though there is much to admire about the intentions of "Benny & Joon," the foundation of the story is not strong enough to support it.

The title itself underscores the film's major structural problem. There are two relationships developed. One is between Benny Pearl (Aidan Quinn), an amiable auto mechanic, and his mentally ill sister Joon (Mary Stuart Masterson), to whom Benny has dedicated himself to protecting and keeping out of institutions. The other is between Joon and Sam, the romance that develops when Sam, through some implausible conceit about a poker bet, comes to live with them.

The second relationship is the most interesting and the best written, but it is the first and weakest that gets the most attention.

It is obvious that first-time screenwriter Barry Berman—no kidding, a former Ringling Bros. & Barnum and Bailey clown was most inspired while inventing Sam; Depp even does serviceable work as a street mime and performing clown in the film. And the movie only comes to life after Sam and Joon meet on that supra-sensory wave length that seems to exist only in the imaginations of writers.

We have to accept the seriousness of Joon's illness on faith. Other than an early comic scene where she directs traffic in a snorkel mask, and a frightening full-blown psychotic episode late in the movie, there is nothing unusual about her, and nothing particularly interesting. At least, not until Sam enters her life, and they both find a purpose outside their isolated lives.

The film that "Benny & Joon" most resembles in theme is the 1963 "David and Lisa," which was based on a true story about two emotionally disturbed teenagers whose romance proved therapeutic. This movie is not as ambitious, and it is downright embarrassing when it attempts to get clinical about Joon's illness. Still, the relationship between the eccentric lovers is the only strength Chechik had to draw on, and he was stuck developing it as a subplot.

"Sam & Joon" would have been both a better title, and a better movie.

NEWSWEEK, 4/26/93, p. 64, David Ansen

In the very whimsical fable *Benny & Joon*, Johnny Depp plays an eccentric, sensitive aspiring clown named Sam who wears a porkpie hat like his idol Buster Keaton, sits in trees and uses an iron and an ironing board to make grilled cheese sandwiches. A shy loner, he finds his soul mate in Joon (Mary Stuart Masterson), bright, articulate, artistic, but mentally unbalanced. Subject to breakdowns at the slightest agitation, she's looked after by her loving but overprotective brother Benny (Aidan Quinn), a handsome mechanic who seems to be using Joon's precarious mental state to avoid his own private life.

Movies that make mental illness cute and poetic tend to give me the heebie-jeebies, and this one doesn't help its case by being evasively vague about the nature of Joon's condition. That said, it should be granted that "Benny & Joon" is one of the more palatable and inventive examples of this suspect genre, its inherent sappiness leavened by screenwriter Barry Berman's wit and director Jeremiah Chechik's clever use of familiar silent-comedy routines. But if audiences clutch this teddy bear of a movie to their breasts, the bulk of the credit goes to the deft and likable cast. In anyone else's hands, the mimelike Sam would be an insufferably fey concoction. But Depp plays him with such conviction that you can't keep your eyes off him. It's not merely Depp's physical dexterity that impresses: he has a melancholic inner stillness that's genuinely Keatonesque. Edgy and tightly wound, Masterson makes a good romantic contrast to his dewy reticence, and Quinn (with his Clift-like quaver) more than holds his own as the straight man in this carnival of quirk. If you can accept it on its fablelike terms, the wishfully rosy resolution will seem heavenly; more skeptical viewers may have an allergic reaction to the whole concept. Your call.

SIGHT AND SOUND, 7/93, p. 37, Claire Monk

Joon Pearl, a mentally disturbed woman in her early twenties, is bright, highly verbal and an enthusiastic painter. She shares a home with her older brother Benny, a car mechanic, who takes care of her. One evening Benny finds Joon throwing something at the part-time housekeeper, who announces her resignation, leaving Joon with no daytime carer. During Benny's weekly poker game, one of his friends, Mike, complains about his cousin Sam, who is boarding with him, and jokingly suggests palming off Sam on Benny as a 'housekeeper'. Joon's psychiatrist Dr Garvey tries to persuade Benny that Joon would be better off in a home. During the next poker game, Mike's bid is that Benny should take Sam off his hands. Mike wins, and Benny and Joon acquire Sam as a member of their household. Benny, Joon and Sam go to a diner, where Sam's plate-skimming and food-juggling skills attract the attention of the waitress, Ruthie.

Benny gets to know Ruthie through Sam and Joon's developing friendship. When he drives her home after a visit she invites him in for a beer; he refuses, but asks her out to dinner. Dr Garvey reminds Benny to tell Joon about his plans to put her in a home; Benny asks for her admission to be deferred. His date with Ruthie goes well, but once again he refuses to come in for a drink and she is hurt by what she sees as a brush-off. Benny's moroseness contrasts with Joon and Sam's increasing happiness, particularly on a trip to the park, where Sam's brilliant clowning draws a crowd, enchants Joon and dramatically raises Benny's opinion of him. That night, Sam and Joon make love, but Joon asks Sam not to tell Benny. Benny arranges an audition for Sam but when he tells Joon and Sam, Joon is upset and Sam is silent. Sam tells Benny about their relationship; Benny reacts violently, and throws Sam out. Joon protests; Benny refuses to listen and shows her the brochure for the home.

That night Joon sends Benny out to buy food while she and Sam, intending to run away, catch the night bus. Without her medication, Joon has a seizure and is taken to the mental hospital, accompanied by Sam. At the hospital, Benny is told Joon won't see him and doesn't want to leave. He sees Sam waiting in reception, and reacts violently again. Sam is visited by a penitent Benny, asking for help in getting to see Joon. They finally gain admission and Benny apologises to Joon, offering her the chance to try living independently. Joon agrees that she'd like to try living in her own flat, and Dr Garvey signs her release papers. Benny is tentatively reunited with Ruthie; and Joon starts her new life in the flat next to Ruthie's, frequently accompanied by Sam.

The idea that getting together with Johnny Depp is an effective therapy for mental illness certainly holds more appeal than, say, *Rain Man*'s vision of enforced contact with an autistic brother as a cure for 80s materialistic values. Hollywood's recent fondness for expropriating mental illness or impairment as a metaphor—homogenising a host of disabilities into a state of innocence which cleanses flawed or corrupt 'normality'—is not entirely absent from *Benny and Joon*, but at least the tone of former clown Barry Berman's debut script is more knowingly comic than selfrighteous. "Benjamin, don't underestimate the mentally ill," Joon warns her brother when she suspects him of cheating at table tennis. But Joon's smart remark has an all-too-predictable double meaning—with the uncanny perceptiveness Hollywood likes to impute to the 'challenged', she has subliminally sussed Benny's plans to betray her by putting her in a home. This inconsistency between endowing her character with real offbeat wit and originality (she dislikes raisins, she explains to Sam, because "they've had their life stolen ... they taste sweet, but really they're humiliated grapes"), then falling back on the low-risk liberal clichés of the American mental illness movie is symptomatic of the film's slightly unsatisfactory hybrid nature.

Unfortunately, *Benny and Joon*'s likeable but flawed magical realist script is weighed down by unmagical direction. Excellent central performances do much to compensate, and the end result has some unusual strengths—an offbeat blue-collar milieu where poker is played not to win cash but to get rid of unwanted household items, and a no-fuss portrayal of the psychological effects of being a carer (Benny's confusion, self-denial and lack of social confidence after 12 years of caring for Joon are superbly conveyed by Quinn). Depp's precision clowning makes for some moments of great visual comedy: as he punts across the kitchen using a mop as a pole and mimes his way into a job in a video store, his role looks increasingly like a consolation prize for not getting to play Chaplin. But Jeremiah Chechik's apprenticeship directing *National Lampoon's Christmas Vacation* (his sole previous feature) and Hall and Oates videos for MTV has clearly taken its toll; moments of high emotion (Sam and Joon weepily make out on her studio floor) and moral reflection (Benny broods next to a moving goods train) are reduced to a rock-video bathos made worse by blasts of John Hiatt and Joe Cocker on the soundtrack.

This directorial heavy-handedness exacerbates the feel-good attitude to mental problems. For instance, the title sequence establishes that Joon is Artistic But Unbalanced by having her paint an impassioned impasto abstract and then destructively smear her hands across the canvas. Her other symptoms include making milkshakes with strange (though not inedible) ingredients while wearing a snorkel, and a pyromaniac tendency when crossed. When Sam confronts Benny with the 'controversial' view that "apart from being a little mentally ill, Joon is pretty normal," we are likely to agree, but not for the reason intended. The implied cause of Joon's condition is as fudged as the cure. A hint in a flashback that her mental distress may have originated in the death of both parents in a road accident makes a crucial difference to our acceptance of the premise that Sam's emotional healing might make her 'well'; yet it remains unclarified.

To its credit, the film makes a belated point (during the getaway attempt which precipitates Joon's hospitalisation) of showing that Sam is no substitute for her regular medication. But by this stage in the story his role as catalyst and twin soul has been so strongly established (we know he's a kindred spirit the moment he starts tasting paint from Joon's canvas and making toast by ironing the bread) that our final impression is that Sam and Joon are just a couple of kooks whose problems are resolved by falling in love. In this fantasy of mutually protective innocence, only the 'normal' Benny is required to confront the complex struggles of adult life.

VILLAGE VOICE, 4/13/93, p. 58, Manohla Dargis

Whimsy is at full throttle in the romantic comedy *Benny & Joon*. A sister-and-brother act without enough laughs, the two sibs live together in a charming house, on a charming street, in some charming burg. She (Mary Stuart Masterson) is a painter and he (Aidan Quinn) is a mechanic. Life would be swell but he's lonely and crazed because she's nuts—certifiable, in fact. When she's not smearing colors on canvas, Joon is breaking dishes, terrorizing the help, and every so often letting loose on the outside world. Her psychiatrist wants her in an institution, but big brother prefers to keep Joon close at hand, even though Saturday night means playing sitter not stud. Then Joon meets Sam (Johnny Depp), a naif whose Buster Keaton moves prove insanity isn't some *Titicut Follies* nightmare, it's some kind of *wonderful*.

It's amazing there are those who still think mental illness is a picturesque adventure. (My own panic attacks were always a laugh riot.) *Benny & Joon* isn't evil, but it sure is screwy. Barry Berman, the clown who penned the script, isn't just ill-informed, he doesn't know what to make of its juiciest bits. (Berman's a graduate of what the movie's press kit calls the "prestigious Clown College.") Not only do he and director Chechik let Benny's creepily close feelings for baby-sister dangle, but Joon reads more like wacky art student than anything else.

The cast is game, though except for Depp they don't know how to pump flat material. A graceful physical comedian, Depp never sinks into preciousness. Even when working a bowler and a fistful of air, he takes the goo out of mime and *Benny & Joon*'s movie madness.

Also reviewed in:
CHICAGO TRIBUNE, 4/16/93, Friday/p. C, Dave Kehr
NEW YORK TIMES, 4/16/93, p. C13, Janet Maslin
VARIETY, 3/29/93, p. 82, Emanuel Levy
WASHINGTON POST, 4/16/93, p. B7, Rita Kempley
WASHINGTON POST, 4/16/93, Weekend/p. 39, Desson Howe

BETTY

An MK2 Productions USA release of an MK2 Productions/CED Productions/FR3 Films coproduction with the participation of Canal+. *Producer:* Marin Karmitz. *Director:* Claude Chabrol. *Screenplay (French with English subtitles):* Claude Chabrol. *Based on the novel by:* Georges Simenon. *Director of Photography:* Bernard Zitzermann. *Editor:* Monique Fardoulis. *Music:* Matthieu Chabrol. *Sound:* Jean-Bernard Thomasson and Maurice Gilbert. *Production Designer:* Françoise Benoit-Fresco. *Art Director:* Jean-Pierre Lemoine and Pierre Galliard. *Costumes:* Cristine Guegan. *Running time:* 103 minutes. *MPAA Rating:* Not Rated.

CAST: Marie Trintignant (Betty); Stéphane Audran (Laure); Jean-François Garreau (Mario); Yves Lambrecht (Guy Etamble); Christiane Minazolli (Madame Etamble); Pierre Vernier (The Doctor).

LOS ANGELES TIMES, 8/27/93, Calendar/p. 4, Kenneth Turan

A well-dressed woman with a haunted look steps almost by chance into a small Paris bar. Hours later she leaves with a man she's picked up, both of them smashed, headed for a place in Versailles he knows. Age 28, without a profession, a nonstop smoker and drinker, Betty, for that is her name, has the look of a one-woman lost generation, a wasted Piaf waif out on the town.

Although we learn a lot more about her during the course of "Betty", it would be a disservice to the sensibility behind this film to say that we ever come to really understand why she acts the way she does.

"Betty," the latest work from Claude Chabrol, functions instead as a fatalistic character study. It is the kind of rigorous slice of dark and obsessive life we've come to expect from the master

French director, best known for films from the 1960s such as "La Femme Infidele" and "Le Boucher."

Chabrol's austerity as a director has kept him from becoming the kind of sentimental favorite his colleague Francois Truffaut was in this country. Yet by returning again and again, as he does in this, his 45th film, to themes of repression and sexuality, Chabrol has achieved a kind of control of his material that is remarkable.

"Betty," which Chabrol scripted, is taken from a novel by the same name by Georges Simenon, a writer whose unsentimental concentration on abnormal psychology is a match for Chabrol's style. The combination has resulted in a decidedly odd but mostly involving two-character study—short on plot but long on the intricacies of unpredictable human behavior.

That dive in Versailles that Betty is taken to is called Le Trou (the Hole), described by the proprietor Mario (Jean-Francois Garreau) as a place where all the regulars are twisted. Betty catches not only Mario's attention but also that of his girlfriend, Laure (Chabrol regular Stephane Audran), a hard-drinking widow who came to the city after her husband's death and never left.

Laure, a former nurse, takes to Betty with an immediate and unsettling intensity. She procures this cipher of a woman a hotel room next to hers, draws her bath, cleans her clothes, finds her a doctor, even places her feet in cozy slippers. All she seems to want in return is Betty's alcoholic companionship.

Laure tells Betty her story, and, gradually, through an intricate series of fragmentary flashbacks and long monologues, Betty's comes out as well. The stifling bourgeois quality of her past life is carefully delineated, although, like most quasi-mysteries, "Betty" (Times-rated Mature) is more interesting and less schematic before we find out all the details of its protagonist's troubling life.

Aside from Chabrol's unadorned direction, the attraction of "Betty" lies in the performances by an accomplished pair of actresses. Audran is polished as usual, but the main focus is on Marie Trintignant as Betty. Trintignant, the daughter of actor Jean-Louis (who was once married to Audran), does a forceful job of creating a woman who, through all her secrets are revealed, is not much less of a mystery when this somber, unsettling film ends than when it began.

NEW YORK POST, 8/20/93, p. 26, Jerry Tallmer

You put Claude Chabrol together with Georges Simenon and what you come up with is one totally amoral film called "Betty." Amoral not immoral—but amoral is I guess, morally worse.

You also come up with high-class soap opera in French.

It also is something to watch, if only for the fugitive smile and great grace, as always, of Stephane Audran, and the question-mark smile and depravity-within-virginity of Marie Trintignant as the younger woman whom Audran drags back from the dregs, and who kicks her in the teeth for the favor. You know, no good deed goes unpunished. *La lecon*, you might say.

Actually it's sort of the same lesson as from "Madame Bovary," the last film Chabrol gave us. This time he's gone to Simenon rather than Flaubert, with results that are cinematically less boring.

Betty Etamble is a homeless beauty in her late 20s, driven out of her home for her misdeeds by her loving husband, drifting from bed to bed, bar to bar, until discovered (and rescued) in La Trou, the Hole, a joint with fish tanks, by Laure Levaucher, a well-to-do widow of 49, one-time trained nurse, who takes drunk, vomiting Betty back with her for R&R to Laure's suite in the chic Hotel Trianon.

Bit by bit, in a scattering of flashbacks, flash-forwards, and flash-sideways—it takes a degree of piecing-out—we learn Betty's story, starting with the death of her chemist father when she was 8. The girl was sent to live with an uncle and aunt in the Vendee, and there, at 15, in the wine cellar, she stumbled on Uncle shtupping Therese, the well-stacked maid, likewise 15. "Tell your aunt and I'll give it to you too," the uncle says, with menace.

He never actually laid a hand on Betty, but "since I was 15 I've been a whore to rival Therese," which is why a grown-up Betty would one day warn Guy (Yves Lembrecht), the younger, non-military son of a stiff military family, not to marry her. "You're crazy," she'd say, wiping the coffee off his suit. "Oui, je suis fou," he'd answer. A nice scene, with Trintignant very lovely.

So they were married. Two children came, two little girls. "But they're not my children now," Betty will presently declare to Laure. "In fact I don't think they ever were, except when I was expecting. Mother love is a thing in books. Even before they were born, I was 'The Mother.' "

When Betty's extracurricular habits with a saxophone player had finally, glaringly, stood revealed, Guy's ramrod mother said one cold word and Guy handed Betty a check for 200,000 francs in return for her instant departure and her signature on a paper that took away her children forever. I know something about documents like that out of my own boyhood without the 200,000; indeed, without Betty. What did not happen in my boyhood was Guy, later pleading for Betty to come back to him, and she almost gently sending him packing; another nice scene.

Besides, Betty had other fish to fry—with the keeper of the fish tank, Mario the bartender (Jean-Francois Garreau), good samaritan Laure's handsome young boyfriend. There is a showdown, a payoff, low-key and fatal. One party perishes, one survives. This is the clinical Simenon case history of a survivor. I don't think they have room for it in heaven, but it passes the time, here below.

NEWSDAY, 8/20/93, Part II/p. 69, John Anderson

Claude Chabrol's "Betty" follows on the high heels of his much-lauded "Madame Bovary," and if the celebrated French director has become fixated on self-destructive women, it's a good thing. And a progressive one. Where "Madame Bovary" was beautiful, stylish but decidedly anemic, "Betty" is full-blooded and dangerous.

Betty, whom novelist Georges Simenon based on a dissipated woman he met one night in a Versailles bar, is the dark side of Emma, if such a thing is possible. Both live comfortable bourgeois existences, both are married to men they find contemptible, and both allow their own wantonness to destroy their lives. The difference is the arsenic: Emma eats it, because, in the end, she has some sense of shame and desperation. Betty, ultimately a predator, has no shame, and therefore never gets desperate.

"Betty" is a disturbing film, because of what it makes us ask ourselves, and *how* Chabrol makes us ask. He establishes Betty, who is given a sensuous, vulpine quality by Marie Trintignant, as an object of pity. And though she ultimately lacks anything we're likely to call virtue, she continues to evoke sympathy—because in her pursuit of pleasurable, and not so pleasurable flesh, she's completely fatalistic and self-destructive, as well as being oblivious to the victims she's leaving in her wake. That these include her two children, whom she "sells" to her husband—in a separation agreement prompted by a flagrant incidence of infidelity—does nothing to make us dismiss her. We keep hoping she's got an alibi.

But even as Chabrol strips her of every dignity, and gives us a heroine devoid of character, we keep investing a certain amount of trust in her. Which tends to make us ask a few too many questions of ourselves.

We're being suckered, of course. We meet Betty, rain-soaked, drunk and hollow-eyed, stumbling out of a Paris bar with a man who could be anyone, but turns out to be a doctor (Pierre Vernier). He takes her to a Versailles restaurant called the Hole, where he notices her rubbing her arm with her fingers. You have an itch? he asks. It's the worms, he tells her, you have worms under your skin. The good doctor then prepares to extract them with a small scalpel he carries with him.

Betty, who doesn't seem particularly disturbed by any of this—or anything else, for that matter—is rescued by Laure (the wonderful Stephane Audran), a widow and Hole habitue who informs her the doctor is a junkie. The Hole is, in fact, full of lost souls; it could be a way station to hell. Full of "twisted" people, as the owner, Mario, readily concedes, it embraces Betty, and she it.

Laure, on whom Audran bestows a great deal of dignity, maturity and sex, has her own problems, including drink. But she takes the sodden Betty back to her hotel like a stray dog, nursing her, keeping her supplied with scotch and cigarettes, until Betty's story comes out.

She's been thrown out by her starchy husband—he and his mother have caught Betty *flagrante delicto*—and as we go back through her life, it's clear that she's a woman who's suffered by living in a man's world. As a young girl, she witnessed her uncle's rape of a maid; as an adult, she's been treated like breeder stock by her husband and mother-in-law. But Chabrol never allows the circumstances of her life to relieve her of culpability for her own acts. She's led a comfortable life; the offenses to her, while insulting, have never been fatal. The rape, in fact, happened to someone else. Her attempts to explain away, or allow others to explain away, her complete lack of scruples makes whatever affection we harbor for her even more pathetic.

The unfolding of Betty's history is a masterly example of stream-of-consciousness storytelling by Chabrol. Lines of dialogue suggest recollections that then appear, with the juxtapositions often very ironic and blackly funny. The director's use of small detail and amorphous morality make this a rich, troubling drama, which in the end is all a matter of control. Chabrol has it; Betty doesn't.

VILLAGE VOICE, 8/24/93, p. 64, Alissa Quart

In *Betty*, Claude Chabrol traces the unraveling of his antiheroine (Marie Trintignant) in yet another melodrama of the *bon chic bon* genre. Betty is discovered by an older upper-class woman, Laure (Stephane Audran), in Laure's boyfriend Mario's downbeat bar, near collapse (and of course all the more sultry) with drink and fear. After waking up mysteriously in Laure's chichi hotel suite, Betty recounts her childhood and failed marriage into the haute bourgeois, amid a steady stream of room service J & B.

Many of the techniques recall those of Chabrol's more successful films like *Le Boucher*. Betty's infirm narrative ripples with uneasiness. Her remembered traumas are played out in flashback over the drone of Laure's polite conversation. Continuity is subtly ruptured. The high-class melodrama is satirized in a nervous, ambience-heavy manner, as rattling glass bottles signify rape and dead fish in a tank business as usual. Chabrol is superb at managing a great deal of visual information, evoking a bar or a dinner party with meticulous economy.

What confounds the satire is that Betty's "moral" transgression is so tame: drink, affairs, a Deneuve-esque stint of prostitution. Her subversion is anatomized through a faux Freudian case study that teeters on the edge of send-up. One wonders why *Betty* goes to such lengths to give Betty a past, even if it is a spoof, ascribing a half-psychology to the classically trite bad girl while the other characters luxuriate flatly in their social types.

Laure's embrace of la waif, putting herself at risk and receiving diffidence in return, is inexplicable, but Chabrol regular Audran gives off the sense of enigmatic self-control that makes Laure's movement toward her almost plausible. Marie Trintignant's Betty is practically anticharismatic: the film locates her immorality in her empty eyes and bashed-tooth smile. In *Betty*, the bad girl dynamites the rules of the chattering classes, creating a tried-and-true opposition, with none of the repressed emotionality or interiority that might allow us to look beyond the cliché. Again this is the troubled no-way-out "feminism" present in Chabrol's *The Story of Women*, which in the end is no feminism at all.

Also reviewed in:
CHICAGO TRIBUNE, 10/1/93, Friday/p. D, Michael Wilmington
NEW REPUBLIC, 9/13/93, p. 28, Stanley Kauffmann
NEW YORK TIMES, 8/20/93, p. C12, Janet Maslin
VARIETY, 4/6/92, p. 167, Lisa Nesselson
WASHINGTON POST, 9/15/93, p. B8, Megan Rosenfeld

BETWEEN HEAVEN AND EARTH

An Arrow Entertainment release. *Producer:* Marion Hänsel. *Director:* Marion Hänsel. *Screenplay (French with English subtitles):* Marion Hänsel and Paul Le. *Director of Photography:* Josep M. Civit. *Editor:* Susanna Rossberg. *Music:* Takashi Kako. *Running time:* 80 minutes. *MPAA Rating:* Not Rated.

CAST: Carmen Maura (Maria); Jean-Pierre Cassel (Editor in Chief); Didier Bezace (Tom); Samuel Mussen (Jeremy); André Delvaux (Professor).

NEW YORK POST, 10/5/93, p. 22, Lawrence Cohn

The issue of women's and babies' reproductive rights is looked at from an entirely new point-of-view in the Belgian movie "Between Heaven and Earth" but result is a half-baked concoction.

Carmen Maura, who's made a terrific impression as the comic heroine of several Pedro Almodovar films, turns highly dramatic as a TV journalist in Brussels who becomes pregnant after being trapped in an elevator with a friend during a power outage.

She never names the father and is determined to have the child, raising it herself. Her maternal instincts get turned on in full force when she befriends young Jeremy (Samuel Mussen), a neighbor whose parents are neglectful.

Filmmaker Marion Hansel turns mystical when Maura's fetus starts talking to her (they converse in the film's language, French, even though Maura is playing a Spaniard living in Brussels). It tells her it doesn't want to be born, recalling an old Joan Collins horror movie on that theme but treated with utmost seriousness here.

Maura's baby turns out to be late and in the 42nd week of pregnancy she's assigned to do a story about overdue babies. This leads her to interview a professor (played by Andre Delvaux, Belgium's leading film director) who philosophizes on the subject, and gets her in trouble when she gets on tv and tells overdue moms to resist doctors' attempts to induce their labor.

Alternating between suicidal thoughts and hope for mankind, Spanish star Maura is very impressive in her histrionics here, well-delivered in French. The performance indicates that this talented star is overdue for serious roles (and a U.S. film assignment to boot).

Ultimately, Maura is left on a beach with the baby begrudgingly agreeing to be born. The notion of the unborn protesting being brought into such a hopeless world as we've created for them is sophomoric at best.

Short running time (the film lasts only an hour and 15 minutes) is appropriate to the essay. The supporting cast, including the great French actor Jean-Pierre Cassel as Maura's boss, has little to do.

NEWSDAY, 10/1/93, Part II/p. 71, Gene Seymour

Were one to mention that Carmen Maura, veteran of such wacky, over-the-top Pedro Almodovar classics as "Woman on the Verge of a Nervous Breakdown," stars in a film about a pregnant woman trying to talk her reluctant child out of the womb, you'd say, "Of course she is!" with the assumption that one was talking about a comedy.

Unfortunately, Marion Hansel, director of "Between Heaven and Earth," is deadly, drearily serious about this story of a Parisian TV journalist (Maura) who believes that all unborn children, not just hers, are choosing to stay unborn beyond nine months because the world is such a crappy place—and getting crappier. The premise is an interesting one, whether played for laughs or not. The communication between a woman and her unborn child offers a wealth of possibilities, any of whose development required a bold and daring imagination. Hansel's film goes no further in aspiration than the average made-for-TV movie about women in peril, complete with that genre's mind-numbing ooze of "sincerity."

In fact, Hansel so fervently believes in the import of her "message" that any humor or menace that might spice up things is forsaken in favor of a queasy frenzy that propels Maura's character in several agitated directions. She smokes and drinks so much coffee and wine during her pregnancy that you start wondering whether it's her poor pre-natal diet that sets off the bad vibes between mother and fetus.

But no. It's Maura's coverage of a terrorist bombing that starts giving the kid qualms about coming out. Eventually, Maura finds out that every pregnant woman she encounters is several weeks late on delivery. When she discloses her belief on TV that it's the babies themselves who are deciding to stay inside, she sets off a nationwide furor. She heads for the shore to talk things over with Junior. If he doesn't come out, she figures, no one else will. What starts out as an intimate drama about a professional woman coming to terms with a major life change mutates into an ineptly handled "Why-won't-anybody-believe-me" fantasy. It's a shame, because Maura could do a lot with a warm, serious role far better conceived than this.

VILLAGE VOICE, 10/12/93, p. 61, Leslie Camhi

Is life desirable? Marion Hansel's *Between Heaven and Earth* offers some provocative answers. Carmen Maura plays Maria, a single Parisian TV journalist who decides to bear the child resulting from casual, amicable sex in an elevator. Late in term, as she gulps down double espressos and rushes to cover bombings at the university, the fetus begins sending out unusual signals. "Nothing obliges us to live," she is informed in dreams.

Imagine that a strange presence suddenly takes root within and refuses to leave your body. The film's uncanny power stems from its exploration of "normal" maternal horror. Maria is not alone: in her 40th week, she uncovers a nationwide epidemic of prolonged pregnancies and induced labors resulting in stillbirths. Experts reach for explanations ranging from tidal irregularities to global warming, but Maria's inside source informs her that fetuses are simply refusing to be born into an inhumane world. It's one thing to tell this to your tranquilizer-prescribing doctor, and quite another to broadcast it on national television.

Maura, an Almodóvar favorite, is vital and regal; the other performances pale next to hers. *Between Heaven and Earth* falters as it seeks to translate into words and images the ineffable yet immediate forms of interuterine communication. It's hard to regard fetal images, at least in this country, without recalling their role in arguments that vilify the rights of women—and I'm not sure why the film's unborn are always already masculine. Still, there's something eerily moving in this portrayal of a fetus's ferocious refusal of life and a woman's troubled romance with the familiar and alien, loved and encumbering presence within her.

Also reviewed in:
NEW YORK TIMES, 10/1/93, p. C5, Stephen Holden

BEVERLY HILLBILLIES, THE

A Twentieth Century Fox release. *Producer:* Ian Bryce and Penelope Spheeris. *Director:* Penelope Spheeris. *Screenplay:* Lawrence Konner, Mark Rosenthal, Jim Fisher, and Jim Staahl. *Story:* Lawrence Konner and Mark Rosenthal. *Based upon the television series created by:* Paul Henning. *Director of Photography:* Robert Brinkmann. *Editor:* Ross Albert. *Music:* Lalo Schifrin. *Music Editor:* Steve McCroskey. *Choreographer:* Brad Jeffries. *Sound:* Thomas Causey. *Sound Editor:* Gary S. Gerlich and Gregory M. Gerlich. *Casting:* Glenn Daniels. *Production Designer:* Peter Jamison. *Art Director:* Marjorie Stone McShirley. *Set Designer:* Lawrence A. Hubbs and Evelyn Barbier. *Set Decorator:* Linda Spheeris. *Special Effects:* Richard Zarro. *Costumes:* Jami Burrows. *Makeup:* Brad Wilder. *Stunt Coordinator:* Mike Cassidy. *Running time:* 90 minutes. *MPAA Rating:* PG.

CAST: Diedrich Bader (Jethro and Jethrine); Dabney Coleman (Mr. Drysdale); Buddy Ebsen (Barnaby Jones); Erika Eleniak (Elly May); Zsa Zsa Gabor (Herself); Cloris Leachman (Granny); Dolly Parton (Herself); Rob Schneider (Tyler); Lea Thompson (Laura); Lily Tomlin (Miss Hathaway); Jim Varney (Jed); Linda Carlson (Aunt Pearl); Penny Fuller (Margaret Drysdale); Kevin Connolly (Morgan Drysdale); Lyman Ward (Chief Gallo); Leann Hunley (Miss Arlington); Ernie Lively (Briggs); David L. Crowley (Danforth); Mike Cassidy (Waters); David Byrd (Mr. Mackey); Patrick Cranshaw (Reverend Mason); Eric "Sparky" Edwards (Fat Elmer); Mickey Jones (Spittin' Sam); Robert Easton (Mayor Amos Jasper); Don McNatt (Billy Bob); James Schmid (Derek); Branden R. Morgan (Jake); Charlie Heath (Lance); James O'Sullivan (Coach); Annalee Spheeris (Girl in Car); Amy Golden (Girl in Bathroom); Eddie De Harp (Guard at Wedding); John Ashker (Guy in Jeep); Tony Dueñas (Gang Member); Nina Beesley (Clampett Maid); Ronan O'Casey (Man at Party); Gary Cervantes (Carlos); Gregory Wallace (Male Nurse); Sid Newman (Gabe); Taylor Gilbert and Marti Muller (Women at Party); Shawn Modrell (Flight Attendant); Gordon Moss (Hank); Carmen Filpi (Frank); Barbara "Babs" Friedkin and Chaille Hamilton Percival (Backup Singers).

LOS ANGELES TIMES, 10/15/93, Calendar/p. 1, Peter Rainer

You can feel your IQ plummeting while watching "The Beverly Hillbillies but since you lose 10,000 brain cells a day anyway, why not have a few laughs?

It's not exactly a ringing huzzah to say this film lives up to the long-running TV show. While that series, which ran on CBS from 1962-1971, was never as awful as its detractors claimed, it wasn't exactly Congreve either. It was a deliberately airhead sitcom with some expert comic actors—Buddy Ebsen and Irene Ryan—poking through the corn. Some of the routines were as old as vaudeville, but its staying power in syndication isn't undeserved: Some of those routines still have their nutball clout.

The film version, directed by Penelope Spheeris, lately of "Wayne's World," doesn't try to "enlarge" the show. Thank God. It plays on the audience's familiarity with the TV series, starting out with "The Ballad of Jed Clampett," and that's a canny commercial approach: there are no jarring new incidents or characters, no serial killers or flying saucers, although Beverly Hills is smoggier than it used to be and Jed has now been upgraded to billionaire status.

The superannuated boomers watching this film can re-experience their childhood gooniness without too much strain while the teens who currently catch the show in syndication can feel as if they're playing with a bigger and brighter version of an old toy. A movie like "The Beverly Hillbillies" (rated PG for "off-color humor") has a way of turning audiences into connoisseurs of pap. You sit there and actually begin to compare the virtues of Buddy Ebsen's Jed versus Jim Varney's, of Lily Tomlin's Miss Hathaway versus Nancy Kulp's, of Cloris Leachman's Granny versus Irene Ryan's.

Of such distinctions are film critics—and madness—born.

Spheeris and her team of writers (Lawrence Konner, Mark Rosenthal, Jim Fisher, and Jim Staahl) aren't real big on plot, which is probably all for the best. In this version of the legend, Jed treks to the hills of Beverly to find a wife—someone with the finishing-school finesse to make a lady out of his tomboy daughter Elly May (Erika Eleniak). Elly is first seen wrestling a bear (the bear loses). Her predilection for critters doesn't seem to extend to most of the male population at Beverly Hills High, where she pins the wrestling team captain. (The gibes at Bev High are sharp, like the shot of the cappuccino cart in the school hallway.)

In the TV show, Donna Douglas' Elly was tastefully bodacious, but Eleniak is closer to hubba-hubba. In fact, the whole revamped Clampett clan seems pumped and Nauticized. Varney, in a bold departure from his "Ernest" movies and "Hey, Vern!" TV commercials, gives Jed a coiled humor. When he sizes up a prospective wife you get the feeling he might want to do more than just listen to Hank Williams records with her.

Diedrich Bader's Jethro is even more galumphingly cloddy and manic than Max Baer's. Traipsing about in his jeans and work-boots, he seems like a refugee from the Village People. (He also plays Jethrine, Jethro's twin brother in drag. Don't ask.) Cloris Leachman, from some angles, is a dead ringer for Irene Ryan, and she has the same vim, though she doesn't really come into her own until the film winds up. She has her best moment in the afterglow of an electroshock therapy session—her hair is buzzed out and she has a supernal glow on her face. She went up against electricity and electricity lost.

Dabney Coleman mostly mugs up a storm as Mr. Drysdale, the banker who—you know this already, don't you?—sucks up to the Clampetts. Rob Schneider, in cahoots with Lea Thompson playing a fake French tutor, mugs even more. Subtlety isn't exactly the order of the day in "The Beverly Hillbillies": These actors must have decided that underplaying would be heresy. There's stiff competition for overplayers, including an orangutan that bowls perfect strikes.

Best in the cast is Lily Tomlin, who brings out Miss Hathaway's furtive, randy side—her thing for Jethro thaws her out. Tomlin is such a whiz at tight-mouthed, officious loons that the role might have been created for her.

Tomlin is a good reason to see the movie even if you're not a "Hillbillies" nut. But there are enough good dumb jokes scattered throughout to keep it fairly funny anyway, even if the shadowland between good dumb and just plain dumb dumb is often unclear in this film.

See it with someone you love—but not with someone you are trying to impress.

NEW YORK POST, 10/15/93, p. 29, Michael Medved

The most amusing moments in "The Beverly Hillbillies" come at the very end of the picture and help to illustrate what's wrong with everything we've seen before.

As the final credits roll, director Penelope Spheeris puts together a series of outtakes involving all the principal members of her talented cast, showing them each as spontaneous, charming, responsive performers.

It's precisely those elements of spontaneity and naturalness—the same elements that made Spheeris' work on "Wayne's World" such a pleasure—that are so sorely lacking in the rest of this picture. "The Beverly Hillbillies" comes across as stilted, forced, almost painfully unfunny—like a high school talent show tribute to "Hee-Haw."

The motion picture faithfully follows the familiar setup of the famous theme song from the beloved '60s TV show, but from the very beginning you know that the movie version will be bigger and broader—but not better—than the original.

When Jed Clampett (Jim Varney), the "poor mountaineer [who] barely kept his family fed," shoots at a rabbit and accidentally strikes oil. he provokes more than "bubbling crude": He absurdly unleashes four huge gushers that cover him with sludge.

A few minutes later, cousin Jethro (Diedrich Bader) makes a grand entrance by driving up in an old car that knocks over an outhouse—revealing Granny (Cloris Leachman) with her drawers down.

This sort of potty humor is typical of the consistent smuttiness that betrays the innocence and charm of the old TV show. The main focus of the movie's plot involves a sexy seductress (Lea Thompson) who wants to lure widower Jed into marriage in order to pilfer his billions.

Thompson, who is far better suited for the young mother role she played in "Dennis the Menace," is woefully miscast as a vamp; she competes with the stiff uncomfortable Varney (better known as his obnoxious alter ego, Ernest P. Worrell) for the distinction of the most embarrassing performance in this altogether embarrassing movie.

The best acting, on the other hand, comes from the least-known members of the cast: perpetually grinning Diedrich Bader as a convincingly lunk-headed Jethro Bodine and the luminous Erika Eleniak (who previously played the stripper who pops out of a cake in Steven Seagal's "Under Siege") as Jed's tomboy daughter, Elly May.

Both of these young players bring energy and freshness to their parts that is entirely absent in the tired work of old pros like Dabney Coleman (who plays banker Milburn Drysdale) and Lily Tomlin (as his ultra-efficient assistant, Miss Hathaway).

Director Spheeris still wrings a few surefire laughs out of the ancient catfish-out-of-water concept, but the idea of the Clampetts as unspoiled noble savages makes even less sense than it did 30 years ago.

With satellite dishes and VCRs regularly popping up in even the most backwoods shacks—and with Varney's Jed Clampett describing himself as a fan of Dolly Parton and Hank Williams we're still supposed to see these people as so naive that they've never before seen anyone expressing disrespect by raising a middle finger.

The film-going audience, on the other hand, is surely sophisticated enough to understand when half-hearted moviemakers are flipping the public the proverbial bird.

NEWSDAY, 10/15/93, Part II/p. 69, John Anderson

Penelope Spheeris oughta get tossed into the *cee*-ment pond.

The director of "Wayne's World," of which too much has already been said, is really grabbing for the brass ring with "The Beverly Hillbillies," a celebration of a television sitcom that was itself a celebration of imbecility. The film doesn't go anywhere the original Paul Henning production didn't; it even recycles some of the same jokes. And while reruns of the TV show might have some nostalgia value (harking back to when we actually enjoyed such idiocy) the movie is completely oblivious to its own irony. That is, with the exception of Lily Tomlin, whose Jane Hathaway is like a creature from another—better—movie.

One of the lamest television comedies ever produced, "The Beverly Hillbillies" was, and is, a sociological curiosity. The characters represent the two ends of America's social spectrum: The Clampetts, an Ozark family who become fabulously wealthy after they strike oil, move to Beverly Hills. The people around them, who were ever aghast at the Clampetts total lack of social grace, are snobbery personified. The great midsection of America, therefore, can laugh—when the jokes were actually funny—at characters they either hate or pity, and all of whom are objects of ridicule.

But while the upper class was devoid of any redeeming qualities, the Clampetts have a certain homespun innocence, especially patriarch Jed, a font of backwoods wisdom. Jim Varney, of the "Ernest" films, plays Jed Clampett with the same mix of naivete and what passes for common sense as Buddy Ebsen (he makes a cameo as Barnaby Jones), who originated the character. Cloris Leachman looks and sounds a lot like Irene Ryan, the first Granny; and Erika Eleniak, onetime Playboy featurette, is the same sweetly innocent sex bomb Donna Douglas was, only more so.

The truly irritating element in a film that generally makes you grit your teeth, is Diedrich Bader, who as Jethro Bodine is so stupid he makes paint look intelligent. Stupidity, though, is what "The Beverly Hillbillies" has always been about. So perhaps Bader's really giving the most effective performance.

The plot, as it were, involves Tyler (the ubiquitous Rob Schneider), an underling of the banker Mr. Drysdale (Dabney Coleman), trying to get Jed to marry his trashy girlfriend Laura (Lea Thompson) and steal all the Clampett money. It doesn't work, of course, but in the meantime we get to watch the Clampetts eat off the pool table, and Dolly Parton (playing herself) contribute her talents to a film that ridicules the same rural people who helped send her to Las Vegas.

SIGHT AND SOUND, 8/94, p. 37, Kim Newman

Accidentally discovering oil on his property, Arkansas backwoodsman Jed Clampett instantly becomes a billionaire and moves to Beverly Hills. There he hopes to find a suitable new wife who will raise his tomboy daughter Elly May to be a real lady. Along with Jed and Elly May come Granny, and Elly May's cousin Jethro. Banker Milburn Drysdale eases the Clampetts into society by buying them a mansion, ordering his son Morgan to look after Elly May in high school, detailing assistant Jane Hathaway to trouble-shoot and giving the lunk-headed Jethro a job as Vice-President.

Although Miss Hathaway originally mistakes the family for intruders, Jed trusts her and lets her take charge of the search for a wife. At school, Elly May helps Morgan out by humiliating the head bully by flattening him in a fight. Tyler, Drysdale's unscrupulous employee, schemes to get hold of the Clampett billions by passing off his girlfriend Laura as a French teacher. Entering the Clampett home to tutor Elly May, she sets out to woo the unworldly Jed. Granny catches on to the scheme just as the wedding is announced, and is packed off by the villains to an oppressive old people's home. As Clampett relations flock to California for the wedding, Miss Hathaway consults private eye Barnaby Jones, who tracks Granny to the home. Miss Hathaway and Granny invade the ceremony in time to expose Laura and Tyler. In lieu of a wedding, Jed decides to throw a party.

As mainstream Penelope Spheeris, *The Beverly Hillbillies* follows *Wayne's World* as an adaptation of a 60s TV sitcom, but it flounders in the wake of the *Addams Family* movies. Under any circumstances, it's a disaster which strains harder for fewer laughs than any non-Blake Edwards comedy in recent memory. The level of wit on display can be grasped from Laura's *'Allo! 'Allo!* French accent, whereby the expression "happiness is hard to find" comes out as "a penis is 'ard to find".

Jim Varney, toning down the obnoxiousness of his 'Ernest' character, is reasonably cast, and room is even found for Buddy Ebsen, the original Jed, by writing in a cameo for his other TV persona, geriatric 'tec Barnaby Jones (his age cruelly emphasised under the end credits in an out-take of him muffing a simple line). However, the Clampetts—except for the annoying Diedrich Bader as Jethro *and* his twin sister—get relatively little screen time, leaving the bulk of the humiliation to Lily Tomlin, who looks alarmingly like Leonard Nimoy in a wig, as the fumbling Miss Hathaway.

Pared down as if a merciless preview had decreed the removal of all excess footage (Elly May's high school sub-plot is especially perfunctory), this still hasn't got a single decent gag, and strains especially with a shot of the White House as 'Cousin Bill' searches for his missing invite to the Clampett wedding. Penelope Spheeris herself, heard briefly forgiving the cast for fouling up in the desperate blooper clips that end the film, is worlds away from her earlier careers. A trace element of her usual concern for music minutiae at least ensures that the classic "Ballad of Jed Clampett" is played mercifully straight, rather than replaced, *Addams Family* style, with a rap. However, the tune-in-next-week optimism of the closing lyric ("You're all invited back again to this locality to have a heapin' helpin' of the hospitality") seems misplaced—this is highly unlikely to be rewarded with a sequel.

Also reviewed in:
CHICAGO TRIBUNE, 10/15/93, Friday/p. N, Michael Wilmington
NEW YORK TIMES, 10/15/93, p. C20, Janet Maslin
VARIETY, 10/18/93, p. 51, Todd McCarthy
WASHINGTON POST, 10/15/93, p. D1, Hal Hinson
WASHINGTON POST, 10/15/93, Weekend/p. 41, Desson Howe

BEWARE OF A HOLY WHORE

An Anti-teater-X-film/Nova International production.   *Director:* Rainer Werner Fassbinder. *Screenplay (English and German with English subtitles):* Rainer Werner Fassbinder.   *Director of Photography:* Michael Ballhaus.   *Editor:* Franz Walsch and Thea Eymèsz.   *Music:* Peer Raben, Gaetano Donizetti, Elvis Presley, Ray Charles, Leonard Cohen, and Spooky Tooth.   *Art Director:* Kurt Raab.   *Running time:* 103 minutes.   *MPAA Rating:* Not Rated.

CAST: Lou Castel (Jeff);   Eddie Constantine (Himself);   Hanna Schygulla (Hanna); Marquard Bohm (Ricky);   Rainer Werner Fassbinder (Sascha);   Ulli Lommel (Korbinian); Margarethe von Trotta (Production Secretary);   Kurt Raab (Fred);   Ingrid Caven (Extra); Harry Baer (Her Husband);   Werner Schroeter (Deiters).

NEW YORK POST, 7/9/93, p. 29, Jerry Tallmer

Toward the end of "Beware of a Holy Whore" the terrible-tempered fellow named Jeff who is the director of the movie inside the movie—the one that they're all gathered here to make in this empty Spanish hotel—screams to the world at large, his co-workers, his bedmates (male and female), his slaves: "If I can't smash something I might as well be dead!"

He really didn't have to tell us. Jeff's been screaming since the first moment he arrived—days late—with an explosion of: "I ask for a palace, you give me a dump." The money from Bonn has run out. Producers come and go, with more interest in horses than film. Everybody's making passes at everybody, of all sexes. There's nothing to shoot with. The cameraman's overdue and so is the star—Eddie Constantine; with a face pickled in mahogany. "For once in my life," Jeff screams, "I wanted to make a movie without responsibilities." Then he smashes a glass.

Later, when somebody asks what the movie's all about, Jeff says icily: "It's about brutality. What else can one make a movie about?

He really didn't have to tell us. Jeff meant political-social-economic brutality, but this movie—the one wrapped around the one inside—reeks with something even crueler, casual personal brutality, the kind that has Jeff cracking a cast-off lover (female) across the face three times, *smack, smack, smack.* "I'm not shooting one foot of film unless that woman's off the set!" Jeff snarls as he hurls two or three more Cuba Libre glasses across the lobby.

Now the interesting thing is that Jeff (actor Lou Castel) is a manifest stand-in, or surrogate for Rainer Werner Fassbinder, the extraordinary young man who would make this film, "Beware of a Holy Whore," in 1970, at the grand old age of 23, would whip out 43 fairly astonishing films in all before drugs and booze and fury snatched him off in 1982, at age 36.

The other interesting thing is that Fassbinder himself is *in* the movie in gleaming white suit and black shirt, playing the disagreeable walrus who is Jeff's aide-decamp and all-purpose production manager, as given to screaming and brutal irrational behavior as his chief. There are many survivors of the Fassbinder dramatic commune who can testify to that behavior. When all's said and done, it is Fassbinder, putting the words in Jeff's mouth—"The worst thing is when one discovers how bourgeois one is oneself"—who passes the harshest judgement on Fassbinder.

NEWSDAY, 7/9/93, Part II/p. 59, John Anderson

Fellini has explored the self-indulgent madness of the filmmaker ("8½," "Intervista") but the point of view has always been from Federico's head. When Fassbinder decided to explode *his* artistic process, though, the point of view was considerably lower.

Rainer Werner Fassbinder, who died in 1982 of a toxic mix of cocaine and alcohol, made "Beware of a Holy Whore" in 1970, a year in which he made six feature films. Shot on a breakneck 22-day schedule, the film concerns a bored, sexually delinquent cast and crew of a film—Fassbinder's "Whitey" was the reputed model—that is short on money, material and patience.

The cast, waiting for its director to show up, gets more and more hysterical, which Fassbinder links to their increased sexual activity, of the hetero-, homo- and bisexual varieties. Small betrayals, both real and imagined, contribute to the nervous atmosphere. Leonard Cohen and Elvis bleat from the jukebox. They need a leader, but when Jeff (Lou Castel, wearing Fassbinder's leather jacket) finally arrives, it's not his guidance that draws the rest of the people together, but his irrational, abusive behavior.

Fassbinder, who plays the ill-tempered production manager Sascha, explores themes that had obsessed him before—including power, sexual power, political power, his own power—and "Whore" is the last film where he deals with them so straightforwardly. His pudgy, decadent, pockmarked face is just one of the many great faces here: Eddie Constantine, playing Eddie Constantine; Hanna Schygulla, Fassbinder favorite, playing "Hanna" and looking like a cross between a teutonic Marilyn Monroe and a corrupt Shirley Temple; plus Kurt Raab, Ingrid Caven, Magdalena Montezuma and other members of the Fassbinder film commune.

In retrospect, Fassbinder seems the most representative example of the New German Cinema, the vanished movement of the late, '60s and early '70s that included Wim Wenders and Volker Schlondorff, if only because he seemed to live with the same license he brought to the screen. Earnestly homosexual, a champion of the working class, he abused substances the way he abused lovers and actors. "Whore" shows how well aware he was of his own nature, the nature of moviemaking, and the impossibility of attaining true collaboration in a medium that needs a singleness of vision. For James Joyce, the cracked looking glass was the symbol of Irish Art; for Fassbinder, the plight of the filmmaker is summed up in the scene in which Jeff Fassbinder's alter ego, stands alone at the middle of a flight of stairs, reading about himself in a newspaper.

VILLAGE VOICE, 7/13/93, p. 56, Hilton Als

Once upon a time, in a hotel by the sea—a sea as blue as a peacock's eye and with white clouds over it—a troupe of actors, a script girl, lighting technicians, producers, and one makeup artist lay in wait for their director. The director had already slept with many of the cast and crew assembled, making, in the process, cheap promises he had no intention of keeping. The promises usually involved future offers of work he had no plan to fulfill. The director was German as were the majority of his crew, many of whom, sitting in the white hotel lobby, ordering Cuba libre after Cuba libre, expounded thoughts (and nonthoughts) on the meaning of community. None of the cast and crew mentioned Marx. Without their director, this community did not seem to function well. They cried, indulged in petty bickering, lied, borrowed money, gossiped. When the director finally arrived and began to indulge in *his* petty bickering, lies, infidelity, the community became one, which is to say everyone made a film whose theme, in this case, was state-sanctioned violence. This scenario-scripted and directed by Rainer Werner Fassbinder and called *Beware of a Holy Whore* (1970)—was according to the director, a "break" from the type of work he had done before, which included a number of plays for the Antiteater in Munich and 11 films.

Beware of a Holy Whore (shot in near-record time: 22 days in Sorrento, Italy) was a coda to his earlier work. That work, which often had a paralyzing effect on me, was stagy and seldom cinematic. Except for the director's consciousness in the mouths of others, nothing stirred on the screen. What Fassbinder relied on before *Holy Whore* was the actors' presence to make the images work, most notably Hanna Schygulla's. What Hanna conveyed: blond churlishness, desire in the seams of her dress, relative muteness.

In *Holy Whore*, Fassbinder began his most interesting experiments with film as medium: cheap stock; faces made up to appear more plastic, immovable, while the actors moved (for the first time) in conjunction with the camera.

Holy Whore ushers in the new film body—Fassbinder's own: bloated, aggressive, seductive, demanding to be seen. That whore (cinema according to Fassbinder) is among the most beautiful he has ever known. Watch her method of seduction most carefully as Schygulla, moving soundlessly in space, hears and conveys what Fassbinder's cinema would become: an amalgamation of violence and formal purity. In it, her shape (Schygulla's) is impervious to the shouts of others as Ray Charles demands, "Let's Go Get Stoned."

Also reviewed in:
CHICAGO TRIBUNE, 10/22/93, Friday/p. F, John Petrakis
NEW YORK TIMES, 11/12/76, p. C8, Vincent Canby

BLACK CAT

A Headliners Productions release of a D&B Films Co. production. *Executive Producer:* Dickson Poon. *Producer:* Stephen Shin. *Director:* Stephen Shin. *Screenplay (Cantonese with English dialogue; Chinese and English subtitles):* Lam Wai-lun, Chan Bo-shun and Lam Tan-ping. *Director of Photography:* Lee Kin-keung. *Editor:* Wong Wing-ming, Kwok Ting-hung, and Wong Chau-on. *Music:* Danny Chung. *Sound:* Leung Lik-tsi. *Art Director:* Fu Tsi-tsung. *Special Effects:* Gary Paller. *Make-up:* Tibor Farkas. *Costumes:* Lau Bo-lam. *Stunt Coordinator:* Owen Waistrom. *Running time:* 91 minutes. *MPAA Rating:* Not Rated.

CAST: Jade Leung (Catherine); Simon Yam (Brian); Thomas Lam (Allen Yeung).

LOS ANGELES TIMES, 10/13/93, Calendar/p. 5, Kevin Thomas

Stephen Shin's "Black Cat" is Hong Kong's answer to "La Femme Nikita"—and also to its American remake, "Point of No Return." As such, it packs plenty of punch and should please devout fans of Hong Kong action flicks. There are several virtuoso set pieces, but John Woo has nothing to fear.

The film divides neatly into three half-hour parts. The first is composed entirely of deftly sustained: nonstop action—with plenty of Hong Kong-style violence—as a truck driver, apparently somewhere in Upstate New York, makes the literally fatal mistake of coming on too strong to a waitress (Jade Leung) at a truck stop cafe. Leung quickly wastes him, then a cop plus several others before she's shot down herself.

When she regains consciousness she finds herself in the hands of the CIA, which has had implanted in her brain a microchip designed to emit periodic jolts of pain that can be relieved only by a medication doled out by the agency.

She has no alternative but to spend the next year in training to become a CIA superagent. This takes up another half-hour of screen time almost as lively as the first section. At last she's ready to be turned loose, and is assigned to Hong Kong, where she is to work as a photojournalist—and where she falls in love with another photographer (Thomas Lam).

It's a long way from slinging hash at that trucker's cafe to an elegant Hong Kong high-rise apartment, but how is Leung to manage a successful love affair and at the same time be on constant call from the CIA? In her film debut, the trim, pretty Leung handles action as adroitly as Schwarzenegger or Stallone, but as appealing as she and Lam are, their romance is conventional and slows down the final third of the film.

Shin certainly is skillful, but "Black Cat" (Times-rated Mature for violence, some sex) is essentially routine, an all-too-obvious kickoff to a series that already has its third installment in production. Not helping matters is that the print being shown is scratchy, worn-out and its color murky in the utmost.

NEW YORK POST, 10/30/93, p. 15, Thelma Adams

Stephen Shin's "Black Cat" is another "La Femme Nikita" clone. The Hong Kong director only forgot two things: coherence and character. The result is a cat full of howlers rather than a trim and compelling thriller on shapely legs.

Tough-girl Catherine (Jade Leung) works a turnpike truck stop. Enter a bad Schwarzenegger imitator, complete with swagger, cigar and garbled Austrian accent. He's horny, she's harassed. He gets served a fork through the back of his hand.

Catherine kills the trucker and lands in a few women-behind-bars brutal matron scenes that leave her so black-and-blue she looks a plague victim. Upon escaping, she takes a bullet in the chest only to be resurrected by the CIA. Apparently, they need chick assassins who look good in spandex.

To keep Catherine obedient the agency plants a micro-chip or "black cat" in her brain. Brian (Simon Yam) teaches his Black Cat the mechanic's trade and turns her loose on the free world to kill and kill again. What could stop this killer cat?

Love. Catherine meets Allen (Thomas Lam), a guy with his heart in the right place (even if the screenwriters insist the pump's on the right side of his chest—can they do that?). Romance softens Catherine's trigger finger. To protect his investment, Brian demands the ultimate loyalty test.

Besides looking good in black, Jade's Catherine is a cipher. By turns sulky and hysterical, she hits her marks, but who knows why? Nikita was a natural-born killer, Black Cat is a puss with attitude. Still, if Hollywood could copycat "Nikita" with "Point of No Return" why not Hong Kong?

This Asian action flick has a "B" movie, trash appeal. For those on the continuity squad, there are abundant laughs. A drive through downtown Manhattan passes the Vancouver Hotel. Catherine heads for a hit in heels, and escapes in flats.

At one point, Brian dispatchs Cat to kill the World Wildlife Fund chief. I still can't figure out why the CIA demands his extinction, but the scene provided my favorite line "Why are you so interested in wildlife?" an edgy reporter confronts the environmentalist.

Look out for Jade's return in "Black Cat II: Assassination of President Yeltsin." The third cat is already in pre-production. We can hardly wait.

NEWSDAY, 11/29/93, Part II/p. 79, John Anderson

Given the presumption among U. S. audiences that they are the center of the film universe (which is actually probably somewhere in India), "Black Cat," is a rather humbling experience.

This virtual remake of "La Femme Nikita" (to say nothing of its illegitimate child, "Point of No Return") was shot largely in the West, but was clearly intended for Hong Kong audiences. As such, it cares about as much for Western perceptions as our films usually do for the East. Continuity? Comprehensible subtitles? Forget about it. You will, however, have to make sense of Australian-accented policemen in Vancouver, which according to "Black Cat" is located somewhere in the Catskills. But there's plenty of action, and the cinematic solecisms add a note of hilarity to the proceedings.

Catherine, who will become Erica (and is played by newcomer Jade Leung), has a bad attitude already when the trucker with the Arnold Schwarzenegger accent pulls into her truck stop, makes his crude advances and all hell breaks loose. Coming to amid the blood and broken dishes of their donnybrook-in-the diner, Catherine—gun still in hand—fires and kills a cop. This, of course, prompts the all-Caucasian police force to beat her Asian backside almost all the way home to Hong Kong.

The CIA, intrigued with Catherine's talents—she consistently breaks out of jail, and delivers delicious retribution on her tormenters—has her officially "killed" and puts her in a rigorous training program, after implanting a microchip called the Black Cat in her brain. Under the tutelage of her mentor Brian (Simon Yam), she becomes an efficient administrator of U.S.-sponsored violence; her first hit is the bride at a Jewish wedding, where all the ushers carry Uzis.

Sent to Hong Kong, Erica finds love, doomed and beautiful, via Allen (Thomas Lam), a photographer she meets while undercover. He knows nothing of her secret life, but you can bet he'll find out. And it won't be pretty.

With the critical success of director John Woo, and the increased American appreciation of Asian film in general, Hong Kong action movies have acquired a certain cachet—and one has to assume that's why this film is being released here. But a film like "Black Cat" has to be approached as what it is—stylish, perhaps, but definitely goofy, simple and aimed straight at the adrenal glands.

Also reviewed in:
CHICAGO TRIBUNE, 12/10/93, Friday/p. B, John Petrakis
NEW YORK TIMES, 10/29/93, p. C10, Stephen Holden
VARIETY, 6/22/92, p. 46, Derek Elley

BLACK TO THE PROMISED LAND

A Blues Productions presentation. *Producer:* Renen Schorr and Madeleine Ali.   *Director:* Madeleine Ali. *Director of Photography:* Manu Kadosh. *Editor:* Victor Nord. *Music:* Branford Marsalis. *Sound:* Yossi Vanon, Amir Boverman, Danny Natovich, and Shai Zauderer. *Running time:* 97 minutes. *MPAA Rating:* Not Rated.

LOS ANGELES TIMES, 10/8/93, Calendar/p. 10, Kevin Thomas

In 1989 Stewart Bialer, a science teacher at the Bedford-Stuyvesant Street Academy High School, escorted 11 of his students, all of them black, to a three-month stay at a kibbutz at the foot of the Golan Heights. Such an undertaking is obviously a natural subject for a documentary, and debuting filmmaker Madeleine Ali, who happens to be both black and Jewish, has done it justice with her lively and thoughtful "Black to the Promised Land."

Not surprisingly, the announcement of such an unusual venture became a media event in New York. This stung the young people, six boys and five girls ranging in age from 15 to 18, for they were instantly characterized as juvenile delinquents because the Street Academy is an alternative school for kids with problems.

In any event, they're bright, articulate and outgoing, especially the girls, who have downright dazzling personalities—but their hosts in Israel are honest enough to admit that they were apprehensive about extending hospitality to "criminals."

The new kibbutzniks from Brooklyn are instantly taken with the peace, quiet and safety of their new crime-free, drug-free environment but initially loathe the highly organized life and exhausting work there. They are expected to get up early and do either farm or factory labor, including, ironically, picking cotton—"I felt like Kinta Kunte," says one girl.

They've also become media savvy: When early on in their visit they're interviewed for Israeli TV, they flash megawatt smiles and insist they love kibbutz living.

Time is on the side of both the Israelis and the African-Americans as they get to know one another. The kids learn the value of structure and discipline in daily life and also the importance of people sharing with and caring for each other. Their experience is not all work and no play, and a highlight for most of the young people is a visit to Jerusalem on Easter.

At the same time they destroy negative stereotypes of American blacks that some of their hosts held and bring fresh life to the kibbutz. One young Israeli boy, expecting the worst "because of their environment," remarks at their departure: "They're great. They're so cool: I love their style."

That departure is bittersweet indeed. Some of the visitors flat out don't want to leave their new friends, almost certainly the only white acquaintances they've ever had. One girl had remarked earlier, "It's like a fairy tale, and I don't want to wake up." '

"Black to the Promised Land" is Times-rated Mature for language.

VILLAGE VOICE, 11/3/92, p. 60, Carolyn Cohen

Black to the Promised Land, straddles two cultures. This documentary, by Madeleine Ali, a Jewish, African American director, follows the trip that 11 black teenagers from Bedford Stuyvesant took with their Jewish teacher to an Israeli kibbutz. It begins with a collage of their life back in Brooklyn: The camera careens through scarred streets and abandoned apartments. "Just say no" is scrawled on walls where kids converge to sell drugs. A school poster—"Are your high school classmates going to kill you?"—is juxtaposed with rap songs about African American heroes.

The film uses interviews to narrate the students' journey. The camera forces them to see themselves as performers in their own lives. Some interviews elicit simplistic, glib responses, but others resonate with ambivalence. In one, a girl mocks her work in Israeli cotton fields; later, she savors the quiet and safety of kibbutz life. The students teach dances to the Israelis, and in turn learn Purim dances. It's mesmerizing to watch how easily bridges can be built between cultures.

But the film ends with harsh truths. Back in Brooklyn, rap music and jazz throb as the students return to their broken lives. One is assaulted; another learns his brother has been beaten. Now they can no longer accept this numbing landscape as home.

Also reviewed in:
VARIETY, 6/15/92, p. 57, Dennis Harvey
WASHINGTON POST, 4/30/93, Weekend/p. 44, Joe Brown
WASHINGTON POST, 5/1/93, p. G3, David Mills

BLUE (France/Switzerland/Poland)

A Miramax Films release of an MK2 Productions SA (Paris)/CED Productions (Paris)/France 3 Cinema (Paris)/CAB Productions (Lausanne)/TOR Production (Warsaw) coproduction with the participation of Canal Plus/Centre National de la Cinématographie, supported by the Fonds Eurimages of the Conseil de l'Europe. *Producer:* Marin Karmitz. *Director:* Krzysztof Kieslowski. *Screenplay (French with English subtitles):* Krzysztof Pisiewicz and Krzysztof Kieslowski. *Screenplay Collaborators:* Agnieszka Holland, Edward Zebrowski, and Slawomir Idziak. *Director of Photography:* Slawomir Idziak. *Editor:* Jacques Witta. *Music:* Zbigniew Preisner. *Sound:* Jean-Claude Laureux, Pascal Colomb, and (music): Rafal Paczkowski. *Sound Editor:* Claire Bez, Bertrand Lancios, and Jean-Claude Laureux. *Casting:* Margot Capelier. *Set Designer:* Claude Lenoir. *Set Decorator:* Marie-Claire Quin, Jean-Pierre Delettre, Christian Aubenque, Julien Poitou-Weber, and Lionel Acat. *Costumes:* Virginie Viard and Naima Lagrange. *Make-up:* Valerie Tranier and Jean-Pierre Caminade. *Running time:* 97 minutes. *MPAA Rating:* Not Rated.

CAST: Juliet Binoche (Julie); Benoît Régent (Olivier); Florence Pernel (Sandrine); Charlotte Véry (Lucille); Hélène Vincent (Journalist); Philippe Volter (Estate Agent); Claude Duneton (Doctor); Hugues Quester (Patrice); Emmanuelle Riva (Mother); Florence Vignon (Copyist); Jacek Ostaszewski (Flautist); Yann Tregouet (Antoine); Isabelle Sadoyan (Servant); Daniel Martin (Downstairs Neighbor); Catherine Thérouenne (Neighbor); Alain Ollivier (Lawyer); Pierre Forget (Gardener).

CHRISTIAN SCIENCE MONITOR, 12/6/93, p. 16, David Sterritt

Polish director Krzystof Kieslowski prefers not to make one movie at a time. Although he has made many stand-alone films, including "The Double Life of Veronique" two years ago, his most celebrated work is the "Decalogue," a series of 10 movies on issues suggested to Kieslowski by the Ten Commandments.

His newest picture, "Blue," is the first part of a trilogy inspired by the colors of the French flag—blue, white, and red, standing for liberty, equality, and fraternity. Blue symbolizes freedom to Kieslowski, but his film is no simple celebration of the satisfactions and challenges of liberty.

Like most of his finest works, such as "No End" and the "Decalogue" spinoff called "A Short Film About Killing," it probes the mysteries of its subject on physical, psychological, and even spiritual levels.

Lending further resonance to the story is the fact that it doesn't deal with freedom in a comforting form but focuses on unwanted freedom, which confers independence at the expense of familiar limits and boundaries.

The picture is not wholly successful, and some reviewers find its delicately crafted images too arty and artificial. It was received enthusiastically by many spectators at the recent New York Film Festival, though, and has won prizes at the Venice and Chicago filmfests; so it's now heading to commercial screens with a fair amount of momentum.

The main character, played with exquisite grace by Juliette Binoche, is a young woman who has just suffered a devastating tragedy: the death of her husband and daughter in a car accident. Since her spouse was a renowned composer—whose latest work, an orchestral piece meant to encourage global peace, was incomplete when he died—the artistic world takes a strong interest in her, and in her plans for sharing the composer's musical legacy with his former colleagues and admirers.

She wants nothing to do with the media-bred sympathy that comes her way in the aftermath of her enormous loss. Her new freedom is something she never asked for or wanted, and her only desire is to return some kind of order to her life.

But this is complicated by a couple of unexpected factors. One is the startling realization that her husband had a lover who meant a great deal to him during the last part of his life. Another is the music world's discovery that she secretly helped her husband compose his music, hiding her assistance, and allowing him to receive all the credit.

Besieged by these developments, she attempts to forge a new life away from the public eye—and to reconcile her own needs with increasingly urgent moral obligations.

"Blue" is at its best when Kieslowski uses cinematic means to express the inner life of its heroine, whose tentative but growing awareness of her right place in the world—no longer dependent on fame, possessions, professional secrets, or even family relations—is reflected in the delicate forms and sensuous colors of Kieslowski's impressionistic images, photographed by Slawomir Idziak.

This effect is enhanced by Zbigniew Preisner's beautiful score, which plays an even more important role in "Blue" than in "The Double Life of Veronique," also about a woman whose personal growth is intertwined with musical activity.

In the end, "Blue" is not as satisfying as Kieslowski's best movies, largely because its finale—optimistic and uplifting, but superficial and a bit arbitrary—doesn't live up to the richly evocative events that precede it. Kieslowski shouldn't be criticized too harshly for falling short of the unusually high expectations he builds, but the ending of "Blue" suggests that he hasn't yet plumbed the depths of the vast philosophical questions that fascinate him so much.

LOS ANGELES TIMES, 12/8/93, Calendar/p. 1, Kenneth Turan

It is a mark of the virtuosity with which director Krzysztof Kielowski has made "Blue" that it is possible to envision its intensely emotional story of a woman's search for meaning after tragedy unhinges her life becoming, with slight tinkering, the plot for a standard-issue Bette Davis "women's picture" of the 1940s.

Yet there is nothing ordinary or banal about the way Kieslowski, a Polish director now working in France, has gone about his business here. Though he starts with conventional story elements, he conveys them with a striking combination of focused acting, unexpected images, music strong enough to be a physical presence, and a sensitivity to light, color (blue, not surprisingly, is a visual leitmotif), and textures.

This kind of complete filmmaking gives "Blue" (Rated R for "some sexuality") a sense of emotion that is both pared down and intensified. Daring in its willingness to risk looking maudlin by dealing with extremes, "Blue" doesn't hesitate to explore spiritual and psychological states that are beyond many films.

"Blue's" official name is "Three Colors: Blue" and is envisioned by Kieslowski (whose previous 10-part "The Decalogue" indicated a proclivity for multiple stories) as the first of three films named after the colors of the French flag and investigating the concepts of liberty, equality and fraternity.

Liberty is in the dock here, but it is not the conventional notions of freedom that Kieslowski and co-screenwriter Krzysztof Piesiewicz are concerned with, but the more philosophical notion of freedom from people, possessions and even ambition, things that to many people define—not limit—life.

To Julie (Juliette Binoche), "Blue's" protagonist, these are not theoretical concerns. In the film's opening segments, she loses both her husband, a celebrated composer, and her young daughter in a terrible automobile accident in which she herself is seriously injured.

When she is well enough to reclaim her life, Julie decides to dramatically cut it back, obsessively wiping out all traces of her past self, from her belongings to human attachments, that she now regards as traps. These include the affection of Olivier (Benoit Regent), her husband's associate, and the score of the Concerto for the Unification of Europe, a major commission her husband was working on when he died. Put in simplest terms, Julie wants to disappear.

Two things stop her, one being the peskiness of life itself, which stubbornly refuses to go away and leave her alone. A series of small moments and unexpected events, insignificant in themselves, ever so delicately combine in "Blue's" careful script to raise the possibility of Julie's reconnecting to the world even as she doesn't want to.

A more powerful force is the music that is in her head, the music for that European concerto (in which Julie apparently collaborated with her husband) that will not leave her alone. Penetrating and transfiguring, it is the kind of work we have come to expect from Zbigniew Preisner, who frequently collaborates with Kieslowski and did the haunting score for his "The Double Life of Veronique."

And this music isn't heard in any ordinary background way. Rather Kieslowski uses it as emotional punctuation, bringing it up in strong, short bursts, accompanied by flashes of light, when it forces itself into Julie's mind. Should she run her finger over the score, we hear what that finger has touched, and should she attempt to destroy the written record, we hear that happening, too.

This unconventional use of music is paralleled by the subjective, expressionistic camera work of Slawomir Idziak, who, along with Binoche and the film itself, took a prize at the Venice Film Festival. Filled with unexpected close-ups—and darting, swooping movements that leave you unsure where the camera will go next, what it will chose to see, Idziak's mysterious cinematography adds to "Blue's" sense of excitement and discovery.

Though after her work in "Damage" and "The Unbearable Lightness of Being" Juliette Binoche can hardly be classed as a discovery, it is always startling to re-experience the glass-shattering honesty and integrity of her performance. The idea of simply walking through a scene is alien to her, and in that sense she is perfect for this artfully made film, dense with feeling, in which no shot is ordinary and no moment taken for granted.

NEW LEADER, 4/11-25/94, p. 20, David Bromwich

Krzysztof Kieslowski's *Blue* had a short run in New York, but it is the most interesting film I have seen in the last year or so, and Kieslowski is one of the most rewarding directors alive. The first of a trilogy in French—whose other parts, *White* and *Red*, will be released by Miramax—*Blue* is a story of oblique energy and intelligence about the work of mourning. A woman in her 30s survives the car wreck in which her husband and child perished. She sees the funeral on videotape during a brief stay in a hospital, and memories of the dead tug at her like an unspoken request.

Her husband was a famous composer; his notes for an unfinished work have to be sorted out. Their house has grown too big for her; she must settle in an apartment somewhere in Paris. None of this is the same as finding a new life or caring to find one. So too, the hero of *Remembrance of Things Past*, after his grandmother's death, took a sip of water and realized that this accidental reflex of continuing life broke the perfectness of his grief. *Blue* is about the second and third sips.

Juliette Binoche plays the heroine, and it is a role she has long been working toward. In *The Unbearable Lightness of Being* and in *Damage*, the lines of her face and even her smile spoke of a life of suffering. *Blue* is a richer film that actually earns the weight of her look. Binoche is in almost every frame, and we see her watching things—with revulsion, then resistance, then with a clarity that is grave without being heavy. She visits her mother, who is mentally dead, and the TV in the convalescent home shows inexplicable soundless images of bungee-jumping: a metaphor eerily resonant with her own suspense between death and life.

In her apartment she hears a squeaky noise, and finds in the broom closet a litter of mice. Since putting a stop to any life is a thought she cannot bear, she borrows a neighbor's cat. The incident is worked for neither pity nor humor. The brutal practicality grates against the tenderness, and the emotions are left at a standoff. Then she makes another discovery, that her husband had a mistress. Visiting the woman, she finds her pregnant with his child: more life, more equivocation.

No End, [see *Film Review Annual, 1988* for reviews] a film Kieslowski made in 1984 lately released on video by New Yorker Films, is a parallel story that sheds a good deal of light on *Blue*. The heroine is another survivor, but one whose mourning leads to suicide. Her husband, Antek Zyro—a name with the half allegorical shading Kieslowski sometimes favors has died in his 30s of a heart attack. He was a lawyer, in the midst of his advocacy of a Solidarity protester, and the wife picks up the loose ends. She connects the protester with an established lawyer who advises the man to soften his dissidence and agree to cooperate with a politically sanctioned labor union. The protester makes his compromise, and gains his freedom. His bowing to pressure is not shown as a defection from love or idealism. The heroine's suicide is not shown as an evasion of the political struggle.

Kieslowski, who was born in 1941, belongs to the first Polish generation to grow up with habits formed in the postwar years. His stories do not concern the prosperous or the life-fulfilled. Ambition, the trait whose assertion or absence shapes all the characters in movies from the commercial democracies, is, for the men and women Kieslowski portrays, simply not one of the relevant properties of life. They appear to strive in human dealings for the effect he aims at esthetically, an ordinary accuracy of vision. When you come to think about it, this quality is miraculous and as rare as any persistent virtue.

The Double Life of Veronique, [see *Film Review Annual, 1992* for reviews] in America the most widely seen of Kieslowski's films, gave a misleading clue to his temperament. It made some people instantly regard him as a piece of French sophistication whose beliefs were possibly mystical and certainly pretentious. There is, in truth, a mystical element in his fascination with death—personified in *The Double Life* in the figure of the marionette artist who keeps contact with a dead Polish woman and her look-alike in Paris. In all his films, death is a nearly personified power of chance and force, the singular fact that proves our lives do not belong to us.

I took *The Double Life* to be partly an allegory of a man who left one country to make films in another, an exiled artist's uneasy act of assent to life in translation. The richness of the images, the suffusions of color that were part of a romance of place as well as person, deflected attention from this premise. In movies, where visual tricks like a single actress playing two parts are legitimately expected to give an account of themselves, the enigmatic relation between the living and dead sharers of the same life seemed a cheat, as it would not seem if you encountered it in a long story by Kleist or Hoffmann. Still, *The Double Life* has a wonderful consistency in its treatment of outward exile and inward affinity, themes close to Kieslowski everywhere.

The better one comes to know this director, the longer one's patience grows. The sense is strong in all his work of people caught in the toils of habit, or brought low by an unspectacular dip of fortune. The physical beauty of his images and the intuitive rightness of his details have been remarked by all his admirers, but Kieslowski's ear is as attentive as his eye in effects of musical scoring and sound mixing. An interior scene of a couple drinking coffee and quietly conversing will be penetrated by dim noises from elsewhere: the sounds of traffic, or feet on stairs, or a door slamming in the night.

Political circumstances in Poland may have left their mark on Kieslowski's style in the form of a reticence one is apt to read as wholly personal. His emphasis on individual scenes and the expository depth of many of them—itself a reaction against the glibness of montage—makes for a family resemblance that his films share mainly with each other. Among influences, I sometimes think I can see traces of Bergman at the abstract extreme of *The Silence*, or the naturalistic extreme of *The Passion of Anna*. The invention that worked so well in the latter film, where Bergman turned the actors toward the camera and had them talk about the characters they played, is imaginable in a film by Kieslowski, but in his version the characters would talk about themselves.

Something like this does happen in *No End*. The heroine, in a coffee shop, glances at an American sitting at a nearby table, whose hands remind her of her dead husband's. The young man reads the glance as a solicitation: "Fifty dollars?" Because she desires not to be known, she nods and takes him to a hotel. After they make love she speaks, in Polish, a soliloquy that comes as close as the film ever does to explaining her feelings about her life. It is important that the man not understand her words, and just as important that the words be said.

Sex in these films is not the subordinate fact most serious films make it out to be. A neighbor of the heroine in *Blue* is a live-sex performer in a disco joint, dismayed when she sees her father once in the audience. Why, asks the heroine, do you do it? "I like to. I think everybody does." Sex can have a motive close to despair, but its exertions come from an irreducible demand that is one of the few things in life beyond suspicion. On the other hand, erotic pursuit and mastery are far from a concern that Kieslowski's people can cherish. "I make films," he has said, "about how hard it is to live." That difficulty belongs to a world of conscious effort and not of drives or hungers.

The moral ground-note of his work can be heard very steadily in *The Decalogue* (now available from Fox Video). This sequence of 10 stories, filmed in the late 1980s, deals with the inhabitants of an apartment complex in Warsaw. One episode goes to each of the ten commandments, but the plots are often at an angle to the transgression named. It is initially hard to place, for example, the story of a young woman tempted by feelings of gratitude and resentment to the brink of incest with her father; the temptation eludes definition and seems so accidental as to defy naming. Again, the episode for "Thou shalt not kill" turns out to refer to the brutal killing of a cab driver by a passenger, but also to the penalty of capital punishment.

The Decalogue is infused with a pity both common and uninsistent-a view taken by one human creature, who happens to be an artist, of the vicissitudes of others. Though his pity is Christian in its bearings, Kieslowski has no more regard for religion than for any other practice of ritual or compulsion. The metaphysical hypothesis in which he sets some store is the idea of magical links between person and person, or between a single person and a fate. This is a hard intuition to get onto film. Writing does it by verbal echoes, repetitions, calculated shifts of mood and tense or hints that belong to rhetoric more than to grammar. Kafka could imply on any page of his books a retrospective self-defeat in acts that carried no apparent token of determinism. Kieslowski has to rely more literally on echoes of face or gesture, visual coincidences that have a shadowy explanation, and now and then quotations from writers.

The prudent old lawyer in *No End*, having obtained the release of his dissident client, reads aloud some lines of poetry to comfort a success that is also an end of defiance. These lines tell about a wolf who has become a mangy dog, with a glint no longer of cunning but of age in his yellow eye. The wolf asks pardon from those who may have expected a more savage bravery. We are even smaller, he says, than our more realistic hopes, but that is how things are. It is a characteristic thought for Kieslowski—impartial in its sympathy for those who accept the pardon and those who ultimately refuse to ask it.

Blue closes with the heroine assisting a friend who is trying to finish her husband's uncompleted work. She knows rather better than he how to compose in her husband's style; there are suggestions that she wrote much of his music all along, so that his death was for her the loss of a mask. The friend, a man of more modest gifts, says of his own additions to the score: "This music can be mine. It will be a little heavy and awkward." She goes back to him, for the time being, and makes love to him. On that strange and familiar gesture—a consolation she can give rather than take—the first part of Kieslowski's trilogy ends. I look forward to parts two and three.

NEW STATESMAN & SOCIETY, 10/15/93, p. 34, Jonathan Romney

Holland also turns up as script consultant in the credits of another Polish expatriate venture. [The reference is to *The Secret Garden*; see Romney's review of that film.] *Blue* is the first of a trilogy by Krzysztof Kieslowski based on the colours of the French flag and the notions of Liberty, Equality, Fraternity. It's hard to know how the other two-thirds will relate to it, but this first part looks incomplete, a suggestive but unfocused pendant to the extraordinary *Double Life of Véronique*.

Once again set in France, it features Juliette Binoche as a woman who loses her husband and daughter in a car crash and ventures out into the world for a life of untrammelled anonymity. The freedom she seeks is, of course a chimera.

Because its theme is so close to the surface, it is much less resonant than *Véronique*, with its often mystifying but always fascinating elaborations on the *doppelgänger* theme. Once again, Kieslowski and cinematographer Slawomir Idziak distort the recognisable world into something imbued with an unearthly charisma. For my money, this baroque approach yields far more than the visual literalism of Kieslowski's acclaimed *Decalogue*, but it also opens him up to the temptations of mysticism. This is what scuppers the film, in a cryptic final sequence that seems to gesture tendentiously at the ultimate unitedness of all souls. *Blue* is far more potent when it just gives you a coffee cup or a hanging lampshade to mull over, or luxuriates in the color of the title. Still, the film coaxes out of Binoche's withdrawn sullenness an enigmatic depth it hasn't had in ages. After her shop-dummy turn in Louis Malle's *Damage*, that's really something.

NEW YORK POST, 12/3/93, p. 39, Thelma Adams

What's intriguing about "Blue" is how few words are spoken and how much of the story is told through sound, music, and visual imagery.

"Blue" is the first movie in Polish director Krzysztof ("The Double Life of Veronique") Kieslowski's tricolor trilogy. Along with "Red" and "White," it will provide variations on the French flag and motto, "Liberty, Equality, Fraternity," with a thrust that is primarily personal as opposed to political.

"Blue" explores liberty in terms of the odyssey of a young French widow (Juliette Binoche). When her husband, a famous composer, and daughter, Anna, are killed in a car crash, Julie is at liberty to remake her life.

Julie burns her husband's unfinished score and gobbles a lollipop left by her daughter. She sells off everything and leaves her chateau with no more than a cardboard box and an inner scream.

The widow cuts her final, compelling tie to her old life: the unrequited love of her husband's apprentice. With a startling technique, Julie seduces Olivier (Benoit Regent) and abandons him. A woman of few words, she gets straight to the point: "I'm like any other woman. ... I have cavities. ... You won't miss me now."

Julie is beautiful, small-boned, doe-eyed, lithe and centered; she is also stubborn and strong-willed, empowered by the self-absorption of the distraught. Binoche delivers an intense performance as a widow in deep denial who discovers that a radical break with the past doesn't necessarily liberate an individual from grief.

Known in America for her roles in "Damage" and "The Unbearable Lightness of Being," Binoche won best actress—and "Blue" garnered best picture—at the 1993 Venice Film Festival, The movie was a serious contender for the best foreign film Oscar until last month, when it was disqualified on a technicality.

This otherwise crystalline film does have trite spots. A prostitute befriends Julie. Awakened in the night by a desperate call, Julie visits the sex shop where Lucille (Charlotte Very) works. While naked performers grind in the background, Lucille reveals why she panicked: Her father sat in the audience that night and nearly saw her live-sex act.

Equally weak is the plot twist that shocks Julie out of her isolationism: She discovers that her husband had a mistress before the crash. Even worse, the mistress is carrying his child.

But Kieslowski strings cliches elegantly. What remains are indelible blue-tinged images: An external shot of Julie and Olivier making love—pressed against a window, as fluid as creatures captured in an aquarium; little girls in water wings leaping into a swimming pool, a flock of angels, a fleeting reminder of Anna; and a death-defying octogenarian bungee-jumping on a blue TV screen.

Binoche herself remains the strongest image in "Blue." The actress creates a portrait of grief and healing, of liberty surrendered to love, expressed through a deep-gazed silence as compelling as any monologue.

NEWSDAY, 12/3/93, Part II/p. 93, Jack Mathews

The declared subject matter of "Blue," the first leg of Polish director Krzysztof Kieslowski's trilogy of colors, is liberty, but the predominant tone is black. The movie is about profound grief, the story of a woman plunged into emotional darkness after the accidental deaths of her husband and young daughter.

This whole "Three Colors" concept—the colors of the French flag equated with the "Liberte! Equalite! Fraternite!" cry of the French Revolution—seems little more than a strained conceit, and we'll have to wait for "Red" and "White" next year to see if they add up to anything more.

In the meantime, "Blue," in French with subtitles, stands shakily on its own legs as a contemporary study in mourning, propped up in large measure by the powerful performance of Juliette Binoche.

Binoche, Jeremy Irons' dangerous lover in "Damage," plays Julie, the wife and musical partner of a famous French composer who is killed in a car crash in the opening scene. Surviving that accident, and a subsequent suicide attempt, Julie attempts to erase her pain by disposing of the possessions she shared with her husband, including the unfinished composition he was writing for a celebration of the Unification of Europe.

Taking an apartment in Paris, Julie attempts to vanish in the midst of humanity, like a single note buried in a symphony, and to drown her sorrows—and herself, if she can get up the nerve—with daily swims in the building's indoor pool.

Soon, she learns there is no escape, either from her personal grief or from the society around her. There are other forces, other egos, at work—the prostitute (Charlotte Very) with the wounded soul who befriends her, the mistress (Florence Pernel) carrying her husband's baby, the associate (Benoit Regent) trying to finish and take credit for his last composition.

All of this moves at the pace of healing itself. "Blue" is a dirge, as much as a story, and Zbigniew Preisner's moody classical score is as important a character in the film as the music of Mozart was in "Amadeus." A couple of scenes, where Julie runs her finger across sheets of music and the notes come alive on the soundtrack, are virtually lifted from "Amadeus."

Kieslowski is also something of a composer. There isn't a scene in "Blue" that doesn't draw your attention to its composition—reflections, shadows, geometric patterns, the movement of the camera, the way the music interacts with the action. The movie is awash in self-conscious artifice, and often to the detriment of the film's moods.

When Julie tosses her husband's sheet music into a trash compactor and the notes on the soundtrack begin to crumple and groan, a moment of intended emotional anguish is suddenly transformed into low comedy.

But if Kieslowski ("The Double Life of Véronique") is too much of an artist and experimenter for his own good, he does make striking images, even when dealing with tragedy.

In that fatal opening sequence, we don't actually see the car crash. We overhear the father telling a joke, during a bathroom break on a country road, while we stare at a fluid dripping—rhythmically, ominously—from one of the car's vital organs. As the car lurches forward, we anticipate the horrible screeching and crunching that follows.

Liberty does play a supporting role in "Blue." Julie learns that grief is her captor and that only by letting go of her past can she be free of her pain. It's not much of a revelation, in the grand scale of human psychology, and it is certainly not what the revolutionaries were hollering about two centuries ago in France.

For the moment, we'll have to consider "Blue" the first installment of a work in progress, and see if "Red" and "Green" will create a full palette.

SIGHT AND SOUND, 11/93, p. 54, Geoffrey Macnab

Julie, a young French woman, loses her husband and child when the family car careers out of control on a remote country lane and crashes into a tree. Badly injured in the accident, she tries to commit suicide on waking up in a hospital bed, but her attempt is thwarted by a vigilant nurse.

At the time of his death, Julie's husband Patrice, a famous composer, had been working on a piece of music to be performed simultaneously by 12 different orchestras in all the EC capitals. While Julie is convalescing in the hospital, a journalist visits her, asking if she will finish the piece herself, and enquiring whether the rumour is true that she wrote all of Patrice's music; Julie refuses to answer. Discharged from the hospital, she returns to the family château, sorts through her belongings, and instructs her lawyer to sell everything. She even destroys Patrice's remaining work. After spending one night with Olivier, a composer friend, she tells him to forget about her. Hiring an anonymous apartment in Paris, she tries to build a new life, away from her past acquaintances and music. She makes occasional visits to her elderly mother, who is living in a nursing home. Otherwise, her time is spent in a daze, as she swims, potters round her flat and grieves. Her one new friend is her neighbour Sandrine, a prostitute whom the other neighbours want to evict. Julie refuses to sign their petition, and Sandrine is allowed to stay.

One night, she receives a call from Sandrine, who had been performing in a striptease joint, and had spotted her father in the audience. As she is consoling Sandrine at the club, she notices her own photo is on television, in a programme about Patrice. Interviewed by the journalist who harassed Patrice in the hospital, Olivier admits he has been commissioned to finish the piece. Julie is amazed that any of the score has survived, and alarmed by pictures showing Patrice with another woman. She searches out Olivier and offers to help him. She also quizzes him about the "other women" and learns that he had been unfaithful for years. Julie tracks down Patrice's mistress, a successful lawyer, eventually confronting her in a restaurant cloakroom. The mistress claims Patrice loved her. Julie accepts this, but is shocked to discover the lawyer is pregnant with Patrice's baby.

Having completed the score, Julie offers it to Olivier. He refuses to accept it, saying he can't take credit for her work. Julie resumes her relationship with him. Learning the château has not yet been sold, she moves back in herself, and begins to make provisions for the lawyer's baby. The lawyer is not surprised by her decision, saying Patrice had always emphasised she was an honourable woman.

After the privations endured by the saints and sinners of Kieslowski's Polish *Dekalog*, where moral choices had to be balanced against political and economic necessity, and where austerity was the watchword, life—at least in material terms—has become very much easier for the protagonists of *Trois Couleurs: Bleu*. The first part of a trilogy, with each film taking as its starting point one of the shades of the tricolour, *Bleu*'s ostensible theme is liberty (equality and fraternity, white and red, are to be its sequels).

It is not freedom of choice or expression that concerns the director here, but a rather more abstract notion of individual freedom. Although the picture is nominally inspired by one of the great revolutionary symbols, Kieslowski and his scriptwriter Krzysztof Piesiewicz are singularly uninterested in invoking the spirits of Danton and Robespierre. Their 'unpolitical', almost Proustian project is to consider how far individuals are able to detach themselves from family, memory and material objects, the very things which give most lives a definition.

The film is seen entirely from the perspective of a recently bereaved woman who, in her grief, tries to sever all links with the past. Our first sight of her, a huge close-up of the side of her face, emphasises this is to be her story. Slowly, she flickers into consciousness. Refracted on her iris as she lies in her hospital bed is the image of the doctor, telling her she has lost her husband and child in the car crash. We are seeing through her eye.

What has been described as Kieslowski's "luminous, numinous and ominous" visual style is much in evidence. As in *The Double Life of Véronique*, reasonably familiar landscapes— French countryside, Parisian city scenes—are given an eerie, uncanny quality. Fields are draped in mist, streets are labyrinthine, and there is the same vertiginous sense of time distorted. It is never really clear whether the story takes place over days, weeks or months. Any narrative progression is haphazard, occurring through chance or coincidence. In a cafe, Julie just happens to hear a street busker playing snatches of her husband's last, uncompleted work on his flute. She just happens to catch a glimpse of herself on television. She just happens find out about her husband's mistress.

The only common thread linking these random events is music. There are frequent, highly stylised moments of near-epiphany when the action freezes as Julie experiences some pang of involuntary memory, and the music blasts out on the soundtrack. At first, she seems overly obsessed with the myth of her husband's genius, and there is a danger the film will become bogged down in a ponderous elegy for the dead composer. But *Bleu* is not so much about celebrating the 'great' man as exorcising him. It turns out that Patrice was far from the model figure she remembers; and there are constant hints that he didn't actually write the music himself.

Perhaps Julie was the composer all along. Perhaps, indeed, Kieslowski is taking a sly dig at the whole cult of the auteur.

Arguably, *Bleu* follows more in the tradition of the French New Wave than of its director's Polish-based work. In particular, it echoes Godard's *Vivre sa vie*, in which Anna Karina was similarly cast adrift in the big city landscape. Not only do Binoche and Karina look remarkably alike, with identical haircuts and the same, mournful stare, but both pictures portray women struggling to live their own lives in a world where men pull the strings. And both directors seem intoxicated by their stars. Like Godard with Karina, Kieslowski risks aestheticising Julie's sense of isolation. With its swirling classical music, sumptuous production values and *la belle* Binoche at its core, there are moments when the movie seems like an upmarket brandy commercial. But it is rescued from the dead end of arthouse chic by a riveting central performance and the director's always idiosyncratic eye for detail. Kieslowski manages to convey Julie's grief most effectively through almost throwaway images. She stares in morbid fascination at a rat tending its litter; her gaze seizes on countless little objects, many of them, predictably enough, blue: under her scrutiny, these take on immense, totemic significance. Although the film veers toward the melancholy, there are moments of mordant humour, notably when we discover Patrice's dying words were nothing more profound than the punch-line to a stale joke.

In the end, *Bleu* seems anti-climactic. Julie comes in from the cold, resumes her relationship with her irritating lover, who has been pursuing her round the city like a droopy St Bernard dog. She completes her husband's score for him and makes provisions for his mistress's child. Yet, banal as this all is, the film finishes with a flourish. The music, so far heard only in staccato fragments, is finally played in full as the camera pans from Julie and her boyfriend, encased like ornaments behind a glass screen, across a series of *tableaux vivants* of the main characters featured in the film—among them Julie's elderly mother and the wide-eyed boy who witnessed the accident. It's a glorious moment, and one which testifies to Kieslowski's ability to startle us with his formal virtuosity, even as his narrative crumbles round him.

Perhaps Kieslowski is, as his supporters so ardently proclaim, the most important film-maker in Europe; but his blithe abandonment of social issues and retreat into a remote, mystical realm where personal experience is all that matters, do not augur well for the future.

TIME, 12/6/93, p. 90, Richard Corliss

Most serious European directors would never admit it—they'd say it's a form of movie idolatry endemmic only to Hollywood—but they love to stargaze. They will pay an attractive actress on-screen for 1½ hours and mostly ... just ... watch ... her. She poses at a window, she listens to the phone ring; in a moment of high agitation she may drag on a Gauloise. A vision of dyspeptic distress, she is a modernist pinup for the monastic voyeur behind the camera. When the woman is lovely, pouty Juliette Binoche, and the director is Krzysztof Kieslowski, the picture can become the X ray of anguish: not stargazing but soul gazing.

Kieslowski, a Polish filmmaker now working in France, has an imposing European reputation from his 10-part series *Tje Decalogue* (still unreleased in the U.S.). His Franco-Polish *The Double Life of Véronique* earned its star, Irene Jacob, the best-actress award at last year's Cannes Film Festival. His new *Blue* won Binoche the best-actress prize this September in Venice. So Kieslowski knows two or three things about showcasing beautiful women. He gives them an identity crisis, locks them alone in a Paris apartment and puts their chic, bleak spirits handsomely on display.

In *Blue*, Julie (played by Binoche) has every reason for her swank suffering. Her composer husband and their young daughter have died in a car crash from which Julie barely escaped. So she hides away from her friends and herself. "I don't want any love, memories, belongings," she says. "Those are traps." It takes her the length of the film to realize that isolation is the deadliest snare, that the only release is art and passion. But the true drama can be found in Kieslowski's meticulous images. Cool and seductive, they are the perfect frame for Binoche's harried glamour.

VILLAGE VOICE, 12/7/93, p. 63, J. Hoberman

Until a few years ago, Krzysztof Kieslowski was one of Europe's poor cousins. The most ambitious director still working in Poland, he seemed condemned to refine his sardonic brand of neoexpressionist mysticism explicating the inner lives of those who dwelt in dreary Warsaw housing projects. Then the Communist state with all its subsidies, crumbled, and, in characteristically reluctant triumph, Kieslowski entered Le Department Store.

With his 1991 co-pro *The Double Life of Véronique* illuminating the far from crowded French sky, Kieslowski became European. (One British critic has proclaimed him the most "truly European" of directors.) *Blue*, which had its local premiere at this year's New York Film Festival, seems a salute to the post-Cold War order. It's the first panel in a triptych of features, each named for a chunk of the French *tricouleur* and meant to illustrate one of its ideals: *Liberté, Egalité,* and *Fraternité*. The idea might have sprung full-grown from former culture minister Jack Lang's brow, but Kieslowski's examination of revolutionary concepts in the postideological world seems ambivalent even in its ambivalence.

The identification of liberty with loss seems inevitable. Euro-freedom per Kieslowski is a purely individual and negative state. Julie (Juliette Binoche), the protagonist of *Blue*, is liberated after her husband—"one of the most important composers of our time"—and their young daughter are killed in a car wreck. The accident was as avoidable as it proves decisive. (In the newly published *Kieslowski on Kieslowski*, the director suggests that all deaths are in some way willed: "one can say it's cancer or a heart attack or that the person falls under a car, but really people usually die because they can't go on living.")

Julie, however, is not yet ready to die. Unable to take poison, she becomes a superbly lit icon of sorrow; free of material want and family obligations, she imagines she is even through with history. She declines to finish and rather chooses to destroy her husband's magnum opus, an incomplete concerto written, with bland Kieslowskian irony, as a celebration for the so-called Unification of Europe. (There is no suggestion that Warsaw was among the 12 European capitals where the piece was to have its simultaneous premiere. In any case, Kieslowski is the virtuoso here.

Blue opens with the camera positioned under the wheel of a speeding car. The crack-up is heralded by absurd omens—a blue foil candy wrapper flutters out the car window, a hitchhiker succeeds in getting a ball in a cup just before the (offscreen) crash. For all the movie's crypto-New Age belief in the power of crystals and transmigration of souls, Kieslowski's fascination with absurd coincidence—the beach ball rolling out of the car wreck—is itself a leap of faith. Few other filmmakers have left so little to chance.

Kieslowski can begin a scene with a close-up of blanket lint or the reflection in a spoon. strike a compositional balance on an impossibly shallow depth of field as though it were a tightrope. His light-bending, space-warping style is predicated on impossible angles, aural shock cuts, and unexplained shifts in illumination. The main beneficiary is his star: Operating within a narrow range of diffidence, determination, and anxiety, Juliette Binoche's slightly smudged features register a dozen shades of icy perfection. (Given Kieslowski's concern for textures, she's almost disturbingly svelte.) Her gaze serves to reproach the world while, with her enigmatic behavior, she herself is an object of contemplation.

Blue's jangling, jarring structure keeps the narrative provocatively off-kilter and the chronology obscure, particularly as Kieslowski has a taste for sensory hallucinations. Even more than *The Double Life of Veronique*, which was also scored by Zbigniew Preisner, *Blue* seems motivated by a desire to make music tangible. Julie's surges of emotion are signaled by a blast of her husband's composition and a quick fade-out and back to the same frozen moment. When she's startled awake by the heavy chords, the music swirls around her as mysterious mini-UFOs of blue light. (Later, the score shrieks in protest as she tosses it into a trash compactor.)

Abandoning her husband's château, the widow moves to a fabulous empty apartment in an obscure part of Paris. *Blue* presents a mockingly gaga, slightly futuristic sense of Western affluence—luxury hospitals, capacious sex clubs, and TV wired right into our life. ("To this day, Kieslowski claims to make features according to documentary principles," reports the introduction to *Kieslowski on Kieslowski*.) A transistor Sony is propped on Julie's pillow so that she can watch her husband and daughter's funeral; when she tells her senile mother that all attachments are "traps," the ubiquitous TV beams out a grotesque image of a free fall.

Living alone, Julie ritually cleanses herself with violent dips in a (naturally, empty) blue pool, doggedly refusing to become involved with the various friends, neighbors, and crime victims who cross her path. The revelation—again via TV—of her late husband's infidelity only frees her from another set of memories. Ultimately confounded by the life-force (memorably embodied by the litter of rats she discovers in her closet), she finds herself doing what she might have done anyway. If Kieslowski seems the most paradoxical of Catholic filmmakers, it is not only because his is a spirituality without God. *Blue* seems to have been made to reconcile the idea of liberty with the director's own mordant notions of predestination.

Too bombastic to read as hopeful, *Blue*'s ending is a sort of claustro-cosmic music video, suturing most of the principals (and even offering an image of the unborn). The ostensible celebration of interconnection comes straight from AT&T, the characters might have stepped out of the pages of *Vogue*, but, if nothing else, the mad brio of the montage renews Kieslowski's commitment to the movies.

Also reviewed in:
CHICAGO TRIBUNE, 2/11/94, Friday/p. C, Michael Wilmington
NATION, 12/20/93, p. 780, Stuart Klawans
NEW YORK TIMES, 12/4/93, p. 16, Vincent Canby
NEW YORKER, 12/13/93, p. 122, Anthony Lane
VARIETY, 9/20/93, p. 28, Lisa Nesselson
WASHINGTON POST, 3/4/94, p. C7, Hal Hinson
WASHINGTON POST, 3/4/94, Weekend/p. 44, Desson Howe

BLUE (Great Britain)

A Basilisk Communications/Uplink production in association with Channel 4/The Arts Council of Great Britain/Opal/and BBC Radio 3. *Producer:* James MacKay and Takashi Asai. *Director:* Derek Jarman. *Screenplay:* Derek Jarman. *Music:* Simon Fisher Turner. *Sound:* Marvin Black and (music) Markus Dravius. *Running time:* 76 minutes. *MPAA Rating:* Not Rated.

VOICES: John Quentin; Nigel Terry; Derek Jarman; Tilda Swinton.

CHRISTIAN SCIENCE MONITOR, 10/12/93, p. 14, David Sterritt

[*Blue* was reviewed jointly with *Raining Stones*; see Sterritt's review of that film.]

LOS ANGELES TIMES, 5/12/94, Calendar/p. 12, Kevin Thomas

As the ravages of AIDS, which claimed Jarman's life Feb. 19, began to rob this most visual of filmmakers of his sight, he took on the most formidable challenge imaginable: to make a movie that would be entirely aural except that the screen would stay a sky blue—for 76 minutes. Jarman may have lost his sight but not his vision, for "Blue" is amazingly involving, an oratorio of soaring and richly varied sound and music as well as prose that verges on the poetic. Jarman charts the progress of his terminal illness with a terse, clinical detachment; these diary-like remarks punctuate an impassioned celebration of life and love in the face of a forthrightly accepted impending death.

NEW YORK POST, 4/8/94, p. 36, Thelma Adams

When you know you're about to die, why buy new shoes?
Derek Jarman knew he was dying of AIDS when he made "Blue." He cast off the visual and narrative trackery of "Caravaggio" (1986) and "Wittgenstein" (1993). Out of a deathwatch candor came the British director's most profound film.
"Blue," though experimental, remains accessible. For the entire feature, the screen is swimming pool blue, a blank canvas for the thoughts of the viewers, as shallow as a billboard, as deep as space.
Blue mood. Blue sky. Blue funk. Blue seas.

The screen serves as a metaphor for the blindness Jarman suffered during his decline. We not only sympathize with Jarman, we enter into his illness. Without visual stimulation, we turn inward. As Jarman's body wasted away, his mind remained "bright as a button."

The movie functions on one level as a Buddhist exercise, an effort to "walk away from illness." But, as a voice, presumably Jarman's, acidly points out, Buddha "wasn't attached to a drip [intravenous device]."

With its textured sound track and brilliant sound editing, "Blue" can't be confused with a minimalist film.

The voices of Jarman and actors who have worked with him in previous films (Tilda Swinton, John Quentin and Nigel Terry) weave together memories, medical history, bits of news (Bosnia is on Jarman's mind), philosophical meditations, and snatches of song.

Simon Fisher Turner composed the moody, other-worldly score. Electronic music whiz Brian Eno also contributed.

Like the hospital waiting rooms which come to signify hell-on-earth for Jarman, he creates a space between living and dying where we can contemplate loss: his and our own. Says Jarman, "This is a hard wait."

The wait is now over for the British director, AIDS carried him off this year. In the end, he had neither time for regrets nor platitudes. The movie celebrates passion between men ("kiss me again ... greedy lips") and expresses the universality of suffering (needles figure large in the fears of all hospital patients).

Jarman bridles at the term "living with AIDS," saying that the virus was "appropriated by the well," and finding no comfort in movements and quilts. His deathwatch is an intimate vigil, uncertainty a personal demon.

As blindness set in, Jarman's vision was never clearer, his work never more honest. The movie begins and ends with prayer bells. The final "Blue" mood is oddly restful, like the pause after a long, tiring swim.

NEWSDAY, 4/8/94, Part II/p. B7, John Anderson

Ironic, isn't it? That Derek Jarman, one of the more breathtakingly dangerous and painterly filmmakers of the last half-century, should be best remembered for a 76-minute film whose only visual content is a brilliant blue screen? It's the kind of twisted epilogue Jarman would have appreciated.

And did, in fact. At last fall's New York Film Festival, Jarman, who knew he was dying, told Film Comment, "It's going to be my most successful movie, which is completely mad."

Not so mad, though. For the director to spend his career creating lush images and homoerotic agitation, and then dispense with "pictures" as we know them, seems a somehow logical and inevitable summing up of a career shortened by AIDS. Perhaps having a fatal disease distills the artistic impulse. It certainly distilled the art.

The disease is as much a subject of the film as Jarman, who died in February—knowing he'd had the HIV virus for the last half-dozen years—and it's a film as deeply personal as it is interactive. Sit as close to the screen as possible; block out the intruding light, the visual detritus and let your eyes be monopolized by the blue. Ostensibly unchanging, the screen will pulse and mutate, as will your mind.

What we see mirrors what Jarman saw, after retinitis started taking his sight. "I have no friends who are not dead or dying," the voice says, after the sound of bells—which also end the film, and lend to it an odd sense of ecclesiastical closure—introduced the narration.

Over the sound track by Simon Fisher Turner, Jarman, through the voices of Nigel Terry, John Quentin, Tilda Swinton—and in one brief moment himself—rages and fantasizes, drips irony and relates anecdotes that are obscurely personal, or maudlin, or moving. The overall effect, though, is fairly devastating.

SIGHT AND SOUND, 10/93, p. 40 Chris Dark

A group of voices, Derek Jarman's amongst them, accompany an unchanging image, a blue that fills the screen completely. These voices, supplemented and punctuated by sound effects and music, relate fragmentary details of the director's treatment for symptoms of the HIV virus, the experience of slowly losing his sight, of meeting others undergoing similar treatment, of living with the virus. The voices also mourn the deaths of friends, consider the plight of those caught up in the war in Sarajevo and relate anecdotes of the travels in mythical lands of a character called Blue. Throughout the film the voices meditate on the colour itself, its place in nature and its spiritual qualities as well as bursting into bawdy song.

Blue is, quite simply, blue, and over the duration of Jarman's film the single colour makes of the frame a combination of canvas, mind screen and eye. *Blue* is the colour of silence, subjectivity and suffering.

To talk of a film that has such a carefully worked and impressionistic soundtrack as 'silent' may seem perverse, but it is a silence that is installed at the level of the image, a strategic silence that Jarman has chosen in response to what he calls "the pandemonium of the image". It is suitably ironic, then, that *Blue* should have been premiered at this year's Venice Biennale where it shared exhibition space with work by Oliviero Toscani, the photographer responsible for the shocktactic images of the infamous Benetton advertising campaign. Toscani and Benetton, and more specifically the notorious campaign image that depicted a dying HIV patient surrounded by his grieving family are perhaps only the most notorious examples of clamorous 'event-images' that serve ultimately to publicise only themselves, losing sight utterly of the specific realities from which they generate their self-serving controversy.

In the face of such images and their heavily mediated profligacy, *Blue* retains the 'silence' of abstract painting—influenced notably by the monochrome work of the French painter Yves Klein, who himself died an early death at the age of 34. But its silence is one pregnant with the subjective responses of artist and spectators alike. For the form of the work provokes an active viewing which the soundtrack has been designed to elicit—its combination of monologue and prose—poem, sound and music occasionally coalescing to lyrical, almost song-like effect. This property will be most fully accommodated by the simultaneous broadcast of *Blue* on Channel Four and Radio Three, the old Brechtian idea of "separation of the elements" receiving here a novel, multi-media twist. The soundtrack works to spark the spectator's own images off the silent blue canvas; this is a film that takes place as much in the spectator's head as it does onscreen—"an infinite possibility becoming tangible", as Jarman puts it in one of the monologues.

The asceticism of *Blue* appears to be a refusal of fictional melodrama and the auto-censorship inherent in demands for 'positive' images, at the same time as constituting a 'less-is-more' *volte face* when confronted with the Benetton imagery. But the film resists being reduced solely to the strategic dimensions of its form. This is because, abstract in conception as it might sound, *Blue* is also a resolutely personal meditation on life with, and on approaching death from, HIV. Incorporating excerpts from the diary Jarman has kept while undergoing therapy at St. Bartholomew's Hospital, the commentaries return repeatedly to his treatment for encroaching blindness. *Blue*, then, is the colour of creeping sightlessness ("the shattering bright light of the eye specialist's camera [that] leaves empty sky-blue after-image ... darkness made visible"); the artist's response to the infection's terrifying robbery of his faculties ("If I lose half my sight, will my vision be halved?"); and of suffering borne with remarkable humour ("The Gautama Buddha instructs me to walk away from illness. But he wasn't attached to a drip"—one of several painful punchlines in the soundtrack's sombre comedy of infection).

The humorous sense of absurdity co-exists with stark anger, particularly directed at government-induced dependency on the work of Aids charities, and tender laments for dead friends. The range of emotional responses emerges as a refusal to be consumed by horror and despair, a defiant gesture of freedom in the teeth of death.

Likewise, *Blue* itself seeks to refuse the already clotted repertoire of images and scenarios resorted to in representing the unrepresentable. For eyes immune to images of agony, *Blue* fulfils the imperative to sometimes turn the gaze away and within, towards an image as 'silent' as that proposed here. But it is an image whose richness and beauty nevertheless make it impossible to forget that *Blue* is also the colour of a shroud.

VILLAGE VOICE, 10/19/93, p. 56, Georgia Brown

"Different," you see, has parameters, an eight-by-10 frame. In truth, a multimillion-dollar fiction about trauma is a contradiction in terms. The difference between this and suffering the real thing is like night and day. At least I hope it is. Personally, if I ever find myself on a plane taking a nosedive, I pray no traces of *Fearless* clutter my final minutes. But I wouldn't care if Derek Jarman's *Blue* popped into mind.

In Britain's *Time Out*, a piece on Jarman by Paul Bruston begins with the director saying, "All I see in AIDS films is sentimentality," and goes on to quote from Jarman's open letter to Greg Araki (*The Living End*) published in *The Guardian*: "You resolved your film in a sympathetic and gentle way with the two boys sitting by the sea. Why didn't you allow them to blow their heads off in the love scene that preceded this?" Dying of AIDS, Jarman is sensitive to misrepresentation.

Blue, which played one night in the NYFF and has no distributor, is different in that its only image, projected for 75 minutes, is a shade of blue. Inspired by Yves Klein's monochromatic series based on the sky above his hometown, Nice, *Blue* is probably Jarman's last film, since he's nearly blind and greatly weakened. He continues, however, to write and (using assistants) to paint.

The specific shade in *Blue* is the intense, deep, bright blue of an evening sky in summer—not here but in the latitudes of northern Europe. As in Jarman's delirious *The Last of England*, the soothing tenor of Nigel Terry dominates. (Out of the blue also come the voices of Tilda Swinton and John Quentin and the music of Simon Turner.) Throughout, everyone in the audience keeps looking rapt at the screen even though it doesn't vary. Except that it deepens, becoming a blue room, a space from which Jarman sets down aspects of his daily regimen, remembers friends who died horribly, rhapsodizes, mocks, and rages. Anyone who's seen *The Last of England* or *The Garden*, or read the published diaries, knows the rich, gripping cadences, the dead-on irony.

In a review of Donald Hall's *Life Work*, Robert Kelly remarked on "a strange new genre: autothanatography." If people are dying at (or before) the peak of their powers, as many are doing with AIDS, it hardly seems strange they would seize dying as a subject and use urgency creatively. Jarman has always had subjects; he didn't need this one. On the other hand, he's always been friendly to apocalypse. There's a sense in *Blue*, after all the rancor, of welcome.

Also reviewed in:
NATION, 10/4/93, p. 365, Stuart Klawans
NEW YORKER, 5/2/94, p. 106, Anthony Lane
NEW YORK TIMES, 4/8/94, p. C13, Stephen Holden
VARIETY, 9/27/93, p. 38, Todd McCarthy
WASHINGTON POST, 2/11/94, Weekend/p. 50, Desson Howe

BLUE KITE, THE

A Kino International rrelease of a Longwick Film Production Ltd. and Beijing Film Studio production. *Producer:* Luo Guiping and Cheng Yongping. *Director:* Tian Zhuangzhuang. *Screenplay (Mandarin with English subtitles):* Xiao Mao. *Director of Photography:* Hou Yong. *Editor:* Quan Lengleng. *Music:* Yoshihide Otomo. *Sound:* Wu Ling and (music) Yoshiaki Kondo. *Art Director:* Zhang Xiande. *Set Designer:* Wang Zesheng. *Set Decorator:* Zhu Baosheng and Li Gang. *Costumes:* Dong Juying. *Make-up:* Hao Xia and Wu Yeyao. *Running time:* 138 minutes. *MPAA Rating:* Not Rated.

CAST: Yi Tian (Tietou as an Infant); Zhang Wenyao (Tietou as a Child); Chen Xiaoman (Tietou as a Teenager); Lu Liping (Mum, Chen Shujuan); Pu Quanxin (Dad, Lin Shaolong); Li Xuejian (Uncle Li); Guo Baochang (Stepfather, Lao Wu); Zhong Ping (Chen Shusheng); Chu Quanzhong (Chen Shuyan); Song Xiaoying (Sis); Zhang Hong (Zhu Ying); Liu Yanjin (Shujuan's Mother); Li Bin (Granny); Lu Zhong (Mrs. Lan); Guo Donglin (Lin Yunwei); Wu Shumin (Street Committee Officer).

CHRISTIAN SCIENCE MONITOR, 10/12/93, p. 14, David Sterritt

[*The Blue Kite* was reviewed jointly with *Raining Stones*; see Sterritt's review off that film.]

LOS ANGELES TIMES, 6/1/94, Calendar/p. 3, Kenneth Turan

Of all the remarkable films to have come out of China over the past few years. "The Blue Kite" could well be the most authentic, the most accessible and, finally, the most powerful. Daring politically and quietly shattering emotionally, it tells the truth in such a completely human way that it hardly seems foreign at all.

Unlike the work of fellow Fifth Generation filmmakers Chen Kiage ("Farewell My Concubine") and Zhang Yimou ("Raise the Red Lantern"), there is nothing theatrical or operatic about this film from director Tian Zhuangzhuang. A welcoming naturalism characterizes his style here, an ability to see great events through the lives of ordinary people caught unawares in the toils of history that is immediately involving.

Set between the death of Stalin in 1953 and the living death of 1968's Cultural Revolution, Xiao Mao's realistic script illuminates that most chaotic period of modern Chinese politics by telling the story of an ordinary woman named Chen Shujuan (popular Chinese actress Lu Liping) and her extended family.

Simple as it is, this idea did not find favor with the powers who run China's film industry. After viewing a rough cut of "The Blue Kite," they forbade shipping the footage to Japan (where most Chinese films go for post-production). The film was spirited out anyway, edited according to the director's detailed notes, and shown to great praise both at Cannes and the Tokyo Film Festival, where the Chinese delegation walked out during the screening and later announced plans to sue the Dutch company that had acquired the world rights.

It may seem unusual for such a quiet film to have stirred up such a considerable fuss, but it is just the discretion and restraint with which "The Blue Kite" was created that makes its points so effective and its indictment of China's past political situation so damning.

Certainly when we first meet Shujuan, everything seems happy and hopeful. Much to the delight of her idealistic sister (Song Xiaoying) and her brothers (Zhong Ping and Chu Quanzhong), she is about to marry librarian Lin Shaolong (Pu Quanxin) and move into a small apartment in a bustling Beijing courtyard. Soon a son, called Tietou or "Iron Head," is born and, true to his nickname, he grows up to be the film's stubborn narrator.

Much of the action of "The Blue Kite" takes place in that busy courtyard and among the members of that family. Director Tian is a thoughtful, nuanced observer, and, helped by Hou Yong's sensitive camerawork, he gets a great deal of poignancy out of intimate family scenes between brother and sister, mother and child, husband and wife.

These moments play out against the turmoil caused by the topsy-turvy political movements of the day. First came Rectification, a call from the Communist Party for honesty and criticism, followed almost immediately by an Anti-Rightist campaign that condemned those who did speak out. Next was the Great Leap Forward, a frantic attempt to increase China's industrial production, which led finally to the mad terror of the Cultural Revolution.

"The Blue Kite" is especially good at showing how difficult it was for ordinary people to try to find space to just survive as the baffling crosswinds of politics caused the loss of jobs, relationships, even lives. "The more I think about it," Shujuan says at one point, more in resignation than in anger, "the less I understand."

This kind of rigorous, unforgiving look at a major span of Chinese history, a willingness to take on political movements that are still off-limits to criticism, is one of the things that got "The Blue Kite" in such trouble with the authorities. The other taboo, apparently never before addressed on film, is official insistence that attractive women in the army eschew steady boyfriends and instead provide escort services for powerful party leaders as "political duties."

The only token of hope in this troubled time is the kite of the film's title. A fragile paper object that keeps getting destroyed or lost and then rebuilt, it symbolizes freedom, beauty, innocence and the hope of escape, all the things that that generation of Chinese, as this film so carefully shows, had to live their lives without.

NEW YORK, 4/11/94, p. 57, John Powers

Ask Americans about politics and they'll talk about Clinton. Ask the Chinese and they'll talk about their own lives. In *The Blue Kite*, the great Chinese director Tian Zhuangzhuang offers a semi-autobiographical portrait of life in Beijing from 1953 to 1967. It's a story of decent comrades betrayed by a roller-coaster revolution that's forever changing direction. Urged to make constructive criticisms of the party, loyal Communists are sent to labor camp when they do so. Ordered to service party leaders, pretty young women soldiers are jailed as "counterrevolutionaries" when they refuse. Having devoted their lives to Mao's teaching, honest bureaucrats are suddenly denounced by Red Guards, who beat them senseless. I've seen no film from mainland China more openly hostile to the Communists than *The Blue Kite*. But the best reason to see this picture isn't its dissident panache but its observation of one family's life, as seen through the eyes of a troublemaking young boy named Tietou. Working in the tradition of Hou Hsiaohsien's masterpiece, *The Time to Live and the Time to Die*, Tian Zhuangzhuang spins a delicate story about the beauty of daily life and the fragility of happiness—symbolized by the soaring blue kites that are forever being caught in the trees.

NEW YORK POST, 4/8/94, p. 37, Thelma Adams

The personal is the political.

No film in recent memory has wedded the two spheres with such earnest grace as Tian Zhuangzhuang's "The Blue Kite." Like its title, this tale of a boy and his mother caught in the crosswinds of Chinese politics from 1953-68 is deceptively simple.

Originally screened last fall during the New York Film Festival, "The Blue Kite" has yet to fly in China where it is banned, presumably for its criticism of communism.

Director Tian is a member of China's Fifth Generation, a group of filmmakers often compared to the French New Wave for lack of a better box in which to toss them. Graduates of the Beijing Film Academy in 1982, they were the first class to graduate after the school reopened post-Cultural Revolution.

Famed alum Chen Kaige received an Oscar nomination this year for "Farewell, My Concubine" but was aced out by "Belle Epoque." Zhang Yimou's "Ju Dou" was also nominated for an Oscar.

More subdued than "Concubine," which had a larger budget and was drawn from a popular novel, "The Blue Kite" is based on an original script by Xiao Mao, another Fifth Generation member.

The movie's style could be called scrubbed realism; the genre, family saga. The impact is the slow burn set by a patient, mature filmmaker who has finally returned to autobiographical material after the ethnographic fictions which put him on the international festival map, "The Hunting Ground" and "The Horse Thief."

The story is told from the point of view of a boy named Tietou (played by three different young actors), which means "iron head." He has been given the nickname in hopes that he will grow up strong, and Tietou is a strong-willed, lovable little troublemaker.

Tietou's thrice-widowed mother Chen Shujuan, played by the wonderful Lu Liping, shares center stage. During the short spring of her first marriage, her husband gives their robust son a blue kite. Where it gets caught in a tree, he says that he cannot get it down but he can make Tietou another.

The kite—and the elusive freedom it symbolizes—contrasts with the red banners and sloganeering of Mao's regime. Rectification, re-education, and the Cultural Revolution are movements that will mold the child's soul as they shred his family.

The untimely exits of Tietou's three fathers shape the drama. His biological father, accused of being a rightist, dies in a labor camp; his stepfather collapses from overwork and malnutrition.

Tietou's mother seeks security with a party functionary, but when the political winds change again after the 1966 Cultural Revolution, the Red Guard brand her third husband as a counterrevolutionary.

Over the course of the film, we watch Tietou evolve from a beloved, sheltered child to an adolescent who boasts of humiliating his principal and burning his school books during the Cultural Revolution.

The man Tietou might have been under another regime is caught in history's tree like a kite.

Shaped by a mother's devotion and tragic loss, confronted by a system that demands absolute loyalty to constantly shifting principles, Tietou's future hangs by a slender thread. Who will this strong-willed boy become?

When a kite gets caught in a tree, you can make another. But how do you rebuild a man?

NEWSDAY, 4/8/94, Part II/p. B7, John Anderson

The content may be Inquisitional, but the timing is pure Hollywood: China's blackballing of the director of "The Blue Kite," just in time for its New York opening.

The Chinese government, of course, is unconcerned with what constitutes good publicity for a film it hates. But cutting the legs out from under Tian Zhuangzhuang and six other filmmaking entities—an "internal memo" reportedly forbids film labs and studios from working with them—marks a significant shift, and disintegration, in the Beijing zeitgeist. Is the action particularly surprising? No. "The Blue Kite" has been agitating Chinese officials for some time, and for good reason.

Beneath all the controversy, the film is basically a soap opera, a sprawling, multi-charactered narrative charting the messy romances and compromised morality of unremarkable people made remarkable through circumstance—in this case, the Cultural Revolution. But it's a thrilling soap opera, rich in heroics and betrayal, that reminds us why this kind of thing ever worked in the first place.

From the opening scene, in which Shujuan (Lu Liping) and Shaolong (Pu Quanxin) move furniture into their new home on Dry Well Lane (the well never had any water) and literally set their own stage, "The Blue Kite" is a pageant of form and metaphor. The kite itself, for instance, which Shaolong makes for his small son Tietou (played at various ages by Yi Tian, Zhang Wenyao and Chen Xiaoman) and remakes, each time it tangles in the trees. A symbol of Tietou's longing for Shaolong himself—a librarian who, caught up in the paranoid intrigue sparked by Maoist caprice, will die in a labor camp—it also signifies the elusive but resilient spirit of the people, occasionally floating, pale blue against a pale blue sky, but more often rent and abandoned.

Tietou's life is central to the film, as is his mother's. A teacher of apolitical leanings, she survives the capricious dictates of Maoist Beijing, as well as three husbands. Shujuan becomes a part of the fabric of the country as it changes, just as the nation's transmutation is part of her domestic life. Nothing is permanent, in the end, except a will to live.

What probably has incensed the Chinese authorities more than anything is the hypocrisy that infects Chinese history over "The Blue Kite's" 14-year span. At their wedding—which had been postponed by the death of Stalin—they sing a song of the motherland: "Our workers love labor ... production soars/We are peace loving and never invade others"; immediately afterwards, Sis (Song Xiaoying), the stridently Marxist sister of Shujuan, recounts her husbands's death on the front. When Zhu Ying (Zhang Hong), girlfriend of Shujuan's brother, protests to a party official that her duties shouldn't include "entertaining" high-ranking Communists, she is demoted and disgraced. The occasional reform marches led through the courtyard that constitutes Shujuan and Tietou's immediate universe are an admitted sham. And when Shujuan's other brother Shuyan (Chu Quanzhong) criticizes policy—during the Rectification Movement, which encouraged such criticism—he is labeled a rightist and shipped to a labor camp.

Unlike the films of Zhuangzhuang's fellow Fifth Generation filmmakers—Chen Kaige, of the epic and ornate "Farewell My Concubine," or Zhang Yimou, whose austere and beautiful "Raise the Red Lantern" constituted political allegory—"The Blue Kite" cannot be divorced from or edited of its political content. Which makes it dangerous. What makes it art is Tian Zhuangzhuang's passion and courage, which invest the film with tears and rage.

SIGHT AND SOUND, 2/94, p. 55, Phillip Kemp

Beijing, 1953. Librarian Lin Shaolong and schoolteacher Chen Shujuan are about to marry, but the ceremony is delayed when Stalin's death is announced. Ten days later, they celebrate their marriage along with members of Shujuan's family: her mother, her older sister 'Sis' (a confirmed Marxist and widow of a revolutionary hero) and her brothers Shusheng, an army officer, and Shuyan, an art student. Shaolong's friend and colleague, Li Guodong, also attends.

Shaolong and Shujuan move into an apartment in a courtyard building owned by Mrs Lan. Their son Lin Dayu, known as Tietou, grows up in the bustling world of the courtyard— which, in accordance with Party doctrine, Mrs Lan has turned into a communal co-operative. Mao Tse-Tung announces the Rectification Movement ("Let a hundred flowers bloom"), encouraging criticism to rid the Party of complacency. Among those who respond are Shuyan, complaining about the exam system at his school, and Liu Yunwei, a colleague of Shaolong's at the library. Liu associates both Shaolong and Li Guodong with his criticism, although they weren't present at the meeting. Shusheng's girlfriend Zhu Ying, a performer in the Army Song and Dance Troupe, objects to being expected to attend dances (and, by implication, to have sex) with top Party leaders. Those who criticised are denounced as 'Rightists' and punished. Under pressure, Li Guodong dissociates himself from Shaolong and Tiu Yunwei, both of whom are sent to labour camps. Shuyan is banished to work on the land. Zhu Ying is first made to work in a factory, then imprisoned as a counter-revolutionary. Shusheng, who has contracted an eye disease that threatens his career, is powerless to help her. The Great Leap Forward is announced, and everybody melts down kitchen implements to help steel production. Tietou enjoys the upheavals, but Shujuan struggles to survive in Shaolong's absence. A letter arrives: Shaolong has died in a forestry accident.

Li Guodong, guilt-ridden over his part in Shaolong's fate, helps support Shujuan. Tietou adores Guodong, and eventually Shujuan marries him; but, overworked and undernourished, he dies of a liver complaint. Shujuan and Tietou move in with her mother, Sis and Shusheng, now almost blind. Sis finds Shujuan a new husband, Wu Leisheng, an elderly senior party member. Both Shujuan and Tietou are unhappy and Tietou gets into fights at school. When the Cultural Revolution breaks out he happily joins in humiliating the school principal. Wu Leisheng, knowing the Red Guard will come for him, tells Shujuan to divorce him. She agrees reluctantly, having grown to feel affection for him, and returns with Tietou to her mother's house, where Shuyan is back from the country with a peasant fiancee, Guiha. Zhu Ying is released but, broken by her experiences, refuses to marry Shusheng. Sis is denounced and humiliated. Worried about Wu, Shujuan goes to his house and finds him, seriously ill, under attack by the Red Guard. She tries to intervene, and is herself arrested. Tietou, rushing wildly to her aid, is brutally beaten up. Wu dies in custody and Shujuan is sent to a labour camp as a counter-revolutionary.

With *Horse Thief*, his first film to gain widespread distribution outside China, Tian Zhuangzhuang established himself as a leading member of the 'Fifth Generation' of Chinese directors. Since then his reputation has faded beside those of his contemporaries Chen Kaige and Zhang Yimou. *The Blue Kits* should restore him to his rightful place.

In terms of narrative, though, the new film has little in common with the exotic, even hermetic otherness of *Horse Thief*, with its minimalist dialogue and mystical Tibetan rituals. Within Chinese-language cinema, the nearest parallel to *The Blue Kite* might be the Taiwanese family sagas of Hou Hsiao-hsien: *A City of Sadness*, or *The Time to Live and the Time to Die*. Like Hou's films, *The Blue Kite* reflects the trials and upheavals of an era through the vicissitudes of one family, showing how the arbitrary stupidities of political dogma attack and erode the modest structures of human happiness.

The kite of the title stands—perhaps just a touch too obviously—for this personal happiness, at once joyful and perilously fragile. We first see it being flown for the infant Tietou by Shaolong; later Tietou himself, a disaffected adolescent, finds unexpected pleasure in flying it for his young step-niece Niu-niu. When, like most kites, it gets caught in a tree, he promises to make her another, but events overtake him. In the final scene, lying bruised and bleeding on the ground, his mother dragged off by the Red Guards, Tietou looks up and sees the kite's tattered remains dangling from the branches.

The Blue Kite is a film about trust betrayed: the trust of people who believed in a wise and benevolent leadership. At the wedding, the assembled company happily bow to Mao's portrait and sing, "On the peaceful soil of the Motherland life gets better every day". But already the omens are gathering. Shaolong's friend—and future unwilling betrayer—Guodong brings the couple a clay horse, symbol of prosperity; as he puts it down, the head breaks off. From now on, at each twist and lurch of the Great Helmsman's erratic steering, another fragment of the family's warm, communal togetherness will be destroyed.

Yet the film, though moving, isn't depressing. Throughout, despite everything, there are still moments of tenderness and even joy. At the start of the film, alone for the first time after the wedding, Shaolong lifts his bride and whirls her round in an impulse of giddy delight. Towards the end, Tietou asks Shujuan what makes her happy; she replies, "Being with you." Happiness is personal, small-scale and doggedly resilient. "Are people still getting married in times like these?" asks Wu in bitter disbelief. But they are, even if it's only Shuyan and his foolish bride, with her red cheeks (as Tietou rudely observes) "like a monkey's arse".

Though full of anger (Xiao Mao's script is based on Tian's own family history), the film never preaches or lectures. Indeed, some allusions are subtle enough to escape non-Chinese audiences. This is said to be the first film to refer to the practice of requiring attractive female soldiers to have sex with Party bosses, but the reference is oblique enough to be missed. And it's never stated that what kills Guodong is the famine caused by Mao's disastrous Great Leap Forward. Most likely there are other nuances that will pass a Western viewer by, but the overwhelming emotional thrust of the film is universal in its impact.

By filtering his story through a child's perspective (it's Tietou who provides the running voice-over), Tian Zhuangzhang combines lucidity of vision with a novelistic richness and complexity of narrative. These qualities are matched by the visuals, subtly framed and lit by Tian's cinematographer Hou Yong, whose domestic interiors often have the quiet luminosity of Vermeer. Tian draws from his actors performances of total, undemonstrative conviction; as Shujuan, Lu Liping holds the still centre of the action with limpid grace. Perhaps not surprisingly, *The Blue Kite* has aroused the fury of the Chinese authorities: denied an exit visa, Tian was forced to complete his final edit at long distance, and has yet to see his own finished film. In a backhanded way, there could hardly be a greater tribute to the power and truth of his work.

TIME, 5/2/94, p. 75, Richard Corliss

When bad things happen to good people: this is a dominant theme of literature and drama through the ages, from the Book of Job to Dostoyevsky novels to most soap operas and TV movies. It is also the story line of the Chinese film *The Blue Kite*—and the story behind the suppression of this bold, masterly work.

Tian Zhuangzhuang's film opens in 1953, with the marriage of lovely Chen Shujuan (Lu Liping), a schoolteacher, and gentle Lin Shaolong (Pu Quanxin), a librarian. The two believe they have much to celebrate: their warm love, to be sure, but also the dawn of a true People's Republic. Their political ardor can't last; what begins in naive hope is crushed against the great wall of Maoist reality.

The couple have a son, Tietou (played by three children in the 15-year course of the narrative), and all seems well. But shortly thereafter, the family begins its run of exemplary bad luck—everything rotten that could have happened to anyone in the plague years of Maoist China seems to happen to them.

During the rectification movement of 1957, when citizens were urged to "let a hundred schools of thought contend," a colleague of Shaolong's innocently implicates him in criticism of their work conditions, and when the official policy reverts back to thought control, Shaolong is banished to a labor camp, later to be killed by a falling tree. Tietou's uncle is going blind, and Uncle's girlfriend, star of an army theater troupe, is sent to jail because she refuses an order to have sex with political leaders. Shujuan's second husband (Li Xuejian) dies from a liver ailment aggravated by the rampant malnutrition of the early '60s. And during the spiteful frenzy of the Cultural Revolution, Shujuan's third husband (Guo Baochang) is humiliated and beaten by the righteous Red Guard. What is worse than young American rebels without a cause? Young Chinese cadres *with* one.

Cataloged like this, the plot may sound like little more than anti-agitprop. And indeed *The Blue Kite* is by far the most excoriating depiction in Chinese film of Mao's ravages. But at its heart it is about domestic dreams, about a hope for better days that flies above the characters as brightly and vulnerably as Tietou's favorite blue kite. The rhythms of this family—the meals and arguments, the worries about money and the sweet moments when a put-upon mom finds bliss playing with her bright child—are handsomely observed and beautifully played. In Lu, Tian found one of those perfect faces from which emotion rises spontaneously, acutely and eloquently.

But to Chinese authorities, *The Blue Kite* was nothing more than an incendiary insult. They approved the script but, when Tian diverged from it, refused to let him edit his film; it languished for a year and was completed abroad by others working from the director's screenplay and notes. The film was banned in China, and last month Tian and six other prominent directors were forbidden to make films in their homeland.

So Tian must feel kinship with the beleaguered brood in *The Blue Kite*. It is now the challenge of the world film community to see that he is not silenced because he told the truth.

VILLAGE VOICE, 4/12/94, p. 51, J. Hoberman

At once reckless and restrained, *The Blue Kite* is not only the most politically bold movie to emerge from People's China but also one of the most formally adroit. Directed by Tian Zhuangzhuang from a script by his Fifth Generation comrade Xiao Mao, *The Blue Kite* is both specific and universal—it's the story of a mother and child and their search for a father in the 14 tumultuous years between 1953 and 1967, the end of the Korean War and the height of the Cultural Revolution.

Like Chen Kaige's *Farewell My Concubine*, which was in production simultaneously at the Beijing Film Studio, *The Blue Kite* examines private life (or, perhaps, its absence) in the midst of political cataclysm. *The Blue Kite* is, however, a less overtly theatrical film. Its milieu is the lower-middle-class intelligentsia; the main stages here are smoky courtyards and crowded kitchen tables. The first sequence, in which an engaged couple—the kindergarten teacher Shujuan and the librarian Shaolong—move their belongings to a small apartment in the Beijing back alley suggestively called Dry Well Lane, is a form of dressing the set.

The Blue Kite rarely leaves the domestic sphere. Nor does it have to. (As Kafka once wrote, "A cage went looking for a bird.") From the early scene in which Shujuan and Shaolong's wedding is delayed 10 days by the announcement of Stalin's death through the various campaigns waged by the neighborhood Committee to the climactic invasion of Shujuan's home, turmoil is ubiquitous. Chinese politics as a form of natural disaster. For the denizens of Dry Well Lane, daily life continues amid constant disruption, just as it does for those who dwell on the flood plain of the Yellow River. The workplace is no less treacherous. Encouraged to offer constructive criticism, as "a hundred flowers" bloom during the 1957 Rectification Movement, an enthusiastic librarian writes a letter to criticize the bureaucracy, generously adding his colleagues' names to his own and thus planting seeds of disaster for all three.

Tian handles historical sweep with remarkable tact. Like that of his Taiwanese contemporary Hou Hsiao-hsien, Tian's mode is economical, the film's multilayered soundtrack suggesting a vast expanse of time and space beyond the courtyard (or the film frame). Best known for the brilliantly stylized ethnographic enigmas of *On the Hunting Ground* (1985) and *The Horse Thief* (1986), provocatively set in inner Mongolia and Tibet, respectively, Tian makes precise use of period detail and household clutter. (In much the same way that these earlier films suffered limited release simply by representing the taboo subject of China's non-Han minorities, so *The Blue Kite*—banned in China and officially a Hong Kong-China production—has short-circuited Tian's career by referencing the political reversals of the 1950s.)

The Blue Kite contains a miniseries's worth of character and incident—the trim and girlish Shujuan is three times widowed by the movie's end—yet, while combining aspects of Socialist Realism *typage* and the Hollywood "woman's film" melodrama, the movie is fiercely understated. Particularly striking is its unsentimental view of childhood. Shujuan's son Tietou, born in March 1954 (two years after Tian), is a willful toddler who grows into an unsmiling, demanding child. Observing that she and Shaolong were themselves so "well behaved," Shujuan wonders how they spawned this particular little devil—as if the individual's relationship to authority were not the subtext of Tian's entire film. Throughout, children are presented as a source of rowdy energy, underfoot yet heedless of adult concerns.

A distant cousin to Oskar, the diminutive, demonic protagonist of *The Tin Drum*, Tietou is apt to comment on his mother's dilemmas by reciting a taunting nursery rhyme. Spanked by Shaolong for breaking a window, he brandishes a paper gun: "Daddy's bad. I'm going to kill him." Not long after, Daddy is deported—in part because he goes to the toilet at the wrong moment during a workplace meeting held to identify the "rightists" in their midst. News of Shaolong's death arrives in suitably detached fashion. Unlike his mother, Tietou never weeps—although the New Year's sparkler he craves is called a "Happy Old Man."

A year or two later, around the time of the Great Leap Forward, Shujuan marries one of Shaolong's former colleagues—"Uncle Li," a kindly man, consumed with remorse for having written the letter of criticism that ultimately sealed Shaolong's fate. In the movie's most mystical moment, Shujuan consoles Uncle Li by telling him that Shaolong's tragedy would have happened anyway—in any case, Uncle Li is never released from his burden of guilt. He works himself to death and, after presenting Tietou with his Happy Old Man, collapses as he holds a tray of never-to-be-eaten New Year's dumplings.

Thereafter, the state of Shujuan's life is signified by the rubble of her empty apartment. In the early '60s, she marries an established, middle-aged functionary, one of her sister's old comrades. ("It was the first time I ever rode in a car," Tietou's adult voiceover recalls as mother and son leave Dry Well Lane for presumably greener pastures.) But life in their new, relatively spacious house—where, in a parody of bourgeois domesticity, Shujuan functions as cook, mistress, and maid—is far more alienated. The 12-year-old Tietou is no less a behavior problem, dumping his rice bowl or spying on Shujuan and his new stepfather through the transom over their bedroom door.

Of course, the Cultural Revolution provides an even more exciting orgy. Red Guards humiliate the head of Tietou's school before a crowd of excited, cheering children. Tietou can't wait to tell his mother that he spat on the principal—he's stunned when she slaps him. Sent to his grandmother's, he explains that "We burnt all our texts, but I go to school every day—it's a lot of fun." More than any previous Chinese movie, *The Blue Kite* suggests the heady thrills that the Cultural Revolution provided. Right up until the last sequence, political brickbats have been flying over Tietou's head. There's a distinctly mordant humor, as well as horror, when one creases his noggin.

Ending with the image of its tattered namesake, the symbol of some unattainable freedom, *The Blue Kite* doesn't have *Farewell My Concubine*'s glitz or pageantry. Still, it's supercharged with metaphor. The wedding in which the nuptial couple bow to a portrait of Mao and sing a Party hymn is "watched" by a wooden animal whose head drops off as someone makes a patriotic remark about China's peaceful intentions.

The political banner that comes loose from its mooring and gracefully descends upon a pair of book-laden librarians, the gaggle of noisy comrades who parade through Dry Well Lane as part of a campaign to exterminate sparrows are, in a sense, the meaning of this superbly controlled and subtly moving film.

Also reviewed in:
NATION, 5/2/94, p. 604, Stuart Klawans
NEW YORK TIMES, 4/8/94, p. C13, Vincent Canby
NEW YORKER, 5/2/94, p. 106, Anthony Lane
VARIETY, 6/14/93, p. 56, Derek Elley
WASHINGTON POST, 8/5/94, p. C2, Hal Hinson

BODIES, REST & MOTION

A Fine Line Pictures release of a Fine Line Features/August Entertainment presentation of a Mindel/Shaw production. *Executive Producer:* Joel Castleberg. *Producer:* Allan Mindel, Denise Shaw, and Eric Stoltz. *Director:* Michael Steinberg. *Screenplay:* Roger Hedden. *Director of Photography:* Bernd Heinl. *Editor:* Jay Cassidy. *Music:* Karyn Rachtman and Michael Convertino. *Music Editor:* Ken Wannberg. *Sound:* Walt Martin, (music) Paul Brown, and Dennis Sands. *Sound Editor:* Per Hallberg and Lon E. Bender. *Casting:* Sunny Seibel. *Production Designer:* Stephen McCabe. *Art Director:* Daniel Talpers. *Set Decorator:* Helen Britten. *Set Dresser:* Thierry Labbe and John McElroy. *Costumes:* Isis Mussenden. *Make-up:* Deborah Larsen. *Running time:* 94 minutes. *MPAA Rating:* R.

CAST: Phoebe Cates (Carol);   Bridget Fonda (Beth);   Tim Roth (Nick);   Eric Stoltz (Sid);
Alicia Witt (Elizabeth);   Sandra Lafferty (Yard Sale Lady);   Sidney Dawson (TV Customer);
Jon Proudstar (Station Attendant);   Scott Johnson (Chip);   Kezbath Weidner (Diner Woman);
Peter Fonda (Motorcycle Rider);   Amaryllis Borrego (Waitress);   Rich Wheeler (Elizabeth's
Grandfather);   Scott Frederick (TV Store Kid);   Warren Burton (Radio Preacher's Voice).

LOS ANGELES TIMES, 4/9/93, Calendar/p. 4, Michael Wilmington

"Comedy is long-shot and tragedy is close-up," Charlie Chaplin once claimed. If that's so, then
the sweetly hip comedy "Bodies, Rest & Motion" may be an in-betweener: sliding in and out of
medium-shot, squeezing out laughs just this side of sobbing, focusing on pains that, from a step
or two farther back, could make us howl with merriment.

In some ways, this brainy romance, adapted by director Michael Steinberg and Roger Hedden,
from Hedden's play, could be led a portrait of a generation. But that makes it sound too pretentious. It's a *goofy* portrait, alternately dappled with sorrow and limpid with laughter. It's
dreamy, tart and sexy; it swings.

The film's title refers to Newton's Second Law—the proposition that bodies in rest or motion
stay that way until acted on by an outside force—and that metaphor seems to control the
characters. Mythical Enfield, Ariz., is their arena: a honey-lit desert city of nondescript malls,
neat little streets and lawns, bare rooms and hot skies. Enfield, created out of bits and pieces of
Tucson, Ariz., is like a Southwestern dollhouse-town, and moving through its charmingly arid
and square topography are four compact characters: Phoebe Cates' pert Carol, Bridget Fonda's
vulnerable Beth, Tim Roth's obnoxious Nick and Eric Stoltz's amiable Sid.

This foursome, all in their late 20's, "in-betweeners" themselves, give "Bodies, Rest & Motion"
its special mix of bite and caress. Cleverly depicted as prototypes of their unsettled time—trapped
between dissolving illusions and elusive new possibilities—they're acted with high relish and
nuance by a cast that seems delighted to be together. And Steinberg, who showed humanity,
precision and depth in his last film, "The Waterdance" (co-directed with writer Neal Jimenez),
shows more here: a bittersweet lyricism that illuminates what could have seemed slight or sordid.

For some audiences, it still may. From one angle, this group is a morally loose, shallow,
egoistic, uncommitted bunch, imbued with everything that made the '80s, for some, a dubious
achievement.

Nick and Beth are a couple—temporarily. Nick, fired from his TV salesman job, plans to leave
Enfield. Carol, Nick's old flame and Beth's best pal, shows up. Nick bugs out early, leaving Beth
with broken dreams and a brand-new TV. Sid, the handyman, unknown to any of them—except
Beth, with whom he flirted at an intersection the night before—comes to repaint the house. Night
falls ...

What's obviously happening is a shifting or reordering. Just as Nick and Beth's old house is
stripped of its furniture, color and character, the quartet is reassembling into new patterns—or
trying to. And just as Nick—whose surly self-absorption is trenchantly caught by the selfless
Roth—keys the *first* half of the film, Sid's entrance slowly shifts the center of gravity. Sid is
Nick's "opposite": a homebody where Nick is restless, in love with the here and now that Nick,
apparently, can't stand.

Does this make the women sound like tag-alongs? Not here. *They're* opposites too. Fonda gives
Beth a fine, raw openness and vulnerability, while Cates encloses Carol in an armor of deliciously
calculated cutie-pie mannerisms, head-bobs and watchfully ironic stares, most of which suggest
she's as manipulative as Nick. Sid and Beth are the dreamers, Carol and Nick are the cynics.
And, as the movie wryly recognizes, they're all closer than they think.

Economic and evocative dialogue, wonderful acting, sprightly humor, emotional suppleness, a
marvelously inconclusive conclusion, an ingenious Michael Convertino score that mixes Indian
incantation with soft syncopation: "Bodies, Rest & Motion" has a lot to offer in a small package.

But perhaps we should give a special nod to its eroticism—something Steinberg also caught with
delicacy and feeling in "The Waterdance." Movie bed scenes have gotten such a satiny overall
sameness, they take the kiss out of sex. Surely, it's not just the fact that Fonda and Stoltz are an
off-screen couple that makes their scenes here so tender, memorable and right, sensual but not
carnal.

NEW YORK POST, 4/9/93, p. 26, Jami Bernard

If Harold Pinter were in his 20s today and had suffered a severe blow to the head, he might have written the script for "Bodies, Rest & Motion," an alarmingly arty movie about listless young things who can't decide what to do with themselves.

Or maybe playwright and first-time screenwriter Roger Hedden is just trying to be Hal Hartley, minus the ironic edge.

At any rate, this is a mainstream movie done up (or down) to look like art-house fare, and the young and the restless may find that appealing—a movie they can rally around when they can't think of anything else to do.

The gorgeous cast (one of the producers is a co-founder of the Click modeling agency) includes Bridget Fonda, who always looks good either at rest or in motion; Phoebe Cates as her boyfriend's ex; Tim Roth as a TV salesman who feels a need to move on to another town and another mall job, and Eric Stoltz as a hometown housepainter who knows what he wants when he sees it. He sees Fonda and he wants her.

The title is taken from one of those Newton laws concerning gravity, the one that says that bodies continue to do whatever it is they're doing, unless they're pushed in another direction. If they're motionless, they stay motionless, and if they're moving, they keep on keeping on. (Another of those laws is the one that applies to those swinging balls on strings that knock each other right and left, and these toys can be glimpsed in the movie as a sight gag every now and then.)

The movie opens amusingly, with Roth and ex-girlfriend Cates lazing about on a sofa completely lethargic. "We're moving," says Roth, when it is apparent they are doing nothing of the kind.

What he means, though, is that he and current lover Fonda are moving to another dead-end town, thus setting into motion what was motionless—and that's about as deep as it gets, although my interest never flagged until an interminably Pinteresque scene in a half-painted room.

"Bodies, Rest & Motion" isn't stupid, merely trying too hard. The enigmatic aura can get stifling once you realize that all this equivocation boils down to a woman's decision between two men—should she stay or should she go? "Come hold me and you'll be happy," says the housepainter. Ah, would that life were so simple.

The movie maintains the static feel of the stage play from which it is derived; not altogether wrong in a movie about stasis, yet unnerving just the same I got the feeling after an hour that the movie hadn't really begun yet—again, not altogether wrong in a movie about how motionless things have trouble getting started.

NEWSDAY, 4/9/93, Part II/p. 52, Jack Mathews

The opening image is a close-up of metal escalator stairs going up. The last image is of a car purposefully moving down a highway, heading east. In between, everything about Michael Steinberg's offbeat comedy "Bodies, Rest & Motion" seems to be moving, while going nowhere.

Such is life, says screenwriter Roger Hedden, who wrote this first as a play, then as a movie, applying Newton's First Law of Motion (bodies at rest or in motion remain in that state until compelled to change by an outside force) to human behavior.

It's a wonderful idea, and the law seems to prove itself in this slight but compelling and occasionally very funny story about four aimless young adults at rest or in motion, waiting for the forces of change, under the baking sun of Enfield, Ariz.

In motion are:

Nick (Tim Roth), a boozy job-hopping drifter convinced that his future awaits him in the next town.

Beth (Bridget Fonda), a waitress whose quality of life is habitual, pegged to whichever man she happens to be living with—at this moment, Nick. "I go home with men, and I stay with them," she laments. "That's what I do."

At rest are:

Carol (Phoebe Cates), Nick's old girlfriend, who has acquired a job, a car and a home in Enfield, hoping to take root there, even though it's settling for a life far below her expectations.

Sid (Eric Stoltz), a painter, romantic, working-class philosopher, and an Enfield native, following his father's advice that if "you stay in one place, luck knows where to find you."

"Bodies, Rest & Motion" cuts a 48-hour slice out of these four peoples' intertwined lives, during which each of them somehow alters the state of one of the others. In life, as in physics, everything is both the object and subject of change, and "Bodies" serves as a drama/lab experiment showing us how the human molecules knock each other around.

Nothing about the movie is as dull as that sounds. Redden wrote three-and-a-half interesting characters—Cates has blossomed into a fine actress, but her emotionally stationary Carol doesn't get as much done in two days as the others—and the actors have a great time bringing them to life.

Roth, a British actor who has slipped comfortably into the skins of American characters (notably the undercover cop in Quentin Tarantino's "Reservoir Dogs"), has the flashiest role, that of a middle-class dropout marinating his demons in whiskey, and you're never quite sure where he's going with it. Is he dangerous, suicidal, bug nuts, or just a charming wastrel?

In the opening scene, he announces to Beth they're moving to Butte, Mont., because he read somewhere that it is "the city of the future." That was a long time ago, he says, "the future may already be there."

The movie takes an odd turn very early when Nick decides to skip off alone, and leave Beth behind. From there on, Steinberg, who co-directed last year's "The Waterdance," cuts back and forth, tracking Nick's experiences on the road, and the unlikely romance that begins to develop at home between Beth and the irrepressible Sid, who comes to paint and falls in love instead.

Fonda and Stoltz, a couple in real life, work well together, and you develop a quiet rooting interest in their characters' relationship. For Beth, still in motion, Sid is like an impetuous one-night-stand, an amiable way to ease her pain. For Sid, at rest, Beth is the girl of his dreams, and the beginning of life.

"Bodies, Rest & Motion" creates more loose ends than it ties together, yet there is not much more you need to know. Nick, Beth and Sid are not different people after two days, but they are moving in different directions, knocked off course by each other, and it is clear that they will end up in different places because of it.

"Bodies" may be dealing with the aimlessness of a specific generation, people coming of age in an era of shrinking opportunities, but its central metaphor is timeless. The laws of motion don't change.

SIGHT AND SOUND, 2/94, p. 48, Nick James

Enfield, Arizona. Beth is driving home from her dead end job. She stops at a set of traffic lights and a man in a pick-up truck lets her go in front. In an unkempt living room, friends Nick and Carol carouse drunkenly. He tells her that he's moving to Butte, Montana. They are indulging in intimate play when Beth walks in. She and Nick are a couple and as they walk over to their house we learn that Carol is Nick's ex-lover.

Next day is Nick's last at his job as a TV salesman and Beth suggests he steal a set. After he has left, Sid, a painter, arrives and starts to decorate the house for the new tenants. He reminds Beth that he is the pick-up truck driver.

Over lunch, Nick discusses his route with Carol. She gives him a present and suggests that, as he is passing near his parents' home and he hasn't seen them for ten years, he should visit them. Carol then calls on Beth and tells her to go to the mall to help Nick steal the TV. At the store, Nick gives Beth a receipt with which to collect the TV. Back home, Beth and Sid watch the new set. Then Carol arrives to announce that Nick has left town. After the two girls have spent a night in a local bar, Beth returns and listens to Sid explain his philosophy of luck and love before they finally kiss.

Nick arrives at his parents' address to find the house is now occupied by a deaf old man and a young girl. The girl has lost her parents and her story completely shatters Nick's nihilistic cool. He tries to call Beth but their phone has been disconnected. He heads back to Enfield.

Meanwhile Beth and Sid are in bed and he is giving her more of his philosophy about being yourself no matter where you go. She then decides to sell all her worldly goods in a yard sale, and a recently bereaved woman offers $300 dollars for the lot. Beth leaves. When Nick returns and finds out about Beth and Sid, he soon comes to the conclusion that Sid should go after her. The film ends with Nick and Carol on the sofa and Sid searching the highway for Beth.

Despite an ensemble cast bearing all the right grunge credentials for serious heart-searching youth, *Bodies, Rest & Motion* is curiously lacking in the anti-glamour required of the disaffected Generation X. The characters all have the requisite dead-end Macjobs and appear to be as laid-back and feckless about their respective fates as they should be, but their movements around each other are wooden and stagebound, and director Michael Steinberg appears to have put little effort into translating this small-scale theatre play for the screen. Thus the street-smart all-American gesturing that Tim Roth is nowadays offering reads more like a desperate effort to inject life into a dead zone.

The slowly unfolding moral of this four-hander would appear to be that flight is useless but inevitable. An alternative reading provided by Eric Stoltz as Sid is that if you stay still, your luck will find you. Since Stoltz goes in search of luck at the end, while Roth returns to find his, the conclusion reached is that movement makes no difference. It's simply a demonstration of Newton's First Law of Motion, one that takes in a fair amount of jaw-dropping banality on the way.

If Stoltz's dewy-eyed, earnest puppy-dog impersonation fails to assist his delivery of greeting card sentiments such as "It's only possible to find true happiness through another", then likewise Roth's cartoon De Niro face-mangling does nothing to enhance his posturings as a tortured soul incapable of love.

Those who are the target of these messages—Bridget Fonda as Beth and Phoebe Cates as Carol—smile grimly and try to make sense of their lives: Fonda taking the real risk of total uncertainty as the antidote to coupledom and Cates opting for the more traditional role of the girl who waits for the wanderer to return. Again the film takes no stance on which option is to be preferred.

Perhaps the most unexpectedly resonant moment occurs when Roth meets a grizzled old hippy biker on the road. We learn later that behind the beard is Peter Fonda. The look of sheer awe on Roth's face could stand either for his incomprehension in the presence of a real American myth or the film's incomprehension in the presence of a representative from a proper road movie.

VILLAGE VOICE, 4/20/93, p. 58, Manohla Dargis

Moody and achingly tender, Michael Steinberg's *Bodies, Rest & Motion* is about the ills that haunt our flesh and spirit. At the center of this ronde in miniature are four people stalled in their twenties—friends, lovers, strangers bumping against one another like atoms under glass. While Nick, that's "Fucking Nick" (Tim Roth), gets revved on bourbon and bile, girlfriend Beth (Bridget Fonda) goes blank at stoplights, so stunned by life she's blinking out. Off to the side is her best friend, Carol (played wonderfully by Phoebe Cates), who just happens to be Nick's old flame. When these three aren't working some mall, they're sitting around trying to squeeze hope from words, words, words.

The film opens as Nick and Beth are preparing to leave Arizona for Nick's city of the future, Butte, Montana. As Beth packs up their belongings, small disturbances scrape at life's languor—a coffee maker fails, a TV is swiped, a painter arrives to ready a house not yet empty. For his part, Sid (Eric Stoltz) comes to paint, but stays to make love, putting a dent in destiny—maybe. Meanwhile, Nick's down the road, and Carol is sitting, watching, waiting.

With its easy, deliberate pace, *Bodies* has the feel of one of those lazy summer days, when pressing a cold beer against your neck defines ambition. It's a cinematic walkabout that makes sense more often than not, though when it doesn't, it's because Steinberg's groping as hard for direction as his characters. It's then that all those words and measured silences take on a Hal Hartley cadence, but without the deadpan. Beth and Sid's heated moments are especially sappy. Draped decorously over one another, bodies misted with sweat, this golden pair flow together like fate. Their sex scenes are needlessly contrived, as if screwing were only a sign of the divine and not sometimes just, well, screwing. In contrast, Nick and Carol's liquor-drenched tears are far more intimate, and strangely more inviting.

Smarter than *Singles*, less arch than *Slacker*, *Bodies Rest & Motion* is not for the impatient. Loose ends remain untied, story lines float like weeds in water. Take that opening shot, a Steadicam glide into a cacti thicket, with African spirituals rising in rapture. Steinberg cuts back to this vision repeatedly; he has a reckless disregard for continuity editing (and the limits of audience patience). Here amid this spiky beauty, he's found joy, hope, rest.

Also reviewed in:
CHICAGO TRIBUNE, 4/30/93, Friday/p. I, Dave Kehr
NEW YORK TIMES, 4/9/93, p. C11, Janet Maslin
NEW YORKER, 4/12/93, p. 111, Anthony Lane
VARIETY, 2/1/93, p. 99, Todd McCarthy
WASHINGTON POST, 4/23/93, p. D7, Rita Kempley
WASHINGTON POST, 4/23/93, Weekend/p. 33, Desson Howe

BODY OF EVIDENCE

A Metro-Goldwyn-Mayer release of a Dino De Laurentiis Communications production. *Executive Producer:* Stephen Deutsch and Melinda Jason. *Producer:* Dino De Laurentiis, Bernd Eichinger, and Herman Weigel. *Director:* Uli Edel. *Screenplay:* Brad Mirman. *Director of Photography:* Doug Milsome. *Editor:* Thom Noble. *Music:* Graeme Revell. *Music Editor:* Dick Bernstein. *Sound:* Keith A. Wester, Kurt St. Amant, and (music) Dan Wallin. *Sound Editor:* Sandy Gendler and Val Kuklowsky. *Casting:* Mary Jo Slater. *Production Designer:* Victoria Paul. *Art Director:* Michael Rizzo. *Set Decorator:* Jerie Kelter. *Set Dresser:* Peter Clarke, Nicholas Parker, and Jim Meyer. *Special Effects:* Dale Martin. *Costumes:* Susan Becker. *Make-up:* Deborah Larson and Patricia Gerhardt. *Make-up (Maddona):* Joe Campayno. *Stunt Coordinator:* David Ellis. *Running time:* 99 minutes. *MPAA Rating:* R.

CAST: Madonna (Rebecca Carlson); Willem Dafoe (Frank Dulaney); Joe Mantegna (Robert Garrett); Anne Archer (Joanne Braslow); Julianne Moore (Sharon Dulaney); Jurgen Prochnow (Dr. Alan Paley); Frank Langella (Jeffrey Roston); Michael Forest (Andrew Marsh); Charles Hallahan (Dr. McCurdy); Mark Rolston (Detective Reese); Richard Riehle (Detective Griffin); D. Scott Douglas (Printman); Mario DePriest and John DeLay (Technicians); Ross Huffman-Kerr (Photographer); Mark C. Vincent (Reporter); Frank Roberts (Minister); Aaron Corcoran (Michael Dulaney); Timi Prulhiere (Waitress); Corey Brunish (Jamie); Stan Shaw (Charles Biggs); Jeff Perry (Gabe); John Chandler (Dr. Novaro); Lillian Lehman (Judge Burnham); Peter Paul Eastman (Jury Foreman); Byron Clark (Clerk).

FILMS IN REVIEW, 4/93, p. 132, Barbara Cramer

The Kamasutra according to Madonna, and likely one of the biggest turkeys of all time—except it's so dumb and stupid, you might have a good laugh in spite of yourself by default.

This courtroom drama has the Material Girl on trial for murdering her older lover. The motive: she's heir to his $8 million, and where there's a will, she finds a way to collect. The weapon: her body. (He had a heart attack.) The legal question: can she be held responsible? The problem for the audience: who really cares?

Lots of kinky sex with her married lawyer Willem Dafoe (who'll probably never live this one down), but since there's no discernible chemistry between them, all their groping and bedding down-up-and-sideways becomes less amatory, more amateur gymnastics.

If you're unfamiliar with Triple-X video stores, take note that hidden behind the film's unaccountable "R" rating lies borderline hard-core porn. Madonna's M.O.A.—strictly FTB (for the birds) requires such S&M hardware as nipple clamps, handcuffs and leather belts. One mise-en-scène, in a dimly-lit public parking garage, has the duo deftly playing Doctor-and-Nurse, bumping and grinding on shards of glass atop an automobile hood. But they don't stop there. There's legitimate concern that another way she gets a rise out of Dafoe (by dripping hot candle-wax down his bare middle—and well below) may result in a rash of real life third degree burn victims who recklessly, fecklessly throw caution to the wind.

Body of Evidence is evidently Madonna's attempt to allure, but she's fatally unattractive. Physically, and a testament to her personal trainer and daily runs around the park, she has the greatest torso this side of Nike (the statue, not the sneakers). Aesthetically, the rest of her ends up onscreen as Mrs. Potato Head. Neither the camera nor lighting are kind to her. And her costumes and makeup—lifted from Jean Harlow movies—don't do her justice. In the past, she may have shown promise as a first rate comedienne, but she's no *femme fatale* of, say, the Lana and Kathleen Turner School of Seduction. Bleached to the bare bones in sheer blondness, she does try awfully hard, but falls well below her hype and our expectations.

In the film, as a sex kitten with a weakness for rich men with poor circulation, she's also no angel and apparently guilty as sin. Just when you think the case against her is clear, red herrings proving otherwise are tossed in—only to be thrown out.

The only thing played straight is the dialogue. But lines which *woulda* been fun if tongue-in-cheekily said (i.e. "They've taken something good between two people in love and made it dirty") are delivered without even an iota of the irony it *shoulda* had. At least that way, you *coulda* laughed *with* her, not *at* her.

Perhaps that's the film's major problem. No humor. None from Madonna nor any of the others. A dreary Anne Archer (who should get a new agent—or at least some new facial expressions) is typecast once again as a "wronged" woman, and the rest, including Joe Mantegna as prosecutor, Lillian Lehman as a one-dimensional judge (angry-angry), and Jurgen Prochnow as a surprise witness, are poorly guided by Uli Edel (*Last Exit to Brooklyn*). It's possible the German born director confused "Eros" with "Ares", or "sensuality" with "sex" (and the raw mechanics of performance). He greatly overestimated our appetite for fore-and-afterplay. In any event, something was lost in the translation.

Worth a mention is that the disgruntled author of a book bearing the same name as the film obviously didn't relish the connection. (Titles can't be copyrighted.) In what might be a movie milestone, pressure was put on MGM to stipulate the following, in credits spelled out larger than life on the screen: "Not based on the novel by Patricia Cornwell."

Still, all things considered, we should mitigate our hostilities toward this atomic sized bomb. The film's 99 minutes certainly offer double that in unintentional amusement value. For the nonce, bashing Madonna takes our minds off subjects of more serious import—like a war with Iraq, or the high cost of medical care, or the trillions in interest we Americans have to shell out to pay off our national debt. For that, we should be grateful.

So I come to praise Madonna, not bury her. After all, I *did* enjoy and appreciate her talents (in *Desperately Seeking Susan*). Maybe it's a generation thing, and Susan Seidelman knew something Edel didn't. Maybe Madonna fans see something here that I can't, but which has made her one of the hottest, most successful properties of the last decade. Critical hoots and howls albeit, she's laughing all the way to the bank. Maybe I'm just too old to relate.

LOS ANGELES TIMES, 1/15/93, Calendar/p. 1, Kenneth Turan

Take a sexually liberated star whose last project was a clothing-optional book that had to be sealed in Mylar. Add a plot line about whether it is possible to, shall we say, love someone to death. Throw in a few scenes involving hot wax, handcuffs and other sex toys borrowed from the Spanish Inquisition. It may sound racy, but the naked truth is that the only thing in "Body of Evidence" that comes close to sizzling is that overheated wax.

Starring Madonna as a "did she or didn't she" murder suspect and Willem Dafoe as the legal eagle who risks his marriage, his reputation and his ability to get a good night's sleep to defend her, "Body of Evidence," promises a great deal more than it can deliver. Yes, there is a lot of talk about passion without limits and the animal side of human sexual behavior, but when it comes to putting the same on screen, "Wild Kingdom" turns out to be considerably more involving.

Like "Basic Instinct," to which it bears a feeble family resemblance, "Body" opens with the death of a prominent and wealthy businessman in sexually super-heated circumstances. His death certificate may read cardiac arrest, but D.A. Robert Garrett (Joe Mantegna) didn't just fall off the turnip truck.

After viewing some spicy home movies the deceased conveniently left behind and hearing what his loyal secretary (Anne Archer) has to say about Rebecca Carlson (Madonna), the dead man's very lively girlfriend and prime beneficiary, Garrett decides that the rather unusual charge of murder by fornication is in order. "She is the worst kind of killer," he thunders to the jury, "because she disguised herself as a loving partner."

Rather than hire Dr. Ruth as a character witness, Rebecca employs defense attorney Frank Dulaney (Dafoe). Though he is supposed to be some sort of legal Sir Galahad, Frank comes across as more oafish than domineering. And he doesn't even blink when Rebecca hits him with a series of venerable lines such as "He wasn't old to me" and the always popular "They're trying to take something good and make it dirty."

Once Frank is hired, "Body of Evidence" proceeds down a pair of equally silly and unconvincing lines. One is the courtroom battle, which, despite lawyers leaping up and down and objecting at the slightest provocation, is remarkably listless. Surprise witnesses and socko testimony are the orders of the day ("Frank, I can explain everything" is one of Rebecca's frequent lines) but the shocks are too arbitrary to be at all convincing.

The same goes for the romance between the nominally married attorney and his girls-just-want-to-have-fun client, a femme fatale who seems to have looked to Torquemada for sex tips. Much to his surprise (if no one else's) Frank turns out to share her taste for the wilder shores of love, and soon he and Rebecca are turning places like the P4 level of the courtroom garage into their own private lovers' lane.

This taste for passion in the most uncomfortable places is shared by the characters in the current "Damage," but the (difference is that while Jeremy Irons and Juliette Binoche bring enough conviction to their roles to involve you in their unlikely situation, the protagonists in "Body of Evidence" (despite its R rating for strong sexuality, language, violence) never do.

Though both Madonna and Dafoe have been convincing on screen in the past, they are too self-absorbed as actors to create the kind of interpersonal chemistry this story demands. She seems too knowing for her role, he too distant for his, and the resulting lack of mutual involvement sinks whatever hopes this vehicle had.

Not that it had that many to begin with. Brad Mirman's script is rife with hollow lines and arbitrary situations and director Uli Edel, whose previous "Last Exit to Brooklyn" was well-received, has been unable to bring any energy at all to the screen. Even the heavy-breathing scenes, about which the press notes reveal, "the collaborators sat and discussed for hours," feel passionless and overrehearsed. Perhaps, like many other overprepared athletes, the players in "Body of Evidence" left their best game in the locker room.

NEW STATESMAN & SOCIETY, 4/16/93, p. 35, Jonathan Romney

Another act of auto-destructive self-parody [the reference is to *Accidental Hero*, see *Film Review Annual, 1993*.] is Madonna's turn in *Body of Evidence*, which belies the popular notions that a) she's a sizzling mass of libido, and b) she knows a good career move when she sees one. In this ignoble non-starter, she's a lukewarm hot babe accused of screwing a rich old geezer to death—stop-me-if-you've-heard-this-onestory that would be laughed out of any courtroom drama worth its oak panelling.

The twist is that everyone acts as if sex had only just arrived in Portland, Oregon. Madonna's character may be on trial for her sexual appetite, but everyone's more interested in her dietary quirks. She likes nothing more shocking than a bit of tastefully lit hanky panky with candle wax, but the jurors gasp at the slightest mention of nipple clamps as if they had never glanced at the *Village Voice* personal columns.

Months after the *Sex* book brouhaha, everyone's dog-tired from theorising about Madonna. This dreary, inept film is way past its sell-by date. But it does confirm that her brand of eroticism is straight out of the old Windmill Theatre, where the nudes never budged. Her raunchiest videos have always essentially been fast-cut selections of stills: it's when she moves, and worse, acts, that you realise how lifeless, humourless and desperately unironic she is.

Body of Evidence could have been made by the Medved lobby as a puritanical corrective to her book: evidence that sex is not what it's cracked up to be, even when it's uncomfortable. Even the masturbation scene is dogged enough to look like a demonstration of the sturdy durability of Calvin Klein panties. But, who knows, maybe that's what they care about in Oregon.

NEW YORK, 1/25/93, p. 54, David Denby

In *Body of Evidence*, Madonna plays a woman named Rebecca who's on trial for murder. But let's not be silly: Madonna cannot create a character; she cannot yield herself to any fantasy except her own—that she is single-handedly liberating America from its hypocrisies and hang-ups. The movie, nominally a courtroom drama, is actually just a pretense to exploit the public's fascination with Madonna's sex life, and perhaps the most pathetic thing about it is that the people who made it think they are doing something really dirty. Every time Rebecca reveals some secret, and the prosecuting attorney (Joe Mantegna) says, "You mean you used ... *handcuffs?*," the extras in the courtroom all murmur *rhubarb kartoffel, rhubarb kartoffel,* or whatever it is that extras are told to murmur in order to create a rumble of consternation. Oooh, shocking! Rhubarb kartoffel!

Onscreen, Madonna is a hot bore, a terrible naked actress. She may pour melted wax on poor Willem Dafoe's privates, but honestly, in *Double Indemnity,* a movie made a half-century ago, the fully dressed Barbara Stanwyck conveyed more dirty lust just by *acting* with her incomparable smoky voice. Since *Body of Evidence* is inept in every way, picking on Madonna may seem unfair, but she obviously wants to be a movie star, and it may be worth saying why she doesn't qualify.

To begin with, her speaking voice is thin and metallic. The director, Uli Edel, is German and may not hear the tin writing in Brad Mirman's screenplay, but surely he can hear the tin in Madonna's voice? Edel doesn't help her there, and his lighting annihilates her. He favors huge swatches of alienating white light, and by the time he and cinematographer Doug Milsome get done illuminating her face, she looks like a gleaming white wafer. There's no depth or range of expression to the face—it's about as sexy as a sundial. In a rock video, she's whirling around and singing, so if you can't see her it doesn't really matter, but in *Body of Evidence* the dramatic effect depends on our "reading" the heroine's ambiguous face (is she telling the truth?), and the harsh lighting reveals only that Madonna cannot hold a close-up. Her face has nothing to say. For a movie actress, that's the point of no return.

Spreading herself out on the floor or climbing atop a car in a parking lot and raising her skirt for Dafoe, she's a coarse, unmysterious object, a seeming escapee from *The Robin Byrd Show.* Madonna plays her self-flattering myth—a naughty girl who's too honest to pretend she's good, a woman so truthful, doing what the rest of us only dream of doing, that she will free us from our lies. But Madonna also makes an attempt to merge her persona with Marlene Dietrich's, wearing a suit and beret at one point, as if she were a dazzling, svelte dish like Dietrich. This is a hapless mistake. Dietrich never relinquished her haughty reserve: The essence of her glamour was the imagined perfection of what she *withheld.* The result was that she was treated as a sex goddess, whereas Madonna, in this movie, is treated as a nasty whore. A pop star can be overexposed, but a movie star cannot. There must be some mystery, or else she doesn't survive onscreen—except in porny flicks.

This movie makes *Basic Instinct* look like a masterpiece. In the cheesy opening sequence, the camera travels up the steps in a stone mansion as lightning flashes through the windows. But all of this menacing atmosphere leads to nothing more powerful than a man sitting in bed looking at a homemade sex video. Is the opening meant to be a parody of gothic thrillers? Where's the punch line? The man is dead the next morning, and Rebecca, his lover and the beneficiary of his will, is accused of murdering him. According to the prosecuting attorney, she knew he had a bad heart yet made love to him so wildly that she killed him. The screenplay is so poorly written that one can't tell at first whether this idea is meant as parody either. But no, the filmmakers are serious, and the prosecutor accuses Rebecca of having attempted to screw other men to death as well. One of them, a survivor, is played by a shamefaced Frank Langella as a mere shell of a man (too much wax put out his candle).

Though millions of men rape and abuse women every year, the cinema has shown a remarkable interest recently in the murdering sexual *woman.* I suppose there is nothing for us to do but thank Hollywood for bringing this pressing social issue to light.

Dafoe gets to play the victim-sap this time, and he makes me realize how good Michael Douglas is. Dafoe has always had a weighted, over-deliberate method of speaking, as if he were prepping for a job as Charlton Heston's dialogue coach, but here, as Rebecca's hotshot attorney, he is ludicrous. Given that Madonna has only one thing on her mind, his tormented face and dawn-of-consciousness delivery seem more than a little out of it. The audience started giggling at his sexual anguish early in the show and never stopped. As for the other actors, Mantegna looks bored, and Anne Archer, as the dead man's secretary and Madonna's rival, is weepy and creepy. A shadow of crude mediocrity hangs over all of them. Really, I don't get it. Did all these people want to work with Uli Edel on the basis of his bleak, antagonistic direction of *Last Exit to Brooklyn*? Edel seems ill at ease with human beings, who, unfortunately, are the material a movie director has to work with.

Does *Body of Evidence* make it as a trash classic, a howl for the ages? No, Edel doesn't have enough fantasy and warmth to make enjoyable trash. The only dream here is Madonna's—that men will become so aroused by her they will begin dropping dead all over the place. The movie might, however, be a gift-wrapped package to those academics who make a career of writing analytical papers about the wealthy sex icon. *Body of Evidence* is so denuded of human interest and plausibility that the power relations in it are as clear as the bones of a skeleton. So much to deconstruct! *Body of Evidence* may die in the theaters, but it should keep the academic quarterlies humming.

NEW YORK POST, 1/15/93, p. 25, Jami Bernard

Never was there a more compelling argument for an actress to sleep with her director than "Body of Evidence." Madonna looks terrible in it. Maybe if she had slept with Uli Edel, he would have lit her better. Remember, Madonna looked fabulous in "Dick Tracy" when she was sleeping with Warren Beatty.

Anne Archer doesn't look so hot herself in "Body of Evidence." Perhaps both actresses should have slept with the director. Maybe that would have given him a heart attack, and then life would be imitating art—or at least it would be imitating the artless "Body of Evidence"—in which Madonna is a beautiful young woman accused of screwing her aged lover to death.

That her character is beautiful you'll just have to take on faith, since she looks weary and dissipated, with a line through her cheek as if too much hard living had just belted her in the jaw.

To be fair, this is the best serious acting that Madonna has ever done; but that isn't saying much. She has a long way, and many acting lessons, to go.

She plays Rebecca Carlson, a woman on trial for using her feminine wiles and her taste for sadomasochistic sex to send her elderly, wealthy lover over the edge. Some of the men out there might be thinking, "Gee, whatta way to go!" But they are not taking into account that first their nipples will be squeezed in a clamp, then their backs will be sliced with shards of glass, and then hot wax will be dripped on their manhoods. *Now* what do you say?

Willem Dafoe, whose cheekbones alone could slice deeper than any shard of glass, plays Frank Dulaney, Rebecca's lawyer. You know how some men get when their around beautiful women—their jaws go slack, their eyes get limpid and their common sense (let alone their memory of their wives and children) gets all fuzzy. Frank not only wants to defend the grieving woman, he also wants to get the handcuffs-&-wax treatment that Rebecca doles out on her windswept houseboat.

Note to S&M fans: If you insist on trying these moves at home, skip the part where Rebecca licks the hot wax off her lawyer's chest. That is truly yucky.

"Body of Evidence" is a trashy potboiler, but not as erotic as the movie's brief flirtation with an NC-17 rating would suggest. The movie seems more like a marketing adjunct to Madonna's "Sex" book than a thing of its own. "It's not a crime to be a good lay," argues Frank in Rebecca's defense at her trial.

There are missed opportunities to explore the relationships among the women in the cast—the spurned wife and secretary, the backlash idea of the single woman as a threat to men's hearts—but basically the message is that lawyers should not get involved with their clients until the trial is over. And even then, bring the Band Aids.

NEWSDAY, 1/15/93, Part II/p. 62, Jack Mathews

There is a glimmer of good news for moviegoers on the opening weekend of Hollywood's 1993 season: After "Body of Evidence," in which Madonna plays a woman accused of lulling a man with sex, there is nowhere to go but up.

"Body of Evidence" is Hollywood's version of amateur night at a topless bar, where some blonde has just climbed on the stage and taken everything off but doesn't know how to dance. So, everyone just sits there dumb-founded, equally embarrassed by her audacity and her incompetence.

Madonna, of course, does know how to dance, and she has everything under control when she gets her clothes off in this movie. But when it comes to reading a line or reacting to a line or simply walking into a room as if she were someone else, no can do.

Madonna's is one of those performances, like Pia Zadora's in "Butterfly," that takes talented people down with it. Stacy Keach and Orson Welles were among Zadora's victims in "Butterfly." The casualty list for "Body of Evidence" includes Joe Mantegna, as the prosecuting attorney, Anne Archer, as the deceased man's troubled secretary, and Frank Langella, as a prosecution witness who claims to have come within an orgasm of losing his own life.

But the primary victim is Willem Dafoe, stuck playing a defense attorney who has to convince a Portland, Ore., jury that his client, and off-duty dominatrix, is guilty of nothing but being "a great lay."

There is no way to overstate the ludicrousness of "Body of Evidence," a "Basic Instinct" wannabe made from a script that 20 years ago could have been promoted as a sequel to "Deep Throat." ("Say, friends, remember that woman whose sex organ was located next to her epiglottis? Well, it's in the right place now, but she's using it to kill men with weak hearts and inherit their estates.")

This is the low-concept, soft-porn plot of the decade. Madonna's Rebecca Carlson is an art gallery owner accused of killing her middle-age lover by revving up his heart with cocaine-laced nasal spray, then handcuffing him to a bed and getting him to blow a valve with some strenuous sex.

"This case should have never gone to trial," Dafoe's Frank Dulaney tells the jury in his opening statement. No kidding, counselor! It should have never gone into development.

The script was turned into a movie because Dino De Laurentiis, the high-flying Italian producer who talked Jessica Lange into letting an animated gorilla feel her up in "King Kong," was looking for something—anything—with which he could further exploit the daredevil slut image of Madonna.

Can't get her to simulate masturbation in front of an audience ... been done.

Can't get her to pose nude in a public place ... been done.

Can't get her to be photographed having rough sex ... been done.

So, along comes first-time screenwriter Brad Mirman with an idea most of us would be loathe to mention, and De Laurentiis has an opportunity to show Madonna doing it all in one place. Forget the Mylar-covered book and the unexpurgated video, just buy a ticket to "Body of Evidence" and ...

Watch Madonna pour hot candle wax on Dafoe's birdlike chest, cool the lava with a splash of champagne, then scarf it up like a hungry buzzard.

Watch her straddle him on the hood of a Buick, and see the expression on his face when he feels the sensuous tingle of broken glass digging into his back.

Try not to laugh as Madonna attempts such lines as, "They've taken something beautiful between two people and made it something dirty."

Win a set of dishes guessing the number of "Basic Instinct" rip-offs, besides the fact that they are both murder mysteries about a sadomasochistic blonde who likes to lure lame-brained lawmen into death-defying acts of bondage.

"Body of Evidence," directed by Uli Edel ("Last Exit to Brooklyn"), is a slick-looking production with lots of genre atmosphere—smoky rooms, rain-dappled windows, a moody, Madonnaless soundtrack by Graeme Revell—but there is no hiding the fact that it is a courtroom drama with no case.

Despite the impassioned theatrics of Dafoe and Mantegna, the usual assortment of hostile and hand-wringing witnesses, plot twists that will have you laughing out loud, and a judge (Lillian Lehman) who likes to play rough herself, you'd have a tougher time—and more fun—trying to figure out who killed Cock Robin.

NEWSWEEK, 1/18/93, p. 59, David Ansen

You may find this hard to believe, but the star of *Body of Evidence*, an actress named Madonna, actually reveals a lot of flesh in this courtroom drama. The exhibitionism, let me hasten to add, is entirely in the service of her character, Rebecca Carlson, a sexpot dominatrix who is accused of murdering her lover, an older man with a weak heart and a big fortune, by exciting him to death. The district attorney (Joe Mantegna) is intent on proving that Rebecca's body is a lethal weapon. Her defense attorney (Willem Dafoe), though a married man, believes in trying out the weapon himself. Discovering the kink in his own lustful heart, the lawyer and his client indulge in some sweaty S&M game-playing themselves: she pours hot wax on his tied-up body; they make love atop broken glass on the hood of a car parked in the courthouse garage; later, she brings out the handcuffs ...

Is Rebecca a murderous material girl, or just a lusty gal with a misunderstood life-style? That's the question that supplies the suspense in Uli Edel's slick thriller, in which "Witness for the Prosecution" cohabits with "The Story of O" and "Basic Instinct." Until it collapses into a silly shambles in the denouement, "Body of Evidence" is a fairly stylish entry in the currently ubiquitous *femme fatale* sweepstakes. As written by Brad Mirman, Madonna's role is so tailor-made for her that one might suspect she is reading outtakes from her best seller, "Sex" (there's lots of talk about liking to be "in control"). Made up in '30s ice-goddess fashion, she's still more an icon than an actress, but there's no denying the avidly smutty *frisson* she brings to the sex scenes. It's Dafoe's quiet conviction, however, that keeps the drama rooted in something resembling reality: he makes a theoretical role intriguingly human. Anne Archer also appears, not as a noble wife this time, but as the dead man's secretary, who seems a little too eager to pin the blame on Rebecca. "Body of Evidence" won't be remembered for classic plotting or brilliant legal gambits. But give it its due: it holds one's attention.

SIGHT AND SOUND, 5/93, p. 48, Julie Wheelwright

Andrew Marsh, an aged millionaire with a weak heart, dies in unusual circumstances in his Oregon mansion. His blood reveals traces of cocaine, and a video of his love-making with gallery owner Rebecca Carlson is found in his bedroom along with his corpse. Suspicion mounts when local detectives find various sex toys and Marsh's secretary Joanne Braslow announces that Carlson murdered him. Frank Dulaney, Portland's top defence lawyer, takes on Carlson's case just before assistant DA Robert Garrett files murder charges against her. Dulaney learns that Rebecca stands to inherit Marsh's $8 million estate, but remains convinced that their relationship was based on a mutual taste for sado-masochistic sex.

When the trial opens, Garrett attempts to prove that Rebecca purposely engaged Marsh in increasingly dangerous sexual acts and laced a nasal spray with cocaine to induce a heart attack. At first, Garrett's arguments are destroyed when Dulaney reveals Joanne Braslow's former cocaine habit, her previous sexual relationship with Marsh and that he had recently reduced her share of his will in favour of Carlson. But as the trial progresses, Dulaney becomes sexually involved with Rebecca, which threatens both their professional relationship and his marriage. When Garrett proves in court that Rebecca had a previous affair with an older business tycoon with a weak heart, Dulaney is outraged by the betrayal and confronts her. Rebecca is saved, however, by her convincing testimony that she broke off with the businessman when she found him in bed with another man.

Dulaney wins the case but returns to Rebecca's houseboat that night to catch her discussing Marsh's murder with her lover Dr Alex Paley, who supplied Marsh with the fatal dose of cocaine. When Paley learns about Rebecca's affair with Frank, he shoots her in a jealous rage and the police arrive in time to arrest the killer.

"Can you really screw someone to death?" Frank Dulaney's precocious son asks his father. "Of course not," replies Frank, flinching from the accusations made against his client. But out of the mouth of babes comes wisdom. When assistant DA Garrett tells the court that Rebecca Carlson is a "ruthless, calculating woman", the question hangs in the air. According to Garrett, Rebecca's luscious body—of which the audience sees much—is as deadly as "a gun or knife". The theme of the female body as weapon is familiar territory and *Body of Evidence* offers no surprises.

An unconvincing plot, with the murder never fully explained, is further hampered by Brad Mirman's clumsy screenplay, thick with clichés and pretentious allusions to sexual liberation. While it gestures towards Madonna's role as a woman on the cutting edge of sexual expression, this posturing quickly buckles under its own contradictions. Rebecca espouses enlightened views on sado-masochism—"have you ever seen animals make love? It's intense, it's violent but they never really hurt each other"—yet she's a manipulative harridan. She may be an expert with nipple clamps but in the tradition of Hollywood vamps, she keeps a cold eye on her lover's bank balance.

With this sexual whirlwind whistling through their lives, neither Frank Dulaney nor Andrew Marsh can be held responsible for getting in bed with Madonna. Rebecca tells Dulaney, "I know I'm irresistible," and it's assumed that male lust knows no moral boundaries. Uli Edel's direction reinforces this antiquated notion by reducing the subtle power dynamics of sexual desire to the visual cliche of Rebecca as "dominatrix", literally the woman on top. And once again, it's difficult to separate Madonna the star from her on-screen character, whose gestures seem to have been lifted from her book *Sex*: her index finger dives below white cotton panties, there's a furtive screw in an underground parking lot and an anal rape. Neither does Willem Dafoe bring depth to these erotic scenes, although he is far more convincing with Julianne Moore as his wife Sharon.

Edel apparently intended the sex scenes to provide the film's action, which they do only by default. Since the murderer's *modus operandi* remains unclear, Garrett's revelations about Rebecca's former lovers with weak hearts have little dramatic impact. The tension is further undermined by a judge who treats the courtroom with all the gravitas becoming a diner, scolding the attorneys and reminding the spectators to "keep your rude mouths shut or get out".

While the film includes a handful of career women—the judge is a black woman, Sharon manages a smart restaurant and Rebecca owns an art gallery—it is mainly a thinly disguised exercise in male bonding. Garrett's prurient questioning of Rebecca's sexual habits, which first sends Dulaney into a fury, is later justified by her involvement in Marsh's murder. At the boathouse the two men watch Rebecca's corpse floating in the river (cf. Alex in *Fatal Attraction*) and congratulate each other on catching the real criminal. For all its reliance on contemporary debates about perversion, *Body of Evidence* indulges a depressingly narrow view of sexual relationships.

VILLAGE VOICE, 1/19/93, p. 45, J. Hoberman

Madonna must covet James Brown's title as the hardest worker in show business. There's no kind of fun that can't be instrumentalized. In *Body of Evidence* she plays a woman put on trial for leaving a dead millionaire and a trademark nipple-clamp in a recently occupied bed. The charge is murder; the lethal weapon, according to the prosecuting attorney (Joe Mantegna), is Madonna herself. She's accused of fucking her lover to death.

Madonna's character owns an art gallery; she lives in a duplex houseboat to rival Cleopatra's Barge, eschews drugs for homeopathic medicine, and gets regular acupuncture treatment in her tawny rump. ("Booty of Evidence"? a colleague suggested.) So why is she constantly under suspicion? "They've taken something beautiful between two people in love and made it dirty," she complains to her lawyer (Willem Dafoe) in the first of the movie's inadvertent, if insufficiently numerous, howlers. "It's not a crime to be a great lay," is Dafoe's first line of defense and that's even before he and his client have taken to having blatantly unsafe sex in dangerous places.

So, is Madonna a demure victim of prejudice or an evil succubus of death? Most of *Body of Evidence* is devoted to a trial in which Mantegna keeps serving up sleazy witnesses and Dafoe and Madonna keep batting them out, (That's literally, as when Madonna outed her brother in *Truth or Dare*.) Is the star a wrongly accused Susan Hayward, a coldly manipulative Barbara Stanwyck, or some tight-wrapped yuppie conflation of the two? Does she prey on rich old men with strong libidos and weak tickers—a modus operandi that gives a new meaning to affairs of the heart—or is she just an innocent fan of semiconsensual s&m? You be the judge (a character who, as played by Lillian Lehman, is herself a scold of dominatrix proportions).

The audience of semioticians that packed the Ziegfeld to interrogate this latest text audibly enjoyed Madonna's protestations of wounded innocence. But they chuckled even louder when Dafoe told her, "You have an inflated opinion of yourself." Whatever she is Madonna presents herself as an irresistible force. Her mere appearance in his life is sufficient to improve the lawyer's conjugal relations. The movie is predicated on the assumption that Madonna has only to crank up her musk-machine and shake her money-maker to bring the world to its knees.

The roughhouse sex suggests gay porn—abrupt and tigerish. Madonna directs the action herself—and, if *Body of Evidence* had half the oomph of *Basic Instinct*, it might have been a minor camp triumph. But, as docilely directed by Uli Edel (*Last Exit to Brooklyn*), it not only fails to go over the top but loudly bangs its head in the attempt. The movie has the inert blandness of a European co-pro—although the would-be collaboration here is between the left and right halves of the brain.

Beyond co-pro is the garish assortment of supporting actors, each schlepping his or her own baggage. It's not just that Joe Mantegna connotes an entire Mamet-world of macho angst. Hair teased into a grotesque pompadour, Anne Archer plays one of several wives obliterated by Madonna's fatal attractions while, in the course of his desecration, Willem Dafoe has to endure more temptations than he did as J.C. The tacky postmodern ambience is reinforced by staging the trial in Michael Graves's salmon-and-turquoise Portland courthouse—this mock-imperial backdrop is the perfect site for Madonna's (no doubt skim) milk bath—and the movie's unique credit "not based on the novel by Patricia Cornwell." But, given that Madonna can only play herself, the movie's weirdest twist is the echo effect achieved by her seeming imitation of Sharon Stone's *Basic Instinct* impersonation of her.

Madonna's repeated failure to make it on the silver screen would be poignant were her desire to succeed not so dogged. Even the sense of s&m her character articulates has a curiously careerminded, joggerlike spin, predicated on the principle "no pain, no gain." (*Body of Evidence* also exhibits a oddly punitive attitude toward sexual pleasure, particularly arriving on the heels of Madonna's apparently celebratory *Sex*.) As leading wannabe Camille Paglia might advise: Relax and be fabulous.

Not tonight, Camille. Madonna only gets a single credit here, but *Body of Evidence* is still a work of total control. (We await her announced collaboration with fellow parochial-school delinquent Abel Ferrara—working title *Ms. Calculation*?) Indeed, for all the acrobatic sex, the star permits herself but a single climax. It's an interesting bit of self-disclosure. Madonna's heavy breathing and orgasmic moans are more heard than seen—and then revealed to be issuing from a videotape, a performance made for TV.

Also reviewed in:
CHICAGO TRIBUNE, 1/15/93, Friday/p. C, Dave Kehr
NEW REPUBLIC, 2/8/93, p. 25, Stanley Kauffmann
NEW YORK TIMES, 1/15/93, p. C3, Vincent Canby
VARIETY, 1/11/93, p. 64, Todd McCarthy
WASHINGTON POST, 1/15/93, p. B1, Rita Kempley
WASHINGTON POST, 1/15/93, Weekend/p. 38, Desson Howe

BOILING POINT

A Warner Bros. release of a Hexagon Films production. *Executive Producer:* Rene Bonnell and Olivier Granier. *Producer:* Marc Frydman, Leonardo de la Fuente, and Patrick Beaufront. *Director:* James B. Harris. *Screenplay:* James B. Harris. *Based on the novel "Money Men"* *by:* Gerald Petievich. *Director of Photography:* King Baggot. *Editor:* Jerry Brady. *Music:* Cory Lerios and John D'Andrea. *Music Editor:* Patrick O'Sullivan. *Sound:* Russell C. Fager and (music) Ernie Scheesley. *Sound Editor:* David Lewis Yewdall. *Casting:* Al Guarino. *Production Designer:* Ron Foreman. *Art Director:* Russ Smith. *Set Decorator:* Rick Caprarelli. *Set Dresser:* Helen Kozora. *Special Effects:* Lou Carlucci. *Costumes:* Molly Maginnis. *Make-up:* Allison Gordin. *Stunt Coordinator:* Chuck Waters. *Running time:* 98 minutes. *MPAA Rating:* R.

CAST: Wesley Snipes (Jimmy Mercer); Dennis Hopper (Red Diamond); Lolita Davidovich (Vikki); Viggo Mortensen (Ronnie); Seymour Cassell (Leach); Jonathan Banks (Max); Christine Elise (Carol); Tony Lo Bianco (Dio); Valerie Perrine (Mona); James Tolkan (Levitt); Paul Gleason (Transaction Man); Lorraine Evanoff (Connie); Stephanie Williams

(Sally);   Tobin Bell (Roth);   Bobby Hosea (Steve);   Dan Hedaya (Brady);   George Gerdes (Henderson);   James Pickens, Jr. (Prison Officer);   Keith Hickles (Cook);   Rick Dean (Bartender);   John Petievich (Hotel Security Officer);   Mark Phelan (Banner);   Nancy Sullivan (Female Clerk);   John Lander (Coroner's Deputy);   Lisa Kaseman (Ballroom Dancer);   Janet May (Vocalist);   John David Sarviss (Helicopter Pilot).

LOS ANGELES TIMES, 4/16/93, Calendar/p. 8, Kevin Thomas

Despite an action thriller ad campaign, "Boiling Point" is writer-director James B. Harris' superior contemporary *film noir*, originally called "Money Men," which is the title of the Gerald Petievich novel upon which it is based.

The ads tell us that Wesley Snipes plays "a cop who's reached the boiling point," where in fact his Jimmy Mercer is a Treasury agent of formidable self-control in pursuit of the person or persons who have killed his partner.

We're being led to expect another "Passenger 57" when what we've got instead is a stylish, effective, deliberately B-scale movie that's more like Hawks' "The Big Sleep" and boasts an ensemble Grade A cast and emphasizes character over action.

"Boiling Point" is taut and crisp, and when it's required, Harris handles violence with swift dispatch rather than the large scale fireworks that have become *de rigueur*.

There's a real danger, however, that action fans will be disappointed while those who are looking for witty adult entertainment that offers the pleasures of *film noir* classics will be put off by the ads.

Alas, "Boiling Point" is the kind of film more likely to get a chance to be appreciated in Paris—it was in fact, produced by a French subsidiary—than in Hollywood, which is its principal setting.

Snipes' Mercer and Dennis Hopper's Red Diamond are men with seven-day deadlines. Mercer has been given a week to close the case himself on his partner's death before being transferred to Newark; Red, a lifelong con man with a taste for counterfeit money, has the same amount of time to come up with the cash he owes a Mafioso (Tony Lo Bianco, in a chilling performance of false bonhomie), an old associate from whom he had hoped to borrow 50-grand to get started after having just finished serving a five-year stretch at Terminal Island.

Although billed second, Hopper is the film's dominating presence, and he gives us one of his best portrayals ever, as a flashy, middle-aged loser, a guy increasingly desperate behind the brass facade typical of a used car salesman. He's like Jack Lemmon's real estate salesman in "Glengarry Glen Ross," but firmly on the wrong side of the law. He's shrewd, seasoned, decidedly dangerous and a shameless liar, but you can plainly see that he's never been very smart.

His mounting panic is all too obvious whereas Mercer, so well played in understated style by Snipes, keeps his cool even when he feels as if he's dying on the inside from loneliness, a feeling intensified by the loss of his partner. (The one place where Red does feel confident is on the dance floor, and he can't go to the Palace often enough to glide and swing to the nostalgic music of an orchestra with a '40s big-band repertoire.)

For 20 years the cliché of the law enforcement officer's personal life is that his wife has left him—or is about to do so, saying inevitably that his work is all wrong for a man with a family.

Typical of the freshness of "Boiling Point" is that just when Mercer receives this deathless remark from his ex-wife, both Diamond and his naive but lethal young protégé Ronnie (Viggo Mortensen) are received with open arms by their women, who know better but care for them anyway.

If Valerie Perrine's attractive waitress is far, far better than Red deserves, Mercer does have the consolation of Lolita Davidovich's elegant and wise high-class call girl, who would consider going off with him but only if he *doesn't* resign from his job.

With its spare, moody score and King Baggot's color cinematography that's lit like it's black-and-white, "Boiling Point" is a smoky, sophisticated pleasure throughout. (With the Hollywood Roosevelt and the Palace as key locales, the film scarcely ever strays farther away than Union Station.)

Contributing strongly to that pleasure are such sterling actors as Dan Hedaya as Mercer's stalwart new partner, Seymour Cassel as a very canny bad guy and Jonathan Banks, a standout as a slick, crooked Century City attorney.

"Boiling Point" (rated R for violence and for language) is the work of a man who knows his way around the crime genre. Harris produced Stanley Kubrick's "The Killing," directed the 1987 "Cop" from James Ellroy's "Blood on the Moon" and is now developing a film of Ellroy's, "The Black Dahlia."

NEWSDAY, 4/17/93, Part II/p. 23, Terry Kelleher

The ads say Wesley Snipes is "a cop who's reached the 'Boiling Point.'" This is not, strictly speaking, true.

Snipes plays a Los Angeles-based Treasury agent in the movie, and his temperature seldom gets more than a degree or two above normal. There's nothing here worth losing one's cool over.

In "Cop" (title says it all) and "Fast-Walking" (prison flick), director-writer James B. Harris showed he can give a genre picture a touch more interest than expected. But then both those films were juiced up by the presence of James Woods.

The actor chiefly charged with responsibility for energizing "Boiling Point" is not Snipes but Dennis Hopper, who portrays the criminal targeted by the hero. Hopper's Red Diamond has his roots in the sort of '40s film noir this movie seeks to emulate. He wears two-tone shoes, dances to the big-band sounds and walks like a drum major. His language is grifter-speak: "There ain't gonna be no heat from the cops ... Trust me—you'll be set for life." Of course, only a fool would fall for this ex-con's con game, but Hopper fails to make the character any more believable than his rap. Though his hand gestures are busy, he never really finds Red's voice.

Snipes' Jimmy Mercer, on the other hand, is rather blah from beginning to end. He carries a torch for his ex-wife, but never lights it. A fine-looking hooker named Vikki (Lolita Davidovich) loves Jimmy enough to favor him with freebies, but they have a relationship so vaguely defined that the movie can't wrap it up without an explanatory postscript.

As for his professional life, the script dictates that Jimmy nail Red and his young triggerman, Ronnie (played with laconic menace by Viggo Mortensen), for counterfeiting and murder if he hopes to stave off a transfer to the Newark office. Despite this compelling motivation, Jimmy uses neither brilliant detective work nor unusually heavy firepower to crack the case. He just makes the obvious moves, waits for a break and girds for the climactic showdown (set, of course, in a ballroom featuring the music of "the fabulous '40s").

During the closing credits, the old standard "Dream" gives way to "Money Men," a rock-and-roll number that takes its name from the novel on which Harris based his screenplay. The original title would be more descriptive than "Boiling Point" if the movie tried to satisfy our curiosity about the business of counterfeiting. But that would entail telling us things we don't already know.

SIGHT AND SOUND, 11/93, p. 37, Tom Tunney

Los Angeles. US Treasury agents Mercer, Brady and Russo mount an undercover operation around a dingy Hollywood motel. However, the bust goes wrong when Russo is shot dead and his $10,000 'buy money' is stolen by Ronnie, an impressionable young crook in league with Red Diamond, a dapper con artist just released from jail. Mercer visits his ex-wife; Diamond visits his waitress wife Mona; and Ronnie visits his girlfriend. All receive frosty receptions. Diamond calls on mobster Tony Dio, gives him $8,000 and is given a mere seven days to raise the balance of $42,000 he owes from the time before he went to jail.

Threatened with a transfer to Newark, Mercer persuades his boss Levitt to keep him on the case so he can catch his partner's killer. Their meeting is in the same hotel in which call girl Vikki plies her trade and which Diamond frequents. A lead takes Mercer first to jail, where he interviews Freddy, an imprisoned counterfeiter, and then to a bar where he poses as a potential buyer of counterfeit money to Virgil Leach, the holder of the imprisoned man's stash. When arrested, Leach refuses to co-operate, even when Mercer threatens action against his girlfriend Connie. Diamond meets Vikki in the hotel bar and invites her to go old-time dancing with him at the Palace ballroom. Walking her back to the hotel, Diamond almost crosses paths with Mercer—who is himself having an affair with Vikki.

Diamond visits Max, a crooked lawyer, and gets the brush off when he asks for $50,000 for keeping his mouth shut about their illicit dealings. Mercer and Brady go to Connie's apartment, but are too late to prevent her killing herself. Ronnie goes to Max's office, posing as a potential seller of counterfeit money. A meeting is arranged for that night between Ronnie and one of Max's men. Ronnie shoots the man, then drives over the corpse. However, the cash he takes from the dead man's money belt also proves to be counterfeit. The next day, Mercer interrogates Max and finally extricates the name he wants: Red Diamond. Realising that time is running out for him to pay back his debt, Diamond lies to Ronnie, claiming that not only has he killed an important Mafia man, but that there are also witnesses to the crime—his plan being to get Ronnie to kill Tony Dio.

Diamond takes Vikki dancing to the Palace again, while Mercer visits his ex-wife and child and discovers her with another man. Meeting Vikki on the street, he asks her to go with him to Newark and she refuses. Diamond visits Mona and says that he'll be free if things go right for him that night, and tells her to meet him at the Palace. Tailed by Mercer and Brady, Diamond and Ronnie go to Tony Dio's place and Ronnie shoots both Dio and a bodyguard while Diamond grabs a substantial amount of cash. The pair separate, agreeing to meet later at the Palace, but Diamond is arrested by Mercer.

Mercer takes Diamond to the dance hall and allows him to approach Ronnie alone. Diamond tells Ronnie that he (Ronnie) has drawn the cops there and says that he should shoot his way out. Ronnie dies in a hail of police bullets, and Diamond is captured and driven away by the police past Mona who is waiting outside. Mercer and Vikki subsequently go to Newark together, while Diamond, sentenced to life imprisonment, plans to appeal.

James B. Harris's films as writer-director-producer characteristically present a murky black comic vision in which the line between right and wrong, cop and criminal is blurred. Rather than dealing in fixed moral certainties, his is a savagely ironic and sometimes subversive world in which everyone manipulates everyone else in a brutal game. There are only two rules: no one can be trusted and a good line of comic dialogue is always worth more than developing the plot or characters in a believable way.

In *Fast Walking* (1981), James Woods' corrupt prison guard, Frank 'Fast Walking' Miniver (so named because of his peculiar dancing gait), is not really very different from Tim McIntire's top-dog convict—and both share the same lover, Kay Lenz. In *Cop* (1988), Woods' sleazy detective tells his little daughter violent bedtime stories and uses a shotgun calmly to blast the defenceless villain in the closing scene. Containing a much-used shotgun, a shared lover (Vikki) and some deft fast walking from Dennis Hopper, *Boiling Point* can be seen as the third part in an unofficial Harris trilogy of black comic crime and punishment. Its opening sequence features a graceful long shot in which all we see are Diamond's feet and flamboyant black and white shoes as he confidently strides along in the street to the strains of an old-fashioned dance number. The implication both here and in *Fast Walking* is the same: the stylish movement defines the man. Both men are colourful, wilfully eccentric individuals adrift in a world of conformity. And, where *Fast Walking* is set in and around a jail, *Boiling Point* features two ex-convicts, Diamond and Ronnie, just released from behind bars. It's an obvious continuation of themes: two ex-cons trapped by their own delusions, following on from a guard and a convict who are similarly imprisoned.

However, compared with *Fast Walking*, which builds a fascinating tension between the amoral guard and the even more amoral convict, *Boiling Point*'s attempt to work up similar parallels between Diamond and the near burnt-out Mercer fall flat. As played by James Woods or Bruce Dern, Mercer could have been interesting. Instead, played straight and without any hint of humour by Snipes, he's merely dull—though he's hardly helped by the fact that the script gives him no memorable lines. By contrast, the relationships between Diamond and Ronnie, and Diamond and his wife are full of sardonic vitality. We constantly ask ourselves who is the most stupid: Diamond for having such hopeless delusions of grandeur or Ronnie for believing him.

Purely on the level of plot, this is a tired and desperately contrived thriller. The tough cop whose dedication to his job has ruined his private life is a limp genre cliché rivalled only by that other formula dimension to Mercer's character: his hunger to avenge his partner's death. However, the film's obvious delight in foregrounding its many bare-faced coincidences is consistently engaging. The casual carelessness of the ending—the title which limply explains what's happened to Vikki and Mercer—is perhaps in keeping with a script which, again and again, trades dramatic credibility in favour of outrageous humour.

Diamond, though, is a genuine comic creation. His nostalgia for old-time dancing might recall such modern *noir*-influenced thrillers as *Hustle* (Burt Reynolds' taste for old movies and Cole Porter) and *Atlantic City* (Burt Lancaster's dapper clothes), except that he's completely lacking in those characters' introspective depth. Furthermore, he's never made to stand symbolically in the way that they do for the supposed decline of a well-ordered past into the sleazy present. He also lacks that other fundamental trait of the *noir* hero—an emotional vulnerability to women. In Harris's scheme of things, it seems, the world has always been a sleazy place; women are mostly victims, and the nearest Diamond comes to self-knowledge is his exasperated cry when he's finally arrested: "What's the use, you can't fucking win!"

Dramatically, *Boiling Point* (the title is never satisfactorily explained) is hardly substantial, but it's also consistently entertaining. Harris skips across the surface of his hackneyed story in much the same carefree way as he introduces Diamond in the opening scene. And, at least when Hopper and Viggo Mortensen are on screen, it's difficult not to skip along happily beside him.

Also reviewed in:
NEW YORK TIMES, 4/17/93, p. 16, Janet Maslin
VARIETY, 4/19/93, p. 46, Lawrence Cohn
WASHINGTON POST, 4/19/93, p. C2, Richard Harrington

BOPHA!

A Paramount Pictures release of an Arsenio Hall Communications production in association with the Taubman Entertainment Group. *Executive Producer:* Arsenio Hall. *Producer:* Lawrence Taubman. *Director:* Morgan Freeman. *Screenplay:* Brian Bird and John Wierick. *Based on the play by:* Percy Mtwa. *Director of Photography:* David Watkin. *Editor:* Neil Travis. *Music:* James Horner. *Music Editor:* Joe E. Rand. *Sound:* Richard Lightstone and (music) Shawn Murphy. *Sound Editor:* Bill Phillips. *Casting:* Jane Warren and Leo Davis. *Production Designer:* Michael Phillips. *Art Director:* Tracey Moxham. *Set Decorator:* Dankert Guillaume. *Set Dresser:* Michael Freeman. *Special Effects:* Rick Creswell. *Costumes:* Diana Cilliers. *Make-up:* Diane Hammond. *Stunt Coordinator:* Gavin Mey. *Running time:* 120 minutes. *MPAA Rating:* PG-13.

CAST: Danny Glover (Micah Mangena); Malcolm McDowell (De Villiers); Alfre Woodard (Rosie Mangena); Marius Weyers (Van Tonder); Maynard Eziashi (Zweli Mangena); Malick Bowens (Pule Rampa); Michael Chinyamurindi (Solomon); Christopher John Hall (Naledi Machikano); Grace Mahlaba (Thokozile Machikano); Robin Smith (Reteif); Julie Strijdom (Lucy Van Tonder); Peter Kampila (Nonsizi); Sello Maake Ka-Ncube (Magubane); Eric Miyeni (Bantebe); Tshepo Nzimande (Mandla); Wilfred Tongarepi (Nkeala); Innocent Ngavaira (Samuel); Gavin Mey (White Policeman #1); Stan Leih (White Policeman #2); Joseph Munyama (Black Policeman #1); Zilla Mamansi (Teacher); Gift Burnett (Philomen); Ackim Mwale (Priest); Eric Nobbs (Police Commissioner); Fidelis Cheza (Josiah Machikano); Anna Manyewe (Mrs. Machikano); Portleen Ben (Thandi Machikano); Mary Makwangwalala (Nomah); Bertha Msora (Mother #1); Jane Nhukarume (Mother #2); Winnie Ndemera (Old Woman); Beauty Mamere (Child in Police Station); Kizito Gamaliel and Alec Ziko (Solomon's Henchmen).

LOS ANGELES TIMES, 9/24/93, Calendar/p. 16, Kenneth Turan

More than any of the world's trouble spots, filmmakers are drawn to South Africa. Because the racial oppression has been so obvious and the oppressors so unrepentant, apartheid has a built-in emotional impact that's had filmmakers practically lining up to take their shot at portraying its agonies on screen.

"Bopha!" is the latest film to be set in that caldron and the fact that it is the latest robs it of a lot of its force. Despite strong and honorable performances from stars Danny Glover and Alfre

Woodard and a creditable first directing job by Morgan Freeman, this film is more predictable than powerful.

Earnest and nonexploitative though it is, "Bopha!" covers ground that has just about been tilled to death. After "A Dry White Season," "A World Apart," "Seraphina!" (which also had African protagonists) and even "The Power of One" and "Cry Freedom" (which didn't), there is very little we haven't already seen about the bad old days when the apartheid system was simultaneously all-powerful and on the verge of coming apart.

And hurting "Bopha!" (rated PG-13 for language and apartheid-driven violence) is more than the fact that we know everything that's going to happen in it from beginning to end. With the release from prison and rise to preeminence of Nelson Mandela, the government's plans for power sharing with the black majority and an increase of fanaticism on both sides, the political situation has changed in ways that are equally dramatic but much less easy to categorize than what this film presents.

Set safely in the past, "Bopha!" (the term means both arrest and detention in the Zulu language) starts with a point of view not seen, before, that of a spit-and-polish black sergeant in the township police, a man charged with defending a system many of his neighbors know from experience as repressive and evil.

And Micah Mangena (Glover) does more than defend the system. He is so passionate in his belief in it that as a taskmaster at the police academy, he teaches new recruits to think of pride, intelligence and guts whenever anyone calls them pigs, This is a formidable part for Glover (still best known to audiences for his role in the "Lethal Weapon" series despite his remarkable work in films like "To Sleep With Anger") and he gets the maximum amount out of it.

Naturally Micah wants his teen-age son Zweli (Maynard Eziashi) to follow in his footsteps. But this is 1980, and even in quiet Moroka Township things are changing. High school students like Zweli are upset at being taught in Afrikaans not English and are increasingly willing to listen to radicals like Pule Rampa ("Out of Africa's" Malick Bowens). Even Micah's benign commanding officer (Marius Weyers) has to deal with two operatives from Special Forces (Malcolm McDowell and Robin Smith) who have first-degree sadism written all over them.

Adapted from the Percy Mtwa play by screenwriters Brian Bird and John Wierick, "Bopha!" inevitably heads toward a confrontation between father and son that will surprise no one, especially since the performance by Eziashi, who was effective in Bruce Beresford's "Mr. Johnson," never seems to get untracked. And though everyone on screen is shocked when crowds of students resist authority and begin to chant in the streets, those who've seen any of those previous South African films will have seen it all before.

Director Freeman, who himself starred in "The Power of One," shows to best advantage during the wrenching scenes between Marius and his wife Rosie (the always exceptional Alfre Woodard) over their son and their future. At the other end of the spectrum are the broad and obvious performances of the Special Forces guys, who do everything but twirl nonexistent mustaches to emphasize their cruel heartless nature. If we'd never seen another film on the horrors of apartheid, all this might have been more impressive, but we have and it isn't.

NEW YORK POST, 9/24/93, p. 40, Michael Medved

"Cry Freedom" ... "A World Apart" ... "A Dry White Season" ... "Sarafina!"

And now "Bopha!," Hollywood's latest attempt at selling the public an anti-apartheid melodrama. Each of the previous projects attracted major American stars, drew mostly respectful reviews, and earned dismal returns at the box office.

"Bopha!" seems destined to follow the disappointing pattern of its predecessors, despite the presence of big names such as Arsenio Hall (executive producer) and Morgan Freeman (who makes his directing debut). Like the other examples of this ill-fated formula, this film is earnest and admirable, full of good intentions and fine performances, but so preachy and predictable that it becomes a chore to watch.

Of course, Paramount insists that "Bopha!" is different, a film about family conflict and tensions between father and son.

Danny Glover plays the father, a tough sergeant in the South African police back in 1980, who wants his boy to one day follow him onto the force. The fine young London-born actor Maynard

Eziashi plays the son, a bright student and soccer star who gets involved in anti-government demonstrations at school.

The film follows an obvious path to its overblown climax: as the sadistic white authorities turn peaceful demonstrations into bloody riots, the father is ordered to arrest his own son. He must choose between his family and his loyalty to a job he's honored for more than 20 years.

This dilemma might have been far more compelling had the filmmakers made some attempt to balance these competing demands.

For instance, they might have shown that at least some of his work involved coping with common criminals, protecting the poor people of his neighborhood from violence or theft. Instead, the film suggests that the only task of the South African police is ruthless political repression.

Morgan Freeman, who has earned well-deserved praise as one of today's most consistently splendid actors, wins mixed success as a first-time director.

Assisted by the distinguished cinematographer David Watkin ("Out of Africa"), he brings raw energy and power to some of the crowd scenes, but for the most part he treats the hackneyed script with such Biblical solemnity that he only calls attention to its stagey confrontations and clunky dialogue.

In one exchange, Glover muses, "I don't know what's happening with the boy, I can't seem to reach him." His long-suffering wife (superbly well-played by the great Alfre Woodard) then helpfully replies, "He's about to become a man. Thinking his own thoughts."

If the people behind the camera had spent more time "thinking their own thoughts," Woodard, Glover and the rest of the gifted cast might have had something to work with. As it is, "Bopha!" (which means "to arrest" in Zulu) reduces both complex political struggle and painful personal tragedy to the level, of comic-book propaganda.

NEWSDAY, 9/24/93, Part II/p. 63, Gene Seymour

It's odd, to say the least, that most of the major Hollywood feature films about South Africa released in recent years have been told primarily from a white central perspective. "Biko" may have drawn its title from the martyred black leader, but the film was mostly about white journalist Donald Woods. "A World Apart's" central character was the daughter of a white anti-apartheid activist. Even black director Euzhan Palcy's corrosive "A Dry White Season" was told from the point of view of a confused white liberal.

All of which makes even the release of "Bopha!," an adaptation of Percy Mtwa's popular play, something of a watershed. This time, a black family occupies the core of a drama that deals with the effect of racist public policy on personal lives. More illuminating still, the head of the family is a black police officer.

It seems not to occur to Sgt. Micah Mangena (Danny Glover), proud veteran of the South African police, that he is caught in crossfire between the system whose laws he upholds and the hardships those laws impose upon those who are black like him. Duty, it seems, is enough for him.

His wife, Rosie (Alfre Woodard), suspects there's something perilous in this contradiction. His son, Zweli (Maynard Ezashi), *knows* there's something wrong with it—and is getting more involved in the kind of anti-apartheid activities his father is charged with breaking up.

The officer arrests a prominent local activist, whose subsequent torture by Special Branch police (led by a sneering Malcolm McDowell) makes Micah Mangena a pariah and potential target of vengeful township residents. His wife is likewise shunned. His son gets more deeply involved in the cause. Crisis and confrontation are not far away.

This is actor Morgan Freeman's first directorial effort and, at times, the staging and visual flow betray his inexperience. But he handles and frames his actors beautifully. Glover is, as always, a striking presence who can ride a character's complexity like a champion surfer on a huge wave. The chemistry that he and Woodard have patented over three movies sets off enough energy to make one wish they were on screen together more often.

The gut-wrenching story absorbs and enrages up to its shattering conclusion (more despairing than the original play's), which leave's you feeling that to be born black in South Africa is to be born dead. Changing the ending took guts, given the feel-good dictum that rules commercial cinema. Still, I, for one, wanted somehow to feel, if not better, at least more.

VILLAGE VOICE, 10/26/93, p. 63, Cameron Bailey

It's tempting to get all flushed by the idea that *Bopha!* could never have happened even 10 years ago. Imagine: Paramount makes a film about South Africa, executive produced by Arsenio Hall, directed by Morgan Freeman, and starring Danny Glover and Alfre Woodard in central roles. Such a pleasing flex of representational muscle. Based on South African Percy Mtwa's play, Freeman's directing debut returns to 1980 for the first big-budget, African American look at the black struggle that's easiest to synopsize and hardest to put onscreen.

As a police sergeant brought down by the system that nurtured him, Glover brings the grace and gravity of his best work, even when the South African accent and culture elude him. He walks through Moroka township like it was Oakland, which may be his point. Woodard is both less present and more convincing, elevating the skimpy role of Glover's wife into the film's richest performance.

Bopha! is noticeably devoid of helpful, heroic white folks. These *blankes* are points along a spectrum ranging from an officer's gray condescension to Malcolm McDowell's ice-blue villainy as a Special Branch übercop. The black characters occupy a parallel spectrum—Glover's cop accommodates white power, his son (Maynard Eziashi) joins a student rebellion. Their conflict reveals that the reality of apartheid makes compromise for blacks not only untenable but dangerous. Another movie might have made that point sharply, visually, but *Bopha!* buries it under melodrama. Freeman falls into the trap set for actors who risk directing strong performances, weak cinema. *Bopha!*'s craft is never less (or more) than competent, but Freeman seems happy just to add his contribution to the existing market of antiapartheid catharsis products. Each time I'm offered another image of masses of stoic, singing South Africans, it gets harder to see it fresh.

Also reviewed in:
CHICAGO TRIBUNE, 9/24/93, Friday/p. C, Michael Wilmington
NEW YORK TIMES, 9/24/93, p. C18, Vincent Canby
VARIETY, 9/27/93, p. 36, Leonard Klady
WASHINGTON POST, 9/24/93, p. C1, Hal Hinson
WASHINGTON POST, 9/24/93, Weekend/p. 42, Desson Howe

BORN YESTERDAY

A Hollywood Pictures release in association with Touchwood Pacific Partners I.   *Executive Producer:* Stratton Leopold.   *Producer:* D. Constantine Conte.   *Director:* Luis Mandoki. *Screenplay:* Douglas McGrath.   *Based on the play by:* Garson Kanin.   *Director of Photography:* Lajos Koltai.   *Editor:* Lesley Walker.   *Music:* George Fenton.   *Music Editor:* Sally Boldt. *Choreographer:* Miranda Garrison.   *Sound:* Thomas Causey and (music) John Richards.   *Sound Editor:* Bobby Mackston.   *Casting:* Amanda Mackey and Cathy Sandrich.   *Production Designer:* Lawrence G. Paull.   *Art Director:* Bruce Crone.   *Set Designer:* Nancy Patton and Philip Toolin. *Set Decorator:* Rick Simpson.   *Special Effects:* Michael Wilmot.   *Costumes:* Colleen Atwood. *Make-up:* Fred Blau.   *Make-up (Melanie Griffith):* Naomi Donne.   *Make-up (John Goodman):* Kevin Haney.   *Make-up (Don Johnson):* Jay Cannistraci.   *Body Make-up (Melanie Griffith):* Nadege Schoenfeld.   *Running time:* 102 minutes. *MPAA Rating:* PG.

CAST: Melanie Griffith (Billie Dawn);   John Goodman (Harry Brock);   Don Johnson (Paul Verrall);   Edward Herrmann (Ed Devery);   Max Perlich (JJ);   Michael Ensign (Phillipe); Benjamin C. Bradlee (Secretary Duffee);   Sally Quinn (Beatrice Duffee);   William Frankfather (Senator Kelley);   Fred Dalton Thompson (Senator Hedges);   Celeste Yarnall (Mrs. Hedges); Nora Dunn (Cynthia Schreiber);   Meg Wittner (Mrs. Kelly);   William Forward (Senator Duker); Mary Gordon Murray (Bindy Duker);   Ted Raimi (Cynthia's Assistant);   Rondi Reed (Victoria Penny);   Matthew Faison (Congressman Hulse);   Kate McGregor-Stewart (Mrs. Hulse);   Arthur

Leeds (Man at Party); John Wesley (Senator Welch); Andi Chapman (Mrs. Welch); Drew Snyder (Senator Dorn); Terri Hanauer (Mrs. Dorn); John Achorn (Senator Banks); Ann Hearn (Mrs. Banks); Gordon Reinhart (Jewelry Store Owner); Selma Archerd (Lois); Catherine Hausman (Valerie); Freda Foh Shen (Maid); Marisol Massey (Waitress); Leroy Perry, Jr. (Dr. Playle); Tony Palladino (Barber); Amanda Hendon (Manicurist); Fritz Sperberg (Jose Perical); Robyn Renner (Hansom Cab Driver); Paul Guyot (Bellman).

LOS ANGELES TIMES, 3/26/93, Calendar/p. 1, Kenneth Turan

While it's not clear that any film really cries out to be remade, "Born Yesterday" needed a second version less than most. And not because the original is such a sainted relic that redoing it is next to sacrilege. On the contrary, despite its elevated reputation, the 1950 "Born Yesterday" had as many pitfalls as pleasures, all of which the current version dutifully stumbles into.

A romantic triangle between a crude millionaire, a handsome, sophisticated journalist (remember, it's just a movie) and the former Vegas showgirl who turns both their heads. "Born Yesterday" is in reality little more than an elaborate showcase for the actress who plays the redoubtable Billie Dawn.

The part made Judy Holliday (who originated the role in Garson Kanin's Broadway play) a star and won her an Oscar as the quintessential dumb blonde who turns out to know a thing or two. Though it's not going to do the same for Melanie Griffith this time around, she is, once again, the best reason to spend any time with this muddled production.

Billie arrives on the scene as the blasé companion of gruff workaholic capitalist Harry Brock (John Goodman), who blusters into Washington on his private plane, screaming "OK, let's do some business" before the engines have even cut off. Billie, whom we first view in a languid shot that emphasizes the state of her legs, has other things in mind. Like finding out what TV stations her soaps are on. "So I don't like new towns," she says in her breathy way, "You have to learn all new channels."

Advised by an aide that favorable press coverage will help the business he has with Congress, Brock agrees to be interviewed by Paul Verrall (Don Johnson), a journalist as powerful as he is cute. "If Paul gives you the thumbs-up," we are solemnly told, "it s a big deal in this town."

Brock, however, soon has other things to worry about. Billie, it seems, is not only so out to lunch she thinks the collapsing Eastern Bloc is some crumbling masonry structure, her lack of savvy is hurting her boyfriend's plans. And when Brock decides to hire someone to smarten Billie up, and teach her how to talk right, guess who gets the job.

Everyone, however, gets more than they bargained for in this little arrangement. Billie not only cleans up her double negatives, she so raises her ethical and moral standards it's amazing Bill Moyers doesn't build a series around her. And both Verrall and Brock find that their professional and love lives get a lot more complicated when Billie gets a few new ideas in her head.

With her little-girl voice and low-cut outfits, Griffith could play Billie in her sleep, and, for all the help she gets from writer Douglas McGrath and director Luis Mandoki, she just about has to.

McGrath's script, based on Kanin's play, has an inert quality to it that leaving in period slang such as "egghead" and "lowdown" doesn't help. And Mandoki, whose last project was "White Palace," seems to resent the fact that "Born Yesterday" (rated PG) is basically a farce. Any chance he gets, the director emphasizes the film's dramatic moments, giving the action a heaviness that becomes increasingly wearying.

But while Griffith has the advantage of playing "Born Yesterday's" only fully drawn part, Goodman and Johnson have to deal with the same character weaknesses that sabotaged their predecessors, Broderick Crawford and William Holden, all those decades ago.

The very able Goodman is trapped as a big lug who may or may not have a heart of gold, and the indecision about whether he is a comic character or a sadistic monster is as frustrating here as it was in the original. Johnson, for his part, looks uncomfortable in his horn-rimmed glasses and has trouble getting a handle on a colorless role, little more than a walking civics lesson, that baffled Holden as well.

As much as Griffith is right for Billie, times have changed enough to make this birth of the not-so-dumb blonde feel tedious. And the actress, who at any rate played basically the same part to much greater effect in "Working Girl," would be better served if screenwriters thought of new ways to use her considerable talents instead of trying to shoehorn her into someone else's golden slippers.

NEW YORK POST, 3/26/93, p. 21, Jami Bernard

If there was a role Melanie Griffith and her little-girl voice were destined for, this is it—the dumb trophy girlfriend who learns to think for herself in the remake of "Born Yesterday."

It has been updated and Hollywooded, but the new "Born Yesterday" maintains most of the original Garson Kanin gags; and it boasts the undeniably romantic casting of real-life husband-and-wife team Don Johnson as a bespectacled investigative reporter trying to teach Griffith some ABCs and Griffith as the dumb one who takes several reels to get through a De Tocqueville tome.

Griffith plays Billie Dawn, former Vegas showgirl—she can still recite the five lines she had in the show—and current bauble on the arm of nefarious businessman Harry Brock (John Goodman). They arrive in Washington, D.C. so Harry can play footsie with some bribable senators in order to further his business interests.

Harry's business interests are also in the interest of Billie, since most of the companies have been put in her name in order to avoid legal loopholes. Billie is handed a sheaf of papers to sign every so often, but she's so ignorant she doesn't read them. She cares only about mink coats, purse-sized TV sets, and doing leg lifts in bed while eating bonbons.

Harry hires journalist Paul Verrall (Don Johnson) as Billie's tutor, hoping he will give her just enough interesting things to say at cocktail parties so she won't embarrass herself. The first thing Paul teaches her is a set of responses she can use in most social situations, just as long as Paul is feeding her the signals, telling her which bon mot to trot out. When it works, she sees how nice it feels to be respected in a conversation, and now she's hooked on knowledge.

By the way, Paul is supposed to be the very soul of journalistic integrity—in fact, public and private integrity were the goals of the original movie—but it is never brought up in either version how a reporter doing a story on a bigwig like Harry could in all conscience be in his employ at the same time, taking his money, accepting his hospitality, and kissing his girlfriend. Details, details. Johnson is very likable as the journalist. He hides Paul's shark-like instincts behind a veneer of gentility and courtliness. Paul immediately recognizes Billie's homespun wisdom—she's not stupid, just uneducated and too depressed to do anything about it.

In another movie, perhaps, a little learning would be a dangerous thing. Here, Billie becomes a little too brilliant a little too fast—but that's the Hollywood thing. This Billie is too charming and kittenish ever to alienate anyone. (The original Billie, played by Judy Holliday, brayed like a donkey and was vulgar even with her newly won book learning, although at the same time it was a cannier performance.)

The most rousing scene—and ever since the "Under the Sea" number in "The Little Mermaid" every Disney movie has a rousing musical number—is when Billie wins everyone over in one fell swoop by teaching a dinner party her mnemonic for remembering the Constitutional amendments. She sings them to the tune of "The Twelve Days of Christmas" and soon everyone is joining in.

Goodman is less the gruff, crude businessman of the original and more like a celebrity doing a hissy-fit; that's certainly a Hollywood interpretation of the corrupting power of money. Harry has someone to shave him and buff his nails at all times. Goodman acts with his usual mix of naivete and distancing irony, when he sees the two other points of the love triangle kissing, he feels left out: "Hello, am I in the room here?" Which sums up how Goodman often distances himself from his own character for comic effect.

As usual, if you grew up on the original movie, you probably won't cotton to this one, but "Born Yesterday" is such good material that it makes for a pleasing update. It's not intellectually challenging, but if that's what you're after, read De Tocqueville.

NEWSDAY, 3/26/93, Part II/p. 66, Jack Mathews

When Billie Dawn, the empty-headed girlfriend of slob millionaire Harry Brock, is asked by a U.S. senator what she thinks about America's responsibilities in light of the collapse of the Eastern Bloc, she is startled by the news.

"When the block collapsed, were people hurt," she asks, "or was it just property damage?"

Given the times in which we live, and the distance American women have tried to put between themselves and post-war stereotypes, reviving "Born Yesterday," the 1946 Broadway play and 1950 movie for which Judy Holliday created the quintessential dumb blonde, is not the best remake idea Hollywood has had lately.

To make Kanin's story hip for today's audience would require a massive overhaul, and first-time screenwriter Douglas McGrath has managed barely a tune-up on it. McGrath and director Luis Mandoki ("White Palace") show a respect for material we're not used to seeing in remakes, but by transporting Kanin's ideas and characters virtually intact into the '90s, they've merely magnified how outdated they are.

"Born Yesterday," as written, was a one-set, three-character play, about Harry Brock (John Goodman), a vulgar self-made millionaire who holes up in a swank Washington penthouse while lobbying a few senators for favorable legislation, Billie (Melanie Griffith), his boozy, abused concubine, and Paul Verrall (Don Johnson), the good-looking magazine reporter hired by Brock as Billie's tutor.

It's "Pygmalion" in the Beltway, with a few notions about corruption in government. Mostly, it's just "Pygmalion," with Paul teaching Billie the power of knowledge, and Billie teaching Paul about love in return.

When the project was first announced, it sounded like an invitation to disaster for Melanie Griffith. No matter how much she may seem like Billie Dawn in real life, it was inevitable that she would be compared, cruelly, to Holliday.

The great surprise is that Griffith's performance is the least of "Born Yesterday's" problems. Griffith invented a completely different character, softer, less theatrical and more vulnerable than Holliday's, and there is no fair comparison to be made. It's a solid, sympathetic performance, Griffith's best since "Working Girl," and it provides what few sparks the film gives off.

In every other way, the '93 edition of "Born Yesterday" is less an adaptation than an exhumation. John Goodman is a little louder and perhaps a little more likable than Broderick Crawford's version of Harry, but adds up to the same cartoonish bozo. And Johnson, as passive as we have ever seen him, seems lost in a role that even William Holden found difficult to enlarge.

If Mandoki, who's never directed comedy before, didn't take the material so seriously, you wouldn't waste a second pondering the plausibility of Billie's transformation from airhead to genius, from sex toy to free spirit, in a matter of weeks. But the movie careens from intellectual slapstick to pompous sermons on ethics, mostly from Paul, who, judging by his willingness to take a $500-a-day job from the man he's writing about, should be the last to judge.

The mix of comic absurdities and puffed-up moralizing cancels each other out after a while, and you're left with nothing much more than Griffith's fresh performance in a role pulled out of a time capsule. It's not enough.

SIGHT AND SOUND, 8/93, p. 41, Lizzie Francke

Washington DC. Millionaire Harry Brock arrives in town on confidential business accompanied by his ex-chorine girlfriend, Billie Dawn. Sensing that there is a story to uncover, journalist Paul Verrall pursues Brock, who is impressed by him. Brock and Billie attend a party at the Secretary of the Navy's mansion. To Brock's embarrassment, Billie is a laughing stock. Brock's financial manager Ed Devery believes she is a liability and advises his boss to send her back home.

Billie is invited by journalist Cynthia Schreiber to talk on a radio show and ends up looking even more foolish. Brock decides that Billie needs educating and persuades Verrall to be her tutor. Offended, Billie is initially reluctant, but changes her mind when she learns that the handsome Verrall is going to teach her. At the end of their first session, Billie makes a tentative pass at Paul which he courteously refuses. As her lessons continue, Billie proves to be an excellent pupil. She puts her new skills to the test at a party and passes with flying colours. Encouraged by Paul, she begins to take her studies seriously, getting to grips with the American constitution.

One morning, Paul arrives at Brock and Billie's hotel suite to find Brock in a meeting with six senators. When Paul questions Brock, the latter warns him off. Brock and Billie hold a dinner party for various important Washington folk, and Billie impresses them with her wit. The following day Billie turns up at the hotel and overhears Brock arguing with a senator. Suspecting that Brock is up to no good, she questions Devery about papers that she is regularly required to sign. Brock does not like her new attitude; he hits her and tells her to leave.

Billie goes to Paul and tells him about Brock's activities. They return to the hotel suite and search it for evidence. It transpires that Brock is bribing the senators to ease a deal and that all his companies are in Billie's name. Paul is pleased with the scoop and asks Billie to marry him, but before she can give him an answer, Brock turns up and Paul has to leave. Meanwhile, Brock also decides that he wants to marry Billie. She refuses him and packs her bags, telling him that Paul is about to expose the scam. Brock is most concerned about her ownership of the companies. Paul returns to the hotel. He confronts Brock and there is an altercation. Billie tells Brock that his shady dealings will not be exposed as long as he behaves himself. She leaves with Paul.

It was a bizarre decision to remake the Garson Kanin-penned *Born Yesterday*. Few actresses could emulate, let alone eclipse, Judy Holliday's twinkling and gracious characterisation of Billie Dawn, the ultimate dumb blonde who proves to have not only a heart of gold but a high IQ. Holliday, who had played the part on Broadway, polishing it until it became completely her own, was coaxed on to the big screen by director George Cukor, whose Pygmalion complex showed both in the choice of story and his approach to actresses. Awkward, even ungainly, the beauty of Holliday's Billie was to be found in her wit. Melanie Griffith goes through the motions along with the rest of the cast, but there is no vitality in her imitation, nor even any passion in the affair with Paul Verrall, played by her husband Don Johnson.

It is left to the mighty presence of John Goodman to carry the film. But unlike Broderick Crawford, who imbued the original Brock with a touch of sympathy, so giving credibility to the fact that Billie had put up with him for so long, Goodman plays the unscrupulous millionaire as a far from cuddly character. There is a shocking viciousness about him which comes to the surface when at one point he slaps Billie's face. This ugly scene is the only one with any spark.

In spite of the irony that contemporary Hollywood has to reach into the past to find a decent role for a woman these days, Billie's turning the tables on the bimbo stereotype that still frequently finds its way into the movies has much to recommend it. Our first glimpse of Billie is of her tattooed and golden chained ankles; the first sound is of her ear-splitting screech "Harry" in broad Brooklyn twang: clearly, this woman is cheap and tacky. In her 1990s manifestation Billie Dawn is inseparable from her Walkman and her TV remote control mainlining her daily dose of soaps. She even exercises along to a fitness programme while munching her way through a bowl of M&M's.

But like Griffith's character in *Working Girl*, Billie's problem is not that she appears stupid but that she lacks class. She is white trash out of her depth in Washington society, finding that her flamboyant earrings are as much of a *faux pas* as her ill-chosen comments. In this respect, Kanin's original intention to satirise spiteful, snobbish Washington still holds, despite screenwriter Douglas McGrath's efforts to modernise the story. Paul tells Billie that there is one line that will always get her out of tight corners at cocktail parties. If in doubt, say, "That's as likely as a democrat being elected president." It's the one joke that one is happy to see fall flat.

VILLAGE VOICE, 4/6/93, 60, Manohla Dargis

Straight from the Hollywood recycling bin comes *Born Yesterday*, a new take on Garson Kanin's 1946 play. This time out Melanie Griffith is Billie Dawn, the live-in rental who's owned body and soul by business thug Harry Brock (the always reliable John Goodman). When Harry lands in D.C. for some high-stakes stratagems, he finds bubbleheaded Billie needs a little cerebral polish to finesse the D.C. circuit. He hires journalist Paul Verrall to do the upkeep, a role Don Johnson has seen fit to sleepwalk through.

Too didactic by half, Kanin's drama was turned into an engaging if stagy vehicle for Judy Holliday by George Cukor in 1950, and it's impossible not to think of that picture while watching this lackluster remake. While Holliday's Billie plowed through Thomas Paine and half a dozen others by the second act, Griffith's girltoy's wattage is far dimmer. Wouldn't a '90s woman, even one who watches soaps for recreation, catch a few CNN minutes here and there?

The major problem with *Born Yesterday* is that the play belongs to a radically different America, one before Watergate and all of history's exhumed corpses, from JFK on. A poignant idealism permeates Kanin's speechifying about democracy, something that now sounds almost quaint, especially in such a cynical rehash as this one (Paul feeds soundbites to Billie, not truth).

The funny thing is that in 1993 hope—still a lovely word—has more currency than anyone predicted when cameras got rolling last June, about the time Bill Clinton was making the rounds.

Also reviewed in:
CHICAGO TRIBUNE, 3/26/93, Friday/p. A, Johanna Steinmetz
NEW REPUBLIC, 4/26/93, p. 28, Stanley Kauffmann
NEW YORK TIMES, 3/26/93, p. C17, Vincent Canby
VARIETY, 3/29/93, p. 82, Leonard Klady
WASHINGTON POST, 3/26/93, p. C1, Hal Hinson
WASHINGTON POST, 3/26/93, Weekend/p. 42, Desson Howe

BOUND BY HONOR

A Hollywood Pictures release in association with Touchwood Pacific Partners I. *Executive Producer:* Jimmy Santiago Baca and Stratton Leopold. *Producer:* Taylor Hackford and Jerry Gershwin. *Director:* Taylor Hackford. *Screenplay:* Jimmy Santiago Baca, Jeremy Iacone, and Floyd Mutrux. *Story:* Ross Thomas. *Director of Photography:* Gabriel Beristain. *Editor:* Fredric Steinkamp and Karl F. Steinkamp. *Music:* Bill Conti. *Music Editor:* Curt Sobel. *Sound:* Edward Tise and (music) Lee DeCarlo. *Sound Editor:* Louis L. Edemann and Paul Timothy Carden. *Casting:* Richard Pagano and Sharon Bialy. *Production Designer:* Bruno Rubeo. *Art Director:* Marek Dobrowolski. *Set Decorator:* Cecilia Rodarte. *Set Dresser:* David Hopkins. *Special Effects:* Larry L. Fuentes. *Costumes:* Shay Cunliffe. *Make-up:* Fred C. Blau. *Tattoo Designer:* Freddy Negrete. *Running time:* 180 minutes. *MPAA Rating:* R.

CAST: Damian Chapa (Miklo); Jesse Borrego (Cruz); Benjamin Bratt (Paco); Enrique Castillo (Montana); Victor Rivers (Magic Mike); Delroy Lindo (Bonafide); Tom Towles (Red Ryder); Carlos Carrasco (Popeye); Teddy Wilson (Wallace); Raymond Cruz (Chuey); Valente Rodriguez (Frankie); Lanny Flaherty (Big Al); Billy Bob Thornton (Lightning); Geoffrey Rivas (Carlos); Karmin Murcelo (Dolores); Jenny Gago (Lupe); Noah Verduzco (Juanito); Lupe Ontiveros (Carmen); Gary Cervantes (Smokey); Victor Mohica (Mano); Tom Wilson (Rollie); Ray Oriel (Spider); Mike Genovese (Sgt. Devereaux); Steven Anthony Jones (Cyclone); Harold J. Surratt (Pockets); Natalija Nogulich (Janis); Ving Rhames (Ivan); Danny Trejo (Geronimo); Jimmy Santiago Baca (Gato); Peter Mark Vasquez (Chivo); Judith Verduzco (Alicia); Sonia Rodriguez (Victoria); Roberto Contreras (Cruz' Grandfather); Evelyn Guerrero (Luisa); Gary Tacon (Clavo); Luis Contreras (Realthing); Paulo Tocha (Apache); Freddy Negrete (Freddy); David Dunard (Gill); Steve Eastin (Hollenbeck Captain); Alina Arenal (Perla); Julie Zamaryonov (Belinda); Daniel McDonald (Gallery Assistant); Gibby Brand (Jared Levinson); Elizabeth Austin (Lois Levinson); Adan Hernandez (Gilbert); Richard E. Butler (Frank Velka); Michael Bofshever (Salesman); Art Snyder (Councilman Snyder); Robert Pescovitz (Surgeon); Primitivo Tapia (Street Kid); Robert J. Juarez (Priest); Eddie Perez (Joker); Claudia Gabriella Colin (Joker's Girl); David Labiosa (Coolaide); Rudy Barrios (Tres Puntos Gangmember); Juan Charles, Charles Guillermo, Eugene Barrios, and Jimmy Chavez (Vatos Locos); René Bontana (5 Puntos Counterman); Dan Vasquez (Warden); Michael McFall and Donald E. Lacy, Jr. (Transvestites); Zandra Hill (Black Cook); George Pereira (Old Con); Angel Romero (Parole Board Member); Joe Schloss (Prison Escort); Chris Chloupek (Prison Photographer); Gill Montie (AV Inmate); Vanessa Marquez (Montana's Daughter); Martin McDermott (Delano Guard); Martha Cardenas (Landlady); Catherine Price (Newscaster); Jerry Perea (Tattooed Lipped Partier); Lindsay Ginter (Officer Young); Victor Koliacos (PCP Kid); Christine Avila (Mother of PCP Kid); Robert Padgett (Doctor to PCP Kid); Rio Hackford (PCP Intern).

LOS ANGELES TIMES, 4/30/93, Calendar/p. 1, Kenneth Turan

"Bound by Honor" is nothing if not ambitious, but sometimes ambitious is all it is. A sincere attempt at epic filmmaking, it has been unable to translate its aspirations into believable, non-clichéd cinema. What unrolls instead is approximately three hours of violent, cartoonish posturing incongruously set in the realistically evoked milieu of East Los Angeles.

Once called "Blood In, Blood Out," this story of three childhood friends—from the barrio and the different paths they take over a dozen years had its name and ad campaign changed after test marketing raised fears it might provoke incendiary reactions. Similar prudence has meant that though the film opens today in San Diego and 29 other cities, its Los Angeles/Orange County debut is at least two weeks away.

The clash between the care that has been taken by director Taylor Hackford to make "Bound by Honor" culturally authentic and its wholehearted embracing of all manner of bogus emotional and dramatic situations is not the film's only curious aspect. In terms of plot, it shares a multitude of similarities with Edward James Olmos' 1992 "American Me" and even ends up giving Floyd Mutrux, one of that film's screenwriters, credit on this script (along with poet Jimmy Santiago Baca and Jeremy Iacone) as well.

But even though both films went so far as gaining unprecedented access to shoot in different California prisons ("American Me" got Folsom, "Bound by Honor" San Quentin) their tones are considerably different. The Olmos film is largely unsentimental and inescapably earnest, a kind of wake-up call to the Latino community, while Hackford's, for all its fervor, is thoroughly slick and commercial, a potboiler more concerned than not with getting an exploitative rise out of an audience.

Also different are the director's great hopes for "Bound by Honor," his desire to turn out a kind of defining saga of Chicano culture. Hackford (who produced "La Bamba" and directed such films as "An Officer and a Gentleman" and "Everybody's All-American") has said he had Luchino Visconti's neo-realistic classic "Rocco and His Brothers" in mind as he worked. A more likely model is Francis Ford Coppola's "Godfather" trio, but except for inordinate length, there is little resemblance between the two.

"Bound by Honor" begins in 1972, with Miklo (Damian Chapa) returning to his Chicano mother in East L.A. after an unsatisfactory encounter with his Anglo father in Las Vegas. As a product of two cultures, called "milkweed" or "the Pillsbury doughboy," Miklo never feels he quite belongs anywhere, but he has come back to the barrio because that's as close to home as it gets for him.

More or less happy to see him are his two best friends and fellow members of a gang called Vatos Locos, Paco Aguilar and Cruz Candelaria. Paco (Benjamin Bratt) is a hot-tempered boxer known as "the Black Rooster," while Cruz (Jesse Borrego) is an aspiring artist.

But before any of this can happen, a conflict with the rival Tres Puntos gang shatters the trio. Paco goes into the Marines, Cruz goes into the hospital and comes out strung out on drugs and angry about the thought of a career spent decorating the living rooms of affluent Anglos. And Miklo, the milkweed, ends up having to cope with the nastiness of San Quentin.

Though the film is nominally about all three men over the next dozen years, Paco just about disappears from the screen until the final hour, and Cruz doesn't fare much better. Most of "Bound by Honor" (rated R for strong violence and language and for sexuality and drug content) ends up focusing on Miklo's time inside. Brutalized by the Aryan Vanguard and the Black Guerrilla Army, he is increasingly drawn to the almost mythical La Onda organization and its charismatic leader, Montana Segura (Enrique Castillo), known as Mero Mero.

And it is inside San Quentin that the film's pulpy sensibility starts to seriously unravel. The overdone parade of leering, cursing, violent prisoners manages to be distasteful without being particularly convincing. And as "Bound by Honor" plod's through an interminable laundry list of graphic, bloody confrontations, criminal pursuits outside the prison, it seems that all it has gained by its extended length is the opportunity to be more than usually convoluted and confusing. Apparently in love with East L.A., this film succeeds only in getting lost in it.

NEW YORK POST, 4/30/93, p. 29, Jami Bernard

In a few weeks, the Public Theater is going to show a movie that runs 26 hours long, the longest movie ever made. It faces stiff competition in the longevity department from "Bound by Honor," a three-hour movie about Chicano gangs that feels like it runs 26 hours.

Director Taylor Hackford's overstuffed, uninvolving saga follows the travails of three Chicanos (two half-brothers and a cousin) in East L.A. who run afoul of the law and of their blood oaths to one another. One, a painter, ends up badly injured in an escalating turf war, and later turns to drugs. Another joins the Marines and takes his tough-guy ways into the police department, where he uses them to better advantage. The third, a half-brother with white ski blond hair and bright blue eyes, has a tough time of it in jail where he looks Anglo but feels Chicano and has the secret tattoo on his hand to prove it. There appears to be an hour's worth of tattooing scenes in "Bound By Honor."

If you've seen Edward James Olmos' very similar "American Me," you've seen it all—the harsh realities of prison life, blood-oath alliances, murders to pay off old debts, drug-running, the striving for identity and a sense of family, the racial tensions and betrayals. There are the obligatory murders in the prison yard, the concealed weapons, the jockeying for position on the cafeteria line.

Except for the painstaking attempt to show prison life as it really is—by now, after several such movies, we get the idea already—"Bound by Honor" is mediocre in every way. The same handful of Latino or vaguely Latino words are repeated ad nauseam, eventually subbing for all semblance of dialogue and losing all meaning. There isn't a sentence that passes between characters without one of them saying either "homeboy" or "loco," and despite the presence of poet Jimmy Santiago Baca on the screenplay credits, the most poetic lines are on the order of "We should help each other, not cut each other's throats!"

Of the three, Benjamin Bratt as Paco, the Marine, stands out for his acting, presence, and movie-star looks. But the lead, newcomer Damian Chapa as the white-skinned Miklo, plays most of his role in a wild-eyed way that could be interpreted either as consternation or fear.

It's clear that the makers of "Bound by Honor" felt they had a Very Important Movie on their hands—hence the three hours—but it takes more than length and a nice budget to make an epic.

NEW YORK POST, 4/30/93, p. 29, Michael Medved

However one responds to the results of Taylor Hackford's efforts in producing and directing "Bound by Honor," one has to admire his "cojones" for undertaking the project in the first place. After all, this is a white-Anglo filmmaker who has obviously poured heart and soul into a plushy three-hour epic that's meant to stand as some kind of summary statement of the Chicano experience in contemporary America.

The press notes released with the picture defensively remind us that despite his lack of Latino background, Hackford once worked as a Peace Corps volunteer in Bolivia and learned to speak Spanish.

He also brings more meaningful qualifications to the task at hand, because Hackford (best known for "An Officer and a Gentleman," "Against All Odds," and "White Nights") is a director who has always been able to generate the sort of raw energy and passionate performances that make up for narrative flaws.

In this case, the story is too simple (and too mechanical) to support the crushing weight of the film's serious intentions and its all-but-interminable running time. The movie follows 20 bloody, brutal years in the lives of three boyhood friends from East Los Angeles, who are linked by blood relationships (two half-brothers, one first cousin) and common gang membership.

One of the boys (Damian Chapa) ends up in San Quentin, where he emerges as a leader of an all-powerful prison gang. Another (Jesse Borrego) squanders his phenomenal artistic ability and nearly destroys himself with drugs. The third (Benjamin Bratt), who had once been the most violent and anti-social of the bunch, joins the Marine Corps and eventually becomes a sensitive, heroic cop.

One of the problems with this picture is that the potentially fascinating transformation of this character received far less screen time than the self destructive excesses of his two "compadres."

We never see how—or why—he managed to transcend his violent past nor do we get even the slightest glimpse of his personal life. Is this dedicated police officer married? Is he even interested in women? Hackford apparently believes that the horrors of prison life and drug addiction are inherently more interesting and important than the miracle of a troubled kid who turns his life around.

This imbalance is even more problematic since the young actor playing the cop delivers such a stunning performance in those relatively rare moments that the movie focuses on him. All of the largely unknown young leads are impressive in this film, but Peruvian-American Benjamin Bratt is a real star, with a smoldering presence that ignites the screen whenever he's on camera.

Bratt is so good, in fact, that he even manages to keep his dignity when delivering flat-footed lines such as: "I shot your leg off, and that's something I'm going to have to live with for the rest of my life. But you're still my blood. And I don't want to see my own blood destroy itself."

This sort of clunky dialogue is surprising since one of the three credited screenwriters is the award-winning Chicano prison poet Jimmy Santiago Baca. Presumably, Baca made his most positive contribution in the truly extraordinary prison sequences perhaps the most authentic and chilling ever filmed. Hackford won approval to shoot these scenes on location at San Quentin and used 300 real-life convicts as especially effective extras.

Unfortunately, he pushes too hard with his attempts to use these behind-bars episodes as a metaphor for all of Chicano life in America. The electrically charged camera work by Mexican-British cinematographer Gabriel Beristain captures the panorama of East L.A. life with too much warmth, spice and diversity, to support the movie's explicit promise that all Mexican-Americans are actually pioneers in this hostile, unjust society.

This preachy point is driven home with such relentless redundancy that by the end of this monstrously over-long but often intriguing film many moviegoers will feel that they have been incarcerated for a long stretch and that their patience should have earned them a chance for parole.

NEWSDAY, 4/30/93, Part II/p. 71, Jack Mathews

Before Taylor Hackford became a movie director, he won two Emmys for work done as an investigative news reporter for Los Angeles public television station KCET, and he was credited with helping TV move into the rock-and-roll generation with his notions for staging broadcast performances.

With that background, you would expect his films to reflect both a sense of dramatic realism and a cutting-edge hipness. Instead, he has made a string of slick, over-the-top major studio movies that wallow in cliché, sentiment and melodrama.

However, none of his previous six films—from the idealized '50s rock-and-roll movies "The Idolmaker" and "La Bamba" to the contemporary dramas "An Officer and a Gentleman" and "White Nights"—was as frustratingly bogus as his three-hour, prison/barrio epic "Bound by Honor."

The convoluted saga, which repeats themes, characters and even dialogue from last year's less polished but more believable "American Me," follows the lives of three Latino cousins, from their late-teens as gang members in East Los Angeles to a point 12 years after a lethal run-in with a rival gang sets the trio on radically different paths.

One cousin, the blue-eyed, half-white Miklo (Damian Chapa), is sent to San Quentin for murder, where, to gain acceptance by a powerful Latino prison gang known as La Onda, he commits a second murder. Another cousin, the talented artist Cruz (Jesse Borrego), emerges from a hospital lame, morphine-addicted and self-destructive. The third, the ex-boxer Paco (Benjamin Bratt), joins the Marines rather than go to jail, and returns to the barrio as a tough undercover cop.

Thus, the scene is set for some traumatic family reunions, and a ton of contrived melodrama.

"Bound by Honor," which is loosely based on the reflections of Latino poet Jimmy Santiago Baca, who co-wrote the screenplay, is at its heart about the importance of family in the Latino culture, and how the deep loyalties inspired in children actually predispose them to dead-end gang life in the barrio.

Exploring that theme is worthwhile, to be sure, and the first half hour of "Bound by Honor" holds out that promise. But once introduced, the theme is relegated to the background, coming forward only when it's needed to provide motivation for intrigue and mayhem that would be monotonous in a movie half its length.

Of the several stories being told, the one that interests Hackford most is the war between black, white and Latino gangs over control of the drug business inside the prison. It's told as a movie within the movie, "Godfather Behind Bars," with Miklo duplicating the feat of Michael Corleone, growing into the role of the San Quentin don.

Hackford even included a Francis Ford Coppola cinematic trick, cutting back and forth from a string of calculated assassinations ordered by Miklo to an ironically festive Day of the Dead parade in East Los Angeles. I suppose it figures that the most interesting scene would be one Hackford borrowed.

To give the director his due, he made a great effort to give his film an authentic look and feel. He shot it mostly within the confines of San Quentin and East Los Angeles, two different kinds of prisons, using inmates/residents as extras. And his choice of having the Latino characters speak naturally, colloquially, blending their Spanish with English (often in the same sentences), gives their dialogue a natural spontaneity.

But Hackford squanders all of that actuality on formulaic tales unworthy of it. The central story—Miklo's transformation from gang hanger-on to wily crime lord—is badly undermined by the inexperience of Chapa. The young actor whips up some ferocious scowls and banty rooster poses, but there isn't a moment when you're unaware of how hard he's working.

The actor we're most likely to see again is Bratt, a Peruvian with a great face and a powerful screen presence. If Hackford had used Paco's transformation as the movie's centerpiece instead of Miklos', we at least would have had an interesting actor to watch.

As it is, "Bound by Honor" is one of the longest three-hour movies you'll ever see.

SIGHT AND SOUND, 10/93, p. 39, Olly Blackburn

East Los Angeles, 1972. Chicano half brothers Paco Aguilar and Cruz Candelaria are joined in the barrio by their half-Anglo cousin Miklo Velka, whose roots are betrayed by his white skin and blue eyes. Cruz is a talented artist, Miklo has just left prison on parole and they are all bound together in Paco's street gang, Los Vatos Locos. When a rumble with the rival Tres Puntos leaves Cruz badly injured, Vatos Locos take their revenge and Miklo kills Spider, the rivals' leader. After pursuit and arrest, Miklo is sent to San Quentin Prison while Paco avoids the fallout by joining the Marines.

San Quentin proves to be a brutal jungle in which the white Aryan Vanguard (AV), the Black Guerilla Army (BGA) and La Onda, the ruling Latino gang, vie for control of gambling and drugs operations. Miklo is introduced into this world by Popeye, a small-time player who abuses Miklo's trust by trying to rape him. In order to win the respect of La Onda, Miklo uses his white looks to take a job with Big N, the prison cook and bookmaking kingpin, so that he can kill him. This he does after uncovering Al's business partner—Sgt. Devereaux, a crooked prison officer. A lieutenant in La Onda's ruling council, Miklo heads the hugely profitable gambling operation, while at the same time educating himself to help speed up his parole.

Back in the *barrio*, Cruz's success as a commercial artist merely fuels his growing heroin addiction. One night, while in a stoned stupor, Cruz's adoring younger brother Juanito slips into the studio and overdoses on a left-over needle. Cruz is banished from the family and the shock turns Paco from the Marines to undercover narcotics operations where he gains a reputation as a successful but ferociously driven cop.

Miklo gets released on parole. His attempts to hold down a straight job at a tyre factory are destroyed by a crooked foreman who skims off his paychecks to cover gambling debts and life in a squalid flat inhabited by Popeye and a coterie of Chicano hoodlums. Miklo takes part in an armed robbery which is busted by Paco, who halts his cousin's escape by shooting him in the feet, one of which has to be amputated. Back in San Quentin, Miklo discovers that La Onda is in danger of being squeezed out by the mushrooming cocaine trade. Montana, the gang's politicised leader, refuses to have anything to do with the trade, but when another lieutenant, Carlos, breaks away from La Onda to start dealing, a war with the BGA flames up, which spreads into the streets of LA.

Recognizing that such fighting simply strengthens the AV, Montana forms a truce with BGA leader Bonafide to stop Carlos. But Montana is killed by a BGA member working off forged instructions. To avert a war, the governor of San Quentin and Paco, who is now a detective, convince Miklo to make a truce with Bonafide. La Onda bides its time, then, in alliance with the BGA, takes the opportunity on the Day of the Dead to wipe out the AV, doing a double-cross and destroying the BGA at the same time .

On the same day, Cruz's stepmother forgives him for Juanito's death. In San Quentin, La Onda is about to be dispersed across the country. Miklo promises that it will just spread wider and then, with Magic Mike, his new blood brother, he destroys evidence that it was in fact he who ordered Montana's murder. Back in LA, Cruz and Paco are finally reunited beneath a mural of them and Miklo that the artist painted years earlier, in the *barrio*.

Initially, *Blood In Blood Out* does not bode well. A three-hour epic on Los Angeles Chicanos, part-*Godfather*, part-*Riot in Cell Block Eleven*, directed by the maker of *An Officer and a Gentleman*—already it sounds like a poisonous recipe. The opening to Taylor Hackford's film, with its bombastic Spanish guitar and all those breast-hugs, seems to confirm our worst fears. When Miklo arrives at his aunt's doorstep, he's already experienced an attack of the flashbacks, some macho tear-jerking and a brief ecstacy with a backstreet Madonna.

But the film triumphs over cliché to sustain its vast length and space. The key to this success lies in its epic size, a mood and scale more akin to a miniseries than grandiose cinema. In fact cinematographer Gabriel Beristain has shunned the operatic, cinemascope feel of most epic cinema in favour of a rougher televisual style that imperceptibly evolves as the years progress—from the flat static style of the 70s sequences to a brasher fluidity a decade on. The small-screen ambience means that the characters are allowed to build, and the story to develop some fibre beneath its immense body. *Blood In Blood Out* doesn't bear the weight of its three hours, which is a triumph of sorts. Such length also helps the film to slowly envelop its audience. The clichés from the first reel are turned to stunning effect as the three leads evolve into figures very different from our presuppositions. Paco's admission, at the film's close, of guilt for the chain of events culminating in Spider's murder and for everything that followed, redefines his own behaviour—he is a man seeking redemption, not revenge.

But the film still stands as cinema. It borrows the texture and proximity of television, but it also contains an urgency best pounded out from the big screen. There is the exoticism of East LA Chicano culture, giving us the feel of being quiet intruders into another world. Cruz sprays a graffiti Aztec Goddess onto his low-rider, and Miklo's revenge at the end of the film is intercut *Godfather*-style with the heaving carnival dancing of the Day of the Dead. Throughout, the film's language veers—mostly in mid-sentence—from bastardised English to Spanish, and the small details, from gang-banger's tattoos to a glass of mescal for Juanito's grave, betray an uncomprehended authenticity. Every frame contains a statuette of the maternal Virgin who, in a movie dominated by men, obsessed with *machismo*, is far and away the most substantial female role.

Blood In Blood Out wasn't made for the Anglos, but geared instead to the relatively untapped Latino market in the US. Hackford produced *La Bamba* (the first major studio movie to be made both in Spanish and English, and given separate promotion campaigns), the entire cast and crew were Latino and the script was co-written by poet, author and ex-con Jimmy Santiago Baca. This presumably provides much of the film's other strength—the visceral realism of its prison scenes. Most of it was shot on location in San Quentin, so as well as institutional sodomy, repeated stabbings and a touchdown with Miklo's prosthetic leg, we have ominously large, bald extras. The close-ups of prison food too look authentically awful—almost as repulsive, in fact, as Miklo's lethal blow-job on Big Al.

This is the sort of movie where every twist is accompanied by a booming guitar lick and someone's face scrunching up with emotion. It has lines like, "I don't want his pork chop, I want his life." There's a lot of shouting. But you're reminded of Buñuel's defence after he made his own slice of Latino street life, *Los Olvidados*, and critics condemned brass bedsteads in paupers' homes as a flight of Surrealist fantasy: he'd seen those bedsteads with his own eyes. Much of what initially seems ridiculous about *Blood In Blood Out* gains credibility with time. The film drives forward with a gnawing momentum, and most of the elements that seem overblown and out of place are steadily melted into the fabric.

The film's cod-operatic acting style is a product of culture rather than poor casting, as becomes increasingly apparent. This is also why it may deliver a bit of a shock to Anglo audiences. This is a movie set in America in which English is a second language and white faces are rare and despised. Miklo's white skin is a cross he has to bear, and that's a big reversal for a Hollywood which likes its epics in the mould of *Dances With Wolves*. But *Blood In Blood Out* is fascinating because it works when it shouldn't; because it's a foreign picture of a place we think we know so well; because it's a Third World film, produced in the heart of the First.

VILLAGE VOICE, 5/11/93, p. 62, Ed Morales

Bound by Honor is Hollywood's second attempt at documenting the Chicano prison gangs that ruled San Quentin in the '70s and '80s. Clocking in at about three hours, the film features even more relentless and graphic brutality than its predecessor, Ed Olmos's *American Me*, but in many ways it is the superior film. While *American Me* centers on the prison gang leader, *Bound by Honor* focuses on two brothers and their half-white cousin in a *Godfather*-like epic tale of betrayal and reconciliation. The script—largely written by the gifted Chicano poet Jimmy Santiago Baca, a high school dropout who became a writer while imprisoned—is not only authentic, but lyrical.

Unfortunately, the actors don't quite live up to the writing. Damian Chapa (who really is half-white, half Mexican) is convincingly fluent in Chicano slang and runs the requisite gamut of conflicted emotions, but doesn't electrify. Benjamin Bratt as the gangsta-turned-cop is equally competent and uncompelling. It's Jesse Borrego's Basquiat-like, drug-addicted painter who provides the best moments—alternating laconic boho cool with screaming art-damaged rages.

Borrego's performance doesn't rescue *Bound by Honor* from its climactic tangle of mixed messages. The moral imperative of loyalty to *familia*, celebrated ad nauseam by the brothers Raza, only serves to destroy a temporary alliance between African Americans and Chicanos. And it rings hollow in a film where women are almost completely invisible.

Also reviewed in:
CHICAGO TRIBUNE, 4/30/93, Friday/p. C, Dave Kehr
NEW YORK TIMES, 4/30/93, p. C8, Vincent Canby
VARIETY, 1/25/93, p. 133, Brian Lowry

BOXING HELENA

An Orion Classics release of a Main Line Pictures presentation. *Executive Producer:* James R. Schaeffer and Larry Sugar. *Director:* Jennifer Chambers Lynch. *Screenplay:* Jennifer Chambers Lynch. *Story:* Philippe Caland. *Director of Photography:* Frank Byers. *Editor:* David Finfer. *Music:* Graeme Revell. *Music Editor:* Dick Bernstein. *Sound:* J. Bayard Carey. *Sound Editor:* Dane A. Davis. *Casting:* Ferne Cassel. *Production Designer:* Amy Stevens. *Art Director:* Paul Huggins. *Set Decorator:* Sharon Braunstein. *Set Dresser:* Karen Young. *Special Effects:* Bob Shelley. *Costumes:* Patsy Chaney. *Make-up:* Nina Port. *Prosthetics:* Bill "Splat" Johnson. *Stunt Coordinator:* Lonnie Smith. *Running time:* 105 minutes. MPAA *Rating:* R.

CAST: Julian Sands (Dr. Nick Cavanaugh); Sherilyn Fenn (Helena); Bill Paxton (Ray O'Malley); Kurtwood Smith (Dr. Alan Harrison); Art Garfunkel (Dr. Lawrence Augustine); Betsy Clark (Anne Garrett); Nicolette Scorsese (Fantasy Lover/Nurse); Meg Register (Marion Cavanaugh); Bryan Smith (Russell); Marla Levine (Patricia); Kim Lentz (Nurse Diane); Lloyd T. Williams (Sam the Clerk); Carl Mazzocone, Sr. (Pastor); Erik Shoaff (Uncle Charlie); Lisa Oz (Flower Shop Girl); Ted Manson (Mailman); Adele K. Schaeffer (Flashback Party Woman #1); Amy Levin (Flashback Party Woman #2); Matt Berry (Young Nick Cavanaugh).

LOS ANGELES TIMES, 9/3/93, Calendar/p. 4, Kevin Thomas

It was probably worth every costly cent for Kim Basinger to get out of doing the dreadful "Boxing Helena"—but you have to wonder whatever there was about it that persuaded her to consider doing it in the first place.

Julian Sands, his pronounced British accent unexplained, stars as Dr. Nick Cavanaugh, a chief surgeon in an unnamed North American city who as a child was extolled to work hard—and was simultaneously taunted by his sexy, amoral mother who flaunted her open nudity and casual affairs. When the mother dies, the doctor is all set to put her elegant mansion up for sale when he encounters the gorgeous but haughty Helena (Sherilyn Fenn), with whom he had once had a one-night stand and is now absolutely transfixed by her.

An awkward pursuit ensues, with her rushing out of the mansion and into the street, where she is struck by a car. When she regains consciousness she finds her legs have been amputated and that she has become the doctor's prisoner. That he does not yet feel she is sufficiently dependent upon him is made overwhelmingly clear by repeated foreshadowing shots of a replica of the armless Venus de Milo.

In her directorial debut, Jennifer Chambers Lynch, who also wrote the script from Philippe Caland's story, reveals her filmmaker-father David Lynch's taste for the bizarre without any of his darkly perceptive humor and sense of style. "Boxing Helena" has been filmed with the straightforwardness of a standard TV movie, which means that it lapses swiftly into a protracted exercise in morbidity and silliness ending in a creaky cop-out device almost as old as the movies themselves.

Devoid of wit and irony, the film becomes merely a simple, blunt expression of extreme fear of women compounded by the preposterous, not to say dangerous, notion that absolute helplessness causes a woman to fall in love with a man for whom she had previously expressed only contempt. At any rate, it would take a great deal more talent and ability than Lynch possesses to enable us to see Nick and Helena's love-hate nexus as some kind of extreme metaphor for *Angst*-ridden contemporary relationships between men and women.

Sands and Fenn seemed to have trusted Lynch completely, and both give selfless, committed portrayals that just might have worked in a more subtle and substantial context. Sands is expert at projecting infantile creepiness, and Fenn excels in the film's one sane passage in which she attempts to explain to Nick what a woman needs emotionally from a man.

The year's most thankless role surely must be that of Betsy Clark as Nick's fiancée, who keeps throwing herself at a man who's clearly terminally weird. Also on hand are Art Garfunkel and Kurtwood Smith, as Nick's fellow doctors, and Bill Paxton, who gamely attempts to work up some humor as Helena's macho boyfriend. "Boxing Helena" (rated R for two scenes of strong sexuality and for language) fails by a wide mark to live up to all the publicity stirred up by its producer's suit against Basinger.

NEW YORK POST, 9/3/93, p. 29, Michael Medved

A few months ago, after a well-publicized trial, a California court fined Kim Basinger more than $8 million for backing out of a commitment to star in "Boxing Helena." Now that the world can see the rancid quality of the finished film, this money may turn out to be the best investment Basinger ever made.

The plot centers on a brilliant but shy surgeon (Julian Sands) who is romantically obsessed with the arrogant, promiscuous Helena (now played by the lovely Sherilyn Fenn, of "Twin Peaks" fame). One afternoon he lures her to his lonely mansion in order to declare his love, but when she tries to run away she's struck and severely injured by a hit-and-run driver.

The demented doc opts for an unconventional course of home care: He amputates both her legs above the knee and holds her prisoner in his house. When she continues to spurn his advances, using her wheelchair to escape his clutches, he proceeds to remove her arms at the shoulder.

With Helena in this "perfected" form, our hero places what's left of her in a polished wooden "box" where he feeds her, brushes her hair, applies makeup, treats her as the beautiful doll of his dreams—and continues the inevitable seduction of his patient.

If a man had created this sordid story, feminists would have been properly outraged, but the producers of the film hope to make the most of the fact that it's the product of the "youngest woman screenwriter/director in Hollywood history." Unfortunately, 25-year-old Jennifer Chambers Lynch (daughter of the always audacious David Lynch), employs a style that makes her movie look like an extended perfume commercial.

There are also three extended sequences of voyeuristic sex. These scenes bear only the most tenuous connection to the plot, and their inclusion identifies "Boxing Helena" as a sickening piece of soft-core porn.

By refusing to portray the torment and pain, the stumps and the scars associated with actual dismemberment, it ultimately glamorizes the process.

And if this weren't enough reason to avoid this tawdry trash, consider Sherilyn Fenn's hapless performance, in which her rage over her lost limbs toward the end of the movie is no more intense than her rage over a lost address book at its beginning. There's also an insipid and infuriating epilogue that lets Lynch have it both ways—suggesting that the whole ugly experience she dramatized for the previous 90 minutes was nothing more than a feverish dream.

It's possible that the "freak factor" may draw crowds to the theaters as the movie opens, but one can be sure that word of mouth will ensure that "Boxing Helena" has no legs.

NEWSDAY, 9/3/93, Part II/p. 62, Ira Robbins

Obsessive love has been a staple inspiration for star-crossed drama at least since Shakespeare, but whether uncontrollable desire is true romance or merely a twisted compulsion to possess is the question. The irony of people hurting each other in the name of love is a paradox that cuts to the center of human existence. And somewhere inside this twisted mess of a film is a true artistic heart grappling with the answer.

This film about a surgeon who reduces the woman he "loves" to an imprisoned torso has already generated lots of press, as much for its controversial subject material as the production's false starts. (Both Madonna and Kim Basinger withdrew from the title part; the latter lost an $8.9 million judgement in a resulting lawsuit.)

But the directorial debut by Jennifer Chambers Lynch, the 25-year old daughter of David Lynch, lacks the sharp creative vision (or Dad's stylized bizarreness) to make its point about the neediness and vulnerability of love. What's more, "Boxing Helena" is loaded down with Oedipal issues, premature ejaculation, the physically challenged and more. And the film's stiff, obvious direction and acting, slow, obvious screenplay and cop-out ending render its intellectual content inscrutable. How many times does Lynch need to show the armless Venus de Milo?

Helena (Sherilyn Fenn) is an imperious, cruel sexpot who uses men and discards them with nary a care. Dr. Nick Cavanaugh (Julian Sands) can't get over a brief affair with Helena. (Blame it on his horrid, cold father and bitch goddess mother.) Nick's neurotic notion of romantic pursuit is, in fact, stalking; any illusions he might have about worshipping her are unrelated to anything like love. It takes a badly staged contrivance—an auto accident that necessitates an impromptu at-home amputation—to get her into Nick's clutches, but once she is, their sparring becomes a stage for provocative suggestions about what men and women really want from each other.

Anyone who's ever had an unrequited crush knows the resentment of foiled attempts to impose needs or desires on an unwilling object of desire. Nick's desperate push to make Helena love him pivots on making her dependent. Slowly, as he forces her to relinquish her prized power, their emotional parrying begins to yield some real ideas on the subject. But Edward Albee this ain't.

To Lynch's credit, it takes courage to undertake a project certain to be misconstrued and attacked for the wrong reasons. Many will view this violence against a woman as an attack on women, which it most certainly is not. Unfortunately: whatever her true goals, they're lost to inexperience and confusion.

SIGHT AND SOUND, 7/93, p. 38, Amanda Lipman

On the day of his mother's funeral, Dr Nick Cavanaugh—who was humiliated by her as a child—leaves the cemetery to go to the hospital and perform a life-saving operation. Meeting his friend Dr Lawrence Augustine in a bar, he glimpses Helena, a woman with whom he has been besotted, and rushes outside to avoid her. Having decided to move straight into his mother's house, he goes there to meet his girlfriend Anne, but ends up spying on Helena while she has sex with her boyfriend Ray. Helena throws Ray out and makes plans to go away, but first she goes to Nick's housewarming party, where she treats him with disdain. Nick makes such a fool of himself over her that Anne walks out on him. The next day, he tricks Helena into coming to his house. When she realises this, she tries to run away and is knocked down by a passing car.

Regaining consciousness, she finds out that Nick, who is tending to her solicitously, has amputated both her legs. They begin a relationship as loving jailer and angry prisoner, though not before Nick has given up his job to a fellow doctor who discovers what is happening. As Nick—beset with memories of his mocking, sexy mother—cuts himself off from the world to be with Helena, Ray starts hunting for her and Anne tries unsuccessfully to make it up with Nick through sex. Nick then cuts off Helena's arms and makes her watch while he has sex with a prostitute. Finally, Helena admits that she loves him and wants him. Just as they are about to make love, Ray bursts in and attacks Nick, who is knocked out. When he regains consciousness, he is in hospital. He visits Helena and it becomes clear that the whole story has been a dream—that after she was knocked down, he brought her to hospital where she was operated on, and that she still has her limbs.

It is certainly a bad sign when a film's biggest claim to fame hangs on the fact that both Madonna and Kim Basinger nearly got involved with it—the latter enough to leave her with a big bill for bailing out too late. But even if the two stars in question have made their own share of inexcusably poor movies, they have shown good sense in not getting involved with this one.

Having established its titular premise, as Fenn's gaudy Helena is 'boxed' by having her legs and then her arms cut off by the adoring but mad Dr Julian Sands, the film goes resolutely nowhere. He dresses her up and feeds her; she mocks his sexual inadequacy. A few characters who have the potential to play pivotal roles disappear. Instead, there are endless short scenes charting bits of daily life, and video-style music breaks that patently play for time. It soon becomes clear that the idea has reached its stunted fruition.

Just how to react to the film is another problem: most of it is so ponderously serious that it's laughable. Though there are plenty of potentially camp elements, from the situation itself to Sands' aesthete-cum-surgeon, they are all given a determinedly po-faced and heavy-handed treatment. Why does Nick have sexual problems and crazed obsessions? Cut to images of his louche, leering mother—courtesy of Freud, by way of unreconstructed trashy '50s psychodramas. With what can we equate Helena's limbless state? Why, with that Venus de Milo-esque statue at which the film so helpfully keeps pointing.

In terms of its sexual politics, this is all even odder, when put next to several gratuitous sex scenes and the platitudes that the formerly sharp-tongued Helena starts to spout about women being soft and gentle and wanting to be loved by a big, strong man. The fact that this all turns out to be some kind of wish-fulfillment dream on Nick's part is never used to cancel out the meaning here, or to put it in any other, more ironic context.

The film is either singularly lacking in irony, or so extraordinarily removed from itself so as to make engaging with it impossible. Not only is the script unbelievably bad—packed with clumsy, forced and often banal dialogue—but some of the acting has to be seen to be believed. Worst, or funniest, of all is Bill Paxton—great as the naive sheriff in *One False Move*—who does a bizarre, leather-clad, lip-curling impersonation of an aging rock star, as Helena's 'wild' boyfriend Ray. Fenn's Helena, (perhaps intentionally) overdressed and overpreened, has a hard job trying to make her sketchy character add up to more than a series of (literally) disjointed utterances. Only Sands seems remotely at ease, playing at his habitual aesthetically fervent madness with an enthusiasm that belies the inanity of his dialogue. His smaller neurotic compulsions—endlessly changing his shirt and washing himself—are more interesting than his larger problems, including, as a bafflingly 'major' plot point, premature ejaculation.

Lynch also borrows bits and pieces from her father David. As if uncertain of its own style, *Boxing Helena* intermittently gives way to white light flashes and menacingly prowling cameras. This would be fine if it added anything to the film. But Lynch would have done better by her movie debut if she had concentrated less on the niceties she has borrowed from psychoanalytical text books and more on essentials like story, script and character. If this were even entertaining, it would be a whole lot more bearable.

VILLAGE VOICE, 9/28/93, p. 66, Kate Tentler

I must say I feel pretty sorry for Jennifer Lynch. It's not that I think she's a self-hating woman because her directorial debut is so steeped in misogyny: an emotionally limited man, Nick (Julian Sands), haunted by his beautiful, abusive, often naked mother, is obsessed with the luscious, verbally castrating, and often naked Helena (Sherilyn Fenn), whose limbs he amputates in a vain attempt to make her need and love him. Classic definition, right? And it's not that Lynch had to fight big bad Hollywood to get her little film made. No, the reason I feel pity for her is that *Boxing Helena* (which she also wrote, poor thing) is just a terrible movie and one that, like too many controversial films that blatantly pander to humanity's worst aspects, isn't really worth the attention it's getting. It's entirely flat and silly, so bad there were times my hands flew up involuntarily to cover my face in embarrassment.

Aside from a couple of mysterious ambient shots that seem pilfered from her dad (director David Lynch), Lynch's unimaginative direction looks borrowed from Showtime's erotic-titillation *Red Shoe Diaries*. There's a lot of Victoria's Secret lingerie, candles, and corkscrew-curled hair that's supposed to suggest sex. The only thing we ever learn about the characters is that Helena is a shrew and Nick is a retarded boy. Now Lynch might argue that *Boxing Helena* is about the power of love, desire, and possessiveness. And these elements are highlighted, over and over again, as motives for the story. Problem is, *Boxing Helena* is more the appearance of something interesting than something interesting.

Also reviewed in:
NEW YORK TIMES, 9/3/93, p. C1, Janet Maslin
VARIETY, 2/1/93, p. 98, Todd McCarthy
WASHINGTON POST, 9/3/93, p. G7, Rita Kempley
WASHINGTON POST, 9/3/93, Weekend/p. 43, Joe Brown

BOY'S SHORTS: THE NEW QUEER CINEMA

A Frameline release of six short films exploring gay themes. *Running time:* 119 minutes. *MPAA Rating:* Not Rated.

RESONANCE: *Director:* Stephen Cummins. *Screenplay:* Stephen Cummins and Simon Hunt.

WITH: Mathew Bergan; Chad Courtney; Annette Evans.

R.S.V.P.: *Director:* Laurie Lynd. *Screenplay:* Laurie Lynd.

ANTHEM: *Director:* Marlon Riggs.

RELAX: *Director:* Christopher Newby. *Screenplay:* Christopher Newby.

BILLY TURNER'S SECRET: *Director:* Michael Mayson. *Screenplay:* Michael Mayson.

THE DEAD BOY'S CLUB: *Director:* Mark Christopher. *Screenplay:* Mark Christopher.

LOS ANGELES TIMES, 11/25/93, Calendar/p. 9, Kevin Thomas

"Boys' Shorts: The New Queer Cinema" might better have been called "Men's Briefs" because there's nothing adolescent about the six decidedly mature films that compose this absorbing two-hour program presented by Frameline, which sponsors the San Francisco International Lesbian & Gay Film Festival.

Indeed, what the six highly varied works have most in common is that they view the gay experience not as something hermetically sealed-off from the rest of society but as being very much a part of the world at large. As a result, this collection is virtually as accessible to straights as it is to the gays to whom it is specifically addressed. Inevitably, AIDS is a central issue in several of the shorts, yet the filmmakers have brought fresh perspectives to the subject.

With images and interior monologues rather than dialogue, Australian filmmaker Stephen Cummins' lyrical "Resonance" tells the love story of two young men—they meet when one of them, a martial arts instructor, rescues the other from a gay bashing—largely in mime and dance, highlighted by a boxing match between the two men that becomes a dance, transforming aggression into affection.

In "R.S.V.P.," the most impressive of all the offerings, Canadian filmmaker Laurie Lynd reveals the impact of the loss of a young man, Andrew (Ross Manson) to AIDS. His lover (Daniel MacIvor) returns home from Andrew's funeral just in time to hear on the radio program "R.S.V.P." Jessye Norman singing Berlioz's "La Spectre de la Rose," which several weeks earlier Andrew had requested, Lind then cuts to Andrew's parents and his sister as they are listening to the same recording on the same program. This link becomes Lind's point of departure for exploring what Andrew meant to his loved ones, and the result is an acutely perceptive film, at once detached and impassioned.

Marlon Riggs' "Anthem" recalls his earlier "Tongues Untied" in its use of poetry and dance to celebrate gay love between black men, but "Anthem" is less lyrical, more like a chant and rap, declaring that such love is revolutionary in its impact and implications. The British filmmaker's ironically titled "Relax" evokes in powerful, surreal fashion the agonizing uncertainty with which a young gay man anxiously awaits the result of his HIV test.

Michael Mayson's "Billy Turner's Secret" is the one film among the six to suggest that it could be a student film which it is—in the lack of coherence and clarity in its narrative. It is moving anyway, capturing an authentic sense of fear and pain, for it deals with the difficulties facing a young black man (Mark D. Kennerly) in revealing his homosexuality to his homophobic straight roommate (played by Mayson himself).

"Boys Shorts" (Times-rated Mature for adult themes) concludes with Mark Christopher's "The Dead Boys' Club," in which a young man (Nat DeWolf), once he puts on a pair of shoes that had belonged to a man who has just died of AIDS, finds himself experiencing the giddy disco years of gay life in the flush of the liberated '70s. In this way Christopher is able to suggest the loss of a substantial portion of an entire generation to AIDS while symbolizing the need to practice safe sex.

NEW YORK POST, 7/21/93, p. 26, Jerry Tallmer

All across the city of Toronto the voice of Jessye Norman is a purifying river that threads together the tears—wept and unwept—of those who loved Andrew Selman. She sings from Berlioz, "Le Spectre de la Rose," rich, dark, exquisitely moving, as is this film, "RSVP.," by the Canadian writer/director Laurie Lynd.

It is Andrew's mate, Sid, returning to the empty apartment, seeing Andrew's unmanned computer, his sweater tossed on a chair, his laughing face in the photos on the wall, who has first put on the radio—a recording, Jessye Norman with the London Symphony, requested weeks ago by the young man who is now dead.

As we hear the aria we see all those whom it is touching, wherever within reach of the radio they are: Andrew's devastated sister, his stoical parents, the bartender—a young black woman—who was his friend, the girl who rips down a scrawled "FAGGOT" over the death notice on the bulletin board in the school where Andrew (Ross Manson) taught. And of course we see Sid (Daniel MacIvor), holding that sweater, thinking his thoughts.

That is all we need to see, in this, by far the best, most sensitive, of the six "Boys' Shorts" of a program that also advertises itself as "The New Queer Cinema" opening today, at Village East.

A less indirect, less poetic, and in fact indecipherable statement about AIDS is Christopher Newby's "Relax," the adventures on and off a rooftop of a young Londoner named Steve (Philip Rosch) and his tough boyfriends.

Still more indecipherable is "Resonance," an 11-minute piece by Stephen Cummins about a gay-bashing in an alley in Sydney, Australia.

"Anthem," by Marlon Riggs, is an angry blast of pseudo-poetry equating black African and Afro-American pride with black homosexual rage and passion.

"Billy Turner's Secret," by Michael Mayson, an NYU Film alumnus from Detroit, is a longer (26 minutes), more amusing work, though pretty confusing if you lose the track at any moment. Set on the basketball courts and streets, in the locker rooms and living rooms of Harlem, it turns macho as well as color inside out. Rugged Billy Turner's secret is that he is gay.

Finally, "The Dead Boys' Club," by Mark Christopher, in which a tender lad from the sticks (Nat DeWolf) learns all about the big town from a couple of studs (Erik Van Der Wilden and Erik Estrada) and a pair of old shoes.

VILLAGE VOICE, 7/27/93, p. 62, David D. Kim

Drawn from the U.S., Canada, Australia, and England, the six films that make up *Boy's Shorts* are a compelling sampler of queer cinema's next wave. Ranging in length from nine to 26 minutes, all have traveled the festival circuit and—like queer culture in general—have finally plugged into a commercial outlet.

One of the strongest films, Christopher Newby's black-and-white *Relax*, captures AIDS anxiety through the hazy nightmares and heightened awareness of a man awaiting his blood-test results. Pacing isn't necessarily Newby's strong point; nevertheless, *Relax* effectively evokes the ticking clock of his protagonist's panic. *Anthem*, by Marlon Riggs, also bears the stamp of an idiosyncratic and inventive filmmaker. Like a music-video version of Riggs's earlier work, *Tongues Untied*, this tightly edited short intersperses spoken verse with quick-cut images. Zulu dancers, empowerment slogans, a fluttering American flag, African American men speaking and embracing identity assumes many rhythms here.

The music plays more slowly in *R.S.V.P.*, Laurie Lynd's elegiac look at a man who's recently lost his lover to AIDS. Carried across radio waves, Jessye Norman's resonant voice (singing Berlioz's "Spectre of the Rose") articulates his unspoken grief while reaching the ears of others affected by the death. The image of an empty hospital bed figures prominently, as it does in Mark Christopher's much hyped, if slightly disjointed fantasy, *The Dead Boys' Club*. When a young man dons a pair of disco shoes given to him by an older relative, he finds himself bumping and grinding with those bad, bad boys of the '70s. Grainy shots of muscle and leather apparently remind us to play it safe, though they also reinforce the gay white iconography of boy-boy sex.

Less wistful, Stephen Cummins's *Resonance* opens with a gay-bashing scene and closes with a series of interpretive dance sequences. The latter are regrettably corny—particularly a boxing-ring duet; then again, filming performance is difficult enough without having to address bias violence. Only straights are bashed in Michael Mayson's gentle comedy *Billy Turner's Secret*. Though it could use more visual juice, this coming-out narrative is appealing and upbeat: Homeboy's a homo, but homophobic roommate doesn't have a clue until girlfriend's cousin strolls in and outs him. Roommate acts out, the gay boyz act up, and roommate eats crow. If only queer life were so simple.

Also reviewed in:
NEW YORK TIMES, 7/21/93, p. C17
VARIETY, 8/16/93, p. 40, Greg Evans
WASHINGTON POST, 2/21/94, p. B7, Rita Kempley

BRONX TALE, A

A Savoy Pictures release of a Price Entertainment presentation in association with Penta Entertainment of a Tribeca production. *Executive Producer:* Peter Gatien. *Producer:* Jane Rosenthal, Jon Kilik, and Robert De Niro. *Director:* Robert De Niro. *Screenplay (based on his play):* Chazz Palminteri. *Director of Photography:* Reynaldo Villalobos. *Editor:* David Ray and R.Q. Lovett. *Music:* Jeffrey Kimball and Butch Barbella. *Music Editor:* Todd Kasow. *Sound:* Tod Maitland, (music) Chris Cassone and Gary Chester. *Sound Editor:* Dan Sable. *Casting:* Ellen Chenoweth. *Production Designer:* Wynn Thomas. *Art Director:* Chris Shriver. *Set Decorator:* Debra Schutt. *Set Dresser:* Anthony Baldesare. *Special Effects:* Steve Kirschoff. *Costumes:* Rita Ryack. *Make-up:* Michael Laudati. *Make-up (Robert De Niro):* Ilona Herman. *Stunt Coordinator:* Doug Coleman. *Running time:* 120 minutes. *MPAA Rating:* R.

CAST: Robert De Niro (Lorenzo);   Chazz Palminteri (Sonny);   Lillo Brancato (Calogero, Age 17);   Francis Capra (Calogero, Age 9);   Taral Hicks (Jane);   Kathrine Narducci (Rosina);   Clem Caserta (Jimmy Whispers);   Alfred Sauchelli, Jr. (Bobby Bars);   Frank Pietrangolare (Danny K.O.);   Joe Pesci (Carmine);   Robert D'Andrea (Tony Toupee);   Eddie Montanaro (Eddie Mush);   Fred Fischer (JoJo the Whale);   Dave Salerno (Frankie Coffeecake);   Joseph D'Onofrio (Slick, Age 17);   Luigi D'Angelo (Aldo, Age 17);   Louis Vanaria (Crazy Mario, Age 17);   Dominik Rocchio (Ralphie, Age 17);   Patrick Boriello (Slick, Age 9);   Paul Perri (Crazy Mario, Age 9);   Tommy A. Ford (Phil the Peddler);   Rocco Parente (Driver, Hey Marie!);   Joe Black (Murdered Man);   Louis Gioia (Last Rites Priest);   Mitch Kolpan (Detective Belsik);   Phil Foglia (Detective Vella);   Richard DeDomenico (Priest);   Max Genovino (Louie Dumps);   Ralph Napolitano (Gino);   Steve Kendall (Red Beard);   A.J. Ekoku (A.J.);   Sobe Bailey (Willy);   Dominick Lombardozzi (Nicky Zero);   Frank Caserta, Sr. (Old Gee);   Ed Derian (Fight Announcer);   Larry Lederman (Racetrack Announcer);   Gianna Ranaudo (Tina);   Philip Garbarino (Sonny's Killer);   Nicky Blair (Jerry);   David Batiste, Derrick Simmons, and Ali S. Abdul Wahhab (Angry Neighbors);   Albert Attansio and Pat Vacaro (Capos);   Rocco Matra and Frank Caserta, Jr. (Soldiers);   Richie Ranieri (Bodyguard);   Sal Cestaro (Coffeemaker);   Larry Liedy (Bartendar);   Elizabeth Abbassi (Lady in Window);   Ida Bernardini (Fish Store Customer);   Frank Conti (Fish Store Owner);   Clem Caserta, Jr. (Pizza Man);   Sonny Hurst (Biker).

LOS ANGELES TIMES, 9/29/93, Calendar/p. 1, Kenneth Turan

Great actors are time bandits, hoarders of pieces of observed reality that can be parceled out to create a performance. And the best thing about Robert De Niro's work behind the camera in "A Bronx Tale" is that he has brought this actor's sensibility, this delight in small and casual moments, to his first film as a director.

Set (where else but) in the Bronx, hardly virgin territory for the movies, "Tale" brings more tangy authenticity to its evocation of the tribal world of New York's ethnic neighborhoods than almost any film you can name. Its re-creation of the primarily Italian Belmont section, home of hoodlums and honest citizens both, is so sweetly and vividly remembered you can almost smell the pepperoni.

The key player (aside from De Niro) in this recapturing of a particular place and time is Chazz Palminteri, a journeyman stage and TV actor who, apparently out of desperation, decided to write a monologue rooted in his childhood in the Bronx. The monologue became a celebrated one-man show that Palminteri turned into a script he refused to part with unless he ended up with a key role himself.

Appealing though it is in its celebration of ambience and mood, however, "A Bronx Tale" (rated R for strong language and several scenes of violence) doesn't have the same tact when it comes to plotting. A film that would have been better off without a melodramatic story line, "Tale" is burdened by no fewer than two, neither one particularly convincing and both feeling as if they were forcefully grafted onto an otherwise charming flowering plant.

While it stars De Niro and Palminteri, "Tale" revolves around the unsentimental education of a third party, Calogero (C for short) Anello, who goes from being a wide-eyed 9-year-old (Francis Capra) when the film opens in 1960 to an only nominally more sophisticated 17-year-old (Lillo Brancato), in the tumultuous year of 1968.

C's father, Lorenzo (De Niro, selflessly taking a not very interesting part), is a hard-working bus driver who frets that "the saddest thing in life is wasted talent." His son, however, can't help but be attracted to the only glamour in the neighborhood, the crime family wise guys who hang out in Chez Bippy, drinking coffee and stronger stuff and gambling the hours away.

Chez Bippy is the kind of place where the regulars have names as colorful as the bar itself. Frankie Coffeecake, so called for his less-than-ideal complexion; JoJo the Whale, whose shadow once killed a dog; and Eddie Mush, the infallible jinx whose presence can mess up any good thing, are all habitues, as are Jimmy Whispers, Danny K.O., Louie Dumps and of course Tony Toupee.

Even if you feel you never want to see another colorful Italian as long as you live, it will be difficult to resist the film's relaxed, unforced way with these locals, who turn a basement craps game into a grimy comic gem. Many of them are played (as is C at both 9 and 17) by non-professionals with whom De Niro the director has a quite effective touch.

Sonny, the kind of guy who already knows the answer when he asks, "Anybody got a problem with that?" Palminteri, who after all wrote the role, knows enough to underplay its excesses, and ends up with a vital, seemingly effortless performance that dominates the film from beginning to end.

Naturally C can't resist Sonny after a violent incident brings him to the great man's notice, but though the ads insist "A Devoted Father Battles the Local Crime Boss for the Life of His Son," that is a totally bogus conflict. For one thing, father Lorenzo mostly ignores his son's infatuation, and for another, Sonny is a more complex character than your ordinary capo. He's read Machiavelli (yes, he read it in prison, but at least he was reading) and he strongly believes young C should go to college and leave the streets behind.

Equally arbitrary is the interracial romance that the 17-year-old C begins to contemplate when he sees African-American Jane (Taral Hicks) talking to friends on his father's bus. Awkward in its sincerity, this forbidden love also strikes a contrived note, as if it were thought up to order when someone felt the situation demand more conflict.

All in all, "A Bronx Tale" is best when it just lets its guys hang out in the neighborhood (really Astoria, Queens, beautifully transformed by production designer Wynn Thomas) listening to the soundtrack's exceptional collection of period music. De Niro's direction is always unassuming in the best sense, and whenever his and Palminteri's film forgets about the supposed demands of plot it remembers the best parts of itself.

NEW YORK, 10/18/93, p. 120, David Denby

A 9-year-old boy, sitting on his front stoop in the Belmont section of the Bronx in 1960, sees something so bizarre it remains imprinted on his mind for years. Two men, each in his own car, are screaming at each other over a parking space. One guy gets out and starts swinging a bat at the other's car, smashing the front window and menacing the man inside. Suddenly, a neighborhood gangster leaves his post at the corner, where he stands monitoring the neighborhood, takes out a revolver, and without a second's hesitation empties it into the guy with the bat. The gangster and his friends hustle the other man away.

Now, what was *that*? An argument over a parking space? Or was it some old, old quarrel, some embedded pattern of rivalry and hatred now working itself out? The camera stays back, at the distance of the boy's view, and the whole thing happens so quickly that it's impossible to sort out. In some way, the little boy, whose name is Calogero, spends the rest of his youth trying to penetrate the codes of adult behavior. *A Bronx Tale*, Robert De Niro's directorial debut, could be called a fable about the difficulty of becoming a man—a story about the traps and delusions of manhood in a tough neighborhood where people get shot without reason (in 1960, this was still considered strange). After the shooting, the police line up the usual suspects against a store, right out on the street, and they ask Calogero, who has curly, soft brown hair and wide-open eyes, to identify the killer. The boy refuses to finger the gangster, whose name is Sonny. "You did a good thing for a bad man," says Calogero's father, Lorenzo (De Niro), a hardworking and entirely honest bus driver.

A Bronx Tale might have turned into a conventional struggle for a boy's allegiance—the good father versus the bad father—but De Niro has something more interesting in mind. The moral values remain up in the air. The good father, Lorenzo, is certainly good, an apostle of hard work, blunt honesty, and intelligent love; and De Niro plays him as a virtuous straight arrow. But is Sonny a monster? Calogero learns to read him. *A Bronx Tale* is a fable without an obvious lesson, except this one: Only the most alert and intelligent boys can truly learn from experience; the rest are doomed to repeat the stupidest behavior of the tribe. Part of the Bronx tale is that some of the boys *don't* grow up.

The movie was written by the actor who plays Sonny, Chazz Palminteri, who first developed the material as a monologue for the Los Angeles stage. Quite a coup: Palminteri has fictionalized incidents from his life and wangled for himself the plumiest role. Palminteri's jet-black hair is swept back, revealing a high, strong forehead and thick black eyebrows. He has a hoarse, insistent voice, and a dark shadow on his chin and cheeks. Sonny is a formidable neighborhood thug—a murderer, an extortionist, an enforcer—but he's also the least mythic, the most rational and calculating of the recent movie mobsters. He's intelligent and watchful; he seems like someone you could talk to. When Calogero refuses to turn Sonny over to the police, Sonny becomes the boy's guardian angel.

Palminteri's nostalgia is bittersweet. In the exceptionally well edited early sequences—as the 17-year-old Calogero (Lillo Brancato) narrates, looking back to his childhood—De Niro introduces the neighborhood in 1960. It's doowop time: The music is lulling and sweet; the Yankees, with their legendary switch-hitting centerfielder, have not yet threatened to leave for New Jersey. The camera travels around the neighborhood haunts—through the alley behind Calogero's building and into the back entrance of the bar and "social club," where the heavy-bellied hoods and encrusted bums, with their scarred faces, their nicknames and peculiarities, hang around talking and gambling. In the small roles, De Niro uses nonactors from New York, men with faces and bodies redolent of an entire way of life. In the neighborhood, the little boys imitate the mobsters: When the hero goes to confession and the priest asks him about "the fifth" (commandment), Calogero tells him it's the right not to incriminate yourself. In defiance of his father, Calogero becomes Sonny's pet.

In part, A Bronx Tale seems a kind of minor-key complement to the Scorese masterpieces, especially GoodFellas, which is also the story of the education of a young man. Palminteri and De Niro don't bring anything like Scorsese's crazy exuberance and menace to the neighborhood milieu; they're much more matter-of-fact and realistic, closer to human uncertainty and failure. Most of Calogero's friends are turning into rather pathetic petty hoods and layabouts—racist slobs obsessed with blacks living in the next neighborhood. Calogero himself isn't cut out to be a gangster—there's too much of his father's straightforward decency in him—and Sonny is smart enough to know that. Victory for this boy means staying out of trouble, so the movie, by its very nature, lacks excitement. Calogero is looking to please his two fathers, and Lillo Brancato, the rather slight young beginning actor who plays him, has a long narrow face, sad eyes, and an abashed manner.

Our interest shifts to Sonny and to Palminteri's idea of what a gangster is and should be. For Sonny is actually a kind of ideal. He's extremely violent, but he doesn't hurt anyone who doesn't deserve to get hurt (you never see him shaking anyone down). He's shrewd, paraphrases Machiavelli (accurately), and gives some of the best advice ever heard in the history of the movies. Is he believable? Not quite, but Palminteri obviously believes in Sonny's tragedy, which is that he can save other people but not himself.

Much of the movie is absorbing, though there are lame passages. The violence, including the interracial violence, doesn't always grow out of the story. Calogero's friendly relationship with a black teenage girl (Taral Hicks)—a bridge over troubled waters—seems like wishful thinking. Also, as Janet Maslin pointed out, De Niro doesn't seem to know what to do with the female characters. But he's made a good beginning: The Bronx neighborhood is alive, and the way the nabe changes over time, the national media culture encroaching on a tiny enclave, is convincing and touching. As a director, De Niro may not be a demon like his friend Scorsese, but he has humor and warmth of feeling, and that already puts him ahead of most of the competition.

NEW YORK POST, 10/1/93, p. 44, Michael Medved

In Robert De Niro's first film as a director you might expect the same strength that have so consistently characterized his work as an actor over the past 20 years—energy, earthiness, passion and an edge of nuttiness and danger.

"A Bronx Tale" delivers all of that and much more.

It's a lyrical, funny, tender, big-hearted piece of work with surprising grace notes of sweetness and nostalgia. Despite some difficulties in bringing his film to a satisfactory conclusion, De Niro turns in a directorial debut that's even more impressive that Mel Gibson's fine work in "The Man Without a Face."

Like Gibson, he helps his own cause with an extraordinarily effective and almost self-effacing performance. He plays a hardworking bus driver who lives in the Belmont section of the Bronx in 1960.

He's worried about bad influences on his bright nine-year-old boy, Calogoro (Bronx-born newcomer Francis Capra), particularly from the elegant, imperious neighborhood crime boss, Sonny (Chazz Palminteri).

One afternoon the boy watches from his stoop as Sonny shoots a stranger in cold blood; when he's later questioned by the police, the lad wisely declines to identify the killer. Despite De Niro's protests, his son is rewarded for his discretion with a new position as mascot to the local mobsters, who congregate at a street corner inner sanctum known an Chez Bippy.

The movie then skips ahead eight years, with the 17-year-old Calogero (now played by an energetic young De Niro lookalike named Lillo Brancato) relating to the lone-wolf Sonny as his role model and father figure, while his real father anguishes over the kid's future. "It's the working man who's the real tough guy," De Niro angrily informs his son. "The guy who gets up every morning to go to work for his family."

Everything in the film works beautifully until the final half hour, when the main story is derailed by a hokey interracial Romeo-and-Juliet subplot involving our teenaged Italian-American hero and an African-American beauty (the radiant 17- year-old model Taral Hicks) he meets in school. It's the only aspect of this tale that doesn't ring true.

The film closely follows the essential elements of the stage performance which Chazz Palminteri based on his own childhood recollections and performed in Los Angeles and New York. That one-man tour-de-force featured Palminteri in more than a dozen different parts, and he must be hugely gratified to see how vividly all these characters emerge on screen.

Using ordinary guys from the neighborhood rather than professional actors, De Niro gives unforgettable life to Jimmy Whispers (Clem Caserta), Tony Toupee (Robert D'Andrea), the hugely obese JoJo the Whale (Fred Fischer), the badly pock-marked Frank Coffeecake (Dave Salerno), and, most memorably of all, Eddie Mush (Eddie Montanaro)—who is such a sure-fire jinx that every bet he makes turns instantly to mush.

It's part of De Niro's triumph that he's won so many splendid performances from first-time actors (especially the two terrific boys who play Calogero), but the best work in the film still comes from Palminteri.

NEWSDAY, 9/29/93, Part II/p. 48, John Anderson

The Bronx of "A Bronx Tale" is a mythic place, the kind that exists in snapshots, taken on sunny days, with one hand shading one eye. It's the kind of place George (Sorry to Go) Steinbrenner would like to see surrounding that large piece of rent-controlled property he currently occupies. And in some ways it's the type of community people were looking for when they fled to the suburbs in the mid-'60s, a place where families of the right color could put their traditional values into practice.

In 1960, when "A Bronx Tale" unfolds, the Yankees are gods, the city is a lot paler, and intolerance, while perhaps no more prevalent than today, is at least more socially acceptable. The Belmont section (which was recreated for the film in Astoria) is on its way to becoming a ghetto within a ghetto, a white Italian island in the dark sea of the borough. And it provides 9-year-old Calogero Anello (Francis Capra) with a 4-foot-high view of the best and worst of New York City. On clean, bustling Belmont Avenue, Calogero lives with his mother, Rosina (Kathrine Narducci), and bus-driver father, Lorenzo (Robert De Niro), who takes him to Yankee games and shares with the boy his limited wisdom. In between intimate family moments, Calogero sneaks off to the local bar, Chez Bippy, to study his idol, Sonny (Chazz Palminteri), the neighborhood hood.

Sonny ignores the kid until the day the kid sees Sonny kill another man in the street. But after Calogero, who's made to go through an impromptu (and improbable) police lineup on the street, tells the cops Sonny didn't do it, he has, from that moment on, two fathers and a lifelong dilemma.

Does he listen to his hardworking, if not particularly inspiring, father? Or to the morally bankrupt Sonny—who calls him C—and his "I-read-Machiavelli-in-prison"philosophy of life? Between the street dramas, coming-of-age rituals, racist violence and the interracial romance between the older Calogero (Lillo Brancato) and Jane (Taral Hicks), "A Bronx Tale" is really about the boy's paternal confusion. That it's a less than absorbing quandary is partly because of casting, and partly due to direction. De Niro has proven himself one of our most adventurous actors, but he's a decidedly run-of-the-mill director, at least his first time out. That he borrows so heavily from his own best director, Martin Scorsese, and from Spike Lee (and from "West Side Story," "American Graffiti" etc.) may be natural, considering his subject matter; he wants that street sense, the spasmodic violence, the city grit and a darkly comedic point of view.

But while De Niro shows some flair for comedy, it isn't dark, and it isn't conducive to the edgy atmosphere he's trying to create through the rest of the film. Nor does he know where to use the jokes, or in what dosage. A scene in which young Calogero shoots craps for Sonny, a crucial moment in his upbringing, becomes a burlesque in which Sonny keeps banishing unlucky gamblers to the bathroom. A scene in which the boy goes to confession and he and the priest do a kind of "who's on first" routine involving the Fifth Commandment and Fifth Amendment is not only in questionable taste but jarringly out of character. And several scenes at the Anellos' dinner table, which might have shored up our belief in Calogero's home life, become shtick.

Chazz Palminteri's story is a male thing, a parable about fathers and friendship and conscience that, while not exactly "The Joy Luck Club for Men," has some important if less than revelatory things to say about families, love, the work ethic and the capriciousness of fate. Women, though, virtually don't exist, and are problematic when they do. When Lorenzo turns down an offer from Sonny to run numbers on his bus, it's his wife, Rosina, who thinks that maybe Lorenzo should have taken the $150 a week. And Jane, the black girl who becomes C's first love, is a cipher, although Taral Hicks is beautiful and sweet. The male actors, particularly Brancato, give generally good performances. It would have been interesting to see De Niro cast as Sonny. On the other hand, that might have given "A Bronx Tale" more volatility than its director could have handled.

NEWSWEEK, 10/4/93, p. 88, David Ansen

Just when you thought you'd OD'd on movies about goombahs and goodfellas in the old neighborhood, along comes *A Bronx Tale*, a deliciously well-observed memory piece about growing up in the '60s that marks the vital debut of director Robert De Niro. Sure, there are echoes of Scorsese, but De Niro and writer Chazz Palminteri put a fresh spin on their story of a young boy growing up torn between two patriarchs—his real dad (De Niro), a hardworking bus driver who wants to save his son from the temptations of the street, and the suave local crime boss Sonny (Palminteri), who takes the 9-year-old Calogero (Francis Capra) under his wing when the boy refuses to rat on Sonny for shooting a man in the street. At the age of 17, Calogero (Lillo Brancato) is reveling in his status as the Machiavellian Sonny's favorite, but he's still got his father's decency. When black/Italian racial tensions come to a boil, his lowlife pals reach for baseball bats but he falls for a lovely black girl (Taral Hicks). Sonny tells him to follow his heart, but only if she passes The Door Test: if she leans over and unlocks his side of the car before he gets in, she's worth pursuing.

It's details like this that give "A Bronx Tale" its vibrancy. It's a generous movie, teeming with great neighborhood characters—like Eddie Mush, who never placed a bet he didn't lose—and with a dynamite selection of '60s music. Both funny and brutal (and only at the very end, a little too melodramatic for its own good) Palminteri's screenplay views the radical social changes of the '60s through the prism of a patriarchal society frozen in its ways. (Sonny's boys make mincemeat of an invading squad of long-haired bikers.) Wonderfully acted by a seamless mix of pros and amateurs, this pungent, bittersweet movie lets us taste the flavors of a warm and dangerous time and place.

SIGHT AND SOUND, 3/94, p. 36, Robert Yates

1960. An Italian neighbourhood in the Bronx. To images of the area and its characters, including local mobster and 'neighbourhood god' Sonny, the voice of Calogero recalls his childhood. Calogero, aged nine in 1960, lives with his family next to the bar which serves as Sonny's HQ and gambling den, a place Calogero's bus driver father, Lorenzo, has always warned him away from. Sitting on the family stoop one day, Calogero witnesses Sonny shoot a man dead; aware of the low status afforded a 'snitch', Calogero chooses not to identify Sonny in a police line-up. As a reward for his son's inaction, Lorenzo is offered a well-paid job running numbers, but turns it down. Sonny sends for Calogero, and soon the boy is making money serving drinks. When Lorenzo finds out, he takes Calogero to Sonny and forces him to return the money.

1968. The racial make-up of the neighbourhood is changing, and blacks have begun to arrive. The 17-year-old Calogero and his friends now have their own haunt. Calogero, however, spends much of his time with Sonny, who regularly dispenses advice. Sonny dislikes Calogero getting mixed up in any violence, and sends him away from a beating he and his gang—and subsequently, Calogero's friends—mete out to a group of Hells Angels. Lorenzo endeavours to maintain his influence, and the struggle for Calogero is underlined at a boxing match when Lorenzo, sitting with his son, refuses Sonny's offer of ringside seats.

In school, Calogero summons up the courage to speak to Jane, a black girl, and they fix a date. Sonny sees no problem in dating a black girl, but Lorenzo reckons each race should stay with its own kind. Before the date, a group of black youths is attacked by Calogero's friends. Calogero does his best to protect one of the youths by only pretending to fight. Later, as Calogero meets up with Jane—in Sonny's car, borrowed for the occasion—this same youth also turns up. He is Jane's brother, and accuses Calogero of full involvement in the fight; Jane cancels the date. Back home, Calogero is set upon first by his father wanting to know what he was doing in Sonny's car, and then by Sonny himself who accuses him of planting explosives in the car.

Meanwhile, the gang war continues, with Calogero's friends deciding to drive to the black neighbourhood, armed with firebombs. A docile Calogero accompanies until Sonny pulls him from the car. Jane, told by her brother that Calogero did in fact defend him, apologises to Calogero. But after a kiss, he remembers what his friends are set to do. He arrives in the black neighbourhood too late—his friends are all dead, destroyed by one of their own bombs. Calogero, realising that Sonny has saved his life, runs to thank him. But before he reaches him, Sonny is shot dead. The killer is the son of the man whose murder the young Calogero had witnessed. In the funeral parlour, Lorenzo joins Calogero in paying respects to Sonny. A third mourner, Carmine—evidently the new local mob boss—offers Calogero all the help he needs.

Robert De Niro's debut as a director is both hackneyed and confused, flaws which are probably related. The confusion lies in the film's intended central opposition between Lorenzo, the decent bus driver, and Sonny, the mafioso. De Niro and principal player Chazz Palminteri, who also wrote the script (from his own play), have said that they wanted to present an Italian-American community which focused on the ordinary hard-working man and not just on the mob. Yet Lorenzo has a cardboard cut-out of a life: he drives his bus, he offers some maxims for moral guidance, and that's about it.

Perhaps the character gives nothing more because the film relies so heavily on cinematic precedent. Guides to what to do with Lorenzo are not as prevalent as models for mapping out Sonny's world or for flagging the street and sentimental education of Calogero. For the former, there are shootings and crap games; for the latter, gangs and love across a racial divide. Indeed, most scenes recall scenes from other movies, with De Niro braving some risky comparisons: the introduction to his film's rogues' gallery puts one instantly in mind of the run through the barful of mobsters in Scorsese's *GoodFellas*. There's nothing original in script or direction, De Niro only managing to convince us that he can put together a guide to stock Italo-Americana.

Giving up on Lorenzo means that the signalled opposition between two sets of values—Lorenzo's decency versus the soiled status and wealth of Sonny—is a non-starter. Sonny, however, ends up fighting from both corners, from both black and white. It is Sonny who looks out for Calogero on the street, who gives him sound advice about his date, and who rescues him from his friends' ill-fated attack on the black neighbourhood. At the end, one almost expects a message to flash up across screen reading, "a nurturing mafioso, just what every boy needs." This is not because Sonny, before his death, had seen the light, but simply because, just as Lorenzo is a hazy protector, so Sonny never seems much of a devil. Hence, no dilemma seizes Calogero; he is not torn between an honest life with modest rewards and one of ill-gotten gain. Merely, he sometimes has a practical problem of keeping two men happy.

Interestingly, the type of conflict the film fails to construct is one which has been realised with some success by several black American films of the last few years, like the recent *South Central*. Here, a father's tussle to hold onto his son—his rival is a powerful drug dealer—is set firmly in a carefully documented and credible milieu. A *Bronx Tale*, on the contrary, suggests a never-

never land assembled from cinematic off-cuts. Shaped into a motley garb, it is only fitting that the jester should show up at the end, and turn out to be Joe Pesci, giving a comic turn to a would-be moving resolution.

TIME, 10/11/93, p. 83, Richard Schickel

Lorenzo (Robert De Niro) drives a bus back and forth across the Bronx he goes, a dutiful and moral man, passionate about two things: his family and the fate of the New York Yankees. Sonny (played by the teller of this autobiographical tale, Chazz Palminteri) leads a life at once more stationary and more glamorous—at least to Lorenzo's nine-year-old son Calogero (Francis Capra). Mostly Sonny stands on a corner doing whispered criminal business with colorfully dubious types.

Then one day, in what looks like no more than an argument over a parking space, Sonny kills a man. Little Calogero witnesses the act—and then refuses to identify the murderer to the police. Sonny thereafter takes are interest in the lad, who in turn begins to take an interest in hoodlum life, becoming errand boy, mascot and, as he attains adolescence (when he is played by Lillo Brancato), a possible wiseguy in the making.

We are once again in Scorsese country (circa 1960), a familiar, comfortable place for De Niro to be for his directorial debut. Yet despite their long-running collaboration, De Niro's manner is not at all Scorsesian. The central conflict, the struggle for Calogero's soul, is stated with a fable's starkness. But the tone of the film, perhaps preserved from the performance piece Palminteri originally wrote for himself to play, is musing, reflective, gently insinuating.

This contrast between an essentially harsh environment and the warmth with which it is recalled sets up odd and original reverberations. Among other things, we are reminded that in a not too distant time it was possible for poor people to sustain decent, respectable lives, although crime and violence lived next door. Toward the film's end, Calogero dares something almost unimaginable for someone of his class and kind: he begins dating a black woman (Taral Hicks) whom he meets in school. Racial violence ensues, but there is also a curious coming together in the conclusion—of his father's basic decency, of Sonny's breakaway boldness.

Hicks' may be the year's most arresting debut, but Capra and Brancato are also treasurable finds, and De Niro and Palminteri are anchoring presences in a film that is clearly more than a "project" for them. Their caring makes us care too, more than we might have imagined we could.

VILLAGE VOICE, 10/5/93, p. 58, David D. Kim

A well-made if many splintered thing, Robert De Niro's directorial debut, A Bronx Tale, burnishes an urban coming-of-age story, revealing both the steely glint of Scorsese and the nostalgic luster of Neil Simon.

"C"., short for Calogero, narrates this tour da Bronx, circa 1960 and 1968. As a nine-year-old boy, he, along with his fellow wiseguy wannabes, mimics the gestures and expressions of the local gangsters, a motley assortment of grotesques with aptly chosen nicknames—Frankie Coffeecake, JoJo the Whale, Tony Toupee. C.'s idol, Sonny (Chazz Palminteri, who also wrote the screenplay and stage version), runs this street-corner fiefdom and eventually takes the boy under his pin-striped wing. This irks C.'s dad, Lorenzo (De Niro), a hardworking bus driver who steers clear of the mob until his inevitable tug-of-war with Sonny over C.'s loyalties.

Dispensing his "do as I say, not as I do" wisdom, Palminteri's Sonny exudes a hard-won charm, and Lillo Brancato plays the 17-year-old C. with a convincing mix of earnestness and wonder. De Niro treats his own role as the film's righteous and restrained, though flawed, moral center. But A Bronx Tale's sure-handed performances suffer from a wobbly narrative setup: halfway through the film, C. suddenly falls for a black girl. Introducing the only full-fledged female and/or black character at this point seems belated, and the ensuing ill-fated-lovers gig never quite segues into what becomes a major plot line: the influx of blacks in C.'s rapidly integrating nabe.

The romance does provide a diversion for those who feel dese-dose-and-demmed out by the film's Goodfella-ish aura, lightly parodied by Joe Pesci's brief walk-on. Otherwise, A Bronx Tale's final race-charged moment, followed shortly by another climactic scene, too neatly pulls C. off the fast lane of his adolescent mean streets.

Also reviewed in:
CHICAGO TRIBUNE, 10/1/93, Friday/p. A, Michael Wilmington
NEW YORK TIMES, 9/29/93, p. C13, Janet Maslin
VARIETY, 9/27/93, p. 35, Todd McCarthy
WASHINGTON POST, 10/1/93, p. C1, Hal Hinson
WASHINGTON POST, 10/1/93, Weekend/p. 52, Desson Howe

BY THE SWORD

A Hansen Entertainment release of a Movie Group presentation in association with SVS-Triumph of a Foil Film/Horizon production. *Executive Producer:* Philip Rose, Robert Straight, and Frank Guistra. *Producer:* Peter E. Strauss and Marlon Staggs. *Director:* Jeremy Kagan. *Screenplay:* John McDonald and James Donadio. *Director of Photography:* Arthur Albert. *Editor:* David Holden. *Music:* Bill Conti. *Sound:* Kim Ornitz. *Casting:* Jay Todd. *Production Designer:* Gary Frutkoff. *Art Director:* Kim Rees. *Set Decorator:* K.C. Fox. *Costumes:* Susan Nininger. *Running time:* 90 minutes. *MPAA Rating:* R.

CAST: F. Murray Abraham (Maximilian Suba); Eric Roberts (Alexander Villard); Mia Sara (Erin Clavelli); Chris Rydell (Jimmy Trebor); Elaine Kagan (Rachel); Brett Cullen (Gallagher); Doug Wert (Hobbs).

LOS ANGELES TIMES, 9/24/93, Calendar/p. 17, Kevin Thomas

"By the Sword" takes us into the largely unfamiliar world of a modern-day fencing academy and thereby into the troubled souls of two very different men. Absorbing and sophisticated, it has a European quality in its willingness to let much go unsaid, trusting in implication, and in building tension slowly. F. Murray Abraham and Eric Roberts are perfectly cast as its stars.

Abraham's Max Suba is a man with a mission, but we don't know that when we meet him. He appears as a somewhat weary and defeated middle-aged man down on his luck when he applies for work at a Manhattan *salle* run by Roberts' handsome, imperious Alexander Villard, who quickly discovers that Suba is too rusty to teach fencing.

With condescension Villard offers him a job as a janitor, which Suba accepts. We watch Suba gradually coming alive, getting in shape, meeting an attractive, vivacious woman (Elaine Kagan) and little by little moving from dusting and mopping to some coaching, eventually winning Villard's grudging respect. It's clear enough, however, that Max has a murky past and that there will be some kind of reckoning between him and his employer, who oddly experiences similar nightmares.

What concerns director Jeremy Kagan and writers John McDonald and James Donadio is not so much the clash of swords but of values. Villard has such an intense "winning-is-everything" philosophy that he insists one of his star pupils (Chris Rydell), almost as arrogant as he is, break up a budding romance with a newcomer to the *salle* (Mia Sara) because she might prove too distracting. Suba, on the other hand, has learned that winning is nothing if it costs a loss of humanity. "By the Sword" further deals with childhood trauma which can result in a tragically distorted view of a lost parent, with the quest for redemption and with the timeless romantic allure of sword-play; it would seem that the picture, which bears a 1991 copyright, has been on the shelf because it isn't easy for exhibitors to slot.

It's gratifying to see both Abrahams, more a man of the theater than of films despite his Oscar for "Amadeus," and Roberts in roles worthy of them. "By the Sword" (rated R for language), which benefits strongly from Gary Frutkoff's imaginative and meticulous production design, is by no means a two-character film, and Kagan, Rydell, Sara and Brett Cullen as Villard's kindly, level-headed assistant, all get the chance to make favorable impressions.

NEW YORK POST, 10/22/93, p. 29, Bill Hoffmann

Fencing isn't a boring or predictable sport, but you'd never know it from watching the low-budget dueling drama "By the Sword."

F. Murray Abraham plays the mysterious Max Suba, who takes a job as a janitor at a fencing school in TriBeCa owned by champion swordsman Alexander Villard (Eric Roberts).

Poorly executed, LSD-like flashbacks reveal that 25 years ago, Suba killed Villard's father during a duel, as the little boy watched in horror.

Now after spending a quarter-century behind bars, Suba is back to see what's become of his victim's kid and to inevitably spark another fight to the finish.

But getting to that climactic moment of battle is a 90-minute-long battle for the audience—against an onslaught of poorly developed characters, mediocre dialogue and a sappy Spanish guitar score (by the usually reliable Bill Conti of "Rocky" fame).

Two romantic subplots—one involving Abraham, the other Mia Sara—go absolutely nowhere and drag down what little suspense there is.

The oh-so-serious script begs for a little comic relief, and the south-of-the-border sound track makes you wonder if there's a bullfighting subplot about to erupt.

Everyone is so damned serious! When a stonefaced Abraham walks out of the Franklin Street subway station and passes El Teddy's restaurant in the film's opening scenes, you already want to say to him: "Hey, pal—go in, sit down, have a drink, relax!"

Abraham does what he can with his lines, but it's sad to watch the man who so deservedly won the best supporting actor Oscar for "Amadeus," gallantly going down with a sinking ship.

Isn't there anybody in Hollywood willing to put this long-neglected talent in a decent movie?

The young, energetic cast playing fencing students, effectively mimic real swordplay—perhaps the most authentic touch here. But even these scenes have the dramatic spark of a Fencing 101 training video because everything else is so bland.

If movies lived and died by the sword, this picture, I hope, would be destined for the latter fate.

NEWSDAY, 10/22/93, Part II/p. 79, John Anderson

The entire sport of fencing is about frustrated intention: The concept is based on how efficiently one can kill another with a sword, but the rules forbid you to actually do it. It's appropriate, therefore, that "By the Sword" so completely lacks a killer instinct.

The title suggests a sequel to "Captain Blood," but we're in modern times. We're even in the subway, whence a ragged and hollow-eyed Max Suba (F. Murray Abraham) emerges into Lower Manhattan and a new life. Just released from prison after having killed his fencing master—which we learn about through repetitive, hallucinogenic flashbacks—he immediately goes to the *salle*, or fencing academy, of Alexander Villard (Eric Roberts), the son of the man he killed, and the world's foremost fencer.

He requests a teaching position, but his skills are rusted; offered the janitor's job by the imperious Villard, he takes it, and is exposed to the younger man's hardened philosophy of life and sport, and his fiercely competitive students: Jimmy Trebor (Chris Rydell), who's Villard's best pupil and knows it; Hobbs (Doug Wert), Jimmy's rival; Gallagher (Brett Cullen), the kindly assistant instructor who lacks Villard's ambition; and Erin Clavelli (Mia Sara), the beautiful and self-assured new student who'll get hurt, with the inevitability of a sunrise, by Jimmy.

You want to like "By the Sword," mostly because of Abraham, who makes Max a credible mix of pride and guilt; his fresh out-of-prison relationship with Rachel (Elaine Kagan), and his confession to her of his past, are genuine. His crankiness, too, seems real, especially after he tries to regain his fencing form. And Roberts is effective, affecting the properly icy and intimidating presence of a somewhat damaged man—he saw his father killed—who's also the best in the world at what he does.

The fault with the film, really, lies with director Jeremy Kagan and screenwriters John McDonald and James Donadio, who haven't probed these characters deeply enough, and set them adrift in enough confusing detail to sink considerably larger ships than this. Max Suba isn't Max' name, for instance, but we don't learn this until we're already at sea about who's who, about why Villard doesn't recognize the name, and why he doesn't know the man who killed his father. The swordplay is fun, though, even if it makes you yearn for Errol Flynn and Basil Rathbone.

Also reviewed in:
CHICAGO TRIBUNE, 5/14/93, Friday/p. F, Dave Kehn
NEW YORK TIMES, 10/22/93, p. C15, Vincent Canby
VARIETY, 10/14/91, p. 246, Susan Ayscough

CALENDAR GIRL

A Columbia Pictures release of a Parkway production. *Executive Producer:* Penny Marshall and Elliot Abbott. *Producer:* Debbie Robins and Gary Marsh. *Director:* John Whitesell. *Screenplay:* Paul W. Shapiro. *Director of Photography:* Tom Priestley. *Editor:* Wendy Greene Bricmont. *Music:* Hans Zimmer. *Music Editor:* Laura Perlman. *Sound:* Don H. Matthews and (music) Jay Rifkin. *Sound Editor:* Don Hall. *Casting:* Lisa Beach. *Production Designer:* Bill Groom. *Art Director:* Sarah Knowles. *Set Designer:* Dawn Snyder and Mindi Toback. *Set Decorator:* Lynn Wolverton-Parker. *Special Effects:* Bill Doane. *Costumes:* Erica Edell Phillips. *Make-up:* Cyndi Reece-Thorne. *Stunt Coordinator:* Jack Gill. *Running time:* 91 minutes. *MPAA Rating:* PG-13.

CAST: Jason Priestley (Roy Darpinian); Gabriel Olds (Ned Bleuer); Jerry O'Connell (Scott Foreman); Joe Pantoliano (Harvey Darpinian); Steve Railsback (Roy's Father); Kurt Fuller (Arturo Gallo); Stephen Tobolowsky (Antonio Gallo); Emily Warfield (Becky O'Brien); Michael Quill (Photographer); Leslie Wing (Ned's Mother); Blake McIver Ewing (6-Year-Old Ned); Michael David Kaye (6-Year-Old Scott); Sean Fitzgerald (6-Year-Old Roy); Maggie Simman (6-Year-Old Becky); Elizabeth Quill and Emily Whitesell (Howdy Doody Moms); Sean Fox (12-Year-Old Ned); Timothy Heath (12-Year-Old Scott); Kevin Michaels (12-Year-Old Roy); Irene Roséen (Nurse); Jerry Brutsche (Pipsqueak); Jason Brown (Young Boxer); Candi Brough and Randi Brough (Twins); Liz Vessey (Sylvia); Lisa Walters (Delphine); Maxwell Caulfield (Man in Bathrobe); Rae Allen (Mrs. Macdonald); Tuesday Knight (Nude Woman); Phil Reeves and Sean Whitesell (Officers); Steve Carlisle (Farmer); Stephanie Anderson (Marilyn Monroe); Chubby Checker (Himself); Joe Dietl and Todd Lemisch (Ushers); Jay S. York (Tattoo Artist); Harry S. Murphy (PCH Officer); Christine Joan Taylor (Melissa Smock); Cortney Page (Marilyn Monroe's Voice).

LOS ANGELES TIMES, 9/3/93, Calendar/p. 6, Michael Wilmington

The three bonded buddies in "Calendar Girl"—zooming off to Hollywood in a sky-blue Galaxy 500 convertible in search of a date with their dreamgirl, Marilyn Monroe—are like most movie bachelor trios. They're star-struck youngsters from the provinces, here small-town Nevada, loose in the big city: here, L.A., with its palms, Grauman's (now Mann's) Chinese Theater and Beverly Hills hideaways.

And the movie they're in—a generally likable, shallow comedy written by Paul W. Shapiro—is like most other Kids-in-the-City movie fantasies. It's not top-notch or unusual—but it's got a crush on pop nostalgia itself, which is one of the likable things about it.

Likable, too, is the central trio. One is brash and daring (Jason Priestley as Roy), one sensitive (Gabriel Olds as historian Ned), one a clown (Jerry O'Connell as smiley Scott). They're all steeped in show-biz culture: meeting at 9 at a Howdy Doody look-alike contest, jointly falling in love with Marilyn—and her famous nude calendar—at 12. When they decide to try to consummate their fantasy, it's the summer after high school—in 1962, the year before J.F.K.'s assassination and the Beatles, a period often described as America's "End of Innocence."

Priestley, Olds and O'Connell interact well, connect with one another. Bickering, wisecracking and "dis-ing" each other, they're still tight as Crazy Glue. The movie pretends to be about their fantasy pursuit, but it's more precisely about how three teen-age guys love each other at the moment they're about to split up: a sunny, dippy epic of a Last Bachelor Fling.

As such, it's a cute picture: if you were looking for the ideal word to describe "Calendar Girl," it might be *watchable*. The director, John Whitesell, did a season of the "Roseanne" show—and he handles the characters and jokes with the relaxed spaciousness that usually works best in TV. He keeps his distance and amiability and doesn't shove the movie in your face.

That doesn't mean the Monroe track-down makes much sense—especially when the threesome crashes at the Hollywood hillside digs of swinger Uncle Harvey, an amazingly accommodating host played by Joe Pantoliano. Or when they moon around M.M.'s bungalow in their convertible. Or even when they try to elude the film's top clowns: played, in a dreamlike stroke of perfect casting, by Kurt Fuller and Stephen Tobolowsky.

"Calendar Girl" is another interact-with-the-icon fantasy, like "Garbo Talks," or "I Wanna Hold Your Hand" (the Beatles). And that's one of the things that's a little off about it: the suggestion that the dream isn't much different than the truth, that real-life Marilyn was exactly as she seemed in the movies. There's another level of irony, perhaps unconscious. Priestley is a current TV heartthrob (on "Beverly Hills, 90210"), who resembles the other great '50s movie romantic icon James Dean—and is dressed and hairstyled to resemble him even more.

In a way, this movie is about a real-life small-town Dean—or perhaps Dean split in three—going after Marilyn Monroe. Perhaps that's why we can't expect much more from "Calendar Girl" (MPAA-rated: PG-13) than likability, watchability, ultra-cute credits sequences. If a movie love affair consists of shoving two long-dead celluloid dreams together, the match-up may give you a tickle, but it usually won't burn.

NEW YORK POST, 9/3/93, p. 29, Michael Medved

Ever since her shocking death on Aug. 5, 1962, millions of men have fantasized that their pure, perfect love might somehow have saved Marilyn Monroe.

This fond, forlorn notion injects a misplaced note of sadness into the badly botched coming-of-age comedy, "Calendar Girl." The flimsy plot centers on three 18-year-old MM fans who take a road trip from their Nevada home town to Hollywood in the fateful summer of '62 in a crack-brained scheme to get a date with their goddess.

As always when today's Hollywood conjures up a trio of adolescent buddies, one of them is a cocky, fast-talking hustler (Jason Priestley, TV heartthrob of "Beverly Hills 90210"); one of them is a solid, shy, straight arrow (New York stage actor Gabriel Olds); and one of them is a lovable loser with a handicap (Jerry O'Connell, who played a similar part at age 11 in "Stand By Me"). Usually, that handicap consists of a weight problem or thick glasses, or both, but here it's a largely unexplained wooden leg. All three of the likable stars deliver reasonably capable performances, with Priestley earning special credit for surviving a script that calls for removing his shirt some half-dozen times.

In any event, the three pals pile into the Galaxy 500 convertible (it's always a convertible in such films, isn't it?) that Priestley has borrowed without permission from his bullying father (Steve Railsback), and they head for the Hollywood hills. Once there, they find Marilyn's home without difficulty and spend their time trying to get past the star's bad-tempered, broad-shouldered housekeeper (Emily Warfield) in order to talk briefly to the queen of their dreams.

The only suspense in this yawn of a movie is whether or not these guys will ever get their dream date with Miss Monroe, and since we know that Marilyn will be dead in a few weeks anyway, this question offers no tension at all. Though it's perfectly plausible that these boys—like millions of Miss Monroe's other fans at the time—knew nothing about her addiction to sleeping pills, her hospitalizations or her deep depressions, we are now so painfully aware of these problems that the movie's failure to even hint at them is not only dumb, it's offensive.

The stupidity hits bottom with a dreadful sequence in which the boys follow the unaccompanied star, disguised only in a brunette wig, on a visit to a nude beach, where she frolics merrily in sun and surf. This episode, along with a similarly asinine set-piece about the guys buying a cow to appeal to Miss Monroe's supposed fondness for barnyard animals falls well below the "I Love Lucy" level and contrasts with an embarrassingly earnest narration about being "pushed into life" and "changing from boys to men."

If ever there were a clear illustration of the old idea that nostalgia isn't what it used to be, "Calendar Girl" would be it. While "American Graffiti" captured the same moment in history with the perfect combination of innocence and anxiety, every period detail in this new film feels hopelessly phony—from the anachronistic R&B sound track to the use of 1990s catch phrases

("Let's boost a cow," "You just don't get it, do you?") to toss-away references to fallout shelters and Howdy Doody look-alike contests.

A number of other films have focused on the interaction between ordinary folks and legendary stars, including Greta Garbo ("Garbo Talks"), The Beatles ("I Wanna Hold Your Hand"), and Elvis ("Heartbreak Hotel"). The problem with all such projects is that the entertainment icons, even when presented from a respectful distance, often seem more compelling than the fictional characters with which the movies surround them.

This is definitely the case here, where the liveliest moments in the entire film arrive during the final credits, when brief clips showing the actual Marilyn Monroe highlight the shortcomings of the rest of this puerile and pallid picture.

NEWSDAY, 9/3/93, Part II/p. 67, Terry Kelleher

Memo to Paul W. Shapiro: Stop—you're making us carsick.

Shapiro wrote the script for last years treacly "Breaking the Rules," about three bonded males in their early 20s who drive from Ohio to Hollywood so the one with terminal cancer can realize his dream of competing on "Jeopardy!" Now Shapiro gets screenplay credit for "Calendar Girl," about three bonded males in their late teens who drive from Nevada to Hollywood in 1962 so they can importune Marilyn Monroe for a dream date.

The road trips are getting shorter, but the movies are getting worse.

The memory of Monroe has been exploited in fiction of every stripe, so we probably should be grateful that "Calendar Girl" doesn't depict her in an orgy with the Kennedy brothers. In this tale, the sex symbol comes across as sweet but, shall we say, unobservant. Monroe (embodied by Stephanie Anderson, whose face remains hidden, and voiced by Cortney Page) finally agrees to go out with the best-looking of the young swains, then appears not to notice when he nobly allows one of his less-studly pals to take his place. Does this count as a blind date?

When the boys aren't bidding for MM's attention by any means necessary—including hosing down a cow outside her window—they're engaged in the sort of bickering that marks undying friendship in these coming-of-age movies. If handsome Roy (Jason Priestley of "Beverly Hills 90210") is especially obnoxious, blame his troubled relationship with his ex-boxer father (Steve Railsback). It's a good thing dad and son eventually settle their differences by—you guessed it—slugging it out in the ring.

Give you an idea of this movie's sense of humor: Roy is menaced continually by a pair of mobster brothers (Kurt Fuller and Stephen Tobolowsky) who communicate in sign language because one is a deaf-mute. Roy's chum Scott (Jerry O'Connell) has an artificial leg, which he's acutely embarrassed to expose on a nude beach.

There might be time for more hilarious handicaps if Ned (Gabriel Olds), the third and most thoughtful of the "inseparables," didn't have so much narrating to do. All this voice-over raises the suspicion that debuting director John Whitesell had to tell us because he wasn't sure how to show us.

Ned's concluding words of wisdom are: "Nothing ever happens if you don't show up." So don't.

VILLAGE VOICE, 9/7/93, p. 62, Kate Tentler

Sometimes celebrity is rooted in a hairdo. Think of Farrah Fawcett, Bon Jovi, Sinéad O'Connor, Princess Diana. Beauty parlor creations are the very embodiment of their famous personas. Every lock is trimmed, molded, or shorn with the care that the grass at Augusta's golf course is clipped.

This is not lost on the makers of *Calendar Girl*, starring Jason Priestley. But while in *Beverly Hills 90210* Priestley's gelled, DA flattop hybrid is sexy and cool in a goody two shoes retro kind of way, in this throwback '60s coming-of-age flick, it does nothing more than make him look like Brandon. Which is perfectly fine with me, since I don't mind wasting time looking upon his sweet, sideburn-framed face.

In *Calendar Girl*, that face is such a welcome distraction because the film is so dim-witted, encouraging comparison with better movies of its ilk (*Fandango, Losin' It,* and György Szomjas's *Mr. Universe*). The plot essentially concerns three lifelong buddies who, just before they make life changes that will jettison them into adulthood (college, marriage, Vietnam), take off on a madcap road trip to meet Marilyn Monroe. They've got a convertible and they're loaded for bear.

While wacky things befall them—they have to strip at a nude beach—they ultimately learn that, yes, fame and fortune are paltry substitutes for true friendship. It's a boring moral, especially since Madonna has proven that for every new coif there are always plenty of fresh, fabulous friends to be found.

Also reviewed in:
NEW YORK TIMES, 9/3/93, p. C9, Janet Maslin
VARIETY, 9/13/93, p. 32, Emanuel Levy
WASHINGTON POST, 9/6/93, p. C7, Peter Gilstrap

CAPTIVE IN THE LAND, A

A Gloria Productions/Gorky Film Studios/Soviet American Films release of a John Berry/Stuart Phoenix production. *Executive Producer:* Peter S. Gold. *Producer:* Malcolm Stewart and John Berry. *Director:* John Berry. *Screenplay:* Lee Gold. *Based on the novel by:* James Aldridge. *Director of Photography:* Pierre William Glenn. *Editor:* Georges Klotz. *Music:* Bill Conti. *Production Designer:* Yurih Konstantinov. *Sound:* Henri Roux and Jean-Michel Chauvet. *Art Director:* Jacques Voizot. *Special Effects:* Philippe Alleton. *Costumes:* Eugenia Chervonskaya. *Running time:* 96 minutes. *MPAA Rating:* Not Rated.

CAST: Sam Waterston (Rupert Royce); Alexander Potapov (Averianov).

NEW YORK POST, 1/18/93, p. 22, Audrey Farolino

A peculiar sort of time disorientation sets in while watching "A Captive in the Land." The movie—about an American meteorologist who parachutes into the desolation of a frozen Arctic ice plain in order to rescue a downed airman—appears to be set in the present.

But all that ice is a perfect setting since the movie is permeated with a Cold War attitude—from the meteorologist's initial dismay when he discovers that the man he's risking his neck to save is, of all things, a Russian ("I'll be damned" he mutters), to lines like "I never met a Communist before and hope to never meet another one" and the $64,000 Question "What were you doing in the Arctic, anyway?" (which elicits the helpful response, "What were you doing?")

Though the movie was a joint Soviet-American production (directed by McCarthy-era blacklist victim John Berry), it began filming in 1989 based on a script written in the 1970s and an even earlier novel, which may explain its outdated politics.

The time vertigo doesn't stop there, though: This is also the sort of movie that often seems as if it should have been made in the 1940s, with, say, Cary Grant.

Instead of Cary, we have Sam Waterston, who gives his usual strong and intelligent performance as meteorologist Rupert Royce. Equally skilled is Russian film star Alexander Potapov as the injured airman.

Royce is aboard an RAF transport plane heading to the U.S. base at Thule, Greenland, when the plane wreck and its lone survivor are spotted. Since the RAF plane can't land there and it's out of radio range for a distress call, Royce volunteers to parachute down with supplies and to aid the survivor until a rescue helicopter can be sent.

Royce's meteorological smarts must have deserted him, though, since he apparently doesn't realize that fog, driving snow and shifting ice will soon all but obliterate the crash site.

Huddled in a makeshift shelter in the wrecked fuselage, Royce and the all-but-paralyzed Russian express their growing desperation through growing exasperation with each other, bickering about everything from poetry to Communism (luckily, the Russian speaks English). When all hope of rescue is gone, they decide their only chance is to trek across the hundreds of miles that separate them from the nearest civilization, with Royce hauling Averianov on a makeshift sled.

Their ordeal contains some truly gripping moments, which, coupled with the actors' abilities, make you wish all the more that the filmmakers had been wise enough to give the useless political overtones the deep freeze.

NEWSDAY, 1/15/93, Part II/p. 67, John Anderson

It's a rather tepid Cold War that's waged between Royce (Sam Waterston), an American meteorologist, and Averianov (Alexander Potapov), a Soviet airman, in John Berry's "A Captive in the Land." Trapped on the Arctic ice, with no hope of rescue, they face not only a murderous environment but mutual distrust and a cultural abyss. And the heat they generate isn't enough to defog your windshield.

For Berry, the project was obviously a labor of love. The screenplay was adapted from James Aldridge's novel by Berry's close associate, Lee Gold, who died in 1985. Berry and his co-producer, Malcolm Stuart, had worked for 15 years, both separately and together, to bring the story to the screen; Gold's brother Peter eventually financed the film, which became the first joint Soviet-American production in 13 years.

But the simple fact remains that the material, whose clash of cultures theme is very familiar, also is dated; the novel and script are products of a period when fear and acrimony flourished between the two superpowers, and it's tough to resurrect that old feeling, even if you wanted to, even if the film could do it for you.

"Captive" isn't helped by Waterston's performance, which is alternately detached and unconvincingly earnest. He is too icy an actor even for the Arctic, which his character is crossing aboard an RAF plane en route to Greenland. The craft passes over the wreckage of another plane, which no one can identify, but they see one body moving. The plane can't land on the craggy ice, and it's out of radio contact with its base. "Somebody's gotta go down there," Royce declares, although why he thinks it has to be him is something we never understand.

What he finds are a number of dead Soviets, and the crippled Averianov. "Russian!" he exclaims; he might just as well have said, "Martian!" Royce drags the man into the wreckage of the Soviet plane, which he proceeds to reinforce and insulate, while waiting for the helicopters to arrive.

It isn't long before they realize, due to the changing weather and the shifting ice, that they'll never be rescued. Averianov is tortured by his inability to help Royce; Royce starts to get a little crazy when the snow seals them in and the air is cut off. He becomes paranoid about the Russian and has some scary moments with a gun, a heavy-handed commentary on American cultural tolerance.

Averianov has the better role, and Potapov gives a much more passionate performance, even if the lines often are trite. "If you're so free," he tells Royce during one of their sophomoric political discussions, "why don't you leave?" Royce has his own moments of obtuseness, such as when Averianov begins speaking to a photo of his wife. "I was telling my wife to forget me," he says. "She can't hear you," Royce says. Thanks for the tip, pal.

Averianov quotes Robert Burns and Admiral Byrd and explains Hemingway to Royce, who seems not particularly well-read. This is just part of a somewhat snide take on American anti-intellectualism: Royce supplies the legs and the technical expertise; Averianov supplies the passion and the poetry. Arctic Siberia supplies the blinding whiteness and stark landscapes, which are at once beautiful and forbidding, passive and hostile. But "Captive in the Land," for all its good intentions, never meets its own expectations.

VILLAGE VOICE, 1/26/93, p. 58, Manohla Dargis

The second movie this month to feature an air disaster swept into snow-choked oblivion, *A Captive in the Land* is an untimely parable about just how chilly ideological warfare can get. When U.S. meteorologist Royce (Sam Waterston) volunteers to parachute from a transport plane onto an Arctic tundra to help a crash survivor, little does he realize the paralyzed victim's a Soviet (Alexander Potapov as Averianov). Bad weather prohibits a landing, so reckless Royce, eager to play hero, takes the fall. The idea, see, is the air force will pick up the pair the next day, only more lousy weather keeps this odd couple stranded and numb—a state not unlike that eventually induced by the film itself. Earnest but inert, *Captive* desperately wants to say something about the universal goodness of man—blah, blah, blah—but unlike, say, *Alive*, doesn't have meat on its bones. Royce isn't only a drag, he's a drag without history or, even worse, a feel for a good story. Irritated because his object of rescue isn't G.I. Joe, Royce refuses to engage in dialogue, which pretty much nullifies any hopes for *My Dinner With Averianov*. For his part, the injured airman does little but recite Robert Burns poetry (with helpful translations) and pump up his faithless partner—"Fight, Royce, you must fight." Helmed by McCarthy casualty John Berry (*Claudine*), this story needed to be told once upon a time, maybe. Even then, though, good intentions would not have been enough.

Also reviewed in:
NEW YORK TIMES, 1/15/93, p. C6, Stephen Holden
VARIETY, 5/13/91, p. 104

CARLITO'S WAY

A Universal Pictures and Epic Productions release of a Bregman/Baer production. *Executive Producer:* Louis A. Stroller and Ortwin Freyermuth. *Producer:* Martin Bregman, Willi Baer, and Michael S. Bregman. *Director:* Brian De Palma. *Screenplay:* David Koepp. *Based on the novels "Carlito's Way" and "After Hours" by:* Edwin Torres. *Director of Photography:* Stephen H. Burum. *Editor:* Bill Pankow and Kristina Boden. *Music:* Patrick Doyle. *Music Editor:* Roy Prendergast. *Choreographer:* Jeffrey Hornaday and Debbie Benitez. *Sound:* Les Lazarowitz. *Sound Editor:* Maurice Schell. *Casting:* Bonnie Timmermann. *Production Designer:* Richard Sylbert. *Art Director:* Gregory Bolton. *Set Decorator:* Leslie A. Pope. *Set Dresser:* Bruce Lee Gross. *Special Effects:* Steven Kirshoff. *Costumes:* Aude Bronson-Howard. *Make-up:* Michael Laudati. *Stunt Coordinator:* Dick Ziker. *Running time:* 141 minutes. *MPAA Rating:* R.

CAST: Al Pacino (Carlito Brigante); Sean Penn (Dave Kleinfeld); Penelope Ann Miller (Gail); John Leguizamo (Benny Blanco); Ingrid Rogers (Steffie); Luis Guzman (Pachanga); James Rebhorn (Norwalk); Joseph Siravo (Vinnie Taglialucci); Viggo Mortensen (Lalin); Richard Foronjy (Pete Amadesso); Jorge Porcel (Saso); Frank Minucci (Tony Taglialucci); Adrian Pasdar (Frankie); John Agustin Ortiz (Guajiro); Angel Salazar (Walberto); Al Israel (Rolando); Rick Aviles (Quisqueya); Jaime Sanchez (Rudy); Edmonte Salvato (Battaglia, Big Guy); Paul Mazursky (Judge Feinstein); Tera Tabrizi (Club Date); Victor Sierra (Kid); Caesar Cordova (Barber); Jon Seda and Ruben Rivera (Dominicans); Sherie Mambru and Brenda Hernandez (Girlfriends); Elliot Santiago (Knifeman); Frank Ferrara (Manzanero); John Hoyt, Chuck Zito, Steven Puente, and Tony Cucci (Club Bouncers); Alfred Sauchelli, Jr., Anthony Catanese, Sam Weber, and Sonny Zito (Bodyguards); Walter T. Meade (Jackson Corrections Officer); Michael Hadge and Richard Council (Diamond Room Men); Lindsey Lombardi (Diamond Room Dancer); James Bulleit (Louie); Crystal Haney (Estate Party Woman); Gregory Misciagno (Italian at Copa); Mel Gorham (Pachanga's Date); Rocco Sisto (Panama Hatman); John Finn (Duncan); Brian Tarantina (Speller); Jaime Tirelli (Valentin); Owen Hollander (Cab Driver); Dean Rader-Duval (Med Tech); Gene Canfield (Train Conductor); Sharmagne Leland-St. John (Woman at Grand Central); Rene Rivera and Orlando Urdaneta (Bartenders); Troy A. Hawkes (Solicitor at Go-Go Club); Kim Rideout (Gail's Friend at Dance Studio); Christina Murphy, Juliette Ortega, and Mary C. Hammett (Waitresses); Debbie Benitez, Roberta Mathes, Freddy Rios, and Mike Ramos (Dancers); Yelba Matamoros (Blanco's Girlfriend); Nelson Vasquez (Blanco Associate); Jason Daryn (Party Waiter); Dan Brennan and Michael Moran (Party Guests); Vinny Pastore and Garry Blackwood (Copa Wiseguys); Cynthia Lamontagne (Woman at Elevator); Bo Dietl and Kato (Casino Men); James V. Miller (Black Jack Dealer); Marc Antony (Latin Band at Disco).

CHRISTIAN SCIENCE MONITOR, 11/12/93, p. 12, David Sterritt

During much of his career, director Brian De Palma has shuttled between two kinds of moviemaking.

Pictures like "The Fury" and "Raising Cain" are exercises in cinema for its own sake, telling fantastic and often violent stories with as many touches of flamboyant filmmaking as the screen will hold. Pictures like "Scarface" and "The Untouchables" are just as violent, but concentrate more on themes and characters.

De Palma's new movie, "Carlito's Way," falls into the second group. It has plenty of cinematic flourishes—unexpected angles, startling cuts, and moments when the camera is turned upside down. But it tells a fairly conventional story, and focuses more on Al Pacino's acting skills than on De Palma's directorial daring.

The result should please a wider audience than more eccentric movies like the recent "Raising Cain," although it may prove too ponderous and long (at 141 minutes) for blockbuster success.

The story begins with the main character, a streetwise Puerto Rican named Carlito, being viciously stabbed in a New York train station by some faceless enemy. The rest of the movie is an extended flashback telling us how Carlito came to this sorry situation.

Along the way we meet his friends, from a would-be ballerina to a shady attorney, and his enemies, from a brash young rival to the vengeful son of a murder victim. We also see much of the mayhem that has peppered Carlito's career—shown with unsettling gusto, but restricted to fewer scenes than in some of De Palma's more gruesome pictures.

What's interesting about David Koepp's screenplay for "Carlito's Way" is that it revolves around a bad guy who wants nothing more than to go straight and start a new life. The upheavals in the story come less from Carlito's mercurial nature than from the influence of the urban jungle around him, which seems determined to drag him back into the underworld for good.

In this respect, "Carlito's Way" resembles earlier films as different as Otto Preminger's classic "The Man With the Golden Arm" and Rainer Werner Fassbinder's epic "Berlin Alexanderplatz," which also show how hard it is for a one-time criminal to carve out an honest life with nothing but good intentions to rely on.

De Palma explores this subject thoughtfully, if not very originally, with solid help from Pacino's earnest performance. Sean Penn is less effective as the corrupt lawyer of the tale, partly because he seems to find his character more amusing than convincing.

LOS ANGELES TIMES, 11/10/93, Calendar/p. 1, Kenneth Turan

"Carlito's Way" is right down the middle of the road, and that is something of a surprise. A mid-level commercial thriller, it is a solid and acceptable if not overwhelmingly exciting piece of work from a star and a director not previously known for their centrist tendencies.

For both Al Pacino (who won an Oscar last time out with "Scent of a Woman") and Brian De Palma ("Scarface," "The Untouchables") are folks who ordinarily spend as much time hanging far above the rim as any NBA all-star. When it comes to the virtuoso aspects of cinematic excess, they have always stood up to be counted.

"Carlito's Way" does have its share of skillfully done surface flash, but the film lacks the energy and originality to make a lasting impression. And its best feature, a finely paced final half-hour, is half an hour too late in coming, victimized by a 2-hour-and-25-minute length it doesn't have the wherewithal to carry.

Definitely not the shy type, Carlito Brigante (Pacino) tells his own story in an extensive voice-over. Introduced (in an elegant prologue beautifully shot in black and white by cinematographer Stephen H. Burum) at a moment of crisis in his life, Carlito flashes back to 1975 and one of his few triumphant days in court.

Released early from a prison sentence because of the work of attorney David Kleinfeld (Sean Penn) in exposing the state's use of illegally obtained evidence, Carlito tells the judge that after 25 years on the street he is finally rehabilitated.

"I am through walking on the wild side," he says with enough flourish to make one think that maybe he has chosen acting as a second career. But no, Carlito's dream is to save enough money to buy into a friend's car-rental franchise in the Bahamas. As he explains to a dubious Kleinfeld

(Penn almost unrecognizable in glasses and a halo of thinning frizzy hair), "Car rental guys don't get killed that much."

Serious enough about going straight to take a job, Carlito ends up managing a hot club called El Paradiso to help raise his getaway money. But as a former legend in the East Harlem drug trade, once known as (no kidding) "the J.P. Morgan of the smack business," he finds it difficult to leave his past behind. "I don't invite this stuff," he says after one particularly violent incident. "It runs after me."

As the volatile Carlito, Pacino also has his ups and downs. While his opening courtroom scenes raise the fear that both his Latino accent and his performance will carom out of control, Pacino for the most part keeps a good grip on his character. He's always had presence to burn, and where he calms down some of his speeches, like his confession that "you don't get reformed, you just run out of wind," are quite effective.

Carlito's story, the tale of a man whose code of honor is outmoded, who comes out of prison to find he doesn't know who he can trust, is as familiar as it sounds. Not helping things are the giveaway lines screenwriter David Koepp (working from a pair of novels by Edwin Torres) keeps putting in people's mouths. Anytime anyone says, "This is going to be no problem" or "I got a good feeling about this" or "I just got to do this one thing," it gets increasingly difficult not to lose control and yell, "Wrong, wrong, wrong!" at the screen.

Equally by the book is Carlito's love affair with Gail (Penelope Ann Miller), an old flame who calls him Charlie and sees that he is a swell fellow underneath the dross of the street. Miller works hard to make the part believable, but finally the role fits too snugly into the traditional "exotic dancer with a heart of gold" category to allow for much genuine impact.

The same thing could be said of the entire production. Although De Palma, always the complete professional, commits no missteps with "Carlito" (rated R for strong violence, drug content, sexuality and language), no major spark of excitement or passion energizes it as it does the best of his work.

This is simply a durable film that won't drive you crazy one way or the other, and, with Brian De Palma, that is not necessarily the best of situations.

NEW YORK, 11/15/93, p. 85, David Denby

In the climactic shoot-out of *Carlito's Way*, Brian De Palma's fluently entertaining new gangster movie, the camera seems to disregard the laws of gravity and mechanics and simply float through the air from one perfect vantage point to another. Carlito Brigante (Al Pacino), a retired East Harlem hood, is trying to leave town from Grand Central station with his girlfriend (Penelope Ann Miller), but first he must escape four heavy-breathing Mafiosi who want to kill him. De Palma outdoes the famous stairway shoot-out in *The Untouchables*. This time he's got escalators, and *everything* is in motion—the characters, the camera, the stairs, and the bullets. The episode is hair-raising.

The trouble with this magnificent bit of filmmaking is that the emotions of it don't come close to matching the virtuosity of De Palma's staging and Stephen Burum's camerawork. Carlito, the former smack king of Spanish Harlem, out of prison and determined to go straight, has got caught up in a debt of honor. Against his better judgment, he helps his lawyer, Kleinfeld (Sean Penn), who has gotten him out of prison, in Kleinfeld's dispute with the mob. But the lawyer is patently unworthy. In an apparent parody of Alan M. Dershowitz, Sean Penn plays him with frizzy hair sticking straight out and an overall manner of squashed hysteria. In three-piece suits, Penn looks tiny—minuscule, almost. Lips damp with excitement, he gives us a wormy, palm-sweating little chiseler and cokehead who longs for the intrigue of the criminal life without having the moves or the courage for it. Kleinfeld is a voyeur, and neither Penn nor De Palma can contain his contempt for a man who's slumming in the streets of violence.

That contempt destroys the emotional basis of the movie. Carlito, as Pacino plays him (fabulously), is a great man, a compound of shrewd, violent skills and philosophical intelligence, and there's no reason for him to spend so much time and take such risks for the disgusting Kleinfeld. His "debt of honor" isn't remotely convincing. Apart from that, *Carlito's Way* is a long, slow, episodic, and atmospheric exploration of criminal life, Latino division, in the New York of the mid-seventies. There are enjoyably hyped-up scenes in glittering clubs, in a poolroom, on the streets. There is much strutting, much sleaze and violence; and through it all, Pacino concentrates fiercely and speaks gangster folk poetry in his gnarled, I've-experienced-everything voice.

NEW YORK POST, 11/10/93, p. 30, Michael Medved

"Carlito's Way" begins with a gripping black-and-white prelude that shows a faceless gunman shooting Al Pacino as he's about to board a train at Grand Central Terminal.

When the paramedics arrive to wheel the wounded man toward an ambulance, his voice-over musings fill the sound track, and the main body of the movie unfolds as a series of full-color flashbacks showing the sequence of events that led him to that train platform.

Perhaps the unusual structure of the film—with the protagonist hovering near death from its opening moments—may help to explain the shockingly lifeless nature of Pacino's performance.

He staggers through his part like a zombie, trying to portray a man who has been beaten down by his hard-luck life, but his dull-eyed, monochromatic screen presence inspires weary indifference rather than empathy.

In "Scarface," his previous collaboration with director Brian De Palma, Pacino went way over the top in a sneering, campy display of actorly excess; this time he may have over-compensated by moving much too far in the direction of understatement and restraint.

Pacino plays Carlito Brigante, a one-time kingpin of the Spanish Harlem drug trade, who emerges from prison after serving five years of a much longer term, when his slick lawyer (Sean Penn) springs him on a technicality.

Carlito is sincerely determined to go straight, but it hardly amounts to the disclosure of some startling twist to report that associations from his former life keep dragging him back toward violence and crime.

This plot is so tired it does everything but wheeze: In fact, it's fair to say the only real surprise in the course of the entire film is Sean Penn's appearance. He is scarcely recognizable behind wire-rim spectacles and a tightly-curled, reddish neo-Afro, while his subtle, eerily effective performance also marks a striking shift from the moody posturing in some of his previous films.

Penn brings both compassion and conviction to the plight of his character—a terminally nerdy Ivy League shyster who develops a nasty cocaine habit and sets out to prove that he can be as tough as any of his underworld clients.

De Palma wins similarly persuasive performances from many of his other supporting players (especially Penelope Ann Miller as Carlito's long-suffering love interest), and he also delivers a thrilling, impressively edited chase scene at the end of the movie, but it comes much too late to redeem the arid, formulaic stretches that preceded it.

The script (by David Koepp, one of the screenwriters on "Jurassic Park") is adapted from two gritty novels by Edwin Torres, a justice of the New York State Supreme Court.

Torres' own story—from his birth on a kitchen table in the East Harlem barrio through service as a defense lawyer for indigent clients to a career as one of the state's toughest and most distinguished jurists (whose harsh sentences earned him the nickname "The Time Machine")—would make a far more interesting movie than this predictable tale of a gloomy ex-con.

With so few films focusing in any way on Latino themes or characters, it's a special shame to see yet another big studio extravaganza that altogether ignores the complexities of that community and offers instead a hackneyed, one-dimensional portrayal of drugs, dysfunction and despair.

NEWSDAY, 11/10/93, Part II/p. 70, Jack Mathews

Al Pacino seems to be giving a "greatest hits" performance in Brian De Palma's "Carlito's Way." He has the feral bearded look of Frank Serpico, the emotional cool of Michael Corleone, the seductive guile of his lonely ex-con in "Frankie and Johnny," and the faintest trace of that hot salsa accent he cooked up for Tony Montana in "Scarface."

The composite Pacino, in the role of reformed Puerto Rican-American heroin dealer Carlito Brigante, is a mellow image. This is a smooth, relaxed star turn from one of the few great actors of his generation, and though "Carlito's Way" is no more than a big-budget B movie, he and his co-stars Sean Penn and Penelope Ann Miller often make it a lot of fun.

De Palma, coming off three of the worst movies any major director has strung together, may be mellowing himself. "Carlito's Way" has plenty of bloody violence, some hot sex, a few showy stylistic camera moves, and an operatically overblown gunfight in Grand Central Terminal. But for the first time since "The Untouchables," De Palma has managed to elevate genre material rather than overwhelm it.

Adapted from a pair of Spanish Harlem potboilers written by moonlighting State Supreme Court Justice Edwin Torres, "Carlito's Way" takes us into the East Harlem of the mid-'70s, where Brigante, freshly sprung from prison by his crafty lawyer (Penn), re-enters society determined to go clean and save enough cash to start a car rental business in a resort town called Paradise in the Bahamas.

Instead, he ends up running a mob hangout called El Paradiso in East Harlem, an atmosphere not exactly conducive to staying clean.

Carlito also finds that he has become a legend in the neighborhood, where old opportunities and young hoods pose equal threats, and he's not back on the streets a day when he blunders into the crossfire of a drug deal gone sour. Later, a favor for a friend makes him a witness to a double murder, and puts him on the most wanted lists of both the FBI and the M-A-F-I-A.

Carlito doesn't have to look for trouble, as they used to say in movies with loud jazz scores, it looks for him.

There is some sharp dialogue scattered throughout David Koepp's screenplay, but it's the glee with which the three stars inhabit their pulp novel characters that keeps "Carlito's Way" moving briskly through its nearly 2½-hour running time.

Penn, in his first screen role in three years, is marvelous as David Kleinfield, a lawyer who symbolizes the easy-sex, easy-drugs excesses of the '70s. With sideburns to here, a frizzy perm and wire-rimmed glasses, Penn is barely recognizable at first, and it takes a while to realize he's not just along as Pacino's sidekick.

Kleinfield, the friend for whom Carlito will do anything, is a time bomb, a man spiraling out of control and making coke-warped decisions that threaten to take his pal down with him. It's the kind of bad-guy role that would turn an actor like De Palma favorite John Lithgow into pure ham, but Penn holds much of the character in and keeps him at least vaguely human to the very end.

As Gail, the stereotyped jilted girlfriend asked to stand by her man one more time, Miller had the good sense to know that the only way to play her was to overplay her, and she has a couple of scenes (a lusty topless number in a Broadway bar) that make her presence known.

It is Pacino, however, who keeps this slight tale bolted to the screen. Like Bogart, Cagney and other stars of the Golden Age of mobster movies, Pacino can entertain us simply by dressing up and running through his repertoire of tough-guy mannerisms.

Here, playing Carlito in both flashback and as the apparently dying narrator, his performance is in stark contrast to the role of the acerbic, alcoholic ex-Army colonel that brought him his first Academy Award in last year's "Scent of a Woman." It's as if the star were making up for putting everyone through that emotional wringer by saying, "Okay, I've got the Oscar, now let's have some fun."

NEWSWEEK, 11/15/93, p. 89, Jack Kroll

Love him or hate him, That's Brian De Palma. Movie buffs love his pure movieness, all tracking cameras, whirling pans, slo-mo, reality as a baroquen dream. Women hate him for his obsession with victimhood, his itch for the orgasm of demolition. His best movies are his coldest and cruelest: "Blow Out" and "Dressed to Kill" are better than the operatically wimpy "The Untouchables." I mean, Eliot Ness is a frat boy with a gun permit, but Carrie the telekinetic avenger is vicious fun. But the time comes when vicious brilliance irritates the eyes and oppresses the heart. On the surface, Carlito's Way looks like classic De Palma; it makes a lot of noise, visual and aural, it centers on an antihero whose vice mutates into virtue. But this big extravagant movie is an empty barrel, even if the barrel is chrome-plated.

The antihero is Carlito Brigante (Al Pacino), a drug dealer from Spanish Harlem. Carlito, just out of jail, is fed up with being the heroin king and decides to go into the rental-car business. While managing a nightclub to finance this move he encounters a new generation of bad guys epitomized by "Benny Blanco from the Bronx" (John Leguizamo). Like an old gunslinger challenged by Billy the Kid wanna-bes, Carlito has to watch his back. He'd rather watch Gail (Penelope Ann Miller), the blond go-go dancer who's his Anglo dream girl. The guy he should watch is Kleinfeld (Sean Penn), the cokehead lawyer who's into gang stuff way over his frizzy head.

This would seem to be a film right up De Palma's scarfaced alley, and in fact it looks and pulsates a lot like his "Scarface." But "Scarface" came at you like a knockout puncher; "Carlito's Way" struts and poses like a charade. The movie is adapted by David Koepp ("Jurassic Park") from two novels about Carlito by Edwin Torres, a native of the New York barrio and a long-time justice of the New York State Supreme Court. The novels have a romantic patina, but behind that there's a hard reality: you learn a lot about a culture and about the criminal-justice system. De Palma doesn't really care about that he's interested, as he's so often told us, in the visual and kinetic possibilities: a billiard ball whacking into a skull, a disco jumping with salsa and sex, a guy shot so bad that he bleeds the color right out of the movie.

Tellingly, the film changes Gail from a teacher and social activist to a topless dancer. To little-boy movie moguls, how can a *teacher* be sexy? The movie Gail is an embarrassment, for the story and for Miller. Kleinfeld is likewise stripped down to a caricature and Penn plays him in a flurry of smirks and snorts. The treasured Pacino himself seems to be doing out-takes from other Pacinos: some leftover Scarface tissue, some hoo-has from "Scent of a Woman." Newer, down-to-gutter directors like Quentin Tarantino ("Reservoir Dogs") and Abel Ferrara ("Bad Lieutenant") make De Palma's moves seem overblown and out of touch. This major talent has become a style in search of a subject.

SIGHT AND SOUND, 2/94, p. 48, Nick James

Carlito Brigante, a convicted heroin dealer five years into a 30-year prison sentence, is freed thanks to his lawyer Dave Kleinfeld. He announces that he will go straight, that prison has changed him. But Carlito no longer recognises the places or the faces in his old neighbourhood. All he wants is $75,000 to buy into a friend's business.

Brigante finds trouble when he goes with his nephew to a drug deal; everyone but Carlito ends up dead, and he suddenly has enough money to buy into and manage a nightclub his lawyer part-owns. While running the club, he meets Benny Blanco, an up-and-coming coke dealer who idolises him. He also sees Gail, a stripper, whom he'd loved before he went to jail. Kleinfeld has trouble dealing with his client Taglialucci, a mafioso who accuses Kleinfeld of stealing the million dollars he had received to bribe a witness. Taglialucci demands that Kleinfeld help him bust out of jail. Kleinfeld plays on Carlito's sense of honour and drags him into his problems. Meanwhile Carlito has a chance to kill Blanco, but doesn't take it. Gail warns Carlito that he should stay away from Dave, but Carlito still believes that he owes Dave. Carlito goes with Dave as backup, but Dave murders Taglialucci and his son Frank. Everybody now wants revenge. The mob tries to kill Dave and the District Attorney wants Carlito to testify against him for Taglialucci's murder. Carlito buys train tickets to Miami for himself and Gail, but before he can escape, the mob comes after him. He defeats them in a shoot-out in Grand Central Station, only to be murdered on the platform by Blanco.

As Al Pacino said in another movie, "Every time I think I'm out, they pull me back in."

Neither an incoherent mess like *Raising Cain* nor a sprawling disaster like *The Bonfire of the Vanities, Carlito's Way* offers an intriguing spectacle. The supporting cast of ultra-New York character actors, the film's catalogue of aggressive-compulsive behaviour, and the occasional explosion into trademarked Brian De Palma set pieces suggest that the director has snuck onto a Sidney Lumet set and directed the big action scenes.

Carlito's Way stands to De Palma's career as *Cape Fear* stands to Scorsese's—it is the work of a man who needs a hit to prove that he can turn in a solid job of work that will make money. If the film fails to profit, and nothing suggests that it will, the failure cannot be laid at De Palma's door. The films differ in that De Palma reins in his natural expressionism and fondness for big gestures—the big action sequences achieve neither the hallucinatory highs of *The Fury* nor the operatic grandeur of *The Untouchables*—where Scorsese pushed his farther to fit more comfortably into the overwrought world of the Hollywood action movie.

On the other hand, *Carlito's Way* may simply be one of those films that force us to confront an uncomfortable fact about people we regard as great directors. A lot of film-makers in the second level of greatness—the level below the Renoirs, Hitchcocks and Buñuels—face enormous difficulties in sustaining their achievements and careers. Half the problem lies with the industrial process of film-making itself. The longer a director in Hollywood sustains his career, the more subject he becomes to the economic imperatives of the business. To step back from big-budget films seems at once a logistical challenge and an admission of failure. The longer a director stays in the business, the more difficult it becomes to make the kind of movies that got him interested in film-making in the first place.

The other half may be in the nature of directorial talent itself. The industrial side of the business demands that a director connect with a public. No audience, no films. A lot of second-level greats—Frank Capra, Anthony Mann, Woody Allen—manage to have a decade when their sensibility and the public's harmonise. Then the zeitgeist shifts and people wonder why the films have declined in quality. Emerging from the extraordinary freedom of the early 70s and working in Hollywood at a time when *The Godfather*, a big expensive project, cost less than $10 million, De Palma's hits didn't have to be terribly big to recoup their cost and his flops were not terribly expensive. In the current economic climate, when the average cost of a Hollywood movie has climbed into the $25 million range before prints and advertising, studio demands are a straitjacket to someone whose greatest challenge has always been to discover movies to fit around his visionary set pieces. We might remember that De Palma began and ended the 80s with flops—*Blow Out* and *Bonfire*. His only real hit in that decade was *The Untouchables*, and his stab at Oscar-winning respectability, *Casualties of War*, flopped badly.

This new De Palma film offers a fierce Pacino performance, a far better one than the flamboyant fraud of *Scent of a Woman*, and a trio of big action sequences as exciting as anything seen on screen this year. One of the most admirable things about De Palma is his refusal to bow to the current trend in action thrillers to cut, cut, cut—he remains one of the few directors addicted to the long take, and to those strange, floating, unstable shots that can be achieved only with the Steadicam, and which in De Palma's hands become the sole aesthetic justification for the device.

Carlito's Way has the assurance of a good film-maker working with good material. But it also feels padded—the entire romance plot could disappear from the film without anybody noticing. Worst of all, it feels like the work of a film-maker marking time until something comes along that he can feel passion for.

TIME, 11/15/93, p. 106, Richard Schickel

As we are told more than once, Carlito Brigante (Al Pacino) gained his education almost entirely on the streets of Spanish Harlem. That is too bad. If he had spent more time at home watching the old *Late Show*, he would have known from the early gangster movies (especially James Cagney's) that there comes a moment in any criminal career when it becomes impossible to go straight no matter how much you want to. It's an image problem with tragic dimensions.

Brian De Palma has, of course, seen *Angels with Dirty Faces* and *The Roaring Twenties*. No director knows the traditions of the violent genres better or is better at bringing them back to rushing life. And in *Carlito's Way* David Koepp has given him a script that works smart variants on the gangster film's classic conventions. Early on we find Carlito in court, about to be sprung after serving just five years of a 30-year rap, making a grandiose speech thanking everyone who has helped him. It's a fine bit, which, as the judge sourly comments, sounds a little too much like an acceptance speech at some show-biz awards ceremony.

This nice comic weirdness signals that business is not going to be conducted as usual. Carlito, like most reform-minded hoods, has a naive vision of the honest life. He hopes to buy into a car-rental agency. He also hopes to rekindle his old flame, Gail (Penelope Ann Miller), once a respectable chorus girl, now working topless in a go-go club.

But Carlito needs more than a good woman to avoid recidivism. He needs Pat O'Brien. You remember Pat O'Brien, Cagney's superego, trying to keep his wayward pal on a righteous path. What Carlito has instead is his friend and shyster lawyer, Dave Kleinfeld (Sean Penn, in a terrific performance). He is in too far with the Mob, and he needs Carlito's muscular help in a cocka-mamie plan to avoid gangland's vengeance. It goes awry, naturally, and Carlito's subsequent flight brings out the best in De Palma—breathless, bravura moviemaking, intricately designed, but playing like a delirious improvisation.

Out of breath is a useful condition to impose on Pacino. Really good movie actors force you to lean in a little in order to catch their meaning. Pacino, instead, leans on you, and though his boldness is sometimes impressive, in its calculated way there is also something overweening about it. There's almost no vulnerability about him, and that quality was what kept Cagney in a viewer's good graces. It is why Cagney's hoodlums seemed touched by tragedy, while Carlito seems touched only by technique. There is an irony here: an actor's bruising desire to transcend type is what prevents a very ambitious and otherwise skillful movie from transcending its genre.

VILLAGE VOICE, 11/16/93, p. 59, J. Hoberman

To watch *Carlito's Way* is to feel the great Ferris wheel of popular culture lurch full circle. This big new Brian De Palma movie begins at the end—a gangland hit, a sense of time congealing, the camera flipping upside down, and Al Pacino's mildly amazed, studiedly Nuyorican voiceover observing that "Somebody's pulling me close to the ground. ..."

Thus established as flashback, *Carlito's Way* unfolds in the mid 1970s-halcyon days for both director and star. Carlito Brigante (Pacino), the onetime heroin king of East Harlem, is released on a technicality after five years in prison. As if to provide a brief recap of his former self, he's introduced in court expansively thanking the Judge, the detective who illegally tapped his phone, and David Kleinfeld (Sean Penn), the hotshot mob lawyer who managed his appeal: "I've been born again ... like the Watergaters." The hyper, hopped-up delivery is evocative of Pacino's own 1975 performance in *Dog Day Afternoon*, and the movie echoes with mellow evocations of past characterizations: Michael Corleone, Serpico, Tony Montana. Pacino himself is the institution.

Based on two novels by New York Supreme Court Justice Edwin Torres, *Carlito's Way* is an extremely cautionary illustration of the gangster flick koan that what goes around comes around. Carlito returns to El Barrio and, after treating the audience to a bloody display of the old ultra v, meekly invests in an East Harlem nightclub. The resurrection of Gerald Ford is surely upon us when *The Brady Bunch* enters the canon, *Saturday Night Fever* returns as a midnight movie, and *Dazed and Confused* is followed by a $45 million evocation of the coke-crazed '70s played out in pastel leisure suits, staged in assorted disco infernos, and scored to nonstop KC and the Sunshine Band.

Pacino shelters his intensity as though cupping a match on a windy night. For a cold-blooded killer and dope-pusher, his Carlito has a surplus of likability—not to mention couth. There must have been a dress clause in the star's contract. While Penn suggests an inflatable toy with a Dershowitz hairdo and everyone else is compelled to plaster ultrawide shirt collars over brightly-colored lapels, Pacino is appropriately courtly and tragic in a dark suit, dark shirt, and dark tie, his voiceover continually hinting at a suitably somber gangster way of knowledge.

John Leguizamo provides the movie with an indigestible mass of malevolent ambition in the role of Bronx cowboy Benny Blanco, but Penn's Kleinfeld (sniveling some lines and shnuffling others) is meant to be the personification of '70s sleaze—the scene of coked-up frenzy out at his Long Island pool party could have been catered by Julia Phillips.

The big question is whether Kleinfeld ripped off a Mafia client currently incarcerated on Rikers, although, given that the movie is structured as Carlito's flashback, one wonders how we even know the tawdry details of Kleinfeld's affairs. Meanwhile, the emphasis on *temps perdu* is accentuated by Carlito's search for his former girlfriend Gail, a corn-fed Kewpie-doll played by Penelope Ann Miller. (Nothing in the movie is less convincing than Pacino's pop-eyed amazement when he finds Gail humping the pole in a Times Square topless club; still, Miller's deadpan response provides one of the comic highlights.) This barely motivated love affair mainly serves to reprise a screaming argument, occasioned by Carlito's return to the life, that is right out of *The Godfather*.

Indeed, De Palma dawdles through the material as though it really were *The Godfather* but there's a near total absence of texture, a complete disinterest in any milieu beyond the dance floor. While the movie has its share of helicopter dolly shots, De Palma is most in his element as a master of suspense, orchestrating scenes that give anxiety a polyrhythmic complexity. Inflated as the first two hours feel, the movie's final 30 minutes are an expert spiral of doom that sweeps the action down by subway and escalator from Carlito's club to a rendezvous at Grand Central—it's a test of De Palma's own nerve in that the tension works despite the forgone ending.

In the end, *Carlito's Way* seems weirdly sentimental—as though De Palma and Pacino were doing penance for their excessive *Scarface*. Given the hero's unwavering desire to go straight, this may be the first 12-step gangster movie. Carlito is just another ghetto dreamer. Is De Palma serious in offering the lugubrious quaver of Joe Cocker's "You Are So Beautiful" as walkout music or is it just his way of putting quotation marks around the concept "sincere"?

Also reviewed in:
CHICAGO TRIBUNE, 11/12/93, Friday/p. A, Michael Wilmington
NATION, 12/20/93, p. 780, Stuart Klawans
NEW YORK TIMES, 11/10/93, p. C19, Janet Maslin
NEW YORKER, 11/22/93, p. 117, Terrence Rafferty
VARIETY, 11/15/93, p. 30, Leonard Klady
WASHINGTON POST, 11/12/93, p. C6, Hal Hinson
WASHINGTON POST, 11/12/93, Weekend/p. 48, Desson Howe

CB4

A Universal Pictures release. *Executive Producer:* Sean Daniel and Brian Grazer. *Producer:* Nelson George. *Director:* Tamra Davis. *Screenplay:* Chris Rock, Nelson George, and Robert LoCash. *Story:* Chris Rock and Nelson George. *Director of Photography:* Karl Walter Lindenlaub. *Editor:* Earl Watson. *Music:* John Barnes and Bill Stephney. *Music Editor:* Earl Ghaffari. *Choreographer:* Jeannette Godoy. *Sound:* Jose Antonio Garcia, (music) Jack Rouben and Earl Martin. *Sound Editor:* Sandy Gendler and Val Kuklowsky. *Casting:* Kimberly Hardin. *Production Designer:* Nelson Coates. *Art Director:* Martin Charles. *Set Designer:* Karen Steward. *Set Decorator:* Susan Benjamin. *Set Dresser:* Marcus Epps, James Harper, and Eric Troop. *Special Effects:* John Hartigan. *Costumes:* Bernie White. *Make-up:* Kim D. Davis. *Stunt Coordinator:* Bob Minor. *Running time:* 83 minutes. *MPAA Rating:* R.

CAST: Chris Rock (Albert Brown/MC Gusto); Allen Payne (Euripides Smalls/Dead Mike); Deezer D (Otis O. Otis/ Stab Master Arson); Chris Elliott (A. White); Phil Hartman (Virgil Robinson); Charlie Murphy (Gusto); Khandi Alexander (Sissy); Arthur Evans (Albert Sr.); Theresa Randle (Eve); Willard E. Pugh (Trustus); Tyrone Granderson Jones (40 Dog); Rachel True (Daliha); Victor Wilson (Lt. Davenport); Richard Gant (Baa Baa Ack); J.D. Daniels (Ben); Stoney Jackson (Wacky Dee); La Wanda Page (Grandma); Louisa Abernathy (Mrs. Otis); Sharisse Jackson (Tamika); Daphne Jones (Tashana); Saba Shawel (Tawana); Vanessa Lee Chester (Talona); Chasiti Hampton (Tee Tee); Wayne Ward (Biscuit Diner); John Walcutt (Director); Jeremiah Birkett (Malik); Christopher Keene (Accountant); Lance Crouther (Well Dressed Man); Shirley Hemphill (976-Sexy); Mari J. Sahley (976-Piss); Al Clegg (976-Diss); Laverne Anderson and Sonee Thompson (Video Set Dancers); Gerard G. Williams and Melvin Jones (Inmates); Cathy Giannone, Bill Haller, Kenneth Menard, Loretta Jean Crudup (Diners); Mary Oedy (Sun); Robin Tasha Ford (Shine); Renee Tenison and Rosie Tenison (Twins); Niketa Calame (Albertina); Jedda Jones (Waitress); Ice-T, Ice Cube, Flavor Fav, Eazy E, Halle Berry, and Shaquille O'Neal (Themselves).

LOS ANGELES TIMES, 3/12/93, Calendar/p. 6, Michael Wilmington

"CB4," a musical comedy about three gangsta rappahs from Locash, Calif., is part satire, part celebration. That's what causes most of its problems.

The movie has bounce and bite, but it skitters around too much. Its needle is hip-hopping around between too many grooves. Co-writer/co-producer/star Chris Rock of "Saturday Night Live" plays the lead role of Albert Brown: a shy, almost fragile-looking middle-class Locash youth who turns himself into the oily-wigged, crotch-grabbing, jailhouse jive rapper, MC Gusto. And though Rock's satiric aim is occasionally deadly, on other occasions his show seems to be turning into a showcase for a lot of major rap songs and records (which isn't bad at all), and a more conventional '80s-style funny-money fairy tale about success which isn't good).

Rock loves rap. That's the first thing that's obvious about this movie—particularly in a droll little montage early on, where Ice-T, Ice Cube, Flavor Flav, Eazy E, Halle Berry and the Orlando Magic's Shaquille O'Neal appear in quick succession to offer testimonials to the gritty-grabby greatness of Cell Block Four: CB4 for short.

These dubious eulogies, part of a puff-piece CB4 documentary being shot by the obsequious and idolatrous filmmaker A. White (Chris Elliot, son of Bob and Ray's Bob), suggest we're in for something in the vein of "This Is Spinal Tap" or "The Rutles"—a "mockumentary," sending up both rap's excesses and media's hype. But Rock and his co-scenarist Nelson George—the essayist and occasional screenwriter-producer—drop this structure soon: a shame. They move the movie into flashback, and then flash-forward, tame it a little—even while they're stripping the masks off their central trio: Albert/Gusto, Euripides Smalls alias Dead Mike (Allen Payne) and Otis O. Otis alias Stab Master Arson (Deezer D).

"CB4" has a terrific comic point: that the "street" overtones of rap can get co-opted by middle-class kids, who have no clear idea of what the street and the underclass really are. The mock-macho gang is a crock: the real street violence comes back to haunt them. Despite their bottle-tipping, dirty-mouthed devil-may-care in the opening scenes, these guys are gag gangsters. Albert has copped both his moniker and his maniacal act from the *real* Gusto: a murderous, misogynist, coke-sniffing, gun-waving dude played by Charlie Murphy—who's a ringer for his younger brother, Eddie.

Murphy's Gusto will eventually break out of jail and try to kill them but Albert, his copycat, is about as dangerous as Kool-Aid. And the rest of CB4 are shams, too, conscious or not. When Dead Mike, the Afrocentric ideologue/idealist of the trio, later records a consciousness-raising solo song, the lyrics sound like "I'm black; I'm black; I'm blackety-blackety-black." And Otis a.k.a. Stab Master is a pudgy rich kid who wants *amour* with a real-life centerfold. They're all from comfortable homes and, at one point, Albert's Pops (Art Evans) reviles his son for pretending to be "street" when he wasn't born poor—like Pops was.

"CB4" is directed by Tamra Davis—and she gives the movie the sizzle and style she put into her rock videos and her recent flashy film-noir update "Guncrazy." Mostly, Davis tries to showcase the cast and the songs: the right ploy, since the cast and songs are the best things about "CB4." Most of the actors give funny, full-bodied performances, the fullest bodied and funniest may be Khandi Alexander's turn as Sissy, a voracious groupie with alligator eyes.

The score—by composer John Barnes and music supervisor Bill Stephney—is full of raucous rap parodies, rollicking rap standards (by Ice Cube, Ice-T, LL Cool J, Public Enemy and others), all mixed up so that no one who watches the movie will be able to say that rap is nothing more than rhymes and brags with a jackhammer beat. One of the more adventurous of the recent African-American comedies, it still gets bogged down in those movie-movie formulas, those phony recipes for success.

NEW STATESMAN & SOCIETY, 11/26/93, p. 34, Jonathan Romney

They used to say that a subcultural phenomenon was dead as soon as it was parodied on TV or the Sunday supplements got hold of it. That may have been the case once, but it stopped being true some short time after punk—probably the last major youth culture that caught the media industry on the hop.

Never again would a sudden eruption of energy and imagery be allowed to slip by without being either assimilated or parodied while in its cradle. Hip-hop as an interesting case in point. For nearly a decade, in cultural domination has spread so wide—even infiltrating the hidebound white rock culture that resisted it for so long—that even its most fervent proponents long ago ceased to take it for granted as a force of insurrection. Individual acts may still muster all of rap's rhetorical weaponry, but from the start there have been enough cash-in merchants, second-raters and bluster jockeys around to turn the music rapidly into a limited repertoire of tattered tropes and worn-out iconography.

That's why *CB4* seems to have come along too late in the day. Or maybe it's just too late in rap's day. The film has been hailed as hip-hop's own *Wayne's World*, and it's as amiably innocuous as that—a story of well-meaning nerds getting in too deep but emerging older and (not that much) wiser.

The trio of the title are swaggering adepts of gangsta rap, wearing prison uniforms, modelling their stance on acts like NWA and their ex-member Ice Cube, and named after the cell block in which they supposedly did time. At the start of the film, a fawning Wasp documentary maker, A White, is giving them the star treatment, swooning at their every gesture: "A material act of defiance by rappers," he marvels, when one of them rips up a parking ticket.

Subsequently it's revealed that "The World's Most Dangerous Rappers" are a bunch of nerdy buffoons, who only a moment before had been sitting at home bullied by their kid sisters. Their spokesman MC Gusto (the amiably manic *Saturday Night Live* alumnus Chris Rock) has stolen his name and act from a real hard case, and it's only a matter of time before the impostors are rumbled.

The jokes are pretty obvious. A record company executive asks them, "Do you glorify violence? Do you defile women in your lyrics? Do you fondle your genitalia on stage?" and they reply, "Whenever possible"—which answer of course wins them the jackpot. It's tame parody, the sort that, for fear of *really* offending its targets, invites them to play along.

Hence the cameos by rappers Ice-T and Ice Cube, whose meaner-than-mean stance is supposedly what the film is parodying. It's the same logic that has stars turning up on *Saturday Night Live* to collude in their own lampooning, and that makes British politicians so inordinately proud of being rubberised on *Spitting Image*.

Directed by Tamra Davis, *CB4* is a sluggish, sophomoric effort, more like *Mad* magazine than real satire. Sharper by far is a similar squib that's just run at the London Film Festival, *Fear of a Black Hat*, which someone really should release here fast. It's created by and stars Rusty Cundieff, a graduate of the Spike Lee academy (he was in *School Daze*). Where *CB4* is *Wayne's World*, *Black Hat* is more like *This is Spinal Tap*, with all that implies about being funnier and more acute.

The fact that the entire film is done as a fake documentary (made this time by a skeptical black woman director) gives the humour a distance that allows its subjects to carve themselves up. The band NWH (Niggaz With Hats) try to be hyper-cool and never slip out of their earnest pose, whereas CB4 are openly played as black Jerry Lewises. *Black Hat* wins out for overkill smartness, and gets an extra lead by points for a very funny piss-take of the mystico-rappers PM Dawn.

What is remarkable, though, is that the same jokes are common to both films. Both bands are inept gangsta posers taken seriously by the media and demonised by the moral right; both come from the archetypal bad side of town (CB4 hail from Locash, NWH from "Tough Neighbourhood USA"); both perform lame-brain anthems—respectively "Sweat on my Balls" and "Suck My Dee Asterisk Cee Kay". Are there really so few jokes in rap culture that they have to be shared?

That may be the case, and that in fact may be *CB4*'s main regret. The film starts with a curiously poker-faced credit sequence. The camera scans contemplatively over a decade's worth of rap memorabilia—sleeves, posters and hats commemorating the Fat Boys, Run DMC, Grandmaster Flash, and further back, funk precursors such as Parliament. Look at rap's rich tapestry, it seems to say ... and then look at this—and gives us CB4's idiot bad-boy posturing. *CB4* is produced and co-written by Nelson George, an acute commentator on black music who has bemoaned its descent from the golden age of Motown and R&B.

What *CB4* is complaining about, albeit ineffectively, is the depleted iconography in today's dominant black music, the too-persistent recourse to machismo and inner-city nihilism. But if the images of gangsta rap have become an easy-to-use template in music, its effect is also being felt in cinema. *Menace II Society* by tyro directors the Hughes Brothers, released in the New Year, is a strict re-run of the ground-breaking *Boyz 'N 'The Hood* bolstered by tough-guy imagery. Like John Singleton's film and the recent Oliver Stone-produced *South Central*, *Menace II Society* works over the now familiar theme of the impressionable boy brought low by urban deprivation, lack of education and the absence of strong father figures, all of which seems to destine them inexorably to gun law.

Menace shows how easy it is to click to automatic pilot once you look for inspiration to gangsta narrative. The airless feel of the film comes not so much from the claustrophobic milieu as from the easy assumption that such work can get by passing itself off is "how it is" reportage—which has always been the common argument about the lyrics of Ice-T and the West-Coast hardman school.

It's possible to take other things from rap than behavourial codes and a quicksilver pace. Films could profitably pick up on its function as a bulletin board. Public Enemy notably turn their records into extended commentaries on their own media coverage. Leslie Harris' *Just Another Girl on the IRT*, for all its considerable flaws, was powerfully aware of the dialogue element in rap, which was why its smart-girl sexual politics got across with some force. Rather than "this is how it is", it asked, "How do you think it is?"

Fear of the Black Hat may seem to have little to do with state-of-things reportage, but it's more revealing about rap culture and its stereotypes than *Menace* could ever be. Its wise-acre flippancy resists the deadness of the open-and-shut case.

NEW YORK POST, 3/12/93, p. 29, Matthew Flamm

Not everyone will get—or like—every joke in "CB4," a rap movie parody aimed squarely at rap music fans. But the comedy does offer this much for the uninitiated: a funny performance by the affable Chris Rock, who is also the movie's co-writer and co-producer.

A collection of skits posing as a "behind-the-scenes" look at the baaadest rappers in history, "CB4" has a try-anything quality that is another of its assets. Rock playing Albert Brown, a.k.a. M.C. Gusto, narrates most of the movie while stuck in an L.A. traffic jam with A. White (the amusing Chris Elliott), a goofy Caucasian who is making a "rapumentary" on the band.

They only look (and sound) dangerous: The three foul-mouthed gangsta rappers who make up CB4 are actually middle-class guys from the fictional town of Locash, Calif. Regular if unsuccessful performers at a local club called Gusto's, they get their break when the club owner (Charlie Murphy, Eddie's older brother, in his movie debut) is busted for narcotics.

Albert decides that a prisoner's work shirt and baggy blue jeans, bad attitude and jerry-curled hair are just what their act needs, They take their name—short for Cell Block 4—from Gusto's new home, and Albert even steals his moniker.

After signing with rap record mogul Trustus Jones (very little is subtle in this movie), CB4 goes to the top of the charts with their hit number "Sweat of My Balls," And the fellows work overtime on their act.

Meek and mild around his girlfriend (Rachel True), Albert now boasts "Must be one of my bitches" when the phone rings in his jeep (yeah, sure it is).

Dead Mike (Allen Payne) becomes a black nationalist who casts everything in terms of racial pride ("Did you know the black man invented ice cream?" he tells a fan).

As directed by Tamra Davis, a veteran of music videos and director of the cult hit "Guncrazy," "CB4" takes care to feature intelligent, articulate women who regularly put the guys in their place. But as much as it sends up the fantasies of testosterone-loaded teen-age boys, "CB4" is also meant for them.

NEWSDAY, 3/12/93, Part II/p. 67, John Anderson

For those still harboring hope that rap is going to go away, "CB4" will be deeply depressing. For the rest, this recklessly irreverent comedy will be mostly hilarious.

"CB4," which stands for Cell Block 4 and concerns the fictional rap group of the same name, may in fact make the moment when rap and the hip-hop culture became permanently cemented in America's mainstream consciousness. It's hard to imagine the script, by writer Nelson George and comedian Chris Rock, not being accessible to almost everyone, even at its most esoteric. And only a very healthy genre can be parodied and stand it, so easily.

The film, which wastes no time going right for the throat, opens with a film within-the-film, "CB4: A Rapumentary" by the dweebish A. White (Chris Elliott), who's trying to tell the true story of the baddest gangster rap group to ever come out of Locash, Calif. Among those who testify on camera about CB4's authenticity, sex appeal and general vileness are Ice T, Ice Cube, Halle Berry, Flavor Flav, Shaquille O'Neal, the Butthole Surfers and Virgil Robinson (Phil Hartman), a weasely politician who will launch a politically loaded campaign against the group.

Its members—MC Gusto, Dead Mike (Allen Payne) and Stab Master Arson (Deezer D)—are portrayed as hardened ex-cons who are the rage of the age. But after a brush with death—the Jeep that White and CB4 leader MC Gusto are riding in comes under fire ("My first drive-by!" White says)—Gusto spills the real story about CB4.

Combining a somewhat cynical attitude toward popular black culture with a sensibility straight out of "Airplane!"—the stoopid sight gags are endless—"CB4" skewers rap, and the combination of machismo and misogyny that often fuels it. There are uncountable jokes about male anatomy, vulgar language and some rotten treatment of women, but it's all in the interest of deflating the pumped-up, crotch-grabbing image of hardcore rap.

MC Gusto, Dead Mike and Stab Master Arson, whose real names are Albert, Euripides and Otis, come from solidly middle-class backgrounds; in their various rap incarnations they've been the Mad Bohemians, the Bagheads and the Overweight Lovers. They're only in it for the women, and only resort to the gangster image after Albert inadvertently causes the arrest of the real Gusto, a gangster played with great energy by Charlie Murphy (Eddie's brother). It's Gusto, now a prison escapee, and his henchman, 40 Dog (Tyrone Granderson Jones), who come gunning for Albert, and who pursue CB4 for the rest of the movie.

The plot of "CB4" sort of spirals out of control, but it really isn't the point; being funny is, and being brave. Dead Mike's wildly facetious Afro-centrism—he comes under the sway of a black nationalist named Baa Baa Ack (Richard Gant)—is going to drive some people crazy, but the question is whether black filmmakers can be free to parody and puncture whatever overripe targets they choose, and not worry about backlash. Rock, George and director Tamra Davis have shown they're not worried.

NEWSWEEK, 3/29/93, p. 65, David Ansen

Is CB4 "the world's most dangerous band?" In a "rapumentary" about them by the hapless filmmaker A. White (Chris Elliott), such heavy-duty hip-hoppers as Ice-T, Ice Cube and Flavor Flav pay tribute to their awesome badness. That fake documentary, which comes at the start of CB4, raises one's hopes that Tamra ("Guncrazy") Davis's satire will do for hip-hop what "This Is Spinal Tap" did for heavy metal. Not quite. Soon we're scurrying off on a long flashback that tells us how three nice, middle-class kids—Albert (Chris Rock), Euripides (Allen Payne) and Otis (Deezer D)—pass themselves off as authentic gangsta rappers and rise to the top of the music biz. Trouble is, Rock has stolen a real gangster's identity, and now he's out of the joint and looking for revenge.

This plot is the least interesting thing about "CB4," a scattershot comedy written by Rock, Nelson George and Robert LoCash that takes aim at conniving groupies, mercenary Afrocentrists, rightwing politicians on anti-rap crusades and middle-class poseurs who think it's hip to act like gangbangers. But sending up the macho, misogynistic postures of rap isn't easy, because so much of the real thing already borders on knowing self-parody. Torn between celebration and sendup, "CB4" misses its big target as often as it hits. Still, it's hard not to chuckle when Rock, in a slow-motion lovers-running-in-the-field montage, trips and falls under an excess of gold chains, or when he experiences a nightmare vision of his future in the "Hip Hop Retirement Home." This isn't a movie for anyone who thinks Ice-T is served with NutraSweet, but rap fans will appreciate its funky, insider's irreverence.

SIGHT AND SOUND, 12/93, p. 42, Louise Gray

Rap trio CB4—"the world's most dangerous band"—are to be the subject of a "rapumentary" made by A. White, a sycophantic TV director. As MC Gusto (alias Albert) drives White through L.A., Gusto—a jail-breaking gangster whose name Albert has stolen—appears; he tries to shoot them. Escaping into a traffic jam, Albert tells White the full story behind CB4.

Albert and fellow band members Euripides (aka Dead Mike) and Otis (aka Stab Master Arson) were middle-class black kids from the L.A. suburb of Locash. They loved rap music, in particular 'gangsta' rap, a hardcore form with a violent vocabulary. After some dismal attempts to win rap talent contests, Albert is inadvertently implicated in the arrest of Gusto, a cocaine-dealing club owner. Albert assumes the gangster's name and the trio remodel themselves in a convict-chic image (CB4 refers to the cell-block where Gusto is held).

Following a deal with record producer Trustus, CB4 hit the big time. Robinson, a conservative politician looking for re-election, denounces CB4's gangsta stance and launches an anti-rap campaign. Dead Mike acquires an Afro-centric guru, Baa Baa Ack, Arson works through the groupies and MC Gusto acts tough. After seeing CB4 perform their song "Sweat Of My Balls" on TV, Gusto is incensed. He breaks jail, kidnaps Albert and forces him to take part in an armed robbery. CB4 temporarily split up, and Trustus chokes to death in a restaurant when Gusto threatens him. Albert and a groupie, Sissy, lure Gusto to a hotel room, where Gusto, waiting in bed, is arrested. CB4 perform a reunion concert in which they announce their departure from gangsta rap in favour of the more melodic, message-based 'old school' rap style.

"Do you glorify violence? Do you abuse women? Do you fondle your genitalia on stage?", Trustus asks CB4. "Yes!" they chorus, and Trustus promptly signs them. In one stroke, the black middle-class kids Albert, Otis and Euripides (who makes pocket money working a 970-GAY phone-in line) take on a swaggering 'gangsta' identity, appropriated from Gusto (played by Eddie Murphy's brother Charlie). Real-life characters—gangsta rappers Ice, Ice Cube and Public Enemy's Flavor Flav—personally endorse CB4's toughness in a series of cameo appearances.

This is all witty parody, giving the same detailed attention to rap that *Wayne's World* and *Spinal Tap* gave to rock music. CB4's two writers Chris Rock and Nelson George come recommended via the *Saturday Night Live* TV show and a series of columns and books respectively. *CB4* shares the aforementioned movies' gag-paced speed, but if this were all it had going for it, comparisons might also be extended to the Hudlin Brothers' lame vehicle for rappers Kid 'n' Play, *House Party*. However, in exploring the conflict between personal and assumed identity, George and Rock have underpinned their script with serious issues.

Most people who view *CB4* will be aware of the political climate surrounding rap. In particular, gangsta rap has been the subject of considerable controversy on both sides of the Atlantic, with its more conservative critics seeing in its violent scenarios evidence of rap's sociopathic tendencies. Its songs are models of outlaw values, punctuated with misogynist and homophobic outbursts.

Gangsta rap is, its defenders claim, a statement of 'how-it-is', a brutal reflection of a brutal society. But is it? Recent features such as *New Jack City, Boyz N the Hood* and *Straight Out of Brooklyn* portray black American society as an underclass which uses violence as its calling card; they perpetuate an image of a homogenised black lawlessness. *CB4* delights in debunking such images and in doing so, manages to reclaim some critical territory from rap's conservative analysts.

For Rock and George, nothing is sacred. The CB4 trio—enamoured of music, confused by everything else—buy into outlaw chic as a way of finding an easy identity. Their efforts go badly wrong: the normally articulate Albert is driven into sullen silence when MC Gusto's vocabulary is challenged by black journalists; Euripides takes up a back-to-Africa babble pedalled by a quack guru; Otis—hitherto a virginal boy always ready to help his sisters—takes refuge in sex.

The relationship between Los Angeles, pop and violence occupies a special place in contemporary history. Charles Manson believed the Beatles were sending him apocalyptic messages through their songs; L.A. punk banks like X and Black Flag had an incandescent ferocity about them; and if the Rodney King riots had had a soundtrack, it would have been a rap one.

If rap represents the fears of white America, it is also a projection based on a concept of black music and community as an undifferentiated mass. *CB4* eloquently points this out, and is also very funny. It deserves a wide audience for this, and for giving the pretensions of gangsta rap a few judiciously aimed kicks.

VILLAGE VOICE, 3/23/93, p. 61, Colson Whitehead

As a fan of the swine, I have to admire MC Gusto, a man who's not afraid to say, "I'd eat a pig's ass if they cook it right." Rap's fascination with the evils of pork is just one of the targets of *CB4*, which details the rise of three middle-class boys—Albert, Euripides, and Otis—from youthful scrubs to platinum-selling gangster rappers.

Written by its star. Chris Rock, and *Voice* writer Nelson George, *CB4* pinions the rap world's favorite postures—sexist, militant, criminal—while maintaining a sentimental fascination with black youth culture. One scene, where the boys are cruising the streets listening to the car radio and vying for who gets to be Run and who gets to be DMC, is a counterpart to *Wayne's World*'s "Bohemian Rhapsody" sequence, a paean to black teenage goofiness.

The band's character growth is marked by its progress toward old-school purity. Dissing alternative rap's ready consumption by critics and crossover fans, *CB4* has the boys start by wearing dreads and tie-dyed shirts, chanting, "We're the bohemians, you got to put us on." When that doesn't work, they go the gimmick-band route, donning shower caps and calling themselves the "Bagheads." Finally, Albert and his friends recognize that gangster rap is the way to go. The film finds closure in the final parody song, a rendition of "Rapper's Delight" that signals the band's renouncement of fads and a return to simplicity.

Within the logic of the music, "Delight" is a tight ending, but the film neglects other niceties, losing sight of characters and subplots—Albert's girlfriend disappears and the band's persecution by a procensorship politician remains unresolved. For all the terror the film's villain is intended to inspire, he never generates enough fear. The drama of *CB4* is forced to take a back seat to its canny satire of rap stereotypes and to Chris Rock's bugging out.

Unlike other films with a heavy rap presence, *CB4* has a long memory, and this proves its greatest asset. As the soundtrack coos Doug E. Fresh's "The Show (Oh, My God)" over the opening credits, the camera pans over a shrine to the glory days: the rainbow swirl of Sugarhill Record covers; the stylized gear of the Fat Boys, and Biz Markie; and a glass case containing, according to a plaque, Grandmaster Flash's platform shoes. Countering these now-kitschy artifacts is CB4's elaborate concert set—the band tosses out gigantic balloon testicles during "Sweat of My Balls"—its grandiosity describing just how far the music has come since days of cutting up Chic in the basement.

Also reviewed in:
CHICAGO TRIBUNE, 3/12/93, Friday/p. B, Dave Kehr
NEW YORK TIMES, 2/12/93, p. C13, Janet Maslin
VARIETY, 3/8/93, p. 60, Brian Lowry
WASHINGTON POST, 3/12/93, p. D7, Hal Hinson
WASHINGTON POST, 3/12/93, Weekend/p. 42, Desson Howe

CEMETERY CLUB, THE

A Touchstone Pictures release. *Executive Producer:* David Manson, Philip Rose, and Howard Hurst. *Producer:* David Brown, Sophie Hurst, and Bonnie Palef. *Director:* Bill Duke. *Screenplay (based upon his stage play "The Cemetery Club"):* Ivan Menchell. *Director of Photography:* Steven Poster. *Editor:* John Carter. *Music:* Elmer Bernstein. *Music Editor:* Kathy Durning. *Choreographer:* Ronald Tassone. *Sound:* Willie Burton. *Casting:* Terry Liebling. *Production Designer:* Maher Ahmad. *Art Director:* Nicklas Farrantello. *Set Designer:* Michael Hanley. *Set Decorator:* Gene Serdena. *Set Dresser:* Amy Shaff. *Special Effects:* Sam Barkin. *Costumes:* Hilary Rosenfeld. *Make-up:* Rosemarie Zurlo. *Make-up (Diane Ladd):* Frances Kolar. *Make-up (Olympia Dukakis):* Tom Brumberger. *Make-up (Danny Aiello):* Deborah Zoller. *Dialect Coach:* Don Wadsworth. *Stunt Coordinator:* Greg Elam. *Running time:* 100 minutes. *MPAA Rating:* PG-13.

CAST: Ellen Burstyn (Esther Moskowitz); Olympia Dukakis (Doris Silverman); Diane Ladd (Lucille Rubin); Danny Aiello (Ben Katz); Lainie Kazan (Selma); Jeff Howell (Paul); Christina Ricci (Jessica); Bernie Casey (John); Alan Manson (Abe Silverman); Sam Schwartz (Irving Jacobs); Stephen Pearlman (Rabbi); Gene Ray (Photographer); Allan Pinsker (Mel); Alice Eisner (Rene); Hy Anzell (Al); Robert Marinaccio (Caretaker); Ben Tatar (Man); Glen Z. Gress (Maitre'd); Roger Serbagi (Bill); Robert Costanzo (Morty); Wallace Shawn (Larry); Louis Guss (Ed Bonfigliano); Irma St. Paule (Theresa); Therese Courtney (Nita); Bingo O'Malley (Judge); Emanuel Matthew Yavne (Cantor); Brett James Kennedy (Customer); Kathryn Fisher (Second Customer); Sean E. Markland (Detective); Etta Cox (Singer).

LOS ANGELES TIMES, 2/3/93, Calendar/p. 1, Peter Rainer

The three recently widowed women in "The Cemetery Club" visit their husbands' gravestones as a trio. They go as an outing; their clubbishness reinforces their shared solitude. Esther Moskowitz (Ellen Burstyn) is the most judicious and becalmed of the trio, her beauty still has its bloom. Doris Silverman (Olympia Dukakis) is an inveterate complainer: Lucille Rubin (Diane Ladd) is perpetually randy.

We're supposed to view these ladies as a kind of tripartite Everywoman—or at least Everywidow. Although much is made of their Jewishness, the film's aim is to "universalize" their plight. They kvetch for a higher cause.

Based on the play by Ivan Menchell and directed by Bill Duke, "The Cemetery Club," set in Pittsburgh, is shamelessly upfront about the ways it attacks our tear ducts. Occasionally, as with the cameos by Lainie Kazan as an oft-married free spirit, and Wallace Shawn as a wedding director, the results are giddy fun. But the sitcom high jinks and the socko sentimentality wear you out because there's little behind it except winks and winsomeness.

Doris and Lucille, in particular, are portrayed as one-note caricatures. Their confabs are exhaustingly predictable because they keep hitting the same keys. Part of the problem is the way the roles have been written: These are "types," not characters. The actresses have been encouraged to play out their miseries so broadly that they might as well be traipsing through an *opéra bouffe*. Ladd had a lyrical loopiness in "Rambling Rose" but there's no lyricism in Lucille's dingbat longingness here. And it may be time for Dukakis to give that tough-tender wised-up act of hers a rest. Her performances have become generic.

Burstyn, who has rarely made it into the movies in the past decade, provides a calm center for the film's shenanigans, but she's lovely without ever being terribly interesting. She plays up her vulnerability in ways that at times are moving and at times unseemly. (Esther is so vulnerable that she seems diaphanous—without a solid bone in her body.) Her romance with Danny Aiello's Ben Katz, a widower who married rather late in life, has a few tentative moments of real feeling, although it's solidly in the early Paddy Chayefsky/"Marty" mode. This "little people" approach is supposed to be humanistic but sometimes comes across as condescending instead. All this sentimental diminution doesn't allow for the exaltation in people's lives.

"The Cemetery Club" (rated PG-13 for sensuality and language) is another in a line of middle-age second-chance-at-love scenarios. "Moonstruck," by far the best of breed, led the way, but lately we had "Used People" and now this. They're more like "Moonstruck Out."

There have been some rumblings that, since "The Cemetery Club" is about a frankly Jewish community, it's odd that no Jewish actors are among the four principal leads. There are plenty of things wrong with this movie but the question of ethnicity is not—should not be—one of them. It would be a shame if critics decided that only Jews should plays Jews in the movies. Isn't it difficult enough to give a good performance without bringing in religion? Besides, isn't the whole point of acting to become something you are not? For an actor, believability is the only valid criterion.

NEW YORK POST, 2/3/93, p. 23, Matthew Flamm

If it achieves nothing else, "The Cemetery Club" should demonstrate once and for all that no matter the economics of filming, Pittsburgh is not New York.

Of course, the biggest problem with this tepid, predictable comedy is its screenplay, which Ivan Menchell adapted from his short-lived Broadway play—in the process moving the setting from Queens to Pittsburgh.

The story of three freshly widowed best friends, "The Cemetery Club" aims to be a geriatric "Moonstruck Meets Steel Magnolias," with a little of television's "Golden Girls" thrown in. It stars three big-name actresses—Olympia Dukakis, Ellen Burstyn and Diane Ladd—whom one feels have signed on in the hope of playing the sort of warmhearted, three-dimensional characters Hollywood is famous for seldom providing.

These Pittsburgh Jewish matrons visit their husbands' graves together every Sunday. It's here—with tombstones marked "FINK," "GOLDBERG" and "GOLDSTEIN" in the background of every shot—that the friends come to terms with their lot as single women. It's also where Burstyn meets her love interest, a Jewish cop turned cabbie, played by Danny Aiello.

The performers are, not surprisingly, the best thing in the movie. When Ladd sings the tangoish standard "Kiss of Fire" at an elderly-singles get-together, "The Cemetery Club" almost seems like a real movie.

"Which brings us back to the setting. There's nothing wrong with non-Jewish actors playing Jewish characters, but why Pittsburgh? "The Cemetery Club," directed by Bill Duke (no, it doesn't matter that he's a black director), works overtime to be authentic. But it has no sense of place, no feeling for its characters' milieu, and no idea of character except as derived, secondhand, from sitcoms and bad movies,

At least if they'd shot in New York, they would have had locations.

NEWSDAY, 2/3/93, Part II/p. 55, Terry Kelleher

The movie may linger less in the boneyard than the play on which it's based, but that doesn't mean "The Cemetery Club" is alive and kicking.

When Ivan Menchell's comedy, about three Jewish widows began a six-week Broadway run in 1990, Newsday's Leo Seligsohn described it as "The Golden Girls' marinated in chicken soup." Ethnic seasoning notwithstanding, the dish certainly seems bland enough to be served weekly in network prime time.

"The Cemetery Club" has only one salient qualification for the big screen—its promotability as a "women's picture" in the laugh-through-our-tears tradition of "Fried Green Tomatoes" and "Steel Magnolias." The ad pitch is certainly similar: Come see "Academy Award winner Ellen Burstyn," "Academy Award winner Olympia Dukakis" and "Academy Award nominee Diane Ladd."

We'll know the shortage of worthy female roles has reached the crisis point if "The Cemetery Club" returns its stars to Oscar contention. The fine actresses do nothing to embarrass themselves, but neither do they rise far above the banality of the material.

Dukakis' Doris is the humorless one, rigidly devoted to the memory of her late spouse. Ladd's Lucille is the horny one, always with an eye out for eligible males. Burstyn's Esther, the most recently widowed of the trio, is the composed, well-balanced type. They visit the cemetery together and address remarks to their husbands' headstones. If the guys weren't already asleep, these little talks would lull them in seconds.

Eventually, Esther attracts the interest of a man—not a pleasant butcher as in the play, but an ex-cop named Ben, portrayed with a few rough edges by "Academy Award nominee Danny Aiello." In the movie's biggest non-surprise, Lucille stops wrangling with Doris long enough to join her in condemning Esther's new relationship. Could it be she's not such a swinger after all?

In writing the screenplay, Menchell obviously decided, (or was persuaded) that his original work needed punching up as well as opening up. Ben gives Esther a driving lesson—a desperate comedy ploy if ever there was one. And then the really outrageous part: The couple has a safe-sex rendezvous in a hotel room, and Ben has a devil of a time—ouch!—putting on his condom. "The Cemetery Club" might have been entirely lifeless if Lainie Kazan hadn't signed on to do her brassy number as scandalous Selma, who marries and divorces elderly moneybags in quick succession. It's a bit of a puzzle, however, why this character was chosen to deliver the obligatory homily about love being more comfortable the second (seventh?) time around.

One could argue that director Bill Duke, with his record of action features ("A Rage in Harlem," "Deep Cover") and TV dramas, was a poor match for this property. One could suggest that the comedy lost flavor when the producers switched the setting from New York to Pittsburgh. But if it's not on the page, it's not on the stage ... or the screen.

VILLAGE VOICE, 2/23/93, p. 56, Amy Taubin

Combining exhausted Broadway and Hollywood formulas, *The Cemetery Club* is girl meets-loses-gets boy for the Medicare set. What's ludicrous here is not that sixtysomethings might have romantic yearnings, but that these characters barely qualify as human. Puerile as any teen comedy, *The Cemetery Club* focuses on a trio of recently widowed women—one who's a little too bawdy (Diane Ladd), one who's a little too staid (Olympia Dukakis), and one who's just right (Ellen Burstyn). Esther, the just-right one, is thoughtful, empathetic, and impulsive enough to get involved with Ben (Danny Aiello), a semi depressed ex-cop who became a cab driver when his wife died.

Adapted by Ivan Menchell from his Broadway play, the film is set in Pittsburgh's Jewish community. The press kit explains that director Bill Duke, who's African American, and the four leading actors, none of whom are Jewish, spent a great deal of time researching Jewish traditions and behavior. About the only thing they seemed to have learned is that during the period of mourning, mirrors are covered.

The problem, however, is not so much with the acting or the directing (though Duke, who made the vastly underrated *A Rage in Harlem* and *Deep Cover*, could have been wiser in his choice of crossover material) as with the screenplay. Among the topics never mentioned in *The Cemetery Club*: home security systems; plastic surgery; TV or radio talk shows; the cost of everything; the condescension of lawyers, doctors, accountants; cooking for one; the government's neglect of the elderly; racial tension; relationships between parents and children; health clubs; and, of course, the daily update on what *they* are doing—*they* referring either to the feared *other* or to friends momentarily, out of favor.

Menchell has zero understanding of how the conversation of the anxiety-ridden shifts between obsession and digression and even less awareness of what's on the minds of middle-class people who've been protected all their lives by marriage and the family and then, suddenly, are forced to fend for themselves.

Also reviewed in:
CHICAGO TRIBUNE, 2/12/93, Friday/p. I, Dave Kehr
NEW YORK TIMES, 2/3/93, p. C14, Vincent Canby
VARIETY, 2/8/93, p. 74, Richard Natale
WASHINGTON POST, 2/12/93, p. C7, Hal Hinson

CHAIN OF DESIRE

A Mad Dog Pictures release of a Distant Horizon film. *Executive Producer:* Anant Singh. *Producer:* Brian Cox. *Director:* Temistocles Lopez. *Screenplay:* Temistocles Lopez. *Director of Photography:* Nancy Schreiber. *Editor:* Suzanne Fenn. *Music:* Nathan Birnbaum. *Music Editor:* Jeffrey Kimball. *Choreographer:* Karole Armitage. *Sound:* Joe Romano. *Sound Editor:* Bernard Hajdenberg. *Casting:* Andrea Stone Guttfreund and Laurel Smith. *Production Designer:* Scott Chambliss. *Art Director:* Michael Shaw. *Set Decorator:* Judy Becker. *Costumes:* Pilar Limosner. *Make-up:* Suzanne Willett. *Running time:* 105 minutes. *MPAA Rating:* Not Rated.

CAST: Linda Fiorentino (Alma D'Angeli); Elias Kotes (Jesus); Angel Aviles (Isa); Patrick Bauchau (Jerald Buckley); Grace Zabriskie (Linda Bailey); Malcolm McDowell (Hubert Bailey); Jamie Harrold (Keith); Tim Guinee (Ken); Dewey Weber (David Bango); Holly Marie Combs (Diana); Seymour Cassel (Mel); Assumpta Serna (Cleo); Kevin Conroy (Joe); Suzanne Douglas (Angie); Joseph McKenna (MC); Karole Armitage, Michael Puleo, Rachel Tucker, Alicia Ho, and Edward Jenkins (Dancers); Iraida Polanco (Woman in Church); Joshua Kaplan (Boy in Church); Antonia Rey (Jesus' Mother); Teodorina Bello (Santera); Mickey Cottrell (Procurer); Sabrina Lloyd (Diana's Friend in Gallery); York Bergin (Tommy); Todd Bailey (Boy in Window); Sarah Newhouse (Girl at Ticket Counter); Edgar Omedo Sandel and John Schnall (Radio Announcers); Brooks Roger (Sgt. Langdon, All the Pres' Women); Lynn Frazen-Cohen (Gloria Insberg, All the Pres' Women); Rica Martens (Woman in Pearls, All the Pres' Women); Ebony Jo-Ann (Laughing Woman, All the Pres' Women).

LOS ANGELES TIMES, 6/30/93, Calendar/p. 3, Kevin Thomas

With his elegant and erotic *Chain of Desire*, writer-director Temistocles Lopez has deftly transposed the structure of "La Ronde" and set it down in contemporary Manhattan. Those who've seen Max Ophuls' memorable 1950 film version of Arthur Schnitzler's 1897 play

"Reigen" will recall that it is composed of a series of vignettes in which one lover moves on to the next who in turn moves on to another until the last lover connects with the first, thus completing a circle.

This ironic device allows Lopez to show how sexual longing and emotional craving in all their permutations reveal the loneliness and isolation that is endemic to modern urban life. A film of wit and compassion, "Chain of Desire" is a serious comedy, spiked with humor that is as hilarious as it is subtle. In only his second feature, Lopez hasn't Ophuls' flawless pacing but arguably his film possesses greater depth. It also possesses a flowing, graceful style, and cinematographer Nancy Schreiber brings a burnished, moody glow to his sleek, sensual images of Manhattan. More realistic than romantic, the film crosses racial, ethnic and sexual lines and socioeconomic levels.

Setting in motion Lopez's "chain of desire" is Linda Fiorentino's sultry singer, a current hit in the club scene but so unhappy in love she finds herself coming on to a husky Latino workman (Elias Koteas) in a church. Koteas' pretty wife (Angel Aviles) in turn is subjected to the kinky advances of her employer (Patrick Bauchau), who in turn is having an affair with the wife of a friend, and so on until we return to Fiorentino a dozen individuals later.

Virtually everyone involved makes an impression, no small accomplishment in a film with 14 principals and more than that number in supporting parts. Especially sharp and amusing is Grace Zabriskie, as a middle-aged woman whose lover proves to be as big a bore in bed as her husband (Malcolm McDowell), who's a closeted gay. Assumpta Serna is another standout as the beautiful but put-upon wife of a highly successful, shamelessly womanizing painter (Seymour Cassel). Lopez casts Dewey Weber as a handsome gay but instead of treating him as a stud shows him to be a reflective cabaret singer specializing in Brecht/Weill-like songs.

With "Chain of Desire" (Times-rated Mature for adult themes and situations), Lopez reminds us that taste and eroticism can be mutually beneficial rather than mutually contradictory. His major coup, however, is alluding to AIDS anxiety only in passing until a finish that reverberates through all that we have witnessed. "Chain of Desire" has more on its mind than sex.

NEW YORK POST, 6/25/93, p. 33, Jerry Tallmer

The subtext of Arthur Schnitzler's "La Ronde," that brilliant and enduring anti-comedy of 10 chain-linked sexual encounters, written by him in Vienna in the winter of 1896-97, was the unseen grinning skull of syphilis. You had to look even harder to detect this shadow skull in the no less brilliant Max Ophuls all-star (Signoret, Reggiani, Simon, Gelin, Darrieux, Gravet, Joyeux, Barrault, Miranda, Phillipe, Walbrook) movie of 1950.

The subtext in "Chain of Desire" a new movie by the Caracas-born, European-educated Temistocles Lopez, has been taken out of the closet and pushed right up in our faces, if by a ghostly offstage telephone voice in the manner of "Letter to Three Wives." There, the homewrecker was dear, sweet sleep-around Addie Ross. Here the bad-news telephone caller is male, and his news to the young woman with whom we begin the chain is: "I don't know how to tell you this but I'm sick" Nobody needs to be told what kind of sick in 1993.

Much else besides AIDS is pushed in your face in "Chain of Desire," not all of it as unwatchable as you might think, though grossness is the order of the day. I don't mean sexual grossness; I mean cinematic grossness. Too big, too loud, too clear, too forced, too manipulated, too obvious, too too.

And yet there are moments, there are always moments. A smile was forced from me by the S-M lady in mock French maid's garb who, breaking a fingernail as she whacks away with a ruler at a rich respectable old party, hangs him out to dry with the first time this was fun, but it's getting f-----g repetitious. Why do I always wind up with weirdos?"

Or how do you like the Jesus/De Niro-type housepainter-cum-bartender who, having just committed adultery with a young woman he'd seen sobbing in church—the one who starts the chain—proceeds home to El Barrio to tell his hotcha little wife, as she lures him into bed, that he's been off trying to start a chain of laundromats where people can eat empanadas and listen to salsa while they sit and wait?

Most of all I enjoyed the scene in which an artist's classy and elegant wife, furious over *his* adultery, conducts a sort of assault from the rear on the husky young assistant who's tacking up her husband's canvases. They wind up thrashing around on the floor on one of the husband's works in progress, its blood-red smearing all over her white summer dress. Yes, again, obvious; you can almost see the wheels gleefully turning over in the Temistocles Lopez brain—but I got some small charge out of it.

All the more so because Assumpta Serna, the Spanish actress who plays the classy wife, indeed stands out in this cast for class. Her husband is the always reliable Seymour Cassel. Also reliable is Malcolm McDowell as a sententious big-shot TV interviewer who keeps his closet homosexuality from his wife—that S-M French maid of a preceding link in the chain. She's the actress Grace Zabriskie; two other key links are Linda Fiorento and Suzanne Douglas. That none of these people is Simone Signoret or Gerard Phillipe goes without saying and isn't their fault.

The movie climaxes, if you'll forgive me, with three people in this great city—two men and one woman—spying on one another through their windows as each and every one of them gratifies himself/herself. Well, that's *one* way to break the chain. Funny that Arthur Schnitzler never thought of it.

NEWSDAY, 6/25/93, Part II/p. 54, Jack Mathews

The idea of updating Max Ophuls' classic 1950 "La Ronde" as a cautionary tale about sex and passing fancies in the high-risk '90s is so smart it's surprising someone hadn't thought of it years ago. But now that it has been done, with Temistocles Lopez' "Chain of Desire," maybe someone should do it again.

Lopez, a Venezuelan making only his second English language picture, has his heart and mind in the right place. His idea for "Chain of Desire" is perfect, just to burrow into a big city and follow a progression of encounters, one person to another to another, and note how easily a number of unrelated people can be linked intimately in just a few days.

Unfortunately, the characters and situations he has created are so glib and cliched, "Chain" never does much more than point out how much better an idea it is than a movie.

The film opens with a helicopter shot of Manhattan, drops us off gently in midtown, then picks us up a couple of hours later and takes us away. In between, we meet 14 people, consecutively, as if we were watching a sexual relay race in which we were the baton.

Not every encounter involves sexual contact, but each one might, and since one of the characters has been exposed to the HIV virus, the risk behind their random nature is always apparent.

The chain begins and ends in a trendy, imaginary club in the tower of the Chrysler Building, introducing us first to Alma (Linda Fiorentino), a husky-voiced chanteuse who, in pain from a dissolved relationship, allows herself to be picked up for an afternoon of sex by a Hispanic painter (Elias Koteas) she meets in church.

Afterward, we follow the painter out of Alma's apartment and go home with him to his wife (Angel Aviles), who puts him through another amorous bout, and the next morning we watch her being sexually humiliated by the perverse doctor (Patrick Buchau) for whom she does housework. And on it goes.

Before the Whitman's Sampler chain is completed, we've met a closeted gay TV newsman (Malcolm McDowell, in the film's strongest performance), a teenage male hustler, a gay couple, a housewife dominatrix, a womanizing artist, a trio of strangers who practice ultimate safe sex (they masturbate while watching each other from facing apartment windows), and—talk about an exotic bird—an adult female virgin! Sexus notyetus manhattaninus.

Lopez' tone ranges from morose sentimentality to goofy bedroom farce, mostly farce, but fails to give us anything like a real character, or a good joke, for that matter. Without the larger context of their lives, his characters come off as a gamey bunch, unconnected by anything but their desperation and vulnerability.

Granted, it's a tough assignment; we're not with any one person for more than 10 minutes. Still, to keep this merry-go-round moving, for its metaphor to take hold as anything more than an abstract idea, a connection also has to be made with the audience.

It doesn't, and the human links of Lopez' chain are exposed as cardboard figures, stereotypes delivering a message as cold, mechanical and fleeting as a table of statistics.

SIGHT AND SOUND, 9/93, p. 42, Emily Caston

New York. Alma, a singer at an underground club, finds comfort from a builder at work on her local church after splitting up with her boyfriend Michael. A "chain of desire" involving 14 people and 28 different types of desire begins when Jesus returns home to his wife, Isa, who works as a maid. When she is assaulted by her rich employer Jerald the following day, she hands in her resignation and Jerald turns to his second lover, Linda. But Linda has grown bored of his "repetitious" S&M games, and uses the affair to try and liven up her marriage to TV presenter Hubbie, who is not only indifferent but mute when questioned about his own secret life: a second apartment for seeing rent boys. Keith, one of the boys, leaves hurriedly after his pimp threatens Hubbie with blackmail. Keith beats up his pimp and is found on the street by volunteer worker Ken, who represents a more committed and altruistic love. Ken invites Keith to stay at his apartment with his flatmate and lover Dave, an up-and-coming singer. Dave begins seeing Diana one night after his show, and Diana meets an eminent and amorous painter called Mel at an art exhibition. Mel's wife Cleo seduces her husband's assistant Joe in revenge for Mel's deception. Later that night, whilst talking on an 0898 contacts' phone-line, Joe discovers the fully safe and far more erotic sex offered by a strange woman in the apartment opposite. "No contact, no commitment," boasts the woman Angie, to her friend the next day. The friend turns out to be Alma. She is preparing to go on stage at the club when her ex-lover, Michael, calls to say that he has tested positive for HIV. No-one knows how many of the 14 others are at risk. Reluctantly Alma sings and tells her audience, "have a wonderful time".

Chain of Desire adheres in structure to *La Ronde*, Max Ophuls' 1950 adaptation of Arthur Schitzler's merry-go-round of alienated love. Temistocles Lopez's inspiration is to turn the 'round' into a cautionary tale about AIDS by revealing—at the end of the film—that the first in the chain of desire is HIV positive. Despite repeated references to safe sex and two of the characters' participation in an 'Undercounting AIDS Kills' demonstration—the film leaves unsaid how many on the chain have been infected, although it is clear that the majority, by deceiving their partners about their second lover, are at risk.

This yields a more original exploration of desire than the film's steamy billing suggests. Lopez comments on voyeurism, alienation, trust, commitment and transgression as well as deception; he avoids the stereotyping found in comparable movies, particularly gender stereotyping; and replaces Ophuls' post-war nostalgia with a cynical humour, a preoccupation with desires labelled 'abnormal' and a determination to 'tell all' about sex rather than leave its detail to the imagination. But Lopez's skill in dissecting them is markedly uneven.

A shorter film might have been more apt for the episodic structure, and might have conveyed more effectively the quite simple message that it carries—do not deceive your partner. The trouble with this structure is the difficulty of maintaining suspense, insight and depth of character; in the first 20 minutes Lopez does not manage this. The encounters between Alma, Jesus, Isa and Jerald are as lacking in depth and cliched in their resolutions as scenes from a crude sex steamer for the sell-through market. Only when Grace Zabriskie enters as Jerald's would-be maid does Lopez really begin to thrash out the emotional and social sources of his characters. When Malcolm McDowell enters as Linda's husband, quite an interesting story unfolds, and we become immersed in a complex network of well-observed phobias about communication, trust and truth held by some interesting and unusual personalities.

From here on, Lopez's characterisation and social commentary improve, although the film remains somewhat diffuse, and the sequences involving Keith have a hurried and cliched feel. But Lopez has an impressive cast; Holly Marie Combs as the incomparably cool Diana and Seymour Cassel as the pathetically charming menopausal painter really bring the script to life (Mel promises to give Diana the "full Lolita treatment" in return for her questionable virginity).

The dry humour bites, but Lopez's direction is less than inspired, with frequent recourse to talking heads, repetitive two-shots, and cluttered frames which take little advantage of the screen and often miss the emotional centre. But the cuts from one sequence to the next work well, and Nancy Schreiber's lighting redresses some of the film's lack of imagination. Nevertheless the direction improves as the film progresses and the sequence involving Joe, Angie and a stranger is not only beautifully shot, lit and acted but raises pertinent questions about safe sex, fantasy and voyeurism.

Also reviewed in:
NEW YORK TIMES, 6/25/93, p. C19, Stephen Holden
VARIETY, 9/7/92, p. 53, Todd McCarthy
WASHINGTON POST, 8/13/93, p. D6, Richard Harrington

CHILDREN OF THE CORN II: THE FINAL SACRIFICE

A Dimension (a division of Miramax Films) release of a Fifth Avenue Entertainment presentation of a Stone Stanley production. *Executive Producer:* Lawrence Mortoff. *Producer:* Scott Stone, David Stanley, Bill Froelich. *Director:* David Price. *Screenplay:* A.L. Katz and Gil Adler. *Based upon a short story by:* Stephen King. *Director of Photography:* Levie Isaacks. *Editor:* Barry Zetlin. *Music:* Daniel Licht. *Sound:* Kim Ornitz. *Casting:* Geno Havens. *Production Designer:* Greg Melton. *Art Director:* Tim Eckei. *Set Dresser:* Christie L. Theorin. *Costumes:* Gigi Melton. *Stunt Coordinator:* Bob Stephens. *Running time:* 93 minutes. *MPAA Rating:* R.

CAST: Terence Knox (Garrett);   Paul Scherrer (Danny);   Rosalind Allen (Angela);   Christie Clark (Lacey);   Ned Romero (Red Bear);   Ryan Bollman (Micah);   Ted Travelstead (Mordechai);   Ed Grady (Dr. Appleby);   John Bennes (Hollings);   Wallace Merck (Sheriff Blaine);   Joe Inscoe (Simpson);   Marty Terry (Mrs. Burke/West);   Dean Bridgers (Jedediah); Aubrey Dollar (Naomi);   Kristy Angell (Ruth);   David Hains (Fraser);   Leon Pridgen (Bobby); Kelly Benett (Mary Simpson);   Rob Treveiler (McKenzie).

LOS ANGELES TIMES, 2/8/93, Calendar/p. 8, Kevin Thomas

Let's hope "Children of the Corn II: The Final Sacrifice" lives up to its title, for if there ever were a film that didn't deserve a sequel in the first place it is the 1984 original.

These "Corn(y)" pictures are based on one of Stephen King's farthest out premises: Adults in the Nebraska farm belt have messed with the ecology so badly that their kids become vulnerable to a disease disseminated by infected corn. (Last time out Iowa stood in for Nebraska, this time it's North Carolina.)

The disease turns them into oddly puritanical worshipers of a vengeful nature spirit they call "He Who Walks Behind the Rows," which they appease by slaughtering their parents (and practically anyone else older than 19).

"Corn II" opens with the discovery of a slough of bodies in a musty cellar. Covering the story is a reporter (Terence Knox) for a tabloid who would like to get back into respectable journalism after having been fired from Newsweek for telling off his editor. He figures—wrongly—that getting to the bottom of the massacre will be a step up from writing about how Rock Hudson was actually yet another of J.F.K.'s many lovers. At the same time he's trying to make peace with his sarcastic estranged son (Paul Scherrer), whom he's brought along; there's also time for both father and son to romance local women.

Along with heavy-handed doses of ecological messages and American Indian mysticism, there is a group of ominous blank-faced teens, dressed vaguely like the Amish or Mennonites. Most of the townspeople are completely oblivious to them, despite all those corpses in the cellar. Those who do take notice meet grisly fates.

It must be said that, stuck with a script full of plot holes, director David Price doesn't flinch. Both he and his key actors are clearly up to better material than "Children of the Corn II: The Final Sacrifice" (rated R for horror, violence, and language).

NEWSDAY, 1/30/93, Part II/p. 23, Terry Kelleher

By now, we're resigned to the idea that everything Stephen King ever scribbled must be turned into a movie. But who passed the law that says each title must have at least one sequel?

Almost nine years have passed since the release of "Children of the Corn," and in all that time nobody could come up with a halfway-coherent rationale for "Children of the Corn II." So they decided to make the movie anyway.

At the start of "Corn II," a couple of yokels discover a basement full of stinking corpses—"50 bodies in various stages of decomposition," as the local TV newsman brightly phrases it. We get a quick fill-in on how the whacked-out youth of Gatlin, Neb., slew the town's adult population.

Well, supermarket-tabloid reporter John Garrett (Terence Knox) is here to cover the gruesome story, with his alienated teenage son, Danny (Paul Scherrer), in tow. And they'll get right on the case as soon as each finds himself a local girlfriend (Rosalind Allen for Dad, Christie Clark for the kid).

OK, ready to investigate, But wait—Danny's so disaffected he actually falls in with the teen killer cult, led by the constantly ranting Micah (Ryan Bollman, perhaps forced by Satan to overact). Or is Danny merely infiltrating the group in the cause of journalism? The movie never bothers to make it clear.

And if you're a sucker for clarity, don't even ask why the young folks are slaughtering their elders, or what kind of help they're getting from the vengeful god of the cornstalks. For a while, the movie hints that the whole thing may be explained by some kind of agribusiness conspiracy, but it turns out the writers can't figure out that angle any better than we can.

Director David Price also has trouble deciding on a point of view. Sometimes we see the victim through the eyes of whoever/whatever is stalking them, but eventually that gimmick is discarded. The fact is, nobody behind the camera seems to know what we're supposed to be watching. They just assume the bleeding and screaming will keep us amused.

The violent, hopelessly confused climax finds one of Micah's minions hurling a spear at Garrett, who calmly catches it and throws it back for a lull. If his tabloid folds, there's always "American Gladiators."

Also reviewed in:
NEW YORK TIMES, 1/30/93, p. 16, Stephen Holden
VARIETY, 2/8/93, p. 74, Lawrence Cohn
WASHINGTON POST, 1/30/93, p. D2, Richard Harrington

CHILDREN OF FATE

A First Run Features release of a Young/Friedson production in association with Archipelago Films. *Executive Producer:* Robert M. Young. *Producer:* Adam Friedson. *Director:* Andrew Young and Susan Todd. *Director of Photography:* Andrew Young. *Music:* Ted Kuhn and John La Barbera. *Sound:* Susan Todd. *Running time:* 85 minutes. *MPAA Rating:* Not Rated.

LOS ANGELES TIMES, 11/23/93, Calendar/p. 6, Kevin Thomas

In 1961, filmmakers Robert M. Young and Michael Roemer made for NBC "Cortile Cascino," a documentary about a woman and her family living in a slum in the heart of Palermo, Italy. The network deemed it too strong to air, but Young managed to get his hands on much of what he and Roemer had shot. Three decades later this footage has been incorporated in their powerful "Children of Fate" by Young's son Andrew and Andrew's wife, Susan Todd, who discovered the woman, Angela, and her relatives still living in or near Palermo.

At 53, the sturdy, resilient Angela is still enduring hardship and tragedy, just as she was three decades earlier, but she has improved her own lot considerably. A woman of much native intelligence but little or no education, she finally found the courage to leave her drunken, abusive husband after 28 years, move to a charming town nearby where she has a nice apartment and supports herself as a cleaning woman (and is amusingly candid about cheating her employers in minor ways).

On the whole, "Children of Fate" is a portrait of an extended family caught up in a vicious cycle of poverty, ignorance and crime, a kind of companion piece to Werner Schroeter's elegiac drama. "The Kingdom of Naples."

Never mind that most of the slum, Cortile Cascino, has been torn down and that Angela and her relatives now live in considerably more material comfort. One of Angela's sons has spent half his life in prison and at 31 feels like an old man; the daughters she strived so mightily to ensure a better life have met even sadder fates than their brother. Angela's husband, Luigi, once a slicked-up petty crook, is now a blubbery, bleary-eyed wreck residing in Cortile Cascino's last remaining building, eking out a living scavenging scrap metal.

Yet even as the film strikes the pessimistic, deterministic note its title suggests, there are little flashes of hope. Angela's younger son, handsome as a movie star, has been saved by a loving wife who works with him cleaning offices; they dream of the day when they can open a grocery store. This son has discovered that being a man means being responsible—and not in being a wife-beater. Maybe even someone born in Cortile Cascino can have some effect over his own destiny after all.

Robert Young and Michael Roemer's black-and-white footage has the lyricism and impact of Italian Neo-Realism as we watch Angela's family and neighbors go about their daily lives in a picturesque rabbit warren of ancient, crumbling structures, picking rags and staving off hunger as best they can while bearing ever more children they cannot possibly afford to feed, let alone educate. Water for the entire community comes from a single pipe; basic modern conveniences are unheard-of luxuries.

Cortile Cascino society is Mafia-permeated and profoundly macho, and, for all the prostitution going on, puritanical: A single kiss upon her cheek from Luigi dictated that Angela marry him regardless of her feelings about him.

Andrew Young and Susan Todd really do not match the quality or style of the earlier footage. Their straightforward work, in color, is more informal, talkier. They film largely in a series of nondescript apartments in place of the highly photogenic, richly atmospheric Cortile Cascino. Even so, their deft crosscutting between past and present is most effective, defining sharply all that has changed in 30 years—and all that has not.

Arguably, the most intriguing figure in "Children of Fate" (Times-rated Mature) is not the forthright, realistic Angela but her brother Gildo. Thirty years earlier he seemed for the world a punk just like Luigi, but today is an antiques dealer—Angela says murkily she wouldn't hazard a guess as to where he gets the stuff—who lives in a tastefully furnished apartment. Gildo is also a philosopher, acknowledging that getting ahead in life can lead to self-absorption and admitting to occasional longings for the camaraderie of the old neighborhood, bad as it was. Material success has its pitfalls, he reflects: "The more you have, the more you want."

NEW YORK POST, 5/26/93, p. 24, Jerry Tallmer

There is one sound like no other in this world—the *shwunk* of a shovelful of dirt hitting a coffin.

In "Children of Fate" the stunning and devastating documentary is heard twice hitting coffins, in two different Sicilian hillside cemeteries 33 years apart: the tiny coffin of 1-year-old Finuccia the ordinary barren box of 33-year-old Anna. These were the daughters, both of them—two of the six children—of a woman named Angela, whose destiny is that of having been injected by birth into Cortila Cascino, the dirt-poor Palermo starvation slum familiarly know as the Well of Death.

Incidentally, though it is only a subtheme of the movie, the Mafia controlled both those funerals, and profited from them.

In 1961, on commission from NBC-TV, filmmakers Robert M. Young and Michael Roemer —inspired by the writings and works of Danilo Dolce, Sicily's "apostle of the poor"—went to Palermo and shot black-and-white footage, the story of Angela and her family, that was considered too shocking by the network for it ever to be aired. Thirty years later, Andrew Young, son of Robert, and Andrew's wife Susan Todd, went back to Sicily and shot the rest of the story.

Everything had changed, and nothing had changed.

Where once the shanties and hovels had stood amid garbage and hogs, there are now high-rises—prisons of another sort for the poor, ridden with drugs and violence. "In those days we didn't know about nice things; now we know and want them." Everybody has TV. "Then, we hardly knew what it was."

The fat blond infant screaming with hunger in the old black-and-white film is now Angela's 31-year-old son Tortucco, who has spent half his life in prison. Daughter Anna we have seen hooked to her IV on the road to death, a cancer victim smoking away, passing a cig to her own little girl. Angela's third daughter, Fina—a drawn, ascetic beauty who in irritation beats her child as her father once beat *her*—has just finished four years of house arrest for robbing a jewelry store with the husband who is now himself dead of an overdose.

Angela herself says she's 7 years old—marking her birth from the day 7 years ago that she finally gathered up the courage to leave her idle brutal sado-macho-masochistic husband Luigi, unemployable alcoholic father of all this brood and take up a new life in Ragusa on the other side of Sicily, "as far away from him as I could get."

Only her sleazy brother Gildo has done well, a dog-eat-dog survivor in the "antiques" business who smugly invites the camera to dwell on his furniture and bric-a-brac as he expatiates on his political and economic philosophy. "There is no altruism in the world ... Life is all one fight ... It all sucks."

Angela too is a survivor—even of the days when more than once I had to do something bad so that my *daughters* wouldn't have to." Only later did I learn from the press kit that Angela has had 28 abortions in her life, and that at last notice she was in jail somewhere in Sicily on charges unspecified.

And Luigi, the husband is a survivor of sorts—once as handsome, Angela thought, as Elvis Presley, now a battered lonely hulk of blubber with female dugs and a scarred body. He, scared of dying alone, wants to get together with Angela again. Fat chance.

Children of Fate" has something in common with Michael Apted's "35-Up" series of lives glimpsed and re-glimpsed over years-apart gaps, something also in common, inversely, more harrowingly, with Federico Fellini's great "Vitelloni." And it belongs in that company.

VILLAGE VOICE, 6/1/93, p. 56, Manohla Dargis

One of the enduring fictions of documentary film is that seeing is not only believing, but understanding. While plenty of docs challenge this fiction, others, such as Andrew Young and Susan Todd's *Children of Fate*, get stuck in a decidedly undialectical groove. Some background: in 1961 upstarts Robert Young and Michael Roemer shot *Cortile Cascino*, about a Palermo slum. Solicited by NBC, their film never hit the airwaves because the material was, apparently, deemed too potent for U.S. palates. Now, Young has returned to Sicily as producer of *Children of Fate*, a follow-up that incorporates scenes from his original with new material by his son Andrew and daughter-in-law Susan Todd.

The vehicle for this trip down memory hell is Angela, a middle-aged woman who three decades earlier had been one of Young and Roemer's back-alley stars. In voiceover, Angela speaks of hard times, weighing her past misery against the relative happiness she's realized since. While certainly compelling (she blesses a family meal with "Eat, get fat, and pray you don't die"), Angela, like many of us, has a rather myopic take on her own history. For her the *whys* of suffering are all but immaterial, chalked up to the mysteries of life. The truth is when this woman stole food to feed her babies, buried her malnourished toddler, felt the blows from her husband, it had nothing to do with "fate." Angela may believe in God, but that doesn't mean Young, et al., need have checked their politics at the church door.

Also reviewed in:
NEW REPUBLIC, 6/14/93, p. 30, Stanley Kauffmann
NEW YORK TIMES, 5/27/93, p. C13, Janet Maslin
VARIETY, 2/15/93, p. 85, Emanuel Levy
WASHINGTON POST, 7/30/93, p. G7, Rita Kempley
WASHINGTON POST, 7/30/93, Weekend/p. 39, Desson Howe

CLAIRE OF THE MOON

A Demi-Monde Productions release. *Executive Producer:* Nicole Conn. *Producer:* Pamela S. Kuri. *Director:* Nicole Conn. *Screenplay:* Nicole Conn. *Director of Photography:* Randolph Sellars. *Editor:* Michael Solinger. *Music:* Michael Allen Harrison. *Sound:* Brian Crain. *Running time:* 105 minutes. *MPAA Rating:* Not Rated.

CAST: Trisha Todd (Claire Jabrowski); Karen Trumbo (Dr. Noel Benedict); Faith McDevitt (Maggie); Caren Graham (Tara O'Hara); Sheila Dickinson (BJ); Damon Craig (Brian); Patricia Blem (Shiloh Starbright); Sherilyn Lawson (Lynn Schroeder).

LOS ANGELES TIMES, 1/29/93, Calendar/p. 8, Kevin Thomas

Nicole Conn's "Claire of the Moon" is a graceful, sensual and persuasive evocation of a growing passion between two very different women.

The setting is a writer's retreat on the beautiful Oregon coast run by a salty, shrewd middle-aged lesbian (Faith McDevitt) who mischievously has booked into the same cottage the elegant, highly disciplined Dr. Noel Benedict (Karen Trumbo), a respected therapist and writer, and Claire Jabrowski (Trisha Todd), a successful satirist who's a freewheeling, statuesque beauty with a strong Georgia O'Keeffe profile.

Despite awkward moments, "Claire of the Moon" winds up the best American-made lesbian drama since "Desert Hearts."

Both women are smart and impressively articulate, something not lost on either, since most of the other women attending the retreat are airheads. However, only when Noel expresses her gayness openly in a group meeting does she commence commanding Claire's respect, gradually attracting her, although Claire has a hard time buying Noel's belief that men and women "speak a different language" and therefore can never be as close as two women. (That belief is open to debate, obviously, but how could Noel, as a lesbian, use such retrograde terms as "sexual preference"—rather than orientation—and "lesbian *sub*culture"?) Is Noel just a passing fancy for Claire, clearly a woman open to all sorts of experiences? Is Claire latently gay? Is she bisexual? Do Noel and Claire have a future together? Conn is too smart to try to answer such questions, instead contenting herself to charting a totally unexpected mutual sexual attraction that builds toward a moment of truth as discreetly presented as it is erotic, and beautiful. (Conn's heterosexual love scenes are also pretty steamy.)

There is an initial archness, a straining for wit and sophistication, at the start of "Claire of the Moon" (Times-rated Mature for adult themes, language, nudity, sex) that gradually melts; it's as if Conn, as a filmmaker, was developing and growing along with Noel and Claire.

What really makes the film work, however, is that Conn, backed by an imaginative cameraman, Randolph Sellars, is able to create a series of poetic images that continually subvert the film's torrent of words. Like a good semanticist, Conn knows the crucial difference between the map and territory. Specifically, Conn also knows what Noel and Claire discover: A time comes when two people who are seriously attracted to each other finally need to shut up and make love.

NEW YORK POST, 4/17/93, p. 17, Matthew Flamm

Made on a shoestring by a first-time and clearly inexperienced director, "Claire of the Moon" nonetheless stands apart. It is, as far as I know, the first soft-core porn film that has ever been set in a writers' colony.

Is that progress, or what?

Oh yes, "Claire" is also an "honest, lesbian love story told by an 'out' lesbian," according to writer-director Nicole Conn, as quoted in the production notes.

Or as explained by Dr. Noel Benedict, the character burdened throughout the film with expressing the director's point of view, "Men and women will never speak the same language. So men and women can never achieve true intimacy."

From the moment the lonely author/shrink sets eyes on Claire Jabrowski, her opposite pole roommate at the Arcadia Women Writers' Retreat, it's clear that the two women will achieve "true intimacy" by the final reel. Typical of soft-core, the plot is just a pretext—transparently so to the viewer, though perhaps not to the well-meaning director.

Of course, the uptight Noel (Karen Trumbo) does need time to drop her guard. And the free-spirited Claire (Trisha Todd), so fond of one-night stands with hunky guys, has to realize she can have even better sex with a woman who loves her. Conn fills out the teases—which include, of all things, a neck massage and a love scene that (surprise!) was only a dream—with dialogue that is little short of astonishing.

"I was pure instinct," says Claire of how she knew to deal with men from her teen-age years. "I didn't have any verbiage for it."

No verbiage, huh? Gee, that's tough.

There are worse things than mistakes in, er, verbiage, but these characters are supposed to be writers (famous, best-selling writers).

But then, what can you expect from a porn film that is also part situation comedy—the inconsiderate, chain-smoking Claire playing Oscar Madison to Noel's Felix Unger? The Arcadia writers' retreat, meanwhile, is run like an encounter group: At a weekly gossip session, the lesbians lecture the straights, who consist most notably of a moron, a bigot and a victim.

I suspect that for Conn this is payback time.

NEWSDAY, 4/16/93, Part II/p. 79, John Anderson

No, there haven't been many feature films dealing positively with lesbianism, and for that reason alone "Claire of the Moon"—which concerns identity through love of another woman—is an important film. And a brave film. But not a particularly good film.

One would assume that Nicole Conn, who wrote, produced and directed what is a rather prolonged and strident story, had more of an objective than just getting lesbians on screen. Certainly, there's enough bad Hollywood attitude to counter, "Basic Instinct" being only the most recent and pernicious example. But instead of avoiding stereotypes, Conn virtually wallows in them, and the result is a film that not only fails to cut to the chase—its most anti-Hollywood aspect is the length of time it takes the two leads to get to bed—it tends to undercut its own otherwise reasonable arguments.

Can a person, the film asks, deny her sexual self and (1) be happy, or (2) realize her full potential? Claire, a blonde bombshell played by Trisha Todd, is author of the lightweight "Life Can Ruin Your Hair" and the veteran of trench warfare in the singles bars; the first scene we get is a gauzy/sweaty memory of her latest one-night stand. She has an aggressively sullen attitude, smokes too much, and is, despite a sharp intellect, oblivious to what's making her miserable.

When she attends the Arcadia Writer's Retreat, she's assigned a room with Dr. Noel Benedict (Karen Trumbo), psychiatrist, academic, and author of "The Naked Truth," a study of sexual behavior. Naturally, the two are like oil and water; naturally, they'll fall in love, with Claire finally realizing who she really is. In the interim, though, they wage small warfare, sniping at each other both in private and before the rest of the motley crew attending the retreat.

They are a particularly annoying lot. Chief among them is Maggie (Faith McDevitt), the director of the retreat, who's like a cross between Popeye and Alice B. Toklas and executes some of the film's more self-conscious sloganeering. But the straight women are worse: One, a writer of bodice-ripping romance novels, is named (yes!) Tara O'Hara (Caren Graham), a cartoonish confection who wears nothing but off-the-shoulder dresses and gets hot reading her own swollen prose; another, Shiloh Starbright (Patricia Blem), is a New-Age pixie who seems to be having a private harmonic convergence inside her head. These, together with the novice writer and housewife Lynn Schroeder (Sherilyn Lawson), are send-ups of heterosexual types and might have had a purpose, and some humor, if the two main characters weren't also straight out of central casting.

Claire may be, as Noel describes her (and not very professionally), "a common, garden-variety slut," but Noel's no rare species either: Her close-cropped hair, supercilious demeanor and repressed body language make her as much a stereotype, as much the realization of some homophobe's imagination, as any other character in the movie. And her doctrinaire pursuit of her own limiting sexual philosophy doesn't help matters.

Between the Hallmark card landscapes, some tiresome dialogue and some stiff performances, "Claire of the Moon" raises interesting questions. Chief among them, however, is how we're supposed to read characters who are so totally unconvincing.

VILLAGE VOICE, 4/20/93, p. 58, Lisa Kennedy

It all depends on whether you are one of those ends-justify-the-means types, or someone who has no problem with self-serious trash—and I mean that in the nicest possible way. *Claire of the Moon* is both the longest tease of a flick to come down the dyke, er, pike, in a dog's age, and very much a lesser version-in-images of the lesbian pulp novels of the '50s. While after more than a seven-year wait we at least deserve a slightly improved (or altogether different) *Desert Hearts*, in *Claire* we get the low-rent doppelgänger of *Lianna*, with all the dourness and didacticism that implies. (Embarrassingly, the Sayles pic had more levity).

When Claire meets Noel, at a woman writers' retreat in the Pacific Northwest. there's no love lost. That's promising. Claire (played pretty winningly by Trisha Todd) is a writer; Noel is Dr. Noel Benedict, shrink and author of Hite-like sex books. She's blond, she's dark-haired; she's promiscuous, she's pent-up and chilly; she's straight, well, bi-, well ... , she's an out lesbian. You see where this is heading. On the way, there's a lot of thwarted desire (just the way we like it) and far too much chatter.

The self-distributed *Claire* has been wowing them at the box offices throughout the country and may, ironically, lead to more interest in lesbian feature films. More power to the filmmakers, I say. Still, will the first question we gals ask after that rare lesbian flick always be, "Was it good for you?" Do lesbian films have to keep reinventing the wheel, trapped on the spokes of yet another coming-out saga? How 'bout sex and a *real* plot? There's too much that's just plain tacky here. That all the women are white, well, think Southampton in August with a gaggle of therapists. All this said, if you go see *Claire* and see it not necessarily on its own terms but as high camp sans humor, it'll probably be good for you.

Also reviewed in:
NEW YORK TIMES, 4/16/93, p. C11, Janet Maslin
VARIETY, 10/26/92, p. 68, Daniel M. Kimmel

CLIFFHANGER

A TriStar Pictures release of a Carolco/Le Studio Canal+/Pioneer production in association with RCS Video. *Executive Producer:* Mario Kasser and Lynwood Spinks. *Producer:* Alan Marshall, Renny Harlin, Gene Patrick Hines, James R. Zatolokin, and David Rotman. *Director:* Renny Harlin. *Screenplay:* Michael France and Sylvester Stallone. *Story:* Michael France. *Based on a premise by:* John Long. *Director of Photography:* Alex Thomson. *Editor:* Frank J. Urioste. *Music:* Tevor Jones. *Music Editor:* Dan Carlin, Sr.. *Sound:* Tim Cooney and (music) John Richards. *Sound Editor:* Wylie Stateman, Gregg Baxter, Robert Batha, and Greg Plotts. *Casting:* Mindy Martin. *Production Designer:* John Vallone. *Art Director:* Aurelio Crugnola and Christiaan Wagener. *Set Decorator:* Bob Gould. *Set Dresser:* Alessandro Gentili. *Special Effects:* John Richardson, Larry Cavanaugh, and Giovanni Corridori. *Visual Effects:* Pamela Easley. *Costumes:* Ellen Mirojnick. *Make-up:* Jeff Dawn. *Make-up (Sylvester Stallone):* Gary Liddiard. *Stunt Coordinator:* Joel Kramer. *Running time:* 118 minutes. *MPAA Rating:* R.

CAST: Sylvester Stallone (Gabe Walker); John Lithgow (Eric Qualen); Michael Rooker (Hal Tucker); Janine Turner (Jessie Dieghan); Rex Linn (Travers); Caroline Goodall (Kristel); Leon (Kynette); Craig Fairbrass (Delmar); Gregory Scott Cummins (Ryan); Denis Forest (Heldon); Michelle Joyner (Sarah); Max Perlich (Evan); Paul Winfield (Walter Wright); Ralph Waite (Frank); Trey Brownell (Brett); Zach Grenier (Davis); Vyto Ruginis (Matheson); Don Davis (Stuart); Scott Hoxby (Agent Hayes); John Finn (Agent Michaels); Bruce McGill (Treasury Agent); Rosemary Dunsmore (Treasury Secretary); Kim Robillard (Treasury Jet Pilot); Jeff McCarthy (Pilot); Mike Weis (Co-Pilot); Duncan Prentice (Treasury Helicopter Pilot); Kevin Donald (Ray); Jeff Blynn (Marvin); Thor (Thor).

LOS ANGELES TIMES, 5/28/93, Calendar/p. 1, Kenneth Turan

Someday they'll make an action picture that manages to do without a plot. Someday they'll figure out how to squeeze so much mayhem into two hours that it won't matter who is doing what to whom. But for now, no matter how spectacular the stunts are, they still have to be connected to a scenario, and as long as that's the case, films like "Cliffhanger" are going to continue to fall short.

Make no mistake, the high-flying stunts in director Renny Harlin's film are definitely state of the art, and while they're going on, the film works up a serious level of excitement. But as soon as the action stops and the inevitable talking begins, "Cliffhanger" falls to earth with a considerable thud.

Though director Harlin has claimed, presumably with a straight face, that he took this project on because it would give him "more in terms of character and relationships" than his previous "Die Hard 2," and despite a rather involved writing credit (screenplay by Michael France and Sylvester Stallone and a screen story by Michael France based on a premise by John Long), "Cliffhanger" has the kind of dramatic texture that would look undernourished in a comic book.

Stallone, obviously, did more than take a pencil to the film's inconsequential script, he also stars as Gabe Walker, mainstay of the Rocky Mountain Rescue Team, specialists in helping those stranded in the unforgiving snows of Colorado.

After a challenging on-site experience that is perhaps "Cliffhanger's" best sequence (so don't come late), Gabe decides the mountains are no longer for him. He wants his sweetheart and fellow rescuer Jessie Deighan (Janine Turner, veteran of TV's equally snow-bound "Northern Exposure") to leave as well, but she thinks that's an offer she can refuse.

While Jessie and Gabe exchange insights about the vagaries of human behavior, "Cliffhanger's" other plot shoe drops. A Treasury jet carrying exactly $100 million is attacked by hijackers, and soon the cases of money as well as the plane come crashing down right in Jessie and Gabe's neck of the woods.

Eric Qualen (John Lithgow), the oh-so-evil genius who heads the hijack crew, decides he needs professional help locating the $100 million, not to mention getting back to town. And, quicker than Jack Frost, Jessie, Gabe and teammate Hal Tucker ("Henry: Portrait of a Serial Killer's" Michael Rooker) all end up on top of the mountain going toe to toe with the desperadoes.

Tucker is initially introduced as a character who bears a fearsome grudge against Gabe (could this have been the "more in terms of character and relationships" that Harlin was talking about?). But once the action gets started, that enmity all but disappears, as does any chance of memorable acting from anyone. Even Lithgow, whose bravura villain role in Jim McBride's made-for-Showtime "The Wrong Man" was one of the delights of the Cannes Film Festival, can only do so much with a plot that seems to have been written for Alan Rickman.

Seeing "Cliffhanger" also underscores what an act of sheer will it has been for Stallone to turn himself into an international action star. His career-making role in the original "Rocky" is still his best work, and its mixture of light action and pathos remains his most successful acting path. Despite having bulked himself up into the appropriate body, Stallone tends to come off as awkward when he does battle, betrayed by a face that seems more sad and sensitive than believably heroic.

Another problem for Stallone, as well as "Cliffhanger's" most offensive aspect, is the way he insists on playing average guy Gabe as if he's more invulnerable than the Terminator. Both Gabe and Hal receive horrendous beatings from the bad guys that are extended well beyond the point of sadism, beatings of a ferocity that would kill almost anyone, yet they survive with hardly a noticeable aftereffect. It is not a pretty picture and, if there was any sense in the ratings system, it would earn this picture an NC-17 instead of its timid R (for violence and language).

If you can survive those beatings and the exposition doesn't excessively bore you, the beauty of the Italian Alps' Dolomite range (which doubled for Colorado in Alex Thomson's crisp photography) and those action sequences (including dizzying climbing and some exceptional midair antics, which are not sadistic) all function as advertised. "Cliffhanger" no doubt makes for a great coming attraction, but as a two-hour movie its claims are much more problematic.

NEW YORK, 6/14/93, p. 65, David Denby

At the beginning of *Cliffhanger*, as Sylvester Stallone was clinging to the underside of an obliquely angled cliff—just swinging back and forth, having a ball—I thought to myself, It's time take up knitting. I could do sweaters, perhaps, or scarves, or even baby booties. Anything that can be produced at home. *Cliffhanger*, I have no doubt, will create a generation of couch-hangers. This is not a movie about the exhilaration of adventure; it's a movie about the pain of adventure.

In two hours of violently nasty thrills, all staged on peaks, Stallone fights gravity, avalanches, and helicopters; he fights the cold, bats, infrared goggles, and six of the most meaninglessly vicious thugs ever assembled for a single movie. Compared with them, the stomach-tearing monster in *Alien* was a peach.

Cliffhanger is the summer season all in one film. Now that I've seen it, I feel that I can just skip to the fall and go back to regular movies. The studios fashion the summer-season movies so they have as little narrative complexity and characterization as possible; indeed, in its purest form; a summer movie wants to break free from meaning altogether and ascend into the stratosphere of oxygen-free thrills. *Cliffhanger* is a balloon heading skyward.

Oddly, it starts like a real movie. In the first scene, as Stallone is up there having fun, a young woman crossing a gorge on a cable gets stuck and needs help. Stallone, who is part of a mountain rescue team, leaves a ledge, moves out on the cable, and tries to save her, but she can't hold on and falls to her death. The Finnish director Renny Harlin (*Die Hard 2*) stretches out the scene for suspense and finally for pain. The woman's anguish as she knows she's going to die is terrifying to watch. Her boyfriend (Michael Rooker), another member of the rescue team, sends murderous glances at Stallone, whom he holds responsible for the fatal accident. As for Stallone, he becomes a guilt-stricken, neurotic mess, and can no longer get along with his own girlfriend (Janine Turner), who flies the helicopter for the rescue team. She urges him back into action, telling him that if he doesn't work, "You're going to be stuck on that ledge for the rest of your life."

Heavy stuff: life and love among a Rockies rescue team. But the filmmakers immediately drop everything they've set up. A gang of thieves steals $100 million in cash from a Treasury Department jet (it's a midair theft), and things quickly go wrong. The money, stored in three cases, falls somewhere into the snowy mountains, and then the thieves' plane crashes into a peak. They survive, and try to use the rescue team to recover the money, but our heroes gallantly refuse, fighting the impolite fellows all the way. The thrills begin, and the whole early business about the girl, the anger between the two men, Stallone's neurosis, etc., gets forgotten.

The rivalry between the two men is just a cliché anyway—you know they will eventually need each other—so I can't pretend to mourn its absence. What's funny, however, is the sense one gets that the filmmakers, catching a glimpse of summer-season box office, abruptly broke free of their own screenplay ("The hell with *that* stuff"). Stallone, to my surprise, doesn't interfere with the process of strategic weightlessness. He must have realized that he could save his career by shutting up and becoming a piece of machinery; he doesn't try to express himself or draw on his persona from past movies. Which is a relief. Since it's cold in the mountains, he doesn't take his shirt off either, which is also a relief. He's just a large, densely packed object, stoically receiving punishment, climbing, falling, hanging from ropes, doing whatever is necessary to keep the ball in play. The next-to-last action hero.

Cliffhanger, as you may have gathered, isn't *about* anything, but at least we're not looking at cars smashing through plate-glass windows. The new setting makes the movie feel fresh. Harlin shot *Cliffhanger* in the Dolomites in Italy, draping the action across a variety of terrain—ledges, sheer rock faces, snowy woods at night, a rope bridge, and so many of the snowscapes are quite beautiful. What happens in these lovely mountains isn't even faintly believable, but after a while I realized that none of it was supposed to be. *Cliffhanger*'s physical excess is exactly the point. Harlin takes up the style of exuberant fantasy that Spielberg developed—in the *Indiana Jones* series, only with an added dose of cruelty. For instance: Stallone slides down a mountain astride a villain, punching him all the way, and then, just before they are both about to sweep off a ledge into nowhere, Stallone swings his climbing hook into the ground—*thunk!*—and hangs on to terra firma, while the bad guy goes rushing over the edge. The whole point of this sequence is Michael Rooker's watching the man fall and saying; "Gravity's a bitch."

Cliffhanger just goes on and on, malevolently exciting us with one bash after another. What the villains do is often so crazily mean that it doesn't even help them get the money back. They are mean for kicks, and the heavy jocularity of the violence is dispiriting. I could have done without the two sadists, one African-American, one British, who enjoy beating people to death and who narrate each blow as they deliver it. It's the old schlock-movie formula: The bad guys have to be cruel enough to justify the audience's enjoying their deaths without feeling guilty. On the other hand, I relished John Lithgow, the head of the thieves, who is a great supervillain. A supervillain always has a foreign accent and takes an aesthetic pleasure in violence. He's beyond perversity;

he turns sadism into wit. Alan Rickman played one in *Die Hard*—the obvious successor to all those monsters stroking pussycats in the Bond films. Lithgow's Eric Qualen is, I suppose, British, but Lithgow adds a vaguely Continental spice to the accent. Is the flavor Swiss? Belgian? Schleswig-Holsteinian? Whatever it is, it's consistently hilarious. Lithgow, flashing his great eyeteeth, enjoys himself so much as the swine that one can pull back from the movie—which, after all, is moronic—and ride along with him. Who needs Rickman or Anthony Hopkins? In this range of high-camp viciousness, Lithgow is the American king.

NEW YORK POST, 5/28/93, p. 31, Jami Bernard

Here's a quote they won't be using on the movie ads, even though it's meant in the nicest possible way—"Cliffhanger" is so exciting I felt sick.

No, really. You want action? Suspense? Suspense in the most literal sense, as in seeing actors suspended off the ledges of Olympian-high cliffs? "Cliffhanger" brings it all home in an avalanche of thrills and never-before-seen photography. Maybe some of it is courtesy of the special-effects lab, but you'd barely know it.

Most people would never suspect that rock-climbing could be so heroic.

Much has been made of Sylvester Stallone doing his own stunts, partly to get his action-movie career back on track. Well, that definitely is Stallone hanging by his knuckles from the side of sheer rock faces. The camera starts out tight on his straining muscles, then pulls back slowly—back and back and back—until this Hollywood star is just a speck clinging for his life on the jagged edge of the Dolomite mountain range, where the movie was filmed (It's set in the Rockies.) I wonder how much they insured him for.

One warning; The dialogue is as flat as the mountain peaks are sharp, so don't expect linguistic miracles.

Stallone plays Gabe Walker, a sensitive member of the Rocky Mountain Rescue team, a group of hardy souls who wisecrack their way up and down from tight vertical spaces to bring home errant hikers and hang gliders. They engage in TV weatherman-type happy-talk, partly to calm the people they rescue and partly to set the stage for the movie horrors to come.

"Cliffhanger" opens with a heart-stopping rescue sequence in which Gabe fails to save his best friend's girlfriend. You know she's doomed when she says while being strapped to a cable suspended over infinity, "So we're still on for dinner?" Cancel those reservations, down you go! It's clearly not Gabe's fault, but he's a *sensitive* guy, and he goes into a blue funk. He may never climb another mountain, he may never ford another stream.

Director Renny Harlin ("Die Hard 2") slows the pace a bit to bring in a strange and not wholly cohesive plot about some vicious Treasury Department hijackers who crash in the mountains and lure in the rescue team to help them track their suitcases of money. Gabe is a sucker for a load of plane-crash survivors, so up he goes again and now the action picks up again.

Harlin indulges in an exciting series of you can top this (yes he can) near-misses, in dizzying succession: the hijackers sliding on a wire from one airborne plane to another, then crashing; Gabe on his misguided mission to save them, surviving avalanches, bat caves, cliffside fistfights, icebound lakes, frostbite, an overturned helicopter, exploding bridges, and archvillain John Lithgow in a devilish performance all the more effective for its restraint.

He's up! He's down! He's falling! He's trapped! He's a goner! He's a hurtin'! Sly has never taken so many lumps, nor look so good. His bulging veins seem like they're about to pop off his arms and hit someone in the eye, yet his character isn't a tunnel-visioned idiot like Rambo.

Good supporting work by Michael Rooker as Gabe's former best friend and Ralph Waite as a sympathetic rescue worker give the story a human framework that this visually consuming movie desperately needs. It's true that many of the humans are brought into the movie simply to be tortured and killed, but in the almost non-verbal context of "Cliffhanger," this constitutes a good time.

Janine Turner gets a little too hysterical as Gabe's usually resourceful girlfriend; at least she's just as good a climber as he. Watch the two of them (in this case, their stunt doubles) grapple in tandem off the mountain during an explosion.

More interesting than Turner is Caroline Goodall as a villain with nerves of steel.

The director borrows strategically from Hitchcock—and even Spielberg for some of the compositions of his scenes, but all is forgiven—"Cliffhanger" is an action-photography lover's dream, and the very lifeline Stallone's career needed.

NEWSDAY, 5/28/93, Part II/p. 63, Jack Mathews

The action sequences in Renny Harlin's Rocky Mountain thriller "Cliffhanger" are so how-in-the-hell-did-they-do-that? spectacular that you'll thank star Sylvester Stallone for co-writing the screenplay and keeping it dumb.

There isn't a complex thought, a real person, a believable interaction or a single compelling plot point to get in the way of the eye-popping action on the craggy slopes, cliffs and peaks of its mountain setting. The movie is said to have cost more than $70 million to make, and after getting a load of its stunts, you figure maybe half the budget was spent on accident and life insurance.

In fact, a lot of the most hair-raising sequences were done on sound stages, where Stallone and his co-stars risked no more than sprained ankles and rope burns. But the film moves at such a furious pace there is no time to look for tell-tale signs of optical trickery, even in scenes where climbers are clearly moving in ways that defy gravity.

Nor is there time, thankfully, to ponder characters and situations that might be rejected as too thin to fill out a comic book. "Cliffhanger" is the only movie I recall with screen credits for a premise, a story and a script. One assumes the distinctions are minor.

Stallone plays Gabe Walker, the ace climber of a Rockies rescue team (the mountain footage was actually shot in the Italian Alps), who is drawn out of his melancholy retirement to save his girlfriend (Janine Turner) and an estranged pal (Michael Rooker) from a gang of international killers searching the snowclad summits for briefcases filled with $100 million in stolen cash.

Seems that the thieves, led by the nefarious psychopath Qualen (John Lithgow) and a bad-apple U. S. Treasury agent (Rex Linn), survived a plane crash after a failed mid-air heist, and plan to kill their would-be rescuers as soon as they collect their scattered dough.

But trying to beat the sure-footed Walker to their money is like trying to beat a crow to a dead raccoon, and as the frustration level of the outlaws rises, so does their taste for blood. The body count is miniscule compared to most Stallone films, but the graphic nature of the violence is at the highest peak of the R rating.

This is good guy-bad guy stuff at the extremes. Stallone's Walker is a muscular, sweet-natured Superman whose only weakness is a conscience that grows mopey over missed opportunities for heroism. In the smashing opening sequence, we see Gabe try, unsuccessfully, to save a woman from falling to her death, and eight months later, when the Qualen gang's SOS is heard, he's still punishing himself.

As for Qualen, nobody plays this kind of comic evil with quite the relish of Lithgow, last seen in the dual role of wacko father-and-son child psychologists in Brian DePalma's "Raising Cain," and by the time the actor, working with an overcooked British accent, finishes chewing the scenery, we're amazed to find a tree left standing in the Rockies. The good news is that Stallone and Lithgow aren't the real stars. This is a case where the talent of a director is evident in every scene, from the choreography of the action to the pace of the editing, and the Finnish-born Harlin ("Die Hard 2") may be the best big-budget action filmmaker in Hollywood.

There must be a dozen breathtaking sequences in "Cliffhanger," and even though they occasionally repeat themselves (twice, Gabe has to hang on for dear life after a suspension bridge collapses over a gorge), they're marvels to watch. In one scene, which ranks with the best of the opening sequences of the James Bond series and which was obviously not shot in a studio, a stuntman playing the Treasury agent slides across a cable connecting one airborne jet to another.

This is one summer popcorn movie that you should watch without the popcorn. You might inhale a couple of kernels.

NEWSWEEK, 6/7/93, p. 66, David Ansen

The classic male action movie is boiled down to basics—action and more action—in Renny Harlin's *Cliffhanger*. From the smashing opening, in which rescue climber Gabe Walker (Sylvester Stallone) watches an inexperienced climber slip from his grasp and free-fall to her death, through airplane hijackings, avalanches, chopper crashes and brutal beatings, "Cliffhanger" does its damnedest to see that the audience gets its money's worth of thrills. But for all the-state-of-the-art stunt work, the movie has little personality; it's ice cream without flavor. The Michael France/Stallone screenplay is a compendium of clichés so familiar that the movie itself loses interest in them (will Gabe overcome his guilt and climb again?). The plot involves $100 million in stolen Treasury money that falls into the Rockies from a hijacked plane. An evil Brit (John Lithgow) and his henchmen lure Stallone up the mountain to find their treasure and Sly, his ex-partner (Michael Rooker) and his estranged girlfriend (Janine Turner) must foil their nefarious plot. Harlin is willing to sacrifice everything from characterization to plausibility to keep his movie hurtling from climax to climax. The result is a movie that manages to be simultaneously thrilling and bland.

SIGHT AND SOUND, 7/93, p. 39, Henry Sheehan

The Rocky Mountains. Rescue team members Gabe Walker attempts but fails to save the life of Sarah, the girlfriend of his partner Hal Tucker. Months later, while treasury officials are ferrying millions of dollars in currency, agent Travers hijacks the money and escapes to another plane, where he joins up with master villain Qualen and gang. But their plane is damaged, and the three suitcases containing the money plummet to the mountains below, where they are scattered. The gang's pilot Kristel crash-lands and fakes a distress call, to which Hal responds. He is joined by Gabe, who had disappeared since Sarah's death but returned under the prompting of helicopter pilot Jessie Deighan.

Gabe and Hal reach the criminals and are taken prisoner. Under duress, they lead the gang to the first suitcase. After Gabe has retrieved the money, Qualen orders him killed, but Gabe escapes, emptying the case into a mini-avalanche before escaping. He joins up with Jessie, who's been alerted by a radio communication from Hal. The two beat Qualen and co, now guided by Hal, to the second suitcase. Gabe escapes the gang, and meets Jessie at a cave where they burn the second load of money for heat.

Next morning, the gang encounters two parachuting teenagers; Qualen has one shot, but the other, Evan, escapes. Gang member Kynette ambushes Gabe at a tower while the gang cross a bridge. Rescue team member Frank, who's discovered Evan, flies overhead; the gang kills Frank and takes his helicopter. Travers and Qualen fight for control of the gang; Qualen kills Kristel, so that he will be the group's only pilot. Gabe, killing Kynette in a struggle, begins to cross the bridge, but trips a device which blows it up, and just makes it back to the tower. He and Jessie escape before the tower explodes. Jessie goes in search of Frank's copter while Gabe reaches the third suitcase, attaching its homing device to a rabbit to distract Travers. Jessie, meanwhile, is captured by Qualen, while Hal fights another gang member. Qualen finally meets up with Gabe, who destroys the rest of the money by throwing it into the rotating blades. Gabe and Qualen fight in the copter, which crashes down the mountain, entangled in its own cable. Gabe barely escapes, while Qualen is blown up.

On an obviously appreciable level, *Cliffhanger* is a remarkably entertaining movie and a vindication for director Renny Harlin. Although his *Die Hard 2* was a huge hit, it was also an ungainly film, overstated special effects and stunts sloppily cobbled together. Yet here Harlin displays perfect pitch, not just with the individual scenes of jaw-dropping stunt work, but in the way those episodes flow into each other with varying degrees of intensity. Even Stallone, in the middle of all the leaping, grabbing, slipping and rappeling, gives what is for him a completely unaffected performance, shorn of his usual tics.

So it's also churlish to complain that about one third of the way in *Cliffhanger* slips from the heights at which it starts and settles on a lower plateau where stunts and peaks dominate actions and personality. If the movie hadn't started so well, it might have spared itself this criticism. The first scene, a little masterpiece of action film-making, is set at the top of a towering crag from which the principals must scurry, via a thin cable and thousands of feet over a rocky floor, to a neighboring precipice; spectacular as they are, the vertiginous settings never overwhelm the characterisations.

The latter may lean a bit on action stereotypes, but the film still manages to churn up the old conflict between easy-going hero Gabe and Michael Rooker's stolid second banana Hal, while feisty love interest (Janine Turner) and loyal comic relief (Ralph Waite) look on anxiously. Any more conflict and the opening scene's drama would have been nearly unbearable. As it is, it's a perfect set-up for the oncoming stakes. Similarly, the second scene, a mid-air skyjacking, is fueled by the sudden reversals that begin when a Treasury agent murders his fellow travellers. Harlin pulls the old action filmmaker's trick of getting you to root for a bad guy pulling off an impossible heist. That's why it's so disappointing that, when the two groups link up, the action also descends from edge-of-the-seat excruciating to merely entertaining. The cast—who seem to be doubling for their stunt people—recede ever more into type, a particularly annoying trend when it comes to Lithgow's Qualen.

To its credit, the film never stops giving you plenty to look at, and few of the possibilities offered by the breathless landscape go unmined. Considerable ingenuity is devoted to the way the caches of cash are destroyed. And Michael France's screenplay is scrupulously fair; it may not have all that many cards to play, but they're all face up on the table. So what if the ending follows the logic of an old serial, in which at some moments tremendous amounts of time are given over to physical feats, while other similarly adventurous tasks are covered with some convenient ending? The title, after all, evokes the predicaments that serial heroes spent seven days of the week trying to escape and from which on Saturday afternoon they slipped effortlessly. Perhaps that old-time innocence is the best thing *Cliffhanger* has to offer.

TIME, 6/7/93, p. 68, Richard Schickel

You worry about Sylvester Stallone. For most of *Cliffhanger* he runs around in a T shirt atop a mountain range in the snow. The absence of parka and mittens is, of course, dictated by the desire to show off his huge, ever straining biceps. Still, you hate to see a guy risking pneumonia for his art, so it's a relief when, a couple of shots after he he's fought a subsidiary bad guy in an icy tarn, his shirt is shown to be miraculously dry.

But we are not at *Cliffhanger* for realism; we're there for the cliffhanging, and there's plenty of it. What gets Stallone up on the rocks is a rescue call from a downed private jet whose passengers are a vicious gang of thieves led by John Lithgow. They've just screwed up the hijacking of another plane carrying $100 million in thousand-dollar bills, which are now scattered all over the dangerous landscape. So Sly and his friends have to worry about psychotically wielded weapons as well as their foot-and handholds. This makes for reasonably good fun. Director Harlin's only large mistake is staging the several violent deaths too authentically. They momentarily mar the highspeed implausibility of a movie that, like his *Die Hard 2*, agreeably combines the edgy and the genial.

VILLAGE VOICE, 6/8/93, p. 60, Gary Indiana

Cliffhanger is a much less convoluted romp through the peaks and abysses of a Hollywood script conference [the reference is to *Sliver*]: Sylvester Stallone, looking more and more like Rock Hudson in *Written on the Wind* albeit slack-lipped and ape-jawed—and Michael Rooker, looking and sounding less and less like Henry the Serial Killer, are tricked into guiding a hilariously evil gang led by John Lithgow through the storm-pestered Rockies in search of $100 million the gang has skyjacked from a Treasury Department airplane but lost because of a midair fuckup.

The background story is that Gabe Walker (Stallone), a year before, flubbed the rescue of Hal Tucker's (Rooker's) girlfriend, who dropped, to her death. Gabe left the area with Hal still blaming him for what's-her-name's fall. Then Gabe comes back to the Rockies, not to stay, but to ask his girlfriend, Jessie (Janine Turner, of *Northern Exposure*), to leave with him. She refuses. As he prepares to leave by himself, Jessie gets a distress call from a group of stranded hikers—actually, the evil gang—and asks Gabe to help in the rescue. Gabe refuses, but a few minutes later has second thoughts, and soon encounters the still-embittered-over-what's-her-name's-death Hal on a small ledge. They struggle. Gabe tells Hal to go ahead and push him off. Hal grumbles, "Naw, you live with it."

Pretty quickly, of course, they are both in mortal danger and each risking his life for the other. Gabe gets separated from the gang, and teams up with Jessie to thwart the villains and save Hal.

It all sounds fairly stupid on paper, but director Renny Harlin is a masterful translator of shit into brilliance. Pure escape, *Cliffhanger* has adrenalin pumping through every frame, and if you have vertigo, it's even more delirious. Everything is shot at a tilted, scarifying altitude, or looks that way. The characters are often seen clinging to little rock outcroppings by their fingernails. The geography of the film is completely unknowable, like the tunnel system in *Alien³*.

There isn't much depth to the characters (though even the kindly old rescue pilot is more complex than anyone in *Sliver*). But it is, as Stallone the scriptwriter claims, a tale of redemption. Because just near the end, Gabe has to relive that horrible moment, this time with Jessie his own girlfriend slipping out of his grasp, clinging to him for dear life, wearing the same type of glove, even ... and ...

Okay, the redemption part is corny. The real fun is watching Lithgow sneer as decent people are killed, wasting his own closest confederate simply to eliminate the number of available helicopter pilots, and telling Michael Rooker: "You'd like to kill me, wouldn't you? Well, take a number and get in line."

Also reviewed in:
CHICAGO TRIBUNE, 5/28/93, Friday/p. A, Dave Kehr
NEW YORK TIMES, 5/28/93, p. C1, Janet Maslin
NEW YORKER, 6/21/93, p. 96, Anthony Lane
VARIETY, 5/24/93, p. 44, Todd McCarthy
WASHINGTON POST, 5/28/93, p. G1, Rita Kempley
WASHINGTON POST, 5/28/93, Weekend/p. 42, Desson Howe

COMBINATION PLATTER

An Arrow release of a Bluehorse Films Inc. production. *Executive Producer:* Jenny Lee and Man Fuk Chan.   *Producer:* Judy Moy, Tony Chan, and Ulla Zwicker.   *Director:* Tony Chan. *Screenplay (English, Mandarin and Cantonese with English subtitles):* Edwin Baker and Tony Chan. *Director of Photography:* Yoshifumi Hosoya. *Editor:* Tony Chan and James Y. Kwei. *Music:* Brian Tibbs.   *Sound:* Bob Taz.   *Casting:* Amanda Ma.   *Art Director:* Pat Summa. *Running time:* 84 minutes. *MPAA Rating:* Not Rated.

CAST: Jeff Lau (Robert); Coleen O'Brien (Claire); Lester ("Chit Man") Chan (Sam); Colin Mitchell (Benny); Kenneth Lu (Andy); Thomas K. Hsiung (Mr. Lee); Eleanora Khilberg (Noriko); James DuMont (James); Ellen Synn (Jennie).

LOS ANGELES TIMES, 2/16/94, Calendar/p. 3, Kevin Thomas

With humor and poignancy, Tony Chan's "Combination Platter" pulls us into the challenging and uncertain everyday life of an illegal immigrant. It's a gritty but warm low-budget film of deceptive simplicity. A first-time director, Chan hasn't much sense of rhythm, and sometimes a feeling of self-consciousness creeps into routine exchanges between people. These aspects of the film matter little, however, in the light of all that Chan accomplishes. Few films explore so thoroughly the role of cultural identity in creating unconscious racism—and with such a subtle, light touch.

Chan's wistful hero, Robert (Jeff Lau, a formidably low-key actor), is a sort of Asian Lyle Lovett, a homely but earnest and likable young man working as a waiter in a Chinese restaurant in Flushing, Queens, which has become New York's second Chinatown. He works hard and unobtrusively, dutifully sending money to his parents in Hong Kong. His main concern is obtaining the all-important green card. His sympathetic employer (Thomas K. Hsiung) feels business is too slow for him to absorb the tax penalties of sponsoring Robert, and even if he were to do so, it would take Robert five years to get his card. Naturally, Robert would like to speed up the process, enabling him to bring his parents to America, but the only way to accomplish this is to marry an American citizen.

When a glamorous Chinese American woman ups her price from $25,000 to $50,000 to marry Robert for convenience, he eventually allows his friend Andy (Kenneth Lu) to set him up with a white woman, the plain but vivacious Claire (Colleen O'Brien). Robert and Claire seem to be a realistic match, but "Combination Platter" unexpectedly turns out not to be a contemporary "Marty" after all. Chan shows Robert and Claire's relationship to be but a part—and a subsidiary one at that—of Robert's life.

Most of the film, in fact, takes place in the restaurant, which gives "Combination Platter" its broad perspective. In his choice of key locale, Chan, whose parents own the actual restaurant in the film, is able to break through the monolithic view whites so often have of Chinese people.

Within the restaurant's staff there is a language barrier between those Chinese who speak only Cantonese and those who speak only Mandarin. Then there's the owner's pretty American-born niece Jennie (Ellen Synn), the restaurant's cashier, who knows neither dialect—and eats Chinese food with a fork instead of chopsticks; she complains good-naturedly that the "Chinese think of me as American, and the Americans think of me as Chinese." (Perhaps because it's a view from within, Chan is awfully hard on the restaurant's white patrons; didn't Chan's parents ever have any polite or pleasant white patrons?)

Ironically, Jennie's unfamiliarity with her ancestral language puts her in a situation similar to that of the restaurant's only white employee (Colin Mitchell), who's razzed by his friends for working in a Chinese restaurant in the first place. All these observations, which are alternately played comically and seriously, provide a crucial, invaluable context for Robert's revealing remark about his feelings for Claire: "If only she weren't American. ..."

At once Chan is able to create suspense—will the relationship go anywhere? Will Claire be hurt?—and to suggest how those so often the targets of racism can be susceptible to it themselves, albeit innocently. And in dealing with the plight of the illegal immigrant, Peter Weir's "Green Card" was a delightful romantic comedy but in comparison, "Combination Platter" comes across as the genuine article.

NEW YORK POST, 11/3/93, p. 36, Thelma Adams

"Combination Platter" is a slight, good-natured independent feature set in Flushing's Chinatown.

Newcomer Jeff Lau stars as Robert, an illegal immigrant from Hong Kong who waits tables at the Szechuan Inn. Through his eyes, we get a look at the relations among Asians, Asian-Americans and non-Asians in a pocket of New York where conflicts arise over whether one speaks Mandarin or Cantonese, much less English.

First-time director Tony Chan (who also produced and co-wrote the script) knows his territory. His primary location was his parents' restaurant. Working with a $250,000 budget, he shot from 10 p.m. to 10 a.m. After the restaurant closed. In 24 days, the movie was in the can.

The result is choppy, but appealing. Robert, the innocent abroad, has a single goal: to get his green card. The movie opens with him negotiating a marriage-of-convenience with a hip Asian-American. When she ups the bribe from $25,000 to $50,000, the deal goes sour. He begins to date a Caucasian but, before long, their friendship sours.

The movie's climax comes when the Immigration and Naturalization Service raids the Szechuan Inn. The white agents look like something out of "Dragnet," but as Robert scurries around the basement in search of a hiding place, our hearts race. Two beefy agents cuff the dishwasher and we realize how tenuous Robert's position really is. All his dreams of prosperity, his ability to send money home to his parents in Hong Kong, hinge on one thing—a green card. Love is a luxury Robert can't afford.

The acting is acceptable. Jeff Lau, a stockbroker by day, won't be leaving his day job soon. Lester Chan delivers the most arresting performance as an arrogant waiter who relishes saying nasty things in Chinese to those who don't understand. If you've ever wondered what your waiter said about you after he returned to the kitchen, you might discover you don't want to know.

In an otherwise tame movie, Chan takes one risk. In the end, nothing is settled. Robert gets neither the girl nor the green card, he's just a little less green himself. It rings true—that's the simple beauty of this film.

NEWSDAY, 11/3/93, Part II/p. 101, John Anderson

Despite being produced on a virtual shoestring, "Combination Platter" is just what it should be: Small, spare and straightforward in its account of a Chinese immigrant's wrestling match with America, and wildly ambitious in its attempt to illuminate some basic and perhaps unpleasant truths.

These include man's uncanny ability to find someone to look down on, even when he's got nowhere to go but up. In the Chinese restaurant where Robert (Jeff Lau) works (Tony Chan filmed in his parent's Flushing restaurant, which saved on catering) and where the threat of an Immigration Services raid is always very real, we find a messy microcosm of life. The waiters are all from Hong Kong—their education and fluency in English gets them the better jobs—while the kitchen help is mainland Chinese. The tension between the two groups is as thick as the egg drop soup and is intensified by their inability to communicate because of differing dialects.

Robert, who offends no one, has his own biases to deal with. Desperately in need of a green card, he agrees to the counterfeit marriage his friend Andy (Kenneth Lu) has arranged with a Chinese-American woman—who tries to extort more money out of Robert than he has. The deal off, and feeling his luck is running out, Robert reluctantly dates Claire (Colleen O'Brien), a Caucasian woman whose name he can't pronounce and who is unaware of Robert's plight. Robert, at the same time, is ill at ease at the idea of dating, to say nothing of marrying, a white woman.

Poisoning the restaurant's atmosphere is Sam (Lester [Chit Man] Chan), the most Americanized of the waiters, who not only vents his contempt for the kitchen staff and constantly insults the white bus boy Benny (Colin Mitchell) in Cantonese, but is also losing heavy money to his bookie and stealing tips.

But while Sam represents a cross-cultural miscarriage, the anxieties director Chan is exploring are really embodied in Jennie (Ellen Synn), the Chinese-American niece of the restaurant's owner, Mr. Lee (Thomas K. Hsiung). The Chinese treat her like an American, she says, Americans treat her as a Chinese. Unlike the illegals her uncle employs, she's a woman with a country, but without a culture. Whether her plight is any better than theirs is something Chan lets us think about. And whether all Americans aren't in the same boat is something we have to think about.

The acting is uniformly good, especially that of Lau. Robert is determined and hardworking, but ultimately sad. He wants things to be different, but you sense he wants to be different, too. When he watches two of the restaurant's regulars—a white American and his Asian date—his reaction is a mix of fascination and loathing, both at the situation and himself.

VILLAGE VOICE, 10/26/93, p. 62, Manohla Dargis

Set in the quiet hum of the Szechuan Inn, in the hectic clamor of Flushing, Queens, Tony Chan's *Combination Platter* is an adventure of the most unlikely kind, a quotidian epic of immigration, assimilation, labor, and romance.

Robert (Jeff Lau), a recent Hong Kong arrival and Inn waiter, is pursuing his green card with all-consuming passion and little luck. There's a marriage prospect who doubles her price, an employer sponsorship that fades from view. In desperation, the hapless, earnest Robert even turns to a boorish and lonely, woman for that flash of green, only to find his own decency an awkward liability.

Aside from cops, detectives, psychotherapists, and the occasional nanny, movie-made America is strangely idle; most screen people simply don't work. In *Combination Platter* they do very little else. Food is cooked, tables cleared, patrons stroked (waiter: "that's a really great story"). There are fights in the kitchen, and small, awkward gestures of hope in the dealings between tribes—Asian and Caucasian, Cantonese and Mandarin, American Born Chinese (ABC) and those Fresh Off the Boat (FOB).

A Sundance discovery, *Combination Platter* is a debut as winning as it is original. Thoughtfully directed (the 24-year-old Chan also cowrote the screenplay) and artlessly acted (newcomer Lau is terrific), it has the expressive face of "real" life but without the deadly downtime. Day folds into night effortlessly, the routine of labor working a quiet counter-point to Robert's anxious quest. As if to compensate for his hero's lack of English, Chan tends to settle in on the details of everyday life, holding its small moments like gifts. Moments that are modest in a film that is anything but.

Also reviewed in:
CHICAGO TRIBUNE, 2/4/94, Friday/p. M, John Petrakis
NATION, 12/13/93, p. 744, Stuart Klawans
NEW YORK TIMES, 11/4/93, p. C22, Janet Maslin
VARIETY, 2/8/93, p. 76, Emanuel Levy
WASHINGTON POST, 1/21/94, p. G6, David Mills

CONEHEADS

A Paramount Pictures release. *Executive Producer:* Michael Rachmil. *Producer:* Lorne Michaels. *Director:* Steve Barron. *Screenplay:* Tom Davis, Dan Aykroyd, Bonnie Turner, and Terry Turner. *Director of Photography:* Frances Kenny. *Editor:* Paul Trejo. *Music:* David Newman. *Casting:* Lora Kennedy. *Production Designer:* Gregg Fonseca. *Art Director:* Bruce Miller. *Set Decorator:* Jay Hart. *Costumes:* Marie France. *Make-up (Coneheads):* David B. Miller and Marie France. *Stunt Coordinator:* Fred Lerner. *Running time:* 87 minutes. *MPAA Rating:* PG.

CAST: Robert Knott (Air Traffic Controller); Jonathan Penner (Captain Air Traffic); Whip Hubley (F-16 Pilot); Dan Aykroyd (Beldar); Howard Napper (Ang Pilot); Jane Curtin (Prymaat); Michael Richards (Motel Clerk); Eddie Griffin (Customer); Sinbad (Otto); Phil Hartman (Marlax); Adam Sandler (Carmine); Grant Martell (Hispanic Man #1); Art Bonilla (Hispanic Man #2); David Spade (Turnbull); Rosa Briz (Hispanic Woman); Michael McKean (Seedling); Cooper Layne (Engineer); Sarah Levy (Hygienist); Drew Carey (Taxi Passenger); Shishir Kurup (Khoudri); Jon Lovitz (Dentist); Sydney Coberly (Nurse); Barry Kivel (Doctor); Terry Turner (Sketch Artist); McNally Sagal (Female Agent); Richard M. Comar (Agent); Nicolette Harnish (Connie, 10 years old); Jason Alexander (Larry Farber); Lisa Jane Persky (Lisa Farber); Michelle Burke (Connie); Joey Adams (Christina); Parker Posey (Stephanie); Chris Farley (Ronnie); Kevin Nealon (Senator); Jan Hooks (Gladys Johnson); Julia Sweeney (Principal); Ellen Degeneres (Coach); Walt Robles (Fire Marshall); Todd Susman (Ron); James Keane (Harv); Sam Freed (Master of Ceremonies); Garrett Morris (Captain Orecruiser); Tom Davis (Supplicant); Dave Thomas (Highmaster); Peter Aykroyd (Highmaster Mentot); Laraine Newman (Laarta); Nils Allen Stewart (Guard); Tim Meadows (Athletic Cone); Mitchell Bobrow (Garthok Combatant); Laurence Bilzerian (Cone Battle Commander); Topper Lilien (Cone Pilot).

CHRISTIAN SCIENCE MONITOR, 8/12/93, p. 11, Marilynne S. Mason

[*Coneheads* was reviewed jointly with *So I Married an Axe Murderer;* see Mason's review of that film.]

LOS ANGELES TIMES, 7/23/93, Calendar/p. 1, Peter Rainer

Family values have rarely looked better than they do in "Coneheads".

Beldar (Dan Aykroyd), wife Prymaat (Jane Curtin) and 16-year-old daughter Connie (Michelle Burke) are probably the most normal and upstanding characters in the movies right now. Sure, Beldar was sent on a mission to conquer Earth, but that was then and this is now. After a detour to the suburban haven of Paramus, N.J., Beldar and Prymaat have settled into manicured-lawn America and raised their daughter with tender loving care. They may not have green cards but Beldar works hard running his Meepzor Precision Discount Driving School and Prymaat scours the supermarkets to keep the family stocked with mass quantities.

The first of 11 Conehead sketches showed up on "Saturday Night Live" in 1976. (Laraine Newman, who is given a cameo in "Coneheads," played Connie.) If you thought those sketches were a one-note joke that couldn't possibly transfer to a feature-length film, you're only half-right. The joke is essentially one-note, but the filmmakers get a lot of music from the reverbs. Director Steve Barron and screenwriters Aykroyd, Tom Davis, Bonnie Turner and Terry Turner don't trot out the Coneheads like relics from the Comedy Hall of Fame. What was funny about them in 1976 is still funny—it's as if they had never gone away.

Beldar and Prymaat are as robotically contrapuntal as ever, their speech patterns as programmatic and flat-toned. (Connie, who grew up in suburbia, speaks and moves like a normal Earthling—it's a parody of how first-generation children break away from their immigrant parents.) The fun in watching Beldar and Prymaat is that, for all their clipped movements and computerese, they're incongruously, intensely human. Watching them, we have the same fun that we have when we try to discern the humanness of Mr. Spock and the other Vulcans on "Star Trek."

Aykroyd and Curtin haven't lost a whit of wit since they first played these roles. They go very deep into the nuttiness, but without camping it up or winking at the audience. What comes through in their performances is an improbable, almost romantic affection for their characters, and that affection sets the tone for the whole movie (rated PG for comic nudity and some double-entendre humor). It's an unusually companionable jape; in this world it makes perfect sense that the Coneheads' friends and neighbors never really register that there's anything terribly different about them. They're all-American eccentrics—even if they happen to come from the planet Remulak.

Aykroyd has always had a genius for playing obsessed characters locked in by their own loopy rigor; this is the quality that links all his best riffs, from his Vegematic salesman to his Tom Snyder and Richard Nixon. Beldar is so rigorous he's (literally) otherworldly, but Aykroyd shows us his furtive, giggly side, his faint ache to be human. When he plays golf with his neighbor (Jason Alexander), he gets a secret thrill from his prowess; as the auto driving instructor to a desperately amorous woman (Jan Hooks), he's blank to her advances but the flattery makes his eyes shine. ("There's a sadness to your wisdom," she tells him as she exits the car.) When Prymaat gets wind of her competition she gamely buys up every supermarket women's magazine for advice on how to hold her man, and then Curtin has her finest moment. She shows us the lovestruck Prymaat in a desperate full-out seduction scene that's so crazily far-out it's poignant. She even dons a wig for the occasion. (She looks much more beautiful without it.)

As Connie, Michelle Burke has a lovely presence. Her cone only seems to add to her beauty. It's no surprise that her burbly suitor, Ronnie (Chris Farley), with his massive body tics and sweaty exasperations, falls for her in a big way. (He's willing to fly back to Remulak with her.) Farley is such an amazing physical comic that every heave of his shoulders and snap of his neck seems to draw on an entire personal history.

Throughout "Coneheads" a steady parade of wildly gifted comics, mostly from "Saturday Night Live," turn up for quick cameos, After awhile, you begin to wait eagerly for them—it's like the boomer's version of the star walk-ons in "Around the World in 80 Days." Besides Hooks and Newman, the list includes Kevin Nealon, Adam Sandler, Phil Hartman, Dave Thomas, Sinbad, Julia Sweeney and Garrett Morris.

Michael McKean has an extended bit as an INS agent hell-bent on deporting the Coneheads—his Earthling's obsessiveness is as robotic in its own way as Beldar's—and David Spade, in a great turn, is his unctuous assistant. (He has a classic moment when, deported to Remulak, he suddenly recognizes a way to slime his way into the Highmaster's good graces.) Jon Lovitz has the best moment of all, playing a dentist faced with the prospect of capping Beldar's teeth—all three rows of them.

"Coneheads" doesn't always make the most of its material. Some of it is a bit too family-entertainment squishy. (On TV, Beldar used to smoke an entire pack of cigarettes—all at once.) The Conespeak exchanges between Beldar and Prymaat are marvelous concoctions—as marvelous in their own way as the newspeak Anthony Burgess invented for "A Clockwork Orange"—but there should be more of them. You can't beat this film for demented heart-tugs though. When Prymaat looks at a big pile of cone-like eggplants in the supermarket and lets out a momentary shriek of horror, you know you're watching nutbrain perfection.

NEW YORK, 8/9/93, p. 76, David Denby

TV skit humor is the guerrilla warfare of entertainment. What you get in a skit—an outrageous collision of attitudes, a sudden flare-up of personality—produces a quick, rude projection of a comic idea. But when repeated and repeated, the idea turns into an assault. The *Saturday Night Live* people have given us great times on television, but in the past the movies made from skit materials developed there have been oppressive. After a decent beginning, *The Blues Brothers* became gross and desperate and finally degenerated into car-chase gags, and *Wayne's World* was altogether hateful—unbearable as much for its cramped repetitiveness as for its "ironic" pretend slob humor, which turned out to be genuine slob humor.

Well, so much for theory, because *Coneheads*, which shouldn't work as a movie, works just fine. Lorne Michaels produced it, and Dan Aykroyd and Tom Davis had a hand in writing it (along with Bonnie and Terry Turner), so the origins in mid-seventies *SNL* material have been preserved. Indeed, not much has been added. The idea, I suppose, has been merely padded out, but the result nevertheless is a very pleasant, goofy movie, consistently funny, likable, and even good-hearted. I thought I had grown tired of them, but there they are again, Beldar (Aykroyd) and Prymaat (Jane Curtin), pink, vaulted, humanoid creatures from the planet Remulak, forced to live on Earth after their spacecraft makes an emergency splashdown in the East River. The movie begins with the landing and presents a kind of struggling-immigrant story—an immigrant story set in a seemingly less truculent America than the present one. No radio-talk-show host jeers at them; no one even notices that they're a bit odd. They fit right in with the Sikh taxi drivers (Beldar wears a turban on his cone when he drives).

Superior beings from a totalitarian planet, they either stand too close to people or bustle about ceremoniously, like fussy courtiers in old movies, and they speak in their adenoidal monotones a weird kind of Remu-English, so bizarrely functional ("metallic-tender disks" for coins) that it's almost poetry.

The joke, of course, is that instead of conquering the Earth, they are conquered by it, and especially by American banality, which suits them just fine. Despite their advanced skills (fixing machine parts, eating ten waffles at once), they become entirely middle-class. Happily, they burrow into a suburban tract house in Paramus, play golf at the local club, and conservatively raise their daughter, Connie (Michelle Burke), a nice, pretty girl in American-flag jeans who just wants to date and go to the mall.

Like many American middle-class couples, they fade into a kind of sodden contentment. Beldar wears plaid jackets and puts on weight, while Prymaat, who has a tendency to primness, like someone's aunt, sticks to the shopping and cooking; her only worry is that Beldar might be losing interest in her cone. An overzealous INS agent (Michael McKean) wants to send them back whence they came, but everyone else accepts them. And why not? The Coneheads are very eager to make things go right. They are conformists in an age in which many people lack the economic security to conform. The closest thing to a satiric idea in the movie is the notion that most Americans wouldn't recognize outer-space creatures if the creatures dressed badly enough.

The large-scale production allows the director, Steve Barron (*Teenage Mutant Ninja Turtles*), to make fun of science-fiction conventions and to stage a few scenes on Remulak itself, which turns out to look like an immense grotto in a Hawaiian resort hotel. Yet the size of the production never overwhelms the affectionate comic tone. This is a *domestic* comedy; that's its charm, and that's also why the skit material still works—it hasn't been blown up to fit someone's notion of the big screen. In one of the loveliest sequences, we see some crudely shot home movies of the childhood of Connie Conehead, and the jokes just whiz by—for instance, a beach sand castle in the shape of a cone—without emphasis or explanation. Barron, who is British and has directed a great many music videos as well as *Ninja Turtles*, trusts the audience enough to keep the comedy genial and deadpan.

The actors, many of them from past and current incarnations of *SNL*, slip easily into limited roles and don't overplay the hand that's been dealt them. Michael McKean, who should get better movie parts after this performance, manages to do a stock comic bit—a madly ambitious bureaucrat—with a nasty hysteria that is funnier for remaining three quarters hidden. And diminutive David Spade, as his sycophantic assistant, lodges himself somewhere under McKean's shoulder and sends up a nonstop stream of assurance and compliments. (We could all use a Spade to get us through the days.) As Connie's chubby paramour, Chris Farley is a mass of ordinary-guy aggressions covering basic timidity. Farley is very funny relishing his good fortune in having a *date* with a pretty conehead girl.

As the unliberated Prymaat, Jane Curtin does her masklike, Pat Nixon-at-a-bake sale thing, but Aykroyd has never been more expressive. Aykroyd's performance has a rare quality in a big pop movie—at times, his eyes are bursting with anxiety. Partly because of his bulk, age seems to have hit him as a sadness. *Coneheads* is a rather mild and sweet-natured movie—the one true family movie of the year. I hate to say this, but it probably won't be a hit for precisely the reason—its gentleness—that I like it so much.

NEW YORK POST, 7/23/93, p. 27, Michael Medved

Paramount Pictures certainly seems to have jumped onto the family-values bandwagon this year, two of the studio's biggest releases portray strong, loving, traditional nuclear families with parents who are kindly and caring toward their kids at the same time they remain passionately devoted to one another.

As it happens one of these exemplary clans is an assemblage of misfit ghouls (featured in the coming "Addams Family Values") and the other is a trio of ultra-domed aliens from the planet Remulak who are otherwise known as Coneheads.

While Beldar and Prymaat (Dan Aykroyd and Jane Curtin) may never quite pass for Ozzie and Harriet, this movie maintains a surprisingly affectionate attitude toward the suburban ideal the Coneheads so ardently pursue.

After they crash-land their spaceship in the East River these intergalactic visitors begin behaving like any other new immigrants, working hard (in an electronics repair shop, driving a cab and running a driving school) while hoping to gradually blend in to the society around them.

That assimilation process—viewed as wholesome and natural here—is treated with gentle and compassionate humor rather than savage satire. We're actively rooting for Beldar to win the golf trophy he covets, or for his daughter Connie (lovely newcomer Michelle Burke) to get her dream date to the prom.

One of the reasons we end up caring so much about these curious creatures is that Dan Aykroyd who first created the Coneheads (together with writer Tom Davis) during the '76-'77 season of "Saturday Night Live," does such a sensitive and remarkable acting job beneath his heavy makeup and impressive latex cone.

Yes, he gets plenty of laughs out of his nasal mechanical voice and some freakish facial effects, but he never loses sight of the warm-hearted, vulnerable character he's supposed to be playing. It is a great comic performance.

The rest of the cast is similarly solid—especially Michael McKean (of Spinal Tap) and David Spade (of the current SNL crew)—as the villains of the piece. They play smarmy, ambitious bureaucrats at the Immigration and Naturalization Service who will stop at nothing to apprehend and deport the Coneheads.

In the face of an unmistakably rising tide of nativist sentiment in this country, the filmmakers leave no doubt that their own sympathies lie entirely with illegal aliens—of both the international and the interplanetary variety.

Director Steve Barron is something of an alien himself—a capable Brit who has directed more than 100 music videos as well as creating the first installment in the series of Ninja Turtle movies. While that wildly successful independent film showed its low-budget background with some slightly cheesy special effects, the production values in "Coneheads" are first rate.

The story even takes us through the galaxies and onto the surface of Remulak, providing awesome spacecraft, elaborate sets, lavish costumes and hordes of conehead extras in the spirit of old-fashioned, full-blooded, sci-fi filmmaking.

This sequence is visually stunning, but conceptually ill-considered: The vicious world of Remulak is so radically different from the gentle visitors we've come to know that you begin to wonder whether they've landed on the wrong planet by mistake.

Amazingly enough, some of this feels like an old TV skit stretched past the breaking point. It will work just as well for moviegoers who've never seen SNL as it does for diehard fans of the show (who are by the way, treated to some dozen cameo appearances by past and present members of its cast).

In order to preserve its child-suitable PG rating, the picture never shows us Beldars plarg (Conespeak for male genitalia), but it will win its audience by displaying an abundance of heart.

NEWSDAY, 7/23/93, Part II/p. 63, Jack Mathews

The best thing I can say about "Coneheads" is that the time passes much more quickly than you would imagine. It's short, only 82 minutes, but still, listening to Dan Aykroyd and Jane Curtin talk in that tinny, robotic monotone for more than five minutes at a stretch promised hard duty.

The movie version of the recurring "Saturday Night Live" TV sketch plays exactly like a movie version of a sketch. The Coneheads, Beldar (Aykroyd) and Prymaat (Curtin), move off the stage and into the American Heartland (well, New Jersey), where they drive cars (with sunroofs that accommodate their peaked noggins), raise a beautiful, bald daughter (Michelle Burke, in for Larraine Newman), and consume mass quantities enough to cause an up-tick in the economy.

Although Beldar and Prymaat are on assignment to conquer a world for their masters on the planet Remulak, they are just too nice, too content with suburbia, to cause mischief, and Aykroyd and Curtin play them with such gregarious innocence, the whole movie takes on a genial E.T.-esque glow.

The film, unevenly directed by Steve Barron ("Electric Dreams"), puts its faith in the Coneheads' family values. They are like a sitcom family out of the '50s, with Beldar the concerned and occasionally wise father, Prymaat the dutiful McCall's/Redbook housewife, and Connie the spirited, saucily rebellious daughter. Dad plays golf, mom shops, the daughter is a high school cheerleader, diver, and rock and roller. Nobody seems to notice that their heads look like pink eggplants, and that Beldar and Prymaat speak in a dialect of computerese as noticeable as Middle English.

In fact, the only thing that gets them noticed is the fact that Beldar, who job-hops from appliance repairman to cabbie to driving instructor, doesn't have a green card. That puts him on the Most Wanted List of the xenophobic chief (Michael McKean) of the Immigration and Naturalization Service, whose tireless search for the illegal aliens provides the slender thread of a storyline.

"Coneheads" provides a few hearty laughs, the best of them in a scene where Beldar opens his mouth to dentist Jon Lovitz and reveals more rows of teeth than you'll find inside a Ferrari transmission. For each good joke, however, we endure three or four ghastly misfires, and by the last reel, which includes an awkwardly unproductive trip to Remulak and back, the skit is running on fumes.

By the way, beware of Conehead nuts. Some guy showed up at my screening wearing a store-bought, latex conehead. It was partially collapsed and looked more like a reservoir-tip condom, but its silhouette drove me crazy.

NEWSWEEK, 8/2/93, p. 55, Jeff Giles

They're not from around here. *Coneheads* is the story of one immigrant family: Beldar (Dan Aykroyd), Prymaat (Jane Curtin) and their lovely daughter Connie (Michelle Burke). Mr. and Mrs. Conehead leave planet Remulak bent on conquering Earth, but after crash-landing they settle for making it in the suburbs. Dredging up the ancient "Saturday Night Live" skits, director Steve Barron ("Teenage Mutant Ninja Turtles") and producer Lorne Michaels deliver an amiable comedy without a thought in its pointy head.

The makeshift plot hinges on Connie's romance with an earthling auto mechanic (Chris Farley), and the family's attempts to dodge two sleazy immigration officials (Michael McKean and David Spade). The INS refuses to believe that their name is "De Cicco" or that they come from France. At times "Coneheads" seems to be about xenophobia—or the nagging suspicion that one's parents are aliens. Mostly, it's about the Coneheads' souped-up verbiage—"Mebs! We must egress immediately!"—and their goofy cones. Beldar's noggin pokes through his sunroof; Prymaat's idea of foreplay is a little ringtoss.

Born on "SNL" in the late '70s, the Coneheads would no doubt be resting in peace if it weren't for the success of "Wayne's World." A host of past and present "SNL" players appear in cameos, which is a comfort as the movie careens toward a muddled third act full of B-movie sci-fi effects.

The Coneheads implore, "Consume mass quantities," and the filmmakers have come bearing junk food.

VILLAGE VOICE, 8/10/93, p. 58, James Hannaham

If Conan O'Brien really did re-write *Coneheads*, that might explain its resemblance to a two-hour *Simpsons* episode (a good episode, mind you, but remember that duration). The similarity is funny (ha-ha and weird) because while both spring from the myth of the dysfunctional family, Beldar (Dan Aykroyd) and genetomate Prymaat (Jane Curtin) are more enraptured than alienated by American culture. Like Homer et al., they delight in gluttony, specifically "mass quantities" of round textured wheat products smeared with bovine secretions"! (buttered Eggo waffles), and encourage their supersmart daughter Connie (Michelle Burke) to lead a sterile suburban childhood (documented meticulously by many strips of sprocketed celluloid). But they have complete mastery over household appliances—Prymaat's inhalations can top her vacuum cleaner's—are fluent in Remulakian, English (albeit prolix), and French, and are respected by their neighbors. They're slumming, like Zippy the Pinhead, not natural "bluntskulls" like Bart.

Still, the setups seem suspiciously Springfield. While living in a trailer park, they're hunted down by immigration officers, one of whom sucks up to authority Smithers-style (never mind that the INS rarely chases illegals, no matter what planet they're from). Beldar opens a driving school (though he'd make an ideal chemistry professor), buys an assumed identity from a crook—the film even indulges *The Simpsons*'s strange obsession with Indian cab drivers. All of this gets superimposed on the classic immigrant's tale, minus the bias crimes. Of the too many jokes about cranial configuration, only one's an insult. No wonder they assimilate so eagerly.

Also reviewed in:
CHICAGO TRIBUNE, 7/23/93, Friday/p. C, Clifford Terry
NEW YORK TIMES, 7/23/93, p. C3, Janet Maslin
VARIETY, 8/2/93, p. 43, Leonard Klady
WASHINGTON POST, 7/23/93, p. C6, Rita Kempley
WASHINGTON POST, 7/23/93, Weekend/p. 44, Desson Howe

COOL RUNNINGS

A Buena Vista Pictures release of a Walt Disney Pictures film. *Executive Producer:* Christopher Meledandri and Susan B. Landau. *Producer:* Dawn Steel. *Director:* Jon Turteltaub. *Screenplay:* Lynn Siefert, Tommy Swerdlow, and Michael Goldberg. *Story:* Lynn Siefert and Michael Ritchie. *Director of Photography:* Phedon Papamichael. *Editor:* Bruce Green. *Music:* Hans Zimmer. *Music Editor:* Laura Perlman. *Sound:* Larry Sutton and (music) Jay Rifkin. *Sound Editor:* Mark Mangini. *Casting:* Chemin Sylvia Bernard and Jaki Brown-Karman. *Production Designer:* Stephen Marsh. *Art Director:* Rick Roberts. *Set Decorator:* Lesley Beale. *Special Effects:* Bill Orr. *Costumes:* Grania Preston. *Make-up:* Norma Hill Patton. *Stunt Coordinator:* Jacob Rupp. *Running time:* 98 minutes. *MPAA Rating:* PG.

CAST: Leon (Derice Bannock); Doug E. Doug (Sanka Coffie); Rawle D. Lewis (Junior Bevil); Malik Yoba (Yul Brenner); John Candy (Irving Blitzer); Raymond J. Barry (Kurt Hemphill); Peter Outerbridge (Josef Grool); Paul Coeur (Roger); Larry Gilman (Larry); Charles Hyatt (Whitby Bevil, Sr.); Winston Stona (Coolidge); Bertina Macauley (Joy Bannock); Pauline Stone Myrie (Momma Coffie); Kristoffer Cooper (Winston); Bill Dow (Registration Official); Jay Brazeau (Kroychzech); Campbell Lane (Shindler); Matthew Walker (German Official); Christopher Gaze (British Official); Jack Goth (Gremmer); David Lovgren (Swiss Captain); Kerwin Kerr (Boy #1); Deamion Robinson (Boy #2); Beverly Brown (Lady #1); Cyrene Tomlinson (Lady #2); Oliver Hunter (Joseph); Fitz Weir (Uncle Ferte); Teddy Price (Drunk); Charles Harvey (Cop #1); Clive Anderson (Cop #2); Michael London (Heckler); Lloyd Roache (Push Cart Darby Starter); Cheryl Kroeker (Hotel Clerk);

Karyn J. Scott (Line Dancer);   Craig Lehto (Bobsled Starter);   Al Trautwig (Himself);   John Morgan (Himself).

LOS ANGELES TIMES, 10/1/93, Calendar/p. 4, Kevin Thomas

Bobsledding is not exactly the first thing anyone would associate with Jamaica, but it's precisely the unlikeliness of that combination that fuels "Cool Runnings," a sweet-natured, high-spirited comedy, that rare movie that plays effectively to all ages. Even rarer, it celebrates genuine sportsmanship, placing the emphasis back on how the game is played in the face of the winning-is-everything philosophy that permeates every aspect of contemporary life.

"Cool Runnings," which takes its title from a Jamaican slang expression meaning "peaceful journey," was inspired by an actual event, but director Jon Turteltaub—and his several writers have taken liberties so creatively that we're left with the good feeling that if the story didn't exactly happen this way it should have.

Tall, handsome, cheerful but absolutely determined track star Derice Bannock (Leon) has every reason to believe he'll qualify for the Olympic tryouts when fellow competitor Junior Bevil (Rawle D. Lewis) accidentally trips him. Derice's late father, also a track star, had as a friend an American who competed in bobsledding in the 1972 Olympics and today is a low-life Kingston bookie. Never mind that Derice has never seen a bobsled, let alone snow, or that the bookie, Irv (John Candy), is somewhat less than enthused to serve as a coach, putting together a Jamaican bobsledding team to compete in the Winter Olympics in Calgary in 1988.

Produced by Dawn Steel, who has nurtured the project since she was Columbia's head of production, "Cool Runnings" swiftly gets its thoroughly enjoyable show on the road. Derice and Junior are joined by Derice's pal Sanka Coffie (Doug E. Doug), whose Jamaican-style pushcart will be turned into a sled, and the brooding, shaven-headed Yul Brenner (Malik Yoba), a muscular young man with a fierce longing to escape Jamaica and its poverty.

The sledding really gets tough in Calgary, and not just because the temperature is 25 degrees below zero. For reasons the Jamaicans, who are themselves treated as a joke and even subjected to all-out racism, do not yet know, Irv is greeted with more coldness than the weather. "Cool Runnings" has an abundance of opportunities to cheer for the underdog, and it deftly hedges its bets in involving us further in the redemption of the troubled Irv, clearly a man with a past.

It also leaves us with the feeling that Turteltaub hasn't missed a beat or a nuance in bringing an exceptional script to the screen. In these fortuitous circumstances, not only do the four actors playing Jamaicans emerge as engaging, well-nigh irresistible personalities but also Candy, in the pivotal role, couldn't be better in one of the most complex portrayals he's ever created. Irv is as sad as he is funny, but he's also got guts and wit. When the script calls for Irv to do some all-stops-out grandstanding, Candy is your man to get away with it.

For a light-hearted, frequently hilarious film, "Cool Runnings" (rated PG for mild language and brief violence) touches adroitly on such serious matters as national pride, self-respect and endemic poverty. The bobsledding sequences are terrifically exhilarating, but the key moment in this handsome, intelligent film occurs in a quiet time when Irv tells Derice that "If you're not enough without a Gold Medal, you're not enough with it."

NEW YORK POST, 10/1/93, p. 44, Lawrence Cohn

That wacky Jamaican bob-sledding team that enlivened the 1988 Winter Olympics is enshrined in the fun Disney feature "Cool Runnings." It's light entertainment that has a definite motivational value for youngsters.

The film boasts quite a lot of slapstick reminiscent of the old-regime Disney features of the '60s. Mainly U.S. talent Leon, Doug E. Doug, Rawle D. Lewis and Malik Yoba portray the Jamaican athletes who, robbed of a chance to compete in track and field, opt to represent their nation in the cold-weather sport of bobsledding.

Leon is the dedicated, handsome one; Doug plays the comic relief cutup; Rawle is the rich kid defying his father; and Malik, called "Yul Brenner," is the bald tough guy with a warm heart. Their predictable antics as fish out of water in wintry Calgary are handled by director Jon Turteltaub with a nice mix of gags and honest emotion. The four leading actors make a sympathetic team.

Looking like he's put on quite a few pounds, John Candy guest stars winningly as their reluctant coach. Always guaranteeing laughs, Candy's irritable, dark side works very well in creating some dramatic friction with the young leads.

The movie plays true to formula creating the requisite "let's root for these underdogs" attitude for the audience. Producer Dawn Steel has learned her lessons well in the genre of making teens feel good about themselves, practically a house style back in her days at Paramount Pictures.

The climax of the quartet finishing the race at all costs, even though in defeat, is inspiring.

The contrasting locations in Jamaica and Canada have been crisply photographed by Phedon Papamichael, and Hans Zimmer has contributed a sprightly, reggae-inflected musical score.

NEWSDAY, 10/1/93, Part II/p. 56, John Anderson

The very idea of a Jamaican bobsled team—the real-life version of which supplies the premise for "Cool Runnings"—is such an improbable and inherently funny idea that it would have made perfect sense for a movie studio to have created and bankrolled such a team in the first place. (Hmmmm ... Nah.)

But that's a far too cynical thought about a movie that makes you feel this good. Not that everything about "Cool Runnings"—Jamaican slang for "peaceful journeys" and perhaps the most unabashedly entertaining film of the year—makes you feel *that* good. In telling the story of the Jamaican team, which really did make it to the 1988 Winter Olympics in Calgary, the filmmakers shed a rather unflattering light on the international athletic community, the major attributes of which seem to be greed, cronyism, the propagation of corporate sponsorships and a sneering attitude toward the very precept the Olympics always wrap themselves in: To represent one's country is the highest honor an athlete can have; winning is secondary. Yeah, right.

But the four members of the team—Derice (pronounced da-reese) Bannock (Leon), Sanka Coffie (Doug E. Doug), Junior Bevil (Rawle D. Lewis) and the shaved-headed Yul Brenner (Malik Yoba)—really do believe it. Which helps make the movie such a kick.

While taking a few liberties with its fact-based story, the film also takes full advantage of its two equally beautiful locales, Canada and the Caribbean. We see the latter first along with the shapely legs of Derice, the son of an Olympic gold medalist and an aspiring Olympian himself—in track. Derice seems to have the necessary talent, even if he has to practice with stones for starting blocks and toilet paper for a finish line. But during the trials, he and two other runners—Junior and Yul Brenner—collide and are disqualified. "You'll have another chance in four years," a protesting Derice is told, and it's small comfort; he wants to be an Olympian even more than he wants to run. So, inspired by the push-cart races in which his Rastafarian friend Sanka competes, Derice makes the unlikely leap to bobsled, and the help of a bar-owning bookie and ex-bobsledding champ named Irv.

Jon Candy, as the ex-"slider" with the dirty little secret (he cheated at the '72 Games), is bitter, slovenly and generally unsupportive; his team, after all, has never seen snow. He runs the four through harrowing paces—their "sled" consists of welded-together oil drums on wheels—that generally end with Derice asking "Sanka, you dead?" and Sanka replying, "Yeah, mon." And while he gradually begins to believe, one of the team's biggest handicaps will be Irv's standing among other Olympians, which causes the Jamaicans even more consternation than they create for themselves.

For all its "Rocky"-esque narrative, the comedy is the main event in "Cool Runnings," which features very funny performances by Doug E. Doug and Candy—even though the latter's serious moments border on the mawkish. Leon, who was so memorable as one of "The Five Heartbeats" and tangled with Sylvester Stallone in "Cliffhanger" this summer, is a charismatic leading man. And although there's a dangerous tendency to make the Jamaicans' fish-out-of-water circumstances the butt of the humor—you know what I mean, mon?—"Cool Runnings" maintains its dignity, even while on thin ice.

SIGHT AND SOUND, 4/94, p. 39, Ben Thompson

Jamaica, 1987. Like his father before him, Derice Bannock is going to be a gold medal-winning sprinter, while his happy-go-lucky friend Sanka Coffie skilfully confirms his dominance in the island's push-cart derby. When the time comes for Derice's Olympic 100m trial, rich man's son

Junior Bevil shakes Derice's hand at the start, but in the race he falls and trips both him and formidable bald hardman Yul Brenner.

Unsuccessfully trying to convince Jamaican Olympic Committee president Coolidge to re-run the race, Derice sees a picture of his father with an American medal winner, Irving Blitzer, who came to try and harness Jamaican sprinting talent in a bobsled team, but failed, and is now an unsuccessful bookie. Realising the bobsled is now his best chance to go to the Olympics, Derice recruits Sanka and goes to persuade a reluctant Irv to coach them. Many hopefuls gather to fill the other places, until Irv shows them a film of horrific sled crashes. Then only Junior and Yul remain. The quartet begins training. The process is painful but they make progress. The Olympic Committee will not give them any money and requests for sponsorship are met with ridicule, but Junior sells his car, and they're off to Calgary.

Arriving in Canada, they struggle to acclimatise to icy conditions. Irv is hated by the bob-sled establishment but manages to pull strings to get his team a rickety sled. Rival competitors give the Jamaicans a hard time, but despite this, and numerous obstacles the authorities put in their way, they manage to qualify. Their first televised run is a disaster, but their second is a triumph. The third and final run starts off even better, but ends in a horrific crash as the rickety sled collapses. The quartet emerges unscathed, and carry their broken carriage over the line to a tumultuous reception.

All hail that rare beast, the novelty Olympian redemption drama with an inter-racial buddy aspect. Trailed as "a new comedy for all audiences", this heartwarming Disney cocktail of sun and snow—filmed on no-expenses-spared location in Calgary and Jamaica—has already gone down well in America. There is no reason why it should not do the same here, though it might benefit from a last minute title-change to *Chariots of Ice*.

Irv, the disgraced bob-sledder who has regained the power to dream, is a role tailor-made for John Candy, and he wears it well, shifting swiftly and with considerable grace out of grouch ("Let me lay out some difficulties: snow, you don't have any") and into serious bonding mode. His four athletic proteges—true Olympian, chirpy slacker, oppressed richboy and complex hard-man—do not have quite such room for manoeuvre within their types, and are required to mug even more shamelessly than Candy is. Leon is the most familiar face among them; he was the saintly statue that came to life in Madonna's "Like A Prayer" video. CVs full of award-winning crack-addict ex-basketball player roles point to an inequality of opportunity in Hollywood that is every bit as great, and rather less mitigated by circumstance, as that in winter sports.

Cool Runnings' plot loses nothing in for being based on fact; the film-makers having, in their own words, "applied creative license to illuminate a unique scenario". The theme is difference—Sanka with a hot water bottle inside his cat-suit, a babble of aggressive Germanic voices wishing the plucky Jamaicans back where they came from—but it's basically the same old story. The film constantly pushes the obvious cultural and climactic buttons, but the longer it goes on, the harder it is not to be moved by it.

Green shoots of corn are frequently visible. But there is something unusual going on here as well. How often does a Hollywood sporting drama actually practise what it preaches in terms of it not being the winning but the taking part that counts? *Cool Runnings* keeps faith with Irv's hard-earned realisation that "A gold medal is a wonderful thing, but if you're not enough without it, you'll never be enough with it", and in so doing earns a real thrill for its coda—"in 1992 the Jamaican bob-sledding team returned to the Olympics, as equals".

VILLAGE VOICE, 10/5/93, p. 58, James Hannaham

With adorably cute fluffiness, almost synonymous with Disney live-action films, *Cool Runnings* tugs at your heartstrings, demonstrates the triumph of the human spirit, sings, dances, and smothers Jamaican culture in ersatz guava jelly. Loosely based on the true story of the 1988 Jamaican bobsled team's not-so-Olympic record (they finished 25th out of 26), *Cool Runnings* follows four frustrated sprinters so desperate for gold that they hound bobsled-hotshot-turned-tub-of-goo Irv (John Candy) into coaching them. Everyone's a "type." Derice (Leon, who was Christ in Madonna's "Like a Prayer" video) is the hunky hero, Sanka Coffie (Doug E. Doug) his dreaded goofy sidekick, Yul Brenner (Malik Yoba) the tough guy, and Junior Bevil (Rawle D. Lewis) the dweeb.

Since they're all "boys" in the worst sense of the word, characters drawn from a room at the Ocho Rios Intercontinental Hotel offering complimentary bad accents who "no problem" their way through the saccharine script, it's up to coach Candy to make them bobsledders (and by extension, men), simultaneously regaining the respect of the officials who demedaled him long ago.

These exploits culminate not in literal victory (the concept of a Jamaican bobsled team winning a medal after only months of training being too dopey even for Disney) but in the kind of achievement engineered for maximum handkerchief wetness that's so obviously manipulative as to seem more than a lickle fooly-fooly.

Also reviewed in:
CHICAGO TRIBUNE, 10/1/93, Friday/p. L, John Petrakis
NEW YORK TIMES, 10/1/93, p. C8, Janet Maslin
VARIETY, 9/20/93, p. 29, Leonard Klady
WASHINGTON POST, 10/1/93, p. C6, Richard Harrington
WASHINGTON POST, 10/1/93, Weekend/p. 52, Desson Howe

COP AND A HALF

A Universal Pictures release of an Imagine Films presentation. *Executive Producer:* Tova Laiter. *Producer:* Paul Maslansky. *Director:* Henry Winkler. *Screenplay:* Arne Olsen. *Director of Photography:* Bill Butler. *Editor:* Daniel Hanley and Roger Tweten. *Music:* Alan Silvestri. *Music Editor:* Kenneth Karman. *Sound:* Joe Foglia. *Sound Editor:* Paul Clay. *Casting:* Meg Liberman and Mark Hirschfeld. *Production Designer:* Maria Caso. *Art Director:* Allen Terry. *Set Designer:* Damon Medlen. *Set Decorator:* Cindy Coburn. *Set Dresser:* Jeffrey Scott Taylor. *Special Effects:* Richard Jones. *Costumes:* Lillian Pan. *Make-up:* Marie Del Russo. *Make-up (Burt Reynolds):* Brian K. McManus. *Running time:* 87 minutes. *MPAA Rating:* PG.

CAST: Burt Reynolds (Nick McKenna); Norman D. Golden II (Devon Butler); Ruby Dee (Rachel); Holland Taylor (Captain Rubio); Ray Sharkey (Vinnie Fountain); Sammy Hernandez (Raymond); Frank Sivero (Chu); Rocky Giordani (Quintero); Marc Macaulay (Waldo); Tom McCleister (Rudy); Ralph Wilcox (McPhail); Tom Kouchalakos (Jenkins); Carmine Genovese (Rio); Sean Evan O'Neal (McNally); Max Winkler (Boy in Bathroom); Steve Carlisle (Mr. Fleming); Annabelle Weenick (Mrs. Boyle); Paul Vroom (Purse Thief); Tim Goodwin (Bobo #1 Artist); Mike Benitez (Bobo #2); Maria Canals (Mrs. Bobo #2); Nils Stewart (Bobo #3 Thug); Chester Grimes (Bartender); Claudette McAdoo (Homeowner); Becky Kluzek (Martha); Amanda Seales (Katy); Nicholas Caruso (Boy #1); Shane Obedzinski (Boy #2); Jennifer Howard and Ashley Howard (Jump Rope Twins); Malia Tuaileva (Maria); Kenneth Taylor (Passing Cop); Nicole Bradley (Watching Cop); Bill Cordell (Mr. Perm); Sandra Itzin Gallo (Police Dispatcher); Amy Stephen Wilder (Lady With Groceries); Alan Landers (Attorney, TV Show); Judy Clayton (District Attorney); Andrew Reynolds (Skateboard Kid); Debra Becker (TV Reporter).

LOS ANGELES TIMES, 4/2/93, Calendar/p. 12, Michael Wilmington

Many movies these days are about "wanna-bes": characters who want to be something they're not, and who amazingly, get their wish.

Here's what we get in "Cop and a Half". A tough Tampa cop (Burt Reynolds). A cute kid who *wants* to be a tough Tampa cop (Norman G. Golden II). A vicious gangster who wants to be a doo-wop idol (Ray Sharkey). An elementary school principal who wants to be Da King.

There's more: A lady police captain who acts like a social worker (Holland Taylor). Playground bullies who want to be gangsters. Thugs who want to be straight men. Cops who want to be clowns.

Almost everybody in this movie aspires to be somebody else, and it's no wonder. If you were stuck in something like "Cop and a Half," you'd probably be dreaming of greener pastures yourself. The movie itself is a sort of "Kindergarten Cop" wanna-be: Burt Reynold's character, a bash-your-head kind of cop named Nick McKenna, suggests Dirty Harry on his way to Dr. Rogers' neighborhood.

Put them all together: add another empty, marketing-hook script, by Arne Olsen; mix in the usual beefy, budget-flexing, rock-the-house production, and polish it off it with over-jolly direction by Henry Winkler—perhaps *he* wants to be Ron Howard—and you haven't got even *half* a movie.

"Cop and a Half" isn't a disaster, but it's something less entertaining: an elongated trailer full of posturing and puffery, obvious gags, programmed sentiment. In this shtick-a-thon, the basic hook is simple: Devon Butler (Golden), an imaginative Tampa tot who plays cop games, witnesses a gang-land execution and then, with the police hot for his testimony, blackmails them into letting him ride, as a "partner," with the force's surliest, sloppiest, let-it-hang cop: Reynolds' McKenna.

When Devon joins Nick, wish fulfillment runs amok. Devon gets to ticket his principal for speeding. Devon lectures surly Nick on police procedure, with texts drawn from the VCR; later the two bond so tightly that they wind up living together, like Oscar and Felix in "The Odd Couple." Devon is chased into his playground, and his schoolmates confound the crooks by jumping up in waves and yelling "I'm Devon Butler!"—which may mean *they* all want to be in "Spartacus." Or "Malcolm X."

This is one of those movies that suggest that the world is a huge TV set, with 100 cable channels that people can program themselves into at will. The characters are all tube-drunk, and the movie seems primarily conceived for a TV-besotted, media-friendly audience. If you argued that nothing in it makes any sense, the filmmakers would probably argue right back that "Cop and a Half" isn't supposed to make sense: it's supposed to make money.

The actors, with the exception of Reynolds, who's lightly burlesquing his old '70s cop parts, all play "cute." That's why 8-year-old Golden has the big advantage. The cutest of the bunch, he doesn't have to try as hard.

Around them, we get cute cops and crooks, cute hairy-chested barroom bikers who get in cute barroom brawls—and Vinnie Fountain (Sharkey), the cute crime czar, a depraved egomaniac who call himself "D. DiMucci," after Dion, and keeps breaking into renditions of "Dream Lover" and "The Wanderer." (If he's such an aficionado, why doesn't he remember the words?) Cuteness is the movie's curse; it's as if everyone in it had been condemned to six months of hard whimsy.

Golden may steal much of "Cop and a Half" (rated PG), but it's only petty larceny. This movie's by-the-numbers story and strange mix of viciousness and coy "lovability"—the same ga-ga hybrid of sadistic schmaltz we got in "Kindergarten Cop" or "Stop! Or My Mom Will Shoot!"—suggests a movie so commercially calculated it wants to be its own sequel: "Cop and a Half II." We should be that lucky.

NEW YORK POST, 4/2/93, p. 29, Audrey Farolino

If there's one formula that Hollywood never seems to tire of, it's the old "tough cop paired with oddball partner" routine.

Of course, it's getting harder and harder to come up with a novel enough oddball, since scriptwriters have already used up everything from a wiseguy con ("48 Hrs.") to an overeager actor ("The Hard Way").

So one can perhaps understand why the creators of "Cop and a Half" felt compelled to go to the absurd extreme of pairing tough guy detective Nick McKenna (Burt Reynolds) with—get this—a third-grader.

"I'm your worst nightmare—an 8-year-old with a badge," intones pint-sized Devon Butler (Norman D. Golden II) as he pulls over his school principal for speeding.

This all sounds, of course, like a moviegoer's worst nightmare. But it isn't—or at least, it's not *quite* that bad—thanks mostly to Golden, are extremely engaging young actor with a gift for low-key comic delivery ("Never let civilians see us disagree—it undermines my authority," he sternly tells McKenna, and the line actually sounds funny given his reading of it).

Credibility, needless to say, isn't the movie's strong suit. We are supposed to buy the idea that Devon, a law enforcement buff who spends his days playing at being a cop and his evenings watching "Miami Vice" reruns, witnesses a drug ring murder and then refuses to give the police information about it unless they allow him to play cop for real.

Topping that on the farfetched meter is this: The department actually agrees, letting the tyke ride around with the foul-tempered McKenna.

As in every movie of this type, McKenna spends a lot of time grumbling about his rotten luck and making nasty remarks to his new partner—but those remarks sound a lot nastier than usual, given that they're aimed at a kid ("Find somebody you recognize or I'm going to rip your little head off," is an example.)

Also true to genre, the mismatched partners get over their initial hostility and begin to bond while on the trail of that drug gang (which, by the way, is led by a bizarre lounge-singer-turned-crook played, appropriately enough, by Ray Sharkey).

Ruby Dee doesn't have much to do in the role of Devon's upstanding grandmother, and Reynolds despite a few amusingly sarcastic moments—mostly just comes across as tired and unpleasant. When McKenna sighs, "I'm too old for this," you get the feeling it's coming from Reynold's heart.

NEWSDAY, 4/2/93, Part II/p. 63, Jack Mathews

It has been 21 years since Burt Reynolds was stiffed out of an Oscar nomination for his one great performance, in John Boorman's "Deliverance," and the quality of his film work has been in something like free-fall ever since. The next sound you hear, "Cop and a Half," is Burt finally hitting bottom.

In this stunningly inept comedy, Reynolds seems to be parodying all his own hard-boiled detective characters, playing a pot-bellied, slow-moving, back-aching veteran homicide detective forced to take on an 8-year-old partner while trying to break up an international drug ring in Florida.

You see, the kid (Norman D. Golden II), is obsessed with TV cop shows and is living out a perpetual authoritarian fantasy. He lives with his grandmother (Ruby Dee), a night nurse, and when she's away, he's Detective Devon Butler, communicating with a pal with toy two-way radios, using snappy TV cop lingo on school bullies and keeping his eyes out for suspicious characters.

When Devon stumbles upon a real murder and overhears singing crime lord Vinnie Fountain (Ray Sharkey) plan a drug deal, he cuts a deal of his own with the police: If they give him a badge and put him on patrol, he'll help them crack the case.

Somebody actually sold that idea to Ron Howard's Imagine Films, which brought us the loathsome "Problem Child" movies, and they made it, with Howard's old "Happy Days" buddy Henry Winkler directing and "Evening Shade" himself playing the reluctant babysitting detective.

Happy Days are not here again.

Reynolds looks appropriately shopworn and out-of-shape for the role, which has him mostly chasing after the kid, then trying to catch his breath and rub the ache out of those old knees. He wears snug shirts and jackets to emphasize his protruding gut, and lets the sweat pour whenever he breaks into a trot.

The self-mockery, the idea that we're seeing Hawk or Dan August in the twilight of his career, would have worked better, at least visually, if Reynolds didn't have that spectacularly healthy looking toupee. But how much humiliation can you ask of a fallen star?

To be fair, "Cop and a Half" is not essentially a Burt Reynolds movie. It's a children's fantasy, with impetuous—some might say bratty—Devon serving as the story's central character, the alter ego of every kid who plays cops and robbers in his mind.

Children his age may get a kick out of seeing Devon show his irascible partner how to calm a domestic dispute with sweet talk, and save his partner by conking a bad guy on the head. But for adults, there is nothing to ease the pain. Arne Olsen's script is an endless string of cliches, bad dialogue and clunky sight gags, and Winkler has no sense of comic pacing or staging. He doesn't even know how to set up a shot so it is interesting to look at.

The clumsiest scene in the movie, a tough category, also is the cheapest joke. After challenging Nick to some sort of urinating target practice, Devon manages to hit the old guy in the leg. Kids probably will find that very funny, but it had me wondering whether Nick is familiar with the laws regarding exposure.

"I'm your worst nightmare," says Devon, in a scene where he gets to write his school's principle a speeding ticket. "An eight-year old with a badge."

It's pretty much my worst nightmare, too.

SIGHT AND SOUND, 7/93, p. 40, Martin Wagner

Tampa, Florida. Eight-year-old Devon Butler dreams of being a cop, trying the tough cop-speak he has picked up from television on friends and foes on his school playground. One day he witnesses tough but disillusioned detective Nick McKenna chasing and arresting a suspect, and notes down the number plate of a car which got away. The next day Devon spots the car again and follows it to a warehouse where he witnesses the killing of a suspected informer by drug dealer and frustrated singer Fountain. When McKenna arrives at the crime scene, he is furious to find that the only witness is a child, and his attitude doesn't improve when Devon demands a badge and handcuffs in return for giving any information.

McKenna reluctantly takes the boy on a shift, which at first is too dull for Devon, who was expecting instant shoot-outs à la *Miami Vice*. But matters improve when he gets to help sort out a domestic dispute and against all odds begins to gain McKenna's respect. However, the shift over, McKenna doesn't invite the kid back. In the meantime, Fountain has instructed his incompetent henchmen to kill the young witness, forcing McKenna to put Devon up in his bachelor pad for protection. Fountain's men almost manage to run Devon over when he is on a routine traffic patrol, but McKenna saves him in the nick of time. He invites Devon back on board as his partner and they track down a suspect in a seedy bar; the pair win a fight against the muscular clientele, but lose their man in the ensuing car chase. Devon still feels that McKenna doesn't respect him enough and runs away to face the criminals on his own. He is caught, but McKenna tracks him down to a harbour warehouse. After a chase on land and water, McKenna and Devon immobilise the criminals. They have become a team, yet Devon decides to concentrate on being a normal boy for the foreseeable future.

"I'm your worst nightmare: an eight-year-old with a badge," says Devon to a motorist as he fines him for speeding. He is not wrong. While young kids will no doubt chuckle appreciatively at the broad comedy, adults will look in vain for any sophistication: *Cop and a Half* unashamedly caters to children's crudest fantasies and leaves the rest of the world at a loss. There are a few adult pleasures to be had from McKenna's one-liners ("I'd like to rip your arm off and wave it at you"), but he soon, too soon, succumbs to the charm of his unwanted protegé. This, cynics might feel, may be due more to the overemotional piano music dropped in without subtlety than to any real charisma on the kid's part. Sadly, young first-time actor Norman D. Golden II lacks any of the endearing qualities we have come to expect even from a *Problem Child*.

Screenwriter Arne Olson goes to great length setting up situations, but doesn't often manage to come up with adequate one-liners to turn them into successful comedy, while director Henry Winkler handles the many action sequences well but leaves the clumsily scripted personal drama to its own devices. Burt Reynolds—back after a four-year break from feature films—plays the part which usually goes to Nick Nolte, whose mere physical presence opposite the young girl in *Three Fugitives* was a joke in itself.

But however grumpy and bad-tempered Reynolds' McKenna might be, we know he never really dislikes his young charge Reynolds' character changes as dramatic rules require: his initial treatment of suspects is more likely to attract the attention of Internal Affairs than the admiration of an impressionable youngster; while his sudden transformation from kid-hating monster to potential surrogate dad, while not in the least surprising, never convinces. McKenna's claim that real-life police-work is dullsville compared to *Miami Vice* is of course immediately proved wrong. After all this excitement, Devon's decision to be a normal boy for the time being comes as a surprise for those adults who have bothered to stay the course, and puts kids watching firmly back into their place after an hour and a half of escapism.

262   FILM REVIEW ANNUAL

Also reviewed in:
CHICAGO TRIBUNE, 4/2/93, Friday/p. B, Dave Kehr
NEW YORK TIMES, 4/2/93, p. C17, Stephen Holden
VARIETY, 4/5/93, p. 176, Richard Natale
WASHINGTON POST, 4/2/93, p. D6, Rita Kempley
WASHINGTON POST, 4/2/93, Weekend/p. 44, Desson Howe

CRUSH

A Strand release of a Hibiscus Films production in association with the New Zealand Film Commission/NFU Studios/NZ On Air. *Producer:* Bridget Ikin. *Director:* Alison Maclean. *Screenplay:* Alison Maclean and Anne Kennedy. *Director of Photography:* Dion Beebe. *Editor:* John Gilbert. *Music:* JPS Experience and Antony Partos. *Music Editor:* Andrew Lancaster. *Casting:* Diana Rowan. *Sound:* Michael Hedges. *Sound Editor:* Greg Bell. *Production Designer:* Meryl Cronin. *Art Director:* Brett Schwelters and David Turner. *Costumes:* Ngila Dickson. *Make-up:* Abby Collins and Dominic Till. *Stunt Coordinator:* Peter Bell. *Running time:* 97 minutes. *MPAA Rating:* Not Rated.

CAST: Marcia Gay Harden (Lane);   Donogh Rees (Christina);   Caitlin Bossley (Angela);   William Zappa (Colin);   Pete Smith (Horse);   Jon Brazier (Arthur);   Geoffrey Southern and Wayne Roberts (Patients)   David Slott (Stephen);   Harata Solomon (Aunty Bet);   Caroline De Lore (Colleen);   Phil McLachlan (Ward Sister);   Alistair McConnell (Doctor);   Terry Batchelor (Taxi Driver);   Martin Booker (Waiter).

LOS ANGELES TIMES, 9/22/93, Calendar/p. 4, Kevin Thomas

Alison Maclean's sinister compelling "Crush" begins so swiftly that it's important to pay close and immediate attention to its stunning opening sequence. It suffices to say here that sequence ends in a car accident, with one woman, Christina (Donogh Rees), nearly killed and the other, Lane (Marcia Gay Harden), walking away with only a scratch on her forehead. "Crush" has so much wit and panache it's important not to give too much away. In any event, it proceeds with such persuasive psychological validity that its every moment rings true.

This taut, sly fable of innocence and corruption takes place in rural New Zealand, where Lane, an American, is visiting Christina, a literary critic and once Christina's classmate. While Christina winds up in the hospital Lane zeros in on Christina's friend, Colin (William Zappa), a struggling novelist, and his motherless 15-year-old daughter Angela (Caitlin Bossley). Blatantly sexy and seductive, Lane first befriends and beguiles Angela, rapidly transforming her from an androgynous tomboy to a pretty young woman; just as rapidly, however, Lane drops Angela to seduce her lonely father, who quickly develops an all-consuming passion for her.

Lane is big-time bad news, clearly a sociopath who gets her kicks from manipulating others, but she doesn't reckon with the depth of Angela's growing rage toward her. She may in fact also be incapable of considering that Angela may proceed upon a course of action with consequences beyond the teen-ager's comprehension.

We may find Lane entirely loathsome, yet her seductive impact on others is all too credible. In her writing (with Anne Kennedy) and in her direction, Maclean takes chances and inspires her actors to go the distance with her. Harden has appeared impressively in "Miller's Crossing" (as a gangster's girl) and "Used People" (as Shirley MacLaine's troubled daughter, who assumed identities of everyone from Marilyn Monroe to Mrs. Robinson), and here she makes Lane captivating and repellent.

In a sense Angela is the film's true central character, and therefore the film itself can be taken as a notably bizarre and drastic coming-of-age story. As Angela, Bossley projects such a youthful naivete, such a justifiable sense of outrage, that she never loses sympathy no matter how vengeful she becomes. Zappa, trim of body but ravaged-looking in his craggy visage, exudes a moody, wounded quality of intellectual macho. Rees is simply amazing as a severely injured woman gradually awakening in mind, body and spirit to a dangerously complete comprehension of the full circumstances surrounding the near-fatal car crash.

"Crush," whose title can refer to Angela's initial feelings for Lane as well as Christina's fate in the accident, is highly sensual. "Crush" (Times-rated Mature for language and considerable sex) is a highly assured and sophisticated venture.

NEW YORK POST, 9/10/93, p. 40, Jerry Tallmer

When you see boiling bubbling mud, like lava, at the beginning of a movie, under the credits, you can make a pretty good guess how the movie's going to end.

Well, I'm not going to tell you how "Crush" a New Zealand film by Alison Maclean, ends. I'll only tell you it's about a young woman named Lane who's no better than she should be—nor should she be driving cars that roll over at 100 mph and almost kill, but in any event de-brain, her best girlfriend. Nor should this Lane, quite a juicy joyous tough-talking brunette in a yellow beret, be rolling in the hay with almost any male who comes in sight here in beautiful rural Rotorua.

Or female either, for that matter—young Angela, for instance, the pretty but spooky 18-ish daughter of dour Colin, a blocked novelist with the pinched face of defeat—pinched even when our Lane puts the blocks to *him*.

Angela doesn't like that very much. Angela used to like Lane, but now she doesn't like Lane, and she goes to the hospital—and keeps going there—to see what she can find out from Christina, Lane's cool blonde girlfriend who was in that red sportscar when it rolled over and over and is now, as I said, still alive but quite emphatically goo-goo-goo inarticulate unremembering debrained.

Until she does start to remember.

So all this clinches, or crushes, together, with unrestrained sensitivity and angst; and one big problem (for me) was the frequent inability to sort Colin, Angela's dour papa, from Arthur, an incidental rascal in the story. They looked alike, skinny and sour with bags under their eyes.

The fellow I could sort out was Horse, a genial husky moustache with his neck and other parts in casts, who gets young Angela to be nice to him in his hospital bed, in between her espionage visits to smashed-up Christina.

Whom she presently brings home for a week's visit. And that's when everybody goes off for walks in the forest, which is also when I won't tell you how the picture ends.

I will say that Colin and Arthur, those lookalike losers, are played by William Zappa and John Brazier; that Christina is Donogh Rees, acting and babbling her head off; that young Angela is Caitlin Bossley with an American baseball cap turned backwards on her head; and that I certainly would not have and did not recognize bold busty redlipped Lane from when last viewed as that morose unfulfilled wife with cockeyed Antarctic visions in "Angels in America."

Which is a tribute to the talents of Marcia Gay Harden, who as the free-thinking sexpot you love to hate is better than this whole movie.

NEWSDAY, 9/10/93, Part II/p. 71, Jack Mathews

The opening image of Alison Maclean's "Crush" is of a reddish-brown mud percolating in a steaming, geothermal pond, and if that metaphor doesn't suffocate you, maybe the movie will do the trick.

That pond is in Rotorua, a rural community in Canadian-born Maclean's adopted country of New Zealand, where a car crash draws three women and one man together into a hothouse of stifled, ambiguous sexual gamesmanship.

The catalyst of the story, which Maclean developed at a workshop at the Sundance Institute, is Marcia Gay Harden's Lane, a femme fatale who protects her fragile ego by acting out as a drunken, bisexual vamp. In ways either implied or implicit, she seduces and scars everyone with whom she has a relationship.

It is Lane's carelessness behind the wheel that leaves book critic Christina (Donogh Rees) hospitalized with brain damage and brings Lane together with Colin (William Zappa), a working-class novelist Christina was en route to interview, and his 15-year-old daughter Angela (Caitlin Bossley).

For reasons buried deep in Lane's disturbed mind, she avoids visiting her injured friend, who it is suggested may also be her lover, and instead insinuates herself into the lonely, awkward lives of Colin and Angela.

The teenager, who has yet to explore her own sexuality, is quickly seduced by Lane's aggressive friendliness and is fascinated by her flamboyant, party girl behavior. But the infatuation ends abruptly when Lane begins sleeping with Angela's hopelessly love-struck father, and a cycle of vengeance is begun that we can be sure will get us back to the thermal spring for another metaphor or so.

For this sort of Freudian fable to work, you have to care deeply about the people involved, and the inspiration just isn't here. Lane is meant to be mysterious and charismatic, but Harden's performance doesn't have a soft or appealing note to it. Instead of coming off as one of the psychologically wounded, she's merely a bad seed, a mundane screen villain heading for a comeuppance.

Bossley's Angela is the only character developed to any extent, and the film is best when we're with her, watching her quietly deal with her anger. But the connection isn't strong enough to justify this study in melancholy, and by the end, we're left with the feeling we've been taken in by a psychological shaggy dog story.

Those, steaming mud bubbles said it all.

SIGHT AND SOUND, 4/93, p. 44, Verina Glaessner

New Zealand. Journalist Christina and her anarchic American friend Lane drive to Rotorua to interview prize-winning novelist Colin. Lane takes the wheel and crashes the car. She escapes uninjured, but Christina is hospitalised with severe brain damage. The stunned Lane retreats to a nearby motel. She decides to keep Christina's appointment with Colin. Outside his house, she meets his fifteen-year-old daughter Angela and makes no secret of her attraction to her. Taking Angela back to the motel, she lends her a provocative dress to wear to the local night-club that evening. Despite her father's disapproval, Angela wears the dress and accompanies Lane.

At the club, Angela is attracted to Maori singer Horse, but it is Lane who seduces him, inviting him and Angela back to the motel. After an intruder attempts unsuccessfully to get into the room, Lane and Angela return to Angela's house to sleep. Next morning, Lane introduces herself to Colin and invites him to the motel on the pretext of giving him a haircut. Colin accepts the invitation and they make love. Later, Lane moves in with Colin and Angela. After Lane openly spends the night with Colin, Angela goes to the hospital to visit Christina. Benefiting from Angela's regular visits, Christina gradually comes out of her coma. Jealous of Lane's affair with her father, Angela primes Christina with hatred of Lane as the person responsible for Christina's injuries.

When Colin, Lane and Angela go to stay at a lakeside cottage, Angela arranges for Christina to join them. Both Colin and Lane are shocked by the appearance of the wheelchair-bound Christina. During a walk in the hills, Angela and Colin leave Lane and Christina alone together. To Lane's surprise, Christina is suddenly able to walk. They arrive at a hill-top look-out, where Christina suddenly pushes Lane over the parapet. Angela, fearing the worst, hurries back to find them, but arrives just too late to witness Christina's act of revenge.

Crush begins well. Director Alison Maclean, whose first feature this is, expertly draws the viewer into the action via the intimate conversations between the two friends Christina and Lane during their drive along the New Zealand backroads in the opening scene. The careful placing of characters within an ambience and lack of melodramatic rhetoric recall Peter Weir's relaxed introduction to *The Cars That Ate Paris*. The script and Marcia Gay Harden's blithely anarchic performance establish Lane's iconoclasm and the ruthlessness with which this American friend flouts conventional morality. It is also hinted, through Angela's sexual ambiguity, that all may not be as it seems.

Maclean has expressed her admiration for the way Buñuel uses sexuality to cut through bourgeois pretension. In Pasolini's *Teorema* a mysterious stranger similarly releases a family's repressed sexuality to disturbing effect. But Maclean, however vivid her portrait of the amoral intruder, never really gives enough substance to the small-town values Lane throws into disarray. Colin's status as a reputed novelist is left somewhat obscure, while only the odd glimpse of suburban life is offered: late-night antics at the club, a few extras at a restaurant, the stunted architecture, and the clipped language of the protagonists. The signs of an incipient tourist industry are given distinctly malevolent implications, from the mannequin dressed in Maori costume to the threatening hiss of the bubbling natural geysers of Hell's Kitchen which suggest a veneer of civilisation in imminent danger of cracking apart. Natural forces have been used as potent symbols in films like Henry Hathaway's *Niagara* or Rossellini's *Stromboli*, where they are matched by characters who possess equal dynamism. Here, it is only Lane's evil intent that manages to convince. Angela's desire for vengeance is both too masked by Caitlin Bossley's placid performance and too heavily sign-posted by the script to be effective,

It might have been better to speed the narrative to its inevitable conclusion as soon as Angela's true purpose in visiting Christina becomes clear. Colin is portrayed as a sexual stooge from the beginning (at one point he clownishly approaches Lane with one leg in and one out of his trousers)—which may sharpen the film's sexual sting, but is hardly enough motivation for the character to hunch angst-ridden in front of his word processor. Nevertheless, *Crush* contains an impressive performance from Harden and provides sufficient evidence of an authentically skewed eye-view to arouse interest in Maclean's future work.

VILLAGE VOICE, 9/14/93, p. 55, Georgia Brown

These days, when movies go all out to ingratiate and are deathly afraid to upset, it takes guts to make a dense, smart, seething little movie like *Crush*. Particularly one with three possessed women warring over a dazed, out-of-his depths artist, a man none of them particularly wants.

When Alison Maclean's *Crush* turned up in the main competition of Cannes '92 (and belated thanks to Gilles Jacob for putting it there), the morning press screening greeted the movie with a ritual spanking—whomp-whomp-whomp went vacated seats in the dark. Critics for the festival's daily mags acted like they were rating dirty diapers. Probably you would never be able to see *Crush* if it hadn't picked up a following at Sundance last spring. And you probably won't be able to see it now, in a theater anyway, if you don't go quick. Lovingly shot by Dion Beebe, it ought to be seen on a big screen.

Obviously, Maclean has a feel for the old B pictures. (In interviews, the Canadian/New Zealand director cites Sam Fuller, Buñuel, Wenders's *The American Friend*, and Jane Bowles as primary influences.) She appreciates cruddy, darkened interiors, sealed off from the prying light. It's been a long time since I've seen such authentic chintziness on screen. While *Crush* may end up being compared to dank films by other women from down under—Jane Campion's *Sweetie* or Jocelyn Moorhouse's *Proof*—it's much more of a genre picture. But while clearly an homage, it is also deeply (deeply) felt.

Crush starts off with a car crash in which two women travelers, who may have started out with crushes on each other, are crushed together inside. (The nature of their previous relationship remains mysterious.) Christina (Donogh Rees), a literary critic, is on her way to interview Colin, a novelist who may be academically celebrated but he's hardly a celebrity. The accident throws the critic (analytic intelligence) into a coma, whereas what survives is far more lethal.

Out of the wreckage, like a swamp thing, crawls Lane (Marcia Gay Harden), the "friend" who was driving. Ignoring Christina's trapped body, this predator walks away from the accident and directly into the lives of Colin, the writing recluse (William Zappa), and his 15-year-old daughter, Angela (Caitlin Bossley). (To some extent this sounds like Losey's *Accident* from three women's point of view.) First, Lane seduces the shy, tomboyish Angela—giving her a short red dress, taking her out of the frumpish house—then she goes to work on Dad, who's instantly and even more uncritically besotted. Having lost both this bright new mom as well as a dull old dad (wary of any budding femininity on his daughter's part), Angela turns to the alternate mother, Christina, presently a grotesque tableau of lumps and contusions. Visiting the hospital each day, Angela begins nursing this wreck to "health." Or something.

Maclean's characters, excepting Angela, are disturbingly unlikable. If Christina turns into a monster of vengeance, Lane is a monster of greed and appropriation, luring people in and then scorching their hands when they reach out. She's also conflicted and tormented. (Harden, who turns in a brave performance, is photographed quite brutally.) Both women are simultaneously surreal and painfully real. Beside the three ladies jockeying over the narrative, men look positively helpless. Horse, a nightclub singer, turns up immobilized in the hospital (he tried to touch Lane, too). Colin, the artist, is a helpless naif, barely socialized, without survival skills. *His* portrait is so real, it's excruciating.

The movie's opening shot is a close-up of thick reddish-brown gook bubbling and steaming. It could be chocolate sauce or a mole. The setting is New Zealand's Rotorua—center both of geothermal wonders and Maori culture—a terrific location for a movie about the return of the repressed. Or three witches brewing poisons in the devil's kitchen.

Crush reminds me of the other first-rate film playing right now—at least I hope it's still around—Chabrol's *Betty*. (In the early '60s, influenced by American crime flicks of the '40s and '50s, some New Wave directors—Chabrol, Rohmer, Rivette, Truffaut—made films with psychological density, shifting sexual triangles and opaque, destructive motives.) *Betty* harks back powerfully to Chabrol's major theme (the one he discovered in Hitchcock): Some people invite others to intervene in their lives and others are compelled to intervene; yet one is conveniently labeled innocent and the other guilty. For all her compulsive betrayals, Marie Trintignant's slouched and sloshed Betty is terribly sympathetic, if only because she assumes all the guilt. The wonder in Chabrol is that his innocents aren't boring.

Like Betty, Lane is driven to destroy, yet she's not invulnerable to consequences. When the young and wounded Angela imitates Lane to get revenge, she uses Christina as her agent. As far as we know, Angela (like Betty) emerges spotless as a lamb.

Maclean's quirky, piquant details aren't just clevernesses. In her first shot of the two women, they're stopped beside the road, and Christina is polishing off what looks like Kentucky Fried Chicken. "Want my skin?" she asks Lane. You bet. A few minutes later, driving like a demon, Lane spots a female mannequin—a homemade sign to hail tourists. What's she seen? A frozen woman? A woman without qualities? Whatever, it's scared her half to death.

Also reviewed in:
NEW YORK TIMES, 9/10/93, p. C8, Vincent Canby
VARIETY, 5/25/92, p. 54, David Stratton

CRUSH, THE

A Warner Bros. release of a Morgan Creek production. *Executive Producer:* Gary Barber. *Producer:* James G. Robinson. *Director:* Alan Shapiro. *Screenplay:* Alan Shapiro. *Director of Photography:* Bruce Surtees. *Editor:* Ian Crafford. *Music:* Graeme Revell. *Music Editor:* Jim Harrison. *Sound:* Michael T. Williamson. *Sound Editor:* Michael Hilkene. *Casting:* Marci Liroff. *Production Designer:* Michael Bolton. *Art Director:* Eric Fraser. *Set Decorator:* Paul Joyal. *Set Dresser:* Steve Houle, Neil Turkington, Tom Bonny, James Purvis and Brian Kane. *Costumes:* Sharon Purdy. *Make-up:* Rosalina Da Silva. *Stunt Coordinator:* Betty Thomas. *Running time:* 110 minutes. *MPAA Rating:* R.

CAST: Cary Elwes (Nick Eliot); Alicia Silverstone (Darian Forrester); Jennifer Rubin (Amy Maddik); Amber Benson (Cheyenne); Kurtwood Smith (Cliff Forrester); Gwynth Walsh (Liv Forrester); Matthew Walker (Michael); Deborah Hancock (Samantha); Beverley Elliott (Tex Murphy); Andrew Airlie (Dr. Pollard); Sheila Paterson (Mrs. Tinkerman); Brent Chapman (Steven Tinkerman); James Kidnie (Attorney); Betty Phillips (Abigail Spaulding); Duncan Fraser (Detective); Paul Bittante (Police Officer); Doug Abrahams (Hospital Room Cop); Mark Acheson (Locksmith); Deryl Hayes (Reporter); Lesley Ewen (Photo Editor); Jennifer Clement (Art Director).

LOS ANGELES TIMES, 4/5/93, Calendar/p. 3, Michael Wilmington

It's nice to know some Hollywood filmmakers have a handle on what's wrong with the world. While the rest of us fret about the economy, crime, disease, war, ethnic cleansing and other "ephemera," "The Crush" points its finger squarely at a menace too long ignored: lustful 14-year-old girls.

This is one more "yuppie-in-peril" movie, just as slick and empty, manipulative and crude, as most of the rest: all those paranoid pictures bent on scaring us with insane roommates, murderous baby-sitters and killer temps. Here, our "hero-victim" is a young journalist, who unwittingly stumbles into a suburban Hades: hounded by the crazed genius girl next door, who's determined to seduce him or ruin his life. The prey: GQ cover-guy-type Nick Eliot (Cary Elwes). The hunter: his landlord's daughter, sexy Darian Forrester (Alicia Silverstone), the rich nymphette from Hell.

What's a poor coverguy to do? Try as he might to preserve his purity, Nick can't evade the pouty-lipped, jailbait temptress. She parades before him in a bikini and Lolita-glasses, breaks into his apartment at all hours, rolls her eyes and licks her lips. She maneuvers him into her closet and forces him to watch a provocative striptease while he reels with fright.

Then, when Nick fails to respond, she turns nasty. Prank after prank, attack after attack, ending with her *pièce de résistance*: a rape charge that sends Nick to the slammer.

Isn't it time the writers of Hollywood started rethinking their whole "yuppie-in-peril" program? This sub-genre has gone from nascence ("Jagged Edge") to over-ripeness ("Fatal Attraction") to decadence in less than a decade. "The Crush" is a prime example.

Writer-director Alan Shapiro ("Tiger Town") shows some shallow expertise. He's hired Bruce Surtees (Clint Eastwood's erstwhile "Prince of Darkness") as his cinematographer, flooded the screen with sunlight and fancy decor, and shaped the film so that, by the end, some parts of the audience will be howling for Darian's blood.

"The Crush" (MPAA rated R, for violence and sensuality) tries to tease up lewd fantasies and then wash things clean with a moralizing rampage, stealing from Hitchcock: a murderous merry-go-round battle out of "Strangers From a Train."

Darian isn't a wholly ill-drawn character—15-year-old Alicia Silverstone gives easily the film's best performance—but she's a crock. Either she's a cold-blooded psychopath, murderously self-confident in her sex appeal, or she's an adoring teen-ager. But both?

Other idiocies abound. We're asked to believe that Darian, to buttress her rape charge, can figure out how to steal Nick's sperm. We're informed that Nick, faced with the computer destruction of a cover article and all his notes, just as a magazine meeting opens, can race back home and rewrite it all—from *memory*—then whip back and hand it to his editor before the meeting ends. (Is that how *this* script was written?)

Most of all, we're asked to believe that a genius concert pianist and writer, world caliber equestrienne and brilliant killer would persist in hopeless infatuation for a character whose major assets seem to be neat housekeeping, a Gap wardrobe and smoking cute cigars.

Come to think of it, that's one of the least of "The Crush's" implausibilities. The heart may never know where it listeth, but only the most die-hard "yuppie-in-peril" fans will want to list up here.

NEWSDAY, 4/5/93, Part II/p. 45, Jack Mathews

If Warner Bros. and the MPAA rating board weren't so uncomfortable with the subject matter, writer-director Alan Shapiro might have had a little hit on his hands with "The Crush." Still may.

The movie, about, a 28-year-old magazine journalist who moves into a wealthy family's guest house and becomes the object of the family's unbalanced 14-year-old daughter's affection, is slicker, better written and better acted than we've come to expect from movies dumped on the market without critics' screenings and with so little advertising.

It is an exploitation thriller, a Junior League version of "Fatal Attraction," without an original idea in it. But, first-time director Shapiro is a good imitator. He has worked up a modicum of tension, and the performances of Cary Elwes and newcomer Alicia Silverstone hold our attention while the plot runs its predictable course.

Elwes' Nick Eliot has no sooner unpacked in his picturesque guest house in Vancouver, Wash., when Silverstone's precocious Darian Forrester begins flirting with him. At first, Nick thinks she's just a little impetuous, but after she gets him in a wet liplock, he reassesses her behavior as a crush, and when his photographer girlfriend (Jennifer Rubin) endures a near-fatal run-in with Darian's pet wasps, he and the audience realize he's tangled up with a combination of Amy Fisher, Lolita and the Bad Seed.

What is uncomfortable, at least for adults (teenagers are likely to love this puberty dream), is the sexual tension between Nick and Darian. Recent events in Long Island and elsewhere have made us all sensitive to adult-child sensuality, evidenced by the film's R rating. Though there are no sex scenes, no graphic violence and minimal nudity (bare behinds, briefly seen), the MPAA gave it the same audience restrictions as the ultra-violent and nearly pornographic "Basic Instinct."

"The Crush" could have been much more commercial with a PG-13 rating, which it almost certainly would have received before Amy and Joey hit the news. Given the mood these days, no studio would dare appeal it.

SIGHT AND SOUND, 10/93, p. 43, Verina Glaessner

Nick Eliot finds himself the unwanted object of the amorous attentions of Darian—the precocious 14-year-old daughter of his new landlords, Liv and Cliff Forrester, whose back garden cottage he rents upon taking up a new job as staff writer for the glossy magazine *Pique*. At a party hosted by the Forresters, Nick finds himself lured by Darian to a beauty spot favoured by courting couples, and in an unguarded moment kisses her. Amy, a *Pique* photographer who befriends Nick, warns him that the girl has a crush on him.

Darian's incursions into Nick's privacy become ever bolder. When a photograph of himself as a child with his father disappears, Nick suspects Darian. Disturbed in her room while searching the supposedly empty house, Nick hides in a cupboard with louvred doors; but Darian, suspecting his presence, strips provocatively. Attempting to flee the house, Nick is stopped by Cliff, who demands he accompany him to the attic, suspicious of his presence in the house. He warns him against showing any sexual interest in his daughter, and shows him the fairground roundabout he bought for Darian but which she has long since outgrown. Unveiling his newly resprayed Valiant to Amy, Nick is shocked to discover an obscenity scratched across the bonnet. Attempts to discuss the matter with Cliff and Liv fail before Darian's feigned innocence.

After Darian's girlfriend Cheyenne attempts to warn Nick about Darian, she meets with an 'accident' at riding school. At a crucial editorial meeting, Nick is horrified to discover his computer disc blank; returning home he discovers the computer wiped. A search reveals a hidden cellar housing an altar Darian has built to him. Frantically Nick attempts to rewrite his piece. After Darian observes Amy in bed with Nick, an 'accident' involving a wasps' nest is arranged for Amy in her darkroom. Nick's attempts to find alternative lodgings are thwarted, and he finds himself under arrest for the sexual attack of a minor. Acquittal seems impossible when physical evidence is adduced linking him to Darian. His editor arranges bail but sacks him. Returning to the house to pack, he is visited by Cheyenne who tells him of Darian's diary—evidence enough to clear him. Searching the deserted house, Nick enters the attic, where he discovers Cheyenne bound to—the roundabout. Darian accuses him of having sex with Cheyenne when he attempts to release her. Cliff arrives and attacks him. Outraged, Darian makes for her father, violently attacking him. Nick recovers sufficiently to level a punch at her. Later, confined to a prison hospital, Darian begins to form a strong attachment to her psychiatrist.

Alan Shapiro, whose first feature this is, is a better director than he is a screenwriter, and *The Crush* is better directed and photographed—by Clint Eastwood's director of photography Bruce Surtees—than its mechanical script deserves. Arguably the American teenager is a horror film waiting to happen, and *The Crush* hardly needs Darian's array of lethal props—the wasps' nest, the riding tackle that invites interference, the fairground roundabout—to make its point. It is surely the thoughtless recycling of generic material that leads to Darian being presented as not only sexually but also intellectually precocious. Only on the other side of the Atlantic could acquaintance with the life-cycle of the wasp invite awed accusations of "knowing stuff", or competence at the piano and a position two grades above one's age group present sufficient cause for emotional trauma. Intellectual vacuity would surely have *increased* the character's fearsomeness.

Improbabilities abound. The altar with its burning candles could surely not have escaped notice for long? And the louvred wardrobe in Darian's room is an all-too-familiar place of concealment. Comparison cannot but be made with *Play Misty For Me* (also photographed by Surtees), likewise a film about female obsession explored from the male victim's viewpoint. *Play Misty For Me* derived its shock value from glimpses of the desperation informing its female protagonist's actions. Against Jessica Walter's playing in that film, Alicia Silverstone's interpretation of Darian cannot but appear superficial. She plays Darian as a deliberate cross between a young Ann-Margret and Sue Lyons' Lolita (Shapiro's references to the film of Nabokov's novel are many but not varied, stopping emblematically at glasses and bikini). Darian becomes less a maelstrom of out-of-kilter desire than merely the engine cranking up narrative devices. She is also over-explained through the existence of her vacuously social-climbing parents and in particular her sexually possessive father.

Somewhere along the line, thanks to Surtees' atmospheric cinematography, a point is made about the tensions between the familiar and ramshackle (the guest house in the garden, the tour of Vancouver architectural vernacular), and the new, stripped-out and glossy world (the office, Amy's apartment, the museum of Indian culture). A point is also made about the opportunity for reinvention of the self offered by a change of location and employment. Cary Elwes gains stubble and horn-rimmed spectacles through the edited title sequence journey to Vancouver and his search for lodgings, recreating himself as a fall guy likeable enough, if cut to a somewhat over-familiar pattern of chinos, Brooks Brothers and Timberlands. Some faint humour is also wrung from the journalistic milieu. That Darian's rewrite of Nick's story gains plaudits confirms suspicions that glossies with titles like *Pique* could only be written by 14-year-olds. Despite narrative predictabilities and the sense of missed opportunity, *The Crush* staves off dullness with well-shot, fresh locations and amiable casting.

Also reviewed in:
NEW YORK TIMES, 4/3/93, p. 17, Janet Maslin
VARIETY, 4/12/93, p. 75, Brian Lowry
WASHINGTON POST, 4/5/93, p. D4, Hal Hinson

DANGEROUS GAME

A Metro-Goldwyn-Mayer release of a Mario and Vittorio Cecchi Gori presentation of a Maverick production. *Executive Producer:* Freddy DeMann and Ron Rotholz. *Producer:* Mary Kane. *Director:* Abel Ferrara. *Screenplay:* Nicholas St. John. *Director of Photography:* Ken Kelsch. *Editor:* Anthony Redman. *Music:* Joe Delia. *Music Editor:* James Flatto. *Sound:* Michael Barosky. *Sound Editor:* Stuart Levy. *Casting:* Randy Sabusawa. *Production Designer:* Alex Tavoularis. *Art Director:* Nathan Crowley. *Set Decorator:* Stephanie Ziemer. *Set Dresser:* Mike Malone, Eric Roemheld, Lisa K. Sessions, Anthony J. DiMeo, and Anthony Pappas. *Costumes:* Marlene Stewart. *Make-up:* Raqueli Dahan. *Make-up (Madonna):* Hiram Ortiz. *Running time:* 105 minutes. *MPAA Rating:* R.

CAST: Harvey Keitel (Eddie Israel);   Madonna (Sarah Jennings);   James Russo (Francis Burns);   Nancy Ferrara (Madlyn);   Reilly Murphy (Tommy);   Victor Argo (Director of Photography);   Leonard Thomas (Prop Guy);   Christina Fulton (Blonde);   Heather Bracken (Stewardess);   Glenn Plummer (Burns' Buddy);   Niki Munroe (Girl in Trailer);   Lori Eastside, John Snyder, Adina Winston, and Dylan Hundley (Party Guests), Juliette Hohnen (Bar Patron); Julie Pop (Morton's Waitress);   Lili Barsha and Robyn B. Ashley (Flight Attendants);   Anthony Redman (Swinger);   Noga Isackson (1st Assistant Director);   Randy Sabusawa (Producer); Mindy Eshelman (Wardrobe);   Jesse Long (Script Supervisor);   Linda Murphy (Boom Operator);   Marta Bukowski (Video Tape Monitor);   Bill Pope and Martin Schaer (Camera Operators);   Jim Fitzgerald (1st Assistant Camera);   Hiram Ortiz (Hair);   Patton Howell Caldwell, IV (2nd Assistant Director);   Phil Nielson (Stunt Coordinator);   Richard Belzer (Himself);   Annie McEnroe (Herself);   Sammy Jack Pressman (Himself);   Steve Albert (Boxing Announcer).

NEW STATESMAN & SOCIETY, 6/3/94, p. 40, Jonathan Romney

As-serious-as-your-life is just not serious enough for Abel Ferrara. His last film but one, *Bad Lieutenant* (a slack remake of *Body Snatchers* came next), was a full-blown hellfire-or-redemption job: a compellingly ghastly picture of a working stiff fatally addicted to spiritual self-mutilation. Ferrara now takes a farther dip into the furnace with *Dangerous Game*.

This is a bizarre film—intermittently fascinating, but probably extremely bad. The game in question is film-making; this is the story of a director shooting a movie. Ferrara's premise is that making movies is the most perilous, soul-endangering occupation going—the usual fatuous hyperbole filmmakers indulge in lest the punters think they're having too cosy a time.

There they are, chilling out in LA in their trailers and hotels, paid vast amounts, plied with sex and booze and coke. You think it's easy? No, it's dangerous! Be grateful. They're doing it for us!

From start to finish, *Dangerous Game* is just this kind of loopy self-aggrandisement. But it's something else too—joyless to the point of being almost abstract, a purely formal essay in endurance. As films about films go, *Dangerous Game* is a little more crazed than the rest. It's *8½* with the fun taken out, *Day For Night* with added night.

Director Eddie Israel (Harvey Keitel) is making a film called *Mother of Mirrors*, starring Sarah Jennings (Madonna) as Claire and Francis Burns (James Russo) as Russell. Claire and Russell are a couple who argue a lot in darkened rooms; so are Sarah and Francis. Russell is a mad bastard who can't get enough sex, drugs, drink, screaming; Claire has given them all up except the latter, and taken to religion. She is the "mother of mirrors", presumably because everyone else sees their reflection in her, or projects on to her the image they want to see. Sounds a lot like Madonna, doesn't it?

In fact, *Dangerous Game* is the first film to use Madonna intelligently, and she comes across far more creditably than either Keitel or Russo, who veer into disturbing Method machismo at the least opportunity. Her casual, wired-up fatigue gives the film its edge, as if suddenly there were a human being in it, alongside all the hyperventilating tragedy masks. It's a remarkable switch on her wax-work presence in other movies, where she has had to play the star and little else.

Here, almost entirely bereft of aura, she provides the most intriguing aspect of the film's play on reality and illusion. Because we can't forget she's Madonna, we can never mistake her for "Claire" or "Sarah". Within the film, her presence stands out as an opaque sliver of reality.

But how can Madonna, whose very purpose is to exemplify pure performance, possibly represent the real in a film? The paradox underpins the movie beautifully.

Eddie, then, is sleeping with Sarah is sleeping with Francis is fighting with Eddie is fighting with his wife Madlyn—who, as the only person around not directly involved in Eddie's film, is viewed as an intruder who therefore has to be pulled into the dramatics. *Dangerous Game* starts with Eddie and Madlyn at home; once Eddie gets on set, the action closes in on itself. Suddenly we're in a cloistered world of sets, hotel rooms, scenes captured on murky video and labelled like documented reality: "LA rehearsals". Outside celluloid, there is no real world.

Everything, therefore, becomes heightened psychodrama. Eddie becomes the third mad actor in his film—which is, Ferrara keeps reminding us, also the film we're watching, At one point during the filming of *Mother of Mirrors*, the clapperboard actually reads, "A Ferrara, *Snake Eyes*": the title the film carried at last year's London Film Festival.

Ferrara keeps switching between the rehearsals for and the filming of Eddie's film, the actual scenes from that film, the comparable scenes between Sarah and Francis, the same scenes with Eddie acting out the parts, Eddie on video delivering waffly exegeses ... None of this is new, but the endless reflections create a hall-of-mirrors effect that is fascinating for two reasons. It is so utterly stifling, and it is bereft of irony.

What's lacking is any critical humour towards these banal excesses. Are we meant to take these people's emotional warfare seriously, all to complete a film that looks misconceived from the start? (*Mother of Mirrors* looks like Bergman's *Scenes from a Marriage* rewritten by David Mamet.) But Ferrara piles on excruciating absurdity after absurdity, unable to control his addiction to angst.

When Russell has a *Bad Lieutenant* moment, getting down on his knees and roaring out his transcendental pain, Eddie directs him: "To God! To God!"; the director-demiurge equation hits us with sledgehammer subtlety. When Sarah asks, "What's the difference between acting and feeling?", you wish Ferrara and screenwriter Nicholas St John had taken advice from someone with a more delicate grasp of Brechtian dialectics.

What *is* fascinating is why anyone would want to make *Dangerous Game*. Why perpetuate the Romantic myth of film-making as suffering? Here, Ferrara's film takes on an uncomfortably personal edge. It becomes that most interesting and least interesting of things, a male director's neurotic couch-kvetch. The film touches a nerve when we're most inclined to titter with embarrassment, when the narcissism goes way too far.

It comes to a head when Eddie tells his wife Madlyn that he's regularly been sleeping with other women on set. "Actresses, models, make-up, wardrobe ... I'm exhausted." At this point, the audience cracks up. This "real" moment looks more like a sloppily written movie than anything in *Mother of Mirrors*. However, the story goes that Ferrara, at a loss for dialogue, simply stuck a tape recorder under his own bed, told his own wife he'd been unfaithful, then reproduced the ensuing row verbatim. That may or may not be true, but the fact remains that Madlyn is played by Nancy Ferrara, Abel's wife. We're treading the fine line between film and family therapy.

Cathartic as it may be for the participants, it isn't for us. We're placed in the position of analysts impatient for these troublesome people to leave the consulting room. But we may get something instructive from *Dangerous Game*: its neurotic investment in the myth of artistic suffering. There *are* questions to be asked here—and one is about supposedly raw emotion being served up on screen.

What's the appeal of unhinged crisis for a film-maker, and what's supposed to be its appeal for us? This is film as Artaudian theatre of cruelty—cruel for the actors, cruel for the characters, cruel for us who have to endure it, cruel for the self-stigmatising auteur. Why, then, isn't it in any way cathartic? Mainly because Ferrara isn't interested in any release: he wants to go deeper into hell and never stop. But all we get is something into which we can never go deeper: the mother of all mirrors, an abyss that we look into and find a dumb, stultified gaze looking back. *Snake Eyes* indeed.

NEW YORK POST, 11/19/93, p. 33, Thelma Adams

The turkey of the year has arrived just in time for Thanksgiving. "Dangerous Game," Abel Ferrara's new film, starring America's favorite female impersonator, Madonna is dangerously dull.

Ferrara built his reputation on stylish splatter flicks about New York's hairy underbelly like last year's acclaimed and reviled "Bad Lieutenant" starring Harvey Keitel.

Screenwriter Nicholas St. John, who also wrote Ferrara's cult classic "King of New York" sets "Dangerous" on the left coast.

It is one of the most self-conscious movies about making movies ever. Ferrara's alter-ego, Eddie Israel (Harvey Keitel), directs Sarah Jennings (Madonna) and Francis Burns (James Russo) in a scenes-from-a-doomed-marriage picture.

Meanwhile, Israel's relationship with his wife, Madlyn (Nancy Ferrara, Abel's spouse) unravels.

St. John's bleak tale plays like No Exit on the Hollywood Freeway. Ferrara's relentless, brooding self-examination can only be termed "Deep Navel." Keitel deserves some slack after his triumph in "The Piano." Here he's over-the-top and nowhere at all. Like "Dangerous Game," Keitel's performance is all climax and no development.

Madonna proved again in "Body of Evidence" that she was no actress. Now she plays a bad actress badly. She has enough trouble handling one role; the dual role of an actress portraying a wife-in-crisis is beyond her. Madonna is so overexposed that her body projects all the sexual heat of a rubber chicken.

In "King of New York," there is a scene in which a mobster shows his disrespect to another man by peeing on his shoe. In "Dangerous Game" Francis tries to get a rise out of Sarah in the film-within-the-film by peeing on their ice-blue shag.

These scenes are an apt metaphor for Ferrara's territory-marking, one-note, testosterone-driven shock-provoking school of filmmaking. With his visual pyrotechnics, Ferrara can bang out a mean crime story. But his spiral into darkness, despair and drugs in Hollywood is a crashing bore.

Ferrara's latest movie shows that earlier signs of Cimino's Disease have become a full-blown infection.

NEWSDAY, 11/19/93, Part II/p. 77, Jack Mathews

Suffering artists often make for the most insufferable characters, and Abel Ferrara's "Dangerous Game," in which art imitates life for a film director and his two stars, delivers some of the most insufferable of them all.

Harvey Keitel, so brilliant in Ferrara's otherwise loathsome "The Bad Lieutenant," stars as Eddie Israel, a seductive, soft-spoken filmmaker trying to prod the demons out of the souls of his two leading actors and into the lives of their characters in a story about a violently collapsing marriage.

The movie within the movie, "The Mother of Mirrors," seems marginally interesting, what little we get to know of it. It's about a middle-class urban couple being brought down by the wife's spiritual conversion and her husband's continuing addictions to drugs, booze and sexual aerobics.

"They lived on the edge," an ad writer might muse, "and then they fell."

Of course, as stars Sarah Jennings (Madonna) and Francis Burns (James Russo) push their characters to the brink of disaster, they push themselves to the brink as well. Under the constant goading of the director, who is using them to lure out his own demons, their performances—a rape, a punch in the face, a swipe of a knife across a neck—become cinema verité.

Ferrara mixes documentary and conventional dramatic footage throughout "Dangerous Game," and much of the former comes off looking like amateur home video, as if some unacknowledged crew member were collecting all the delicious byplay on a camcorder for the wrap party.

The intention of the movie is to delve into the madness that befalls some filmmakers, makes them believe that what they are doing is more important than it is. Certainly, it's not infrequent that filmmakers and stars take themselves and their work too seriously, but they are really taking themselves too seriously when they dramatize their own delusions.

"Dangerous Game," which is ultimately more about the rotting of the director's soul than the self-destruction of his stars, wallows in this sort of egocentric melodrama, and does it with three not very interesting people. Russo and Madonna (much better here than in "Body of Evidence") give their all for both Eddie Israel and Abel Ferrara, but Russo's character is so self-absorbed, and Madonna's such a willing victim, that we don't much care what happens to them.

As for the philandering, abusive and intellectually shallow Eddie Israel, let's hope screenwriter Nicholas St. John didn't base him on Ferrara. Or if he did, that Ferrara, who cast his own wife (Nancy Ferrara) as Mrs. Israel, didn't take it as a compliment.

SIGHT AND SOUND, 6/94, p. 45, Amanda Lipman

Film director Eddie Israel spends a final evening with his wife and young son in New York before flying to Los Angeles to make a film, *Mother of Mirrors*. There, he discusses the motivation of the characters in the movie with its leading couple Sarah and Frank, and shoots a scene from the film. In it, Frank's character, Russell, a decadent yuppie, berates Sarah's character, Claire, for her change of attitude; she has given up her debauched lifestyle and become a strict, almost mystical Catholic. At dinner that night, Sarah charms Eddie, telling raucous jokes. Later Eddie, watching the day's rushes, calls Frank to tell him that he thinks Sarah, a TV actress, is good in the part. Frank, lying in bed with Sarah, refers to her as a whore; furious, she leaves.

In a montage of documentary-style discussions about the film between Eddie and his actors and of scenes of the film in progress, it becomes clear that Frank is fairly close to the character he plays and that his combination of desire and hatred for Sarah is real. In one scene, as Russell, he tears Claire's dress, cuts her hair roughly and shows her videos of their past sexual exploits while mocking her saintliness; she remains silent. Eddie asks Sarah out for a drink and she accepts. They dance together by a deserted swimming pool before going back to his hotel room. Just after Sarah has left, Eddie's wife Madlyn and their son pay him a surprise visit. Shocked, he tries to cover up any sign of his infidelity.

Eddie continues filming. In one scene in which Russell rapes Claire, Sarah becomes upset and acuses Frank of really having intercourse with her. Eddie warns him about his behaviour. Frank is sullen and angry. Later, Sarah tells Eddie about once being attacked by a stranger. Eddie and Madlyn drive up to the hills at night where they make love in the back of the car. Afterwards, he grows silent. When she asks what the matter is, he becomes angry. Later that night, Madlyn receives a phone call to say that her father has died; she leaves for New York.

Eddie and Sarah work on a scene in which Claire finally responds to Russell's taunts. Eddie flies back to New York for the funeral. When he arrives, he confesses his affair with Sarah to Madlyn. She is furious and throws him out. On the plane back to LA, he eyes up the stewardess with whom he later has sex. In his hotel room, he has a vision of Madlyn coming towards him while he asks her what she wants him to do. Later, he is slumped over the lavatory, having thrown up. The final scene shows Russell/Frank and Claire/Sarah together. He comes up to her with a gun. She tells him to shoot and he shoots.

Abel Ferrara's *Bad Lieutenant* telescoped the themes of sin and redemption into the study of one corrupt cop. In *Dangerous Game* (shown at the LFF as *Snake Eyes*), Ferrara has spread these concerns through a handful of characters—Eddie, the movie director, Frank and Sarah the actors, and Russell and Claire, the characters they play. Painted in crude strokes of degradation and guilt, *Bad Lieutenant* had a curiously moral feel. *Dangerous Game* engages less with moral absolutes—Claire's fatalistic piety in the film *Mother of Mirrors* does not signify only salvation but also retreat or even, as Russell would have it, cowardice. But it is also a less striking film. Where *Bad Lieutenant* was full of appalling but bold images, *Dangerous Game* is wordy and confused.

Much of this confusion is conscious: Ferrara mixes 'straight' dramatic narrative (Eddie and his family) with documentary-style video (Eddie and his cast discussing the film's characters) and stylised scenes from *Mother of Mirrors* in the making, so that it is sometimes hard to know which you are watching. A shot of a brutal exchange between James Russo and Madonna will eventually pull back to show cameras filming them or Eddie observing them (at one point, the clapperboard for *Mother of Mirrors* reads, "*Snake Eyes*/Ferrara").

And as the film progresses, the events in *Mother of Mirrors* are seen to mirror reality. Eddie's quasi-religious directorial creed that "the ultimate is pain and suffering—that's what it takes to survive" turns into a general dictum. Frank really is the debauched coke fiend he plays; Sarah accuses him of actually raping her in one extraordinarily tense scene made no less harrowing by the figure of Eddie presiding over it.

The relationships are also muddled. Eddie and Frank are old friends who eventually fall out. Frank and Sarah are lovers who fall out badly while playing an estranged husband and wife. Eddie is a tender lover to Sarah, a substitute sadistic Russell (when getting her to act her part), a deceitful husband still in love with his wife (played, perhaps to add an extra frisson, by Ferrara's own wife) and a combination of God and voyeur who watches closely, though apparently objectively, over the horrific scenes between Russell and Claire. Although he is not one of the actors, it is Eddie who appears to be playing the most roles. As he journeys from the devoted husband of the first scene to the comatose wash-out lying in his own vomit at the end, more echoes of *Bad Lieutenant* can be heard. But there is a difference. The anti-hero of that film was granted redemption after a moment of epiphany. The 'spiritual' experience Eddie has with a ghostly Madlyn in *Dangerous Game* leaves him less able to take control of his life than ever. Many things to many people, he is unable to be anything to himself.

Undoubtedly powerful at times, *Dangerous Game* seeks to overwhelm with negation. As a result it has a curious, merry-go-round quality: as long as you go with it, it seduces you into playing along with its circuit of sex, drugs, anger, confusion, fear and deception. If you let go, it becomes easy to ask why you should bother watching these brittle, self-engrossed people whose unmitigated self-disgust is not simply depressing but irritating. And what is most irritating is the fact that so many strands are plaited into what is essentially a one-trick pony. Eddie and Frank do not change so much as take us deeper into their drear, passive psyches. The novelty wears off—as does the allure of Russo's endless chemically-induced paranoid outbursts and of the usually brilliant Keitel's heavy-lidded sloppiness.

By contrast, Madonna finally proves that she can act without vamping. Where Keitel and Russo remain rooted in the same self-indulgent displays, she plays about in a far more challenging way with the boundaries between her two differently wilful characters. But in the end, even that does not matter. It is the film's final act of negation that as Sarah and Madlyn attempt to deal with their lives, those lives are pulled from under them by the men in yet more acts of sheer, stupid crudity.

VILLAGE VOICE, 11/23/93, p. 59, J. Hoberman

Admirably uniniatiating despite its lurid star power and coyly self-reflexive premise, *Dangerous Game* is another Abel Ferrara vision of the pit. The action is poised on the edge of violence with a group of volatile performers scraping each other raw. Hell in this ensemble piece is other actors.

Ferrara is a master of cine upchuck, and *Dangerous Game*, which originally had the more flavorsome title *Snake Eyes*, is unadulterated guts-spill. It's a movie about the moviemaking process, and if Ferrara (who, despite his newfound quasi-respectability, is unlikely to be adapting Edith Wharton any time soon) understands something about that, he knows at least as much about enacting solitude, emptiness, and rage.

Although the movie's claustrophobic Actors Studio premise suggests degenerate Cassavetes, the atmosphere is characteristically down and dirty. Harvey Keitel plays a two-fisted director who takes off from a wife, child, and comfortable town house on a snowy West Village street for wildest Los Angeles, there to film the aptly titled *Mother of Mirrors*—a two handed melodrama starring a pair of flaming neurotics played by world-class ranter James Russo and an alternately diffident and tearful Madonna.

The line between art and life is blurred from the getgo. Is it the Russo character who throws a tantrum on set or his character's character (who then climaxes one scene by pissing on the floor)? In *Mother of Mirrors*, Madonna and Russo play man and wife: She has returned to the Catholic church after a life of sexual and pharmaceutical dissolution; he feels abandoned. That the Russo and Madonna characters are sleeping together offscreen only adds to the confusion—as does Madonna's real-life role as the movie's de facto producer.

Considering the improvisational nature of the project, *Dangerous Game* is rigorously analytical in its grungy way—and not only because the script requires Madonna to ponder "the difference between acting and feeling." Scenes are repeated with variations throughout. Ferrara employs two film stocks—one for onscreen and the other for "offscreen" action—albeit treating both realities as quasi-vérité. One suspects that a number of videotaped rehearsals found their way into the final cut; the slate for a scene in *Mother of Mirrors* has Ferrara's name chalked on as director.

The movie-within-the-movie might have been dreamed up by punk *maîtresse* Beth B. (who, a decade ago, co-directed Russo in *Vortex* opposite Madonna doppelgänger Lydia Lunch), but it's far less cool. From the moment he appears, Keitel's director is hungry for breakdown performances: "Either do more coke and more booze or do less, but you gotta give me what I need," he tells Russo. Ferrara is scarcely less ruthless, cutting from the Madonna character recalling a rape to a close-up of an inflatable frog floating in a swimming pool.

Madonna is scarcely unwilling to take abuse—let alone deconstruct herself as an actress. "I'm not having my picture taken by Richard Avedon," she exclaims in one of her convincing "offscreen" moments; it's as if in some post-parochial-school support group, she and Ferrara found each other. There's a sense in which tormenting the star is the spectacle, indeed the ritual, of *Dangerous Game*. This is one exploitation film that knows its name.

In the movie (as in life), Russo plays a pugnacious secondario to Madonna's sacred monster. Not only does he verbally lambaste her, slap her around, rape her (in front of the crew), and slice her with a knife (after the director has yelled "cut!"), there are even "homemade" videotapes of Madonna—or rather the Madonna character's character—participating in some sort of grotesque orgy. (In one of the movie's prize moments, the overly pleased Russo character starts arguing with his director who orders him off the set while the VCR continues to blast out visual blasphemies in the background.) Meanwhile, Keitel attacks her as "a commercial piece of shit."

As movie and "movie" wear on, Keitel grows increasingly distracted. *Mother of Mirrors* merges with his own breakdown; his very features seem to dissolve—his nose a blob on the seamed slab of his face. Filming the breakup of a marriage inevitably affects his own. His wife (played by Nancy Ferrara, the real director's spouse) visits him in L.A., then gets the news that her father has died and returns to New York—thus setting the scene for a series of inappropriate admissions and naturalistically agonized domestic arguments. Mrs. Ferrara's feistiness in the role of directorial wife underscores her reported walkout on *King of New York* when it was shown at the 1990 New York Film Festival. ("I hated every thing about it," she later told *New York* magazine.)

Snow-covered New York is positively quaint by comparison to the neon maw of L.A., but it's the act of filming that seems most insane. Somehow, Ferrara manages to integrate a clip of Werner Herzog in the middle of the Amazon jungle discussing the madness of making *Fitzcarraldo*: "Maybe I should check into a lunatic asylum." The implication is that the director of *Mother of Mirrors*, if not *Dangerous Game*, is already there.

Emerging from the emotional lower depths, Ferrara's confession seems as anguished as the dry heaves. *Dangerous Game* may not pack the same wallop as *The Bad Lieutenant*, but it's no less ambitious. The movie gropes for meaning like a cave dweller toward the light.

Also reviewed in:
NEW YORK TIMES, 11/19/93, p. C14
VARIETY, 9/27/93, p. 41, David Stratton

DANGEROUS WOMAN, A

A Gramercy Pictures release of an Amblin Entertainment presentation of a Rollercoaster production. *Executive Producer:* Kathleen Kennedy. *Producer:* Naomi Foner. *Director:* Stephen Gyllenhaal. *Screenplay:* Naomi Foner. *Based on the novel by:* Mary McGarry Morris. *Director of Photography:* Robert Elswit. *Editor:* Harvey Rosenstock. *Music:* Carter Burwell. *Music Editor:* Adam M. Smalley and Tom Kramer. *Sound:* Stephen D. Halbert. *Sound Editor:* Norval D. Crutcher. *Casting:* Amanda Mackey and Cathy Sandrich. *Production Designer:* David Brisbin. *Art Director:* Kenneth Hardy. *Set Designer:* Mary Finn and Renato Franceschelli. *Set Decorator:* Margaret Goldsmith. *Set Dresser:* Helen Kozora, Phil Briggs, and Chris Parker. *Special Effects:* Larry Fioritto. *Costumes:* Susie DeSanto. *Make-up:* Deborah Larsen and Brad Wilder. *Stunt Coordinator:* Dan Bradley. *Running time:* 101 minutes. *MPAA Rating:* R.

CAST: Debra Winger (Martha Horgan); Barbara Hershey (Frances Beecham); Gabriel Byrne (Colin Mackey); David Strathairn (Getso); Chloe Webb (Birdy); John Terry (Steve Bell); Jan Hooks (Make-up Girl); Paul Dooley (Tupperware Salesman); Viveka Davis (Mercy); Richard Riehle (John); Laurie Metcalf (Anita Bell); Maggie Gyllenhaal (Patsy); Jacob Gyllenhaal (Edward); Myles Sheridan (Paul); Brad Blaisdell (Wesley); Warren Munson (Gately); Rebecca Arthur (Checker); Philip McNiven (Young Man); Breon Gorman (Heidi); Anna Mathias (Singer); Jack Riley (Bandleader); Brandis Kemp (Female Caterer); Charyl Wright-Roberts (In-Mate); Martine Wood (Female Security Guard); Joel Randel (Male Security Guard); Cassidy Ann Thomas and Chelsea Thomas (Martha's Daughter).

LOS ANGELES TIMES, 12/3/93, Calendar/p. 1, Peter Rainer

Folksy movies about "disturbed" and possibly stunted screwballs are usually phony and patronizing, but "A Dangerous Woman" is the intelligent exception. It's about Martha Horgan (Debra Winger), who lives in the guest house of a ranch owned by her aunt Frances (Barbara Hershey) and wears thick eyeglasses and seems perpetually addled by the endless guile of humanity.

Martha herself is guileless: she speaks the truth at all times not so much by choice as by instinct. Her slight backwardness—the doctors have never come up with a clinical name for it—sets her apart from the townsfolk, but what really sets her apart is her improbably pure spirit. What drives her and everyone else a little batty is that her childlike openness is crossed with the privacies of a grown woman.

The film, adapted by screenwriter Naomi Foner from the 1991 Mary McGarry Morris novel and directed by Stephen Gyllenhaal, doesn't undervalue Martha's strangeness, it just sees beyond it. So does Winger. The material is booby-trapped with high-flown sanctimony about Martha's "otherness" but, except for a couple of sequences, most notably near the end, the film never turns Martha into a saint or a standard bearer. It doesn't cutesy-fy her torment. (Neither did the novel.)

Gyllenhaal places Martha at the film's center and gives Winger the space to create a full-out characterization (for one of the few times in her career). She's wonderful without being showy. She doesn't play down to the audience or let us know she's only kidding around. It's a supremely unself-conscious portrayal of a woman who is supremely self-conscious. Martha observes everyone with a voyeur-like intensity but she also carries herself like someone who is constantly under surveillance. Wariness palls her features.

There's an interconnectedness to people's lives in this film, a buzz of shared emotion. The communal miseries are always in danger of teetering into "Peyton Place" territory but Gyllenhaal and Foner approach them from the inside, and that helps to give the film—rated R for "graphic sexuality, strong language and a scene of violence"—a freshness. (So does the plangent cinematography by Robert Elswit, which gives everything a warm, almost overheated glow.) Even when you can see where the film is going, it often catches you off balance, particularly in the ways in which it gets inside the ache of Martha's sexual longings. It's these longings that set "A Dangerous Woman" apart from most similarly themed movies. The film doesn't "humanize" Martha by pretending she's asexual.

Martha isn't the only character in the film who aches. Frances, who watches over Martha with ferocious hawk-like vigilance, is a deeply unhappy woman caught in a sordid, humiliating affair with a married state assemblyman (John Terry). She's too smart for the fix she's in and she knows it. But her weaknesses are the underside of her ferocity; that's one reason she's so protective—overprotective—of Martha. She understands the dangers or frailty.

When Mackey (Gabriel Byrne), an itinerant handyman, talks his way into patching up her ranch, he sets up an attraction with both women. Mackey is a bit too metaphorical a conceit for such a naturalistic movie—he's like a D. H. Lawrence interloper, all Masculine Life Force—but he fits into this universe anyway. Maybe it's because he turns out to be just as bollixed as everyone else. His scenes with Martha are tender and scary, these two walking wounded are captivated by intimacy but they can't really handle the emotional fallout.

The black comedy in "A Dangerous Woman" is that Martha, who lives by the "truth," is, in a sense, the sanest person in the movie—yet it is her unwavering fixation on honesty that stigmatizes her. That's what makes her a dangerous woman. (Without it, she'd just be the town screwball.) Through her eyes you see other townspeople—including her best friend Birdy (Chloe Webb) and Birdy's wandering-eyed boyfriend Getso (David Strathairn)—for what they are, not for what they pretend to be.

The filmmakers don't take the material into the most upsetting and severe emotional regions the way, say, a Flannery O'Connor or a Carson McCullers might have, and that's probably a limitation. There's a feel-good falsity to parts of the film, particularly at the end, that doesn't do justice to the sadness of Martha's life. But the filmmakers are trying to transmute that sadness into something redeeming—something heroic—and it's an understandable impulse. They prize Martha and, by the end, so do we.

NEW STATESMAN & SOCIETY, 5/20/94, p. 32, Jonathan Romney

A *Dangerous Woman* is a small, smart miracle of a film, and part of the miracle is that it got a cinema release at all. Everything about it suggests that in the normal course of events it might have crept out on video only, disguised as one of those "problem of the week" TV movies. Remorselessly downbeat, it has a beautifully ambivalent ending that's one in the eye for the very concept of the "feel-good" movie.

This is a rare example of that almost extinct genre, the Hollywood melodrama. By that I mean *real* melodrama, which crams all the world's infernal passions into a kitchen sink, and not one of those big-budget dewy-eyed numbers that Hollywood occasionally bangs out to boost Kleenex sales. And it's also a low-concept movie whose subject absolutely resists summing up in a neat two lines.

So it's about a dangerous woman. And presumably that woman is Debra Winger. Well, yes and no, but nothing in this film can be pinned down that easily. This is the sort of movie that makes studio executives put down their chequebooks in despair, and critics pick up their notepads.

Ostensibly, the woman of the title is Martha (Winger), whose undefined, and seemingly undefinable, mental problems have caused her to be in the care of her young aunt Frances (Barbara Hershey): a glamorous, neurotic high-flyer who acts at once as Martha's mother, sister and wayward daughter. They live together but apart in separate wings of a secluded house, and although Martha is to all intents and purposes independent, she's also under Frances' subtly domineering sway. It's in Frances' interests to keep Martha dowdy, de-sexed, fitting both the stereotypes of the old maid and the eternal child.

Martha's problem, at bottom, is with adulthood. She's surrounded by it, in the form of other people's obsessive drives—their childish urges, which they're able to cover with a veneer of sophistication. Her troubles begin when she's working in a dry-cleaner's and spots her best friend's sleazy partner Getso (an impeccably insidious David Strathairn) stealing from the till. When she reports him, it's partly with the voice of a child who won't join in, partly with the voice of absolute moral authority. She is shocked when she finds that worldly authority won't play her game.

What's brilliant about Naomi Foner's screenplay (from Mary McGarry Morris' novel) and her husband Stephen Gyllenhaal's direction is the devilish ease with which it blurs the distinction between the childish and the adult, the trivial and the earth-shattering. *A Dangerous Woman* is about monstrous passions, but also about decorum and the manoeuvres people go through to persuade themselves and the world that all is in order.

And what makes the film so effective as melodrama is the way that it deals with embarrassment. It begins with a wonderfully explosive scene. Frances is at home entertaining the politician with whom she's having a discreet liaison. Suddenly, in bursts his wife Anita (Laurie Metcalf), a raging fury of a woman who smashes her car into the porch then rushes in demanding vengeance. That's when Martha who has been watching, herself bursts in to protect Frances.

Suddenly, we're not sure whose irruption is the more unsettling: the angry wife or the gawky half-child among these stormy grownup wills. The residue is the smashed porch that looms through the film, a symbol of the broken home—the sort of *embarrassing* symptom that gives neighbours something to talk about.

Throughout, embarrassment is the measure of Martha's inability to fit in. When the entire world seems to close ranks over her denunciation of Getso, it's embarrassing for all concerned. When she climbs into Getso's car and catches him with another woman, it's embarrassing. And when she tries to fit in by braying heartily at all the wrong jokes at a Tupperware party, it's excruciating. As viewers, we're embarrassed more than anyone, caught between society's misunderstanding of her and her misunderstanding of it.

But we're caught out in other ways too. We're lulled into seeing Martha as others see her—as a bumbling, sexless figure in need of protection. When suddenly her sexuality emerges undisguised, as she finds herself turned on by simmering handyman Colin (Gabriel Byrne) and starts masturbating vigorously, our reaction is one of absolute unease—as if she has broken her contract with us. It's partly because of our habitual unease with any signs of sexuality in the mentally ill; partly because we realise we've been seeing her as others see her when we thought we had got close enough to see her otherwise.

Martha is no more or less dangerous than any other woman in this story, or any man. Everyone's passions are dangerous, either through intensity or simply inertia—as in the case of feckless Colin, whose deadbeat charm rides carelessly roughshod over everyone he comes into contact with. But the film is particularly concerned with attempts, by men and women alike, to pack away neatly the dangerous nature of women.

Frances has her passions carefully packaged, and presents the cool front of the professional political mistress; but when she can't package Martha as well, she goes bananas. Her ruthlessly infantilising hold on her fails when Martha goes into town and gets herself a make-over at the behest of a monstrous beautician (a relishable gusher of a cameo by *Saturday Night Live* veteran Jan Hooks). It's one of the film's many pointed moments. Suddenly, Martha's her own woman—but she's not. She's a terrible botched creation of Helena Rubinstein.

It's quite miraculous how many strands Foner and Gyllenhaal keep running consecutively, right to the genuinely shocking climax (all the more heartening in that Gyllenhaal's previous *Paris Trout* and *Waterland* were so wayward with their narrative). They're helped, of course, by a choice cast—a magnificently loathsome David Strathairn, Barbara Hershey playing cannily on the expectations of coolness that her persona usually carries, and Gabriel Byrne ... well, he was always the least invisible of actors. But here, considering his inability to merge totally into a less than convincing part, he's pretty successful.

Of course, it's Debra Winger's film, and it proves once again that she's too much of a difficult case ever to fit the bland template of the Hollywood lead. Winger has always kept her distance from conventionally flattering parts and homed in on those that give conflicting signals. Check out, if you can find it, her unsettling *femme fatale* in the Arthur Miller-scripted *Everybody Wins*, a weird, overlooked diamond of a film. Winger's Martha keeps you guessing, and everyone else. The crowning twist is that she seems to be keeping herself guessing as well. Uncertainty, in a Hollywood movie, tends to be as dangerous as it gets.

NEW YORK POST, 12/3/93, p. 45, Michael Medved

"Dangerous Woman" is intensely well acted handsomely shot, solidly directed—and absolutely impossible to recommend. This is the sort of infuriatingly aimless downer that raises two un-answerable questions: Why did so many talented people agree to participate in making it, and why in heaven's name should moviegoers part with their hard-earned money to see it?

The story centers around a quaint collection of desperately unhappy loners living out their bitter lives in a dusty town in rural California. Debra Winger plays Martha the "Dangerous Woman" of the title, a bespectacled misfit who may be mildly retarded and whose childlike sensibility leaves her painfully vulnerable to the conniving adults around her.

She lives in the guest house on a ranch owned by her aunt (Barbara Hershey), a bored widow who is conducting a hopeless affair with a married politician (John Terry), despite the destructive rages of his jealous wife (the formidable Laurie Metcalfe). Gabriel Byrne plays an alcoholic, homeless handyman who gets a job fixing up the porch that Metcalfe has destroyed, and ends up moving in for a while with Hershey and Winger.

Nothing much happens with these people, though Byrne does, at long last, finish his work on the porch. Winger also manages to lose her job at a local laundry when she's falsely charged with pilfering money from the cash register, the accusations are made by a vicious, sleazy low life named Getso (David Strathairn) who is of course, the real thief.

At the very end of the movie there's a sudden blast of violence that's supposed to come as a complete shock but the filmmakers go to such great lengths to portray it as an accident that the occurrence seems arbitrary rather than inevitable, and it does nothing to illuminate the characterizations that have been the picture's main focus.

Meanwhile, Winger's courageous performance is undermined by her underwritten part. This always adventurous actress will receive a great deal of praise for so dramatically deglamorizing herself: With her protruding jaw, her squinty eyes behind impossibly thick glasses, her pathetic clothes and convincingly klutzy movements, it's hard to believe that this same performer ever played sex symbols.

Martha indeed comes across convincingly as one of those lost souls you might see on the street, but since we know so little about her we don't up caring any more than we would for a passing stranger. We know even less about Byrne and Hershey, leaving us little chance to empathize with their drunken blubberings.

The spare and distant screenplay is by Naomi Foner, best known for the intriguing (and Oscar-nominated) script for "Running on Empty." The director here is her husband Stephen Gyllenhaal, who previously crafted the critically respected "Paris Trout" (with Barbara Hershey and Dennis Hopper) and "Waterland" with Jeremy Irons.

Like those previous films "A Dangerous Woman" seems to exalt style over substance; its portentous moodiness never adds up to anything, except for an insipid epilogue that evokes Hollywood's latest cliche about redefining "family" as any assemblage of people thrown together by affection or circumstance.

The only real danger in "A Dangerous Woman" is that the audience will suffer a massive attack of boredom, mixed with mounting irritation that so much skill should be wasted on so empty and pointless a vehicle.

NEWSDAY, 12/3/93, Part II/p. 86, John Anderson

Martha, the dangerous woman of "A Dangerous Woman," is in many ways the perfect woman, the perfect person. She doesn't lie. She's loyal to her friends. She tries hard to please. And when all is said and done, she does the right thing.

Naturally, she's the local oddball. Kids make fun of her when she walks down the street, her body a jumble of inconclusive intentions. Her salary at the dry cleaner's is paid by her wealthy aunt and guardian Frances (Barbara Hershey), because Martha, whose mental "illness" has never actually been diagnosed, wouldn't work otherwise. People are either pitying of Martha, like her good friend Birdy (Chloe Webb) or cruel, like Birdy's boyfriend Getso (David Strathairn), who frames her for stealing the money he's palmed from the dry cleaners case register. Her trusting nature constantly betrays her. Calamitous events will befall her, but it seems almost redundant, because her life is a calamity.

Debra Winger, giving one of her most involved performances, imbues Martha with a catalog of nervous tics and self-conscious mannerisms that might have been maddening delivered by a lesser actress. But Winger, who's had considerable experience playing characters who are slightly off-center, is canny: She makes Martha much more than an object of pity, endowing her with a combination of traits—innate kindness and learned shrewdness—that elevate her to the poignant.

Much of "A Dangerous Woman," though, is just too irritatingly predictable. Frances' affair with Steve, a married politician (John Terry), is never going to work out; his alcoholic wife, Anita (an effective but brief performance by Laurie Metcalf) has already driven her car through Frances' porch during a drunken tantrum. When Mack (Gabriel Byrne), an itinerant, inebriate handyman is hired by Frances to fix the porch, you know that both Martha and Frances are going to succumb to his charms, as pungent as they may be. And that tragedy will occur seems a foregone conclusion, given the foreboding pace of Martha's story.

But Stephen Gyllenhaal, dealing with a far simpler tale than he rendered in the sadly unappreciated "Waterland," has a sturdy grasp on what makes Martha work, which is the hard reality of her story. There are no grandiose gestures, no sentimental adornments—when Mack and Martha have sex, it's brutish and short, punctuated by his post-coital lurch into the darkness and her assumption of the fetal position. The white-trash misdemeanors of Getso are tawdry but banal; he's an insignificant worm. We know he'll get his comeuppance, although not quite so violently, and not with violence so coolly and realistically portrayed.

"A Dangerous Woman" is really a very small story; I'm not familiar with the book, but movies don't tend to embellish on a novel. The characters really shouldn't be of any interest, and aren't, except for Martha. She's an unpleasant mirror on our petty intolerances, and Winger puts her in a frame that both dazzles and bewilders.

SIGHT AND SOUND, 6/94, p. 46, Lizzie Francke

Martha Horgan, a woman in her late 30s, lives with her young aunt Frances on a large country estate. Martha's undiagnosed mental condition keeps her slightly separate from the world. Frances is having an affair with a local married politician, Steve. One night while the two lovers are together, Steve's wife Anita turns up in an alcoholic stupor at Frances' and Martha's house, crashing her car into the front porch. Later Frances advertises for a handyman to repair it. Meanwhile Martha, who works at a dry cleaner's, is fired after being accused of taking money from the till. She explains that the real culprit is Getso, her best friend Birdy's boyfriend, but no-one will believe her. Back home, she tries to contact Birdy, but Birdy won't take her calls.

Colin Mackey, an alcoholic drifter, turns up in answer to Frances' ad. Frances refuses to give him work. Later Martha storms off after an argument with Frances, and is met by Colin, who offers her a lift into town. There Martha bumps into Getso who starts taunting her, and Colin chases him away. He drives Martha back home and starts working on the house. When Frances returns she is first annoyed but she can see that Colin is doing a good job. Colin stays and Frances sets about organising a surprise party for Steve. Later Martha is upset when Frances buys her a dress for the party. She wants to prove that she can do something for herself and goes into town, where she buys a dress and gets a make-over. On the way home she has another altercation with Getso.

Later, Frances upsets Martha with a disparaging comment about her new look. That night a drunken Colin visits Martha and they end up making love. The party for Steve goes well until Anita turns up. Frances is devastated to see Steve and Anita dancing together, and she hits the bottle. Colin finds Frances crying on the kitchen floor; mistaking him for Steve, she encourages his advances. Later Colin tells Martha that he will soon be leaving. Upset, she seeks out Birdy for advice. She discovers Getso at Birdy's apartment; the two get into a fight and Martha stabs and kills Getso. Martha is arrested. It turns out that she is pregnant. Frances tries to persuade her to state that she was raped by Getso and killed him in self-defence. Martha refuses to agree to this or have an abortion. Colin tells Frances he is the father of the baby. Martha pleads guilty to murder and is put into care. She has the baby which Frances looks after. Martha is regularly visited by her aunt, her young daughter and Colin.

With an opening sequence that lunges immediately into complex and ambiguous territory, *A Dangerous Woman* marks itself as a film of intense emotional force, a crash trauma condensed into elliptical fragments. It also begs the question of who might be the dangerous woman of the title, as Anita looms out of the darkness and drives her car into Frances' and Martha's homestead, set in a small orange grove in an almost desert-like patch of America. There is a sense of great damage and dislocation in the brief eruption of Anita's terrible grief.

There is also the suggestion that the anger which she is able to display so defiantly may be imploding in Martha and Frances. In this respect, the film shifts between these women. It is to Laurie Metcalf's credit that she brings such substance to her cameo, which in its own way matches the brilliance of Hershey and Winger's performances. Anita may appear only briefly, but those moments are saturated with an intensity that make them pivotal. Such is the party scene in which Anita arrives once again out of the darkness to claim and dance with her husband. They dance closely, obviously needing each other. Frances looks on, prevented by circumstance from displaying any feeling, but it is the saddened expression on Martha's taut face which intimates how embroiled in each other's confusion these characters are.

The film is concerned with the slippage between people—emotional attachments evolved out of substitution. Director Stephen Gyllenhaal and screenwriter Naomi Foner evoke a certain realism, but then very subtly undercut it with spare, slightly disjointed dialogue that seems looped at times in order to disorientate. In such a way the film is about relationships refracted and distorted through a lens. This enmeshment is most specifically found between Martha and Frances. Frances is only a couple of years older than Martha, yet she is her aunt. Here the notion of family is as collapsed as the front porch—a theme picked up at the end when Frances in effect becomes mother to Martha's daughter. This doubling is also marked in Frances' opening voice-over explaining Martha's condition—"She was always odd, but there was nothing that they could label ... so she became mine."

Martha might therefore be conceived as the cypher for resistance. She can't be labelled or tacked down. She refuses to be socialised, in the sense that she divines the truth at great cost to herself. Yet, curious about the world, she forces herself to learn about the conventions of 'good' and acceptable behaviour. There is poignancy in her desire, though the protocol is presented as rather ludicrous. Reading a 'How to be Popular' manual before attending Birdy's Tupperware party, she learns the socially acceptable lines, dresses in bright colours and laughs at the salesman's bad jokes. Yet, so studied, it is all out of kilter. The scene in which she has a beauty salon makeover is also conceived as somewhat satirical, as the beautician hard-sells her cosmetics; yet, as she waves her wand like some sugar-plum suited fairy, the process effects a positive change in Martha.

But the film does more than rework the cliché of the frumpy duckling learning to swan about. For Martha's make-over, plus her decision to pick a dress for herself rather than acquiesce to Frances' choice, is seen to be part of her move towards articulating her own sexuality. In a previous scene, she is observed discreetly masturbating, an activity which seems to have been prompted by her watching Colin work in the garden.

Certainly Frances would seem to feel threatened by this altered Martha, as is apparent in her desperate put-down after she returns in her new guise, "How could you do this, this is just like you," Frances exclaims—though it is exactly not like the secretive, isolated Martha. She is now refusing to be the child that Frances had to put an invisible rein on, or the innocent that Colin earlier sought religious blessing from. Socially wayward and now sexual, there is the potential for her to become a dangerous woman indeed. Thus the film tilts towards an uneasy and disruptive conclusion, its own power being in its oddness, its refusal to be categorized.

VILLAGE VOICE, 12/7/93, p. 63, J. Hoberman

An even more drastic spectacle of personal reinvention, [The reference is to *Blue*; see Hoberman's review.] *A Dangerous Woman* presents Debra Winger as a puffy superfrump, the universal object of derision for a small, central California town. Winger's Martha is a thickly-bespectacled nerd who can hardly answer the phone without knocking off her glasses, transforming even a neighborhood Tupperware party into an exploration of the outer limits of geekdom.

Touchier than the most hypersensitive adolescent yet prone to childlike blurting, Martha is supported by a wealthy, unhappily distracted aunt (Barbara Hershey), who underwrites her nominal job in a Main Street dry cleaner. The store is filled with petty corruptions but the dangerous thing about Martha is—she doesn't lie. Neither does the camera: Winger's contrived hunched-over waddle, her abundance of tics and surplus of techniques, bring to mind Dustin Hoffman, even as her flat, whiny drawl and scrunched-up face suggest a role that could easily have been played for laughs by Gilda Radner.

Indeed, the *Saturday Night Live* connection is irresistible after the exceedingly broad scene wherein Martha gets a makeover from a drugstore cosmetician inanely played by Jan Hooks. Further transformations are promised once an itinerant Irish handyman (Gabriel Byrne) materializes out of the gloaming: "I get hangovers now before I finish drinking," this dark angel gloomily confesses to the innocent Martha, whose eyes widen and skin clears once she removes her glasses and receives a real kiss. Before long the mercurial handyman is teaching her how to dance and from there it only takes a bit of slap and tickle to restore an approximation of the lusty old Debra Winger.

Made by the wife-husband team Naomi Foner (writer-producer) and Stephen Gyllenhaal (director) from the novel by Mary McGarry Morris, *A Dangerous Woman* is an engrossing but lopsided stunt—ultimately stumbling from the realm of mega-performance and modest character drama into the land of lurid fairy tale. It's there that David Strathairn, Byrne's evil twin and the most accomplished of the performers who orbit the film's periphery, manages to eclipse the hardworking star in the most violent sequence through skillful underplaying.

Also reviewed in:
CHICAGO TRIBUNE, 12/3/93, Friday/p. A, Johanna Steinmetz
NEW REPUBLIC, 12/20/93, p. 36, Stanley Kauffmann
NEW YORK TIMES, 12/3/93, p. C19, Janet Maslin
NEW YORKER, 12/13/93, p. 125, Anthony Lane
VARIETY, 9/27/93, p. 37, Todd McCarthy
WASHINGTON POST, 12/3/93, p. G7, Rita Kempley
WASHINGTON POST, 12/3/93, Weekend/p. 58, Desson Howe

DARK HALF, THE

An Orion Pictures release.   *Executive Producer:* George A. Romero.   *Producer:* Declan Baldwin.   *Director:* George A. Romero.   *Screenplay:* George A. Romero.   *Based on the book by:* Stephen King.   *Director of Photography:* Tony Pierce-Roberts.   *Editor:* Pasquale Buba. *Music:* Christopher Young.   *Music Editor:* John Lasalandra.   *Sound:* John Sutton and (music) Eric Tomlinson.   *Sound Editor:* Michael Hilkene and Eric W. Lindemann.   *Casting:* Terry Liebling.   *Production Designer:* Cletus Anderson.   *Art Director:* Jim Feng.   *Set Decorator:*

Brian Stonestreet. *Set Dresser:* Greg Jones. *Special Effects:* Carl Horner, Jr. *Visual Effects:* Peter Kuran. *Costumes:* Barbara Anderson. *Make-up:* Jeannee Josefczyk. *Make-up Effects:* John Vulich and Everett Burrell. *Stunt Coordinator:* Phil Neilson. *Running time:* 122 minutes. *MPAA Rating:* R.

CAST: Patrick Brannan (Young Thad Beaumont); Larry John Meyers (Doc Pritchard); Beth Grant (Shayla Beaumont); Christina Romero (Little Girl); Rohn Thomas (Dr. Albertson); Molly Renfroe (Hilary); Judy Grafe (Head Nurse); John Machione (Male Nurse); Amy Madigan (Liz Beaumont); Timothy Hutton (Thad Beaumont/George Stark); Erik Jensen (Male Student); Robert Joy (Fred Clawson); Tom Mardirosian (Rick Cowley); Rutanya Alda (Miriam Cowley); Kent Broadhurst (Mike Donaldson); Glenn Colerider (Homer Gamache); Christine Forrest (Trudy Wiggins); Royal Dano (Digger Holt); Michael Rooker (Alan Pangborn); Nardi Novak (Pangborn's Receptionist); Zachery "Bill" Mott (Norris Ridgewick); William Cameron (Officer Hamilton); David Butler (Trooper #1); Curt De Bor (Trooper #2); Drinda Lalumia (Dodie); Lamont Arnold (NYC Cop #1); Lee Hayes (NYC Cop #2); Julie Harris (Reggie Delesseps); John Ponzio (Todd Pangborn); Chelsea Field (Annie Pangborn); Jack Skelly (Man in the Hallway); Marc Field (Donaldson Cop #1); Rik Billock (Donaldson Cop #2); Bruce Kirkpatrick (Officer #1); David Early (Officer #2); Jeff Monahan (Wes); Jeffery Howell (Dave); Melissa Papp (Rosalie); J. Michael Hunter (Garrison); Therese Courtney (Receptionist); Marty Roppelt (Young Officer); Sarah Parker (Wendy Beaumont); Elizabeth Parker (William Beaumont).

LOS ANGELES TIMES, 4/23/93, Calendar/p. 12, Michael Wilmington

There are two Timothy Huttons in the "The Dark Half," the kitschily gory new Jekyll-Hyde thriller from Stephen King's 1989 novel. And it's hard to tell which is scarier: the Hutton who plays Thad Beaumont, small-town teacher and father and failed writer of serious novels, or the *other* Hutton—the one who plays George Stark, the killer from redneck Hell. That Stark is a sneering, leather-jacketed sadist, who roars out of the graveyard with a razor and a bad attitude, and, commandeering a black Toronado, leaves a trail of fear and corpses behind him.

As Mississippian George, Hutton suggests a Dixie demon in lizard-skin boots: Elvis' "Are You Lonesome Tonight?" is his nightmare signature tune. As Thad from Castle Rock, Maine—the character King obviously modeled on himself—Hutton looks glassy-eyed, checker-shirted, "normal." Surrounded by concerned wife Liz (Amy Madigan) and their kids—twins, naturally—he's almost a monster of niceness.

Does Thad's inner evil focus his energies? In the story, which director George Romero has adapted with his usual dark skill, George Stark is the pseudonym Thad invented for a series of bloody bestsellers, written in the hard-boiled style of Jim Thompson or Shane Stevens. And when Thad, threatened with exposure by a scummy little blackmailer ("Atlantic City's" Robert Joy), decides to kill off "George," and get on with his serious, *unsellable* stuff, his inner self comes hellishly to life and won't let him.

King's story is full of zingers, all aptly visualized by Romero. There's Thad's dead twin, who turns up as a tumor, or an eye, in his brain. There's the "Wrong Man" investigation of Thad by shrewd Sheriff Pangborn (Michael Rooker). And there's a hair-raising grab from Hitchcock's "Birds": flocks of thousands of sparrows, or "psycho-pomps," that keep mantling the landscape, like vast multi-wringed harbingers of *Angst*.

The movie's *other* George, "Dark Half's" writer-director Romero, is, like King, a specialist at mixing the mundane with the gruesome. And, though Romero often seems to be working this material too gingerly, carefully, he gets the right tone of gradually rising menace. King and Romero are a natural match, and though this isn't the best of the King-derived horror movies—"The Shining" and "The Dead Zone" probably are—it's close.

Violent and credibility-straining it may be, but it's not cheap or thoughtless. The film captures the best part of the book, and since it's more compact—at 467 pages, the novel was a slightly gaseous over-read—it may be more effective. Romero prunes the story, revs it up. He gets a gleam and smoothness that offset the gore: the tony photography by Tony Pierce-Roberts

("Howards End"), the presence of classy Julie Harris, as Delesseps, Thad's pipe-smoking colleague.

In a good acting ensemble, Hutton shines in both parts—though, as Thad, he doesn't always suggest the kind of shaggy introvert who might idealize a swaggering, maniac bully like George. Yet, if "Dark Half" has a major flaw, beyond simple overkill, it's something deep in the original book itself. Romero and King, who once had a pseudonym of his own (the "late" Richard Bachman), keep Stark too emotionally *separate* from Thad. The story might be more terrifying if it showed more mutual attraction and sympathy between the good and dark halves.

Thad Beaumont represents the author as he'd like to be seen, and George is what he secretly dreams of being: the cold-eyed wanderer and hell-raiser. In a way, the two mirror a great schism in American literature: the tendency of male writers to fail at home life and succeed with tales of the outlaw country, or what Huck Finn called the "territory ahead."

Using this split, "The Dark Half" (MPAA rated R for violence and language) performs a private exorcism on a huge super-movie stage. It gives us thrills, shocks, works us over. But it doesn't really touch us much—and, deep down, that's probably what King and Romero most wanted. Maybe the real tears and pain are in the side they don't show. Maybe they're in the *other* movie.

NEW YORK POST, 4/23/93, p. 31, Jami Bernard

As I'm writing this, I'm eating snacks, washing them down with chemical-saturated diet colas, and being nasty to people who call me on the phone. I guess that's my Dark Half. Watch out, the sparrows are flying again!

In "The Dark Half," Thaddeus Beaumont (Timothy Hutton) is a mild-mannered English professor who is struggling to write quality fiction. In his off hours, he's a nasty son of a gun who writes pulp fiction under the pseudonym George Stark. When he's George, he writes with a special pencil, drinks heavily, smokes like a chimney. His handwriting gets bad, his thoughts worse, and the dark clouds over his eyes are nothing compared to the dark swarm of sparrows that fills the skies whenever a new Stark novel is about to hit the best-seller list.

The beast within is a familiar concept in literature and movies, but "The Dark Half" is about something more specific to artists—the occasional fear or megalomaniacal fantasy that the artist's own imaginings are so vivid they can actually spring to life and wreak havoc.

"The Dark Half" is directed by George Romero, who adapted the Stephen King book for the screen. King has traversed this territory before with "Misery," in which (in the movie version) writer James Caan finds he cannot kill off the character he has created for a series of trashy books because an ardent fan is holding him hostage and forcing him to write the character back to life. "Misery" was about the trap writers get into of creating characters their readers won't let them get rid of.

"The Dark Half" is virtually the same theme, only this time the invented character himself won't let Thaddeus kill him off. King may have been inspired by his own experience of working under the pseudonym Richard Bach.

In the larger sense, the problem is Thad's own reluctance to give up his lucrative pseudonym in order to try his hand at art—which is not only harder to write but also doesn't pay as well. In the smaller sense—and "The Dark Half" is nothing if not literal and particular—Thad is really two people, twins, one of whom is the pleasant intellectual, the other a junkyard dog of a guy.

Most people have the occasional bad mood, but Thad has a lot more than a bad mood brewing in his skull—in fact, he has a whole other unborn twin living inside his head! (This doesn't spoil anything for you; it's in the first 10 minutes of the movie.)

As a child, Thad gets headaches; and when the doctors open him up they find inside the twin who never got born yet is advanced enough to have blinking eyes and a cavity in one of his teeth. The doctors remove the twin and Thad grows up feeling incomplete, unconsciously rubbing the area from where they surgically removed his alter ego long ago.

As an adult, Thad and his Rock of Gibraltar wife (Amy Madigan) have twins of their own—lots of goo-goo reaction shots. So far, neither of the twins is showing signs of those headaches Thad used to have, and yet those sparrows are continuing to fly. Flocks of computer-animated birds keep swerving and swooping as if they have lost their way en route to some long-ago Hitchcock set, where they properly belong.

Thad and wife "kill" the George Stark alter ego by exposing him in People magazine, and then a series of real murders begins, all bearing Thad's fingerprints. The sheriff (Michael Rooker) is puzzled but doesn't arrest Thad because, unlike the killer, Thad doesn't wear pointy shoes and whistle "Are You Lonesome Tonight?"

As in "Misery," "The Dark Half" is in awe of the process of writing itself—the supplies, the ritual. Like many artists, Thad has self-loathing for his compulsion to keep his audience happy, while simultaneously wondering whether his creations are superior to him. Thad must face up to his inner demons, and if "The Dark Half" isn't always as gripping as one would like in a horror movie, at least it has an intriguing premise and the opportunity to see Timothy Hutton break out of his clean-cut image to play both roles.

NEW YORK POST, 4/23/93, p. 31, Michael Medved

The good news is that thanks to some dazzling visual effects and Timothy Hutton's top-notch performance, it's the best dumb evil-twin movie we're likely to see this year.

Hutton stars as a standard-issue mild-mannered professor of English at a picturesque college in central Maine. As the story unfolds, his colleagues are shocked to discover that he's been using a pseudonym to write bloody, macho best-selling novels. With his secret discovered, Hutton resolves to kill off his embarrassing alter ego, but this "dark half" isn't quite ready to go gentle into that good night.

It turns out that the tough-guy personality the hero has invented to suit his pseudonym has become psychically connected to a gigantic, throbbing tumor that was removed from the teen-aged Hutton's head in an especially gross and unsettling prologue to the story. Now this ambulatory mass of murderous flesh, outfitted in black leather jacket, slicked-back hair and pointy-toed cowboy boots, goes on a rampage of mayhem and mutilation, ultimately threatening the professor, his twin infant sons, and his saintly, long-suffering wife (Amy Madigan).

All the slit throats, puncture wounds and beating deaths are additionally (and incoherently) accompanied by the periodic appearance of a squawking swarm of thousands of bad-tempered (and ultimately flesh-eating) sparrows, whose main function seems to be to demonstrate how far movie special effects and avian acting have progressed since the days of Alfred Hitchcock's "The Birds."

As soon as any self-respecting horror fan hears that this story takes place in central Maine and involves some soft-spoken guy confronting an unspeakable, supernatural terror, he'll know that he's arrived in overly familiar Stephen King country—even though director George Romero here uses his own home base of Pittsburgh to stand in (unconvincingly) for rural New England.

Romero, still best known for the 1968 cult classic "Night of the Living Dead," describes the project as a "Jekyll and Hyde story"; but this material owes far more to classic German "Doppelganger" tales of the Romantic era—with the civilized hero suddenly confronting a look-alike monster comprised of pure Id.

However you construe this character, Hutton does a remarkably good job with both halves of his performance. Ever since his Oscar-winning role in "Ordinary People" Hutton has made a specialty of shy, All-American guys with some off-center, self-destructive streak lurking just below the surface.

It comes as no surprise that he handles the tormented teacher part of his role with effortless aplomb, but the real revelation here is the gleefully sadistic, perfectly calibrated menace that he brings to his moments on screen as the murderous spirit, George Stark. Hutton's total transformation in these scenes suggests that this gifted (and often undervalued) actor might enjoy a highly profitable career playing vicious bad guys, if he so chooses.

Of all the score of movies based on King's work, the most interesting to date have been those (such as "The Shining," "Stand By Me" and "Misery") that depict psychological rather than supernatural struggles and terrors. And it's too bad that Hutton didn't get the chance to apply his talents to that sort of project

"The Dark Half" offers yet another illustration of the generally reliable rule of thumb that the horror movie with the weakest, most predictable story line comes up with the most vivid and gut-churning special effects. The filmmakers make a special point of hitting you over the head with technical virtuosity because there's not much else to keep you awake.

NEWSDAY, 4/23/93, Part II/p. 70, John Anderson

"The Dark Half" might have been the horror junkie's horror film, given the pairing of a Stephen King story with the direction of George ("Night of the Living Dead") Romero.

But this Jekyll-and-Hyde story about a writer's murderous pseudonym coming to life is too long to sustain King's lukewarm introspection about his own motives as an author—the 1989 book followed the author's revelation that he also was the non-horror-writing novelist Richard Bachman. And it's too psychologically pretentious for Romero's tongue-in-cheek approach to terror.

The film has its moments, of course, some provided by the star, Timothy Hutton, some by the director: As the story begins, young Thad Beaumont (Patrick Brannan) suffers a series of blinding headaches. When a shard of his skull is surgically removed—with the kind of loving detail you'd expect from Romero—we see a latent eye peering out at us. And part of a nose. And a tooth. With a cavity. These are the remains, we're told, of Thad's twin, a not-fully-formed fetus that was absorbed into Thad's own body before birth. It's questionable medicine, *a la* King, but quintessential Romero, with humor and gore thriving symbiotically—much the way the older Thad (Hutton) and his alter ego, George Stark (Hutton again), will thrive later.

Thad grows up to become a college professor and "serious" writer who invents George so he can write sadistically violent and lucrative crime novels without tainting his own name. Romero wants us to accept all the armchair psychiatry about Thad's repressed id at face value, when it's really more of King's armchair quackery. But it does provide for some genuine suspense early on, as Thad speaks of George and lapses into the latter's malevolent personality. As his wife, Liz (Amy Madigan), watches with rising apprehension, there's even a fleeting feeling of momentum. But Romero doesn't sustain it, settling instead for isolated moments of mayhem and visual exhilaration.

When Thad's secret is about to be exposed by a blackmailer, he decides to come clean, "kill off" George and reap a torrent of publicity; People magazine even runs a shot of Thad and Liz in a cemetery, standing over a George Stark headstone. But George, straight razor in hand, is not about to go gently into that good night. Instead, he starts cutting throats, beginning with those of the People reporter, the photographer, Thad's agent and the agent's ex-wife, all to the strains of Elvis singing "Are You Lonesome Tonight."

It's unfortunate that Hutton's last outing was in "The Temp," a particularly hare-brained thriller, because doing two such movies in a row looks like a trend (though this is a 1991 production, apparently held up by Orion Pictures' problems). Even though Thad is typical Hutton, George—whom the actor plays as a cross between Willem Dafoe in "Wild at Heart" and Michael Keaton in "Beetlejuice"—shows how comically liberated an actor can be when he wraps himself in black leather and Brylcreem.

One of the better performances in "The Dark Half" is by Michael Rooker (who played the title role in "Henry: Portrait of a Serial Killer") as the cop who lets Thad remain free while he investigates the case. The fact the murders continue with increased frequency doesn't make his leniency very logical of course, but Rooker almost makes us forget all that. Romero, however, can't convince us to buy his story, even with the kind of suspended belief one usually takes along to a film like this. And the flocks of sparrows Thad hears in his head whenever George is on the prowl, and which swarm in great Hitchcockian waves, only serve to remind one how scary a good movie can be.

SIGHT AND SOUND, 11/93, p. 39, Kim Newman

Castle Rock, Maine, 1968. Young Thad Beaumont, an aspiring writer, is operated on for a brain tumour which turns out to be the residuum of an unborn and incompletely absorbed twin. As the tumour is excised, the hospital is besieged by a freak flock of sparrows. 1991. Thad has become a critically acclaimed but commercially unsuccessful author of literary novels and is teaching creative writing. After class, he is approached by Fred Clawson, a blackmailer who has learned that Thad is also George Stark, the pseudonymous author of a series of successful and violent thrillers. Rather than pay Clawson, Thad arranges for an article in *People* magazine exposing his Stark identity and appears in a photograph with his wife Liz, posing with a mock gravestone for Stark. The remains of the unborn twin, buried in the same graveyard, evolve into an incarnation of Stark, who emerges from the earth to embark on a vengeance spree, murdering all who were a party to his 'death'.

Because Stark leaves Thad's fingerprints, Sheriff Alan Pangborn has to suspect that the writer is the murderer but, convinced by vague alibis, refrains from arresting him. Stark makes contact with Thad and tries to force him into writing another Stark novel, claiming he is literally falling apart and that further books will allow him to coalesce. Thad, talking with his colleague Professor Delesseps, learns that sparrows, which still flock unnaturally around Stark, are psychopomps, entities come to carry one of the pair off to the afterlife. Stark kidnaps Liz and Thad's twin children and returns to the family home in Castle Rock. Thad follows and confronts his decaying alter ego. The sparrows attack the house and tear Stark to shreds.

Most horror trades on universal fears, but here, as in several other book-to-film translations (*The Shining, Misery*), Stephen King trades on the fears of a novelist. Specifically, he explores the fears of a popular novelist unable or unwilling to subscribe either to the belief that genre writing is the equal of, say, John Steinbeck, or to the pop criticism that holds mass-appeal genres as expressions of a reader's wishes if not an author's intentions. As a novelist, especially as one who sometimes writes under a pseudonym (Jack Yeovil), I should find *The Dark Half* hitting home with me. But, for all the knee-jerk shocks in the kill scenes and Timothy Hutton's unsettling mildness as Thad, I remained only vaguely disturbed at odd moments. As a writer, I was more inclined to get irritated by lapses like Sheriff Pangborn's refusal to lock Thad up, in defiance of all rational characterisation, simply because the story would end if the hero weren't free to continue his duel with the monster. King and George A. Romero are too good at their trade/art to fall over like this, but the book and film of *The Dark Half* are littered with stumbles which could come from the merest paperback original or direct-to-video dodo. Like *Misery*, which King originally intended to publish under his 'Richard Bach' pseudonym, *The Dark Half* deals with the writer's intensely personal professional problems. Far less successful than his earlier novel, which benefits from the lack of King's sometimes fuzzy supernatural contraptions, the book draws on the impulses that led King to create Bachman and explicitly echoes the circumstances of his 'exposure'. The vital difference, of course, is that King, unlike Thad Beaumont and like George Stark, is the half of the partnership who reaches and pleases huge audiences with books that might be construed as simply gruesome entertainments. Sadly, like Stark, the novel opens coherently and gradually falls apart. After the interesting process of establishing Stark's separate existence has been dispensed with, the new-born entity contents himself with the simplistic-monster business of slaughtering a succession of marginal characters before the final confrontation.

Romero's careful adaptation of an unwieldy tome tries hard to correct King's slapdash plotting, but is ultimately yoked to the novel's trite story and unable to articulate the more intriguing issues raised. Far less effective than his concise *Monkey Shines, The Dark Half* finds Romero away from his usual concerns (although he works in the horror genre, Romero's films prefer science fiction to the supernatural) and doing his best to embody another man's ideas. That Romero remains one of the most underrated craftsmen in genre cinema is proved yet again by the way he almost pulls off much of King's silliness. Stuck with an absurd finale, Romero carefully works in the eerie sparrows as a recurring theme from the first sequence, almost but not quite justifying the avian *deus ex machina* with the ominous build-up.

The film's major success is in the area of characterisation, with Hutton delivering complementary performances almost on a level of Jeremy Irons in *Dead Ringers*. There is a scripted confusion about the villain, who never decides whether he is a pseudonym come to life, the ghost of a dead twin, or another incarnation of that malignant Elvis currently stalking American popular culture. Evoked by a snatch of "Are You Lonesome Tonight", and with pointy boots, ominous quiff and Mississippi accent, Hutton's Stark is a potent monster, with his polite threats and razor slashes. But he never remotely suggests a writer, and sadly disappears under open-sore make-up as the plot falls apart around him.

There are frightening early hints—Thad lovingly explains to his toddler that he'd like to cut off Clawson's penis and shove it down his throat—that the monster is not entirely externalised. But when he learns that Stark has done exactly this to the creep, he is properly horrified and our sympathies are restored. Amy Madigan, heroically making something of a thankless role, indicates that she has always known about the dangers of letting Stark loose. However, the film, in tidying up King's confusion about where Stark comes from, tends to exonerate Thad by making the villain an 'other' rather than a manifestation of the writer's unhealthy impulses. The abrupt cutoff after Stark has been pecked apart robs the film of King's downbeat conclusion—that the marriage will be unable to survive Liz's realisation that the monster is as much a part of Thad's personality as the gentle father.

The film's 'happy' ending is oddly unsatisfying. On the evidence given about both men's books, it's hard not to go along with their agent's claim: "I read George Stark because it's fun, but I read Thad Beaumont because it's my job." Without Stark, one fears for the future career and sanity of Thad.

VILLAGE VOICE, 4/27/93, p. 62, Colson Whitehead

A decade ago, you could count on being subjected to two or three horror releases a month. Nowadays, low-end horror goes straight to video, and the mainstream "thriller" has taken over as outlet for the public id. Today's monsters aren't anonymous Jasons, Freddys, and Chuckys, but familiar, if testy, babysitters, roommates, and office temps.

George Romero, who made his mark with *Night of the Living Dead*, has survived this winnowing of the horror market; with *The Dark Half* has crafted that rare object, a moody, polished horror film, and that even rarer thing, a successful Stephen King adaption. Once you've accepted this film's conceit—that when "serious" author Timothy Hutton kills off his pulp-writing, but income-generating, pseudonym, George Stark, Stark comes to life looking for trouble—Romero delivers the shocks, peppered with gallows humor.

Romero always made a virtue out of genre and monetary restrictions, but with *The Dark Half's* Hollywood-sized budget, he doesn't have to rely on splatter and lurching zombies. *The Dark Half* ditches the entrails for stock, but well-wielded, suspense effects: the strategic red herring, the unseen threat just outside the frame, the Hitchcockian flourishes straight outta *The Birds*.

Hutton portrays both the writer and his doppelgänger, mouthing corny dialogue about the "dark side" of humanity. His dark side, the razor-swinging Stark, is proof that Elvis still walks among us—he torments his victims to "Are You Lonesome Tonight?" and sports the trademark 'do and cracker accent. In this film, the evil that lurks in the heart of men is the King.

Also reviewed in:
CHICAGO TRIBUNE, 4/30/93, Friday/p. H, Dave Kehr
NEW YORK TIMES, 4/23/93, p. C10, Vincent Canby
NEW YORKER, 5/3/93, p. 105, Terrence Rafferty
VARIETY, 4/26/93, p. 68, Todd McCarthy
WASHINGTON POST, 4/23/93, p. D7, Richard Harrington

DARK AT NOON

A Sideral/Animatografo coproduction with Canal Plus. *Producer:* Leonardo de la Fuente. *Director:* Raúl Ruiz. *Screenplay (French with English subtitles):* Raúl Ruiz. *Director of Photography:* Ramón Suárez. *Editor:* Helene Weiss-Muller. *Music:* Jorge Arriagada. *Production Designer:* Luis Monteiro. *Special Effects:* Alain Le Roy. *Running time:* 100 minutes. *MPAA Rating:* Not Rated.

CAST: John Hurt (Anthony); Didier Bourdon (Félicien); Lorraine Evanoff (Inés); David Warner (Ellic); Daniel Prévost (The Priest); Myriem Roussel (The Virgin of Imitations); Filipe Dias (The Child); Rosa Castro Andre (Francisca); Maria Joao Reis (Ana); Adriana Novais (Paula).

NEW YORK POST, 8/21/93, p. 17, Jerry Tallmer

There was a land where men are silent and the dogs bark, where people walk in trances with their arms out stiff before them, where the trees have legs for branches and the gates squeak in

B-flat, where a chateau looks like El Greco's towering Toledo, where horsemen ride veiled in black like the Lone Ranger.

To this never-never land, somewhere vaguely in Portugal, there comes young Dr. Felicien Pascal, fresh from an internship in a Paris insane asylum, in search of his late father's fortune. "I have two passions," he announces. "Languages and miracles."

Both passions will be gratified in short order. Abandoned by the drayman who's conveying him to his destination, the doctor encounters a priest. "Which way to the Village of Dogs?" the doctor asks. "Simple," says the priest. "Follow the crutches." In an instant we see the traveler lugging his suitcases up, down, through, across fields and hills sprouting with crutches everywhere, thank you, Mr. Dali.

Presently, after the doctor has been sifted out of a premature grave, glowing apparitions of the Madonna appear over rooftops, over the river, the chateau. "She's there!" cries the doctor, spotting his miracle. "What difference does that make? *C'est moi* got you out of that hole," is the priest's caustic reply; thank you, Mr. Bunuel.

Languages. "Dark at Noon" for that is the name of this movie—thank you, Mr. Koestler—is half in French with English subtitles, half in English with French subtitles, all of it freely, casually intermingling. Actually, the French name of the movie is better. "L'Oeil Qui Ment," The Eye That Lies.

Ringmaster (or miracle-maker?) of this whole sub-Surreal circus is that 52-year-old Chilean-born *wunderkind*, the ultra-prolific Raul Ruiz, last seen in these parts when shooting "The Golden Boat" in and around SoHo three or four years ago. Technically speaking, visually, aurally, in camera world focus, performance, etc., "Dark at Noon" is to "The Golden Boat" as well, as noon is to midnight.

And it has a story—of sorts. The big cheese of the Chateau is a marquis who has a factory. with which he hopes to corner the world market in prosthetic devices. One of those Madonnas looms over the factory as a strikebreaker. "The Marquis enjoys a good draft," we are informed—in a nice line—when the wind stirs. He also has a double, a certain Anthony, who ravages a chicken leg a la Henry VIII.

One or the other of these people—both are played by John Hurt, looking ever more like Ronald Reagan—wrap the doctor (Didier Bourdon) in cobwebs to keep him from the beautiful but remote Ines (Lorraine Evanoff), a "schoolgirl from Chicago" who is the great-great-niece, if I have this right, of St. Just, zealot of the French Revolution.

Then there is Ellic, a painter and snob; his paintings eat people; he's David Warner, once the zany hero of "Morgan." Later the priest (Daniel Prevost) is prematurely buried. "You're all excommunicated!" he cries to his unearthers. I leave it to you to unearth your own deep meanings from "Dark at Noon," but one of them, I can tell you is my own most prevalent long-term recurring nightmare.

VILLAGE VOICE, 8/24/93, p. 64, Leslie Camhi

A Chilean surrealist who has lived for 20 years in Paris, Raúl Ruiz makes home a disembodied condition. *Dark at Noon (L'Oeil qui ment)* is set in Portugal, at the close of World War I, where a Parisian doctor specializing in miraculous recoveries is summoned to assume his father's legacy. Walking through fields of sleepwalking peasants, lined with rows of crutches and dotted with apparitions of "Our Lady of Imitations." our man of science makes his way to a château, where a farsighted entrepreneur (John Hurt), anticipating legions of war-wounded, has invested the doctor's inheritance in a factory producing prosthetic devices.

What has the Father left us, and what are we going to do about it? The entrepreneur's own vicious little family drama is played out between lines, a disturbing Chilean fantasy of pampered, blond Chicago beauty; Ellic, an artist who must feed his perpetually famished paintings; and an aging, ailing Marquis, whose bad manners extend to literally burying his guests.

Ho hum, another hermaphrodite, long-standing fans of this inimical auteur of the unconscious may mutter, finding the austere estrangement of Ruiz's early work missing from the amber tones of this lush production. But the words and images still bear the imprint of his uncanny touch; also, they're extremely funny. "I used to be interested in astronomy, but now I use my eyes instead," a character explains. So should we all.

Also reviewed in:
NEW YORK TIMES, 8/20/93, C12, Stephen Holden
VARIETY, 5/25/94, p. 50, David Stratton

DAVE

A Warner Bros. release of a Northern Lights Entertainment/Donner/Shuler-Donner production. *Executive Producer:* Joe Medjuck and Michael C. Gross. *Producer:* Lauren Shuler-Donner and Ivan Reitman. *Director:* Ivan Reitman. *Screenplay:* Gary Ross. *Director of Photography:* Adam Greenberg. *Editor:* Sheldon Kahn. *Music:* James Newton Howard. *Music Editor:* Jim Weidman. *Sound:* Gene Cantamessa and (music) Shawn Murphy. *Sound Editor:* Robert Grieve. *Casting:* Michael Chinich and Bonnie Timmermann. *Production Designer:* J. Michael Riva. *Art Director:* David Klassen. *Set Designer:* Joseph Pacelli, Jr., John Dexter, Darrell Wight, and Steve Arnold. *Set Decorator:* Michael Taylor. *Set Dresser:* Lee Orlikoff. *Special Effects:* David M. Blitstein. *Visual Effects:* Harrison Ellenshaw. *Costumes:* Richard Hornung. *Costumes (Sigourney Weaver):* Ann Roth. *Make-up:* Ron Berkeley, Linda De Vetta Richmond, and Robert Norin. *Running time:* 112 minutes. *MPAA Rating:* PG-13.

CAST: Kevin Kline (Dave Kovic/Bill Mitchell); Sigourney Weaver (Ellen Mitchell); Frank Langella (Bob Alexander); Kevin Dunn (Alan Reed); Ving Rhames (Duane Stevensen); Ben Kingsley (Vice-President Nance); Charles Grodin (Murray Blum); Faith Prince (Alice); Laura Linney (Randi); Bonnie Hunt (White House Tour Guide); Parley Baer (Senate Majority Leader); Stefan Gierasch (House Majority Leader); Anna Deavere Smith (Mrs. Travis); Charles Hallahan (Policeman); Tom Dugan (Jerry); Alba Oms (Lola); Steve Witting (Secret Service); Kellen Sampson (David); Lexie Bigham (White House Guard); Frederic W. Barnes, Ronald Brownstein, Eleanor Clift, Senator Christopher Dodd, Senator Tom Harkin, Bernard Kalb, Larry King, Michael Kinsley, Morton Kondracke, Jay Leno, Frank Mankiewicz, Christopher Matthews, John McLaughlin, Senator Howard Metzenbaum, Justice Abner J. Mikva, Robert D. Novak, Thomas P. "Tip" O'Neill, Richard Reeves, Arnold Schwarzenegger, Senator Paul Simon, Senator Alan Simpson, Ben Stein, Oliver Stone, Kathleen Sullivan, Jeff Tackett, Helen Thomas, Nina Totenberg, Sander Vanocur, and John Yang (Themselves); Stephen Root (Don Durenberger); Catherine Reitman (Girl at Durenberger's); Dawn Arnemann (Mom at Durenberger's); Marianna Harris (Clara); Sarah Marshall (Diane); Ralph Manza (White House Barber); George Martin (President's Physician); Laurie Franks (White House Nurse); Tom Kurlander (Trauma Doctor); Dendrie Taylor (Trauma Nurse); Joe Kuroda (Japanese Prime Minister); Genevieve Robert (Vice-President's Wife); Jason Reitman (Vice-President's Son); Ruth Goldway (Secretary of Education); Frank Birney (Director of OMB); Paul Collins (Secretary of Treasury); Peter White (Secretary of Commerce); Robin Gammell (Postmaster General); Heather Hewitt (Judy); Gary Ross (Policeman); Jeff Joseph (Ellen's Aide); Bonnie Bartlett (Female Senator); Robert V. Walsh (Speaker of House); William Pitts (Congressional Doorkeeper); Dan Butler (Reporter); Wendy Gordon, Ben Patrick Johnson, and Steve Kmetko (Announcers).

FILMS IN REVIEW, 8/93, p. 261, James M. Welsh

So far, the best comedy of 1993 is Kevin Kline's *Dave*, directed by Ivan Reitman and developed from a nicely crafted screenplay written by Gary Ross, that recalls the populist idealism of Frank Capra. Mr. Dave Kovic (Kevin Kline) goes to Washington under false pretenses in this movie, but he doesn't have far to go. Dave, a good hearted common man, runs a temporary-employment agency in Baltimore and is taken to Washington by the Secret Service because he looks just like

President Bill Mitchell (also played by Kevin Kline, naturally, and made up to resemble George Bush).

Dave is hired to double for the President at a formal dinner, after the President himself gives a speech. President Mitchell, a less than honorable man, wants to sneak away for a carnal tryst with a pretty secretary, one last fling, it turns out, since the President suffers a stroke in bed and lapses into a coma. The President's chief of staff, Bob Alexander (Frank Langella in an icy performance), sees this misfortune as an opportunity for a palace coup. The comatose President is secured away out of sight and Dave's impersonation becomes a full time job. Only the chief of staff, White House press secretary Alan Reed (Kevin Dunn), and a few trusted underlings know the switch has been made.

Fortunately for Alexander, President Mitchell and his First Lady (Sigourney Weaver) are not on the best of terms, live in separate quarters, and barely see each other, except at affairs of state. But Ellen Mitchell is no one's fool, and during those required joint appearances begins to notice a difference, since Dave is far more decent and compassionate than her husband.

Alexander's conspiracy involves removing Vice President Nance (Ben Kingsley), since Nance is too decent and too honest to allow himself to be manipulated by Alexander's greed and lust for power. Alexander manages to implicate Nance in a savings-and-loan scandal in order to put the machinery of impeachment in motion. The plan is to have Nance impeached, then have Dave name the sinister Alexander as his Vice President. Afterwards, Alexander will engineer a second "stroke" and the comatose President will be taken to the hospital and proclaimed unable to govern. The Machiavellian Alexander will then become President.

The problem is that Dave begins taking his acting job too seriously. After he discovers that Alexander has manipulated him into vetoing a jobs bill that would have helped the poor, he acts on his own to reverse the veto and pass the legislation. Alexander is furious about this but Dave earns the gratitude of the First Lady, who has by now figured out that Dave is an impostor, forcing Dave to confess to her and explain the situation. At first Ellen is ready to pack up and leave the White House, but decides instead to stay on a while to help Dave save Vice President Nance's reputation and to double cross the power hungry Alexander.

The screenplay is a little far fetched but amusingly worked out and nearly believable. Writer Gary Ross believes that some White House chiefs of staff tended to be megalomaniacal, and, he told the *New York Times*, "as powerful as the President, if not more so. So I wondered what would happen if one of these guys did not want to let go, if the horse they rode suddenly collapsed but they didn't want to collapse with it." Frank Langella plays the role of Bill Alexander with just the right touch of egotism and cynical contempt and is convincingly dangerous.

His cynical view of the Presidency is effectively counterpointed by Dave's populist optimism and good nature, as Dave proves to be far more decent, honest, and popular than the ailing President. The film's rapid pace and continuity detract attention away from the elaborate contrivances of the plot. Ultimately *Dave* is a feel-good movie, but one that also works as top rate satirical entertainment.

LOS ANGELES TIMES, 5/7/93, Calendar/p. 1, Kenneth Turan

"Dave" is the best kind of comedy, one whose jokes can't be given away. Though replete with amusing situations and clever lines, its strongest suit is the delicately pitched comic performances of its actors, most especially star Kevin Kline.

As "Soapdish," "A Fish Called Wanda" (for which he won an Oscar) and his celebrated stage performance in "The Pirates of Penzance" demonstrated, Kline has a magnificent talent for farce. No one can slip out of a chair or take a fall quite like he does, and his way with both the simplest facial expressions and the broadest physical gestures is unendingly funny. So to allow him, as "Dave" does, to fool around with two characters in the same film can't help but be pleasing.

It is the premise of this light-on-its-feet political satire (written by Gary Ross and directed by Ivan Reitman) that William Harrison Mitchell, the humorless President of the United States, has a double. That would be Dave Kovic, the hang-loose owner of a temporary employment agency who wears funny ties and isn't averse to riding a pig if the situation demands it.

Though President Mitchell is a ruthless policy wonk whose political philosophy seems to be "when I kill something, it always dies," he does have a weakness for philandering after hours. Which is why Secret Service agent Duane Stevensen (Ving Rhames) is always on the lookout for an executive lookalike, someone who can stand in for the President when he feels like slipping away.

Dave is naturally recruited, but events transpire to turn what everyone thinks will be a one-night stand into a longer engagement. "We want you to extend things a little," is how Bob Alexander, the President's icy chief of staff (Frank Langella), carefully puts it, and so the most ordinary of guys gets to see what it's like to be the major-domo of the free world.

While its look-alikes in politics premise echoes everything from "The Prisoner of Zenda" to "The Prince and the Pauper," "Dave's" theme of an innocent confronting and mastering experience has more than a little in common with the Oscar-nominated screenplay for "Big," which Ross co-wrote with Ann Spielberg.

And while director Reitman ("Ghostbusters," "Kindergarten Cop", "Twins") has not been known as the most subtle of filmmakers, the combination of his sure commercial sensibility and Ross' fastidious writing has resulted in a smoothly professional comedy that has an appealing air of low-key ridiculousness about it. Especially well-done are the scenes of Kline as Dave trying to get used to the perks of the White House, wondering nervously if, for instance, he needs to dial 9 before making an outside call.

And since Ross is something of a political junkie, the film was not only able to get august Washington figures from Sen. Alan Simpson to the perpetrators of PBS' "McLaughlin Group" to appear, it also came up with witty and appropriate things for them to say. One of "Dave's" sharper conceits is that far from going unnoticed, the difference in the post-Dave presidency is chewed over by Capitol Hill pundits to a gleefully ridiculous extent.

But aside from Oliver Stone (who makes a very funny conspiracy theorist appearance), the only person who is truly suspicious about the President's change in demeanor is his wife, Ellen (Sigourney Weaver). An outspoken social activist who barely speaks to her husband, she starts to wonder why he has become so warm and personable just as, in yet another twist, bachelor Dave starts to think that the First Lady is an extremely attractive woman.

Though as a veteran of Reitman's "Ghostbusters" Weaver knows just how to behave in these films, she is pretty much overshadowed by the premier *farceurs* she is surrounded with. Besides Kline, Frank Langella has his power-mad power behind the throne act down perfectly, Kevin Dunn is equally adept as a prevaricating press secretary, and Rhames seems much too funny to be the same actor who played Cinque in "Patty Hearst." Best of all, though, is Charles Grodin as Dave's perplexed friend Murray Blum, an accountant whose stony double-takes are things of wonder.

Despite all these good things, "Dave" (rated PG-13) does sag a bit in the middle when it goes soft and teary à la "Mr. Smith Goes to Washington" about the swell virtues of good government. But this is just a momentary blemish on the face of what otherwise looks to be the most coolly refreshing comedy of the season.

NEW LEADER, 6/14-28/93, p. 21, David Bromwich

Dave—a political comedy with a big heart—is fluff just a bit too ponderous to waft before it sinks. The manager of a temp agency, Dave (Kevin Kline) looks like and talks like the President. He is recruited as a stand-in by the White House Chief of Staff when the President—who is really his aide's front-man—suffers a stroke. Some way into the high-stakes impersonation, Dave turns out to be a better-natured man than the comatose leader, as well as a cleverer executive, and—anyone can work it out from there.

The director, Ivan Reitman, goes at the broad material with constraint, an inexplicably reluctant farceur. A scene where the fake President and real First Lady (Sigourney Weaver), trying to escape from Washington, get arrested for a traffic violation, is worked for a single soft perfunctory joke. Another one, where the fully dressed First Lady pulls open the shower door to reproach the naked Dave for his veto of a bill, risks not a shadow of visual humor and trails off with no punch line at all.

Kevin Kline has a nervous gift for comedy but, like almost everybody in this one, he avoids anything that might resemble an adventurous touch. His chances are confined to short stretches of delicate mischief. Told to explain Dave's absence to the folks back home, he picks up the phone ("Do you have to dial 9?") and cooks up a line about a girl he met: "She's Polynesian. Half Polynesian and half American. She's Amnesian."

But overall the script has slender verbal resources. The show appears waiting to be stolen by a face and a voice, and both belong to Frank Langella, the corrupt and magisterial and infinitely Roman Chief of Staff. When he upbraids his press secretary, reminding him that "I was a Senator," one thinks: "Of course you were." When, with all his weight, now massive and distinguished, Langella pounds to the fake President's office in a fury of execration, it seems too small a thing to praise him for inhabiting the part. One fully expects to see him in Washington somewhere, hovering in a portico, or behind an important chair whose levers he watchfully presses.

Sigourney Weaver finds no surprises as a First Lady stiff with virtue and sexual resentment. Her smile, pleasant when it happens, seems to come from far away. A lot of miscellaneous talent is kicking around the edges of the film: Ben Kingsley as the good, square Vice President; Charles Grodin as an accountant friend of Dave's, to whom he can say, "Murray, I can't tell you the whole story, kind of a national emergency kind of thing, but—you gotta help me cut the budget a little."

Once Murray does help, the truth seems to be that everybody wants to help; they were just timidly hiding behind bad habits, without a worldly motive. Looked at as a liberal fantasy, Dave is less wised-up than any film of its kind from the '30s or '40s. But it gives a clue to the mental life of the people who now divide their time between Hollywood and Washington.

This impression is confirmed by the number of political celebrities with cameo roles. Senators Dodd, Harkin, Simpson, and Simon all comment characteristically on the prospects of Dave's budget. Several Washington talking heads and political reporters are likewise trotted out in force. The gimmick is a steal from the documentary clips of real intellectuals analyzing Zelig—already itself a send-up of the mugging Witnesses of Reds—and one can't help wondering if the mix hasn't gone from funny to something else. The display of celebrities certainly makes a curious handshake with Dave's message about the average good guy being able to do some good. Mr. Smith Sneaks into Washington, they should have called it.

NEW YORK, 5/17/93, p. 78, David Denby

Who is Kevin Kline? As a screen presence, I mean. Talented man, serious man, with a large streak of silliness, too (that great bit in Soapdish). But who is he? When I think of Kline's movie performances, from Sophie's Choice on through The Big Chill, Violets Are Blue ..., A Fish Called Wanda, I Love You to Death, and Grand Canyon, I have no sense of specific personality. He comes off as genial and intelligent but not as anyone in particular. He lacks specific gravity, definition—whatever it is that such disparate actors as, say, Jack Nicholson and Jack Lemmon have (and Danny DeVito has too much of). Egotism is probably the word I'm looking for, a sense of himself so inviolable that it shows up in every movie.

In Ivan Reitman's new comedy, Dave, Kline uses his lightweightedness very cleverly. He plays twin roles—President William Harrison Mitchell and Dave Kovic happy-go-lucky Baltimore employment counselor—as two kinds of physical impersonation. He lends his body to each. Wearing frameless glasses and dark-blue suits he's exceptionally funny as the hollow, power-mad Bill Mitchell, forty-fourth president of the United States, who hacks the air vertically with his palms, Mitchell's presidency is in decline, and he's become a sour, reactionary fellow; Kline makes him, literally, a stiff, a man so rigid with calculation that he seems alienated from the movements of his own plank-like body. Everything about him is willed, flat, abrupt.

But then, playing Dave, good-hearted supplier of office temps, Kline is loose and gangly, with a sappy smile and a voice that wanders alarmingly when he sings. Dave the dope is offered a peculiar job. The president, it seems, has the habit of capping a speech at a hotel by bedding down in one of the rooms with a White House secretary. Someone is needed to "double" for him—someone who can wave to the crowd and step into a limousine while the president is still plowing the fields upstairs. That person becomes Dave, presidential look-alike. Only one thing goes wrong: The engorged president has a stroke and goes into a coma. At that point, the White House chief of staff, Bob Alexander (Frank Langella), and the adroit communications director, Alan Reed (Kevin Dunn), decide that they will not inform the virtuous vice-president (Ben Kingsley) but will take power themselves, using the dummy substitute as the real thing. Dave takes the Oval Office.

As long as Reitman and screenwriter Gary Ross are setting up their premise and getting Dave established in the White House, the movie is great fun. Reitman, director of the *Ghostbusters* films, has a practiced hand, and the large-scale yet smooth Hollywood production he puts together is well suited to the movie's subject, which is the way that power operates at the highest levels. The premise of a fake president is unlikely to put it mildly—but the filmmakers throw themselves into it, making all the externals as realistic as possible, and we eagerly go along with them, hoping for laughs. J. Michael Riva, the production designer, has created a superb mock-up of the swank White House interiors—formal yet airy, with lots of red and white. There's a real fascination in what the rooms look like and how people move in them, the atmosphere of bustling secrets and high importance.

What does power do to people? Reitman has actors who can tell us this. Sigourney Weaver is a perfect First Lady, a haughty yet wounded woman whose husband has betrayed her so many times she has retreated deep inside. Weaver has the stature and the formality for the role; she wears pensively uncomfortable clothes, clothes designed for public viewing, but she wears them proudly. Langella, as the evil chief of staff, is heavy yet shorn—practically bald. Gone are Langella's early liquid good looks, replaced by the deformations of face and body that power brings. He gives an utterly serious performance as a recklessly driven man. He's all lips and eyes now, with a soft voice—pure ambition.

All this is very entertaining, but once Dave gets into the president's chair, the movie lets us down brutally. Bob Alexander prepares his protégé, Dave, for his supreme role, but the filmmakers don't really show us how the simpleton pulls it off—how Dave fakes his way through meetings, say; and is just on the verge of exposure, only to recover with some wild bit of improvisation. Mostly Reitman gets by with montage—jumping from one scene to the next of the president performing on some public occasion. It's as if the chief executive really were a ceremonial figure without ideas or brains. In Reitman's conceit, Dave is a great success: Suddenly the president is no longer a sour-spirited loser but a vibrant young man, and the Washington press corps and the country fall in love with him.

Dave turns out to be punchless, as if Dave himself had designed it. The movie doesn't even have pace: Reitman, forgetting that he's making a farce, slows everything down, and he turns all earnest and soft. Dave, a good-hearted liberal, wants to "do" something, to "stand up for what's right," so he gets a full-employment bill passed—just like that. (Good timing, Ivan: You're releasing the movie just after Clinton's job-creating economic-stimulus bill was defeated.) Reitman and Ross, it turns out, are trying to exploit the softheaded Perot populism—the idea that all we need is a few honest men with their hearts in the right place and the "mess" in Washington will go away.

The filmmakers have no ideas, so inevitably they turn to formula. The First Lady falls in love with her new husband, though a less likely couple than Sigourney Weaver and Kevin Kline would be impossible to imagine. Since nothing is written for them, they sit on the banks of the Potomac staring at the White House at night. In the end, Kline's tentativeness hurts the movie. He's physically adept, but his being such a blank makes Dave a blank. One thinks of all the ways the movie might have been better—for instance, if Dave himself, under the pressure of power, had slowly metamorphosed into Bill Mitchell. But such a sobering idea isn't even suggested. A good part of the American public wants to believe in innocence, and in *Dave* it's getting a big hunk of it—a nice movie, with a nice man at its center.

NEW YORK POST, 5/7/93, p. 27, Jami Bernard

When a presidential lookalike finds his one-night gig in Washington turning into an extended stay because the real President has suffered a stroke, government truly gets into the hands of the little people in "Dave," a delightful comedy that happens to fit the national mood of the moment.

Most people will want to compare it to "Mr. Smith Goes to Washington" and other vaguely political feel-good movies of yesteryear, in which the commoner triumphs over the political system to preserve democracy the way it was intended. It certainly fits that mold.

And yet its emotional success is on a much more personal level—the man who by impersonating someone else finds his own identity. Therefore, "Dave" is closer in spirit to recent comedies on the same theme—"Moon Over Parador," for example, in which a failing actor finds his greatest role in impersonating the deposed dictator of a banana republic, or "The Distinguished

Gentleman" in which Eddie Murphy runs for Congress on a dead man's name but finds a new calling for public service.

So the joy of "Dave" is less in its exposure of political corruption—yes, yes, we all know that the accountant around the corner can do a better job with the national budget than the guys in power—than in the fact that it is a rich, unpretentious comedy about a man who learns he can truly rise to the occasion.

Kevin Kline is absolutely perfect and physically graceful as Dave. an ordinary guy with a big heart who just happens to look like the President of the United States (also played by Kline). The man in office is a George Bush type—pompous, elitist, an opportunist who cuddles his wife and dogs only when there are photographers present. The lookalike, who is kept on after the real President has a stroke in the boudoir of his mistress, is more of the Clinton variety—sunnier, relaxed, so happy to be in the famed Oval Office that he swipes an ashtray.

It's the presidency as the ultimate male fantasy, a playing ground where you get to throw out the first ball of the season, meet heads of state, order anything you want for lunch, and be married to First Lady Sigourney Weaver.

Frank Langella has some delightful moments as the pernicious, scheming chief of staff who regards the highest office in the land as his own property. And in a small but stellar supporting role, Charles Grodin is the disapproving, slightly shambling accountant around the corner who as a favor to Dave balances the nation's books overnight.

Thus the stage is set for Dave, the Everyman to segue from merely impersonating the President's mannerisms to making decisions that affect the country.

Director Ivan Reitman and writer Gary Ross wisely keep the humor away from the bumbling—surely the impersonator could have spent most of the movie calling people by the wrong name. The humor is human—Dave is unsure whether he needs to dial 9 to get an outside line from the Oval Office; when confronted in the shower by an angry First Lady, he struggles with his conscience about whether to turn around and face her while naked.

Real politicians and journalists have fleeting roles as themselves, including Oliver Stone whose conspiracy theory for once is really on target.

The message of "Dave" is no deeper than you'd find in the average fortune cookie, but there are simple laughs galore, something as rare as honesty in government.

NEWSDAY, 5/7/93, Part II/p. 66, Jack Mathews

All right, you nostalgic Frank Capra fans who are always complaining that "They don't make 'em like they used to," here comes Ivan Reitman's "Dave," and it's just like they used to make 'em. Or, at least, as Capra occasionally did.

Reitman's film, written by Gary Ross (co-author of "Big", is warmly romantic, shrewdly funny, politically savvy, a tad cynical and anchored by a comedy performance by Kevin Kline that ranks among the best of those given for Capra a half-century ago.

Kline, of course, is Dave, a big-hearted, hardworking, slightly goofy manager of a Baltimore employment agency whose spitting-image resemblance to the ruthlessly calculating President Bill Mitchell lands him a temp job in the Oval Office. Hired as a stand-in for Mitchell at a public appearance, Dave is promoted to full-time puppet after the president suffers a stroke while doing the Kennedy with a blond aide on a hotel room floor.

OK, so it's not *exactly* like they used to make 'em.

The plot of "Dave" is as old as "The Prisoner of Zenda," an 1894 Anthony Hope novel first made into a movie in 1913 and three times since. A common man is installed in power and rises to the occasion. Dave, at first a naive innocent being manipulated by a corrupt White House chief of staff (Frank Langella) and toady press secretary (Kevin Dunn), comes to like the job, the power, and—not least—the first lady (Sigourney Weaver).

Moreover, he's a better leader. He's honest, sensitive, charming, and, while the real president lies in a post-coital coma, Dave's effervescence sends the president's public approval rate soaring.

"Dave" is unabashed political and romantic fantasy, and though its White House sets and Capitol scenes are impeccably accurate, it won't stand a second's scrutiny. Before enemies and events conspire against him, Dave doesn't do much more than occupy the White House and have a fine time at a series of choice photo ops, playing with dogs on the White House lawn, singing "Louie, Louie" with workers at an assembly plant, doing magic tricks for a homeless child.

And not even the first lady is able to detect a physical difference between Dave and Bill, though she gets a good look at the imposter when she interrupts him in the presidential shower. No, the First Couple have not been intimate for a while, but some things you don't forget.

Still, it's a fantasy worth your unconditional surrender. Ross, as he and cowriter Anne Spielberg did with Tom Hanks' child-man in "Big," creates such an interesting identity crisis, makes you root so hard for the lamb among wolves, that the story takes on its own reality.

In the film's most satisfying sequence, Dave asks his accountant friend Murray Blum (a brief, hilarious turn by Charles Grodin) to help him find $650 million worth of fat in the federal budget so he can save a homeless shelters project, and then begins carving away in front of his startled Cabinet, the press, and his furious chief of staff, Bob Alexander (played with superb shifty-eyed villainy by Langella).

Nothing about the scene is real, except our desire to see Dave's impetuous honesty rewarded, and to see him derail Alexander's plans for assuming the presidency himself. Dave is not only the surrogate president in the story, but the surrogate ideal of what we'd like our president to be, a person acting solely on conviction.

The truism that the film ignores is that politics is by nature a game of leveraged compromise, and that the president, if one were inclined to do the right thing, would not be able to. Witness the hazing of Bill Clinton.

On that score, "Dave" offered so little threat to real politicians that Reitman got senators from both parties to appear as themselves, offering partisan commentaries on Dave's ambitious jobs program. Among them, Sens. Tom Harkin, Christopher Dodd, Howard Metzenbaum and Alan Simpson.

The film also has some fun with the media, following the president's remarkable personality change through the musings of "The McLaughlin Group," "Crossfire," and Jay Leno. Oliver Stone even shows up on TV, telling a bemused Larry King that the new improved image of the president is part of a White House conspiracy.

Reitman, whose "Twins," "Stripes," "Meatballs," "Kindergarten Cop," and two "Ghostbusters" movies have made him the most successful commercial comedy director in history, is moving up in class here. At the expense perhaps of that teenage audience he has owned in the past, Reitman is aiming at sophisticated adults, playing cerebral over visual jokes, and is dead on target.

Still, as good as the writing and directing is on "Dave," it's hard to imagine the film working as well with any other star. Kline, who is a better actor than Steve Martin and less smug than Bill Murray, has developed into perhaps the screen's best comedy actor, and his performance here, growing from a genial naif who would be content with a White House souvenir to a take-charge guy eager to alter the nature of American politics, is sublime.

"Dave," we're with you.

NEWSWEEK, 5/10/93, p. 59, David Ansen

Nice guy Dave Kovic (Kevin Kline), who finds temporary jobs for the unemployed, is a dead ringer for the president of the United States (Kevin Kline). When approached by the Secret Service he takes a temp job himself as a one-time stand-in for the prez. But when the president has a stroke while boffing his secretary, the power-mad chief of staff (Frank Langella) and communications director (Kevin Dunn) stage a little coup d'état. Wouldn't Dave like to play his role a bit longer? Their unwitting tool agrees and discovers that he has his own ideas of how to run the government—and that the First Lady (Sigourney Weaver) turns him on.

Screenwriter Gary ("Big") Ross may have borrowed his look-alike premise from "The Prince and the Pauper" and "The Prisoner of Zenda," but Dave is delightful proof that old tables can be wittily recycled. Under director Ivan Reitman's surprisingly delicate hand, "Dave" goes more for charm and chuckles than for the political jugular. This is cleverly updated Capracorn with a common-man hero whose genuine concern for the people makes the legitimate incumbent look bad.

Self-mocking cameos by real pols, media folk and celebs, including Newsweek's Eleanor Clift and a conspiracy-sniffing Oliver Stone, provide bonus fun. But it's the spritely comic timing of the fine Hollywood ensemble that keeps "Dave" percolating. This affable, well-built comedy is Reitman's best since "Ghostbusters."

SIGHT AND SOUND, 11/93, p. 40, Phillip Strick

Dave Kovic, who runs a small employment agency in Baltimore, bears an uncanny resemblance to the President of the United States, whom he impersonates occasionally for laughs at local fund-raising events. When President Mitchell needs a stand-in while he enjoys an assignation with Randi, one of his secretaries, Dave finds himself recruited to make a brief appearance as 'President' at a massive reception. His impersonation is suddenly extended when Mitchell has a stroke in Randi's arms, and his Chief of Staff, Bob Alexander, seizes the opportunity to further a scheme to discredit the Vice-President and put himself in line for the presidency. Dave is carefully coached by Alexander and his reluctant accomplice, Communications Director Alan Reed, to continue a hoax that will fool the White House executives, the media, and even the First Lady, Ellen, who despises her husband. Nervously accepting the role as an opportunity to serve his country, Dave settles into the routine of presidential duties and by sheer innocence and warmth of character begins to transform the Mitchell image.

Noting his new-found concern about the plight of the homeless, Ellen begins a fresh appraisal of her 'husband'—until Alexander's dismissal of a funding project convinces her that the President is still resorting to his usual trickery. Confronted by her, Dave starts to question the actions being taken by Alexander supposedly on his behalf. Alexander tells him that $650 million has to be cut from the federal budget, and Dave calls on his friend, accountant Murray Blum, to help him understand government finances. Together they examine the figures, and to Alexander's astonishment Dave steers his next cabinet meeting through a number of budget revisions which enable him to reinstate the welfare programme. Ellen tricks Dave into revealing that he is an impostor and demands to see her husband; they visit the vault where Mitchell lies on a life-support system. Unwilling to partner a fake President, Ellen prepares to leave the White House but relents after an evening of discussion with Dave about what the Presidency might yet achieve.

Dave summons a press conference, and fires Alexander when he tries to intervene; the President's announcement that employment will be found for every American provides a major topic for the startled media. Returning from the overseas tour that has kept him out of circulation, Vice-President Nance refutes the allegations initiated against him by Alexander, and when Dave checks with the repentant Reed he learns that it was indeed Mitchell, not Nance, who was guilty of malpractice. Alexander announces at a news conference that the President is implicated in scandal, and Dave responds by admitting to a shared guilt with Alexander. The President then collapses from another apparent stroke, and Dave returns to his employment agency while Mitchell is buried and Nance is sworn in as his successor. As Dave's friends begin to campaign for his entry into politics, Ellen turns up in Baltimore to give him her loving support.

Gary Ross's king-for-a-day fantasy would seem a rewarding topic for a screenwriter with an active political background (a Kennedy and Dukakis supporter, Ross has composed a host of campaign speeches). There are moments when *Dave* seems poised in readiness to remind us of the simple humanitarian truths, formerly articulated by Mr Smith and Mr Deeds, by which a government might inspire its people. But the mood proves to be comical with only the slightest of allegorical veneers, and the opportunities are allowed to slip away. In the end, national management is restored to the grip of the professionals (many of whom play themselves in the film, doubtless to the enthusiasm of their electorate) while the silver-tongued newcomer, having proved little more than the possibility of bluffing one's way into anything, is returned to the bottom of the ladder to attempt a more conventional ascent. By reinforcing the popular belief that government is largely in the hands of incompetents (such as its own hero), Dave stays ingratiatingly subversive. It is much easier after all—as Norman Lamont may have noticed—to raise a laugh by observing, "If I ran my business this way I'd be out of business" than to balance the books while staying in office.

Ross's screenplay for *Big* similarly plunged an innocent into a role of perplexing sophistication, allowed him a brief triumph based on disruptive non-conformism, and extracted him when the going began to get rough. Inexplicable magic (*Big*) and outrageous coincidence (*Dave*) are cynically employed to point the stories where Ross wants them to go: both offer a split personality theme, man and child in the same body, a struggle for accelerated maturity in an environment of suddenly major issues. The awkward reward in each case is the love of a mature woman, an eventuality which leaves *Big* in disastrous confusion, but which makes marginally better sense in *Dave* if no questions are asked about the hero's pre-Presidential career (what, no ties?) or, for that matter, about the tastes of the First Lady. Strikingly, both films conclude with the feel-good premise that it is in the natural order of things to work out for the best. Otherwise, the only cause they promote is that of discomfiture: there is scarcely a character in either one who is not required at some point to pop the eyes and drop the jaw.

Dave makes comfortable material for Ivan Reitman, whose comedies are a catalogue of double-takes and disruptive innocents (Murray in *Stripes*, Schwarzenegger in *Twins*, practically everybody in *Ghostbusters*). The film has been unobtrusively put together with a lot of close-ups and a minimum of effects. There's a cunning moment when the President confronts his double for the first time, the camera movement 'proving' that it's incontrovertibly the same actor twice over; but the style is mostly formal rather than flashy, some rather obvious backdrops augmenting a generally plausible White House. The director's trademark—a soundtrack noisily compiled from rough-hewn chunks of orchestration—here gets a Spielbergian top-dressing of romantic strings.

But the play's the thing: always generous to his cast, Reitman finds a perfect villainy in the troubled eyes of Frank Langella, who splendidly emotes a Svengali influence until forced by the script into lugubrious dementia. And the whole adventure is carried shoulder high by the performances of Sigourney Weaver and Kevin Kline, their subtlety steering the narrative through most of its translucent moments. Both Ross and Reitman share an interest in stories of partnership (the Rushton-Hanks alliance in *Big* becomes the Grodin-Kline unit in *Dave*, in turn a variation on the ill-matched duo of *Twins*), and *Dave* is a highly polished and evasively untroubling illustration that they have every reason to celebrate the benefits of teamwork.

TIME, 5/10/93, p. 65, Richard Schickel

The President, the press secretary reports blandly, has suffered "a slight circulatory problem of the head." That's spin doctor—better yet, parody spin doctor—for a stroke that has left the Commander in Chief an aspiring kumquat.

Time for an orderly transition of power, right? Wrong. Time for a coverup. Time for Dave Kovic (Kevin Kline), a presidential look-alike, to step into President Bill Mitchell's not exactly unfillable shoes. Dave is the owner of a soft (not to say bleeding-) hearted employment agency whose uncanny resemblance to The Man has led to a nice little sideline, impersonating him first at the openings of car dealerships and other lowball promotional fests, then, at the Secret Service's behest, at a real presidential function.

Hey, Dave—how'd you like to make a full-time job of it? This suits the Machiavellian purposes of chief of staff Bob Alexander (played with joyously evil relish by Frank Langella). As his name suggests, he combines the less attractive traits of Bob Haldeman and Alexander Haig. He's been running Mitchell (whom Kline also plays), and he's not about to abandon power gracefully. Besides, this putz should be a pushover.

Obviously, Alexander has never seen *Mr. Smith Goes to Washington.* He is therefore ignorant of Hollywood's potent, immemorial belief (and the nation's wistful hope) that innocence can reform the capital's swampy soul. It's a dear dream, and working off it Ivan Reitman and Gary Ross have fashioned a dear and funny movie.

Once Dave has mastered the President's swivel chair (he has a tendency to tip too far back in it), he starts mastering the other instruments of power as well. Budget reform, an improved day-care program, a bold new jobs program, even the banishment of corruption—all these he achieves by the simple assertion of guileless right thinking. He even manages to woo Mrs. Mitchell (Sigourney Weaver) out of the separate bedroom and angry silence into which her real husband has forced her to retreat.

There is some sentimentality in this, but it is lightly, genially stated. And it is balanced with a sharp comic shrewdness. Reitman has succeeded in recruiting all sorts of prominent people—ranging from sitting Senators to the McLaughlin Group to Oliver Stone, contributing a paranoid slant on good-heartedness—to satirize their own and, more important, the media's self-importance. They impart to *Dave* just the topical edge it requires.

Not that one wants to take anything away from its professional actors. The Bushiness of Kline's President is well-observed, and the woolliness of his Dave contains bristles too. He's warm without being entirely cuddlesome. Weaver has a veteran wife's weary wariness down perfectly. Ving Rhames as a Secret Service man allowing Dave to melt his professional steeliness, Kevin

Dunn as the press secretary for whom "no comment" is a moral statement, and Charles Grodin as a CPA appalled by federal accounting practices complete one of the best comic ensembles in years. Under Reitman's unforced and confident direction, they ground improbable fantasy in very human, very winning believability.

VILLAGE VOICE, 5/11/93, p. 60, Georgia Brown

When Capra's *Mr. Smith Goes to Washington* came out in 1939, that bootlegger-gone-to-London Ambassador Joseph P. Kennedy, cabled Harry Cohn of Columbia Pictures urging the studio to cancel its European run. He thought the movie made the American system look sick. (Maybe he found Edward Arnold's villain a little too close for comfort.) Senators like Alben W. Barkley despised the film for depicting "the Senate as the biggest aggregation of nincompoops on record!" According to Capra, the Washington press corps hated it not only because the picture's chief reporter was a lush but because they didn't want Hollywood horning in on their territory. Protests fizzled, however, as the verdict of the "little people" came in.

Post-Vietnam, Watergate, Iran-gate, Reagan/Bush, today it's hard to find a movie pol who isn't venal or a movie anchorperson who's anything other than a narcissistic ass. With *JFK*, Oliver Stone demonstrated how easy it is to make people believe in rottenness and the most bizarre convolutions of chicanery. In Ivan Reitman's charming new comedy *Dave*, Stone, appears on *Larry King Live* hawking another wild conspiracy theory. Only this time he's right.

The adorable, brazenly corny *Dave* is written by Gary Ross, cowriter of another tale of imposture or double identity. Here Ross takes one big truth—the average citizen's moral superiority to the politician—and runs with it. Instead of a child playing a grown man (*Big*), here a manchild impersonates the president of the United States. (As one citizen caller quizzed *Larry King* guest Kevin Kline recently: "What I want to know is how this plot differs from *Moon Over Parador, King Ralph, The Distinguished Gentleman?*" I forget the answer.)

It takes just a few broad strokes to establish just how, well, evil, President William Harrison Mitchell is. He's indifferent to his dogs (corgis!), to his regal, intelligent wife (Sigourney Weaver), to the office and its charge. Kevin Kline's impersonation leans toward George Bush—President Mitchell is lean, went to Yale, wears wire-rimmed glasses, favors the thumbs-up gesture, although he's a slightly more persuasive public speaker. "God Bless America" is a standby refrain. Like JFK's, his eye is on the ladies-in-waiting, and in order to take time-out with them, he uses a double for routine public appearances.

The stand-in hired for such occasions is salt-of-the-earth Dave Kovic, who runs a temp placement office in Baltimore. Dave looks just like President Mitchell (since both are played by Kline) except that Dave's hair is tousled, he doesn't wear glasses and he has a sweet, open demeanor. When Mitchell lays eyes on this boyish image of himself, he remarks, "You're a very handsome man. Just get rid of the grin. You look like a schmuck." Of course, we know what's coming: This mean and craven Prez is going to be out of the picture shortly (we can guess in what manner he will go, too), giving Dave his chance to show that a good man can do a better job, with the dogs, the wife, the country.

Let me just say I'm glad they didn't ask Robin Williams to play Dave/Prez. Kline's Dave may resemble Williams at times, but the role isn't hostage to excruciating mannerisms. Kline plays this almost straight. The flakiness is in check, limited to homespun exuberances like singing "Oklahoma" while riding his bike or doing regular Joe things like snitching an ashtray from the Oval Office. One truly shameless scene in a homeless shelter has Dave working magic on a lonely child, but I didn't even mind it.

The movie's villain is the towering chief of staff, former senator Bob Alexander. Frank Langella gained 25 pounds for the part but maintains his penetrating Count Dracula stare. The haircut is *echt* Haldeman. Obsessed with protocol and power, Alexander considers the horny president his puppet. His assistant in the cover-up is a far less Manichaean aide, played by Kevin Dunn. A good many of the movie's jokes come in seeing Dave's inner Washington peopled by the TV ghosts, the aggregation of nincompoops, we know so well: Senators Simpson, Harkin, Dodd, and Metzenbaum; Kinsley and Novak, McLaughlin and his coven. What Washington movie these days would be complete without Nina Totenberg?

If the Washington of *Mr. Smith* was a foul and nasty place (the only good men are marble), *Dave*'s really is quite sunny. The president's wife really does care about the homeless, his VP (played by Gandhi, er, Ben Kingsley) is a former shoe salesman and a Boy Scout in the old, Jimmy Stewart sense. Charles Grodin does a hilarious turn as Murray Blum, a shy accountant who comes to the White House to help balance the nation's books.

Reitman like Capra may have been a child immigrant (at four his family left Czechoslovakia for Canada; Capra left Sicily when he was nearly six), but as directors the two haven't much in common. Capra's pictures grew increasingly dark with a thick river of hysteria running through them. Reitman makes silly comedies, enjoyable and ephemeral. After the early Bill Murray vehicles *Meatballs, Stripes,* and *Ghostbusters* he's gone on to direct Arnold Schwarzenegger in *Twins* and *Kindergarten Cop*. In 1984, he was voted Director of the Year by the National Association of Theatre Owners.

Dave's charm and limitation, like its main character's, lie in its stunning simplemindedness. After confirming our worst fears about who's in charge and the utter unreliability of public image, it goes on to reassure our childish faith that what's wrong can be rectified quite easily, by the ever-available pure in heart.

Also reviewed in:
CHICAGO TRIBUNE, 5/7/93, Friday/p. A, Ddave Kehr
NEW REPUBLIC, 5/31/93, p. 30, Stanley Kauffmann
NEW YORK TIMES, 5/7/93, p. C12, Janet Maslin
NEW YORKER, 5/17/93, p. 101, Terrence Rafferty
VARIETY, 4/26/93, p. 68, Brian Lowry
WASHINGTON POST, 5/7/93, p. B1, Rita Kempley
WASHINGTON POST, 5/7/93, Weekend/p. 50, Desson Howe

DAZED AND CONFUSED

A Gramercy Pictures release of an Alphaville production in association with Detour Films. *Producer:* James Jacks, Sean Daniel, and Richard Linklater. *Director:* Richard Linklater. *Screenplay:* Richard Linklater. *Director of Photography:* Lee Daniel. *Editor:* Sandra Adair. *Music (soundtrack assembled by):* Richard Linklater. *Sound:* Jennifer McCauley. *Casting:* Don Phillips. *Production Designer:* John Frick. *Art Director:* Jenny C. Patrick. *Set Decorator:* Deborah Pastor. *Costumes:* Katherine (K.D.) Dover. *Make-up:* Jean Black. *Stunt Coordinator:* Fred Lerner. *Running time:* 97 minutes. *MPAA Rating:* R.

CAST: Jason London (Pink); Joey Lauren Adams (Simone); Milla Jovovich (Michelle); Shawn Andrews (Pickford); Rory Cochrane (Slater); Adam Goldberg (Mike); Anthony Rapp (Tony); Sasha Jenson (Don); Marissa Ribisi (Cynthia); Deena Martin (Shavonne); Michelle Burke (Jodi); Cole Hauser (Benny); Christine Harnos (Kaye); Wiley Wiggins (Mitch Kramer); Mark Vandermeulen (Tommy); Esteban Powell (Carl); Jeremy Fox (Hirshfelder); Ben Affleck (O'Bannion); Jason O. Smith (Melvin); Christin Hinojosa (Sabrina); Parker Posey (Darla); Matthew McConaughey (Wooderson); Catherine Morris (Julie); Nicky Katt (Clint).

LOS ANGELES TIMES, 9/24/93, Calendar/p. 1, Peter Rainer

The high school "experience" ought to be a cinch to capture on film but it rarely is. Those dawdly, dithery days and nights too often come across as coy, mannered—worse, *meaningful*. Most high school movies are made by adult filmmakers who don't remember that, when you're young, you don't comprehend your life as a series of coming-of-age revelations. You're too busy being dazed and confused.

Richard Linklater, who has made the aptly titled "Dazed and Confused" as his follow-up to "Slacker," understands this. One of the film's constant pleasures is the way it avoids the coming-of-age syndrome. His high schoolers go through changes in the course of the film, but without fanfare. We watch them on the last day of school—it's 1976—and observe their tribal tantrums on into the night.

The cast of characters is large but remarkably differentiated. We may be looking at a congregation of types—including Pink (Jason London), the star quarterback, O'Bannion (Ben Affleck), the bully who hazes freshmen, Slater (Rory Cochrane) the doper, Wooderson (Matthew McConaughey), the hoody graduate who keeps hanging around the high school, and Cynthia (Marissa Ribisi), the red-headed brain who falls for the hood—but Linklater has too much affection for them to type them. These kids are individuals, and yet no matter what high school era you passed through, they're immediately recognizable. (You also recognize yourself in them.)

The mid-'70s, of course, are basic to Linklater's game plan; set a few years earlier or later, the film's mood would have been not so subtly altered. These students are on the crest of the era of lowered expectations, caught in the time warp between the hectic rebellious '60s and the greed-is-good '80s. They're in a dulled-out limbo but they seem to accept their fate with an almost comic aplomb. When they toke a joint or chug a beer they do it with mock abandon; they know they can't hope to be rebels without a cause a la James Dean. The times don't allow for that kind of vehemence. So they loiter and jive and wait for the new era to kick in and define them. (The terrific soundtrack, ranging from Aerosmith to Dylan, is their anthem.)

And yet one of the best jokes of the film is how close these kids seem to teen-agers today. For one thing, the fashions are back in style. But, on a deeper level, the tribal rituals are essentially the same. (That's why they're tribal.) Linklater doesn't go very far into these rituals but he doesn't keep things at a sitcom level either. "Dazed and Confused" (rated R for pervasive continuous teen drug and alcohol use and very strong language) isn't the creepy, floating jag that his first film, "Slacker," was. For all its originality, that film was like David Lynch on downers or, maybe, uppers. The personal stories in "Dazed and Confused" aren't over-dramatized or weird, but they retain a slightly hallucinatory quality because Linklater keeps everything, on the same wide-eyed level. Keg parties and scuffles and dope-smoking all enter into the same convivial blur.

The cast is studded with standouts. Adam Goldberg, playing a junior who wants to become a lawyer and join the ACLU except he can't stand the people he's supposed to help, is right on target. Wiley Wiggins, as a much-hazed freshman, turns his lanky lope into a strut by the film's end. Sasha Jenson's Don is the kind of footballer who can't resist dispensing headlocks to those less fortunate than he. Ribisi turns her character's bemused attraction for the hood into something almost poignant. (She brings out his own bemused gallantry.) Linklater, who went through high school in the mid-70s, is still close enough in spirit to these actors to draw them out.

"Dazed and Confused" isn't the "American Graffiti" for the mid 70s generation. It's a highly enjoyable spree that doesn't add up to a whole lot by the end. But you don't necessarily *want* it to add up to anything—that's part of its charm. Linklater knows his limitations, which is another reason why his connection to his characters is such a perfect fit.

NEW STATESMAN & SOCIETY, 9/16/94, p. 34, Ben Thompson

"Withdrawing in disgust is not apathy." This seemingly simple line form Richard Linklater's 1990 film debut *Slacker* turned out to lead in a number of different directions. When the film—a languorous trawl through the twisted minds of a 100 or so youthful residents of Austin, Texas—was first shown in Britain at the 1991 London Film Festival, it felt like a cool breeze from somewhere new: a first attempt to put something on the screen that had been out there in real life for some time without anybody with a camera bothering to notice it.

By the time distribution companies overcame their initial lack of interest and the film went on general release here, a year or so later, it was already well on the way to becoming a historical landmark of alleged youth ennui. *Slacker* had become a term of abuse rather than an underground ideal, and the original idea of being as creative as possible within a framework of massive social alienation was being swept away on a tide of ill-informed comment and commercial exploitation. What options are left open for those whose lives have become a marketing category?

The self-debasing idea of "Generation X" did not originate with Douglas Copland, nor with a bad English punk band, but with the book the latter party got their name from, Charles Hamblett and Jane Deverson's pioneering insight into youthful anomie, first published in Britain in 1964. As if sensing that what was needed was some historical perspective, 31-year-old Linklater decided, with his second film *Dazed and Confused*, to go back to his own mid-1970s roots.

This, as it turns out, was a productive move. The film did well in America after a slow start, hindered rather than helped by its studio-controlled publicity's pitiful attempt to cash in on the marijuana revival ("The film everybody's taking about").

In Britain, there were similarly ill-founded moves to have *Dazed and Confused* released straight to video on the grounds that it was "too American" to do well in Britain—perhaps recalling such other well-known UK box-office flops as *Grease* and *Saturday Night Fever*. Reason ultimately prevailed however, and the film arrives without quite such an agonising delay as that suffered by *Slacker*.

Dazed and Confused is a much easier film to watch than its predecessor, where the action baton is passed from character to character like an endless relay on a track with no curves. Not only are its disparate groups of characters tied together into what might fairly be called an ensemble, but there are even signs of a narrative. The action takes place on the last day (and night) of school in an anonymous middle American town in Bicentennial Year, 1976. It centres on Pink, the handsome popular football quarterback who faces a choice between signing a no-drink-and-drugs pledge for the sake of next year's team, or embracing the mellower lifestyle of a full time pot-head: and Kramer, a gawky but charismatic junior high graduate who finds himself suddenly swept into senior-high society.

American film makers can hardly be accused of neglecting the high school environment, so Linklater's achievement in making it feel vibrant and new is all the more to be respected. The colours seem to glow. The familiarity of the music—a 1970s rock odyssey of Bad Company, Aerosmith (semi-ironic totems in *Wayne's World*, but the real thing here) and others—breeds delight not contempt, and the soundtrack winds in and out of the story with sinuous glee. But it's in *Dazed and Confused*'s characters that its real strengths lie.

There are some 25 distinct personalities in this film. They begin as types: jerks, nerds, stoners—but don't we all? Even if most of these actors and actresses have better skin than any three-dimensional teenager has any right to expect, they do manage to capture that feeling you get at school of people struggling to fit the suit that destiny has knitted them. The memorably-named Wiley Wiggins (a teenage computer buff who wants to be a film director) stands out a bit as Kramer, but otherwise there is no hierarchy, just a lot of good, funny acting.

The desire for acceptance is the main communal motivating force, and Linklater focuses an unflinching moral gaze on the gruesome "hazing" initiation rituals whereby graduating junior high students are received into the society of their new senior peers. Boys have it easy. They are merely chased and beaten with special bats. Girls are forced to grovel on the ground, covered in eggs and flour by their cheerleading elders chanting "fry, little piggies, fry", and then obliged to propose marriage on bended knee to senior males who will probably see this as an opportunity for obscene innuendo.

Even those, like Pink and Kramer's sister Jodi, who seek to mitigate the severity of these ordeals by offering the hand of friendship to their victims afterwards, still seem to be slightly degraded by them: and in the eagerness with which they embrace the adult world of necking and beer-busts, hazing graduates like Kramer and his female counterpart Sabrina are seen to be turning their backs on their innocence.

Grown-ups who choose to remain stuck in adolescent grooves, like the radical teacher ("The 1968 Democratic Convention was probably the most bitchin' time I've ever had in my life") or the ageing predator Wooderson ("That's what I love about high school girls—I get older, they stay the same age") are no better off.

This sense of bewilderment and even loss adds colour to what might have been a plain old nostalgic haze. "The 1970s suck," observes cerebral, red-headed Cynthia, preparing to surrender herself to the dubious charms of Wooderson, "maybe the 1980s will be radical". Richard

Linklater's *Dazed and Confused* somehow manages what its characters can't—to be knowing, without losing its innocence.

NEW YORK, 10/4/93, p. 104, David Denby

The American teenagers in Richard Linklater's satirical sketchbook movie *Dazed and Confused* like to bash mailboxes. They like to do *what?* They bash mailboxes with the garbage cans they pick up at night while cruising around their suburban town; they also smoke dope with a variety of hookahs ("bongs") and spend a lot of time pretending they want to get laid. The climax of the movie—and the school year—is a beer bust. *Dazed and Confused* is set in 1976, when American youth were stranded between the political passions of the sixties and the material passions of the eighties. The kids have no causes to fight for, not much personal ambition, and a lot of bad music (Kiss, Foghat, Alice Cooper). The music keeps them jumping even when they're waiting for something to happen, which is virtually all the time.

Feminism hasn't yet taken hold among the girls, who engage in bizarre hazing rituals with the younger girls—covering them with sugar and ketchup and getting them to propose on their knees to the boys. Humiliating other people while avoiding humiliation yourself seems to be the main preoccupation. Like every American generation since World War II, these seventies teens signify the End of Civilization as We Know It. And yet they're not so bad. Most of them are rather funny. And the movie, for all its aimlessness and its seeming celebration of moronic time-wasting, is often charming. Richard Linklater knows that he and his friends were too silly to get outraged about.

A critic getting impatient with Linklater risks sounding like an adult telling one of these teenagers to shape up. There's not much point to the activity: In time, they'll learn. Linklater, 32, doesn't like to structure a movie too tightly; he's looking for the magic in anecdotes and vagrant moments—a pothead's funny way of using his hands as he talks, a bizarrely alive phrase rising out of the muck of youth jargon, a touch of poetry in the plastic past. Linklater has a nice, gentle touch, and he's free of false nostalgia. But he doesn't have much dramatic sense, and at times the movie falls to the level of its not very inspired characters.

His first film, the acclaimed *Slacker* (1991), was a deadpan portrait of a lumpen intellectual class—the benumbed college dropouts and eternal graduate students of Austin, Texas, philosophers of the laundromat stuck in their dope habits and their "theories" about this and that. The picture was organized serially, from anecdote to anecdote, from rap to rap, a multiple-shaggy-dog-story movie. This time, Linklater has gone back, in the manner of George Lucas in *American Graffiti*, to his own youth.

Linklater's nostalgia, however, has a neutral tone. He and his friends were nothing great; they were teenagers. *Dazed and Confused* is also a collective portrait, casually organized as a series of interlaced tales—pranks, hazing, small matters of honor—all taking place on the afternoon and night of the last day of school.

In 1976, the nation was 200 years old, an event memorialized in *Dazed and Confused* by the rapturous fantasy of the pothead Slater (Rory Cochrane), who is convinced that George Washington cultivated weed as a southern cash crop. There is also a mock revolution: The hero, a pretty-faced football player (Jason London), won't sign a demeaning document concocted by the head coach that calls for the players to abjure drugs and alcohol. The only other signs of spirit are shown by the two self-conscious nerds (Adam Goldberg and Anthony Rapp) who reject the general mediocrity and try to escape. These two hyperarticulate boys feel like freaks, and they're heading out; everyone else is trapped.

Linklater, unlike Lucas, is not out to sell anything, yet thinking about *American Graffiti* may suggest what's limited about *Dazed and Confused*. The aimlessness of Linklater's movie isn't stylized enough to amount to an aesthetic interpretation of the past. Lucas worked in a specific place (the central valley of California), and he gave the movie a geographic center (Mel's Drive-In), a mythic hero (Wolfman Jack), a specific look (red and blue neon), and a layer of dreams. His town had an unconscious. But Linklater sets his film nowhere in particular—Suburbia, U.S.A.—and puts everything on the surface. The movie is funny, but after a while, one begins to sink under the general demoralization. One longs for a little more variety, a girl with some spirit, a sense of why these dopey kids, however graceful their antics, are worth a lingering look.

NEW YORK POST, 9/24/93, p. 41, Michael Medved

Millions of Americans who attended high school in the mid 1970s are now approaching the dangerous age of 40, suddenly vulnerable to unreasonable spasms of nostalgia for their wild and crazy youth.

This is the obvious target audience for a surprisingly bland new movie "Dazed and Confused," which tries to inspire the same sort of enthusiastic recollections of the year 1976 that "American Graffiti" generated for 1962. To that end, writer-director Richard Linklater slavishly follows the set-up and structure of that earlier film, leading a dozen disparate teenagers through all-night adventures that culminate at dawn the next day.

In this case, the action begins on the last day of school at the end of junior year (as opposed to "Graffiti"'s end of summer after graduation) and takes place in a comfortable suburb somewhere in Texas. The school's star quarterback Randy "Pink" Floyd (played by Jason London, who made such a strong impression in "The Man in the Moon") can't decide whether he will sign his coach's pledge of abstinence from booze and pot; if he doesn't he may not be allowed to play for the team in senior year.

As it turns out, all the other players—and the rest of the high school student body—are too stoned to care much about the issue. Heaving trash cans at mail boxes to knock them off their posts represents the height of excitement to this inventive crew.

Despite a sound track that features the immortal works of Alice Cooper, Aerosmith, Ted Nugent, Peter Frampton and other stalwarts of the period, the '70s nostalgia remains fatally unfocused. Director Linklater (whose only previous feature was the artsy, incoherent "Slacker," about an angst-ridden group of 20-something Texans) insists on treating his characters' high school experience in timeless universal terms, but the theme falls flat due to the excessive focus on some of the bizarre folk ways of this particular Texas town.

An attractive and capable young cast make all of this reasonably watchable, though the characters remain so appallingly under-written, with so few distinguishing characteristics that it's hard to care much about any of them.

Released in 1973, just 11 years after the season it celebrated, "Graffiti" touched a poignant chord with its presentation of an innocent world that already seemed irrevocably lost. No such chasm seems to separate us from 1976. No one could describe that moment in history as innocent, so if this film doesn't mourn lost innocence, what can it lament—lost decadence?

Linklater makes an attempt in that direction, but his prettified portrayal of the era's indulgence in illegal substances as nothing more than carefree, old-fashioned good times doesn't ring true.

In commenting on the finished film, its creator seems almost apologetic. "I just remember telling the entire cast that they were playing extraordinary people living in an unextraordinary place at an unextraordinary time." Linklater recalls. It is hardly surprising that the result is an unextraordinary motion picture.

NEWSDAY, 9/24/93, Part II/p. 65, John Anderson

For all the attitude that flavors his films—both of them—it's really the hypocrisy of the hip that fascinates Richard Linklater. The straitjacket of nonconformity that youth slips on so casually. The mortifying confines of cool.

"Slacker," Linklater's 1991 debut, concerned the post-collegiate, pseudo-bohemian subculture of Austin, Texas, and had an unorthodox structure that was well-suited to its subjects: Characters would occupy the screen for a few moments, long enough to relate some screwball anecdote, and then disappear forever. By dismissing his characters so abruptly—their pretentions were often too much for too long anyway—Linklater also paid homage to a nation's vanishing attention span. With "Dazed and Confused" he adopts a more conventional approach to storytelling, while still exploring the wonders of optional reality.

And what better time to set his tale than 1976, a year of bicentennial bombast, post-war Nixon withdrawal and the sneaking suspicion that the quality of life in the United States was going the way of the economy. And what better place to examine the clash of '60s and '80s ethos than a high school in small-town Texas, where pot and football are on a collision course (all to the accompaniment of Alice Cooper, Black Sabbath and Peter Frampton).

And where, on the last day of his junior year, Randall (Pink) Floyd (Jason London), school quarterback, is facing a dilemma: Does he sign the pledge sheet being given all returning players, demanding they not indulge in drugs or alcohol? Or risk his football career and those of his team-mates?

"What are they going to do next? Give you guys urine tests?" someone asks, in one of Linklater's many wiseguy lines, but moral decisions are alien to these kids. Pink isn't sure what's bothering him about the pledge. What's right is usually what everyone else does, despite the rebellious pose most of them assume.

This includes the brutal hazing that the soon-to-be seniors inflict on the incoming freshmen. Mitch (Wiley Wiggins), whose constant hair-flipping with his fingers is perfect, gets a particularly brutal paddling, precisely because his older sister, Jodi (Michelle Burke), asked the guys to go easy on him.

"Dazed and Confused," which takes place over an 18-hour period (call it "American Graffiti: The Dark Side") is much more about adolescent self-absorption and countercultural affecta-tions—which here consists mostly of the enormous consumption of marijuana and beer—than it is about plot.

In brief, there's supposed to be a party at Pickford's (Shawn Andrews) but the beer delivery arrives before his parents leave, so they don't, and the end-of-school celebration becomes a beer-bust in the woods. Several psychodramas are played out. The pursuit of freshmen continues. Mitch gets "adopted" by Pink and the other seniors, as does Sabrina (Christin Hinojosa), a freshman girl who gets attached to Tony (Anthony Rapp), who along with Mike (Adam Goldberg) and Cynthia (Marissa Ribisi) comprise the school's pseudo-intellectual clique.

"We should be ready for anything," says Mike. "'Yeah, we are," says Cynthia. "But what?" They don't know, but their characters, like all the others in "Dazed and Confused," are instantly, recognizable. Linklater uses kids who look as if they belong in high school, not on "Beverly Hills 90210."

And while making a very funny film, fully evocative of its era, Linklater also proves that things don't really change that much. "Hey," someone asks, "you still driving to Houston tomorrow to get those Aerosmith tickets?

NEWSWEEK, 10/4/93, p. 85, Jeff Giles

It was bound to come up sooner or later. Richard Linklater was screening "Dazed and Confused"—his crushingly funny and knowing ode to misspent youth, set in the much-maligned '70s—when studio executives interrogated him about a certain scene. It's an inconsequential bit: some high-school girls sit around drinking beer and flicking bottle caps. One girl says, "Do you want to do something else?" Another says, "Yeah. Like what?" Which says it all, or nothing at all, depending on how you look at it. "In the film business, you have to justify everything," says the 32-year-old director. "Everybody said, 'This scene doesn't mean anything. It doesn't advance the plot.' I was like, '*What* plot?'"

In 1991, Linklater debuted with the small independent film "Slacker," a celebration of life on the fringes shot in his hometown, Austin, Texas. The director had dropped out of Sam Houston State University. He had parked cars and worked on an oil rig. He'd helped found the Austin Film Society, which screened the works of Fassbinder. "Slacker," not surprisingly, was out there. Roughly 100 misfits breezed in and out of the movie's revolving door, the most memorable of which was a hyperanimated young woman trying to fence Madonna's Pap smear.

For "Dazed," Linklater jumped to a $6 million budget and a big-time partner, Universal Pictures. But his style remains wonderfully idiosyncratic: talky, character driven and almost entirely without artifice. "Dazed" visits familiar teen themes like authority, boredom, young love and social climbing. Still, it's one of those rare movies that don't talk down to teenagers, but speak for them. After a study showed that films rated PG and PG-13 were better investments than films rated R, the folks at Universal wondered if "Dazed" had a shot at a PG-13. "Well," Linklater told them, "we have 78 'f---s' in the script, pot smoking all the way through and teenagers drinking and driving. I don't think so."

You would think that Hollywood would be wary of a film so steeped in drug culture. But the pot smoking takes place at a safe remove, the '70s. "You could set this movie today," says Linklater, "you just couldn't get it made." Even dressed in '70s threads, however, "Dazed" has managed to create controversy. The Motion Picture Association of America recently got into a scuffle with the distributor, Gramercy Pictures, demanding this ad line be killed: "Finally! A movie for everyone who *did* inhale."

"Dazed" begins on May 28, 1976, the last day of classes at a Texas high school. It ends 18 hours later, after a night of hazings and keg parties, petty crimes and crying jags. At the center of the first-rate ensemble cast, all of them unknowns, there's the kindly quarterback Randy "Pink" Floyd"(Jason London) and the wide-eyed freshman Mitch Kramer (Wiley Wiggins). Mitch, with his loud floral shirt, is an innocent who wants in. Pink, with his cool white bell-bottoms and puka-shell choker, is a jaded-jock who wants out: "If I ever start referring to these as the best years of my life, remind me to kill myself."

Orbiting around Pink and Mitch are a yearbook's worth of characters. Wooderson (Matthew McConaughey) is a skanky, lascivious, aging graduate; Don Dawson (Sasha Jenson) is a live-wire football hero.

Slater (Rory Cochrane) is a hilarious, analytical pothead who insists that George and Martha Washington "toked weed" and considered it "a good cash crop for the Southern states." The actors inhabit their roles so easily that they give the movie a documentary feel-though most are too young to remember the '70s as more than a blur. Says Linklater, "In rehearsals, I'd have to tell them, You don't say *dude*, you say *man*."

As a '70s flashback, "Dazed" has everything but a drum solo: macramé belts, wide-body muscle cars, Alice Cooper tunes. But Linklater never plays the decade for laughs. He soft-pedals the movie's current trendiness—the '70s revival meets the pot revival—just as he resists the exploitation and high drama common to most high school flicks. "I just wanted to capture what I remember: the rhythm of being a teenager. It was a *lack* of drama that I was going for."

With "Dazed" launched, Linklater is drumming up interest in new scripts. One concerns a couple that meets on a train; another, two construction workers in the '80s. Linklater figures he can make the movies with or without Hollywood. "I'm not a part of the club," he says. Recently, he took money he made on "Dazed" and bought a '68 GTO. Hollywood types prefer a Lexus, but Linklater's driving a muscle car.

SIGHT AND SOUND, 10/94, p. 39, Ben Thompson

The last day of school, 1976. Students of Lee High school prepare to terrorise the junior high school kids who will be joining them next year. Footballing seniors Don, Tony, Benny and Pink are given a pledge of abstention from drink and drugs, which they are supposed to sign by the end of the day. Their classmate Jodi asks them to go easy on her younger brother Mitch, but this only hardens their resolve to make him suffer.

Mitch and three of his friends initially escape the attentions of bat-wielding seniors, notably the brutal O'Bannion. Later in the day they are tracked down one by one, with Mitch suffering a particularly severe fate as he is apprehended leaving the baseball field. Impressed by his fortitude, Pink asks Mitch to go with them to the party planned for that evening. The junior high girls too are humiliated, forced to grovel in the dirt and propose marriage to various seniors. One of them, Sabrina, is treated with unusual courtesy by the gawky, cerebral Tony. Like Mitch, Sabrina is adopted by a glamorous senior, as Jodi invites her to the party as well.

Unfortunately, the party is cancelled when the host's parents find out what he had planned and decide to postpone their holiday. Mitch hangs out at the pool hall, buys beer for the first time, gets in scrapes with Don and Pink, and catches the eye of one of his sister's social circle. With some of his younger friends, he also engineers O'Bannion's humiliation by covering him in paint. Suave older guy Wooderson arrives in a flash car, announces a 'beer bust' out at the point, and sets his cap at Tony's red headed, intellectual friend Cynthia.

At the point, Sabrina and Tony's friendship deepens; Tony's uptight friend Mike gets into a fight with a vicious greaser; Mitch drinks, smokes marijuana with the school's stoner/philosopher Slater and gets driven home, with a romantic stop-over in a field, by his sister's friend; Pink is pressurised by his team-mates to sign the pledge. He gets kissed by Jodi, but leaves with his official girlfriend Simone and a stoner posse including Slater, Don and Wooderson, to watch the sun rise on the football field. They are apprehended, and when Pink's football coach tells him he is mixing with the wrong crowd, he crumples up the pledge and throws it away. Mitch too is apprehended by his mother, but manages to convince her he has done nothing wrong.

As if knowing that the zeitgeist baton he picked up with his first film *Slacker* would be carried off by those less nimble of intellect (mentioning no names, but see *Reality Bites*), Richard Linklater has taken a step back in time. But this vibrantly laid-back comedy of mid-70s high school manners is also a massive step forward. It might not have a plot, but it certainly has a story, and *Slacker*'s conveyor belt of kooky mid-twenties ne'er-do-wells has given way to a tightly bound ensemble of funny and believable adolescents: imagine an early John Hughes film shifted half a decade back to the pre-Reagan era and remade by a human being.

The high school characters in *Dazed and Confused* are just as inclined towards philosophical reflection—feminist analyses of *Gilligan's Island*, stoner's meditations on the probability of George Washington being a big dope smoker—as their elder forebears in *Slacker*, but the fact that they actually are at a crossroads instead of merely perceiving themselves to be at one gives their musing much-needed momentum. Summer heat seeps from the screen, ambition goes up in a gentle haze of marijuana smoke and the film swaggers and lollops along to the beat of a supremely cheesy 70s rock soundtrack—Black Sabbath's 'Paranoid' has never sounded so jaunty.

This is no mere nostalgia trip. Linklater refuses to romanticise adolescent cruelty—the camera does not flinch from the bullying, and lingers on a couple of bat-thwacking incidents to unsettling effect—but shows rare perception in dealing with the nuts and bolts of teenage power negotiation. Watching this film in an American cinema, the waves of recognition were almost oppressive; on the other hand, the film seemed to make a British preview audience slightly nervous, as if wanting to remember things this way but not quite being able to. US film-makers can hardly be accused of neglecting adolescence, but few if any have previously approached it with the winning blend of knowingness and innocence with which Linklater here reclaims teen knowledge (the girls get to drink and drive and smoke drugs too) from the exploitative clutches of post-*Animal House* first-fuck cinema.

In this endeavour he is aided by a charismatic cast, notably Wiley Wiggins as the cheeky young tyke Mitch and Matthew McConaughey as the hilariously predatory Wooderson. And if Pink's central dilemma—whether to be the handsome football hero with all the girls after him or the handsome free-thinking waster with all the girls after him—will not strike a chord with everyone, his ability to see himself as the centre of all human drama ("If I ever start referring to these as the best days of my life, remind me to kill myself") might be more recognisable.

Dazed and Confused has the odd flash of ironic hindsight, for example in Cynthia's alternate decade theory—"Everyone knows the 70s suck, so maybe the 80s will be radical"—but it is mercifully free of that "and then I grew up to become a film-maker" feeling that scars so many cinematic insights into adolescence. Few of these people are going anywhere, but they are not going anywhere with style and dignity.

TIME, 10/11/93, p. 83, Richard Corliss

Randall "Pink" Floyd (Jason London) is the nearest thing Lee High School—or this engagingly vaporous movie—has to a hero. He's a decent guy, a star quarterback, a rebel with a cause. He is also his idea of a realist. Scanning a party-hearty nightscape of dopers, predatory jocks, ineffectual intellectuals and girls auditioning to be meat, Pink sighs, "If I ever start referring to these as the best years of my life, remind me to kill myself."

Pink has a point, for the locals (the film was shot in Austin, Texas) are an eccentric bunch. In a town-honored tradition, the new seniors submit the new freshmen to hazing: the younger girls get pacifiers in their mouth, the younger boys paddles on their butt. Then, as a reward, they "take you out and get you drunk." What a dear ritual this is, mixing mandatory hedonism with the cracker camaraderie rampant in certain football-worshipping, cousin-marrying sectors of the American heartland. Paris, France, comes to Parris Island.

Well, that was 1976, this is 1993, and somewhere Pink is being reminded of his words and handed a Ginsu knife. Who could not be nostalgic for those heady days when a gallon of gas or a pack of cigarettes cost 60¢, when songs still had chord changes, when Gerald Ford was a nation's jovial punch line of a President? The '70s was the last pre-rehab decade: you could do cool stuff and not worry about dying from it. So despite Richard Linklater's attempts to be sharp-eyed about the period, *Dazed and Confused* is doomed to look as romantic as an old prom portrait.

Linklater's problem here—as in his 1991 *Slacker*, a goofy *La Ronde* of layabouts and conspiracy theorists—is that he is incapable of drawing characters who are only caricatures. They always wriggle smartly to life, from the narco-lunatic (Rory Cochrane) convinced that George Washington "toked weed" to the brainiac (Adam Goldberg) who decides he doesn't want to be an A.C.L.U. lawyer after all because he can't stand the people he would be defending. O.K., but what's the alternative? "I wanna dance!"

The movie's advertising was modified after industry censors objected that it promoted drug use. Linklater is surely no ham-fisted moralist, and his film has lots of attitude to shake a finger at. But it also has enough buoyant '70s music to shake anybody's tail feather, and a kind of easy jubilance of narrative and character. Bet it makes you wanna dance.

VILLAGE VOICE, 9/28/93, p. 58, Joe Levy

The deep saturation of mall-land America by clogs, bell-bottoms, and Lenny Kravitz is as sure a sign as any that the '70s revival is over and done. Already *Details* editors weepy for the early '80s have begun printing new wave nostalgia notices, neckwear is slimming down toward the inevitable return of the skinny tie, and former East Village hipsters are scouring Red Hook second-hand stores for gear from Ocean Pacific, the Stüssy of 1982. So Richard Linklater's second feature, set on the last day of high school in 1976, arrives at a strange crossroads. Though I expect much of the celebration of *Dazed and Confused*—and if there's been a film more worth celebrating this year, I've missed it—to center around its frighteningly accurate costumes, cars, and soundtrack, this has a lot more going for it than another reclamation of "our" history, "our" music, and "our" fashion. Sweetly intoxicating and stunningly detailed as Linklater's journey through the past may be, minus the dope smoking and the Frampton, you can sniff most of that baby-buster diaper residue in *Brady Bunch* re-runs. But there's no whiff of infantilism to *Dazed and Confused* like the 1969 Zeppelin song for which it's named, it hits a timeless vein of youth joy and frustration. It could just as easily be set in 1986 and named for a 1964 Chuck Berry song, "No Particular Place To Go."

The story is simple, but those frustrated by the constant wandering of *Slacker* will be glad it's there: on the afternoon school's out for summer the new seniors torture the incoming freshmen, and then everyone cruises around looking for a party until it's time to drive to Houston the next morning for Aerosmith tickets. Like *Slacker*, *Dazed and Confused* draws its narrative energy from its characters and their interplay, but unlike *Slacker*, these characters are more than performance-art spiels. A disunified collection of jocks, stoners, and nerd intellectuals, they revolve around the film's nominal hero, Randy "Pink" Floyd, a lanky babe with a Leif Garrett do whose status as star quarterback gives him license to run with anyone he chooses. He plays poker with the social misfit smart kids—Mike, Tony, and Cynthia—goes on dope runs with the perpetually stoned Slater, and hangs, natch, with his buddy Don and the rest of his teammates, who urge him to sign a coach's pledge letter promising not to indulge in any substance abuse. Randy, who like everyone else in *Dazed and Confused* treats cannabis smoke like teenage oxygen, just isn't sure about that pledge sheet. ("I didn't know things were so bad they had to resort to neo-McCarthyism," spouts perpetually wired nebbish Mike. To which Cynthia—in one of the intellectual anachronisms that Linklater, looking back through the lens of the '80s, can't resist—adds, "What are they going to do next, give you guys urine tests?")

"It's the old age-oppressing-youth thing," Mike says of the pledge, though he could just as easily be talking about the hazing rituals his classmates turn loose on the new freshmen: the boys get paddled savagely, the girls have it even worse. Carted to the high school parking lot, they're doused in mustard and ketchup, feathered, and led around on leashes. Singled out as potentially cool kids during their hazing—maybe it's the studied nonchalance of their doe-eyed stares—Mitch and Sabrina are offered rides to the big party later that night, and they spend the evening cruising the strip with the older crew, learning the traditions of teen transcendence. There's an eerie quality of endless indoctrination laced throughout *Dazed and Confused*, and though it's all about the pursuit of cool, it all sadly, oddly comes back to that old age-oppressing-youth thing—when one senior girl tells her charges during the hazing, "I went through it as a freshman and you'll do it as a senior"; when Mitch is sent on a beer run and scores a sixer by parroting an older asshole's line of bull; when a leisure-suited dad takes glee in foiling plans for that night's big party, imprinting on each kid who rings his doorbell an evil you're-busted grin like a die-press stamps metal.

"You ever feel like everything we do, everything we're taught, is just to service the future?" asks Cynthia, driving around with Mike and Tony looking for something to do once Evil Dad has stomped their party buzz. "I'd like to stop thinking about the present as a *preamble* to something." Not quite aimless but certainly not focused, hardly apathetic but certainly not a call to action, it's a perfect statement of the sum zero of suburban life, and it speaks for every character in *Dazed and Confused*. Stuck inside of Linklater's nameless 'burb (presumably Austin, Texas, but quite purposely unspecified), each of them can spy the glories of the future and the past, and they drive all night looking for a way to bring them into the present, going for spin after spin and always ending up back at the same pool hall. "It's the girls in the class ahead of us that were wild," gripes Slater between tokes, recalling someone else's heyday. "The girls in our class are all prudes. Wait'll I get to college. I can't wait to get to college." "That's what I love about high school girls," drawls Wooderson, who's in his twenties and pursuing a postgrad doctorate in GTOs and jailbait. "I get older, but they stay the same."

He sounds like a vampire, or the kind of nostalgic loser Bruce Springsteen worried about becoming in "Glory Days." And maybe he is, but Wooderson's also the guy who pulls together that night's beer bust, a creative act that shows how he earned his rep (he'll score a date with class brain Cynthia by the time things wind down—go figure). There are no heroes or villains in *Dazed and Confused*—and that's perhaps Linklater's greatest accomplishment: he's given us the rare teen movie that sees these kids as they'd see themselves.

In part, that's because of the ensemble acting, enormously felt and true to the experience. Their eyes burning bright with visions of the palace of wisdom, the cast releases wave after wave of high school memories—particularly Jason London as Pink, whose face captures the quiet drama of a hometown hero who knows there's more to life than juvenile kicks, and Wiley Wiggins as Mitch, whose mask of adolescent indifference can never fully disguise the raw exuberance of his innocence. But it's also in how Linklater presents his cast. The relentless hand jive, slang, and sartorial splendor—all of which make *Dazed and Confused* seem too perfect at first blush—spring directly from the sort of adolescent self-mythologization, equal parts Byronic and moronic, that kids use to fill the emptiness of the suburbs with *something*, some sense of history, even if it's only their own.

Linklater's other great accomplishment is putting the same loose-to-lazy, it's-not-a-movie-it's-*life* vibe that made *Slacker* run like Laurie Anderson on 'ludes in the service of a tightly paced and smoothly crafted movie. Restless and giddy, mirroring in its construction the choogling boogie that blares from the soundtrack, this isn't in the least a tale of teen anomie. These kids are a different sort of merry prankster, knocking over mailboxes and breaking car windows as they wander the space between hippie and punk without ever being conscious of doing so—and they smoke so much pot, it's a wonder they're conscious at all. Like contemporary hip hop, *Dazed and Confused* takes great pleasure in stunts and blunts and the way they flaunt authority (and like contemporary hip hop, it ain't nothing but a G-thing—despite some honest attempts at *Foxes*-like girl talk, this is a boy's movie through and through, though that does, of course, entail showing what dickheads boys can be).

But unlike contemporary hip hop, *Dazed and Confused* has no dark side. Aside from one fight at the beer bust (and Linklater's camera refuses to linger on the tears of its aftermath), there's no downside, no trouble, nothing worse than the portrayal of survival as an end in itself. At times, it seems a bit too romanticized. Linklater tends to remember the '70s the way rock groups like Urge Overkill and Teenage Fanclub do: as better than they were, all Kiss, Black Oak Arkansas, and Foghat, no Carpenters, "Seasons in the Sun," or disco (and I don't recall everyone in high school—even the nerd intellectuals—being quite this cute). But by the end, it's the fact that nothing and no one is changed by the film's events—an easy stasis echoing suburbia's ceaseless, unchanging rhythm—that's Linklater's trump card. Full of references to teen movies past—one butthead gets a bucket of paint dumped on him in a *Carrie* homage, and the yellow hot rod from *American Graffiti* is conspicuously seen cruising the strip—*Dazed and Confused* pulls off one trick rarely, if ever, managed by a teen flick: it refuses to teach a lesson, to portray a transformation, to celebrate growth.

Oh sure, there's Pink's struggle over signing that pledge sheet—"If it ain't that piece of paper, it's some other choice they're gonna try and make for you," Wooderson lectures him as they smoke a joint on the empty football field waiting for sunrise. But consider where breaking all the rules has left Wooderson: on the 50-yard line with a bunch of high school kids, recalling his past football glories. If this is Pink's stand, it's an awfully forced, small, even silly one—"You act like you're so oppressed." Pink's sometime girlfriend Simone bitches as that joint makes the rounds, "but you guys are like kings of the school"—and it ends up seeming like a parody of the after-school-special type of "difficult decisions" so many teen movies pose. Unlike most every other adult who's looked back on their adolescence, from Nicholas Ray and George Lucas to John Hughes and John Singleton, Linklater resists the urge to moralize. The kids he puts up on the screen couldn't have asked for anything more.

Also reviewed in:
CHICAGO TRIBUNE, 9/24/93, Friday/p. L, Clifford Terry
NEW YORK TIMES, 9/24/93, p. C12, Janet Maslin
NEW YORKER, 10/4/93, p. 214, Anthony Lane
VARIETY, 6/21/93, p. 41, Ken Eisner
WASHINGTON POST, 10/22/93, p. C7, Hal Hinson
WASHINGTON POST, 10/22/93, Weekend/p. 48, Desson Howe

DEAD ALIVE

A Trimark Pictures release of a Wingnut Films production. *Producer:* Jim Booth. *Director:* Peter Jackson. *Screenplay:* Peter Jackson, Stephen Sinclair, and Frances Walsh. *Story:* Stephen Sinclair. *Director of Photography:* Murray Milne. *Editor:* Jamie Selkirk. *Music:* Peter Dasent. *Sound:* Tony Johnson and (music): Neil Maddever. *Casting:* Frances Walsh. *Production Designer:* Kevin Leonard-Jones. *Art Director:* Ed Mulholland. *Set Dresser:* Brad Mill. *Special Effects:* Steve Ingram. *Creature and Gore Effects:* Richard Taylor. *Costumes:* Chris Elliott. *Make-up:* Debra East. *Prosthetics Designer:* Bob McCarron. *Stunt Coordinator:* Peter Hassall. *Running time:* 97 minutes. *MPAA Rating:* Not Rated.

CAST: Timothy Balme (Lionel); Diana Penalver (Paquita); Elizabeth Moody (Mum); Ian Watkin (Uncle Les); Brenda Kendall (Nurse McTavish); Stuart Devenie (Father McGruder); Jed Brophy (Void); Elizabeth Brimilcombe (Zombie Mum); Stephen Papps (Zombie McGruder); Murray Keane (Scroat); Glenis Levestam (Mrs. Matheson); Lewis Rowe (Mr. Matheson); Elizabeth Mullane (Rita); Harry Sinclair (Roger); Davina Whitehouse (Grandmother); Silvio Fumularo (Father); Brian Sergent (Vet); Peter Vere-Jones (Undertaker); Tina Regtien (Mandy); Bill Ralston (Stewart); Tony Hopkins (Winston); Tony Hiles (Zoo Keeper); Duncan Smith (Drunk); Tich Rowney (Barry); George Port (Lawrence); Stephen Andrews (Spike); Nick Ward (Spud); Kenny McFadden (Gladstone); Angelo Robinson (Courtney); Johnny Chico (Head Chief); Fijian Rugby Club (Tribesman); Peter Jackson (Undertaker's Assistant); James Grant (Tram Driver); Michelle Turner (Blonde Woman); Jim Booth (Lionel's Father); Sam Dallimore (Young Lionel); Anna Cahill, Kate Jason-Smith, and Frances Walsh (Mothers at Park); Norman Willerton (Tramp); Robert Ericson (Boy on Bike); Morgan Rowe and Sean Hay (Baby Selwyn); Vicki Walker (Selwyn Voice); Chris Short (Customs Official); Jamie Selkirk (Father at Zoo); Brad Selkirk (Son at Zoo); Forrest J. Ackerman (Forry).

LOS ANGELES TIMES, 7/14/93, Calendar/p. 5, Peter Rainer

How delicately can I put this? "Dead Alive" is the most hilariously disgusting movie ever made. It makes something like "Re-Animator" seem like a UNESCO documentary about Mother Teresa.

It highlights more headless torsos and detached limbs and suppurating wounds and wriggling innards than you'll probably ever want to see again for the rest of your life unless you're a surgeon or a coroner. The director, Peter Jackson, seems to have ingested the grossest sequences from every schlock cheapie of the past two decades—from "It's Alive" to "Child's Play" to

"Lawnmower Man"—and then spewed them across the screen in thick, scudding swaths of crimson, green and yellow.

There's no point decrying this film for being yucky. That's like criticizing professional wrestling for being unsubtle. "Dead Alive" isn't easy on the stomach but, if you can get past the glop, it's a wallopingly good time. Jackson, a New Zealander, makes a sick joke out of the audience's squeamishness by carrying things so far you have to make a choice to giggle, throw up or walk out. He has a great instinct for what will drive us into squeals of giddy disbelief. If there's a blender in a scene, you can be sure someone will be Mixmastered; if a head is severed it will soon be blubbering its lips.

Jackson sets his slapstick gorefest in a quiet New Zealand town in the 1950s, where the milquetoast Lionel (Timothy Balme) lives with his overbearing horror of a mother (Elizabeth Moody). When a Spanish girl (Diana Penalver) whose migrant family runs a corner shop becomes infatuated with him, he incurs the wrath of Mum, who tails them to the zoo where she is bitten by the dread Sumatran rat-monkey. The monkey gets whomped but almost immediately Mum starts acting big-time weird: At a luncheon for a charity organization her ear demurely plops into her pudding. (Great taste, less filling.) She turns into a humongous, lipsticked zombie and Lionel, ever the dutiful son, can't quite put her to rest. Pretty soon a vast community of zombies has taken up a gurgly residence in his basement, while his girlfriend tries to figure out why Lionel seems to be acting so, well, *distracted* lately.

Jackson, with his co-screenwriters Stephen Sinclair and Frances Walsh, works in a lot of fairly sophisticated subversive satire about everything from the church (a kung fu minister who chops his zombied flock) to momism (Lionel's Mum attempts to get her son to re-enter her womb-literally. He shrieks back at her, "All my life you told me nothing but lies!").

There are probably political jabs in this film that only New Zealanders will pick up on but most of the ultra-*eeeuuh* stuff is all-too-accessible. Jackson keeps everything on such a high-low plane of nuttiness that just about everything in this film seems inevitably, ghoulishly right. The pre-zombie characters are already overscaled so grotesquely that, when they turn into a bloody bundle of boils, the transformations are like a higher form of evolution. These folks are never more alive than when they're dead. "Dead Alive" (Times-rated Mature for just about everything) is a groaner of cultclassic dimension. After you see it, you want to race out of the theater and recommend it to your sickest friends right away.

NEW YORK POST, 2/12/93, p. 32, Jami Bernard

One of the most overused lines in screenplays is: "I've got a bad feeling about this." But the line can be forgiven, seeing as it is uttered during the preamble to "Dead Alive," and proves as apt a description as any.

I've got a bad feeling about even *telling* you about this movie. It is for gore fans only, and even they face being slimed to death in this goofball effort from New Zealand.

On the surface, it is a story about a Latin girl (Diana Penalver) and the awkward boy (Timothy Balme) whom the tarot cards say she is going to marry. Their love plans are thwarted by his mother, who is left in a sort of dead-alive state by a bite from a rare "rat monkey" at the zoo. Under the surface—but just barely—it is about how boys must make a psychological break from their mothers before they can have a relationship of their own.

Further under the surface, the movie is about slime. Mother's rat-monkey bite begins to ooze, and soon pieces of her face are falling off into her pudding. Eyeballs pop, innards squeeze themselves outward, and pus, drool and goo abound to the accompaniment of sucking sounds.

Sonny can't get mom to stay dead, so he injects tranquilizers up her nose every so often. "Dead Alive" borrows gleefully from such predecessors as "King Kong," the Godzilla movies, "Night of the Living Dead" and "Eraserhead," any one of which I'd rather see right now.

While it's true that the rat monkey is nicely animated, "Dead Alive" boasts no advances in the special-effects department and no discernible ingenuity. It will mainly appeal to those who fondly recall playing with their diapers.

NEWSDAY, 2/12/93, Part II/p. 79, Terry Kelleher

Gushing blood, oozing guts, severed limbs—meant to be scary.

Gushing blood, oozing guts, severed limbs—meant to be funny.
The distinction is key in reckoning the entertainment value of "Dead Alive," a horror spoof from New Zealand. But after a while, it's a distinction without a difference.
Director Peter Jackson, whose style was proclaimed by the title of his first film—"Bad Taste"—here aims to out-gross all the gore that's gone before. The publicity for "Dead Alive" offers it as "positive proof that nothing succeeds like excess." Rather, the movie proves that comedy cannot live by excess alone.
Look at the scene in which luckless Lionel (Timothy Balme) serves lunch for his domineering mother (Elizabeth Moody) and representatives of Wellington's elite Ladies Welfare League. Mum, you see, is turning into a flesh-eating zombie after being bitten by a Sumatran Rat Monkey. She's also shedding her skin, a condition Lionel has tried to remedy with household glue. Well, the dessert course is marred somewhat when Mum's ear plops into the custard and she obliviously spoons it into her mouth.
One of the lunch guests excuses herself to upchuck, and a few audience members may be thinking along the same lines. But for stronger-stomached viewers, this should be a high point of the comic gross-out. Outraged propriety is always good for a laugh. Unfortunately, the scene comes far too early in the movie. It's just a warm-up, a comparatively dry run, before the screen is awash in gore.
In fairly short order, Lionel has a "family" of undead monsters locked in the basement—Mum, a nurse, a priest, a punk and a demon infant who emerged from an old radio. Of course, Lionel has a love interest as well, but Jackson shows no sustained appreciation for the awkward humor of that relationship. Paquita (Diana Penalver) comes into her own only when she must join her boyfriend in battling the zombies, whose numbers grow exponentially after Lionel's scabrous Uncle Les (Ian Watkin) throws a beer bust in the house and the many revelers somehow get undead.
As the blood spatters and the body parts fly, Jackson casts any sense of pace or proportion to the winds. The effects are sometimes extraordinary—the head spinning in the blender! the torso trapped in the toilet!—but quantity numbs us to quality. As for the gags that don't require technical wizardry, how many times can Uncle Les take a kick to the groin and lose his toupee?
The game is "Can You Top This?"—and Jackson winds up beating himself.

SIGHT AND SOUND, 6/93, p. 48, Farrah Anwar

1957, Skull Island: a New Zealand zoologist loses both his arms and is then beheaded because the rare specimen of rat monkey he's carrying accidentally bites him. Wellington, New Zealand: Paquita, a young Spanish shopkeeper, is told by her taro-reading granny that she is due to have a long romance with a man whom she will recognise by the symbol of the star and the moon. Her next customer, Lionel, knocks over a stand, causing liquorice to assume a crescent and star configuration; Paquita asks him out to the zoo. They are followed on their date by Lionel's widowed mother Vera, intent on sabotaging her son's romance. While hiding, she is bitten by a rat monkey, and becomes progressively more ill over the next few days. Despite being ministered to by Lionel and Paquita, whose dog she manages to eat, Vera is declared dead by district nurse McTavish, who is then decapitated by an undead Vera. Lionel manages to push his mother and Nurse McTavish—who also becomes re-animated—into the cellar.
Lionel visits Paquita at the shop and is given a mystic pendant for luck by her granny. He is followed by a fast-decomposing Vera, who is hit by a tram and assumed to have died from the accident. Although she returns to life again just before her funeral, Lionel tranquilises her long enough for a successful burial. Realising that she may still be undead, Lionel attempts to exhume her, only to be attacked by a gang of teddy boys. When one of them urinates on Vera's grave, he suffers a surprise castration at her hands. As the gang turn into zombies, the parish priest, Father McGruder, is awakened and helps Lionel fend them off, losing his own life in the process.
Lionel now has several undead in his cellar, where the carnally aroused McGruder and McTavish manage to conceive a zombie foetus. Vera's brother Les discovers the sedated zombies and, thinking that Lionel is a necrophile, blackmails him into giving up Vera's estate, an event he celebrates by inviting friends to a party at Lionel's house. When a zombie is accidentally let out, Lionel and Paquita decide that the inhabitants of the cellar must be killed off permanently, but their plan backfires and all the guests end up zombified and hungry. Lionel discovers his

father's remains in the attic and remembers that he witnessed Vera drowning him in the bath as a child. Freed from his guilt about her death, he successfully kills all the zombies with a lawnmower. He and Paquita are confronted by a gigantic, grotesquely decayed Vera, who manages to pull Lionel back into her womb. Just as she is about to kill Paquita, Lionel slices his way out with his lucky pendant. As Vera falls into the burning house, the reunited couple at last walk away free and unharmed.

In 1984, when the DPP drew up a list of video titles for prosecution under the Obscene Publications Act, at least 15 of the works in question were either zombie films or were heavily influenced by the genre. The list, of course, included Sam Raimi's *The Evil Dead*. Although he was never successfully prosecuted, the 'video nasty' publicity was enough to make Raimi shy away from the unsettling mood of the original in favour of comic set pieces for his sequels *Evil Dead II* and *Army of Darkness*. It is arguable that *Braindead* (which owes a heavy debt to Raimi) would have found itself on the DPP's hit list less than ten years ago. However, unfettered by any legal worries, it arrives in the UK just as Tom Savini's remake of the seminal *Night of the Living Dead* slinks off the big screen, having barely registered at the box office.

Biographical production notes allude to Peter Jackson's lifetime desire to make a zombie film, and *Braindead*, his most coherent and technically accomplished film to date, certainly fulfils that ambition. But his film may just deliver a *coup de grâce* to a genre still reeling from the video nasty debate and the subsequent Video Recordings Act. With George Romero unable to find commercial or critical favour with his uncompromisingly bleak *Day of the Dead* (the only zombie film to extend the mythology of the monster in a halfway decent manner), the undead have repeatedly found themselves shuffling down the dirt track marked 'gross humour' (cf. Dan O'Bannon's *Return of the Living Dead*). With *Braindead*, they have reached a dead end, because it's impossible to imagine anyone out-grossing the New Zealander's effort, or wanting to. It seems that a serious treatment of the zombie as a monster for our times, encompassing what Thomas Pynchon called "the dreamer's own horror of isolation", is now well nigh impossible.

Witness how, despite a final half-hour of delirious mayhem, in which lawnmowers, meat cleavers, garden shears and chef mixers unite to purée an army of zombie extras, *Braindead* has been passed uncut, while Romero's sequels and Raimi's *The Evil Dead* all suffered punishing trims at the hands of the censor. This is not to discredit the BBFC, which has recognised the film's EC Comics credentials, and thus dismissed its potential as a tabloid pot-stirrer. In doing so, however, they have unwittingly aligned themselves with those who know and perhaps love the zombie (as appears to be true of audiences at several festivals worldwide, where *Braindead* has been enthusiastically received), rather than those who do not. Members of the latter group, stumbling into *Braindead* unprimed by at least one Romero/Raimi work, or by O'Bannon's jokey film, will find plenty to reinforce recent concern and bewilderment about screen violence.

Their reaction will be heightened by the fact that Jackson and his co-writers Walsh and Sinclair take an adolescent zit-squeezers' delight in pushing the audience head first into their bloody, muciferous, eviscerated images. While some of the orifice-puncturing, head-splitting prosthetics fail to come up to scratch, other efforts—like a dinner guest unknowingly gulping down custard laced with a newly burst boil—have a genuine emetic quality.

It's a measure of Jackson's audacity that he juxtaposes moments like this with footage of Elizabeth Windsor (with 'God Save the Queen' on the soundtrack) without breaking his stride. Among all the carnage is a sly dig at New Zealand's Commonwealth heritage (underlining the Antipodes' current republican mood) and the need to maintain a stiff upper lip as others are literally losing theirs. The film knowingly breaks into the *Archers* theme tune, just as Vera and a semi-decapitated Nurse McTavish are hurriedly pushed into the cellar to save appearances. Lionel's despair as he acquires an extended underground family resolutely intent on flouting decorum is made funnier by the fact that he is more embarrassed than horrified by his predicament. Unfortunately Jackson cannot maintain this level of wit and relies heavily on set pieces, including a rather ham-fisted nod to Larry Cohen's *It's Alive* (Lionel taking the zombie baby to the park) and a more successful martial arts piss-take, which sees Father McGruder fly-kicking the undead teds with the fervour of a born-again Bruce Lee.

But the film's finest moment is the climactic variation of an old Freudian chestnut: Vera, reincarnated as a gigantic, hyper-oestrogenised distortion of motherhood, opens up her pudendum to accommodate her son's re-entry providing a memorable Oedipal (w)retch for our times, and a highly unsuitable epitaph for the zombie monster.

VILLAGE VOICE, 2/9/93, p. 60, James Hannaham

Only someone from a very bad home could have made a film at once so inventive and stupefyingly gory as New Zealander Peter Jackson's *Dead/Alive*. Only a dedicated lunatic could mix hilarity and dismemberment so successfully.

The plot could make Freud wake up—from the dead—screaming: As Lionel Cosgrove (Timothy Balme) experiences his first kiss, his domineering mother gets bitten by the accursed Sumatran Rat-Monkey, a bite that kills and then turns her into a drooling, leprous zombie with a lust for human flesh. After Mum munches on a nurse, the guilt-ridden Lionel hides the bodies in his basement. In no time, he has a dysfunctional family of neo-cadavers living with him, which he keeps docile with tranquilizers.

Hyper-aware of its own trashiness, *Dead/Alive* has breakneck pacing (Lionel's girlfriend decides she loves him before their first date) that feeds the ridiculous, Pythonesque situations, but also seems designed to leave time for the final smorgasgore, a half-hour sequence jam-packed with motile body parts, blood-soaked protagonists, and a corpse with a light bulb stuck—no, I won't give that away. This bloody climax (probably where most of the budget was spent) contains some of the most excessive evisceration I've seen outside of snuff films. That it's hysterically funny shows how comedy is really tragedy with its limbs ripped off.

Also reviewed in:
NEW YORK TIMES, 2/12/93, p. C16, Stephen Holden
VARIETY, 5/25/92, p. 51, David Stratton

DEAD FLOWERS

An Upfront Films release of a Wega Film production. *Executive Producer:* Veit Heiduschka. *Producer:* Gebhard Zupan and Michael Katz. *Director:* Peter Ily Huemer. *Screenplay (German with English subtitles):* Peter Ily Huemer. *Director of Photography:* Walter Kindler. *Editor:* Eliska Stibrova. *Music:* Peter Scherer. *Sound:* Thomas Szabolcs. *Production Designer:* Tommy Vögel. *Costumes:* Heidi Melinc. *Running time:* 90 minutes. *MPAA Rating:* Not Rated.

CAST: Thierry van Werveke (Alex); Kate Valk (Alice); Tana Schanzara (Oma, Grandmother); Dominique Horwitz (Willy d'Ville).

NEW YORK POST, 4/30/93, p. 33, Jerry Tallmer

It isn't every romance that starts with the guy telling the girl on the morning after: "I have to go off to poison a few rat traps, gas a few beetles, smoke out some mice."

The guy, you see, is an exterminator—a tall, beefy, emotionless hulk who never (well, almost never) takes off his hat, even in the bedroom, and will remind you of several of the slob heroes in Jim Jarmusch films.

The girl who has flagged him down in his van on the road in the rain at night and been taken home by him to where he lives with his Grandma in the suburbs of Vienna, gives her name as Alice and says that some very bad people—CIA types, but worse—are after her. She also says she's the daughter of an American U.N. diplomat. The guy, Alex (Thierry van Werveke), tries to get rid of her, but once she does a striptease on the road—to change into one of the dresses his Granny wore as a young woman—Alex is hooked emotionless or not.

Thus the premise of "Dead Flowers" a film by the 34-year-old Viennese-born Peter Ily Huemer, an NYU Film School graduate last seen hereabouts with the 1988 "Kiss Daddy Goodnight".

"Dead Flowers" is a far less pretentious and better movie, though it's not all that unpretentious either. I'd call it a marriage of Wim Wenders and Jean Cocteau—of those Wenders road movies and the great "Orpheus" by Cocteau in which death comes on motorcycles and the search through Hades is for the lost Eurydice.

In "Dead Flowers" death comes by bicycle, and its herald is not the soulful sensitive Heurtebise of the Cocteau masterpiece but a scroungy weasel of a hit man in shades—a character named Willy d'Ville played by an actor named Dominique Horwitz, try that on your pianola.

The Alice/Eurydice is Kate Valk, a not altogether wooden actress—oh, hell, she's better and more attractive than that, but subtle she's not—out of the Wooster Group down in SoHo.

The actual heart and star of the movie is the old Grandmother who grieves over her dead husband and gets him mixed up from time to time with grandson Alex. High point of the movie for me is when Granny feigns remembering the disappeared Alice for fear of being put away as senile. The Germans have a way of producing memorable *alte damen* for such roles, and Tana Schanzara is one of them. Maybe in this picture weirdly featuring an exterminator, she's the exterminating angel.

Also reviewed in:
NEW YORK TIMES, 4/30/93, p. C8, Stephen Holden
VARIETY, 12/14/92, p. 47, Eric Hansen

DECEPTION

A Miramax Films release of a Majestic Films production.   *Executive Producer:* Haruki Kadokawa.   *Producer:* Lloyd Phillips.   *Director:* Graeme Clifford.   *Screenplay:* Robert Dillon and Michael Thomas.   *Story:* Robert Dillon.   *Director of Photography:* Laszlo Kovacs.   *Editor:* Caroline Biggerstaff.   *Music:* John Barry.   *Music Editor:* Robert Randles and Clif Kohlweck.   *Sound:* Dom Summer and (music) Shawn Murphy.   *Sound Editor:* Dody Dorn.   *Casting:* Jennifer Shull.   *Production Designer:* Richard Sylbert.   *Art Director:* John King.   *Set Decorator:* Jim Erickson and Lisa Fischer.   *Costumes:* Rudy Dillon.   *Make-up:* Marie-Gabrielle Selarque.   *Running time:* 90 minutes.   *MPAA Rating:* PG-13.

CAST: Andie MacDowell (Bessie Faro);   Liam Neeson (Fergus Lamb);   Viggo Mortensen (Johnny Faro);   Jack Thompson (Ed);   LOS ANGELES: Paul Spencer (Johnny Faro, Boy);   Chad Power (Niles Faro);   Monica Mikala (Alexandra Faro);   Kaelynn Craddick and Sara Craddick (Cleo Faro);   Luis Cortes (Hermes #1);   Amy Van Nostrand (Marge Swimmer);   Pedro Gonzalez-Gonzalez (Uncle Jorge);   Lucy Rodriguez (Tia Lupe);   Jeff Corey (Joe Dick);   Miriam Reed (Renee Dick);   Kimberley LaMarque (Mailwoman);   Francine Lee (Lily);   Mariachi & Tecalitlan (Mariachi Band);   VERA CRUZ: Alberto Estrella (Hermes #2);   Jorge Fegan (Undertaker);   Paco Mauri (Coroner);   Sylvia Short, Sage Allen, and Montrose Hagins (Fergus Groupies);   Lolo Navarro (Hotel Proprietress);   Rodrigo Puebla (Bank Teller #1);   Juan Antonio Llanes (Bank Teller #2);   BERLIN: Gunter Meisner (Herr Bruchner);   Thomas Frey (Bank Teller #3);   Monica Simon (EDK Receptionist);   ATHENS: Natassa Manisalli (Melina);   Nikos Kouros (Kolatos);   Aristidis Nikoloudis (Hotel Concierge);   CAIRO: Lydia Lenossi (Miss Abousief);   Mandana Marino (Miss Hakim);   Hosni Hasham Zahram (Taxi Driver);   Salh Abu El Asem (Warehouse Foreman);   Maisa El Rafai (Woman in Church);   Negm El Deen Mohammed Afifi (Iman, Mosque);   Robin Lee (Priest at Funeral);   Hannaa Hamed Ibrahim (Young Mother, Crypt);   Folkloric Art Group (Ramadan Musicians).

LOS ANGELES TIMES, 11/1/93, Calendar/p. 9, Kevin Thomas

As a travelogue, "Deception" is terrific; as a romantic adventure, it could scarcely be slighter, pleasant-enough escapist fare for the easily nourished. With gorgeously photographed locales ranging from the blue-collar L.A. County neighborhood of Lennox to Cairo in all its ancient, shabby splendor, "Deception" has production values worthy of a far more substantial movie.

Andie MacDowell stars as the unsophisticated wife of a pilot (Viggo Mortensen) with a struggling airplane salvage business transport company with ramshackle offices near LAX and in

Veracruz. When he is reported killed when his plane explodes outside Veracruz, MacDowell goes down to investigate, finding his cache that, via a secret code on them, allows her to collect more than $800,000 in bank accounts in Veracruz, the Bahamas, Berlin and Athens.

Needless to say, Mortensen, whose business is made clear from the film's production notes rather than the film itself, has been into something definitely shady, and MacDowell's pursuit of the truth culminate in Cairo.

MacDowell is ever the charmer, but writers Robert Dillon and Michael Thomas have given her little to work with—or rather, against. Except for a brief encounter in Veracruz with MacDowell, Liam Neeson's director of an international famine relief fund is off screen for the first 50 minutes of the movie's 90, eventually crossing paths with her once again in Cairo.

Neeson is simply too good to waste on the most meager of leading man roles; the same could be said for Jack Thompson, as Neeson's Cairo shipper, in a supporting role. Worse yet, for all the film's mysterious and menacing touches along the way, MacDowell ultimately experiences amazingly little danger.

Laszlo Kovacs cinematography is the film's glory, and it's hard to think of any film that has captured Cairo's rich, pungent atmosphere so extensively.

Directed smoothly by Graeme Clifford, "Deception" has been rated PG-13 for a shooting and brief language, it had originally been rated R under its previous title "Ruby Cairo" for a scene of strong sexuality, and for violence.

NEW YORK POST, 12/3/93, p. 45, Thelma Adams

Is the world ready for an Andie MacDowell vehicle?

MacDowell, a high note in the "Short Cuts" ensemble, is a handsome actress with a surprising steely quality beneath her cover-girl looks. But she is still not strong enough to carry the limp romantic thriller, "Deception."

The actress plays Bessie Faro, a Putumayo-wearing, coupon-clipping mother of three turned code-busting, globetrotting single white female. (The kids are more accoutrements of Bessie than characters in their own right). While MacDowell is believable in the part, the role is unbelievable.

Bessie met her pilot husband, a GQ cover boy named Johnny (Viggo Mortensen), while wait-ressing in Cairo, Ky. In stilted voice-over—a sure sign of narrative damage control—Bessie described being with Johnny as a ride in a car with no brakes. "Ladies," she says, "I like the ride."

That ride takes her all the way to Cairo, Egypt after Johnny's plane crashes in Mexico and the housewife-turned-sleuth suspects foul play. Along the way, she encounters squidgy new-age hero Dr. Fergus Lamb (Liam Neeson).

A reformed brandy-swilling oil millionaire (is there a 12-step program for that?), Lamb now heads "Feed the World," a world hunger organization. For a while I hoped Neeson ("Husbands and Wives") would turn into an evil food guru, but white knight was all they wrote.

Like an overloaded plane, the movie takes way too long to get off the ground. From Cairo, Ky., to Cairo, Egypt, scene after scene of exposition pass, with lots of crayon marks on maps and shots of jets overhead, as Bessie investigates Johnny's death.

This lavishly boring tour of exotic places depicts the kind of Mexico where all locals talk with their hands and men, young and old, are suspicious lechers. The Arabs don't fare much better, despite Lamb's exultation of their spiritual side.

"Deception" is a talent dump, a project that is promising on paper only. Director Graeme Clifford ("Frances"), noted Director of Photography Laszlo Kovacs ("Frances," "New York, New York" and "Easy Rider," among many others) and co-screenwriters Michael Thomas ("Scandal") and Robert Dillon ("Revolution") fail to deliver a movie that either thrills or romances.

Opening "Deception" quietly amidst the Christmas rush is like burying the movie in the flooded Nile.

NEWSDAY, 12/3/93, Part II/p. 93, Jack Mathews

Supposing somebody offered to pay you to travel from Los Angeles to Veracruz to Berlin to Athens to Cairo. No strings attached, except that you might have to work some long hours. Would you go?

Being asked that question is the only explanation for the existence of "Deception," a thriller (not!) that reunited, on a globe-hopping junket, director Graeme Clifford, production designer Richard Sylbert and cinematographer Laszlo Kovacs, teammates a decade earlier on the fine biographical film "Frances."

It would also help explain the presence of Andie MacDowell and Liam Neeson, two romantic leads whose stars seemed, just moments ago, to be in ascension.

MacDowell, hot off of her co-starring role in "Groundhog Day," is a housewife-turned-detective in "Deception," a woman who leaves her three small children with babysitters in L.A. while she follows a trail of money left in banks throughout the world by her late husband, a pilot quick-fried in a plane crash in Veracruz.

After raising plane fare with a yard sale, MacDowell's Bessie shows up in Veracruz to bury her husband, and while there, finds a handful of his most prized baseball cards, whose markings she miraculously recognizes as coded international bank accounts.

Seems her husband had been up to more than salvage, and had stowed his ill-got gains in banks all over the world. All she has to do is get a power of attorney and a Mileage Plus account and be on her way.

In flashbacks, we see MacDowell's Bessie being swept off her Kentucky feet by the dashing Johnny Faro (Viggo Mortensen), who, for reasons as murky as anything else in the story, calls her Ruby Cairo. The movie was originally titled "Ruby Cairo," which not only has a nicer ring to it than "Deception," but which possibly could have kept the film's secret a little longer.

As it is, there's not much question Bessie buried the wrong briquet in Veracruz, especially after she meets the handsome Dr. Lamb (Neeson), a vibrant fellow devoted to getting food to people in Third World countries. As you can imagine, this romance buds in the oddest places.

The story may not hold you enthralled, but the film features some of the year's best travel footage. The sequence showing Dr. Lamb and Bessie climbing the Great Pyramid of Cheops at sunset, and the view of Cairo from the top, are stunning.

For cast and crew, "Deception" must have been an excellent adventure.

SIGHT AND SOUND, 6/93, p. 63, Christopher Bray

Bessie Faro, wife and mother of three, lives a hand-to-mouth existence in Los Angeles. She spends her days watching television and tending to the kids, while her husband Johnny struggles to keep his airplane salvage business going. This quiet routine is disturbed when Johnny is reported dead in a plane crash in Mexico, leaving Bessie with nothing but a mortgage and a stack of unpaid bills. With what little she has Bessie travels to Vera Cruz for the funeral.

In Mexico she encounters Dr Fergus Lamb, a globe-trotting humanitarian who works for Feed The World, an organisation dimly connected with Johnny's increasingly shady-looking business. In Johnny's office she finds some baseball cards he has marked with a code. Translated, these lead her to a string of massive international bank accounts which, by forging her husband's signature, she clears out. Her travels end in Egypt where she discovers that the sacks of grain imported by Feed The World are actually stuffed with a deadly chemical. She accuses Lamb of subterfuge but he convinces her he knows nothing of the smuggling. Problems at a Cairo bank lead Bessie to suspect that Johnny might still be alive, and eventually she tracks him down. He tells her that he had to fake his death in order to escape murder at the hands of an organisation he had conned. This organisation has been trailing Bessie, however, and now they actually do kill Johnny. Bessie returns home a rich woman. As she and her children pack up to leave their run-down house, Dr Lamb arrives and they all depart together.

Like last year's *Deceived*, *Ruby Cairo* is an entry in the deceptive spouse genre. Alas, also like *Deceived*, *Ruby Cairo* is not only not an investigation of marriage per se, it is not even an investigation of a particular marriage.

Since we do not meet Johnny until five minutes from the end of the film, and since Andie MacDowell is an actress with a tight curfew on range (whoever cast her against type as an impoverished working-class mom?), we have no idea what kind of marriage we are dealing with. Even the film's title—Ruby Cairo is Johnny's nickname for Bessie—is left unexplained until the closing moments. One is left suspecting that a sizeable expository chunk has been removed from the beginning of the film.

Perhaps by way of compensation, other things are over-explained. Like sub-standard Billy Wilder, the film uses an irksome double narration mode. Director Graeme Clifford is not content to show us something, he tells us about it as well. When Bessie discovers her husband's hidden baseball cards, we zoom into a close-up of their mysterious markings; meanwhile she tells us in voice-over that "it looks like the way Johnny marks his cards ... it must be a code". It is hard to believe that Clifford edited the sublimely subtle *Don't Look Now* and *The Man Who Fell to Earth*.

With its voice-over, the search for a missing partner, the exotic locations, and the smuggling of poison, the film owes a great deal to *The Third Man*. Johnny even gets a Malthusian-Nietzschean speech in which he tries to excuse his running poison all over the world (Viggo Mortensen is no Orson Welles). Yet nothing is made of the opposition between his weary cynicism and Dr Lamb's right-on humanitarianism; in fact the film is such a mess that these two characters never even get to meet. The wonderful Liam Neeson is badly underused, cast as a cut-price Jeff Bridges with nothing to do but look tall.

The scenery, likewise, has nothing to do but look good. Yet there's no gainsaying the fact that look good it does. Cairo takes on the pungent colour of late Matisse, and in Vera Cruz, Berlin and Athens, Laszlo Kovacs's photography is as sumptuously eerie as ever. He is helped in his task by John Barry, who contributes one of his finest scores for years. One might argue that Barry's is the controlling intelligence behind the film: it is not accidental that all the scenes which work are backed by his music and that most of the ones that don't aren't. Between them Barry and Kovacs give the narratively unnecessary ascent of the Pyramid of Cheops a power beyond its functionless beauty. This scene almost makes up for the fact that *Ruby Cairo* is nothing but a plot and the plot nothing but predictable. Almost, but not quite.

Also reviewed in:
CHICAGO TRIBUNE, 12/3/93, Friday/p. D, Michael H. Price
NEW YORK TIMES, 12/3/93, p. C10, Janet Maslin
VARIETY, 5/10/93, p. 236, Derek Elley
WASHINGTON POST, 12/4/93, p. F2, Hal Hinson

DEMOLITION MAN

A Warner Bros. release of a Silver Pictures production. *Executive Producer:* Steven Bratter, Faye Schwab, Craig Sheffer, and Aaron Schwab. *Producer:* Joel Silver, Michael Levy, and Howard Kazanjian. *Director:* Marco Brambilla. *Screenplay:* Daniel Waters, Robert Reneau, and Peter M. Lenkov. *Story:* Peter M. Lenkov and Robert Reneau. *Director of Photography:* Alex Thomson. *Editor:* Stuart Baird. *Music:* Elliot Goldenthal. *Music Editor:* Christopher S. Brooks. *"Demolition Man" performed by:* Sting. *Sound:* Tim Cooney. *Sound Editor:* Robert G. Henderson. *Casting:* Joy Todd and Ferne Cassel. *Production Designer:* David L. Snyder. *Art Director:* Walter Paul Martishius. *Set Designer:* Mark Poll, Natalie V. Richards, and Carl Stensel. *Set Decorator:* Robert Gould and Etta Leff. *Special Effects:* Joe D. Ramsey. *Visual Effects:* Michael J. McAlister and Kimberly K. Nelson. *Costumes:* Bob Ringwood. *Make-up:* Scott H. Eddo. *Stunt Coordinator:* Charles Picerni and Steve Picerni. *Running time:* 120 minutes. *MPAA Rating:* R.

CAST: Sylvester Stallone (John Spartan); Wesley Snipes (Simon Phoenix); Sandra Bullock (Lenina Huxley); Nigel Hawthorne (Dr. Raymond Cocteau); Benjamin Bratt (Alfredo Garcia); Bob Gunton (Chief George Earle); Glenn Shadix (Associate Bob); Denis Leary (Edgar Friendly); Grand L. Bush (Zachary Lamb, Young); Pat Skipper (Helicopter Pilot); Steve Kahan (Captain Healy); Paul Bollen (TFR Officer); Mark Colson (Warden William Smithers, Young); Andre Gregory (Warden William Smithers, Aged); John Enos (Prisoner); Troy Evans (Tough Cop); Don Charles McGovern (Prison Guard); Bill Cobbs (Zachary Lamb, Aged); Patricia Rive, Anneliza Scott, and Dean Minerd (Police Officers); Kristopher Logan (Troubled Guy); Paul Perri (Squad Leader); Susan Lentini (TV Reporter); Casey Wallace (Little Girl); Michael Tennessee Lee (Boggle Guard); Chris Durand and Brett Jones (Museum Guards); Dan Cortese

(Taco Bell Entertainer); Lara Harris, Sam Nehira, and Claude Oatts (Taco Bell Patrons); Alex Chapman (Taco Bell Scrap); Brandy Sanders (Fiber Op Girl); Rosemarie Lagunas (Hamburger Stand Scrap); Ken Baldwin, Jack Black, Michael Buice, and Carlton Wilborn (Wasteland Scraps).

LOS ANGELES TIMES, 10/8/93, Calendar/p. 1, Kenneth Turan

Clearly undecided about whether to be a loud movie or a dopey movie, "Demolition Man" has ended up being both a loud movie and a dopey movie, a resolution that does not give the art of compromise a very good name.

Starring Sylvester Stallone and Wesley Snipes as a cop and a criminal (guess which is which) whose rivalry extends deep into the future, "Demolition Man" was intended at one time to do no more than live up to its R rating "for nonstop action violence and for strong language."

And when the film begins, in the terminally chaotic Los Angeles of 1996, it seems "Demolition Man" will be testosterone-driven enough to make "Cliffhanger" look like the movie version of "Remembrance of Things Past."

Stallone is LAPD Sgt. John Spartan, the umpteenth take-no-prisoners cop who allows nothing to get in the way of his rescue of the innocent. The innocent this time around are 30 hostages happy-go-lucky psychopath Simon Phoenix (Snipes in dyed-blond hair) has hidden away in a desert warehouse in an urban war zone.

As staged by Marco Brambilla, a commercial director making his theatrical debut, Spartan's rescue mission is an impressive action sequence that features enough body blows and explosions to incapacitate an army.

The rescue attempt goes awry, however, and both Phoenix and Spartan end up being put into spanking new cryonic prison, frozen into blocks of ice for a very long time. Unfortunately for action fans (we know you're out there), the movie itself pretty much goes into the deep freeze as far as mayhem is concerned, making do with penny-ante action sequences until the finale more than an hour down the road.

In place of battles, "Demolition Man" unaccountably offers a goof-ball piece of science-fiction parody, a played-for-laughs version of life in the year 2036 that presents a society so harmonious, its people seem next door to brain dead.

Under the leadership of Mayor/Gov. Raymond Cocteau (Nigel Hawthorne), the principality of San Angeles has recovered from both disease and earthquake devastation and become a land of peace, love and understanding. Except for the grungy Scraps, rebels who live underground, citizens are little more than walking happy faces, content to say things like "all is serene" and "mellow greetings" to each other and live by Cocteau's squeaky-clean rules.

So, when Simon Phoenix unaccountably gets defrosted and goes on a crime rampage, no one in San Angeles has a clue how to handle him except Barbie-doll police lieutenant Lenina Huxley (Sandra Bullock). She suggests thawing out Spartan as well, and soon enough he and Phoenix are trading bullets and baleful looks just like the bad old days.

Though the original story for "Demolition Man," such as it is, is credited to Peter M. Lenkov and Robert Reneau, the half-baked satiric sense of humor of the science-fiction sequences is doubtless the responsibility of the third credited screenwriter, Daniel Waters.

After the success of the anarchic "Heathers," Waters' career took a curious turn. He became the house wit of over-budget action movies, providing a layer of fatuous humor for "Hudson Hawk," "Batman Returns" and now this. Though some of the jokes in "Demolition Man" are actually funny, its quasi-facetious tone is overall more trying than entertaining.

As for the acting, there is not much of it. Nigel Hawthorne, the hottest actor in London off his stage performance in "The Madness of George III," seems barely awake here, and Snipes spends much of his time laughing, presumably at how much money he's getting paid for so little acting. As for Stallone, with so much silliness going on all around him, you actually miss his reliable figure when he's off the screen.

The only other thing of interest about "Demolition Man" is the various ways it steals from "Blade Runner," presumably even shooting a chase in downtown's Second Street tunnel as a kind of homage. Those hungry for futuristic action dramas would be well advised to watch that film on video or laser disc and leave "Demolition Man" to self-destruct on its own.

NEW YORK POST, 10/8/93, p. 45, Thelma Adams

Beef on beef. Stallone and Snipes. Together again for the first time in "Demolition Man." This movie is about as much fun as a kick in the head, but if you like those kind of kicks, there are plenty of them.

"Demolition Man" opens with what used to pass for a climax, so that everything that follows is anticlimactic. The premise, which Stallone repeats twice for those in the audience who are pitch-impaired, is: "send a maniac to catch one." Los Angeles in 1996 is one big burning pit, a post-riot, paranoid-fantasy theme park. Arch-villain Simon Phoenix (Wesley Snipes) has taken a busload of hostages. John Spartan (Sylvester Stallone), rogue cop, goes on a solo mission to nail Phoenix and free the passengers.

Some people are hard on shoes; Spartan's hard on property. That's why he's known as the Demolition Man. He collars Phoenix, but the hostages die and the factory where the standoff took place burns down. Sentenced to 70 years in cryostasis (the deep freeze) for the manslaughter of the innocents, Stallone is put on ice along with Snipes.

Cut to 40 years later. As a result of social engineering, LA. has become a basin of peace and harmony. The people talk in mellow future valley speak, sex is virtual reality, profanity a misdemeanor, and the gadgets look straight out of a 1996 AT&T trade show.

When Phoenix murders his way out of jail during a parole hearing, the local cops, unaccustomed to violence, can't handle him. The police defrost Spartan to catch Phoenix. The cat-and-mouse continues with better toys. The two beef cakes chase each other around the future until the final inevitable standoff, which isn't all that different from the first.

Any rapport the two leads might develop is interrupted by them bashing each other. Stallone's all jaw as usual. He shoulders his way through his scenes with a one-in-three chance of hitting a punch line. He's pumped his body into a flesh sculpture, but he's wasted on me.

As Phoenix, Snipes seems to be enjoying himself. It's a turn on his "New Jack City" drug kingpin without the searing anger and hate that made that role memorable. Here he's intentionally cartoonish, with a blond thatch that makes him look like a Mohawk beautician.

The supporting cast is lively, aided by a script that doesn't take itself too seriously. As the 21st-century policewoman in thrall with the 20th, Sandra Bullock is perky and animated. She gets some good lines and delivers them amiably. Comic Denis Leary spews a few mini-monologues as an underground leader who finds peace and harmony discordant.

"Demolition Man" is part "Total Recall," part "New Jack City," and part "Flash Gordon," and it's completely stale. This bash-by-numbers is for die-hard action-adventure fans only.

NEWSDAY, 10/8/93, Part II/p. 82, John Anderson

Sylvester Stallone comedy? One approaches such a creature as one would approach an Arnold Schwarzenegger ballet, with a general sense of dread. But by not trying to be funny, Stallone helps make "Demolition Man" one of the funniest films of the year, a consistently entertaining action-comedy with little pretension and more than a few biting observations about modern life.

It's the year 2032, and the amalgamated municipality of San Angeles is in a state of dire pleasantness. Freedom of choice, freedom of speech and anything unhealthy have been outlawed. "Be well" is the post-millennial mantra, everyone calls everyone else by both their first and last names, and ubiquitous devices issue summonses for violations of the Verbal Morality Statute. It's a colorless but peaceful world, where police approach criminals with "extreme assertiveness." If they can find any.

They do, of course. Into this lobotomized Shangri-La comes Simon Phoenix (Wesley Snipes), an escapee from the sub-zero cryo-prison where he was put on ice in 1996. Back then, felons were frozen rather than executed, and the major criminals of the 20th-Century are in cold storage. So is John Spartan, a cop known as the Demolition Man before he was framed by Phoenix and given his own 70-year sentence. When Officer Lenina Huxley (Sandra Bullock, a 20th-Century history buff, suggests that her superiors thaw out Spartan to battle Phoenix, they do. But the ensuing mayhem makes them wish they hadn't.

"I'm not sure he's any different than Simon Phoenix himself," sniffs George Earle (Bob Gunton), the officious chief of the previously unnecessary police. And it's a good point. The carnage—good-natured, high-tech carnage—is almost enough to convince you of the rightness of San Angeles.

Stallone's had plenty of experience playing Neanderthals, and does so again, relatively, in "Demolition Man." Spartan, in the '90s, is a fully modern man; thirty years later, he's become an anachronism. As a man out of his time (there's a bit of borrowing from "Time and Again," "Sleeper" and the work of "former president Schwarzenegger") Stallone is amusing, but the screenplay is so clever, and the jokes so pointed about our fears and expectations, that you can't help laugh out loud. And many of the laughs are bolstered by hard truths about urban life: When evil genius Dr. Raymond Cocteau (Nigel Hawthorne) tells Phoenix that people are terrified of him, and the golden-blond black man answers, "People have always been terrified of me ..." it's pretty obvious what he's talking about.

And so, Stallone has delivered the unexpected, an intelligent, often hilarious film with a conscience, and a performance that doesn't get in the way of his very capable co-stars. Bullock, for instance, who's so perky you can't stand it. And Snipes, the villain you can't quite bring yourself to hate, turns out to be the kind of natural comedian Stallone will never be, and doesn't have to be, for "Demolition Man" to work so well.

NEWSWEEK, 10/18/93, p. 85, David Ansen

Demolition Man is a movie that should have been fun, and isn't, John Spartan (Sylvester Stallone), a "maniac" cop from the anarchic bad old days of 1996, is released from his cryogenic prison sentence in the year 2032 to pursue the similarly defrosted "maniac" criminal Simon Phoenix (Wesley Snipes), his archenemy. The cops in the future can't handle the job because "San Angeles" in the 21st century is a peaceful, crimeless, utterly sterile place—a fascist Eden of unending banality where cocktail pianists sing old commercial jingles, fines are given for profanity, where sex and cholesterol are illegal and all restaurants are called Taco Bell. Leave it to Sly to teach these geeks the virtues of vulgarity, rebellion and brute force. It sounds a lot better than it plays. Marco Brambilla, a novice director, can't begin to mesh the schizy mixture of head-banging violence, future-shock satire and Hollywood in-jokes. The actors have no characters to play and scramble haplessly for a consistent style. The exuberantly bad-ass Snipes at least seems to be enjoying himself. Sly gets to maim, kill, take his clothes off and, in one of the movie's actually funny moments, knit. He makes a lovely red sweater.

SIGHT AND SOUND, 12/93, p. 44, Michael Atkinson

In the crime-ravaged urban inferno of Los Angeles circa 1997, supercop John Spartan is coptered in to defuse a hostage situation engineered, as Spartan alone guesses, by super-villain Simon Phoenix. The two face off in an empty warehouse that Phoenix has already soaked in gasoline, and in mid-fight, the arch-criminal sets the place ablaze. Unknown to Spartan, Phoenix's 30-odd hostages were in the building, and Spartan stands accused of their manslaughter. Both men are incarcerated in a cryoprison, where they will wait out 70-year sentences while computerised rehabilitation programmes are drummed into their sleeping brains.

35 years later, Phoenix is woken for his parole hearing, utters the code word for his computerised shackles and kills everybody in the room. The futuristic city he escapes into—San Angeles—is the angelic twin of the 1997 city: the freeways are clear, nearly everybody wears neo-Buddhist robes, violence is unknown and physical contact of even a sexual nature is taboo. "Be well" is the interpersonal greeting of choice. Thus the police are not equipped to deal with homicidal maniacs from the past. To make things worse, Phoenix seems to possess a thorough foreknowledge of how this computerised utopia works, a fact that baffles even him. Lenina Huxley, a perky young policewoman with a love of late twentieth-century trash culture and a yen for even the mildest excitement, tracks Phoenix's movements and eventually suggests they thaw Spartan out to deal with the villain.

Once awake and dazed by his new surroundings, Spartan continually tracks and combats Phoenix until losing him in the city's underground caverns. Soon, the city's self-appointed mayor/guru Dr Cocteau reveals himself to be the architect of the whole mess, having engineered Phoenix's freedom and knowledge so that he may find and assassinate the leader of the homeless underground, Edgar Friendly. Spartan eventually enters the world beneath the city, meets Friendly, and faces off yet again with Phoenix, returning to the cryo-prison for a final showdown.

High-horsepower action movies all are a peculiar breed of mass entertainment, at once dauntingly low-brow, smirkingly self-reflexive and infatuated with haphazard destruction. Having evolved from the gene pool fed by James Bond, Dirty Harry and the *Star Wars* trilogy, and truly taking to land in *The Terminator*, the artillery-expending blockbuster genre has certainly reached some sort of critical mass, if 1993 is any indication. Half of the summer's big Hollywood releases were predicated on comparatively gritty and literate concepts and characterisations (*In the Line of Fire* and *The Fugitive*), while the other half, most prominently *Cliffhanger* and *Last Action Hero*, were simultaneously preposterous hyperextensions of action-movie aesthetics and self-parodying trashings of the same. *Last Action Hero*, especially, is a smoking ruin of Brechtian tropes, disassembling the genre in a fit of bratty cleverness and leaving it in pieces on the floor.

This may seem like a textual dead end, but there are plenty of laughs to be had, as *Demolition Man* also bears out. Less self-parody than a ferociously irreverent comedy (and science-fiction satire) that just happens to entail a lot of *mano-a-mano* gun violence, Sly's newest slice of turkey turns the tables on the *Terminator* films' wholesale-mayhem-from-the-future strategy. Here, the agents of destruction pass from a nightmarish past/present into an absurdly peaceful future, wreaking havoc. *Demolition Man* wears its only-a-movie comic book bravado on its sleeve—in the very first shot of the film, we see the post-Rodney King L.A. purgatory of 1997 in a wry, swooping helicopter shot that passes *through* the flames engulfing the famous HOLLYWOOD sign.

Of the several credited writers on the film, the recognisable voice of *Heathers* author Daniel Waters is prevalent; one character actually greets another with "Greetings and salutations," a quote from the earlier film. Presumably thanks to Waters, the movie is chock-a-block with hilarious present-mocking futurisms, from the empty L.A. freeways, the oldies radio stations (and lounge singers) playing ad jingles as if they were yesterday's Top 40 hits, and the President Schwarzenegger Memorial Library, to someone answering a phone with, "If you'd prefer an automated response to your call, push 'one' now."

Given the goofy wit of the film's script, the actors either rise to the occasion or, in the case of Stallone, simply lurch about dimly. Phoenix is as pure a comic book villain as any dreamed up by Marvel Comics, and Snipes chews each matte painting and neo-modernist set like the damned on holiday. Comedian Denis Leary, as the irascible nonconformist Friendly, is a brilliant bit of casting, digging into his trademarked firecracker routine to fire off some pro-vice *bon mots* at San Angeles' utopian new-ageism. Though imbued with all the personality of a lump of coal, Stallone manages occasionally to find the right moment amid the firefighting and explosions, as when he hungrily digs into an illegal rat burger, or presents Sandra Bullock, his ersatz partner in the twenty-first century, with a sweater he knitted in one night, thanks to the rehab programming he got in cryo-prison.

Frankly, *Demolition Man*, like nearly all films of its genre not directed by James Cameron or John McTiernan, an enjoyable mess. Its plot makes little sense (Friendly is hardly formidable enough a threat to San Angeles to warrant Cocteau's excavation of one-man shitstorm Snipes), and its action sequences inevitably become repetitious and crisscrossed with narrative errors. It floats thanks to its consistency, and the gutsiness of its humour—how many other films would dare to re-enact and somersault the Rodney King beating scenario? Here, of course, it's seven wimpy, white future cops well versed in etiquette, trying to take in a single black man, and he kicks their asses. On the one hand, this may seem to excuse the LAPD's use of excessive force; on the other, this is the moviest of movies and there's nothing wrong with a little payback.

TIME, 10/18/93, p. 98, Richard Schickel

Of the many nightmarish futures that have been imagined for us on the screen, none is more hellish than the year 2032 as envisioned in *Demolition Man*. It posits the total triumph of every kind of correctness that is urged on us today—political, dietary, linguistic. It is not merely that all of San Angeles (the Southern California metro area stretching from Santa Barbara to San Diego and embracing Los Angeles) has been declared a no-smoking area. It is also legally salt free. And alcohol, red meat and sex free too. If you cuss in public, you are issued a ticket by all-hearing, omnipresent machines. If you need to find out something about the past, you look it up at the Arnold Schwarzenegger Presidential Library.

You can imagine how Sylvester Stallone's basic screen character would react to an environment like that. Perhaps the word violently springs to mind. And if you're up to here with '90s cant, there is a certain rude satisfaction in watching him blow it away—along with a wide as assortment of villains.

Villains? How did they get loose in this gun-free Utopia? Therein lies the simple tale *Demolition Man* has to tell. For all its sanctimoniousness, San Angeles is a fascist state. Its smooth-spoken leader, Raymond Cocteau (Nigel Hawthorne), is annoyed by a persistent band of rebels, living where such folk always do in fictions like this, in the cities underground passages. There they cook hamburgers (well, actually, they're ratburgers), swill beer and dream of cholesterol's restoration. To deal with the outlaws, Cocteau frees a killer named Simon Phoenix (Wesley Snipes) from cryogenic prison (they took to deep-freezing criminals as early as 1996, during the last convulsive phase of urban warfare). To deal with him, his wimpy cops, not knowing Phoenix is in league with their boss, warm up his old nemesis John Spartan (Stallone), who's been doing chilly time for overly enthusiastic police work in the bad old days.

Soon enough the protagonists have acquired heavy weapons and are going at each other as people do in films produced by Joel Silver, he of the *Die Hards* and the *Lethal Weapons*—i.e., frequently, spectacularly, preposterously. Stallone and Snipes both play this nonsense tongue-in-cheekily. Sandra Bullock has an attractive naivete as a scholarly policewoman who hangs out with Sly. But ultimately the script's often sharp social satire is drowned out by the noise and confusion. It is also undercut by casting virtually all the psychopathically murderous criminals as minority-group members. A little political correctness in that matter would have prevented this movie from playing right into the dismissive hands of the forces it most wants to criticize.

VILLAGE VOICE, 10/19/93, p. 51, J. Hoberman

Demolition Man—the latest megamillion-dollar potlatch to come from Joel Silver—is your basic comic-book clash of the titans. Sylvester Stallone, reworking his tough-cop Cobra persona for humorous dinosaur potential, is pitted against the equally billed Wesley Snipes, a mad criminal sporting a chiseled sneer and a blond mushroom do.

The makeup on these meat puppets may not be as striking as the Basil Wolverton cum Big Daddy Roth gross-outs on display in the current Looney Tune Grand Guignol *Freaked*, but the performances are no less stylized. Stallone is barely articulate; Snipes overcompensates by mugging and cackling like a bionic Little Richard. Mortal enemies in a suitably apocalyptic fin de siècle Los Angeles, the two are sentenced to cryostasis and defrosted in the year 2032 to continue their epic battle-discovering, as Snipes puts it, that reality has become "a pussy-whipped *Brady Bunch* version of itself."

Sly, for his sins, has been reborn into a post-earthquake, p.c. L.A. where ineffectual, nonviolent cops spout New Age jargon and electronic Michael Medved-inspired thought police issue tickets for violations of the "verbal morality standard." (This, of course, is self-servingly self-reflexive. One of the movie's big laff lines is a seven-year-old girl's juicy "Fuck you, lady!") Among the other extrapolated trends are hideously overwrought computer graphics, oldies radio stations that play ancient advertising jingles for Ken-L Ration and Armour hot dogs, and safe, secretion-free telepathic sex.

The world is run by the effete Dr. Cocteau and his fat sissy sidekick (Tim Burton regular Glenn Shadix). All resistance is literally underground—a nominally Third World mix of homeless substance abusers living on rat-burgers and staging periodic raids to spray-paint graffiti on the pristine upper world. It only remains for Sly to restore a healthy balance of masculine aggression and self-destructive energy, with the help of an overenthusiastic ingenue (Sandra Bullock) who is not only "addicted to the 20th century"—and the comic mangling of its colorful slang—but pays her partner the ultimate compliment: "You are even better live than on laser disc."

Although the film's a showcase for Stallone, who has recently discarded his trademark glasses and can be seen posed nude and bronzed bright orange in a pensive mode on the cover of the current *Vanity Fair*, screenwriter Daniel Waters (*Heathers, Hudson Hawk, Batman Returns*) is most likely responsible for its jocular attitude, creative newspeak, and rampant movie references (the only ones that make any sense are those to Sly's perceived rival, Arnold Schwarzenegger). Nearly as facetious as it is violent, stocked with ambitious sets, *Demolition Man* aspires to the pomo pizzazz of such well-beloved Reaganite dystopias as *Robocop* or the original *Terminator*. The combination of goonish comedy and massive fire power are, however, more suggestive of *The Coneheads Die Hard*.

What can you say about a movie that opens with the star parachuting into a flaming L.A. riot and winds up endorsing underclass violence as healthy self-expression, that decries idiot commercialization and posits museums stocked with live ammo, that (while gratuitously homophobic) ends with the star sporting a dainty AIDS ribbon? The more Sly pumps up, the easier it must be for him to operate behind his own back.

Also reviewed in:
NEW YORK TIMES, 10/8/93, p. C23, Vincent Canby
VARIETY, 10/18/93, p. 50, Emanuel Levy
WASHINGTON POST, 10/9/93, p. D5, Hal Hinson

DENNIS THE MENACE

A Warner Bros. release. *Executive Producer:* Ernest Chambers. *Producer:* John Hughes and Richard Vane. *Director:* Nick Castle. *Screenplay:* John Hughes. *Based on characters created by:* Hank Ketcham. *Director of Photography:* Thomas Ackerman. *Editor:* Alan Heim. *Music:* Jerry Goldsmith. *Music Editor:* Darrell Hall and Scott Stambler. *Sound:* Jim Alexander and (music) Bruce Botnick. *Sound Editor:* Michael D. Wilhoit and Wylie Stateman. *Casting:* Jane Jenkins and Janet Hirshenson. *Production Designer:* James Bissell. *Art Director:* Michael Baugh and Steve Wolff. *Set Designer:* Karen Fletcher. *Set Decorator:* Eve Cauley. *Set Dresser:* Dan Clancy. *Special Effects:* Michael Wood. *Visual Effects:* Rebecca Marie. *Costumes:* Ann Roth and Bridget Kelly. *Make-up:* Linda Melazzo. *Running time:* 110 minutes. *MPAA Rating:* PG.

CAST: Walter Matthau (Mr. Wilson); Mason Gamble (Dennis Mitchell); Joan Plowright (Martha Wilson); Christopher Lloyd (Switchblade Sam); Lea Thompson (Alice Mitchell); Robert Stanton (Henry Mitchell); Amy Sakasitz (Margaret Wade); Kellen Hathaway (Joey); Paul Winfield (Chief of Police); Natasha Lyonne (Polly); Devin Ratray (Mickey); Hank Johnston (Gunther); Melinda Mullins (Andrea); Billie Bird (Edith Butterwell); Bill Erwin (Edward Little); Arnold Stang (Phtographer); Ethel Gerstein (Gaggle Lady #1); Rebecca C. Hogan (Gaggle Lady #2); Leona Toppel (Gaggle Lady #3); Peggy Goldberg (Gaggle Lady #4); Jack McGuigan (Gaggle Man); Corey Vane (Mike); Casey Gamble (Hide and Seeker); Daiana Campeanu (Babysitter); Robert A. Saunders (Broken Arm Babysitter); Beverly J. O'Donnell (Elderly Babysitter); Betty (Ruff).

LOS ANGELES TIMES, 6/25/93, Calendar/p. 1, Peter Rainer

Alfred Hitchcock once said that a thriller is only as good as its villain, so shouldn't a "Dennis the Menace" be only as good as its menace?

Well, yes and no. As the infamous Dennis Mitchell in the new film version, little Mason Gamble isn't very menacing, but his bemused peskiness is a welcome relief after the hyperenergized Macaulay Culkin of the "Dennis"-style "Home Alone" films. He's almost recognizably human. This John Hughes production based on the Hank Ketcham comic strip is pretty tepid tomfoolery but at least it's not assaultive in the way that most kids' films are nowadays. It's trying for giggles instead of guffaws.

The "Dennis" comic strip, early '60s TV show and currently syndicated animated series all opt for an Everytown U.S.A. blandness—pipsqueak rebellion in a '50s time warp. The movie, directed by Nick Castle from Hughes' script, is still caught up in that warp (with a few concessions, like the fact that both of Dennis' parents now work). This means that Dennis doesn't get into any high-tech shenanigans. No computers, no video games, no laser guns. The film pretty much sticks to the old-fashioned basics: Dennis spills a jar of paint, Dennis wrecks the dentures of his grumpy nemesis and neighbor, Mr. Wilson (Walter Matthau), Dennis accidentally clonks a scurvy thief (Christopher Lloyd). Since this Dennis is only 5 years old, perhaps the decision was made to keep things slapstick-simple. Or could it be that the filmmakers regard Dennis as a "classic"—like, say, Huck Finn or Penrod?

This sort of misplaced reverence probably won't do much for young audiences accustomed to a little more zap and bounce in their heroes. Parents might be grateful, though. The shenanigans in "Dennis the Menace" (rated PG for comedic mischief) are mostly so mildly conceived and executed that kids aren't likely to try them out on their families when they get home from the theater. Mom and Dad won't have to lock up the frying pans.

Walter Matthau is perfect casting as Mr. Wilson and he seems to know it. He enjoys being a crotchety grouch. Of course, he always has, even when he was too young to be playing old coots. Matthau doesn't turn Wilson into a darling; he's a sourpuss who snorts in his sleep and hasn't a kind word for anyone except his infinitely patient wife (Joan Plowright). Matthau's performance seems to be out of Charles Dickens and not Hank Ketcham or John Hughes, and he makes a lot of Dennis' scenes possible. Also, his vocal whine has never sounded closer to W.C. Fields', and this must be some sort of tribute. Fields, that great lover of child actors, would have elevated the role of Mr. Wilson to heights of ecstatic nastiness.

If Hughes was expecting this film to create another pipsqueak franchise for him, he may have miscalculated. "Dennis the Menace" seems more like a rest period in between Culkin-ized tantrums. It's not much—just one goofy little foul-up after another—but its lack of crassness is rather sweet.

NEW YORK, 7/12/93, p. 54, David Denby

"Cheek pinchers!" cries Dennis (Mason Gamble) as a brace of elderly garden-club ladies descends on him in *Dennis the Menace*. At its (occasional) best, John Hughes's rambunctious production (directed by Nick Castle) captures the essence of what children find intolerable in adults. The way they sleep, for instance. Trying to ward off the little pest, Walter Matthau's Mr. Wilson emits a barrage of snarfing fake sleeping noises, right up to the moment Dennis slingshots an aspirin into his mouth. Dennis lives a pre-media existence in a perfect small town with a river and a moon; he lives, that is, on the street and in the backyard, in a paradise of mischief. (Some of his pranks may make parents grateful for Nintendo.) He is innocent but relentless, a child who sends panicked cats crashing into each other.

NEW YORK POST, 6/25/93, p. 32, Michael Medved

At his best ("Planes, Trains, and Automobiles," the original "Home Alone"), prolific filmmaker John Hughes combines energetic slapstick with touches of old-fashioned sentimentality to send audiences home both amused and satisfied. At his worst ("Dutch," "Curly Sue," "Home Alone 2: Lost in New York"), his movies have a joyless, mechanical feel to them as they rattle through their predictable paces—often leaving viewers with a nasty aftertaste.

Though it may earn considerable money at the box office due to Warner Bros.' aggressive marketing campaign, "Dennis the Menace" definitely follows the pattern of Hughes' worst efforts.

He's credited aa writer-producer, but director Nick Castle ("The Last Starfighter") seems all but irrelevant, due to the picture's slavish recycling of Hughes' "Home Alone" formula. This time, the two burglars from that mega-hit have been fused into one nasty thief called "Switchblade Sam." Played with genuine menace and inappropriate intensity by Christopher Lloyd, this grimacing villain is a filthy, homeless thug with rotting teeth who is frightening rather than funny. When he gets his inevitable, sadistic comeuppance at the hands of 6-year-old Dennis, the lengthy sequence is both boring and ugly—with the howling bad guy set on fire, and his face ultimately pounded to a bruised and bloody pulp. At the end of the process you might think you had accidentally walked into "Menace II Society" rather than "Dennis the Menace." All of this is a world away from the easygoing innocence of Hank Ketcham's beloved comic strip, which first appeared in 1951. Hughes' main nod to this original "Dennis the Menace" comes through the physical recreation of the boy's comfortable village as a suburban idyll straight out of Norman Rockwell. But he then proceeds to undermine the sense of familiarity and nostalgia with several "cutting edge" '90s touches. Not only do we see "Switchblade Sam" entering houses at will and pilfering cherished possessions, but Dennis' baby-sitter (who appears to be no more than 12) is shown aggressively and graphically groping her boyfriend—an overweight, loutish Lothario with an earring. Meanwhile, the younger children engage in three different, gross and utterly gratuitous conversations about sex that left my own 6-year-old daughter puzzled and vaguely disturbed.

The prevailing vision of a 1950s picket-fence paradise, where comfortable conventions mask some deep inner rot, seems to have been borrowed from "Blue Velvet"—hardly the tone you'd expect in a "feel good" film for the kiddies.

Worst of all, Dennis himself is transformed into a spoiled, nasty little brat. In the comic strip, he is an active, likable kid who gets into trouble with mud and mischief, but he is never mean. Here, he attacks his elderly neighbor Mr. Wilson by, among other things, refilling Mr. Wilson's mouthwash bottle with toilet bowl cleaner, taking his false teeth from his bathroom and breaking them, and shooting an aspirin into the man's sleeping mouth with a slingshot. The slapstick indignities inflicted on the unfortunate old man include two different assaults aimed directly at his private parts.

Walter Matthau handles his role as Mr. Wilson with such convincing crustiness and warmth, and with such masterful comic timing that he makes all of this almost endurable to watch. His characterization is easily the best thing in the movie and makes one long for a more appropriate context to back up his consummate professionalism.

Mason Gamble, the 7-year-old actor chosen to play the title character after a nationwide talent search, is an undeniably pretty and appealing child, whose self-conscious cuteness counteracts his charm.

This picture marks the first feature film officially offered by Warner Bros.' much-heralded new Family Entertainment division; it is a singularly inauspicious beginning.

NEWSDAY, 6/25/93, Part II/p. 50, John Anderson

You have to give John Hughes, the screenwriter on "Dennis the Menace," credit for one thing: He's hooked into the dark side of Hank Ketcham's classic comic strip, the nightmare subtext of a man who, having retired after years of service to the U.S. Post Office, finds that his twilight years are going to be besieged and beset by a 5-year-old from hell.

George Wilson (Walter Matthau) is such a man. He's a bit of a grouch, sure, but you would be too if you lived next door to Dennis Mitchell, especially as played by tow-headed cutie-pie Mason Gamble. The child is a pint-sized sociopath; there are no motives for his actions other than the resultant suffering of his aging, badly toupeed neighbor. When George suggests to Dennis' father, Henry (Robert Stanton), that corporal punishment might not be out of the question, I think I heard Mother Teresa let out a cheer in the back of the theater.

Dennis has been done before—by Jay North in the old '60s TV series, in a badly animated Japanese version, in a 1987 William Windom movie—but Gamble's arrival on screen has been heralded as something like the second coming of Macaulay Culkin (and if that doesn't increase your heart rate, we sympathize). The very blond child is cute, but he's no actor. And under Nick Castle's direction, his "technique" actually backfires: When he's supposed to be softening Mr. Wilson's hardened heart—hardened, as it happens, by Dennis' quasi-criminal antics—Gamble still sounds like a short con man. The effect isn't pathos, it's irritation. And a lot of sympathy for Mr. Wilson.

He's a wonderful vehicle for Matthau's long-suffering, basset-hound face. He's a little meaner than previous Mr. Wilsons, though. When he finds Dennis using a spy to cheat at hide-and-seek, he sends the accomplice child home by telling him his father wants to take him out for ice cream. "He's going to be disappointed," says Mrs. Wilson (Joan Plowright). "Disappointment's going to be a big part of his life," George replies. "He's a foot short for his age and he's crosseyed." "Dennis the Menace" exists in a strange kind of time warp, where people wear '50s clothes and drive '90s cars. Where Dennis' mom, Alice (Lea Thompson), newly returned to the work force and fighting corporate politics, might have been dropped out of June Cleaver's kitchen. Where a malodorous thief like Switchblade Sam (a Hughes creation played by Christopher Lloyd) can commit a one-man crime spree because the town has never had any crime before. You'd want to move there, if only Dennis would move out. The plot, as it were, involves Sam's robbing of Mr. Wilson's house while he is hosting a garden party to celebrate the blooming of his prized 40-year-old plant. And Mr.Wilson's subsequent condemnation of and reconciliation with Dennis. And, of course, Dennis capturing Sam, in a sequence that is so overly cruel parents might consider less violent movies for their offspring, like "Jurassic Park" or "Last Action Hero."

SIGHT AND SOUND, 9/93, p. 44, Leslie Felperin Sharman

Dennis Mitchell, a six-year-old problem child, lives with his parents Alice and Henry next door to curmudgeonly Mr Wilson and his kindly wife Martha. Alice has had to take a job to help with family finances, so Dennis spends time with his friends Margaret and Joey in their treehouse, and later stays with the Wilsons while his parents are away.

Meanwhile, the nefarious Switchblade Sam has begun a spree of thieving in the town. One night he breaks into the Wilson house and steals a coin collection. Dennis raises the alarm just as Mr Wilson's 40-year orchid blooms, spoiling the flower's ten-second moment of glory, which his gardening club has gathered to watch. Furious, Mr Wilson banishes Dennis from his sight. Wandering in the woods, Dennis is taken hostage by Switchblade Sam, and in his innocently motivated desire to help ends up subjecting Sam to a series of painful ordeals. Upon discovering the stolen coins, Dennis escapes, turns Sam over to the police, and is reunited with his parents and a contrite Mr Wilson.

Dennis is distilled from Hank Ketcham's American comic strip *Dennis the Menace*, an enduring Sunday newspaper serial whose version of suburban Americana provides a missing link between the adult-centered *Blondie* of the 1940s and the all-child cast of the 60s *Peanuts*. Its main comic heat source is generational friction, fuelled with copious bouts of slapstick. In fact it's the same energy on which the Home Alone machines are run, which were also manufactured by *Dennis'* producer John Hughes. As with well-made video games, adults might decry the product's violence, sentimentality and addictiveness, but there's no denying the fact that Hughes makes some clever little gadgets.

Known as Dennis the Menace in the States, in Britain the film has been retitled simply Dennis in order to avoid trademark infringement with the D.C. Thompson character of the same name. It seems hardly likely that anyone could confuse this Dennis with the British proto-punk who launched a thousand New Age travellers' tatty black-and-red jumpers. Thompson's Dennis is an anarchist in almost every sense of the word, while the American's more anodyne mayhem is usually confined to nothing more scandalous than losing his frog among the pews during Sunday Service and accidentally maiming grown-ups. It's all clean, wholesome, unrelenting violence.

After a cartoon series that updated Dennis' milieu to the present day, complete with skateboards and video games, this latest film incarnation cheerfully recaptures the original quasi-50s setting. While cars and other props are contemporary, the costumes and sets are all Sputnik-era style, a self-consciously anachronistic melange of bouffant hair and pastel-coloured kitchens. Even the sexual politics are retro: Margaret, Dennis' tot friend, is obsessive about playing house, while Alice, his mother, is guilt-racked about neglecting her home, and colludes with Dennis to wreak retribution on the film's only real baddie, a childless career woman who plays a marginal role. Eventually, it becomes clear that this is a film designed for baby-sitting grandparents to take their progeny to—it's really their sense of nostalgia that is being appealed to, while only manageable younger children will feel seduced by a hero with only a slingshot for armour and not a single ninja kick to his repertoire.

The fast pace and pleasures of *Dennis* are not well served by its star Mason Gamble, who despite having been selected from a much-hyped nationwide talent search, is a rather colourless little sprite. All gloopy toilet-tissue ad eyes, he fails to convey what little pugnacity Ketcham's original character possessed. Inevitably he is beggared in any comparison with Hughes' other protegé, Macaulay Culkin. Still the film is forever redeemed by Walter Matthau's classic performance of cantanker, worth every penny of the admission price. His comic timing is exquisite as he runs through a gamut of grouchy gestures, horrified mugs, and mournful moues of resignation. Overall, there are worse ways for a kid to keep his or her grandparents occupied on a summer afternoon.

VILLAGE VOICE, 7/6/93, p. 52, Kathy Deacon

In *Dennis the Menace*, writer/producer John Hughes returns to the brat-*mit*-schmaltz genre of his box-office juggernaut, *Home Alone*. This time the setting evokes the now obsolete ambience of middle-middle-class backyard family life in WASP Middle America, where a retired postal clerk like old Mr. Wilson could be a respected member of a garden club. Mason Gamble manages to translate the diabolical energy of Dennis, and Walter Matthau the fathomless irritability of Mr. Wilson, from Hank Ketcham's arch-'50s comic strip.

But unlike the roly-poly tyke of the strip, Gamble's Dennis has a fragile elfen vulnerability that makes him a comely foil for Switchblade Sam (Christopher Lloyd), whom he must dispose of in his parents' absence, just as Kevin totals the intruders in *Home Alone*. With Sam, middle-class respectability is challenged by a creature even lower on the social spectrum, a derelict with god-awful teeth who discovers he's no match for a kid from a good home. Of course, two-thirds of the film deals with the sadomasochistic thing Dennis has going with Mr. Wilson—whose constipated heart breaks when the boy disappears—but this is mere child's play compared to the wanton violence visited upon the homeless thief who is stabbed, shackled, garroted, and repeatedly set aflame by our spunky wunderkind.

A regressive suburban fantasy, *Dennis the Menace* also sends up bitchy, dreadful little girls who won't just play by themselves, childless career women vindictive toward moms, and an undersize kid with a physical impairment. Children in the audience took particular delight in the fart the hobo emits after he's force-fed by Dennis. Adults might be amused by one or two other moments, though in general the slapstick (paint regurgitated from vacuum cleaners and the like) is well-paced, but tired.

Also reviewed in:
CHICAGO TRIBUNE, 6/25/93, Friday/p. B, Mark Caro
NEW YORK TIMES, 6/25/93, p. C12, Vincent Canby
VARIETY, 6/28/93, p. 22, Todd McCarthy
WASHINGTON POST, 6/25/93, p. C1, Rita Kempley
WASHINGTON POST, 6/25/93, Weekend/p. 42, Joe Brown

DIVERTIMENTO

An MK2 release. *Producer:* Pierre Grise. *Director:* Jacques Rivette. *Screenplay (French with English subtitles):* Pascal Bonitzer, Christine Laurent and Jacques Rivette. *Director of Photography:* William Lubtchansky. *Editor:* Nicole Lubtchansky. *Production Designer:* Manu De Chauvigny. *Running time:* 126 minutes. *MPAA Rating:* Not Rated.

CAST: Michel Piccoli (Frenhofer); Jane Birkin (Liz); Emmanuelle Béart (Marianne); Marianne Denicourt (Julienne); David Bursztein (Nicolas); Gilles Arbona (Porbus).

[*Divertimento* is an abbreviated version of *La Belle Noiseuse*. See *Film Review Annual, 1992*, for reviews.]

NEW YORK POST, 9/17/93, p. 40, Lawrence Cohn

"Divertimento" is one of the best films New Yorkers will see this year, but it doesn't qualify as a must-see. That's because art house devotees have already watched "La Belle Noiseuse" two years ago and the new feature is essentially a condensation.

Beginning with Steven Spielbergs 1980 "Special Edition" of "Close Encounters of the Third Kind," the concept of releasing director's cuts or "original versions" of films has caught on to promote videos and laser discs, such as "The Abyss" and "Blade Runner." Even "Lawrence of Arabia" and "Spartacus" earned ink in the press by virtue of restoring missing footage.

In France the same trend has made box-office hits of significantly longer versions of "The Big Blue" and "Betty Blue." Director Jacques Rivette goes the other direction by taking his four-hour "La Belle Noiseuse" and making it more conventional by reduction to just over two hours of running time. "Divertimento" hits all the high points of its predecessor. Michel Piccoli stars as a burnt-out artist, living with his wife Jane Birkin in a lovely mansion in the provinces. When young painter David Bursztein comes to visit, accompanied by his girl-friend Emmanuelle Beart, a chance suggestion that she model for Piccoli sets in motion a fascinating battle of wills.

Reluctantly, Piccoli moves from sketching the beautiful Beart to taking up a famous project he abandoned 10 years ago—painting the nude "La Belle Noiseuse." That means eradicating the image of Birkin, who was Piccoli's model for the original work, and replacing it with Beart's.

In the 1991 film, Rivette used the technique of his best feature to date, 1968's "L'amour fou"—in which film time approximates real time. We saw Piccoli painting (with closeups of the hands of real-life artist Bernard Dufour) for over an hour all told, forcing Beart into painfully contorted poses. It wasn't till the second half of that four-hour opus that the worm turned, Beart asserting herself and a highly charged drama unfolding.

With "Divertimento," Rivette has eliminated almost all the painting footage as well as the extraneous preamble, so the film gets to the point in just 40 minutes. Instead of his trademark lengthy takes, the director cuts from scene to scene, creating a more conventional drama rather than the previous unfolding of a slice of life.

The result retains those plentiful nude scenes of Beart (which were the first full nudes permitted for Japanese audiences when the original film played in Tokyo). For "Noiseuse" fans it's half a loaf.

The main change is Rivette's playful use of some alternative takes in which the actors break up. No, it's not "Smokey and the Bandit" style out-takes but an in-joke technique Rivette has used in several of his games-playing features, such as "Celine and Julie Go Boating"—the closest thing to a U.S. hit for the New Wave veteran.

Piccoli and Beart are tops, while Birkin retains her classic scene telling off her husband in the final reel. The supporting cast, especially Bursztein and his possessive sister Marianne Denicourt, has been deemphasized in the film's pruning to the point of merely delivering exposition.

NEWSDAY, 9/17/93, Part II/p. 73, Jack Mathews

Usually, when a filmmaker who favors the long form has a chance to re-edit one of his movies, he will lengthen it—go back to the film vault, recover all those fabulous scenes he had to leave out the first time, and put them back in.

Jacques Rivette, one of the original French New Wave directors, has taken his last film, the 1991, four-hour "La Belle Noiseuse," and cut it in half!

The production notes for "Divertimento," the title Rivette gave to his shortened version, explains that instead of trimming "La Belle Noiseuse" down for a contractually committed two-hour TV version, he changed the point-of-view of the story, used different scenes for different effects, and re-crafted an entirely new film.

Well, not quite. Rivette has certainly shifted the emphasis of the story, about a famous retired artist and the young model who inspires him to complete his masterpiece. The new version focuses on the artist, the original on the process of his work. But the movie's themes are fundamentally unchanged.

And though "Divertimento" is worth seeing, particularly if you missed the original, more than mere footage was lost in the editing.

"La Belle" may have been two hours too long to begin with, but which two hours? The first film, adapted from a Balzac short story, ambles on for an hour just setting up its premise and introducing its characters, a process that still seems long at half the time in "Divertimento."

In the hills of southern France, young Parisian artist Nicolas (David Bursztein) and his girlfriend, Marianne (Emmanuelle Beart), have come to visit the master Frenhofer (Michel Piccoli) at his centuries-old stone chateau. Expecting inspiration, Nicolas instead finds resignation. Frenhofer hasn't worked in 10 years, since abandoning in frustration a painting he called "La Belle Noiseuse," and he now speaks of his talent as if he were, recalling an old, passionate affair.

Frenhofer is quickly captivated by the beauty of the aloof Marianne, but it is not until she off-handedly explains the meaning of "noiseuse," a French-Canadian word for a woman who causes men heartache, that he associates her with his own invented temptress, a 17th Century courtesan he'd found in a book and nearly destroyed himself trying to paint.

When Nicolas, to the indignation of Marianne, volunteers her as Frenhofer's model for La Belle, the dangerous game of deconstructing a human psyche in order to create an image on canvas begins.

The power and essence of the first film are the long, painstakingly detailed sessions between Frenhofer and Marianne, evolving from awkward silence to reluctant collaboration to full-blown emotional combat. That cycle is repeated in "Divertimento," but gone completely are the sequences devoted to the actual artistic process.

In "La Belle," which is about to be released on video, there are five- and 10-minute stretches where no words are spoken, where we watch Frenhofer sketch and doodle while Marianne, nude as a berry, struggles to maintain the tortuous poses demanded of her. We see the sketches come to life, a line, a dab, a smear of ink at a time, in seamlessly blended inserts of work done for the camera by French master Bernard Dufour. Dufour's work is fascinating to watch, and Rivette integrates it in a way that gives substance to both Frenhofer's character and Piccoli's performance. As Frenhofer frets over his inability to find his subject, to draw "the blood, the fire and the ice" out of Marianne, we can see the panic guiding his hand, and at the same time see the layers peeling away from her fragile ego to expose what it is he's after.

Those dynamics are in the new film, as well, but they are stated rather than implied, talked about instead of demonstrated; and the difference is crucial. In attempting to make a more conventional film, Rivette has ignored the distinction Frenhofer himself draws between art that is good and that which is great. It is the willingness of the artist to take risks, to search for the essence of his subject, and attempt to create something with a life of its own.

"Divertimento" is a beautiful look at an artist's life. "La Belle Noiseuse" had the blood and the fire and the ice.

Also reviewed in:
NEW YORK TIMES, 9/17/93, p. C16, Vincent Canby
NEW YORKER, 9/20/93, p. 111, Anthony Lane

DJEMBEFOLA

An Interama Films release of a documentary in French, English, and African dialects with English subtitles.   *Producer:* Laurent Chevalier.   *Director:* Laurent Chevalier.   *Director of Photography:* Laurent Chevalier.   *Based on an idea by:* Pierre Marcault. *Running time:* 65 minutes. *MPAA Rating:* Not Rated.

NEW YORK POST, 9/15/93, p. 27, Matthew Flamm

When the African drummer Mamady Keita was born the voice-over tells us at the beginning of "Djembefola" he cried so hard that his worried parents took him to a witch doctor.

"He saw a great future ahead of him, and that's why he cried," the narration continues.

"Djembefola" a documentary portrait of the Guinean-born, Brussels-based djembe (drum) player, has no bone to pick with the witch doctor. Director Laurent Chevalier approaches his subject with the sort of reverence a Hollywood publicist reserves for his favorite superstar.

Fortunately, it hardly matters. "Djembefola" which means "someone who makes a djembe speak"—is still a vividly detailed look at a vital figure in African culture. The film opens today for a one-week run at the Film Forum, on a double bill with "Mizike Mama," a documentary about the Zaire-Belgian singing group Zap Mama.

"Djembefola" follows Keita as he travels from Brussels to Conakry, the Guinean capital and then on to his tiny native village of Balandugu, which he left as a teen-ager 26 years ago. On his return he is so overcome by emotion that the village elders have to scold Keita—who apparently does nothing half-way—to stop bawling.

There are great shots of the ebullient drummer rehearsing and performing with the Guinean national ballet. There are also hints, though not enough of them, of what life was like under the Guinean strongman Sekou Toure, who has coddled the country's dancers and musicians.

"Mizike Mama," directed by Violaine de Villers, with the collaboration of Denise Vindevogel, is the more reflective of the two films. Whereas Keita seems a kind of natural phenomenon, Marie Daulne, the mixed-race, Belgian-Zairean leader of Zap Mama, has produced her art carefully and deliberately out of her own conflicts.

"My music is a fusion, like myself," says the singer, who—working with a multitrack home recording system—has combined the polyrhythmic pulse of the Pygmies with European choral traditions.

The documentary succeeds as both personal portrait and portrayal of how art gets made.

Also reviewed in:
NEW YORK TIMES, 9/15/93, p. C26, Stephen Holden

DR. BETHUNE

A Tara Films and Filmline International release with the participation of Telefilm Canada in association with China Film Co-Production Corp. *Producer:* Nicolas Clermont and Pieter Kroonenberg. *Director:* Phillip Borsos. *Screenplay:* Ted Allan. *Director of Photography:* Raoul Coutard and Mike Molloy. *Editor:* Yves Langlois and Angelo Corrao. *Music:* Alan Reeves. *Running time:* 115 minutes. *MPAA Rating:* Not Rated.

CAST: Donald Sutherland (Dr. Norman Bethune); Helen Mirren (Frances Penny Bethune); Helen Shaver (Mrs. Dowd); Colm Feore (Chester Rice); Ronald Pickup (Alan Coleman); Anouk Aimée (Marie-France Coudaire); Guo Da (Dr. Chian); James Pax (Mr. Tung); Harrison Liu (Dr. Fong).

FILMS IN REVIEW, 11-12/93, p. 416, Suzanna Turman

Dr. Norman Bethune is not a familiar name to the average movie-goer. The controversial Canadian doctor who began making waves during the 1930s has fascinated Donald Sutherland, a fellow Canadian, for a number of years. He has already played him in two previous television films.

Born in 1899, Dr. Bethune came from traditional medical training in Canada, but became concerned not only with medicine itself, but also with the corollary problems of affordable, accessible medical care, until he became an early advocate of socialized medicine.

Attracted to the tenets of the Communist idealism which was widespread among intellectuals in the 1930s, Bethune travelled to the trouble spots where he felt his medical skills were serving an ideal at the forefronts of the battle against fascism. Leaving behind his comfortable life in Canada, he pursued the dream across the world—to Spain, where he served as surgeon for the Loyalist forces during the civil war, and later to China. It was in China, finally, where, crusading for better medical care, supervising a makeshift mobile wartime medical unit by appointment by Mao Tse Tung, Bethune found happiness and fulfillment, despite the primitive conditions, earning the respect and esteem of all who came to know him there.

As told by director Phillip Borsos and screenwriter Ted Allan (who was a comrade of Bethune), the story is somewhat disjointed, especially with the flashbacks and flashforwards between Bethune's early years, the narrative by his long suffering wife (Helen Mirren) and the time in China which is the centerpiece of the movie. Nevertheless, the versatile Donald Sutherland, always a pleasure, plays Bethune with an intensity born of long thought, and his portrayal of this complex character—charming, seductive, idealistic, temperamental, impatient, imperious, confrontational—is the chief reason to see the film. (Bethune as army surgeon will of course recall an earlier Sutherland role.)

By a fortuitous fluke, although this project has been in the works for 50 years (Ted Allan's efforts date from 1942, which is probably why this has a serious core rarely seen today), the film happens to arrive just at a time when Bethune's impassioned opinions about medical care make it particularly topical.

LOS ANGELES TIMES, 3/9/94, Calendar/p. 6, Kevin Thomas

"Dr. Bethune," an often absorbing and intelligent film biography, boasts one of Donald Sutherland's best portrayals, as the Canadian legend Dr. Norman Bethune. Bethune, born in 1890, was a brilliant, tempestuous physician who pioneered socialized medicine and introduced blood transfusions on the battlefields of the Spanish Civil War, though he was ultimately driven away by the Republicans for his hard drinking and incessant womanizing. He ended up finding contentment and respect at last as chief medical officer to Mao TseTung and his 8th Route Army, dying in China in 1939.

There are the makings of a distinctive, "Schindler's List"-scale saga here, but instead we get a genteel treatment typical of the English-speaking Canadian cinema. It has been directed briskly by "The Grey Fox's" Phillip Borsos, but with not nearly as much panache as a headstrong genius rake, like Bethune deserves. "Dr. Bethune" is far too conventional a film for so unconventional a hero.

Ted Allan, Canada's most honored screenwriter, a man who actually knew Bethune, wrote his script in 1942, which Darryl Zanuck was to produce. Best known for the autobiographical 1975 Canadian production "Lies My Father Never Told Me" and for John Cassavetes' last film, "Love Streams," Allan has come up with pithy dialogue, some sharp characterizations and a classic, "Citizen Kane"-like structure, an intricate interweaving of flashbacks triggered by a reporter's interviews with people who had been important in Bethune's life.

To pull this off with maximum clarity and impact, you need a stronger, more dynamic personality than Borsos possesses; you need a director who could have given the film more shape and distinction. The result is a movie that is good when it needs to be great. You come away sorry that Norman Jewison, who tried, didn't get his "Dr. Bethune" off the ground.

Yet "Dr. Bethune" is well worth seeing as a refreshingly adult, socially conscious drama, especially for Sutherland's persuasive, charismatic portrayal, which is well-matched by Helen Mirren's Frances Bethune. The physical attraction between the Bethunes is tangible, their love intense and enduring, but they were spectacularly ill-matched in temperament. Frances is far too prudish and traditional for Norman, who probably would have been bad husband material for practically any woman. Even so, Frances is no fool, and she is probably right to regard her husband as "politically naive."

Sutherland and Mirren work up plenty of fire, but they're the film's only truly vivid presences; all Anouk Aimee, as a beautiful French-Canadian who deals with Norman with far more sophistication and calm than his wife, gets to do is look soulful and sympathetic. As a writer, Allan laid a solid foundation, but needed to have been inspired—or given the chance—to flesh out the subsidiary characters more fully.

"Dr. Bethune" has been on the shelf undeservedly for several years, but that's understandable to a certain extent, given its subject's lack of familiarity in the U.S. and the film's serviceable, yet overly prosaic style. It certainly possesses scope, spanning the last decade or so of the doctor's life and stretching from Montreal to Madrid to actual remote Chinese locales. What Norman Bethune did and had to say is of enduring importance, and it may well be that his message will come across more effectively if the film eventually winds up on television.

NEW YORK POST, 9/17/93, p. 41, Jerry Tallmer

It was Mrs. Dowd, the good-looking Protestant missionary in China, who said it best: "He's a rude, arrogant, completely unpleasant man," That was before she, like all the other women he ever looked at, fell under his spell.

Norman Bethune was in fact, an impossible man. He was also one of the heroes of our time.

Here is an image of him, fleshed out by Donald Sutherland: a tall, gaunt, eggheaded, halo-fringed, hot-eyed figure in a ragged old black overcoat, collar up, racing through a shattered landscape under Japanese fire carrying a small limp Chinese child, probably dead, in his arms.

The movie is "Dr. Bethune," and for some of us it is certainly deja vu all over again. For the rest, I hope it's both instructional and exciting. I mean how many movies do you go to where the hero quotes from e.e. cummings: "Buffalo Bill's defunct, who used to shoot one two three four five clay pigeons just like that ...."?

Born in Ontario in 1890, dead in China, 1939, of septicemia from a finger-prick of his own scalpel—"Have you people never heard of sepsis?" we have earlier seen him raging—Bethune was a surgeon saint of anti-fascist battlefields from Guadalajara to Tang-Hsien. Among all else, as the film says, he "revolutionized battlefield medicine forever as the first person ever to do blood transfusions in combat."

It is a didactic film for what was, after all, a didactic time, Auden's "low dishonest decade" of the 1930s, when men of good will were being sold out and slaughtered all over the world. In the beginning Bethune the crusader, rebel with a cause, was as intolerably opposed to Soviet communism as to all other tyrannies. "I am a comrade in the more traditional sense." In the end, when pressed by howling reporters: "Are you a red?" he merely murmured: "Yes," and lifted his fist for the International.

Between—in this movie directed by Phillip Borsos from a long-embattled 41-year-old old script by Ted Allan—we get the full turbulent kaleidoscope, not always easy to follow—in a jumble of flashbacks. We certainly get the idea that Bethune was not an easy man for his wife Frances (Helen Mirren) or Mrs. Dodd the missionary (Helen Shaver) or Marie-France the beautiful French-Canadian admirer (Anouk Aimee) or any other woman to live with, even be with.

Or man either, for that matter, from the conventional old head of the hospital to Mr. Tung (James Pax), the loyal interpreter assigned to Comrade Bethune by Mao himself, to Dr. Fong (Harrison Liu), the inept Chinese medico Bethune demotes from surgeon to orderly and much later apologizes to—before the entire cadre—for that humiliation "The fascist I did not recognize is the fascist within myself, and within everybody," he humbly says. Too humbly.

So it's that kind of movie. I've never really warmed up to Donald Sutherland, but he's this man to the bone. And how do you like your blue-eyed boy now, Mr. Death?

NEWSDAY, 9/17/93, Part II/p. 78, John Anderson

Donald Sutherland is becoming a Michael Caine for the '90s, appearing in what seems to be every other movie released and occasionally making a good one. "Dr. Bethune" for instance.

While Sutherland's performance has its uneven moments—once in a while, he seems to be conserving energy, perhaps for his next feature—it is, like the film, sturdy, uncompromising and quite fascinating. And given the complex nature of its subject, this is a considerable accomplishment.

Norman Bethune, a Canadian surgeon with Marxist leanings, fought against prejudice and a politically entrenched medical establishment—and accusations that he was a "red"—in his attempts to revolutionize his nation's health system. He introduced modern surgical techniques into '30s China, and provided his services to the Loyalists during the Spanish Civil War. An epic womanizer and prodigious drinker, he was also a visionary, and like most visionaries could entertain few visions other than his own, something "Dr. Bethune" makes quite clear. Rather than go for the standard cinematic lionization, Sutherland and director Phillip Borsos make Bethune a monumental egomaniac, one with a great deal of genuine pride, and who consistently infuriates those around him.

Borsos keeps quite a few balls in the air while telling Bethune's story, which we get from newspaperman Chester Rice (Colm Feore). His voice-overs and interviews with Bethune's friends and lovers provide part of the film, while the rest focuses on Bethune himself at various stages of his life: his early romance with Frances (a wonderful Helen Mirren) the woman he marries twice; his often frustrating experiences in war-torn China and Spain; his equally frustrating attempts to introduce medical reform back home, and an affair with Marie-France Coudaire (Anouk Aimee).

Despite the low-key and occasionally dry tone of the film, there are some marvelous moments: Bethune making a plea for medical reform on a movie theater stage, while wartime newsreel footage plays behind him; panoramic shots of China's interior (the film is a Canadian/French/Chinese co-production); Dr. Bethune's public apology to Dr. Fong, a self-taught surgeon whose incompetence infuriates him, but whose dedication eventually wins him over. And, of course, there are the scenes with Mirren, an actress who should be at least as busy as the hard-working Sutherland.

VILLAGE VOICE, 9/21/93, p. 66, Kathy Deacon

Halfway through Phillip Borsos's visually poetic bio-pic, Dr. Norman Bethune declares himself a "red." The Canadian surgeon and boulevardier, a committed advocate of socialized medicine during the Depression, abandons his conviction that "the Russians have exchanged one tyranny for another." Alas, after joining the Loyalist forces in Spain and heroically performing transfusions on the battlefield, he is expelled as a "bad Communist" for drinking and womanizing. But he ultimately trades in the good life for the good fight, and devotes the rest of his years to helping bring modern medicine to China.

Dr. Bethune begins and ends with Bethune's 1939 funeral; parallel flashback sequences shot on location in Montreal, Spain, and China—and accompanied by selections from Bethune's own writing—trace the slow process of his personal and political transformation. He ends up as a battlefield doctor alongside Mao's partisans fighting the Japanese. In charge of all the hospitals in the liberated area, he introduces mobile training units and antiseptic procedures that prove instrumental in saving thousands of lives.

In an age where "looking beyond" communism is very much the thing, this romantic look back is the oddly timed result of a Canadian-Chinese coproduction deal. Ted Allan's 1942 script tells of Communist China's "better world at birth," and the producers have left it at that—with no added irony or presentiment. It's just as well. The film's atmospheric scenes create an extraordinary sense of reality, and of history recreated in the buff.

Donald Sutherland is an attractive Bethune, with vivacious unselfconsciousness. His wife (Helen Mirren) and comrade (Anouk Aimée) are complex minor characters, subtly underplayed. To the film's credit, we get an even more vivid understanding of the Chinese partisans, such as Bethune's colleague Dr. Chian, played by Guo Da, a popular Chinese actor. The sheer physical grandeur of China, though, finally steals the picture.

Also reviewed in:
NEW REPUBLIC, 8/2/93, p. 32, Stanley Kauffmann
NEW YORK TIMES, 9/17/93, p. C13, Stephen Holden

DRAGON: THE BRUCE LEE STORY

A Universal Pictures release.   *Executive Producer:* Dan York.   *Producer:* Raffaella De Laurentiis and Rick Nathanson.   *Director:* Rob Cohen.   *Screenplay:* Edward Khmara, John Raffo, and Rob Cohen.   *Based on the book "Bruce Lee: The Man Only I Knew" by:* Linda Lee Cadwell.   *Director of Photography:* David Eggby.   *Editor:* Peter Amundson.   *Music:* Randy Edelman.   *Music Editor:* Robert Randles.   *Sound:* Leslie Shatz, Reinhard Starger, Steve Nelson, (music) Elton Ahi, and Dennis Sands.   *Casting:* Jane Jenkins and Janet Hirshenson.   *Production Designer:* Robert Ziembicki.   *Art Director:* Ted Berner.   *Set Decorator:* Dayna Lee.   *Set Dresser:* Cathy Mantych and Danny Butch.   *Special Effects:* William H. Schirmer.   *Visual Effects:* Kevin O'Neill.   *Fight Coordinator:* John Cheung.   *Demon Fabricator:* Peter Bohanna.   *Costumes:* Carol Ramsey.   *Make-up:* James Ryder.   *Stunt Coordinator:* Merritt Yohnka and Steve Lambert.   *Running time:* 119 minutes.   *MPAA Rating:* PG-13.

CAST: Jason Scott Lee (Bruce Lee);   Lauren Holly (Linda Lee);   Robert Wagner (Bill Krieger);   Michael Learned (Vivian Emery);   Nancy Kwan (Gussie Yang);   Kay Tong Lim (Philip Tan);   Ric Young (Bruce's Father);   Louyong Wang (Yip Man);   Sterling Macer (Jerome Sprout);   Sven-Ole Thorsen (The Demon);   John Cheung (Johnny Sun);   Ong Soo Han (Luke Sun);   Eric Bruskotter (Joe Henderson);   Aki Aleong (Principal Elder);   Choa-Li Chi (Elder);   Iain M. Parker (Brandon);   Sam Hau (Young Bruce);   Michelle Tennant (Shannon);   Clyde Kusatsu (History Teacher);   Alicia Tao (April);   Kong Kwok Keung (Mr. Ho);   Johnny Cheung, Anthony Carpio, and Chan Tat Kwong (Chefs);   John Lacy (Nunnemacher);   Harry Stanback (Benny Sayles);   Michael Cudlitz (Tad Overton);   Forry Smith (Green Hornet);   Van

Williams (Green Hornet Director); Sean Faro (Assistant Director); Alan Eugster (Propman); Paul Raci (Bad Guy); Ed Parker, Jr. (Ed Parker); Shannon Lee (Party Singer); Robert D. Garrett (Krieger's Butler); Lala Sloatman (Sherry Schnell); Fu Suk Han (Cha Cha Dancer); Nick Brandon (Boswain); Louis Turenne (Maitre d'); Paul Mantee (Doctor); Jonathan Penner (Studio Executive); Calvin Bartlett (Stunt Coordinator); Jan Solomita and Shannon Uno (Hecklers); Lau Pak Lam ("Big Boss" Director); Rob Cohen ("Enter the Dragon" Director).

CHRISTIAN SCIENCE MONITOR, 5/7/93, p. 15, David Sterritt

Near the beginning of "Dragon: The Bruce Lee Story," someone makes an offhand reference to Fred Astaire, the great Hollywood musical star.

It seems like a throwaway moment. But if you followed the real-life career of action-movie star Bruce Lee in the early 1970s, you may remember that he was compared to Astaire in some contemporary reviews.

On the surface, this was an odd connection to draw since Astaire danced his way through light-hearted romantic entertainments, and Lee made his name in violent kung-fu melodramas. What inspired the comparison was the extraordinary gracefulness, suppleness, and inventiveness of Lee's performances.

The genre he specialized in, often called "chop-socky," by skeptical critics, was a minor and dubious one. If it accomplished nothing else, however, it produced one memorable star whose career might have branched out in different directions had he not died in 1973 in his early 30s.

The film traces Lee's ups and downs in the two worlds he knows best—martial arts and show business—without neglecting the challenges he faced as an Asian-American in a white-dominated society.

Much of the story has obviously been tailored for slick entertainment purposes rather than fidelity to Lee's actual life, and a disclaimer in the final credits indicates that one of the movie's key episodes is pretty much a fiction dreamed up by the filmmakers. Still, the picture has important things to say about subjects as different as interracial romance and the importance of education, and it makes its statements with enough wit and energy to make "Dragon" an engaging diversion, if a hokey and predictable one.

The movie gets under way in Hong Kong, with a fight scene that's so stagey and gratuitous that I expected the rest of the picture to be a total loss. This episode paves the way for a much better portion of the story, however, in which Lee learns that he was born in the United States and that he'd better return there soon, since his life may now be in jeopardy. We follow him to California where he works as a dishwasher, realizes that college is the path to a better life, and sets up as a martial-arts instructor to pay his bills.

Conflicts arise when white bigots mock his ethnicity and his Anglo girlfriend's mother objects to their marriage, despite their obvious devotion to each other. Dissatisfied with the traditions of martial-arts training in the Chinese-American community, Lee also stirs up big trouble there: by teaching ancient Asian secrets to non-Asian students, and by developing his own self-defense system in opposition to the strict heritage of conventional disciplines.

The most enjoyable parts of the movie are in the last portion, as Lee moves to Hollywood and becomes a supporting actor on "The Green Hornet" television show, where he plays Kato, the hero's chauffeur. Bolstered by this small success, he throws himself into developing the "Kung Fu" series as an "Eastern western" with the potential for huge popularity—only to find himself replaced by a non-Asian star, David Carradine, before the first episode is filmed.

Disgusted with Hollywood, he takes his family to Hong Kong, where he finds that "The Green Hornet" is known as "The Kato Show" and has earned him a devoted following. He parlays this into stardom in kung-fu movies shot in Asia and then breaks into the domain of the white-controlled Hollywood studios. His death occurs as he awaits the premiere of his first big-budget American production.

"Dragon" would be a better film if it didn't rely so frequently on the action-movie formulas that made Lee's own pictures less worthwhile than they should have been, given the vigor of his performances. Jason Scott Lee does an uncanny job of recreating Lee's style and personality, though. It's a busy time for him, since he's also in "Map of the Human Heart" this season. The supporting cast includes Lauren Holly and Nancy Kwan, among other likable performers.

The story moves at a rapid clip, thanks to director Rob Cohen.

LOS ANGELES TIMES, 5/7/93, Calendar/p. 1, Peter Rainer

The problem with most movie biographies of famous stars is that the wattage of the imper-sonators is rarely as bright as the originals. The exceptions—Barbra Streisand as Fanny Brice, for example, or James Cagney as George M. Cohan—only prove the rule.

What's exciting about "Dragon: The Bruce Lee Story" is that, in Jason Scott Lee, the movies have created a new star out of an old star. The film is a tribute to Bruce Lee but it's also a tribute to the transforming powers of performance. Lee does justice to Bruce Lee while, at the same time, creating a character out of his own fierce resources. He is, quite literally, smashing.

Jason Scott Lee is such a kinesthetic actor that, even in repose, he seems charged up. He has the kind of larger-than-life athleticism that Burt Lancaster had, or Marlon Brando in films such as "Viva Zapata!" and "The Wild One." In Bruce Lee's most famous movie, "Enter the Dragon," he lectured a martial arts student about the need for an "emotional content" to his kick. Jason Scott Lee has heeded the lesson; in him, physicality and soulfulness are twinned. His emotional expressiveness is bound up with his physical expressiveness.

This explosive physicality isn't necessarily the most subtle kind of performing but it's intensely alive on the screen in a way that the more scaled-down kinds of acting can't touch. And it justifies the hero-worshippy tone of "Dragon," a movie that treats Bruce Lee as a legend from the get go, with all the trimmings. You can enjoy all the cornball confrontations and pumped-up melodramatics, you can forgive the way the film concocts and inflates incidents in Lee's life, because, at its core, it showcases the real thing. That's the way it is with larger-than-life actors: They prime you for larger-than-life stories.

"Dragon"—directed by Rob Cohen from a script he wrote with Edward Khmara and John Raffo based on the book "Bruce Lee: The Man Only I Knew" by Lee's widow, Linda Lee Cadwell—begins with Lee's boyhood in Hong Kong in the late '40s and then moves on to his migration to America, his founding of a martial arts school specializing in his innovative style of kung fu—*jeet kune do*, or "way of the intercepting fist"—and his break with the Chinese-American martial arts Establishment for taking non-Chinese students.

One of the students, Linda (Lauren Holly), quickly evolves into Lee's archetypal stand-by-your-man mate; she defies the wishes of her mother (Michael Learned), who fears a brood of "half-breeds" if they marry. Then she defies Lee's own demons, which, in their most mystic form, appear to him periodically as a fiend in full battle armor. When he gets his back busted in a fight and sits immobile in a hospital with little hope of ever walking again, Linda doesn't fulfill his worst fears and skedaddle; instead, she inspires his recuperation. (In reality, Lee's back injury came from lifting weights.)

Most of Lee's film forays are here: his appearance as the sidekick Kato in the TV series "The Green Hornet;" his disappointment when "Kung Fu," the series he conceived, went to David Carradine; his decision to make martial arts movies in Hong Kong, leading up to the Hollywood-Hong Kong co-production "Enter the Dragon," which opened in 1973 three weeks after his death at the age of 32 and created an international cult of posthumous pop stardom that rivals James Dean's or Elvis Presley's.

The fight scenes in "Dragon" (rated PG-13 for martial arts violence and sensuality) are more flamboyant and theatrical than most of the ones in Bruce Lee's movies, even though a number of them are based on sequences from his films. They top each other, each face-off in "Dragon" is just a little bit freakier and more jet-propelled than the one before. Jason Scott Lee, who studied martial arts for the role, builds on the florid, almost comic powerfulness of karate stars like Jackie Chan; he's ingratiatingly lethal. (Bruce Lee was more like a lean destroyer—balletic and ballistic.) The movie—without being coarse about it—plays around with the racial angle in Bruce Lee's confrontations. (This angle is the subtext of many a karate movie.) Against the monstrous Chinese-American pummeler Johnny Sun (John Cheung), Bruce plays David to his Goliath, but when he reacts to a white jock's racist baiting by playing pat-a-cake with his pecs, it's a great comic moment. Bruce is like a one-man rescue mission for Asian manhood; he gleefully over-throws the buck-toothed wimp caricature. (In one sequence we observe him watching Mickey Rooney as a Japanese yammerer in "Breakfast at Tiffany's" and averting his eyes in shame. It makes Lee's pay-backs seem all the sweeter.)

The movie peaks with Bruce exulting in his own prowess on the set of "Enter the Dragon." Rob Cohen thankfully doesn't work in a dreary post-mortem, but, of course, since this film was completed, Lee's son Brandon was killed on the set of his own movie. Since Brandon is portrayed in "Dragon" as his father's spiritual heir—and the beneficiary of his father's successful struggle with his demons—the film takes on an unexpected sadness. Our recognition of Brandon Lee's death suggests that a larger story is being played out than this movie can account for. Brandon Lee might have become the first international Asian-American movie star since his father. Instead, as a result of "Dragon," that legacy will probably confer to Jason Scott Lee.

It's in good hands.

NEW YORK POST, 5/7/93, p. 23, Jami Bernard

Bruce Lee is fending off a pack of attackers, when suddenly he tastes his own blood. Now he's *really* mad. His face balls up into a dense mask of anger, and his hands become fists of fury.

"Dragon: The Bruce Lee Story" may not be wholly faithful to the life and times of the martial arts martyr—it is based only on his widow's fairly rosy version of their life together—but the fight scenes are so faithful to the style and spirit of Lee's movies it's like seeing lost footage.

In fact, the movie's most brilliant aspect—aside from the uncanny casting of the exceptional Jason Scott Lee—is the use of stylized, wittily choreographed fight scenes to punctuate and elevate the biographical material. In a dance hall fight at 18, Lee does a series of back flips onto a banquet table and pauses for a bite of cake; these filmmakers know their Bruce.

Inasmuch as he is knowable, anyway. He died young under mysterious circumstances, just like his son, Brandon, a few weeks ago on a movie set of his own—which adds a poignant and also chilling aspect to "Dragon" which as much as anything is a foreshadowing of Brandon's own doom. In one scene, Bruce fights his inner demons (which manifest themselves outwardly) while yelling at little Brandon to flee. Anyone who buys into the Bruce Lee myth—and Elvis has nothing on him there—will be in thrall.

Lee's life may have been short—he died at 32 of a brain edema—but his impact was enormous. A popular child actor and volatile adolescent, he was born in the U.S., raised in Hong Kong, and returned to the U.S. to establish his own less regimented form of kung fu (called jeet kune do). He was popular (if forcibly restrained) as Kato in the "Green Hornet" series, and narrowly lost the lead of TV's "Kung Fu" to David Carradine—ostensibly—because of his accent.

Yet he became the first international Asian movie star with only a handful of films, and grandfathered today's phenomenal boom in Hong Kong action pictures.

Actor Jason Scott Lee (no relation) captures all of Bruce's salient qualities—his charisma, concentration. sense of whimsy, even his trademark caterwauling. Whatever Jason Scott is paying his personal trainer, it's not enough—his body is chiseled into a precise replica of Bruce's lean, mean machine, well-muscled but wiry. During the high kicks, his legs and arms torque and lock like steel cable.

The movie's weak link is Bruce's all-American wife, Linda, played insipidly by Lauren Holly. Since the real Linda obviously exerted some creative control over the project, her character is a bland cipher, and the movie won't even discuss the non-mystical aspects of Bruce's death. (He died in the home of his mistress, but you'd never know it from watching this.)

"I prefer to remember the way he lived," narrates Linda. But Lee fans will flock to see "Dragon" as much for the cult of his death. And—there's no getting around it the movie derives extraordinary power from its intimations of mortality for Brandon, to whom the film is dedicated.

NEW YORK POST, 5/7/93, p. 23, Michael Medved

The thrilling and crowd-pleasing new film "Dragon" not only portrays the late martial arts star Bruce Lee as a fearless and unstoppable fighting machine, but also wants us to accept him as the most significant Chinese thinker since Confucius.

In this version of his life, the one-time back-street brawler from Hong Kong turned into a secular saint—an aspiring teacher, crusader against prejudice, ideal lover and devoted father, who, had he been granted a few more years of life, would surely have cured cancer—or at least won the Nobel Peace Prize.

The film's dialogue even informs us (twice) that Lee's white-hot ambition for big-screen success had less to do with any craving for fame and fortune than it did with his altruistic desire "to show

America the beauty of our culture." The beauty of Chinese culture as depicted in chop-socky cinematic bloodbaths such as "Fists of Fury" or "Game of Death"?

Well, never mind, because despite its preposterous pretensions, "Dragon" works like gangbusters due largely to an altogether remarkable performance by its 26-year-old star. Jason Scott Lee (no relation to the legendary character he plays here) is a one-time Hawaiian surfer of mixed Chinese-Hawaiian ancestry who brings to the movie's eight major fight scenes an unforgettable combination of punishing power and balletic grace—Jean-Claude Van Damme blended with Mikhail Baryshnikov.

The fact that he had no martial arts training before his work on this film makes his achievement all the more astonishing; even Bruce Lee's most devoted admirers will be delighted with the way that this picture captures the explosive charisma of their idol.

In addition to his sinewy athletic grace, Jason Scott Lee Is also an accomplished actor of great subtlety and range—as evidenced by his other current release, man of the "Map of the Human Heart." In "Dragon," he manages to make Lee into such an irresistibly attractive life that for once in a film celebrating the martial arts, the love scenes are no less thrilling than the fight scenes.

These lavishly romantic interludes are aided incalculably by the participation of Lauren Holly, who plays Bruce Lee's glamorous blond wife, Linda. Holly, perhaps best known for her TV role in "Picket Fences," had previously demonstrated remarkable acting ability by pretending to find Andrew Dice Clay irresistible in the execrable "The Adventures of Ford Fairlane." Luckily for her (and for us), this new picture provides her with a leading man far more worthy of her affection.

Director/co-screenwriter Rob Cohen displays real genius in coping with the most serious challenges in any film biography of Bruce Lee: How do you deal with the haunted, doomed quality of this brief life that ended at age 32, when Lee, just on the verge of international stardom, fell into a mysterious coma and died of edema of the brain?

Cohen (whose only previous credit as a director was the understated—and underappreciated—"A Small Circle of Friends") brings this ominous casualty to life through creation of a mystical demon in the form of an ancient Chinese warrior in imposing armor, who stalks Lee from childhood. In the film's climactic struggle, the hero battles this faceless helmeted force while urging his frightened little boy, Brandon, to run away and escape. Since Brandon Lee himself died in March 29 of this year in a tragic accident on the set of his own new film, these moments in "Dragon" become almost unbearably poignant.

Audiences will love this picture, and will scarcely notice its heavy-handed and totally gratuitous subtext: relentless political preachments about America's disgraceful past (and present) record of anti-Chinese racism. It's as if the filmmakers couldn't feel satisfied with making a fastmoving piece of populist entertainment, but felt called upon to deliver a more serious "message" by incongruously including more than a dozen illustrations of our allegedly ubiquitous bigotry.

In one embarrassing scene, our hero Lee tearfully declares that he once felt attracted to America's "mountain of gold" but later discovered the fine print that said it was restricted to "whites only." Bruce Lee's own experience in winning lasting popularity that cut across all racial lines, along with the impressive success achieved by literally millions of other Asian immigrants, stands as definitive rebuttal to such predictable and politically correct indictments that turn up all too often in today's Hollywood films.

NEWSDAY, 5/7/93, Part II/p. 71, John Anderson

During the first fight sequence in "Dragon: The Bruce Lee Story," drunken sailors have broken up a Hong Kong dance, mauling the Chinese men, pawing the women. A bespectacled Bruce (Jason Scott Lee, no relation to the late star) enters the fracas like some Far-Eastern Clint, demolishes his first sailor, does handsprings through the room, lands on the banquet table and crouches there eating a sandwich. And then he smiles, with lethal intent.

The scene, like the climactic moments in Bruce Lee's best movie, "Enter the Dragon," is a reflection in a mirror reflected in a mirror reflected in a mirror. Are we watching Jason Scott Lee as Bruce Lee? Or a Bruce Lee movie? Or the character Bruce Lee making a Bruce Lee movie.? Or ...? No, it's simply director Rob Cohen making the movie about Bruce Lee that Bruce Lee might have made himself.

Like Bruce's glasses—which seem to disappear—"Dragon" is all artifice in the service of art, a shrapnel-studded case of exploded reality. But this is why the film works so well—unlike that other recent film-star biography, "Chaplin," which didn't work at all. The high-minded Richard Attenborough jammed his film with every factual datum he could and never came close to the kind of grace Chaplin embodied. Cohen, on the other hand, embraces every kind of Hollywood fight-film cliché and action/ adventure *tchotchkes* and captures the essence of his subject's screen image.

What he doesn't do is treat the man—the American-born, Hong Kong-raised martial artist who achieved global celebrity—with much depth. In the script by Cohen, Edward Khmara and John Raffo, Lee's congenitally wise, superhumanly skillful, temperamentally even. He bristles at injustice, loves his wife, Linda—played by Lauren Holly as a cross between Talia Shire in "Rocky" and Greer Garson in "Mrs. Miniver"—and smites the forces of evil. Only near the end of the movie, when his film career erupts, does he neglect his family. And after an epiphany out of central casting, he realizes what really matters.

But in spite of its almost shameless collection of plot clichés, "Dragon" moves along flawlessly, thanks mostly to Jason Scott Lee. Bruce Lee's films might have been action intensive, but his performances, which balanced humor with a sense of genuine rage, lifted their hackneyed storylines to another level. Jason Scott Lee gives us all of this, adorning his performance with all the physical tics that were his character's trademarks. And the fight scenes, artfully choreographed by John Cheung (who also plays Bruce's nemesis, Johnny Sun) are thrilling dances that re-create the excitement of "Fists of Fury," "The Big Boss" or "The Chinese Connection."

Although we might not get depth, we do get dreams—about demons, and about America. "Tell me you'll make a big noise there," his father says, "so I can hear it over here ..." In America, he gets his wife and an education, but he also encounters small-mindedness—his mother-in-law (Michael Learned) strenuously objects to his and Linda's marriage—and betrayal at the hands of Hollywood. It's not till the disappointed Bruce returns to Hong Kong that he makes it really big.

"Dragon" is about the struggle for success, triumph over doubt, mixed marriage, etc. But it does right by Bruce Lee, who died under mysterious circumstances in 1973, just three weeks before "Enter the Dragon" opened. There's no telling how big he might have been.

But after his death, unfinished footage and screen tests became whole films, "Green Hornet" episodes were combined for another feature, and martial-arts movies fans were beset by Bruce Li, Bruce Le and Bruce Lei.

SIGHT AND SOUND, 9/93, p. 45, Verina Glaessner

Hong Kong, 1949. Superstitiously afraid that the death of his elder son bodes ill for the destiny of his younger son, Bruce Lee's father has the boy trained in the martial arts discipline Wing Chun. Throughout his life, Bruce is to remain haunted by a recurring hallucination of a demon warrior, which represents an inner fear he must conquer or pass to his own son. As Lee enters his teen years, his fanatical and exhibitionist devotion to martial arts makes life in Hong Kong difficult. In 1961, Lee attacks a group of sailors molesting Chinese women at a dance hall. When one is seriously injured, Lee's father gives him his American birth certificate (the boy was born while the family were on tour with a opera troupe) and the fare for passage to the States.

San Francisco, 1962. Lee washes dishes in Gussie Yang's restaurant, where the attraction that develops between him and a waitress provokes tension with the other kitchen staff, ending in a fracas after which he is fired. Before he leaves, Yang gives him a loan and advises him to invest it in education. Lee enrolls in college and becomes increasingly aware of racism. Hassled by a group of athletes in the college gym, he fights back, earning their respect, and agrees to teach them martial arts. His classes soon attract Linda and despite general disapproval of inter-racial relationships they start dating. Lee opens what he hopes will become the first in a chain of martial arts institutes.

Oakland, 1964. Lee's classes have become increasingly popular and attract the attention of the Chinese community who demand he stop teaching the non-Chinese. When he refuses, the community bosses arrange a tournament between him and the deadly Johnny Sun. Lee defeats him, but Sun strikes back after the match, crippling him. While he is in traction, Linda suggests he dictate to her his book on the new martial arts style he has evolved. At an international karate meeting at Long Beach, Lee's exposition of his style is booed. He issues an open challenge, and Johnny Sun responds. This time Lee defeats him, injuring him fatally. Lee is spotted and signed up to play Kato in the *Green Hornet* television series. He works on the idea for a new series, *Kung Fu*, but is not cast. Returning to Hong Kong for his father's funeral, Lee is signed up by 'Pearl of the Orient' studios.

1970, Thailand. Luke, Johnny Sun's brother, tracks Lee down and attacks him on set. Lee responds by killing him, and noticing the camera still running, exposes the film. *The Big Boss* Big Boss makes Lee a star but his family life is neglected. He is offered the starring role in a Warner Brothers-Hong Kong co-production, *Enter the Dragon*, but during shooting he suffers another hallucination, in which the demon warrior threatens his son Jason. He fights and finally kills him. Three weeks before the film opens, he dies.

There is a story of some pith and poignancy to be told about Bruce Lee, the former child actor who became an international martial arts star, and who died (of a swelling of the brain) in somewhat suspicious circumstances. It is a story that could offer insights into the more unsavoury aspects of the Hong Kong industry and the ambiguous realities of Chinese immigrant experience, as well as into contradictory aspects of Lee's own character. *Dragon: The Bruce Lee Story* opts instead to "print the legend".

Dragon is ostensibly based on the biography by Lee's American wife Linda—its title *Bruce Lee: The Man Only I Knew* offering itself as both a riposte to gossip about his affair with Hong Kong actress Ting Pei in whose flat his body was found, and as carrying a monopoly of the truth. But the film makes little of the tiny amount of fresh information that it contains (e.g., Lee's father dressed him as a girl in his early years to avoid detection by the demon who had snatched his elder brother).

What the film does do is to make a martial arts movie of Lee's own life, tailoring the genre to current fashions for ethnocentrism—Lee asserts his desire to become a Chinese hero with a Chinese culture and new age metaphysics. In making a theme of the bigotry Lee confronted, it feeds back to source a subject Lee himself explored in *Fist of Fury*, in which he memorably kicked to pieces a sign reading "No Dogs or Chinese". Much of this is par for the generic course. Some is kitsch: Linda, changing for a date with Lee, shocks her friend by telling her she would "go all the way" with a nonwhite. But some is pointed: the couple's initial enthusiasm for *Breakfast at Tiffany's* dies on appearance of the film's Oriental caricature, and we wince at the *Green Hornet* producer's instructions that Lee should not remove his mask lest his Oriental appearance become visible.

The film also ducks the opportunity to tell us much about Jeet Kune Do, the martial arts style Lee adapted from Wing Chun. Cohen's choice of genre cannot help seriously constraining any genuine biographical impulse. Conflicts have to be played out as tournaments, whether with bigoted whites or conservative Chinese. Lee's own angst has to be played out as his recurring fantasy of the Chinese warrior, a hallucinatory figure appearing at times of stress, caused on one occasion by a college assignment on Hegel. The demon warrior metaphor removes the need to deal either with the contentious psychological problems. Thus Rob Cohen, the director of this film, playing Robert Clouse the director of *Enter the Dragon*, keeps the viewer firmly within the parameters of Lee's own fantasy. "Lost touch with you for a while there, buddy," is his only comment, as Lee emerges aghast from the final life-and-death struggle with his phantom adversary. On what Clouse saw, and others knew, Cohen remains tantalizingly silent.

Much of *Dragon* is predictable, awkwardly written and scant advance on the clutch of 70s film biographies which traded fairly shamelessly on Lee's name and notoriety. The lacunae are many and varied: Lee's experience as a Cantonese child star is not mentioned; *Fist of Fury, The Way of the Dragon* and the unfinished *Game of Death* are barely or not at all mentioned. There is no attempt to account for the crassness of *Enter the Dragon*, made when Lee was visibly unwell, and which misunderstood both the nature of the martial arts film and the particular contribution Lee made to it.

Apart from the shock of Jason Scott Lee's (no relation) boss-eyed appearance as the protagonist, the actor yields an account of his role which dispenses with any need for comparison. He is aided in the hyperbolic fight sequences by John Cheung, a stunt man who worked on *Enter the Dragon*. More poignancy than the project deserves is lent it by the recent death of Lee's son Brandon.

TIME, 5/17/93, p. 64, Richard Schickel

A poor immigrant lad arrives in the U.S. with nothing in his luggage but talent, a dream and the capacity for hard work. He overcomes prejudice, stuffy conservatives in his profession and a debilitating accident that should have left him crippled for life. Along the way, he acquires a sweet and understanding wife who not only comforts him but also inspires him in adversity.

But—and here comes the really inspired part—every 10 minutes or so, circumstances require him to kick a little butt. This he does with a panache that ensures the yipping, pleasure of all the young males in the house and, since this heroic figure is also a really cute guy, the gurgling approval of their dates.

Is this the ultimate biopic or what? It has all the romantic and celebratory moves of the genre, in addition to which its subject is no bearded duffer moping around a laboratory or gallant, tear-streaked lady belatedly triumphing over a dismal affliction, but a movie star (of sorts) who specialized in doing a highly cinematic thing—namely a form of kung fu, all lightning reactions and fluid, swirling choreography. Moreover, the movie retains that air of breathless awe and dauntless approval that has always made movie biographies such a pleasant relief from the gloomy ambiguities of written ones.

No sooner does Bruce (Jason Scott Lee, no relation) conquer the little world of kung fu than he moves on to the larger—well, anyway, flashier—world of show biz. And, of course, more troubles that need braving out: he plays Kato on *The Green Hornet* TV series, but it gets canceled; he has a million-dollar idea for another series, which is swept out from under him because the network doesn't want the Chinese hero played by a Chinese actor (hence the lead in *Kung Fu* goes to David Carradine). Bruce returns to his roots, from which he draws the beginnings of a new career as the protagonist of cultishly successful martial-arts movies. Soon, however, he is paying the accustomed costs of stardom: turning into a temperamental workaholic, neglecting his family. Just as it seems that superstardom is about to end his problems, a cerebral edema ends his life at a mere 32 years of age.

It is, putting it mildly, a crowded life. And putting it mildly again, this is an entirely uncritical movie. And yet a surprisingly likable one. Part of this quality derives from the lively innocence of Jason Scott Lee's performance, and the sweet spunkiness of Lauren Holly as the all-American coed Bruce marries in college. Part of it derives from the go-ahead conviction of Rob Cohen's direction. He foreshadows his hero's early death by having his dreams haunted by fate (giddily yet scarily represented as a warrior figure out of China's ancient past) and proposes that Lee ran so hard, so fast in an attempt to outdistance this grim stalker. It's an incautious conceit, and some of its effectiveness may derive from the recent, equally sudden, equally premature death of Lee's son Brandon on a film set. One begins to think that perhaps the family really is haunted. But even in happier circumstances, one could succumb to the charged-up romanticism of this dippy, entrancing movie.

VILLAGE VOICE, 5/18/93, p. 60, J. Hoberman

The most entertaining thing about *Dragon: The Bruce Lee Story* is its *faux naif* premise that Bruce Lee actually lived a Bruce Lee movie. Five minutes into the picture, teenage Bruce (Jason Scott Lee, no relation) is defending a Hong Kong dance hall—leaping, kicking, chopping, spinning, stomping, pausing only to insure that his shirt gets correctly torn off or to scarf down a chunk of pineapple, as he demolishes half a dozen drunken, racist, knife-wielding Caucasian sailors.

As myth, *Dragon* has its giddy pleasures. The idea that Lee settled a blood feud on the set of *The Big Boss*, the camera rolling, then ripped the film out of the gate to obliterate the footage of his greatest fight is like candy for paranoids. Breezily directed by Rob Cohen, *Dragon* is as full of pseudo-Chinese bromides as it is punctuated by amplified thuds. But the movie is so likably comic that you can forgive its monotonous insistence on family values. Even the most nouveau *Karate Kid* inspirational moments—a wheelchair and baby stroller limned against the sky—have their wide-eyed charm.

The son of Chinese actors—born while his parents were on tour in San Francisco in 1940—the real Bruce Lee was a juvenile star of the burgeoning Hong Kong movie industry (20 films between 1946 and '58), as well as a sometime boxer, and the Crown Colony cha-cha champ. He came to the U.S. to study in 1959 but wound up in Hollywood teaching martial arts to the likes of Lee Marvin and Steve McQueen. Lee played an Asian sidekick in the TV series *The Green Hornet* then, his movie career thwarted by American racial taboos, returned to HK in 1971 to star in the first modern-dress martial-arts flicks.

The Big Boss and subsequent Lee vehicles made unarmed combat the genre norm. In each, the hero wades into a crowd of villains without a weapon—save his fists, elbows, and feet. Lee's fighting style was an acrobatic mixture of judo, kick boxing, tae kwon do, and the Ali shuffle, endearingly punctuated by the star's trademark squawk. Lee eschewed body doubles; his movies imbued stuntman authenticity with cartoon hyperbole. Such was the temper of the times that he was frequently compared to Fred Astaire—an analogy *Dragon* maintains by cutting from dojo to dance floor and choreographing its most spectacular fight (erupting from the kitchen of the restaurant that employs Bruce as dishwasher) to the bar-band staple "Green Onions."

Here as elsewhere, Asian American hunk Jason Scott Lee exhibits more charm if less smolder than his namesake (he's more of a U.S.-style jock), but he undeniably has the moves down. A tour de force of physical training, the JSL performance combines self-parodic hypervigilance with an impressively vein-popping torso. When he and Lauren Holly, who plays Lee's wife, Linda, are filmed making love, it's his body on which the camera bestows its most tender caresses.

Throughout *Dragon*, Lee repeats that he wants to show the world the beauty of Chinese culture, and the movie configures his career as a victory over racial prejudice. He runs a racist gamut—restaurant, movie-show, mother-in-law-to court campus queen Linda and brings down the wrath of San Francisco's Chinese elders through his willingness to instruct whites and blacks in the "secrets" of the mystic East. For the latter sacrilege, he must engage in single combat in a subterranean pit somewhere beneath Grant Avenue. (Despite the movie's ritual obeisance to "spiritual discipline," virtually every conflict is resolved by violence.) Fifteen minutes later, with splendid irrationality, we learn that Lee's controversial teachings have become the scandal of the martial-arts world—now abruptly administered by whites.

Although Bruce Lee's narcissism and obsession with physical self-improvement make him a particularly contemporary figure, *Dragon*'s racial logic is hardly inappropriate. Lee was a potent figure for Chinese audiences because he appeared to be a teacher, rather than a student, of the West. His celluloid opponents were often foreigners (white or Japanese) whom he beat at their own aggressive game. In the U.S., Lee movies opened in Chinatowns but soon crossed over to a black/Latino/inner-city audience. Given this international, interracial Third World solidarity, it's significant that Lee's breakthrough occurred at the moment the Vietnam War was recognized as unwinnable and China reentered Western "history." Indeed, six months after Nixon went to China, *Kung Fu*, a project Lee had brainstormed before leaving California, was ABC's *Movie of the Week*, while Warner Bros. signed him to appear in the English-language *Enter the Dragon*.

Lee both fed and fed off the 1972-74 worldwide kung fu craze, during which the mode *Variety* dubbed "chopsocky" interfaced with popular forms from biker flicks to spaghetti westerns to soul music. *Enter the Dragon* returned some $100 million worldwide on a $600,000 negative (plus half again as much spent on publicity) and made Lee the species' single most celebrated individual, after Muhammad Ali and before Sylvester Stallone. What's more, three weeks before *Enter the Dragon* opened in August 1973, Lee was mysteriously dead.

There hadn't been a comparable necro-star since James Dean, who suffered his fatal car crash well before the opening of *Rebel Without a Cause*. (*Dragon* acknowledges this mystic connection by having the young Bruce keep a picture of James Dean in his room.) Lee's divinity was consecrated by about a billion posters and a raft of hastily contrived exploitation films, ranging from *Bruce Lee and I*, which starred the HK actress in whose apartment he expired, to a feature-length mish-mash of old *Green Hornet* episodes. Such counterfeit and cobbled-together films, including one centered on footage of Lee fighting Kareem Abdul-Jabbar, were still being released a decade after his death—an anniversary also commemorated by Albert Goldman's suitably tawdry two-part exposé in *Penthouse*. *Dragon* is no less than Lee's third coming.

Although it uncannily seems to predict the death of Lee's son, Brandon, the one thing on which this sanitized bio-pic doesn't wish to speculate is the lurid tale of Lee's demise. *Dragon* ends by citing his "mysterious coma," echoing Linda Lee's preference for remembering the way her husband lived rather than how he died. Was it sex, drugs, the iron fist, HK producer Run Run

Shaw? You needn't have trained in a Shaolin Temple to sense the presence of a half dozen TV schlocku-mentaries aquiver in the wings.

Also reviewed in:
CHICAGO TRIBUNE, 5/7/93, Friday/p. C, Dave Kehr
NEW YORK TIMES, 5/7/93, p. C19, Vincent Canby
NEW YORKER, 5/19/93, p. 102, Terrence Rafferty
VARIETY, 5/3/93, p. 40, Leonard Klady
VARIETY, 9/28/92, p. 79, Fred Lombardi
WASHINGTON POST, 5/7/93, p. B7, Richard Harrington
WASHINGTON POST, 5/7/93, Weekend/p. 50, Desson Howe

EL CID

A Miramax Films release of a Samuel Bronston production. *Producer:* Samuel Bronston and Anthony Mann. *Director:* Anthony Mann. *Screenplay:* Philip Yordan, Fredric M. Frank, and Ben Barzman. *Director of Photography:* Robert Krasker. *Editor:* Robert Lawrence. *Music:* Miklos Rozsa. *Art Director:* Veniero Colesanti. *Costumes:* John Moore. *Running time:* 180 minutes. *MPAA Rating:* Family.

CAST: Charlton Heston (Rodrigo Diaz de Vivar/El Cid); Sophia Loren (Chimene); Raf Vallone (Count Ordonez); Genevieve Page (Princess Urraca); John Fraser (Prince Alfonso); Herbert Lom (Ben Yussuf).

LOS ANGELES TIMES, 8/20/93, Calendar/p. 10, Michael Wilmington

With all its colors and visuals returned to their original splendor, the current re-release of the 1961 "El Cid," is the kind of super-spectacle they don't make anymore, maybe *can't* make anymore. This restored print, another of Martin Scorsese's invaluable reclamation projects, shows why.

It's a vast, teeming pageant, loaded with decor and furious action. History, romance, legendary, adventure, swashbuckling jousts, sword fights and grand battle scenes—with 5,000 soldiers of the Spanish Army acting as extras in the overpowering climax, the oceanside Valencia siege sequence—all these combine for close to the quintessence of the "cast of thousands" historical extravaganza: the genre that began with Griffith and DeMille and, in the '60s, reached its physical peak.

Shot in Spain by producer Samuel Bronston, "El Cid" (Times-rated Family) is a marvel of historical reconstruction. The original 11th-Century castles were used, 35 ships of the Moorish fleet rebuilt, costumes and settings re-created with lavish care; even Miklos Rozsa's score uses medieval modes. The script, by Philip Yordan, Fredric M. Frank and the uncredited blacklist victim Ben Barzman, is out of the ordinary too. It paints a corrupt, obsessive Spanish court, filled with cruel intrigue and perverse psychological undercurrents, as a dark backdrop for the shining, pure force of El Cid's nobility.

If the chivalric ideal is at the heart of Corneille's classic drama, "Le Cid"—whose events make up much of the film's first half-honor beyond death keys the historical legend itself, especially its grisly, necrophile climax: the corpse's last charge at the Battle of Valencia. Director Anthony Mann, assisted here by Yakima Canutt and the brilliant cinematographer Robert Krasker ("Henry V," "The Third Man") was a recognized master of action and landscape in 1961. His work in "El Cid"—the long shots of mountainous vistas and turreted castles, the close-ups of furious brawling—now seems an extension of his classic '50s Jimmy Stewart Westerns ("Winchester 73," "The Naked Spur") rather than a departure from them. And the film's Rodrigo (El Cid) and Chimene, paradigm historical star Charlton Heston and Sophia Loren—supported by Raf Vallone,

Genevieve Page, Herbert Lom and others—are at *their* physical peaks too. They help make the film seethe with excitement and beauty.

This movie may lack humor to counterbalance its intensity, and it's sometimes less successful in intimate scenes: When these stars kiss, it's like Zeus and Hera smooching. But, torn from its time and restored to ours, "El Cid" has overpowering scale, blackhearted villains, pure knights and ladyloves, breathtaking grandeur. It's an ode to heroism, idealism and romance that still sweeps us away.

NEW YORK POST, 8/20/93, p. 28, Lawrence Cohn

Restored to pristine condition, the spectacle "El Cid" is not the greatest of the epics, an honor reserved for "Lawrence of Arabia." Yet it's still an exciting drama produced on a grand scale in 1961 by Samuel Bronston, who also made "King of Kings" that year.

As its star Charlton Heston said at the Aug. 5 reissue premiere, "'Spartacus,' 'Ben-Hur' and 'El Cid' have additional importance because they can't afford to make them anymore." In fact, to re-create the "El Cid" cast of thousands, fabulous Spanish sets and locations plus a superstar cast today would surely cost well over $100 million.

Heston, well-accustomed to larger-than-life characters like Moses and "Ben-Hur," portrays Rodrigo Diaz de Vivar, a patriotic hero in 11th-century Spain who's christened "El Cid" (meaning "the Lord") by a respectful Moorish leader played by British actor Douglas Wilmer, Rodrigo consistently does what's right no matter what. His selflessness is such that other characters frequently react with wonderment, saying the equivalent of "what's with this guy?" every few reels.

That's the main stumbling block to a 1993 audience appreciating "El Cid" and its relentless spirituality. The melodramatic situations scriptwriters Philip Yordan and Fredric Frank put Rodrigo through are always well-defined with motivations made crystal clear, but the character remains too good to be true. It takes an actor the stature of Heston to pull it off. By film's end his heroism is moving, especially as he rides off into the mists of legend in the classic final shot set on the beach of Valencia.

More successful at creating a living, breathing character is Sophia Loren, cast as Rodrigo's bride-to-be Chimene. Her beauty is amply captured by cinematographer Robert Krasker on wide screen, using the same 70-millimeter Super Technirama process as "Spartacus.". Loren alternates fire and ice in expressing her passion for Rodrigo, tempered by a call for vengeance. Rodrigo has killed her father in a fair fight of honor and has also been branded a traitor to Spain by the testimony of Count Ordonez (Raf Vallone), another of Chimene's suitors.

Director Anthony Mann and second-unit director (of "Ben-Hur" fame) Yakima Canutt deliver arresting compositions and vivid battle scenes.

The film boasts an excellent villainess played by French actress Genevieve Page, as the princess who schemes with her incestuous brother Alfonso (John Fraser) to take over the kingdom. Herbert Lom, still playing Clouseau's adversary in Blake Edwards' "Pink Panther" movies, is striking with dark makeup as the evil Moorish leader Ben Yussuf who has pledged a holy war to conquer first Spain, tomorrow the world.

Also reviewed in:
CHICAGO TRIBUNE, 8/27/93, Friday/p. B, Richard Christiansen
NEW YORK TIMES, 12/15/61, p. 49, Bosley Crowther
WASHINGTON POST, 8/27/93, p. C7, Richard Harrington

EL MARIACHI

A Columbia Pictures release of a Los Hooligans production.   *Producer:* Robert Rodriguez and Carlos Gallardo.   *Director:* Robert Rodriguez.   *Screenplay:* Robert Rodriguez.   *Story by:* Robert Rodriguez.   *Director of Photography:* Robert Rodriguez.   *Editor:* Robert Rodriguez. *Music:* Marc Trujillo, Alvaro Rodriguez, Juan Suarez, Cecilio Rodriguez, and Eric Guthrie.

Music Editor: Robert Rodriguez. *Sound:* Robert Rodriguez. *Special Effects:* Robert Rodriguez. *Stunt Coordinator:* Manuel Salinas and Mario Hernandez. *Running time:* 84 minutes. *MPAA Rating:* R.

CAST: Carlos Gallardo (El Mariachi); Consuelo Gómez (Domino); Jaime De Hoyos (Bigotón); Peter Marquardt (Mauricio, "Moco"); Reinol Martinez (Azul); Ramiro Gomez (Cantinero); Jesus Lopez (Viejo Clerk); Luis Baro (Domino's Assistant); Oscar Fabila (The Boy); Poncho Ramon and Fernando Martinez (Azul's Rats); Manuel Acosta (Bodyguard); Walter Vargas and Roberto Martinez (Prisoners); Virgen Delgado, Juanita Vargas, and Yolanda Puga (Female Bodyguards); Alfredo Cisneros (Keyboardist); Alejandro Peña (Piña/Loco); Israel Reyes (Taco); Clara Scott (Moco's Manicurist); Maria Castillo, Samuel Quiroz, and Roberto Delgado (Jail Guards); Fermin Barron (School Bus Driver); Tito Tortuga (La Tortuga).

LOS ANGELES TIMES, 2/26/93, Calendar/p. 1, Peter Rainer

The 24-year old director Robert Rodriguez has an instinctive feeling for pace and movement. His first feature, "El Mariachi," reportedly made for $7,000, doesn't tell you much about what he might be able to do with actors and a strong, complex script—it's basically a cinematic exercise that provides a shoot-out or a chase scene every few minutes.

But from moment to moment it keeps you watching. Shot in 16mm, in 14 days, the film was transferred to 35mm by Columbia Pictures and has a refurbished soundtrack. Even by micro-budget standards that $7,000 figure seems suspiciously on the low side, but the film (rate R for strong violence) is still an example of what you can come up with on next to nothing. Technically, in terms of how the shots go together, "El Mariachi" is prodigious.

It would be a mistake, however, to make too much of Rodriguez's budget. Once you get over the fact that this movie was made for the equivalent of lunch money on most studio productions, you're faced with what it actually is: A tall-tale shoot-em-up that draws on a whole arsenal of styles, including those of Peckinpah, Scorsese, Spielberg, Leone and Hill. It's a movie made by a talented tyro who, judging from what's on the screen, hasn't yet lived much of a life.

It's about a mariachi (Carlos Gallardo) who wanders into a Mexican border town and is mistaken for a hit man (Reinol Martinez). Both carry around a guitar case but the hit man's is chock-full of weapons. In the ensuing clash of mistaken identities, the musician shacks up with the former girlfriend (Consuelo Gomez) of the local drug lord (Peter Marquardt) who is also the hit man's target. Her protection is the world's sleepiest pit bull.

That's about it for story development or emotional nuances. The script, by Rodriguez and Gallardo, is a series of mock-comic confrontations that allows the director to shoot the works. The actors are non-professionals, which is probably just as well: Too much emoting in these roles would be painfully inappropriate.

When the drug king lights his stogie on the sandpapery skin of one of his henchman, you can hear the amplified scratch as the match bursts into flame, just as you hear the amplified blows whenever anyone is hit. Rodriguez sets up this sleepy, deranged border town with every buzzing fly intact. He's good on atmosphere.

If all we wanted from the movies was derring-do we wouldn't need to go to the movies. TV commercials would do just fine. Rodriguez has the technique to make first-class-looking movies on grade A budgets but, with his skills and his humor, he should aim for more than a career of fancy pyrotechnics.

NEW STATESMAN & SOCIETY, 8/13/93, p. 33, Jonathan Romney

[*El Mariachi* was reviewed jointly with *Laws of Gravity*; see Romney's review of that film in *Film Review Annual, 1993.*]

NEW YORK POST, 2/26/93, p. 21, Jami Bernard

The Story of how 23-year old Robert Rodriguez got picked up by Columbia Pictures and ICM as the latest hot young director is a four-star story in and of itself. But first, "El Mariachi."

"El Mariachi" is an exciting, unpretentious, very funny action picture about a mariachi singer who comes to a small dusty border town at exactly the same time as a vicious hit man. They are both dressed in black and carry guitar cases, except that El Mariachi's case contains the real article.

The sweet, hapless singer, wanting only some steady work in a bar, gets chased all over this one-horse town by people thinking he is the hit man. Meanwhile, he falls in love with a beautiful bar owner who is otherwise spoken for by the meanest man in town.

Simple, no? Simple, yes. Rodriguez made this movie for the Spanish action-video market for the incredibly tiny sum of $7,000, $3,000 of which he raised by offering his body to science in a month-long cholesterol-reducing experiment. Cholesterol-lowered and wallet-improved, he gathered together his best friends as actors and wrote a script. He also produced, photographed, and edited.

The noise of the clunky camera drowned out the dialogue, so Rodriguez hand-synched a separately recorded soundtrack. When the synching didn't match, he substituted yet another shot of a friend's pit bull, whose role in the movie is just that—something they could cut to when the soundtrack went awry.

One of his actors didn't even speak any Spanish, but all of them were fed their lines one at a time—Rodriguez read them the line with the inflection he wanted, they parroted it back once, then he rolled the camera. There was no budget for second takes. For the action sequences, Rodriguez held the camera in a wheelchair while the lead actor, a good friend of his, rolled him around. Unless, of course, it was one of the lead actor's own scenes, in which case Rodriguez had to run with the camera himself.

"El Mariachi" is first of what was planned to be a trilogy; the next two will have budgets like $6 million, thanks to a two-picture deal with Columbia, which also bought the rights to the El Mariachi character.

Rodriguez isn't hot only because his "back story" is so fantastic. "El Mariachi" looks like it had a budget 100 times bigger, which is to say that although it looks low-budget, and doesn't always look so good blown up from 16mm, it shows an expert stretching of the budget. Because there was no money or film stock to spare, the whole movie, with its 2,000-or-so cuts, had to be planned minutely, and Rodriguez's choices show a born director's skill with the medium.

The important thing is that "El Mariachi" is a refreshing piece of work, with or without its shaggy-dog history.

NEWSDAY, 2/26/93, Part II/p. 67, Jack Mathews

Calling 24-year-old Robert Rodriguez' "El Mariachi" a little movie is an insult to its minis-culinity. Shot in Mexico on 16mm film for about the cost of an '85 low-mileage Toyota, this Spanish-language action spoof about a vagabond musician who gets caught in the crossfire of a gang war has to be the tiniest major studio release in history.

Of course, how Rodriguez' $7,000 home movie got on to Columbia Pictures' release schedule already is the stuff of Hollywood legend. Ambitious young Texan enters a medical clinic as a paid guinea pig for a cholesterol study, writes a script between blood tests, then skips across the border with his fee, borrowed equipment and an unpaid cast and returns 14 days later with a feature-length motion picture.

The capper: An agent takes the project to Columbia Pictures, which signs Rodriguez to a long-term contract and decides to blow his little movie up to a grainy 35mm print size and send it out, as is. The only thing missing from this fairy tale now is a standing ovation at next year's Oscar show.

No question, getting a picture made for $7,000 is a remarkable feat, and as a calling card, the movie equivalent of a demo tape, "El Mariachi" deserves the attention it got in Hollywood. But whether it deserves the attention of moviegoers now being asked to pay sticker price, for a homemade jalopy depends on how badly they want to follow the career of Robert Rodriguez.

Rodriguez obviously is a very confident filmmaker, and, given the limitations of time and money, he managed a dazzling array of stylistic flourishes, many of them derivative of either Sam Peckinpah (the bloody, slow-motion shoot-outs) or Sergio Leone (the sweaty close-ups and squinty stares).

He even got a reasonably convincing performance from his childhood buddy Carlos Gallardo, as the amiable mariachi who, after being mistaken for a guitar case-carrying killer and falling in love with a ganglord's girlfriend, is forced to get tough and shoot a lot of people himself. Mariachismo?

The film's greatest strength is its sly sense of humor—a pit bull watchdog that lays around like a rag, a gringo madman (Peter Marquardt, whom Rodriguez met at the cholesterol clinic) who's so tough he lights matches on *other* people's necks, a saloon's one-man mariachi band. But it is comedy in relief of comedy. For all its endless chases and gory shoot-outs, there isn't a moment of real tension in "El Mariachi."

It is not even clear that Rodriguez, a one-man band himself (he is the film's writer, producer, director, editor and cinematographer), intended anything more than a personal exercise. The action sequences often are laughable for both their excess and their clumsiness, and probably were meant to be. If you have time to do something only once, parody is safer than reality.

In one sequence, shown in slow-motion, the mariachi runs directly toward two gunmen in a pickup truck and manages to dodge their bullets as he leaps between them and causes them to shoot each other. Rodriguez could be spoofing Rambo or "Lethal Weapon" or Hollywood itself.

More likely, he was just trying to keep his camera in focus.

SIGHT AND SOUND, 9/93, p. 50, Cynthia Rose

In a north Mexican town, a villain named Azul engineers a breakout from jail, with the help of henchmen, who bring him a guitar case filled with weapons. Local crime boss Moco—who had withheld ill-gotten gains from his ex-sidekick—is alerted by phone. Meanwhile, a young *mariachi* (musician) walks into town, hoping to secure a job in one of the local bars. The first bar he enters already has a 'band': one man with a keyboard. As the mariachi leaves, Azul enters and shoots four customers; the bartender telephones Moco, warning him of a lethal 'musician'. The young man makes his way to another bar, whose owner Domino says she will employ him. He checks in at a hotel, whose proprietor phones Moco; his sleep is interrupted by a posse of Moco's gunmen. A chase ensues, in which two men shoot each other by accident, and other members of the gang are killed. The mariachi defends himself, first with his guitar case, then with a weapon belonging to one of the dead men. Domino hides him in her apartment.

Moco phones Domino's barman to warn him about the guitar case. Domino confronts her guest in the bath, and he convinces her of his true identity by singing her a song. That night, he performs to an enthusiastic crowd at Domino's. The next morning, he entrusts his precious instrument to her, while he returns to his hotel for a refund. Azul, visiting Domino's for a beer, picks up the wrong guitar case. Confronted by Moco's men, Azul finds his only weapon is a guitar. Azul makes it home, and sends his men to find the missing case of weapons. At Domino's, the mariachi is having his wounds tended to, when Moco rings. The mariachi learns that her bar was a gift from Moco, who continues to woo her. The musician accepts money from Domino to replace his guitar. Again, there is an attempt on his life; he jumps into a pickup, which happens to be headed for Moco's. When he is discovered, Moco informs his men they have the wrong man, and the mariachi is returned to town. Meanwhile, Domino agrees to take Azul to Moco's so that she can rescue the 'hostage: Remembering the motorbike, the mariachi follows them, but arrives at Moco's too late: Moco kills both Domino and Azul, and wounds the musician in his playing hand. The mariachi manages to kill Moco, and he is left facing the gangster's henchmen. But they simply walk away, leaving the mariachi to ride off.

Richard Rodriguez, 24, is one of ten children from Texas—a former film student and cartoonist whose editing skills shine in this, his debut feature. He and partner Carlos Gallardo (who plays the movie's hapless protagonist) raised $9,000 with which to make their quickie pic—intending to sell it in the Spanish-language marketplace. Using one borrowed camera, with Gallardo's mother as caterer, they shot *El Mariachi* in Mexico over 14 days, bringing it in with $2,000 to spare. Like Leslie Harris' *Just Another Girl on the I.R.T.*, the team used a sample reel to attract wider attention. This trailer sold Richard Rodriguez to ICM, who then sold his movie to Columbia.

Its edges are frayed and it has no production values: But *El Mariachi* boasts a neat and clever dynamic: its hero stumbles into a saga which replicates those fatalistic *corridos* he sings. *Corridos* have played a linchpin role in evolving a Mexican-American culture and identity. Descended from Spanish romance ballads, they grew into a form which depicts and eulogises current events. The personal 'I' is as central to them as a concern with romance and politics, thus the song format offers a perfect framework for genre film.

Mexican-Americans, of course, will see this right away (as scholar Maria Herrera Sobek wrote recently, through *corridos* the US-bound immigrant "consciously wills himself or herself into the pages of history"). One American film that has notably utilised the form before is Robert M. Young's *The Ballad of Gregorio Cortez* in 1982, but that simply re-enacted one very famous song-story.

Rodriguez's energies are much more cinematic, and two facets of *El Mariachi* seem especially fresh. One is the aforesaid editing, using hundreds of creative cuts. The other is a subtle but pervasive Chicano aesthetic. This often parodies spaghetti-Western machismo, as in the recurring joke about villains who, as power shifts, strike their matches on different portions of each other's anatomy. Generally, the film operates with the kind of verve which heralds a confident stylist. Tough guys who demand beers always thank the bartender—even when, to their horror, he presents a glass with each bottle. The cost-effective Casio keyboard stands in for the more romantic mariachi ensemble. And our hero ponders why his nemesis is called Azul, when he is never seen wearing blue.

Much of this humour is what Mexicans themselves decry as *pocho*—a polite term for 'gringoised'. And, though *chicanismo* is well-established in US life, it has rarely made the transition into American movies. Despite serious projects such as Edward James Olmos' *American Me* (1992) or Robert Redford's *The Milagro Beanfield War* (1987), *chicanismo* is still best glimpsed in the under-rated 1987 Cheech Marin comedy *Born in East L.A.*

Rodriguez, though, is more serious than comic. The whole set-up of *El Mariachi* is that of a pastiche Western. It may be a one-plaza, rather than a one-horse town. But *Gunsmoke* rules obtain—the sole female character is a sympathetic saloon owner, and a single gangster (here a *gringo*) owns everything. Rodriguez uses the cliches to make an interesting point: his hero's *mejicano* dream—his familial destiny of carrying on as a mariachi—has lingered past its expiry date (this subtext is clear from the moment he enters town, when he passes a dusty bust of the one-time revolutionary President, Francisco I Madero).

In his search for soulfulness, the would-be mariachi refuses to smoke and drinks only soda pop (anything else would hurt his voice, he asserts proudly). Yet, in the end, he loses both his girl and his playing hand, without having enjoyed a single moment of manly action. Rodriguez uses a broad genre to make subtle points: about change and tradition, about Mexicans and Chicanos with separate values and voices. Despite its superficial sense of low-budget genre-as-usual, this project offers something truly new for American film. There will be high expectations for its forthcoming follow-up *El Mariachi: Corrido Dos (The Second Song)*.

VILLAGE VOICE, 3/2/93, p. 50, Georgia Brown

El Mariachi is the justly famous $7000 movie made by Robert Rodriguez, a 24-year-old from Austin, Texas, subsequently signed by Columbia to a two-picture deal. Although surrounding hype may have created something of a backlash against this small, entertaining action picture originally intended for the Mexican video market, the deflationary perspective is useful. Don't expect too much and you won't be disappointed. *El Mariachi* is a witty, energetic genre picture that pushes its materials for all they're worth.

Written by Rodriguez and his lead actor, Carlos Gallardo, the story follows another No Name who hitchhikes into a not-so-sleepy border town, gets embroiled in a mistaken-identity duel and rises (or falls) to the occasion: The guitar he totes gives way to guns. An itinerate mariachi like his father and his grandfather, all he asks is space in a bar and a chance to earn some tips. But now another man in black, carrying a cache of arms in a guitar case, stalks the same streets, intent on killing the resident drug lord—a suave playboy who recently tried to have him rubbed out. So a comedy of errors is hatched, and violence (much of it slapstick) ensues. In the course of things, the mariachi is befriended by a sad-eyed lady bartender, who happens to occupy a prominent place in the drug lord's affections. This is a love story, too. And it has good dreams.

Using a handheld camera, just one take (the number East European directors use), and minimal dialogue, Rodriguez has done very nicely by his scanty means and materials. Apparently, he's now making a $5 million version. The pressure is on to do it better.

Also reviewed in:
CHICAGO TRIBUNE, 3/12/93, Friday/p. J, Dave Kehr
NEW YORK TIMES, 2/26/93, p. C6, Janet Maslin
NEW YORKER, 2/22/93, p. 169, Terrence Rafferty
VARIETY, 9/14/92, p. 48, Todd McCarthy
WASHINGTON POST, 4/3/93, p. C1, Hal Hinson

EQUINOX

An I.R.S. release off a Nicholas Stiliadis and Syd Cappe presentation of a SC Entertainment International production. *Executive Producer:* Nicolas Stiliadis, Syd Cappe, and Sandy Stern. *Producer:* David Blocker. *Director:* Alan Rudolph. *Screenplay:* Alan Rudolph. *Director of Photography:* Elliot Davis. *Editor:* Michael Ruscio. *Sound:* Susumu Tokunow. *Sound Editor:* John Nutt. *Casting:* Pam Dixon. *Production Designer:* Steven Legler. *Art Director:* Randy Eriksen. *Set Decorator:* Cliff Cunningham. *Set Dresser:* Hather McElhatton. *Special Effects:* Paul Murphy. *Costumes:* Sharen Davis. *Make-up:* Kathryn Bihr. *Stunt Coordinator:* Greg Walker. *Running time:* 108 minutes. *MPAA Rating:* Not Rated.

CAST: Matthew Modine (Henry Petosa/Freddy Ace/Immanuel); Lara Flynn Boyle (Beverly Franks); Fred Ward (Mr. Paris); Tyra Ferrell (Sonya Kirk); Marisa Tomei (Rosie Copa); Kevin J. O'Connor (Russell Franks); Tate Donovan (Richie Nudd); Lori Singer (Sharon Ace); M. Emmet Walsh (Pete Petosa); Gailard Sartain (Dandridge); Tony Genaro (Eddie Gutierrez); Angel Aviles (Anna Gutierrez); Dirk Blocker (Red); Kirsten Ellickson (Young Helena); Pat Clemmons (Helena); Debra Dusay (Judith Hammer); Les Podewell (Jerome Hammer); Megan Lee Ochs (Bess); Carlos Sanz (Harold); Leonora Finley (Maye); Isabell Monk (Apartment Superintendent); Billy Silva (Sabujii); Tom Kasat (I.M. Stong); Dane Wheeler-Nicholson (Self-Defense Victim); Paul Meshejian (Ralph); Robert Gould (Mel); Shirley Venard (Villa Capri Waitress); Willis Burks II (Willie); Pancho Demmings (Morgue Worker); Jack Walsh (Newspaper Man); Martin Marinaro (Attendant); Elizabeth Ann Gray (Large Woman on Bus); Wayne A. Evensoe (Large Woman's Companion); Randy Gust (Bus Punk); Matthew Dudley and John Sargent (Toughs); Diane Wheeler-Nicholson (Drunk Woman); Frank Davis (Marsh); Mark Modine (Cook); Ken Earl (Banker); Vinnie Curto (Gangster); Chris George (Villa Capri Pianist); Kerry Hoyt (Kerry); Rebecca Sabot (Paris' Girlfriend); Suzette Tarzia (Charlene).

LOS ANGELES TIMES, 6/16/93, Calendar/p. 3, Michael Wilmington

Does every wimp dream of being a gangster? And are gangsters wimps with guns and an attitude? In Alan Rudolph's dreamy, sinuous "Equinox", Matthew Modine shakes us up in a double role that spins both sides of this coin. Modine plays a pair of twins separated at birth: one who grows up good but impotent, the other virile and bad.

Like Timothy Hutton's two sides in "The Dark Half," these two "selves" are dark and light, yin and yang: the "good" Henry Petosa bumbling through his futile routine as an introverted mechanic, while "bad" killer-winner Freddy Ace rakes in the chips as driver and silken torpedo for the local mob.

"Equinox" is not exactly a cautionary fable or psychological study, and it's certainly not a conventional thriller. More obviously, it's a *film noir* fairy tale, a beautifully articulated jazz rhapsody of a movie, full of stunning imagery and daffy jokes. In it, Rudolph plays around with the thriller form and the themes of duality and good/evil, using the plot to comment on alienation, romantic loss, the emptiness and corruption of modern life. By now an expert at this oddball subgenre, he is freely embellishing the notes, just like a good sax man noodling on "Body and Soul" or "Solitude."

Rudolph keeps weaving together the two stories: while the twins pass each other on parallel tracks and a sort of private eye, Tyra Ferrell as the inquisitive morgue janitor Sonya, tracks them down. Henry quails behind a double-locked apartment door, going shy with the sprightly hooker down the hall (recent Oscar winner Marisa Tomei in a juicy turn), and courting the equally introverted poetry-loving civil servant Beverly (Lara Flynn Boyle). Meanwhile, cold-as-ice Freddy kills without a qualm, and treats his sleek blond wife, Sharon (Lori Singer), with distant, hard-edged cool.

Each has a buddy and a father figure: Henry's twitchy pal Russell (Kevin O'Connor) and his barmy vaudevillian stepdad, Pete (M. Emmett Walsh): Freddy's one-armed, psycho cohort Richie Nudd and his super-rich mob-man boss Paris (Fred Ward). The two even hang out in the same Italian ristorante—Henry eats there, Freddy is shaking it down—while, never, for most of the film meeting or seeing each other.

But since the film deals with the equivalent of "equinox," the day when darkness and light are equal, a reckoning is obviously imminent.

Rudolph sets "Equinox" in the mythical city of Empire—actually Minnesota's Twin Cities—which Rudolph, designer Steven Legler and the remarkable cinematographer Elliot Davis ("The Moderns," "King of the Hill") refashion into a drizzly evil wonderland.

At the center, Modine, though he may be pushing the "nerd" button a little heavily, gives us the dark and light sides with wit and passion, irony and deep emotion. As an actor, he hits his own equinox, balances the role effortlessly. And, as filmmaker, Rudolph once more takes us into those smoky, lyrical, mesmerizingly daft realms of which only he seems the ace.

NEW STATESMAN & SOCIETY, 7/9/93, p. 28, Jonathan Romney

Equinox is a dream of a film. Like a dream, it has its own perfect logic—but a logic that can't easily be pinned down. That's par for the course for director Alan Rudolph, one of American cinema's great non-conformists.

Rudolph makes extremely strange films, but they don't have the wilful demonism-by-rote aberrations of the David Lynch school. Rather, Rudolph uses all the cherished conventional codes of US cinema—romance, *noir*, mainstream comedy—and scrambles them just enough that they stay the right side of dysfunction. Most of Rudolph's films have these curious spaces and ellipses written into them. They're spaces for contemplation—but contemplation of the dreamiest, most bittersweet-romantic variety.

It's hard to pin the label "dreamer" on a film-maker without giving the impression of pastel-pale vapidity. With Rudolph, that's almost true, but there's a test case: his 1987 film *Made in Heaven*. That expressly took on the soft-focus language of metaphysical Mills and Boonery (two love-struck souls part in heaven, to be reunited on earth), only to give it a steely undercurrent of irony that so foxed the studio that it insisted on imposing an unambivalent glutinous ending.

With *Equinox*, Rudolph makes things easier for us by making things darker from the outset, but he's still playing with the fluff of fantasy. Identical twin brothers are separated at birth, and grow up unaware of each other to pursue different but complementary destinies until fate takes a hand. Fate is played by a medical orderly (Tyra Ferrell) who one day comes into possession of a mysterious letter gripped by a dying bag-lady and decides that it's her passport to a literary career: she's going to make it the basis of a "fairy tale". Sonya effectively narrates the film, but we can't be sure whether she's investigating the brothers' story, unravelling its thread, or actually writing it, spinning the tale's frayed, scattered fabric.

At one end of the thread is Freddy (Matthew Modine), a small, murderous cog in the empire of crime king Mr Paris (Fred Ward). Apparently a worldly success, Freddy is one of Rudolph's characteristic fantasising strays, but he's a Walter Mitty on the dark side: a cheap-shot pretender, fantasising desperately about overthrowing Mr Paris's Napoleon.

At the other end of the thread is the impossibly meek and nervous Henry (Modine again), whose dreams are of travel and love. His inamorata is the equally tongue- and heart-tied Beverly (Lara Flynn Boyle), who sits at home muttering over her Emily Dickinson until such time as her knight errant learns how to shine up his armour.

There's no link between the two brothers except a restaurant they both occasionally visit (Henry for love-lorn goulash, Freddy to lean on the owner), and an absurd dream of origins. The backstory that Sonya uncovers is a dippy Ruritanian romance about a fabulous legacy, a European prince and heart-rent ballerina. It's what Freudians call a "family romance", except that the romance is soured by its location in a hellish, loveless city, while the families are either half-invented (the improbably glorious parents) or makeshift surrogates (The mob for Freddy, E Emmet Walsh's big-hearted galoot of a garage owner for Henry).

But there's no chance of mistaking the film's romantic strain for mere soft-heartedness. A definite streak of cruelty underwrites its sense of regret, just as the lean-spirited plotter Freddy is the flip side of Henry's listless dreamer. Star-crossed Henry and Beverly may be, but they're also crossed by their own hopelessly negative idealism. It leaves them ditched in an anachronistic world of their own—of flat caps, lace doilies and hideously stuffed sofas—while the world outside thrusts breakneck towards some unimaginable "future" represented by the lottery advertised on every wall of the hellish city.

None of this is spelled out so much as limned in every strange, anomalous touch of decor and characterisation. Everything seems slightly wrong, out of time and place, as if left behind by one of the splits that run through the film—right up to the vertiginous aerial shot of the Grand Canyon that ends it with a sweeping stroke of ostentatious allegory.

Equinox is an extraordinary piece of narrative crazy-paving that, against all odds, leads you to a very definite heart-rending pay-off. Rudolph's jigsaw approach is helped by a typically eclectic soundtrack (Nordic jazz, West African blues) and a matching cast. Modine works beautifully off what could have been a virtuoso trick part, with Boyle's nervy, desiccated ingenue, a vibrantly sly cameo from Marisa Tomei, and a scene-stealing, tear-jerking turn from that grand curmudgeon M Emmet Walsh. It's the only film so far this year to exercise both your unconscious and your Kleenex box.

NEW YORK POST, 9/8/93, p. 26, Lawrence Cohen

Iconoclastic filmmaker Alan Rudolph has created the intricate "Equinox" a bizarre saga of twins separated at birth who are fated to meet with violent results. Fans of Rudolph's introspective films, especially his similar 1985 "Trouble in Mind," will enjoy this exercise but it will seem mighty cryptic to the uninitiated.

Matthew Modine has two of his best screen assignments playing the twins. We first see him as the mousy, downtrodden Henry, living in a strange, futuristic urban jungle where he works at his crazy dad's car repair shop. He can't even get home with the groceries without getting mugged by roving gangs.

Modine has a crush on his best friend's sister, Lara Flynn Boyle, but she's even more timid than he is. In a performance that nearly dominates the film, Boyle is outstanding at suggesting a repressed personality, seething with pent-up passion and talking about herself in the third person.

Modine's evil twin, Freddy, is a small-time hood working for gangster Fred Ward's protection racket. His wife is played earthily by Lori Singer, who also was the lead actress in Rudolph's "Trouble in Mind."

Aspiring writer Tyra Ferrell comes upon a dying homeless woman at the beginning of "Equinox," and using a letter she's found investigates the woman's long missing twin sons. Her efforts tie together the film's loose ends, but Rudolph relies too much on this device to alternately feed the viewer information or withhold it during the course of the picture.

A great ensemble cast keeps "Equinox" worth watching even at its most indulgent moments. Especially notable is Oscar-winner Marisa Tomei who's quite touching as a prostitute neighbor of Henry's. Rubber-faced M. Emmet Walsh also creates a unique character as Modine's former vaudevillian father, always cracking dumb jokes.

The weakest element of "Equinox" is the uninteresting gangster subplot presided over by Fred Ward as a caricature of a kingpin. This material is obviously introduced in order to set up the film's violent climax, but Rudolph's direction of the fateful meeting of the twins is awkward and phony. Far better is a classic final aerial shot of Modine standing overlooking the Grand Canyon.

NEWSDAY, 9/8/93, Part II/p. 55, Gene Seymour

If human doormats were a hot investment, garage mechanic Henry Petosa (Matthew Modine) would be on easy street. But with Henry's lousy luck, he'd probably find some way of blowing that too. The poor shlub's so pathetic that, even with bejeweled dowagers walking around him, he gets mugged for his sack of groceries. In a rare moment of eloquence, he laments, "My whole life seems to be taking place without me."

Henry doesn't know it, but he's got an identical twin brother in another part of gloomy Empire City who's everything he wishes he were. Freddy Ace (Modine) is cool, tough and confident. A swaggering, enigmatic aide to mob boss Mr. Paris (Fred Ward), Freddy is married to a beautiful, adoring woman (Lori Singer), while Henry can barely summon the nerve to call his best friend's shy sister (Lara Flynn Boyle) for a date.

Freddy doesn't know he has a twin brother either. But unbeknownst to both, an aspiring writer (Tyra Ferrell), who found their mother's body is close to putting the pieces together. Meanwhile both brothers' penchant for finding trouble edges their diametric destinies closer together.

Such is the curious tale spun by writer-director Alan Rudolph, who's developed a cult following for such moody fables of urban serendipity as "Choose Me," "Remember My Name" and "Trouble in Mind."

As with those films, "Equinox" has an off-kilter narrative texture that keeps your attention riveted even when you don't quite get what Rudolph's doing or why. In his imaginary universe, Rudolph seems to bend reality and the way people struggle to express their feelings.

"I've seen the best and I've seen the worst," says M. Emmett Walsh as Henry's adoptive father and garage boss. "But I can still sit up in the morning and count ten toes." Who *talks* like that?, you wonder. And then, you think, who cares? Rudolph's playful, over-the-top imagination carries you along like a lush and loony jazz solo.

What weakens the film is its central performance. Modine, while appealing as Henry, doesn't quite convince as the charismatic Freddy. Most likely, the role was originally conceived for long-time Rudolph leading man Keith Carradine, who would have had just the right mix of innocence and menace to pull it off.

Rudolph's bewitching atmosphere of dreamy grittiness makes up for a lot—as do the supporting performances. Walsh, Ferrell and Ward are each funny and frantic by turns. Boyle, best known for her work with the equally idiosyncratic (and better-known) cult director David Lynch, is becoming quite adroit at balancing wistfulness and sensuality.

And in a too-brief turn as a prostitute and single mom living in Henry's tenement, Marisa Tomei displays the kind of knockout versatility and presence that won her an Oscar for "My Cousin Vinny."

SIGHT AND SOUND, 7/93, p. 41, Ian Penman

Empire City, the future. Helena, a bag lady, dies on the way to hospital, clutching a sealed envelope. In the morgue, Sonya, a young black nurse and aspiring writer, pockets the envelope and begins to research Helena's story. In the same city, Henry Petosa and his friend Russell discuss social plans and Russell's sister Beverly, with whom Henry has been having a romance crippled by mutual shyness. After being mugged for his groceries, Henry arrives home at his apartment and calls Beverly, but puts the phone down without speaking.

Elsewhere in Empire, Freddy Ace—who is Henry's double—argues with his fellow gangster Richie, on their way to the Villa Capri restaurant to meet their higher-up Dandridge. Dandridge coerces the owner Eddie to join their 'family'. Freddy and Richie tussle, with Freddy coming out on top. Henry is visited by his neighbour Rosie, who lives downstairs with her pimp Red; she contrives to leave Henry with her baby while she goes out to 'work'. Freddy arrives home to tell his wife that he has been made the personal driver of his boss Mr Paris.

The next day, Henry's adoptive father Pete tells him that the bank has made him an offer for the garage he owns and they both work in. Meanwhile, Mr Paris hints that he wouldn't be displeased to see the back of Richie. Henry is 'paid back' for his babysitting with a sexual favour from Rosie.

Red arrives and, furious, hits Rosie; Henry scuffles with Red, who falls downstairs.

Sonya discovers that a blind trust account had been set up in Helena's name. Posing as a biographer, she visits a firm of attorneys and learns that Immanuel, a European count, deposited the money 30 years earlier. He had an affair with Helena, then a ballet dancer; she fell pregnant and gave birth to twin boys (Henry and Freddy) who were separately adopted and are unaware of each other's existence: Immanuel, already married, returned to Europe, where he died in a racing car accident; Helena had a breakdown. The attorneys also discover that the account includes a retainer for the firm, and they agree that in the event of a withdrawal they will split with Sonya 10% of a sum which is now $4m.

Over dinner at the Villa Capri, Henry tells Russell and Beverly of the potential sale of the garage, and his plans to travel abroad. Richie arrives to intimidate Eddie, and Russell, who is besotted with Anna, ascertains that there is something wrong. Richie spots Henry and, mistaking him for Freddy, taunts him before being dragged away. Later, Freddy shoots Richie dead. He is received by Paris and Dandridge for a celebratory drink, but is sullen, and only grudgingly accepts a cash reward. Henry returns home to find that an enraged Red has killed Rosie.

Sonya finds Henry's adoption papers, and when she confronts Pete, he gives a veiled affirmation. Henry dines with Beverly and they once more discuss leaving. She is not entirely persuaded, but says she would like to visit the Grand Canyon. Later, Russell badgers Henry to help him sort out Anna and Eddie's troubles with the gangsters. Henry gives Beverly a necklace and they arrange to meet later that night to leave.

Henry meets Russell at the Villa Capri, where Freddy and Dandridge soon arrive. While Freddy talks to Eddie, Anna slaps Dandridge, who knocks her over; Russell attempts to come to her rescue. Dandridge sees Henry and is startled by his resemblance to Freddy; Anna shoots Dandridge, then threatens Freddy with the gun. Stunned by the sight of Henry, Freddy is shot by Anna. Henry finds Freddy slumped in an alleyway; they stare at each other, before Henry rushes off.

Stopping at the garage to take money and a car, he calls for Beverly. She won't come down and begs him to come in, but he drives away. Four days later, Beverly and Sonya discuss the events of the fateful night; Freddy has died and Henry has disappeared. En route for the Grand Canyon, Henry sees two young twin boys in a diner and realisation dawns on him. He stands and looks out over the Grand Canyon, alone.

Equinox could be *Made In Heaven*—which Alan Rudolph saw taken away from him and disastrously rejigged by a studio—remade, with derailed genetics instead of destinal romance as its keynote. This is one of Rudolph's 'own' projects, as opposed to those he serves up to preserve his niche in the Hollywood hierarchy. At this point in his career—especially given the storyline of *Equinox*—it would have been very easy for Rudolph to do a *Cape Fear* and simplify his style into self-denigrating Lynchian strangeness.

But the Rudolph fan club need not fret. *Equinox* is like espresso for the eyes, it's Rudolph *in excelsis*. Even bridging scenes are limned with oneiric detail, look-twice touches. The streets of his low-key sci-fi metropolis (actually Minneapolis) are dotted with clusters of strange hooded figures, and omnipresent posters for the chance game Lotto. Rudolph films his flashback tale like a laid-back pupil of Roeg, all elegantly faint echoes and wisps of worrying detail. *Equinox* has enough inventiveness in its audacious little Moebius script to furnish four normal Hollywood projects.

Rudolph takes his literally conventional storyline (think *Twins* remade by Jacques Rivette—everything hinges on deferral rather than immediate resolution) and glosses it with a persistent stutter of visual symbolism. Leitmotifs of darkness and light, convergence and duality, might have been predicted from the titular off, but *Equinox* wears Rudolph's intelligence lightly. He includes *in* all the things Hollywood seems compelled to ignore these days—things like racial diversity, social failure, real ardour, unreal awe. He may seem far removed from the description 'political film maker', but 'politics'—as an overview of how different people(s) overlap—is there in his films: America is pictured as a polyphonic, multiracial patchwork.

This white boys' story is traced and written by a young black woman, and this fact alone seems to make the film (and its tall but potentially thin tale) resonate outward from the centre, in a slowly accumulating but sharply registered dissonance. Even the music reinforces this fundamental, quavering split: hung between the icy jazz of Terje Rypdal, and the shimmering black-jewel sound of Malian bluesman Ali Farka Toure (heard every time Tyra Ferrell comes on screen). Ferrell might be the oddest on-screen alter ego Rudolph has yet given himself. At the beginning, she tells a colleague, "I'm writing a story. It's a fairy tale, kinda." Rudolph has described his films as urban fairy tales, and this one flirts with disastrous overload—what with the glaring symbolism, the Mills & Boon flashbacks, and the constant switches between daft humour and grim dystopian reality.

It's easy to forget just how hard-edged Rudolph's multi-nuanced plotlines can be, and how bruised, misbegotten and derelict the lives of his characters. Modine—like Tom Berenger in *Love at Large* and Kris Kristofferson in *Trouble in Mind*—plays his tough guy philosopher as a subtle pastiche, but never takes it too far into empty irony: his Freddy Ace seems a real (hurting, rather than hurtful) presence. Each twin could have had a film to himself, and the scenes Modine's bumbling Henry has with both Lara Flynn Boyle (cast—in a long, simmering, sexless relationship—as something like Louise Brooks' Lulu turned into a safe-sex era spinster) and M. Emmet Walsh (as his putative daddy) are a joy.

From the opening credits (a simple, subtle change from light to dark), Rudolph contrives varying degrees of eloquent luminosity. The boys, it transpires, were born on September 23—one of the two days in the year when an equinox can take place. "Equinox" is the code word which opens the secret bank account, but it's also the idea upon which hang the film's overlapping moods. Typically, Rudolph lets a peripheral character spell things, late in the proceedings. "That's when light and dark are equal," wheezes the corpulent Dandridge, thinking about himself but in reality talking about the tragic equinoctial night ahead.

By the end of the film it's safe to assume that Rudolph is mapping not just a personality split, but a national one. US cinema was founded on genres (the Western, *noir*) which betray a restless, querulous worry about questions of origin, identity, birthright. What starts out as a banal Romantic confusion (only Rudolph could get away with this stuff about dashing European counts and tragic ballerinas) ends in a climactic scene which you will find either unutterably resonant, or a pseudo-cosmic cop-out.

As Henry stands perched on the edge of realisation (an empty realisation, for this is a life emptied four times over in one go: his lineage, his brother, his lover, his own identity), Rudolph's camera describes a breathtaking open-air pirouette, away from Henry and around the arid American beyond. The Grand Canyon stands for the birth(s) of the past, and the desolation of the present; it is, in other words, a dried up Empire.

VILLAGE VOICE, 9/14/93, p. 68, Amy Taubin

Genre mixes with a longing for hypertext in *Equinox*, Alan Rudolph's most piquant depiction of free-floating anxiety since *Choose Me*. A kind of low-rent *Batman*, *Equinox* is a separated-at-birth tale set amidst the sewer vapors and lotto billboards of a wannabe Gotham City where the poor and the middle classes prey on one another while wraithlike women in ankle-length furs stride heedlessly through the carnage as if walking a runaway.

Matthew Modine plays twin brothers Henry Petosa and Freddy Ace, who are unaware of each other's existence until they meet in the back alley of the Villa Capri (specialties: goulash and teriyaki turkey); by then, it's too late, Henry, a timid social retard, works in his adoptive father's garage and spends his after-hours dodging women (Lara Flynn Boyle and Marisa Tomei) who are as peculiarly attractive and disconnected as he is. Freddy, on the other hand, is predatory, power-driven, and supremely discontented. The personal driver of a bigtime gangster (Fred Ward), he fancies himself as Rommel, undervalued by Hitler.

Hardly a plot-driven film, *Equinox* moves scattershot among three stories: Henry's, Freddy's, and that of a would-be novelist who's either investigating the origins of the twins or making them up as she—and the film—goes along. Rudolph employs the loaded psychological situations of adoption and twinning as metaphors for a more encompassing millennial malaise. "My whole life seems to be taking place without me in it," says Freddy, and he's not the only one afflicted with the desperate sense that a part of them is missing. The women still look to the hapless men to fix things; paralytically depressed or plain hysterical, the men barely know the women exist.

Despite its inexplicable whimsies and compulsive digressions, the film has a queasy bad-dream punch that lasts long after it's over. Modine is achingly vacant—it's one of his best performances. Rudolph manages to put the camera where it's least expected and move it in seemingly impossible ways. *Equinox* ends with a three-minute helicopter shot of the Grand Canyon as it's never been shown before. It puts everything in place by leaving one hanging at the edge of the abyss.

Also reviewed in:
NEW YORK TIMES, 9/8/93, p. C20, Stephen Holden
VARIETY, 5/25/92, p. 53, Todd McCarthy
WASHINGTON POST, 10/15/93, p. D7, Hal Hinson

ERNEST RIDES AGAIN

An Emshell Producers Group release.   *Executive Producer:* Coke Sams.   *Producer:* Stacy Williams.   *Director:* John R. Cherry III.   *Screenplay:* John R. Cherry III and William M. Akers.   *Director of Photography:* David Geddes.   *Editor:* Craig Bassett.   *Music:* Bruce Arntson and Kirby Shelstad.   *Sound:* Rich Schirmer.   *Casting:* Sid Kozak.   *Production Designer:* Chris August.   *Art Director:* Helen Veronica Jarvis.   *Set Decorator:* Mary Lou Storey.   *Costumes:* Martha Snetsinger.   *Running time:* 93 minutes.   MPAA Rating: PG.

CAST: Jim Varney (Ernest P. Worrell);   Ron K. James (Abner Melon);   Linda Kash (Nan Melon);   Tom Butler (Dr. Glencliff);   Duke Ernsberger (Frank);   Jeffrey Pillars (Joe).

LOS ANGELES TIMES, 11/12/93, Calendar/p. 6, Kevin Thomas

It is downright scary to realize that "Ernest Rides Again" is the *fifth* in a series of comedies starring Jim Varney as Ernest P. (Powertools) Worrell, that zany weirdo that Varney created as a TV pitchman back in 1980. The humor in this film is so elementary, so numskull, it defies description or extended discussion.

It's hard to believe that anyone ever age 5 would be amused by Ernest's goofy shenanigans, but clearly the guy, who has some 2,000 commercials to his credit, has a following somewhat older; apparently, John R. Cherry III, the film's director and co-writer (with William Akers), most know what he's doing, appalling as that might seem, "Ernest Rides Again" (rated PG for slapstick violence) as the first in the series not made in association with Disney's Touchstone Pictures.

Since in his own mind Ernest, now a janitor at a small-town college, is more than a match for Indiana Jones, it is not surprising that he buys the theory of the college's history professor (Ron James) that the actual Crown Jewels of England are not in the Tower of London after all but are buried somewhere in the vicinity inside a giant Revolutionary War cannon. (How about that for a comic premise?) Not surprisingly, the prof is widely regarded as a crackpot, yet he's less than thrilled with the prospect of Ernest determinedly coming to his aid with his Rube Goldberg metal detector.

Varney probably deserves some credit for throwing himself so wholeheartedly into playing the geeky, rubber-faced Ernst. It's quite a contrast to the weedy charm Varney exudes as Jed Clampett in the new big-screen version of "The Beverly Hillbillies"—a film, incidentally, which shows how much fun cornball humor can be when it's done with an affectionate wit and sophistication.

NEW YORK POST, 11/13/93, p. 15, Bill Hoffmann

Be prepared to be annoyed—very, very annoyed.

In "Ernest Rides Again," Jim Varney returns for his fourth (!!!) go-round as the bumbling, in-your-face handyman, Ernest P. Worrell.

And with the sole exception of one decent gag, this picture gets about as close to comedy as a cat does to water. As you remember (but would probably like to forget) Varney created Worrell as a rubber-faced pitchman ... for various products on TV in the mid-1980s.

Disney's Touchstone Pictures division then turned this vapid video stooge into the star of three "Ernest" comedies.

They made money, but someone at Touchstone got wise and pulled the plug on further Worrell opuses.

Now comes a company called "Emshell," which has resurrected Ernest—and given him a budget that could probably fit into a kid's piggy bank.

But it makes no difference, because Varney is everything here.

Shamelessly mugging through every scene and shoving his face right into the camera, the wide-eyed, good ol' boy wants desperately for us to like him.

But within five minutes you want to squash him like a bug.

For the record, the plot concerns Ernest's discovery of a giant cannon containing the crown jewels of England and how an evil professor tries to wrest it away from him.

Along the way, Ernest gets chased by a buzzsaw, attacked by a nailgun, eats a steel wool sandwich, destroys a country fair, takes a pie in the face, gets hooked by a fisherman and steals a tractor.

Get the picture?

Very small children might get a bang out of Ernest's adventures but even they'll eventually begin fidgeting.

Just so you know, the one funny line happens when Ernest gets severely battered at a construction site. "Are you dead?" he's asked. "I guess I would be if I weren't so close to being an actual cartoon!" Ernest quips.

Even if this latest Ernest effort bombs, don't rest easy. Another one is on the way.

How do I know this? Varney comes on screen at the end of the film to pitch "Ernest Goes To School"—scheduled for release next summer.

For a while it looked like Varney was hanging up his Ernest act. Especially after he got decent notices in "The Beverly Hillbillies" and "Wilder Napalm." But apparently that's not going to happen.

I guess with Varney, once a pitchman, always a pitchman.

NEWSDAY, 11/12/93, Part II/p. 81, Terry Kelleher

Just when Jim Varney was stretching as an actor (OK, we're stretching the truth) in "Wilder Napalm" and "The Beverly Hillbillies," he turns up at the multiplex in another of his idiotic "Ernest," movies. Is this good for the image, Vern?

The opening-credit sequence, with its mock-heroic theme song and slightly Monty Pythonish visuals, inspires hope that "Ernest Rides Again" may be more entertaining than the four previous big-screen adventures of hayseed TV pitchman Ernest P. Worrell. But no. No indeed.

In "Ernest Rides Again," Ernest warms up with 10 minutes of laborious slapstick at a construction site, then teams with a squeaky-voiced history professor (Ron K. James) to discover a five-ton, pre-Revolutionary War cannon in which are hidden the real crown jewels of England (as opposed to the phony ones on exhibit in the Tower of London).

The search for the cannon is not entirely without amusement. Ernest has a moment of striking self-awareness after taking a fall that would spell serious injury for a more serious man. "Are you dead?" the professor inquires. "I guess I would be," Ernest says almost thoughtfully, "if I weren't [so] close to being an actual cartoon."

Regrettably, as soon as Ernest finds the cannon, he gets his empty head stuck in its mouth. Once extricated, he rides the monstrous weapon all over creation, with treasure-coveting villains, British agents, vacuum-cleaner salesmen and the professor's obnoxious wife (Linda Kash) in hot but inept pursuit. The chase seems longer than the New York City Marathon, and about as funny as a subway breakdown.

Yes, Varney repeatedly sticks his nose into the camera for those extreme closeups that make the viewer feel foully breathed upon. Yes, Ernest says lots of dumb stuff like: "I had a finding device once. I lost it." However, within the confines of his overfamiliar character, Varney occasionally feels entitled to do a quick Peter Lorre impression or break into a British accent. Hey, Vern! Are ya sure Robin Williams started like this?

Whatever else the future holds for Varney, "Ernest Goes to School" (filmed back-to-back with "Ernest Rides Again") opens next summer come hell or high water.

Also reviewed in:
NEW YORK TIMES, 11/12/93, p. C10, Stephen Holden
VARIETY, 11/29/93, p. 31, Daniel M. Kimmel
WASHINGTON POST, 11/12/93, p. C6, Hal Hinson

ESPECIALLY ON SUNDAY

A Miramax Films release of a Basic Cinematografica-Titanus/ParadisFilm-Intermedias/Dusk Film coproduction in association with RAI-2 and Eurimages.. *Producer:* Amedeo Pagani, Giovanna Romagnoli, and Mario Orfini. *Screenplay:* Tonino Guerra. *Music:* Ennio Morricone. *Running time:* 86 minutes. *MPAA Rating:* R.

THE BLUE DOG: *Director:* Giuseppe Tornatore. *Director of Photography:* Tonino Delli Colli. *Sound:* Christian Vallais. *Production Designer:* Attilio Vitti. *Art Director:* Francesco Bronzi. *Costumes:* Beatrice Bordone. *Make-up:* Maurizio Trani.

CAST: Philippe Noiret (Amleto).

ESPECIALLY ON SUNDAY: *Director:* Giuseppe Bertolucci. *Director of Photography:* Fabio Cianchetti. *Sound:* Stephane Kah. *Production Designer:* Attilio Vitti. *Art Director:* Nello Giorgetti. *Costumes:* Mariolina Bono. *Make-up:* Mario Di Salvio.

CAST: Ornella Muti (Anna); Bruno Ganz (Vittorio); Andrea Prodan (Marco); Nicoletta Braschi (Booth Girl).

SNOW ON FIRE: *Director:* Marco Tullio Giordana. *Director of Photography:* Franco Lecca. *Sound:* Frank Struys. *Production Designer:* Tullio Lullo. *Art Director:* Gianni Silvestri. *Costumes:* Metka Kosak. *Make-up:* Pierantonio Mecacci.

CAST: Maria Maddalena Fellini (Caterina); Chiara Caselli (Bride); Ivano Marescotti (Don Vincenzo); Bruno Berdoni (Husband).

ADDITIONAL SEQUENCES: *Director:* Giuseppe Bertolucci

CAST: Jean-Hugues Anglade (Motorcyclist).

LOS ANGELES TIMES, 8/13/93, Calendar/p. 10, Michael Wilmington

The Italians may not have invented the episode film—the multipart movie united by a single theme, writer or director—but, beginning in the 1950s, they certainly perfected it. That tradition is splendidly continued in "Especially on Sunday," a trio of short films pulsing with passion, wry detachment and a bit of despair. Their unifying factors are a brilliant screenwriter, Tonino Guerra, and his thrice-repeated subject of love, seen from peculiar slants.

These stories—models of compression, beautifully written—each maintain a core of melancholy and irony. A dog worships a lonely shoemaker-barber who scorns him ("The Blue Dog"). Another man becomes catalyst for a sexless relationship between a troubled young couple ("Especially on Sunday"). An elderly woman finds her only solace by spying on the lovemaking of her newlywed son and daughter-in-law—who becomes her willing accomplice ("Snow on Fire").

Guerra, who wrote eight films apiece with Michelangelo Antonioni and Francesco Rosi and others with Fellini, De Sica, Bertolucci, Tarkovsky and Angelopolous, may be Italy's greatest living screenwriter; indeed, in that country's history, only Cesare Zavattini can easily be ranked with him. But Guerra has such a seemingly self-effacing style—he blends in so easily with the world view and emotional/psychological rhythms of his collaborators—that it may take a film like this, interpreted by three different directors, to show how consummate a craftsman he is.

Each director—"Cinema Paradiso's" Giuseppe Tornatore in the first tale, Marco Tullio Giordana in the third and Giuseppe Bertolucci (Bernardo's brother)—in the second aid also in the linking sections—has a recognizable style and attack. Tornatore lets the film breathe with warmth and sentiment, Bertolucci is more baroque; Giordana creates a mood of hushed anxiety.

Yet the voice and themes are Guerra's. Love—wounding, ecstatic or absurd—rises in unexpected places. Sorrow and disappointment may be inevitable: passion a brief match-flare illuminating darkness. He tells us this with breathtaking economy and clarity, writing for the screen as Chekhov's suicidal young playwright Konstantin wished to write in "The Sea Gull"—not self-consciously, preciously or, bombastically, but simply, "so that the words flow freely from the heart."

The actors are excellent. Shaggy-bear Philippe Noiret in "Blue Dog," haunted Bruno Ganz and sumptuous Ornella Muti in the second, daughter-in-law Chiara Caselli and mama Maria Maddalena Fellini (Frederico's sister) in the last, all have grand gestures, privileged moments. And in the best film of the trilogy, Tornatore's "Blue Dog," the memorable images are many: the scruffy little mutt, brow spotted with blue paint, howling at the "master" who rejects him. The cavernous streets through which dog pursues master, and master later tries to find his "pet." And the last, harrowingly ambivalent scene—which is either a crazily happy ending or a retreat into a madness that is life's shield against grief and guilt.

Watching "Especially on Sunday" reminds us of the major tradition of the Italian episode film—"Love in the City," "Yesterday, Today and Tomorrow," "Boccacio '70"—and also carries us back to earlier literary galleries, like Boccacio's "Decameron." Yet the mood here isn't ribald. These are films about love by an observer who has lost his illusions, but still clings to the memory of passion, finding solace in those bursts of empathy that, however improbably, break through walls of indifference or pain. The view may seem bleak, but the artistry of its telling warms the heart.

NEW YORK POST, 8/13/93, p. 26, Jerry Tallmer

An exquisite little Italian movie sneaks into town today at the Angelika. Well, I should say two-thirds exquisite, because "Especially on Sunday" ("La Domenica Specialmente") is a three-part picture, and I liked the first and third parts, "The Blue Dog" and "Snow on Fire," better than the one in the middle.

The whole thing has been written by one man, Tonino Guerra, screenwriter for Antonioni, Fellini, De Sica, the Tavianis, etc. etc., on several dozen pretty great films of the past 3½ decades, all the way from "L'Avventura" to "Ginger and Fred" and beyond. Here the directors are three of a younger generation, Giuseppe Tornatore, Giuseppe Bertolucci (Bernardo's brother), and Marco Tullio Giordana.

In "The Blue Dog" Guerra and Tornatore pay tribute of a sort to another film about an old man and a pooch, De Sica's 1952 masterpiece, "Umberto D." But Amleto, the shoemaker /barber of this opening vignette, isn't as old as Umberto D., or externally as lonely. Internally—well that's what the story is all about.

He's played, and my God, how he's played, with only the barest ration of words, most of them saying how much he hates dogs, by marvelous Philippe Noiret, the projectionist of Tornatore's "Cinema Paradiso." He may detest dogs, may do all he can to get rid of this one, this red/brown stray with a blue spot on its forehead, an animal who even creates a scandal in church, but when it comes to pulling the trigger on a shotgun, Amleto—at 2:20 in the morning—can't do it. Somebody in another window does it. And that's when the barber dons hat, scarf, overcoat and, cigar clenched in mouth, goes looking down cobblestoned alleys and up country roads for the mutt with the loving eyes, who haunts him.

Tornatore and his cinematographer, Tonino Delli Colli, make a poem of those cobblestones, those shuttered windows, the shoemaker's lasts and lathes, laundry on a line, sheep on a windy hillside, one lone tree, one human being's stoic face.

"Snow On Fire," directed by Giordana, the cautionary tale, I guess you'd call it, that closes the film, has a woman named Caterina confessing to a young priest about how she has spied on the lovemaking of her son and his bride—a couple of kids who wed and bedded in snowtime and liked it so much they would only emerge when Mama put dinner on the table.

She, Caterina—an impressive movie debut by Maria Maddalena Fellini, Federico's sister—had pried up a brick in the floor when kept from sleep by cries of arousal, only to find herself staring straight into her daughter-in-laws face at the moment of orgasm. And the girl had stared back. And this went on night after night. It takes a death and another troubled confession to illuminate what these two had so deeply in common.

"Especially on Sunday," the middle piece, directed by G. Bertolucci, brings together the stolid Bruno Ganz and the inexpressibly beautiful Ornella Muti with two other players, Andrea Prodan and Nicoletta Braschi, in a double-paired oddball romantic quadrille that includes a slide show of women *a toilette* and is a bit too schematically symbolic (or something) for me. But the rest, including a framing bit with a boy, a motorcyclist, and some birds, is very, very nice indeed.

NEWSDAY, 8/13/93, Part II/p. 67, John Anderson

A mix of the cerebral, the bittersweet and the unabashedly trite, "Especially on Sunday"—the collective title of three stories from screenwriter Tonino Guerra ("Blow-Up," "Amarcord"), as well as the name of the second of the trio—is set in Guerra's home in the Marecchia valley, and are meant, according to Guerra's prelude, to celebrate the "intense love" that emanates from that voluptuous locale. The three stories, each handled by a different young director, do concern themselves with love. But it's love that has to fight to be born, and must resort to surrogates, third-party seduction and voyeurism to make itself heard.

"The Blue Dog," which reunites "Cinema Paradiso" director Giuseppe Tornatore with the star of that Oscar-winning film, Philippe Noiret, finds the actor playing a lonely, crusty loaf of Italian manhood named Amleto, a combination barber and shoemaker. The cranky peace of his existence is disturbed one day by a mangy little cur with a blotch of blue across his forehead, who decides Amleto is the one for him. Amleto, of course, wants him gone and abuses the mutt unabashedly.

If the message about the lonely dog-lonely man matchup weren't clear enough we have Amelto's acquaintances pointing out that since he has no wife, he needs a dog. Is this kinky? No, forget the socio-sexual nuances. Simply rest assured that when the dog finally leaves Amleto alone, the cobbler pines for his companionship.

Coming out of "The Blue Dog's" matter-of-factness we get the far more ethereal terrain of "Especially on Sunday" (directed by Giuseppe Bertolucci, Bernardo's brother) with its meditative, Antonioni-esque blue skies and the opaque interplay of its three principals: Anna (Ornella Muti), her eccentric contemporary Marco (Andrea Prodan) and Vittorio (Bruno Ganz), an older man who happens upon the odd couple one afternoon, after stopping to right an upended turtle that's lying in the middle of a sunbleached country road. Anna is torn between the worldly, sensitive Vittorio and the tortured, sensitive Marco, who lacks the nerve to seduce her. Only after Vittorio makes his move is the holding pattern resolved. It's anti-romance, with considerable heat flowing between Ganz and Muti.

The last installment is "Snow on Fire" (directed by Marco Tullio Giordana), which stars Maria Maddalena Fellini (Federico's sister) as a lonely, very Catholic widow who's taken to watching her younger brother (Bruno Berdoni) and his wife (Chiara Caselli) make love. Lifting a brick from her upstairs room, she looks down through the floor, into the eyes of her sister-in-law and relives her own young passion, while burdening her soul with sin. The beauty of the story, the most emotionally involving of the three, lies in Guerra's recognition of romantic passion as no province of youth, but rather the food of life, no matter how or where you find it.

VILLAGE VOICE, 9/7/93, p. 65, Marco Spino

The four tales that comprise *Especially on Sunday* are set in Italy's Marecchia Valley, which, the narrator informs us, "finds its beauty in its landscape and in the strong emotions of the people." For the next hour and 30 minutes we're treated to bittersweet cinematography, flute and accordion music, and characters who cry more than Demi Moore.

Filled with allegories, allusions, and paradoxes, two of the stories focus on people's relationships with animals (a bird and a dog)—while the others tackle love triangles. Writer Tonino Guerra attempts to weave all this together into a seamless, dreamy landscape, but the result is somewhat convoluted. None of the three directors manage a distinctive style. Yet two performances shine. Ornella Muti as Anna struts like a marble Venus, tangoing and making enigmatic quips, much like Monica Vitti in Michelangelo Antonioni's films. Anna seduces two men, then pits them against each another, all the while enjoying her power.

Chiara Caselli's Sposa, in contrast, matures from a nubile woman to an estranged wife; she has such a young and playful sexuality that her deterioration is tragic. Sposa's guilt stems from allowing her mother-in-law to watch her have sex. The two women confess their "sin" to a priest, though they do not talk about it with each other—a wild improbability, but then nothing in this film is to be taken literally.

Like many folk tales, *Especially*, uses exaggeration to provide insights into desire, yet these insights remain dense and ambiguous and are muddled by the film's overriding sentimentality.

Also reviewed in:
CHICAGO TRIBUNE, 8/20/93, Friday/p. H, Clifford Terry
NEW YORK TIMES, 8/13/93, p. C14, Stephen Holden
VARIETY, 10/21/91, p. 73, Deborah Young
WASHINGTON POST, 8/20/93, p. D6, Rita Kempley

ETHAN FROME

A Miramax Films release of an American Playhouse Theatrical Films production in association with Richard Price/BBC Films. *Executive Producer:* Lindsay Law and Richard Price. *Producer:* Stan Wlodkowski. *Director:* John Madden. *Screenplay:* Richard Nelson. *Based on the novel by:* Edith Wharton. *Director of Photography:* Bobby Bukowski. *Editor:* Katherine Wenning. *Music:* Rachel Portman. *Choreographer:* Patty Smith and Chip Hedler. *Sound:* Paul Cote. *Sound Editor:* Campbell Askew. *Casting:* Billy Hopkins and Suzanne Smith. *Production Designer:* Andrew Jackness. *Art Director:* David Crank. *Set Decorator:* Joyce Anne Gilstrap. *Set Dresser:* Catie Dehaan, William Bonn, Robert L. Bartell, Jim Russell, and Timothy Moulton. *Costumes:* Carol Oditz. *Make-up:* Kathryn Bihr. *Stunt Coordinator:* Jery Hewitt. *Running time:* 107 minutes. *MPAA Rating:* PG.

CAST: Liam Neeson (Ethan Frome); Joan Allen (Zeena Frome); Patricia Arquette (Mattie Silver); Tate Donovan (Reverend Smith); Katharine Houghton (Mrs. Hale); Stephen Mendillo (Ned Hale); Jay Goede (Denis Eady); George Woodard (Jotham); Deborah Ayer (Young Ruth Hale); Rob Campbell (Young Ned Hale); Burt Porter (Harmon Gow); Robert Nutt (Church Elder); Louise DeCormier (Mrs. Varnum); Edsel Hughes (Mr. Varnum); Patty Smith (Mrs. Homan); Tom Todoroff (Conductor 1910); Rusty De Wees and Paul Donlon (Men at Post Office); Darri Johnson (Customer at Eady Store); William Graves (Denis Eady's Father); Phil Garran (Mr. Howe); Virginia Smith (Mrs. Howe); Margie Vaughan (1st Young Woman); Joanne Rathgeb (1st Mother); Deborah Bremer (Funeral Woman); W. Clark Noyes and Howard Boardman (Men at Funeral); Gil Rood (Conductor); Dennis Mientka (Andrew Hale); David Dellinger (Minister); Kristin Collins, Annie C.Z. Nesson, and Sarah Yorra (Hale Party, Young Girls).

CHRISTIAN SCIENCE MONITOR, 3/12/93, p. 13, David Sterritt

Literary adaptations are back in style, and if you haven't noticed the trend, "Ethan Frome" is here to nudge your attention. Based on a 1911 novel by Edith Wharton, it's the latest in a string of recent films that take their stories, characters, and themes from well-known books that preceded them by decades or even centuries. Examples range from "The Last of the Mohicans" and "Of Mice and Men" to "The Lover" and "Malcolm X," not to mention "Bram Stoker's Dracula" and "The Muppet Christmas Carol."

The fact that a movie is based on a respected book doesn't mean it's a good movie, of course. Hollywood history is littered with low-grade adaptations of excellent novels and stories—and conversely, many a second-rate book has yielded a first-rate movie version.

ANNUAL

It has even been suggested that bad books make better movies, since filmmakers don't feel tied down by the original and can let their imaginations fly. Auteurs from Orson Welles to Alfred Hitchcock have made masterpieces from "Touch of Evil" to "Vertigo" based on novels that few spectators ever found reason to read.

Yet it's still heartening when American filmmakers turn to literary sources as they've been doing lately, since it proves that remakes and "high concept" gimmicks aren't all the industry is capable of nowadays. "Ethan Frome" is no groundbreaking film, but its arrival is a refreshing antidote to the big-budget emptiness that marked so many of the holiday season's releases.

The plot of "Ethan Frome" is lurid enough, in its austere and chilly way, to make a juicy-sounding movie project. The title character lives with his perpetually sick and dominating wife, Zeena, on a desolate New England farm. Into their home comes Zeena's young cousin, Mattie Silver, who captures Ethan's heart in a way he's never known before. Passion flares, but in this setting and among these people it's obviously doomed from the start. The climax is predictably tragic—leading to a denouement worthy of a B-movie melodrama in its hopelessness.

Wharton was being rather adventurous when she wrote this tale in the early years of the 20th century, flouting the advice of a professorial friend who warned her—overlooking scores of classics—that "no great work of literature has ever been based on illicit passion." Literary critic Alfred Kazin quotes this remark in an essay on "Ethan Frome" that stresses Wharton's fascination with "the risk and ultimate tragedy of the illicit, even though she usually treats it more as a matter of temptation than of actual behavior. She plunges directly into this feverish territory in "Ethan Frome," perhaps emboldened by the story's distance from the circumstances of her own life. The novel has undeniable power even if it lacks the subtlety of her most resonant writing.

As directed by John Madden, the movie version of "Ethan Frome" is crafted with a care and seriousness that suit the spirit of Wharton's book. The chief difference between reading the novel and watching the film is the sensory impact of the motion-picture screen, which gives an ironic visual beauty to the wintry atmosphere that broods over the home where Ethan works out his sad destiny. The movie's other chief contribution is a set of solid performances, most notably by Liam Neeson.

And now let's wait for the next Edith Wharton-based movie due in theaters soon: "The Age of Innocence," adapted from her extraordinary novel by director Martin Scorsese, in a radical change of pace from his usual contemporary concerns. Many movie lovers are breathless with anticipation.

FILMS IN REVIEW, 2/93, p. 53, Barbara Cramer

Rarely have characters been lifted from the pages of a book and set to film so faithfully and flawlessly: "He was a part of the mute melancholy landscape, owner of a failing sawmill in Starkfield." So began *Ethan Frome*, Edith Wharton's 1911 classic novella, a somber, tragic tale of wasted lives. So too begins this exquisitely rendered film, as those words are echoed in visual terms.

Told in flashback, it's a story of thwarted dreams and frustrated love, and the viewer expects the unhappy ending. But to director John Madden's credit, he sustains the tension and mystery of "why" and "how the tragedy came about up to the very last frame. Considering the subject matter, it's a formidable achievement. Seldom in recent memory has a movie so filled with sadness and heartbreak emerged as such an energizing, satisfying entertainment.

The setting is the New England village of Starkfield early in this century; a town defined by Calvinist stoicism and the amount of snowfall; where everyone says exactly what's on his self-righteous mind, and where private affairs are public domain.

The Fromes' misfortunes were common knowledge to everyone but Rev. Smith (Tate Donovan), the newly-arrived preacher from Boston. When he first sees Ethan (Liam Neeson), shuffling, lame and bent, along a desolate country road, he's curiously bothered. (Just who is that old, darkly wretched man, he wonders, with the anguish of the universe reflected in his every expression?) Gradually, as Smith becomes part of the insular community, the tale unfolds: of Ethan's loveless marriage to Zeena (Joan Allen) and his passion for their hired girl Mattie Silver (Patricia Arquette) who became the love of his life.

Like Job, Ethan never had much luck. Years before, just as he was set to move to Florida to study engineering, his mother became terminally ill and he was forced to stay home. Zeena, a distant cousin, moved in to help. After the funeral, out of a misguided sense of kinship and affection toward Zeena, Ethan made the decision he would live to regret. *Maybe if it'd been spring, it would have been different. But it was winter, so they married.* He was 25.

From the start, it was a disaster. Zeena, a self-indulgent harpy eight years his senior, is never well. After five years pass, ones filled with her interminable complaining, she sends for Mattie, a young girl from Connecticut without family and with only $50 from the sale of her old piano. *Mattie needed somewhere to live, Zeena needed someone to help, and so those three were brought together.*

Zeena treats her like an indentured servant, but Ethan thrives on Mattie's joy of life. It would be only a matter of time before the virtuous pair fall deeply in love. (Though that passion onscreen is implied rather than explicit, a powerful undercurrent of sexuality and eroticism pervades their moments together. It's electrifying.) Without divulging the film's stunning, harrowing conclusion, suffice to say there are obstacles blocking their dreams.

Ethan Frome is a high water mark for everyone involved, from Richard Nelson's carefully crafted adaptation to Bobby Bukowski's cinematography and lighting, so consciously influenced by the art of 17th Century French painter Georges De La Tour. Nothing seems left to chance. The movie has no padding. Life in Starkfield is created handsomely, with an economy in approach that only enhances the film's realism. You can feel the mid-winter chill and taste their hardscrabble existence. From scenario to staging, from music to lighting, everything meshes.

Best of all is the acting, altogether credible portrayals by a highly accomplished cast. Neeson (*Leap of Faith*) is unforgettable in the title role, as he grows from an earnest, vigorous young man into an older, severely ravaged one.

As his wife, Joan Allen (*Tucker*) sidesteps the obvious. Horrid as Zeena is—and she's perfectly awful—Allen elicits an understanding and sympathy for that miserable woman with a bile duct where her heart should be.

Completing the marital triangle, Patricia Arquette (*Wildflower*; and yes, she's the sister of actress Rosanna) brings an enchanting fragility and vulnerability to her role as the sweetly innocent Mattie. Without resorting to obvious cliches or wiles, she delicately blossoms before your eyes. Notable also is Katharine Houghton as the preacher's landlady and film's narrator, who knew them all before the trouble began.

Though filmmakers generally avoid such heartbreakers like the plague (they're usually unprofitable), this property was special. Aside from Wharton being the first woman to win a Pulitzer Prize (for *The Age of Innocence*), her novella has long been regarded a masterpiece of American literature. Over the years, many tried to bring it to the screen—MGM once, Warner Brothers twice, in the '40s with Gary Cooper and Bette Davis, and then again in the '50s, with Jane Wyman and Charlton Heston. None succeeded.

At present, Wharton seems to be supplanting E.M. Forster on the screen as the "in" novelist for the nineties. When *Ethan Frome* entered the public domain in 1989, four film companies announced plans to do it. (Disney commissioned director Martin Scorsese to develop a screenplay, but he deferred that to film *The Age of Innocence* her Pulitzer novel for Columbia, starring Michelle Pfeiffer and Daniel Day-Lewis, now in post-production and slated for release next fall.)

Of the group, the only one to stay with it—and ultimately succeed—was Lindsay Law, executive producer of American Playhouse. With colleague Stan Wlodkowski as producer, he turned Peacham, Vermont into *Ethan Frome*'s Starkfield; and after over 80 years—Edith Wharton's literary classic finally arrives on screen. It should become a screen classic as well.

LOS ANGELES TIMES, 3/12/93, Calendar/p. 14, Peter Rainer

Edith Wharton's 1911 novella "Ethan Frome" is a powerhouse downer. In little less than 200 pages, she conveys a sense of bleakness so complete that it borders on the sadistic. Wharton's finely limned sentences are deceptively decorous; she uses her sensitivities to spook you.

The movie that has been made from the novella, starring Liam Neeson as Ethan, has been a long time coming. Hollywood has been trying to film it for more than half a century. (Bette Davis and Gary Cooper, for example, were involved in an aborted project in the '40s.) It's easy to understand why "prestige"-minded movie producers might be attracted: The novel is a "classic" tragic love affair—rapturously desolate.

Ethan, whom we are first introduced to as a crippled man in his 50s, hobbles about his hometown of Starkfield, Mass., and keeps to himself. We move back in time to discover the source of his mute agony, He once had dreams of leaving the village to become an engineer but family circumstances held him down. His wife, Zeena, who cared for Ethan's ailing mother, has become an embittered hypochondriac. Zeena's distant cousin, Mattie, who arrives to help out the household, is such a fragile soul that Ethan falls desperately in love with her. Their fugitive moments together are wracked with doom because they recognize their passion is futureless. They can't conquer the fated circumstances of their lives.

This sort of thing can work as literature but as a movie, the relentless gloom and long, frozen stares and one-second-at-a-time pacing can make you a little batty. The characters in "Ethan Frome" are working out a kind of penance, and that feeling transfers to the audience. The moroseness we experience is meant to serve a higher cause.

Wharton may not have endorsed the spiritual benefits of despair but the filmmaker's, director John Madden and screenwriter Richard Nelson, certainly do.

As Ethan, Neeson first hobbles into view with a world-class limp—it's the kind of limp that can win you an Oscar. He's better in his pre-limp mode, in the flashback portion of the film. Neeson doesn't try for a star-turn, he wants to convey Ethan's banked longings, and if he's not totally successful, it's probably because the role is so lumpish and reactive, so full of thwarted emotions, that it never really allows the human being to emerge.

With Wharton, the three characters were so emblematic with grief that they (intentionally) never quite come to life. They have the gravity of hooded figures in a passion play. (When you read the book and imagine it as a movie, it calls up a slow, silent classic.) The movie (rated PG for thematic content) softens these sufferers and, in the case of Zeena, even works up a bit of sympathy for her severities. Joan Allen is such an extraordinarily subtle actress that Zeena's sickness comes across as a kind of last-ditch flirtation: it's her only way of securing Ethan's indulgence. Zeena in the movie seems less cruel than desperate; she's sick all right—soul sick.

As Mattie, Patricia Arquette lacks the ethereal fragility that one imagines from the book but her ruddy-cheeked ripeness doesn't seem out of place beside Neeson's long-boned frame. They have a transcendent pioneer ruggedness together. There's a lovely moment when she sings to Ethan and he's dumbstruck; he's stricken by the disparity between her winsome desire to please and the glum, boxed-in life he leads.

"Ethan Frome" needed a more poetic approach to keep it from descending into a dreary funk. Madden, a stage director who also worked for British television and American Playhouse (where this project originated), doesn't have a wide imaginative range. He's content to film the story in a straight-forward way that makes it seem less gruesome and creepy than it really is. Classic works of American literature are often weirder and more disturbing than the movies that are derived from them: what often survives in an adaptation of, say, Faulkner, Poe or James, is the bare bones of plot. What's missing from the films is the author's way of seeing.

"Ethan Frome" is so bare to begin with that it might have survived its transfer to the screen if the filmmakers had sought to express the lyricism in Wharton's stark, dark moodiness. Instead they opt for dank, dogged realism. You watch these people suffer without wanting to suffer right along with them.

NEW YORK POST, 3/12/93, p. 29, Jami Bernard

The way airplanes will not be showing the plane-crash movie "Alive" on their in-flight screens, Vermont probably won't be using "Ethan Frome" to boost tourism. Filmed there to portray the unforgiving winters of Starkfield, Mass., "Ethan Frome" features more snow and cold than "Nanook of the North."

Starkfield is a pretty good name for this town. Everywhere you look is hardship, poverty, plainness, lack of opportunity—and of course, snow. It never melts, never gives into spring. The stooped, beaten man named Ethan Frome would have broken his back working a lifetime even if he hadn't broken it another way.

The fabulous Liam Neeson plays the title character of the Edith Wharton book in which forbidden passions take a heavy toll. The picture's framing device is a youthful minister who gradually learns about the mysterious Ethan through a series of flashbacks to the final, desolate, "Jane Eyre"-like ending.

The viewer (or reader of the book) can view Ethan one of two ways—as a man whose own limitations cause the women around him to wither and sicken, or as a good, strong man saddled with a succession of neurasthenics who make his life a living hell. The movie version tends to take the latter view.

First Ethan cares for his sickly mother, with the help of his cousin Zeena (Joan Allen in a remarkably rigid, unforgiving performance). He marries Zeena less by choice than by the feeling he has no choice, and she turns into a replica of his mother, always ailing, complaining and bedridden.

When Zeena's own cousin, Mattie (Patricia Arquette) comes to live with the snowed-in couple, at first she seems sickly too, but gradually the bloom of youth and health upon her attract the hapless Ethan. But in an emotional and physical landscape where everything is blanketed over thickly, Ethan's feelings cannot come out of hibernation without hell to pay.

The acting is uniformly good, with Neeson's exaggerated bowshape a cruel reminder of the twisted passions of his character's youth.

Although I long for the days when unhappy or enigmatic endings were acceptable, "Ethan Frome" is so relentlessly downbeat and depressing you'll want to warm yourself by the fire. Just because it's based on a "classic" novel doesn't make it required viewing.

NEWSDAY, 3/12/93, Part II/p. 62, Jack Mathews

With all the handcuffs, hot wax and nipple clamps accompanying foreplay in movies these days, its refreshing to see a man lose his wits over a woman by the look of her in a new dress or by the scent of her hair. By simply being in her presence.

Of course, the title character of Edith Wharton's 1911 novella "Ethan Frome" was having his passion stirred at a time when a glimpse of stocking, as Cole Porter would say, was looked on as something shocking. The question now, as John Madden's supremely tasteful adaptation of Wharton's novel moves to the screen, is whether audiences accustomed to looking up women's skirts will respond to its dolefully reticent sexuality.

The casting of Liam Neeson as the sturdy Ethan and Patricia Arquette as his wife's spirited young cousin Mattie Silver aids the cause immensely. Neeson, who combines a powerful physical presence with an amazingly gentle manner, has more sex appeal wearing a farmer's grungy winter rags than Michael Douglas or Willem Dafoe have running around buck naked, and Arquette, Rosanna's more talented younger sister, has the ability to express complex emotions without uttering a word.

Their sympathetic styles are essential to Wharton's theme. "Ethan Frome" is a romantic tragedy about forbidden love among farm people in rural New England, and though there is more physical acting out between Ethan and Mattie in the film than Wharton could bring herself to imply, the story still gets its power from the furtive glances, the body language and the thick silences that express the characters' simmering internal passions.

The film's most remarkable scene, the best depiction of pure romantic tension you're likely to find in any film these days, comes when Ethan and Mattie are left alone for the first time, and spend an agonizing evening *resisting* their impulses. If we were in the age of interactive movies, where audiences could make these decisions, Ethan and Mattie would get a 98 percent "Go for it" rating. But all we can do now is ache for them.

"Ethan Frome" was an oddity for Wharton, an excursion into the mores of far simpler people than she knew growing up among the New York sophisticates who supplied the detail of most of her novels. But her concerns were the same in the New York of "Age of Innocence" as in the fictional Starkfield of "Ethan Frome"—the dignity and civility of individuals weighed against the moral and social pressures of their day.

In the turn-of-the-century setting of "Ethan Frome," restraint and sacrifice are greater virtues than sexual and emotional fulfillment, and the air crackles with the thunder of temptation. Ethan's problem, after his sick wife, Zeena (Joan Allen), asks Mattie to live with them and care for her, is not that he's in a bad marriage, and that he might have a better one. But that he's in a marriage, at all. Adultery has no mitigating circumstances.

Madden, and screenwriter Richard Nelson, have devised a rather clunky way of telling the story, as a flashback mystery. In the opening scene, we see a man badly crippled, hunched over as if his back had been snapped in two, and dragging a leg behind him that looks as heavy as a ball and chain.

The man is Ethan, and the town's new minister (Tate Donovan), who has just arrived by train, eyes him like a ripe soul to be saved. Riper still, when he notices that the Starkfield locals look at him as if he were their own worst memories. Driven as much by curiosity as by his calling, the minister hires the impoverished farmer as his coachman, for the handsome sum of 50 cents a week, and begins probing him for answers.

Finally, the minister's landlord (Katharine Houghton), fearing that Starkfield's lack of Christian charity will drive the reverend away, fills in for him, and for us, the tragic events that left Ethan Frome a crumpled mass. If you'll forgive Mrs. Hale the laconic pace—her story is too simple to be hurried—you'll be rewarded both by its emotional detail and its surprising punch line.

"Ethan Frome" is rated PG-13, for implied sensuality certainly. There is no nudity, profanity or violence. In 1911 Starkfield, it would have been banned.

NEWSWEEK, 3/15/93, p. 74, David Ansen

Edith Wharton, one of the greatest American novelists, is also one of the sexiest, which is not the least of the reasons filmmakers have been gobbling up her books for the screen. While we wait for the anticipated feast of Martin Scorsese's "The Age of Innocence," we have this American Playhouse production of her tragic love story *Ethan Frome*—a solid appetizer. Abandoning her usual New York high-society haunts, Wharton turned her exquisite eye on a doomed triangle amongst laconic 19th-century rural New Englanders. Ethan Frome (sensitive hunk du jour Liam Neeson), the strong, silent Massachusetts farmer, is trapped in a joyless marriage with his hypochondriacal distant cousin Zeena (Joan Allen) and falls in love with their spirited young housekeeper Mattie (Patricia Arquette).

Blanketed in New England snowdrifts, director John Madden's solid but somewhat prosaic film seems a little stiff in the joints at first. Screenwriter Richard Nelson's frame for the story, in which a young minister (Tate Donovan) tries to discover why the townsfolk shun the old, crippled Ethan, is little more than portentous drum rolling. But "Ethan Frome" blossoms when the two lovers, left alone in the house, spend their first evening together. In this erotically fraught sequence, charged with inarticulate longing, the long wintry months of repressed passion briefly, gloriously thaw. Neeson and Arquette have a touching, lovely chemistry, and Allen, drawn and haggard, makes Zeena a complex passive-aggressive figure. Once the love story kicks in, the steel trap of Wharton's narrative descends; no matter how well you know this tale, it still packs a wallop.

SIGHT AND SOUND, 7/94, p. 56, Stella Bruzzi

Winter. Reverend Smith arrives from Boston to take up his new position in the small Massachusetts town of Starkfield. On his way from the station, he passes a crippled man, Ethan Frome. The backwater farming community is reluctant to talk about Ethan and his wife Zeena, and after his first sermon, the disillusioned clergyman is on the point of packing his bags. To prevent him from leaving, Ruth Hale takes him to the Frome household and on the way recounts Ethan's story ... Ethan lives with his ailing mother and a distant cousin, Zeena, who looks after her. After his mother's death, Ethan and Zeena marry. But it is a loveless marriage, and Ethan, relinquishing his plans to study engineering, resigns himself to life looking after Zeena.

Zeena takes in an orphaned relative, young Mattie Silver, to help her. When the increasingly hypochondriac Zeena visits a specialist in a nearby town, Mattie and Ethan are left alone in the house overnight; they become lovers. Their joy turns to despair when Zeena returns home unexpectedly early. Sensing something, Zeena hires a girl to replace Mattie, insisting that she leave the next day. That night, Ethan goes to Mattie's room. The next day, Ethan drives Mattie to the station, buying her a keepsake hairpin on the way. As a final gesture, the two go tobogganing. Their sledge hits a tree, leaving both of them lying motionless in the snow ... Ruth and Reverend Smith arrive at Ethan's house. Ruth asks to see Zeena, and they are ushered in to find a woman lying in bed. Smith is astonished to discover that this is Mattie, attended by a frail but able-bodied Zeena.

In the other recent Edith Wharton adaptation, *The Age of Innocence*, fate and society conspire to prevent Countess Olenska and Newland Archer from consummating their relationship. *Ethan Frome* suggest that if the would-be lovers had actually met, the outcome would have been disastrous. The deformed, asymmetric figure of the older Ethan testifies to the perils of transgression in the conformist society of early twentieth-century East coast America. His tortured, debilitated frame lumbering across the snow is a grim symbol of guilt, repression and unvoiced pain.

We are offered no hope of enduring happiness—we know how Ethan ends up, so even the flashbacks are overshadowed by tragedy. Paradoxically, it's rather a relief to escape the restrained bonhomie of the early scenes, in which the congregation diverts Smith's concern for Ethan and poverty by plying him with tea and presenting him with a gaggle of marriageable girls. By contrast, the flashback is something of a liberation. Ethan's emerging love for Mattie is lovingly and lingeringly charted—as when he peeks in at her dancing with a luckless suitor and quietly turns away in bemused jealousy.

The film hinges, inevitably, on a disproportionately long sequence when Zeena is away visiting her doctor, the only night that Ethan and Mattie spend alone. Oddly, the moment of recognition and fulfilment—when Mattie's bedroom door creeps open and Ethan enters to kiss her—is an anticlimax, cut abruptly away from to the jollity of the following day. Up to this point, the suppressed attraction between the two has been expressed through a series of veiled mundanities—Ethan complimenting Mattie on her cooking, Mattie crying over a smashed dish. As if playing at being husband and wife, Ethan lights an after-dinner pipe while Mattie takes up her sewing. The scene is both poignant and faintly ridiculous.

This use of small gestures to convey large emotions is ultimately inadequate for getting across the intensity of the characters' feelings—but perhaps this is the point. After all, Ethan and Mattie snatch only a few hours of intimacy before Zeena returns. *Ethan Frome* is a bleak story, its pessimism not alleviated by the relentless pace of the adaptation. The acting, editing and camerawork follow in the same resigned footsteps towards the catastrophic denouement.

In order for the audience to feel loss, there needs to be a more positive and engaging sense of what might have been than is offered here. *Ethan Frome* doggedly suggests that it could not be any other way, closing with Ethan dragging his useless leg behind him like a burden. This is the nemesis meted out to those who seize the day and live to face the consequences: no cathartic release, just drudgery and memories of the past.

VILLAGE VOICE, 3/16/93, p. 54, Georgia Brown

Given the rule of thumb for adaptations—trashy books make the better movies—you wonder why anyone adapts even a minor classic. (Please don't offer me *Howards End* as an exception.) When I heard *Ethan Frome* was coming soon, I thought maybe someone was aiming to capture something like a Monarch Notes video market: with *Ethan Frome* plus *Of Mice and Men*, two are down in *Silas Marner* to go. How else explain that when rights to *Ethan Frome* passed into the public domain in 1989, something like four companies raced to begin production? Even Martin Scorsese considered directing it until settling on Wharton's *The Age of Innocence* instead.

Like many others, I imagine, I've harbored a long-standing aversion to this little 1911 text, so that rereading it now feels like a revelation. I have come to tell you that despite Lionel Trilling's crabby verdict ("not a great book or even a fine book, but a factitious book, perhaps even a cruel book"), *Ethan Frome* is actually a gripping page-turner with a firm, Simenon-like grasp on human behavior.

The grisly, gothic tale centers on Ethan, a loner with a spooky repetition compulsion: turning successive loved ones, beginning with his mother, from pleasant nurturers into ugly, quarrelsome, dependent invalids. And while periodically wrecking the thing he loves, Ethan retains the sympathy and awe of spectators (readers) by spectacularly wrecking himself as well. One of the book's eeriest effects comes from the silent intercourse between the living and their counterparts lying beneath the town's ubiquitous tombstones. This is a land that never thaws. *Ethan Frome* also grimly describes a quintessential duel between American men and women. The novel's final clause, "the women have got to hold their tongues," seems to come as a dire warning from a woman writer who barely escaped the common fate.

Screenwriter Richard Nelson (nominated for a Tony Award for *Two Shakespearean Actors*) adapts Wharton's book with no particular felicity. He changes the story's narrator from an engineer (who works, significantly, for a *power* company) stuck in the desolate rural area for the winter into the town's new minister fresh up from Boston. The earnest, boyish Reverend Smith (Tate Donovan) is a recognizable type: the well-meaning meddler plopped into a situation he can't comprehend. Struck by the spectacularly maimed Ethan, Smith sees a potential beneficiary of his charity. He reproaches his parishioners for avoiding Frome and even starts packing his bags in a fit of pique. (Not much sticking power here!) Lost in this change is Wharton's conception of the narrator observing a shadow self, sensing in Ethan (a former engineering student) a deadly, almost physical pull toward inertia.

Directed by John Madden, the movie opens with Liam Neeson bent sideways in a C-curve, dragging across an icy clearing. In Darkman mode, Neeson projects the pathos of a powerful man rendered helpless by a secret wound and committed to isolation. Like the book, the movie is mostly flashback—telling how Ethan got this way—with a revelatory shock coming at the end. The flashback begins many years earlier when Ethan's mother dies and he marries his cousin, Zenobia, or Zeena (Joan Allen), who had come to care for her. But quickly Zeena herself turns petulant and neurasthenic and in turn hires her own young cousin, Mattie Silver (Patricia Arquette). Arquette is especially winning as the pretty but rather confused Mattie, whose vivacity quickly attracts Ethan. Several awkward, tentative scenes, where she and Ethan inarticulately grope toward declarations, are very compelling. But the modest movie itself is not, over all. There's no vision here besides a tepid respect for a classic, and so when the climax comes, it's neither thrilling nor devastating. Sadly, the movie has the look and feel of an American Playhouse production, which it is.

It may be worth noting how chilling Wharton's portrait of a doomed ménage à trois is compared to the one in *The Last Days of Chez Nous*, where everyone ends up putatively better off, even though their solutions are self-deceived all around. (In *Chez Nous* too, a husband abandons his wife for her younger, dancing sister, while the older woman broods about her shrewish disposition.) Trilling blamed *Ethan Frome*'s critical popularity on the accident of its appearance in an age when literature was relentlessly sunny. Well, there's lots to be said today for a properly cruel ending.

Also reviewed in:
CHICAGO TRIBUNE, 3/12/93, Friday/p. I, Clifford Terry
NEW REPUBLIC, 4/12/93, p. 28, Stanley Kauffmann
NEW YORK TIMES, 3/12/93, p. C8, Vincent Canby
NEW YORKER, 3/29/93, p. 103, Anthony Lane
VARIETY, 1/18/93, p. 78, Todd McCarthy
WASHINGTON POST, 3/19/93, p. F7, Rita Kempley

EXECUTION PROTOCOL, THE

A First Run Features release of a Worldview Pictures/West End Films production. *Executive Producer:* Paul Baker. *Producer:* Stephen Trombley and Mitch Wood. *Director:* Stephen Trombley. *Director of Photography:* Paul Gibson. *Editor:* Peter Miller. *Music:* Robert Lockhart. *Sound:* John McCormack. *Running time:* 90 minutes. *MPAA Rating:* Not Rated.

NEW YORK POST, 4/28/93, p. 28, Jami Bernard

In the documentary "The Execution Protocol," you'll learn more than you ever wanted to know about the lethal injection machine that is used to send Missouri death-row convicts to their final reward, or lack thereof.

"The Execution Protocol" is a systematic look at the process by which the Potosi Correctional Center executes its mission—to house, and occasionally kill, convicted murderers who have drawn death sentences. Director Stephen Trombley uses interviews with both prison officials and a few well-spoken prisoners to create a grim portrait of an ecosystem behind the prison walls, where one type of murderer patrols another type of murderer with the sanction of the state—or so Trombley sees it.

"Issue" documentaries cannot help having a point of view, and Trombley's is against capital punishment. His case is not made so firmly that it will win over the fence-sitters, yet everyone can have a good laugh at the expense of the pompous prison officials, like the warden who always looks like he's smiling even when he's discussing how to kill a man by the book.

Of the hundreds of inmates at Trombley's disposal, he chose three extraordinarily rational-seeming ones who wisely stick to issues like legal and ethical rights rather than referring back to the grisly crimes that put them in prison stripes in the first place.

Yet whenever they discuss the emotional strain of living under a death sentence, or not being able to see their wives and children again, or the inanity of getting a medical checkup before being killed, it's impossible not to wonder how many of these rights they had afforded their own victims.

Trombley takes a clinical, almost cerebral approach to the subject—which may not be the best way to win converts in this emotional issue, if that was his aim. His main point seems to be that the government has no legal or moral credentials to be in the killing business, and that it should face up to the hypocrisy.

And then there's the machine, which takes a starring role. Trombley loads his documentary with portentous portraits of the sterile-looking machine, underscored with even more portentous music.

The three-step injection process—which first sedates the prisoner before killing him, and through its complexities allows the machine's operators to escape personal culpability—is the perfect objective correlative for the lumbering prison bureaucracy that employs it and constantly frets over its efficiency. Some of the more gruesomely funny scenes involve staff meetings where the officials attempt to revise the minutiae of the procedures.

A bizarre interview with the mild-mannered man who invented the machine—he brings the camera crew down to his basement to inspect the device—concentrates on the instrument's technicalities without any mention of the cosmic dimension of its purpose.

Trombley could have taken a page from Lily Tomlin, who in her one-woman Broadway show (and movie) pointed back and forth from a Warhol poster to the real thing, saying, "Soup ... art! Soup ... art!" Trombley could have juxtaposed images of the injection machine with that of a handgun, since that is the effect he is trying to pull off, with only middling results.

NEWSDAY, 4/28/93, Part II/p. 57, Jack Mathews

According to recent polls, more than 70 percent of Americans support capital punishment, and British filmmaker Stephen Trombley's "Execution Protocol," a documentary that equates Missouri's lethal injection system with torture and premeditated murder, isn't likely to change a single mind.

It's not that Trombley doesn't make a case. The prison officials at Potosi Correctional Center, where the 16-mm. film was shot, are so clinically matter-of-fact about the killing machine they use to carry out executions they send chills up your spine, and the psychological horror of living under a death sentence comes through with painful clarity in interviews with condemned men.

But the notion that showing people the equipment and the by-the-book procedures used in carrying out the death penalty will somehow turn them against it is naive. And no one on the yes side of the capital punishment issue will miss the fact that Trombley purposely omits the nature of the murders committed by his interview subjects, lest they be abstracting.

"Execution Protocol" is itself so emotionally cold, so methodical in its presentation that it has the impact of a feature in Popular Mechanics. Yes, there is grisly fascination in seeing exactly how a programmed stainless steel machine feeds three potent drugs—one to anesthetize, one to paralyze, one to finalize—into a tube that leads from one room into another, and finally into a vein, causing the death of a human being.

However, we don't see a person executed, or even prepared for it. None of the three condemned men (of 77 on Potosi's death row) interviewed on camera had an execution date, though one of them tells us what it was like to have come within three hours of being strapped down before a reprieve came through.

If the subject wasn't so profoundly disturbing, "Execution Protocol" would be as dull as a tour through a smelting plant. We spend most of our time listening to prison officials explain that they're just doing their jobs, or to a prison chaplain justifying executions with his own hand-picked biblical citations. We meet the designer of the injection apparatus, who runs us through its features as if it were a laptop computer, and the dispassionate prison doctor, who reveals the ingredients of the killing machine's secret sauce.

The only thing like a sensible debate on the issue of the death penalty is provided by the men condemned to it, and their argument—that the punishment does not fit the crime—is rendered moot by our ignorance of the crimes.

In the final section, Trombley abandons his neutral approach and, to Robert Lockhart's abominably heavy-handed musical score, carries out a mock execution, cutting back and forth from a ticking clock and a pulsating electrocardiogram printout to the whining and thumping of the injector. Flat line, fade to black.

Included in the press materials for "Execution Protocol" were letters from Amnesty International, endorsing it as an educational tool in the fight against capital punishment, and from the Missouri Department of Corrections, which apparently plans to use it as a training film.

I'd call that a tie.

VILLAGE VOICE, 5/4/93, p. 61, Jimmie Briggs

"You cannot commit a clean murder. It's impossible." So says Joe, #CP48, a seven-year resident of death row at Potosi Correctional Center in Southern Missouri. Promoted as a "real-life horror film," *Execution Protocol* presumes to take viewers on a 90-minute descent into the American justice system's "clean murders."

The title draws its name from the Missouri Protocol, guidelines for carrying out capital punishment designed to ease the burden of responsibility of those doing the job by breaking it down into an assembly line of smaller tasks. One of the assistant superintendents at Potosi describes capital punishment as a "nonconsumptive industry" that has been a boon for the economically depressed area in which he works.

Stringing together a compilation of interviews with inmates and prison personnel, as well as lingering shots of the Leuchter Lethal Injection Machine, Stephen Trombley's bleak, humorless documentary traces the events leading up to a death-row inmate's execution with striking restraint except for an overbearing, creepy score, which sounds like it's out of some dated slasher film.

What is most interesting about the film is what it doesn't say. The "execution technologist" who speaks in several brief moments in the film, Fred Leuchter, is none other than the author of *The Leuchter Report*, which stated that there were no gas chambers used in the Holocaust, and who has assisted in the defense of right-wing wacko Ernst Zundel. Leuchter has a virtual monopoly on supplying equipment and training for executions throughout the United States.

Also reviewed in:
NATION, 5/17/93, p. 676, Stuart Klawans
NEW YORK TIMES, 4/28/93, p. C13, Vincent Canby
VARIETY, 11/23/92, p. 51, Derek Elley

FALLING DOWN

A Warner Bros. release in association with Le Studio Canal +, Regency Enterprises, and Alcor Films. *Executive Producer:* Arnon Milchan. *Producer:* Arnold Kopelson, Herschel Weingrod, and Timothy Harris. *Director:* Joel Schumacher. *Screenplay:* Ebbe Roe Smith. *Director of Photography:* Andrzej Bartkowiak. *Editor:* Paul Hirsch. *Music:* James Newton Howard. *Music Editor:* Jim Weidman. *Sound:* David MacMillan and (music) Shawn Murphy. *Sound Editor:* Charles L. Campbell and Louis L. Edeman. *Casting:* Marion Dougherty. *Production Designer:* Barbara Ling. *Art Director:* Larry Fulton. *Set Designer:* Jann K. Engel and Brad Ricker. *Set Decorator:* Cricket Rowland. *Special Effects:* Matt Sweeney. *Costumes:* Marlene

Stewart. *Make-up:* Tom Lucas and Steve Abrums. *Stunt Coordinator:* Michael Runyard.
Running time: 112 minutes. *MPAA Rating:* R.

CAST: Michael Douglas (D-Fens); Robert Duvall (Prendergast); Barbara Hershey (Beth);
Rachel Ticotin (Sandra); Tuesday Weld (Mrs. Prendergast); Frederic Forrest (Surplus Store
Owner); Lois Smith (D-Fen's Mother); Joey Hope Singer (Adele, Beth's Child); Ebbe Roe
Smith (Guy on Freeway); Michael Paul Chan (Mr. Lee); Raymond J. Barry (Captain Yardley);
D.W. Moffett (Detective Lydecker); Steve Park (Detective Brian); Kimberly Scott (Detective
Jones); James Keane (Detective Keene); Macon McCalman (Detective Graham); Richard
Montoya (Detective Sanchez); Bruce Beatty (Police Clerk); Mathew Saks (Officer at Station);
Agustin Rodriguez (Gang Member One); Eddie Frias (Gang Member Two); Pat Romano
(Gang Member Three); Fabio Urena (Gang Member Four); Karina Arroyave (Angie); Irene
Olga Lopez (Angie's Mother); Benjamin Mouton (Uniformed Officer at Beth's); Dean Hallo
(Uniformed Officer's Partner); James Morrison (Construction Sign Man by Bus Stop); John
Fleck (Seedy Guy in Park); Brent Hinkley (Rick, Whammyburger); Dedee Pfeiffer (Sheila,
Whammyburger); Carol Androsky (Woman Who Throws Up); Margaret Medina (Lita the
Waitress); Vondie Curtis-Hall (Not Economically Viable Man); Mark Frank (Annoying Man
at Phone Booth); Peter Radon (First Gay Man); Spencer Rochfort (Second Gay Man); Carole
Ita White (Second Officer at Beth's); Russell Curry (Second Officer's Partner); John Fink
(Guy Behind Woman Driver); Jack Kehoe (Street Worker); Valentino D. Harrison (Kid With
Missile Launcher); Jack Betts (Frank, Golfer); Al Mancini (Jim, Golfer); John Diehl (Dad,
Back Yard Party); Amy Morton (Mom, Back Yard Party); Abbey Barthel (Trina, Back Yard
Party); Susie Singer (Suzie the Stripper); Wayne Duvall (Paramedic); Valisha Jean Malin
(Prendergast's Daughter).

CHRISTIAN SCIENCE MONITOR, 3/1/93, p. 13, David Sterritt

"Falling Down" begins with a traffic jam. And our hero, played by Michael Douglas, is stuck
in it. His name is William Foster, although he's sometimes called "D-FENS" after his vanity
license plate, and the movie's promotion has latched onto this as a way of making the story sound
even more macho and exploitative than it is.

Bill is an ordinary guy with ordinary problems—like a broken marriage and a layoff from his
job—until that traffic jam touches off extraordinary anger. He abandons his car and heads for
home on foot, getting into fights with all kinds of irritating people along the way. It's a crazy
thing to do, and sure enough, Bill appears to have lost his mind.

But has he really? Or could it be that his current difficulties have simply put him under too
much stress? Or maybe—just maybe—his explosive condition could be considered a reasonable
response to the malfunctions in today's society?

One problem with "Falling Down" is that it never makes up its mind what Bill's problem is.
If the movie had selected one set of motivations for his behavior (or integrated *all* the motivations
into a lucid and logical whole), it might have amounted to a clever analysis of a troubled
personality, or a poignant lament for a broken family, or a telling indictment of city life.

As it stands, though, the picture is a jumble, willing to spice its story with anything good for
a momentary thrill.

It's also a distasteful jumble that stirs up the worst instincts of its audience by heaping abuse
on Bill, encouraging us to identify with him, then prodding us to enjoy his bursts of venom and
violence. After all, the movie constantly hints, he's not *half* as bad as the people who keep
irritating him.

Especially revealing about the film's lack of goodwill is the fact that many of its villains fit
stereotypes right out of Hollywood's most racist and xenophobic mold. From a Korean
storekeeper to Hispanic gang members, Bill's most memorable enemies are nonwhites with
"funny" accents and hostile attitudes; even a homophobic anti-Semite who tries to befriend him
is inspired by Hitler and "foreign" sources.

The movie offers token "balance" by including a smart Hispanic woman and a likable Japanese
man among the cops who eventually track Bill down. But in most theaters, these "normal"
characters won't erase the fearful and derisive responses the villains are designed to provoke from
audiences.

Bill himself isn't overloaded with good instincts, for that matter. Once his adventure has begun, it takes very little to set him off on some kind of rampage. But the movie does pile terrible provocations on the poor fellow to make it easier for us to sympathize with him. Hispanic thugs, scary panhandlers, pushy construction workers, and other creeps are typical inhabitants of today's urban scene, the movie tells us, and they'd push *anyone* over the edge.

And of course Bill has individual problems, from his wife's hostility to his lack of employment. Perhaps we're meant to think of these as sad reflections of society's deep malaise, but again, the movie doesn't make any such point in a clear and coherent way. In the end, it just wants to stir up a ruckus on the screen and in the emotional responses of moviegoers.

Its attempt to pass itself off as social criticism is far from convincing, and makes the whole project seem completely cynical.

"Falling Down" has a few ingredients worth praising. These include thought performances by Barbara Hershey and Tuesday Weld as the wives of the main characters; Rachel Ticotin as the Hispanic cop; and especially Robert Duvall as the police officer who realizes there's a method to Bill's madness.

Even here, though, the movie can't suppress its mean-spiritedness. At the preview screening I attended, the most applause came when Duvall's character stands up to his obviously troubled wife by telling her to shut up and cook supper. Add sexism to the movie's list of moral failings.

CINEASTE, Vol. XX, No. 1, 1993, p. 39, Tom Doherty

The leisurely long take zeroes in on a man's face—tight mouth, eyes encased behind nerdy eyeglasses, droplets of sweat on his nose and forehead, vertical tufts of a really bad haircut. Veering around to assume his point of view—from the driver's seat of a late model, limited legroom automobile, stuck in the gridlock purgatory of an on-ramp traffic jam—the camera scans the sights in his immediate field of vision. Amidst a soundtrack of car horns and hot curses from frazzled, frustrated motorists, he spies two in-your-face bumper stickers ("He Died for Your Sins" and "How Am I Driving! Dial 1-800-EAT SHIT"), a Garfield suction doll leering like a gargoyle from behind a windshield, and a busload of squealing, repellent kids. By the time the camera completes its 360-degree track and swings back around on the man behind the wheel—bedeviled now by a persistent fly buzzing about a shabby interior with busted air conditioning and broken window—any act of senseless violence suddenly makes perfect sense.

Joel Schumacher's *Falling Down*, from a pissed-off screenplay by Ebbe Roe Smith, is a film in the grand demagogic tradition of *Dirty Harry, Death Wish, Walking Tall, First Blood* and *Thelma & Louise*. The evil twin to earnest left coast liberalism, Hollywood's vigilante strain—agitpopulism?—burrows directly into the animal brainstem of American culture. No less than talk radio or grassroots uprisings, the agitprop genre expresses the deep-seated discontent of a disenfranchised demos. Listening to the war whoops of encouragement from audiences in the throes of vicarious retribution, one can't help but appreciate how much more full-throated they sound against the clucks of concern from editorialists in defense of due process. As Aristotelian catharsis or incitement to riot, social barometer or gasoline on the fire, such films are really quite breathtaking in their way.

The title alone indicates that *Falling Down* is more deeply deranged and hopelessly disturbed than its take-no-prisoners predecessors. The anger it vents really isn't against anything so specific as Miranda warnings, multiethnic sociopaths, duplicitous bureaucrats, or redneck rapists. Its gripe is against the whole human condition, or at least the human condition as lived in the nation's second largest metropolis. A trend setter in psychosis as well as style, LA breeds its own line of crazies with suicidal tendencies. Against the laser-beam focus of New York maniac violence, the LA breakdown seems more diffused and existential, a West Coast vibe best summed up in the succinct explanation offered by that California girl whose murderous rampage at high school one morning was immortalized by the Boomtown Rats: "I don't like Mondays."

Michael Douglas plays the flipped out motorist who chucks it all in and sets off on a deliberate rampage through the greater LA area. His representative status and vehicular affinities are underscored by the vanity license plate which becomes his monicker: D-FENS. Ostensibly D-FENS wants to get back home, patch things up with his ex-wife Elizabeth (Barbara Hershey), celebrate his daughter's birthday party, and restore the nuclear family triad. In reality, that end is but the means to cut a swath through the dysfunctional infrastructure, human and architectural, of urban life.

While D-FENS is walking amok, a parallel life via parallel editing finds retiring policeman Prendergast (Robert Duvall), a henpecked cop on his last day on the job, putting the puzzling pieces of the one-man crime wave together as his menopausal harpy of a wife (Tuesday Weld) nags him about skinless chicken and Kitty Litter. Save for his affectionate female partner, Sandra (Rachel Ticotin), the cops at the station house are a notably unsupportive and obnoxious crew. In truth, Prendergast seems to have every bit as much reason to go off the deep end as D-FENS. His sane decency is a cross-cut juxtaposition to his quarry's seething anger, but since he's knee-deep in just the kind of crap that D-FENS is blasting out of—bad home life, rotten job, the very same traffic jam—it is the cop, not the criminal, who seems pathetic and deranged.

As Schumacher and Smith see it, to live and die in LA is to experience an endless run of days of the locusts. The Sixties Shangrila of sun, fun, and blonde-bedecked T-Birds has assumed the mantle of America's iconic urban hellhole, a title New York once had locked up. The landscape is homegrown Calcutta-graffitied walls, boarded-up shops and going out of business sales, sidewalks strewn with the homeless and the hapless. In Lawrence Kasdan's Grand Canyon two men reach across the boundaries of race and class to agree that the City of the Angels is an apt metaphor for apocalypse now. "This neighborhood has gone to shit," says one. "This country has gone to shit," corrects the other.

Schumacher gives El Lay no quarter. His widescreen compositions hug the horizontal space of a city picture—imperfect for the Panavision frame, a blighted landscape of steamy asphalt and steel panels, a Third World trenchtown with no productivity, no community, no hope, graffiti-ridden, squalid, fetid, laden with exhaust fumes that ride waves of heat and give the atmosphere a smothering weight and density. Set during one of those sizzling, oppressive summer days when justifiable homicide greets the next comment about heat and humidity, Falling Down is surely the most socio-politico-meteorologically uncomfortable film since Do the Right Thing.

Contributing to the Saharan atmospherics is the fact that D-FENS goes through his paces on foot, that most aberrant mode of transportation through LA. In his daylong hegira crisscrossing southwest through South Central, Hollywood, and Beverly Hills to reach the beach at Venice, he is almost heroic in his ambulatory stature, incongruous in his dogged pedestrian determination to get home. The quality of classical tragedy imbues the odyssey: the unity of time and place in a morning-to-dusk diurnal journey, dead reckoning his way through a pavement wasteland. The final destination would be Venice—the cynosure of Old World decrepitude, reborn in the New World, now as broken down and corrupt as its parent.

Falling Down sprays its automatic fire-power wide and far, with no names on the bullets, but that doesn't mean the casualty rate is distributed evenly. D-FENS's targets are a Korean grocer, Latino thugs, toothy food service workers, foul-mouthed passersby, neofascist swine, pushy panhandlers, potbellied construction workers, geriatric duffers, and a family of hapless barbecuers. The list checks off a fair sampling of white collar, white male hate objects and the vigilante vignettes serve up goodly portions of rabble-rousing raw meat. The pièce de résistance occurs in a Whammy Burger joint where, refused breakfast at 11:33 a.m., D-FENS pulls out an M-10 from his gym bag and demands service from sparkly manager Rick and smart-ass counter girl Sheila. (What is it about fast food restaurants—cf. Five Easy Pieces—that so angers the Hollywood elite? No reserved seating!) Another satisfying set piece finds D-FENS driving a septuagenarian golfer into cardiac arrest ("Now you're gonna die wearing that stupid little hat!," he gloats), a deliciously nasty sop to working stiff boomers resentful at subsidizing the social security of leisure class retirees.

Falling Down is equally wily about the groups it exempts from D-FENSive aggression. Although a video-smark black youngster helpfully tutors D-FENS in the care and operation of a bazooka, African-Americans never walk into his cross hairs—a cagey agitprop strategy reminiscent of the moment in Walking Tall when a Deep South sheriff approaches a black man with seeming hatred, only to embrace him as a boon companion. One likely reason Falling Down played so well in urban action centers is that it taps into not just white male anger but also African-American animosities toward other stripes of the rainbow coalition. In fact, black and white can share a common interracial bond of racist loathing against linguistically challenged Korean-American shopkeepers and Uzi-toting Chicano gang bangers, through for one half of the audience the two ethnic targets can also serve as surrogates, a shade removed, for loathing of the other half.

Likewise, D-FENS refuses to bash another group with a high sensitivity to media portrayals and a low boiling point, gay Americans. When the manager of an Army Navy surplus store rails at his "fag" customers, D-FENS reacts with disgust to the presumption of manly, Aryan kinship. "You're not like me," he says to the nativist nabob (played by Frederic Forrest, seemingly in the grip of post-traumatic stress from *Apolcalypse Now*). "I'm an American. You're a sick asshole." As if to say: 'I am no born-to-lose white trash—I am an avatar of responsible middle class rage.' Part of this is just cynical calculation, a device to bind the spectator closer to D-FENS by keeping him just this side of beyond-the-pale loony. Yet the neo-Nazi at least has a target for his venom. D-FENS will fire at anything that cuts across his bow.

The historical resonance of D-FENS's destruction is a game of connect the dots: *fin de siècle* America spelling finis to the average American Joe in the not-so-gay Nineties. As a leading economic indicator, D-FENS incarnates Perotista rage at the decline of high wage manufacturing jobs linked to the defense industry in post Cold War America. Set in relief against the rising expectations of the world of their fathers, the limited options and lost control of white-collared white men make for a wrenchingly painful acquaintance with cultural marginalization.

Hence the alternating euphoria and torment in this tale of a lifelong rule-player and clock-puncher savoring his spontaneous deviance ("I'm having a really rare morning") and yet bewildered at the moral turn-about ("I'm the bad guy!"). For the really dense spectator, the film provides a visible signpost: a black man—D-FENS's doppelganger in a matching white shirt and tie—pickets a bank with a sign that says "Not Economically Viable." Taken away by the police, the protester fixes his gaze on his alter ego and intones, "Remember me."

Assuring an unforgettable memory of its own, *Falling Down* locks the spectator into a point of view death grip. The film is packed with crisp, admiring shots of the protagonist—in low angle close-up, surveying a road construction site; in long shot, walking across country club greenery like the angel of death. To take another example: at the beginning of the film, D-FENS walks into a Korean grocery seeking change for a phone call. The shopkeeper tells him to buy a soda. He strides over to the freezer and opens the door. The patented UCLA Film School reverse-angle shot from inside the freezer shows D-FENS clutching a Coke can to his head, to relieve the heat and his headache, as the refrigeration hums on the soundtrack conjure his interior sensorium. Ironically, detailed craftwork is evident everywhere in the film, especially in the supporting roles and minor bits. Hollywood is *still* one West Coast industry that manufactures a product where Made in the U.S.A. is the mark of quality control and world class value. It makes one proud to be an American, even if the Japanese are holding the studio purse strings.

As D-FENS's arsenal escalates—from baseball bat to switchblade to automatic weapons to bazooka—the level of his anger intensifies. Having enticed spectators into identification with the mad avenger, Schumacher presumably intends participant observers to fall away from the vigilante posse at some point, as the true depth of D-FENS's derangement becomes clear, as the estranged husband, devoted father, and beset Everyman exposes himself as a trigger-happy stalker and abusive father. But once the blood is up, once cinema has locked and loaded ninety minutes worth of spectator identification, it's difficult not to go along for the full ride, to partake of the sheer adrenaline rush of letting off steam and blowing all circuits, the palpable enjoyment of savoring, with the protagonist, that oh-so-rare morning when everything is permissible. The climax of *Falling Down*, the end of the road for D-FENS, evokes *Dirty Harry*, with the perpetrator floating in the water, shot by a cop in a final *mano a mano* faceoff, his harmless water pistol floating beside him, shooting blanks, his wad shot, followed to the very end, right off the pier into his death in Venice.

FILMS IN REVIEW, 6/93, p. 186, Edmond Grant

These days "responsible" moviemakers can't bear to leave us alone with an anti-hero. Rather than place us squarely in the mind of an unhinged character, mainstream Hollywood now feels that when making a movie about the nature of violence, it's not enough to simply show the chaos and carnage it causes—you've got to add perspective.

Falling Down is a case study in this sort of narrative compromise. Scripter Ebbe Roe Smith and director Joel Schumacher clearly felt uncomfortable remaining focused on their antihero, a white, middle class man (Michael Douglas) who goes berserk while "just trying to get home" from Los Angeles to Venice, Calif. So we have a second protagonist, a lovable, upstanding, white middle-class cop on his last full day on the job (Robert Duvall).

The film is deeply disturbing at times and oddly moving at others, but its central source of fascination proves to be its weirdly uneven tone, which swings from black comedy to realistic contempo-tragedy to an almost self-righteous explanation of William Foster's psychological background. Foster is Douglas's character, who's been fired and blows a gasket on the way home. It begins with a killer traffic jam, and is helped along by a succession of high stress urban encounters. Eventually, we begin to suspect that D-FENS (Foster's personalized license plate, and the nickname eventually given him by Duvall's character) is seeking out potentially explosive situations on the way to his stated goal: his daughter's birthday party (his estranged ex-wife, played by Barbara Hershey, and his little girl find this an unhappy surprise). With the introduction of certain details about his past (he abused said ex-wife, acted strangely in recent weeks around his mother, and is a Viet-vet, naturally), it becomes apparent that D-FENS isn't intended as a positive figure, but there's no denying that the film is primarily constructed like a comedy (a sort of darker version of *The Out-of-Towners'* disaster upon disaster structure), and that we're supposed to identify with, and enjoy, his actions: "rolling back the prices" at a deli; mouthing off to volatile streetscum; making sure his meal is served "his way" at a fast-food burger joint. Every so often, however, the picture confronts the dramatic fact that he's terrorizing innocent bystanders as he goes about his righteous rampage. Smith and Schumacher do add additional perspective on his condition by showing that he is not alone in his outrage (via a protesting black man who's literally his mirror image).

On the acting side, it's refreshing to see Douglas discarding the preening quality that distinguished his recent performances (and off-screen interviews) for a bittersweet sense of confusion and loss. The ever-impeccable Duvall makes his comforting stick-figure character as real as possible; even during the final faceoff, which the film envisions as a showdown between separate sides of white middle-class manhood.

A final note: given the catalogue of contemporary ills depicted in the picture, and the circumstances under which it can be viewed, there seems one major exclusion from Douglas' lethal encounters: the scene in which he makes talkative multiplex moviegoers shut up during the feature.

LOS ANGELES TIMES, 2/26/93, Calendar/p. 1, Kenneth Turan

It all starts with a fly. A fly buzzing around in a car with failing air-conditioning and non-functioning windows, stuck on the L.A. freeways in the Mother of All Traffic Jams on the hottest day of the year. If this sounds like a setup, you're beginning to get the picture.

There is a man inside the car, an ostentatiously average citizen with a white shirt and tie, brush haircut and clunky glasses, even a pen shield in his shirt pocket and a patriotic "D-Fens" personalized license plate. The heat, the traffic, the fly, the futility of his no doubt miserable life, everything combines to overwhelm the man, and as "Falling Down" opens, he abandons his car, "announces "I'm going home," and starts to walk away from it all.

This, you may be sure, is not fated to be an ordinary walk. For as D-Fens (Michael Douglas with a scowl surgically implanted on his face) heads west toward the ocean, he embarks on a Cook's Tour of urban decay, progressively experiencing every insult and indignity known to modern man. But passive no more, in fact Everyman turned Terminator, he gives as good as he gets, wreaking vengeance for the slights of a lifetime on anyone who has the temerity to get in his way.

As written by Ebbe Roe Smith and directed by Joel Schumacher, "Falling Down" is more than anything else a greedy picture. Charles Bronson's "Death Wish" with a bogus social conscience, it is eager to have things both ways, to spinelessly pander to a mass audience on the one hand while piously calling attention to pressing urban problems on the other.

The first person D-Fens meets, for instance, is a surly grocer who not only doesn't have the decency to give him change to make a phone call, but also has shamelessly overpriced everything in his convenience store and is a pain in the neck in the bargain. But never fear, D-Fens is about to teach him a lesson he is never going to forget.

The same holds true for everyone else who crosses the man's path, from turf-proud gang members, pushy panhandlers and a bigoted neo-Nazi (Frederic Forrest) to "Dig we must" street repair crews who could care less about the inconvenience they cause, and intractable fast-food employees who won't serve breakfast to customers who just miss the cutoff. "Aren't you ashamed of yourself?" D-Fens tells these folks, an armed and dangerous Miss Manners intent on restoring civility to the world even if he has to frighten people half to death to do it.

Yet "Falling Down" isn't content with having audiences laugh at its simplistic jokes and mindlessly cheer D-Fens on, it also wants us to cluck disapprovingly at what a loose cannon he is, to sympathize with the terrorized ex-wife (Barbara Hershey) he wants to visit and the quietly heroic cop (Robert Duvall) who has to first figure out what D-Fens is up to and then track him down while dealing with his own high-strung and whiny spouse (Tuesday Weld). And all this, wouldn't you know it, on his very last day on the job.

Most galling of all, "Falling Down" (rated R for violence and strong language) seems eager to get credit for the way it uses serious social problems as shallow window dressing in an urban fantasy. Throwing in shots of homeless people, of a man holding a "Dying of AIDS" sign and another protesting at a failed savings & loan is supposed to convince us this film is serious about making a difference, when all it is serious about is putting money in its own pockets.

"Falling Down's" script and direction are slick and commercial (Smith is an actor turned screenwriter, Schumacher's credits include "Flatliners," "Cousins" and "The Lost Boys"), and the film is certainly adept at pointing out the areas of stress and irritation in modern city life. But "Falling Down" appears to be totally oblivious to the ways it is at best capitalizing on a difficult situation and at worst making it even more intractable.

Rather than admit that the very real problems D-Fens encounters are not capable of simplistic solutions, the film wants to safely pin every trace of trouble on those nameless others who always seem to do so much damage. Happy to have found a way to cash in on society's miseries, "Falling Down" encourages a gloating sense that we the long-suffering victims are finally getting our splendid revenge. The ultimate hollowness of that kind of triumph reflects the shallowness of a film all too eager to serve it up.

NEW STATESMAN & SOCIETY, 5/28/93, p. 31, Jonathan Romney

When *Falling Down* was released in America, it sparked a volatile debate. Everyone had something to say about the film, which follows the downfall of a redundant defence worker, played by Michael Douglas—nicknamed D-Fens after the licence plate on his abandoned car—as he finally snaps one blistering June day in Los Angeles, and goes on a frenzied walk-about through the city.

The thrust of most of the reviews in the "quality" broadsheets and magazines was that this story of a 1990s trigger-happy Willy Loman was nothing more than a base vigilante movie in artful guise. Richard Schickel of *Time* described it as a "dangerous and morally stupid movie". Gene Siskel of the *Chicago Tribune* judged that "... explosions and not ideas are what *Falling Down* is all about", while Kenneth Turan of the *Los Angeles Times* derided it as "Charles Bronson's *Death Wish* with a bogus social conscience".

Indeed, the *Death Wish* series became a handy reference point for reviewers to lob at the film. Needless to say, America's self appointed monitor of media ethics, Michael Medved, was not going to join the crowds who were queuing to see it.

Importantly, the film also scored low points with various minority campaigning groups, which took it to task for the much discussed and, indeed, inflammatory scenes in which D-Fens beats up a Korean store owner, then belligerently confronts members of a Chicano gang. Jeana Park of the Korean American Advocates for Justice called the film: "Immoral. Unjustifiable. Unbelievable." Violent, and racist to boot.

With this indignant reception in mind, I went along to the British preview, nervously expecting a boorish right-wing diatribe. The odds were against *Falling Down*'s director Joel Schumacher (a former production designer), but partly because so far he had hardly proven to be the most sophisticated of cineastes.

His last film, *Dying Young*, was a flash, but shallow and sentimental tale, about a poor little rich boy dying of cancer who falls in love and subsequently plays Pygmalion to his down-at-the-heels nurse. Starring Julia Roberts, it seemed like a sick *Pretty Woman,* glorified with arty references to give it the illusion of depth. From this, it was quite conceivable that Schumacher's latest project could be more about explosions than ideals.

But the fact is that *Falling Down* is rich with ideas and not all palatable, especially if you happen to be an American white middle-class male with an attachment to your homeland. For the film rummages through a particular state of mind and airs the ugly fears lurking there. The frayed white-collar man, who has always presumed his claims to status to be irrefutable, is shown to be the last to wake up to the fallacies of the American dream.

The clues are there for the taking. In an outburst over the price of produce in the Korean-owned store, D-Fens harks back nostalgically to 1965. That was the time of LBJ, just before the 1960s were soured with the truth about the Vietnam war. Indeed, D-Fens has just lost his job at an ammunitions plant, where, as his mother puts it, he "built important things to protect us from the communists". In the new world order, with no discernible outside enemy for America to define itself against, it's not just D-Fens who is cracking up, but his country. It is the status of the States that's under question here.

This is something that the American critics seemed to avoid. The literal, politically correct interpretation that Jeana Park follows is far from flexible. *Falling Down* does not condone D-Fens' dangerous arrogance towards the Koreans and Hispanics, but rather unravels racist attitudes. With its picaresque structure, the film is like an exaggerated cartoon. Indeed, Schumacher's propensity for visual allusion is finally marshalled into a coherent and resonant schema.

At one point, the irate D-Fens is in a ludicrous Whammyburger joint. Pointing to the discrepancy between the illustration of a fat juicy burger tucked into a fluffy white bun and the shrivelled object he is served with, he asks: "What's wrong with this picture?" It's a question to be asked throughout *Falling Down*, as one scans the screen for signs.

Within the opening shots, a double trajectory can be traced. As D-Fens stews in his gridlocked car, he glances up to a hoarding by the freeway. A poster for sun-tan oil displays a bikini-clad woman languishing in the heat. The advert's legend reads: "White is for laundry." But look at the image again and one sees that someone has graffitied in a little man peeking out of the woman's cleavage. "Help me," he cries, seemingly trying to scrabble free.

The billboard is like a huge think bubble that siphons off and puts on display D-Fens' anxieties. The film's most manifest concern is that white might indeed be in for a scouring; but its other crucial consternation (and few of the American male critics addressed its sexual politics) concerns women.

The object of D-Fens' angry odyssey is to get back home to his wife and young daughter. But it transpires that D-Fens, who proved to be a difficult husband, is divorced and thus disenfranchised from his family. Another presumed right to have and to hold has gone bung.

Meanwhile, D-Fens' shadow, a cop called Prendergast, on his last day of duty before retirement, is interrupted constantly with calls from his anguished, invalid wife. She is presented as a bit of a "nag", though her worries for her husband's safety would seem to be totally legitimate.

Too suffocatingly close or too far away, women are not happily positioned in relation to the men in the film. This is another source of ire. Look past *Falling Down*'s showdown ending to its final shot, where Schumacher fills the screen with a video image of the all-American happy family that never was. It begs the question: what's wrong with this picture? The American critics didn't seem to get that. Perhaps it's too explosive an idea.

NEW YORK, 3/8/93, p. 64, David Denby

Falling Down, which stars Michael Douglas as a true-blue American who runs amok, is aptly titled. Actually, the movie is worse than a downer; it's a concentrated dose of recessionary despair, a sort of poison-pen letter conceived in the late, unlamented Bush era. *Falling Down*, which has received advance praise for courage in the *Times*, confronts the American urban mess. Yet it quickly converts what's serious and ambitious in its themes into exploitation, reminding one of such earlier social-drama/exploitationfantasies as *Joe* and *Death Wish*—pummeling, demagogic movies that knew how to take over the audience's anxieties and then push them over the edge.

Falling Down is about the trashed surface of American city life—the callousness and meanness, the astonishingly pointless violence. On a suffocating Los Angeles summer day, when the heat hangs in the flatlands and everything turns yellow, a laid-off defense worker (Michael Douglas)—an everyman with no name—sits in his automobile, stuck in a freeway jam. As hostile faces stare at him from behind closed windows and a fly buzzes around his head, he suddenly loses it. Abandoning the car, he decides to visit his ex-wife, Beth (Barbara Hershey), and his little daughter, who live in a house in Venice. His terrified wife doesn't want to see him—there's a restraining order—but he walks there anyway, all the way across the city, from Pasadena to Venice, which the movie presents as a journey through hell. He's a sympathetic figure, but he's crazy and infinitely dangerous.

Douglas's hair has been shaped into a brush cut, his face converted to a rectangle by fifties-dork glasses. He's ... Robo-Square!, the ultimate Mr. Straight, a man who appears never to have noticed that the ethnic and social composition of Los Angeles has been changing. Judged apart from the screenplay and direction, Douglas's performance has a certain pathos. This malevolent man honors the idea of reasonableness in himself (he thinks he's just a normal family guy). Speaking in a forced, even voice, Douglas suggests a nostalgia for sanity; he'd *like* to be sane, but he just can't hang in there any more. He's too disappointed: *Someone lied to him.* He's meant to be the kind of blandly literal-minded psycho glimpsed in a CNN newsbreak—a seemingly upright man who snaps, and then empties a gun into a schoolyard.

You can see the artistic ambition here. The cinematographer, Andrzej Bartkowiak, heightens L.A.'s summer glare into the yellow terrors. The panorama of human scumminess, the hostile or indifferent faces, suggests familiarity with the classics of alienation: It's a fair bet, for instance, that Bartkowiak, director Joel Schumacher, and screenwriter Ebbe Roe Smith (a former actor) have read Camus's heat-maddened classic *The Stranger* and have seen Fellini's *8½*, which also begins with a man's nauseated fear of expressionless faces behind windows. The screenplay is classically structured and resonant with familiar big themes. For instance, Douglas is a man who runs and runs until he reaches the end of the American frontier (the picture comes to a climax on the Venice pier). Meanwhile, a retiring detective in the L.A.P.D., Prendergast (Robert Duvall), is set up as an elaborate parallel case. Prendergast has undergone terrible times, too, but he's kept himself together. Like Douglas, he loves his wife (a neurotic shrew, played by Tuesday Weld) and his little girl, who died. Each man is an Odysseus trying to reach a home that is no longer there. A humane and intelligent policeman, Duvall is the positive to Douglas's negative.

But structural rigor without sensitivity or intelligence doesn't count for much. Douglas begins his journey by trying to get change for a phone call from a Korean convenience-store owner, who refuses the change, asking him to buy something. So Douglas, grinning evilly, starts baiting the Korean, asking him how much things cost, carrying on as if the store owner were at fault for every penny of inflation since 1965. Soon he's smashing up the store with a baseball bat. The scene may have been conceived well before the Los Angeles riots, but Schumacher was still shooting when the riots broke out. Didn't he notice what was going on? This disgraceful episode effectively blesses the near-pogrom that was conducted against Korean property. Schumacher and Smith are plugging into the hostile atmosphere: Bash the mothers; they're leeching on us.

Joel Schumacher (*St. Elmo's Fire, Flatliners*) may not have accomplished much as a director, but he's been around long enough to know that inner-city and suburban-mall audiences are likely to cheer Douglas's ecstatic outbursts. The trick of the movie is to make the victim-hero crazy enough that his behavior will be rejected but sympathetic enough that his rancor appears halfway justified. Then audiences will say, "He may be cracked, but the guy won't take s--- from anybody." (The TV ads for the movie suggest not a nut on the loose but a man who won't be pushed anymore, a populist hero.)

Sitting in a vacant lot in a gang-controlled Latino neighborhood, Douglas gets accosted by two thugs, and he turns on them and clubs them, too. And when they try to kill him from a moving car, what happens to them can also—and will also—be cheered as the fate they deserve. The movie conveys the anxiety of a white guy who fears becoming a member of the minority—the exasperation of living with strangers. As John Avildsen did in *Joe*, Schumacher increases the audience's anger and then lets it out in bursts of violence. And he directs crudely; the encounter with the Latino toughs, for instance, might have worked if it were more ambiguous—if the violence weren't inevitable.

Just when you might be getting down on Douglas, he meets someone who's loonier than he is—a gay-baiting Nazi, played by Frederic Forrest in open-mouthed-loco style. So our hero may be crazy, but he's not an anti-Semite or a homophobe. Which certainly makes him more palatable, doesn't it? Instead, Douglas attacks the idiotically cheerful employees of a burger chain; he frightens some rich old fools at a golf course. No doubt there are many annoying people in the world, but a filmmaker contriving occasions to tell them off isn't doing much to address alienation. After a while, Douglas seems like Howard Stern with a brush cut, a loudmouth making himself feel good. Only blacks are spared his wrath. Apart from a sympathetic fellow refused a bank loan and a little boy on a bicycle, blacks hardly appear on the street. Is it possible that Schumacher's courage is lined with calculation? After all, blacks form a major part of the inner-city movie audience.

As Douglas gets closer to his wife, who rightly fears for her life, Prendergast, evidently the only intelligent person in the city, closes in on him. Duvall gives a small-scale but shrewd performance as the disciplined, wily old cop, and Barbara Hershey is extremely effective in suggesting the terror of a not very bright woman who has suffered at the hands of a violent man. The final scenes are decently written and well played. Yet what's moving in *Falling Down* gets lost in roistering blather. The movie is of a piece with reactionary radio call-in programs, in which legitimate complaint collapses into paranoia, the blind leading the blind in a folly of miscomprehension. *Falling Down* adds to this hapless din. It may get a rise out of its audience, but it's a movie made by—and for—the spiritually exhausted.

NEW YORK POST, 2/26/93, p. 21, Jami Bernard

There was a report earlier this week of a rise in incidents of disgruntled former employees coming back to shoot up the place. Had they somehow seen advance screenings of "Falling Down" or is "Falling Down" merely on the cutting edge of social pathology?

Michael Douglas has never been better—and that's pretty scary—as a straight-arrow guy who veers from the straight and narrow after losing his job, his family, and his sense of reality. We know him only by his vanity license plate, which reads D-FENS.

The movie opens rather fabulously with Douglas stuck in traffic, sweating, getting paranoid and claustrophobic, menaced by a bee and a window that won't roll down, going quietly insane behind the wheel of a car that can't go anywhere.

Eventually he just abandons his car and walks away across the highway, and so begins a movie in which Douglas' character episodically does all the things many people secretly dream of doing whenever life gets inconvenient—smashing up a store whose prices are too high, shooting an attacker point-blank while making fun of him, punishing bureaucrats and functionaries who make daily urban life a living hell.

The trouble is, this character is a white male, and all the victims in the movie happen to be recognizable minorities. This is a "Death Wish" movie for white folks who feel the minorities came in and ruined everything for them. In this, it is rather shocking.

Robert Duvall is cast opposite Douglas as a retiring detective—how come movies always seem to catch detectives on their last day of work before the pension kicks in?—who has a lot in common with the perp. They both feel boxed in (Duvall has a strange, nagging wife, played by Tuesday Weld) and they both feel under-appreciated.

"Falling Down" continues the trend begun by Kevin Costner in "The Bodyguard" of featuring a hunky actor in a terrible haircut. Douglas looks like one of those '60s nerds, with a buzz cut, black-rimmed glasses and a pen pack in his white shirt pocket. A lot of this movie, while apparently serious, is having its own little bit of fun. "I'm just standing up for my rights as a consumer," he says after busting up a Korean deli.

"How's the food?" he asks his stunned hostages at a fast-food burger joint whose rules about when they serve breakfast are impenetrable.

Douglas goes around picking up a succession of weapons people try to use against him, using them in turn against his next victims. The capper occurs when he takes out his frustrations on a condescending road-repair crew with a rocket launcher.

While we would all like to use a rocket launcher on whomever it is who has been tearing up Sixth Avenue for the last few years for no apparent reason and without making any visible repairs, "Falling Down" appeals to its audience's worst instincts in a winking sort of way that has little to do with movie art and a lot to do with exploitation.

NEWSDAY, 2/26/93, Part II/p. 62, Jack Mathews

As a recent emigré from Los Angeles, I watched Joel Schumacher's paranoid view of that city in "Falling Down" with a combination of recognition and revulsion. Yes, the traffic is hell, the gangs are terrifying, and the influx of foreign populations has rearranged the physical and cultural landscapes.

But will the frustrated white middle class represented by Michael Douglas' berserk engineer really identify with a man who destroys a Korean's grocery store because of his accent, who terrorizes the staff and customers at a fast-food restaurant because they stopped serving breakfast three minutes before he arrived, who fires a bazooka shell at a busy construction site because one of the workers is rude to him?

"Don't you want to do this?" the film's TV commercial asks as Douglas' crewcut wacko commits a variety of violent felonies.

Sadly, the answer for too many people will be yes. The frustrations that Schumacher and screenwriter Ebbe Roe Smith tap into are real. But the last thing Los Angeles, or any other urban center, needs is a movie that feeds into the paranoia of one demographic group's anxieties, connects all the emotional dots and seems to conclude that even though violence is wrong, it's an understandable response.

If "Falling Down" is intended as a fable about the failure of the American Dream, as seen by L.A.'s displaced white minority, it doesn't quite get there. There are obvious parallels to Frank Perry's "The Swimmer," in which Burt Lancaster played a disoriented man crossing town by way of his wealthy neighbors' backyard pools, and Sidney Lumet's "Network," with its madder-than-hell TV newsman urging Americans not to take it anymore.

However, there are no gradual revelations in "Falling Down," nothing to explain the man's madness in terms of his environment. When Douglas' character, known only by the name on his license plate ("D-FENS"), abandons his car on the freeway in the film's opening scene and begins his crosstown journey, his lunacy is in full bloom. God help anybody—black, white, Hispanic, Asian, rich, homeless or as frustrated as he is—who gets in his way.

The filmmakers seem to be gambling that we'll stick with this character because, hell, Michael Douglas is playing him. And for a while, Douglas does whip up some irresistible furies. Since "Fatal Attraction," Douglas has played nothing but borderline creeps, and this time he's simply crossed the border.

But 10 or 15 minutes of him is all you can take. There is no character beneath this ranting madman, and following him on a series of foot-bound adventures from East Los Angeles to Venice beach is like spending the last hours with someone about to turn a McDonald's into a shooting gallery.

Through the movie's squishy subplot, about a milquetoast detective (Robert Duvall) trying to stay out of trouble on his last day on the job and get home safely to his neurotic wife (an obese Tuesday Weld), we do learn a little about D-FENS' background. About his job at a defense plant and his relationship with his mother (Lois Smith) and his ex-wife (Barbara Hershey).

Even then, he seems less a victim of urban upheaval than someone genetically programmed to lose his wits, circa 1993.

Schumacher ("St. Elmos' Fire," "Flatliners") has never tackled material remotely as difficult as this, and occasionally allows the film's angry tone to drift into demented fantasy. A long sequence involving Douglas' character and the neo-Nazi war-surplus store owner (Frederic Forrest) who sees D-FENS as his kind of Aryan nut is so far over the top the film almost has no chance of recovering.

What "Falling Down" reminds me of more than any other movie is Michael Winner's "Death Wish," which played to the same kind of middle-class frustrations in New York by glorifying vigilantism. D-FENS is no hero, vigilante or otherwise, but when he takes a bat and a gun to the stereotyped street-life of L.A., too many people will be getting too much pleasure from watching him.

NEWSWEEK, 3/1/93, p. 80, David Ansen

Joel Schumacher's slick, deeply confused exploitation movie *Falling Down* is a thriller of urban paranoia. Michael Douglas plays a divorced, unemployed defense-industry worker who gets stuck in a hellish Los Angeles traffic jam, abandons his car, pops his cork and proceeds to go on a violent rampage across the city. His final destination: the home of his terrified ex-wife (Barbara Hershey) and child. The only man who can stop him: a mild-mannered desk cop named Prendergast (Robert Duvall) who is, as we are told too many times in Ebbe Roe Smith's none-too-subtle screenplay, serving his last day before retirement.

Sounds like a standard psycho-on-the-loose setup, right? Wrong. "Falling Down" wants to be taken as a Major Statement about middle-class frustration in a deteriorating multicultural society. Though the Douglas character (called D-Fens after his license plate) is clearly bonkers, we're meant to identify with his rage against a world that has crushed his white, middle-class dreams. Like Howard ("I'm mad as hell") Beale in " Network" crossed with Charles Bronson in "Death Wish," "Taxi Driver's" Travis Bickle and the real-life Bernie Goetz, he's supposed to be a cracked Everyman gone gun crazy for our sins.

A real artist could make something incisive or darkly hilarious out of this moral tightrope act. Schumacher, veering recklessly between social satire, kick-ass fantasy and damsel-in-distress melodrama, play's the game for opportunistic cheap thrills. One moment D-Fens, with his glasses and geek wardrobe, is a dangerous sicko, the next he's Supernerd the avenger. His rampage begins when he assaults a Korean grocery owner and trashes his store after the guy refuses to give him change for a phone call. Why are we supposed to identify with this jerk? Because he's played by a star? It would help if we saw what D-Fens was like before he went over the edge, but "Falling Down" doesn't have time for little things like character development.

The movie's solution to this problem is to make D-Fens's victims even more vile than he is. So Douglas gets to whomp menacing, machine-gun-toting Latino gangbangers, drive a rich, snooty golfer to a heart attack (a comic touch, I presume) and terrorize the officious employees of a fast-food joint with his arsenal of weapons. We're not allowed to feel anything for them. In the most ludicrous sequence, he blows away a surplus-store manager (Frederic Forrest), but we're meant to cheer because this miserable dude is a homophobe, a racist and a Nazi. Schumacher's touch is not light.

"Falling Down" rants with forked tongue. While solemnly condemning racism and violence, it doesn't miss an opportunity to play on the audience's most paranoid instincts. It would be easy enough to dismiss this as simply a dumb (though expertly photographed) junk movie. But its pretensions render it pernicious. Pandering to the Zeitgeist, it becomes part of the problem it pretends to address.

SIGHT AND SOUND, 6/93, p. 52, Cynthia Rose

On a June morning in Los Angeles, two men are caught in the same traffic jam. One abandons his car and walks away; the other announces himself as a cop, Detective Martin Prendergast, working off his last day of duty. He orders the car to be shoved to the side of the road, revealing license plates which read 'D-FENS'. Its driver walks into a nearby grocery, ostensibly asking for change to use a pay phone. When the Korean owner, Mr Lee, tells him he must make a purchase, he uses Lee's baseball bat to trash the shelves before exchanging his dollar bill for two quarters and a Classic Coke.

At work, Prendergast is taunted by his colleagues, who regard him as a desk jockey. The exception is his ex-partner Sandra Torres, who asks Prendergast to meet her for lunch. Meanwhile, in a Venice Beach bungalow, Beth, the divorced wife of 'D Fens' is organising a birthday party for her daughter Adele. D-Fens is trying to reach her on the phone, but keeps finding it engaged. Sitting down to drink his Coke, he is interrupted by two Latino gang members, who try to commandeer his briefcase. He fends them off, relieving one of a switchblade. Downtown, Prendergast gets the first of a series of complaints from his nervous wife, followed by a call from Mr Lee, who tells him about the "man in the white shirt and tie." The gang members, looking for revenge, spot D-Fens and spray the entire street with gunfire, but fail to injure him. As their car piles into another, D-Fens commandeers their weapons. As reports hit police HQ Prendergast is receiving a cursory last-day speech from his contemptuous captain. Beth, panicked by her ex-husband's call, asks for police protection.

After being panhandled by a con-man, D-Fens carries his growing arsenal into a local Whammyburger, where, told it is minutes too late to buy breakfast, he terrorises staff and customers. Prendergast is watching his colleagues quiz the gang members' girlfriend Angelina, who tells them about the "man with a white shirt and tie"; later, he is having lunch with Sandra when she is called out to the Whammyburger. Torres tracks the culprit to a surplus store, where the owner covers for him. The owner then reveals himself to be a homophobe and neo-Nazi with his own weapons; menaced by him, D-Fens kills him and exits dressed in combat gear.

Convinced that one man is behind the same crimes, Prendergast and Torres team up to find him. Prendergast remembers the man with the D-FENS licence plates; finding his name is William Foster, he and Torres call at his home, where they find his frightened mother. Crossing a private golf course, Foster scares an old man into a heart attack. Torres discovers Foster has been unemployed since being fired by a defence plant a month earlier. She and Prendergast trace Beth's residence. Foster has now reached Beverly Hills, where he terrifies the caretaker and his family at a plastic surgeon's mansion. Unable to get police protection, Beth races out with Adele, moments before Foster arrives. Foster suspects they have fled to Venice Pier, but before he can leave, is ambushed by Torres and Prendergast. Torres is wounded while Foster escapes, but armed with her gun, Prendergast tracks him to the pier, tricks him into setting his gun down and holds him at bay. Bluffing with Adele's water pistol, Foster forces a fatal shoot-out and topples into the bay. Prendergast returns the family to their bungalow, where the guests are beginning to assemble for Adele's party. Then he has the small pleasure of telling his Captain "fuck you" in front of news cameras.

Falling Down has been heavily hyped as a controversial blockbuster—a "crude vigilante picture" stalking the mall disguised as satire; "the Michael Douglas film which goes beyond *Basic Instinct*"; an orgy of violent wish-fulfillment aimed at America's white middle class (who, in Clintonian budget terms, earn circa $100,000 per year and do not constitute the mass of multiplex escapists). *Newsweek* used a shot of Douglas as D-Fens on its cover, for a story entitled 'White Male Paranoia; and last month's *Sight and Sound* deconstructed the film over three pages.

Of course, Douglas and director Joel Schumacher seize any credit for handling issues of moment. They clearly wanted to make a *Taxi Driver* for the 90s, to update the toll of urban stress on the 'working man''s psyche. To this end, *Falling Down* is paced and shot idiosyncratically, cleverly scripted and structured (details about its characters unreel very gradually) and wonderfully lit by Andrej Bartkowiak. Yet its driving force is the same old shameless Hollywood formula: horror pic meets urban-anxiety thriller. Added to this is a level of product placement (masquerading as irony) which would shame even Nike.

The film means to be different by not letting any one of its genre elements dominate. Instead, that domination is distilled into Michael Douglas. He plays a stylised character, half surreal, half real bad guy: a sociopath called Billy Foster, laid off by an LA defence firm, Notech. Critics have painted Foster as a kind of crash-and-burn finale for the USA's White Hero. But he's hardly the first Anglo-American male in movies to walk away from problems, bully people without regard to race, creed or colour, and project a warped sense of affection onto his own daughter. He's simply the first one to be played by showbiz dynast Douglas. And, however hard Douglas works, he brings an overkill of aura to the very idea of what it means to be 'working class'.

Not that he gets any help from his character. D-Fens is a composite of the media's nightmare projections, a Frankenstein who is part Oprah, part network news and part 'reality programming' (US TV such as *Cops, Hard Copy* and *Unsolved Mysteries*). He's not passed off as surd evil, yet his outlines remain fuzzy. Why was he fired from the job? Where *has* he been going every day? How come a 'working stiff' talks like a Beverly Hills *bon viveur*? Foster is supposed to crack under the burden of outsize resentments and deep confusion. But all we get is Michael Douglas, weighed down by those Big Themes he thinks his character carries. Douglas transforms every outburst into a comic punchline, and so much wants to be 'understood' that he practically winks at the audience. But he understands the 'working class' less than they understand Hollywood.

This is why Robert Duvall walks away with the film, turning it into a fairly absorbing drama about a cop who has more secrets than his sociopath. While Douglas cruises along on single-gear star charisma, Duvall slowly unveils a complex and real working-class hero, raunchy and fallible, worn and gutsy. Prendergast was written as the converse of his quarry: a cop whose final day at work collides with Foster's last shred of sanity. Foster terrorises his wife (Barbara Hershey, excellent at suggesting the messy links between desire and violence) and Prendergast coddles his (Tuesday Weld, excellent too as a woman defeated first by the loss of her child, then the loss of her beauty). A traffic delay explodes Foster; but, trapped in the very same gridlock, Prendergast chuckles over a billboard at the side of the road. Foster cannot see people—to him, they are merely obstacles. But Prendergast is revealed as tolerant and ultra-observant; he is an exceptional cop, an experienced psychological handler. Prendergast is a man not because he carries a gun and blows away disrespect; he is manly because he doesn't need anyone else to acknowledge his fortitude. Duvall shows us a well of solitude far scarier, but far truer, than any of the film's overblown urban spectres (drive-by shooters out of Peckinpah, panhandlers who sound like prime-time comedians, a sexist Nazi homophobe with a David Koresh-size arsenal).

Prendergast accepts that life is tough and luck is random; he's the only character who calls Foster what he is—an "ordinary" whiner. Cornered on Venice Pier, Douglas gestures limply over the waters, mumbling that plastic surgeons have stolen the American dream. Playing on the irony of Michael Douglas saying this, Prendergast almost shakes the screen with his incredulous laughter. "You're mad because they lied to you? They lie to everybody! They lie to the FISH!"

A whole life has gone against Duvall's character. Yet somehow Prendergast gets the most out of everything—whether it's solving his final crime or anticipating a Mexican meal. Humour has proved his saving grace: Prendergast laughs to explode pain, to relate with contempt from his captain and colleagues, to expiate the terrible range of human acts cops must witness. It's fascinating to find that such laughter packs more visceral power than either D-Fens' weaponry or Douglas' star presence. Along with Hershey, Weld and Rachel Ticotin (as Prendergast's quick-to-judge ex-partner Torres), Duvall turns a by-the-numbers thriller inside out.

TIME, 3/1/93, p. 63, Richard Schickel

It's hard to know how to respond to *Falling Down*: deplore it's crudeness or admire its shrewdness. But it is occasionally the movies' job to plunge into the national psyche, root around in its chaotic darkness and return to the surface with some arresting fantasy that helps bring our uglier imaginings into focus. In that sense, this often vulgar and exploitative movie has some value.

It begins in a place we've all been—a hopeless traffic jam—and it proposes a solution most of us have entertained: dump the damn car and proceed on foot. Of course, most people think twice. But the figure played by Michael Douglas, and identified (from his customized license plate) only as D-FENS, is not at the moment into mature reflection. Recently separated from his job and his wife, he's a bundle of hot-wired nerves. And today is his young daughter's birthday. He has not been invited to the party, but he means to crash it.

When he steps out of that automobile and heads for his sometime home far across Los Angeles, D-FENS steps into a contemporary urban nightmare. It's all here: panhandlers and drive-by shootings, a terrorized fast-food restaurant, even a neo-Nazi skinhead spewing hate. In effect, director Joel Schumacher is recreating, quite artfully, all the horrific images on the 11 o'clock news. And it is impossible to distance yourself from these pictures the way you can when they are surrounded by weather and sports.

Much the same thing happens with D-FENS, whose portrayal by Douglas is more finely tuned than Ebbe Roe Smith's script. When we meet him he is a sort of Everygeek—flattop haircut, half horn-rims, a pocket protector fully armed with ball-points. You expect his anger to be ineffectual, especially since he starts out armed only with paranoid righteousness. But, as we all know, weaponry is easily acquired in the jungle of our cities, and by the time D-FENS nears home, he has acquired a bazooka. More important, he is no longer the nightmare's victim, but rather its logical extension and principal ogre, the guy the neighbors always describe as "quiet" or "well behaved," after his shooting spree is over.

Falling Down attempts to balance his imbalance with the presence of a cop named Prendergast (Robert Duvall). He, too, is something of a loser, due to retire prematurely from the force at the end of the day. But he has the qualities everyone needs to survive in the city these days—good humor, patience, some compassion. These, however, are quiet virtues, and even though they are expertly embodied by Duvall, they are passive. They are not, at least, cinematic virtues. He can't really compete for the camera's attention. Or ours. When the film is over, it's hard to remember him.

For, let's face it, there is an element of truth in the character of D-FENS. But it is, finally, tabloid truth. His motives and psychology are not, to say the least, subtly set forth. The menaces lurking in the city he traverses are exaggerated. And the people who drive him over the edge are all racially or socially stereotypical, the broadly drawn "others" imagined by the uninformed middle class, quaking behind the walls of their gated communities, talking at cocktail parties about buying guns and insisting—not entirely persuasively—that they wouldn't be afraid to use them. To the degree that *Falling Down* encourages this mind-set, it is a dangerous and morally stupid movie.

VILLAGE VOICE, 3/2/93, p. 50, Georgia Brown

The writer of *Falling Down*, Ebbe Roe Smith, must've been an English major in pre-Derrida days. The title is not only one of those '60s—*Going Away, Making It, Letting Go, Fucking Up*—but it resuscitates the key metaphor of the era: Remember the Fall (i.e., of man). Throw in a Christ complex and along the path sprinkle apocalyptic messages (here, a "He died for your sins" bumper sticker), and it's, New Critic, do yo' stuff.

Sealed in his car in a traffic jam, a lone figure (Michael Douglas) watches the steam rise; his engine is heating up. It's a day of record heat in L.A. and in surrounding cars, assorted passengers stare blankly ahead. Directly in front, a little girl—a Chicana angel, a Madonna (before the tainting of the word)—looks back at the man with pity and compassion. A fly begins to buzz this stranger's pate. Suddenly he deserts his car, Just walks away.

Despite the echoes above, *Falling Down*, directed by Joel Schumacher, is less *8½* than it is *Grand Canyon* or even *Bonfire of the Vanities*, both of which take off from a car's breakdown in an urban no-man's-land, an event that has come to signify the onset of a contemporary male's mid-life crisis. Face to face with fear, the white man's little habitat begins to crack. Except that this Mr. White, as I'll call him (he's the Man With No Name for most of the movie), is fearless. The humor here is that he's not quaking but standing tall and kicking butts.

Sheathed in righteous indignation, rendered invincible by wrath, this guy's a superhero who hasn't revealed his secret identity. Carrying his Samsonite briefcase, wearing nerdy specs and a plastic pocket protector, the man can go anywhere in the city. Bullets whiz by, felling innocent and guilty alike, but not him. He could walk the streets of Sarajevo.

Mr. White's adversaries, or foils, are chosen with care. The first is a sullen Korean grocer. (Who's counting the Korean audience?) Perhaps the idea is that African Americans who may be tired of finding their neighborhoods depicted as dead zones will be mollified seeing Mr. White getting royally ticked off at the Asian's fussy ways: Like, you have to buy something to get change for the phone. Then charging 85 cents for a Coke, which doesn't leave a quarter. Furious, Mr. White wrests the baseball bat from the Korean and starts smashing the merchandise. Even more exciting, Mr. White lets fly certain anti-immigrant retorts, like "You don't even have the grace to speak my language," and—when quoted the price of an item—"Do you have any idea how much money my country has given your country?" (Not because we like you, cockroach, but to fight the commies.)

What's got into this harmless-looking fellow? For some time into the movie, White's motives are opaque, thereby allowing us to read into him what we wish. He's an emboldened Citizen K., a lonely Odysseus (always saying he's "going home"), a consumer who's paid for one too many shoddy products. One of the fed up and not going to take it anymore. (Even later, when he comes into possession of an arsenal, by and large Mr. White only shoots people who deserve it.)

But while the film's publicity bills him as an everyman—"The adventures of an ordinary man at war with the everyday world"—the fact is that Mr. White is not J.Q. Citizen pushed over the edge but a psycho in the middle of his break. And except for a despicable Latino gang, the everyday world is not all that horrid either. He goes into a burger chain and can't get an omelet because it's a few minutes past the breakfast hour. Big deal. And so what if his Whammy special doesn't look like the color photo. It's just fast food, for heaven's sake. The social critique here isn't very incisive. And it gets more forced and didactic. When he comes to an army surplus store run by a neo-Nazi commando (Frederic Forrest), the whole setup is a cliché any juvenile TV-watcher could write.

Gradually we learn that White has lost his defense industry job and his wife has left him, taking the kid. The first seems not to be his fault (he's a casualty of the Wall's falling down), but the second certainly is. Currently he resides with his dotty mother (a timid bird straight out of Tennessee Williams with her precious glass menagerie). White's estranged wife (Barbara Hershey) knows perfectly well he's a danger to her and the child. (If Douglas weren't such a cold actor to begin with, his character might not lose quite so much sympathy along the way. The more we see of him, though, the less we identify, making the ending far less tragic than it might have been.)

Cleverly, Ebbe Roe Smith has bolstered his narrative with an intriguing subplot. This counter-point to White's odyssey involves a modest LAPD detective who takes it upon himself to track the errant psycho down. Detective Prendergast (Robert Duvall) is spending his final day before retirement cleaning out his desk and fending off desperate calls from his panicky wife who can't bear one more minute alone. When he begins hearing about the trail of violence, we're primed to believe that Prendergast's intimate experience with personality disorder (his codependency) equips him to anticipate the suspect's moves.

While one wife screeches "Come home!," the other is crying, "Don't you dare come home!" To continue the parallel, both men have lost a beloved daughter (read, innocence). Playing the henpecked, old-fashioned paternalist, Duvall comes off as immensely sympathetic. As Douglas's trajectory flattens out, Duvall takes over the picture. At one point, during a farewell interview with the precinct's chief, when the bullying younger boss tactlessly reveals that he neither knows nor cares about this man before him, the camera lingers on Prendergast's downcast eyes and the remains of a polite smile. In Duvall's sly expression, we read hurt but also veiled contempt—an emotion he gets to vent later in the day.

Almost parenthetically *Falling Down* slips in one piquant allusion to time's cruelty. Trying to explain his wife to Sandy, his pretty ex-partner, Prendergast says, "She was once very beautiful." Sandy, who's very fond of Prendergast, can't understand how the loss of beauty could drive a woman to such a state. But because the raging wife is played by a virtually unrecognizable Tuesday Weld, we who are old enough know very well what he means.

Also reviewed in:
CHICAGO TRIBUNE, 2/26/93, Friday/p. C, Dave Kehr
NEW REPUBLIC, 3/22/93, p. 30, Stanley Kauffmann
NEW YORK TIMES, 2/26/93, p. C3, Vincent Canby
NEW YORKER, 3/8/93, p. 98, Terrence Rafferty
VARIETY, 2/15/93, p. 83, Brian Lowry
WASHINGTON POST, 2/26/93, p. C1, Hal Hinson
WASHINGTON POST, 2/26/93, Weekend/p. 32, Desson Howe

FAMILY PRAYERS

An Arrow Entertainment release of a Sugar production. *Executive Producer:* Larry Sugar. *Producer:* Mark Levinson and Bonnie Sugar. *Director:* Scott Rosenfelt. *Screenplay:* Steven Ginsberg. *Director of Photography:* Jeff Jur. *Editor:* Susan R. Crutcher. *Music:* Steve Tyrell. *Production Designer:* Chester Kaczenski. *Art Director:* Marc Dabe. *Set Decorator:* Judi Sandin. *Costumes:* Johnny Foam. *Running time:* 105 minutes. *MPAA Rating:* PG.

CAST: Tzvi Ratner-Stauber (Andrew Jacobs); Joe Mantegna (Martin Jacobs); Anne Archer (Rita Jacobs); Paul Reiser (Dan Linder); Patti LuPone (Aunt Nan); Julianne Michelle (Fay Jacobs); Allen Garfield (Cantor); Conchata Ferrell (Mrs. Romeyou); Shiri Appleby (Nina).

LOS ANGELES TIMES, 7/16/93, Calendar/p. 14, Peter Rainer

"Family Prayers," set in Los Angeles in the 1960s, tries to get inside a 13-year-old boy's day-to-day struggle to save his father from his gambling addiction.

Andrew (Tzvi Ratner-Stauber) isn't a take-charge kid, but he has plucky determination. He hangs around while his dad (Joe Mantegna) is gambling with garment center co-workers or placing bets on the phone, and the look on the boy's face is politely accusatory. Andrew is trying to be his father's conscience, but he doesn't realize that the man is too far gone to be helped.

For a movie with so much potential drama, "Family Prayers" is too wan and plodding. The script by Steven Ginsberg has some good ideas: It's a movie about a boy who tries to save his family in order to save himself.

Ginsberg has in even-handed, noncoercive approach to character: there are no villains in this tragedy. But director Scott Rosenfelt doesn't have the skills—this is his first feature—to draw much emotional texture from these everyday lives. (If he did, the lives wouldn't seem so everyday.) There's too much glum virtuousness on display in "Family Prayers" (rated PG). Everybody seems touched by how sufferingly decent they are. It's humane all right, but it's boring.

Mantegna gives a reasonably involving performance; he doesn't try to turn this gig into Willy Loman, though the script sometimes pushes him in that direction. But we never see the crazy compulsiveness that would compel a man who loves his family to place them in such jeopardy, (A couple of goons trail him periodically and trash his home, but shouldn't a movie about a gambler carry more of a sense of risk?)

The other performances, with two exceptions, are unmemorable, Ratner-Stauber lacks charge and inner tension. Anne Archer is the suffering wife, a role she has played at least thrice too often. Paul Reiser, as the hippie who tutors Andrew for his bar mitzvah, is cloyingly avuncular.

But Allen Garfield has a few all-too-brief moments as a cantor that ring true, and Patti LuPone, as the boy's aunt, injects some real, razzing energy into all the plodding sorrowfulness. If she was the gambler in the family, she'd be all aces.

NEW YORK POST, 2/19/93, p. 27, Jami Bernard

I've been to some lackluster bar mitzvahs, but this one takes the cake, and the floral arrangement too. Not even Joe Mantegna can save the picture; at least he doesn't have to read from the Torah.

Tzvi Ratner-Stauber is a newcomer who plays Andrew, a boy on the brink of manhood—at least according to Jewish law. It's time for his bar mitzvah but he's not interested. He's not even interesting.

Because Tzvi is a newcomer and a child, it would be better not to say anything that will give him a complex later in life. So let's just say the camera shouldn't have spent so much time home alone with him.

Mantegna plays Andrew's father, a gambler whose addiction is costing the family dearly, not only in money but in emotion. Sometimes bad men come and knock at the door, demanding payment. The sacred roll of bills that's buried in the freezer in aluminum foil is marked for Andrew's bar mitzvah, but daddy's problem is getting in the way of family health and happiness. (Go see "A Tree Grows in Brooklyn.")

Andrew isn't too interested in studying for his bar mitzvah, what with all this *mishigass* going on at home. Actually, Andrew doesn't seem too interested in anything, including the movie, but that's where we bring in Paul Reiser in hopes of giving the proceedings a zany touch.

Reiser plays a caring hippie-ish bar-mitzvah tutor—is that a full-time line of work?—who senses the boy is worth saving, even though his listlessness is putting everyone to sleep at least in *my* row).

Try and guess who Anne Archer plays. Would it be a sweet, earnest, concerned wife and mother, whose face collapses every time her husband disappoints her? Yes, it would.

The story's structure seems odd and distended, the dialogue uninvolving. There aren't too many movies about the Jewish experience, so it's too bad that we'll have to sit shiva for "Family Prayers."

NEWSDAY, 3/19/93, Part II/p. 67, Jack Mathews

It is at the critical juncture in an Orthodox Jewish boy's life—that crowded emotional intersection where physical change, social awkwardness and the pressures of a coming bar mitzvah collide in a hail of testosterone sparks—that Andrew Jacobs takes on the additional task of trying to keep his family from crumbling under the weight of his father's gambling addiction.

First-time screenwriter Steven Ginsberg reportedly pulled "Family Prayers" together from his own scarred bar mitzvah memories, and its emotional detail leaves little doubt as to its sincerity.

But heartfelt is not a movie, and despite the fine performances of such veterans as Joe Mantegna, as the self-destructive Martin Jacobs, Anne Archer, as his long-suffering wife, and Patti LuPone, as his wealthy, intrusive sister-in-law, "Family Prayers" is undone by its rookie enthusiasm.

Besides Ginsberg, a former Daily Variety editor and film critic, "Family Prayers" is the first feature for director Scott Rosenfelt and for young Tzvi Ratner-Stauber, who as Andrew must shoulder the bulk of the film's hefty emotional baggage.

The movie's most memorable image is of Andrew staring, with a mixture of pain, betrayal, disappointment and hope, at a father who is helpless against his own addiction. Unfortunately, what makes that image memorable is not its power so much as its frequency. Whenever Rosenfelt wants to point out the real losers of Martin's gambling, he cuts to a close-up of Andrew staring at him, like a kicked dog, from around a corner or across the room.

Part of the problem seems to be Rosenfelt's confusion as to where to focus the story. While it's clear we're following the fate of this family in late '60s Los Angeles from Andrew's vantage point, he almost disappears from the screen whenever an adult is around. It's as if Rosenfelt, a Hollywood producer ("Home Alone," "Mystic Pizza"), couldn't stand having all those high-priced actors around playing second banana to a kid, and expanded their screen time beyond their usefulness to the story.

As enjoyable as those performances are—particularly that of LuPone, who hams it up to the point of cliche as the pushy sister-in-law, and Paul Reiser, as Andrew's sensitive tutor—they throw the film's center off balance. Rosenfelt has to keep reminding us, with those shots of the doe-eyed adolescent, that "Family Prayers" is really about coming-of-age in a dysfunctional family, not about the psychology of gambling addiction.

VILLAGE VOICE, 2/16/93, p. 60, Alyssa Katz

Hard as it is to stomach the fact that people still try to make boys-coming-of-age films, it's even tougher to ponder how much cliché and condescension Hollywood might pack into a bar mitzvah. But in between indulging in a lot of dated bull about the power of manhood, Steven Ginsberg, the film publicist who "loosely based" the script for *Family Prayers* on the nerve-wracking weeks leading up to his own bar mitzvah, actually works in some fresh perspectives on Jewish domestic life shrouded in daintily diffused 1969 light.

His painfully sullen alter ego in flood-water pants (Tzvi Ratner-Stauber, a Semitic Fred Savage) refuses to pass into manhood, ceremonially or otherwise, because his father (Joe Mantegna), a compulsive gambler, doesn't exactly offer the best role model. Dad renders the matter moot anyway by squandering the bar-mitzvah fund—he keeps betting against the Mets.

Yet again Anne Archer plays the suffering wife, a role she's been synonymous with since *Fatal Attraction*. Someone, please, write a script for this woman. Paul Reiser exudes a much more enjoyable vibe as a Marxist peace-activist bar-mitzvah tutor who has his tone-deaf student listen to the blues for inspiration. He also teaches the kid a little ethnic pride, remarking after a *Planet of the Apes* matinee that "Herschel Bernardi's brother was in that." Regrettably, his antiwar teachings don't stop the boy from carrying out the genre's requisite decking of the school bully.

Also reviewed in:
NEW YORK TIMES, 3/19/93, p. C16, Stephen Holden
VARIETY, 1/25/93, p. 135, Emanuel Levy

386 FILM REVIEW ANNUAL

FAMINE-33

A Dovzhenko Feature Film Studio production. *Producer:* Oleksy Chernishov. *Director:* Oles Yanchuk. *Screenplay (Ukrainian with English subtitles):* Serhij Diachenko and Les Taniuk. *Based on the novel "The Yellow Prince":* Vasyl Barka. *Director of Photography:* Vasyl Borodin and Mykhajlo Kretov. *Editor:* Natalia Akajomova. *Music:* Mykola Kalandjonak and Victor Pacukevych. *Running time:* 95 minutes. *MPAA Rating:* Not Rated.

CAST: Halyna Sulyma (Odarka); Georgi Moroziuk (Myron); Kostyk Kazymyrenko (Mykola); Olenka Kovtun (Olenka).

NEW YORK POST, 12/15/93, p. 43, Bill Hoffmann

Rewards often come through demanding, painful work. Such is the case with audiences watching the searing new docu-drama from the Ukraine. "Famine-33."

This may be the most painful motion picture you will ever sit through—and it's something you must truly work at watching all the way through.

But if you can stomach the graphic, often horrifying images, this impressive re-enactment of one of history's greatest atrocities provides one of the most rewarding movie experiences of the year.

It is an incredibly moving, invaluable document of man's neverending inhumanity to man.

The year was 1933. The place, Russia's desolate Ukraine.

Communist Party boss Joseph Stalin instituted a mindboggling program in which peasants had to export all their grain. Since most ignored the order, rifle-toting soldiers were dispatched to pillage tiny villages and confiscate the food supplies of the masses.

Thus began an artificially induced famine that ended in the starvation deaths of more than 7 million people—one in four of every Ukrainian man, woman and child.

Director Oles Yanchuk focuses on the plight of Myron Katrannyk, his wife, elderly mother and three kids, who scrape by from meal to meal with little more than watery broth.

The family's fate is sealed when local Communist officials discover Myron's wife has secretly hidden a gold chalice from the local church to keep it out of the hands of party thugs.

Myron's scenes with his doomed family are heartbreaking.

He talks openly of death and dying as his children eat their tiny meals. He speaks half-heartedly with his son about trying to catch sparrows to eat. And he watches in horror as his ailing mother is shoved to the ground and dragged by a ruthless soldier.

It's hard to describe the emotional impact of watching "Famine-33."

Disturbing shots of soldiers pillaging the countryside, banging down the doors of starving families and shooting peasants who approach them for food are devastating.

There are scenes of cannibalism, of half-dead villagers being hurled into mass graves and of brutal torture.

The powerful black-and-white photography is interspersed with lush color shots of the characters' hallucinations of better times.

I don't want to discourage anybody from seeing "Famine-33."

But be warned: It is not for the fainthearted or anybody looking for an evening of light historical drama.

TIME, 12/27/93, p. 70, Richard Corliss

On a flatbed train, the soldiers survey their stock—a pole of emaciated bodies, hundreds of men, dead or near dead—and begin their work. With brute efficiency they toss the bodies into a deep, burning pit. Down the hill the bodies roll, toward incineration. They don't slide with the burly grace of stunt men; they topple clumsily, bumping into one another, robbed of dignity even in their dying. For agonizing minutes the carnage continues, until the soldiers' job is done and the pit smolders with an almost visible stench.

This is the climactic scene of Oles Yanchuk's *Famine-33*, a scarifying film about the real-life murder and starvation of more than 6 million Ukrainians by Stalins bureaucrats in 1932-33. Not many Americans will see this picture, which opened last week in one New York City theater; stark, iconic, black-and-white Ukrainian movies, especially when their subject is "the hidden Holocaust," have limited mall appeal. But in its meticulously brutal imagery, in its theme of humanity enslaved and justice outraged, in its Manichaean categorizing of people as holy victims or soulless villains, *Famine-33* has important similarities to Hollywood-financed pictures coming this Christmas to a 'plex near you.

Yuletide at the movies is often grim; *Sophie's Choice, Scarface, Ironweed, Hoffa* and most of Oliver Stone's psycho-dramas were December releases. The reason is coincidence: Christmas Day also marks the start of the last eligible week for the year's Oscar nominees to be released, and that's the cue for superserioso films. So audiences in search of vigorously vacant entertainment this holiday season will find *Mrs. Doubtfire* and not much else. The rest is state torture, mortal prejudice, mass death. Instead of tidings of joy, Hollywood offers the writhings of Job.

Steven Spielberg's *Schlindler's List*, which opened last week, has already, provided the elevated downer of the decade. But wait, there's more. Trailing *Schlindler*, and in the line of *Doubtfire*, is a trio of high-minded horror shows:

• *Heaven & Earth*. Oliver Stone is back for a third tour of Vietnam, after *Platoon* and *Born on the Fourth of July*. But for once in an American movie, the focus is on the Vietnamese, and on the sufferers: the land and the women. Phung Le Ly (played by newcomer Hiep Thi Le), growing up in the idyllic rice farmland of central Vietnam, becomes the victim of every possible atrocity as civil war heats up in the late '50s. She is tortured with knives, electric prods, snakes, even ants; she is brutalized by the republican army and raped by the Viet Cong. She is a stand-in for her lovely country, despoiled by successive invaders like a slave princess by jealous pashas. And when she escapes to the U.S. with her sergeant husband (Tommy Lee Jones), life doesn't improve. It's still sexual rapacity, guns and ammo, war games by other means.

• *In the Name of the Father*. Daniel Day Lewis stars as Gerry Conlon, the Belfast man who, while on a London spree in 1975, was unjustly arrested, convicted and jailed as an I.R.A. terrorist. The British police in charge of the case were no Miss Marples; they tortured the four major suspects to extract bogus confessions. In director Jim Sheridan's tense retelling of this shameful chapter in British jurisimprudence, the lads are smacked, threatened and humiliated. And Gerry's saintly father (Pete Postlethwaite), jailed with him, is allowed to die slowly, with little medical attention. By the end of the movie, whether or not you're a member of Sinn Fein, the Brits' brutality toward the Conlons will get your Irish up.

• *Philadelphia*. Andy Beckett (Tom Hanks), a lawyer who is quietly gay and controllably HIV-positive, learns he now has AIDS. The partners in his firm find out too. When they confect a phony excuse to fire him, Andy sues for wrongful dismissal and hires a skeptical, cut-rate attorney (Denzel Washington) to defend him. Can the case against these powerful solons be won? And if so, will Andy be alive to savor the victory? *Philadelphia*'s agony lies less in these questions than in Andy's drastic deterioration. Hanks so scrupulously, heroically mimes the wasting wrought by the disease, from chest lesions to a 30-lb. weight loss, that Jonathan Demme's film ultimately becomes a documentary on the ravages of AIDS—and on the masochistic machismo of Method acting.

In theory, all these pictures should be cheered. Films, even American films, needn't be only a baby sitter or a roller coaster. They can aspire to edify, to pry minds open to moral indignities around the world and in our own cranky hearts. Why can't directors aim high—not just for an Oscar but, hey, maybe a Nobel Peace Prize? And why shouldn't moviegoers, like everyone else during the holidays, be subject to compassion overload? Or be confronted by purposeful screen suffering until they shout, like Wayne and Garth, "We're not worthy"?

No reason at all. But often, when smart directors tackle a "controversial" issue like Vietnam or the Irish question or AIDS, they forget some of their art. Instead of building scenes deftly, allusively, they accumulate horrific detail to make sure you get the point. The films get longer, more ponderous; they sit on your chest until you finally surrender to their good intentions. In the process, they may become sentimental, cautionary fables of mistaken identity, compiling atrocities and piling them on photogenic victims. Suffering sanctifies Le Ly and Gerry's dad and Andy, makes them objects of veneration to the faithful; everyone wants to kiss the hem of their torment.

In the '30s and '40s, Hollywood made "controversial" films about lynching. But the victim was always innocent; no one dared say that even a guilty man deserved due process. In 1947, when

Elia Kazan was making *Gentleman's Agreement*, about a writer who discovers anti-Semitism while pretending to be Jewish, a crew member told Kazan he got the moral: We should be nice to Jews because they might turn out to be Gentiles.

Today's corollaries are no more subtle. Police shouldn't torture men suspected of terrorism, because they might not have done it. Soldiers should not rape girls, because they might be as cute as Bambi. Corporate lawyers (Hollywood's new villain, here and in *The Firm* and *The Pelican Brief*) should not railroad a man with AIDS, because he might be Tom Hanks.

Hanks' Andy is a wonderful fellow: chipper, supremely competent, lavishing genial respect on colleagues high and low. He also seems a good subject for a sensibly daring film about AIDs. And for its first hour, *Philadelphia* is a pretty fine social comedy about private pain; it lays out the dilemma with a grace almost worthy of Hanks' bravely understated playing. But then it becomes much too timid. It says that the death threat hanging over gays commands our sympathy for them. It renounces character shadings for easy good guys (Andy's huge family, each one of them amazingly accepting) and crumb-bums (his bosses, who can only mutter and sputter). Nothing in the real world is quite so simple as this.

And, to tell the truth, no ambitious movie is quite so simple as magazine trend pieces may try to make it seem. Certainly not *Heaven & Earth*, which is thematically grotesque but visually gorgeous: the camera takes in the spectacle of Southeast Asia (Thailand mostly, stunt-doubling for Vietnam) with the rapture of an intelligent lover. Because it traces Phung Le Ly's life story, the film is dramatically misshapen: its most singing moments are in the first half. And audiences may be as weary of Stone's haranguing about Vietnam as they are afraid of people with AIDS. But if Stone simplifies and distorts, he often does so brilliantly, like a cartoonist with a Fauvist's eye for the drama in color and character.

In the Name of the Father showcases a different kind of art. Sheridan (*My Left Foot*) is a bricklayer among directors; you can see the mortar between scenes. But he dares to make his hero something more, or rather less, than a plaster saint; Gerry is a scurvy thief who is guilty of every social crime but the one he's charged with. The drama here is eventually located not in the young man's battle against the Brits but in the coming to terms with his father, and thus his place in his family and his haggard country. It's a jailbird love story of two men bound by blood.

By the end, the conventions of all three films are exposed. They mean to shock and then inspire, with the revelation that good people can triumph. They amount to a tiny ray of Hollywood sunshine in the storm of 20th century chaos. While seeming to look clearly at the world, they ignore the bitter, deprived existences of most people who live in it: in Ukraine or Ireland or Vietnam, or in the death camp of an AIDs ward.

VILLAGE VOICE, 12/21/93, p. 63, J. Hoberman

Here for the holidays, Oles Yanchuk's *Famine-33* is an accomplished low-budget first feature, as well as the first fiction film to treat the catastrophic famine that accompanied the collectivization of Ukrainian agriculture, starving over 7 million to death during the winter of 1933-34.

Whether or not the decimation of the Ukrainian population was deliberate genocide or a monumental blunder rendered monstrously punitive by Stalin's cruelty: its evil has been amplified by strenuous denials within and without the Soviet Union. In the absence of a Ukrainian *Shoah*, *Famine-33* (which was given its world premiere over Ukrainian television on November 30, 1991, the night before the former Soviet republic voted overwhelmingly for independence) is programmatically modest. Like the Ukrainian-language movies produced in the U.S. during the 1930s, it was initially funded through small individual donations; its scope is that of a single peasant family.

Shot in misty black and white, the movie is deliberate and incantatory, bordering on lugubrious. The spare score is a spooky mix of organ, violin, and tinkling bells. The famine is presented with stark religiosity as a Massacre of the Innocents—the doomed Katrannyk family is entrusted with hiding a golden chalice after their village church is broken up by CP thugs. There are no Schindlers here. With the exception of a *kolkhoz* leader who blows his brains out rather than turn over 90 per cent of the collective harvest to the state, the Communists are blatantly diabolical—munching on confiscated goodies as they torment their victims.

If the peasants' purity borders on listlessness, *Famine-33* is set, as the Katrannyk grandmother puts it, on the threshold between this world and the next. Straining under its moral burden, the movie continues the specifically Ukrainian folkloric mode developed by Alexander Dovzenko, revived by Sergei Paradjanov, and extended by Yuri Illyenko. Visions rise like vapors from the iconography of frozen corpses and mass graves. By the end, the deceptively still Ukrainian landscape is a graveyard haunted by intimations of cannibalism and worse, as Red soldiers of the Antichrist harvest death in the fields.

Also reviewed in:
NEW YORK TIMES, 12/15/93, p. C23, Stephen Holden
VARIETY, 8/10/92, p. 58, Emanuel Levy

FAR OFF PLACE, A

A Walt Disney Pictures and Amblin Entertainment release. *Executive Producer:* Kathleen Kennedy, Frank Marshall, and Gerald R. Molen. *Producer:* Eva Monley, Elaine Sperber, and William W. Wilson, III. *Director:* Mikael Salomon. *Screenplay:* Robert Caswell, Jonathan Hensleigh, and Sally Robinson. *Based on the books "A Story Like the Wind" and "A Far Off Place"* by: Laurens van der Post. *Director of Photography:* Juan Ruiz-Anchia. *Editor:* Ray Lovejoy. *Music:* James Horner. *Music Editor:* Thomas Drescher. *Sound:* Colin Charles and (music) Shawn Murphy. *Sound Editor:* Larry Kemp and Michael D. Wilhoit. *Casting:* Shari Rhodes, Sally Stiner, Christa Schamberger, and Paul Tingay. *Production Designer:* Gemma Jackson. *Art Director:* Carine Tredgold and Jonathan McKinstry. *Set Decorator:* Ian White. *Special Effects:* Dave Harris. *Costumes:* Rosemary Burrows. *Make-up:* Norma Hill. *Stunt Coordinator:* Roly Jansen. *Running time:* 104 minutes. MPAA Rating: PG.

CAST: Reese Witherspoon (Nonnie Parker); Ethan Randall (Harry Winslow); Jack Thompson (John Ricketts); Sarel Bok (Xhabbo); Robert Burke (Paul Parker); Patricia Kalember (Elizabeth Parker); Daniel Gerroll (John Winslow); Maximilian Schell (Col. Mopani Theron); Miles Anderson (Jardin); Fidelis Cheza (Tracker); Taffy Chihota (Warden Robert); Anthony Chinyanga (Doctor); Brian Cooper (Store Keeper); Magdalene Damas (Nuin-Tara); John Indi (Bamuthi); Sebastian Klein and Kessia Randall (Children on Sand Dune); Isaac Mabikwa (Poacher); Bertha Msora (Koba); Japan Mthembu (Carfax); Charles Pillai (Mr. Tang); Andrew Whaley (Warden Gerald); King George Ziki Moyo Group (Matabele Dancers).

LOS ANGELES TIMES, 3/12/93, Calendar/p. 16, Kevin Thomas

Disney's "A Far Off Place" a wondrous African adventure epic opens with a succinct pre-credit sequence showing poachers slaughtering elephants for their tusks. It then launches its story with so little exposition we know no more what's happening than do its two 14-year-olds, Nonnie (Reese Witherspoon) and Harry (Ethan Randall), who promptly find themselves fleeing for their lives over the Kalahari Desert, accompanied by a young Bushman named Xhabbo (Sarel Bok).

Judging from their accents, Nonnie and her parents (Robert Burke, Patricia Kalember) seem to be either Americans or Canadians, living in a present-day unnamed African country in a landed gentry splendor recalling the colonial era. Nonnie's father, however, is a progressive who operates his estate in partnership with the natives.

It is his vociferous protests of elephant poaching, an illegal but enormously lucrative enterprise, that propels his daughter and Harry to head for the desert. Freshly arrived from New York with his own father for a visit with Nonnie's family, Harry hasn't even had time to change out of his preppy blue blazer and khakis before he's trudging through sand with Nonnie and Xhabbo.

Right away "A Far Off Place," which was adapted from two Laurens van der Post books, announces that it's a different kind of family film, aiming for older children and adults. Its PG rating is appropriate: That pre-credit sequence—and some subsequent events—are too brutal for small children, and its narrative throughout is too elliptical not to confuse little kids. Still, the film does leave us wishing for more information along the way, specifically about the young people, who after all have just met, and their families. However, its strategy of not letting us know much more than do the teen-agers and their bushman friend pays off in generating suspense and uncertainty. Indeed, you may well find yourself as shocked as they are at learning the identity of their enemy and pursuer.

Much of the film is taken up with the 1,000-plus miles trek, at once a display of Xhabbo's ancient survival wisdom and a testing of the children's resilience and capacity to mature. But the film is shrewdly structured so that as time goes on it can provide respite from a gorgeous but potentially monotonous landscape by increasingly cutting away to events that could determine whether or not Nonnie and Harry live or die should they make it across the Kalahari.

Clearly, director Mikael Salomon, in his theatrical feature film debut, has resisted taking the easy way out at every turn. That Salomon comes to directing as a formidably gifted Oscar-nominated cinematographer (for the undersea "Abyss" and also for "Backdraft's" scary visual effects) doubtlessly accounts for the film's intense sense of the visual. Africa is always the most photogenic of locales, and through the lens of Juan Ruiz-Anchia's camera the Kalahari's sand dunes—it's actually the Namib Desert—take on a superb sculptured look.

The film constantly engages your heart as well as your eyes, and its images are counterpointed by James Horner's magnificent score, ever-shimmering and majestic, supplying emotion and even narrative force throughout.

Meanwhile, Witherspoon and Randall emerge as very likable young people, smart and resourceful—and on the brink of first love and sexual attraction. Bok's Xhabbo lends a witty, gentle presence. Elsewhere are Jack Thompson and Maximilian Schell, both friends of Nonnie's father and eager to find out what happened to her and Harry.

As a historic collaboration between Disney and Steven Spielberg's Amblin Entertainment, "A Far Off Place" (rated PG for violence and mild language) spins its tale filled with all the traditional adventure elements with the utmost sophistication.

NEW YORK POST, 3/12/93, p. 29, Matthew Flamm

"Out of Africa" it isn't. But this yarn about a boy and girl and their Bushman friend who cross the Kalahari desert by foot has its own kind of grandeur. Shot in Zimbabwe and Namibia, "A Far Off Place" entertains so well with romping elephants, wind-carved dunes and shimmering heat-struck plains that one can all but forgive the creaky dialogue and predictable plot.

The movie opens today on a double bill with the latest Roger Rabbit-Baby Herman cartoon short, "Trail Mix-Up." Both films go easy on the eyes.

According to the production notes "A Far Off Place," based on the novels "A Far Off Place" and "A Story Like the Wind," by the South African author Laurens van der Post, has been updated from a tale of mercenaries to one about elephant poachers. It's the brutal murder of a Western anti-poaching activist and his wife that sends their spirited daughter 2,000 miles across the desert.

Nonnie (played by the attractive young actress Reese Witherspoon) is joined in her trek by Harry (Ethan Randall)—a teenage visitor from New York whose father was also killed in the raid—and her faithful dog. They're guided by Nonnie's bushman pal, Xhabbo (Sarel Bok), who had had a "tapping," or premonition of the violence, and hid them in a cave.

"If the wind can cross it, we can cross it," Xhabbo assures his friends, who are about to set out on a rest-stop-free hike with nary a change of clothes or a spare canteen between them. By now, of course, they have no other means of escaping the bad guys, who will continue the hunt with planes and helicopters.

The filmmakers are full of good intentions: Nonnie, who has lived in Africa all her life, takes Xhabbo at his often mystical word. Nature-loving platitudes abound. ("Only kill for food; only kill what you must," the charmingly played Bushman tells Harry after the New Yorker has bagged his first buck with bow and arrow.)

All the animals, a title card informs us at the opening, were well cared for during filming.

But "A Far Off Place" is no more nor less than a children's adventure tale (well-matched with the amusing madly kinetic, almost 3-D "Trail Mix-Up," which plays like a ride through a theme park); the conservation message just fills out the plot. The indomitable trio dodge bullets, outwit villains and escape across a crevice in a literal cliffhanger.

Fortunately, they're doing so against one of the world's most spectacular backgrounds. Mikael Salomon, a cinematographer making his feature directing debut, has a keen sense for keeping landscape interesting—and the help of the red, orange and yellow sands of the Namib desert, which stands in for the Kalahari.The crisp cinematography is by Juan Ruiz-Anchia.

"A Far Off Place" may be too violent for very young children, with a grizzled, rifle-toting Maximilian Schell blowing away poachers in the opening scene. But the film does offer three sweetly engaging young leads, who seem as natural in their roles as the landscape.

NEWSDAY, 3/12/93, Part II/p. 67, John Anderson

Along the way from white-dominated Africa, through the Kalahari Desert and into a kind of interracial/spiritual oneness, "A Far Off Place" (1) separates the men from the boys; (2) the women from the girls; (3) the boys from the girls and, occasionally, (4) the weak-of-stomach from the hardened fur-wearing.

The film, a Disney adventure about three young people—two white, one black—fleeing murderous ivory poachers, accomplishes (1) and (2) by killing off most of the grownups right away. Paul Parker (Robert Burke), notable among his countrymen for being the first white landowner to share his profits with his black workers; is also an active, ardent foe of the poachers. One night they take their revenge, killing him, his wife Elizabeth (Patricia Kalember), their friend John Winslow (Daniel Gerroll), and whoever else happens to be in the house. Fortunately for the film, this does not include the Parkers' daughter, Nonnie (Reese Witherspoon), or the visiting Harry Winslow (Ethan Randall).

At the time of the murders, the two teenagers are out in the dark with Xhabbo (Sarel Bok), a young Bushman, who through a "tapping"—spiritual experience during which he taps his chest with his fingers—predicted the carnage at the Parker house. This capacity to predict danger and conjure up defenses against it will save them later. It is Xhabbo who provides much of the humor and charm in the film; like N!Xau, the star of "The Gods Must Be Crazy," he is a Bushman, whose speech is punctuated by tongue clicks and who espouses the pantheistic credo that propels "A Far off Place."

Pursued by the killer-poachers—one of whom, to no one's surprise, is Parker family friend John Ricketts (Jack Thompson)—two young people accomplish (3) in a neat switch of sexual-role playing: Nonnie is a crack shot, an expert with dynamite, a cocky and self-assured young woman who doesn't suffer fools gladly; Harry, besides being a foolish, self-absorbed lout with a large amount of intolerance for cultures other than his own, is both intimidated by and admiring of Nonnie's abilities.

This role reversal—which would have been a lot more effective if it had been treated nonchalantly—is the freshest element in a fairly predictable film. When the trio decides to cross the Kalahari—a feat Harry compares to walking from New York to Miami—you're pretty sure they're going to make it, and that their friend Col. Theron (Maximilian Schell), a policeman who takes a certain amount of glee in shooting poachers, is going to rescue them. All the audience will need to fear is how belabored the trip is going to be, how thirsty it's going to make them, and whether Xhabbo is ever going to stop delivering Bushman platitudes.

The photography is often stunning; the Kalahari is reduced to its basic geometry in a way Edward Weston might have appreciated. But the acting is generally atrocious; Witherspoon was a lot more natural in "The Man in the Moon."

And there's also the issue of brutality to consider: When the poachers, in the opening moments of the film, take chainsaws to the tusks of the elephants they've just killed, it might turn a few stomachs, as will some of the other scenes involving animals (although, we are told, none were hurt in making the film). These moments seemed to bother adults at the screening I attended much more than the children, but some discretion might be advisable.

SIGHT AND SOUND, 9/93, p. 46, Paul Tarrago

Present-day Botswana. Paul Parker is blasting a drainage ditch for his home when his old friend John Winslow arrives from New York, with his son Harry reluctantly in tow. After almost blundering into one of the explosions, Harry mooches around feeling out of place. That night he follows Paul's teenage daughter Nonnie to a secret meeting with Xhabbo, a young bushman. Xhabbo insists that they both remain with him overnight; he has had a premonition. At daybreak Nonnie sees smoke coming from her house and rushes back to find that ivory poachers—against whom her father had been campaigning—have laid waste to everything and everyone. She and her companions set off on the run across the Kalahari desert.

Family friend Mopani Theron, head of the anti-poaching squad, vows to find the culprits. A colleague, John Ricketts, offers to search for the children by helicopter. Meanwhile the fleeing Xhabbo 'asks' a herd of elephants to follow in their wake and obscure their tracks. A helicopter appears but Nonnie insists they hide. They lay out their clothes as decoys, and the helicopter shoots at the inert forms—their would-be assassin is John Ricketts. Now dead in the eyes of their enemies, the fugitives continue across the desert. They learn from one another, and though reluctant to show it, Nonnie begins to care about Harry, who in turn becomes respectful of Bushman culture. Ricketts learns of the teenagers' continued existence through a bracelet dropped by Nonnie. Stung by a scorpion, Xhabbo again has a premonition, and despite his delerium is able to summon up the wind to cause a sand storm, which forces their pursuers away. The sea lies just over the next dune; the children are found and saved.

Mopani, Nonnie and Harry find the ivory hoard in one of Ricketts' mines; he turns up and there is an armed struggle, and Ricketts is killed in an explosion. Bidding goodbye to Xhabbo and Harry, Nonnie returns to her homestead. Harry arrives carrying a cage of birds, the one thing on their journey that Nonnie had admitted to missing.

Last year, John C. Avildsen's *The Power of One* showed just how awry teen pics set in Southern Africa could go, so a Disney/Amblin co-production set in the same locale could be grounds for righteous indignation. The combination of great natural beauty and overt injustice have a storybook straightforwardness to them; unfortunately *The Power of One* wanted a storybook hero too, a nice white boy hero to lead the humble indigenous folk. Fortunately, *A Far Off Place* is as far removed from this ethos as you could reasonably expect; adapted from two Laurens van der Post novels, this story of good teens chased by bad adults has an old-fashioned Disney ring pumped up with Spielbergian liberalism. With the lead teen recast as female and the story transposed to the present day, the script has every opportunity to be contemporary in its ruminations. (Post's mercenaries are rewritten as poachers), but manages to avoid any sociopolitical conflicts, as the young heroes mostly spend their time together in the wilderness, outside any social structures.

In Harry's description of twentieth-century technology (satellite TV and Walkman culture) and in Ricketts' commercial practice (the coveted tusks graphically lopped off with chainsaws), Western culture signifies excess and rupture; it uses dynamite to dig drainage ditches and routs opponents by massacre. It's nature, then, and not just the Kalahari itself, that is the 'far off place' of the title. At the same time the film is an account of an adult world in which Harry and Nonnie still occupy only marginal positions. They occupy a position somewhere between this world and Nature. Nature prevails, though, and in its quasi-mystical manifestations undermines the presumptions of the adult world. As the film moves towards closure—the children's parents dead and Ricketts accordingly punished—Harry's decision to stay represents a prodigal-son return to a preelectric world.

In its downplaying of technology and its leisurely pacing, lack of heroics and nominal episodes of tension, *A Far Off Place* seems boldly old-fashioned, almost a travelogue dressed up in dramatic form. Spectacle of never-ending red sands is intercut with the teenagers' exchanges, and a brief interlude in a crocodile-infested swamp followed by a near-fatal leap across a crevass, a scene apparently tacked on to spice things up. It's unnecessary, though, because on top of Juan Ruiz-Anchia's dizzying photography (of the Namib desert, standing in for the Kalahari), Nonnie, Harry and Xhabbo make engaging characters, strongly played and equipped with some wellscripted banter. In all that it sets out to do, this is an affectionate and accomplished film.

TIME, 4/5/93, p. 60, Richard Corliss

[*A Far Off Place* was reviewed jointly with *The Adventures of Huck Finn*; see Corliss' review of that film.]

Also reviewed in:
CHICAGO TRIBUNE, 3/12/93, Friday/p. C, Dave Kehr
NEW YORK TIMES, 3/12/93, p. C15, Janet Maslin
VARIETY, 3/15/93, p. 62, Brian Lowry
WASHINGTON POST, 3/12/93, p. D1, Rita Kempley
WASHINGTON POST, 3/12/93, Weekend/p. 42, Desson Howe

FARAWAY, SO CLOSE

A Sony Pictures Classics release of a Road Movies and Tobis Filmkunst production. *Executive Producer:* Ulrich Felsberg. *Producer:* Wim Wenders. *Director:* Wim Wenders. *Screenplay (German with English subtitles):* Wim Wenders, Ulrich Zieger, and Richard Reitinger. *Story:* Wim Wenders. *Director of Photography:* Jürgen Jürges. *Editor:* Peter Przygodda. *Music:* Laurent Petitgand. *Music Editor:* Peter Przygodda. *Sound:* Günther Kortwich and (music) Gareth Jones. *Sound Editor:* Barbara Von Weitershausen. *Casting:* Catherine Coste. *Production Designer:* Albrecht Konrad. *Set Decorator:* Martin Schreiber. *Special Effects:* Ulrich Netzer and Michael Luppino. *Costumes:* Esther Walz. *Make-up:* Hasson von Hugo and Christine Atar. *Stunt Coordinator:* François Doge. *Running time:* 140 minutes. *MPAA Rating:* Not Rated.

CAST: Otto Sander (Cassiel); Peter Falk (Himself); Horst Buchholz (Tony Baker); Nastassja Kinski (Raphaela); Heinz Rühmann (Konrad); Bruno Ganz (Damiel); Solveig Dommartin (Marion); Rudiger Vogler (Phillip Winter); Lou Reed (Himself); Willem Dafoe (Emit Flesti); Mikhail Gorbachev (Himself); Marijam Agischewa (Kirsten); Henri Alekan (Captain); Tom Farell (Jack); Monika Hansen (Hanna and Gertrud Becker); Aline Krajewski (Raissa); Günter Meissner (Falscher); Ronald Nitschke (Patzke); Camille Pontabry (Doria); Udo Samel (Security Officer #1); Gerd Wameling (Security Officer #2); Matthias Zelic (Liquor Store Owner); Hanns Zischler (Dr. Becker); Martin Olbertz (Dying Man); Tilmann Vierzig (Young Konrad); Antonia Westphal (Young Hanna); Ingo Schmitz (Anton Becker); Frédéric Darie (Maurice); Jean-Marie Rase (Jules); Lajos Kovacs (Lali); Bruno Krief (Paul); Armance Brown (Paula); Hugues Dolforge and Claude Poncelet (Elastonautes); Susanne Jansen (Woman at Gallery); Bob Rutman (Artist); Yella Rottländer (Winter's Angel); Alexander Hauff (Cab Driver); Johanna Penski (Florist); Steffi Hiller and Eberhard Knappe (Passers-by); Shefqet Namani (Street Gambler); Klaus-Jürgen Steinmann (Policeman); Andrzej Pieczynski (Czomsky); Natan Fedorowskij (Russian); Louis Cochet (Louis); Daniela Nasincova (Angel); Günter Kelm and Heinz-Peter Graubaum (Museum Security Guards); Claude Lergenmuller (André); Melanie Pontabry (Melanie); Alfred Sczczot (Grumpy); Nadja Engel (Woman Slapping Cassiel).

CHRISTIAN SCIENCE MONITOR, 5/25/93, p. 14, David Sterritt

In a modest but significant trend, some American filmmakers have been paying increased attention to religious matters lately.

Examples range from a high-profile epic like "Malcolm X" to an offbeat drama like "The Rapture. " While they vary widely in their ideas and attitudes, these films give the lie to alarmist critics who claim that American film has been taken over by crass materialism.

A number of movies at this year's Cannes Film Festival indicate that the same tendency is affecting European cinema. A good example is *Faraway, So Close* by Wim Wenders, a major German director.

Made as a sequel to his well-liked "Wings of Desire," it again tells the story of an angel who falls to Earth and becomes an ordinary man—not because he rejects his angelic mission, which is to carry the message of love and hope to unhappy people, but because his affection for humanity becomes so great that he can't help embracing it all the way. He takes up his new life

394   FILM REVIEW ANNUAL

with enthusiasm, determined to do good deeds and leave the world a more decent and caring place than he found it.

As in his earlier film on this subject, Mr. Wenders is more interested in spinning a gossamer fantasy than exploring profound issues; still, he seems sincere in his acknowledgment of a spiritual dimension in human experience, and in his hostility toward images and behaviors that chain people to the lower aspects of their existence.

And once more he has assembled a marvelous cast to enact his story. It includes Otto Sander as the angel who becomes a man; Peter Falk and Willem Dafoe as angels with very different personalities; Bruno Ganz as another of their colleagues; Nastassja Kinski as an angel who remains angelic; and rock star Lou Reed as himself.

Despite such an interesting subject and so many talented collaborators, however, it must be said that Wenders has made regrettably little of the opportunities offered by this film.

After a glorious beginning, in which his camera evokes a sublime sense of transcendence and wonder, he steers the movie into more than two hours of unfocused drama, limp comedy, and pointless adventure scenes, spiced with homilies as philosophically rich as the average fortune-cookie slogan. Wenders's impulses are laudable, and the best moments of his new picture are magnificent. But he has not carried the "Wings of Desire" saga to a lofty new stage of development.

LOS ANGELES TIMES, 12/12/93, Calendar/p. 6, Kevin Thomas

With the shimmering, elegiac "Faraway, So Close", Wim Wenders continues the magnificent spiritual odyssey he commenced six years ago with "Wings of Desire." It was so fortuitous that Wenders introduced in the first film two angels, both eager to become human and each worthy of his own story, that you have to wonder whether he didn't have the possibility of a sequel in mind at the outset. The film's title refers to its angels' ability to be close to humans without being visible to them or being able to affect their destinies.

In any event, the reunification of Germany that occurred in between the two films is the clear source of the inspiration for "Faraway, So Close." On the most profound of its many levels it can be taken as an allegory on the coming together of the two Germanys and the sacrifice involved in accomplishing it. It even features Mikhail S. Gorbachev, the former Soviet president, pondering the meaning of life.

A meditation on what it means to be alive today, and in Germany specifically, "Faraway, So Close" seems a considerably more complex film than "Wings of Desire." Wenders has so much to express through such a complicated, heavily populated plot that his film can be wearying in its leisurely pacing, despite the constant awesome beauty of its images and miraculous use of sound.

Wenders' ideas, emotions—and his characters—eventually do converge in a stately manner, rewarding the patient with a stunning, enlarging vision of human experience, a melding of the material and spiritual worlds. "Faraway, So Close" can be very tough going in its first half, but given its overall scope, passion and brilliance it is, arguably a great film all the same.

Those who've seen "Wings of Desire" will recall that it concerned the angel Damiel (Bruno Ganz), who falls in love with Marion (Solveig Dommartin), a beautiful trapeze artist, and who craves to become human. This time it's his fellow angel, Cassiel (Otto Sander) who has the urge. But Cassiel is considerably more reluctant, and he finally becomes human only in order to catch a child (Aline Krajewski) falling off an apartment balcony. Whereas Damiel and Marion seem to be living happily ever after, Cassiel, who now calls himself Karl Engel, discovers how tough it can be to be human: very swiftly he plunges from elation to despair, drowning his poverty and loneliness in drink.

Karl's progress toward redemption, his determination to learn how humans see and hear, will serve to connect many different people who in turn represent a cross-section of modern Germany. The mother of the child Karl saves, Hanna (Monika Hansen), and their unofficial guardian, the elderly Konrad (Heinz Ruhmann), once Hanna's family's chauffeur, are sought by a seedy private eye (Rudiger Vogler, star of Wenders' early films "The Goalie's Anxiety at the Penalty Kick," "Kings of the Road" and "Alice of the Cities").

He is in the hire of a brash, breezy and decidedly shady German-born Detroit businessman (Horst Buchholz), to whom Karl, in his naivete, becomes a sidekick. Hovering over Karl in her concern is fellow angel Raphaela (Nastassia Kinski).

Dogging Karl at every turn is Willem Dafoe's menacing, enigmatic Emit Flesti—"Time Itself" in reverse, apparently the universe's Time-Keeper, who has another destiny in mind for Karl, who only wants the simple kind of life Damiel has with Marion; unlike Cassiel, Flesti can move back and forth between being a human and an angel. Besides Gorbachev, also passing through Berlin and impinging upon Karl's story, are Lou Reed (he's also seen in concert) and Peter Falk, who appeared in "Wings of Desire" as himself, a true mensch who cannot see angels but can sense their presence as few other humans can.

Through the interactions of these individuals plus many others, Wenders spins an up-to-the minute fable about the eternal struggle of good and evil, and its implications for Germany—and mankind, for that matter—past, present and future. Although Jurgen Jurges this time takes over for legendary cameraman Henri Alekan, "Faraway, So Close" is just as luminous as "Wings of Desire" in its richly modulated black-and-white sequences and equally beautiful color sections—it's Wenders' notions that angels are color blind. (Alekan this time appears as the captain of a ship in the film's final sequence.) Wenders observes his many people with the kind of wit, compassion and sophistication that Robert Altman brings to his films. "Faraway, So Close" really kicks in and comes alive when Buchholz appears on the scene as a classic good-bad guy, a rascally charmer with as much warmth as irony.

In handsome middle age Buchholz retains the charisma and presence that first brought him international acclaim on stage and screen three decades ago. There's resonance in his performance as there is in those of others, especially the veteran Ruhmann, Falk and Dafoe. Quizzical, wistful and wise, Sander's Cassiel rightly dominates the film with an essentially and appropriately passive presence.

Forbidden to shoot in East Berlin for "Wings of Desire," Wenders is now able to balance his portrait of Germany's key city in all its vitality, grandeur and scars of its tragic past. Wenders takes us to such heroic structures as the Pergoman Museum and down the restored Unter den Linden—and even atop the Brandenburg Gate as well as the Angel of Victory statue with which Wenders commences both films.

The film's visual sweep is matched by Laurent Petitgand's glorious romantic score, which contrasts with sharply contemporary songs not only by Lou Reed but also Laurie Anderson, U2 and Nick Cave, whose "Cassiel's Song" provides "Faraway, So Close" its eloquent end-title accompaniment. Although passed over as Germany's official entry into the Oscars, the demanding but truly rewarding "Faraway, So Close" significantly did take the grand jury prize at Cannes.

NEW STATESMAN & SOCIETY, 7/8/94, p. 20, Jonathan Romney

It ought to be obvious that a man who makes films about angels might turn out to be religious. But somehow it never hit me about Wim Wenders, until he declared himself in a recent interview. Wenders' films are chronically hung up on notions of grace and redemption. But when filmmakers talk about the soul, you tend to assume they mean the soul of celluloid.

Because *Faraway, So Close*, the follow-up to *Wings of Desire*, carries its anxiety about grace so much on the sleeve of its angelic overcoat, its simplicity sometimes comes across as dumbness—just as its hero, the fallen angel Cassiel (Otto Sander), comes across as the ultimate holy fool. Wenders himself is cinema's last holy fool (or the last *convincing* one: does anyone still give Godard the benefit of the doubt?). He's ready to walk into a morass of metaphysical perplexity. Here is a man who, in his underrated essay film *Notebook on Cities and Clothes*, agonised at length about the soul of his shirt.

Faraway, So Close has had a rough ride ever since it was screened last year in Cannes, in a version some 20 minutes longer. It had a reception of bemused shrugs. British critics have written it off as a further step into irreversible dementia after the aptly titled rambler *Until the End of the World*. It's been called formless, sentimental and pretentious, and the fact that it has taken so long to be released here only adds to the wearied indifference.

I can't see how you can be indifferent to a film as heady as this, and I'm putting *Faraway, So Close* right into my list of great misunderstood films. Part of the trouble lies in the deep suspicion that surrounds an art-film director dirtying his hands with a "sequel". Despite Wenders' protests that this is *not* a sequel to *Wings of Desire*, it quite patently is; the only difference being that it didn't start out as one. Wenders simply wanted to make a film in East Berlin, just as *Wings* was made in the West. Inevitably, he ended up with the same cast of characters.

Since *Wings*, the Wall has fallen and former angel Damiel (Bruno Ganz) has taken up a contented earthly residence as a pizza chef, living with his wife Marion (Solveig Dommartin) and their multilingual daughter. This time, it's the turn of Damiel's friend Cassiel (Otto Sander, above) to make the descent to earth, losing invisibility, ubiquity and contact with fellow-spirit Raphaela (Nastassja Kinski). Once on earth, he wanders aimlessly, yielding to booze and melancholia until, stirred improbably by a song at a Lou Reed concert, he starts thinking how he can use his association with a German-American racketeer (Horst Buchholz) and "be good".

The cosmology is the same. Angels still hover over Berlin in black-and-white, tuning in to the waves of consciousness that waft around the full-colour mortal sphere. But this time the film is shot through with anxiety: is it still possible to make *Wings of Desire* after the Wall? Clearly not, and that's where the abiding sense of loss comes from. Although the sense of the miraculous is pretty much intact (Jurgen Jurges' airily gliding photography is every bit as sublime as Henri Alekan's), things can no longer be unfamiliar.

Wings looked forward to a dream of walls falling—not just *the* Wall, but walls between men and women, heaven and earth. *Faraway, So Close* may have nothing striking to say about the new Germany, but in its spirit of stunned post-fall melancholia, it is of its time. Damiel came in search of love; Cassiel is after nothing in particular. Walls have tumbled, but rather than separated realms rushing together, the result is a hungover disorder.

A taxi driver doesn't even know he's in East Berlin; the city itself is an unreadably scrambled map. American gangsters are the returned spirits of German gangsters. At one extraordinary point, Cassiel wanders into an art gallery, and in a dream is transported back to the same spot when Nazi officers are hooting with derision at the exhibition of "Degenerate Art".

There's an often piquant randomness about what Cassiel finds. Lou Reed sits strumming a fragment of his 1973 Berlin album, and wondering why he doesn't write them like that any more. Mikhail Gorbachev is there, pondering on the poet Tyuchev and his utopian vision of reconciliation. He's there because he happened to be in town and gave Wenders three hours of his time; his presence adds to the film's curious scrapbook quality. Gorbachev is not only an element of the real incorporated into the fiction, but a living, faded remnant of an interrupted dream.

Willem Dafoe, written in after four weeks of shooting, looms large as "Emit Flesti", a passion-play demon straight out of Oberammergau. Complaints that he makes an unconvincing evil presence are beside the point; he's purely and simply Willem Dafoe lending a hand to a project that is reluctant to congeal into a fiction proper. These elements give the film a transparency that it shares with Wenders' "essays", like *Cities and Clothes* and *Lightning Over Water*.

The result is massively flawed, but gloriously so, whereas *Until the End of the World* made you cringe. One mistake in its 20-minute trimming has been to lose certain political specifics—its references to gun-running and racist firebomb attacks are now vestigial. This apart, the fact that there is so little sense of place, structure or narrative in *Faraway, So Close* is beside the point.

The marvellously baggy, quizzical Sander is really Wenders' representative on earth—a lost soul uncertain what to do or where to go. But what redeems him, and redeems the world for Wenders, is the grace of the look: the possibility of looking at the world in a way capable of transforming it. What you can't ignore in this film is his enduring passion for that look, which floats with a consistently heady, alarmed curiosity. There are tracking shots here to die for.

Faraway, So Close isn't a fully-formed movie like *Wings of Desire*, which is why I rather prefer it. It's a semi-improvised, drunken notebook of jottings, if an incongruously sumptuous one. It may not make much sense as a film, but as cinema—another thing entirely—it has grace to spare.

NEW YORK POST, 12/22/93, p. 45, Michael Medved

When a film features Peter Falk and Lou Reed playing themselves in key roles, and presents the movie debut of a promising actor named Mikhail Gorbachev, you know you're in for an unusual experience.

"Faraway, So Close" definitely delivers on that promise: It is a bizarre, uneven, often captivating piece of work, and an intriguing sequel to one of the most stunningly original films of the 1980s.

In "Wings of Desire" (1987), German director Wim Wenders (best known in this country for "Paris, Texas") portrayed Berlin—not Los Angeles—as the real "City of Angels."

Heavenly messengers lurked in its alleyways or perched atop its monuments, silently watching the rush of humanity around them. These silent, sympathetic, unseen presences could hear the private thoughts of all passing people, and witness the passion and folly of their lives, but they had no power to change the course of events.

When one especially compassionate angel, Damiel (Bruno Ganz), fell in love with an earthly trapeze artist (Solveig Dommartin), he gave up his status as an immortal and made the fateful transition to ordinary human existence.

In the new film, Damiel is living happily with his family in what used to be East Berlin, and running a pizza parlor appropriately named Casa del'Angelo.

Meanwhile, his former companion, Cassiel (played by Otto Sander, a veteran German actor with a marvelously expressive face), is still performing his heavenly functions, "far away, so close" to the mortals around him.

His new angelic partner is played by Nastassja Kinski, who projects a solemn, soulful, haunting beauty in this film that is truly otherworldly.

In spite of her companionship, Cassiel feels a powerful longing to participate in the everyday life of the city, and at a moment of crisis he steps in to protect a little girl from tragedy—finding himself instantly transformed into a human being.

His main obstacle in adjusting to his new status involves interference from a celestial timekeeper (played by a sneering, out-of-place Willem Dafoe), who shifts between the worlds of angels and humans, determined that Cassiel should return to the heavenly host.

The best part of the film is its first half, where Wenders presents his heartbreaking, black-and-white angel's-eye view of humanity with even more poetic force than he did in "Wings of Desire."

The film's second half, shot mostly in grimy, grainy color, is far less impressive, and centers on Cassiel's all-too-human adventures as a manservant to ruthless German-American gangster Horst Buchholz.

There's also a subplot involving the secrets of a former Nazi chauffeur—played by a spry 91-year-old actor named Heinz Ruhmann, who doesn't look a day over 70. The big climax to all this involves a guerrilla raid by a band of trapeze artists and former angels who capture a cache of deadly black market weapons and blow up a warehouse of violent porno videos.

Much of this action feels like the product of improvisation, or last minute inspiration—as if key scenes came together without too much conscious plan. Nonetheless, the movie's sprawling, off-the-wall, self-indulgence is part of its appeal.

Wenders has created a weighty, wacky picture that's as odd, tender, surprising—and frustrating—as life itself; no wonder his angels long for this passionate mortality.

NEWSDAY, 12/22/93, Part II/p. 59, John Anderson

In the gospel according to Wim Wenders, angels can observe their human charges, counsel them, console them, sympathize with them, and of course invade their privacy. But they can't influence their destiny. Which is where angels part company—unfortunately in this case—from film directors.

In his quasi-classic "Wings of Desire," Wenders used a gloriously free camera, spectacular imagery and divine anguish to create a positive statement about the human condition. It was a spiritual film, naturally, as well as a visual feast that posed intellectual quandaries.

"Faraway, So Close," the sequel Wenders apparently doesn't consider a sequel—at a recent Manhattan screening, he urged the audience to "forget you saw 'Wings of Desire'"—borrows its best conceits from the earlier film: The panoramic views from atop Berlin's Angel of Victory; the black-and-white camera work that depicts the angelic dimension, and the color that depicts the temporal world; and the way Wenders marries the interior dialogue of his human characters with the mind's voice of the angels.

But for a filmmaker who eschews "beautiful imagery"—in an interview in Paris last year, he declared such pictures "nothing"—he relies on such pictures almost exclusively to keep our attention.

The story of Cassiel (Otto Sander), an angel who longs to be human, just as Bruno Ganz did in "Wings," isn't new, and isn't compelling. And it seems to be presented in a tongue-in-cheek manner, as if Wenders were trying to parody Wenders, or create some kind of "Wings" pastiche, and an implied tribute. The earlier film's use of pop cultural touchstones—Peter Falk, for instance, who again plays a former angel named Peter Falk—has hit its saturation point in "Faraway," with Lou Reed performing, U2 contributing to the sound track and an appearance by "special guest" Mikhail Gorbachev.

Ganz is back as ex-angel Damiel, who we first see riding a bike down the street in his capacity as pizza delivery boy (and if this scene wasn't consciously constructed as a "Wings of Desire" joke, Wenders is letting his subconscious get away from him). Damiel is married to the trapeze artist Marian (Solveig Dommartin), and they have a daughter Doria (Camille Pontabry). Cassiel also meets Hanna (Monika Hansen) and her daughter, Raissa (Aline Krajewski), whose plunge from an apartment terrace prompts Cassiel's decision to become human and save the girl. The chauffeur Konrad (Heinz Ruhmann) is Hanna's protector, whose memories of Nazi Germany will be explored with something less than probity. And Horst Buchholz portrays Tony Baker, a shady businessman whose relationship with the evil Patzke (Ronald Nitschke) will predicate the "Murder, She Wrote"-style suspense sequence that climaxes the film.

Wenders may want us to forget "Wings of Desire," but I don't want to. And "Faraway, So Close" isn't the film to make anyone forget it.

SIGHT AND SOUND, 7/94, p. 46, Philip Kemp

Cassiel, one of the invisible angels who watch over the people of Berlin, confides to his colleague Raphaela his longing to know what it's like to be human. Meanwhile he moves among the citizens, listening to their thoughts and sympathising with their joys and sorrows. Among those he watches over are Damiel, a former angel turned human who runs a pizza parlour, his trapeze-artist wife Marion and their daughter Doria; Mikhail Gorbachev, visiting Berlin to give a speech; Hanna, a single mother, her daughter Raissa and Konrad, an old man who used to be Hanna's chauffeur; Phillip Winter, a private eye keeping tabs on Hanna, Raissa and Konrad; Winter's employer Tony Baker, a shady German-born American business-man; Patzke, Baker's criminal rival; and the actor Peter Falk, another former angel, who is visiting Berlin for an exhibition of his drawings.

When Raissa, alone in her high-rise flat, falls from the balcony, Cassiel chooses this moment to become human and catches her. He visits Damiel, who joyfully welcomes his fellow ex-angel. Taking the name 'Karl Engel', Cassiel sets out to explore the human world, only to find it full of loneliness and indifference. Getting drunk, he sinks rapidly into petty crime and degradation. His progress is tracked by a mysterious, sinister figure, Emit Flesti, who alone is able to move freely between the human and angel worlds, and is determined to get Cassiel killed.

Cassiel is rescued from destitution by Tony Baker, who takes a liking to him and makes him his right-hand man. When Patzke takes Baker captive, Cassiel rescues him; in gratitude, Baker offers him a percentage of his activities, which include massive arms-dealing. Horrified, Cassiel runs off, only to come upon the dying Winter, shot by Flesti. Konrad comforts Cassiel and explains Baker's history: he is Hanna's brother, taken to America in 1945 by his escaping Nazi father, while Hanna and her mother remained behind in Konrad's care.

Enlisting the help of his friends, including Marion's acrobatic troupe, Cassiel contrives to hijack Baker's arms cache and spirit it away on a barge, taking Hanna and Raissa along too. Patzke, getting wind of the plan, kidnaps Baker and takes over the barge, holding Raissa at gunpoint to ensure everyone's good behaviour. Cassiel, aided by Flesti, snatches Raissa to safety, but Patzke shoots him dead. In the ensuing commotion, Patzke and his thugs are overpowered. Cassiel's friends mourn his death, consoled by knowing that he is once again an angel and reunited with Raphaela.

What makes it all the more infuriating is that Wenders' command of cinematic technique seems to increase in direct relation to the sogginess of his content. Jürgen Jürges' swooping, lyrical cinematography is no less heart-stoppingly exhilarating than that of the veteran Henri Alekan (who photographed *Wings*, and shows up this time round in a gruff cameo as the barge captain. In fact Jürges' black-and-white scenes are so exquisitely toned that it feels like a letdown when the film switches into colour. (The convention, as before, is that angels see in monochrome and humans in colour.) Wenders' sense of editing is as acute as ever, and from his players—especially Bruno Ganz and Peter Falk—he draws performances of relaxed, engaging charm. To see so much technical mastery placed at the service of such banality might well make the angels weep.

Wings of Desire had to be shot mostly in what was then West Berlin. Post-Wall, Wenders was able to shoot *Faraway, So Close* in the former East Zone where ruins and bomb damage, long since tidied away in the West, still evoke the trauma of the war years. Placing the action in the liberated area of the city is also apt, since what the film addresses is the sense of bleak disillusion that followed the euphoria of reunification. Cassiel—and Wenders too, it seems—sees the people of Berlin sunk in a sterile materialism: "Human eyes can only take—they no longer give," muses the ex-angel. Even Mikhail Gorbachev, in his acting debut, is wheeled in to reinforce the message, quoting the writer Fyodor Tyuchev: "Some say a country can only be forged in blood and steel. We shall try to forge it with love. Then let's see which lasts longer."

At a time when the quick-fix of market forces is destroying Gorbachev's own homeland, it would be hard to quarrel with Wenders on what's wrong with Berlin—and with the world. The problem comes with the triteness of his proposed solutions. Like Bertolucci, he seems to have swapped political acuity for fuzzy moral uplift, and thrown in his sense of narrative drive. Big terms like Time and Memory are tossed around (*"Zeit ist Kunst"*—time is art—reads one wall poster) but rarely pinned down. In *Wings of Desire*, Peter Handke contributed a toughness to the script that ballasted the film's windy abstractions. Lacking Handke's collaboration, the sequel abandons any pretence at narrative coherence, let alone structure.

Plausibility, of course, is beside the point in a fantasy, but internal consistency isn't too much to ask. The first half of the film, in which Otto Sander ambles round peering benignly at everybody, is amiable enough—although anyone who hasn't seen the earlier film, and doesn't know that Damiel also used to be an angel, may have trouble working out what's going on. But after Cassiel opts for full-colour humanity, we are pitchforked into a garbled pastiche of a gangster thriller, tricked out with occasional dollops of Nazi war-guilt; its bland disregard for motivation suggests that Wenders made the whole thing up as he went along. This is a depressingly long way from the taut, ironic reworking of *noir* conventions he gave us in *The American Friend*.

The most ill-conceived element is Willem Dafoe's character, archly named Emit Flesti (try spelling it backwards). Dafoe brings far more style than it warrants to the role of this cut-rate Mephistopheles, who has apparently engineered the whole affair in order to end Cassiel's human life. Yet at one point he simply produces a crossbow and kills off a minor character. Why he couldn't do the same with Cassiel—and why, come to that, he is so determined to see off Cassiel while quite unbothered by Damiel's human state—is anybody's guess.

Yet if *Faraway, So Close* is frequently irritating, it's rarely boring. And it has moments of delight: the troupe of acrobats, turning bungy-jumping into an aerial ballet; Bruno Ganz bowling along on his pizza trike belting out "Funiculi Funicula" in outlandish Italian; Dafoe, warned his malicious behaviour will pall in the long run, snapping back, "I *am* the long run." There's also some neat comedy of confusion with Falk trying to gain entry to a guarded building, causing puzzled debate among the guards over why *Columbo* is showing on their entry-phone circuit. But in the end *Faraway, So Close* founders under the weight of its own self-indulgence. Let's hope some kind angel will protect us from a further sequel in which Nastassja Kinski goes human.

TIME, 1/10/94, p. 69, Richard Corliss

The three rules of movie sequels:

1) *If the original movie is really special to you, the filmmaker, don't make it over.* A sequel is essentially a commercial venture, designed to extend a product's shelf life. Not wanting to taint the memory of their most personal films, Steven Spielberg left *E.T.* alone, and Frank Capra refrained from making *Son of a Wonderful Life*. But Wim Wenders felt no such scruples about redoing *Wings of Desire*, the 1987 philosophic fantasy that is his masterpiece. This try-everything director correctly saw *Wings* as an open-ended excuse for considering the changing state of his

native Germany. So here, with no apologies, is the fascinating sequel: *Faraway, So Close*, or *Wings 2*.

2) *Bring back the old stars and add a big new one.* Bruno Ganz and Otto Sander are back as Damiel and Cassiel, the angels come to Earth. Peter Falk returns as an ex-angel, and Solveig Dommartin as the trapeze artist who'll meet any heavenly body halfway. But here's a casting coup: Mikhail Gorbachev as himself. He sits at a desk, pondering the meaning of life and the purpose of the, universe. "I'm sure that a secure world can't be built on blood, only on harmony," opines the former Soviet leader, now available for smaller roles. "If we can only agree on this, we will solve the rest."

3) *Don't elaborate on the original film's story; instead, remake it.* Rocky always fought a guy; Indiana Jones saved yet another buried treasure; the *Lethal Weapon* lads kept blowing stuff up. Here Cassiel, the second angel, follows Damiel's lead and becomes human, a brand-new Candide. But Wenders actually has a new idea, courtesy of recent history. In *Wings of Desire*, two angels hovered over divided Berlin, invisibly consoling its citizens. In the sequel, written by Wenders, Ulrich Zieger and Richard Reitinger, angels patrol a Berlin that is politically united but even more fractious—a city of gangsters and gun runners, of the homeless and spiritually helpless. *Wayne's World 2* this ain't.

What is the same in both Wenders films is the notion of angels as bestowers of grace on a secular landscape. Wenders' view is traditional and strangely powerful. He sees angels as invisible consolers, gentle kibitzers in the monologues that run endlessly through our mind. They are the eternal observers, God's night watchmen, holy voyeurs. Wenders would probably say they are moviegoers, eavesdropping for a few privileged hours on a world more perilous and beautiful than our own. In a lovely scene, Cassiel comforts an old chauffeur (Heinz Rühmann, a German movie star since 1926) with memories of his childhood. The angel's knowledge validates these reveries, brings the faraway into reassuring emotional close-up.

There is folly aplenty here: klutzy drug lords, nattering detectives, angels on bungee cords. Oh, and Willem Dafoe as a death figure named Emit Flesti—which makes sense only when spelled backward, and then not nearly enough. But Wenders has always worked on the wild side; even his previous film, the botched *Until the End of the World*, was a misstep so grand and elaborate it was like a clown's jig on a high wire. In *Faraway, So Close* the dance lasts almost until the end of the film. And for those two hours it seems almost seraphic.

VILLAGE VOICE, 1/4/94, p. 45, J. Hoberman

Wim Wenders used to be considered the most "American" of New German cineastes. He's since reformed and is currently chairman of the European Film Society. Still, *Faraway, So Close* suggests that if Wenders never quite succumbed to Hollywood's siren song, he's nevertheless been infected by the Hollywood disease—the opportunistic parasite known as vacant sequelitis.

Wenders's *Wings of Desire*, released here almost six years ago, was one of the most original movies of the 1980s and, despite its downward trajectory toward a staidly, cornball conclusion, one of the most satisfying. Wenders's vision of a Berlin brooded over by angels and haunted by unseen forces provided him the occasion for some remarkable camera pyrotechnics even as it offered a remarkable metaphor for the German condition—better than any movie I've ever seen, it conveyed the isolation and melancholy of divided Berlin.

When Wenders made *Wings of Desire*, German unification seemed outside the realm of possibility. But *Faraway, So Close* is a kind of *Wings of Desire 2* and what was fresh and resonant is now routine and bizarrely arbitrary. Shot mainly in the former Soviet sector, as if to provide a geographic complement with the camera swooping through the apartment blocks around Alexanderplatz, the sequel has lost the original's Cold War orientation. Even the aerial pirouettes are less sublime than silly.

Like its predecessor, *Faraway, So Close* begins with a somber seraph (Otto Sander) perched atop Berlin's Angel of Victory, tuning in on the thoughts of the city's mortal inhabitants. (In the Wenders schemata, angels are sensational moviemakers—cosmic voyeurs.) And, as did Bruno Ganz in *Wings of Desire*, the craggy-faced Sander falls to earth and becomes human. "It's so vivid here," he muses as the film stock changes from angelic black and white to garish color. Sander is reunited with Ganz, now a singing pizza baker married to the circus acrobat Marion

(Solveig Dommartin), and, like an eager upperclassman, Ganz turns Sander on to coffee and olives to initiate the comedy of his comrade's adjustment to human status.

Faraway, So Close is looser and wackier and more comic than *Wings of Desire*—Wenders can be said to do comedy. (The effect is light-headed without actually being funny.) It's also blatantly star-struck. The benignly smiling Peter Falk is back, as tuned into angels as he was in *Wings of Desire*, and a dour but decent Lou Reed is in town, pondering the nature of Berlin without the wall. The most bizarre cameo has Mikhail Gorbachev contemplating the meaning of life, as one of Wenders's angels throws a comforting arm over his shoulder—Wenders means to pay homage to the man who deconstructed the wall, but it only certifies the last Soviet leader as a has-been.

Wenders stretches his mythology a bit, providing Sander, while an angel, with a solemn female sidekick named Raphaela (the suitably beatific Nastassja Kinski) and confounding him, once human, with enigmatic Willem Dafoe as a metaphysical conceit called Emit Flesti. (Spell backwards, as the Serutan commercials used to say.) Oppressed with the most impossible part and worst dialogue in the movie, Dafoe gets Sander going on an extended bender and thus precipitates the most affecting sequences. Alone and afraid, calling on the unseen Raphaela, the ex-angel climbs monuments, begs in the street, and collapses in an art museum (which inexplicably carries him back to the 1938 Nazi exhibit of "Degenerate Art").

Ultimately, Sander finds employment working as guardian angel for a mysterious businessman (Horst Buchholz), who has returned to German from America. Here, Wenders concocts a scenario with a halfhearted resemblance to *The American Friend*, enabling him to play out the drama of German unification in thriller terms. The crass Nazi-bred, America-raised operator is brought together with his long-sundered East German sister as ex-angels and their beaming circus cronies happily join forces to rescue Germany from the pollution of imported video porn. As in *Wings of Desire*, albeit on a more global scale, all you need is love.

Faraway, So Close, feels even longer than its 140 minutes—although it has evidently been shortened since its stormy premiere at Cannes last May. It's less arduous to sit through than Wenders's aptly titled *Until the End of the World* and the director manages to contrive some arresting images right through to the last shot of a boat disappearing in the mist. There are even moments when Wenders's nutty metaphysics approaches a loopy grandeur. But the convoluted mythology is more often a distraction from the filmmaking and, as forced and precious as the material feels, it's ultimately an encumbrance. The fantasy that liberated *Wings of Desire* is the sequel's ball and chain.

Also reviewed in:
NEW YORK TIMES, 12/22/93, p. C15, Caryn James
VARIETY, 5/24/93, p. 46, Todd McCarthy
WASHINGTON POST, 2/11/94, p. B7, Rita Kempley
WASHINGTON POST, 2/11/94, Weekend/p. 48, Desson Howe

FAREWELL MY CONCUBINE

A Miramax Films release of a Tomson (HK) Films Company Limited presentation in association with China Film Co-production Corporation and Beijing Film Studio. *Executive Producer:* Hsu Bin and Jade Hsu. *Producer:* Hsu Feng. *Director:* Chen Kaige. *Screenplay (Mandarin with English subtitles:* Lilian Lee and Lu Wei. *Based on the novel by:* Lilian Lee. *Director of Photography:* Gu Changwei. *Editor:* Pei Xiaonan. *Music:* Zhao Jiping. *Sound:* Tao Jing and Ilu Ilc. *Art Director:* Yang Yuho and Yang Zhanjia. *Set Decorator:* Wang Chunpu, Zhang Ruihe, Song Wanxiang, and Cui Xiurong. *Set Dresser:* Liu Zhiping, Xie Xinsheng, and Zhang Jungui. *Costumes:* Chen Changmin. *Make-up:* Fan Qingshan and Xu Guangrui. *Director, Peking Opera:* Shi Yansheng. *Music Designer, Peking Opera:* Tang Jirong. *Stunts, Peking Opera:* Diao Li and Li Yan. *Running time:* 154 minutes. *MPAA Rating:* Rated R.

CAST: Leslie Cheung (Cheng Dieyi); Zhang Fengyi (Duan Xiaolou); Gong Li (Juxian); Lu Qi (Guan Jife); Ying Da (Na Kun); Ge You (Master Yuan); Li Chun (Xiao Si, Teenage); Lei Han (Xiao Si, Adult); Tong Di (Old Man Zhang); Ma Mingwei (Douzi, Child); Fei Yang

(Shitou, Child); Yin Zhi (Shitou, Teenage); Li Dan (Laizi); Jiang Wenli (Douzi's Mother); Zhi Yitong (Aoki Saburo); David Wu (Red Guard).

CHRISTIAN SCIENCE MONITOR, 10/13/93, p. 12, David Sterritt

China's leaders should be proud that their country has produced some of the world's most exciting filmmakers in recent years. Yet fear seems to outweigh good sense where movies are concerned.

When the superb film "Ju Dou" was nominated for an Academy Award two years ago, Chinese authorities tried to yank it from the race, complaining that Zhang Yimou's powerful drama—banned in China—painted too unflattering a portrait of Chinese life.

More recently, Chen Kaige's epic *Farewell My Concubine* shared the Cannes Film Festival's top prize. And again the officials showed more pique than pride, barring the movie from exhibition in China because of some political implications and because one character—a male opera star specializing in female roles—is apparently a homosexual.

Happily, the spirit of Chinese cinema refuses to be squelched, and the atmosphere surrounding it may now be improving. "Farewell My Concubine" has been approved for release after a small amount of editing, albeit with a warning from censors that they are not reducing their vigilance toward future films.

And a healthy number of Chinese filmmakers keep working vigorously despite the bureaucratic obstacles they are liable to confront with each project.

This was demonstrated anew at last month's Montreal World Film Festival, which presented no fewer then seven movies listed as Chinese productions or coproductions. Among them were at least two that deserve high praise: "Farewell My Concubine," having its first North American screenings, and Xie Fei's exquisite drama *The Women From the Lake of Scented Souls*, which came to Montreal after winning the Berlin festival's top award. [This film has not had a theatrical opening.]

The quality that links these movies most closely is a vivid sense of Chinese historical evolution. "Farewell My Concubine" examines this on a grand scale, using the careers of two opera stars as a vehicle for tracing Chinese life from the 1920s through the 1970s.

The film's first hour concentrates on experiences under the old feudal system, showing how the chance for artistic training serves as both a difficult burden and a promising opportunity for the young protagonists. The second hour becomes more melodramatic as one of the main characters falls in love with a beautiful but dissolute woman, sparking an emotionally complex rivalry with his partner. The final portion of the film takes place during the Cultural Revolution, when art and ideology become inextricably mingled.

Of the movie's three main sections, the first and third are the strongest, using personal and cultural events to illuminate broad social and historical issues. The middle hour is less brilliant.

This is a minor quarrel with a major film, however—directed by Chen with extraordinary energy, and superbly acted by a talented cast including the magnetic Gong Li, known for her starring roles in Zhang's most exciting movies.

"The Women From the Lake of Scented Souls" is more intimate and even more stirring. It takes place in a provincial village where a sesame-oilmaker is thrilled to learn that a wealthy Japanese woman wants to invest in her operation, upgrading its technology and increasing its output.

Another story line deals with the oilmaker's son, beset with mental and physical ailments, and with a young woman who is forced—through a financial debt—into becoming the man's wife.

At first, the film's two narrative lines appear to be unrelated except for their occurrence in the same village. But the movie's unity soon becomes apparent, since all of its elements are connected to the difficulties of adapting to a modern style of living—and more specifically, the impossibility of simply erasing the social and psychological habits that dominated premodern life for centuries.

On a social level, the townspeople think foreign investment and improved equipment will bring them squarely into the modern age, but they learn that progress is a less dramatic process than they'd hoped.

On a personal level, the sesame-oilmaker remembers with desperate grief how she was sold into marriage under the old society. She utterly fails to recognize that her money-based scheme to acquire a daughter-in-law is merely an updated version of the same sad scenario. She eventually sees the error of her plan and decides to reverse it, but it's clear to everyone that damage has been done and any correction will be hopelessly inadequate.

Directed and edited by Xie with uncommon thoughtfulness and sensitivity, "The Women From the Lake of Scented Souls" deserves a worldwide audience.

FILMS IN REVIEW, 1-2/94, p. 49, Harry Pearson

All in all, the Year of the Boar has proved most propitious for Asian filmmakers and their American counterparts. And it's about time, judging from the works we have at hand here, for with these filmmakers comes a vitality and, as much—if not more—needed, a far different perspective on the basics in human relationships, particularly those to do with friendships, families, and love affairs than we ever get from American movies.

Of the three movies under review, only *The Joy Luck Club* seems a whiter shade of pale, reduced as it is to a more Hollywood approach to the complications of the mother-daughter relationship. Viewed without comparison to *The Wedding Banquet* and *Farewell My Concubine* (the way most Americans who see *Luck* will take it), the movie may seem more different than it is, simply because there are so few depictions, in American cinema that is, of the generational tensions between mothers and daughters. Because the characters are so dangerously close to the cardboard cut-outs of attitudes, rather than the psychological complexities of character, *Luck*, instead of earning the profuse tears shed in the nation's screening rooms and theatres, simply pushes the right manipulative buttons, high toned though they may be, in a sort of *Classics Illustrated* approach to the subject. In time I suspect, the characterizations in this movie, appealingly acted though they are, will come to seem to be unacceptably stereotypical (though positively so, which is why no one is marching in protest). But stereotypes of whatever stripe only reinforce attitudes, instead of breaking them down so that we may see our fellow humans in all their glorious complexity and unpredictability.

Which is exactly what happens in *The Wedding Banquet*, the kind of bittersweet comedy of character you seldom see in American films. Here we have a group of people (only one a white American, though gay), no one's a stereotype, and all seem to act from their own inner motivations, which we, the audience, are sometimes left to guess. The laughs, and there are many of the quieter kind, come from expressions of character, and from the characters' reactions to the situations in which they find themselves (instead of, as happens so numbingly often, the other way round). If you find yourself misty eyed at points in *this* movie, it won't be because someone has found the right buttons to push, but rather it will be in recognition of the difficulties the members of our species have in communicating with one another. There is, evident here, a genuine affection for the quintet of ensemble actors, each of whom gives a performance that seems less like acting than living inside the characters' skins, from the inside out.

The basic plot will illustrate what I mean: Wai-Tung, a yuppified Asian American, is happily mated to Simon (Mitchell Lichtenstein, son of the glorious Roy) and just as happily in pursuit of the almighty buck—he even has a derelict warehouse space he rents, in this case to Wei-Wei (May Chin) who finds him attractive, though she is well aware of his domestic situation. Wai-Tung's parents (played superbly by Sihung Lung and Ah-Lea Gua, well-known Taiwanese actors), back home in Taiwan, want to see him married off, and are relentless about it, even sending out computer dating forms for their son to fill in. In one of the movie's best quirky touches, Wai-Tung and Simon fill in the blanks with what they think will be impossible requirements—she must have two PhD's, speak five languages, and be an opera singer. No sooner written, though, than—bingo—she's on the way from Taiwan and her name is Sister Mao. Simon then suggests that since Wei-Wei needs a green card and Wai-Tung a bride-in-name-only that a marriage of convenience might be arranged to keep the parents happy. And so it is arranged. The folks show up from Taiwan—Simon is passed off as Wai-Tung's landlord and Simon, a mean hand with a Chinese dish, allows Wei-Wei to pass off his cooking as her own. A city hall marriage is arranged, much to the folks' horror. At a Chinese restaurant after the ceremony, the group accidentally encounters, in the form of the restaurant owner, one of Mr. Gao's army days subordinates, who is only too happy to arrange a "proper" wedding banquet, an uproarious and bawdy affair in which the newlyweds are pushed into sex, a one time affair that produces a pregnancy, and brings all the unspoken assumptions and misunderstandings to a head, though not quite all out into the open. (There are more complications and nuances than I am presenting here.)

While this movie has, at its center, a gay couple, it is not really about being gay. It is, rather, about the expectations that parents have of their children and how the children will try to fulfill those expectations without sacrificing their own individuality. It is about love and friendships, about, at its heart, what we so disparagingly call family values in an era in which the concept of the family has taken on startling new forms. That is, the older generation's expectations versus the reality in which the younger generation finds itself—precisely the sort of conflict that *The Joy Luck Club* attends to only on the surface, and with the safest sort of conventional view of the new family. *Banquet* is a wonderful portent for the future of its director, Ang Lee, whose work we shall follow with interest. As I said, it is distinguished by its ensemble acting, but an especial nod must be given to Lichtenstein who has the most difficult role to play—he is the loving mate whose good nature is stretched past the snapping point, in part because his Chinese isn't good enough for him to understand what is being said most of the time, and in part because he, a control freak, must surrender to a kind of absolute trust, or lose his man.

I saved the very best till last.

Farewell My Concubine is as close to being a masterpiece as any film within recent memory. It is a long film and attempts the impossible—that is, showing the impact of huge cultural upheavals and revolution upon the inner lives of individuals and upon their relationships with each other—and it almost succeeds at that. Its principal failing, a choppy final twenty-or-so minutes may be the result of mainland censorship (the director, Chen Kaige, isn't helpful on this point since he says he hasn't seen the film since it was "cut" by the authorities) since this is the point at which the criticism of contemporary China is at its most ferocious. Don't think for a second that Kaige doesn't take the dimmest sort of view of politics and the "authorities" who make up the political establishment. China's Cultural Revolution is presented with such contempt it's a wonder the dictators there didn't burn the negative.

Farewell is essentially a love story. And it is about a kind of love—one of unshakable commitment and devotion—that doesn't seem to exist much in the West anymore. The two self-sacrificing lovers, both in love with the same man (who becomes less and less worthy of their unwavering troth as he grows older and less daring), could not be more distinctively different. One Cheng Dieyi (played by the striking Leslie Cheung, who should have played M. Butterfly) is a man who sings female roles in Chinese operas; the other, Juxian (played by Gong Li), is the tough minded prostitute who marries the man in question, Duan Xiaolou (Zhang Fengyi). Cheng and Duan have grown up as apprenticed opera singers thrown together at the All Luck and Happiness Academy (which is anything but) as young boys. (Indeed, the scenes at the Academy are reminiscent of the best of Charles Dickens. You can hardly take your eyes from the screen, partly in disbelief at the abusive treatment meted out to each and every boy.) Duan becomes the protector of the gentle and rather passive Cheng, and eventually his lover, a relationship that is to continue, on and off, for the next 50-odd years. The relationship is seriously strained when Duan takes up with Juxian, and, awkwardly, lets himself get trapped into an unwanted marriage. What complicates this is that the two men are among the most popular of Chinese stars, Duan playing a warrior king, Cheng his faithful-till-death concubine. The intricacies of their relationships, one to another, are played out in counterpoint with the deteriorating political situations—from the invasion of the Japanese to the rise of Mao and Communism to the atrocities of the 1966 Cultural Revolution (an 11-year reign of terror within China's political system). What is unusual is that the inner lives of the characters are played out on the stage of public events, indeed, those events give rise to the expression of feeling and deep ambivalences that have few other outlets given the social structure of Chinese society. This makes for some wonderful cinematic moments, and Kaige's near-novelistic structure for his tale thus becomes spellbinding. Leung and Gong Li carry off the acting honors. If this were a Hollywood product, Gong Li would be a shoo-in for a Best Supporting Actress nomination, so vivid is her portrayal of an independent soul, used to living by her wits and by her ability to sometimes intimidate others into doing what's best for her. You come to believe in this character and understand, through the moments of tenderness and sympathy she shows over time, the greatness of her soul. (And, of special worth is the photography, done by Gu Changwei, whose visual palette proves a feast for the eyes.) Beautifully directed by Kaige, and, for once, worthy of the prize at Cannes for best film.

Do yourself a favor and make it a point to see this film.

LOS ANGELES TIMES, 10/22/93, Calendar/p. 1, Kenneth Turan

"Farewell My Concubine" is a slow boat through China, and why shouldn't it be? An unhurried journey on the great tide of modern Chinese history, this gorgeous, intoxicating epic is confident enough of its visual and narrative power not to rush the telling. Old-fashioned in form but modern in psychological dynamic, it's a film that you can lose yourself in, that washes over you like a warm and enveloping mist.

"Concubine's" selection as co-winner (with Jane Campion's "The Piano") of the Palme d'Or merely confirmed what everyone at Cannes felt, that this remarkable film marked the coming of age of Chinese cinema both artistically and politically, and that its subject matter, panoramic scope and stately length (here trimmed to a relatively svelte two hours and 36 minutes) marked it as the "Gone With the Wind" of modern Chinese cinema.

Directed by Chen Kaige, one of the most prominent of China's current "Fifth Generation" of directors and featuring Hong Kong heartthrob Leslie Cheung, mainland star Zhang Fengyi and the alluring Gong Li, "Concubine" concerns itself with more than half a century of the most turbulent political doings.

Starting in the warlord era of 1925 and expanding through the war with Japan, the return of the Nationalists, the eventual triumph of the Communists and the horrors of the Cultural Revolution before it ends in the relative tranquillity of 1977, "Concubine" not only covers a lot of territory, its sense of visual pageantry brings all of it vividly to life.

But "Concubine" is more than just another dazzling face. It also traces the complex emotional relationship between its three protagonists, shaped and reshaped in response to both political events and the demands of their own hearts. But here "Concubine," written by Lilian Lee and Lu Wei from Lee's novel, throws in something of a twist. Rather than the usual romantic triangle, it has both a man and a woman passionately in love with the same man.

"Concubine" opens with a brief prologue set in 1977. Into an empty arena totter a pair of beautifully costumed Peking Opera stars, Duan Xiaolou (Zhang Fengyi) wearing the broad black beard of the King of Chu and Cheng Dieyi (Leslie Cheung) exquisitely dressed as the Concubine Yu. They have not worked together for 22 years, not seen each other for 11, but on this day they will once again perform the finale from the opera that made them famous and gives this film its name.

Having established the longevity of this relationship, "Concubine" now flashes back to 1925 and its beginnings. A shy and slender boy (the future Cheng) is apprenticed to a harsh school for potential opera actors and singers by his prostitute mother. His origins lead the others to tease him, but the group's bluff natural leader (the future Duan) takes a liking to the new boy and good-heartedly takes him under his wing "Concubine" does not hesitate to spend time showing this bond developing, a stratagem that pays off emotionally once they become adults.

Though unfamiliar to most Westerners, Chinese opera has been a popular art form for centuries, combining as it does furious acrobatics, stunning costumes and elegant, stylized gestures and singing in a spectacle that fully lives up to the word. Unfortunately, Chinese opera also believes in physical typecasting and Cheng is literally forced to train for exclusively female parts while Duan is allowed to sing as a robust male.

When we see Duan and Cheng as adults in 1937, time and training have beautifully suited them to their trademark yin and yang performances in the title opera, which tells of a loyal concubine who refuses to abandon the defeated King of Chu even though to stay and dance for him and pour his wine will inevitably mean death.

Generally good-natured and easy-going, though with a pugnacious streak, Duan considers Cheng a "stage brother" he feels a great deal of familial affection for. Cheng, however, who onstage "blurs the distinction between theater and life, between male and female," has begun to live his opera role offstage and fallen in love with the man who plays his king.

Into this volatile mix comes Juxian (Gong Li), the top prostitute at the House of Blossoms brothel. Partly out of love and partly out of calculation, she maneuvers to have the affable Duan marry her, an act that so enrages Cheng that he announces, almost at the same moment as Japanese troops enter the city, that he will never sing with Duan again.

For the rest of the film, through all that political turmoil, Juxian and Cheng scramble, with sporadic success, to undercut each other, one trying to break up the marriage, the other intent on killing the partnership, and both having to deal with that childhood bond that can never totally go away.

Given that this film is set in the world of opera, it should be no surprise that "Concubine's" script makes considerable use of melodramatic plot elements, including such standards as the foundling, the convenient pregnancy and even the lecherous eunuch.

Keeping things honest, however, are two factors, one being the depth of feeling and skill the actors bring to the three principal roles. Zhang Fengyi is casually powerful as the man everyone is in love with, and Gong Li, the star of "Ju Dou" and "Raise the Red Lantern," puts her steely temperament and expressive face to excellent use. Most memorable is Leslie Cheung, who gives an exceptional performance that manages to gracefully emphasize the feminine in Cheng's nature without descending into camp.

Finally, the high level of filmmaking skill of both director Chen and cinematographer Gu Changwei (who shot "Ju Dou" and "Red Sorghum" for director Zhang Yimou) provide a kind of momentum that is difficult to resist. In its superb use of composition, color and light, "Concubine" is practically a textbook of lush visual pleasures.

Though they were not the only cause of "Farewell My Concubine's" (rated R for language and strongly depicted thematic material) celebrated battles with the Chinese censors, some of the strongest and most memorable scenes in the film concern the brutal humiliations and denunciations of the "struggle sessions" that marked the Cultural Revolution.

Director Chen, who as a teen-aged Red Guard publicly denounced his own father (director Chen Huaikai, who works as artistic director here), clearly had a deep personal stake in making those sections of "Concubine" as honest and powerful as possible. That concern has infused the rest of his film as well, turning it into a vision of another time and another place that won't be forgotten any time soon.

NEW STATESMAN & SOCIETY, 1/7/94, p. 33, Jonathan Romney

Chen Kaige's epic *Farewell My Concubine* looks set to clean up as the first art-house blockbuster of the year, and it's a monolith of a movie. Having shared the 1993 Cannes Palme d'Or with *The Piano*, it certainly deserves all its accolades. But who knows whether, a few years ago, the sheer scale of the film and its references to modern Chinese history and the Chinese opera tradition might not have proved a bit too formidable for western audiences?

If *Farewell My Concubine* now seems marketable, it's partly because we have been softened up for it by the success of Chen's ex-cinematographer and supposed rival Zhang Yimou. Zhang's films *Red Sorghum, Raise the Red Lantern* and especially *Ju Dou* struck a chord in the west with an ebullient, highly coloured style that matched a stately feel of apparent timelessness (*Ju Dou* appeared mediaeval, although set in the rural 1920s) with a grandiose emotional sweep that at times seemed like pure Douglas Sirk melodrama.

Farewell My Concubine, though more demanding and austere, has something of the flash and dazzle of that style, at odds with the starker, more contemplative tone of earlier Chen films such as the village drama *King of the Children* or *Life on a String*. (Zhang Yimou, meanwhile, confounded expectations with his most recent film, *The Story of Qiu Ju*: a naturalistic drama that seemed a stone's throw from Ken Loach country.)

Farewell My Concubine belongs in a familiar epic tradition, lying somewhere between *Gone With The Wind* and Bertolucci's *The Last Emperor*, which dealt with the same setting and period, and in which Chen Kaige briefly appeared. With the splendours and rigours of the Peking Opera as its central metaphor, *Farewell* tells the story of two boys who start out together training for the opera in the 1920s. It follows them through the vagaries of history—through stage success and the marriage of one of them, to the mass denunciations of the Cultural Revolution.

The opera background makes for a flamboyant but peculiarly apposite variant on the perennial theatre-of-life metaphor. While history goes through its turbulences, the Opera remains the same, or at least aspires to. The two performers—Xiaolou (Zhang Fengyi) who plays the stage

King, and Dieyi (Leslie Cheung), his drag Concubine—always take the same roles in the opera that gives the film its name. Their whole being is identified with the strictly codified costumes and make-up—but their roles' apparent impermeability won't protect them from change.

The film is framed explicitly as spectacle, a staged marvel. It starts in 1977, as two figures shuffle into a darkened arena, and an unseen figure recognises them as the players returned their greatest, and only, routine. The actors kick into their parts, and the action blossoms into a sinuous Steadicam tour of a 1920s marketplace, in which a troupe of child performers do their act before exploding into thunderous anarchy. There's a great shot when Chen flashes in on one face, thereby signalling one of his key themes—a pancake-faced child mugging joyously among the tightly regimented ranks.

The next time we see the boys, we learn the price of their explosive grace: the daily rigours of the opera school, run by an implacable headmaster of the Wackford Squeers variety whose idea of a short, sharp shock for the boys is balancing a bowl of cold water on the head all frozen night long.

The latest recruit is the androgynous Douzi (later named Dieyi), who is admitted only on pain of having his "monstrous" extra finger severed. As a child, the future drag diva is already getting tangled up in the words to a song that requires him to state whether he's a boy or a girl "by nature". Somehow, they always come out muddled. The point is not whether he's "really" a boy or a girl; it's that he is forever caught between having to be one thing and play another.

The young "girl" has to go through a gruelling masculine discipline in order to become a man fit to masquerade as a woman. As an adult, his homosexuality has no clear status. It can't be identified either as a side product of the role he has been trained to, or as a rebellious subversion of that role, pushing it to the extreme by identifying himself with the Concubine. The idea of a "true" nature is ruled out entirely. Dieyi is a volatile substance contained only by the mask he wears.

As Dieyi, Leslie Cheung's remarkable performance exceeds the bounds of camp to suggest the elusive blankness of the obsessive thespian. As Juxian, the prostitute Xiaolou married, Gong Li—Chinese cinema's one undisputed international star—takes rather more than a support slot. Juxian is a mirror-image of Dieyi, his real-life rival for his stage partner, and a performer every bit as adept as him. There's a wonderful scene where she comes into her own and gives the old teacher some angry lip, leaving her respectful husband dumbfounded.

The opera theme may suggest that Chen is invoking a "timeless" art, like the recently re-released *Les Enfants du Paradis*. But he wrings considerable irony out of his characters' desire for the opera to be timeless, a desire at odds with the realities of history. These highly drilled conservatives, supple in body, can't be supple in attitude, and get left behind at every political turn.

One minute, the opera is a harsh, immutable discipline; the next it's viewed publicly as a decadent indulgence. Later, the very form is overhauled, its old stories booted out in favour of parables of agricultural victory. As the old opera bigwigs shuffle out sheepishly in their new Communist mufti, they shrug it off as "a costume change". And even the roles aren't immutable: Dieyi's greatest trauma comes when his own persona as Concubine Yu is stolen by a young protégé.

The film's cynical insight is that politics, too, is pure performance, an ever-changing floor-show in which what matters is not what you do but what you're seen to do and, more importantly, who you're seen doing it with. When the first denunciations come, we're shown a flag-waving session at which Xiaolou uneasily takes part. And in the final bout, the demonised opera artists are herded together and forced to re-apply their stage slap before they do their most spectacular and most ambivalent turn of all—a massive three-ring circus of mutual abnegation.

What distinguishes the film is not just the scale and seriousness, but the way that small moments, apparently trivial epiphanies, fit into the bigger picture. There's Dieyi's brief opium reveries, his bitching session with Juxian, and a heady sequence when the boys leave the school to learn what their art destines them for: a world of glorious razzle-dazzle, kites and candy apples.

The way that details and memories are threaded through it all makes the film not just an epic, but a Proustian epic (which used to be Bertolucci's forte, for all his pomp). It's something of a baggy monster on first viewing, but *Farewell My Concubine* is considerably richer beneath the surface fire than you would immediately suspect. And God knows it's rich enough even then.

NEW YORK, 10/25/93, p. 84, David Denby

Dieyi (Leslie Cheung), a male singer in the Peking Opera, has the painted white face and tender ruby lips of a concubine; Xiaolou (Zhang Fengyi), his partner and friend, wears fierce black and white face paint and yellow robes as the concubine's lover and king. The two performers want only to be left alone to practice their stylized, exquisite art, but inevitably they are battered by the catastrophes of modern China—the rule of the warlords in the twenties, the Japanese invasion and occupation in World War II, and the various depredations of Maoist rule, culminating in the Cultural Revolution of 1966. At the end of the movie's epic time span, in 1977, Dieyi and Xiaolou appear in full costume in an empty theater. Their audience has vanished; their society, which values political rectitude more than art, has betrayed them. But they still want to perform the same roles they always have.

The award-winning Chinese epic *Farewell My Concubine* is sure to become a success here. Though often violent and tumultuous, the movie celebrates such gentle themes as the persistence of art and love, the preeminence of personal destiny in a society collectivized and massified into a state of brutal inhumanity. But *Farewell My Concubine* is also about spectacle, and for me that's a problem. To Western eyes—or at least to one pair of Western eyes—the way every emotion in *Concubine* gets pressed into pageant, including the most personal feelings, is an oddity that cuts away half the film's meanings. The movie deserves the success it will likely have, but I did find a few things puzzling in its dramatic method (and I've noticed similar stylistic flourishes in other Chinese films). What follows is not so much a negative judgment as a measure of cultural distance. Western eyes could be lying eyes.

Farewell My Concubine is based on a novel by Lilian Lee, a novelist and journalist in Hong Kong who has also written screenplays. Lee, who adapted the novel with Lu Wei, and director Chen Kaige (*Yellow Earth*) work in broad strokes, throwing together personal and national crises (the two seem always to coincide), hammer-blowing every point two and three times. Much of this is fun: Kaige and Lee are entertainers of great vitality, with a powerful sense of the harshness and cruelty of life. Yet in some way, they embody that harshness and cruelty themselves. They jam their violent moods together, without sorting things out.

At the beginning of the movie, Dieyi's mother, a prostitute unable to maintain the child herself, deposits him at the Peking Opera School. Informed that the school cannot take in a boy who has six fingers on one hand, she quickly chops off the extra finger. The act is not only emotionally shocking; it's dramatically shocking—abrupt, decisive, iconic almost. The images are brief: swinging knife, crying child, bloody hand, new pupil at the school. Kaige does very little preparation for the moment and even less follow-up. The school itself is Spartan and punitive, a gray-walled prison in which the boys, many of them orphans or castaways, are ruthlessly trained in movement and voice. Those with superior skills will take fixed roles in the legendary material that makes up the Peking Opera repertory—heavily costumed and artificial dramas in which the performers either tumble about or stand and sing, the voices working within a narrow tonal and melodic range. In contrast with Mozart or Verdi, Chinese opera seems violently physical but also inflexible. What's prized is perfection of execution within precisely defined traditions. When a performer masters those traditions, which may be tiny movements or minute vocal inflections, the audience responds with frenzies of appreciation.

At the school, the master whomps the boys on their butts for the slightest infraction. *Whomp! Whomp!* He hits them for things they do wrong and things they might do wrong in the future. He does more punishing than teaching, but Lee and Kaige seem fascinated by spanking, which is presented as the key to discipline—painful, no doubt, but more personal than, say, the humiliations inflicted in the Communist period by party cadres. You would have to say the movie is pro-spanking. Years later, when Dieyi and Xiaolou are established stars, they come back to the school, willingly take down their pants, and even ask to be whomped some more.

Which brings us, in a way, to sex, about which the filmmakers seem rather confused. As a teenager, the strong and thick-bodied Xiaolou is given masculine roles, while tiny, delicate Dieyi is made to dress as a nun and recite the line "I am by nature a girl, not a boy"—except that he always stumbles and says "boy, not a girl." *Whomp!* Is the movie a protest against the way a child was forced into an unsuitable sexual role? At first we think so: When still a boy, Dieyi is abused by a repulsive, ancient palace eunuch who admires his performing style. Yet Dieyi is in love his entire life with Xiaolou. Is he meant to be homosexual or not? The mature Dieyi comes under the protection of a "decadent" theater patron, Master Yuan, who has the thin-lipped hauteur of a Hollywood sadist from about 1944. The way the moviemakers present it, there's something creepy about homosexuality itself. What exactly did they think Dieyi lost when his finger got chopped off? The movie has squashed, even unconscious, sensuality—many scenes of men spanking both boys and men but a shocked attitude toward sex. At least gay sex.

The two men stand on the stage and sing, accompanied by the Chinese orchestra with its wailing gongs and sudden, stinging blows of the stick, and Dieyi's whitened face, in close-up, has an infinitely tender delicacy. Leslie Cheung, the popular Hong Kong actor who plays him, is genuinely touching; his Dieyi believes entirely in art, and is therefore entirely vulnerable to life. He's crushed when Xiaolou, a crude extrovert, a virile, "normal" man, falls in love with and marries a beautiful prostitute called Juxian (Gong Li). Dieyi wants unity of life and art—he wants to be his partner's concubine offstage, too, and at times he's so absorbed in his role that we can't tell if he has any genuine emotions of his own. Juxian, a shrewd cookie, holds on to her husband, and keeps the two men performing together; but inevitably, as events crash in, sometimes literally marching right into the theater, these three begin to betray one another. Revolution and war destroy both art and private life.

I think we're meant to believe that Dieyi, the one who lives for art, is the truest and bravest of the three—the least compromised—but the ending of the movie is so overwrought I couldn't be sure. In *Farewell My Concubine*, tragic material is handled in a pop style—or rather, a spectacular style. The Peking Opera has had a real effect on Kaige. His movie is all presentation, all surface. He works with a startling physical freedom, but the physicality of the movie is often close to the hyperbolic high jinks of the Hong Kong school of action-film-making. Emotions change very suddenly; everything is externalized—anguish, for instance, which is expressed in violent outbursts. For me this is confusing because the filmmakers seem to be perpetrating exactly the sin they complain of in Chinese life—the constant violation of the private self by public pressures. *Farewell My Concubine* is a powerful experience, but there's no sense that any of the characters has an interior life. After two and a half hours, I still didn't understand either man. Is this a weakness or an irrelevance? I could be asking for meanings that signify nothing to Chinese filmmakers or audiences. Either way, this vivid movie left me overstimulated but dissatisfied.

NEW YORK POST, 10/15/93, p. 29, Thelma Adams

"Farewell My Concubine" refers to the Peking Opera about the king of Chu. Threatened by a rival and tricked into believing that all is lost, the king begs his concubine to leave and save herself. She remains. Dancing one final dance for her king, she slits her throat so that she will be loyal to him alone.

"Farewell My Concubine" is the opera within Chen Kaige's vibrant and operatic film. Don't be put off by a subtitled Chinese film about the Peking Opera. It's never less than completely entertaining, a visual feast gripping to the end. Epic in proportion, it's a Chinese "Gone With the Wind" with a gender-bending twist.

At this year's Cannes Film Festival, "Concubine" shared the Palme D'Or with Jane Campion"s "The Piano." The movie opens in 1977, and then flashes back to 1925 to chart the fate of two opera legends.

Cheng Dieyi (Leslie Cheung) and Duan Xiaolou (Zhang Fengyi) meet as boys, achieve stardom, and continue to play King and Concubine for half a century. The themes of passion, loyalty, politics and fate at the opera's heart resonate in the lives of these two stars and in China's sweeping political changes.

As oppressed schoolboys learning the opera trade, Dieyi and Xiaolou vow to "stick together to the day we die." It is 1925. Warlords rule Peking. At the opera, all roles are played by men and a player is trained for a single type of role. Xiaolou is destined to play the male. Wan and beautiful, Dieyi is prepped for female roles, despite his insistence that he is a boy.

Dieyi's transformation from boy to Concubine is brutal. When his prostitute mother first brings him to the school, the master rejects Dieyi because he has six fingers. His mother chops off the offending finger with a cleaver.

When Dieyi resists singing the female lyrics correctly, substituting boy for girl and offending the school's patron, it is Xiaolou who bloodies him. And once Dieyi has accepted the role of Concubine on stage, a rich and powerful old man molests the beautiful boy, leaving him dazed and disturbed.

By 1937, Dieyi and Xiaolou are stars. Handsome and living a luxurious life particularly sweet after their boyhood deprivation, they are oblivious to the impending Japanese invasion. While being photographed together in Western and traditional dress, they are a team, a couple of sorts.

It is clear that, at least in Dieyi's eyes, their roles of Concubine and King continue even when their faces are scrubbed of the mask-like stage make-up. Dieyi is passive, Xiaolou aggressive; one nurtures, the other protects. Xiaolou's engagement to Juxian (Gong Li), a high-class prostitute, wrecks the balance.

Dieyi's unrequited passion for Xiaolou ignites into jealousy and rage. Juxian, as manipulative as she is beautiful, exacerbates the breach between the stars. The love triangle continues in full force through the war of resistance against the Japanese, the rise of the Communists, and the Cultural Revolution.

The passion and personal betrayal of the lovers is intensified by the witch hunts of each succeeding regime. Political events might hasten their fates, but it is the strength or weakness of each man or woman, the character under the mask, that seals their destiny.

Director Kaige has made a film of grand ambition and matching achievement. The acting is universally first-rate. In a vibrant, visually exciting work overflowing with operatic costumes and sets, Kaige always has his thumb firmly planted on his characters' emotions. Never for a minute does the tide of history, the yen for historical accuracy, sweep the lovers and their plight from center stage.

NEWSDAY, 10/15/93, Part II/p. 64, Jack Mathews

A few years ago, Italian director Bernardo Bertolucci's Chinese spectacle "The Last Emperor" swept up nine Academy Awards, making it the third most celebrated movie in Oscar history. Chinese director Chen Kaige's "Farewell My Concubine," the epic story of two life-long partners in the Peking Opera, may have to settle for simply being a better movie.

"Farewell," as lovely to look at as "The Last Emperor" and infinitely more entertaining and informed, may be nominated for Best Foreign Language film, but that award would merely isolate it further from the mass audience that would love it.

Experts in Asian films tell me the sudden emergence of accessible Chinese movies is due to the need to recoup growing costs from Western markets. The filmmakers are giving their stories more structure, and the subtitles are being written in a livelier, more colloquial style, all of which seems true of "Farewell My Concubine."

But if Kaige has compromised his art in any way, it's not apparent. "Farewell" delves into the political and social subtleties of a half-century of modern Chinese history with a clarity as sharp as the most linear Western epic.

The culture is limitlessly exotic, but we are drawn in and moved around there with ease.

Framed by scenes between the two old opera stars in an empty auditorium in 1977, the film carries us from the 1920s and the era of warlords, though the Japanese invasion of China in the late '30s, to the rise of Maoist communism, to the end of the Cultural Revolution. All of this historical context serves as a finely tapestried backdrop, against which the human drama—as in opera itself—is played out.

The key, as with any successful narrative, is the characters at its core, and Kaige, with a script adapted by Lu Wei and Lilian Lee from Lee's novel, has three sensational figures, the two men of the Peking Opera, Dieyi (Leslie Cheung) and Xiaolou (Zhang Fengyi), and the prostitute Juxian (Gong Li, of "Raise the Red Lantern"), who enters their lives and tests the bond between them.

It's a love triangle at its most potent. Dieyi, the self-sacrificing concubine to Xiaolou's king in the parallel opera within the movie, is forced as a boy of ambivalent sexuality to assume the roles of women while training for the opera, and spends the rest of his life soul-deep in love with his swaggering, unresponsive partner.

For Dieyi, the hope of drawing Xiaolou into a romantic commitment in real life vanishes with the arrival of Juxian, whom Xiaolou brashly proposes to in a moment of impetuous, macho showmanship in front of a pack of would-be clients at her brothel.

The opera that Dieyi and Xiaolou repeat constantly is about choosing your own fate, and it ends in tragic self-sacrifice. Tragedy marks the lives of its stars, too. There are ill-fated affairs, drug addiction, a miscarriage, suicide, political persecutions, acts of courage, and loyalty offset by moments of spectacular weakness and betrayal.

Through it all, you never stop caring for Dieyi, Xiaolou and Juxian, and Cheung, a popular Hong Kong rock star who in operatic drag makes Jaye Davidson look like a bar fighter, gives the most emotionally powerful performance you may see anywhere this year.

But if all this sounds heavy, it is bouyed by its lush opera sequences, Zhao Jiping's music, and by a marvelously wry sense of honor, particularly in the early stretch where the two boys (played by child actors) connive to endure together the rigors and tortuous discipline of their opera training.

"Farewell" runs two hours and 34 minutes, but don't worry, you won't want to take your eyes off the screen long enough to look at your watch.

NEWSWEEK, 11/1/93, p. 74, David Ansen

Chen Kaige's ravishing epic *Farewell My Concubine* should be the movie that opens American eyes to the new wonders of Chinese cinema. The first Chinese film to win the Palme d'Or in Cannes, a smash at the recent New York Film Festival, Chen's big, beautiful movie has the lushness of Bertolucci and the sweeping narrative confidence of an old Hollywood epic. It is the latest, and perhaps most stunning, in a string of films from the People's Republic, Taiwan and Hong Kong that have swept all the grand prizes at festivals from Venice and Berlin to Locarno and Tokyo, a cinematic grand slam that confirms that the boom in China is not limited to economics.

Where much of Western film has reached the decadent phase of rehash, Chinese filmmakers are burning to tell their untold stories. Chen's remarkable movie uses an unusual love triangle to telescope more than 50 years of tumultuous Chinese history. Beginning in 1925, during the warlord era, and progressing through World War II, the Communist victory over Chiang Kai-shek and up through the Cultural Revolution, Chen's tale is told through the intimate focus of two Beijing Opera stars. They meet as children at the harshly disciplinarian opera academy. Cheng Dieyi, with his feminine features, is trained to play the Concubine who dies for her King in the traditional opera "Farewell My Concubine." Duan Xiaolou plays the King. For the fanatical esthete Dieyi (the amazing Leslie Cheung), life and art, male and female, blur dangerously into one: in love with his friend, oblivious to politics, he lives only for the Opera and is devastated when Xiaolou (Zhang Fengyi) marries a real-life concubine, the gorgeous and opportunistic prostitute Juxian (Gong Li).

In the timeless world of the Beijing Opera, the rules of performance never change; the Concubine is always faithful to her King. In the frenzied political world around them, everything is in flux, power shifts and betrayal is the only way to survive. This tortuous love triangle lulls us with its sumptuousness, but its message is unrelievedly tragic. In the climactic nightmare of the Cultural Revolution, when the opera stars are dragged through the streets by the Red Guards, the last remnants of personal loyalty are shredded in an orgy of recrimination. Yet the film leaves one with hope: out of China's bitter history comes this triumphant testament. In movies at least, art has the final word.

In China, "Farewell My Concubine" has met a different fate. The schizoid nature of the current regime, as it embarks on its new capitalist adventure, was evident in the official reaction to Chen's victory in Cannes. While trying to court the Olympics to Beijing, the government was touting "a more open China." But though Chen got a hero's welcome when he returned to Beijing after Cannes, no government officials came to greet him, and the 100 journalists at the airport were instructed not to report on the film. Because of its horrific depiction of the Cultural Revolution, and its frank look at homosexuality, the movie was banned. Only after crucial cuts could the film be shown. Officials were particularly upset by a character's suicide in 1977, at the brink of Deng Xiaoping's era of reform. Who would dream of killing himself at such a moment? "I was not angry," says Chen, "just very, very sad. It's a pity that art and politics still cannot be separated in China."

The explosive creative fever in Chinese film was inevitable: when liberalization began in the '80s, after years of turgid, socialist-realist filmmaking, a new generation of filmmakers leapt to make up for lost time. The Beijing Film Studio (where "Concubine" was shot) was reopened. The new economic reforms encouraged an infusion of film financing from Hong Kong, Taiwan and Japan. Filmmakers still have to get their scripts approved by officials (the bolder ones submit sanitized versions and shoot from a real script). Though "Concubine's" script had passed muster, the power of the finished film obviously proved too much for the fickle bureaucrats.

"Whether or not your script is approved is often just a matter of luck," says Zhang Yimou, whose films have won two Oscar nominations ("Ju Dou" and "Raise the Red Lantern") and the grand prize in Venice ("The Story of Qiu Ju"). "The same script that gets approved in June can be rejected in July." His colleague Tian Zhuangzhuang, whose "The Blue Kite" unflinchingly depicts the grim political realities of China in the '50s and '60s, has given up hope that his movie will ever be shown in his country. Last month the Chinese delegation stormed out of the Tokyo film festival to protest its showing; later it won the top prize.

Chen, Tian and Zhang are the best-known members of the so-called Fifth Generation of Chinese filmmakers, who all graduated from the Beijing Film Academy in 1982. "What distinguishes my generation of filmmakers is that we grew up during the Cultural Revolution," says Chen. "We are still angry about it." The teenage Chen, who was sent to the countryside to work on a rubber plantation, denounced his own filmmaker father. "There was no human dignity at that time. Later I apologized to my father. Still, I cannot forgive myself."

Though encouraged by recent reforms, Chen wonders how deep the changes go. "A quarter of a century ago, we were crazy about politics. Now we are crazy about making money. Our thinking has not really changed. I am afraid one day we will become money hooligans, without culture."

The culture is there, resplendently, in these potent new movies. But not for Chinese eyes.

SIGHT AND SOUND, 1/94, p. 41, Tony Rayns

Beiping (now Beijing), 1925. Effeminate and frail, Douzi is indentured at Guan Jifa's Peking Opera Academy by his mother, a prostitute no longer able to raise him; Guan accepts the boy only after an extra finger on one of his hands has been chopped off. Other boys vilify Douzi, but the athletic Shitou becomes his friend and protector. Life for the boys is harsh, and Douzi one day runs away with classmate Laizi, but a visit to the Peking Opera entrances them and leads them to return; their punishments provoke Laizi's suicide. Douzi triumphs in an amateur performance at the home of Zhang, a former imperial eunuch, and is afterwards sexually molested by the host. He is traumatised, but now accepts that his destiny is to play female roles.

1937. The Japanese army is approaching Beiping. Shitou and Douzi are now stars of Na Kun's opera troupe under the stage names Duan Xiaolou and Cheng Dieyi. Xiaolou specialises in male martial roles and Dieyi in female roles; they are famous for playing the embattled King of Chu and his concubine Yu in the opera *Farewell My Concubine*. Dieyi resists overtures from wealthy opera patron Yuan Shiqing until Xiaolou falls for Juxian, a prostitute from the House of Blossoms. Dieyi's jealousy and moral disapproval of Juxian lead him to visit Master Yuan's house, where he accepts the gift of an antique sword and succumbs to Yuan's sexual advances. That night, Japanese troops enter the city. Dieyi interrupts Xiaolou and Juxian's engagement party to announce that their stage partnership is over. But when Xiaolou is arrested for insulting a Japanese officer, Dieyi wins his release by singing for the Japanese. Xiaolou, ungrateful, accuses Dieyi of betraying his race; Dieyi turns to opium for solace. Their estrangement is ended by their former teacher Guan, who dies telling them how to comport themselves. They adopt a young trainee from Guan's academy, naming him Xiao Si.

1945. Soon after the Japanese surrender, Dieyi is charged with being a collaborator. Juxian, who has miscarried Xiaolou's child, urges Xiaolou to intercede for Dieyi, so that they will no longer owe him anything. Dieyi, dazed by opium, blows his chance of an acquittal in court; but he is released anyway on the orders of a Kuomintang officer who wants to see him perform. By 1948, with Dieyi still lost in opium dreams, Xiaolou is reduced to selling fruit on the streets.

1949. The Communists take the city, renaming it Beijing. Yuan is denounced at a mass meeting. Xiao Si, now an eager young militant, enlists the aid of Xiaolou and Juxian in curing Dieyi's opium addiction, but soon after turns against his adoptive 'parent' and steals his stage role as Concubine Yu. Dieyi abandons the theatre.

1966. The Cultural Revolution erupts, and Xiao Si leads a group of young Red Guards in interrogations of Xiaolou and Dieyi about their past political 'crimes.' Under extreme duress, Xiaolou and Dieyi betray each other, and Xiaolou is pressured into saying that he never loved the former prostitute Juxian. Soon after, Juxian hangs herself. 1977. As China begins to recover from the Cultural Revolution, Xiaolou and Dieyi are reunited on an opera stage for one last performance of *Farewell My Concubine*. At the play's climax Dieyi, identifying totally with the character of the concubine, commits suicide with the sword he received from Master Yuan.

Covering much the same historical period as *The Last Emperor*, and with much the same Steadicam sweep, *Farewell My Concubine* looks very much like a political corrective to Bertolucci's epic. *The Last Emperor* (in which Chen Kaige had a prominent cameo role) moved from Qing Dynasty imperial exotica to Japanese-fascist decadence to a benign view of the Communist 'reinvention' of Chinese society, faithfully reflecting Party-line cliches at every stage of the historical pageant. Chen's film, however, offers a diametrically opposed reading of China's modern history. It starts out with grass-roots hardships at the Peking Opera Academy in the 1920s; the emphasis on poverty and on physical and emotional pain effectively blocks any underlying impulse to romanticise the 'old society'. It sails through the nightmare of the war and the years of Japanese occupation with the minimum necessary denunciation of Japanese militarism, preferring to stress the indifference of art to politics, and to note that there were Japanese officers perfectly capable of appreciating the finer points of Chinese culture. And it views China's decades under Communist government as a rising tide of lies, hypocrisies and betrayals, with the 'new masters' behaving at least as badly as their Japanese predecessors. This is a strong (and, for a made-in-China film, brave) account of China's agony, and it has recognisable roots in Chen Kaige's four earlier features.

In other respects, of course, this is a major departure for Chen. His first big-budget, studio-shot film, it also marks his first work with established movie stars and his first hesitant engagement with the demands of melodrama. It seems fitting that the result shared the Cannes Palme d'Or with *The Piano*, since Chen, like Jane Campion, had suffered a bruising in previous years at Cannes. *King of the Children* and *Life on a String* both played in competition without winning prizes; neither attracted the kind of critical hostility that *Sweetie* did at the festival, but both ran aground on the general ignorance of Chinese history, politics and culture. Critics and audiences were unable to supply the larger perspectives needed to make sense of Chen's subtle and aesthetically refined allegories. *Concubine* confronts that ignorance head-on, using Lilian Lee's popular novel as the basis for a flagrantly unrealistic drama of love, treachery and death that is readily accessible to any audience willing to watch a subtitled movie. Miramax's acquisition of rights for all English-speaking territories, concluded before Cannes, has clinched Chen's shift from small art-house audiences to a broad public. It has also resulted in some Hollywood-style 'fine tuning': Miramax has negotiated 14 minutes of cuts with Chen since the Cannes showing, and the original English title *Farewell to My Concubine* has been abridged.

Purists are already lamenting Chen's 'sell-out' to commercialism without, however. suggesting what other way forward he might have found as a Chinese director needing a global audience to survive. It's true that *Concubine* is a much less 'personal' film than Chen's previous ones. This time, no character represents the director's point of view, and the sprawling storyline resists being reduced to any level of metaphor or allegory. As in Zhang Yimou's *The Story of Qiu Ju* and Tian Zhuangzhuang's *The Blue Kite*, events here mean exactly what they seem to mean; there is no resort to ambiguity or evasion. Unlike his contemporaries, however, Chen has opted for high artifice rather than 'realism' in his approach to China's unresolved traumas.

Although the storyline spans some five decades and the background chronology respects historical fact, Chen makes no attempt to age his main characters convincingly and plays fast and loose with historical credibility. Chen's point is that the film's central *gestalt*, the eternal tension between male and female, between adults and children, between people and the roles they play, is essentially timeless. Xiaolou, Dieyi, Juxian and Xiao Si are all semi-detached from their historical roots; they are in their own time warp, fated to act out their passions and conflicts oblivious (or, better, impervious) to most of what happens around them. The main characters are represented ahistorically because they measure themselves against operatic archetypes, not everyday role models. Their reality, one could say, is purely existential.

Where this concept becomes problematic is in the depiction of homosexuality. Lilian Lee's original novel (since rewritten to bring it into conformity with the screenplay) was straightforwardly a gay love/hate story, squarely centred on the relationship between Xiaolou and Dieyi. Chen Kaige's major change to the book was to boost the part of Juxian from a two-page walk-on to a full scale role for Gong Li; this is perhaps justified by the resulting sharp contrast between Concubine Yu as a courtly female archetype and Juxian as a brassy and opportunistic hooker. But the inflation of Juxian's role also prevents the film from dealing with Dieyi's homosexual feelings for Xiaolou; in fact, it helps it to evade the issue altogether. The introduction of Douzi/Dieyi as a child with six fingers on one hand suggests that he is a freak of nature (biological determinism?), but the following scenes in which the boy is forced against all his instincts to accept female roles seem designed to offer ammunition to the Clause 28 lobby: ruthless cultural conditioning is shown to 'promote' homosexuality in the boy. As a child, Shitou/Xiaolou is sensitive to the plight of his effeminate friend and becomes a virile young protector, sharing his blanket and caressing Douzi tenderly in the bath; but the adult Xiaolou is crassly insensitive to Dieyi's feelings in a way that makes nonsense of the boyhood scenes. Whether this evasion of the gay issues is evidence of directorial homophobia, as some critics are claiming, or whether Chen Kaige simply failed to think through the implications of his borrowed storyline remains moot. Either way, the resulting blockage leaves a major dent in the film's credibility as psychodrama.

Much less controversial is the overall success of the film's visual and aural aesthetics. Cinematographer Gu Changwei and sound designer Tao Jing achieve wonders in creating the fictional space for the film's abstracted characters, giving the film a persuasive unity and coherence. It is their contribution that enables Chen to pull off the feat of simultaneously rooting his story in the historical process and abstracting his main characters from that process. Fittingly, the film's sense of the push-pull of history comes to a head in the Cultural Revolution scenes of betrayal and mutual recrimination. These are undoubtedly the scenes that have the strongest personal meaning for Chen, who here publicly makes amends for denouncing his own father at the time by crediting the man himself, Chen Huaikai, as the film's 'artistic director'. These same scenes, with Dieyi and Xiaolou confronting each other across a bonfire of opera libretti, also contain the film's key image: an inserted close-up of Xiao Si experiencing something like orgasm at the moment that Xiaolou cannot bring himself to say that Dieyi was Master Yuan's lover, All of the film's tensions, contradictions and evasions come together in that one shot, making the film more than worthy of the director of *Yellow Earth* and *King of the Children*.

VILLAGE VOICE, 10/12/93, p. 49, J. Hoberman

Beijing will have to wait for the Olympics, but Chinese movies are muscle-flexing on an international scale unseen since the emergence of the *Neue Deutsche Kino* some 20 years ago.

Fashionably decentered, Chinese cinema is produced not only throughout the People's Republic but in Hong Kong and Taiwan, Southeast Asia and North America—with new hybrids and permutations forming all the time. HK hasn't just spawned a movie industry able to withstand our own, it's begun to cast a spell on Hollywood. Even before spring's Bruce Lee bio-pic, the cognoscenti spotted traces of cult favorite *A Chinese Ghost Story*. Three years ago, it was tough to get *Premiere* to run a piece on John Woo; after *Hard Target* this summer, it was tougher to find a slick without a Woo profile—his publicity dwarfing that of star Jean-Claude Van Damme.

Now the buzz has Stallone touted for *The Killer*'s American remake and genre-master Tsui Hark following Woo to Hollywood. Perhaps it's not too late for HK's amazing, but aging, Jackie Chan, whose *Police Story III* opens Friday for a limited run north of Chinatown. (Would you believe me if I told you that the stunt-mad denouement—Jackie and costar Michelle Yang dangling from a helicopter as it wheels over the flaming bumper cars of downtown Kuala Lumpur—packs more thrills than the climax of *Terminator 2*?)

China isn't near, as was said in the '60s, it's here. Over the 1992-93 season, Chinese art movies won the equivalent of racing's triple crown—successive top prizes at Venice, Berlin, and Cannes.

It may be a coincidence that *The Joy Luck Club* is posting the highest per-theater grosses of any current release (with *M. Butterfly* a potential challenger, but it's no surprise that the current New York Film Festival boasts three highly impressive Chinese movies—two of them showing this week.

Directed by "Fifth-Generation" stalwart Chen Kaige, produced by former kung fu star Hsu Feng, based on a bestseller by Lilian Lee, featuring international glamour icon Gong Li and an army of extras, starring Canto-pop idol Leslie Cheung, evoking *The Children of Paradise* even as it draws on the spectacle of the Beijing opera, and unfolding over the course of a tumultuous half-century, *Palme d'Or*—cowinner *Farewell My Concubine* is the most cannily packaged Chinese art film to date. Combining PRC scope and HK glitz, this sumptuous romantic epic suggests '30s Hollywood born again. It's David O. Selznick's dream of a red chamber, the old MGM alive and kicking the gong around. The ornate brocade and smoky interiors are multiplied by numerous mirror shots, the atmosphere so heavy Yves St. Laurent ought to name a perfume after it.

Total pop compared to Chen's previous features, *Farewell My Concubine* is an extravagant gloss on broad cultural archetypes—the director once cited *Batman* as an American equivalent. A tale of two actors—one a player of male roles, the other (Cheung) an impersonator of women—it takes the title of a Beijing opera that ends with the double suicide of a defeated ruler and his favorite mistress. Chen's two protagonists are trained from childhood to inhabit these parts, and the identification transcends theater. It's basically a love story and, for all the coy sexuality, Cheung creates a more androgynous being than the opera star John Lone plays in *M. Butterfly*, blurring gender as his character merges art and life. When the "ruler" marries a real concubine (Gong), the jealous stage "concubine" gives himself to a wealthy patron—nervous thunder in the background presaging the series of mutual betrayals that will climax amid the Cultural Revolution.

Farewell My Concubine emphasizes the brutal training of the Beijing opera, where both Jackie Chan and John Lone served apprenticeships: "How many beatings does it take to become a star?" one child wails. But this harsh discipline is scant preparation for the hard knocks of Chinese history—the characters suffer through war, occupation, prison, and cataclysmic shifts in the political line. The movie is not devoid of irony—in 1949, an actor optimistically reasons that "even the Communists have to have opera"—but it's even more stuffed with grand gestures. The stage-concubine storms into his partner's engagement party, chucks an antique sword at the happy couple, and breaks into a star-fit cut short by the frantic news that "the Japanese have invaded the city!" *Farewell My Concubine*, hello Beverly Hills.

Also reviewed in:
CHICAGO TRIBUNE, 10/29/93, Friday/p. A, Michael Wilmington
NEW YORK TIMES, 10/8/93, p. C22, Vincent Canby
VARIETY, 5/24/93, p. 46, Derek Elley
WASHINGTON POST, 10/27/93, p. C10, Hal Hinson
WASHINGTON POST, 10/29/93, Weekend/p. 44, Desson Howe

FATAL INSTINCT

A Metro-Goldwyn-Mayer release of a Jacobs/Gardner production. *Executive Producer:* Pieter Jan Brugge. *Producer:* Katie Jacobs and Pierce Gardner. *Director:* Carl Reiner. *Screenplay:* David O'Malley. *Director of Photography:* Gabriel Beristain. *Editor:* Bud Molin and Stephen Myers. *Music:* Richard Gibbs. *Music Editor:* Will Kaplan. *Sound:* Petur Hliddal and (music) Armin Steiner. *Sound Editor:* Bruce Fortune. *Casting:* Renee Rousselot. *Production Designer:* Sandy Veneziano. *Art Director:* Daniel Maltese. *Set Designer:* Stan Tropp. *Set Decorator:* Chris A. Butler. *Set Dresser:* Douglas M. Vaughn. *Special Effects:* Clay Pinney. *Costumes:* Albert Wolsky. *Make-up:* Stephen Abrums and Hallie D'Amore. *Stunt Coordinator:* M. James Arnett. *Running time:* 89 minutes. *MPAA Rating:* PG-13.

CAST: Armand Assante (Ned Ravine); Sherilyn Fenn (Laura); Kate Nelligan (Lana Ravine); Sean Young (Lola Cain); Christopher McDonald (Frank Kelbo); James Remar (Max Shady); Tony Randall (Judge Skanky); Clarence Clemons (Clarence); Michael Cumpsty (Laura's Husband); John Witherspoon (Arch); Blake Clark (Milo Crumley); Edward Blanchard (Restroom Patron); David Greenlee (Restroom Stall Patron); Tim Frisbie (Guy in Bumper Car); Michael MacLeod (Freckle-Faced Kid); Carl Reiner (Judge Ben Arugula); Laurie Lapinski (Frightened Woman); Eartha Kitt (First Trial Judge); Harvey Levine (Blind Guy); Christopher Darga (Prison Guard); Bernard Hiller, Lucy Lin, Jane Lynch, and Casey King (Prison Reporters); Jacob Vargas (Flower Delivery Man); Alex Zuckerman (Jeff); Ronnie Schell (Conductor); Bunny Summers (Train Passenger); Judy Nagy, Julie Donatt, Pauline Arthur Lomas, Suli McCullough, and Bernard Hiller (Reporters); Bob Uecker (Sportscaster); Mark Anthony (Sports Announcer); Kevin Michael Richardson (Bailiff); Susan Angelo (Lana's Prosecutor); Gregory Sporleder (Court Clerk); Joseph Attanasio (Jury Foreman); Savannah Smith Boucher (Woman Juror); Steve Houska (Courtroom Usher); Roger Reid (Court Reporter); Barry Eisen (Press Room Reporter); George Lopez and Keith Campbell (Murder Investigators); Doc Severinsen (Guest Musician); Vito Mirabella (Hot Dog Vendor).

LOS ANGELES TIMES, 10/29/93, Calendar/p. 10, Chris Williams

If you somehow managed to miss any of the erotic murder thrillers of the last five years or so, "Fatal Instinct" offers a quick—though not painless-primer in virtually every psychosexual one of them.

A more pointed genre parody intent on proving there's *noir* business like show business could've been ripping fun. But director Carl Reiner is more intent on offering Cliff's Notes for VCR couch spuds than satire. It's the kind of endlessly referential, toothless spoof that sticks an elbow in your side every 20 seconds or so: "Now we're doing the 'Body of Evidence' candle wax scene! Recognize the funny-hats montage from 'Sleeping With the Enemy'? Get it?"

By the time you've been thus poked and prodded through patchwork re-creations of most of "Fatal Attraction," "Body Heat" and "Cape Fear," your charity for caricature is pretty much rousted by rib fractures.

The picture's original shooting title was "Triple Indemnity," though the change was just as well, since the movie doesn't give its audience enough credit for remembering old movies to spend more than a few token moments referencing anything pre-'80s. Armand Assante stars as Ned Ravine. (a combination of tough-talking suckers William Hurt and Michael Douglas), who has an ill-fated, adulterous fling with blond-bewigged temptress Sean Young (doing Kathleen Turner, Glenn Close, Sharon Stone, and Madonna).

Assante is also being stalked by psychotic ex-con James Remar (as Robert De Niro) *and* his insurance money-hungry wife Kate Nelligan (who actually resembles Barbara Stanywck, from a certain angle). His only true friend is loyal secretary Sherilyn Fenn, who's in a spot of stalking trouble herself after feigning death at sea to hide from her abusive husband (á la Julia Roberts).

This manic jumble takes its cues, of course, from the anything-goes absurdity that's been the hallmark of all movie parody since the runaway success of "Naked Gun." The crucial difference is that the Zucker-Abrahams-Zucker team (at its triadic, pre-split best, anyway) usually approximated the form and not so much the specificity of its sources. "Airplane!" will still be a riot a hundred years from now, but "Fatal Instinct" runs the risk of leaving even its immediate target audience adrift during fleeting homages to flops like "Body of Evidence," "Body Double" and "The Temp."

The casting has its benefits, with Assante an unlikely enough *farceur* that you have to laugh when he sinks to doing the mambo in high heels, and with Young so very game to make light of her own popular nutso-*fatale* image.

And Reiner and writer David O'Malley do rack up a few chuckles in the early going: a not-so-high-speed chase in bumper cars; the *noir* hero who has a ceiling fan in his own auto; even a nice bit of Blake Edwards-style slapstick that takes place in Nelligan's overly populated bedroom.

But, through most of the hobbled homage in "Fatal Instinct" (rated PG-13), Reiner's own best instincts take a turn for the terminal. The man who created "The Dick Van Dyke Show"—and who did similar femme-fearing misogyny and *noir* spoofery in "The Man With Two Brains" and

"Dead Men Don't Wear Plaid" far more successfully—deserves better than to wind up feeding off the Zucker brothers' spoils.

NEW YORK POST, 10/29/93, p. 29, Michael Medved

As you might guess from its title, the new Carl Reiner comedy "Fatal Instinct" simultaneously satirizes "Fatal Attraction" and "Basic Instinct," but its ambitions hardly stop there.

This frenetic and frequently funny film also spoofs "Sleeping With the Enemy," "Cape Fear," "The Postman Always Rings Twice," "Body Heat," "Chinatown," "Double Indemnity," "A Kiss Before Dying" and many other titles.

The story centers on a typically hard-boiled hero, (Armand Assante), who works as a cop by night and a lawyer by day, often defending the same crooks that he's just arrested.

Despite his claims of an instinctive ability to sort out "the rotten apples and the peaches" among women, he fails to notice that his wife (Kate Nelligan) is conducting a torrid affair with a bumbling auto mechanic (Christopher McDonald) who she enlists in a scheme to murder her husband for his insurance money.

At the same time, Assante must deal with a potentially fatal distraction in the form of a mysterious panty-free sexpot (Sean Young), and a vengeful ex-client (James Remar) who's just been released from prison, while his only reliable ally is his plucky, infatuated legal secretary (Sherilyn Fenn).

This story plays itself out with so much inane energy that it's easy to get caught up in the gross, childish spirit of the piece. When impassioned defense attorney Assante declares, with his most earnest poker face, that "the prosecution arguments are illogical, irrelevant, immaterial and caca-poopie-doodoo!" it is shamelessly stupid, but also very funny.

The hugely elaborate sex scene between Young and Assante—involving spinning plates, contortions inside refrigerators, electronic buffing of bare buns, and other innovations—is both outrageous and hilarious.

Director Reiner's wide range of satirical targets makes for some problem in focus: the films he references have nothing in common with one another beyond the vague designation "thriller."

Some of these pictures are film noir classics (previously borrowed by Reiner in the amusing "Dead Men Don't Wear Plaid"); others are contemporary melodramas (or recent remakes) that only dimly reflect the old format.

Unlike the prolific Zucker-Abrahams team (which created the "Airplane!," "Naked Gun" and "Hot Shots" Series) Reiner isn't satisfied to take aim at one sort of film at a time: As a result, you're never sure what's coming next and there's no sense of beating a dead horse with satiric overkill.

Amazingly enough, "Fatal Instinct" may represent career high points for both Assante and Young—neither of whom has previously been known for dramatic (or comedic) range.

Beyond his brilliance in "The Mambo Kings," Assante has looked stiff and stagey in many movie roles, but here his dull-witted straight man is a comic triumph—even funnier that Leslie Nielsen in the "Naked Gun" films.

Young also shines, suggesting that tasteless, nut-case comedy may provide that ideal vehicle for this often ill-used actress.

The gorgeous camera-work and atmospheric lighting by Gabriel Beristain ("Caravaggio") captures her with an appealing air of old-fashioned glamour, and she has never come across as warmer—or sexier—than she does here.

Reiner proudly describes "Fatal Instinct" as "the most beautifully photographed silly movie ever made," and he may be right.

In any event, after his disappointing outings with "Sibling Rivalry," "Bert Rigby, You're a Fool," "Summer School" and other feeble flops, it's a genuine pleasure to see this beloved institution of American comedy once again resorting to his own fatally funny instincts.

NEWSDAY, 10/29/93, Part II/p. 74, Jack Mathews

The quality of Carl Reiner's movies has often drifted, like a shopping cart with a bad wheel, over the line separating intelligent comic invention from sophomoric slapstick.

Maybe it was his early association with Mel Brooks, or the fact that, he spent so many of his developing years cranking out jokes and sketches for TV. But few comic minds have been put to as uneven use as Reiner's and none has had the range to reach both the height of his brilliance ("All of Me") and the depth of his banality ("The Jerk").

Both hemispheres of Reiner's brain were engaged on "Fatal Instinct," a pun-filled, hour and a half send-up of Hollywood thrillers, done in the blatantly imitative style of "Airplane!," "The Naked Gun" and "Hot Shots!" And though the banal side of him is in firm control, there are, among the hundreds of jokes attempted, a few good laughs.

"Fatal Instinct" is more than a parody of its namesakes, "Fatal Attraction" and "Basic Instinct." It's a Frankenstein's monster of a comedy, with scenes, characters and dialogue summoned up from such mysteries and thrillers as "Double Indemnity," "Chinatown," "Body Heat," "Sleeping With the Enemy," and "Cape Fear" (the Scorsese version).

The sketches and sight gags are interlaced with a story about Ned Ravine (Armand Assante), a cop who moonlights as a defense lawyer for those he arrests, and the three women—his scheming, unfaithful wife (Kate Nelligan), a sociopathic one-night-stand (Sean Young) and his lovestruck secretary (Sherilyn Fenn)—who threaten to addle his simple mind.

Reiner, with a script by stand-up comic and former "Mork and Mindy" writer, David O'Malley, doesn't stick with any plot theme very long. The real inspiration here is not the movies being mocked, but the success the Zucker brothers—David and Jerry. and Jim Abrahams have had with this brand of loopy cartoon humor, beginning with "Airplane!"

No one ran sustain a 20-jokes-per-minute pace, not even the "Airplane!" gang, but the success ratio has to be higher than in "Fatal Instinct." Even when Reiner introduces a fresh idea, the image of a beautiful woman in a slinky evening gown with napkins and candy wrappers stuck to her heel, he ruins it by repeating it a half-dozen times.

The bigger problem is that O'Malley and Reiner are trying to mock sequences from films that were more than a bit self-conscious when they were done the first time, and the effort is often painfully strained. Twice they try to outdo the "speeding" metaphor ("How fast was I going, officer?") that served as foreplay between Barbara Stanwyck and Fred MacMurray in "Double Indemnity," and you simply can't spoof dialogue written (by Billy Wilder and Raymond Chandler) with its tongue that deeply in its cheek.

In the opening sequence, Assante and Sean Young replay the scene from "Body Heat" where Kathleen Turner gets William Hurt worked up with a string of sultry double entendres. That was pretty much a send-up itself, of the Bacall/Bogie "put your lips together and blow" scene from "To Have and Have Not," and having Assante and Young get steamed up over the shape of a hot dog doesn't do much for anybody.

It is understandable for someone of Reiner's facile wit to want to follow "Naked Gun" and "Hot Shots!" These are movies that make all of us think we could make a living writing in Hollywood, and Reiner and Mel Brooks, with their hilarious "2,000 Year Old Man" albums, captured some of the same lunacy more than three decades ago.

But it is not easy to come up with fresh material by cannibalizing old movies, as the Zuckers/ Abrahams team did, and as Reiner and O'Malley have shown with "Fatal Instinct," it's impossible to do it by imitating the cannibals.

Also reviewed in:
NEW YORK TIMES, 10/29/93, p. C8, Janet Maslin
VARIETY, 10/18/93, p. 50, Brian Lowry
WASHINGTON POST, 10/29/93, p. B7, Rita Kempley

FATHER HOOD

A Buena Vista Pictures release of a Hollywood Pictures production. *Executive Producer:* Jeffrey Chernov and Richard H. Prince. *Producer:* Nicholas Pileggi. *Director:* Darrell James Roodt. *Screenplay:* Scott Spencer. *Director of Photography:* Mark Vicente. *Editor:* David Heitner. *Sound:* J. Bayard Carey. *Music:* Patrick O'Hearn. *Casting:* Michael Fenton and Allison Cowitt.

Production Designer: David Barkham. *Art Director:* Dins Danielsen. *Set Decorator:* Suzette Sheets. *Costumes:* Donfeld. *Stunt Coordinator:* Charles Picerni. *Running time:* 84 minutes. *MPAA Rating:* PG-13.

CAST: Patrick Swayze (Jack Charles); Halle Berry (Kathleen Mercer); Sabrina Lloyd (Kelly Charles); Brian Bonsall (Eddie Charles); Michael Ironside (Jerry); Diane Ladd (Rita); Bob Gunton (Lazzaro).

LOS ANGELES TIMES, 8/27/93, Calendar/p. 14, Michael Wilmington

When a foreign-born director starts making films in the United States, he or she often gets high on the physical landscape. Energized, they show us things that American filmmakers—often obsessed instead with turning landscape into *metaphor*—take for granted.

In "Father Hood", Darrell James Roodt, the fine young South African director of "A Place for Weeping" and "Sarafina!" slips into that tradition—although his material is slim. It's another chase movie, a family fugitives tale about a lovable crook of a dad (Patrick Swayze) springing his kids from an abusive child care institution and vamoosing on a cross-country chase with hordes of cops in hot pursuit—and the social messages about systemic flaws rattling along behind like a trail of tin cans tied to the bumper.

Novelist Scott Spencer, the author of "Endless Love," wrote the script from an idea by producer Nicholas ("GoodFellas") Pileggi. And neither of them are pushing hard. It's as if they've deliberately scaled themselves down: trying to cover the formulas, think and write cute, press all the right buttons. The script shows only a dim sense of how newspapers are written, how ordinary people talk. The only dialogue that rings true is the public-speak drone of the judges and the bureaucrat bad guys.

But Roodt plainly relishes the chance to get out on the road, to show us the high hot sky over Nevada highways and Hoover Dam; skitter through L.A.'s alleys and the Glenrose limestone tunnels of Texas' Cascade Caverns: blaze through Mojave and—like Hong Kong's John Woo in "Hard Target"—nose around New Orleans.

"Father Hood" works on a pure travelogue level. As shot by Roodt's South African cameraman, Mark Vicente, it's wonderful to watch. Most of the characters may be trapped in programmed spontaneity, but you can get a real lift out of the landscapes, the crisp sunlight splayed over gas stations and billboards, and the cannonade of '50s and '60s rock oldies that keeps surging out of outlaw dad Jack Charles' car radios. Critics often use a lazy cliché for action movies: They call them "rides." But that's what "Father Hood" is: a fast ride, in congenial company.

Like the ex-Iron Curtain directors who get smashed on American pop culture, Roodt comes from repressive environs; you can tell he's firmly on the side of crazy, reckless Jack in his war with the law. But Spencer doesn't really make these characters tick. What accounts for Jack's odd notion that kidnaping his kids at gunpoint won't affect his upcoming court date? The dialogue is slick and unsurprising; when people get into arguments, it's like a screaming game show.

Even so, there's a smartness to the writing that the actors catch. Swayze the dancer does Jack, small-time crook who tries to think positive, as if the role was a dance: an exuberant swagger-strut full of mean chuckles, yells and flamboyant hair-combs. It's a shame there aren't better jokes in this script, because Swayze gives the part a sunny, slap-happy bounce that makes some of his fellow cast members look a little sleepy.

The two children—Sabrina Lloyd and Brian Bonsall—are fun but unremarkable. Halle Berry is stunningly pretty in the slight part of "Los Angeles Post" reporter Kathleen Mercer. Diane Ladd isn't given much either—just a grotesque gambling grandma turn in the Las Vegas scenes.

Not until we get to Orleans and Michael Ironside's part as Jerry, Jack's gun-happy partner, do we find an actor who's figured out how to *live* the part. With his leather, wild eyes and matted mane, Ironside's Jerry looks scary-volatile, strung out on paranoia and weaponry. He practically reeks of doom.

When a movie shows you the sights as nicely as "Father Hood" (MPAA rated PG-13), it may seem petty to ask for better talk. But, to a degree, "Hood" points up its own flaws: planting the child care theme, then blasting off into the Wild Hot Yonder with Jack. That's not a bad place to be—with Swayze behind the wheel, Marvin Gaye on the radio and Roodt calling the shots—but, like far too many movie rides, this one doesn't carry any aftershocks or reminiscent shine. When it's over, it's over.

Also reviewed in:
VARIETY, 9/6/93, p. 27, Brian Lowry
WASHINGTON POST, 8/27/93, p. C7, Rita Kempley

FEARLESS

A Warner Bros. release of a Spring Creek production.   *Producer:* Paula Weinstein and Mark Rosenberg.   *Director:* Peter Weir.   *Screenplay (based on his novel):* Rafael Yglesias.   *Director of Photography:* Allen Daviau.   *Editor:* William Anderson.   *Music:* Maurice Jarre.   *Music Editor:* Dan Carlin.   *Sound:* Charles Wilborn and (music) Shawn Murphy.   *Casting:* Howard Feuer.   *Production Designer:* John Stoddart.   *Art Director:* Chris Burian-Mohr.   *Set Decorator:* John Anderson.   *Special Effects:* Ken Pepiot.   *Visual Effects:* William Mesa.   *Costumes:* Marilyn Matthews.   *Make-up:* Ed Henriques.   *Stunt Coordinator:* Chris Howell.   *Running time:* 125 minutes.   *MPAA Rating:* R.

CAST: Jeff Bridges (Max Klein);   Isabella Rossellini (Laura Klein);   Rosie Perez (Carla Rodrigo);   Tom Hulce (Brillstein);   John Turturro (Dr. Bill Perlman);   Benicio Del Toro (Manny Rodrigo);   Deirdre O'Connell (Nan Gordon);   John De Lancie (Jeff Gordon);   Spencer Vrooman (Jonah Klein);   Daniel Cerny (Byron Hummel);   Eve Roberts (Gail Klein);   Robin Pearson Rose (Sarah);   Debra Monk (Alison);   Cynthia Mace (Cindy Dickens);   Randle Mell (Peter Hummel);   Kathryn Rossetter (Jennifer Hummel);   Craig Rovere (FBI Agent #1);   Doug Ballard (FBI Agent #2);   Molly Cleator (IHOP Waitress);   Rance Howard (Bald Cabby);   Schylar Gholson (Sam Gordon);   Trevor Gholson (Benjamin Gordon);   Anne Kerry Ford (Mother of Baby);   Michael Mulholland (Red Cross Volunteer);   Cliff Gober, Jr. (Paramedic);   Sally Murphy (Jackie);   Steven Culp (Emergency Doctor);   John Towey (Wilkenson);   Stephanie Erb (Lisa);   Cordis Heard (Flight Attendant);   Paul Ghiringhelli (Reporter);   Ryan Tomlinson (Jonah's Friend);   Eric Menyuk (Sears Salesman);   Don Amendolia (Male Survivor);   Rondi Reed (Woman Survivor);   Elsa Raven (Grey-haired Lady);   William Newman (Elderly Man);   Jeanine Jackson (Redhead);   Don Boughton (Middle-aged Man);   David Carpenter (Young Man in Group);   Rome Owens ("Bubble" Rodrigo);   Kevin Brophy (TV Reporter);   Joe Paulino (Reporter #2);   Michael Ching (Doorman);   Roger Hernandez (Priest);   Antoinette Peragine (Laura's Sister);   Ramoncita Hernandez (Abuela);   Isabel R. Martinez (Tia);   I. Rodrigo Martinez (Tio);   Mel Gabel (Reflecting Can Hobo);   Jama Smith (Flight Attendant #2);   Donna Keegan (Flight Attendant #3);   Trisha Brittenham (Flight Attendant #4);   Linda Lee (Flight Attendant #5);   Daryl Hemmerich (Flight Attendant #6);   Gerald L. Kersey (Pilot);   Randy Danekas (Co-Pilot);   Gene DeAngelis (Intercity Captain);   Danielle Clegg (Young Survivor);   Joan Murphy (Ice Cream Mom);   Shannon Ratigan (Harassed Husband);   Adelaide M. Wolf (Harassed Wife);   Loyd Catlett (Texan);   Rebecca Hardt (Ballet Student);   Suzanne Q. Burdeau (Danielle's Mother);   Maria Bembenek (Jackie's Sister);   Richard Blum (Passenger #1);   Ashley Cemo (Passenger #2);   Norman Fessler (Passenger #3);   Lisbeth Rasmussen (Passenger #4);   Ken Mofhitz (Passenger #5);   James E. Flannigan (Passenger #6);   LaVina Wilkerson (Passenger #7);   Robert "Bobby Z" Zajonc and Mike Tamburro (Helicopter Pilots).

LOS ANGELES TIMES, 10/15/93, Calendar/p. 4, Kenneth Turan

"Fearless" ought to be the cause of unconditional celebration, but it's not. A provocative look at disaster's aftermath, at what it can mean to survive a near-death experience, "Fearless" is compellingly directed by Peter Weir and features a performance by Rosie Perez that is remarkable even by her standards.

Yet despite all these good things, despite even a strong and illuminating conclusion, "Fearless," a film that so wants to be inspirational, instead leaves a feeling of irritation in its wake. Hamstrung by a key miscalculation and an unfortunate loss of nerve, it achieves a good deal but falls short of its own aspirations.

What "Fearless" is more than anything is the story of one man's spiritual odyssey. Max Klein (Jeff Bridges), a San Francisco architect, is discovered by the camera in a central California cornfield, holding an infant and leading a child but with a look of troubled disorientation on his face.

As this powerful sequence unfolds, it becomes suddenly and awfully clear (helped by Allen Daviau's focused cinematography) that a major plane crash has just taken place. Instead of experiencing the impact, we view the site from the air and from the ground, strewn with the detritus of lives that will never be the same. Suddenly, flames are seen, Carla Rodrigo (Rosie Perez) screams, "My baby's in there," and everything erupts.

None of this, however, much concerns Max. The child and the infant are not his but strangers he has led from the wreck. Disposing of them, he stealthily flees the scene, taking a taxi to the nearest hotel, where he strips and, amazed, runs his hands down his intact body, murmuring to himself, "You're not dead."

This realization soon becomes the driving force in Max's life. Once a nervous flier, he shocks airline representatives by insisting on taking a plane home. And when the airline seats him next to Dr. Bill Perlman (John Turturro), a psychiatrist specializing in crash survivors, Max airily dismisses his concern.

Back in San Francisco, Max more or less shrugs at the emotional greeting of his wife, Laura (Isabella Rossellini), and their son. Neither can he connect with the hysterical wife of his partner, a fellow passenger who did not survive the crash. Completely full of himself, and feeling, as he later tells Perlman, that the crash was the best thing that ever happened to him because it opened him to "the taste and love and beauty of life," he considers himself a member of a club no one else can possibly join.

Though much of the point of Rafael Yglesias' screenplay (and presumably of the novel it is based on) is to illuminate this change in Max, the hard fact is that in simplest terms the crash has turned Max into a total jerk, smug, insufferable and pompous, possibly acceptable on paper but not on screen.

Feeling he has moved to some high astral plane, Max becomes the most tedious man on the planet, and it is, so deeply unpleasant to experience his act that spending long periods of time in his company, as "Fearless" insists we do, makes considering the moral implications of his situation, as the film probably wants us to, impossible.

Though Jeff Bridges is one of the best of American actors and does everything here that Weir and the script asks of him, it feels like a mistake to have cast him as Max. Because Bridges brings a kind of innate swagger to many of his roles, the end result is to make Max so intolerable and impervious to empathy that it becomes difficult not to wish he'd died in that crash after all.

While it is possible to argue that this unpleasantness in Max's character is the whole point of "Fearless," the canvas that trait is played out on is not so easily defended. For, in typical Hollywood fashion, "Fearless" has lost its nerve and pulled the implications of its punches where Max's world is concerned.

For the most honest impact, Max would be acting like an oaf in an environment that clearly did not deserve it. But, perhaps concerned that he would look even more like a jerk than he already did, the filmmakers decided to indicate that he has good reason to act badly, turning Max into one of those "King of Hearts" wise fools who understand things sane folks do not.

So for most of the picture, the only foils Max has are either venal, like the hero-worshiping press; corrupt like the lawyer Brillstein (Tom Hulce), well-meaning but helpless like Perlman or weak like Max's wife. By stacking the deck with these real-world excuses, the filmmakers encourage the audience to think less badly of Max, to say, "See, he's right to act self-satisfied and dismissive; he is the only strong and honest soul in a world full of deceivers, weaklings and cowards."

The only person who doesn't fall into this category is Carla, and it is no accident that the scenes with her are almost uniformly "Fearless'" most solid and affecting. Carla, acutely played with a fine-tuned sadness by the usually rambunctious Rosie Perez, has never gotten over the death of her baby in the crash. Introduced to Max by Perlman, at his wit's end about both of them, they form an unexpected bond that has repercussions no one anticipates.

Aside from the Carla-Max friendship, the second half of "Fearless" (rated R for language and airplane crash realism) features a remarkable series of flash-backs, parceled out in small but effective doses, to the crash itself. As with much of the film, these scenes are adroitly done and bring to mind director Weir's memorable early Australian work like "'Picnic at Hanging Rock" and "The Last Wave." But finally these moments only cause regret that all of this adventurous, frustrating film is not up to the standard its best sections set.

NEW STATESMAN & SOCIETY, 4/15/94, p. 32, Jonathan Romney

From the very start of Peter Weir's *Fearless*, we're excluded, unable to figure out where we are, or why. The camera drifts through a dense, high cornfield. Then we see Jeff Bridges striding through the growth, in slow motion, dishevelled but confident. He's holding a child, and there is a train of people following him, looking as dazed as we're already beginning to feel. We emerge into the clear, to see the debris of a crashed aeroplane and the flurry of activity round it.

For a split second, we see a charred body, before it's hurriedly covered over with a shroud. A champagne bottle rolls across the ground. Then Bridges walks up to a taxi and calmly asks: "Take me to the nearest hotel."

What's so audacious about this sequence is that we know what's going on, but it's not what we're used to. We're witnessing the aftermath of a plane crash, but there's nothing to tell us this is a plane-crash movie. We're presented with a spectacle, but it's held at a distance; everything is silent, slowed down, with the atmosphere somehow hanging heavy. This is not a scene that we recognise from *Airport* or *Alive*. We realise we have entered the drama after the drama proper has happened, and throughout the film there's the sense of having arrived just too late ever quite to understand things.

Fearless positions us with beautifully poised ambivalence towards its hero Max, an architect who survives a disaster and is immediately transformed. The film takes us close enough to him to allow us to feel his change, but also distances us enough to conceal its meaning. From the bag of nerves that he has been on the flight, Max is transformed by crossing the unthinkable barrier. "This is it," he tells himself, "this is the moment of your death." Then it dawns—"I'm not afraid, I have no fear."

Put in these black-and-white terms, *Fearless* has all the makings of cheap Hollywood psychology, and stands to be read as part of the current school of borrowed-time melodramas that respond to an intensified fear of mortality. (Aids? The *fin de siècle*? The LA earthquakes? Choose your own favourite motivation.) In *Regarding Henry*, Harrison Ford began to glow after a near-death experience; in *My Life*, terminally ill Michael Keaton greeted the advent of the "distinguished thing" by reaching for his camcorder. A cosy coming-to-terms is guaranteed every time.

Fearless, however, earns its name by daring to look into the void and stay silent. So Max is fearless—then what? We don't really know. The film is painstakingly reluctant to diagnose his condition. He visits an ex-girlfriend and announces that, suddenly, he's able to enjoy strawberries, to which he was once allergic. As he tucks into a dishful, he looks up at the waitress' name-tag: "Faith". Normally, it would be a ruinously significant moment, but here it isn't. What does the word mean anyway? Is it presented for us to read meaning into, or to understand that Max is reading meaning into it? Or is it what it appears to be—a name on a name-tag? Even here, the film is scrupulously economical with its meanings. Nothing we see chimes unequivocally with the significance we expect from a plane-crash drama.

Then Max is pulled back into his life. The FBI arrive to remind him that he hasn't contacted his wife. From then on, everyone seems to be conspiring to pull him back in to a normal context. His wife (Isabella Rossellini) is desperate at the way he's eluding her; his ambulance-chasing attorney (a relishably unctuous Tom Hulce) can't understand why Max won't conform to the angry-victim role he has mapped out for him. And a trauma psychiatrist (John Turturro, playing up the comic-neurotic shrink only a tad too much) can't see why Max doesn't need him more. The rest of the film is about these clinical attempts (ours included) to *define* Max.

The film's finest irony—and here's where it makes an elegant compromise with the Hollywood imperative to be "high-concept"—is that, although the nature of Max's experience can be easily summed up in a one-word title, its *meaning* can't. This is one of the few Hollywood movies in recent memory that dares to keep us so tantalisingly at a loose end. So elliptical is it, in fact, that it comes as close as Hollywood could imaginably get to achieving the numinous tone of Kieslowski. (Perhaps Weir should embark on a trilogy and retitle this *Three Colours: Strawberry*).

Apparently deadened by his experience, Max sometimes seems not to respond to the world. But, rather, the world doesn't respond to him. His experience is so singular that he can't find it echoed in anyone else. He doesn't find it in his wife (Rossellini seems absolutely to have found her tenor here, playing a tenacious but bitter compassion). He doesn't find it in a survivors' group, which turns out to be a chaotic, bitter parody of palliative "shared-experience" culture.

Instead, he links up with Carla (Rosie Perez), a traumatised young mother who lost her child in the crash and blames herself. Perez is absolutely commanding in the control with which she plays the extremities of grief. But her episodes with Bridges, the film's centrepiece, are its least interesting moments. They're about recognisably real experience, when we've become more interested in the intangible. They verge on true-life psychodrama, something that Hollywood conventionally handles more or less well.

Carla's experience is given its most illuminating slant when she and Max visit a shopping mall, and effectively start mourning themselves by playing invisible angels. The moment when Perez touches a baby in slow-motion, quite unnoticed, is a magical, perfectly judged piece of *trompe-l'oeil*.

As *Fearless* proceeds, a certain self-importance encroaches (words encroach, too, and it begins to smack a bit of the well-made play). Having deferred the great apocalyptic moment, Weir seems unable to hold off the big transcendental pay-off for too long. Hence the misjudged climactic spectacle of the crash itself, an orgasmic epiphany in glorious slow-motion, complete with Gorecki soundtrack. Here's where *Fearless* gives up the ghost and accepts that it can no longer withhold the traditional rewards. Special effects flash, there's a dollop of awe and a privileged leap into Max's skull. But the assumption that suddenly we can *understand* his experience is over-literal, not to say intrusive.

I'm less sure about the ending, which I thought had been patched on to placate preview audiences—but no, the novel by Rafael Yglesias (who adapted it himself) really ends like that. It's a shame the final moment isn't much darker. I'd like to think that there's some ambivalence left. Like its iconic scene of Bridges poised precariously on a ledge overlooking the city, *Fearless* perches between two realms: one in which there are always easy reconciliations, and a far riskier world in which nothing is quite readable.

The film is understandably nervous about the balance. It seems to want finally to step down off the high wire and opt either for metaphysical kitsch or for the banality of a delayed-trauma case study. For the most part, it doesn't do either. It looks in on Hollywood emotions and explanations, but the thin partition that keeps it outside is glassy enough to make it a very singular work indeed.

NEW YORK, 11/1/93, p. 74, David Denby

Peter Weir has long been the most mystical and intuitive of feature directors, a man eager to put his ear to the ground, or stare at the sun, or listen in wonder to the tales of Australian aborigines. The wind speaks to him; it speaks mighty significances unavailable to the rest of us, who are held in the deadening grip of mere material reality. In *The Last Wave* (1977), the skies seem poised between apocalypse and revelation. Were we doomed or saved? Weir created moods quivering with expectation, a silence haunted by blasts of unheard trumpets.

If you were perched on the same wavelength as Weir, you might have found all this suggestive and powerful. If not, as Gertrude Stein said, not. A material guy myself—indeed, the one man in all of Northern California who never got stoned in the late sixties—I had little patience for

Picnic at Hanging Rock and none at all for *The Last Wave*, with its occult visions, its higher mumbo jumbo. God, Weir was serious—humorless, some of us said, and anti-intellectual as well. At the same time, no one could say that he was not highly talented, a master of ominous, overloaded visual imagery. In his films, one feels the power of nature and the uncanny.

When he left Australia and began working here in 1985, he wisely headed for the severe yet radiant Amish community in Pennsylvania; there he made *Witness*, a curiously becalmed thriller set in an idyllic society of otherworldly people. Life as it's lived in the feverish American cities and car-fumed suburbs interested him not, and if such soft-brained commercial movies as *Dead Poets Society* and *Green Card* can be taken as an indication of Weir's hold on social reality, it's just as well that he looked elsewhere.

The trouble with Peter Weir's movies, in short, is that they're awfully impressive up to the moment in which they become unbearably stupid; and his new film, *Fearless*, which is filled with challenging scenes and moments, goes spectacularly wrong before it's over. Nevertheless, it deserves a break: Weir takes risks almost no one else is taking, and some of the film is fascinating. Once again, the hushed landscape speaks to those who have ears to hear it.

Jeff Bridges is a San Francisco architect, Max Klein, who survives an airline crash in a Southern California cornfield. In the worst moment, as the plane is going down, Max begins helping and reassuring people; later, he leads the survivors out of the wreckage. How did he become so brave? We see the crash itself in terrifying fragments throughout the movie, each fragment taking us closer to the moment of impact, and all we can tell is that his terror suddenly gave way to bliss. He didn't care whether he died or not. Back in the world again, he feels that he's passed through death. A ghost, he calls himself. And the ghost can no longer take seriously the world's business and social rituals, including the love of his family. He becomes a saint and a truth-teller—in other words, a son of a bitch. Hostile, unnerving, and largely indifferent to other people's feelings, he looks sourly at his family and friends and lawyer, as if their caring about money or work were a form of madness. For weeks, he can't talk to anyone but Carla (Rosie Perez), another survivor, who's in a pitiable state. She blames herself for the death of her son in the crash.

The movie is based on a novel by Rafael Yglesias, who did the adaptation himself. I was impressed by the tough-mindedness of the filmmakers' approach. Max is not meant to be a Robin Williams figure—a nice fellow going through a small attack of whimsy. On the contrary, we get the impression that he never was easygoing and that his current crisis is one he might not come out of. Jeff Bridges gives him a nasty edge but also, at times, a remarkable detachment, as if his spirit had retired to a place deep within him. Traumatized, Max has been delivered into happiness: He doesn't care about anything. Bridges keeps the tone light; he can do abstracted and bemused moods without getting supercilious, and borderline-psychotic episodes without frightening us, and at times he lets a trace of sympathy for other people break through Max's self-sufficiency. He's certainly the most likable son of a bitch in recent movies.

For stretches, the film is impressive. Weir, working with the great cinematographer Allen Daviau, creates moments of physical wonder and spiritual unease—the appalling mess of litter and broken bodies in the cornfield, for instance, with Max walking silently through the wreckage, wondering if he's really alive; or the vastness of the California mountains and desert on the day afterward, when Max, rather than calling home, drives out to the wilderness to stare at the sky. He sits on the ground with a few grains of dirt in his hand and loses himself in the distance—a lapsing out into the ineffability of life. The metaphysical high is well earned.

The camera captures what this euphoric but damaged man feels: It stares at things obsessively, in extremely bright light, as if everything had suddenly become lucid. Traveling about, Max visits an old girlfriend and finally goes home, only to dodge his son and his wife, who, in the person of Isabella Rossellini, is definitely not someone to run away from. Eyes wide open, her spirit surging toward her man, Rossellini gives a passionate performance—easily her best work in movies. Her outrage when Bridges shuts her out is the strongest thing in *Fearless*.

The movie has an off-center brilliance here and there, but the big plot movement in it—Max's obsessive relationship with the working-class Hispanic wife and mother Carla—feels forced and unconvincing. These two, having been through hell, "understand" each other, but they don't have all that much to say as they wander around San Francisco in Max's Volvo. By the time they start buying Christmas presents for their dead family members, you begin to wonder if Weir hasn't gone over the edge himself. The Brooklyn-born Rosie Perez has a likably game quality, but with her small frame and tinny voice, she's not right for big emotions like grief and anguish and deep spirituality. Anyway, she and Bridges just don't go together; he's polite to her, but nothing catches fire.

A second death and resurrection involving the Volvo and a brick wall is, I'm afraid, the crash that breaks the moviegoer's back. (For Jesus it was enough to be reborn once.) Peter Weir falls all too easily from the uncanny to the foolish, and there's probably nothing to be done about it: His strength as a maker of mystical moods is inextricably tied to his intellectual weaknesses. Yet there may be hope for him. He makes the Rossellini character so intelligent and appealing that you wonder if some day he won't stop listening to the spirits altogether and rise to the cinematic embrace of an obviously superior woman.

NEW YORK POST, 10/15/93, p. 23, Thelma Adams

Bummer without a cause. "Fearless," Peter Weir's drama about plane crash survivors, is deadly.

Jeff Bridges plays Max Klein, the reluctant hero. On a routine flight, his plane goes down. During a moment of grace, he thinks: "This is it. This is the moment of your death ... I'm not afraid. I have no fear."

Director Weir has made a successful career with entertaining, adult movies about spiritual crises edged with the mystical. "Witness" plopped tough cop Harrison Ford in Amish country where he fell for a local lass and confronted his Yankee cynicism. In "The Year of Living Dangerously," Mel Gibson chucked his skepticism in strife-torn Indonesia when he encountered supernatural forces he couldn't explain.

"Fearless" starts strong. Weir's visual imagery is abbreviated and poetic: the wound of the crash site; a single red boot on scorched earth. Carla (Rosie Perez), held aloft by two men, twists back towards the plane, ripping at her rescuer's scalp while wailing for her missing child. Max's face is the determined mask of a hero as he leads passengers to safety, a baby in one arm, a boy by the hand.

Max walks away from the crash euphoric. He has faced death and survived.

The scenes that follow are hallucinogenic. From desert sand to his own nipple, Max looks at everything anew. Driving down the highway, he sticks his head out the window, doglike, experiencing pure joy. He reads the name on a waitress' badge—Faith—like a sign from beyond.

But there's no room for this euphoria when he returns home where his wife (Isabella Rossellini) awaits him with a lawyer in tow. Max cannot go back to life-as-usual. He turns instead to Carla whose transforming grief over her son's death equals his own renewed passion.

As Carla, the young Catholic whose faith has been ripped apart, Perez ("White Men Can't Jump") has her best role yet. She's flown the flygirl routine. Her streetwise humor is a grace note here, rather than a crutch, and she demonstrates a startling range and intensity. The beautiful Rossellini, in a part that is woefully underwritten, is no match for Perez.

"Fearless" also features Tom Hulce and John Turturro as the Tom and Jerry of professionals, Hulce plays an ambulance-chasing lawyer; Turturro is a therapist hired by the airlines to counsel crash survivors, With slicked-back hair and a greedy glee, Hulce seems to be doing a Nixon riff. Turturro seems uncomfortable, and hence unbelievable, as the shrink. I always love these guys. Both are great character actors, but they appear here like brothers from another movie.

Bridges does a good job—but don't go making room for Oscar on that mantel yet. He can't overcome a script that crash lands after a strong start.

In a screenplay based on his novel. Rafael Yglesias succeeds in defining Max's spiritual crisis but doesn't have enough control over plot and conflict to sustain the audience's interest. Max survives the plane crash, but the movie dies halfway through.

NEWSDAY, 10/15/93, Part II/p. 64, Jack Mathews

Of all the potential disasters of modern life, the one that may create the most universal anxiety and empathy, the one we take most personally, is the airplane crash.

Air travel is a crapshoot in the sky, a negative lottery with millions-to-one odds. But, hey, you never know. And as we hear survivors describe those terrifying seconds before the crash, we try to imagine our own feelings and behavior in that situation, and wonder how surviving it would affect *us*.

It is the psychological reaction to such an event that holds the morbidly fascinating center of Peter Weir's "Fearless," a movie that better than any I can think of forces the viewer to feel the terror of near-death and the exhilaration of survival.

For Max Klein (Jeff Bridges), an architect whose partner and best friend is decapitated in their interrupted flight from San Francisco to Houston, the experience is transcendant, "the best thing that ever happened to me." A worry-wart nearly paralyzed by the fear of flying when his plane takes off, he is, soon after the hydraulic system fails and panic sets in around him, suddenly becalmed.

After saving several other passengers from fire and smoke, he literally walks away from the crash site. He tells a taxi driver to deliver him to the nearest hotel, where he takes a shower, examines his nearly unscathed body, and says to the image in the mirror, "You're not dead!"

We're never quite sure whether Max actually believes he is not dead. With his fearlessness comes a sense of immortality. He boldly wolfs down strawberries, to which he is deathly allergic, and nothing happens. He walks across a busy street and isn't hit. He dances on the edge of a skyscraper and is intoxicated by the conquest of the mortal anxiety attack that put him there.

Whether he is psychotic, or touched by the hand of God, Max loves where he has gone and doesn't want to lose or share the feeling. Not with his increasingly frustrated wife (Isabella Rossellini), his young son (Spencer Vrooman), the airline company shrink (a miscast John Turturro) assigned to counsel the crash survivors, or the media that want to profile his heroism.

As his marriage crumbles and he becomes more and more isolated, Max seems to thrive in a spiritual cocoon, increasingly convinced on that plane he passed into another dimension, through a tunnel of light that he obsessively tries to recreate on his drafting table.

Throughout this strange, unsettling film, which was adapted by Rafael Yglesias from his own novel, we revisit the cabin of the crippled airliner to learn more about Max' transformation, contrasted with the more typical panic of the fellow survivor Carla (Rosie Perez), with whom Max, on a mission of salvation, eventually becomes bonded.

No one can suggest as many conflicting internal emotions behind a stoic mask as Bridges, and Max, both maddeningly aloof and irresistibly charming, is one of his finest performances.

Weir, who dabbled in metaphysical subjects before abandoning Australian films ("The Last Waye") for Hollywood ("Witness"), leans a little too heavily to the spiritual side. It's our confusion about Max' behavior that makes him so compelling, and Weir nearly blows the mystery.

Still, it is a fascinating portrait of life after near-death, and there is barely a moment when we are not wondering how we would have been changed by the same experience.

NEWSWEEK, 10/18/93, p. 85, David Ansen

Max (Jeff Bridges) is an architect who has always been afraid of flying—until he's in a plane crash. In the air, at the moment when death seems a certainty, he transcends his fear and achieves something like a state of grace; his unearthly calm enables him to rescue several passengers. Back on terra firma, where he is proclaimed a hero, he finds it impossible to slip back into his old life. He is, in the title of Peter ("Witness") Weir's strange and unnerving movie, *Fearless*. Dazed but elated, he can no longer relate to the pettiness and mendacity of everyday life. He withdraws from his loving wife (Isabella Rossellini) and turns away from his son. Instead, he is powerfully drawn to a fellow powerfully drawn to a fellow survivor, Carla (Rosie Perez), who lost her child in the crash, and has become almost catatonic in her grief and guilt. The airline's psychologist (John Turturro) can't reach her, but Max has the power to bring her back to life.

How are we supposed to regard Max's altered state? An ambiguity, rare in Hollywood movies, hangs over Weir's film, which screenwriter Rafael Yglesias adapted from his own novel. Has Max become a kind of angel—enlightened, spiritually purified—or has he become monstrous in his arrogance, his delusion of immortality? Clinically, he's suffering from posttraumatic-stress syndrome, but in illness he discovers ecstasy, and is loath to give it up.

The intense, portentous, quasi-mystical atmosphere of "Fearless" is reminiscent of Weir's early work in his native Australia, "Picnic at Hanging Rock" and "The Last Wave." A gifted stylist, his re-creations of the airplane crash (scattered throughout the story in flashback) have a queasy visceral impact. At its best, the movie has the unsettling ability to make the viewer see the world from Max's heightened, unbalanced point of view. The manic conviction of Bridges's performance holds us, but the film isn't always able to sustain its hypnotic tone. When Max and Carla go shopping for presents for his dead father and her dead son, the whimsy threatens to get out of hand. And when he tries to cure her of her guilt by driving a car into a wall (to show how she couldn't have held onto her baby), you may wonder if it's Max or the movie that has gone bonkers. Still, "Fearless" is the rare commercial movie that raises more questions than it answers. You leave it in an altered state yourself—moved, not quite satisfied, but certain you've seen something out of the ordinary.

SIGHT AND SOUND, 5/94, p. 41, Philip Kemp

Max Klein, a San Francisco architect, is flying to Houston with his friend and partner Jeff Gordon, when their plane crashes into a cornfield outside Bakersfield. Just before the crash, Max, hitherto terrified of dying, experiences a feeling of peace and total lack of fear. Jeff is killed but Max survives unscathed. He rescues a baby and a young boy, Byron, from the wreck, and leads other passengers to safety. Still in a beatific state, he makes his way to a motel, hires a car, and looks up an old flame; while with her he happily eats a bowl of strawberries, to which he used to be allergic. Not until the FBI trace him does he think to contact his wife, Laura.

Max is publicly hailed as a hero, but during the subsequent weeks he seems locked off in a world of his own where Laura is unable to reach him. As if believing himself invulnerable, he walks through speeding traffic and balances perilously on high parapets. His detached attitude frustrates both Brillstein, a lawyer eager to win damages for the Kleins and for Jeff's widow Nan, and Dr Perlman, a psychiatrist counselling the crash survivors. Hoping to elicit some response, Perlman introduces Max to Carla Rodrigo, a young woman whose two-year-old son died in the crash, and who is devastated by grief and guilt.

Max and Carla establish a close, though platonic, friendship. Helping her come to terms with her son's death, he finally exorcises her guilt by driving full tilt into a wall to prove the impact must inevitably have wrenched the child from her arms. Both Max and Carla are injured, but not seriously. His sense of immortality enhanced, Max becomes even more remote from Laura, who resents his relationship with Carla. Brillstein shows up, ecstatic over the huge damages he hopes to secure. Listening to him, Max deliberately chokes himself on a strawberry, and finds himself back in the wrecked fuselage, walking peacefully towards a bright light. At the last moment he hears Laura's voice begging him not to die, and returns to life.

The conventions of the air-disaster movie are well established. First we're introduced to a stock company of passengers and crew (nervous old lady, pompous businessman, etc.), then they're all herded on to a plane marked 'Destination: Catastrophe' *Fearless*, living up to its title, jettisons this whole weary scenario. Instead, it plunges us straight into the aftermath of a crash, with Jeff Bridges wandering out of a cornfield into a scorched-earth desolation of shattered fuselage, burst luggage and dismembered human fragments. (This film, it's fair to bet, is unlikely to do great business on the inflight movie circuit.)

The uncompromising opening is typical of a film which rarely takes the expected route or the easy option. Its central crux—the liberating epiphany experienced by Max Klein in the last moments before the crash—is never explained, still less explained away. Peter Weir and Rafael Yglesias (scripting from his own novel) offer us various hints, but in the end what's happened to Max remains as enigmatic as what became of the vanished schoolgirls in Weir's first hit, *Picnic at Hanging Rock*. It's refreshing to see a mainstream Hollywood film that so resolutely refuses to manipulate its audience, but rather invites us to watch and reflect and make up our own minds.

The metaphysical dimension is neither endorsed nor ruled out. Sometimes Max seems to be conducting a feud with a vindictive deity ("You want to kill me, but you can't!" he yells triumphantly at the sky, having walked unscathed through hurtling traffic), at other times he comes close to setting up in competition. "So there's no god, but there's you?" Carla asks half-jokingly when he expounds his ideas, and taking a shower soon after the crash he thoughtfully fingers a small, stigmatum-like wound in his left side. In a diner he gazes enraptured at a waitress's name-tag inscribed 'Faith; but whether he's found faith, and in what (himself, or some outside principle?) is left undefined.

The one certainty is that Max has freed himself from his previous phobic, inhibited self. "I can't get back. I don't want to," he tells Laura. But where a more glib film might present this as pure gain, a man liberated to "live life to the full", *Fearless* makes clear that in many ways Max (Played by Jeff Bridges with something of the same disquieting ambiguity, at once affable and remote, that he brought to the alien in John Carpenter's *Starman*) has become a lesser human being. The young boy, Byron, may see him as a hero and second father, and Carla feel "it's like God sent him to me"—but to his wife and son he's a monster of selfishness, blandly shutting off the pain he's causing them. He talks of feeling more alive than ever, but part of him—a good part, in both senses—has died.

Another reading of the film, of course, would be that Max has in fact died in the crash, and that everything bar the flashbacks is his moment-of-death experience. "We're safe because we died already," he assures Carla, and on his drawing board Laura finds a series of mysterious vortices that resolve themselves into two celestial images: Dore's depiction of the heavenly host from Dante's *Paradiso*, and Bosch's 'Ascent into the Empyrean'. These images are echoed in the final scene, where the dying Max finds himself walking though the tunnel of the fuselage towards a brilliant light. Here as in *The Last Wave* (which offered its own unorthodox take on death and visions), Weir taps into mystic levels.

If religion gets sceptical treatment in *Fearless*, the same goes for the secular alternatives. At one point Dr Perlman (subtly portrayed by John Turturro as a man hamstrung by his own sense of inadequacy) stages a group therapy session for the crash survivors. Far from offering us reassuring scenes of traumas being sobbed out on supportive shoulders, the session degenerates into an agonised mess, with angry accusations tearing the group apart and leaving everyone in a worse state than before. Facile comfort, once again, is not on offer.

The film sounds only one false note, when in its final moments Max is brought back to life. Dramatically and emotionally it would work far better if he died, and the last-ditch reprieve smacks of a loss of nerve on somebody's part. That apart, though, *Fearless* strikes audaciously out on its own individual track, and it's a melancholy thought that it will probably fare far worse at the box-office than Weir's meretricious crowd-pleasers like *Green Card* and *Dead Poet's Society*.

TIME, 10/18/93, p. 98, Richard Schickel

They stumble silently out of a cornfield, tattered, battered survivors of some disaster either natural or unnatural. The almost hallucinatory opening sequence does not tell us what befell them. No one speaks. There is no sound except an eerie musical theme. But these stunned faces are familiar to us. We see them every day on television, in newspaper and magazine photos. They haunt our century. And our anxious imaginings. For these are the faces of those whom cataclysm has inexplicably spared and who must not pass their borrowed time contemplating fate's enigmatic workings.

In the case of *Fearless*, the cataclysm is a plane crash. Among the survivors is Max Klein (Jeff Bridges), an architect. He comes out of that field leading a young boy and cradling a babe in his arms. We learn later that he led others to safety as well, despite the fact that his partner and best friend died horribly just a few feet from him. Max's opposite number is Carla Rodrigo (Rosie Perez), whose baby was wrenched from her arms and killed on impact.

Max soon develops a near Godlike sense of immortality. He imperturbably noshes strawberries, to which he previously had a deadly allergy. He stands on the edge of high buildings daring the winds or a misstep to carry him away. He deliberately crashes his car into a wall at high speed. Nothing can touch him—except the plight of Carla, who has been reduced to an almost catatonic state by grief. He feels compelled to bring her back to life, and he is quite obnoxious in this, his final rescue attempt.

His arrogance alienates him from his wife (Isabella Rossellini) and son. They—like John Turturro's determinedly patient psychiatrist, a specialist in traumatic stress, and Tom Hulce's determinedly impatient tort lawyer, trying to extract a settlement from the airline—would prefer a more humble and malleable response to a near death experience.

For that, finally, is what this remarkable movie is about. We discover that Max has literally seen the light, that blinding white light that features in so many reports of out-of-body experiences. He has walked some way down the tunnel to the afterlife that is also a convention of these tales. Arrogance, a belief that he is of the elect, is an entirely plausible, if quite unexpected, response.

That's the great thing about *Fearless*—its unexpectedness. The most one might expect these days in a movie about a plane crash is *Airport '93*. The best we might hope for in a study of survivors is psychological faith healing. But Rafael Yglesias has written that amounts to a meditation on mortality. In the process, he has provided director Peter Weir with a route back to his best vein, that of *Picnic at Hanging Rock* and *The Last Wave*, those curiously creepy movies in which ineffable, quite insoluble mysteries slowly insinuate themselves into ordinary life. Together the filmmakers have given Bridges a singular figure—beamy, spooky, secretive—to play and provided Perez, a ferociously real, marvelously touching actress, with a role that should make her a star.

VILLAGE VOICE, 10/19/93, p. 56, Georgia Brown

The buzz on *Fearless* is as loud as Hell's Angels on the block. At the IFP awards dinner (where all awards but one went to big-time stars and filmmakers), a tall blond woman raved about the movie: It's so *different*, she said. she'd never seen anything like it. It's good that this woman is editor of a premier magazine (not mentioning any names) whose function it is to tout Hollywood movies; probably buzz is permanent in her eardrums. So all the way through *Fearless* I was sitting there wondering, what's different?

Jeff Bridges—such a pleasure recently in *American Heart*—plays Max, a passenger on a plane that crashes into a Midwest cornfield. The opening shot of the cornfield looks like it's out of *Field of Dreams*, with dazed and confused ghosts wandering out to be met by awed spectators. Max, who's carrying a baby and leading a kid (neither of them his), has helped passengers from the wreckage. You may think he's like Dustin Hoffman in *Hero*, but *Fearless* is different since Max was on the plane. Now he's experiencing post-traumatic stress syndrome, a bit like Tim Robbins in *Jacob's Ladder*. The difference is that Max isn't dead, he's alive and changed. No, not exactly like Harrison Ford in *Regarding Henry*. (Did I say that Max is an architect, like every sensitive movie male in the last two years?)

Okay, I'll cut it out. Directed by Peter Weir and adapted by Rafael Yglesias from his novel (which I haven't read), *Fearless* takes off from a flyer's frequent fantasy: How would I behave if this plane suddenly conked out? Would I be suffused with inner peace, or would I spoil my finale with a panic royale? In *Fearless*, Max is overcome by a great calm and behaves heroically, like an incarnation of the patron saint of travelers. As one woman puts it later, "God sent him to me—my own angel!" Except for one special thing, which we see him do at the end, it isn't clear what feats Max actually performs, but grown men and women worship his shoes while children don't want him out of their sight.

Since Max survives with only a flesh wound—unlike his best friend and business partner who's been decapitated—he subsequently develops a messiah complex. Back home in San Francisco, he strolls into traffic, does Harold Lloyd stunts on top-story ledges, dares to eat strawberries which he was once deathly allergic to. He yells at God. He thinks he might *be* God. (This is different from Bill Murray's deity complex in *Groundhog Day*, because Max is serious.) Reentering daily life is the real difficulty. His wife (Isabella Rossellini) and kid, not having survived a crash, are strangers. He's only at home with other survivors, like the tortured Carla Rodrigo (Rosie Perez), who lost her baby in the crash. A shrink (played by John Turturro) hired by the airline has brought Max over to Carla's to see if he can get her out of bed. Max speaks to her, she responds, and together the two create their own little mad, grieving world. The trick is to get these two to the point where they don't have to keep crashing, testing their invulnerability. (Max's reentry comes via just the little agent you think it will.)

About a month ago, on a screening room elevator, two suits were raving about Rosie Perez's *Fearless* performance; one predicted an Oscar. Well, Rosie here is a delight as Rosie always is. She plays a hysteric in *Fearless* too, but the difference is that the character is given reason—she's lost her Bubble (which comes out like Bubbo). Rosie does look different with no makeup.

Like Weir's *Dead Poets Society, Fearless* is a sincere, inspirational melodrama, which could easily move you to tears. The tears, however, will not be different. When people from the business say "different," they mean reassuringly the same. But maybe I should be touched by their enthusiasm.

Also reviewed in:
CHICAGO TRIBUNE, 10/15/93, Friday/p. A, Michael Wilmington
NEW YORK TIMES, 10/15/93, p. C12, Vincent Canby
NEW YORKER, 10/25/93, p. 120, Terrence Rafferty
VARIETY, 10/18/93, p. 49, Todd McCarthy
WASHINGTON POST, 10/29/93, p. B1, Hal Hinson
WASHINGTON POST, 10/29/93, Weekend/p. 44, Desson Howe

FEMALE MISBEHAVIOR

A Hyena Films production in association with Hamburger Filmburo and Kampnagelfabrik. *Producer:* Monika Treut. *Director:* Monika Treut. *Director of Photography:* Elfi Mikesch. *Editor:* Renate Merck. *Sound:* Tonike Traum. *Running time:* 80 minutes. *MPAA Rating:* Not Rated.

WITH: Camille Paglia (Herself); Annie Sprinkle (Herself); Carol Macho (Herself); Max/Anita Valerio (Herself).

LOS ANGELES TIMES, 5/20/93, Calendar/p. 3, Michael Wilmington

[*Female Misbehavior* was reviewed jointly with *Nitrate Kisses*; see Wilmington's review of that film.]

NEW YORK POST, 4/23/93, p. 33, Matthew Flamm

One must be grateful to Monika Treut, the New York-based German director, who in her explorations of the sexual fringe takes us where few other filmmakers visit.

The question is, how grateful? In her new film, which consists of four short documentaries collectively titled "Female Misbehavior," Treut follows her subjects so far past the boundaries of conventional good taste that the most sympathetic viewer may wonder if the trip is worth it.

To her considerable credit, Treut avoids any traces of sensationalism, whether she's interviewing a female-to-male trans-sexual in "Max," a lesbian sadomasochist exhibitionist in "Bondage," or the New Age performance artist Annie Sprinkle in "Annie."

One can admire Treut's bravado without necessarily enjoying it. The director, whose last film was the somewhat easier to take comedy "My Father Is Coming," shows the audience no mercy even when filming Sprinkle's outrageously gynocentric "act."

The sight of the jovial ex-porn star self-administering a speculum—followed by close-ups of her cervix—certainly rates among cinema's more unusual moments. And as the critic Camille Paglia argues in the amusing opening documentary "Dr. Paglia," "wherever there's a taboo, it's the obligation of the artist to step on that taboo and shatter it."

What we gain from the experience is another issue. Sprinkle may think she's pushing the aesthetic envelope ("Isn't it beautiful?" she asks one spectator with a flashlight) rather than catering to some new kind of anatomical voyeur. But the more detached viewer is likely to be repelled, not least by her unbridled narcissism.

"Bondage," too, has its hard-to-watch scenes.

Treut herself is no disinterested observer but a sexual-political provocateur committed to gender-bending. That's her weakness and her strength: Like any avant-gardist, she plays the hypocritical game of wanting us to be uncomfortable while implying we *shouldn't* be.

In any case, the most revelatory moments in "Female Misbehavior" are also the easiest to stomach: Max, a modern day Tiresias, describing the differences between male and female, or the S&M aficionado explaining how bondage makes her feel "warm and secure."

NEWSDAY, 4/23/93, Part II/p. 83, Gene Seymour

Scholar-provocateur Camille Paglia, arguably the era's most outrageously self-promoting academic, irritates so many with her critique of conventional feminist doctrine that mainstream TV interviews and magazine profiles have tended to cushion her high-octane patter with "opposing viewpoints," thus containing her free-wheeling persona within the easily digestible role of "Strong Woman that Strong Women Love to Hate."

But whether you think Paglia is hopelessly overexposed or (from whatever ideological standpoint) Satan's stepchild, you will still find something fascinating in "Dr. Paglia," the first in Monika's Treut's quartet of documentary shorts depicting "misbehaving women.

Treut simply lets Paglia rap on and on, not only about her idiosyncratic sexual politics, but also about her childhood, her lifelong obsession with paganism, her ease in talking with children as opposed to grownups, her unapologetic egotism, her hangups about her looks and clothes.

The approach is shrewd because it opens the possibility for Paglia's detractors to be beguiled by her exuberant, if calculated, candor. Meanwhile, for those who believe Paglia to be the outrageous libertine that is her public pose, her confessions of being a bit of a basket case when it comes to her own sexuality betray faint traces of latent Puritanism. Either way, you won't feel quite the same way about Paglia after you've seen Treut's film.

The jaunty tone set by "Dr. Paglia" is continued in "Annie," a whimsical portrait of porn star Annie Sprinkle whose live act includes a "bosom ballet" atop audience members' heads.

"Bondage," the 1983 film that helped make Treut's reputation, is a sustained interview with a leather-garbed lesbian named Carol who talks at length about how "warm and secure" she feels when she's all tied up and tortured. Despite a jolt or two (like a painful trick she performs with her microphone and her right nipple), the monologue becomes redundant and tedious after a while.

The last movie, "Max," is the most poignant portrait. It depicts a Native American woman named Anita Valerio who, after several operations, is now Max Valerio. Like "Bondage," this film, too, seems to drone and sag under the weight of its relentlessly penetrating impulses. But besides finding out more about such transitions than you ever knew before, you find Max himself to provide the kind of witty, curiosity-inducing company that Paglia does, albeit in a different way.

VILLAGE VOICE, 4/27/93, p. 62, Manohla Dargis

Now that the saucer-eyed Keene Kid has pushed Amazon Barbie off the runway, how long before the vogue for angry women and bad girls runs its course? Consider then the curious historical footnote from Monika Treut, *Female Misbehavior*. An anthology of four short films reveling in naughty and nasty women, it's one artifact that goes a long way toward proving we haven't come that far, baby. Both *Annie* (Miss Sprinkle to you) and the superior *Bondage* have been making festival rounds for years. Each has its considerable charms, but post-*On Our Backs*, seems a bit recherché. Far more engaging, or enraging, are the two newer films that bookend *Misbehavior*, the opening harangue, *Dr. Paglia*, and closing volley, *Max*.

Exhausting and only mildly insulting, *Paglia* is a brief chapter out of The Gospel According to St. Camille. Once again, it's Paglia against the spurious monolith "feminism," Paglia who stands alone—imagine her taking anything lying down because she loves fucking and dirty pictures of naked ladies. It's easy to dislike this motormouth, though not everything she says is quite as dumb as her tiresome self-promotion. Paglia's biggest sin is that she thinks to be powerful you must play by patriarchy's rules.

That line of thinking is carried further in *Max*, about a pre-op female-to-male who thinks biology may be a feminist defense of transsexualism, but you won't find it here. At the core of Max's desire to be an anatomically correct man is a profound rejection of the feminine: After all, what's so fabulous about being soft, simpering, powerless? If that sounds simplistic, you're right. There's a world of difference between sex and sex roles, something neither Max nor Treut considers. Flying high on testosterone and bravado, Max walks around shadowboxing at the camera. By the time s/he starts in on the joys of not being able to cry anymore, I get pretty misty.

Also reviewed in:
CHICAGO TRIBUNE, 1/22/93, Friday/p. F, Dave Kehr
VARIETY, 11/30/92, p. 69, Susan Ayscough

FIFTY/FIFTY

A Canon Pictures release of a Raymond Wagner/Maurice Singer production. *Producer:* Maurice Singer and Raymond Wagner. *Director:* Charles Martin Smith. *Screenplay:* Dennis Shryack and Michael Butler. *Director of Photography:* David Connell. *Editor:* James Mitchell and Christian A. Wagner. *Music:* Peter Bernstein. *Sound:* Cameron Hanza. *Casting:* Ellen Lang and Anna Lim. *Production Designer:* Errol Kelly. *Special Effects:* Conrad Rothman. *Stunt Coordinator:* Hubie Kerns, Jr. *Running time:* 100 minutes. *MPAA Rating:* Rated R.

CAST: Peter Weller (Jake Wyer); Robert Hays (Sam French); Charles Martin Smith (Martin Sprue); Ramona Rahman (Suleta); Kay Tong Lim (Akhantar); Dom Magwili (Gen. Bosavi); Azmil Mustapha (Col. Kota); Ursala Martin (Liz Powell).

LOS ANGELES TIMES, 3/1/93, Calendar/p. 6, Kevin Thomas

"Fifty/Fifty" is an above-average modestly budgeted action-adventure that teams Peter Weller and Robert Hays as a devil-may-care pair of mercenaries blackmailed by the CIA into leading the overthrow of an oppressive island regime somewhere in Malaysia.

Although the material is inherently familiar and predictable, writers Dennis Shryack and Michael Butler, director Charles Martin Smith and the stars successfully freshen up the formula. Clearly designed for the international market, the film comes across with more wit and intelligence than is usual with such fare.

The filmmakers' key strategy is to introduce Weller and Hays as a couple of boisterous guys in it for the loot, men who have the earmarks of male chauvinists and white supremacists—your standard issue Ugly Americans. Yet the film moves toward an enlightened contemporary tone. Gradually, the two men, led by the more reflective Weller, find themselves committed to the cause of the freedom fighters of the fictional country of Tengara.

Weller and Hays don't take themselves too seriously, and that impression is contagious. Smith also appears as their CIA boss, a smart, decent type caught between Washington directives and the desire to see Weller and Hays succeed. The film's leading lady, Ramona Rahman, plays a feisty freedom fighter. "Fifty/Fifty" was shot almost entirely in Malaysia, half of it in Penang, and it benefits from its exotic locales.

The big news in "Fifty/Fifty" (rated R for scenes of violence and for language) is the impressiveness of Smith's firm direction—lively, brisk and sharp, in what is only his third outing behind the camera.

NEWSDAY, 3/1/93, Part II/p. 41, Terry Kelleher

"I've got a plan," says the soldier of fortune portrayed by Peter Weller.

"Yeah," says the soldier of fortune portrayed by Robert Hays. "Plan A for Awful and Plan B for Bad."

Both plans are in operation throughout "Fifty/Fifty," a woeful action-adventure-comedy that occasionally alludes to "Butch Cassidy and the Sundance Kid" but plays more like your unfavorite episode of "The A-Team."

Directed by Charles Martin Smith, who also takes the role of a CIA agent, "Fifty/Fifty" lurches from lame humor to stock violence to spurious moral conflict and all the way back again. It's not exciting even for a moment, and about the only time it's intentionally funny is when Hays flirts with the idea of sexual contact with a goat. He's desperate for fun, and we know the feeling.

Though they've been double-crossed by the CIA before (hey, who hasn't?), Weller and Hays accept the agency's gold to overthrow an Asian dictator whom Weller recently served as a hired gun. Of course, the coup is just a "money gig" for the boys—until they get a load of the rebel leader's fiery but comely niece (Ramona Rahman). Weller wins her over by turning on to her idealism, after Hays strikes out with an approach better suited to four-legged females.

The CIA sells them out, their Joan of Arc dies for the cause, yet our heroes refuse to quit. Get the drift? This time it's personal.

"Fifty/Fifty" never seems to figure out what it's up to. First we get TV-approved epithets ("cheese-face," "brickbrain"), then a sudden outbreak of the "f" word. First it's the kind of movie in which the protagonists keep on bantering even when strung up by the ankles; then it's the kind of movie in which army thugs brutalize innocent peasants. One minute, Weller and Hays are going out in a blaze of suicidal glory; the next, their condition is anything but serious.

There's only one constant: We don't care.

Also reviewed in:
VARIETY, 3/8/93, p. 60, Lawrence Cohn
WASHINGTON POST, 3/1/93, p. B6, Hal Hinson

FIRE IN THE SKY

A Paramount Pictures release. *Executive Producer:* Wolfgang Glattes. *Producer:* Joe Wizan and Todd Black. *Director:* Robert Lieberman. *Screenplay:* Tracy Torme. *Based upon the book "The Walton Experience" by:* Travis Walton. *Director of Photgraphy:* Bill Pope. *Editor:* Steve Mirkovich. *Music:* Mark Isham. *Music Editor:* Tom Carlson. *Sound:* Henry Garfield and (music) Stephen Krause. *Sound Editor:* Joseph A. Ippolito. *Casting:* Rick Pagano, Sharon Bialy, and Debi Manwiller. *Production Desinger:* Laurence Bennett. *Art Director:* Mark W. Mansbridge. *Set Designer:* John Leimanis. *Set Decorator:* Daniel L. May. *Special Effects:* Alan Edward Lorimer. *Costumes:* Joe I. Tompkins. *Make-up:* Ken Chase. *Make-up (James Garner):* Charlene Roberson. *Stunt Coordinator:* Chuck Waters. *Running time:* 98 minutes. *MPAA Rating:* PG-13.

CAST: D.B. Sweeney (Travis Walton); Robert Patrick (Mike Rogers); Craig Sheffer (Allan Dallis); Peter Berg (David Whitlock); Henry Thomas (Greg Hayes); Bradley Gregg (Bobby Cogdill); Noble Willingham (Blake Davis); Kathleen Wilhoite (Katie Rogers); James Garner (Frank Watters); Georgia Emelin (Dana Rogers); Scott Macdonald (Dan Walton); Wayne Grace (Cyrus Gilson); Kenneth White (Buck); Robert Covarrubias (Ray Melendez); Bruce Wright (Dennis Clay); Robert Biheller (Ellis); Tom McGranahan, Sr. (Dr. Wilson); Julie Ariola (Dr. Cayle); Peter Mark Vasquez (Ramon); Gordon Scott (George); Mical Shannon Lewis (Mary Rogers); Courtney Esler (Emily Rogers); Holly Hoffman (Cathy); Marcia MacLaine (Nurse); Glen Lee (Geiger Counter Man); Vernon Barkhurst (Bill Grant); Jerry Basham, Teresa Fox, and Travis Walton (Citizens); Susan Neifert (Anchorwoman); Jane Ferguson (Lurae Jenkins); Nancy Neifert (Cathy's Mom); Charley Lang (Jarvis Powell); Lynn Marie Sager (Ida); Mari Padron (Thelma); John Breedlove (Balding Man); Frank Chavez (Orlando); Louis A. Lotorto, Jr. (Paramedic); Ronald Lee Marriott (Digger); Shinichi Mine (Japanese Reporter); Scott M. Seekins (Emergency Room Doctor); Eric Wilsey (Claude).

LOS ANGELES TIMES, 3/13/93, Calendar/p. 4, Peter Rainer

"Fire in the Sky," a UFO movie, doesn't fly. It claims to be based on an actual case of alien abduction but the movie is as phony as a $3 bill.

The opening, at least, is peppy. A clearing in a nighttime forest slowly brightens as the credits roll. When the scene shifts abruptly to a pick-up truck charging wildly along the dirt roads before screeching to a halt in front of the local saloon. Its occupants—four loggers—straggle zombie-like inside. They've just witnessed a spectacularly horrific event: One of their mates has been zapped by a flying saucer.

It's a motley bunch. Mike (Robert Patrick) is a good ol' boy with problems supporting his wife and two snugly daughters. Bobby (Bradley Gregg) wears a cowboy hat most of the time and has a Cantinflas mustache. David (Peter Berg) has wire-rims and goes to church, Allan (Craig Sheffer) is a bully with a headband and a police rap sheet. Greg (Henry Thomas) is callow and fearful. (Thomas, the child star of "E.T." has seen better days with aliens.) The missing abductee, Travis Walton (D.B. Sweeney)—who claimed this experience in 1975 and subsequently wrote a book about it—is Mike's best friend and his sister's boyfriend.

Travis is portrayed as a Huck Finn-type sport. In his pre-abduction mode, he scoots through his hometown of Snowflake, Ariz., on his motorbike without a care in the world. He scampers up the side of Mike's house to regale his paramour at her window with a package of doughnuts before proposing marriage. He's such a rambunctious all-American kid that it's clear something bad is in store for him. The aliens, you see, aren't abducting just *anybody*. They're airlifting America's finest.

Director Robert Lieberman and screenwriter Tracy Torme lay out the long, dull, predictable scenario. The loggers are widely ridiculed as liars. The grandfatherly local sheriff (Noble Willingham, out Brimley-ing Wilford Brimley) and a skeptical police investigator (James Garner, hyper-relaxed) pursue clues and order up lie-detector tests. Clean-cut UFO-ologists show up and hand out their calling cards. Media hordes descend. Why, we are made to feel, can't the aliens abduct a few of these pesky camera-toting jerks?) When Travis, naked and traumatized, turns up after five unaccounted-for days, the focus of the investigation switches from murder to hoax.

Since we see the initial UFO contact through the eyes of all five loggers, there doesn't seem to be much room in this movie for the possibility that these guys made it all up, or that the whole thing is one big mass hallucination. When, after what seems like an eternity, the big moment comes and we relive Travis' experiences aboard the mother ship, the results are disappointingly goopy. He awakens in a bed of membranous glop and then works his way through the fuselage, which looks like a gigantic elevator shaft, into the operating room. There, the aliens—who look like snoutless, bug-eyed pencil erasers—are waiting for him with their probes and sensors. It's an icky outing.

There isn't much in the way of hard evidence in this movie (rated R for sci-fi violence). Travis doesn't swipe the captain's log or come back spouting Martian Urdu. Once he unloads his phenomenological baggage it's not long before he's his old sporty self again and then the movie ends. We never get inside Travis' terror—the aliens do a much better job of probing him than the filmmakers do. And there's a sneaky condescension at work in "Fire in the Sky." Even though the film takes the side of the loggers, the implication is unavoidable: These guys are such rubes that they *must* be telling the truth.

NEWSDAY, 3/13/93, Part II/p. 23, John Anderson

Faced with a mammoth, throbbing, angry-looking UFO hovering over the wooded mountains of Arizona, why does Travis Walton (D.B. Sweeney) jump out of a truck full of his fellow loggers, run under the UFO and dance around like a moron? It's not the only question "Fire in the Sky" raises, but it's certainly the largest.

We know Travis is a flaky kind of guy; he wants to open a motorcycle shop with his best pal Mike (Robert Patrick) and call it M.T. Motors. Mike is an earthier sort, with a wife, kids, a mortgage and a sister, Dana (Georgia Emelin), whom Travis wants to marry. Which is one reason why, when Travis is promptly knocked on his butt by a blast of light and disappears for five days, Mike and his co-workers come under suspicion of murder. Part "Close Encounters," part, "Ox-Bow Incident," "Fire In the Sky," which is based on Travis Walton's (true?) story, doesn't know what it wants to be, although the individual parts work fairly well on their own. Robert Patrick, who was Arnold Schwarzenegger's futuristic nemesis in "Terminator II," is a little tough to take as Mike Rogers; his temperament makes inexplicable hairpin turns, but that's probably director Robert Lieberman's fault. Sweeney is a bit of a dim bulb but likeable. And James Garner, as state investigator Frank Watters (who never does believe the story of Travis' extraterrestrial encounter) operates on his now-standard blend of country common sense and dyspepsia.

Some truly gripping moments come after Travis is found, trembling and dehydrated, outside a rundown gas station. He can't remember anything about the missing five days at first, but at a welcome-home party, it all comes back: The gelatinous cocoon where the aliens kept him, the weightless trip through the huge space station, and particullarly the torture at the hands of his withered, noseless captors. Those few frantic and frightening moments are almost worth the price of admission. Not so the lengthy buildup, nor the flaccid postscript to Travis' story. But sci-fi buffs will probably revel in the film's rendering of Travis Walton's recollections.

SIGHT AND SOUND, 7/93, p. 42, Nick James

November 5, 1975. Special investigator Frank Watters is called to Snowflake, Arizona to interview a five-man logging team who claim to have survived an uncanny and terrifying experience. A sixth member of the team is missing and their leader Mike Rogers describes how his best friend Travis Walton disappeared. After a hard day's lumbering, the crew are travelling home in a pickup truck when they notice a strange red light in the sky and see a large, saucer-shaped object hovering above the ground. Before Rogers can stop him, Travis approaches the object, whereupon a beam of white light lifts him, then dashes him to the ground. Convinced that Travis is dead, the others persuade Rogers to drive on, but he decides to go back for his buddy. Rogers returns alone to the scene, but there is no trace of Travis or the object.

Unimpressed by this story, and suspecting foul play, Watters orders a search of the woods. No body is found but the townsfolk are convinced that the loggers murdered the popular Travis, while even Rogers' kid sister Dana (Travis's girlfriend) and his wife Katie are skeptical. With the arrival of UFO fanatics and autograph hunters, media harassment, local hostility and Watters' pressure tactics begin to rattle the team. They take polygraph tests, but Rogers refuses to undergo a second one when the results prove inconclusive. Five days after the incident, Rogers receives a phone call from Travis, who is found huddled naked in the corner of a gas station office. As he recovers the ability to communicate, he experiences memory flashes of his extra-terrestrial experience. In the longest of these nightmare flashbacks, Travis is entombed in the bowels of a honeycombed atrium. When he tries to escape, tadpole-headed creatures drag him to an operating table and attempt to drill his temples.

Travis eventually recovers and Watters moves on, swearing that he will one day crack the case. Some years later, Travis, having married Dana, fathered two children and set up a long-cherished motorcycle business, goes looking for Rogers, who has lost his house and is estranged from his own family. Returning to the site of the incident, they are reconciled.

Scenes of backwoodsmen squaring off while brandishing chainsaws or erect digits turn this flimsy true story of UFO sighting into something resembling an outdoor prison movie. Although a conspiracy is initially hinted at when the loggers agree to stick to the same story, any suspicion that they might not be sincere is banished when their close encounter is reverently depicted in flashback. While this 'it's-all-true' approach validates the startling nightmare sequence at the film's climax, the very power of that sequence exposes the 'Waltons-on-steroids' treatment of the earthbound scenes.

This hesitancy of mood is exacerbated by an ambivalence about the Mike Rogers character. In simultaneously celebrating and punishing the sullen macho values behind his role as an honest but tight-lipped pillar of the community, the script exposes the full range of actor Robert Patrick's baleful glances. In contrast, D.B. Sweeney as Travis is allowed to play up his function as the film's literal dreamer and all-round most popular person without question.

Appropriately enough, 'real' issues—hard work, nosy neighbours, devious policemen and rural poverty—fill out the background. Yet judging by their behaviour, Rogers and his crew are permanently scarred more by living in a town called Snowflake than by working for a living or seeing their workmate zapped by a flying saucer. It's as if being accused of having an overactive imagination leaves them open to the charge of being soft, flaky and capable of melting.

VILLAGE VOICE, 3/30/93, p. 60, Erik Davis

A muddled, aimless UFO tale, "based on a true story," *Fire in the Sky* concerns a crew of scruffy burnouts from Snowflake, Arizona, who encounter an alien spacecraft in a national forest. The spaceship, which resembles a volcanic pacifier, abducts Travis Walton, and most of the film concerns his neighbors' suspicious reaclion to his disappearance. Girlfriends and shopkeepers get ornery while James Garner—playing a detective with a turquoise bolo tie—brings down the forces of secular reason on our friends' unlikely tale. About the only pleasures during all this run-around are the low-life, mid-'70s sets and the burnouts' grungy Sub-Pop aesthetic of plaid shirts, sweaty bandanas, and scraggly facial hair.

By the time Travis returns as a traumatizcd nude whimpering in the rain, the audicnce had already started making their own noises—giggling, doing bird imitations, gathering their things to leave. And though the "climactic" examination scene in the alien spaceshlp was decent horror (Cronenberg's *Dead Ringers* crossed with *Reservoir Dogs*), it literalized what better abduction films like *Communion* wisely leave as undefined delirium. The withered appearance of the aliens did give some credence to the theory that the aliens are abducting humans to revitalize their own gene pools, but that's only interesting if you dabble in such notions. And even then, it's not that intertesting.

Also reviewed in:
NEW YORK TIMES, 3/13/93, p. 16, Vincent Canby
VARIETY, 3/15/93, p. 63, Lawrence Cohn
WASHINGTON POST, 3/13/93, p. D1, Rita Kempley

FIRM, THE

A Paramount Pictures release. *Executive Producer:* Michael Hausman and Lindsay Doran. *Producer:* Sydney Pollack, Scott Rudin, and John Davis. *Director:* Sydney Pollack. *Screenplay:* David Rabe, Robert Towne, and David Rayfiel. *Based upon the book by:* John Grisham. *Director of Photography:* John Seale. *Editor:* William Steinkamp and Fredric Steinkamp. *Music:* Dave Grusin. *Music Editor:* Ted Whitfield. *Sound:* David MacMillan and (music) Don Murray. *Sound Editor:* J. Paul Huntsman. *Casting:* David Rubin. *Production Designer:* Richard MacDonald. *Art Director:* John Willett. *Set Decorator:* Casey Hallenbeck. *Set Dresser:* Lisa Miller, David Weathers, Joseph McAfee, Jr., and Spencer Register. *Costumes:* Ruth Myers. *Make-up:* Ben Nye, Jr. and Richard Dean. *Stunt Coordinator:* Andy Armstrong. *Running time:* 154 minutes. *MPAA Rating:* R.

CAST: Tom Cruise (Mitch McDeere); Jeanne Tripplehorn (Abby McDeere); Gene Hackman (Avery Tolar); Hal Holbrook (Oliver Lambert); Terry Kinney (Lamar Quinn); Wilford Brimley (William Devasher); Ed Harris (Wayne Tarrance); Holly Hunter (Tammy Hemphill); David Strathairn (Ray McDeere); Gary Busey (Eddie Lomax); Steven Hill (F. Denton Voyles); Tobin Bell (The Nordic Man); Barbara Garrick (Kay Quinn); Jerry Hardin (Royce McKnight); Paul Calderon (Thomas Richie); Jerry Weintraub (Sonny Capps); Sullivan Walker (Barry Abanks); Karina Lombard (Young Woman on Beach); Margo Martindale (Nina Huff); John Beal (Nathan Locke); Dean Norris (The Squat Man); Lou Walker (Frank Mulholland); Debbie Turner (Rental Agent); Tommy Cresswell (Wally Hudson); David Kimball (Randall Dunbar); Don Jones and Michael D. Allen (Attorneys); Levi Frazier, Jr. (Restaurant Waiter); Brian Casey (Telephone Installer); William J. Parham (Minister); Victor Nelson (Cafe Waiter); Richard Ranta (Congressman Billings); Janie Paris (Madge); Frank Crawford (Judge); Bart Whiteman (Dutch); David Dwyer (Prison Guard); Mark Johnson and Jerry Chipman (FBI Agents); Jimmy Lackie (Technician); Afemo Omilami and Clinton Smith (Cotton Truck Drivers); Susan Elliott and Erin Branham (River Museum Guides); Ed Connelly (Pilot); Joey Anderson (Ruth); Deborah Thomas (Quinn's Maid); Tommy Matthews (Elvis Hemphill); Chris Schadrack, Jeffrey Ford, and Jonathan Kaplan (Lawyer Recruiters); Rebecca Glenn (Young Woman at Patio Bar); Terri Welles (Woman Dancing with Avery); Gregory Goosen (Vietnam Veteran); Jeane Aufdenberg (Car Rental Agent); William R. Booth (Seaplane Pilot); Lannie McMillan Quartet (Peabody Musicians); Ollie Nightingale (Restaurant Singer); Teenie Hodges (Restaurant Lead Guitarist); Little Jimmy King (Memphis Street Musician); James White (Singer at Hyatt).

CHRISTIAN SCIENCE MONITOR, 7/6/93, p. 12, David Sterritt

Lawyer movies have been around for ages, ranging from first-rate pictures like "Witness for the Prosecution" to scruffier melodramas like "Body Heat" and the recent "Cape Fear" remake.

"The Firm," starring Tom Cruise and Gene Hackman, aims for the higher end of that spectrum. The cast is sensational, the photography looks great, and the story has interesting characters and plenty of built-in suspense.

If the film isn't as compelling as it wants to be, it's because the narrative is more superficially clever than intelligent, and wears thin before its 2½ hours are over. Still, the first half of the picture is smartly entertaining, and even the draggy last hour has enough surprises to compensate for confusion in the plot and too many chase sequences.

"The Firm" is also fairly restrained by today's standards—earning its R rating with some foul language but holding sex and violence to lower levels than in many current offerings.

Cruise plays Mitch McDeere, a top-of-his-class Harvard Law School grad who's being courted by every high-grade firm in the land. He chooses a little-known outfit in Memphis, not because it promises more opportunity or stimulation than the others but because he likes the warmly old-fashioned people who work there—and the six-figure salary they offer him.

The firm has peculiarities though, and Mitch's wife starts noticing these before he does. Wives of employees aren't "forbidden" to have their own jobs, she's told—which makes her wonder what *is* forbidden. And what kind of firm aggressively encourages its partners to have children, so the ensuing responsibilities will ensure lasting dependence on their employer?

Deeper mysteries start surfacing when Mitch plunges into his new job. Some are technical, such as the eagerness of a senior partner to bend the law precariously far on behalf of a client. Others are more serious, and more frightening. In the past few years, Mitch learns, four members of the firm have met untimely deaths. Coincidence? Maybe. But how to explain their "missing" files in a secret room at a faraway resort?

With knowledge like this, Mitch can't shake the suspicion that something is terribly wrong. Then he hears from the FBI, which confirms his fears and demands his help in exposing the firm's connection with organized crime. He finds himself in a triple bind: leave the firm and risk being murdered, or stay and be arrested, or help the FBI by breaking his oath of confidentiality, which means he'll never be allowed to practice law again.

All this is only the setup for the overlong action sequences in "The Firm," and for the many plot twists—some ingenious, others not—that result when Mitch dreams up a way to beat the bad guys and solve his own predicament.

The end of the story is satisfying in a Hollywoodish way, complete with fast-moving climax and victorious conclusion. But it portrays Mitch as more interested in salvaging his professional future than in cleaning up all the evil he's encountered; and it encourages us to accept his shortcuts as a reasonable compromise. While this isn't bad enough to be called an inexcusable ethical failing in the movie, it suggests that "The Firm" resembles the law firm in its willingness to hedge on moral issues.

There's little to complain about in the film's acting. Cruise outdoes the mature performance he gave in "A Few Good Men" not long ago, and Hackman is his usual convincing self as Mitch's mentor. Jeanne Tripplehorn conveys both strength and vulnerability as the hero's wife.

The supporting cast includes a long list of appealing talents. Among them are Hal Holbrook as the firm's top attorney; Ed Harris as a belligerent FBI agent; Gary Busey as a hard-boiled private eye; Holly Hunter as his feisty assistant; Steven Hill as a government official; and Wilford Brimley, cast against type, as the firm's nasty security expert.

Special credit goes to Terry Kinney as one of Mitch's fellow employees and David Strathairn as Mitch's brother, a likable jailbird. Paul Sorvino also makes an uncredited appearance in a marvelously minimalistic turn as a Mafia hood.

"The Firm" was capably directed and produced by Sydney Pollack, whose long career includes many Hollywood films with a serious edge, from "Tootsie" and "Three Days of the Condor" to "The Way We Were" and "They Shoot Horses, Don't They?"

The screenplay is credited to David Rabe and the team of Robert Towne and David Rayfiel, based on John Grisham's bestselling novel; it's at its best when snappy dialogue, not expansive action, is the main focus. John Seale did the colorful cinematography, and Dave Grusin composed the neatly jazz-inflected score.

FILMS IN REVIEW, 10/93, p. 336, Andy Pawelczak

Everybody in *The Firm*, Sydney Pollack's disappointing new legal thriller based on John Grisham's bestseller, keeps telling Mitch McDeere (Tom Cruise) that he deserves all the best things in life, and the refrain is the best thing in the movie: in America we all feel that we deserve the best, and the movie's major break with realism is that Mitch stops believing it sooner than most. After graduating near the top of his Harvard law class, Mitch takes a job with a Memphis law firm that treats him like a visiting movie star: house in the country, Mercedes, six-figure salary, endless praise of his superior talents. It would take a bear stronger man than Tom Cruise's Mitch to resist such blandishments, and in the early part of the movie he's in yuppie hog-heaven though his wife Abby (Jeanne Tripplehorn), a girl-next-door type who's the film's icon of decency, chastity and upper-class noblesse oblige, smells something rotten.

The movie's first half hour is very promising. The firm is the image of conservative respectability, the senior partners lathered in unostentatious affluence and Old South gentility. For anyone less dazzled than Mitch, though, there are some disquieting signs: there are no divorces in the firm, wives are discouraged from working and encouraged to bear children, drinking is frowned upon, and the partners constantly reiterate that the firm is one big happy family. It's like a company run by Ross Perot with Dan Quayle as V.P. in charge of family values, and this part of the movie has a sly satirical edge and at the same time builds an atmosphere creepy enough that it's a let-down when it turns out that the firm isn't a coven but merely a money-laundering operation for the mafia.

Unfortunately, once Mitch realizes the truth the energy goes out of the movie and it degenerates into a standard thriller. An F.B.I. agent (played by Ed Harris) lays out Mitch's choices: he can testify against the firm, which will cost him his license for violating client confidentiality and put him in the witness protection program for the rest of his life; or, he can resign, which will cost him his life—three previous junior partners who attempted to leave ended up dead under suspicious circumstances. The rest of the movie is devoted to the complicated but not very interesting plot Mitch devises to play both ends against the middle, and at a two and a half hour running time it's a long trek to the end.

As Mitch, Tom Cruise has the right ingratiating, upwardly mobile smile, but once the plot machinery takes over the movie he doesn't really have much to do—he's what Graham Greene used to call a "director's dummy." The same can be said for Jeanne Tripplehorn with the additional caveat that her love scenes with Cruise are peculiarly inert. Gene Hackman, as a senior partner who acts as Mitch's rabbi in the firm, does his usual professional job, bringing a suggestion of angst-ridden depths to an otherwise aggressively superficial movie. Hackman is a proven master of middle-aged and desolate romantic pathos, and the movie's few moments of genuine feeling all belong to him. Gary Busey as a good-old-boy private detective has a few funny moments, and David Strathairn as Mitch's brother is laid back and enigmatic. Holly Hunter, who has gotten a lot of good press lately as a result of a best actress award in Cannes for *The Piano*, is a welcome divertissement as a secretarial bimbo who turns out to have a heart of gold and an unexpected surplus of brains.

Sydney Pollack's direction is plodding and unimaginative, and he lards the picture with cliches. Yes, there's the familiar robotic hit man with shoulder length hair (God, what kind of movies have we been watching?), and here comes the Godfather with the heavy impastoed face of an ethnic caricature and an accent straight out of Brooklyn. At one point Pollack even throws in a leaden little symbol in the form of a dog race in which the dogs are lured around the track by a motorized bone. We get the point: run, Mitch, run after that ever receding American Dream. In the end, Mitch gets his bone, but the film, after a lot of strenuous huffing and puffing, doesn't go anywhere at all.

LOS ANGELES TIMES, 6/30/93, Calendar/p. 1, Kenneth Turan

When a book sells 7 million copies and is translated into 29 languages, who can doubt that it is doing something right? So the inevitable film adaptation has to decide whether to play it perfectly safe or take risks with what is close to a sure thing.

The powers behind "The Firm" have avoided the dilemma by splitting the difference. They have carefully protected the core qualities of the John Grisham novel while radically rejiggering its plot line. The result is a top-drawer melodrama, a polished example of commercial movie-making that manages to improve on the original while retaining its best-selling spirit.

Clearly, Paramount Pictures, which purchased the movie rights to this story of lawyers on both sides of the law even before it was sold as a novel, wanted the best for this project, and when Hollywood wants the best in mainstream directing, Sydney Pollack is always on the list.

Though "Havana," his last film, was a misfire, Pollack remains the total professional, an actors' director and one of the foremost practitioners of the kind of nicely calibrated work that is so smooth there is a danger of discounting the amount of skill that goes into it.

Casting was a similar gold standard production. As hotshot attorney Mitch McDeere, Tom Cruise, the heartthrob of the moment, was the obvious choice, and "The Firm" not only pairs him with Gene Hackman as legal mentor and Jeanne Tripplehorn as loving wife, but also fills in the background with the strongest and most varied group of supporting actors in memory.

"The Firm's" most intriguing credit, however, is the one for screenplay, divided as it is between a trio of exceptional writers who are as accomplished as any mob hit men: playwright David Rabe ("Streamers," "Sticks and Bones"), four-time Oscar nominee Robert Towne ("Chinatown," "Shampoo") and longtime Pollack collaborator David Rayfiel, who also worked on the director's similarly themed "Three Days of the Condor."

If "The Firm's" intention was to simply replay the novel, this much talent wouldn't be necessary. But what's been done here is similar to rebuilding an engine: The book's best-selling plot has been taken apart and put back together again in noticeably better shape. Subplots have been strengthened, characters switched around to make the jeopardy more emotionally involving, and increased physical action has been added to the mix, all of which ratchets the excitement level up a number of notches.

"The Firm's" narrative focus, however, has been kept intact, and that involves the trials of lawyer McDeere. The film's opening sections quickly establish him as a top prospect at Harvard law, a loophole-loving tax lawyer whose days of waiting on tables and riding the bus home to patient spouse Abby are soon to end in a welter of big-money proposals from fancy firms.

But the offer McDeere ends up being unable to resist comes not from New York or L.A. but rather courtesy of a small, 41-lawyer outfit in Memphis named Bendini, Lambert & Locke. Not only do they propose to pay top dollar, but they throw in a low-interest home loan and a new Mercedes, color to be determined later, as extra added incentives.

A visit to Memphis and lots of talk about how everybody in Bendini is one cheery family clinches things for McDeere. Though Abby is put off by the Stepford quality of some of the corporate wives and thinks maybe things are too good to be true, the ambitious Mitch, clearly too busy a young man to read many novels, is unworried by the surface perfection.

The first blemish on McDeere's dream comes when two members of the firm die violent and unexpected deaths. Then he gets rousted by a pair of surly men who just might be government agents. Gradually, much against his will, McDeere comes to suspect that Bendini is not exactly the paradise it appears. But like Harry Houdini, bound in chains and tossed overboard, his situation is one from which escape seems impossible, and every move he makes only serves to tighten his bonds,

Though Mitch McDeere can never quite escape being more a cog in a thriller machine than a character, Tom Cruise goes a surprising distance toward making him believable. The actor's charisma has never been in question, but under Pollack's guidance his charm, though evident, has been so muted that when he's called on to be awkward and in jeopardy it is convincing.

Also plausible is his relationship with wife Abby, as Cruise and actress Tripplehorn (Michael Douglas' wretched girlfriend in "Basic Instinct") make a much more charming romantic pair than Cruise and real-life companion Nicole Kidman did in "Far and Away."

Even more impressive is the range and quality of performances "The Firm" (rated R for language and some violence) has gotten from its supporting players. Usually star-driven vehicles have one or two smaller roles that are worth commenting on, but here attention must be paid to more than half a dozen ensemble bits. Included are Gene Hackman's major turn as McDeere's troubled associate, Wilford Brimley as the firm's ominous head of security, David Strathairn as McDeere's brother, Gary Busey and Holly Hunter as private investigator and loving secretary, Ed Harris and Stephen Hill as government operatives, even fallen mogul Jerry Weintraub as the disreputable Sonny Capps and "Wide Sargasso Sea's" Karina Lombard in the small but critical role of a young woman on the beach.

When so much of the acting in a film is quietly effective, an extra nod must be given to the director. Sydney Pollack has not only taken the risk of letting his film run the two and a half hours needed to include relevant characterization, he has demonstrated how emotional shading and subtlety can be worked into big-ticket items. Contrary to so much of what we've seen this summer, "The Firm" proves that a presold blockbuster doesn't have to be the dumbest film on the block.

NEW LEADER, 8/9-23/93, p. 21, David Bromwich

The premise of *The Firm* is that lawyers are specialists in running the world. Fresh out of Harvard Law School, Tom Cruise accepts an every-wish-is-granted offer as an associate with a firm in Memphis, and glows with rewarded merit while his wife grows puzzled at certain signs. The company wives are kept in the dark about the business, encouraged to have many children, and, what is more unusual and disconcerting, "No one's divorced in the firm." Two partners die mysteriously in a swimming accident; the woman who brings the news is observed to be "not sad, but scared—there's a difference." Studying for the bar in a greasy-spoon restaurant, Cruise is hectored knowingly by a detective with a shaved head. A well-placed source informs him that no partner has ever left the firm alive.

The joke lying in wait here, which the director, Sydney Pollack, never properly tags, is that Bendini, Lambert & Locke of Memphis differs only in degree from countless other firms. You *literally* do not leave it alive. Cruise's strategy, elaborately refined, is to play off the firm's inside security unit against an outside investigative agency, and he carries it through with broken-field assurance and unqualified success. The self-satisfaction is made to look generous because in saving his skin he is also saving his marriage.

Sydney Pollack directed *Three Days of the Condor*, one of the best conspiracy-thrillers of the '70s, but his style has slackened cooperatively with the times. The screenplay of *The Firm* is 50 bite-size lumps, the dialogue rigorously held to four exchanges per bite. To eke out the hour-long chase, morsels are spliced together from a great many undernourished plotlines, the average scene length holding steady at 15 to 45 seconds: the span of a TV commercial. Someone said about Hemingway that his descriptions were so exact you could keep alive as a hunter if you read them carefully. It is doubtful that anyone watching *The Firm* could learn to make a multiple Xerox. The easy rush of wasted shots has less to do with narrative conventions than with in-flight showings, and the plot grows terminally snarled when the audience can bear it, between after-lunch coffee and immigration cards.

In a swank movie like this, the real stars are the decor, the music and the sound-mixing. Any threat of unscheduled emotion would lose its edge in the Dave Grusin score, a nonstop upbeat cocktail-lounge blues for acoustic piano. Life is digestible, the music says—see how easy it goes down? Gene Hackman, as a senior partner "decent and corrupt and ruined," rises alone from the mass of youthful pretense and mobile attitudes. "You've earned a good dinner and a night out," he tells Cruise once man-to-man, with a mocking shake of his hips *cha cha cha*, and the coarseness and the delicacy of his touch seem inseparably human.

NEW YORK, 7/12/93, p. 53, David Denby

My experience, I suppose, was fairly typical: I bought John Grisham's *The Firm* at a chain bookstore, intending to read a little of it at lunch. I read it through my tuna fish and coffee; I read it through my entire afternoon work time and then through dinner. At 3:20 A.M., bleary-eyed, I turned off the light next to my bed; I was on page 438. After a few hours' sleep, I picked up the book again and finished it. Exhausted, I stepped to the window and looked outside. Trees, cars, children! I could have been Jonah emerging from the fish. My body felt numb and rubbery, so I poked myself a few times to see if the nerve endings were still there.

What accounts for this extraordinary, worldwide compulsion to turn the pages? The hero of *The Firm*, Mitchell McDeere, is a hungry young man graduating near the top of his class at Harvard Law School. Wooed by many prestigious firms, he decides instead to sign on with Bendini, Lambert & Locke, a prosperous but relatively small outfit in Memphis, Tennessee, that specializes in tax law. The firm fusses over him and offers him many nice things—terrific pay, a certain nifty German sports coupe, a house with a low-interest mortgage. The novel grabs one initially because it presents, with almost erotic intensity, the American fantasy of overwhelming and immediate success.

Yuppie beware! For at the same time Grisham, who has a rather malignant sense of humor, develops a sinister, cocoon-like atmosphere. The firm seduces Mitch and infantilizes his wife, Abby, encouraging her to sink into a life of shopping and decorating. Within months, Mitch realizes he's been pulled into a criminal conspiracy, overpaid to keep his mouth shut and do his job. The firm does legitimate business, but it's also a front, laundering huge amounts of cash for a Chicago Mafia family. Once you agree to join, you can't leave—anyone who tries it quickly finds himself in a fatal accident. When Mitch gets sandbagged by the FBI—forced to gather evidence for it against the firm—he rebels and looks for a way to ace out everybody.

The book offers money, success, crime, sex—the four pillars of best-sellerdom—and a relentlessly paranoid story, in which everything closes in on the hero and he struggles to break free. Grisham provides only the simplest elements of characterization. Mitch, less a person than a machine, barely sleeps and never makes a mistake. We don't even get to see his legal skills; we have to take them on faith. Is the book any good? Well, no, it isn't, but it's very entertaining, and most of all, it's efficient: Grisham provides just enough matter to keep you screwed to your seat but *never anything more*. There are no reverberations, no implications, and what passes for an ethical dilemma is resolved in a burst of movieish euphoria. Writing the book in 1989, Grisham may have started out to skewer the eighties carnival of greed, but he leaves the hero a rich man at the end.

I realize I may sound naive here, almost like someone who never noticed the traffic and then got hit by a car. After all, this blanking out, this wash of fantasy, is the only thing many people want from fiction. But for anyone who wants more, reading a Grisham, a Ludlum, a Clark—any of the chain-store classics—is like spending a debauched weekend with low companions, pleasurable but vaguely guilt-inducing.

Which is not to say we don't want to prolong the weekend. The Firm was practically a movie between covers, so I don't know how the actual movie version could have been screwed up. But it has been. *The Firm*, directed by Sydney Pollack and written by David Rabe, Robert Towne, and David Rayfiel, has been turned into a rather high-minded adult thriller. The movie tries to produce real emotions and even, God help us, a few real people. Some of it is exciting, and it's all well acted and smartly written, but the brazen pop fascination has been drained out. I find myself in the bizarre position of asking for a trashier approach. The way Pollack and company have adapted the material, it no longer makes sense. The movie retains Grisham's pop structure but denies the audience a pop payoff; *The Firm* now feels priggish and self-deluded.

The filmmakers don't seem to have understood what 7 million readers enjoyed. For instance: Grisham's malicious suggestion that in a crooked law firm, extreme decorum and criminality go together perfectly. Grisham lays on the farcical corporate pomp, the Masonic-temple rituals of a closed society in which everything is cloaked in secrecy (a great temptation to fraud). His lawyers are like corrupt medieval bishops, smoothly intelligent keepers of the rules who themselves obey only those rules that gratify their own interests.

Amazingly, Pollack underplays the insinuating, velvet-coffin atmosphere of the firm. He must have thought such stuff would be corny, so he makes the plushly designed law-office scenes rather curt.

But done this way, the movie lacks color and atmosphere, especially since Pollack has also dropped Grisham's Florida honky-tonk settings and most of the Cayman Islands raffishness. Worse, he never develops the kind of spreading *noirish* dread that, say, Alan Pakula employed so devastatingly in *All the President's Men*. There are fine moments, but Pollack's direction is too brisk in scenes that call for languor and suggestiveness. Since the movie is very tightly edited, the fine moments never expand emotionally.

Many of us also enjoyed the journalistic side of the book—the details of the money-laundering operation (the flight of green to the Caymans, the wire transfers to dummy accounts, and so on). This has been dropped altogether. I shall not give you the details, but the nature of Mitch's rebellion against the firm and the FBI has been materially altered. The filmmakers' version may be more plausible, less cynical, but it's also far less satisfying. Damned if Tom Cruise doesn't once again discover his integrity; he discovers, you know, the *law*, and begins making speeches, as if he were still playing his part in *A Few Good Men*. One would think that Cruise was too old to still be clinging to his moral virginity, but that's the way everyone wants to use him.

What's left is taut and by summer-season standards extremely intelligent. The triumvirate of screenwriters has brightened up the dialogue and tried to give the anguished husband-wife exchanges some emotional density. Cruise, running through Memphis in his suit, holding his briefcase, generally gives a more convincing impression of intelligence than he has in the past. As Abby, Jeanne Tripplehorn (from *Basic Instinct*) appears to be a competent, serious, and utterly humorless actress who bears an alarming resemblance to Harry Hamlin. The more vivid person-alities are stationed out at the edges: That great actor David Strathairn plays Mitch's brother, a con, with fierce, silent intensity, and Holly Hunter is chipper and touching as Mitch's vulgar but shrewd accomplice Tammy.

The most vivid of all is Gene Hackman, consistently the finest American screen actor over the past quarter-century. Hackman is Mitch's mentor, Avery Tolar, a saddened older lawyer, a joker whose cynicism arises from loneliness and self-disgust. Hackman goes from strength to strength: He was brilliantly nasty as the brutal sheriff in *Unforgiven*, and here the mockery and lechery give way to flickering moments of decency. Hackman is always lucid but never obvious, and I can't imagine ever getting tired of him. In *The Firm*, he gives a three-dimensional portrait of corrupt middle age. I looked at him with admiration and also with disbelief, because he really doesn't belong in this material. Sometimes you can't fight the power of pop; you just have to go with it. Instead, Pollack and his crew have turned a terrific piece of escapist fiction into an earnest seminar on the dangers of greed. Given what Hollywood filmmakers are paid, this may be a more poignant lesson for them than it is for us.

NEW YORK POST, 6/30/93, p. 23, Michael Medved

After I read the book, I was beside myself," director Sydney Pollack ("Tootsie," "Out of Africa") confessed to a reporter about his first encounter with the literary inspiration for his new movie "The Firm." "It had so many characters and such a convoluted plot that it'd need a 300-page script that would translate into a five-hour movie."

The finished film isn't quite that long, but at times it feels like it is. At 2 hours and 34 minutes, Pollack's ambitious adaptation of John Grisham's hugely popular best seller (7 million copies in print) runs out of gas at least 40 minutes before it coughs and sputters to its unsatisfying conclusion.

The legal details and intricate twists and turns that helped make the book so fascinating and persuasive to read might have worked well in a television miniseries, but in the context of this frustrating feature film they come across as fragmentary, confusing and ultimately implausible.

It's impossible to blame the large and distinguished cast for what goes wrong. All the major players deliver superb performances, with the significant exception of the lackluster star turn by leading man Tom Cruise.

He plays the brilliant young lawyer Mitch McDeere, an arrogant, hard-driving, ambitious kid who faces a crisis and ends up developing new depths of integrity and sensitivity. It's precisely the part that Cruise has played so often and so well—in the past that he ought to be able to do it in his sleep; and on occasion in the course of the film he seems badly in need of a wakeup call.

For one thing, this marks the second film in a row (following "A Few Good Men") in which Cruise plays a glib, self-assured attorney who's just graduated from Harvard Law School. Perhaps that august institution should consider awarding him an honorary degree so he can now feel free to go on to other roles.

In "The Firm," the young hotshot takes his Harvard credential and his beautiful wife (Joanne Tripplehorn, the sexy police psychologist in "Basic Instinct") down to Memphis for a job with a small stuffy but conspicuously prosperous law firm that's offered him far more money than any of the better-known outfits in New York, Chicago or L.A.

Only after he settles into his new job and begins investigating the mysterious deaths of four of his predecessors does he begin to get the idea that the firm functions as an elegant well-paid front for organized crime.

Meanwhile, the FBI (in the person of a bullying agent played by the always effective Ed Harris) is on the case and will stop at nothing to bust these pompous crooks. Cruise must decide whether to cooperate with the feds, violating legal ethics by betraying his colleagues and his clients, or else stick with the firm and run the risk of jail and disgrace.

The movie is gripping and watchable as it constructs this dilemma for its central character, but far less convincing as it shows the way he tries to deal with it. An especially notable weak point is the violent and climactic confrontation between the hero and two murderous thugs. Its stagy resolution relies on the sort of ridiculous, convenient cliches that make audiences groan.

Whenever Gene Hackman's on screen playing McDeere's cheerfully corrupt, hard-drinking and incorrigibly womanizing mentor at the firm, he provides the depth and warmth that are sorely lacking in the rest of the movie. Against all odds, this amazing actor makes his difficult character more engaging and sympathetic than the two-dimensional hero—further throwing the picture's emotional balance out of whack.

"The Firm" is never an outright embarrassment—like Sydney Pollack's disastrous last outing, "Havana." But considering the hype and the talent involved and the fact that audiences may find the film a very long trial to sit through, we have a right to expect something better than a hung jury.

NEWSDAY, 6/30/93, Part II/p. 49, Jack Mathews

John Grisham's best seller "The Firm" was the perfect no-brainer airplane book, a thriller whose characters reminded you of no living humans, whose premise and clever plot twists masked their huge implausibilities, and whose head-long narrative force seemed to get you from New York to Chicago in half the time.

In attempting to flesh out Grisham's unfounded characters, and legitimize his fanciful story about an ace Harvard law grad who becomes an associate at a firm servicing the Mafia, director Sydney Pollack and his trio of screenwriters have turned it into something that's often as dull, detailed and sluggish as the Senate budget debate.

And at 2 hours and 34 minutes, the movie seems to take longer to watch than the book did to read.

Credit Pollack with good intentions. He is an intelligent, tasteful filmmaker who, with the spectacular exception of "Havana," has one of the best records of any major studio director for delivering slick, star-driven mainstream pictures. Of all sorts: comedy ("Tootsie"), tragedy ("They Shoot Horses, Don't They?"), epic romance ("Out of Africa").

"The Firm" is as slick as any of them, and with Tom Cruise and Gene Hackman in key roles, it certainly has marquee value. But it has none of the heart, romance and psychological depth we have come to expect from Pollack's movies, and which he and high-powered writers Robert Towne ("Shampoo"), David Rabe ("Casualties of War") and David Rayfield ("Three Days of the Condor") tried so hard to create.

Pollack didn't so much rewrite the book as he recast and reformed it. He played up some characters, downplayed others and gave it a new, more complex (and less satisfying) ending that does away with the book's ambiguous ethical moral. Otherwise, it is reasonably faithful to Grisham's story.

It follows Mitch McDeere (Cruise) and his school teacher wife Abby (Jeanne Tripplehorn) from the poverty of college life in Boston to the flush suburbs of Memphis, where Mitch has followed a too-good-to-be-true job offer from the folksy partners at Bendini, Lambert & Locke.

Pollack drags out the early part of the story, as Mitch and Abby get to know the firm and the cultish control it asserts over the associates and their families. Abby is much quicker than her enthusiastic husband to see trouble brewing.

"You're not forbidden to work and the firm encourages children," one of the other lawyer's wives cheerfully advises Abby early on. "They promote stability."

While Abby is home, steaming about Mitch's long hours and pondering her apparent role as a Stepford wife, Mitch is bonding with his cynical, hard-drinking tutor Avery Tolar (Hackman) and relishing his status as the firm's rising star.

Other than a disintegrating marriage, all is well with Mitch until two associates on firm business in the Grand Caymans are killed in a mysterious boat explosion.

After learning that there have been other mysterious deaths among associates (the firm's boast that no one has ever left it is only technically true), Mitch begins his own investigation and is soon caught between the Justice Department, some pushy FBI agents, his bosses and the mob, and is faced with a decision.

Does he become a snitch, blow his career and live out his life in a witness relocation program? Or adopt a go-along, get-along attitude, and hope the firm is never busted?

As readers of the novel know, Mitch came up with another alternative, one that draws in an assortment of colorful characters: Mitch's imprisoned brother Ray (David Strathairn), eccentric private eye Eddie Lomax (Gary Busey), Eddie's able assistant Tammy (Holly Hunter) and a mob boss (Paul Sorvino) who seems to have wandered in from a Scorsese movie.

Pollack got some wonderful performances out of these supporting players, and it is not until that third act reaches speed that the movie approaches the level of suspense and tension that pervaded the book.

Obviously, Pollack hoped to make his characters interesting enough to allow a long, leisurely buildup, but it didn't happen. He had no characters to work with, and certainly mega-star, mini-talent Cruise is not an actor who can make something from nothing, even with the best direction.

Pollack's attempt to create a love story where there was none involved beefing up Abby's role and turning her into both a suffering and conquering hero, a betrayed wife whose love for her husband overrides her pain and has her ultimately risking her life for him.

Tripplehorn, the troubled psychologist in "Basic Instinct," gives a forceful, passionate performance and dominates her scenes with both Cruise and the unusually laconic Hackman, playing a character weighted down with guilt and sadness. This is not a "fun" Hackman performance, and it's a big disappointment after his Oscar-winning role in "Unforgiven."

The emphasis placed on the McDeeres' relationship, and on Tolar's unlikely attempts to seduce Abby, sacrifices the pacing that made the book such a compelling read.

In the end, "The Firm" is neither the fast-paced summer thriller it might have been, nor the character-driven drama Pollack tried to make of it.

It's that strangest of all summer concoctions, a no-brainer that wants you to give it some thought.

NEWSWEEK, 7/5/93, p. 57, David Ansen

Mitch McDeere, the hero of *The Firm*, is definitely a Tom Cruise kind of guy. He's a smart, hungry Harvard Law School grad whose aspiring Yuppie-dom is redeemed by his dirt-poor background, which gives him a slight chip on his shoulder and an outsider's defiance. In other words, he looks as comfortable in a black leather jacket as in a lawyer's suit. The Cruise hero is always on the verge of insufferable cockiness, until life tests his mettle (in the air, on a racetrack, in a courtroom) and he learns that there are higher values than fame or fortune.

This formula, which is wearing a bit thin, works better in Sydney Pollack's spiffy adaptation of John Grisham's best seller than it has in a while, because here it's not the whole show. There's a lot more going on in this convoluted thriller than the spectacle of a handsome lad transcending his callow nature. Pollack treats Cruise as a team player, surrounds him with a smashing team of actors and sustains the suspense for a taut two and a half hours.

McDeere is a bright young man in one whopping jam. Courted by all the big law firms, he accepts an irresistibly cushy offer from the small Memphis firm of Bendini, Lambert & Locke, specialists in tax law. This cozy, familial firm seems too good to be true—and it is. His wife (the sexy, smart Jeanne Tripplehorn) is suspicious from the start, and the mysterious death of two lawyers in a boating accident doesn't help. No one, in fact, has ever left the firm—alive. He soon finds out the reason, when FBI agents inform him that his employers are run by the mob ... and that McDeere will end up in the pen if he doesn't turn over Bendini, Lambert's files to the Feds. But if he cooperates his days are numbered.

Grisham readers may think they know how McDeere gets out of his dire predicament, but Pollack and his three big-name screenwriters—David Rabe, Robert Towne and David Rayfiel—have added a major new twist, clever but not entirely plausible, to the tale. Without giving anything away, let's just say that a firm this paranoid and security conscious would never have such a convenient Achilles heel.

"The Firm" is far from water tight, but if it doesn't quite match Pollack's crackerjack '70s thriller "Three Days of the Condor," it's a classy contender. Gene Hackman adds rich nuances to the role of Avery Tolar, Mitch's duplicitous, self-loathing mentor; Ed Harris is wonderfully short fused as a tough-guy FBI agent who's not as sharp as he'd like to be; Wilford Brimley is cast nicely against type as the firm's head of security, and Gary Busey has great fun with the brief, splashy role of a seedy detective investigating the case. But best of all (so good you want more of them) are Holly Hunter as Busey's gum-popping secretary, who becomes Mitch's secret weapon, and David Strathairn as Mitch's low-life brother, whom he springs from jail as part of his deal with the Feds. A summer genre movie for grown-ups, "The Firm" helps restore faith in Hollywood professionalism.

SIGHT AND SOUND, 10/93, p. 44, Nick James

Newly graduated law student Mitch McDeere, wooed by top law firms, assumes he is heading for the big city. But Memphis firm Bendini, Lambert and Locke outbids all rivals, dangling a leased black Mercedes as bait. Mitch is impressed with the firm's family atmosphere and ignores his wife Abby's concern that their private life might fall into the firm's paternal embrace.

Mitch is soon the keenest rookie on the roster, working 90 hours a week for his new mentor Avery Tolar. He soon learns of the deaths of two of the firm's associates in a diving accident in the Cayman Islands where the firm owns a couple of condos and does a lot of offshore work. During a lunch break in a local diner, Mitch is accosted by FBI agent Wayne Tarrance, who tells him that the deaths were no accident and that the firm is a money-laundering operation for the mob. Mitch goes to Avery and tells him of the approach but not what was said. Senior partner Oliver Lambert tells him that the FBI are always dogging the firm because the government is always losing tax cases against them. Later the mob's on-site man Devasher says he thinks they should get some "insurance" on Mitch and suggests that they send him with Tolar to the Caymans.

Once in the Caymans, Tolar flouts all the company rules about booze and philandering. Mitch too is approached by a bikini-clad woman, but he turns her down and takes a walk along the beach. In the shadows he sees a woman beating off a persistent man, and chases the assailant away. The woman wishes to express her gratitude, and Mitch fails to resist. Next day he visits diving instructor Barry Abanks, whose son lost his life with the two associates, and learns that the circumstances were suspicious.

Returning to Memphis, Mitch drives to the penitentiary to see his brother Ray, whose existence he has kept from the firm. Later he and Abby argue about his continual absence from home, and Mitch tells her his concerns. He contacts a private detective friend of Ray's, Eddie Lomax, and asks him to investigate the deaths. Eddie is killed by a Nordic thug and his death is witnessed by his secretary/lover Tammy.

At a seminar in Washington, Mitch is again approached by Tarrance who tells him about Lomax and introduces him to FBI chief Denton Voyles. Either Mitch works for them or he will be indicted when the FBI finally crack the mob connection. Mitch agrees a price of a million dollars plus freedom for Ray. Mitch copies the secret files in Tolar's office, setting up Tammy in a nearby office where she can make multiples. But Devasher finds out, and decides to scare Mitch by showing him photos of Mitch making love to the beach girl. Mitch confesses his infidelity to Abby, and she resolves to leave him.

Abby is visited by Tolar, and turns down his offer of a trip to the Caymans. Tolar is flying in the company Lear jet; its hold is stuffed with cash. Remembering a secret file room in the condo, Mitch arranges for Tammy to plunder it while Tolar is out, but Tammy learns that Tolar has cancelled his diving lesson and her emergency call to warn Mitch is intercepted by Abby. Abby flies to the Caymans and, having drugged Tolar's drink, joins Tolar in his room. Before passing out, he confesses his disappointment at her complicity.

An FBI informer tells the mob that Mitch is the leak. Fortunately, Tarrance finds out in time to save him. Mitch refuses FBI protection and flees to Mud Island with the Nordic thug in pursuit. Devasher sends a hit squad to the Caymans, then joins the pursuit of Mitch. In a darkened room Mitch engineers Devasher and the thug's mutual destruction. With Ray released and the documents copied, Mitch confronts the mob bosses. He explains that confidentiality prevents him from revealing what he knows as long as he remains unharmed. But he also tells them that the firm are guilty of mail fraud. Mitch bargains his safety for theirs, providing the firm is destroyed in the process. Later, Mitch gives Tarrance the mail fraud evidence and he and Abby drive away to a new life.

The Firm is a peculiar hybrid in that it began life as a film script and yet became a best-selling blockbuster novel long before a film emerged. Author John Grisham has published two more such money-spinners about the legal profession since. The delay may explain why the novel and the script have such divergent narratives, albeit starting from the same premise. However, the differences ought to be instructive about what is currently acceptable in mainstream fiction but not in the cinema.

Prominent among many plot changes between novel and film is the way that the hero Mitch is allowed to come away from his ordeal almost unscathed. The novel is truer to the inflexible come-uppance of the Faustian pact: Mitch is allowed no way back into 'normal' society but has to become a permanent fugitive from the mob, cruising the obscure parts of the Caribbean on a never-ending limbo holiday. That the Tom Cruise character learns his moral lesson at so little cost suggests a star flexing his box-office muscles at the plot's expense.

The casting of Gene Hackman may likewise explain the unlooked-for frisson between Tolar and Abby. If Jeanne Tripplehorn had had some of the small-town hunger about her that Mitch and Abby are meant to exude, then her tacit fascination with him might be in character. Instead the two co-stars look too much at home in their *Hello*-spread house, even after they know it's bugged. It's as if the 80s had never finished and greed still seemed the smarter option.

Grisham's novel offers a particularly stark set of formula parameters: a large and powerful institution, a young independently-minded go-getter, and a sinister conspiracy that draws our hero into morally dubious territory. Pollack approaches the simple but event-stuffed page-turner (as rejigged by, among others, Robert Towne, who has scripted many a drama of festering immorality) as an edifice to be climbed at frantic pace, fired up by star-power and a blues piano score. However, the pacing is lumbered by such rambling spellings-out as the whispered exchanges on the McDeeres' front porch.

On the plus side, a legal thriller has for once avoided the pitfalls of a static and talky genre—there are no courtroom scenes. Yet *The Firm*'s production values are so thick-pile that they tend to suppress the excitement. Furthermore, even a cast as prestigious as this one can't paper over Grisham's one great logical plot hole, which has survived into the film: why, if they're flying money out of the country in a Lear jet, do the mob need an expensive firm of lawyers to launder their money?

TIME, 7/5/93, p. 58, Richard Schickel

Adapting a best seller for the movies is like carving flesh down to the bone. You keep the skeleton, then apply rouge and silicone until the creature looks human. Any screenwriter adapting the 500-page novel, *The Firm*, John Grisham's tort thriller about tax attorneys fronting for the Mafia, would try to streamline the story, infuse action into a narrative that is mostly lawyers chatting, give an emotional history to characters who are basically plot props and ... please, a new ending. Grisham spun a lovely yarn—the venality, the conspiracy, the flypaper guilt—then let it unravel at the denouement. His climax had the hero in a Florida motel waiting for a FedEx package!

The Firm was one of those "it-kept-me-up-all-night" page turners for which there is no equivalent in movie hype. "I sat all the way through it" just doesn't have the same zing. But that is what to expect from the film of *The Firm*, which clocks in at 2½ hours—barely shorter than the audiocassette version of the novel. It's more bustle than brio.

The movie begins sharply, laying out the panoply of privilege: the sleek cars, the comfortable faces (Gene Hackman, Hal Holbrook). It's like going on a shopping spree at Neiman Marcus and then getting whacked with the bill: here is the middle class's Faustian bargain of big money and sapping compromise, of anxious wives and Stepford lives. How handsome the paneling on a lawyer's desk—as handsome as the paneling on a lawyer's casket. At Bendini, Lambert & Locke, death is the penalty for abusing the rule of confidentiality. Harvard Law whiz Mitch McDeere (Tom Cruise) will break that rule and many others honored by his firm, the Mob, the FBI and his resilient wife Abby (Jeanne Tripplehorn).

So far, so good. Cruise, like Robert Redford two decades ago, is a Hollywood hunk who has played it smart by playing smart guys: young men with cute brain waves who can make intelligence and idealism sexy. He and the pricey cast (Ed Harris, Holly Hunter, Wilford Brimley) make the machinery purr. The writers have corrected the book's dangling threat—how to confront and cleverly resolve Mitch's brief disloyalty to Abby—and its stodgy ending. The movie's moral is that however corrupt the Mob is, these lawyers are worse. Better for Mitch to cut a deal with a don than to let the firm stay in business.

Too often though, Sydney Pollack, whose swank and care energized the Redford thriller *Three Days of the Condor* in 1975, surrenders to genre goofiness, setting up bad guys who are omnipotent at the start and impotent at the end. Like a complex lawsuit, the movie gets buried in paperwork; there's too much walking and talking. (See Tom think. See Tom brood. See Tom make photocopies. See Tom amble across his living room—in slow motion.) And at the end, too much running and gunning. Maybe every thriller demands a chase, but a clever thriller deserves a better one. On that endless, aimless run, Mitch loses his way, and *The Firm* goes flabby.

VILLAGE VOICE, 7/6/93, p. 45, Georgia Brown

Like 7 million others, though in the line of duty, I bought *The Firm*. But then I restrained myself after 46 pages—just as Mitch and his wife head south for the new job, new friends, new troubles—because I didn't want to spoil the movie. John Grisham is an effectively trashy writer and I must say he had me dying to know what that spooky ol' Memphis law firm's secret business was. Now I find out from the movie and what a dreary little secret it is. Not knowing was a lot more fun. What Grisham's story has going for it is the horror subtext: a novice's growing dread that s/he has unwittingly checked into some sort of sinister asylum. There're also those dire threats to the individual hidden by Middle America's tree-lined streets. (I kept hoping for something like Stepford partners.) The premise really is right out of Lewton: Like the ghost ship, the firm sails far out to sea commanded by its lunatic captains. As one by one the crew drop overboard, the untried mate fights to survive.

Directed by Sidney Pollack, *The Firm* stars Tom Cruise and Jeanne Tripplehorn as the golden couple, Ed Harris (with shaved head, a really inconspicuous undercover FBI agent), Holly Hunter as a hillbilly secretary, and Gene Hackman as Mitch's burned-out, sad-case mentor in the firm. The movie begins as a thriller and turns into a caper. It capers on and on and on. The running time is 154 minutes. The final hour, with its parallel chases, seems endless and often incoherent. (Test audiences, where were you?) For anyone dying to see a lawyer in pinstripes run for his life, briefcase in hand, this should satiate. A journey by monorail to some place called Mud Island seems inserted merely for an attractive distance shot of the chase.

Judging from statements in publicity materials, Robert Towne (screenwriter with David Rabe and David Rayfiel) was the one who determined Mitch should find respect for the law. A valiant effort was rewriting the ending, finding a way he can get out of the firm legally—and *not take a penny for himself*. Towne calls the law "the most sacred thing there is in a secular world," adding, "If you follow the law, it will be your salvation." Even if the author of *Chinatown* and *Shampoo* has now got religion, I doubt that all the firm's lawyers could make this case.

Also reviewed in:
NEW REPUBLIC, 8/2/93, p. 32, Stanley Kauffmann
NEW YORK TIMES, 6/30/93, p. C15, Vincent Canby
VARIETY, 7/12/93, p. 52, Todd McCarthy
WASHINGTON POST, 6/30/93, p. D1, Rita Kempley
WASHINGTON POST, 7/2/93, Weekend/p. 31, Joe Brown

FLESH AND BONE

A Paramount Pictures release of a Mirage/Spring Creek production. *Executive Producer:* Sydney Pollack. *Producer:* Mark Rosenberg and Paula Weinstein. *Director:* Steve Kloves. *Screenplay:* Steve Kloves. *Director of Photography:* Philippe Rousselot. *Editor:* Mia Goldman. *Music:* Thomas Newman. *Music Editor:* Bill Bernstein. *Sound:* Danny Michael and (music) John Vigran. *Sound Editor:* Scott Hecker. *Casting:* Risa Bramon-Garcia and Juel Bestrop.

Production Designer: Jon Hutman. *Art Director:* Charles Breen. *Set Decorator:* Samara Schaffer. *Set Dresser:* John D. Kretschmer, Marcus Lee Brown, Jerry King, Shane Patrick, J.P. Schwan, Joe Self, and Lisa K. Sessions. *Costumes:* Elizabeth McBride. *Make-up:* Leonard Engelman and Dorothy J. Pearl. *Stunt Coordinator:* Andy Armstrong. *Running time:* 127 minutes. *MPAA Rating:* R.

CAST: Julia Mueller (Sarah Willets); Ron Kuhlman (Clem Willets); Jerry Swindall (Young Arlis); Ryan Bohls (Scotty Willets); James Caan (Roy Sweeney); Dennis Quaid (Arlis Sweeney); Ez Perez (Boy in Suit); Craig Erickson (Tiny Ted); Barbara Alyn Woods (Cindy); Gwyneth Paltrow (Ginnie); Joe Berryman (Plump Man); Mag Ryan (Kay Davies); Scott Wilson (Elliot); James N. Harrell (Woody); Gerardo Johnson (Juan); Hector Garcia (Nestor); Betsy Brantley (Peg); John Hawkes (Groom); Vic Polizos (Pudge Riley); Nik Hagler (Earl); Travis Baker (Sullen Kid); Christopher Rydell (Reese Davies); Angie Bolling (Woman with Crying Baby); Joe Stevens (Kyle); Libby Villari (Waitress); Gail Cronauer (Emma).

LOS ANGELES TIMES, 11/5/93, Calendar/p. 1, Kenneth Turan

"Flesh and Bone" proves what "The Fabulous Baker Boys" postulated, that writer-director Steve Kloves is a bred-in-the-bone filmmaker. Up to a point. For though this finely made movie displays remarkable virtues, including the most moving performance of Dennis Quaid's career, it is also good money sent after bad, a series of impressive accomplishments recruited to serve a questionable plot.

Like "Baker Boys," Kloves' celebrated debut film, "Flesh and Bone" reveals a natural filmmaker who does so many things well it's difficult to know where to start, a gifted creator who refuses to be fenced in and do the obvious stories the obvious ways.

From its very first frames, Kloves (with the potent assistance of "A River Runs Through It" cinematographer Philippe Rousselot) shows an almost casual ability to create tension and mood. "Flesh" opens in the emptiness of Texas farm country on a quiet night 30 years in the past, a night that looks placid but feels, for no reason you can name, both menacing and unnerving.

After this brief but critical prologue, "Flesh" switches to a convincingly bleak and barren West Texas present and a character from that night, Arlis Sweeney (Quaid), who seems as at home in the arid landscape as a sand lizard.

Self-employed as a servicer of vending machines dispensing condoms and crackers on a rural route, the caretaker of a flock of tick-tack-toe-playing chickens known collectively as Brainy Betty, Arlis has the most regular and predictable of lives and he wouldn't have it any other way. Perhaps because of what transpired 30 years ago, he is uneasy with human contact, nervous in the presence of emotion.

Kloves has a knack for making this kind of offbeat, on-the-edge character very real, and Quaid inhabits the role as he never has anything before. It is an interior, laconic performance, one that couldn't be further from his trademark effervescent "Big Easy" persona, but Quaid, intensely masculine as always, plays it with so much force and conviction he wipes all his other roles off the slate.

Like a confident chef, Kloves gradually blends other characters into his mix. First comes the case-hardened Ginnie (a striking performance by Gwyneth Paltrow), a shoplifter, con artist and worse, glimpsed out on the edge of Arlis' world. When there is Roy (James Caan), with ties to Arlis' past. And finally there is Kay Davies (Meg Ryan, her bubbliness effectively muted), optimistic with little reason to be, fleeing from a bad marriage and worse luck with men.

Not surprisingly to anyone but each other, Arlis and Kay feel a wary attraction to each other, and, as "Baker Boys" demonstrated, one of the things Kloves conveys well is sexual tension and longing.

While many directors get jittery when romantic connections have to be made, Kloves seems to relish them, relaxing into the situations in a natural, involving way.

As these people's lives unfold and combine, "Flesh" manages the pleasant sense of a movie that might at any moment head off in unexpected directions. A writer of on-target dialogue that often carries a playful twist to it, Kloves is a filmmaker who enjoys crossing genre lines, turning in a mixture of romance and dark, despairing psychological thriller that is agreeably difficult to pigeonhole.

However, "Flesh and Bone" (rated R for language, some sexuality and a scene of intense violence) does finally pick a predominant direction to head off into, and it is an unfortunate one. For this film turns out to revolve around a whole series of whopper coincidences, even one of which would be difficult to swallow. Not even a film this accomplished can work up enough suspension of disbelief to enable audiences to ingest them all, and just making the attempt is painful.

One could make the case that this film, reminiscent of the dead-end writings of Jim Thompson and Cornell Woolrich, is similarly concerned with the workings of immutable fate, not flimsy coincidence. But in fact "Flesh" originated in an idea Kloves first had when he was much younger, a time when contrived plots have a regrettable tendency to appear profound. Which makes it understandable, though just as much of a pity, that a director whose abilities are so varied and so tangible should have been undone by his allegiance to such a trifling plot line.

NEW YORK, 11/15/93, p. 84, David Denby

In *Flesh and Bone*, the new film written and directed by Steve Kloves (*The Fabulous Baker Boys*), you can hear the nasty silences of the night. The movie is set in the arid plains and spooked, empty towns of West Texas. Not much is going on down there: The towns are so rudimentary that they've barely established themselves on the cheerless terrain. Kloves and his great cinematographer, Philippe Rousselot, concentrate on a few fragments—an old motel or gas station poised despondently at the edge of nowhere; a woman holding a baby; a tall girl with sunglasses robbing a corpse in a funeral home and slipping away. Life hasn't quite come up to speed. A man and woman (Dennis Quaid and Meg Ryan), each at loose ends, struggle to have a love affair.

I realize that comparing a movie to a great exhibit of still photographs is not paying it the world's highest compliment. Nor is it strictly accurate: Some of the finest moments in *Flesh and Bone* could be achieved only in the movies, an art form in which one can track the incomparable menace of time merely passing, second after second. But in *Flesh and Bone*, the spare, eccentric beauty of individual compositions is often stunning, and some of the most powerful scenes are also some of the stillest. *Flesh and Bone* is an odd case—a gothic family drama, complete with murder and mythic evil, done in dry modernist style. Kloves, whose first movie was so exuberant and likable, hasn't quite figured out how to bring the material fully alive. The overall tone is somber and emotionally recessive. Strictly speaking, *Flesh and Bone* is a dud. But who wants to speak strictly? The movie shows more talent than many a successful work.

In a frightening prologue, a silent little boy, seemingly lost, is taken in by a friendly family; later that night, the boy opens the front door of the house so his father can come in and clean the place out. Silent, dark, and deadly: The robbery goes awry, and the father winds up killing the entire family except for a wailing baby somewhere upstairs. Years later, the little accomplice has grown up into a taciturn, rather remote man, Arlis (Quaid), who drives a truck from one dead town to another, servicing candy and condom machines. Arlis, horribly guilty over his part in the murder long ago, has gratefully sunk into a transient existence. He doesn't want too much life, too much activity; the dead towns suit him fine. Dennis Quaid, hiding under a hat and dampening his natural arrogant charm, keeps his voice low, his lips drawn down. Quaid goes too far, I think, in reining himself in (there are moments in which you may want to tickle him with a feather). But the performance is affecting as a physical realization of a man who wants to live without living.

A funny girl falls into Arlis's lap—Kay (Ryan), who is running away from her dork of a husband. Arlis doesn't give Kay much, but he's solid and honest and handsome (when he takes his hat off), and she falls in love. Meg Ryan, half suppressing her floppy-tailed, smiling adorableness, brings traces of sadness and courage to this orphaned woman. We can't tell if Arlis and Kay are going to make it. Nothing in this part of the world seems to support intimacy. People are just barely hanging on to their little piece of tobacco chaw; and at times, the banality of the truck-and-motel life teeters on the edge of madness. Kloves creates odd spaces in the conversations, as if language had decided to retreat and let the void take over.

Just as Arlis and Kay are beginning to put something together, Arlis's murdering father, Roy (James Caan), shows up, a man worse than anyone can imagine—tricky, manipulative, witty, and shameless. He has a young hustler in tow, Ginnie (Gwyneth Paltrow), the tall thief we've seen operating around the edges of earlier sequences. Gwyneth Paltrow (Blythe Danner's daughter), who has acted in only a few plays and movies, gives odd, unnervingly "right" readings. At first, she seems cold and vague and soulless—a pale, thieving, almost beautiful Western girl. But there are flickers of fear around the bitten-off tough lines.

The movie doesn't quite break free: It's gripped by silence and art consciousness. Quaid and Ryan need a big emotional scene together, and they don't get it (cut-off people can defeat a director). *Flesh and Bone* would have benefitted from a looser, more volatile style. In this somber context, we don't know how to take some of the whimsical southwestern oddities—Arlis spray-painting a performing chicken, for instance. An emblem of absurdity? A sign of life? The audience sits quietly, waiting for the joke.

Yet *Flesh and Bone* is incomparably more interesting than that overpraised dry-gulch misery *Tender Mercies*. Kloves has a real eye and an idiosyncratic sense of character. Once I got used to the movie's peculiar halting rhythm, I leaned in toward the screen, and many of my doubts disappeared into the wide-open spaces. I will always remember a couple of scenes—father and son, reunited after years, looking at each other with acute understanding and mutual loathing; the two hostile young women walking across an endless field of hay while the men settle their old scores in the house where they once committed murder together.

NEW YORK POST, 11/5/93, p. 35, Thelma Adams

I'm on the fence about "Flesh and Bone"—and that's because it can't decide what kind of movie it is. It's part thriller, part rowdy white trash jamboree, and part atmospheric romance.

The first 10 minutes are the tensest. Writer-director Steve Kloves patiently follows a desperate crime unfolding in an isolated West Texas farmhouse. Here's another movie that opens in climax. Kloves ("The Fabulous Baker Boys") strives for authenticity by setting his story in the West Texas plains where he was born.

"Flesh and Bone" is atmosphere-rich, an externalized country-western ballad. With cinematographer Philippe Rousselot ("A River Runs Through It"), Kloves paints a parched landscape of cheap motels, bus stations, pool halls and abandoned houses.

The sleekness of Rousselot's camera work contrasts with the tumbled-down territory of the heart the story seems to demand. Never has a Greyhound bus looked so gorgeous. The scenery sings when it should be squawking. It's another mixed message.

Kloves has cast four attractive actors in his romance-thriller-road movie, and Rousselot never loses their best sides. Rednecks and rascals never looked so good. How do you recognize white trash in a Hollywood movie? They drink bourbon and beer, straight from the bottle, but their hair never looks slept in.

As Roy Sweeney, James Caan gives his most chilling performance in years. Sweeney's a cold-blooded killer. He believes in family when it suits his criminal schemes, and will travel three states to cut off any loose ends. Roy's son Arlis (Dennis Quaid) has traded in the family business for a quiet life. With a hat on his head, and a truck full of Mars bars and condoms, he's a vending machine cowboy with outlets in two counties.

Arlis is a troubled, quiet man. Quaid suppresses his abundant charm and twists his lips into a knot. It's a good performance up to a point, but the set of his mouth gets old. He's just too dry; the mask never cracks.

Still, Quaid's never less than watchable. He sure looks good in jeans; that's one man I'd never let walk away from me.

Quaid's real-life wife, Meg Ryan, plays Kay Davies. Kay's a waif fleeing an abusive husband and completely ripe for the picking.

Ryan has a terminal case of the cutes. Her hard-girl act seems to come more out of the script than her character (she can't even hold a cigarette). Still, when Kay takes on her big-haired husband with a pistol, Ryan grabs the moment and runs away with it.

Ginnie (Gwyneth Paltrow) rounds out this oddball quartet. She's a dubious character with no past, a nubile petty criminal who'll steal the ring off a corpse.

She has the stealthy sensuality of a cat as posed to Ryan's cheerleader charm. Paltrow seems to be walking through some other, grittier movie—Ruby's evil twin from "Ruby in Paradise" or a member of the posse in "Drugstore Cowboy."

Ginnie's just another unlikely piece in this puzzling movie. Why would Arlis follow Ginnie into the pounding rain and an unwanted reunion with Roy when Arlis knows she's a shifty character and he's placed this ruse himself? Beats me.

Kloves has built his plot on a web of coincidences that stretch credibility. While "Flesh and Bone" is highly watchable, it's as emotionally flat as the West Texas landscape—and even less memorable.

NEWSDAY, 11/5/93, Part II/p. 82, Jack Mathews

When Meg Ryan makes her appearance in writer-director Steve Kloves' "Flesh and Bone," it's from a cake. A giant, hollow cake at a stag party in a Texas kicker bar. She's the drunken babe inside in the red stripper outfit with a sequined "Boo" over each breast, and she no sooner pops out of the cake than she barfs on one of the ol' boys up front and passes out.

This may not be the most crucial scene in "Flesh and Bone," but it's worth an early mention be as hard as it may be to imagine Meg Ryan playing a smoker, it's one of the film's *least* incongruous moments.

Kloves, who made such a potent directorial debut with the sensuously rich "The Fabulous Baker Boys," has gone off the deep end with his follow-up, a story that hangs murder, romance and fate from a thin strand of outrageous interlocking coincidences and illogical conclusions.

"Flesh and Bone" stands in odd contrast to "Baker Boys," a film with an atmosphere as thick as the moody piano riffs Jeff Bridges played in those smokey jazz bars, and which had enough sexual tension between Bridges and costar Michelle Pfeiffer to raise the humidity in theaters.

The heat in "Flesh and Bone" is as dry as the air over the West Texas plains where fate brings Kay (Ryan), a lonely woman taking a vacation from her abusive husband, together with Arlis (Dennis Quaid), the quiet businessman who has the local condom machine and juke box concessions and maintains a troupe of colorfully dyed, tic-tac-toe playing chickens.

Kay's and Arlis' attraction is one of opposing dynamics. She is searching, he is settled. She's open, he's closed. She likes surprises, he likes patterned predictability. She's effervescent, he's duller than his dusty pick-up truck.

When Arlis asks Kay about the word "Boo" on her chest, she stretches her bra to reveal the missing "b" at the end of each word and says, "It's the story of my life." He doesn't get it.

If this sounds like farce, it occasionally is. But it is comedy indelicately balanced against the darkest backdrop. In the disturbing opening flashback sequence, we see a farm family slaughtered in the middle of the night by an intruder, and the memory of that event hangs over the horizon of the film like a thunderhead.

What do those killings 30 years ago have to do with Arlis and Kay, who seem to be having one of those uncomplicated rural romances that begin and end on a bar stool? And who are these other characters on the fringe, the repulsive drifter Roy (James Caan, in a throw-away performance) and the dead-eyed young woman (Gwynneth Paltrow) we see stealing jewelry from corpses at funerals?

Kloves certainly knows how to drag out the answers and build suspense, but when he connects all the characters and all the dots in the final reel, they add up to a preposterous picture. In a movie year remarkable for its number of failed endings, this one may take the prize.

Still, there is much to admire within "Flesh and Bone." Philippe Rousselot, the Oscar-winning cinematographer on "A River Runs Through It," has a gift for framing rural America, and though "Flesh" seems as bleak and dusty as "River" was lush and clean, its images are often stunning.

Quaid and Ryan, who are married, may not produce as many sparks on screen as (for their sake, it is hoped) they do at home, but they are wonderfully matched in the lighter sequences, and any director who can control the actors' most annoying mannerisms—her Goldie Hawn smile, his Jack Nicholson—hasn't totally wasted his time.

SIGHT AND SOUND, 12/94, p. 47, Amanda Lipman

One dark night, a Texan couple, living on a remote farmhouse with their son and baby daughter, take in a strange boy who says he is lost. The boy has a star tattooed onto his temple. When they are asleep, he lets in his father, and the two set about burgling the house. They are interrupted by the farmer, but the intruder shoots the whole family, except the baby, dead.

Thirty years later, Arlis Sweeney, who runs novelty and vending machines, drives into a roadside bar/shop. He sees a young woman steal from the shop; later, he keeps glimpsing her around. In the local church, the woman steals jewellery from the corpse that has been laid out for the family. Then, on a bus out of town, she steals money from a woman lying asleep next to her. That night, Arlis goes into a diner, where a stag night is being held, to pick up his vending machine takings. A stripper comes out of a wedding cake, and collapses, drunk. He takes her back to his motel and puts her to bed. The next morning, the stripper, Kay, explains that she was only stripping because her money had been stolen on the coach. Arlis takes her home. Her loudmouth husband Reese turns up and, accusing Kay of sleeping with Arlis, hits her in the face; she turns the tables by putting a gun to his head. She packs her bags and leaves with Arlis, travelling around with him on his jobs and staying with him in motels. Soon they become lovers. Kay notices that Arlis has a star tattooed on his forehead.

One night, Arlis' father Roy turns up with the woman pickpocket. He is wounded and Arlis grudgingly cleans him up. Roy and Ginnie, the young woman, drive off the next morning, and Ginnie recognises a house on their way as the one in a photograph of Kay's parents. She innocently tells Roy. Meanwhile, Arlis has also found Kay's photograph and realises that she was the baby that was left alive that night. He decides he must leave her.

By the afternoon, he is filled with remorse and phones her. But she has gone off with Ginnie to her family's house. He races after them, and finds Kay, Ginnie and Roy there. Roy explains to Arlis that he has brought Kay there to kill her and tie up "loose ends". Arlis is horrified and shoots his father dead. Ginnie steals Roy's watch and they all leave. Back at the motel, Kay asks Arlis for an explanation but he will not say anything. They say goodbye and he drives away, leaving her behind.

There is a certain hard-bitten touch of Jim Thompson in Steve Kloves' second film. Its handful of characters are alienated and disconnected: in the effort to keep his past at bay, Arlis deals with vending machines and tic-tac-toe-playing chickens rather than human beings; the hard-smoking-and-drinking Kay has no family, and is running away from a loveless marriage; Roy's criminal activities have set him apart from the rest of the world and from his son; and Ginnie is a wandering thief with no roots.

Arlis and Ginnie prefer it that way, although the entertainingly disdainful Ginnie's two moments of near sentimentality are both centred round family matters—Kay's mother and the murder of Kay's family. But Kay and Roy believe, in their different ways, in the strength of human relationships: Kay, in her constant optimism in looking for the right man; Roy, in his endlessly stated conviction of the bond of flesh and bone. Both are proved wrong. Kay's desire for togetherness keeps leading her to the very men she should avoid—first Reese, then Arlis. And Roy is so convinced of the ties that bind that he taunts Arlis into killing him.

But Roy's relationship with his son is a very twisted kinship: when Arlis is a child, Roy uses it to inspire fear. Now, there seems to be a certain amount of mutual loathing. Once he has seen that Arlis and Kay are happy, Roy's suggestion that Arlis not only be present but even take part in Kay's murder seems sadistic in the extreme. Arlis, for his part, is torn between the kinship his father insists on and hatred of his father's way of life and what it has done for him.

Where does that lead the film but to the notion of transgression? How can Arlis ever make up for what he has done? However law-abiding and disconnected from other people he has become, every baby's cry makes it plain that he never ceases to be haunted by his past. So when his father makes it possible, Arlis pays for his past transgression through another murder, that of his father, and ends up losing not just Kay but Roy too. The Biblical tone here is echoed in Arlis' own words. Asked by Kay what happened at the farm, he replies, like the most macho of film heroes, "Some things are better left unsaid." His father's blood, staining his shirt, he refers to as "just a little blood"—Arlis has made his sacrifice and the ties have finally been cut.

This could be pretty powerful stuff, yet the film remains surprisingly flat. Dennis Quaid, returning to a serious role after several years of fooling around, is convincingly clamped-jawed and diffident, but never much more. Although the film does not opt for crude psychology in explaining Arlis' past and present, neither does it offer any clues as to what happened to turn the mute, sullen, tattooed little devil child at the film's start into the man he has become. The ambivalence in his relationship with his father—growlingly played by James Caan as a charmer with a very nasty streak—is never expressed enough to make an impact. Only one moment, when

Roy pulls him close to him on a motel bed and Arlis automatically jerks away, almost in pain, gives a sense of what goes on between them.

Meg Ryan's Kay is also part of the problem. Her variation on the ditsy, gutsy lady may please or turn stomachs, depending on your preference, but her place as the ever-hopeful innocent seems overly schematic. Despite her shows of independence, she keeps coming across as part of the plot mechanism rather than part of the film, and the result is not altogether engaging.

Flesh and Bone misses the lightness of touch of Kloves' first feature, *The Fabulous Baker Boys*, but it is not without its moments of humour, such as the spectacle of Arlis grimly blow-drying his brightly coloured hens in a motel room crammed with vending machine items; or Ginnie greasing her fingers with Vaseline from her lips in order to steal a corpse's ring more easily.

What is more, the film's sour pessimism is graced by the down-at-heel motels, bars and diners that, in turn, perfectly offset the ugly Texan landscape, which only becomes beautiful at the farmhouse, a place desecrated by Roy. And if *Flesh and Bone* never quite works as a mystery or as a psychological drama, it ends up strongest as an atmospheric, parodic, if overlong, depiction of lonely lives in a lonely place.

VILLAGE VOICE, 11/16/93, p. 67, Devon Jackson

For the first 30 minutes of this small-town-in-Texas murder drama, writer-director Steve Kloves (*The Fabulous Baker Boys*) and cinematographer Philippe Rousselot establish an odd momentum and tension (and pull off one of the more quiet, well-paced opening scenes in recent film), and then, well, Meg Ryan, perhaps too close on the heels of *Sleepless in Seattle*, starts mugging it up *big-time*. And there ain't a damn thing Kloves and Rousselot do to stop her. Too bad, because *Flesh* has plenty else going for it, with an ambitiousness to be admired.

It's the type of character-rich drama Bob Rafelson or Sam Shepard would've written in the early '70s. A boy and his father wipe out nearly an entire family after botching a simple burglary. Jump ahead a few decades to a now withdrawn vending-machine operator (nicely underplayed by Dennis Quaid) whose charmingly evil dad (James Caan) appears out of nowhere, and with him his girlfriend and petty-thief protégé, Ginnie (Gwyneth Paltrow, who shows up everybody). Coincidentally, Quaid has just taken up with Kay (Ryan), the one survivor of the mass murder.

But, just as the somber mood begins to deepen (via Mia Goldman's metronomic editing) and we start to reflect on an arresting sequence (Paltrow, all legs, sneers, and sunglasses, appearing and reappearing like a bad omen) or a theme like blood ties, Ryan turns on the perky charm. If that's not frustrating enough, we have to suffer through too many hackneyed love scenes. If only Ryan's character came off a bit more traumatized or had just a wisp of Paltrow's streetwise edge, then Kloves might've had a film as intense as its opening scenes.

Also reviewed in:
CHICAGO TRIBUNE, 11/5/93, Friday/p. I, Michael Wilmington
NATION, 12/13/93, p. 744, Stuart Klawans
NEW YORK TIMES, 11/5/93, p. C10, Janet Maslin
VARIETY, 11/8/93, p. 26, Todd McCarthy
WASHINGTON POST, 11/5/93, Weekend/p. 50, Desson Howe
WASHINGTON POST, 11/8/94, p. B10, Rita Kempley

FLIGHT OF THE INNOCENT

A Metro-Goldwyn-Mayer and Rocket Pictures release of a Cristaldi Film/Fandango production in association with RAI-TV/Fildebroc. *Executive Producer:* Massimo Cristaldi and Bruno Ricci. *Producer:* Franco Cristaldi and Domenico Procacci. *Director:* Carlo Carlei. *Screenplay (Italian with English subtitles):* Carlo Carlei and Gualtiero Rosella. *Story:* Carlo Carlei. *Director of Photography:* Raffaele Mertes. *Editor:* Carlo Fontana and Claudio di Mauro. *Music:* Carlo

Siliotto. *Sound:* Roberto Petrozzi and Adriano di Lorenzo. *Sound Editor:* Aurelio Pennacchia. *Production Designer:* Franco Ceraolo. *Special Effects:* Zed Special Images. *Costumes:* Mariolina Bono. *Make-up:* Alessandro Bertolazzi. *Running time:* 105 minutes. *MPAA Rating:* R.

CAST: Manuel Colao (Vito); Francesca Neri (Marta Rienzi); Jacques Perrin (Davide Rienzi); Federico Pacifici (Scarface); Sal Borgese (Vito's Father); Lucio Zagaria (Orlando); Giusi Cataldo (Giovanna); Massimo Lodolo (Rocco); Anita Zagaria (Vito's Mother); Isabelle Mantero (Police Woman); Nicola Di Pinto (Questor); Severino Saltarelli (Scarface's Driver); Gianfranco Barra (Porter); Giovanni Pallavicino (Vito's Grandfather); Anna Lelio (Vito's Grandmother); Beppe Chierici (Don Silvio); Veronica Del Chiappa (Stefania); Sandro Barletta (Simone).

LOS ANGELES TIMES, 10/29/93, Calendar/p. 4, Kevin Thomas

"Flight of the Innocent" plunges us immediately into 15 minutes of breath-stopping bloodshed and terror. In a beautiful pastoral setting in Calabria in Southern Italy, three men brutally gun down another man; in retaliation an entire family is wiped out with the exception of one 10-year old boy, Vito (Manuel Colao), who abruptly find himself running for his life.

In his feature debut, writer-director Carlo Carlei creates an entire world so completely and so cinematically, and with such absolute conviction, that suspension of disbelief becomes total. Carlei has such bravura, such furious energy, we don't even want to question the credibility of all that happens.

Even after the film is over, when we realize that Vito has truly astonishing stamina and smarts for his age, we're not in a mood to question anything, so thoroughly has Carlei engrossed us.

What he has done so excitingly, in short, is to bring an innately Italian grace and passion to bear upon a solidly constructed Hollywood thriller plot. The gap between rich and poor, the way in which dire economic conditions breed the worst kind of savagery—these and other concerns emerge along the way, but at heart "Flight of the Innocent" is a jolting, suspenseful and richly satisfying chase picture.

It rests squarely—and easily—on the narrow shoulders of the sober, angelic-looking Manuel Colao, who has formidable poise and powers of concentration and expression for so young an actor.

Carlei and his co-writer Gualtiero Rosella do such an excellent job of not giving anything away that reviewers really ought not reveal much of the plot. During a brief respite in his desperate dash to reach Rome, where an adult cousin lives, Vito does see on TV a couple (Francesca Neri, Jacques Perrin) pleading for the safe return of their kidnaped son. Instinctively we know that Vito, who is about the same age as the missing boy, and the distraught couple will somehow connect, for Vito has recognized in the wife's anguish his own fear and pain.

No one could accuse Carlei of subtlety—indeed, Vito's chief tracker (Federico Pacifici) is heavily menacingly scarred—but he's so assured and confident he gets away with one grand flourish after another.

For example, we know that Vito's mother, hidden by the sheet she has hung out to dry, has been shot when a blood stain rapidly expands over the sheet, which in turn becomes her shroud as she grabs at it while falling. It's a poetic slo-mo beauty-in-carnage image right out of Peckinpah and samurai movies. Even though it seems flashy here, it does epitomize the film's assault on the emotions; Carlei appeals boldly to the visceral rather than the rational.

Yet Carlei is capable of irony, which gives his film its depth, for he leaves us realizing that wholesale slaughter of Vito's family has saved the boy from an almost certain life of crime.

Provocatively, Carlei, amid much bloodshed, suggests that people are inherently good—that Vito instinctively knows right from wrong and is capable of acting bravely upon that knowledge precisely because he's still too young to have been corrupted by his family. You may not entirely agree with Carlei on this and still be beguiled by "Flight of the Innocent" (rated R for sequences of graphic violence, and for some language).

NEW YORK POST, 10/22/93, p. 29, Thelma Adams

The Mean Streets of Southern Italy. Calabria Vice. Italian director Carlo Carlei reveres Martin Scorsese and Michael Mann (along with Kubrick and Spielberg). "Flight of the Innocent" is a foreign movie for American tastes.

Like Mann, Carlei employs a heightened realism. He films compelling scenes of violence against patiently composed, beautifully lit backdrops. If the brutality upsets you, scan the landscape: the mountains' golden cleft, the gilded clouds, the gorgeous rolling hills.

The first-time director rips his story from the Italian headlines. In the economically depressed South, kidnapping-for-profit has become an alternative industry. Since 1966, Italy has recorded 689 of these crimes—127 in Carlei's native Calabria alone. The offspring of northern wealth are easy prey for bandit families who kidnap and feud.

"Flight of the Innocent" opens in the countryside. Two men shoot a pair of shepherds. They, in turn are avenged by their kin who kill an entire family, grandma included. The boy the family was holding for ransom also dies. One son, Vito (Manuel Colao), survives, a witness to the mass murder.

Carlei paints with blood. Between the two killing sprees, Vito peeks under the family dinner table. He sees the stain of fresh blood on the toe of his father's boot and knows the score.

The death of Vito's mother (Anita Zagaria) as she hangs a sheet is unforgettable. A blood moon appears on the white sheet. It waxes until, with the succeeding shots, the sheet pulls away, and the mother rolls down the hill, wrapped in white cotton.

Vito becomes the innocent in flight. Shouldering the kidnapping victim's backpack, the 10-year-old runs just ahead of the scar-faced man who slaughtered his family. Scarface (Federico Pacifici) pursues Vito to Rome.

When the killer has Vito within shotgun range, he tells the boy: "Take a good look. This is death." Vito escapes the double barrel but not his nightmares. He dreams it is his own father carrying the gun aimed at his head.

In a psychological twist, Vito becomes both the last man in his family and the alter-ego of the dead rich boy. Vito's survival depends upon whether he will continue his family's blood feud, perpetuate the resentment behind their life of crime, or break free and take a moral stand. He must span the gap between north and south, rich and poor, citizen and bandit.

This fast-paced Italian suspenser, seen through the eyes of a traumatized child, never lets up. Carlei rejects "the expression" international moviemaking. "I want to make mainstream movies for an audience all over the world."

If his American-influenced thriller is another result of cultural imperialism, what's a monster to the French is great stuff in the hands of Carlo Carlei.

NEWSDAY, 10/22/93, Part II/p. 71, John Anderson

Blood, metaphorical and otherwise, runs fast and thick through "Flight of the Innocent," first-time director Carlo Carlei's thriller/parable based on the real-life kidnaps of his native Calabria.

Initially, there's the blood of Christ: In the dead calm of a sunbleached afternoon, two shepherds are executed on a southern Italian hillside, the bearded of the two assuming a crucifixion pose as he's shotgunned to death. The lambs around him, in keeping with the liturgy, scatter.

The bloodletting continues as the killers—the family of young Vito (Manuel Colao)—are pursued to their home by a rival gang and murdered wholesale: Grandma gets it mid-scream in the kitchen; Mamma is gunned down while hanging laundry, the white sheets turning scarlet as they wrap themselves around her lifeless body, like a shroud. Vito—unaware his father is a ruthless kidnaper until he sees the still-fresh blood on his shoes—survives the massacre. But as the killers pursue him across the country and he makes a valiant effort to atone for his family's crimes, he's haunted by his inheritance, the "bad blood" of his patrimony.

Carlei generates considerable tension during Vito's chase scenes, but aspects of the film are confused. After the massacre, for example, Vito flees to a cave where his father's hostage, the child Simone (Sandro Barletta), was being held, only to find him dead already; if Vito didn't know about the kidnapings, why did he think Simone was in the cave? And Carlei also ornaments his story with so much Christian imagery that it weighs the fleeing Vito down. Having him hide overnight in a mausoleum is one thing. Having him rise like Lazarus the next morning is another.

It's easy to get swept up in Vito's plight, however, as his circumstances make him the consummate outsider. His parents not only are dead, but in death they've become strangers to him. He can't seek aid from the authorities. The rival gang, led by the frightening Scarface (Federico Pacifici) wants to kill him. Dashing by foot and by train to Rome, he finds his cousin Orlando (Lucio Zagaria) and what he thinks is sanctuary, only to see Orlando blown away, because he, too, is part of the criminal network.

Vito represents the possibility of redemption, and therefore the sinner, as well as the innocent. He seeks out Simone's parents, Marta (Francesca Neri) and Davide (Jacques Perrin), and dreams of taking Simone's place among them, either as their child or as a blood sacrifice to the killers. One of those dreams, the film's best moment, in fact, is a devastating denouement, and might have been a crushingly sad finale. But Carlei—who since making "Flight of the Innocent" has been adopted by Hollywood—pushes it a little further, makes the movie a little longer, and in the end strips his story of the pathos it might have had.

SIGHT AND SOUND, 4/94, p. 40, Peter Aspden

Calabria. Two shepherds are shot down by a group of bandits. The following day, a gang wielding machine-guns arrive at the house of ten-year-old Vito, whose father was one of the bandits. They wipe out the entire family, except for Vito, who manages to hide. He runs to a cave in the hills, where he sees one of the attackers leaning over the body of his dead brother, as well as another dead child. He picks up a small rucksack belonging to the child, but is pursued by the man, who has a heavily scarred face. After a chase through a nearby village, Vito escapes on a train.

Vito's family had kidnapped the young child, Simone Rienzi, for ransom. On the train, Vito is fascinated as he leafs through Simone's schoolbooks in the rucksack. In another village, he sees Simone's parents on television pleading with the ransomers to return their son. They have already paid two billion lira and clearly think their son is still alive. Arriving in Rome by truck, Vito tracks down a cousin, Orlando, who tells him the bandits will not find him there. But one day the two of them return to Orlando's flat and find it ransacked. Orlando recovers a packet of money and gives it to Vito. The two of them leave the flat, but Scarface is waiting for them outside, and shoots Orlando. Vito is able to escape with the ransom money in his rucksack.

Next day, Vito is spotted by two policewomen and, after hiding his rucksack, allows himself to be taken in. He is sent to a children's home, pending investigation, but a friend of Orlando turns up and takes him away, determined to get his hands on the money.

Vito gives him the slip, picks up his rucksack, and makes for the Rienzi home, near Siena. Breaking into the house, he is spotted by Simone's mother, who, in her grief, thinks he is her son. Vito tells them that Simone is dead, but they do not want to believe him. Simone's father Davide is due to meet the kidnappers that night to pay a further instalment in return for his son; Vito hides in the back of his car. At the rendezvous, Scarface and an accomplice turn up aiming to trick Davide into giving them the money, even though Simone is dead. But Vito emerges from the car to tell Davide of the trick. The kidnappers capture Vito and demand the other sack of money, but once more he gives them the slip. They give chase and Scarface shoots him before the police arrive and capture the kidnappers. As Vito lies wounded, he has a vision of his family sitting at a long dining table with Simone's family. The ambulancemen take him away. Finally, Vito sits at Simone's desk, having taken the place of the dead child.

Carlo Carlei's misguided attempt to fuse the racy realism of American film-making with the rural poetry of his native country's tradition threatens at several points to turn into something a good deal more interesting. But his film is ultimately scuppered by the absence of an incisive screenplay and the resort—sadly, not uncommon in today's Italian cinema—to a sentimental ending which would surely have curled the toes of Carlei's neo-realist forefathers. The avowed aim of the director may be a Scorsese-meets-the-Tavianis on a sultry afternoon in Calabria, but none of the figures so admired by Carlei would have the effrontery to end such a profoundly violent movie on the complacent, doe-eyed expression of a ten-year-old boy happily settled into a new life of bourgeois comfort.

Things start well enough, with a tense, edgy opening vaguely reminiscent of Leone's *Once Upon a Time in the West*, but replacing Ennio Morricone's fuzz-boxed electric guitar with screaming crickets, violently flapping birdwings and a natural habitat which pays scant respect to innocence. The opening salvo of murders is convincingly-paced and disturbing; but once Vito has his first close escape—and there are far too many of these throughout the film—the tension is dissipated and there is nothing of substance to take its place. There is certainly a missed opportunity here, for there is still plenty to be said about the complex relationship between Northern and Southern Italy, a feature which continues to dominate the country's rapidly-changing political landscape. As the film moves from the barren fields of Calabria to the sumptuous luxury of the Rienzis' Tuscan villa, via a hectic interlude in Rome, we are barely made aware of the transition between what could be said to be two different countries, beyond the shifting visual backdrops. The nearest we get to a state-of-the-nation report is in cousin Orlando's speech to Vito on the power of money to intimidate and protect, but this is too isolated and clumsy an example to be effective.

Less successful still are Carlei's attempts to get metaphysical. Even if one accepts that children can save the world—and this depth of insight is probably best confined to Coca Cola advertising—too little is made of the symbiotic relationship between the privileged Simone, killed in the name of greed and resentment, and the poorly-educated Vito, who in determining to tell the truth to Simone's parents, finds in himself the delicate sensibilities required to end once and for all the interminable cycle of violence of North-South mutual hatred.

Carlei's heroes, such as Olmi or Tarkovsky, would surely have made more of the film's few genuinely dislocating moments such as Vito's wandering about in a deserted chemical plant which stands as a testament to political corruption and scandal. And they would never have countenanced the wildly over-the-top performance of Federico Pacifici as the ubiquitous (and apparently very stupid) Scarface. The film's final moments veer even more uneasily between comic-book brevity and pseudo-surrealism; a pallid dream sequence and the ultimate doppelganger effect of the closing scene are laughable in their attempt to resolve the preceding blood-baths. Italian directors be warned: your happy shiny people and well-scrubbed toddlers are giving innocence a bad name.

TIME, 11/1/93, p. 90, Richard Schickel

In movies this has been the year (possibly the decade) of the threatened child. The stories told about such children—abused or abandoned, in some way forced to cope prematurely with life's terrors—can be read in a couple of ways. They may represent a revival of interest by moviemakers in one of fiction's archetypes, that of the child alone and improvising in a world he didn't make and doesn't understand. They may also reflect our relatively new sensitivity to child abuse.

Whatever the case, no youngster has lately, or perhaps ever, been placed in more deadly peril than 10-year-old Vito (Manuel Colao) in *Flight of the Innocent*. And no director has more vividly realized the plight of an innocent than youthful Carlo Carlei (who wrote the screenplay with Gualtiero Rosella). One fine warm day in Calabria, in southern Italy, Vito's entire family (and a boy they have mysteriously sequestered in a cave nearby) is massacred, and Vito narrowly escapes execution at the hands of a scarfaced man who will stalk him (and his nightmares) for the rest of the film.

Neither Vito nor the audience entirely understands what's happening to him. All he (and we) know is that he must flee for his life. And therein lies the key to this film's success. For Carlei wants to thrust us into the mind of this almost completely silent boy. He gives us no more information than Vito acquires, in bits and pieces, as he flees to Rome in search of something, somebody—we're not sure. Carlei's camera is often radically subjective, seeing through Vito's eyes as the boy rushes panicked through the streets. Equally often it is radically objective, tracking a small, lonely figure in landscapes mysterious and menacing to him.

These things we learn in due course: that Vito's sole surviving relative is a small-time crook in Rome; that the dead boy in the cave had been kidnapped by Vito's family and was being held for ransom; that the family's slayers were members of a rival clan (though their precise motives remain obscure). Vito catches glimpses of the dead boy's parents on TV, making anguished pleas for his return. Eventually he feels compelled to make his way to them, and attempts to crawl into their son's bed, into his very life. The moviemakers note that there have been nearly 700 kidnappings for ransom in Italy since 1986. They also observe that murderous clan warfare is a continuing fact of life in Calabria. But *Flight of the Innocent* is not primarily a sociological tract nor an exercise in save-the-children sentiment. Little Vito has no time for such abstractions. His life depends on the correctness of hasty impressions, silent intuitions of danger. The result is something much better than sentiment. It is something quite close to the high emotions classic tragedy is supposed to evoke—quite close, that is, to pity and terror.

VILLAGE VOICE, 10/26/93, p. 58, Georgia Brown

Carlo Carlei's *Flight of the Innocent* is a bird of another color. [The reference is to *La Chasse Aux Papillons*.] This debut feature is a tense, bloody thriller, rather crudely effective because of a very loaded ingredient: endangered children, Told through the wide, solemn eyes of a traumatized 10-year-old, sole survivor of a family of Calabrian bandits, the film is one long, grueling flight to the north. If the boy's ongoing escape from body snatchers recalls *Pinocchio*, Vito (Manuel Colao) differs from the wooden one in that he's a singularly good and honest boy.

Just where Vito's virtue comes from is a matter not touched upon. The movie's opening shows his father committing a gory, cold-blooded murder. It turns out that the family is in the business of kidnapping children of rich families to the north and holding them for huge ransoms. Right now, an older brother, Santo, guards a smartly dressed Siena schoolboy, Simone, in a nearby cave. But when a rival bunch, bent on vengeance, massacres Vito's whole family, in the blood-bath, Simone gets it, too.

Picking up the other boy's knapsack, Vito flees his home, dreams of the privileged Simone dancing in his head. He gapes at a Snoopy pencil transfixed. Seeing the kid's attractive, immaculate parents (Francesca Neri and Jacques Perrin) on TV appealing for Simone to come home, he begins fixating on the warm bed, the blue fairy mama tucking him in. When we finally glimpse the actual bed in the princely room, it looks like it's been done by decorators to the Medici. It's the child consumer's heaven. And the obscenity of this opulence is never questioned.

The dope has it that Carlei, a former Calabrian himself, is now in Hollywood picking his next project and may never work in Italy again, It figures.

Also reviewed in:
CHICAGO TRIBUNE, 4/1/94, Friday/p. H, Michael Wilmington
NEW REPUBLIC, 11/15/93, p. 26, Stanley Kauffmann
NEW YORK TIMES, 10/22/93, p. C8, Vincent Canby
VARIETY, 10/5/92, p. 64, Deborah Young

FOR A LOST SOLDIER

A Strand Releasing release of a Sigma Film production in cooperaton with Avro-TV Holland. *Producer:* Matthijs van Heijningen. *Director:* Roeland Kerbosch. *Screenplay (English and Dutch with English subtitles):* Roeland Kerbosch. *Adapted from a novel by:* Rudi van Dantzig. *Adaptation:* Don Bloch. *Director of Photography:* Nils Post. *Editor:* August Verschueren. *Music:* Joop Stokkermans. *Sound:* Marcel de Hoogd. *Production Designer:* Vincent de Pater. *Costumes:* Jany Temime. *Running time:* 92 minutes. *MPAA Rating:* Not Rated.

CAST: Maarten Smit (Young Jeroen Boman); Andrew Kelley (Walt Cook); Jeroen Krabbe (Old Jeroen Boman); Feark Smink (Hait); Elsje de Wijn (Mem); Derk-Jan Kroon (Jan); Valerie Valentine (Laura).

LOS ANGELES TIMES, 8/6/93, Calendar/p. 12, Kevin Thomas

The Dutch film "For a Lost Soldier" resembles many other European pictures in its coming-of-age theme set against World War II. Writer-director Roeland Kerbosch and his adapter Don Bloch have brought choreographer Rudi van Dantzig's autobiographical novel to the screen with the warmth, intimacy and sensitivity we have come to expect in subtitled movies.

In its first half hour, Kerbosch's film is altogether typical, but then it ventures into exceedingly risky territory with daring and taste. (As a period piece, the film boasts a few anachronisms; "Sha-boom," for example, is a song of the '50s, not '40s) Finally, though, Kerbosch undercuts the chances he takes with a frustrating vagueness and evasiveness.

In the so-called Winter of Hunger in 1944, 12-year-old Jeroen Boman (Maarten Smit) is sent by his parents along with a group of other Amsterdam children to foster homes in Friesland because there is still an abundance of food along the North Sea. Jeroen is lucky in the family he has been assigned. The father Hait (Feark Smink), a fisherman, a strong, loving man, and his wife had requested a girl, as a companion for their daughter, the youngest of their three children, but the couple are as forthright in making him welcome as they are honest in expressing their initial disappointment. This hearty family is as earthy as it is religious, devoutness is a matter of spirituality rather than moralizing or passing judgment.

Time passes uneventfully with Jeroen hanging out with Jan (Derk-Jan Kroon), a friend from Amsterdam several years older than he and very conscious of the opposite sex. However, Jeroen, now that he's experiencing the onset of puberty, finds himself very aware of Jan when they go to the beach. Not long after this, the boys encounter the first troops of liberation, Americans and Canadians. Among them is a handsome, sturdy Canadian named Walt (Andrew Kelley), who looks to be about 20. The attraction between them is immediate.

Kerbosch is adroit in depicting both Jeroen and Walt as two lonely individuals far from home. Because both are such regular guys and because Walt's fellow soldiers realize that they'll soon be moving on, it is credible that the two could spend so much time together without raising eyebrows. Friendship, however, gives way to stronger emotions.

While Kerbosch proceeds with as much discretion as courage in dealing with such potentially explosive material, the truth is that "For a Lost Soldier," as well-acted as it is, lacks crucial clarity. This may have something to do with the language barrier, although about half the film is in English (and the Dutch is subtitled). We have to wonder how Walt manages to be so completely at ease with his homosexuality, especially in the era in which this film is set. He's presented as a sunny, easygoing, spontaneous young man without a care in the world—and that's the trouble: He may be kind and gentle with Jeroen but seems not to consider how his lovemaking could affect a boy who could not be more than 13, a boy he soon will be bidding farewell.

Since Kerbosch's role is after all to illuminate rather than to judge, he really needs to have revealed not only considerably more about Walt but also—and especially—the totality of his impact upon Jeroen, whom we meet in middle age in the film's prologue. A choreographer, Jeroen (Jeroen Krabbé) finds himself blocked in creating a ballet dealing with themes from his youth. He comes to realize that he must confront what happened between him and Walt so long ago, which he seems to have suppressed and which clearly has left him traumatized.

Has the adult Jeroen been able to have successful relationships with others, male or female, or both? Kerbosch leaves us to assume that Jeroen is gay just as he leaves us to assume that he and Walt fully engaged in sex in the first place. "For a Lost Soldier" (Times-rated mature for adult themes, language) delves into issues far too serious and controversial for such questions to go unanswered.

NEW YORK POST, 5/8/93, p. 14, Jami Bernard

The stock visual of a strapping soldier giving chocolate to a kid in a country he has just helped liberate takes on new meaning in "For a Lost Soldier," a sweetly rendered Dutch film about a subject that may give you indigestion.

Jeroen Krabbé plays a choreographer with choreographer's block—he can't seem to get his modern dancers to portray the liberating feeling of Liberation, World War II style. He thinks back to his wartime boyhood, when he was hidden in the North Holland countryside until the war was over because there wasn't enough food or safety to be found in Amsterdam.

Despite the kindness of his rural foster family, young Jeroen (Maarten Smit) feels like an outsider, especially because of his incipient homosexual yearnings.

These yearnings are soon gratified by a Canadian soldier, who comes to town with the Allies after beating Germany. The soldiers are polite but randy; one of the film's interesting moments occurs when a local girl comes out of a soldier's room half-naked and crying after her initiation into sex, only to find Jeroen and his soldier-boy in the bloom of romance.

Walter the soldier (Andrew Kelley) becomes Jeroen's pal, mentor, and eventually his lover—even though they don't share the same culture or language.

The friendly, casual way in which Walter indoctrinates the impressionable adolescent is the stuff of a potential training film for the Man-Boy Love Association. The relationship makes sense in the context of the movie, and yet no one with any knowledge of psychology can overlook the unpleasant ramifications of sex between an adult and a child, however intrigued or willing that child may seem, and however well the adult rationalizes it, including in a film.

VILLAGE VOICE, 5/11/93, p. 62, James Hannaham

Q: What country other than Holland could produce a Disney movie about man-boy love? A: The Netherlands. In fact, *For a Lost Soldier* looks like it came from Uranus, not because a 12-year-old boy and an older soldier are its romantic leads, but because director Roeland Kerbosch treats their liaison like Family Channel fare. Witness the sappy premise: The film is framed by scenes of the boy, Jeroen, years later. He has become a choreographer of bad dance to worse music. (The effects of prepubescent bunga-bunga?) Choreographer's block and the death of his father inspire him to return to the scene of his deflowering.

Young Jeroen (Maarten Smit), a somewhat sissified lad sent to the Dutch countryside to escape harm during the German occupation, alienated by his host family, takes to running off with a chum who's rapidly turning het. But jumping into the gene pool isn't on Jeroen's mind. He's developed a crush on Walt (the mouth-watering Andrew Kelley), a canadian liberator of Holland (and its boys). Walt supplies Jeroen with chocolates, teaches him to drive, clean a gun—call it "male bonding plus." Jeroen starts fantasizing about doing the Lindy with Walt.

Cautiously, the film affirms that Jeroen's a willing partner in his seduction—it's boy-man love, too—but isn't afraid to take the possible love-scene risks. However, risks alone do not a good film make, and though it's touching yet bizarre to see the sexual underpinnings of a *Boy's Town* sensibility exposed, *Soldier* oversimplifies its characters and neglects the details that could make this "true story" more truth than schmaltz.

Also reviewed in:
CHICAGO TRIBUNE, 3/11/94, Friday/p. F, John Petrakis
NEW YORK TIMES, 5/7/93, Stephen Holden
VARIETY, 1/18/93, p. 79, David Stratton

FOR LOVE OR MONEY

A Universal Studios release of an Imagine Films presentation. *Executive Producer:* David T. Friendly. *Producer:* Brian Grazer. *Director:* Barry Sonnenfeld. *Screenplay:* Mark Rosenthal and Lawrence Konner. *Director of Photography:* Oliver Wood. *Editor:* Jim Miller. *Music:* Bruce Broughton. *Music Editor:* James Flatto and Patricia Carlin. *Sound:* Peter F. Kurland. *Casting:* John Lyons and Christine Sheaks. *Production Designer:* Peter Larkin. *Art Director:* Charley Beal. *Set Decorator:* Leslie E. Rollins. *Set Dresser:* Joseph "Pepe" Bird, Joseph F. Proscia, Gilbert Gertsen, Gordon H. Gertsen, John P. Oates, John Oates, Gary Levitsky, Glenn Jones, and Greco. *Costumes:* Susan Lyall and David Carl Robinson. *Make-up:* Bernadette Mazur, Bron S. Roylance, and Paul Gebbia. *Stunt Coordinator:* Charles Croughwell. *Running time:* 95 minutes. *MPAA Rating:* PG.

CAST: Michael J. Fox (Doug Ireland); Gabrielle Anwar (Andy Hart); Anthony Higgins (Christian Hanover); Michael Tucker (Mr. Wegman); Bob Balaban (Mr. Drinkwater); Isaac Mizrahi (Julian Russell); Patrick Breen (Gary Taubin); Udo Kier (Mr. Himmelman); Simon Jones (Albert); Dianne Brill (Gloria); Dan Hedaya (Gene Salvatore); Fyvush Finkel (Milton); Mike G. (Charlie); Saverio Guerra (Carmen); Daniel Hagen (Vincent); La Chanze (Nora); Paula Laurence (Mrs. Vigusian); Donna Mitchell (Eleanor Hanover); Debra Monk (Mrs.

Wegman);   Sandra Reaves-Phillips (Marie);   Susan Blommeart (Charlotte);   Nicole Beach (Julian Russell Girl);   Susan Ringo (Mrs. Brinkerhoff);   John Cunningham (Mr. Brinkerhoff); Ann McDonough (Mrs. Nimkoff);   Richmond Hoxie (Mr. Bailey);   Alice Playten (Mrs. Bailey); Erick Avari (Benny);   Douglas Seale (Freddy);   David Lipman (Man in Elevator);   le Chanché du Rand (Woodsy Woman);   Anne Lange (Tiffany Saleswoman);   Salem Ludwig (Customer); Louis Cantarini (Cab Driver);   Hikari Takano (Leon);   Jed Krascella (Stage Manager);   Gabor Morea (Maitre d');   Beverley Peer and Robert Scott (Musicians);   Mark Zimmerman (Pilot); Al Cerullo, Jr. (Co-Pilot);   Dan Brennan (Tiffany Guard);   Francis Dumaurier (Husband); Bobby Short (Himself);   Suzann O'Neill (Tatiana);   Tim Gallen (Eliot);   Steven Randazzo, Steve Ames, and Harry Burgin (Gangsters);   Alvin Alexis (Bicyclist);   Nick Cosco (Piano Player);   Jane Deacy (Traffic Policeman).

LOS ANGELES TIMES, 10/1/93, Calendar/p. 8, Peter Rainer

Michael J. Fox is the right actor to play a high-powered concierge for a ritzy New York hotel. As Doug Ireland in "For Love or Money," he has the fast moves and all-seeing eyes that keep him right on top of his guests' every whim. If you're staying at the Bradbury Hotel; Doug can get you anything—for a generous tip, of course.

The concierge role brings out the desperation in Fox's scampering, eager-to-please persona. He's a first-rate comic actor with suggestions of something deeper. But the movie doesn't do him justice. It's trying for swank bubbliness—Billy Wilder's "The Apartment" crossed with "Breakfast at Tiffany's." But director Barry ("The Addams Family") Sonnenfeld and screenwriters Mark Rosenthal and Lawrence Konner are more suited to slapdash nutso comedy. The swings between clunky slapstick and "heartfelt" moments are jolting. (They'd be even more jolting if the slapstick or the heart tugs were effective.)

Doug grew up in a Catskills resort where his father worked as a bellhop, and it's been his dream to one day ditch his concierge gig and open his own snazzy hotel. He's scrimped for years to put together the plans—he's even picked out a plot on Roosevelt Island. When a rich investor (Anthony Higgins) agrees to front the money if Doug "baby-sits" his mistress Andy (Gabrielle Anwar), Doug doesn't hesitate—even though he's been trying to date Andy on his own. Doug and Andy slowly warm to each other. His conflict is loud and clear: Does he choose love or money?

The filmmakers encourage us to buy this fairy tale by downplaying the smarminess of the conception. Doug is, after all, essentially a procurer, and Fox certainly has it in him to be hard-bitten and double-edged. But he's wedged into sitcom situations here: parts of the film play like tonier versions of "Love American Style." Gifted, funny actors turn up in small roles—like Michael Tucker as a mollycoddled husband staying at the hotel, or Bob Balaban as a predatory IRS agent, or Fyvush Finkel as an ancient bellhop—but Sonnenfeld gives them about as much weight as the performers on TV commercials. (Fashion designer Isaac Mizrahi, playing essentially himself, turns up for a giddy cameo.)

What's missing from this film (rated PG for "elements of sensuality and mild language") is any awareness of its own anything-for-a-rise shamelessness. The filmmakers just plow ahead with the clonks and the heart tugs. Unlike their concierge hero, they have no conflicts about reaching for love *and* grabbing for the gold.

NEW YORK POST, 10/1/93, p. 45, Michael Medved

"For Love or Money" is one of those mercilessly mediocre movies that might be pleasant enough to watch late one night on TV, or to use as a time-killer on a transcontinental flight, but in no way is it worth seven bucks at your local Bijou.

This picture is both tired and tiresome, a flabby romantic comedy that's neither romantic or comic enough to keep the attention of its audience.

Michael J. Fox plays Doug Ireland, the unstoppable concierge at a posh midtown hotel called "The Bradbury" (they actually shot the exterior of The Pierre). While providing theatre tickets and hotel reservations for the hotel's guests, he dreams of opening an exclusive hostelry of his own on Roosevelt Island.

To make this noble ambition a reality all he needs is a few million bucks of unconditional backing, and he hopes to win it from powerful entrepreneur Christian Hanover (a sneering Anthony Higgins).

While Hanover considers the plucky lad's proposal, he asks him to perform a few discreet favors—like providing comfort and companionship at inconvenient moments to the rich man's increasingly demanding and temperamental mistress (British actress Gabrielle Anwar).

With this obvious set-up, the romantic leads would have to generate real sparks to make their inevitable attraction watchable, and Fox and Anwar just don't cut it. Anwar made an indelible impression last year as Al Pacino's lovely tango partner in "Scent of a Woman," but in that role she benefitted mightily from the fact that she hardly spoke.

The camera loves her—with her slightly pouty, intensely vulnerable, little-girl's face and her powerful athletic body—but when she delivers her lines you somehow lose interest. She brings an unpleasant whiny quality, and a deadly lack of humor to her role as a department store perfume girl so stupid that she accepts all her cruel lover's many explanations for standing her up, and believes his repeated promises that he's leaving his wife.

The film's feeble attempts at humor feature a cartoon mafioso (Dan Hedaya) permanently ensconced in the hotel with a blonde bimbo; a relentless IRS man (Bob Balaban) investigating our hero for unreported tips; and some painfully funny scenes featuring Yiddish theatre veteran Fyvush Finkel as a senile bellhop. There's also a bit part for noted fashion designer Isaac Mizrahi in his acting debut, playing (what else?) a noted fashion designer as an insulting gay stereotype complete with "hissy fit."

Michael J. Fox has shown that he can be a serious and compelling performer ("Casualties of War"), but his comedic roles as slick-talking but sympathetic manipulators have developed a deadly, cookie-cutter sameness. Beyond the success of the "Back to the Future" trilogy, and the easy-going comedies "Secret of My Success" and "Doc Hollywood," his movie career has consisted of a series of spectacular flops, including "Bright Lights, Big City," "Light of Day," "The Hard Way," and, most recently, "Life with Mikey."

He is now making his directorial debut in a fantasy called "Thirty Wishes", and one can only wish that this picture is paced more crisply than the soft, sluggish "For Love or Money."

The director here is noted cinematographer Barry Sonnenfeld ("Misery", "When Harry Met Sally"), who won his only previous directorial credit with last year's smash hit "The Addams Family." That picture also suffered from flat-footed timing and clumsy staging, but nifty special effects and affection for the old TV series more than made up for its shortcomings.

This time out, he's fashioned a dead-in-the-water dud that will generate little love, and no money.

NEWSDAY, 10/1/93, Part II/p. 61, Gene Seymour

Though its delayed release prompted smirks and raised eyebrows from film industry pundits, "For Love or Money" isn't the disaster many anticipated. It's far from being a great, or even a good, movie. But the thing would bark, scratch for fleas and roll around in the dirt it weren't for Michael J. Fox.

As Doug Ireland, the concierge of a Central Park South luxury hotel, Fox exudes the kind of ingratiating vigor and swaggering grace that made many believe, only a few years ago, that he was cloned from a cell of James Cagney's. Once again, he's playing a cute and cunning hustler with a heart of gold. He can do this trademark role in his sleep by now; to his credit, he doesn't.

Doug orchestrates the fulfillment of his guests' wishes with terrifying efficiency. He knows how to get good seats at the theater, a good suit for a night on the town, a great gift for your mate. Needless to say, he's rolling in tips, all of which he pours into the fulfillment of his own fondest wish: opening a luxury hotel called "The Doug."

Doug sees his chance when the city's hottest capitalist of the moment (Anthony Higgins) asks that a room be made available to him for an extra-marital liaison. In return, Doug's hotel plans will be pushed towards development by the billionaire's manicured hands. Doug is too happy to oblige—until he finds out that his benefactor's babe (Gabrielle Anwar) is a young lady he himself had been trying to date without success.

Shades of "The Apartment." (In fact, Fox could stake a claim on Jack Lemmon's legacy as much as—maybe more than—Cagney's.) But compared with that acerbic classic of love vs.

ambition, "For Love and Money" offers very little complexity or even deep tones in its characterizations.

The movie also piles on more cute complications than its flimsy structure can carry. Director Barry Sonnenfeld, whose touch for low comedy was well-served in "The Addams Family," seems less sure-footed here. A dodo-brained sequence in which he's trying to discreetly remove Anwar from the East Hampton mansion of her lover serves no real purpose except to let Fox indulge in some gratuitous pratfalls.

There's also something vaguely retro about "For Love or Money's" slick coating and ambition-driven plot. Casting Fox as yet another variation of Alex Keaton makes the film seem as if it was supposed to have been made four or five years ago. But the '80s are already slipping into the realm of nostalgia—and they seem to be taking Fox with them.

"For Love or Money" offers solid proof that Fox can carry a movie by himself. But unless he does something completely different (and soon) it's doubtful he may have too many more chances to dominate others.

SIGHT AND SOUND, 12/93, p. 43, Ben Thompson

By day, New York based hotel concierge Doug Ireland swaps front row seats for sold-out shows and rides around in limousines buying outrageously expensive jewelry. At night, he goes home to his poky flat and surveys his dream: a cardboard model of a hotel of his own. Every last cent he has earnt from lavish tips has gone on an option on a derelict riverside site, and time is running out. But still, Doug finds time to help out guests who are not big tippers, and to save aged bellhop Milton from getting the sack.

Doug contacts a potential investor, English multi-millionaire Christian Hanover. Keen to get on Hanover's right side, Doug secures him a room for an extra-marital assignation. The object of Hanover's roving eye turns out to be Andy Hart, a young woman from the perfume counter, whom Doug had been prone to idealise. Doug's day worsens when he is cornered by an IRS investigator, who finds property speculation inconsistent with his declared income. Hanover pressurises Doug into acting as a minder for Andy. He has to watch her sing in a club, and make excuses when the millionaire is late for their dates. When these backfire and Andy turns up at a party given by Hanover and his wife, Doug flies in by helicopter to get her out, then tells Hanover how to talk her round.

The deal is progressing, but Doug's feelings for Andy are starting to get in the way. One afternoon he shows her his site and his plans, and explains how his father worked all his life in a hotel and died young. There is a spark between them but they ignore it. The deal is finally clinched, with Hanover persuading Doug to turn the lease of the hotel over to him to confound the IRS. He also convinces Andy that he intends to leave his wife. Each realises the other is being tricked—the IRS man was working for Hanover, who not only has no plans to split with his wife, but also maintains other paramours. Doug tears up the contract and, after a frantic chase, catches up with Hanover's car just as a furious Andy gets out of it. They get married, and, thanks to a mistake by Milton, a low-tipping millionaire whose marriage Doug had saved gets sent his hotel plans and decides to invest.

Every time Michael J. Fox is in another film you think it must be his last in his current skin, but it never is. And thank goodness for that, because this man is an entertainer. Director Barry Sonnenfeld compares him to Cary Grant, which may be going a bit far, but there is a similar generosity in the way he controls the screen, even though everything is unfairly weighted in his favour.

The Concierge has several strings to its bow. The first is a very American theme: the relationship between material and spiritual goals. This is familiar ground for Fox after The Secret of My Success and Bright Lights, Big City, but it's interesting to see how the way he treads it has changed, now that the 80s are just a bad memory. Few other actors can make the hunger for material advancement seem so innocent, but there is a new caring and sharing gloss on Doug's ambition. The comic confusion at the heart of this film is the idea that capitalism can be benign and reward virtue. Its hero might know all the angles, but he wants to run his dream hotel "like a family". After all, exploitation killed his dad.

To those not well versed in the pleasures of real estate, Doug's reality—surfing the Brooklyn traffic, bucking the Broadway ticket market—often seems more vivid and exciting than his dream (oh great, just what New York needs, another hotel). But there is a nice scene where he visits the site and produces a beautiful architectural drawing from under a stone, which he superimposes over the ruin by balancing it between two sticks.

The film's selling angle, the romance, is its weakest, and much respect is due to *L.A. Law*'s Michael Tucker as the middle-aged out-of-town ingenu struggling to make a success of his second honeymoon, for making it work. It's not Gabrielle Anwar's fault that her character is wet enough to irrigate the Mojave Desert, but her performance does not help. You might just be able to maintain sympathy for Andy after seeing her taken in by the smarmy Hanover (a nicely oleaginous Anthony Higgins in what you might call the Roger Rees role), but once you've heard her sing, it's all over. This woman's hopes of a career as a chanteuse are excruciatingly ill-founded; in nightclub siren terms, she is more Timothy than Mae West.

In satisfying contrast with the dewy-eyedness of its romantic aspirations, *The Concierge* is also a fast-moving and surprisingly abrasive New York comedy. Sonnenfeld's direction is very pacey, with a snappy visual style that feels less sub-Tim Burton than it did in *The Adams Family*. The eye for the grotesque, which he demonstrated to such good effect as director of photography on *Blood Simple* and *Raising Arizona*, roves gleefully about the Metropolis. The dialogue does not feel as though it's been screen-tested in Kansas. There is a lot of name-dropping, some sharp lines—"You think these people are happy? They'll still be smiling six months after they're dead"—and a surprisingly broad undercurrent of racial comedy. Michael J. Fox, the kindly WASP, buzzes through a gallery of ethnic stereotypes. There's the serene Milton, for example, played by Yiddish theatre legend Fyvush Finkel, and Udo Kier as an effetely fascistic maitre d: This will leave many people feeling slightly uneasy, but I suppose that's what New York does too.

Also reviewed in:
CHICAGO TRIBUNE, 10/1/93, Friday/p. L, Johanna Steinmetz
NEW YORK TIMES, 10/1/93, p. C8, Janet Maslin
VARIETY, 10/11/93, p. 73, Leonard Klady
WASHINGTON POST, 10/1/93, Weekend/p. 52, Desson Howe
WASHINGTON POST, 10/2/93, p. G8, Richard Harrington

FORBIDDEN LOVE: THE UNASHAMED STORIES OF LESBIAN LIVES

A Women Make Movies release of a National Film Board of Canada Studio D production. *Executive Producer:* Ginny Stikeman. *Producer:* Rina Fraticelli. *Director:* Aerlyn Weissman and Lynne Fernie. *Screenplay:* Aerlyn Weissman and Lynne Fernie. *Director of Photography:* Zoe Dirse. *Editor:* Cathy Gulkin and Denise Beaudoin. *Music:* Kathryn Moses. *Sound:* Justine Pimlott. *Casting:* Nadia Rona. *Art Director:* Denis Boucher. *Costumes:* Nicoletta Massone. *Running time:* 85 minutes. *MPAA Rating:* Not Rated.

CAST: Stephanie Morgenstern (Laura); Lynne Adams (Mitch).

LOS ANGELES TIMES, 8/4/93, Calendar/p. 2, Kevin Thomas

Aerlyn Weissman and Lynne Fernie's warm and informative documentary "Forbidden Love" introduces us to nine Canadian women who dared to fulfill their lives as lesbians in the homophobic '50s and '60s. Ranging in age from their 40s to early 70s, they are all blessed with hearty survivors' humor.

Otherwise, they vary in appearance and race, several have children and have been married. What they have in common is their determination in seeking out the few lesbian-friendly bars and nightclubs, generally located in the Skid Row areas of Canada's largest cities, which were the only places lesbians could gather and meet each other.

It's quite clear early on that most of these women come from sufficiently conservative backgrounds to make us aware that had they not been lesbians they would not have ever ventured into such dicey districts, at once dangerous and exciting. Much of what the filmmakers document applies to the gay experience in the United States in the same decades, although in the '50s and even earlier at least New York's Greenwich Village was hospitable to homosexuals.

The filmmakers' point of departure, however, is not gay gathering spots but the lurid lesbian-themed paperbacks of the era, which the women tell us were their first connection with lesbian lifestyles; as such, they were cherished even though the mores of the times dictated unhappy endings. A key exception to the rule were the six paperback novels Ann Bannon wrote between 1957 and 1962: Bannon today tells the filmmakers that her publisher, Gold Crest, did not force the negative formula upon her but because she was then married with small children she finally felt forced to give up writing. Indeed, Weissman and Fernie effectively frame their interviews with a gentle tongue-in-cheek dramatization of a paperback lesbian novel from which their documentary derives its title.

Much of the interviews are given over to discussing first loves and the lively bar life, but there are inevitably frightening accounts of the brutal police raids that could strike the nightspots or even private parties at any time. The filmmakers, who intersperse their interviews with an apt and generous selection of archival footage, include a newsreel of such a raid.

One of the key issues under discussion is the polarized roles lesbians, even more than gay males, were then expected to play. One woman after another attests that she was supposed to choose to be either a butch or a femme, and several speak of realizing that they found themselves strait-jacketed into the very roles they were escaping when they left their husbands. A Canadian Indian and a black singer speak of the special difficulties of being double-minority individuals. The one crucial question the filmmakers inexplicably leave unasked is whether their interviewees, once past their first loves, ever managed to establish long-term relationships.

Upbeat, entertaining and good-natured, "Forbidden Love" (Times-rated Mature, for adult issues) offers beyond the special challenges presented by homosexuality an affirmative portrait of women who found the courage to live their lives as they pleased.

NEW YORK POST, 8/4/93, p. 27, Jerry Tallmer

By their titles ye shall know them: "Odd Girl Out," "21 Gay Street," "Private School," "Queer Patterns," "Women's Barracks," "Girls' Dormitory," "A Forbidden Affair" ...

These and dozens of others were the lesbian Gold Medal novels of the 1950s, and Ann Bannon, the classy-looking suburbanite who wrote many of them, talks in the film "Forbidden Love" of how these epics for all their trashy/banal movie-poster covers, spread the bracing word to lonely ladies of the fellowship everywhere: "We are sisters. This is how we are."

Ms. Bannon is one of the 10 women, femmes, butches, white, brown, tall, short, stout, thin, stunning, not so stunning, some now with white hair, who go before the cameras of Aerlyn Weissman and Lynne Fernie to recollect, with equanimity, humor, and a few traces of rage, what it was like to be growing up (in Canada) and finding out you were a lesbian in the 40s, 50s, 60s.

It is wonderfully wry stuff, for the most part. Several of these women back in their teens or 20s decided for instance, that all the lesbians lived in New York, so it was off to Greenwich Village for a week at a time—"in my best butch clothing," one recounted—looking for lesbians. "Never did find them."

Another recalls an early exploratory conversation with a girlfriend. "She said: 'I think I'm like that.' I said: 'Oh no, not *that*'—whatever 'that' was. Eventually I felt, well, maybe I'm like that too.'"

Another, older, a touch of Irish on her tongue, took a book out of the library when she was 15 or 16—"Serenade," by James M. Cain. "I thought it was about music. Gee, was I surprised ... My first affair was with an office worker. It was just dynamite. Like being run over by a 10-ton truck."

An extraordinarily handsome woman on horseback in western Canada speaks of how it all began for her with her teacher. "Kids started peeking in the window. Ultimately she had to leave the school." A gorgeous girl who suffered vicious discrimination as an Eskimo—okay, native American—"decided to go the other way, to go bad, and I was *really* bad."

There is the account of an infuriated husband condemning wife and beloved daughter—lesbians both to burn side by side in hell; the tale of an infuriated butch driving her motorcycle right through the door of a famed lesbian hangout and up to her rival's table. "Femmes went out and got jobs and cooked and cleaned while butches just had to hang around and be butches." Sound familiar?

All of this testimony is interspersed with a little staged drama of a lesbian seduction as in one of those Gold Medal paperbacks. But the documentary testimony is drama enough, and better.

NEWSDAY, 8/4/93, Part II/p. 63, John Anderson

It's a classic scene: the station platform, the impatient train, one suitcase, two lovers—one leaving, one staying, torn by circumstance and society, forced to part, their paths never to cross again ...

It's pap no matter how you slice it, even when the parting lovers are both women. Which is much of the point of "Forbidden Love: The Unashamed Stories of Lesbian Lives," a film that mixes standard documentary footage with a tongue-in-cheek dramatization of an imagined 1950s lesbian novel called "Forbidden Love." By contrasting the pulp-novel version of homosexual women with the real thing—Canadian lesbians, ages 40-70, telling what life was really like for them in the '40s, '50s and '60s—filmmakers Aerlyn Weissman and Lynne Fernie make a valuable statement about how low-slung pop culture may have helped warp the straight world's perception of gays and by extension how it warps perceptions at large.

What they don't do to any particular degree is show how these novels—with titles like "Women's Barracks," "Girls' Dormitory and "Man Hater" ("They hide their claws under nail polish!!")—might have warped the women's perceptions of themselves. We meet Ann Bannon, an author of these books, who was unusual in that she provided her characters happy endings (retribution for sexual trespasses was a big theme in these novels). But rarely are the books referred to by the interviewees in any substantive way.

The dramatizations, though, are funny and uncomfortably accurate in what they send up: the sweet and almost-innocent Laura (Stephanie Morgenstern), traveling to the big city, venturing into a lesbian bar and meeting the knowing Mitch (Lynne Adams). Afraid, frightened of Mitch's advances, Laura yearns to explore this side of herself ("If she left now, would there be a next time????"). Fighting her fear, she goes to Mitch's place for a very steamy and beautifully shot sex scene that provides some relief after the overly talky stretches that interrupt the Laura-Mitch installments.

These interviews, while frank and occasionally illuminating, lack cohesion. And their limited focus—on gay life in Toronto and Montreal—may make the film a bit parochial for non-Canadian audiences. Add to this the fact that this year we've seen at least two films—"Last Call at Maud's" and "Nitrate Kisses"—that covered a lot of the same territory and more directly. "Forbidden Love" (the movie, not the book) also seems to have an attitude about its subjects' reminiscenses: What some audiences might perceive as tawdry actually is. It's inadvertent, of course, but the pulp runneth over.

VILLAGE VOICE, 8/10/93, p. 58, Stacey D'Erasmo

Now that cheap, hot love is back in fashion, the lesbian pulp novels of the '50s and early '60s—those lurid dime-store paperbacks, like *Women's Barracks, Lesbians in Black Lace, Private School*, and the superb Ann Bannon series—seem like how-tos for you and your sweetie(s). *Girls' Dormitory*? Isn't that a special night at the Clit Club? But the real thing—as demonstrated by this charming documentary about the days when life imitated pulp by necessity, not choice—was at once shyer, tougher, and wilder.

Blending interviews with Canadian lesbians who had no place to go in the '50s and '60s but skidrow dives and beer parlors with a pleasant but unthrilling original pulp movie, *Forbidden Love* reveals that the steamy, punishing narratives of pulp fiction—frequently the only information and company these women had—shaped their lives. As interviewee Lois M. Stuart, who was a teacher by day and a knife-packing, cross-dressing butch by night, puts it, "If you're going to lead a double life, lead a double life."

The joys of the double life in the days when femmes wore their dresses tight and butches drove their motorcycles right into the bar to fight over them are on swaggering display here. These, after all, are the survivors. Underneath, you can also hear the quieter refrains of abuse, sadness, and loss. But from the brave woman who walked into her first lesbian bar when she was seven-and-a-half months pregnant to the acerbic, lean rancher who looks like the Marlboro man if the Marlboro man were a sixtyish lesbian (and my choice for butch pin-up of the year), these survivors are living proof that not all endings are tragic, and not all attractions fatal.

Also reviewed in:
CHICAGO TRIBUNE, 12/3/93, Friday/p. H, John Petrakis
NEW YORK TIMES, 8/4/93, p. C18, Janet Maslin
VARIETY, 5/3/93, p. 41, David Rooney

FORTRESS

A Dimension release of a Davis Entertainment Company and Village Roadshow Pictures production. *Executive Producer:* Graham Burke and Greg Coote. *Producer:* John Davis and John Flock. *Director:* Stuart Gordon. *Screenplay:* Steve Feinberg, Troy Neighbors, and Terry Curtis Fox. *Director of Photography:* David Eggby. *Editor:* Timothy Wellburn. *Music:* Barry Levine. *Music Editor:* Virginia Ellsworth. *Sound:* Paul Clark. *Sound Editor:* Robert Mackston. *Casting:* Mike Fenton and Maura Fay. *Production Designer:* David Copping. *Art Director:* Diaan Wajon. *Special Effects:* Tad Pride. *Mechanical Effects:* David Pride. *Costumes:* Terry Ryan. *Make-up:* Karla O'Keefe. *Stunt Coordinator:* Glenn Boswell. *Running time:* 91 minutes. *MPAA Rating:* R.

CAST: Christopher Lambert (John Brennick); Kurtwood Smith (Poe); Loryn Locklin (Karen Brennick); Lincoln Kilpatrick (Abraham); Clifton Gonzalez Gonzalez (Nino); Jeffrey Combs (D-Day); Tom Towles (Stiggs); Vernon Wells (Maddox); E. Briant Wells (Friendly Border Guard); Carolyn Purdy-Gordon (Zed); Denni Gordon (Lydia); Alan Zitner (Camper); Peter Marshall (Travel Agent); Dragica Debert (Bio Scanner Guard); Troy Hunter, Harry Nurmi, and Peter Lamb (Border Guards); Michael Simpson (Medical Trustee); Heidi Stein (Pregnant Woman); Josephine MacKenroth, Nancy Grande, and Tracy Martin (Women Prisoners).

LOS ANGELES TIMES, 9/6/93, Calendar/p. 3, Michael Wilmington

"Fortress," a science fiction movie about an impregnable high-tech jail in an overpopulated fascist future world, is a surprise.

For a film that first seems a throwaway, it has unusual intensity and grip. It's not another over-reaching, under-financed "Terminator" or "Total Recall" wannabe. Right from the opening scenes—a border-crossing shoot-out that contrasts rotting, scavenging homeless hangouts below a bridge with ultra-efficient sterile police car searches above—"Fortress" delivers something extra. For a picture that seems stamped with "low expectations"—it was dumped into a Friday L.A. opening without critics' screenings—it shows some quality and ambition.

Not in the script: That's another tag-team job lacking surprise or punch. But director Stuart Gordon and his company get tension, mood and style into "Fortress" anyway.

Gordon—whose tackily ingenious low-budget horror movies for Empire ("Reanimator," "From Beyond") offered some of the more robust guilty pleasures of the 80s—is telling another dystopian story here: the nightmare of an outlaw future couple (Christopher Lambert and Loryn Locklin) whose crime is having a second baby when one only is allowed, and who are thrown into a sexually segregated super-prison, a fortress surrounded by desert, controlled by an omnipotent computer and a super-voyeur warden/director named Poe (Kurtwood Smith in corpse--like makeup). The prison *pièce de résistance:* explosive devices called "intestinators" implanted in prisoners' guts.

This obvious parable of fascism has as its villains huge corporations, bottom-liners, anti-abortionists and soulless science. The conspiracy seems strained, but the passion is palpable. Working with more opulent means than usual—Australian facilities, a $14-million budget, lavish effects—Gordon widens his arena. "Reanimator" was a cute, scrappy, wickedly funny shock-comedy that stretched the boundaries of low-budget horror, but Gordon's previous science fiction epic, "Robojox," looked chintzy, budget-strangled. This one has more visual aplomb.

In his college days, Gordon was a big admirer of Stanley Kubrick; this most Kubrickian of his movies has a stately pace, huge, sterile trap-like interiors that remind you of "2001," and gaudily anarchic violence and flashy mind control scenes that recall "Clockwork Orange." There's a family connection too: Gordon's wife, Carolyn Purdy-Gordon, plays a computer named ZED—a distant cousin of "2001's" outwardly beneficent, inwardly crazy HAL.

"Fortress" suffers from problems beyond its script. Lambert once again plays too American: His French accent makes his "John Brennick" as bizarre a hybrid as his "Sanderson" was in the ridiculous "Knight Moves." Couldn't he play Canadian immigrants named LeBeau or LeFleur?

The movie never really explores or exploits its flashy central locale: the multileveled "Metropolis"-like prison. Gordon's darkly genial humor is also largely absent—except in the vibrating role and performance of "Reanimator" veteran Jeffrey Combs as wiggy demolition expert "D-Day," a seeming '60s refugee, who still yells "Right On!" in moments of emotion.

"Fortress" (MPAA rated R) has the theme of the great dystopian science fiction stories: novels like Zamyatin's "We," Huxley's "Brave New World" and Dick's "Man in the High Castle"; movies like "THX-1138" and "Blade Runner." But it doesn't have their elaboration or richness of psychological detail. Its script is the jail in which the project rots; its clichés are the computer program that won't let it escape, run free. But there's something there anyway: the thrill of nightmare, a hologram of paranoia, a seed cracking the concrete.

NEWSDAY, 9/6/93, Part II/p. 29, Terry Kelleher

As if the latest scandal in New York City's Parking Violations Bureau weren't enough to cause uneasiness about the privatization of government functions, along comes this movie called "Fortress."

It's set in a 21st-Century prison owned and operated by the Men-Tel Corp. The government pays the company $27 a day per inmate, and in return Men-Tel maintains maximum security by means of "intestinators" forcibly implanted in the cons' guts. If a prisoner makes waves, an all-seeing computer activates his intestinator and he doubles over in extreme discomfort. When the institution's coolly cruel director (Kurtwood Smith) orders a "random intestination," every other inmate looks as if he just took a low blow from Mike Tyson.

Pretty inhumane, but then the director's not exactly human. He's a humanoid, with just enough feeling to enjoy watching the inmates' sex dreams on his wall of video monitors.

Watching Smith (the soft-spoken sadist of "RoboCop") portray this strange corporate soldier is one of the small pleasures offered by "Fortress." Another is filmmaker Stuart Gordon's way of interweaving tomorrow's sci-fi technology with big-house cliches from the day before yesterday. Although this prison is equipped with a state-of-the-art "mind-wipe chamber," the inmates still say things like "The scared don't survive inside" and "Nobody makes it outta this place."

"Fortress" isn't as clever as Gordon's "Re-Animator," but it's not as gory, either. (Come on, only a couple of stomachs actually explode.) Most of the blood is shed in good, old-fashioned brawling, and Gordon seems somewhat more concerned with keeping up the pace than dwelling on the carnage.

With a more interesting actor in the lead, Gordon might have made a movie that went rather well with a box of popcorn. Unfortunately, Christopher Lambert brings so little life to his part that three days of sustained mind-wiping torture leave the hero appearing only slightly more dead-eyed than usual.

Not content to take a dim view of future trends in penology, "Fortress" also raises the side issue of state-imposed birth control. What lands the hero and his pregnant wife (Loryn Locklin) behind bars is their attempt to violate the odious one-child-per-motherlaw. The message here is muddled, but at least Gordon checks himself before a late scene in the prison delivery room grows *too* distasteful.

SIGHT AND SOUND, 8/94, p. 40, Caren Myers

The USA, the not too distant future. To curb over-population, a law has been passed that no woman shall give birth to more than one child. Former Black Beret captain John Brennick and his wife Karen, pregnant for the second time after the loss of their first child, are caught trying to cross the border. She escapes, but he is sentenced to 31 years in the Fortress, a 30-storey maximum security prison built underground and run by a private corporation, Men-Tel.

On arrival, each man is forcibly implanted with an intestinator, a device which automatically triggers unbearable pain if its host crosses a yellow line, and causes the stomach to explode if he crosses a red line. A surveillance machine monitors the men's dreams and relays them on video to the offices of prison director Poe, who punishes them if they have pleasurable thoughts.

Brennick is assigned a cell with Nino Gomez, an impulsive kid; Stiggs, a nervous boffin; D-Day, a nasty thug; and Abraham, a wise old prisoner who acts as Poe's personal valet. Brennick soon learns that Karen has been captured as well. He makes enemies with Maddox, the joint's resident tough guy, and is forced to fight him, to Poe's voyeuristic amusement. When Poe orders him to execute Maddox, Brennick refuses and stands by helplessly while the computer blasts a hole through Maddox's stomach. He does, however, retrieve Maddox's intestinator, which he slips to Gomez.

Poe, smitten with Karen, orders Brennick to be electronically lobotomised, but offers to stop torturing him if Karen will become his consort. She accepts, and Brennick, now a vegetable, is returned to his cell. The now heavily pregnant Karen discovers that Poe is an 'enhanced' human being who doesn't eat or sleep, and can't have sex. Plying him with champagne, she is able to access Brennick's dreams through the computer and restore his sense of self.

Re-established, Brennick plans an escape. Stiggs discovers a way of removing the intestinators, and Abraham smuggles a map back from Poe's quarters. As they break out, pursued by androids and killer robots, D-Day is killed, while Poe murders Abraham and sends Karen to have a lethal Caesarean. Poe is caught in crossfire and explodes. Stiggs is shot, but manages to corrupt the security computer before he dies. As the prisoners stage a mass break-out, Brennick, Karen and Gomez escape across the Mexican border. As Karen goes into labour, the truck comes alive and mows Gomez down. But Karen and the baby are unharmed and the family is reunited.

So paranoia is in: *Fortress* is only the most recent of futuristic prison movies sent to warn us that we are becoming a society under surveillance. While it is true that you can't go for a day's shopping any more without being caught on video camera, the fantasies of total intrusion posited by such movies are so hysterical that they end up having, at best, no more than a kitsch appeal to anyone over 12.

The current formula was established five years ago by John Hillcoat's *Ghosts ... of the Civil Dead*—prisoners are stripped of their civil rights and held in facilities owned by faceless corporations which are accountable to no-one. The conspiracy theory prison is run with a kind of institutionalised sadism that either allows a Darwinian *laissez faire* policy where the inmates duke it out among themselves (as in the rather entertaining Ray Liotta vehicle *No Escape*) or attempts utter domination—as in this film, where the prisoners' very thoughts are invaded.

The twist provided by both *Fortress* and *No Escape* is the introduction of the invincible ex-army hero (a direct descendant of Kurt Russell's eyepatch-wearing Snake Plissken in John Carpenter's *Escape From New York*), the only man, as it happens, who can take on the system single-handedly. Whatever a 'Black Beret' may be, Christopher Lambert, here sporting the regulation unwise action man haircut, is that man—which means that he is strong, silent (which, in Lambert's case, is a good idea) and handy with a machine gun.

While this is strictly routine material, there is no excuse for it to be turned into a film as laughable as *Fortress* without even being funny. It is just about possible that the director, Stuart Gordon—who in happier days made the gleefully ghoulish *Re-Animator* was flummoxed by a script that appears to have been written by a pair of computer nerds who haven't seen daylight since 1975. But Gordon doesn't even try—he lets the film look as though it is taking place in a hangar, and laboriously pulls the plot strings with no suspense, no humour, and a few derisory special effects lifted from *Alien*. *Fortress* is so shabby, it makes *No Escape* look like *Apocalypse Now*, and with its bizarre fixation on the stomach—pregnancy, exploding bellies, crippling intestinators—might leave an audience feeling somewhat nauseated.

Also reviewed in:
NEW YORK TIMES, 9/4/93, p. 11, Stephen Holden
VARIETY, 2/1/93, p. 97, David Straiton
WASHINGTON POST, 9/6/93, p. C7, Richard Harrington

FREAKED

A Twentieth Century Fox Films release of a Tommy production. *Producer:* Harry J. Ufland and Mary Jane Ufland. *Director:* Tom Stern and Alex Winter. *Screenplay:* Tim Burns, Tom Stern, and Alex Winter. *Director of Photography:* Jamie Thompson. *Editor:* Malcolm Campbell. *Music:* Kevin Kiner. *Music Editor:* Jay Richardson. *Sound:* Lee Orloff. *Sound Editor:* Michael Hilkene. *Casting:* Artz & Cohen. *Production Designer:* Catherine Hardwicke. *Art Director:* Kim Hix. *Set Designer:* Theodore Sharps. *Set Decorator:* Brian Kasch. *Set Dresser:* Jenny Baum. *Special Effects:* Martin Bresin. *Creature & Visual Effects:* Thomas C. Rainone. *Costumes:* Malissa Daniel. *Make-up:* Julie Hewett. *Creature Make-up Effects:* Screaming Mad George and Steve Johnson. *Stunt Coordinator:* Rick Barker. *Running time:* 80 minutes. *MPAA Rating:* PG-13.

CAST: Brooke Shields (Skye Daley); Alex Winter (Ricky Coogin); William Sadler (Dick Brian); Eduardo Ricard (George Ramirez #1); Henry Carbo (George Ramirez #2); Deep Roy (George Ramirez #3); Mihaly "Michu" Meszaros (George Ramirez #4); Brian Brophy (Kevin); Michael Stoyanov (Ernie); Morgan Fairchild (Stewardess); Alex Zuckerman (Stuey Gluck); Megan Ward (Julie); Randy Quaid (Elijah C. Skuggs); Jaime Cardriche (Toad); Nicholas Cohn (Bob Vila Look-A-Like); Derek McGrath (Worm); Jeff Kahn (Nosey); John Hawkes (Cowboy); Mr. T (The Beared Lady); Karyn Malchus (Sockhead); Lee Arenberg (The Eternal Flame); Patti Tippo (Rosie the Pinhead); Tim Burns (Frogman); Bobcat Goldthwait (Sockhead as Tourist/Voice of Sockhead); Don Stark (Editor); Arturo Gil (Clown); Alex Winter (Sensitive Man #1); Tom Stern (Sensitive Man #2); Gibson J. Haynes (Cheese Wart); Pamela Mant (Nun); Joe Baker (Prof. Nigel Crump); L.S. Kruse (Peasant woman #1); Marilyn Garcia (Peasant Woman #2); Rick Le Clair (Screaming Hippie); Georgina Valdez (Screaming Woman); Calvert Deforest (Larry "Bud" Melman); Tom Stern (Milkman); Michael Gilden (Eye); Joseph Griffo (N. Eye); Jack Yates (Security Guy); Ray Baker (Bill Blazer); J.D. Silvester (Biker); Jon M. Chu (Giant Stuey Monster); Vincent Hammond (Giant Rick Monster); David Bowe (EES Assistant); Chuck Bulot (FBI Chief); David Roberson (FBI Guy); James Baxter Rogers (Another FBI Guy).

LOS ANGELES TIMES, 10/4/93, Calendar/p. 2, Chris Willman

One does hesitate to mention the words "Freaked" and "for Academy consideration" in the same breath. But if Oscar voters could be dragged—kicking and screaming—to this exercise in wiseacre grotesqueries, it might at least get a nod in next year's makeup effects category. Or in a special latex subdivision dubbed Best Disfigurements Not Applied to Mel Gibson.

"Freaked" has less in common with earnest men without faces, of course, than with the Garbage Pail Kids at play on the Island of Lost Souls. Alex Winter—the only half of Bill & Ted—stars as an unctuous young TV star who winds up in a spot of trouble on a promotional visit to South America. He and a pair of equally obnoxious pals wander into a sinister freak show, run by Randy Quaid in Buffalo Bill regalia, and immediately get turned into gooey prime attractions.

Those already transformed include a human worm, a toadman with a 25-foot tongue, Mr. T as the bearded lady, Bobcat Goldthwait as a guy with a sock-puppet for a head and an unbilled Keanu Reeves as the dog-faced boy (who runs off for most of the movie upon seeing a squirrel).

Winter co-directed and cowrote with Tom Stern, joined by third writer Tim Burns in a reunion of the team behind MTV's shortlived "Idiot Box" series. Here, as there, the lads have a desperate try-anything approach to black comedy that mixes potty-level humor with enough absurdist pop culture references to rival Dennis Miller. (Best moment: Quaid is seen laughing maniacally—at a Family Circus panel.)

Combined with the terrific creature effects, this smug stew results in at least a couple-of-dozen moments of wildly inventive fun and roughly twice as many puerile groaners. "Freaked" (rated PG-13) *is* a whole lot more entertaining than most films that open in a single theater without press screenings, but neither Tod Browning's nor Monty Python's reputation is in danger just yet.

NEWSDAY, 10/2/93, Part II/p. 23, Terry Kelleher

Yes, there is something to be said for a movie in which a bearded but rouged Mr. T declares with quiet satisfaction: "I am woman, and I like me."

So we're here to tell you that the movie is called "Freaked," and it may be a sleeper hit if those stories are true about hallucinogens making a comeback.

"Freaked," which concerns a carnival of mutants in a South American country named for a dessert, attempts a cross between Monty Python and MTV, with an added pinch of genetic material from the "Bill and Ted" comedies.

Alex Winter, co-star of B & T's "Excellent Adventure" and "Bogus Journey," plays the lead in "Freaked," as well as collaborating with Tom Stern—on the writing and direction. Previous Winter-Stern works include a horror-spoof short and MTV's "The Idiot Box."

What they're after here is comic anarchy or, as the publicity puts it, "rebellious lunacy." They wisely chose a veteran loony in Randy Quaid for the role of Elijah C. Skuggs, the freak-show proprietor who captures insufferable actor-spokesperson Ricky Coogin (Winter) and two cohorts and turns them into his newest attractions. Ricky is transformed into a revolting creature—half-jerk, half-beast. Julie (Megan Ward), a sloganeering feminist-environmentalist, is Siamese-twinned with Ricky's buddy Ernie (Michael Stoyanov), a sexist dope. OK, not exactly razor-sharp social satire.

Still, the makeup people had fun fashioning the supporting mutants, especially the Worm (pince-nez seems the perfect accessory for a human-annelid) and Nosey (face it—a man-sized schnozz is going to have a few unsightly hairs), Sock Head (voiced by Bobcat Goldthwait) resembles a frantic reject from the Muppet factory, and the big, bad T-man looks—dare we say it?—quite comfortable as that carny fixture, the Bearded Lady.

At about an hour and a quarter, "Freaked" is short—but definitely not too short. Considering the rapid-fire pace and the modest store of good ideas, 22 minutes might have been a nice running time. Talk about limping to the finish line: The story is told in flashback as Ricky gives an interview to a vapid talk-show host (Brooke Shields), and the climax is interrupted by a lame commercial parody.

But there's something to be said for a movie in which the Toad Man eats bunnies whole and reads the National Review.

Also reviewed in:
NEW YORK TIMES, 10/2/93, p. 14, Stephen Holden
VARIETY, 9/27/93, p. 39, Leonard Klady

FREE WILLY

A Warner Bros. release in association with Le Studio Canal +, Regency Enterprises, and Alcor Films. *Executive Producer:* Richard Donner and Arnon Milchan. *Producer:* Jennie Lew Tugend and Lauren Shuler-Donner. *Director:* Simon Wincer. *Screenplay:* Keith A. Walker and Corey Blechman. *Story:* Keith A. Walker. *Director of Photography:* Robbie Greenberg. *Editor:* O. Nicholas Brown. *Music:* Basil Poledouris. *Music Editor:* Tomas Milano. *Sound:* Clark King. *Sound Editor:* Tim Chau. *Casting:* Judy Taylor and Lynda Gordon. *Production Designer:* Charles Rosen. *Art Director:* Diane Yates and Charles Butcher. *Set Designer:* Harold Fuhrman. *Set Decorator:* Mary Olivia-McIntosh. *Special Effects:* Tom Ward. *Whale Effects:* Walt Conti. *Costumes:* April Ferry. *Make-up:* Pamela Westmore. *Stunt Coordinator:* Dennis R. Scott. *Running time:* 112 minutes. *MPAA Rating:* PG.

CAST: Jason James Richter (Jesse); Lori Petty (Rae); Jayne Atkinson (Annie); August Schellenberg (Randolph); Michael Madsen (Glen); Michael Ironside (Dial); Richard Riehle (Wade); Mykelti Williamson (Dwight); Michael Bacall (Perry); Danielle Harris (Gwenie); Isiah Malone (Vector); Betsy Toll (Passerby #1); Rob Sample (Passerby #2); Merrilyn Jones (Passerby #3); Mickey Gaines (Waiter); Justin R. Hall, Robert M. Duque, and Sam Samson (Fish Throwers); Willis Van Dusen (Fish Vendor); Tom Lasswell (Brody); Moultrie Patten and Ed Murphy (Homeless Men); Jim Michaels (Announcer); Keiko (Willy).

LOS ANGELES TIMES, 7/16/93, Calendar/p. 1, Michael Wilmington

For Herman Melville in "Moby Dick," the white sperm whale was a vast, mysterious monarch of the seas, a Godlike being dispensing destiny to the puny humans trying to catch it. For the makers of "Free Willy", the Orca or "killer" whale, a more predatory cetacean, becomes their symbol of nature exploited, ultimate victim of man's greed and rapacity.

And though, like whale Willy himself, trapped in a park, the theme is imprisoned in a movie fairy tale—a slightly sentimental adventure story of Boy meets Whale—somehow its majesty comes through anyway. Children's movies shouldn't be asked for the sophistication and verisimilitude we demand of adult films. And "Free Willy" is for children and families, first and foremost.

For them, it should be one of the treats of the year. There's a muscular sincerity to this movie, a power and spread to its imagery that triumphs over the occasional candied purple patches or strained plot twists. At its best, "Free Willy", gets some of the primal emotion of a "Lassie Come Home," "White Mane" or a "Yearling": those "corny" or fanciful animal movies that stick in our minds for years. And whether you cheer or jeer at its wildly over-the-top cliff-hanger climax—with the good guys desperately speeding a kidnapped whale to the ocean in a repair truck, while bad guys fiendishly try to stop them—"Willy" still often captures honestly a sense of the wonders and terrors of nature.

Perhaps that's because the producers have been so lavish: The prelude wildlife whale ballet was shot by the famous whale photographer Bob Talbot. Perhaps it's due to our knowledge of the current danger to whales, a species slaughtered, according to Jacques-Yves Cousteau, at the staggering rate of 40,000 a year between 1929 and 1979. Perhaps it's because "Free Willy" as written by Keith A. Walker and Corey Blechman, keeps mostly within an "innocent eye." It follows the perspective and experience of a 12-year-old protagonist, Jason James Richter as urban street kid Jesse, whose delinquency lands him in a part-time job at the local sea world.

Jesse is consciously portrayed as a kid with an edge, surly, rebellious and suspicious of his guardians, nice-guy car mechanic Glen (Michael Madsen, in his "Thelma & Louise" mode) and his artsy journalist wife, Annie (Jayne Atkinson). And suspicious too of his park employers, an American Indian myth-spinner (August Schellenberg, from "Black Robe") and a collegiate feminist seal-handler (Lori Petty).

The mixture of races and types—Jesse's youth-officer is African-American (Mykelti Williamson) and the villains are pinch-faced money-mad park entrepreneurs Dial and Wade (Michael Ironside and Richard Riehle)—stamps this movie as not just a fairy tale but a liberal one, a "Save the Whales" fantasy of seemingly impeccable political "correctness."

It's a tribute to the movie's makers that they never let the pattern obtrude. Music brings boy and whale together—Jesse's bluesy harmonica, Willy's plaintive whale song—and there's both magic in the encounter, and a weird believability in their blossoming friendship.

Partially, this comes from adroit casting. Richter, who has never acted in a movie before, may have the blond, Beatle-hair good looks of a Sitcom child but he's not cutesy or sticky. His surliness never seems put-on, and there's a rapt absorption when he and Willy interact. Willy himself—impersonated by the marvelous Mexico City performing whale Keiko—is a genuinely lovable Orca. "Killer" whales, like dolphins, are brainy and sociable enough to be ace performers, and though Keiko is sometimes doubled by Walt Conti's ingenious animatronics whale, it's only in the dangerous or out-of-water scenes.

Simon Wincer, who directed "Willy," has been stuck in a kind of action-movie rut since he emigrated to Hollywood from Australia. But his one great American movie, the 1989 "Lonesome Dove," probably started the Western movie renaissance that led to "Dances With Wolves" and "Unforgiven." And "Dove's" considerable virtues—its unforced rhythm and wonderful feel for landscape and place, the casual density of its background detail, the understated low-key intensity of its performances—are present here, too.

In the end, how we respond to "Free Willy" (MPAA-rated PG) is a matter of taste and temperament. Anti-ecology jokesters of the P. J. O'Rourke stripe will find the movie ludicrous. But children and adults willing to succumb to its wonders, and even its absurdities, may have the last laugh. There's something to be said, after all, for innocence, the interconnectedness of life, the ocean's awesome sweep. There's something to be said for fairy tales—when they're done with breadth and emotion. At its best, "Free Willy" jumps that barrier.

NEW YORK, 8/16/93, p. 58, David Denby

At the ridiculous conclusion of *Free Willy*, a large tear formed itself in my eye, rolled down my cheek, and landed with a plop on my critic's Steno pad. So much for criticism. I cried despite my hating every cheap trick the movie played on me—the orphan boy rejecting his kindly foster parents by throwing a baseball through the window; the captured whale moaning for his family and the family out at sea moaning back; the Indian whale trainer murmuring old tribal prayers. Still, when the kid frees the mammal, well, those orca-liberation stories get me every time.

NEW YORK POST, 7/16/93, p. 27, Michael Medved

If you're going to make a contemporary message movie, you could hardly pick a safer, less controversial message than "Save the Whales."

A few conservative curmudgeons might grumble, taunting environmental true believers with their intentionally outrageous slogan "Nuke the Whales!," but even the most incorrigible right-wing skeptic must melt with some combination of awe and affection when confronted with the reality of these magnificent mammals. Talk about family values!

As "Free Willy" helpfully informs us, orcas (or "killer whales," the clever predators featured in this film) stick with stable family groupings for a lifetime, sometimes remaining with their own mothers for more than 50 years.

Such endearing orca information helps establish our emotional bond with Willy, a young whale taken from his doting parents at the beginning of the movie and confined in a seedy "Adventure Park" somewhere in the Pacific Northwest.

Willy adjusts poorly to his life in captivity, skulking around his lovely, undersized tank and stubbornly refusing to cooperate with his trainers or to learn the crowd-pleasing tricks they try to teach him. He's a brooding, sullen, sea mammal-without-a-cause—a juvenile delinquent who invariably frustrates his exploitive owners.

Needless to say, Willy eventually meets his human counterpart Jesse, a cynical street kid, who's arrested one night during a graffiti raid on the adventure park where Willy lives. Instead of going to juvenile hall, Jesse agrees to do penance by cleaning up the aquatic theater he's defaced, and so begins the inter-species friendship at the center of the film.

When the whale's unscrupulous owners realize that the insurance policy they've taken out on the beast may be worth more than their 7,000-pound animal guest, it's only a matter of time before Jesse and his friends make a daring decision to (you guessed it) free Willy.

The two stars at the heart of this story are a pair of 12-year-olds—one of them, Keiko, is a 22-foot-long veteran performer from an aquatic park in Mexico City and the other, Jason James Richter, is an inexperienced actor from Hawaii.

Unlike so many of today's smooth and relentlessly cute young stars, Richter shows us some of his rough edges and manages to convince you that Jesse is, indeed, an obnoxious self-destructive, even dangerous kid. Under the skillful guidance of director Simon Wincer (who previously did the stunning Australian racehorse saga "Phar Lap" and TVs magnificent "Lonesome Dove"), Richter never overdoes the underlying sweetness and innocence bit, so the picture generates unexpected emotion when it comes to the sub-plot about Jesse's relationship with his would-be foster parents (Michael Madsen and Jayne Atkinson).

The only real surprise in this creaky material is how well it all works—especially for kids. Young moviegoers above the age of 5 will find themselves crying and cheering at appropriate moments, together with the more sentimental and susceptible among their parents.

Along the way to its truly spectacular climax, "Free Willy" misses no chance at scoring points for political correctness: There's a special "Save the Whales" 800 number that flashes on screen at the movie's end, an all-knowing Native American mystic ("Black Robe's" formidable August Schellenberg), who just happens to work at the adventure park, and a greedy, evil capitalist ("Making lots of money—that's what we're all about!") sneeringly played by Michael Ironside.

Fortunately, none of these preachy touches seriously interferes with the forward momentum of the story, until the very conclusion of the picture, when the credits roll and the soundtrack's embarrassingly awful original song ("Will You Be There") by that noted animal lover Michael Jackson. This panting, whining, sobbing, hyper-emotional hymn seems to focus on the Christ-like elements in Willy's personality. It is so breathtakingly ridiculous that its worth sitting through the very long credits to hear the number in all its appalling entirety.

NEWSDAY, 7/16/93, Part II/p. 56, Jack Mathews

By the time you get to the end of this sentence, which describes "Free Willy" as a fable about a troubled boy who befriends a killer whale and attempts to free him from captivity, you'll know how it ends.

But that's OK. If it ended any other way, it wouldn't be the summer's *perfect* family movie, the one picture you can count on to exhilarate your kids and put a bounce in your own step. The audience I saw it with was cheering the final scenes, and some of those voices sounded pretty husky.

"Free Willy," directed by Emmy-winning Australian Simon Wincer ("Lonesome Dove"), follows the adventures of 12-year-old Jesse (Jason James Richter), a bitter street waif who is placed in a foster home in a Northwest coastal town and compelled to clean up the graffiti he and a friend spray-painted on the walls of an aquatic park or face a stretch in juvenile hall.

Jesse is a hard case, as is Willy, the depressed 7,000-pound orca living in the park's claustrophobic show tank, and they prove to be kindred spirits.

Both were separated from their parents—Jesse's abandoned him years earlier, and Willy was snatched from his family by poachers—and neither is interested in behaving the way strangers want them to.

A quick bond is established and soon Willy is doing everything but jumping through hoops for the kid. Both suddenly have some purpose in their lives, and all is well until Jesse learns of the park owners' scheme to kill Willy for insurance money.

Wincer, working with a script by Keith A. Walker and Corey Blechman, keeps the story simple and focused, but still manages to develop themes about trust, friendship and respect for nature.

No question, Willy is the whale of every boy's dream, Lassie of the sea, but the film leaves a clear message that it's wrong to keep big, smart animals like whales in captivity. They are lonely, they don't have enough room and their life expectancy is halved.

Inevitably, "Free Willy" makes that point with some embarrassment. The filmmakers used models and an "animatronic" whale for many scenes, but to show Willy's amazing assortment of tricks (he leaps, rolls, flaps, sticks out his tongue, does hot laps around the pool with Jesse on his back), they had to exploit one of the real things. Willy's best scenes are played by Keiko, a 7-year-old performing orca from Reino Aventura in Mexico City.

At the end of "Free Willy," just as Michael Jackson's theme song "Will You Be There" is brought up on the soundtrack, an 800-number for a friend-of-the-whales helpline is flashed on the screen.

And at that moment, as Willy heads out to rejoin his family, we can all agree that the amiable giants should be free. But it would be naive to expect this movie to do anything other than promote business at aquatic parks around the country.

The performances by the human actors pale next to Keiko's energetic work. Richter, a 13-year-old making his film debut, evinces an Oliver-like quality, a pickpocket with a good heart, and although he oversells his bad boy "attitude" in his scenes with adults, he is obviously having a great time with the whale.

The story didn't leave much room for anybody else. Michael Madsen, the sadistic killer in "Reservoir Dogs" seems emotionally cramped in the role of Jesse's eager-to-please foster father. And Lori Petty, Geena Davis' sister in "A League of Their Own," barely registers as the whale trainer who stands back and lets Jesse take over.

On the other hand, Michael Ironside, a perennial heavy, is deliciously malevolent as the park's greedy owner, and August Schellenberg, a Canadian actor who is half-Mohawk, is warmly engaging as the Indian handyman who becomes Jesse's friend, mentor and, finally, his ally in the rescue mission.

"Free Willy" is a first-class production and a bit of a miracle among modern action films. There is tension, suspense and a bang-up chase sequence, yet minimal violence, no blood and hardly a sour note.

I was disappointed by the film's climactic moment, when Willy leaps to freedom. After seeing those dinosaurs gallop across the plains in "Jurassic Park," you'd think Wincer's special-effects crew could show us a whale leaping over a wall. Instead it's done in the editing, with quick cuts, close-ups and overdramatized music to effect the illusion, and it's not worthy of the rest of the film.

But it does make the point, and for families looking to be enriched by a movie, it's the high point of the summer.

SIGHT AND SOUND, 3/94, p. 38, Leslie Felperin Sharman

In the American Northwest, a whale is captured by a fishing boat, the Pequod. Later, in a nearby city, a young homeless boy, Jesse, and his friend Perry break into an amusement park while running from the police. Perry spray-paints the tank in which the whale is being held. He escapes, but Jesse is caught and is fostered out to a young couple, Glen and Annie. Forced to clean up the tank as restitution, Jesse grows increasingly fond of the whale, now named Willy, who seems only to like him. Under the guidance of two park employees, Rae, a young woman trainer, and Randolph, a Native American whale attendant, Jesse becomes increasingly close to Willy, and learns to trust adults, even Glen, who until now has kept his distance emotionally from Jesse.

Unfortunately, Dial, the amusement park officer, wants Willy to turn a profit by performing, or else he will have him killed in order to collect the insurance. Jesse trains Willy to do the tricks. On the day of his first show, Willy refuses to perform. Jesse is mortified and withdraws emotionally.

Planning to run away, Jesse goes to say goodbye to Willy, but spots Dial's henchmen sabotaging the tank. He rounds up Randolph and Rae, and they decide to release Willy into the ocean so he can rejoin his family. They prepare Willy for travel and escape the park, only to suffer a minor accident on the road. Glen and Annie come to their assistance, and they all race to the marina to deposit Willy in the water before he dies of dehydration. They succeed in the nick of time.

Although just a modest, sentimental little story about one boy and his whale, *Free Willy* must be a headache for Warner Bros' publicity department. While the title is perfectly anodyne in the US, in the UK it suggests a gay porn film for the especially stingy. Even more embarrassingly, the theme song is sung by that famous lover of children and animals, Michael Jackson.

Until very recently, when it came to sea animals larger than a dolphin, Hollywood subscribed to the *Moby Dick* approach, i.e. they were vicious monsters of the deep, to be conquered in the name of progress—see, for example, *Jaws* or *Orca the Killer Whale*. Greenpeace has changed all that and ever since *Star Trek IV: The Voyage Home* these huge mounds of blubber have become cuddly symbols of man's inhumanity to nature.

Now the villains are not so much the whalers but the irresponsible theme park managers who treat animals as 'commodities'. Yet *Free Willy* skirts away from questioning the underlying ethics of animal performance—a smart move, as analysis might undermine the political correctness of the film itself. In mixing its climactic *Born Free* ending with lots of impressive stunts by an exploited animal, the film's ideology remains confused. The analogy between Willy the jailed whale and Jesse the captured kid is also problematic. Finally freed, Willy is able to rejoin his 'family'. Jesse, on the other hand, although seemingly happy, still has a family imposed on him—like an animal in captivity, forced to bond with strangers.

Meanwhile, the men do a lot of getting in touch with their feelings. As Glen, Michael Madsen swaps the cutthroat razor he brandished in *Reservoir Dogs* for a friendly baseball glove, while August Schellenberg looks soulful as the noble Indian lackey who guides Jesse's understanding of whale spirituality. There is so much patronising beatification of Native Americans that the film might have been retitled *Dances with Whales*.

With its relatively slow pace and weepy quality, *Free Willy* ought to hold the attention of docile 5-to-8-year-olds, but one has doubts whether the older youth of today will really like it, unless they are zealous environmentalists or budding zoologists. Like many children's films, *Free Willy* is easy to be cynical about, but being so excessively trite, it is also hard to like.

TIME, 7/19/93, p. 59, Richard Corliss

If you were a 12-year old boy on a solo Save the Whale campaign, well, you'd slap your favorite marine mammal into a truck for a drive to the Pacific Ocean. And to keep him refreshed, you'd probably run him through an automatic car wash. And then, like an animal tamer who uses love instead of a whip, you'd get your adorable orca to leap over a high jetty so he could be reunited with his pod. You'd go that far for a friend. Where there's a whale, there's a way.

Here comes *Free Willy*, this month's feel-good sleeper. Preview audiences have gone wild for *Willy*, the story of two 12-year-olds separated from their folks. Jesse (Jason James Richter) is a troubled boy who, while cleaning up the graffiti scrawled on the walls of a seaquarium theme park in the Pacific Northwest, bonds mystically with a 7,000-lb., 22-ft.-long killer whale named Willy. Aided by his foster parents and two sympathetic adults at the park, the sweet boy makes it his mission to free the sweet beast.

The film, written by Keith A. Walker and Corey Blechman and directed by Simon Wincer (TV's *Lonesome Dove*), has a no-fault recipe for success. Start with *Jurassic Park's* fondness for huge, dangerous, pet-worthy creatures and its cunning use of special effects to make the fauna realistic. Add a dollop of Hollywood eco-mania, portraying the park officer as a predatory capitalist who would kill Willy for the insurance money. And wrap this around the summer's favorite icon: the fatherless boy who teaches everyone else—surrogate parents, adult friends and a nearby cetacean—how to be human. The movie hits every emotional button with a firm fist. It makes the phrase feel-good sound like a command from the industry's P.C. Patrol.

There's no denying, though, that *Free Willy* is a clever movie toy for the kid market. Most of the time Willy is played by Keiko, a killer whale (actually a type of dolphin) that the company found in a seaquarium in Mexico City. But frequently Keiko is spelled by a stunt double: a high-tech robot coated with 3,000 lbs. of eurythane rubber. (There is also a Turbo Willy—essentially the top of the whale, with mammoth hydraulic propellers on the bottom.) How real were the fake Willys? Persuasive enough so that the real Willy got the hots for them. "Whales are well-endowed animals," notes Walt Conti, the effects magician who created the seductive stand-ins. "It's pretty obvious he was attracted."

Free Willy has other attractions. Richter is an appealing, unaffected young performer; and Willy, with his black-and-white shading and fine Deco design, is a handsome brute. He's smart enough to understand complex English sentences, nodding an appropriate yes or no to Jesse's questions. And like any ingratiating adolescent, Willy knows how to make bad manners look cute. The children who giggled in *Jurassic Park* at the sight of a paleobotanist elbow-deep in triceratops doody will love the moment when Willy uses his blowhole to whisk away a huge wad of whale snot. Most important, he has a sweet disposition—lets the boy stroke his tongue—and is fiercely loyal to his human sibling. By film's end, a million tots in the audience will be tearfully whispering Jessie's climactic words: "I love you, Willy."

Who could not love *Free Willy*, aside from a grouchy movie critic? Perhaps the people at Sea World, the chain of popular marine parks in San Diego; Orlando, Florida; San Antonio, Texas; and Aurora, Ohio. Its curators are steamed at the film's depiction of an animal theme park as an inhumane cesspool. "The movie is not a fair portrayal of whales in captivity," argues Jim Antrim, general curator at Sea World in San Diego. "The trainer seems to be feeding the animal an inferior type of fish and often walks by the animal in an uninterested manner." Sea World execs charge that the movie is inaccurate on many levels, from the miraculously rapid affinity between Jesse and Willy to the malicious characterization of trainers, park staff and visitors. In one scene, dozens of customers bang interminably on the glass wall of Willy's tank, inciting the whale to a destructive frenzy. No security guard is in sight.

"If I had my druthers, these places wouldn't even exist," says *Free Willy*'s executive producer, Richard Donner (*Lethal Weapon, Radio Flyer*). "There are those who'll argue the aquatic parks are like zoos, that they teach children and others about animals. But I'm against zoos too." Donner's wife, Lauren Shuler-Donner, who co-produced the movie, says, "We didn't set out to make a movie condemning aquatic parks. We set out to make a movie about a boy and a whale and family and friendship and freedom. But personally, I've never liked zoos, seaquariums or even birds in cages. If people want to see a whale, they can see it on television or in movies or go on a whale-watching tour." Two of the *Willy* whales may soon go on tour. Animatronic Willy is set for a promotional jaunt. And real Willy—Keiko—will have to find less confining quarters. It is in danger of growing too large for its Mexico City tank. As co-producer Jennie Lew Tugend notes sadly, "It's a 22-ft. whale in a tank that's only 15 ft. deep." Activists, unite against Hollywood's neglect of a new star. Save this whale!

VILLAGE VOICE, 7/27/93, p. 62, Lisa Kennedy

After one dispenses with the obligatory joke about the porniness of its title, there are still things to be said about Warner Family Entertainment's (the Bros.' new kiddie division) debut, *Free Willy*. An Orca-sized whale of a tale, the movie follows Jesse, an abandoned Seattle street kid more *Hook*-Lost-Boy than *Streetwise*-tough, and Willy, the enslaved "killer" whale he befriends. Of course, while Jesse still has the requisite chip on his shoulder, he is no longer street-bound, having been placed into foster care with the Greenwoods, Annie and Glen (played by the yummy Michael Madsen). And it's not the mere fact of Willy's captivity that suggests his enslavement—this is not an anti-Sea World flick—so much as his mistreatment and his craven exploitation by Northwest Adventure Park's smarmy owner.

But even as they bang out familiar sentimental notes, movies that feature animals (the whale, Keiko, is billed too low for my taste) also provide strangely moving liberating metaphors. While we are forced by our bodies to identify with the human in these films, we might ache for a freedom beyond our wordiness, a sort of whale whistling, clicking and splashing freedom, a dumb and full freedom.

In the end, Willy's drive to an ocean of his own initiates Jesse into that all-too-human world where certain allegorical resolutions—reuniting Willy with his pod, his community—will heal all wounds. His foster parents' love will be accepted; his mother, now gone for six years, will be relegated to a less harmful place in his memory; and, my friends, he will come to know Iron John.

Okay, if there is one frustrating thing to be reported about this otherwise fleeting, endearing movie, it's that *Free Willy* continues Hollywood's fixation on white (preferably blond) boy protagonists. A Native American friend (August Schellenberg), a gal marine biologist (Lori Petty), and a black social worker (Mykelti Williamson) don't get *Willy* off the hook.

Also reviewed in:
CHICAGO TRIBUNE, 7/16/93, Friday/p. A, Clifford Terry
NEW YORK TIMES, 7/16/93, p. C12, Vincent Canby
VARIETY, 7/19/93, p. 71, Leonard Klady
WASHINGTON POST, 7/14/93, p. D1, Hal Hinson
WASHINGTON POST, 7/16/93, Weekend/p. 38, Desson Howe

FROM HOLLYWOOD TO HANOI

A Friendship Bridge Productions film. *Producer:* Tiana (Thi Thanh Nga). *Director:* Tiana (Thi Thanh Nga). *Screenplay (English, French and Vietnamese with English subtitles):* Tiana (Thi Thanh Nga). *Director of Photography:* Michael Dodds, Bruce Dorfman, and Jamie Maxtone-Graham. *Editor:* Roger Schulte. *Music:* Allan Gus. *Sound:* Gordon J. Grinberg and Zeborah Tidwell. *Running time:* 78 minutes. *MPAA Rating:* Not Rated.

CINEASTE, Vol. XX, No. 3, 1994, p. 45, Gitta Reddy

Now that Oliver Stone's finely tuned epics 'about' Asian women—*Heaven and Earth* and *The Joy Luck Club*—have hit the screens, the sharp and thoroughly engrossing *From Hollywood to Hanoi* sneaks in a more personal voice. It opens like an ominous fairy tale, with cartoonlike, redneck bad guys standing on a dock, one of them fingering a cigar. A young Southeast Asian woman pulls a gun on them. "You're under arrest!," she exclaims. "For smoking?," they snap back, and try to escape, dodging our heroine's swift kick. She pursues them by motorcycle, wrestling them on the hood of a truck, fearlessly battling until she's thrown with a scream of "NO!" into the water. "My career was going nowhere," intones Tiana in voice-over, and as the B-movie clip ends, the pursuit of Asian-American identity is on.

Director-writer-producer Tiana's Hollywood acting career interestingly punctuates her feature directorial debut, carving out a unique niche among documentaries as well as documentarians searching for their roots. With a surprisingly self-mocking tone at the onset, although sidestepping obvious political stands, *From Hollywood to Hanoi* is nonetheless an overt treatise on national and ethnic identity and one of the few feature length personal-identity-as-politics films to appear on commercial screens recently. Born Thi Thanh Nga, Tiana's previous filmography is under telling aliases: after debuting in Sam Peckinpah's *The Killer Elite* (1975), she became Tiana Alexandra to appear in such fare as the World War II miniseries *Pearl* and an Aaron Spelling Christmas special, and as Tiana Banana she made three music videos for Warner France, including *Lust in de Jungle* and *Free As I Want 2B*.

Using what must be some of her most embarrassing film clips, Tiana acknowledges and plays off of her previous 'identities' right off the bat. A journey in both a geographical and psychological sense, *From Hollywood to Hanoi* manages a tour through the many realities of the filmmaker's life as she presents them, a media-savy rumination for those who have never been to today's Vietnam as well as for those who do not live with the many dualities Asian Americans face in the U.S. Interviewing three clearly 'Amerasian' teens standing in front of a school, Tiana asks, "Do you consider yourself American or Vietnamese!" As if acknowledging the media take on what it means to be from a time and two places marked by the same war, bomb explosions are intercut while they respond. Their difficulty yet eagerness in answering her parallels the filmmaker's own complex approach to identity throughout the course of the film.

A breezy but poignant overview of Tiana's privileged childhood in a South Vietnamese government family leads into their continual effort in the U.S. to be the "perfect Americans." But it is her later decision to return to Vietnam that defines the film. There, amid emotional meetings with relatives and visiting places she excitedly remembers or has only heard about, the camera bears witness to Tiana's reunion with a proudly Vietnamese Vietnam, the oasis of her quest to find what it can mean to be Vietnamese.

Billed as the first American film about Vietnam actually shot in that country, the footage is, indeed, quite remarkable. Tiana interviews a Texas-trained doctor at a Saigon Agent Orange ward, the camera lingering on research lab jars of grossly malformed babies in the film's most straightforward critique of American imperialism. She gossips with cousins on her hotel bed while they raid her cosmetics case, and endures when they dig up "one of my worst movies from the local bootleg video place." Her north Vietnamese coverage belies rather biased ethnography, using commentary from passing interview encounters as constant reminders of her otherness in this apparently more bleak land forbidden to her childhood years. Ardent to the point of ecstatic Ho Chi Minh supporters dot the landscape of Tiana's northern journey, but her interaction with the brass remains in the realm of the poetic, literally. It was Tiana's poem, "Dear America, Dear Vietnam," which so impressed Vietnamese officials that she gained the difficult permission to return. Reciting poetry to compliment her, Senior Politburo Advisor Le Duc Tho refers to Tiana as "niece" and explains that he declined the Nobel Peace Prize awarded him (and Henry Kissinger) after the war because it was given to both sides, both the "aggressors" and the "people who fought for peace."

Both sides, both homes to Tiana remain elusive by the end at a glitzy suburban Christmas on her return to her family's home in northern California. Her father, who was the head of the South Vietnamese Ministry of Press and to whom the film is dedicated, remains staunchly against her visit to their homeland. He refuses his daughter's souvenir gift of a helmet, although agreeing to hold it for the camera. He himself "will not return until the country changes direction." Characterizing herself as the rebellious daughter, Tiana and her film's primary emotional concerns are charted through just such returns—to Ho Chi Minh City (which Tiana remarks is still called Saigon by everyone), to the forbidden Hanoi, to her family in San Jose's Little Saigon, and, presumably with this film, back indeed to Hollywood. Where to find home, here or there?, is an underlying though never definitively answered question. In Saigon, Tiana finds in the many abandoned Amerasian children and the young Viet and Duc, Siamese twins born victims of Agent Orange, analogies to her split self—is she Vietnamese, or is she American? In encounters along her route in northern Vietnam, where people remark on Tiana's appearance versus accent, the question becomes *how* is she Vietnamese, *how* is she American.

From Hollywood to Hanoi, despite its amazing seamlessness from location to location, amplifies the idea that, like many immigrants, Asian-Americans returning home after an era, or a generation or two, may face a blinding wall to what they seek. As with *The Joy Luck Club*, implied and almost celebrated is a mythologizing wall between the seeker and the 'homeland' that is never addressed. Though not pointedly addressed here either, Tiana's wall is obviously built of media images of violence and the kind of equally violent caricatures she has been asked to portray by the first city of her film s title. An ongoing victim of 'serious' tomes comprised of white liberal guilt and nostalgia during its existence as an American obsession, Vietnam emerges in Tiana's film as a home, and one still considered a home to many Asian-Americans who are survivors of the war, immigration, and the everchanging difficulties of acculturation and assimilation.

Tiana's interwoven strands form a surprisingly easy, though seemingly unholy, alliance. From her former niche as Hollywood martial arts tough cookie, fast on her draw and her "hi-ya's," to interviewing survivors of the My Lai massacre, is a big jump. Her authorial approach is friendly and familiar, narrating with a conversational gusto pleasant even to those more accustomed to a TV talk show host than a PBS ethnographer. Although both Tiana's father and uncle held prominent positions in the South Vietnamese administration—her uncle was Defense Minister—she belies her own less than political steamroller approach by referring to them informally as "the head cheese" and her "feisty" uncle. The recounting of her years before the making of the film are engagingly humble, with lively tales of her childhood in Vietnam when she was coaxed into finishing her dinner by threats of Ho Chi Minh tearing her up, and later naively agreeing with her classmates in America that all the "gooks" were bad.

Visually Tiana often reads more as interviewer than participant, reliant as one may be on how war and Third World documentarians usually conduct themselves onscreen. When the filmmaker appears in a bright red jeans ensemble while interviewing in North Vietnam, she reveals herself to be as much a child of Hollywood as she is of anywhere else. "I felt like an outsider," says Tiana in voice-over. "I didn't look the same [as the North Vietnamese]—I didn't talk the same." Even in her familial South Vietnam, among people she once knew or communicates more kinship with, Tiana remains a visitor and moderator, her manner and relation to the people her camera encounters disturbingly ambiguous. But what are war, Vietnam, or biographical documentaries supposed to be like, anyway! And how does a first-person documentarian fit herself into these narrow genres most often defined by white male liberal guilt and nostalgia!

From Hollywood to Hanoi introduces a promising new filmmaker with powerful subject matter. With a sequel ready to be cut, and Oliver Stone himself on the board of her Southeast Asian/European/American cultural arts board, Tiana's new career should be something to watch.

NEW YORK POST, 7/21/93, p. 26, Matthew Flamm

Born in Vietnam and raised in the United States, Tiana Thi Thanh Nga—a.k.a. Tiana Alexandra, Tiana Banana and just plain Tiana—claims a certain confusion about her identity. Viewers of "From Hollywood to Hanoi," may be less inclined to wonder.

In the course of her offbeat, personal yet politically engaged documentary, Tiana finds she is both Vietnamese and American. Really, she is pure immigrant, a rebellious daughter of a traditional family, whose roots-discovering journey "home" is as American a ritual these days as finding oneself was in the '60s.

The issue is complicated, however, because Vietnam is complicated. Tiana, a quasi-successful singer and actress, becomes the first member of her very extended family to go back, and it's against her father's wishes. It's also against the U.S. government's wishes (a visa to Vietnam must be obtained abroad).

Tiana serves as our emissary whether she's tearfully reuniting with a relative in a dusty quarter of Saigon or speaking French with a silver-haired and courtly Gen. Vo Nguyen Giap, who engineered the defeat of both the French and the Americans. It almost doesn't matter what she says; she's all we've got.

Tiana films on her own terms, too. Her personal odyssey begins with her privileged childhood as the daughter of a South Vietnamese government honcho in Saigon, President John Kennedy, she recalls, once sent her a Chatty Cathy doll.

Even so, it was no ordinary privileged childhood. "I still remember the robes and the smell of burning flesh," she says over footage of self-immolating Buddhist priests.

Her family moving to the States in 1966, Tiana chooses the most American path of all: At 16, she boards a Greyhound for Hollywood. Clips from the B-movies in which she starred as a karate princess provide wonderful, self-mocking comic relief.

"From Hollywood to Hanoi" is not always successful in the attempts it makes at "Roger & Me"-style humor. But it does pick up some genuinely absurd bits along the way: Gen. William Westmoreland interviewed in a straw peasant's hat at a "Miss Saigon" benefit, and the director tangoing with Oliver Stone in a Hanoi lounge.

The main virtue of "Hollywood" is in the heartfelt way it confronts a devastating past, be it in the director's own family, a pair of Siamese twins (courtesy of Agent Orange) or Amerasian teenagers in a Saigon orphanage. Tiana may find her Vietnamese soul, but her ability to challenge custom and reinvent herself seems 100 percent American.

VILLAGE VOICE, 7/27/93, p. 60, Manohla Dargis

One year after U.S. combat troops landed in Vietnam, Thi Thanh Nga landed in the United States. It was 1966, and as foreign forces swept across her homeland, Nga and her family settled down in California, where when "kids said they hated the gooks, I did too." Politics by way of the personal, *From Hollywood to Hanoi* is the documentary story of how Thi Thanh Nga became Tiana, the chop-socky vixen of exercise and music videos (as well as some lowly budget films), and how this woman with two names, two identities, two countries eventually came home not just to Vietnam, but to herself.

Developed over the course of five years, *From Hollywood* is a dazzling postvérité whirl of original material buoyed by home movies, still photos, newsreel footage, and prime U.S. military propaganda (listen quick for some Jack Webb nasality). It's a heady fusion, one in which a clip of Nga's favorite childhood movie, *The Wizard of Oz* ("There's no place like home"), is followed by images of the "red faced, big noses" of newly arrived GIs ("I was in love," gushes Tiana in voice-over) and the casual aside that Dad was "the head cheese in the foreign ministry" in charge of press in South Vietnam.

Perky, brisk, and eager to please, *From Hollywood* is a welcome tonic for exposition drear, though at 78 minutes it's a bit too economical. This is especially evident when the film plays fast and loose with chronology, as it does when setting its framework. During an early sequence, Tiana explains what drove her back to Vietnam by cross-cutting her Hollywood years with the countdown to war's end, in the process shifting the personal and political out of synch. She narrates, "I tried to tune out the war but I couldn't," while on screen, history shuffles from the notorious execution of a Vietcong prisoner by a South Vietnamese police chief ('68), to a clip of Tiana in a cheapster with Rod Steiger ('87), then back again to the fall of Saigon ('75). There's nothing wrong with this temporal sleight of hand, but it underscores the film's scattershot style, as well as its occasional—and occasionally irritating—inattention to detail. This historical blurriness is most conspicuous when the spotlight hits Tiana's own family. Maybe we don't need to know it's a *South* Vietnamese official who wielded the gun in that '68 clip, but the fact that Tiana's "favorite uncle" was the defense minister for South Vietnam ("left behind" during the fall of Saigon) seems reason enough for more context. It may be unfair to demand hard facts and harder feelings from this likable, diaristic work (what *did* you do in the war, Daddy?), but Tiana can be an unreliable witness to history. When she finally catches up with her uncle the moment is undeniably moving, but I wish she'd asked him something other than whether or not he hates the communists, something about his role in the military, his thoughts on the U.S., the CIA, Westmoreland. Then again, perhaps that's another movie altogether.

As touching as *From Hollywood to Hanoi* is—and the film does convey extraordinary pathos—it's frustrating Tiana isn't, well, tougher with family and foe alike. In a perverse twist, her interview with Le Duc Tho, Kissinger's sparring partner at the Paris peace talks, is (slightly) more illuminating than anything either her father or favorite uncle offer up. Even more startling is her dialogue with General Vo Nguyen Giap, the military genius behind the North Vietnam victory. Giap doesn't speak long here but he speaks well. Conversing in French (as all the politburo vets do); Giap explains that "the Vietnamese, no matter where they live, dream about their country. For example, you. Right?" Tiana doesn't need to answer, and, she doesn't.

As she travels Vietnam, visiting relatives and talking with peasants and politicos alike, Tiana encounters hardship upon hardship. She resists placing the easy burden of blame on 100 years of French colonialism, 30 years of U.S. military intervention, or the communists, but her images of weeping women, mangled Agent Orange casualties, as well as the legless, the sightless, and the sorrowful, say it all. Given such material, Tiana can "be a trite, disappointing guide. (Too often she reminds us of her background in acting by hamming it up.) Every so often, though, she hits hard and deep, as during her interview with a My Lai massacre survivor, a woman who simply won't—can't—look Tiana in the eyes.

In moments like this another film emerges in *From Hollywood*, one that breaks through the crust of naive tourism and makes for something truly wondrous. One of the documentary's finest sequences begins during a walk with that favorite uncle. "Dear Dad," she voices, "I wish you were here with us," as the scene cuts—in a stunning oedipal gambit—to an Amerasian woman describing the brutality visited on Vietnam's biracial children. One more edit, and suddenly it's the grainy black-and-white '60s, featuring a cast of jokey, impossibly young GIs. "Is there anything this beach lacks?" the newsman pumps the crowd. "American girls!" they cry in unison, 'cause Vietnamese girls are "gooks, you know, slant-eyed, they're no good."

From Hollywood to Hanoi perches gingerly somewhere in between history and autobiography, wisdom and oblivion. Like its maker, it's a film very much divided, something that, I suspect, makes it all the stronger. One of General Giap's most famous maxims is, "When the enemy attacks, retreat, when he retreats, harass him." (Ask any kid and they'll say the same thing about handling parents.) Tiana has dedicated her film to her father, who opposed her return to Vietnam passionately. Whether it's a question of ideology, or something more complex, more personal, his daughter leaves open. Still, whether she knows it or not, Tiana (Thi Thanh Nga) has followed General Giap's counsel, and in the process turned filial piety into guerrilla filmmaking of the very finest order.

Also reviewed in:
NEW YORK TIMES, 7/21/93, p. C13, Vincent Canby
VARIETY, 11/23/92, p. 51, Derek Elley
WASHINGTON POST, 6/1/93, p. C1, Hal Hinson
WASHINGTON POST, 10/4/93, p. B7, Hal Hinson

FUGITIVE, THE

A Warner Bros. release.   *Executive Producer:* Keith Barish and Roy Huggins.   *Producer:* Arnold Kopelson.   *Director:* Andrew Davis.   *Screenplay:* Jeb Stuart and David Twohy.   *Based on characters by:* Roy Huggins.   *Story:* David Twohy.   *Director of Photography:* Michael Chapman.   *Editor:* Dennis Virkler, David Finfer, Dean Goodhilll, Don Brochu, Richard Nord, and Dov Hoenig.   *Music:* James Newton Howard.   *Music Editor:* Jim Weidman.   *Sound:* Scott D. Smith and (music) Danny Wallin.   *Sound Editor:* John Leveque, Bruce Stambler, and Becky Sullivan.   *Casting:* Amanda Mackey and Cathy Sandrich.   *Production Designer:* Dennis Washington.   *Art Director:* Maher Ahmad.   *Set Designer:* Ann Harris and Nancy Mickelberry. *Set Decorator:* Rick Gentz.   *Special Effects:* Roy Arbogast and Tom Ryba.   *Costumes:* Aggie

Guerard Rodgers. *Make-up:* Peter Robb-King. *Stunt Coordinator:* Terry J. Leonard. *Running time:* 128 minutes. *MPAA Rating:* PG-13.

CAST: Harrison Ford (Dr. Richard Kimble);   Tommy Lee Jones (Samuel Gerard);   Helen Kimble (Sela Ward);   Julianne Moore (Dr. Anne Eastman;   Joe Pantoliano (Cosmo Renfro); Andreas Katsulas (Fred Sykes);   Jeroen Krabbé (Dr. Charles Nichols);   Daniel Roebuck (Biggs); L. Scott Caldwell (Poole);   Tom Wood (Newman);   Ron Dean (Detective Kelly);   Joseph Kosala (Detective Rosetti);   Miguel Nino and Tony Fosco (Chicago Cops);   Joseph F. Fisher (Otto Sloan);   James Liautuad (Paul);   David Darlow (Dr. Lentz);   Tom Galouzis and James F. McKinsey (Surgeons);   Mark D. Espinoza (Resident);   John E. Ellis (Anesthesiologist); Gene Barge and Thomas C. Simmons (11th District Cops); Joseph Guzaldo (Prosecutor);   Dick Cusack (Walter Gutherie);   Nick Kusenko (Assistant Defense Attorney);   Joan Kohn (Assistant Prosecuting Attorney);   Joe D. Lauck (Forensic Technician); Joseph V. Guastaferro (Coroner); Andy Romano (Judge Bennett);   Richard Riehle (Old Guard);   Thom Vernon (Carlson);   Ken Moreno (Partida);   Eddie "Bo" Smith, Jr. (Copeland);   Frank Ray Perilli and Otis Wilson (Jail Officers);   Pancho Demmings (Young Guard);   Jim Wilkey (Bus Driver);   Danny Goldring (Head Illinois State Trooper);   Nick Searcy (Sheriff Rawlins);   Kevin Crowley (State Trooper); Michael James (Head Welder);   Michael Skewes (Highway Patrolman);   Ila Cathleen Stallings (Duty Nurse);   Linda Casaletto (Rural Hospital Nurse);   Cody Glenn (Paramedic);   Cynthia Baker (Woman in Car);   Johnny Lee Davenport (Marshall Henry);   Mike Bacarella (Marshall Stevens);   Bill Cusack (Tracing Technician);   David Hodges (Marshall David);   Lillie Richardson (Copeland's Girlfriend);   Peter J. Caria, IV (Billy);   Tighe Barry (Windshield Washer);   Monika Chabrowski (Polish Landlady);   Lonnie Sima (Landlady's Son);   Oksana Fedunyszyn (Myoelectric Receptionist);   Orlando Garcia (Desmondo);   Afram Bill Williams (Salesman);   Bruce L. Gewertz (Dr. Bruce);   Jane Lynch (Dr. Kathy Wahlund);   Joseph Rotkvich (Officer Joseph);   Steven Lilovich (Officer Steve);   Noelle Bou-Silman (Myoelectric Technician);   Roxanne Roberts and Alex Hernandez (Trauma Doctors);   Theron Touche Lykes (Orderly);   Joel Robinson (Patient);   Greg Hollimon (Skating Orderly);   Cheryl Lynn Bruce (OR doctor);   Marie Ware (Nurse Gladys);   Bernard McGee (Man);   Ann Whitney (Myoelectric Director);   Lily Monkus and Willie Lucas (Desk Clerks);   Turk Muller (Clearing Officer);   Ann Marie Alvarez (La Cubana);   Eugene F. Crededio (Visitation Guard);   Maurice Person (Clive Driscoll);   Terry Hard (Officer Hormel);   Pam Zekman, David Pasquesi, Lester Holt, Jay Levine, and John Drummond (Newscasters);   Brent Shaphren, Stephen A. Landsman, and B.J. Jones (Doctors at Bar);   Drucilla A. Carlson (Gerard's Secretary);   Margaret Moore (Nichol's Assistant);   Manny Lopez (Seminar Doctor);   John M. Watson, Sr. (Bones Roosevelt); Kirsten Nelson (Betty);   Juan A. Ramirez (Man on "El");   Neil Flynn (Transit Cop);   Allen Hamilton (Host);   Eric Fudula (Hotel Security Guard).

CHRISTIAN SCIENCE MONITOR, 8/9/93, p. 13, David Sterritt

Every dedicated watcher of 1960s television knows the story. Our hero is Dr. Richard Kimble, a privileged and prominent man who suddenly finds himself in a very tight spot. His wife has been murdered, and he's been convicted of the crime.

But he manages to escape just before the prison door clangs shut, and the only way he can stay off death row is to track down the real killer by himself—while also evading the tenacious cop who has vowed to track him down.

"The Fugitive" made its debut on ABC in 1963. It enjoyed a four-year run, culminating in a final episode that drew more viewers than any series episode ever had.

More than 25 years later, Hollywood has finally taken on Dr. Kimble and company in its own '90s fashion.

The movie version of "The Fugitive" is tough, noisy, and violent—barely staying within the confines of a PG-13 rating for its medical material as well as its bursts of gunplay and fighting.

But while it won't win Oscars for subtlety, it might win them in other categories. It's as powerful as it is bruising, with more surprises than "Jurassic Park" and more sheer energy than any action movie this season.

There's also an interesting theme—which is suggested rather than probed, but gives "The Fugitive" an edge over the fluff that Hollywood normally concentrates on during the warm-weather months. Kimble is a physician, and it turns out that his wife's murder resulted from big-money skullduggery in the medical and pharmaceutical worlds; this idea is developed by the movie's images and dialogue, which contrast humane doctors (like Kimble) with others who care about profits more than patients.

I'm not suggesting that this subplot makes "The Fugitive" into an intellectual event, but the screenplay's interest in a real problem like money-driven medical care is commendably thoughtful alongside the backward-looking fantasies of a "Jurassic Park."

"The Fugitive" was directed by Andrew Davis, whose career has been anything but distinguished, consisting mostly of Chuck Norris and Steven Seagal exploitation pictures. While he deserves credit for pulling the elements of "The Fugitive"into a tidy package, it's impossible to watch the movie without recognizing the capable contributions of others.

Chief among them are stars Harrison Ford as Kimble, and Tommy Lee Jones as the deputy marshal on his trail. Advance word had that Jones gives the performance of his career and steals the picture from under Ford's nose.

I'm not convinced that Jones outdoes his weirdly excellent work in "J.F.K." or his vivid portrayal in "The Executioner's Song," but he is certainly in top form here—and so is Ford, who really does give the performance of his career, particularly in the early scenes.

Behind the camera, top credit goes to Michael Chapman, whose rich cinematography recalls the extraordinary work he did on Martin Scorsese's classics "Taxi Driver" and "Raging Bull," among other pictures. His nighttime views of Chicago are especially vivid, surrounding the film's shoot-'em-up aspects with an atmosphere of dark mysterious beauty.

No fewer than six editors stitched his shots together, giving the most hard-hitting scenes a furious rhythm that contributes greatly to their impact.

Like so many of today's movies, "The Fugitive" goes on too long; it's well over two hours and could easily be trimmed by 30 or 40 minutes. It's also more violent than it had to be. But it delivers the goods that summertime audiences demand, and I expect it will be one of the year's major hits.

FILMS IN REVIEW, 10/93, p. 328, Andy Pawelczak

The Fugitive, Andrew Davis' intelligent new thriller, is based on a mid-sixties TV series about a man wrongfully accused of killing his wife. The TV show, perhaps because it went on and on for four years with basically the same plot, had a dreamy, timeless feeling (or perhaps it just seems that way in the alchemical theater of memory)—darkness, pursuit, pursuer and pursued like figures on a frieze eternally frozen in mid-step. Davis' film takes the opposite tack: almost from the beginning the pace is furious. *The Fugitive* is another big Hollywood thrill machine, but within its genre limitations it's frequently compelling and has two excellent performances by Harrison Ford and Tommy Lee Jones.

Ford plays Richard Kimble, the rich doctor falsely convicted of murdering his wife (we see the murder in grainy fragmented flashbacks). For the movie's first fifteen minutes, Kimble is in a trance as he's tried and sentenced to death, but when the other inmates on a prison transport bus stage an escape he wakes up and stays fiercely awake for the rest of the movie as he evades the police and tries to clear his name. The escape scene, one of the movie's big set-pieces, involves a spectacular train wreck and is followed soon after by a death defying leap from a high dam. Davis choreographs these scenes very skillfully (audiences tend to applaud the train wreck), but basically they're just higher intensity versions of things we've seen before, and I began to worry about what he would do for the rest of the movie. Once Kimble gets back to Chicago, however, things settle down as he searches for a mysterious one-armed man who is the real killer. Ultimately, the denouement involves medical skulduggery and a big pharmaceutical company, appropriate objects for our contemplation in this Age of Hillary.

As Kimble, Harrison Ford achieves the seemingly impossible, making a rich doctor into a sympathetic point of identification. Despite the superhuman heroics early on, Kimble is a vulnerable, wounded hero. Through most of the movie's second half, as Kimble hides out from the police and tracks the one-armed man, he's the-man-alone-in-a-crowd of 20th century existentialist mythology, the impenetrable monad sitting opposite us on the subway whose real life takes place somewhere well outside of our lines of sight. The triumph of Ford's performance is that with minimal dialogue and acting he lets us see both Kimble's anxiety and his intelligence—he even makes the cliche of tapping into a computer's data base seem interesting.

Davis splits the film's focus between Kimble and Sam Gerard (Tommy Lee Jones), the picture's other point-of-view character, a federal marshal who relentlessly pursues the fugitive. As Kimble searches for the one-armed man, Gerard, just a heart beat behind, predicts his every move, and Davis builds tension through adroit cross cutting between cop and fugitive. (As in *In the Line of Fire*, the two principals don't connect until the end.) Gerard is just as smart and determined as Kimble but has a very different style. Where Kimble is all bottled up anguish and cerebral inwardness, Gerard is a wise cracking extrovert who wades into crowds and instantly takes command. We first see him in the chaos of the train wreck, taking over the investigation with a few barked orders and imperious gestures. After awhile, Gerard's imperiousness becomes the film's best joke; his characteristic gesture is a wave of the hand as he orders his subordinates to clear the area. As Gerard, Tommy Lee Jones has just the right authority leavened by flashes of ironic self-awareness. At one point, he calls himself the big dog, but with his leonine grace and oddly beautiful mask-like face he's really a big cat.

Andrew Davis up until now has been a genre director—his best known previous films were with Chuck Norris and Steven Seagal—but with this movie he's pushing the envelope. Without straying far from the laws of the contemporary big-budget action thriller (a lot of action, elaborate special effects, minimal distracting character development etc.), he gives *The Fugitive* more depth than we're accustomed to in this kind of movie, mostly through the nuanced and contrasting acting styles of Ford and Jones but also through his mise en scene. The movie eschews a high-contrast film noir look in favor of a gray diurnal Chicago cut up into pieces of a jig-saw puzzle (we frequently experience a slight lag of consciousness as we wonder where we are). *The Fugitive* doesn't have anything as resonant as the famous scene in *North by Northwest* (a film very different in tone but with a similar archetypal, Kafkaesque theme—the pursuit of a falsely accused man) in which Cary Grant is chased across an open field by a crop-duster as persistent as an angry horsefly, but it has a few moments that will stay with me and the picture as a whole has a dark, suggestive nimbus. I'll remember a scruffy, cold forest impeding Harrison Ford's escape, the everyday chaos of a hospital in which Kimble adopts the protective coloration of a maintenance worker, Tommy Lee Jones' mysterious face, Ford walking into the dark maw of a railroad tunnel and later on walking out of a flophouse into a neon-studded skid row somewhere in the dangerous labyrinth of the city.

NEW YORK, 8/16/93, p. 57, David Denby

The art of the movies, once celebrated as the wonder of the twentieth century, has become in the nineties a subject for nostalgia and fond hopes; and mere professionalism in moviemaking has begun to count for more than it used to. *The Fugitive*, like the beautifully disciplined thriller *In the Line of Fire*, is a case of skill and dedication transforming clichéd material into something freshly exciting. *The Fugitive* may not be art, but it displays craft of the highest order. Before the credits sequence is over, you know you're in more than capable hands, too: *The Fugitive* could be described as a nonstop chase. But if this sounds like something you would like to avoid, consider that *The Fugitive* has two remarkable men in it and a mystery at its heart. Inventive and spectacular as it is, the movie is also a brazenly enjoyable celebration of high intelligence.

I wish I could say something—anything—about the old David Janssen TV series *The Fugitive*, which played for four successful seasons back in the sixties and serves as the basis for this movie; but the truth is I can't remember ever sitting through an episode. That voice! That face! David Janssen's heavy rumble cast a spell of sanctimony over sixties TV. This time the main character, Dr. Richard Kimble, is played by Harrison Ford, who himself has contributed little to the gaiety of American life in recent years. But Ford, in his grim and troubled way, is a genuine movie star—his presence is heroically haggard. Do you remember the story? Kimble, a Chicago surgeon ... falsely convicted of murdering his wife ... escapes from imprisonment and eludes his pursuers while attempting to track down the real killer ... who is ... um ... a one-armed man. Sounds idiotic, I know, but Ford's nemesis—a U.S. marshal—is Tommy Lee Jones, that unknown great American actor, and the movie turns into a duel between two superior men.

The essence of thriller-making is to push past ordinary realism, push, push, but not too far—that is, not to the point of flagrant implausibility. A great director of thrillers knows how to make physical fantasy convincing. Andrew Davis, the American who has done good genre work with Chuck Norris (*Code of Silence*) and Steven Seagal (*Under Siege*), may be a new master of this tricky game of I've-seen-it-but-I-just-barely-believe-it. There are no higher meanings in *The Fugitive*, and no Hitchcockian perversities either; the movie is about force hurtling through space, about movement. Yet Davis is an inventive and witty man; he's mastered the intensity of momentum without producing the boredom of momentum.

In Chicago, at Richard Kimble's townhouse, Richard's wife (Sela Ward) is killed by a mysterious assailant. The scene, in black-and-white, plays in nightmarish fragments through the opening of the movie. In these early scenes, the cinematography (by Michael Chapman) and the editing (by Dennis Virkler and David Finfer) are so precisely calibrated for ambiguity that the event yields its full truth only gradually. Convicted of the murder on the basis of circumstantial evidence, Kimble is riding in a prison bus when some of the other prisoners start a revolt. And that's when the movie really takes off. The bus goes over a ravine and lands on a railroad track as a freight train pulls into sight. *Push, push, but not too far* ... Davis places cameras in both the bus and the train, and cuts back and forth between the two as they converge; there's a terrific impact, and the train jumps the rails and, still going hard, crashes through the woods, right on the tail of the escaping Ford. It's as if the untracked engine were chasing him. Can paranoia get any wilder than that?

Tommy Lee Jones shows up, as U.S. marshal Sam Gerard, and the movie notches to a higher level of intensity—and then stays there. Jones has a large forehead, deep-set dark eyes, rough skin, and a rather frightening smile that suggests a skull forcing itself into mirth. He's too unnerving-looking to play ordinary roles, and over the years, he has developed his own offhand way of doing things, a devastating style of delivery, rapid, casual, terse. As Sam Gerard, he sends out orders to his staff at lightning speed but with just enough stress or humor so that each order seems to fit into a long personal relationship. He knows these people; he can control them with a slight shift in intonation. They are held together by jokes, past experience—but everything flows from him, the coolest boss in the world. One of the most fascinating things in the movie is the way this very tough man soothes a badly frightened young federal agent (Tom Wood) who has a sweet face and a ponytail. Mastering him, gentling him, he takes control, but not in the cornball, drawling, paternal style of John Wayne. Jones is coolly malevolent, and he does a superbly witty impersonation of a man in total command. His speed and lightness are like a tap dancer's elegance; he throws things away—words, gestures, props.

Gerard's job is to catch an escaped prisoner, not to settle a matter of guilt or innocence, and so there's a suggestion of mischief in Jones's happiness, an amoral pleasure in the hunt. All the actors working as his staff (including Joe Pantoliano) catch this sense of slightly vicious fun: We're smart, and we're perfectly happy hounding this poor son of a bitch who claims he didn't kill his wife. They chase Kimble through the woods, in a sewer, over a waterfall, in hospitals, in Chicago buildings, in a parade, on and on, each time coming closer but never actually getting him.

While the pursuers are enjoying their professional expertise, Kimble is out there hiding, running, and scrounging, and Harrison Ford makes him more and more angry. About ten years ago, a baffling heaviness settled into Ford's manner. In his mysteriously solemn performances in *Working Girl* and *Presumed Innocent*, there seemed to be some irony, some joke that we weren't getting. Maybe he wasn't getting it, either: He began to look almost haunted. But this time, the manner fits the role. More spooked and furrowed than ever, he unleashes his impressive strength and endurance, his capacity for suffering. If he doesn't find his wife's killer, Dr. Kimble will either be executed or spend the rest of his life in hiding. Instinctively, he does what a dedicated doctor is used to doing—he hangs around his hospital in Chicago. It's his home turf, and, carelessly disguised, he insinuates himself into the building, slipping into and out of different roles, even practicing a little medicine on the run, all the while looking for clues to the identity of the one-armed killer.

The movie becomes an exhilarating duel between matched intellects. Gerard the supercop, as inexorable as Inspector Javert in *Les Misérables*, says he doesn't care whether Kimble murdered his wife or not. Yet he can't catch Kimble, smart as he is. It finally occurs to Gerard that the only way to bring in Kimble is to find the actual murderer. Unwavering will gets overtaken by something like wisdom. At the end, hunter and quarry confront each other as brothers: An emotional bond has developed between them. Yet the end of *The Fugitive* wouldn't be as satisfying as it is if the ruthless chase had not been told, moment by moment, with such superb Hollywood professionalism.

NEW YORK POST, 8/6/93, p. 23, Michael Medved

"The Fugitive" is so good that watching it leaves you physically exhausted.

Some films challenge the mind or stir the emotions, but this one connects at a more visceral level, producing shortness of breath and racing heart. It makes no logical sense, but, so help me, after two hours of running alongside Harrison Ford through some of the most spectacular chase scenes ever filmed, you feel as if you've just completed a significant aerobic workout.

To give this picture its due, you should put aside any thoughts of the 30-year-old TV series that inspired it. Starring the late David Janssen, that show ran on ABC from 1963 through 1967, and the movie has borrowed the basic setup from the old series, but little else.

Dr. Richard Kimble is a prominent physician wrongly convicted of the murder of his wife. He escapes from custody, and sets out to find the real killer—a mysterious one-armed man—in order to clear his name.

The main obstacle in his quest for justice is a ferociously formidable lawman who's pursuing him. Deputy U.S. Marshall Gerard as played by Tommy Lee Jones, is a consummate professional who isn't interested in Kimble's guilt or innocence; he's merely concerned with doing his job, and that means putting the collar on an escaped con.

When the two men confront each other in a drain pipe (a reminder that the whole "Fugitive" concept was originally borrowed from Victor Hugo's "Les Miserables," with its famous chase through the sewers of Paris), Harrison Ford shouts out that he's innocent.

Jones answers back with total conviction, "I don't care!" His performance, perfectly combining menace, brilliance and fierce dedication to duty, is a stunning achievement that may well earn him an Oscar nomination as best supporting actor.

Harrison Ford, for all his mastery of the tremendous physical demands of his role, isn't quite up to that level. He goes through the movie communicating one emotion—grim determination in the face of pain and tragedy—but he does project that emotion well.

Meanwhile, the chase scenes and special effects are so mind-bogglingly impressive that you won't have much time to notice acting. Early in the film, when the prison bus carrying Kimble skids off a road, then is flattened by an on-rushing train, the movie features a sequence that is such a stunning combination of cinematography, bone-chilling sound-recording and brilliant editing that preview audiences have been greeting the screening with wild applause.

The most serious quibble anyone could have with "The Fugitive" involves the way it finally explains the mysterious murder of Kimble's wife; the plot that the good doctor uncovers turns out to be both absurdly complicated and, unhappily, unconvincing.

Meanwhile, there's a showy, overblown climax involving Kimble, Gerard and the guilty mastermind who set all this unhappiness in motion that goes on much too long.

Despite these shortcomings, the film is a major triumph for director Andrew Davis. In the past, he has created hard-hitting action films for Steven Seagal ("Above the Law" and "Under Siege") and Chuck Norris ("Code of Silence"), but this time out he shows what he can do when he's finally given a good script (co-written by the creator of "Die Hard") and a leading man who can deliver lines as well as he delivers blows.

The violence here is chilling when it needs to be, but never sadistic; there's none of the cartoon-ish or gratuitous cruelty you saw in "Cliffhanger," for instance.

Throughout the film, Davis handles characters as skillfully as he handles stunts, so you come to care deeply about Dr. Kimble and his fate. That's why you go home feeling personally drained, since you've run many torturous miles in his heroic shoes.

NEWSDAY, 8/6/93, Part II/p. 54, Jack Mathews

Looking ahead to this summer's movie schedule, you might have thought Hollywood was holding an Action Directors World Championship. There was "Die Hard's" Renny Harlin, with

"Cliffhanger," "The Hunt for Red October's" John McTiernan with "Last Action Hero," "Das Boot's" Wolfgang Petersen with "In the Line of Fire," and the Grand Master himself, Steven Spielberg, with "Jurassic Park."

In addition, Sydney Pollack and Philip Kaufman, directors whose tastes run toward more sophisticated fare, were trying their hands at popcorn thrillers being adapted from pulp novels, respectively John Grisham's "The Firm" and Michael Crichton's "Rising Sun."

Now that all of the summer's action movies are in the theaters, we can declare a champion, and it is ... none of the above. The best directed action film this summer, one of the best in years, is relative newcomer Andrew Davis' "The Fugitive."

Davis got this job the hard way, by making a good action movie starring one of the most wooden actors of the 20th Century, Steven Seagal ("Under Siege"). By casting great villains and making them the focus of that film, Davis turned a B movie into an A movie. With Harrison Ford and "The Fugitive," Davis has A material all the way, and he uses his opportunity to put on an action director's clinic.

From the spectacular opening combination bus/train wreck sequence to the rooftop finale, "The Fugitive" is a study in protracted thrills, tension, suspense and hair-breadth escapes, a nonstop chase film with people on the run you actually care about, Hollywood melodrama doesn't get any better than this.

The quick pace of "The Fugitive" contrasts sharply with the TV drama of the mid-'60s. That ABC series moved haltingly, partly because of the late David Janssen's laconic portrayal of Dr. Richard Kimble, and partly because of the episodic nature of TV itself.

The movie solves both problems. Ford, an actor who projects both rugged physicality and penetrating intelligence, plays the good doctor as if he were prescribing himself amphetamines, and the script, by Jeb Stuart ("Die Hard") and David Twohy, tells in two hours a mystery that kept TV viewers hanging for four repetitive seasons.

And, no, if you were among the 72 percent of American TV viewers who tuned in to the last show on Aug, 29, 1967, the movie does not end the same way.

The general circumstances, however, are familiar, Dr. Kimble is a well-regarded Chicago surgeon who, after being convicted of murdering his wife, escapes custody and starts off in quest of the one-armed man he saw leaving his house after his wife's death. From the moment of his escape, Kimble is pursued by a relentlessly obsessive cop, in this telling Deputy U.S. Marshal Sam Gerard (a career performance by Tommy Lee Jones), and the race is on to see who catches whom first.

The Stuart-Twohy script compacts the double chase into a time frame of a few days, most of it set in Chicago, where Kimble returns to stalk his wife's killer.

If you step back from the story for a moment, little of what occurs is plausible. Kimble turns out to be not only a great doctor and a great humanitarian, finding time in his own crises to make lifesaving medical prognoses for ailing strangers, but also a sleuth of Sherlockian proportions. And the way Deputy Gerard and his federal agents browbeat the local police defies the muscular reputation of Chicago's finest.

But you won't be able to step back. Davis sets the hook so quickly and so deeply in the opening minutes of "The Fugitive"—for my money the most energetically orchestrated opening act of any film since "Raiders of the Lost Ark"—that you just hang on and ride it out.

Before the opening credits have rolled, we have met Kimble and his wife (Sela Ward), learned much about their relationship and life-style, seen scenes from the murder and have attended the interrogation, trial and conviction of the wrong man. Moments later, an attempted escape by fellow convicts sends their prison bus tumbling down a hill into the path of an oncoming train, leaving Kimble just seconds to clear his head, rescue an injured guard and leap to safety.

That train/bus collision was shot on a real track, with a real train and bus, and photographed from as many angles as an NFL touchdown pass. There were even cameras inside the two vehicles. The only thing faked was Kimble's jump from the bus. The squealing of the trains' metal wheels, the impact, the numbing noise of crunching metal, all real, all edited into a tight few seconds of footage that rank among the great action sequences on film.

Davis obviously goes for realism wherever possible. Later in the movie he has Gerard chase Kimble through the streets of Chicago during the St. Patrick's Day Parade. The actual parade. Davis just sent the actors and camera crews into the streets and told them to get what they could.

Still, it is the characters who make "The Fugitive" work so well. Kimble and Gerard are not traditional opponents; they are both good guys following their instincts. The sadistic glee with which Gerard stalks Kimble taints his goodness a little, but Jones, one of Davis' marvelous "Under Siege" villains, leavens Gerard's dark side with enough humor to keep him sympathetic.

All in all, Hollywood has made this a great summer for action fans, and with "The Fugitive," it saved its best for last.

NEWSWEEK, 8/9/93, p. 57, David Ansen

For four seasons on ABC in the mid-60s, they chased down escaped prisoner Dr. Richard Kimble, the physician unjustly convicted of murdering his wife. Three decades later, they're still after the poor guy—and he's still desperately using his wits to find the one-armed man who committed the crime. Only now Kimble is played by Harrison Ford, not David Janssen, and his worthy adversary, the federal marshal obsessed with capturing him, is Tommy Lee Jones. Yes, The Fugitive is back, compressed by writers Jeb Stuart and David Twohy and director Andrew Davis into a fast and furious feature film that starts at a gallop and never stops to catch its breath.

Davis, who made the underrated thriller "The Package" and the clever Steven Seagal hit "Under Siege" (in which Jones's villain stole the movie from Seagal's clunky hero), favors gritty settings and a rough-edged style. His action movies are slick and charged with energy, but not in the sleek manner of John McTiernan ("Die Hard"); his quasi-documentary style lends power to this paranoid "wrong man" fantasy, and helps us forget just how farfetched the plot really is.

Ford and Jones, like Eastwood and Malkovich in "In the Line of Fire," anchor the flamboyant suspense in reality. The secret of good action movies this summer seems to be stars who aren't afraid to show their mileage. Battle scarred, brainy and equipped with a healthy quota of irony, these two veterans give "The Fugitive's" plentiful thrills a sense of soul. Only at the drawn-out ending does this cunning entertainment wear out its welcome. But by then you may be too wrung out to notice.

SIGHT AND SOUND, 10/93, p. 45, Kim Newman

Chicago. Richard Kimble, a respected vascular surgeon, returns home to find his wife Helen has been murdered by a one-armed man who struggles with him and escapes. On circumstantial evidence, Kimble is convicted of murder and sentenced to death. En route to prison, another convict fakes illness and stabs a guard, causing the bus to plunge off the road and on to a railroad track. The driver uncuffs Kimble so that he can see to the guard's wound and it falls to him to haul the man free when a train ploughs into the bus. Kimble makes his way to a rural hospital where he shaves off his beard and tends his injuries, while deputy marshall Samuel Gerard and his team take over the escape case.

Gerard picks up the trail and runs Kimble to ground, pursuing him into the tunnels behind a dam and confronting him at a precipitous outlet. When Gerard tells him he does not care if his quarry is innocent, Kimble jumps and is assumed dead by everyone but Gerard. In Chicago, Kimble contacts Dr Charles Nichols, a colleague, for a hand-out and impersonates a hospital janitor to gain access to computer records about prosthetic arms. Nichols admits to Gerard that Kimble is still alive. Gerard, following in his quarry's steps, also examines the records of men with prostheses. Kimble visits an imprisoned one-armed man who turns out not to be the killer; Gerard nearly catches him in the county lock-up but he escapes into a St. Patrick's Day parade. Kimble learns that the murderer is Fred Sykes, an ex-cop employed by a pharmaceuticals firm which wants to market the drug Kimble was involved in testing.

Kimble realises he was the intended murder victim and that Nichols, hoping to conceal the harmful side-effects of the drug, was instrumental in setting him up. Kimble phones Gerard from Sykes' apartment, knowing the call will be traced, and Gerard begins to piece together the evidence. Sykes attacks Kimble on an elevated railway train and is overpowered and left handcuffed to a pole. Kimble goes to a hotel where a medical conference is in progress and confronts Nichols during a speech. Kimble and Nichols fight and Kimble wins. Gerard catches up with them, finally admitting that Kimble is innocent. Vindicated, Kimble is taken back into custody.

Devised by Roy Huggins and produced by Quinn Martin, *The Fugitive* TV series ran from 1963, when David Janssen's Dr David Kimble was first convicted of the murder committed by the one-armed man, to 1967, when Barry Morse's Lieutenant Gerard finally caught up with him and was forced to admit he had been pursuing the wrong man. A surprisingly subtle rethink of *Les Misérables*, the show was, while it was on the air, uniquely open-ended. Its hero faced problems that could not be solved within the 47 minute running time of a typical episode.

Sadly, the most disturbing aspect—the possibility that Dr Kimble, like successors such as Smith and Jones or the Incredible Hulk, would be left running in limbo without ever clearing his name—has inevitably been dropped in this feature version, which simply sticks together the plots of the pilot and the famous two-part story that wound up the series. What was interesting was the way a quirk of justice forced the middle-class Kimble to become an itinerant blue-collar worker, constantly dropped into situations that revealed social injustice. Despite his brief spell as a hispanic janitor, Harrison Ford's Kimble focuses resolutely on his own problem, never distracted, as Janssen was, by other people's plights. Four years of television, only a fraction of which dealt with Kimble's case, are here compressed into the hardly unfamiliar story of the innocent man on the run, trying to clear his name.

Given that it is shorn of much of its original purpose, *The Fugitive* is a remarkably successful Hollywood product, with a brilliantly contrived star double act pursuing different paths through the central plot. There is much pleasure to be had in the way Kimble and Gerard, respecting each other as the heroes and villains of Budd Boetticher Westerns used to, continually keep each other abreast of their investigations, solving the mystery together while rarely meeting. Andrew Davis, a newly promoted action man who has worked fruitfully with Tommy Lee Jones in *The Package* and *Under Siege*, makes the huffing and puffing chases seem fresh and surprising, managing with ingenuity such coups as the perilous bus crash that lands the survivors in the path of an oncoming train.

Early on, the film takes a tricksy approach in undercutting Kimble's interrogation with his memories of the evening of the murder, not quite revealing enough information for us to judge what has actually happened until we are well into the chase. A medical conspiracy appears out of nowhere after about an hour of action, which gives rise to a few groaning moments and a confused expository sequence involving several subsidiary crimes. A whiff of 90s minority awareness can be detected in the needless complication which reveals the handicapped Sykes to be a lesser villain in the employ of an unconvincing mastermind.

Having suffered through the meretricious seriousness of *Regarding Henry* and the equally fudged pulp of *Patriot Games*, Harrison Ford finally gains back respect as the improbably hardy Dr Richard Kimble, grimly surviving certain death and dropping years when he shaves off his white-tinged beard. The most interesting character, as in the series, is Gerard; while Barry Morse's cop was a near-psychotic loner, Jones' marshall is surrounded by a Hawksian team he alternately cajoles and abuses with a delightful stream of patter. It is Gerard's professionalism which keeps him on the case even when the quarry is almost certainly dead ("That'll make him easier to catch, then") and forces him finally to concede not only that Kimble is innocent but that his innocence matters.

TIME, 8/9/93, p. 57, Richard Schickel

A smart federal law enforcement officer, his wit informed by years of experience and buttressed by all the latest crime-fighting technology; a cunning, daring criminal managing always to stay just an infuriating half step ahead of his pursuer; a final confrontation that begins at a large, celebratory public occasion, proceeds to vertiginous grapplings along the edge of a big-city high-rise and ends with justice done by the narrowest, scariest of margins.

Old news, you say. You've already seen and loved *In the Line of Fire*. Well, here comes another movie that deploys similar elements, including deeply satisfying star performances and high-energy directorial craftsmanship. The difference between them arises from a couple of simple role reversals. In *The Fugitive* the criminal is actually an innocent man: Richard Kimble (Harrison Ford), a surgeon falsely accused of murdering his wife. The lawman—a U.S. marshal named Sam Gerard (Tommy Lee Jones)—is the character in the grips of a dangerous obsession, namely to capture the eponymous escapee.

The best measure of this movie's merits is that the cross-reference that springs most readily to mind is another well-made current movie. But everyone knows *The Fugitive* derives its title, protagonist and basic situation from the 1960s television series in which David Janssen, as the luckless Kimble, was pursued across many years and many states by Barry Morse's implacable detective. It was *Les Misérables* in prime time, and that overtone is lost in this adaptation, which compresses the pursuit and confines it mostly to Chicago. But the tension and realism that result from permitting Kimble less running room amply compensate for the diminishment of the original's romantic aura.

Not all that was good about the old Kimble has been lost. He can still spare risky time to help others, like a child being ignored, at peril to his life, in an emergency room. He still has the recklessness that comes to people who have nothing left to lose (the most spectacular of his hairbreadth escapes is a dive into the torrent coursing over a dam hundreds of feet high). And he still has his own pursuit to pursue—of the one-armed man whom he alone knows is his wife's actual murderer.

Busy fellow, and nobody plays harried better than Harrison Ford. He plays other things well too, notably in the scene in which, as he is interrogated by the police, he comes to realize that he is their chief suspect. Grief, outrage, incomprehension, terror—what a rich mixture of emotions he registers in a matter of seconds. Jones may have a somewhat simpler line to play in the movie, but he is a marvelously incisive actor, and he brings his character right up to the edge of the demonic without falling into the psychotic abyss. He is playing the role of a man playing a role—tough omnicompetence—and the little flickers of ironic self-awareness he permits himself as he judges his effect on others are delicious.

Which brings us back to a final comparison with *In the Line of Fire*. Both these movies are tightly wound duels between vividly contrasting characters who match up only in the quality of their intelligence. Both more than satisfy the most primitive demand of the action genre, which is, of course, for plenty of action. But unlike most films of their kind these days, they do not feel machine-made. They take the time (and it doesn't require much) for the digressions that enlist real concern—not just in what's going to happen next, but in the fates of their characters as well.

VILLAGE VOICE, 8/17/93, p. 56, Joe Levy

Maybe there actually are a finite number of tales to be told, but *Batman*, *The Addams Family*, *The Flintstones*, *The Jetsons*, *The Beverly Hillbillies*,—what's next *The McLaughlin Group: Men in Tights*? (Brian Dennehy, call your agent.) No, it's *The Fugitive* another in a chain of small-to big-screen jumps, the emerging film archetype of the '90s: You know the story, now see the stunts. But *The Fugitive* doesn't fit the mold. For one thing, the TV series it's based on isn't exactly a big deal to the PG-13s that'll be lining up around the block for this precisely wrought action film. For another, at its center it's a parody of every "reality"-based cop show on the air: The U.S. marshals keep cornering their prey, only to find he's slipped through their net, time after time.

There seems to be real intelligence at work here, as if in trying to make *Die Hard* with pathos, director Andrew Davis couldn't just go for bigger and deffer, he had to struggle with the action-flick conventions he'd executed faithfully on Steven Seagal's behalf in *Above the Law* (as, bad as you think) and *Under Siege* (better). Things don't start well for him, though: He leads with a murder, filmed in slow-mo grainy black and white, and though its languid connection to choreographed Hollywood sex may be meant as disquieting, it's more disgusting. The exposition that follows is laced with flashbacks of the violence—Dr. Richard Kimble's wife has been murdered by a one-armed man, and as his story is told, first to the Chicago police, then to the judge, it comes to life for us, in bits and pieces.

It's only after the murder, the investigation, and the trial have been gotten out of the way and Dr. Kimble (Harrison Ford) is on his way to prison—all of 15 minutes in—that Davis uncorks something fresh. What's more special an effect, he asks, than Harrison Ford running from that gargantuan marble in *Raiders of the Lost Ark*? The answer is an audaciously overstated visual allusion: Harrison Ford hopping around in leg irons, fleeing from a runaway train in *The Fugitive*. This train wreck is magnificently out of scale, goofy in its grandeur, at once playing to the Hollywood dictum that shit oughta blow up shortly after the opening credits and playing with that same impulse for immediate apocalyptic gratification. The crash transforms Kimble from prisoner to fugitive, and it signals that things are off and rolling just the way that big marble did 12 years ago, but it does so with an explosive energy that Spielberg was foolish enough to save for the *end* of his movie.

Davis sustains that energy, delivering the requisite spills and thrills, but something more: a jagged paranoia that's the downside to the rush of every big stunt. Soon, what began as conventional Hollywood shit clicks into place, as if to say, as they do about certain drugs, that this is *really great* shit. Davis's fondness for skycam shots of Chicago's towers, for instance, seems at first little more than expensive. But as Kimble goes underground—fleeing through drainage pipes, sleeping beneath leaf piles, renting a basement room—those helicopter pans become a release from all the mounting tension. And when that slow-motion murder footage replays in Kimble's dreams, it merges—strangely, sadly—with half-remembered tender moments, slashes of sexual pleasure, and flashes of light in a sex/death connection that is disquieting. Before long, everything begins to resemble the bad speed trip of those dreams. Grimy, overamped, unrelenting, *The Fugitive* is given to an excitement that's always a cover for fear, and that's just one of the ways it reroutes expectations. Though Harrison Ford has top billing here, he spends more time looking over his shoulder than he does speaking; he's not this movie's hero, he's its victim. Maybe that's why *The Fugitive* is the only summer action picture that doesn't feel like a James Bond descendant—Fritz Lang's *Fury* is more like it.

The Fugitive's real hero doubles as its villain, or one of them. As U.S. Marshal Samuel Gerard, Tommy Lee Jones pursues Ford with unexplained obsession, pausing only to crack wise with screwball wit or *noir* terseness. He's a charismatic urban cowboy—"Call me deputy," he corrects someone who's made the mistake of addressing him as "officer"—in command of a conspicuously multicultural posse (the U.S. marshals, evidently, take affirmative action much more seriously than the Chicago cops, who are, here at least, uniformly white, male, and stupid). Jones swaggers lovably, leaking compassion around the edges, and his performance—charged with a particularly American mythos—steals the show. You don't know who to root for, Kimble or Gerard.

Kimble, of course, in part because he's unable to go almost anywhere without saving someone's life (usually with a cop standing by watching, but not recognizing him), but mostly because he gets the better of the authorities. There's a distinctly antiauthoritarian bent to *The Fugitive* one of its advantages over in *In the Line of Fire*, though the lack of directorial missteps doesn't hurt, either). It's not just the cop, walking down a hospital hallway with a fax of Kimble stopping the good doctor and telling him to zip his fly, it's that fax, too. Gerard and his marshals have at their disposal all the tools of the information age, but Kimble's no-tech beats out their hi-tech every time. It's as if Davis had embedded a little lesson about the action film—always eager to soak up a new toy in search of a bigger bang—way down inside his movie: Use all the technology you want, nothing tops ingenuity driven by basic terror.

Also reviewed in:
CHICAGO TRIBUNE, 8/6/93, Friday/p. A, Clifford Terry
NEW REPUBLIC, 9/20 & 27/93, p. 36, Stanley Kauffmann
NEW YORK TIMES, 8/6/93, p. C1, Janet Maslin
NEW YORKER, 8/16/93, p. 93, Anthony Lane
VARIETY, 8/9/93, p. 34 Leonard Klady
WASHINGTON POST, 8/6/93, p. D1, Rita Kempley
WASHINGTON POST, 8/6/93, Weekend/p. 33, Desson Howe

GARDEN OF SCORPIONS

A Film Forum presentation of a Lenfilm/Experimental Studio/Cineclub Zer Kala production. *Director:* Oleg Kovalov. *Screenplay (Russian with English subtitles):* Oleg Kovalov. *Director of Photography:* Anatoly Lapschow. *Editor:* Subeava and A. Karelin. *Music:* Carl Orff, Bela Bartok, and Dmitri Shostakovich. *Sound:* Garri Velenki. *Special Effects:* L. Krasnova. *Running time:* 96 minutes. *MPAA Rating:* Not Rated.

NEW YORK POST, 3/17/93, p. 23, Matthew Flamm

First the Berlin Wall comes down. Then the Soviet Union dissolves. And now—experimental films from the former land of socialist realism.

Is nothing sacred?

"Garden of Scorpions," a self-described "optical poem," is a kind of fever dream of the Cold War, combining clips from newsreels and dizzyingly weird but official Soviet movies from the 1920s through the 50s. The Russian film, which provides an appropriate if overwhelming complement to the Sergei Eisenstein program also at the Film Forum.

Some of the material is frightening—much more so than anything in an American Red Scare movie. An endless field of North Korean troops—spookily well-behaved—greets a Russian friendship committee. Carl Orffs "Carmina Burana" comes up on the sound track, its exaggerated choruses the perfect background to a totalitarian vista.

Some of the material is funny, in an unsettling way. A madman in a Soviet pseudo-documentary on mental health explains that he wrote "all 10 of Shostakovich's symphonies" (*and* he wrote all of Mayakovsky's poems).

There's also a quality of (slightly smug) hindsight to the film: We're shown—over and over—who collaborated. A very young Yves Montand eagerly sings and dances before a Soviet audience (a very beautiful Simone Signoret looks on). The wonderful Italian actress Giulietta Massina accepts an award.

Eisenstein—whose theories of montage provided the blueprint for "Scorpions"—prances ridiculously as a London bobby in a 1930 documentary. I wasn't sure what the point was here—sometimes the intentions of "Scorpions" writer-director Oleg Kovalov remain obscure.

Self-consciously experimental and much too long, "Garden of Scorpions" is not without narrative: The films flash in and out of "The Case of Corporal Kotschetkov," a 1955 melodrama in which a naive soldier falls for a pure-Russian beauty, who turns out to be working for a ring of capitalist secret agents.

The clunky spy story is so loopy and paranoid that it could be the sustained hallucination of J. Edgar Hoover's opposite number.

Though not nearly as innovative or effective as "The Interpretation of Dreams," another recent Russian collage, "Scorpions" does peel away context to expose the absurdly banal fantasy life of Stalinism. It's a cinematic trip behind the mirror, a compendium of awful mistakes.

It just needed to be edited down a little.

NEWSDAY, 3/17/93, Part II/p. 59, John Anderson

An "optical poem" is how Oleg Kovalov describes "Garden of Scorpions," his acerbic compilation of footage from Soviet films of the '20s to '50s, and it's an apt description. The best poetry works on more than literal or logical levels; it makes its own rules. And to fully appreciate "Garden of Scorpions," the viewer has to adapt to Kovalov's party line.

That line is, at best, an anarchic one: Kovalov turns Soviet righteousness on its head by using large chunks of mediocre, soapish Soviet melodrama full of Stalinist blather, intercutting scenes from the classic "Potemkin," "Storm Over Asia," "The Man With the Movie Camera," and some 30 other films, and creates a coherent narrative, and some riotously satirical commentary on the suffocating nature of the Soviet zeitgeist.

In telling what is ostensibly a story about a soldier, who, through love, becomes a capitalist tool, Kovalov works in the tradition of Sergei Eisenstein—seen playing a cop in one rare segment—and, particularly, avant-gardist Lev Kuleshov, who changed the order of film segments and thus changed their meaning. Kovalov not only changes meanings, he reverses them. The sermons on drink delivered to Corporal Kotschetkov (much of the footage comes from a run-of-the-mill romance titled "Corporal Kotschetkov's Case"), juxtaposed with scenes ostensibly promoting anti-individualistic Soviet policy, make hypocritical what must have once been simply overweening. When Kovalov creates sequences in which the masses are deliriously cheering the sprouting of wheat, or two vaudevillians sing paeans to potato production, it seems far more devastating to pre-Gorbachev attitudes that any Solzhenitsyn-esque diatribes.

"Garden of Scorpions" follows—or rather, manufactures—Corporal Kotschetkov's travails with love, espionage and paranoia, and while showing us some incredible, rarely seen "educational" films and propaganda footage, frightening in its banality, and newsreel footage, too—a well-shod Nikita Kruschchev in New York meeting Frank Sinatra and Shirley Maclaine is deliciously decadent. Best of all, though, is an apparently never-before-seen performance by Yves Montand before an audience of worshipful Soviet students, with Simone Signoret looking on from the wings. It's a bizarre scene, and thus fits perfectly into "Garden of Scorpions."

VILLAGE VOICE, 3/23/93, p. 53, J. Hoberman

Montage may be a French word but it was a Soviet concept—the fruit of experiments in editing dictated by a post-revolutionary combination of material shortage and, particularly in the case of imported movies, ideological deficiency. Reediting preexisting footage was a Soviet art form: Esther Shub assembled the first compilation documentary in 1926, the same year newsreel images of American stars Douglas Fairbanks and Mary Pickford were appropriated to star in a Soviet comedy.

In that sense, *Garden of the Scorpions* is a return of sorts to the brave new world of the 1920s, even as it reinterprets the post-Stalinist '50s for the post-Soviet '90s. This self-identified "optical poem"—the first feature by Olag Kovalov, a 42-year-old film critic from former Leningrad—mixes and matches archival footage in a kind of stately delirium. Against the solemn triumphalist themes of Shostakovich, Bartók, and Nino Rota, it sifts through the rubble of official truth, reassembling the facts with a distinctively, Russian sense of grandiosity and disorder.

Opening with a newsreel of a 1959 political rally—marching formations, ecstatic spectators, a parade that celebrates Soviet cinema with a float of the Battleship Potemkin—*Garden of Scorpions* segues, or else disintegrates, into a documentary on the treatment of alcoholism. The hypnosis applied to one patient then serves to trigger episodes from the movie *The Case of Corporal Kotschetkov*, an obscure 1955 feature (apparently the Soviet equivalent of a Cold War cheapster like Republic's *Red Menace*) by Alexander Razumny, a filmmaker who was cranking out p.c. comedies in the early 1920s.

The burgeoning of a chaste and patriotic romance between innocent Corporal Kotschetkov and the equally wholesome Comrade Valya, who sells sundries from a kiosk located just beyond the military base, unreels interrupted by clips from *Storm Over Asia*, from a study on film on the Socialist Realist classic *How the Steel Was Tempered*, from an inexplicable movie of toddlers striking poses on a turntable and kissing the Soviet flag, from propaganda movies impossible to describe. Any given montage sequence might be bracketed by shots of some glowering guy in hospital pajamas, as though to suggest it's all in the mind of a mental patient. Describing his methodology for a German audience. Kovalov cited the so-called Kuleshov effect—the notion that context is everything. An individual shot has no fixed meaning; its significance is a factor of the shots that precede and follow it.

Although Kovalov's rules seem inconsistent and his editing can be slack, his film sets up an intricate system of associations. Footage alternately coalesces into narrative or dissolves into a montage of discrete attractions. Valya and her genial grandmother stuff Corporal Kotschetkov with food: the girl then plays the guitar as the corporal sings patriotic folk songs that blossom into a vision of official parades in Red Square. When, after a subsequent meal (or maybe the same one) the baffled corporal develops food poisoning, the movie bursts into a queasily colored hallucination of Western "decadence": Time's Square, *Jailhouse Rock*, Marilyn Monroe singing "Heat Wave" and then shmoozing with Khrushchev on his 1959 visit to Hollywood.

Much of *Garden of the Scorpions* consists of comic vaudeville turns: a red Sullivan Show. A big band celebrates those romantic Odessa nights. Sergei Eisenstein clowns in the guise of a British bobby. Giulietta Massina flits by, dewy-eyed. The most extensive performance belongs to the young Yves Montand, who appears on stage in the jaunty persona of a Citroen mechanic while wife Simone Signoret gazes adoringly from backstage. That Montand and Signoret were among the first Western European celebs to visit Moscow after the 1956 invasion of Hungary is underscored by an abrupt cut to Budapest.

Throughout, Kovalov interpolates bits of the natural world (gila monsters, constellations, desert landscapes) as if to locate these disconnected shards of Soviet social reality in some organic context. Valya picks up a book, rather than of Marx and Engels, the interpolated illustrations are of dinosaurs, perhaps the same monsters whose bones we later see scientists excavate. In its intermittent sense of capricious, pseudo-factual filmmaking, *Garden of the Scorpions* suggests Buñuel and Dali's *L'Age d'Or* (which initially posed as a documentary on scorpions) even more than it does our own *Atomic Cafe*.

When Montand and Signoret's tour of the Soviet capitol is intercut with the obvious miniatures representing a 1938 dream of the "new" Moscow, or when a boat filled with heedless jitterbuggers seems to cruise past a statue of Stalin, Kovalov effects a form of socialist surrealism. Meret Oppenheim's fur-lined teacup and Man Ray's cosmological eye are insinuated into the montage—the latter when Corporal Kotschetkov is picked up and interrogated as a traitor by a sleazy KGB operative who informs him that Valya and her grandmother are a "nest of spies" but who subsequently turns out himself to be a double agent ... maybe.

In the end, the nest of spies is arrested and happiness runs amok. Montand sings "Autumn Leaves" as tanks roll toward Budapest. Full mobilization brings storms, explosions, disasters, earthquakes. Crowds can scan the skies. Animated planes fly over the never-built Palace of the Soviets. A proletariat and peasant strike a heroic pas de deux: another crew of workers resist a tank. Khrushchev rides a tank through New York. Brezhnev applauds. Who the hell are these guys? The decomposition of Soviet reality takes a chunk of our own with it.

Also reviewed in:
NATION, 4/5/93, p. 464, Stuart Klawans
NEW YORK TIMES, 3/17/93, p. C16, Vincent Canby
VARIETY, 2/17/92, p. 68, David Stratton

GEORGE BALANCHINE'S THE NUTCRACKER

A Warner Bros. release of an Elektra Entertainment/Regency Enterprises presentation of a Krasnow/Milchan/Hurwitz production. *Executive Producer:* Arnon Milchan. *Producer:* Robert A. Krasnow and Robert Hurwitz.   *Director:* Emile Ardolino.   *Adapted from the Stage Production by:* Peter Martins.   *Director of Photography:* Ralf Bode.   *Editor:* Girish Bhargava. *Music:* Peter Ilyitch Tchaikovsky.   *Music performed by the New York City Ballet Orchestra under the direction of:* David Zinman.   *Music Editor:* Paul Zinman.   *Choreographer:* George Balanchine.   *Sound:* Frank Stettner.   *Sound Editor:* Dennis Leonard.   *Production Designer:* Rouben Ter-Arutunian. *Lighting Designer:* Alan Adelman. *Visual Effects:* Eric Brevig. *Ballet Master-in-Chief:* Peter Martins.   *Ballet Mistress:* Rosemary Dunleavy-Maslow.   *Children's Ballet Mistress:* Gabrielle Whittle. *Costumes:* Karinska. *Make-up:* Craig Lyman. *Running time:* 93 minutes. *MPAA Rating: G.*

CAST: Darci Kistler (The Sugarplum Fairy); Damian Woetzel (Her Cavalier); Kyra Nichols (Dewdrop);   Wendy Whelan (Coffee);   Margaret Tracey (Marzipan);   Gen Horiuchi (Tea); Tom Gold (Candy Cane); Lourdes Lopez and Nilas Martins (Hot Chocolate); William Otto (Mother Ginger);   Peter Reznick (Fritz);   Karin Von Aroldingen and Edward Bigelow (Grandparents);   Robert Lafosse (Dr. Stahlbaum);   Heather Watts (Frau Stahlbaum); Bart Robinson Cook (Herr Drosselmeier); Jessica Lynn Cohen (Marie);   Macaulay Culkin (The Nutcracker); Kevin Kline (Narrator); TOYS: Katrina Killian and Roma Sosenko (Harlequin and Columbine);   Michael Byars (Soldier);   Robert Lyon (Mouse King);   THE GUESTS: Heléne Alexopoulos, Lauren Hauser, Melinda Roy, Stephanie Saland, Simone Schumacher, Deborah Wingert, Lindsay Fischer, Kipling Houston, Peter Naumann, Alexandre Proia, Jock Soto, and Erlends Zieminch (Parents); Kimberly Cortes, Eve Harrison, Petra Hoerrner, Miriam Peterson, Ashley Siebert, Kielley Young, Misha Braun, Alexander Levine, Igor Odessky, Andrei Vitoptov, and Alex Wiesendanger (Children);   Priscilla Pellecchia and Robert Wersinger (Teenagers); Zippora Karz and Julie Michael (The Maids).

LOS ANGELES TIMES, 11/24/93, Calendar/p. 13, Peter Rainer

Macaulay Culkin has bright red candy lips in "George Balanchine's The Nutcracker." They're practically phosphorescent. They could turn out to be the most famous pop star lips since Mick Jagger's.

Clearly this is not the insight one is supposed to take away from this film. But whenever Culkin, playing the Nutcracker Prince, turns up, the bottom tends to drop out of the ballet. It's not that he's bad really, it's just that he keeps flashing that "Home Alone" smirk: You fear he may try to bop the Sugarplum Fairy.

The Tchaikovsky ballet is such a great old warhorse that it survives all this and more. The famed New York City Ballet production, derived from the choreography of George Balanchine and staged by Peter Martins, transfers to the screen relatively intact. Director Emile Ardolino, who died on Saturday at age 50, worked with Balanchine and directed many dance documentaries before he switched gears with such films as "Dirty Dancing" "Sister Act." He doesn't provide much visual excitement compared to Carroll Ballard's lyrical, underrated "Nutcracker: The Motion Picture," which was designed by Maurice Sendak, this G-rated film version is stodgy.

But Ardolino keeps the focus on the dancers, and it is they, and not the camera, who provide the real lyricism. Isn't that the way it should be in a dance film?

LOS ANGELES TIMES, 11/24/93, Calendar/p. 12, Lewis Segal

When George Balanchine choreographed in Hollywood during the 1930s and 40s, he utilized every kind of movie trickery—from fancy optical and editing effects to substituting a dance double for a non-dancing actor. His interest in how the camera could extend the fantasy of ballet affected even those sequences supposedly taking place on a theater stage.

Made a decade after his death, the stagebound "George Balanchine's The Nutcracker" can't begin to suggest his creative fascination with film. Indeed, its origin and destiny are in television. The director, editor and others on the creative team work in the same style they pioneered on the PBS "Dance in America" series beginning in the mid-'70s, while the co-producers head a record company with a growing dance-video catalogue.

One hopes that the eventual Elektra laser disc (already mentioned in the film's credits) allows viewers to switch off the plot summaries spoken on top of the music by actor Kevin Kline. Unfortunately it's too late to do anything about the music itself: a relentlessly fast, high-pressure performance led by David Zinman that doesn't resemble anything Balanchine sanctioned in his lifetime so much as the approach to Tchaikovsky that Peter Martins enforced in his production of "The Sleeping Beauty."

Local balletomanes with cable could see seven different productions of "The Nutcracker" last year on television alone. This version will do as well as any other for people who merely want a holiday dance-fantasy about a little girl with a big doll. For those with a taste for inspired choreography, however, it's pretty near the only choice.

Balanchine and Tchaikovsky, Balanchine and New York City Ballet: These are pairings that opened new chapters in dance history not so long ago. Led by the radiant Darci Kistler and the buoyant Damian Woetzel, the sunny, all-American principals here make it easy to see why.

NEW YORK, 12/6/93, p. 120, David Denby

Two things are extraordinary in *George Balanchine's The Nutcracker*: David Zinman's conducting of the Tchaikovsky score, and the great pas de deux, at the end, of Darci Kistler's Sugar Plum Fairy and Damian Woetzel's Cavalier. Apart from that, I can't see any particular reason New Yorkers, who have ready access to the live experience, should bother with the film at all. Peter Martins, who staged the ballet, and the late director Emile Ardolino haven't reimagined the work for the camera; they haven't even recorded it well. Staged at SUNY Purchase, the dance is viewed entirely from out front; the view cuts from high to low, from close to far, but it holds the same angle, thereby losing the magic of the movie camera, which is that it can go anywhere. The lighting may work onstage, but in the movie, it's too dull to bring life to Rouben Ter-Arutunian's sets, which look faded. As the Nutcracker Prince, Macaulay Culkin is an embarrassment. In a word, the movie is a bore, a case of mediocrity embalmed in self-congratulation.

NEW YORK POST, 11/24/93, p. 33, Michael Medved

There's so much that's delightful and enchanting about the new movie version of "The Nutcracker" that the best thing to do is to confront the picture's major flaw right way, then move on to words of praise. The bad news, in fact, can be summarized in two words: Macaulay Culkin. This pre-teen star is many things—a likable screen presence in the "Home Alone" movies, and even an impressively intense young actor in "The Good Son." He is not, however, a world-class ballerino—despite the fact that he once studied at the School of American Ballet and performed the mimed role of the younger brother, Fritz, in previous New York City Ballet productions of "The Nutcracker."

The crucial part of the Nutcracker Prince, is, however, another matter entirely, and Master Culkin's tentative, half-hearted attempts at dance—accompanied by a vaguely sneering, Little Lord Fauntleroy pout—are to put it bluntly, embarrassing.

Asking him to hold his own as the lead in this Tchaikovsky/Balanchine classic makes as much sense as asking Elvis to play Richard III, or Michael J. Fox to sing "Boris Godunov."

One of the reasons that Culkin looks so bad is that everyone around him looks so spectacularly good, including 12-year-old Jessica Lynn Cohen—an unaffected charmer who plays Marie and displays precisely the sort of effortless athletic grace that her costar so conspicuously lacks.

The great Darci Kistler is, of course, a gravity-defying wonder as the Sugarplum Fairy, while Wendy Whelan dances "Coffee" with such sinuous sexiness that you can be sure this is one hot beverage that would wake you up in the morning.

All of the performers seem to be thoroughly enjoying themselves during every moment of this lavish production—and their enthusiasm helps the picture avoid the tired sense of dutiful display that often creeps into productions of "The Nutcracker" around the middle of the second act.

You know that this act is set in a dream world, by the way, because the colorful sets (designed 30 years ago by the great Rouben Ter-Artunian) depict every manner of fattening sweet-toothed delight but the only inhabitants of this magical land are tall, willowy, muscular dancers with not so much as an ounce of extra flesh on their bodies.

Director Emile Ardolino (who, sadly, died just this week) is best known for uncomplicated popcorn movies like "Sister Act" and "Dirty Dancing," but he also directed or produced 29 programs for the award-winning PBS series "Dance in America."

Here, his editing and camera work are just about ideal, paying at least as much attention to the dancers' faces as to their feet, and presenting ballet as a heartfelt form of communication rather than a cold, empty spectacle.

Aiding substantially in that communication is one of this production's unsung heroes—conductor David Zinman, who whips the feisty New York City Ballet Orchestra into an edgy, splendidly energetic performance that never sugarcoats the music, giving full rein to Tchaikovsky's passion and occasional frenzy.

Kevin Kline's few sentences of narration are altogether unnecessary ("Such a tree it was, surrounded by the most tantalizing gifts!") and delivered in a sleepy drone, but this will do little to interfere with the substantial satisfactions this movie provides.

My own kids loved it without reservation, and have already begun begging for the chance to see it again; this remains, on balance, the best film for children released so far this holiday season.

NEWSDAY, 11/24/93, Part II/p. 62, Janice Berman

Director Emile Ardolino, who died Saturday, was a master at making dance look wonderful on film; think of "Dirty Dancing" and his TV documentary, "He Makes Me Feel Like Dancing." I wish I could say his final effort, too, had succeeded. But sadly, "George Balanchine's The Nutcracker," starring Macaulay Culkin and the New York City Ballet and staged by ballet master-in-chief Peter Martins, is at most a competent replica of the stage ballet.

The production notes say the creative team wanted to preserve Balanchine's version rather than generate a new one. But stage versions of great ballets such as this one include magic. If that were not the case, people would simply rent dance films instead of going to the real thing. There is evidence here of massive technical efforts to make magic. A three-dimensional tree was brought in to substitute for the flat stage Christmas tree that grows to a height of 40 feet, and the folks from Industrial Light and Magic photographed it the way the spaceships of "Star Wars" were. So instead of watching a tree grow, it seems as if we're watching it blast off. It even roars. Talk about telling Tchaikovsky the news! The orchestra, incidentally, is well conducted by David Zinman.

At the film's end, the flying sleigh has animated streams of stardust coming out of its runners, but it looks like an after-burning afterthought.

The movie was filmed at the State University of New York at Purchase, because there was enough room for camera cranes and such. But it looks like there wasn't enough room for lights. The beauty of Rouben Ter-Arutunian's sets and Karinska's costumes is muted by the gloomy lighting.

Not compromised in the least, however, is the dancing, led by Darci Kistler (who as usual seemed lighted from within) as the Sugarplum Fairy and Damien Woetzel as the Cavalier. Bart Cook is an intriguing Drosselmeier. The Waltz of the Flowers, led by Kyra Nichols' quicksilver Dewdrop, was superb, and the party scene kids were just fine.

As for young Culkin, maybe you've heard about that fight his father, Kit, had with the producers, ostensibly because dad objected to the Kevin Kline narration. Narration should be the least of his worries. The narration is gratuitous, but it's not offensive.

No. The real problem is that Macaulay Culkin, 13, as the Nutcracker Prince, is wearing too much lipstick. His co-star, the enchantingly natural Jessica Lynn Cohen, doesn't wear any.

The other worm in the sugarplum is that he's out of place. Even though he danced with the City Ballet in 1989 and '90 as the mischievous little brother Fritz, it's clear his dancing days are behind him; his big moment, a mime sequence, that's charming when properly done, was as flat as a rat's ear.

It looks as though Macaulay Culkin was told, "OK, put on this pink suit and patent-leather pumps. And whatever you do, don't act." It's totally out of kilter with what his fans have come to expect. Can't you just see his "Home Alone" character checking out those threads, putting his hands to the sides of his face and screaming?

SIGHT AND SOUND, 2/95, p. 44, Trevor Johnston

As the first feature film to be produced by Elektra Entertainment, the newly formed video operation of Elektra Nonesuch records, *George Balanchine's The Nutcracker* is exactly the kind of project you'd imagine might come from the classical arm of a major multi-media conglomerate. A filmed record of the New York City Ballet's much-loved production of the Tchaikovsky masterpiece, it is for the most part admirably straightforward and respectful of composer and choreographer's intentions. Yet the casting of Macaulay Culkin in the key child role of old uncle Drosselmeier's heroic nephew at times adds a 'crossover' spin to the proceedings. His presence, although doubtless intended as a hook for parents and kids alike who might otherwise be turned off by the notion of a full-length classical ballet comes off as something of an awkward distraction, with the attention-grabbing *modus operandi* of the Hollywood child star chafing against the ensemble tradition of the ballet company.

That said, Culkin's appearance can't be completely ascribed to the synergistic connivance of the marketing department, for in his previous life as a mere mortal, 'Mac'—then a student at the School of American Ballet—took part in the NYCB productions of 1988 and 1989. Then, significantly, he was cast in the bit part of the brattish Fritz, who petulantly smashes the magical nutcracker in the first act prelude to the fantasy adventure later undertaken by Marie and Drosselmeier's nephew, himself in turn revealed as the Nutcracker Prince. It is in the latter role—which father Kit Culkin performed with the same company in the 50s—that we now find the million-salaried *Home Alone* star. He has a small mime element to deliver and does so with neither more nor less accomplishment than you might expect from any ordinary member of the *corps de ballet*—it's only the half-smirking close-ups that become rather cloying after a while.

Culkin apart, the only other aspect of the film to be less than seamlessly integrated is the accompanying narration, an attempt to clarify Tchaikovsky and Hoffmann's slightly episodic fantasy for a wider audience. Cheerily intoned by Kevin Kline, it is rather over-obvious, telling us what we can see already (apparently Culkin pere was so outraged he withdrew his son from proposed promotional duties).

Industrial Light and Magic provide only a fantastically growing Christmas tree and the flying bed which whisks Marie and the nephew to the snowy land of the Sugar Plum Fairy. For the rest, the use of the sets and costumes familiar from NYCB's annual Balanchine revival sets the seal on a generally faithful screen preservation of a long-running seasonal favourite in the Big Apple. Even non-balletomanes could hardly fail to be impressed by the grace and discipline of Darci Kistler's Sugar Plum Fairy, the high spirits of Tom Gold's leaping Sugar Cane or the controlled exuberance of the 'Dance of the Snowflakes', while David Zinman conducts the NYCB orchestra in a slow-starting but climactically resplendent reading of an endlessly delightful score. All in all, this *Nutcracker* stands as the sort of holiday treat for well-behaved children that the adults will enjoy just as much as, if not more than their young charges.

Also reviewed in:
NEW YORK TIMES, 11/24/93, p. C11, Stephen Holden
VARIETY, 11/22/93, p. 33, Todd McCarthy
WASHINGTON POST, 11/24/93, p. C3, Susie Linfield
WASHINGTON POST, 11/26/93, Weekend/p. 60, Joe Brown

GERONIMO: AN AMERICAN LEGEND

A Columbia Pictures release. *Executive Producer:* Michael S. Glick. *Producer:* Walter Hill and Neil Canton. *Director:* Walter Hill. *Screenplay:* John Milius and Larry Gross. *Story:* John Milius. *Director of Photography:* Lloyd Ahern. *Editor:* Freeman Davies, Carmel Davies, and Donn Aron. *Music:* Ry Cooder. *Music Editor:* Bunny K. Andrews. *Choreographer:* Desmond F. Strobel. *Sound:* Lee Orloff. *Casting:* Reuben Cannon. *Production Designer:* Joe Alves. *Art Director:* Scott Ritenour. *Set Decorator:* Richard C. Goddard. *Special Effects:* Larry Cavanaugh. *Costumes:* Dan Moore. *Make-up:* Gary Liddiard. *Stunt Coordinator:* Allan Graf. *Running time:* 115 minutes. *MPAA Rating:* PG-13.

CAST: Jason Patric (Lt. Charles Gatewood); Gene Hackman (Brig. Gen. George Crook); Robert Duvall (Al Sieber); Wes Studi (Geronimo); Matt Damon (Lt. Britton Davis); Rodney A. Grant (Mangas); Kevin Tighe (Brig. Gen. Nelson Miles); Steve Reevis (Chato); Carlos Palomino (Sgt. Turkey); Victor Aaron (Ulzana); Stuart Proud Eagle Grant (Sgt. Dutchy); Stephen McHattie (Schoonover); John Finn (Capt. Hentig); Lee de Broux (City Marshall Hawkins); Rino Thunder (Old Nana); Hoke Howell (Billy Pickett); Richard Martin, Jr. (Apache Medicine Man); J. Young (Hawkins' Deputy); Raleigh Wilson (Yaqui Dave); Jackie Old Coyote (Apache Vision Woman); Monty Bass (Dead Shot); Pato Hoffmann (The Dreamer); Scott Crabbe (Courier at Ball); Patricia Pretzinger (Woman at Ball); Roger Callard (Sgt. Mulrey); Juddson Keith Linn (Bronco Apache); Mark Boon Junior (Afraid Miner); M.C. Gainey (Unafraid Miner); Michael Ruud (Chaplain); Michael Minjarez (Dandy Jim); Burnette Bennett (Skip-Hey); Davina Smith (Dead Shot's Wife); Jonathan Ward (C.S. Fly); Luis Contreras (Rurale Officer); Jaquelin Lee (Apache Woman); Jim Manygoats (Ailing Apache); Scott Wilson (Redondo); Eva Larson (Catina Waitress); Greg Goossen, Sonny Skyhawk, Michael Adams, Walter Robles, and Anthony Schmidt (Schoonover Gang); Jim Beaver (Proclamation Officer).

LOS ANGELES TIMES, 12/10/93, Calendar/p. 8, Kenneth Turan

What becomes a legend most? "Geronimo: An American Legend" chooses the path of cool classicism and mostly makes it work. A handsome and respectful Western that wants to simultaneously echo and modernize the myths of the past, it is an impressive piece of work that, perhaps inevitably, ends up being more than a little cold around the heart.

Inevitably, because Geronimo himself was less interested in gaining sympathy than demanding respect and the right to do as he pleased. An implacable war leader of the Chiricahua Apache, he was one of the last Native American commanders to agree to be restricted to a reservation, and when he escaped its confines in 1886—a breakaway that is at the film's heart—the event made news nationwide.

Director Walter Hill has made Westerns before ("The Long Riders"), but nothing on as epic a scale as this. And it is as a physical piece of filmmaking that "Geronimo" is most successful. Photographed by Lloyd Ahern and filled with gorgeous panoramas that both recall and amplify the Westerns of John Ford (who also shot around Moab, Utah), the film never lets you forget its story's spectacular scale. And when Hill's acknowledged facility with action sequences is factored in, "Geronimo" ends up being one of the director's most impressive films.

As written by John Milius and Larry Gross from a story by Milius. "Geronimo" focuses not so much on one character as several. And though it differs in tone from "Dances With Wolves," it uses the same device of having a participant/narrator reading from his own somewhat stilted prose to get us into the story.

That would be Britton Davis (Matt Damon), a second lieutenant newly out of West Point whose first assignment out on the Western frontier of Arizona and New Mexico is to assist Lt. Charles B. Gatewood (Jason Patric) in the surrender of Geronimo. A variant of John Wayne's Ethan Edwards in "The Searchers," Gatewood is the son of a Confederate veteran, knows heaps about the Apache ways, speaks their language, but also respects them as both fighters and men.

And as played by Wes Studi, himself a member of the Cherokee Nation and memorable in both "Dances With Wolves" and "The Last of the Mohicans," Geronimo exhibits a cold hauteur that would elicit respect from a stone. A proud man with a hard and arrogant scowl that is authentically frightening. Geronimo ends up taking a liking to Gatewood, for whom he seems to feel a warrior-to-warrior respect.

The great non-compromiser also admits to a grudging appreciation for two other White Eyes who have long been on his trail, Brig. Gen. George Crook (Gene Hackman) and Al Sieber (Robert Duvall), the sturdy chief of scouts who has not let 17 gunshot and arrow wounds interfere with his soldierly duties.

But though everyone would like nothing more than for Geronimo to spend the rest of his days peacefully growing corn on the Turkey Creek Reservation, that is not to be. The great man acts involved with some subversive ghost dancers and takes off again, and the time is not long before Gatewood is plucked out of the ranks and ordered to try to bring him in.

All this back and forth naturally involves traditional exploits of the hard-riding and deadly shooting variety, and "Geronimo" shows that Hill remains a model where action is concerned. His gunplay sequences are crisp, forceful and to the point, examples, especially in a showdown in a Mexican cantina, of filmmaking that knows enough not to overdo things.

From a thematic point of view, what Hill and "Geronimo's" writers are after is a melding of traditional themes of fatalism and honor and venerable "Death to all White Eyes/Lieutenant, you have your orders" dialogue with a more up-to-date reading of Western situations that emphasizes the inevitable conflict of cultures and the tragedy of the Chiricahua's subjugation.

"Geronimo" even manages to be somewhat historically accurate, if you discount the fact that the real Geronimo was in his late 50s or early 60s at the time and looked more like an angry Ross Perot than the magnetic Studi. But it has paid a price for its virtues, and that price is empathy.

For as much as "Geronimo" earns our admiration, it is a difficult film to warm up to. Consciously cool and unemotional in tone, it also has to deal with a performance by Patric, the main audience surrogate, that is more distant than it needs to be and a plot that similarly does not facilitate involvement.

The closest thing to a hero "Geronimo" allows, Patric's Gatewood, with his whispery Southern accent and brooding demeanor, is irritating in his stoicism when he doesn't need to be. Though setting out to make a classic is hard to argue with as an aim, getting things exactly right turns out to be a tricky business.

NEW YORK POST, 12/10/93, p. 49, Michael Medved

As a history lesson, "Geronimo: An American Legend" leaves a great deal to be desired, but as an example of slick and stirring cinematic entertainment, it's an impressive piece of work.

The subject is the U.S. Army's Geronimo campaign of 1885-86, in which Washington deployed some 5,000 troopers—one fourth of its total strength at the time—to capture a single Apache renegade, who had escaped from an Arizona reservation with a few dozen followers.

Wes Studi, the Cherokee actor who made such a strong impression as the brooding, vicious Magua in "The Last of the Mohicans," plays Geronimo and provides this picture with its most formidable asset.

Studi is so good, in fact, that he could have made Geronimo compelling even if the script hadn't felt the need to reduce the fascinating and complex historical figure into a two-dimensional poster boy for Native American rights.

The other leading members of the cast deliver similarly superb performances, especially Robert Duvall as a veteran Army scout whose long decades of battling the Chiracahua Apache have left him with a body covered with scars and a love-hate relationship with his wily adversaries.

Gene Hackman plays Gen. George Crook, the capable, conscientious commander who wanted to use the Army to keep an impartial peace between settlers and Native Americans, while Jason Patric is a sympathetic cavalry lieutenant who learns to trust and admire Geronimo.

The major characters are based on historical figures, and they emerge for the most part as decent, even heroic participants in a sad chapter of history, rather than caricatured racists and sadists who are pointlessly persecuting the Chiracahua Apaches.

While Geronimo's real-life brutality is greatly de-emphasized, the filmmakers do dramatize one of his many massacres; the warriors in this film are a long way from the insipidly sweet and sensitive quiche-eaters of "Dances With Wolves."

Director Walter Hill ("The Long Riders," "48 Hours") is a specialist in tough, stylish action films, and handles this material with unaccustomed depth and nuance; the battle scenes have been staged with appropriate flair.

But Hill also does a sensitive job delineating character and developing relationships.

The immensely atmospheric musical score by Ry Cooder (who deserves an Oscar nomination for his work on this film) and the sweeping, monumental canyon locations near Moab, Utah, lend the picture a quality of epic grandeur: Hill has journeyed to John Ford country, both geographically and cinematically.

It's only in the last 15 minutes that this handsome picture quite literally loses its balance and collapses in an orgy of predictable, trendy and weepy political preachments—leaving the audience with a sour, sanctimonious aftertaste to an otherwise superior western.

NEWSDAY, 12/10/93, Part II/p. 94, John Anderson

"Dances With Wolves" might have helped resurrect the western, but it also slipped a noose around its neck. Judging by "Geronimo: An American Legend," filmmakers henceforth will be so busy perfecting American Indian dialects, fine-tuning the socio-political landscape and putting the *wickiups* in the proper positions that they'll have no time for drama.

"Geronimo" is a curious beast: A film that makes much of its adherence to historical fact, but not to the point where its subject's atrocities might make him unsympathetic. It's subtitled "An American Legend," even though it was America that destroyed Geronimo's world. And despite its staunchly revisionist posture, the film still can't shake its Euro-centric worldview. "It's a morality, once you understand it," Lt. Charles Gatewood (Jason Patric) tells an underling referring to Geronimo's fierce will to fight.

All this would be forgivable if the film were engrossing, which it's not. The producers should be credited, I suppose, with casting an actual Indian—Wes Studi, the villainous Pawnee warrior of "Dances with Wolves"—even if he only gets fourth billing. As Geronimo, who fought and eluded a U.S. Army force of 5,000 men in the mid-1880s, he is a strong and noble presence, but the star of the film is Patric.

His Gatewood is the Apache-ologist under Gen. George Crook (Gene Hackman), who also sympathizes with Geronimo, but is obligated to track him down after the Apache leads an reservation uprising, killing a number of U.S. officers and heading for Mexico. Among the Army force on hand is Al Sieber, a much-wounded veteran of the Indian wars (Robert Duvall, reprising "Lonesome Dove's" Gus McRae). "You don't love who you're fighting for," he admonishes Gatewood, "and you don't hate who you're fighting against." Compared to Gatewood, Sieber is frontier machismo personified, all red blood and red hands. He can't stand not to fight and in this, he has an ally in his old nemesis, Geronimo.

The action sequences are exciting and sharply executed, even if they owe quite a bit to director Walter Hill's predecessors. The landscapes—Hill shot among the same Utah canyons John Ford used in some of his best films—seem drained of color and life, much like the story itself. And the attempts to adorn Geronimo's tale with mysticism—his occasional black-and-white flashes of his own spiritual power—are off-handed and trite.

All too much of the story is delivered via the narration of Lt. Britton Davis (Matt Damon), a green young officer abruptly thrust into the chase for Geronimo. The effect of his stilted words and stiff speech are intended to evoke a young, overly formal military man, but the fact remains that too much narration means there's a deep need for some visual storytelling.

SIGHT AND SOUND, 11/94, p. 47, Tom Tunney

1885, the American Southwest. A small band of Chiricahua Apaches led by Geronimo are the last Indian tribe to defy to the US Government. Lt Britton Davis is newly assigned to the command of Brigadier General George Crook, whose Sixth Cavalry have the task of tracking them down. Davis and Lt Charles Gatewood meet with Geronimo in the desert, and he agrees to give himself up. Crook accepts Geronimo's surrender and the Indians are consigned to the barren reservation at Turkey Creek. Crook assures Geronimo that the tribe will be under the protection of the US Army.

The noisy rituals of a medicine man incite a US Army patrol to open fire and a battle ensues. Three Indian scouts are subsequently hung for switching sides. Crook is told that Geronimo has broken out and orders an expedition, led by Gatewood and chief of scouts Al Sieber. Geronimo's war party massacres a group of copper miners, sparing only one man who stood up to them. Gatewood shoots dead an Apache brave who challenges him to single combat.

Crook meets Geronimo in Mexico and accuses him of breaking his word. Geronimo still refuses to surrender and Gatewood subsequently resigns. His successor, Brigadier General Nelson Miles does not believe in using Apache scouts. Though some 5,000 men are employed to track down just 35 Apaches, they fail. Miles orders Gatewood to find Geronimo and present him with favourable terms which Miles has no intention of adhering to. Gatewood's three-man expedition comes across a massacred Yaqui Indian settlement. The expedition subsequently encounters the Texan scalp hunters responsible and in the shootout that ensues, all the scalp hunters and Sieber are killed.

After meeting him in his mountaintop lair, Gatewood returns with Geronimo to San Carlos. The US Army's Apache scouts, including Chato, are summarily disarmed and put with Geronimo and his men on railway wagons for the long trip to a Florida reservation. Gatewood is assigned menial duties. Britton tenders his resignation, accusing the army of breaking its word. On the train east, Chato tells Geronimo he was right to fight the white men. Britton's voice-over tells us that Geronimo lived for a further 22 years but was never allowed to return to his homeland.

The latest in the crop of post-*Dances With Wolves* Westerns has nothing new to say; white men speak with forked tongues and Indians are treated shamefully. The shadow of *Ulzana's Raid* falls heavily over the film, but where Robert Aldrich adopted a deeply ironic view of the struggle between two cultures, the aim here is simply to embellish the myth. The phrase 'An American Legend' in the title is a telling pointer. It allows the co-option of the real Geronimo into a patriotic scheme of things in which he represents all that is best and most enduring in the American spirit. It's an idea wholly in keeping with the consistently heroic themes in scriptwriter John Milius' work, in which great Americans do not so much represent society as violently define themselves in opposition to its dominant values.

Like Sean Connery's Arab chieftain in *The Wind and the Lion*, Patrick Swayze's guerilla leader in *Red Dawn* nd Nick Nolte's renegade sailor in *Farewell to the King*, Wes Studi's Geronimo is a warrior who lives according to his own heroic code. Milius filters praise for these warriors though the device of an admiring secondary character. *Farewell to the King* had Nigel Havers' sensitive British officer; *Red Dawn* a thoughtful Cuban Colonel; *The Wind and the Lion* President Theodore Roosevelt. *Apocalypse Now*, which Milius also worked on, is similarly organised around the responses of Captain Willard to Colonel Kurtz.

Thus the confessional voice-over of naive young Lt Davis is vital for our understanding of both Geronimo and Gatewood. However, here the device seems shopworn and fundamentally flawed. Davis' tedious observations diminish the Apache leader to a supporting player in his own movie. Also the fact that Davis is morally spotless—he makes a point of telling us that he didn't kill any Apaches—lets the audience off the hook.

Structuring the film around Gatewood or the cynical Sieber would have been a more challenging route. Better still would have been to focus directly on Geronimo himself, the technique adopted by the superior 1993 TV movie *Geronimo*, whose hard-hitting closing sequence—in which Geronimo confronts long-time Milius icon Theodore Roosevelt—could almost be a deliberate riposte to the idea of Geronimo as an *American* legend.

In comparison, Walter Hill's film is an annoying muddle. His main strategy, the voice-over, has two complementary focuses of admiration: Geronimo and Gatewood. These characters have to be presented as kindred spirits to enforce the Americanising impetus and the film does its best to comply. Both are treated badly by the US Army, and both spurn conventional military tactics: Gatewood finds Geronimo with a mere three men, Geronimo defies 5,000 with less than 40.

Unfortunately, unexplained ambiguities in Gatewood's character constantly interfere with our understanding of Geronimo. As a Southerner, he is presented as an expert on lost causes. "Don't love what you're fighting for and don't hate what you're fighting against," is Sieber's succinct summing up of his nature. And how to explain his selling out of Geronimo? The film refuses to put a Judas slant on his behavior, giving him a line which sounds hopelessly inadequate: "We're trying to make a country here—it's hard." It is impossible to match those sentiments with Geronimo's stark line, "Once I moved around like the wind, now I surrender." *Geronimo and Lt Gatewood* might have been a more accurate title for the film. But only if granted the caustic irony of, say, Robert Altman's *Buffalo Bill and the Indians* could it have done justice to either of them.

TIME, 12/13/93, p. 79, Richard Schickel

It's about the last thing you expect to see in the '90s: an old-fashioned cavalry-and-Indian western, not so very different from the kind John Ford and many others used to turn out regularly. All the classic elements are here: a harshly beautiful Southwestern landscape; the eponymous warrior chieftain (Wes Studi), noble, misused and off the reservation because promises have been broken; an idealistic young officer (Jason Patric) who respects his enemy; and a greenhorn (Matt Damon) who wants to learn more about him; an honorable general (Gene Hackman) and a bloody-minded one (Kevin Tighe). There's even a grizzled scout (Robert Duvall), wise in the ways of the enemy.

Above all, this genre is about manliness and different ways of achieving its basic requisites—honor, stoicism and freedom of movement. *Geronimo: An American Legend* takes a tragic view of those values. Everyone who tries to live by them ends up dead, imprisoned or disgraced. In that sense, it is very much a '90s movie, a conscious metaphorical backlash against newer, softer definitions of masculinity. Here good soldiers and Apaches are equally the victims of compromising, "civilizing" forces.

Director Walter Hill's combat sequences are short and sharp, but there are not quite enough of them. The script, by Hollywood's last rogue males, John Milius and Larry Gross, devotes too much time to parlay and palaver—to self-justification, if you will. Depending on your point of view, that's either a necessity or a sad commentary on the state of traditional male ways of being.

VILLAGE VOICE, 12/14/93, p. 65, Georgia Brown

Give me any day a good old western (please don't call this revisionist) like Walter Hill and John Milius's *Geronimo*, with its brooding, end-of-an-era, last-of-a-breed poignancy, its touching trust that honor matters. (I'm reviewing the film second and in brief because it screened late.) Written by Milius and Larry Gross, *Geronimo* too is told from the white man's vantage, although the Chiricahua Apache leader is presented as a complex personality with a philosophical bent. Like Paul in *Six Degrees*, he ends up, with his band, being carted off to prison, but at least their last words aren't wistful tributes to the treacherous White Eyes.

Mixing fact and myth, the movie opens in 1885, when Geronimo (Wes Studi), who's fled to Mexico, surrenders to the U.S. Army under General George Crook (Gene Hackman), and he and the remnants of his tribe are relegated to a narrow plot called Turkey Creek. They're told to grow corn on the unfertile land. Eventually when the cavalry kills a medicine man, they rebel and many flee with Geronimo toward Mexico. Thus begins the legendary Geronimo campaign, where, by the end, a band of 35 starving Apaches eludes a force of 5000 soldiers.

Honoring history, the filmmakers have opted for an episodic narrative rather than a classic plot leading to a final battle. Basically, Geronimo's action moves from massacre to massacre until the intentionally anticlimactic ending, where it trails off into ironies. Appropriate ironies, if not especially dramatic.

The character of Lieutenant Charles Gatewood (Jason Patric) is the movie's moral center. A Southerner who says he has plenty of his own reasons for hating the Blue Coat, the handsome, tight-lipped, blue-eyed Gatewood is the western's godlike white hero: Here he's heroic for prowess and bravery, for revering the native people and their ways, bonding with Geronimo, and believing with the best of the officers (like Crook) that he's saving the Apaches from extinction by bringing them in. Of course, in the last he's disillusioned.

Robert Duvall plays the hard-bitten Sieber, the Army's chief scout, a more contradictory breed and perfectly recognizable as a western type. He's fascinated by Apache brutality—the nation's survival struggle unhindered by Christian ethics. The irony is that Christians conduct wholesale extermination while pretending that it's accomplished cleanly.

Filmed in the red-gold desert of John Ford territory (the canyons near Moab, Utah), *Geronimo* succeeds in putting Geronimo at the center by making him right. He's also, as he must be, an exceptional warrior (with a great ravaged face), a faithful keeper of the code. Every time Studi's onscreen, he commands attention with his stern gaze, his accusing eyes. In fact, he's very nearly a match for his counterpart, the perfect white man.

Also reviewed in:
CHICAGO TRIBUNE, 12/10/93, Friday/p. C, Clifford Terry
NEW YORK TIMES, 12/10/93, p. C21, Janet Maslin
NEW YORKER, 1/10/94, p. 81, Terrence Rafferty
VARIETY, 12/13/93, p. 36, Todd McCarthy
WASHINGTON POST, 12/10/93, p. B7, Richard Harrington
WASHINGTON POST, 12/10/93, Weekend/p. 55, Desson Howe

GET THEE OUT

A First Run Features release of a Lenfilm Studios production. *Producer:* Rafik Zamanov and Dimitri Astrakhan. *Director:* Dimitri Astrakhan. *Screenplay (Russian with English subtitles):* Oleg Danilov and Dimitri Astrakhan. *Adapted from stories by:* Sholem Aleichem, Isaac Babel and A. Kuprin. *Director of Photography:* Yuri Worontsov. *Editor:* Dimitri Astrakhan. *Music:* Alexander Pantichin. *Production Designer:* Alexander Kikivkin and Marya Petrova. *Running time:* 90 minutes. *MPAA Rating:* Not Rated.

CAST: Otar Mengvinetukutsesy (Motl); Elena Anisimova (Golda); Tatyana Anisimova (Beyelka); Alexander Likov (Peter); Valentin Bukin (Trofim).

CHRISTIAN SCIENCE MONITOR, 2/16/93, p. 12, David Sterritt

Directed by Dimitri Astrakhan, this Russian production is based on stories by such authors as Aleichem and Isaac Babel, whose themes are woven seamlessly into a lively screenplay. The main character is a dairy farmer named Motl, who tries his best to live a happy and hearty life despite domestic challenges, such as his daughter's secret marriage to a husband who isn't Jewish, and more frightening signs of the times, such as smoldering anti-Semitism in the area around Motl's small community.

"Get Thee Out" is much folksier and funnier than "Labyrinth," [This film has not had a theatrical opening in the United States.] but it's no less serious in its warnings about the insidiousness of bigotry.

Stunningly photographed by Yuri Worontsov, it is distributed in the United States by First Run Features, a releasing company based in New York, and began a regular run at the Walter Reade theater.

NEW YORK POST, 1/27/93, p. 21, Jerry Tallmer

You come away from "Get Thee Out," the Russian film with a headful of swarming, opposing images of the Ukrainian countryside at the turn of the century: scenes and moments of exquisite beauty, indoors and out, and everywhere, everywhere, very subtly at first, lying against a barn door, stuck in a block, almost inconsequentially, axes.

There is a chilling little poem by Robert Frost a deceptively childlike fragment of advice from a crow that suddenly veers from banality into "... and look for skunk tracks in the snow, with an ax." The axes of "Get Thee Out" are for killing Jews.

This movie, most astonishingly made two years ago by the then 34-year-old director Dimitri Astrakhan, also intermixes rich raucous scenes in full color for the story of Motl Rabinovich, his family, and his neighbors, with still, silent sequences in old-rotogravure sepia—bestrewn with the corpses of women and children and old people—for Motl's flashback memories of pogroms he lived through as a boy, to soul-stirring Felliniesque/Nino Rota music by Alexander Pantichin.

But now Motl (Otar Mengvinetukutsesy) is a man, and a man of substance, a lusty blue-eyed bearded sardonic dairyman and big wheel in his stetl, who might be Tevye and indeed *would* be in a more sentimental venue, such as a smash Broadway musical. Does he find a note in his wagon: "Tonight will be the end of all the Yids, including you"? He shrugs it off.

This is the new Russia of Turgenev and Tolstoy and a Czar who has declared pogroms to be against the law. Why, Motl's best friend, Trofim (Valentin Bukin)—the guy who roisters with him in whorehouses—is a non-Jew. Even the local constable is not unfriendly. And that good Russian peasant who eats at Motl's table and asks "Why couldn't I be a Jew?"—he is a friend, no?

Until several things happen. Trofim's feckless painter son, Peter (Alexander Likov), falls in love with Motl's daughter, beautiful Beyelka (Tatyana Anisimova). A horse-thief gypsy is beaten to death under unclear circumstances. This could reverberate. And then the constable shows up. During a new fever of anti-Semitic violence throughout the province, he has orders to start a pogrom here.

Trofim—still a friend—helps Motl stage a mock-pogrom, complete with a fake fire (in an outhouse), the smashing of dishes, the strewing of thousands of feathers in slow-motion a la "Zero de Conduite." The cop gets the idea, and is satisfied "Now everything is all right," says Motl.

That's before Motl goes to town to buy wine and gets pushed around by a murderous bully. Before the good Russian peasant shows up drunk, ax in hand, blood in his eye, yelling: "Kill the Yids!" Before the pogrom reaches out, from the sepia stills of old memory to the here and now, hammering on the doors of the stetl, Motl's door, or looming up out of the fog as a monstrous pair of headlights on a half-seen truck atop which there looms a ferocious, unidentifiable figure brandishing ... an ax.

Here the movie turns into "On the Waterfront"; more yet, a Warner Bros. brotherhood-and-no-surrender drama of the 1940s. One might wish it were all so easy, even today, a century after Tolstoy, a half-century after Adolph Hitler. But "Get Thee Out"—and I haven't even told some lovely things about the young people's romance—is one hell of a movie for all that.

VILLAGE VOICE, 1/26/93, p. 53, J. Hoberman

Set a bit further east on the eve of an earlier revolution, the Russian *Get Thee Out* is another, if less virtuoso, carnival of state sanctioned, alcohol-fueled violence. [The reference is to *The Oak*; see Hoberman's review.] Dimitri Astrakhan's first feature dramatizes the uneasy relationship between a Jewish dairyman and his Gentile neighbors in a remote Ukrainian village.

Astrakhan's Jews are an earthy bunch—his hero Motl is something like Sholom Aleichem's Tevye as he might have been reconfigured by Isaac Babel, a full-bearded patriarch who celebrates his new success with a night at a brothel and who advertises his dairy with a hand-painted sign of bare-breasted milkmaids. Still, the situation is ominous; the lusty idyll is interspersed with sepia footage of Motl's premonition of his former shtetl aflame, streets littered with Jewish corpses. The locals have already beaten a gypsy horse-thief to death, and when word comes down to attack the Jews, they stage a mock pogrom to fool the authorities, smashing selected crockery and torching only Motl's outhouse. (One effective touch: a vodka-addled neighbor who arrives too late for the action has to abruptly switch gears, dropping his brandished ax and wheedling a drink.) Meanwhile, Motl's daughter is in church, marrying the son of the local constable; the couple returns as a harbinger of the anti-Jewish terror engulfing the countryside.

The new Russian cinema has brought a number of Jewish-theme films—one would have to go back to the late '20s to find a comparable effusion. Then, as now, most are period pieces; the difference being that the "traditional" past the new films recall is virtually beyond recollection, Thus, despite its setting, *Get Thee Out* is a no less self-conscious pastiche than the American performance artist Eleanor Antin's ersatz Yiddish silent *The Man Without a World*. Indeed, in some respects, Antin's San Diego-built shtetl and its inhabitants seem more authentic—or at least more authentically postmodern—than Astrakhan's.

Still, although sometimes coarse, *Get Thee Out* is far from the worst Russian movie to excavate Jewish history. If the unconvincing closer seems a paradoxical, perhaps Pavlovian, nod toward proletarian internationalism, the film is nevertheless remarkable for the bluntness with which characters articulate their anti-Semitic paranoia. In this, unfortunately, *Get Thee Out* is less postmodern than contemporary. Such sentiments have scarcely dated; nor are they restricted to the former Soviet Union.

Also reviewed in:
NEW YORK TIMES, 1/26/93, p. C14, Vincent Canby
VARIETY, 12/23/91, p. 45, Amy Dawes

GETTYSBURG

A New Line Cinema release of a Turner Pictures and Mace Neufeld/Robert Rehme presentation of an Esparza/Katz production. *Producer:* Robert Katz and Moctesuma Esparza. *Director:* Ronald F. Maxwell. *Screenplay:* Ronald F. Maxwell. *Based on the novel by:* Michael Shaara. *Director of Photography:* Kees Van Oostrum. *Editor:* Corky Ehlers. *Music:* Randy Edelman. *Sound:* Stephen Halbert. *Casting:* Joy Todd. *Production Designer:* Cary White. *Art Director:* Mike Sullivan. *Special Effects:* Matt Vogel. *Military Choreographer:* Dale E. Fetzer, Jr. *Historical Advisor:* Brian Pohanka and Pat Falci. *Costumes:* Michael T. Boyd. *Make-up:* Michael Spatola. *Stunt Coordinator:* Steve M. Boyum. *Running time:* 248 minutes. *MPAA Rating:* PG.

CAST: CONFEDERATE CAST: Tom Berenger (Lieutenant General James Longstreet);   Martin Sheen (General Robert E. Lee);   Stephen Lang (Major General George E. Pickett);   Richard Jordan (Brigadier General Lewis A. Armistead);   Andrew Prine (Brigadier General Richard B. Garnett);   Cooper Huckabee (Henry T. Harrison);   Patrick Gorman (Major General John Bell Hood);   Bo Brinkman (Major Walter H. Taylor);   James Lancaster (Lieutenant Colonel Arthur Freemantle);   Morgan Sheppard (Major General Isaac R. Trimble);   Kieran Mulroney (Major G. Moxley Sorrell);   Patrick Stuart (Colonel E. Porter Alexander);   Tim Ruddy (Major Charles Marshall);   Royce Applegate (Brigadier General James L. Kemper);   Ivan Kane (Captain Thomas J. Goree);   Warren Burton (Major General Henry Heth);   Macintyre Dixon (Major General Jubal A. Early);   Joseph Fuqua (Major General J.E.B. Stuart);   Tim Scott (Lieutenant General Richard S. Ewell);   George Lazenby (Brigadier General J. Johnston Pettigrew);   Alex Harvey (Major Hawkins);   Charles Lester Kinsolving (Brigadier General William Barksdale);   Ted Kozlosky (Confederate Lieutenant);   Henry Atterbury (Lee's Aide);   Graham Winton

(Major General Robert E. Rodes);   Curtiss Bradford (Another Officer);   Daniel Chamblin (Confederate Officer);   Patrick Falci (Lieutenant General Ambrose Powell Hill);   Greg Ginther (Rodes' Courier);   George Heffner (Another Officer);   Tom Landon (Texas Soldier #2); Michael Tennessee Lee (Rebel Prisoner);   Rick Leisenring (Confederate Voice);   Steve Leone (An Officer);   Tom Mays (Early's Courier);   Frank McGurgan (Old Sergeant);   Peter Miller (Pender's Courier);   Arnold Nisley (Sergeant);   Ted Rebich (Dr. Cullen);   Curtis Utz (Texas Soldier #1);   C. George Werner (Another Officer);   Joe Ayer and Eric Ayer (Banjo and Guitar Players);   FEDERAL CAST: Jeff Daniels (Colonel Joshua Lawrence Chamberlain);   Sam Elliott (Brigadier General John Buford);   C. Thomas Howell (Lieutenant Thomas D. Chamberlain); Kevin Conway (Sergeant "Buster" Kilrain);   Brian Mallon (Major General Winfield Scott Hancock);   Buck Taylor (Colonel William Gamble);   John Diehl (Private Bucklin);   Josh Mauer (Colonel James C. Rice);   John Rothman (Major General John F. Reynolds);   Richard Anderson (Major General George G. Meade);   William Campbell (Lieutenant Pitzer);   David Carpenter (Colonel Thomas C. Devin);   Maxwell Caulfield (Colonel Strong Vincent);   Donal Logue (Captain Ellis Spear);   Dwier Brown (Captain Brewer);   Herb Mitchell (Sergeant Andrew J. Tozier);   Emile O. Schmidt (Brigadier General John Gibbon);   Daniel Baumann (Private #2); Ken Burns (Hancock's Aide);   Michael Callahan (Beared Man);   Scott Allan Campbell (Captain Atherton W. Clark);   David Cole (Buford's Aide);   Mark Z. Danielewski (Private);   Brian Egen (Cocky Lieutenant);   Tom Fife (2nd Maine Man);   David Fiske (Courier);   John Fitzpatrick (Old 2nd Maine Man);   Vee Gentile (Private);   Gary Gilmore (Union Rider, Voice #1);   John Hadfield (Vincent's Courier);   John Heffron (Sergeant Charles H. Veil);   Con Horgan (Officer #1);   Richard Kiester (Devin's Aide);   Matthew Letscher (Young 2nd Maine Man);   Robert Lucas (Guard, 118th Pennsylvania);   Reid Maclean (Private Jim Merrill); Jonathan Maxwell (Private Bill Merrill);   Barry McEvoy (2nd Maine Soldier);   Scott Mehaffey (Lieutenant, Buford's Staff);   Mark Moses (Sergeant Owen);   Russell Starlin (Officer #2); Leonard Termo (Corporal George F. Estabrook);   Frank Moseley (Soldier #1, 20th Maine); Brian Resh (Soldier #2, 20th Maine);   Lawrence Sangi (Soldier #3, 20th Maine);   Michael Phillips (Soldier #4, 20th Maine);   Adam Brandy (Soldier #5, 20th Maine);   Sandy Mitchell and John Durant (Fiddle and Guitar Players).

CHRISTIAN SCIENCE MONITOR, 10/8/93, p. 13, Frank Scheck

No one has any reason to doubt media magnate Ted Turner's devotion to Southern History, but if further proof is required it is provided in the new film "Gettysburg," which opens in theaters around the country today. Turner originally made it as a miniseries for his TNT network, but was so pleased with the results that he decided to release it theatrically. This, despite the film's 4½-hour running time.

The film is written and directed by Ronald Maxwell, and based on the Pulitzer Prize-winning novel "Killer Angels" by Michael Shaara. It is the most exhaustive re-creation of the Civil War ever made on film; for that matter, it is one of the most spectacular depictions of warfare ever committed to celluloid. Filmed on the original locations with thousands of extras playing soldiers, its verisimilitude is positively spooky. Which is not to say that it belongs on the big screen, despite its large budget, lavish production, and 70-gun presentation. The film, in attempting to document every aspect of the conflict, goes into so much detail that dramatic momentum is lost. At times the pacing is so slow that we wish the South had won the war.

"Gettysburg" is best when it veers away from talkiness (there are several long, philosophical conversations about the meaning of the war) and concentrates on the battles, which it goes into with enough detail to satisfy even the most stringent military historian. Particularly fascinating are the re-creations of the siege of Little Round Top, and of Pickett's Charge, the most legendary battle of the war. In scenes such as these, stirringly filmed, the movie transforms itself from a classroom exercise into gripping drama.

A large cast of notables appears, including Turner himself in a cameo as a Confederate soldier who meets a quick death. Strong performances are provided by Tom Berenger, Jeff Daniels, and Sam Elliott as various commanders; Kevin Conway as a spunky soldier continuing to fight despite a number of wounds; and Martin Sheen, who, as Robert E. Lee, effectively portrays decency and dignity. And Richard Jordan, in his last screen appearance, gives one of the best performances of his career.

"Gettysburg" may not appeal to everyone, but history buffs and the thousands of people who visit the tragic historic site every year (the film may be shown continuously there), will no doubt ensure that it will have a permanent place in the annals of historical films.

LOS ANGELES TIMES, 10/8/93, Calendar/p. 6, Peter Rainer

At a bit over four hours, "Gettysburg" has a TV miniseries pacing and spaciousness. That's not surprising, since it was originally planned as a miniseries—and will air in a six-hour version on Ted Turner's TNT network next year.

Director-screenwriter Ronald F. Maxwell, adapting Michael Shaara's 1974 Pulitzer Prize-winning novel "The Killer Angels," keeps the action confined to the three climactic days in the summer of 1863 when 150,000 Northern and Confederate soldiers squared off in the bloodiest battle of the Civil War. He's aiming for epic drama with intimate shadings.

As in Shaara's book, most of the personages in the movie are officers, and this gives it a somewhat Olympian tone—except the dialogue is often stilted, as if Robert E. Lee and the others were already aware of their places in history. They carry on like Men of Destiny.

Maxwell introduces each of these men in heightened cameos that set off their personalities in a flash, On the Confederate side, Lee (Martin Sheen) is gracious and revered by his men, Lt. Gen. James Longstreet (Tom Berenger) is rough and ready, as defensive a tactician as Lee is offensive; Brig. Gen. Lewis Armistead (Richard Jordan) is valiant and deep-souled—he fears for his friend Union Gen. Winfield Scott Hancock (Brian Mallon), against whom he will charge.

The North has its own legend-toned lineup, including Col. Joshua Lawrence Chamberlain (Jeff Daniels), who knows his Bible and his Shakespeare and defends Little Round Top against crushing odds: Brig. Gen. John Buford (Sam Elliott), whose knowledge of terrain is almost primeval—it is he who saves the high ground for the Union army, and Sgt. Buster Kilrain (Kevin Conway), a tough Irishman whose view of humanity is unremittingly bleak. ("There is no divine spark," he says.)

Maxwell's view of these men—these "killer angels"—is not so unremitting. He takes an even-handed approach, carefully balancing out his scenes between North and South. The logistics of battle are lucidly sketched, and so are the various arguments for war on both sides. But very little truly objectionable material intrudes, which gives the film a placid sheen. Lee, for example, is quoted in Shaara's book as saying that he does not believe "the Negro, in his present stage of development, can be considered the equal of the white man," but this sort of stuff doesn't make it into the movie. Lee is portrayed less as a racist than as a high-minded bungler of genius who tragically did not heed Longstreet's warnings about Gettysburg.

The battles themselves, while they have panorama and authenticity, are rather mild in their depiction of violence. Maxwell goes in for long tracking shots and sprawling tableaux, but there's not much kinetic spring in his war sequences. We feel we're observing the battles rather than being right inside of them.

And yet the battles are the best part of "Gettysburg." Whenever the action stops while the officers plot and wheedle and ruminate, the film sinks into animated waxworks. A few of the actors, notably Jeff Daniels and the late Richard Jordan, manage to inject some real feeling into all the historical posturing. They bring the human drama into intense focus, and we fear for them when the bullets and the cannonballs start flying. Some of the other performances are undone by fake beards. Lee's isn't so bad, though it gives him a St. Nick look. But Tom Berenger is saddled with a thatch that makes him look like an Amish elder on a bad beard day.

After Ken Burns' PBS series "Civil War," and the shelves of books that have been written about the Battle of Gettysburg, this full-scale re-creation sometimes seems like a species of pageantry—the ultimate boys' dress-up game, complete with uniforms and fake rifles. When the film is at its best, though, Maxwell makes us forget the fakery, and the enormity of what we're witnessing sinks in. (It has the time to sink in.) "Gettysburg" (rated PG for language and battle scenes) isn't a work of great feeling or depth but it lays out its story with a minimum of bluster, and that has its own integrity. It doesn't close off your interest in the Civil War, or in warfare.

NEW YORK POST, 10/8/93, p. 39, Michael Medved

The new Civil War epic "Gettysburg" is such a noble, even heroic, undertaking that you end up wishing passionately that it provided a more satisfying cinematic experience than it does.

Though it will no doubt captivate TV viewers when it airs next year as a six-hour miniseries on Ted Turner's TNT network, as a feature film it comes across as earnest but unfocused—a shapeless, sometimes clumsy disappointment.

Part of the problem is the sheer length of the piece: The theatrical version runs for four hours and eight minutes, and is made to seem even longer by an intermission inserted at an especially awkward point in the proceedings.

It's virtually impossible to sustain dramatic tension for that long when everyone in the audience already knows how the story will turn out; this could be the only movie of the year where a critic doesn't have to worry about giving away the ending.

Of course, the chief selling point for this project—particularly in its big-screen version—is the purportedly spectacular battle scenes, which have been presented with admirable concern for historical accuracy and have been filmed for the first time ever on the actual "hallowed ground" at Gettysburg, where 150,000 Union and Confederate troops struggled for three fateful days in July of 1863.

Despite a few stirring moments, the intended crowd scenes in the film fall flat—due in large part to mediocre camera work and editing. During the climactic restaging of Pickett's charge, for instance, we seem to see the same few bodies blown into the air by Union artillery some half-dozen times.

The music is also a major problem: To make elaborate battle scenes crackle with significance and excitement, you need the kind of haunting, heartfelt and heroic strains provided by composer James Horner for the great Civil War film "Glory." Here, Randy Edelman's painfully pedestrian score relies too heavily on electronic synthesizers, and contributes to the ho-hum atmosphere in even the most important moments.

Through shot, shell and snores a large, distinguished and deeply committed cast struggles mightily to bring this material to life. Martin Sheen would hardly seem a logical choice to play Confederate commander Robert E. Lee, but his performance is altogether inspired—highlighting the vulnerable, deeply spiritual, almost mystic cast of mind behind the great man's stoic mask.

Tom Berenger, as Lee's skeptical lieutenant James Longstreet, and Jeff Daniels, as college professor-turned-Union hero, Colonel Joshua Lawrence Chamberlain, are also outstanding —utterly convincing and unfailingly passionate behind the sometimes tacky-looking false whiskers they are required to wear.

The problem is that writer-director Robert Maxwell (a veteran of PBS and several respected TV movies), like Lee himself on the final day of the battle, doesn't really know what to do with his magnificent troops.

"Gettysburg" is based on Michael Shaara's remarkable Pulitzer Prize-winning novel "The Killer Angels," which explores the innermost thoughts and emotions of commanders on both sides, but when the movie script attempts similar revelations it comes across as so much stilted speechifying. The picture is also highly selective and sometimes misleading in its role as a living history lesson.

For all its sprawling screen time and epic ambitions, it inexplicably omits some of the most significant incidents and fascinating personalities of the actual battle of Gettysburg.

For instance, we never even meet Gen. Dan Sickles, a fiery New York politician who had won headlines by murdering his wife's lover before the war, and whose ineptitude (and insubordination) nearly lost the battle for the Yankees.

In the end, the movie version of "Gettysburg" will probably be remembered like the real-life Pickett's charge: a gallant effort, complete with bugle calls, battle flags, and stunning displays of individual excellence, all in the service of a flawed battle plan and a lost cause.

NEWSDAY, 10/8/93, Part II/p. 66, John Anderson

In 1913, as part of the 50th anniversary observance of the battle of Gettysburg, elderly survivors of that encounter re-enacted Pickett's Charge, the suicidal southern attack that resulted in thousands of Confederate losses. And as they crossed the once blood-soaked field, and rushed into the breach of memory, the old soldiers suddenly broke, and fell weeping into the arms of their old enemies.

As recounted by Ken Burns' epic PBS documentary "The Civil War"—with no footage, just narration—it was not only an unforgettable moment, but a defining one in our lingering fascination with that terrible war. And it was the kind of thing "Gettysburg" tries and tries to fashion for itself with virtually no success.

Clocking in at a daunting four hours and eight minutes, this Turner Pictures enterprise—Ted must have wanted to make the Civil War epic that *doesn't* show Atlanta burning—strives for historical accuracy and probably achieves it: As the studio points out, more than 5,000 Civil War re-enactors were used in the film, and those guys are murder with minutiae. Someone should have pointed out to them, however, that during the battle scenes—Pickett's Charge, for example—they were supposed to be staring into the face of death, not discussing the Braves' chances in the playoffs.

Rich in precarious beards and inconsistent accents, campfire banjos and swollen orchestrations, "Gettysburg" gives us all the main players, and does so with flair. As Gen. James Longstreet, who would take the blame for the Confederate loss, Tom Berenger is a bravado-less leader with a conscience. As his commander, Robert E. Lee, Martin Sheen gives us a deeply revisionist southern icon, who looks like U.S. Grant and sounds like a cross between King Ludwig and Blanche DuBois. There's the southern general Lewis Armistead (Richard Jordan), his federal counterpart and good friend Winfield Scott Hancock (Brian Mallon), and, in the film's most convincing performance, Jeff Daniels as Col. Joshua Lawrence Chamberlain. A college professor and volunteer ("We thought it might be fun ...") Chamberlain takes an undersized battalion, including a hundred mutineers he's inspired to join him, and succeeds in holding the hill called Little Round Top against a much larger and better armed Confederate force. It's the film's most exciting sequence, and Daniels always makes Chamberlain likable, a man under fire who's trying to preserve his dignity.

But even when the fighting is at its most terrible, "Gettysburg" is a curiously bloodless affair, which makes it feel even more like a TV movie—a six-hour version of which reportedly will air on TNT next year. It may also work well as an educational tool. Director/writer Ronald F. Maxwell certainly strives to make the strategic aspects of the battle—in which 43,000 died—accessible. But he also does a lot of recycling. The notions the film puts forth about the causes of the war are almost quaint ("Why are we fighting?" someone asks. "To free the slaves, of course," he's told). And, with the regularity of commercial breaks, the larger action is interrupted for one-on-one discussions that fill in the political theories behind each side's grievance.

"Gettysburg" also has a kind of Hollywood-brand heroism about it that you don't see anymore, or want to. It's about old-time division, old-time religion, old-time tradition, and about men being Men and never questioning their duty. And each time the music swells, we know something significant is happening.

SIGHT AND SOUND, 10/94, p. 43, Tom Tunney

Part One: June 1863. The small town of Gettysburg, Pennsylvania, becomes the focus for the biggest and most crucial battle of the American Civil War. A Union army column approaches the encampment of Confederate Lieutenant General Longstreet, and Confederate commander General Lee decides to organise his forces around Gettysburg. On the Union side, the commander of the 20th Maine regiment, Colonel Joshua Chamberlain, convinces nearly all of the mutineers from another regiment to rejoin the fight; Chamberlain also has the responsibility of looking after his younger brother, Lieutenant Thomas Chamberlain, who is one of his officers. In the vanguard of the Union advance, Brigadier General Buford realises that if the Confederates take the high ground around Gettysburg, the situation for the Union side will be hopeless. While awaiting reinforcements, Buford orders the high ground to be held at all costs.

July 1. Lee orders Lieutenant General Hill to advance and dismisses Longstreet's suggestion to disengage their forces. The Confederate push fails and an emotional Major General Trimble asks to be relieved of his command; Lee refuses. In the Union HQ Meade confers with Buford over his strategy.

Lee decides on a two-pronged assault, including an attack on the hill of Little Round Top; Major General Hood is put in the command of this attacking force. Defending the area is Chamberlain's unit. Three of the remaining mutineers decide to join the fight with him. The Confederate advance up the hill is again and again repelled by Chamberlain's men, who resort to a bayonet charge when they run out of ammunition. The battle is a crucial victory for the Union side.

Part Two: July 2, evening. In the Confederate camp, Brigadier General Armistead reflects on his pre-war friendship with Union commander Major General Hancock. Confederate cavalry Major General J.E.B. Stuart arrives at HQ and Lee berates him for not keeping him informed of his whereabouts. July 3. Lee orders an assault across open ground into the centre of the Union line. Longstreet is convinced the attack will fail but goes along with his commander's wishes. On the Union side, Chamberlain receives orders to redeploy to the centre of the battlefield.

Longstreet tells his men that the battle will decide the fate of their country; privately, he predicts to his fellow officers that the attack will fail. The Confederate assault is preceded by a massive artillery barrage. At first, Chamberlain cowers, but is inspired by the sight of an unperturbed Hancock. The Confederate troops move up through their own artillery positions, but then shells and rifle fire exact a devastating toll. Armistead's men are savagely cut down and the advance is reduced to a shambles, before degenerating into a piecemeal retreat. Lieutenant Chamberlain finds the dying Armistead on the battlefield. Already a broken man, Armistead is further upset to hear that his friend Hancock has also been wounded.

In the aftermath of the Confederate retreat, Lee suggests to his subordinates that the defeat was all his fault, but they vociferously deny it. Lee orders Longstreet to organise a withdrawal and expresses a pessimistic view of the Confederacy's prospects. The Chamberlains are reunited in a silent embrace.

Filmed on the actual locations of the 1863 battle, *Gettysburg* features, as the press notes put it, "the largest-scale motion picture sequences filmed in North America since D. W. Griffith's *The Birth of a Nation.*" The comparison can be made in other ways too. Ronald F. Maxwell's film certainly lacks both the cosy romantic interest and the rampant racism of the Griffith epic, but it does offer a similar vision of the Civil War as an arena in which the civilised and pre-eminently honourable men of both sides somehow found themselves killing each other.

Like the Yankee Stonemans and the Confederate Camerons in *The Birth of a Nation*, Armistead and Hancock are still close friends although they fight on opposite sides. But how could they and their once united country have come to this? Griffith's film notoriously blamed not so much the institution of slavery but the slaves themselves for the outbreak of the Civil War. Gettysburg offers something equally absurd—it blames no one at all. The war's bloodiest battle is wholly detached from its social and political contexts and presented simplistically as a monument to the honour and endurance of the combatants on both sides: sterling qualities which, by implication, helped forge the modern American character.

As a large-scale reconstruction, the film's very narrow focus on nothing but the key historical figures involved in the battle is understandable. But its eagerness to present almost all the officers of both sides in a positive light means that *Gettysburg* is more like a military pageant than a living, breathing drama. It covers all the historical ground, but unlike Edward Zwick's Civil War film *Glory*, for instance, has no discernible point of view. The absence of preening Southern belles and plantation mansions is to be commended, but the film's reluctance to go beyond the honourable surfaces of its officer class, and in particular to probe into the more dangerous recesses of the Southern white psyche, is its biggest failing.

In script terms—though the performances sometimes hint at more—the officers on both sides are presented as life-size electronic puppets one would expect to find in the theme park that will surely some day be erected on the Gettysburg site. They may be historically accurate in the details of uniforms, manners and fulsome facial hair, but they are completely lacking in psychological complexity. These are all courageous, honourable men, who believe in God and the rightness of their cause, but how many of them on the Southern side owned slaves? How did they achieve and sustain their positions of power and, more to the point, how could they manage to persuade thousands of poor whites to fight and die with them in the cause of slavery? This is a rich vein of thought which the novels of William Faulkner in particular have exploited to the full: the huge gap between the chivalric code of the 'Southern gentleman' and the savage economic and racist realities which underpinned his social pretensions. *Gettysburg* consistently shies away from engaging with this issue, in favour of a mind-numbing litany of platitudes about the nobility of the human spirit.

Gettysburg is more like a traditional officers-only British war movie than the more democratically-inclined American model. The ordinary soldiers are canon fodder for the cameras and their point of view is never more than a positive reaction to their leaders' words. One longs for at least some token dissent from the ranks, but the film avoids any such jarring notes.

The movie's made-for-TV status also militates against a convincingly brutal presentation of the battle scenes. These sequences finally attain an impressive momentum, with the camera tracking past lines of ear-splitting artillery and following thousands of men into the climatic charge. Unfortunately the rigorous censorship of US TV doesn't allow for an accurate depiction of the horrendous death and dismemberment exacted. And because of the film's focus on the officers, these thousands of soldiers are just so many ciphers who tidily fall over and die. This is a sanitised warfare that succeeds as spectacle, but which is badly lacking in urgency and personalised danger. Frequently many of the 5,000 extras involved (recruited from battle re-enactment enthusiasts from across the USA and Europe) can be seen looking lost while waiting their turn to be killed; the director also has the persistent bad habit of putting his camera in front of rather than behind his men's weapons. A key factor in the visual aesthetic of the war movie genre is the extreme difficulty of filming an actual battle. In real combat, the camera is hardly ever in front of the guns—if it were, the cameraman wouldn't be alive for very long. The low prowling camerawork in Lewis Milestone's *All Quiet on the Western Front* and Stanley Kubrick's *Paths of Glory* are both informed by this fundamental matter of the cameraman's life and death, and gain immensely in impact as a result. Gettysburg is sadly lacking in such power.

That said, there are real virtues in almost all the performances. Nineteenth-century stolidity, simple faith and common decency are marvellously conveyed by Jeff Daniels in particular, and the dashing enthusiasm of Stephen Lang's Pickett genuinely seems to belong to another far off, far more naive time. If the film's glaring lack of irony has a positive side, then it surely lies in the strength, commitment and full-bearded quality of its cast.

TIME, 10/25/93, p. 80, Richard Schickel

There are three compelling reasons to see *Gettysburg*. The first is General Robert E. Lee, the second is Colonel Joshua Lawrence Chamberlain, and the last is Brigadier General Lewis Armistead. They don't embrace all the contortions imposed on the human spirit by military necessity, but they'll do for a potent, dramatic start. And their existence as well-drawn figures amid the hubbub of a four-hour epic speaks well for writer-director Ronald Maxwell's sober intentions and very creditable achievements in this film.

Of the three, Martin Sheen's Lee is the most startling. In our folklore (and in the hearts of his troops) the Confederate leader has been granted near saintly status. Sheen gives us the dark side of the holy warrior, a man of courtly manners who is possessed by a vision of a vainglorious, straight-ahead assault on the enemy's center—the vision that produced Pickett's disastrous charge. It was a course of action that defied reason (personified here by Lieutenant General James Longstreet, who is underwritten and underplayed by Tom Berenger).

Lee's opposite number in the film's dramatic scheme is Colonel Chamberlain, commander of a ravaged regiment assigned to defend the Union flank on the hill known as Little Round Top. A college professor and, as played by Jeff Daniels, a soft-spoken humanist-idealist, he is democratic man at his best. And a commander of steely resolve. Almost out of ammunition, unable to withstand another Confederate charge, he mounts a bayonet assault of his own, downhill and through heavy woods (in the film's best combat sequence). Finally, there is the late Richard Jordan's Armistead, the film's great romantic, haunted by the fact that he must meet his best friend in battle—haunted too by his unrequited love for the man's wife. "Virginians! Who will go with me!" he cries, rushing to his gallant doom.

All these performances are touched with a sense of rue, a sense of lives caught up in forces they cannot master. This, together with our knowledge of the dreadful cost of the battle, lends a terrible poignancy to the film. The fact that Maxwell struggled for a decade to realize the project (even mortgaging his home to retain the rights to Michael Shaara's Pulitzer-prizewinning novel,

The Killer Angels, on which he based his screenplay) lends a certain critical tolerance to one's view of the film, which lingers too long over the preparations for engagement, contains perhaps too many couriers galloping up with exposition and concludes with a battle that is handled rather distantly and bloodlessly. These flaws, though, are minor compared with the acuity of the film's best characterizations, the vaulting scale of its design and, above all, its old-fashioned belief that history, besides being instructive in itself, can—and should—be a great movie subject.

VILLAGE VOICE, 10/26/93, p. 64, Tom Kertes

"Is today Friday?" General Robert E. Lee inquires of his faithful attendant. "Yes, sir." "Friday, July the third?" "Yes, General." "Then tomorrow," Lee announces triumphantly, "is July the Fourth!!"

With such analytical minds to lead them, it's small wonder the rebels lost the Civil War. And with such scintillating dialogue, it'll be even less surprising when *Gettysburg* follows the South southward. This movie is *Tora! Tora! Tora!* without the kamikazes, *Battle of the Bulge* minus the bulge. It joins the too-long list of bloated war epics—a discourse on military strategy sans a single character to care about or relationship to relate to.

If ever a film cried—bellowed!!—for a subplot, *Gettysburg* is it. I kept hoping one of the reb generals would come up with marriage problems. Or chide a cheating mistress. Heck, by the end of the third hour of this four-hour-plus film I'd have settled for Ulysses S. Grant going out on a blind date.

The plot: The Confederates arrive at Gettysburg. The Federals arrive at Gettysburg. The North takes up positions on the battlefield. Lee does the same, but not nearly as well. The rebs charge, foolishly. The rebs lose, decidedly. While all this unfolds, we learn more about flanking, pincer movements, ammunition, muskets, the joys of reloading, and the heartbreak of getting shot in a vital part than we've ever cared to know. The actors (and there are some major talents here in Jeff Daniels, Tom Berenger, Martin Sheen, and C. Thomas Howell) appear to vacillate between attempting to take a nap and trying to camouflage their embarrassment.

Also reviewed in:
CHICAGO TRIBUNE, 10/8/93, Friday/p. C, Michael Wilmington
NEW REPUBLIC, 11/8/93, p. 32, Stanley Kauffmann
NEW YORK TIMES, 10/8/93, p. C16, Stephen Holden
VARIETY, 10/4/93, p. 37, Daniel M. Kimmel
WASHINGTON POST, 10/8/93, p. D6, Hal Hinson
WASHINGTON POST, 10/8/93, Weekend/p. 36, Desson Howe

GHOST IN THE MACHINE

A Twentieth Centiry Fox release.   *Producer:* Paul Schiff.   *Director:* Rachel Talalay. *Screenplay:* William Davies and William Osborne.   *Director of Photography:* Phil Meheux. *Editor:* Janice Hampton and Erica Huggins.   *Music:* Graeme Revell.   *Music Editor:* Richard Bernstein.   *Sound:* Mark Weingarten.   *Sound Editor:* Bruce Richardson.   *Casting:* David Rubin and Debra Zane.   *Production Designer:* James Spencer.   *Art Director:* Jim Truesdale.   *Set Designer:* Jann Engel.   *Set Decorator:* Sarah B. Stone.   *Special Effects:* Richard L. Thompson and John Richardson.   *Visual Effects:* Eric Henry, Richard E. Hollander, Craig Barron, and Michael Pangrazio.   *Costumes:* Isis Mussenden.   *Make-up:* Sheryl Berkoff-Lowe.   *Make-up Effects:* Tony Gardener.   *Stunt Coordinator:* Mickey Gilbert.   *Running time:* 104 minutes. *MPAA Rating:* R.

CAST: Karen Allen (Terry Munroe);   Chris Mulkey (Bram);   Ted Marcoux (Karl);   Wil Horneff (Josh Munroe);   Jessica Walter (Elaine);   Brandon Quintin Adams (Frazer);   Rick Ducommun (Phil);   Nancy Fish (Karl's Landlord);   Jack Laufer (Elliott);   Shevonne Durkin (Carol);   Richard McKenzie (Frank Mallory);   Mimi Lieber (Marta);   Mickey Gilbert (Mickey the Driver);   Ken Thorley (Salesman);   Carl Gabriel Yorke (Safety Technician);   Richard Schiff (Scanner Technician);   Clayton Landey (Mel);   Walter Addison (Veteran Cop);   Matthew Glave (Rookie Cop);   Carlease Burke (Woman Cop);   Michael Laguardia and Charles Haugk (Cops); Chris Ellis (Lieutenant);   Robert Lamar Kemp (Yuppie);   Dom Magwili (Doctor);   Haunani Minn (Nurse);   Charles Stransky (Cop at Police Station);   Alix Koromzay (Punk Girl);   Helen Greenberg (Customer);   Nigel Gibbs (Detective);   Andrew Woodworth (Home Security Men); Zack Phifer (Priest);   Don Keith Opper (Man in Office);   Mitchell R. Parnes (Bartender); Edwina Moore (Newswoman);   Rick Scarry (Newsman).

LOS ANGELES TIMES, 12/31/93, Calendar/p. 29, Kevin Thomas

"Ghost in the Machine" deftly envisions a dead serial killer living on as a computer virus. As a technological thriller, this 20th Century Fox release has superior special effects, maintains a clear story line through a thicket of computer mumbo-jumbo, but its machinery tends to be more interesting than its people. To her credit, director Rachel Talaly pulls everything together sharply and briskly.

Karen Allen stars as a Cleveland divorcée, a TWA office worker who goes to an electronics store to buy a present for her ultra-organized boss. She hits upon a scanning device, which the salesman demonstrates by showing how easily it can scan her address book. In a rush she forgets her address book, which is promptly snagged by the store's weirdo repairman (Ted Marcoux), who is in fact an elusive serial killer.

Never mind that Marcoux dies in a car accident rushing off to kill Allen; the way in which writers William Davies and William Osborne have his evil mind live on behind the grave is ingenious and even creepily credible. Marcoux, in short, has accidentally become plugged into the brain of an elaborate mainframe computer. Electrical circuitry enables him to have limitless possibilities in turning even the most mundane household appliance into a deadly weapon.

The film's special-effects teams under coordinator Richard L. Thompson—Richard Hollander and his company VIFX handled the optics, John Richardson and his people the physical aspects—can't be praised enough. All the ways in which the killer's evil spreads and manifests itself are consistently dazzling. The trouble is that they show up the film's human relationships as drab and conventional in comparison.

Allen is your typical stressed-out single mother, her 13-year-old son (Wil Horneff) the usual bright but troubled fatherless adolescent. The film's biggest contrivance is not technical but in having maverick computer genius Chris Mulkey show up out of the blue just at the right moment.

There's a chemistry between Allen and Mulkey, fine actors both, but there's no time for it to develop. There's probably enough technical wizardry to satisfy sci-fi/horror fans, but the depictions of various grisly deaths through electrocution—and other terrible means—rule out "Ghost in the Machine" for youngsters.

NEW YORK POST, 12/30/93, p. 25, Thelma Adams

What evil lurks in the hearts of men—or machines—or an unlikely combination of both?

"Ghost in the Machine" is an occasionally funny techno-thriller. When a serial killer (Ted Marcoux) gets vaporized during an MRI, his maniacal intelligence goes on-line. Karl becomes the hacker from hell.

Rachel Talalay ("Freddy's Dead: The Final Nightmare") directs this nerd-driven byte-sized scarefest. Computer paranoia runs rampant in the suburban Ohio never-never land where sons love their laptops and mothers shrug their shoulders and hug their Filofaxes.

Unfortunately for computerphobic mom Terry (Karen Allen), Karl (a.k.a the address-book killer) gets hold of her Filofax just before he goes electric. It turns out Karl has a bug in his caring systems—and wants to delete anyone he likes and their network of loved ones.

Terry reluctantly accepts the help of Bram (Chris Mulkey), a computer hacker for good, not evil. It's this reconfigured family—divorced mother, son Josh, and surrogate father—who battle the evil bachelor.

"Frankly, Terry, I'm sick of all this family values crap," are killer Karl's last words as this exercise in suburban terror takes a campy turn.

Against the backdrop of back-lot ranch houses, Allen shines as the suburban mama who just wants to enjoy her (apparently ample) alimony in peace. The actress drew sparks with Harrison Ford in "Raiders of the Lost Ark," Jeff Bridges in "Starman," and Bill Murray in "Scrooged."

Now the brown-eyed, freckle-faced Allen appears to be in career dry dock. Why? Who knows? But she's the best thing going in "Ghost in the Machine" giving an otherwise flimsy movie a little weight.

NEWSDAY, 12/30/93, Part II/p. 55, Gene Seymour

As you always knew it would, the psycho-killer sub-genre has gone high-tech with the release of "Ghost in the Machine." And yet, some things in motion.

Specifically, it's a bolt from an electrical storm that affects a hospital's MRI machine. It happens that the shattered body being scanned belongs to a computer repairman (Ted Marcoux), who spends his off-hours butchering innocent families. He crashed his car on the way to the home of his next victims, a divorcee (Karen Allen) and her rap-loving, computer-hacking teenaged son (Wil Horneff).

The storm causes a power surge in the MRI machine sending the killer's internal atoms into the city's electrical circuitry and computer systems. Legally he's dead but he's not an interfacing psycho: If you can plug it in, he can kill you with it. Sticking to his original plan, he goes after Allen by messing up her bank account, drowning her dog, harassing her son and microwaving her boss. It's up to a super hacker (Chris Mulkey) to try and outwit the killer.

The movie works on a superficial (and not terribly original) level as a cautionary tale of our overdependence on technology and what could happen if the machines bite back. There's also a nice little generational clash woven lightly into the relationship between Allen and Horneff.

But beyond the premise and the computer-generated special effects, there's not much extension in imagination or audacity. Director Rachel Talalay, who also did "Freddy's Dead: The Final Nightmare," brings some of the old "Elm Street" brio to a few of the uglier moments. (It'll be hard to face your faithful microwave oven with the same ardor after you've seen the movie) But this is basically a hacker's overheated idea of Grand Guignol suspense. It leaves you with the same kind of languid light-headedness one gets after an afternoon wandering a mall, looking, not buying.

Also reviewed in:
NEW YORK TIMES, 12/30/93, p. C11, Caryn James
VARIETY, 1/3-9/94, p. 54, Leonard Klady
WASHINGTON POST, 12/30/93, p. C2, Richard Harrington

GIFT

A Warner Reprise Music and Video release. *Producer:* Allan Wachs. *Director:* Perry Farrell and Casey Niccoli. *Screenplay:* Perry Farrell and Casey Niccoli. *Running time:* 83 minutes. *MPAA Rating:* Not Rated.

CAST: Perry Farrell (Perry); Casey Niccoli (Casey).

NEW YORK POST, 9/3/93, p. 28, Dan Aquilante

They don't lie, cheat or steal—Casey and Perry are the nicest junkies you'd ever want to meet. Yeah, heroin is the monkey on their backs, but what they're really addicted to is love.

"Gift" is a wonderful narrative film that fuses performance footage from Farrell's now-defunct band, Jane's Addiction, with the fictional story of the day he discovers his wife, Casey, dead of an overdose in their home.

It's the Beatles' "A Hard Day's Night" on smack, in how it explores the behind-the-scenes of rock stardom with a detached sense of comedy and Farrell's deadpan, wise-guy humor.

"Gift" documents Perry's and Casey's constant search for ecstasy through their love of each other and their lust of the needle and the spoon. The parallel of both addictions is disturbing and appealing at the same time.

On the surface you want to say the message of "Gift" is live fast, die young, make a pretty corpse. But this thought-provoking black comedy—that owes a major debt to Dali's surreal film, "An Andalusian Dog"—is really a celebration of living life as art. Like Dali, Perry and Casey are trying to establish a greater reality through love and dope.

Parents should not let their kids see this film, because of how it glorifies narcotics and the junkie's flight with euphoria.

But adults who are smart enough to realize "Gift" is fiction will find Farrell as engaging an actor as he was a singer for Jane's Addiction and is as the frontman for his current group, Porno for Pyros.

There are a few oddities in "Gift" that I still can't fathom, such as the duet Farrell sings with Ice-T during the closing credits. The song, "Don't Call Me Nigger, Whitey," a verbal fight between the two singers, is a fantastic musical moment that has nothing to do with the rest of the picture.

NEWSDAY, 9/3/93, Part II/p. 75, Ira Robbins

It was the Sex Pistols who sang, "We're so pretty, we're so pretty ... vacant," but it took Perry Farrell, the singer and mastermind of the late band Jane's Addiction, to try to put such nihilistic rock narcissism on film.

In what can be seen as an attempt to prove the self-fulfilling irony of "Nothing's Shocking" (the title of the band's 1988 album), Farrell and wife Casey Niccoli have written, directed and starred in (as themselves) "Gift," an incoherent and self-amused vanity project that attempts desperately to be outrageous but succeeds only in being obnoxious.

Upholding the standard trinity of sex, drugs and rock and roll, "Gift" jumps between a number of disconnected elements. There's a thin story about the couple scoring dope, Niccoli dying of a heroin overdose and Farrell being arrested for her murder. There are scenes of Farrell and Niccoli being wed in a Mexican Santeria service, Farrell surfing and Jane's Addiction performing onstage and in the studio. Also in the mix is an inexplicable segment in which a therapy group of hospital patients discuss their addictions, a comical drug sketch in a doctor's office and Farrell's walk on Venice Beach with a performance by a roller-skating musician. The whole mishmash ends with what looks like a cheap rock video of Farrell and rapper Ice-T duetting on Sly Stone's 1969 plea for racial tolerance, "Don't Call Me Nigger, Whitey."

Shot with varying levels of technical quality (some of the Mexican footage is grainy enough to have begun as Super 8), "Gift" benefits from skillful editing, which at least offers its free-association logic a clear field in which to ramble. But in reaching for an aura of decadence by joking about substance abuse, displaying graphic scenes of injection and staging mock scenes of sadomasochism and necrophilia, the couple who would be this decade's Sid and Nancy dilute their home movies in a shower of cheap thrills, self-indulgence and self-consciousness. But then those values also drove Jane's Addiction, and the group certainly had its fans. This, then, is for them.

GOD IS MY WITNESS

A Headliner Productions release. *Producer:* Manoj Desai and Nazir Ahmed. *Director:* Mukul S. Anand. *Screenplay (Hindi with English subtitles):* Santosh Saroj. *Director of Photography:* W.B. Rao. *Editor:* R. Rajendran. *Music:* Laxmakant Pyarelal. *Running time:* 180 minutes. *MPAA Rating:* Not Rated.

CAST: Amitabh Bachchan (Badshah Khan); Sridevi (Benazir, Menhdi); Nagarjuna (Raja); Shilpa Shirodkar (Henna).

LOS ANGELES TIMES, 6/11/93, Calendar/p. 2, Peter Rainer

"Khuda Gawah"—or "God Is My Witness"—is must-viewing for audiences who prize the grand-scale nuttiness of Bombay epics at their most redolently romantic. If you've never seen one of these Indian extravaganzas—a distinct possibility since the Four Star theater stopped showing them locally several years back—you may not be prepared for the monumental impasto of Hindu folklore and Hollywood hyper-kitsch. (and the current crop is actually far tamer than the epics of several decades past.)

Subtle is not the first—or even the 16th—word to spring to mind in thinking about the acting. Or the directing, the score, the musical numbers. The numbers are the best: They erupt out of nowhere and knock your socks clean off. They're a welcome entry in the annals of the musical—Busby Beserkely.

"God Is My Witness" probably makes more sense if you're Indian, but maybe not. Clearly making sense is not Job One here. The delirium sets in early and never lets up. The action begins in Afghanistan between two rival clans with a race to the finish between competing horsemen carting a goat hide—or something like that. The game is called "Buzkashi," and it's like a cross between Olympic field hockey and the chariot race scene from "Ben Hur." When our hero Badshah Khan, played by Indian superstar Amitabh Bachchan, makes it to the finish line toting his half of the hide, he's in for a shock; his chief rival for the goat turns out to be a *woman*—the sultry veiled Benazir (Sridevi, another Bombay superstar). No one in Hollywood ever met this cute.

Badshah Khan would like to marry Benazir but first he must avenge her father's death by journeying to India and bringing back the cranium of his killer. This section of the film (Times-rated Mature for violence) might be subtitled "Bring Me the Head of Habibullah." Just to make sure Khan's blood lust is properly stoked. Benazir engages her paramour in an elaborate dance that owes more than a little something to hoochie-coochie. She scratches him on the cheek in mid-cooch, and he laps the trickle of blood like it was holy water, while all around them turbaned minions shimmy and shake their silken rumps. By the time he recoups Habibullah's head—his whole carcass, actually—Badshah Khan has run into the kind of trouble that only a 3-hour (not including intermission) movie can resolve.

The largely poor and illiterate Indian audiences for whom movies like "God Is My Witness" are made are as demanding (or, pejoratively, undemanding) as the denizens of our own multiplexes. The impossibly romantic scenarios, with their paeans to sacrifice and blood revenge, are both crass and elating; the escapism on display is unabashed. No kissing is allowed in these movies, no piquant show of flesh. And yet the whole shebang is sensual; life is presented as a series of pageants inspired by desire.

Bachchan and Sridevi (who plays two roles) are a combustible pair even though—or maybe because—their acting range seems limited to various degrees of smolder. Sridevi looks a bit like a darker Morgan Fairchild while Bachchan, particularly as he grows more bearish and hirsute, resembles Topol in "Fiddler on the Roof," though his guttural rant—his normal speaking voice—sounds more like Al Pacino in "Dick Tracy." He has the heroic presence of a true matinee idol. He's impassioned by his own grandiosity and so is this movie. It's deliriously beyond camp, beyond kitsch.

NEW YORK POST, 8/24/93, p. 28, Jerry Tallmer

The central fact about "God Is My Witness," the Indian film is this: Running time, 180 minutes.

More than once in my notes I see I've jotted down about some action or another—probably when people are singing passionately, eye to eye, how much they hate and love one another —"This goes on quite a while—like forever." Here is a sample of the song.

HE: "Enemies are felled by arrows, not by piercing glances."

SHE: "I am not a butterfly. I destroy."

He is Badshah Khan, a Pathan warrior in Afghanistan, she is the beautiful Benazir, a name I have formerly only associated with Benazir Bhutto of Pakistan. They'd clashed as opponents—she veiled in a *buzkashi*, a game so called in which two teams from rival clans conduct a sort of violent polo match over the body, which soon becomes the corpse of a poor battered goat.

They'd immediately fallen in love, and now Benazir requires that Badshah ride across the border into India (shouldn't it be Pakistan?) to bring her back the head of Habibullah, the man who'd killed her father. Then only will she consent to marriage.

From that event stems the entire three-hour melodrama of song, dance, dust, fire and fury, very much like an American Western—a hokey posturing one beyond belief—full of grandiloquent macho boasts and braggadocio and betrayal and triple-cross and fistfights and firefights and bodies rolling down mountains only to turn up in the next reel in amazing revival from absolute death.

Also spectacle, lots of spectacle; and although I like buttes and canyons and deserts as much as the next guy, I'm not much of a party for spectacle. Blandly mixed in at random with all this period stuff are modern automobiles, jet planes, walkie-talkies, cellular phones.

Well, years pass, Benazir goes gaga with grief over the absence of her jailed husband, there's a thankless daughter, at least two full-blown villains, two good buddies, God knows what else. For my part you can't even tell the players *with* a scorecard, but I guess you don't go to movies like this one for logic or clarity. You go for emotion, of a sort.

My favorite line is the daughter's "Don't show me your morbid face, go!" The actress named Sridevi, who plays both wife and daughter, has something of the eyes and smile of Elizabeth Taylor—and something of the immobility too.

NEWSDAY, 8/20/93, Part II/p. 71, Jonathan Mandell

My mouth dropped open near the beginning of "God Is My Witness." This was after the hero falls in love with the heroine while they are fighting over a dead goat, but before the dancing chorus of saber-wielding, fire-blowing Afghanis, and way, way before the howitzer-and-dagger climax with everybody and their in-laws tied up in the desert.

I could not figure out whether I was supposed to laugh at this three-hour bloody tandoori western and musical melodrama from Bombay, in Hindi, which could reasonably be described as Romeo and Juliet played like Rambo and Ophelia by Nelson Eddy and Madonna in a Robin Hood setting from a "Days of Our Lives" script directed by Sam Peckinpah, except that description doesn't quite cover it. It's too simple.

The mutated Hollywood mishmash is apparently a concrete genre in India (which has the world's largest movie industry) and is eaten up by the masses there, who also adore its two stars.

Sridevi plays the sultry, heavily mascaraed Benazir, who tells Badshah Khan (Amitabh Bachchan), a bearded, dewy-eyed member of a rival clan in Afghanistan, that she will marry him only if he goes to India to kill Habibullah, who killed her father. He finds Habibullah, who is about to be executed by the Indian authorities, abducts him on horseback from the gallows, is ambushed by Habibullah's gang, slices Habibullah up and is saved by the honorable Indian jailer from whom he stole the now-dead killer. He honorably promises the honorable Indian jailer that he will return in a month to serve time in prison for the abduction. He goes back (with dead Habibullah) to Afghanistan to marry Benazir, but he returns as promised to the Indian prison, where he stays for decades, which drives Benazir insane. I'm leaving out a lot. There are also about eight musical numbers. (A typical lyric, or at least subtitle, is: "Of your intoxicating gaze do not make me drink.")

Then, after the intermission, we meet the now grown-up sons and daughters of the characters in the first act, one of whom, also played by Sridevi, is a giggly, teenage, gun-toting race-car driver.

The plot becomes increasingly berserk, confusing and illogical—though not much more so than, say "Cliffhanger." Despite its evident earnestness, "As God Is My Witness" has got to be at least an inside joke. Maybe that's why the hero dropped his jaw, about when I did; at first I thought he was trying to express his love or joy or nobility, but maybe he too was just in shock.

VILLAGE VOICE, 8/31/93, p. 62, Erik Davis

Representing the largest film industry in the world. India's popular movies are chockful of over-blown emotionalism, seriously sublimated lust, and gaudy musical numbers. But beyond the Indian diaspora, they haven't much penetrated the West. So the three-hour epic *God Is My Witness* is a double treat: an example of the Third World's most resolutely popular cinema and a delirious hunk of folkloric camp. The film opens with high-fiving Afghanis playing *buzkashi*—basically, polo with a goat corpse—during which Badshah Khan falls in love with the maiden Benazir (Sridevi). What follows is accurately described by the film's ad as "a sweeping tale of love, honor, and passion."

Sridevi is magnificent in her dual roles as pluckish coquette and long-suffering wife, but Amitabh Bachchan as Badshah Khan is the largest presence here. A burly man with a voice that seems to emerge straight from his solar plexus, Khan sobs, thumps his chest, and follows a code of honor that would put a samurai to shame. He's the kind of guy who, when crossing the border into India, stops and introduces himself to the land personally.

Like nearly all of its Bombay kin, *God Is My Witness* poaches moves from Hollywood epics, westerns, and Busby Berkley musicals while elaborating them into India's unique film lingo. Particularly odd is the magical lack of continuity in the song sequences, when lip-synching lovers are instantly and inexplicably transplanted from cities to lush forests where they go through numerous costume changes before finishing the tune. The hip-shaking numbers they perform are as cheesy as any flashdancing cheerleader, but it's not American cheese.

The release of *God Is My Witness* is a clear attempt to siphon off the rising popularity of Hong Kong's violent ballets. Fans of John Woo and Tsui Hark will be disappointed by the film's production quality and lack of kinetic direction. But *God Is My Witness* has the advantage of Bombay's voluptuous erotic play (the fact that, as a rule, lovers never kiss only juices up the tease).

Perhaps the most provocative image, though, is the portrait of Benazir that Khan paints on the wall of the prison cell where he spends much of the movie. Simultaneously sexy and sublime, the portrait resembles nothing so much as a movie poster.

Also reviewed in:
NEW YORK TIMES, 8/20/93, p. C8, Stephen Holden

GOOD EVENING, MR. WALLENBERG

A Sandrew Film production with Scansat/TV3, The Swedish Film Institutre, Filmhuset and Film Teknik in association with Hunnia Film Studios. *Executive Producer:* Klas Olofsson. *Producer:* Katinka Farago. *Director:* Kjell Grede. *Screenplay (Swedish, German and Hungarian with English subtitles):* Kjell Grede. *Director of Photography:* Esa Vuorinen. *Editor:* Darek Hodor. *Music:* Janos Solyom and Frans Helmersson. *Sound:* Bjorn Gunnarson. *Production Designer:* Laszlo Gardonyi. *Costumes:* Inger Pehrsson. *Running time:* 115 minutes. *MPAA Rating:* Not Rated.

CAST: Stellan Skarsgard (Raoul Wallenberg); Erland Josephson (Rabbi in Stockholm); Katharina Thalbach (Marja); Karoly Eperjes (Szamosi); Miklos B. Szekely (Ferenc Moser); Franciszek Pieczka (Marja's Papa); Jesper Christensen (Officer); Laszlo Soos (Eichmann).

NEW YORK POST, 4/23/93, p. 33, Jerry Tallmer

There are 52 Jews to be got off this train, and only five passports in Wallenberg's hand.

"Five passports for 52 Jews," says Szamosi, the man at the wheel of the truck, a Hungarian Jew, pretending to be from the Spanish Embassy. "Put on the fur hat," he says to Wallenberg. "Without the fur hat, you're lost." They have 30 seconds, these two, to complete the whole operation.

Wallenberg, blandest of men, puts on the fur hat, steps out beside the train, and in an instant—as Szamosi slams the truck backwards up against the open door of the boxcar—turns into a raging dragon.

"These men are needed for *very urgent* repair work at the Spanish Embassy," he yells in German at the sergeant in charge, out-Naziing the Nazis in volume and ferocity. Do you *understand* me, Sergeant? Why are you not cooperating? I want the names of all your men. What's the matter with you, can't you speak German???"

The 52 Jews on the train jump, pour, spill onto Szamosi's truck, the truck roars off, Wallenberg and his fur hat leaping into the truck at the last moment, "You took too long," he snaps at Szamosi. But they have their 52 Jews, and the sergeant and his soldiers still don't know what hit them.

Thus one of the gripping moments—one of dozens—in "Good Evening, Mr. Wallenberg," a film by Kjell Grede of Sweden about the Swedish playboy-turned-diplomat who by sheer guts and selfless heroism saved perhaps 100,000 Jews from being shipped off to the Holocaust from 1944 Budapest, only to be shipped off himself to some terminal form of non-existence in Soviet Russia.

Very little in the movie is as clear-cut as the rescue from the train; much of it in fact is totally confusing—just as confusing, discontinuous, mismatched, inexplicable, brutally absurd as was, I suspect, day-to-day, moment-to-moment existence itself in Nazi Hungary or Nazi anywhere. A program note in fact declares: "All the people in this film really existed. Everything in the film is true. Unreal perhaps, yet absolutely true." And the film bills itself as "A passion taken from reality."

That it is, and I think the most passionate and best re-creation of Wallenberg and his moment that I've yet seen or read. Stellan Skarsgard is merely perfect as the blue-eyed zero of a traveling salesman—importer of delicacies from Germany and Hungary—who can only answer No and No and No again to the sour, suspicious Swedish rabbi (Erland Josephson of the Bergman stock company) who demands: "Are you an idealist? Do you believe in God? Am I altogether wrong in judging you—hardly anyone of note—mediocre for this mission?"

Also perfect is Karoly Eperjes as cock-of-the-walk caustic Szamosi, and Katharina Thalbach as a living ghost of a young woman driven half-mad by seeing the Germans slaughter her two small daughters before her eyes. It is this Marja who haunts the movie, and Wallenberg, with four or five hungers all mixed together—hatred, terror, fatalism, need for affection, revenge. And there is an Eichmann in the film who—with his murderously icy "Good evening, Mr. Wallenberg"—might for a change really be Adolf Eichmann.

Indeed, everything here is brilliantly executed except its—or Wallenberg's—obsession to rescue yet another 20 Jews from yet another truck, this one held hostage by a dogfaced homegrown Hungarian Nazi (Miklos B. Szekely). The incident seems to go on forever, reel after reel, and it is not one of Wallenberg's triumphs. Twenty Jews—against 60,000 who are about to die in the Budapest ghetto, unless ...

Unless Wallenberg can throw a little blackmail around; a tired Wallenberg, an exhausted Wallenberg, stoking up the inner fire one more time. In the end, when the Russians come, perhaps he's just tired enough to let his guard down. That rabbi back in Stockholm must have spent the rest of his life wondering how he could so badly have miscalculated the importer of delicacies who wasn't anyone of note. So, I guess, should we.

NEWSDAY, 4/23/93, Part II/p. 75, John Anderson

Raoul Wallenberg, the Swedish diplomat who saved thousands of Hungarian Jews from the Nazi death camps, was arrested by the Soviets on June 17, 1945, and is presumed to have died in a Moscow prison in 1947. A cruelly unjust end, and one that deprived the world the chance of perhaps redeeming itself in some small way by acknowledging his courage. But it also provided the world with a perfect hero, an idea rather than a man.

Swedish filmmaker Kjell Grede has tried to make the idea flesh, and he's succeeded almost entirely. By avoiding any urge to sentimentalize, and making the unformed, callow Wallenberg (Stellan Skarsgard) such a mediocre character, he makes what Wallenberg did all the more remarkable, because the man is so flawed. It's an exceedingly depressing trip Grede takes us on, each time your hopes are raised, he dashes them. But in the end, the film sparks the same hopefulness, tenuous though it may be, that one gets just considering Wallenberg's existence.

Although the film begins with the subject's epiphany—an importer of gourmet foods from Hungary, he's on a business trip through eastern Europe when he witnesses the dumping of Jewish bodies from a train bound for the camps—most of the action takes place in Budapest in 1944. The outcome of the war is clear, and the Nazis are in a defeat-fueled murderous frenzy; Wallenberg, a decidedly unqualified diplomat, has been sent to do what little he can.

Even though Wallenberg's use of Swedish passports to save lives makes him a near-legendary figure among the Jews of Budapest, the man himself is an ambiguous figure, and is treated ambiguously by the people he's trying to save. He can't save them all, and for that they hate him. And it makes him hate himself; for every life he snatches from the Nazis' jaws, an untold number are killed.

Grede wisely shows Wallenberg operating on two "fronts": a tenement where 20 Jews have somehow escaped the systemic killing, and the ghetto, which has been targeted for mass destruction by Adolf Eichmann. The latter is a lopsided confrontation between the twin angels of mercy and death; the former serves to closely analyze the dynamics of imminent death—the small cruelties, the fear, the utter madness.

In this age of Schwarzenegger, et al., we may have become numb to cinematic violence of the goriest sort. But the virtually bloodless murders committed by the Nazis in "Good Evening, Mr. Wallenberg" serve to blunt their impact. And while we're not calling for more bloodshed on-screen, here it might have been appropriate, especially in a film that is otherwise so consistently frank and uncompromising.

VILLAGE VOICE, 4/27/93, p. 62, Leslie Camhi

Eichmann visited Budapest with a staff of 16 in the spring of 1944, and by summer half a million Hungarian Jews were dead. When news of the killings reached Sweden, Raoul Wallenberg, a well-bred but mediocre young businessman (an importer of delicacies) from a prestigious family, was sent to Budapest as humanitarian attaché. *Good Evening, Mr. Wallenberg* chronicles the six desperate months during which this unlikely hero overstepped diplomacy, and with a relentless combination of bribery, blackmail, fraud, and collaboration, saved perhaps 100,000 Jews.

Swedish director Kjell Grede has shot the familiar cinematic vocabulary of hopelessness in beautifully modulated browns and grays: a young couple marry on the eve of deportation. a baby is born, a child's toy rolls across the floor and stops. More moving is his careful re-creation of the unreal sensations of surviving under insane conditions and the surreal images that the totalitarian exercise of power produces. So, in a ghetto courtyard, people hold their paintings for a German officer who barks, "We only want Watteau!" while a woman, half-mad, voluntarily foregoes her clothing for the nakedness proper to victims.

Wallenberg's presence in Budapest paradoxically served his enemies by calming the Allies' conscience, while his passion and compassion became a diplomatic embarrassment, a responsibility, no government wanted to claim. At the war's end, he was taken to Moscow by Soviet authorities and mysteriously disappeared. *Good Evening, Mr. Wallenberg* highlights the existential in his struggle, with which history still contends.

Also reviewed in:
CHICAGO TRIBUNE, 6/11/93, Friday/p. F, Patrick T. Reardon
NEW YORK TIMES, 4/23/93, p. C12, Stephen Holden
VARIETY, 10/29/90, p. 53

GOOD SON, THE

A Twentieth Century Fox release. *Executive Producer:* Ezra Swerdlow and Daniel Rogosin. *Producer:* Mary Anne Page and Joseph Ruben. *Director:* Joseph Ruben. *Screenplay:* Ian McEwan. *Director of Photography:* John Lindley. *Editor:* George Bowers. *Music:* Elmer Bernstein. *Music Editor:* Kathy Durning. *Sound:* Susumu Tokunow and (music) Dan Wallin. *Sound Editor:* Stan Bochner. *Casting:* Deborah Aquila. *Production Designer:* Bill Groom. *Art Director:* Rusty Smith. *Set Decorator:* George DeTitta, Jr. *Set Dresser:* Peter Nauyokas, Tempest S. Farley, Ray Fisher, Arthur Pottie, Paul Richards, Bob Schnieg, and Donald Wilson. *Special Effects:* Neil Trifunovich. *Costumes:* Cynthia Flynt. *Make-up:* Bernadette Mazur. *Stunt Coordinator:* Jack Gill. *Running time:* 87 minutes. *MPAA Rating:* R.

CAST: Macaulay Culkin (Henry);   Elijah Wood (Mark);   Wendy Crewson (Susan);   David Morse (Jack);   Daniel Hugh Kelly (Wallace);   Jacqueline Brookes (Alice);   Quinn Culkin (Connie);   Ashley Crow (Janice);   Guy Strauss (Arizona Doctor);   Keith Brava (Doctor in Blackport);   Jerem Goodwin (Factory Worker);   Andria Hall (Woman Reporter);   Bobby Huber (Axe Man);   Mark Stefanich (Ice Man);   Susan Hopper (Woman at Rescue);   Rory Culkin (Richard in Picture).

LOS ANGELES TIMES, 9/24/93, Calendar/p. 1, Kenneth Turan

"The Good Son" is an ending in search of a movie. Its climactic scene (fear not, it won't be revealed here) is the kind of high concept predicament that is supposed to send audiences out of theaters with a buzz on their lips. Instead it can do no more than point up how flat what's come before has been.

With a script credited to novelist Ian McEwan ("The Cement Garden," "The Comfort of Strangers"), though in sore need of his usual ambiguity and edge, "The Good Son" is yet another reworking of familiar "Bad Seed" themes, in which very evil thoughts come in very small packages.

Rated R for "acts of violence and terror involving a disturbed child," "The Good Son" will also be known as the movie where young Macaulay Culkin, the CEO of the billion-dollar "Home Alone" industry, decided, either with or without adult urging, that he was tired of playing a cute urchin with a friendly grin. Eager to deepen and darken the scope of his roles, he chose this picture to do it in, not, as it turns out, the wisest of decisions.

Though Culkin's name is listed first on the credits "The Good Son" is really the story of another 12-year-old boy, Mark Evans, played by the sturdy, saucer-eyed star of "Huck Finn," Elijah Wood.

Mark's lot in life is not a happy one. No sooner does the film open but his mother dies, though not before she takes the time to promise that she'll always be with him. And Mark's dad, Jack (David Morse), finds he has to leave for a once-in-a-lifetime business opportunity in Japan just after the funeral ends. What to do with young Mark?

Not to worry, says Mark's uncle Wallace (Daniel Hugh Kelly). The lad can live with my wife and our two children in our typically photogenic New England town of Rock Harbor. "It'll only be for two weeks," Dad promises. Need one say that they will be the longest weeks in young Mark's life?"

Wallace used to have three children, Mark discovers, but toddler Richard unexpectedly drowned in a tub. That leaves 8-year-old Connie (Quinn Culkin) and her older brother Henry (Macaulay Culkin), on the surface, the good son every father would like to have.

But though he seems like a regular kid, Henry, Mark soon discovers, has a, shall we say, scientific side. For this young man is fascinated by death, wants to learn all he can about it, even took notes (notes!) when he saw his baby brother in his fatal tub. Ever the conscientious researcher, Henry soon embarks on some experiments of his own, but when an unsympathetic, not to say terrified, Mark tries to spill the beans, he finds no one wants to hear his tale.

Director Joseph Ruben ("Sleeping With the Enemy," "True Believer," "The Stepfather") is a capable, energetic filmmaker who has been successful with this kind of pulpy material in the past. And he tries hard here, even throwing in enough dizzying crane shots to unnerve a tightrope walker.

But the unsurprising, one-note nature of "The Good Son," the fact that it's a bump-in-the-night movie where all the bumps are visible a mile ahead, sorely constricts any possibility of excitement. Mark may get increasingly frantic at Henry's doings, but nobody in the audience is likely to share his concern

Macaulay Culkin is not what's wrong with "The Good Son," but in all honesty his performance doesn't help. Not every actor, no matter what the age, can convey the dark side, and Culkin comes off more sullen and pouty than evil. He works at it, but he can't overcome the fact that he is simply miscast.

All this is especially ironic given the fact that "The Good Son" was delayed a year so Culkin, not the original choice but a power at the studio due to "Home Alone," could fit it into his schedule, even though that meant that the original producer and director and even some of the cast ended up being replaced. While this film may be beneficial for the Culkin clan (sister Quinn makes her film debut and even brother Rory gets a screen credit for appearing as a photograph of the deceased Richard), it will not do the holder of the family franchise nearly as much good.

NEW YORK, 10/4/93, p. 104, David Denby

Joseph Ruben, the director who started so well with *The Stepfather* and *True Believer*, has turned himself into a commercial formalist of no great interest. *The Good Son* is better than Ruben's paint-by-numbers thriller *Sleeping With the Enemy*, but only a little bit better. The movie is gripping; it quickens one's pulse when it should and releases the audience into reasonable satisfaction at the end. But it's a movie with very few dimensions. Watching it, I couldn't escape the feeling that Ruben had solved a number of limited formal problems in his head in advance—involving a treehouse, some snowy woods, a rocky point over water—and had then shot the movie without passion, without wildness or wit. Hitchcock also solved problems in his head, but he set himself more complex ones.

The Good Son is one of those flatly unbelievable things about a bad seed, a 12-year-old boy (Macaulay Culkin) who is "pure evil" and who kills people and animals who annoy him. Only his little cousin (Elijah Wood), a good boy who has lost his mother, can perceive the true nature of the little murderer; everyone else is taken in by Macaulay's sweet lips and reasonable manner. As in *Sleeping With the Enemy*, Ruben makes things easy for himself by working with two-dimensional characters, and he's not helped by an inexpressive performance from the high-priced tow head. I'm afraid that I, too, can see through Macaulay Culkin. As W. C. Fields said when he spiked Baby LeRoy's drink, "The kid's no trouper." Culkin appears to be just basking in the attention. The actor here the true potential star is Elijah Wood, who has the most powerfully tragic face I can remember seeing in a little boy; Wood understands the emotional significance of what he's doing. I'm not sure the same is true of Joseph Ruben. The screenplay, by the English novelist Ian McEwan, provides some psychological interest that Ruben has only half developed. Vital feelings are missing from this movie, and Ruben's coldness throws us back on the distastefulness of the subject—a child murdering other children, served up as entertainment.

NEW YORK POST, 9/24/93, p. 41, Michael Medved

The biggest problem faced by the new thriller "The Good Son" is the "Aw, Come On" factor.

As soon as people hear that it stars "Home Alone,"'s incurably cute Macaulay Culkin as some sort of murderous monster, the natural reaction is, "Aw, come on! That makes about as much sense as casting Tom Cruise as a vampire!"

Though no one can say at this point how Mr. Cruise will ultimately acquit himself in the upcoming "Interview With The Vampire," it is now possible to grade young Master Culkin for his first-ever role as a vicious villain. Despite persistent rumors of trouble behind the scenes, I'm amazed to report that the kid deserves an "A"; his performance as diabolical Henry Evans is complex, convincing and utterly chilling.

In fact, Culkin comes across as a good deal more natural and comfortable in this role than he did in either of the "Home Alone" movies—where at times he seemed to be visibly acting—which raises the intriguing possibility that the real-life Mac may have more in common with the heinous Henry than with the cuddly Kevin.

In any event, this tow-headed tyke is one subtle and accomplished actor, who now deserves to stand alongside the masterful John Malkovich in "In the Line of Fire" as one of the most frightening big-screen bad guys of the year.

Part of the secret of his success in this eerily effective shocker is the unusually intelligent screenplay by respected British novelist Ian McEwan. The story begins when a genuinely sweet and decent child, Mark, (played by Elijah Wood of "Huck Finn," "Avalon" and "Forever Young") goes off to spend a few weeks with his aunt and uncle, following his mother's death from a wasting illness.

At first, Mark has a marvelous time with the two first cousins he hasn't seen in years (played by Culkin and his spunky real-life sister, 9-year-old Quinn Culkin), but then the young visitor begins to notice strange, sadistic aspects to cousin Henry's sense of fun. Killing a vicious dog and deliberately provoking a freeway pile-up are only the beginning.

They say that the devil is in the detail and it's the telling details here that make Henry's devilish nature so believable and terrifying. You can understand how his parents could remain blind to his true nature in contrast to the scarcely credible situation in the campy, creepy 1950s play and movie the "Bad Seed" to which "The Good Son" inevitably will be compared.

Director Joe Ruben and cinematographer John Lindley (who previously worked together on the mediocre melodramas "The Stepfather" and "Sleeping With the Enemy") here provide perfect pacing and a series of indelible images; the Norman Rockwell coziness of the wintry, coastal Maine setting (actually shot in Cape Ann, Mass.) heightens the sense that his unsuspecting family is painfully vulnerable, to Henry's menace.

The only sequence that strikes a false note is the overwrought climax at the edge of a sheer, 120-foot cliff, since such spectacular heights are in short supply on the New England coast, they staged the scene some 1,500 miles away on the Minnesota shore of Lake Superior.

"The Good Son" is one of those exceedingly rare thrillers that not only makes you sweat, it makes you think.

NEWSDAY, 9/24/93, Part II/p. 58, John Anderson

If Macaulay Culkin were more than 12 years old, and there hadn't been such unpleasant advance word about how he got this role, you might call his appearance in "The Good Son" a bold attempt to plot a new career path. Misguided, as it turns out, but bold.

This updated, R-rated "Bad Seed" casts Macaulay—the prince of PG, the Midas of mall movies, the sweet-faced screamer of "Home Alone" and "HA 2"—as a prepubescent sociopath with homicidal impulses who terrorizes his cousin and sister, cons the adults around him, kills a dog with a homemade gun, and maliciously causes an 10-car pileup. He's a very primal kind of monster—the child with an angel's face, and no soul, who uses the presumption of childhood innocence to commit horrible crimes. And he should strike at a very primal kind of fear. Macaulay, however, doesn't so much strike as gnaw.

The young actor's face has been his fortune, but there's never been a cause for him to display much on it, besides a smirk or a shriek. And the vapid look he wears in "The Good Son" almost works to his advantage. There's so little on the surface, you suspect there must be something else going on behind it, perhaps something malevolent. But blankness doesn't prove to be enough, especially when the film's basic question is whether pure evil actually exists.

Mark (Elijah Wood) certainly thinks so. After his mother dies—she dies, an eagle flies, it's that kind of film—and his father is sent on an extended business trip, Mark gets packed off to live with his aunt Susan (Wendy Crewson) and uncle Wallace (Daniel Hugh Kelly), and his cousins, Henry (Macaulay) and Connie (Quinn Culkin). It's tough enough being uprooted after losing your mother, but Mark's also toting a huge load of guilt. He promised his mother he wouldn't let her die, and then she did. He bonds, though, with Susan, who's carrying her own guilt: A few years earlier, she lost her baby Richard, who drowned in the bathtub when she left him for just a minute (hmmmm ...).

Henry—whose interests include constructing a weapon that fires 5-inch steel bolts, and throwing a dummy off an overpass in the middle of rush hour—takes full advantage of Mark's problem. No one, he rightly assumes, will believe a troubled boy like Mark when he claims Henry's a sick puppy. In fact, why not blame Mark for the very crimes he accuses Henry of committing?

Mark Lehmann, the film's original director, resigned rather than direct Macaulay (whose father reportedly held up production of "Home Alone 2" until Macaulay was given the "Good Son" role). His replacement, Joseph Ruben ("Sleeping With the Enemy"), seems to be casting about for something to give the film suspense, since he can't generate it through his young actors (Elijah Wood is the real star of the film, and gives a very capable, but dull-edged performance). A shot of Susan asking "How about some breakfast?" is given the same dramatic emphasis as one in which someone's life is threatened. And the music, often, is simply wrong.

There are some gripping moments, but many more that smack of manipulation and convenient developments in plot and character. Would a mother ever believe that her son could do what Henry does? And, for that matter, do we believe in a child as spiritually malformed as Henry?

No, we all need more proof than "The Good Son" provides that pure evil, if not opportunism and cinematic manipulation, actually exists.

NEWSWEEK, 10/11/93, p. 59, Jack Kroll

Macaulay Culkin has been called the Shirley Temple of the '90s, a kid superstar who breaks the box-office records and commands Stallone-size wages. But the comparison has more interesting levels. Temple beguiled a Depression-mauled audience with her eerie ebullience, her inadvertent parody of song, dance and sex. So sacred an iconette was she that Graham Greene was sued for libel for a review that spoke of her "dimpled depravity," her "dubious coquetry," noting that "adult emotions of love and grief glissade across the mask of childhood." Reviewers of Culkin's new thriller (instant top box office), *The Good Son*, who referred to Mack's "sweet lips" and "bedroom eyes" no doubt delighted Twentieth Century Fox, the very studio that hauled Greene into court.

But if Greene's pre-Nabokovian analysis raised hypocritical hackles, at least, as he pointed out, it was "emotions" that animated Temple's. What makes Culkin a scary devil-doll in "The Good Son" is the absolute lack of affect that becalms those 12-year-old eyes and lips. Culkin plays Henry, a homicidal homunculus who kills his little brother, dispatches a dog with his homemade crossbow, causes a 10-car smash-up by tossing a dummy onto the highway, tries like hell to polish off his sister and his mother—and feels absolute zero. When Mark (Elijah Wood), Henry's cousin who's staying with his family, tries to stop the one-tot crime wave, Henry says: "You just don't know how to have fun."

So who is Henry and why does he like making people dead? This movie, like Henry himself, doesn't give a damn. Unlike the "Bad Seed"-type films in earlier, more Freudian decades, "The Good Son" provides no context for understanding the little creep. Henry's mom and dad are candidates for an OPY Award (Obvious Parents of the Year)—they just dress Hammering Henry in his cozy L.L. Beanish woolies and miss every sign that he's thinning out the local populace. The script is credited to British novelist and screenwriter Ian McEwan ("The Comfort of Strangers") but, clearly, uncredited rewriting has gutted it of McEwan's usual texture. The original director, Michael Lehmann ("Heathers"), left the film when Kit Culkin, Mack's father and manager, reportedly said that his tyke wouldn't make the sequel to "Home Alone" unless he got the role of Henry.

The new director, Joseph Ruben ("Sleeping With the Enemy"), has come up with an exercise in button-pushing exploitation. He's like a poor man's Brian De Palma, finding glossy visuals and scary angles: Henry and Mark climb to a rickety tree-house; Henry sends his kid sister through thin ice on a frozen pond; Henry corners his mom on a dizzying cliff. Let's not kid ourselves, "The Good Son" is child pornography with violence rather than sex as the hook. It's funny how steamed up grown-ups can get when Sharon Stone uncrosses her legs, but Mack Culkin can hack away at his family for no discernible reason and he's just an adorable predator in Pubescent Park. Culkin is less like the infernally talented Shirley Temple and more like the celestially untalented Brooke Shields. He's not really an actor but a model, the mini-embodiment of some unsavory fantasies in this age of emotional entropy. Elijah Wood, however, is a terrific actor. But he'll never make $5 million a movie.

SIGHT AND SOUND, 1/94, p. 45, Leslie Felperin Sharman

After his mother dies, ten year-old Mark Evans is sent to New England to stay with his aunt and uncle and their two children—Henry, who is about Mark's age, and his little sister Connie—while his father goes away on a business trip. Mark's aunt Susan is still mourning for her youngest child Richard, who died in a bathtub accident some time ago.

At first, Mark and Henry have fun playing together. However, Mark gradually realizes that despite his innocent guise in front of grown-ups, Henry is violent, vicious and frighteningly amoral. Mark becomes complicit in an escalating series of Henry's cruel pranks, from smashing windows to killing a local dog, and finally causing a major road accident with a stuffed dummy thrown from a bridge. When Mark threatens to expose him, Henry attempts to kill Connie by contriving an accident while skating, but she is narrowly rescued. Mark tells Henry's mother what has been going on, but she attributes his seemingly irrational behaviour to grief at his mother's death. After fighting with Henry, Mark is confined to the house.

Meanwhile, Susan investigates Henry's secret shed and finds evidence which supports Mark's accusations. She and Henry go for a walk, during which she openly asks if he killed Richard. He admits his guilt, but runs away, apparently upset. Susan follows him to a cliffside, where he pushes her off. Mark, who has broken out of the house, wrestles with Henry on the precipice. Susan crawls back up onto the ledge and catches each boy by a hand, just as they fall off the edge. Able to save only one, she chooses Mark, despite Henry's glib appeals to mother love, and drops her son onto the fatal rocks below.

Based on a screenplay by Ian McEwan, *The Good Son* is bound to suffer from routine comparisons with the recent cinematic adaptation of his first novel, *The Cement Garden*. Against the latter's edgily English treatment of incest, all look-at-me camerawork and startling editing, *The Good Son* looks far too Hollywood-slick, a bog-standard thriller which everyone, especially McEwan, probably did only for the money. In fact, though by no means excellent, it is in many ways the more interesting film. While *The Cement Garden* peddles grotesquerie and prurience, like an adolescent eager to shock its parents, *The Good Son* is a more mature, yet ultimately more subversive movie, asking more difficult questions about childhood and familial love. If this film were a teenager, it would be one who always did his homework, never pranged the family car, and then one day quietly shot everyone with a rifle made in his metalwork class.

Which is precisely the kind of child that Macaulay Culkin plays in it—a cherub who, without much of a cause, is ruthlessly malevolent, a Charles Manson in size four Reeboks. As with his recent fiction, McEwan's script here is portentously concerned with the Nature of Evil. This Manichean perspective works better in the chiaroscuro world of the thriller film than it does in his pretentious attempts at the Novel of Ideas. The film offers a range of optional explanations of Henry's psychopathology—sibling rivalry, the corrupting violence of video games and horror movies—but in the end, Henry's taste for violence is ultimately inexplicable. Like the eponymous anti-heroine in Maxwell Anderson's play, which *The Good Son* recalls in theme as well as details, Henry is also simply a 'bad seed'.

It's an unfashionable conclusion for the mainstream cinema, which usually prefers behaviouralist explanations for all aberrations from normality, like the psychiatrist's remarks at the end of *Psycho*. If anything, the film suggests that Henry is but an extreme manifestation of the cruelty inherent in all children, a point clunkingly underscored when he and Mark wear identical masks. Unlike Kit Culkin, Macaulay's own father and manager, the parents here are hardly to blame, being simply as blinded as the rest of us by the dazzling ideology of childhood innocence. Like the numerous shots of children behind windows, and at one point clear ice, our perception of childhood is always filtered. The shock ending, with Wendy Crewson setting the ultimate example of Tough Love, is perhaps so satisfying because it taps adults' own unspeakable feelings of hatred towards their progeny.

Never have I seen the death of a character applauded so heartily by an audience, as when Macaulay Culkin plummets to his death in this film. No doubt this was more an indication of their aversion to the actor than their engagement with the story. Nonetheless, the casting of Mac as the baddie is thought-provoking for several reasons. Firstly, laying his performance against Elijah Wood's excellent one as Mark makes it apparent what a mediocre actor Mac is. Henry hardly seems to differ from Kevin in the *Home Alone* films—voice flat, gestures precocious, presence annoying. But this has the remarkable effect of illustrating how similar this film and the other pair really are. Just as in *Home Alone*, Mac's character uses his devious imagination to play tricks and defend himself, only here the result is real injury rather than slapstick. In all three films, Mac is a cute, sadistic, irritating little bastard who deserves to die; in *The Good Son* he finally does. Parents and disgruntled babysitters everywhere will applaud.

TIME, 9/27/93, p. 84, Richard Schickel

Joseph Ruben's apparent mission in life is to turn the commonplaces of family dysfunction into worst-case scenarios. Everyone at some time or another imagines comfortable domesticity going radically wrong. Ruben gives this uneasy feeling—that we all may be no more than a mischance or two away from reading our names in a tabloid headline—grabby if sometimes almost comically simple life on the screen. In Ruben's *The Stepfather*, that eponymous figure turns out to be—his stepchildren guess it!—a serial killer. In *Sleeping with the Enemy*, Julia Roberts' character fakes her own death trying to escape the husband from hell.

In *The Good Son*, the director taps yet another nasty, not entirely uncommon fantasy. What if a child's normal mischievousness—a compound of forgivable prankishness, a bit of secretiveness, some expectable sibling rivalry—is not just a boyish phase? What if it is actually the first sprouting of a very bad seed? Meet Henry Evans (Macaulay Culkin). Who would believe that polite, sweet-smiling Henry is actually the devil's spawn? Not his doting parents, who are still grieving over the presumably accidental death of his younger brother. Not his visiting cousin Mark (Elijah Wood), who is also in mourning for his recently deceased mother and eager at first to overlook a few scary eccentricities. Not the audience—not for a while, anyway. We want Culkin's screen character to remain the beleaguered, adorable innocent of the *Home Alone* pictures.

As he does in his bleak, spare novels, screenwriter Ian McEwan uses very simple means to establish an air of menace. The death of a neighborhood dog, a spectacular multi-vehicle auto accident, the near death of Henry's little sister in an ice-skating incident—Henry's role in all these can be explained away by people with a vested interest in maintaining their tranquillity. Ultimately, cousin Mark awakens Henry's mother (a very believable Wendy Crewson) to long-suppressed suspicions, which leads to a stark and indescribable climax—literally a cliffhanger, but one so nervy and straightforward that it puts you in mind of old-fashioned B movies.

That's what's good about Ruben. He doesn't mess around with nuance. He sticks to the psychological basics and the most primitive scare tactics. Nothing distracts him from arriving, via the shortest possible distance, at some not exactly subtle but inescapably gripping point. It ain't art. Nobody's ever going to call him the new Hitchcock. But there's something admirable in his disdain for high, fancy stepping, his heedlessly efficient drive to put us in touch with the primal ooze of our worst imaginings.

VILLAGE VOICE, 9/28/93, p. 66, Alyssa Katz

Macaulay Culkin's eerily lush lips and bedroom eyes work magic in *The Good Son*, broadcasting the psychosis that drives Henry, his portrait of a minuscule killer. Who needs a performance? Some may say he's miscast, but the delirious novelty of the towheaded wonder in gruesome action really hits the happy bone. Dangling his cousin Mark (Elijah Wood, a child actor who can act) from a nosebleed-high treehouse, playing Malkovich to Wood's Eastwood, deadpanning, "If I drop you, do you think you could fly?" Culkin's Henry works *The Good Son* into a peppy *Bugsy (Ho) Malone* take on the psycho-bitch movie. (Those psycho-bitches are, after all, children with breasts.) It's not camp, but close, maybe day camp.

At first, Henry and Mark, a soulful young thing who's been sent to live with his aunt's family on the Maine coast after his mother dies, have a blast together, smashing windows, playing combat games, shooting household pets with a homemade crossbow. Then things get rough. The melding of children's games with adult-style malevolence—hide-and-seek (in a vast pitch-black house), rubber ducks (cum murder evidence)—tweaks the genre thrills as the bad kid torments the good.

Threads about the role of fear in children's lives and on the existence of pure evil get stalled by the *noir*-thin construction of Culkin's self-styled Übermensch. Why ask why? XYY? Who knows—Henry's just the Bad Hat, the Bad Seed, Bad. As with Macaulay's friend Michael Jackson, his inner life remains mysterious.

Also reviewed in:
CHICAGO TRIBUNE, 9/24/93, Friday/p. A, Michael Wilmington
NEW YORK TIMES, 9/24/93, p. C12, Janet Maslin
VARIETY, 9/27/93, p. 40, Brian Lowry
WASHINGTON POST, 9/24/93, p. C1, Hal Hinson
WASHINGTON POST, 9/24/93, Weekend/p. 42, Desson Howe

GROUNDHOG DAY

A Columbia Pictures release. *Executive Producer:* C.O. Erickson. *Producer:* Trevor Albert and Harold Ramis. *Director:* Harold Ramis. *Screenplay:* Danny Rubin and Harold Ramis. *Story:* Danny Rubin. *Director of Photography:* John Bailey. *Editor:* Pembroke J. Herring. *Music:* George Fenton. *Music Editor:* Sally Boldt. *Sound:* Les Lazarowitz and (music) John Richards. *Sound Editor:* George H. Anderson. *Casting:* Howard Feuer. *Production Designer:* David Nichols. *Art Director:* Peter Lansdown Smith. *Set Designer:* Karen Fletcher-Trujillo. *Set Decorator:* Lisa Fischer. *Special Effects:* Tom Ryba. *Costumes:* Jennifer Butler. *Make-up:* Dorothy Pearl. *Stunt Coordinator:* Rick LeFevour. *Running time:* 103 minutes. *MPAA Rating:* PG.

CAST: Bill Murray (Phil Connors); Andie MacDowell (Rita Hanson); Chris Elliott (Larry); Stephen Tobolowsky (Ned); Brian Doyle-Murray (Buster); Marita Geraghty (Nancy); Angela Paton (Mrs. Lancaster); Rick Ducommun (Gus); Rick Overton (Ralph); Robin Duke (Doris the Waitress); Carol Bivins (Anchorwoman); Willie Garson (Phil's Assistant Kenny); Ken Hudson Campbell (Man in Hallway); Les Podewell (Old Man); Rod Sell (Groundhog Official); Tom Milanovich (State Trooper); John Watson, Sr. (Bartender); Peggy Roeder (Piano Teacher); Harold Ramis (Neurologist); David Pasquesi (Psychiatrist); Lee R. Sellars (Cop); Chet Dubowski (Bank Guard Felix); Doc Erickson (Bank Guard Herman); Sandy Maschmeyer (Phil's Movie Date); Leighanne O'Neil (Fan on Street); Evangeline Binkley, Samuel Mages, and Ben Zwick (Jeopardy! Viewers); Hynden Walsh (Debbie); Michael Shannon (Fred); Timothy Hendrickson (Waiter Bill); Martha Webster (Waitress Alice); Angela Gollan (Piano Student); Shaun Chaiyabhat (Boy in Tree); Dianne B. Shaw (E.R. Nurse); Barbara Ann Grimes, Ann Heekin, and Lucina Paquet (Flat Tire Ladies); Brenda Pickleman (Buster's Wife); Amy Murdoch (Buster's Daughter); Eric Saiet (Buster's Son); Lindsay Reinsch (Woman with Cigarette); Roger Adler (Guitar Player); Ben A. Fish (Bass Player); Don Rio McNichols (Drum Player); Brian Willig (Saxaphone Player); Richard Henzel and Rob Riley (D.J. Voices); Terry Fryer (Piano Hand Double).

LOS ANGELES TIMES, 2/12/93, Calendar/p. 1, Kenneth Turan

"Groundhog Day" may not be the funniest collaboration between Bill Murray and Director Harold Ramis, and it doesn't have a chance of being the most financially successful. Yet this gentle, small-scale effort is easily the most endearing film of both men's careers, a sweet and amusing surprise package.

Though endearing is not an adjective often associated with the deadpan, abrasive, almost misanthropic style of humor Murray is known for, it is his comic hostility that makes "Groundhog Day" as agreeable as it is. Taking the bitter with the sweet is more than a venerable cliché, but it is also a recipe for making sentimentality palatable on screen.

Much of the credit for this charm ought to go to first-time screenwriter Danny Rubin, who came up with the original idea (and shares script credit with Ramis). There is a romantic innocence about his concept that survives the overreliance on Hollywood shtick that weighs down the film's first part and makes us believers by the close.

Murray stars as Phil Connors, a Pittsburgh TV weatherman who is so self-involved he's convinced he doesn't just report the weather, he creates it. Jaded and cynical, Connors hates nothing more than having to journey to rural Punxsutawney once a year and participate in the unsophisticated shenanigans centering on whether a certain groundhog does or does not see his shadow.

But on this particular Feb. 2, some things turn out to be different for Phil. For openers, he has a new producer, the cheerful, good-natured Rita Hanson (Andie MacDowell). For another, Phil discovers that, much as he dislikes it, Feb. 2 is a day he just can't escape. Ever.

Upon awakening in Punxsutawney on what should be Feb. 3, Phil gradually realizes that everything about this day, from the clock radio playing "I Got You Babe" at precisely 6 a.m. to the chitchat of total strangers, is exactly the same as it was on Feb. 2. But while everyone else is living this day for the first time, Phil is not only repeating it, he seems destined to repeat it again and again and again until the end of time.

What would you do if there were truly no tomorrow, if you knew everything that was going to happen on a given day and nothing you did ever had even a hint of consequences? As he comes to understand, if not accept his situation (which, like all fairy tales, is offered blessedly free of explanation); Murray's Phil quickly disposes of the obvious choices. He pigs out on pastries, drives with abandon, seduces women and flouts the law. Does any of this make him happy? No, it does not.

Then, almost in desperation, Phil remembers Rita, and decides, for want of something better to do, to use the knowledge he can accumulate about her as he keeps reliving Groundhog Day to seduce her. It is a clever conceit, and one that has life-changing consequences that even Phil can't begin to imagine.

A lot of things can go wrong when the repetition is the essence of a film, not the least of which is that seeing the same situation over and over sounds like a considerable bore. And, in the opening stages of the PG-rated "Day," when moments like stepping into a puddle of ice water are given more than their due, it looks as if Murray and company won't be able to escape that trap.

But Rubin's story has more warmth than you might anticipate, as well as its own kind of resilience, and having the gruff Murray (rather than some more fuzzy and cuddly actor) endure a change of heart makes the softer emotions easier to accept. With MacDowell as the pleasant foil, Murray turns "Groundhog Day" into a funny little valentine of a film. It won't overwhelm you or change your life, but after all the more obvious laughter is over, it may just make you smile.

NEW STATESMAN & SOCIETY, 5/7/93, p. 34, Jonathan Romney

The film *Groundhog Day* is based on the double-edged premise of living the same day over and over again. If you were an idealist, you would know that, whatever went wrong, you could always get it right next time around. If, on the other hand, you were a cynic, you might feel as if you were in for endless identical sequels to the same movie.

Groundhog Day's cynicism taps right into the cynicism of sequel-era Hollywood itself—the kind of cynicism that will one day give us *Home Alone 23*—and goes one better. Imagine if, instead of a string of sequels, you crammed a film full of all its own possible sequels, and turned a one-joke skit into an infinite regress of repeated gags, each folding into the next. *Groundhog Day* tells us early on that we're going to have the same gag thrown at us time and time again. The challenge is to keep finding new ways to laugh.

So the first time cynical TV weatherman Phil Connors (Bill Murray) wakes up on Groundhog Day in the impossibly congenial hick town of Punxsutawney, Penn, and the radio's playing Sonny and Cher, we laugh, because God forbid it should happen to us. The second time it happens, we laugh but this time nervously, because God forbid it should happen twice. The third time, we're already breaking out in a cold sweat, anticipating a water-torture effect—we know that director Harold Ramis and co-writer Danny Rubin will feel no compunction about milking this gag *ad infinitum*.

Fresh hell is one thing Phil doesn't get. Every day, he stumbles downstairs to be greeted by an indefatigably chirpy hotel keeper, ambushed by the town bore (the peerless Stephen Tobotowsky), and subjected to the awful annual ceremony in which a small rodent emerges to "forecast" the weather. From then on, he has to make his own amusements— overeating, reckless driving, meticulously planned seductions, the gradual acquisition of godlike powers.

Groundhog Day may be the purest nightmare movie Hollywood has ever produced—potentially endless repetition, just for its own sake—but it's also the most formalist. It's like a dare between Rubin and Ramis to see how many variants they can work on one theme before 101 minutes are up. They go about it with fiendish ingenuity, undercutting our expectations when we least expect it, but also confirming them just when we're getting as weary as Murray is of having them confirmed; they like to make sure that from time to time it feels like hell for us too.

Or they divide the repetitions up into series of routines, and series within series—a series of seductions, a series of good deeds, a series of (successful) suicide attempts. Phil ends up living the same principle that gag-writers operate by—if a routine doesn't work, try again, and when you've tried till you're heartily sick of it, find a new routine. Then there are all the fine gradations of pacing; sometimes the film assaults us with knowing monotony, sometimes the repetition takes on a delirious speed-spiked rhythm.

Bill Murray is probably the only comic who could last the course. Imagine Robin Williams or Tom Hanks reacting for all they're worth, and trying to milk the situation for its human element. But Murray's transcendent langour makes him perfect casting for a man whose daily hell starts the second he wakes up. He has always excelled in treating every situation like a bad Budweiser dream; he's a slow-burning somnambulist who reacts with stony disdain as disasters mount. But here, he's got something new to deal with—*nothing* happens, unless he makes it happen.

The fact that there is absolutely no explanation for Phil's predicament makes *Groundhog Day* unique in contemporary Hollywood, where everything has to be justified to the point of absurdity. Look how fastidiously *Home Alone* films set up ways for Macaulay Culkin to be left behind, not once but twice. Here, though, the basic premise *needs* no justification.

Actually, that's not *quite* true. There is a moral justification, if you choose to see it. Early on, Phil snarls, "I *make* the weather." Well, he thinks he does, and in this respect, the time-loop is laid on purely for his moral edification—time will be out of joint until he realises that actually it's the weather that makes him. So everything seems to be set up for a dainty little moral homily ending in a grouch's rehabilitation.

In fact, *Groundhog Day* has a more cynical agenda. Sure Phil is improved, but for all the wrong reasons, and in all the wrong ways. He can become the perfect man purely because he has nothing else to do, having exhausted all the day's other possibilities. Given time, he becomes a god, omniscient and omnipresent, and when that's driven him mad, maybe then he'll settle for being a nice guy. But he's only officially a nice guy when the woman he's lusted after all along (Andie McDowell) recognises him as one. And that's where the film ends up, in a perfect have-your-cake-and-eat-it male fantasy. Yes guys, even a repellent jerk can get off with Andie McDowell in 24 hours flat.

The probable reasons for *Groundhog Day*'s massive US success is that it appeals at once to absolute idealism and to absolute cynicism. It comes packaged as a moral lesson about human perfectability, but its deep structure allows for total amorality. Phil gets to do horrible things to other people with impunity, because the next day it'll all be undone. That's the principle behind *Tom and Jerry* violence, but *Groundhog Day* is a first in applying that principle to the comedy of manners.

I've neglected to point out just how brazenly funny *Groundhog Day* is. But it's funny because, instead of spoon-feeding you, as most Hollywood comedies do, it actually tests your endurance, putting you in the same claustrophobic eternal present as its hero, and constantly daring you to rethink your habitual conceptions of cinematic time. Who'd have thought the director of *Ghostbusters* would prove the rightful heir of Alain Resnais?

NEW YORK, 3/1/93, p. 110, David Denby

Groundhog Day might have been a mere gimmick movie, but it isn't; it's something better—a gentle fantasy of both paralysis and liberation. This is a comedy about a man who gets stuck in time. Bill Murray plays a dyspeptic TV weatherman, working out of Pittsburgh, who goes to the small Pennsylvania town of Punxsutawney to do the annual cornball story on Groundhog Day. The next morning he wakes up, and it's still February 2. The groundhog has seen his shadow, but time has stopped. No matter what happens to Murray—sex, death, sleep—he keeps waking up in his hotel at 6 A.M., February 2, with Sonny and Cher singing "I Got You, Babe" on the clock radio. This is a nightmare, obviously, because the same things happen every day; and a blessing, because Murray knows everything that will happen on Groundhog Day.

What if you wanted to impress a girl, and you were able to ascertain, through infinite practice, all her favorite moods? Murray wants to get in bed with his producer, Andie MacDowell. The day repeats itself, and he tries over and over, each approach a little closer to the mark, but he still gets rebuffed each time. When God invented the cinema, He must have known He was placing in man's hands an unparalleled instrument for the manipulation of time, and His servants Danny Rubin and Harold Ramis, who wrote the screenplay together (Ramis directed), take splendid advantage of this possibility. They engage in some drastic narrative foreshortening, finally overlapping the same moment of each repeated day—Murray getting slapped across the kisser again and again as he fails.

When he finally breaks through, it's because he becomes a new person. The movie is a kind of Scrooge/Groundhog Day story: A man realizes that winter is not death but just a season that is part of the cycle of life and that eventually ends. He sees the end of winter in himself; he opens himself to the world. A benevolent streak comes out in Bill Murray: *Groundhog Day* becomes a comedy of goodness. Aware of everything that's going to happen, Murray catches a kid falling out of a tree and tries to keep a homeless old man alive. The device allows Bill Murray to reveal more of himself than he ever has before, and he gives his most intimate and detailed performance yet. He seems not only an intelligent man but intelligent enough to be a benevolent man.

NEW YORK POST, 2/12/93, p. 31, Audrey Farolino

Praising a movie that stars Bill Murray and a groundhog isn't something you should do if you want to enhance your intellectual standing.

Nevertheless, at the risk of destroying what little reputation I have left in that department, I must confess that I liked "Groundhog Day." Very much.

People to whom I have made that statement tend to look at me with grave concern, and some feel compelled to point out that the movie's trailer is egregious. Which it is, since it focuses on sillier moments like the groundhog driving a pickup truck.

What the trailer fails to capture is the movie's caustic wit, Murray's perfect deadpan delivery and the plot's cleverness: It's about a man who finds himself living the same horrendous day over and over again.

As a reporter, I can identify only, too well with someone assigned to cover Groundhog Day once too often. That's the fate that befalls Phil Connors (Murray), a vain lout of a TV weatherman, who finds himself dispatched to Punxsutawney for the fourth year in a row ("For your information, hairdo, there is a major network interested in me," he snarls at a colleague who snickers at his fate).

Making matters worse, Connors is accompanied by wisecracking cameraman Larry (Chris Elliott) and Rita (Andie MacDowell), a hopelessly upbeat producer. When Rita tries to convince Connors that people actually like Groundhog Day, Connors replies, "You know, people like blood sausage, too—people are morons."

Connors drags himself through the assignment and the trio sets off for home, but a blizzard traps them in Punxsutawney. Thus the nightmare begins: Connors awakes in his hotel the next morning, only to realize, with growing confusion and horror, that somehow it's Groundhog Day all over again. As it will be every succeeding day, though Connors is the only person aware of the time freeze.

The premise is fertile ground for laughs, and they're mined expertly. But it also offers a look at human psychology in the absence of that great motivator known as "tomorrow."

Connors progresses from frustration ("Well, what if there is no tomorrow? There wasn't one today," he fumes at a phone operator), to recklessness ("I don't worry about anything anymore—I don't even have to floss") to despair (he makes numerous suicide attempts, and tries to off the groundhog as well) to a kind of numb wonder if maybe he isn't "a god ... not *the* god, I don't think."

Connors is also falling in love with Rita. But no matter how much progress he makes each day in winning her over, when the next day replays itself he is right back to what he was originally in her eyes—a jerk.

The movie's premise is rather Kafkaesque, but its message is more Capraesque: Even if you're stuck in the same place with the same people doing the same things every day, you can find salvation of a sort through little acts of kindness and selflessness.

Oh dear—have I actually mentioned Kafka and Capra in connection with Bill Murray? I'd better stop here before I really go too far.

NEWSDAY, 2/12/93, Part II/p. 66, Jack Mathews

What would you do if you woke up tomorrow and it was today, all over again? The song playing on your clock radio, the, people you meet on the way to work, the blizzard moving in from the Southwest ... everything the same, except for your behavior, and everything forgotten by everyone but you?

That is the marvelous fantasy device of Harold Ramis' "Groundhog Day," and with Bill Murray delivering the most mature performance of his career, it has a romantic charm to match its freshness and its constant good humor.

Its plot is a gimmick, to be, sure, and Ramis and his co-writer Danny Rubin don't even attempt an explanation for Pittsburgh TV weatherman Phil Connors' predicament. One day he and his film crew are in Punxsutawney, Pa., covering a corny small-town ritual, and the next day they're at it again.

For Connors (Murray), an ambitious egotist who belittles everyone from the town bum to his brightly sincere producer Rita (Andie MacDowell), spending eternity with the piteously cheerful rubes of Punxsutawney is like sharing a cell with Mister Rogers. In the hands of less skillful filmmakers, the movie might have had the same effect on us.

But beneath the simple notion of "Groundhog Day" are layers of good ideas. Like "Heaven Can Wait" and all memorable romantic fantasies, "Groundhog Day" is at its heart a life lesson, a story of self-discovery and change, and done in a way that gives us an immediate rooting interest.

All the way through the movie, your mind play's a game of "What would I do-What will he do?" And as Connors goes through the cycles of panic, anger, playfulness, depression and acceptance, he inevitably tries everything you can imagine. The main thing working against him is that there is no escape. Whether he commits suicide or ends up in jail, he awakes in the same bed listening to Sonny and Cher sing "I've Got You Babe." On the other hand, "tomorrow is another day" takes on a whole new meaning.

Within the confines of his 24-hour prison, Phil can accomplish whatever he wants through trial and error, from robbing an armored truck to seducing women, with total immunity.

Ramis, who directed Murray in "Caddyshack" and worked with him as either an actor or writer on several other comedies, managed to engage his best comic instincts here—without resorting to the sophomoric high jinks that have marked all of Ramis' previous work. He's taken an absurd set of circumstances and refused to fill it with absurdities. Every character and action in the story follows a certain logic, even the months-in-the-making whirlwind romance between Phil and Rita.

"Groundhog Day" is an actors' sandbox. Not only do the recurring characters all appear in big scenes, but in several versions of them, revealing a little more (if themselves in each one. Every performance besides Murray's necessarily reacts to his, but the chemistry works, particularly with MacDowell, who shows a confidence we've never seen in her before.

Murray's natural style, a wisecracking smugness that borders on condescension, is ready-made for the self-absorbed TV personality we first meet. However, his performance really takes off after Phil enters the time warp and is forced, by the boredom of his own company, to reach out for other people.

His character learns a lot about the real qualities of life under those circumstances, and between the smiles and robust laughs this smartly executed movie delivers, so do we.

SIGHT AND SOUND, 5/93, p. 50, Ben Thompson

Phil Connors, a cynical Philadelphia TV weatherman, is less than happy when he is despatched for the fifth time to the small town of Punxsutawney to cover the annual Groundhog Day ceremony. A snowstorm threatens too, though he predicts that it will miss the area. The great day—February 2nd—dawns and the groundhog duly emerges from its box. According to the local dignitaries, the rodent seer has predicted six more weeks of winter. Phil's idealistic producer Rita Hanson extols the town's simple virtues, but he remains unconvinced, and when the snowstorm duly materialises to prevent his departure, takes to his bed in disgust. He wakes up next morning to find that it's February 2nd again. At first he is incredulous and seeks help from Rita, from a doctor and from a psychiatrist. The next morning it happens again: it's a new day for everyone except Phil. He gets drunk and ends up in jail after driving a car down a railway track. He wakes up as usual in his guest-house bedroom. Over successive February 2nds, he uses the knowledge he is able to acquire about the town's people and events for sexual and financial gain, seducing women and robbing banks. He devises a devious plan to have his way with Rita, but it consistently fails.

Despondent, Phil steals the groundhog and commits suicide by driving off a cliff. He wakes up as usual to Sonny and Cher on the radio. Having exhausted all possible suicide routes, he manages to get Rita to understand what has happened to him and, after they spend a glorious day together, he tells her that he loves her. Next day, she remembers nothing. After unsuccessfully trying to save the life of an old tramp, Phil starts to use his power of hindsight for the good of the community—catching falling children, performing Heimlich manoeuvres—building up a daily regime of life-saving 'chores'. One Groundhog night he goes to the post-ceremony party that he'd spurned on his first February 2nd. The townspeople treat him like a hero and Rita is so impressed she buys him for the night in a charity auction. Next morning, February 3rd dawns at last for Phil. Blissfully happy, he decides to set up house with Rita in the town he now knows so well.

Groundhog Day is that rarest of cinematic pleasures—a major studio Hollywood comedy that both delights and surprises. It's based on a story by Danny Rubin, who co-wrote the screenplay with director Harold Ramis, and although it's the original idea that is initially so startling, the inventiveness and delicacy with which it is realised are finally just as impressive. There's not much in Ramis' career to suggest a talent for subtle, character-based comedy—he started out as jokes editor of *Playboy* and went on to co-write *Animal House* and direct *Ghostbusters* (on the plus side, he also made *Caddyshack*). But that, within the framework of a very high concept, is what he delivers.

The idea of the endlessly repeating day is in fact such a high concept—if Samuel Beckett or Philip K. Dick had thought of it, they could have retired early, their work complete—that the film is in danger of catching a nosebleed. The first repetition is crucial; too many big laughs too soon and the film would be over in its first 15 minutes. Ramis wisely gives it time, going for chuckles rather than belly laughs. It is the gradualness of Connors' awakening to the different ramifications of his predicament that is so affecting. Bill Murray's world-weary weatherman redeemed by magic has none of the self-conscious showiness of Steve Martin's character in *L.A. Story*. Murray starts out small and expands the character to fill the space allowed, which, as it turns out, is substantial.

The scenes in which he painstakingly constructs a complete psychological profile of the object of his desire, Rita, in order to get her into bed, only to be repeatedly frustrated, are among his funniest ever. When the material is right, no one can do cheap and deep at the same time like Murray. To their credit, the supporting players never appear bored with their secondary status. Even Andie MacDowell manages to make something worthwhile out of her role as bewildered nice girl, while the townspeople seem to revel in their function as mere pawns.

The film's dark underside (Murray's repeated attempts at suicide are genuinely disturbing) ensures that its humanist message—if forced to stay long enough in the place you most hate, you could come to love it—does not leave a saccharine after-taste. Happily, the streak of misanthropy in Murray's character survives to the end. *Groundhog Day* pays lip-service to Capraesque redemption conventions, but it is refreshing that the weatherman seems to become a better person more out of boredom than anything else. In a way, this film gives the small town due restitution for the savage assaults of the Lynch-mob—instead of peeling away the gloss of a too-perfect facade, it transforms Connors' blistering contempt into admiration.

TIME, 2/15/93, p. 61, Richard Corliss

SHE: Do you ever have déjà vu?
HE: Didn't you just ask me that?

For most folks, déjà vu may provoke a momentary shudder, the creepy sense of having side-stepped into the twilight zone. For Hollywood, though, it is a guiding principle. The industry wants audiences to feel they have seen this thing before but don't know where or when. Nearly every movie plot is a reprise of a story that has already worked. Recombinant familiarity means box office; originality is an orphan, subversive and suspect.

So let's all cheer the emergence of *Groundhog Day*, a very original comedy about déjà vu. A Pittsburgh weatherman (Bill Murray) visits Punxsutawney, Pennsylvania, home of the Groundhog Day Festival, and finds himself forced to relive that particular Feb. 2 over and over, maybe forever—or at least until he gets it right. You might describe the film as Son of *The Exterminating*

Angel (1963), Luis Buñuel's surrealist movie prank about a dinner party no one can leave. But, not to worry, it ends up as *It's a Wonderful Life*. And it has Murray, who, ever since his debut on *Saturday Night Live* in 1976, has been defining the would-be-hip U.S. male—the frat fellow with wit. The cool jerk.

Since TV's birth, the funny weatherman has been the medium's primal infotainment guy, a stand-up comic who uses lively banter and cute graphics to sell a lot of dull data about isobars. Phil Connors (Murray) is an ace at his job; he has the patter down pat. But he's been working under his own high-pressure system too long. Off camera, to his producer, Rita (Andie MacDowell), and his cameraman, Larry (Chris Elliott), Phil is a captious creep. They would be thrilled to hear that he has been lost in space.

Instead he is trapped in time. He wakes up the next day to discover it is still Feb. 2. The same people he saw on Groundhog Day say the same things; the same unforseen snowstorm blows into town; Punxsutawney is Brigadoon. Phil is angry, then reckless, then depressed, then suicidal. Yet he can't die, he can't escape. He can only change. So in the dozens of Groundhog Day replays, he puts his familiarity with the town to humane use: a child falls from a tree and, because Phil knows it will happen, he can catch the boy. "I'm a god," Phil decides. "Not *the* God, I don't think." The real God, he muses, may not be omnipotent. "Maybe he's just been around so long, he just knows everybody."

Danny Rubin's story is a clever metaphorical fable about moviemaking. Actors endure endless retakes of the same scene, with new improvs, trying to keep it fresh on the umpteenth take. Eventually, Phil knows the action so well, he can literally direct it: "A gust of wind. A dog barks." And finally he is the writer, changing history by anticipating it. But this Chinese-puzzle-box movie has a deeper message inside. It says that most folks' lives are like Phil's on Groundhog Day: a repetition, with the tiniest variations, of ritual pleasures and annoyances. Routine is the metronome marking most of our time on earth. Phil's gift is to see the routine and seize the day.

Murray's gift is to make the appalling appealing. As the gonzo journalist in *Where the Buffalo Roam,* the blissed-out war veteran in *The Razor's Edge,* the sadistic TV executive in *Scrooged* or the crazed hypochondriacs in *Little Shop of Horrors* and *What About Bob?*, Murray always imparted a blithe, loosey-goosey air of getting through life on his terms, in his own high style. He has the natural actor's charm of making manners matter. He carries *Groundhog Day* with his uniquely frittery nonchalance and makes the movie a comic time warp anyone should be happy to get stuck in.

VILLAGE VOICE, 2/16/93, p. 54, Georgia Brown

Simplicity versus pretension is a theme of *Groundhog Day*, a magical psychological comedy starring Bill Murray as a man undergoing an intense course in behavior modification. Directed by Harold Ramis, the movie is such a gem, it's probably a shame to say anything but Go!

Basically, Murray reprises his role in *Scrooged*, although his "before" character, Phil Connors, is not an ogre but merely one of those unbearable creatures known as TV weathermen. One of those local heroes who gets by on openly displayed narcissism, pompous Phil just can't say anything that isn't vacuous. His new producer, Rita (Andie MacDowell), and Larry, the channel's roving cameraman (Chris Elliott), think he's a pig. Larry (equipped with Elliott's wit) regularly mocks him. Rita, who majored in 19th-century French poetry, keeps her distance.

Will the tin man get his heart! Phil doesn't go to Punxsutawney PA, for the annual Groundhog Day Festival for that purpose, but the gods are kind enough to contrive an ingenious method of auto-analysis. After the ceremony, when the threesome get caught in a blizzard (one Phil didn't predict), he goes back to the inn for the night. Mysteriously, however, the day keeps repeating over and over, maybe hundreds of times—whatever the number it takes for Phil to get things right. The first few trys, he's merely bored by the repetition. He doesn't even know enough not to step in the same puddle twice. Next, he finds freedom from tomorrow liberating: he can live for the moment—take in all the calories he wants, for example. At a further stage, he uses his superpowers to bed the local chicks: He can find out things about them one day to use to woo them the next. When he uses these tricks on Rita, she soon sees through him. He wants to die and tries to. Only when he goes through several more stages of despair and begins really to change will she give him a chance. Spring comes when it's time.

No, we don't have to relive each of Phil's Sisyphean days with him. The script by Danny Rubin is cleverly fashioned to make the succession of "same days" play as a series, the focus changing from one to the next, with various small-town characters waxing and waning in importance. Though the premise lends itself nicely to certain gags (like playing along with *Jeopardy!* while knowing the answers in advance), the moral of this story is that each day is what one makes it. The potential exists for many scenarios, if only we weren't hindered by myopia and rotten character.

Though the movie is grounded in an unusually fresh conceit, it's hard to imagine it working this smoothly without Murray, who's capable of moving at imperceptible points from simp to cad to romantic lover. Strange to say, but this droll, blasé, lumpy-faced man may be the Cary Grant of our time.

Also reviewed in:
CHICAGO TRIBUNE, 2/12/93, Friday/p. C, Dave Kehr
NEW REPUBLIC, 3/15/93, p. 24, Stanley Kauffmann
NEW YORK TIMES, 2/12/93, p. C3, Janet Maslin
NEW YORKER, 2/22/93, p. 170, Terrence Rafferty
VARIETY, 2/8/93, p. 73, Richard Natale
WASHINGTON POST, 2/12/93, p. C1, Hal Hinson
WASHINGTON POST, 2/12/93, Weekend/p. 50, Desson Howe

GRUMPY OLD MEN

A Warner Bros. release of a John Davis/Lancaster Gate production. *Executive Producer:* Dan Kolsrud.   *Producer:* John Davis and Richard C. Berman.   *Director:* Donald Petrie. *Screenplay:* Mark Steven Johnson. *Director of Photography:* Johnny E. Jensen. *Editor:* Bonnie Koehler. *Music:* Alan Silvestri. *Music Editor:* Kenneth Karman and Andrew Silver. *Sound:* Russell Fager and (music) Dennis Sands. *Sound Editor:* Mark P. Stoeckinger. *Casting:* Sharon Howard-Field.   *Production Designer:* David Chapman.   *Art Director:* Mark Haack.   *Set Decorator:* Clay Griffith. *Special Effects:* Peter Albiez. *Costumes:* Lisa Jensen. *Make-up:* Rick Sharp. *Stunt Coordinator:* Ernie Orsatti. *Running time:* 105 minutes. *MPAA Rating:* PG-13.

CAST: Jack Lemmon (John Gustafson); Walter Matthau (Max Goldman); Ann-Margret (Ariel Truax);   Burgess Meredith (Grandpa);   Daryl Hannah (Melanie Gustafson);   Kevin Pollak (Jacob Goldman); Ossie Davis (Chuck); Buck Henry (Snyder); Christopher McDonald (Mike); Steve Cochran (Weatherman);   Joe Howard (Pharmacist);   Isabell Monk (Nurse);   Buffy Sedlacheck (Punky);   John Carroll Lynch (Moving Man);   Charles Brin and Ollie Osterberg (Fishermen).

LOS ANGELES TIMES, 12/25/93, Calendar/p. 2, Peter Rainer

Watching Jack Lemmon and Walter Matthau sparring each other in "Grumpy Old Men" is like watching an old vaudeville routine for the umpteenth time. They play off their tics and wheezes with the practiced ease of old pros but there's something a bit too chummy and self-congratulatory about it all. They're enjoying themselves more than we are.

Lemmon's John and Matthau's Max live side by side in a small Minnesota town and have been feuding for decades. (We're never quite sure why.) They greet each other every morning with such endearments as "putz" and "moron." They go ice-fishing—the film takes place between Thanksgiving and Christmas—and finagle ways to sabotage each other's catch.

When a New Age-y widow, Ann-Margret's all-too-aptly-named Ariel, moves in across the street, she heats up the duel between the two crotchety widowers. She favors them with her life lessons.

Ariel is so blissed-out she seems lobotomized but we're supposed to think she's a free spirit who gives these men back their lives. It's a relief when Burgess Meredith, playing John's 94-year-old father, shows up. He's a funny, randy old coot; his attempts to paw Ariel are the only real signs of life in the movie.

Director Donald Petrie and screenwriter Mark Steven Johnson—who's still in his 20s—are trying for a holiday perennial. That's why they throw in the hearts and flowers along with the whoopee cushions. The dinky subplot involving the children of John and Max—played by Daryl Hannah and Kevin Pollak—seems to exist only to skew the age demographics for this film a bit downward.

That may be a shrewd move. If you're young enough to have missed some of the better Lemmon-Matthau pairings, like "The Fortune Cookie" or "The Odd Couple," then "Grumpy Old Men" won't seem so grumpy.

NEW STATESMAN & SOCIETY, 5/27/94, p. 33, Jonathan Romney

[*Grumpy Old Men* was reviewed jointly with *Naked Gun 33⅓*; see Romney's review of that film in *Film Review Annual, 1995*.]

NEW YORK POST, 12/24/93, p. 35, Michael Medved

Some 18 years ago I regularly attended a *minyan* (a Jewish prayer quorum) composed entirely of grumpy old men.

Two of them, Kalman Saltzman and Benny Weiner, both over 80, invested so much energy in their ferocious and incomprehensible rivalry that I sometimes worried they would beat each other to death with their canes. Then another member of the group reassured me. "Actually, they enjoy this," he said. "They need each other. Hating each other's guts is what they live for."

That is precisely the relationship of John Gustafson and Max Goodman (Jack Lemmon and Walter Matthau), whose 50-year feud provides the focus for the thoroughly entertaining comedy, "Grumpy Old Men."

Next-door neighbors in a picturesque Minnesota town the two widowers exchange snarling obscenities every morning and toss smelly fish into one anothers cars.

Their cantankerous competition remains cozy and comfortable until the day a new neighbor moves in across the street a free-spirited painter and professor played by the radiant Ann-Margret. The boys, both of whom have led entirely sexless lives for the many years since their wives died, begin a frenzied fight for her attention.

Lemmon and Matthau bring surprising freshness and bite to this thin material. "Grumpy Old Men" marks their fifth on screen pairing (following triumphs in "The Fortune Cookie" and "The Odd Couple" and disappointments with "The Front Page" and "Buddy Buddy"), and by now they play off one another with such perfectly tuned finesse that even some of their throwaway lines generate lusty laughs.

The supporting cast also helps, led by the hilarious Burgess Meredith as Lemmon's foul-mouthed, beer-guzzling, 94-year-old father, appalled at the bickering between the two "crazy kids," and lusting after Ann-Margret for himself.

Ossie Davis brings warmth and dignity to his role as a local businessman who sells bait to Lemmon and Matthau to fuel their ice-fishing obsession, while Daryl Hannah and Kevin Pollak are winning as their respective children.

Most Hollywood treatments of Midwestern villages are either idealized or contemptuous, but the view of wintry Wabasha presented here avoids both extremes.

This is, after all "Lake Woebegone" country and the first-time script by Minnesotan Mark Steven Johnson blends wry humor and affection in a way that Garrison Keillor himself might recognize. Director Donald Petrie shows the same gifts for warm-hearted characterization and local color he displayed on "Mystic Pizza" and the snowy locations add an element of seasonal magic.

The movie's biggest problem involves the Ann-Margret character, who comes across as a convenient figure of male fantasy rather than as a realistic individual. She is so smashingly attractive and vital that it's hard to imagine why she'd be interested in either of the Grumpy Old Men—let alone both of them.

Moreover, the plot depends on one of these guys making a self-sacrificing gesture toward the end of the film that is so utterly out of character that you groan in disbelief.

By that time, however, most moviegoers will be so caught up in the spirit of the proceedings that they'll stick with the story until it arrives at not just one, but two romantic razzle-dazzle, feel-good endings. Leaving us with this sweet aftertaste may annoy some jaded critics, but for most movie-going civilians it will help to insure that this is one new film, for all its delicious nastiness, that will actually add to the jolly spirit of the season.

NEWSDAY, 12/24/93, Part II/p. 43, Jack Mathews

It is apparent that old friends and frequent co-stars Jack Lemmon and Walter Matthau had a great time working on Donald Petrie's "Grumpy Old Men," their first film together since Billy Wilder's 1981 "Buddy Buddy." It is apparent because at the end of the movie, we are shown outtakes of them having a great time.

We see the two naturally funny men turn blown lines into little comic sketches, invariably funnier than the mistake-free versions used in the movie. Sometimes the cameras just kept rolling when the actors, and their riotous co-star Burgess Meredith, decided to screw around.

In one shot, a close-up of Matthau looking down the street, supposedly at a car carrying Lemmon's character away, Lemmon suddenly appears next to him and cracks him up saying, "Who are looking for?"

Would that the movie had as many spontaneous moments. It has some, and for those who get the giggles just seeing Lemmon and Matthau interact, it may have enough. But through most of the film, it is like watching two old vaudeville partners trying to shake the dust off their favorite skits.

In "Grumpy Old Men," conceived for them by first-time writer Steven Mark Johnson, they are "The Odd Couple" recast as two bickering old coots in Wabasha, Minn., lifelong next-door neighbors and fellow ice fishermen who fill their lonely days and nights with boyish pranks meant to make each other miserable.

The stakes are raised dramatically in their one-upmanship: when Ann-Margret's high-spirited; seductive Ariel Truax, a middle-aged widow with a schoolgirl's energy, moves in across the street and causes the old fellows to check the testosterone levels in their libido tanks.

After days of peeking out through their curtained windows, watching Ariel roar down the street on a snowmobile and pop out of her steaming sauna to cool down in the snow, Max (Matthau) and John (Lemmon) get up the nerve to compete for her attention.

John charms her first, but after spending a night with her (his first sex since the '70s, he acknowledges nervously), thinks better of it and breaks the relationship off, conceding the field to Max, who quickly moves in.

I suppose the movie needed some conflict beyond the posturing hostility between Max and John, but this device sets the story's feet in concrete. "Grumpy Old Men" is way too light a situation comedy to support such melodrama, even for the one awkward scene it takes to set up, and the movie never quite recovers.

Ann-Margret has a lot of fun mugging as Ariel, but she doesn't convince us for a minute that this vibrant, warm-hearted and beautiful woman would fall quickly in love with either of the grumpy walnut heads snarling at each other across the way. Nor does the coy romantic subplot between Daryl Hannah, as John's daughter, and Kevin Pollack, as Max' lovesick son, do much to fill out the picture.

Meredith, still vigorous at 88, is strapped onto the ride as the dirtiest old man in Minnesota, giving son John raunchy pep talks about his sex life and threatening to take over if he can't get the job done. I don't think vulgar old people are intrinsically funny, as so many filmmakers do, but in Meredith's case, particularly in the outtakes used at the end, I have to make an exception.

The idea of using outtakes over the final credits is not new. Peter Sellers was hilarious in the botched scenes tagged onto the end of Hal Ashby's "Being There." But those played as a bonus to a good movie. With "Grumpy Old Men," they're like a last-ditch effort to make you think you had a better time than you did, and it nearly works.

SIGHT AND SOUND, 6/94, p. 48, Louise Gray

Minnesota. John Gustafson, a retired teacher in his sixties, is heavily in debt to the tax authorities. While eluding Snyder, an IRS tax inspector, John bumps into Max Goldman, his neighbour and long-time enemy. Delivery men carry an odd assortment of items into a nearby house. Next morning, John goes to his ice shanty on the frozen lake to fish, where he meets Grandpa, his 94-year-old father. That night, the new arrival, Ariel Truax, visits John to use his bathroom. She is a middle-aged widow with a predilection for new age ideas. John's daughter Melanie informs her father that she and her husband Mike are to separate. Jacob, Max's son, who is running for mayor, delivers an election notice. Jacob has had a crush on Melanie since school days. Max plays a series of tricks on John, who retaliates by hosing Max with water and hiding a rotting fish in his car. Max loses his favourite fishing rod under the ice. At Thanksgiving, John and Max both dress up to woo Ariel, but Max gets to her house first. Grandpa retrieves Max's rod and gives it to John, who later breaks it. John comes home to find Ariel cooking a gourmet Chinese meal. After a jaunt on Ariel's snowmobile, they go to bed. Next morning, John delivers the rod, now repaired, to Max's shanty, but the latter is unmollified. Max shunts John's shanty into the lake, then attacks him with a frozen fish. Grandpa intervenes to break up the fight. Max tells John he has nothing to offer Ariel. That night, after a row, John and Ariel split up. It is Christmas Eve; Max rides the snowmobile with Ariel. Melanie, Mike and their child arrive to see John. They have decided to give their marriage another chance. John flares up and leaves to go to a bar. At Melanie's request, Jacob asks Max to make up with John. Max finds John in the bar and apologises awkwardly. As John leaves, he collapses from a heart attack, whereupon Max takes him to hospital. Ariel visits John and they are reconciled. Max fails to stop Snyder from putting John's house on the market, but Jacob, now mayor, turns up with a desist order. At John and Ariel's wedding, Grandpa gives the bride away and Max is best man. Max has organised loans to pay off John's debts. John finds that Max has planted a rotting fish in the wedding car as a joke.

Grumpy Old Men really an excuse to recapitulate the success of *The Odd Couple*—opened to rave reviews in the US. This is a measure of the affection in which Jack Lemmon and Walter Matthau, who are responsible for some of American cinema's best comic moments over the last 40 years, are held. Hence director Petrie's decision to run a series of out-takes—missed cues, alternative funny lines—at the end. And, indeed, this film depends on moments rather than plot. The storyline is simple. An adolescent feud over a woman destroys Max and John's friendship, which remains fixed on anxieties surrounding betrayal and rivalry. The advent of the daffy Ariel, in threatening to repeat the original scenario, revitalises and intensifies their fight. The real issue, of course, is love. The absence of a significant female character—John's first wife is barely named and Ariel, despite being an eccentric recycled Californian, remains profoundly uninteresting—indicates that the important relationship is between Max and John. They bitch about ways to die, about fishing and their ailments, in set-pieces at which Matthau and Lemmon are supremely adept. A surreal touch has Matthau attack Lemmon with a frozen fish, and the sardonic humour is carried over into the soundtrack, which, despite the wintry weather, reprises Irving Berlin's "Heat Wave".

Sub-plots and secondary characters inevitably get short shrift. The potentially intriguing relationship between Melanie and Jacob never gets off the ground, and despite strong performances from Burgess Meredith as the goatish Grandpa and Ossie Davis as Chuck, they remain part of the background. Matthau and Lemmon dominate, consummately conveying the loneliness and anger of their roles with looks and gestures. The strange, mutual dependency of their relationship recalls *The Odd Couple* and, like that film and its TV series spin-off, *Grumpy Old Men* makes for peculiar comedy. Max and John are tragic characters whose antics often veer towards the pathological.

It is a credit to the strength of the central performances that the happy ending rings hollow. Having delivered his sparring partner to hospital, Max is asked by a nurse whether he is a friend or relative. "Friend," Max replies after a lengthy pause. John and Ariel's wedding is followed by a scene in which Max tells John about the loan he has arranged to pay off the latter's debts—finishing the movie with another marriage, of sorts.

TIME, 1/10/94, p. 58, Richard Schickel

Old guys. They fill their long, fixed-income days and their TV-dinner nights wistfully recalling past potencies. If we are to believe two new movies, they also spend a fair amount of time plotting new conquests—and not necessarily of age-appropriate ladies either. The rest of their long hours they pass bickering.

Walter Matthau and Jack Lemmon are awfully good at this sort of thing. You might say they've been practicing since they were (relatively speaking) kids. By this time they instinctively know how to bring out the comic best in each other—Matthau's bullying misanthropy, Lemmon's melancholic good cheer. It follows that they invest *Grumpy Old Men*, in which they play querulous neighbors, with an appeal that is nostalgic and, if you are a devotee of well-practiced shtick, technically seamless.

Maybe it's the fact that the pair are working in the frozen north—the film is set in a small Minnesota town—that ensures that the comedy is fairly crisp. Or maybe it's that the script by Mark Steven Johnson and the direction by Donald Petrie (both young shavers) keep sentiment within reasonable bonds. Or maybe, God love them, it's that the filmmakers allow one of their leads to be something more than a dreamer, sexually speaking. It helps too that the object of his successful affections is Ann-Margret, all peaches and cream, playing a free-spirited new neighbor. In a movie about old age, the gambit is virtually unprecedented.

By contrast, *Wrestling Ernest Hemingway* takes place in hot, muggy Miami. The old gentlemen here are Richard Harris as Frank, a sometime seafarer who once brawled with Papa, and Robert Duvall as Walt, a fastidious Cuban barber, now retired. Harris has fun overacting, Duvall has fun underacting, but nobody has any fun with the opposite sex. Frank has a snappish relationship with his landlady, played by Shirley MacLaine, and is too raffish for Piper Laurie, who is excellent as a dignified lady he meets at senior-citizen matinees. Meanwhile Walt moons over a young waitress (Sandra Bullock). Also written by a sprout, Steve Conrad, and directed by Randa Haines (*Children of a Lesser God, The Doctor*), who specializes in the woes of isolation, *Wrestling Ernest Hemingway* aspires to be serious about its subject. Yet in a curious way this sobriety works against it. Frank and Walt turn into schematically contrasting case studies, and the movie's sympathy for them eventually becomes patronizing.

Grumpy Old Men avoids both queasiness and boredom by throwing only sharp, sidelong glances at old-age issues like straitened circumstances and the death of friends. And the fact that Matthau and Lemmon are playing men of their own ages (73 and 68), which Harris and Duvall (61 and 63) are not, adds authenticity and an element of gallantry to the movie. It also suggests a solution to the problem of old age: if you're healthy, keep working.

Also reviewed in::
CHICAGO TRIBUNE, 12/24/93, Friday/p. D, Michael Wilmington
NEW YORK TIMES, 12/24/93, p. C16, Caryn James
VARIETY, 12/13/93, p. 38, Brian Lowry
WASHINGTON POST, 12/24/93, Weekend/p. 36, Desson Howe
WASHINGTON POST, 12/25/93, p. B10, Hal Hinson

GUELWAAR

A New Yorker Films release of a Film Domireew (Dakar)/Galatee Film (Paris) co-production with the participation of FR-3. *Producer:* Ousmane Sembène and Jacques Perrin. *Director:* Ousmane Sembène. *Screenplay (Wolof and French with English subtitles):* Ousmane Sembène. *Director of Photography:* Dominique Gentil. *Editor:* Marie-Aimée Debril. *Music:* Baaba Maal.

Sound: Ndiouga Moctar Ba. *Production Designer:* François Laurent Sylva. *Running time:* 115 minutes. *MPAA Rating:* Not Rated.

CAST: Omar Seck (Gora); Ndiawar Diop (Barthélémy); Mame Ndoumbé Diop (Nogoy Marie Thioune); Thierno Ndiaye (Pierre Henri Thioune, "Guelwaar"); Isseu Niang (Véronique); Myriam Niang (Hélène); Moustapha Diop (Aloys); Marie-Augustine Diatta (Sophie); Samba Wane (Gor Mag); Joseph Sane (Father Léon); Coly Mbaye (Alfred).

CINEASTE, Vol. XX, No. 2, 1993, p. 48, Françoise Pfaff

At a time when Western media frequently display starving, helpless Third World people 'saved' by benevolent foreign aid, Senegalese filmmaker Ousmane Sembene sends out a bold and disquieting message: Foreign aid perverts rather than nurtures. Food and other relief items may not reach their intended goal. Grain and rice can be bartered, sold, or distributed as celestial manna by local government officials. Foreign aid destroys the fabric of African societies and allows corrupt individuals to buy votes and retain power as the managers of their countries' dependency and economic bankruptcy. Such is the theme of *Guelwaar*, Sembene's eleventh motion picture and one of his most explicit political films to date.

Shot in both French and Wolof (the African language spoken and understood by most Senegalese), *Guelwaar*'s plot is initiated by an administrative error, resulting in the burial of a Catholic in a Muslim cemetery and almost triggering a local religious war. This incident, set in contemporary Senegal, unveils the manipulative and exploitative ways of some of the nation's political and bureaucratic elite. As the film unfolds, viewers discover that *Guelwaar*'s eponymous protagonist Pierre Henri Thioune, called "Guelwaar" ("the noble one" in Wolof, did not die from natural causes. He was killed because of his strong public stand against tainted Senegalese leaders and degrading dependence on foreign food assistance which turns recipients into beggars.

Sacrifice of "the noble one" is not in vain. His words will be brought to action one day by his disciples, the community's younger and purer generation, who literally trod over the rice dumped from foreign aid bags—a daring and even sacrilegious act in the sporadically famine-ridden Sahel region of Africa. Thioune died, but his indomitable spirit lives on. "We can't live and grow up beggars," proclaims Etienne, the group's young leader.

The idea for *Guelwaar*'s script derived from a Dakar newspaper article about a burial mistake involving Christians and Muslims. Sembene later grafted the issue of foreign aid to the initial story. As he explained to me in 1992, "For more than thirty years we've been plagued with foreign aid and food assistance. People can be helped for a little while, but not for thirty years!"

Senegal's reliance on foreign aid started soon after the country's independence in 1960 and has increased ever since. Economic aid comes primarily from the European Economic Community, the U.S., and some oil-rich Arab nations (interestingly, Sembene doesn't allude to the latter in this film). *Guelwaar* is based on certain historical facts, recreated into a new and provocative fictional reality by Sembene's vivid imagination and Marxist philosophy. Here, as in many of his other cinematic and literary works, Sembene sides with the impoverished masses and advocates his country's self-sufficiency, national unity, cultural and moral integrity, all of which he believes should be achieved through regenerative collective action.

With *Guelwaar*, Sembene has remained faithful to the notion of cinema as a didactic tool rather than an escapist device. Indeed, the film's political urgency more than counterbalances minor flaws in casting and scriptwriting. The stilted performance of some of the nonprofessional actors, for example, hampers the credibility of their characters, most notably the police commissioner and Thioune's son, Barthelemy, who travels to his father's funeral from his new-found home in France. And Bartholomy's reassumption of his Senegalese identity in response to a benevolent policeman's admonishments seems almost miraculous.

Guelwaar will assuredly be termed by some a political manifesto, but Sembene defines it, in the superimposed titles at the end of the film, as "An African legend about Africa in the twenty-first century." (He obviously doesn't expect Senegal's immediate self-sufficiency.) As in other works, the director identifies himself as an African *griot*, the traditional bard who tells legends and morality tales, and whose work reflects and synthesizes the problems, struggles, and aspirations of his people.

Aspects of Senegal's oral tradition also can be noted in *Guelwaar*'s narrative. Its many subthemes (prostitution, adultery, cultural alienation), which may appear superfluous or even disturbing to Western audiences, recall the digressions commonly found in the *griot*'s delivery. The film's repetitive elements (such as the police officer's recapitulation of the story we have just witnessed) and polyphonic statements (the evils of foreign aid are vehemently denounced by at least three characters) resemble the *griot*'s repetitive gestures, enactments, and words used with a pedagogical intent. *Guelwaar*'s farcical sequences are reminiscent of situations a *griot* might use as comic relief in a pathetic or heroic story. A case in point is Thioune's visit to his lover disguised as an old woman and his subsequent escape, naked, after being surprised *in flagrante delicto* (the hero's mind is strong, but his human flesh is weak). Moreover, *Guelwaar*'s many solemn greetings, discourses, and palavers, which also can be linked to Senegal's oral tradition, elevate the film's contemporary reality to that of an epic, as befits its legendary ending.

While the film advocates the end of foreign aid, it does not suggest the actual means of Senegal's economic recovery. In this respect, *Guelwaar* also parallels African dilemma tales, the outcome of which is debated and decided by spectators. Indeed, *Guelwaar*'s abrupt final freeze-frame invites viewers to draw their own conclusions. Sembene uses the Western medium of film within the context of African esthetics, and this should be taken into consideration when assessing his works.

As a *griot*-filmmaker, Sembene mixes realism with varied metaphorical levels of meaning. Grueling realism (i.e., the exhumation of Thioune's decayed corpse) precedes a shift to symbolism. Only after Thioune's body is removed from the Muslim cemetery does his community find the strength and direction for its moral and ethical rebirth. Significantly, two of the most striking and meaningful sequences appear at the beginning and end of *Guelwaar*. Both forcefully punctuate the importance of the drastic changes advocated by Sembene through Thioune.

In *Guelwaar*'s initial scenes, light and sound effects evoke mystery and disquietude, revealing the mood of the story that will ensue. At first, viewers are faced with an almost totally dark screen out of which emerges the eerie white shirt of a slowly limping character. The irregular sound of his steps, later coupled with the shrieking noise of a rusty gate, immediately creates uneasiness and tension. From the very beginning, the disturbing sound of the character's gait prefigures the main concern of the film—the somber aspects of a corrupt and figuratively dismembered society, handicapped by a limping, dependent economy.

The barely lit front of a house, in the second scene, allows a more precise perception of the character, a black male. As he enters the house and switches on the light, the man's features and body are fully visible, as well as the details of the room where a picture of Christ hangs, indicating a Catholic home in a country eighty percent Muslim. When he responds to his mother's call, we learn his name, Aloys. Sembene's progressive presentation of Aloys in the first sequence parallels that of Thioune, his father, whose physical and psychological portrait is gradually developed through flashbacks.

In contrast to its beginning, *Guelwaar* ends with a long shot of men, women, and adolescents wearing colorful, vibrant attire which stands out against a stark, sandy background bathed by the scorching sun. The people marching alongside the horse-drawn cart with Thioune's exhumed body represent the Catholic community to which the Thioune family belongs. Led by Etienne, the procession crushes foreign aid underfoot as it moves onward in a slow, orderly manner, announcing the community's steady but probably difficult socioeconomic progress. It is interesting to note here that Sembene, born a Muslim but now a proclaimed atheist, chooses his country's Christian minority to perform what could be termed a Senegalese theology of moral and economic liberation. This quasi-Biblical march becomes the epic image of a people in the process of regaining control over their destiny, made explicit as words from Thioune's last speech are heard in voice-over, connoting a West African animistic tradition in which the world of the ancestors sustains and stimulates the living: "This aid they're distributing to us will kill us. It has killed all our dignity and pride. What humiliation!"

Thioune's words are followed abruptly by a voice-over song that perpetuates and exalts his memory and his humanitarian legacy. In contrast to its gloomy first sequence, *Guelwaar*'s hopeful ending, well served by Baaba Maal's musical score, reflects Sembene's inherent faith in humanity. By the twenty-first century, Thioune will become a legendary and mythic symbol of courage, dignity, and pride, all values embodied in the Wolof word *jom*, which Thioune repeatedly uses in his last speech. The work of a political activist and skillful griot, *Guelwaar* is a bold and unremitting indictment of foreign aid to Senegal, Africa, and Other Third World areas.

NEW YORK POST, 7/28/93, p. 26, Jerry Tallmer

He was a hero with feet of clay, like most heroes. Guelwaar, they called him, "the Noble One," his full name being Pierre Henry Thioune, Senegalese orator, rebel, bit of a demagogue, womanizer, leader of his people.

Now he is dead, but his body is missing. When it turns up buried in a Moslem village graveyard—Guelwaar (Thierno Ndiaye) having been a Christian—there's all hell to pay.

Thus the premise of "Guelwaar," the new movie by Ousmane Sembene, 70-year-old "father of African cinema." Before we're through, two hours later, the film has laid bare a host of the contradictory cross-currents and conflicts of a multi-tribal, multi-religious, post-colonial nation ridden with poverty, hunger, corruption, tyranny, petty bureaucracy, vested ignorance, etc., etc., as only an African would know it.

"What do the women talk about?" one character asks another. "The usual things: family, drought, embezzlement, scandals, birth, death, the Christian faith." Or as Guelwaar's oldest son, a Parisian come back for the funeral, keeps saying, or sighing: *"Quelle Afrique!" ... Quel pays! ... C'est ca, l'Afrique!"*—"What an Africa, what a country, that's Africa for you!"

"I am *French*," this Barthelmy (Ndiawar) furiously exclaims, waving his passport at the police chief who's investigating the case. "Okay," replies the sardonic, hard-bitten officer, "and I'm your ambassador." To a third party the policeman explains: "This one [Barthelmy] is white." "A white so black?" is the astounded response.

It's the cop, a Graham Greene character named Officer Gora (Omar Seck, in a superb performance), who will, like Pilate, wash his hands of the whole affair while yet trying to mediate it.

There's not much action, give or take a few stick-waving mobs of Moslems or Christians howling for one another's blood, but there are some strong human scenes to remember. Guelwaar's wife (Mame Ndoumbe Diop) grieving over the funeral suit that's lying flat as a pancake on their bed—grieving and cursing his memory and her lot. The priest, Father Leon (Joseph Sane), entangled in sober-sided dialogue with the stunning, underdressed young woman (Myriam Niang) who, like her friend Sophie—Guelwaar's daughter—has come up for the funeral from Dakar, where both of them are prostitutes whose earnings (shh!) support their families. "Don't judge lest you be judged," she remarks, which may be taken as the movie, and its maker's motto.

In the end, of course, everybody, even Barthelmy, finds his own—African—soul.

NEWSDAY, 7/28/93, Part II/p. 73, Gene Seymour

Rare is the filmmaker of any age, on any continent, who dares to pull a whole society into the range of his vision, expose its many contradictions and follies *and* goad it to change without seeming strident, mean-spirited or clumsy.

With "Guelwaar," 70-year-old Ousmane Sembene, the Senegalese-born "father of African cinema," has taken on this imposing task with the equally imposing serenity and confidence of a grand master. This latest work not only serves as worthy opener to the Film Society of Lincoln Center's monthlong African film festival, it also is a worthy introduction to—and summation of—Sembene's 30-year body of work.

"Guelwaar's" title character is a corpse, a political activist who rabble-roused for most of his life in a poor, drought-prone Senegal town before meeting a violent death (the circumstances of which remain murky throughout the film). The morning of his funeral, his family discovers that his body has been taken from the morgue.

The local police find that Guelwaar, a baptized Catholic, has been accidentally interred in a Muslim cemetery. The process of setting things right becomes a microcosm of the dueling pieties, petty squabbling and blithe corruption that Sembene believes to be gnawing away at his country's soul—and subverting the dream of a united, self-sufficient Africa.

You don't for a minute doubt Sembene's conviction. And yet, he massages more than punches the viewer. No one is given a completely one-sided depiction, not even Sembene's martyred hero, whose virtues and vices are revealed through flashbacks. Filmmakers with similar didactic impulses could learn a lot from Sembene's shrewd attentiveness to human complexity.

The film moves at an almost leisurely pace. So much so that some conversations, like one between a Catholic priest and a prostitute, seem to have drifted in from nowhere with faint connection to the central plot. Still, even with these digressions it holds your attention the way few "more polished" films do these days.

VILLAGE VOICE, 4/6/93, p. 56, Georgia Brown

Prophets are often without honor in other countries too. Ousmane Sembène of Senegal is one of the great living filmmakers, yet you wouldn't know that in these parts. His 1992 *Guelwaar* was turned down by the New York Film Festival (which wouldn't know a masterpiece if it bit the committee in its collective bootie), as was his extraordinary film, *The Camp at Thiaroye*. Now the Film Society redeems itself (partly) by mounting a splendid month-long African Film Festival, with a Sembène retrospective on the side. The exceptional, tremendously moving *Guelwaar* will open the series and show eight times throughout the month.

Such intelligence shines out of Sembène's films, yet this is a man virtually without formal education. He was expelled from school at 12, worked as a bricklayer, fought for the French in World War II, spent many years in France, though not in the elite circles frequented by *assimilés* like Leopold Senghor. (Later, back in Senegal, Senghor would ban Sembène's *Ceddo* in a dispute over the *title's spelling*.) Sembène was in his thirties and a docker in Marseilles when he published his first novel and nearly 40 when he took up filmmaking. He knew that his novels, written in French, would only reach the educated few—a group his works were generally critical of. The movies, usually in Wolof and French (for officials), are made for ordinary Africans and make no special concessions (like simplicity of plot) for Western audiences. Their increasing inventiveness makes Western films look especially codified—or stultified.

Sembène is a little like Noam Chomsky (to take a recent example) in that he consciously sets out to compile a kind of counter-history, a corrective to the official record. Since colonialism (in new and old forms) suppresses history, Sembène knows it's necessary to continually refresh the collective memory. Many of his films are based on actual events. Moving backward and, on one stunning occasion (in the epic *Ceddo*), forward in time, his feature films conduct increasingly complex debates around a range of vital issues. And although they clearly, passionately, take sides, the later films rarely feel didactic because they earn their positions dramatically. Certain questions are always central, like, Where did we come from? and, How did Africa get into this mess?

In *Guelwaar*, a murdered political activist is to be readied for his funeral when suddenly his corpse is missing from the morgue. A sympathetic police investigator learns that the body has been mistakenly taken off to a village and given a Moslem burial. That the dead man was Catholic is just one problem. The film follows the family's effort to retrieve the body (a holy war nearly breaks out), and in the course of things we learn not only why the man was beaten to death but much more—thanks to Sembène's deft, idiosyncratic management of many characters (who may emerge or drop from sight with stunning ease). At the end comes a wrenching cry against Western aid—the latest form of debilitating, humiliating, corrupting paternalism.

VILLAGE VOICE, 8/3/93, p. 53, Georgia Brown

Guelwaar returns. Reviewed in this space last spring when it was featured in the Walter Reade's superb (and mostly sold-out) African series, Ousmane Sembène's masterpiece is now opening at Lincoln Plaza. Seeing it again, I am moved anew by Sembène's rare and honest talent, his obstinate, frame-by-frame refusal to commit to commercial moviemaking.

A murder mystery, too, the film opens with Guelwaar's crippled son slowly making his way in the night to his mother's house bearing tidings of his father's death. A political activist, Guelwaar has been assassinated, it turns out, though the circumstances emerge very slowly. It seems that Sembène's movie moves like this despised son, steadily, at its own pace.

Some may see Sembène's method as naive. I see it as a highly sophisticated adaptation of the medium to the task. Although stylistically the two have little in common, I would link Sembène with Bresson for the way his story gathers to a powerful, spirit-cleansing close.

Specifically, Guelwaar has spoken up against aid, welfare, and the corruption that always attends the dole. "If you want to kill a man of dignity," he says, "give him each day what he needs to live." "Thank you" corrupts. As another character observes, "Theft, embezzlement of public funds have become heroic virtues." So colonialism continues its reign. Independence must be radical. Meanwhile, religious spats and wars distract people from the true evils.

Killed for his threat to local powers, buried wrongly, then disentombed, Guelwaar is no mythic God but a real man. Between his urban Christian family and followers and the rural Muslims who've taken the body, there seems an impossible breach. Equivalent in moral stature to Guelwaar is the imam who cuts through ideology to effect a healing. ("What's happening to our people?" he laments.) The spare use of liturgical music is extraordinarily effective as the end brings a miracle, a spontaneous uprising.

Also reviewed in:
CHICAGO TRIBUNE, 4/22/94, Friday/p. J, Michael Wilmington
NEW REPUBLIC, 9/6/93, p. 30, Stanley Kauffmann
NEW YORK TIMES, 7/28/93, p. C18, Janet Maslin
VARIETY, 11/30/92, p. 76, David Stratton
WASHINGTON POST, 2/4/94, p. C6, Richard Harrington

GUERRILLAS IN OUR MIDST

A Women Make Movies release.   *Producer:* Amy Harrison.   *Director:* Amy Harrison. *Director of Photography:* Ellen Kuras.   *Music:* Gary Shea.   *Running time:* 35 minutes. *MPAA Rating:* Not Rated.

CINEASTE, Vol. XX, No. 1, 1993, p. 47, Cynthia Lucia

Amy Harrison's documentary, *Guerrillas in Our Midst*, echoes the energy and wit of its subject—the sassy, self-proclaimed "conscience of the art world," the Guerrilla Girls. This stealthy band of women, all visual artists, first organized to protest the under-representation or total absence of female artists and artists of color in New York's major museums and galleries. The call-to-arms resounded in 1985, when the Museum of Modern Art's "International Survey of Contemporary Painting and Sculpture" exhibited the work of 169 artists, less than ten percent of whom were women.

Cross-cutting from a New York museum gallery to the dark, dank streets where the 'Girls' exhibit their work (their stylish, consciousness-raising posters have now become collector's items), Amy Harrison playfully establishes the unacknowledged 'half-truth' upon which the 'universal' art market has thrived. Complete with grainy film stock, *film noirish* lighting, frantic pacing, and Gary Shea's mock gangster-film score, her documentary leads us to believe we are witnessing a crime (or at least a misdemeanor), as the 'Girls,' in their trademark gorilla masks, pound the midnight cobblestones of New York's SoHo gallery district, peevishly plastering their posters over stenciled admonitions to "Post No Bills."

An abrupt cut brings T. S. Eliot to mind when we are situated back inside the museum with its muted colors and with classical music on the soundtrack, as "... the women come and go/Talking of Michelangelo ..." or very likely of a *contemporary* male artist. It is here where the real crime (and a serious one) is committed. In a stroke of terse metonymy, Harrison's museum evokes the sealed interior of the white, male-dominated art establishment, from gallery owners, consultants, dealers, and critics, to the writers of art histories and the artists themselves.

Harrison extends her style of clever counterpoint throughout the film. Interviews with stilted, self-important members of the art establishment reach levels of self-parody when juxtaposed with interview footage of the Guerrilla Girls (masked, of course) and Guerrilla Girl supporters such as artists Elizabeth Dworkin and Lauren Ewing, *The New York Times* art critic, Roberta Smith, a convert who admits, "They've made me more aware of what the breakdown of my coverage is." Featured throughout are the witty but pointed posters designed by the Guerrilla Girls, including "The Advantages of Being A Woman Artist: Working without the pressure of success; Not having to be in shows with men; Not being stuck in a tenured teaching position; Having the opportunity to choose between career and motherhood ..."

The film gloats more than a little, as do we, when Guerrilla Girl target Mary Boone, a prominent gallery owner with a long record of grossly under-representing women and artists of color, initially proclaims, "I think the Guerilla Girls have had a very negative impact upon women," only later to waffle and stumble when attempting to defend her position in light of powerful Guerrilla Girl influence. As the film closes, we learn that Boone now represents fifty percent women artists.

We likewise can't help but giggle over the fortuitous ironies that crop up. Art consultant Jeffrey Deitch, for instance, sits in his spacious, high rise office, overlooking midtown Manhattan, while criticizing the Guerrilla Girls: "I've been surprised and a little amused that their focus seems to be so careerist. For me, it's about art." In response to growing Guerrilla influence, Deitch later insists, "You know I support the Guerrilla Girls."

He can hardly say otherwise, since national press and television attention to the Guerrilla Girls' project has established the group as a viable and visibly nagging presence. The result: invitations to sit on museum boards and to speak as panelists in a variety of contexts. As one Guerrilla Girl points out, "You have to get into a position of power before you can change things, and that's what we're trying to do."

And it is exactly at this juncture where Harrison's admitted valentine to the Guerrilla Girls (and nothing wrong with that) could have taken an interesting, if somewhat pesky, turn. As part of a panel, the same Guerrilla Girl suggests that one way museum-goers can help to change things is by asking to see more work by women. To this plea one young woman responds: "What you're asking for ... all of us is to be able to play *their* game." An important issue, to which the Guerrilla Girl replies, "It would be one thing if there were another game to play, but for me the only other game ... is word processing." Although the conference participant chose not to follow up on this reply, it seems that Harrison should have in her own discussions with the Guerrilla Girls. Shouldn't these inventive guerrillas be asked at least to imagine an alternative or a parallel game, or perhaps to create one! *Guerrillas in Our Midst* misses an opportunity here to explore an issue at the core of feminist debate.

It is, indeed, hard to imagine why the Guerrilla Girls want to become part of the art establishment after so much time is spent exposing the network of manipulation and secretive bidding in the art world. Stimulated by Reagan/Bush policies which led investors to seek unregulated investments, such bidding amounts to "insider trading," as one Guerrilla Girl explains. The Guerrilla Girls have formulated their own "Code of Ethics for Art Museums" in response to the burgeoning corruption within this system: "Thou shalt not be a Museum Trustee and also the chief stockholder of a major auction house; Thou shalt not give more than three retrospectives to an artist whose dealer is a brother of the chief curator; Thou shalt not keep curatorial salaries so low that curators must be independently wealthy or willing to engage in insider trading." While funny and playful, the "Code" rightfully points out the fact that insiders in the art world have been stealing the show in more ways than one.

The nudging yet noncombative style of the Guerrilla Girls certainly has met with success, and "today nothing succeeds like success," one Guerilla Girl tells us frankly, from a real, feet-on-the-ground position. The Guerrilla Girls *have* been successful in raising the consciousness of the art world, resulting in practical, positive changes, and they have been successful in achieving their goal of making "feminism fashionable again." In light of their success, perhaps it isn't fair to ask that the film press the Guerrilla Girls a bit. But, then, again ... *Guerrillas in Our Midst* may have missed the opportunity to paint an original, radical landscape, not merely informing us about the Guerrilla Girls' project, but also intervening in a meaningful attempt to provide a new vision of possibilities.

NEW YORK POST, 4/14/93, p. 24, Jerry Tallmer

[*Guerillas in Our Midst* was reviewed jointly with *Joan Mitchell: Portrait of an Abstract Painter*; see Tallmer's review of that film.]

NEWSDAY, 4/14/93, Part II/p. 67, John Anderson

[*Guerillas in Our Midst* was reviewed jointly with *Joan Mitchell: Portait of an Abstract Painter;* see Anderson's review of that film.]

VILLAGE VOICE, 4/20/93, p. 58, Kathy Deacon

[*Guerrillas in Our Midst* was reviewed jointly with *Joan Mitchell: Portrait of an Abstract Painter*; see Deacon's review of that film.]

Also reviewed in:
NEW YORK TIMES, 4/14/93, p. C14, Stephen Holden

GUILTY AS SIN

A Hollywood Pictures release.   *Executive Producer:* Don Carmody and Bob Robinson. *Producer:* Martin Ransohoff. *Director:* Sidney Lumet. *Screenplay:* Larry Cohen. *Director of Photography:* Andrzej Bartkowiak. *Editor:* Evan Lottman. *Music:* Howard Shore. *Music Editor:* Suki Buchman. *Sound:* Bruce Carwardine. *Sound Editor:* Ron Bochar. *Casting:* Lynn Stalmaster. *Production Designer:* Philip Rosenberg. *Set Decorator:* Enrico Campana. *Set Dresser:* Bill Wood. *Special Effects:* Martin Malivoire. *Costumes:* Gary Jones. *Make-up:* Patricia Green. *Make-up (Rebecca De Mornay):* Ann Lee Masterson. *Make-up (Don Johnson):* Jay Cannistracci. *Stunt Coordinator:* Dwayne McLean. *Running time:* 107 minutes. *MPAA Rating:* R.

CAST: Rebecca DeMornay (Jennifer Haines);   Don Johnson (David Greenhill);   Stephen Lang (Phil Garson);   Jack Warden (Moe Plimpton);   Dana Ivey (Judge Tompkins);   Ron White (Diangelo);   Norma Dell'Agnese (Emily);   Sean McCann (Nolan);   Luis Guzman (Lt. Bernard Martinez);   Robert Kennedy (Caniff);   James Blendick (McMartin);   Tom Butler (Heath); Christina Baren (Miriam Langford);   Lynne Cormack (Esther Rothman);   Barbara Eve Harris (Kathleen Bigelow);   Simon Sinn (Mr. Loo);   John Kapelos (Ed Lombardo);   Tom McCamus (Ray Schiff);   Harvey Atkin (Judge Steinberg);   Anthony Sherwood (Ken Powell);   Chris Benson (Arraignment Judge);   Melanie Nicholls-King (Receptionist);   Johnie Chase (Clerk); Brigit Wilson (Rita Greenhill);   Albert De Rosa (Plasterer);   Yanira Contreras (Woman at Cleaners);   Shelley Young (Woman at Supper Club);   Sandi Ross (Postal Supervisor);   Peter Blais (Handwriting Expert);   Denis Akiyama (Lab Technician);   Lili Francks (Nurse);   Roland Rothchild (Intern);   Jack Newman (Jury Foreman);   Gene Mack (Security Guard);   Tom Quinn (Squash Player).

LOS ANGELES TIMES, 6/4/93, Calendar/p. 1, Michael Wilmington

If recreational sex these days is a battlefield, then Rebecca De Mornay and Don Johnson, the stars of "Guilty as Sin," come off as a couple of erotic samurai.

Playing a hotshot female defense attorney and her randy client, an accused wife-killer, these two use sexiness as a weapon: ripping each other with a glance, thrusting with an innuendo, parrying with a smile. The movie—directed by Sidney Lumet in his coolest, smoothest, most punctilious style—is an "erotic thriller" of some bloody accomplishment, and some flaws, but it's also funny. And the humor turns precisely on the easy grace and playfulness with which these actors, public sex objects of long standing, manipulate their on-screen allure.

Not all of "Guilty as Sin" works. The movie doesn't have much of the gaudy égore and Adrian Lyne gloss audiences expect from "erotic thrillers." But, courtesy of Lumet and screenwriter

Larry Cohen, it has something most of the others lack: an interesting center, characters that intrigue us and draw us in.

It's almost a two-person show. There are some good minor roles—Jack Warden as an avuncular shamus, Dana Ivey as a steely-prim judge, Ron White as a prosecutor-patsy and Stephen Lang as the boyfriend-in-the-background—but it's DeMornay and Johnson, two professional flirts in a deadly game, who carry the weight.

She's at her best, he's close to it. DeMornay's Jennifer Haines seduces juries and judges in the service of evil clients—murderers, mobsters—many of whom she knows are guilty. Johnson's David Greenhill *is* guilty, of something, but so overwhelmingly manipulative and arrogant that he thinks even outright confession can't hurt him. He's the stud without alibis, a man who *brags* that he lives off women. She's the woman who gets evil men off. It's a match made in courtroom hell.

That may be "Guilty's" problem. It finally succumbs to all the bogeyman-will-get-you clichés of the "Fatal Attraction" and "Basic Instinct" school, when it's onto something better, riskier.

David Greenhill has some of the comic, deadpan evil of that king of American literary Don Juans, Harry Diadem in Calder Willingham's "Eternal Fire": the role the young Paul Newman was born to play but didn't. Like Harry, mean mama's boy Greenhill is coldly self-infatuated, a first-rank liar and game-player, a ruthless sadist when the game goes sour. Jennifer, whom we often see through his eyes, is his "greatest score," a chilly, bemused, gorgeous perfectionist. Johnson gives Greenhill's seductions a fey, slightly screw-loose charm and his quiet, impacted rage is terrifying. The fact that there's no onscreen sex between the two of them only spikes the tension more.

The early tête-á-tête scenes, set against chilly rich backdrops, have the crisp bite of high-style romantic comedy, an "Adam's Rib" played between a killer and a shyster. It's a comedy of sex-role reversal—with Greenhill the object, Jennifer the icily appraising gazer. But the laughs are always underpinned with something darker: the voluptuous unease of two shining sex-sharks circling each other in a dark and perilous sea. Even when "Guilty" shifts into its trial scenes, or its Grand Guignol mode—bringing on the blood, terror and cliffhangers—that steely humor always seems an inch or two beneath, a knife poking through silk.

Lumet is usually superb with courtroom movies ("Twelve Angry Men" and "The Verdict"), but he's not always at top form with thrillers, and he's tended to enclose this one too much. Like Woody Allen's dramas, "Guilty as Sin" needs ventilation, exteriors. Though set in Chicago, it was shot in Toronto—and, unusually for Lumet, there's little sense of place.

But Lumet's direction of the actors, as always, is exemplary. With his quiet, almost motionless camera and his emphasis on contained emotion, he makes it real, even when it's clearly not. It's a good show, but if there's something dissatisfying here, perhaps it's because the director isn't as fascinated with genre tricks as screenwriter Cohen. He doesn't revel in the trashy nightmarish aspects of the plot, try to pull off the bravura little stylistic touches Cohen, as director, would have gone for.

Like John Schlesinger and the other "class" directors forced into big-budget yuppie-in-distress thrillers, Lumet may not be engaged enough. At this stage, he should probably be stretching himself dramatically, adapting books like Malamud's "The Assistant" or Bellow's "The Victim." But who would finance them? "Guilty as Sin" (MPAA-rated R for violence, language and some sexuality) *is* finance-able, a compromise. A compromise by pros: a sleek, in-and-out shocker about foreplay on the edge of an abyss.

NEW YORK POST, 6/4/93, p. 27, Michael Medved

In recent years Hollywood has released a fetid flood of films about killer bimbos: psychotic beauties who use their womanly wiles to lure unsuspecting men to great sex and cruel death "Guilty as Sin" tries a gender switch to breathe some new life into this tired old formula—it's "Basic Instinct" with a role reversal.

This may not be the world's most promising premise for a motion picture, but it needn't have been the mess that it is except for the disastrous decision to cast Don Johnson as the seductive serial killer.

In the past, in under-appreciated films like "Cease Fire" (1985) and "Paradise" (1991), Johnson has turned in some solid sensitive performances, but here he is so hysterically over the top, so hopelessly confused that you can't help feel sorry for the poor guy. If you were watching on home video you'd turn it off to save the lost lamb from further embarrassment.

In one outrageously intense scene, the supposedly irresistible seducer, clad in a fluffy white bathrobe, shrieks plaintively and wiggles his dark eyebrows up and down in a manner that simultaneously suggests Groucho Marx and Joan Crawford or at least Faye Dunaway impersonating Joan Crawford in "Mommie Dearest."

The character he's trying so hard to play is David Greenhill, a sophisticated predator accused of pushing his wealthy wife off a high-rise balcony to her death. He claims the entire case is a deliberate frame-up by the dead woman: She wrote an incriminating letter to the police then committed suicide, to punish him for his compulsive womanizing.

This explanation sounds plausible enough to persuade a hotshot defense attorney (Rebecca De-Mornay) to take the case, but once Johnson has entangled her in the web of the lawyer client relationship he begins to manipulate the situation for his own nefarious purposes.

Part of the problem with "Guilty as Sin" is that DeMornay, who always brings a haunted edge to her performances, comes across as far more dangerous than her murderous client. Fresh from her own commercially successful killer bimbo role (as the vengeful nanny in "The Hand That Rocks the Cradle"), she seems far too formidable to ever feel menaced by this preening, prancing clown.

Director Sidney Lumet seems to understand that their silly thrust-and-parry will never scare audiences, so he throws in one scene of utterly gratuitous, horribly sadistic violence (directed against the lawyer's boyfriend, Stephen Lang) in a last-minute attempt to get our attention. In the past, Lumet has created some of Hollywood's most memorable courtroom dramas, from "12 Angry Men" to "The Verdict," but the trial here offers so little tension that you expect to see Judge Wapner presiding.

Lumet is also noted for his gritty feel for New York streets, but this story, set in Chicago, was actually filmed in Toronto, and emphasizes so many cold, high-tech surfaces that it seems as if all the characters have been mysteriously trapped in a giant suburban mall.

Fortunately, few moviegoers will be trapped into seeing this miserably misguided movie, whose only virtue is the timing of its release: It appears while the memory or the even more frustrating "Sliver" is still fresh, and just one week before the onrushing dinosaurs of "Jurassic Park" stomp all such annoyances into well-deserved obscurity.

NEWSDAY, 6/4/93, Part II/p. 64, Jack Mathews

Do you know how to tell when a lawyer is lying to you? His lips move.

Do you know why sharks won't attack lawyers who fall overboard? Professional courtesy.

Did you hear the one about the defense lawyer who was too ethical to snitch on a guilty client, so she planted false evidence on him, hoping he'd be convicted of the murder charge she was being paid to defend him against?

Wait, that last one isn't a lawyer joke, it's a Hollywood joke. It's a major plot point in Sidney Lumet's inadvertently amusing psychological thriller, "Guilty as Sin." The title is also the plea that Lumet and screenwriter Larry Cohen should cop when accused of turning law, logic and ethics upside-down while making a silly summer movie.

Rebecca DeMornay, the mad nanny from last year's hit "The Hand That Rocks the Cradle," plays Jennifer Haines, a brilliant Chicago criminal lawyer who's just dumb enough to take on a cunning, professed gigolo (Don Johnson) accused of murdering his rich wife.

David Greenhill looks guilty, sounds guilty and acts guilty—guilty as sin—but there is something about his GQ style, his swagger and his mischievous smile that intrigues Jennifer, challenges her to prove to herself and her skeptical colleagues that she can both withstand his seductive hustle and prove him innocent in the bargain.

Jennifer, of course, is the only person in Chicago, or in your local theater, who doesn't have this guy's number on sight. You know the word "rakehell?" It refers to someone so evil you have to rake hell to find him. That's Greenhill, the Devil in an Armani suit, and no sooner is he out on bail than he begins taunting Jennifer, terrorizing her, masquerading as her deluded would-be lover while setting her up as an unwitting accomplice.

More than once, Jennifer explains to someone that lawyers cannot ethically reveal their clients' secrets, and you can see why. The movie would be over in 20 minutes if she went to the judge and said, "I am defending a serial killer, get me out of this."

It is only when Jennifer sends an old crony (Jack Warden) to investigate Greenhill's background, then commits a whopper of a felony herself—planting fake evidence, of all the cheap tricks—that you begin to doubt both her smarts and her sense of ethics.

Cohen, whose only funnier script was about a dessert gelatin that eats people ("The Stuff"), wrote this with an apparently straight face, Lumet directed it that way, and everyone but the surprisingly clever Don Johnson performed as if they were in a sequel to "The Verdict," Lumet's great 1982 courtroom drama.

Johnson's performance is so sly and whimsical, he almost makes the rest of the picture worthwhile. You have to have a sense of humor, not to mention copious gall, to play a man so drop-dead gorgeous women will drop dead for you, and Johnson, who has undoubtedly weakened a few knees in his time, relishes the opportunity. He uses his face and smile as a weapon—aims, fires, hits 'em.

"Can I buy you a drink?" a good-looking young lady asks him at a bar.

"I've already got one," he says, gigolo-like, "but you can pay for it."

If looks could kill.

SIGHT AND SOUND, 1/94, p. 46, Phillip Strick

As Chicago defence attorney Jennifer Haines negotiates another triumphant acquittal for a client of dubious character, she notices the scrutiny of an unknown admirer among the courtroom observers. At her office next morning, he introduces himself: David Greenhill, wanted on suspicion of murdering his wife, and in need of a brilliant attorney to help prove his innocence. Claiming to be unimpressed by his blatant tactics of charm and flattery, Jennifer turns him over to the law, but quickly has second thoughts; persuading herself that this is a case which could further enhance her reputation, she agrees to represent him. She realises her mistake almost immediately: the ruthlessly manipulative David attempts to alienate her boyfriend Phil with hints that Jennifer has fallen for him, and infuriates the rich benefactress who has been paying his bills. Jennifer tries to drop the case but her petition to the court is refused and she finds herself trapped.

Making himself increasingly at home in her office, and openly claiming that she has seduced him, David admits to her that he has disposed of a number of past wives, knowing that she will be unable to divulge this privileged information. Desperate, she turns for guidance to her friend, veteran private investigator Moe Plimpton, who agrees to delve into David's past. As the trial begins, Jennifer is convinced that her life is in danger as David might decide at any time that she knows too much. The case against him depends on whether he could have been in the building when his wife fell from a window, and whether a letter accusing him of intent to murder, sent from his wife to the police, is authentic. Experts pronounce the letter a fake, but Jennifer, investigating the building, realises that David could have disguised himself as a workman in order to enter and leave unobserved. Buying overalls and other painting gear, she arranges for them to be discovered as incriminating evidence.

Seeing through Jennifer's trick and learning of Moe's investigations, David beats up Phil as a warning. He also produces an alibi: the attractive Mrs Bigelow confirms that he was with her and that, in full painting gear, he helped to redecorate her apartment. The jury is out for a week, but fails to agree on a verdict. The case is dismissed, and in the empty courtroom David tells Jennifer how, on first seeing her, he worked out how his wife's murder could be made to appear the result of their joint planning. Scared but furious, Jennifer decides to take Moe's file on David to the State Attorney's Office, regardless of the risk to her career. But before Moe can copy it for her he is visited by David, and both Moe and the file go up in flames. Intercepting Jennifer on her way to rejoin Phil, David attempts to push her over a balcony, but she drags him with her. David is killed by the fall, but Jennifer lands on top of him and survives.

With its immaculate villain, its culpable (and blonde) heroine, and its ambivalence towards the efficient workings of the law, Larry Cohen's screenplay evokes the kind of thriller that Hitchcock would have enjoyed, something along the lines of a high-gloss *Shadow of a Doubt*, with innocence and guilt in turbulent complicity. Unexpected as it is to find the maverick Cohen in such fine-trimmed territory, one might concede that many of his characters—the Invaders of the 60s TV series, say, or the small-time conman of *Q: The Winged Serpent*—occupy a Hitchcockian shadowland where bravado is the only defence against an inevitable retribution. In *Guilty as Sin* the hunt for punishment continues: the arrogant lawyer pays for achieving the release of one obvious crook by submitting to the clutches of another. In turn, the client plans ever riskier crimes that bring him closer to his downfall. He eventually topples, in the tradition of Hitchcock's lost souls, from a vertiginous height.

Cohen's parables tend appealingly towards the overheated, and *Guilty as Sin* bubbles with notions to spice up the main ingredients. It is a cheerful irony, for instance, that after manipulating the legal system to suit herself Jennifer is drawn into a predicament where justice depends on her own law-breaking—and even then lets her down. Introducing the wondrous Mrs Bigelow as if in supernatural intervention to provide an inexplicable alibi, Cohen invalidates the entire trial by wrapping an intertitle over a week of deliberation by the jury, finally dismissed for being unable to make up its mind and charmingly thanked by the defendant in person. Formerly self-confident and proud of it, Jennifer has by this time discovered in the urbanely subversive ladykiller—to whom she succumbs with every glance—an alter ego who has already rewritten her past and infected her future. Committed to his defence, which with simple, demonic accuracy is that women behave irrationally when he's around, she must logically fall with him when, like the rest of his victims, she is forced into an assisted suicide. The film's concluding image should have been of the two of them, jointly destroyed, but in deference to the upbeat, the lady is scraped decorously off the floor. Her compliant and long-suffering boyfriend, perhaps foreseeing the possibility of a more balanced partnership, reassures her with a profoundly ignorant "You're gonna be fine, darling". We're not likely to believe that, either.

Left to his own devices, Cohen could have been expected to film all this with a vibrant delirium, but with Sidney Lumet at the helm the production becomes, despite itself, a class act. Curiously uncritical of the story's absurdities which, if presented with energy and pace, might just about pass muster, Lumet's serene style achieves the paraphrase of Hitchcockian elegance while never quite mastering the art of divine intervention. A number of suspense scenes clearly invite editing in the manner of the dropped-shoe sequence in *Marnie*—the furtive investigation of a locker just as its owner is returning from the squash court, the scraping together of evidence in a bedroom as the butler prepares to emerge from the kitchen. But Lumet is as always more interested in immediacy than in anticipation, and persistently undercuts the tension as if recognising its irrelevance. When the villain brandishes a knife while carefully preparing a sandwich, the only blood he sheds is his own; and when he confesses his wrongdoings into a microphone in an empty courtroom the door crashes open to reveal not an accusing horde but a solitary cleaning trolley. Lumet's soundtrack assails us with such crashes, echoing the judge's gavel in the opening scene; sadly, they soon begin to sound like attempts to keep us awake.

A primary weakness is the casting of Rebecca DeMornay in a role that demands another Barbara Stanwyck or at least an Angie Dickinson—someone capable of delivering her lines with enough parodic edge to bring them to life. Hampered by her cradle-rocking image of instability, DeMornay comes across more as petulant teenager than as seasoned courtroom fighter, and at first ogle from the shameless Don Johnson she is gone with a gulp. Hugely enjoying himself, Johnson plays monster with ingratiating transparency, fooling nobody but his rich and shark-like admirers who all look as if they could snarl more effectively in any court than his tremulous defence attorney. Shrugging away these clownish figures, Lumet employs his usual team, Bartkowiak (camera) and Rosenberg (designer), to explore a more personal geometry. Where *The Verdict* was constructed visually from an intricate series of boxes, and *The Morning After* was portrayed in a succession of horizontal bands of colour, *Guilty as Sin* concentrates on vertical perspectives befitting its multiple falls from grace. From the beautifully graded columns of beige provided by the walls of the Greenhill apartment to the varied staircases that seem to trap their users in cages of steel and glass, the film is a frustrating combination of the exquisite and the banal, of opportunities transcended or briskly overlooked. Offsetting the superb shot of the grieving heroine alone on a black screen—which reminds us that Lumet's most consistent theme is that of remorse—there are too many malevolent camera movements leading nowhere and too many jarring interpolations like the workman who, for a couple of flash shots, suddenly turns into Don Johnson. With story and style in such a state of collision, *Guilty as Sin* itself hovers in free fall, lost for a parachute.

Also reviewed in:
CHICAGO TRIBUNE, 6/4/93, Friday/p. C, Johanna Steinmetz
NEW REPUBLIC, 7/5/93, p. 26, Stanley Kauffmann
NEW YORK TIMES, 6/4/93, p. C8, Janet Maslin
VARIETY, 6/14/93, p. 55, Lawrence Cohn
WASHINGTON POST, 6/4/93, p. C7, Rita Kempley
WASHINGTON POST, 6/4/93, Weekend/p. 44, Desson Howe

GUNCRAZY

A Zeta Entertainment release in association with First Look Pictures. *Producer:* Zane W. Levitt and Diane Firestone. *Director:* Tamra Davis. *Screenplay:* Matthew Bright. *Director of Photography:* Lisa Rinzler. *Editor:* Kevin Tent. *Music:* Ed Tomney. *Sound:* Daniel D. Monahan. *Production Designer:* Abbie Lee Warren. *Art Director:* Kevin Constant. *Costumes:* Merrie Lawson. *Running time:* 97 minutes. *MPAA Rating:* R.

CAST: Drew Barrymore (Anita Minteer); James Le Gros (Howard Hickock); Billy Drago (Hank Fulton); Rodney Harvey (Tom); Joe Dallesandro (Rooney); Michael Ironside (Mr. Kincaid); Ione Skye (Joy); Robert Greenberg (Mr. Sheets); Jeremy Davies (Bill); David Eisenstein (Chuck); Dick Warlock (Sheriff).

LOS ANGELES TIMES, 1/20/93, Calendar/p. 1, Kenneth Turan

Passionate women and unstable men, trapped in doomed romances by an uncaring world, have proved an irresistible lure for generations of filmmakers. But no matter how often we've seen it, if it's done right there's something endlessly watchable about violence-prone young lovers facing off against a fatalistic universe. And "Guncrazy" does do it right.

Borrowing its title (here shortened to one word) and some broad conceptual outlines from Joseph Lewis' classic 1949 film noir, much of its spirit from Terrence Malick's "Badlands," and bits and pieces of its ethos from everything from "They Live by Night" to "Bonnie and Clyde"; "Guncrazy" is nothing if not derivative.

But first-time director Tamra Davis and screenwriter Matthew Bright have brought a refreshingly empathetic approach to this latest version, and in actors Drew Barrymore and the protean James Le Gros they have the performers who can carry out their intentions. Made with sureness and authority, this film doesn't condescend to either its characters or their relationship, and that counts for a lot.

"Guncrazy" is set in the mythical central California town of Helm, a pocket of fringe housing so drab the local dump is excitement central (the drive-in has been closed for 10 years). The place is so listless that many of its male members view 16-year-old Anita Minteer (Barrymore) as their primary source of entertainment.

Living in a tiny trailer with the sexually predatory Rooney (Joe Dallesandro), her absent mother's ex-boyfriend, Anita is a study in isolation and despair and a prime target for local scuzzballs who call her *sperm bank* and regularly exploit her. Barrymore, who was allowed to drift over the top in "Poison Ivy," is much more in control here, and her portrayal of someone so deeply in need of even artificial affection that she allows herself to be sexually coerced is genuinely moving.

Things start to change for Anita when, in response to a high school assignment, she begins a pen-pal relationship with the equally bereft Howard Hickok (Le Gros), a prisoner in Chino with a violent past. "I always dreamed of a girl who liked guns," he writes her. "I feel something bigger than us both is bringing us together." A sample reply: "I love you more than words can ever know; my darling."

These fantasy-laced letters are soon replaced by action. Anita convinces the local snake-hand-ling preacher (Billy Drago) to sponsor Howard for parole, and suddenly there he is getting off the bus, an awkward study in polyester. But Anita knows just how to break the ice: She's brought him his favorite gun, a handsome 9 mm job, and soon he is all smiles.

Anita and Howard are attracted to more than each other; they are both hopelessly infatuated with automatic weapons. Guns seem to empower them, make them feel special, provide them with a way to take control of their otherwise frustrating lives.

But that control is illusory, for the weapons they so love ultimately overstimulate Anita and Howard, leading to results neither could anticipate and no one can come close to handling. Like Adam and Eve thrust from the Garden, this pair of hopeless lovers, as naive as they are pathological, slowly stumble to Armageddon.

While it is traditional in these films to portray the woman as the instigating bad seed, as in fact she was in the original "Gun Crazy," Davis and Bright have very sensibly put things on a more even keel here, making Howard into a more than equal partner where carnage is concerned.

A key factor in making this conception believable is the performance of Le Gros. One of the best of young actors, with fine work in "Drugstore Cowboy" and "My New Gun" behind him, Le Gros hits the right combination of sweetness and violence to make Howard, who turns out to have considerable problems of his own, a memorable creation.

Though "Guncrazy" (rated R for strong violence, sensuality, language) is very efficiently made (and stylishly photographed by Lisa Rinzler, one of a very few women cinematographers) it does occasionally overreach, going a little heavy on the rural grotesques as well as the romantic nature of the Anita/Howard relationship.

On the other hand, it is the film's ability to mostly show us that relationship on its own terms, to reveal both why these two are made for each other and why their very closeness inevitably leads to disaster, that is its strongest suit. With moments of odd, dark humor sprinkled among the violence, this traditional study of psycho kittens in love breaks just enough new ground to be an impressive piece of work.

NEW YORK, 2/22/93, p. 60, David Denby

I wish I could share the critical euphoria over the independent film *Guncrazy*, but most of the movie, I thought, was brainless and synthetic. Anita (Drew Barrymore), a bored and ignorant 17-year-old, lives with her mother's old boyfriend in a California dirt town. Beautiful but defenseless and still overweight, as if her spirit were locked in baby fat, Anita has a cowlike passivity—she accommodates the town louts at the dump—until she meets, through the mail, a shy, polite convict at a California state prison. The convict, Howard (James Le Gros), is a deferential young man with an ungovernable violent streak. Anita helps arrange his release, and though he's impotent (at first), she doesn't care; his abashed politeness is intensely romantic for her. Helplessly, but not quite against their will, they are drawn into violence.

It's almost a primal movie subject—the childlike lovers who are despised by society but remain utterly gentle and true to each other. But not every version of the myth is as sentimental as this one. *Guncrazy* is like the original *Gun Crazy* or *Badlands* filtered through the glib romantic sensibility of MTV. The director, Tamra Davis, has made documentaries and also music videos, and much of the movie is conceived as a series of depressed visual moods. The talented cine-matographer Lisa Rinzler uses richly saturated colors and a restlessly moving camera to create a junk-strewn paradise from which beauty and meaning have been mysteriously withdrawn. The spectacular California light doesn't make people cheerful; it makes them crazy, and the lowing, ever-present music, a draggy, druggy presence on the soundtrack, tells us that bad times are inescapable.

Guncrazy, which was written by Matthew Bright, is drenched in unthinking fatalism made hip by extreme violence. Howard and Anita clutch huge revolvers but seem astounded when the guns go off and hurt people. As the movie would have it Anita and Howard are too brutalized by society to do anything else *but* kill. The movie approves of helplessness and finds it romantic. Drew Barrymore may be an extraordinary image of sexuality and trouble, but she's an image out of fashion ads and music videos, and she doesn't get the help she needs to shape her looks into a performance. James Le Gros, on the other hand, is extraordinary. Husky, with eyes that flash dangerously, he stays within the humble, beaten-down manner, a sincere boy who's never been given a thing and who takes refuge from trouble in deference. *Guncrazy* has a few startling moments—the couple attempts to rob a diner, only to have Anita give back the money to men who have families to support. But such original conceits are rare. *Guncrazy* resolves murder into visual mood, and when Howard heads into a fusillade, blowing away cop after cop while taking countless bullets in the chest, *Guncrazy* joins the corrupt conventional entertainments it purports to react against.

NEW YORK POST, 1/27/93, p. 21, Jami Bernard

Because "Guncrazy" is an artifact from the land of trashy B movies, it is only fitting that its star, Drew Barrymore, was up against Katharine Hepburn for a Golden Globe award this past weekend. If it had been any of Barrymore's noble antecedents up against the great Kate, it simply wouldn't have been as much fun.

The teen-age Barrymore has cornered the market on cinematic sluts. Before she was one of the three Amy Fishers, she was the seducer of an entire family in "Poison Ivy." Now she is the town tramp who after an adolescence of taking male abuse develops a taste for guns in "Guncrazy." From the moment she uttered the immortal words "penis breath" in "E.T.," a star was born.

Barrymore as *ueber*-slut is enchanting even when she's being ridiculous, as she is bound to be in a movie in which she has sex in a drainpipe and is raped by her mother's no-good boyfriend. James Le Gros plays another laconic type, a sleepy-lidded ex-con who becomes Barrymore's pen pal, husband and personal savior. He may be impotent in the sack, but he's a helluva shot with a gun; together they go on the lam for some assorted slayings. Their love for each other saves their souls, more or less.

Guns in this movie are used as casually as a pocket comb. Although Barrymore very purposefully shoots her first victim, the rest of them just sort of happen; they say the wrong thing or get in the way or prove too annoying, so they get a bellyful of lead. Neither Barrymore nor Le Gros can help it, despite true regret. This is what happens when middle-American life gets too bland, the movie seems to say, when it is trying to say anything. Barrymore's character lives in one of those humorless trailers, the kind that's not attached to any vehicle. In an area without even a mall, the town dump will do as the place to hang out and have sex. It's a wonder more of the townsfolk don't take to shooting guns, so stifling is the atmosphere.

Barrymore and Le Gros take a sexy shower together in which their bonding is signaled by the mingling of dead men's blood that washes off them. It's a love story, you see.

What this feature-film directing debut by Tamra Davis is most notable for is establishing and sustaining an infectious B-movie spirit. A woman at a recent screening laughed nervously at a scene where a corpse is carried from a beer cooler to the town dump. Stranger still is the killing couple lying abed watching excitedly as their story unfolds on television as if they were watching a cool vid clip on MTV, or "The Amy Fisher Story,"

"Guncrazy" appeared first on cable TV, where its true trashiness went underappreciated. Now you can catch Barrymore in a skimpy tank-top undershirt on the big screen.

NEWSDAY, 1/27/93, Part II/p. 53, Jack Mathews

The scene that perhaps best defines the darkly comic tone of first-time director Tamra Davis' "Guncrazy" comes on the wedding night of Drew Barrymore's 16-year-old Anita and James Le Gros' 24-year-old Howard, somewhere in the desert of central California.

With Howard unable to perform in bed, Anita suggests they consummate their vows instead by revealing their deepest secrets to each other. Howard begins by admitting he's never been able to have sex with a woman, and Anita, who's been sexually abused and humiliated most of her life, calmly leads him to a trash bin behind her trailer for a little show-and-tell.

"I'll consummate for you now," she says, lifting the lid and revealing the decomposing corpse of her mother's boyfriend Rooney (Joe Dallesandro), whom Anita shot to death a month earlier after being raped by him.

If honesty counts for anything in a marriage, this one's off to a roaring start.

"Guncrazy" is as warped a version of the Bonnie and Clyde outlaw lovers myth as any in a long procession that includes the 1950 "Gun Crazy," "Badlands," "Thieves Like Us," "Dirty Mary, Crazy Larry," "Drugstore Cowboy" and "Bonnie and Clyde" itself.

What sets this one off is that it's neither a romantic joyride nor a character study of sociopaths. Anita and Howard kill people and drift into the abyss, but they don't have a mean streak between them. They're a couple of emotionally abandoned children who haven't been given a proper clue as to how to behave or protect themselves.

Matthew Bright's lean, uncomplicated script and Davis' stylish, sympathetic direction throws these lopsided, previously unloved characters together and lets us watch them head down the road, like a pair of wounded animals destined to be caught in society's headlights.

Whether the film is intended as an exercise in nihilist comedy or as a modern fable about the consequences of child abuse, "Guncrazy" cares passionately about its odd couple and forces us to care, too.

The trick of this film is its perverse, Lynchian humor. Anita's hometown is a lowland Twin Peaks, an expanse of scorched earth inhabited by a local mechanic (Billy Drago) who runs a side business preaching the gospel with fire, brimstone and poisonous snakes, a parole officer's daughter (Ione Skye) who's a potsmoking outlaw wannabe, and a sheriff (Dick Warlock) who inexplicably carries around a teddy bear.

How Anita and Howard get together redefines the phrase "meet cute."

Misunderstanding a class assignment to find pen pals, Anita begins corresponding with a lonesome inmate—Howard—at the state pen. When Howard responds with earnest declarations of love and promise ("I always dreamed of a girl who liked guns, perhaps it was you I was dreaming of"), both their lives suddenly have purpose.

While waiting for Howard's release, Anita studies handguns, becomes a sharpshooter, rejects Rooney's sexual advances and refuses to provide any more "favors" for the local tom cats down at the town dump.

"I've got a boyfriend now," she tells them.

When Howard shows up, there's a brief period of bliss, then events and local prejudices combine to turn Anita and Howard into killers and fugitives on the run. Barrymore, whose real life reputation nearly overwhelmed her character in one of last month's network TV movies about Amy Fisher, has played several teen tramps in low-budget movies, but this is her first substantial screen character, and she does wonders with it. Anita is a desperate kid, abused and abandoned, living in a dirt-poor town whose citizens pay no more attention to lost kids than to lost dogs.

Le Gros, Matt Dillon's sidekick in "Drugstore Cowboy," has a way of appearing both harmless and lethal, a gentle guy with a Class A addiction to guns. If he could just get that job he wants as a test shooter for a gun company.

"Guncrazy" was made originally as a Showtime premium channel TV movie but, after some success at festivals, is getting a theatrical release. Whether it finds the cult audience it's looking for, it's already a winner for Davis, a former rock video director moving up to features.

"Guncrazy" may be imitation David Lynch, but it's a good imitation.

VILLAGE VOICE, 2/2/93, p. 49, J. Hoberman

Rescued by Film Forum from released-to-cable limbo, Tamra Davis's luridly sensitive *Guncrazy* is a neo B indie with the cultural cachet of a night at the bowling alley. The ambience is low-rent, the characters mainly blockheads. The thud and clatter of their fate seems the result of an improbable, slow-motion strike-one pin inexorably knocking down the next.

The belle of the gutter ball is Drew Barrymore. Doughy features framed by a corona of mousse-encrusted hair, Barrymore plays 16 (her own age when she made the movie). As in *Poison Ivy* and *The Amy Fisher Story*, she portrays an adolescent with a surplus of sexual knowledge—a bad girl. But here, she's been hit broadside and stupefied by life. Living in a cramped trailer where she is regularly abused by the oafish consort her wayward mother left behind, Barrymore's Anita is a member of the erotic lumpen so baffled by existence and eager for affection that she's a slut entranced—readily banging the scurviest of her classmates, several at a time, amid the construction debris of the town dump.

Anita's life changes when, creatively misunderstanding a class assignment, she starts to correspond with a 24-year-old convict named Howard Hickok, played with convincing feeblemindedness by James Le Gros. As in *My New Gun*, Le Gros is the symbol of liberation, the master of the Gun—he even tells his parole officer that his ambition is to be a "test-shooter" for a small arms manufacturer. And as in Stacy Cochran's film, Le Gros is not exactly what he first seems. He's sweeter and nuttier—trying his best to cope when excited Anita secures him a job as an unpaid assistant to the snake-handling garage mechanic who presides over a one-room church and believes the IRS to be the vehicle of demonic possession.

Tamra Davis has made both music videos and documentaries; her first feature combines the iconic characterizations of the former mode with the observational camera of the latter. *Guncrazy* is played out against the same central California hills that served as the backdrop for a thousand cheap westerns and open-air films noir—the landscape seems brighter and more degraded, but it has something of the same emptiness. In the best B tradition, the supporting cast is inspired: Joe Dallesandro's rancid performance as Anita's abuser is complemented by Billy Drago's turn as the ferally charismatic snake-handler, and Ione Skye's avid cameo as the grouch parole officer's cheerleader daughter.

Despite its title, *Guncrazy*—directed from an eight-year-old script by Matthew Bright—is less a remake of the Joseph H. Lewis classic than an updated downscaling of the tradition from which Lewis's *Gun Crazy* springs. Drawing on Bonnie and Clyde for its sexual pathology and evoking *Badlands* in its adolescent confusion, *Guncrazy* imbues the outlaw lovers with the what-me-worry? affect associated with the onetime blank generation. The dialogue is poignantly brain-dead. The movie opens with the high school teacher reminding his charges of their own recent history: "Remember the beginning of the year, when most of you thought Japan was in Europe?"

Guncrazy is characterized by unsubtle, occasionally irrational exposition, solid production values, and a few extraordinary instances of directorial tact, as when Anita wreaks vengeance on her rapist. Of course, one rapist scarcely makes a difference in this world. The movie swarms with rampaging authority figures, including the one who lives in Howard's brain. The ex-con is tightly wound and sexually impotent. ("It's OK, you can still come in my mouth," Anita comforts him to no avail.) Guns are compensatory for both; as Howard will later tell an erstwhile tormentor, "As long as I have this gun I'm smart, you're stupid." Once they become partners in crime, Anita tells Howard that she doesn't care if they "never do sex." She considers herself free.

Of course, freedom in this depressed world is purchased with violence and only brings destruction. A succession of unpremeditated killings leads to an inept flight, heading for the bright lights of Fresno, where Anita imagines her mother has gone: "Our lives are over now," Howard broods. The pair's one attempted stickup is classically bungled. Still, as in *Bonnie and Clyde*, celebrity confers worth and serves as sexual therapy. Far more than the overtly leftist *Bonnie and Clyde*, however, *Guncrazy* is haunted by the specter of class. "That dog lives better than we do," Howard tells Anita, with more amazement than rancor, after they nearly run over a suburban pet and then, sincere Good Samaritans, return it to its owner.

In the film's final minutes, the fugitives effectively ascend to heaven. They break into a suburban house, doll themselves up, watch a vacation slide show, express an idiotic delight when they find they're the subject of the 11 o'clock news (which comes complete with Howard's father offering to throw the switch when his son is electrocuted). The final camera move into the nighttime sky confirms their stardom—it's as if *Guncrazy* is the docudrama for a crime spree that hasn't yet happened.

Truly, those looking for an embodiment of nascent '90s zeitgeist could do worse than analyze Drew Barrymore. When E.T. extended his bony finger, touched her little forehead, and croaked a solemn injunction to "be good," he created a seven-year-old Mary Magdalene. This golden child turned alkie jailbait not only lived out every Reagan-era excess, she also lived to confess them all in a suitably precocious memoir. A goddess for Wayne's World, but also made for Oprah, young enough to be Madonna's daughter, Drew posed naked for *Interview* (hailed in the magazine as "a national treasure")—and that was well before she celebrated her upcoming 18th birthday by effortlessly fulfilling Amy Fisher's destiny.

What can you say about an actress who survived the simultaneous onset of a midlife crisis and puberty? For pure Oedipal prurience, *Damage* is totally outclassed by *Poison Ivy*, with Barrymore as an outrageously provocative teen temptress, complete with nose ring and thigh tattoo. Indeed, from *Aladdin* to *Chaplin*, from *The Bodyguard* to *Body Evidence*, it's difficult to think of a current movie that wouldn't be improved by Drew's presence.

Also reviewed in:
CHICAGO TRIBUNE, 2/12/93, Friday/p. F, Dave Kehr
NEW YORK TIMES, 1/27/93, p. C17, Vincent Canby
VARIETY, 6/1/92, p. 68, Todd McCarthy
WASHINGTON POST, 2/5/93, p. B1, Hal Hinson

HAPPILY EVER AFTER

A First National Film Corporation release of a Filmation presentation. *Executive Producer:* Milton Verret. *Producer:* Lou Scheimer. *Director:* John Howley. *Screenplay:* Martha Moran and Robby London. *Director of Photography:* Fred Ziegler. *Editor:* Jeffrey C. Patch and Joe Gall. *Music:* Frank W. Becker. *Sound:* Steve Pickard and Louie Montoya. *Art Director:* John Grusd. *Running time:* 80 minutes. *MPAA Rating:* G.

VOICES: Irene Cara (Snow White); Edward Asner (Scowl); Carol Channing (Muddy); Dom DeLuise (Looking Glass); Phyliss Diller (Mother Nature); Zsa Zsa Gabor (Blossom); Sally Kellerman (Sunburn); Malcolm McDowell (Lord Maliss); Tracey Ullman (Thunderella); Michael Horton (The Prince).

LOS ANGELES TIMES, 5/28/93, Calendar/p. 12, Kevin Thomas

Filmation's "Happily Ever After," an uninspired sequel to Disney's 1937 classic "Snow White and the Seven Dwarfs," is scarcely a happy occasion for the audience or for Snow White and her Prince.

"With the Wicked Queen gone who would harm us?" asks the Prince (voice of Michael Horton) as he and Snow White (voice of Irene Cara) walk through the woods to invite the Seven Dwarfs to their wedding. The answer writers Martha Moran and Robby London have come up with is the Wicked Queen's evil brother Lord Maliss (voice of Malcolm McDowell)—pronounced Malice—who can transform himself into a dragon at will and who vows vengeance for the demise of his sister, who had been the innocent Snow White's nemesis. Lord Maliss swiftly swoops down on the betrothed couple, with Snow White escaping and her Prince whisked off to the Realm of Doom.

Making her way to the Seven Dwarfs' cottage, Snow White finds that it is now the home of their cousins, the Seven Dwarfelles, each of whom has been bestowed by Mother Nature (voice of Phyllis Diller) with a power that controls an aspect of life on Earth. Accompanied by the Dwarfelles—voiced by Carol Channing, Zsa Zsa Gabor, Sally Kellerman, Linda Gary and Tracey Ullman, with the last two actresses playing two roles—Snow White plunges into a perilous mission to rescue her Prince.

Produced by animation veteran Lou Scheimer, "Happily Ever After" is nothing if not consistent in its mediocrity. Backgrounds are so indistinguishable from countless other animated fairy tales as to seem generic. The film's humans and creatures similarly lack a distinctive look, with Snow White and the Prince seeming especially bland. The film's several songs are instantly forgettable.

Under the direction of John Howley, only a spunky Phyllis Diller and McDowell, a gleeful villain, are able to create a strong sense of personality. It would be unfair to slough off "Happily Ever After" (G-rated—despite a strong dose of animation's traditional violence) on to youngsters.

NEW YORK POST, 5/28/93, p. 34, Michael Medved

When a G-rated animated feature stars the voices of both Phyllis Diller and Carol Channing, you know you're in some kind of trouble.

The new kiddie movie "Happily Ever After" not only includes the vocal stylings of these two hotter-than-hot superstars, it also features a streetwise, cutting-edge rap number (called "The Baddest") performed by that well-known champion of hip-hop culture, Edward Asner.

When you add to this an environmental-consciousness ditty called "Mother Nature's Song" as sung by Diller, and a phoned-in, phonetically assembled performance (as "Blossom") from that beloved children's favorite, Zsa Zsa Gabor, then you get some idea of the bizarre and outrageously tacky atmosphere that pervades this well-meaning production.

The story dares to ask the question "Whatever happened to Snow White?" and provides its own inane answers.

The action begins with our comely heroine (portrayed by the voice of Irene Cara) and her handsome prince riding off together to get married. Rather than exploring their difficulties in keeping that romantic spark alive during many years of marriage and children, the story introduces Lord Maliss (Malcolm MacDowell), who is the "even wickeder brother" of the late, lamented wicked queen and who captures the prince before he can make an honest woman of Snow White.

The plot then heads in a trendy, feminist direction: This time it's the fair maiden who must rescue her imprisoned prince. To complete this politically correct arrangement, the heroine is aided not by seven dwarfs (who, we are told, have decided to work a new mine in another part of the forest); but by their cousins, the seven female "Dwarfelles."

With names like "Sunburn" "Muddy," "Thunderella," "Moonbeam" and "Critterina" these crudely drawn munchkins resemble squat, pint-sized and punk-haired washerwomen, and will make moviegoers long for Grumpy, Bashful, Dopey and the rest of the bunch.

In fact, one of the major challenges facing this new family-friendly offering is that it appears on the scene just five weeks before the heavily hyped re-release of a spiffy, fresh-looking, color-adjusted version of the original "Snow White" and "Happily Ever After," hardly benefits from comparisons to that 1938 Disney classic.

Though the press materials boast of more than "100,000 animation cels that were individually painted, by hand, in intricate detail," the images on screen seem no more detailed or lifelike than standard kid-vid fare on TV.

In fact, the fluffy, cutie-pie images and garish colors bear an unfortunate, resemblance to the "Rainbow Brite" series, and even to the dreaded "Care Bears," who have driven so many parents of pre-schoolers into saccharine-overdose fits.

The ultimate question on this sort of picture is, of course, will it play to the peanut gallery and the answer here is a qualified yes. The story has just enough scary moments and surprises to keep the attention of most youngsters, and the music (with a busy score by Frank W. Backer) is bland but serviceable.

One number, "Thunderella's Song," as performed by the ever-versatile Tracey Ullman is significantly better than that—so producer Lou Scheimer (creator of such TV abominations as "He-Man/SheRa," "Aquaman," and the "Batman" and "Superman" animated series) obligingly repeats the lively aria for all who missed it the first time around.

As for my own kids, they certainly enjoyed the picture—though not nearly as much as they liked any of the recent Disney titles or the just-released Japanese import "My Neighbor Totoro."

When I asked my 4-year-old, Shayna, if she would like to see "Happily Ever After" a second time, she shyly replied, "Maybe we can go home and watch a Barney video instead."

NEWSDAY, 5/31/93, Part II/p. 33, Jack Mathews

With the success Disney has been having with animated musicals, it was inevitable that a third-rate animation company like Filmation would try to grab some of the action, and "Happily Ever After," Filmation's continuation of "Snow White and the Seven Dwarfs" is just what you'd expect—third rate.

The musical numbers are pale imitations of the show-stoppers in "The Little Mermaid" and "Beauty and the Beast," and the listless, washed-out animation is a bare cut above the quality of Saturday morning TV.

Still, there is enough broad action to keep toddlers in their seats through most of the 84-minute running time, and parents may be amused by the efforts of writers Martha Moran and Robby London to reverse the damsel-in-distress formula and turn the sequel to "Snow White" into a post-feminist fairy tale.

In this story, it is Snow who must rescue her Prince, after the weenie is abducted by the evil Lord Maliss and taken to the Realm of Doom, and it is the powerful Mother Nature and her assistants—the Seven Dwarfelles!—who help steel her nerve.

The voices are nicely performed by Irene Cara (Snow), Michael Horton (Prince), Malcolm MacDowell (Lord Maliss), Phyllis Diller (Mother Nature), Dom DeLuise (the Looking Glass), and Ed Asner (as Scowl, a cigar-chomping owl).

Among the Dwarfelles, you'll hear the unmistakable rasps of Carol Channing and Zsa Zsa Gabor, as well as the voices of Tracey Ullman and Sally Kellerman.

Would that the filmmakers were as imaginative in their images as in their casting. Aside from the nice trick dreamed up for Lord Maliss—he transforms himself into a flying red dragon at will—"Happily Ever After" is about as stimulating as a night at the Smurfs.

Also reviewed in:
NEW YORK TIMES, 5/29/93, p. 13, Stephen Holden
WASHINGTON POST, 5/29/93, p. D9, Rita Kempley

HARD-BOILED

A Rim Film Distributors release with East Coast distribution by Peter Chow of a Milestone Pictures production.   *Producer:* Linda Kuk and Terence Chang.   *Director:* John Woo. *Screenplay (Chinese with English subtitles):* Barry Wong.   *Director of Photography:* Wong Wing-Heng.   *Editor:* John Woo, Kai Kit-Wai and David Woo.   *Music:* Michael Gibbs and James Wong.   *Music Editor:* David Wu.   *Choreographer:* Cheung Juhluh.   *Sound (music):* Max Rose.   *Art Director:* James Leung and Joel Chong.   *Special Effects:* Lau Hon-Cheung. *Costumes:* Bruce Yu and Janet Chun.   *Make-up:* Bernadette Cheng.   *Stunt Coordinator:* Philip Kwok.   *Running time:* 127 minutes. *MPAA Rating:* Not Rated.

CAST: Chow Yun-Fat (Inspector Yuen, "Tequila");   Tony Chiu Wai Leung (Tony);   Teresa Mo (Teresa);   Philip Chan (Superintendent Chan);   Anthony Wong (Johnny Wong);   Kwan Hoi-Shan (Hoi);   Bowie Lam (A-Lung);   Tung Wai (Little Koi); John Woo (Barman in Jazz Club).

LOS ANGELES TIMES, 4/30/93, Calendar/p. 6, Kenneth Turan

John Woo's time is now. Known as the director who never leaves you begging for more, Woo is a veteran of the rowdy, populist Hong Kong cinema who's been embraced both by fickle critics and the financiers of Hollywood. "Hard-Boiled" not only demonstrates why, it doesn't keep you waiting to find out.

This newest Woo film (not counting his English-language debut, the Jean-Claude Van Damme-starring "Hard Target," due later this year) has barely begun before the excitement begins. The setting is a Hong Kong tea house, an early morning rendezvous for bird fanciers and, as it turns out, a nefarious gang of gunrunners. Checking them out are a squad of plainclothes police, lead by Inspector Yuen, nicknamed Tequila (Chow Yun-Fat), a toothpick-chewing, jazz-playing cop with a hyperactive trigger finger.

Suddenly a signal is given and for the next 10 minutes an intoxicating Bacchanalia of balletic violence fills the screen. For Woo, a natural filmmaker with an eye for arresting images, is also one of the premier orchestrators of large-scale mayhem ever to fill a screen.

It's not just that bullets uncountable ricochet around, along with assorted bird feathers and bric-a-brac, or that the dead pile up like cordwood: It's the dazzling way Woo, director of photography Wang Wing-Heng and action coordinator Cheung Juhluh pull it all together and put it on display.

Alternating restless, supple camera movements with dynamic cutting, multiple angles and frequent use of slow motion, Woo and company turn out dazzling, energetic action sequences that are as close to pure cinema as anything on the market today. When a survivor of one of Woo's carnivals of carnage describes it to police as "too quick, like a dream," there's no one in the audience who won't know what she means.

More than that, Woo manages to imbue all this mass destruction (shown here in the original director's cut) with an air that is almost whimsical. Despite the use of weapons powerful enough to make even NRA members feel secure, the action in "Hard-Boiled" is more fanciful than disturbing and leaves you with the sense that it's all been quite imaginary. Like the Hong Kong martial arts films they bear a family resemblance to, Woo's works are lightly playful and inventive in their violence, especially when compared to nominally childish but essentially nasty films like "Home Alone 2."

"Hard-Boiled's" script, written by Barry Wong from an original story by Woo (who also has a hand in the editing and a small part as a philosophical bartender) is a not unfamiliar tale of conflicting loyalties and betrayal. At first it centers on the rivalry between competing arms dealers, the old-style paternalistic Mr. Hoi (Kwan Hoi-Shan) and an up-and-coming psycho named Johnny Wong (Anthony Wong) who is given to somber pronouncements such as "Everything will end but war" and "He who holds a gun holds the power."

But, like other Woo films, including 1989's knockout "The Killer," "Hard-Boiled" can't resist the lure of male bonding, focusing on the against-all-odds friendship of Tequila with an enigmatic hit man named Tony (Tony Leung) who broods all alone on a boat filled with the origami cranes he fashions every time he puts someone away.

Finally, of course, it is the action that draws you to "Hard-Boiled" (Times-rated Mature for violence), everything from the small-scale stuff like a single-shot mob hit in a library to the film's serio-comic finale in a major hospital, where comically reverent shots of babies being rescued alternate with bursts of automatic weapons fire.

NEW YORK POST, 6/18/93, p. 31, Matthew Flamm

This is one tough cop. It's not enough that "Tequila" Yuen shoots his way through a gunfight with a pistol in each hand rolling over tables in a crowded Hong Kong teahouse, skidding along its floor, sliding down a banister and never running out of bullets. He can also keep a toothpick dangling through it all from the corner of his mouth.

"Hard-Boiled," the new film from the noted Hong Kong action director John Woo ("The Killer"), could have been called "Over the Top." It has the bodycount of a whole summer's worth of Hollywood sequels, firepower to rival the Pentagon's, and more balletically staged, geometrically arranged, multi-party shootouts than a Sam Peckinpah festival.

Gunpowder, after all, was invented in China. And guns are pretty much all that "Hard-Boiled" is about. The improbable story—conceived by Woo and written by Barry Wong—concerns Triad gun smugglers who have been turning Hong Kong into the sort of killing field one associates with American cities.

It's not hard to see what the problem is. When Tequila—a cop so cool he moonlights as a jazz musician—and his partner raid the bad guys in the spectacular opening teahouse scene, they kill as many waiters and patrons as gangsters. ("You were supposed to take them alive!" complains Tequila's always irate chief.)

The gun-smuggling story, which soon involves gang warfare, is really little more than an excuse for Woo's set-pieces. "Hard-Boiled" is about gunplay as fantasy; it may try for hard-boiled, but it feels like cops and robbers as played by 8-year-old boys.

The movie pushes the buddy-action formula to comic extremes. Tequila (the amusingly smooth Chow Yun Fat), pledged to avenge his partner's death in the teahouse, becomes a one-man army—until he teams up with an equally trigger-happy undercover cop. (Their bickering friendship is so blatantly homoerotic, it would make Martin and Lewis blush.)

There's no limit to the havoc they wreak. Woo sets the film's bloody, bravura climax in a hospital owned by the gangsters. Tequila, shot in the shoulder, blasts away at the bad guys—cradling a newborn baby with his good arm.

NEWSDAY, 6/18/93, Part II/p. 67, John Anderson

John Woo, Hong Kong's master choreographer of cinematic violence, has blasted the action genre onto a whole new level. His shootouts are a ballet; his fire-bombings are poetry. And while he lets the body count get away from him, he constantly fascinates, through a combination of chaos and an excruciating control over what we're allowed to see.

"Hard-Boiled," Woo's latest effort, is a gaudy, gory pyrotechnical display, and not just because he delivers more firepower per frame than any other director. He's playing at much higher stakes here as far as gambling with what his audience can handle, higher than in his best-known films, "The Killers" or "A Better Tomorrow." The situations in which he places his characters are more precarious, his victims more vulnerable, and his lethal dances are packed with far more numerous and complicated pas de deux than most filmmakers—especially in this overworked genre—would bother to attempt. But Woo pulls it off, in high style.

Take the opening blood bath, the teahouse shootout—which may soon become The Teahouse Shootout among hard-core action aficionados. Maverick police inspector Tequila Yuen (Chow Yun-Fat), arrives with partner A-Lung (Bowie Lam) to sabotage an arms-smuggling ring, while the criminals eat dim sum and dote on the caged birds that occupy each table (a common sight in Hong Kong). It's a particularly nerve-wracking setup; the birds are as fragile as the peace, the camera itself is edgy. You know something's going to happen, you almost don't want it to. And then again, you do. And then they start blowing the place to smithereens.

Where other action films seem to have self-imposed limits about who and what gets demolished, "Hard-Boiled" goes beyond anyone's expectations. One gunman, trying to flee through a panicked crowd, simply shoots down each customer in his way and runs over his or her body. Tequila, trying to stop two other thugs, slides along a banister while simultaneously firing two pistols and chewing a toothpick. During a particularly frenetic sequence in the restaurant's kitchen, he takes an acrobatic trip down a flour-covered table and lands with his gun pressed to the forehead of the last remaining criminal, rendering him helpless. Then, of course, he pulls the trigger.

Caught in the teahouse battle—a far classier melee than the hospital siege that ends the film—is Tony (Tony Chiu Wai Leung, not to be confused with the other Chinese actor Tony Leung, of "The Lover"). Tony is in deep cover, having joined one of the two rival "triads" or gangs that control the illegal arms market in Hong Kong.

When Tony accidentally kills another cop during the fight, it exacerbates his existing recriminations about his job, how it forces him to kill innocent people, how he doesn't feel like a real cop. He's set up as a counterweight to Tequila, the consummate renegade, played with sneering charm by Chow (proclaimed in the ads as "The Next Action Hero"), a Woo favorite. Tequila plays clarinet, and says he always plays a song when a colleague dies; Tony makes origami cranes, one for every life he's taken. The artistic sides to their personalities are merely a concession to dramatic form, although in the course of crushing the megalomaniacal arms kingpin Johnny (Anthony Wong), they achieve a kinship of blood.

Woo imposes no rules on himself regarding space or time, or even logic. Cops and robbers alike recover miraculously from the most debilitating wounds whenever it's convenient; they accomplish remarkable bits of marksmanship and then can't seem to hit someone who's standing right in front of them. But Woo is not about reality in any sense. He's about action. Period. And the way he limits our perspective, letting closeups linger on, tantalizing us with a sense of impending eruption behind or around the characters, puts an edge of hysteria on the entire picture.

Woo surrenders to the maudlin more than occasionally; characters are melodramatically freeze-framed before dissolving into other scenes; moments of introspection by Tony or Tequila are just sappy. And Woo sets a pace for himself from the outset that he can't maintain. But his action sequences are so artfully handled and his sense of humor is so outrageous—Tequila invents a new form of skeet-shooting at one point, plinking gunmen off their flying motorcycles—that it's difficult not to be tickled, and thrilled.

SIGHT AND SOUND, 10/93, p. 47, Tom Tunney

Hong Kong. Police detectives Inspector Yuen (nicknamed Tequila) and A-Lung attack a gang of gun-running gangsters in an extended shoot-out, during which A-Lung is killed. Yuen is reprimanded by his Chief Superintendent for his excessive use of force. Gangster hitman Tony—in reality an undercover detective—assassinatesLittle Mustache, a member of gunrunner Hoi's gang, who was supplying information to Hoi's rival Johnny Wong. Tony joins forces with Wong's gang, which includes Little Koi, also a police informer. This group is confronted by Yuen, who attempts to arrest Tony; Little Koi saves Yuen's life by knocking him to the ground. Later, Yuen meets Little Koi and is told that Wong is planning to attack Hoi's warehouse arsenal that night.

Wong and Tony oversee the assault, in which gun-wielding motorcyclists massacre Hoi's workers. Hoi and his minions arrive and are surrounded by Wong's men. Hoi attempts to do a deal with Tony, asking that his people be spared in exchange for his own life. Tony pretends to agree, shoots Hoi, then massacres his surviving underlings. Yuen, who has been hidden, now swings into action and another gun battle ensues. After Tony has declined to shoot Yuen, Yuen realises he must be an undercover cop, and surprises him at his boat, where they join forces repelling a further gun attack. Tony is wounded, and Yuen hides when Wong arrives; Wong promises medical aid for Tony in the hospital he owns—which also houses his main weapons store.

Ordered to kill Little Koi by Wong, Tony intervenes when he sees Koi set upon by Wong's gunman Mad Dog. Tony arranges for Koi to survive the shooting; Koi then tells Yuen about the hospital arsenal and is taken there for treatment. Tony goes to the hospital to save Koi with Yuen's help. Koi, attempting to escape, is killed by Mad Dog. Tony and Yuen sneak into the basement armoury, but attempting to break in, Tony is electrocuted. Yuen revives him but Mad Dog appears and another battle ensues.

Amid the mayhem, Mad Dog objects to Wong's attempt to demolish the building with explosives; he tries to kill him, but is shot by Wong. Yuen goes back to help his sweetheart Teresa rescue a baby left behind in the building; Wong takes him prisoner and drags him out of the hospital to confront Yuen and the police. Tony grabs Yuen's gun and shoots him by firing the gun through his own body. Yuen then shoots Wong. At police HQ Tony's file is ritually burned.

Hard-Boiled's press kit carries quotes from the likes of James Cameron, Quentin Tarantino (who calls John Woo "the most exciting director to emerge in action cinema since Sergio Leone") and *Variety* ("the Mozart of Mayhem"). This lavish quoted praise signals an intention on the part of the film's British distributor to market the film both as an 'action' spectacular and as the work of an *auteur* whose boldly kinetic style has already achieved much critical approval. This approach will probably reap dividends despite the fact that, compared to Woo's 1989 *The Killer*, *Hard-Boiled* is a disappointment. The energy, wit and panache with which Woo stages his massively extended action scenes remain as potent as before, but what the film fatally lacks—as the absurdly contrived plot indicates—are characters and a story which would invest these scenes with a worthwhile moral impact. Instead, the emphasis is on action as an end in itself.

In *The Killer*, much is made of the friendship between Chow Yun-Fat's character Jeff and the cop on his trail; Jeff is granted a definite moral and emotional stature despite the patent absurdities of the storyline. *Hard-Boiled* trades in similar ideas, with nowhere near the same success. Tony makes a paper crane every time he kills; he also says he wishes to escape from his 'dark' life (to the North Pole!) and there's some budding respect between him and Yuen. But here these laboured kinship notions seem secondhand and merely incidental to the main business of setting up the next spectacular action set piece. Whereas in *The Killer*, the shoot-outs served to define the characters and the relationship between them (and allowed Woo to have much fun at the expense of genre conventions), here such elements have a musty off-the-peg quality—they're simply a loose framework from which to hang the big production numbers.

The action numbers certainly are immense, with a prodigious body and bullet count and a dynamic fluency in their choreography, editing and sheer speed that is frequently stunning. Perhaps no other director can currently match Woo's heavy calibre finesse in combining gun-play and movement. Characters almost always run, leap and dive while firing. Bullets weave intricate patterns of blasted bodies, windows, furniture and fluttering masses of paper. Slow motion frequently extends pivotal moments and emphasises the grace of destruction, the beauty of disintegration and the raw power of pyrotechnics. The film's musical-like choreography and the overall rhythmic quality of the destruction suggest a directing style that has as much in common with Busby Berkeley as it does with Sam Peckinpah. It's an essentially decorative aesthetic of destruction in which pyrotechnics and firepower are celebrated for their own sake. In absurdly close proximity to each other, the leading characters shoot less to kill than to sustain their perverse dance-of-death courtship for as long as possible. In *Hard-Boiled* this is best illustrated in the scene in which two characters run alongside either side of a shattering glass partition while harmlessly blasting at each other. As in a dance routine, it's the performance rather than its goal that's important. The killing zone in front of camera is like the endlessly extended stage in a vintage musical, its many disposable villains arrayed much as the scores of anonymous showgirls in a Busby Berkeley revue. On the evidence of *Hard-Boiled*, John Woo fits snugly and unproblematically into the same straightforward 'action' category as workaday straight-to-video directors like Aaron Norris and Craig R. Baxley, rather than with such films as *Taxi Driver, The Wild Bunch* or John Milius' *Dillinger*. These films all have their pivotal action sequences, but they're also more than 'action' films, because their directors use the 'action' as a way to explore their characters and the social milieu in which they struggle—through violence—to define themselves. Such films creatively blur the distinction between safely synthetic screen action and the kind of gut-wrenchingly physical violence that we recognise as real. *The Killer* at times moves into this dangerous territory, but *Hard-Boiled* signally lacks such an exploratory urge. Though the stunts are magnificent, the casual plotting, low comic asides and thin characterisations most often recall the busy but emotionally sterile antics of James Bond or The Man from U.N.C.L.E.. The implausibly foolish villain Wong is especially mundane and derivative.

Perhaps the scene that best sums up *Hard-Boiled*'s moral timidity is the one in which Yuen blasts at least six anonymous gunmen while holding a baby, then exclaims, "Hey, X-rated action!" before wiping a victim's blood off the child's face. That line is a wink to the audience that Woo is sending up the action genre, but it's also an admission that the movie won't stray out of that genre's bloody but bland parameters. The baby won't get its head blown off—if it did, we'd be in a much more dangerous, far more interesting film.

As it is, *Hard-Boiled* is a little like what *The Wild Bunch* might have been if William Holden's character hadn't been killed at the end; or *Taxi Driver* if Travis Bickle hadn't been mentally unstable; or *Dirty Harry* if the lead had been played by Elvis Presley or Glen Campbell. On this evidence, John Woo is indeed "one of the best action movie directors working in the world today." However, that's as much a criticism as a compliment, because *The Killer* had strongly suggested that he could also be much more than that. His forthcoming Hollywood debut, *Hard Target* with Jean-Claude Van Damme, will hopefully confirm he can be again.

VILLAGE VOICE, 6/22/93, p. 63, David D. Kim

"He who holds the gun," one of *Hard-Boiled*'s black hats intones, "holds the power." Maybe. But he who holds two guns and comes screeching down a banister without ever getting so much as a splinter in his invincible butt holds the secret to Woo!Woo!Woo!mania: the heroes are hard-boiled, and the shit is raw.

By my estimate, 185 people are wonton meat by the end of John Woo's latest bloodbath, but who's counting? What matters is death as style: the arc of a motorcycle as it crash-lands on someone's face, the whirl of bodies blasted across a teahouse kitchen. Despite a few cheesy freeze-frames and editing that sometimes looks as if it were done under crossfire, massacre scenes are pumped up yet graceful, eloquent if messy.

This time, Woo's ballistic ballet features two cops—jazz buff Tequila (Chow Yun-Fat) and undercover man Tony (Tony Leung, *not* of *The Lover*—whose electric pas de deux bespeaks that intense love between men, albeit the kind best expressed through the unbridled spray of bullets. Their target is gangster boss and number-one-son-of-a-bitch Johnny, who's stashed his smuggled weapons in a hospital's basement morgue. When Tony 'n' Tequila discover it, Johnny threatens to blow the place up. Enter Tequila's love interest, Teresa, who plays tag-team rescue by frantically escorting droves of limping, confused patients (gunshot victims, perhaps?) from the burning hospital before it ... Wait! The babies! What about all those squirming babies?

Oh. The humanity. Woo automatically shifts into hyperkitsch. One of his many pristine goddesses, Teresa wears virtue like a bulletproof vest and glides through the maternity ward without ever breaking a nail. Tequila, however, gets to squeeze the last drop of melodrama. Clearly, this director understands resilience: whether Hollywood (as in *Hard Target*, his upcoming Van Damme vehicle) or Hong Kong, Wooville is a place where over-the-top pathos always survives the splatter.

Also reviewed in:
NEW YORK TIMES, 6/18/93, p. C12, Vincent Canby
VARIETY, 9/28/92, p. 82, Susan Ayscough
WASHINGTON POST, 8/20/93, p. D6, Richard Harrington
WASHINGTON POST, 8/20/93, Weekend/p. 42, Desson Howe

HARD TARGET

A Universal Pictures release of an Alphaville/Renaissance production. *Executive Producer:*
Moshe Diamant, Sam Raimi, and Robert Tapert. *Producer:* James Jacks and Sean Daniel.
Director: John Woo. *Screenplay:* Chuck Pfarrer. *Director of Photography:* Russell Carpenter.
Editor: Bob Murawski. *Music:* Graeme Revell. *Music Editor:* Dick Bernstein. *Sound:* Al Rizzo,
Kenny Delbert, and (music) Danny Wallin. *Sound Editor:* John Dunn and George Simpson.
Production Designer: Phil Dagort. *Art Director:* Philip Messina. *Set Decorator:* Michele Poulik.
Set Dresser: David Schlesinger and Michael Martin. *Special Effects:* Dale Martin. *Costumes:*
Karyn Wagner. *Make-up:* Anne Hieronymus. *Make-up (Jean-Claude Van Damme):* Zoltan.
Stunt Coordinator: Billy Burton. *Running time:* 92 minutes. *MPAA Rating:* R.

CAST: Chuck Pfarrer (Binder); Bob Apisa (Mr. Lopacki); Arnold Vosloo (Van Cleaf); Lance
Henriksen (Emil Fouchon); Yancy Butler (Natasha Binder); Lenore Banks (Marie); Douglas
Forsythe Rye (Frick); Michael D. Leinert (Frack); Willie Carpenter (Elijah Roper);
Jean-Claude Van Damme (Chance Boudreaux); Barbara Tasker (Waitress); Kasi Lemmons
(Carmine); Randy Cheramie (Shop Steward); Eliott Keener (Randal Poe); Robert Pavlovich
(Police Detective); Marco St. John (Dr. Morton); Joe Warfield (Ismal Zenan); Jeanette
Kontomitras (Madam); Ted Raimi (Man on the Street); Sven Thorsen (Stephan); Tom Lupo
(Jerome); Jules Sylvester (Peterson); Dave Efron (Billy Bob); Wilford Brimley (Douvee).

LOS ANGELES TIMES, 8/20/93, Calendar/p. 1, Kenneth Turan

There's one on every John Woo production, a sequence of such intoxicating, delirious violence,
with bullets and bodies dancing around in feverish combination, that you almost cannot
comprehend, let alone believe, what you are seeing. When it comes to putting large-scale,
explosive action on film, Woo is the new gold standard.

And action is what he's been directing in Hong Kong, where enormously popular Chinese-
language films like "Hard-Boiled," "The Killer" and "A Better Tomorrow" have helped him to
gain a reputation so considerable that where "Hard Target" was recently screened to mayhem
aficionados, his name got a noticeably bigger round of applause than kick-happy star Jean-Claude
Van Damme.

"Hard Target" is Woo's 23rd film but also something new: his first English-language
Hollywood production. This much-anticipated melding of East and West was no simple thing, as
the film's seven trips to the MPAA before it managed to eek out an R rating (for a great amount
of violence and for language) will attest.

And though it has its share of boggling action sequences and will serve as an acceptable
introduction to domestic fans not familiar with Woo's work, "Hard Target" is an awkward
mixture, not on the level of the director's best work, and leaves open the question of how well
his style can adapt to Hollywood.

Certainly Woo has had no difficulty bringing over his trademark visual apparatus intact. Set in
New Orleans, not Hong Kong, "Hard Target" is nevertheless filled with most of the director's
favorite things: black-helmeted motorcycle riders, fiery explosions, symbolic doves, shattered
glass and loving shots of larger-than-life rifles and handguns.

Woo's particular brand of idiosyncratic sentimentality, however, is largely absent (a victim,
apparently, of the testing process), as is Chow Yun-fat, the star of all of Woo's most recent films
and the director's alter ego. Van Damme, the erstwhile "Muscles From Brussels," turns out to

be an insufficient replacement, woodenly stymieing all of Woo's persistent attempts to mythologize him via careful use of slow-motion photography.

Also, the fact that Van Damme's weapons of choice are lethal karate kicks gives this picture an uncomfortably hard edge that is unusual for Woo. Though victims are machine-gunned by the gross in his films, sheer numbers give their deaths a balletic, almost fairy-tale grace. By contrast, the violence here is initially up close and personal. Perhaps that's what American audiences expect, but it is unpleasant nevertheless.

It all starts with Chance Boudreaux (Van Damme) minding his own business in a greasy spoon when he notices innocent Natasha Binder (Yancy Butler) attracting the wrong kind of attention. She is in town looking for her dad, a combat veteran down on his luck. Chance shows no interest in her quest until, in a typically cockeyed plot twist, he turns out to need some money to pay his union dues. Really.

What Chance and Nat stumble upon is a knockoff of "The Most Dangerous Game," a well-funded operation in which wealthy men stalk the human animal. Running things is Emil Fouchon (the reliably nefarious Lance Henriksen), a droll sort who believes "it has always been the privilege of the few to hunt the many." Just to make things more sporting, victims are selected from down-on-their-luck combat veterans, but once Chance gets involved, the challenge level gets considerably higher.

Though this scenario (written by Chuck Pfarrer) is not noticeably complex, fully half of "Hard Target" is taken up laboriously setting it in motion and stolidly demonstrating Van Damme's martial arts prowess.

When the second half kicks in, so to speak, Woo partisans will finally be on familiar ground. A kinetic shootout on a bridge becomes a chase through the bayous to a Mardi Gras warehouse/graveyard, the setting for (at last) one of the director's dazzling, can-you-top-this roller coaster sequences, made with so much panache that fans will be tempted to forgive the false starts that came before. Or if not quite that, to at least suspend judgment till John Woo's next crack at the Hollywood machine comes around.

NEW YORK POST, 8/20/93, p. 25, Lawrence Cohn

In his first assignment for a world-class filmmaker, Jean-Claude Van Damme delivers just another Van Damme picture. "Hard Target" has plenty of action scenes for the faithful but little else to recommend it.

Hong Kong director John Woo successfully auditions for Hollywood with this made-in-New Orleans exercise, piling on the slow-motion, exploding blood packs, tricky editing and fancy camera angles. The visual distractions (such as endless repetitions of the "Robin Hood" tracking arrows) and digital stereo sound effects almost fool the viewer into thinking something of interest is happening.

Van Damme's an unemployed sailor hired by pretty Yancy Butler to find her missing dad. We've already seen daddy murdered by evil Lance Henriksen and his bloodthirsty hunters in the opening scene, with the in-joke that papa is played by "Hard Target" screenwriter Chuck Pfarrer.

His one-note script is the umpteenth variation on the classic Richard Connell story "The Most Dangerous Game," in which human prey is considered the ultimate thrill for macho hunter types. Henriksen gives would-be sportsmen a chance to track down and kill homeless ex-servicemen for $500,000 a pop. Yancy's pop is one such case, and after an hour of preamble, ex-Marine Chance Boudreaux (played by Van Damme with his usual fractured English dialogue but no attempt at a Cajun twang) becomes the quarry.

The slow-motion and able stunt men make Van Damme look good in action, alternating fancy kicks with the John Woo specialty of automatic weapons. For once he's not the worst actor on screen, as Butler (who played a robot nicely in TVs "Mann and Machine") is so relentlessly bug-eyed that she's stuck for an extra effect when confronted with a mean-looking rattlesnake (actually a puppet).

Henriksen is way too hammy as a villain who likes to tell off his henchmen and clients.

The movie's technical effects are awesome at times, but nowhere does maestro Woo get a chance to show the skill with actors he demonstrated seven years ago in his breakthrough thriller about male bonding "A Better Tomorrow." Hopefully his next U.S. assignment will be more challenging.

NEWSDAY, 8/20/93, Part II/p. 64, John Anderson

In "Hard Target," his first Hollywood production, John Woo, the king of Hong Kong action films, is teamed with Jean-Claude Van Damme, the Belgian-made fixture of American martial-arts features. It's a nice matchup, like Fred and Ginger: Woo has the class, Van Damme has the sex.

Woo probably wanted to be John Ford, but wound up a cross between Sam Peckinpah and Akira Kurosawa: a maker of wildly violent films that have grandeur because they're rooted in a classical sense of good and evil. "Hard Target" may not contain the restrained violence of Woo's Hong Kong work—the current "Hard-Boiled" for instance—but the evil may be better defined.

Chuck Pfarrer's screenplay is part western, but is clearly based on the old Richard Connell story "The Most Dangerous Game." There, rich men hunted humans for sport. Here, in what may be a Woo nod to the economic anxieties of the New World, they hunt homeless men. And, just to keep things sporting, they prefer their game to be vets with combat experience.

Most Woo movies open with a frenetic siege of some kind, but here he gives us two. Before the credits finish rolling, we've watched a bearded, bedraggled man chased through New Orleans by truck, motorcycle and high-velocity arrow; the closeups of the arrows, spinning toward their prey, make the slow-moving man not only doomed but pathetic. He's tough, though. It takes three arrows, and innumerable bullets, to bring him down. But down he comes—just as "Directed by John Woo", appears on screen.

The second fight, a rare one for Woo since no guns are fired, comes soon after and involves Chance (Van Damme) an itinerant merchant seaman from the bayou who takes on some local toughs when they try to rob a young woman who's just gotten to town. It's a sequence with as much poetry as broken bones, and just as much coincidence: The woman, Natasha (Yancy Butler), is looking for her long-lost father, a homeless man who's just about to turn up dead, the assumed victim of a suspicious fire. When Chance finds he's really been killed by an arrow, he's attacked by thugs. And then he goes looking for their boss.

Lance Henriksen is a nasty bit of goods as Fouchon, the malevolent entrepreneur who arranges all this organized and very expensive man-hunting for his high-income clients. In a way, he and his equally lethal henchman, Van Cleaf (Arnold Vosloo), are like Anne Rice's vampires, alighting in whatever "unhappy little corner of the world where we can ply our trade." When things get too hot in New Orleans, they start looking toward Eastern Europe. "We can work there for years," Fouchon says, in the kind of cynical evaluation of the world you don't usually get in a Van Damme movie.

Nor do you get the kind of poignancy that accompanies the killing of Elijah (Willie Carpenter), another homeless man and a friend of Chance, who's seduced by Fouchon's offer of $10,000 to run for his life. Elijah's chased, wounded, manages to kill his main pursuer, but is finally gunned down after making futile pleas for help to people on the street. "Hey man! I don't have any spare change, man!" one yuppie screams at him. And so, Elijah simply stands up before his executioners, a double victim of voracious capitalism.

By this time, Fouchon and Co. are ready to move to Sarajevo, but they have to get Chance off their trail first—the movie's noteworthy for how much time it doesn't focus on Van Damme—and this of course is impossible. But they try.

Along the way, which passes through the Louisiana bayou, Wilford Brimley makes a pre-posterous appearance as Chance's Uncle Douvee, spouting Cajun aphorisms and firing more arrows at a dozen guys with automatic weapons. This leads to the final showdown, a pyro-technical assault that ends in a old warehouse full of macabre Mardi Gras floats.

It's good, but "Hard Target's" most exciting sequence is the one in which Chance, Natasha and Detective Mitchell (Kasi Lemmons) wage a small war on the streets of the French Quarter that seems to last 15 minutes, and is probably much shorter—just like your nails, by the time the whole thing is over.

SIGHT AND SOUND, 11/93, p. 42, Verina Glaessner

New Orleans. The wealthy and refined Emil Fouchon runs an exclusive business organising the hunting and killing of men. Aided by South African ex-mercenary Pik Van Cleaf, he gives his clients access to sophisticated weaponry and a lethal team of armed motorcyclists. The quarry is chosen from ex-Navy men, combatants out of work, down on their luck and without living relatives. These men are procured for them by Randal Poe who uses the cover of his flyposting business to make contact with likely victims. Their latest victim, Binder, is killed with a sophisticated crossbow as he flees. But Randal has slipped up, and shortly afterwards Binder's daughter Natasha arrives in New Orleans looking for her father. When she is attacked by a group of thugs, an out-of-work sailor, Chance Boudreax, comes to her defence. She offers to pay him to help her find her father. With the help of Roper, another ex-serviceman and a habituee at the mission Natasha's father frequented, his possessions are located. Natasha lodges a missing person's form with Carmine, a woman police officer and soon after she is given the news of the discovery of her father's body, identified by dental records and service dog tag. Leaflets among Binder's possessions lead Chance and Natasha to Randal Poe, and a visit to the scene of the fire leads Chance to the discovery of a dog tag matching the one in the police's possession—this one bearing marks suggesting a shooting. Carmine orders an autopsy.

Pik meanwhile punishes Randal, slicing off one of his ears. Morton, a police doctor who has been helping Fouchon by faking autopsy, results, is shot in the eye by Pik. Randal meanwhile makes contact with Roper, offering him work, but is subsequently by Fouchon and Pik if he can use his military training to escape an armed pursuer and make his way across the river. Fouchon's new client Zenan is terminally clumsy and is himself shot by Fouchon while Roper, wounded and bleeding, makes his way downtown. There his cries for help go ignored by passers-by and he is finally dispatched in an orgy of gunfire: Carmine herself is later shot, and Chance—with Natasha in tow—himself becomes Fouchon's next quarry.

Chance and Natasha make their way through the bayou to his Uncle Douvee's illicit whiskey still, which they wire with explosives against the imminent arrival of the gang. While Fouchon in a helicopter pursues Chance, who is now on horseback, Douvee and Natasha lie low. The final battle—with Natasha and Douvee taking part—is waged in a vast hangar used to store Mardi Gras costumes; Pik and Fouchon are killed in the onslaught of grenades, heavy weaponry and physical dexterity.

The dream of breaking into the international—meaning American—market has been a potent one for the Hong Kong film industry for the past 30 years. Director John Woo seems better placed than most to realise it. Woo has made the transition from the conventions of a resolutely low-tech martial arts genre—he trained with Shaw Brothers' most impressive martial arts director Chang Cheh, working on two of his best films, *Vengeance* and *Blood Brothers*—to a high-tech one of super stunts and sophisticated weaponry, without losing touch with the gut reality of the physical struggle the genre explores and embodies. But he has also garnered a swathe of plaudits from some of Hollywood's most bankable names, including Martin Scorsese and Quentin Tarantino, who admits Woo's influence on *Reservoir Dogs*, and who is writing a script for him. The current film, however, most noticeably does not have a Tarantino script, but the fact that it is a reworking of Ernest Schoedsack's 1932 film *The Most Dangerous Game* should be some compensation. Schoedsack's way with fairytale, nightmare and myth is not actively antagonistic to Woo's own mix of naive genre and nightmare. The theme of killing for sport and the struggle to resist the extinction of the self is close enough to Woo's previous film *Hard-Boiled* to bode well.

Beneath a thick wrapping of wordless and extended scenes of destructive mayhem, that earlier film contains a meditation on personal and national identity and its loss. It suggests itself as a kind of nightmare about Hong Kong's, and indeed China's, future. Menace is generated not merely from stunt pyrotechnics but also from Woo's Oshima-like awareness of the threat contained in sterile modernist spaces and the fragility of the human body. No favours have been done Woo's thesis by the relative bloodlessness of *Hard Target*. An awareness of physical frailty has been turned into a mere felling of trees. If vulnerability is of central importance, then the casting of Jean-Claude Van Damme poses problems. Here is an actor of small range, not given to suggesting self-doubt, and his presence in the lead ensures that the kind of drama that can be enacted is strictly in the Superman vein. When someone reassures Natasha that "he'll be all right—we know he will—hence the array of daring stunts involving motorbikes, cars and trains, all travelling at full speed.

This leaves only the two villains Fouchon and Pik as bearers of self-doubt and vulnerability, marginalised by the script, but at once more interesting in themselves and in their relationship with each other than the protagonist. Arnold Vosloo gives a suggestive account of Pik, the killer proud of his professionalism, although he is not called upon to question his beliefs as the villain of *Hard-Boiled* is. It is only in the closing moments that Lance Henriksen, distraught as he closes the eyes of his dead friend amid the chaos, is able to suggest very much beyond an aesthete of violence given to pounding through Beethoven's Appassionata at his grand piano.

Hard-Boiled's seamless and impressive merging of the personal and the national finds no coherent development here. Instead the script takes pains to point out the un-Americanness of the two villains, rootless and cosmopolitan, who make plans to ship out of New Orleans for some of the world's more notorious trouble spots. What price then Henriksen's frequently uncanny resemblance to a recent American president and the fact that he is shown to live in a very white house indeed? But traces of a harsher moral critique do remain in places, in a sequence filmed amid the squalor of St Louis' homeless, and in the facile use by Fouchon of the language of democratic choice and market economics to mask his own and others' corruption. He is, he argues, only extending to civilians options open to the professional soldier.

There are clumsinesses in the dialogue, in the performances, in the scenes involving Uncle Douvee and in the throwaway comic ending. But Woo is a director with something to say and an eye for the poetic and resonant. One has to admire the daring stunt work and the intense bravura of the opening sequence, in which a New Orleans street in darkness and rain becomes as threatening and insubstantial as a nightmare. There's also considerable horror in the scene in which the wounded Poe is shunned as he lurches through the brightly lit downtown streets. At this particular point in history, however, we cannot but ask whether the use of ultra-violence in film can still be taken as mere hyperbole; and whether the use of weaponry—however excessive and fetishised—can still be seen as a simple 'empty sign' to be given meaning through the genre in which it occurs or by the auteur who uses it.

VILLAGE VOICE, 8/31/93, p. 51, Georgia Brown

Having recently revisited *The Killer* at the Quad, I can see that it's going to be hard to watch John Woo in theaters north of Chinatown. Too much nervous tittering and ill-timed laughter. In a recent *New Yorker* piece on Woo, James Wolcott describes a showing of *A Better Tomorrow* with "fans" whooping "Woo! Woo!" at the screen. It sounds like trying to watch something good at a college film series. (Reportedly the same idiots are ruining Film Forum retrospectives.) Clearly, as Flannery O'Connor put it, the only cure is for someone there to shoot every time they open their traps.

Typical. No sooner has John Woo arrived than the wrong crowd has claimed him. And even Wolcott, a polite but obviously unimpressed tourist, has misunderstood. *The Killer*'s climactic scene, where the two blinded lovers crawl past each other, he characterizes as a prime example of Woo's "goofy black humor." Woo fans he calls "movie nuts who prize sensation over sensibility." (Which sensibility? The one not grounded in sensation?)

But there is far more to Woo than delirious violence, and those woo-woo kids are not the treasurers, and certainly not the makers, of Woo's reputation. The Chinese (at least ones from abroad) don't find Woo hilarious or a crock, and neither do movie people I know. Maybe it's that most Americans prefer their violent melodramas cold and cynical, like *The Godfathers*. Which is why none of the summer thrillers betrays a shred of real pathos. They're all made by pastiche artists, some more skillful than others, bent on raising a debased vocabulary of "realism" to meaningless heights.

John Woo is different in that he has a true lyric vision. In Hong Kong, speaking the vernacular, he's found a way to make contact. His killer-heroes are less nihilists than radical romantics, who shoot up the world because they despise its mercenary aspect and desperately love what it could be, and perhaps was. In the same way, they long to get away from Hong Kong's glittering corruption yet are tied to or pine for home. His films reek of sad utopianism, vast religious melancholy, and oceanic pity for us all.

The hyperbolic, indiscriminate violence with its faceless victims is intended to open us up. This is how the films can feature balletic displays of gore and yet celebrate brotherly love and outmoded ideals of loyalty, honor, and professionalism. (The male bonding often gets translated by critics into various thoughts about homoerotic subtext.) When those two blind worms in *The Killer* (reminiscent of Sirk's *Magnificent Obsession*) inch past each other in the leaves, in front of the flaming white church, the sight isn't cynical but (laugh if you like) terribly tragic. Those earlier bittersweet close-ups of the world-weary gangster, played by Chow Yun-fat, really are meant to break your heart.

Woo uses close-ups as vessels of infinite tenderness, the way Leone and Fassbinder did, and Fuller and Sirk before them. He's taken slo-mo and the bloodbath from Peckinpah, the freeze—stop-action feeling—from the New Wave. His bright, hard-edged pop surface is drawn from Godard and Sam Raimi (an executive producer on *Hard Target*).

In Woo's passionate epic, *Bullet in the Head*—an update of Leone's *The Good, the Bad, and the Ugly* (just listen to the music), with the Vietnam War supplanting the Civil War—Woo's famous image of two men holding a gun to each other's heads gets exhaustively explicated. (What two four-letter words begin with *K-i* followed by double letters?) At various times each of the three buddies is asked to shoot one of the others, and either does or doesn't. But the three are only converted to guns after witnessing the event made famous by the news photo of a VC's street execution—another bullet in the head. Woo here is dealing in substantive issues, the chaos and treachery of societies turning against each other.

In *Reservoir Dogs*, Quentin Tarantino appropriates both the drawn-guns-all-around image and one of Woo's drawn-out bleed-on-me love affairs (ending with a bullet in the head). But all this talk about the relation between Harrison and Tommy Lee in *The Fugitive*: What have we here but two cute guys? *In the Line of Fire* attempted some *Tightrope*-style connection between Clint and Malkovich, or Clint and JFK, but it's essentially a hollow love.

Unfortunately, Woo's recently released *Hard-Boiled*, though it did have Chow Yun-fat and that baby, is comparatively ordinary. It misled a lot of people who hadn't seen the best into thinking Woo is merely in the business of making bigger, more fiery explosions.

Which brings me to *Hard Target*, the director's first U.S. effort, and a studio vehicle for that Belgian hunk of cheese, Jean-Claude Van Damme. In the first place Woo didn't write it (Chuck Pfarrar who wrote *Darkman* did). In the second, it's not even the film Woo shot and which reportedly was jeered by test audiences and then recut by studio butchers. Woo, I've heard, says the movie isn't his. Still, mercifully, it has a signature, even if smudged with some letters erased.

Starting with its opening from the point of view of a trapped quarry—staggering around looking for mercy and finding none—*Hard Target* has a strong and distinctive look. I love the shot of the homeless camp on the Plaza d'Italia and the way Woo uses Yancy Butler primarily as a pretty face (she's searching New Orleans for her lost father). The villains (Lance Henriksen and Arnold Vosloo) come on like satanists. Their game is staging high-priced hunts where jaded businessmen can track humans. They lure homeless vets into being the prey, tempting them with money to make yourself a man again." "It's a drug, isn't it?" Henriksen asks one successful hunter, "bringing a man down." I must say, this isn't a question usually asked in Woo's movies.

The subsequent hunting of the tall, sympathetic Elijah (Willie Carpenter) contains most of the movie's tenderness. (All the movie's good guys are Viet vets down on their luck yet men of honor.) As in the opening hunt, Elijah ends staggering, wounded—though this time on a busy, night-time Bourbon Street—begging for help, and no help comes. Finally, facing his executioner, all dignity, he shows he always was a man. Soon the movie repairs to the neighboring bayous, though most of the final action takes place in a vast backwoods warehouse filled with Mardi Gras props. Minding his still, Wilford Brimley turns up as Jean-Claude's crazy-as-a-fox Cajun uncle. The girl is dragged along so she can be scared silly by a snake.

I can't help it if you'd just as soon see curlylocks Van Damme cremated in one of Woo's fiery furnaces. (No Eastwood, Cruise, Connery, or Ford for this director to play with. The accomplishment is that he makes Van Damme watchable.) Though a dove flutters down at a crucial juncture, the essentials of a true Woo drama-passion, pietà, pathos—are missing. Even so, *Hard Target* has real style as well as terrific kinetic sequences, and I'll take it over all other summer pix any humid day.

Also reviewed in:
CHICAGO TRIBUNE, 8/20/93, Friday/p. C, Richard Christiansen
NEW YORK TIMES, 8/20/93, p. C8, Janet Maslin
VARIETY, 8/30/93, p. 19, Emanuel Levy
WASHINGTON POST, 8/20/93, p. D6, Richard Harrington
WASHINGTON POST, 8/20/93, Weekend/p. 42, Desson Howe

HARVEST, THE

An Arrow Releasing Company release of a Morgan Mason/Jason Clark production. *Executive Producer:* Ron Stone, Carole Curb Nemoy, and David A. Jackson. *Producer:* Morgan Mason and Jason Clark. *Director:* David Marconi. *Screenplay:* David Marconi. *Director of Photography:* Emmanuel Lubezki. *Editor:* Carlos Puentes. *Music:* Dave Allen and Rick Boston. *Sound:* Alex Silvi and Salvador de la Fuente. *Casting:* Rick Montgomery and Dan Parada. *Production Designer:* J. Rae Fox. *Set Decorator:* Graciela Torres. *Costumes:* Ileane Meltzer. *Running time:* 97 minutes. *MPAA Rating:* R.

CAST: Miguel Ferrer (Charlie Pope); Leilani Sarelle (Natalie Caldwell); Harvey Fierstein (Bob Lakin); Anthony John Denison (Noel Guzman); Henry Silva (Detective Topo); Tim Thomerson (Steve); Matt Clark (Hank).

NEW YORK POST, 11/5/93, p. 35, Bill Hoffmann

Charlie Pope's career is on a respirator. Divorced, popping Prozac and suffering from writer's block, Pope is unable to bat out the screenplay he owes a demanding, foul-mouthed movie producer.

Given one last chance to redeem himself, Pope flies to Mexico to research the murder his floundering story is based on.

In the intriguing new thriller, "The Harvest," Pope encounters plenty to prod his writing skills into high gear—and nearly loses his life in the process.

He's mauled by a vicious dog, seduced by a gorgeous blonde (female), chased by a sadistic blond (male) and ultimately has one of his kidneys surgically removed by ruthless organ transplant salesmen.

Writer-director David Marconi has created a tense tough little low-budget movie with enough twists and turns to keep us guessing and caring even when his script shortchanges us on character development and plot coherence.

As played by Miguel Ferrer, (best known as Albert, the know-it-all fed on "Twin Peaks"), Pope is a man on the edge with few choices but to dive further into danger, catch those who victimized him and finish his script.

Ferrer, who rarely turns in a bad performance, is the major asset here—helping the movie over its rough edges. Many other performers couldn't have.

Leilani Sarelle is appropriately sexy as the femme fatale who may or may not have set Ferrer up. The pair have two sizzling love scenes—including one where they get it on in a car as Ferrer drives. Don't try this one in traffic folks.

If the sex scenes seem more convincing than some of the dialogue, maybe it's because Ferrer and Sarelle fell in love on the set and got married.

Fine location photography by Emmanuel Morgenstern Lubezki (who lensed "Like Water For Chocolate") gives the film a claustrophobic look and helps to stretch the suspense.

There's no question that more money, better writing and bigger stars could have turned this quirky production into a major Hollywood thriller.

But despite its problems, "The Harvest" keeps you on your toes and guessing until the end.

NEWSDAY, 11/5/93, Part II/p. 91, Terry Kelleher

Cop: "Anything missing?"
Crime victim: "Just my watch, my ring ... and my kidney."
This exchange alone earns "The Harvest" one star for novelty. In fact, let's go out on a limb and credit writer-director David Marconi with making the first movie to feature "forced nephrectomy" as a major plot element.

Miguel Ferrer plays a struggling screenwriter trying to tell a supposedly fact-based script about murder in Mexico. A contemptuous producer (Harvey Fierstein) raspily orders him south of the border to research a rewrite of the third rewrite. While trysting on a Mexican beach with a blonde temptress (Leilani Sarelle), Ferrer is knocked cold and dragged off. He regains consciousness several days later, crudely stitched and one kidney short.

An unsympathetic police detective (Henry Silva) suggests that opportunists removed Ferrer's organ for sale on the black market, but then strong-arm men come after his *other* kidney, explaining that their unidentified employer's initial transplant didn't take.

The scenarist escapes the thugs and again hooks up with the blonde—a liaison that allows Ferrer and Sarelle to simulate various forms of sexual gymnastics, including a slow-motion precis of the Kama Sutra and an advanced lesson in how to pleasure one's partner while operating a motor vehicle. (Ferrer's supporting role in "Revenge" may have given him a chance to study the similar automotive exploits of Kevin Costner and Madeleine Stowe.)

We're happy, and not at all surprised, to note that their artistic collaboration on "The Harvest" led to real-life marriage for Ferrer and Sarelle. He makes an interesting anti-hero and she manages to be both sultry and rather sweet, except when she's forced to say things that are stupid: 'You like shadows? They're great. They show the dark side of things."

Unfortunately, "The Harvest" grows sillier and less suspenseful as it progresses. Marconi and cinematographer Emmanuel Lubezki offer enough tight closeups of Ferrer's eyes to make us wonder whether the film's medical specialty is nephrology or ophthalmology. There's so much improbability and inconsistency that Marconi has little choice but to rationalize it all away with a trick ending.

Hmm, what have we here? Mediocre thriller or satiric metaphor? Movie or movie-within-a-movie? Does it matter when neither is very good?

Also reviewed in:
NEW YORK TIMES, 11/5/93, p. C30, Janet Maslin
VARIETY, 1/18/93, p. 78, Todd McCarthy

HAWK, THE

A Castle Hill Productions release of an Initial production in association with BBC Enterprises/Screen Partners. *Executive Producer:* Mark Shivas, Eric Fellner, Larry Kirstein, and Kent Walwin. *Producer:* Ann Wingate and Eileen Quinn. *Director:* David Hayman. *Screenplay (based on his novel):* Peter Ransley. *Director of Photography:* Andrew Dunn. *Editor:* Justin Krish. *Music:* Nick Bicat. *Sound:* Graham Ross and Roger Long. Sound Editor: Kant Pan and Ian Fuller. *Casting:* Leo Davis. *Production Designer:* David Myerscough-Jones. *Art Director:* Charmian Adams. *Special Effects:* Stuart Brisdon. *Costumes:* Pam Tait. *Make-up:* Magdalen Gafney. *Stunt Coordinator:* Peter Brayhman. *Running time:* 86 minutes. *MPAA Rating:* R.

CAST: Daryl Webster (Woman Driver); Thomas Taplin and Joshua Taplin (Boys in Car); David Harewood (Sergent Streete); Clive Russell (Chief Inspector Daybury); Pooky Quesnel (WPC Clarke); Marie Hamer (Jackie Marsh); Helen Mirren (Annie Marsh); Christopher Madin (Matthew Marsh); George Costigan (Stephen Marsh); Rosemary Leach (Mrs. Marsh); Owen Teale (Ken Marsh); Melanie Till (Norma); Helen Ryan (Mrs. Crowther); John Duttine (John); Joyce Falconer (Woman in Capri); Caroline Paterson (Jan); Jayne Mackenzie (Eileen); Naddim Sawalha (Bahnu); Sean Flanagan (Harry); Rachel Moores (Susan); Margery Mason (Greengrocer); Sydney Cole (Weighbridge Operator); Frazier James (Crane Operator).

LOS ANGELES TIMES, 5/13/94, Calendar/p. 6, Kevin Thomas

More likely than not, the international acclaim accorded Helen Mirren for her portrayal of a hard-edged London police detective in the "Prime Suspect" miniseries on PBS has triggered the American theatrical release of the 1992 BBC production "The Hawk." It's a gratifying psychological thriller with a glorious Mirren as a blue-collar Manchester housewife who begins to suspect her husband may in fact be the elusive serial killer who has been terrifying the area by savage, apparently random killings of wives and mothers not unlike Mirren's own Annie Marsh.

Peter Ransley's adaptation of his novel not only keeps you guessing—every time you think the plot's telegraphing itself you're left confounded—but also enables director David Hayman to come through with a film that's exceptionally fluid and visual for a British production.

"The Hawk," which takes its title from its serial killer's grisly signature of putting out his victims' eyes, is also a deft, shrewd observation of a woman too modest to be fully aware of her innate superiority to her crass husband (George Costigan), her nosy mother-in-law (Rosemary Leach) and insinuating brother-in-law (Owen Teale). Self-reliant, hard-working and forthright, Annie is a firm believer in knowing one's place and in being a conscientious wife and mother— she has two children. She may be at a loss as to say whether she and her husband are truly in love but is quick to assert that they are happily married.

The instant, however, that Mirren starts allowing herself even to consider the possibility that her husband may be a serial killer she is confronted with an overwhelming sense of self-doubt. How can she even begin to think of trusting her instincts when it has not been that long since she experienced postpartum depression in the wake of the birth of her last child severe enough to require institutionalization? She finds escalating fear and uncertainty in a mounting war with her natural assertiveness and common sense.

Mirren plays the likable, intelligent but beleaguered Annie with absolute conviction and sympathy while "The Hawk" gradually increases its suspense until it has you on the edge of your seat before you realize it. Hayman wisely resists pretension at every turn; that "The Hawk" is so resolutely a genre film through and through serves only to enable it to deliver all the better its traditional-style thrills and chills.

NEW YORK POST, 12/10/93, p. 48, Thelma Adams

"The Hawk" shouldn't be so affecting, but it is. David Hayman's British thriller covers movie-of-the-week territory. A suburban Manchester housewife, Annie Marsh (Helen Mirren), gradually convinces herself that her husband, Stephen (George Costigan), is a murderer.

Is Stephen the Hawk, so-called because the killer pecks out the eyes of his victims after he molests them, or isn't he? From the opening image—the serpentine red and white lights of cars on a highway—the tension is palpable. It never lets up. Even the sound of the rain takes on an urgent, rattler's hiss.

Mirren, who played Chief Inspector Jane Tennison in public television's addictive "Prime Suspect," delivers yet another masterful performance. She invades a character and makes it her own, submerging her persona in the part.

As Mirren ages, the lines of character in her face become more prominent, her beauty tempered by experience. But even as a drab housewife moving hazily through household chores and child rearing, she surprises.

On a night out with Stephen, her hair curled and her face made up, Annie has a burst of glamour downplayed until that moment. If a killer prowls within Stephen, a woman suppressed lurks within Annie.

Peter Ransley's tidy script turns on the development of Annie's character. As her suspicions escalate, the sleepwalking mum's life begins to clarify. Ransley uses a past episode of postpartum depression to undermine Annie's credibility, a fissure of instability that Mirren aptly underplays.

Hayman and Ransley exploit the tension between the diary of a mad housewife and the killer within to the very last car chase, casting suspicions one way and then the other like the serpentine lights on the highway. With an exceptional performance from Mirren, they have created a spare, taut thriller that shouldn't be missed.

NEWSDAY, 12/10/93, Part II/p. 99, John Anderson

A young mother stranded in the rain on a crowded English highway, leaves her two children in the car and walks off to use a roadside callbox. You know she won't be back: The bleeding red taillights are foreshadowing her fate. And the police crime-scene tape, whipping in the breeze of the following morning, confirms it.

Meanwhile, Annie Marsh (Helen Mirren), a suburban housewife with a spotty past, finds her husband's hammer missing from its place on the pegboard. What we already know, and what she soon realizes, is that the Hawk—so-called because his sex-murders are punctuated by the plucking of his victims eyeballs—has used such a tool in carrying out the string of vicious homicides that have terrorized the area.

Now, you have to ask yourself: Is a missing hammer enough to make a wife suspect that her husband is a vicious fiend. In real life, it might be more than enough. But in the movies, shouldn't a loyal spouse, even one as edgy as Annie, need more than a misplaced tool to make her think her husband's engaged in rape and slaughter?

Director David Hayman does nicely with what he has, which is an only moderately successful screenplay by novelist Peter Ransley. He also, however, has Mirren, one of the better actresses alive, and whom I'll watch in just about anything. Ironically, her major impact on American audiences was probably through the two "Prime Suspect" detective series that have aired on PBS over the last couple of years. And that's really where "The Hawk" belongs, on "Mystery!" during an off week.

Without giving too much away, the film does delve with some effect into Annie's twin plights: a former mental patient with a bit of the agoraphobe about her, she's also married to a man who's living multiple existences. Stephen (George Costigan) is an earthy family man, but he travels a lot—his job route, wouldn't you know, coincides remarkably with the Hawk's pattern of mayhem. And when Stephen is home, he spends many evenings at the Royal Hotel, a place frequented by pimps, prostitutes and Stephen's slimy brother Ken (Owen Teale).

Annie decides to visit the pub with Stephen to find out about his life, and while there makes a friend of Jan (Caroline Paterson), whom Annie is unaware is a prostitute. When Jan becomes the Hawk's new victim, and she's reduced by the newspapers into just one more dead hooker, Annie is appalled, both by the degradation of the victim and the limitations of her life.

Melanie Till is good as Annie's friend Norma. So is Rosemary Leach, as Annie's abrasive mother-in-law. And Mirren, of course, as always nice to see, even while riding a featherless creature like "The Hawk."

SIGHT AND SOUND, 12/93, p. 46, Emily Caston

Annie Marsh's contented suburban life with her husband Stephen is marred only by unwelcome visits from his protective mother and brother Ken. But one day a brutal motorway rape signals the start of a series of horrific local murders. Noticing tools missing from the garden shed, Annie remembers the murderer's trademark of using blunt tools to put out his victims' eyes. Although he calmly deflects Annie's interrogation, Stephen's aggressive behaviour at dinner with friends unnerves her. She realises that he is going out more than usual, often for the weekend. Accompanying him on one outing, she finds herself at a seedy pub, chatting away to Jan, a young woman friend of Ken. Comments dropped by Ken and the fact that Stephen was not at home on the nights of the murders strengthen her suspicion. But two spells in psychiatric hospital, severe post-natal depression and the return of old nightmares have undermined Annie's confidence in her sanity; she calls her old psychiatrist, but he has left the hospital.

Alone and frightened, Annie goes to the police. Under pressure of questioning, she realises that she has confused the dates and retracts her allegations. Later, however, she realises that the dates were correct and, on hearing that the latest victim is Jan, the woman from the pub, becomes certain that Stephen is 'The Hawk'. He tries to strangle her and Annie takes the children to the country but returns when he finds them. Now unwilling to return to the police, Annie takes justice into her own hands. She cuts short Stephen's threats by stabbing and killing him with a kitchen carving knife. She is arrested but with no physical evidence of Stephen's guilt to defend herself. Bail is granted, and Annie finds the stolen 'G' registration car used by Stephen during the murders and bought, hidden, and stolen by his brother Ken.

David Hayman's story of a woman discovering that her husband is a serial killer invites attention because it tells the story entirely from the woman's point of view. In the wake of films such as *The Silence of the Lambs* and John McNaughton's *Henry: Portrait of a Serial Killer*, this is a fresh and potentially interesting point of departure. The great problem is that it fails to break through the detailed sequence of events to establish Annie Marsh's character and plight. When Annie first discovers the hammer missing, she believes too quickly that her husband is responsible—or at least too quickly when we've not been told that anything has made her distrust him in the past. Why has she never suspected her husband before? Perhaps more pointedly, why has she had psychiatric problems? Barring cursory and cliched reference to a children's home and post-natal depression, the audience is kept in the dark. The result is that, despite his clear intention of reversing them by placing the woman at the centre of the film, Hayman and script-writer Peter Ransley—from whose novel the script was adapted—leave in place the media-created stereotypes surrounding rape and serial killing.

The Hawk sets itself up as a film offering social comment on the nature of serial killing, but in comparison to films such as *Henry* offers little to illuminate its characters' backgrounds. There are few clues as to the nature of the couple's relationship before the murders began or to the sudden eruption of Stephen's violence against women. The influence of his protective mother and rough background (personified by his tattooed, sexist car mechanic brother Ken) is gestured toward but in no more than a token manner.

Some of those shortcomings might have been averted by sharper direction, greater visual observation of the characters' environments and a clearer focus on the emotional centres of the scenes. Hayman uses interesting camera movements and, in the early sequences, braves long, difficult handheld shots that follow rather than force the action into frame. But the constant use of close-ups eclipses clues lurking on the set, as well as much of Helen Mirren's acting. This may be a deliberate attempt to convey the claustrophobic nature of suburban life, but it backfires, obscuring what it seeks to show. This said, the opening shot of The Hawk's first victim—seen through pouring rain and windscreen wipers driving to her death—works well, and Mirren's performance is impressive albeit occasionally too strong. The children too are good, particularly Marie Hamer as the daughter struggling to be adult and supportive despite the pains of a child's vulnerability.

To say *The Hawk* is more suited to TV than cinema is less to fault it than to comment on the waste of the potential of the widescreen. Its heavy dependence on dialogue rather than action also bears the mark of its BBC origins. But the conclusion is hard to avoid, as is the fact that, ultimately, the film never comes to grips with the intense and complex psychology involved.

VILLAGE VOICE, 12/14/93, p. 77, Amy Taubin

A crook-winged vehicle for Helen Mirren, *The Hawk* soars ominously, then plummets off the mark. Mirren plays Annie Marsh, a suburban mother of two, married to a dead-eyed, affectless fellow whom she suspects is the serial killer dubbed "the hawk" for the way he gouges out the eyes of his female victims after raping and bludgeoning them to death. Annie has scant evidence to support her fears—only some missing tools and the fact that hubby's business trips match the dates and locales of the murders. Moreover, her history of mental illness makes her doubt her own suspicions.

A psychological thriller, *The Hawk* is most compelling when it's expressive of Annie's panicky, alienated point of view. For much of the film, however, the all-too-familiar plot mechanics of is-he-or-isn't-he-the-killer get in the way. Director David Hayman, who knows how to nuance the movement of a handheld camera to give us a visceral sense of seeing through Annie's eyes, too often chooses to withhold character information in the interest of maintaining suspense.

Mirren, best known for her portrayal of Inspector Jane Tennyson in the TV series *Prime Suspect* (about to begin its third season on PBS), gives Annie the nervous hypervigilance of a woman who's lived her life under siege. Like Tennyson, Annie comes to realize that the enemy is not merely a serial killer, but the law itself.

Also reviewed in:
NEW YORK TIMES, 12/10/93, p. C21, Caryn James
VARIETY, 9/27/93, p. 40, Derek Elley

HEAR NO EVIL

A Twentieth Century Fox release in association with Great Movie Ventures.   *Executive Producer:* David Streit.   *Producer:* David Matalon.   *Director:* Robert Greenwald.   *Screenplay:* R.M. Badat and Kathleen Rowell.   *Story:* R.M. Badat and Danny Rubin.   *Director of Photography:* Steven Shaw.   *Editor:* Eva Gardos.   *Music:* Graeme Revell.   *Music Editor:* Dick Bernstein.   *Sound:* Mark Ulano.   *Sound Editor:* Mark P. Stoeckinger and Wylie Stateman.   *Casting:* Glenn Daniels.   *Production Designer:* Bernt Capra.   *Art Director:* John Myhre.   *Set Decorator:* Susan Mina Eschelbach.   *Set Dresser:* Deborah Emmel.   *Special Effects:* Rick H. Josephson.   *Costumes:* Fleur Thiemeyer.   *Make-up:* Bonita DeHaven.   *Stunt Coordinator:* Greg Elam.   *Running time:* 97 minutes.   *MPAA Rating:* R.

CAST: Marlee Matlin (Jillian Shananhan);   D.B. Sweeney (Ben Kendall);   Martin Sheen (Lt. Philip Brock);   John C. McGinley (Mickey O'Malley);   Christina Carlisi (Grace);   Greg Elam (Cooper);   Charley Lang (Wiley);   Marge Redmond (Mrs. Kendall);   Billie Worley (Tim Washington);   George Rankins (Roscoe);   Karen Trumbo (Nadine Brock);   Candice Kingrey (Police Interpreter);   Mary Marsh (Mrs. Paley);   Ron Graybeal (Porsche Driver);   Bill Pugin (Doctor);   Pat Codekas (Ms. Younger);   Mary Ann Marino (Museum Guard);   Clay Luper (FBI Cotton Candy Vendor);   Joe Ivy (FBI Agent #1);   Rick Jones (FBI Agent #2);   Mahon Kelly (Alex);   Marvin LaRoy Sanders (Grocery Checker);   Kathy McCurdy (Sign Language Instructor);   Merrilee Dale (Museum Guide);   Timothy Harper, Marlon Irving, Brian Sims, and Craig Warren (I-ZAYA Acappella Band).

LOS ANGELES TIMES, 3/29/93, Calendar/p. 2, Michael Wilmington

In "Hear No Evil," when director Robert Greenwald wants to convey the terror and isolation of a deaf woman pursued by killers, he uses two strategies. He either has the sound vanish, or he jacks it up so wildly that footsteps hammer out like a Wagnerian kettledrum.

Corny devices, but they work. And "Hear No Evil," dumped unceremoniously into theaters last Friday, without critics' screenings, works better than you'd expect.

Not without a struggle, though. In many ways, it's another flashy trailer-movie, with a marketing-hook premise, a tag-team script and a narrative flow pasted together with rock, shock cuts and chic photography. The setup is obvious: beautiful, deaf athletic trainer Jillian Shananhan (Marlee Matlin), chased by fascistic cops and a mysterious masked menace, after a reporter friend (John C. McGinley) slips a priceless Alexandrian coin into her beeper.

Every once in a while, the screenwriters trap Jillian in a closet or blind alley, send her racing down a lonely road at night, or put her in an abandoned lodge while the killer prowls around. And sound, or its lack, are the key to her fears. The faintest noise, magnified, becomes her incessantly repeated death knell.

Yet "Hear No Evil's" ultimate fate may not simply be sharing double bills with the 1971 "blind woman-in-peril" shocker, "See No Evil." This picture has some life. It doesn't always give off the stale, dead, manipulative feel of the usual yuppie-in-peril genre thriller: hyped-up, high-tech, over-programmed movies like "Fatal Attraction," "Single White Female" and "The Hand That Rocks the Cradle." If you accept the fact that it's nothing more than a standardized 1993 Hollywood product, you can enjoy yourself.

The director, Greenwald ("Sweet Heart's Dance"), has a sure, vivifying touch with actors. Here, we can get pleasure in the way super-sensitive Matlin and the shaggy, ultra-boyish D.R Sweeney play their love scenes together: tentatively, warily, full of buoyant give-and-take and sly wit. Or the way Martin Sheen knifes into his villain role of Brock, the slick, sadistic police lieutenant who tortures witnesses by turning up the sound on his favorite opera arias. Sheen plays Brock the way Eddie Albert used to play heavies for Robert Aldrich: as a smiling, graying winner, a snappy dresser with no morals.

Then there's John C. McGinley, of the Oliver Stone stock company, who plays doomed reporter Mickey O'Malley—with such on-the-edge intensity that he cranks up the whole movie. More than that, there's the film's look. Normally, yuppie-in-peril shockers have glossy, barely-lived-in interiors. The decor's message seems to be: Don't let scum into your life because they'll kill people and depreciate the property. But the, production designer here—Bernt Capra, who directed "Mindwalk"— knows how to suggest personality by messing up a room; when he does have an immaculate interior, it belongs to Brock, a man who probably aspires to a life of erotic thriller elegance.

"Hear No Evil's" soundpeople—who include mixer Mark Ulano, supervising sound editors Mark P. Stoeckinger and Wylie Statemen and six *other* sound editors—make the most palpable contribution—not just in the distortions that let us "share" Jillian's deafness but in the way they use that sonic emblem of urban paranoia, noise from the street. The rushing traffic and helicopters outside the windows—or their sudden, eerie absence—become as much a presence as the characters.

Finding a good role for Matlin, the hearing-impaired actress who won an Oscar for her debut, at 21, in "Children of a Lesser God," is obviously the *reason d'etre* of this movie. And, here, it's a case of the actress bursting the bounds of her role, giving more than she was given, making Jillian lively, ultra-responsive, self-sufficient. "Hear No Evil" (MPAA rated R, for violence, language, sensuality) is basically a standard genre piece where cast and crew are more active than usual, where they try not to let the old, slick, stale guidelines kill their creative delight in making scenes play. That isn't enough, but it's something.

NEWSDAY, 3/27/93, Part II/p. 23, Terry Kelleher

Only viewers for Quality Television can save us now. If NBC doesn't renew "Reasonable Doubts," Marlee Matlin may have more time for bad movies like "Hear No Evil." Stripped to its essentials (what an indecent thought), "Hear No Evil" is "Wait Until Dark" with a deaf heroine. Other than the star's actual hearing impairment, this would-be thriller has no connection with reality.

Matlin plays Jillian, a marathon runner and personal trainer who unwittingly comes into possession of a valuable stolen coin when a jittery journalist (John C. McGinley) hides it inside her pager. A rogue cop named Brock (Martin Sheen) and his henchmen want the coin intensely enough to spend three-quarters of the movie menacing Jillian and Ben (D.B. Sweeney), her emergency ally and love interest. When Brock is unavailable, a masked meanie takes over the terror campaign. Either way, Jillian has a lot to scream about.

The script by R. M. Badat and Kathleen Rowell is casually contemptuous of plausibility, and the movie's concept of romance is exemplified by a bedroom scene in which Ben asks Jillian how to sign the words "breasts," "horny" and "orgasm."

Director Robert Greenwald and cinematographer Steven Shaw make us dizzy with free-floating camera work—that is, when they're not giving us a crick in the neck with gratuitous low-angle shots. The moviemakers also monkey with the sound so the audience can experience peril from Jillian's point of view. But just so we'll know the theater's speaker system is still in working order, the silence in the heroine's head is frequently interrupted by the tinkling of bells. On the "I Love Lucy" side of deafness, Jillian burns the toast, sets off Ben's smoke alarm and hears nothing amiss.

Although Brock is supposed to be a genuinely scary guy, he tortures suspects by forcing them to listen to opera—indicating he learned interrogation methods by watching Woody Allen's "Bananas." Sheen presumably took the money and ran.

SIGHT AND SOUND, 3/94, p. 39, Olly Blackburn

Portland, Oregon. After a priceless coin is stolen from a local museum, reporter Mickey O'Malley is contacted by the frightened thief who reveals that corrupt police lieutenant Philip Brock masterminded the robbery. O'Malley obtains the coin and secretes it inside the beeper of his fitness trainer Jillian Shananhan, who is deaf. Brock and his sidekicks find and torture O'Malley, giving him till the end of the day to return the coin. Terrified, O'Malley borrows a car from his friend, restaurateur Ben Kendall and, attempting to flee town, is blown up and apparently killed.

When Jillian and Ben are interviewed by Brock, their suspicions are aroused by his aggressive interest in the coin's whereabouts. That night a masked man breaks in to Jillian's flat and while searching for the coin nearly kills her friend Grace. Jillian hides in Ben's apartment and together they go after Brock, stealing incriminating surveillance video tapes from his house and giving them to the FBI.

Brock is arrested and Ben and Jillian leave town for a romantic weekend in a remote country lodge. While Ben is out, Jillian discovers the coin hidden in her beeper. The same masked man who attacked Grace breaks in and pursues Jillian through the lodge until she pushes him out of a window to his doom: the man turns out to be Mickey O'Malley—he had faked his own death intending to retrieve the coin and retire in luxury. Jillian and Ben return the coin to the museum, where they are celebrated as heroes.

The credits to *Hear No Evil* open over aerial views as Marlee Matlin jogs through Portland in pink leotards to a soft rock soundtrack. This is the cinematic equivalent of middle-of-the-road rock: homogeneous to the point of anonymity, relentlessly mainstream, slickly produced in a sterile, styleless way and, allowing for token exceptions, one hundred per cent white.

Hear No Evil is a shocking trip to the blandside, a place in which everything, especially the hairdos, is mercilessly trapped somewhere in the mid-80s. The men look like extras from *Cocktail*, while the women, uniformly dressed in clashing lycra, look and act as if they've stepped out of a TV ad for mail order chest-presses.

Every single element of the script is hitched with unerring predictability to some future plot demand. We first see Ben Kendall training as a climber, ergo Lt. Brock will live in a house up a mountainside. Brock videotapes his victims, therefore those tapes (which are stored next to the CD rack on his home entertainment system) will be the evidence that sinks him. And if the tapes have no sound and Jillian is deaf, it therefore follows that during the film's third act she will lip-read them. This is filming by numbers, the algebra of the inane in which even the central gimmick of having a deaf heroine does no more than provide an excuse for including vibrating beepers and hand-miming the word for 'orgasm'. The fact is that *Hear No Evil* is so wooden the only characterisation the film can possibly conceive of is tightly cuffed to a transparently ridiculous plot which is cauterised of any humour, let alone any irony.

Even Martin Sheen, as Brock, looks more like a wide-boy accountant than a cop on the loose. He listens to arias while rearranging people's fingers and is quick to pull a Glock from his cummerbund when he returns home to find an intruder at his video collection. But all this is merely paying lip service to the post-Bond villain who traditionally combines gentlemanly hobbies with nonchalant ultra-violence. This thriller can't even turn Sheen into a good villain, but then it's the sort of movie that conveys its idiom of evil by showing a close-up of the baddie's feet stomping over a child's stick of candyfloss.

The responsibility for the film's painstaking mundanity must lie finally with director Robert Greenwald. Certainly the dialogue is shameless, as characters speak lines like "I have a story that is so big it'll blow your mind" with absolute sincerity. The acting is of the pretend-the-camera-isn't-there school and it all looks like a Budweiser commercial. But that's no excuse—recent muted classics like *One False Move* or *Deep Cover* managed to transform perilously generic material into small gems on a shoestring budget. However, where someone like Bill Duke can pull off quality hackwork, Greenwald (who made the Olivia Newton-John vehicle *Xanadu*) doesn't even pass by hack standards, and this is only worth seeing as an object lesson in state-of-the-art mediocrity.

Also reviewed in:
NEW YORK TIMES, 3/29/93, p. C16, Stephen Holden
VARIETY, 3/29/93, p. 83, Lawrence Cohn
WASHINGTON POST, 3/27/93, p. G4, Rita Kempley

HEART AND SOULS

A Universal Pictures release of an Alphaville Stampede Entertainment production.   *Executive Producer:* Cari-Esta Albert and James Jacks.   *Producer:* Nancy Roberts and Sean Daniel.   *Director:* Ron Underwood.   *Screenplay:* Brent Maddock, S.S. Wilson, Gregory Hansen, and Erik

Hansen. *Story:* Gregory Hansen, Erik Hansen, Brent Maddock, and S.S. Wilson. *Director of Photography:* Michael Watkins. *Editor:* O. Nicholas Brown. *Music:* Marc Shaiman. *Music Editor:* Scott Stambler. *Sound:* Richard Bryce Goodman and (music) Joel Moss. *Casting:* Pam Dixon. *Production Designer:* John Muto. *Art Director:* Dan Webster. *Set Designer:* Lauren Polizzi and John Berger. *Set Decorator:* Anne Ahrens. *Set Dresser:* Daniel Ross Harpold and John H. Maxwell. *Special Effects:* Steven Galich. *Visual Effects:* Mike Chambers. *Costumes:* Jean-Pierre Dorleac. *Make-up:* Ken Chase. *Stunt Coordinator:* Mic Rodgers. *Running time:* 104 minutes. *MPAA Rating:* PG-13.

CAST: Robert Downey, Jr. (Thomas Reilly);   Charles Grodin (Harrison Wilson);   Alfre Woodard (Penny Washington);   Kyra Sedgwick (Julia);   Tom Sizemore (Milo Peck);   David Paymer (Hal the Bus Driver);   Elisabeth Shue (Anne);   Bill Calvert (Frank Reilly);   Lisa Lucas (Eva Reilly);   Shannon Orrock (Woman at Audition);   Michael Zebulon (Singer at Audition);   Chasiti Hampton (Shirley Washington, Age 7);   Wanya Green (Diane Washington, Age 8);   Janet MacLachlan (Agnes Miller);   Javar David Levingston (Billy Washington, Age 4);   Robert William Newhart (Bob Newhart);   Sean O'Bryan (John McBride);   Steven Clawson (Bartender);   Joan Stuart Morris (Wanda);   George Maguire (Music Director);   Marc Shaiman (Piano Accompanist);   Richard Portnow (Max Marco);   Jacob Kenner (Duane Dortmueller, Age 10);   Janette Caldwell (Woman in Cadillac);   Eric Lloyd (Thomas Reilly, Age 7);   Janet Rotblatt (Mrs. Brodsky);   Bill Capizzi (Race Track Ticket Clerk);   Will Nye (Frank's Football Buddy);   Eric Poppick (Mr. Polito);   Susan Kellermann (Noelle);   Robert Parnell (Mitchell);   Ed Hooks (Jim);   Michael Halton (Motorcycle Cop);   Wren T. Brown (Sgt. Wm. Barclay);   Lorinne Dills-Vozoff (Anne's Mom);   Richard Roat (Anne's Dad);   Bob Amaral (Duane Dortmueller);   Luana Anders (Records Bureaucrat);   John Goodwin (Security Guard);   John Durbin (Stage Manager);   B.B. King (Himself);   Walter King, Melvin Jackson, Leon Warren, James Toney, Michael Doster, Calep Emphrey, Jr., Tony Coleman (B.B. King's Band);   Kymberly Newberry (Angela Barclay);   Jamilah Adams Mapp (Samantha Barclay, Age 3);   Tony Genaro (Man at Farmhouse).

LOS ANGELES TIMES, 8/13/93, Calendar/p. 12, Michael Wilmington

How can you stay whimsical when your theme, buried under several tons of Hollywood slick, is the spiritual crisis of modern man? Trust the stars.

"Heart and Souls" is a Big Time Cute movie about ectoplasmic chums and last-minute redemption, a bright fantasy-comedy about humanizing yuppies and reviving empathy in the moral wreckage of the '80s. It wins a few, loses a few. It makes us laugh, gets mileage out of the Four Seasons' "Walk Like a Man." In the end, the actors save it, especially *two* of the actors: star Robert Downey Jr., who may have moved into the Robin Williams-Steve Martin-Whoopi Goldberg category, and supporting actor David Paymer, who never hits a false note.

Downey's Thomas Reilly is the heart of "Heart": a slick-haired corporate clone who lives on his phone, thrives on the deal. And Charles Grodin, Alfre Woodard, Kyra Sedgwick and Tom Sizemore play the four souls trapped with him—all killed in a San Francisco bus crash at the moment Reilly was born, en route to the maternity ward. Paymer is the departed bus driver who pops up 27 years later to zip the spectral quartet off to the great Uptown or Downtown—after informing them, a little late, that, through Reilly, they had a shot at redeeming their "wasted" lives. And still do.

Comedies with supernatural premises either float buoyantly up through a blizzard of implausibility or drown in their own whimsy. "Heart and Souls"—which would like to move us as "It's a Wonderful Life," or even "All of Me" once did—almost makes it.

But the picture has two big problems. First: There's nothing very visually arresting, amusing or exciting about four people, whom no one else can see, hanging around together within six feet of Downey. And even *that* situation isn't milked for the right kind of voluptuous, crazy fun.

Second: Though the script, the soulful quartet and apparently Heaven itself give their blessing to the union of Reilly and girlfriend Anne (Elisabeth Shue), we may have qualms. Why does Anne nag Reilly not about bottom-line sliminess but about giving her his room key? Why does she get mad when she catches him playing hooky from their date by belting out the national anthem at a B.B. King concert—something you'd think might crack her up? Shue's extraordinary prettiness make us like Anne, but it's a chore, since the main value the writers give her to trumpet is "normality." Is she the spiritual heir of Warren Harding?

There's one great opportunity for virtuoso fun here: the chance handed Downey to impersonate the mannerisms of his co-stars whenever one takes over his body. With the delicate, precise mimicry he showed in "Chaplin," he slips delightfully into Woodard's feline assurance, Sizemore's swagger, Sedgwick's sexiness or Grodin's repressions. The character he's playing—the same kind of languid, self-obsessed, inwardly anxious hedonist he played throughout the '80s—isn't deep, but Downey digs something comic out of his superficiality. He's an empty vessel, waiting to be filled up with soul.

"Heart and Souls" was directed and partially co-written by the Ron Underwood-S.S. Wilson-Brent Maddock team and it has some of the virtues of their previous collaborations. "Tremors" and "City Slickers": breezy, sunny liveliness, casual humanism, an attitude of "They may be clichés, but we love 'em anyway!"

"Heart and Souls" (MPAA-rated PG-13 for some sensuality) tries to awaken our sympathies. And sometimes does. It's probably no accident that the movie's heavenly ferryman is a punctilious Jewish bus driver, or that the four souls satelliting around Reilly are all somewhat "outside": a single black woman (Woodard), a blue-collar burglar/macho-man (Sizemore), a would-be bride fleeing marriage (Sedgwick) and Grodin's opera-aspiring recluse—who suggests, at least partially, a gay sensibility. Do nice comedies finish last? Not necessarily. Like most Big Time Cute movies, this one winds up wearing its heart on its sleeve and its soul in its pocket.

NEW YORK POST, 8/13/93, p. 27, Michael Medved

"Heart and Souls" takes such a long time to introduce its characters and to set up its plot, wasting so much energy on an elaborate, unwieldy and ultimately irrelevant prelude, that you may be tempted to give up on the film before the main story even gets started.

And that would be a shame, because once it hits its stride, "Heart and Souls" turns out to be a sweet, likable little picture with diverting performances from a distinguished cast.

The movie opens in San Francisco in 1959 with a brief sketch presenting four people from different walks of life (aspiring opera singer Charles Grodin, struggling single mother Alfre Woodard, petty thief Tom Sizemore and cocktail waitress Kyra Sedgwick) who have nothing in common other than the fact that they're all facing some quiet crisis in their lives.

They also happen to board the same late-night bus, then die together in an impressively orchestrated crash that results from the cheerful incompetence of a distracted driver (David Paymer) who will win no posthumous safety awards from the local transit company.

Before the victims can find themselves a good liability lawyer in the Great Beyond, their souls are instantly and inexplicably attached to a new baby, born in a car on the way to the hospital at the precise time and place of their fatal accident. For the next 34 years, the spirits are forced to remain within a few feet of this growing boy, who's the only one in the world who can see them.

Unfortunately, the cute kid eventually develops into a shallow yuppie played Robert Downey Jr., and the souls discover that the only way they can ever move on to some higher realm is by persuading the selfish snot to let them borrow his earthly frame to complete the unfinished business of their lives.

Downey's deft performance makes this process fun to watch: As amply demonstrated in "Chaplin," he's an enormously gifted physical comedian who here accomplishes a series of amusing transformations to show three souls commanding his body.

The problem is that there's too much of a good thing, and the movie seems at times mechanical and repetitive. Why did there have to be four souls, with four separate stories? Wouldn't three have done the trick? The best candidate for elimination would be Kyra Sedgwick, usually an edgy and interesting actress (as shown in "Singles") but whose bland presence in this film can't compare to the charm and weight provided by old pros such as Grodin and, most especially, Alfre Woodard.

On several occasions, contemporary Hollywood has attempted to recapture the magic of Golden Age comedies about life after death. "Here Comes Mr. Jordan" achieved successful reincarnation as Warren Beatty's "Heaven Can Wait"; "A Man Named Joe" became Steven Spielberg's disappointing "Always." The obvious inspiration for "Heart and Souls," with its fun-loving guardian ghosts enlivening the otherwise stuffy existence of a dull mortal, is 1937's "Topper."

The sprightly spooks here may not be as elegantly entertaining as Cary Grant and Constance Bennett, but they are still thoroughly pleasant company, thanks in large part to director Ron Underwood. As he did in "City Slickers," and even in his man-eating-earthworm epic "Tremors," Underwood demonstrates easygoing assurance with his actors and an unmistakable fondness for the characters they're creating. That affectionate attitude provides this movie with a warm heart, and even some soul, but a bit more brains would have helped a great deal.

NEWSDAY, 8/13/93, Part II/p. 62, Jack Mathews

Take a little "Ghost," a little "All of Me," a little "Heaven Can Wait," a little "Switch," and a little of every other ghost movie you've seen, and you have Ron Underwood's "Heart and Souls," a grab-bag spiritual comedy that doesn't add up to the sum of any one of its parts.

A shame. With a little more invention, this could have been one of the year's more amiable movie entertainments, and given that this is Underwood's first film since "City Slickers," that's pretty much what we expected.

But it's doubtful any director could have made much of this gallumphing, committee-written script. The credits list four different writers, two sets of two, which is tantamount to a confession that the project was probably never worth doing.

The storyline is about as thin an excuse for metaphysical musings as one can imagine. In 1959 San Francisco, four people rushing to complete some personal, business are killed in a bus crash, and their spirits are consigned by a Higher Authority, for reasons known only to Him, to hanging within a few invisible feet of a child born at the scene and at the moment of their deaths.

When that child becomes a man, self-absorbed yuppie Thomas Reilly (Robert Downey Jr.), the spirits, wearing the same clothes they died in, learn they have only a short time to enter his body, one at a time, and finish up their mortal chores before the Afterlife Express whisks them away.

As dopey as that sounds, it might have worked, if the four spirits—two men and two women—and their host were interesting characters. None is.

Downey, attempting to build on his post-"Chaplin" reputation as a physical comedy actor, has a few good scenes acting out the ghosts' mannerisms and personalities. But it takes half the movie to get to those pantomimes, and when they arrive, they are either obvious (if you can picture a man in a suit strutting like a drag queen, you've got half of Downey's performance) or, worse, uninteresting! Reilly, poor soul, got stuck with a pathetic set of spirits.

There is, foremost among the ciphers, Julia (Kyra Sedgwick), a waitress who was rushing to accept her boyfriend's wedding proposal when the bus crashed. Hard to imagine what business remains for her three decades later, and you'll be sorry you asked.

Milo (Tom Sizemore) was a low-level thief who once ripped off a kid's stamp collection. When he's not taking advantage of his invisibility to look up women's skirts, he's trying to figure out how to retrieve the stamps and return them. Hell of a guy.

Harrison (Charles Grodin), a milquetoast librarian and closet tenor, didn't have the guts to sing solo in public, and he is vaguely hoping to cut loose with Reilly's vocal chords just once before joining the great choir in the sky.

And there is Penny (Alfre Woodard), a hard-working, single mom whose death left the fate of her children in doubt, a fact that will lead us to a reunion scene stolen directly from "Ghost." You know an idea is heavy when it takes four writers to lift it.

On the plus side, "Heart and Souls" sets new visual effects standards for mortals/ghosts interaction. Its spirits are not transparent figures; they are as opaque as Reilly, and when they enter his body, they seem to simply move forward and snap into place. The illusions were achieved with the same process used in "Terminator 2," and they are fascinating.

If the writing were only half as good ...

TIME, 8/16/93, p. 58, Richard Corliss

Sometimes critics are human or a reasonable facsimile thereof. They like a good cry at the movies. They can get all sniffly and teary, just like real people, when somebody falls in love or dies. The candy shell of their heart can melt into chocolate when a kid hugs a whale. What separates critics from you is that inside the chocolate they must nurture the hard nut of cool judgment. They must know the difference between a good cry—emotion earned by film artistry, as in *E.T.* or Greta Garbo's *Camille* or, for that matter, *The Secret Garden*—and a bad one.

No question, *Heart and Souls* is a cry movie in every stitch of its elaborate plot. In 1959 four strangers—a working mother (Alfre Woodard), a petty thief (Tom Sizemore), a waitress in love (Kyra Sedgwick) and a timid opera singer (Charles Grodin)—board a San Francisco bus and die when the driver swerves to avoid a car. In that car, at that moment, a woman gives birth to a boy, Thomas; and in his body the spirits of the four dead passengers are trapped. Today the ghosts have learned that Thomas (Robert Downey Jr.) can perform one act for each of them that will write a happy ending to their interrupted life stories. One by one, the spirits take over his body so that, as their agent, he can reunite a family, return stolen property, track down a missing sweetheart and have a musical triumph.

Heart and Souls could itself be a low sort of triumph. At a sneak preview the audience cheered when one spirit got his star-spangled wish, and they applauded at the end. The house was so streaked with humid tears it nearly had to be hosed down. But this movie is a bad cry, for calculation steams off it like skunk musk. It is packed with stale "sure-fire" routines, like the rendition of a rock-'n'-roll oldie (here *Walk Like a Man*) and a funny car crash (which comes a reel or two after the fatal crash—*yikes*). The screenplay's big achievement is to create four people who are already dead and then give each a death scene.

Buried in this vat of feel-good glop are two piquant themes. One is a child's need to believe that invisible friends are real. Early on, when the four ghosts desert child Thomas and tell him, "Just be with your mommy and daddy," you can read the panic in his eyes; he is as bereft as Baby Jessica. The other theme is an adult's need to believe that our final worldly departure might come only after we have made peace with others and, thus, ourselves. That's worth a tear. Even a critic will cry for what might have been: a nice film inside a bad one, like a ghost of its better self.

See? Critics can be human, even when they watch a movie that isn't.

VILLAGE VOICE, 8/17/93, p. 54, Georgia Brown

More complicated than your normal paranormal comedy, Ron Underwood's *Heart and Souls* commits the cardinal error: Its premise can't be put into three words, or a paragraph, or a review. Its exposition unspools like Dante's list of the damned. One scene in which the convoluted rules of the game are laid out is so excruciatingly prolonged it makes you blush for everyone involved. You want to hold this movie's hand. Yet just when you think it's more or less disintegrated before your eyes, it bounces back. For a picture about four dead people, I guess that's about par.

Okay, try to follow. First, four unrelated San Franciscans (Charles Grodin, Kyra Segdewick, Alfre Woodard, and Tom Sizemore) are shown bopping around in 1959, when, by chance, they all board the same city bus and die in a crash. Simultaneously, at the site, a woman gives birth and the four souls (but not the dead driver! He goes elsewhere!) attach themselves to the baby. It's not usual dying procedure; something has gone awry. So this kid, Thomas (Eric Lloyd, the cutest movie kid you've seen), is supplied with four imaginary friends able to intervene in his daily rounds. Then they have to leave, or stop intervening, and there's a wrenching separation. (First cry.)

Why do they have to leave? Why do they reappear some 20-odd years later wearing the same outfits? Well, the green bus comes ghosting in and the same driver announces, "Let's go, dead people." If nothing else, this introduces a much-needed urgency into the proceedings. Though Thomas (grown up to be Robert Downey Jr.) resists the fact that his four angels need to inhabit him successively to make good on one last bit of unfinished business, he submits, giving Downey the chance to do a few strained impersonations.

You won't believe it, but the idea for *Heart and Souls* was taken from a nine-minute film-school short by Erik and Gregory Hansen. That must have been one busy nine minutes.

This stupendously messy amalgam of *All of Me*, *It's a Wonderful Life*, *Heaven Can Wait*, *Ghost*, and *Chances Are* (to name a few) is saved by the angelically recessive Grodin—formerly a timid man who wants to sing in front of an audience—and a beatific Woodard, as a mother who just wants to find out what happened to her babies. Amazingly, Underwood (who directed *City Slickers*) makes each of the characters' finales pay off in laughs or tears.

Also reviewed in:
CHICAGO TRIBUNE, 8/13/93, Friday/p. C, Johanna Steinmetz
NEW YORK TIMES, 8/13/93, p. C14, Janet Maslin
VARIETY, 8/16/93, p. 39, Leonard Klady
WASHINGTON POST, 8/13/93, p. D6, Rita Kempley
WASHINGTON POST, 8/13/93, Weekend/p. 36, Desson Howe

HEAVEN AND EARTH

A Warner Bros. release in association with Regency Enterprises, Le Studio Canal +, and Alcor Films of an Ixtlan/New Regency/Todd-AO/TAE production. *Executive Producer:* Mario Kassar. *Producer:* Oliver Stone, Arnon Milchan, Robert Kline, and A. Kitman Ho. *Director:* Oliver Stone. *Screenplay:* Oliver Stone. *Based on the books "When Heaven and Earth Changed Places":* Le Ly Hayslip and Jay Wurts and *"Child of War, Woman of Peace":* Le Ly Hayslip and James Hayslip. *Director of Photography:* Robert Richardson. *Editor:* David Brenner and Sally Menke. *Music:* Kitaro. *Music Editor:* Carlton Kaller. *Sound:* Bill Daly and (music) Bruce Botnick. *Sound Editor:* Wylie Stateman. *Casting:* Risa Bramon Garcia, Billy Hopkins, and Heidi Levitt. *Production Designer:* Victor Kempster. *Art Director:* Alan R. Tomkins and Woods Mackintosh. *Set Designer:* Jack G. Taylor, Jr. *Set Decorator:* Merideth Boswell and Ted Glass. *Set Dresser:* Alice Baker. *Costumes:* Ha Nguyen. *Make-up:* Matthew Mungle. *Special Make-up:* Greg Cannom. *Stunt Coordinator:* Phil Neilson. *Running time:* 135 minutes. *MPAA Rating:* R.

CAST: Haing S. Ngor (Papa); Bussaro Sanruck (Le Ly, Age 5); Supak Pititam (Buddhist Monk); Joan Chen (Mama); Thuan K. Nguyen (Uncle Luc); Hiep Thi Le (Le Ly); Lan Nguyen Calderon (Ba); Thuan Le (Kim); Dustin Nguyen (Sau); Mai Le Ho (Hai); Vinh Dang (Bon); Khiem Thai (Brother In Law); Liem Whatley (Viet Cong Captain); Michelle Vynh Le (Viet Cong Cadre Woman); Tuan Tran (Rapist); Aron Starrat (Helicopter Soldier); Peter Duong (Republican Colonel); Hieu Van Vu (Teacher); Phil Neilson (Marine in Helicopter); Michael Lee (Ky La Wizard); Thanh Vo (Grenade Girl); George Roarke (U.S. Advisor); Michael Paul Chan (Interrogator); Dave Cooper (Bald Onlooker); Irene Ng (Torture Girl #1); Thuc-Hanh Tran (Torture Girl #2); Vu Anh Phan (Snakeman); Mai Le (Steward); Vivian Wu (Madame Lien); Long Nguyen (Anh); Term Saefam (Herbalist); Stephen Polk (G.I. #1); Keith Smith (G.I. #2); Brad Rea (G.I. #3); Tran Huy (Danang Cop); Robert John Burke (G.I. Paul); Timothy Guinee (Young Sergeant); Yeun Yong Dumda (Jimmy, Age 1); Timothy Carhart (Big Mike); Kevin Gallagher (Tall Marine); Brian Helmick (Short Marine); Catherine Ai (Bar Girl); Tommy Lee Jones (Steve Butler); Somsak Hormsombat (Siclo Driver); Nuttikit (Jimmy, Age 3); Don Ho, Jr. (Tommy, Age 2); Phuong Huu Le (Jimmy, Age 6); Dale Dye (Larry); Scott Barkwill (Staff Sergeant at Embassy); Conchata Ferrell (Bernice); Debbie Reynolds (Eugenia); Jennifer Low Sauer (Supermarket Shopper #1); Gina Sheri Tavizon (Supermarket Shopper #2); Chitra Mojtabai (Supermarket Check-out Girl); Annie McEnroe (Dinner Guest #1); Marianne Muellerleile (Dinner Guest #2); Marshall Bell (Dinner Guest #3); Le Ly Hayslip (Jewelry Broker); Huynh Cao Nguyen (Landlord); Willie Nark-Orn (Tommy, Age 5); Lester Gopaoco (Jimmy, Age 8); Toby Vu (Alan, Age 2); Andy Reeder (Alan, Age 4); Chau Mao Doan (California Monk); Vivien Straus (Neighbor's Wife); Mai Nguyen (California Wizard); Melinda Renna (Police Woman); Robert F. Marshall (Detective); Tai Thai (Jimmy, Age 20); Tom Nam Ly (Tommy, Age 15).

CHRISTIAN SCIENCE MONITOR, 12/28/93, p. 14, David Sterritt

Oliver Stone knows a lot about Vietnam and its modern history. In the 1960s, he dropped out of college to fight in the war there. Years later, he used that experience as the basis for

"Platoon," the 1986 hit that made him a major Hollywood figure. He turned again to the Vietnam War in "Born on the Fourth of July," about a war veteran who became an antiwar activist.

Stone has long promised a third movie to round out his Vietnam trilogy, and now it has arrived: "Heaven and Earth," based on autobiographical books by Le Ly Hayslip, a Vietnamese woman whose life has traversed an enormous range of tragic and triumphant events.

Stone uses her story as a metaphor for the wrenching changes Vietnam itself has gone through during the past several decades. At the same time, he tries not to lose sight of his heroine's odyssey as a touching human drama in its own right.

His goal is certainly ambitious to weave the personal and the historical into a single tapestry that's at once emotionally moving, viscerally exciting, and intellectually enlightening.

Unfortunately, his filmmaking skills aren't up to the challenge. For all its good intentions, "Heaven and Earth" must be counted with the season's major disappointments—especially since it comes right after "JFK," the boldest and brightest picture of Stone's career.

"Heaven and Earth" begins in a rural Vietnamese village called Ky La, where Le Ly lives contentedly with her family in the early 1950s. Their lives undergo a tumultuous change when Vietnam's growing political unrest—sparked by opposition to French colonization—erupts into military violence.

The people of Ky La are surprised by this, since French rule has always seemed rather distant and abstract to them. But these developments are impossible to avoid, and Le Ly soon finds herself caught in a confusing web of conflicts involving her traumatized neighbors and the French, South Vietnamese, American, and rebellious Viet Cong armies. Later, an American marine woos her and whisks her off to the United States, where she confronts a new set of challenges.

Le Ly's story poignantly illustrates the extraordinary difficulties, ranging from frustrations and irritations to flagrant crimes and outrageous horrors, that Vietnam endured during its protracted struggle for independence. Her tale also has an important feminist dimension, since her travails often have as much to do with her gender as the generalized chaos and brutality of the war.

This is especially clear in a harrowing sequence that shows her undergoing torture by South Vietnamese forces and rape by Viet Cong rebels and in another episode that shows her submitting to the sexual blandishments of a well-to-do Saigon employer.

By focusing on Le Ly not just as a symbol but as a complex and authentic human being, Stone avoids the mistake Brian De Palma made in "Casualties of War, " which also explored the intersection of combat machismo and gender oppression in Vietnam, but seemed more schematic than compassionate.

In other areas, Stone has been less successful. What attracted him to Le Ly as a character was evidently her blend of intelligence and sensitivity with an outlook on life that's almost naive in its poetic idealism.

Stone's attempt to capture this naiveté is unsophisticated and heavy-handed, though, giving the film a veneer of superficial sentiment (especially in its narration) that has all the insight of a greeting card.

Things get worse when Le Ly arrives on American territory and Stone veers into social satire. Here he piles one overcooked device upon another, from exaggerated settings and hyperbolic acting to fatuous dialogue and distorting lenses, all to make the far-from-original point that '60s suburbanites were less smooth and savvy than Stone would have liked.

Some talented performers wrestle with the uneven material "Heaven and Earth" offers them, and they deserve credit for their good-faith efforts. Hiep Thi Le, born in Vietnam and now living in California, makes an earnest and often persuasive attempt to portray Le Ly in all her diversity, from peasanthood in Vietnam to middle-class life and eventual business success as an American citizen.

Her father is sturdily played by Haing S. Ngor, known for his good acting in "The Killing Fields" and the current "My Life." In addition, Joan Chen follows her work in "The Last Emperor" and "Twin Peaks" with a heartfelt performance as Le Ly's mother.

Tommy Lee Jones is below his best as Le Ly's deeply troubled American husband, but much of the blame goes to his poorly written part. Debbie Reynolds and Conchata Ferrell are among the misused supporting players.

Stone wrote the screenplay, based on the books "When Heaven and Earth Changed Places" and "Child of War, Woman of Peace," both written by Hayslip with a co-author. Japanese composer

Kitaro wrote the film's appropriate music, and regular Stone collaborator Robert Richardson did the lush cinematography.

CINEASTE, Vol. XX, No. 3, 1944, p. 56, Pat Dowell

With *Heaven and Earth*, Oliver Stone departs from the territory he knows best, and it shows. Vietnam now hangs around Stone's neck like a virtual cinematic albatross, but his turf is really America, in every sense of the word. And yet *Heaven and Earth* attempts to show the Vietnam war from a Vietnamese perspective. Straying even further from his ground zero, Stone has chosen a story with a woman at its center.

You have to give him credit for tackling what no other Hollywood director can be bothered with and for trying to correct his faults (critics routinely point out how unconvincing are the women he creates on screen). This is the first Oliver Stone movie, however, that leaves a fan feeling only indifference. It's tempting to think that when putting this one together he was still a little shellshocked from the *JFK* firefight, which was, after all, the biggest film controversy since *Birth of a Nation* was released. Whatever the reason, *Heaven and Earth* is Ollie Lite, despite depictions of torture, rape, domestic violence, combat, and the hair-raising spectacle of unfettered American consumer culture circa 1970.

It is the Oliver Stone movie you could take your mother to see (in fact, Stone dedicates it to his mother) because its visions of torment are all carefully funneled into emotional channels familiar to anyone who has ever seen a soap opera or *Gone With the Wind*. It registers, finally, as the blandest movie in Stone's oeuvre (*Wall Street*, another drama that reverberates with the filmmaker's filial love, runs a close second).

The woman caught between heaven and earth is Le Ly Hayslip, who was a teenaged peasant in Vietnam when the American intervention began. She worked with the Viet Cong, was imprisoned by the South Vietnamese, married an American, and emigrated to Southern California. She suffered just about every indignity that war presents, and Stone has crammed most of what she reported in her two volumes of memoirs (*When Heaven and Earth Changed Places* and *Child of War, Woman of Peace*) into a film of just over two hours.

As a guide through this headlong string of calamities and courage, Stone provides his main character with a voice-over narration. "One day in 1953 the French came," we hear in actress Hiep Thi Le's colorless, syrupy voice, and "then in 1963 the pleasant countryside changed forever," and so on—an unrelenting vocal pointer to spell out what is felt or seen or when it happened or what she thought of it.

The voice-over creates a stifling emotional mold for the images, and serves to Americanize the story by taming its more uncertain ideological moments. "The ant became our moral model," we hear when the village begins to work happily with the Viet Cong who have come to organize them. Visually the film's heaven, the village of Ky La, is full of golden vistas, saffron robes in a green landscape, and then the flares of war. Stone uses recurring motifs—a cone-shaped hat tumbling across green, undulating fields or a fireball shooting directly overhead—to suggest the serenity and beauty of the village world, even when war comes to it.

The Viet Cong are as much an interruption to this heaven as their enemies, but the peasants are more sympathetic to them because they at least, Le Ly says, "lived their lives with the earth." Stone carefully picks his way across the political minefield of a Hollywood Vietnamese movie by showing the peasants caught between two ruthless forces.

'A pox on both your houses' is the methodology that Stone employs, demonstrating Le Ly's dilemma with parallel scenes that comprise one of the film's few effective uses of narration. "One night they came for me," Le Ly relates when the South imprisons her. The electroshock torture scene that follows is vintage Stone—quick cuts, vivid close-ups, intimacy through big emotions. The soldiers even torture Le Ly with honey and ants and snakes (the movie adds to the book's account a laughing American Army bystander who is oblivious to her distress). Then Le Ly's mother bribes her out. The villagers and the VC don't believe it. "Finally the Viet Cong came for me," she says, echoing the army's arrest. The VC condemn her to death but her assigned executioner rapes her and sends her away instead.

Then it's the city, family disintegration, seduction by an employer, childbirth, prostitution and all barely outlined before the movie is half over. Le Ly does everything but say, "As God is my witness, I'll never go hungry again." Eventually The American enters the picture in the person of Tommy Lee Jones, who is saddled with the entire catalog of Vietvet hang-ups.

He eventually confesses to having been in black ops and psy ops—a killer haunted by murdered men and brutalizing employers. The Pentagon types, who promised him a lucrative gun running job, betray him even in civilian life back in the States. Jones looks like a shell hollowed out from the inside, but still there's only one place for his ultimately abusive and suicidal character to go, and it's neither heaven nor earth.

When the movie touches down in the States, which Le Ly in her book said she thought would be heaven, *Heaven and Earth* is briefly jolted into something wild. Stone depicts with savage sarcasm a smug family of American idiots, led by Debbie Reynolds! They stand as contrast, of course, to Le Ly's own self-sacrificing and loyal mother and father (Joan Chen and Haing S. Ngor). By this point it becomes clear that *Heaven and Earth* presents the Oliver Stone version of family values, and that it isn't going to rise above the liberal cliché of imbuing ethnic characters with a warmth and humanity that whites have lost.

To be fair to Stone, Hayslip s books reflect the most traditional views of men and women, even if her entrepreneurial life seems to have been at odds with such prescriptions for living. "A woman may do many things," she wrote in her book, "but the first thing god equipped her for is to bring forth and nourish life, and to defend it with a warrior's strength. My task, I was beginning to see, was to find life in the midst of death and nourish it like a flower." In the movie her marriage to the composite, floundering American fails as she builds economic independence in a new world that is an old, festering parody of home to him.

Hayslip's autobiography was also filled with the undigested details of everyday life, from the ordinary to the bizarre, from her husband's false teeth to the feel of a rapist's penis (memorably, "like a thumb"). The need for movie glamour washes those redeemingly grubby details out of Stone's film; all that's left are the glistening platitudes. This is one reason the film seems overwhelmingly formulaic as it pursues the inevitable course of taking Le Ly back to Vietnam to touch her heavenly base once again.

The great irony of *Heaven and Earth* is that it never comes to life as a Vietnamese story or as a woman's story. Stone brings great energy to the parts of it devoted to American absurdities and to troubled manhood. Those are his specialties, and *Heaven and Earth* does nothing to broaden his horizons.

FILMS IN REVIEW, 3-4/94, p. 55, Andy Pawelczak

Oliver Stone's latest movie, *Heaven and Earth*, is being billed as the third part of his Vietnam trilogy, along with *Platoon* and *Born on the Fourth of July*. In the first two movies he dealt with the grunt experience on the ground in Vietnam and the protest movement back home, and now in the new movie he tries to give us the war from the point of view of its chief victims, the Vietnamese peasants. It's an admirable goal, but the movie is cluttered with cliches gleaned from such disparate sources as what used to be called "women's movies" and even *The Good Earth*, the Pearl Buck thirties opus about the tribulations of Chinese peasants. Sadly, its central character never comes to life.

Based on two books by its real life heroine, *Heaven and Earth* tells the story of Le Ly Hayslip (Hiep Thi Le), who, during the course of the movie, undergoes an unbelievable series of ordeals and misadventures. The opening shots of a pre-war, 1953 Vietnamese village—misty mountains, pastoral rice fields, Buddhist monks padding around under colorful umbrellas—establishes the mood of a paradise soon to be lost. First the French invade, then the Viet Cong, followed by the South Vietnamese army and the Americans. Le Ly is tortured by the South Vietnamese for aiding the Viet Cong, raped by a Viet Cong cadre as a suspected collaborator, impregnated and abandoned by a wealthy Vietnamese, and eventually married to an American GI who turns violent and alcoholic. It's enough trauma for several lives and for several movies.

At one point in the movie, a crass American refers to Le Ly as a "beautiful China doll," and I'm afraid she never becomes much more than that. As played by Hiep Thi Le, a California college student discovered by Stone, she's more a witness to and victim of history than an active participant in her own drama. Even when Le Ly is struggling to survive as a black market peddler in Da Nang and speaking a brutalized street patois ("Me good girl" etc.), Hiep Thi Le never shakes off a bland sweetness and light. Nor is she any more believable as a slightly lacquered suburban matron and successful real estate dealer in the film's American sequences.

Americans take a beating in the film—well deserved no doubt, but rendered less powerful by their crudely caricatured portrayal. In Vietnam they laughingly collaborate in the torture of Le Ly, and in America they're dumb, insensitive consumers. In the film's most gimmicky visual, Le Ly's fat sister-in-law initiates her into American society by unveiling the contents of a huge, stuffed refrigerator, and we're asked to view the scene simultaneously from Le Ly's point of view as a hallucinatory vision of American plenty and from the perspective of a sophisticated critic of crass American consumerism. Stone makes the point again later in a supermarket scene that looks like it was designed by Andy Warhol: stacks of Coca-Cola bottles and Campbell's soup cans stand like ambiguous monuments to the American Way.

Tommy Lee Jones as Le Ly's husband has to carry the burden of American guilt for the war. Jones is an actor who can evince both an almost feminine tenderness and an unshaven, phallocentric brutality, and here he has an opportunity to do both, though the script doesn't adequately prepare us for the transformation. When we first see him in Vietnam, he's an immensely sensitive GI who wants to take care of Le Ly and her child, but once he's back stateside he descends into a miasma of agonized guilt—he tells Le Ly that he was a specialist in murder in Vietnam—and booze fueled pathology.

Stone is just about our only political filmmaker, and he has staked out Vietnam as his special territory, but none of his films really comes to terms with the war—they're too concerned with self-flagellation and expiation, which, in a strange twist, almost becomes exoneration. In *Heaven and Earth*, he presents a conventional vision of history as chaos in which the innocent little people are engulfed by successive waves of violence. That's okay as far as it goes, but it doesn't go very far in accounting for the still troubling extremes of American arrogance and triumphalism. Any film about Vietnam has to compete with the images we saw on TV during the war—summary street executions, self-immolated Buddhist monks, napalmed children. The subject calls for surrealism, not melodrama, and *Heaven and Earth*, though an honorable effort, doesn't add anything to the collective image reservoir as indelible as Kubrick's icy, interplanetary mise-en-scene in the first half of *Full Metal Jacket* or Robert Duvall in Coppola's *Apocalypse Now* celebrating the smell of napalm in the morning.

LOS ANGELES TIMES, 12/25/93, Calendar/p. 1, Kenneth Turan

Without the passionate interest of writer-director Oliver Stone, "Heaven and Earth" and its woman's point of view on the trauma of Vietnam might not have made it to the screen. But Stone is this film's burden as well as its champion. His presence and his style are so overwrought and insistent that the most lasting impression the movie makes concerns not Vietnam or even women but the sensibility and technique of Oliver Stone himself.

No one has ever accused Stone of being too subtle, but neither can he be faulted for not caring or caving in to popular taste. In fact, when he harnesses his particular passions to his gift for polemical filmmaking, as he did with "Platoon," "Born on the Fourth of July" and "JFK," he has made such subjects as the Vietnam War and the Kennedy assassination the subject of intense national discussion.

And while this is Stone's third Vietnam film, which may be more than people think they want to see, he shouldn't be faulted for returning to that time and place any more than Indian-born Ismail Merchant and American James Ivory would be for turning again to England's golden age. The problem is not the story Stone wants to convey but the way he is impelled to tell it.

Even when, as in the case of this largely true story of the enormously eventful Vietnam-to-America life of Le Ly Hayslip, Stone has a strong and intrinsically interesting tale to relate, he can't help acting as if he had to twist your arm to get your attention. This film's emotions are so big they tend to wear you out, uncomfortably forcing audiences to feel something they would probably just as willingly embrace on their own.

Based on the memoirs by Hayslip, "When Heaven and Earth Changed Places" and "Child of War, Woman of Peace," Stone's film covers nearly four decades of chaotic life experience for Hayslip during an equally cataclysmic period in her country's history. Although telling the story from a woman's point of view is a welcome departure for Vietnam films, as is its desire to be evenhanded about the Vietnamese, Stone's epic, operatic style has survived unchanged from his earlier films.

Hayslip begins her story in the 1950s, in a lushly photographed (by Robert Richardson) countryside that is as visually romanticized as anything in "The Secret Garden." Although the people of Ky La lived in bucolic oneness with the Earth, that peace was not fated to last, as "the most beautiful village on Earth" is burned to the ground by the French even before the opening credits are done. And there is more to come.

After the French the Viet Cong show up, angry and armed and speaking passionately about the need to reunite the two halves of their country. Although her father (Haing S. Ngor) is suspicious, knowing that "freedom is never a gift, it must be won and won again," Le Ly's brothers join up and go north and she herself becomes a devoted cadre.

Taken into custody by the South Vietnamese and their inept American advisers, Le Ly (played by the nonprofessional but very capable Hiep Thi Li) is beaten and graphically tortured. But no sooner does she manage to get out than the VC find her sudden freedom suspicious and proceed to take their own sadistic vengeance on her. Everywhere she goes, even to a nominally cushy job in a rich man's house, trouble has no difficulty following.

Stone (working with production designer Victor Kempster) is quite good at the physical recreation of Vietnam, especially the savage, anything-goes urban jungle atmosphere that the American occupation created, but he is so busy trying to beat the drum for this parade of horrors that he doesn't allow a more natural and lasting kind of emotional connection to form between the characters and the audience.

Only when Le Ly meets the American in her life, Sgt. Steve Butler (Tommy Lee Jones), does "Heaven and Earth" stop for breath. Terribly earnest and sweet at first, although prone to troublesome nightmares, Butler (who is a composite of several Americans) wins the heart of Le Ly. But Butler and his nightmares turn out to be more complicated than anticipated, and Le Ly can't be accused of exaggeration when she says at one point "me and men, we have bad karma."

Although it has its share of strong moments, "Heaven and Earth" does not have enough quietly touching ones, as if Stone felt the story were too important and the world too hard a place to clutter up with the likes of that. And though nominally told from the Vietnamese point of view, a look at the forthcoming "The Scent of Green Papaya," Vietnam's Oscar entry, shows how far from that country's sensibility Stone's hectoring methods are. While the passion and verve he brings to filmmaking are enviable, more trust in the audience would also be nice.

NEW STATESMAN & SOCIETY, 1/21/94, p. 34, Jonathan Romney

Heaven & Earth is the proverbial tale told by an idiot, full of sound and fury and signifying nothing. The idiot, I should say, is not the film's narrator and subject Le Ly Hayslip, on whose two autobiographical books the film is based. But it's a safe bet that early on in his career, director Oliver Stone was taken by the phrase "visual pyrotechnics" in a film review, and ever since has barely been able to shoot a scene without a couple of dozen Roman candles to hand. *Heaven & Earth* is pure Independence Day razzamatazz, rockets'-red-glare from start to finish. The irony is that this time, he *thinks* he's not telling an American story at all.

Heaven & Earth is billed as the third chapter of a Vietnam trilogy, following on from *Platoon* and the compelling *Born on the Fourth of July*, American stories to the hilt. I was never much impressed with *Platoon*, which consolidated the stereotype of self-regarding 1960s angst. But its follow-up was extraordinary, precisely because its earnestness knew no censorship and its symbolism no subtlety. *Heaven & Earth*, though, swamps its subject in heavy-artillery bombast, and from the start, when the heroine's voice-over is effectively defused by the credits its runs against, you know it's no contest.

Le Ly Hayslip, *née* Phung Thi Le Ly, is a woman who, as she puts it, has had more that her share of bad karma, (I can imagine a studio conference in which the execs think, "Who's man enough to take on this much bad karma? Oliver Stone, that's who.") Born in Central Vietnam in the early 1950s, the young Le Ly (Hiep Thi Le) enjoys an idyllic life in her secluded farming village, until the tanks start to roll. She joins up with the Viet Cong, but is captured by the South Vietnamese and tortured, in a remarkably unpleasant scene, with ants and snakes. She returns to her village only to be treated just as harshly by the VC, and raped by the side of what she's told is her own grave. Either it's grotesque pathetic fallacy, or this really happened in pouring rain—but this is a dreadful scene, not so much harrowing as embarrassing, as if the camera can't quite believe what it's seeing. It's the "can-such-things-be?" element that makes it so awful.

Working as a bar girl in Saigon, Le Ly meets Steve Butler, a sad, lonesome GI, who will whisk her off to a new life. Of course, the minute you realise that he's Tommy Lee Jones, you just know that a reel later, he'll be having cold sweats and crashing into the furniture and those dried-raisin eyes will be popping out of his head, while Stone flashes up black-and-white flashbacks from Butler's own personal hell ("Psy-ops, baby!").

Heaven & Earth invites a cynical response because you can see so clearly what the film wants to do, and what it ends up doing. A truism about Stone's films is that he's the lyric poet of the US foreign policy guilt trip, and this film does nothing to give that truism any extra depth. It's so manifestly a penance not only for the war, but also for making two films about the war centred entirely on the wounds of American youth. *Heaven & Earth* attempts to redress the balance not only by representing the Vietnamese experience, but by being twice as bombastic as *Platoon* and *Born on Fourth of July* put together.

From the start, the film is shackled to the stylistic weight of its precursor and the inescapable dazzle of what remains the most monolithic and most problematic Vietnam movie, *Apocalypse Now*. Stone is far more high-minded than Coppola, but he's equally besotted with spectacle. He knows no other way to convey the irreducibly foreign experience that is Le Ly's story than by filtering it through American movie lore.

Hence an opening sequence that spells out the *Paradise Lost* image with staggering preciousness. We see gorgeous sunsets and flat picture-postcard shots of the rice fields; as a million strings swoon, the young Le Ly asks, "Where did I come from?", her mother replies, "from my belly-button," and the two exchange winsome giggles. It's like some glutinous parody of *The Good Earth*.

But Stone is stuck in a rut as he decants his own tropes. From *Platoon*, we get the swoops of crossfire, the fiery arcs shooting across the screen. From *JFK*, we get the flashes of monochrome footage. Then there's a sequence in which the Viet Cong visit the village, trying to mobilise it; there's a hoedown, and Le Ly's dancing with flowers in the firelit night; suddenly the camera tilts, and we're right in the middle of a Venice Beach freakout from *The Doors*.

When Le Ly goes to the States, Stone unleashes his wildest effects to show us just, you know, how *unreal* that country is. Steve's mother is Debbie Reynolds, perfectly pink and egg-like, with a flock of gremlin-like dogs. Everything is round, cornucopian—the drive-in fridge stuffed with the fat of the land ... No wonder thin, angular Le Ly is out of place. And her drift from her own identity begins when she acquires a very un-Vietnamese buffant hairstyle. When she returns home, years later, it's that formidable Dolly Parton confection that marks her irrevocable estrangement from her ravaged mother (Joan Chen under drooping prosthetics).

Stone is remarkable for his ability to make political movies that are only political in that they aren't political at all. That is, he can take a subject like Vietnam and turn it into a lament for lost boys, or make of the Kennedy assassination a drunken disquisition on the paranoid nature of filmmaking. But because they couldn't tackle their ostensible themes in any other way, these films suddenly became immensely powerful statements about a national *Zeitgeist* that can only get a purchase on historical realities through a blurred, solipsistic optic.

Addressing war, Stone can only function through the notorious observation expounded by Michael Herr, Coppola and others that Vietnam was a "rock'n'roll" war—a notion ultimately reassuring for the way it domesticates the issue. With that in mind, Stone's 'Nam cycle is about bringing it all back home. Here too, there's a palpable swell of relief when Le Ly hits Saigon, and we get bursts of "Mellow Yellow" and "Judy in Disguise"—phew, home at last!

Stone isn't able to say much about Vietnam except that it's not America, or much about Hayslip that isn't about his own fantasies of otherness and oriental "wholeness". In this month's *Premiere*, Stone muses about Hayslip, "She's my counterpart. She's a mirror image, all the things that could have happened to me if my soul had been a woman's." In the end, Stone is looking to her to assuage all his own bad karma as well as his country's.

Le Ly herself, despite Hiep Thi Le's tenacious performance, is lost in the ensuing firestorm. It's too much, as if an over-eager Stone had pledged to his subject to use *all the resources* at his disposal to tell her story. The result is neither heaven nor earth but the big, dumb banging of purgatory.

NEW YORK, 1/10/94, p. 44, David Denby

In *Heaven and Earth*, Oliver Stone's unrelenting epic about a Vietnamese woman's experience of war, Le Ly, the young heroine, is walking in the fields near her village when she's suddenly battered by wind and rain, What's going on? She's as baffled as we are. When she's knocked down, the tall grass around her shakes wildly. It turns out that a helicopter is landing, and virtually on top of her. Watching this sequence, I thought, Who else but Oliver Stone could conceive of such an experience? Or film it so powerfully? The tragedies and grotesque physical violence of Vietnam seem to have left a huge repository of images in his memory.

A few years later, Le Ly is supporting herself and her little boy by selling blackmarket goods near an American Army base, and she's approached by a friendly MP, who asks her, as a favor and for a great deal of money, to perform some routine sexual services for two GIs who are about to go home. It's clear that the MP, who likes her, is trying to help her survive and has no idea how humiliating his request is. The man is so much taller than Le Ly that Stone can barely keep them both in the frame, and as Le Ly walks toward the two soldiers, also tall, and Stone struggles to find an angle to keep all three of them in the shot, the physical awkwardness of the scene becomes an emblem of the director's shame and sincerity. He wants us to feel what this tiny woman feels, even if it means making a clumsy shot.

It's because of such moments of power and empathy that I can't dismiss *Heaven and Earth*, though a good part of me wants to. For years Oliver Stone has been buzz-bombed (by me, among others) for his ruffian indifference to women. Well, with *Heaven and Earth* the great man seems to be saying, "You want a women's movie? *I'll* give you a goddamn women's movie." *Heaven and Earth* is an attempt to make the women's movie to end all women's movies—as if all of female experience could be crammed into one film.

Le Ly (Hiep Thi Le) grows up in a small village near Da Nang and suffers one violent, painful, and alienating experience after another. Her brothers are "recruited" by the Vietcong, and the village is ravaged and brutalized in turn by the French, the South Vietnamese government troops, the Vietcong, and the Americans. Briefly a VC guerrilla, Le Ly is tortured by the South Vietnamese; then, after she's released, she's terrorized and raped by the VC. She becomes the mistress of a wealthy man in Saigon—a gentle weakling—but gets thrown into the street when she conceives a child. As her village and her country are destroyed, she marries an American Marine sergeant (Tommy Lee Jones) who seems benevolent but who is revealed, once home in America, to be a miserably unhappy psychotic. And so on: everything *including* the hounds snapping at her heels.

I intend no mockery of the tumultuously painful life that destiny has forced on women like Le Ly. *Heaven and Earth* is based on a true story—the experience of Le Ly Hayslip, set down in two published memoirs. But what is historically true and what can be gracefully (or even ungracefully) fitted into a work of art may be two different things. The movie has a brute, hectoring quality, with one extreme experience slamming into the next, all of them linked by Le Ly's incongruously earnest voice-over narration ("And then the French came. ..."). Hiep Thi Le, a college student who has never acted before, is tiny and beautiful, with the warmest smile seen in recent movies. She's really not a bad actress, but Stone's punitive scheme turns her into a punching bag. Of course a punching bag always swings back to get hit again, and that's Stone's point—Le Ly is indomitable. But the repeated blows don't make for much dramatic interest. And what a workout Hiep Thi Le gets! In short order, she runs through all of the fluttering, orphan-in-a-storm, waif-victim roles that Lillian Gish performed for D. W. Griffith, and she ends up as a version of the fortyish Joan Crawford—a Southern California entrepreneur with a bouffant hairdo.

She has exactly one moment when she seems like a person we might know rather than an icon of enduring womanhood. Tommy Lee Jones, as the Marine sergeant Steve Butler, pursues her into her apartment in Saigon. He's sweet, but there's something too insistently nice about his approach; he's desperate, maybe. As Hiep Thi Le puts him off—another big American, she thinks, looking for sex—she has a moment of slyness, her voice floating upward sarcastically. The rest of the time, she's Woman. (Stone dedicated the movie to his mother.)

It's not just life and history that won't let up on Le Ly; Oliver Stone won't, either. The soundtrack is punctuated with screams and thuds in the night; spearheads of flame shoot across the sky. Le Ly dreams of being tortured and raped; she dreams of the VC being thrown out of helicopters, something she couldn't know about. The film is her nightmare, but it's Oliver Stone who's inside her head. When she goes with Jones's Marine sergeant to San Diego, Stone mounts a Kubrick-like satire of American excess, with fatso relatives opening monstrous refrigerators. Some of this is funny in a gross sort of way. But soon people are shrieking at one another, and Steve is falling apart from shame over his foul deeds in Vietnam and sticking a gun in his mouth. The suffering becomes lurid, almost gothic.

As far as Stone is concerned, there's been no remission of sin for America's behavior in Vietnam; he wants to stick a gun in our mouths too. He's powerful and serious—he always has been—but he so overloads the medium that he seems nearly hysterical, a left-wing tabloid moralist with a strong sense of imagery. (It's as if he doesn't feel fully alive unless his moods bring him close to death.) This violent and stressful women's movie turns out to be one of Stone's most macho works.

Covering his bets somewhat, Stone gives *Heaven and Earth* the look and sound of a big commercial movie, with an epically banal score and repeated crane shots of a beautiful Vietnamese valley (most of the film was shot in Thailand). *Heaven and Earth* is about an idyll destroyed. The endless war wipes out the traditional religious and family structures; it eviscerates the lovely village, with its thatched-roof buildings and lush fields. Le Ly—ravaged, violated, betrayed—is a metaphor for Vietnam itself. The movie comes full circle at the end, when Le Ly, a survivor, an American business success, returns to the village and is subjected to a stunning tirade from her brother, a Vietcong veteran. The Vietnamese fought for independence and freedom, he says, and they have known only great suffering. The Americans caused much of this suffering, and she's an American now—another blow to the chops. But is it Le Ly's fault that the Communist victory has produced little but misery? (There are some things, even in Vietnam, that America is not responsible for.) She may be rich and successful, but that helicopter is still bearing down, the blades coming ever closer.

NEW YORK POST, 12/24/93, p. 29, Michael Medved

Whenever studio marketing departments trot out phrases like "A Triumph of the Human Spirit!" it's a sure sign that the movie they're trying to sell is an ordeal to watch.

That's certainly the case with Oliver Stone's "Heaven and Earth", in which his unfortunate heroine is beaten, raped, tortured, starved, prostituted, and endlessly insulted, assaulted and abused.

Stone renders these horrors with the visceral energy and fierce conviction that characterize all his work. But despite some fortune-cookie philosophizing ("A child without a father is like a house without a roof"; "Different skins, same suffering"), his new movie adds up to nothing more than three hours of pointless pain.

The film dramatizes the story of Le Ly Hayslip, a Vietnamese-American activist and author, and is loosely based on her two volumes of memoirs. Stone provides a lovingly detailed re-creation of her home village of Ky La and depicts its ancient, bucolic way of life—before the French and then the Americans arrive—in absurdly idyllic terms.

With waving rice and swelling music (part of a soupy, intrusive, symphonic score by Japanese composer Kitaro), this is old-fashioned "happy peasant" stuff, where even the water buffalo seem to smile.

To his credit, Stone (who also wrote the screenplay) shows some balance in depicting the disruption of this Eden with the Viet Cong engaging in wartime atrocities along with the Americans and their South Vietnamese allies. The cruelty of the pro-Western forces, however, gets by far the most attention including a torture sequence so sadistically specific that most moviegoers will turn from the screen.

Eventually, Le Ly (played by an appealing and sensitive Vietnamese-American college student named Hiep Thi Le) leaves her village for Saigon, where she has an impact on Le Ly in real life.

Jones does an impressive job playing a character who's initially kind but reveals far darker elements in his personality after he brings his Vietnamese bride to California following the fall of Saigon. It turns out, of course, that the source of his problems is the CIA—Oliver Stone's favorite three-letter abbreviation for evil.

A long, mumbling, high-camp confessional in which the fictionalized character talks about secret participation in bloody, horrific "black ops" is too much for an actor of even Jones' indestructible abilities.

Unfortunately, the movie shows very little of Le Ly's life in America beyond the violent crack-up of her troubled husband—which is a shame, because in her books these are the most intriguing aspects of her story.

As in Stone's previous Vietnam-theme film, "Born on the Fourth of July," the main character's rise from long-suffering victim to activist hero is announced but never dramatized.

We do see a nostalgic return visit to her village, where Stone would have us believe that life has settled back into its old, happy norms. But to understand the long journey the character has experienced we are given only enigmatic statements that might best be described as Hollywood Zen.

"Your circle of growth is now complete," Le Ly learns. "Your past is completed."

Promotional materials for the film promise "four decades of turbulence, despair, enlightenment and triumph." There is plenty of well-stated turbulence, despair, enlightenment and triumph—and no enlightenment at all.

NEWSDAY, 12/24/93, Part II/p. 38, Gene Seymour

It doesn't matter whether the movie is 90 minutes or just under four hours. It doesn't matter whether the movie is any *good* or not. There comes a point in every Oliver Stone film when you just want to put your hands over your ears and yell back at the screen, *"SHUT UP! SHUT UP! SHUUUUUUT UUUUUUUPPPP!!!":*

Not that Stone's feverish, declamatory style is, by itself, a bad thing. In an age of slick packaging and market-driven cowardice, commercial cinema needs all the shouters and iconoclasts it can get, and the one thing even his detractors must concede is the see the-hill-take-the-hill courage of Stone's convictions.

Still, one hoped that for "Heaven and Earth," Stone would ease up just a little on the gas pedal. The third, and—maybe—last of his Vietnam epics provided the most daunting challenge of all: a chronicle of the war from the Other Side. That the story's point of view belonged to a sensitive young Vietnamese girl would have required delicacy and subtlety from a director not (to say the least) known for either.

Still, for parts of the first half-hour or so, you think, maybe he'll pull it off. He gets excessive in his rolling vistas of unspoiled Vietnamese farmland, but this is balanced by the tenderness displayed toward the central character, Le Ly (Hiep Thi Le), and her parents (Haing S. Ngor and Joan Chen.)

Even after Stone begins to grind these characters' fate into history's maw, there are moments of harrowing filmmaking. The brutality visited upon Le Ly by both the Viet Cong and the South Vietnamese is harsh and unrelenting enough to make you, once again, wonder: Now *what* was it we were supposed to be doing over there? Grabbing your gut and forcing such re-evaluation down your throat is what Stone does best.

Once he has your gut, however, he never lets go. He just keeps squeezing. It isn't enough for Stone to let the true story of Le Ly Hayslip (adapted from two volumes of memoirs) speak for itself. He has to steam-fit it into an allegorical vision of what was done to her homeland.

Granted, the elements are all there, given that Le Ly was born a farm girl, grew up in sympathy with the Viet Cong, was tortured and degraded in various ways by the South Vietnamese and the Americans and eventually entered a troubled marriage with an American serviceman (Tommy Lee Jones).

But, as always, Stone gets so caught up in his passion and rhetoric that he loses his grip on the human elements. Le Ly is acted upon so often that you barely notice when she begins to take control of her life. Conchata Ferrell and Debbie Reynolds (!) as Jones' sister and mother, respectively, are forced to sacrifice dignity for Stone's ham-handed contrast of bumptious, slovenly Americans with Le Ly's wise and noble family. The most serious and ironic consequence of such overcooked allegory is that it ultimately resembles the exploitation and dehumanizing aspects of the war Stone so virulently attacks.

Stone usually is lucky enough to have good actors to save him from his own excesses. Hiep Thi Le is appealing, but her presence isn't strong enough to overcome Stone's ponderous design. Chen and Ngor bring as much subtlety and grace to the film as their relatively marginal roles allow.

It's left to Jones, as Steve Butler, to save the show, and he climaxes a huge year with a riveting, haunting portrayal of a warrior desperate to subdue his demons. Stone's script is inept at tracking the soldier's emotional collapse. Jones takes what he's given and runs with it like the heavyweight champ he is.

NEWSWEEK, 12/27/93, p. 47, David Ansen

You can't accuse Oliver Stone of playing it safe. His third attempt to wrestle with the demons of Vietnam—after "Platoon" and "Born on the Fourth of July"—is the first Hollywood movie to tell the story of the war from a Vietnamese perspective. For that alone he merits a salute. And in this highly charged adaptation of two memoirs by Le Ly Hayslip, a Vietnamese peasant girl who saw her family torn apart by the war, suffered atrocities committed by both North and South, and suffered again in southern California as the wife of an abusive American soldier, Stone is also attempting his first woman's epic. But don't effect his cinematic manners to change; the narrator may be female, but the vision is *echt* Stone. He remains the Mike Tyson of directors, satisfied only with knockout blows.

"Heaven and Earth" comes at you in angry flurries: whatever ghastly indignity Le Ly (Hiep Thi Le) or anyone in her family endured, Stone's camera won't miss a queasy detail—her protracted torture by the South Vietnamese, her rape by a Viet Cong officer. This is powerful stuff (as the overbearing Kitaro score reminds you) but it yields diminishing returns. As her saga leaps over the years and continents, Stone loses his grip on a great, harrowing story. Years pass in the blink of an eye. She's the servant in a rich man's house, a peddler of cigarettes to GIs, a bar hostess, a prostitute, a mother. Children appear who are barely accounted for. In San Diego, where she becomes a successful entrepreneur, the doting husband (Tommy Lee Jones) she met in Nam goes psycho and kidnaps her children. There's enough material here for a mini-series. Crunched into 2¼, hours of spasmodic narrative, Le Ly's extraordinary life is reduced to its lurid highlights. Stone's so eager to get to the good stuff (i.e. the bad stuff) that the movie plays like the longest coming-attractions trailer ever made.

Some of the parts are undeniably gripping; what gets lost are the characters themselves. Jones's now charming, now desperate, now cuckoo soldier barely makes sense, and for good reason—he's a composite of four different men in Hayslip's books. Hiep makes an assured debut, but Stone's script never discovers the real woman behind the symbolic martyr. In the end, back in Vietnam, we know what has happened to Le Ly, but we don't who she is. Nor, one suspects, does Stone.

SIGHT AND SOUND, 3/94, p. 39, Philip Strick

Sixth-born child to the Phung family, Le Ly spends her infancy at the rice-farming village of Ky La, near the Central Vietnamese town of Da Nang. Although briefly terrorised by the French in the 1950s, the village remains a haven of peace until, in 1963, when Le Ly is 12, the Viet Cong arrive from the North with warnings against the South Vietnam government and its American allies. Le Ly's brother is recruited by the Viet Cong, and goes north with them to Hanoi. Then Government helicopters move in, the villagers are ordered to help destroy the Viet Cong, and the teenage Le Ly finds herself with divided loyalties. She is arrested and tortured by Government soldiers for her suspected Viet Cong sympathies, but her mother uses Le Ly's dowry to buy her release. Her sudden freedom arouses the suspicions of the Viet Cong, who prepare to execute her. As a last-minute reprieve, she is raped instead.

Le Ly flees with her mother to Saigon where her sister Hai finds them jobs as domestic staff to the wealthy Anh Lien; fascinated by his new young servant-girl, Anh begins an affair with her, and she is soon pregnant. Madame Lien, however, is Catholic and refuses to let her husband acquire a concubine: Le Ly is packed off to Da Nang. Living at first with another sister, Kim, a night-club dancer, Le Ly hustles the American troops who throng the town and—for the sake of the family pride—tries to avoid prostitution. She revisits the village, now a military outpost, to see her father again before he dies; he tells her she must fight to raise her little son Jimmy as best she can. After the funeral, Le Ly returns to work as a waitress at the Korean Casino in Da Nang. Catching the eye of weary U.S. Marine Steve Butler, she gradually warms to his attentiveness and they become lovers. Over the next three years, as she bears his child and the struggle for Vietnam intensifies, she begins to believe his promises that America offers a kind of paradise. At last they escape from Vietnam and fly to California.

Warmly received by Steve's mother Eugenia and elder sister Bernice, Le Ly is astonished at the profligacy of American consumerism, but the magic soon wears thin. Steve already has a wife, who receives half his pay-checks, he is reluctant to let Le Ly go out to work for a place of their own, and he is quickly bored by inactivity. Vietnam has made him an adventurer, eager for weaponry and bloodshed; to Le Ly's horror, he wants to raise their three sons, who refuse to learn Vietnamese, as survivalists in his own image. As Le Ly becomes self-supporting, Steve is increasingly unstable; he moves out, kidnaps the children, and after several rows he despairs of his own sanity and commits suicide. Some 13 years later, in the 1980s, Le Ly has become a successful businesswoman and revisits Vietnam with her sons. In Ho Chi Minh City (formerly Saigon) she introduces Jimmy to his father Anh, now working in a laundry, and is reunited with her relatives at Ky La. Her brother Sau scorns her capitulation to the American way of life, but her mother is proud of what Le Ly has achieved, and in a dream Le Ly also senses her father's approval. She accepts that her destiny is to be never wholly Vietnamese or American but to strive for some form of balance between the two extremes.

Despite appearances, the case can be made that with the third of his Vietnam stories Oliver Stone for the first time pays some attention to the Vietnamese voice. His opening salvo, *Platoon*, at heart the study of a moral dilemma, could as easily have been a Western; and *Born on the Fourth of July* quickly showed its colours a part of Stone's manifesto against American self-betrayal. It is only now with *Heaven & Earth* that the 'real' Vietnam—reconstructed in various Thailand locations—emerges fragmentarily from the mists of guilt. What has been habitually "a state of mind" (Stone's frequent description of Vietnam) at last has the chance to acquire some screen sense of its proper physical, historical and philosophical identity.

The new mental state, unfortunately, is less than lucid; Stone is an impressionist, dealing in detail and detour en route for accuracy, and the film retreats to familiar vantage points—the bedlam of battle, the plight of servicemen returning home—whenever possible. But as an attempt to restore the balance, to show the non-American side, it offers a spectacular, palliative portrait of a beautiful country chronically afflicted with the blight of military destruction. Less ingratiatingly, it contains an underlying message of jaded fatalism: that the American invaders got no more than they deserved, while the Vietnamese people endured no more than they expected. This revisionist approach, showing how the Viet Cong committed atrocities against their own race while the American forces largely resigned themselves to indolence, derives not from a military apologist, but from the autobiography of a Vietnamese survivor.

Accustomed to adapting true-life memoirs to suit his own persuasions, Stone finds the strikingly symbolic Le Ly a manageable heroine in her early years but slowly loses her as maturity sets in. Partly, one suspects, this is because of her very ambiguity as a political cypher, but there is also a more fundamental problem. Stone's innocents impaled on experience have previously all been male; the women in his films function awkwardly as furniture, victims or audience, haunting the margins of a distinctly masculine conclave. Where they demand greater attention, as with Jim Morrison's partner in *The Doors*, or the activist hometown sweetheart in *Born on the Fourth of July*, Stone allows plenty of admiring close-ups but little of substance. Mysterious and unsecured, they have dropped out of the narrative without making much of an impression on it.

No surprise, then, that the ingenuous Le Ly is dominated by a series of men, including her father and brother, until firmly elbowed from any claim to the film's spotlight by the arrival of Steve. He has the advantage not only of being played with ravenous skill and subtlety by Tommy Lee Jones but also of being a composite of at least four Americans who shaped the events of her life in reality. In the grip of this fascinatingly unstable force, Le Ly continues to play victim until released by his suicide; Stone then casually discards the next 13 years of her American independence to bring the story back to village basics, with Le Ly's sons already beginning to do the talking. Since those evaded years represent the culmination and reportedly the triumph of Le Ly's talent for self-sufficiency, their dismissal would be inexplicable were it not, firstly, that there could be no easy way to film them, and secondly, that Stone is evidently intent on a different destination.

In dedicating *Heaven & Earth* to his mother, Stone seems to be atoning for a lack of filial respect in his past work, where the matriarchal voice, if heard at all, is something of an embarrassment. Le Ly's mother sets an enduring example of fortitude: as well as saving her daughter's life she had a miraculous last-second escape of her own. Played with a discretion bordering on invisibility by Joan Chen, her advice largely ignored and with no evidence to offer for the potent gulf of Le Ly's American years, she would nevertheless seem to be the secret of Le Ly's resilience if we take at face value the film's careful circle of motherhood, culminating in the mother's valedictory blessing to her daughter.

But the allegiance is hollow: naturally enough, Stone identifies far more with Steve than with Le Ly, and the film's other mother, chubby, affable and irrelevant (Debbie Reynolds), is sketched with typical dismissiveness. It is to her father that Le Ly constantly defers, 'seeing' him again at the end in one of the brief monochrome visions that punctuate the film. "From my father I learned to love God," she says, and draws from him much the same lesson in saintliness as the young voyager gained from his elders in *Wall Street*, dedicated by Stone to the absent, perversely heroic father of his own teenage years.

In the sense that one parent is concerned with Le Ly's physical well-being, the other with her spiritual growth, *Heaven & Earth* ingeniously translates the Vietnamese/Buddhist concept of Father Heaven and Mother Earth to Le Ly's dilemma of filial loyalties and, through her, to Stone's. Wandering between the two, Le Ly produces an uneasy parallel between the paternalistic paradise of America and the maternal stoicism and fecundity of Vietnam, a notion that Stone wisely refuses to dwell on. If Le Ly's view of the middle ground comes from being emotionally stretched between two 'home' countries, Stone's appears to rest somewhere between an idyllic childhood and a disillusioned adolescence, with Vietnam being the point where it all went wrong.

We are, as a result, treated to a prologue and epilogue of questionable rustic serenity, with images of a girl balancing on a water-buffalo, orange-robed monks strolling through paddy-fields, the mountains and meadows and streams of a long-lost horizon to which Le Ly at last returns. Stone films the valley with the devouring hunger of a tourist avid for sunsets, rendering it as suspect and temporary as the intricately parodic shots of American supermarkets and crassly furnished homes, no expense spared or truly comprehended. His skill at filming a diabolical chaos remains impressive but Le Ly's story leads only to a passionless conclusion despite its lurid accompaniment of shrieking strings. Protesting too much that this is an authentic Vietnam, Stone seems after all to have ended up in some other frame of reference, somewhere between Le Ly's domestic purgatory and his own.

TIME, 12/27/93, p. 70, Richard Corliss

[*Heaven and Earth* was reviewed jointly with *Famine-33*; see Corliss' review of that film.]

VILLAGE VOICE, 12/28/93, p. 82, Georgia Brown

Oliver Stone's epic-scale historical romance, *Heaven and Earth*, is based on Le Ly Hayslip's two autobiographical chronicles, *When Heaven and Earth Changed Places* (written with Jay Wurts) and *Child of War, Woman of Peace* (written with James Hayslip). I've not yet read the second but the first is a richly detailed account of an excruciating coming-of-age in war-torn Vietnam. If Stone had included half of what happens to this resilient warrior woman, the movie would've run a week.

When the Vietcong begin arriving in Phung Thi Le Ly's village, the situation is not unlikely Belfast's. The people may have allegiances (they support the VC over the government), but essentially they're pawns caught between two masters who show up alternately, ruthlessly demanding fealty and suspicious of enemy influence. At one point, Le Ly (Hiep Thi Le) is imprisoned by the government and tortured, then, when she's released, she's raped and nearly killed by the VC, who accuse her of being a spy. When she has to leave her village for good, she and her mother (Joan Chen with blackened teeth) luckily find positions with a rich Saigon family; unluckily, Le Ly gets pregnant by the husband. They're shipped off to Danang where Le Ly peddles cigarettes and whiskey to GIs and occasionally (when the price is right) takes money for sex.

The above summarizes just the movie's first half. Unfortunately, the sheer breadth of the plot overwhelms character. Le Ly is more like a puppet—Judy rolling with a series of Punches (she sure pops up quick). Attractive in a Western, baby-doll way, Hiep's onscreen presence is alternately wispy and brittle; her voiceovers lack gravity. (The scenic vistas also are bland in their Western prettiness.) For all of the Sturm und Drang of Hayslip's odyssey (you half expect her to cry, "I'll never eat rice balls again!"), it's strangely without affect.

So, when Tommy Lee Jones, as Sergeant Steve Butler, suddenly appears midway through the epic, he sweeps in like a monsoon, or Mr. Rhett Butler, flattening all in his path. Even at first, as a war-weary basket case, his heartsickness blankets the screen like a massive cloud formation. Apparently, Le Ly has a healing effect because Steve sincerely wants her as his wife. And the GI is faithful, 100 per cent: When she's lost in a refugee exodus, he finds her, and when Saigon falls, he whisks her and her two sons (one his) back to San Diego. There they join his mother and sister in a tract house, shop at giant supermarkets, and pack the freezer with frozen peas. (We're now into Hayslip's second volume.) Back in the States, Le Ly struggles to make a new life as Steve cracks up.

Jones is immensely touching, and when he's around, Stone fashions a terrifically stirring drama. It's as if he meets his real emotional subject here. But if initially it seems that the American elements easily overpower the Vietnamese, the long view might be that Eastern subtlety has once more subverted Western "knowhow." The same old story. Stone gets points for trying.

Also reviewed in:
CHICAGO TRIBUNE, 12/24/93, Friday/p. A, Michael Wilmington
NATION, 1/3-10/94, p. 30, Stuart Klawans
NEW REPUBLIC, 2/7/94, p. 26, Stanley Kauffmann
NEW YORK TIMES, 12/24/93, p C1, Janet Maslin
NEW YORKER, 1/17/94, p. 87, Anthony Lane
VARIETY, 12/27/93, p. 50, Todd McCarthy
WASHINGTON POST, 12/24/93, Weekend/p. 36, Desson Howe
WASHINGTON POST, 12/25/93, p. B1, Hal Hinson

HEIMAT II

A Edgar Reitz production in association with WDR/HR/NDR/BR/SFB/SWF/BBC/TVE/TV-1/YLE/DR/NRK/ORF. *Producer:* Edgar Reitz. *Director:* Edgar Reitz. *Screenplay:* Edgar Reitz. *Director of Photography:* Gernot Roll, Gerard Vandenberg, and Christian Reitz. *Editor:* Susanne Hartmann. *Music:* Nikos Mamangakis. *Sound:* Heiko Hinderks, Haymo Heyder, Manfred Banach, and Reiner Wiehr. *Casting:* Robert Busch. *Production Designer:* Franz Bauer. *Costumes:* Billie Brassers and Nikola Hoeltz. *Make-up:* Mia Schoepke. *Running time:* 1532 minutes. *MPAA Rating:* Not Rated.

CAST: Henry Arnold (Hermann); Salome Kammer (Clarissa); Anke Sevenich (Schnüsschen); Daniel Smith (Juan); Michael Schönborn (Alex); Franziska Traub (Renate); Hannelore Hoger (Elisabeth Cerphal); Hanna Köhler (Frau Moretti); Gisela Müller (Evelyne); Michael Seyfried (Ansgar); Armin Fuchs (Volker); Martin Maria Blau (Jean-Marie); Lena Lessing (Olga); Peter Weiss (Rob); Frank Röth (Stefan); Laszlo I. Kish (Reihard); Susanne Lothar (Esther); Veronika Ferres (Dorli); Franziska Stömmer (Frau Ries); Manfred Andrae (Gerold Gattinger).

NEW STATESMAN & SOCIETY, 5/7/93, p. 32, Martin Chalmers

The first *Heimat*, a chronicle of a fictional German village during the 20th century, ended on an apocalyptic note. It was 1982, a time of an accelerated arms race and fears of nuclear war.

Features of village community appeared to survive the "economic miracle", but the Hunsrück hills were being tunnelled for cruise missile installations. Even the funeral of Maria Simon, the village matriarch, was disturbed by low-flying jets. A feeling of helplessness in the face of these developments was accentuated by condemning the viewer, for what seemed an interminable time, to being the only sober person at a German village *kirmes*.

Die Zweite Heimat, now three episodes into its run on BBC2, goes back in time to cover only one decade. Director Edgar Reitz's setting is no longer invented Schabbach, but the real city of Munich. However, if *Heimat* took a mere 16 hours to get from 1919 to 1982, the 1960s as experienced by Maria's illegitimate son, Hermann Simon, and his friends extends to 13 two-hour films-within-a-film.

One of the more affecting episodes of the earlier film dealt with the intolerant response of mother and village to the teenage Hermann's relationship with an older woman. It was impressive, not least, because of its depiction of the oppressiveness of family and village life in the 1950s.

The vision of rural idyll that *Heimat* tended to slide into, despite its critical intentions, was effectively undermined. This slippage was perhaps an honest reflection of ambivalence. It was also a consequence of the sheer duration of the film, of the use of the conventions of the TV soap, which establish the familiarity of the circumscribed location and of interlocking lives.

Hermann, however, leaves the village behind. A musical prodigy at school, he is determined never to love again and never to return to the "horrible Hunsrück. He enrols at the conservatory in Munich to train as a composer. Hermann despises his past so much that he even takes elocution lessons to get rid of his rural accent.

Die Zweite Heimat becomes the (auto)biography of a generation. It shows the excitement of moving away from home, of becoming part of a peer group at college or university—a new home that will inevitably dissolve—and of making intellectual, artistic, emotional and sexual discoveries. At the same time, this is a generation coming together in a very particular place; Germany in the 1960s, made up of young people who were still small children at the end of the war, many of them the first in their families to enter higher education.

Although individual episodes focus on other figures, Hermann remains very much the central character. However, this novel-like concentration on subjective experience is balanced in the early episodes by the context of the conservatory, a kind of village within the city. It lends *Die Zweite Heimat*, at times, the air of an avant-garde *Fame*. But the occasional mawkishness of the dialogue is, in turn, more than compensated for by exhilarating, virtually wordless flights of cinematic fantasy, which at once punctuate and condense the more naturalistic scenes.

The film successfully rescues the thrill at the invention (and rediscovery) of avant-garde gestures in art at the last moment when the avant-garde still mattered. If there is something specifically German to this, then it lies in the importance of the challenge, of artistic modernism to the conservative "restoration" atmosphere of West Germany in the 1950s and early 1960s.

Die Zweite Heimat recapitulates with affectionate mockery both the musical experiments of the time, and the early years of the New German Cinema, when Reitz first came to prominence. Tribute is paid, above all, to the writer and film-maker Alexander Kluge, without whom the revival of German cinema would be difficult to imagine. This ranges from trade-mark devices such as the speeded up sequence during the opening credits to the prominent role given Hannelore Hoger, one of the few professionals in *Die Zweite Heimat* who starred in several of Kluge's films.

Also preserved, along with a noble sense of seriousness and an enthusiasm for experimentation, is the routine sexism of the male characters. Reitz records this in an almost naive way, though it must be granted that here, as elsewhere, he has the courage to be naive. In later episodes, Reitz somewhat clumsily tries to portray the rise of a feminist consciousness among women. The clumsiness is perhaps an index of his own discomfort.

As a portrait of a generation emerging before the 1960s (as they are remembered) got going, *Die Zweite Heimat* has some of the feel and pleasures of an old serial novel. Even more than its predecessor, however, despite all the moments are purely visual and musical.

Is it good? Probably. Reitz is not a great film-maker. What he did discover, quite late in his career, was a way of combining a talent for telling stories in film that also left space for the avant-garde enthusiasms he recollects in the earlier episodes of *Die Zweite Heimat*. If, however, the viewer is looking to the film for answers to the great questions posed by German history, then he or she should not expect too much—and, in any case, not expect too much of any one artist.

NEW YORK POST, 6/4/93, p. 31, Jerry Tallmer

It isn't the longest movie ever made. A 1987 "The Cure for Insomnia," by J.H. Timmis IV, would seem to be that, at 85 hours. But at 26, "Die Zweite Heimat," or "Heimat II: Chronicle of a Nation," qualifies as a pretty strong runner-up. It also beats its predecessor, the 15-hour "Heimat" of 1985 by 11 hours.

Both these novelistic epics, the overlapping story of a village, a people (the Germans) and a nation (Germany) through the convulsive half-century of 1919-1970, were written and directed by the (now) 60-year-old Edgar Reitz, one of the pioneers of the New German Cinema.

We see the story through the eyes, first, of the inhabitants of the fictional village of Schabbach in the Palatinate—that was the 1985 portion—and now for 26 hours we focus on young Hermann Simon as he strikes out in heartbreak and rebellion in 1960 (his mother has destroyed a juvenile romance) for the big cosmopolitan city, Munich, humming with culture, politics, and available women.

Indeed, though Hermann has taken a sacred vow never to fall in love again, women of all sorts and varieties keep throwing themselves at his head and elsewhere. "God's sword flashes over Munich, city of pleasure," a passing philosopher-cynic quotes from Thomas Mann—it was also the city of Hitler—and in fact it is the breadth and texture of Thomas Mann that this film, like its forerunner, reaches for and in many ways attains.

God, they say, is in the details, but so is Satan. The mass of detail of this work is fabulous and impressive, but I do not know that we need to follow *every* cup and saucer and buzzing fly or *every* train-window reflection throughout the 10 long years of Hermann's angst and maturation. On the other hand not loving been able to spare but a few hours to taste from all 26 of this very long trip, I do not think you will find any minute of it boring. I did not.

The acting throughout is impeccable, even if Henry Arnold, its long lean soulful Hermann, is a bit old to pass for 20 at the beginning. Of the ladies I managed to catch, the one that quite tickled my fancy, as she did Hermann's, was the Renate (Franziska Traub) who he felt was too ugly when she took him to bed as a homeless young greenhorn in Munich.

Reitz made these "Heimats" in rage over "the crocodile tears of our nation." That rage is captured here, in soft pedal. You have to wait for it. Let me know, when you see all 26 hours—in 13 installments, if it wasn't worth it.

VILLAGE VOICE, 6/15/93, p. 56, Manohla Dargas

Heimat II: Chronicle of a Generation starts modestly enough, given that Edgar Reitz's follow-up film to his 1984 *Heimat (Homeland)* clocks in at 26 hours. It's 1960 and 18-year-old Hermann Simon (Henry Arnold) is thrashing on his bed renouncing love, mother, and his hometown of Hunsbruck. A gifted musician and aspiring composer, Hermann wants to leave Hunsbruck for Munich, to experience "the freedom of will." He's a baby Nietzschean on his way, searching for fame but finding metaphysics at every turn.

Once in Munich, Hermann meets the strange and talented Juan, who plays as many instruments as he speaks languages. Later, Hermann meets the strange and talented Clarissa, a cellist with whom he falls in tormented love. And still later, Hermann meets many, many other strange, talented, and brooding young souls, like Helga and Stefan and Alex and Volker (the principal cast numbers 39).

If this sounds vaguely like *As the Zeitgeist Turns*, that's only half right. While soaps are a fugue of exposition and high drama, *Heimat II* is weirdly monotonal. Events unfold, then unfold, then unfold some more. People come and go, details pile up, yet for all the love, occasional death, ever-present angst, the accent is fixed. One reason for this may be that most of the young characters are variations on the same theme. Despite their eccentricities, they mouth similar platitudes—a few, like Alex, more elegantly than others—and wallow in solipsism. Every so often someone intones *the war, Nazis, Hitler,* but the words float in the air, unmoored from history or memory. In fact, most of the young don't seem scarred, much less touched, by the recent past. They live in an aesthetic bubble, finding refuge in one another, in music, in art.

Early in *Heimat II* a drunk asks Hermann if he's familiar with Adorno's theory of 12-tone music. Hermann brushes the man off; he doesn't have time for the question, but Reitz clearly does—26 hours, in fact. Adorno considered music a form of critical thinking, but found fault with

12-tone serialism because "the new ordering of 12-tone technique virtually extinguishes the subject." In *Heimat II*, Reitz is determined to restore the subject, the German subject, that is. Where this leaves everyone else, of course, is another question, one currently playing itself out in the *Heimat*. The quotation Reitz really should have cited is blunt, but would have represented the philosopher refugee better. "To write poetry after Auschwitz," lamented Adorno, "is barbaric."

Also reviewed in:
VARIETY, 12/7/92, p. 72, Eric Hansen

HERMAN

A Herman Films release through RKO Distribution. *Producer:* Petter J. Borgli. *Director:* Erik Gustavson. *Screenplay (Norwegian with English subtitles—based on his novel):* Lars Saabye Christensen. *Director of Photography:* Kjell Vassdal. *Editor:* Martin Asphaug. *Music:* Randall Meyers. *Sound:* Kari Nytro. *Production Designer:* Frode Krohg. *Costumes:* Inger Derlick. *Running time:* 100 minutes. *MPAA Rating:* Not Rated.

CAST: Anders Danielson Lie (Herman); Frank Robert (Herman's Grandfather); Elisabeth Sand (Herman's Mother); Kar Remlow (Jacobsen); Sassen Krohg (Mrs. Jacobsen); Harald Heide-Steen, Jr. (Fatso the Barber); Bjorn Floberg (Herman's Father); Jarl Kulle (Panten); Linn Aaronsen (Rudy).

NEW YORK POST, 5/12/93, p. 26, Jerry Tallmer

Once upon a time not so long ago there was a nice Swedish movie called "My Life as a Dog." Now there is a nice Norwegian movie called "Herman" which would be all the nicer if there had never been a movie that it somewhat resembles called "My Life as a Dog." Still, "Herman" directed by Erik Gustavson, is not a bad movie on its own terms, once you get past the fact that it's also about an oddball misfit 11-year-old boy.

Herman is the kind of loner who often talks in the third person and does things like stagger down the sidewalk toward the grocer's wife, a termagant in furs, shielding his eyes. When she calls him a brat, he replies: "One isn't a brat, one's blind and very much lost"

He also gets picked on by his classmates, coaches and teachers, and this time, when he arrives late as usual and the teacher bawls him out, Herman offers the excuse that he was attacked by a fox. "And how did you handle this beast?" the teacher demands. "It appeared to be death" the boy answers. "It was wrapped around Jacobsen's wife."

Anders Danielson Lie gives Herman just the right insouciance for rebellious wisecracks like that—a glib patina of course, over insecurity, anxiety, pain. But Herman's mother, unlike Ingemar's in "My Life as a Dog," will not die; it's Grandpa who dies, *that* pain, in a beautiful scene in which Herman in Santa Claus mask comes to visit the old man (Frank Robert), Herman's mother (Elisabeth Sand) works for Jacobsen the grocer and this comes out subtly, late in the film—has to fend off his attentions. Herman's father (Bjorn Floberg) is a husky, hearty guy—too hearty and a bit too cliche—who works high overhead in the cabin of a construction crane. Throughout the movie he keeps offering to give Herman a ride on the crane, and the kid keeps stalling. Dad also gives Herman the present of a comb, and what could be a more obvious symbol than that?

It's Fatso the barber who spots the little patch on Herman's scalp that leads everybody to the doctor and presently to the news that Herman will lose all his hair to a rare skin disease—alopecia areata, according to the press kit, though if they said that in the movie, I never heard it. Mother knits him a woolen cap with tassel, which solves nothing. In a classroom confrontation the teacher tears off the tassel—and later regrets it.

Herman, in his grief, and subject to a lot of bullying—"Baldy! Skull!"—goes a bit crazy. He heaves a stone through Fatso's plate-glass window, solving nothing. He mimes an absurd suicide, giving the teacher a near heart-attack. He runs away in his yellow oilslicker. Actually his real fears, over and above—or beneath—the baldness, are Dad's crane, and the grocer's hungry eyes on Mother.

The bewigged boy gets solace from three quarters: an old drunk played by the great Jarl Kulle of "Smiles of a Summer's Night"; Grandfather's tall tales about Waldemar, a WW II prisoner comrade who stole Tut-ankh-Amun's wig from under the Great Pyramid at Giza; and Ruby, the pretty little redheaded classmate who beats Herman in running but bucks him up with affection. There was a girl much like that in "My Life as a Dog" too, but, as I say, you have to take the thoughtful pleasures of "Herman" in their own right.

NEWSDAY, 5/12/93, Part II/p. 53, Gene Seymour

"Herman" is a dry, sweet concoction spritzed with a somewhat bizarre twist: Its title character, an 11-year-old Norwegian boy, is afflicted with a skin disease that is causing his hair to fall out.

But what gives the film its merit is that director Erik Gustavson and scriptwriter Lars Saabye Christensen (adapting from his novel) don't milk any unnecessary pathos or peculiarity from this affliction. Instead, the disease becomes a device for exploring the bittersweet nature of a boy's isolation from those around him.

Played with unassuming charm by Anders Danielson Lie, Herman, who has an annoying habit of referring to himself in the third person (as in "One is very well, thank you."), is so keenly aware of his gift for vivid pretending that he wears his imagination like a fortress.

This fortress travels with him to and from school and back home again to his bemused, doting parents (Elisabeth Sand, Bjorn Floberg). But for all their love and indulgence, not even they gain passage into the fortress. That honor goes almost exclusively to Herman's dying grandfather (Frank Robert) and the neighborhood dipsomaniac (Jarl Kulle), from whose tall tales Herman fashions the particulars of his own inner world.

Then reality bumrushes Herman when the local barber finds thinning patches of hair on his scalp. A series of tests finds nothing wrong with Herman except the rapid, inexplicable loss of hair. Suddenly, Herman finds his isolation from his family, teachers and schoolmates (who already thinks he's weird) deepening beyond his control. His effort to win his way back into the world while retaining some hold on his imagination becomes the film's driving force.

The 1950s ambiance gives the film a passing resemblance to "My Life as a Dog," while lacking the latter film's larger, darker dimensions. Yet, "Herman's" sunnier texture in no way shortchanges its own modest virtues of shrewd observation and wry grace.

VILLAGE VOICE, 6/1/93, p. 56, Regina Raiford

Herman, Norway's Academy award candidate for Best Foreign Language Film of 1991, at first seemed a lightweight Scandinavian takeoff of the *Peanuts* comic strip. But in fact this romance between a roundheaded boy and a little red-haired girl is a subtle, somber tale about growing pains. Herman, who has suffered an unexplained and rapid loss of his hair, initially refuses to accept his condition but eventually embraces it as a manifestation of his quirkiness. Moving from his family home to the terrors of the playground to his dreams of Zorro, he navigates through the confusing, contradictory landscape of childhood.

Based on Lars Saabye Christensen's bestselling novel, the film is framed within Herman's 11-year-old perspective. All of the characters and events seem glazed in a golden glow, like old photos, though director Erik Gustavson avoids sentimentality. His visuals may seem plucked from children's book illustrations, each one idyllic, yet the plain, sharply detailed acting, especially by Anders Danielson Lie as Herman, keeps the story grounded.

Herman captures that elusive time in life when one is young enough to wish on globes but old enough to know life is unfair.

Also reviewed in:
NEW YORK TIMES, 5/13/93, p. C20, Janet Maslin
VARIETY, 9/3/90, p. 78

HEXED

A Columbia Pictures release of a Price Entertainment/Brillstein-Grey production. *Executive Producer:* Bernie Brillstein and Howard Klein. *Producer:* Marc S. Fischer and Louis G. Friedman. *Director:* Alan Spencer. *Screenplay:* Alan Spencer. *Director of Photography:* James Chressanthis. *Editor:* Debra McDermott. *Music:* Lance Rubin. *Music Editor:* Joanie Diener. *Sound:* Michael Haines and (music) Steve Hallmark. *Sound Editor:* Barney Cabral. *Casting:* Cathy Henderson and Tom McSweeney. *Production Designer:* Brenton Swift. *Art Director:* Albert Locatelli. *Set Designer:* Mary Finn. *Set Decorator:* Sara E. Andrews. *Special Effects:* Jack Bennett. *Costumes:* Joan S. Thomas. *Make-up:* Magdalena Nena Smarz. *Stunt Coordinator:* Russell Towery. *Running time:* 90 minutes. *MPAA Rating:* R.

CAST: Ayre Gross (Matthew Welsh);   Claudia Christian (Hexina);   Adrienne Shelly (Gloria O'Connor);   Ray Baker (Victor Thummell);   R. Lee Ermey (Detective Ferguson);   Michael Knight (Simon Littlefield);   Robin Curtis (Rebecca);   Brandis Kemp (Ms. Strickland);   Norman Fell (Herschel Levine);   Pamela Roylance (Jennifer);   Billy Jones (Larry);   John Davies (Henry Pratt);   Fred Mata (Bellman);   Marilyn Staley (Nurse);   Julio Cedillo (Officer Sanchez); Woody Watson (Officer Gillis);   Randy Means (Policeman);   Phyllis Cicero (Officer Novak); Tasha Auer (Officer Turner);   Shelley Michelle (Body Double);   Terry Poland (Mime);   Joe Berryman (Southern Businessman);   Gil Glasgow (Priest);   Jonathan Dorn and Erin Kempe (Teens);   Mark Walters and Tony Brownrigg (Cops);   Spencer Lucas and Bob Hess (Detectives);   Roy Metcalf (Junkie);   Francis Silmon (Singing Dishwasher);   Hector Garcia (Hispanic Newscaster);   Alan Ackles (Newscaster);   Suzanne Moss (2nd Newscaster);   Elaine Long (Intro Reporter);   Linda Edwards (Female Reporter);   Maria Arita (Reporter);   Laura Banks (1st Reporter);   David Sederholm (2nd Reporter);   Teresa Ganzel (3rd Reporter); Michele Russell (T.V. Reporter);   Geoffrey Garza (Party Bartender);   John William Galt (Obese Slob);   Gary Moody (Desk Sergeant);   John B. Wells (SWAT Commander);   Doug Small (Bus Driver);   Lisa E. Seyfert (Deaf Woman in Bar);   Georgia Lambron (Pedestrian).

LOS ANGELES TIMES, 1/25/93, Calendar/p. 7, Michael Wilmington

"Hexed" more than lives up to its title. Cursed with a lack of inspiration from start to finish, this vastly unamusing action-comedy finds director Alan Spencer desperately trying to pump up his stale script at every turn. Once again, you're left to wonder not only how a studio could justify the expense of releasing "Hexed" but also how the project managed to get a green light in the first place. Direct-to-video would have seemed the logical route for this loser.

A talented young comedian, Arye Gross, who hopefully will survive this debacle, stars as a 30-year-old hotel desk clerk, indulges in reasonably harmless mischief to relieve the boredom of 12 years on the job. Overlooking his pert colleague (Adrienne Shelly, the delectable leading lady of Hal Hartley's "The Unbelievable Truth" and "Trust"), who adores him, he daydreams about America's most photographed model of the moment, the sexy and statuesque Hexina (Claudia Christian). When she unexpectedly checks into the hotel, and the desk clerk even more unexpectedly lands a date with her, his life swiftly turns into a nightmare. Hexina, it turns out, is a homicidal maniac intent on dispatching a blackmailer—and anyone else who gets in her way.

There's no point in further belaboring the hopeless "Hexed" (rated R for sexuality and language), which is itself already so labored.

Also reviewed in:
NEW YORK TIMES, 1/23/93, p. 16, Janet Maslin
VARIETY, 2/1/93, p. 97, Lawrence Cohn
WASHINGTON POST, 1/25/93, B7, Richard Harrington

HIGHWAY PATROLMAN

A First Look Pictures release of a Together Brothers/Ultra Films production. *Executive Producer:* Sammy O. Masada, Kuniaki Negishi, and Naoki Tachikawa. *Producer:* Lorenzo O'Brien. *Director:* Alex Cox. *Screenplay (Spanish with English subtitles):* Lorenzo O'Brien. *Director of Photography:* Miguel Garzon. *Editor:* Carlos Puente. *Music:* Zander Schloss. *Sound:* Roberto Munoz and (music) Carlo Nuccio. *Casting:* Miguel Sandoval and Claudia Becker. *Production Designer:* Cecilia Montiel. *Art Director:* Bryce Perrin and Homero Espinoza. *Set Decorator:* Brigitte Broch. *Special Effects:* Federico Farfan. *Costumes:* Manuela Loaeza. *Make-up:* Maria Eugenia Luna. *Running time:* 104 minutes. *MPAA Rating:* Not Rated.

CAST: Roberto Sosa (Pedro Rojas); Bruno Bichir (Anibal Guerro); Vanessa Bauche (Maribel); Zaide Silvia Gutiérrez (Griselda Marcos); Pedro Armendariz, Jr. (Sergeant Barreras); Malena Doria (Abuela); Towi Islas (Emilio); Ernesto Gomez Cruz (Commander Navarro); Mike Moroff (Commander Sanchez); Jorge Russek (Mr. Mateos); Ana Bertha Espin (Mrs. Sanchez); Eduardo Lopez Rojas (Mr. Rojas); Maricruz Najera (Mrs. Rojas); Adjari Chazaro (Isabel); Carlos Alvarez (Luis); Karl Braun, Alex Cox, and Ron Stoliar (Gringos); Guillermo Rios (Lieutenant Perez); Arturo Farfan (Trucker); Damian Alcazar and Alejandro Bracho (Suspects); Gabriel Pingarron (Assistant Inspector); Jorge Fegan (Bus Driver); Rene Pereyra (Mechanic); Gerardo "Chiquillin" Zepeda (Guard); Mauricio Rubi (Drunk Driver); Sergio Calderon (Passenger); Moises Ivan (Governor's Son); Alonso Echanove (Dr. Bolanos); Magda Rodriguez (Beautiful Woman); Regino Herrera (Old Barman); Gerardo Moscoso (Governor); Claudia Becker (Mother Consuelo); Dolores Heredia (Radio Dispatcher); Victorino Porcayo (Operator); Ana Rittner (TV Reporter).

LOS ANGELES TIMES, 2/4/94, Calendar/p. 2, Kevin Thomas

"Highway Patrolman" is maverick director Alex Cox's finest film to date and represents his best work since his terrific debut feature, the funky, surreal 1984 "Repo Man." This film, in Spanish with English subtitles, opens just the way one would expect of Cox—with a darkly satirical take on his subject, an idealistic young Mexican's training at the National Highway Patrol Academy in Mexico City. But the British-born Cox and his producer-screenwriter, Lorenzo O'Brien, a Peruvian raised in Mexico, gradually get more serious once their wiry, wistful hero (Roberto Sosa) takes up his first assignment in a remote town in Durango.

It would seem that working in a foreign language has given Cox the necessary freedom and detachment not to worry about being hip and to take the plunge into classic screen storytelling, backed by O'Brien's superbly structured script.

While it rightly skewers American hypocrisy and complicity in Mexican drug-trafficking, "Highway Patrolman" abounds in the timeless virtues of traditional filmmaking. Indeed, there is an epic quality, moral as well as visual, to the hero's odyssey that recalls the Westerns of John Ford and such John Huston films as "Treasure of the Sierra Madre" and "Under the Volcano."

Almost immediately Sosa's earnest, likable Pedro Rojas discovers the impossibility of adhering to the straight and narrow. On the one hand, he's too underpaid to resist accepting the occasional "mordita" once he's a husband and father; on the other, a strict enforcement of the law becomes a hardship and injustice upon people who are simply struggling to survive. If he is to survive, Pedro must learn to steer a sensible course between extremes and discover within himself his own strength and his own code of behavior.

To be sure, he will be put to the test time and again, and in the process he discovers his sticking point is drugs, which are transported regularly through the region and which are all too available to the locals. Although he marries the hearty, plain-spoken Griselda (Zaide Silvia Gutierrez, who has the looks and personality of Mercedes Ruehl), he is drawn to the beautiful but drug-addicted prostitute Maribel (Vanessa Bauche).

Sosa is such a focused actor that we're able to believe firmly in Pedro—to never lose sight of the fact that he is an ordinary man, dogged in his determination and intense in his concentration, but in no way a superman. In its way, "Highway Patrolman" is a coming-of-age film, both for its hero and for Cox himself.

"Highway Patrolman" is also a beautiful, gritty film, shot by Miguel Garzon and scored evocatively by Zander Schloss. It's steeped in the atmosphere of vast, desert-like vistas slashed by highways sizzling in the heat. A lurid, seedy "Zona Rosa" brothel contrasts with Griselda's large and inviting old family home. While it's a sad commentary on the state of foreign-language film distribution that "Highway Patrolman," which surfaced at UCLA in November, 1992, as part of a contemporary Mexican film series and which bears a 1991 copyright, is only now being released, we can only be grateful that it has arrived at last.

NEW YORK POST, 11/17/93, p. 31, Thelma Adams

Anyone who has seen a movie by Alex Cox ("Repo Man," "Sid and Nancy") will be ready for a wild ride when they get pulled over by "Highway Patrolman," his latest. They're in for a surprise.

"Highway Patrolman" is a spare, lean character study of a cop—in Spanish with subtitles. This odd road movie plays out on one dusty stretch of asphalt in the Mexican interior, the road to nowhere.

With limited material, Cox plumbs astonishing depths. He has reined in his usual excess and opted for a parched realism. The results are as offbeat and unexpected as anything he's directed.

Patrolman Pedro Rojas (Roberto Sosa) has something in common with Cox's rogues' gallery of repo men and murderers and rebels. By trying to enforce a strict moral code in a lax society, Rojas the lawman is also an outsider. He could be a sheriff in a western, a samurai on the border of anarchy.

Rojas is a stiff, trim young man with an unexpressive face. One cheek is marred by a jagged scar. His dream is to wear the badge and drive the car of a highway patrolman.

In the academy, Rojas learns the patrol's cardinal rule: first the officer pulls the offending car over, then he figures out what law has been broken. This isn't Dragnet, although Sosa plays Rojas as straight as Sergeant Friday.

Upon graduation, Rojas proudly assumes his position on the Durango highway. He starts out with the patrolman's swagger, the toreador's strut. He relishes his newfound authority and its external signs: the driving gloves, the shiny handcuffs at his waist, the big car with the powerful engine.

Events soon chip away at the patrolman. He marries Griselda (Zaide Silvia Gutierrez), and she pressures him for money; he accepts a bribe; he roughs up the governor's son and takes the heat; he turns to booze and a prostitute; in a moment of inattention, he receives a bullet in the leg. The shot reduces his swagger to a limp from which he never fully recovers.

In a great scene, the pregnant Griselda turns on Pedro when he returns home from a brothel. Inflamed, she stomps into the kitchen and selects a knife. She flicks the blade through an apple to test its sharpness. Satisfied, she applies the knife to Pedro's throat. The tension and timing are pitch perfect, never melodramatic.

Roberto Sosa won the best actor award at the San Sebastian (Spain) Film Festival last year for his portrayal of Pedro. He delivers a taut performance as the man behind the shades who is diminished but not beaten by the road, the highway patrolman who surrenders his badge and, perhaps, his dreams.

NEWSDAY, 11/17/93, Part II/p. 63, John Anderson

The implacable march music that opens Alex Cox' "Highway Patrolman" is perfect accompaniment for its hero's moral lock-step. He'll be stumbling by film's end, but early on one suspects that police cadet Pedro Rojas' failure to recognize evidence when he sees it may make him the perfect candidate for the inherently corrupt police force he's about to enter.

What, he is asked by an instructor, is the first rule about the motorists he'll soon be pulling over on highway patrol?

"They've always broken the law?" Pedro (Roberto Sosa) asks.

"Correct!" the instructor responds. "Stop them and *then* figure out what they've done."

Despite all this, Pedro takes his dreams and ideals with him as he heads out to maintain law and order on the Mexican highways. But he's burdened quickly by emotional baggage: His father, a no-show at his graduation, has disowned him for passing up medical school. His best friend, Anibal (Bruno Bichir), succumbs quickly to the graft that fuels the force. Griselda (Zaide Silvia Gutierrez); the ranch owner he marries, pressures him for the very money he's try to resist. And he finds little solace with Maribel (Vanessa Bauche), the coke-addicted prostitute he frequents.

Cox, the Liverpudlian director of this Spanish-language picture who has made deft explorations of the societal and moral fringes in "Repo Man," "Sid and Nancy" and the violently controversial "Walker," gives us small victories, stripped-down heroics and story that's so unadorned it's lush. Steering his hand-held camera (and the hands of cinematographer Miguel Garzon) through extended take after extended take, he compounds the sense of impending doom that permeates Pedro's story. Like Antonioni without the self-indulgence, Cox' lingering stare generates dread.

But while Pedro's is a world in which the sun, and avarice, have baked things hard, there's also humor, sometimes just in how inevitable some things are. The first person he pulls over, a blonde who's driving like a lunatic, cries and embarrasses him and gets off without a ticket. Assigned to the pig-trucking route for being too fair to meet his ticket quota, he then takes his first bribe—and watches some happy peasants butcher the diseased pig that's been tossed off the driver's truck. The Third World sexual dynamic is upside down: the wife is a harpy, the whore is a saint. Pedro, whose father was crippled by police bullets during a strike some years before, is himself shot through the knee and crippled after pulling over some well-armed reckless drivers.

There's really very little, though, that's predictable about "Highway Patrolman" outside of the miserable way Pedro is treated, both by the people who pay him and the people he helps. Pedro, the devout believer in the system—and who's given an engrossing portrayal by Sosa—finds his salvation by losing his religion. It's a very modern and precise story, far from uplifting but brutally honest.

SIGHT AND SOUND, 9/94, p. 45, Robert Yates

After graduating from the National Highway Patrol Academy in Mexico City, Pedro Rojas is sent to work the isolated roads of northern Durango. At first, he attempts to strictly enforce the law, despite the Academy's teaching, and the common belief among patrolmen—articulated by his colleague and friend, Anibal—that they can hardly get by without accepting bribes.

When Pedro pulls over a young woman, Griselda, she talks her way out of a fine and swiftly seduces him. Soon, Pedro and Griselda are married, and the birth of a daughter quickly follows. Griselda begins to complain about the meagreness of Pedro's earnings; while, at work, Pedro's superior upbraids him for not hitting the required quota of tickets, and gives him the patrolman's short straw—the pig road. There Pedro's resistance to bribes weakens. Depressed, he visits a local club, gets drunk and sleeps with a prostitute, Maribel. When he finally gets home, Griselda's anger is quietened when he shows her his illicit takings.

At work, after catching up with the drivers of a wayward, speeding car, Pedro lets his guard slip and is shot in the leg. Barely conscious, he sees a vision of his father, who insists that Pedro give up his patrol job. After a spell in hospital, Pedro learns that his father has died. His problems get worse: he insults Maribel, whom he is getting close to; crashes his car; and arrests the governor's son, making trouble for his superiors. Then, when Anibal springs a trap on some drug dealers, Pedro's car breaks down and by the time he reaches his friend, he can only watch him die. Pedro determines to catch the drug gang.

Doing some routine work, he is asked by a woman to come and visit her ill daughter. The daughter turns out to be Maribel, suffering cold turkey; she refuses to reveal who her drug supplier is. However, Pedro tracks down the gang; he lets the runners go but takes the load and stashes it, all apart from the drugs he takes to Maribel, with which carrot he persuades her to go home to her mother.

Pedro follows up his catch by intercepting a drug delivery by helicopter, in the process shooting one of the drug gang. For his achievement, he is honoured, but he decides to resign from the force, sick of the corruption. His job now is to take care of Griselda's family ranch. He also agrees to support Maribel after she threatens to return to the brothel.

About Alex Cox's films, one thing that can be said with certainty is that they are unusual. *Walker* (1987) told the tale of an 1850s American mercenary in Nicaragua through 1980s anachronisms (*Newsweek* covers, limousines). Its predecessor, *Straight to Hell* (also known as *Straight to Video*) endeavoured to parody the spaghetti western with a cast of rock stars and rag mag jokes. Next to these tortured attempts at novelty, his punk biopic *Sid and Nancy* (1986) seems a positively straight and competent piece of work.

His debut *Repo Man* apart, the wilful novelty has not amounted to much. In *Repo Man*, the off-the-wall, whimsical approach to its account of the L.A. auto-repossessions trade worked as an apt and witty short-cut into the absurdities which can arise between men and their toys. Otherwise, Cox's experiments, rather than furnish us with enlightening hybrids, have tended to produce clumsy monsters.

The most curious element of his latest hybrid, filmed in Spanish, is its 'magic realist' touches. The film is shot, for a large part, with an eye to making its realism as dirty as possible—eg. a close-up of a rotten pig sliced up on a dusty roadside—but the 'magic' occasionally intrudes. Most bizarrely, during Pedro's session with a shrink, a Day of the Dead emblem suddenly materialises on the carpet. What this offers beyond an easy (dis)embodiment of the exotic—we're in Mexico, where things don't happen quite the way they do in Kent—is not clear. Since the film's writer Lorenzo O'Brien, also Cox's partner in Together Brothers Productions, was born in Peru and raised in Mexico, he might have avoided cultural cliché. In his defence, it seems that the Mexican public did take to the film.

El Patrullero's style is otherwise marked by extensive use of hand-held camera and scenes shot in 'real time'. The two combine well when tracking Pedro's vain attempt to reach Anibal, who has been attacked by a drug gang. Rather than underline the discovery of the body, Cox wisely chooses to draw the scene's emotional force from the limping Pedro's struggle. He is frustrated, guilty, and already half convinced he will arrive too late, and the camera stays with his desperate on-foot chase: Pedro struggling, dragging his injured leg, the camera struggling with him. Elsewhere, for example when Griselda jumps on her drunken husband, swift, sharp movements are caught as if by a well-placed, nimble documentarist. Effective use is also made of the Mexican locations, especially when characters are followed moving from the sleazy town with its gaudy show of worldliness to the vast, arid landscape beyond.

The script is hardly as compelling. Apparently, the Japanese financiers who backed the film explained their interest to Cox and his team by identifying a samurai story within the script. They noted its central character struggling to hold onto a code of honour in a corrupt world. Parallels can indeed be forced out—our hero fights against temptation; weak, he succumbs; later, he repents and falls on his (metaphorical) sword. Still, the Japanese backers are to be envied their imaginative leap.

The film is not particularly poor, simply unengaging. O'Brien and Cox set out to portray the life of a little, muddled man, coming to terms with life's compromises. There's nothing wrong with muddled characters; they are, after all, the stuff of drama. The trouble is that Pedro's concerns, his work, his soul searching are made to seem all too little. He is put through all the right hoops, his progress tracing the classic curve of the decent man who resists and later succumbs to temptation; and yet there is little to wrestle with. It is as if all the moments which provoke changes of mind are skipped over. Certainly, reasons are given—Pedro is under pressure from his wife and lover—but they are presented cursorily. We are shown him changing, but never given reasons to persuade us why this should happen.

Perhaps to lament the absence of psychological meat is to long for the sort of film Cox and O'Brien were determined not to make. A theme of their stated intentions is to create something different from a Hollywood film, "more naturalistic." In their terms, that might mean avoiding the all too simple shape of melodrama, but here it also results in something inconsequential.

VILLAGE VOICE, 11/23/93, p. 64, Georgia Brown

Maybe the best film at Cannes 1992 was Alex Cox's *Highway Patrolman*. It certainly wasn't noticed by distributors squabbling over *Strictly Ballroom*, NYFF scouts, or the strictly mainstream *New York Times*. And while it's nice to know that Cox won Best Director at a discerning Santa Barbara Film Festival, the point is that New York audiences could have easily missed out on *Highway Patrolman* entirely. (And by the way, whatever happened to Jon Jost's *Sure Fire*?)

The Oxford-educated Cox sure must have a rebel soul to make his best movie in another language.

Still, a year and a half later—*gracias a Dios* and Film Forum's Karen Cooper—*El Patrullero* arrives, and any New York film student (theory or production) who misses this beautiful, wacky, utterly self-assured film should be expelled to the other, charred coast. A lesson New York film schools should be teaching is that filmmakers who resist Hollywood's overwrought grammar and corrupt syntax have a far better chance of reaching the heart.

In *Highway Patrolman*'s case the heart is drawn Mexican-style: a blood-red muscle with arteries sticking out like little stumps. This valiant organ belongs to the movie's hero, Pedro Rojas (the wonderful Roberto Sosa), who appears in almost every scene. As an earnest, hardworking recruit training to be a highway patrolman, Pedro already has troubles. When the instructor calls on him with a hypothetical question about pulling someone over, Pedro stutters out something about the law. Wrong: "They've *always* broken the law. ... First, stop them. *Then*, figure out what they've done wrong." Poor Pedro has an incorrigible honest streak bound to get him nowhere.

Pedro graduates, goes out into the field (the thirsty Durango desert), and falls into the time-honored system of bribes, quotas, and petty theft. He participates but suffers, and, instead of being paid (like his buddy Anibal who prospers), Pedro pays. The system begins taking its revenge. Most of Pedro's adventures are presented as a subtle comedy of errors.

Early on, he stops a woman (Zaide Silvia Gutierrez) who knows where she's going, rather abruptly marries her, and finds himself enmeshed in another dolorous system. Ending up, after one loony, guilt-induced binge, with a pretty prostitute, Maribel (Vanessa Bauche)—addict and mother of two—he gets engaged in still another set of sticky obligations. Plus, he gets shot in the leg and crashes his car. But the wound, the woman, the wreck he drives, as well as the murder of his partner, inspire Pedro to new heights of resistance, and he goes up solo against a gringo-backed drug-smuggling ring. In the long and glorious tradition of the limping hero, Pedro has his moment.

Throughout, Pedro is haunted by the specter (literally) of his father—a man he wants desperately to please but whose heart is hardened. Papa wanted his son to become a doctor, not a "petty bribetaker." Like Hamlet's father, Pedro's appears only as a ghost—that is, as a figment of the son's conscience.

You can call *Highway Patrolman* a black comedy, but its underlying (understated) vision is more melancholy and fatalistic than bitter. Starting from classic comedy's sad-little-man point of view, Cox and scripter Lorenzo O'Brien succeed in taking the little guy seriously psychologically. They also are unusually open about everyday civil ethics south of the border. Although everyone in the movie's Mexico is casually corrupt, the film, astonishingly, has no villains. Gracefully, it conveys a sense of right and wrong without tacking on conventional morals.

What I love about *Highway Patrolman* is how everything about it celebrates the humble, the funky, the honorable. Using a handheld camera (the talented cinematographer is Miguel Garzon), long takes (there are only 187 cuts in the whole film), with delightful excursions into real time (the most flagrant of which is painfully funny), Cox indicts the whole Hollywood force.

Also reviewed in:
CHICAGO TRIBUNE, 3/18/94, Friday/p. K, John Petrakis
NEW YORK TIMES, 11/17/93, p. C26, Stephen Holden
VARIETY, 5/25/92, p. 52, David Stratton

HOCUS POCUS

A Walt Disney Pictures release.   *Executive Producer:* Ralph Winter.   *Producer:* David Kirschner and Steven Haft.   *Director:* Kenny Ortega.   *Screenplay:* Mick Garris and Neil Cuthbert.   *Story:* David Kirschner and Mick Garris.   *Director of Photography:* Hiro Narita. *Editor:* Peter E. Berger.   *Music:* John Debney.   *Music Editor:* Nancy Fogarty.   *Choreographer:* Peggy Holmes and Kenny Ortega.   *Sound:* C. Darin Knight and (music) John Richards.   *Sound*

Editor: George Watters II.   *Casting:* Mary Gail Artz and Barbara Cohen.   *Production Designer:* William Sandell.   *Art Director:* Nancy Patton.   *Set Designer:* Martha Johnston and Brad Ricker. *Set Decorator:* Rosemary Brandenburg.   *Set Dresser:* James Meehan.   *Special Effects:* Terry Frazee.   *Visual Effects:* Peter Montgomery.   *Cat Animation:* Chris Bailey.   *Costumes:* Mary Vogt.   *Make-up:* John M. Elliott, Jr.   *Make-up (Bette Midler):* Lee C. Harman.   *Make-up (Bette Midler, Old Age):* Kevin Haney.   *Stunt Coordinator:* Glenn Wilder.   *Running time:* 93 minutes. *MPAA Rating:* PG.

CAST: Bette Midler (Winifred); Sarah Jessica Parker (Sarah); Kathy Najimy (Mary); Omri Katz (Max);   Thora Birch (Dani);   Vanessa Shaw (Allison);   Amanda Shepherd (Emily); Larry Bagby III (Ernie, "Ice");   Tobias Jelinek (Jay);   Stephanie Faracy (Jenny);   Charlie Rocket (Dave);   Doug Jones (Billy Butcherson);   Karyn Malchus (Headless Billy Butcherson); Sean Murray (Thackery);   Steve Voboril (Elijah);   Norbert Weisser (Thackery's Father); Kathleen Freeman (Miss Olin);   D.A. Pawley (Fireman #1);   Ezra Sutton (Fireman #2);   Don Yesso (Bus Driver);   Michael McGrady (Cop);   Leigh Hamilton (Cop's Girlfriend);   Devon Reeves (Little Girl "Neat Broom");   Joseph Malone (Singer);   Jordan Redmond (Little Angel); Frank Del Boccio (Lobster Man);   Jeff Neubauer (Boy in Class);   Teda Bracci (Calamity Jane); Peggy Holmes (Dancer).

CHRISTIAN SCIENCE MONITOR, 8/12/93, p. 11, Marilynne S. Mason

[*Hocus Pocus* was reviewed jointly with *So I Married an Axe Murderer*; see Mason's review of that film.]

LOS ANGELES TIMES, 7/16/93, Calendar/p. 1, Kenneth Turan

The most important thing to remember about "Hocus Pocus" is not its celebrated co-stars but the traditional label it's going out under. Logos don't lie, and by releasing this film under the Walt Disney Pictures banner (as opposed to its racier Touchstone and Hollywood divisions), Disney is telegraphing that this PG-picture's heart and soul belong to the world of well-scrubbed youth movies the studio used to specialize in.

But isn't this the film with Bette Midler, Sarah Jessica Parker and Kathy Najimy in much-publicized roles as 17th-Century witches come back to bustling life in modern times, camping and vamping it up in a way few toddlers are of an age to appreciate? What are they doing in the same picture with a talking cat and bad guys who can think of nothing worse to do than steal candy on Halloween?

The answer is that "Hocus Pocus" apparently aims to be a family movie of a calculating kind, offering a little something for every demographic group within reach of the price of admission. Younger children can identify with the 8-year-old heroine, adolescents can enjoy either the plentiful special effects or the film's photogenic teen-age protagonists, and parents can watch Bette, Sarah and Kathy romp and stomp around.

A very commercial idea, and "Hocus Pocus" is sporadically successful at making it work, at least on the kids' film level. But after setting up the situation, screenwriters Mick Garris and Neil Cuthbert (working from a story by David Kirschner and Garris) have a hard time coming up with interesting places for the plot to go. So even at 96 minutes (and padded out with pointless, uncredited cameos by Garry and Penny Marshall) "Hocus" feels thin and undernourished from an adult point of view.

The story opens in ye olde Salem, Mass., circa 1693, where the three Sanderson sisters—forceful Winifred (Midler), airhead Sarah (Parker) and eager Mary (Najimy)—are in the process of extracting the life force from a hapless little girl, the better to appear young and nominally beautiful themselves.

Things don't quite work out for the trio, but before they depart this life, they emphatically vow to be back. Cut now to 1993, where high schooler Max Dennison (Omri Katz), newly moved to Salem from free-thinking Los Angeles, goes on the record as believing that the Sandersons' by now celebrated promise is a bunch of hooey.

More open to the legends however, is Max's fetching classmate Allison (Vinessa Shaw), and Max is nothing if not open to getting to know her better. So when he and younger sister Dani (the captivating Thora Birch) run into Allison on Halloween, a trip to the old Sanderson house to check out the tale can hardly be avoided.

The house is suitably dark and creepy and before you can say, well, hocus pocus, the Sandersons are back in business, "three ancient hags versus the 20th Century," as one of the kids puts it. Their mission is to recover their spell book and draw the life force out of every child in sight before the rising sun of a new day turns them forever to dust.

All three actresses, most especially Midler, clearly had a fine time as the sisters of Satan, complete with comically convincing chants and incantations. Their energetic version of "I Put a Spell on You" is breezy and cheerful, which is the tone director Renny Ortega, responsible for the ill-starred "Newsies," has tried for throughout.

But though children may be satisfied (if the witch stuff doesn't scare them) adults will have a harder time with the by-the-numbers confrontations between the witches and the plucky youths.

NEW YORK POST, 7/16/93, p. 27, Michael Medved

Every year, Halloween provides Americans with one of our most cherished excuses for acting silly.

Otherwise reasonable people will wear ridiculous costumes and ghastly makeup, while attending wild parties and behaving like overgrown children.

"Hocus Pocus," which takes place entirely on Halloween, 1993, serves the same function for its three capable stars, Bette Midler, Sarah Jessica Parker, and Kathy Najimy (the giggly nun from "Sister Act"). It gives them the chance to overact in an especially grotesque and childish way, but they're obviously enjoying this silliness so much that it's difficult not to share in the fun.

The three leading ladies play the Sanderson sisters of Salem, Mass., who, in a prologue set in 1693, are justly accused of witchcraft and executed for their crimes. The action then skips three centuries to modern-day Salem, where three kids (teen-agers Vinessa Shaw and Omri Katz, and the adorable 11-year-old Thora Birch) are fooling around in the Sanderson house, now a witch-craft museum, on Halloween. They light a mystical black-flamed candle that inadvertently brings the Sanderson sisters back to life, but in order to stay alive they must suck the life force out of some innocent child before dawn breaks.

The all-night battle between the kids and the coven is hardly the stuff of edge-of-your-seat suspense, but it does provide a few clever twists. When Kathy Njimy discovers that her old reliable broomstick has been stolen she soars into the sky (very convincingly, by the way) on an upright vacuum cleaner. Much of the humor centers on the confusion inspired by Halloween. At one point, the Sanderson sisters themselves are taken in by a middle-aged couple who are dressed up as Mr. and Mrs. Satan—and played by the distinguished directors, brother and sister Garry and Penny Marshall, in amusing but uncredited cameo roles.

Director Kenny Ortega keeps the action moving along at an athletic pace, while slashing the screen with a riot of outrageously tacky colors and garish lighting effects as if to assure us that none of this should be taken too seriously. He manages to recapture some of the energy that characterized his stellar career as a choreographer (for the movie "Dirty Dancing" and countless pop music stars), escaping from the stodgy stupidity that characterized the disastrous "Newsies," his one previous directorial credit.

The most serious problem with "Hocus Pocus" is its inappropriate PG rating (it ought to be PG-13) and its designation as a "Walt Disney Picture"—which may lead parents to the mistaken assumption that it's suitable for small kids.

Children below the age of 10 could be seriously frightened by some of the scarier special effects (a walking, moldering corpse, and a talking black cat that's graphically squashed by a truck, then brought back to life) and they might also be puzzled by utterly gratuitous sexual references. Was it really necessary in a PG picture for a 15-year-old boy to repeatedly show his embarrassment over the fact that he's still a virgin or for his kid sister to tell his would-be girlfriend that the boy's been lusting after her "yabbos" beneath her sweater?

Fortunately, "Hocus Pocus" isn't nearly as disturbing for children as Hollywood's other recent witchcraft extravaganza—Nicholas Roeg's repellent, artful and totally terrifying "Witches" with Anjelica Huston—but it is still intense enough to raise real questions about its intended audience. Since it's too gross for little ones, and much too goofy for most adults, that leaves a narrow audience appeal focused squarely on pre-adolescents. No matter how negative the reviews, they'll no doubt come to the theaters to enjoy this picture and then rent it on home video every Oct. 31 as part of the annual silliness of Halloween.

NEWSDAY, 7/16/93, Part II/p. 60, Jack Mathews

Bette Midler looks more like a dressed-up lab rat than a witch in "Hocus Pocus," and that's about the best that can be said for this misfired Halloween spoof. Every time, Midler turns toward the camera, with those shellacked upper incisors protruding from her pinched lips, a little giggle escapes.

But little giggles aren't what Walt Disney Pictures was hoping for. "Hocus Pocus," which stars Midler, Sarah Jessica Parker and Kathy Najimy as sibling witches in modern Salem, Mass., was to be the summer's surprise family hit, this year's "Sister Act" or "Honey, I Shrunk the Kids."

Instead, it is a sub-juvenile, feature-length Halloween skit, so overacted and obvious its audience has been narrowed to trick-or-treaters.

Midler was quoted recently grumbling about the state of movies, saying most of them are made by callow young men "with no life experiences and no point of view" and that actors have "to make things work."

She may have been talking about this picture, which is nothing more than an idea vamped on for 93 minutes. The idea being that the Sanderson sisters, who were hanged 300 years ago, have been brought back to life in modern Salem on Halloween and have until dawn to achieve immortality by inhaling the souls of the town's children.

Standing between them and their mission are the three kids who accidentally brought them back, and the talking cat Binx, actually the youth the witches turned into a cat before their execution three centuries ago.

After setting all this up, director Kenny Ortega ("Newsies") and writers Mick Garris and Neil Cuthbert couldn't come up with anything interesting to fill it out. The witches fly, they cackle, they even sing and dance, but they don't really *do* anything.

And if Midler thought she and Parker and Najimy were making things work, they were mistaken.

What the actresses created was the Three Stooges of witchcraft. Midler spends most of her time plowing an elbow into one of the others, or bopping them on the head. Between gasps, Najimy (the fat nun in "Sister Act") mumbles out of the right side of her mouth, as if she'd suffered left hemisphere damage while dead, and Parker bounces around and squeals as if she were conjuring the spirit of the beach babe she played in "L.A. Story."

The fact is that actors cannot save a bad script, no matter what they do, and while this one has good intentions and a few good moments, it is more trick than treat.

SIGHT AND SOUND, 11/93, p. 43, Leslie Felperin Sharman

Salem, Massachusetts, Halloween, 1693. Three evil witches, Winifred, Sarah and Mary Sanderson, use a magic spell book to sap the lifeforce out of little Emily Binx to make them young, and turn her brother Thackery into an immortal black cat. The villagers hang the witches, but they prophesy that should a virgin ever light their black-flamed candle, they will return to life.

Halloween, 300 years later. A teenage boy named Max has just moved to Salem from Los Angeles. He scoffs at Halloween and the legend of the Sanderson sisters. His little sister Dani demands that he accompany her trick-or-treating while their parents go to a ball. En route, they meet Allison, a girl from Max's class whom he wants to impress. He convinces them to visit the Sanderson sisters' house, now a museum. While there, Max lights the black flame and conjures up the sisters. With the help of Binx the cat, they steal the sisters' spell book and narrowly escape. The sisters fly out to regain the book so that they can steal the life-force from more children and so live forever, but they must do so before sunrise or they'll turn to dust.

In town and at the ball, Max, Dani and Allison try to get help, to no avail. They trap the witches in a kiln at school. Thinking they have burned them up, they rest at Max's house, but the witches snatch Dani and the book and escape to their cottage. Max and Allison trick the witches and regain Dani. In the final showdown at the cemetery, the witches almost succeed in sapping Max's life-force, but the sun comes up in time and they are obliterated. Binx's spirit is set free from his cat body at last to join his sister in heaven.

Max, the sceptical teenage lead of *Hocus Pocus*, cynically observes that "everyone knows" Halloween was invented by candy companies to boost sales. The jaded heart might add the film and television industry to the list of conspirators. After Christmas, Halloween—in the States especially—is one of the most commercialised pagan festivals that Christianity has ever adapted to its own purposes. On the consumer shelf along with the toffee apples and fake fangs this All Hallows' Eve, Disney is offering *Hocus Pocus*. For all its machine-tooled edges and plastic moulding, its campy sense of fun sticks like Silly String to a hired costume. Its timing is prescient; not least in terms of release date. After the waning of Teenage Mutant Ninja Turtles, sonic hedgehogs and other contemporary flavoured icons, children's products are resuscitating favourite demons of the past. After all, if dinosaurs can be raised from the dead, why not witches.

Hocus Pocus should offer a resurrection to the flagging career of Bette Midler, which was badly wounded by the flop *For the Boys* and the missed opportunity of starring in *Sister Act*. Back on divine form here, this star vehicle showcases her real talents for burlesque comedy and lung-straining musical numbers. Her version of Screaming Jay Hawkins' "I Put a Spell on You" doesn't bury the original so much as transform it into a Broadway show-stopper, complete with sister witches Sarah Jessica Parker and Kathy Najimy singing back-up. There are only a few more songs in the film, but it still has a strong musical comedy flavour which will particularly appeal to parents. "Oh no, I think I've left the cauldron on!" cries Bette/Winifred, just as the sisters are about to be hanged. Director Kenny Ortega's background as a choreographer must have been an asset here. Like the film's ball-goers, bewitched to dance all night, he never lets the pace flag.

Inevitably, a film about witchcraft such as this relies heavily on special effects. After a glut of technology-intensive films this summer, *Hocus Pocus* wisely avoids overdoing things. On the evidence of this film, one would think techniques had barely improved since Disney's 1970 witch-flick *Bedknobs and Broomsticks*.

Apart from the expertly animated talking cat, who also reinflates after being run over by a car, it's all pink smoke, routine flying sequences, and highly stylised matte photography. The pantomime artificiality of most of the effects undercut the plot's subtextual menace, which taps children's fear of strangers and abuse.

Conversely, the realism of the unkillable cat appeals to the fantasies of feline lovers of all ages. When Binx seems to be dead at last, the pathos is surprisingly potent. The use of the slushy strains of "Ave Maria" as he ascends to heaven—recalling the final sequence of *Fantasia*—is strangely moving, for all its calculation. Mixing candy corn with just enough creepiness. *Hocus Pocus* delivers more treats than tricks.

Also reviewed in:
CHICAGO TRIBUNE, 7/16/93, Friday/p. C, Johanna Steinmetz
NEW YORK TIMES, 7/16/93, p. C16, Janet Maslin
VARIETY, 7/26/93, p. 29, Brian Lowry
WASHINGTON POST, 7/16/93, p. C1, Rita Kempley
WASHINGTON POST, 7/16/93, Weekend/p. 38, Desson Howe

HOLD ME, THRILL ME, KISS ME

A Mad Dog Pictures release. *Executive Producer:* Martin Ira Rubin. *Producer:* Travis Swords. *Director:* Joel Hershman. *Screenplay:* Joel Hershman. *Director of Photography:* Kent Wakeford. *Editor:* Kathryn Imhoff. *Music:* Gerald Gounet. *Sound:* Robert Sheridan. *Production Designer:* Dominic Wymark. *Art Director:* David Willit. *Set Decorator:* Terry Whitaker. *Costumes:* Cathy Cooper. *Running time:* 92 minutes. *MPAA Rating:* Not Rated.

CAST: Adrienne Shelly (Dannie); Max Parrish (Eli, Bud, Fritz); Sean Young (Twinkle); Diane Ladd (Lucille); Andrea Naschak (Sabra); Bela Lehoczky (Laszlo); Ania Suli (Olga); Timothy Leary (Mr. Jones); Mary Lanier (Lucille's Mother); John Auxier (Lucille's Son).

LOS ANGELES TIMES, 7/30/93, Calendar/p. 4, Kevin Thomas

"Hold Me, Thrill Me, Kiss Me" is not nearly as funny as it means to be, yet as a minor diversion it's breezy and fast-paced. In an encouraging feature debut, director Joel Hershman proves to be a good storyteller, capable of creating distinctive characters and catching them up in an ingenious plot. It's just that his dialogue and his jokes could be funnier.

After an amusingly zany opening, hunky but feckless hero Bud (Max Parrish) holes up in a seedy El Monte trailer park inhabited by a bunch of colorful characters. Bud, who's on the lam, has landed there after having been picked up by one of its residents, an aggressive, blunt-talking topless dancer (Andrea Naschak). However, it's not Naschak's statuesque Sabra who captivates Bud, but her demure teen-aged sister Dannie (Adrienne Shelly).

The film is at its best as a romance, as Bud and Dannie fall in love amid the screwball shenanigans. Both Parrish, in his film debut, and Shelly are highly appealing actors.

The real find of "Hold Me, Thrill Me, Kiss Me" however, is Naschak, a onetime child actress who moved on to Shakespeare festivals but spent 1990-92 as porn star April Rayne. Naschak's varied background has served her well. She's totally uninhibited—and satirical—when it comes to sex and exhibiting her spectacular body. But she also has a trained comedian's sharp timing and delivery. She understands well that what's so funny about Sabra is that this kinky sexpot has absolutely no sense of humor, especially about herself.

Among the other vivid trailer-park residents are Ania Suli and Bela Lehoczky, a real-life mother and son, who play an eccentric mother and son constantly bickering over the fact that the mother's last husband, an agent, has made off with $150,000. The elegant Suli, like her character in the movie, was a prewar star of films and opera in her native Hungary.

There's more than a bit of repetitiousness in the shrill carrying-on of these two. Hershman should have spent less time with them and more with Diane Ladd as a loveless middle-aged woman who wrangles with her mother (Mary Lanier, her real-life mother) and is stuck with a goofy son (John Auxier, an actual inhabitant of the trailer park where the film was shot). Ladd must have done the picture as a favor to Hershman, who in turn should have given her more to do. As it is, she does have one terrific scene with Parrish.

Appearing throughout "Hold Me, Thrill Me, Kiss Me" (Times-rated Mature for sex and language) is a running gag, Sean Young as a crazed, dangerous heiress who sets the plot in motion. Timothy Leary also turns up as a decidedly shady type.

NEW YORK POST, 7/30/93, p. 25, Michael Medved

"I guess killing your sister and burying your dog and losing your virginity all in one day can be hard on a girl."

So says the murderer-on-the-lam hero (Max Parrish) to his 17-year-old trailer-park sweetie (Adrienne Shelly) in a rare, reflective moment in "Hold Me, Thrill Me, Kiss Me," the altogether outrageous (and illogically endearing) film that's aptly summarized by its 32-year-old writer-director, Joel Hershman, as "a sweet, nasty love story."

Oddly enough, the action begins with a wedding. When our muscular, biker-burglar hero, Eli, hesitates before saying "I do" to a spoiled heiress played by Sean Young, she pulls out a gun and holds it to his head. In the ensuing struggle over the weapon, she's the one who's accidentally shot, and he becomes a fugitive.

Eventually he makes his way to a grungy trailer park in El Monte, Calif., where he's sheltered by a sexually insatiable stripper and part-time porno star (played by the spectacularly statuesque real-life porno star, Andrea Naschak, a.k.a. April Rayne) who's dangerously addicted to chocolate milk. Eli, however, is more interested in the stripper's tomboy kid sister (Adrienne Shelly), a dreamy teen who's only friend is her Great Dane, Gus. The film also features strong supporting work by Diane Ladd (as a fading Southern belle and trailer-park neighbor) and Timothy Leary (as a mysterious, white-clad figure who will help the hero get the fake passport he needs to flee the country).

Part of the fun with this film is the way the well-known people, who appear in it make reference to their own public reputations. Readers of the major tabloids, for instance, know that Sean Young is notorious for her obsessive, unstoppable pursuit of her leading men, so that's precisely the sort of role she gets to play here. At one point Timothy Leary testily reminds us, "I'm no dummy. I went to Harvard, you know!"

With its parade of offbeat semi-celebrities, its plastic surfaces, garish colors and deliberate trashiness, "Hold Me, Thrill Me, Kiss Me" will remind some observers of the work of John ("Pink Flamingos") Waters, but there's a crucial difference. Waters often condescends to his characters, presenting them as cartoonish, larger-than-life figures, but Joel Hershman generates genuine affection for the earthy eccentrics who populate his world. Here, it's the settings and the situations—and not the characters themselves that are hopelessly tacky.

There's also an all-but-irresistible romanticism at work here that eventually overwhelms all the deliberately grotesque touches, like the abundance of vibrator and dead-dog jokes. Newcomer Parrish (identified in the press material only as a "surfer/model") has an easygoing charm and a brooding, smoldering presence that suggests that he might be a long-lost Baldwin brother.

Adrienne Shelly, who previously starred in "The Unbelievable Truth and Trust" for iconoclastic director Hal Hartley, is one of the few actresses working today who can convey innocence effectively. This is essential to this film's purposes. As director Hershman declares. "A romantic at heart, I wanted to present a story of innocent love. I mean, Adrienne Shelly loses her virginity as the title song plays in the background!"

The sound track also features the work of such sensitive and poetic artists as Elvis Hitler, King Missile, the Honey Buzzards and Violent Femmes. This accompaniment should help the picture achieve instant cult status among the midnight movie crowd, while more conventional moviegoers can appreciate it as a guilty pleasure.

NEWSDAY, 7/30/93, Part II/p. 69, Jack Mathews

In the opening scene of Joel Hershman's loony black comedy "Hold Me, Thrill Me, Kiss Me," a wedding at a roadside chapel is interrupted when the groom spits in his fiancé's face and she pulls a gun on him, demanding that, he say, "I do."

"Well, I don't!" he says,

"Maybe you folks should discuss this and come back at another time," says the justice of the peace.

Moments later, the gun goes off during a struggle, and the groom hurries off, leaving his near-bride for dead, and the audience wondering what in the world will come next.

Hershman, a recent NYU film school grad, claims to have written the script for his first feature in 10 days and to have shot the movie in less than three weeks. No argument here. Both gestation periods seem about right.

But as rushed and amateurish as much of the film is, it offers more interesting characters, and certainly more laughs, than "Hocus Pocus," "So I Married an Axe Murderer" and most other comedies coming from the major studios these days.

"Hold Me" plays itself out in the low-rent Southern California trailer park where the reluctant groom Eli (Max Parrish) takes refuge among an assortment of oddballs, each of whom is nurturing an urgent fantasy.

Sabra (Andrea Naschak), a topless dancer and nymphomaniac, is hoping to save up enough money through porn movies and Hustler layouts to become a gym teacher at the local YWCA.

Her sister Dannie (Adrienne Shelley) is a 17-year-old virgin who sleeps outside each night, dreaming of appearing on TV game shows while her sister entertains a parade of cops and pickups.

Their neighbor Laszlo (Bela Lehoczky) is a failed drug dealer who rips off his mother's Social Security checks to play the horses, while his mother (Ania Suli) hosts daily tag sales, trying to make enough money to claim her late husband's ashes from a local crematorium and return with them to Budapest.

Hershman devoted some of his 10-day writing time to developing a romantic triangle for Eli, Dannie, and Sabra, as well as a couple more murders, a resurrection and two robberies of the same money. His best hours, however, were spent writing outrageous lines of dialogue, which were to be delivered deadpan.

"Down deep, I'm a sensitive and vulnerable girl," Sabra tells the skeptical Eli. "Don't let my dildos, vibrators and handcuffs fool you."

At this point, Hershman is a better writer than a director. His scenes are funnier in concept than in execution, and most of the performances are the quality of those in the films Sabra aspires to star in. Laszlo has the best lines in the movie, but Lehoczky never reads them in anything less than a full scream.

Its guest stars—Sean Young as Eli's fiance Twinkle, and Diane Ladd as a hypochondriacal trailer park resident—have a great time mugging it up, without raising the overall level of performance. Only Shelley, a veteran of Hal Hartley movies, and Parrish, a model making his acting debut, were able to create anything resembling real people.

Still, "Hold Me" is full of dark surprises and delightfully malevolent humor. It's "Mickey and Maude" on the cheap, and a nice calling card for Hershman. Who knows what this guy could do if he had a whole month.

VILLAGE VOICE, 8/3/93, p. 56, Manohla Dargis

Speaking of pigs and slop [the reference is to *La Vie de Boheme*; see Dargis' review], Joel Hershman's *Hold Me, Thrill Me, Kiss Me* is cinematic flatulence of the worst kind—sour, flat, rank. When a hunk named Eli (Max Parrish) accidentally shoots his monstrous bride-to-be (Sean Young, sigh), he disappears into the obscurity of a trailer park. There, amid plastic lawn ornaments and fugitives from David Byrne's *True Stories* (does anyone still think hair curlers and obesity funny?), Eli finds sex with a stripper named Sabra (Andrea Naschak) and love with her sister, Dannie (Adrienne "I did it for the money" Shelly).

Shrill and wildly disjointed, Hershman's script jumps from one set-up to another in a panicked search for laughs. Needless to say, it's a losing proposition. In one trailer, there's a washed-up Hungarian diva at the mercy of her sadistic spawn; in another, a lonely woman (Diane Ladd) passing away the time with her brood. For the most part, Hershman lets these bewildered souls twist in the wind, they're just cinematic noise for pretty-boy Eli's tortured stratagems.

From first frame to last, Hershman is clueless. He's clearly cribbing from John Waters, but this debut feature shows none of the Baltimore auteur's wit, style, or intelligence. Most damning is the fact Hershman just doesn't get that Waters actually loves his characters, the "filthiest people alive." No matter how gross, vile, or shameless the circumstance, his empathy is as bottomless as Divine's talent was vast. In contrast, Hershman presents almost everyone but his two leads as cretins, slobs, shrews, losers; he's slumming and it shows. *Pink Flamingos* may feature dog shit but make no mistake, *Hold Me, Kiss Me, Thrill Me* is dog shit, pure and steamy.

Also reviewed in:
CHICAGO TRIBUNE, 8/20/93, Friday/p. I, John Petrakis
NEW YORK TIMES, 7/30/93, p. C12, Janet Maslin
VARIETY, 6/8/92, p. 52, Maggie Brown
WASHINGTON POST, 9/17/93, p. D8, Rita Kempley

HOME OF OUR OWN, A

A Gramercy Pictures release of a PolyGram Filmed Entertainment presentation of an A & M Films production. *Executive Producer:* Patrick Duncan. *Producer:* Dale Pollock and Bill Borden. *Director:* Tony Bill. *Screenplay:* Patrick Duncan. *Director of Photography:* Jean Lépine. *Editor:* Axel Hubert. *Music:* Michael Convertino. *Music Editor:* Ken Wannberg. *Sound:* Steven Laneri and (music) Dennis Sands. *Sound Editor:* Patrick Dodd and John Nutt. *Casting:* April Webster, Cate Praggastis, Alison Zimet, and Ray Simm. *Production Designer:* James Schoppe. *Art Director:* Marcia Calosio. *Set Decorator:* Steven A. Lee. *Set Dresser:* Debbie Farrar and Kee L. Miller. *Special Effects:* Rick Josephson. *Costumes:* Lynn Bernay. *Make-up:* Darcy Knight and Cheryl Voss. *Running time:* 104 minutes. *MPAA Rating:* PG.

CAST: Kathy Bates (Frances Lacey); Edward Furlong (Shayne Lacey); Soon-Teck Oh (Mr. Munimura); Tony Campisi (Norman); Clarissa Lassig (Lynn Lacey); Sarah Schaub (Faye Lacey); Miles Feulner (Murray Lacey); Amy Sakasitz (Annie Lacey); T.J. Lowther (Craig Lacey); Melvin Ward (Father Tomlin); Dave Jensen (Mr. Hilliard); H.E.D. Redford (Mr. King); Michael Flynn (Mr. Wolters); Don Ré Simpson (Gas Station Attendant); Frank Gerrish (Mr. Whitman); George Sullivan (Dave Pollock); Rosalind Soulam (Ilene); Tamilisa Wood (Raymi); Joshua Schaefer (Boyd); Frank Kanig and John Rixey Moore (Cops); Tom Nibley (Mr. Nardin); David Nieman (Owens); Jeff Olson (Bowling Alley Patron); Berit Winge (Pamela); Jasmine Trinnaman (Esther); Micaela Nelligan (School Bus Driver); Whitney Porter (Pigtail Girl).

LOS ANGELES TIMES, 11/5/93, Calendar/p. 10, Kevin Thomas

"A Home of Our Own" would be unimaginable without Kathy Bates, for she brings a tart presence and an unassailable authority to what would be otherwise an overly predictable and sentimental saga about a single mother packing her six kids into a beat-up Plymouth and winding up in a tiny Idaho town. Always a pleasure to watch, Bates is so absolutely real and natural, and is so totally captivating an actress, that the film becomes a touching, involving experience.

It's Los Angeles 1962, and Bates' Frances Lacey has just been fired from her potato chip assembly line job for fighting back when her boss grabs her buttocks. Deciding that she and her kids have about as much a chance of making it in L.A. as an "ice cube in a frying pan," she gathers up her "Lacey tribe" and heads Northeast, destination unknown. Just as her car is about to give out once and for all, she spots an unfinished shack on the outskirts of an Idaho town and swiftly works out a deal to obtain it from its owner, a kindly nursery owner (Soon-Teck Oh).

Frances may well remind you of someone in your own family, the kind of unstoppable woman you're lucky to have as a grandmother—by then she will have mellowed rather than as a mother. She is a proud, determined realist, a look-you-straight-in-the-eye,tell-it-like-it-is, lay-down-the-law survivor with ironclad principles; a firm disciplinarian with high disdain for anything that smacks of charity.

She's also a profoundly loving, caring parent, but sometimes her pride and strictness, her over-whelming sense of responsibility, short-circuit her affections. She's caught up in such an intense, all-absorbing struggle for survival that it's hard for her to unbend, although at times she's capable of laughing at herself, having fun with her kids and, when pressed, of owning up to her mistakes. (When Bates, never slimmer, laughs and smiles, she becomes beautiful.)

But being besieged by poverty and bone-tiredness, she has such a struggle to get a roof over her head and food on the table that it's difficult for her to see that she and her children may need beyond such basics.

Frances is of course admirable, especially in the philosophy of honesty and self-reliance she tries to instill in her kids, but she can be hard to live with. That's especially so for her oldest, 15-year-old Shayne (Edward Furlong), who finds it increasingly difficult to buy into her dream of eventually prevailing over adversity, to submit to her authority and to do without so much of what the other kids at school take for granted.

Drawing from his own experiences as one of 12 children whose single mother took off from L.A. in 1961 to build a new life for her family in the rural Midwest, writer/executive producer Patrick Duncan brings a special edge to Frances and Shayne's spiky relationship.

"A Home of Our Own" has been directed lovingly and unpretentiously by Tony Bill, who elicits marvelous performances not only from Bates and Furlong but also many others, particularly Clarissa Lassig as Bates' sweet-natured eldest daughter and Tony Campisi (Bates' husband in real life) as Frances' would-be suitor, a seeming nice guy who turns brutal when Frances resists his crude sexual overtures.

As pleasing as "A Home of Our Own" (rated R for some mild language and violence in a family drama) is, in so many ways we're nevertheless left with the feeling that there's a grittier story here—that Duncan's own story, if only as one of 12 rather than six children, was lots tougher and maybe not quite so heartwarming as the one he's chosen to tell. Such grittiness would also have helped distinguish this film more sharply from much similar fare on television.

NEW YORK POST, 11/5/93, p. 31, Michael Medved

"A Home of Our Own" is burdened with a bland and boring title, an insipid ad campaign and a star who, despite her Oscar-winning acting abilities, is hardly a glamorous box-office draw.

These handicaps inspire an awful sinking feeling that suggest that despite all the good things conscientious critics may say about it, moviegoers will probably pass up this earnest, admirable little picture.

And that would be a shame because "A Home of Our Own" is full of moving moments and heartfelt performances, Kathy Bates is superb as a single mom who, when fired from her assembly-line job in 1962, loads her six children into a battered Plymouth and drives north from Los Angeles with no specific destination in mind.

She's hoping to find a location that will provide the family with a permanent home, and she thinks she has found the right place when she spots a half-finished shack outside a small town in Idaho.

She persuades the owner of the property, an initially skeptical Japanese-American nursery operator (beautifully played by Soon-Teck Oh), to let the "Lacey Tribe" live there in return for free labor in fixing up the place.

The rest of the movie follows the family's struggles to construct "A Home of Our Own," with mom toiling as a waitress in a bowling alley and spending every spare penny on building materials. To her great credit, Bates never makes her character too saintly or heroic; this is a sympathetic but painfully flawed woman who at times faces problems of her own making.

One of those challenges involves the smoldering resentment of her oldest child who, at age 15, is angry over the fact that he's asked to be "the man of the house." The story is narrated from the point of view of this boy some 30 years later, and is based on the real-life reflections of screenwriter Patrick Duncan who grew up in similar circumstances in a fatherless family of 12 children.

Unfortunately, the key role of this troubled kid is assigned to Edward Furlong, whose performance might best be described as vintage whine: He brings to bear the same brittle, self-pitying tone so evident in his previous work in "American Heart" and, to some extent, in "Terminator II."

The movie also indulges an unfortunate flirtation with political correctness, neglecting to inform us until it's nearly over that Bates is actually a widow, not an unwed mother or an abandoned wife.

This blurring of an important distinction allows screenwriter Duncan to describe his own film in trendy terms as an affirmation of single mothers "who do a fine job of it" and rebuke to "people trying to impose their family values on someone else." Actually, his picture movingly describes the most traditional sort of family values: self-discipline and cooperation and sacrifice.

In films such as "My Bodyguard," "Five Corners" and "Untamed Heart," director Tony Bill has made a specialty of handling quirky material in poetic, compassionate style.

"A Home of Our Own" is his most handsome and lyrical film to date, aided considerably by a marvelous film score by little known composer Michael Convertino. Those who make the mistake of ignoring this release will be passing up one of the more satisfying cinematic experiences of the season.

NEWSDAY, 11/5/93, Part II/p. 82, Jack Mathews

An unemployed widow with six kids, a rattle-trap car, a day's supply of egg salad sandwiches and enough pride to fill a canyon hits the road in the opening moments of Tony Bill's "A Home of Their Own," and though she has no idea where they're headed, we've seen enough of these trials of indomitable spirits to know it's not a place she's looking for, it's a condition.

Frances Lacey (Kathy Bates) thinks it's merely a house she needs, a permanent shelter that will envelope and protect her children, give them the security they haven't felt since their "vagabond Irish Catholic------" father died and abandoned them. Spotting the weathered, unfinished shell of a house in the middle of Nowhere, Idaho, Frances takes it as a God-given sign and is determined to settle right there. After talking the landowner—the sympathetic Japanese-American (Soon-Teck Oh) who runs the business across the highway—into letting her and the kids work off the rent, the Laceys move in and, with the ingenuity of pack rats building a nest, begin adding the walls, roof and windows to Mom's ramshackle dream.

"A Home of Our Own" is a reminiscence piece, a frontier tale set in 1962 and filtered through the memory of screenwriter Patrick Duncan, who re-creates himself as 15-year-old Shayne (Edward Furlong, from "Terminator 2"), the oldest and most put-upon of the Lacey children.

Duncan did not do well by himself. Shayne, who provides the narrative voice, is not as compelling as his circumstances, and he provides no perspective for the period. The family is moving from urban California in the era captured in George Lucas' "American Graffiti," but when they squat in Idaho, it might as well be 1862.

Like many stories from writers inspired by their own family albums, "A Home of Our Own" encourages our involvement almost solely on the author's assurance that, although little may seem to be happening, it is an epiphany in the lives of wonderful, worthwhile people, and there will be a lesson in it for us all. What keeps the audience at a distance is that the lesson seems unique to Frances Lacey. It is quickly apparent how deeply bonded her family is, and her confusion between a home and a house—love versus comfort—is hers alone. Her ample will is calcified with a layer of stubbornness that threatens more harm to her family than good, and which diminishes rather than strengthens her character.

Bates is a potent screen presence, most effective in diluted doses, as she was in "Fried Green Tomatoes" and other ensemble films. Frances is probably the best developed and most central role she has had, but Bates fills her with such aggravated force the character nearly bursts at the seams. Bill's direction, thankfully, doesn't strain for the sentimentality that would have done it in altogether. We can easily understand why this woman would be remembered so fondly by her grown children, and we admire her. But in the end, she remains a distant figure, a face and a memory from someone else's family album.

SIGHT AND SOUND, 6/94, p. 51, Richard Skinner

Los Angeles, the early 60s. Frances Lacey unfairly loses her job in a potato-chip factory after being subjected to sexual harassment. She returns home to her family of six children to find that her eldest son, Shayne, has been caught stealing nickels from phone booths. Having no-one to lean on—her husband died some time earlier—and finding no reason to stay, Frances decides to head east in search of a new life. After a long drive, she finally sees a house she likes—a half-built structure owned by a lonely Asian man, Mr Moon. Initially reluctant, he finally agrees to let the Lacey family live there in exchange for work around his house and nursery. The children attend the local school and find part-time jobs within the small rural community.

Frances finds work herself in a bowling-alley cafe and goes about the business of building her house bit by bit. There are tensions within the family, however: Frances' refusal to accept charity leads to hardship, while her excessive promises of happiness cause arguments between herself and Shayne, culminating in him being beaten with his father's belt.

Frances responds to the advances of Norman, who also works at the cafe. She agrees to go on a date with him and he reveals to her that he has booked a motel room for the night. Angry at his presumption, she rejects him, and he strikes her. That night, she nails her husband's belt to a tree. Next day, Frances goes to work thinking she will have to quit, but she learns that the owner has already sacked Norman.

Just when everything seems to be going well, the house catches fire accidentally and is burnt to the ground. The next morning, the community drives over and starts to build a second house, one in which the family stays.

A Home of Our Own begins and ends with some snapshots of Kennedy-era nuclear families standing against clapboard houses. A rostrum camera slowly picks out toothy smiles while a voice-over announces the film's main theme of family togetherness during hard times. Barely five minutes in and the orchestra's sweltering. Openings like this do not augur well, over-used as they have been for too long in American TV films. Indeed, easy options are the keywords to the movie, the softer the better. After an overlong sexual harassment scene and a few over-detailed shots of depressed L.A., the family hits the road in (naturally) a clapped-out Plymouth.

Braking to a standstill, Frances sees her dream house and badgers Mr Moon into letting her live there. No doubt she would have given him her wedding ring if she hadn't already sold it to fix the car. And so her family begin their gradual, cutesily eccentric integration into the archetypal

Norman Rockwell community. However, what started as a flight of fantasy soon becomes an object of obsession for Frances. Her dream house is to be built at all costs, including overlooking her family's most basic emotional needs and rejecting all offers of help. For Christmas, her children are given a selection of tools and she is genuinely surprised at their disappointment. The scene's punch is pulled, however, by our (and the children's) knowing beforehand what she is going to give them. Basic dramatic tension gives way to slushy sentiment.

This is a far cry from director Tony Bill's role as producer on *Taxi Driver* and chaperone to the careers of Terrence Malick and Paul Schrader, among others. Writer Patrick Duncan has revisited his own past in the writing of this film and it falls into the concomitant nostalgia trap. The L.A. intro is too underdeveloped for us to gauge the family's inner tensions and the film, anecdotal and incidental, hops from one drippy story to another without a solid through-line to guide us. Consequently, there is little real catharsis at the pyrotechnic finale, while the second denouement—in which town and family club together to build the second home—seems to be taken straight from *Witness*.

Also reviewed in:
CHICAGO TRIBUNE, 11/5/93, Friday/p. B, Johanna Steinmetz
NEW YORK TIMES, 11/5/93, p. C29, Vincent Canby
VARIETY, 11/1/93, p. 37, Emanuel Levy
WASHINGTON POST, 11/5/93, p. G7, Hal Hinson

HOMEWARD BOUND: THE INCREDIBLE JOURNEY

A Walt Disney Pictures release in Assiciation with Touchwood Pacific Partners I.. *Executive Producer:* Donald W. Ernst and Kirk Wise. *Producer:* Franklin R. Levy and Jeffrey Chernov. *Director:* Duwayne Dunham. *Screenplay:* Caroline Thompson and Linda Woolverton. *Based on "The Incredible Journey" by:* Sheila Burnford. *Director of Photography:* Reed Smoot. *Editor:* Jonathan P. Shaw, Jay Cassidy, Michael Kelly, and Brian Berdan.. *Music:* Bruce Broughton. *Music Editor:* Patricia Carlin. *Sound:* Bayard Carey and (music) Armin Steiner. *Sound Editor:* David McMoyler. *Casting:* Susan Bluestein and Marsha Shoenman. *Production Designer:* Roger Cain. *Art Director:* Daniel Self. *Set Decorator:* Nina Bradford. *Costumes:* Karen Patch. *Makeup:* Carla Roseto Fabrizi. *Animal Coordinator:* Joe Camp. *Make-up (Special Animal Effects):* Barry Demeter. *Stunt Coordinator:* Monty Cox. *Running time:* 85 minutes. *MPAA Rating:* G.

CAST: Ben (Shadow); Rattler (Chance); Tiki (Sassy); Michael J. Fox (Chance's Voice); Sally Field (Sassy's Voice); Don Ameche (Shadow's Voice); Don Adler (Molly's Father); Ed Bernard (Desk Sergeant); Kevin Chevalia (Jamie); Anne Christianson (Research Assistant); Ted D'Arms (Vet); Woody Eney (Forest Ranger "Mark"); Kim Greist (Laura); Rich Hawkins (Forest Ranger); Robert Hays (Bob); Nurmi Husa (Caterer); Jane Jones (Molly's Mother); Veronica Lauren (Hope); David MacIntyre (Foote); Kit McDonough (Female Foret Ranger); Mary Marsh (Laura's Mother); Nick Mastrandrea (Hal); Glenn Mazen (Minister); Mariah Milner (Molly); Janet Penner (Bob's Mother); William Edward Phipps (Quentin); Dorothy Roberts (Peter's Teacher); Frank Roberts (Laura's Dad); Jean Smart (Kate); Virginia Spray (Grace); Gary Taylor (Frank); Mark L. Taylor (Kirkwood); Benj Thall (Peter); Peggy West (Jamie's Teacher).

LOS ANGELES TIMES, 2/3/93, Calendar/p. 6, Kevin Thomas

"Homeward Bound: The Incredible Journey," which stars two dogs and a cat, sounds like a throwback to old Disney, and in fact Uncle Walt made it the first time around 30 years ago. However, this variation on Sheila Burnford's 1960 novel improves vastly on the original, in which we watched three pets trek interminably through the rugged Canadian High Country in search of their masters accompanied only by cowboy star Rex Allen's off-screen narration. The animals were lovable, of course, but their incredible journey became incredibly dull.

Writers Caroline Thompson and Linda Woolverton have remedied this problem in two ways, by bringing their family into the story and by providing voices for the pets. Anthropomorphism on the screen is a painstaking art and craft, and "Homeward Bound" is a fine, heart-tugging example. Thompson and Woolverton have provided delightful personalities for Shadow, a wise and mature golden retriever; Chance, a frisky American bulldog puppy, and Sassy, a fastidious, weight-conscious Himalayan cat. Their voices are supplied, respectively, by none other than Don Ameche, Michael J. Fox and Sally Field.

The film opens in the High Sierra—annoyingly, the film is hazy on geography and other details. Bob (Robert Hays) and Laura (Kim Greist) have just married, bringing together pets and children from previous marriages. Since Bob, a professor of some sort, has a temporary gig in San Francisco, the family closes up its nice old home in the Sierra and leaves the pets with a friend (Jean Smart). After some credible glitches, the homesick Shadow, Chance and Sassy escape and commence their adventure-filled odyssey.

Director Duwayne Dunham effectively crosscuts between the animals and the worried family in San Francisco. The result is that on one level the film is about three children—well-played by Benj Thall, Kevin Chevalia and Veronica Lauren—whose adjustment to a new family arrangement in a new place is made more challenging by their awareness that they may never again see their beloved pets, on another level, it's a pure adventure for the animals.

The writers have been especially deft with the animal sequences, allowing us to view the world from the pets' point of view from time to time and suggesting that, although the animals are all intelligent, there are some things that humans can know and they cannot. Animal trainer Joe Camp and his colleagues, in turn, have performed miracles with the many cats and dogs that play Shadow, Chance and Sassy.

Formerly an editor for David Lynch, who gave him a chance to direct three episodes of "Twin Peaks," Dunham acquits himself impressively in his feature debut, blending fantasy and reality seamlessly and melding effectively his on-screen actors with his offscreen cast. "Homeward Bound: The Incredible Journey" (rated G) is that rare family film that really ought to please the entire family.

NEW YORK POST, 2/3/93, p. 24, Audrey Farolino

Imagine a movie about a bickering male/female duo (sort of like Regis Philbin and Kathie Lee Gifford) setting off on a dangerous wilderness trek along with a wise and kindly gentleman (sort of like Mr. Rogers). Now further imagine that instead of Philbin, Gifford and Rogers you have a frisky bulldog puppy, finicky Himalayan cat and stalwart golden retriever playing those roles.

The result is "Homeward Bound: The Incredible Journey," based on Sheila Burnford's popular children's novel.

Not having seen Disney's 1963 version of the same story, I'm not equipped to compare this one to the original. But since the intended audience wasn't even born back then, comparisons hardly seem necessary. And judging from the reactions of the small fry around me at a recent screening, this version more than passes muster.

Chance (the bulldog puppy), Sassy (the cat) and Shadow (the retriever) are living the carefree lives of domesticated pets—eating shirts, slippers and scrounged food, then merrily throwing it all up—until the day their family temporarily relocates to San Francisco, leaving the pets at a friend's remote ranch. Increasingly worried by the family's disappearance, our furry friends decide to make their own way home across miles of wilderness.

How do I know the pets were worried? Because these animals "talk" courtesy of human voices that articulate their thoughts (Michael J. Fox is the bulldog, Sally Field the cat and Don Ameche the retriever). A typical exchange: "Cats rule and dogs drool," Sassy informs Chance; "Oh go hock up a hairball," Chance retorts. The device seems silly at first, but it grows on you, especially if you're surrounded by kids howling delightedly at their one-liners.

The animals encounter the usual array of wilderness perils (mountain cats, plunging waterfalls, etc.). Meanwhile, the family (Robert Hays as the father, Kim Greist as the mother, Benj Thall, Kevin Chevalia and Veronica Lauren as the kids) is rapidly losing hope of ever seeing their beloved pets again.

The humor is sometimes fresh, sometimes juvenile, and at times surprisingly gross (should the line "flat-faced butt sniffer" really be in a children's movie?). Likewise, the sentiment teeters between touching and syrupy—but bring a hankie, since even adults might shed a tear or two at the shamelessly heart-tugging ending.

NEWSDAY, 2/3/93, Part II/p. 50, Gene Seymour

Once upon a time, the humans who make movies for Walt Disney were as adroit with real-life animals as they were with the animated ones. This inspired anthropomorphism is one of the more recognizable, if least appreciated aspects of the Disney legacy. Put another way, I bet more people remember "The Love Bug" and "The Absent-Minded Professor" than "White Wilderness," "Peri," or even "The Three Lives of Thomasina."

"Homeward Bound: The Incredible Journey" almost recaptures the spirit of those lovingly crafted stories. A remake of the successful 1963 adaptation of Sheila Burnford's novel, the film's protagonists are a wise old golden retriever, an impetuous bulldog pup and a fastidious Himalayan cat whose family moves from the woods to the city without them.

Though the pets are left in the good hands of a rancher ("Designing Woman's" Jean Smart), the old dog gets to thinking about his pet boy. (You know how it is. We say we own them, but they *know* they own us.)

The old dog decides to make his way back to their old house. The cat and the pup follow suit.

And that's when these guys start running into a succession of things most homebound animals never see in a couple dozen dog years: a set-to with a porcupine, a tangle with a raging river, a duel of wits with a mountain lion. Meanwhile, the three children grieve for their lost critters while the parents (Robert Hays and Kim Griest) do whatever they can to ease the pain. We speak, in short, of "Lassie Come Home" times three.

In the original film, all one needed was the caramel-coated narration of cowboy star Rex Allen to tell you what the animals were thinking as they ran away from bears. This screenplay, co-written by Linda Woolverton ("Beauty and the Beast") and Caroline Thompson ("The Addams Family"), kicks up some freewheeling banter between the animals in the form of voice-overs by Don Ameche as the retriever, Sally Field as the cat and Michael J. Fox as the pup.

Much of this inner dialogue gives the film a scruffy, sometimes coy hipness. (When the pup sees a chicken coop, Fox' voice is heard exulting, "Hallelujah, I've died and gone to Kentucky!") Even at its most self-conscious, however, the device wins you over.

As, for that matter, does the whole movie, despite its grainy texture and go-for-the-tear-ducts sentimentality. One's own memories of the simple virtues of Disney animal adventures of the past—the austerity of the design, the unadorned storytelling—keep getting in the way of wholehearted endorsement of this new venture, which tries almost too hard to ingratiate itself to a new generation of parents and children. But then, how many of them are even going to remember that Thomasina was a cat or that Peri was a squirrel?

SIGHT AND SOUND, 11/93, p. 44, Jill McGreal

Chance, an American bulldog, Sassy, a Himalayan cat and Shadow, a golden retriever, belong to three children—Peter, Hope and Jamie—who live with their mother in a ranch house in the Californian mountains. Chance has recently been adopted by the family after being abandoned and impounded. He is mischievous and energetic, baiting Sassy and ignoring the advice of the older and wiser Shadow. The idyll is interrupted when Laura, the children's mother, remarries. Bob, her new husband, has taken a job in the city and the family must leave their home temporarily. The pets are left behind at the mountain ranch of a family friend, Kate. When she leaves for a few days to pasture her animals, Shadow feels that something is wrong and decides that he must find Peter, and so sets off followed by Sassy and Chance.

Shadow leads the two other pets into the mountains. Chance leaps excitedly into this new adventure but when night falls he seeks Shadow's protection from the unfamiliar sounds and conditions. The next day, both dogs rely on the fishing skills of Sassy for their first meal. On a subsequent fishing expedition, Chance chases off two baby bears but is nearly mauled by their enormous parent. At a river crossing, Sassy falls into the current and is swept over a waterfall. When she fails to reappear, the two dogs continue without her and are chased by a lion.

Meanwhile, Sassy has been found bedraggled on the banks of the river by a mountain man who takes her back to his cabin and nurses her back to health. The next day, Sassy hears Chance and Shadow barking nearby, and rushes to join them.

Later, Chance encounters a porcupine which sheds several of its quills; into the dog's jowls. Hurt but undeterred, Chance carries on and the animals come across a little girl who is lost. They protect her until she is found and the search party recognises the animals from a flyer that Bob has circulated through the county. They are captured and driven to the local pound where they must wait to be collected. The pets fail to understand that they are being rescued and after Chance has been treated they escape back into the mountains. Finally they reach the ranch, to which the family has now returned and the pets are reunited with their owners. Chance's adventures have taught him about loyalty and friendship and he has learnt to consider the ranch and its occupants as his home and family.

Homeward Bound: The Incredible Journey is the way I remember Disney in the 50s when Sunday afternoons around the television consisted of programmes featuring animals and plants in their natural surroundings accompanied by warm, kindly male voice-overs projecting on to the subjects every kind of human thought and desire. Even the Venus fly trap chattered to itself about the juicy flies passing just out of reach while the flies scolded themselves for flying too close to danger.

Homeward Bound moves one step further than these Disney originals, replacing the voice-over with dialogue. It's a daring move because, unlike the animated version, there can be no lip-synch and the first few minutes are distractingly different from other live action feature films, with the dialogue—unrelated to lip movement—being strangely disconnected from the action and the characters. However, with nearly all feature films these days being re-recorded, lip-synch is simply a convention governing the audience's relationship with the screen. It's a relationship which *Homeward Bound* successfully flouts. It helps that the actors turn in good performances; Michael J. Fox is particularly well cast as Chance, injecting just the right puppyish feel into the character and speaking the lines in dog-like yelps with great gusto.

But any sense of innovation is quickly dispelled by a reassuring Disney formula of friendship, loyalty, courage and honour. Set in a mythic version of contemporary America, in which values are simple and wholesome, *Homeward Bound* is irredeemably old-fashioned. Its subtext is Laura's remarriage and its effect on her eldest child, Peter. He cannot reconcile himself to his mother's new husband and sees his enforced separation from Shadow as Bob's fault. It's an old story about pain, jealousy and fear of loss with the relationship between Peter and Shadow presented as a metaphor for love, security and trustworthiness. But it's a pure conceit when the reappearance of the pets at the end of the film puts the situation right. Life just isn't like that.

There are echoes of *Bambi* when Sassy disappears over the waterfall, but it doesn't have the same impact as the death of Bambi's mother. Neither does the film have the same magical visual qualities or simple directness of the Disney animated *oeuvre*. Live action emotions are more complicated and opaque, and I doubt whether Chance's personal journey from friendly but rootless pup to mature, home-loving, trustworthy best friend has much moral sticking power for under-tens.

Homeward Bound comes from Sheila Burnford's novel *The Incredible Journey*. Rudyard Kipling tried his hand at a dog subject in his extraordinary novella *Thy Servant a Dog*: "Please may I come in? I am Boots. I am son of Kildonan Brogue—Champion Reserve—V.H.C.—very fine dog; and no-dash-parlour-tricks." At some points in *Homeward Bound* the writers try unsuccessfully for a Boots-style character in Chance. But the pets have an emotional range and a developmental psychology which parallels that of human beings. Kipling's Boots never develops a conceptual apparatus; he learns through behaviour, as dogs do. He will never understand the "kennel that moves" (his master's car) but it seems implausible that the infinitely wise Shadow should not understand the telephone. For all this, *Homeward Bound* is a bland but pleasing film for young children, and their parents will marvel at the superbly trained animal stars.

TIME, 4/5/93, p. 60, Richard Corliss

[*Homeward Bound* was reviewed jointly with *The Adventures of Huck Finn*; see Corliss' review of that film.]

Also reviewed in:
CHICAGO TRIBUNE, 2/12/93, Friday/p. G, Dave Kehr
NEW YORK TIMES, 2/3/93, p. C15, Janet Maslin
VARIETY, 2/8/93, p. 74, Brian Lowry
WASHINGTON POST, 2/12/93, Weekend/p. 50, Desson Howe
WASHINGTON POST, 2/13/93, p. G12, Megan Rosenfeld

HOT SHOTS! PART DEUX

A Twentieth Century Fox release. *Executive Producer:* Pat Proft. *Producer:* Bill Badalato. *Director:* Jim Abrahams. *Screenplay:* Jim Abrahams and Pat Proft. *Director of Photography:* John R. Leonetti. *Editor:* Malcolm Campbell. *Music:* Basil Poledouris. *Music Editor:* Curtis Roush. *Choreographer:* Lester Wilson. *Sound:* Thomas Causey and (music) Tim Boyle. *Sound Editor:* Gary S. Gerlich and Gregory M. Gerlich. *Casting:* Jackie Burch. *Production Designer:* William A. Elliott. *Art Director:* Greg Papalia. *Set Designer:* James F. Clayton, Sr. *Set Decorator:* Jerie Kelter. *Set Dresser:* Glenn "Spanky" Roberts, Mike Holowach, Michael Vojvoda, Doug Sieck, Roger Abell, Alan Baptiste, Jr., and Kai Blomberg. *Special Effects:* John Frazier. *Visual Effects:* Erik Henry. *Costumes:* Mary Malin. *Make-up:* Ronnie Specter. *Make-up (Charlie Sheen):* David Anderson. *Running time:* 87 minutes. *MPAA Rating:* PG-13.

CAST: Charlie Sheen (Topper Harley); Lloyd Bridges (Tug Benson); Valerie Golino (Ramada Rodham Hayman); Richard Crenna (Colonel Denton Walters); Brenda Bakke (Michelle Rodham Huddleston); Miguel Ferrer (Harbinger); Rowan Atkinson (Dexter Hayman); Jerry Haleva (Saddam Hussein); David Wohl (Gerou); Mitchell Ryan (Gray Edwards); Michael Colyar (Williams); Ryan Stiles (Rabinowitz); Rosemary Johnston (Lavinia Rodham Benson); Gregory Sierra (The Captain); Andreas Katsulas (Rufshaad); Clyde Kusatsu (Prime Minister Soto); Ben Lemon (Team 2 Leader); Buck McDancer (Richard Nixon); Larry Lindsey (Gerald Ford); Ed Beheler (Jimmy Carter); Daniel T. Healy (George Bush); Jay Koch (Ronald Reagan); Charlie Haugk (Navy Seal); Dian Kobayashi (Mrs. Rodham Soto); Bob Vila (Himself); Stuart Proud Eagle Grant (Geronimo); J.D. DeKranis (Michael Corleone Look-Alike); Bob Legionaire (Captain McCluskey Look-Alike); Corey Rand (Sollozzo Look-Alike); Tony Edwards (Limo Driver); James Lew (Kick Boxer Opponent); Gerald Okamura (Corrupt Kick Boxing Referee); Chi-Muoi Lo (Thai Kick Boxing Sportscaster); Ron Pitts (Black Kick Boxing Sportscaster); Norm Compton (Phil); Kelly Connell (Radio Operator); Wayne Satz (News Anchorman); Pat Harvey (News Reporter); Joseph V. Perry (Singing Waiter); Oz Tortora (Singing Busboy); Judith Kahan (Veiled Woman); Shaun Toub (Sleeping Guard); Mark Steen (Adrian Messenger); Carey Tall, Sr. (Train Conductor); Don Miloyevich (Cab Driver); Edward Nassaney (Iraqi Door Guard); Andy Siegel (Iraqi Soldier); C. Ransom Walrod (Iraqi Boat Driver); John Arthur Escobar (Necktie Guard); Nancy Abrahams (Mother Whose Baby is Snatched); Charlie Abrahams (Snatched Baby); Jane Butenhoff (Slim Woman at Banquet); Louise Yaffe and Eleanor Schiff (Grey Edwards' Concubines); Pamela Thompson, Karen "Boom Boom" Proft, and Nancy Steen (Nuns Not in This Movie); Don Gruenberg, Alice Gruenberg, and Jamie Abrahams (Backyard Family); Joseph "Bambi" Abrahams (Basketball Player); Alison Anne Abrohams (Chain Skimmer); Jack Bernstein (Cop); Deborah Hwang-Marriott (Kick Boxing Mother); William Haig Marriott (Kick Boxing Child); Siren and Zap (American Gladiators).

LOS ANGELES TIMES, 5/21/93, Calendar/p. 8, Kevin Thomas

In the divertingly silly "Hot Shots! Part Deux," our first glimpse of Charlie Sheen has us squinting for evidence of special-effects trickery. Surely Sheen's head has been attached via camera magic to a torso far more muscular than his own. But no, it soon becomes clear that

Sheen really has been working out mightily in order to send up Sylvester Stallone and his "Rambo" movies.

Sheen's sculptured physique is virtually the only evidence of effort exerted in the making of this often hilarious film, a fizzy summer comedy concocted by director Jim Abrahams and his co-writer Pat Proft, past masters at the art of disguising their efforts. Actually, there are no fewer than 30 movies spoofed in the course of "Part Deux's" swift 89 minutes, but they come so thick and fast you can't hope to catch all the references. This film is every bit as funny—perhaps even funnier than the first "Hot Shots!" (1991), which skewered "Top Gun."

It seems that Saddam Hussein not only has taken American hostages but also captured two sets of unsuccessful rescuers. What to do but send for the one man capable of saving the day—the indomitable, hopelessly square, sober-sided Topper Harley? But first, CIA agent Michelle Rodham Huddleston (Brenda Bakke)—all the women in the film have Rodham as their middle name—must track him down in a Southeast Asian monastery, where he's in a spiritual retreat that permits him to engage regularly in violent martial arts contests for the pleasure of the locals. (And where the sex-starved monks stop at nothing to try to attract the Sharon Stonelike Michelle, who arrives in spike heels and micro-mini.)

The care with which "Hot Shots! Part Deux" has been made is revealed early on, with our introduction to Hussein (Jerry Haleva, a burly Saddam look-alike). Hussein's stronghold is fabulous, a lush aerie done in movie palace Moorish, stylish with just a soupçon of vulgarity. A mere glimpse at the contents of his refrigerator is good for laughs, and when he takes off his shirt …!

Abrahams and Proft's nonstop throwaway humor keeps spirits lifted and a smile on our faces, and it also has the admirable effect of deflating those action movies that exploit violence in the name of a pious, if dubious, patriotism. It would seem that it's a little late in the day to poke fun at Rambo, not exactly the most current of targets, but this is where the filmmakers' shrewdness comes into play.

Topper and his true love, Ramada Rodham Hayman (Valeria Golino), are back from the first film, and they are endearing in their dense but intrepid earnestness. Even more dense is Lloyd Bridges' Tug Benson, an admiral the first time around who, terrifyingly enough, is now no less than the President of the United States. One of Hussein's captives is a colonel played by Richard Crenna, who played a colonel in all three Rambo movies.

"Hot Shots! Part Deux" looks good without looking over-inflated. William A. Elliott's production design, John R. Leonetti's camera work and Basil Poledouris' score are as sharp and crisp as the actors' performances. "Hot Shots! Part Deux" (rated PG-13 for sexual spoofs and language) generates lots of happy nonsense, but there's no nonsense in its steadfast, unpretentious craftsmanship. Those who stay for the hefty end credits—yes, there is a personal trainer listed for Sheen—will be rewarded with gags strewn throughout.

NEW YORK POST, 5/21/93, p. 25, Michael Medved

If you've ever seen "Blazing Saddles," then there's an easy way to predict how you'll respond to the outrageous new comedy, "Hot Shots! Part Deux."

All those who loved the notorious campfire scene in that earlier film will surely enjoy this ridiculous new picture. If on the other hand, you felt disgusted and embarrassed with Mel Brooks' vulgar version of cowboy flatulence, then you should definitely save your money and stay home.

As for me, I'll confess that I laughed out loud at the "Blazing Saddles" bean-eaters—and also got a kick out of "Hot Shots! Part Deux." Make no mistake; This movie could never be described as a meaningful contribution to Western Civilization. It is gross, dumb, tasteless, silly and immature—in other words, it gives the audience exactly what it wants in a fast-paced parody of this sort. "Part Deux" also happens to be one those very rare sequels that is more energetic, innovative, and entertaining than the original film.

Partially, that's because director/co-writer Jim Abrahams (co-creator of the "Airplane" and "Naked Gun" movies) takes aim at a more promising target this time around. The first "Hot Shots!" spoofed "Top Guns" with Charlie Sheen playing a brilliant but rebellious fighter pilot named Topper Harley. The new film takes its inspiration from the "Rambo" pictures—and all those other deadly serious (and unintentionally hilarious) epics about moody, muscular killing machines (played by Stallone, Norris, Schwarzenegger, Willis and other Hollywood hunks who are recruited for some desperate, top-secret mission.

The assignment this time involves the rescue of hostages who've been rotting in Iraq since the end of the Gulf War. Lloyd Bridges, a senile and demented admiral in the first "Hot Shots!," has naturally been promoted to Commander-in-Chief and as President of the United States he calls Lt. Topper Harley out of his retirement in a Buddhist monastery to handle this super-secret Middle Eastern mission.

Also returning from the first film is Valerie Golino as the gorgeous psychiatrist, equestrienne, torch singer (and now secret agent) who serves as Topper Harley's love interest, Golino has previously co-starred with some of Hollywood's most charismatic leading men; from Tom Cruise ("Rain Man") to Pee-wee Herman ("Big Top Pee-wee"), but she seems to enjoy a special loosey-goosey rapport with Charlie Sheen. One highlight here involves a brilliant take-off of the romantic Italian restaurant serenade from "Lady and the Tramp." When Golino commands Sheen to "Kiss me like you've never kissed me before!" he rises to the challenge with erotic originality.

And so it goes, with non-stop nods to an oddball assortment of fondly remembered films including "Casablanca," "Apocalypse Now" (with a memorable cameo by Charlie Sheen's father, Martin Sheen), a Sharon Stone look-alike named Brenda Bakke who delivers off-the-scale sexiness (and flawless comic flair) that put to shame the overhyped superstar she is spoofing. Richard Crenna, gamely reprising the role he played in all three "Rambo" films as the hero's compassionate commanding officer, is also enormously amusing, when he's taken prisoner in Iraq, his utterly straight-faced intensity help to create the most hilarious hostage videotape in history.

Of course, not all the movie's gags work nearly this well, but there's more than enough in this densely packed 87 minutes to keep you constantly laughing—and appalled. Along the way, filmmaker Abrahams and his collaborator, co-writer and executive producer Pat Proft, have accomplished a miraculous rescue of their own, saving this tired format and making you actually look forward to a third installment in the series.

NEWSDAY, 5/21/93, Part II/p. 62, John Anderson

There's something vaguely encouraging about the way we can laugh at a film like "Hot Shots! Part Deux," where so much of the humor is based on the assumption that Americans can't do anything right. At the same time, that there's so much to laugh at makes you a little uneasy.

"Part Deux" is the sequel, of course, to "Hot Shots," which followed in the pun-and-sight-gag encrusted tradition of "Naked Gun," "Police Squad" and the granddaddy of them all, "Airplane!" To truly enjoy it, the viewer must abandon his or her dignity for at least 90 minutes, and accept the inherent silliness. If you can't do that, stay home and laugh along with "McNeil/Lehrer."

"Hot Shots! Part Deux" (hereafter referred to as "HS!PD") also demands that you accept what is strictly a Bush administration movie, which carries a certain unavoidable staleness. Saddam Hussein (Jerry Haleva) is back, with a lisp and a bad temper, holding American gulf war hostages, plus two teams of would-be rescuers who couldn't get out of each others way. The president, Tug Benson (a hilarious Lloyd Bridges, who's become a fixture in this kind of film) wants Topper Harley (Charlie Sheen), the perfect soldier, to go in and bring those boys back. "You're the best of what's left," he tells Topper.

The problem is, Topper's living in a Tibetan monastery, the kind you only find in a movie by Jim Abrahams (one of the original "Airplane!" team). Where they hold kick-boxing matches in a setting that resembles the Russian roulette scenes in "Deer Hunter." Where they serve runny pig nose sandwiches. Where CIA agent Michelle Rodham Huddleston (Brenda Bakke) inspires the presumably celibate monks to do backflips.

To explain many more of the gags in "HS!PD" would be a disservice. The point, after all, is to see how many can be jammed into one movie, not tell a story, which in this case is pretty obvious. Topper and Michelle share romance and a beauty mark—she gives it to him as a memento when he leaves for Baghdad. In Iraq, Topper reunites with his old love Ramada Rodham Hayman, played by Valeria Golino ("It was a sequel ... I had to come"). And Saddam gets whupped.

Some of the jokes seem tired and predictable; the references to "Casablanca" are overdone and the takeoff on Sharon Stone's interrogation in "Basic Instinct" seems almost obligatory. But there are plenty of solid laughs, none of which we're cruel enough to reveal.

It's probably OK to give a few of the end credits though, which include Fun Facts ("Actor Richard Crenna invented tartar sauce"), a quote from Michael Bolton ("I GOT A LOT OF HAIR FOR A BALD GUY AND IF I WEAR IT LIKE THIS YOU'LL NEVER NOTICE") and the secret to "The Crying Game."

And if you want to know what *that* is, you can go see "HS!PD."

SIGHT AND SOUND, 9/93, p. 47, Nick James

A special forces mission to free US hostages from the en suite prison camp of a mad Middle Eastern dictator's palace is ambushed, panicking the dictator into accidents with machine guns, domestic appliances and finger food. Back in the US, demented President Tug Benson orders a mission to rescue the mission to rescue the mission. His top advisor Colonel Denton Walters suggests Topper Harley, "the best of what's left."

In a Far Eastern gambling shack, Harley has a kick-boxing bout with an oriental, closely watched by Walters and a team of cheerleaders. The Colonel and CIA mission head Michelle Huddlestone follow him to him to help. He recalls his desertion by the love of his life, Ramada, which drove him into the monastic life. Meanwhile the sex-forsworn monks queue to impress Michelle.

At a Presidential dinner, Michelle's knee-crossing brings steam to Harley's ears; in a limousine afterwards, their activities are lovingly videoed by the chauffeur. The following day, having joined a marine unit, Topper is sent to the Middle East where they are met by the local guerilla contact, who turns out to be Ramada. As they sail under disguise in a fishing vessel towards their target, Ramada explains that she left Harley because she was married, and that her husband Dexter Hayman is now a prisoner of the dictator. After destroying a gunboat, the team arrive at the camp and storm it. Meanwhile, President Benson himself swims ashore in a wet suit and proceeds to duel with the madman. Harley rescues Dexter, and nobly defers to him with Ramada. However, Dexter steps off a cliff and once Michelle is discovered to be a spy who betrayed the former missions, Topper and Ramada are re-united.

If, as much reported, Hollywood is currently in a sweat of self-loathing about the quality of its product, then what better barometer of contempt than a Jim Abrahams spoof? *Hot Shots!* was neither particularly venomous towards its model *Top Gun*, nor all that irreverent once it had underlined the lame ideas and stock situations; but it did give some sense of the cynicism behind the gung-ho military blockbusters of the 80s. That Hollywood now feels inclined to disavow the violence that characterised so many Reagan era movies makes this a convenient moment for Abrahams to pump chisel-jawed hero Topper Harley up to Rambo proportions. If the result feels as much an act of bad faith as the Stallone originals, then that's just another layer of symptomatic irony to compound the guilt that studio executives apparently feel about indulging the more visceral pleasures of adolescent boys.

The anxiety which has led to Schwarzenegger's fiscally floppy bout of self-analysis *Last Action Hero* (in which Arnie's 'loose cannon' cop is much like Emilio Estevez's in *National Lampoon's Loaded Weapon*) is evidenced here in the speed and disdain with which film source references are disposed of, sometimes much faster than the actual gags. There's also a strong whiff of nostalgia about some of the sources chosen: the spaghetti-eating scene from *The Lady and the Tramp*, the airstrip conclusion to *Casablanca* (already spoofed famously by Woody Allen in *Play It Again Sam*). Of course it's in the nature of a spoof to flaunt its neuroses, but *Hot Shots! Part Deux* shows surprisingly scant interest in its *Rambo* model. All our amazement is concentrated onto whether Charlie Sheen's new-found bulk is fake or not.

In the era of morphing and animatronics the question may be irrelevant. He looked totally convincing but I'd rather believe that Sheen's miraculously sculpted sinew is fake than accept that he would muscle-bind for a mere spoof. Yet, straight original movies have begun to incorporate elements of self-parody (Nora Ephron's *Sleepless in Seattle*, for example) and some blockbuster concepts are already too spoof-like to bear spoofing (*Super Mario Bros.*) In that context, maybe *Hot Shots! Part Deux* is as close as Sheen can get to *Raging Bull*.

Also reviewed in:
CHICAGO TRIBUNE, 5/21/93, Friday/p. B, Clifford Terry
NEW YORK TIMES, 5/21/93, p. C6, Janet Maslin
VARIETY, 5/24/93, p. 44, Brian Lowry
WASHINGTON POST, 5/21/93, p. B1, Rita Kempley

HOUSE OF ANGELS

A Sony Pictures Classics release of a Memfis Film and Television production. *Producer:* Lars Jonsson and Lars Dahlquist. *Director:* Colin Nutley. *Screenplay (Swedish with English subtitles):* Susanne Falck. *Director of Photography:* Jens Fischer. *Editor:* Perry Schaffer. *Music:* Bjorn Isfalt. *Sound:* Asa Lindgren-Davidson and Berndt Frithiof. *Sound Editor:* Eddie Axberg and Lasse Liljeholm. *Production Designer:* Ulla Herdin. *Costumes:* Sven Lunden and Britt-Marie Larsson. *Make-up:* John "Janne" Kindahl. *Stunt Coordinator:* Rolf "Nicke" Niklasson. *Running time:* 119 minutes. *MPAA Rating:* R.

CAST: Helena Bergstrom (Fanny); Rikard Wolff (Zac); Sven Wollter (Axel Flogfalt); Jakob Eklund (Morten); Reine Brynolfsson (Fleming Collmert); Ernst Gunther (Gottfried Petersson); Viveka Seldahl (Rut Flogfalt); Per Oscarsson (Erik Zander); Tord Peterson (Ivar Petersson); Ing-Marie Carlsson (Eva Agren); Jan Myrbrand (Per-Ove Agren).

LOS ANGELES TIMES, 10/1/93, Calendar/p. 6, Kevin Thomas

The spirit of Jean Renoir seems to hover over Colin Nutley's funny and endearing "House of Angels," which is set in a Swedish country village, the perfect spot to observe timeless human comedy.

In a darkly zany accident the local elderly squire (Per Oscarsson) has been killed and is to be buried in proper formality. Just as the young bearded minister (Reine Brynolfsson) is extolling the eccentric dead man's virtues a stunning young blonde (Helena Bergstrom) enters the church, strides down the aisle and takes a seat in a front pew.

After the services the townspeople are astonished to learn that the stranger, whose name is Fanny, is the dead man's granddaughter, who they never knew existed. It seems that Fanny's late mother, Alice, was something of a free spirit who left town to pursue a career as a singer. Fanny, who has followed in her mother's footsteps as an entertainer, has no idea who her father was.

Fanny and Zac (Rikard Wolff), her show-biz partner and companion from childhood, are completely uninhibited types. Mostly, they're on the road, constantly touring on the lower rungs of the continental cabaret circuit, and they think it would be fun to kick back and rest up in the magnificent, though seedy, manor house Fanny has inherited from her grandfather, who turns out to have been a wealthy landowner with extensive holdings.

Both Fanny and Zac, who is gay, cadaverous and favors black leather, are thoroughly likable, genuinely kind, friendly and outgoing. Yet they might as well be creatures from Mars as far as most of their new neighbors are concerned, especially the women, who are at once shocked by Fanny's frank Marilyn Monroe-like sexuality and intensely jealous of her.

Nutley, a Briton long in Sweden, and his writer Susanne Falck take pains to acquaint us with an array of townspeople and their foibles. The key couple are the Flogfalts, Axel (Sven Wollter) and Rut (Viveka Seldahl). Axel is a virile, taciturn middle-aged farmer who has coveted Fanny's property for years, and Rut is the epitome of small-town small-mindedness, declaiming hysterically that Fanny is a drug-taking harlot.

In a sly, amusing way the filmmakers make it clear that hypocrisy runs rampant in the community, and Fanny finds herself sorely tempted to pick up the gauntlet the community has thrown down at her. However, Nutley et al have ultimately set their sights higher, and in the tradition of Renoir, extend compassion to one and all, insisting upon seeing good even in the awful Rut.

Nutley directs his ensemble cast as well as Falck writes for them, and in Bergstrom he has made a real discovery, a vibrant beauty with Dietrich legs, a stunning figure—and a great sense of humor and presence. What's more, although "House of Angels" (rated R for nudity, sex-related material and language) is primarily in Swedish, it's clear that Bergstrom's English is just fine.

NEW YORK POST, 8/6/93, p. 26, Jerry Tallmer

She must have been a heart-breaker, that Alice. All we know about Alice in "House of Angels" is that she has been dead nearly 20 years when the movie opens in an idyllic, troubled Swedish countryside. And we know that old Erik (Per Oscarsson)—bizarrely dead on his motorized pedal-pusher as the result of a shot at a rabbit—was her father.

Who will get to take over the 250 acres of fields and timber that surround old Erik's big yellow manor house? Well, Axel Flogfalt (Sven Wollter), big-time farmer, power broker, hunter of rabbits, has his cold eyes focused right there, hard.

Axel's wife, Rut (Viveka Seldahl), is a bigoted busybody, and she has a lot to busy-bigot about. Their loafish son Morten (Jakob Eklund), whose talents mostly run to fixing windows, is carrying on with hot-blooded, petulant Eva (Ing-Marie Carlsson), wife of storekeeper Per-Ove Agren (Jan Mybrand), a meek mild chap who takes out his pleasures in secret porno-viewing. Not until much later will we learn how crazy Per-Ove is. Or how crazy everybody in this idyllic landscape is, except perhaps, for Fanny.

Fanny? Who's she? Why, she's the scrumptious peaches-and-cream blonde who has motor-cycled over the hill and into town without announcement in black leather and high heels along with her friend and life comrade, Zak, a sharp-faced, quick-witted beatnik type (Rikard Wolff, film's best).

She's also the granddaughter of Erik, the daughter of Alice. Fanny (Helena Bergstrom) doesn't know who her father was, or is. But she knows that Grandfather Erik's land and house belong to her.

Before the film is completed all hell will have broken loose, all sorts of joyous upsets will have happened as a subversive consequence of Fanny and Zac, including the mass nude singing of "Auld Land Syne" on a riverbank and laughing Fanny will discover herself blessed with not just one confessing papa, but two. We're blessed too.

NEWSDAY, 8/6/93, Part II/p. 59, John Anderson

They certainly know about sin in the little Swedish village at the center of Colin Nutley's "House of Angels." The wife of the town's richest man, Axel (Sven Wollter), is cavorting with the pastor; her son is doing it in his Land Rover with the local shopgirl, and her brother watches porno on his VCR all day long. Axel spends his days coveting Angels Farm, owned by his aged and soon-to-be-dead neighbor Erik (Per Oscarsson). And everyone is blind to the others' peccadillos.

Evil, however is another story. The villagers think they recognize it when Erik's granddaughter, the beautiful, blond cabaret entertainer Fanny (Helena Bergstrom), arrives to claim Angels Farm. And why not: She's trashed Axel's plans, distracted all the men and driven the women into a jealous tizzy. She's darkness with a smile, so hard to hate the villagers are convinced she's dangerous.

Their intolerance is the only evil, of course, and director Nutley and screenwriter Susanne Falck have devised a farcical morality play that remains gentle and warm in its evocation of rural life, even when the townspeople are at their most vitriolic, and the film is at its most obvious.

This third feature by Nutley ("The Ninth Company," "Black Jack") owes a lot to Bill Forsythe's fabled "Local Hero," although the roles are reversed: Here, the visitors to the countryside are enlightened, rather than vice versa. But the same kind of affection for human foible ameliorates the characters vicious small-mindedness, to the point where you might even want to move there.

"House of Angels" is also a journey of self-discovery, for everyone. Accompanied by the large, leather-clad Zac (Rikard Wolff, her boyfriend and fellow performer (their sexual tastes are flexible, it seems), Fanny has come looking for her roots, as well as her land. Her late mother, a fondly remembered local favorite, never told her who her father was, so she hopes to find something out. Along the way, she brings the reclusive Petersson brothers, Gottfried and Ivar

(Ernst Gunther and Tord Peterson) out of their shell; brings Axel and his wife, Rut (Viveka Seldahl), up short, and, with all the angst and ill will she has generated among his congregation, provides Fleming, the pastor (Reine Brynolfsson) with a genuine mission.

Along the way, there are some comic scenes, propelled largely by the magnetic presence of Helena Bergstrom, who is hard not to look at. The way she lets the village gossip roll off her back is charming; when she finally loses it, her responses—having a visiting troupe of Berlin performers bathe naked before the well-mannered but brutish Axel, laughing in his wife's face when Rut goes on a spectacular tirade and flaunting her superior sexuality before the frumpish local women—make her a heroine of understated but epic proportions.

That Fanny is troubled makes her all the more attractive, as does the way Nutley lets the shadows slowly grow around her. All the characters, in fact, develop in a natural, convincing way that makes "House of Angels" very human and very warm.

SIGHT AND SOUND, 7/93, p. 36, Tom Charity

A small village in Western Sweden. No sooner has eccentric widower Erik Zander presented his will to the local solicitor, Ragmar, than he is killed in a bizarre motor accident involving the parish priest. The man who owns the neighbouring farm, Axel Flogfalt, can barely disguise his glee at the prospect of getting his hands on the valuable surrounding woodland at the forthcoming auction.

He and his wife are shocked when an heir appears out of nowhere to take up the claim: Erik's mysterious granddaughter Fanny. A cabaret artiste, she arrives mid-funeral on the back of a Harley Davidson with her leather-clad friend Zac. The small, insular community is immediately scandalised by Fanny's bleach-blonde appearance and forthright behaviour. She and Zac move into the Zander house. Fanny is prepared to sell, but the alacrity with which Axel makes his offer gives her pause. She is also sure that one of the villagers is her father, though her mother never revealed his identity. The most likely candidate is the taciturn Ivar Petterson, who lives with his brother Gottfried. Ivar won't be drawn, but Fanny befriends Gottfried, who is happy to recollect the golden summer days before Fanny's mother quit the village so suddenly. Many of the other villagers, however, are not so amiable. Local housewives are jealous of the attention she attracts from their menfolk, and the Flogfalts are particularly vituperative in their condemnation.

The antipathy is such that the parish priest feels he has to intervene. He inveigles Fanny and Zac to invite their friends from the cabaret circuit to put on a show in the church, so that the villagers may understand and appreciate what they do. Despite its outre nature, the show is a great success, and the community is reconciled. Mrs Flogfalt is moved to show her husband a letter nearly three decades old. It is from Fanny's mother to the father of her daughter—Axel. Fanny sells him the land and determines to get back to her career, but she keeps the house so that she may return.

British-born director Colin Nutley must now consider himself a Swedish film-maker. After a brief career in TV in this country (most notoriously the series *Annika*, about a Swedish au pair), he moved to Sweden to make a series of documentaries, one of which inspired this, his third local feature film. One would be hard put to identify a specifically 'British' intelligence at work here, although it is probably worth pointing out that the movie concerns an insular community coming to terms with a foreign interloper, and one who works in showbiz at that (Fanny and Zac work the cabaret circuit in Germany).

The theme is a familiar one, and the treatment is nothing if not leisurely. Nutley pictures a warm pastoral idyll, and gears his film to a suitably rural pace. Even the bizarre motor accident which instigates the action takes place at no more than 30 mph. This may be a study of small-town bigotry, but the director's instincts are generous: he allows his characters their foibles. That said, at about half an hour too long, the film cannot really afford its sketchy development, and it is seriously let down by the facile homilies which comprise Nutley's dramatically suspect conclusion. The local priest painstakingly spells out the relevant lesson—love thy neighbour—before taking the unconventional step of handing over his church to a troupe of drag artists and cabaret performers in the (vindicated) belief that they will win over his conservative congregation. Even Nutley must have entertained doubts about such a schmaltzy showbiz epiphany, since he cuts away from the performance for an equally phoney climax in which a degenerate villager attempts to burn down the Zander farm—the extent of this character might be summed up, *Dances With Wolves*-style, as 'Impotent Dramatic Scapegoat who Watches Porn.'

VILLAGE VOICE, 8/10/93, p. 49, Georgia Brown

Likewise a bid for tolerance and the extension of cultural boundaries [the reference is to *The Wedding Banquet*] is Colin Nutley's *House of Angels*, recently the most popular film in Sweden. Written by Susanne Falck, this didactic social comedy is based on an old story: Fast urban life intrudes into the backcountry where values are strict (if secretly flouted), prejudice reigns, and people have been this way for centuries. The theme is specifically European, though it sometimes surfaces in this country, too.

Even before old Erik has died, his neighbor Axel (Sven Wollter) has dibs on his vast property. No one in the village realizes Erik had a granddaughter, and certainly no one could imagine one as provocative as Fanny (Helena Bergstrom), who shows up for the funeral in racy black leather on a motorcycle. She's accompanied by a fellow cabaret performer—lanky, hirsute (and gay?) Zac (Rikard Wolff), whose wont it is to grin wolfishly. The two look alarming but are really quite harmless.

House of Angels doesn't avoid a typical flaw of this sort of picture: The city visitors—supposed to represent (sexual) liberation from stodgy or perverted ways—aren't really very appealing, or talented. Furthermore, the country bumpkins are often so simplistically caricatured, the critique seems smug. Maybe if you're Swedish it's more trenchant.

Also reviewed in:
CHICAGO TRIBUNE, 11/12/93, Friday/p. I, Michael Wilmington
NEW YORK TIMES, 8/6/93, p. C10, Janet Maslin
VARIETY, 2/17/92, p. 70, Gunnar Rehlin
WASHINGTON POST, 1/7/94, p. B6, Rita Kempley
WASHINGTON POST, 1/7/94, Weekend/p. 34, Desson Howe

HOUSE OF CARDS

A Miramax Films release of a Penta Pictures production. *Executive Producer:* Vittorio Cecchi Gori and Gianni Nunnari. *Producer:* Dale Pollock, Lianne Halfon, Wolfgang Glattes, and Jonathan Sanger. *Director:* Michael Lessac. *Screenplay:* Michael Lessac. *Story:* Michael Lessac and Robert Jay Litz. *Director of Photography:* Victor Hammer. *Editor:* Walter Murch. *Music:* James Horner. *Sound:* Thomas Brandau. *Casting:* Mali Finn. *Production Designer:* Peter Larkin. *Art Director:* Charley Beal. *Set Decorator:* Leslie E. Rollins. *Costumes:* Julie Weiss. *Running time:* 108 minutes. *MPAA Rating:* PG-13.

CAST: Kathleen Turner (Ruth Matthews); Tommy Lee Jones (Jake Beerlander); Asha Menina (Sally Matthews); Shiloh Strong (Michael Matthews); Esther Rolle (Adelle); Park Overall (Lillian Huber); Michael Horse (Stoker); Anne Pitoniak (Judge); Joaquin Martinez (Sectenel); Jacqueline Cassel (Joey's Mother); John Henderson (Bart Huber); Craig Fuller (Roy Huber); Rick Marshall (Frank Stearson); Reuben Valiquette Murray (Reuben); Emily Russell (Emily); Joseph Michael Sipe, Jr. (Joey); Yvette Thor (Melissa); Connie Mashburn (Teacher); Samuel David Miller (Samuel); Michael McDaniel (Michael); Robert W. Lyon (Robert); LuChera Huntley (Luchera); Issac J. Banks (Issac); Eric Coble (Eric).

LOS ANGELES TIMES, 6/25/93, Calendar/p. 14, Kevin Thomas

"House of Cards" is the latest in the "Lorenzo's Oil"/Mother Knows Best genre in which a parent defies traditional medical wisdom in treating her mysteriously ailing infant.

As such, the film projects a powerful and original vision, only to undercut it constantly by a trite and tedious battle of wills between the mother (Kathleen Turner) and a child psychologist

(Tommy Lee Jones). It is further undermined by a persistent aura of contrivance and a crucial lack of clarity. Since "House of Cards" actually gets somewhere, it's too bad it wasn't thought out more fully.

Turner plays Ruth Matthews, a wife and mother who witnessed her husband falling to his death from a pyramid in Mexico while on some kind of archeological project. (The professions of husband and wife aren't clear; production notes tell us they're architects).

Just before returning home to the United States, Ruth's bright, inquisitive 6-year-old daughter Sally (Asha Menina, a grave, wistful presence and the film's key strength) has a parting, conversation with a mystical archeologist who draws upon Mayan beliefs to comfort her, telling her that her father has gone to live on the moon.

By the time Ruth, Sally and her older brother Michael (Shiloh Strong) have arrived at their home, a large Victorian in a rural setting—production notes reveal that it's somewhere in North Carolina—Sally seems to be in a trance.

"House of Cards" now commences its drawn-out collapse. To begin with, it's hard to understand how Michael, established swiftly as an otherwise mature, responsible adolescent, would induce his sister, by now a virtual sleepwalker, to retrieve a baseball by walking in—not along—a gutter bordering the roof. Soon both Sally and her mother, who tried to rescue her, are in danger of falling.

Ruth, however, remains in deep denial about her daughter's condition even after they both have been rescued by Jones' Dr. Beerlander. It's even harder to understand why Ruth, established as a smart, gutsy woman; refuses to hear out Beerlander in his understandable concern for Sally.

Presumably, writer-director Michael Lessac wants to plug into the widespread distrust of the medical Establishment, but a more profitable strategy would have been to move beyond this cliché to present mother and doctor as partners for whom the occasional disagreement is understandable in their pursuit to reach Sally.

Far too often Turner and Jones are required to fall back upon their movie-star charisma in participating in a verbal Ping-Pong match that threatens to lower "House of Cards" to the level of routine TV-movie fare. Beerlander endlessly reiterates his philosophy that "normal is awesome" in regard to the goals he sets for the children in his care, while Ruth stubbornly insists that his traditional methods might well shatter her child's uniqueness.

"House of Cards" (rated PG-13 for theme), which has an insistently eerie James Horner score, picks up considerably when Ruth hits upon an idea that may enable her to enter her child's hermetic world and retrieve her from it. This inspiration, to which the film's curious title refers, is expressed imaginatively yet is marred by needless confusion at key moments of its unfolding. "House of Cards" is admirable in its persistent ambitiousness but is finally too flawed to be satisfying.

NEW YORK POST, 6/25/93, p. 32, Matthew Flamm

There are scenes in "House of Cards" in which the film—about a disturbed, gifted child—seems like the real thing: a sensitive little drama that doesn't use mental aberrations merely as a hook.

It even seems for a while that the characters are following their own dictates, rather than being pushed around by the plot. The child's mother is the picture of parental fear and concern as she resists the common sense arguments of the child psychologist, who wants the little girl brought in for tests.

Ruth Matthews (a pudgy Kathleen Turner), recently widowed and just back home after three years digging in the Mayan ruins, can barely handle her own grief, let alone her daughter's. So it seems that she *could* talk herself into believing there was nothing wrong with little Sally, who hasn't spoken since they returned to the States.

Sally, a precocious 6-year-old (played affectingly by 8-year-old newcomer Asha Menina), has also taken to climbing sleepwalker-like up trees and atop buildings. Beerlander, the psychologist sent out by the girl's school, makes his entrance at the household just as Ruth is trying desperately to coax her child off the roof.

Tommy Lee Jones plays the tough-minded shrink with a directness that makes his first scenes with the equally convincing Turner absolutely credible. It's only later, when he has to shout lines at her like "Do you think you're the first person to see God in the face of a child?" that they seem to be in a movie-of-the-week.

And Ruth never does get the message that her daughter might be autistic—nor does she need to, which is one of the ways "House of Cards" turns out to be so much smoke and mirrors.

Ruth, in the tradition of movie mothers who believe faith out-weighs knowledge, thinks Sally is sending signals. These include the giant house of cards the girl builds one night out of family photos, Tarot and playing cards. Unfortunately for the air of suspense the film tries to create, the signals can be read by the audience long before their meaning dawns on Ruth.

"House of Cards" has altogether too much meaning. It's too bad that Michael Lessac, making his feature directing debut from his own script, didn't have more of a story. Or that he couldn't resist exploiting real heartbreaking problems—and, in a tour of an actual mental health center, real life victims—for the sake of a movie whose connection to them is dubious at best.

NEWSDAY, 6/25/93, Part II/p. 54, John Anderson

What writer-director Michael Lessac *seems* to be trying to tell us in "House of Cards" is that the parent of an autistic child can ignore the advice of experts, ignore the best interests of the child and exhibit a self-absorption that borders on the neurotic, because everything will work out as long as she loves the child enough. Which seems like a gross insult to any parent who's had to deal with this problem, and is certainly a waste of time for the rest of us.

Ruth Matthews (Kathleen Turner), isn't a totally unsympathetic character, but she's no heroine. An architect, she's spent the last several years working on an archeological restoration in Mexico—during which time she watched her husband fall to his death from a pyramid—and now she has returned with her two children to their home in North Carolina. It isn't long before daughter Sally (Asha Menina) starts exhibiting signs of autism.

Sally's symptoms include a recurrent howling, prompted by any change in the familiar. When her brother Michael (Shiloh Strong) moves her dolls out of order, for instance, she howls. She also has no fear of heights: Retrieving a baseball for Michael from the roof of their house, she's silent and placid, until her mother comes out the window to "rescue" her and the howling starts. Making a timely arrival is psychologist Jake Beerlander (Tommy Lee Jones), a specialist in autism sent by Sally's school. Jake asks what's different, Michael says it's Ruth's baseball cap—which she has put on backward—and by turning it back around, she turns Sally off.

If it were left to Ruth, Sally would still be out there howling. But Ruth rejects Beerlander's diagnosis of her daughter, denies there's anything wrong, chalks up all Sally's strange behavior to the girl's grief over her father. Only the intercession of the courts can get professional help for the girl.

When Sally builds an intricate, delicate house of cards—playing cards, Tarot cards, old photos of her father—it's clear to Ruth that she's reaching out, that she's saying something worth listening to. As Jake points out, it might be nice if she and the other autistic kids could tie their shoes, but Ruth is more concerned with the creative energies the child is displaying, and how it connects to Ruth.

What are we to think about all this? Ruth is virtually an abusive parent, one who's in chronic denial about her own child, and so fascinated by the other idiot savants Jake treats at his center that she intrudes on their treatment. Her position is that a Sally saved by Jake's brand of psychology wouldn't be Sally anymore. "She isn't Sally now," Jake tells her. But it doesn't seem to sink in.

When Ruth builds a giant replica of Sally's house of cards in the woods near their home, it proves to be the spark needed to bring Sally back from her mental prison. It's not only a ludicrous finale, it's a jumbled mess of dream sequences in which Ruth and Sally apparently visit each other's subconsciouses. It hardly matters, though, nor do the performances: Turner does a lot of sighing to signify her sad plight, and Jones, whose patient, dedicated Jake should have been the hero of the piece, has his legs cut out from under him by an absurdly contrived ending and a mentality that reduces a child's mental illness to a dramatic device.

VILLAGE VOICE, 7/13/93, p. 58, James Hannaham

Little Sally (Asha Menina, owing much to Dominique Dunne) won't talk or respond to stimuli after returning home from Mexico, where her architect father died several months before while working at an ancient Mayan ruin. She's mysteriously developed a heightened sense of balance (which she demonstrates on her unstable rooftop), a newfound architectural savvy and a damn good fastball. Her mom, Ruthie (a refreshingly frumpy Kathleen Turner), and child psychologist Jake T. Beerlander (Tommy Lee Jones) can't agree on an approach to returning Sally to "normal," whatever that means. Ruthie's approach includes an attempt to understand the meaning of the playing-card palace Sally obsessively constructs by building a similar structure on a much larger scale.

The negative buzz this movie generated from its lengthy shelving isn't entirely deserved. In a strong dose, and one of its elements could have made for a high degree of revulsion; the virtual reality sequences in particular, though an excuse for rad visuals, couldn't suspend a seven-year-old's disbelief. The hokey idea that Mayan mystics have transformed Sally into a "child who sees things" could have gotten stale fast, ditto the sentimental home-for-children bits.

But stitched together in a way that doesn't suggest either as a definite answer, *House of Cards* manages to sustain the same kind of feminine, symbol-laden suburban spookiness that made me love last year's Belly LP, *Star*. I only wish it had been made by people more adept at exploring its two interesting themes—that one might understand someone or otherwise "bring them back" by duplicating their artwork, and that only a thin line separates artistic expression from autistic expression.

Also reviewed in:
CHICAGO TRIBUNE, 7/2/93, Friday/p. M, Clifford Terry
NEW YORK TIMES, 6/25/93, p. C18, Vincent Canby
VARIETY, 2/15/93, p. 84, Todd McCarthy
WASHINGTON POST, 7/2/93, p. B7, Rita Kempley
WASHINGTON POST, 7/2/93, Weekend/p. 32, Desson Howe

HOUSEHOLD SAINTS

A Fine Line Features release of a Jones Entertainment Group/Newman-Guay production. *Executive Producer:* Jonathan Demme. *Producer:* Richard Guay and Peter Newman. *Director:* Nancy Savoca. *Screenplay:* Nancy Savoca and Richard Guay. *Based on the novel by:* Francine Prose. *Director of Photography:* Bobby Bukowski. *Editor:* Beth Kling. *Music:* Alex Steyermark. *Music Editor:* James Flatto. *Sound:* William Sarokin. *Sound Editor:* Skip Lievsay. *Casting:* John Lyons and Julie Madison. *Production Designer:* Kalina Ivanov. *Art Director:* Charles Lagola. *Set Designer:* Jeff McDonald. *Set Decorator:* Karen Wiesel. *Set Dresser:* Timothy Pope and Gordon Robert Keath. *Special Effects:* Greg Hull. *Costumes:* Eugenie Bafaloukos. *Make-up:* Kathryn Bihr. *Stunt Coordinator:* Eliza Coleman. *Running time:* 124 minutes. *MPAA Rating:* R.

CAST: Tracey Ullman (Catherine Falconetti); Vincent D'Onofrio (Joseph Santangelo); Lili Taylor (Teresa); Judith Malina (Carmela Santangelo); Michael Rispoli (Nicky Falconetti); Victor Argo (Lino Falconetti); Michael Imperioli (Leonard Villanova); Rachael Bella (Young Teresa); Illeana Douglas (Evelyn Santangelo); Joe Grifasi (Frank Manzone); Dale Carmen (Father Matthias); John DiBenedetto (Augie Santangelo); Marie DeCicco (Rita); Nancy Marie (Cindy Zagarella); Sam Josepher (Lorraine); Elizabeth Bracco (Fran); Jessica DiCicco (Young Cindy Zagarella); Mabel McKeown (Judy); Robert Stoke (Host); Marianne Leone (Sr. Cupertino); Thomas A. Ford (Vincenzo Santangelo); George Teng (Mr. Shen); Mary Portser (Mrs. Harris); Dzeni Teng (Pat Shen); Elizabeth D'Onofrio (Mary); Phyliss Wenderlich (Sr. John Xavier); Schelli Barbaro (Sr. Agnes); Ann Tucker (Sr. Philomena); Sebastian Roche (Jesus); Dorothy Hughes (Mrs. Angela Linari); Beatrice Boyle (Nun/Receptionist); Chalotz Lagola (Johnny); Dawn Saito (Mme. Butterfly); Loretta Bassani (Antoinette); Caterina D'Alessio (Rossina); Marta Fensore (Maria); Caolgero Savoca (Louis);

Anthony Manzo and Vincent Fensore (Neighbors);   STORYTELLERS: Irma St. Paul (Mary); Leonardo Cimino (Mario);   Rosemary De Angeles (Older Mother);   Dianna Salvanto (Young Mother);   Max Fetner (Little Boy);   Christina Rosa and Gabriella Rosa (Baby).

CHRISTIAN SCIENCE MONITOR, 9/21/93, p. 14, David Sterritt

One movie at a time, women continue to challenge the long-held male domination of American film. Recent examples of this effort, from "The Ballad of Little Jo" to "The Joy Luck Club" and "Boxing Helena," show female directors and writers tackling difficult subjects that relate to women on social as well as cinematic grounds.

These include family relations, issues of equality and independence, and freedom from both oppression and idealization by power-wielding men. While far from perfect, the films raise questions and provoke thought in ways that few pictures from Hollywood's old-boy network care to do.

The most fascinating of the latest woman-made movies is "Household Saints," directed by Nancy Savoca from a screenplay she wrote with Richard Guay, based on a novel by Francine Prose.

This film has a structural flaw—its first and second halves are not well-integrated with each other—that may confuse moviegoers and prevent the picture from finding the audience it deserves. For spectators who open their hearts to its deeply felt story, however it offers rich rewards.

The story begins as a comedy-drama about broadly drawn Italian-American characters, showing how a butcher named Joseph Santangelo wins the hand of young Catherine Falconetti from her father in a late-night pinochle game.

Catherine doesn't like the idea of an arranged marriage—this isn't the Old Country, she spiritedly reminds her dad—but no better prospects have come along. So she marries Joe, moves into his home, and sets about coping with his strong-willed mother, who has a story, a saying, and a superstition to suit every conceivable occasion.

The first half of "Household Saints" focuses on these characters and a few others in the neighborhood, sketching a frequently amusing portrait of Italian-American folkways without breaking any new ground. But the movie undergoes a major shift when Catherine and Joe have a daughter named Teresa, who proves to be a most unusual child.

From her earliest years, she is preoccupied with questions about her Roman Catholic faith, and by high school age she's determined to become a nun. Joe rigidly opposes this—he's a religious man, but very skeptical about the church—so Teresa decides to honor God through fastidious devotion to ordinary daily activities, particularly the household tasks often thought of as thankless "women's work."

She carries her self-sacrifice to extremes that are obviously unwise, as when she goes through a period of refusing to eat for religious reasons. Yet she manages to function in the everyday world—going to college, finding a boyfriend, discovering sex—until she has a mystical visitation one afternoon over her ironing board. She is convinced she's been specially blessed; everyone else is convinced she's lost contact with reality. The end of the story is either tragic or triumphant depending upon one's view of Teresa and her quest.

It would have been easy for the filmmakers to give definitive answers about Teresa, either signalling that she has become insane or showing some kind of miracle to prove that her visions are real and true. By demanding that each moviegoer come to an individual conclusion about this, "Household Saints" challenges its audience to think about matters that most commercial films consider too difficult, sensitive or simply unfashionable to handle.

Equally bold is the movie's strong feminist orientation, framing Teresa's enigmas in a context of domestic chores and suggesting that even the most ordinary of these may point to a spiritual dimension.

There are numerous things wrong with "Household Saints," from its two-part construction to its weak handling of subplots. Yet it remains a touching and stimulating experience, showing depths in filmmaker Savoca that were only hinted at in the finely drawn "True Love" and the unfortunately ragged "Dogfight," her previous features.

Lili Taylor gives a brave and inventive performance as Teresa; other solid work comes from Tracey Ullman as her mother, Vincent D'Onofrio as her father, and Judith Malina as the old Italian matriarch. Jonathan Demme was the executive producer.

LOS ANGELES TIMES, 10/1/93, Calendar/p. 16, Peter Rainer

Most movies are locked into a single mood from the first shot but "Household Saints," directed by Nancy Savoca from Francine Prose's novel, moves gracefully from knockabout high spirits to a kind of austere sublimity. It's a difficult movie to get a fix on, but the difficulty is what makes it special.

The shifts in tone correspond to its portrayal of three generations of Italian-American women in New York's Little Italy following world War II. The three women are temperamentally and spiritually quite different from one another and yet they form a triumvirate: They are each indomitable in their own way.

Carmela (Judith Malina) is the deeply superstitious mother of Joseph Santangelo (Vincent D'Onofrio), the neighborhood butcher, who wins his 17-year-old wife, Catherine (Tracey Ullman), in a pinochle game. Carmela has more than the usual mother's suspicions about her new daughter-in-law, in between schooling her in domestic chores and teaching her the family secret of sausage making, she casts a dim eye on her pregnancy and considers the woman bad luck.

Carmela is like a creature out of urban folklore, and Malina makes her rituals and fears shockingly alive. Her conversations with her dead husband aren't jolting because she lives in a continuum of fantasy anyway. Catherine, who is brought into the family as a rather simple, down-to-earth woman, lives outside Carmela's continuum and yet she's drawn into the old woman's way of seeing.

When Catherine and Joseph have a daughter, Teresa (Lili Taylor), the film settles into a tone of easygoing domesticity for a while. But Teresa turns out to be as fanatic in her way as Carmela—it's just that she's much more blissed-out about it. As a child in Catholic school she accepts with wide-eyed wonder the stories of visits by Our Lady of Fatima. Later, she wins first prize for an essay "Why Communism Is the Anti-Christ." She wants to join a nunnery but her father is incensed at the idea. (He would much rather she marry a nice Catholic boy than Christ.)

Teresa moves inexorably out of her parents' realm—out of her earthly realm altogether—but Savoca keeps her case deliberately ambiguous. She regards Teresa's devotionalism as eerie, possibly insane, and yet in touch with the miraculous. And she manages to give Teresa her due while at the same time doing the same for her parents. Their concern has its gravity, and the most touching moments in the film are those in which Catherine, who has no affinity for the spiritual, tries to embrace her daughter. (Tracey Ullman makes us see that Catherine's effort is, in its way, a spiritual gesture.)

Savoca, with her co-screenwriter Richard Guay, doesn't bring out enough of the richness in this generational saga (rated R for scenes of sexuality). It moves gracefully from moment to moment but Teresa's story leaves a chill, and the lives of some of the characters, particularly Catherine, are skimped. It's genuinely unsettling, though, and that counts for something. It's trying to perplex audiences in new ways.

NEW YORK POST, 9/15/93, p. 27, Jerry Tallmer

There are two movies in one in "Household Saints"—the rich and funny one, that's the first half, and the spare and serious one that is married to it for the second hour. Though I loved the first half and liked the last half, and even though Jesus appears in the second half, I'm not sure it's a marriage made in heaven.

Actually "Household Saints," directed by Nancy Savoca, produced by Jonathan Demme, is a movie all about marriage—the flesh and blood kind when a strapping, macho sausage butcher in Little Italy wins a wife in a pinochle game and that other kind which has to do with a young woman's burning thirst to be a bride of Christ.

Here on Earth it is the great unbearable heat wave during the San Gennaro Festival of 1949, and Joseph Santangelo (Vincent D'Onofrio), sausage-selling son of Carmela Santangelo, has taken a fancy to stoic, saturnine Catherine Falconetti (Tracey Ullman), the gum-chewing young customer who spots him weighting the scale with his thumb. "You know what I can do with that thumb?" he says, demonstrating with a sausage.

He wins her from her father (Victor Argo) with a heart flush in exchange for wafts of cold air from the meat locker, and everybody is happy or reasonably happy except Joe's little old fireball of a mama, in her little black dress and little black hat.

Also triumphant is the gorgeous full-blooded performance of this terror by Judith Malina, giving every wonderful rolling juicy ounce of worldly-wise urban scorn to Carmela's every moment, even in prayers to her dead husband and St. Anna. The prayers are that the drip of a daughter-in-law should not give birth to a chicken. When St. Anna betrays the prayers by way of a miscarriage, mama burns St. Anna's picture.

There is however, a later miracle, the healthy birth of a daughter who grows up in her teens to be the exquisite Teresa (Lili Taylor). When Teresa wins from the nuns as a school prize "The Study of a Soul," and reads therein what St. Therese of Lisieux had said—"To ecstasy, I prefer the monotony of daily toil"—the girl's mind is set forever. She, too, must become a nun. "Over my dead body," butcher Joe Santangelo shouts.

She falls in love, moves in with a boyfriend, but when the boyfriend's at work, Christ appears and works a miracle—a whole apartment full of the red shirts Teresa's ironing. I'm afraid you may be able to guess how the passion of this namesake of St. Therese's turns out, at the expense of making the movie longer than it should be.

What is not longer than it should be is the joy of watching Judith Malina, fiery Living Theater pillar of the avant-garde for 35 years, come into her own as a movie star. Judith, I always told you—when you didn't want to hear it—that your strong point in acting was comedy. And here you are.

NEWSDAY, 9/15/93, Part II/p. 63, Gene Seymour

God, as the expression goes, is in the details. And it is in the details, that "Household Saints," a magical-realistic family epic set in New York's Little Italy, achieves its best moments. Director Nancy Savoca ("True Love") displays a large heart, a keen eye and an engaging feel for personality in this quirky, uneven film, which she and producer-husband Richard Guay adapted from a novel by Francine Prose.

It begins on a sweltering summer night shortly after World War II. At the tail end of a long, wine-soaked pinochle game, roguish neighborhood butcher Joseph Santangelo (Vincent D'Onofrio) makes a wager with Falconetti (Victor Argo), the radio repairman across the street. If the butcher's hand is good, he'll marry the repairman's dreamy, sullen teenage daughter, Catherine (Tracey Ullman.)

Falconetti loses. But as far as Joseph's mystic-minded mama, Carmela (Judith Malina), is concerned, her son is the loser. She can't even make a decent antipasto, Carmela mutters of her new daughter-in-law. Nonetheless, Catherine is guided through all the Italian matriarch's sacred rites—especially the fine art of making sausage. (Don't be surprised if, while watching Savoca's rich sequences of rolling and seasoning meat, your mouth starts to water.)

Shortly after Carmela dies, Joseph and Catherine are blessed with the birth of a daughter, Teresa, who, as she grows up in the '50s and '60s (Lili Taylor plays her as a teenager), is blessed-cursed with a religious faith as mystical as—and far more overpowering than—Carmela's.

Watching Savoca handle this thick and spicy mix is almost as engrossing as watching Carmela make her sausage. One gets an authentic feel of the '40s, '50s and '60s, right down to Ullman's hairstyles and the apartment decor, that is in no way mitigated by the occasional fantasy sequences that sprout in the middle of the story.

The problem comes when Savoca tries to maintain a narrative structure solid enough to contain all the intriguing particulars. Somewhere toward the middle, as the story's focus shifts almost entirely to Teresa, the story line starts to wobble and trip over itself much like the awkward adolescent Taylor plays with such affecting grace.

The focus on Teresa becomes so intense, in fact, that it blurs the other characters into near-insignificance. One wonders, in fact, if the novelistic nature of the story would have been better served in a mini-series form. (Except that no network, public, private or cable, would know what to do with it.)

If the characters remain vivid throughout, it's because of the performances. Ullman's mimetic and empathic gifts are the stuff of legend by now. But it is the way D'Onofrio handles his character's evolution from youthful swagger to middle-aged befuddlement that provides the film's subtle charge—and maybe its most gratifying surprise.

If, by the end of "Household Saints," one feels somewhat stuffed and logy, it may be because Savoca herself became overwhelmed by the ingredients she had and felt compelled to jam as many of them in as possible.

VILLAGE VOICE, 9/21/93, p. 60, Gary Indiana

Joseph Santangelo, a meat vendor on Mulberry Street in the '40s, wins Catherine Falconetti from her father, Lino, in a pinochle game, during a record heat wave. After they marry, Catherine moves in with Joseph and his mother, Carmela, a wizened harridan steeped in Catholic superstition. Catherine becomes pregnant. Carmela tells Catherine that because she's helped Joseph kill Thanksgiving turkeys in the shop, she's going to give birth to a chicken. The baby, in fact, is born dead. A while later, after Carmela dies, Catherine has a healthy child, Teresa, who begins at an early age to emulate St. Therese, "the Little Flower."

Nancy Savoca's *Household Saints* is surely one of the most beautifully photographed and ponderously structured movies of the year; though it really is a straightforward study of three generations of Italian women in Little Italy, its segue from the story of Catherine's marriage to that of Teresa's childhood and adolescence makes it feel like two films. The period details are conspicuous and pleasurable: Mercury-head dimes on a card table, vintage radio sets, the stuffy, icon-haunted interior of the Santangelo apartment under the reign of Carmela and its brightly colored, tacky renovation by the modern Catherine.

The film is quietly and consistently inventive, from the placement of the camera to the timing of scenes, and the acting is so intelligently nuanced that the occasional sliver of ham doesn't damage it even slightly. Tracey Ullman, as Catherine, proves for the millionth time that she's a brilliant naturalistic actress as well as an inspired mimic and comedienne; Vincent D'Onofrio, last seen getting offed by Tim Robbins in *The Player*, plays what could have been a slightly oafish Joseph as a shrewd, agreeably opportunistic, life-loving guy. Lili Taylor plays Teresa enigmatically, with flashes of wicked humor, and enough inner silence to keep the absurd question of whether she really is a saint alive in the viewer's mind. Finally, as Carmela, Judith Malina at last has a film role that lets her cut loose and create a whole character: Carmela is triumphantly complex, believable, exasperating, hilarious, and at very unexpected moments lovable, a stereotype transformed by a gorgeous script, and by Malina's talent, into a sublime oddity.

Also reviewed in:
CHICAGO TRIBUNE, 10/1/93, Friday/p. B, Michael Wilmington
NEW YORK TIMES, 9/15/93, p. C15, Janet Maslin
VARIETY, 9/27/93, p. 38, Todd McCarthy
WASHINGTON POST, 10/2/93, p. G3, Hal Hinson

IL LADRO di BAMBINI

A Samuel Goldwyn Company release of an Erre Produzioni/Alia Film in association with RAI-TV Channel 2. A co-production with Arena Films (Paris). A joint venture with Vega films (Zurich). *Executive Producer:* Enzo Porcelli. *Producer:* Angelo Rizzoli and Stefano Munafo. *Director:* Gianni Amelio. *Screenplay (Italian with English subtitles):* Sandro Petraglia, Stefano Rulli, and Gianni Amelio. *Director of Photography:* Tonino Nardi and Renato Tafuri. *Editor:* Simona Paggi. *Music:* Franco Piersanti. *Music performed by:* Amit. *Sound:* Alberto Doni, Giorgio Agazzi, Gianni Zampagni, and Alessandro Zanon. *Sound Editor:* Benedetto Atria. *Casting:* Ofelia Garcia, Marco Spoletini, Umberto Enzo Castagna, Adriana Sapone, and Antonio Sapone. *Production Designer:* Andrea Crisanti. *Set Decorator:* Giuseppe M. Gaudino. *Costumes:* Gianna Gissi and Luciana Morosetti. *Make-up:* Esmé Sciaroni. *Running time:* 108 minutes. *MPAA Rating:* Not Rated.

CAST: Enrico Lo Verso (Antonio);   Valentina Scalici (Rosetta);   Giuseppe Ieracitano (Luciano);   Florence Darel (Martine);   Marina Golovine (Nathalie);   Fabio Alessandrini (Grignani);   Agnostino Zumbo (Priest at the Children's Home);   Vincenzo Peluso (Neapolitan Carabiniere);   Santo Santonocito (2nd Carabiniere);   Vitalba Andrea (Antonio's Sister);   Massimo De Lorenzo (Papaleo);   Celeste Brancato (Girl at Dinner);   Renato Carpentieri (Police Chief).

CINEASTE, Vol. XX, No. 1, 1993, p. 37, Peter Bondanella

It has become almost as fashionable for Italian critics to compose an epitaph for contemporary Italian cinema as it was some years ago for American writers to declare that the novel was dead. And yet, in recent years a number of films by relatively young directors have achieved considerable success abroad, notably Giuseppe Tornatore's *Cinema Paradiso* and Gabriele Salvatores's *Mediterraneo*. While I would not rank *Il Ladro di Bambini* (American release title, *Stolen Children*) quite so high as its European enthusiasts, Amelio's film deserves serious attention as further evidence that the announcement of the Italian cinema's demise may well be premature.

Given the powerful hold Italian neorealism has exerted over the development of the Italian cinema in the postwar period, it would be surprising if a relatively uncomplicated work such as *Stolen Children*, which boasts a minimal budget and employs nonprofessional actors, would not be cited as evidence of a trend among young Italian filmmakers labeled by some Italian critics as 'neo-neorealism.' Supporting scriptwriters Sandro Petraglia and Stefano Rulli, who have provided noteworthy scripts for a number of the most interesting contemporary films by young Italian filmmakers, deserve a great deal of credit for the success of *Stolen Children*, for, unlike so many scriptwriters, they realize that too much unnecessary dialog, even in the service of a powerful message, may hinder rather than assist the persuasive powers of the camera. The film's plot also recalls traditional neorealist predilection for focusing the camera's gaze upon the underprivileged and the lower classes, especially those of southern origin.

In a filthy tenement on the outskirts of Milan populated mostly by Sicilian immigrants, a mother is arrested for prostituting her eleven-year-old daughter, Rosetta (Valentina Scalici). A young Carabinieri official named Antonio from Calabria (Enrico Lo Verso) is charged with escorting Rosetta and her ten-year-old brother, Luciano (Giuseppe Ieracitano), to a religious institution for orphans in Civitavecchia. There, Rosetta is recognized as the infamous child-prostitute whose picture has appeared in all the tabloids and is callously turned away, leading Antonio to decide (without proper authorization from his superiors) to return the children to Sicily, the land of their birthplace. The film traces in a simple and eloquent fashion this journey, which ends with a reprimand for Antonio for his kindness, while the children are directed toward a foster home.

Some contemporary assessments of the golden years of Italian neorealism point to the melodramatic use of children in such works as *The Bicycle Thief, Umberto D, Paisan,* or *Rome, Open City* as evidence of sloppy sentimentality or defective ideological commitment to the class struggle or the possibilities of revolutionary social change. Such arguments are patently absurd when applied to the masterpieces of Rossellini and De Sica, and there is certainly nothing sentimental about the portrayal of the children in this film. The very idea of child prostitution precludes such sentimentality. Amelio's dispassionate camera style and his effective but laconic script offer little chance of a better life for the children during this bleak journey to the south of Italy. In fact, Amelio may well intend *Stolen Children* as an ironic reversal of the positive emotional direction we encounter in Rossellini's epic journey from Sicily to northern Italy, a journey that promised both moral regeneration and national rebirth in a new Italian future so unforgettably portrayed by *Paisan*, one of Italian neorealism's most enduring films.

Amelio's camera work recalls that of Vittorio De Sica in his penchant for long shots in corridors (usually found in hostile public institutions) or his sometimes too static framings of the unhappy children within tawdry surroundings. Indeed, the environment becomes almost as important in this film as in the best work of Michelangelo Antonioni, but whereas Antonioni's architectural monuments usually embodied a love for abstract design and a modernist style in the buildings he photographed, Amelio underlines the sordid side of Italy's contemporary society—tawdry neighborhood bars, endless streets surrounded by dirty yards or enclosed by wire fences, heart-rending expanses of tacky, hastily built structures that manage to ruin even the beautiful coastline of the Mediterranean shore. This barren urban landscape, the perfect setting for a world devoid of positive human values except for the simple kindness of Antonio toward the two children, dominates the picture even more than do its protagonists and is relieved only once in the entire film when, for a brief but fleeting moment, the trio take a plunge in the gorgeous Mediterranean waters and are bathed in a halo of pure, pagan sunlight.

The positive values that do emerge from Amelio's film underline Italy's past—the sense of family solidarity once associated with the south that has now been shattered in the northern tenements by greed, moral corruption, and the debasement of children. If neorealist cinema exalted children as the symbol of future hope in a rebirth of democratic, nonfascist Italy, Amelio's dismal exploration of the corruption of youth paints an ugly picture of how spurious and naive such hope may have been. To his credit Amelio deals with the bitter reality of a much changed Italian society where comfortable myths about the sanctity of the family and the benevolent relationship between parents and children so firmly held in the Italian consciousness yield to an analysis of the kinds of social problems American viewers will more easily associate with our own fragmented family structure. Only briefly, when Antonio stops at his sister's restaurant in Calabria and the visitors meet his ancient grandmother, are we allowed to catch a glimpse of a more idyllic family in Antonio's background. But the grandmother's photograph of a young and obviously happy Antonio in a cowboy outfit serves the two children as a bitter reminder of the kind of privileged life they will never enjoy.

Amelio's skill in obtaining masterful performances from nonprofessional child actors appearing in their film debuts can only recall a similar mastery in the greatest neorealist films directed by Vittorio De Sica. Rosetta and Luciano do not appeal to us because of any cheap 'cuteness.' In many respects, they are unattractive and initially evoke not sympathy but repulsion. Not only do brother and sister dislike each other intensely, but the opening of the film also suggests that Luciano may actually have been the source of the information the police obtained to arrest his mother (who, in the opening sequence of the film, criticizes him severely for being effeminate while treating Rosetta, the source of her income, in an entirely different manner). Through the simple gestures of kindness and hospitality shown to the pair by the young Calabrian policeman, however, the two children come to realize an important lesson. It is not the sugarcoated, optimistic message that their lives will be radically changed in the future, but rather that they have only each other to rely upon in their forthcoming battle with a heartless society that cares little for their survival.

Antonio is the catalyst for this change in the two children, whose performances reveal an astonishing range of emotions that more experienced professionals would envy. But Antonio cannot really assist the two children in any meaningful way. As he sleeps in the car in a vacant lot just before taking them to the foster home, the two children sit silently on a curb. Rosetta's only gesture is to cover her frail brother's shoulders with his jacket in the early morning cold, but her action is sufficiently eloquent to convince the viewer that, in the future, the bonds of family may well rescue them from what seems to be an unpromising life of negation and solitude. Thus, while Amelio's film chronicles the breakdown of the traditional nuclear family even among the southern Italians who have always considered family ties sacred, *Stolen Children*, like many other neorealist classics, implies that only family ties may ameliorate the desperate situation reflected in the film's storyline.

Italy's postwar cinema has always served a civic function. In its best moments, it has represented the country's conscience. Italian neorealism set a standard in this regard, and the best of Italy's filmmakers have never forgotten neorealism's sense of moral indignation and its championship of the poor, the friendless, and the downtrodden. Gianni Amelio deserves to be counted as a worthy successor to this noble cinematic tradition, and he emerges as a young director who should be expected to produce even more impressive results if Italy's chaotic film industry ever resolves its persistent inability to provide adequate capital and international distribution for its best works.

FILMS IN REVIEW, 6/93, p. 193, Eva H. Kissin

Accompanying two children from Milan to a children's "Home" in Sicily doesn't sound like a favorable plot for a movie. However, this special assignment of Antonio, a young officer in the

Carabinieri, to escort Rosetta, an eleven-year-old prostitute and her eight-year-old brother, Luciano, is ultimately a fascinating journey.

The three travel through the gray underside of Italy in second and third class trains. The children are distant, uncommunicative, recalcitrant and all around difficult. Antonio must pull a runaway Rosetta out of the ladies room in the railroad station, and Luciano's asthma attacks constantly slow down their progress. The first "Home" in Milan will not take them, and the children are assigned to a place in Sicily. The trio heads south missing trains and becoming increasingly irritable.

At one point, Antonio is so frustrated that he stops to visit his family in Southern Italy and pretends the children belong to a high official in the Carabinieri. Here, the kids unbend a bit under the protection of their borrowed background and the warmth of his Italian family until the devastating reason for their destination is revealed.

The children retreat into themselves again until Antonio "steals" them away for a few days at the seashore. Here, in the sunshine, he attempts to teach the frightened city boy to swim, and begins to reach the feelings of the girl who is learning to trust him.

The journey is a rite of passage for the two children, non-professional actors who give brilliant performances. The range of their expressions from the profound cynicism only children can experience—to the open delight of childhood itself—is remarkable.

The film is as spare as the journey, but there is a profound lesson in human relations in this social document. Watching Antonio surrounded by his family, we understand the source of his warmth and decency. When his ninety-two-year-old smiling toothless grandma shows his boyhood pictures to Luciano, we have our first inkling of the child inside the hard-bitten little boy.

This is a film to treasure in the great Italian neo-realist tradition of the fifties. See it and feel it. You won't forget it easily.

Gianni Amelio's direction has exactly the right tone. Enrico Lo Verso is splendid as the young officer and Valentina Scalici's Rosetta and Giuseppe Ieracitano's Luciano speak the international language of children.

LOS ANGELES TIMES, 3/12/93, Calendar/p. 1, Kenneth Turan

"Il Ladro di Bambini" translates as "Stolen Children," but what is really stolen in this spare, faultless and almost magisterially melancholy Italian film is childhood itself. Eleven-year-old Rosetta and her younger brother Luciano are sullen, mistrustful and withdrawn, and it is the business of writer-director Gianni Amelio to quietly reveal not only what went wrong but also what if anything can finally be done about it.

In even its title, which echoes Vittorio De Sica's landmark 1949 "Ladri di Biciclette" ("The Bicycle Thief"), this film is a return to the classic simplicity of Italian neo-realism, a style of filmmaking that emphasized real-world settings, non-professional actors, documentary-style cinematography and a strong social conscience. But what is impressive about "Bambini" is not just its roots but how effectively Amelio has updated the style and made it forceful, relevant and moving.

A major box-office hit in Italy despite its somber tone, "Bambini" has also been deluged by awards, winning Italy's David di Donatello prize, the Grand Jury Prize at Cannes and the Felix for best European film of 1992. However, its measured pace and refusal to oversentimentalize its story did not win it any friends in the motion picture academy, where it was denied so much as a nomination for best foreign language film.

In a prologue set in a working-class area of Milan, "Bambini's" characters are quickly and elliptically introduced. Rosetta (Valentina Scalici) is a child prostitute turned out by her mother when she was 9. A police raid puts the mother in prison and sends Rosetta and Luciano (Giuseppe Ieracitano) to an institution near Naples.

Assigned to escort them by train are a pair of paramilitary Carabinieri. But the job seems so simple that one of the men decides to take care of some personal business instead, leaving Antonio (Enrico Lo Verso) in sole charge of the expedition.

Shy, lacking in confidence, with the big ears and doubtful face of a bargain-basement John Travolta, Antonio is far from happy with his assignment. The taboo nature of Rosetta's past life unnerves him, as does Luciano's refusal to talk and the resentful attitude neither child is shy about assuming.

Making things worse, this simple assignment soon turns into a quagmire. The institution that is supposed to accept the children refuses them point blank, a recurrence of Luciano's asthma makes for further delays, and the intrinsically decent Antonio finds himself almost forced into taking an interest in his companions.

The developing of the relationship between the Carabinieri and this morose pair is the heart of "Bambini" (Times-rated Mature) and its area of greatest stylistic rigor. As the trio embark on what turns into a trip down the entire length of Italy, we see not an artificial cute-meet bonding, but one that is formed so gradually and tentatively it seems to be happening in real time. Ever so slowly, Antonio (who the film hints may have been raised without parents himself) comes to be increasingly drawn into the predicament of these tiny lost souls, a process that is echoed by the audience's growing involvement in their plight.

Several factors go into making this delicate operation a success, starting with picture-perfect casting. While Lo Verso has had limited acting experience, the two children had none and were no doubt chosen for their personal spirit and for the extraordinary expressiveness of their faces, the look of very old and careworn souls they carry with them despite their lack of years.

And Amelio (whose last film, "Open Door," was nominated for an Oscar) is exceptional in his ability to work with this non-professional cast. Nothing ever feels forced, from the camera placements to the smallest dramatic details, leading to that rare sense of observing life as it happens. Amelio and his co-screenwriters Sandro Petraglia and Stefano Rulli in fact modified the dialogue from day to day to take advantage of the changing natures of their neophyte performers.

Just as underplayed as the acting, but very much there, is the film's pointed but unobtrusive social concerns. For the backdrop for these children that no one wants is a society in disarray, callous, corrupt, materialistic and unconcerned about human relations. That "Il Ladro di Bambini" can make such a statement without pounding a Hollywood-style drum about it is a measure of both its sophistication and its success.

NEW YORK, 3/15/93, p. 61, David Denby

The coming attractions for *Stolen Children* (*Il Ladro di Bambini*) aren't very appealing, and in any case the subject of lost, unloved, or abused children seems booby-trapped with unearned sentiment. So I was amazed—and thrilled—to discover that the movie was actually wonderful. Gianni Amelio, the director, works in a way that can only be called clean. *Stolen Children*, which won most of the major awards in Italy, is strong and unsentimental. Most of the emotions develop without words, in looks and silences, in moods tentatively offered and hesitantly extended. Amelio's control is extraordinary; his emotional intelligence is extraordinary, too.

Amelio plucked a brutal story from the headlines and then set about treating it raptly, tenderly, with all the grave attention of a Renaissance master. Outside Milan, a little girl, Rosetta, 11 years old, is put to work by her mother as a prostitute. Amelio doesn't show us much: just the mother standing at a stove; a single shot of the girl's back; a man's hand reaching toward hers. The meaning of the episode emerges from the stony-faced dismay of Rosetta's 10-year-old brother, Luciano, who sits, as the girl works, in the family's kitchen and then outside the apartment, locked in misery and in hatred of his mother and sister. Something vital to life has been destroyed in both children. When the mother is arrested (the father has long since fled), the children are turned over to a pair of officers from the carabinieri—the state police—for transportation to a Catholic orphanage near Rome. On the train, one of the officers peels off (presumably to visit a girlfriend), leaving the children in the care of Antonio (Enrico Lo Verso), a very young man who feels trapped by the job.

Antonio has decent instincts, but like many young men he's baffled by children. Rosetta and Luciano won't eat; they have the infuriating habit, in a train station or a park, of silently wandering off in different directions. Anyone who has ever spent an afternoon taking care of kids, even happy kids, will identify with Antonio's helplessness. And these two are far from happy. The girl is defiant and mean (she really has been corrupted in some way), the boy utterly silent. When they arrive at the orphanage, they are turned away: Rosetta's reputation makes it impossible to admit her. More and more desperate, Antonio drives the children to an institution in Sicily, but he takes his time, making many detours. He never says what he's doing, but we can see that his official duty has been overtaken by something else—the unspoken and perhaps unadmitted intention of pulling the two children back from the emotional death they have entered into. The movie ends ambiguously—in sadness but with the possibility of hope.

Neither child has acted before. Amelio discovered Valentina Scalici, who plays Rosetta, at an Italian resort (she's Sicilian), and he gets from her a performance of peculiar bitter melancholy and distance, with many small intimations of experience beyond her years. Scalici, who is 13, has a disturbingly unhappy face—her eyes seem to be looking inward—while the 12-year-old Giuseppe Ieracitano has such exquisite features that it is impossible to feel anything for him but love. The exceptional beauty of the children has the effect of purifying—in the sense of raising to the ethical and spiritual level—the movie's themes of betrayal, loneliness, and fear. This way of using the iconography of childhood may be familiar from Italian religious art, but Amelio does it without kitsch. There's nothing soft or ingratiating in the shape of the movie or the performances.

Antonio is a young man not quite formed, but one can see why he's a carabinier: He believes in some vague, barely articulate way that life should have dignity; he's genuinely shocked by disorder. Lo Verso, who has acted in small film roles and onstage, has full, curved lips, ears that stick out, powerful dark eyes; he's awkwardly attractive, with a swarthy Italian-prole face that lights up every now and then in pure joy. When he smiles at some French girls who flirt with him, one can see how, in a different week, he might have been a conventional, happy young man. But this week, he goes almost as far as his responsibilities as a parent—too far to go back without suffering.

Amelio, whose somber movie about justice in the Fascist period, *Open Doors*, played here in 1989, works intuitively, with a minimum of dialogue. *Stolen Children* is all moment-to-moment delicacy, the emanation of mood, Amelio's sense of the correct balance of affection, withdrawal, and engagement between Antonio and the two children seems to me uncannily accurate. Much of the time he just studies the children, and some of the most eloquent shots are among the simplest—the moment near the end, for instance, when the three travelers, exhausted after several restless nights, are finally relaxed enough in one another's company to fall asleep. Amelio doesn't give the material the fable-like definition that the neorealist masters Rossellini and De Sica achieved in the forties in such films as *Open City* and *The Bicycle Thief*. He doesn't want that kind of overwhelming emotional pull, and although a few episodes could have been more firmly shaped, I didn't mind the tentativeness. *Stolen Children* is about fleeting and unacknowledged emotions; it *should* be exploratory and anecdotal.

The different emotions have also been produced by a different Italy. Postwar Italy was desperately poor and dispirited by the moral calamities of wartime. This movie suggests the moral callousness of a richer country, but a country out of balance. Every building the trio visits is either half built up or half torn down. Italy is cracking, and the children have fallen through. An American, of course, is likely to envy a country in which people can still be shocked by parentless children. In America, the fate of Rosetta and Luciano would not be considered news. Or it would be news of the wrong kind: A little girl whose mother turned her into a prostitute would attract the interest not of a kindly policeman but of Oprah Winfrey.

NEW YORK POST, 3/3/93, p. 24, Jami Bernard

At first it seems that the withdrawn, quietly praying 11-year old girl is simply being obstinate in not coming out of her room to join her mother and little brother in the kitchen. But gradually and nearly wordlessly, through an extended opening sequence of unusual power, it becomes clear that the child is sitting on the bed awaiting her next paying customer; her mother has prostituted her.

"Il Ladro di Bambini" (Stolen Children) is a return to the Italian neo-realist tradition by director Gianni Amelio. It is not about the horrors of child prostitution but of the growing trust and concern that develop between the brother and sister as they are taken on a long, emotional journey to a foster home by an initially reluctant military officer.

The home won't accept the girl because of her scandalous situation, so the officer (Enrico Lo Verso) is forced to trek the kids down to Sicily, to a much tougher home.

The girl (Valentina Scalici) is understandably suspicious of adults. She's difficult, withdrawn and sometimes emptily flirtatious in a way she has been taught to be. But the soldier understands that she is just a child, and she gradually responds to him when she is treated like one; he makes her wash her hands before eating, whereas the last man to take an interest in her hands was the john who placed his over hers on her bed.

The boy (Giuseppe Ieracitano) is an asthmatic whose bouts seem to be brought on by a particular and acute sense of isolation: although the story is mostly told from an omniscient point of view, the camera stays closest to the little boy. The three actors all newcomers, are very natural and unaffected.

The journey grows longer as the pleasure of it deepens. Although that may be giving the soldier's superiors cause to think that he has stolen the kids, what has really been stolen is their childhood—hence the title. You may think the film is heading toward a reinstatement of that precious commodity of childhood, but neorealism doesn't thrive for long in direct sunlight.

NEWSDAY, 3/3/93, Part II/p. 48, John Anderson

Poor Luciano. His mama abuses him terribly. "Have you become a girl?" she asks, trying to shame him out of the house to play. But the child just grows more mute and sullen till his mother forces a thousand lire on him and sends him off to buy ice cream.

His sister, meanwhile, receives nothing but verbal bouquets from Mom, who calls her "darling" through her bedroom door, and then takes money from a man who wants sex with the girl. Eleven-year-old Rosetta (Valentina Scalici) prays to her guardian angel while we see an arm, naked—except for wedding band and wristwatch, reach across the bed for her. Out in the kitchen, Mama stares dumbly at her money. Out in the street, Luciano stares at his.

"Il Ladro Di Bambini," the Grand jury Prize winner at last year's Cannes Film Festival, is a sly bit of business: uncompromising and complex in its portrayal of abused children, it teases us with possibilities—chiefly, whether innocence can ever be retrieved. After their mother's horrific arrest for prostituting Rosetta, the children are assigned to a young *carabiniere* named Antonio (Enrico Lo Verso), virtually a child himself, who is to take them to a children's home. En route, the needy three play a game of emotional tag that's resolved with each finding love in the other. But despite the tantalizing feel-good elements of the film, there looms the inescapable fact that some things that are stolen can never be replaced. And this elevates the film from melodrama to genuine tragedy.

His young actors give what may be the most moving juvenile performances ever, and director Gianni Amelio doesn't waste them on maudlin purposes. Instead, he employs their innate sentimentality to engender genuine despair. Lo Verso may give a wonderful performance as Antonio, whose sense of duty can't supersede his sense of goodness, but it is the children's movie, and more specifically, 13-year-old Valentina Scalici's.

Looking like a young, streetwise Natalie Wood, Scalici combines her character's unnatural sexuality with a child's confusion; Rosetta carries the burden of the female world on her back, and her own broken heart in her eyes. And the men who used her are always with her—when a religious home rejects her because of her past; when Antonio's friend offers kindness and she reads it as a proposition; and when, at a First Communion party at Antonio's sister's home, she watches the other children and knows she really isn't one of them.

The relationships that result among Rosetta, Luciano and Antonio are everything they should be—intricate, irrational, thoroughly human. Antonio can't decide if he's a father figure, a governmental apparatus or just the third kid in the group. Luciano, who spends much of the film not talking, hates his sister, but it's just misdirected rage at the abominations of his life. Rosetta seesaws between toughing it out and collapsing in her own shame. After the rejection at the first home they make their way toward another in Sicily, and in one stunning scene (through which Amelio evokes his Italo-cinematic predecessors), the girl, in a dress of aqua, yellow and tan, walks across a striated backdrop of ocean, sky and beach and is virtually absorbed back into nature. Which is where she belongs, and whence she's been stolen.

"Il Ladro di Bambini"—"stolen children"—pushes all our injustice buttons. Antonio will get in trouble for bending his soldierly rules and the children will feel the arbitrary cruelty and weight of a society—a world—that doesn't want to help them, but doesn't want to be blamed for them either. Theirs is the kind of story which, as related in a newspaper, might make you think twice. In this film, and with these two children acting, it doesn't go away.

SIGHT AND SOUND, 12/93, p. 48, Leslie Felperin Sharman

Milan. A woman is arrested on a rundown housing estate for pimping her 11-year-old daughter. The girl, Rosetta, is taken into care with her nine-year-old brother Luciano. Antonio, a *carabiniere* (paramilitary policeman), is assigned to accompany the children to an orphanage up North. The orphanage refuses to accept the children because certain papers are lacking. Antonio is told to take them to a Sicilian children's home instead, so they journey south over a period of three days.

Despite their initially strictly official relationship, Antonio and the children grow gradually closer. They stop off in Calabria at Antonio's sister's house where his niece is having her First Communion party. The happy family atmosphere is shattered when a guest matches Rosetta's face to a tabloid photograph and confronts her. They leave for Sicily. Dallying before he must finally take them to the children's home, Antonio spends an idyllic day on the beach with the children. He tells two French girls that the children are his own, partly to protect them and partly out of affection. When a thief steals a camera from one of the French girls, Antonio tackles him and hands him over to the police. At the station, he is horrified to discover that, rather than praising his heroism, the authorities think he has kidnapped the children over the last three days and that his career as a *carabiniere* is now seriously threatened. The spell of intimacy between Antonio and his charges is finally broken as he drives towards to the children's home at last.

Back in 1953, Cesare Zavattini, one of the foremost scriptwriters and advocates of Italian Neo-realism, called for 'socially important' cinema in the pages of *Sight and Sound*. "The time has come to tell the audience that they are the true protagonists of life," he thundered, in the quaintly existential humanist way of the times. "The result will be a constant appeal to the responsibility and dignity of every human being." Thirty years later, while the visual mannerisms of Neo-realism have been incorporated into the cinematic international mainstream (long takes, grainy stocks, etc.), the humanitarian ideals and zealotry which informed the movement are relegated mainly to the realms of the television docu-drama. The films of Gianni Amelio, the director of *Il Ladro di bambini*, have consistently attempted to retie the severed threads connecting these two remnants of the Neo-realist tradition. Usually funded by and premiered on television, Amelio's films transmute the alloy of TV issue-based melodrama into steely cinematic products, often hard-edged and brutal, but imbued with the very appeal to human responsibility and dignity that Zavattini called for long ago.

Despite Italian cinema and culture's tendency to sentimentalize childhood and the family (cf. *Cinema Paradiso*), ever since his first feature, *La fine del gioco* (1970) which dealt with borstal children, Amelio's films have rooted through the moral trash cans at the back of the domestic habitat. *Il Ladro di bambini* is no exception, raking as it does over the fetid mess that child prostitution makes of young lives. The material is sensational, but the treatment is anything but—we never see a second of sex on screen.

A typical problem-of-the-week TV film would end where this one begins. Instead of showing how Rosetta was coerced onto the game, it depicts the equally bleak existence that lies ahead for children put into care, encapsulated in the orphanage scene where the children sit in tidy rows of desks, listening to a nun's platitudes about life being a gift. And just when you think the film is starting to go soft, the seemingly warm community of Antonio's home town discloses its seeds of small-mindedness.

Like the leads in *Bicycle Thieves*, which *Il Ladro di bambini* wistfully recalls, the young actors playing Rosetta and Luciano are as affecting as only unprofessional actors can be. Victims but hardly innocents, their photogenic faces convey pain with the barest of blank looks. The occasional slackness of the editing gradually builds up a sense of something missing until it suddenly hits you at the end what the title hints at: rather than the children themselves, it is their childhoods which have been stolen.

TIME, 4/5/93, p. 60, Richard Corliss

[*Il Ladro di Bambini* was reviewed jointly with *The Adventures of Huck Finn*; see Corliss' review of that film.]

VILLAGE VOICE, 3/16/93, p. 56, Manohla Dargis

In *Il Ladro di Bambini* (*Stolen Children*), the road back from hell is wet with tears. When 11-year-old Rosetta and her 10-year-old brother, Luciano, are yanked from Mom it's because she's been prostituting Rosetta. Treated like criminals, the two kids are put under military guard and shipped out to a children's home. En route, however, one of their escorts goes AWOL, and they're left alone with Antonio, a fledgling whose naïveté is a minor miracle. Left to their own devices, the unlikely trio invent a world unto themselves, and slip into a pocket of comfort, intimacy, and hope.

Heavy-going from reel one, this may sound like made-for-TV manna, or a handy excuse for another Valium, but it's not. Shot in a rigorously spare style and brilliantly acted by its three leads, *Il Ladro di Bambini* is as restrained as it is powerful. Pain isn't packaged here, tied with a bow and explained away with platitudes about child abuse, bureaucracy, or the good old days no one ever really had. Instead, terror is in the details, in the chipped polish of a girl who can't stop gnawing her fingers, in the gasps of an asthmatic boy for whom breath itself means anguish. Just like faith, suffering minus cheap sentiment is a tough sell. Which is one reason why *Il Ladro di Bambini* is a work of such uncommon grace, one that brushes at the soul even as it refuses to break the heart.

Also reviewed in:
CHICAGO TRIBUNE, 4/30/93, Friday/p. D, Johanna Steinmetz
NEW REPUBLIC, 3/22/93, p. 30, Stanley Kauffmann
NEW YORK TIMES, 3/3/93, p. C13, Janet Maslin
VARIETY, 5/11/92, p. 119, Deborah Young
WASHINGTON POST, 3/26/93, p. C6, Hal Hinson
WASHINGTON POST, 3/26/93, Weekend/p. 43, Desson Howe

IN ADVANCE OF THE LANDING

A Cineplex Odeon Films Canada release of a Cygnus Communications production. *Executive Producer:* Don Haig. *Producer:* Dan Curtis. *Director:* Dan Curtis. *Based on the book by:* Douglas Curran. *Director of Photography:* Don Hutchison. *Editor:* Kevin Schjerning. *Music:* Fred Mollin. *Sound:* Brian Avery. *Running time:* 90 minutes. *MPAA Rating:* Not Rated.

WITH: Ruth E. Norman; Betty Hill; Larry W. Bryant; Gabriel Green; John Shepherd; Evan Hayworth; Paul Eichenberg; Alan Moseley; Marcello Truzzi; Sherrie Rose.

NEW YORK POST, 1/29/93, p. 29, Jerry Tallmer

One can only hope that with all the other problems foreign and domestic that President Clinton inherited this week, he won't have to worry about any zooming in from outer space on the wings of the Archangel Uriel.

Archangel Uriel is (or was, when photographed) a lady with the formidable aspect and high starched collar of Queen Elizabeth I who tells us "we can change bodies, which I expect to do very soon; I have lived in this body 90 years."

She also tells us she was in one of those former incarnations "Mary of Bethany to Jesus of Nazareth" and that with the power of the light Jesus gave her—a cosmic generator—she has often journeyed in and served as a part-time pilot of spaceships. "They do not fly, they oscillate," she informs us.

Uriel, founder of the Unarius Academy of Science, might be considered the doyenne of "In Advance of the Landing," a documentary about UFO-believers made—without comment—by Dan Curtis, a Canadian who based this film on a 1985 book by photographer and fellow Canadian Douglas Curran.

I too shall report without comment.

Here's a lady in a pink sweater, with pearls. Betty Hill of Portsmouth, N.H. who tells us she saw a spaceship crossing the railroad tracks. It looked like two soup plates put together." She "opened it up and heard the sound of a rooster crowing. This frightened me, because I have two roosters."

Here's Allan Mosely, a red-robed young priest in the LA branch of the Aetherius Society, leading a congregation of people in business suits going *"Ommmmmmmm,"* just like Allen Ginsberg. "I'll eat meat," Mosely tells us "Drive a car. If necessary, even watch a television program. Goodness gracious, we're just ordinary people, What makes us special is what we do."

What they do is send out "messages of cosmic intelligence" through "prayer-pack batteries," each of which—he shows us one—represents "hundreds of hours of thought energy." The Aetherians "used one such battery to get a ceasefire on Cyprus in '74." He does not cite other accomplishments.

Here's a note on a kitchen table, I forget where: "Folks. Gone to Venus. All is well. Lee."

Here's a lady from Vancouver, B.C. telling us about taking pictures of a UFO—"like a diamond in the sky, like a ferris wheel"—and wanting to show them to her husband, who was watching a hockey game and said: "Oh, sure." We see a couple of the photos. Rather more like halos in the sky.

Here's a clip from "The Arrival," a Unarian movie that begins as follows: "The time is 160,000 B.C. Based on a true story." We see a caveman at his fire "started by a blue spaceship." The caveman speaks English of a sort. He says: "I do not understand what is heppining."

And here, finally—I mean finally for all the space *I* have, not for all the space out there or in the movie—is Gabriel Green, president of the Giant Rock Flying Saucer Club of America, who tells us he was aboard a flying saucer in Nevada "on 11 different occasions," that they are peaceful people from another planet they call Flarion," and that in 1960—the year of Kennedy vs. Nixon—he ran for President of the United States to spread the word. "But they [the Flarions] asked me to withdraw and support Kennedy."

Well, I know a man, and a very serious man, named C.D.B. Bryan, who a few years ago wrote a very serious book called "Friendly Fire" about the family of an Iowa boy who was killed by his own artillery in Vietnam. Bryan is now at work on a book about people all over the country who have seen or think they've seen, UFOs. He takes them quite as seriously as his earlier subjects. Hey, you never know.

NEWSDAY, 1/22/93, Part II/p. 68, Gene Seymour

It's difficult to know from watching "In Advance of the Landing" what we're supposed to think of its subject, which is the belief in extraterrestrial life and its varied, exotic manifestations.

On the surface, Canadian filmmaker Dan Curtis seems to view his assorted interview subjects with tender solicitousness, whether it's the priests of a space-oriented religion in California who encourage their flock to pray to storage batteries or the hippie-loner who sends out signals from his private radio tower in Northern Michigan hoping, like Cliff Robertson in the first "Outer Limits" episode, to make contact with an electro-wonk in another galaxy.

What Curtis wants to convey is the texture of a folk sub-culture comprising people who have developed their own view of the cosmos and have fashioned their own belief systems with their own icons and rituals.

But the film seems content merely to show these people talking and acting out their obsessions. It's as if, just by looking at them in their split-level hovels and homemade space artifacts, we're supposed to feel as emotionally moved as Curtis was by their devotion to a dream.

The approach backfires because, often as not, we're moved to snicker and howl at such outrageousness as that personified by an elderly woman who, for several years, has won followers by portraying herself as a sort of interplanetary goddess who, through her good works, wants to lead fellow extraterrestrials trapped on earth to a new sense of universal harmony and peace. It sounds harmless enough and not *altogether* bad. But on screen, it comes across as tacky.

My favorite of the bunch is Betty Hill, a New Hampshire woman whose alleged kidnaping with her husband Barney by aliens in the mid-'60s, is perhaps the most celebrated. She sticks to her story and she says she maintains contact. Whether you believe her or not, her dry wit and sense of perspective toward the phenomenon is sadly lacking in Curtis' overview.

VILLAGE VOICE, 1/26/93, p. 56, Georgia Brown

Anyone who believes extraterrestrials are hovering around, even making occasional contact, should stay away from Dan Curtis's mocking documentary, *In Advance of the Landing*. Curtis says in production notes that he really doesn't know if UFOs exist, but his film sure does make believers look like a motley collection of flakes, dimwits, and raving crackpots.

At a party about 10 years ago, I spent some time with the painter Budd Hopkins, an unlikely Ancient Mariner, who clearly does believe that abductions have taken place. I haven't seen Hopkins since (nor read his book), and for all I know he's an amiable crank, but he sure kept me occupied for a half hour with some amazing stories. And though he appears briefly in Curtis's film, he doesn't get to tell any tales here because he's used merely to set up more of Curtis's ridicule. Likewise, a Pentagon employee who sued the government for access to its UFO research is made to seem like a pretty silly warrior: He's filmed walking up the steps of the courthouse with martial drumrolls deflating his mission. The teasing way Curtis treats subjects like these, I would call unethical. Some others, I must admit, look like their fair game.

If you wish to laugh at nut cases, the movie provides much to snicker, or at least smile, at. Curtis has dug up some weird archival footage. There's a sect, for example, that prays fervently to storage batteries—probably while somebody's bilking somebody out of his or her life savings. (Its priests have suspicious British accents.) Then there are the terminally pathetic tapes, such as the middle-aged hippie waiting patiently for a radio signal from above. Many reasons may occur to you why the presence of aliens may be comforting or otherwise, but Curtis does no psychologizing or investigation and certainly no analysis, implicit or otherwise. There's a movie to be made here, but he has taken the easy way out.

Also reviewed in:
NEW YORK TIMES, 1/22/93, p. C7, Vincent Canby
VARIETY, 2/1/93, p. 96, Lawrence Cohen

IN THE LINE OF FIRE

A Columbia Pictures release. *Executive Producer:* Wolfgang Petersen, Gail Katz, and David Valdes. *Producer:* Jeff Apple. *Director:* Wolfgang Petersen. *Screenplay:* Jeff Maguire. *Director of Photography:* John Bailey. *Editor:* Anne V. Coates. *Music:* Ennio Morricone. *Music Editor:* Bill Abbott. *Sound:* Willie Burton and (music) Franco Patrignani. *Sound Editor:* Wylie Stateman and Gregg Baxter. *Casting:* Janet Hirshenson and Jane Jenkins. *Production Designer:* Lilly Kilvert. *Art Director:* John Warnke. *Set Designer:* Jann K. Engel. *Set Decorator:* Kara Lindstrom. *Special Effects:* Rocky Gehr. *Costumes:* Erica Edell Phillips. *Make-up:* Jim McCoy and Werner Keppler. *Stunt Coordinator:* Buddy Van Horn. *Running time:* 126 minutes. *MPAA Rating:* R.

CAST: Clint Eastwood (Frank Horrigan); John Malkovich (Mitch Leary); Rene Russo (Lilly Raines); Dylan McDermott (Al D'Andrea); Gary Cole (Bill Watts); Fred Dalton Thompson (Harry Sargent); John Mahoney (Sam Campagna); Greg Alan-Williams (Matt Wilder); Jim Curley (President); Sally Hughes (First Lady); Clyde Kusatsu (Jack Okura); Steve Hytner (Tony Carducci); Tobin Bell (Mendoza); Bob Schott (Jimmy Hendrickson); Juan A. Riojas (Raul); Elsa Raven (Booth's Landlady); Arthur Senzy (Paramedic); Patrika Darbo (Pam Magnus); Mary Van Arsdel (Sally); Ryan Cutrona (LAPD Brass); Lawrence Lowe (FBI Technician); Brian Libby (FBI Supervisor); Eric Bruskotter (Young Agent); Patrick Caddell (Political Speaker); John Heard (Professor Riger); Alan Toy (Walter Wickland); Carl Ciarfalio (CIA Agent Collins); Walt MacPherson and Robert Peters (Hunters); Tyde Kierney

(Police Captain Howard);   Anthony Peck (FBI Official);   Rick Hurst (Bartender);   Doris E. McMillon (DC News Anchor);   Robert Sandoval (Bellboy);   Joshua Malina (Agent Chavez); William G. Schilling (Sanford Riggs);   Michael Kirk (Computer Technician/Bates);   Richard Camphuis (Party Fat Cat);   Marlan Clarke (Marge);   Robert Alan Beuth (Man at Bank);   Susan Lee Hoffman (Woman at Bank);   Donna Hamilton (Reporter at Dulles);   Bob Jimenez (Reporter at Hotel);   Cylk Cozart (Agent Cozart);   Michael Zurich (Agent Zurich);   Rich DiDonato and Jeffrey Kurt Miller (Undercover Agents);   Kirk Jordan (Agent).

CHRISTIAN SCIENCE MONITOR, 7/16/93, p. 11, David Sterritt

Clint Eastwood belongs to that sturdy group of movie stars who grow more interesting as they grow older. Like his contemporary Robert Redford, he has never been particularly bold or expressive as an actor. But also like Redford, he has aged in fascinating ways—taking on more complexity as an artist, an icon, and a personality with each year and every new crag that arrives on his ruggedly handsome face.

Another thing Eastwood shares with Redford is a willingness to poke good-natured fun at his own screen image. Redford did this in his recent "Sneakers," and Eastwood has done it in a number of pictures—including the popular western "Unforgiven," where he played an over-the-hill farmer who had more trouble getting on his horse than vanquishing the bad guys. Frank Horrigan, the Secret Service agent played by Eastwood in "In the Line of Fire," isn't so far gone. But he's a far cry from the energetic up-and-comer he was in his early days. The decades have taken their toll—especially since the moment in 1963 when he and his fellow agents failed to save President John F. Kennedy from assassination. Horrigan has stayed in the Secret Service, trudging through a reasonably successful career. Bad memories have never left him, though, and his lonely personal life reflects his lingering sense of guilt.

This acquires renewed force when the current president (not modeled on any real-life politician) becomes the target of a would-be assassin. This killer, as crazy as he is dangerous, regards his deadly plot as a sinister sort of game. He draws Horrigan into the game by contacting him and revealing aspects of his evil scheme—along with taunts about Horrigan's past, and challenges to do his job more capably this time around.

In the scenes that focus on Horrigan's life, "In the Line of Fire" gets marvelous spice from Eastwood's gift for not taking himself too seriously. As in some of the movies he made with Sondra Locke, the character he plays is a macho he-man who can't quite pull off the self-centered posturing that comes with this territory. His encounters with a female Secret Service agent are delicious to watch, as his wisecracks fall flat and his attempts at charm wear thin—leading her to end one of their conversations by cheerfully observing, "Time flies when you're being annoyed!"

In the scenes focusing on Horrigan's duel with the assassin, the movie grows far more somber and aggressively violent at times. Credit for the power of these episodes goes largely to John Malkovich, whose skill and conviction serve him grimly well as one of the most demented characters to reach the screen since the horrifying villains of "The Silence of the Lambs," whom Malkovich's psychopath occasionally resembles.

"In the Line of Fire" was directed by Wolfgang Petersen, the versatile German filmmaker whose credits range from "Das Boot," a hard-hitting war picture that earned international acclaim about 15 years ago, to "The Neverending Story," a likable children's movie. He keeps his new film hopping at a lively pace, and he shows sensitivity to the look and feel of American politics.

Both the humorous and sober aspects of the story have slack moments during the last half-hour or so, however, and Petersen shares responsibility for this along with Jeff McGuire's screenplay. One can't help suspecting that "In the Line of Fire" would have more depth if Eastwood himself had directed it, since his work behind the camera—in pictures as varied as "Bird" and "White Hunter, Black Heart," to name just a couple—has established him as one of Hollywood's most invigorating stylists.

Other collaborators on the movie include two of the best in the business: John Bailey, who did the vivid cinematography, and Ennio Morricone, who composed the effective score. Rene Russo and Fred Dalton Thompson round out the good supporting cast.

FILMS IN REVIEW, 10/93, p. 329, Harry Pearson

In the Line of Fire is the sort of high concept thriller that, when both the ingredients and the auguries are right, Hollywood does best. And, for *Fire*, more than just the auguries were right; so were the elements necessary to the transmutation of concept to reality.

Consider: In terms of its plot, *Fire* incorporates just about every cliche known to the makers of modern thrillers. And yet herein, thanks both to the crisp and tightly constructed screenplay (from Jeff Maguire, a rookie) and a happy blending of many diverse talents, these cliches are played with such resonance that they nearly acquire the power of myth.

Were it not for a significant moral hole in the construction of the narrative, the guiding hands behind this movie might well have produced a genre masterwork. That gap robs the movie of its moral weight and, finally, conscience.

First, though, the good stuff.

Let's begin with the performances. Which are, with the exception of Fred Dalton Thompson's Harry Sargent, uncommonly good. Consider: Patrika Darbo, in the small but crucial role of a gabby bank teller who comes to no good end: You don't, for a second, doubt her. Then there's the most underrated of our young leading men, Dylan McDermott, playing the troubled sidekick to Clint Eastwood's wizened Secret Service agent. McDermott is pivotal to the tale; it is a thankless role, but one to which he brings the breath of reality, which he achieves by underplaying: note how realistically he manages to suggest fear in two crucial sequences. You believe the character, not the actor. Eastwood is simply wonderful in his role as a man for whom the world changed when John F. Kennedy was assassinated (and, indeed, as the movie makes clear, it did change with that killing). He holds himself responsible, thinking had he acted more quickly after hearing the first gunshot, he might have thwarted the murder. (We accept this convention as the film postulates it, although there is no reason to believe anyone could have done anything after the first shot—the time interval was too small—hence the necessity for a single bullet theory). Failing that, we have to believe that Eastwood's character has an overweening notion of his own importance, and later on, because of the gap, that we do. Eastwood's agent is aging, not in top physical condition, and, it would seem, living a life without much meaning. Eastwood projects a frail vulnerability, and, at moments, a kind of crinkly unassuming charm unlike anything you've seen out of him before. And so his heroism here becomes the ordinary man's heroism, not what we're used to, the superhero who has only special effects to overcome. Last but hardly least, we have John Malkovich's brilliant, creepy, and seductive (just as evil should be) performance as the would-be assassin, whose motive in assassinating a president is "to punctuate the dreariness"—a skin-crawling line. Indeed, Malkovich is very nearly too good in this role. It could be, like Brad Dourif's crazy in *One Flew Over the Cuckoo's Nest* and Anthony Perkins' Norman Bates, a hard one to live down. (Malkovich is, by all evidence, far too much the smartie to ever allow himself to become typed in this fashion. Still, with that face, one wonders if he ever will quite capture the popular imagination so powerfully in any other way again). One of his most brilliant bits during the movie's most critical scene—putting Eastwood's pistol in his mouth—was entirely improvised, and, all the more eerie for that. Malkovich, just after this bit of foreplay, then shoots down Eastwood's partner, McDermott, adding powerful implications to an already troubling encounter, on the rooftop.

To this, we must add the technical credits: Wolfgang Petersen's trim direction (so nice to see him lean and mean again, especially after *Shattered* and *Enemy Mine*); John Bailey's startlingly fresh look for the film and his intelligent use of the Panavision screen; Bailey manages to suggest the monolithic mass of Washington (as a perceptive critic elsewhere has noted), which he colors in moody modern art style (intentionally). In certain venues, however, the film looked less sharply edged than it is in fact, thanks to the current and lousy state of the projection art (same thing happened to *The Crying Game* in certain theaters). I thought Ann V. Coates editing in no small way responsible for the movie's headlong thrust and near relentlessness. Even its "quiet" moments has a kinetic feeling. And, in the appropriately equipped theaters, the soundtrack exhibited very wide frequency response, though not much in the way of imaginative use of surround.

For all this, I found the computer "enhancements" of reality (inserting Eastwood into the Kennedy-Dallas newsreels and an actor's head onto Bill Clinton's body politic during last year's campaign) *obviously* fake. Ditto for the climactic finale, which could and should have been a lot more fierce—I'm thinking of the *pas-de-deux* in the glass elevator and Malkovich's plunge—and a lot less phony.

Neither these technical blips, nor an uninspired score by Morricone, seriously injure the film's pacing. But there are certain questionable aspects of the script: Where does Malkovich get all his money? Is telephone tapping technology that easily confounded by CIA-style digital switching devices? Why don't Eastwood and McDermott call for back-up?

These pale into silence beside the film's most troubling lapse (a lapse that actually invites audience questioning, say, notably, on the point of back-up and Eastwood's motivations). A brief plot synopsis first:

Eastwood, in checking out what seems to be a routine sort of call, runs into evidence that a potential assassin is about to strike the president, who is in a desperate bid for re-election, hence, inclined to ignore Secret Service strictures in an effort to appear more accessible to the public. Soon enough, the would-be assassin is telephoning Clint to taunt and tease him, particularly about the Kennedy assassination. By the way, this president is no John F. Kennedy and thus, in Malkovich's enlightened view, hardly worth the saving. Eastwood, who shares Malkovich's contempt for this president, is paid by the Secret Service to protect him.

At the heart of the movie is the rooftop confrontation which involved Eastwood, Malkovich, and McDermott. There has been, immediately subsequent to this, a painful scene in which McDermott tells Eastwood he wants to quit the Service, and gives him good reason why. (So you know he's going to be killed, since the script skips no cliches.) Eastwood prevails upon him to stick with it. Malkovich makes another of his calls (during which he violently loses his temper for the first time—an improvisation also—watch Eastwood's reaction if you don't believe he's become *the* consummate actor), only this time, he stays on too long and—bingo—they've traced him through the phone call. Minutes later, McDermott spots Malkovich walking away from his boarding house (in disguise) and he and Eastwood give chase. This leads to the justly praised rooftop sequence. Eastwood is just behind Malkovich when he jumps a gap between two buildings, a leap that the aging agent barely makes: he is left hanging almost literally by his fingernails. Malkovich grabs Eastwood's hand, saving him from a three-story fall into an alleyway. Eastwood, with his free hand, pulls out his gun as if to shoot Malkovich. Malkovich says: "The only way for you to save the president is to shoot me. Are you willing to do that? To give your life for his?" And Eastwood doesn't shoot. (After all, the fall might *not* have killed him.) McDermott, who has been watching all this, can do nothing. Malkovich swings Eastwood to the side, releases him so that he lands on a third floor fire escape, and then, after a feint, shoots McDermott. Twice.

You'd expect Eastwood's agent, tortured with guilt for (circa) 30 years for failing to save Kennedy, to be tormented by his failure to act—a failure that might mean this president's death and certainly meant his partner's death (one doubly needless since McDermott was on the verge of resigning). At this point, you might well wonder why, when Malkovich put his mouth around Eastwood's pistol, he didn't just blow off the back of his head. After this, nothing happens. There is no reaction. Eastwood doesn't demonstrate much in the way of grief, nor anything in the way of self-doubt or self-questioning. We don't even know if he has words of comfort for McDermott's offstage wife and children. Nor is any of this in the script (which I had hoped, since Maguire seemed otherwise to be covering all bases). This moral failure on his character's part robs the audience of its sympathy for Eastwood and turns the movie, more or less, into what it had, up until this point late in the tale, assiduously avoided becoming, that is, just another thriller with an invincible and morally insensitive hero. And it is after this point, that the life and elan go out of the picture. If we are held in place, it is because of the momentum of the plot's mechanics and a post-assassination sequence that induces a rush of adrenalin—this scene of the president being removed, by Secret Service men, from the hotel through its elaborate kitchen and back hallways is truly electrifying. But the rest is pretty much pulp. Too bad, too.

LOS ANGELES TIMES, 7/9/93, Calendar/p. 1, Kenneth Turan

Used to be that all a hero needed to operate was a weapon, a partner and a code of honor, with maybe a good woman thrown into the mix. In these more uncertain times, however, a hero is hardly worth saluting without a villain of stature on the other side, standing mockingly in his path and matching him strength for strength.

And when the hero is played by Clint Eastwood, this requirement becomes even more critical. For Eastwood, no ordinary good guy, is a paradigm of virile qualities, a man who has been so invulnerable for so long he's become a one-of-a-kind icon whose movies are built around him with all the care and discernment of a necklace fabricated for the Hope Diamond.

So with Eastwood starring as a veteran Secret Service agent in Wolfgang Petersen's crisply entertaining "In the Line of Fire", the key question is who gets to play the implacable assassin sworn to drop the President in his tracks. The choice was John Malkovich and it's difficult to think of a better one.

It's not just that Malkovich is an excellent actor with credits ranging from "Dangerous Liaisons" to "Of Mice and Men." It's the kind of actor he is, an Obie-winning veteran of the prestigious Steppenwolf Theater Company who is at home even on the stages of London's West End.

With a background so spiritually different from Eastwood's "Rawhide"/spaghetti Western origins, Malkovich makes the best kind of villain for this piece, providing the kind of intrinsically adversarial presence that James Dean, for instance, did for Raymond Massey in "East of Eden." And Malkovich's insinuating, carefully thought out delivery is in the same way an ideal foil for Eastwood's bluntly straightforward habits.

Eastwood's Frank Horrigan is not protecting anyone at first, he is working with partner Al D'Andrea (Dylan McDermott) on the services anti-counterfeiting detail and taking less guff than anyone in the federal government. One night, called on to investigate a suspicious lodger, he and Al discover enough disturbing evidence to make Frank sure they've stumbled onto an executioner's lair.

But not only has Frank recognized a potential killer, the killer has recognized Frank as well. For Horrigan is not just any Secret Service agent he was John F. Kennedy's favorite, on the scene in Dallas and traumatized from that day to this (and for all we know in a support group with Kevin Costner's similarly disturbed "Bodyguard") because he wasn't able to stop the bullet that found the President.

All this comes out in a series of phone calls that the assassin, who airily asks to be called Booth (as in John Wilkes) because that man "had flair, panache," makes to Frank out of sheer dark glee that this legendary agent is on his trail. "Going up against you raises the game to a much higher level." Booth says in his oily, menacing way. "Fate has brought us together. I can't get over the irony."

Booth's feeling of connection with Frank, his desire to simultaneously admire and taunt him, is the strongest point in "In the Line of Fire's" script, which ends up giving many of its best lines to the predator. (It was written by Jeff McGuire on the suggestion of producer Jeff Apple, a Secret Service buff since he was a teen-ager whose continued fascination apparently led to extensive agency cooperation.)

More or less a genius of a hit man, master of weapons, phone trickery, disguise and no doubt much more, Booth is especially good at driving Frank crazy, messing with his head with all those needling phone calls. Hobbled by encroaching age, doubting superiors, pain-in-the-ass politicos who just don't get it, even a bad case of the flu, Frank manages to get himself reassigned to the presidential protection detail and perseveres. Still smarting over Dallas, he knows that Booth is going to make a try at this President and he wants to be there when it happens.

Given that everyone in the theater knows the same thing, to say that director Petersen completely involves us in the action is saying a great deal. The first first-rank director Eastwood has agreed to work with in at least 10 years, Petersen (best known for the splendid "Das Boot") brings many of the same qualities as Eastwood himself would to the project, including a lean, unadorned style, a concern with pace and an emphasis on keeping the audience intrigued. With his professionalism and his understanding of genre, Petersen is as good a match for Eastwood on his side of the camera as Malkovich is on his.

As for Eastwood himself, his laconic mastery of screen acting has become such a given that "Line of Fire's" script feels free to have some gentle fun with his durable persona by having Horrigan claim "a good glare can be just as effective as a gun." In truth, every part of this film trades so heavily on Eastwood's presence that it is impossible to imagine it with anyone else in the starring role.

"In the Line of Fire" (rated R for violence and language) has also tried, with some success, to broaden Eastwood's appeal, to make him less Dirty Harry and more Jimmy Stewart by entangling him romantically with a feisty female agent engagingly played by Rene Russo, who was similarly matched with Mel Gibson in "Lethal Weapon III."

Eastwood, whose light comedy flair was evident as far back as "Bronco Billy," is quite adept at the stretch, but unfortunately this May-December liaison is the least well-written and creatively imagined part of the story. We are patient through it all, however, because when the bullets fly, there is no one but Eastwood we'd rather see pumping them out for our side.

NEW STATESMAN & SOCIETY, 9/3/93, p. 35, Jonathan Romney

How much mythic resonance can one man carry? Last year, Clint Eastwood single-handedly gave the Western back all its tight-lipped integrity in *Unforgiven*; now here he is making something fresh out of the stale old action movie with *In the Line of Fire*. He didn't direct this time—that honour goes to Wolfgang Petersen, redeeming himself magnificently after the rambling idiocy of his cod-Hitchcockian *Shattered*. But Eastwood's presence, which grows more iconic as each hair turns grey, dominates the film and gives an already tight, intelligent piece of work a real sense of pathetic stature.

As ever, Eastwood doesn't have to do that much—he's rarely had to emote, *Unforgiven* notwithstanding. Usually it's just a case of running, firing, staying mum and exuding some kind of unspecific intent. Here, he's taken on a nicely acidic self-deprecating humour, miles from the jokey, cigar-chomping, cartoon he's allowed himself to become on occasion. He's reticent here, but his reticence gets more eloquent as his characters get older; it's not so much *substance* he's taken on, but rather a patina, like the moss that grows on old statues and makes them twice as august.

Here he's helped in any case by Jeff Maguire's well-honed script, which gives him a complex character and a familiar but inventively reworked premise—he's the good cop trying to stop a crazed killer getting to the president. But the story packs both a mythic dimension and a personal one. Eastwood's character, Frank Horrigan, is an ageing presidential security man who's regarded by colleagues as a "dinosaur", a "borderline burn-out". Of course, he's been dragging around 30 years of torment—he was in JFK's car the day he got shot, and part of him is stuck in Dallas (a young Eastwood has actually been sewn magically into film of the motorcade). Not only is he living on borrowed time (he's convinced he could have stopped the bullet), but he's also living in a world he has no place in, and one he feels responsible for. Like much of middle America, he's convinced that US history (as a *utopian* myth) ended with JFK's death. "Everything," he muses, "would be different today, if ..."

What is all that guilt and impotence, if not the flip side of a megalomaniac fantasy of omnipotence? If Horrigan seems to embody all that's still noble—albeit scarred—in modern America, it's because he sees himself as noble but scarred. There's a self-aggrandising pathos in him that is destined to meet its match; and that comes in the form of an all-knowing enigma on the other end of the phone. Horrigan enters into a sort of telephonic, telepathic tag match with a mysterious would-be assassin (John Malkovich) who's obsessed with presidential killings, but who likes to call himself "Booth" rather than "Oswald". "Booth had more style," he says and you can see why. Like the Booth who shot Lincoln in a theatre, this Booth is a performer *and* a spectator—he likes to watch the spectacle from afar, but he loves to be part of it too. In addition, he's a master of disguises, seeing his mission as a game, a grand performance (indeed, he seems to wear disguises purely for his own amusement). A multiple, feminised foil to Eastwood's male, monolithic self-identity, Malkovich is superb, playing up his own narcissistic tendencies to the hilt, glacial one minute, on the edge of histrionics the next—a prissy, sardonic face in the crowd, lips pursed with murderous intent.

They're doubles, of course—"Booth" and Horrigan turn out to have similar misgivings about post-JFK America. But his similarity makes Booth a remarkably effective psychoanalyst, too. He knows everything there is to know about his foe, knows how to hit the right buttons to get the responses he wants, how to manipulate silences. This is, after all, an analytic game all the way.

What Horrigan's after is a cure, and that's only possible through repetition. He needs to relive his trauma to get close to the bullet again, but properly this time, maybe destroying himself in the process (his is a death wish on a historical scale). In effect, Horrigan needs to grow up: he's a case of arrested development. He can't get over being a young man who outlived a symbolic father; now he's an old man, but a father-figure *manqué*, who thinks he can only achieve patriarch status by defeating one younger man and saving (dying for?) another. That's why the part of America's post-JFK trauma seems to have been sparked off again by the advent of Clinton and the popular desire to see him as Kennedy *redivivus*. There's certainly plenty of scope for trauma when a nation obsessively invests the hopes associated with youth into a role that's so fundamentally regarded as a patriarchal one. It's no accident, then, that the one resounding—albeit confused—attempt so far to paint a state-of-the-nation picture of Clinton-era America has been *Falling Down*, in which social breakdown is equated with a crisis in the state of fatherhood itself.

NEW YORK, 7/19/93, p. 48, David Denby

Like Michael Jordan turning midair variations on a simple dunk shot, *In the Line of Fire* transcends its own clichés as it goes along. This exciting, intelligent, and even deeply felt movie is easily the best American thriller since *The Silence of the Lambs*. It's a surprise, too, because there's nothing wonderful in the idea itself: The theme of a Secret Service agent longing to take a bullet for the president—and fulfilling himself by getting shot—was turned into moist and redolent garbage only recently in *The Bodyguard*, in which ex-agent Kevin Costner, having failed the Gipper at his moment of need, became the stern protector and lover of a cranky pop star. ("And I ... ee ... I ... ee ... I will alwayyyss love yooouuou... .") *That* pop star.

But the screenwriter Jeff McGuire, working from an idea by producer Jeff Apple, has dug deeper in the same mine and has discovered a vein of high-grade ore; and Wolfgang Petersen, the German-born director who made *Das Boot*, works with startling power. Clint Eastwood, his physical skills slowing, his breath running shorter, is Frank Horrigan, an agent haunted by the events of Dallas, 1963. Close to Kennedy when the first bullet hit, Frank froze for an instant and failed to save the president from the second bullet. For the past 30 years of Frank's life, he has languished in the shadow of that moment's hesitation. Within the Secret Service, he's known as a sorehead and a loser, with a tendency to screw things up.

The stoic loner whose pride covers deep wounds is, of course, familiar from Hemingway and from everything that descended from Hemingway—hard-boiled fiction and Humphrey Bogart's heroic grimace and some of the earlier, less convincing performances of Clint Eastwood himself. It's one of the staples of American popular culture, but what makes the character live in this case is the challenge he faces—a threat to kill the current American president that comes from someone considerably smarter than Frank.

Mitch Leary (John Malkovich), an ex-assassin for the CIA who has snapped, is a nasty tease with a malicious sense of irony. When Frank and his partner answer a complaint and break into Mitch's Washington apartment, they stare at a wall filled with pictures of the Kennedy motorcade and quotations from Sirhan Sirhan. The obsessions of a hapless fantasist who kills presidents in his head—that's what Frank is meant to think (there are indications that the pictures were left there for Frank to find). But it's a ploy, a feint, and quickly Mitch lets the Secret Service know that, on the contrary, he's a wacko who can kill the president, and whenever he wants to. He's willing to die; he just wants to be famous. He plays with Frank's suspicious anxiety, questioning his courage, telling him on the telephone that *another* American president is going to fall right in front of him.

This man of many disguises shows up at a rally as the president gives a speech, risking getting caught. Only afterward does Frank realize that Mitch has been there, mocking, taunting, watching him. The filmmakers have turned the usual kind of movie supervillain into a hipster intellectual, a chameleon of sinister wit and perverse imagination, like Nabokov's Clare Quilty from *Lolita*. And Mitch loves teasing Frank, the ultimate square, who carries his pained, noble sense of duty around with him like a sack. Both men are drawn, mothlike, to the president, who is nothing more than a hollow pol running for re-election: Frank because redemption for his past sins will arrive only through his protecting this man; Mitch because the president is there to be killed.

It's great fun watching these two actors of utterly different temperament go up against each other. Malkovich has pulled together all his malevolent skills—the drawling mock innocence, the slow, shiv-edged sarcasm, the donkey-foolish smile that turns mean. Malkovich could make an invitation to a children's birthday party sound like the creepiest of insinuations, and he has some giddy moments—his rag-doll walk, for instance, when Mitch, standing in Lafayette park (just across from the White House), poses as a bum with long hair and a gold tooth; his eager smiles when he dresses as a suave, wealthy businessman trading pleasantries at a fund-raiser. Mitch is himself a kind of actor, and the link between acting and nasty black magic has never been clearer.

In the past, when Clint Eastwood wanted to show us he was a fallible man—in *Every Which Way but Loose*, say—he would scowl furiously, pretending to be outraged that a monkey, a woman, a child, remained outside his control. People would be shocked: Clint is acting! Clint has a sense of humor! But he was still granite, alas, and he would quickly retract into myth, two dimensions acknowledging that a third might be out there somewhere. In this movie, however, he gives an essentially realistic performance; and he's actually quite touching. His flirtation with a coolly beautiful Secret Service agent (Rene Russo), who genuinely dislikes him in the beginning and has to be won over, is full of awkward mishaps. His tears of shame when he recalls the Kennedy assassination—tears mixed with love for JFK—complete the transformation to a man whose grace is now moral rather than physical.

Wolfgang Petersen has great skill with detail (remember the rivets popping when the submarine went too deep in *Das Boot*?), and here he captures what the Secret Service agent sees—the unaccountable movements, the crush of fools trying to get near to the president in public, each one a potential assassin. I was fascinated by the minutiae of the agents' routine, by the frantic security procedures—the agents hustling the president through hotel corridors after Mitch gets a shot off, holding his arms and pushing him as if he were the assailant rather than the victim. There's nothing like fresh physical observation to bring a thriller to life. Petersen keeps the tension high through the many telephone conversations between Frank and Mitch, and their direct confrontations are thrilling, especially a chase across rooftops ending in a physically bizarre and morally logical scene that is worthy of Hitchcock.

Of course, Eastwood gets there in the end—he gets back to myth. His Frank has to take the bullet regardless of his feelings for the officeholder: His heroism is almost impersonal—it's an ideal of service—but the hero is now a man at last.

NEW YORK POST, 7/9/93, p. 25, Michael Medved

Where were you the day JFK was shot?

If you put that question to veteran Secret Service agent Frank Horrigan, the character Clint Eastwood plays so well in the new thriller "In the Line of Fire," then you're asking the wrong guy.

According to the smart, snappy script (by previously unknown screenwriter Jeff Maguire), Horrigan spent that fateful day in Dallas, assigned to protect the president, and even 30 years later he hasn't gotten over his failure to do his job.

In '63 he was a slick young hotshot, Jack Kennedy's favorite agent; but after three decades he's a burnout case—with his wife and kids long departed and his fellow agents treating him as an object of pity. He spends his off-duty hours drinking alone, or playing jazz piano in dark, smoky bars.

The story kicks in when Horrigan stumbles across evidence of a methodical maniac who's determined to kill the current chief executive. If the aging agent can stop this new assassination, he'll somehow redeem himself for Dallas; this time, he's determined that he'll do what he failed to do 30 years before, and take the bullets intended for the President of the United States.

It's part of the special genius of this movie that director Wolfgang Petersen portrays this current president as hardly worth the trouble: He's a paunchy, middle-aged mediocrity (Jim Curley) in the midst of a floundering reelection campaign who's identified only by his Secret Service code name "Traveler."

The point of Eastwood's dedication isn't the defense of some worthy prince (or principle), but rather reclaiming his own lost honor. This raises the strong implication that if he can only foil this new killer then he can somehow make up for what went wrong for the whole country in November 1963.

Eastwood, fresh from his Oscar-winning triumphs in "Unforgiven," has never played a more complex, vulnerable and compelling hero; and in scheming killer John Malkovich he more than meets his match.

Hannibal Lecter can now move over and make room at the top: Malkovich's Mitch Leary is one of the most memorable movie villains of recent years. This is a great performance, investing this creepy, brilliant psychotic with so much intensity and flair that we almost come to root for pure evil—as we did with Lecter.

The other star of the film, former Vogue model Rene Russo, plays essentially the same role she handled effectively in "Lethal Weapon III"—a tough, no-nonsense law enforcement professional who provides the love interest for the hero.

Here she's presented as part of a new breed of dedicated female recruits to the Secret Service (dismissed as "window dressing" by the curmudgeonly loner, Horrigan), But she is ultimately moved by Horrigan's quirky charm, piercing loneliness and single-minded pursuit of the killer.

Their brief love scenes offer no nudity or graphic details, but an abundance of genuine passion and tenderness; Eastwood has seldom struck such sexy sparks with one of his female co-stars.

The film has so much going for it that its shortcomings are easily overlooked. Chief among these is a big climax that turns out to be unexpectedly ordinary and sharply disappointing after all the expertly calibrated suspense that leads up to it. There's also a silly and unnecessary back story about evil machinations by the CIA.

But German director Wolfgang Petersen handles even the script's weakest elements with consummate skill and perfect pacing, never allowing showmanship or self-conscious "artistry" to interfere with the story's momentum.

In the past, even his American-made box office flops ("Enemy Mine," "Shattered") featured scattered moments of brilliance and poetry; but "In the Line of Fire" recaptures the taut intensity of Petersen's unforgettable World War II epic, "Das Boot."

Like the German U-Boat crew in that harrowing 1982 classic, his Secret Service heroes aren't supermen—they're just ordinary guys trying desperately to do their jobs under increasingly insane and menacing circumstances. These movies seem to suggest that this quiet professionalism is the essence of true heroism—as it is of superior movie-making.

NEWSDAY, 7/9/93, Part II/p. 54, Jack Mathews

In Wolfgang Petersen's brilliant new thriller "In the Line of Fire," John Malkovich plays a would-be presidential assassin who nicknames himself Booth, out of admiration for the "panache" of the lunatic who killed Abraham Lincoln.

Clint Eastwood is Frank Horrigan, a Secret Service agent whose inability to protect John F. Kennedy from an assassin 30 years ago nearly destroyed his life and left him so guilt-ridden, he's ready to accept the blame for even Lincoln's death.

"I wish I could have been there for you, Abe," Horrigan mumbles at one point to the Lincoln Memorial.

Booth, in fact a disenchanted ex-CIA agent, knows every nuance of Horrigan's torment, empathizes with him, as one civil servant to another, and offers him a chance to atone for his and every other blown attempt to protect a leader. In the first of many calls to Frank, Booth announces his intention to kill the president, and invites the Secret Service man to try to stop him. The cat-and-mouse game that ensues is a model of filmmaking efficiency, from the writing and casting all the way through to the perfectly paced final edit and Ennio Morricone's evocative score. The movie is two hours long, but seems to zip by in half the time of Sydney Pollack's lead-footed adaptation of "The Firm."

This is the best movie Eastwood has hired himself out for in 22 years, since Don Siegel's "Dirty Harry," and, like his role in last year's "Unforgiven," it's a character seasoned by both his years and his past movie lives.

Horrigan, by his own description, is a borderline burnout "with questionable social skills." He is who Dirty Harry might have become if he'd gotten a better education and gone into the Secret Service instead of the San Francisco PD.

He's calmer, deeper and less political than Harry, and his emotional range has expanded to allow in some amiable wit, an occasional smile and in one surprisingly moving scene, a few tears.

But Horrigan is very much the same sort of department rebel, more interested in getting the job done than in following the book, and he can provoke a superior in a wink.

Petersen seemed to know exactly how far he could go with Eastwood's tough-guy image and mannerisms without lapsing into cliché, and by transporting Eastwood's own musicianship and love of jazz to Frank's character, he gave him a layer of personality that fits him like an old suit. Eastwood, who often resembles the oak he swung from in "Hang 'em High," has never looked looser or more comfortable in front of a camera.

The tempered performance was essential to this material, because there is only one bad guy for Eastwood to confront, and he's no do-you-feel-lucky kind of punk. Booth is deranged but brilliant, and the pursuit of him, and the race against the clock to save the president, works on the audience like a long, furiously burning fuse.

What "In the Line of Fire" lacks in number of bad guys, Malkovich more than makes up for in pound-for-pound evil. Booth's reasoning is twisted by spite against a government that made a killer of him, but the relish he takes in taunting Frank and prepping for the big day is pure, malevolent sport.

It is hard work creating suspense and tension through telephone conversations, but Malkovich makes those the most compelling scenes in the picture. Booth, using his CIA savvy to elude traces, coolly toys with Frank and the others listening in on the phone, badgers him about his past, tweaks his conscience, questions his willingness to "take a bullet" for his boss.

Malkovich masters this character almost entirely through inflection, and it's an extraordinary "voice" performance. One moment, he's attempting to lull Frank with soothing assurances that he understands what he's going through; the next, he's on a mad rant, demanding to be treated with respect. "In the Line of Fire" has plenty of other things going on—a dramatic rooftop chase, a spectacular high-rise finale, two double-murders—but the real psychological action is over the phone.

If the film has a weakness, it is in the romantic subplot between Frank and fellow Secret Service agent Lilly Raines (Rene Russo). It's essential that Frank have someone who can draw out the real source of his pain, and Russo (Mel Gibson's love interest in "Lethal Weapon III") gives Lilly the right combination of grit and compassion to give credence to both her career role and her relationship.

However, having established the romance, Petersen seems to think better of it and take it back. Frank expends a lot of energy and charm seducing Lilly, but after their first passionate encounter is interrupted by a phone call, it's as if they forget where they left off.

Maybe you will, too. It is a thriller, not a love story, and the second half rushes us headlong toward the inevitable assassination attempt.

In a season of near misses—"Jurassic Park" has great dinosaurs and ridiculous people, "Cliffhanger" had great action and a ridiculous story—"In the Line of Fire" is the most satisfying thriller yet.

NEWSWEEK, 7/12/93, p. 60, David Ansen

It remains to be seen how Clint Eastwood the director-producer is going to try to follow that tough act "Unforgiven." But Clint the actor-star returns in full stride in *In the Line of Fire*, a crisp and lean cat-and-mouse thriller that is, pound for pound, the most accomplished Hollywood entertainment so far this summer. He's playing a tough, cranky, aging Secret Service agent named Frank Horrigan. Frank's a bit of an anachronism, a jazz-loving leftover from another generation. He's still got great loner instincts, but he's damaged goods: he was on duty protecting JFK in Dallas that day in 1963, and his failure to take the bullets intended for the president has been gnawing at his conscience ever since. Now there are new death threats against a new president, and Frank wants a chance to redeem himself. The strange thing is, the assassin, a man of many names and disguises (John Malkovich), seems to have handpicked Frank as his opponent. As the president, campaigning for re-election, crisscrosses the country, a creepy game develops between the two men: the one willing to give his life to save the president, the other willing to sacrifice his to kill the president.

Eastwood played with this theme in "Tightrope," blurring the psychological line between virtuous hunter and depraved prey. It's an old riff, but Jeff McGuire's deft screenplay plays smart variations on the theme. And Eastwood and Malkovich, though they may seem to come from two different acting traditions, prove a brilliant pairing, less cat and mouse perhaps than lion and snake. The slippery, soft-spoken Malkovich is a master of wormy menace. Like Peter Lorre, the paradigm of twisted, dead-behind-the-eyes psychos, he has the delicious gift of showy understatement. Eastwood is never showy, but his laconic simplicity has never been so sly. Age has deepened him: it gives the strain in his face resonance, and wit to his romantic fervor. One of the pleasures of "In the Line of Fire" is the grace with which it meshes the suspense with Frank's amorous pursuit of a younger Secret Service agent (Rene Russo), a woman who'd like to write Frank off as a sexist dinosaur but can't resist his seasoned charm. The tough-tender chemistry between them feels lived in, comfy.

The man behind the camera is Wolfgang Petersen, returning to the gripping form of "Das Boot." You can sense he's made a careful study of Eastwood's movies, but he brings his own special flair to the action scenes—there's a cliffhanging rooftop-chase sequence that pumps new blood into that oldest of conventions—and he shifts the comedy and the tension with no gear-stripping. Maybe it takes a German director, an English editor (the accomplished Anne Coates) and an Italian composer (Ennio Morricone) to make a movie in the classical Hollywood style these days. Generously exciting, "In the Line of Fire" is mercifully free of that artificial energy that makes so many new movies look as if they were created with steroids. To use a word that Malkovich's psycho is anachronistically fond of, this thriller has panache.

SIGHT AND SOUND, 9/93, p. 48, Tom Tunney

Having busted a gang of counterfeiters, veteran US Secret Service agent Frank Horrigan investigates a possible threat to the life of the US President—an abandoned Washington DC apartment in which the walls are covered with photos of John F Kennedy and other assassination victims. Horrigan later takes a telephone call at his apartment from a man calling himself 'Booth', who intimates that he's planning to kill the President; 'Booth' shows a close knowledge of Horrigan's career and his presence on duty during JFK's assassination.

At an abrasive meeting with his bosses, Horrigan is introduced to his new colleague Lilly Raines, with whom he later develops a relationship. Horrigan suggests that Booth's threat should be taken seriously, and asks to be assigned back to presidential protection duty. Escorting the presidential limo on foot, Horrigan is watched by Booth. Booth calls Horrigan again, taunting him about his inability to save JFK, and showing a detailed knowledge of Horrigan's life—his drink problem and the fact that his wife left.

Booth opens a bank account using a fictional company name and then, to cover his tracks, feels obliged to murder the bank clerk and her flatmate. Booth uses the account to make donations to the President's campaign fund, which later ensures an invitation to the presidential banquet in LA. During escort duty, Horrigan recognises a disguised Booth and gives chase. Booth escapes, but leaves his fingerprints behind; but his prints and identity are deemed to be classified information, and withheld from Horrigan.

At an indoor rally, Horrigan causes a scare when he mistakes a bursting balloon for a gunshot—Booth is responsible. A lead takes Horrigan and his partner Al D'Andrea to Booth's home in Phoenix, where two CIA agents reveal Booth's true identity—Mitch Leary, a top CIA assassin who was made redundant. Out practising with a homemade plastic gun, Leary is approached by two men and kills them both. Tracing Leary's latest call, Horrigan and D'Andrea pursue him over the rooftops; Horrigan almost falls and is caught by Leary, who gives him the option of killing them both. Saving Horrigan, Leary kills D'Andrea and escapes.

Posing as a businessman, Leary appears at the fund-raising junket in LA. Horrigan, arresting an innocent waiter in front of the TV cameras, is reassigned to the next presidential destination, San Diego. There, he realises that a note found at Leary's house refers to the bank where Leary opened his account. Investigating, he returns to the banquet in time to put himself between Leary and the President. A struggle concludes with Leary dangling from a great height. Horrigan offers to save him, but Leary chooses to fall to his death. Hailed as a hero, Horrigan announces his retirement and returns home with Lilly to hear a final message from Leary, which they choose to ignore.

One of the watersheds of Clint Eastwood/s movie career was his role as the maverick detective Harry Callahan in Don Siegel's *Dirty Harry*. The crucial symbolic watershed in postwar US history was the assassination of John F Kennedy. The value of *In the Line of Fire* lies in the way it adroitly unites these two elements. The film functions both as a formidable star vehicle and as a sophisticated cultural sponge, soaked to capacity with enlightening allusions to other movies.

Even down to his similar-sounding name, Frank Horrigan is a close relative of Harry Callahan: he's a professional with his own personal code, short on words and long on actions, a social and moral dinosaur who's accurately distrustful of authority. Unlike Harry, though, he also has a strong streak of self-pity, which goes back to his guilt about his perceived role in the death of JFK.

Much of the emphasis in Siegel's direction lay on bringing out the similarities between Harry and his adversary, the serial killer Scorpio. Both define themselves through violence, both live isolated lives in a city depicted as a nightmarish wasteland. The authorities Harry work for are morally bankrupt: his own life is purposeless but for his job; and the film's conclusion sees him blasting Scorpio into oblivion, then throwing away his badge of office in disgust. *Dirty Harry* is a profoundly pessimistic film, graphically conjuring the loss of direction that was seen to pervade US life in the years following JFK's assassination.

A superb villain, Mitch Leary in *In the Line of Fire* is a direct descendant of both Scorpio and *Taxi Driver*'s Travis Bickle. A disillusioned ex-CIA assassin, he's decided to take his revenge on the system that he feels has betrayed him. He's a man who's been morally destroyed by the time he's lived through and the discredited policies he's helped to implement. In his phone calls to Horrigan, Leary tries to persuade him that they share a common sense of betrayal. He wants Horrigan to acknowledge that society is now beyond redemption and that merely playing out a violent ritual is now all that's left to them both: "There is no cause worth fighting for. All we have is the game."

The world Leary talks about here is precisely the world of *Dirty Harry*, in which San Francisco became a gigantic game board for Harry and Scorpio to act out their struggle. The master stroke in *In the Line of Fire*, however, is the way in which it at first engages with the issue of Leary and Horrigan both being mentally scarred, but then deftly changes tack and organises itself around Horrigan's dismissal of the comparison. What Leary fails to understand is Horrigan's concept of honour—obviously, for a man who worked for the CIA in the 60s and 70s, that would be a difficult idea to grasp.

Horrigan is less the near-psychotic Callahan of the original *Dirty Harry* than a low self-esteemed version of the socially more relaxed hero of that film's first sequel, *Magnum Force*—a man who is prepared to work within 'the system' because it's all there is. In every area except his professional code, where no compromise is allowed, Horrigan is a pragmatist, prepared to accept imperfection—in others, if not in himself. He sees JFK's assassin not in terms of conspiracies and cover-ups, but as a simple follow-on from his own lapse from his professional high standards. "If only I'd reacted," he tells Lilly, "I could have taken that shot." Nothing else is important; Lee Harvey Oswald and the 'magic bullet theory' don't even rate a mention—which surely must be a first in any movie to include real footage of the Kennedy motorcade.

It's a gloriously absurd idea, particularly coming in the wake of Oliver Stone's *JFK*, but it's also a concept perfectly in keeping with Eastwood's star image and the way in which this image was first established in the Western genre. Stone's film might be seen as the *High Noon* of Kennedy movies, with Kevin Costner's Jim Garrison as a Gary Cooper/Marshall Kane figure, vainly asking questions, pleading for support from, then pointing an accusing finger at the corrupt social and political order. *In the Line of Fire*, however, takes a Hawksian, *Rio Bravo* approach to the subject. Horrigan isn't concerned with anyone else's behaviour: almost all officials are fools, the world is full of bad guys, the CIA employs killers—all this goes without saying.

However, the crucial difference between Horrigan and Harry is that Harry lives by his heroic code, while Horrigan guiltily believes he's failed in his life by not saving JFK. Saving the President 30 years on redeems him in much the same way that Dude—the Dean Martin character in *Rio Bravo*—is rehabilitated by helping John Wayne's sheriff hold out against the bad guys. It's the code of the professional lawman that Horrigan reaffirms, but it's also the behaviour of a hero who neither expects nor requires perfection from the world around him. Unlike both Dirty Harry and *High Noon*'s Marshall Kane, Horrigan doesn't throw his badge away, but retires happily and gracefully. He is a much more mellow Eastwood hero than Callahan—not a cynical avenger, but someone who's content again with his place in the world. It's a cosily redemptive ending.

A film as full of remarkable and rewarding resonances as *Unforgiven, In the Line of Fire* shows that the continuing potency of Eastwood's star image lies in his ability to redefine it self-consciously and subtly within the context of his other films and of earlier genre landmarks. Here, courtesy of Wolfgang Petersen's lean direction and Jeff Maguire's astute script, he achieves this within the crime thriller genre, finally breaking free after several flawed attempts (*Tightrope*, the several *Dirty Harry* sequels) from beneath Siegel's mantle. This is a fascinating reaffirmation and modification of his seminal role, by a star who could well be the last action hero to emote with his eyes rather than his muscles. Howard Hawks would be proud of him.

TIME, 7/12/93, p. 62, Richard Corliss

Clint Eastwood has always been an old man. Even in the '60s, as the gunslinger in Sergio Leone westerns, Eastwood had the squinty eyes, sour mouth and weary walk of a soldier who had been in too many wars. The six-day stubble hid countless psychic scars; the cigar butt stuck between his teeth suggested a world gone up in smoke; the poncho he wore could have been a shroud. As Dirty Harry and a passel of creepy cowboys, Eastwood carried himself with the slow, wily grace of the living dead. Idealism had been blasted out of him—only a grim irony stirred inside. *Unforgiven*, his Oscar winner and $100 million smash, was not a valedictory to the Clint persona; it was the latest verse in a career-long elegy to the faded American Dream.

Next stanza: *In the Line of Fire*, a just above-par melodrama about a Secret Service agent haunted by having botched his protection of John F. Kennedy nearly 30 years ago in Dallas and now assigned to shield the current President from a would-be assassin. Frank Horrigan (Eastwood) is your basic borderline burn-out with questionable social skills. He's a beast from the past, *Clintosaurus rex*, who believes that the things he knows about people will compensate for his diminished physical resources. His opponent, Mitch Leary (John Malkovich), is your basic twisted genius, a rogue warrior with dead eyes and a killer grudge.

The movie can exasperate when it embraces—and this is the last time we'll point this out, Hollywood, so listen up—the cockamamie conventions of the thriller genre: the buddy-partner who announces his retirement, then dies violently; the smart female officer who's around for window dressing and romantic relief; the pot-bellied villain who is more athletic than the slim, trim hero; and the mandatory climactic chase, in which the bad guy loads his gun, the good guy careers across town, and the moviegoer checks his watch.

At heart, though, *In the Line of Fire* is a conversation between two sides of a smart, troubled mind. In a series of phone chats, Leary toys with Horrigan, hovers like a dark angel or a guilty conscience, lets the agent see his fun-house mirror image in an assassin's paranoid logic. Why kill the President? "To punctuate the dreariness." At the end of the cold war and the American century, Leary says, "there's no cause left worth fighting for. All that's left is the game. I'm on offense; you're on defense."

The real battle here is between two generations of acting styles: meticulous method vs. star quality. On offense is Malkovich the master thespian, building a character with wigs and fake noses, gunning the menace by alternating a spooky stillness with violent shifts of his wispy, lispy voice. On defense is Clint the listener, the reactor, whose worn, handsome face is his technique. In these moments, you see agitated Actor and aging Star in a hot war of wits. The shoot-out is wonderful to watch.

VILLAGE VOICE, 7/13/93, p. 49, Georgia Brown

As a thriller, *The Bodyguard* may've been a joke, belly flopping like Kevin Costner taking one of several asinine flying leaps, but it surely did appeal to women who love Whitney (too much). Looking for the former, I was blind to the latter. This is how reviewers often miss the point next to the point. Little did I see how a dumb movie would reduce to a thrilling music video.

Not that I'm immune to the basic promise: that bodyguards wear lacy hearts over their brass balls. Donald Sutherland was never so sexy as in *Klute*, playing a depressed, lonely guy, a strict and grim puritan who watched over but couldn't touch. He will keep her safe while she will stir him awake. Patty Hearst wasn't the first poor rich girl to marry her bodyguard, but she had the best reason, to remind him of the time he wasn't there. *In the Line of Fire* is also a story of a bodyguard who wasn't there. Well, he was, but he didn't take the bullet. The second bullet, that is. Of course we're talking about the trauma *JFK* betrayed. Oh what a burden Frank Horrigan (Clint Eastwood) has borne. So when a clever, fanatical nutjob who's stalking the current president knows intimately the details of Frank's past failure, it's hard to tell if the guy is really fixated on the president or on Frank. And when Frank flubs his chances to eliminate the evil blot, it's hard to tell what his priorities are either.

But the real appeal of *In the Line of Fire* is that this very tense thriller stars the real last action dinosaur, our Clint, and that in Malkovich it has an actor capable of creating a commensurate (cartoon) villain. The movie is directed by Wolfgang Petersen, who has had bad luck since he came to Hollywood following the success of *Das Boot*, but who once made a fine little movie about a chess player. (It starred Bruno Ganz and was called *Black and White Like Day and Night*.) Also, the film's score is by Ennio Morricone, though I can't say it weaves its usual magic spell.

Shrewdly the movie just hints at the character of the president Frank is assigned to protect. He could be the caliber of the guy replaced by Dave (in *Dave*), except we don't get close enough to know. The silver hair and slick, bland good looks—suggest a swifter Senator John McCain. The point is, since he's in trouble and at the end of his first term, the head of his reelection committee (played by Watergate minority counsel Fred Dalton Thompson) is a nasty, desperate fellow.

That he's pledged to take the bullet for a fellow he doesn't necessarily like or approve of shows the kind of game Frank plays. A company man, sworn to an oath of service, he's still characterized by a thick shield of cynicism. Agent Frank is also over the hill. As he has since his grizzled Gunny in *Heartbreak Ridge*, Eastwood plays heavily on the age thing—the lone wolf, too old and too ornery-to-get-it-right-with-women thing. The marriage? Yup, she walked again. And, yes, there was a drinking problem.

So, Agent Frank rents rooms in a frugal bungalow, spends money only on (you guessed it) jazz CDs. Late at night, he tickles the ivories at a local watering hole. At the office, he affects an unhousebroken mode. Introduced to a female colleague, Agent Lilly (Rene Russo), he remarks that the secretaries are getting prettier. "And the field agents are getting older," she smart-mouths back. But the female agent is experienced enough to realize that the geezer (lots of geriatric jokes here) is more man than all the p.c. youngbloods around her. Wisely, fledgling screenwriter Jeff Maguire has merely adapted Eastwood's established persona. The scene where Frank sits, eating a dixie cup and watching Lily walk away, is un-forgettable.

Fine. Except the moviemakers have ruined it all! (Although what I'm about to report will be highly general, anyone who likes to avoid plot should skip this paragraph.) The film's opening sequence has Frank snatching his young partner, agent Al (Dylan McDermott)—Clint's latest rookie—from the jaws of death. A family man, Al finds his anxieties mounting about the profession—or is it about being fearless Frank's backup? Finally, he announces he's quitting and Frank (uncharacteristically) begs him to stay on: "I need you." Of course we sophisticates recognize this as a dire threat to Agent Al's welfare. Well, get it he does—with Frank in about four different ways responsible for his being killed. And since the movie absolutely fails to deal with this betrayal—to acknowledge it, to compensate for it—the betrayal becomes the movie's. Saccharine tears are spent for the mythical John Kennedy, but there's only one further, cursory, mention of poor Agent Al.

My notes after the incident above are strewn with remarks like, *Stupid, Stupid*, and then again *Stupid*. I started wishing Agent Frank would die. It was the only way he could redeem himself. (In the old days, kids, they sometimes died. And we got the deep satisfaction of grieving for flawed and fallen heroes.) I suppose it's a tribute to the movie that it upset me, at least worked me into some fit of pique, something no other "big" summer movie (*Last Action Zero, The Farm*) has remotely approached.

Actually, we're not meant to dwell on Frank's relationship with his buddy, which all along is overshadowed by his obsession with Malkovich's creepy, analytical, brutal villain. It's their mano a mano duel, their love bouts (mostly phone sex, though at one point Mitch takes Frank's gun in his mouth) that are the heart of the movie. A former assassin for the CIA, a master of disguise, this Doberman turned on his corporate master sees himself as Frank's soulmate. Scriptwriter Maguire is thinking doppelgänger (and *Tightrope*).

Perversely, I take solace from this new evidence that Eastwood's mere presence, his persona, can't make a picture. How much more intelligent Eastwood's own pictures are. Clint in charge would never be so indifferent to the integrity of character.

Also reviewed in:
CHICAGO TRIBUNE, 7/9/93, Friday/p. A, Clifford Terry
NEW REPUBLIC, 8/9/93, p. 28, Stanley Kauffmann
NEW YORK TIMES, 7/9/93, p. C1, Vincent Canby
NEW YORKER, 7/12/93, p. 93, Terrence Rafferty
VARIETY, 7/19/93, p. 71, Todd McCarthy
WASHINGTON POST, 7/9/93, p. B1, Hal Hinson
WASHINGTON POST, 7/9/93, Weekend/p. 42, Desson Howe

IN THE NAME OF THE FATHER

A Universal Pictures release of a Hell's Kitchen/Gabriel Byrne production. *Executive Producer:* Gabriel Byrne. *Producer:* Jim Sheridan. *Director:* Jim Sheridan. *Screenplay:* Terry George and Jim Sheridan. *Based on the autobiographical book "Proved Innocent" by:* Gerry Conlon. *Director of Photography:* Peter Biziou. *Editor:* Gerry Hambling. *Music:* Trevor Jones. *Music Editor:* Bill Abbott. *Sound:* Kieran Horgan and (music) Roger King. *Sound Editor:* Ron Davis. *Casting:* Patsy Pollock and Nuala Moiselle. *Production Designer:* Caroline Amies.   *Art Director:* Rick Butler. *Special Effects:* Joss Williams. *Costumes:* Joan Bergin. *Make-up:* Toni Delany. *Stunt Coordinator:* Bill Weston. *Running time:* 127 minutes. *MPAA Rating:* R.

CAST: Alison Crosbie (Girl in Pub);   Philip King (Guildford Soldier);   Emma Thompson (Gareth Peirce);   Nye Heron (IRA Man 1);   Daniel Day-Lewis (Gerry Conlon);   Anthony Brophy (Danny);   Frankie McCafferty (Tommo);   Paul Warriner, Julian Walsh, and Stuart Wolvenden (Soldiers);   Jo Connor (Bin Lady);   Karen Carlisle (Female Rioter);   Seamus Moran (IRA Man 2);   Billy Byrne (IRA Man 3);   Maureen McBride (Mother);   Jane Nolan (Girl with Baby);   Laurence Griffin and Jason Murtagh (Boys in Riot);   Kelly McKeavney (Young Girl);   Joanna Irvine (Ann Conlon);   Fiona Daly (IRA Woman);   Catherine Dunne (Woman on Balcony);   Pete Postlethwaite (Guiseppe Conlon);   Anna Meegan (Granny Conlon);   Marie Jones (Sarah Conlon);   Leah McCullagh (Bridie Conlon);   John Lynch (Paul Hill);   Beatie Edney (Carole Richardson);   Saffron Burrows (Girl in Commune);   Mark Sheppard (Paddy Armstrong);   Jamie Harris (Deptford Jim);   Britta Smith (Annie Maguire);   Don Baker (Joe McAndrew);   Barbara Mulcahy (Marian);   Mick Tohill (Man in Bookies);   Peter Sheridan, (Manager of Bookies);   Joe McPartland (Charlie Burke);   Stanley Townsend (Hooker's Driver);   Corin Redgrave (Robert Dixon);   Gerard McSorley (Belfast Detective Pavis).   Rachael Dowling and Tina Kellegher (Policewomen);   Ronan Wilmot (Paddy Maguire);   Maclean Burke (Young Vincent Maguire);   Joe Jeffers (Young Patrick Maguire);   Alistair Findlay (Forensic Scientist);   Aidan Grennell (Trial Judge);   Daniel Massey (Prosecutor);   Bosco Hogan (Defense Counsel);   Kenneth Edge (Jury Foreman);   Aine O'Connor (Dixon's Wife);   Guy Carleton (Prison Admissions Officer);   John Benfield (Chief PO Barker);   Dave Duffy and Martin Dunne (Prison Officers);   Larry Murphy (Old Prison Officer);   Frank Harper (Ronnie Smalls);   Jer O'Leary (Prisoner John O'Brien);   Paterson Joseph (Benbay);   Malcolm Tierney (Home Office Official);   Iain Montague (Leader of Delegation);   Paul Raynor (New Chief Prison Officer);   Clodagh Conroy (Dixon's Secretary);   Peter Sheridan (Priest);   Darren McHugh (Dixon's Son);   Peter Campbell (Government Official);   Alan Barry (Archivist Jenkins);   Jonathan Ryan (Scottish Governor);   John Pickles (Procedural Court Judge);   Liam O'Callaghan (Archvist 2);   Tom Wilkinson (Appeal Prosecutor).

CINEASTE, Vol. XX, No. 4, 1994, p. 44, Martin McLoone

In Ireland, Jim Sheridan's *In the Name of the Father* has been a box office phenomenon, racking up admissions to a point where it is now second only to Spielberg's *Jurassic Park* in the list of all-time top grossers. Indeed, when the film was released originally throughout Ireland, it did so much business in its first few weeks that its box office returns for Northern Ireland alone were sufficient to get it into the U.K. top ten *before* its British opening. Needless to say, when the film was finally released in Britain, this success was not repeated. Despite decent reviews in the main, and an impressive London opening performance, the film slipped into the art-house circuit where it was only moderately successful.

This contrast is interesting in itself, especially for what it can tell us about the difference between Irish and British perceptions of the film (and of the monumental miscarriage of justice which is its focus). The British opening was accompanied by a major controversy over the film's portrayal of real people and real events. This controversy was originally raised by serious jour-nalists in both Ireland and Britain who had covered the events over many years but it was later exploited by a hostile tabloid press in Britain whose main object was to deflect attention from the film's criticism of the British police and judicial system. To some extent, this tabloid attack was successful, contributing to the fact that the film was not the popular audience success in Britain that it was in Ireland. The controversy also served to deflect critical attention away from the film *as film* and onto the more barren terrain of measuring its representation of reality against the known facts. As a result of all this frenetic critical activity, *In the Name of the Father* remains a curiously misrecognized film which has suffered from being construed within an inappropriate and unrewarding critical discourse.

Now it would appear that the film is suffering the same critical fate in the U.S. as well. Consider this curious item which appeared in the popular British film magazine, *Empire*:

> *In an only-in-America turn of events, a resident of Alameda, California, has issued proceedings against Universal Pictures, distributors of* In the Name of the Father, *for wrongly billing the film as a true story. Jane Cutolo demands that every cent of the $20 million U.S. box office take accrued thus far be returned to moviegoers duped by posters for the film. 'The billboards promised that we would be told the truth,' the eccentric Ms. Cutolo insists. 'Instead we were given a hyped-up dramatised version of events as they* didn't *happen.'*

This bizarre item, of course, might well be some kind of April Fool's jape or even a rather tasteless publicity stunt dreamed up by someone connected with the film. It is nonetheless interesting, though not in the way suggested by the arrogant and very British manner in which it has been written up by the *Empire* correspondent. Rather, in its very absurdity, Ms. Cutolo's quoted remark illuminates the inadequacies of the stance taken by many British (and some Irish) critics of the film.

In the Name of the Father has been constructed as a work of mass entertainment and, as a consequence, the real events on which it is based have been shaped to fit the needs of the genre. All mass entertainment films, especially those financed by Hollywood, are hyped-up, dramatized versions of the real world. That has always been popular cinema's great strength and, if the criterion of quality is how closely art mimics the real world, then it is popular cinema's great fail-ing as well. The accusation could just as easily be leveled at Spielberg's version of the Holocaust in *Schlindler's List* (and no doubt it has been by some critics) but, in the end, one suspects that those who attack popular cinema's treatment of real events in this literal and pedantic manner do so to avoid facing up to the issues which the films raise. This predilection has motivated many of the attacks on Sheridan's version of the Gerry Conlon story, and especially those orchestrated by the tabloid press in Britain.

What has been even more surprising, however, is the way in which respected political correspondents and film reviewers in the national newspapers of both Ireland and Britain have also taken the filmmakers to task over the liberties they took with the strict facts of the case. Even the British Film Institute's journal, *Sight and Sound*, commissioned lawyer Michael Mansfield to write a legalistic albeit sympathetic piece about the film. As a result, the country's leading film monthly failed to deal *filmically* with *In the Name of the Father*. It approached the film almost

as if it were a piece of television news or investigative reporting rather than a fiction feature conceived for popular cinema consumption. The problem, of course, is that the question of fact and
fiction is central to the events which the film depicts. And, by any standards, these are true events
which almost defy belief.

In 1974, at the height of their bombing campaign in Britain, the IRA exploded a bomb in a pub
in the town of Guildford, near London, killing five people and injuring many more, some of them
seriously. The justification for this atrocity was that the pub was frequented by off-duty British
army personnel and was, therefore, a legitimate military target. In truth, though, many of the
dead and injured were young people out for an evening's enjoyment and the indiscriminate nature
of the bombing sickened the majority of people in Ireland (including many of the IRA's own
supporters) and outraged public opinion in Britain. The British police were under enormous
pressure to find the bombers and assuage the wave of public anger and revulsion which swept the
country. These were not good days to be publicly Irish in Britain.

In the end, three young Northern Irish men and the English girlfriend of one of them were
arrested and charged with the crime. Subsequently, in an enlarged investigation, seven members
of one family were convicted as the bombers' accomplices. There was widespread suspicion in
Ireland that these were innocent people, a suspicion strengthened when, a year later, the British
police captured an IRA unit after a siege at an apartment in London. This IRA unit admitted
having carried out the Guildford bombing and confirmed that those charged were innocent. The
British authorities chose to ignore the IRA claim, and so began a fifteen year campaign on behalf
of the innocent accused (who were commonly referred to in Ireland and Britain as the Guildford
Four and the Maguire Seven). *In the Name of the Father* is based on the book written by one of
the Guildford Four, Gerry Conlon's *Proved Innocent*. Conlon's father, Giuseppe, was one of the
Maguire Seven, arrested while staying with Gerry's aunt, Annie Maguire, when he went to
England to help his son. Eventually, the entire Maguire family was convicted as accomplices.

The Maguire convictions were secured on flimsy forensic evidence, later comprehensively
discredited, and the Guildford Four convictions rested on confessions beaten out of them by police
torture and threats to their families. These innocent people spent up to fifteen years in prison
(Giuseppe Conlon eventually died there) proclaiming their innocence and fighting the convictions.
Gradually a campaign grew up around the case which embraced journalists, lawyers, politicians,
and clergymen in both Ireland and Britain. By 1990, the convictions were quashed (though in the
case of one of the Four, Paul Hill, the last charge was dropped only earlier this year). It must
surely rank as one of the most outrageous miscarriages of justice in legal history, an injustice that
could only have been sustained by a conspiracy and cover-up at the highest levels of the British
establishment.

The story of the Guildford Four and the Maguire Seven has been told often on Irish and British
television. Many of the investigative documentaries made by British TV, in particular, played a
crucial role in awakening public consciousness to the enormity of the injustice and the scale of
the cover-up which sustained it. There have also been a number of fictional (or more accurately
'factional') accounts of the story, including an Irish TV film, *Dear Sarah*, based on Giuseppe's
letters to his wife. Throughout the years of the campaign, the emphasis has been on the search
for truth and the systematic distortion of the facts perpetrated by the British establishment. In
these circumstances, the unease which many people have expressed about Sheridan's compression
of details and his license with strict accuracy is understandable. Such dramatic methods are the
requirements of the genre, however, and so rather than continue the inventory of facts against
fictions which has dominated discussion of the film, we should consider the esthetic and political
implications of Sheridan's use of these genre conventions.

Hollywood films are driven by either character (preferably involving big-name stars) or action,
often involving an array of stunts and special effects. In most cases, there is a clear-cut division
of labor between these two elements in establishing narrative momentum. Thus, some films are
largely driven by, and some film stars are largely associated with, one or the other of these basic
elements. *In the Name of the Father* is character-driven, involving two high-profile stars in Daniel
Day-Lewis and Emma Thompson and an array of accomplished Irish and British character actors,
headed by an impressive performance from Pete Postlethwaite as Giuseppe Conlon. In adhering
to this basic requirement, something has to give and, in this case, it is strict documentary realism
and an engagement with the politics of the situation.

Sheridan has chosen to emphasize the central father-son relationship between Giuseppe and Gerry Conlon and to concentrate on how their joint ordeal rescues their strained relationship. In this regard, it taps into the 'men-without-women' prison drama genre, where the quest for justice becomes a journey of self-discovery—a kind of *Cool Hand Luke* for the Nineties. There is, however, a fundamental difference between Paul Newman's Sixties antiestablishment prison hero and Daniel Day-Lewis's Gerry Conlon. *Cool Hand Luke* is a celebration of one individual's refusal to conform, even in the face of a rather meaningless death. Indeed, his extreme individualism and unrepentant rebellion is a source of inspiration to his fellow inmates. Gerry Conlon's imprisonment, on the other hand, is presented as a form of personal and spiritual redemption—a journey from petty criminal nonconformist to embracing the law of the father. The character of Giuseppe is central here.

Giuseppe's ill health and frailty is contrasted with his own inner strength and spiritual vitality. He is the center of a film which constructs a moral rather than a political universe. In the early scenes, Gerry's unstructured adolescent rebellion is shown to be a pathetic, self-defeating act of defiance. He is presented with three alternatives to his own dysfunctional and antisocial actions. He can bow down to the corrupt authority of the British, the first 'law of the father' which attempts to rein him in. Although his rejection of this option is never in doubt, within the moral universe which the film constructs this is essentially a moral rather than a political choice. In the character of the British policeman, Dixon (Corin Redgrave), Gerry confronts his first father-figure on a journey towards moral redemption. In prison, he meets his second father-figure in IRA leader Joe McAndrew, under whose influence he falls for a while. For Gerry, this is a question of virility—McAndrew's single-minded attachment to physical violence and his capacity to fight back offers a clear-cut alternative to his own father's seeming impotence in the face of adversity.

Gerry's eventual rejection of McAndrew leads him back to his own father. The moral strength of Giuseppe's pacifist resistance to the injustice is finally recognized by the prodigal son. There is no moral ambiguity in Gerry's acquiescence to his father's will. The overtly religious theme is emphasized by Giuseppe's devout Catholicism (mocked earlier in the film by Gerry) and, when he dies in prison at the point of Gerry's redemption, the Christian theme is complete. Indeed, Gerry's spiritual journey from the iconoclastic Seventies to the moral Nineties is marked on the soundtrack by the musical journey from Jimi Hendrix to Bono. In all the sound and fury over the film's lack of documentary realism, the fact that it is one of the most overtly Christian films to emerge in popular cinema in recent years has largely been missed.

In the Name of the Father emerges as a moral rather than a political film largely because of the narrative structure and visual style employed by Jim Sheridan. The relative underuse made here of Emma Thompson in the role of the campaigning solicitor, Gareth Peirce, is significant. One could imagine a different telling of the Guildford Four story which made greater use of the investigation plot, one in which the uncovering of injustice, conspiracy, and cover-up would require at least some direct encounter with the political forces which have shaped the situation in the first place. This plot device has been a staple of popular cinema over the years, using either a campaigning journalist, attorney, or cop as the nemesis of injustice and corruption. The political possibilities of the device are exemplified in the French *policier*, although it has a strong pedigree in classic Hollywood cinema as well. It is Costa-Gavras's favored narrative structure, especially in his American films like *Missing* and *Music Box*, although it is most effectively employed for political purposes in his 1972 study of CIA involvement in Latin America, *State of Siege*.

Despite the undoubtedly key role played by the campaigners in breaking open the case, however, Sheridan eschews such an approach and the Thompson character is used largely as a device which allows Conlon to tell his own story, through her, to the audience. Certainly, she gets two rousing set-pieces in the film—her accidental discovery of suppressed evidence corroborating Conlon's alibi and her emotional outburst when producing this at the appeal hearing. In other regards, though, the investigation plot is very much secondary to the central father-son relationship.

Visually, too, Sheridan closes down the epic scale of the film after the opening scenes of street riots in Belfast. Driven by Hendrix on the soundtrack and shot with real verve and style, these scenes are myth-making cinema of a high order. After that, the film is shot largely in a claustrophobic shot/reverse-shot style, the highly stylized opening replaced by a series of head-to-head encounters between father and son in prison. Sheridans' great strength, of course, is his ability to coax convincing performances from his cast. Six Oscar nominations and two wins (Daniel Day-Lewis and Brenda Fricker for *My Left Foot*) is a remarkable achievement in only three films, and is testament to his years of apprenticeship in the Dublin theater. The problem, though, is that his cinema is often very stagebound and static (the first encounter between Gerry and Giuseppe is particularly stagey, relying on that old theatrical device of having one character remind the other in detail of some incident in the past which he must well remember—"And then you said ... And then you did ... Remember, Da!").

These prison scenes work well enough for the oedipal tensions in the relationship and for establishing the moral universe in which they are played out. On one hand, the resulting emphasis on character limits the political potential of the film and renders it unsatisfyingly poised between oedipal melodrama and political thriller. On the other hand, even though the politics of the situation are subsumed into the moral universe which the film constructs, they are not entirely contained within it. There are leakages and interesting contradictions.

To understand these better, it is important to remember that *In the Name of the Father* exists in relation not only to the real world of Irish politics, but also to other cinematic representations of Ireland and the Irish and, indeed, to much older traditions of repregentation. In their classic study of the subject, *Cinema and Ireland*, Rockett, Gibbons, and Hill have argued that because, until relatively recently, most cinematic images of Ireland were the product of either the American or British cinemas, they tended to portray the country in primitivist terms, reinforcing prejudices and perpetuating outrageous stereotypes. Hill goes on to argue that this is particularly disabling when these cinematic images work against an understanding of Irish politics and society and especially of the nature of political violence in Ireland. It could be argued that despite the creative input from Ireland, Sheridan's film prolongs such a disabling myth—that violence in Ireland is basically irrational, flowing from an innate tendency or character flaw in the national psyche.

In the film, there is no doubt that the portrayal of McAndrew, the IRA leader, is a chilling one, effectively realized by Don Baker in another performance that is a credit to the director. In the pivotal scene which marks Gerry Conlon's final turning away from violence, McAndrew viciously attacks a prison guard using an ingeniously improvised blowtorch. Since the film has slowly built up audience empathy with the guard, the cold-blooded nature of this assault hits home. Audience revulsion is mirrored in Gerry's response of going to the guard's aid, and Gerry's subsequent distancing himself from the IRA leader again reinforces the subject position which the film constructs for the audience. The fact that this brutal attack takes place during a prison screening of *The Godfather* is suggestive, to say the least. Part of British government strategy over the years has been to deny that violence in Northern Ireland is politically motivated. Indeed, government ministers have consistently used terms like 'gangsterism' or, more pertinently, 'godfathers of terrorism' in condemning the IRA. The structure of this scene would seem to reinforce this attitude.

And yet, *The Godfather* reference suggests another interpretation. In *The Godfather, Part II*, Michael Corleone is in Cuba, about to conclude a deal with the Miami crime bosses to carve up the island between them. At a military roadblock, he witnesses a futile act of bravery by one of Castro's young insurgents and immediately decides against the deal. These are not people he can do 'business' with, precisely because they are not gangsters. They are motivated by politics rather than the greed and self-interest which he understands. There is something of the same aura about McAndrew in his confrontation with a prison full of hardened criminals, seething with anti-Irish prejudice. One word in the ear of the toughest prisoner, pointing out the power of the IRA to reach his family, and the prison is his. This is not a man with whom mere criminals can do business.

McAndrew's political acumen is well established later when he effectively organizes the disparate prisoners into collective action to protest prison conditions. Thus, the film's rejection of him is not on the grounds of his criminality or gangsterism, as some critics have suggested in relation to *The Godfather* reference. Rather it is a rejection of his chilling and uncompromising politics (a situation which incidentally mirrors the opinion of about ninety-five percent of the Irish people, if the vote for Sinn Fein in the recent European Parliament elections is any guide). But the political motivation of the IRA is at least acknowledged in the film, a considerable difference from dominant cinematic representations (and an acknowledgement belatedly made by the British government itself when it admitted in 1993 that it had opened "channels of communication" with Sinn Fein).

One final political reference in the film is worth mentioning. At the beginning of his incarceration, when Gerry must deal with anti-Irish sentiment among the English prisoners, he is able to make common cause with the black West Indian inmates who suffer similar abuse. There is a clear reference here to a kind of postcolonial solidarity among peripheral and marginalized cultures, but, like the film's treatment of the IRA, this political notion slips out in an unguarded moment in the film's otherwise controlling moral vision. Sheridan is undoubtedly a director who has politics—this was evident years ago in his work in Dublin's avant-garde cinema—but he is not a political filmmaker and In the Name of the Father is not a consciously political film.

So what, finally, are we to make of In the Name of the Father as a work of Irish cinema! It is well to remember that this film comes along at a time of frenetic film activity in Ireland. For schematic purposes, it is useful to classify the plethora of Irish-theme films which have recently emerged into three types defined by the level of Irish input into the creative process. The greater the involvement of Irish creative talent, the less likely, one assumes, the films will perpetuate dominant myths and representations. The first type is the Hollywood blockbuster, like Far and Away or Patriot Games, which, since the box office is their primary concern, are content to peddle the expected myths. The second category, of which Sheridan's film and Neil Jordan's The Crying Game are prime examples, operates on medium-sized budgets allowing for greater creative input from Irish talent but which nonetheless demand certain generic concessions to ensure their 'recognizability' with American audiences. These films can be a lot more adventurous in their tackling of sensitive Irish themes than can the blockbusters, but, for their filmmakers, it nonetheless involves a potentially debilitating process of negotiation with commercial imperatives. Finally, there is a lesser known 'third cinema' coming out of Ireland itself—an independent, indigenous cinema that works on very small, even minuscule budgets, and which aims to make critically engaged and challenging films which explore the realities and contradictions of contemporary Irish life. As in the U.S. at the moment, the most radical and adventurous cinema is to be found not in the mainstream but in this independent sector.

It would be churlish to deny the emotional power of In the Name of the Father or to decry the considerable craft which went into its making. It undoubtedly succeeds in bringing the enormity of the injustice to popular cinema audiences, but it also points out the need for a more challenging and critically engaged cinema. One hopes that the success of Sheridan's (and Jordan's) film will generate greater cultural support in Ireland for indigenous film production. The critical issue concerning In the Name of the Father, therefore, is not the extent to which it takes license with the facts of the real case, but how the esthetic strategies it employs hold lessons for those indigenous Irish filmmakers attempting to forge a new cinematic esthetic.

LOS ANGELES TIMES, 12/29/93, Calendar/p. 1, Kenneth Turan

If the world had been created without injustice, Hollywood would have invented it by now. Fueled by a righteous "j'accuse" kind of anger, the movies enjoy nothing more than fulminating against miscarriages of justice and defending the ill-treated and falsely maligned.

"In the Name of the Father" is a model of this kind of engaged, enraged filmmaking, a politically charged "Fugitive" that uses one of the most celebrated cases of recent British history to steamroller an audience with the power of rousing, polemical cinema.

"In the Name of the Father" also reunites the formidable creative team responsible for "My Left Foot," director Jim Sheridan and star Daniel Day-Lewis. Strongly tied to a powerful underlying reality (though it inevitably tends to simplify), this film has the additional advantage of being concerned with the emotional truth of its key relationships, adding an unusual father and son story to its incendiary mix.

Sheridan hits us almost at once with a shocking component of the film's reality, the 1974 IRA bombing of a pub in Guildford, a town just outside of London. Five people were killed, but the damage done to a nervous Britain's sense of internal security was greater still.

In the climate of near-hysteria that followed, the Draconian Prevention of Terrorism Act was passed, allowing the police to interrogate suspects for up to seven days without bringing charges or allowing access to an attorney. A young man named Gerry Conlon (Lewis) and three pals were arrested under this measure, and, soon to be known as the Guildford Four, all were charged with the bombing.

A brief prologue places Conlon in prison, introduces us to his new lawyer, Gareth Peirce (Emma Thompson), and then flashes back to his past, back to Belfast in the early 1970s, where Conlon precipitates a blood-stirring riot, Giuseppe sends him off to England, where Conlon heads straight for a hippie commune looking for drugs, free love and all the trimmings.

It is on a visit back to Belfast that Conlon is suddenly arrested for the Guildford bombing. And it is in its powerful, unsettling re-creation of how the British police psychologically bludgeon a confession out of him that Sheridan's cracker-jack visceral filmmaking begins to unerringly pull us in, totally involving the audience on the side of this classic wrong man.

Bad as Conlon's situation is, it gets worse. When his poor father comes over to England to try to help him find a lawyer, he is arrested, too, as is Conlon's royals-loving aunt and assorted other unlikely relatives. And, after an investigation controlled by the ruthless Inspector Dixon (presumably a pseudonym), Conlon is sentenced to 30 years to life imprisonment for a crime there seems to be no doubt he did not commit.

Most of "In the Name of the Father" takes place behind the walls of the various prisons Conlon is incarcerated in over nearly 15 years, and the film's script (written by Terry George and Sheridan from Conlon's autobiographical "Proved Innocent") follows his situation from both legal and personal perspectives.

Though the various attempts, ultimately spearheaded by lawyer Peirce (a small role for Thompson, but one with a big payoff), to have Conlon freed are gripping, they gain much of their strength from the film's ability to emphasize how this feckless youth changes as an individual and in relation to his father.

Persuasively played by veteran British theater and TV actor Postlethwaite (startling as a different kind of father in Terence Davies' "Distant Voices, Still Lives"), Giuseppe Conlon is an ordinary-seeming dad whose strengths are only visible gradually and under duress.

As the son whose eyes are opened, Daniel Day-Lewis gives another one of his extraordinarily convincing performances. Of Irish descent, he may have come by his character's melodic accent naturally, but more demanding were not only the chilling interrogation sequences (the actor went without sleep or food for several days to prepare) but also the transformation in personality Conlon undergoes.

Starting as a callow malcontent, Conlon visibly matures during his years inside, interacting with not only his father but also fellow prisoners Joseph McAndrew (Don Baker), an IRA stalwart, and Benbay (Paterson Joseph), a mellow Rastafarian. And Day-Lewis changes along with his character, his body and even the rest of his face altering in the course of this rich, screen-owning presentation. It is a piece of acting that makes us feel we are living those harrowing years right along with him.

While "In the Name of the Father" leaves you with no doubt as to Conlon's innocence, it should be noted that the case remains a controversial one in Britain, with trials pertaining to it still going on and one conservative newspaper going so far as to say that Thompson's decision to take the role was "not perhaps the wisest decision a British actress could make."

As for the real Conlon, he closes his book with the hope that he won't "spend the rest of my life being known only as one of the Guildford Four."

Whatever else it does, and it does quite a lot, "In the Name of the Father" puts that hope a lot further off into the future.

NEW STATESMAN & SOCIETY, 2/11/94, p. 35, Jonathan Romney

If the success of a political film can be judged by the amount of publicity it affords an issue, then *In the Name of the Father* is a remarkable achievement. It has already stirred up massive controversy in Britain, Ireland and the US, and it certainly can't do the film any harm to be released just when the spotlight of the international press has fallen with new intensity on the status of the IRA. And it's certainly surprising in the current nostalgist state of mainstream cinema to find a film about a specific recent event—the trial and unjust imprisonment of the Guildford Four—getting such a spectacular airing.

But other than its power to generate headlines and draw attention once more to the questionable state of the British justice system, it's doubtful whether Jim Sheridan's film is that much of a success. Its political impetus is pretty much skin deep—and Sheridan has suggested that it's as much about the fraught relations between fathers and sons as about those between England and Ireland.

It is clear from the beginning that this is not, strictly speaking, a film about the Four, but about one of them, Gerry Conlon, whose memoir *Proved Innocent* forms the basis of the narrative. Conlon was one of the four who in 1975 were tried and judged guilty, on suspect evidence, of the Guildford pub bombing, and who were finally released after the judgment was quashed in 1989. His father Guiseppe was one of several more—the so-called Maguire Seven—who were additionally imprisoned. The story deals little with the Maguires, or with the rest of the Four.

What we get is neither a dramatisation of the Guildford Four's story, nor a dramatised inquiry into the way in which such a manifest fit-up job could have been perpetrated. Instead, it's Conlon's sentimental education—a real-life *bildungsroman* taking him from his early days as a self-confessed "disreputable chancer" to the wiser, resilient survivor that prison and injustice made of him. That's not to underplay the horror of his ordeal, nor the charisma and intensity of Daniel Day-Lewis's performance. But what we get is an emotional spectacle that we're asked to *feel*, without being persuaded to think through, or to ask any questions about.

The film begins with a boisterous bit of scene-setting roughly equivalent to the opening chapters of Conlon's book, in which he reminisces about youth on the Lower Falls Road. Presented as an exuberant, maverick Jack-the-Lad stealing lead off a roof, he's mistaken by British troops for an IRA sniper, and ends up sparking off a riot. Subsequently, he is threatened with knee-capping by the IRA for being such an uncontrollable liability. He's clearly the last person who would ever be taken seriously as IRA material, which makes his accusation entirely absurd. When he and Hill are accused of the bombing, it seems to be purely on the grounds that they're Irish and have been denounced by a peevish hippie in the squat they pass through.

How this charge ever gained credence, and how it was built on by the police is never made clear. Because the whole course of the story is known, and its eventual conclusion foreseeable from the outset, there's no real narrative, other than the simple enactment of what happened.

Sheridan generates drama by concentrating on character, on an image of human improvability and endurance that could apply equally to a thousand prison dramas; and, more controversially, by taking a considerable degree of poetic licence with the facts. The circumstances in which solicitor Gareth Peirce (Emma Thompson) found the suppressed documents that confirmed Conlon's alibi were, by all accounts, less dramatic then they are here. Indeed, the alibi itself is given a discreet but significant tweak: Charles Burke, whom Conlon met in a hostel, and who was able to account for his whereabouts, here becomes a tramp on a park bench who gives Conlon and Hill an object lesson on the perils of being Irish in England. It's a small but pertinent example of the way that Sheridan can't resist making things just that little bit more sentimentally pointed. And this is where the film falls out of politics and into melodrama.

The law here is a bunch of shadowy, unnamed men in suits. The most memorable example in British cinema of these shady figures is the ending of the otherwise persuasive 1985 thriller *Defence of the Realm* (starring Gabriel Byrne, executive producer of *In the Name of the Father*). As with that film, the powers-that-be are embodied in a sinister figure in pin-stripes—here an apocryphal, upper-crust policeman named Dixon (Corin Redgrave) who turns up briefly in Conlon's interrogation acting the proverbial Good Cop, easing the way after the bonehead Bad Cops have given Conlon hell.

In the final courtroom scenes, when the sentence on the Four is quashed, Sheridan cuts to an extreme close-up of Dixon's pursed lips, the point being clear: the system struck dumb; it cannot speak the truth. By pinpointing Policeman X as the cause of all Conlon's travails, Sheridan gives up the possibility of a more investigative look at the case. Instead, the film becomes a Manichean allegory—prissy English anal retentives versus the Irish spirit—given full reign in Gerry's somewhat *Iron John*-ish emotional showdowns with his doomed father (Peter Postlethwaite) whose undemonstrative, consistent strength makes an excellent foil for Day-Lewis's compelling range across the emotional gamut.

The film benefits from Sheridan's reigning-in his penchant for stage Irishness, which so dogged *My Left Foot*. Here, there's only a touch of that, but it hits the emotion button with barefaced directness: when Guiseppe dies, all the other prisoners toss little burning papers out of their windows. As they float down in the darkness, a wistful Gaelic theme strikes up.

The film's one stab at subtlety at last founders in melodrama, but it briefly works. It's the ambivalent role given to the IRA man McAndrew, whom Conlon meets in prison and who briefly becomes a surrogate father, until his summary revenge on a guard. The character is flawed because he's so much a function of Conlon's feelings towards authority and his own father, and because he embodies two polarised popular images of the IRA at once—total controlled intent, total uncontrollable savagery. The gamble doesn't quite come off but, for a while, Sheridan seems to be taking on an element of genuine indeterminacy in playing one image off against the other. It's the only interesting question mark in a film that otherwise tells us what to think and feel.

As ever, you feel churlish complaining about a film like this, as you do when Oliver Stone or Costa Gavras makes an equally hamfisted stand on a pressing issue. The argument for the film is that it needed to be made; but it didn't need to be made like this. *In the Name of the Father* doesn't ask the questions it could have asked. How could such a thing happen? How can it be prevented from happening again? Where does the problem lie—with the British legal system, with the courts' relation to the police, with the police's relation to British policy on Northern Ireland? Or with one or more unidentified men in pinstripe suits? By not bothering to coax us into asking such questions, *In the Name of the Father* is no less an open-and-shut case than the one concocted against the Four.

NEW YORK, 1/17/94, p. 54, John Powers

Indignant and harrowing, *In the Name of the Father* is the most engrossing movie I've seen about the mess in Northern Ireland since Marcel Ophüls's *A Sense of Loss* two decades ago. It's based on the autobiography of Gerry Conlon, a scrappy Belfast punk who, along with his father and several others, was wrongly convicted of the 1974 pub bombings that killed five people in the London suburb of Guildford. Although the verdict immediately became a cause celebre (the "Guildford Four" were championed by everyone from Lord Devlin to the Pogues), it wasn't overturned until 1989, when the Conlons' lawyer finally proved that the English authorities had wantonly suppressed evidence pointing to her clients' innocence. Gerry Conlon had already been in prison for fifteen years.

With its victimized hero and inarguable moral lesson (cops shouldn't railroad innocent men), Conlon's story could easily have become another message-laden pachyderm like *Philadelphia*. It has been spared this lumbering fate by Jim Sheridan, the big-hearted Irish writer-director who first made his name with *My Left Foot*. Sheridan doesn't have a quarter of the cinematic flair of Brian De Palma or Adrian Lyne, but he also has none of their cynicism. His movies vaunt emotional truth over stylistic filigree; they have the roughhewn directness of a great Irish bar band. *In the Name of the Father* cares less about scoring easy partisan points—though it notches up quite a few—than about mapping Gerry Conlon's belated moral awakening.

When we first meet Gerry (Daniel Day-Lewis), he seems an unlikely hero for a Hollywood film about the miscarriage of justice. Scruffy, thoughtless, and blithely amoral, he's the sort of boyo who snickers when his father tells him that "honest money goes further"—Gerry would rather steal the sheet metal from his neighbors' roofs. Never one to trouble his head with politics, he leads precisely the sort of lumpen existence that gives him, ironically, the profile of an IRA bomber. After gleefully robbing a prostitute's flat in London, he's hauled in on terrorism charges, bullied into making a false confession, convicted of murder, and, in a droll touch worthy of Buñuel, packed off to a prison cell with his father, Giuseppe (Pete Postlethwaite), a quiet, frail man whose homily-spouting saintliness has always driven his son crazy.

This pairing starts out as sheer torture for the embittered Gerry, who, scorning his old man's painstaking efforts to win their freedom in court, does whatever he can to get by—dropping acid with beaming Rasta prisoners, falling under the spell of a convicted IRA bomber, Joe McAndrew (Don Baker), whose coiled confidence only shows up Giuseppe's mousiness. But this is a movie filled with false father figures, including the Crown, and once Gerry witnesses McAndrew's coldblooded brutality, he begins to understand that his principled, nonviolent, dying father is the patriarch he should have respected all along. His heart belongs to Da.

What stops all this from being unbearably corny is Daniel Day-Lewis's characteristically headlong performance. Prone to actorish self-regard, if not actual self-absorption—a quality neatly exploited by Martin Scorsese in *The Age of Innocence*—Lewis dives into his roles with such Method intensity that he often threatens to burst them at the seams. In Gerry Conlon he's found a character who keeps stretching to fit his ambition. Whether lolling against a wall or springing into action, giggling at his own wisecracks or sobbing piteously in the interrogation room, Day-Lewis captures Gerry's contradictions in all their sloppy extremity, undergoing a transformation so subtle that you register it subliminally. It's only at the film's end that you realize how everything about Gerry has become different—his posture and facial expressions, the lilt of his language. He's gone from a slouching bit of riffraff who scoffed at the word *honesty* to an upright, well-spoken activist whose ill-starred life has taught him to cherish the truth.

The truth is often ugly in the not-quite-post-colonial struggle over Northern Ireland. *In the Name of the Father* surges with righteous fury at the double-dealing bigotry of the English police and the Draconian terms of Britain's Prevention of Terrorism Act, which allows the authorities to detain (and browbeat) suspects for a week without filing charges or letting them see a lawyer. Still, Sheridan's no bomb-thrower. He carefully distances himself from the IRA, both in his horrifying depiction of the Guildford slaughter and in his handling of McAndrew, whose grim, eye-for-an-eye ruthlessness is shown to be a kind of icy dementia. If Sheridan's pro-Republican sentiments emerge anywhere, it's in niceties of style: McAndrew has a samurai charisma that does not excuse his violence but does make him seem far more dignified than Robert Dixon (Corin Redgrave), the dishonest English cop whose every appearance is a thesaurus of shifty mannerisms.

Dixon gets his comeuppance in the final reel, when Emma Thompson mugs her way through a showy speech about British justice that was doubtless her reason for taking on the otherwise mingy role of the Conlons' solicitor. When her words carry the day, the courtroom explodes and we're all supposed to exult cathartically at Gerry's triumph. That's fair enough: He's earned every bit of sympathy we give him. But leaving the theater, I felt a niggling disappointment that a movie that begins by conjuring up the bloody, baffling morass of "the troubles" should wind up making us feel something so simple. Unlike most polemics, *In the Name of the Father* never has more sting than when it's complex—teasing out the passions and allegiances that turn a layabout into a man. And it's never emptier than when it asks us to feel superior to cartoonishly wicked English cops, as if they weren't prisoners of the same tortured history that Gerry Conlon is.

NEW YORK POST, 12/29/93, p. 32, Michael Medved

From "The Count of Monte Cristo" to this year's smash hit "The Fugitive," there's something incomparably dramatic about the plight of an innocent man convicted of a crime he didn't commit.

"In the Name of the Father" makes that familiar situation seem almost unbearably disturbing because it tells its true story in such direct, straightforward style. Irish director/co-writer Jim Sheridan (who previously earned acclaim with "My Left Foot" and "The Field") understands that the events he re-creates here are horrifying enough that they require no hint of melodramatic hokum.

His hero, Gerry Conlon (Daniel Day-Lewis), is hardly a paragon of virtue; he is an unemployed petty thief in Belfast whose dippy, irresponsible behavior would qualify him for the clinical designation "putz." When he tires of dodging British soldiers and IRA gunmen, he heads for London in 1974 and finds a temporary home in a hippie commune.

This aimless existence is rudely interrupted when he and three friends are suddenly arrested on charges that they tossed terrorist bombs into London pubs and killed five people.

Armed with newly enacted legislation allowing prolonged interrogation without formal charges or access to legal counsel, police brutalize Conlon and his pal Paul Hill (John Lynch) into signing false confessions—which they later recant.

Nevertheless, the authorities (led by the officious Corin Redgrave) suppress evidence that would clear the accused and succeed in imposing life sentences.

Even worse, they arrest Conlon's unsuspecting aunt and cousins as accessories to murder, along with his long-suffering father, who has come to London to seek his release.

Veteran British stage and TV actor Pete Postlethwaite plays the senior Conlon and delivers a performance so profoundly impressive that it deserves consideration for the supporting actor Oscar.

He enables us to see his character's unselfish nobility; at the same time we can understand why his son would fail to recognize the ailing old man's true stature.

Playing that son, Daniel Day-Lewis advances his claim to recognition as the most versatile actor on Earth. There's no trace here of his heroics in "My Left Foot," "The Last of the Mohicans," or "The Age of Innocence," yet he is utterly compelling as an immature but somehow likable loser who grows up gradually during 15 years in prison.

In portraying that appalling stretch of suffering, this fine film falters: The long prison sequences in the middle of the film never seem to pay off, and even interchanges between father and son, locked for years in the same cell, offer little dramatic jolt.

Deliverance seems almost arbitrary when it finally arrives, in the form of determined new defense attorney Emma Thompson (in yet another fine, ferocious performance) who manages to get the case reopened.

That case remains intensely controversial in Britain today where, four years after Gerry Conlon's release, three police officials accused of framing him recently won acquittal.

Given Jim Sheridan's Irish origins, the English press assumed his film would amount to one-sided propaganda for the IRA; instead the only Republican terrorist who actually appears in the picture is depicted as ruthless and brutal.

Though Sheridan highlights anti-Irish prejudice in much of the British establishment, this is no Oliver Stone-style work of political pamphleteering.

"In the Name of the Father" remains something less ambitious but far more substantial than that: a searing, unforgettable account of a personal, painful and ultimately pointless injustice.

NEWSDAY, 12/29/93, Part II/p. 57, John Anderson

Jim Sheridan can, apparently, have it both ways: Make a film decrying the British government's manipulation of the truth, distortion of fact and shameless exploitation of public emotion, by manipulating truth, distorting fact and shamelessly exploiting public emotion.

"In the Name of the Father," which Sheridan ("My Left Foot," "The Field") has admitted is a "dramatic interpretation of the truth," concerns the injustices perpetrated against the so-called Guildford Four. Convicted for the vicious IRA bombings of two pubs near London in 1974, they saw their convictions overturned in 1989 because police detectives were determined to have altered or suppressed crucial interviews with the defendants. By that time, however, Gerry Conlon, the centerpiece of this story, had already served 15 years. And his father, Giuseppe, had died in prison.

It's a potent piece of history, and Sheridan has warped it. He wants to make people angry, and he does: His story is rife with blatant injustices perpetrated by a nation maintaining an army of occupation in Northern Ireland, and whose minions were more than content to imprison the innocent in order to appease a public enraged by senseless murders. But the anger Sheridan generates is completely reliant on the audiences assumption that the story is true; he does very little else, stylistically or dramatically, to move us. And since many of the facts are either misleading or counterfeit, so is the emotion.

The film's best extended scene is its first: At a time when Catholic-Protestant tensions were at their worst, Conlon—rendered in passionate if overly mannered terms by Daniel Day-Lewis—is spotted stealing scrap metal off a Belfast roof by British soldiers. Mistaking him for a sniper, they pursue him, and their pursuit turns into a riot, with children hurling rocks, their elders hurling Molotov cocktails, and Jimi Hendrix playing a hot guitar smear across the soundtrack. The sequence is disgusting in its intergenerational venom, and something of a false advertisement for the rest of the film.

Nothing ever matches it visually, although it does eventually establish Conlon's troubled relationship with his father, played with studied anguish by Peter Postlethwaite, which will serve as the film's dramatic underpinning.

Having enraged the Irish Republican Army with his continued thievery, because it attracts British Army attention—this time, Gerry led the soldiers right through an IRA safe house—they're about to kneecap him when Giuseppe intervenes. There's little gratitude; Gerry is resentful of his devout and unassertive father, although the son and heir is in no position to cast aspersions on anyone.

It's after he and future co-defendant Paul Hill (John Lynch) go to London that the sky falls in. And where Sheridan starts setting us up: While the Guildford Pub is being blown to bits, Gerry is seen robbing the apartment of a high-priced London hooker, something that actually happened 10 days after the Guildford blast. But this fictitious alibi serves as the heart of Sheridan's argument for Conlon's innocence.

The outcome of the case, too, is a figment of Sheridan's imagination: There was no dramatic courtroom refutation of the British case, as enacted here by Emma Thompson, as Conlon's attorney Gareth Peirce. Their case was won on technicalities. And there was no Detective Dixon (Corin Redgrave), the unscrupulous policeman and embodiment of English cruelty, who orchestrates the coerced confessions of the Four and suppresses the admission by IRA terrorist Joseph McAndrew (Don Baker) that he pulled the Guildford bombing. Then again, McAndrew is an imaginary character, too.

In between the trumped-up trial of Conlon and Co., and their very dramatic exoneration, is some very standard prison drama, replete with Conlon's gradual politicization, Giuseppe's private purgatory and premature death and attorney Peirce's stalwart efforts to get Conlon freed. Thompson contributes her usual charming self, although her character is rather undefined. What's missing entirely is something to make "In the Name of the Father" more than a self-righteous screed that does little but undermine the Irish cause, while perpetuating a particular brand of fraud.

NEWSWEEK, 1/3/94, p. 63, David Ansen

Guaranteed to get your blood boiling, *In the Name of the Father* relates the true story of Gerry Conlon (Daniel Day-Lewis), one of the "Guildford Four" wrongly convicted of planting IRA bombs in two English pubs in 1974. As tales of injustice go, this one's a doozy. Not only did Conlon and his Irish mates spend 15 years in jail before their sentences were overturned, but seven other innocents—including his father and his aunt—served time on trumped-up charges. It was one of the English judiciary's most shameful hours. The political pressure to find a culprit for the bombings turned the criminal-justice system criminal itself: evidence, was willfully suppressed, torture used to extract confessions, and when the actual terrorists admitted their guilt, their testimony was ignored. Twenty years later the "Irish problem," as ugly and unresolved as ever, the case—and now this film—are still arousing angry passions in England.

Director Jim Sheridan (who made the memorable "My Left Foot" with Day-Lewis) tells his gripping tale with a fury that stokes up an audience the way early Costa Gavras movies ("Z") used to do. But there's more to his story (co-written by Sheridan and Terry George) than good, scruffy Irish victims and rabidly bad English heavies—though there's plenty of that. It's also the story of Gerry Conlon's relationship with his father (Pete Postlethwaite), a man he despises until, by cruel fate, they become cellmates in prison and are forced to hammer out a radical change of heart.

Day-Lewis's Gerry is a rich creation. A hotheaded flake and petty criminal more interested in getting loaded than in politics, he flees to London after falling into trouble with both the Brits and the IRA in Belfast, spends time in a hippie squat (the "free love" era is swiftly, hilariously evoked) and on the night of the bombing makes a big score robbing a prostitute's apartment. One can understand why his father has contempt for him, and why he can't tolerate his sickly, oppressively upright dad. In jail he's politicized by the IRA terrorist Joe McAndrew (Don Baker), a kind of surrogate Bad Father he must reject before he can make his peace, with his real father. Day-Lewis takes us through Gerry's turbulent conversions with fierce, unsentimental conviction. Emma Thompson plays Gareth Peirce, the lawyer who, five years into the Conlons' incarceration, takes up the case and slowly wins Gerry's trust. It's not a big role, but like everything involved in this fleet, impassioned movie, it's lit with fervor.

SIGHT AND SOUND, 3/94, p. 41, Martin Bright

On the evening of October 5, 1974, an IRA bomb rips through a pub in Guildford. A decade later a woman solicitor, Gareth Peirce, is listening to the testimony of one of the four people convicted of the bombing—Gerry Conlon, one of the 'Guildford Four'.

Conlon is seen in flashback as a young man with a group of friends stealing lead from a roof in Belfast. He is mistaken for a gunman by some British soldiers who chase him through the streets of Belfast. He narrowly escapes knee-capping from the IRA for the trouble he has caused thanks to the intervention of his father, Guiseppe. Gerry decides to try his luck in England and on the ferry he meets an old school friend, Paul Hill. In London, Paul introduces Gerry to another Belfast boy, Patrick Armstrong, who lives in a squat with his English girlfriend Carole Richardson. But following an argument about the war in Northern Ireland Paul and Gerry are thrown out of the squat.

They spend the night of the Guildford bombing sleeping in a park with an Irish down-and-out, Charlie Burke, who warns them of the perils of London. After stealing some money from a prostitute, Gerry decides to lie low in Belfast for a while. Meanwhile, the squat in London is raided by the police. Soon after, the police come to Belfast for Gerry. During interrogation, Paul Hill confesses to the bombing and advises Gerry to do the same. Gerry holds out until one of the police officers says that his father will be shot if he does not confess. In court, the prosecution base their case largely on these confessions and those of Patrick Armstrong and Carole Richardson. All four are given life sentences.

In prison, Gerry shares a cell with his father who has also been framed on terrorist charges. While Guiseppe starts a campaign to prove his innocence, Gerry sinks into the prison's drug culture. The monotony of prison life is broken; the IRA man Joe McAndrew, one of the gang that really planted the Guildford bomb, takes Gerry under his wing. Gerry is impressed by the discipline of the older man, who leads the prisoners in a protest about conditions. The head prison officer, Barker, calls in the riot squad. McAndrew later takes his revenge on Barker with a makeshift flame-thrower. Horrified by the incident, Gerry distances himself from McAndrew and throws himself into the campaign to prove his and his father's innocence. When Guiseppe dies in prison it only serves to harden Gerry's will.

Gareth Peirce continues pursuing Gerry's case, and gains access to the police archives where she finds a file marked, "Not to be shown to the defence". It contains a statement from Charlie Burke confirming that he was with Hill and Conlon on the night in question. In 1989, Peirce produces this file at the appeal hearing. The sentences against the Guildford Four are quashed and they walk free from the courtroom. Amid scenes of jubilation Gerry Conlon pledges to fight on to clear his father's name.

One of the central absurdities of Gerry Conlon's case was that the IRA wouldn't have touched him with a bargepole. At the time of his arrest he was a petty criminal and a drug user, immature, unreliable and out for a good time. Throughout his long imprisonment, those campaigning for Conlon's release emphasised the fact that he was not IRA material. This presents a problem for Jim Sheridan, for the very character flaws that made Conlon an unlikely leader of an IRA active service unit also make it difficult to turn him into a convincing movie hero (though casting Daniel Day-Lewis in the part obviously helps).

Sheridan gets round this by means of a redemption scene of some note. It happens during a prison film show. A fairly appalling act of violence from the Republican prisoner, Joe McAndrew, leaves a prison officer writhing on the floor, his clothes consumed by flames from a home-made blow-torch. Until now, Gerry has been a waster even in prison, grudgingly resigned to his fate. But in the face of real human suffering it is Gerry who comes to the screw's rescue—an act of kindness which is his salvation.

Sheridan's films to date have all hinged on violent set-pieces that illuminate the central relationship of the film—the astonishing fight scene when Bull McCabe and his son confront the American in *The Field* and the restaurant scene in *My Left Foot* when Christy Brown declares his love for Dr Eileen Cole. The film-show scene has just this function in *In the Name of the Father*—and just to drive home the Oedipal point, the film the prisoners are watching is *The Godfather*.

This film is not really about Gerry Conlon's fight for justice. It is much more concerned with the relationship between Gerry and Guiseppe. Sheridan has said that after *My Left Foot*, which is essentially about Christy Brown's relationship with his mother, he was on the look-out for a script about a father-son relationship. He had not really thought about making a film about the Guildford Four, but when he saw the script of *In the Name of the Father* it fitted the bill perfectly. Thus Sheridan makes every figure of authority in the film into some kind of surrogate father to Gerry. He begs the commanding police officer, Dixon, to "stop these men hurting me", and after Gerry confesses, Dixon gives him a cuddle as if he had just been a naughty boy. He is similarly drawn to Joe McAndrew because he is a man of action where his own father seems like a sickly old fool.

By far the best scenes in the film are the claustrophobic head-to-heads between Gerry and Guiseppe. Their confinement together allows Gerry to unburden himself of all the feelings of hatred and embarrassment. He tells of the time his father told him off for cheating in a game of football. Furious with Guiseppe, he drew his father's name in the mud and pissed on it. This is stirring, primal stuff.

After his transformation, Gerry grows to recognise the genuine moral strength of his father. This even takes on something of a religious dimension as Guiseppe becomes a messianic figure towards the end of his life. The scene immediately after Giuseppe's death parallels the torching of the prison officer. One by one, prisoners drop sheets of lighted paper into the snow-covered prison yard in tribute to the man and his struggle, until hundreds of tiny flames float away into the winter sky. The idea is that these gentle flames, which mark the beatification of Guiseppe, represent a more genuine form of solidarity than the scorching heat of McAndrew's revolutionary passion.

The story of the Guildford Four is pretty riveting as it is, but in Jim Sheridan's hands it becomes a great yarn to be retold and embellished. Never one to shy away from stereotypes of his countrymen, Sheridan makes his Gerry Conlon the archetypal loveable Irish rogue, while McAndrew is the murderous Republican psychopath that we read about all the time in the tabloid press. The portrayal of McAndrew is a strange kind of tribute when you think that it was the man who was presumably the real life model for McAndrew—Joe O'Connell, the leader of the Balcombe Street Group—who calmly pleaded the innocence of the Guildford Four at his own trial instead of offering a defence for himself.

As for Gerry's relationship with Guiseppe, in reality it seems that the two men were hardly ever in the same prison, let alone the same cell. And where, for the sake of Freudian neatness, the film has Gerry confessing after the police say they are going to kill his father, Conlon himself has always claimed it was his sister and mother they threatened.

Like Sheridan's previous features, *In the Name of the Father* is unashamed Irish myth-making. But considering the sensitivity of the issues involved, it is a bit odd that Sheridan has taken quite such liberties with the truth. This is, after all, a film about a man who spent 14 years in prison because people made up stories about him.

TIME, 12/27/93, p. 70, Richard Corliss

[*In the Name of the Father* was reviewed jointly with *Famine-33*; see Corliss' review of that film.]

VILLAGE VOICE, 12/28/93, p. 82, Georgia Brown

My favorite studio-released film this season—since *Groundhog Day*, to be exact—is Jim Sheridan's *In the Name of the Father*. Drawing from a true story—Gerry Conlon's memoir of wrongful imprisonment for an IRA bombing—Sheridan fashions not merely a gripping thriller but a delicately nuanced father-son story. *In the Name of the Father* effectively examines the gross injustices perpetrated in the Father's name—bringing to trial such paternalistic authorities as the Crown, the Law, the IRA, the Church—but in the end what counts is the simple decency of one lowly man, one good-enough father.

The movie opens with a bang. Almost. The few frames preceding the white blast are ideologically critical: A happy foursome walks down a block and enters a noisy Guildford pub; then a bomb blows the place apart. Showing us these young people sauntering toward death or maiming, Sheridan removes any doubts (apparently the London press has been voicing many) that the film might be sympathetic to terrorists.

Daniel Day-Lewis plays Conlon from his days as a carefree Belfast punk (stealing sheet metal from roofs), through a brief hippie phase in London, to his arrest and an abomination of a trial for the Guildford bombing, 15 years served of a life term, and on to a second trial. It's a smashing performance by Day-Lewis, possibly his best. (It's my favorite anyway.) The character grows from a snotty, strutting lad, a rebel with no cause, into a man of substance, "the truth" as his standard. A pretty rare transformation for a mere movie to undertake.

Guiseppe Conlon, Gerry's unfortunate da (the superb Pete Postlethwaite, the fascistic father in *Distant Voices, Still Lives*) at first seems merely the generic parent—someone for the young hero to vent against and leave behind. Worried about his wayward son's nonfuture in Belfast's streets, Guiseppe manages to send him off to London. (The IRA has nasty ways to deal with petty thieves who attract cops to their hideaways.) To Gerry, his da is an embarrassment: A runty guy, he's neither attractive nor powerful, and his principles seem outmoded, a sign of weakness in an age of war. Guiseppe's the sort to worry about the breaking of eggs, killings of innocents.

Anyway, London isn't a haven but a trap for Irish layabouts. Following the pub bombing, the police round up Gerry, his friend Paul Hill (John Lynch), as well as a wide-eyed couple from their squat. The newly enacted Prevention of Terrorism Act allows the police to hold suspects seven days without counsel. The short of it is that the Guildford Four, as they're called, are framed and convicted. So are the Maguire Seven—the alleged bombmakers—who include Gerry's father, his aunt Annie, and her two young sons. The Four get life. The judge says he wishes he could give them death sentences.

What if, in the prime of your callow young adulthood, you went to jail and mum or dad were thrown in as your cellmate? Cruel and unusual punishment? Well, this borderline hilarious situation is the one in which the Conlons, *père* and *fils*, find themselves. *In the Name of the Father* may be ostensibly focused on the corruptions of the English patriarchy, but its heart, wisely, lies in the thrashing out of differences between one parent and one child. (The film evolves from invoking "*The* Father" to Gerry's passionate evocation of "*my* father.") When a charismatic IRA hard-liner (Don Baker) enters the prison, Gerry eagerly becomes his acolyte. Guiseppe not only is unimpressed, he's revolted. A thrilling war for the child's soul is begun.

I love this movie and hope its light doesn't get buried under the bushel basket that is *Schindler's List*. Unfortunately, both films are being released by Universal, which must be primarily committed to Spielberg.

Also reviewed in:
CHICAGO TRIBUNE, 1/14/94, Friday/p. C, Michael Wilmington
NEW REPUBLIC, 1/3/94, p. 28, Stanley Kauffmann
NEW YORK TIMES, 12/29/93, p. C11, Janet Maslin
NEW YORKER, 1/10/94, p. 81, Terrence Rafferty
VARIETY, 12/27/93, p. 50, Todd McCarthy
WASHINGTON POST, 1/14/94, p. G1, Rita Kempley
WASHINGTON POST, 1/14/94, Weekend/p. 44, Desson Howe

INDECENT PROPOSAL

A Paramount pictures release.   *Executive Producer:* Tom Schulman and Alex Gartner. *Producer:* Sherry Lansing.   *Director:* Adrian Lyne.   *Screenplay:* Amy Holden Jones.   *Based on the novel by:* Jack Engelhard.   *Director of Photography:* Howard Atherton.   *Editor:* Joe Hutshing.   *Music:* John Barry.   *Music Editor:* Clif Kohlweck.   *Sound:* Keith Wester and (music) Shawn Murphy.   *Sound Editor:* Alan Robert Murray.   *Casting:* Victoria Thomas and Barbara Harris.   *Production Designer:* Mel Bourne.   *Art Director:* Gae Buckley.   *Set Decorator:* Etta Leff.   *Set Dresser:* Richard Garcia, James Halstead, Craig Heine, and David Snodgrass.   *Special Effects:* David Kelsey.   *Costumes:* Bobbie Read, Bernie Pollack, and Beatrix

Aruna Pasztor.   *Make-up:* Ben Nye, Jr., Dennis Liddiard, and Richard Dean.   *Stunt Coordinator:* Walter Scott.   *Running time:* 118 minutes.   *MPAA Rating:* R.

CAST: Robert Redford (John Gage); Demi Moore (Diana Murphy); Woody Harrelson (David Murphy); Seymour Cassel (Mr. Shackleford); Oliver Platt (Jeremy); Billy Bob Thornton (Day Tripper); Rip Taylor (Mr. Langford); Bily Connolly (Auction Emcee); Joel Brooks (Realtor); Pierre Epstein (Van Buren); Danny Zorn and Kevin West (Screenwriters); Pamela Holt (David's Girlfriend);   Tommy Bush (David's Father);   Mariclare Costello (David's Mother);   Curt Odle (David's Boss);   Jedda Jones, Myra J, and Edwonda White (Craps Women);   James Migliore (Craps Stick Man); Nick Georglade (Croupier); Ritamarie Kelly (Dress Shop Saleslady); Sam Micco (Sam);   Joseph Ruskin (Pit Boss);   Joe La Due (High Roller); Ben W. Fluker (Roulette Croupier); Carleen Shordone (Coffee Shop Waitress); Toru Nagai (High Roller Card-man); Steven Dean (Craps Pit Boss); Frank J. Allison (Craps Box Man);   Dana Williams (Jeremy's Secretary); David Cousin (Craps Dealer); Catlyn Day (Wine Goddess); Irene Olga Lopez (Gage's Maid); Dru Davis (Bernice); Rudy Morrison (Maitre D'); Richard B. Livingston (Mike); Joe Bays (Jeffrey); David Rees (Businessman); Françoise Bush (Woman in Restaurant); Elizabeth Gardner (Real Estate Receptionist); Robert "Bobby Z" Zajonc and Alan Purwin (Helicopter Pilots); Sheena Easton (Herself); Herbie Hancock (Himself).

FILMS IN REVIEW, 8/93, p. 263, Keith Edwards

Would She? Could She? Wouldn't You? The million dollar question. It is resolved relatively early in the film and from there on it is simply filler to flesh out the time slot. Given the participants, the huge offer is absurd. Robert Redford has not weathered the years with the best of them (like Cary Grant or Douglas Fairbanks) and therefore has to be photographed through gauze, lit from behind or shot in the dark like Gary Cooper in *Love In The Afternoon.* Those decades on the slopes have taken their toll on his princely visage, yet he is not Ross Perot and one would think it possible for him to get a partner in his sumptuous bedroom for a lesser sum, if not "on the house."

Demi Moore and Woody Harrelson really do punish the parquet in their model kitchen with explosively explicit sex, yet Ms. Moore is a pretty, wistful little lady like Maggie McNamara or Millie Perkins and this ante seems a trifle high for her services. It is curious in this script that the wager for the wife's body is offered to the husband which equates her bartered status with a prized pony or a side of beef.

The tale is being touted as a lovely old fashioned film which it is, but if you are going to recycle old formulas, let's plunge forward into the Clinton Nineties.

Redford should have offered the big bucks to Demi for a night with Woody.

LOS ANGELES TIMES, 4/3/93, Calendar/p. 1, Kenneth Turan

Every once in a great while a movie comes along that is so unintentionally silly, so thoroughly implausible, all you can do is bow your head in bemused astonishment. "Indecent Proposal" is such a film.

The first joint venture of producer Sherry Lansing and director Adrian Lyne since "Fatal Attraction," "Indecent Proposal" aims at a similar kind of potboiler intensity, a parallel peek into the trashy lives of the rich and fatuous.

Not afraid to ask the tough questions, "Proposal" wonders what would happen if an idyllic but suddenly impoverished young couple (Demi Moore and Woody Harrelson) ran into an unabashed billionaire (Robert Redford) who offered $1 million for a very close encounter with the Mrs. "The night would come and go," the billionaire says suavely, "but the money would last a lifetime." Not at today's prices.

One obvious problem "Proposal" has is that another film has already asked that same question in a very different way. Andrew Bergman's "Honeymoon in Vegas" involved Nicolas Cage, Sarah Jessica Parker and James Caan in the identical situation, but treated it as absurd farce, not one of the ponderous moral dilemmas of the age.

But even if "Honeymoon in Vegas" had never existed, this particular film would be in trouble. Though some of its moments are intentionally humorous (especially those involving Oliver Platt as the couple's opportunistic lawyer), mostly "Indecent Proposal" wants you to feel deeply for the plight of this morally stricken young couple, skewered by an offer they just can't seem to refuse, when all you want to do is giggle at how ridiculous it all is.

Sweethearts since high school, Diana and David (yes, they call each other D) tell most of their story in dueling flashbacks that begin in the present with the two of them alone and sad. She is sitting on an L.A. bus (how's that for tragic?) talking about setting free the one you love, while he is moping around the pier at Paradise Cove, mumbling that "losing Diana was like losing part of me. I thought we were invincible." Not quite.

David is a passionate architect for a local firm who liked to point out the finer points of local car washes when he could take time out from "putting everything he knows" into the plans for their future dream house. Then the recession hits and David fears he could lose it all.

Even Diana's work as a real estate agent can't tide them over, and, in danger of losing their dream house in what appears to be an imaginary part of Santa Monica, the two Ds make a gutsy, if not particularly logical, decision. They take all their cash and head out for Las Vegas, determined to win enough to keep the foreclosures from their door.

Unfortunately, the Ds have picked the same day to visit Vegas as womanizing billionaire John Gage, a high roller who tosses around $10,000 chips like they were styrofoam coasters. Naturally, the fetching Diana catches his eye, and when he offers to buy her an outfit she's been wishing for, she frostily replies, "The dress is for sale, I'm not." Well, intuition never was Diana's strong point.

Though getting the picky Redford to play Gage must have seemed like a coup at the time, his performance, a variation of his bland "The Great Gatsby" outing, is not what "Indecent Proposal" (rated R for sexuality and language) needs. Redford's Gage is so busy being exquisitely sensitive and polite he neglects to project any energy, and without it the crucial morning-after part of the movie gradually collapses under the weight of its own self-importance.

Victims of a group delusion, Lansing, Lyne and screenwriter Amy Holden Jones (who is not above purloining one of Gage's key speeches from "Citizen Kane") have overestimated the power of the "my money for your wife" situation and underthought what the lasting consequences of that wager might be.

Without creditable motivation or convincing acting (Harrelson and Moore look alternately dreamy, cranky and confused), the more desperately the filmmakers want to involve you in the plight of the Ds the more preposterous everything becomes. It may not be polite to laugh at other people's troubles, but "Indecent Proposal" doesn't leave you much choice.

NEW STATESMAN & SOCIETY, 5/21/93, p. 30, Jonathan Romney

Demi Moore and Woody Harrelson are a young couple who have it all, looks, love and money—that is, until the recession hits, and their dream home looks like falling foul of the repro man. Then along comes Robert Redford and offers them a million dollars in exchange for one night with Demi. Tag line: "He liked her so much he bought her company".

Indecent Proposal is visually and dramatically anaemic, a high-concept film based on a wafer-thin premise, and shot with all the fussy, over-lit Tampax-ad glitz that's made Lyne the last word in the Lifestyle school of cinema. But the film's gone down a storm at the US box office and on *Oprah*-type chat shows, where its subject has been mulled over as if it had the sort of philosophical gristle that would qualify it for *The Moral Maze*. The argument is aimed fairly and squarely at Mr and Mrs Married America, especially if they deem themselves a bit liberal, a bit adventurous, but responsibly adult with it. Ladies, would *you* sleep with Robert Redford for a million dollars? And guys, how would *you* feel if she did?

Dumb questions. Of course she would. And of course he'd be down at the club bragging to his buddies about it. Now, if they'd given the Redford part to Danny DeVito, the question might have been more interesting, but not that much. A million dollars is a million dollars. The film doesn't go for complex stakes, just the highest ones it can think of. Even *Fatal Attraction* had some degree of complexity and ambiguity; what's striking about *Indecent Proposal* is the way it thinks entirely in absolutes.

So the Murphys are a *blissfully* happy couple, *totally* in love, who have (and therefore stand to lose) *everything*. Redford is *absolutely* staggering, a fairy-tale prince who's not just loaded, but *infinitely* loaded. One single act, and the couple can have *everything* back, *immediately*. The trouble is, although everything is charged with absolute value, nothing has any depth: it's a film of flat, unambivalent signs, which mean nothing more than they seem to.

Diana and David's conjugal bliss is practically represented by a drawing of a house with a squiggly line to signify smoke. They live in one beautiful home and dream of building another. When they split up, poor Woody sees his architect's model of a dream house lit from inside by a beatific white glow. Marriage isn't a complex of transactions between two people: it's a house, full stop.

Similarly, money doesn't represent any of the things that it gives access to, like power, or the illicit, or security; it represents dollar signs. One Million Dollars is the film's bottom line, its absolute self-referring signifier. When the Murphys go to Las Vegas and win the jackpot, Lyne doesn't actually show them swanking around in dressing gowns emblazoned with dollar signs, or have their eyeballs roll around like cash registers; but they do throw sheaves of greenbacks around their bedroom and roll around in it.

Then enter Redford, surrounded by penthouse apartments, yachts, helicopters: all the badges of infinite wealth that might look ostentatious in an episode of *Dynasty*. He's called John Gage, but he might as well have been called Daddy Megabucks. God knows, there are more interesting ways to represent powerful money and its trappings. But this drama of comic-book symbols is less about ideas and things that can be charged with meaning, more about the mathematics of pure value.

It's significant, though, that a film that spells everything out so blankly refuses to tell us about one thing—the intimate transaction at the film's centre. We're treated to plentiful saccharine sex between the Murphys—endless backlit marital romping between bouts of tidying up. But the secret sex that (apparently) takes place between Diana and Gage on his yacht remains a mystery, and she and David swear never to discuss it. What happens between them is taboo, because it has happened outside the bounds of marriage. It's indecent to be more accurate, obscene, in the sense of taking place offstage, off the scene of marriage.

Read that way, *Indecent Proposal* turns out to be not at all the "women's film" that it has been sold as—that is, a film appealing to women's fantasies of what it would be like to have a dream lover as a change from boring old hubby. Rather, the film's turning point comes when David no longer knows exactly what's happening in his wife's life—when she becomes unknowable. From this point on, *Indecent Proposal* is effectively a "man's film", addressing male anxieties about the unknowable sexuality of the little woman at home.

David may love Diana, but he has no idea what she's *worth* until another, more powerful man tells him. And he finds out exactly what she's worth; the film's a *reductio ad absurdum* of the phrase "Babe, you look a million dollars". But it doesn't simply tell us that in a marriage the wife is a liquid asset, it tells us in a way that replicates the star system. If David's biggest asset is Diana, the film's is Demi Moore, currently one of Hollywood's hottest properties (sic). The film presents Gage's purchase of her as a rich man's whim, but it also tells legions of adoring Demi-fans what they already know—that a night with her must be worth a million dollars.

In fact, the film is entirely about Moore as a star, an adorable, value-able object of desire. As a star, Demi-Diana is the object of negotiation between the fan (her husband) and the system, or if you like, the agent (the all-powerful, all-knowing dealer who names her price).

Some commentators have seen Gage as a JFK figure; but he's really a Mike Ovitz. And it's true that only when a value is placed on a star's head does she become a star. She becomes one when she becomes unknowable, fabulous; thus Diana to David, thus Demi Moore to her audience.

The film's really an allegory of the unstoppable rise to glory of Demi Moore, but at the price of an old-fashioned sentimental fetishisation of marriage. The institution has never emerged from a melodrama as glowingly coated with holy meaning as it does here. At the end, when David gets his property back, as he surely must, that's one hell of a pedestal he's going to put her on.

NEW YORK POST, 4/7/93, p. 17, Jami Bernard

A few years ago, there was a spate of body-switching comedies coming out of Hollywood. There was no particular public clamor for body-switching comedies, and yet they kept on coming.

Now we are having a nasty outbreak of sell-your-spouse-in-Vegas movies. The latest one, "Indecent Proposal," is "Honeymoon in Vegas" but without the Elvises.

In "Honeymoon in Vegas," Nicolas Cage ran up so many gambling debts that he had to rent his fiancee to rich, sentimental James Caan for a night. After a few drinks by the pool, Cage thinks better of it, but a lot of zany situations and Elvis impersonators stand between him and retrieving his true love. Meanwhile, the fiancee is truly touched by Caan's attentions, proving in movieland that women's hearts can indeed be bought in exchange for an expensive night out on the town.

It's not like "Honeymoon in Vegas" broke the bank or anything, but apparently the money-men saw a hole that needed to be filled—more movies about wife-bartering in Vegas.

"Indecent Proposal" is virtually the same movie. The role of the rich guy is essayed by Robert Redford, who has been lit so peculiarly that his face looks pink—too much Vegas sun, perhaps. Redford plays John Gage, a man so rich that all he has to do is whisper the word "one" to a minion, and within moments, one million dollars in gold chips is wheeled over to his blackjack table like a treat on a dessert cart.

Woody Harrelson and Demi Moore play the debt-ridden couple whose passion for each other is not so undying that it can't be interrupted for a million-dollar night. Redford pays Harrelson the million, gives Moore a nice dress to wear on her date, then whisks her off to his yacht.

Is this a distasteful premise or what? The kids' marriage never fully recovers from it and neither does the movie. Harrelson, who was so sexy in "White Men Can't Jump," looks sleepless and imbecilic. Moore looks lovely in repose, which is just as well since she spends most of the movie reposing in one man's arms or another. The two of them make the least compelling couple possible, their life together consisting of spats over who left the toilet seat up.

Redford has an untenable role, in which he has to look suave but not oily, flash money without being ostentatious, and be so confident of his sexual skill that he believes Moore will fall in love with him after a single night. He adopts a stance out of the "I'm a Handsome Man" gag routine from "Saturday Night Live."

I'm a fan of director Adrian Lyne and the way he synthesizes pop-culture film techniques, notably in "Flashdance," "9½ Weeks" and "Fatal Attraction." But his attempts to spice up this movie range from the sub-Lyne (overstated reaction shots in the casino) to the ridiculous (bouncy sex on a waterbed full of paper money).

The movie rushes past the actual night of paid-for passion, which is too bad—because the implication is that the Redford character is so good in bed that Moore should have paid *him* for the privilege.

At least "Honeymoon in Vegas" tempered its cynical story with humor. "Indecent Proposal"—aside from some amusing supporting work from Oliver Platt as the lawyer who must finesse the particulars—takes itself very seriously, and tries to be ultra-romantic with creamy cinematography, dreamy music and nice clothes. It's not "The Way We Were" but perhaps "The Way We Whore."

NEW YORK POST, 4/7/93, p. 17, Michael Medved

If a great-looking stranger offered you $1 million in exchange for the chance to spend one night with your spouse, would you agree to the deal?

If this question intrigues you, then try talking it over with your partner, discussing it with your closest friends, or raising the issue with your therapist; but do not, under any circumstances, go out to see "Indecent Proposal," the hapless new release from Paramount Pictures.

It's hard to imagine that any real-life conversation about sex or, for that matter, about the pennant prospects of the Philadelphia Phillies or the coming mayor's race in New York—would prove less titillating and less satisfying than this soggy, stodgy mess of a movie.

The picture begins with a shot of a lonely pier shrouded in mist, with seagulls flapping their way across the screen to add to the mournful atmosphere. We soon hear not one but two characters (Woody Harrelson and Demi Moore), both providing voiceover narration to tell us that their marriage is in trouble; but it takes forever for the flashbacks to unfold and to finally reveal the nature of this difficulty.

It turns out that these two high-school sweethearts are deeply in love. We experience the depths of their affection through an interminable scene of lovemaking, shot in the classic, quick-cutting, upbeat, rock-accompanied MTV style, hinting at a half-dozen different positions on their kitchen floor and delivering considerably less erotic charge than most aerobics videos. We are also supposed to recognize these two as warm, wonderful human beings because they live in a funky, cluttered home near the beach with a sad-eyed mongrel while Harrelson, a brilliant architect, struggles to build their dream house.

Unfortunately, the recession promptly punctures their hopes, so this lovable pair does what any thoughtful and responsible couple would do under the circumstances: They go to Las Vegas to gamble away their last $5,000 in the world.

In the course of this fateful visit they conveniently encounter the bemused billionaire John Gage (Robert Redford), who makes them the provocative offer described in the title. No sooner do they agree to his terms than Harrelson begins feeling seller's remorse, banging his head on elevator doors, bellowing his wife's name down hotel corridors and otherwise registering his displeasure with the situation.

One of the key problems with this flimsily constructed concoction is that you feel no sympathy whatever with the sufferings of this jerk; as he tearfully rips apart all photographs of his lovely wife (which he later reassembles with Scotch tape) one can only hope that she leaves him once and for all. Harrelson plays the sort of obtuse and egocentric lunkhead he created in "White Men Can't Jump," without a hint of that previous character's energy or egocentricities; in fact the clinical name for the sort of personality he portrays here is "putz."

Redford, meanwhile, doesn't even have that much to work with when it comes to his character, and he strolls through most of the picture as if he's merely an empty suit, striking poses for Gentleman's Quarterly. His motivation remains not so much a mystery as a muddle, while we learn absolutely nothing about his personal history or even how he has earned his fabulous wealth.

In several scenes, he seems to be harking back 20 years to his ironic and understated performance in "The Great Gatsby"; when he takes Moore for a tour of his elegant but lonely mansion you half expect him to point out the green light at the end of his dock. After several characters have commented on how this dashing billionaire could command the attention of anyone he wants, there's no explanation whatever as to why there are no other romantic interests in his life, or why he's suddenly selected Moore as his Daisy Buchanan.

Alone among the principals, Demi Moore escapes for the most part without serious embarrassment: She deftly manages numerous changes of wardrobe and even a few changes of mood in the course of her performance. Ultimately, however, she too is undermined by the fatuous direction of Adrian Lyne, ("Flashdance," "Fatal Attraction"), which constantly recalls the woozy romanticism of TV ads for expensive perfume.

In fairness, not even the most brilliant direction could have done much with the shallow and altogether lifeless script by Amy Holden Jones, who previously crafted screenplays for the commercial hits "Beethoven" and "Mystic Pizza," and directed the cult classic "The Slumber Party Massacre."

By the time this picture staggers to its unspeakably annoying ending, much of any audience will be enjoying a slumber party all its own. Director Lyne and producer Sherry Lansing (who was recently appointed chairman of Paramount Pictures) fail miserably in their attempt to combine the same elements that made such a conspicuous success of their previous collaboration, "Fatal Attraction."

Perhaps recognizing that their misfired melodrama ought to offer some deeper lessons, its creators have tried to suggest a political significance to their cinematic statement. Sherry Lansing, for instance, says in the movie's press kit that she hopes the film "will signal the end of an era—a time when greed and the desire for material possessions overwhelmed people and they began to lose sight of human values." Along similar lines, Robert Redford suggests that "Indecent Proposal," is a postmortem of the '80s "when greed was licensed in the United States as a way to be and a way to go."

Ronald Reagan and his notorious "Age of Greed" have been blamed for many sins in recent months—ranging from homelessness and the AIDS epidemic to teen acne—but it would be especially unfair to hold him responsible for this irredeemably awful motion picture.

NEWSDAY, 4/7/93, Part II/p. 62, Jack Mathews

There is a cynical old joke about a rich lecher and a young woman that goes like this:

He: Will you sleep with me for one million dollars?
She (after reflection): Yes, I will.
He: Will you sleep with me for one dollar?
She (outraged): What kind of woman do you think I am?
He: I know what kind of woman you are. I'm trying to find out what your price is.

Tall tales from cruel little jokes grow, and the misogynistic notion behind that transaction—that every woman can be bought—has blossomed into a major moral dilemma in Adrian Lyne's artificial and ponderously introspective "Indecent Proposal." Lyne has used moral issues to peddle some flesh before in such films as "9½ Weeks" and "Fatal Attraction," but he's never taken his material quite this seriously.

"Indecent Proposal," which is unrelated to last year's almost identically plotted "Honeymoon in Vegas," stars Robert Redford as John Gage, a dashing, womanizing billionaire who offers to pay $1 million for one night with a married woman he spots stealing candy in a Las Vegas hotel.

In these recessionary times, there is no haggling over price. Diana Murphy (Demi Moore), a Los Angeles real estate broker, and her husband, David (Woody Harrelson), a free-lance architect, have come to Las Vegas in a last-ditch effort to stave off bankruptcy, and having had no luck at the tables, they accept Gage's first offer.

"It's only my body, not my mind or my heart," says Diana, as she and David talk themselves into a Faustian deal they think will shore up their otherwise deliriously happy marriage. (Moviegoers who have observed Moore's cleavage expand cosmetically over the years may add that it's not exactly her body, either.)

Of course, it is much easier to keep the flesh and the spirit separate before one has been rented out, and Diana's one-night stand as a Forbes 500 hooker enters the bloodstream of her marriage like a fatal virus. The question afterward, as David's guilt gives way to suspicion, jealousy and rage, is not what money can buy, but what it cannot buy back.

In a way, the movie suffers the same fate as the Murphys' marriage; it starts to fall apart the morning after Diana sleeps with John Gage. Almost nothing that happens from then on seems a logical extension of what happened before, least of all the erratic behavior of David and the impetuous courtship of Diana by her lovesick John.

The premise and set-up of the story is better suited to screwball comedy than romantic bathos, and that is how they were used in Andrew Bergman's hilarious "Honeymoon in Vegas," which starred James Caan as a mobster who offers to square a young gambler's debt in exchange for some time with his fiancée. The moral question is the same in both movies—what does it take for decent people to sell themselves?—but by casting Redford as the buyer, and then making him sensitive, polite and sincere in the extreme, "Indecent Exposure" undermines the dilemma.

Agreeing to sleep with Robert Redford for money may be more moral than agreeing to sleep with, say, Howard Stern, but the idea creates an entirely different fantasy. And price structure!

This is a very passive performance by Redford, who seems content to model his expensive wardrobe while letting his killer smile stand in for charm. His John Gage is a totally fabricated character, like Cary Grant's angel sent to earth in "The Bishop's Wife" to test a troubled marriage and tempted to stick around for a little earthly romance himself. In "Indecent Proposal," however, it's played as straight as a nervous breakdown.

There are some light moments in the early going, and a very funny performance by Oliver Platt as the Murphys' greedy lawyer ("Don't negotiate without me ... I could have gotten you $2 million"). But once the moral issues and the rivalry between David and the billionaire kick in, the movie catches up in an emotional whirlpool that takes it right down the drain.

NEWSWEEK, 4/19/93, p. 64, David Ansen

You're a pretty Los Angeles real-estate agent (who looks like Demi Moore) blissfully married to an up-and-coming architect (who looks like Woody Harrelson). You have a picture-perfect life until the recession hits. Now the money's gone, the debts are piling up and you find yourself in Vegas (not like you, but what the heck) down to your last desperate dime when suddenly a glamorous billionaire (who looks exactly like Robert Redford) offers you a million dollars to spend one night with him, no strings attached. What's a newly poor girl to do?

That's the hook, farfetched but catchy, of Adrian Lyne's *Indecent Proposal*. Granted, it's the same hook as "Honeymoon in Vegas," but you can bet the serious fellow who brought you " "Flashdance," "Fatal Attraction" and "9½ Weeks" isn't going to stock his movie with flying Elvises. Too bad: this solemn clunker could have used *something* that flew—wit, Wallendas, woodpeckers or maybe a decent plot. To be fair, there is a helicopter that whisks Moore off to Redford's yacht for her million-dollar night. But all we get to see of this is a kiss, then a cut to the following morning as Demi returns to her husband, who has been transformed overnight into a jealous, surly toad. Can their marriage survive this devil's bargain?

At this point you might expect the story to get interesting. It doesn't. The marriage falls apart, Demi takes up with the ardent billionaire (the nature of his obsession is inexplicable, and nothing about Moore's performance conveys irresistibility) and we wait through an eternity of digressions for Woody to rediscover his ideals and win her back, which he does by bidding a million dollars on a hippopotamus. Don't ask.

Director Lyne frantically flexes his technique, turning a mundane household quarrel over the laundry into a food-throwing donnybrook, whipping up MTV-style sex scenes utterly devoid of passion. But not once in the whole silly exercise does he approximate a genuine emotion. Unable to dramatize marital love, he sells it, as if he were pitching perfume. Having nothing credible to play, Moore and Harrelson strike poses of love and anguish, and try not to look embarrassed. Neither radiates much star wattage. Redford does his suave, twinkly-eyed charm act as only he can. He's perfect, and perfectly unreal.

For connoisseurs of daffily gratuitous movie moments, however, "Indecent Proposal" does offer some gems. My favorite is when Demi, our narrator, abruptly announces that she's taken a job "teaching citizenship just to keep myself busy." This allows Lyne to stage a "cute" schoolroom courtship scene in which the nattily attired Redford woos the dressed-to-the-nines teacher from the back of the class while the appreciative ethnic types ooh and aah at the glamorous white lovers. Lame as Amy Holden Jones's screenplay is, you can bet this scene was written at studio gunpoint. (Presumably Demi's class flunks, for she is never again seen at work.) Then there's that hippo-auction scene, but never mind ... If you're not napping by the end, you may be forced to concede that "Indecent Proposal" didn't need flying Elvises after all. Its mirth is all its own.

SIGHT AND SOUND, 6/93, p. 55, Lizzie Francke

Seven years into their marriage, college sweethearts David and Diana Murphy are still very much in love. They live together in Los Angeles where David pursues a successful career as an architect and Diana works as a real estate agent. When the recession creeps up on them, David loses his job, Diana finds her business slowing down and the half-built dream home that David has designed is threatened with repossession by the bank. The Murphys go to Las Vegas, hoping to win the extra $50,000 that they need; on their first day they win $25,000. Later, browsing in a clothes shop, Diana is approached by an elegant older man; he offers to buy her a dress, but she refuses. The next day, David and Diana lose all their money. Heartbroken, they tour the gambling dens, and find the mystery man—John Gage—playing at one of the tables. He asks to borrow Diana for luck in a one million dollar gamble; she reluctantly agrees and Gage wins. Gage invites Diana and David to be his guests, and sends Diana the dress that she liked. Gage offers the couple a million dollars in exchange for one night with Diana; after much soul searching, they agree and a contract is drawn up by their lawyer friend Jeremy. David has second thoughts and tries in vain to chase after Diana, but Gage has already whisked her away by helicopter to his yacht.

Diana and David return home, agreeing never to discuss the incident, but find their efforts have been in vain, as the house is repossessed. Later, David suspects that Diana is still seeing Gage, and the couple's relations deteriorate. Diana decides to try and buy back their land; she discovers that it has been bought by Gage and confronts him. When David learns that she has seen him, he believes his suspicions to be founded and moves out. Gage turns up at Diana's office and she is forced to show him around some properties. Diana finds the insistent Gage hard to shake off, and eventually becomes his lover. David still grieves for Diana and attempts unsuccessfully to win her back, but later learns that she wants a divorce. At a charity auction, David bids a million dollars for a hippo in Diana's name, and presents her with the signed papers; the two talk while Gage looks on. While driving home, Gage tells Diana that she is the best of the 'Million Dollar Club' and that he has struck similar deals before. Diana asks to finish their affair and is dropped off on the highway. She takes a bus to the pier where David once proposed to her; David is also there and they pledge their love for each other.

Halfway through this *Honeymoon in Vegas* without the gags (or the flying Elvises), we catch a 10-second glimpse of a young woman reading Susan Faludi's *Backlash: The Undeclared War Against Women*. Product placement for last year's feminist bible? More like Adrian Lyne's sly little nod towards a book that rumbled his much-debated *Fatal Attraction*. Faludi joined other critics in taking the film to task for its demonizing portrayal of the independent career woman and its beatification of the family. The film was emblematic of the 'backlash' movement that Faludi believed erupted in America in the 80s, with its idea that "women were unhappy because they were too free; their liberation had denied them marriage and motherhood."

Perhaps Lyne is hoping that *Indecent Proposal* will merit a mention in *Backlash 2*, since it so cockily invites feminist censure and so baldly attempts to be of its moment by playing with the current preoccupation with the demise of 80s-style pecuniary values. But zeitgeist movies cannot be so easily fabricated. The bland and transparent *Indecent Proposal* fails to be controversial; it also fails to be the erotic thriller that it is trailed as.

In a film that could use a few twists and turns, the most surprising thing is that it is written by Amy Jones, who wrote and directed *Love Letters*, a low-budget movie that merited considerable critical attention when it was released in the mid-80s. Originating from the Roger Corman exploitation stable (which dictated some obligatory nude scenes), it was an ironic play on the conventions of the 'woman's movie', that followed a brilliant young career woman's obsessive affair with a married man. Jones' heroine, rather than being consumed by the dangerous liaison, comes to a self-understanding that enables her to walk away bereft but wiser. An intimate film full of careful observations on the hazards of relationships, *Love Letters* rewrote the romance genre.

Indecent Proposal, however, sets itself up as an old-fashioned (read: regressive) 'love story' with a high-minded moral that makes it supposedly hip to the 90s. You've heard the one about how "money can't buy love"? As Gage says, "let's test the cliché". Dangerous words to use in a film riddled with them. The threat to Diana and David is not impending death, or another lover, but cash and the lack of it. Their prettily bohemian 2CV lifestyle masks the fact that they are still entrenched in 80s values and the dream of a luxury home by the sea. They have overreached themselves already. So their cards are surely marked as they drive to the neon hell of Las Vegas to gratify all their worldly desires.

Lyne spares us the subtleties; this is the Faustian pact writ large, and no doubt Gage's hand-made leather shoes hide well-manicured cloven hooves. When it comes to the devil, the male of the species is always immaculate, and ideally dressed by Cerruti or Armani. Compare and contrast with Alex the unkempt temptress in *Fatal Attraction*. Gage plays the same tricks as Alex, sinisterly popping up in Diana's life in his attempts to lure her. But unlike her, Gage is the acceptable, dimpled face of adultery. Redford plays him as President Charming, ready to whisk Diana away from it all—surely a self-made Perot figure but with the Clinton smile that women are supposed to go wild for. His 'Million Dollar Club' is supposedly the only sicko chink in his otherwise shining armour.

Gage is the archetypal Mills and Boon romantic hero, but is this film the substance of every girl's dreams? One could speculate on a little role reversal: imagine a Cerruti-clad Catherine Deneuve offering to buy David the well-cut pair of trousers that he covets. Imagine on; once again it is the woman who is the object of the raw deal and the currency of the exchange. Despite her protestations that she is not for sale, Diana is the modern manifestation of the bartered bride, a sign of one man's spending power over another. While David and Diana engage in the kitchen and bathroom sex obligatory in a Lyne movie, Gage's prowess is measured in what he can buy. Sex between Gage and Diana is fetishised into a dressing-up routine as Diana is turned into another pretty woman that he can adorn more than adore.

What then of the decent proposal? In a champagne-ad beach tryst at the beginning of the film, David asks Diana to marry him. Seven years and x months later, the two conveniently return to their romantic haunt, and it's another advert. The pack shot frames their entwined hands with their wedding rings sparkling in the dawn light. As every girl knows, the truest riches are to be found in that band of gold.

VILLAGE VOICE, 4/13/93, p. 49, Georgia Brown

Adrian Lyne's *Indecent Proposal* begins with moving shadows cast on a blank surface: So, we might say, do all movies, *did* all movies, begin (back in the flickering light of Plato's cave). The mysterious shadows, it turns out, are thrown not by human figures but shifting letters of the title. PROPOSAL is blunt and hard-edged, unequivocal—which proposals in initial stages tend to be. As befitting a word that efficiently locates the center of the movie's appeal, INDECENT is indistinct, vaporous, as if formed out of fog. Already we're anxious.

A quintessential movie-movie, the stunningly skillful, thrillingly romantic *Indecent Proposal* has everything to do with Hollywood—and, by extension, with that larger culture of dancing images, this America. (When they put those stars on the flag, who could have foreseen what they'd come to signify?) Besides stars: deals and property, pimps and whores. Money. Indecency.

And decency? Perhaps. If you believe in decency, clap your hands.

From out of the shadows and fog, the smoke and the mirrors, stride such a wholesome young couple. Maybe not the sacrosanct family of Lyne's *Fatal Attraction*, but the incipient sacrosanct family. Demi and Woody. She, sorta wooden; he, kinda dim. (Diana and David are their movie names.) Bright young things, former high school sweethearts. He's an architect, she (*quel* disappointment!) a real estate agent: two sides of the coin of property. His god is Louis Kahn. Hers ... Leona Helmsley? Both, however, in their respective spheres, are involved in style. They drive a battered *deux cheveaux*, for godsake. She knows mortgages; they snap up a piece of Santa Monica oceanside to build their dream house on. The house is half done when the recession hits. Hey, we know when that was.

Having trained in creating those minidramas called commercials, Lyne is a master of efficient exposition—particularly of ellipses (the most brilliant and daring ones here, I can't disclose). The goal is to communicate the basics instantly, or, as Ruth Prawer Jhabvala didn't say, Only connect the groin and the nerve endings. As if they're the most natural things in the world, Lyne foists on us improbable events and far-fetched situations, makes us believe without questioning. He's a magician. Not only the main plot, but almost every scene in *Indecent Proposal* is preposterous or close to it. (If Lyne had directed *Damage*, what a harrowing film it would have been!)

For example: A few minutes into the movie, this smart, professional, savvy pair takes off for a Vegas casino to turn $5000 into $50,000. The first day they rake in $25,040. They plan to get the other half the next day!

Strolling in a fancy casino boutique, Demi, the picture of urchin-chic, helps herself to a Godiva chocolate put out for customers. Through the glass partition she's observed closely by billionaire Robert Redford. He continues to watch as she furtively scoops up a handful. Next, she's posing with a $5000 dress. He steps in and offers to buy it for her. "You earned it." (Giving him pleasure *watching*.) "The dress is for sale. I'm not," she replies. Flattered? Suspicious? The sullen Demi keeps her secrets. (The audience's gut response—Take it!—finds expression soon enough in the crude mercenary cracks of a yahoo spectator at Redford's blackjack table.)

Given this deep-in-debt but happy young couple and a rich but melancholy, and predatory, older man, any media-literate dunce can predict what comes next. They have what he wants, he has what they want. Why not make a bargain? On the surface, what he wants is not them, but her. The classic woman-as-chattel business. She's choice property. It's just her body. Why not? What is the body to the soul? She tells her husband (and herself): "I'm doing it for you." But the bargain requires the young husband's assent—i.e., complicity. He gives reasons (excuses) too. But there's no getting around the fact that he'll be the one to suffer. He's sold the other, not himself. To make his love credible, he must get cold feet. Too late, of course. Hellfires burn.

Has money come between the perfect couple, obliterating their shared past as well as their future? Is this movie about the couple? It threatens not to be.

For his part, the Redford character wants the wife to admit that she has chosen. *We* know she's chosen. That is, if you agree with me that Redford, not Moore, is the real object of desire here. Redford's appeal blurs the issues. Shot through what looks like one layer of gauze for each decade, he doesn't look younger (he actually looks ancient) so much as he looks radiant—all aura. Tenderness personified. Like the word indecent in the titles, he's a vapor trail. Gatsby's ghost.

Would you take $1,000,000 to spend the night with Robert Redford? Is this the question? Is the bargain a macguffin? Of course it will fuel much after-the-movie argument. (*This* is the best dating movie in some time.) Would you let your wife, husband, significant other go? Depends, is the only answer. Name your variables. Could you stand being left behind? Can you say no? Louis Kahn said, "A good question is better than the best answer."

Having posed a classic question (albeit in a fairly absurd form), Lyne subtly, dutifully, opens the possibility that Redford's John Gage *may* be the devil. Is this woman in danger? What can we expect of a man exercising naked monetary power? (And if he fails to wield power malevolently, does that make him less sinister?) Maybe Gage diabolically runs a $1,000,000 Woman Club the way the Spur Posse conducts its points-for-sluts competitions. Lyne sprinkles doubts and stirs gently. Very gently.

In the classic Hollywood romance one has to give up the money to get the real prize. Usually, in the end, the money is included as a bonus. The unwritten rule is that those who give up riches freely will get something wonderful back. (Don't try this at home.) What happens here I'll leave you to find out.

It's easy to spot elements from Lyne's previous films: sex in the kitchen with a burner on, a sexually liberated woman with a fresh (or foul) mouth who's passionate enough to destroy a man's property (throw a brick through the mansion window, pour acid on his car, yank off the tablecloth during his business lunch), eros and wealth, eros and corporate success, women's bodies and their un-coverings (legwarmers to short-shorts), offbeat details in home furnishings. Auspiciously, *Indecent Proposal* reminds us of recent blockbusters, *Pretty Woman* (rich man buys poor woman, shopping, Roy Orbison) as well as *Ghost* (yuppie love and homemaking nipped in bud, Demi Moore).

This movie is so clean it's close to fable, fairy tale, or morality play. It's peopled with archetypes rather than characters. It's less real-life than hyper-life. The script—credited to Amy Holden Jones and adapted from a novel by Jack Engelhard—has been pared down to clipped, insinuating repartee (She: "You can't buy people." He: "But I buy people every day.") and charged one-liners: "I bought you because you said you couldn't be bought." The film contains just the right proportion of brisk comic scenes. The requisite fool is a crass young lawyer named (what else?) Jeremy. Oliver Platt's performance hovers precariously between odious and ludicrous.

Lyne knows how to make wonderful use of reactive expression, perfectly casting and directing a few crucial "faces." In just a second or two these wise outside observers—a waitress in a Vegas diner, a croupier at a roulette table, and especially Seymour Cassel's Mr. Shackleford—bestow looks of great pity while managing to convey the melancholy peace made with their own bondage.

Finally, Lyne may not have wholly succeeded in working his own variation on a classic comic plot (Harrelson's limitations, rather than Redford's charisma, may be the bottom line) but he's convinced me he's some kind of genius. No Goethe, Hawthorne, or Eric Rohmer, but, since he calls his movies "page-turners," I'll grant him O. Henry.

Also reviewed in:
NEW REPUBLIC, 5/3/93, p. 29, Stanley Kauffmann
NEW YORK TIMES, 4/7/93, p. C13, Janet Maslin
NEW YORKER, 4/26/93, p. 107, Anthony Lane
VARIETY, 4/12/93, p. 75, Todd McCarthy
WASHINGTON POST, 4/7/93, p. D1, Rita Kempley
WASHINGTON POST, 4/9/93, Weekend/p. 38, Desson Howe

INDIAN SUMMER

A Touchstone pictures release of an Outlaw Production.   *Producer:* Jeffrey Silver, Robert Newmyer, Caroline Baron, and Jack Binder. *Director:* Mike Binder. *Screenplay:* Mike Binder.

Director of Photography: Tom Sigel.   *Editor:* Adam Weiss.   *Music:* Miles Goodman.   *Music Editor:* Nancy Fogarty.   *Sound:* Ed Novick, Freddy Potatohead, and (music) Joel Moss and Dennis Sands.   *Sound Editor:* Patrick Dodd.   *Casting:* Richard Pagano, Sharon Bialy, and Debi Manwiller.   *Production Designer:* Craig Stearns.   *Art Director:* Rocco Matteo.   *Set Designer:* Diane Bald.   *Set Decorator:* Jane Manchee.   *Set Dresser:* Julian Peters.   *Costumes:* Jane Robinson.   *Make-up:* Jeanne Van Phue.   *Stunt Coordinator:* Steve Lucescu.   *Running time:* 98 minutes.   *MPAA Rating:* PG-13.

CAST: Alan Arkin (Unca Lou); Matt Craven (Jamie Ross); Diane Lane (Beth Warden); Bill Paxton (Jack Belston); Elizabeth Perkins (Jennifer Morton); Kevin Pollak (Brad Berman); Sam Raimi (Stick Coder); Vincent Spano (Matthew Berman); Julie Warner (Kelly Berman); Kimberly Williams (Gwen Daugherty); Richard Chevolleau (Sam Grover); Robert Feldmann (Man in Canoe); Anne Holloway (Cook); Diane Lane (Claire Everett); Cliff Woolner (Ranger Thaddeus Clay); Emily Creed (Young Jennifer); Brad Deutch (Young Jamie); Jesse Felsot (Adam Randall); Gabriel Gunsberg (Young Rick); Brian La Pointe (Young Matthew); Jeremy Linson (Young Brad); Heidi Marshall (Young Kelly); Noah Plener (Young Jack); Rebecca Rumsey (Young Beth); Ashley Williams (Ida Heinken).

LOS ANGELES TIMES, 4/23/93, Calendar/p. 16, Peter Rainer

What would it be like to go back with your bunk-mates from 20 years ago to the summer camp of your youth? If "Indian Summer" is any indication, the results would be a lot like a sappy thirtysomething comedy-drama replete with scenes of campfire readings and sheet-shorting.

Writer-director Mike Binder actually went back to his childhood camp deep inside the woods of Ontario's Algonquin Provincial Park to film. It's the same camp that, the press notes say, Chevy Chase and Gilda Radner attended, which probably merits a footnote somewhere. (Maybe it was something in the drinking water.)

Binder obviously has deep feelings for the auld lang syne of summer camp, but his reverence tends to take the form of postcard-pretty vistas of Camp Tamakwa in full autumn foliage. His ensemble of ex-campers and mates—including Vincent Spano, Julie Warner, Bill Paxton, Elizabeth Perkins, Kevin Pollak, Matt Craven, Kimberly Williams and Diane Lane—blend jarringly into the surroundings with their various shticks and tics. They're an overqualified bunch for the shenanigans they're called upon to perform—over and over again. (Perkins, for example, falls out of bed for reveille twice—two times too many.) As the camp director, Alan Arkin shuffles about like he was ready to move into Wilford Brimley's slippers; he turns himself into an old poop.

One big reason this film's auld lang syne seems a bit out of key is because the ex-campers don't seem old enough to be mooning about the missed possibilities in life. Thirtysomethings certainly have these longings but surely the joke ought to be that such lives are still green. A little irony in "Indian Summer" (rated PG-13 for some drug content, sensuality and language) would have gone a long way; it seems to have been written for superannuated fortysomethings. And the big emotional moments don't resolve anything—except, of course, the need to resolve the plot. The dumbest "relationship" moment comes when Matthew (Spano), whose been on the outs with his wife Kelly (Warner), finds himself being punched out by her in the camp's boxing ring. Strindberg it's not.

On the plus side, this is probably the only film ever made that credits a "Moose Unit." There are some great shoots of moose.

NEW YORK POST, 4/23/93, p. 30, Jami Bernard

Unless as a child you attended Camp Tamakwa—and evidently many famous people did, including Chevy Chase and directors Sam Raimi and Mike Binder—you may feel left out during the festivities and forced hilarity of "Indian Summer," a sort of "Big Chill Goes to Camp."

Chevy Chase is not in this movie. But Raimi is, as an inept camp attendant, while Binder wrote and directed. As soon as you see a summer-camp setting—especially during the off-season—you expect a horror flick where lusty campers get their heads lopped off on the volleyball court. If

Raimi and Binder had switched places, that's probably what we would have gotten—and personally, I'd have had more fun.

That's because this 20-year reunion from Camp Tamakwa's "golden years" necessarily begins with everyone knowing everyone else, and having so many shared memories that it's like that gag about longtime prisoners who know each other's jokes so well all they need to hear is the number of the joke, instead of the punch line, to burst out laughing.

Therefore, the audience is baffled and maybe a little resentful at being left out of the nostalgia-fest. Binder is counting on viewers to dredge up their own summer-camp memories with which to fill in the blanks. (Calling Camp Minisink!)

A bunch of former campers returns for a week in the off-season to reminisce and, by drenching themselves in the well of nostalgia, to cure themselves of the rigors of adult life by recognizing the child within (or maybe simply by seeing a real-live moose again). However they turned out as adults appears traceable right back to that last golden summer at Tamakwa when they canoed and learned life lessons in miniature.

Each of them has achieved adulthood by developing some annoying personal trait—one of the guys is attracted only to bimbos, one of the girls is perpetually lonely—and it doesn't take a merit badge to know that a return to lost youth is going to help everybody get over every little thing.

Meanwhile, they indulge in such ritual juvenilia as short-sheeting beds and stealing toilet paper. It wasn't all that funny back then, and it's not so funny now, but "Indian Summer" milks it for all it's worth.

Old sweethearts rekindle the fires without a match, new sweethearts get in the boxing ring, and Alan Arkin as the irascible old camp manager wakes everyone up with that infernal clanging bell from the good ol', bad ol' days.

Once you get to know the baby-booming former campers, the movie grows on you. Like a fungus, sure. But by the end of "Indian Summer" I finally had that warm glow that would have helped the movie at its start.

The enthusiastic cast includes Vincent Spano, Elizabeth Perkins, Kevin Pollak, Bill Paxton, Matt Craven and Diane Lane. The dialogue is typically banal, the bright spots being Raimi's little bits of business as the bumbling caretaker. If only Raimi had gotten behind the camera and really stirred things up, "Indian Summer" would be more memorable than looking at someone else's precious scrapbook.

NEW YORK POST, 4/24/93, p. 15, Michael Medved

The single most impressive feature of the new comedy/melodrama "Indian Summer" is the utterly shameless way in which it steals from Lawrence Kasdan's 1983 hit "The Big Chill."

It's not just the basic setup that's the same; the entire cast of characters is virtually identical.

There's an unmarried career woman with a loudly ticking biological clock (played by Mary Kay Place in the original film and by Elizabeth Perkins here); a moody, romantic hunk who's wasted his youthful promise and become a rootless hippie wanderer (William Hurt/Bill Paxton); a hard-working husband and father slightly bored with his prosperous respectable life (Kevin Kline/Vincent Spano); his earthy, bright endlessly understanding wife (Glenn Close/Julie Warner); and a pushy, sarcastic, compulsive Jewish talker (Jeff Goldblum/Kevin Pollack). Of course, no "Little Chill" could be complete without a much younger outsider who enters the group of anxious Yuppies by virtue of her sexual involvement with one of its members who inspires much jealousy due to her unspoiled youthful outlook and her supple body. Meg Tilly played that role 10 years ago, and the radiant 21-year-old Kimberly Williams (Steve Martin's daughter in "Father of the Bride") handles the chore this time.

These resemblances may seem mechanical as they unfold; but keeping track of the way the new characters match up with their prototypes actually lends "Indian Summer" a resonance it otherwise wouldn't have. The main problems with this picture involves its differences from "The Big Chill," not its countless similarities.

The old friends here aren't college buddies form the University of Michigan, as they were in that earlier project; this time they are pals form sleep-away camp (though still Michiganders, by the way!) who shared a few summers at a rustic Canadian retreat whey they were children. We're repeatedly told that those brief, pleasant weeks at Camp Tamakwa meant a great deal to each of the characters, but writer-director Mike Binder never even begins to show us why.

Recollections of athletic contests and hiking expeditions and bunkhouse practical jokes among 12-year-olds can never convey the same universal echoes—or hint of social significance—as memories of counter-cultural college years in the turbulent '60s.

Binder, who showed an intriguing flair for quirky autobiographical filmmaking in his one previous film, "Crossing the Bridge," seems aware of the trifling nature of this material, and accordingly sets up a corny plot contrivance that's supposed to make us care.

The crusty, gray-haired camp proprietor "Unca Lou" (portrayed by Alan Arkin in a sleepy, phoned-in performance) reveals that he is going to close Tamakwa after some 40 years unless one among a handpicked corps of his former campers, summoned in early fall for a final reunion, agrees to take over the enterprise. We're supposed to bite our nails as the precious camp teeters on the brink of extinction.

Will Tamakwa close forever, or will some bewildered Yuppie find new meaning in life by keeping the place open for future generations of lucky kids? What do you think? Does the bear sit in the woods?

Even though it is utterly lacking in tension or emotional depth of any kind, the film is still pleasant enough to watch, thanks to an abundance of pretty scenery (photographed at the real-life Camp Tamakwa in a golden autumnal haze by cinematographer Tom Sigel) and due to the efforts of the likable and competent cast. Elizabeth Perkins and Kevin Pollak are especially good, wringing the last drops of life out of their under-written characters and giving some of their scenes an unexpected edge.

Prominent director Sam Raimi (best known for "Darkman" and the "Evil Dead" movies) here takes a holiday from horror to play the camp's klutzy handyman; he displays a surprising gift for slapstick and easily earns the picture's biggest laughs.

An utterly gratuitous and jarring note amid all this sweetness and autumn light involves the picture's unequivocal endorsement of marijuana—even as a drug of choice for 12-year-olds. During their reunion the former campers renew and deepen their friendships by getting high together, while fondly remembering pre-teen summers in which they all most definitely inhaled.

The major studios reportedly resolved some years ago to show greater restraint when it came to glamorizing recreational drugs; but that policy appears to have gone up in smoke in this PG-13 project, giving this bland diversion from Touchstone/Disney its only big surprise.

NEWSDAY, 4/23/93, Part II/p. 70, Jack Mathews

Mike Binder, the writer-director of the latest ensemble buddy movie, "Indian Summer," is a former stand-up comedian, and his film, about a handful of anxious young adults returning to the summer camp where they met in childhood, often substitutes jokiness for character, punch lines for revelations.

That's not all bad. I saw Binder work at the Comedy Club in Los Angeles in the early '80s, and he was a good standup. He came out of Detroit full of energy and fresh ideas, and with a hip sense of social irony that provided a solid foundation for routines he worked up about his circle of friends.

"Indian Summer," set in the same picturesque Canadian camp where Binder and his pals spent many summers of their youth, is an attempt to stretch those observations into a feature-length movie. Place the accent on "stretch."

The film is done, in the style of John Sayles' "Return of the Secaucus 7" and Lawrence Kasdan's "The Big Chill," and some of Binder's material rates the comparison. When one of his characters observes that married men with vasectomies who get divorced these days "still have to wear condoms," it comes out as a throwaway line in a conversation, just a thought surfacing on someone's lips. But in the context of these characters' generation, its implications reverberate like a gunshot in a canyon.

Binder also has some of the Kasdan-Sayles-Barry Levinson gift for writing naturalistic dialogue for group scenes, when friends are just sitting around shooting the breeze, and it is in those moments where "Indian Summer" is at its best. An early sequence when the reunited campers raid the kitchen at Camp Tamakwa and sit around smoking pot, reminiscing and battling the munchies is an inspired piece of filmmaking.

The scene is very funny, but it also very effortlessly introduces us to each of the major characters, fills us in on the nature of their various relationships as kids in the camp, and sets us up for the conflicts that will inevitably develop.

The group includes: The couple, Matt (Vincent Spano) and Kelly (Julie Warner), who met at Camp Tamakwa 20 years earlier and are now in a shaky marriage; Jennifer (Elizabeth Perkins), Matt's childhood sweetheart, now grown into a cynical, lonely adult; Beth (Diane Lane), a competitive showboat mourning the recent death of her husband; Brad (Kevin Pollak), the one--time camp prankster spoiling for a second childhood; Jack (Bill Paxton), who was kicked out of camp all those years ago and is here to reveal the mystery behind it, and self-absorbed Jamie (Matt Craven), whose beautiful girlfriend Gwen (Kimberly Williams) will give him a major lesson in humility.

It is, as movie cliques go, an interesting cast of characters, and there are some nice performances, particularly those of Perkins, Paxton and Williams, in her first role since "Father of the Bride." But the conflicts that Binder creates for them, and the resolutions, are as contrived as a list of camp activities. Swim, fish, hike? Huh-uh. Talk, fight, make up.

Even the thing that reunites them, an invitation from nostalgic old camp owner Unca Lou (Alan Arkin), strains the imagination. Why the class of '72 out of more than 40 in Unca Lou's past? For no apparent reason other than it represents the adult generation Binder best understands.

Camp life, from canoeing to short-sheeting, never changes, but being in your late 20s in the early '90s is unique.

Binder obviously has some talent to share, but it's a raw talent he brings to the screen. "Indian Summer" opens with a black and white flashback of Unca Lou and the kids staring at a moose in the woods. That Binder repeats this scene—twice!—with the kids and the moose 20 years later is a joke on both Bullwinkle and the audience.

VILLAGE VOICE, 5/4/93, p. 58, Anne Glusker

There are certain movies that you know you shouldn't like, but you do anyway. The music swells, your tears well, your chain is jerked, and you sink deliciously into the warm bath of bathos. *Indian Summer* would like to be one of those movies. Planted firmly in *The Big Chill* reunion genre, it's the extremely flimsy tale of eight friends in their early thirties who return to the summer camp where we all, supposedly, had those seminal early adolescent experiences; first moose sighting, first kiss—you get the idea. But when the music swells in this movie, instead of welling tears, all you get is a slight shiver of embarrassment.

The poignancy and bittersweetness that the title means to evoke are driven home with a sledge-hammer. The red and yellow leaves of the eponymous season seem to be in every scene, in every shot. Characters brush past them, moose peer out from between them; they are underfoot and under credits, in impossibly punched-up, heightened hues.

The human scenery, always a crucial part of the-movie-you-shouldn't-like category, isn't bad. Vincent Spano isn't my cup of tea, but some go for him. And Elizabeth Perkins has a face that radiates intelligence. Spano's and Perkin's respective characters almost rekindle an old camp passion during a midnight tryst in a deserted cabin, but are saved by the bell in the form of Lou, the camp's director (Alan Arkin), who incidentally seems more like a used-car dealer from the Bronx than a molder of young minds and bodies in the Ontario wilderness.

The film throws in the obligatory songs of the bygone era—and yes, anyone who was anywhere near adolescence during the '70s probably will feel at least a tiny tug at the heart when "Spinning Wheel" plays. But that's nowhere near enough. A good, button-pushing, bad-for-you movie needs some kind of plot.

Also reviewed in:
CHICAGO TRIBUNE, 4/23/93, Friday/p. B, Dave Kehr
NEW YORK TIMES, 4/23/93, p. C10, Vincent Canby
VARIETY, 4/26/93, p. 69, Emanuel Levy
WASHINGTON POST, 4/24/93, p. D2, Hal Hinson

INSIDE MONKEY ZETTERLAND

An I.R.S. Releasing release of a Coast Entertainment production. *Executive Producer:* Louis J. Perelman and Jefery Levy. *Producer:* Tani Cohen and Chuck Grieve. *Director:* Jefery Levy. *Screenplay:* Steven Antin. *Director of Photography:* Christopher Taylor. *Editor:* Lauren Zuckerman. *Music:* Rick Cox and Jeff Elmassian. *Sound:* Craig Felberg and Stephen Tibbo. *Production Designer:* Jane Stewart. *Set Decorator:* Wendy Weaver. *Costumes:* Stephen Earabino and Hayley Marcus. *Running time:* 92 minutes. *MPAA Rating:* R.

CAST: Steve Antin (Monkey Zetterland); Patricia Arquette (Grace Zetterland); Sandra Bernhard (Imogene); Sofia Coppola (Cindy); Tate Donovan (Brent Zetterland); Katherine Helmond (Honor Zetterland); Bo Hopkins (Mike Zetterland); Debi Mazar (Daphne); Martha Plimpton (Sofie); Rupert Everett (Sasha); Ricki Lake (Bella); Lance Loud (Psychiatrist); Frances Bay (Grandma); Luca Bercovici (Boot Guy).

LOS ANGELES TIMES, 8/25/93, Calendar/p. 5, Kevin Thomas

Imagine being a fledgling screenwriter working on a project that reveals the corruption that brought about the demise of L.A.'s streetcar system, the beloved big Red Cars in particular.

You might think it a topic best suited to "Chinatown's" highly experienced Robert Towne, but the feckless hero of the quirky and amiable "Inside Monkey Zetterland" forges ahead with the project despite the nonstop litany of distractions that make up virtually the entire film.

Steven Antin's Monkey has scarcely a moment's peace and quiet in his Spanish-style flat in the Fairfax area. He's forever being interrupted by his high-strung, possessive mother (Katherine Helmond), a veteran soap-opera star in constant fear of being written out of her show. Then he gives comfort and temporary shelter to his sweet-natured gay sister (Patricia Arquette), whose lover (Sofia Coppola) has deliberately become pregnant without consulting her.

Then there's an aggressive, neurotic neighbor (Sandra Bernhard) who throws herself at him continually, and there are some new politically radical tenants (Martha Plimpton and Rupert Everett). Also dropping by are Monkey's hippie father (Bo Hopkins), who shows up annually; his thin-skinned grandmother (Frances Bay); his hairdresser brother (Tate Donovan) and even a super-intense fan (Ricki Lake) of his mother.

The one person who's leaving rather than arriving is his bored lover (Debi Mazar), and even she is perpetually returning to pick up more of her stuff and give Monkey yet another piece of her mind. No wonder the guy's in therapy (with shrink Lance Loud), but even there his privacy is being invaded, for in return for free treatment he must submit to being observed by a bunch of medical students from behind a one-way mirror.

Antin, who also wrote the film, has a sharp ear for flaky dialogue and a bead on human foibles L.A. style, but he might well have considered going a bit further outside Monkey and suggested what role this highly impersonal city has in affecting behavior and an individual's sense of security (or lack of same).

Although "Inside Monkey Zetterland" is very much a writer's film, director Jefery Levy has managed to draw a quality of freshness from everyone in a very large cast. Along with Antin, the film's likable linchpin, Helmond, who plays against the clichés of the Jewish mother, and Plimpton, whose role is comically outrageous, have the showiest parts. "Inside Monkey Zetterland" (rated R for language) is modest yet undeniably distinctive.

NEW YORK POST, 10/15/93, p. 28, Michael Modvod

Monkey Zetterland (Steven Antin) is a part-time Hollywood actor and aspiring screenwriter who's supposed to be facing a dramatic crisis in his life, but his problems don't really amount to much.

Someone has stolen his favorite gold curtains from the bedroom window and his hairdresser brother (Tate Donovan) ruins his hair. His girlfriend (Debi Mazar) leaves him because he's boring, and his whacked-out opera singer neighbor (Sandra Bernhard) begins following him.

His sister (Patricia Arquette) breaks up with her pregnant girlfriend (Sofia Coppola), his mother (Katherine Helmond), a soap-opera star, shows little confidence in his unfinished movie script, and his long-absent father (Bo Hopkins) suddenly shows up for Thanksgiving dinner.

None of this is either hilarious or overly dramatic, but is consistently amusing, undeniably engaging in its easy-going eccentricity. Director Jefery Levy, whose previous film, "Drive," proved a favorite on the festival circuit in 1991, handles every component of this odd assemblage with the proper touch of whimsy.

At times the material recalls the work of novelist John Irving (brought to film in "The World According to Garp" and "The Hotel New Hampshire"). Unlike the Irving adaptations, however, "Monkey Zetterland" never strains for seriousness or symbolism. Leading man Antin (who also wrote the original screenplay) wisely portrays Monkey as a bland, bemused Everyman, not some suffering victim.

"Monkey Zetterland" is one of those artful little trifles that should advance the careers of all concerned, even though it is neither important nor memorable in its own right.

NEWSDAY, 10/15/93, Part II/p. 77, Terry Kelleher

"Isn't it the small details in life that really, really matter?" asks the protagonist in "Inside Monkey Zetterland."

Depends on what they amount to. In this movie, it's something less than a hill of beans.

Steven Antin wrote the script and stars as Monkey, a sometime actor currently working on a screenplay about the arrested development of public transportation in Los Angeles (as if "Who Framed Roger Rabbit" didn't cover that subject in sufficient depth). Monkey is a bland, rather diffident fellow. We understand only too well why his on-and-off girlfriend, Daphne (Debi Mazar), complains of boredom. So the movie attempts to surround the central cipher with eccentricity.

Monkey's mother, Honor (Katherine Helmond), is a meddlesome, insecure soap-opera actress who prattles constantly about her hemorrhoids. His sister, Grace (Patricia Arquette), is a lesbian who's angry with her lover, Cindy (Sofia Coppola), for getting pregnant. His neighbor, Imogene (Antin's friend Sandra Bernhard), is a self-styled conceptual artist who follows him around and favors him with photocopies of her feet. According to Monkey's voice-over, his father, Mike (Bo Hopkins), is "a dictionary of '60s cliches," although the moviemakers unaccountably forget to let us hear the man talk.

Two of the secondary characters actually provide amusement: an antagonistic acquaintance named Sofie (Martha Plimpton), a woman on a mission to "expose closeted homosexuals," and Monkey's brother, Brent (Tate Donovan), a hairstylist preoccupied with his own hair. But Antin and director Jefery Levy overestimate the viewer's tolerance for desultory conversation. "Don't get me started," Monkey and his mother like to say. Take the hint that you'll have to wait three-quarters of an hour for anything to happen.

The late jumble of events, none of them plausible, includes a terrorist bombing, the theft of Monkey's script (like so many foolish writers in the movies, he keeps only one copy), and some gunplay by Bella (Ricki Lake), a deranged fan of Honor's. It's as if Levy, who had seemed content to film dead-end arguments at a polite distance, were suddenly determined to whip the small, scattered details into some sort of dramatic shape.

What emerges, however, is merely a facile irony, vague in form and empty of content. There's nothing inside "Inside Monkey Zetterland."

VILLAGE VOICE, 10/19/93, p. 60, Manohla Dargis

Jefery Levy's *Inside Monkey Zetterland* has all the familiarity of an alien visitation. In this case, the invaders hail from Los Angeles, a world in which idiosyncrasy is as studiously affected as DKNY grunge.

At the center of this teapot tempest is Monkey Zetterland (Steve Antin, who also wrote the script), a washed-up actor who spends his days and nights massaging his psyche in an experimental therapy program and braving a tsunami of chattering castraters (Katherine Helmond, Debi Mazar, Martha Plimpton, Ricki Lake, Sandra Bernhard). When Monkey isn't negotiating women or copping a quick Ferris Bueller at the camera, he—wouldn't you know it—is busy searching for the holy grail (via a screenplay called *The Red Car*).

In this post-Woody period, it takes considerable nerve to think anyone would find the combination of neurotic women, analysis, Grossinger's gags, and Hollywood quite as entertaining, or fresh, as do Levy and his cinematic cohorts. Since there's no real narrative to anchor Monkey's shtick, the film works best when it steers clear of hemorrhoid jokes and gets its anxious eponym off our backs. The amazing Patricia Arquette (as Monkey's sister, Grace) and Sofia Coppola (as Grace's Valley-meets-Edie sweetie) are unexpectedly good, though for entirely different reasons (Arquette because she's so talented, Coppola because she's so peculiar). Cheaper than a round-trip plane ticket, the film is a trip in itself, though whether it's worth the ride is strictly up to you.

Also reviewed in:
CHICAGO TRIBUNE, 11/26/93, Friday/p. I, John Petrakis
NEW YORK TIMES, 10/15/93, p. C12, Stephen Holden
VARIETY, 7/27/92, p. 60, Emanuel Levy
WASHINGTON POST, 12/3/93, p. G7, Rita Kempley
WASHINGTON POST, 12/3/93, Weekend/p. 58, Desson Howe

INTO THE WEST

A Miramax Films release of a Little Bird production in association with Parallel Films/Majestic Films/InternationalMiramax Film/Film Fair International/Newcomm. *Executive Producer:* James Mitchell. *Producer:* Jonathan Cavendish and Tim Palmer. *Director:* Mike Newell. *Screenplay:* Jim Sheridan. *Based on a story by:* Michael Pearce. *Director of Photography:* Tom Sigel. *Editor:* Peter Boyle. *Music:* Patrick Doyle. *Music Editor:* Roy Pendergast. *Sound:* Peter Lindsay. *Sound Editor:* Bob Risk. *Casting:* Ros Hubbard and John Hubbard. *Production Designer:* Jamie Leonard. *Art Director:* Mark Geraghty. *Special Effects:* Gerry Johnston. *Costumes:* Consolata Boyle. *Make-up:* Morna Ferguson. *Make-up (Ellen Barkin):* Aileen Seaton and Norma Hill. *Stunt Coordinator:* Tony Smart. *Running time:* 92 minutes. *MPAA Rating:* PG.

CAST: Gabriel Byrne (Papa Riley); Ellen Barkin (Kathleen); Ciarán Fitzgerald (Ossie Riley); Ruaidhri Conroy (Tito Riley); David Kelly (Grandpa Ward); Johnny Murphy (Tracker); Colm Meaney (Barreller); John Kavanagh (Noel Hartnett); Brendan Gleeson (Inspector Bolger); Jim Norton (Superintendent O'Mara); Anita Reeves (Mrs. Murphy); Ray McBride (Mr. Murphy); Dave Duffy (Morrissey); Stuart Dannell (Conor Murphy); Becca Hollinshead (Birdy Murphy); Bianca Hollinshead (Angela Murphy); Owen O'Gormon (Cafferty); Mark O'Regan (Welfare Man); Phelim Drew (Sergeant Brophy); Sean Madden (School Inspector); Vinnie McCabe (Video Shop Owner); Tony Rohr (Traveller); Brendan O'Duill (Barman); Dave Carey (Resident); Joan Sheehy (Woman with Pram); Lana Citron (Sophie); Clive Geraghty (Smiley); Charles Ruxton (Tommo); Stanley Townsend (Rico).

LOS ANGELES TIMES, 9/17/93, Calendar/p. 12, Michael Wilmington

At the opening and close of "Into the West", there's an archetypal, radiant movie image: a snowy white horse streaking or cantering across a moonlit Irish beach. That horse-white mane flying, hoofs clopping a fiery tattoo—becomes the movie's dominant metaphor: an equine image of freedom, beauty, supernal power and grace. And, even though that's the sort of highly charged, overused symbol that can soar into poetry or tumble into cliché, in this film it works.

As envisioned by writer Jim Sheridan and director Mike Newell, the mysterious white horse whose name in Gaelic means "Land of Eternal Youth"—turns into a true fairy-tale harbinger: romanticized, heroic. And the picture itself leaps over all its obstacles and becomes splendid family entertainment. Packed with keening witchery and wild delight, "Into the West" should delight the susceptible, even as, perhaps, it annoys the jaded. Yet this picture gives us what we expect from an Irish fairy tale. It opens up the whole vein of humor and darkness mined by writers from Lord Dunsany to Synge and Yeats: grit and lyricism, earthiness and exhilaration, the tear that tumbles down past a smile.

"Into the West's" magical white horse is the property of its main child protagonists, Ossie and Tito Reilly, played by the marvelously engaging, rowdy and scapegrace pair Ciaran Fitzgerald and Ruaidhri Conroy. Here, Ossie and Tito become an outlaw pair on the run, pursued from city to countryside to sea, by a variety of authority figures: the boy's drunken, loving father (Gabriel Byrne as Papa Reilly), the brutal cops who track them down, and the evil entrepreneur who wants to steal their horse and clean up at the steeplechase races.

We may suspect early on that the horse has supernatural origins: It emerges on a moonlit beach and actually seeks the boys out. But, for Ossie and Tito, their horse also embodies the movie fantasies they love best—American cowboy pictures.

The movie puts the animal in one outlandish place after another—from the Reilly's shabby apartment to hectic city streets to an empty movie-house, where boys and horse take in a car-chase thriller. And these weird settings underscore one of the main anachronisms of modern life: the fantasies of freedom and flight, engendered in a world scarred by poverty and urbanization.

The actors are all fine: a crisp, fierce crew headed by the boy protagonists and their majestic horse, including Byrne, David Kelly as a ferocious grandfather, Ellen Barkin as Reilly's gutsy Gypsy wench.

Yet there's something that doesn't jell completely in the director-writer team: Newell, who made the dark class-crossing romance "Dance With a Stranger" and the blithe feminist "Enchanted April," and Sheridan, the writer-director of "My Left Foot" and "The Field." Sheridan probably wanted to direct this script as well—and the virtuosic shine and brilliance of the images Newell gets with his excellent cinematographer, documentary veteran Tom Sigel, may be a bit more lush than he would have wanted.

But together they've crafted a wind-swept tale that suggests that in a terrible world, freedom, even though pressed, may magically break through. In a movie year strangely dominated by the perspectives of childhood, "Into the West" (MPAA-rated PG) suggests something else too: It tells us that the instincts and intuition of those children are vital—especially in a world gone rotten, cruel or corrupt, packaging its dreams, marketing and exploiting its magic.

It's a view both sentimental and harsh. Yet, in the end, there's something crazily comforting in its mix of pessimism and dreaminess, The movie's lyrical energy eases us along, until, as in many fairy tales, dream fuses with nightmare. The dream does win out in the end, perhaps only because it has to, because, here, "happily ever after" is one of the rules of the game. But, it's no cliché, since the nightmare remains as well: the pain that sweeps over the boys and us on the high scary cliffs, even as freedom and the sea beckon in the distance.

NEW YORK, 10/4/93, p. 108, David Denby

Jim Sheridan, the director of *My Left Foot*, has written a fierce and dark modern fairy tale called *Into the West*, and Mike Newell has directed it in a style that can only be called brooding. Two motherless but far from defenseless little boys, children of Irish gypsies ("travelers"), fall in love with an extraordinary white horse. The boys, obsessed with American Westerns, ride the horse, which seems to protect and understand them, into the West Country of Ireland, a dark-gray-green landscape of flat plains, thick forests and rocky bluffs. After them come their estranged, alcoholic father (Gabriel Byrne), a variety of travelers (including Ellen Barkin), and half the Irish police. Children sit through this film in rapt fascination, perhaps because the fanciful and lyrical parts of it are grounded in something raw and elemental—the myth-haunted anger of excluded people, the implacable desire of children and parents to find each other.

NEW YORK POST, 9/17/93, p. 39, Michael Medved

"Into the West" is one of those well-intentioned something-for-everybody projects that tries hard to enchant kids while impressing their parents, but fails miserably at both goals. Sitting through the film is like attending a pretentious seance that's an obvious fake, or watching a clumsy magician at a kid's party whose trick cards keep spilling out of both sleeves.

Gabriel Byrne plays an alcoholic widower who lives with his two sons in a dreary public housing project in Dublin. We're told that Byrne and his boys are members of an ancient Celtic gypsy tribe known in Ireland as "the travelers," but he's betrayed his heritage by living among "the settled people."

The boys' grandfather (David Kelly) speaks for the traveler traditions and shows up one day with a magnificent wild white horse that instantly bonds with the younger boy, 8-year-old Ossie (Ciaran Fitzgerald). He takes the magical steed to live with them in their 16th-story flat, but before the story can degenerate into a Gaelic version of Mr. Ed, the police confiscate the horse.

When an unscrupulous cop sells the handsome animal to a wealthy industrialist who wants to exploit its remarkable jumping abilities, the kids liberate Tir na nOg and, following the example of their heroes from American cowboy movies, escape with him "into the west."

Along the way there's a great deal of mystical blarney about the horse representing the "spirit of Eternal Youth" and coming "from a land under the sea," at the same time he's supposed to be the reincarnated soul of the boys' dead mother.

To track down his missing sons, Byrne reunites with his traveler pals, including a feisty single mother played by Byrne's real-life wife, Ellen Barkin.

Barkin is on screen too briefly to significantly embarrass herself, but Byrne's performance is so hammy and exaggerated that he seems to have infected the rest of the cast. By the end of the picture, the "Into the West" players could organize their own chapter of Overactors Anonymous.

Amazingly, this maudlin mess could be the product of some of the finest talent in films today: Irish screenwriter Jim Sheridan previously scripted "My Left Foot" and "The Field," while British director Mike Newell is best known for the spellbinding thriller "Dance With a Stranger" and the gorgeous romance "Enchanted April," which I (and several other critics) selected as the best film of 1992.

That picture offered just the right touch in handling its elements of magic realism—a wistful subtlety that allowed the mystical themes to inexorably gather force. Here, however, the storytelling is melodramatic and ham-handed from the beginning—helped not at all by the huffing-and-puffing score by Patrick Doyle, who previously crafted the lovely music for Kenneth Branagh's "Much Ado About Nothing."

NEWSDAY, 9/17/93, Part II/p. 73, John Anderson

The concept of The West looms large in Irish consciousness. There's the west of immigration, the feral western coast of Ireland itself, and even the semi-fictional American West of stage, screen and "Bonanza." And there's a little of each in "Into the West," a gritty, tattered, fractured fairy tale and a low-altitude flight of fancy.

The film brings together director Mike Newell ("Enchanted April"), screenwriter Jim Sheridan ("My Left Foot," "The Field") and actor/producer Gabriel Byrne, who also enlisted his wife, Ellen Barkin, for what was clearly a pet project. But it's not their movie. It belongs to Ciaran Fitzgerald and Ruaidhri Conroy, the young actors who play Ossie and Tito Riley, and give the kind of natural performances that are ultimately saddening, because the chance that they could do it again seems so remote.

The film, which opens with a beautiful white horse galloping along a beach and the clumsy progress of an ancient-looking wagon making its way through an Irish forest, rockets into the 20th Century with the sudden appearance of a jet plane, and modern times is where it will stay. But the conflict between old and new is a constant in the film, which maintains a distinct bias toward the old.

The new, after all, is represented by the Dublin slums where Papa Riley (Byrne), a widower drowning his lingering grief in alcohol, lives with and neglects his two young sons, Tito (Conroy) and Ossie (Fitzgerald). Once a member of the Travelers, a clan of roving Irish gypsies, Papa has abandoned his old life for the city. But it comes back to haunt him, as does his reproving father (David Kelly), who's been driving that wagon to Dublin.

The white horse—his name is Tir na nOg (Land of Eternal Youth), grandfather says—arrives with him. The boys immediately take to the horse, the horse takes to the boys, and the boys take the horse home and give him a shower, invoking the rage of neighbors and the board of health. After some comedic moments in the apartment, the horse is taken into custody, and before Papa can bail him out he's been sold by a malicious policeman named Bolger (Brendan Gleeson) to an unscrupulous horse breeder named Hartnett (John Kavanagh). When the boys steal the horse back, it sparks a nationwide hunt, and a flight that continues till the end of the movie.

The boys imagine themselves cowboys and are overjoyed to learn there's a price on their heads; they see a fox hunt and imagine it's a posse. One rainy night, they hole up in a movie theater, run the projector, feed popcorn to the horse and in the morning narrowly escape by riding Tir na nOg through someone's kitchen, where they're handed breakfast by the sympathetic homeowners.

There's a lot of action, a lot of humor and perhaps too many slo-mo shots of Tir na nOg jumping over things. But there's also the sense that these are kids who've lost their mother and are in a kind of situation that's way beyond their ken. "Let's get a hotel," Ossie says at one point, as they travel west, bringing their father—who is pursuing them along with most of the Irish authorities—back to the Travelers, and to his own history. Newell's finest work here, though, is with the kids, who are never not believable. Finding themselves at their mother's grave—yes, there's a little magic here—Ossie asks, "Did mommy ever see me?" and although the moment is perilously close to becoming maudlin, it remains genuine and real, like most of the film.

SIGHT AND SOUND, 1/93, p. 48, Claire Monk

Eire. Grandpa Ward, a traveller, is alone by the sea when a white horse appears. It follows him to a travellers' encampment in the middle of Ballymun Flats, a dilapidated high-rise estate in Dublin where his young grandsons Tito and Ossie live with their father Papa Riley, one-time traveller king and widower of Grandpa Ward's daughter Mary. When Mary died giving birth to Ossie, Papa Riley's grief led him to reject the travelling life and flee to the 'settled' world, to Grandpa Ward's disapproval. Grandpa Ward tells the children that the horse's name is Tir na nOg, meaning land of eternal youth, and that it comes from the sea. It forms an instant attachment to Ossie and moves into the Rileys' flat. Following complaints from other residents, the police arrive and Tir na nOg is taken away and illegally sold by the corrupt police inspector Bolger to Noel Hartnett, a wealthy businessman.

The boys discover Hartnett's identity when Ossie spots Tir na nOg and sees his 'owner' interviewed on a TV racing programme. Papa Riley is dragged in for questioning by the Garda and shown video footage of another race at which his sons take the horse and ride away on it. The boys and Tir na nOg head west into the countryside with a £5,000 reward on their heads. Papa Riley seeks out the travellers to ask for their help in tracking down his sons. His old friends Kathleen and Barreller agree to join his search and the three set off on horseback.

As they near the coast, Tir na nOg leads the boys to their mother's grave. The three adults later find Grandpa Ward at the same spot. As the police close in, Tir na nOg carries the boys to a beach, where Papa Riley, Grandpa Ward, Kathleen and Barreller are waiting. The police advance on the horse with a net, but it carries Ossie out to sea and they trap Papa Riley instead. Beneath the water, Ossie is reunited with his dead mother. Papa Riley fights free and carries Ossie out of the water. Ossie tells him about his meeting with his mother. The police retreat, but the horse has vanished. As the family and their traveller friends gather round the campfire that night, the caravan bursts into flames. Tir na nOg emerges from the fire and gallops away.

Scripted by Jim (My Left Foot) Sheridan from a story supplied by the producers, this road movie gives itself several tricky hurdles to negotiate. Aside from the difficulties faced by any director whose central characters are a horse and two children, Newell takes on the delicate task of adopting the viewpoint of the travellers, whose nomadic culture is misunderstood, mistrusted and xenophobically abused in Ireland, and of striking a balance between authenticity and magical realism.

This mix works potently in the early city scenes, where the anachronistic Tir na nOg, led through Dublin's crowded shopping centres, crammed into the Ballymun council block lifts, or leaping magically over police vans, serves as a humorous comment on the poverty and instability of urban life and the travellers' ambiguous status in the 'settled' world. The Rileys are shown as victims—as when Papa is abused and beaten up in police custody—but they are also manipulators. In one very funny scene, the boys have little luck begging in the city centre until Tito orders Ossie to make his rendition of "Danny Boy" more heartrending by breathing asthmatically.

In the film's best moment, the restive horse, cornered in the box-like flat by the Garda, kicks its way through the flimsy wall into next-door's living room where the startled neighbours are watching *Butch Cassidy and the Sundance Kid* on television. As its title suggests, *Into the West* draws conscious parallels between the travellers' life-style and Western motifs. When Ossie, Tito and Tir na nOg shelter overnight in a small-town picture house towards the end of their journey, the film which runs when they fiddle with the projector is another example of the genre; the horse's giant shadow across the screen suggests a reciprocity between the two worlds, and the cinema itself seems to belong to a Western set.

Newell's achievement is to give the horse a snorting, clattering physical presence to match the weight of myth and metaphor it carries, and filling the screen with expanses of dilating nostril or watery eye to create an uncanny semblance of equine acting. But as the film settles down into a repetitive rural chase, it offers diminishing returns. Byrne is believable in both tower block and tent, but the carefully realised authenticity of the travellers' milieu is unbalanced by the presence of Ellen Barkin as Kathleen, her personal makeup artist all too clearly in tow and her sexual chemistry with real-life husband Byrne simmering at all the wrong moments. "The boys need a mother", she tells him. In an ironic reversal, *Into the West* proves not to be a paean to the nomadic life after all but to the domestic stability the travellers' traditional values are made to represent.

Nor is Sheridan's script an entirely corn-free zone. "Are the travellers cowboys or Indians, Papa?" shrewd Tito asks towards the end. The cop-out reply now that a happy ending looms recalls the lame maxims of television's *The Wonder Years*: "There's a bit of traveller in everybody, Tito. Only a few of us know where we're going".

TIME, 9/27/93, p. 85, Richard Schickel

Two cute kinds, their mother dead, their father sunk in despair. A splendid white horse who adopts them. Cruel adults who try to separate boys and steed. A comical-adventurous attempt by the innocents to escape their wicked—or at least unfeeling—oppressors.

Oh God, family fare. Well, yes and no. That is to say, you could safely bundle the brood off to *Into the West* and no harm would come to them. But a grownup could sneak off to it all alone and have an extremely rewarding evening. For stallion and friends are Irish, meaning that an aura of Celtic mysticism surrounds the horse and a rebellious, wandering spirit moves in eight-year-old Ossie (Ciaran Fitzgerald) and 12-year-old Tito (Ruaidhri Conroy).

They are, in fact, the adorable inheritors of a threatened Irish subculture, that of the Travellers, or Celtic Gypsies. It is their grandfather, who continues to follow the old, threatened ways, who brings the animal he calls Tir na nOg (Land of Eternal Youth in Gaelic) to them in the unhappy Dublin housing project where they live with their father (Gabriel Byrne), who abandoned his free-roving heritage after his wife's death.

The kids don't know much about that. But never mind. Televised westerns have filled the gap, imbuing them with the spirit of benign outlawry. They assert it first in the richly comic sequence in which they try to hide their horse from the police (who are in league with a rich man who wants to turn Tir na nOg into a champion jumper) in their tiny apartment. They maintain it as they move on into the west, where one of their refuges is, appropriately, a movie theater closed for the night. The sweetly funny improvisations of their flight through the Irish countryside all help them to resist sentimentality and symbolic schematization.

In the best sense of the word they—and the movie—remain wayward, unpredictable. For this, credit the blarney-proof script of Jim Sheridan (*My Left Foot*) and the wintry imagery and emotional firmness of the direction by Mike Newell (*Enchanted April*). There are no leprechauns sitting on their shoulders. Their fantasy is firmly grounded in the austere reality of modern Ireland, and that reality adds poignance to the mythic yearnings of the characters.

VILLAGE VOICE, 9/21/93, p. 55, Georgia Brown

"The old ways are dead," growls Gabriel Byrne ominously in the first few minutes of *Into the West*. So you know he's got to refind those old ways, recapture whatever it is he's drinking his way under tables to forget. And you've got a good inkling that his two chipper, motherless lads, Ossie and Tito (Ciaran Fitzgerald and Ruaidhri Conroy), will provide the means to force him back into the past.

Written by Jim Sheridan (director of *My Left Foot*) and directed a bit showily by Mike Newell (*Enchanted April*), *Into the West* is an enchanting, manageable, tense adventure for kids and their grownups. Set partially in gloomy Dublin, partially, in the lush countryside, it draws on a bit o' Celtic lore as well as traditions of a gypsylike tribe called the Travelers—itinerant tinkers who live in caravans and are ostracized by townspeople. When the boys' wizened grandpa—*he's* still clinging to the old ways—brings back a wild white horse into their Dublin project, the creature represents more than just the spirit of their mysteriously lost mother. (Ellen Barkin isn't the mother, but she turns up as a Traveler.) Also under the spell of John Ford westerns, the pint-sized runaways-on-horseback manage to become the object of a nationwide police hunt. These resourceful kids are dear, and when the dark and dour Byrne finally cracked a smile, it made my day.

Also reviewed in:
CHICAGO TRIBUNE, 9/17/93, Friday/p. H, Michael Wilmington
NEW YORK TIMES, 9/17/93, p. C1, Janet Maslin
VARIETY, 12/21/92, p. 60, Derek Elley
WASHINGTON POST, 9/17/93, p. D7, Rita Kempley
WASHINGTON POST, 9/17/93, Weekend/p. 53, Desson Howe

IT'S ALL TRUE: BASED ON AN UNFINISHED FILM BY ORSON WELLS

A Paramount Pictures release of a Les Films Balenciaga production in association with the French Ministry of Culture, Canal +, the French National Center for Cinematography, La Fondation GAN pour le Cinéma, and R. Films. *Running time:* 89 minutes. *MPAA Rating:* G.

IT'S ALL TRUE—Four Men on a Raft: *Director:* Orson Welles. *Director of Photography:* George Fanto.

WITH: Manuel "Jacaré" Olim Meira; Raiamundo "Tata" Correia Lima; Jerônimo André de Souza; Manuel "Preto" Perei da Silva; Francisca Moreira da Silva; José Sobrinho.

IT'S ALL TRUE—*Producer:* Régine Konckier, Richard Wilson, Bill Krohn, Myron Meisel, and Jean-Luc Ormières. *Director:* Richard Wilson, Myron Meisel, and Bill Krohn. *Screenplay:* Bill Krohn, Richard Wilson, and Myron Meisel. *Director of Photography:* Gary Graver. *Editor:* Ed Marx. *Music:* Jorge Arriagada. *Sound:* Jean-Pierre Duret.

NARRATOR: Miguel Ferrer.

THE STORY OF SAMBA (CARNAVAL)—*Screenplay:* Robert Meltzer. *Director of Photography:* Harry J. Wild. *Choreographer:* Herivelto Martins.

MY FRIEND BONITO:—*Producer:* Orson Wells. *Director:* Norman Foster. Story: Robert Flaherty. *Director of Photography:* Floyd Crosby.

CAST: Jesús Vásquez (Chico).

FILMS IN REVIEW, 1-2/94, p. 52, Andy Pawelczak

In 1941, Orson Welles, the *enfant terrible* of cinema, was recruited by Nelson Rockefeller, then working for the Office of International affairs, to make a film in Latin America as part of President Roosevelt's Good Neighbor Policy with the purpose of wooing Latin Americans away from their flirtation with European fascism. Welles rushed through the final production stages of *The Magnificent Ambersons* and *Journey Into Fear* in order to take off for Brazil as soon as possible. (Welles, and film audiences everywhere, paid for this dearly; the studio, reneging on a promise, took over the final cut of *Ambersons* and eliminated crucial footage. The film we have today, as great as great as it is, shows only signs of Welles' much darker vision of American life.) Once in Brazil, Welles threw himself into shooting but was soon overtaken by the first of the catastrophes that were to dog him for the rest of his life—the studio underwent a change in administration, and his funds were cut off. Some of the footage he shot, forgotten for fifty years in a studio vault and eventually elevated to the mythical status of a "lost masterpiece," has now been resurrected and pieced together to form the centerpiece of the new documentary *It's All True: Based On An Unfinished Film by Orson Welles.*

From the footage assembled here, we still don't know if the film envisioned by Welles would have been a masterpiece; except for one extended, half-hour segment, it's too fragmentary, and Welles' greatest films have a specific architecture that adds aesthetic grandeur and emotional resonance to the film's separate parts. The filmmakers, Richard Wilson (who worked with Welles in Brazil), Myron Meisel and Bill Krohn, have put together original Wellesian footage and interviews with Welles at different ages and with his Brazilian and American assistants. Unfortunately, the interviews don't add much to our understanding of Welles' method and intentions—they're short and superficial—or capture the sense of adventure and fun (for which Welles had a great capacity) that must have accompanied the whole project. Shooting with minimal equipment and faced with the sometimes violent hostility of the right wing Brazilian government that feared the movie would aid and abet subversive elements, Welles improvised as he slowly discovered his subject through the process of shooting the film. In one of the movie's nicer interview moments, an ancient samba singer (with the wonderful name of Grande Othelo) who worked on the original film explains, in response to a question about the non-existent script, that Welles' didn't write, he had ideas.

From the evidence in this movie, the ideas were quintessentially cinematic. Welles intended the film to have three parts: a Mexican sequence and two Brazilian sequences, one about carnival (which he eventually decided was to be a history of the samba) and the other about four fishermen's real life epic sea journey to Rio on a primitive raft in order to protest social conditions in their village. Welles didn't actually direct the Mexican sequence but functioned as the absentee spiritual auteur. The piece that we see, about the blessing of the young animals in a small village, has a powerful Eisensteinian ambiance in its expressionistically angled shots of peasants converging on a church. The Rio carnival footage is particularly fragmentary, but it has a technicolor elan that make me wish Welles had been able to do more. It also reminds us that Welles was at least partially a political animal who knew Roosevelt and wrote a syndicated liberal newspaper column. In one of the interviews, he makes it clear that he had an intuitive and sympathetic understanding of the samba's political meanings insofar as it was the music of the favelas, the makeshift slums that covered Rio's hills. Although Welles came out of a period that produced a spurious stage Africanism, his interest in black culture was genuine and long-lived; in his New York theater days, he directed an all-black production of *Macbeth* in Harlem and produced a stage version of Richard Wright's *Native Son.*

The heart of the movie is a 22 minute reconstruction of the third sequence, "Four Men On A Raft." As one of the interviewees says, this was a truly Homeric journey, and Welles captures its mythic size in both his pacing and compositions. Like the Mexican footage, this sequence has an Eisensteinian quality: somber faces that bespeak five hundred years of oppression shot from a low angle against shifting skies. The skies in this film form a virtual encyclopedia of the heavens, ranging from the smudgy to those that intimate immortality, and the shots of the sea capture a "seaness" that reminded me of Murnau's *Tabu.* But it's the human drama that really catches fire and shows that Welles could have been a great documentarian. The shots of the villagers engaged in their everyday tasks have an anthropological realism in addition to an aesthetic luminosity, and a funeral sequence is just about as good as anything in Welles' oeuvre. Welles used the actual villagers in the movie, many of whom had never even seen a film, and the parts of the four voyagers, who had become national heroes in Brazil, were played by the men who actually made the journey. When one of them drowned during a mishap in the shooting, Welles vowed he would finish the film as a homage to all of them and spent the next four years unsuccessfully trying to raise money through acting, a routine that was to become a regular part of his creative life.

Although Welles' *It's All True* fails in its interview sequences (there's one scene in which two samba performers sing together that is so stagy and false that it's almost embarrassing). I'm grateful to the filmmakers for giving us the original footage. In addition to its intrinsic aesthetic value, it underlines Welles' interest in melding realism, for which Andre Bazin so lavishly praised him, and myth, reminding us that Charles Foster Kane is one of the great, bigger-than-life mythical creations of the 20th century. And the interviews with Welles himself, however brief and teasing, are more than welcome. It's always a pleasure to see this great artist and raconteur slyly gaze into the camera as he tells us about his fabulous, disastrous, mythical life-in-film.

NEW YORK POST, 10/18/93, p. 22, Thelma Adams

In 1941, Orson Welles was Hollywood's boy genius. "Citizen Kane" premiered. He began shooting "The Magnificent Ambersons." By 1942, Welles was a Hollywood pariah. His production company, Mercury Pictures, was kicked off the RKO lot. "Ambersons" opened on a double bill with "Mexican Spitfire Sees a Ghost." What happened?

Welles went to Brazil. With the U.S. on the brink of entering WWII, there was concern about Nazi influence in Latin America. According to "It's All True," a documentary, Nelson Rockefeller (an RKO shareholder) urged Welles to fly to Rio as a cultural ambassador. Welles rushed to finish shooting "Ambersons," with the agreement that his editor would follow and they would follow cutting the picture there (a deal RKO later welshed on).

Welles decided to shoot "It's All True," a Latin American trilogy. It could begin with "My Friend Bonito," a film he had already begun in Mexico. In Brazil he would shoot "Carnaval." Welles was confident that the third story would emerge eventually.

Things went awry immediately. The lights didn't arrive from Hollywood in time to shoot "Carnaval," which forced Welles to borrow anti-aircraft lights from the Brazilian army. Meanwhile, a coup at RKO decimated his support in Hollywood. RKO ultimately pulled the plug on Welles' "It's All True."

In the documentary, Welles tells the story of his intention to film a voodoo ceremony. When he had to renege on his arrangement with a voodoo doctor due to lack of funds, the doc was hostile. Welles left the room to plead his case with RKO. When he returned, the doctor was out but there was a long silver needle with a red thread driven through his script. Voodoo or not, the project was cursed.

Meanwhile, Welles had decided on the third part of his omnibus film. He would shoot a sequence about four fishermen who had sailed on a raft along the Brazilian coast for 61 days. These populist heroes arrived in Rio to plead the case for fishermen's rights to Brazil's president.

The choice to film "Four Men on a Raft," was politically sensitive, and alienated both the Brazilian government and RKO.

Long believed lost, the footage was rediscovered in 1986. The main function of the documentary, written and directed by Richard Wilson, Myron Meisel, and Bill Krohn, is to frame and provide the context for the found footage. "Four Men on a Raft" is 22 minutes of pure Welles—and it is breathtaking.

With a $10,000 budget, black-and-white stock, a borrowed silent Mitchell camera and a Hungarian cinematographer, Welles made his film. Pared down in the extreme, directing Brazilian non-actors, Welles showed what he could do without elaborate camerawork or Joseph Cotten.

Welles drew a star-making performance from an illiterate 13-year-old girl. The black-and-white photography was pure poetry. He injected the bare bones of the fishermen's plight with the added drama of a tragic love, and captured the beauty and danger of their relationship to the sea with stark simplicity.

The lost footage is a reminder that behind the virtuoso was a true genius.

Welles claimed that he never recovered from the RKO slap. "Of course," he tells the camera, "we all live with our pasts, but I try to encourage it not to misbehave."

VILLAGE VOICE, 10/26/93, p. 53, J. Hoberman

There's a deep irony to the title *It's All True*—particularly as taken from the unfinished movie by Orson Welles and applied to the belated presentation of that long-lost footage. A trickster of genius, the first American artist to take what we call "the media" for his medium, young Welles panicked the nation with a fictional newscast and popularized the fake documentary in *Citizen Kane*; old Welles sold himself as a voice of authority and wound up his movie career with a documentary that further mystified the making of an earlier film.

The earliest of the five incomplete features Welles left to posterity, as well as the first to receive posthumous release, *It's All True* was commissioned by the State Department, underwritten by RKO, and shot mainly in Brazil. Like the Hollywood career of Carmen Miranda and Walt Disney's *Saludos Amigos*, it's an artifact of FDR's "Good Neighbor Policy," the wartime wooing of Latin America that dates from Warner Bros.'s 1939 *Juarez* and ended, more or less, with Betty Garrett singing, "Take back the rhumba-AY, the mambo-AY, the samba AY-AY-AY!" in Broadway's 1946 paean to demobilization, *Call Me Mister*.

It's All True is also an episode in the undoing of Orson Welles. Two weeks after Pearl Harbor, the still untarnished 26-year-old wunderkind was recruited by Nelson Rockefeller, then State Department coordinator for Inter-American Affairs (as well as a major RKO stockholder) to become a "special ambassador" to Brazil even as he improvised a movie there. (One is reminded of the Diego Rivera mural that Rockefeller commissioned and destroyed, as well as the state intervention that derailed the careers of pop idols Elvis Presley and Muhammad Ali.) Sacrificing his subsequently butchered *Magnificent Ambersons* on the altar of patriotism, Welles flew to Rio in time to film Carnaval—using anti-aircraft searchlights lent by the Brazilian government.

In addition to celebrating Brazil's prime tourist attraction, Welles began poking around the Rio slum districts called *favelas* and became interested in the story of the *jangadeiros*—four fishermen who had recently undertaken an impossible 60-day voyage, sailing a six-log raft from their northeastern village 1500 miles to Rio to dramatize their demand for social reform. In this way, Welles managed to lose the sympathy of the Brazilian regime as well as the support of RKO, which underwent its own palace coup and, in the summer of 1943, pulled the plug. Welles would recall that "for the new men who came to power in RKO it was all too easy to make this giant, scriptless documentary in South America look like a crazy waste of money. ... A truly merciless campaign was launched, and by the time I came back to America my image as a capricious and unstable wastrel was permanently fixed in the industry's mind."

Welles spent the next four years in a fruitless search for financing to finish the movie, and, until the footage was rediscovered moldering in a Paramount vault a month before his death, *It's All True* was even more elusive than such other "tropical" disasters as Eisenstein's unfinished *Que Viva Mexico* or Maya Deren's never-completed Haiti footage. As assembled by a team of knowledgeable film scholars and Welles buffs, including original crew member Richard Wilson, it emerges from cinema purgatory as a heady, hopelessly impure concoction of edited rushes, explanatory newsreels (real and fake), and interviews with the project's aged veterans.

The centerpiece is the 20-minute reconstruction of "Four Men on a Raft," itself the restaged story of the *jangadeiros*, which cost one of the fishermen his life. As edited by Ed Marx from Richard Wilson's notes, it might be the missing link between the aestheticized lyrical-heroic quasidocumentaries of the late 1930s (Eisensteinian *typage*, Strand-like patternings; heroic low-angles alternating with figures in formation, limned against the sky or rendered insignificant by vast landscapes) and the grittier neorealism of the late 1940s. Shooting on location with limited raw stock and a cast of nonactors (and without sound), Welles applies his mastery of the Hollywood fakebook in a manner that forecasts the delirious pragmatism of *Arkadin* and *Othello*.

Inevitably, the 1993 *It's All True* raises many more questions than it ever answers. A pulsatingly vivid carnival montage jumps crazily from day to night, from the streets to a studio set—is it Welles's or was it pulled together by editor Marx? Is the *favela* footage about Welles or by him? The movie's labor of love is somewhat compromised by a combination of Wellesian fantasy and marketplace realism. From beyond the grave, the maestro regales the camera with anecdotes that sympathetic researchers have taken pains to debunk, even as commercial considerations dictate that his footage (some of which he never saw) be edited, scored, and somehow "finished."

It would have been fascinating to see Welles's actual rushes, although what's been provided is certainly better than nothing—and it could have been a lot worse. Still, if ever a movie needed footnotes, it's this one. The picture has been repainted to suit the frame. It makes a compelling two hours but it's not all true.

Also reviewed in:
NEW REPUBLIC, 11/15/93, p. 26, Stanley Kauffmann
NEW YORK TIMES, 10/15/93, p. C8, Vincent Canby
NEW YORKER, 11/1/93, p. 122, Anthony Lane
VARIETY, 10/25/93, p. 79, Todd McCarthy
WASHINGTON POST, 10/27/93, p. C10, Rita Kempley
WASHINGTON POST, 10/29/93, Weekend/p. 46, Desson Howe

JACK THE BEAR

A Twentieth Century Fox Films release of an American Filmworks/Lucky Dog production. *Executive Producer:* Ron Yerxa.   *Producer:* Bruce Gilbert.   *Director:* Marshall Herskovitz. *Screenplay:* Steven Zaillian.   *Based upon the novel by:* Dan McCall.   *Director of Photography:* Fred Murphy.   *Editor:* Steven Rosenblum.   *Music:* James Horner.   *Music Editor:* Jim Henrickson.   *Sound:* Jeff Wexler.   *Sound Editor:* Gregory M. Gerlich.   *Casting:* Mary Goldberg.   *Production Designer:* Lilly Kilvert.   *Art Director:* John Warnke.   *Set Designer:* James Truesdale.   *Set Decorator:* Cricket Rowland.   *Set Dresser:* Joanna Gilliam.   *Special Effects:* Dick Wood.   *Costumes:* Deborah L. Scott.   *Make-up:* Zoltan Elek and Katalin Elek. *Stunt Coordinator:* Loren Janes.   *Running time:* 98 minutes.   *MPAA Rating:* PG-13.

CAST: Danny DeVito (John Leary);   Robert J. Steinmiller, Jr. (Jack Leary);   Miko Hughes (Dylan Leary);   Gary Sinise (Norman Strick);   Art LaFleur (Mr. Festinger);   Stefan Gierasch (Grandpa Glickes);   Erica Yohn (Grandma Glickes);   Andrea Marcovicci (Elizabeth Leary); Julia Luis-Dreyfus (Peggy Etinger);   Reese Witherspoon (Karen Morris);   Bert Remsen (Mr. Mitchell);   Carl Gabriel Yorke (Gordon Layton);   Lee Garlington (Mrs. Festinger);   Lorinne Vozoff (Mrs. Mitchell);   Justin Mosley Spink (Dexter Mitchell);   Jahary Bennett (Michael); Lillian Hightower Domio (Mrs. Sampson);   Troy Slaten (Edward Festinger);   Jessica Steinmiller (Katie Festinger);   Douglas Tolbert (Ray);   Christopher Lawford (Vince Buccini);   Cliff Bemis (Detective Marker);   Charles Dugan (Mr. Strick);   Marion Dugan (Mrs. Strick);   Sam Freed (Mr. Morris);   Dorothy Lyman (Mrs. Morris);   Kevin McDermott (Cop);   Rob Dunn (Construction Worker);   Christy Botkin (Nursery School Teacher);   Vonna Bowen (Nurse); Steven McCall (Studio Technician);   Donovan Leitch, Sarah Bork, and Dena Goodmanson (Grad Students);   Paul S. Wilson and Scott Thomson (Street Workers);   George E. Clayton, Jr. (Backhoe Driver);   Monica Calhoun (Sondra);   Kelly Connell (Fireman).

CHRISTIAN SCIENCE MONITOR, 4/6/93, p. 12, David Sterritt

There is such a shortage of artistic ambition in Hollywood that we should probably be grateful for any picture that tackles a difficult subject with a modicum of skill and sincerity.

"Jack the Bear," starring Danny DeVito, is such a movie. Through a dramatic story, it suggests the provocative idea that anger and violence lurk in the hearts not only of obvious villains, but also of ordinary people with ordinary lives; and it tries to be constructive by exposing these bad qualities for what they are.

The movie's strategies for accomplishing this, however, are uninspired and counterproductive. In the end, the gap between its inspirations and its achievements is too great for comfort.

Mr. DeVito plays John Leary, a single father who's doing his best to raise two children, 12-year-old Jack and 3-year-old Dylan, in a Northern California town during the early 1970s.

John's effort to be a good parent is complicated by a couple of factors. For one, he himself isn't that much of a grownup. His behavior is often immature, and even his job is embarrassing for his family, since he earns his living as a childish comedian on a local television show. In addition, he's disturbed by lingering grief over his wife's accidental death and by a drinking problem he has developed as a result.

It isn't only being a single father when you have failings of your own to reckon with; and being a child in such a household can be quite a challenge, too. Making matters worse for the Leary clan, there's a weird and scary man living in their neighborhood, and the kids are genuinely afraid of him—adding yet another pressure to their young and impressionable lives.

For a while, "Jack the Bear" appears to be a fairly conventional coming-of-age story. Jack copes with his flawed but loving dad, falls in love with a pretty schoolmate, tries to remember what life was like with mom, and suppresses his fear of the family's menacing neighbor.

But it's that neighbor who changes the movie into more of a horror story than a nostalgia picture. We discover that he's not just eccentric but psychopathic, with Nazis sympathies and a streak of criminality in his nature.

On top of this, the film doesn't make him the only purveyor of rage and violence in the children's lives. Other people, from a father down the block to John and even Jack himself, turn out to be capable of violence toward those smaller than themselves.

"Jack the Bear" clearly wants to convey a useful message by telling us that hurtful qualities may take root in ordinary, well-meaning people if they aren't alert to prevent this. Yet the filmmakers contradict their own message by making their main villain, the Nazi-like neighbor, a blatant and unmistakable weirdo who'd terrify just about anyone. It's also unfortunate that Jack's eventual victory over the villain is more physical than moral. We may cheer the bad guy's downfall, but we learn little of value from the manner of his defeat.

Other failings of "Jack the Bear" are its overwritten music, and its slick cinematography, which makes every scene look artificial and eye-catching no matter what mood it's trying to convey. The ending is especially unconvincing, swamping the story in a wave of sentimentality that's as gushy as it is contrived.

The subjects of dysfunctional family life and child abuse are certainly worthy of cinematic treatment. "Jack the Bear" marks an advance over the recent "Radio Flyer," which turned its confused story into an unwitting argument for suicide as a solution to childhood problems; and coming soon is "This Boy's Life," which treats similar material with a fair amount of sensitivity and intelligence. Still, it doesn't appear that Hollywood is ready yet to tackle this difficult topic with the credibility it deserves.

"Jack the Bear" was directed by Marshall Herskovitz, one of the creators of "thirtysomething" on television. Steven Zaillian wrote the screenplay based on Dan McCall's novel.

The supporting cast includes Gary Sinise as the sinister neighbor and Andrea Marcovicci, in flashbacks, as Jack's fondly remembered mother. Robert J. Steinmiller and Miko Hughes are fine as the title character and his little brother.

LOS ANGELES TIMES, 4/2/93, Calendar/p. 10, Peter Rainer

The face of 12-year-old Jack Leary (Robert J. Steinmiller Jr.) he's nicknamed Jack the Bear by his father, John (Danny DeVito), the host of a monster movie show on late-night television.

His mother (Andrea Marcovicci) who had already separated from John, was killed a few years back in a car accident, and Jack's memories of her, which we see in honeyed, slowed-down flashbacks, reappear to him in moments of stress. He lives with his father and his 3-year-old brother Dylan (Miko Hughes) in an Oakland neighborhood slowly going to seed—the time is 1972—and he longs for solace without quite knowing how to get it.

"Jack the Bear," directed by Marshall Herskovitz from a script by Steve Zaillian based on the 1972 novel by Dan McCall, comes out at a time when Hollywood is aswarm with rampaging tots whose motto seems to be "Clonk or Be Clonked." It focuses on the boy's pain without apology. It's almost revolutionary: a kid in the movies who actually possesses a nervous system.

Herskovitz, directing his first feature after a career in television that included co-creating "thirtysomething," makes Jack's game, beseeching face his film's centerpiece, and his instincts pay off. We keep discovering more to look at, more even, perhaps, than the young actor is able to consciously reveal.

The film is about how Jack, whose father camps it up as a monster not only to his TV audience but to the local kids, comes to recognize the real monsters of life. It's a self-conscious fable, more languorous and conventionally "sensitive" than McCall's antic, hippy-dippy, free-flowing book, with its reverbs from Twain and Salinger. The film of "Jack the Bear" (rated PG-13 for its theme) is closer to the movie version of "To Kill a Mockingbird," but with a deep-toned luster in its best moments that makes it a stranger, less categorizable film than that one. (The superb cinematography is by Fred Murphy.) It even has a Boo Radley-type character: Norman Strick (Gary Sinise), the calmly crazy neighbor who twists the plot into sinister byways.

There are all sorts of sharply observed psychological details, like the sullen, unfussy moment when Jack breaks up with his girlfriend (Reese Witherspoon), or the scenes between Jack and his grandfather (Stefan Gierasch), a bitter man who was blacklisted as a screenwriter and refuses to relinquish his imperious pride.

The film, which seems truncated in places, could stand to be even more shaggy and adventurous, more poetically stylized to approximate Jack's state of aggravated apprehension. (That would have made some of the melodrama seem less melodramatic.) Herskovitz's principled modesty doesn't often pull us into Jack's way of seeing. Except for a few sequences near the end, when Jack's terror overwhelms him, we don't really view the world through his blinkered, fevered gaze.

A bigger problem is DeVito. The actor one thinks of for John in reading McCall's book is somebody like the young Jon Voight, but you can see why DeVito was cast here. His squat, squalling presence is all-of-a-piece with the horror movies he introduces, and he's just enough of a goof to reinforce the notion that John can't take care of his kids because he's too much the kid himself.

But DeVito's John doesn't really seem to be a part of this family, even a broken-off part, you don't sense a deep link between him and Jack, and that may be because as an actor DeVito doesn't have much of an inner life. He's not doing Danny DeVito shtick in "Jack the Bear"—he makes a stab at subtlety—but for the most part we assume the bond between John and his son far more than we feel it.

The reason this flaw is not fatal is because the movie really belongs to Jack, and, ultimately, his feelings of loss for his mother. His father, just like his baby brother and the motley ragtag neighborhood kids and his grandparents and girlfriend and grade-school teacher and all the others, is part of a passing parade of distractions, they both taunt and mollify his aloneness. Herskovitz keeps the focus on what's most important: Jack the Bear's longing for succor. Even in moments of reconciliation we can feel the chill of his unprotected solitude.

NEW YORK POST, 4/2/93, p. 21, Jami Bernard

Although it rather heavily makes its point about the monsters that lurk within the human heart, "Jack the Bear" is a moving and surprisingly funny evocation of the horrors one little boy must face as he comes to terms with his childhood.

It's based on the book of the same title by Dan McCall, but it has "To Kill a Mockingbird" written all over it.

Jack Leary (Robert J. Steinmiller Jr.) and his younger brother, Dylan, are being brought up by their fun-loving, hard-drinking father, John (Danny DeVito). Dad is a sort of professional monster—in pancake makeup and an ax through the skull, he introduces horror movies on late-show TV. He is a fixture also among the neighborhood kids, who love coming by the disheveled Leary house for a scare or two.

Jack loves staying up late to watch his dad on TV, but gradually the scary movies begin to cast a pall over real life as well. There's an odd menacing neighbor (Gary Sinise, with hypnotically sinister eyes, in the Boo Radley role), a local kid whose lack of parental care is making him susceptible to all manner of vices, and dad's gradual deterioration from drink. In this movie, a child's nightmare possibility of monsters lurking under the bed is as close as Jack gets to cheery nostalgia.

Worst of all, there is the hole in Jack's heart ever since his mother died. The evocative flash-back scenes featuring Andrea Marcovicci as the remembered mom are especially haunting.

"Jack the Bear" lumbers, bear-like, under the weight of its many elements—Jack's first infatuation with a classmate who is way too hormonally advanced for him (Reese Witherspoon); the problems of a single father raising two boys; dad's drinking problems on the set of his television show; the possibly evil Boo Radley next door; an act of reprisal that makes you forget most of the movie has been a comedy up until then.

Yet it finally manages to integrate these elements into the general melange of Jack's childhood.

First-time feature director Marshall Herskovitz, who seems to have the same fondness for old-time movie schlock as Joe Dante ("Matinee," "Gremlins 2"), cheerfully ranks out a few sacred cows. The neighborhood children, far from being sweet and adorable, are mini-monsters themselves, a junior Fellini festival. And Jack's New Age-type school teacher is a horror show of a different kind.

Herskovitz manages to get some excellent performances out of the child actors, and De Vito shows a more intelligent dramatic range than his comedies usually allow him (although his funny bits are still the high points). There is something so simple yet hilarious about a moment in which the younger son pries a stale cookie off his sleeping dad's shoulder, summing up the kind of simple rapport between childish dad and somberly adult kids in the haunted house of their childhood.

Just when "Jack the Bear" is too much like "To Kill a Mockingbird" to bear, it comes into its own again, shining light in the dark places of childhood and memory.

NEWSDAY, 4/2/93, Part II/p. 58, Jack Mathews

Think about it. If Danny DeVito showed up at your door on Halloween dressed head-to-toe in a bunny outfit and mumbled "trick or treat" through a pair of plastic buck teeth, would you wonder what a middle-aged man is doing playing a kid's game, or would you give him a handful of M & Ms and tell him how cute he is?

I don't mean to be cruel. I like DeVito, and I can suspend my disbelief as much as anyone. But movies in which the roly-poly half-pint is miscast are becoming a genre. In "Other People's Money," he played love scenes with Penelope Ann Miller. In "Hoffa," he was a thug Teamster throwing his weight around. Now, in "thirtysomething" creator Marshall Herskovitz' "Jack the Bear," he's embarrassing his 12-year-old son by going trick-or-treating?

Kid, no one would notice!

DeVito's size isn't the only problem. Once he's out of that bunny outfit, he appears much too old to be playing John Leary, a young widower trying to raise two children in 1974 Oakland. In Dan McCall's novel, from which Steven Zaillian's screenplay is adapted, Leary is an adult stuck in suspended intellectual adolescence, a man caught up in the youth cult of the '60s and unwilling or unable to grow out of it.

Despite a thick toupee, the 48-year-old DeVito has been around the sun a few too many times to pass for thirtysomething.

"Jack the Bear," told from the point-of-view of Leary's son Jack (Robert J. Steinmiller Jr.), is set during the traumatic year after the accidental death of Leary's wife (played in increasingly chilling flashbacks by Andrea Marcovicci). The father, Jack and 3-year-old Dylan (Miko Hughes) have moved from New York to a rundown neighborhood in Oakland populated, in Jack's imagination, by a variety of oddballs and villains, not least the lame, expressionless loner (Gary Sinese) who lives across the street.

Leary, an alcoholic with a checkered career history, is a former TV clown now doing a ghoul shtick as Al Gory, host of a local midnight TV horror show. Although dad is a hoot to be around when he's sober, and catnip to the neighbor kids for whom he portrays various monsters, his late hours and long hangovers leave troubled, pubescent Jack as the man of the house.

"Jack the Bear" is at its best trying to untangle Jack's emotional confusion—over the loss of his mother, over the dawning romantic urges stimulated by an aggressive classmate (Reese Witherspoon), over his ambivalent feelings for his loving but immature father.

These sections, particularly in the early going, have an irresistible nostalgia about them, "Wonder Years" crossed with "To Kill a Mockingbird." As our narrator, Jack filters his new neighborhood and its characters through a child's fervid imagination, creates his own horror stories and monsters and keeps us guessing as to where the line is drawn between reality and invention.

That one of the neighbors actually turns out to be something of a monster, however, shoves the family drama aside and hurls "Jack the Bear" into mundane melodrama. A flat-footed thriller.

While it is self-destructing, the story becomes so tangled in its emotional ambitions, it's hard to know what's being resolved. The nature of Jack's mother's death? Whether the kids would be better off with their responsible but boring grandparents? Whether John can pull out of his dipsomania and become a real father?

As miscast as he is, DeVito has his moments, particularly as the campy TV host, and in one long scene where he entertains his son's girlfriend with impressions of Quasimodo. But it is hard to get past the feeling that he's only in this movie because he was hot when the producers were trying to strike a deal.

On the other hand, the convincing performances of the child actors Steinmiller and Hughes are in the realm of miraculous. A scene where Jack punishes Dylan by making him stand next to a fence with three agitated Dobermans on the other side is as terrifying and real as anything you'll ever see kids do in a movie.

NEWSWEEK, 4/5/93, p. 56, David Ansen

[*Jack the Bear* was reviewed jointly with *The Adventures of Huck Finn*; see Ansen's review of that film.]

SIGHT AND SOUND, 6/93, p. 56, Amanda Lipman

Oakland, California, 1972. After the death of his mother, 12-year-old Jack ('the Bear') Leary, haunted by memories of her, has moved to a new house with his father John and young brother Dylan. John is a horror comedy actor, round whom the local kids swarm to make him do his act. Through Jack's narration, details are revealed about the entertaining, disorderly Leary household, presided over by a heavy-drinking father in mourning for his wife. Their street is equally full of strange people, including 'Norman the psycho', who manically polishes the car in which he crashed and lost a leg. One night, the kids decide to sneak into Norman's house; he chases them off, injuring himself in the process, and persuades John to take him to hospital.

John, meeting with disapproval from his producer over his work, and from his parents-in-law over bringing up his kids, starts drinking even more. On the first day of school, unable to wake John, Jack has to take Dylan to school himself. At his own school, he falls for a girl called Karen whom he invites round to dinner where she is charmed by the antics of his father.

At Halloween, Norman turns up, asking for a donation for a racist political candidate. That night, blind drunk on his show, John acts out a parody of Norman's fascistic leanings, and as a result, is put on enforced sick leave. The next morning, Norman's dog is found poisoned on the Learys' front lawn. Norman is convinced that John has killed his dog and kidnaps Dylan. The child is found, abandoned and unable to speak. Jack's grandparents take both children away to Los Angeles but Jack cannot stand the censorious atmosphere and goes back home. Norman is waiting for him but, after a chase, ends up falling out of a tree. Dylan comes home too. One evening, Jack is playing a piano piece, called 'Jack the Bear', taught to him by his mother. He and his father talk about the past and the future, and suddenly Dylan starts to talk again. When the local children next come round asking to see monsters, John tells them that there is no such thing.

Following in the footsteps of Edward Zwick, his other half in the *thirtysomething* creative team, Marshall Herskovitz has taken to the big screen. And anyone expecting the winsome, liberal coziness of the Philadelphia-set soap will not be disappointed. In many ways, though, this is more like the TV series *The Wonder Years* meeting *To Kill a Mockingbird*. If the period feel, soundtrack, comic details—such as an earnestly ridiculous hippy teacher—and pubescent romance stuff belong to the former, the idea springs from the latter.

Except that this film's Boo Radley really is a monster. While *To Kill a Mockingbird* proves that fear is the basis of prejudice, this superficially more politically conscious film ironically seems to end up saying the opposite. Gary Sinise's blank-faced loner Norman is a fantasy hybrid of psycho Norman Bates, bogey man Michael Myers, child-snatcher and crazed Nazi. As such, were he the product of Jack's fevered imagination, he would make considerably more sense to the film than he does. Instead, by representing a real 'evil', he is so incredible as to undermine any of the issues that his behaviour raises.

This may be partly because the viewpoint in the film—Jack's—is there in name only. His narration does no more than fill in details. And although he is supposed to be working through his grief over his mother, anger at his father and alienation in a new neighbourhood, there's remarkably little subjectivity here; things actually are as he perceives them. Despite the constant references to his fear (of monsters), visualised through him watching his father playing TV monsters in between late-night horror shows, the quasi-Freudian links the film seems to ask us to make between real and imaginary monsters are never satisfactorily played out.

Jack's luridly-coloured flashback memories of his mother are similarly frustrating; the bitty nature of the film makes it hard to fit them in to Jack's experiences and relationships. In fact, much of *Jack the Bear* is purposelessly episodic: the Learys' neighbours, whose desperate psyches are just glimpsed, may provide a refreshing angle on the usual happy images of suburban childhood but their effect is of throwaway background detail.

Danny DeVito puts on his best serious performance as the child-like father, as unable as his son to come to terms with the death of his wife. Too much of this, though, consists of sad, sidelong looks backed up by fiddly 'emotional' music and imperceptible sighs. Playing up his decent, funny side leaves little room to explore the negative emotions that Jack keeps talking about, but which only rise to the surface—briefly and efficiently—at the end of the film.

Although Robert Steinmiller Jr as Jack does his best to hold all the threads together, the film rambles between glycerine sentimentality (where it has anything to do with Jack's little brother Dylan), dealing partly with such issues as Norman's racism and sloughing through emotions in a annoyingly knowing, post-therapy manner. Its effect is that of a TV series that has been telescoped and packed, with each of its rather glib resolutions, into an hour and a half. Despite a surfeit of material, nothing is thorny enough to sustain and the result is a long haul.

TIME, 3/29/93, p. 63, Richard Schickel

We are supposed to take John Leary (Danny DeVito) warmly to heart. He has a childlike nature, at its best whimsical and gallant, at its worst careless and a little dim about the relationship between cause and effect. A recent widower, he is doing his best to single-parent two young boys (Robert J. Steinmiller Jr. and Miko Hughes) and to make good in his cute new job (as the comically ghoulish host of midnight horror movies) in a new town (Oakland, California, circa 1972).

Had the people who made this movie been content to develop that situation lightly, they might have made an inconsequential domestic comedy. But they are abustle with larger, if entirely inchoate, ambitions. They have invested John with a real problem—alcoholism—and they have plunked the Learys down on a block that is a sort of dumping around for the damned of the lower middle class. Among their new neighbors are a neo-Nazi, a drug-addict mom who dies of an overdose and someone who keeps a pack of killer Dobermans in the yard next door. For a family teetering on the brink of dysfunction, this environment seems bound to push them over the edge. Sure enough, Dylan, the younger son, is kidnapped and rendered speechless by the trauma.

This crisis is purely arbitrary. So is its eventual resolution. It comes out of nowhere and goes nowhere interesting. But that's the way of this film. The possibly admirable intention is to avoid the false good cheer of the typical family drama. But it has been replaced by the equally false gloominess that often passes for seriousness in Hollywood. *Jack the Bear* plays as if Maxim Gorky had for some reason been asked to try his hand at a sitcom.

The direction by Marshall Herskovitz, one of the creators of television's *thirtysomething*, is at least true to the spirit of the script—at once ponderous and digressive—but without a clear, clarifying attitude toward it. DeVito's performance is characteristically strenuous, but he is lost—who wouldn't be?—among the story's conflicting moods and emotional claims. They should have called it *Jack the Unbearable*.

VILLAGE VOICE, 4/13/93, p. 56, J. Hoberman

[*Jack the Bear* was reviewed jointly with *This Boy's Life*; see Hoberman's review of that film.]

Also reviewed in:
CHICAGO TRIBUNE, 4/2/93, Friday/p. H, Johanna Steinmetz
NEW YORK TIMES, 4/2/93, p. C12, Janet Maslin
NEW YORKER, 4/5/93, p. 102, Terrence Rafferty
VARIETY, 2/22/93, p. 66, David Stratton
WASHINGTON POST, 4/2/93, p. D6, Rita Kempley
WASHINGTON POST, 4/2/93, Weekend/p. 45, Desson Howe

JACQUOT

An Sony Pictures Classics release of a Cine-Tamaris production with the participation of Canal Plus, La Sept, La Sofiarp, and CNC. *Producer:* Agnès Varda and Perrine Baudoin. *Director:* Agnès Varda. *Screenplay (French with English subtitles):* Agnès Varda. *Story:* Jacques Demy. *Director of Photography:* Patrick Blossier and Georges Strouvé. *Editor:* Marie-Jo Audiard. *Music:* Joanna Bruzdowicz.   *Sound:* Jean-Pierre Duret, Nicolas Naegelen, and Jean-Pierre Laforce.   *Sound Editor:* Aurique Delannoy.   *Casting:* David Pinchon and Sophie van Baren. *Production Designer:* Robert Nardone and Oliver Radot.   *Costumes:* Françoise Disle.   *Running time:* 118 minutes. *MPAA Rating:* Not Rated.

CAST: Philippe Maron (Jacquot 1);   Edouard Joubeaud (Jacquot 2);   Laurent Monnier (Jacquot);   Brigitte de Villepoix (Marilou, Jacquot's Mother);   Daniel Dublet (Raymond, Jacquot's Father);   Jacques Demy (Himself);   Clement Delaroche (Yvon 1);   Rody Averty (Yvon 2);   Hélène Pors (Reine 1);   Marie-Sidonie Benoist (Reine 2);   Julien Mitard (René 1); Jeremie Bader (René 2);   Jeremie Bernard (Yannick 1);   Fanny Lebreton (Geneviève, the Young Refugee);   Edwige Dalaunay (Bella);   Jacques Bouret (Mr. Bonbons);   Jean-Françoise Lapipe (Uncle Marcel);   Chantal Bezias (Aunt Nique);   Jean-Charles Hernot (Guy, Workman); Marie-Anne Emeriau (Grandmother);   Véronique Rodriquez (Singer);   Henri Janin (Clogman); Marie-Anne Hery (Clogman's Wife);   Christine Renaudin (Aunt from Rio);   Yves Beauvilin (Design Teacher);   Francis Viau (Night Visitor);   Yvette Longis (Luce, Butcher);   François Vogels (Monsieur Debuisson);   Françoise Lenouveau (Madame Bredin, Upholsterer);   Philippe Lenouveau (Monsieur Bredin, Upholsterer).

This film was shown at the 1991 New York Film Festival under the title *Jacquot de Nantes*. For the earlier reviews, see *Film Review Annual, 1992*.

LOS ANGELES TIMES, 9/1/93, Calendar/p. 4, Kevin Thomas

Near the beginning of "Jacquot", Agnès Varda's enchanting tribute to her late husband, director Jacques Demy, Varda tells us that Demy's "childhood was his treasure and the source of inspiration for his films." She aptly describes her film as "an evocation"—a biography of Demy's early years in Nantes in Western France, on the Loire River. It is seamlessly punctuated with clips from his films and with loving glimpses of the gaunt-looking but still gallant Demy, who occasionally comments on his own life and work.

The heart of the matter is how as a boy Demy, who was born in 1931 and died of leukemia in 1990, evolved into a filmmaker by the time he had reached his teens, Demy seems to have had a truly happy childhood, living with his parents and a younger brother in a tiny apartment over his father's garage—the actual garage seen in the film.

It is altogether fitting that the man whose most famous film, "The Umbrellas of Cherbourg" (1964), unfolds entirely in song, had parents who occasionally would start singing as they worked—the father (Daniel Dublet) as an auto mechanic, the mother (Brigitte de Villepoix) as a hairdresser.

When little Jacquot saw a puppet show, he was inspired to make his own puppets and put on his own show. When he was given a primitive hand-cranked projector and a couple of Chaplin shorts, he discovered the need to try his hand at making his own movies and to present them in a kitchen cabinet shelf whimsically transformed into a miniature movie screen, complete with proscenium and red drapes. Dogged in his persistence and endless in his resourcefulness in creating his own tools and teaching himself every aspect of elementary filmmaking, Demy transformed a small attic, also used by his father to store tires, into a miniature studio for his experiments in animation; in a very real sense he was learning to master the cinema by reinventing it.

Meanwhile, he thrilled to such movies as Marcel Carne's "The Devil's Envoys" (1942) and "Children of Paradise" (1945) and Robert Bresson's "Les Dames du Bois de Boulogne" (1946);

not even World War II, which at times came perilously close to the Demys, undermined his perseverance.

The meticulous depiction of Demy's quiet, dedicated pursuit of his passion become's the film's sturdy spine, allowing Varda to make her digressions enrich her husband's story rather than to distract from it. Her use of the adult Demy is disciplined and succinct and her use of clips swift and inspired.

We discover that "a country cousin turned into an upscale tart by a Brazilian millionaire" provided the inspiration years later for Jeanne Moreau's peroxided compulsive gambler in Demy's "Bay of Angels" (1962) as Varda cuts from the cousin to Moreau. Of special importance is Nantes' elegant 19th-Century arcade, the Passage Pomeraye, where in a second-hand shop Jacquot traded five children's books and his Erector set for his first camera (9.5 mm); it is seen not only in Varda's film but in clips from Demy's "Lola" (1960) and "Umbrellas of Cherbourg."

"Jacquot" itself is essentially in black and white, but whenever the budding artist's imagination starts soaring it switches to color.

United in their passion for filmmaking, Demy and Varda were otherwise as much a study in contrasts as their films. The earthy, intellectual Varda is a short, ample woman, as direct and brisk as her films, Demy was a slim, handsome man, perhaps as romantic in his nature as in his elegant, swirling pictures. They complemented one another in life as they do in "Jacquot," the only time they ever worked together in the more than 30 years they shared.

French filmmakers pay more attention to children than most do, and Varda, always wonderful with youngsters, directs the three boys—Philippe Maron, Edouard Joubeaud, Laurent Monnier, all of whom resemble the adult Demy—to play Jacquot to perfection.

"Jacquot" (rated PG for mild sensuality and language) is a heartfelt homage to the memory of Demy and his work, but it is emphatically an Agnès Varda film, neither husband nor wife would have wanted it any other way.

NEW YORK POST, 6/25/93, p. 35, Jerry Tallmer

A man—not an old man, but a man nearing 60 and the end of his life, a gray grizzled handsome Frenchman—lies on a beach, in blue jeans, sifting sand. He was a filmmaker; now he is a painter; we see his painting of two undressed adults who love one another. We see him at his desk, pushing aside his cat to start writing, remembering.

His name is Jacques Demy, and what he remembers—and what his wife for 30 years, whose name Is Agnes Varda, will make into *this* movie—is the imperishable secret golden time, the boyhood in and around Nantes that, despite war and the German occupation, was seedbed for all the creative flowering of the Jacques Demy who was to grow up to give us works like "Lola" and "The Umbrellas of Cherbourg" and "Les Demoiselles de Rochefort."

The Varda movie about the boy who became the man she loved is called "Jacquot," and it is exquisite. It intercuts memory, which is to say reconstructed memory, with snatches from some of Demy's films of passages that somehow sprang out of that memory—Anouk Aimee as a chanteuse, Catherine Deneuve making an omelet, Jeanne Moreau at the roulette table, the clogmaker making his clogs, Jean Marais as the devil ...

Ingmar Bergman had his magic lantern. Demy had his marionette theater, built from a big cardboard carton, and then his first rudimentary camera, barely more than a toy. For Jacquot's first few feet of already used film he trades away his precious viewpiece of the S.S. Normandie under steam, then soaks and scrubs the celluloid clean.

For a more advanced camera a bit later, he trades his even more precious Erector-set model of the bridge at Mauves, the town on the Rhone where mama and papa had sent Jacquot and kid brother Rene to stay with a *sabotier*—a clogmaker—and his family when the air raids hit Nantes.

It was there, by that bridge over the Rhone that a parachutist had dropped out of the sky from a dogfight right outside the classroom one fine day during grammar lesson—an incident that 14-year-old Jacquot will transpose into a stop-motion animated short, "Raid sur le Pont de Mauves," his first triumph after fuzzy or totally unexposed earlier disasters.

If that were all, that would be enough. But it is far from all. This is a movie suffused with tenderness, beauty, idiosyncracy, joy, occasional pain—and of course the terminal pain that is its given. Mama (Brigitte de Villepoix) singing in her kitchen, papa (Daniel Dublet) in his garage singing as he bangs away on a recalcitrant engine, the hired-hand mechanic singing away on "La

Cucaracha" from the grease pit—never was there such a singing family, but it is not slush. It is gaiety, courage.

Three actors play Jacquot, the best and sweetest of them being the youngest, Philippe Maron, one of those adorable little French boys. Numbers 2 and 3 grow taller, gawkier, coarser, even if I liked it when one of these gawkier Jacquots is called upon—"Hey, tell us what to see; he always knows"—by his older classmates. (Go see Danielle Darrieux, he tells them.) In case you haven't figured it out, by now, I loved this movie—everything except the little pointing hand to tell you when it's switching from new footage to old. For slow readers, as Norman Mailer used to say.

NEWSDAY, 6/25/93, Part II/p. 54, Joseph Gelmis

Agnes Varda's "Jacquot" is a modest little biography, a tribute to her late husband, Jacques Demy, warm and generous to a fault. Its generosity, alas, stunts its possibilities.

"Jacquot" is about Demy's childhood in late 1930s and early to mid-'40s France. Varda shot the film in the garage Demy's father owned and the family's adjoining apartment in Nantes. Three different youths play Demy from ages 8 to 18; Philippe Maron, Edouard Joubeaud and Laurent Monnier.

Much of the action takes place during the German Occupation. So there are interesting sidelights, such as Demy and his pals' boycotting the German-made color adventure "Baron Munchausen," which they dearly want to see; and settling instead for the black and white French-made "Visitors of the Night."

Despite its wartime setting, "Jacquot" is a chronicle of trite adventures and experiences. The basic conflict in the film is Demy's resistance to following in his father's footsteps. Forced to go to mechanic's school, he obsessively struggles to create amateur films with home movie cameras and puppets and stop-action animation in his attic.

"Jacquot" stops frequently to show a sequence from one of Demy's films—for the purpose of documenting its source or inspiration, from a scene or a character or an event in Demy's childhood. Varda cuts, for instance, from young Demy watching a puppet-theater production of "Donkey Skin" to a snippet of Catherine Deneuve's fairy godmother coaxing her to wear a donkey skin in Demy's 1970 fantasy of the same name.

This technique might be more meaningful to American audiences if Demy had had a more interesting childhood or if he had been a master whose movies deserved closer scrutiny or even if the creative transformations of his life into art were ingenious. On all these counts, "Jacquot," comes up short. Varda's doting, uncritical memoir is more worthy of respect as an act of love than as entertainment or a portrait of an artist as a young man.

VILLAGE VOICE, 6/29/93, p. 53, Georgia Brown

Jacques Demy (1931-90) was not an extraordinary talent, just a special one whose lyric sensibility left a small but distinct mark on the cinema of the New Wave. This achievement was almost entirely confined to four charming features of the '60s: The first two, *Lola* and *Bay of Angels*, were his best; then came those idiosyncratic pastel musicals, *The Umbrellas of Cherbourg* (everyone sings) and *The Young Girls of Rochefort* (they dance). After '68, his career went downhill.

Whereas other New Wave directors were influenced by gangster pictures and psychological thrillers (Hawks and Hitchcock), Demy's taste ran to Hollywood musicals, especially ones with sailors and Gene Kelly. The son of an auto mechanic and a hairdresser (the marriage of beauty and technology?), he grew up in Nantes, where there must have been sailors since it is situated at the mouth of the Loire just before it reaches the Atlantic. Here, as in the rest of France, the war came and went but the cinema kept going. The Nazis lined up with the rest of the town.

In *Jacquot (Jacquot de Nantes)* it was called originally), the story of Demy's childhood, his coming into a vocation, is told by his fellow filmmaker and wife of almost 30 years, Agnès Varda. Better known than Demy today, Varda started as a photographer and then began making documentaries—perhaps still her best work. She also wrote and directed successful fiction films—like *Cleo From 5 to 7; One Sings, the Other Doesn't; Vagabonde*—and films that combine the two modes, like *Jacquot*. All her movies tend to intersect with her life and the best are at least semi-autobiographical—likethe 1958 *L'Opéra Mouffe*, a poetic evocation of the Rue Mouffetard as seen through the eyes of a pregnant woman (which Varda was at the time). As Richard Roud wrote, "Documentary is transformed into a visual commentary on love and death, birth and old age."

In *Jacquot*, three young actors re-create stages of Demy's childhood, but Varda also interweaves shots of Demy, her own commentary, and clips from his films. Impressively, she refuses to let *Jacquot* turn slick, thereby keeping true to the subject, the consuming passion of amateurs. The quality she honors is naïveté, the quality Demy at his best (and worst) was known for.

As an artist Demy remained faithful to his childhood, drawing subject matter and sustenance from memory and the media of the era-fairy tales, puppet shows, theater, circuses, and finally the movies. He said his was a happy childhood and who are we to wonder about a dark side? The story Varda tells is one of enchantment. At a puppet show, the boy becomes entranced and doesn't want to leave. At home he keeps the experience alive, cutting out his own paper puppets and making a stage. And when, finally—with Disney's *Snow White*—the movies take over, he's not only inspired to make his own movie but the theater as well—a miniature stage and screen (significantly?) in his mother's cupboard.

During the war he trades a kid some ball bearings from his father's garage for discarded scraps of film stock. A treasure! Someone gives him a projector and a short to show on it. When he gets tired of the one film, he scrapes off the emulsion and paints on the celluloid. When he finally trades for a secondhand 9.5mm camera, he organizes the neighborhood to dramatize the story of a kidnapping. Like Shakespeare, he has boys play the girls. Eventually his father grows impatient and insists on sending him to technical school. Still, he's consumed with one goal. The film ends when he finally gets his wish—to go to Paris and train in filmmaking.

Jacquot is an ambitious elegy made while the subject was still alive, but dying. (Nothing in the movie indicates what he died from, but obituaries said leukemia.) Varda films Demy sitting on the shore, sand sifting through his fingers. She focuses close in on spots on his skin, the terrain of a square inch of flesh, as if she wants to preserve the body, to hold on to him. He looks awkward, perhaps uncomfortable being a subject—his melancholy expression a contrast to the movie's focused, energetic boy and to the cheerfulness of his famous films.

Also reviewed in:
CHICAGO TRIBUNE, 9/3/93, Friday/p. J, John Petrakis
NEW REPUBLIC, 7/19 & 26/93, p. 28, Stanley Kauffmann
NEW YORK TIMES, 6/25/93, p. C21, Vincent Canby
WASHINGTON POST, 8/6/93, p. D6, Hal Hinson
WASHINGTON POST, 8/8/93, Weekend/p. 34, Desson Howe

JAMÓN JAMÓN

An Academy Entertainment release of a Lolafilms production. *Producer:* Andres Vicente Gomez. *Director:* Bigas Luna. *Screenplay (Spanish with English subtitles):* Cuca Canals and Bigas Luna. *Director of Photography:* J.L. Alcaine. *Editor:* Pablo Del Amo. *Music:* Nicola Piovanni. *Sound:* Miguel Rejas. *Sound Editor:* Francisco Peramos. *Casting:* Consol Tura. *Art Director:* Chu Uroz and Noemi Campano. *Set Designer:* Pep Olive. *Set Decorator:* Pedro Gaspar. *Special Effects:* Reyes Abades. *Costumes:* Neus Olivella. *Make-up:* B. Villanueva. *Running time:* 90 minutes. *MPAA Rating:* Not Rated.

CAST: Penélope Cruz (Silvia); Anna Galiena (Carmen); Javier Bardem (Raúl); Stefania Sandrelli (Conchita); Juan Diego (Manuel); Jordi Molla (José Luis); Tomas Penco (Raul's Friend); Armando Del Rio (José Luis' Friend); Diana Sassen (Silvia's Friend); Chema Mazo (Silvia's Father); Isabel De Castro Oros (Silvia's Sister); Marianne Hermitte and Maria Renio (Girls in Puticlub); Nadia Godoy (Singer in Puticlub); Susana Koska and Miguel Garcia (Friends at Disco); Roberto Bermejo (Bullfighter).

FILM QUARTERLY, Fall 1993, p. 30, Marsha Kinder

Bigas Luna's *Jamón Jamón* (1992) opens with a stunning shot of a desolate Spanish plain seen through the silhouette of one of those gigantic black bull billboards (advertising Osborn brandy) that have long punctuated the Iberian landscape. Without a word being uttered (or printed), this sign brings to mind for most Spaniards not only the name of the product but also its well-known slogan, "Osborn es cosa de hombres" ("Osborn is a man's thing"). The shot is dominated by the bull's giant cojones looming over the foreground, slightly detached from the rest of the beast and making a strange creaking sound. This composition immediately tells us not only that the film will be blatantly phallocentric but also that it will go for big emotions which verge on parodic excess, perceptions that are strengthened when this traditional sign of Spanish machismo is rivalled by an equally giant post-Franco billboard with a crotch shot of sexy Samson-brand briefs.

Yet we soon learn that it is female desire that drives this fast-paced melodrama, for the hyperplotted narrative follows three beautiful sexual women over the top. First, there is young Silvia (Penelope Cruz), who works in the Samson factory cutting out patterns of the men's underwear; she has been impregnated by her boyfriend José Luis (Jordi Molla), the son of the factory owners who are the wealthiest family in town. Second, there is Silvia's loving, hardworking mother, Carmen (Anna Galiena), who, after having been abandoned by her drunken, abusive husband, became the town whore to support her three daughters; her lovers include both her prospective son-in-law José Luis and his businessman father, Manuel. And finally there is Silvia's arch antagonist, Conchita (Stefania Sandrelli), José Luis's seductive, devouring mother, who not only opposes the class-crossed match but even hires a handsome young hunk to lure Silvia away from her son. Conchita literally chooses the cojones of Raúl González (Javier Bardem), who is *not* a relative of Spain's ruling Felipe but a 22-year-old would-be bullfighter who delivers salamis and hams for Hernán Cortés's Los Conquistadores Company. She picks this over-determined Spaniard out of a line-up of desirable young studs who are auditioning for her company's jockey-shorts billboard, but she loses control of the "plot" when she fails to resist her own hired *jamón*. In this consumerist world of overblown, stereotyped images, it is hardly surprising that all three women have similar tastes. For that matter, so do the men. What is more surprising—is that this film's sexy images; like the billboards, are clearly addressed to the erotic tastes of both genders.

As if acknowledging the current challenges to concepts of the nation, *Jamón Jamón* blatantly parodies several stereotypes of Spanishness, particularly those associated with sexuality. Mocking the sacred cult of masculinity that surrounds the bullfight, one hysterical scene shows José Luis literally attacking the fetishized *cojones* of the gigantic Osborn bull, which come crashing down from the sky. Ever the adaptive *bricoleur*, Silvia scoops them up and uses them as a shield against the drenching rain. In several scenes, the emotionally stunted men eagerly gnaw on the women's breasts (*tetas*), as if to recapture the pleasures of maternal plenitude and, as one of them puts it, to indulge their hispanic taste for Spanish omelettes (*tortilla española con jamón*). The film plays with the sexual implications of the pride Spaniards take in their gastronomic passion for garlic, which is used like an aphrodisiac, and for *jamón*, which comes in many varieties from the diverse regions of the nation (in fact, one of Spain's most popular retail chains of ham shops is called Museo de Jamón).

In addition to *cojones, tetas*, and these national gastronomic favorites, the film also plays with the fetishistic power of the shoe, which has been given a distinctive Spanish inflection worldwide by Buñuel's movies. Despite her emotional sincerity, Silvia longs to have a big closet totally devoted to footwear, a fetishistic fantasy of phallic empowerment that her rich archenemy Conchita has already fulfilled. This implies that Conchita's suspicions are not entirely wrong, for one of Silvia's motives for marrying José Luis is apparently to be in the expensive shoes of his phallic mother. This shoe fantasy derives as much from Hollywood consumerist melodramas like *Written on the Wind* and *Vertigo* (where Technicolor luxury is a turn-on) as from Buñuel's perverse parodies of this genre like *El* and *That Obscure Object of Desire* (where the ideological implications of these erotic obsessions are deconstructed).

In *Jamón Jamón*, this exaggeration of the shoe fetish is part of the broader parody of the eroticizing power of consumerism—a theme that was also central to Bigas Luna's earlier film, *Bilbao*. In the first comical sex scene between Conchita and Raúl, where she successfully gets a rise out of his limp penis with the promise of a new Yamaha 600 motorcycle, the film even borrows a specific fetishistic shot from *Bilbao*: a downward-angle shot of the rutting couple with her black-and-white high-heeled pumps provocatively jabbing into the foreground.

As in previous films by Bigas Luna, the process of fetishization is stylistically dependent on a heavy use of huge, fragmenting close-ups. Yet these extremely close shots also cultivate the kind of ironic distance that is usually associated with long shots, a strategy of disruptive perspective that Ortega y Gasset (in the context of modernist literature) has called "infra realism."

Reality can be overcome, not only by soaring to the heights of poetic exaltation but also by paying exaggerated attention to the minutest detail. The best examples of this—of attending, lens in hand, to the microscopic aspects of life—are to be found in Proust, Ramón Gómez de la Serna, and Joyce.[1]

An ironic interplay between extreme close-ups and long shots is characteristic of the cinematic adaptation of *esperpento*, that distinctively Spanish form of absurdist humor which is associated with the modernist plays and novels of Ramón de Valle-Inclán and which has strongly influenced the visual style of Buñuel, Almodóvar, and Bigas Luna.

In earlier Bigas Luna films like *Bilboa, Lola,* and *Las edades de Lulú*, extreme close-ups evoke the erotic obsessiveness of the perverse protagonists, but here in an ensemble piece like *Jamón Jamón* (whose style and structure otherwise seem fairly conventional) these disruptive close-ups characterize the perverse perspective of the whole narrative and its consumerist context. Moreover, the close-ups and long shots are frequently linked by the assertive camera moves of José Luis Alcaine (who was also the cinematographer on Almodóvar's 1987 breakthrough film, *Women on the Verge of a Nervous Breakdown*)—moves that are so strikingly purposeful that they seem to be ardently pursuing the camera's objects of desire.

From the very opening of the film, this visual dynamic is associated with consumerism, for we go right from the close-up of the dangling *cojones* in the Osborn sign to graceful sweeping pans across the desolate landscape, to a close-up of the parched earth, and then to even closer shots of Raúl's buttocks and crotch. In the factory sequence that immediately follows, extreme close-ups of female fingers doing piecework on the textured fabric of the briefs precede the first facial close-up of Silvia, who is introduced as one of the workers. Within the same sequence; large close-ups also pick out the crotches and faces of the young men auditioning for the Samson billboard. As if to make certain that we notice these visual dynamics, we see the auditions being videotaped, with the cameraman repeatedly kneeling for the crotch shot and then standing up for the facial close-up in one fluid movement that sweeps across the male torso, and then we also see a facial close-up of Conchita watching the live footage of these fetishized close-ups on a video monitor with rapt attention. As she tells her husband, these ads are primarily addressed to women because they buy the briefs. Not only do these two opening sequences literally refer to advertising discourse but the strong graphics and rapid cutting of their visual style also evoke the kind of audacious television commercials for which Spain became known in the 1980s, when the annual revenue for television spots reached close to two billion dollars. (In his 1990 "Global Report on Spain," *Variety*'s Madrid correspondent Peter Besas observed that between 1980 and 1989, advertising sales for Spanish television increased sevenfold, a faster rate of growth than any other nation during that same period.[2])

Though *Jamón Jamón* is Bigas Luna's eighth feature and winner of the Silver Lion Award at the Venice Film Festival, the film is being promoted on the coattails of Almodóvar's international success. It is praised in the press kit for proving "there is innovative film-making outside the Almodóvar stable." José Juan Bigas Luna is a Catalan film-maker from Barcelona who made his first feature *Tatuaje (Tattoo)* in 1976 at the age of 30 and his controversial masterwork, *Bilbao,* in 1978, two years before Almodóvar emerged on the Spanish film scene with *Pepi, Luci, Bom y otras chicas del montón.* Though notorious for the outrageous excesses of his films (the droll bestiality of *Caniche,* 1978; the masochistic eroticism of his thriller, *Lola,* 1985; the witty, reflexive violence of his multinational parodic horror film, *Angústia [Anguish],* 1987; and the pornographic explicitness of *Las edades de Lulú [The Ages of Lulu],* 1990), Bigas Luna is seriously regarded by several noted Spanish critics (including Román Gubern) as one of Spain's most original film-makers. What is most remarkable about his films is that the excessiveness of their outrageous content is balanced by the brilliance of their aesthetic rigor and conceptual boldness—a combination that leads to a disturbing ambiguity of tone.

For example, *Bilbao* depicts the erotic obsessions of an infantilized man in Barcelona who fantasizes about escaping his repressive family by kidnapping a prostitute named Bilbao and making her float like Jesus—a vision that is at least partially inspired by Ribera's paintings of martyred saints. Convinced that she is the "best object," he becomes inflamed with consumerist desire. Though he merely wants to possess her, he nevertheless "accidentally" kills her. This claustrophobic "story of love" is totally dominated by his obsessive point of view, which is expressed through dehumanizing extreme close-ups (that evoke both the detail from the fine art of painting and the insert shot from pornography) and through his confiding voiceovers (that are delivered in hushed tones with no affect). Though this film caused a scandal at Cannes, it is regarded by Spaniards as one of the most brilliant works of the post-Franco era.[3]

Yet Bigas Luna is still not well known abroad, even though his underrated *Reborn*, 1981 (a cross between Huston's *Wise Blood* and Rossellini's *Miracle*, with touches of Godard's *Hail Mary*), was made in the U.S.A. (with Dennis Hopper in a leading role). In this crosscultural sacrilegious melodrama, Hopper plays a phony television evangelist from Houston who is joined on his "Miracle Tour" across America by an Italian vestal virgin with authentic stigmata (Antonella Murgia) who turns into a postmodern Madonna; she was bought from the Vatican by an Italian mobster (Francisco Rabal) who (echoing Coke commercials) claims to know "the real thing." Bigas Luna's crosscultural casting and humor also failed to draw large North American audiences to *Angústia*, although the film was a big commercial success in Spain. It stars Michael Lerner as a Norman Bates-type killer oculist who is manipulated into murder by his demonic mother (played by Zelda Rubenstein, fresh from her success in the Spielberg blockbuster, *Poltergeist*). Just when the gore gets unbearably grisly, we learn that their story is an inset East European horror film called *Mommy*, which is now being screened in a movie theater on Hollywood Boulevard, where it inspires another sexually repressed serial killer to go on a murder spree that is finally stopped by an L.A. SWAT team. This reflexive premise enables Bigas Luna to compare how violence is represented in different cultures and genres. The director may finally reach a global audience with *Jamón Jamón*, which should appeal to fans not only of Almodóvar but also of Sirk and Lynch.

Jamón Jamón plays on a wide range of intertextuality. Like Saura's debut feature, *Los golfos (Hooligans*, 1959), its opening evokes the first scene in Buñuel's *Los olvidados* (1950), showing young low-life buddies practicing bullfighting passes (without a bull) on the outskirts of town, but here Bigas Luna's long shots are punctuated with the kind of blatantly erotic crotch shots that can also be found in Almodóvar's *Matador* (1986). Not only does Raúl look like a handsome version of Buñuel's villainous Jaibo, but he provokes an equally surrealistic nightmare of castration and death in Silvia and robs his young rival (José Luis) of his mother, an erotic encounter that is also associated with meat (*jamón* rather than beef).

In its violent climax, *Jamón Jamón* uses a pair of ham bones to parodically reproduce Goya's famous painting, "Duel with Cudgels." In the process it also evokes Saura's serious adaptation of this image in *Llanto por un bandido (Lament for a Bandit*, 1963), with its overly dramatic music and its stylized movements between distancing long shots and brutal closeups—an alternation that makes it difficult for us to miss the studied allusion. Yet Bigas Luna's bathetic choice of weapon also brings to mind Almodóvar's murderous ham bone in *¿Qué he hecho yo para merecer esto? (What Have I Done to Deserve This?*, 1984).

Jamón Jamón also has many allusions to Bigas Luna's own earlier works: the promise to the poodle that he won't be eaten evokes carnivorous scenes from *Caniche*; the *jamón* warehouse (where Raúl works and lives) brings to mind both the warehouse where Bilbao is murdered and the sausage factory where her corpse is turned into ground meat; and the rivalrous incestuous couplings between fathers and daughters and mothers and sons are reminiscent of similar yet less explicit rivalries in *Lola*.

The film's ubiquitous incest is pushed to the point of parodic humor by its excess (not one, but *two* rival incestuous mothers, "the mother whore" and "the whore mother," as they are labelled respectively in the final credits!). Yet as in Almodóvar's comic melodramas, these sex scenes still retain their erotic power, only here the humor is more corrosive and less celebratory of pleasure, for Bigas Luna's films seriously question whether the effects of Spain's historic shift to democracy and postmodern consumerism are really as liberating as advertised. They seem to imply that just as in the 1960s, when the Franco regime promoted images of a modernized Spain abroad to woo Western tourists and investors for its economic miracle at home while still subjecting Spaniards to fascist repression, the post-Franco images of a super-liberated Spain now being promoted in the 1980s and 1990s are similarly bogus and exploitive. For the new commercial stereotypes of transgsessive sexuality have merely replaced those earlier Spanish clichés of gypsies, flamenco dancers, and matadors—a substitution that has been most successfully promoted in the world market by Almodóvar's outrageous comedies.

In *Jamón Jamón*, this substitution of images is overseen by the businessman, Manuel—played by Juan Diego, the Communist actor who was the first to represent Franco on screen in a fictional film (Jaime Camino's *Dragón rapide* [1986], a popular Catalan docudrama about the outbreak of the Civil War). As if to make the connection to his fascist heritage explicit, Manuel emphatically refuses to change his company's advertising slogan because (like the well-known Osborn brandy slogan) his family "has used it successfully for three generations."

In contrast to Almodóvar's works, Bigas Luna's films are not populated by recently emancipated women, homosexuals, and transvestites; rather, his emotionally stunted characters retain an internalized repression which turns pathological in a consumerist context. The one exception may be *Las edades de Lulú*, which opens with the heroine's birth and immediately moves in for a fetishized close-up of her powdered pristine genitals, which remain the obsessive focus both of the camera and of her own transgressive pursuit of pleasure across all boundaries of gender and sexuality. Although the film's tone remains ambiguous, Lulu's liberated quest leads to heavy bondage, which is depicted as far more dangerous than it was in Almodóvar's *Atame (Tie Me Up, Tie Me Down*, 1989).

Though the eroticism of *Jamón Jamón* violates boundaries of class and generation, it is strictly heterosexual—despite the fact that Raúl obviously has homoerotic appeal and in one scene (where he pursues Silvia into the women's toilet) even quips, "I'm a bit of a *maricón*!" Instead, the film's sexual deviations verge toward incest and bestiality, deviations that are dependent on repression and that are very difficult to celebrate.

I do not mean to suggest that the characters in *Jamón Jamón* literally have sex with animals (as they do in *Caniche*) but rather that they themselves are identified with various animal species, perversely implying not only that their own incestuous behavior is "natural," but also that it is exogamous coupling (with a different species or class) that is truly transgressive. Virtually all of the main characters are associated with a different animal. The best example is Carmen, who "does the parrot" for José Luis as he masturbates; she imitates the bird with her words, her moves, and her tongue (an impersonation that actress Anna Galiena makes wonderfully erotic) while her lewd parrot, Guaca, keeps shrieking "polla" (prick) like a sexual mantra. As in a bestiary, the men are differentiated and defined by the animals with whom they are symbolically linked. Infantilized by his bitchy mother, José Luis seems to identify with a lapdog, designing panties for she-dogs that they can wear when they are in heat. His father dismisses the idea with contempt, reminding him, "Our line is ... for human beings!" Yet in the first incestuous embrace between Silvia and her prospective father-in-law, Manuel, who is also her mother's longtime lover, a fly crawls across his stony, lifeless face with its drone dominating the sound track, making us question whether he is human at all. This embrace is in marked contrast to an earlier hysterical scene where we see Carmen's handsome wayward husband trying to break into the house he long ago abandoned, perhaps to molest his oldest daughter, Silvia, who stands on the other side of the glass door sobbing, passionately declaring her love but still keeping him out. Though he beats against the door like the big bad wolf wielding a huge club in his hand, instead of using it to break through the glass he turns it against his own truck, which is teeming with terrified chickens.

The macho hunk Raúl (who physically resembles Silvia's father) is also associated with two animals, the bull and the hog. Not only is he introduced to the audience quite literally under the phallic sign of the bull, but later he and a friend prove they have balls by clandestinely sneaking into a bull pen—naked and with a hard-on—to do passes with a bull in the dark. Yet, to gain entry to Silvia's house and heart, Raúl bathetically chooses to identify with pigs (rather than with chickens or the big bad wolf like her father). To make Silvia open her door, he sticks a clove of garlic up the ass of her family pig and then provides the grunting sound effects; together they subdue the beast and save it from an oncoming truck, a communal act that leads them to adopt ever-after the endearing epithets "Cerdo" (pork) and "Jamona" (ham) respectively. Later, when he falls off his motorcycle as it runs down her younger sisters' darling pet piglet, Pablito, Silvia declares her undying love not for the dead swine (who soon will be eaten) but for the surviving Raúl.

In the daylight barroom scene where Silvia and Raúl have sex for the first time, their reckless abandon is as wild as that of the lovers in Lynch's *Wild at Heart*. Yet, despite the swelling music, the symbolic dissolves, and the orgasmic jackpot on Raúl's slot machine, the romantic ecstasy is deflated by the other customers, who flee the bar as if they were watching two copulating beasts, and by the lovers' final climax, which takes place under the castrated sign of the bull. This scene displays a masterful control of tone as the perspective shifts abruptly from inside to outside the romance, undercutting the erotic climax with *esperpento*.

As I have argued elsewhere, the Spanish oedipal narrative frequently conflates Oedipus and Samson, who are mirror images of each other, eroticizing incest and exogamy respectively as reversible sexual taboos.[4] In *Jamón Jamón*, the advertising slogan that Manuel's family has used successfully over three generations for its briefs is: "You've a Samson inside!"—a slogan that appears on the billboard which prominently displays Raúl's genitalia securely encased within a fashionable polka-dotted crotch. Within this consumerist oedipal narrative, Raúl plays the exogamous Samsonite jock who threatens to rupture the patrimonial line of these philistine capitalists and leave his family in ruins. Yet, consistent with melodrama, despite all the violence and hysteria nothing of substance really changes. With the final sweeping camera movement the film merely reshuffles its six transgressive characters into three incestuous pairs artfully posed for a final melodramatic triptych. Not only does this painterly tableau evoke traditional Christian iconography (with a double Pietà), but it also restores power to the rich incestuous patriarch. Instead of being barred from the door like Sylvia's lowlife father, Manuel stands upright like a rock, supporting his son's pregnant fiancee with his embrace, ready to finance and appropriate his post-Franco Madonna and child.

NOTES

1. Ortega y Gasset, José, "The Dehumanization of Art," in *Velázquez, Goya and the Dehumanization of Art*, trans. Alexis Brown (New York: W. W. Norton, 1953), p. 77.
2. Peter Besas, "TV ad sales grow 7-fold in 10-years," *Variety* (September 24. 1990), p. 58.
3. For a detailed analysis of *Bilboa*, see my essay "The Spanish Oedipal Narrative from *Raza* to *Bilbao*," *Quarterly Review of Film and Video* 13, no. 4 (1991), pp. 67-94. A longer version of this essay appears as chapter 5 in *Blood Cinema*.
4. "The Spanish Oedipal Narrative," pp. 75-76.

LOS ANGELES TIMES, 10/29/93, Calendar/p. 8, Kevin Thomas

Comedies don't come much darker than Spanish filmmaker's Bigas Luna's breezy, outrageous sex farce "Jamon Jamon". It has a pow-in-the-kisser finish you may hate for seeming to spoil your fun, but upon consideration—or a second viewing —it becomes clear that the ending has the quality of inevitability.

Far from puritanically punishing the participants for their entangled sexual shenanigans, Luna, long an explicit chronicler of sexual obsession, is merely observing in bemused fashion the way in which passion tends to rage out of control. From its opening shot, a view of a stretch of arid highway framed by an immense anatomically correct roadside silhouette of a bull, "Jamon Jamon" has fun with the obsession with male sexual endowment. We're in a desert-like region that is the site of a nearby men's underwear factory, where its owner's attractive but shrewish wife Conchita (Stefania Sandrelli) sizes up a lineup of young men trying out for a modeling job.

Conchita is as concerned with selecting the man who best fills out the merchandise as she is over her son's affair with one of her factory workers, the beautiful Silvia (Penelope Cruz), who is not only pregnant by him but also the laughter of the still young and equally beautiful Carmen (Anna Galiena), proprietress of the local roadside brothel. Quick to put two-and-two together, Conchita decides that the model she picks, Raul (Javier Bardem), a local stud who drives a ham delivery truck and aspires to bullfighting, is just the guy to bribe into seducing Silvia away from her pouty, ineffectual son José Luis (Jordi Molla). But what if she is to fall under the spell of Raul's bold, earthy charms herself?

Long before anyone in America had ever heard of Pedro Almodóvar, Bigas Luna was gleefully shaking up audiences. With his disturbingly powerful 1978 "Bilbao," which inevitably brought to mind "The Collector," Luna worked in a gritty, naturalistic style yet made completely credible the increasingly distorted imaginings of a young man obsessed with a voluptuous, uncomplicated, hardworking prostitute.

If "Bilbao's" hero went too far, Luna himself lapsed into the thoroughly nauseous the following year with "Caniche" (Poodle), a revolting tale about an extravagantly decayed brother and sister who get carried away with their passion for their dogs and each other.

Luna was last heard of five years ago with "Anguish," a horror picture that for all its Grand Guignol grisliness was a serious consideration of the power of movies in the blurring of reality and fantasy in which a crazy mother and son (Zelda Rubinstein and Michael Lerner) echo the brother and sister in "Caniche." Although Luna, With his darkly outrageous view of sex, has lots in common with Almodóvar, he is an idiosyncratic filmmaker if there ever was one.

Without a doubt "Jamon Jamon," which was among Spain's 10 top box-office hits last year, will become Luna's best-known movie to date. It also may be his best, for it proceeds with an assured nonchalance, its vigorous rhythms punctuated with cuts to trucks roaring down that highway and buoyed by Nicola Piovani's score, which alternates between the jaunty and the plaintive, depending on the mood of the scene.

While Galiena, Cruz and Molla are entirely admirable, Sandrelli, the elegant Italian actress now in her gorgeous 40s, and the well-muscled Bardem have the roles that acquire them to carry the picture, which they do with ease. While Bardem, who recalls the young Jean-Paul Belmondo in his ability to take humorous pleasure in his unabashed sexiness, plays the happy-go-lucky boor, Sandrelli is the ultimate hypocritical bourgeoisie.

With "Caniche," Luna was heavy-handed in his attack on the bourgeoisie; here, he lets us take his social commentary or leave it, yet it is undeniable that what makes "Jamon Jamon" so explosive is its clash between sex and class. "Jamon Jamon's" distributor rejected an R-rating—you would think it would draw an NC-17—and it is Times-rated Mature for considerable sex and nudity, and for language.

NEW STATESMAN & SOCIETY, 6/4/93, p. 34, Andy Robinson

The Spanish film-maker Bigas Luna could have chosen a *butifarra* sausage as the emblem of his latest celebration of signs and surrealism, Barthes and Buñuel, *Jamón, Jamón*. But instead he chose a cured ham.

The Catalan director's choice of meats was not just a question of taste. *Jamón, Jamón* (poorly translated: cured ham, cured ham) is a homage to *la España profunda*: the deep Spain of bulls, balls, paella and potato omelette (with or without onion).

Given the chance, some Catalans would probably run Bigas out of Barcelona for creating such a unified "Spanish" semiology when the Catalans have their *butifarras*, the Gallegos their *lacón* (boiled ham), and while the other nationalities in the Spanish state are scouring their regions' history for gastronomic symbols to support their claims to nationhood.

But Bigas has opted for that quintessential Spain—the country that is best experienced when you drive through such Baudrillardian vacuums as the Monegros desert in Aragon and stop at one of the roadside bars where the lorry drivers eat.

Here in the middle of nowhere is Bigas Luna's Spain: the black silhouette of the Osborne sherry advertisement hoarding, a towering, sheet-metal bull with protruding horns and dangling bollocks; the glimmering green and pink lights of the *puticlub* brothel; log-shaped Manchego cheese *bocadillos* which give you jaw ache; bullfighting paraphernalia on the walls; paella on Thursdays; and pig's legs hung from the ceiling. This is *jamón* versus Balkanisatian.

Nor is it the first time that ham has been chosen as a symbol of nation and sex in Spanish movies. Bigas acknowledges being influenced by the dream sequence in Buñuel's *The Discreet Charm of the Bourgeoise*, in which a man finds a ham in the street, devours it like an animal, wakes up, goes to the kitchen and eats a slice of ham from the fridge.

Indeed, the best images in *Jamón, Jamón* are deliciously surrealist. Scavenging dogs lick a massive paella pan clean in a desert rainstorm. Penelope Cruz, Bigas' Nastassja Kinski, dreams of lizards poking their heads through dolls' eyes and bulls' horns being sawn through as the object of their lust, the brawny ham-seller Javier Bardem, hangs lifeless from goal posts in the middle of the desert.

Almodóvar is there too; not only that brilliant scene from *What Have I Done To Deserve This?* in which Carmen Maura, the desperate, high-rise housewife, batters her husband to death with a ham bone, but also in the close-ups of hard-ons in the first bullfighting scene of *Jamón, Jamón* (not, I should add, the *naked* moonlit bullfighting scene just before Bardem persuades Cruz to clean his feet with olive oil).

The "ham as weapon" theme is picked up by Bigas towards the end of the film in his caricature of Goya's *A Garrotazos*, when Bardem and his rival for Cruz's love, the rich kid Jordi Molla, beat each other about the head with *jamónes*.

But if a cured ham has to be a phallic symbol and a club, at least Almodóvar put it in the hands of a woman. In *Jamón, Jamón*, it's the *cojones* (balls) that count. Bardem wins the battle for Penelope Cruz thanks to his bollocks and his penchant for raw garlic. "Garlic excites me," he says.

The crucial scene for *Jamón, Jamón*'s doubtful plot is the one where Jordi Molla (son of a wealthy underpants manufacturer whose products are modelled by Bardem) finds out that Penelope is not interested in him and rips the balls from the Osborne bull. The piece of sheet metal that had been the bull's balls then acts as an umbrella for Penelope as she makes her way through another rainstorm to meet her butch lover.

And all because Jordi's mother, a snobby businesswoman who is spiritually a whore (*la puta madre*), put the young ham seller up to it; and Penelope's mother, a whore who is spiritually a lovely woman (*la madre puta*) couldn't stop the dénouement of this Greek tragedy.

If the plot of *Jamón, Jamón* isn't on a par with Bigas' visual imagination, the moral of the story is frankly banal. As it turns out, the po-faced underpants manufacturer (jilted Jordi's dad) represents the threat of northern Europe and Brussels to "deep" Spain.

Bigas intends to write a political epilogue to *Jamón, Jamón* that gives some (well, actually not much) food for thought: "Juan Diego (who plays the underpants man) will take Penelope Cruz off in his Mercedes towards the north, towards Europe," he says. "But the Osborne bull which is, of course, the Minotaur, comes down from the hills, grapples with the Mercedes and carries the girl off towards the south.

"It's the story of the abduction of Europe ... the bull, of course, has no balls by then because the future that awaits us could be difficult": submerging ourselves in Europe, he explains, "has its advantages and disadvantages."

Bigas could call the epilogue *Chopped* (pronounced shop-éd), which is Spanish for chopped ham with pork.

NEW YORK POST, 9/24/93, p. 44, Jerry Tallmer

Sex and food, sex as food. The Spanish director Bigas Luna is not the first to work with that equation, but he may be the looniest. In any event "Jamón Jamón" is pretty loony.

"Jamón Jamón" means Ham, Ham, and whenever one of the lovers of beautiful Silvia the oppressed teen-age omelette maker savors her upper adornments he tastes one as ham, the other as potatoes.

He's Jose Luis, the poor little rich boy, and they're making love out in the nowhere just off the highway under the tin silhouette of an enormous black bull, a roadside sign that's one of the strongest visual elements in the affair at hand. "When we get married, can I have a closet just for shoes?" she asks. This is the kind of movie in which beautiful Silvia (Penelope Cruz) slowly sags to the ground to indicate pregnancy. Jose Luis (Jordi Molla) pledges their engagement with the pop-up ring from a soda can.

But his terrible-tempered mama isn't having any. She's Conchita (Stefania Sandrelli, if you can believe that), boss lady of the Samson jockey-shorts factory—not only terrible-tempered but sexually tempestuous. The second big visual symbol in "Jamón Jamón" is the roadside billboard of a well-bulged Samson product, and the model for the bulge was a proletarian stud named Raul.

It is with this Raul (Javier Bardem) that mama arranges a contract. She'll give him his heart's desire, a Yamaha; he'll seduce sweet Silvia and thus wreck sonny boy's infatuation. Thing is, mama also has a yen of her own for Raul the rough-and-ready.

Silvia goes home in tears to *her* mama, beautiful worldly-wise much-abused Carmen (Anna Galiena), the town barkeep, town whore, topless dancer from the age of 13. Mama's been sleeping off the record with her daughter's wimpy boyfriend's papa. As a matter of fact, wimpy Jose Luis has been sleeping with Carmen too—his girlfriend's mother.

Raul the bulge goes after Silvia in a number of predictable ways; and she keeps predictably telling him to Get Lost, until at last she doesn't. To him, she tastes, right and left, like ham and garlic, two of his favorite romantic stimuli. Raul and terrible-tempered Conchita inevitably get together and make loud music, and *this*, I guess, is when she gives him the Yamaha. It all ends up in a mano-a-mano of Raul and Jose Luis trying to kill one another—with a degree of success—by way of a slugfest with hams.

I could only think of the late Newman Levy's encapsulation of "Hamlet": "The King dies, the Queen dies, and Ham dies, I calls it a hell of a play." It may be noted that director/co-writer Luna isn't too proud to steal from "Network" (intercourse gabfest) and "The Wild One" (motorcycle-enforced courtship). A final preposterous tableau of corpses and hams in the desert sums the whole thing up.

NEWSDAY, 9/24/93, Part II/p. 65, Jonathan Mandell

In "Jamón Jamón," Raul is a sexy underwear model and aspiring bullfighter who also delivers hams for a living, drives a ham-shaped truck, lives in a ham warehouse and eats ham to increase his sex drive. He meets a young woman named Silvia by rescuing her hog from the highway, though he has driven it out there in the first place. When later he pushes his way into the ladies room of a disco to grab hold of Silvia and kiss her, she breaks away from him and calls him a pig. He calls her a pig, too, though he means it affectionately. "You're tastier than ham," he tells her, face on unclothed breast, when lust finally triumphs.

But their romance—as if you couldn't guess—is not kosher. Raul was paid to seduce Silvia.

"Jamón Jamón" means ham, ham in Spanish, and director Bigas Luna makes sure we never forget it. But even without the props, "Jamón Jamón" would be a piggish film. Luna has laced his surreal exercise with sex and nudity, vulgarity (e.g. crotch shots), and a sexist view of men and women clearly designed to shock and titillate.

Silvia (Penelope Cruz) becomes the target of Raul's seduction after she tells her spoiled boyfriend, Jose Luis (Jordi Molla), that she is pregnant and Jose Luis proposes marriage. But there are complications. Silvia is the daughter of the town prostitute; even Jose Luis is a client. He is also the son of the owners of the big (men's underwear) factory in town; his mother Conchita (Stefania Sandrelli) wants this marriage stopped. So she hires one of her models, Raul (Javier Bardem), to stop it in the best way she knows how. Raul falls genuinely in lust with Sylvia.

What follows is an ever-more complex matrix of seductions. If this were a French farce, it would all be played strictly for laughs; there are indeed a few well-formed comic moments. But "Jamón Jamón" is unmistakably Spanish, with touches of melodrama and cruelty, of symbolism, of arresting images—stray dogs scrounge a plaza-sized pan of leftover rice in the sparse, poor desert countryside. As well-crafted as it often is visually, so is it well-acted; the actors make their characters more credible than they deserve. The result is a strange kind of stateliness that acts in counterpoint to the adolescent tone, and thus paradoxically, undercuts the whole enterprise.

SIGHT AND SOUND, 6/93, p. 57, Philip Strick

In the arid region of Los Monegros, village girl Silvia lives with her mother Carmen, who runs a roadside brothel. Silvia works at the nearby underwear factory and has become pregnant by José Luis, son of factory owners Manuel and Conchita. Although José Luis is willing to marry Silvia, their wedding plans are opposed by Conchita, who is convinced that Silvia is only after their money. She recruits Raúl, a young man who works at a ham warehouse and hopes to become a bullfighter, to seduce Silvia into forgetting about José Luis. Confident of success, Raúl finds his attempts to get acquainted firmly repulsed: he helps Silvia recover a pig, offers her a lift in his ham-promoting trailer, and embraces her at the local dance-hall, but she rewards him with no more than a hearty clout.

José Luis proposes an inspired marketing scheme to his father Manuel: underwear for dogs. When this is received with derision, he turns for consolation to Carmen, who has no qualms about giving him a warm welcome. Raúl and a friend practise their bullfighting skills at night in a cattle compound, adding to the risk by performing nude; chased off by the owner, they take refuge at Silvia's home. She lends them clothes and throws them out when Raúl again tries his luck. Meanwhile, Conchita has decided that she wants Raúl for herself; getting him into bed, she promises him a motorbike if he gives up the pursuit of Silvia. He is happy to accept, but when he falls off the bike and Silvia rushes to his aid, they both realise the extent of their feelings for each other. Silvia accuses José Luis of immaturity, and consummates her love for Raúl during a thunderstorm.

Distraught at losing Silvia, José Luis reveals to his mother that the girl is pregnant. Equally upset at losing Raúl, Conchita makes moves to get him back: she tells Silvia that Raúl was bribed into making love to her, and tells Raúl that Silvia is pregnant by José Luis. The promise of a Mercedes, along with Conchita's sexual favours, proves a seductive argument, and Raúl yields to Conchita. José Luis, however, pays another visit to Carmen while Silvia, left alone, is unexpectedly consoled by Manuel. Finding his mother with Raúl at the ham warehouse, José Luis attacks his rival with the only available weapon, a side of ham, and the two men batter each other until José Luis is felled. Over his corpse, cradled by Carmen; the participants in the tragedy, silently contemplate the consequences of having yielded to their appetites.

The teasing humour of Bigas Luna, industrial and interior designer turned film-maker, has won him a number of European festival mentions and a growing notoriety, but as yet no unanimous international recognition. This could have something to do with his taste for the unconventional, often exposed in clinical detail, as with his second film *Caniche* (1978), about a wife whose passion for her pet poodle drives her husband to extremes of infidelity with a stray Alsatian, or his third, *Bilbao* (1978), about an amateur photographer so obsessed with a prostitute that he kidnaps her, shaves off her body hair and empties a bottle of milk over her unconscious form. Contrary to such surprises, the best of Luna is intriguingly elliptical: in *Reborn* (1981), featuring Dennis Hopper as a hell-fire television evangelist, the idea of God patrolling the urban skies in a helicopter has more to offer than the film is finally prepared to confront; but even in its evasiveness *Reborn* is a vision to be taken seriously.

By contrast, the problem with *Jamón, Jamón*, is that it can't be taken seriously on any level. Luna has reverted to domestic fantasy, the mood for his earlier films, but not this time in a spirit of eccentric exploration; instead, he is intent on satire of the broadest kind, incorporating what he calls "six magnificent characters, prototypes of our country". In his notes Luna exuberantly prepares us for trouble: Silvia "represents what's best in the world". Raúl is a "parcel bomb, the obscure object of desire". Manuel personifies "the new European imperialism". Conchita is "a wonder, one f--- of a mother", and so on.

If, by some Godardian method, he had introduced these observations into the film, Luna's derisive undermining of his characters might have forestalled his audience's bewilderment; but without commentary his storytelling wanders too arbitrarily between slapstick eroticism and an exaggerated neo-realism to achieve any clarity of focus. It is evident enough, from the heavy symbolism of the giant cut-out bull on the hillside, its potency at risk from every strong breeze, that an overview of the Spanish predicament is being offered; but that Luna's prototypes, with their farcical innocence and ungovernable hungers, are more Spanish than universally human (if humanity deserves to be viewed with such cynical affection) remains unsubstantiated.

In Luna's doctrine, Spanish sexual and eating habits are closely linked, so that his osculating couples sample each other with avid comments on the flavour of various bits of anatomy; Silvia tastes of potato to one admirer, of onion to another, and even when not being consumed she invites appreciation as *"una mujer jamona"*, a nice bit of meat. The cast abandons its dignity to these gastronomic excesses with admirable generosity—although less conducive to nausea is the embrace in which a stud and his mistress discuss what kind of motorbike he'll get in return for his services. But it is disconcerting to watch actresses of the calibre of Stefania Sandrelli and Anna Galiena (the 'ideal' woman from *The Hairdresser's Husband*) resorting to such levels of overstatement.

Luna films them in laudatory Panavision, along with the lugubrious wastes of the Monegros region, a desert bisected by a single uncaring highway. But apart from his final tableau of lip-smacking despair (a Buñuelesque flock approaches from the horizon as the distraught lovers clutch each other in terminal paralysis) is less interesting visually than usual. Rather, he has seized upon an assortment of scatological diversions—an 'audition' of men's briefs, a nude bullfight, a Coke can as a target in a urination contest—to prepare the way for his climactic irony, a battle to the death with sides of ham as cudgels. As demonstrated in his best-known film, *Anguish* (1986), a Chinese-box horror film about horror films, he can be more inventively outrageous than this, and with better reason.

VILLAGE VOICE, 9/28/93, p. 53, Georgia Brown

Of all national cinemas, Spain's is the kinkiest and raunchiest, the most obsessed with perversity. Watching an erotic parable like *Jamón Jamón* sitting in an American movie theater feels more than slightly surreal. (Except for a recent fling with that imp Almodóvar, it's astonishing how seldom we see anything from post-Buñuel, post-Franco Spain.) Whereas the French—as well as the Belgians and the Dutch—turn out lots of coy, ultra-suggestive tragicomedies like *The Hairdresser's Husband* and *Monsieur Hire*, the Spanish seem compelled to go all out and roll in the barnyard. For a time, this was put down to those years of fascist repression.

The controversial Catalan director José Juan Bigas Luna moved to film from graphic design and his films have a stark, hard-edged handsomeness and a penchant for fetishistic close-ups. The chilling *Bilboa* ('78), once the object of a mini-uproar in Cannes, traced the daily round of a voyeur named Leo who enlisted a blow-dryer, an electric razor, and an electric toothbrush in the service of his drives. In the '80s, Bigas Luna began turning to international casts: He made one film with American midget Zelda Rubinstein (*Anguish*) and another with Dennis Hopper (*Reborn*).

His new film, *Jamón Jamón*—which translates as *Ham Ham*—concocts a spicy paella of bulls' balls, pigs' haunches, garlic, and the sausages featured in men's underwear ads. It's a movie consciously immersed in cultural semiotics—advertising, technology, and the local cuisine. Its targets: paternalism, empty cults of manliness, and the harm done by overbearing mothers.

Jamón Jamón is the story of two families and a Marky Mark-type loner. In the Monegros, a parched and poor region, at least one family is rich and vulgar. The husband-and-wife CEOs of an underwear business, Manuel (Juan Diego) and Conchita (Stefania Sandrelli), have staked everything on their one spoiled prince, José Luis (Jordi Molla). Working in the family factory is the lithe, luscious Silvia (Penelope Cruz), who has just discovered she's pregnant by José Luis. Silvia's mother, Carmen (Anna Galiena, the hairdresser in *The Hair Dresser's Husband*), runs a roadside whorehouse and counts José Luis and his father among her clients. Her estranged husband, a truck driver (his rig carries live chickens), we see just once, pounding furiously on the door and begging his daughter to let him in. She obviously wants to open the door.

But many trucks like Papa's roar back and forth along a central highway, stirring the dust and creating hot tailwinds. Men, Bigas Luna intimates, define themselves by what they ride. It's the old *Gas Food Lodging* syndrome with women stuck in place, minding the stations (feeding and breeding), and men in motion, practicing their moves, as if virility itself is a vocation.

The outsider in this is a dim-witted, sleepy-eyed hunk named Raul (Javier Bardem), a layabout delivery boy for the region's famous hams and an amateur matador—activities that make him a satire on Andalusian machismo. Raul eats lots of ham, chews raw garlic for potency, and likes getting naked and practicing on the bulls.

When Raul auditions his bulge for an underwear ad, the chief judge, Conchita, is *muy* impressed. Later on, she hires him to seduce Silvia, in an effort to separate the girl from her son. Proud possessor of an Imelda-type shoe closet, Conchita assumes Silvia is merely after the family fortune. Knowing that boys like motors, she offers Raul a Yamaha bike and later, a Mercedes. On his new bike, Raul whips up and down a side road, just as the truck drivers do on the highway.

Both young men prefer Silvia, but this doesn't stop them from screwing the moms—*la puta madre* and *la madre puta*, as the credits put it. Not to be outdone, José Luis's father has his eye on Silvia as well as her mother. In an incestuous culture, older women are predators and young men are studs. Is Carmen's generosity less damaging than Conchita's rapaciousness? The movie's emphasis on tit-sucking seems a comment on infantilized males.

Although Silvia and Carmen (famous for their tasty potato omelettes) are less crass and far more attractive than their bourgeois counterparts, no one here is particularly sympathetic. Bigas Luna's grotesquerie seems impelled by the same moral fervor that inspired the old illustrators of purgatory. In his films. a coldblooded intellectual fastidiousness wars with hot-blooded eroticism. *Jamón Jamón* is sardonic, furious, and very disturbing. I staggered out feeling I'd been flattened by a rolling semi.

Also reviewed in:
NEW YORK TIMES, 9/24/93, p. C18, Vincent Canby
VARIETY, 9/7/92, p. 51, Peter Besas
WASHINGTON POST, 10/23/93, p. D4, Rita Kempley

JASON GOES TO HELL: THE FINAL FRIDAY

A New Line Cinema release. *Producer:* Sean S. Cunningham. *Director:* Adam Marcus. *Screenplay:* Dean Lorey and Jay Huguely. *Story:* Jay Huguely and Adam Marcus. *Director of Photography:* William Dill. *Editor:* David Handman. *Music:* Harry Manfredini. *Music Editor:* Jack Tillar. *Sound:* Oliver L. Moss and (music) Jerry Lambert. *Sound Editor:* Phillip Seretti. *Casting:* David Giella. *Production Designer:* W. Brooke Wheeler. *Set Decorator:* Natali K. Pope. *Special Visual Effects:* Al Magliochetti. *Mechanical Effects:* Bellisimo Bellardinelli and Tom Bellisimo. *Costumes:* Julie Rae Engelsman. *Make-up:* Kimberly Greene. *Stunt Coordinator:* Kane Hodder. *Running time:* 88 minutes. *MPAA Rating:* R.

CAST: John D. LeMay (Steven Freeman); Kari Keegan (Jessica Kimble); Kane Hodder (Jason Voorhees); Steven Williams (Creighton Duke); Steven Culp (Robert Campbell); Erin Gray (Diana Kimble); Rusty Schwimmer (Joey B); Richard Gant (Coroner); Leslie Jordan (Shelby); Billy Green Bush (Sheriff Landis); Kipp Marcus (Randy); Andrew Bloch (Josh); Adam Cranner (Ward); Allison Smith (Vicki); Julia Michaels (Elizabeth Marcus F.B.I.); James Gleason (Agent Abernathy); Dean Lorey (Assistant Coroner); Tony Ervolina (FBI Agent); Diana Georger (Edna, Josh's Girlfriend); Adam Marcus (Officer Bish); Mark Thompson (Officer Mark); Brian Phelps (Officer Brian); Blake Conway (Officer Andell); Madelon Curtis (Officer Ryan); Michelle Clunie (Deborah, the Blonde Camper); Michael Silver (Luke, the Boy Camper); Kathryn Atwood (Alexis, the Dark Haired Camper).

LOS ANGELES TIMES, 8/16/93, Calendar/p. 3, Michael Wilmington

"Jason Goes to Hell: The Final Friday" is no occasion for bloody Auld Lang Syne. The "Friday the 13th" series, nine movies and innumerable corpses after its 1980 debut, here comes to a supposedly permanent dead-end, as we watch the second of its resident maniacs, truculent Jason Voorhees, repeatedly shot, hacked, blown to bits, vivisected—by a coroner who also eats his heart—and dragged off to hell by what seems to be the local chapter of the Night of the Living Dead.

Somebody with a sense of symmetry is operating here. Thirteen years after the original Camp Crystal Lake blood bath, the "last"—produced by the original's producer-director, Sean S. Cunningham, directed by newcomer Adam Marcus and scored by "13th" mainstay Harry Manfredini—was released, without press screenings, on Friday the 13th.

Does this mean that the filmmakers are really closing the circle? That the long, bloody and mostly dumb career of Jason, a rampaging hulk in a hockey mask who loves to kill lecherous teenagers *in flagrante delicto*, is finally over? That, after deluding us with "Friday the 13th: The Final Chapter" in 1984, thumbing their noses at us with "Friday the 13th, Part 5, The New Beginning" the very next year, and then hacking and bashing their way, in fairly quick succession, through Parts 6, 7 and 8, Jason's employers—now New Line Cinema rather than Paramount—have finally decided that enough is enough?

Don't bet the cemetery on it. There's only one sure way to kill Jason, and that's to stop going to his movies.

Actually "Jason Goes to Hell", gives us plenty of reasons to quit. On the movie's feeble plus side are Richard Gant's acting (as the coroner), Manfredini's music and one funny joke in the last half-minute. On the minus side: ludicrous characters. Garbled nonstop gore. Persistent loud, clanging noises that give you the impression of being trapped inside a malfunctioning radiator. Shadowy lighting that makes you feel as if you're staggering around in the dark.

And more: Scene after scene where supposedly "normal" human beings behave with monumental stupidity—and are promptly tortured and killed, sometimes in elaborate S & M rituals. Dialogue and performances that might convince you English is your second language—or third. Innumerable close-up shots of insane murderers grabbing victims and French-kissing them with black, snakelike tongues.

Obscene shouting matches between repulsive dimwits. Police that make the Keystone Kops look like a convention of Nobel laureates. One "hero" who molests waitresses and breaks fingers for kicks: another who spends most of the film running around frantically, trying to catch up with the murders. Great gory spews of bloody entrails, photographed in loving detail.

If all that isn't enough to make you quit Crystal Lake, nothing will. But then, nothing ever did before.

"Jason Goes to Hell: the Final Friday" (rated R, for violence, sensuality and language) does have a new wrinkle—though new only to *this* series. Probably by way of John McNaughton's underrated "The Borrowers," the script writers have lifted the old John W. Campbell "Who Goes There?" gimmick of the monster hopping from one new body to the next—giving us not one maniac, but a batch of them, each new "Jason" lurching off with murder on its mind as soon as the old one gives it one of those snake-tongued soul kisses. Beyond this horror-show variant of "La Ronde," it's business as usual: One synthetic shock after another, designed to drive teenagers on dates to grapple each other, and teen-agers without dates to snicker at the fates of those who have them.

What do they mean "Jason Goes to Hell?" If hell isn't a series of "Friday the 13th" movies, repeated into eternity, then "Halloween's" Michael Myers is a pacifist and Elm Street's Freddy Krueger is a Noble Peace Prize candidate. As for Jason, if it's really time for him to hang up his ax and get a day job, there's always Wall Street. Or maybe even movie criticism.

NEW YORK POST, 8/14/93, p. 13, Matthew Flamm

It has been 13 years since the very disturbed Jason Voorhees made his first appearance at Crystal Lake. You would think by now that any of the young women visiting the region would know not to shower or bathe or take off their clothes for any reason when they're alone.

But maybe they believe Jason is really dead. After all, "Jason Goes to Hell: The Final Friday," which is the ninth edition of the "Friday the 13th" shock-horror series, isn't the first to claim it's the last.

The movie, which opened yesterday with no advance screenings for reviewers, boasts the return of producer Sean S. Cunningham, who produced and directed the original "13th" in 1980 and has had the good sense to stay away ever since. He has come back only because this one really is the last—it *really, really is*, say the production notes.

If so, Jason and his hockey mask will have gone out with somewhat of a bang.

"Jason Goes to Hell" could never be confused with "Psycho" (despite the shower scenes). And perhaps it benefits from the comparison with its predecessor, the really wretched "Jason Takes Manhattan."

But in its primal, hormone-driven, slightly cheesy way, this latest sequel seems to work.

Its smartest trick may be in keeping Jason out of most of the movie. Before the opening credits come up, the now-middle-aged, world-famous serial killer gets blown away by SWAT-team cops (who, clever fellovs, use a shapely young woman at her bath to lure him).

Jason is just a collection of charcoal-broiled bits when he's wheeled into the federal morgue. But by the time the unsuspecting coroner (Richard Gant) realizes that the heart is still beating, it's too late. He's somehow driven to eat the disgusting mass of muscle, and then he goes out and kills people all the way to Crystal Lake.

"Jason Goes to Hell" has a body count to match "Terminator 2" but, with less money for special effects, it employs something like a story. Jason will hop from body to body by means of that force-fed heart, until he can find a certain host—I won't reveal the secret ingredient—in which he can live forever.

The hockey mask reappears selectively; mixing "Dracula" with "Invasion of the Body Snatchers," "Jason" has its clones look like the real Jason whenever they're seen in a mirror.

As directed by twentysomething first-time director Adam Marcus, "Jason Goes to Hell" weaves it's way rather awkwardly through genres. It's part western (there's a black-hatted bounty hunter with not enough to do), part soap opera (the Voorhees family entanglements are like something out of "Days of Our Lives"), part sado-voyeuristic teen slasher movie.

What the hell, it made me scream.

NEWSDAY, 8/14/93, Part II/p. 21, Terry Kelleher

Thirteen years after he started his killing spree, Jason Voorhees at last shows a sense of social responsibility.

If you've seen any of his screen adventures—from the original "Friday the 13th" (1980) to "Friday the 13th, Part VIII (1989)—you know the hockey-masked hulk particularly relishes dispatching healthy young couples on the verge of intercourse. But in the new "Jason Goes to Hell: The Final Friday," the ogre punctuates murder with a public-service message, slaughtering two frisky Crystal Lake campers only *after* they've tossed away the condom and elected to gamble on unsafe sex. It's a hard lesson, but somebody's got to learn it.

Yes, "Jason Goes to Hell" offers a little humor. There's the enterprising Crystal Lake diner, run by a foul-mouthed termagant (Rusty Schwimmer), that has a two-for-one special on "Jasonburgers." There's "American Case File," a reasonably on-target parody of tabloid TV. There's the clever closing shot, an in-joke sure to please horror fans and New Line Cinema stockholders.

Unfortunately, first-time director Adam Marcus and writers Dean Lorey and Jay Huguely have a story to tell as well. And it's a confusing mess. Turns out the lumbering Jason (Kane Hodder) has the ability to "jump into" other people's bodies, sort of like Scott Bakula's character on the television series "Quantum Leap." When he wipes out the aforementioned campers, for example, he does so in the skin of an unlucky coroner (Richard Gant) who made the mistake of assuming a dismembered, bullet-riddled Jason was a dead Jason—and made the further mistake of eating Jason's heart, though a Jasonburger would have been cheaper and more digestible.

So Jason could be anybody—the sheriff of Crystal Lake (Billy Green Bush), even the slick anchorman on "American Case File" (Steven Culp). Only Creighton Duke (Steven Williams), the noted bounty hunter, fully understands Jason's power of instant reincarnation. Creighton alone can explain why Jason must be killed only with a glowing dagger wielded by another Voorhees—such as his sister, Diana (Erin Gray), or his niece, Jessica (Kari Keegan). Meanwhile, everybody's trying to pin a murder rap on poor Steven Freeman (John D. LeMay), Jessica's erstwhile boyfriend and the father of her imperiled baby.

Add substandard sound and lighting, and you have a movie that's awfully difficult to follow. But at least this is "The Final Friday." They wouldn't lie to us ... would they?

Also reviewed in:
NEW YORK TIMES, 8/14/93, p. 12, Stephen Holden
VARIETY, 8/23/93, p. 22, Greg Evans
WASHINGTON POST, 8/14/93, p. D3, Richard Harrington

JIT

A Northern Arts Entertainment release of a Film Africa/Mukuvisi Films. *Executive Producer:* Neil Dunn and Michael Raeburn. *Producer:* Rory Kilalea. *Director:* Michael Raeburn. *Screenplay:* Michael Raeburn. *Director of Photography:* Joao "Funcho" Costa. *Editor:* Justin Krish. *Music:* Oliver Mtukudzi. *Sound:* Esko Metsola. *Casting:* Paul Tingay. *Production Designer:* Lindie Pankiv. *Costumes:* Lindie Pankiv. *Make-up:* Susan Hains. *Running time:* 98 minutes. *MPAA Rating:* Not Rated.

CAST: Dominic Makuvachuma (UK); Sibongile Nene (Sofi); Farai Sevenzo (Johnson); Winnie Ndemera (Jukwa); Oliver Mtukudzi (Oliver); Lawrence Simbarashe (Chamba); Kathy Kuleya (Nomsa); Jackie Eeson (Gift); Cecil Zilla Mamanzi (Police Neighbor); Zanape Fazilahmed (Oliver's Wife); Taffy Marichidza (Hotel Manager); Jones Muguse (Taxi Driver); Fidelis Cheza (Barman); Emmanuel Boro (Worker); Shoyai Chikombah and Bertha S. Nesora (Travelers); John Chin (Taxi Drunk); David Chiganza (Eliot); Emmerson Chitakatira (Golf Club Manager); Aaron Nusekanevama (Mini Football Player); Alfred Chitanda (Parker); John Two Sos (Beggar); Tarcisious Sanyika (Waiter); Simpson Kovera (Emergency Taxi Driver); Barbara Nkala (Chamba's Wife); Neville Gonbah and Rudi Manupete (Gang Members); Elias Mukunyadze (Sidecar Driver); Brian Cooper (Bakery Boss); D. Hoyd (Furniture Salesman); Taffy Chiota (Auto Exhaust Manager); Jane Kilalea (Housewife).

SIGHT AND SOUND, 3/93, p. 42, Mark Sinker

UK, a country boy, lives in Harare, Zimbabwe, with his uncle Oliver. He's there to make his way in the world, but his idea of a career is cycling around delivering copies of his uncle's latest record to local bars—that is, when he's not battling with his ancestor spirit the Jukwa, a beer-loving old ghost-woman, who only cares to look after him when he's providing the libations.

Sofi works answering phones at Prime Records, the company Oliver is signed to, and goes out with the smooth, monied Johnson. When UK falls out of a taxi and hits his head, he comes round to find a concerned Sofi leaning over him; instantly smitten, he decides to marry her, but Sofi's cheerful gambler father Mr Chamba will allow the marriage only if UK can raise his desired bride price of a hi-fi and 500 dollars in cash. UK sets to, taking on a variety of unpromising get-rich-quick jobs, but they're mostly disastrous: he keeps getting fired, and when he's finally able to stump up the bride price, Chamba gambles the money away, and then demands a refrigerator as well, insisting it will help sway Sofi.

It's clear that all this is happening because UK is not attending to his Jukwa's welfare, so she in turn is neglecting his. When he buys her a whole crate of beer, things start to go right. His jobs don't improve—flower peddler, one-man bus service—but his general likeability and earnest endeavour get people helping him. His mooning around Sofi annoys Johnson, who begins to show his true criminal colours. After a showdown, Johnson's sidekick Gift makes a bogus offer to help UK get the better of Gift's boss—a trick to get UK ensnared in a robbery he didn't commit. But when the fridge arrives at the Champa household, Gift is found inside it, bound and gagged, and the police arrive, tipped off by UK, to arrest a protesting Johnson. Reluctant at first, then enthusiastic, Sofi embraces her husband-to-be.

In the classic fairy-tale, the poor boy has to perform some task to win the hand of the princess. Sometimes the king's all for it, sometimes the plot hinges on his jealousy. *Jit*, which in all other respects has few pretensions to avant-garde status, gets its spin from Sofi's father. He loves the goofy notion that UK—who's hopeless, except that everyone loves him—might win his hyper haughty daughter's hand; but he really does want that money, those appliances.

Billed as Zimbabwe's first feature film, *Jit* is so engagingly simplistic—its plot Boy-Meets-Girl-And-Gets-Girl-The-End—and so uncomplicatedly engaging that it would be easy to miss its shrewdness. The characters are all the stuff of light comedy—even the criminals are entirely unthreatening, hardly more than truculently impolite. *Jit* certainly makes the best of slim resources, with untried and enthusiastic amateurs for cast, and the Harare citizenry going about their business unconcerned as the backdrop in many shots. Special effects? Jump cuts—and the Jukwa magically appears.

Director Michael Raeburn insists he's very much aware of the challenges and pitfalls facing a non-African filming African city life in Africa (he cites Nabokov in America as proof that something worthwhile can result from outsiders storytelling in a country not their own—which is perhaps not the analogy that springs to mind as you watch, but he has a point). How much the look of the film is down to him and how much down to his host country, which provided crew and actors, would be hard to say. Certainly the cut of his clothes, for extras and stars (Dominic Makuvachuma, with his grin and simpleton artlessness, is nothing if not a star) has the thrift-store realism look of early 70s British cinema; the 16mm filming only emphasises that. *Jit* hasn't had the *vérité* storyboarded out of it; you feel the actors turned up for the shoot in what they'd be wearing anyway. Sofi's elaborate going-out hairdo, for example—just suddenly there before our eyes, an unsignalled detail—might be Sibongile Nene's own favoured hairdo, pure uncalculated serendipity.

At the same time, the film acts as a kind of video showcase for the country's front-rank pop groups. Sound-track music is an almost constant primary-colour pulse-lilt, dropping back behind dialogue only a little—and plenty of the action actually takes place in bars with bands playing in real time. Oliver Mtukudzi's participation is probably a coup for them, as probably the second top figure in ZimPop (which is known as *jit*, from two similar Shona words, one meaning 'dance in a circle' the other 'jump up and down'—the Bhundu Boys brought it to these shores five or six years ago, although they don't appear in the film). The first song you hear is Thomas Mapfumo's 'Mhondoro'—Mapfumo being the top figure in ZimPop, Zimbabwe's own Bob Marley and creator of a sound more distinctly indigenous than the frankly Brit beat-group-derived rock 'n' roll of *jit ordinaire*. It may be that this factor more than any other made it a hit in Zimbabwe itself.

The music's fine; especially if we don't have the language, it has a power which we're drawn to, an innocence, Beatlish and unspoiled—probably deceptively. But the bottom line of this fairy tale is money. The realist aspect of *Jit*'s magical realism goes beyond the Jukwa's alcoholic bent; she disapproves of UK's crush, thinks marrying for love is stupid. African sorcery is thoroughly unromantic, a practical and businesslike affair. UK is so called because his schoolmates thought he'd go far; Johnson seeks to persuade Sofi by offering her a real trip to London; she scoffs, not in thrall to higher thoughts (true love over mere baubles), but because he's never yet taken her anywhere.

There is a welcome bonus in the film's quite unnecessary willingness to make its cartoon figures more than just one-dimensional. UK as bread delivery-man is straight Benny Hill, in a speeded-up series of bewhiskered but very funny slapstick sight gags; but the speech he gives earlier to persuade the baker to hire him (about a bike's unpricy flexibility in city traffic) persuades us too. It's a neat little surprise when it turns out to be pure bullshit. There's UK's unfazed decision to propose to Sofi while she's picking out suppertime chickens. There's her father's unmasked glee at UK's beating out his richer rival (the denouement is really no more than a fairy godmother flourish, to say the play's ended). There's Sofi's own girl-talk scenes with her best friends, her Tracy Chapman poster pin-up, her modern-girl suspicion and reluctance ("Getting the bride price is not the same as getting the bride," she warns before the closing clinch). These are all serendipity—not of acting, not even of observation especially, just of a story running pleasantly against the grain.

VILLAGE VOICE, 3/30/93, p. 51, J. Hoberman

From another part of the old British empire, namely Zimbabwe, we have *Jit*, a (mainly) English-language 16mm feature that had its local premiere last week at "New Directors" and is currently ensconced at the Public Theater.

Jit's director, Michael Raeburn, is a bit more programmatically multiculti than Srinivas Krishna. The lengthy, first-person pressbook he wrote for *Jit* includes the following dialogue: *"Where are you from, Michael Raeburn?"* Africa. *"But you're white?"* Yes, I admit my coulour is pale, but my features are negroid, my blood is red and carries genes that come from men and women who were olive, red, white, black—who were Arabic, Italian, Turkish, Belgium [sic] and celtic and *other. I am everything and nothing—I am what I am."* Although this Whitman- (or perhaps Popeye-) esque stance suggests a promising exploration of African identity, Raeburn's aspirations are actually more generic.

Named for "jit jive," the local variant of Afro-pop, *Jit* tells the tale of a ferociously cheerful young black man who leaves his village to become a bike messenger in the city. There, the indefatigable UK, so nicknamed by his neighbors because they imagined he would go far, falls in love with a willowy clotheshorse who not only looks like a fashion model, but appears to be a head taller and five years older than her persistent suitor. In order to win this prize, UK must not only outwit her gangster boyfriend but pay her father's exorbitant "bride. price" (a new sound system, a new refrigerator, and $500).

In the film's most original touch, UK is alternately helped and hindered in his quest by a shape-shifting, beer-swilling old crone who represents the spirits of his ancestors. Still *Jit* slips from the pleasantly two-dimensional into the willfully dull, kept alive only by the soundtrack and occasional band gig. Otherwise we watch UK fail as a waiter, as a messenger, as an apprentice mechanic, as a caddy, and as a door-to-door salesman. In most cases, he's fired for creating some sort of havoc—often shown as speeded-up slapstick. When in doubt, Raeburn pumps up the volume and undercranks the action. After a while, it's the same old jit.

Also reviewed in:
CHICAGO TRIBUNE, 12/17/93, Friday/p. J, John Petrakis
NEW YORK TIMES, 3/20/93, p. 16, Stephen Holden
VARIETY, 12/31/90, p. 36

JOAN MITCHELL: PORTRAIT OF AN ABSTRACT PAINTER

A Christian Blackwood Films release. *Producer:* Christian Blackwood and Marion Cajori. *Director:* Marion Cajori. *Director of Photography:* Ken Kobland. *Running time:* 58 minutes. *MPAA Rating:* Not Rated.

NEW YORK POST, 4/14/93, p. 24, Jerry Tallmer

It was never my privilege to meet Joan Mitchell, the first-rank abstract artist and fascinating, complicated woman who spent most of the years between 1955 and 1992 in France, but now, despite her death in Paris last October, I feel that I've known her at least a little, and maybe quite a lot more than that.

It must have been shortly before her death that she herself sat for a portrait—the canvas being the camera and questioning of filmmaker Marion Cajori.

Perhaps the first thing you notice in the 58-minute "Joan Mitchell: Portrait of an Abstract Painter is the contrast between the subject's weathered, once-beautiful face—the face, in tree bark, of a survivor—and the delicate floral weave of a whole shimmering sequence of her paintings.

"She has a burning sensibility, one that is skinned alive," says some critic or other within the film, a Frenchman—I did not catch the name. Mitchell herself reduces her artistic contribution, with a shrug, to: "A mixture of love and death and all that crap, you know." Earlier on, she has said: "They call me *sauvage* ... and there are lots of things women can't do. Being a *sauvage* is one of them." Again: I don't paint well out of violence or anger. I don't like that at all. Hitler doesn't inspire me."

But she has, if not her angers, then her formidable tartness, her distinct and manifest will. She does not suffer fools gladly, not even foolish questions from the maker of this film.

She was a product, Joan Mitchell, first of Chicago ("all my paintings start with Lake Michigan") and of a self-made, highly competitive father ("I thought painting would take me completely out of competition, free me from him forever"), then of the great, exciting Cedar Bar era of the 1950s.

"De Kooning, Kline, I thought they were marvelous, I wanted to be part of them. In Washington Square I would walk my dog. [Hans] Hofmann would go by and tip his hat.

'Mitchell, why aren't you working?' ... People were nice to me because I *was* a female, and no threat to anybody."

But being female, "you do what the man wants, don't you?" After marriage to and from publisher Barney Rosset, there was the painter Jean-Paul Riopelle. "I never wanted to move here"—to France, but France was where Jean-Paul wanted to stay. "He was my 24-year live-in, okay? And then he took off with the dog sitter. That's the way it was."

She lived and worked in Vetheuil, overlooking Monet's gardens on the Seine, and always denied that Monet had anything to do with her own work, though to more eyes than just mine it clearly did. But so did Van Gogh, Cezanne, Matisse. "You love Matisse?" the filmmaker plods on, and earns by way of a pained response: "He's one of the few painters who has color *and* light—oh, he's fabu ... I wouldn't *look* at it. Come on baby."

Paired on the program with Joan Mitchell is Amy Harrison's "Guerrillas in Our Midst," a 35-minute report on the radical female underground that in 1984 started invading galleries and museums in gorilla masks and postering the city with such as:

"The Advantages of Being a Woman Artist 1. Working without the pressure of success. 2. Not having to be in shows with men. 3. Having an escape from the art world in your free-lance jobs. 4. Knowing your career might pick up after you're 80 ..."

What they do is a pain in the ass to the Establishment—some of it voiced here—and considerable fun for all the rest of us. Serious fun, as the saying goes.

NEWSDAY, 4/14/93, Part II/p. 67, John Anderson

There are few stylistic parallels to draw between "Joan Mitchell: Portrait of an Abstract Painter" and "Guerrillas in Our Midst." but the two documentaries make for a near-perfect double bill: a cool, confidently-wrought picture of a pioneering female artist, and a funny/angry protest by women in gorilla masks against discrimination in the Art World. Regardless of the order in which you watch them, they validate each other's point of view.

Joan Mitchell, who was a kind of second-generation Abstract Expressionist, died in Paris last October, but left a wealth of paintings that, although abstract, evoke the Impressionists in their potent use of color and light. And director Marion Cajori is more than generous with those pictures, allowing them to dominate the film while even Mitchell's acerbic self is forced to play a secondary role.

And that isn't easy: Mitchell was not, we see, an easy person, although the interviewers in "Portrait of an Abstract Artist" purposely push her past her limited reserve, to a point where the laconic, no-nonsense Mitchell, using one crutch to get around, has to explain things she feels should be obvious: How each letter of the alphabet has its own color, for instance, or how her paintings work. She doesn't suffer fools gladly, it's clear, but the questions, and Mitchell's re-action to them, take us beyond the artist's imperious facade.

Where Cajori is so wonderful is getting Mitchell to explain her life without, wringing it out of her, or hammering it into our heads. One of the more splendid moments in a splendid film comes when Mitchell tells about her parents, her mother, she says, was a poet, and deaf; she often wondered what it was like to be in her soundless head. We wonder, in turn, whether the mother's deafness sparked the daughters visual genius. The father, a man ungenerous with love, invites no such musings. Mitchell turned to abstract paintings, she says, so he, wouldn't be able to dispute what her paintings were about.

Although she speaks with affection for fellow New York painters like Franz Kline, Ad Reinhardt and Hans Hofmann, she was never "one of the boys." Nor did she receive, during her lifetime, the kind of recognition she deserved. And this is the kind of thing that has the Guerrilla Girls, a clandestine band of women artists and poster-hanging museum terrorists, so upset.

In "Guerrillas in Our Midst," they use humor to torpedo the political and financial moorings of New York's fabled art establishment (galleries, agents and people with money). And they turn the words of gallery owners like Mary Boone, who insist that the black, Hispanic and female artists simply aren't out there, against the speakers themselves.

A playful and polished 35-minute film, "Guerrillas in Our Midst," fails to show us much of the art it's promoting, but it makes a couple of button-pushing points: that there is a white male-run system in place through which artists, mostly white and male, make their way through the ranks to gallery and museum shows; and that there is a romantic fascination among art collectors with the idea of the *male* artist, probably drunk and starving in a garrett, turning out brilliant, tortured works of art.

But the Guerrilla Girls, who use their hairy gorilla masks and unknown identities to exploit the same hype-propelled system they condemn, don't quite follow through: They may want the business someday, but it seems clear that the real problem is buyers and sellers who wouldn't know good art if it jumped up and hit them on the wallet.

VILLAGE VOICE, 4/20/93, p. 58, Kathy Deacon

Wearing gorilla suits and kinky gorilla masks—and stockings—the Guerrilla Girls targeted the corrupt art gallery/museum cartel that reached its zenith in the boom-boom '80s. Their posters plastered about Soho cited grim statistics about the art world's virtual exclusion of women artists, and its racism. Amy Harrison's *Guerrillas in Our Midst* is a fleeting 35-minute documentary about this rare bit of '80s effrontery.

In one of the film's priceless interviews, 80s art mogul Mary Boone attempts to describe her m.o. for selecting the artists she will promote. "It has a lot to do with the work, even more with the artist," she says. "Sometimes you meet them at a party." This ad hominem approach produced the decade's sexy male art stars. Yet somehow the only stock-in-trade for women and blacks was their art, which the prominent art dealers who talk to the camera assert wasn't good enough.

Too bad the film is not longer because it raises so many issues: the nepotistic bonds between the galleries and the major museums' society-ridden boards of directors; the use of art by the rich to fudge the value of their assets; the art world conspiracy to promote neo-expressionism as the dominant style of the 1980s. Harrison is in complete sympathy with the Girls' attempts to reform a system that should possibly be nuked. "Salon des Refusés" anybody?

Guerrillas is paired with an hour-long documentary tribute to a woman who did obtain a measure of art world success. *Joan Mitchell: Portrait of an Abstract Painter* was filmed in Mitchell's home in France before her death from lung cancer last year. Having attained the inner sanctum of the New York School in the '50s and perfected her luminous style of abstract expressionism, she is a lonely uprooted soul, leading a solitary existence with her beloved dogs, amused yet slightly disappointed by interviewers' attempts to get her to intellectualize her purely emotional art. As the film progresses the focus gradually shifts to the work itself; there is frame after frame of Mitchell's canvases of magnificent liberated color. You don't read it, it just is.

Also reviewed in:
NEW YORK TIMES, 4/14/93, p. C14, Stephen Holden

JOEY BREAKER

A Skouras Pictures release.   *Producer:* Amos Poe and Steven Starr.   *Director:* Steven Starr. *Screenplay:* Steven Starr.   *Director of Photography:* Joe DeSalvo.   *Editor:* Michael Schweitzer. *Music:* Paul Aston.   *Music Editor:* Ray Palagy.   *Sound:* Tom Paul and (music) Todd Gerard. *Sound Editor:* Janet Lund Robbins.   *Casting:* Deborah Aquila.   *Production Designer:* Jocelyne Beaudoin.   *Art Director:* Noemi Di Corcia.   *Set Dresser:* Monica Bretherton and Philip J. Clarke.   *Costumes:* Jessica Haston.   *Make-up:* Chris Laurence.   *Running time:* 92 minutes. *MPAA Rating.* R.

CAST: Richard Edson (Joey Breaker); Cedella Marley (Cyan Worthington); Fred Fondren (Alfred Moore); Erik King (Hip Hop Hank); Gina Gershon (Jennie Chaser); Philip Seymour Hoffman (Wiley McCall); Mary Joy (Esther Trigliani); Sam Coppola (Sid Kramer); Michael Imperioli (Larry Metz); Olga Bagnasco (Karina Danzi); Laurence Mason (Lester White); Seth Gilliam (Jeremy Brasher); John Costelloe (Randy Jeter); Sunday Theodore (Morissa Marker); George Bartenieff (Dean Milford); Parker Posey (Irene Kildare); Christopher Logan

Healy (Mike Dale);   James Dickson (Hollywood Producer);   Alison Moir (Actress on Street);
Joe Gioco (Karina's Manager);   Larry Mart (Agent in Audience);   Beverly Burchett (Mineola
Waitress);   Anthony Ventola (Astro Waiter).

LOS ANGELES TIMES, 8/20/93, Calendar/p. 8, Kevin Thomas

Steven Starr's "Joey Breaker" is a jaunty little movie that's full of surprises and, beneath its
humor, an unexpected and refreshing seriousness. Richard Edson has the title role as a brash
Manhattan-based talent agent for whom a telephone is virtually an appendage. Having worked
his way up from the mail room, Joey, after 10 years, is nearing the top of a tough profession he
clearly loves: the man gets a terrific charge out of the constant wheeling and dealing.

Joey seems contented when a series of events impact upon his life more than he—or we—at first
realize. One of the senior agents (Mary Joy) successfully coaxes him to come along with her to
have lunch with her friend Alfred (Fred Fondren), a librarian now housebound with AIDS. He
doesn't really have all that much contact with Alfred, but the dying man does make him aware
of his own mortality and that life can be a matter not of regretting what you have done but what
you haven't done.

Then there's the ambitious colleague (Gina Gershon) who his warmly paternal boss (Sam Coppola) has ordered him to get along with but whom he inadvertently insults, with serious
consequences. Most important, however, is his chance meeting with Cyan (Cedella Marley), a
lovely young Jamaican working as a waitress to put herself through nursing school. Much to his
shock he finds himself falling in love with her just at the point that she wants to back off, dead
certain of her own career goals and feeling that he really doesn't know who he is.

For all the fun Starr has with the inside show-biz tactics and strategies, he confronts, via Joey,
all workaholics by questioning values and priorities. Starr, a former William Morris agent, is
clearly a man who has thought through what's important to him, and this quest informs his entire
film.

In its modest and engaging way "Joey Breaker" challenges the way so many of us live our
lives. In the course of the film he manages to present his show-business types as real people,
hard-driving and ruthlessly competitive, but not the usual stereotypical barracudas. He also reveals
how AIDS has affected the entertainment industry in ways that might not occur to us: He maps
out a TV career for a promising client, Hip Hop Hank (Erik King) only to discover that the man,
an ex-con, is terrified of taking a standard insurance exam because of what it might disclose about
his HIV status.

Starr is to be congratulated for filling the screen with smart people who speak intelligently and
for the ensemble performances he draws from his cast. Marley is appealing in her film debut, and
the role of Joey shows that Edson, in his biggest screen role to date, has what it takes to carry
a picture; also notable, Philip Seymour Hoffman as Joey's sharp, eager assistant.

As solid as it is, "Joey Breaker" (rated R for language) not surprisingly bears the marks of a
debut feature. Granted that this is a New York movie, which means it's going to be highly verbal,
but even so it tends to get bogged down with too much trade talk in its first third or so. Also,
Joey's entire odyssey could have been more fully developed and contained a bit of foreshadowing.
Nevertheless, "Joey Breaker," which features Bob Marley songs and a reggae score, possesses
a welcome and engaging substance along with its humor.

NEW YORK POST, 5/14/93, p. 33, Jami Bernard

Joey Breaker is a fast talker who embodies the best and worst of what it takes to be a New
York entertainment agent—a slickness that borders on self-parody and the ability to get the deal
done. You won't be sure whether to laugh at Joey or hire him.

If you hire him, you'll get the best deal in town—lots of money, points, exposure. Unless
you're terrible at what you do, in which case Joey will gladly take your money while doing
nothing for you. The game is to get dibs on the hottest properties, end of game.

If you choose instead to laugh at Joey, the laughter will get tiresome, because Joey Breaker—his
name sounds like a CB handle—is one of those awkward but uniquely talented people for whom
agenting is the only sensible big job. He's not good with people, but he's a mover and a shaker,

so he may as well be moving and shaking on behalf of someone's career than let all that narcissistic energy go to waste.

From the look of the posters on his walls, Joey either works for Miramax or this is some sort of joke at the indie film company's expense.

Richard Edson, a very distinctive-looking actor, talks the talk and walks the walk. There is never a restful moment for him. When he is not thoroughly enjoying a vicious bidding war over a script, he is cruising the room for new clients. It's hard to believe that the beautiful, principled waitress Cyan (Cedella Marley) would fall for such a man. But hey, director Steven Starr wrote the script, and it's based loosely on his own experiences as an agent-turned-filmmaker, so he gets to say that the waitress falls for Joe, and so be it.

In Starr's favor, and largely due to the charisma of Marley (yes, she's Bob's daughter), the waitress is a fully functioning character—at least as interesting as Joey, if not more so.

There is a whole subplot having to do with Joey's learning his humanity through bringing meals to an AIDS sufferer, these scenes dwelt upon uncomfortably, like public service announcements. Although the film is not technically about AIDs, it appears to be inspired by the fear of it—if the end is coming soon, you may as well live more happily in the meantime.

"Joey Breaker" makes agents seem like pond scum, but you have to admire the rapid-fire, almost exotic insiders' dialect they use. "Ciao," says one on leavetaking, "Double ciao," says another. "Bye'...," they purr lingeringly into their telephones, letting expletive-filled conversations lapse into an insidious New Age lull. It's like the brunch scene from Steve Martin's "L.A. Story" extended into a feature-length movie.

Luckily, the movie doesn't buy into the ridiculous concept that leopards, change their spots so easily; the ending is more realistically rewarding than you'd guess.

By the way, the movie is chock-a-block with "agent" jokes. What's the difference between a catfish and an agent? One is a bottom-feeding mudsucker. The other is a fish.

NEWSDAY, 5/14/93, Part II/p. 77, John Anderson

"This cup of coffee could change your life ..."

"Jenny, we own this town ..."

"Stars come and go, but agents are forever ..."

"Open your eyes, Joey, there's more to life than making a deal ..."

"Who are you, Joey Breaker?"

Yes, who are you, Joey Breaker. A man? A lifestyle? A subculture? A Christmas catalog from Cliches 'R' Us?

"Joey Breaker" is actually a kind of East Coast version of "The Player," without the direction, the acting, the script or the dark view. Not exactly a glimpse inside the high-powered world of creative management, it isn't exactly a character study either. Or a comedy.

Perpetrated by former William Morris agent Steven Starr, the film concerns "Morgan Creative" agent Joey Breaker (Richard Edson), a cutthroat New York script agent who loves no one and lives for the deal. In the course of being a weasel he comes to learn something about himself, to appreciate others' feelings, to fall in love. And we learn how to sleep in public places that smell like rancid popcorn.

The problem with the film, besides the execution, is that Joey is never established as anything to begin with. He's certainly not smooth, charming or particularly savvy; he's awkward, and not familiar with either human nature or popular culture. So how did he become such a hot shot in his kind of business? And how can we appreciate the changes he goes through when he's such a cipher to begin with?

"Joey Breaker" is the kind of movie that makes you tired, thinking about the waste. Cedella Marley, daughter of Bob, makes her screen debut with precocious assurance; Edson does what he can with very little, as does Gina Gershon, as Joey's rival, Jenny. (Gershon, coincidentally, played a similar character in "The Player.") And Fred Fondren, in the movie's best moments, plays Alfred, an AIDS patient who brings out Joey's humanity. But it's for naught. "Joey Breaker" has a popping, Bob Marley-intensive score, but all the reggae in the world isn't moving this baby.

VILLAGE VOICE, 5/18/93, p. 66, Beth Coleman

A movie agent meets a wise but angry PWA, a beautiful waitress training to be a nurse, and a talented but poor comic, and becomes a nicer guy. It's as earnest as it seems: Joey Breaker (Richard Edson), white, straight, leaves the shark-eat-shark world of film and $$$ and retires to a tropical island with Cyan (Cedella Marley), his bonny Jamaican GF, after he discovers that you can't buy happiness.

Writer and director Steven Starr left a cushy power gig at William Morris Agency himself to follow his bliss and make his movie. It seems unkind to mock such a sincere Rousseauian dream. So I'll just stand befuddled. Perhaps Starr didn't see *Unforgiven* and doesn't have a clue as to how to decenter a patriarchal subject to make an intriguing flick. Or maybe Starr just really liked *Something Wild* and wanted to remake it interracial, this time with Sister Carol getting the guy instead of Melanie.

It is nice to see a film in which there are more than two gay men without it being solely about AIDS, or *La Cage aux Folles*. Beware, though, of liberalism bearing gifts. Joey struggles with his homophobia, but replaces his former fear with a friendly patronizing.

As much as Richard Edson's sad face soothes the eye, the ¾ distance from which much of the film is shot, the hokiness of a corporate guy being saved by the broke, the overall banal wistfulness of Joey counteract the film's smaller goods. For the luv of Pete, he arrives at a costume party in a Rasta Man outfit and Cyan says without flinching, "Yah look great, man!"

Also reviewed in:
NEW YORK TIMES, 5/14/93, p. C19, Stephen Holden
VARIETY, 3/22/93, p. 53, Lawrence Cohn

JOSH AND S.A.M.

A Castle Rock Entertainment release in association with New Line Cinema of a City Light Films production. *Executive Producer:* Arne L. Schmidt. *Producer:* Martin Brest. *Director:* Billy Weber. *Screenplay:* Frank Deese. *Director of Photography:* Don Burgess. *Editor:* Chris Lebenzon. *Music:* Thomas Newman. *Music Editor:* Bob Badami and Bill Bernstein. *Sound:* Douglas Axtell and (music) John Vigran. *Sound Editor:* Teri E. Dorman and John Larsen. *Casting:* Carrie Frazier and Shani Ginsberg. *Production Designer:* Marcia Hinds-Johnson. *Art Director:* Bo Johnson. *Set Designer:* Keith Neely. *Set Decorator:* Jan Bergstrom. *Set Dresser:* Katherine Lucas, Rick Lambert, and Peter M. Gurski. *Costumes:* Jill M. Ohanneson. *Make-up:* Hallie D'Amore. *Stunt Coordinator:* Gary Combs. *Running time:* 98 minutes. *MPAA Rating:* PG-13.

CAST: Jacob Tierney (Josh); Noah Fleiss (Sam); Martha Plimpton (Alison); Stephen Tobolowsky (Thom Whitney); Joan Allen (Caroline); Chris Penn (Derek Baxter); Maury Chaykin (Pizza Man); Ronald Guttman (Jean-Pierre); Udo Kier (Tanning Salon Manager); Sean Baca (Curtis Coleman); Jake Gyllenhaal (Leon Coleman); Anne Lange (Ellen Coleman); Ann Hearn (Teacher); Christian Clemenson (Policeman); Allan Arbus (Businessman on Plane); Kayla Allen (Annette at Reunion); Nada Despotovich (Susan at Reunion); Brent Hinkley (Bill at Reunion); Jay McNally (Red Haired Kid #1); Daniel Tamberelli (Red Haired Kid #2); Don R. McManus (Calgary Airline Officer); Amy Wright (Waitress); Tyler Gurciullo (Kickball Pitcher); Raye Birk (Hotel Manager); Susan Norfleet (Reunion Coordinator); Annie McEnroe (Woman at Laudromat); Pamella D'Pella (Daughter on Bus); Harry Caesar (Father on Bus); Frank Dent (Canadian Father); Kate Benton (Canadian Mother); Valerie Wildman (Dallas Airline Officer); Bill Dunlevy (Dallas Desk Attendant); Bonnie Burgess (Flight Attendant #1); John Voldstad (Gas Station Attendant); Dhiru Shah (Bus Driver); Jason Edwards (Truck Driver); Deryn Warren (Calgary Ticket Agent).

LOS ANGELES TIMES, 11/24/93, Calendar/p. 4, Kevin Thomas

In its first 15 minutes the thoroughly winning "Josh and S.A.M. reveals just how painful divorce can be for children as poignantly as any movie imaginable. Joan Allen's elegant, brittle Caroline Whitney probably does love her two sons, 12-year-old Josh (Jacob Tierney) and 8-year-old Sam (Noah Fleiss), with whom she lives in California, but her top priority is to land a new husband, even if it does mean dumping them on her ex-husband Thom (Stephen Tobolowsky), who lives in Orlando with his second wife, who has two older sons by an earlier marriage.

Thom, however, is so intent upon creating in one instant one big opportunity he's oblivious to how badly his stepsons are treating Josh—not helping matters, of course, is his own declaration that he's disappointed that his older son has not become a macho, athletic type. With this one-two punch Josh and—Sam too—discover just how unimportant they can be to their parents.

Is it any wonder that Josh and Sam are soon heading for the Canadian border? Not surprisingly, they're plunged into a grand adventure. What is surprising—and gratifying—is the seriousness with which writer Frank Deese and director Billy Weber take Josh and Sam and their plight.

These are real kids with real challenges to overcome in their attempt to make a new life for themselves—not the least of the obstacles is their own very different and constantly clashing personalities. Sam is a sturdy but withdrawn youngster, a terrific athlete for whom sports has proven to be an inadequate outlet for his rages.

Both boys are exceptionally bright, but the older, more intellectual Josh has developed into a master storyteller, which more often than not means that he's become simply a highly skilled liar. Indeed, he persuades Sam to take off with him by convincing his appalled younger brother that he is in fact a Strategically Altered Mutant (S.A.M.), sold to the government by his parents as a child warrior.

Along their bumpy journey they're joined by Martha Plimpton's Alison, a resourceful runaway who's just enough older than Josh to seem a woman of the world to him. What these kids encounter is too diverting and ingenious (yet persuasive) to give away. The point is that the two brothers, forced to survive by their wits, come to care for each as they perhaps never would have otherwise.

While it's true that Alison and the brothers are breathtakingly articulate, they are believable because they are so exceptionally well-written and played. By now Plimpton's skill at playing smart, independent-thinking young women is well-known, but both Tierney, a Canadian in his U.S. film debut, and Fleiss, in his feature debut, are a revelation. Their brothers are so resilient, yet so vulnerable, so worthy of the affection and attention that they've been denied; the film does make you ponder about how incalculable the number of neglected kids must be.

Along with Allen and Tobolowsky, an experienced portrayer of jerks, Chris Penn makes a strong impression as a partying drunk the boys have the misfortune of meeting in the course of their trek. "Josh and S.A.M." (rated PG-13 for kids in jeopardy) is the kind of film that's likely to appeal to those who would never dream of seeing the "Home Alone" movies.

NEW YORK POST, 11/24/93, p. 34, Thelma Adams

Peculiar. That's the word that best describes "Josh and S.A.M."

It's not quite a kid's movie. There are too many odd and unpleasant touches: a discussion of death by lethal injection; a harrowing drive with a nasty drunk driver; and a mother who's an alternate selection of the shrew-of-the-month club.

And "Josh and S.A.M." doesn't have the star power, story line, or sophistication to satisfy adults. However, the movie has its brighter moments.

Twelve-year-old Josh (Jacob Tierney) and 8-year-old Sam (Noah Fleiss) are brothers. Their mother lives on the bad side of Beverly Hills and their father has a new family in Florida.

Generally unhappy about this development, Josh convinces his younger brother that Sam's a "Strategically Altered Mutant (S.A.M)," a child warrior created to fight America's secret wars. To escape their fate, the boys flee north to Canada.

First-time director, and longtime editor, Amy Weber paddles through a script by Frank ("The Principal") Deese. Since both young actors are making their American movie debut, the movie suffers from collective lack of experience.

Jacob Tierney, a young Canadian who appears in "Are You Afraid of the Dark?" on Nickelodeon, has the biggest part and must carry the movie on his shoulders. That Tierney doesn't quite cut it is not damning for an adolescent, but it doesn't help the film. The puffy-lipped actor is somewhat charm-impaired. Noah Fleiss as the chipmunk-cheeked toughie, Sam fares better and scores a higher cuteness quotient.

Actress Martha ("Parenthood") Plimpton appears like the shooting star Sam sees over Colorado. As the runaway Alison, she hooks up with the boys on the road.

Plimpton lifts the movie up. For the 20-odd minutes she's on screen it seems like "Josh and S.A.M." will actually take off. A scene outside of Timmy B's Reptile Ranch with Josh, Sam, and Alison is a genuine hoot, shaggy and funny and fresh.

Then, as suddenly as she arrived Alison hitches a ride going in the opposite direction of the boys and the movie sags anew. A talent is a terrible thing to waste, Martha. Tony Award winner Joan Allen is also squandered as the self-involved mother who tells her troubled 12-year-old "I need to take care of myself now."

This family picture is dysfunctional.

NEWSDAY, 11/24/93, Part II/p. 65, John Anderson

It's difficult to say who's more disturbed: 12-year-old Josh Whitney (Jacob Tierney), a sexually confused and deeply sarcastic child who hates shuttling between his divorced parents' homes; his 8-year-old brother, Sam (Noah Fleiss), who's sullen, withdrawn and prone to violence; or the makers of "Josh and S.A.M.," who apparently made a film about children without ever having met any.

One basic flaw is Sam's belief in anything Josh says. Another is Josh's rather loathsome personality. It's difficult to create a totally dislikable child character, so perhaps "Josh and S.A.M." has accomplished something. Other problems, though, include dialogue that might have been funny on paper, but sounds incredibly pretentious in the mouth of a 12-year-old, and a story that's on unsteady ground from the start.

The boys' problem, after all, is pretty basic to the late 20th Century, while their reactions are beyond extreme. Mom (Joan Allen), is neglectful, sure, and absorbed in her romance with Jean-Pierre (Ronald Guttman)—who seems like a gratuitous slap at the French. Their father, Thom (Stephen Tobolowsky), lives in Florida with his new wife and simian stepsons (Sean Baca and Jake Gyllenhaal), who call the unathletic Josh a "homo." One man's family.

Sam, who is athletically inclined, allies himself with the two apes, until Josh lures him back with a fantastic tale: Sam—or S.A.M.—is a "strategically altered mutant," Josh says, imbued with special powers and sold by his parents to the government as a "child warrior." This explains Sam's behavior to himself, although no 8-year-old would buy it as long as Sam does.

While in Florida, the boys learn that mom is going to marry Jean-Pierre and live for a year in Europe, and they'll be stuck with dad and the chimps. As they're en route to California to say goodbye to mom, their plane is forced to stop in Dallas, where the boys take off. At a hotel, they scam their way into a high school reunion, where Josh, who really is a liar, convinces Derek (Chris Penn) that he's Derek's son. When Derek, who's a little drunk, realizes the truth, he gets violent and Josh hits him over the head with a pool cue. Fearing he's dead, the boys hit the road in Derek's car.

So (puff, puff), anyway, this wants to be the prepubescent "Thelma & Louise" but nowhere near as involving. Noah Fleiss is endearing as Sam, Martha Plimpton does a nice turn as a hitch-hiker who becomes part of Josh's "S.A.M." story, but otherwise, it's a less than charming piece.

SIGHT AND SOUND, 6/94, p. 52, Louise Gray

Twelve-year old Josh and his eight-year old brother Sam are coping with life after their parents' divorce. When their mother Caroline goes on holiday with her fiance Jean-Pierre, the boys are shipped off to their father's house in Florida. Their father Thom is remarried with two more sons: they practise football passes together and Josh is teased for his unsporty demeanour. Sam sides with his stepbrothers Curtis and Leon. News arrives from Caroline that she and Jean-Pierre have married: they are spending the year abroad, and Josh and Sam are to remain in Florida until her return. Flying home to California to collect their things, Josh tells Sam that he is not a normal boy but a Strategically Altered Mutant—a kind of super-soldier—and that his parents have sold him to the Pentagon. Sam—or S.A.M., as he believes himself to be—has been activated for war. Frightened by his destiny, Sam is told that escape is possible via the intervention of the mysterious Liberty Maid, who runs an escape route to Canada.

When the boys' plane makes an unscheduled overnight landing in Dallas, they escape. Josh convinces a man at a high school reunion that he is their real father. The man, Derek, is furious when he finds out the truth and tries to attack them. Josh hits him with a snooker cue. Believing him dead, the boys steal Derek's car and set out for Canada. They meet Alison, a runaway hitchhiker, who takes on the role of Liberty Maid.

Alerted by Thom, the police are looking for the runaway boys. They reach the Canadian border, and Josh tells Sam that the story about S.A.M. is fictional. They are returned to their father, and their step-brothers are dissuaded from further bullying by stories of Josh and Sam's exploits.

"Adolescence is a confusing time in any boy's life," reads the blurb accompanying *Josh and S.A.M.*, and, if the truth be told, its heroes cope with it like any other boys found in the psychopathology textbooks. Josh is an accomplished liar, capable of spinning out such wild stories that truth and fiction merge confusingly. He's a loner: a computer whizz who can hack into electronic cash tills, and who uses the credit card numbers of his absent father to buy computer games, if not a paternal presence. Sam is similarly sidelined; classmates call him "alien" and "robot-man". "See, Mom!" shrieks Josh, as Sam's exasperated teacher returns the younger, belligerent boy home, "This is what happens when you drink while you're pregnant!" Happy families, indeed.

This is what's known as a feel-good movie. It tells us: hey! we've all felt alienated and unsure of our identities; we've all hated team games; sibling rivalry, ambivalent feelings about parents are normal; we've all had the experience of sexuality as a wobbly, frightening thing. Josh's stepbrothers think he's homosexual (evidence: he avoids their relentless, butt-slapping buddy-buddy football games). Interestingly, it is to escape being labelled homosexual that Josh is spurred to run away. And it is the same issue that resolves the movie. Returned to Florida, Sam tells the step-brothers that Josh beat up a guy. "He didn't like being called homosexual," says Sam. In the face of such overwhelming masculinity, the step-brothers retreat. Sam and Josh may not need therapy, but there's always a sequel to be made about Curtis and Leon's paranoiac ability to detect homosexual tendencies in anyone but themselves.

Running away is a perennial theme of children's fiction, and in this respect Josh and S.A.M. is no different from numerous texts in the literary and cinematic canon. Running away is a rite of passage, an entree into the world. What is different in this otherwise rather twee film is its savvy approach to psychological conflict. Sam's mute anger at his parents' separation finds in Josh's mutant story, a ready explanation for his aggressive feelings. The police and the Pentagon, *in loco parentis*, are perceived by the boys as persecutory agencies.

All this said, *Josh and S.A.M.* is hardly a *Night of the Hunter*. It is designed for a youngish audience and the dark, psychopathic world of Laughton's movie is kept carefully at bay. The good fairy in all this is Alison, the runaway teenager who assumes—for reasons that are never explained—the role of Liberty Maid. In fact, Alison is so sketchy a character that we learn precisely nothing about her. Presumably this is a piece of verisimilitude meant to reflect life on the road. Even so, such arbitrary realism seems rather out of place. As far as the plot is concerned, Alison exists for two reasons: to give Josh a cursory contact with females (no, nothing happens, but at least it puts paid to the implicit homosexual theme) and to transmogrify the brothers' sibling hostilities into a wholesome state of love.

What today's kids, weaned on weightier stuff than this, will take from this film is another matter. They'll soon realise that most Nintendo games have better plots than this, and *Home Alone* certainly has better jokes. Parents may be attracted to *Josh and S.A.M.* for the simple reason that a child's film ticket is considerably cheaper than a 50-minute hour with a juvenile shrink. Either way, don't hope for much.

Also reviewed in:
NEW YORK TIMES, 11/24/93, p. C12, Stephen Holden
VARIETY, 8/9/93, p. 35, Leonard Klady

JOY LUCK CLUB, THE

A Hollywood Pictures release. *Executive Producer:* Oliver Stone and Janet Yang. *Producer:* Wayne Wang, Amy Tan, Ronald Bass, and Patrick Markey. *Director:* Wayne Wang. *Screenplay:* Amy Tan and Ronald Bass. *Based upon the novel by:* Amy Tan. *Director of Photography:* Amir Mokri. *Editor:* Maysie Hoy. *Music:* Rachel Portman. *Music Editor:* Bill Abbott. *Choreographer:* Michael Smuin. *Sound:* Curtis Choy and (music) John Richards. *Sound Editor:* Rick Franklin, Albert Gasser, and Bill Angarola. *Casting:* Heidi Levitt and Risa Bramon Garcia. *Production Designer:* Donald Graham Burt. *Art Director:* Diance Kunce, Kwan Kit "Eddy" Kwok, and Jian Jun Li. *Set Decorator:* Jim Poynter. *Special Effects:* Frank W. Tarantino. *Costumes:* Lydia Tanji and Shu Lan Ding. *Make-up:* Valli O'Reilly and Guo Fang Ma. *Running time:* 135 minutes. *MPAA Rating:* R.

CAST: THE MOTHERS: Kieu Chinh (Suyuan); Tsai Chin (Lindo); France Nuyen (Ying Ying); Lisa Lu (An Mei); THE DAUGHTERS: Ming-Na Wen (June); Tamlyn Tomita (Waverly); Lauren Tom (Lena); Rosalind Chao (Rose); CAST: Chao-Li Chi (June's Father); Melanie Chang (June, Age 9); Victor Wong (Old Chong); Lisa Connolly (Singing Girl); Vu Mai (Waverly, Age 6-9); Ying Wu (Lindo, Age 4); Mei Juan Xi (Lindo's Mother); Guo-Rong Chen (Huang Tai Tai); Hsu Ying Li (Matchmaker); Irene Ng (Lindo, Age 15); Qugen Cao (Lindo's Father); Anle Wang (Lindo's Brother); Yan Lu (Lindo's Brother 2); Boffeng Liang (Pedicab Driver); William Gong (Tyan Yu); Diana C. Weng (Lindo's Servant); Yuan-Ho C. Koo (Matchmaker's Friend); Zhi Xiang Xia (Huang Tai Tai Servant); Dan Yi (Servant's Boyfriend); Christopher Rich (Rich); Nicholas Guest (Hairdresser); Kim Chew (Mrs. Chew); Jason Yee (Waverly's Brother); Ya Shan Wu (Lindo's Husband); Samantha Haw (Shoshana); Yu Fei Hong (Ying Ying, Age 16-25); Russell Wong (Lin Xiao); Grace Chang (Lin-Xiao's Opera Singer); Michael Paul Chan (Harold); Phillip Moon (Ken); Melissa Tan (Jennifer); Yi Ding (An Mei, Age 9); Emmy Yu (An Mei, Age 4); Vivian Wu (An Mei's Mother); Lucille Soong (Popo); You Ming Chong (An Mei's Uncle); Fen Tian (Auntie #1); Lena Zhou (Auntie #2); Jeanie Lee Wu (Auntie #3); Andrew McCarthy (Ted); Jack Ford (Mr. Jordan); Diane Baker (Mrs. Jordan); Tian Ming Wu (Wu Tsing); Elizabeth Sung (Second Wife); Eva Shen (An Mei's Nanny); Sheng Yu Ma (Suyuana's Twin daughter 1); Sheng Wei Ma (Suyuan's Twin Daughter 2).

CHRISTIAN SCIENCE MONITOR, 9/16/93, p. 11, David Sterritt

Asian movies and Asian themes are unusually prominent in world cinema just now.

On the international front, two Chinese films—"Farewell My Concubine" and "The Women From the Lake of Scented Souls"—have won top prizes at major festivals. On the theatrical circuit, American audiences are seeing "The Wedding Banquet" and preparing for the Broadway-based "M. Butterfly" and the exquisite South Korean drama "Why Has Bodlu-Dharma Left for the East?"

Of all the new Asian attractions, none has been more eagerly awaited than "The Joy Luck Club," based on Amy Tan's popular 1989 novel. It has now arrived, in a carefully produced adaptation that showcases Chinese talents on both sides of the camera—including director Wayne Wang, an experienced Chinese-American filmmaker, and Tan herself who wrote the movie with Hollywood screenwriter Ronald Bass.

The film is likely to please admirers of Tan's book, since it focuses on the same basic theme: the delights, disappointments, and dilemmas faced by Chinese-American mothers and daughters who grew up on opposite sides of the Pacific under vastly different circumstances.

Like the novel, the movie does a good deal of jumping around in time and space, telling not a single story but an interrelated group of tales, anecdotes, and reminiscences.

Also like the novel, the film never quite coalesces into a fully unified work, but uses its own fragmentation as a metaphor for the diversity of Chinese-American experience. Talky, episodic, and ripely sentimental, it invites us to understand its characters more through our emotions than our intellects. It's an appealing movie, but no more insightful than the bestseller that inspired it.

The title of "The Joy Luck Club" refers to a group of Chinese émigrés in San Francisco who have regular meetings to keep in touch, talk over their lives, and play rounds of mah-jongg in the traditional Chinese way.

The movie begins when young June is asked by the club to take the place of her mother, Suyuan, who recently died. This leads to June's discovery that her twin half-sisters, long thought to have perished during the Japanese occupation of China in the 1940s, are alive and hoping for a visit from their rediscovered American relatives.

June's preparations to meet them in China provide a framework for the rest of the film, which spends most of its time on numerous other yarns. Some are modern, revolving around June's contemporaries, while others look back to Asia and the early lives of the young women's mothers.

The movie is nothing if not varied, skipping between subjects ranging from forced marriage and domestic brutality in old China to unfulfilled ambition and the inequality of women in America today. The challenge of sustaining strong mother-daughter relationships is a constant concern, however.

Tan's novel is better at describing emotions, and the outward conditions they're connected to, than at probing the deeper mental and spiritual roots of her characters. The same can be said of Wang's movie, which substitutes engaging performances and picturesque images for the psychological analysis and social commentary he might have attempted.

While there is much to enjoy in the film, there is little to be learned from it beyond capably filmed details of Chinese dress, custom, and attitude.

Nor does it have the cinematic adventurousness that Wang revealed in his first feature, "Chan Is Missing," but hasn't equaled in his four subsequent pictures.

What entertainment value and emotional appeal the film does boast—and it's a lot—can be traced largely to its Asian and Asian-American cast. Besides Ming-Na Wen as June and Kieu Chinh as Suyuan, the performers include Tamlyn Tomita, Lauren Tom, and Rosalind Chao as the other young women and Tsai Chin, France Nuyen, and Lisa Lu as the mothers.

Amir Mokri did the camera work, which seems more authentic in intimate scenes than in occasional attempts at sweeping grandeur, and Rachel Portman composed the rather commonplace music. Oliver Stone and Janet Yang were the executive producers.

FILMS IN REVIEW, 1-2/94, p. 49, Harry Pearson

[*The Joy Luck Club* was reviewed jointly with *Farewell My Concubine*; see Pearson's review of that film.]

LOS ANGELES TIMES, 9/8/93, Calendar/p. 1, Kenneth Turan

If "The Joy Luck Club" doesn't make you cry, nothing will. In an age of contrived and mechanical sentimentality, its deeply felt, straight-from-the-heart emotions and the unadorned way it presents them make quite an impact. No matter how many hankies you bring with you, it won't be enough.

Though feeble attempts will be made to pigeonhole it as a women's picture, "The Joy Luck Club" is more accurately a humane film, one that makes a point of being honest and compassionate about its characters and unashamed about their feelings. If men think this is of no interest to them, the species is in worse shape than we thought.

A story of distance and how to bridge it, of painful gaps between both mothers and daughters and immigrant parents and U.S.-born children, "The Joy Luck Club" gets its strength and clarity from the best-selling novel by Amy Tan it is based on.

Working as a creative troika, Tan, co-screenwriter Ronald Bass (an Oscar winner for "Rain Man") and director Wayne Wang ("Chan Is Missing") have kept the quiet simplicity of style that is the core of Tan's book, honed and focused its emotional impact, and not attempted to soften the bitterness of the conflicts it portrays. (This has apparently led to a perplexing R rating for "strong depiction of thematic material.")

The film has also taken advantage of the powerful chord it struck in the Asian-American community in general and among performers in particular. While their names are largely unfamiliar to general audiences, the eight actresses who play the film's four pairs of mothers and daughters are not only the pick of several generations of acting talent but also women who understand these characters from the inside and know how to take advantage of the opportunities the roles present.

Though Hollywood conventional wisdom says that eight people's stories are too many for an audience to handle, especially if recognizable faces aren't involved, "The Joy Luck Club" manages to preserve each tale's individuality while bringing them all together with an almost casual skill.

Though each woman's experience is involving, it is what these experiences say en masse about the drama behind the fabled golden door of immigrant dreams that is most moving. "Joy Luck" shows what happens to hope in America, how inevitable the estrangement is between parents who came to save their children from suffering and children who, without that kind of distress, can't begin to imagine what made their difficult parents the way they are.

The film's tone is set by its opening voice-over, taken from the book's fable-like first paragraphs, where an old woman remembers a swan she once bought in Shanghai. The bird first symbolized her hopes for America, for a daughter who "would always be too full to swallow any sorrow" and finally her bafflement at ending up with an uncomprehending child who grew up "swallowing more Coca-Cola than sorrow."

"The Joy Luck Club" opens at a going-away party in San Francisco (Amy Tan is the first guest seen on screen) for June (Ming-Na Wen), leaving the next day for a trip to China. Together with three other Chinese women, each the mother of an American-born daughter, June's late mother Suyuan had begun the club, a weekly mah-jongg gathering of wives who considered the hope of getting lucky their only joy.

This party is the hub from which the stories of each of these eight women (including Suyuan, portrayed in flashback by Kieu Chinh, Vietnam's preeminent actress) radiate out like spokes. A chance remark will trigger a reverie, and mothers and daughters then tell their stories in voice-over and flashback. With as many as three actresses portraying the protagonists at different ages, this may sound complex, but Wang and editor Maysie Hoy (who worked on "The Player") bring it off with perfect naturalness and comprehension.

The mothers' stories are invariably the harsher ones, taking place as they do in the old country, a hopeless nightmare society where a woman was taught, in the words of one, "to desire nothing, to swallow other people's misery and eat her own bitterness."

Suyuan's tale involves the abandonment of children, that of Auntie Lindo (celebrated Chinese actress Tsai Chin), Suyuan's "best friend and archenemy," of an unfortunate arranged marriage. In their turn Auntie Ying Ying ("South Pacific's" France Nuyen) and Auntie An Mei (Lisa Lu, a veteran of both "One Eyed Jacks" and "The Last Emperor") tell equally agonized tales.

While Suyuan's daughter June and Auntie Lindo's daughter Waverly ("Come See the Paradise's" Tamlyn Tomita) get to relate stories of childhood rivalry, all four daughters, including Lena (Lauren Tom) and Rose (Rosalind Chao), talk of more adult difficulties, especially problems with the feckless men in their lives, troubles that stem in one way or another from the way their mothers have formed them. "I like being tragic, Ma," one of them says bitterly. "I learned it from you."

So the mothers, who became hard to survive their pain, are surprised to find their daughters uncomprehending and resentful when that strength of will is turned on them. "Nothing I can do can ever please you," says one daughter; "my mother always does this, she has the perfect countermove," says another. The mothers, accused of turning their eager hopes into stifling expectations, likewise feel misunderstood and unappreciated by children who have not experienced the past.

All this may sound too much on the soap opera side, but the film is saved from that by its absence of sentimentality (though not sentiment) and by the evenhanded but caring direction of Wayne Wang, who has done a notable job and even fit a location trip to China into a modest $10.6-million budget. If studios like Disney continue to be serious about cutting costs, "The Joy Luck Club" is evidence that giving films to experienced independent filmmakers like Wang rather than the usual indifferent rent-a-directors are the way to go.

NEW YORK, 9/20/93, p. 64, David Denby

The Joy Luck Club is an intimate epic about women: The faces of beautiful Chinese women, mothers and daughters, gaze across the generations searching for signs of love and the fulfillment of hopes. Adapted from Amy Tan's 1989 best-seller, this large-scale Hollywood production, which was directed by Wayne Wang, written by Tan and Ronald Bass, and cast with Chinese American actresses, has been constructed as if the entire meaning of life could be conveyed in the expressions of these extraordinary-looking women. The mothers, in particular, appear as powerful as goddesses, giving or taking away life, undermining or setting their daughters straight with just a few words.

Men are out of it, irrelevant; most of the world is irrelevant, too, mere static noise interrupting the essential, momentous communication between mothers and daughters. The female line is the main line, the power line. The movie could be dismissed as feminist wish fulfillment if it weren't so cunningly told.

The filmmakers have arranged the material as symmetrically as a Chinese courtyard: Four elderly women, having suffered immense hardships in pre-Communist China, escaped years ago to San Francisco; in the New World, each has raised one daughter, now in her thirties. The ruling metaphor of *The Joy Luck Club* is a folktale, gravely enunciated over the titles, about a duck that tried to become a goose and stretched its neck so far it became, instead, a swan—something more than hoped for. The daughters are creations of hope, but the mothers, consumed with old sorrows, mentally living in the Old Country as much as the new, cannot easily give them the approval they long for. Rigid perfectionists, the mothers leave the young women in a stew of self-doubt; until, that is, they magically give them their blessing. *The Joy Luck Club* is certainly a very unusual Hollywood movie, rigorous yet delicate, and I wish I could truly love it. But its tone remains relentlessly earnest, its meanings limited or wanly inspirational, and my emotions, rather than welling up, remained small.

The four elderly women of the Joy Luck club, meeting regularly to compete at mah-jongg and cooking, tell stories, the same stories over and over, sometimes about themselves as children in China, sometimes about *their* mothers. Then their daughters tell stories, too, of childhood miseries, of good and bad marriages. Each story centers on a moment of creation or self-destruction in a woman's life, the moment when her identity becomes fixed forever. A stunning, slender Chinese beauty, raped by a wealthy merchant and then rejected by her own family, accepts her role as the least prestigious of the rich man's four wives, and sacrifices herself to make her little daughter strong; two generations later, in America, her daughter's daughter gains strength by hearing this tale. At the climax of the stories, some transaction with a mother—an experience conveyed, a lesson made explicit—produces a transforming act by a daughter.

Formally, *The Joy Luck Club* is a superb achievement. The narrative moves serenely yet forcefully from one story to another, from mother to daughter and then back again, and the endless lines of fable are like powerful cords wound together. Amy Tan has a gift for curt, almost folkloric narration, for minimal but electrifying details and abruptly powerful emotions; and the movie preserves her gifts and her tone.

Wayne Wang, the Hong Kong-born director whose earlier films were good-natured but slight, has pulled together some impressive visual skills. In old China, a rigidly hierarchical society, women of the mothers' generation are controlled by a morality of denial and self-sacrifice. Yet a few rebel. Betrothed to a fleshy teenage boy who doesn't want her, Lindo (Tsai Chin) uses her wits to escape; Wang tells her story swiftly, setting it in starkly discomforting spaces. A recurring scene of refugee misery takes place in a dark-hued war landscape, with tufts of mist arising from sharply peaked mountains. Even in America, the older women speak against solid-color backgrounds, the colors reducing life to the essentials of choice, ego, act. There is something severe, exacting, and will-driven here, a refusal of sensuality, a flinty moral attitude toward experience—Chinese character, perhaps, or at least a Chinese tonality. Despite their bourgeois American trappings, the older actresses (including France Nuyen, from *South Pacific*) are lionesses with teeth and claws intact.

Yet the male characters, with one exception, are caricatures—heartless studs, prigs, or ham-fisted American louts who can't manage a pair of chopsticks. The gorgeous, suffering women marry these losers because they've been schooled not to value themselves. In America, however, there's a remedy: The mothers teach the lesson of self-worth. As far as we can see, that's all they teach their daughters. What a disappointment! The whole tremendous story of Chinese immigration to America, the struggle of cultures and values, comes down to *this*, to contemporary American banalities about self-esteem. *Don't let yourself be undervalued. Don't block out your own desires.* Self-esteem is the upbeat commercial message, and the young women, hearing the magic words from Mom, square their shoulders and face their difficulties. But can this be the only kind of strength or wisdom that mothers convey to daughters? If that's it, why not just give them a copy of Gloria Steinem's latest book?

NEW YORK POST, 9/8/93, p. 23, Michael Medved

"The Joy Luck Club" is such an audacious and honorable effort that most moviegoers will be willing to overlook its significant shortcomings.

For one thing, it's the first major studio film in memory to deal seriously with the Chinese-American experience. And it handles the tension between new world memories with such warm-hearted universality that, everyone with immigrant ancestors will instantly identify.

It's also that rarest of contemporary Hollywood projects: an intergenerational melodrama that focuses on relationships between mothers and daughters, not fathers and sons.

Like the handful of other recent women's pictures that explore these complex feminine connections ("Terms of Endearment" and "Steel Magnolias" come readily to mind), this film is both moving and manipulative. By its end the eight hard-working actresses who play the lead roles have spent so much of their screen time crying their eyes out that audience members will either be annoyed or (more likely) be enthusiastically weeping along with them.

Novelist Amy Tan collaborated with gifted screenwriter Ronald Bass ("Rain Man," "Gardens of Stone") to adapt her own best seller for the screen, and they've been remarkably respectful—perhaps too respectful—of the denseness and complexity of the book.

The movie begins with a going-away party in San Francisco for the beautiful and sensitive June (Ming-Na Wen), who is about to make her first trip to China to meet her long-lost half-sisters. Her mother has just died, and at the party June for the first time takes her mother's place in the "Joy Luck Club"—the group of four indomitable China-born ladies who have been gathering every week for decades for mah jong and conversation.

There follows a series of flashbacks that tell the story of each of these women in turn, and of joy and heartache with their headstrong American daughters. These tales involve a lurid, splashy range of events and emotions, including romance and betrayal, starvation and war, suicide and divorce, abandonment and reunion, sale into virtual slavery, and even the horrifying murder of an infant in order to punish a faithless husband.

It's all carried off with conviction and artistry thanks to the loving direction of Wayne Wang, who, in contrast to the spare, ironic style of his previous films ("Chan is Missing," "Eat a Bowl of Tea") displays a gift for larger-than-life story-telling.

"The Joy Luck Club" dazzles the eye with rich, colorful scenes literally bursting with life, and achieves a grandeur that is altogether astonishing in view of its modest $11 million budget.

The major problem with the film is that all its richness of plot and character will amount to a great deal of confusion for moviegoers who are unfamiliar with Amy Tan's novel. It's hard to keep the characters straight—not for the old racist reason that "all Asians look alike," but because the eight women in the story are played by some 17 different actresses who portray the characters at different stages in their lives.

Though the sheer scope of its ambitions makes "The Joy Luck Club" less than totally successful, it's hard to thing of a recent picture that has tried harder, or dared more.

NEWSDAY, 9/8/93, Part II/p. 50, Jack Mathews

The distribution arm of Walt Disney Pictures needs to pay closer attention to the calendar. The studio opened its Halloween film, "Hocus Pocus," in mid-summer, and now it's releasing the ultimate Mother's Day movie in September.

Women who harbor a regretful moment about their relationships with their mothers are advised to take a full box of Kleenex with them to Wayne Wang's "The Joy Luck Club," and those who take their mothers with them risk a double-drowning.

It didn't affect me quite that way, so to the editor who asked, "Is it a chicks' movie?," I guess it is. Amy Tan's best-selling novel, from which the story of four immigrant Chinese women and their Chinese-American daughters was adapted, burrows so deeply into the unique nature of the mother-daughter experience that it does close us boys out, at least at the deepest emotional level. Call it payback time for "Field of Dreams."

But the appeal of the individual stories being told transcends the gender gap, and though Wang ("Dim Sum") and Tan, who wrote the script with veteran screenwriter Ronald Bass ("Rain Man"), have not quite overcome the novel's disjointed structure, "The Joy Luck Club" has more than four times the power of the typical Hollywood family drama.

The title refers to a group of Chinese women who gather weekly in one of their four San Francisco homes to feast, laugh, play Mah Jong and weave tales, mostly to escape the memories of their harsh youths in China, and to find hope for the future.

Both the book and the movie open, perfectly, with the first Joy Luck Club meeting after the death of its founding member. The instant that June Woo (Ming-Na Wen) sits down to take over for her deceased mother, it is clear how great a culture gap exists between the two generations. And when June is told by her "Aunties" Lindo (Tsai Chin), An Mei (Lisa Lu) and Ying Ying (France Nuyen) that her mother's long-lost twin daughters, June's half-sisters, have been found in China, and that she must go to meet them, the journey begins for all of us.

An amazing journey it is, particularly those chapters set in China, where the Joy Luck four spent the first 20 or 30 years of their lives surviving a range of personal, political and social crises re-enacted in episodic flashbacks.

Each of the mother's stories is powerful enough for a movie of its own. One is forced to abandon her babies during a Japanese invasion. Another marries an abusive philanderer, whom she strikes out at in a way that maims her own soul. Another is forced into an arranged marriage with an impotent husband and beaten by her mother-in-law for not producing grandchildren. The fourth spends part of her childhood in the palace of a man who had raped and degraded her mother, then forced the mother to become one of his concubines.

The focus of these stories is also on the relationships between mothers and daughters, in this case on the knowledge and spiritual strength handed down in traditional Chinese culture. Later on, we see how those experiences helped shape the women's personalities and created the inevitable conflicts with their American-born daughters.

As a piece, "The Joy Luck Club" is the story of three generations of women, the first two from a Chinese culture where daughters are taught to trust, obey and reveres their mothers, the third from an American culture where rebellion and declarations of independence are rites of passage.

The clash between the four mother-daughter sets in the United States is palpable. The mothers resent their daughters' independence, and the daughters are embarrassed and frustrated by their mothers' loyalty to the past.

June's journey, which provides the dramatic thread for the string of stories, is much more than a trip across the Pacific; she follows a trail of personal discovery, learning, as the other daughters (played by Rosalind Chao, Lauren Tom and Tamlyn Tomita) will learn to varying degrees, that to really know their mothers, they first have to understand how their heritage has affected their own lives.

Hong-Kong born Wang, whose early, low-budget films were heralded for their honest depictions of Chinese-American families, and Tan, who is a contemporary of the four daughters in her novel, were a perfect team for this improbable major studio assignment. Together, they have dug right into the heart of the novel, and managed, on an obviously undersized budget, to get most of the book's rich detail on the screen.

The movie is less successful in telling the individual daughters' stories, and in cutting from one to the other, it begins to feel as murky and overwrought as a daytime soap. But the theme that is always there is that the women's lives are complicated by a Chinese heritage they are reluctant to appreciate or understand.

There are other problems. The China stories cry out for scope that the budget wouldn't allow. And Wang's reliance on trite flashback devices (zoom in tight on the face of someone lost in thought, lather on some loud sentimental music ...) is clumsily repetitive.

Still, "The Joy Luck Club" is cause for celebration. In an era when we're lucky to get four good women's stories a year from Hollywood, we're getting four—make that eight—in one movie.

NEWSWEEK, 9/27/93, p. 70, Laura Shapiro

Bring tissues, bring a whole box, you'll be passing it down the row to your sniffling, nose-blowing, red-eyed neighbors. "The Joy Luck Club," based on Amy Tan's 1989 best seller, wasn't particularly sad as a novel, but as a movie—get ready to cry yourself a river.

Four mother-daughter relationships are at the heart of the film. The mothers, born in China, have been playing mah-jongg together in San Francisco's Chinatown for years. Back in China, each was torn from her mother or child by war, madness or simply and horribly by custom. They rebuilt their lives in America, but their American-born daughters, now grown, have suffered losses of their own, trying to juggle the teachings of the old world and the new. All these stories unfold in flashback at a wonderfully unhurried pace. It makes for a long film—two and a half hours—but time flies when you're bawling your eyes out.

Not surprisingly, the mothers' stories are the most powerful. Their daughters' problems—identity crises and failed relationships suffered in gorgeous examples of Bay Area real estate—pack less of a wallop. With Auntie Lindo (Tsai Chin), for instance, we revisit a childhood of poverty. She's 4, round and bright-eyed, and her mother has been forced to promise her in marriage to a wealthy family. We see mother and daughter huddled over their bowls and chopsticks in a dark cottage. "Stop stuffing yourself," her mother chides. "No girl should eat so fast." And she takes a morsel from her own bowl and drops it into Lindo's. The child's face is solemn; she knows she is being trained and how much she is loved. At 15, she is delivered to her fate, mother and daughter in wordless agony. The marriage is disastrous; ultimately Lindo engineers a most resourceful escape. But years later she can't communicate the same message of love and discipline to her own daughter, Waverly (Tamlyn Tomita). In America there's a lot more interference on the line. Instead of an intimate shot of those two faces in a dark cottage, mother and daughter wrapped in mutual understanding, we see Lindo and a young Waverly (Vu Mai) arguing fervently in the streets of Chinatown.

Eventually, Waverly and her mother get through to one another, and so do the other mothers and daughters. These scenes of reconciliation—in a beauty parlor or over the kitchen sink—are a bit contrived, but they help to bring home, literally, the themes of loss and self-discovery first raised in the exotic locales of old China. Yet moments as gripping as Lindo's last look at her mother, or when a sick and desperate Suyuan leaves her babies under a tree in wartime, hardly need to be updated. Anguish on this scale is universal.

Melodramatic? Manipulative? Sure, at times, but great storytellers can get away with anything, and the trio behind this film are in that class. Director Wayne Wang ("Chan Is Missing") and screenwriters Ronald Bass ("Rain Man") and Tan herself have come up with a shamelessly irresistible tale. The first-rate cast is another treat. Indulge yourself.

SIGHT AND SOUND, 4/94, p. 44, Leslie Felperin Sharman

A *bon voyage* party is held for June, a young Chinese-American woman about to visit China to meet her long lost half-sisters, the daughters of her recently deceased mother, Suyuan. Scenes from the party are intercut with long flashbacks to episodes in the lives of June, her mother, her mother's three friends Lindo, Ying Ying and An Mei, and their respective daughters Waverly, Lena, and Rose.

The first flashback shows June as a child, giving a piano recital at which she performs badly, providing the genesis for her feelings of inadequacy in the face of her mother's expectations for her. Like their mothers, June and Waverly have a lifelong rivalrous friendship that resurfaces later in life. Another sequence reveals that Suyuan had to abandon her twin baby girls, June's half-sisters, during the war.

The next twinned pair of flashbacks concerns Lindo and Waverly. Lindo's story reveals how she was forced into an arranged marriage in China that she managed to escape through the clever ploy of invoking ancestral warnings. Waverly had been a chess prodigy as a child. As an adult, she struggles to get her mother to accept her independence, symbolised by her marriage to a Caucasian man. In the third pair of flashbacks, Ying Ying's unhappy marriage in China, which ended with her drowning her own son, is contrasted with her daughter Lena's sterile marriage to an affluent architect. Ying Ying helps Lena become strong enough to leave her marriage and find happiness with a new man.

An Mei, whose concubine mother committed suicide so that An Mei might have a more secure position in the extended family, is compared to her daughter Rose, whose marriage withers because of Rose's passivity. The marriage is shown to have been saved by Rose learning to be more assertive through guidance from her mother. At last, a more extended version of Suyuan's story is shown, explaining the terrible hardships she endured escaping Kweilin during the Japanese invasion, and why she abandoned her babies in the hope that they might be found by someone more capable of caring for them. Bearing presents and mementos of her mother, June goes to China where she meets her now middle-aged sisters and promises to tell them all about their mother, who they feel is still with them in spirit.

The cliched opinion with which Westerners often malign Chinese food is that no matter how much you eat, you never feel completely full. This slander isn't always true in culinary terms, but the analogy seems apt in the case of *The Joy Luck Club*. It's a rich, multi-course movie, with plenty of tasty bits, but by the end its sweet and sour sentimentality becomes a little cloying, and you find yourself still yearning for something a little more substantial on the end of your chopsticks.

Part of the problem is that Amy Tan's novel, on which it is faithfully based, though often quite likable, is not that meaty a work to begin with. The fascination induced by the stories of the mothers' lives in China is dulled by the rather more banal tales of the daughters' American lives. The prose style's mix of Sino-accented narration and self-help group confession tends towards monotony, despite efforts to create a sense of multi-accented diversity. The same dilemma afflicts the film. The Chinese sequences tend to form a homogenous tapestry of brightly-coloured suffering, while the American sections, though more visually differentiated, end up sometimes seeming like scenes from an uneventful soap opera. Tan collaborated closely on the screenplay and so must be held partly responsible both for sharpening the dialogue and for cranking up the melodrama in some of the stories. Though the use of voice-over narration is generally effective, some passages incorporated verbatim from the book—like a metaphor which likens family patterns to a flight of stairs—sound painfully literary when spoken. In fact, it should have been faced that it was a little trite the first time round.

The intricate emotional tugs-of-war between mothers and daughters would be a challenge to any film-maker, and given the ethnic profile of the film, Wayne Wang is probably better qualified than anyone else to meet it. His previous work, including *Dim Sum, Eat a Bowl of Tea*, and *Life is Cheap ... But Toilet Paper is Expensive* has displayed an acute sensitivity to character and the subtleties of Chinese, American and Chinese-American cultures, shot through with a wry sense of humour. Backed this time with big bucks from Oliver Stone and Walt Disney, his unique style is muffled in favour of a glossy, mainstream aesthetic that's always highly competent, if not a little bland. Still, small quirky touches shine through, like a split-second shot of Wang regular Victor Wong and a minor character asleep during a fiery argument at a dinner table, or the bouncy exuberance of the scene where Lindo, bursting with pride, carries a copy of *Life* magazine with Lena's face on the cover down the street so that everyone can see it. In light of the breadth of material, Wang keeps things ticking along very nicely.

Considering how few movies with almost all-Asian casts have been made in the US, perhaps one ought to be more grateful to *The Joy Luck Club* for breaking the ground with such an accessible story. It has also provided an opportunity for an impressive roster of women actors to do more complex roles than the usual sort of parts written for Asians. A droll mention of 'racist movies' like *The World of Susie Wong*—in which Tsai Chin, Lisa Lu, and France Nuyen have all performed in the past—is a reminder of how much the representation of Asian women has progressed since the 50s. This, as well as Oliver Stone's own *Heaven & Earth*, has provided some modest reward for whole careers spent largely as walk-on washerwomen, Liat in *South Pacific*, and extras in *M*A*S*H*. The strength of the performances, especially Tsai Chin's, ameliorates many of the film's faults as a whole. Though a slight debt to Chinese film-makers like Zhang Yimou and Chen Kaige is felt in the texture of the cinematography, at heart *The Joy Luck Club* remains an old-fashioned Hollywood woman's picture, the kind I'd go see with my mother and a big box of hankies.

VILLAGE VOICE, 9/21/93, p. 64, Manohla Dargis

A Chinese ghost story by way of Hollywood, Wayne Wang's *The Joy Luck Club* is about mothers and daughters haunted by history, maternal and otherwise. Based on Amy Tan's runaway bestseller, it's a stately, silky juggling act, one that asks but never quite answers what we talk about when we talk, whisper, and lie about love.

The multigenerational weepy opens with an apocryphal story about a swan feather a woman carries from China to show her daughter, a sign she claims of "all my good intentions." The woman was Suyuan (Kieu Chinh). Now, months after her death, her daughter June (Ming-Na Wen), a woman who knew her mother even less than she knows herself, has gathered together with family and friends on the eve of a trip to China.

The Joy Luck Club is the name Suyuan and her three best friends, June's adopted "aunties," gave themselves when they joined together for weekly rounds of mah-jongg, gossip, history, and hope. Like her friends, Suyuan left her spirit in China, a wound she would try to fill with hope for the American-born June. Over the years, Suyuan would tell June about lost twin girls, babies she'd left behind in the war-torn countryside, babies her daughter accuses her of murdering. As the film unfolds, June tries to reconcile her past by returning, as it were, to the motherland.

Multigenerational stories are tough to pull off, and *The Joy Luck Club* risks narrative overload with eight intertwining stories. Unfortunately the results are needlessly, numbingly schematic (the screenplay was written by Tan and Ron Bass). Unlike the book, *The Joy Luck Club* movie lumbers from one mother-daughter dyad to another, producing a sensation not unlike watching a freight train pass, boxcar by boxcar. It's disappointing Wang doesn't brandish some of the formal virtuosity here that he exploited in his loopy *Life Is Cheap ... But Toilet Paper Is Expensive*. Instead, confined to a structure that prevents great flings of cinematic fancy, he lavishes attention on individual anecdotes, shaping and polishing them into epics in miniature. Which is one reason why the China tales, especially Suyuan's and An Mei's (Lisa Lu), are far more successful than the ones stateside.

Wang has a feel for historical nuance, whether the backdrop is a peasant home, a traditional wedding, or something far more ambitious, say, fleeing multitudes. What he can't salvage are the daughters or their stories. Each loses ground, though this has less to do with Wang's sturdy hand than his material. No wonder. After all, a child's yuppie agonies just don't hold up next to a mother's arranged marriage, her brutal husband, or lost babies.

One of the truest lessons in *The Joy Luck Club* is how the past fuels the future. Auntie Lindo's adventures in matrimony are wildly diverting, but while they gave her character they sucked the life out of her daughter, Waverly (Tamlyn Tomita). A chess prodigy who once made the cover of *Life* ("Could Bobby Fischer Destroy the Chinese Terror?"), the adult Waverly can't shake disappointment, hers or mother's. Starved for approval, she monitors Lindo's every gesture for the smallest sign of love, acceptance, consent. Their turning point occurs during a showdown at a beauty parlor, as mother and daughter each stake a claim to righteousness, unveiling psychic wounds like opposing martyrs. From childhood to childhood, misery to misery, the film scales a pyramid of suffering in which nothing and no person is to blame, neither the culture that promised Lindo into a loveless marriage, nor the mother who crammed so many good intentions into her daughter there was no room left for the child.

"You don't know the power you have over me," Waverly laments. "Now," smiles Lindo, swallowing the canary, "you have made me happy." At times like this, the film is a terrible cheat, dissolving into an encounter session with some half dozen women, all of whom radiate the feel-good glow of successful therapy. As it smooths out the rough edges and stitches up misery, *The Joy Luck Club* smothers hurt, forcing down pain like a pillow on a mewling baby.

Also reviewed in:
CHICAGO TRIBUNE, 9/17/93, Friday/p. C, Johanna Steinmetz
NATION, 10/4/93, p. 365, Stuart Klawans
NEW YORK TIMES, 9/8/93, p. C15, Janet Maslin
VARIETY, 9/13/93, p. 32, Todd McCarthy
WASHINGTON POST, 9/24/93, p. C1, Hal Hinson
WASHINGTON POST, 9/24/93, Weekend/p. 42, Desson Howe

JUDGMENT NIGHT

A Universal Pictures release of a Largo Entertainment presentation in association with JVC Entertainment. *Executive Producer:* Lloyd H. Segan and Marilyn Vance. *Producer:* Gene Levy. *Director:* Stephen Hopkins. *Screenplay:* Lewis Colick. *Story:* Lewis Colick and Jere Cunningham. *Director of Photography:* Peter Levy. *Editor:* Timothy Wellburn. *Music:* Alan Silvestri. *Music Editor:* Kenneth Karman. *Sound:* Don Johnson and (music) Dennis S. Sands. *Sound Editor:* Bob Newlan. *Casting:* Judy Taylor and Lynda Gordon. *Production Designer:* Joseph Nemec, III. *Art Director:* Dan Olexiewicz. *Set Designer:* Duncan Kennedy and William J. Law, III. *Set Decorator:* John Dwyer. *Special Effects:* Terry Frazee. *Costumes:* Marilyn Vance-Straker. *Make-up:* Rick Sharp. *Stunt Coordinator:* Walter Scott. *Running time:* 109 minutes. *MPAA Rating:* R.

CAST: Emilio Estevez (Frank Wyatt); Cuba Gooding, Jr. (Mike Peterson); Denis Leary (Fallon); Stephen Dorff (John Wyatt); Jeremy Piven (Ray Cochran); Peter Greene (Sykes); Erik Schrody (Rhodes); Michael Wiseman (Travis); Michael DeLorenzo (Kid); Relioues Webb (Dre); Will Zahrn (Charley); Eugene Williams (Buck); Christine Harnos (Linda Wyatt); Galyn Gorg (Clarissa); Angela Alvarado (Rita); Lauren Robinson (Angie); Doug Wert (Freeway Driver); Rachel Watt (Driver's Girlfriend); Diedre Kelly (Neighbor); Kathleen Perkins (Bus Driver); David L. Crowley (Rent-A-Cop #1); Stuart Abramson (Rent-A-Cop #2); Mark Phelan (Cop #1); Nigel D. Gibbs (Cop #2); Sean O'Grady (Announcer); Lydell Cheshier (Shop Owner); Donovan D. Ross (Kid on Swing); Michael Scranton (Policeman); Robert S. Neville (Paramedic #1); Hank McGill (Paramedic #2).

LOS ANGELES TIMES, 10/15/93, Calendar/p. 10, Peter Rainer

The perils of taking a wrong turn on the freeway are old hat to any Angeleno but apparently Chicagoans have a lot to learn. In "Judgment Night," four guys in an RV on their way to a boxing match exit the expressway during a traffic jam and descend into a creepy-crawly off-ramp night-world. They were psyched for vicarious violence—a boxing match—and end up victims of the real thing.

For a movie with not too much on its mind, "Judgment Night" is awfully arch. During the course of the film each of the four guys has his day, er, night, of reckoning. Frank (Emilio Estevez) has a loving wife and kids and lives in a tree-lined suburban paradise: his younger brother John (Stephen Dorff) is punkish and hot-tempered; Mike (Cuba Gooding Jr.) is expansive and good-natured; Ray (Jeremy Piven) is craven and filthy rich. (It's his RV.) When they find themselves pursued through abandoned streets and dead-bolted housing projects by a lethal, supercilious drug-lord (Denis Leary) and his lunky minions, they discover what they're really made of.

Of course, the discoveries aren't very startling, since nobody really undergoes a big change. The good guys get better, the cowards get more cowardly, the nuts get nuttier. Fallon, the drug lord, spouts the kind of fancy dialogue that might sound better coming out of the mouth of a James Bond villain, or Patrick McGoohan. He's so highhandedly ga-ga that you're surprised he deigns to talk to *anybody*. (Like any good villain, he saves his best *bon mots* for the moments just before his kills.)

You get the feeling that Fallon is the bad guy because he's well-read and witty, not because he kills people. And Ray is a creep because he's wealthy. In this movie, only the dogged, middle-class family man comes across as a hero. It's the filmmakers' way of passing judgment.

Given the opportunities for gratuitous mayhem, director Stephen Hopkins, working from a script by Lewis Colick, is reasonably restrained. He's aided by his cinematographer, Peter Levy, who gets some real variation out of what might have been undifferentiated darkness.

Recent stalk-and-kill fantasies like "Trespass" and "Hard Target" were snazzier, though. "Judgment Night" (rated R for strong violence, brutality and language) would have been better off trying to be a solid B picture instead of aiming for a B-plus. Nobody loves a teacher's pet.

NEW YORK POST, 10/15/93, p. 28, Michael Medved

"Judgment Night" is a slick, efficient thriller that, if nothing else, should make any husband think twice the next time he wants to spend a rowdy evening of male bonding "out with the boys."

At the beginning of the picture, a hard-working suburbanite (nicely played by the reliable Emilio Estevez) says goodbye to his disapproving wife and infant daughter before heading to a downtown Chicago boxing match in the company of three of his hard-drinking, irresponsible and unmarried pals.

Within minutes, these yo-yos face a world of trouble. Like the ill-fated Sherman McCoy in "Bonfire of the Vanities," they make a wrong turn off the expressway, get lost in a menacing, unfamiliar part of town, and end up striking a pedestrian they've scarcely seen. Unlike McCoy, they stop to pick up their victim and try to find him a hospital emergency room, but it turns out this poor fellow is being simultaneously pursued by a gang of drug-dealing thugs.

Sure enough, these crooks are no ordinary bad guys; They are sophisticated psychopaths who accompany their violent outbursts with witty references to "I Love Lucy," "Webster" and other pop-culture staples. They are led by Denis Leary, best known for his scorched-earth comedic commentaries on MTV, who makes a funny and fascinating villain for this film.

He's not only determined to rub out the former associate who's been cheating him, but he also wants to murder the four frightened yuppies who've witnessed the crime.

The rest of the movie is one long chase scene, but Australian director Stephen Hopkins (who previously guided such shlocky projects as "Predator II" and "Nightmare on Elm Street 5") keeps the action moving along in such a brisk, breathless style that he doesn't give much chance to fret over the story's many implausible elements.

Together with screenwriter Lewis Colick (cowriter of the recent "Unlawful Entry"), Hopkins has obviously spent a lot of time watching "Deliverance"—the stunning 1972 movie adaptation of James Dickey's novel about four suburban guys on a river-rafting expedition whose merry adventure turns into a brutal nightmare, testing their ability to survive and fight back.

Each of the characters in "Judgment Night" mirrors one of the principals of "Deliverance," including the capable, macho tough guy who's injured at a crucial moment (Burt Reynolds in the first film and "Boyz N The Hood"'s Cuba Gooding Jr. here), and the soft-spoken family man (Jon Voight and Emilio Estevez) who must somehow rise to the occasion to rescue his friends.

In place of the cruelties of nature and the vicious hillbillies in "Deliverance," director Hopkins presents an overdone vision of today's dangerous urban jungle. There are entirely too many shots of deserted streets with discarded newspapers blowing in the chill wind, and foolishly extended stretches where our heroes tramp down big-city streets without encountering any signs of life.

The filmmakers are trying to tap into the deep-seated middle-class fear of the horrors that lurk in the big, bad city, but the heroes are too stupid and irresponsible to hold our sympathy, and the colorful villains are too eccentric and irrational to convince us that they're real.

"Judgment Night" delivers its measure of thrills, but to enjoy them you've got to do more than suspend disbelief. You really have to stop thinking altogether.

NEWSDAY, 10/15/93, Part II/p. 69, John Anderson

"Judgment Night" might have been a propaganda film, courtesy of George Steinbrenner Productions: Don't go to the city, you suburbanites, 'cause you'll either be killed, or wet your Gap chinos.

It's also a Boys' Night Out as might have been conceived by Stephen King: Four overage adolescents head out for a boxing match, get lost in the inner-inner city of Chicago while trying to avoid a traffic jam, witness a murder and are chased by the killers through an unfamiliar and inhospitable urban landscape. But what begins as an atmospheric and evocative film—the quartet's first moments on the seemingly deserted city streets are as comfortable as a cold sweat—deteriorates into the standard fugitive melodrama, in which the outgunned suburbanites have to reach deep within themselves to find the testosterone needed to finish off the bad guys.

Yes, we've seen this before, from the plot to the odd and unlikely mix of old school pals at its center: Frank Wyatt (Emilio Estevez), a guy who's rapidly settling into couch-potatohood; his hot-headed younger brother John (Stephen Dorff); Mike (Cuba Gooding Jr.), ex-jock and aging adolescent, and Ray (Jeremy Piven), the yuppie hustler of the group, who cons a car dealer into lending them the large and luxurious camper van they manage to wedge in a Downtown alleyway.

From the back of the van they see the psychotic gangster Fallon (Denis Leary) execute a disloyal soldier. And then Fallon, a relentless predator, turns his sights on them.

The chase becomes increasingly ridiculous, until you want it to be over even more than they do. And forget the acting. Let's just say that Estevez will do a lot less damage if he sticks to comedy. As Frank, the leader of the pack, he's a thoroughly convincing overfed husband and homeowner; as a vehicle of outrage, he's stuck in park.

But "Judgment Night" is really about exploiting the fear of the American city, without really getting into any of the racial or economic foundations for those fears. We certainly get a guided tour of the nation's urban woes, though: Fallon, for one thing, is the product of the prison system. Seeking refuge in a freight yard, our four heroes are set upon by a pack of mentally ill homeless. Denied help in a decaying housing project (where the terrorized residents look like fashion models, by the way) they're also betrayed by the police, who simply never respond, nor probably ever do in this part of town.

It's a consistent movie, though, consistently unconvincing, and something of a slap to the cities, especially Chicago, whose Chamber of Commerce may want to consider a slander suit.

VILLAGE VOICE, 11/2/93, p. 67, Paul Miller

It seems like there's been a bunch of movies lately in which the soundtrack has been much, much better than the visuals. *Judgment Night* is one of those. It is the tale of four buddies—two jock types (Cuba Gooding Jr. and Stephen Dorff) a semi-regretful father (Emilio Estevez), and an annoying yuppizoid (Jeremy Piven)—who become fugitives from a death-bent, doom-seeking underworld figure—played by Denis Leary!

The action takes off as the four leave the clogged "mainstream" of the highway for a shortcut to the boxing match they're dying to see. They blunder into Chicago's decomposing industrial zone, where they encounter bums and also, poor lost souls, witness Leary's execution of a turncoat employee. They're then hunted by Leary through the concrete jungle of the projects toward a twin-barrels-blasting apocalyptic finale in a dilapidated shopping center.

The slammin' soundtrack, by a virtual who's who of alternative music and hip-hop artists, has more impact than the cliché tale of four kids fleeing annihilation. Frantic conga drums and wild disco violins float down over the walls of the projects and out of Doppler-effected moving boom boxes and car radios like incandescent sound particles. All in all, this '70s inner-city blaxploitation gangsta tale updated and recast as a '90s happy-camper-adventure-gone-wrong hits, but in all the wrong places.

Also reviewed in:
CHICAGO TRIBUNE, 10/15/93, Friday/p. L, Johanna Steinmetz
NEW YORK TIMES, 10/15/93, p. C8, Janet Maslin
VARIETY, 10/25/93, p. 80, Leonard Klady
WASHINGTON POST, 10/15/93, p. D7, Richard Harrington
WASHINGTON POST, 10/15/93, Weekend/p. 4, Desson Howe

JURASSIC PARK

A Universal Pictures release of an Amblin Entertainment production. *Producer:* Kathleen Kennedy and Gerald R. Molen. *Director:* Steven Spielberg. *Screenplay:* Michael Crichton and David Koepp. *Based on the novel by:* Michael Crichton. *Director of Photography:* Dean Cundey. *Editor:* Michael Kahn. *Music:* John Williams. *Music Editor:* Kenneth Wannberg. *Sound:* Ron Judkins and (music) Shawn Murphy. *Sound Editor:* Richard Hymns. *Casting:* Janet Hirshenson and Jane Jenkins. *Production Designer:* Rick Carter. *Art Director:* Jim Teegarden and John Bell. *Set Designer:* John Berger, Lauren Polizzi, and Masako Masuda.

Set Decorator: Jackie Carr.   *Full-Motion Dinosaurs:* Dennis Muren.   *Live Action Dinosaurs:* Stan Winston.   *Dinosaur Supervisor:* Phil Tippett.   *Special Dinosaur Effects:* Michael Lantieri. *Women's Costumes:* Sue Moore.   *Men's Costumes:* Eric Sandberg.   *Make-up:* Christina Smith. *Stunt Coordinator:* Gary Hymes.   *Running time:* 123 minutes.   *MPAA Rating:* PG-13.

CAST: Sam Neill (Grant);   Laura Dern (Ellie);   Jeff Goldblum (Malcolm);   Richard Attenborough (Hammond);   Bob Peck (Muldoon);   Martin Ferrero (Gennaro);   B.D. Wong (Wu);   Joseph Mazzello (Tim);   Ariana Richards (Lex);   Samuel L. Jackson (Arnold);   Wayne Knight (Nedry);   Jerry Molen (Harding);   Miguel Sandoval (Rostagno);   Cameron Thor (Dodgson);   Christopher John Fields (Volunteer #1);   Whit Hertford (Volunteer Boy);   Dean Cundey (Mate);   Jophery Brown (Worker in Raptor Pen);   Tom Mishler (Helicopter Pilot); Greg Burson ("Mr. D.N.A." Voice);   Adrian Escober (Worker at Amber Mine);   Richard Kiley (Jurassic Park Tour Voice).

CHRISTIAN SCIENCE MONITOR, 6/11/93, p. 12, David Sterritt

It is well known that going to a typical Steven Spielberg movie is like attending an amusement park. So it's not surprising that Mr. Spielberg has now made a movie *about* an amusement park—and no ordinary park, but a walloping extravaganza stuffed with thoroughly, Spielbergian thrills.

I suppose it was inevitable that Spielberg would crank out an entertainment like "Jurassic Park," given the trajectory of his career. And it's probably just as well that he has turned his talent in this direction—flighty and frivolous though it is—at this stage in his development.

After earning a reputation as one of Hollywood's most dependable money-spinners, with pictures like "E.T. The Extra-Terrestrial" and the Indiana Jones epics, Spielberg has been trying to wax mature in his more recent films. For all their ambition, however, the romantic drama "Always" and the mythical free-for-all "Hook" seem to strain at their grown-up agendas rather than slide gracefully into them. There's only one kind of movie that Spielberg has truly mastered: the kind that looks like a wide-screen video game complete with loony plot twists and mind-bending special effects.

And that's "Jurassic Park" down to its bones. Vivid and violent enough to stretch the PG-13 rating to its limit, it will delight Spielberg fans, reassuring them that he isn't trying *too* hard to grow up, but still has time to put them on a rollercoaster ride now and then.

Based on Michael Crichton's novel (1992, Alfred A. Knopf), the film takes place on an island where an eccentric zillionaire named John Hammond has realized an amazing dream: Using cells extracted from mosquitoes preserved in prehistoric tree sap, he has cloned a colony of dinosaurs that live, breathe, and clomp around exactly as their ancestors did before their species became extinct. His motive is less to advance the cause of science than to provide exotic entertainment in the most audacious theme park ever built.

Hammond's idea may sound great, but as the old science-fiction cliché says, there are things mankind wasn't meant to tamper with. Before the park opens its doors, its computer-controlled operation goes kerflooey—thanks to a greedy employee who's trying to smuggle dinosaur embryos off the island—and the genetically engineered giants run amok.

Caught in the chaos are Hammond's two grandchildren and some scientists he's invited to give the park their seal of approval. Can the handsome paleontologist, the pretty paleobotanist, and the witty but cynical mathematician save the youngsters (and themselves) from the wily Diplodocus, the terrifying Tyrannosaurus Rex, and the dangerously klutzy Brontosaurus? No sweat—but only after two hours of chills, spills, and harrowingly close shaves.

Still working on the adult image he wants to acquire, Spielberg has injected "Jurassic Park" with a few serious questions. The movie asks whether humanity has lost respect for nature to a dangerous degree; whether we now think of science as an intellectual game rather than a key to understanding; whether there *are* things mankind wasn't meant to tamper with. Regrettably, the film never gets around to exploring these issues, since chases, races, and hairbreadth escapes are its main concern in virtually every scene.

Another interesting question raised by "Jurassic Park" is whether Spielberg consciously intended it as a symbolic study of his own life as a filmmaker, or whether this dimension crept into the movie without the director's awareness. Hammond's park isn't sort of like a Spielberg production, it's *exactly* like a Spielberg production—complete with exotic settings, marvelous creatures, and marketing tie-ins like lunchboxes with Jurassic Park logos. It even has a Spielbergian budget: "We've spared no expense!" crows Hammond over and over, taking childlike pride in the sheer hugeness of his enterprise.

Since, everything goes wrong in Hammond's prehistoric playground, should we conclude that Spielberg is criticizing the notion of devoting vast resources to escapism and spectacle, rather than to developing knowledge and improving the world—a statement that would amount to a surprisingly mature self-criticism of his own cinematic career to date?

Apparently not. Hammond's sin, the movie eventually makes clear, is not his ambition to be the ultimate impresario. Instead it's the fact that he dared to create something real, like a world of living creatures, instead of something fake, like a glitzy Spielberg movie.

Truth may be stranger than fiction, Spielberg and company tell us, but fiction is a lot more safe and comfy—and can earn you a fortune without the unpleasant possibility of risking anything but your producers' money. Faced with the choice of spectacle or substance, Spielberg still favors spectacle by a wide margin.

As pure spectacle, "Jurassic Park" works as well as anything else Hollywood's high-tech wizards have given us lately. It's derivative in spots—the classic "King Kong" and the amusing "Gremlins" obviously inspired some of its better dinosaur ideas—but the special effects are simply astounding, with utterly life-like monsters jostling humans who sometimes don't seem half as convincing.

The acting is also on target, within the limitations of a movie that cares more about action and fantasy than credible motivation and well-rounded characters.

Sam Neill and Laura Dern make a nice couple as the paleontlological heroes, and Jeff Goldblum brings his unique humor to the mathematician whose knowledge of chaos theory proves too theoretical to help much.

And it's a pleasure to see Richard Attenborough on screen for the first time in 14 years. He's a first-rate character actor when he isn't busy being a third-rate movie director, and he makes Hammond a surprisingly engaging character.

The supporting cast includes Josh Mostel and Samuel L. Jackson as well as Ariana Richards and Joseph Mazzello as the threatened kids of the story. The rich cinematography is by Dean Cundey, and the split-second editing is by Michael Kahn, a regular member of Spielberg's team. David Koepp and Mr. Crichton wrote the screenplay. John Williams composed the rip-roaring music.

FILMS IN REVIEW, 8/93, p. 259, James M. Welsh

"Welcome to Jurassic Park!" This is a good, ironic line, since the Park turns out to be inhabited by monsters that science has created and technicians, however gifted, cannot control or contain. Steven Spielberg's movie gives the line to kindly old John Hammond, a megolomanical billionaire that the movie reinvents as merely a nice old man who is spared the horrible fate he suffers in Michael Crichton's novel as payment for his prideful, presumptive sins. In the novel after all hell (and fifteen dinosaur species) breaks loose, Hammond unwisely wanders off from the security of his central compound, breaks his ankle, and is eaten by scavenger dinosaurs—poisonous little fellows called "compys," who are about the size of a chicken. Serves him right in the novel, but you won't find a single compy in the movie.

The movie's John Hammond, as played by Sir Richard Attenborough, is a bit balmy and befuddled, but he means well. The screenplay gives him a little speech that allows him to explain how as a young lad he came down to London from Scotland to run a flea circus. No mention of this in the novel. And in the movie Hammond actually seems worried about the fate of his grandchildren, trapped in the Park with deadly carnivorous dinosaurs on the loose. In the novel Hammond thinks mainly about himself and his dream.

The kids are also different in the movie. Lex, the girl, is older than she is in the novel, less given to whining, more aware of the danger, and able to put the computer system back on line after a total shutdown—a plucky, politically correct little heroine. Tim, her precocious brother, is the older sibling in the novel, who fixes the computer system and a take-charge little guy. Spielberg makes him younger, and cuter. No surprise here.

The most important character in the novel who is reduced to almost nothing in the movie is the chemical engineer Henry Wu (B. D. Wong), who unsuccessfully argues with Hammond (only in the novel) about designing more domesticated dinosaurs. Henry isn't even on the island when the storm comes in the movie and things go berserk. His absence reduces the ethical subtext, making the story less interesting. Dennis Nedry (Wayne Knight), the turncoat computer wizard who attempts to steal dinosaur embryos for a rival genetic engineering firm, is an even more disagreeable slob in the movie and justly turned into dinosaur bait.

The paleontologist Alan Grant (Sam Neill) and his assistant Ellie (Laura Dern) are near the mark, but in the movie they seem to have thoughts of matrimony, and Grant needs to develop a more positive and tolerant attitude toward children, as he does as a result of his adventures in Jurassic Park with Lex and Tim, who pesters him with dinosaur questions when they first meet.

Ian Malcolm (Jeff Goldblum), whose reservations about Hammond's tampering with nature by experimenting with dinosaur DNA, gives the novel its moral framework, is made more eccentric in the film and also has a yen for Ellie. He is wounded in the movie, as he is in the novel, but his injury, like the whole film, is less serious. Spielberg attempts to save as many of the good guys as he can, and if the novel is distorted, well, it's not quite the same as tampering with Tolstoy. Entertainment and profits are the bottom line here, and Spielberg certainly knows how to entertain.

It's hardly surprising that Spielberg turns the novel into an action-adventure story calculated to generate a thrill or a surprise every five or six minutes. Instead of a car chase, he offers an open-topped Jeep filled with puny mortals being chased by a T-rex that can run up to 60 miles per hour, fast enough to keep the chase interesting.

The movie is a well constructed scare machine that utilizes state-of-the-art special effects to make it the ultimate monster movie—Big Birds with teeth, *Jaws* and legs, as they say in the industry. It's just too bad that the adaptation was not closer to its source, that so much of the dinosaur lore is abridged, and that the science lesson here is so rudimentary. Those who see the movie will not be bored, but those who have read the novel will expect more. Certainly, those who have not read the novel should give it a try. Spielberg's movie will do, but it's only a movie.

LOS ANGELES TIMES, 6/11/93, Calendar/p. 1, Kenneth Turan

Do the dinosaurs work?
Indeed they do.
Does anything else?
Not really.
The greatly anticipated "Jurassic Park," it turns out, is the poor little rich kid of this sunniest movies. Everything that money can buy has been bought, and what an estimated $60 million can purchase is awfully impressive. But even in Hollywood there are things a blank check can't guarantee and the lack of those keeps this film from being more than one hell of an effective parlor trick.

Ever since director Steven Spielberg began to work on Michael Crichton's futuristic novel of catastrophe in a theme park stocked with flesh-and-blood dinosaurs from the Jurassic Period, the anticipation about what the beasts would look like has been intense. And in that area "Jurassic Park" does not disappoint.

Brought to life by a consortium of four separate effects units, including live-action expert Stan Winston, who created the original "Terminator," and Industrial Light & Magic wizard Dennis Muren, responsible for "Terminator 2's" computer-generated morphing effects, the dinosaurs are wondrously realistic.

Ranging from the kindly brachiosaurus, a 77-ton vegetarian that might crush a flea but wouldn't think of eating it, to the difficult *Tyrannosaurus rex* and the downright nasty velociraptor, some six kinds of dinosaurs come to life with a verisimilitude that is humbling and that also blends seamlessly with the film's considerably blander and less interesting human characters.

All the imagination and effort (including 18 months of pre-production) that went into making the dinosaurs state-of-the-art exciting apparently left no time to make the people similarly believable or involving. In fact, when the big guys leave the screen, you'll be tempted to leave the theater with them.

Not that anyone was expecting "Jurassic Park" to be the dinosaur version of "Howards End." In fact, it was Spielberg himself who created the model for this kind of picture 18 summers ago when he directed the enormously popular "Jaws," a film in which strong acting and concern for character added considerably to its creature-on-the-loose suspense.

One looks in vain, however, for performances as good as those of Robert Shaw or Richard Dreyfuss or patches of writing as memorable as Shaw's monologue about a World War II shark attack. With the exception of Richard Attenborough, who is energetic and fun in the role of Hammond, the entrepreneur who dreamed up the park, "Jurassic's" acting is unengaging and simplistic. Combined with Spielberg's unexpectedly flat directing style, the result is a standard-issue jeopardy picture with (very realistic) dinosaurs plugged into all the appropriate gaps.

Written by novelist Crichton and "Death Becomes Her" co-screenwriter David Koepp, "Jurassic Park" actually starts out with some of the pep and vigor of an old-fashioned B-movie, moving quickly between different locations as if it can't wait to set up its story.

First stop is Isla Nublar, a speck off the coast of Costa Rica and the on-to-be-opened park's locale, here we (and an unlucky worker) get a first-hand glimpse of how ornery those dinos can be. We also get to visit with a nervous attorney, a secretly traitorous park employee, on a dig in Montana, two of the world's preeminent dinosaur experts, handsome paleontologist Dr. Alan Grant (Sam Neill) and his attractive colleague, paleobotanist Dr. Ellie Sattler (Laura Dern).

The link between all these folks is empire builder Hammond, who the nervous lawyer says, can't open his park unless he can persuade scientists that what he's doing is safe. So Hammond prevails on Grant and Sattler (as well as eccentric mathematician and chaos expert Ian Malcolm, played by Jeff Goldblum) to accompany him and his two young grandchildren to Isla Nublar and become his attraction's first visitors.

But, as if possessed by a mysterious tropical lethargy, "Jurassic Park" slows to a crawl once the island is reached. Aside from the ingenious explanation of where the dinosaurs come from (they've been created from dino DNA locked in the stomachs of preserved bloodsucking insects), the film spends almost all its time on false alarms and cute moments emphasizing how much stuffy Dr. Grant can't stand to be around kids.

The action, which takes up most of the second hour, is certainly impressive when it happens, especially when the jumbo-sized *T. rex* goes on a rampage. But because much of the jeopardy involves those young children, parents should treat "Jurassic's" PG-13 (for intense science-fiction terror) rating as if it were an absolute ban on pre-teen admittance. These dinos are the furthest thing from cuddly when they choose to attack.

Though thrilling in the abstract, the battles in "Jurassic Park" suffer, as the rest of the film does, because they're not connected to anything that isn't the emotional equivalent of baby food. For Spielberg, the director who brought it all together in "Jaws," "E.T." and "Sugarland Express," seems, like an out-of-control toy, to be spinning off in a pair of different but equally unfortunate directions.

On the one hand, Spielberg's acceptance of an indifferent level of performance from his actors indicates an increasingly mechanical, uninvolved approach to the non-effects parts of filmmaking, making "Jurassic Park" play like it was directed by one of those special-effects computers it makes such prominent use of.

And whatever emotion does find its way into this film reeks of suitable-for-children sentimentality, which is paradoxical given how unsuitable for children all the action is. It's tempting to call "Jurassic Park" "Father Knows Best: The Early Years," because the sole point of all the carnage appears to be to increase Dr. Grant's appreciation for young people, turning him from a gruff curmudgeon into someone who has the makings of a considerate parent.

Finally though, the problem with "Jurassic Park" is that Spielberg has chosen to make an amusement park instead of a motion picture, so much so that it is difficult to separate what the script says about the park (We're going to make a fortune with this place," etc.) from what the filmmakers must have thought about the project.

"Jurassic Park" will doubtless make that fortune and solidify Spielberg's position as the Pied Piper of popular entertainment. But those who remember when the director didn't sacrifice everything to childish sentiments and special effects will view it as a further step along the familiar road of a talented individual unnerved by success.

NEW STATESMAN & SOCIETY, 7/16/93, p. 34, Jonathan Romney

One of the most memorable images in Steven Spielberg's *Jurassic Park* comes when a Tyrannosaurus rears up in triumph and a banner flutters down, reading "When Dinosaurs Ruled the Earth". It's a nice self-congratulatory touch, reminding us how far saurian cinema has come in sophistication since the 1969 film of that name. But it also points out that *now* is the time when the big scaly ones reign supreme. Much of *Jurassic Park* is charged with messages—not so subliminal either—directly concerning the film's own status as an unvanquishable monster. It was a foregone conclusion that the huge marketing industry attached to the film would make *Jurassic Park* and its subject matter a worldwide preoccupation. So it's tempting to suggest that *Jurassic Park* isn't really about dinosaurs at all. Perhaps the dinosaurs are simply the incarnation of whatever it is that the film's really about: the unthinkable, the sublime, or maybe just the downright bloody huge. It's certainly plausible to see them as the latest manifestation of that transcendental object of awe that keeps appearing in Spielberg films: the shimmering phantoms released at the end of *Raiders of the Lost Ark*, the angelic aliens in *Close Encounters* or more portentously, the Hiroshima mushroom cloud that the young hero of *Empire of the Sun* mistakes for a soul rising up to heaven.

There is indeed a brief transcendental moment in *Jurassic Park*, but it comes towards the beginning, when the scientists visiting the dinosaur theme park run by jolly billionaire John Hammond (Richard Attenborough) gape in awe at a herd of long-necked saurians grazing in the sun.

Their immediate reaction, and ours, is "Can such things be?"; then we think "How do they do it?" and the spell is dissipated. We know we're dealing with a special effects demonstration, and the only question is what other tricks the film will go on to pull (remarkable ones, as it happens, not least a thundering herd of ostrich-like gallomimuses).

But there's no real sense of awe in *Jurassic Park*. Nothing's unveiled as it is in the other films (remember the excruciating slow buildup of *Close Encounters*?). There's something oddly casual about the film, like a mountebank revealing the Eighth Wonder of the World, then showing you a bigger, better one. It has a curious agenda; it knows its job, which is to present breathtaking illusions, but it also wants us to know they're illusions so that we don't get too impressed and forget the other more serious topics on its mind.

Foremost among those are, of course, questions of the environment and of nature. At heart, *Jurassic Park* is an old-fashioned science-gone-too-far movie, and the role of its scientist heroes (Sam Neill, Laura Dern and chaos theorist Jeff Goldblum) is to wave a warning finger about how you just can't mess with nature. At one point, it's discovered that the dinosaurs on Attenborough's island, cloned from DNA and designed to act artificially, are spontaneously doing odd things such as changing sex, thus eluding their programmed behaviour. Horror of horrors, they're turning natural. So Jeff Goldblum was right when he fulminated, "Life will not be contained! Life finds a way!"

In case we're not sure what kind of life the film has in mind, there are plenty of children on hand to remind us. Early on, Neill's character, a confirmed infantophobe, lectures a boy on the horrors of being eaten alive and cautions him "Have some respect". For the rest of the film, he's obliged to swallow his child-loathing and protect Hammond's cute, computer and fossil-literate grandchildren.

The film's real story is about his learning to love kids: to stop being a big kid himself and become a daddy, tender, protective and in touch with nature. Clearly, this is a complex running through Spielberg's films. As in his irksome Peter Pan fantasy *Hook*, they always scratch at the itchy problem of boys becoming men.

Of course, you always know that Neill will get in touch with the daddy within. You can tell right from the beginning when he's carping away about how he hates kids, and Laura Dern gives an indulgent little smile, because she—his destined mate—knows him better than he knows himself. And when the final image of the film is a redemptive flight of storks, you hold your breath waiting for the nappies to be unpacked. (An ornithologist friend points out that they are in fact pelicans. That may be true, but I recognise a symbolic stork when I see one.)

Curiously, though, Neill also confesses to hating computers (which kids, of course, love). The film itself hates technology, too. It can't wait to jettison the computer graphics and hardware and get to grips with the thrill of prehistory. Paradoxically, everything that's modish is condemned as old-hat, commonplace sci-fi stuff.

What makes the film "new"—hyper-modern—is its embrace of the ancient. There's another similar distinction at work between the unimaginably huge dinosaurs and the inconceivably small scale on which they're created. These monsters are the product of *microgenics*, cloned out of DNA taken from the blood of prehistoric mosquitos.

In fact, Spielberg's monsters are created in much the same way. Many of these lumbering titans are actually computer-generated—built out of thousands upon thousands of minuscule pixels, artfully manipulated—just as Hammond's scientists manipulate the DNA chain. So the film is supremely conscious of the process of its own making, which it reproduces in its subject matter. But it's also curiously embarrassed. Like Neill, the film *hates* computers, although it's obliged to use them.

Wouldn't it be better, it implies, if this all *were* real? Hammond himself, reminiscing about a flea circus he once ran, says he created Jurassic Park because he wanted to show the world "something that wasn't an illusion"; to which Dern retorts, "It still is a flea circus ... It's all an illusion."

Hence the film confesses to its own rather pathetic bad faith. *Jurassic Park* marvels at its own image-making, but hates the means it uses to achieve it. It revels in the act of creation, but despairs at the idea that it's all bread and circuses. Making artificial monsters is no kind of creation, the film suggests; natural reproduction is. Spielberg gives us the time of our lives treating us like impressionable kids; but at heart he feels we should be concerning ourselves with more adult business. His next film is about Auschwitz.

NEW YORK, 6/21/93, p. 60, David Denby

Among the many frightening and wonderful spectacles in Steven Spielberg's *Jurassic Park*, the most frightening and wonderful is a noise—the mighty yell of *Tyrannousaurus rex* after it has eaten. The roar has been worked up from a recording of an elephant's trumpet blast, except that (to my ears) it's louder, much deeper, and longer, the sound rushing from immense cavities and spreading out for miles. It is the happy bleat of the all-time king of beasts. Spielberg imagined it as a noise that has the power to appall.

No doubt about it: The dinosaurs in *Jurassic Park* are fabulous. There's none of that awkwardness, the comic-book flimsiness we remember from old movies. The *T. rex* walks ponderously, shaking the ground, but when it swings its neck and jaws to chomp on something, it moves with frightening speed. These beasts are hungry. The smaller *velociraptors*, or raptors, lean forward with their tiny front legs dangling in the air, and suddenly hop, propelled by the back legs; this graceful lean-and-hop movement becomes unimaginably sinister. The dinosaurs are always convincing, even when they smash through fences and intrude into a modern industrial kitchen. They are searching for their food—the human beings who become their prey. *Jurassic Park*, based on the Michael Crichton best-seller, is an evolutionary joke: Man, the master of the universe, has become mere flesh, consumed by animals allegedly too stupid to survive. In its mixture of excitement, wit, and fear, *Jurassic Park* comes close to *Jaws*, though the calculation involved in Spielberg's recent big-machine approach to moviemaking can be depressing.

On a tiny Caribbean island near Costa Rica, a megalomaniacal tycoon (Richard Attenborough) has set up an animal preserve that is half theme park, half monstrous Bronx Zoo. The main feature: actual dinosaurs, re-created in the laboratory from DNA strings preserved for 65 million years in the bodies of blood-sucking mosquitoes. The huge creatures are ... what? Post-extinct? Resurrected?

Before the park can open to the public, however, the tycoon brings scientists to the island to give their approval and help him raise money, There's Alan Grant (Sam Neill), a paleontologist rather remote from humanity; his warmhearted colleague and lover, Ellie Sattler (Laura Dern); and a hipster mathematician, Ian Malcolm (Jeff Goldblum), who dresses entirely in black and talks darkly of chaos theory—the notion that large systems are bound to pass out of human and technological control. Also two of the tycoon's grandchildren, little fairy-tale blondies just made to be eaten. Within the park, a saboteur shuts down the computer systems, and all hell breaks loose. The animals attack the visitors' center. *Feed me!*

As you're watching, you have the sense that you've seen lots of this before. The reptilian head, the jaws with sharpened teeth have menaced people in *Aliens, Gremlins, Predator,* and other movies. To some degree, *Jurassic Park* is an exercise in conventional big-budget thrills—a machine for making money that has been programmed to work in a certain way, with certain built-in elements that have proved themselves in the past. Surely Spielberg's belief in chaos is only philosophical: Nothing like spontaneity is going to interrupt *this* large system's march to a half-billion-dollar worldwide gross.

Spielberg sets things up cunningly, teasing us, but we know his tricks, and emotionally he breaks no new ground. The elements of his style, good and bad, are all in place. In the movie's prologue, the raptors, so vicious that they have to be caged (we can't see them yet), devour a man, which recaps the opening of *Jaws,* when a young female swimmer is mysteriously thrust up out of the water by an unseen force and then violently pulled below. From *Close Encounters of the Third Kind,* we recognize the mood of thunderstruck anticipation, the camera rising on awed faces, the prolonged silences before the revelation of the apocalypse. The low-brow ghoulish mockery is also familiar. A man so frightened he rushes to the toilet stays nailed to his seat right down to the moment when the *T. rex* smashes the bathroom flat and devours him. As the beasts approach, some sort of shaking liquid—water in a glass, Jell-O in a spoon—serves a repeated premonitory function, like the thudding music in *Jaws.*

But Spielberg does deliver; he delivers thrills with all his genius for the mechanics of movement and the psychology of fear. When the *T. rex* attacks a car holding the two little children, and the children haplessly flash a powerful light at the animal—just the thing that is attracting him—the vulnerability of the boy and girl is deeply upsetting. Dinosaurs, of course, are monsters that children love. They're huge and scary, but they're extinct, so they have a certain pathos for children—perhaps for anyone. After Grant and the children escape the tyrannosaur, they wander into the lush forests; and although Grant hates children, he feels a link with the kids. He has the same curiosity as they do. Mesmerized, he wants to walk among the beasts, and he forgets to get scared. In the loveliest moment in the movie—a moment to equal anything in *Close Encounters*—a herd of *gallimimuses* comes hopping toward the three of them, and they're so transfixed they don't get out of the way until the last minute.

Is *Jurassic Park* just another cautionary tale about science? The movie could be seen as the outsize grandchild of all those cheesy sci-fi/horror films from the fifties in which scientists went mad and created gigantic mutated ants. But *Jurassic Park* is also a pastoral idyll. The beasts inspire not only fear but wonder, and the place in which they play is as much a garden as a killing field. Perhaps Spielberg is split himself. Part of him is like the starry-eyed paleontologist, awed by the creatures he's dreamed about, and part of him is a sardonic black prince of chaos like Goldblum's Malcolm, who expects the worst of any situation. Malcolm suggests—and the movie seconds him—that there are some things in nature that you can't cuddle up to. "They're just animals," Dern says to the children, trying to reassure them. Yeah, and as animals, they just go on eating, like the shark in *Jaws.* In Spielberg's best joke, the raptors chase the kiddies into a gleaming industrial kitchen, jumping over the shiny metal counters, scrambling for their dinner.

There's a bit of earnest preaching going on here. Two lessons: Don't muck around with the evolutionary sequence; the dinosaurs had their time and can't adapt to the human epoch. And don't sentimentalize the rapacity of nature. I suppose those things are worth hearing, but a day after the movie, when I no longer shuddered from the roar of the *T. rex,* I couldn't help feeling that there was something stupid about going to all this effort to create dinosaurs on-screen only to turn them into big-toothed heavies in another scare movie. Spielberg is unkind to his own creations. After the humans leave the island, who and what is going to feed the animals?

NEW YORK POST, 6/9/93, p. 27, Jami Bernard

"Jurassic Park" is clearly the event movie of the summer, and you won't be disappointed—if you like event movies. It's a carnival ride in the emotional sense and the blueprint for a carnival ride in the physical, marketing sense, but then that was the promise offered by Michael Crichton's intense, pseudo-scientific novel in the first place.

The Crichton novel was about genetic engineering gone awry thanks to human limitation and mathematical principles. The Steven Spielberg movie is about a paleontologist who is made ready to start his own family by bonding with two kids during a series of hair-raising adventures.

Both feature a fabulous found world of dinosaurs.

Will the wily velociraptor be up for an Oscar next March? Or the stalking T. rex, or the peace-loving "veggie-saurs"? Maybe not, but the special-effects crew sure will be. Even if the movie had not a shred of plot, these dinosaurs would trample all over the box-office competition this summer. They are a seamless combination of animatronics, computer animation, technology and sound effects.

It's hard to say why humans have such a vestigial fascination with these extinct critters—does our own DNA resonate with faint memory when we ponder them?—but it's certain that kids will love the concept, if they don't first have a heart attack during the scary scenes, of which there are many.

The script has sifted away a lot of the technical stuff that made the book so rich, and left the bare bones of the story—a rich man who is funding a tropical theme park featuring real dinosaurs invites a small group to inspect the premises before opening to the public. The group includes a paleontologist (Sam Neill), his paleobotanist girlfriend (Laura Dern), an eccentric mathematician (Jeff Goldblum), a lawyer, and the owner's two inquisitive grandchildren.

The dinosaurs have been manufactured by cloning their DNA, which has been found preserved in the remains of mosquitoes who once bit them and in turn became preserved in amber. Various DNA gaps have been filled out with eye of newt and whatnot, but basically they are the dinosaurs of musty museums come to life, hatching on schedule and eating hearty meals of full-grown cows.

The mathematician's "chaos theory," so chilling in the book, is barely explained, but it's clear that the best-laid plans of mice and brachiosaurs often go astray. Soon the electrified fences that contained the various dinosaur species have broken down and the human visitors are trapped in the wilds of the theme park along with creatures from different stages of evolution. And, boy, are they hungry—it's been eons since they've stalked something juicy.

On a recent radio show, I was asked whether there was anything left for movies to exploit for shock value, and I predicted that the next taboo to be broken systematically would be regarding the integrity of children. Right on schedule, Spielberg (of all people) puts the two children in his movie at peril. They are attacked, nearly electrocuted, trapped in plummeting cars, stalked, terrorized, abandoned—and all this with a PG-13 rating.

These are the same kids who are going to buy all the commercial product tie-ins—the movie's funniest scene is a tender cheesecake shot of all the dino mugs and T-shirts in the gift shop, thrown in without a trace of irony—yet the movie can be strong stuff. "Let's put it this way," Neill instructs a little boy at the site of an archaeological dig, demonstrating how the velociraptor seasons his meal by gutting your stomach with his claw. "You're still alive when they start to eat you."

Goldblum is the most refreshing of the humans, and the vicious velociraptors are the most impressive of the dinosaurs, but the supporting casts of both species make this a frightening and entertaining movie.

NEW YORK POST, 6/11/93, p. 27, Michael Medved

The hordes of eager moviegoers who are jamming theaters for the opening of this year's most heavily hyped motion picture aren't looking for dramatic subtlety, probing character development or profound new insight into the meaning of life.

What they want from "Jurassic Park" is old-fashioned edge-of-your-seat adventure along with some genuinely scary dinosaurs—and until his picture falls apart in its final three minutes, director Steven Spielberg definitely delivers the goods.

By now, only those who have spent the last two months in sensory deprivation tanks could possibly remain unaware of the ingenious premise behind this motion picture. Closely following the details of Michael Crichton's intoxicatingly readable best seller, the film (which Crichton himself co-wrote) depicts an ambitious theme park that uses cloning technology to bring dinosaurs back to life.

The eccentric entrepreneur who masterminds this project, John Hammond (Sir Richard Attenborough) hatches his dinos on a remote island off the coast of Central America, where he hopes to exhibit them to swarms of tourists. Meanwhile, impatient investors worry about potential glitches in the elaborate plans for the park, with its electrified enclosures and high-tech tours.

They dispatch a group of distinguished visitors to determine whether the nearly completed attraction is safe enough to open to the public. When Richard Attenborough tries to assure a skeptical visiting mathematician (Jeff Goldblum) that Jurassic Park is fundamentally similar to Disneyland, Goldblum pointedly observes, "But if the Pirates of the Caribbean breaks down, the pirates don't eat the tourists."

The eclectic cast members who handle these various roles could hardly be better: For once the characters in a movie seem more compelling, more convincingly fleshed out, than the figures in the novel that inspired it.

Spielberg has made a few strategic changes to enhance our connection with these people: In contrast to the book, for instance, there are references to romantic involvement between two visiting paleontologists (Sam Neill and Laura Dern).

In a bow to political correctness, there has also been a role reversal in the depiction of John Hammond's two young grandchildren. This time it's the girl, not the boy, who is the self-reliant, plucky and ultimately heroic computer whiz.

The real stars of the piece remain, however, the dazzlingly detailed dinosaurs—in particular an awe-inspiring, 20-foot-tall Tyrannosaurus rex who's featured in one unforgettably frightening sequence that will be remembered as one of the most suspenseful confrontations ever captured on film.

As crafted by Stan Winston (who also did the universally admired special effects for the "Terminator" movies), together with other masters of visual magic, the dinosaurs are not only amazingly lifelike, they are also thoroughly reptilian.

Like the famous shark in Spielberg's "Jaws," these creatures are a primal, unstoppable force of nature all the more frightening because they are merely following instincts, and there's nothing personal or anthropomorphic in their pure menace and malice.

At the same time, the director manages to project a sense of wonder—and occasionally, even of poetry—as the human spectators behold these amazing beasts.

Unlike many of his previous triumphs, however, "Jurassic Park" is unequivocally unsuitable for small children: Any parent who brings a kid below the age of 10 to see this film is guilty of a form of unconscionable child abuse.

The movie's single most serious shortcoming involves its lack of any satisfying climax or conclusion. This picture never ends, it just stops, as the state-of-the-art thrill machine screeches to a sudden halt in an unforgivably abrupt and arbitrary manner.

For one thing, there is not the slightest hint as to the final fate of the hungry dinosaurs the film has so painstakingly brought to life. Spielberg, in fact, leaves so many untied loose ends, so many annoyingly unresolved plot points, that one can only assume that he has already begun to think sequel.

NEWSDAY, 6/11/93, Part II/p. 65, Jack Mathews

The answer is yes. The only question on anyone's mind when Steven Spielberg agreed to adapt Michael Chrichton's dinosaurs-are-back best-seller, "Jurassic Park," was whether the inventive director of "Jaws," "E.T." and "Close Encounters" could make Crichton's reptilian menagerie look real.

Yes!

The horned Triceratops lying on the ground in a tranquilized stupor, her stomach heaving like a sick elephant's. The gentle, long-necked Brachiosaurus, grazing at the leafy peaks of 80-foot-tall trees. The voracious, shark-jawed Tyrannosaurus rex, wolfing down whole goats. The flightless Gallimumus birds, stampeding across an open plain like a flock of jet-propelled ostriches. The cunning, two-legged Velociraptors, using their razor-sharp claws to kill for the sport of it.

Breathing, walking, hunting, running, feeding, fighting ... the exotic prehistoric animals—some created in computers, others by hand—move with a lifelike realism no imagined screen creatures have ever approached, and with a fearsomeness that will have compliant audiences shrieking as if they were on a runaway roller coaster.

Just the point, of course. "Jurassic Park" is a theme park of a movie with a theme park setting, designed for summer tourists who like their thrills visceral. We watch the actors as if we were all on the same Universal Studios tour team, aware at all times that we're reacting to engineered illusions—but reacting nonetheless.

The script, co-written by Crichton and David Koepp, softens a couple of characters, reduces the violence and has a new, anticlimactic ending, but otherwise follows the novel fairly closely.

An ambitious billionaire (Richard Attenborough), looking for scientific endorsements to comfort nervous investors, invites a pair of dinosaur experts to Isla Nubla, an island off Costa Rica where he has been secretly developing a combination zoo/theme park populated with dinosaurs cloned from DNA preserved in petrified tree sap.

When the park's opportunistic computer whiz (Wayne Knight) disarms the electronic security system so he can make off with a variety pack of frozen embryos, the dino experts (Sam Neill and Laura Dern), a sardonic mathematician (Jeff Goldblum), and the park owner's two grandchildren (Joseph Mazzello and Ariana Richards) are stranded in a time warp, potential scraps of fossil fuel for the awakened giants.

It takes about 40 minutes to get to this point, and it's a disappointingly leaden passage. Spielberg, the past master of the kick-start action/adventure, gives us one spectacular early scene, when we and the touring guests get our first look at a grazing Brachiosaurus. But we spend most of the time getting to know the boring cast or attending lectures on vertebrate history.

Hey, just get us to the park, Steven, and turn the dinos loose!

"Jurassic Park" is Spielberg at his best and worst. The dinosaurs are wondrous, and the action sequences, almost nonstop for the last hour, recall the pulse-pounding pace of "Raiders of the Lost Ark" and some of the sense of impending doom in "Jaws." When the T-rex walks, each step creates a thunderclap and a tremor that puts ripples in ponds a mile away.

The delayed roller coaster ride begins with a long sequence with a T-rex trying to tear apart a tour car to get to the kids cowering inside, and then cuts back and forth from the separated humans as they try to hike past the agitated giants and return to the park's center.

Those who make it find that the center itself is overrun with birdlike, bear-sized "Raptors," meanest of the mean.

Unfortunately, Spielberg did not create human characters anywhere near as lifelike as the dinosaurs. The white-bearded Attenborough gives Dr. Hammond a jolly St. Nick quality, and Goldblum gets off some great lines in the early moments. But they fade quickly.

Spielberg, whose best movie remains "Jaws," has become too nice, too rich and too institutional a fellow to make a truly dangerous movie. You can do a head count when everyone arrives at Jurassic Park and know who will come out alive and who will not (hint: one of the guests is a lawyer), and that emotional safety net undermines both the suspense and the tension.

"Jurassic Park," rated PG-13, may still be too intense for children under 10, but the shocks are mostly funhouse stuff, things popping out at you that just happen to be dinosaurs. Yeah, you see one person scooped up by a T-rex, and someone's detached arm appears at a particularly scary moment, but the actual violence occurs behind bushes or inside cars, out of view of the camera.

In the final analysis, "Jurassic Park" is a movie that will achieve classic status on looks alone. It has no characters to match those in "Jaws," no sentiment to match that of "E.T.," none of the spiritual wonder of "Close Encounters."

Spielberg is too mindful of his success to venture into new territory, too eager to contrive "Spielberg moments," like the sequence where Neill and the kids are awakened in a treetop by a harmless Brachiosaurus, who promptly sneezes dino snot all over them.

Still, Spielberg is the master at provoking awe with creatures from other worlds and other times, and with the immense talent of his teams of computer and model designers, he has come closer than anyone—certainly in Hollywood—to bringing dinosaurs to life.

NEWSWEEK, 6/14/93, p. 64, David Ansen

Steven Spielberg's *Jurassic Park* is nothing more—and nothing less—than the world's most extravagant Godzilla movie. The filmmakers may insist this isn't a monster movie, but as any dinosaur-obsessed 8-year-old can tell you, these prehistoric giants are the ur-monsters of all our nightmares. Without them, half the gnarly demons in movie mythology would never have been dreamed up. And if Spielberg's P.C. horror movie—that's paleontologically correct—turns into the mega-blockbuster everyone expects it to, it's simply because it has the dream cast of the summer: toothy T-rex; the long-necked *Brachiosaurus*; a sickly, armor-plated *Triceratops*; the poison-spitting, gremlinesque *Dilophosaurus*; a stampeding *Gallimimus* herd, and the consummately villainous *Velociraptors*, the smartest, meanest flesh-eaters in the park.

All these stars, it should be pointed out, are female. (Who said there were no great roles for gals this summer?) You see, to prohibit his dinosaur population from reproducing outside the lab, John Hammond (Richard Attenborough), the billionaire impresario of the tropical-island theme park, has cloned only female creatures. Naturally, since he is afflicted with incurable hubris, his best-laid plans go awry: as every cautionary scientific fable since "Frankenstein" has warned, don't mess with Ms. Nature.

When the dinosaurs go on their rampage midway through "Jurassic Park," Spielberg and his special-effects aces rev up the terror with a cutthroat efficiency that will be too intense for most kids under 9. Good as the bone-crunching mayhem is—an enraged *Tyrannosaurus* overturning a car, a spectacular shot of a velociraptor leaping off a kitchen floor toward the camera—Spielberg is especially canny in his buildup to horror. The thumping tread of an unseen beast, its massive weight eerily conveyed by the turbulence in a water glass ... the thrashing of trees and the cries of predator and prey when an ox is dropped into a raptor's pen for lunch—at such moments "Jurassic Park" has the spine-tingly magic of Spielberg's best work.

The parts, however, are better than the whole. When Spielberg is cooking on all burners—in "Jaws," in "Close Encounters" or "E.T."—he can transform genre conventions into a seamless, visionary whole. "Jurassic Park" doesn't have that organic flow; it can't disguise its clunky, B-movie soul. Following Michael Crichton's novel, screenwriters Crichton and David Koepp round up their unlikely gaggle of characters, each of whom has to carry a heavy load of scientific exposition, and none of whom makes any deep claims on our affections.

Hammond assembles a trio of experts to give his park their seal of approval: we meet paleontologist Alan Grant (Sam Neill), whose aversion to children will be predictably reversed when he must save Hammond's two movie-brattish grandchildren from becoming the dinosaurs' hors d'oeuvre. As his paleobotanist girlfriend, Laura Dern radiates strenuous enthusiasm. It's never clear why Hammond wants the opinion of the moralizing mathematician Ian Malcolm (Jeff Goldblum), but Goldblum's manic line readings add a quirky pleasure to the setup. Hammond himself, played by Attenborough with plummy theatricality, is transformed from Crichton's evil fanatic into a more avuncular presence: the true bad guy is the obese, mercenary Dennis Nedry (Wayne Knight), who's selling pirated dinosaur embryos to an outside concern. Spielberg tweaks profiteers again (or is he tweaking hmself?) when he shows us rows and rows of Jurassic Park souvenirs at the park's gift shop: merchandise just like the products that will be spun off this movie.

"Jurassic Park" hits all the patented Spielberg marks—humor, thrills, heart—but not without strain. There's a gooey, lyrical interlude when Neill and the kids bond with a grazing Brachiosaurus (in the movie's New Age scheme of things, the good dinosaurs are vegetarians), but it feels like a pumped-up Kodak moment. These battle-scarred kids should be *terrified*. Oh, well. Is there any point in complaining that this $60 million fun-house ride is less than a classic? All we really ask is that it be scary (it is) and that the dinosaurs set a new standard in suspension of disbelief (they do). Go, tremble and enjoy.

SIGHT AND SOUND, 8/93, p. 44, Kem Newman

When one of his workers is killed, leisure tycoon John Hammond is advised by lawyer Donald Gennaro to have outside experts survey and endorse his latest venture, Jurassic Park. Palaeontologist Alan Grant, palaeobotanist Ellie Sattler and chaos theoretician Ian Malcolm are taken to an island off the coast of Costa Rica and given a tour of facilities where dinosaurs have been genetically engineered. With Hammond's grandchildren Tim and Alexis, the team are sent on an automated 'ride' through areas in which various species of dinosaur are penned. It soon becomes apparent that, beyond the successful recreation of the dinosaurs, the park is rife with design flaws, with the animals stubbornly refusing to conform to Hammond's plans.

As a storm hits, Dennis Nedry, who designed and operates the park's computer systems, shuts down the security programmes so that he can steal a selection of dinosaur embryos he intends to sell to a rival corporation. The ride breaks down and Gennaro is eaten by a tyrannosaurus rex which tries to get at the children, who are rescued by Alan while Ian is wounded distracting the beast. Nedry, lost in the storm, is blinded and killed by a venom-spitting dilophosaurus while Hammond is forced to shut down the power to get around blocks Nedry has integrated into the control systems.

Ellie, accompanied by Robert Muldoon, a game warden who has always distrusted dinosaurs, ventures out to reactivate the power from a generator, while Alan and the children make their way back to the control centre. Muldoon is killed by velociraptors, a vicious and intelligent pack animal; Ellie turns the power on just as Tim is clambering over an electric fence. Alan, who has formerly hated children, manages to save Tim, but the survivors discover that the velociraptors have breached the control centre. Alan, Ellie and the children are menaced by the persistent velociraptors, who are only defeated when the tyrannosaurus intervenes and kills the smaller beasts. The survivors flee the island.

The narrative motor of *Jurassic Park* is the overlap of irreconcilable agendas: the creation and ultimate failure of the theme park requires the input of caring paleontologists, wide-eyed children, Frankensteinian genetic engineers, chaos doomsayers, 'bloodsucking lawyers', ferocious predators and a fatherly multi-millionaire. Similarly conflicted and contrasting motives power the conversion of Michael Crichton's best-selling novel into an 'event' movie by Steven Spielberg. The stresses between the plot and the circumstances of its depiction are what make this blockbuster at once an all-but-infallible entertainment and a demonstration of its character Ian Malcolm's theory that things go wrong exponentially.

After a decade of literary adaptations, Indiana Jones sequels and oddments like *Always*, Spielberg needs to re-establish himself as the commercial and creative giant of the 70s and early 80s. Given this circumstance, *Jurassic Park* has almost all the elements of an identikit 'Spielberg': the paring-down of a monster best-seller into a suspense machine (*Jaws*); the tackling of a popular-science childhood sense of wonder perennial with state-of-the art effects that reimagine 1950s B science fiction (*Close Encounters of the Third Kind*) the all-action jungle adventure littered with incredible perils and gruesome deaths (*Raiders of the Lost Ark*); and big-eyed creatures who range from beatifically benevolent to toothily murderous (*Gremlins*, *E.T.: The Extra Terrestrial*). Add such tropes as a John Williams score; glowing wonder (Laura Dern as much as the children is called upon to gape in tearful amazement); textbook suspense (Tim clinging to a dead electric fence as Ellie unknowingly switches on the power); one all-too-true key speech ("you can't think this through, there are some things you have to *feel*"); and slapstick sadism involving caricatures nobody cares about (the gross Nedry blinded and gutted, the pockmarked Gennaro plucked from the toilet).

However, in a minor key, we note the input of Crichton, a novelist who is himself a director (albeit in career stall after *Physical Evidence*) and who laid down the basics of this plot with his first feature, *Westworld*. As in all of Crichton's SF, in print (*The Andromeda Strain, The Terminal Man*) or on film (*Coma, Looker, Runaway*), complex technical achievements are ultimately dangerous because human motives and skills are incapable of keeping pace with pure scientific advances. Ian Malcolm played with scene-stealing glee by Jeff Goldblum, is Crichton's signature character: a scientist who actually has a theory about why nothing ever goes right. As in the films of James Cameron (a director demonstratably influenced by *Westworld*), Crichton's technophobic visions, like Spielberg's anti-intellectual wonder, can only be brought to the screen by triumphs of technology no less astonishing than genetically recreating dinosaurs or constructing androids in the image of Yul Brynner.

Jurassic Park will be seen by millions for its effects alone, and the combination of puppetwork and animation certainly goes beyond the previous high water marks of Willis H. O'Brien's *King Kong* or Ray Harryhausen's *The Valley of Gwangi*. However, just as a group of diverse experts under the direction of a showman are responsible for the genetic engineering here (rather than the Frankenstein figures of 50s SF or Roger Corman's *Jurassic Park* cash-in, *Carnosaur*), lone visionaries like O'Brien and Harryhausen have been replaced by teams of multi-skilled employees whose collective achievement lacks the individual heart of *Kong*. A further irony is that *Jurassic Park* makes extensive use of the robotics and image-engineering processes Crichton himself predicted (and saw disastrous consequences for) in *Westworld* and *Looker*.

The most significant change between Crichton's novel and Spielberg's film is the transformation of John Hammond from an unsympathetic capitalist into a cuddly cod-Scots visionary played by

Attenborough (irresistibly recalling *Dr. Doolittle*). While the novel is an Awful Warning with a 'gosh-wow-*dinosaurs!'* undercurrent, the film is quite properly in love with its beasties, both as a narrative necessity and as a prelude to the inclusion of a *Jurassic Park* ride on the Universal Studio Tour. In tune with Spielberg's mind numbingly ignorant proclamation that "this is not science fiction, it's science eventuality", the film takes its prehistoric animals seriously, employing advisers to ensure that the dinosaurs act more like real ones than the *Jaws* shark did a real Great White. Alan Grant's explanatory lectures—about the way saurians probably had more in common with the birds than the reptiles—smugly underlines the film's authenticity. Even the saur-hating Muldoon, as he is about to be devoured, breathes "clever girl" (all the monsters are female) in appreciation of the trick the velociraptors have used to trap him. Just as *Close Encounters* crossbred 'true life' UFO stories with 50s Jack Arnold, *Jurassic Park* is informed by dino-buff Spielberg's genre heritage: images and lines deliberately recall *King Kong*, Ray Bradbury's story 'The Foghorn' (filmed as *The Beast From 20,000 Fathoms*), *Dinosaurs!* and *When Dinosaurs Ruled the Earth*. No matter how syrupy the kid-hating Grant's transformation into a fantasy father might be, it's hard to resist such primal moments as his calling to a herd of brachiosaurs with a Bradbury-ish honk only to be answered by a charming animal who takes the sugar off the scene by sneezing quantities of slime over Alexis.

Many annoying things about the film probably constitute survival traits in an international marketplace that would like a new monster to depose *E.T.* in the quarter-billion-dollar club. The softening of the novel so that only secondary characters are killed; the switch from nightmare horror to clean chase; the down-playing of any critique of entertainment capitalism and the pointless science (Crichton's Hammond has a lengthy speech about why it makes more economic sense to recreate dinosaurs than cure cancer); the inclusion of Laura Dern in shorts; and the abandonment of internal script logic in favour of a storyline which demonstrates its own chaos theory—all these factors compromise the film as drama but widen its appeal. The surprise is that painstaking effects coexist with extraordinary clumsiness: in the process of adaptation, many sub-plots are pruned but some extremely awkward factors (the ability of the dinosaurs spontaneously to change sex and thus breed beyond their controlled populations) are confusingly retained, though they serve no narrative function.

Like Jurassic Park, *Jurassic Park* is ultimately unable safely to contain its attractions, but the dinosaurs are still magnificent: the tyrannosaurus attack during a night storm, a fleeing herd of gallimimuses, the gremlin-like collared dilophosaurus cautiously killing its prey and the game of velociraptor hide-and-seek must stand as definitive. However, the most deeply-felt and emotionally complex shot of the film—a pan from a rack of now-unsalable cutesy dinosaur merchandise to the dejected Hammond—raises issues that the media monolith of a 90s studio blockbuster could never address.

TIME, 6/14/93, p. 69, Richard Corliss

John Hammond is a man in love with an idea. Inspired by motives of applied science and pure profit, he has pursued a scheme to clone dinosaurs from their preserved DNA and show off the brand-new bemoths on an island preserve. He has imperiled some noted scientists, and even his two young grandchildren, by inviting them to inspect the park before it is ready. Dino disaster awaits.

Hammond might be an ogre, twisting genetic research into capitalist exploitation, creating the ultimate carnival sideshow, where the freaks eat the gawkers. That is pretty much how Michael Crichton sketched the old man in the novel *Jurassic Park*. But the Hammond played by Richard Attenborough in Steven Spielberg's movie version is another fellow altogether; the director calls him "a cross between Walt Disney and Ross Perot." Hammond is certainly a visionary, a fabulous showman, an enthusiast, an emperor of ice cream, a kid with a great new toy. "Top of the line!" he chirps. "Spared no expense!" Why, he might be Spielberg as a foxy grandpa.

Top of the line? *Jurassic Park*, like every other Spielberg movie, is couture for the masses: a cunning design, elegantly tailored. Spared no expense? Just ask the picture's sponsor, Universal, which has not had a $100 million winner at the domestic box office since 1989 (with the Spielberg-produced *Back to the Future Part II*) and urgently needs a megahit—Hence the marketing tie-in with McDonald's, the imminent *Jurassic Park* ride at Universal's theme parks, and the saturation of action figures, jammies and cologne. The director did cut costs with a decent, modest cast of nonstars, and he tried shooting every dialogue scene in no more than five takes. But the expert exertions of the 483 other artists and technicians listed in the credits ensured that *Jurassic Park* would cost about $65 million, or $1 for every year since dinosaurs became extinct.

But enough money talk. This is a monster movie. So how are they?

Amazing. Dinosaurs live. You are there, once upon a time, before mammal walked or man dreamed. You can pet a triceratops and, if you wish, examine its droppings. You can feed a vegetarian brachiosaur, whose movements are graceful, endearing. At times the beasts (animated, mostly, by the computer sorcerers from Industrial Light & Magic) move in a hazier space than the humans in the foreground, but in the intimate scenes the dinos are utterly convincing. Spielberg loves to mix wonder with horror, and he has fun creating a living Museum of Natural Fantasy.

Then he scares you witless. Here come a nosy tyrannosaur and a fan-faced, bilious dilophosaur. Nastiest of all are the velociraptors, smart, relentless punks in packs—Saurz N the Hood. They have a special appetite for kids, just like the great white shark in the movie that made Spielberg's rep. Now it has some worthy successors: primeval creatures with personality and a lot of bite. *Jurassic Park* is the true *Jaws II*.

Like the films to which it pays elaborate homage—*Gertie the Dinosaur, King Kong* (and its Universal theme-park spin-off, Kongfrontation), *The Beast from 20,000 Fathoms, Godzilla, Bringing Up Baby*—this one sometimes creaks when it's not playing with the beasties. For the first half-hour—the pre-show before the thrill ride—you are advised to bide your time. Screenwriter David Koepp's subplot, in which a paleontologist (Sam Neill) is force-fed lessons in fatherhood by his paleobotanist girlfriend (Laura Dern), is laid on with a trowel. And the plot occasionally beggars belief. If you were up a huge tree and a van were teetering on the branch above you, would you race down the side of the tree just ahead of the plummeting vehicle, or would you move sensibly to the other side of the tree? But that is just another horror-movie tradition Spielberg observes: smart people doing really dumb things.

So what? This is at heart a picture about animals doing really smart things. The dilophosaur can inspire dread just by staring at its prey; the raptors by breathing on a window or opening a door. The *T. rex* goes for broader gestures: tipping over that rickety van, gobbling half of a lawyer, and shaking the other half like a cat with a mouse between its teeth. (And if you miss the book's creepiest scene, where the *T. rex* curls its tongue around a child hiding inside a waterfall, it's not here because, Spielberg says, "the tongue we made just wasn't convincing. It looked like Dino from *The Flintstones*.").

Most of the movie eschews overt violence for its much more satisfying alternative—the threat of violence. The guts and gore are seen mostly in the viewer's lurid imagination. That is why *Jurassic Park* slips so neatly into its PG-13 rating. "I do think this movie is inappropriate for children under 13," Spielberg says. "In general, though, I think children are more traumatized by violence that can be re-created in a natural setting: a movie about child abuse or a movie about murder. This is a movie that not only can't happen, but can't even be emulated. Even if audiences buy into the notion that dinosaurs are back, they still have the reassurance that they won't be attacked by a tyrannosaur on the way home. I guarantee that won't happen."

Ever since the director hit it big with *Jaws*, people have been telling him to grow up. They want him to tackle more personal themes, to address adult subject matter, to please stop making Steven Spielberg movies. Perhaps *Schindler's List*, the Nazi-era drama he has already completed shooting for Christmas release, will satisfy those who want Spielberg to enter an auteur rehab clinic.

But no film could be more personal to him than this one. With its next-generation effects and its age-old story line, this is a movie whose subject is its process, a movie about all the complexities of fabricating entertainment in the microchip age. It's a movie in love with technology (as Spielberg is), yet afraid of being carried away by it (as he is). The film even has a resident conscience, chaos theoretician Ian Malcolm (Jeff Goldblum), who insists that what God has put asunder, no man should join together.

Of course, if Hammond listens to him and shuts down the park, there's no film. The director of such beautiful dramas as *Empire of the Sun* and *Always* knows Malcolm is right; the director of *E.T.* and the Indiana Jones movies knows he must be ignored. Spielberg needs the dinosaurs to run amuck, as they so handsomely, plausibly do.

Yet Malcolm's words are a warning to all directors dazzled by the great new toys of filmmaking. "Dennis Muren and the ILM team," Spielberg says, "have perfected the dinosaur. Now what we need are stories. Without them, technology is an orphan. Without a good yarn, it's just a bunch of convincing pictures."

Thanks to Crichton, Spielberg had a good yarn to work with. Thanks to his effects wizards, the pictures were convincing. But it was the director who put the drama in every snazzy frame. For dinosaurs to rule the earth again, the monsters needed majesty as well as menace. And Spielberg got it all right.

VILLAGE VOICE, 6/22/93, p. 53, Georgia Brown

Relax. The trailers deceive: *Jurassic Park* isn't another cutesy, cuddly family entertainment. Nor is it a barbed attack on runaway science as the ever-vigilant *Times* keeps intimating. (Squash those critters before they hatch!) Thin but exciting in an old-fashioned way, Steven Spielberg's latest concentrates on movie basics: fear, excitement, and suspense. While not as primal as *Jaws*, *Jurassic Park* seems a prudent retreat to Spielberg's earlier, commercial, thrill-packed mode.

At the Ziegfeld screening, the friend on my right strained a muscle trying to save others from his flailing arms; on my left, a young man recently registered with the Selective Service cried out more than once, like a helpless child, Oh, Mom!

Like *Jaws*, *Jurassic Park* is based on a blockbuster novel—this time, Michael Crichton's pretentious muckraker aimed at unregulated biotechnology. Crichton and David Koepp have slanted the movie script, however, to reflect Spielberg's métier. The villain of this piece is not so much run-amok science as the grandiose entertainment business. As soon as impresario John Hammond (Richard Attenborough) announces, "Welcome to Jurassic Park!" he seems to be speaking for Spielberg: the director as enthusiastic host. A little later, in an interactive info-merical, Hammond reiterates his intent: "capturing the imagination of the entire family," bringing them all "into the theater."

And here we are, Steven, but minus the youngsters. Though the dinosaur hook will have every kid over two dying to see it, *Jurassic Park* is too terrifying for tender psyches. Amazingly, it really roughs up its two picture book perfect child protagonists. After *Hook*'s nauseating tribe of Lost Boys, many will appreciate this new coldness.

Picking Attenborough, director of cinematic dinosaurs, to play the entrepreneur is a clue that Spielberg is mocking self and the profession—at least mildly. (In *Close Encounters*, he had Truffaut playing the director of another secret project, but one we were to approve.) Here he even spoofs merchandizing tie-ins: Cut to Jurassic Park lunchboxes for a laugh. Attenborough—who started out as an actor—plays a childish, self-absorbed, and incompetent guru, a shallow Prospero tenuously ruling over obstreperous forces in his island kingdom.

As the movie opens, this "dark Walt Disney," as Crichton's novel put it, is about to invite some experts, a test audience including two children, to try out the rides in his theme park. Given the feat he's performed, he expects rave reviews.

The party consists of two paleontologists snatched from their dig in the Badlands (Dr. Grant and Dr. Ellie, played by Sam Neill and Laura Dern); a black-clad, hipster mathematician heavily into chaos theory (Jeff Goldblum); and a Milquetoast investigator sent by the project's concerned investors. Along with Hammond, this foursome flies into the jaws of a lush green canyon heliport—supposed to be Costa Rica but actually Hawaii. Getting directly to business, they're stunned to discover that the park's attraction is actual dinosaurs cloned by DNA extracted from mosquitos preserved in amber. I think everyone knows how to do this by now.

Of course, it's the given of the genre: Mad scientist awakens destructive forces dormant since before the dawn of time. Just before leaving on an, umm, eventful tour of the park, the eager if skeptical group is joined by Hammond's two grandchildren, Tim and Lex. The kids look so bland, they're surreal. They look like their prototypes in the movies of the '40s and '50s.

For his part, Hammond looks like twinkly Kris Kringle except for his yellow teeth. Obviously, teeth and oral craving enjoy a certain prominence in a movie featuring T. rex and the Raptors (velociraptors). By alternating between the mealtimes of humans and beasts, the movie plays off normal appetite and excess. In an opening scene harking back to *Jaws*, a park worker (one more black sacrificial lamb) is devoured, sort of sucked into a cage, by a hidden something, obviously quick and powerful, and very hungry. Two scenes later we meet the movie's comic baddie (Spielberg is reluctant as ever to create real villains), and he's very fat and pictured craving sweets and money. Another technician (played by Samuel L. Jackson) is a nonstop smoker. At one point, the two battered kids gleefully pig out at a sumptuous feast as the shadow of a raptor falls across the buffet table. Another suspenseful episode takes place in a kitchen. What goes in must come out, you say. Well, the movie covers that side too. Maybe its wildest sight comes after someone's stomach rebels and he flees to the toilet.

How do the creatures look?

Well, the first one we see is a bit faint and placed too near the foreground figures, making us think the illusion (created by robotics and computers) isn't really going to convince us. But it's almost as if this awkwardness is a playful way of loosening us up for shocks to come.

The eventual success of the illusion makes it all the more disappointing that Hammond—standing in for moviemakers trying to turn dream into reality—isn't a more sinister or complex figure. Part fool, part charlatan, he's another defanged Captain Hook. While his traumatized grandchildren are lost in the tyrannosaurus-infested jungle, Gramps sits up eating ice cream and telling the story of his first show, a flea circus—actually a trick perpetrated with tiny props and wires. So, he got his start in special effects.

Once more Spielberg injects his theme of the absent or weak father. If Hammond is the kids' monumentally negligent grandpa, Sam Neill's Dr. Grant becomes their reluctant dad. Established in the beginning is the fact that Grant has an aversion to kids, and it's this perhaps that keeps him and Ellie (Dern) from tying the knot. In the spirit not just of classic sci-fi but also of the Spielberg oeuvre, not a whiff of passion blows between these two. Goldblum's engaging Ian Malcolm comes on as the potentially randy one, though there's no one around to make, as he puts it, "the next ex-Mrs. Malcolm." A gloomy pontificator in the novel, he's the movie's welcome comic relief. But no one here has much to do except tremble with fear and run.

While it's nice to find *Jurassic Park* devoid of cuddly dinos, the movie could be darker, particularly since it isn't for the wee ones anyway. These are frightening times and pulp culture has its work cut out. But I know I shouldn't expect $56 million to buy either pulp or autocritique.

VILLAGE VOICE, 6/29/93, p. 62, Mim Udovitch

Okay, you've laughed, you've cried, you've admired Jeff Goldblum's superior ability to get a tongue into a groove over Sam Neill's. In other words, you've seen *Jurassic Park*, and you've realized that it is little more than maudlin sentimentality punctuated with awe-inspiring special effects: in short, a Spielberg movie. But not so fast. What with all the lunch-box hoopla, it has been largely overlooked that all the dinosaurs are female except for the ones who are mutating into males; *Jurassic Park* is yet another movie in which in which females with a same-sex or transsexual orientation run murderously rampant. Donald Suggs of the Gay and Lesbian Alliance Against Defamation comments: "Ha, ha, ha, ha, ha. Who are you writing this for? Well I'd say there's a tremendous amount of misperception about the transgendered even within the lesbian and gay community, and these misperceptions are really based on ignorance and a lack of fair or balanced portrayals of the transgendered in the mass media. It doesn't surprise me that these prejudices would go as far back as the Jurassic period."

Also reviewed in:
CHICAGO TRIBUNE, 6/11/93, Friday/p. A, Dave Kehr
NATION, 7/19/93, p. 115, Stuart Klawans
NEW REPUBLIC, 7/12/93, p. 26, Stanley Kauffmann
NEW YORK TIMES, 6/11/93, p. C1, Janet Maslin
NEW YORKER, 6/28/93, p. 96, Terrence Rafferty
VARIETY, 6/14/93, p. 54, Todd McCarthy
WASHINGTON POST, 6/11/93, p. G1, Rita Kempley
WASHINGTON POST, 6/11/93, Weekend/p. 42, Desson Howe

JUST ANOTHER GIRL ON THE I.R.T.

A Miramax Films release of a Truth 24 F.P.S. production. *Producer:* Erwin Wilson and Leslie Harris. *Director:* Leslie Harris. *Screenplay:* Leslie Harris. *Director of Photography:* Richard Connors. *Editor:* Jack Haigis. *Music:* Eric Sadler. *Sound:* Harrison Williams. *Casting:* Tracey Moore. *Production Designer:* Mike Green. *Set Decorator:* Robin Chase. *Costumes:* Bruce Brickus. *Make-up:* Karen Robinson. *Running time:* 96 minutes. *MPAA Rating:* R.

CAST: Ariyan Johnson (Chantel);   Kevin Thigpen (Tyrone);   Ebony Jerido (Natete); Chequita Jackson (Paula);   William Badget (Cedrick);   Jerard Washington (Gerard);   Karen Robinson (Debra Mitchell);   Tony Wilkes (Owen Mitchell);   Johnny Roses (Mr. Weinberg); Shawn King (Andre);   Kisha Richardson (Lavonica);   Monet Dunham (Denisha);   Wendall Moore (Mr. Moore);   Laura Ross (Woman Customer);   Rashmella (Woman in Welfare Office); Ron L. Cox (Clinic Doctor);   Richie Carter (Rashawn);   Mwata Carter (Amiri);   Gary Perez (Store Manager);   Lynn Franklin (Social Worker);   Erwin Wilson (Policeman #1);   Louis Thomas, Jr. (Policeman #2);   Nicholas B. Carter (Child Who Opens Bag);   Jasmine Thomas (Chantel's and Ty's Baby);   Moise Dominque (New Born Baby).

CHRISTIAN SCIENCE MONITOR, 3/15/93, p. 14, David Sterritt

There are two items of special interest in the credits of "Just Another Girl on the I.R.T.," the new movie written, directed, and coproduced by Leslie Harris.

One is the presence of Ms. Harris as the triple-threat filmmaker of the project. Not only is she a newcomer to the feature-film world, but she is one of the extremely rare African-American women who have managed to crack the white-male establishment in American film.

Also noteworthy in the credits is the acknowledgement of a substantial number of not-for-profit organizations that helped Harris complete her movie and bring it to commercial distribution. These range from the American Film Institute and the National Endowment for the Arts to the Jerome Foundation and the BACA/Brooklyn Arts Council, among others.

The system of big-business entrepreneurship that governs Hollywood has few provisions for the extra support needed by independent-minded mavericks like Harris. The groups that kicked in for this project deserve thanks not only from the filmmakers, but from everyone who cares about a diversified American movie landscape.

This doesn't mean the picture is a perfect achievement. Like most of its characters, it's rough and sometimes raw to visit with, blending sharp insights into the world of inner-city youth with a weakness for melodrama and touches of silly humor. But to see it is to visit a world rarely touched by mainstream movies.

The heroine of "Just Another Girl on the I.R.T." is Chantel, a teenager who doesn't want to be just another kid on the inner-city path to nowhere. She's proud of her intelligence, earns the highest grades in her calculus class—although this would be more credible if we saw her doing homework—and can't wait to attend medical school and become a doctor.

But her ambitions run into problems, and while many are caused or heightened by the hardships of her environment, others are brought on by nobody but herself. She has an "attitude," as she and her friends would say, that leads her to disrespectful behavior and rude outbursts in school. Her friends are far less serious about life and work than she is, and distract her constantly. And sex is a frequent temptation—despite her awareness of the dangers it poses and the dead-end future that a teen-age pregnancy is likely to bring.

"Just Another Girl on the I.R.T.," named after the New York subway that Chantel rides, follows her through a few months of her 11th-grade life. She hangs out with companions, scuttles an unglamorous boyfriend for one with a handsome face and a classy car, and eventually faces pregnancy—a difficult situation for any single youngster, and particularly for Chantel, who's far less mature and sophisticated than she allows herself to believe.

The story culminates in a childbirth scene of harrowing suspense and horrifying danger. The ending is quiet and downbeat, holding few illusions about Chantel's future but hinting that her life may not be entirely routine in the years to come.

The most lively virtues of Harris's filmmaking style are its incredible energy—the screen positively bursts with color and motion, reflecting the youthful buoyancy of Chantel herself—and its cleverness in blending music, dialogue, and the noise of urban life on the soundtrack, which is an artful achievement in itself. The performances are also distinctive, especially by Ariyan Johnson as Chantel and Ebony Jerido as her best friend, although some of the acting has a sameness and shrillness that make it wearying after a while.

"Just Another Girl on the I.R.T." is too boisterous and obstreperous to be a likely contender for best-of-the-year honors from the filmmaking establishment. Those very qualities, however, are what make it a compelling echo of an authentically new voice in American film. Harris may have an attitude of her own, but it's a vigorous and original one that demands to make itself heard.

LOS ANGELES TIMES, 4/2/93, Calendar/p. 4, Peter Rainer

Chantel (Ariyan Johnson) is 17 and all attitude. A home-girl who lives with her parents and two younger brothers in a Brooklyn high-rise, she flaunts her sass. She loves the idea that she can dis her teachers and still get the highest grades in her class. She'll need them: Her dream is to go to med school.

Leslie Harris, 32, who wrote and directed "Just Another Girl on the I.R.T.," is one of very few black women making feature-length movies in this country. As ragged and uneven as her movie is—it's her first feature—it does occasionally move into areas of experience that we haven't seen on a screen before. The lives of black women, after all, haven't exactly been mined in the movies.

What Harris is trying to do is give us a closer look at the kind of girl we might not ordinarily look at twice. Chantel is a child of the hip-hop generation, and the movies rap soundtrack is like her pulse beat. Harris wants to celebrate her sizzle but she also wants to demonstrate how it can get her into trouble—teen-age pregnancy trouble.

This is the part of the film that seems least original. Once Chantel discovers she's pregnant by her smooth new boyfriend (Kevin Thigpen)—he has a Jeep and lives in a brownstone—the film (rated R for language and sexuality) becomes a bit too cautionary and heavy-handed. It wears its social conscience on its tattered sleeve. It tries to be "educational."

Harris is at her best when she just lets her actors jangle together. As an actress, Ariyan Johnson is pretty much all attitude too, but she's a real dynamo. The scenes with Chantel and her girlfriends trading folklore about birth control, or the ones where Chantel confounds her stolid suitor Gerard (Jerard Washington) at a dance, are both funny and original.

Most movies about black inner-city life have been so male-oriented that "Just Another Girl on the I.R.T." seems like a bulletin from the other side of the tracks. It's more of a harbinger of better things to come than a solid achievement in its own right, but it's moving in a fresh, invigorating direction.

NEW YORK, 4/5/93, p. 60, David Denby

Chantel (Ariyan Johnson, the black high-school student from Brooklyn who is the heroine of *Just Another Girl on the I.R.T.,* tells off her teacher, Mr. Weinberg, early in the movie. Why study the Holocaust? she demands. Why not study the death of young black men in cities?

(The issue is presented as if these were the only two alternatives, and the implication is that Jews are trying to keep blacks down.) Chantel also tells off a haughty woman who shops in the gourmet deli in which she works; she tells off the school principal, her boyfriend, her mother, her father. Who's left? Clarence Thomas? Chantel is supposed to be a great student, though we never see her reading or even listening to anyone. Her aggression is celebrated so openly—she's meant to be sassy and irresistible—that you might think the point of life was to defeat every person you met in verbal sparring. Ariyan Johnson, the young dancer who plays Chantel, jerks her head from side to side as she talks, driving the point home.

Just Another Girl, the first film written and directed by Leslie Harris, has the rhythm of New York—rap music by Nikki D and Cee Asia and other girl rappers, the quick movement and cutting of the restless city. In the press notes for the film, Harris says, "It's time that we start seeing characters on the screen that are real." But apart from the street atmosphere, reality is the opposite of what Harris puts on the screen. *Just Another Girl* consists of little lessons in indomitability. In the end, Harris's kind of self-infatuated fantasy requires ignoring what women like Chantel are actually up against.

The trials of a teenage black girl is a great new movie subject, and this movie betrays it. There isn't a thought that's worked out, a dramatic situation perceived clearly and told truly. Chantel, for instance, wants to go to college; she sees pregnancy as a trap she must avoid. When she does get pregnant, she vacillates, unwilling to have an abortion. This is a fascinating issue: What would lead a young black woman, especially one as allegedly ambitious as Chantel, to have the child? But Harris short-circuits her own movie. I won't tell you how it ends, but let's say that Chantel manages to triumph without losing or learning anything. I applaud anyone who can beat the odds, but I'd also like to know how she does it. Harris, from the evidence of *Just Another Girl on the I.R.T.*, doesn't have a clue.

NEW YORK POST, 3/19/93, p. 29, Jami Bernard

The black woman's voice in film has been silent for so long that it comes out in a big, sassy blast in Leslie Harris's fine and funny "Just Another Girl on the IRT," the first of what I hope will be a long line of movies to explore the urban female experience.

With a splashy debut by Ariyan Johnson—who joins the ranks of Marisa Tomei and Rosie Perez in the exciting new category of Actresses with Attitude—"Just Another Girl on the IRT" follows the home, school, dating, and commuting-by-subway life of 17-year-old Brooklyn girl Chantel Mitchell (Johnson).

"I'm gonna tell you the rear deal," Chantel says in several confrontations with the camera and you get the impression that it is the real deal, indeed.

Chantel is smart, quick, opinionated, and can mow down the competition with her big mouth. But on the subway, and outside her own insulated world, she is perceived by the rest of society as either invisible or a nuisance—just as black women have been depicted for the most part in all movies, including those made by black men.

She works in a yuppie supermarket where the white women want their Brie with caraway seeds. There is a segment in a high school history class that is bound to be perceived as anti-Semitic, in which Chantel makes a case for the Holocaust being less important than black studies because 6 million dead Jews have less impact on her than today's acts of job discrimination. The scene made me uncomfortable and yet stayed true to Chantel's character.

Harris directs the sloe-eyed Johnson and the women who play her pals in a bawdy, shrieking discussion of sex, boys, and AIDS that is more the way women talk among themselves than most anything else you'll find on film.

For the complacent, judgmental-folks who wonder how all those black teenagers can get pregnant and lose the thread of their lives so easily, "Girl on the IRT' gives a rare insight into the context of a life like Chantel's—the social pressures, the psychological denial. When she gets pregnant, her inability to make a decision is what makes her decision for her. Her denial is complete, and full of intricacies: she buys larger sizes of the same clothes so that her family and friends won't notice. ("Mama thought I was a pig, not pregnant.")

Unlike the spate of black male films that have taken women for granted or depicted them as peripheral characters in the service of the male leads, "Girl on the IRT" draws several strong portraits of the men in Chantel's life. Chantel herself is full of inconsistencies, and so are the guys—but everyone's basic decency shines through.

The movie is also quite funny, and yet it was disheartening to see how many people at a recent screening laughed inappropriately at parts that were the most emotionally wrenching. Perhaps the black woman's experience has been so absent from public view that folks have trouble knowing just how to react.

Writer/director/producer Leslie Harris is a major new talent and should get the same accolades they'd give a man for this jazzy, streetwise, soulful girlz 'n the hood.

NEWSDAY, 3/19/93, Part II/p. 67, Gene Seymour

As Chantel, the Brooklyn teenager in "Just Another Girl on the IRT," Ariyan Johnson talks trash a mile a minute and doesn't care at all what you think of her rude, insouciant, turbo-charged rap, whose sound meter seems frozen in the upper reaches.

Yet you not only don't mind that she's in your face for much of the movie, you miss her those few seconds when she's out of the frame. Johnson loves the camera and the camera loves her back even more. Of such transactions are movie stars made.

Johnson's juicy performance deserved a better film. Not that first-time director Leslie Harris doesn't make a good try. Short-circuiting the stereotypes that too often govern mainstream perceptions of black teenagers was a valuable—and still necessary—impulse to pursue.

And for at least the first part of this tour through a topsy-turvy year in Chantel's life, both Harris' hip-hopping dialogue and Johnson's authoritative delivery conspire deliciously against, among others, the strap-hangers who flinch at the boisterous patter of Chantel and her high school girlfriends. "When I'm with my friends, I act like it don't matter," Chantel says in Ferris Bueller-esque asides to the audience. "because it *don't!*"

She goes on to say that these "people be trippin' when they find out how smart I really am." Indeed, beneath Chantel's freewheeling and flirtatious manner is the soul of a true grind. She pulls down A's in school, works hard after school, both at a Manhattan gourmet shop and at home caring for her kid brothers while her parents work long, overlapping hours.

Though it's hard to imagine what she'd be like as a doctor, medical school is where she says she's headed. But then, this subway-riding sister from the projects is swept off her feet by a dreamy, jeep-driving brownstone dweller named Tyrone (Kevin Thigpen), with whom she gets unexpectedly pregnant.

Too suddenly, too abruptly, this brash, smart, confident young woman becomes a confused, frightened and wilfully self-absorbed child, denying her pregnancy to the point where she is able to conceal it from all but Tyrone, who struggles to figure out what she wants to do about the situation.

Chantel follows her student's instincts and bones up on reproductive lore. And yet, she remains in a state of panicky denial up to the end—and even afterward, when she gets desperate enough to consider the unspeakable.

Harris should be commended for trying to make Chantel's character complex and unpredictable enough to risk losing the audience's sympathy.

But when the audience asks, "Well, if she's so smart, how come she acts so dumb about her baby?," it deserves better and deeper explanations than Harris provides.

Worse, Harris makes everything "work out" in the end with such peremptory carelessness that you feel more than a little cheated.

The best you could say about "Just Another Girl on the IRT" is that it gives you a view of life you don't often see in movies. But as the African-American film movement continues to grow in ambition and achievement, just getting these stories on screen won't be enough. Thinking them through and making them sturdy will.

SIGHT AND SOUND, 8/93, p. 45, Cynthia Rose

Every Saturday, 17-year-old self-described "tough girl" Chantel Mitchell takes the IRT subway from her home in the Brooklyn projects to a job on the West Side of Manhattan. She works in a specialty food shop, and after work window-shops with her friend Natete. On the IRT home, they meet another friend, who has had a baby; she confides that the father has given her no help and she depends on her mother. At home, Chantel is kept awake by her parents' arguments, as she dreams of a better life. At school, when her teacher Mr Weinberg brings up the Holocaust, Chantel demands he teach history more "Afrocentrically". Sent to the principal, she informs him she plans to graduate early; he warns that, if she really wants to be a doctor, she must "tone down" her mouth.

Chantel's father complains about her seeing her boyfriend Gerard, who is from the same project. In the park, Chantel and her girlfriends discuss sex, Aids and contraception. At a party, Chantel meets a stranger, Tyrone; learning he has a jeep, she deserts the party and Gerard for a ride with him. She begins asking Natete to cover for her with her family, so she can spend nights with Ty. During their first interlude, he laughs off her suggestion that he wear a condom. Soon, Chantel is throwing up in the ladies' room at school, and a home pregnancy test proves positive. She visits a clinic, where she consults Paula, a counsellor; then she waits in the welfare office, only to find she does not qualify. Chantel decides to deal with her pregnancy as "a dream", even telling Natete she has got her period. She confides in Ty, but he insults and then leaves her; later, more contrite, he offers her the money to finance an abortion. Instead, Chantel buys a girdle and takes Natete on a shopping spree. When Ty discovers what she has done with his money, she avoids his calls. Finally, he corners her and angrily tells her she must make some decision.

By autumn, Chantel is still avoiding reality. Since Ty has been avoiding her, she seeks him out. Although shocked by her size, he seems happy to see her. But their reunion is interrupted by the onset of labour. Ty telephones Paula, who is unable to summon an ambulance. She and her partner speed to the rescue, but Chantel delivers her child before they arrive. Terrified, she instructs Ty to hide her baby in a rubbish bin; it is found by a child, who runs for help. Coaxing the truth out of Chantel, Paula runs to the bin, where she finds the police but no baby. Back at Tyrone's, however, Paula and her partner find the whole family (Tyrone, out of guilt, went back after the baby). One winter later, Chantel is well-dressed and walking around a community college, with her growing, equally well-attired infant; she announces, "We're getting our shit together".

Just Another Girl on the I.R.T. begins as a film about the pros and cons of teenage 'attitude'. But, before it is half way complete, didacticism has drained this timely idea of all potential. The girl of the title is the personality-packed product of a Brooklyn housing project. Chantel is framed as a self-help paradigm out of the hip-hop universe—'consciously'-dressed, upwardly mobile and full of lofty dreams. She wants to graduate high school early, finish college and study medicine. But, in reality, these visions serve the same purpose as her 'fly' wardrobe—they confer the bravado which gets her through each day.

Viewers are shown successive chunks of the problems which forged Chantel's defences: the pal whose boyfriend disappeared the moment she had his baby; the troublesome customers at her workplace; the worried parents struggling with menial jobs and terrible hours. But most of these presentations are messages on legs. Livelier, and delightfully real, is Chantel's giggly posse of girlfriends, a cadre whose advice about sex, Aids and contraception is less reliable than their knowledge of name-brand sneakers.

Just as it starts to zero in on the debits of hip-hop posture, however, *Girl* shifts its focus completely; Chantel's saga becomes a means to 'educate' the viewer. Trying to impress her schoolmates with Afrocentric moxie, Chantel dismisses the Holocaust, and snubs a Jewish teacher. Then she drops her homeboy squeeze Gerard for the flashier Tyrone (when Gerard demands to know what his rival can really offer, Chantel pauses only a nanosecond before she answers, "a jeep"). These scenes may be intended as honest portraits of immaturity. But they are so crudely handled that they reinforce stereotypes: such as the notion that 'Afrocentricity' has to be Louis Farrakhan's turf, or the idea that young black women are the gold-digging 'skeezers' of rap.

Once Chantel engineers her connection with Tyrone, the plot gets even wobblier. With her positive pregnancy test, the clinic visit, and Tyrone's anger, we enter the schematic world of television problem pics. Chantel, however, clings to her tough-girl persona, with Ariyan Johnson making her stubbornness so perverse it commands attention. Chantel may drag herself to see counsellors and welfare officers, even accept the $500 Tyrone gives her to buy an abortion. But she denies her pregnancy with incredible force of will, lying to friends and stuffing her growing tummy into a girdle. With her closest friend Natete (a wonderful debut by singer and dancer Ebony Jerido), she even blows Tyrone's money during an all-day shopping spree. Finally, she has the baby—prematurely, as she is trying to reconcile with Tyrone. But even then she orders the frantic father to hide it in the rubbish.

By this point (after a scene of sustained screaming which outranks Marilyn Burns in *The Texas Chainsaw Massacre*), *Girl* has long since abdicated any plot dynamic. The movie's only strong point is its sharp and zappy cast. But hazy vision finally saps even their energy—just as the pasted-on happy ending mocks their efforts to keep things real. When we reach Chantel's *deus ex machina* transformation, one could be forgiven for thinking that Tipper Gore had final cut.

VILLAGE VOICE, 3/23/93, p. 58, Greg Tate

Leslie Harris's *Just Another Girl on the I.R.T.* gets two snaps up on G.P. alone. When was the last time you saw a black woman carry a picture? When was the last time you saw a sister given the chance? Granted, Julie Dash did put a panoply of diva-dom to work in *Daughters in the Dust*, but that was an ensemble thing. Leading lady Ariyan Johnson holds court up in here with rude-girl authority, flygirl couture, and underdeveloped mother wit. *Just Another Girl* is Johnson's show and she bumrushes it with all the obnoxious buoyancy of a double-platinum rapper. She runs her cocky and too-cute mouth for nearly the whole film, her high-pitched repartee becoming as infectiously annoying as the noisy hook in a Hank Shocklee mix.

Harris will probably have to endure *Girlz N Hood* taglines ad nauseam from reviewers, but this rites of passage essay slices through the meat of easy teen sexploitation to get at the marrow of teenage ignorance, shame, and confusion about contraception, STDs, abortion rights, and parenting. To artfully deliver the pedagogical load Harris relies heavily on Johnson's shit-talkin', eye-cuttin', neck-rollin', Brooklyn flygirl. She is both stereotype and anti-stereotype. Though she resides in the projects, she works hard (at school and after school—her parents hold down steady jobs); though we meet her as a flirt, she's still a virgin. Later we learn that this hiphop baby knows more about Mother Africa than she does about her own reproductive system. The scenes that deal with her denial of pregnancy manage to be hilarious, harrowing, and edgy. Harris gets points for having the nerve to turn the audience ambivalent and then straight-up against her plucky, charismatic principal. The film's frightening dramatic center induces painful tension because while the heroine's self-centered actions are in character they're also unexpected and thoroughly despicable.

Made in 17 days on a shoestring, the movie has a few sync sound problems and photography that ranges from pretty good to passable to kinda funky in places, but Harris's dialogue and Johnson's in-your-eye-sucka attitudinizing give craft critiques the gas face. The conversations on contraception between Johnson's Chantel and her good girlfriends Paula (Chequita Jackson) and Natete (Ebony Jerido) rival Richard Pryor for socially conscious porntalk and the *National Enquirer* for accuracy.

Harris writes for teenagers like somebody who listens to the pathos between the lines of the latest slang rather than somebody who wants to pump up their script's cool quotient. Directed to a black teen audience, *Just Another Girl on the IRT* manages the rare feat of being an instructive, confrontational and loving riff on their sexual manners and mores that is not didactic, patronizing, or morally aghast. The filmmaker's unblinking sense of responsibility to both story and society shows up in the science she drops on her core audience. In that respect *Just Another Girl* rivals the best hiphop for riveting realness, then goes hiphop one better by offering some useful adult wisdom too.

Also reviewed in:
NEW REPUBLIC, 4/19/93, p. 30, Stanley Kauffmann
NEW YORK TIMES, 3/19/93, p. C12, Vincent Canby
NEW YORKER, 3/22/93, p. 102, Terrence Rafferty
VARIETY, 9/21/92, p. 84, Todd McCarthy
WASHINGTON POST, 4/2/93, p. D1, Hal Hinson

KALIFORNIA

A Gramercy Pictures release of a Polygram Filmed Entertainment presentation of a Propaganda Films production. *Executive Producer:* Jim Kouf and Lynn Bigelow. *Producer:* Steve Golin, Sigurjon Sighvatsson, and Aristides McGarry. *Director:* Dominic Sena. *Screenplay:* Tim Metcalfe. *Story:* Stephen Levy and Tim Metcalfe. *Director of Photography:* Bojan Bazelli. *Editor:* Martin Hunter. *Music:* Carter Burwell. *Music Editor:* Adam Smalley. *Sound:* Jose Antonio Garcia. *Sound Editor:* Paul Clay. *Casting:* Carol Lewis, Pat Golden, and Shay

Griffin. *Production Designer:* Michael White. *Art Director:* Jeff Mann. *Set Designer:* Robert W. Harbour. *Set Decorator:* Kate Sullivan. *Set Dresser:* Don G. Smith, Riley "Sean" Jones, and Margaret Hungerford. *Special Effects:* Michael Shorr and Jeff Knott. *Costumes:* Kelle Kutsugeras. *Make-up:* Michelle Buehler. *Stunt Coordinator:* Dan Bradley. *Special Make-up Effects:* Thom Surprehant and Andre Freitas. *Running time:* 117 minutes. *MPAA Rating:* R.

CAST: Brad Pitt (Early Grayce); Juliette Lewis (Adele Corners); David Duchovny (Brian Kessler); Michelle Forbes (Carrie Laughlin); Sierra Pecheur (Mrs. Musgrave); Gregory Mars Martin (Walter Livesy); David Milford (Driver); Marisa Raper (Little Girl); Catherine Larson (Teenage Girl); Bill Crabbe (Middle-aged Farmer); Loanne Bishop and Ron Kuhlman (Officers); Brett Rice (Police Officer); Sarah Sullivan (Bar Waitress); Patricia Sill (Carol); J. Michael McDougal (John Diebold); Tommy Chappelle (Old Man); Judson Vaughn (Parole Officer); David Rose (Eric); John Dullaghan (Mr. Musgrave); Eric Stenson (Young Cracker); Mary Ann Hagan (Waitress); Patricia Hunte (Newscaster).

LOS ANGELES TIMES, 9/3/93, Calendar/p. 8, Kenneth Turan

While it's hard to remember any groundswell of demand for yet another trendy, high-gloss movie depicting in graphic detail the grisly doings of a serial killer, someone must have asked for one, or else why would "Kalifornia" be around, messing up an otherwise nice day?

Maybe it's because screenwriter Tim Metcalfe, didn't want to be pigeonholed as one of the co-authors of "Revenge of the Nerds." Or because director Dominic Sena didn't want to be stuck in music videos forever. Or because stars and real-life couple Brad Pitt and Juliette Lewis wanted something they could act in together. Whatever the reason, "Kalifornia" is here and that is not a cause for celebration.

Set in an unnamed Atlanta-like Southern city, "Kalifornia" is narrated by Brian Kessler (David Duchovny), a writer who thinks nobody knows the trouble serial killers have seen. "They have minds of children, the answer is research and treatment, not imprisonment," he says, practically with tears in his eyes. Naturally, Brian's pals think his elevator doesn't go all the way to the top.

Brian's girlfriend is Carrie Laughlin (Louise Brooks look-alike Michelle Forbes), a sultry photographer who is partial to black underwear and explicit pictures that are too out-there for the local galleries. Infected with terminal ennui, she wants more than anything to get out of town.

Wait, says Brian. Remember that book contract I have on serial killers? Why don't we drive to California and stop along the way at sites of famous mass murders? You'll take your provocative photographs and I'll babble pseudo-profundities like "serial killers live their whole lives somewhere between dreams and reality" into my tape recorder. Won't we have fun?

Carrie agrees with as much enthusiasm as her ennui will permit. The only problem is that they can't afford the gas for the trip. So Brian puts a "riders wanted" sign on a local bulletin board, and Early Grayce (Pitt), another man looking for a change, pulls it off and answers it.

Early, his name will inform you, is not a member of the with-it class. Looking like a young and restless Gabby Hayes, he is an ex-con who lives in a rancid trailer park with his violent temper and waitress girlfriend Adele Corners (Lewis), a simple soul who keeps pet cacti in her purse.

Hard as it is to believe, these four merrily set out together for California in Brian's '61 Lincoln. Carrie takes a strong dislike to Early, who has the disconcerting habit of simultaneously leering and cleaning his feet at the table, but Brian, fascinated by the way "Early lived in the moment," tells her she has nothing to worry about. Right.

Not only are none of these characters particularly fun to be with, but the inevitable violence that enters their lives is strong and unpleasant. Director Sena and cinematographer Bojan Bazelli have given "Kalifornia" (understandably rated R for strong violence, and for sexuality and language) a slick and stylish look but that doesn't make the encroaching mayhem any easier to take.

Lewis and Pitt are two of the best young actors around, but in this film they have gotten lost in a welter of thick accents and cross-cultural slumming. Without a strong hand guiding them, their performances seem mannered and even a trifle repetitive.

Revisiting territory that everything from "Badlands" to the recent "Guncrazy" have worked to better effect, "Kalifornia" appears convinced it is saying something profound or funny or both. Serial killers, it seems, are not the only folks operating under very serious delusions.

NEW YORK, 9/20/93, p. 65, David Denby

In *Kalifornia*, two aesthetes of violence—poseurs—meet up with the real thing. Brian (David Duchovny), a pretentious magazine journalist, is writing a book about serial killers, but poor Bri doesn't understand that killers, you know, *kill*. (He's supposed to be a liberal, but boy, does *he* wise up fast.) His girlfriend, Carrie (Michelle Forbes), who looks like a downtown person out of *Interview* magazine—short, spiky black hair, black bra and undies—does photographs of herself and other women in flagrante with African-American males (sort of a hetero female Mapplethorpe with a participatory thing?). Heading west, they pick up two hicks: Early (Brad Pitt), a pleasant psycho, who kills whenever he feels like it, and his girlfriend, Adele (Juliette Lewis), whom he calls "Mother." Adele, a clear descendant of the innocent played by Sissy Spacek in *Badlands*, is a child-woman trying to deny what her boyfriend does to people. Pitt's snorting, mumbling performance never quite makes it out of his furry beard, but Juliette Lewis, reading her lines in a rapturous singsong, shaping the air with her hands, is funny and even touching.

Director Dominic Sena (another music-video fellow) and writer Tim Metcalfe create tensions among these four that become fascinating in a creepily erotic way. This arty movie is far from boring; like other music video types, Sena composes his movie in striking visual moods (Can it be a coincidence that several of these up-from-video directors have made movies about serial killers? Murder, I've often thought, is at the heart of so many music videos.) But soon enough the question becomes, Does Brian have enough man in him to kill Early and reclaim his girlfriend from Early's grip? (It's what these movies always come down to.) You find out the answer in the climactic scene, which is set in a dummy house in the nuclear-testing range on the California-Nevada border, a house filled with mannequins. Out there in nuke-house, in the great symbolic American desert, everyone gets down and dirty with handcuffs and blood and broken mannequin limbs. *Kalifornia* wants to be a midnight-movie cult hit in the worst way; it about half makes it.

NEW YORK POST, 9/3/93, p. 25, Michael Medved

"Kalifornia" the movie, like California the state, is an intriguing mess; it's full of impressive elements, but the total package adds up to less than the sum of its parts.

David Duchovny (a suave and accomplished young actor who has appeared in everything from kiddie fare like "Beethoven" to cult films such as "The Rapture" and "Julia Has Two Lovers") plays a hip, politically correct graduate student who's struggling to finish a book about the psychology of serial killers.

His girlfriend (played by supremely sexy newcomer Michelle Forbes) is a chain-smoking photographer who specializes in shocking black-and-white images in the style of Robert Mapplethorpe, showing her own athletic body in various compromising positions.

They decide to make a new life for themselves in California, driving across country in a '61 Lincoln convertible and stopping at famous murder sites, where Forbes will shoot photographs for her lover's book. To help pay for this ghoulish joy ride they place a ride-share notice on a bulletin board and turn up two tag-alongs who might stand as textbook definitions of what used to be called "white trash."

Early Grayce and Adele Corners (played by real-life romantic partners Brad Pitt and Juliette Lewis) are down on their luck, since good ol' Earl has just jumped his parole and murdered his trailer park landlord. Meanwhile, the bubble-brained A-dell (who lives in deep denial of her man's violent nature) dreams of the glamorous thrills that await them on the Left Coast.

"When we get out to California," she whines, "I want you to take me to that Chinese restaurant with all them footprints in the cement."

The actors acquit themselves surprisingly well in this silly story—particularly Brad Pitt, who will be totally unrecognizable to those who admired his superb work in "A River Runs Through It" or as the hitchhiker in "Thelma and Louise." Here, with a ragged beard and long stringy hair beneath a cap emblazoned with a Confederate flag, he plays a redneck so coarse and primitive that he makes Gomer Pyle look like Alistair Cooke.

In addition to fine performances, "Kalifornia" benefits from intensely atmospheric camera work (by veteran Bojan Bazelli) and perfectly chosen, dramatically lit locations: you feel as if you're personally enduring these grimy gas stations and run-down country motels. Debuting director

Dominic Sena has built a formidable reputation in creating slick music videos and commercials, and his film remains visually fascinating long after interest in the predictable plot has flagged.

Ultimately, the film in undone—like many others—by its own pretensions at profundity. "Help me out, Early. I don't know s--t about killing," David Duchovny tells his brutal traveling companion. "Does it make you feel good? Powerful? Are you angry at your mother? Do you feel superior?"

The filmmakers clearly do feel superior merely raining such questions, despite the fact that they provide no answers whatever. Instead they deliver increasingly graphic doses of sadistic violence.

At the same time, the lack of a police presence—or any serious manhunt as Early Grayce leaves a bloody, obvious trail on his way west—stretches credibility past the breaking point.

The picture also wallows in its own kutting edge kuteness—like the kurious "K" in the title (which is never explained) or the fact that the klimactic konfrontation (all right, enough already!) takes place in an abandoned nuclear testing range. In the end, this picture offers an ordeal that is not only pointless but also implausible, and as far its central psycho is concerned—this Early worm gets the bird.

NEWSDAY, 9/3/93, Part II/p. 67, Ira Robbins

Imagine a good picture in which the Bob Hope role is played by Charles Manson and you'll have an inkling of this offbeat travelogue. Fueled by the provocative idea of a journalist who writes about murders unwittingly traveling with the genuine article, "Kalifornia" packs two horribly mismatched couples off on an uneasy ride to a place way, way south of the promised land.

While one member of the quartet attempts to investigate violent crimes, another is busy committing them in this brutal tale of innocents being sucked down a sinkhole of increasing mayhem. This mixture of "Something Wild" and "Henry, Portrait of a Serial Killer" gives Brad Pitt—who also hitchhiked in "Thelma & Louise" and chewed the surrealist scenery in "Johnny Suede"—the opportunity to rev up one of the most luridly colorful screen villains since Robert De Niro's Max Cady in "Cape Fear."

Smart, sleek yuppies Carrie Laughlin and Brian Kessler (Michelle Forbes and David Duchovny, whose eyes have the same expressionless animal quality as Richard Gere's), a photographer and a writer, are spinning their career wheels in some unspecified northeastern city. She's anxious to head West, where the art galleries might be more open to her strongly erotic images. When he concocts an idea to drive to California to research a book on America's most infamous mass killers, she jumps at the chance. But while, they've got the wheels (a fine Continental convertible), they lack the cash. Solution: Get someone to share the driving and the expenses.

Who they find, through a simple and credible plot coincidence, is big trouble in the persons of Early Grayce and Adele Corners (Brad Pitt and Juliette Lewis), grubby trailer park trash so low that they've just been evicted from their trailer. He's a spacey southern thug on parole (and not even for the catastrophic bit of casual mischief he performs in the shocking opening scene); she's a pitiful, dimwitted scrap of a child-woman who says "we wuz" a lot, Plays with a yo-yo and makes friends with cacti. By the time Brian and Carrie pick up their blind-date traveling companion, it's abundantly clear who's being taken for a ride.

While Brian plots the course through America's most colorful murder sites, sociopath Early—unbeknownst to the others—makes his own contribution to the nation's crime statistics. As the evidence of Early's malevolence mounts, it's only a question of when gullible Brian, whose primal side is—to Carrie's chagrin—warming to Early's macho swagger, will finally figure out what she quickly suspects.

With four distinct perspectives in the car, the smoothly moving film's sympathies are a little muddled. Adele is a sweet and simple bystander. Early may be a sadistic cold-hearted killer, but he's fun, friendly and does save Brian's hide in a drunken bar fight. And while Carrie is tough and a bit bitchy, she's perceptive, realistic and, after all, right. Brian is the obvious good guy, but he's portrayed as a weenie who spouts liberal dogma about murderers being the product of their families and their environment. There's certainly grounds for debate on the subject, but he comes off as a simple-minded bleeding heart. At his worst, he interviews Early, trying to uncover what made him evil.

The film further plays Brian for a fool, with gratuitous voice-over narration that asks questions like, "What's the difference between a killer and any one of us?" and offers reflections like, "I don't know if I was fascinated by him or frightened by him." It's not until the pace quickens and the action thickens that heroes and villains come out fighting.

"Kalifornia"'s pivotal concept—introducing an effete murder aficionado to the genuine article in a friendly setting—is never mined for anything deeper than the most superficial irony. Director Dominic Sena (whose background is music videos) repeatedly settles for action when suspense is needed, letting the excitement supplant any development of ideas. Ending with a violent climax that's all too familiar (despite its witty choice of setting—a house in a Nevada nuclear test range)—"Kalifornia" gets where it's going without having much to show for the trip but some bad memories.

SIGHT AND SOUND, 4/94, p. 45, Chris Drake

Writer Brian Kessler needs to honour a book contract and decides to undertake a voyage through several southern states of the USA, visiting infamous murder sites along the way. Accompanied by his girlfriend Carrie Laughlin, an unsuccessful art photographer, he intends to compile his written impressions with her images to produce the manuscript. In this way they hope to break out of their unfulfilling lifestyle and head for California. To finance the journey, they advertise for a ride-share and pick up Early Grayce and his girlfriend Adele Corners. Unknown to the other three, Early, on parole for other crimes, is an amoral killer fleeing after the recent murder of his landlord.

At the first of the murder sites, the new tenants of the house that Brian wants to visit refuse him entry, while Early steals a bag from the house. Carrie's misgivings about Early mount after Adele tells her that he beats her, when he savagely cuts Adele's hair in a messy approximation of Carrie's own bob, and when he begins to express a sexual interest in Carrie. At the next gas station, short of money, Early stabs a customer to death out of view of the others. Stopping at a motel, Early and Brian go out to play pool while Carrie stays in with Adele to fix her haircut. At the pool hall, Brian is harassed by an aggressive customer, whom Early sees off with a brutal beating. Back at the motel, Adele tells Carrie how she was gang-raped at the age of 13 and that her relationship with Early now makes her feel secure.

At the next murder site, Early gives Brian a lesson in gunmanship, much to Carrie's disgust. At another site, while exploring inside, Carrie and Brian argue. Storming out, Carrie observes Early and Adele in the car having sex and photographs them from a distance; Early notices her, smiles and carries on. At the next service station, Carrie sees a TV broadcast declaring Early to be a wanted criminal; when Early realises this he threatens her, intimidating her by torturing, then killing the attendant. Stopping at the next site, a disused mine-shaft, they are disturbed by the police. Early kills one of the officers, injures the other and attempts to make Brian kill the injured officer. Brian refuses, so Early finishes him off himself.

Early imprisons Carrie and Brian at the next house they stop at, and kills the elderly husband of the house. When Adele helps his widow escape, he kills her. With Adele dead, Early takes off with Carrie. Brian tracks them to an abandoned house on a former nuclear test-site and, after a battle with Early, kills him and escapes with Carrie. They make it to California and move into a beachfront house.

In the light of *Kalifornia*, Jean-Luc Godard's recipe for film-making as being "a girl, a car and a gun" now calls for one crucial extra ingredient: a primer in Cultural Studies. Dominic Sena loads up his road-movie star vehicle so visibly with all the extra baggage that the genre is these days expected to deal with—identity politics, issues of sexuality and class—that its narrative motor can only splutter along under the weight. Not that Brad Pitt doesn't put in a show stopping performance as Early Grayce, the killbilly hick from hell, with an accent as thick as a mouthful of chewing tobacco and body language straight from *A Streetcar Named Desire* Brando.

But that is precisely one of the film's major problems—it is such an over-the-top performance that Early simply dominates the film and its other characters, making them little more than fellow passengers caught in his murderous tail-spin. At least in *Wild at Heart*, one of *Kalifornia*'s generic cousins, David Lynch gave his characters a kind of cartoon equality and dialogue that could have been sitting in balloons above their heads. Likewise, in *Reservoir Dogs*, Quentin Tarantino delivered dialogues whose geeky insistence on repetition and detail took them straight back to a sense of the everyday absurd. In *Kalifornia*, however, the dialogues and by extension the characters—except for Early, who doesn't so much speak as slobber eloquently—do not really go in either direction. Instead, a voice-over appears to serve the numerous functions of being simultaneously a homage to Terrence Malick, adding a writerly textual density and most nauseating of all, providing an Olympian moral perspective on matters of Good and Evil.

One of the reasons that *Reservoir Dogs* was dragged so often through the talk-show mud was because of its refusal to go for this easy option on violence, moral responsibility and point-of-view in film; it preferred to provide multiple point-of-view and hence a complex perspective. Not so *Kalifornia* which culminates in Brian's sanctimonious 'them and us' discriminations by the time he and Carrie have reached the safety of their Californian hideaway. So much for the socially-conscious baggage; the film travels from liberal bad faith to Darwinian natural law with precious little pathos en route.

Stylistically, Sena can handle two registers of images, both of which he employs to the fullest extent—the insouciance of lifestyle-chic ads, where the camera prowls low through loft apartments just to make absolutely sure that none of that gorgeous diffused lighting goes missing in the shot; and the kinetic enthusiasm of the rock-video register that shows up, predictably, during sequences involving speeding cars and fighting. These approaches provide a sheen that serves to distract from the emptiness of the characters. But Brian and Carrie, Early and Adele go no further than being unsuccessful second-degree embodiments of ideas about the recto and verso of the serial killer: the real thing and its victim (Pitt and Lewis), and the media-encouraged rapacious voyeurism that pursues it, taking shape in word (Duchovny) and image (Forbes). Readers of *The Modern Review* will love this movie.

VILLAGE VOICE, 9/14/93, p. 68, Lisa Kennedy

For such a seemingly brief time, the road belonged to two gals on the lam in a turquoise convertible. Now it appears the road's reverted to its rightful owner—the crazy-sonuvabitch-guy-with-a-gun. Case in point: the fairly middling, careening toward lousy, *Kalifornia*. This movie, the script of which is better than its superficial direction, follows Brian, Carrie, Early, and Adele on an unpleasant, downright deadly, excursion.

Brian (played by *Rapture* doll turned *Red Shoes Diaries* hack David Duchovny) is a postgrad writer looking to spin his thesis on serial killers (whom he regularly confuses with mass murderers) into a Zagat guide of murder sights complete with photos by Carrie, his black-clad, somewhat sullen, definitely out-o'-water-in-the-Midwest girlfriend. Early Grayce (Brad Pitt) and Adele Corners (the ubiquitous Juliette Lewis) are the hicks who answer their ad for riders to California. Unbeknownst to everyone, including sweetie-pie Adele, Early is a killer—one of those mean, irrational types Brian so enjoys empathizing with. Once the tires hit the pavement, things quickly get eerie, then sad and violent.

The lesson of *Kalifornia*—that a smug writer doesn't know the first thing about the killing he valorizes—is not an especially bad one to impart to the scads of folks who idolize Manson, Gacy, et al., but even a good lesson can't survive Duchovny's horrid voiceover or the "haven't we seen this before and better" quality of the whole enterprise. *Badlands. In Cold Blood.* Hello! Except for Lewis, whose too little, too late epiphany that Early is not such a nice guy belongs in a better flick, there's nothing new here, and the old is, well, old.

Also reviewed in:
CHICAGO TRIBUNE, 9/3/93, Friday/p. C, Mark Caro
NEW YORK TIMES, 9/3/93, p. C11, Janet Maslin
VARIETY, 9/6/93, p. 27, Leonard Klady
WASHINGTON POST, 9/3/93, p. G7, Richard Harrington
WASHINGTON POST, 9/3/93, Weekend/p. 43, Joe Brown

KING OF THE HILL

A Gramercy Pictures release of a Wildwood/Bona Fide production. *Executive Producer:* John Hardy. *Producer:* Barbara Maltby, Albert Berger, and Ron Yerxa. *Director:* Steven Soderbergh. *Screenplay:* Steven Soderbergh. *Based on the memoir by:* A.E. Hotchner. *Director of Photography:* Elliot Davis. *Editor:* Steven Soderbergh. *Music:* Cliff Martinez. *Sound:* Paul Ledford, Dave Moreno, Matthew C. Belville, and Mark Coffrey. *Sound Editor:* Larry Blake. *Casting:* Deborah Aquila. *Production Designer:* Gary Frutkoff. *Art Director:* Bill Rea. *Set Decorator:* Claire Jenora Bowin. *Set Dresser:* Matthew R. Altman, Marty McManus, Andy Amann, Mike Bender, and Tim McDonald. *Special Effects:* J.D. Streett, IV. *Costumes:* Susan Lyall. *Make-up:* Elaine L. Offers. *Stunt Co-ordinator:* Noon Orsatti. *Running time:* 109 minutes. *MPAA Rating:* PG-13.

CAST: Jesse Bradford (Aaron Kurlander); Jeroen Krabbé (Mr. Kurlander); Lisa Eichhorn (Mrs. Kurlander); Karen Allen (Miss Mathey); Spalding Gray (Mr. Mungo); Elizabeth McGovern (Lydia); Cameron Boyd (Sullivan); Adrien Brody (Lester); Joseph Chrest (Ben); John McConnell (Patrolman Burns); Amber Benson (Ella McShane); Kristin Griffith (Mrs. McShane); Chris Samples (Billy Thompson); Peggy Friesen (Mrs. Thompson); Katherine Heigl (Christina Sebastian); John Durbin (Mr. Sandoz); Lauryn Hill (Elevator Operator); Jesse Zeigler (Jealous Kid); Remak Ramsey (Principal Stellwater); Fred Cherrick (Woodbine Owner); Joseph Moynihan (Woodbine Waiter); Don Richard (Mr. Farley); Mark Takano (Mr. Yamo); Craig Hawksley (Golfer in Orange Pants); Aelred Rosser (Other Golfer); Jason Feiner and Jared Joplin (Marble Bullies); David Jensen (Front Desk Clerk); Harry Governick (Second Policeman); Sarah Mermelstein (Girl at Graduation); Kimberly Jenkins (Girl at Party); Gabriel Levinson (Boy with Apple); Ron Yerxa (Donald Millee).

CHRISTIAN SCIENCE MONITOR, 8/20/93, p. 12, David Sterritt

Steven Soderbergh's return to the Cannes Film Festival was more low-key than it might have been.

He won the festival's grand prize in 1988 with "sex, lies, and videotape," which went on to great box-office success. But his next picture—the eccentric thriller "Kafka," with Jeremy Irons—never caught on with audiences and dampened expectations that his career would continue to soar without a hitch.

Hoping to recapture his early magic, Soderbergh arrived at Cannes this year with "King of the Hill," a quirky comedy-drama with a 12-year-old hero and an off-beat perspective on family life during the Depression years. It won no awards and sparked no fireworks in the tradition of Soderbergh's debut film, but many festival-goers found it genial and absorbing. It's now opening in American theaters.

"King of the Hill" is based on memoirs by A.E. Hotchner, who grew up during the 1930s in a St. Louis family that faced more than its share of economic and emotional challenges.

The movie's main character, Aaron, is a lively boy with affectionate parents and decent prospects for the future—until hard times begin tearing the household apart, removing each family member from the home until Aaron find himself surprisingly and alarmingly alone. Fending for himself in a third-floor room of the extraordinarily seedy Empire Hotel, he learns more about human nature than many people twice his age could claim.

What attracted Soderbergh to Aaron and his adventures? "There's no rational reason for it," the filmmaker told me in an interview at Cannes in May, shortly before the movie was unveiled there. "I just felt very connected to the kid in Hotchner's book. He's someone who lives inside his head to a large extent, and I relate to that. He's also a bit of a fibber—prone to prevaricating and adapting to circumstances, depending on who's involved in them. As a filmmaker, I relate to that, too!"

Another motivation for making "King of the Hill" was Soderbergh's eagerness to try a more directly emotional kind of storytelling than his earlier pictures allowed. "I feel both my first films were kind of cerebral," he says, "more so than I would've liked. I was interested in dealing with material that was inherently a lot more volatile in its feelings—and this was, since it was all about a kid."

"King of the Hill" has a style as unusual as its story. Many of the images have a larger-than-life, almost surrealistic quality closer to the audacious "Barton Fink" than to a conventional comedy like "Lost in Yonkers," the recent Neil Simon film about a family wrenched apart by the Depression.

"We tried to maintain a 12-year-old point of view," says Soderbergh about the look of his movie. "Adults are somewhat mysterious and unknowable to him. He's confused by their behavior, because it seems inconsistent and even inexplicable at times.

"Some of that we tried to conjure with camera placement," he continues, "and other times it had to do with how things were lit. We tried to come up with a childlike point of view without resorting to distortion and wide-angle lenses ... I didn't want things to get too ornate, because I wanted to stay very close to Aaron all the time. Beyond that, I kind of made things up as I went along, as usual."

Although it has many gentle and humorous moments, "King of the Hill" also has strange and scary aspects, earning its PG-13 rating as it confronts Aaron with some bizarre people and frightening predicaments. One of the things that appealed to Soderbergh about his hero is that the boy has a knack for surviving whatever comes his way.

"But it's one of those situations where he doesn't know enough to be scared," the filmmaker muses about his main character. "If he had any real sense of how much danger he's in at a certain point, things might have turned out much worse for him ... It's his childlike resilience and innocence that keep him going. It never occurs to him that he won't get through, and that's probably what keeps him going."

The able performers in "King of the Hill" include young Jesse Bradford as the protagonist, Lisa Eichhorn and Jeroen Krabbé as his parents, Cameron Boyd as his brother, and Spalding Gray and Elizabeth McGovern as two weird people in a hotel room down the hall.

This is a strong lineup, but despite it, the movie could prove a hard sell—since it's too inventively filmed for an ordinary Saturday-night entertainment, but not exotic or unorthodox enough to be marketed as an art film.

Soderbergh agrees that his movie presents a marketing challenge. "It has a child at the center but it's not for children," he acknowledges. "There are no big stars, and there's no central idea that's easily grasped ... It seems to be the kind of film that 20 years ago would be sort of common, but is less so now. It's rare in America to see films about kids that aren't made for kids."

All this notwithstanding, Soderbergh decided not to waver from telling the story in his own way and on his own terms, letting the commercial chips fall where they may.

"When you know going in that a film is of a certain nature," he says, "you're better off making it undiluted. If you do dilute it to make it more 'palatable,' there's still no guarantee it'll go over with the public. So you might as well just make it, and feel good about that. And years from now you can look back and say, well, at least we made it the way it should be made."

LOS ANGELES TIMES, 8/20/93, Calendar/p. 4, Michael Wilmington

Aaron Kurlander, the boy protagonist of Steven Sonderbergh's heart-stirring new movie, "King of the Hill", is the plucky, all-around kid many of us would like to have been: precocious writer, academic star, dead-eye marble champ, devoted son and brother, dauntless neighborhood explorer. He's a *mensch* of 12; king of his shining little hill.

A hill about to fall.

As Soderbergh brilliantly recreates Aaron's world—the events of writer A.E. Hotchner's autobiographical 1972 novel—we see everything more clearly. His hotel, the Avalon, is a deteriorating fleabag in 1933 St. Louis, taken over by the bank and slowly being converted into a bordello with dance hall annex. As tenants fall in arrears, they're locked out by a sadistic bellhop (Joseph Chrest).

Aaron's father (Jeroen Krabbe) is a glib, threadbare huckster peddling unsellable glass candles, months behind in the rent and one step ahead of the car repossessors. His mother (Lisa Eichhorn) is fragile and work-worn, hospitalized with consumption. His younger brother Sullivan (Cameron Boyd) has been farmed out to relatives.

His neighbors are a gallery of alcoholic lawyers, lovelorn epileptics and indigents. His one hero, Lester (Adrien Brody), is an endlessly resourceful Jewish 15-year-old down the hall with a magical pocket knife and lots of angles. Aaron is a great prevaricator—endlessly fibbing on his background to his snob classmates—but his lies are a battered screen. As he's abandoned in the Avalon, life and the bellhop close ruthlessly in.

Or do they? "King of the Hill" is one of the finest American films of the year—and one of the few which is really *about* America. It's a story—at once humorous, heartening and harrowing—of a world going nightmarishly haywire. The setting and time explain this: the Great Depression, with the nation in the grip of a remorseless economic juggernaut, hobo jungles and "Hoover-villes" swallowing up the victims. Is it paradoxical that this summer of hardship brings out the best in some—or the worst in others—and that this reminiscence of terrible times takes on a honey-eyed, shimmering, nostalgic glow?

Soderbergh, famous for his Cannes Grand Prize-winning low-budget debut, "sex, lies, and videotape," alienated some critics with his artsy film noir follow-up, "Kafka." But, here, he's in command; working with another man's memories, he makes them resonate.

Hotchner's book was lightly sarcastic, deceptively stoic and flip. It was written as if by a youngster—supposedly 13-year-old Aaron a summer later—and, fittingly for a tale by one of Ernest Hemingway's *cameradoes*, the pathos was husked over with "toughness." Soderbergh's storytelling has more overt sensitivity. And the images he gets, working with Alan Rudolph's cinematographer Elliot Davis, are huge, luminous and summery-ripe. It's a visual style, like "Barton Fink's," reminiscent of Roman Polanski's, full of uneasy subjective shots, grotesque aestheticism, a fascination with innocence ravaged.

Jesse Bradford, the young actor who plays Aaron, is refreshingly bright and alert, with just the resilience Hotchner described. Around him, the rest of the cast—everyone above, plus Spalding Gray as cross-hall neighbor Mr. Mungo, Amber Benson as epileptic Ella McShane, Karen Allen as a teacher and Lauryn Hill as Arletta the elevator girl—make a precise, joyously rich gallery.

But, more than anything else, it's the *attitude* of "King of the Hill" that makes it special: its mingled apprehension and delight, In some ways, the story resembles the blockbuster "Home Alone"—also about a child abandoned, locked in and beset by terrors—but "King of the Hill" makes that situation more real and dreamlike, its terrors undismissible.

Soderbergh doesn't include the flashback that explains Hotchner's title: a grisly anecdote in which Aaron and his friends play "king of the hill" on a rainy day and get trapped in mud slides so severe that two of them are buried and one killed. The movie reflects a gentler vision than the novel, but tenderness and compassion aren't always in abundance, we should treasure them when we find them.

Because, like anything else, they vanish. Like all the small or "foolish" things that make life precious to Aaron—his collection of cigar bands, his glassies, canaries, Lester's knife, the magazine pictures of roasts and cakes that he cuts out and eats, when he's starving "King of the Hill" gains its meaning by the love it endows upon its images and words. This beautiful, limber, surprising movie has the glow of great sadness recalled and triumphed over. In its small world, on its dangerous unsteady hill, it wears the crown.

NEW YORK POST, 8/20/93, p. 29, Jerry Tallmer

In room 326 of the Empire Hotel in St. Louis in 1933, the height of the Depression, their lives, in a state of siege, the Kurlander family, pop, mom, 12-year-old Aaron, and kid brother Sullivan. It is a scrungy hotel with a scrungy bellboy, Ben, who also serves as management spy and rat, with a supply of padlocks to slap on the doors of out-of-cash roomers like Mr. Sandoz, the artist down the corridor.

A.E. Hotchner, who once wrote a book called "Papa Hemingway," also wrote a memoir about his own life as a boy, calling the boy Aaron, and Steven Soderbergh, who crashed into movies a few years ago at not much more than Aaron's age with "sex, lies, and videotape," has now put the Hotchner memoir to film as "King of the Hill."

Aaron (Jesse Bradford) is one of those smart young outsiders who are cinematically all the rage at the moment. He has a secret life of communication with his good friend Charles Lindbergh, pilot of The Spirit of St. Louis, and on occasion plays "True or False?" with Mom (Lisa

Eichhorn) along these lines: "Today after school I snuck into Sportsman's Park and saw Pepper Martin at the water fountain and he threw me a piece of gum, true or false?"

Pop (Jeroen Krabbe, the devilish gravedigger of Soderbergh's "Kafka") is a salesman of candles that won't light. He says he's lining up a job with the Hamilton Watch Co. and another with the WPA. In short Pop is a loser. When Mom starts coughing and has to go away to a sanitorium, the kid brother (Cameron Boyd) is packed off to relatives. Then Pop suddenly has to go out on the road and Aaron is left to shift for himself as willy-nilly self-reliant king of the hill in Room 326 and environs.

His chief ally, Lester Silverstone, a tall brassy-yet-sensitive older boy who knows the ropes, is sharply portrayed by Adrien Brody. I also liked Joseph Chrest as the obnoxious bellboy and Amber Benson as sweet somber Ella McShane, the pigtailed girl across the hall who keeps making a play for Aaron that he stolidly resists. Then one fine day she scares the hell out of him with an epileptic seizure. It changes his attitude.

Aaron's and everybody's chief enemy, next to the bellboy, is a bigoted bullying Komedy Kop. I did not like this caricature, in performance or in the script, or a dumb cliche downhill brakeless dash in a speeding car—even if it once maybe really happened—or the stilted quality of much of Soderbergh's dialogue, even for instance, when Aaron amusingly lies about his parents being archaeologists off somewhere on a dig.

There is also a total fakeness in the look and feel of almost everything in the film from automobiles to NRA posters to Hoovervilles to the prize-giving moment in a school auditorium. What was not fake, or what was in any event a good joke, was Aaron concocting dinner out of warm water and ketchup, a la the immortal Joe Gould of Greenwich Village bohemian legend.

There's a quirky offbeat sequence involving Spalding Gray as an unpleasant wayfarer in the Empire Hotel who has contracted for the "customer services" of caustic call girl Elizabeth McGovern and the even more offbeat interjection of semi-sequiturs from time to time by a good-looking, gum-chewing black elevator operator played by Lauryn Hill.

Come to think of it, I think I liked her better than the whole picture. But I must tell you in fairness that I heard people raving on the way out.

NEWSDAY, 8/20/93, Part II/p. 64, Jack Mathews

Movies based on personal memoirs arrive at theaters having gone through a double filtration process that invariably renders them into myths. The stories, by their nature, are distilled through the selective memories of their writers, and the events, characters and nuances that emerge from that process get another going-over by the filmmakers.

At the end of the days, the question is not how historically accurate the film is, or whether it is even believable, but how well it conveys the true feelings and sentiments that inspired it.

Steven Soderbergh's excellent "King of the Hill," adapted from A.E. Hotchner's reminiscence about sharing a one-room flat with his family in a Depression-era St. Louis hotel, has the veneer of myth all over it.

Elliot Davis' cinematography has a colorful prettyness that defies the gritty, gray mood of the Depression. The residential Empire Hotel, where 12-year-old Aaron (Jesse Bradford) lives with his self-deluded father (Jeroen Krabbe), ailing mother (Lisa Eichhorn) and younger brother (Cameron Boyd), is romantically rundown, with a self-conscious seediness that seems to have been inspired as much by old movies as by real life. And Aaron's adventures in the hotel and in the streets of St. Louis, while terrifying enough to knock most kids senseless, leave an almost jaunty air to them.

Still, all this feels exactly right, as memoir. Hotchner is reflecting on a terrible time, and on harrowing personal experiences, but when he wrote "King of the Hill" in 1972, it was from a vantage point 40 years removed, after he had become a lawyer, magazine editor, author and pal/confidant to Ernest Hemingway. He was remembering events that helped shape an obviously successful life, and in such people adversity is often recalled with fondness.

Hotchner's book covered a period of about 18 months in the early '30s when his family lived in the Empire (actually, the Avalon). During that time his brother was bused off to live with relatives, his tubercular mother was placed in a sanatorium and his father hit the road for several weeks, selling watches door-to-door, while Aaron stayed behind to protect the family possessions from hotel-keepers fuming over unpaid rent.

The movie compresses these events into a few busy weeks during one endless heat spell in St. Louis, with Aaron navigating his troubles like Huck Finn on the Mississippi, a comparison that Soderbergh seems to invite. The incidental characters of the Empire—an amiable prostitute (Elizabeth McGovern), a suicidal alcoholic (Spalding Gray), the rowdy delinquent Lester (Adrien Brody)—become even larger figures in a story that has been simultaneously condensed and blown up.

But the real focus, of course, is on Aaron, a bright, imaginative kid who, even in these terrible circumstances, finds joy in being the neighborhood marble champion, in adding to the collection of cigar bands on his hat, in writing about his ongoing fantasy of being Charles Lindbergh's personal adviser.

He is also a kid who can invent a solution to almost any problem, even hunger. When Macaulay Culkin was left home alone, the first thing he did was raid the refrigerator and pig out on sweets. Aaron treats himself to a fantasy meal made from clippings of magazine food ads.

Bradford is the most experienced of all the child actors in this summer's wave of boyhood tales, and he carries the film with a confidence rare even among seasoned adults. But Soderbergh, who wrote the script, may have been a little too ambitious with Aaron's character.

The problem isn't that Aaron is too good to be true, though he certainly is, but that what he often does isn't true to his character. The trap that memoir writers often fall into is investing themselves at a young age with traits that explain their later successes, then exaggerating them in a way that undermines who they really were.

That happens to some extent with "King of the Hill," when Aaron's precociousness as a writer becomes a plot point. The strength of the story is the rich detail with which Hotchner recalled the effects of hard times on his family, and the emotional turmoil he endured while trying to survive it.

Hotchner may have been a precocious writer, but in the movie Aaron becomes so intellectually glib we are reminded that he is a figment of his own imagination, that he is being invented from some point off in the future and imbued with an understanding of his times he couldn't possibly have had.

Still it is a fascinating story, from perhaps the most ignored period of recent American history, and though it is a sugar-coated myth, it leaves an aftertaste that is potently bittersweet.

SIGHT AND SOUND, 1/94, p. 48, Nick James

St. Louis, 1933. Over-imaginative 12-year-old Aaron Kurlander lives with his salesman father, his nervously ill mother and his beloved younger brother Sullivan on a half-deserted floor of the run-down Empire Hotel. Times are tough. While Mr Kurlander works in vain selling door-to-door, Aaron divides his time between being a model school student, keeping an eye open for the repossession men who are after his father's car, and dodging the local flatfoot cop. Soon Aaron's father is forced to send Sullivan away to relatives. All the other residents of the Hotel floor are in similar straits, and Ben the bellhop operates a lock-out policy on those who fall too far behind with the rent.

Aaron's main scheme to help out his family—breeding canaries—turns out to be a flop. Then Mrs Kurlander's health breaks down and she is sent away to a sanatorium, just as her husband finally gets a new job selling watches out of state. Left alone to cope on no money with the responsibility of their threatened room, Aaron prepares for his graduation. Aaron's hustling street friend Lester helps him break into Ben's store of confiscated goods and they steal a smart outfit for the graduation. After the ceremony, in which he wins a prize, he is invited to a party by his rich classmate Christina Sebastian, but the extraordinary tales he tells the other children to cover up his family history are exposed and he runs away.

The hotel manager calls Aaron in for a final warning and so he appeals to his sleazy but friendly neighbour across the hall, Mr Mungo, for help. The half-drunk Mungo, embroiled with 'customer service' girl Lydia, promises to put the manager straight for him. Meanwhile Lester is arrested, but is allowed to give Aaron the knife which he uses to pick locks. When the boy returns, however, he realises that he is about to be locked out, so he shuts himself into his room. Later, looking through the window above his door, he sees a pool of blood seeping from Mungo's room. On investigation, he finds Mungo has slit his throat.

A letter written to the relatives brings Sullivan back, and shortly afterwards Mr Kurlander reappears, newly prosperous with a salary. He wants to just leave their belongings behind, but Aaron is determined that Ben should not have them. He and Sullivan lower their stuff into the back alley on sheets tied together into ropes, and then he breaks into Ben's basement and steals all the keys from Ben's collection of padlocks. Finally the entire family are re-united at their huge new apartment house.

The career of Steven Soderbergh highlights the degree to which film reviewing in Britain has to take reputations on trust. All we have seen of his work in this country is his debut, the Cannes Palme d'Or winner *sex, lies and videotape*, which was greeted as a critical and popular triumph of economical film making. Yet Soderbergh's reputation is at a low ebb, simply because consensus has it that his follow-up—she reputedly bizarre and bigger-budgeted *Kafka*—is unreleasable. His third feature *King of the Hill* therefore has a lot riding on it, in that the former young upstart is perceived as needing a comeback to recoup his bankability.

That Soderbergh should choose perhaps the softest of film options—a rites-of-passage movie—might be an indication of just how badly he wants to be king of the hill again. This impression is amplified by the feeling that, in terms of emotional manipulation, the film is a world away from his impressive debut. Where *sex, lies and videotape* was all low-key sensitivity, its modish minimalism emphasising an atmosphere of high sexual anxiety that explicitly includes the audience as voyeur, *King of the Hill* is distanced by nostalgic high-density colour images borrowed from that treasure-house of 30s Americana, the painting of Norman Rockwell.

Such loving use of period charm is, in a Depression context, deeply ironic, although it does nothing to gainsay the sentimentality that is a given with films taking a child's point of view. Soderbergh, however, keeps his young actor Jesse Bradford on a limited diet of winning smiles, and the boy's voiceover, adapted from the memoir by Hemingway sidekick A.E. Hotchner, has a laconic matter-of-fact edge that keeps any incipient drippiness at bay.

However, the studied weirdness with which the adult characters are presented—reminiscent of that king of all children-in-peril films, *Night of the Hunter*—signals that Soderbergh is still anxious to appear the auteur, but in a way that fits too snugly into the American independent tradition. You get the feeling that the Empire Hotel may be one of a chain that includes the Earle in *Barton Fink* and the Arcade in *Mystery Train*. Take away its moody *mise en scène*, however, and *King of the Hill* is otherwise a purely conventional tale of a kid who wins through against the odds. It is curiously underwhelming despite its successful hallucinatory depiction of Aaron's perceptions. And maybe the one thing that it didn't need that it has in common with Soderbergh's debut is its deadpan sense that nothing really matters very much.

TIME, 8/23/93, p. 67, Richard Schickel

We encounter Aaron Kurlander (Jesse Bradford), 12, reading a paper to his school class in St. Louis, Missouri, in 1933. It's a very persuasive fantasy in which he imagines Charles Lindbergh calling him for advice on what food to take on his transatlantic solo flight. The boy suggests that cheese sandwiches are always good.

In that sequence Steven Soderbergh, working territory far removed from his *sex, lies, and videotape*, efficiently reveals the sweet blend of imagination and practicality that animates his principal character and the sympathetic yet unsentimental approach with which he will recount his subsequent adventures.

For Aaron will soon be soloing himself. First his younger brother (Cameron Boyd) is sent off to relatives so that the family can save money. Next his mother enters a tuberculosis sanatorium. Finally his father hits the road selling watches—the only job he can get in the Depression. That leaves Aaron, who hides his survivor's wit under a deadpan demeanor, to fend for himself in the shabby hotel where the declassed Kurlanders have washed up.

The kid has much to contend with: a hotel management that wants to evict him, a slimily threatening bellhop, the sadistic cop on the beat, not to mention the dawning mysteries of sex and some sudden deaths and dislocations among his friends. The wary reserve of Bradford's performance has a crystalline quality in which you can read in his response to his father's bluster and mother's passivity. You sense in him a future manliness that will avoid both modes.

Soderbergh's adaptation of A.E. Hotchner's novel-memoir is episodic, and that mutes the melodrama inherent in Aaron's encounters with crime, illness and loss. Aaron must improvise his response to events without fully understanding them, and that comes closer to the truth about boyhood than most movies do. It was a directorial mistake to bathe the images in a soft glow. But that visual error is not compounded psychologically. The film has a tough core, and in a time when movies about the troubles of little boys are a sentimental subgenre and dysfunction is being too easily overcome, there is something exemplary about this smart little movie.

VILLAGE VOICE, 8/31/93, p. 60, Chris Goffard

It's rare to find an American film that deals as unflinchingly with childhood as *King of the Hill*. Director Steven Soderbergh does not debase the children in his film by trying too hard to make them cute or rob them of their dignity by trivializing their pain.

The film chronicles the Depression-era coming of age of Aaron Kurlander (Jesse Bradford), abandoned by his family and surviving alone in a cheap hotel where he struggles to keep from being thrown into the streets by a malicious matchstick-chewing bellhop. Particularly memorable is the scene in which Aaron, on the threshold of hunger-induced feverdreams, carefully removes pictures of food from a cookbook, arranges them on a plate, cuts them with a knife and fork, and chews, pretending to suck flavor from the paper. The moment captures his ability to blunt the sting of his situation by using imagination, one of his few weapons.

King of the Hill's only real weakness is that some minor characters are caricatures—the bellhop and a brutal cop, for instance, are empty of discernible humanity. Spalding Gray, however, manages to bring true feeling to the small role of Mr. Mungo, a pasty-faced alcoholic who lures hookers to his hotel room by promising them meals.

Soderbergh's eye for lighting proves acute in the film's climactic scene, where Aaron finally stands up against his unknowingly cruel, emotionally remote father. Aaron's face is seen in a hard, stark glow that suggests the loneliness of a bitterly won independence. It's unclear whether Aaron will embrace his father or spit in his face; we sense both impulses warring inside him.

Also reviewed in:
CHICAGO TRIBUNE, 9/10/93, Friday/p. A, Clifford Terry
NEW YORK TIMES, 8/20/93, p. C1, Janet Maslin
VARIETY, 5/24/93, p. 45, Todd McCarthy
WASHINGTON POST, 9/10/93, p. G7, Richard Harrington
WASHINGTON POST, 9/10/93, Weekend/p. 45, Desson Howe

KNIGHT MOVES

An Interstar Releasing release of a Lamb Bear Entertainment & Ink Slinger presentation of an El Khoury/Defait/Geisslerproduction. *Executive Producer:* Brad Mirman and Christopher Lambert. *Producer:* Ziad El Khoury and Jean Luc Defait. *Director:* Carl Schenkel. *Screenplay:* Brad Mirman. *Director of Photography:* Dietrich Lohmann. *Editor:* Norbert Herzner. *Music:* Anne Dudley. *Sound:* Ralph Parker and (music) Roger Dudley. *Sound Editor:* André Bendocchi-Alves. *Casting:* Michelle Allen. *Production Designer:* Grame Murray. *Art Director:* Gary Pembroke Allen. *Set Decorator:* Michael O'Connor. *Set Dresser:* Patrick Kearns and Clive Edwards. *Special Effects:* Gary Paller. *Costumes:* Deborah Everton and Trish Keaton. *Make-up:* Margaret M. Solomon. *Stunt Coordinator:* Bill Ferguson. *Running time:* 111 minutes. *MPAA Rating:* R.

CAST: Christopher Lambert (Peter Sanderson); Daniel Baldwin (Andy Wagner); Tom Skerritt (Frank Sedman); Diane Lane (Kathy Sheppärd); Charles Bailey-Gates (Willerman); Arthur Strauss (Viktor Yurilivich); Katherine Isobel (Erica Sanderson); Ferdinand Mayne (Jeremy Edmonds); Codie Lucas Wilbee (David, Age 9); Josh Murray (Peter, Age 14); Frank C. Turner (Doctor); Don Thompson (Father); Megan Leitch (Mother); Alex Diakun (Grandmaster Lutz); Mark Wilson (Newscaster); Rehli O'Byrne (Debi Rutledge); Blu Mankuma (Steve

Nolan); Monica Marko (Miss Greenwell); Walter Marsh (Chess President); Suzy Carby (Desk Clerk); Sam Malkin (Doctor Fulton); Elizabeth Baldwin (Christie Eastman); Dwight McFee (Technician); Pat Bermel and Holly Chester (Officers); Elizabeth Barclay (Lorraine Olson); Rebecca Toolan (Mayor); Andrea MacDonald (Mary Albert); Freda Perry (Attractive Girl); Marilyn Norry (Homesearcher); Donna Yamamoto (Reporter); Tom Heaton (Detective); Rachel Hayward (Last Victim); Kymberly Sheppard (Detective Janet McLellan); Deryl Hayes (Officer Harton).

LOS ANGELES TIMES, 1/25/93, Calendar/p. 7, Kevin Thomas

Occasionally a movie flips over into such off-the-hall absurdity that it stuns you. How did this happen?

The new "erotic thriller" "Knight Moves" is a case in point. It's about a Vancouver chess tournament in which a feral, sexy international grandmaster, played by French star Christopher Lambert, spends his off-time playing a cat-and-mouse game with a psychopathic serial killer, a maniac who taunts him over the phone, dribbling out opaque "clues" to his future crimes.

Can you buy that? How about a sudden romance between the grandmaster and a bosomy psychiatric investigator (Diane Lane), highlighted by dreamy walks across drizzly beaches and newspeak romantic exchanges: "You make me feel things I've never felt before." "You should face your feelings." How about those quizzical or scowling cops Tom Skerritt, and Daniel Baldwin, who keep manhandling Lambert and tossing him in the clink? How about Lambert's dimpled little daughter, Erica? Or Ferdy Mayne, of Polanski's "Vampire Killers," as the mysterious, blind chess guru?

How about the serial killer's *modus operandi*: putting clown makeup on his victims, draining their blood and writing cryptic messages on the walls? How about the grandmaster's loony opponents? Or that climax in a leaky basement, with everybody bashing and thrashing around in what seems to be a small indoor lake?

How about ... But why go on? "Knight Moves," which isn't played for laughs, hurls common sense out the window as soon as it introduces star-producer Lambert, with his French accent, as "Peter Sanderson." (Of the Cannes Sandersons?)

This isn't a movie with one or two lapses of logic. It's a movie where logic itself would be a lapse—from a screenplay, by executive producer Brad ("Body of Evidence") Mirman, of such near-perfect silliness that not a single incident or exchange of dialogue is believable. "Knight Moves" is a movie for people who perceive the world only through other movies. Bad ones. It's about the world of chess in the same sense that "Rambo III" is about international diplomacy, or "Friday the 13th" is about facing your feelings.

Faced with this nonsense, director Carl Schenkel, who made the zingy 1989 reggae thriller "The Mighty Quinn," opts for stylistic overkill—and he only succeeds in the opening flashback sequence, with his showy monochrome shots of a violent chess tournament and its bloody aftermath. When the dialogue starts, Schenkel is in trouble, and he probably knows it. There's so much wild energy and so many scenes punctuated with screams or slamming doors it's as if the entire movie were a nonstop temper tantrum.

Should we give "Knight Moves" points for destroying the old cliché about chess players being kooky introverts, and replacing it with a new cliché that shows them as chic, sex-mad, two-fisted, gun-slinging studs and suspected serial killers? Writer Mirman keeps suggesting that life is a game, that movies are a game, And, in some ways, he's right. "Knight Moves" (MPAA rated R, for language, sensuality, violence) *is* a game—but it's closer to three-card monte or tiddlywinks than chess.

NEWSDAY, 1/23/93, Part II/p. 23, John Anderson

If "Knight Moves" were a chess game, it would have to be played with hand grenades. But despite a distinct lack of subtlety, and some glaring flaws—beginning with a title that really doesn't mean anything—the film moves along considerably faster, and is a lot more fun, than the last Fischer-Spassky match.

And speaking of Bobby Fischer: Wasn't it in 1972 that he took a powder after winning the world championship? That's the year "Knight Moves" opens, at a junior championship being held in Washington State: In a sequence that owes a lot to George Romero, two kids, one good looking and self-assured, the other fat and wearing what looks like terminally chapped lips, face off; when the fat—make that calorically challenged—kid loses, he leaps over the table, and stabs his opponent in the hand with a fountain pen. After a short stay in the hospital, presumably for a sportsmanship transplant, he goes home, his father leaves, his mother kills herself, and as she lies in a pool of blood he has milk and cookies and plays a game of chess with himself.

What suspense there is comes after we're flashed forward and meet Peter Sanderson (Christopher Lambert), a grandmaster competing in a world championship in Washington State. Is he the fat kid grown up? There are plenty of indications that he is, beginning with the "fact" that he's the last person to see the first murder victim alive. She's found in her bed, over which a message is scrawled in her blood; she also has lipstick smeared around her mouth as if to imitate chapped lips—or whatever that kid suffered from. It's a point that's never mentioned, but to begin collecting the loose ends in "Knight Moves" would require a large vehicle.

SIGHT AND SOUND, 10/92, p. 53, Nigel Floyd

1972: During a junior chess championship, a defeated competitor stabs his opponent with a pencil. The boy is referred to a child psychiatrist, his father leaves home and his alcoholic mother kills herself. Twenty years later: Having forfeited a major championship three years before, chess player Peter Sanderson makes his comeback at a world-class tournament held on a small North-West Pacific island. His blind coach, Jeremy Edmonds, warns him that he is in danger of alienating his young daughter Erica, as he did his now dead wife. A woman, Debi Rutledge, with whom Sanderson has sex, is then found murdered, her face grotesquely made up and the word 'Remember' scrawled in blood on the wall. Questioned by Chief of Police Frank Sedman and detective Andy Wagner, Sanderson initially denies having been with the victim. But when a mystery phone caller challenges him to a game, and sends him a polaroid of the murdered woman, Sanderson contacts the police. Psychologist Kathy Sheppard is called in to construct a personality profile of the killer. Two more murders occur: the words 'Eventually' and 'Revenge' are written in blood. A fault on Sanderson's chess computer is fixed by local electronics expert David Willerman. The police set up a phone tap in Sanderson's basement, to monitor the killer's calls. But after she and Sanderson make love, Kathy is alarmed to find the victims' names ringed in his phone book. He reassures her; a fourth murder then yields the word clue 'Is'.

Plotting the killer's chess-like moves on a map, the police anticipate his next murder. However, soon after a faulty electronic display board forces Sanderson to abandon a game against his arch rival, Viktor Yurilivich, another woman is killed elsewhere: the word clue is 'Carefully'. Sanderson tells Kathy that his wife's death three years before caused him to shut down emotionally; he then opens a note left by her which proves, as he feared, to be a suicide note. But Kathy suspects him again when he reveals that he already knew the last clue word. After she is attacked by a masked figure, and Jeremy Edmonds is found dead—with evidence indicating that he and Sanderson were accomplices—Sanderson is arrested.

Kathy then finds that a chess-book reference Sanderson claims to have used to deduce the last clue checks out. Meanwhile, Sanderson deciphers the word clues: Remember, Eric-. Realising that his daughter Erica is in danger, he escapes from the police. At his apartment he finds detective Wagner with his throat cut. During a taunting phone call from the killer, Sanderson recognises a background sound as the water pump in the flooded basement where the phone tap is set up. Kathy and Sedman are embroiled in the ensuing struggle, during which Erica is saved and David Willerman—after revealing himself to be the boy who attacked the young Sanderson with a pencil—is shot dead by him.

Despite an absurdly convoluted plot predicated on the idea that the hero (Christopher Lambert) might be a serial killer, this over-heated and over-stylised thriller is devoid of any real suspense. The unlikelihood that the leading man could be the callous and calculating killer of five young women is rendered doubly unthinkable by the fact that Lambert and his real-life wife Diane Lane were involved in this American-German co-production from an early stage, making it virtually a vanity project.

This crippling structural fault aside, Brad Mirman's original screenplay is well constructed, with some neat touches: for example, the reference to Anton Berger's book on how to play chess, which allows Sanderson to deduce the next word clue from the Grandmaster's advice to play

"Carefully, carefully and carefully". Carl Schenkel, who directed the tense 1984 'lift' drama *Out of Order*, seems determined to distract us from the film's essential implausibility by blinding us with flashy camerawork and needlessly elaborate visual design. Ultimately, the efforts of the expressionless Lambert and all concerned are rendered risible by a finale in which the barely glimpsed murderer pops up to resolve the would-be ambiguities.

Also reviewed in:
NEW YORK TIMES, 1/23/93, p. 16, Stephen Holden
VARIETY, 4/27/92, p. 81, David Stratton
WASHINGTON POST, 1/22/93, Weekend, p. 32, Joe Brown
WASHINGTON POST, 1/25/93, p. B7, Hal Hinson

LA CHASSE AUX PAPILLONS

A New Yorker Films release of a Pierre Grise Productions/Sodaperaga/France 3 Cinéma/Metropolis Films/Best International Films coproduction. *Producer:* Martine Marignac. *Director:* Otar Iosseliani. *Screenplay (French with English subtitles):* Otar Iosseliani. *Director of Photography:* William Lubtchansky. *Editor:* Otar Iosseliani. *Music:* Nicolas Zourabichvili. *Sound:* Holger Gimpel, Alix Comte, Gérard Lamps, and Axel Arft. *Sound Editor:* Anne-Marie L'Hote. *Art Director:* Emmanuel De Chauvigny. *Costumes:* Charlotte David. *Running time:* 115 minutes. *MPAA Rating:* Not Rated.

CAST: Narda Blanchet (Solange);   Pierrette Pompom Bailhache (Valérie);   Alexandre Tcherkassoff (Henri de Lampadère);   Thamar Tarassachvili (Marie-Agnès de Bayonette); Alexandra Liebermann (Hélène von Zastro);   Lilia Ollivier (Olga);   Emmanuel De Chauvigny (Father André);   Sacha Piatigorsky (The Maharajah);   Annie-Marie Eisenschitz (Marie); François Tsouladze (Yvonne);   Maimouna N'Diaye (Caprice);   Yannick Carpentier (Monsieur Carpentier);   Otar Iosseliani (The Ghost);   Alexander Askoldov (Drunk);   Pascal Aubier (Quarrelsome Man).

NEW YORK POST, 10/22/93, p. 28, Thelma Adams

"La Chasse aux Papillons (Chasing Butterflies)" is a chocolate bonbon with a mustard center.

Director Otar Iosseliani spoils a delightful confection with a crabby indictment of greed and the global village. The gripe that the more things change, the worse it gets, might play well over the mah-jongg table, but it's not exactly news.

This French comedy of manners by a Georgian director (Iosseliani insists he's no Russian) takes on the decline of rural life in modern France. It is by turns nostalgic, humorous, and surprisingly bitter.

At the center of Iosseliani's village are the ladies who church and the sodden priest who prays over them. Also on hand in this anarchic narrative are a venal notary, a mysterious maharajah, a thieving housekeeper, squabbling spouses, materialistic Muscovites, acquisitive Japanese, blissful Hare Krishnas and an extended aristocratic family likened to a "pack of dogs."

The only fully-realized character, Solange (Narda Blanchet), is delightful. Middle-aged, dressed in cape and sensible shoes, Solange bikes through the disjointed scenes and, while she does, the movie meanders pleasantly.

Charged with the care of her elderly cousin, who owns a local chateau, Solange is the embodiment of rural pleasures, hard work, and family loyalty. She plays the church organ, chides the hung-over padre, buys leeks at the market, hunts fish with a bow and arrow, plays pinball and nurses her cousin—her days are enclosed and full.

Solange listens to the news on her Walkman—a bombing in Lima another in Madrid—but she pedals through her life, unscathed. She might sell off her cousin's legacy one chair at a time to raise cash, but she is rooted in the past and guards it fiercely. She fends off attempts by Japanese businessmen to buy the chateau. When the businessmen offer to wait until the old lady dies, Solange cries, "She has no intention of dying."

However, the old lady dies halfway through "La Chasse aux Papillons." The energetic force of Solange seems to get buried along with her cousin, and the cemetery dirt is tossed over the narrative as well. No longer content to float on the delights of rural life, Iosseliani must show that the sky is falling over rural France.

The director summons the hounds of hell to tear down the old order. As the notary, the next of kin, and the Japanese conspire to shift ownership of the chateau and all it represents, the movie becomes one big, dull muddle. For Iosseliani, the global village is no village at all, but a moral wasteland. Strangled by nostalgia, alienated from modern life, the director loses his sense of humor. The movie strains and fails.

"La Chasse aux Papillons" starts out chasing butterflies and ends pushing up daisies.

NEWSDAY, 10/22/93, Part II/p. 79, Gene Seymour

"La Chasse aux Papillons" is a bon-bon with a jalapeño in the middle. The film's leisurely pace, deadpan humor and gentle eccentricity may lull you into thinking it little more than a dreamy pastoral lightly frosted with social satire. But the full impact of writer-director Otar Iosseliani's portrait of Western Civilization's whimpering decline sneaks up on you like a cat burglar and knocks you over before you know quite what's hit you.

The story is set mainly in a French chateau occupied by an old Russian woman, her housekeeper Valerie (Pierrette Pompom Bailhache) and her cousin Solange (Narda Blanchet), also old, also Russian, but far livelier. Solange plays organ for the church and second trombone with the town band. She fishes for supper with a bow and arrow and shoots pistols at targets like a commando. She loves to listen on her Walkman to what she calls the "delicious news" of violence and chaos at home and abroad.

Next door lives the town's prim notary and realtor (Alexandre Tcherkassoff), who is entertaining an old school chum, the Maharajah of Mukallah. The potentate and his grim entourage fit right in with the notary's sullen son and his statuesque African wife (Maimouna N'Diaye).

Meanwhile, the notary, whose off-key basso singing is, at one point, hilariously augmented by the impromptu tenor of his butler, does business with such diverse clients as the local Hare Krishna group and a contingent of Japanese businessmen eager to buy the old woman's chateau. Solange says her cousin isn't selling anything until she dies, adding, "She has no intention of dying!".

But the old woman does, indeed die. Thus setting off a tangled sequence of family squabbles and nocturnal visits from ancestral ghosts. The manse is inherited by the old woman's sister and dance-teacher niece from Moscow, the latter of whom is all-too willing to take in all the attendant luxuries. The Japanese, by the way, haven't gone away. And there are ominous sounds of discord on streets far away from the countryside that lead to the jolting and (literally) explosive, ending.

Iosseliani, a cult favorite in Europe, was born in the former Soviet republic of Georgia, but like, his characters, exiled himself to France. His skill at visual composition carries reminders of his Soviet film teacher Alexander Dovzhenko while his dry comic touch stirs echoes of the French comic master Jacques Tati.

The director's bi-cultural sensibility also gives him the perspective to make a comedy-of-aristocratic-manners that is, at once as humane as Jean Renoir's "Rules of the Game" and as scathing as Luis Buñuel's "The Discreet Charms of the Bourgeoisie." Make no mistake, though. This "butterfly chase" (a loose translation of the title) stands on its own as a species of fluffy farce, with sharp teeth.

VILLAGE VOICE, 10/26/93, p. 58, Georgia Brown

I've been making a list: reasons to despair for film culture in New York. One such might be that most of us have never seen a film by Otar Iosseliani. For this one, though, there's a corresponding reason for hope: New Yorker Films has picked up *La Chasse aux Papillons*, or *Chasing Butterflies*. The decline of culture, period, is the subject of Iosseliani's enchanting, totally eccentric comedy of manners. The title appears to come from the way the film moves, lighting here, lighting there, following the color. Iosseliani's touch is so deft, his eye so alert, then down drops the net.

Beauty is fragile and dying. If it isn't dead yet, its head is gray and bent. Born in Russian Georgia in 1934, Iosseliani (pronounced, if I've got it right, Yo-sel-yonni) was close enough in time and place to the old ways. He studied in Moscow under Dovzhenko and Boris Barnet, then returned to the Georgian studios, eventually completing four features. In the early '80s, he emigrated to France and looked up, so they say, Jacques Tati—much closer to Iosseliani in his view of progress than were Soviet directors. Of course, Tati died too. In *La Chasse aux Papillons*, the oldest have not only borne most but now they're taking their riches with them when they go. The difference between our time and former times, Iosseliani suggests, is that nothing truly valuable survives.

An old woman lives in a château. She's attended by her housekeeper, Valérie (Pierrette Pompom Bailhache), and her aging but active cousin, Solange (Narda Blanchet). The blunt, doleful, and very droll Solange is the butterfly the camera is most fond of—following her as she pedals off to play the organ for mass (the all-female congregation arrives and departs by bike), does her marketing, fishes for supper with a bow and arrow, rides away with her trombone to band practice, plays a game of *boules* in the village square. A devotee of the news ("delicious news," she calls it), Solange wears a Walkman or, when at rest, puts on the radio. Bulletins from the cruel, chaotic outside world punctuate her daily rounds.

In a neighboring château lives Henri de Lampadère (Alexandre Tcherkassoff), notary, realtor, and general chargé d'affaires. Unlike the old ladies, he keeps his premises spic and span, requiring even the dogs to wear socks on the parquet. (Some of the film's most hilarious, Tatiesque scenes take place in M. de Lampadère's castle. My favorite features an enthusiastic singing butler.) De Lampadère's rather slimy son is married to Caprice (Maimouna N'Diaye), a statuesque French African who conducts offhand house tours for foreign visitors—usually flocks of Japanese women. Japanese men arrive separately, in identical black suits, seeking to buy up the best châteaux; they have their sights on the one inhabited by the old ladies. Nonconforming in the East, Iosseliani isn't about to be p.c. in the West. Doesn't the man know there was a revolution? Is he a supporter of Le Pen? Well, he's safe because the French-French—the old woman's relatives in particular—are such a horrid, greedy lot.

Once the old lady dies (an extraordinary sequence), the camera begins great, swooping (magical) journeys. We discover a sister living in Russia, in one of those quarrel-infested communal warrens, along with her dance-teacher daughter. Ah, we think, the heroines of the story! Untainted by capitalist crassness, they'll turn out to be pure and noble spirits. Ha-ha, guess again. The portrait of Russian émigrés in Paris is wicked.

Iosseliani keeps all his subjects discreet middle-distance. His actors, apparently, are nonprofessionals; the script is so underwritten it provides virtually no exposition. He's made, in a sense, a silent comedy. All we need to know, he implies, is what we gather without being told, with common sense. (Be attentive if you want to know anyone's name or what relation they bear to someone else.) A tolerance for ambiguity helps. Then—in a lovely, lyric burst of East European mysticism—Iosseliani springs his magnificent ghosts.

Initially, *La Chasse* seemed to resemble certain affectionate social comedies. I was all prepared to call it "charming." I figured I could predict, generally, how things would end up (the good triumphing). But almost none of my expectations were fulfilled. In fact, they were exploded. Iosseliani keeps sentimentality at such a distance, his heart is either stone or as tough as a biddy's gizzard. "This is a logical film, not a pessimistic one," he's quoted on *La Chasse*. Ha-ha, good joke.

A friend who knows Iosseliani's earlier, Georgian films says they too are wonderful. One of these, *Once Upon a Time There Was a Singing Blackbird*, played in New Directors nearly 20 years ago. His first French film, *Minions of the Moon* (1984), had a brief American run, I'm told. No wonder he's cynical; his obscurity proves his point.

Also reviewed in:
NEW YORK TIMES, 10/22/93, p. C10, Vincent Canby
VARIETY, 10/5/92, p. 65, David Stratton

LAST ACTION HERO

A Columbia Pictures release. *Executive Producer:* Arnold Schwarzenegger. *Producer:* Steve Roth and John McTiernan. *Director:* John McTiernan. *Screenplay:* Shane Black and David Arnott. *Story:* Zak Penn and Adam Leff. *Director of Photography:* Dean Semler. *Editor:* John Wright. *Music:* Michael Kamen. *Music Editor:* Christopher S. Brooks and Eric Reasoner. *Sound:* Lee Orloff. *Sound Editor:* Jerry Ross. *Casting:* Jane Jenkins and Janet Hirshenson. *Production Designer:* Eugenio Zanetti. *Art Director:* Marek Dobrowolski and Rick Heinrichs. *Set Designer:* Peter J. Kelly, Natalie Richards, Carl Stensel, and Elizabeth Lapp. *Set Decorator:* Cindy Carr. *Special Effects:* Tommy Fisher. *Costumes:* Gloria Gresham. *Make-up:* Jeff Dawn. *Make-up Special Effects:* Thomas Burman, Bari Dreiband Burman, and Jeff Dawn. *Stunt Coordinator:* Fred M. Waugh, Joel Kramer, and Vic Armstrong. *Running time:* 122 minutes. *MPAA Rating:* PG-13.

CAST: Arnold Schwarzenegger (Jack Slater);   F. Murray Abraham (John Practice);   Art Carney (Frank);   Charles Dance (Benedict);   Frank McRae (Dekker);   Tom Noonan (Ripper); Robert Prosky (Nick);   Anthony Quinn (Vivaldi);   Mercedes Ruehl (Mom);   Austin O'Brien (Danny);   Ian McKellen (Death);   Toru Tanaka (Tough Asian Man);   Joan Plowright (Teacher); Jason Kelly (Lieutenant Govenor);   Noah Emmerich (Rookie);   Tina Turner (The Mayor); Billy Lucas (SWAT Cop);   Ryan Todd (Andrew Slater);   Apollo Dukakis (Polonius);   Patrick Flanagan (Punk);   Donald C. Llorens (Monoghan);   Michael Chieffo (Monroe);   Mike Muscat (Cop in LA Station);   John Finnegan (Watch Commander);   Bobbie Brown-Lane and Angie Everhart (Video Babes);   Bridgette Wilson (Whitney/Meredith);   Jeffrey Braer (Skeezy); Anthony Peck (Cop at Ex-Wife's House);   Paul Gonzales (Cop #2 in LA Station);   Anna Navarro (Cop in Station);   Dex Sanders (Mitchell);   Nick Dimitri (Doctor, Funeral);   Sven-Ole Thorson (Gunman);   Rick Ducommun (Ripper's Agent);   Wendle Josepher (Candy Girl); Michael V. Gazzo (Torelli);   Lee Reherman (Krause);   R.C. Bates (Rabbi);   Colleen Camp (Ratcliff);   Donna Borghoff (Hooker);   John McTiernan, Sr. (Cigar Stand Man);   Tiffany Puhy (Autograph Seeker);   CAMEOS: Keith Barish, Jim Belushi, Chevy Chase, Chris Connelly, Karen Duffy, Larry Ferguson, Leeza Gibbons, Hammer, Little Richard, Robert Patrick, Maria Shriver, Sharon Stone, Jean-Claude Van Damme, Melvin Van Peebles, Damon Wayans.

CHRISTIAN SCIENCE MONITOR, 6/25/93, p. 14, David Sterritt

"Last Action Hero," the new Arnold Schwarzenegger movie, is such a megaproduction that even the rumors about it are grabbing major press coverage.

Is it true the budget mushroomed to nearly $120 million, a walloping amount even by big-studio standards? Was the picture really completed long after its target date, in a race to the wire for its premiere last week? Did an alarming number of spectators really turn their thumbs down and their noses up when a rough-cut version was test-marketed last month—suggesting that legendary bombs like "Howard the Duck" and "Hudson Hawk" may have new company soon?

Whatever the answers may be, Columbia Pictures has a lot riding on Mr. Schwarzenegger's super-charged project, which certainly cost a bundle even if it hasn't set an all-time record. Like many a production outfit, Columbia has been in this position before. In 1977, for instance, its survival hinged on the success of "The Deep" and "Close Encounters of the Third Kind," both of which turned into instant hits and propelled the studio into a new era.

Will history repeat itself. The answer is "yes," if Schwazenegger's track record is the deciding factor. His movies have reportedly grossed more than $1 billion during the past decade, capped by the big-buck success of "Terminator 2: Judgment Day" two years ago. The answer is "no," however, if the actual quality of "Last Action Hero" has anything to do with it.

True, movies I don't enjoy often turn into box-office bonanzas, which is one reason I'm a critic instead of a studio boss. But those movies usually have something that I can identify as a marketable commodity—a thought-provoking plot, a lovable star performance, an ability to stir up powerful feelings.

By contrast, "Last Action Hero" has a gimmicky plot and a monotonous star performance. As for feelings, the strongest emotion it whips up is an overwhelming desire to stop your ears against the stupid dialogue, bombastic sound effects, and atrocious music that assaults you every second—courtesy of Dynamic Digital Sound, a diabolical new development in technological overkill. Surely no good movie would feel the need to be so loud.

In fact, everything about "Last Action Hero" seems overdone, beginning with the fact that it serves up Schwarzenegger in a dual role: as Jack Slater, an action-movie star, and as himself playing that character in real life.

The story begins when Slater's biggest fan, a preteen boy named Danny, gets hold of a magical "ticket" that transports him into the latest Slater picture. He and Slater battle various villains, winning every fight and conquering every obstacle because, hey, it's only a movie.

Then the two heroes find themselves together in the real world, where good guys can lose, gunshots can kill, and fistfights really hurt. The movie makes a stab at poignancy here, but that has never been Schwarzenegger's strong point. There's also some foolishness about Slater and Schwarzenegger meeting up with each other,

During the first few scenes, I thought "Last Action Hero" might poke enough fun at its own genre to succeed as a self-mocking satire. There's a hilarious vignette with Joan Plowright as a schoolteacher trying to convince her pupils that "Hamlet" was an "action picture and Laurence Olvier was a super-cool star; and Schwarzenegger does an amusing bit as Jack Slater on the loose in a Shakespearean world, blasting through Elizabethan intrigues with Hollywood-style weapons.

But the cleverness quickly palls, and the movie's promising signs turn out to be highly misleading. Most of the parody is aimed not at lofty icons like Shakespeare and Olivier, but at easy pop-culture targets like Schwarzenegger's own image, which is close to self-parody anyway. The reflexive play with illusion and reality sinks into nonsense so far-fetched that the legendary Houdini has to be dragged into the story to give it some logic. The film-within-a-film is apparently supposed to be a *bad* movie—yet we're forced to watch enormous amounts of it, as part of the movie *we* came to see.

And don't be gulled into "Last Action Hero" by its excellent cast. Schwarzenegger is all over the screen, but Ms. Plowright disappears after one scene—and Art Carney, Anthony Quinn, Robert Prosky, and Mercedes Ruehl don't do much better. Only the talented Charles Dance and F. Murray Abraham, both playing conspicuously nasty characters, stick around long enough to make an impression. Cameos by everyone from Maria Schriver to Little Richard also don't help much.

The film's violence puts the cavernous "Jurassic Park" to shame. If this summer's movie fare does nothing else, it should spark a vigorous debate over the PG-13 rating, and how ineffective the guidelines are in shielding young spectators from mayhem-filled epics like these.

Action specialist John McTiernan directed the picture from a screenplay by Shane Black and David Arnott, with Schwarzenegger as executive producer. Dean Semler did the gaudy cinematography and Michael Kamen composed the aggressive music.

LOS ANGELES TIMES, 6/18/93, Calendar/p. 1, Kenneth Turan

Never kid a kidder, the proverb says, to which those who survive "Last Action Hero" will want to add, never parody a parody. An awkward mixture of overproduced action and underwhelming comedy, this ponderous joy ride is more notable for how strenuously it's been promoted than for how much pleasure it delivers.

Which is especially a shame, because under all the unnecessary hardware that too big a budget inevitably guarantees there are traces of an idea that was appealing once upon a time. Like the very different "Cinema Paradiso" of a few years back, the original story by neophyte writers Zak Penn and Adam Leff must have been something of a mash note to movies, a valentine to the emotional attachment we can feel for what's seen on the screen.

But once an entity of Arnold Schwarzenegger's dimensions became attached to the project, any chances of it being done on an appropriate scale went south. In came big-deal action director John McTiernan ("Die Hard," "The Hunt for Red October") and the flagrantly commercial rewrite team of Shane Black ("Lethal Weapon") and David Arnott ("The Adventures of Ford Fairlane") and everyone started to anticipate grosses that would cover the Earth.

But in their attempt to cleverly corner all the action market money, the filmmakers made some fundamental mistakes. They misunderstood the nature of Schwarzenegger's considerable appeal, and they misjudged the effectiveness of the audience attack weapon they felt they were building.

Though we aren't let in on the news immediately, "Last Action Hero" begins with a film within a film, the newest action movie to focus on Jack Slater (Schwarzenegger), a monolithic L.A. cop who is part Rambo, part Dirty Harry, and all business.

Watching Slater in a nearly deserted New York theater is his biggest fan, 11-year-old Danny Madigan (Austin O'Brien). A movie junkie who regularly cuts school to check out his heroes, Danny is aided by his friendship with Nick (Robert Prosky), the theater's kindly old projectionist.

Nick turns out to be a duffer with clout, able to offer Danny the chance to be the first on his block to see the newest Jack Slater movie. He also gives Danny a special magic ticket he has been hoarding since Harry Houdini himself gave it to him when he was a boy. "It's a passport to another world," Nick says reverentially, and so it turns out to be.

For just as "Jack Slater IV" starts to get going, with Jack fated to take on the villainous team of Anthony Quinn and Charles Dance, the ticket starts to vibrate and turn colors. And a dazed and confused Danny suddenly finds himself right in the middle of the movie, riding in the back seat of Slater's trademark Bonneville convertible as the big guy trades lead with some unidentified desperadoes.

The notion here, one that films ranging from Buster Keaton's "Sherlock Jr." to Ralph Bakshi's "Cool World" have played with, is that film exists in a kind of parallel universe, one that can be entered, with a little help from unspecified forces, by just about anyone.

But though Danny knows he's in a movie, Jack thinks he's acting out in the real world, and a lot of "Last Action Hero's" time is spent in Danny's stubborn attempts to persuade him he's wrong. Finally, events force the two of them to cross back over and the boy and the hero have to cope with New York City's nominally more realistic set of problems.

While this is certainly an acceptable premise, "Last Action Hero" does not manage to live up to its potential, and its biggest asset from a commercial point of view turns out to be one of its problems.

Arnold Schwarzenegger's success as an action hero, as indicated by trademark one-liners like "I'll be back" and "Hasta la vista, baby" is based partly on the way he winks at the audience at the same time he's thrilling them. To turn that implicit mockery explicit, to have him do the kind of out-and-out spoofing much straighter actors like Charlie Sheen and Leslie Nielsen can manage perfectly well, is to simultaneously misjudge and squander the qualities that make Arnold Arnold.

Speaking of letting Arnold be Arnold, it seems at times that this movie, which is filled with cutesy homages to "Basic Instinct," "E.T," "Amadeus" and a whole lot more, has too many Arnolds to go around. Schwarzenegger not only plays the fictional Jack Slater, he also plays the Arnold who plays Jack Slater, which means playing himself, complete with real-life wife, Maria Shriver, as a fictional character.

If that isn't enough to give you a headache, the movie's loud and tiresome stunts are sure to finish the job. Things explode in "Last Action Hero" with a predictable regularity and cars almost never stick to the road, but none of the fuss is up to the standards James Cameron set for Schwarzenegger in the "Terminator" films. And, like someone who shouts English at a foreigner in the hopes that the volume will make him understand, the filmmakers appear to believe that the more assaultive the sound, the more effective the sequence.

And the heart of the film, the joy we are supposed to share with Danny as he lives out his fantasy, never comes off either. "Last Action Hero" (rated PG-13 for strong action sequences) does have occasional moments of humor, including a clever Schwarzenegger-as-Hamlet parody ("There's something rotten in the state of Denmark, and Hamlet is taking out the trash!"), but overall it is lacking in fun or magic. When one of the movie Arnolds says his next film will be "a good story, with emotions," one can only hope that this isn't the one he had in mind.

NEW STATESMAN & SOCIETY, 7/30/93, p. 34, Jonathan Romney

I've recently heard people bat around a chilling prognosis for the next millennium: the idea that future generations will have no use for irony. That may be because the current generation has used it all up. If so, it has all gone into the latest Arnold Schwarzenegger film, *Last Action Hero*.

And it may be that the world is already ushering irony into an ignominious grave by greeting the film with unalloyed disdain.

Last Action Hero has so far been panned almost unanimously by critics. They have seen it as a grotesque lapse into bad faith, as misjudged hubris, and as a gesture of out-and-out contempt for its audience. Its crime is to parody a Schwarzenegger movie under the guise of a Schwarzenegger movie. Arnie has as many bullets in his ammo belt as ever, but this time they are satiric ones targeted at his own persona, at the action genre and its conventions, and at the reasons people go to see Arnie movies in the first place.

The film could arguably be accused of short-changing its public by promising but not providing a proper Arnie film. But if you take a "proper" Arnie film to be one in which he has an unassailable iron-man persona, a mere handful of monosyllabic lines and a multi-million-dollar special effects budget, that simply begs the question of how "proper" such films were in the first place. As far back as *The Terminator*, Schwarzenegger was already creating an implicit parody of his persona by taking the idea of tungsten-tough immutability to ludicrous extremes.

Any film that includes him automatically becomes a part of a flexible genre called the "Arnie movie", simply because the man cuts a figure so totally incommensurable with any notion of the real. All of them, whether "serious" such as *Total Recall* or "comic" such as *Twins*, are entirely about the need to rework normal concepts of realism to accommodate a body and an accent that have no place in any fiction dealing with reality.

But *Last Action Hero* is not a straight self-parodic romp like *Kindergarten Cop*. Instead, it's the closest we may get to abstract Arnie: a meditation on the phenomenology of what it's like to watch an Arnie movie. As the film begins, we think we're watching a segment of the apocryphal *Jack Slater III* through the eyes of 11-year-old Danny, sitting in a Times Square fleapit. It turns out that Danny isn't so much a Schwarzenegger fan, but a Jack Slater fan. When he gets to see a sneak preview of *Jack Slater IV*, and magically falls into the film, he's able to help Slater out by recourse to the conventions of the genre. He finds he can live life as if he has read the script.

There's nothing new about this sort of cinematic trick. It was last and most spectacularly pulled in *Gremlins 2*, in which Joe Dante committed directorial hara-kiri by debunking all the premises of his earlier hit, *Gremlins*. Among his coups was to have his host of snickering hobgoblins mock their incarnation in the first film—which is after all a similar trick to the one Cervantes pulled in Part Two of *Don Quixote*.

Last Action Hero plays the same sort of pranks, removing the walls between the real and the fictional, between knowledge of the world and knowledge of the movies. It could indulge them even more, but often gets bogged down in pedantic niggling about conventions. The boy Danny is a real pain in this respect, a genre diehard who wants everything to conform to a fictional template. The joke's good when it refers to other films—he's able to warn Slater that F Murray Abraham is a bad guy, because he killed Mozart in *Amadeus*. But it gets irritating when Danny thinks the conventions out loud.

During a death-defying stunt, he reasons: "I'm a good guy, it's going to work," then realises: "I'm a comedy sidekick, it's not going to work!". Danny, you can tell, will grow up to be a seen-everything, liked-nothing trainspotter critic. These critics, of course, will loathe *Last Action Hero* because it's all loose strands, because the logic of its Russian-doll structure isn't consistent.

But it doesn't have to be. Once you have removed the fourth wall of illusion, you might as well demolish the entire cinema. What's impressive about *Last Action Hero* is that while it has no more idea of what the real is than any other Hollywood film, it uses the unreal to plumb the questions of what reality might be and how movies might deal with it.

There's immediately a sense that we might want to reconsider our notion of what's tolerable when *Jack Slater*'s impeccably evil British villain (Charles Dance) steps out of the screen and into Times Square. As he looks around at the everyday horror, you can see a faint thrill of revulsion as this cartoon Mephistopheles realises that he isn't quite on a par with what *this* world has in store.

The film's choicest paradox is to bring the fictional Arnie fact to face with the real one—or at least, the most convincing simulacrum of a real Arnie it can muster. As Jack Slater, now exiled in the real world, arrives at the premiere of *Jack Slater IV*, he meets "Arnold Schwarzenegger" himself, but as *Spy* magazine might parody him. He's a 2-D lunk with nothing on his mind but fatuous remarks about halving his films' body count, and desperate to plug his restaurant. When

Slater appears, Arnie nonchalantly greets him with a deliciously obtuse flourish of megastar vanity, congratulating him on being his convincing double. But who's the double of whom? And which one are we rooting for?

You can see why the film struck a dead note in the US. Its hugely entertaining excess of *Looney Tunes* invention strains the bounds of a manageable narrative, just as its star's non-charismatic oddness and bulk strain the dimensions of the realist screen. And it's true that much of the satire is on a one-note level. All the jibing at genre conventions will quickly make the film seem as date-tied as, say, a 1660s skit on Racinian versification.

What *Last Action Hero* does most successfully is dismantle the star persona as a product only marginally related to a real person; but intimately tied to a set of rules that govern how it's presented and consumed. A Schwarzenegger film is only possible if you find a framework strong enough to contain its star: the *Jack Slater* writers seem just about to have managed this.

But once Danny has worked through the rules of how a Schwarzenegger film works—that is, how to watch one—there's no further need for Schwarzenegger. In the end, the image of Arnie that seems most real is not the Jack Slater persona, nor the strutting Austrian at the movie premiere, but the Arnie that stands *outside* the premiere: an 80-foot inflatable Jack Slater effigy. It was this effigy, bobbing placidly out at sea, that at Cannes this year caused more of a stir than either the "real" Arnie or the preview of *Last Action Hero*. And this season, Arnie as a giant-sized logo of himself is the only star likely to give Spielberg's dinosaurs a run for their money.

NEW YORK, 7/12/93, p. 54, David Denby

In *Last Action Hero*, a movie-struck boy with a "magic" ticket jumps right into a movie, encounters his favorite action hero (Arnold Schwarzenegger), and says things like "You can't die until the grosses go down." *Last Action Hero* is an example of executive-suite wit, Hollywood division. The young audience wants to be enchanted, but in this parodistic monstrosity, it is sourly played with; it's as if director John McTiernan and the executives of Columbia Pictures had mistaken their own boredom and self-disgust for the audience's mood. They try to spoof a big, empty action movie, but they can do nothing else but make ... a big, empty action movie. In the movie inside the movie, cars crash and explode in the background of shots, and we are supposed to be amused by the meaningless waste. But what are these mock explosions but more meaningless waste? *Last Action Hero* is a scandal and a bore, an evacuation of a corrupt system that hasn't any idea what it wants to do with the extraordinary art form placed at its disposal. It deserves to be a flop (the grosses *have* gone down).

NEW YORK POST, 6/18/93, p. 31, Michael Medved

The funniest sequence in the new adventure-comedy "Last Action Hero" comes near the very beginning of the film? The great British actress Joan Plowright, widow of Lord Laurence Olivier, plays an elderly teacher who tries to introduce her restless New York City students to the classic film version of "Hamlet," starring her late husband.

Austin O'Brien, a bright, likable 11-year-old who plays the lonely, fatherless Danny Madigan, fidgets as he watches Olivier and imagines how Shakespeare's play might be improved if his movie hero, Arnold Schwarzenegger, played the title role. Suddenly, Arnold appears bulging out of Olivier's costume, chomping his macho cigar, lifting the guilty Claudius over his head and growling. "You killed my father. Big mistake!" Then a stentorian narrator intones, "Something is rotten in the state of Denmark and it's Prince Hamlet's job to take out the garbage!"

The rest of the film only intermittently reaches this level of inventiveness, but director John McTiernan (who worked with Big Arnold before on "Predator," and created the original "Die Hard") keeps the uneven gags and stunts moving along at a brisk enough pace to leave the audience reasonably entertained.

The plot centers on a magical movie ticket that one night manages to blast young Danny out of his theater seat and into the action that's unfolding on screen—a predictable thriller starring Schwarzenegger as Jack Slater, a tough-guy L.A. police officer fighting drug-dealing mobsters.

This idea of a movie fan entering the fictional world of his big screen idol reverses the setup of Woody Allen's "The Purple Rose of Cairo," where film character Jeff Daniels came down off screen to savor reality. It also recalls "Who Named Roger Rabbit?," where human detective Bob

Hoskins discovered the alternate reality of Toon Town, which operated according to bizarre rules established in countless cartoons.

In this film, the world of contemporary action movies is also shown as a cartoon—or a comic book—with a police captain (Frank McRae) who is always furious at the lonewolf hero, bad guys (the elegant, sneering Charles Dance and the earthy Anthony Quinn) who are powerful paragons of pure evil, and a brooding, superhuman, relentless main character (guess who?) who takes generous doses of brutal punishment and still comes back for more.

At one tense moment in the film-within-a-film, Danny tries to reassure Slater/Schwarzenegger by explaining that in action movies the good guys always win—but this knowledge only serves to drain suspense from the film's elaborate set pieces, such as the sequence where Slater dangles from a giant crane 17 stories above a small park that's decorated with tacky mechanical dinosaurs (take that, "Jurassic Park"!)

The satire occasionally falls wide of its mark: Since the picture is basically a sendup of recent action films, every scene ought to feel hauntingly familiar to movie fans—reminding us of hackneyed elements we've watched in the past. Instead, McTiernan has lavished considerable energy on creating images that look like nothing we've seen before—including outer-space leather-and-vinyl outfits for all the gorgeous women who stroll through every scene and a huge teaming, futuristic police station that serves as Slater's headquarters. As Arnold himself might say, "Big mistake!"

In this summer's fierce competition for box-office dollars, hard-core action fans may well opt for "Cliffhanger," with its sweaty, spectacular stunts, overly earnest acting and excesses of sadistic gore, but I prefer this funny, frisky new film—with its relatively restrained blood-and-guts and appropriately awarded PG-13 rating. Even when its gags don't work, "Last Action Hero" maintains a suitably skeptical and breezy attitude toward a tired movie formula that's become a sour joke whenever it tries to take its own conventions too seriously.

NEWSDAY, 6/18/93, Part II/p. 66, Jack Mathews

In a scene near the end of "The Last Action Hero," star Arnold Schwarzenegger dangles from a crane over the famed La Brea Tar Pits in Los Angeles, its black grease pond decorated with cheesy life-size replicas of the dinosaurs whose bones were uncovered there.

The scene, coming after dozens of other inside Hollywood jokes, seems a friendly jab at "Jurassic Park," "Last Action Hero's" chief summer rival, and I was half-expecting to see Arnold land on one of the creatures and flatten it. So that's how dinosaurs became extinct.

Instead, he splashes into the goo, and in the process turns a murky sight gag into a laser-sharp metaphor.

"Last Action Hero" has landed in the goo itself, and is certainly no threat to "Jurassic Park." Not because it is a badly made movie—never has a live-action cartoon looked better—but because its commercial fate is so inextricably bound to the dual personas of Arnold Schwarzenegger, the stone-faced hulk of "Kindergarten Cop" and "Terminator 2," and the tirelessly affable self-promoter of real life.

Schwarzenegger isn't merely the star of "The Last Action Hero," he is its inspiration, its heart, its humor, its premise, its raison d'etre.

The movie couldn't have been made without him any more than "Jurassic Park" could have been made without T-rex, and only those already under his spell will fully appreciate it.

Even the story, about an 11-year-old action fan who is magically transported into a movie starring his idol, is *Arnold's* fantasy. He plays himself, the world's most popular star, playing somebody else, a stone-faced hulk named Jack Slater.

He also plays himself as himself, showing up with wife Maria Shriver for a premiere of the movie within the movie.

For a few eerie moments, Schwarzenegger's Slater and Schwarzenegger's Schwarzenegger are on screen together, and the illusion is complete. They're all the same guy. Take that Steven Spielberg, Arnold has cloned himself.

The gang-written, purposely cliched script for "Last Action Hero" rips off so many other movies, it would take a full page to list them.

But two that deserve special mention are Woody Allen's "The Purple Rose of Cairo," in which a movie fan seems to will a matinee idol off the screen and into her life, and the recent "Cop and a Half," about a dyspeptic detective who is forced to take on a half-pint, know-it-all partner.

"Last Action Hero" combines those two notions when movie-mad Danny Madigan (Austin O'Brien) is handed a magic ticket by an old projectionist (Robert Prosky) at a Times Square movie palace and is whisked into the midst of a chase scene on the streets of a Jack Slater movie shot on the streets of downtown Los Angeles.

Quicker than you can say "cheap movie gimmick," Danny is riding shotgun with Jack Slater, driving the fictional hero nuts with movie references while using information he learned watching the first half of the picture to help his hero root out a gang of killers.

When a fellow cop played by F. Murray Abraham approaches them at police headquarters, Danny advises Slater not to trust him. "He killed Mozart," the kid says, referring to Abraham's role in "Amadeus." Slater won't be the only one who doesn't get it.

A lot of imagination went into the effort of stretching one joke into a two-hour and 10-minute feature, and though the joke is exhausted long before it's over, much of it is good fun.

There is a marvelously inventive sequence showing us how "Hamlet" might look on film if a cigar-chomping, Uzi-packing Schwarzenegger were to play the sweet prince, and its best moments have a kind of nutty "Naked Gun" quality to them.

Director John McTiernan ("Die Hard," "Predator") staged some dramatic stunts and action sequences, and it is safe to say his movie out-explodes, out-chases, out-puns and out-shoots most of the action films he is spoofing.

He has two super-villains, one who wears designer glass eyes (Charles Dance), another (Tom Noonan) with a cadaverous face and a penchant for throwing children off tall buildings.

Without following anything like a compelling plot, the villains and the heroes all end up on the other side of the screen, spilling out into the streets of New York where the premiere of the same film is about to begin, and where "Last Action Hero's" belated message—real violence hurts!—is labored over.

Because we are constantly reminded that the movie within the movie is just that, a movie, there is no tension to anything that occurs in it. The whole thing is just a huge and enormously loud put-on, with Schwarzenegger eagerly aping his own image.

I like Schwarzenegger as an action star, and I figure anyone with the confidence and stick-to-itiveness to become both Mr. Universe and Mr. Box Office has earned the right to flex and gloat, and he does it with irresistible charm. To imagine how awful this would be if the star's appeal didn't match his ego, think back no further than "Hudson Hawk."

Still, as the savvy producer Robert Radnitz once said, you cannot parody a parody, it's redundant. In making the contemporary Hollywood action movie look silly, in having Schwarzenegger become a flesh-and-blood comic strip character, "Last Action Hero" has merely gone to a lot of trouble to state the obvious.

NEWSWEEK, 6/28/93, p. 64, David Ansen

Among other things—too many other things—Arnold Schwarzenegger's *Last Action Hero* is the first $70 million-plus deconstructionist action movie. Admittedly, Columbia Pictures is not selling it as a postmodernist opus (" Quel plaisir! You haven't lived until you've seen Arnold decode his own text!"—Jacques Derrida, " Sneak Previews"). Nonetheless, the Big Guy's legions of fans may be a bit baffled to find, side by side with myriad explosions, machine-gunnings and cars barreling through walls, clips from Ingmar Bergman's "The Seventh Seal," a "Hamlet" parody with Arnold as a not-so-sweet prince, Laurence Olivier jokes (delivered by his widow, Joan Plowright) and the weirdly masochistic moment when the fictional Schwarzenegger character called Jack Slater confronts the real Arnold at a movie première and announces: "I don't really like you. You've brought me nothing but pain."

Just what kind of a would-be summer blockbuster is this? The concept, as old as Buster Keaton's silent masterpiece "Sherlock, Jr." (or Woody Allen's more recent "The Purple Rose of Cairo"), is that a movie-mad kid named Danny (Austin O'Brien), entrusted with a "magic ticket," is transported from the audience *into* an Arnold Schwarzenegger movie. The thing is, the character Arnold's playing, Jack Slater, doesn't know he's fictional, and Danny can't convince him. "You can't die till the grosses go down," the movie-wise child reassures the worried action hero, which may give you an inkling of the movie's pervasive tone of inside-joke self-consciousness. When the kid sees that an FBI agent is played by F. Murray Abraham, he instantly distrusts him. "Watch it—he killed Mozart!" More amusingly, Danny takes Slater to a video store to show him old Schwarzenegger movies—only to find that "Terminator 2" now stars Sylvester Stallone.

I was rooting for director John ("Die Hard") McTiernan to pull off this gargantuan jape: at least it's attempting something different. But "Last Action Hero" fatally outsmarts itself. You simply can't care about the "Jack Slater" movie your stuck watching—some nonsense about a crime boss (Anthony Quinn), his evil British hit man (Charles Dance) and a rival gang they're planning to rub out—when everything in it is a generic joke. If the filmmakers don't believe in what they're making, how can we? By the time Slater and Danny are rescued from death by an animated cartoon cat in a trench coat, you know "Last Action Hero" has lost control of itself. Cartoon characters *don't belong* in Arnold Schwarzenegger movies—nor do computer-generated images of Humphrey Bogart. The film has entered the desperate, anything-goes realm of "Casino Royale." It never recovers, even when Slater and Danny, pursuing the "fictional" villain Dance, burst through the other side of the screen and into the "real" world, where good guys don't always win, and death supposedly stings. But it's too late—nothing can touch us now.

Dreamed up by two young writers just out of college (Zak Penn and Adam Leff), rewritten by action specialist Shane Black and David Arnott, then doctored by an uncredited William Goldman is a vain attempt to give it heart, "Last Action Hero" aims for so many different constituencies—little kids, action-movie fans, hip *cinéastes* and French philosophers—that it will likely satisfy none of them. The sheer size and strenuousness of the effort tends to squelch even the best jokes: this deafening movie defines the term overproduced. And what are we to make of "Jack Slater's" last-minute *mea culpa*: "I don't want to shoot people anymore"? After serving up thunderous portions of screen mayhem, Schwarzenegger wants to let us know he's *sorry* he's the world's most popular action star? Thanks for sharing, Arnold, but we're not buying. Rarely has a movie used so much heavy artillery to shoot itself in the foot.

SIGHT AND SOUND, 8/93, p. 46, Henry Sheehan

Supercop Jack Slater pushes aside a phalanx of cops surrounding a skyscraper and punches his way to the top where he confronts the Ripper, an axe-wielding psycho holding Slater's young son hostage. Although the Ripper has him covered, Slater gets the drop on him and the killer totters off the roof.

Just then the screen goes blank. The action has been taking place in an Arnold Schwarzenegger movie, *Jack Slater III*, screened in a dingy, almost deserted Times Square movie theatre, and watched by Slater's Number One fan, 11-year-old Danny Madigan. When Danny upbraids Nick, an ageing projectionist, for letting the screen go dead, Nick tells him to come back at midnight for a private preview of the brand new *Jack Slater IV*.

Disobeying his Mom's orders to stay safely locked up in their tiny apartment, Danny, after being mugged, goes to the theatre. Before starting the film, Nick hands Danny a ticket, which he says he got from the magician Houdini, who told him it had special powers. In *Jack Slater IV* the cop is up against mob don Vivaldi and his disdainful English hitman Benedict. When Danny is watching a particularly lethal chase, the ticket twinkles and Danny is transported into the action, landing in the back seat of Slater's car. Danny uses his viewer's special knowledge to help out a skeptical Slater (who, like all the other characters in the movie, doesn't believe he's not real and has never heard of Arnold Schwarzenegger). Despite some bumps in the road, the two are able to foil Vivaldi's booby-trapping of another mobster's funeral and expose corrupt FBI agent John Practice. But Benedict gets Danny's magic ticket and moves over into the real world.

Danny and Slater pursues Benedict, even though in the real world the wounds Slater laughed off in the movies will be dangerous. Discovering a public indifference to violence and the powers he now possesses, an uninhibited Benedict plans to bring movie monsters to the real world and so rule it. He begins with the Ripper, whom Slater encounters at the premiere for *Jack Slater IV*, where he also runs into Arnold Schwarzenegger. Slater must relive the climax of *Jack Slater III* once more before dispatching Benedict. He is shot in the process and receives a visit from Death; but with the help of Danny and the magic ticket, is able to return unscathed to his movie.

It should have been enough to say that *Last Action Hero* suffered from over-inflation. After all, the movie is built on a puny gimmick—the notion that the conventions of hi-tech action adventure will look silly when contrasted with, if not *life* exactly, then the conventions of more ordinary melodrama. But no amount of cinematic steroids could turn this into a muscular premise. Not that there's any want of trying. for the film's first 45 minutes or so, it seems that director John McTiernan (*Die Hard, Predator*) is trying to meld *Weekend* with the Keystone Cops, sending a fleet of cars careening and crashing from unexpected heights to unanticipated depths. Freed from the restraints of believability, the action expert launches his rubber-soled missiles from a succession of impossibly-located moving ramps, using downtown LA's over-photographed tiers of bridges, roads and paved riverbeds to refreshing effect.

But there are already warning signs aplenty that this hero's odyssey will be bogus. The whole sequence in which the kindly old projectionist (an overemphatic Robert Prosky) presents young Danny with the magic ticket that effects his passage to Slater-land is too sugary, its lip-smacking anticipation of fantasy at odds with the sardonic presentation of action that begins with the film's very first shot. And the film's supposedly realistic moments, those that deal with Danny's living conditions, are hopelessly compromised by typical big-studio calculation. There may well be some white kids living with single moms in the Times Square area (though perhaps not so white as the blond pale-skinned Californian, Austin O'Brien, who plays Danny), but the poor kids so situated are far, far more likely to be African-American or Puerto Rican. But poor black kids don't sell tickets, and so the 'real' section of the film, which is supposed to offer such a bracingly satirical contrast to the action fantasy, is already compromised by demographic marketing fantasies of its own.

Soon enough, even the film-within-a-film, *Jack Slater IV*, loosens its moorings. Danny keeps trying to tell everyone that they're not real, that they're movie characters and he can tell them what their best move will be, since he's watched the start of the movie and knows who and where the bad guys are. This is a good enough joke if the villains are foiled by inexplicably foresighted cops. But these crooks, despite some delightfully haughty sadism from Charles Dance, are bozos themselves. And when their great coup turns out to be booby-trapping the corpse of a dead mobster known for his propensity to break wind, the storm of fart jokes takes the action right into the toilet. *Jack Slater IV* ends up perched uncomfortably between *Airplane* and the most recent (and already self-mocking) *Lethal Weapon*.

A lot of this can be put down to miscalculation and some egotism on the part of the film-makers, who seem eager to distance their own intelligences from the body of their work. However, it's cynicism that ultimately does in *Last Action Hero*. The first showdown between Slater and the Ripper is mocked for its reliance on excessive stylization to jump-start emotion. Then, just when Slater is bemoaning the action-hero tendencies of his daughter, the Ripper's hostage—who turns out to have died—is revealed as Slater's son, all the better to generate some sympathy for what is an avowed stereotype.

The kitsch turns from undercurrent to raging flood when Slater makes it to the 'real' New York, where he runs into Schwarzenegger and berates him for ruining his life. We've just seen Arnold arriving at the movie premiere with wife Maria Shriver, who angrily cautions him against promoting the restaurant chain he co-owns with other movie stars. Of course, Arnold can't keep himself from pushing the burgers, but the kidding is not as pointed as it looks. After all, Arnold winks, sells, winks, sells and winks again, and it's the selling that keeps its force while the wink turns into a tic.

But then, without shame, the film climaxes on the very same scene that climaxed *Jack Slater III*, the encounter between the Ripper and Slater—only this time Danny is the hostage. In other words, every cliche that the film had mocked for being cheap and sentimental is suddenly resuscitated long enough to bring the movie to a supposedly emotion-packed end. This is a film that cannot imagine existing without the very same stock situations and characters it denigrates. It's a perfect example of cinematic self-hatred.

TIME, 6/21/93, p. 67, Richard Corliss

In *Jurassic Park*, Hollywood apparently has a dinosaur-size hit. Now the town thinks it smells a dog. *Last Action Hero*, the Arnold Schwarzenegger adventure opening this week, has spurred, doomsday rumors because of its ballistic budget (estimates run up to $120 million), a reputedly disastrous sneak preview last month, and the subsequent three-day shooting of a new sequence.

Columbia Pictures, anxious about its huge investment, quickly sent in the spin doctors. The studio did get "slightly panicked" at the preview, says co-writer David Arnott. "Clearly the movie was too long, and the jokes needed timing tweaks. But a lot of people liked it." The new sequence was just "Arnold never giving up on anything," says director John McTiernan. "He guilted us all into shooting it." Now he has to hope that, oh, 40 million Americans will be guiled or guilted into seeing it.

Danny (the appealing Austin O'Brien) is a lonely New York City kid who lives for the movies. He is about to live *in* them, when a "magic ticket" propels him through the screen and into the latest action epic of his film hero, Jack Slater (Schwarzenegger). "We're perfect buddy movie material," the boy tells his reluctant new partner. "I'll teach you to be voluble. You'll teach me to be brave." Having seen part of the picture Danny knows that Jack is in peril from a bull's-eye assassin (Charles Dance). There's a lot that Jack, poor simple muscle-bound dear, doesn't know—including that he's a fictional character. When he chases the assassin out of movieland into the "real" world, he finds that other rules apply. Heroes get hurt. People could die.

Since Buster Keaton's *Sherlock, Jr.* in 1924, Hollywood has often toyed with the looking-glass motif, though never on *Hero's* mammoth scale, where so many cars crash that the audience becomes rubberneckers. Schwarzenegger, a live-action cartoon in the flesh, and McTiernan, who made the brains explode on time in *Die Hard*, might seem just the team to send up the dizzy conventions of the action genre. At first they do so, smartly. A wounded cop mutters, "Two days to retirement," and promptly dies. And Arnold's version of *Hamlet* is even funnier than Mel Gibson's. "To be, or not to be," he says, lighting his trademark cigar stub. "Not to be." And Elsinore goes *boom!* But after a while, as the facetious film references (to everything from *E.T.* to *The Seventh Seal* pile up, *Hero* turns into the industry's all-time costliest inside joke. Watching it is as enervating as being on a real movie set. You see all of the sweat and none of the starlight.

The picture fails on a common Hollywood fallacy: that because people lap up celebrity tattle and flock to movie-studio tours, they must be fascinated by the nuts and bolts of filmmaking. *Last Action Hero* (which is the ultimate studio tour as surely as *Jurassic Park* is the ultimate theme-park ride) starts out mostly nuts, and winds up mostly bolts. Or, rather, winds down. That's a problem with pastiche: it must be constantly jump-started with ingenuity, and even that ultimately pales. By the end, nothing matters.

In this movie's final reel, Jack begs Danny, "Believe in me." But by then he has forfeited the right to ask. Moviegoers can pretend to care about screen heroes; it's called suspension of disbelief. But they can't *pretend* to pretend to care. So when Danny confidently tells Jack, "You can't die till the grosses go down," we must wonder if that pertains to Schwarzenegger too. He needs *Last Action Hero* to be as big as *Jurassic Park*. And our guess is: Not to be.

VILLAGE VOICE, 6/29/93, p. 59, Gary Indiana

Last Action Hero poses the oft-asked contemporary question: if an imbecile exhibits self-consciousness, should we consider this postmodernism in action? The answer is yes, no, maybe, and so what? *Last Action Hero* pokes would-be fun at itself by pushing the ultraviolence of an Arnold Schwarzenegger movie into the realm of goony parody. But this film is too complacent about its star's popularity, and too contemptuous of its audience, to forego the Schwarzenegger formula. Parody, in this case, simply means getting rid of what little narrative verisimilitude is usually required as an excuse for two hours of incredibly loud, brainless visual trauma, huge objects hurling through glass facades, atriums, and crowds of people, barrages of heavy-weapons fire, exploding buildings, high-speed chases along crowded streets, frequent collisions, and bulky motor vehicles tumbling off bridges and overpasses.

A cross between *The Purple Rose of Ciaro* and *Total Recall*, *Last Action Hero* sends irksome, ungifted child actor Austin O'Brien, playing Danny Madigan, into the make-believe world of Jack Slater, a bigger-than-life hero played by Arnold Schwarzenegger, via a "magic ticket." Danny gets the ticket from a kindly old projectionist at the crumbling, condemned movie palace where he often skips school, escaping the mean streets and deadly tenement hallways of New York City where he, Danny, feels powerless.

Danny, naturally, lives with his widowed mom (played with merciful brevity) by Mercedes Ruehl) and therefore lacks a Male Role Model. As everyone from John Singleton to Phyllis Schlafly will tell you, single-parent families where there is no strong father figure are the number one cause of crime in our country. Like *Jurassic Park,* this movie is really a heartfelt plea for responsible adult male role models to rescue today's kids from a world full of badass mother-fuckers whether they be genetically resurrected giant dinosaurs or just psychotic mobsters.

Recent studies show that people who spend an egregious number of hours in front of the television set perceive the world as a far more terrifying and dangerous place than those who watch TV infrequently. Danny is clearly a TV kid. The Jack Slater films give him a sense of vicarious omnipotence. Once sucked inside *Jack Slater IV* he confounds its fictional beings with his detailed knowledge of *Jack Slaters I-III.* It comes as no surprise that this kid knows very little besides the plot devices of action movies, and the film quickly milks this thin form of preciosity dry. Unlike *Terminator 2's* talented Eddie Furlong, Austin O'Brien has a terminal case of the cutes.

When, after what feels like decades inside the film inside the film, Danny and Jack migrate to the real world in pursuit of villain Charles Dance (Sigourney Weaver's abbreviated love interest in *Alien³*.), the fertile brains of all four screenwriters kick into overdrive. We get Schwarzenegger confronting his fictional alter ego at the premiere of *Jack Slater IV.* We get the psycho killer from *Jack Slater III,* released by Dance from celluloid purgatory into actual Times Square. We get myriad sight, sound, and other gags that score off Schwarzenegger's much-advertised, self-deprecating humor. (He can afford it.) The least appealing, most protracted gag is the appearance of Death (Ian McKellen), who's whisked from a screening of *The Seventh Seal* by the chance landing of the magic ticket outside the theater. This would almost have class, if Bergman's Death hadn't already been appropriated by Bill and Ted. Would the writers of this movie sail a single reference above the sub-brow altitude of the average 10-year-old? *And why would they want to?*

This film, a veritable quote-o-rama, closes with a long visual steal from *Blade Runner.* In his final scene, Dance boasts that by using the magic ticket he can recruit accomplices from any movie, which might've given *Last Action Hero* the postmodern zest of Wes Craven's *Shocker.* Even without such a bravura coda, *Last Action Hero* has all the fun and excitement of a multiple-car pile-up, followed by a 7.5 earthquake.

Also reviewed in:
CHICAGO TRIBUNE, 6/18/93, Friday/p. A, Mark Caro
NATION, 7/19/93, p. 115, Stuart Klawans
NEW YORK TIMES, 6/18/93, p. C1, Vincent Canby
NEW YORKER, 7/5/93, p. 94, Anthony Lane
VARIETY, 6/28/93, p. 22, Todd McCarthy
WASHINGTON POST, 6/18/93, p. G1, Hal Hinson
WASHINGTON POST, 6/18/93, Weekend/p. 42, Desson Howe

LAST BUTTERFLY, THE

An Arrow release of a Cinema et Communication/Studio Barrandor coproduction in association with HTV, CTE and Filmexport. *Executive Producer:* Boudjemaa Dahmane, Jacques Methe, and Patrick Dromgoole. *Producer:* Steven North. *Director:* Karel Kachyna. *Screenplay:* Ota Hofman and Karel Kachyna. *Based on the novel by:* Michael Jacot. *Director of Photography:* Jiri Krejcik. *Editor:* Jiri Brozek. *Music:* Alex North. *Choreographer:* Radomil Cech. *Sound:* Jiri Maudry. *Production Designer:* Zbynek Hloch. *Costumes:* Ester Krumbachova. *Running time:* 110 minutes. *MPAA Rating:* Not Rated.

CAST: Tom Courtenay (Antoine Moreau); Brigitte Fossey (Vera); Ingrid Held (Michèle); Freddie Jones (Rheinberg); Linda Jablonska (Stella); Josef Kemr (Stadler); Milan Knazko (Gruber); Lubek Kopriva (Laub); Daniel Margolius (Samuel).

NEW YORK POST, 8/20/93, p. 26, Lawrence Cohn

The difficult subject matter of survival in a World War II concentration camp is given a tasteful but unmoving treatment in "The Last Butterfly."

Tom Courtenay portrays Antoine Moreau, a world-famous mime who dreams in 1944 of opening his own Parisian theater to entertain the expected liberators. Currently he's forced to perform for the German occupiers but manages to slip political statements into his routine.

When his beautiful girlfriend, chorus girl Ingrid Held, is killed as an accused spy in a Gestapo raid, Moreau is suspected of being her accomplice. He's given a chance to retain his freedom if he'll stage a performance at Hitler's mock "City of the Jews," the Terezin concentration camp.

Moreau naively agrees and soon learns many lessons about survival and responsibility. The performance is just a phony show to impress visiting Red Cross delegates, and Moreau finds himself playing God as he determines which adult and child inmates will work on the show and be in the audience, thereby being spared from immediate transport to the death camps.

That plot line is similar to that of Jerry Lewis' never-released 1972 feature "The Day the Clown Cried." Unfortunately, Czech director Karel Kachyna's kid-gloves approach to the material keeps the viewer at a distance and fails to wrench the emotions. Having much of the supporting cast dubbed into English (including Ingrid Held) doesn't help.

As he's done in the title roles of "Billy Liar," "One Day in the Life of Ivan Denisovich" and "The Dresser," Courtenay underplays magnificently and his performance of mime routines choreographed by Boris Hybner is expert.

NEWSDAY, 8/20/93, Part II/p. 71, Jonathan Mandell

In the Czech town of Terezin, some of the most accomplished and intelligent Jews of Europe lived for a time during World War II in apparent comfort and culture, entertained by concerts, dining in cafés, strolling well-tendered gardens.

But Terezin was really a town of horror, set up by Hitler as a "model ghetto" in order to fool International Red Cross inspectors and counter growing rumors of Nazi death camps. In truth, most of the Jews of Terezin were sent off to be murdered in Auschwitz ovens, many of the others died of starvation or brutality in the town itself; of the 140,000 Jews (including children) who passed through Terezin while the Nazis were in charge, only about 16,000 survived.

It is a story that has not been told enough, though there was a noteworthy documentary two years ago called "Terezin Diary," and there have been exhibits and concerts of work by Terezin inmates, as well as books by Terezin survivors.

It is told once again in "The Last Butterfly," a feature film about a (fictional) famous mime from Paris named Antoine Moreau, played by the English actor Tom Courtenay. The Nazis force Moreau in 1944 to travel to Terezin for a one-night performance of fairy tales, enlisting some of the children from the town for his cast. Discovering the truth behind the facade of Terezin leads Moreau to an act of courage.

"The Last Butterfly" was an international effort: In addition to Courtenay, the lead actress Brigette Fossey is French; the director, Karel Kachyna, is Czech, and the film itself, which is based on a novel by Canadian Michael Jacot, was shot in Czechoslovakia in the midst of the successful popular overthrow of the Communist government. It won first prize at the Vienna Film Festival.

For anybody who knows nothing about the true story of Terezin, "The Last Butterfly" is an important film. But it is not a particularly good one. Much of it seems rote and predictable; the pacing is poor, the horror somehow muted, almost underwater. As professional as Courtenay is, it is hard to believe his talent for mime could ever have won his character international acclaim, and the acting of too many of the bit players is just plain bad.

Although filmed in part on location in the still-existing town, the setting is nearly wasted. "The Last Butterfly" fails to deliver a full sense of the real place and its terrible, unbearable ironies. Perhaps no work of art could. But the story of Terezin deserves a better try.

LAST BUTTERFLY, THE 793

Also reviewed in:
NEW YORK TIMES, 8/20/93, p. C23, Stephen Holden
VARIETY, 2/11/91, p. 110
WASHINGTON POST, 1/21/94, p. G6, David Mills

LAST CALL AT MAUD'S

A Maud's Project release. *Producer:* Karen Kiss and Paris Poirier. *Director:* Paris Poirier. *Director of Photography:* Cheryl Rosenthal and Gary Sanders. *Editor:* Paris Poirier and Elaine Trotter. *Music:* Tim Horrigan. *Sound:* Loretta Molutar. *Running time:* 75 minutes. *MPAA Rating:* Not Rated.

WITH: Gwenn Craig; Jo Daly; Sally Gearhart; Judy Grahn; JoAnn Loulan; Phyliss Lyon; Del Martin; Pat Norman; Rikki Streicher; Mary Wings.

CINEASTE, Vol. XX, No. 1, 1993, p. 46, Patricia Leonardi

"I can think of no place better to have suspense and a real eerie feeling of decadence than a lesbian bar, because lesbians are outlaws, we've always been outlaws and I hope we always stay outlaws, and lesbian bars are our secret hiding places." With these remarks by lesbian mystery writer Mary Wings, *Last Call at Maud's* begins its descent into the underground "secret sorority" of the lesbian bar scene from the 1940s to the present. For the next seventy-five minutes, both drinks and conversation are free flowing, as a who's who list of lesbian luminaries and local bar regulars recount tales of coming out, first bar visits, pick ups and affairs, police raids, hippie lesbians, the women's movement, Castro Street clones, Anita Bryant, and AIDS.

The occasion and setting for this documentary by first-time director Paris Poirier is the closing of Maud's, the world's oldest and longest-running lesbian-owned bar, located in San Francisco's Haight Ashbury. *Maud's* is the most recent in a growing subgenre of historical documentaries within queer cinema (*Silent Pioneers, Before Stonewall, Tiny and Ruby: Hell Divin' Women, Comrades In Arms, Women Like Us,* and the classic *Word Is Out*) that reconstruct pre-Stonewall gay and lesbian his/her stories using oral histories, personal photographs and memoirs, home movies, and archival materials. Within this tradition, personal stories and social histories blend and blur in an attempt to make real for audiences the not-so-distant, but often hidden or ignored queer past in a homophobic America.

In *Last Call at Maud's*, the memories of the women interviewed are frequently accompanied by personal photographs of younger selves and lovers. When Rikki Streicher, owner of Maud's, describes the post-World War II bar scene crowded with butches with their slicked-back hair and femmes with their lipsticked mouths and drop-dead dresses, youthful photos of Streicher in earnest boy drag serve to both illustrate and verify her reminiscences. The film displays a fascinating wealth of archival material testifying to repressive police actions and media coverage which, in those days, had no qualms of 'outing' those arrested in bar raids by listing their names and addresses. These events and counter-strategies are fleshed out through individual accounts given by Phyllis Lyon and Del Martin (founders of the Daughters of Bilitis, the first international organization of lesbians) and political activist Sally Gearhart. Gearhart remembers going to 'mixed' bars (gay and lesbian) that had panic alarms alerting patrons to possible raids. By the time the police arrived, they found a myriad of 'heterosexual' couples dancing sedately. The most 'arresting' moments of the film are those which powerfully remind viewers not only of the sanctioned police harassment and the Alcoholic Beverage Control's threat to revoke the liquor license, but also of the risk every lesbian ran simply by patronizing the bar.

While *Maud's* tends toward the maudlin at times, its historic reevaluation of the lesbian bar scene as both a site of cultural and sexual exchanges and as a space of growing political activism puts the post-Stonewall spectator firmly in her place. Poirier describes *Maud's* as a "maternal cuffing" at a younger generation of lesbians that she feels has taken for granted certain freedoms, such as having a safe social space for lesbians. Judy Grahn, author of *Another Mother Tongue*, drives this point home in the film when she remarks, "It wasn't just about loving women, but it was about a whole cultural underground that didn't exist anywhere else except in that milieu which at the same time was dangerous to us."

It is this image of Fifties dykes as rebels with a cause that younger 'lipstick lesbians' are increasingly reconsidering as compelling historical 'role' models (evidenced in part by a renewed interest in butch/femme role playing). Many older lesbians may find this outlaw image reaffirming after bearing much criticism by second wave feminists who argued that such roles merely reproduced heterosexual norms.

Yet, for all its claims of representing lesbians as outlaws, the film remains conventional, glossing over internal conflicts within the lesbian communities, particularly regarding race and class, in favor of a seamless and linear historical narrative in which the butch/femme couples are suddenly and effortlessly replaced by psychedelic, longhaired, braless hippie dykes who are just as suddenly eclipsed by Harvey Milk's assassination, Anita Bryant's antigay crusades, and AIDS. (Historical transitions are conventionally made through photo montages with appropriate accompanying music.) The historical interactions and conflicts between lesbians and gay men are somewhat more fully sketched out, but are uncomfortably subsumed under the AIDS epidemic where lesbians appear as comforting supporters (which they have been), but do not seem to be at risk themselves.

Thus, the film's balance between the personal and the social, between memory and history, between revision and nostalgia, is at best precarious. The choice of subject matter, the closing of Maud's, provides the film with a sense of urgency that asks important questions about what effects these bar closings will have on lesbian culture. (Streicher recently shut down Amelia's, another prominent San Francisco lesbian bar.) At the same time, its narrow focus is at times claustrophobic (all the interviews and moving footage take place in or around the bar) and the spectator is limited to only tantalizing peeks outside Maud's of the broader historical, social, and political issues of the time.

The film's publicity package comments on its blind spots stating, "Because Maud's was a 'talking bar;' Paris let the conversation dictate the structure. If something historical is missing in the narrative, well, it's just because it didn't come up in conversation." One thing that doesn't come up during these conversations is the matter of who is speaking. The film defers on-screen credits till the final scroll, missing the opportunity to connect these women to their specific contributions to lesbian history and politics (as with the founders of The Daughters of Bilitis, noted authors, community activists, scholars, police commissioners, and so on).

Talking head documentaries are popular because they give a greater voice to the subjects they depict, avoid authoritarian narration, and function as important oral/visual recordings. One of their major limitations, however, is their inability to address complex historical arguments and issues. The scope and perspective of the documentary depends heavily on what the filmmaker can 'get' from the interviewee and what the filmmaker is willing to ask. While documentaries like *Last Call at Maud's* are important in continuing the feminist tradition of 'the personal as political,' relying completely on the conversation of others can reduce the political to the simply personal.

LOS ANGELES TIMES, 9/29/93, Calendar/p. 8, Kevin Thomas

Paris Poirier's "Last Call at Maud's" at once bids a fond farewell to a cherished San Francisco landmark and documents a social revolution. Warm without being overly sentimental, this consistently entertaining and engaging film invites its interviewees to range far beyond barroom reminiscences to tell us what it was like to be a lesbian in postwar America. As a filmmaker Poirier is as focused as she is informative, for "Last Call at Maud's" is both incisive and comprehensive in its mere 75 minutes, drawing upon a treasure trove of stills and home movies.

Opening in April, 1966, in the Haight Ashbury district and closing in September, 1989, it may well have been the longest-running women's bar in the world, as its owner Rikki Streicher and her friends believe. Unpretentious in its decor as any neighborhood bar, Maud's was clearly a friendly spot from the start at a time when lesbians, like gay males, had virtually no alternatives to bars as meeting places.

For a number of years after Maud's opened Streicher had constantly to be on the alert for vice raids, couldn't hire women as bartenders until 1973 and, for several years beyond that, was vulnerable to being shut down if the police caught a woman so much as touching another woman's shoulder. Not until the latter part of the '70s were gay and lesbian bars free from harassment, says one of Maud's longtime customers—even in San Francisco. Nevertheless, Maud's weathered all storms to become a true community center that sponsored numerous special events and even had its own softball team.

Interestingly, Maud's customers, which includes San Francisco police commissioner Gwenn Craig, suggest strongly that lesbian bars have always been a great deal more democratic and inclusive than gay male bars, many of which have been blatantly racist and ageist in their admission policies.

Two of Maud's best-known patrons in its earlier years were Del Martin and Phyllis Lyon, pioneering lesbian activists, lovers for 40 years and founders in 1955 of the Daughters of Bilitis, the first major lesbian organization. They and others talk of the incredible secrecy in which gay men and women had to live their lives in the conservative '50s.

Streicher tells us that when she opened the bar bouffant hairstyles were in full force, soon to be swept away in the impact of the hippie invasion that flowered famously in Haight Ashbury itself, affecting not only the way lesbians looked but also the way they thought and felt about themselves and each other.

Indeed, Poirier excels in encouraging her subjects to explain how changes in American society at large transformed the lesbian community in particular—from involvement in the anti-war and women's movements as well as gay liberation to the AIDS epidemic of the past 12 years. AIDS, in fact, is cited as one of the numerous reasons contributing to the demise of Maud's. Soaring overhead costs and declining business did Maud's in, but the underlying causes, along with more conservative sexual behavior dictated by AIDS, seem to include a growing trend toward sobriety and people being more "into themselves," as one woman puts it.

As much as it surely has been missed by its regulars, Maud's may simply have outlived its usefulness, for as one woman points out, there are now many places for a lesbian to be public about her sexual orientation. Even so, you can't help but suspect the loss of Maud's reflects the loss of sense of community that permeates so much of American society today. (Times-rated Mature for adult themes, suitable for teen-agers.)

NEW YORK POST, 3/19/93, p. 29, Matthew Flamm

Among the more peculiar theories advanced by Camille Paglia—that self-promoting literary critic and professed bisexual—is the idea that lesbians aren't sexual enough. She should only get a load of "Last Call at Maud's," a documentary set around the closing in 1989 of the world's oldest lesbian bar.

"There were women standing in line for you," recalls a now-middle-aged bartender, speaking with scarcely-concealed relish of the San Francisco bar's heyday in the late '60s and '70s. Another veteran bartender, explaining that she's often asked if any marriages got their start at Maud's, quips, "Fifteen or 20 a night."

The feature-length documentary, produced and directed by first-time filmmaker Paris Poirier, opens today at the Cinema Village.

Made with no money and little technical skill—sound and picture are distractingly out-of-synch—"Last Call at Maud's" nonetheless succeeds as a history of postwar lesbian life and an intimate portrait of a community institution.

"I had never heard about lesbians" is one refrain that sounds through the interviews, as bar regulars—many of them writers and activists—tell their stories of coming out. One older couple talk of founding the international lesbian organization Daughters of Bilitis in 1955, and of not even knowing there were other homosexual advocacy groups like the Mattachine Society.

In the '50s and '60s, we're told, the only hangouts for lesbians were male gay bars like the Black Cat Cafe. Men would dance with men, women with women—until the police were spotted about to raid, and everybody found an opposite-sex partner.

When a Haight-Ashbury watering hole called Maud's Study became vacant in 1966, Rikki Streicher—an aficionado of lesbian night life—took it over.

"I have always been a bar person," the pleasantly practical Streicher says. "I wanted it to be a composite of all the bars I've been to—all the good things."

"It was better than home," one veteran testifies. Maud's became a place to play pool ("Ladies Only" reads the sign on the wall), pick up other women, talk, dance, fight and drink. Through home movies, snapshots and archival photographs, "Last Call" moves through the bell-bottomed, acid-dropping late '60s, free-wheeling '70s and increasingly sober '80s.

AIDS cast its shadow on Maud's, not only in the grief the women express for its victims but in the lifestyle changes that have accompanied the epidemic. The bar's patrons stopped drinking and sleeping around. Lesbians, it may also be, no longer needed a refuge.

Or perhaps, as Streicher says, 23 years is enough.

NEWSDAY, 3/19/93, Part II/p. 75, John Anderson

Maud's, the long-standing San Francisco lesbian bar that closed in 1989, was like home to a lot of people. And "Last Call at Maud's" is a lot like a home movie.

Which means that this documentary is going to mean more to the people who were there than to those approaching it as disinterested observers. In her efforts to make "Last Call at Maud's" a valentine to a vanished institution—complete with testimonials, scenes from the bar's closing night, and a familiar attitude toward the bar's habitues—director Paris Poirier leaves a lot of us out.

And by broadening her target to include the sexual-political climate of the '50s to mid-'60s, a period that made Maud's important, she loses her original focus.

But somehow, her intentions are so sincere, you want to let her get away with being alternately, irrelevant and digressive.

Poirier intends "Last Call at Maud's" to seem as much like an evening at a bar as she can, so we meet a lot of anonymous people: Unfortunately, none of the many "witnesses" to Maud's history are identified until the end of the film. You figure out who owner Rikki Streicher is, but it would be nice to know we're seeing and hearing Gwenn Craig, the current city police commissioner, or the poet/historian Judy Grahn, or Mary Wings, writer of lesbian mystery novels ("She Came Too Late," "She Came in a Flash") who makes one of the film's stranger declarations: "We've always been outlaws and I hope we [lesbians] always stay outlaws." The political right would certainly have no problem obliging her.

Some of the more touching moments are generated by couples like Phyllis Lyon and Del Martin, long-time partners and founders of the Daughters of Bilitis, the first international lesbian organization, who reminisce about just how difficult it was for them to be a couple. Through still photos, newspaper headlines and other memorabilia, we get a sense of the repressive attitude that prevailed at the time.

Certainly, the homosexual world will never be as it was when Maud's opened. The bar saw extraordinary social changes during its tenure, including the one that spelled its demise: The whole movement toward clean and sober living, accelerated by the AIDS crisis and a general concern for better health, effectively put Maud's out of business. And romance may also have been a casualty. One old-timer, asked during the closing hours whether any marriages ever took place at Maud's, gave the perfect answer: "About fifteen or twenty a night."

VILLAGE VOICE, 3/23/93, p. 61, Martha Baer

Not everyone loves the pungent warmth and claustrophobia of a good, dark, beer-flowing bar, but those who do often call it home. And for those whose clothes are safest seen in the shadows and whose desire could bring on a police raid, perhaps these homes are most cherished of all.

Such is the case of Maud's, mother of lesbian bars, staunch little San Francisco hangout that persevered until 1989, when its memorabilia was auctioned and its passing mourned. A plainly structured documentary (save for the exclusion of its interviewers names, a weird form of anonymity amidst the film's recapitulation of intimacies), *Last Call at Maud's* exhumes the beloved in an exercise interesting in its historical breadth yet limited in its sentiment.

For younger dykes, this doc is a cornucopia of information, with grown-up celebs like Del Martin, Phyllis Lyon, and JoAnn Loulan recounting the sexy secrecy of the early "scene," and with tidbits about extinct legalities and outsmarting law enforcement. But what the movie doesn't do is look beneath the extraordinary camaraderie and question the problem of clique. On the other side of adventurousness, there is a cloying safety, the construction of a timeless other-free zone, so that one finds oneself watching *Maud's*, impatient with the "ingroup" and eager to move on. After all, how many parties can a few queers have for themselves?

That said, what makes *Last Call at Maud's* so interesting are the intersections of the sweep of history with the smallness of one social circle. It's as if, in this film, the cultural moment and the tiny bar stand off, each alternately throwing down a card across the notion of history, each card changing the game. Now-familiar lesbian coming-out stories here are dressed up in stretch pants and bouffants; run-of-the-mill images of '40s nightclubs are distorted with odd accounts of sexual discovery.

Though *Last Call at Maud's* may not inspire the simple nostalgia it means to, it creates a history pleasantly ornate with the hatch marks of private life and sexuality.

Also reviewed in:
NEW YORK TIMES, 3/19/93, p. C6, Stephen Holden
VARIETY, 3/15/93, p. 66, Derek Elley
WASHINGTON POST, 10/29/93, p. B7, Rita Kempley

LAST DAYS OF CHEZ NOUS, THE

A Fine line Features release. *Producer:* Jan Chapman. *Director:* Gillian Armstrong. *Screenplay:* Helen Garner. *Director of Photography:* Geoffrey Simpson. *Editor:* Nicholas Beauman. *Music:* Paul Grabowsky. *Sound:* Ben Osmo and (music) Robin Grey. *Sound Editor:* Karin Whittington. *Casting:* Liz Mullinar. *Production Designer:* Janet Patterson. *Art Director:* Catherine Silm. *Set Decorator:* Kerrie Brown. *Costumes:* Janet Patterson. *Make-up:* Lesley Vanderwalt. *Running time:* 96 minutes. *MPAA Rating:* R.

CAST: Lisa Harrow (Beth); Bruno Ganz (J.P.); Kerry Fox (Vicki); Mirando Otto (Annie); Kiri Paramore (Tim); Bill Hunter (Beth's Father); Lex Marinos (Angelo); Mickey Camilleri (Sally); Lynne Murphy (Beth's Mother); Claire Haywood (Janet); Leanne Bundy (Susie); Wilson Alcorn (Man in Cafe); Tom Weaver (Thief); Bill Brady (Mayor); Eva Di Cesare (Waitress); Danny Caretti (Waiter); Olga Sanderson (Singing Woman); Joyce Hopwood (Clinic Nurse); Steve Cox (Stranger); Harry Griffiths (Old Man Desert Tourist); Amanda Martin (Desert Waitress).

LOS ANGELES TIMES, 3/10/93, Calendar/p. 1, Kenneth Turan

Because its concerns are emotional, because its subject is the often devastating texture of ordinary life, the thoughtful and finely drawn "The Last Days of Chez Nous" takes a bit of getting used to. For films usually do not care to be this honest about the nature of relationships, do not want to risk being truthful about what people do to each other and, most especially, to those they nominally love.

To audiences who remember "My Brilliant Career" and "High Tide," it will not be a surprise that "Chez Nous," nominated for 11 Australian Film Institute Awards, was directed by Gillian Armstrong. Though her Hollywood output has been erratic, on her home territory Armstrong has shown a gift for realistically exploring the core of people's lives without over-dramatizing what she finds there.

What drew Armstrong back to Australia was novelist Helen Garner's exceptional original screenplay dealing with what looks to be a mildly eccentric family living in bohemian ease in contemporary Sydney. But though it starts out like a celebration, "Chez Nous" turns inevitably into an examination of the way people grow apart, of how, through nobody's fault, missed connections and levels of resentment, turn loving relationships suddenly angry and sour.

The life force of this particular family is Beth (Lisa Harrow), a successful novelist who, on the surface at least, is the picture of assurance and self-reliance. Though both her French husband J.P. (Bruno Ganz) and her teen-age daughter Annie (Miranda Otto) may grumble at her bossiness, they also take the competence and compulsiveness that keep the family together very much for granted.

Disturbing this psychological balance is the arrival of Vicki ("An Angel at My Table's" Kerry Fox), Beth's complex younger sister who simultaneously idolizes Beth and is resentful of her success. Irresponsible and self-dramatizing, an energetic free spirit who doesn't function well in the real world, Vicki's presence exposes the fissures in life as it has been lived and makes it increasingly difficult for things to go on as before.

But to describe "Chez Nous" (Times-rated Mature) only from Vicki's point of view is to short-change it, because the film's strength is the way it non-judgmentally examines this family from any number of perspectives. J. P., for instance, more and more feels overwhelmed and left out by Beth's forcefulness, resenting mightily the very qualities that probably attracted him to her in the first place.

And Beth herself, while juggling all of this, is increasingly concerned with her prickly relationship with her cantankerous father (Bill Hunter, currently in "Strictly Ballroom"). Indulging in what J. P. scornfully calls her "mania for resolution," she decides to abandon her family and take a three-week drive with her father into the outback, a decision that has repercussions that no one anticipates but that are foreshadowed by what has gone before.

Garner's polished script believes in the power and relevance of small domestic moments, and director Armstrong makes sure the texture of scenes such as J. P. exploding because someone has eaten his prize cheese before its time is strong and accurate. The hostility and anger endemic to loving relationships, the difficulty of emotional communication, the stubbornness of people even when it's self-destructive—this film manages to capture it all.

"Chez Nous" is well-served by its cast, all of whom, especially Lisa Harrow as Beth, respond with grateful delicacy to a film that offers no resolutions or solutions, only a portrait of fallible people trying to get along as best they can. In its intimacy and agonizing honesty, this quiet film's greatest accomplishment may be the way it gives the cliched field of family drama back its good name.

NEW YORK, 3/15/93, p. 62, David Denby

Beth (Lisa Harrow), the novelist at the center of an irregular Sydney household in *The Last Days of Chez Nous*, is going crazy from trying to be four things at once—wife to her envious French husband (Bruno Ganz); mother (from a former marriage) to a lively teenage girl (Miranda Otto); adviser to her ebullient, directionless kid sister (Kerry Fox); and daughter to her nastily withdrawn father (Bill Hunter). Many of us are caught—sometimes happily caught—in multiple relationships, but Beth's are more unstable than most, and she is expected in every case to hold things together. The movie, directed by Gillian Armstrong, has the same theme as all of her movies—the absolute necessity of female independence.

Lisa Harrow, who is full-bodied and beautiful, matches well, as a much older sister, with Kerry Fox, who has dark, flaming-red hair, a petulant lower lip, and a long-limbed gracefulness. Armstrong directs in a spirit close to Fox's—loose and easy, with solid colors and lots of sunshine—but her sympathies remain firmly aligned with the burdened Harrow. The movie's volatile spirit offers giddy pleasures collapsing into sudden hurt. The husband, who is a self-pitying egotist, shifts his attention to the younger woman, and Beth gets crushed and liberated at once. In this movie, women have positive energy; men withhold and withdraw. The question Armstrong doesn't answer is, if a man like Ganz's selfish husband is so worthless, why do such extraordinary women fall in love with him?

NEW YORK POST, 2/26/93, p. 25, Jami Bernard

When Australian director Gillian Armstrong burst on the international scene in 1979, her film "My Brilliant Career" ended with Judy Davis rejecting marriage so that she could pursue a writing career. That and "An Unmarried Woman," a year earlier, exist in a relative vacuum of movies in which women walk away from marriage triumphantly.

In the intervening years Armstrong has made successively more complex studies of women's relationships; and in her new one, "The Last Days of Chez Nous," there are no easy answers to the problems in the marriage of Beth and J.P. (Lisa Harrow and Bruno Ganz).

Beth and J.P. are an attractive middle-aged couple with a teenage daughter, who live in a warren of apartments in Sydney. J.P. a Frenchman, feels displaced, and longs for another child, but Beth is busy juggling work and family and puzzling out her identity, trying to separate the myths that men have told her about being "bossy, greedy and a spendthrift" from the truth of herself as a compassionate, sturdy, adventurous woman.

There are already stresses apparent when Beth's ebullient younger sister, Vicki (Kerry Fox) comes to visit and changes their lives. Beth is trying to sort things out at the source, by taking her crotchety dad on a sightseeing trip so they can forcibly get to know each other (in Armstrong's movie "High Tide," an estranged mother and daughter do something similar). J.P.'s rootlessness causes displaced rage when Beth ruins his gently ripening Brie cheese by thoughtlessly taking a bite.

The beauty of the film is in its closely observed details of human foibles and relationships, leaving blame out of the mix entirely. Even when J.P. begins an ill-advised affair, this isn't motivated by malice but by a childlike need to recapture some lost part of himself. The movie is aware of how our ability to love is shaped by our preconceptions; in the background, a television show gives the day's romantic horoscope for its predominantly female audience.

"We'll show you what it means to be a woman!" cry Beth and her sister as they pounce on Beth's teen-age daughter (Miranda Otto) and paint her face in a grotesque version of accepted adult makeup. Which is why, perhaps—now that she is forewarned—the daughter sits tirelessly at the piano, working out a duet with her first serious boyfriend, as if practicing to get their relationship right before life's big lies set in.

There are also interesting undercurrents about sisterly and maternal relationships. A childbirth video is met with different responses in different households, including one in which the heavy-breathing sounds of labor suggest at first a porn movie.

Armstrong is a more mature director now, and resolution in the "Last Days of Chez Nous" is full of the bittersweet taste that comes with knowing there are no easy answers and that love, while often a many-splendored thing, can also be a deterrent to real happiness.

NEWSDAY, 2/26/93, Part II/p. 75, Jack Mathews

There may be plenty of reasons for people to appreciate Gillian Armstrong's "The Last Days of Chez Nous," but the only thing that kept this portrait of a disintegrating marriage from being as painful as divorce for me was the luminous presence of Australian actress Lisa Harrow.

This is one of those performances, like Judy Davis' in Armstrong's "My Brilliant Career" 13 years ago, that dominates every scene and every action, whether she's directly involved or not, and makes you see every other character through her eyes, whether it's intended or not.

Harrow, who studied at London's Royal Academy of Dramatic Art and has devoted most of her 24-year career to theater and television in England, seems to have thrown Helen Garner's script off its axis. The story was clearly written as a three-character study, about the self-effacing Australian novelist Beth (Harrow) her charming and selfish French husband, Jean-Pierre (Bruno Ganz), and her flighty young sister (Kerry Fox).

Actually, there is a fourth major character, the colorfully eccentric suburban Sydney house that shelters and connects the threesome along with Beth's teenage daughter (Miranda Otto) and their gawky, jazz-immersed tenant (Kiri Paramore).

The script itself seems as interested in Jean-Pierre, a philandering romantic who feels culturally isolated in a country where you can't even buy a decent brie, and Vicki, a woman equally driven by energy and loneliness. In the first 15 or 20 minutes we get the notion that "Chez Nous" is their story, two free-spirited people tethered to a house and an inert relative.

To Vicki, who has just returned pregnant from a trip to Europe, Beth is the wise older sister who gives her counsel and comfort. To Jean-Pierre, who flaunts his affairs with young women, Beth's solidness and optimism (her novels aren't "destructive" enough for him) have made her an unlovable bore.

Once those issues are out of the way and we've gotten to know the characters, Beth is the only interesting one among them. Being grounded is not the same as being dull, and the only thing keeping Beth's spirit tamed is her dogged determination to hold the family together.

Ganz, one of the angels in Wim Wenders' delightful "Wings of Desire," is an engaging actor (German, not French), and gives Jean-Pierre a quality that makes Beth's tolerance of him marginally understandable. Still, even he disappears into the shadow of Harrow's performance.

During one segment of the film, Armstrong cuts back and forth between the Australian outback, where Beth is on a holiday with her dyspeptic father (Bill Hunter), and the house, where the restless Jean-Pierre and Vicki are discovering how much they have in common.

The dynamics of these parallel events, a daughter trying to make peace with her father while her relationships with her sister and her husband are being threatened at home, are enormous. Yet, the scenes between Jean-Pierre and Vicki are almost a nuisance. Harrow has given Beth's character so much more depth and complexity by then that hers are the only needs we care about.

SIGHT AND SOUND, 3/93, p. 43, Lizzie Francke

Sydney. Late one summer, Vicki, an impetuous drifter, returns from her travels in Italy to stay with her elder sister Beth, a novelist, her French husband J.P. and teenage daughter Annie. There is much celebrating, but the relationship of Beth and J.P—lovers who married only so that J.P. could stay in the country—is on a fragile footing. Beth voices her concerns to her best friend Sally. The two muse on a spire that Beth can see from her porch; Beth explains that she has never found its base. Much to J.P.'s disgust, Vicki lazes about at home, not apparently very intent on finding a job; but Vicki would also like to be a writer and is encouraged by Beth. Beth takes in a lodger, Tim, to help pay the bills. Vicki confides to Beth that she thinks she is pregnant. Meanwhile the household goes to visit Beth and Vicki's parents, and Beth arranges with her father to go on a short holiday. At home, relations between Beth and J.P. deteriorate, while Vicki's pregnancy test proves positive. Beth accompanies Vicki to the abortion clinic where she is mistaken for her mother. Later Beth and J.P. go to visit their friends Sally and Angelo who have just had a baby, and J.P. cradles the child. Beth and her father go on their trip to the outback, but start to argue as soon as they hit the road.

Back at Beth's house 'Chez Nous', the atmosphere is more playful as Vicki and Annie run riot. While watching a documentary about birth, Vicki breaks down, and is comforted by J.P., who tells her she should have told him about the pregnancy as he would happily have adopted the child; later they sleep with each other. Meanwhile, Annie and Tim get together. Out in the desert, Beth and her father resolve their differences. When Beth returns she finds that things have changed at 'Chez Nous'. J.P. finally becomes an Australian citizen, and tells Beth of his affair with Vicki. Beth declares that she never wants to see Vicki again, and Vicki and J.P. move out of 'Chez Nous'. Sitting on her porch and contemplating these traumatic events, Beth catches sight of the mystery spire, and strides off in search of its base.

Following an unhappy sortie to Hollywood for the now-buried Greta Scacchi/Jimmy Smits romance *Fires Within*, Gillian Armstrong returns to home territory—in more ways than one—to direct this poignantly observed and dry-humoured account of emotional blundering and bruising, from an original screenplay by novelist Helen Garner, who scripted Jane Campion's first featurette *Two Friends*. It makes a fine companion piece to Armstrong's last Australian-set feature *High Tide*, which also dealt with a shifting and perplexing nexus of female relationships in a fragmented family.

In both films, the setting tempers the story in an almost organic fashion. In *High Tide* the mood was shadowed by the bleak coastal trailer-park setting, while the focus of *The Last Days of Chez Nous* is a seemingly inviting open house, ramshackle and bohemian, cluttered with and held together by bric-a-brac and mementoes—a treasure trove to be ransacked. It is a home with its fair share of delights, and different types of play run throughout the film: people draw, paint faces, practice bubbling Jelly Roll Morton standards on the old upright piano, or dance about with pots and pans on their heads. Vicki and Annie even plunder Beth's wardrobe while she is away and toy with its contents as if they were castoffs in a kindergarten dressing-up box.

The atmosphere in me *Last Days* is ostensibly that of a balmy late summer with the sky washed flamingo pink (the film is evocatively lit and photographed by Geoffrey Simpson). It turns thunderously close, however, after the arrival of Vicki, a flame-haired lightning bolt with a gawky sensuality about her. Brilliantly played by Kerry Fox—from Jane Campion's *An Angel At My Table*—who is emerging as one of the key actresses of her generation, Vicki is an intense and wilful young woman testing the boundaries of that will, while her elder sister is hitting a moment of self-doubt. Sauntering into a dusk-lit empty house at the beginning of the film, Vicki immediately proves impetuous and destructive as she lunges at a pink-iced heart-shaped cake that has been prepared for her homecoming, and cuts a slice for herself. It is symbolic of her greedy desire, a hunger that makes her careless of others.

In this way food and meals play a significant part in the film, revealing much about the characters and their particular tragedies. Beth mirrors Vicki's impulsive act when she carves herself a wedge of J.P.'s special brie, which is not yet ripe; J.P. castigates her, precipitating another row. Later, when Beth and her father are on the road, an argument brews as Dad struggles to open a crisp packet and obstinately refuses to heed his daughter's constructive advice. Food brings people together, but also tears them apart.

Armstrong and Garner are attentive to the mundane nature of relationships that can be built on or, conversely, collapse over the smallest of details. The film is composed of snatches of dialogue and gestures that betray much more than is apparent, as when Beth, lying in bed with J.P., tells him, "Your skin is cold"; he is indeed dying away from her. There is a sense of loss in Beth's life which is not so much exacerbated as disclosed by the arrival of her younger sister. "She is your mirror, your little echo," comments J.P. of Vicki. The relationship between the two sisters, however, is better described as vampiric and sadly destructive. Vicki is encouraged to be a writer by Beth, but finds that her sister steals her lines, while she retorts to Beth on the discovery of her affair with J.P., "am I always to stand back and not take things just because they are yours?" Beth's relationship with J.P. may have been everything to her, while it is suggested that Vicki may only be looking for a momentary experience with him. The new couple move into an uncluttered but sombre house, their relationship already ill-fated by a misunderstanding.

If *The Last Days of Chez Nous* is about the fatal collapse of a household, it also tells how Beth salvages a sense of herself in the process. She finally begins to reach an understanding with her father; the scenes between Beth and her curmudgeonly dad have a raw honesty to them, as Dad is made to realise that his 41-year-old daughter is no longer a child to destroy with his vinegary admonitions. With this afflicted relationship on the mend, Beth can find some real hope to build the future on. She goes in search of the base of her dreaming spire in the knowledge that has found a sure foundation for herself—bricks and mortar, not bric-a-brac.

VILLAGE VOICE, 3/9/93, p. 55, Georgia Brown

Trollope's title *The Way We Live Now* expresses a basic bourgeois, certainly feminine, appeal. Who doesn't respond to the promise of finding intimate lighting cast on domestic routine and relationships? But for all the interest in seeing ourselves as we are, next to nothing substantial comes our way. After Lessing's *Golden Notebook*, what piddly pickings. Ann Beattie's lifestyle manuals, *thirtysomething*, Lawrence Kasdan? Woody Allen and Yvonne Rainer? Nevertheless we can celebrate the project, which is how I'd like to introduce Gillian Armstrong's *The Last Days of Chez Nous*.

Three women again. Their relationships look fluid, deliberately ambiguous: Sometimes, the three could be taken for sisters; other times they act like a mother and her daughters. Actually, they are two sisters and the child of one. (All, as we shall see, are definitely daughters.) Beth (Lisa Harrow) is the mother of Annie (Miranda Otto) and the much older sister of Vicki (*An Angel At My Table*'s Kerry Fox). When Vicki returns to Sydney, dragging her red suitcase, she goes to Beth, not to their staid, out-of-it parents. "Welcome Home," reads the homemade, heart-shaped cake on the table. She cuts a piece, wolfs it down, and vomits.

If Vicki's arrival is the drama's catalyst, it's Beth who's *Chez Nous*'s center in that she holds the manage together. Still, either Beth or Vicki could serve as point of view, depending on how or with whom one identifies. Although each of the women takes her turn as odd man out, the real stranger here is J.P. (Bruno Ganz), Beth's quirky, demanding husband. He's male in a female household, a Frenchman in Australia; he's not Annie's father either. J.P. gives the impression of passing through, of not sticking around for the duration. Early on you might find yourself wondering if he'll make a play for the ripe, unstable Vicki or if he'll resist, either out of loyalty to Beth or his own fastidious predilections. (A possible but more unlikely Woody Allenish scenario is forestalled when the blossoming Annie gains her own, age-appropriate love object.) Still, J.P. likes to stick a colander on his head and dance with the younguns. (A huge Bruno Ganz fan from way back, I must say I can't stand him as this sententious fool.) Both Beth and J.P. know it's over: The question is who will take the step.

Armstrong is a director who tailors mise-en-scène to the project. She's moved from the elegant mansions and vistas of *My Brilliant Career* to the mobile homes and strip joints of *High Tide*, and now *Chez Nous* looks as cluttered and claustrophobic as its messy Sydney habitat. When Vicki spies the cake on the table, we see the crumbs. The movie gives the impression of having caught things exactly as they are, of having no set dresser-though it has. Beth's career may be almost brilliant—she's supposed to be a successful novelist (like Helen Garner who's written the script)—but she's a basket case in the home. If it's difficult to tell just what talent or sensibility Beth brings to her art, we recognize that she's like many professionally competent women who are unable to order their lives. This discrepancy between what she can do in one sphere and can't in the other will undoubtedly have wide appeal.

For example, Beth cleans up everyone else's messes but when she hurls a sugar bowl at J.P., no one else gets out the broom. (Apparently, they just track sugar around the house until she gets up the next morning.) Usually, somewhere in the corner of the frame, we can see Beth engaged in some chore, like polishing boots. The others, like carefree children or grasshoppers, fiddle the summer away. Meanwhile, Beth flagellates herself for being a control freak and works hard, if unproductively, at trying to get to the heart of her "problem." A current project is taking her stubborn father into the desert to confront the origins of her quarrelsome nature. (Frankly, I think she should've taken a cue from the father in *Walkabout* and just pulled a rifle on the grumpy geezer.)

Yes, it can be refreshing to observe blind, confused, imperfect creatures messing up, the way we do now and then. For some, the movie's strength and charm may even lie in the fact that so much earnest self-analysis misses the mark. We all have blind spots. (Though anyone—like the new *New Yorker* reviewer—who sees a love story here should have his heart examined.)

Such, such are the joys of relationships. Still, the bottom line of this kind of domestic realism is that it appeals to those who identify and alienates those who don't. So to finally put it bluntly, these people really flayed my nerves. Watching two women in thrall to a man who mouths such flawed, self-serving analysis—and who seems finally affirmed, not exposed—is some kind of torture. But if both Beth and Vicki try my patience, so, I remember now, did the heroines of *My Brilliant Career* and *High Tide*—even though both of those at least were played by the charismatic Judy Davis.

I guess Chez Armstrong is one of the last places I'd choose to settle in. Even an overnight might be a strain.

Also reviewed in:
CHICAGO TRIBUNE, 4/16/93, Friday/p. B, Johanna Steinmetz
NEW REPUBLIC, 3/29/93, p. 32, Stanley Kauffmann
NEW YORK TIMES, 2/26/93, p. C6, Vincent Canby
NEW YORKER, 3/1/93, p. 105, Anthony Lane
VARIETY, 2/24/92, p. 250, David Stratton
WASHINGTON POST, 4/2/93, p. D1, Hal Hinson
WASHINGTON POST, 4/2/93, Weekend/p. 44, Desson Howe

LAST PARTY, THE

A Triton Pictures release of a Campaign Films and Athena Group production. *Executive Producer:* Samuel D. Waksal and Elliott Kastner. *Producer:* Eric Cahan, Donovan Leitch, and Josh Richman. *Director:* Mark Benjamin and Marc Levin. *Director of Photography:* Mark Benjamin. *Editor:* Wendey Stanzler. *Music:* Diane DeLouise Wessel. *Sound:* Pamela Yates. *Running time:* 96 minutes. *MPAA Rating:* Not Rated.

WITH: Robert Downey, Jr.; Robert Downey, Sr.

LOS ANGELES TIMES, 9/10/93, Calendar/p. 1, Kevin Thomas

In the provocative "The Last Party" actor Robert Downey Jr. introduces himself as a member of the generation born during Vietnam and matured (hopefully) by the time of the Gulf War. He gives us the impression that he partied away the '80s but is wide awake and asking questions in the '90s. And what better way to get involved than by documenting the 1992 presidential campaign?

At first the film threatens to be much more about Downey, who was nominated for an Oscar for his remarkable portrayal of Charlie Chaplin, than the state of America during a critical election year, but he and directors Marc Levin and Mark Benjamin (who is also the film's lively cinematographer) are just letting us get to know him. Downey can be flip and abrasive but also sharp and thoughtful. He can be a showoff—the man is an actor, after all—but when it comes to asking questions he's an out-front, in-your-face interrogator.

What's most important is that he asks questions of just about everyone he can get to give him the time of day. He questions the homeless and the unemployed as well as the famous and powerful. He gets sensible observations from actor Sean Penn on the importance of participating in the political process and from actress Mary Stuart Masterson on her abortion-rights stand. He doesn't cover the conventions in the usual sense but instead zeros in on participants and spectators.

At one point barred from the Republican convention in Houston, Downey finds out what's going on in the city. He talks to a black man in a ghetto who warns him that if African-Americans can't live in "fancy houses" then whites won't be able to either; in the prosperous-looking suburbs he finds a family reduced to living on food stamps because the husband has lost his job. Meanwhile, Olivier North complains to Downey about how Ice T's "Cop Killer" song is endangering the lives of law enforcement officers, and Jerry Falwell assures him that conservatism is a youth movement. At no time does Downey attempt to disguise the fact that his sympathies lie with the Democrats rather than the Republicans.

All told, what Downey discovers is not at all surprising—that people, regardless of political affiliation or religious conviction, believe that America is going downhill but, on a more encouraging note, that minorities are prepared to fight for their rights. Indeed, Downey tells us that the most stirring moments for him were the AIDS demonstrations and rallies he witnessed in both New York and Houston.

Although a worthy effort, "The Last Party" may have a tough time attracting an audience. How many people are prepared to sit still for yet another rehash of the presidential elections, no matter how personal and idiosyncratic its presentation? How many people are that interested in the political awakening of Downey, as fine an actor as he is? "The Last Party" (Times-rated Mature for language, topless dancer nudity) ends with Downey and his father, Robert Downey Sr., the pioneer underground filmmaker, rejoicing in the election of Bill Clinton. You're left to wonder what they think of him today.

NEW YORK POST, 8/27/93, p. 27, Jerry Tallmer

If he were my son ... If he were my son ...

Well, thank God somebody else has to cope with that, and the somebody else is Robert Downey, who once made a very funny stick-it-up-the-Establishment movie called "Putney Swope." In a few short years Robert Downey Jr. has become, as an actor—notably the actor of "Chaplin"—a great deal more famous than his father, and now he turns moviemaker himself with a documentary ego trip called "The Last Party." Pop is in it from time to time, with love and wit.

What Junior has done is take a camera and crew to the 1992 Democratic and Republican conventions, making a general showoff and nuisance of himself as he interviews any and all celebs within reach.

The film is in fact a search for self-justification. "I've been in a hurry for a long time," young Downey says, "to accomplish what? Recognition, appreciation, money."

The interviews run from Bill Clinton all the way to Willie D. driving Downey through a black ghetto to the menacing tones of: "If we can't have, then y'all can't have either, know what I mean?" Downey doesn't quite know how to handle it, not for the first time when he bumps up against a non-celeb.

In between, we get, for a few:

Patti Davis (Reagan): "My father came in and said: 'Everything's fine,' and then we went to sleep ... The same way my father existed in the family, he existed as President of the United States."

Spike Lee running through his routine about America, land of "baseball, apple pie and racism."

Roger Clinton telling how big brother Bill saved Roger's life "when things got tough ... by telling me to, suck it up." Rapper AZ saying how "whoever has the nice cars, [sleeps with] the most girls" is top dog, also how he's been shot in the head twice.

Oliver Stone saying: "Bull----" with professional contempt to almost everything.

Al Sharpton Al Sharptoning.

Sen. John Kerry (D-Neb.) saying: "Our government lies."

Various blue-collar guys and gals sneering at the homeless ("Years ago they were called bums") and cheering free enterprise ("Money makes the world go round"); various spokesmen of the underclass deploring violence while spouting the mantra of our time: "But I can understand the frustration."

We also see Downey Jr., who I admit has one of the most malleable faces you can imagine, prancing around on all fours on the floors of two conventions in the manner of a goat swimming down a public fountain; doing an Alan Ginsberg "Ommmmmmm"; crashing an ON AIR control room in search of sandwiches; talking about his problems with vaginas. In a word, a Class A smartass.

His film is distinguished by two moments of wisdom: Robert Sr. declaring of the politics of '92: "This is the worst I've ever seen, and if you don't vote this time you shouldn't be alive." And Sean Penn of all people, murmuring, with quiet intensity: "There's this French phrase: If you don't do politics, politics will do." Amen.

NEWSDAY, 8/27/93, Part II/p. 77, Gene Seymour

"The Last Party" rambles, drifts, gets the jitters, ties itself in knots and generally bounces all over the place in its struggle to get a precise fix on what remains of American idealism in a crucial election year.

And there's something endearing, in a retro, '60s sort of way, about the static, fuzzy ambience of this nonfiction film in which actor Robert Downey Jr. spends his 1992 summer vacation attending both the Democrats and Republican conventions, collecting errant vibes inside and outside their respective locales.

The range of people Downey talks to is staggering: Olivers Stone *and* North, Bill *and* Roger Clinton, Patti Davis, Curtis Sliwa, Richard Lewis, Al Sharpton, Sean Penn, John Kerry, Spike Lee, Jerry Falwell, Peter Jennings, G. Gordon Liddy, Jerry Brown, Downey's underground-filmmaker dad Robert ("Putney Swope") Sr., and various rappers, rockers, homeless people, AIDS activists, Wall Street brokers (on whom the irony of the "greed is good" chant is lost) and middle-class homeowners.

So vast is the cross-section yanked into view by Downey and directors Mark Benjamin and Marc Levin that they even manage to get a few words with—let's see if I have this right—a black male celibate Republican rapper (probably the closest thing the GOP has to a rainbow coalition). Putting this bulging grab-bag of attitude and opinion together is itself an earnest, if ultimately futile search for common ground.

Throughout, Downey, who portrays himself as the prototypical hippie-child-turned-indulgent-yuppie, claims he is making contact with as many folks as possible so he can jar himself out of the self-absorption of the '80s and evolve into a more "informed and involved" mode in the '90s.

Yet such highly personalized concepts, buttressed by analogies of *fin de siècle* America to a dysfunctional family crowded with rehab cases, promotes the kind of ditzy solipsism the film supposedly challenges.

After a while, I became less interested in Downey and his fellow celebrities and more engaged by less famous interview subjects like the homeless youth who believes a "black lesbian mother" should be elected president. ("At least, she'd get something *done!*" he says.) Or the suburban Houston couple forced to live on food stamps, I wanted more of these people. But this is Downey's show, not America's.

VILLAGE VOICE, 8/24/93, p. 58, Manohla Dargis

A few years back, a child of Los Angeles, Robert Downey Jr., all but walked away with the movie of the book that diagnosed his generation with clear and brilliant violence: "If you want something, you have the right to take it. If you want to do something, you have the right to do it." In the movie version of Bret Easton Ellis's *Less Than Zero*, Downey plays Julian, a coke addict whose degradation climaxes when he starts to hustle men. In the documentary, *The Last Party*, Downey again plays Julian, only this time by way of 12 steps that would take him through the American political machine as it creaked and groaned through last year's presidential race.

"It's quite a 12-step platform this year," Downey comments early during the Democratic convention. "We have all these recovering men and women, it's kind of like one nation under rehabilitation." Though not exactly earth-shattering, that's about the sharpest bit of analysis in the entire film, even if Downey (a recovery veteran) and company don't have a clue where to take it. Consequently, overwrought and overinvested, the film inverts the familiar adage that the personal is the political and turns it into something along the lines of the political isn't just personal, it's solipsistic. According to this logic, the divorce of Downey's parents is synergistically hooked to the fact Reagan was the son of an alcoholic father and that under him America (in Patti Davis's words) worked like a "dysfunctional family."

True confessions are noble but don't exactly get at such cultural tics as race, sex, and class. Which is why *The Last Party*, MTV-ready with a bullet, is content to be an affable hash of picturesque footage ("Save the Planet Kill Yourself" bumper stickers, strippers, Oliver Stone), interviews, and Downey's own scattershot confessions about everything from politics to impotency. In one sequence, the film jumps from the actor sweating it out on a Stairmaster to him bounding about Chaplin's old soundstage ("my hero's church") to working the Democratic convention to getting his tarot cards read to interviewing Patti Davis to speaking about his own parents' divorce and hugging his dad.

While it's clear why Downey is doing *Donahue*, it remains pretty much of a mystery why anyone should go along for the ride, especially this late in the political game. The film has the feel of an eager-to-please juggler (or son) who tries to dazzle but drops the ball instead, usually for cheap laughs. So even when Downey and company do happen upon a choice avenue, they don't have the patience (or is it brains?) to follow through. Case in point: a delirious sequence that begins with a Goldfingers' stripper who, insists, "I'm conservative in my real life," even as she soberly hoses down her saluting breasts. This teaser is furiously followed by Downey confessing past problems; with women, some sexy shots of the WAC drum corps (!), and the actor quizzing Jerry Brown on how he's managed to mix the personal with the political. Brown explains his strategy with the metaphor that there are "no virgins in a whorehouse," a ripe moment that exposes all the psychosexual fevers of politics, personal and otherwise.

Unfortunately the moment is just another blip on the zeitgeist, as camera and crew rush on to the next subject, the next speaker, the next spew of image and sound. At the Republican convention, they cannily insert an image of a Ku Klux Klan school bus with a "Thank God for AIDS" banner outside the Astrodome, and lavish too much time on Downey deriding square-dancing Republicans. The attitude may be clearly progressive—traders are scum, the homeless are people, too—but the film is as confused and thick with contradiction as its ideology is.

The limits of liberalism are made aggressively, spitefully explicit when, midway through, *The Last Party* returns to Los Angeles from the Democratic convention. As he drives along the freeway, Downey offers how his house was almost burglarized and though he can understand "things are tough ... it makes me want to go and make sure that I know, like, how to use my gun." This libertarian reflex might be palatable if the film had, for even a single minute, paused to wonder just how implicated some of us are in all that history. So why shouldn't Robert Downey Jr. know how to shoot anyone who dares break into his beautiful house with his beautiful wife? After all, he paid for all those nice things—didn't he?

Also reviewed in:
NEW YORK TIMES, 8/27/93, p. C14, Stephen Holden
VARIETY, 9/13/93, p. 33, Brian Lowry

LEON THE PIG FARMER

A Cinevista release of a Leon the Pig Farmer production. *Executive Producer:* Paul Brooks. *Producer:* Gary Sinyor and Vadim Jean. *Director:* Vadim Jean and Gary Sinyor. *Screenplay:* Gary Sinyor and Michael Normand. *Director of Photography:* Gordon Hickie. *Editor:* Ewa J. Lind. *Music:* John Murphy and David Hughes. *Sound:* Paul Hamblin, Stuart Wilson, and (music) Keith Andrews. *Sound Editor:* Danny Hambrook. *Production Designer:* Simon Hicks. *Art Director:* James Helps. *Costumes:* Justine Luxton. *Make-up:* Pebbles and Mariska Vennema. *Stunt Co-ordinator:* Helen Caldwell. *Running time:* 98 minutes. *MPAA Rating:* Not Rated.

CAST: Mark Frankel (Leon Geller); Janet Suzman (Judith Geller); Brian Glover (Brian Chadwick); Connie Booth (Yvonne Chadwick); David De Keyser (Sidney Geller); Maryam D'Abo (Madeleine); Gina Bellman (Lisa); Vincenzo Ricotta (Elliot Cohen); Jean Anderson (Mrs. Samuels); John Woodvine (Vitelli); Annette Crosbie (Doctor Johnson); Stephen Greif (Doctor in Restaurant); Neill Mullarkey (Waiter in French Restaurant); Burt Kwouk (Art Collector); Sean Pertwee (Keith Chadwick); Barry Stanton (Peter the Vet); Bernard Bresslaw (Rabbi Hartmann); Peter Whitman (Rabbi Johnson); Jack Raymond (Gordon); Claudia Morris (Lawyer); Neal Foster, Howard Kitchner, and David Altschuler (Estate Agents); Howard Attfield (Plaintiff); Stanley Davis (Gutterman); Cyril Varley (Mr. Goldman); Frank Lee (Mr. Samuels); Thelma Ruby (Mrs. Bernstein); Robbie Gringras (Harvey Geller); Danny Scheinman (Nat Geller); Edward Halstead (Uncle Benny); Lesley Rubenson (Uncle Ernest); Stan Pretty (Uncle Louis); Rachel Fielding (Bowling Alley Blonde); Paul Simpkin (Lift Operator); Edward Denith (Old Man); Lois Penson (Old Woman); Francesca Hall (Medical Centre Receptionist); Clive Panto (Morris); Ted Valentine and John Guerrasio (Jimmy's Men); Ruth Posner (Jimmy's Woman); David Graham (The Chef); Martine Ritchie and Sara Mansfield (Naked Cellists); Fiz Marcus (Mrs. Gutterman); Hana Maria Pravda (Jewish Woman in Restaurant); Gordon Reid (Jewish Man in Restaurant); Michael Normand and Claire Sinyor (Guests at Wedding); Steve Kenis (Uncle); Reuben Anderson (Little Boy); Maria Altschuler (Little Girl); Steve Rubie (Rabbi Fink); Gary Ellis (Groom); Ray Boot (Photographer); Simon Phillips, Alllan Gilchrist, and Kim Hicks (Artists in Gallery); Ralph Lawton (Shepherd); Tricia Sawczyn (Keith's Mother Beryl); Rodney Webb (Beryl's Husband's Terry); David Ash (Brian's Brother Morgan); June Smith (Yvonne's Sister Jane); Peter Sampson (June's Ex-husband and Fiance John); Virginia Scott (Brian's 2nd Ex-Wife Cynthia); John Phillips (Cynthia's Boyfriend Trevor); Pamela Hutchinson (Keith's Girlfriend Cathy); Daniel Rothchild (Cathy's Teenage Son Luke); Martin Poole (XP Van Driver); Matthew Salisbury (Motorist at Service Arms); Sarah Shackleton (Cashier); Mathew Collins (Hitchhiker); Stephen Savage (Jeremy); Simon Katz (Violinist); Robert Harley (Piano Delivery Man); Diana Eskell (Girl Outside Restaurant).

LOS ANGELES TIMES, 9/21/94, Calendar/p. 4, Kevin Thomas

"Leon the Pig Farmer" is a conventional, minor British comedy of limited interest that could just as easily have been set in America with virtually no changes.

Mark Frankel is the film's appealing star, a young London Jewish realtor who finally walks out on his rapacious firm only to wind up working for his mother's catering business. It's a familiar story of being pressured to get married; of having a fling with a free-spirited shiksa (Maryam D'Abo) but of finally accepting himself, as the nice but dreamy Jewish girl (Gina Bellman) who thought she wanted a more exciting guy accepts him. But feature debuting co-producer-directors Vadim Jean and Gary Sinyor (Sinyor wrote the script with Michael Normand) throw a monkey wrench in the love-hate view of a Jewish enclave where everybody knows everybody else's business. This occurs when Frankel's Leon Geller discovers he was sired by a sperm bank donor who turns out to be a well-off Gentile Yorkshire pig farmer (Brian Glover), a larger-than-life type with an eccentric and complicated extended family who embrace Leon warmly.

At this point the filmmaker's resort to a silly gimmick that is supposed to spin a moral and tie everything up but that instead bulldozes a comedy already strained and overly familiar.

NEW YORK POST, 9/10/93, p. 40, Lawrence Cohn

The dietary taboos of the Jewish religion form the unlikely premise for this satirical British comedy, a one-joke effort that will definitely separate viewers into two camps: one that's laughing and the other that's storming the exits.

Leon's a nice Jewish boy working for mom Janet Suzman's catering business, who finds out he's the result of artificial insemination. Lab director Annette Crosbie (one of many top British stage talents in the cast) informs him of a mixup: His real father is not the veddy, veddy Jewish David De Keyser but rather a pig farmer in Yorkshire, Brian Glover.

Leon heads for the farm and quickly bonds with Glover and his wife Connie Booth. The duo try to make him feel at home by adopting exaggerated Jewish mannerisms and it's at this point that the audience's tolerance for poor taste is really put to the test.

The plot heads south when Leon accidentally crossbreeds a pig and a sheep to create a supposedly kosher hybrid which is never shown on screen. What constitutes "kosher" in this case is not addressed by Gary Sinyor's and Michael Normand's facetious script, which instead thinks it's clever to give equal time to shellfish and pork-product jokes.

Clearly it would take a manic genius and visual stylist like Mel Brooks to bring this naughty material to life. Neophyte directors Sinyor and Vadim Jean have staged this nonsense unwisely against a dark-toned, highly realistic backdrop of North London and Yorkshire. One note of whimsy is having innocent bystanders confide in Leon as if they were his conscience, a device that quickly becomes tiresome.

Also detracting from the intended mirth is Mark Frankel as Leon. The young actor comes on brooding and heavy as if auditioning for the role of Jimmy Porter in "Look Back in Anger."

Best performance is by Maryam d'Abo, who escapes here from a recent string of erotic thrillers to deliver a genuinely funny turn as Leon's hippie-dippy shiksa girl friend. Also appealing is Gina Bellman (seen in America as the star of Dennis Potter's "Secret Friends") as, you guessed it, Leon's hippie-dippy Jewish girlfriend.

NEWSDAY, 9/10/93, Part II/p. 79, Jonathan Mandell

Leon Geller, a guilt-ridden if honest *shlemiel* from North London, has a problem. He has found out that he owes his life to a test tube: His father, Sidney, a net-curtain salesman with a low sperm count, arranged with a fertility clinic 30 years ago to have Leon's mother, Judith, artificially inseminated. That's not Leon's problem. The problem is that the clinic mixed up test tubes. Sidney is not Leon's real father. Leon, the good Jewish boy, was really fathered by a pig farmer from Yorkshire.

This is the premise and the plot—the basic shtik—of "Leon the Pig Farmer," a slight, sprawling British comedy full of what would be considered Jewish humor except that too much of it is not funny.

By unfunny, I don't mean the jokes are offensive, or self-deprecating, or sacrilegious, which of course they are. Could it be Jewish humor otherwise? After all, Mel Brooks built one of his funniest films around the idea of the veneration of Adolph Hitler, and Philip Roth sells lots of books that make fun of Jews who criticize him for making fun of Jews.

Given such a tradition, is it such a crime that Leon (Mark Frankel) leaves his Jewish family and his mother's kosher catering business ("To You We Deliver/Salt Beef and Chopped Liver") to move in with his biological father (Brian Glover) and take up pig-breeding? His *goy* family tries to make him feel at home; they barge in on him while he's taking a bath; they take down the mounted pig heads from the mantel and replace them with a photo of him and an Israeli flag (although they leave the porcelain pig angels in the bathroom); they read "Portnoy's Complaint" and "The Joys of Yiddish" (while holding a piglet) and dine on matzoh ball soup while speaking to each other with Yiddish inflections.

Later, they even try to be understanding when Leon makes a big mistake, crossbreeding a pig with a sheep. Has he created a kosher pig? He consults two rabbis, one traditional, one hiply modern. "On the one hand, it's a very difficult question," the bearded rabbi finally replies. "On the other hand, it's a very difficult question."

The Mel Brooks-like scattershot lunacy and vulgarity mix uneasily with a half-developed romantic subplot full of themes and even specific routines that are lifted straight from (the "Annie

Hall" era) Woody Allen: Seduced by a *shiksa*, obsessed by a nice Jewish neighbor, searching for meaning in his life, Leon is accosted by complete strangers on the street or in an art gallery who glibly remark on his most intimate problems.

All of this should produce more laughs than it does. But the ideas are funnier than the execution. "Leon the Pig Farmer" is understated, nearly lethargic, in a low-budget British way, lacking Mel Brooks' (or Monty Python's) manic comic energy. We are more than halfway through the 98-minute movie before we even find out about the pig farmer.

A slower pace might make sense in a work with much subtle wit, but "Leon" also relies too heavily on the most obvious aspects of Jewish culture—e.g. "oy"—without the deeper insight that underlies the more authentic, savage satire of works like Philip Roth's "Goodbye Columbus" or that of Mordecai Richler. Hamming it up has not made "Leon the Pig Farmer" one continual squeal.

SIGHT AND SOUND, 3/93, p. 44, Robert Yates

Leon Geller, a young Jewish estate agent from North London, resigns after a series of bad turns convinces him he is too conscientious for the profession: his colleague Elliot Cohen closes a deal that Leon has been working on, and an Italian speculator is planning to turn Charles Dickens' house into a leisure centre. Taking a temporary job with his mother's catering firm, he discovers while delivering to a fertility clinic that he was conceived by artificial insemination. Leon is further disturbed by the suggestion that his father's low sperm count might be hereditary, and returns to the clinic for tests. Anxiously driving away, he knocks down a pedestrian, Madeleine. Attracted to Leon, she asks him to take her home, where she shows him her art: erotic stained-glass windows. Leon impresses her by telling her he sculpts. While out at dinner, Madeleine, a well-bred Gentile, is further excited to learn that Leon is Jewish, and seduces him. Back at work, at a wedding where his mother is catering, he bumps into Lisa, a Jewish neighbour he has long courted in vain; this time they sleep together.

Leon returns to the clinic and learns that his sperm count is fine. However, at the time of his conception his father's sperm was mixed up with that of Yorkshire pig farmer Brian Chadwick, Leon's 'biological' father. Told the news, Leon's distressed father can offer no sympathy; nor can Madeleine who, feeling—despite Judaism's rule about descent via the mother—that Leon is not properly Jewish (nor, she discovers, a sculptor), no longer wants to see him, and has taken up with Elliot. Lisa, aloof once more, is too busy to offer any comfort. Leon drives to Yorkshire, tells his story to the Chadwicks' extended family and is warmly welcomed. Pig farming, however, is not his metier, and his first morning's work ends prematurely when he faints. The Chadwicks try to make him feel at home, cooking Jewish food and adopting stock Jewish phrases and gestures. Leon's stay ends in disaster when it emerges that he confused test tubes when helping the local vet, causing a sow to be inseminated with sheep sperm; a hybrid is the result.

After a pair of rabbis judge that the hybrid is possibly kosher, Leon returns to London, with the creature in a holdall. The Chadwicks follow; over drinks at the Gellers, each couple plays at the other's culture and debates over Leon's future. Leon escapes into the countryside taking the hybrid with him, and is followed by the four. Leon sets the creature free and the party, in better spirits, repairs to London and the local Jewish restaurant. From within, Leon sees Lisa, her face against the restaurant window. He runs out, catches up with her, and they kiss.

Billed as the first of its type, a British-Jewish film comedy, *Leon The Pig Farmer* aspires to cover classic Jewish-American ground. Indeed, the Chadwicks consult Philip Roth's *Portnoy's Complaint* and use it as a primer, when attempting to make Leon feel at home. Early on, the territory is sign-posted: conscience-stricken, in thrall to a seemingly inaccessible woman and subjected to the verbal incontinence of his family, Leon is the very model of a Jewish hero. The trouble is that the film never moves beyond dot-by-dot cultural delineation. The crudeness in characterisation is underlined when the Chadwicks' adopted Jewish routine proves not that different from the routines the 'real' Jewish characters have been doing throughout the film. The Gentiles too are flagrant types. Madeleine, the libidinous artist hooked on the 'exotic' (Compared to Jews, other men seem like dead meat"), expresses her free-thinking ways by hating estate agents and not wearing knickers.

With cracks this stale and oppositions this contrived, the signals of *chutzpah*—Janet Suzman does an energetic, nagging mother complete with windmilling arms—remain empty gestures. Nor is there any injection of pace from the stolid filming which, for what is the feature debut of the young production/direction team of Jean and Sinyor, shows precious little pleasure in the process.

As Leon, Mark Frankel (also a feature debutant) rarely shifts from playing bemused, which creates something of a disjunction. Is he not meant to be beset by swirling emotions? Perhaps the film's remorseless stylistic tic is designed as compensation; this dramatises Leon's internal conflicts by having his own misgivings voiced by friends and strangers who stop him in the street. The advice comes from so many angles that one forgets Leon is supposed to be especially neurotic and instead marvels at how efficient the grapevine is in Golders Green.

With no narrative drive offered by Leon's ventures, the film is shaped by the principle of racing from one scene of would-be cultural clash to the next, with links as perfunctory as those in a pornographic film intent on reaching its next set-piece. Here the set-pieces demand hammy acting, with some amusingly grotesque results: notably when Brian Glover's Chadwick makes a cabaret of his attempts to shift his sodden Yorkshire accent into a Yiddish swing. A resolution of sorts does come about when the hybrid appears, or rather, doesn't appear: we see it only as a bulge in a holdall—one failing that the small budget (£160,000) can excuse. For reasons not immediately obvious, Leon begins to take control and even gets the girl. It is possible that herein lies a message: so inspired is he by the wonders of the pig-sheep that he realises the advantages of his own 'cross-breeding'. As a guide to the strength of the film's insights into culture and identity, a bulge in a holdall is just about apt.

VILLAGE VOICE, 9/21/93, p. 67, Paula Bernstein

In sync with the media onslaught over Baby Jessica and other child-custody tugs-of-war, an unlikely cinematic subgenre is in the making—sperm bank foul-up comedies. First, there was *Made in America*, the cloying biracial Ted-Whoopi vehicle, and now, *Leon the Pig Farmer*—a bireligious British-Jewish comedy about Leon, a kosher young Jew (Mark Frankel) who learns, while delivering deli to an infertility clinic, that his genetic father is a Yorkshire pig farmer.

More insightful and witty than its big-budget predecessor, *Leon* explores parental rights and cultural affinity through a suggestive metaphor. In a second sperm foul-up—this time, in the pigpen—Leon mistakenly creates a pig-sheep hybrid that may or may not prove kosher. A surreal showdown between WASP and Jewish culture ensues with both sets of Leon's parents playing reverse stereotype one-upmanship in the battle to claim him.

Sure to be likened to vintage Woody Allen, the film relies on *Annie Hall*-brand reflexive interludes and a laundry list of Jewish jokes, with sexual hang-ups and overbearing parents ("not married yet?") topping the list. Apart from his monumental guilt complex ("guilt isn't a word, it's a way of life"), Leon is too blandly sullen and unequivocably handsome to be a true neurotic—at least in the New York sense. Still, his haphazard flight toward self-realization and his awkward charm make him a mensch in any culture.

Also reviewed in:
CHICAGO TRIBUNE, 2/18/94, Friday/p. L, Johanna Steinmetz
NEW YORK TIMES, 9/10/93, p. C8, Stephen Holden
VARIETY, 9/7/92, p. 52, Derek Elley

LEPRECHAUN

A Trimark Pictures release. *Executive Producer:* Mark Amin. *Producer:* Jeffrey B. Mallian. *Director:* Mark Jones. *Screenplay:* Mark Jones. *Director of Photography:* Levie Isaacks. *Editor:* Christopher Roth. *Music:* Kevin Kiner. *Sound:* Michael Florimbi and Geoffrey Patterson. *Casting:* Lisa London. *Production Designer:* Naomi Slodki. *Costumes:* Holly Davis. *Make-up (Leprechaun Effects):* Gabe Z. Bartalos. *Stunt Coordinator:* Dave Kindlon. *Running time:* 92 minutes. *MPAA Rating:* R.

CAST: Warwick Davis (Leprechaun); Jennifer Aniston (Tory); Ken Olandt (Nathan); Mark Holton (Ozzie); Robert Gorman (Alex); John Sanderford (J.D.); Shay Duffin (Dan O'Grady); Pamela Mant (Leah O'Grady); John Volstad (Pawn Shop Owner); William Newman (Sheriff Cronin); David Permenter (Deputy Tripet).

LOS ANGELES TIMES, 1/11/93, Calendar/p. 3, Michael Wilmington

Even if you're in the mood for a low-budget horror movie about a maniacal leprechaun in bloody quest of a crock of gold, you'd do well to pass on "Leprechaun". This dingy, drab, pointless little movie—a would-be shamrock shocker about four teen-agers menaced by the Irish super-scamp while renovating a North Dakota farmhouse—is made without flair or imagination, seemingly enervated by its own bad taste and low intentions.

"I want me pot of gold!" the movie's fiendishly jolly little leprechaun screams endlessly, impersonated by "Willow's" Warwick Davis under lots of latex. And all the while, he cackles, grins, swings his bloody shillelagh, maims or disembowels victims, or endlessly chases them around a disheveled farmyard while they try, futilely, to paint the front porch.

"Me pot of gold! *Me pot of gold!*" It might be the filmmakers' cry as well. Where's the pot o' box-office someone snagged out of "Child's Play," "Gremlins," "Critters" or every other cutie-pie horror show of recent years? As empty, one hopes, as the crock at the end of every other '80s rainbow.

Writer-director Mark Jones strains mightily to achieve cliché level, but the movie isn't dumb enough to be fun. The settings are drab, the plot creaks, the dialogue is full of empty chirps. And the cast of victims is the usual all-formula grab-bag: a saucy L.A. feminist wench in short-shorts (Jennifer Aniston), a bemused hunk (Ken Olandt), a slow-thinking slobbo (Mark Holton) and a Spielbergian quick kid, aided by a dull-witted cop or two and the hapless O'Gradys, who bring the leprechaun back from Erin.

The movie's murderous Irish elf, notable for his atrocious dental hygiene and his tendency to run amok, drives around in kiddie cars or tricycles and apparently can only be killed with a four-leaf clover. He seems to have been inspired not by pungent types like Barry Fitzgerald or Arthur Shields, with their twinkles' of malice or wily ferocity, but by the cartoon on the Lucky Charms cereal box: the one who screams "Where's me Lucky Charms?" As if to confirm this link, the director includes a scene where Davis devours a cob-webbed box of Lucky Charms and then spits them out.

Is Jones making a subconscious comment on his own movie? In an age that has already given us killer Santas ("Silent Night, Deadly Night"), killer dolls, killer babies, killer toys—everything, it seems, but serial-killing Easter Bunnies and homicidally deranged fuzzy ducklings—maniac leprechauns may be the next logical step. But is it a step we should follow?

"Leprechaun" (MPAA rated R for language and leprechaun violence) tries to scare us all green, but it only bores the bejeebers out of us.

NEWSDAY, 1/11/93, Part II/p. 41, John Anderson

In recent years, the horror genre has been blessed by killer babies, killer dolls, a killer Santa Claus. Why not a killer leprechaun?

Because it's stupid. The concept itself—imbuing a benign fantasy figure with evil—isn't new, of course, and it might have worked. It might even have played havoc with our collective id. But there needed to be a deft hand behind the scenes, instead of the mitten-wearing muttonheads who made "Leprechaun." Is the film boring and inane? Only so far as it's insulting and ridiculous.

"Try as they will / Try as they might / Who steals my gold / Won't live through the night," cackles our repulsive Irish nightmare (Warwick Davis). His gold gone, the demented dwarf follows it to the American Southwest, gives the thief a stroke, but is trapped inside a wooden crate where he remains for 10 years until freed by Tory (Jennifer Aniston), a recently transplanted Californian yearning for watercress in a world of meatloaf. Neither she nor Nathan (Ken Olandt) her hunky/earthy housekeeper, knows where the gold is, but that doesn't stop the Big L from attacking them like a sawed-off embodiment of the IRA.

As it turns out, Nathan's younger brother Alex (Robert Gorman) and his slow-witted friend Ozzie (Mark Holton) have found the Lep's coin-stuffed sack in an old pickup truck, and Ozzie has accidentally swallowed a coin. Which is unfortunate: When the Leprechaun says he wants his gold back, he means *all* of it. And he doesn't plan to wait on Ozzie's digestive tract.

"Leprechaun" milks a variety of horror film cliches. The Leprechaun is repelled, like, Dracula and his crucifix, by a four-leaf clover. He eats bugs. He bites. His face looks like hardened food. He kills one victim with a pogo stick ("This old man / He played one / He played pogo on his lung ..."). Someone should call the Hibernians.

To tell any more about the plot would not only be incredibly tedious, but unnecessary. Anyone out there not know what's going to happen? There's going to be a certain amount of gore, some chase scenes, some heated looks between Nathan and Tory, and the kid's going to be imperiled. The disgusting little brute is going to go down in flames. That much we know. The question is why "Leprechaun," which isn't scary, wasn't at least funny, although nothing about the film is going to preoccupy anyone for long. What, was that question again?

Also reviewed in:
NEW YORK TIMES, 1/9/93, p. 17, Vincent Canby
VARIETY, 1/18/93, p. 77, Lawrence Cohn
WASHINGTON POST, 1/9/93, p. G3, Richard Harrington

LIFE WITH MIKEY

A Touchstone Pictures release.   *Producer:* Teri Schwartz and Scott Rudin.   *Director:* James Lapine.   *Screenplay:* Marc Lawrence.   *Director of Photography:* Rob Hahn.   *Editor:* Robert Leighton.   *Music:* Alan Menken and Mark Shaiman.   *Music Editor:* Thomas Drescher.   *Choreographer:* Diane Martel.   *Sound:* David Lee and (music) Michael Farrow.   *Sound Editor:* Skip Lievsay.   *Casting:* John Lyons.   *Production Designer:* Adrianne Lobel.   *Art Director:* Dennis Davenport.   *Set Decorator:* Gordon Sim.   *Set Dresser:* Richard Ferbrache.   *Special Effects:* Martin Malivoire.   *Costumes:* William Ivey Long.   *Make-up:* Donald Mowat.   *Make-up (Michael Fox):* Bron Roylance.   *Stunt Coordinator:* Charlie Croughwell.   *Running time:* 94 minutes.   *MPAA Rating:* PG.

CAST: Michael J. Fox (Michael Chapman);   Christina Vidal (Angie Vega);   Nathan Lane (Ed Chapman);   Cyndi Lauper (Geena Briganti);   David Krumholtz (Barry Corman);   David Huddleston (Mr. Corcoran);   Victor Garber (Brian Spiro);   Frances Chaney (Mrs. Cantrell);   Kathryn Grody (Mrs. Corman);   Mary Alice (Mrs. Gordon);   Annabelle Gurwitch (Debbie);   Kathleen McNenny (Allison Jones);   Jonathan Charles Kaplan (George);   Tony Hendra (Cookie Commercial Director);   Mario Todisco (Driver);   Michael Rupert (Harrison);   Christine Baranski (Carol);   Sean Power (Lenny);   Laura Bundy (Courtney Aspinall);   Chris Durang (Santa);   Barbara Walsh (Commercial Mother);   Brenda Currin (George's Mom);   Heather MacRae (Mrs. Tobin);   Wendy Wasserstein (Mrs. Wasserman);   Ryan Kent (Evan);   Tim Progosh (Norman Feller);   Aida Turturro (Officer Moran);   Paula Garces (Janice);   Ralph Small (Mr. Wasserman);   Kevin Zegers (Little Mikey);   Tracy Spindler (Cynthia);   Dylan Baker (Mr. Burns);   Kate Burton (Mrs. Burns);   Stephen Bogardus (Man #1);   William Finn (Man #2);   Ann Lawrence (Concerned Woman);   Kelli Fox (Marilyn);   Robin Byrd (Bambi);   Hrant Alianak (Cereal Commercial Director);   Jerry Lawler (The Lobotomizer);   Jeff Jarrett (Evil Eye);   Anaysha Figueroa (Kimberly Denise Jackson);   Michelle Moffat (Kimberly's Mom);   Frank Crudele (Passerby);   Carlton Watson (Galaxy Waiter);   Sandra Caldwell (Corcoran Receptionist);   Eve Crawford (Courtney's Mom);   Marcell Rosenblatt (Tiffany's Mom);   Silvio Oliverio (Marker);   Janet Metz (Employee);   Mandy Patinkin (Irate Man);   Barbara Hollander (Judy Wasserman);   Giannetta Savarino (Baton Twirler);   Shayna Rossin (Tiffany);   Richard James MacDonald (Impressionist);   Samson Benen (Boy);   Joey Allen (Hockey Player);   Holly Bohl and Kristen Bohl (Tobin Twins);   Vanessa Wilson (Ventriloquist);   Ashley Brown (Eric the Magician);   Chantel Leblanc (Cristin);   Tara Pearson (Erin);   Elan Rivera (Spanish Singer);   Jessica Wilson (New York Singer);   Phoebe Lapine (Andrews Sister #1);   Anna Rose Menken (Andrews Sister #2);   Ali Caplan (Andrews Sister #3);   Jacob

Reynolds (Baseball Boy);   Kristen Simpson (Bluebird Singer);   Shatim Welch, Kai Reevey, and Ashley Canterna (Rap Kids);   Damian Gryski (Juggler);   Veronica Wappel and Victoria Wappel (Hippie Sisters);   Chelsie Lamie (Violinist);   Syreeta Neal (Steel Drummer);   Blake McGrath and Tina Pereira (Acrobats);   Soliella Cole and Angela Cole (Stilt Walkers);   Billy Joel Ablaza (Party Boy);   Stephanie Berntson (Opera Singer);   Stefanie Gnys (Tap dancer);   Adrienne Canterna (Belly Dancer);   Erica Yamada (Erica);   Camille Harrison, Christine Muir, and Gigi Uson (Cookie Dancers).

LOS ANGELES TIMES, 6/4/93, Calendar/p. 1, Peter Rainer

In "Life With Mikey," Michael J. Fox plays a former child TV star who peaked at 15 and now runs a third-rate kids' talent agency. It's a terrific piece of casting—maybe too terrific. The role fits Fox like a glove but perhaps at this point in his career he should be scouting for something less form-fitting.

Fox wasn't exactly a child star when he did "Family Ties" on television, but he was still young enough for audiences to mark his progress into adulthood. He's made it in the movies by essentially keeping his spunky kid's core intact: he's capable of real dramatic depths, as he demonstrated in "Casualties of War" and "Light of Day," but for the most part he's a whiz at playing adults as overgrown manic types. His whirling, hot-footed energy links the games of childhood with the games of adulthood. With Fox at the center of your movie, life is one big playpen.

The main reason to see "Life With Mikey" is for Fox's all-out performance—as familiar as it is by now. As Michael Chapman, he has the haggard look of an actor who played out his childhood on television without ever having played it out in his own life. He lives like a slob in his dumpy apartment and eats Froot Loops for breakfast: he watches taped reruns of his TV show—"Life With Mikey,"—and stares at the kid on the screen in sodden disbelief. He winces when people recognize him on the street because the recognition only reinforces his own sense of worthlessness. By doggedly running the talent agency with his brother Ed (Nathan Lane) and their addled gum-popping secretary (Cyndi Lauper), Michael is, in a sense, trying to replay his childhood all over again but this time from the driver's seat.

The movie's adorableness quotient works its way into the red zone when 10-year-old Angie Vega (Christina Vidal) shows up as the answer to the agency's dreams. She first takes Michael's acquaintance by picking his pocket in the subway; when this foul-mouthed waif sweet-talks her way out of another picked pocket a short time later, Michael offers to represent her. She turns out to be a natural—and, because of her quasi-orphan status, she ends up sharing Michael's apartment too. We're meant to see their relationship as mutually enhancing; Angie, precocious, wised-up, discovers the joys of kid-dom in the process of teaching Michael how to be a caring adult.

This isn't quite as syrupy as it sounds because Vidal, who has never acted professionally before, isn't the twinkling twerp we've become accustomed to in these kid-o-ramas. Compared to, say, the moppet in "Curly Sue," she's practically Anna Magnani. But Angie's spunk is in the movie only to be sentimentalized, just as Michael's funk is the kind that gets dispelled with a wink and a smile. Fox and Vidal have a nice rapport: There's a funny moment when Michael pours milk onto his cereal and the curdled stuff comes plopping out of the carton while Angie looks on in saucer-eyed disbelief.

But "Life With Mikey" (rated PG for language and thematic elements) never breaks out of its sitcom confines. Director James Lapine and screenwriter Marc Lawrence don't entirely want to break those confines; their ambition is to show how these people's lives mimic the sitcoms and commercials they work in. But this is not all that stunning a concept, and, anyway, it backfires. The "real" drama in this movie—like Angie reuniting with her father—isn't on a much higher level than the soapy stuff. Life with Mikey merges with "Life With Mikey."

NEW YORK POST, 6/4/93, p. 27, Jami Bernard

At a recent dinner party, a guest confided that sometimes he just wanted a movie that's pleasant but that doesn't require any thought. This man joins the legions who fall into that gray area between film buff and plain old movie-goer, and luckily for them, Hollywood heeds their clarion call.

Today, for instance we love the opening of "Life With Mikey," a no-brainer with undeniable charm and appeal even a few laughs.

Michael J. Fox perhaps harkening back to his "Family Ties" days, plays a former child actor who still lives vicariously through his old TV success. The effortless, boyish charm that got him through the "Life with Mikey" sitcoms—a kind of "Leave It to Beaver" with a tiny edge—is paying off less and less as Mikey ages and his fame stales.

Michael and his brother, Ed (Nathan Lane), struggle to make a living by agenting child actors. Very bad child actors, that is. We meet them in a number of "open auditions" much like the sequence in "The Fabulous Baker Boys." There's a lugubrious boy who agitates his way through a Strindberg soliloquy, smarmy kids who have been taught to overact by their overweening parents and the "cereal king" who requires actorly motivation on the set of a breakfast-food commercial.

Then Michael finds the perfect future child star in Angie (Christina Vidal), a street urchin who picks his pocket and kicks him in the shins. Angie is fresh, feisty, and able to make up stories well enough that she even fools Michael about her real family situation. He takes her in to groom her for a cookie commercial.

"Life with Mikey" a formula all the way, with only one big change—although it is clear that Michael and Angie will bond eventually and change each other's life for the good. Angie is indubitably a child (and of different ethnicity to boot), so that the romantic possibilities are quashed early on. Little orphaned Angie lives in sin with Michael, only there's no sin. (And yet, if I were their neighbor, I'd be pretty suspicious.)

Cyndi Lauper has a small bit as a dumb secretary and is probably responsible, because of her personal ties, for bringing in a scene involving wrestlers. Fox and Lane are good eggs as the agent brothers, and newcomer Christina Vidal does have exactly the kind of raw talent a guy like Michael would have been looking for.

With nothing particularly fresh to recommend itself, "Life With Mikey" still disports itself admirably for its 94 minutes. The guy from the dinner party will be very happy this weekend—satisfied, yet unchallenged.

NEWSDAY, 6/4/93, Part II/p. 69, Jack Mathews

Michael J. Fox and writer Marc Lawrence worked together for a few years on the hit TV sitcom "Family Ties," and their first collaboration on a feature film, "Life With Mikey," is more than a personal reunion. They're back in the sitcom business.

Lawrence's script, about a children's talent agent (Fox) and his relationship with the troubled street urchin (Queens sixth-grader Christina Vidal) who becomes his star client, would have made a better pilot for a TV series than a feature film.

It works okay as a feature, at least for the PG crowd in the mood for something sweet, bright and sentimental.

It just feels as if it should have been shot in a studio before a live audience, with pauses after every joke for a pulse of laughter, and after each tug at the heart for a few warm oohs and ahs.

But Fox is an A-list movie star these days and it's the big screen or bust.

Directed by Broadway's James Lapine ("Falsettos"), "Life With Mikey" is set primarily in the low-rent Times Square offices of brother agents Michael (Fox) and Ed (Nathan Lane) Chapman, whose livelihood hangs from the slender thread of one client star, the mega-brat cereal king Barry Corman (David Krumholtz).

Ed is the workhorse and the worrier of the pair, spending his days either toadying to the relentlessly demanding Barry, or trying to pick out another potential star from the passing parade of auditioning children.

Meanwhile, Michael is laying about in his pig-sty apartment, eating TV dinners, chain-smoking and watching himself in reruns of his hit TV series, "Life With Mikey," that ended 15 years ago.

Mikey, now 31, needs to get a life, and so does Angie Vega (Vidal), a 10-year-old Brooklyn truant Mikey meets in a situation so boldly cliched it's like staring at the sun.

She picks his pocket, and when he catches up with her, she puts on a poor-little-me performance that has passers-by weeping.

Bingo! Here's our new star, Mikey thinks, and though Angie is about as cuddly as a scorpion, Mr. Big at the Corcoran Cookie Co. (David Huddleston) is soon offering her the lead spot in a new national TV ad campaign. But first, Mikey and Angie have to prop each other up and get their lives in order.

The on-again, off-again relationship between Mikey and Angie is painfully predictable, and Vidal, though she has amazing confidence for an 11-year-old who's never acted before, has neither the extraordinary looks nor skills so apparent to everyone who meets Angie in the movie.

Still, there are plenty of high moments to enjoy. Fox is very good at playing child adults, and he certainly knows where Mikey has been. It would have been nice to know how Mikey managed to become broke, after spending his childhood in a hit series (I was hoping to learn that his folks had run off with his trust fund, a dose of cynical realism), but the detail was omitted.

In their sitcom roles, Nathan Lane (Nathan Detroit in the reprised "Guys and Dolls" on Broadway) brings a certain charm to Mikey's gloomy brother, and Cyndi Lauper is great fun as Geena, the brothers' devoted, ditzy secretary.

Many of the biggest laughs are provided by the kids at the open auditions at Chapman and Chapman. There's one boy with a dark soul who recites Strindberg in hopes of landing cereal commercials.

There are accident-prone baton twirlers, a group who does a rap version of "Zip-A-Dee-Doo-Dah," a mini-Ethel Merman, and one girl with a lisp (Shayna Rossin) whose booming, beautiful rendition of "Lullaby of Broadway" would earn four points on "Star Search."

There's also a nice score from Alan Menken, which includes two original songs, "Cold Enough to Snow" and the "Life With Mikey Theme." If the movie's a hit, you may hear that theme again. On television.

VILLAGE VOICE, 6/15/93, p. 59, Regina Raiford

Why do we buy it? That's the question running through *Life with Mikey*. In a role he was born for, Michael J. Fox is Mikey Chapman, a former child actor turned ineffectual talent agent for kiddie stars. Christina Vidal plays Angie, the 10-year-old pickpocket he hopes will save his failing agency. Predictable plot twists aside, the film is from top to bottom an indulgence in cuteness, chock-full of darling yet insufferable child actors.

Mikey mocks the superficiality of the sugary sweet child actors companies use to sell everything from soup to nuts while using those same kids to sell tickets. Case in point is Barry Corman (David Krumholtz) as the 12- year-old cereal king looking for a new realm. Barry, the agency's star client, is the image of a wholesome kid but with the personality of Don Rickles. The foil to Krumholtz's razor-tipped shtick is Angie. Sure she's a wise-ass but her character is mush on the inside; it's this vulnerability that's the emotional hook. When Angie finally sheds her hostile exterior and visits her father on Christmas in a rehab clinic, it almost comes across as believable. As for Fox, he's the perpetual manchild, embodying the child-actor mixture of the ideal, the ridiculous, and the sincere.

Life With Mikey also appeals to our weakness for Hollywood movies about Broadway. The open audition scenes, in which an endless stream of children parade by with increasingly lousy acts, are a sendup of musicals past. Nathan Lane as Mikey's continually exasperated brother and business partner and Cyndi Lauper as the quirky, bighearted secretary play all too familiar characters. Each has the timing to carry the recycled jokes, but the question remains, Why do we buy it? The Broadway movie formula is no more real than these bratty children who joke and heal with great skill. Still, for reasons unknown we do suspend belief, slip into a pair of comfortable storylines and giggle over their antics, maybe just because it's nice to hum "Lullaby of Broadway" all the way home for a change.

Also reviewed in:
CHICAGO TRIBUNE, 6/4/93, Friday/p. F, Clifford Terry
NEW REPUBLIC, 7/19 & 26/93, p. 28, Stanley Kauffmann
NEW YORK TIMES, 6/4/93, p. C8, Janet Maslin
VARIETY, 6/14/93, p. 54, Brian Lowry
WASHINGTON POST, 6/4/93, p. C7, Rita Kempley

LIKE WATER FOR CHOCOLATE

A Miramax Films release of an Arau Films International production in association with Cinevista Inc./Aviacsa/National Council for Cinema and the Arts/Mexican Institute of Cinema/National Tourist Development Fund/Government of the State of Coahuila Kinema Development Fund. *Producer:* Alfonso Arau. *Director:* Alfonso Arau. *Screenplay (Spanish with English subtitles):* Laura Esquivel. *Based on the novel by:* Laura Esquivel. *Director of Photography:* Emmanuel Lubezki and Steve Bernstein. *Editor:* Carlos Bolado and Francisco Chiu. *Music:* Leo Brower. *Choreographer:* Farnesio De Bernal. *Sound:* Marcus Welch, Juan C. Prieto, and Juan Castro. *Sound Editor:* Aurelio Lopez and Bill Markle. *Casting:* Claudia Becker, Felipe Fernandez, and Juan C. Alatorre. *Art Director:* Marco Antonio Arteaga, Mauricio De Aguinaco, and Denise Pizzini. *Set Designer:* Emilio Mendoza, Ricardo Mendoza, and Gonzalo Ceja. *Special Effects:* Raul Falomir. *Costumes:* Carlos Brown. *Make-up:* Julian Tejeda, Robert Billafuerte, and Sergio Espinoza. *Stunt Coordinator:* Javier Lambert. *Running time:* 113 minutes. *MPAA Rating:* R.

CAST: Lumi Cavazos (Tita); Marco Leonardi (Pedro); Regina Torne (Mama Elena); Mario Ivan Martinez (John Brown); Ada Carrasco (Nacha); Yareli Arizmendi (Rosaura); Claudette Maille (Gertrudis); Pilar Aranda (Chencha); Farnesio De Bernal (Priest); Joaquin Garrido (Sergeant Trevino); Rodolfo Arias (Juan Alejandrez); Margarita Isabel (Paquita Lobo); Sandra Arau (Esperanza); Andres Garcia, Jr. (Alex); Regino Herrera (Nicolas); Genaro Aguirre (Rosalio); David Ostrosky (Juan de la Garza); Brigida Alexander (Aunt Mary); Amado Ramirez (Pedro's Father); Arcelia Ramirez (Great Niece, Narrator); Socorro Rodriguez (Paquita's Friend); Rafael Garcia Zuazua (Godfather); Rafael Garcia Zuazua, Jr. (Young Alex); Edurne Ballestros (Young Tita); Melisa Mares (Baby Rosaura); Gabriela Canundas (Young Rosaura); Natalia De La Fuente (Baby Gertrudis); Beatriz Elias (Young Gertrudis); Rodolfo Mejia (Vererable Master); Ricardo Mendoza (First Vigilante); Orquesta De R. Lombra (Musicians); Artemio Cruz (Juan Alejandrez's Assistant); Simon (Pulque); Chester (Tequila).

FILMS IN REVIEW, 6/93, p. 191, Kenneth L. Geist

The magic realism of Gabriel Garcia Marquez and his South American school has been perfectly captured in Alfonso Arau's film, *Like Water for Chocolate*, based on a novel by his wife, Laura Esquivel, who also contributed the adroit screenplay. (The title is drawn from the Mexican phrase for extreme agitation or sexual arousal.)

This fable-like film, which takes place during the Mexican Revolution, is bathed in the orange light of dawns, sunsets, and candlelight redolent of the fiery, suppressed passion of Tita (Lumi Cavazos), who looks just like a Renaissance Madonna. Sweet natured Tita is the youngest of the three daughters of Mama Elena (Regina Torne), a widowed and tyrannical owner of a ranch isolated in the northern plains of Mexico.

Elena forbids Tita's marriage to her beloved and adoring Pedro (the humpy Marco Leonardi of *Cinema Paradiso*), because Mama demands that her youngest care for her alone until her death.

Like Isak Dinesen's bewitching chef, Babette, Tita pours her thwarted passions into her inspired cooking. (Food preparation is the film's continuous motif). Tita's emotionally tainted dishes variously cause incendiary, emetic, or powerfully lustful reactions in her diners.

One sequence is emblematic of the miraculous nature of the film. The middle sister attempts to cool her sexual ardor, occasioned by Tita's quail in rose petal sauce, in an outhouse shower, only to find it magically consumed by the flames of her passion. Running naked through the scrub brush to escape the conflagration, the inflamed maiden is swept up by an ardent and hot looking revolutionary on horseback who lifts her onto his saddle and carries her away.

The sight of Tita's obsessively knitted quilt, unfolding from the carriage that spirits her away like the endless train of a fantastic bridal gown, is another unforgettable image of this truly fabulous film.

LOS ANGELES TIMES, 2/6/93, Calendar/p. 7, Michael Wilmington

If ever a movie looked good enough to eat, it's "Like Water for Chocolate."

Set mostly in the Coahuila desert area of Mexico, in an elegant hacienda where a nutty upper-class family play out their madness against backdrops of revolution and illicit love, it's one of the most sensuous and visually alluring Mexican films in years. It's a 10-course feast of magic realism, a rapt tale of sexual repression exorcized in sumptuous feasts, while rebels roam outside and lovers wait a lifetime for a moment of candlelit bliss. And it's a movie where *everything*—sex, hatred, family spats, politics—has been sublimated into cooking and eating. In "Chocolate," the kitchen is, quite literally, a battleground.

Novelist-screenwriter Laura Esquivel and her director-husband, Alfonso Arau, are out to arouse our appetites, and they succeed. Arau and his cameramen bathe the screen in creamy or crystalline light, through which we see romance, murder, ghostly visitation and the most lip-smacking on-screen cuisine since "Babette's Feast."

"Like Water for Chocolate" is essentially a revolutionary film—but a gentle one. In the first scene, our narrator, while peeling onions, explains her tale as a tragic love story in the form of a cookbook—and, like Vladimir Nabokov's pastiche poem and footnotes in "Pale Fire," the recipes or banquets become the latticework through which we see life, love and death.

"Like Water for Chocolate"—a double entendre that compares sexual excitement to the boiling point of cocoa—is about an interior revolution, matching the Pancho Villista revolt outside. The heroine, Tita de la Garza, has been sentenced to a life in the kitchen by her brutally patrician and prudish Mama Elena (Regina Torne), who, invoking an old family custom, makes Tita her lifelong drudge.

Tragedy and absurdity ensue. Tita's love, Pedro, forbidden to court her, marries instead her flatulent older sister Rosaura, creating a trio of misery. Tita sublimates passion into a lifetime of enchanted cookery. When she cries into the wedding cake batter, the entire party bursts into passionate despair. When she cooks for Rosaura, she destroys her sister-rival's kidneys. And, when she prepares her *piece de resistance*, Quail in Rose Petal Sauce, flavored with the blood of unrequited love, the diners all swoon in lust.

Much of "Chocolate is told in an ironic off-screen narration nearly as deft as anything in "The Magnificent Ambersons" or "Barry Lyndon." Like Marquez's "Love in the Time of Cholera," "Chocolate" carries the theme of separated lovers to majestic extremes, makes repressed passion a metaphor for a human spirit writhing under tyranny or convention. And Arau is a more sumptuous stylist than the usual Mexican filmmaker—even the great iconoclasts such as Luis Bunuel, or runners-up such as Hermosillo or Ripstein.

The acting is over-ripe, too. As Tita, Lumi Cavazos believably stirs up toughness and sensitivity. As Pedro, Marco Leonardi, the teenage Salvatore in "Cinema Paradiso," projects magnetic pretty-boy spinelessness. And the actors who won three of the film's 10 Mexican Oscars (or "Ariels") give us broad hits of pristine goodness or hellfire villainy: Mario Ivan Martinez as Tita's devoted doctor-swain, Claudette Maille as the fiery Gertrudis, and Regina Torne as Mama Elena, an iron matriarch of infuriating witch/bitchery, her lips curling with theatrical disdain, the key to her dark secrets locked in a heart pendant on her breast.

Like most magic-realist tales—including the denser, more brilliant stories of Marquez and Llosa—Esquivel's super-culinary saga has a tone of childlike wonder. Through all this dark whimsy and fairy-tale splendor, "Like Water for Chocolate" (MPAA-rated R, for sexuality) has a shine, a panache. It tells a dark, sad, horrific but heartening story in sweet, gleaming images that tickle ribs, quicken senses and awaken hungers. There's just one word for it: Scrumptious.

NEW STATESMAN & SOCIETY, 10/1/93, p. 33, Jonathan Romney

The press kit for *Like Water For Chocolate* comes complete with menus for such delights as hot chocolate (using three different varieties of bean), Chabela wedding cake, and quails in rosa petal sauce ("Twelve roses, preferably red ..."). It also tells you how to make your own matches ("One ounce of powdered potassium nitrate, one dram of phosphorus"), in case you're so frustrated by fruitless grappling with the quails that you feel like setting the whole thing alight.

It's all considerably more appetising than Alfonso Arau's film. Based on the bestselling novel by Laura Estluivel, who's adapted it here, this Mexican schlockbuster—which has grossed over

$15 million in the US—is an example of that rare but eccentric genre, the food movie. The genre seems to exist less on screen than in the pages of lifestyle magazines, which celebrated it amply during its peak in the 1980s. In theory, the label covers everything from gourmand fancies like the silver-service slap-up pomp of *Babette's Feast* to the more snack-like ingenuity of the Japanese "noodle Western" *Tampopo*, to more dyspeptic horrors like *La Grande Bouffe* and *The Cook, The Thief, His Wife and Her Lover*.

By rights, food movies should be the most subversive genre going, because they express the Great Repressed of cinema—the fact that people actually eat, even though they rarely do in films. No one pointed up better the implications of this odd taboo than Luis Buñuel, in the famous scene that had elegant party-goers sitting round on toilet bowls, then discreetly repairing to little cubicles to feed themselves in privacy. The sheer versatility of food as metaphor for all human activity was never better celebrated than in Juzo Itami's portmanteau *Tampopo*, which packed in food and sex, food and death, food and metaphysics, the lot, appetisingly presented in bite-size packages for cinematic grazers.

But food movies can often be self-congratulatory in a peculiarly cloying way. Imagine a chef laying a sumptuous *pièce de résistance* before a banquet—the spectacle on the platter actually presents itself as the perfect metaphor for the diners' desire. It claims to anticipate exactly what your appetites are, and to reveal those appetites to you in all the glory of their ambition—it's the consummate celebration of your cravings, and because it is, it immediately belittles you, puts you in awe of it; it becomes too good to touch.

That's what's wrong with *Like Water For Chocolate*. Most obviously, it presents food in a spectacular, showy way, with all the schmaltzy, over-glazed sumptuousness of a bad-taste patissier's window. But it also congratulates itself for its aptness in representing the forces of desire and the pleasures of appetite. Set during the Mexican revolution of 1910, it's the story of a family whose matriarch, the fearsome widow Elena, has condemned her youngest daughter to a life in the kitchen, watching her older sister steal the feckless man she loves. Tita therefore sublimates her desires, making a series of dishes that, miraculously, are the perfect translation of her feelings and communicate them directly from heart to gut.

The wedding cake she makes for her lost Pedro and her sister contains a few shed tears, and induces fits of vomiting in the assembled crowd, in would-be Rabelaisian scenes of communal discomfort that compare unfavourably with the massed farting cowboys in *Blazing Saddles*. And when she projects her passion into the quails in rose petal sauce, she brings about an outbreak of satyriasis, pandemic swooning and spooning, eventually causing her older sister Gertrudis to be carried away naked on horseback by lusty revolutionaries (all the more unsettling because the woman's a dead ringer for the Duchess of York).

What's irksome about these episodes is not just that they're predictable and schematic, but that, in their set-piece bombast, they represent themselves as being the perfect correlative to the feelings they represent—just as the dish aspires to being perfectly adequate to the appetite. For sorrow, tainted wedding cake, for passion, quails and roses—it could hardly be a neater fit, and the comic consequences just naturally follow. There's a terrible, automatic obviousness about the imagery, symptomatic of the fag-end of magic realism, which, at its worst, tends to look for the single "miraculous" image that conveys its meanings transparently. Hence the awful contrived moment when we at last see the shawl that Tita's been knitting all through the years of her bitterness, and that of course trails after her wagon for miles and miles ...

There's no irony in these images—which may explain the astounding success at the US box office of something that in most other ways looks like an archetypal "art film". The film is mired in unashamed, literal kitsch, in stilted soap-opera acting and music, and Mills and Boon cinematography (Arau tries to convey an air of story foreboding by low-lighting the film so that it looks as if it's actually been steeped in chocolate).

The worst moment for me, when I saw it at the Latin American Film Festival, came when one of the wise old grannies and trusty female servants who appear throughout gave a little smile and snort of benevolent approbation, and someone sitting near me gave a similar snort in return. The film does indeed ask you to concur in its cosy hearth-side wisdom, which it presents as being passed down by grannies and servants from time immemorial—and with all these faithful family retainers around, there's a terrible ring of *Upstairs, Downstairs* about it. The recipes are apparently completely authentic and handed down from generation to generation in the Esquivel household.

In the final scene, a modern-day woman sits in her own kitchen winding up the story for us, as phantom matriarchs look on approvingly. But this insistence on timelessness and tradition makes it seem as though the Mexican revolution and 80 years of subsequent history had left no traces, other than a shaggy-dog love story and a fancy poultry dish. But then, there are few cultural productions more suspect than "traditional" cuisine. *Like Water* comes across as ready-to-serve exoticism, like a restaurant that slaps the word "authentic" all over its menu to show that it's catering for an exclusively tourist market (this feeling subsists even if, as may well be the case, the film was made primarily for a domestic market).

Maybe Mexican food doesn't agree with me, or maybe it just doesn't agree with cinema. Certainly there's something cloying and over-spiced about the dishes Tita prepared—they're drenched in metaphoric sauce. Maybe Mexican food really is this rich in metaphor—Italo Calvino certainly thought so, but then his own culinary Mexican travelogue, a story called "Under the Jaguar Sun", was the worst thing he ever wrote, a humourless victim of its own taste for exoticism.

May I recommend instead Richard Rodriguez's Tex-Mex budget dish *El Mariachi*, still on the circuit—guacamole straight up, and infinitely more nutritious.

NEW YORK, 4/5/93, p. 61, David Denby

The lovely Mexican fantasy *Like Water for Chocolate*, based on Laura Esquivel's celebrated novel, has been spreading its charm for some time, and I'm glad I finally caught up to it. Nothing in this golden dream of cooking and sex completely makes sense, but everything in it shines. Watching it, I was first lulled, then amazed. In this female-centered world, the men are seen for their erotic possibilities, and cooking becomes the magic and mystery of life—at once witchcraft, aphrodisiac, and food. The movie spans decades, and none of the actors seems to get older. The director, Alfonso Arau, plays at filmmaking, plays at everything, yet the movie has surprising force.

NEW YORK POST, 1/17/93, p. 19, Jami Bernard

The relation between food and love has never been as clear as in "Like Water for Chocolate," a bittersweet Mexican film about people boiling over with passion.

The title refers to the agitated state of hot water before it is mixed with chocolate, and the characters either boil over entirely (if they're lucky), or put such a lid on their emotions that they steep in bitterness over the years.

Tita (Lumi Cavazos) is born in a cascade of tears in her mother's kitchen, and there she is doomed to stay, because family tradition has it that the youngest daughter cannot marry, so that she may tend to her mother until her mother's dying day. Her mother, Elena intends to keep things that way.

Tita's beloved, Pedro (Marco Leonardi), therefore marries her oldest sister so that at least he'll be near Tita.

Mama Elena (Regina Torne) is a widow who, despite a wild youth, gives new meaning to the concept of rigidity. She forces Tita to bake the wedding cake for her sister's nuptials. Tita's tears poison the batter; the wedding party weeps and then throws up, and thus the loveless marriage between Tita's sister and Tita's boyfriend is cursed.

In fact, although Mama Elena tries everything to keep Tita and Pedro apart, Tita can express many emotions through her cooking. Take her rose-petal quail, for instance, made with the buds of a bouquet from Pedro. The quail drives everyone at the dinner table into a sexual frenzy. The middle sister's passions are so inflamed she causes spontaneous combustion in the shower shed and winds up riding naked on horseback with a dashing revolutionary into the sunset.

In this movie, only true love can provide nourishment, so Tita is the one who breast-feeds her sister's baby, while the sister languishes away with a mortal tummy-ache.

Director Alfonso Arau's funny, sensitive movie is adapted from the novel by Laura Esquivel. There is much detail about the relationship among sisters and supportive females in the household—Tita's primary care-giver is the old cook (Ada Carrasco), and her initiation into the wonders of womanhood is through the cook's magical recipes. It is not sudden bursts of action but the comforting routine of household chores that gives life its shape.

There are some images in the movie just as magical as anything the rose-petal quail might induce—such as the endless quilt flowing from Tita's shoulders as she is sent away after a breakdown, or the loving preparation of foods that would make gods weep and young lovers swoon.

NEWSDAY, 2/17/93, Part II/p. 49, John Anderson

In "Like Water for Chocolate," Alfonse Arau's elegant interpretation of his wife Laura Esquivel's popular novel, the usual manly characteristics of the epic film—gratuitous bloodshed, ludicrous heroics, swollen machismo—are forsaken in favor of magic, a freewheeling abandonment of reality, and a lyrical sense of romance. The result is a kind of woman's epic, one that makes matriarchy mythic, that elevates the soupspoon into a scepter.

Food is the fuel and love is the motor in "Like Water," and the engineer/sorcerer is Tita (Lumi Cavazos), youngest child of mother/martinet Elena (Regina Torne), and the product of an illicit liaison with a man we know only as "the mulatto." When Elena's husband finds out about Tita's patriarchy, he has a fatal heart attack; Elena is left—in 1910, as the Mexican Revolution rages—to run the de la Garza ranch with her daughters and female staff. Tita, as family custom dictates, is fated never to marry or have children, but instead must care for her mother until her death.

"Like Water ..." spends much time celebrating custom and tradition in the Mexican culture, but this one undoes Tita's life. She becomes a south-of-the-border Cinderella, repressed and slighted by her mother, who caters to her other daughters—Rosaura (Yareli Arizmendi) and the beautiful Gertrudis (Claudette Maille). When Pedro (Marco Leonardi) asks for Tita's hand, Elena refuses, offering him instead marriage to the homely Rosaura, which he accepts because it affords proximity to Tita.

The broken-hearted Tita, meanwhile, is ordered by her mother to prepare Rosaura's wedding feast—and when Tita cooks, she really cooks. Her tears, having fallen into the batter for the wedding cake, cause the guests to cry and retch uncontrollably; later, when Pedro and Rosaura take up residence with the rest of the family, she combines rose petals with quail and creates a dish that generates lust in all who eat it. Through this meal she "invades Pedro's body" but it's Gertrudis who becomes so overheated she sets the shower stall on fire; the resulting odor—of roses—attracts a revolutionary (Rodolfo Arias) who abducts the naked girl and escapes on horseback. They will return as co-generals in the revolutionary army.

The novel, which Esquivel structured in 12 monthly installments "with recipes, romances, and home remedies," acknowledged the noble qualities of simple domestic pursuits, and celebrated the links between tradition and food, food and memory, memory and immortality. Arau's visualization, gentle but powerful, is rich in earthy tones, and the entire film has a sense of a golden past.

Less convincing than the visual aspects of the film is Tita and Pedro's love story; he's basically a good-looking weakling, she's too good for him. When Tita's mother drives her temporarily crazy—a magic beef broth will restore her sanity—her doctor (Mario Ivan Martinez) falls in love, proposes and the absurd situation with Pedro seems ready to expire. But Tita's life is not fated to be simple. Savory, yes, bittersweet perhaps. But even in a fantastic world of wonder women, there are certain male hazards that apparently can't be avoided.

NEWSWEEK, 3/15/93, p. 74, David Ansen

In this generous serving of Mexican magic realism, taken from Laura Esquivel's acclaimed novel, the kitchen is the source of sorcery and passion. Tita (Lumi Cavazos), the youngest daughter of a stern aristocratic matriarch (Regina Torne), is expected to continue the family tradition of serving her mother until her death, which means that Tita is forbidden to marry the man she loves, pretty boy Pedro (Marco Leonardi). He marries her sister Rosaura instead, to be near the one he really loves. Confined to the kitchen of the family ranch near the Rio Grande, circa 1910, Tita transforms her passions into her cooking. She's a culinary magician—when she weeps into a wedding cake, all who consume it are overcome with tears and grow nauseous with grief. When her hot blood accidentally mingles with her *pièce de résistance*, quail in rose-petal sauce, her libidinous sister Gertrudis literally smokes with lust and runs naked through the brush, where she is scooped off her feet by an amorous revolutionary on horseback who's gotten a whiff of rose petal.

Directed by Esquivel's husband, Alfonso Arau, "Like Water For Chocolate" is an extravagant, playful romantic fable that celebrates passion, liberation and the spirit of women but never forgets that unbridled ecstasy comes at a cost. Tita's battle against her mother's repressive traditionalism drives her to a breakdown, but she recovers under the loving care of a Texas doctor who loves her more wisely than Pedro, but to no avail. The heart must run its combustible course in this ghost-ridden tale, which takes the epic fabulations of Garcia Marquez, adds a soupçon of "Now, Voyager" and mixes with a comic sensibility all its own. Call it Magic Realism Lite. In Arau's sensuous but ironic hands, the flames of passion that consume his characters are more apt to tickle than scorch. It's a *Liebestod* that makes you laugh.

SIGHT AND SOUND, 10/93, p. 42, John Kraniauskas

Mexico, 1895. Born, literally, in a flood of tears on the kitchen table, Tita is condemned by family tradition never to marry. As the youngest daughter of the family, she must rather care for her mother. Tita becomes bound to the kitchen, where she learns the secrets of traditional culinary arts from the servants. However, she falls in love with Pedro, a young neighbour who asks for her hand. Elena, Tita's mother, refuses and offers him her eldest daughter Rosaura instead. He accepts so that he can be near Tita.

Food now becomes a weapon in Tita's hands. Forced to make the cake for her sister's wedding, she cries into the mixture: those who eat it cry uncontrollably and are then seized by nausea. A year later she makes Quails in Rose Petal Sauce: everyone at the table is seized by sexual desire and Gertrudis, Tita's other sister, is carried off naked to join the Revolution by a soldier attracted from the heat of a battle nearby by the scent of roses.

Aware of the electricity between Tita and Pedro, Elena sends him, Rosaura and their newly born son off over the border to live with a relative in Texas. On hearing of the death of her baby nephew soon afterwards, Tita suffers a breakdown and the local doctor, John Brown, insists on removing her from the household so that he can look after her. In gratitude, Tita agrees to marry him.

Meanwhile the ranch is attacked by bandits and Elena is killed. Tita and Dr. Brown return and are joined by the rest of the family. Rosaura gives birth prematurely to a baby daughter and asks Tita if she can be named after her, since she too will be condemned to a similar fate in the name of family tradition. Tita refuses and the baby is named Esperanza (Hope). Tita also discovers the reason for her mother's bitterness: a love affair which produced Gertrudis.

Pedro and Tita consummate their long-standing passion and Gertrudis returns, now a general of the Revolution. Tita stands up to the ghost of her mother that has been tyrannising her. Elena now disappears for good and Rosaura dies from chronic indigestion: Esperanza is free. Dr. Brown, aware of the situation, tells Tita that he only wants her happiness and that she does not have to marry him.

Years later, Esperanza weds Alex, John's son from a previous marriage. Finally alone, Tita and Pedro make love and Pedro dies in ecstasy. Tita decides to follow him and eats matches. The flames of desire envelop the couple and burn down the ranch: Pedro and Tita are united for eternity. All that Esperanza finds when she returns from her honeymoon is Tita's book of recipes.

Like Water for Chocolate has repeated the success of Laura Esquivel's novel of the same name in both Mexico and the United States. This is quite appropriate for a film whose action takes place at the border between both countries. It is also the most financially successful of the films associated with the much heralded renaissance in Mexican cinema that has emerged with a new generation of film-makers, independent producers and, perhaps most importantly here—because the director, Alfonso Arau, is not himself part of this generation—a middle-class public interested in local film production.

The main action of the film takes place during the Mexican Revolution and tells the story of a woman's struggle for affective freedom against authoritarian maternal law and tradition. And this is what marks the film off from the majority of films of the Mexican Revolution and the Westerns that constitute their US counterpart. *Like Water for Chocolate* retreats from the masculinized terrains of high politics and the battlefield and concentrates our attention on the so-called private sphere of a household run by women (the men are either dead, like Tita's father, or mere objects of desire, like Pedro himself). It presents itself, apparently at least, as a 'woman's film'.

The most important place in this home is the kitchen, where Tita is born and learns her culinary skills (and weaponry), and which in the context of violent change represents an important site of continuity. Indeed, from the point of view of the Mexican Tourist Board and the National Council for Cinema and the Arts that partially financed the film, the practice of cooking that takes place there probably constitutes a 'national tradition' worth promoting—especially since the relation to food is deprived of all dangerous connotations of excess. The film is told in flashback by the daughter who still possesses Tita's recipe book—and which, no doubt, she will pass on to her own daughter as a safe sign of female solidarity and past rebellion.

Like Water for Chocolate is not an example of Latin American 'third' or 'imperfect' cinema. Rather, it forms part of that international series of films about food fetishism associated most recently with *Babette's Feast, Tampopo* and *La Grande Bouffe*. Even here, however, it lacks the dangerous obsessiveness of these: instead of bringing politics and sex together via food, so as to subject them to visual analysis, Arau's images religiously separate them out and purify each of these activities from mutual contamination. Tita's passionate sister Gertrudis ignites only to leave the household, join the Revolution and return with a husband; whilst Tita herself is born in a flood of tears in a kitchen stinking of onion, only to die in her lover's arms in a barn converted into an altar. The cleanliness of the images, enhanced by good production values, thus serves its function here by domesticating fetishism.

A counter-Western in the form of a family romance, *Like Water for Chocolate* also functions quite explicitly as a national allegory, and it is the place that it accords women here that probably explains its success. There is, however, another reason: the sentimentalized relation between Tita and the female servants Nacha and Chencha (their names clear signs of social class in Mexico). What is so disturbing about this aspect of the film is that its representation of domestic servitude echoes the classical pre-war Hollywood racism of films such as Gone With the Wind.

Despite the violent struggles for power going on both in and outside the household, the servants' own loyalties remain remarkably stable. Moreover, it is they who provide Tita with her culinary skills, their recipes which fill her recipe book. In exchange they come to embody a now tamed tradition and provide the new family emerging from the revolution with its cultural roots, its links to a mythic past connoted by food. What is so interesting about this film is that it registers this history without, however, acknowledging it.

Like Water for Chocolate is a 'feel-good' melodrama. The fact that the film refuses to reflect on its own social contents may seem remarkable, but is in fact merely a reflection of real social relations in contemporary Mexico itself—and their relative lack of discussion. From this point of view the film acts as a kind of palliative for the middle-class audiences with which it has been so successful. Despite all the changes brought about in Mexican society by the Revolution and its aftermath, they can still feel comfortable with those things that have remained the same: the servants in their kitchens.

TIME, 4/5/93, p. 61, Richard Corliss

Nothin' says lovin' like somethin' from the oven. The extra ingredient is care. Just like Mom used to make it.

It's a pity that the folk wisdom of food has degenerated into commercial slogans—for the kitchen is a place of remembered magic. What are spells, if not womankind's oldest recipes? What is a caldron but a pot for witches' bouillabaisse? Snow White's stepmother was Apple Annie with a grudge, and Macbeth's Weird Sisters were the souschefs of Destiny. If a woman's place is at the stove, then it is there she spent millenniums perfecting her potions. She let her power simmer over a low flame; then she served up the concoction, a work of art from the hearth, to charm those who would love her and poison those who would enslave her.

Tita (Lumi Cavazos), the heroine of *Like Water for Chocolate*, is one such kitchen magician. It is said that she cried even in her mother's womb and that the salt from her tears at birth filled a 40-lb. sack that spiced the family meals for years. She has so much love to give—especially to Pedro (Marco Leonardi), a handsome rancher—but upper-class convention would strangle it. Her tyrannical mother Elena (Regina Torne) decreed that as her youngest daughter, Tita must care for her and never marry.

Denied her life's love and condemned to the serving life, Tita finds in cooking the steam of sorcery. When Pedro marries her sister Rosaura (Yareli Arizmendi) simply to be near Tita, she bakes a wedding cake that leaves the celebrators sick or spellbound. When Pedro dares to give her a bouquet of roses, she presses them ecstatically to her chest—the scratches are as close as she can get to Pedro's caresses—and then prepares a heady quail with rose-petal sauce. Her culinary witchcraft will affect many births, marriages and deaths. But they will not stanch her tears.

In her first novel, *Like Water for Chocolate*, Mexican screenwriter Laura Esquivel brought Gabriel Garcia Marquez's brand of magic realism into the kitchen and the bedroom, the Latin woman's traditional castle and dungeon. The film version was written by Esquivel and directed by her husband Alfonso Arau, known to U.S. audiences for his performances in funky-flaky westerns. In *The Wild Bunch* he played a punk gunslinger and in *¡Three Amigos!* the malefic El Guapo, who spits out the immortal line "A plethora of piñatas!"

There is a plethora of primal romance in *Like Water for Chocolate*, set mostly in Mexico's turbulent 1910s. While the eldest sister (mesmerized, of course, by Tita's food) runs off naked to join Zapata's forces of independence, Tita stays at home to mix her own sweet subversion into her food. As the movie proves, the most profound revolutions are the oldest—the ones women have been cooking up since the cave days.

Acted with subtle ferocity, directed with expansive tenderness, *Like Water for Chocolate* is a story of passion in bondage and death in a fire storm of desire too long withheld. Viewers need not feel so constrained; they can enjoy the emotional splendor, gasp at the ghosts, cry with as much good cause as Tita. By comparison with this banquet of feelings, most other movies are trail mix.

VILLAGE VOICE, 2/23/93, p. 51, Georgia Brown

If movies are fairy tales for the 20th century, for the most part they're seldom as embedded in tradition as Laura Esquivel's beguiling *Like Water for Chocolate*. Directed by her husband Alfonso Arau, the movie starts out as a classic three-sisters story, and, while ultimately exploding outward in its own directions, one of its main objectives is to celebrate creative ancient remedies and recipes. Eschewing the realism of a three-sister film like Brigitte Rouan's *Overseas*, wherein each sister gets her due, *LWFC* goes with the premise that the third and youngest—the one who slaves in the kitchen and sits by the stove—is the story's point of view and conquering hero.

As the last daughter of the de la Garza family, Tita (Lumi Cavazos) is despised, deprived, and secretly extraordinary—she's the gifted child who gets to undertake the exhausting search for the true self. (Third-ness needn't be taken literally but as signifying the child's status in relation to the two parents.) According to Mexican custom, the youngest is forbidden to marry and have children since her assignment is to stay home and care for her mother in her old age. (Lest you should consider this as an anachronism or quaint Third World practice, think hard and you can no doubt come up with at least one dutiful daughter rendered unmarriable by some form of unconscious self-mutilation.)

In the movie's frame, Tita's niece Esperanza recounts her aunt's history while sitting in the kitchen chopping onions. This culinary setting introduces the film's central preoccupation with food and its preparation. (The title, a term for sexual passion, refers to boiling water used to make hot chocolate.) Tita herself grows up in the kitchen, reared by the family cook—another woman sentenced to childlessness—who imparts the secrets of ancient arts. Tita is saved by her talent as a cook and her alliance with working women, particularly the household servants. (Her sexy middle sister, Gertrudis, runs off with a Villista, taking another way.)

Magically, Tita discharges her feelings (particularly jealousy and longing) through her food, which then affects the diners in ways that fit their characters. Esquivel's bestselling novel, sporting a rapturous blurb by Diana Kennedy, prefaces each chapter with a recipe that plays a role in the text. The movie is better than the book in a number of ways—one is that we get to see the great-looking feasts Tita whips up.

When Tita falls for Pedro (played by Marco Leonardi, *Cinema Paradiso*'s teenage projectionist) and the two want to marry, her widowed mother—a handsome tyrant known as Mama Elena (Regina Torne) says, forget *that*. Instead, Mama offers Pedro her eldest daughter, Rosaura. Pedro accepts—the better, he confides to his father, to live near his true love, Tita. (Rosaura appears to have no qualms about marrying her sister's beau.) If this development gives the viewer trouble, it may be helpful to see the arrangement as the oedipal one once removed: Tita's real adversary is her powerful mother and her passion for a husband in the house defies the witch's strongest taboo. The pity is that Pedro, whose sole occupation is being husband to Rosaura, doesn't come off as much of a prize. This is a world, actually, in which men scarcely exist. Still, I wish Pedro had more stature, since it would have given the love story, and the movie's climax, a bigger kick.

Magic realism—the style not just of Central and South Americans but also of such writers as Angela Carter and Jeanette Winterson—reigns here, but to better effect than in the novel. Esquivel isn't much of a stylist; her prose is flat, literal, and explicit, explaining perhaps why the book was Mexico's 1990 No. 1 bestseller. Despite a few heavy-handed moments of its own, the movie is more successful simply because we don't have to listen to running explanations for everything Tita thinks and does.

LWFC gallops along at a steady clip and is thoroughly engaging. Its magic is unobtrusive for being matter-of-fact (no special effects). My favorite shot is of a long, long afghan—the product of compulsive knitting during times of stress—trailing behind the wagon that carries Tita off after a breakdown. At the end I found myself very moved—inexplicably though, since it was not by the final turn of events. Maybe there's something to Tita's claims for magic. Or maybe I was in a trance brought on by prolonged salivation.

Be warned: Almost every scene in *Like Water for Chocolate* contains food and everything looks sumptuous. It might be a good idea to make interesting dinner plans in advance.

Also reviewed in:
CHICAGO TRIBUNE, 4/2/93, Friday/p. J, Clifford Terry
NEW REPUBLIC, 3/1/93, p. 24, Stanley Kauffmann
NEW YORK TIMES, 2/17/93, p. C13, Janet Maslin
VARIETY, 4/27/92, p. 82, Paul Lenti
WASHINGTON POST, 3/5/93, Weekend/p. 38, Desson Howe
WASHINGTON POST, 3/6/93, p. B3, Rita Kempley

LONG DAY CLOSES, THE

A Sony Pictures Classic release of a British Film Institute and Film Four International presentation of a BFI production.   *Executive Producer:* Ben Gibson and Colin MacCabe. *Producer:* Olivia Stewart. *Director:* Terence Davies. *Screenplay:* Terence Davies. *Director of Photography:* Michael Coulter. *Editor:* William Diver. *Music:* Robert Lockhart. *Sound:* Moya Burns and Aad Wirtz. *Sound Editor:* Alex Mackie. *Casting:* Doreen Jones. *Production Designer:* Christopher Hobbs.   *Art Director:* Kave Naylor.   *Costumes:* Monica Howe. *Make-up:* Aileen Seaton and Heather Jones. *Running time:* 82 minutes. *MPAA Rating:* PG.

CAST: Marjorie Yates (Mother); Leigh McCormack (Bud); Anthony Watson (Kevin); Nicholas Lamont (John); Ayse Owens (Helen); Tina Malone (Edna); Jimmy Wilde (Curly); Robin Polley (Mr. Nicholls); Peter Ivatts (Mr. Bushell); Joy Blakeman (Frances); Denise Thomas (Jean); Patricia Morrison (Amy); Gavin Mawdsley (Billy); Kirk McLaughlin (Laborer/Christ); Marcus Heath (Black Man); Victoria Davies (Nun); Brenda Peters (Nurse); Karl Skeggs (Albie); Lee Blennerhassett (1st Bully); Peter Hollier (2nd Bully); Jason Jevons (3rd Bully).

CHRISTIAN SCIENCE MONITOR, 6/15/93, p. 12, David Sterritt

Terence Davies talks with intelligence, passion, and wit about music, poetry, and other forms of expression that have deeply influenced his life.

But his greatest love in the world of art—his "raison d'être," as he calls it—is cinema.

He has been making films in his native England since 1973, and his newest work, "The Long Day Closes," promises to boost his reputation higher than ever among moviegoers who share his affection for visual gracefulness and sensitivity—and his disdain for conventional notions of plot and character development.

Like all of Mr. Davies's works, "The Long Day Closes" is autobiographical. Its hero is Davies as a child, discovering the world of beauty and expressivity that he would later explore as an artist.

In its vivid sense of childhood memory and its exquisite use of form, color, and movement, it resembles his previous film, "Distant Voices/Still Lives," which played in American theaters five years ago. That movie was dominated by the terrifying figure of Davies's father, however, who brutalized his family until his untimely death when Davies was seven years old.

By contrast, "The Long Day Closes" is charged with feelings of family togetherness and warmth—even though Davies considers it a rather sad movie in ways, reflecting not only childhood bliss but also the seeds of adult awareness and the inevitable loss of innocence.

"My childhood fell into two parts," Davies told me in a recent interview. "For the first seven years my father was alive, and he was incredibly psychotic ... My mother wasn't allowed to go out, for instance; and I never slept in a bed, but slept with my mother on a small couch."

After this tumultuous period, Davies experienced his father's absence as a great liberation. "We began to live," he recalls. "Those years between 7 and 11 were so happy. I discovered the world every day, running out into the street and saying, "Isn't it wonderful the way it looks today!" It was like being completely released, and I felt so loved by my family, and so completely secure. I thought they were the most wonderful in the world."

The smallest of pleasures took on enormous meaning for Davies during this time. "My mother could only afford butter on the weekend," he says by way of example, "and then just two ounces; but I was always allowed to have a crust with butter on it. Bliss! As you can see, I was very easily pleased. And still am, at 47!"

One of those pleasures—which loomed ever larger as his life continued—was moviegoing. "The first film I saw was 'Singing in the Rain,' at 7," he remembers with a smile. "Can you imagine? I didn't know what films were, and then to see that. It made me intoxicated with cinema, particularly American musicals—and anything with Doris Day in it!" Under the influence of such pictures, Davies came to see the United States as "the land of Technicolor and magic," while England was "the land of comedy" with such gifted performers as Alistair Sim and Margaret Rutherford.

"The Long Day Closes" is Davies's effort to "take the quintessence of all that, and show paradise—but a paradise that's already been lost," since adult concerns are lying in wait to change childlike feelings and perceptions.

Like his life at that time, the film is "a combination of experiencing that paradise, and the innocence of that paradise, and the not knowing that it is going, although it is going even as it is being experienced. But still, the ecstasy of experiencing that world!"

In other conversations with Davies over the last five years, I have been struck by his extraordinary capacity for remembering the distant past in immediate and sensory terms.

Asked about this gift, Davies compares himself with "people who can speak many languages—they can just do it. I can remember very vividly. But the drawback is that very often the memories are so subjective. I'm also ultrasensitive to atmosphere, to the point where I'll completely misread it at times."

Davies began his career as an aspiring writer and actor. He became a director "quite by accident," when the British Film Institute gave him an unexpected opportunity to try his hand. "I looked through the camera for the first time," he recalls, "and I knew this was what I was put on this earth for. Even if I do it badly, this is why I'm here!"

It is not surprising that film appealed so strongly to Davies, with its ability to conjure up memories by capturing many impressions of sight and sound at the same time.

Yet cinema also leaves out many things—perceptions of touch, taste, and smell—that are integral parts of our most vivid recollections. Davies takes a realistic view of film's assets and limitations.

"I think it has the same quality that music has," he says, "since it's able to capture the quintessence of something in a single image, or series of images. Obviously there are problems with any art form. I happen to like cinema, but there are things you can't do, such as the internal monologue, which you can only do in a novel ... Film is most powerful when it captures a truth, whatever that truth might be—dramatic truth is not the same as real truth—and people recognize it.

"It's like listening to music," Davies continues, "and hearing with your inner ear the harmonic that the piece is going to resolve to. You feel replete, because it's what you've wanted. If you recognize a truth, you may not particularly understand it ... but you know what it means in your heart.

"No art form can give a complete picture of anything; you can only create a world which is true for you, but may have resonances for other people ... And in an odd way, the more specific it is for you, the greater the resonance for others."

LOS ANGELES TIMES, 7/2/93, Calendar/p. 8, Peter Rainer

British filmmaker Terence Davies is such a meticulous and self-conscious craftsman that his movies don't seem directed exactly—they seem calibrated. He deals in powerfully emotional subjects drawn from his own life but he slows the energy level down to a crawl.

In his new film, "The Long Day Closes," set in Liverpool in the years 1955 and 1956, there are long stretches where we just watch the sunlight shift on a carpet, or observe people being slowly enveloped by shadow. Nothing that Davies does is ordinary or artless but his craftsmanship has its suffocating side too. In this movie about the supposedly happy-go-lucky life of an 11-year-old boy, there isn't much of his happiness on view.

Davies is more temperamentally suited to agony. Maybe that's why his previous autobiographical film, "Distant Voices, Still Lives," which dealt with his father's brutality, seems stronger. At least his jeweled dreariness made more sense in that film. In "The Long Day Closes", we've entered a nightworld where everybody is jubilant yet bloodless. It's a crypt comedy.

Bud (Leigh McCormack) spends his days in a bemused swoon: his doting mother and brothers and sister indulge his quietude. He doesn't have many friends but he's comfortable in his own comfy lower-middle-class universe bounded by family and the movies. He escapes to the cinema and sits rapt before the screen.

In case we didn't recognize that moviegoing is a religious experience for Bud, Davies at one point intercuts shots of him watching a movie and attending Mass. This high-toned religiosity is deeply felt yet spurious: There's something self-serving about the way Davies equates movie-making with a holy crusade—it confers on "The Long Day Closes" (rated PG for thematic elements and mild language) a moral importance it doesn't quite earn.

If only the pasty-faced Bud were more expressive and animated. He's supposed to be living out the most exuberant time of his life but he spends most of the movie as a blank. Bud's gravity is perhaps intended as a way of conveying how we look back on ourselves through the scrim of adulthood. But he's the only one who comes across with such somberness. The effect is a bit like a variation on "Hope and Glory" with a zombie at its center.

Davies uses the popular songs and movies of the time for a raucously forlorn effect; it's similar to what Dennis Potter has achieved in his scripts but without Potter's poisonousness or wit. The songs create an echo chamber of mood and memory, though, and so do many of the images, like Bud's mother (Marjorie Yates) cradling her son and singing a song her father taught her, or the shadows of rain flowing against Bud's window. (It looks like weeping.) Davies is an acquired taste, all right. It helps if you like the taste of ashes.

NEW STATESMAN & SOCIETY, 5/22/92, p. 36, Anne Billson

[*The Long Day Closes* was reviewed jointly with *Wayne's World*; see Billson's review in *Film Review Annual, 1993*.]

NEW YORK POST, 5/28/93, p. 35, Jerry Tallmer

Finer sensibilities than mine will sing raptures over "The Long Day Closes," the autobiographical film memoir by Terence Davies about a boy growing up lonely and dreaming in a large, exuberant Roman Catholic family in working-class Liverpool in the mid-1950s.

Eleven-year-old Bud (Leigh McCormack), the filmmaker's remembered self, sits all day at the window, staring out through lace curtains at life on the streets, his big brother going off with their girlfriends, the sparklers of Guy Fawkes Day, the rain, the clouds, the night sky, the imagined heroisms and demons.

The camera stares too, interminably, at the rain, the clouds, the night sky, the way light falls and changes on a carpet, at Mum hanging laundry, at Mum going upstairs, then at the stairs she's just gone up, at the iron grillwork between sidewalk and basement at a crowd of old-timers singing and dancing to "Auld Lang Syne" on New Year's Eve—at the sky, the clouds, the rain, the rain, the rain.

I know these are the visceral, Proustian memories of writer/director Davies, and that we all have these memories—I certainly have my own and to spare—but I do not know that they make a movie, even when sparked up by Bud's getting caned across the palm for being late to school again or by the fascistic schoolmaster who drills the kids in The Processes of Erosion (River, Rain, Glacial, Wind, Marine), or by the spiteful school nurse who goes through the kid's scalps ("Lice ... Clean ... Lice ... Clean"), or by the wonderful fat neighbor lady (Tina Malone) who complains: "I never go anywhere, I'm the bleedin' Prisoner of Zenda."

Long ago somebody told me the first and only rule of movies: A movie should move. That's not really true, but I mean, well, I'd rather watch grass grow, rather watch paint dry.

And yet there are rewards in this film, rich ones. Mum (Marjorie Yates) has a hum for every contingency in or out of life, and these hums, and the music, the songs, from first to last throughout "The Long Day Closes" are in themselves a magical tapestry of nostalgia and memory, yours as well as mine. In the several days since I saw the screening I cannot get out of my head "I Don't Know Why I Love You, I Just Do." Or, for just a few of several dozen others:"Bongo, Bongo, Bongo," "On a Slow Boat to China," "Once in Love With Amy," "Me and My Shadow," "Oh, You Beautiful Doll," "If You Were the Only Girl in the World," and the silken chocolate Nat King Cole "Stardust."

Then there's young Bud and his big sister Helen (Ayse Owens) doing "We're a Couple of Swells" at a family gathering. "We would sail up the avenue, we would sail up the avenue, *we would sail up the avenue*, but we haven't got a yacht ..." Last time I saw that it was Fred and Judy, and I loved it then too. I guess Bud and his sis saw the same flicks I did, you did. This is where that long day, for all its sensitivity, comes alive.

NEWSDAY, 5/28/93, Part II/p. 66, Gene Seymour

Be warned that "The Long Day Closes," isn't an easy-access highway to the past. You may find yourself at times trying to force and prod the film toward the kind of easygoing vitality and light-fingered insouciance from a film promising to convey what director Terence Davies calls, in his program notes, "the state of ecstasy ... about being happy about nothing in particular."

Some of that's there, of course. But it's clear that Davies, who directed a previous autobiographical film, "Distant Voices, Still Lives," is after weightier game. Through the eyes of his 11-year-old surrogate Bud (Leigh McCormack, who resembles Jeremy Irons in miniature), Davies presents more than a simple account of being a Liverpool kid in 1955 and 1956. He is offering a meditation on the nature of memory itself.

There is no plot to speak of. Just a series of deep-focus impressions that begin with a dark, rain-soaked pan to a vacant, gutted rowhouse in a dank corner of Liverpool. In the background, one hears the haunting, almost scary opening to Nat King Cole's rendition of "Stardust."

Davies fades to the same house almost 40 years before, with Bud plaintively asking his widowed mum (Marjorie Yates) for movie money. The languid, studied pace of this scene, the flow of soft noises within and outside the house, define the nature of the whole film. Davies wants to draw us deeply into the texture of what he remembers.

Each scene is a rendering of memory and the images are often heartbreakingly effective. When Bud, a boy quite accustomed to being alone with his own thoughts, moves downstairs from the dimly-lit shadows of his room Christmas Day, he walks into a luminous tableau of his mother, brothers and sisters sitting at a table in their best clothes, murmuring and chatting softly. It's such a gorgeous still-life you wonder if this really is what Bud/Davies actually saw or how Davies himself remembers it.

Other impressions follow, all of them contained within the street corner that constitutes Bud's whole universe. By letting his camera linger and wander randomly and unobtrusively around this street, its residents, its parties and conversations, Davies triggers so many moods and impressions that it challenges a viewer to think just as deeply and broadly about his or her own past.

Perhaps the best display of this style comes when Bud, feeling lonely and hurt because his best friend has gone to the movies with someone else, starts swinging by himself on a basement railing as Debbie Reynolds' "Tammy" swells in the background. The overhead shot of Bud at play moves to another overhead shot of an audience at a cinema, then to a church congregation, then to rows of schoolchildren leaving class row by row. It's an amazing sequence whose daring disorients because it's not what one is used to when visiting a '50s childhood. Like the rest of the film, it gives authentic, ennobling grandeur to pop sentiment.

SIGHT AND SOUND, 6/92, p. 44, Raymond Durgnat

As nocturnal rain thrashes derelict homes, a flashback to eleven-year-old Bud sitting quietly on stairs opens a mosaic of moments from a Liverpool childhood, 1955-6. His home life is illumined by his mother's friendly smiles, her tear at a photograph of his dead father, the glowing torso of big brother Kevin chatting while mending a bike, and a vivacious quartet of grown-up sisters. He wheedles shillings for the pictures, hangs around a cinema's exit doors, and implores adult strangers to take him in to 'A' certificate films.

At his new, Catholic, school he gets the cane for lateness, becomes prey for three playground bullies, and is shamed by a nurse who, inspecting heads, loudly declares "Clean" or "Lice". Often friendless, aimless, he gazes at working brickies, who mock him (with a hint of sexual suggestiveness). His mind echoes with film soundtrack quotes, mostly nostalgic; as a daydream light bathes an empty desk near his, a sailing ship glides by. But in a nightmare, his bedroom wall extrudes brutal male hands that grip his face.

During family visits, he hovers uncertainly between the women and the men, before drifting back with the women, who contemplate, indulgently, the coarser sex. A neighbouring housewife, Helen, constantly but fondly nags her husband Curly for his unending imitations of Hollywood actors; Bud performs alongside his pleasantly tipsy sister as she impersonates Judy Garland. When his mother suggests that he run out to join two schoolmates walking by, he can only flinch in despair at having no friends. In a rare bout of physical activity, he swings mournfully from an iron bar over a basement staircase.

Art, sacred or profane, affords him epiphanic moments, as when Curly's off-key singing starts a family sing-song, or when God's-eye-views of picture palace and school chapel intimate order and community. Certain soundtrack voices, however, are ominous: George Minafer Amberson getting his comeuppance and being forgotten by all; Miss Havisham's eerie unfamiliarity with the word 'play'. In class, a teacher's turned back, and dry voice cataloguing the processes of erosion, epitomise global indifference. None the less, the eponymous vespers, sung by a woman's voice over cloudscape with glittering moon, revere cold, distant, precious light.

Terence Davies' best film yet testifies to the vigour and flexibility of cinematic realisms. It's intensely 'realist' in three common senses: in bending, not subject to form, but form to subject; in generating 'the shock of recognition' at experiences privately powerful but culturally neglected; and in exploring the lives of ordinary people without foreshortening their sufferings and constraints. Davies' especially delicate realism requires a rigorous fidelity to raw experience, carefully protected from conventional discourse, although conveyed by artifice. Davies' style is so closely geared to one individual child, in a largely unique situation (local-and-family micro-culture), as to constitute a sort of 'micro-realism; akin to the micro-history now subverting Marxist stereotypes of class and culture and their "abolition of the subject".

Davies' double focus, on a vanished world and on subjectivity, far from diluting realism, only extends it. As with Proust and Joyce, subjective remembrance and documentation interweave. A sprinkling of self-reflexive touches (a music teacher telling a percussionist, "Just tap it, you're not introducing a film"), and the many looks at, or just off-camera, are not alienation but, on the contrary, complicity effects. Davies' aesthetic is utterly un-Brechtian, expecting consummate identification with an ever-pathetic protagonist, much wronged by life and unable to hurt a fly.

The visual style might be described as 'Wenders intensified'; its frames-within-the-frame, flat planes, and painterly textures constrict the normal perception of spaces (as flexibly defined arenas for activity). A recurrent composition (a vertical split of stairs and hallway) emblemises the boy's Limbo-land; ultimately, perhaps, it relates to the perpendicular overhead shots spectacularly bracketing a cinema's projection beam with a chapel's aisle.

The colours range from iodine hues to greens so luminous they're almost white. Every pose, every group, seems on the verge of becoming a still life, embalmed by the very purity of its emotion. The exquisite play with looks ranges from Bud's quick glance up at a faceless teacher about to cane his hand to adult gazes which, slightly averted from camera, and us, seem cruelly refused or well-meaningly blind. It's as if only musical form—the songs—allow an emotional follow-through. The pressbook speaks of a 'joyous' film, but Bud's friendlessness and inactivity implies a steady misery, heavy with dire potential. Eerie, too, the way Bud is barely encouraged, even by loving adults, in ego-building activities. Around this too-impeccably cherubic boy cluster glaring gaps and lacks. Certainly Davies' 'miniaturism' contrasts with, say, *Les 400 Coups*, whose interactions weave broader perspectives.

Bud and family are evidently different persons from those in previous Davies families. But Davies' autobiographical remarks virtually conflate the screen families, so that the fearsomeness of Bud's father will be widely assumed. However, the marginalisation of any one big obvious threat by more varied and subtle material helps to soften Davies' gross miserabilism. It should also nudge spectators to seek, not some single cause or deep structure which would determine everything, but a conjunction of independent factors (as per common sense and chaos theory).

In some pluri-causal view, Bud's family position, at the tail-end of many siblings, might be as crucial as favourite targets like punitive school discipline or paternal violence (which Political Correctness has confused with 'patriarchy'). Chiselled and delicate, the acting ranges from memory-vignettes akin to 'magic realism' (especially for women) to an easier flow (for men). Helen and copperknob Curly could have popped in from a next door by Mike Leigh—another, albeit less precise, microrealist.

VILLAGE VOICE, 6/1/93, p. 49, J. Hoberman

The credits to *The Long Day Closes*, Terence Davies's mesmerizing follow-up to his 1988 *Distant Voices, Still Lives*, have the ceremonial look of an engraved wedding invitation—yet the film itself is profoundly solitary. It's as though the union Davies has in mind is a marriage of individual and collective memory consecrated by the movies.

The Long Day Closes, is the bridge between the prenatal memories of Davies's two-part *Distant Voices, Still Lives* and the anguished homosexuality of his earlier *Trilogy*. Set during World War II, *Distant Voices* revolved around family memories of a stubborn, furious father as framed by the marriage of his oldest daughter; *Still Lives* picked up the thread of the daughter's unhappy married life, refracted through a succession of celebrations in which the entire family comes together in the local pub to quarrel with their spouses and sing popular songs. *The Long Day Closes*, which Davies says will be his last autobiographical film, takes place a few years later, in 1955-56, with the hero, Bud, a severe-looking, friendless child of 11.

No less than Davies's previous movies, *The Long Day Closes* is charged by a love for the ineffable—in this case, Bud's fascination with that world on the screen we never see. The play of light on transfixed faces, the austere illumination of the projector beam, are counterpointed by something blatantly material—the hurdygurdy waltz from *Carousel* or a sound-clip from *Kind Hearts and Coronets*. Representing daily life as the series of heroic friezes that link one bijou epiphany to the next, Davies's mise-en-scéne combines hyperrealist clarity with stylized theatrical lighting—much of the action staged from the head-on perspective of a viewer in the sixth row.

For those who have seen *Distant Voices, Still Lives, The Long Day Closes* will scarcely seem exotic. Davies repeats many of the lessons of the earlier film. Here again are the etched period details and intensely subdued colors, the a cappella group sings and voluptuous gestures: The first scene uses the 20th Century Fox fanfare to underscore a close-up of a soggy, disintegrating movie poster in a rain-drenched back alley, Nat King Cole crooning "Stardust" as the camera dollies forward, around the corner, and up some stairs to light upon Bud plaintively asking his mother for money to go to the pictures. But *The Long Day Closes* is less bound by narrative than Davies's earlier films—the disappearance of the oppressive father has freed the movie to become a chain of associations.

The youngest of 10 children, born in working-class Liverpool in 1945, and thus a younger contemporary of the Beatles, Davies deals in re-creation, constructing his films out of the sharp shards of childhood memories, assembling his own rarefied world of precious objects and sacred presences. His studio Liverpool is usually cold and dark and as hermetic as a bell jar. (In one evocative bit of business, the family is frightened by the appearance of a black West Indian at their front door.) There are no street noises. The weather is a near perpetual monsoon—the set more drenched with precipitation than the MGM backlot where they shot *Singin' in the Rain*, the film Davies remembers as the first he saw.

Introverted and uncompromising, Davies treats each remarkably studied image as though exhuming some sepia-tinted relic from the archaeological site of Catholic, working-class Liverpool. "I try to celebrate Englishness with the panache of the Americans," Davies told *Sight and Sound*. *The Long Day Closes* occasionally mutates into a fairy-tale England—the fantasy of snow for Christmas, a candlelight vigil, and the mass singing of "Auld Lang Syne" on New Years Eve 1956—but there's a stillness here that distinguishes Davies's reconstructions from those of Hollywood nostalgists like Steven Spielberg and Joe Dante.

As a director, Davies exhibits a startling absense of hubris. (His excavation of childhood wonder suggests the Fellini-esque without the overbearingly expansive Fellini personality.) The Davies mode is a controlled, perhaps depressed, ecstasy. It's a fundamentally religious worldview whose characteristic camera maneuver is a slow lateral pan that gazes down on the action like a low-flying angel. He's a humble devotee with a sense of the audience as the conglomerate of intensely focused solitudes. When Bud's mother sings "Me and My Shadow" she's providing the anthem for the entire movie.

The Long Day Closes is not only haunted by the soundtrack from *The Magnificent Ambersons* but the way in which movies get mixed up with life—the lumpy neighbor who embarrasses his acid-tongued wife with imitations of Edward G. Robinson and James Cagney. As Bud is a permanent observer, Davies keeps finding ways to create visual metaphors for the movie screen (sometimes even in CinemaScope) within the family's drab row house. Indeed, Davies's most remarkable visual epiphany redeems what would seem to be the most hopeless material. An overhead shot of an uncharacteristically playful Bud swinging Tarzan-style on a rusty piece of scaffolding somewhere outside the movie theater cues Debbie Reynolds's tremulously saccharine rendition of the title song from *Tammy*. The stately camera continues to track over the head of a rapt movie audience match-dissolved into first a church congregation, then children in a schoolroom, and finally a landscape of corroded metal and worn stone.

Although *The Long Day Closes* is undeniably beautiful, it's the purity of Davies's concentration that's ultimately most heartbreaking—the distillation of events, the sense of mental performance. For Davies, the projected shaft of light is a form of divine radiance. But *The Long Day Closes* is as tactile as it is ethereal. More redemptive than nostalgic, the movie is a celestial vaudeville in a fastidiously grubby heaven.

Also reviewed in:
CHICAGO TRIBUNE, 7/30/93, Friday/p. D, John Petrakis
NEW YORK TIMES, 5/28/93, p. C12, Stephen Holden
VARIETY, 5/11/92, p. 121, Derek Elley

LOOK WHO'S TALKING NOW!

A TriStar Pictures release.   *Executive Producer:* Leslie Dixon.   *Producer:* Jonathan D. Krane.   *Director:* Tom Ropelewski.   *Screenplay:* Tom Ropelewski and Leslie Dixon.   *Based on characters created by:* Amy Heckerling.   *Director of Photography:* Oliver Stapleton.   *Editor:* Michael A. Stevenson and Harry Hitner.   *Editor:* Michael A. Stevenson and Harry Hitner.   *Music:* William Ross.   *Music Editor:* Jim Harrison.   *Choreographer:* Mary Ann Kellogg.

Sound: Rob Young. *Sound Editor:* Larry Mann and Uncle J. Kamen. *Casting:* Michelle Allen, Lynne Carrow, Sally Dennison, and Patrick Rush. *Production Designer:* Michael Bolton. *Art Director:* Alexander Cochrane. *Set Decorator:* Jim Erickson. *Set Dresser:* Perry Battista, Allan Dervisevic, and Steve Lamare. *Special Effects:* David Gauthier. *Visual Effects:* David Sosalla. *Flying Effects Supervisor:* John Thomas. *Costumes:* Molly Maginnis and Mary E. McLeod. *Make-up:* Victoria Down.   *Stunt Coordinator:* Betty Thomas.   *Running time:* 92 minutes. *MPAA Rating:* PG-13.

CAST: John Travolta (James Ubriacco);   Kirstie Alley (Mollie Ubriacco);   David Gallagher (Mikey Ubriacco);   Tabitha Lupien (Julie Ubriacco);   Lysette Anthony (Samantha);   Sandra Grant (Accountant);   Olympia Dukakis (Rosie);   Danny DeVito (Voice of Rocks);   Diane Keaton (Voice of Daphne);   George Segal (Albert);   Charles Barkley (Himself);   John Stocker (Sol);   Elizabeth Leslie (Ruthie);   Caroline Elliott and Vanessa Morley (Kids at Schoolyard); Sandra Grant (Accountant);   Sheila Paterson (Old Waitress);   Amos Hertzman (Pimply Faced Kid);   Mark Acheson (Burly Dad);   Gerry Rousseau (Homeless Guy);   Kyle Fairlie (Kid on Santa's Lap);   Victoria Brooks (Bratty Girl);   Ron Gabriel (Seedy Santa);   Frank Turner (Dave); Serge Houde (Maitre D');   Michael Puttonen (Dog Catcher);   Roger Cross, Ryan Michael, and Phil Hayes (Pilots);   Miriam Smith (Tipsy Secretary);   Robert Wisden and J.B. Bivens (Rangers);   Tegan Moss (Girl with Puppy);   Chilton Crane (Girl's Mommy);   Alicia Bradsen (Mollie at 12);   Gina Chiarelli (Young Rosie);   Ghislaine Crawford and Justine Crawford (Reindeer Girls);   Andrew Airlie (Co-Pilot);   Andrea Nemeth (Babysitter);   Campbell Lane (Mollie's Dad).

LOS ANGELES TIMES, 11/5/93, Calendar/p. 14, Peter Rainer

"Look Who's Talking Now" is an early November release but it's all about Christmas cheer. As a preemptive strike on the Christmas movie trade, it's cheerily inconsequential. In this third in the series of "Look Who's Talking" movies, it's the dogs' turn to talk. What's next? Will David Lynch take over the series and make the sofas and the garbage disposals talk?

John Travolta and Kirstie Alley re-team as James and Mollie, the couple with two twinkly kids, Mikey (David Gallagher) and Julia (Tabitha Lupien), who acquire two pooches—the scruffy Rocks (voice by Danny DeVito) and the effete poodle Daphne (voice by Diane Keaton). James is now a well-paid pilot for the curvy president (Lysette Anthony) of an international cosmetics firm: Mollie works as an elf for a department-store Santa.

Mollie can't stand the family's new dogs, one of which, Daphne, was a present from the cosmetics prez. The dialogue between Rocks and Daphne is deliberately corny Lady and the Tramp stuff, but it beats most of the adult dialogue.

(DeVito's vocal cords are so gratingly distinctive that, after a while, you just think of Rocks as DeVito, not as DeVito's voice.) Despite the talking-dog gimmick, the enterprise is a continuation of the mood of the first two films in the series: It's all about the joys of family.

The reason that the film (rated PG-13 for off-color dialogue) is borderline pleasant is because, even more than in the first two films, Travolta and Alley are a marvelous team. They're both such remarkably gifted comic actors that they manage to have a good time even though they're way too talented for this taffeta. They prove that you can glide through a retread like this and still retain your dignity as an actor.

Now how about teaming Travolta and Alley in a romantic comedy that's really *about* something?

NEW YORK POST, 11/5/93, p. 34, Michael Medved

If anyone demands proof that good movie parts are hard to find, consider the fact that some of our most notable actors have recently devoted their vocal talents to expressing the innermost thoughts of dogs.

In Disney's delightful "Homeward Bound" earlier in the year, Don Ameche provided the voice for an elderly, faithful golden retriever, while Michael J. Fox delivered the lines of a rambunctious mutt.

In the disappointing new Christmas concoction "Look Who's Talking Now," it's Danny DeVito who takes the part of the spunky mongrel, while Diane Keaton is a pampered poodle.

These two dogs are simultaneously (though reluctantly) adopted by John Travolta and Kirstie Alley, the same likable New York couple featured in the first two "Look Who's Talking" movies.

They are now struggling to raise 6-year-old Mikey (David Gallagher) and 4-year-old Julie (Tabitha Lupien), whose baby thoughts had been expressed in the previous films by the voices of Bruce Willis and Roseanne Barr.

This time, the meager plot kicks in when the little family falls on hard times, as Mommy loses her job as an accountant and Daddy's new position as private pilot for a scheming, sexy cosmetics tycoon (Lysette Anthony) takes him away from home almost constantly.

One of the reasons that this sitcom stupidity falls flat is that the two hounds who dominate much of the action have been so badly cast and poorly coached.

While I'm not quite ready to criticize these animal actors for their lack of emotional range, it does seem that the filmmakers could have done a better job sorting through the millions of adorable canines in this country (including my own gifted golden retriever) to select a cute and charismatic pair. Instead, the two irredeemably dull dogs that they chose provide an especially awkward contrast to the hammy, high energy voice-over work by DeVito and Keaton.

The inevitable attraction between the two pooches (painfully familiar to all viewers of "Lady and the Tramp") generates no sparks, but it is far less disturbing than the movie's other romance—between Travolta and his gorgeous boss, Lysette Anthony (who was last seen as Sydney Pollack's airhead girlfriend in Woody Allen's "Husbands and Wives").

Her determined attempts to seduce the movie's hard-working father figure will make no sense to adults, and may be deeply troubling to young moviegoers. Who ever came up with the bright idea of building a "feel-good" kiddie Christmas movie around themes of potential adultery, jealousy and family breakup?

Other needlessly offensive elements display the same absence of sensitivity. For instance, when Travolta and his DeVito-voiced dog confront a pack of vicious wolves in the woods on Christmas Eve, was it really necessary to give those snarling beasts exaggerated African-American accents?

And then there's the scene when Mikey sees a department store St. Nick behind the scenes, cursing and shouting on the phone about a debt to his bookie.

As he walks away with his parents, they try to reassure the disillusioned kid by saying: "That's not the real Santa Claus. That's just his Jewish cousin, Sydney."

Director Tom Ropelewski (who co-wrote the script with his wife, executive producer Leslie Dixon) took over the "Look Who's Talking" franchise from its creator, Amy Heckerling, after the truly despicable "Look Who's Talking Too" in 1990.

NEWSDAY, 11/5/93, Part II/p. 91, John Anderson

Here's a new twist on an old cliché: Beat a dead horse, and it barks.

"Look Who's Talking Now," the third in the Kirstie Alley-John Travolta series of purported comedies, provides us the opportunity to hear dogs think, rather than babies. This is not an improvement. That the inner life of a mutt like Rocks sounds like Danny DeVito will not endear people to strays and curs. In fact, that the film is set at Christmastime might put people off the holiday season entirely.

Rocks and Daphne (voice of Diane Keaton) simultaneously become part of the Ubriacco household—James (Travolta), Mollie (Alley), Mikey (David Gallagher), who whines about wanting a dog, and Julie (Tabitha Lupien), who has a Charles Barkley fixation (don't ask). In a display of fatherly abandon, James brings Rocks home from the pound on the very day Daphne—a French poodle with a Wedgwood water bowl—has arrived, compliments of Samantha D'Bonne (Lysette Anthony). She's the slinky corporate exec who has hired James as her personal pilot—on the same day Mollie loses her own high-paying position.

Fiscal serendipity? Oh, sure. Among the more offensive devices in this decidedly charmless film is the role reversal provided for Mollie. In the other two films, she was the corporate cutthroat, and James was a shlumpy cab driver. Thanks to her layoff, Mollie can now stay home and be a domestic drone—which is perfect for Alley, who always gives the impression she has either just stopped or is about to start crying. Samantha, her nemesis, represents the predatory evil of ambitious womanhood. She also has sexual designs on James. Don't ask me. I was beginning to think this was science-fiction.

Rocks and Daphne share pleasantries. When she calls him a "tick magnet," his delightful riposte is "... like *you* never sniffed a butt." This should have the preschoolers on the floor—where they'll find their parents, who'll be napping, or cringing.

Writer-director Tom Ropelewski lifts shamelessly from "Lady and the Tramp," although for a few minutes I thought Rocks and Daphne were going to stage a canine "Swept Away." That, of course, wouldn't fit the "Look Who's Talking" *ouevre*, which is more concerned with the wholesome subjects of class and bodily functions—human and otherwise.

SIGHT AND SOUND, 6/94, p. 55, Caren Myers

The Ubriacco family is back, and though the children, Mikey and Julie, have now learned to speak, their parents, Mollie and James, are as frazzled as ever. James is soon hired as private pilot by Samantha, the vampy president of a cosmetics company, while Mollie is fired from her job as an accountant. With the festival season approaching, she takes a job as an elf for a department store Santa. The kids take the opportunity to place their Christmas orders: Mikey, in particular, wants a dog.

As it happens, the neighbourhood spaniel has just had a rather mixed litter after an indiscreet liaison, and the scruffiest of the puppies, Rocks, catches Mikey's eye. But Mollie vetoes the idea, so Rocks, after escaping from the Hell's Angels who buy him, becomes the streetwise companion of a homeless person and ends up in the dog pound. Fortunately, James has relented, and he and Mikey save Rocks from being destroyed.

Coming home, they are surprised to find that Samantha has seen fit to offload her pampered poodle Daphne upon them—for an indefinite stay. The dogs take an instant dislike to each other, as the un-housetrained Rocks nauseates the fastidious Daphne.

Oblivious to the constant canine bickering, the humans are having their own problems. Mollie doesn't trust Samantha, who keeps James increasingly busy. While James flies all over the world, Mollie struggles with holiday preparations and her jealous imagination. One night while she is sleeping, the dogs sneak out and bond over the contents of a Chinese restaurant's garbage can.

But on Christmas Eve, the scheming Samantha tricks James into taking her to a luxurious and remote cabin in the woods on the pretext of an emergency business meeting. Mollie discovers that the meeting is bogus, but is reassured by her mother that James would never be untrue. She resolves to drive the kids and the dogs up to see him in time for Christmas (leaving her parents, whom she had invited to dinner, to fend for themselves). But a mishap on the snowbound roads sends their car crashing into the woods, where Rocks fends off a marauding wolf, and Daphne summons the forest rangers. James unmasks Samantha's perfidy in the nick of time and, guided by Rocks, is eventually reunited with his family at the rangers' cabin, where they have themselves a happy little Christmas.

The quality of novelty was plenty strained in *Look Who's Talking*, which enchanted millions by having a wisecracking Bruce Willis voice an infant's thoughts, and was scarcely improved upon in a sequel (*Look Who's Talking Too*) which featured Roseanne Barr as the boy's baby sister. Now that the current instalment is reduced to putting glib comments in the metaphorical mouths of wisecracking canines, there are not a whole lot of options left, unless the toaster starts talking. Possessed of the kind of plot which would barely fuel an episode of *Who's the Boss?*, *Look Who's Talking Now* is a film exhausted even before the opening credits finish rolling.

Nothing in this film works: the hairier scenes aspire to a *Lady and the Tramp* style charm, but come across more as an extended advert for Pedigree Chum, and the humans (who, if anything, are less interesting than their dogs) have their domestic drama usurped by the glutinous question of Santa's existence. To crown it all, Diane Keaton has to play against type as the snooty rich bitch Daphne, effectively ruining the only chance the movie has to be funny. By the time Mollie is having fantasy sequences that spoof *An American in Paris*, you realise that the film-makers have nothing further to say and are desperately hoping that you won't notice. Believe me, you do.

Also reviewed in:
CHICAGO TRIBUNE, 11/5/93, Tempo/p. 3, Johanna Steinmetz
NEW YORK TIMES, 11/5/93, p. C12, Stephen Holden
VARIETY, 11/15/93, p. 31, Dan Cox
WASHINGTON POST, 11/8/93, p. B10, Rita Kempley

LOST IN YONKERS

A Columbia Pictures release of a Rastar production.   *Executive Producer:* Joseph M. Caracciolo.   *Producer:* Ray Stark.   *Director:* Martha Coolidge.   *Screenplay (based on his play):* Neil Simon.   *Based on a play by:* Neil Simon.   *Director of Photography:* Johnny E. Jensen.   *Editor:* Steven Cohen.   *Music:* Elmer Bernstein.   *Music Editor:* Kathy Durning.   *Sound:* Lee Orloff.   *Sound Editor:* Tom C. McCarthy and Roxanne Jones.   *Casting:* Jennifer Shull.   *Production Designer:* David Chapman.   *Art Director:* Mark Haack.   *Set Designer:* Thomas H. Paul and Mark Garner.   *Set Decorator:* Marvin March.   *Set Dresser:* Jack Eberhart.   *Special Effects:* Daniel Ottesen and Bill Myatt.   *Costumes:* Shelley Komarov.   *Make-up:* Dan Striepeke.   *Make-up (Mercedes Ruehl):* Carol Schwartz.   *Running time:* 110 minutes. *MPAA Rating:* PG.

CAST: Richard Dreyfuss (Louie); Mercedes Ruehl (Bella); Irene Worth (Grandma); Brad Stoll (Jay); Mike Damus (Arty); David Strathairn (Johnny); Robert Guy Miranda (Hollywood Harry); Jack Laufer (Eddie); Susan Merson (Gert); Illya Haase (Harry's Crony); Calvin Stillwell (Gas Station Attendant); Dick Hagerman (Truck Driver); Jesse Vincent (Danny); Howard Newstate (Kid in Store); Peter Gannon (Cop); Lori Schubeler (Teresa); Jean Zarzour (Flo); Mary Scott Gudaitis (Celeste).

CHRISTIAN SCIENCE MONITOR, 5/18/93, p. 13, David Sterritt

"Lost in Yonkers" is one of Neil Simon's childhood stories. The time is the early 1940s, the place is metropolitan New York, and two of the main characters are kids—bright, brash youngsters apparently modeled on Mr. Simon in his early years.

Their names are Jay and Arty, and they're surrounded by enough eccentric grown-ups to supply a future playwright with a lifetime of material. Dad is a wistful widower in debt to a loan shark. Grandma is a German-born dowager who survived the Nazi horrors by permanently turning off her emotions. Uncle Louie looks like a gangster, but we know that deep down he's—well, a gangster, but a relatively harmless one.

And then there's Aunt Bella, the *really* odd duck of the family: pretty, energetic, and afflicted with a mental disability that makes her all the more lovable yet hinders her ability to fend for herself. Her running feud with Grandma is the stuff of local legend. But nobody knows whether she'll cut the apron strings and carve out an independent life.

The movie adaptation of "Lost in Yonkers," which won Simon a Pulitzer Prize in its Broadway version, is at its best when it focuses on Jay and Arty and their impressions of family life. Martha Coolidge, who directed the picture, amusingly captures the blend of magic and uneasiness that an unfamiliar setting—and a crowd of unfamiliar housemates—can have for youngsters who are smart enough to cope with new surroundings, but not mature enough to be sure they're doing it right.

Unfortunately, the movie goes terribly wrong when Simon cranks himself up to be Serious about Major Emotional Issues, which happens in the second half of the story.

Simon is an able comic writer, and when thoughtfulness or sentiment grow naturally from the situation and characters he's developing—as in "The Sunshine Boys," probably his best movie ever—the result is genuinely touching as well as entertaining. But when he forces the issue, tackling a subject that's too weighty and complex for his brand of comedy, the outcome can be mighty distressing.

That's what happens in "Lost in Yonkers," which turns out to be the story not of Jay and Arty, but of Aunt Bella's struggle to become a grown-up despite the expectations of everlasting childhood that her family has settled on her. This is an absorbing subject, and Bella is a fascinating person to embody it. But two problems arise in Simon's treatment.

First, he spends an hour developing Bella as an endearing but incompetent woman who can literally forget to walk through her own doorway when she arrives at home. Yet in the movie's later scenes, she starts addressing her household with speeches that couldn't be more eloquent if *she* were a prize-winning playwright. Perhaps we're meant to think her passionate feelings have unlocked new capacities in her mind and spirit; but Simon doesn't suggest this, much less explain it.

In a further miscalculation that's still more damaging, Simon fails to follow through on these emotional fireworks. The highest point of Bella's struggle is interrupted by an incredibly stupid scene involving Uncle Louie and a stolen car; and the outcome of her dilemma is wrapped in a goopy layer of all's-well-that-ends-well sentimentality, which denies the seriousness of everything we've just been watching. It's meant to have a fashionable feel-good effect, but it's false and superficial.

Mercedes Ruehl fails to make Bella fully real despite a vigorous and sincere performance, providing final proof that Simon has done a poor job of constructing this character. Among the rest of the cast, Irene Worth has powerful moments as Grandma, and Brad Stoll and Mike Damus are solid as the youngsters of the story.

Richard Dreyfuss is amusing as Uncle Louie, although his role is more cute than convincing. David Strathairn is excellent as Bella's sadly inadequate boyfriend. Most of the supporting players are capable, except Susan Merson, who's saddled with a ghastly role (an aunt with breathing problems) that would defeat anyone.

Simon wrote the screenplay, and Johnny Jensen—who collaborated with Ms. Coolidge on "Rambling Rose," her previous picture—did the fetching cinematography.

FILMS IN REVIEW, 8/93, p. 265, Keith Edwards

Martha Coolidge has done a splendid job in shepherding Neil Simon's award winning play *Lost In Yonkers* to the screen. The director realized that the Mercedes Ruehl character was the heart of the matter and has placed her front and center, creating a film that is at once touching, warm and witty in ways the stage play never achieved.

The addition of the previously unseen movie usher who awakens Miss Ruehl's passion was inspired and David Straithairn is sadly moving in this role of arrested development. The two are poignantly paired, unlike the contrived lunacy of the couple in *Benny And Joon*.

Richard Dreyfuss does his familiar used car salesman turn which is well suited to the role of gangster brother. The young sons are blessed with Simon's sharpest barbs and perform like troupers. My problem with the stage piece was the presentation of Grandma Kurnitz, since she remained an indomitable presence like Mount Rushmore from entrance to final curtain. Miss Coolidge has Irene Worth (repeating her stage role along with Ms. Ruehl) make a dominantly dramatic entrance reminiscent of *Fantasia*'s Sorcerer or Otto Preminger in *Stalag 17*—a foreboding shadow followed by thunderous steps. With the aid of film closeup, the director has Ms. Worth reveal subtle shades of pathos after the final round with her liberated daughter. For one brief moment she bites her handkerchief as she stifles a gasp and her eyes gently brim with tears and then it's back to her stoic world. This, however, is the breakthrough that was missing on Broadway. I may be giving Martha Coolidge more credit than is due for this achievement but the original stage team had the opportunity and failed to ignite the material.

LOS ANGELES TIMES, 5/14/93, Calendar/p. 8, Peter Rainer

Aunt Bella (Mercedes Ruehl) in "Lost in Yonkers" is in her mid 30s but still lives with her mother (Irene Worth) above the family candy store. She wears dresses that are too florid for her; she's trying to look more gamin-like, but instead the tactic ages her. She's sad in a flamboyant, trying-to-be-happy way. Bella isn't stupid exactly, but her unyielding mother has stunted her will. She's like a womanly child, and what makes her such a sympathetic character is that she keeps pushing on even though she's desperately aware of her doubleness.

When Neil Simon's play opened on Broadway in 1991, it was greeted with the kind of furrowed-brow raves that help rack up awards. (It went on to win the Tony and the Pulitzer.) Simon's play was supposed to be his most hard-bitten and least self-consciously jokey; he was congratulated for dampening the comedy that made his reputation.

But "Lost in Yonkers" (rated PG for thematic elements and mild language) is essentially deep-dish Neil Simon, which is, after all, not so very deep. But neither is the play negligible: it has a felt, melancholy undertow, and Ruehl and Worth, who both won Tonys for their performances on Broadway, bring out its full, racking sadness.

The drama, which takes place almost entirely in the Westchester, N.Y., suburb in the summer of 1942, begins when the 15-year-old Jay and his 13-year-old brother Arty (the engaging Brad Stoll and Mike Damus) are deposited by their recently widowed father (Jack Laufer) with his unaccommodating mother while he hits the road selling scrap iron to pay off his debts. To the boys, Grandma Kurnitz, with her thick German accent and her brusque scowl and her weapon-like cane, is a character out of a spooky children's fairy tale; they get a perverse kick out of trying to outwit her, or filch candy without being caught. (They always are.) They're amused by her but she also scares them.

Aunt Bella is their sidekick protectress, even though she can't protect herself very well. In interviews, director Martha Coolidge has talked about how she wanted to make audiences view these situations and think of Hansel and Gretel, or Cinderella trapped in her stepmother's house, and, to some extent, she succeeds. The steel-trap whimsy of the play, with its comfy middle-class insights about how families self-destruct, prevents the fantasia from really taking off. But Coolidge draws out the characters' most fervent fantasies and keeps them spinning in mid air. The atmosphere inside that Yonkers apartment where much of the action takes place is thick with dreams: deferred, dashed, rejuvenated.

The other major dreamer besides Bella is her brother Louie (Richard Dreyfuss), a petty hoodlum with a cock o' the walk strut who hides out for a time in the apartment. Louie is as transparently boisterous as Bella. He's probably just as afraid of his mother as she is, but he swaddles his fear in his nattering hood act, dispensing tough guy aphorisms to the two boys. (It's probably what he wishes someone had done for him when he was a boy.) Louie is the most shticky character in the play but Dreyfuss keeps him honest. There's a childishness to his swagger that links him with Bella—their infantilism is their defense against their mother. In their own very different ways they feel valorous about their infirmities.

Simon makes it clear how psychologically abused these people were as kids but he doesn't go deep enough. In a way, this new anti-sentimentality is just the flip side of his old sentimentality. Grandma Kurnitz, who never cracks a smile and is proud that she never cries, is a species of ogre. Worth gives this German-Jewish matriarch a deep-down bitterness that's fiercely authentic but, still, there's something unshaded and monolithic about her. She's the villain of the piece, and her children are her victims. (Besides the boys' father, there's another sister, played by Susan Merson, who can barely take a breath in her mother's presence without choking.) The film doesn't account for the ways in which they might have aggravated their own miseries. The blame is all on one side, as it never is in the great family dramas (think of "Long Day's Journey Into Night" or "Death of a Salesman"). Maybe this is why Coolidge tries to palm the play off as a fairy tale. She pushes the piece into realms where character becomes symbolic, larger-than-life.

Fortunately, Mercedes Ruehl thrives in this expansive setting because she has the ability to make Bella's desperation hyperbolic. When she's sneaking a rendezvous with her stammering suitor (well played by David Straithairn), her desire for their threadbare romance to match the romances in the Bette Davis movies she adores is deeply painful. And yet Bella's passion is her salvation. The play may be set up for her to be a mopey, agitated "little person"—a female Marty—but, the way Ruehl plays her, she's a hellion for happiness, and a true heroine.

NEW YORK, 5/31/93, p. 55, David Denby

I can see no great originality or interest in Neil Simon's *Lost in Yonkers*, which is about a family yearning to be free of a tyrannical matriarch—a suffering woman with a hardened view of life. Yet the actors assembled by producer Ray Stark and directed by Martha Coolidge grab at their roles so eagerly that you stay involved. Richard Dreyfuss as a forties Jewish gangster laughs a bit too maniacally, and Mercedes Ruehl does a feverish impersonation of a goofy yet wise maiden aunt eager for life (to my eyes, Ruehl mostly looks eager to act). The two little boys, Brad Stoll and Mike Damus, say their sardonic lines like practiced troupers, and Irene Worth manages to extract the last amount of wit from the Germanic inflections of the loveless boss lady.

NEW YORK POST, 5/14/93, p. 27, Jami Bernard

When movies are adapted from theater, they usually suffer from "phantom limb" syndrome—sensations and tremors coming from the part that is amputated, which is the live theater experience itself. Watching "Lost in Yonkers," I wondered what it was like to see the original Neil Simon Pulitzer Prize-winning play, whether scenes that were vaguely emotional would have been more so in the stark claustrophobia of a stage set, whether the grandmother's ferocity would be less so without the aid of close-ups.

Even without the means of comparison, "Lost in Yonkers" keeps its aura of having once been a stage play, and however nicely it has turned out on film, it suffers just enough phantom-limb syndrome that finding its audience may prove difficult.

Simon's script has plenty of humor, a very old-fashioned kind, and yet the overall feel of the material is one of misery.

Two bright boys are left in the care of their formidable and impossibly rigid grandmother for a year while their father tries to find some work. I would say they are surrounded by an assortment of equally loony relatives, but that would make it sound as if they had lots of company—actually, living at grandma's over her candy shop (look but no touch) is a fairly solitary enterprise. The boys are terrified by granny and feel isolated in her Old World world.

There is, of course, their Aunt Bella, an overgrown kid with a lopsided grin and a rosy forgetfulness bordering on Alzheimer's even though she is just in her mid-30s. Mercedes Ruehl reprises the role that won her a Tony on stage. The movie seems slightly undecided about whether to tell the story from the boys' point of view or from Bella's, so it does a little of both.

Director Martha Coolidge might have done better to cast SNL's Mike Meyers as the second aunt, the one who talks on an intake of breath so that she's wheezing. Meyers does that to perfection in his "Coffee Talk" skits—"I'm *farklempt!*—while actress Susan Merson doesn't seem to have the knack or maybe no Jewish relatives, *farshtaist?*

The boys (Brad Stoll and Mike Damus) are droll little wiseacres, and Irene Worth is appropriately dread-inspiring as the grandmother who withholds love from her family like the IRS withholds taxes. Her mouth is a thin tight line, like the slash that means "no" on road pictograms.

Ruehl is irrepressible, David Strathairn is sweet as the movie usher Bella falls in love with, and Richard Dreyfuss comes on like gangbusters—kind of disquieting in such a quiet movie—as a nefarious uncle.

And so the individual performances are finely tuned—Coolidge last directed "Rambling Rose" and is able to get strong stuff from her actors—and the material is handled well. Some of it is very emotional, and the back row of the screening where I sat was a chorus of muffled sniffles (including mine).

As for the material itself, it is depressing without the uplift of discovery. Dreaded relatives are familiar emotional terrain. Who really wants to revisit them—especially to find out that they were indeed as nasty and unyielding as we had imagined? It's enjoyable—and a rarity—to see a movie about people and emotions and not about car crashes. This is tempered by the damp melancholia that clings to the skin after the movie is over.

NEW YORK POST, 5/14/93, p. 27, Michael Medved

When you start with a Pulitzer Prize-winning play by America's most popular playwright, recruit a marvelous cast studded with Oscar and Tony winners, then add a skilled, sensitive director whose last project earned well-deserved critical acclaim in 1991, what could possibly go wrong?

Nothing much does go wrong with "Lost in Yonkers," but nothing goes particularly right, either. This is a drab, dutiful production, lacking not only in emotional depth but missing the warmth and wit that his legions of fans would normally expect from Neil Simon.

The story enters on two brothers, aged 15 and 13 (adequately played by newcomers Brad Stoll and Mike Damus) whose widower father takes a job in 1942 that sends him constantly on the road. Reluctantly, he leaves the boys with his iron-wilied, intimidating German-Jewish mama (portrayed by three-time Tony winner Irene Worth) who lives above a candy store in Yonkers. Before the end of the picture the brothers discover that beneath Grandma's cruel, nasty, joyless, exterior lurks a cruel, nasty, joyless inner soul.

Perhaps director Martha Coolidge (who did such a magnificent job with "Rambling Rose") deserves credit for avoiding easy uplift and refusing to hint that Grandma actually possesses a heart of gold, but the resulting portrait is so uncompromisingly negative that it provides little insight or sympathy for the character.

The only one in the family who can stand up to this embittered old tyrant is her black sheep son, Louie (Richard Dreyfuss), a penny-ante hoodlum who comes home to the candy store to hide out for a while from some vengeful Damon Runyon-style colleagues who are looking for stolen loot.

With his exaggerated Brooklyn accent and his angry, defiant swagger, Dreyfuss commands the screen as always and delivers his usual high-octane performance, but you can't for one moment forget that he is strenuously *acting*.

In his previous Neil Simon movie role. Dreyfuss won the Oscar for playing a struggling, slightly pretentious, hopelessly hammy young actor in "The Goodbye Girl"; his self-consciously "colorful" Uncle Louie in this film is the sort of overdone performance *that* thespian would offer, but it's hardly worthy of one of today's most accomplished movie stars.

Mercedes Ruehl, reprising the role that won her a Tony in the stage version of "Lost in Yonkers," is far more convincing as the other bright spot in the boys' bleak life: their scatter-brained, childlike, but warmhearted Aunt Bella. In adapting his play for the screen, Simon (and his longtime collaborator, producer Ray Stark) decided to make Bella the center of this movie, "opening up" the story to follow her romance with a mentally handicapped theater usher (David Strathairn).

This results in a disastrous loss of focus: The picture can't work as a nostalgic memory piece from the point of view of an adolescent protagonist (in the style of "Brighton Beach Memoirs") when it presents so many key scenes that this teenage character never sees.

One of those scenes involves a stagey, souped-up, private confrontation in which Bella declares to Grandma, "I feel pretty empty inside—like you feel all the time!" At the end of the film the audience is left with much the same hollow sensation.

The marketing people are naturally downplaying the dark nature of this material with an advertising campaign that is singularly tacky and outrageously misleading. "A movie that will win your heart!" the radio spots declare. "A feeling like home!"

This last boast is true only if home to you feels dull, desolate and dysfunctional.

NEWSDAY, 5/14/93, Part II/p. 66, Jack Mathews

In the press notes for the movie adaptation of Neil Simon's Pulitzer Prize-winning play "Lost in Yonkers," Simon is quoted as saying, "Comedy based on comedic situations has no weight to it … You can laugh at it, but you forget it the minute you're out of the theater."

I did not see "Lost in Yonkers" on stage, so I'll have to take the word of Simon and the Pulitzer committee that, its heft weighed on audiences long after it ended. However, with the exception of the reprised Tony performances of Mercedes Ruehl and Irene Worth, the filmed version, directed by Martha Coolidge from Simon's script, doesn't linger much beyond the allotted minute.

More than most of his previous films, "Lost in Yonkers" gives us plenty to think about *while* we're watching. Its central story, about the child-woman Bella (Ruehl) and her ungainly at,-tempts to liberate herself from the emotional cruelty of her mother (Worth), is almost painfully compelling.

Where the movie goes wrong is in Simon's uncertain narrative structure. Everyone in the story is figuratively lost in Yonkers, but it is the learning-disabled Bella, a woman of 36 with the emotional development of an adolescent, whose rescue interests us most. Yet, Simon tells the story from the clumsily alternating points of view of Bella and (for way too long) her 15-year-old nephew Jay (Brad Stoll).

The story takes place almost entirely in and around the two-story home, and candy store of Grandma Kurnitz, (Worth) in Yonkers, where, in 1942, Bella's widowed brother Eddie (Jack

Laufer) deposits his sons Jay and Arty (Mike Damus) while he scoots South for a few months to earn some money.

For the likable kids, it is like being dropped off at a summer camp in purgatory. Grandma Kurnitz, lamed by a horse in her youth and steel-tempered by the early loss of her husband and two of her six children, is the witch in "Hansel and Gretel," minus the warmth.

"Lost in Yonkers" sets us up for *that* story, Jay and Arty's sweet-and-sour summer working in and living above Grandma's candy shop. The other family members—Bella, her brother Louie (Richard Dreyfuss), a small-time hustler on the lam with some mob money, and speech-impaired sister Gert (Susan Merson)—seem subordinate to the relationship between the boys and their grandmother.

Coolidge ("Rambling Rose") underscores that expectation by treating the grandmother as a classic movie monster, using foreboding music and the thud of her cane against the hardwood to let us know she's coming, then shooting her with harsh lights and low angles to deepen a scowl already fearsome enough to chase fleas off a dog's back.

Much of this is played for laughs, and the child actors are both very good, particularly 13-year-old Damus, who sounds like Humphrey Bogart before his voice changed. But these scenes are precisely what Simon was referring to as weightless situation comedy. So are those with Louie, played with cartoonish flair by Dreyfuss, and Gert, whose inability to complete a sentence without taking a convulsive gasp of air grows quickly tiresome.

But when the film finally settles on Bella and holds its focus on her determination to bring love into her life, "Lost in Yonkers" gets its bearings. Bella is a wonderfully written character, an innocent living a hell of her mother's making, and her struggle to understand it, and break free of it, is the only story Simon needed to tell here.

Bella is too naive to understand why she is denied her mother's love, and too naive to think she won't still have it. As played by the marvelously expressive Ruehl, Bella becomes an emotional battering ram, trying to knock down both the barriers between her and her mother and those limiting her own intellectual growth.

It is Bella's relationship with a slow-witted, deeply withdrawn movie usher (David Strathairn), and her hopes for a real romance, that lead Bella to finally confront her mother. The force of that scene—the anguished plea of Bella contrasted with the stubborn coldness of her mother—will stay with us for a long time, if little else does.

SIGHT AND SOUND, 7/94, p. 49, Caren Myers

New York, summer of 1942. Fifteen-year-old Jay and his younger brother Arty are taken by their father Eddie to visit their grandmother, who owns a candy store in Yonkers. Grandma, who lives with her simple-minded daughter Bella, is not pleased that Eddie, forced by circumstances to take a travelling job in the south, is proposing to leave the boys with her. But Bella, in an unusual show of spirit, overrides her objections.

The boys settle into their new life, performing a variety of chores for their severe, eagle-eyed Grandma, acting as semi-willing confidants to the exuberant Bella—who has begun a tentative romance with John, a mentally handicapped usher at the local movie theatre—and spending their free time searching for Grandma's legendary stash of cash. One night, creeping down to the store, they stumble upon Grandma's son, Uncle Louie, a two-bit gangster on the run from a petty hood named Hollywood Harry. The boys are enchanted by Louie's tough-guy bravado, and he, in turn, shows them a secret passage out of the basement and teaches them poker. Though he clashes frequently with his mother, he explains to the boys how the hardships she endured in the past made her so tough. But Hollywood Harry and his sidekick are staking out the house, and Louie has to give them the slip. This he does successfully, but not before Bella makes him attend a family showdown, where she announces her intention to marry John and open a restaurant. To Bella's dismay, Grandma refuses to give her approval, and neither Louie nor her sister Gert back her up. Determined to marry anyway, Bella runs away but John is too scared to leave his parents. She returns to confront her mother, who admits to shutting down emotionally after the death of her first two children. After a first few months, Eddie, having saved enough money to pay off his debts, comes back to collect the kids. Though Jay and Arty have learned to respect, if not like, their grandmother, they are sorry to leave Bella, who is becoming more independent. Later, they learn that Bella has left home and started a new life in Florida.

Lost in Yonkers is Neil Simon in gently nostalgic *Brighton Beach Memoirs* mode, and as such is exactly what you'd expect: a bitter-sweet home movie drizzled with wisecracks and wry observations, flawlessly acted and utterly predictable. This is the fourth or fifth time Simon has revisited his childhood, and his generic 15-year-old protagonist is beginning to seem mighty familiar—though Jay here is not an aspiring writer, just an ordinary, reasonably sane Jewish kid in a world of wacky adults. Thirty years ago, Simon used to write bitingly funny farces such as *The Odd Couple*; these days he seems to have retreated into a haze of comfortable memories, where all characters are colourful and no-one is truly bad, just misunderstood. There is something to be said for such a decent, humane world-view, and many people respond to it: as a Broadway play, *Lost in Yonkers* won a Pulitzer Prize. But it is so relentlessly even-handed, it's exhausting. The film starts out promising a villain of epic proportions in Grandma Kurnitz, and even uses the hokey device of keeping her off-screen until her fearsome reputation is established. Eddie, nervous and sweating, dreads asking her to keep his sons, and he frets and fusses at the boys until they get jumpy too. By the time they reach the candy store they are too scared to touch anything, even to eat the hot fudge sundaes that Bella eagerly whips up for them. But when Grandma finally appears, she is not a monster—just a tough, capable woman with a German accent. She won't make allowances for other people's weakness because she won't admit her own, and she mocks Eddie precisely because he's not like her. Irene Worth makes you feel that she's earned that right, and even gives her a sly sense of humour to flaunt it with. Her actual selfishness and cruelty towards Bella, therefore does not seem as awful as it should. And without someone to loathe, the picture just burbles along—like Jay and Arty's ten-month visit, it's no more than a diversion.

Once the boys and Grandma settle into a live-and-let-live routine, the crux of the film shifts to Bella's struggle for independence. Simon is nothing if not professional, and he makes Bella's hopeful marriage announcement poignant enough. His grip only slips when Bella tells her mother that massaging her legs all these years has been like touching "cold, unfeeling marble", and you wonder whether the words belong to Bella or to the old playwright. But this is hardly fresh material, and Bella's loving nature and mental limitations—she's a teenage girl in a woman's body—add a dangerous extra layer of pathos. Fortunately, Mercedes Ruehl gives the character a jaunty optimism that prevents her from becoming cloying—she strides down the street in flimsy, figure-hugging dresses and ankle socks as if she's expecting something good to be right around the corner. Still, there is something a little ingratiating about the scenes between Bella and Johnny; you can't quite shake the feeling that the film-makers are trying to sell you a view of the mentally handicapped as somehow unspoiled, innately more honest and open-hearted than corrupt, self-serving normal people.

Just as things are getting irredeemably cosy, the arrival of Uncle Louis gives the film a lift. Louie's the kind of fast-talking show-off the picture needs, and Richard Dreyfuss, his foxy little eyes gleaming with mischief, barrels onto the scene as if his were the only performance that mattered. But then he leaves without having contributed substantially to the story, and you wonder whether he was meant as anything other than mid-movie entertainment.

In fact, none of the elements of the story seem to amount to much. Martha Coolidge, whose previous film was the well-received *Rambling Rose*, is fast becoming known as an 'actors' director'; which means that she imposes no particular style on the proceedings. She does a sober, unobtrusive job that's also a little dull—she gives the actors their head and respects Simon's prose. You laugh a little, you cry a little, you admire the skill with which everything is put together. There is no doubt that *Lost in Yonkers* is a quality product. But then, so is a good piece of luggage.

TIME, 5/24/93, p. 80, Richard Schickel

One mean mother (Irene Worth); her 36-year-old daughter (Mercedes Ruehl), whom the mother has contrived to keep in a state of childish dependency; and a rebel son (Richard Dreyfuss), who has become a gangster: confine just these three most colorful members of the Kurnitz family in a small space (the apartment above Mom's candy store in Yonkers, circa 1942), and claustrophobia begins to itch at one's soul. Add a couple of lively boys, Jay and Arty (Brad Stoll and Mike Damus), forced by circumstances to live with Grandma for the worst part of a year. All are damaged in less than amusing ways, and after a couple of hours it begins to feel as if they've pumped all the air out of the theater.

Neil Simon's adaptation of his Pulitzer prizewinning play is, as one might expect, entirely respectful of the original (his boldest creative stroke is working his own name into the movie's title). Director Coolidge, who did a fine job with another eccentric family in *Rambling Rose*, moves quite gracefully within the confines of a piece only minimally "opened up" for the screen. Ruehl has two poignant arias announcing her realization of what her mother has done to her. Dreyfuss spritzes high-spirited resentment, and Worth's steely old woman, determined not to show softness to anyone, is a powerful presence. Such suspense as the film displays derives from the question of whether someone, somehow can crack her open.

Nevertheless, for all its professionalism and occasional felicities, you suspect that *Lost in Yonkers* worked better on the stage. One generally wants to maintain a certain distance from dysfunction; you don't want it leaping across the footlights to land, falsely grinning, falsely ingratiating, in your lap. But it is, of course, precisely the camera's business to facilitate such leaps. Even so, if these people had any real charm, if their oddity were cloaked in wit, if their rather chilly creator brought some real compassion to these sealed-off lives, we might take them more readily to heart. If they suggested some generalized insights about lower-middle-class life, we might more readily forgive their dreary excesses. And if wishing could make it so, Neil Simon would be Anton Chekov's authentic, instead of his merely aspiring, heir. Which would make this a much better world to live in.

VILLAGE VOICE, 5/25/93, p. 54, Georgia Brown,

Cut to the New World, 1942. [The reference is to *Sofie*; see Brown's review.] In Neil Simon's *Lost in Yonkers*. Bella Kurnitz (Mercedes Ruehl), 36-year-old Jewish maiden and designated spinster, stays home caring for her sadistic mother (Irene Worth), a Jewish dictator who talks like Henry Kissinger. This apparently semi-autobiographical film is based (was I surprised!) on a Pulitzer Prize-winning play. It takes place during the extended visit to grandma's house of Jay and Arty, teenage sons of the timid, defeated Eddie, who has left to chase a job selling scrap metal The gist of this magnificently cliché-ridden Martha Coolidge-directed movie is that Jay and Arty learn valuable lessons from the generous, childlike Bella and from their gruff but lively Uncle Louie (Richard Dreyfuss), a small-time gangster who comes home to hide out. The boys even learn from Grandma. This, I gather, is the way things go in the theater.

About the time her nephews arrive, Bella, a child in a woman's body, falls for Johnny (David Strathairn), usher at the local Bijou and a very young child in a man's body. (Poor Strathairn, one of the sexiest-looking actors, has been stuck recently playing very backward gents; he was Rennie in *Passion Fish*.) Anyway, his speed and Bella's initially seem not all that incompatible, but then it seems they are.

One of the script's ironies is that Erich von Grandma—she specializes in reducing people to tears and then mocking them for crying—is the proprietor of the ultimate old-fashioned candy shoppe. So she's a witch, of the Hansel and Gretel variety. Reputedly, her rotten disposition was formed when a horse fell on her leg and she suffered much pain. Although the kids make a lot of noise about how fearsome she is, they seem generally impervious.

Lost in Yonkers will probably be a hit in Florida malls but it's hard to imagine the young and movie-literate relishing such hokey theatrics. One repeated convention requires a character to break into an extended, impassioned monologue telling off one of the other characters and defending his/her own right to exist. Then he/she is praised by the one he/she has just told off, congratulated on having gumption, grit, guts, or, worst of all, "moxie." The moxie bit—first performed by Dreyfuss and then imitated by one of the kids—is truly revolting.

Also reviewed in:
CHICAGO TRIBUNE, 5/14/93, Friday/p. A, Dave Kehr
NEW YORK TIMES, 5/14/93, p. C10, Janet Maslin
VARIETY, 5/10/93, p. 236, Todd McCarthy
WASHINGTON POST, 5/14/93, p. B1, Rita Kempley
WASHINGTON POST, 5/14/93, Weekend/p. 44, Desson Howe

LOVE YOUR MAMA

A Hemdale Communications release of an Oliver Productions film. *Producer:* Ruby L. Oliver. *Director:* Ruby L. Oliver. *Screenplay:* Ruby L. Oliver. *Director of Photography:* Ronald Courtney. *Editor:* Joy L. Rencher. *Music:* John Van Allen, Jr. and Markian Fedorowycz. *Sound:* Jacob D. Collins. *Casting:* Ruby L. Oliver. *Set Decorator:* Ruby L. Oliver. *Costumes:* Patsy Maxson. *Make-up:* Anna Intravartolo. *Running time:* 93 minutes. *MPAA Rating:* PG-13.

CAST: Carol E. Hall (Leola); Audrey Morgan (Mama); André Robinson (Wren); Earnest III Rayford (Sam); Kearo Johnson (Willie); Artavia Wright (Lois); Jacqueline Williams (Barbara); Kevin C. White (Bob); Norman D. Hoosier (Zeek); Glenn B. Collins (Jimmy); Linda Roberson (Helena); Mario Andre (Bartender); Pat "Soul" Scaggs (Candy); Darryl A. Reed (Dr. Penn); Tina M. Wright (Hospital Clerk); Charlotte Bitoy (Hospital Nurse #1); Meg Guttman (Hospital Nurse #2); Jan Branion Wethers (Community Clinic Nurse); Clinton B. Fields, Sr. (Car Driver); Michael Martin (Car Driver's Helper); Alyson G. Marsalis (Crying Lady); Pauline U. Lampkin (Neighbor); Michael D. Lampkin (Neighbor's Baby); Cliff Frazier (Church Minister); Edgar C. Douglas (Deacon Green); Delores Jones Hudson (Church Singer); Clifford Bradley (Church Piano Player); Brenda Mathews (Church Lady #1); Glorisa J. Jackson (Church Lady #2); Janet Jackson (Nursery School Teacher); DeLiece M. Keenon (Leola's Baby); Janielle Gooden and Danielle Gooden (Leola's Preschool Child); Debra J. Stone (Ms. Higgins); Cliff Frazier (Mr. Craig); Alison D. Halstead (High School Teacher); James C. Jackson (Big Daddy); Oscar Carr (Postman); William J. Ammons (Banker #1); Arthur J. Benjamin (Banker #2); Tamara M. Tombs (Teenager #1); Joan B. Ruffin (Teenager #2); Dan Zellner (State Director, DCFS); Jackie Samuel (State Supervisor, DCFS); Leona W. Toppel (State Worker, DCFS); James E. Files (Noisy Man); Frank Dominelli (Policeman); Patrick M.J. Finerty (Detective #1); David M. Daniels (Detective #2); Karel King (Detective #3); Michael Brazil (Detective #4).

LOS ANGELES TIMES, 3/5/93, Calendar/p. 12, Michael Wilmington

Pity the poor, all-too-jaded critic confronted with a movie like "Love Your Mama." Bashing it would be like trashing Santa Claus. Or your mama.

It's about motherhood, sticking together and fighting for your dream; about the seemingly endless trials and tribulations of a struggling African-American family in Chicago's ghetto and how they finally break through. And it's the feature debut of filmmaker Ruby L. Oliver, who spent more than 23 years operating day-care centers in that same ghetto, then retired, worked her way through Columbia College Film School, graduated with honors and, finally, scrapped together the $500,000 budget to make "Mama."

Talk about awesome energy. Not only did Oliver produce, direct and write the movie, but she scouted the locations and decorated the sets. And her intentions are the best: "Love Your Mama" details the plight and triumph of the Brown family—which include an alcoholic, philandering father: an unwed pregnant daughter; a car-boosting son paralyzed in a police gun-down—and it's intended to instill faith, hope and courage in its audiences, help them battle through the dangers and frustrations of big-city ghetto life.

How can you say anything bad about a project like this, without coming across like one of the grouches in the movie. all those over-smug bank officers who keep turning down the loan applications of Mama and her daughter Leola for *their* day-care center?

Fortunately, "Love Your Mama" is a movie that wears down your resistance. When I saw it last year at AFIFEST, it struck me as amateurish and overstated, awkwardly written and far too obviously staged and acted. Seeing it again, I'm convinced I was hasty, culturally and morally wrong, and maybe artistically wrong as well.

"Love Your Mama" simply shouldn't be judged by the standards we use for polished medium or big-budget professional productions, because that's what it *isn't*—though, in her photography (by Ronald Courtney) and editing, Oliver has succeeded admirably in getting it to *look* like one. It was shot in the area around 35th and 40th streets in Chicago's Lower South Side and the female lead, Carol E. Hall as Leola, is a Chicago first grade teacher who does acting and modeling on the side.

Most of the rest of the actors, including wonderful, full-throated Audrey Morgan as magisterial Mama, are making their film debuts. And, considering that, the cast—especially Hall, Morgan, André Robinson, Earnest III Rayford, Kearo Johnson and Artavia Wright as the Brown family and Jacqueline Williams as Leola's bumptious buddy—deserve praise.

"Love Your Mama" is not exactly sophisticated or deep. Its dramatic style is more clearly influenced by TV soap operas than anything else. The delivery of the actors is often so measured—and so loud—that they suggest an enthusiastic little theater group playing to the back of a very large house.

But it's got heart and drive and spirit, and it doesn't hold back. If Oliver isn't speaking in the cadences of the savvy pro, at least she's talking about what she sees and knows. If there's melodrama or overstatement in that speech, and a kind of fairy-tale wish-fulfillment in the magical climax—the key, apparently is finding the right bank officer—then somehow it fits.

What the movie does have is a crystal-clear style, in which everything seems bathed in sharp sunlight: warm, open, unabashed, truly sincere. Oliver often holds her camera tight and still on an actor in a heavy emotional scene and the actors, especially Morgan and Hall, break down, weep real tears.

Something in Oliver's dramatic style probably reflects her background in day care. As a filmmaker, she speaks in the same cheerful, careful, over-enunciated tone teachers use with their small charges; it's probably no accident that one of "Love Your Mama's" best scenes is *in* a day-care center, full of lively, happy kids. Is it objectionable for a movie to speak to us as if we were children? Not necessarily. Remember where "Love Your Mama" (MPAA-rated: PG-13) came from, and whom it's talking to, and its spirit-raising, uplifting little ghetto song will reach you.

NEW YORK POST, 3/5/93, p. 32, Jami Bernard

The only reason why it would be unfair to call "Love Your Mama" the worst movie ever made is that awful movies are usually fun in their own way. This one isn't.

Anyway, I am not so sure this is a bona fide movie. Yes, it has been executed with the aid of a camera and presumably, a script, but "Love Your Mama" has no relevance to the world of film as we know it. That it was financed by a church and by a day-care center that appears in the film shows it to be a vanity production of the worst order.

The material is very earnest and well-intended, which only heightens the cringe factor.

Ruby L. Oliver, a day-care center entrepreneur who overcame many obstacles in her own life to achieve her goals, has turned her attentions to writing, producing and directing this movie. There are so few movies about the black urban female experience that I hate to discourage her, but Ruby, keep your day-care job. The rest of you, save your money until "Just Another Girl on the IRT" opens.

"Love Your Mama" is about a black teen-ager (Carol E. Hall) who wants to finish school and open a day-care center, but is mired in the pitfalls of lower-class family life, racism, pregnancy and an extremely literal-minded and stultifying script. Her mama—Audrey Morgan, showing emotion by alternately slitting and rolling her eyes while shouting a lot—is trying to make a go of things with a no-good husband and some no-good kids. One of those kids goes into a coma and recovers fully.

"I gave birth to you, I know your smell and your handwriting!" screams the supposedly wise mama at her dull, thieving children.

Scene after relentless scene shows mama setting a poor example for the kids and then yelling at them, when she is not kneeling at a crackpot storefront church to pray for "a miracle." The camera is always in the wrong place and the movie has no clear point of view, among its endless list of faults.

Even the lousiest exploitation movie at least has some style. "Love Your Mama" should be shown to legislators to convince them to take video camcorders off the market; in the wrong hands, a camera can be a deadly weapon.

NEWSDAY, 3/5/93, Part II/p. 65, Gene Seymour

If "Love Your Mama" were a human being instead of a movie, it would be this sweet, gawky adolescent, tripping on its feet and bursting with so many important and earnest things to say that it can barely contain the urge to shout them all out in a torrential clutter of unbuttoned feelings.

As with such awkward-age children, you keep trying to goad "Love Your Mama" to get a grip, chill out. But this tale of an African-American family's struggle to survive on Chicago's mean streets sprawls, sags and bends all over the place. First-time director Ruby L. Oliver, who also produced and wrote the script, doesn't always seem to know what to leave in her story and what to take out.

The four children of stoic, devout and long-suffering Mama (Audrey Morgan), aren't alone in wondering why she continues to let her ne'er-do-well husband (Earnest III Rayford) stay in the same house after brazenly, if drunkenly inviting his girlfriends home to visit. Nor is it clear why, after finding a car-break-in tool she suspects belongs to her teenage son (André Robinson) and his kid brother (Kearo Johnson), she doesn't put them both under house arrest.

In the meantime, we know all we need to about taking high-school equivalency tests as they affect the uncertain future of her daughter (Carol E. Hall), the good student and aspiring day-care, entrepreneur, whose plans are clouded when she becomes pregnant by the neighborhood musician.

A few of Oliver's observations strike home. (One of Mama's more telling threats to an unruly son is, "I'm gonna kill you before the white man does!") And she is fortunate to have Morgan, whose presence alone brings authenticity to the film. But the characterizations, like the plot, lack the focus and careful construction that would earn the film the uplifting response it so desperately seeks from its audience.

VILLAGE VOICE, 3/23/93, p. 61, Carol Cooper

You might think that if you've seen one black bootstrapping melodrama you've seen 'em all (beginning with Lorraine Hansberry's archetypal *A Raisin in the Sun*). But, in *Love Your Mama*, writer-director-producer Ruby L. Oliver handles this well-worked terrain with flair, confidence, and a sense of humor.

There's a school of contemporary black filmmaking that for the sake of expediency I'll call hyper-realism. It pushes "social realism" to an extreme undreamt of by generations of earnest lefties, and can be a little hard to take if you're not fond of pathos as an aesthetic motivation. There is, unfortunately, much about black reality that is pathetic, and hyper-realism is the Easter-pageant deification of that reality. Most black people don't like being reminded that they are only one or two relatives removed from "the ghetto." Indigent relations pepper the families of almost everyone we know, so that the convenience of "forgetting where you came from" is an impossibility.

What Oliver brings to this dynamic is a conviction that familial pathology can be transformed by love and hard labor. At the point where the average soap opera would have characters die off, give up, or eject dysfunctional family members in disgust, Mama forces her brood to work within the fact that they have only each other to depend on. Religion is slyly critiqued, but is also depict-ed as a comfort. Oliver, herself a preacher's daughter, obviously has read her Job.

Although this movie has the virtue of being about things and people its director knows well, it lets a few laughably two-dimensional performances slip in amongst the supporting cast. In its imperfect execution, *Love Your Mama* has much in common with traveling black community theater pieces like *Mama Don't, Whatever Happened To Black Love?*, and *Beauty Shop*, parts one and two. Made for working-class audiences who like their humor broad and their stories simple, these serve up Sunday-school moralizing laced with self-help propaganda and down-home attitudes in an unstable world. What they lack in production values they make up for in sincerity—and steady ticket sales. Which is why college-trained sophisticates who might ordinarily chortle at corn-pone culture like *Love Your Mama* are advised not to scoff.

Also reviewed in:
NEW YORK TIMES, 3/5/93, p. C14, Vincent Canby
VARIETY, 1/7/91, p. 26
WASHINGTON POST, 3/6/93, p. B8, Rita Kempley

M. BUTTERFLY

A Warner Bros. release of a Geffen Pictures production. *Executive Producer:* David Henry Hwang and Philip Sandhaus. *Producer:* Gabriella Martinelli. *Director:* David Cronenberg. *Screenplay (Based on his play):* David Henry Hwang. *Director of Photography:* Peter Suschitzky. *Editor:* Ronald Sanders. *Music:* Howard Shore. *Music Editor:* Suzana Peric. *Sound:* Bryan Day and (music) John Kurlander. *Casting:* Deirdre Bowen, Joanna Merlin, Doreen Jones, and Karoly Kupics. *Production Designer:* Carol Spier. *Art Director:* James McAteer. *Set Decorator:* Elinor Rose Galbraith. *Costumes:* Denise Cronenberg. *Set Dresser:* Clive Thomasson, Peter Nicolakakos, and E.C. Whelan. *Special Effects:* Georges Demetrau. *Costumes:* Denise Cronenberg. *Make-up:* Suzanne Benoit, Allen Weisinger, Ava Stone, Julia Fenyvessy, and Antoine Garabedian. *Stunt Coordinator:* Bela Unger. *Running time:* 100 minutes. *MPAA Rating:* R.

CAST: Jeremy Irons (René Gallimard); John Lone (Song Liling); Ian Richardson (Ambassador Toulon); Annabel Leventon (Frau Baden); Shizuko Hoshi (Comrade Chin); Richard McMillan (Embassy Colleague); Vernon Dobtcheff (Agent Etancelin); Barbara Sukowa (Jeanne Gallimard); David Hemblen, Damir Andrei, and Antony Parr (Intelligence Officers); Margaret Ma (Song's Maid); Tristram Jellinek (Defense Attorney); Philip McGough (Prosecution Attorney); David Neal (Judge); Sean Hewitt (Ambassador's Aide); Peter Mesaline (Diplomat at Party); Michael Mehlmann (Drunk in Paris Bar); Barbara Chilcott (Critic at Garden Party); George Jonas (Mall Trustee); Carl Zvonkin (Surveilance Technician); Victor Fulop (Marshall); Cadman Chui (Accordian Player); Beijing Opera Troupe (Beijing Opera Performers); Maria Teresa Uribe (Paris Opera Madama Butterfly).

LOS ANGELES TIMES, 10/1/93, Calendar/p. 1, Kenneth Turan

Dazzling and multicolored as a play, "M. Butterfly" has unaccountably been turned into a drab moth of a film. Despite starring Jeremy Irons and being directed by David Cronenberg, whose entire out-put from "Scanners" and "The Fly" to "Dead Ringers" and "Naked Lunch" has been an attempt to get one step beyond the ordinary, "Butterfly" is a determinedly pedestrian affair, sure to make anyone approaching the material for the first time wonder what the fuss was about.

And a great deal of fuss there certainly, has been. When a French diplomat was arrested and accused of spying in 1986, the news that he had no idea that his Chinese co-conspirator and lover for 20 years, the woman he thought had borne him a son, was in fact a man, made headlines around the world and didn't do much for France's reputation as the home of savoir-faire.

Playwright David Henry Hwang was so taken by that tale that he used it as the basis for his drama "M. Butterfly," a multiple Tony winner (including best play) for its Broadway production and subsequently performed in more than 30 countries.

What was good enough for all those sovereign nations, however, was regrettably deemed insufficient for Hollywood. The problem is not the presence of anything sacred in the play, but that in the process of turning it upside down and reversing its focus Cronenberg and Hwang, who also wrote the screenplay, have managed to misplace all the considerable magic the original possessed.

The key to the play's success was its joint audacity and theatricality. It opened with the diplomat, renamed Rene Gallimard, admitting that the public revelations of his private life have made him an international laughingstock. But instead of being timid about things, Gallimard is brash and confrontational, insisting that he will persuade everyone that "in China I once loved, and was loved by, the perfect woman."

What follows is as much an exciting philosophical meditation on the nature of love and sexuality as a blow by blow retelling of Gallimard's relationship with Chinese opera singer Song Liling. The story is further energized by the conflict between what your eyes tell you are seeing and what you know the truth to be.

For reasons that are more shrouded in mystery than Song Liling's sexuality, the movie has chosen to reverse all of this, carefully taking the tension out of the story by telling it in a straightforward way. The result is a kind of Asian "Crying Game" except that everyone who cares knows the secret going in. And that wonderful line about being loved by the perfect woman doesn't set things up, but comes as a kind of limp coda at the tepid finale.

Even the film version's nominal advantage of being able to re-create the physical world "M. Butterfly" (rated R for sexuality and a brief bloody sequence) took place in does not add any excitement. Gallimard is introduced on site as a functionary at the French Embassy in Beijing in 1964, a low-level bureaucrat who vets the expense accounts of more senior men.

Complacently married to Jeanne (Barbara Sukowa, wasted like everyone else), Gallimard stops off at an embassy party one night and sits transfixed as Chinese opera singer Song Liling (John Lone) runs through some arias from Puccini's "Madama Butterfly." Meeting the singer afterward, he is entranced by her tart analysis of why Westerners all love the opera. "I've never seen a performance as convincing as yours," he says, which turns out to be a considerable understatement.

As presented by Cronenberg and Hwang, the relationship between these two plays out like a conventional extramarital affair. After bulling his way through Song Liling's protestations of sexual innocence (though always allowing her to remain fully clothed), Gallimard starts to delude himself that he knows something about Eastern ways of thinking, a situation his surprising promotion at the embassy only encourages. It is all fated to end badly, and it surely does.

Jeremy Irons, who gave perhaps the performance of his career as identical twin gynecologists in Cronenberg's "Dead Ringers," plays Gallimard in a kind of a daze. And though B.D. Wong, who won a Tony as Song Liling (and was last seen on the big screen as a scientist in "Jurassic Park"), gave the role an engaging sauciness on stage, John Lone ("Iceman," "The Last Emperor") has chosen to play it quite somberly, which further deadens a not very lively film.

Also hampering Lone is the fact that movies are a more realistic medium than theater, and the illusion that he is she is harder to create. Lone looks androgynous at best on the big screen, never totally feminine, which makes the filmmakers' attempts to mask that fact seem especially silly. After sitting through "M. Butterfly," you'll wonder why they even bothered to try.

NEW YORK, 10/18/93, p. 121, David Denby

In *M. Butterfly*, a French diplomat (Jeremy Irons) falls in love with someone whom he takes to be the perfect woman (the highly male John Lone), makes love to her for years, and discovers that she's a man. In the movie that David Henry Hwang has written from his own play, only the cattily amusing Ian Richardson seems to understand that the material cannot be done poker-faced. Apart from Richardson, there's not one joke, not one moment of wickedness—nothing but muffled romanticism and sterile aperçus about "imperialism" and a laughably academic manipulation of Puccini's kitsch masterpiece. David Cronenberg's direction is solemn and dead, and Irons, miscast again as an obsessive lover, seems so uneasy in his own body that one can almost believe he would become confused when exploring another's.

NEWSDAY, 10/1/93, Part II/p. 61, John Anderson

China, 1964, and Rene Gallimard (Jeremy Irons), wartless, antiseptic French embassy drone, is backstage at the Peking Opera, walking a gauntlet of painted faces startled by his presence. He's startled, too: startled to be there, startled to be in illicit romantic pursuit of a Chinese opera star and, under it all, thrilled to be making this libidinous cross-cultural leap.

Culture, of course, isn't the only line he's crossing.

"M. Butterfly"—David Henry Hwang's successful Broadway play, and now David Cronenberg's curiously icy film—is based on the true-life scandal, which concerned a French diplomat who ended up spying for the Chinese during an 18-year affair with a lover he never realized was a man. We realize it, however, and immediately. To all but the cheerfully deceived, John Lone, as Rene's love interest, Song Liling, is as convincing a transvestite as Winona Ryder in a lumberjack outfit. But Cronenberg has dispensed with any "Crying Game" subterfuge, going so far as to give us closeups of Lone's beard stubble. The real point is Rene's western fantasies, so overripe he'll believe anything, including Song Liling.

Rene, pathetic dope that he is, has no idea he's harboring these fantasies—about the pliant, adoring "Oriental" woman and love slave—until Song Liling plays him like a well-oiled zither.

"Madama Butterfly," which Rene hears Song sing one night at an embassy affair, is an imperialistic sex dream, she tells him, a hegemonious hot flash. He demures, but it's clear from their ensuing romance that Song, who is a spy, is right, and that her intentions for him are treasonous.

While Song is setting him up for the professional kill—he'll tell her about American troop movements in Vietnam, she'll mislead him about Asian political sentiment—he thinks he's playing expert sexual politics: Receiving letters that are progressively pleading, angry and desperate, he ignores her, then relents, and finally becomes Song's lover. Gentleman that he is, Rene remains ever respectful of Song's modesty, which is concealing quite a bit.

"China is a culture whose soul is rooted firmly two thousand years in the past," Song tells him. "Even my pouring you tea has implications ..." Rene is swept away. His colorless existence—he's basically an accountant whose colleagues hate him for rejecting their expense reports—becomes full-blooded. His Peking nights take on the gauzy quality of a cold dream. When his wife (Barbara Sukowa) questions where he's been all night, he instinctively lies, telling her he was out drinking. But he's really drunk on lust, and the affirmation, via Song's feigned adoration, of his manhood. "Are you my Butterfly?" he asks her. "I want you to say it ..." Rene comes to life via this affair, which is good, because Hwang and Cronenberg don't give us very much about him to start with. The humiliation of Rene—Song eventually makes him think he's fathered their child—is relentless, but it would have been more effective if Rene had been more of a person first, an object of ridicule second. Irons does accomplish something neat, by making us painfully aware of his character's lack of self-awareness. And the film is moving, precisely because his realization of his own self-deception comes so tragically late.

Lone, who is alternately sinister and grieved, plays a problematic Song Liling: Although he's being coerced into spying by the Communists, his sense of satisfaction in betraying Rene seems very real. And it makes their final confrontation absolutely chilling. By then, however, there's been enough chill in "M. Butterfly." Cronenberg should have given us more passion, maybe more Puccini.

SIGHT AND SOUND, 5/94, p. 44, John Harkness

Beijing. René Gallimard, a mid-level functionary in France's legation to China, attends a diplomatic reception. At the party, he is struck by the beauty of a rendition of Cio-Cio San's aria from Puccini's *Madame Butterfly* by a performer from the Beijing Opera. He has never heard the opera before, but the performance and the music move him. He meets the performer, Song Liling, and compliments her. She belittles his taste as the product of a bourgeois colonialist mentality, and invites him to attend the Beijing Opera—"to further your education." Returning home, he discusses the evening with his wife, not mentioning his attraction to Song Liling.

Gallimard begins to pursue Song Liling, attending her performances at the Beijing Opera, visiting her home, exchanging letters. At his work, the intelligence operatives belittle him as a mere accountant, but his diligence does not go unrewarded, and he rises in the embassy. His promotion emboldens him, and Gallimard pursues Song Liling more diligently, apparently never wondering why the woman of his dreams will not remove her clothes in his presence, even while they are having sex. Song Liling is visited by her control; her affair with Gallimard is being controlled by Chinese intelligence, who find the imposture repugnant. She tells Gallimard that she is pregnant, and produces a child in the midst of the Cultural Revolution, at the very moment when Gallimard returns to France and she is sent to a re-education camp.

Now separated from his wife, Gallimard mopes around Paris, living in a pathetic room and attending performances of *Madame Butterfly*. One night, following a riot by Parisian Maoists, he returns to his apartment to find Song Liling. He finds work as a government courier, carrying sensitive documents and passing them to Chinese intelligence. Gallimard and Song Liling are arrested and tried. The prosecutors are dumbfounded by the idea that Gallimard did not know that Song Liling was really a man. In prison, before an audience of convicts, Gallimard paints his face as a Beijing Opera performer, delivers a monologue on his suffering, and commits suicide.

David Cronenberg's film of Henry David Hwang's hit play *M. Butterfly* stands as the director's most perverse gesture towards the mainstream. *M. Butterfly* falls into the broad genre of award-winning film-making—an impeccably literary subject adapted by the original author using exotic location, and starring both Academy Award-winning Jeremy Irons and John Lone, star of Bertolucci's *The Last Emperor*, the biggest Oscar winner of the modern era.

In its longing for respectability, *M. Butterfly* has a certain kinship with Scorsese's *Age of Innocence*, but if Scorsese's characters create their problems by repressing their emotional impulses, Cronenberg's create their problems by giving in to them. Discussions of *M. Butterfly* have tended so far to centre on what the film lacks, but rather, the real problem lies in what it *has*—in the way that the chill of Cronenberg's work here achieves a truly cryogenic quality. Cronenberg's problem with audiences derives less from the strangeness of his material than from the clinical detachment of his style, and his fondness for such emotionally remote actors as Christopher Walken, James Woods and Jeremy Irons. The typical Cronenberg chill was offset by the considerable warmth of Jeff Goldblum and Geena Davis in what turned out to be his biggest hit, *The Fly*.

Based on the true story of a French diplomat who had a 20-year affair with a female impersonator from the Beijing Opera who worked for Chinese intelligence, David Henry Hwang's play functions as a didactic reply to the West's Madame Butterfly stereotypes about Asian women. Hwang's play has a preaching quality absent from Cronenberg's work, and one wonders where Hwang has found this obsession with submissive Asian women in Western culture. Usually, if something exists within the popular consciousness, it will somewhere be manifest in the popular culture, yet it's hard to see that the stereotype and obsession have shown up in Anglo-Saxon culture since the late 50s (*South Pacific, The World of Susie Wong*). One wonders what Hwang thinks of the films of Mizoguchi and Naruse, so many of which concentrate on submissive, stoically enduring women.

The easy comparison would be to *The Crying Game* (apparently, the diplomat never realised that his butterfly, like all the Beijing Opera performers, was a man). But where the surprise revelation in Neil Jordan's film has a narrative function and emotional importance, Cronenberg makes no attempt to convince the audience of John Lone's femininity. Cronenberg offers the spectacle of a man creating an imaginative universe in his own image—which for all the film's Broadway roots puts *M. Butterfly* in the same thematic boat as *Videodrome* and *Naked Lunch*. One admires the result—the precision of Irons' performance, Carol Spier's extraordinary art direction, which makes Beijing look like a suburb of *Naked Lunch*'s Interzone, and the seamless privacy of the film's world. But one doesn't enjoy it, and I speak as someone who enjoys Cronenberg's films very much.

Cronenberg and Hwang's sensibilities offer as startling a mismatch as Bernard Haitink's recordings of Shostakovitch's symphonies—the playing has an impeccable polish, but there's all this stuff trapped underneath, screaming to get out. Cronenberg has an abiding interest in the structure of repression rather than in currently fashionable questions of multiculturalism and gender, and in his best films, all that stuff gets out, usually in the form of mutation and/or madness. The infant assassins of *The Brood*, the paranoid universe inhabited by James Woods in *Videodrome* and Peter Weller in *Naked Lunch*, the *folie à deux* of the doctors in *Dead Ringers*, all demonstrate what happens when people suppress their darker impulses—they emerge on their own.

The film's final confrontation between Lone and Irons tries to get the bad stuff out, but it doesn't really succeed. *M. Butterfly*'s climactic scene, which seeks admission into the world of Cronenbergian transformation, works as a *coup de théâtre*, but seems miles removed from the world of the film that we've seen.

TIME, 10/4/93, p. 87, Richard Corliss

When East meets West in movies, everything can get blurred: male and female, sex and love, performance and reality. In two new films about China, the gender lines are so tangled that it's hard to tell yin from yang. But it's easy to tell hit from miss. *Farewell My Concubine*, Chen Kaige's Chinese film that won a top prize at Cannes this year before being briefly suppressed by the Chinese government, is a gorgeous, galvanizing epic with starmaking turns. *M. Butterfly*, the David Cronenberg film of David Henry Hwang's Broadway play, fumbles its romantic and political metaphors and loses the game.

Hwang's play was based on the incredible-but-true story of a French diplomatic attaché in Beijing who conducted a 17-year sexual affair with a Chinese spy posing as an opera singer and never suspected that the lady was a man. (According to *Liaison*, Joyce Wadler's fascinating new biography of the diplomat, the opera singer was able to fold his genitals inside his body, thus giving the naked illusion of femininity.) From this *International Enquirer* item, Hwang spun a phantasm of multiple myopia: a man preposterously blinded by love, a European culture blinkered by imperialist prejudice in its view of the mystic East.

On the stage, John Dexter's sumptuously stylized production transformed tabloid headlines into a potent truism: that the heart sees what it sees. On-screen, the opera singer's gender is never in question; his 5 o'clock shadow gives him away to everyone but the diplomat. Jeremy Irons tries manfully, and John Lone womanfully, to give real life to the characters, but the close-ups defeat them. So do some unlikely plot points: the defendant and his accuser are put alone to undress and wrestle in a police wagon; the diplomat daubs himself as Madama Butterfly before a rapt audience of French convicts! Cronenberg is unlikely to find other spectators as gullible as they.

If only Leslie Cheung, the beautifully androgynous star of *Farewell My Concubine*, had been cast as the singer in *M. Butterfly*; in his delicacy and passion, he is enough woman for any man to fall for. But then Cheung, a Hong Kong actor living in Vancouver, might not have been available for the role of his career. As Cheng Dieyi, a homosexual star of the Peking Opera who is driven by jealousy when his "stage brother" Duan Xiaolou (Zhang Fengyi) marries a call girl (Gong Li), Cheung is both steely and vulnerable, with a sexuality that transcends gender—a Mandarin Michael Jackson.

Three pairs of actors play Cheng and Duan: as children and then teenagers in the Peking Opera School and finally as adults. Imagine that one of those showbiz sagas about performers who can harmonize only on stage—*For the Boys* or *The Sunshine Boys*—had begun when the main characters really were boys, and continued for 53 years of love, comradeship and betrayal. *Concubine* (cut by about 15 minutes for U.S. release, but still a rich and savory 2½-hour banquet) hopscotches from the warlord era to the Japanese occupation to the Cultural Revolution and beyond. And under each regime, the artist is a pampered slave: flogged by his teachers, adored by his audience, toyed with by the élite, denounced by Mao's vindictive masses—and always asked to do that showstopper, the fable about the king and his faithful concubine, just one more time.

Concubine is an Eastern film whose subject, scope and nonstop bustle will be agreeable to Western moviegoers. Anyone can appreciate the splendor of the theatrical pageantry or the dagger eyes of Gong Li, as a dragon lady whose only commandment is survival. The scenes in the Peking Opera School, where boys are caned for doing wrong *or* right, are no less horrifying than the later tableaus of public humiliation at the hands of the Maoists. But Chen clearly sympathizes with the schoolmasters. From such brutality, he suggests, artists are created. *Concubine* offers another moral: From the crushing cultural restrictions of the People's Republic, vibrant popular art like this can emerge.

VILLAGE VOICE, 10/5/93, p. 49, J. Hoberman

The only shocker in David Cronenberg's adaptation of the Broadway hit *M. Butterfly* is its overall sobriety. For an interracial, gender-bending love story laden with political implications and directed by the erstwhile "king of venereal horror," *M. Butterfly* has a marked lack of affect—let alone delirium.

M. Butterfly, which Warners opens here Friday, comes scarcely free of cultural baggage. The movie reworks David Henry Hwang's widely praised play, a fiction itself inspired by an international hoot, the notorious Boursicot scandal: a French junior diplomat was driven to spying during the course of an 18-year-long love affair with a Chinese transvestite who, as he told the court and *People* magazine, he never realized was actually a man.

Cronenberg's first feature to be wholly financed by a Hollywood studio and first to be made outside Canada, *M. Butterfly* is also one of the few he's directed on which he doesn't have a writing credit, and only the second that can't be characterized as horror or sci-fi. (The previous exception was a reasonably disreputable drag racing movie.) But as impersonal as *M. Butterfly* appears, it recapitulates nearly the sum total of Cronenbergian concerns: body horror, womb

envy, the sense that sexuality is a construct, the promise of the New Flesh, the fear of colonization by an alien life-form. In Cronenberg terms, *M. Butterfly* picks up approximately where *Naked
Lunch* left off, with the male Dr. Benway emerging from the discarded rind of the female Fadela.
  Maximally intertextual, Hwang's play juxtaposed Chinese opera and Puccini, sitcom and
Kabuki, Broadway glitz and tabloid docudrama. Whatever its flaws, it was an astute
popularization of current cultural theory—a satire of phallocratic heterosex combined with a
critique of Orientalism—as well as a lively rehash of the '60s scenario (both the Vietnam War and
Cultural Revolution in the background), and a fabulous star-vehicle for a pair of male actors,
complete with an Act III coup de théâtre anticipating *The Crying Game*'s "surprise."
  As staged here in 1988, *M. Butterfly* was a blatantly theatrical conceit that dramatized an
essentially theatrical situation. The diplomat, Gallimard, falls in love with an image of femininity
as idealized and compliant as a *Playboy* centerfold. The deception succeeds because, as the female
impersonator Song Liling remarks, "only a man knows how a woman is supposed to act." The
film, however, is not only thoroughly dour and doggedly linear but compulsively naturalistic as
well. It's shot, for example, in the actual People's Republic—a needless extravagance in that its
China is so evidently an invented one.
  Literal-minded as it is, this *M. Butterfly* is not *The Crying Game*. One is encouraged from the
onset to recognize that this is a love between two men. Yet, too handsome and assured to play
the pathetic Gallimard that John Lithgow created on stage, Jeremy Irons seems even more
bizarrely naive—without a past, he might have hatched, full grown, at his embassy desk. Despite
a cultivated veneer, the movie Gallimard knows neither the plot of *Madame Butterfly* nor the fact
that all female roles in the Beijing opera are played by men. Smitten to obsession when he first
hears Song Liling (John Lone) perform Puccini at a diplomatic function, he is driven to track the
diva down.
  It is, as David Lynch might say, a mystery of love. Whereas the sex-starved stage Gallimard
refers to himself as "patron saint of the socially inept," his celluloid cousin has a movie-star wife
(Barbara Sukowa, albeit deglamorized with a killer head-cold), a potential stable of embassy
women, and the smooth moves of a practiced seducer. As the object of Gallimard's desire, Lone
is far less coquettish than was B. D. Wong on the stage. He fizzes without effervescence—his flat,
metallic voice is the movie's most evident special effect. But the easy observation that Lone is
no Jaye Davidson is made superfluous by Cronenberg's perverse fondness for presenting the
actor's lightly stubbled features in close-up.
  Lone's masculine appearance might almost be a deliberate alienation-effect. (Indeed, one of the
hits of the Toronto Festival of Festivals, where *M. Butterfly* had its world premiere, was an
American independent with the Cronenbergian title of *Suture*, predicated on the joke of a black
actor perceived throughout as the perfect double for a white man.) The scene in which Song
Liling ponders vintage movie magazine pictures of the old Hollywood's one Asian sex-star, Anna
May Wong, only makes sense if we appreciate the character as Lone.
  "For me, *M. Butterfly* is a mainstream film. For Warner Bros. it's practically an underground
movie," Cronenberg told an audience in Toronto. Humorously misleading, Warners's trailer sells
the movie as ersatz David Lean, shots of teeming Beijing dramatize the momentous observation
that "It was a time of turbulent change ... Two people meet." The real meeting, however, could
be Hollywood cowardice and Cronenberg's hitherto latent streak of Canadian film board super-
responsibility.
  Asked if he was constrained by shooting in Beijing, Cronenberg replied that the Chinese attitude
toward the production was "don't tell us what it's about and then we don't have to say no." The
same principle of denial is recapitulated after a fashion, not only by Cronenberg's protagonist but
also by Cronenberg in his own disinclination to characterize Gallimard and Song Liling's affair
as homosexual. (Auteurists may note a corresponding pattern of attraction/repulsion in the elision
of homosexuality in the factual story that inspired *Dead Ringers* as well as the enhanced
heterosexuality of *Naked Lunch*.)
  Cronenberg treads lightly on the logistics of the couple's physical relations but, however
undefined their affair founders during the Cultural Revolution—among other things, a p.c. unisex
nightmare of undifferentiated gender. Song Liling is arrested and Gallimard sent back to France
in semi-disgrace (in part because his creative misunderstanding of the Orient led him to grossly
overestimate American success in Vietnam). Back in Paris, he haunts the opera for performances

of *Madame Butterfly*, eyes welling up, while outside French cops teargas students brandishing placards of Mao. But as the lovers come unglued, the movie comes together.

Despite Gallimard's insistence that he has '"known and been loved by the perfect woman," and for all the underlying parallels to *Vertigo, M. Butterfly* feels far more congealed than sublime. Yet, with 10 minutes to go, this most conventional of Cronenberg films breaks its cocoon. (The spasm of a smile that flicks across Irons's face when he first sees Song Liling as a man is the signal.) Irons's climactic solo—Butterfly *c'est moi*—not only improves upon the stage production but, darkly virtuosic as it is, carries an unexpected jolt of terminal bereavement. Could the movie's prosaic anti-poignance, its detached, almost strangulated pace, be the strategic buildup to a cosmic punch line?

Given that Cronenberg is one of the most intelligent filmmakers working in North America, it's not impossible that he chose to defamiliarize a lurid story by deliberately dulling it down. (Were he more faithful to the text, Hwang's or Boursicot's, *M. Butterfly* might be the willful "withholding of a Straub-Huillet flick.) The question that remains, of course, is whether a movie concerned with repression, loss, and deep denial should also have to illustrate it.

Also reviewed in:
CHICAGO TRIBUNE, 10/8/93, Friday/p. A, Michael Wilmington
NEW REPUBLIC, 11/1/93, p. 26, Stanley Kauffmann
NEW YORK TIMES, 10/1/93, p. C3, Janet Maslin
NEW YORKER, 10/11/93, p. 121, Terrence Rafferty
VARIETY, 9/20/93, p. 26, Todd McCarthy
WASHINGTON POST, 10/9/93, p. D5, Hal Hinson

MAC

A Samuel Goldwyn Company release of a Macfilm Productions film.   *Producer:* Nancy Tenenbaum and Brenda Goodman.   *Director:* John Turturro.   *Screenplay:* John Turturro and Brandon Cole.   *Director of Photography:* Ron Fortunato.   *Editor:* Michael Berenbaum.   *Music:* Richard Termini and Vin Tese.   *Music Editor:* Todd Kasow.   *Sound:* Billy Sarokin.   *Sound Editor:* Dan Sable.   *Casting:* Todd Thaler.   *Production Designer:* Robin Standefer.   *Art Director:* John Magoun.   *Set Decorator:* Amelia Battaglio.   *Set Dresser:* Joel Barkow.   *Costumes:* Donna Zakowska.   *Make-up:* Sharon Ilson.   *Stunt Coordinator:* Danny Aiello, III.   *Running time:* 118 minutes.   *MPAA Rating:* R.

CAST: John Tururro (Mac); Michael Badalucco (Vico); Carl Capotorto (Bruno); Katherine Borowitz (Alice); John Amos (Nat); Olek Krupa (Polowski); Ellen Barkin (Oona); Steven Randazzo (Gus); Matthew Sussman (Clarence); Nicholas Turturro (Tony Gloves); Joe Paparone (Papa); Dennis Farina (Mr. Stunder); Kaiulani Lee (Mrs. Stunder); Richard Spore (Francis); James Madio (Young Mac); Stephi Lineburg (Young Alice); Herbert E. Weitz (Auctioneer); Stretch "Raul Merced" (Joe Brown); Mike Starr (Fireman); Michael Glynn (Bricklayer #1); Harry Bugin (Patient); Angelo Florio (Paulie Bay); Anthony Alessandro (Young Bricklayer); Sandor Tecsy (Fat Joey); Kent Broadhurst (Mr. Tabin); Abe Altman (Mr. Deutscher); Joseph Marino (Joe the Plumber); Jayne Haynes (Bum); Ruth Maleczech (Burgess); Shirley Stoler (Customer); Doris Gramovot (Cook); Katherine Turturro (Gus's Mom); Robert Proscia (Wounded man); Jeff Braun (Husband); Aida Turturro (Wife); Amedeo Turturro (Child); Patrick Pisano (Young Vico); Anthony Capotorto (Young Bruno); Efren Andaluz (Mac's Son); Judith Roberts (Woman on the Bus); Mario Todisco (Joe the Mule); Jared Matesky (Junkman); Jason Dunchin (Mental Patient); Morton Tenenbaum (Mr. Deutscher's Friend).

CHRISTIAN SCIENCE MONITOR, 2/25/93, p. 13, David Sterritt

Five years have passed since John Turturro supercharged the movie "Five Corners" with his fierce performance as a vengeful psychotic on the loose in a modest Bronx neighborhood. In those years, Mr. Turturro has fulfilled his promise as a talented and versatile young actor.

His most brilliant work is found in Spike Lee's masterpiece "Do the Right Thing," where he plays a bigoted pizza-parlor worker in an African-American neighborhood, and in Joel Coen's inventive "Barton Fink," where he gives uproarious intensity to the title character, a brooding New York playwright trying to give Hollywood an artistic touch in the 1930s. The latter role earned him the Cannes Film Festival's award for best actor two years ago.

His performance in "Mac" is not on a level with those inspired appearances, but the new picture marks a turning point in his career for another reason: It is Turturro's debut as a movie director and also as a screenwriter, since it's based on a script he began writing more than a dozen years ago.

A tribute to the life, work, and values of his late father—an Italian immigrant who earned his living as a carpenter—the movie is clearly Turturro's labor of love. Its honesty and sincerity are unquestionable, and carry the tale through various rough spots that Turturro's filmmaking skills aren't strong enough to avoid.

The hero is Mac, the oldest son of a carpenter much like Turturro's father must have been. At the beginning of the story, Mac and his two brothers are working for a dishonest contractor who will cut any corner and ignore any regulation to get a job done more quickly and cheaply. Eventually he tears himself loose from this corrupt situation—making a forceful point about his dedication to top-quality work—and sets up his own business in partnership with his brothers.

Their adventures range from a high-tension land auction, which turns disastrous when Mac gets into a bidding war with his former boss, to the challenge of building and selling houses in a suburban area where cows rather than people are the primary population. Mac must also deal with the wavering commitment of his brothers, neither of whom shares his bedrock devotion to hands-on labor as a way of life.

As written by Turturro and Brandon Cole, the final version of the screenplay for "Mac" is not always completely clear about the emotions and motivations of its characters, and Turturro's directing style is heavy-handed at times.

While the film never fails to convey Turturro's passionate feelings about the subject of his story, it makes some of its points with a lack of gracefulness that Mac himself would be quick to criticize in the work of a carpenter or a bricklayer on a construction site. Michael Badalucco and Carl Capotorto give earthy performances that don't match the steaming energy of Turturro's acting in the title role; and the editing by Michael Berenbaum seems too emphatic at times.

There is good acting by John Amos as one of Mac's most valuable workers, however, and by Ellen Barkin as a young woman whose offbeat beauty exercises a strong attraction on Mac's easily distracted brothers. The ambience of New York City's outlying Queens borough in the mid-1950s is convincingly captured by cinematographer Ron Fortunato, as well. "Mac" is a minor film in many ways, but the strength of its conviction gives it an unpolished power that's not easily brushed aside.

LOS ANGELES TIMES, 3/3/93, Calendar/p. 5, Kevin Thomas

"Mac" gives us a pretty good idea of where John Turturro's manic intensity comes from. Whether playing the nebbishy, idealistic New York playwright turned loose in Golden Era Hollywood in "Barton Fink" or the petty crook pleading for his life in "Miller's Crossing" or in his various roles in Spike Lee films, Turturro is the archetypal blue-collar ethnic guy, unhandsome and put upon, who at the end of his tether gets a wild, frozen look in his eyes just before exploding.

This happens a lot in "Mac," at once a labor of love 12 years in gestation and an exorcism, for in his directorial debut Turturro is playing a man based on his own father, a bombastic, hard-driving first-generation Italian-American carpenter. It couldn't have been easy growing up the son of the late Nicholas R. Turturro, but "Mac" is suffused with a clear-eyed love and respect. It is also that rarity, a movie about work.

"You know what I think happiness is?" asks Mac Vitelli (Turturro). "To love your job. Not many people know this—that's why they take vacations—but it's the truth. If you hate your work, you hate your life. I like my work."

It's Queens, 1954, and Mac and his two brothers, the sweet, Paunchy Vico (Michael Badalucco) and the reflective art student Bruno (Carl Capotorto) have just buried their father. They're all working in construction for Polowski (Olek Krupa), a cynical, corner-cutting contractor who enjoys making his men miserable. Inevitably, the day comes when Mac has had his fill and persuades his brothers to take the big gamble of going into business for themselves.

There is a great deal of broad humor as well as warm sentiment in the briskly paced "Mac," which Turturro first developed as a play with his co-writer Brandon Cole. There is also much concern for detail and nuance, as in the way he introduces the three brothers. Each is given a distinct identity through the flashback memories triggered as they pause at their father's casket.

Every frame of "Mac" bespeaks great care, with Turturro exploring the creative possibilities of sound and image to convey precisely what he feels. (Turturro is indebted to his resourceful cameraman Ron Fortunato and especially to composers Richard Termini and Vin Tese for their insistent yet richly varied score.) Such care allows "Mac" to move unobtrusively from humor to a tone of increasing seriousness as Mac's dogged, single-minded devotion to make his particular American dream come true increasingly alienates his brothers.

For Mac there is no conflict between love of work and of family, and it is one of Turturro's signal accomplishments that he shows us that the tough perfectionist who can inspire a fierce loyalty from his men (well-played by John Amos and Steven Randazzo, among others) can also instill massive resentment in his brothers, who are, after all, his partners. Mac is such an admirable man, so determinedly honorable in all his dealings yet so oblivious to his bullying impact upon his own flesh and blood. It never occurs to him that they may have dreams of their own, that they may not love carpentry as much as he does or that they could take his outbursts personally. What Turturro is telling us is that there can be a price exacted upon those constantly immersed in work.

The men in this film are seen in the round, and Vico and Bruno are as three-dimensional as Mac. Wistful, kindly Vico sees himself as a Lothario despite his awkwardness with women. Bruno, the quietest of the three, may well be the most talented and brightest of his brothers.

Although played by fine actresses, the women in the film do not fare as well. Turturro has cast his own real-life wife, Katherine Borowitz, as Mac's wife. Borowitz's Alice is strong, plain-spoken, and Borowitz is so skilled she's able to let us see Mac through her loving, respectful eyes. But we want to know more about what makes her devoted '50s wife tick.

Ellen Barkin is always a vivid presence, but the picture would have been better without her brief appearances. Turturro so severely caricatures her poetry-spouting beatnik, who becomes more or less involved with Mac's brothers, that instead of setting off the nobility of Mac's work ethic she makes it seem needlessly smug and sanctimonious.

"Mac" (rated R for strong language and for some sexuality) probably could well have sacrificed a couple of Mac's arias of rage in return for more time spent on its women, but it's easily sustained by the sheer eloquence of its passion. You don't often come by a film extolling the very real rewards of giving an honest day's work for your wages.

NEW YORK POST, 2/19/93, p. 23, Jami Bernard

There was a time when people were valued by the good work they did, not by their money or status symbols. That is the world remembered nostalgically by actor John Turturro in his proficient directorial debut "Mac."

Turturro co-wrote the script in memory of his late father, Nicholas, who was a carpenter. In it he plays himself—his father's son—one of three who carry on their father's legacy of quality craftsmanship in varying degrees.

Set in 1954 Queens after the father's funeral, "Mac" is about one man's attempt to preserve Old World values in a New World order. Mac and his brothers hire on to build cheap tract houses, but Mac sneaks in extra wall supports whenever he can; it is against his nature to skimp on quality. That and his big mouth get him into trouble with his cheerfully corrupt boss (Olek Krupa) and eventually send him into business for himself. The only carpentry he is satisfied with is his own.

The cheap plot of land he buys is no bargain—he is tricked into overbidding on it, only to find it bordered by cow dung on one side and an insane asylum on the other. "Mac" is full of such over-the-top details, the cinematic equivalent of Mac's explosive temper, which in turn is a Turturro acting specialty cultivated by his work in the Coen brothers' movies.

The two younger brothers, played by Michael Badalucco and Carl Capotorto, are similar to Mac, yet different enough—like the same pieces of glass rearranged slightly by the barest twist of a kaleidoscope. One brother is an artist of a different kind, a painter, the other a connoisseur of women. It is only Mac who echoes his father's famous words: "There are two ways to do it—my way and the right way, and they're both the same."

Mac is a visionary, but also a petty tyrant who shuts out his family and his wife (played by Turturro's real-life wife, Katherine Borowitz). Ellen Barkin appears briefly as a bohemian artist's model who gets the younger two brothers all hot and bothered.

"Mac" is very hands-on, low-to-the-ground. The movie opens with the voluptuous, messy pouring of the concrete. There are bathroom scenes and cursing fits and a shot of Mac strapping on his jockstrap as part of his morning ritual. Turturro uses a handheld camera that runs after the actors as if trying to keep up with their energy.

The film is dedicated to the memory of Turturro's father, who is heard over the closing credits on John's answering-machine tape, trying to make sense of this newfangled contraption that keeps him at a distance from the son he loves. That is the most moving part of the film; John has indeed followed in his father's footsteps, trying to make a caring, quality film (even if his beginner status shows sometimes) in an age of cookie-cutter convenience.

NEWSDAY, 2/19/93, Part II/p. 61, John Anderson

You can feel the wet cement, the ringing two-by-fours and the rain that falls on the working men of "Mac," John Turturro's directorial debut and his paean to a time when pride in workmanship meant something more in this country—or at least to more people—than it does today. And you can feel Turturro's devotion to his subject: The film is dedicated to his father, Nicholas, who himself spent a life in the construction trades.

But what you don't get is a real feel for what motivates the characters who populate this often funny, occasionally moving, but ultimately one-dimensional film about a working man's struggle to maintain his standards and still succeed in a cut-throat business and an indifferent world.

Mac (Turturro), the oldest of the three Vitelli brothers, is single-minded and stubborn and exhibits a love of what he does—not the stuff of a very complex character, although that may have been what Turturro was after: a man defined by his work alone. His tenacious pursuit of his dreams is palpable, his values are clear.

The problem is that when Mac eventually alienates his brothers/partners—the youngest, Bruno (Carl Capotorto), a good-looking, good-natured ladies man and art student, and the earthy, round Vico, whom Michael Badalucco portrays with great humor—it doesn't make sense, because Turturro has spent too much time telling us why they love each other to convince us they could ever break apart.

The brothers are introduced at the funeral of their father, whom they recall as a taskmaster and masterbuilder who instilled in his sons, particularly Mac, an appreciation of good work. It's a richly ethnic scene, a darkly funny one that at the same time celebrates pride in heritage.

But throughout the film there's also a sense that self-respect—the kind that makes you do a job properly just because you're doing it—is the private domain of a particular group, and that group is Turturro's.

The Irish with whom the Vitellis do battle on a job site are drunks who bounce bricks off unsuspecting heads; the corrupt builder for whom they work—he frames his houses 24 inches on center, rather than 16, which is anathema to any homeowner—is Polowski (Olek Krupa), who sneers at Mac's standards and does his best to undo his rival's plans to go out on his own. As the picture's embodiment of evil, though, Powloski can't be much more than a caricature, something that plagues the film as a whole.

The aspect of "Mac" that rings most true is in the relationship between Mac and Alice (Katherine Borowitz), who helps him begin his own construction business, and eventually marries him. Turturro and Borowitz, real-life husband and wife, make the couple a genuine partnership; he breaks down her natural reticence, she tempers his native explosiveness.

The way they face the pedestrian but daunting challenges of starting a family, starting a business, coping with crazy relatives and dealing with self-doubt comes across as authentic and loving.

In fact, Mac and Alice represent what Turturro tried and almost succeeded in doing with the rest of "Mac"—celebrate family, workmanship and self-respect, and make a film that was 16 on center.

SIGHT AND SOUND, 1/94, p. 49, Robert Yates

Queens, New York, 1954. The three Vitelli brothers pay their respects to their dead father, laid out in his coffin. A fantasy scene follows in which the father sits up and complains about the quality of the coffin. The two oldest sons, Mac and Vito, work on a construction site, where Mac is regularly in battle with Polowski, the foreman: Mac believes in doing a job well, Polowski insists on cutting corners. The youngest son, Bruno, is at art college and the three still live in the family home with their mother.

Mac visits Alice, who has caught his eye. He reminds her of how, when he was a boy, Alice's father refused to pay for work his own father had done: this serves as his approach to a chat-up line. Bruno, his college term complete, joins his brothers on the site, and is soon caught up in a fight caused by Mac barking at another labourer for his carelessness. Differences settled, Mac determines to rebuild the frame of a house to his own standards. The three brothers are sacked, and Mac convinces the other two that they should set up a family business.

At a party for Bruno's graduation, while Oona—an artist's model with fanciful notions—wins centre stage, Mac and Alice drive to the land Mac intends to buy for the Vitellis' first construction project, a row of houses. Alice offers to contribute by giving Mac all of her savings. At the auction for the land, Polowski induces Mac into a bidding war, tricking him into agreeing to an absurdly inflated price; Mac faints. Resting in hospital, however, he finds out that the sale has been made invalid by the city's hold on the land. Between arguing with other patients, Mac asks Alice to marry him, and she agrees.

Work begins on the land Mac eventually buys and, as boss, he makes sure everything meets his standards. He rarely rests, working on the accounts by night, and Alice has to fight for his attention. Things sour at the site: one of the labourers falls off a roof, and Mac finds Vito taking short cuts. As Mac pushes himself and the others still harder, Bruno tells him he's sick.

After Mac is again duped by Polowski—this time into giving him a key to one of the Vitelli houses, which he uses as a model to sell the houses he himself is building—Mac completes the sale of his row. His reputation growing, a second, larger project, is lined up. However, Bruno and Vito decide that they can no longer work with their brother and the three split bitterly. Mac is left alone muttering about having to do everything himself.

In a post-script, several years later, Mac takes his son along to visit the houses, and tells him that they date from a time when what mattered was the "doing".

John Turturro's debut as a director invites a critical language that fits with the subject matter. It is well crafted, carefully assembled, and never less than solid. If these virtues sometimes seem modest ones, that is also apt since Turturro, feeling his way behind the camera, does not over-reach. While this produces little that's forced or fake, it can result in stolid direction: a great deal happens in close-up, and encounters tend to involve the camera swivelling from one impassioned face to the other. Given the director, an 'actors' film might seem an easy tag. But if by that we mean film using performance, particularly as shown in faces, as the principal carrier of emotion, then that's just what *Mac* is. As such, it is exemplary, with the acting uniformly excellent.

Turturro has been working on *Mac*—(largely inspired by the experience of his immigrant father) since 1980, developing scenes in the theatre and refining the piece with actor friends, many of whom feature in the film's cast. This genesis might have contributed to what is so much of an ensemble piece that characters seem to queue up for their turn to shine. There are also plenty of opportunities for Turturro to perform signature routines: the bug-eyed, manic stare; the rigid limbs; the sudden explosion that comes from nowhere.

An actors' film, then, and also one with a pronounced theme: the value of good work, which Mac defends from the likes of Polowski, who advises that "business is better than work." For the former you need only your mouth. What's more, beauty costs, he says; ugly work is cheap. Arthur Miller's recent play, *The Last Yankee*, dealt with a similar subject, and the loss of the ability to make things (as opposed to talking them up) seems increasingly to be seen as a cause of social malaise. There is great scope for romance in such an analysis—particularly for American cinema, nurtured on the wilful hero—and it is to Turturro's credit that his focus is as much on obsession and the fall-out from Mac's ideals. The two brothers can switch off, Mac cannot. He is a martyr who sees everything in black and white and who is apt to make all disagreements into Biblical encounters.

The 'theme' is seldom obtrusive, embedded as it is in a light, humorous portrait of a carefully drawn time and place. If Turturro can be said to already show signs of a directorial style, it is in the way that he slips nicely from standard naturalistic drama into the exaggerated or the grotesque. Polowski is a demon we enjoy, whom we laugh with; while Oona, played by Ellen Barkin, is the Boho from hell, reciting free form poetry, covering herself in toast—the antithesis of the worker and a clever counter to the film's pull towards sentimentality.

VILLAGE VOICE, 2/23/93, p. 51, Georgia Brown

What looks appetizing in *Mac* is wet cement. An opening shot of steady rain on newly poured concrete is especially tantalizing. Behind the credits we're treated to close-ups of said rain falling on a sopped suburban construction site: work boots slog through mud, a filled wheelbarrow bogs down. Oh man, you just want to shuck those caked brogans and jump into a hot shower. If Esquivel depicts a woman's world as a warm, steamy interior where spicy concoctions are stirred up, John Turturro has created a homage to his father's universe that associates masculinity with heavy labor, foul weather, and a cold, gray, fecal mush.

Here's another ancient tale. Once upon a time an old man dies and leaves three grown sons: The first is a workaholic, the second an aspiring playboy, and the third a would-be artist. The focus, in this biographical case, is on the first. *Mac* opens in 1954 at the father's funeral, somewhere in the vast, undifferentiated borough of Queens. The eldest son, Mac (Turturro) is the one who has internalized Papa's values—hard work, exacting craftsmanship, self-assurance—and who goes into the world to follow his path. Like the third little pig (who was probably the eldest), Mac works from dawn to dusk and builds his house with bricks and mortar. A carpenter in the beginning, he turns into a contractor because he needs to be a boss. The other two sons, Vico (Michael Badalucco) and Bruno (Carl Capotorto) prefer girls and art and fooling around and will probably get eaten by some wolf like Oona (Ellen Barkin), the beautiful, self-absorbed beatnik poet who stirs the boys' blood. In his own crude and straight-ahead fashion, Mac woos the plainer, tomboyish Alice (Turturro's real-life wife, Katherine Borowitz). Alice proves a perfect wife for Mac, loving, loyal, and resourceful. (The brothers' mother is merely a nagging off-screen voice.)

The winner of Cannes's Camera d'Or for best first film, *Mac* has its hero's earnest, straightforward energy. Turturro isn't sentimental about his father. Co-written with Brandon Cole, the script makes clear what a pain Mac must have been—how impossible he was to work for, how little he knew himself, and, though it barely touches on this, what a difficult father he must have been. When, at the end, Mac shows his own eldest son, Johnny, about five, what fine houses he constructed with such loving craftsmanship, we see the huge doubts behind his pride and the kid's bewilderment. In enlisting the boy as witness, he assigns him the task of understanding what he can't grasp. Here, Turturro lovingly discharges his duty, though the film implies that he may never feel done with it.

Also reviewed in:
CHICAGO TRIBUNE, 3/5/93, Friday/p. J, Clifford Terry
NATION, 2/15/93, p. 210, Stuart Klawans
NEW YORK TIMES, 2/19/93, p. C17, Vincent Canby
VARIETY, 5/25/92, p. 53, Todd McCarthy
WASHINGTON POST, 3/5/93, p. C7, Hal Hinson

MAD DOG AND GLORY

A Universal Pictures release. *Executive Producer:* Richard Price. *Producer:* Barbara De Fina and Martin Scorsese. *Director:* John McNaughton. *Screenplay:* Richard Price. *Director of Photography:* Robby Müller. *Editor:* Craig McKay and Elena Maganini. *Music:* Elmer Bernstein. *Music Editor:* Joseph S. DeBeasi. *Sound:* James J. Sabat and (music) Alan Silverman. *Sound Editor:* Philip Stockton. *Casting:* Todd Thaler. *Production Designer:* David Chapman. *Art Director:* Mark Haack. *Set Decorator:* Leslie Pope. *Set Dresser:* Harry B. Hoynes and Timothy W. Tiedje. *Special Effects:* Edward Drohan. *Costumes:* Rita Ryack. *Make-up (Robert De Niro):* Ilona Herman. *Make-up (Bill Murray):* Nena Smarz. *Make-up (Uma Thurman):* Gunnar Swanson. *Make-up (special):* Neal Martz. *Stunt Coordinator:* Doug Coleman. *Running time:* 97 minutes. *MPAA Rating:* R.

CAST: Robert De Niro (Wayne); Uma Thurman (Glory); Bill Murray (Frank); David Caruso (Mike); Mike Starr (Harold); Tom Towles (Andrew); Kathy Baker (Lee); Derek Anunciation (Shooter); Doug Hara (Driver); Evan Lionel (Dealer in Car); Anthony Cannata (Pavletz); J.J. Johnston (Shanlon); Guy Van Swearingen (Cop); Jack Wallace (Tommy); Richard Belzer (M.C./Comic); Clem Caserta (Guy at Table); Fred Squillo and Chuck Parello (Frank's Gang); Tony Fitzpatrick, Eric Young, and Bruce Jarchow (Detectives at Crime Scene); Bob Rice (Uniform Cop); William King and Kevin Hurley (Dealers in the Park); Richard Price (Detective in Restaurant); John J. Polce (Dispatcher); Dick Sollenberger (Saul); Paula Killen (Irene); Eddie "Bo" Smith (Big John).

FILMS IN REVIEW, 8/93, p. 268, Edmond Grant

It seems some time has passed since that period, not so long ago, when our finest actors (De Niro, Hoffman, Nicholson) appeared in only one picture a year. Now, our best and brightest performers sign up for back-to-back movie deals ensuring that, where we could previously count on one exquisite performance per year, we now have to keep up with 2-3 pieces of fine work done in occasionally exceptional, but most often only average, mainstream productions. Items like *Mad Dog And Glory*.

It may be that Robert De Niro's non-stop film activity is helping subsidize the intriguing work done by his Tribeca production company; otherwise how can we explain his workmanlike manner here (a first for this consummate chameleon)?

Mad Dog's plot is as inconsequential as they come, an obvious attempt to revive the beloved Damon Runyon tradition of cute, quirky cop/crook fables. It concerns a cop who helps save a mobster's life, and receives a peculiar "thank-you present" in return, a winsome dame named Glory. The weak sister cop, of course, falls for the girl, and who knows what'll happen when the gangster comes to reclaim her after the week is up?

A fine premise for a master like Runyan, but not for a gritty realist like screenwriter Richard Price, and a skilled but dour filmmaker like John McNaughton (*Henry: Portrait Of A Serial Killer*); one wonders why producer Martin Scorsese became involved in the first place.

Mad Dog's problems arise from the juxtaposition of a '30s-'40s storyline with contemporary details and concerns. Even more problematic are miscalculations in characterization and comic timing. The latter is underscored by the dead spaces that follow several comic moments (spaces cleared for more downbeat "detail"); the characterization problems clear up as we get to know and like mild-mannered Wayne, jokingly nicknamed "Mad Dog" (De Niro), and Glory (Uma Thurman), the girl up for grabs (we'll leave the rather obvious questions of sexism aside—the film has enough troubles); the same can't be said for gangster Frank Milo (Bill Murray), whom we first encounter at length as a stand-up comic (?) doing schtick for a mob-packed audience. This odd piece of detail undercuts the film's later tense sequences—it's hard to feel scared by his presence once we've seen his act.

Still, the movie does have its bright spots, nearly all occurring in the Murray-less midsection, which details the inevitable bonding of Wayne and Glory, complicated by their awkward attempts at sex. De Niro's consummate skills take over at this point (it's his best clumsy-lovemaking scene since *Falling In Love*) and Thurman's character becomes slightly more than the stick figure she's meant to be.

Supporting performers must register with scant screen time: Kathy Baker is wasted as Wayne's perennially victimized neighbor, but both David Caruso and Mike Starr deserve credit for fleshing out the picture's only truly Runyonesque figures, Wayne's hard-as-nails, loyal-as-anything cop partner, and Milo's dimwitted but likeable stooge.

For all the talented involved, though, it's for sure that *Mad Dog* will wind up as just one more entry in the ever-expanding De Niro filmography. Honorable mention will go to the afore-mentioned Wayne-Glory interludes, and the splendid moment where a lovestruck "Mad Dog" photographs a corpse while singing along to Louis Prima's "Just A Gigolo."

LOS ANGELES TIMES, 3/5/93, Calendar/p. 1, Kenneth Turan

"Mad Dog and Glory" is a romance for the cynical and a comedy for those who laugh most when the jokes are hardest to get. A gentle fable put together by people whose previous work has been anything but nice, the film takes strength from its contradictions and becomes a small gem of deadpan humor and yearning hearts.

The hearts belong to the diffident Wayne "Mad Dog" Dobie (Robert De Niro), a cop who hasn't drawn his revolver in 15 years, and an intrepid young bartender named Glory (Uma Thurman). Unattached residents of Chicago—both come under the irresistible influence of Frank "The Money Store" Milo (Bill Murray), part mobster, part fairy godfather, a loan shark in therapy who does stand-up comedy on the side because what he really craves is recognition.

Perfectly suited to Murray's cynical, seen-it-all hauteur, Frank Milo is merely the most flamboyant of novelist-screenwriter Richard Price's collection of daft yet dangerous eccentrics. Unlike most cookie-cutter cop movies, "Mad Dog and Glory's" script has an idiosyncratic sensibility, more Damon Runyon than "RoboCop," and in John McNaughton it has a director who can both understand it and bring it to life.

If Price's previous works ("The Color of Money," "Sea of Love," the best-selling novel "Clockers") have not always looked on the bright side of things, McNaughton's debut film, "Henry: Portrait of a Serial Killer," went Price and everyone else one better. Having them both combine on a romance may be unexpected, but it certainly keeps things from getting uncomfortably mushy.

Also unexpected is "Mad Dog's" low-key tone. Unafraid of starting slow and building, this film takes awhile to get started, and its humor is so uncompromisingly low-key that when the jokes do show up it's not immediately clear if you're meant to laugh or not.

Nicknamed "Mad Dog" by ironic friends on the Chicago police force, Wayne Dobie is an unflappable evidence technician who works the night shift, sleeping by his desk and investigating bloody crime scenes before the bodies are moved. "You're a sensitive, intelligent human being," his brash partner Mike (David Caruso) tells him somberly. "If I ever had an intelligent thought, it would die of loneliness."

One night, while searching for Twinkies near a crime scene, Wayne stumbles upon a conven-ience store robbery. As he calmly tries to talk the perpetrator out of killing a customer lying face down on the floor, the potential victim is mouthing off to the gunman, nearly getting blown away in the process, and Wayne ends up saving him in spite of himself.

A few days later, Wayne is summoned to the Comic Cazie club, where, after a nervous bartender spills boiling coffee on him, he meets Frank Milo, formerly the man on the floor. A not-quite-made member of the mob ("I know guys, guys know me") who's been told by his therapist that he ought to be grateful to Wayne, Frank is a master of menacing (and often comic) eloquence. "I can be the expediter of your dreams," he grandly tells Wayne, but if circumstances change, "your life will become a raging sea."

After a night of inebriated camaraderie with Frank, Wayne is awakened far too early the next morning by Glory, the bartender who spilled the coffee, who has been sent by his new best friend to (a) make sure Wayne's burned hand is OK and (b) make sure any other wants Wayne has for the next week are gratified. "It's not a sex thing," she tells him earnestly. "I'm like a thank-you present. A seven-day singing telegram."

Totally self-sufficient, or so he thinks, Wayne is completely dumbfounded at Glory's arrival, and De Niro's continual befuddlement is easily the funniest he's been since "Greetings" and "Hi, Mom!," his very first films with director Brian De Palma. Always the best of actors, De Niro's work is more interior than usual here, and his role as the most reluctant, inarticulate swain in town gets funnier as his confusion about what to do about this major break in his routine increases.

Matching him scene for scene is Murray, an overly grateful lion who absolutely refuses to leave Androcles alone. And Thurman, though the script has her functioning more as a catalyst than a major player, is exactly right as well. Especially notable in a supporting role is Mike Starr as Harold, Frank's stolid man-of-all-work, who drinks Chivas and milk and thinks he sees celebrities behind every lunch counter.

Though its unhurried pace and ultimately sweet nature give "Mad Dog and Glory" (rated R for sexuality, language, violence and drug content) the feeling more of a diversion than a major work, those who get into its eccentric comic rhythms will definitely be charmed. Watching De Niro's Mad Dog cheerfully prepare to examine a corpse to the strains of Louis Prima singing "I Ain't Got No Body" on a restaurant jukebox may not be to everybody's taste, but, like the rest of this genially cracked endeavor, it can't help but make you laugh.

NEW YORK, 3/22/93, p. 68, David Denby

Mad Dog and Glory, not to put too fine a point on it, is a dud. The film may have been doomed once Richard Price, who wrote the original screenplay, and Martin Scorsese, who produced, decided that John McNaughton, the director of the horrific *Henry: Portrait of a Serial Killer*, should direct this low-key comic story. The movie starts well with a couple of frightening street murders followed by our introduction to a curiously timid character played by Robert De Niro—a police photographer who unintentionally helps a gangster (Bill Murray) and finds himself subject to the gangster's generosity. The bad guy is also a stand-up comic in his own club—a hip idea—and Murray, his hair swept back, looks suave and menacing.

But once Murray deposits Uma Thurman at De Niro's apartment as a return of favor, the movie collapses. De Niro and Thurman fall in love, but their fumbling scenes together are more embarrassing than anything else. The movie could have worked only as a wild comedy, but De Niro, becalmed, is dull, Thurman unfocused, and a deadly air of indecision hangs over most of the scenes. McNaughton can't get a comic rhythm going; he keeps wheeling in Murray, looking as sleek as a Lexus, but Murray never really does anything, and the movie just peters out.

NEW YORK POST, 3/5/93, p. 25, Jami Bernard

There's a lot of talent jockeying for position in "Mad Dog and Glory," and although sometimes all that talent pulls the movie like taffy, for the most part it shows a lot of guts. And like the movie says, no guts, no glory.

Robert De Niro stars as Wayne "Mad Dog" Dobie, a gentle, somewhat insecure Chicago cop who is more comfortable poking for clues among dead bodies than facing up to real-life confrontations. He longs to be like his dimmer but scrappier partner, memorably played by David Caruso,

Wayne forms an uneasy friendship with mobster and sometime stand-up comic Frank Milo (Bill Murray) after saving him from a holdup. Milo in turn—"I'm the expediter of your dreams," he repeats insidiously—sends Wayne an attractive club bartender (Uma Thurman) as a sort of thank-you gift.

The acting in "Mad Dog and Glory" is particularly strong and iconoclastic, helped along by a unique, chewy script by Richard Price ("Sea of Love") and some really interesting, hands-on directing by John McNaughton ("Henry: Portrait of a Serial Killer"). It's easy to see why producer Martin Scorsese recommended McNaughton for his poetically violent imagery, facility with the camera, and macabre sense of humor.

De Niro and Murray could easily have switched roles, but that very possibility makes their screen relationship so funny and fraught. Murray, a first-rate comic, plays a second-rate comic.

De Niro, who played a comic in "The King of Comedy," swears he has the mind "of a civil servant" yet feeds jokes and one-liners to Murray's character.

Journalists who have had brushes with the real-life Murray's arrogance might say that in this movie, as a humorless, vengeful bastard, he comes closest to playing his real self. Regardless, it is a chilling, funny performance, much better for his career than some of those inane comedies Hollywood throws his way.

There is a certain elegance to all the performances, with all scenes getting the cinematic equivalent of a punch line. A bruiser (Tom Towles) beating up a neighbor woman (Kathy Baker) whips out his own cop's badge in his defense. Uma Thurman, as a woman too innocent and nervous to be a call girl, tries to make conversation out of pre-digested TV dialogue. De Niro, ecstatic at having sex after a two-year hiatus, puts a quarter in the jukebox at a crime scene and sings "Just a Gigolo" while examining the corpse. Two men brutally beating on each other in a third man's apartment spare an expensive glass door out of an innate courtliness.

The ways in which the movie doesn't work, particularly the last half-hour, don't detract substantially from the overall picture. "Mad Dog and Glory," flaws and all, will bear the kind of repetition and scrutiny bestowed on great movies.

NEWSDAY, 3/5/93, Part II/p. 50, John Anderson

It's full of mouth, this "Mad Dog and Glory." Bill Murray's congenital smirk. Uma Thurman's voluptuous moue. Robert De Niro's maniacal grin—a scary thing, seldom seen—A lot of interesting mouths. If only what came out of them was half as interesting.

De Niro has never played as nerdy or as unconvincing a character as Wayne Dobie—a police photographer facetiously nicknamed "Mad Dog" because, among other things, he's never drawn his gun. When he eventually does, he wets his pants. He's a very timid fellow, whose loveless lot in life is supposed to generate the pathos in a film that may or may not be a comedy.

Bill Murray's portrayal of Frank Milo, part-time loan shark and part-time stand-up comedian, supplies most of the laughs—several of his lines are hilarious—but he also provides whatever tension the film contains. Murray is still doing shtick, his patented combination of affected lethargy and smarmy condescension, but he's also, on occasion, quite menacing. When Wayne saves his life during a convenience-store holdup, he decides he wants to be Wayne's friend, and Wayne can't say no—either to Frank or whatever gifts he decides to bestow on the placid policeman.

What he gives Wayne is Glory (Uma Thurman), who is sent to spend a week in Mad Dog's apartment, and thus serves as both the sex object and the catalyst for his weenie-to-he-man metamorphosis. Glory has put herself in debt to Frank to protect her brother and has to do whatever he says—or so she says. By the end of the film, we don't know what to believe about her, although it's clear she makes Wayne think she loves him just so he'll get her out of Frank's clutches.

Nothing is particularly compelling about "Mad Dog and Glory," although the opening sequence is disturbing: a crack deal gone awry, with two men dead in a bloody shootout. The killer, the same thug who will rob the convenience store and threaten Frank and Wayne, is eventually found in a garbage can, which Wayne presumes to be Frank's work. He doesn't act on this suspicion, though; his reluctance to be a real cop, or a real man, is the thread that runs through "Mad Dog." As a photographer of corpses, he doesn't need to deal with the living, only the dead, and he's a little dead inside; once Glory opens him up, he admits envisioning himself as a kind of Weegee-esque figure, finding art in the vicious, tawdry corners he prowls. But we never get inside Wayne enough to make his catharsis—climaxed in a vicious as well as preposterous fist-fight with Frank—mean much of anything.

Produced by Barbara De Fina and Martin Scorsese, "Mad Dog and Glory" feels like a pit stop: Murray is coming off his big hit, "Groundhog Day"; De Niro, who simply seems to be adding to his oeuvre with a macholess character, has "This Boys Life" opening soon; Scorsese may be preoccupied with "The Age of Innocence,"; John McNaughton, who directed the horrendous and fascinating "Henry: Portrait of a Serial Killer," doesn't seem comfortable with comedy, so the film seesaws between mining the malevolence in Frank and doing a character study of Wayne.

Uma Thurman, meanwhile, who has a particularly thankless and somewhat sexist role, operates in her own orbit. All three stars, in fact, seem to be operating in different galaxies.

SIGHT AND SOUND, 7/93, p. 46, Ian Penman

A Chicago ghetto. A crack deal goes fatally wrong, and two dead bodies are left in an abandoned car. While at the scene of the crime, police evidence technician and photographer Wayne 'Mad Dog' Dobie is caught up in a nearby supermarket robbery; the perpetrator of the crack murders has called the store's manager and is holding a gun to a customer's head. Although indecisive, even craven (his 'Mad Dog' sobriquet is ironic), Dobie diffuses the situation. Later, he discovers that the customer whose life he inadvertently saved is local crime boss and club owner Frank Milo. The grateful Milo sends a henchman to escort Dobie to his club, where he performs an occasional stand-up routine. The lonely, isolated Dobie becomes caught up in Milo's aggressive bonhomie, and over the course of a drunken night, they confess their respective dreams and disappointments.

Milo ends the night with a vague promise that he can realise Dobie's dreams, but the cop thinks no more of it until Glory, a young girl who tends the bar at Milo's club, turns up at his apartment—a 'gift' from Milo for seven days. Disturbed by this intrusion into his well-ordered world, the ineffectual Dobie fails to act. Milo continues to worm his way into Dobie's life, and takes to turning up at his office with cake and comedy routines for Dobie's fellow officers. Only Dobie's hot-tempered and decisive partner Mike sees through Milo's front.

Glory pleads with Dobie not to 'return' her, as she is working out a form of contract with Milo, in order to pay off a debt her brother owes. Dobie and Glory sleep together, and Dobie wonders if he is in love. When he decides that he is, he tries to annul the 'seven-day contract' with Milo, who is put out, but willing to accept financial recompense. Dobie tries but fails to raise the money, and when Mike works out what is going on, he is enlisted as Dobie's own bodyguard. After various contretemps, Dobie challenges Milo himself to a fist fight to decide the outcome. Glory, who has left in exasperation at the men's bartering over her, returns to embrace the bruised but not beaten Dobie.

Like the recent *Night and the City*—also developed by and starring Robert De Niro, also written by Richard Price, also based on the barroom spiels and bartered fantasies of small-timer US street life—*Mad Dog and Glory* is a tender-hearted paean to flawed guys with fond hearts, gimpy guys with redemptive goals. It's an urban fairy tale—with Uma Thurman as the princess in the loft-conversion tower, De Niro as the Knight in Shining Armour and Bill Murray, craftily cast against type, as a manipulative Mafia boss, the dark *deux ex machina* who brings together the clean-souled lovers.

De Niro's forensics expert worries over his evidential police work and settles into a safely stalled midlife slump. A chance meeting with Murray's sharkskin-suited Mephistopheles changes everything. Price's script makes Dobie take a succession of hairpin transitions through a bottleneck of registers—police-procedural; wiseguy badinage; a cooped-up and lonely cop; a poor sap pricked by the rejuvenescence of love.

McNaughton kicks off with a swerve across the generic crime scene, cleverly deploying Dobie's own lens: he seems to be setting us up for another edge-city game of crazy gazing (cf. the appallingly effective video lo-jinks in *Henry: Portrait of a Serial Killer*). Then McNaughton's hold on *Mad Dog and Glory* just seems to go. He can't seem to hook Price's points-spread of proliferating games onto any holding rhythm—there's literally no sense of transition here, with the actors shuttled artlessly from set piece to set piece (at times, it feels like a parody of David Mamet's sometimes staginess). The mood veers from outbreaks of modish violence—clod's law—to anachronistic and gormless sentimentality. There is a patently misjudged sex scene—doubly superfluous, because the erotic charge between 'Mad Dog' and Glory has already been subtly (dis)played. Elmer Bernstein's noir-ish score—capably retro, wearingly strident—also comes across as misplaced.

There are some compensatory pleasures in the minor roles. David Caruso, as Wayne's fiery partner Mike, is as badgeringly intense as he was in a similar role in Ferrara's *King of New York*. Mike Starr as Frank's physically hulking but mentally limping bodyguard is also fun. And Bill Murray is impetuously apt as Frank—that gamey face giving off an air of serene reptilian malevolence. He seems to have *straightened up* into the part, losing the slouchy ballast of old and gaining streaky inches, so that his snidey eye-line always seems high above De Niro's blinky little boffin. De Niro does his now patented—patently off-the-peg—Mr Normal routine (familiar from *Falling in Love, Stanley and Iris, Awakenings*) and is all too convincingly dull. You're not exactly burning to see further inside Wayne's world, and Glory's conversion to this sweet-natured plodder is implausible. Price's macho fantasy smells way past its sell-by date.

McNaughton seems to be laying out a critique of homogenised movie machismo, but he ends up colluding in Price's delusions rather than cauterising their flow: the tough guys just end up coming to blows; the tender girl just ends up a quiescent (g)love puppet. Price is not exactly renowned for his memorable female characters, and *Mad Dog*'s is par for the course. And although McNaughton gets all coy about not showing Uma Thurman nude—he comes across as simultaneously furtive and nervously noble New Man—the film degrades her thoroughly enough anyway in the passive thrust of her Glory role.

Mad Dog and Glory has enough competing vectors to fuel at least three other, potentially more convincing movies; it is frustratingly haphazard, speared on its inability to choose a single, singular way to go. There's no sign that McNaughton gets in to this material to move it, guide it, and no alienation-effect riffing, either, as in his *Henry*. There's no stylistic vigour, outside of the edgily violent opening minutes, whose every texture (a pared-down monochrome which lasts only as long as the prologue) might be seen as a sad referential nod to the lost independence of *Henry*, and to a *Mad Dog and Glory* McNaughton maybe once envisaged but somehow lost.

VILLAGE VOICE, 3/16/93, p. 51, J. Hoberman

A timid Chicago police detective ironically nicknamed "Mad Dog" saves the life of neurotic loan shark Frank Milo and finds himself gifted with a tootsie half his age—a "a seven-day singing telegram" in the person of the winsome barmaid bluntly called Glory. If *Mad Dog and Glory* were to have a patron saint, his name would be Marty—not just for coproducer Martin Scorcese, but the homely, middle-aged Bronx butcher who, in Paddy Chayevsky's 1955 heart-warmer, found true love with a mousy librarian.

Of course, given *Mad Dog*'s creative personnel, this loser club is a bit more two-fisted. Indeed, the protagonists—Robert De Niro's Mad Dog, Bill Murray's Milo, Uma Thurman's Glory—are positively clenched. As directed by John McNaughton from Richard Price's script, *Mad Dog and Glory* is an uneasy but not altogether unlikeable mixture of character comedy and lowlife vérité—a romantic fable from Scorseseland that opens with a brutal multiple murder in the sort of charnel house ghetto environment where McNaughton's serial killer Henry would be something like a god, then, returning to the world of white people, turns almost whimsical.

Depressed rather than manic, De Niro is the Sad Lieutenant—stolidly dragging his square haircut and beefy scowl home at dawn to watch naked young people pose across the airshaft as though auditioning for Calvin Klein. Having rescued Milo from the unlikeliest of situations (personally collecting a debt in a bodega of death), he's invited to the thugs' comedy club to be nonplussed by Milo's unfunny stand-up spritz. Hair slicked back past the point of no return, a bandage further accentuating his forehead, the putty-faced Murray makes a frighteningly humorless tough guy—and never more so than when invoking his "therapist."

The drunken bonding of these two boiled potatoes is too glum to generate much warmth, even once they wind up at Mad Dog's. He shows Milo his exhibit of sub-Weegee police photos—just a lonely cop with the soul of an artist. "I am the expeditor of your dreams," Milo tells Mad Dog, and the next morning, the cop finds flustered Glory on his doorstep. This angelic creature has no self; she's defined by her relation to men. Milo owns her because she's working off her brother's debt; Mad Dog has her so that she can work off Milo's. Of course, Mad Dog can never forget who gave him this compliant dish and it ruins his appetite.

Mad Dog and Glory is thus a triangle with the inert Mad Dog at its apex. Fortunately, in the submerged simian romance between Mad Dog and Milo, each has a vividly acted second: Mad Dog's hotdog partner (David Caruso, who was Christopher Walken's NYPD nemesis in *King of New York*) is played against Milo's ulcer-ridden, star-struck minion (Mike Starr), a gorilla who drinks Chivas with milk and hallucinates Phil Donahue perched on a stool at some scuzzy White Castle. These proxies mix it up as a prelude to the main event. The most intricate pas de deux, however, belongs to De Niro and Thurman. The pair watch a monster movie on TV, tension mounting through an ominously scored rondo of snuggle, near-kiss, and recoil—a tango of longing and discomfort capped by Mad Dog's confession that he hasn't "made love" in two years.

This scene is McNaughton's most delicate. (His other unmistakable touch: a bloody corpse shrouded in a red-checkered tablecloth and artfully festooned with spaghetti.) Still, the movie could well lose anyone's sympathy once Mad Dog begins putting his own dollar value on Glory's services. What was the original concept here? According to the puff that ran last year in *Premiere*, the final cut tested so poorly, the movie had to be recalled for additional shooting and the opening pushed back from last April to last August to last week. Could Mad Dog have been even less appealing?

By all accounts, De Niro had his choice of roles and so he and Murray are both acting against type—most blatantly when Mad Dog gives Milo lessons in stand-up comedy. Murray's performance is successfully skewed but in the De Niro oeuvre, Mad Dog is one more doughy characterization, flecked with a few tasty raisins. One moment he's a paralyzed nerd; the next (inflamed by the koan "No guts, no glory"), he's a gun-waving loonie. How many times did De Niro rework the character? By the time Milo drifts back into the plot singing an old Tony Orlando song, Mad Dog has a whole new affect. No wonder Milo bangs his head on the building in his frustration.

As the token of exchange, Uma Thurman seems particularly uneasy although, for much of the movie, it goes with the role. Slightly stooped, delicately arranging herself around De Niro, Thurman acts like the world's youngest earth mother. She dignifies an underwritten part, at the cost of constricting her performance. It's as if her dress got caught in the machinery of the plot—she's afraid to bolt, the clothes might rip from her back like a gag in an old Mack Sennet film.

Also reviewed in:
CHICAGO TRIBUNE, 3/5/93, Friday/p. A, Dave Kehr
NEW REPUBLIC, 4/12/93, p. 28, Stanley Kauffmann
NEW YORK TIMES, 3/5/93, p. C3, Vincent Canby
NEW YORKER, 3/15/93, p. 119, Anthony Lane
VARIETY, 3/1/93, p. 56, Todd McCarthy
WASHINGTON POST, 3/5/93, p. C1, Rita Kempley
WASHINGTON POST, 3/5/93, Weekend/p. 38, Desson Howe

MADE IN AMERICA

A Warner Bros. release of a Le Studio Canal+/Regency Enterprises/Alcor Films presentation of a Stonebridge Entertainment/Kalola Productions film.   *Executive Producer:* Nadine Schiff and Marcia Brandwynne.   *Producer:* Arnon Milchan, Michael Douglas, and Rick Bieber.   *Director:* Richard Benjamin.   *Screenplay:* Holly Goldberg Sloan and Nadine Schiff.   *Story:* Nadine Schiff, Holly Goldberg Sloan, and Marcia Brandwynne.   *Director of Photography:* Ralf Bode.   *Editor:* Jacqueline Cambas.   *Music:* Mark Isham.   *Music Editor:* Richard Whitfield.   *Choreographer:* Lester Wilson.   *Sound:* Richard Lightstone.   *Sound Editor:* Mike Dobie and Jeff Bushelman.   *Casting:* Reuben Cannon.   *Production Designer:* Evelyn Sakash.   *Set Decorator:* Hilton Rosemarin.   *Set Dresser:* George Mauricio and Eugene Texeira.   *Special Effects:* Thomas F. Sindicich.   *Costumes:* Elizabeth McBride.   *Make-up:* Michael Germain and Daniel Striepeke.   *Stunt Coordinator:* David R. Ellis.   *Running time:* 70 minutes.   *MPAA Rating:* PG-13.

CAST: Whoopi Goldberg (Sarah Mathews);   Ted Danson (Hal Jackson);   Will Smith (Tea Cake Walters);   Nia Long (Zora Mathews);   Paul Rodriguez (Jose);   Jennifer Tilly (Stacy);   Peggy Rea (Alberta);   Clyde Kusatsu (Bob Takashima);   David Bowe (Teddy);   Jeffrey Joseph (James);   Rawley Valverde (Diego);   Fred Mancuso (Bruce);   Charlene Fernetz (Paula);   Shawn Levy (Dwayne);   Lu Leonard (Clinic Nurse);   Joe Lerer (Hospital Doctor);   Janice Edwards (Hospital Nurse);   Michael McFall (Hospital Intern);   Phyliss Avery (White Woman

#1);   Frances Bergen (White Woman #2);   O'Neal Compton (Rocky);   Michael Halton (Stew);
William John Murphy (P.A. #1);   Ross Benjamin (P.A. #2);   Mel Stewart (Principal Rockwell);
David E. Kazanjian (Mr. Alden);   Jim Cranna (Person at Car Lot);   Shannon Orrock (Wife at
Car Lot);   Alexandra Joy Cuccia (Child at Car Lot);   Chikako Felper (Japanese Woman #1);
Patricia Jow (Japanese Woman #2);   Raquel Osborne (Woman in Sushi Bar);   James Anthony
Cotton (Man with Beer);   Miyuki Takei (Sushi Waitress);   Akihide "Bo" Fujiyama (Sushi Chef);
Gregory Fields, Meashell McCann, Antoine Foote, and Jeffrey Russell (Rappers, Y-T Style).

LOS ANGELES TIMES, 5/28/93, Calendar/p. 1, Kevin Thomas

Talk about chemistry: In "Made in America," Whoopi Goldberg and Ted Danson go together
like Clark Gable and Carole Lombard—or Lucy and Desi. On the surface, of course, they seem
like polar opposites, but they're well-matched in their ability to move deftly from slapstick to
seriousness, rage to tenderness, indomitability to vulnerability. Best of all, beyond the characters
they're. playing, Goldberg and Danson seem to have the ability to take each other by surprise,
constantly keeping each other on his or her mettle.

Goldberg plays the capable, successful Sarah Mathews, owner of a Berkeley bookstore devoted
to African culture and a single mother to Zora (Nia Long), a pretty 17-year-old who's an achiever
with a bright future. By chance, Zora discovers from a blood-typing classroom project that
Sarah's late husband cannot have been the father she never knew, Sarah confesses that Zora was
conceived via a sperm bank donation—she had specified that the donor be "smart, black, not too
tall." Zora becomes determined to find the unknown sperm donor/father.

Danson's Hal Jackson is about the last white man either mother or daughter would want to be
the donor, and they wouldn't be much happier if Hal were black, which is naturally what they
expected. Surely inspired by local fixture Cal Worthington, Jackson is the San Francisco Bay
Area's gaudiest, hardest-selling car dealer, constantly on view in commercials wearing glitzy
cowboy attire and teamed up with one exotic animal after another. Hal exudes a crass, calculated
folksy quality in his commercials that is a turnoff to smart women like Sarah and Zora.

The idea that he really could have fathered Zora has an unexpected impact upon Hal, twice
divorced without children and now sharing a big house with a sweet airhead gymnast (Jennifer
Tilly). He suddenly feels very lonely. If Zora longs for a father, then Hal may be longing for
a child. What's more, Hal and Sarah sense a totally unexpected mutual attraction beneath their
sparring.

Very early on writer Holly Goldberg Sloan, working from a story she wrote with Marcia Brandwynne and Nadine Schiff, moves us beyond conventional interracial romantic comedy. Once Hal
accepts that he is in fact Zora's father, he wants to get to know her and become part of her life,
but the fiercely self-reliant Sarah insists that a donation of sperm does not make man a father. The
truth is that Sarah, proud of her independence, doesn't want to share the child she has raised so
successfully. At the same time the mother, like her daughter, is forced to admit that Hal can be
more sensitive and intelligent than the oafish guy he is on TV. Hal and Sarah also discover they
both possess a wild, spontaneous sense of humor and a bold, uninhibited sexuality.

Any successful comedy must have its serious side if it is to have any weight or substance, and
director Richard Benjamin displays a mastery of the film's ever-see-sawing shifts of tone. Hal and
Sarah both emerge as real people because the film allows them many opportunities to calm down
and get serious. Heading a large and formidable supporting cast with Will Smith as her witty
boyfriend, Long in particular is impressive.

Instead of self-consciously worrying about being politically correct, the makers of "Made in
America" reveal the true multicultural diversity of our society through imaginative characteriza
tion and casting, and they raise important questions about what constitutes a family and what
defines a parent in this age of increasingly non-traditional households.

The film shows, without comment, that a woman can sell a car as well as a man, that a
handsome young Latino just might ask out a pretty young African-American woman, that a gay
black man might prefer Judy Garland to the African music he's supposed to identify with—even
if he's conforming to a homosexual stereotype. Exceptionally well-crafted, "Made in America"
(rated PG-13 for sexual situations and language) is the kind of picture Hollywood often aspires
to but rarely succeeds in bringing off—smart and sophisticated with a wide appeal.

NEW YORK, 6/14/93, p. 66, David Denby

When did Richard Benjamin's directing become so crude? Was it with *The Money Pit*? The director of *My Favorite Year* and *Racing With the Moon* wasn't always desperate for laughs. In *Made in America*, Benjamin takes one roundhouse swing after another and almost always misses. It's the kind of movie in which people are constantly bursting in on one another screaming. Over and over, Whoopi Goldberg rides a bicycle right through San Francisco traffic without stopping for lights—that one cracks me up every time—and Ted Danson mounts an elephant and gets pawed by a bear. Danson's character, Hal, a clownish truck salesman, makes a fool of himself and then, knowing that he has come off badly, covers his chagrin with bluster, swinging his arms and shooting. A man who can't stop himself from acting like a jerk—yet remains acutely aware of what he's done—could be a touching figure if anything were written for him to say, but Danson has to do everything with his big, clumsy frame and lugubrious sunken eyes, and Ted Danson is a very tedious clown.

Made in America is a sperm-bank comedy. Seventeen years earlier, Sarah (Goldberg), the owner of an African-culture bookstore in Berkeley, bought some of the stuff and conceived a wonderful, gifted black child, Zora (Nia Long), who is now about to graduate from high school and go off to MIT. But after a blood test, Zora realizes that her mother's late husband, who was black, could not have been her father, so she sets about discovering who her father is. And he turns out to be white and vulgar; he turns out to be Hal, who does TV ads with chimpanzees and other animals. Yet after meeting his daughter, this shallow hedonist, who sleeps with a dumb aerobics instructor, suddenly feels the stirrings of parental instinct. Of course, snobby Sarah is disgusted. She has no respect for him, and they flail at each other in a long series of mirthless scenes in which differences between two people are exacerbated in order to postpone the inevitable moment of the couple's coming together.

After a while, they calm down and begin to like each other. Goldberg and Danson are visibly enjoying themselves, but in terms of their characters, the attraction is only half worked out. We can see that his longing for dignity touches her. But mainly, they click because he accidentally swallows a gob of green mustard in a Japanese restaurant. Now, this moment of communion may possess some mystical significance for the actors, but the sight was not enough to convince *me* that either of these two was a human being. The romance might have worked if the salesman and the bookstore owner had talked more about their lives, giving us something deeper than we're-all-human, some way of making sense of them as an interracial couple. *Made in America* is too clownish for intimacy. Throughout, Benjamin directs it as if someone were sticking needles in him. Most of what he does isn't direction, it's lunging.

NEW YORK POST, 5/28/93, p. 35, Matthew Flamm

She's smart. He's obnoxious. She runs a bookshop. He sells cars. She lives with her loving, charming teen-age daughter and reveres the memory of her dead husband. He lives with a bimbo-of-the-moment and has two ex-wives.

Oh yeah, she's black, he's white. With "Made in America," the opposites attract comedy-romance formula has been rejigged to include the potentially explosive ingredient of race. Unfortunately, and perhaps inevitably, even with Whoopi Goldberg and Ted Danson in the leads, the recipe still seems stale.

"Made in America" is so broadly drawn and so badly overcalculated, it could have been written by their agents.

The film, directed by Richard Benjamin ("Mermaids"), almost works as the story of a young girl's desperate longing for a father, Zora Mathews (Nia Long), Goldberg's perfectly brilliant and beautiful daughter, discovers in her high school biology lab that her blood type matches neither her mother's nor her (long-dead) father's.

Informed that papa was in fact an anonymous donor at a local Bay Area sperm bank ("I asked for the best they had," Goldberg jokes to her, "... black, smart, not too tall"), Zora gets hold of the computer records and makes the big mistake of looking him up.

That evening, after having been rudely rebuffed by Hal ("Hal's Your Pal") Jackson, she can barely break the news to mom. "You haven't heard the worst part," Zora says, leading up to it "He's a car salesman ... a *white* car salesman."

There is something mildly funny about Sarah (Goldberg)—whose devoutly Afrocentric bookshop is called The African Queen—doing a sort of reverse "Guess Who's Coming to Dinner" ("He's *white?!* What do you mean he's white?!"), And Danson isn't bad as the crude, ur-white huckster (with the roughest edges smoothed off: He shows not a hint of racism).

But the script doesn't know where to go. A contrived comic face-off in Hal's office, in which Sarah gets drunk and argues with both her daughter and her "father," misfires completely. The salespeople on the lot as well as Zora's harmless, somewhat amusing best friend ("Fresh Prince of Bel-Air"'s Will Smith), seem borrowed from the nearest sitcom.

The film's funniest moments hardly concern the stars, coming out of the slapstick that results from Hal's shooting a television commercial with an ill-tempered bear.

Of course, Hal eventually softens, and it becomes touchingly apparent Zora doesn't care what color he is, as long as she can have a dad. When the romance begins between Hal and Sarah it seems all three long to unscramble the egg and create an old-fashioned family. (In their long make-out scene, Danson and Goldberg are believably affectionate, if not the least bit combustible.)

The forced, mawkish wind-up can partly be blamed on Goldberg, who gives in to her old need to play a saint (remember "Clara's Heart"?). In any case, the filmmakers stop at nothing in their pursuit of sentiment and a happy ending.

NEWSDAY, 5/28/93, Part II/p. 62, John Anderson

"Funny thing, sperm," muses Hal Jackson (Ted Danson). Yes, the very thought of it causes us fits of hilarity. Unfortunately, its full comedic depths have not quite been plumbed by "Made in America."

This lightweight comedy, which despite dusty gags and numbing predictability still has a certain charm about it, concerns the four-wheel-drivin', 10-gallon-hat-wearin' car dealer Jackson, who utters the line above sometime after being told he's the father of a 17-year-old black girl. It seems his little white swimmers, donated to a sperm bank 18 years before, somehow found their way into Sarah Mathews (Whoopi Goldberg), a decidedly black lady, and produced her daughter, Zora (Nia Long). Now, they're producing a series of racial, sexual and other identity crises, and far too few laughs.

Despite its sit-com quality, "Made in America" raises some potent issues: Sarah's life as a single mother, and why, after her young husband died, she decided to go to a sperm bank so she could have a child. "I'd just lost the biggest, love of my life," she tells Zora, who's found Hal's name alongside her mother's in the sperm bank's computer, "and I thought maybe I could make myself another one." And there's the question of Hal's life and what he's done with it: A rather buffoonish character, thanks to the ads he does on cable TV, he lives with a woman who might be called Super-bimbo, played by—who else?—Jennifer Tilly. He looks at Zora, a prize-winning science student and wonders what he might have done with his own life.

While there are other weighty matters in "Made in America," there's also a runaway elephant: As part of his dealership's publicity campaign, Jackson gets atop a pachyderm whose trainer controls him with a little bell. Then an irate Sarah, demanding satisfaction from Hal, pulls into the lot on her bike, ringing *her* little bell, and driving the elephant to distraction. En route to the riverfront, where Hal will be unceremoniously dunked, the frantic animal nearly tramples a group of Hare Krishnas ringing *their* little bells ... you get the picture. Throw in a car crash or two and what we have, basically, is a film based on a very adult theme that will have children laughing uproariously.

The publicity campaign for "Made in America" has been much augmented by the reported love affair between stars Danson and Goldberg. And though they're as odd a couple on screen as off, they also manage to make Sarah and Hal sweet enough that you want to believe in them, even if it's tough. This, despite the fact that the two are doing what they always do: He burlesques the irresponsible stud; she plays cute as the don't-muck-with-me, Afro-centric buster of chops.

Sweetness aside, the jokes don't hold up, although there are some good bits from Will ("Fresh Prince of Bel-Air") Smith as Zora's friend Tea Cake Walters, and a very smart performance by Nia Long, who's really the film's bright light. "Made in America" is just too long, and stands on very tired legs.

NEWSWEEK, 6/21/93, p. 65, Jack Kroll

Last week's No. 2 box-office movie (behind "Cliffhanger") is also the No. 1 nominee for Dumbest Movie of the Year: *Made in America*. Concept: Sarah Mathews (Whoopi Goldberg) has had a daughter, Zora, by artificial insemination. She asked the sperm bank for a black donor, but Zora (Nia Long), now 17, finds out her test-tube daddy is a white guy, Hal (Ted Danson). Sarah is outraged. Hal is flabbergasted. Zora just wants a daddy, no matter who, or hue. Switcheroo: Sarah and Hal fall for each other. So what's wrong with a nice comedy that brings the races together? How about (1) unfunny, (2) idiotic and (3) embarrassing? Here's "proud Afro-centrist" Sarah (studio blurb) who runs a bookstore specializing in black culture. So she de-Afrocenters herself by falling for not just a white guy, but a cowboy-hatted used-car dealer who makes screeching TV commercials with bears, elephants and chimpanzees; drives a pickup littered with beer cans, and is shacking up with the mother of all dumb blondes who talks like Betty Boop and does nude cartwheels to express the joy of sex (Jennifer Tilly). See? Unfunny, idiotic, embarrassing. Goldberg won't talk about her apparent real-life romance with Danson. That's classy and dignified. Which is more than can be said for her reel-life romance with Cowboy Hal. Whoopi, can we talk?

SIGHT AND SOUND, 8/93, p. 48, Leslie Felperin Sharman

Sarah Mathews is a black, widowed single mother who runs a bookstore called *The African Queen* in Berkeley, California. Her daughter Zora accidentally discovers that she has AB blood type, which means that Sarah's dead husband was not her father. Sarah admits that she used a sperm bank, so Zora, with the help of her ex-boyfriend Tea Cake, sets out to discover her real father's identity. She learns that the donor is a car salesman, Hal Jackson. Stunned but undeterred by the fact that he's white, she tells him who she is, but he refuses to acknowledge any relationship. After Zora tells a horrified Sarah what she's learned, Sarah goes to the car lot and insists that Hal stay away from her and her daughter. At first, he is happy to comply, but has second thoughts after watching a Shirley Temple movie.

After a chase through the streets of Berkeley involving an elephant and a bicycle bell, Sarah and Hal spend an enjoyable evening, almost ending up in bed. They are interrupted by Zora, who is aghast at their behaviour. Sarah and Hal quarrel and, while driving off in a fury on her bicycle, Sarah is hit by a car. At the hospital, Hal is asked to give blood and learns that he is type O, and therefore not Zora's father. He and Sarah part amicably. Sometime later, on Zora's graduation day, she is called upon to give a speech after winning a coveted science scholarship. She invites Sarah on stage to thank her, and Hal steps forward to help her on to the podium. Zora introduces him as her 'Dad', and all three join in a rousing rendition of "Stand" with the school choir.

Like Onan, recent movies centering on sperm banks have spilt their seed on fallow ground. Both George Miller's *Frozen Assets* and the British *Leon the Pig Farmer* suffered from stunted growth, blighted by screenplay defects and clumsy directorial nurturing. *Made in America* is a somewhat better bred specimen, but it still suffers from a certain sterility, eschewing its initial promise to confound race relations with eugenics in favour of a bland and abrupt happy ending. None the less, it's a likeable effort, good enough for a sultry summer evening at the multiplex when the film you came to see is sold out.

There are moments when one can glimpse the remains of what might have been a spikier, more complex movie. For example, when Zora and Sarah argue about the embarrassment of Hal's whiteness, Zora suggests that she has, and still can, 'pass' as black, just like the kids on *The Cosby Show*. "Don't talk to me about those kids!" fumes Sarah, subtly indicating the anger that many Afro-Americans feel about the dominance of lighter-skinned black actors in the media mainstream. It becomes clear that the Berkeley/Oakland location was chosen because Berkeley, especially the University of California campus that Sarah cycles through in the opening sequence, was one of the cradles of the multiculturalist philosophy—encapsulated in a T-shirt that proclaims "Jesus was a black man"—that her bookshop espouses. That Hal is a quasi-redneck, and thus her cultural opposite, is signalled by his cowboy hats, pickup trucks, and blindingly blonde girlfriend. The clunkingly obvious irony is that both Sarah and Hal are 'made in America', but apart from the aforementioned scene the tensions inherent in their situation are never explored beyond the level of props. Unlike *Jungle Fever*, this film shies away raising any really controversial questions in favour of the homiletic 'answers' that family values, read as universal, provide.

Director Richard Benjamin began his career as an actor, perhaps most memorably as the perplexed lead in *Goodbye Columbus*. The brittle charm of his persona translated well into his delightful directorial debut, *My Favorite Year*. Since then, his career has been rather disappointing, but *Made in America* at least shows that he can coax performers (even animal ones), even if all else is a little lacklustre. Goldberg and Danson are not particularly deep actors, but both are affable and endowed with excellent comic timing. It's hard not to imagine a frisson between them generated by their off-screen romance. The tabloid hullabaloo about their love affair has probably done more to challenge taboos about mixed race relationships than the film itself; but then again, screwball comedy and social commentary do not make comfortable bedfellows.

TIME, 6/14/93, p. 72, Richard Schickel

She's a celibate single mom; he's a shiftless stud, currently shacked up with a dimwitted aerobics instructor. She's the owner of an Oakland, California, bookshop specializing in black studies; he's the proprietor of, and TV pitchman for, a car dealership. She wears authentic African garments to work and rides a bicycle everywhere; he favors inauthentic cowboy duds and hogs the road in a four-by-four. Oh, yes, she's black, and he's white.

But *Made in America* sees this, the most obvious difference between Sarah Mathews (Whoopi Goldberg) and Hal Jackson (Ted Danson), as the least of their problems. It's not so much the discovery that, because of a mix-up at a sperm bank, Hal may be the father of her child that sends Sarah into orbit. It's the notion that after he is identified and tracked down, this particular white man, so trashy, so hopelessly incorrect politically and socially, could have provided half the genetic material for her talented, pretty daughter Zora (Nia Long).

It's hard to think of a more widely appealing comic strategy than this. By banishing the issue of racial conflict, the movie remakes the world as every person of goodwill wishes it really were. And by making all the conflicts between Sarah and Hal purely cultural and therefore subject to good-humored behavioral modification, the movie implies that everything else dividing us today can be worked out with equal simplicity.

It appears to be Goldberg's mission in life to redeem improbable situations. It's what she did so profitably last summer in *Sister Act*, and she's awfully good at it. There's something about her—a gritty, down-to-earth straightforwardness—that tends to promise some realization of our wan hopes that potentially explosive circumstances can be defused—at least for the running time of a movie.

Of course, it helps if the picture contains plenty of distracting farce and an equal measure of disarming sentimentality. It helps too if you can partner Goldberg with someone as agreeable and unthreatening as Danson, if you can find a director as comically inventive as Richard Benjamin, and if you can figure out a way to cast Will Smith. He plays Zora's best friend, Tea Cake, and his marvelously freewheeling choral effects—a muttered aside here, a strangled warning there—give the movie a waywardness it desperately needs.

For *Made in America* is basically one long evasive action, a nice little entertainment designed to whisper sweet nothings in our ear about two very edgy matters, race and sex. Because it's so comforting, it will probably make a ton of money. But bitter truth—anyway an occasional touch of it—can be funny too and, these days, quite useful.

Also reviewed in:
CHICAGO TRIBUNE, 5/28/93, Friday/p. C, Dave Kehr
NEW YORK TIMES, 5/28/93, p. C5, Janet Maslin
VARIETY, 6/7/93, p. 38, Brian Lowry
WASHINGTON POST, 5/28/93, p. G1, Rita Kempley

MALICE

A Columbia Pictures release of a Castle Rock Entertainment presentation in association with New Line Cinema. *Executive Producer:* Michael Hirsh and Patrick Loubert. *Producer:* Rachel Pfeffer, Charles Mulvehill, and Harold Becker. *Director:* Harold Becker. *Screenplay:* Aaron Sorkin and Scott Frank. *Story:* Aaron Sorkin and Jonas McCord. *Director of Photography:* Gordon Willis. *Editor:* David Bretherton. *Music:* Jerry Goldsmith. *Music Editor:* Kenneth Hall. *Sound:* Robert Eber and (music) Bruce Botnick. *Sound Editor:* David E. Stone. *Production Designer:* Philip Harrison. *Art Director:* Dianne Wager. *Set Designer:* Sydney Litwack, Alan Manzer, Hugo Santiago, and Harold Fuhrman. *Set Decorator:* Garrett Lewis. *Set Dresser:* Gary Isbell, Scott Garrett, William Derham, and Donald Chafey, Jr. *Special Effects:* Cliff Wenger. *Costumes:* Michael Kaplan. *Make-up:* Bob Mills. *Stunt Coordinator:* Chuck Waters. *Running time:* 107 minutes. *MPAA Rating:* R.

CAST: Alec Baldwin (Jed); Nicole Kidman (Tracy); Bill Pullman (Andy); Bebe Neuwirth (Dana); George C. Scott (Dr. Kessler); Anne Bancroft (Ms. Kennsinger); Peter Gallagher (Dennis Riley); Josef Sommer (Lester Adams); Tobin Bell (Earl Leemus); William Duff-Griffin (Dr. George Sullivan); Debrah Farentino (Tanya); Gwyneth Paltrow (Paula Bell); David Bowe (Dr. Matthew Robertson); Diana Bellamy (Ms. Worthington); Michael Hatt (Neighbor Boy); Paula Plum (Neighbor Boy's Mother); Sara Melson (Girl on Bike); Ken Cheeseman (Code Blue Operator); Richard Rho (Anesthesiologist); Joshua Malina (Resident); Christine Wheeler (Scrub nurse); Sharon Albright (Circulating Nurse); Tom Kemp (Bartender); Robin Joss and Patricia Dunnock (Dart Players); Brenda Strong (Claudia); Michael Bofshever (Desk Sergeant); Laura Langdon (Desk Clerk); David Candreva (Cab Driver); Ann Cusack (Waitress).

FILMS IN REVIEW, 11-12/93, p. 414, Andy Pawelczak

First *The Fugitive*, now *Malice*—doctor bashing is in this year of Clinton's health plan. It's enough to revive the Republican fantasies of a liberal Hollywood conspiracy, but they don't have much to fear from *Malice*. It's not exactly a bad picture—most of the pieces are in the right places—but it's all very familiar and oddly perfunctory, as though everybody involved knew in advance this wasn't a terribly good movie but might be a serviceable little thriller that would add a credit to their resumes.

Andy (Bill Pullman) is the Dean of Students in a college in a Boston suburb that looks like the all-American town in Hitchcock's *Shadow Of A Doubt*—big handsome houses, tree shaded streets, and fresh faced young people who are the prey of the devil in this paradise, a serial rapist. Andy lives in connubial bliss with his wife, Tracy (Nicole Kidman), who was his student before their marriage, in a big Victorian house that they're renovating. When Jed (Alec Baldwin), a supremely arrogant surgeon, comes to work in the local hospital, Andy impulsively invites him to move into his vacant third floor. Andy went to high school with Jed and, as his wife suggests, has never quite gotten over his hero worship of the bright, distant football champion. Before long there's another rape and murder, tension develops between Tracy and Jed who comes on to her and might even be the serial rapist, and Tracy undergoes an emergency operation for an ovarian cyst. In the course of the operation, Jed removes her healthy ovary which sets the stage for the movie's twists and turns as Nicole sues Jed for malpractice and abandons Andy for permitting the operation. Nothing more can be revealed without spoiling the picture's surprises.

The movie's plot has one major red herring and several holes (unless I missed something) big enough for a whale to swim through. It also cannibalizes several other films, which is perhaps appropriate for a medical thriller whose central event is the surgical removal of an organ. The movie borrows heavily from the unwelcome-tenant plot of the recent *Pacific Heights* and the rite of passage theme of Peckinpah's *Straw Dogs*. In the beginning, Andy is a mild mannered wimp helplessly besotted with his beautiful young wife and dazzled by the macho, over achieving Jed, but by the end he finds his manhood through a little of the good old hyper-violence.

As Andy, Bill Pullman does what he can under the circumstances—there's not much room for character complexity in this plot-driven movie. Recently seen as the jilted fiance in *Sleepless In*

Seattle, Pullman seems to have been type cast as the nice guy victim, though in this film he gets the chance to display a little angst and ferocity. Alec Baldwin is the real star of the show as the doctor with a god complex who explains, in the movie's best scene, that when people pray for their sick loved ones, they're really praying to him, the surgeon. Though it's a one dimensional role, Baldwin, with his raspy voice and demonically good looks, is creepy and convincing. Nicole Kidman, I'm afraid, is still serving her apprenticeship. The film gives her the opportunity to work with two radically different personae, but nothing very striking comes through in either one. George C. Scott, in a cameo role, is adequate as a distinguished doctor, and Anne Bancroft seems to be having fun as a whiskey guzzling old woman. Bebe Neuwirth, with her anti-Hollywood looks and an odd accent that sounds faintly Brooklynese, adds an element of interest as a police detective who at one point suspects Andy as the serial rapist.

The movie's director, Harold Becker, whose previous film was the much more compelling *Sea Of Love*, doesn't do much to invigorate his material. The picture is full of stock footage including a gothic house on a cliff on a stormy night, a search through a dark basement, and a shadowy voyeur silhouetted in a window. Becker and his screenwriter, Aaron Sorkin, try to give the movie a film noir patina, but it's about as deep as Nicole Kidman's eye shadow, and we're a long way from such a film as *Double Indemnity* which, in addition to a strong plot, had characters so memorable that they've entered movie mythology. Nor does *Malice* have the tragic sense of life we associate with film noir, which I for one grievously miss in contemporary film. In the end, *Malice* feels prefabricated, artificial, like a prosthetic device.

LOS ANGELES TIMES, 10/1/93, Calendar/p. 12, Peter Rainer

"Malice," the new thriller starring Alec Baldwin and Nicole Kidman, doesn't have a whole lit on its mind except other thrillers. The borrowings or quasi-borrowings—ranging from Hitchcock to Hitchcock derivatives like "Pacific Heights"—give the film a peculiar kind of comfiness. It's supposed to scare the wits out of you but the plethora of prior associations make it seem more like Old Home Week.

The setting is the archetypal sleepy New England college town—a sylvan glade waiting to be despoiled. A serial murderer has been terrorizing the co-eds and Andy (Bill Pullman), the dean of students, is alarmed. So it the local police investigator (Bebe Neuwirth), who talks tough and suspects everybody—even the rumply bookish Andy.

The plot kicks into gear when Jed (Baldwin), a former high school classmate of Andy's, moves into the community as the new star surgeon. Jed is so supremely self-assured, inside the operating room and out, that he seems to be walking on water for most of the movie. When things get tough later on, he's accused of having a God complex, to which he replies, only half-facetiously, "I *am* God."

Andy's wife, Tracy (Kidman), his former pupil and a volunteer in a children's ward, dislikes Jed at first sight, which doesn't, however, stop him form becoming a tenant in the couple's spacious home. (Aren't surgeons making enough these days to rent their own place?) When Tracy starts experiencing abdominal pains, Jed is pressed into service, which leads to the question: Is this the kind of guy you want rummaging around your innards?

Harold Becker, directing from a script by Aaron Sorkin and Scott Frank, is proficient at keeping things taut despite the bagginess of many of the plot points. In an effort to keep the thrills coming the screenwriters scatter about too many loose ends; they don't provide the precise cat-and-mouse plotting that used to be the hallmark of the well-made thriller but is now virtually nonexistent.

Instead the filmmakers throw in a lot of old standbys, including a lonely house on a cliff high above the hissing ocean, and cinematographer Gordon Willis keeps everything appropriately dark, for that *noir*-ish effect. "Malice" (rated R for sexuality, language and some violence) at least has the *look* of a first-rate thriller.

The performances are serviceable enough to at least keep you guessing for a while who's on the level and who isn't. Baldwin is fairly amusing when his character's ego is puffed to bursting (which is most of the time). He makes Jed into a familiar monster: the doctor as self-anointed Savior. Anne Bancroft and George C. Scott turn up in separate cameos and they contrast perfectly—she overacts like crazy and he underplays to the point of somnolence.

There's no pressing reason to see "Malice" because, in a sense, you've already seen it. And, if you wait a year or two, chances are you'll be seeing bits of pieces of "Malice" in the next batch of so-so thrillers. And so it goes.

NEW STATESMAN & SOCIETY, 1/14/94, p. 34, Jonathan Romney

In its playfully devious way, *Malice* could have been designed expressly to test the descriptive resources of film critics. Not that it's in any way *avant-garde:* it's a manipulative Hollywood hack job, but it has more going for it than the automatic deployment of Hitchcockian suspense strategies suggests. Harold Becker's jolly box of tricks is an extraordinary anomaly at a time when most thrillers consider it a waste of time to double-cross the audience when you can have Sharon Stone cross her legs instead.

Malice is a classic Chinese dinner of a movie. You've practically forgotten it the minute you leave the cinema, even though it has tweaked most efficiently at your entrails. But here's the rub: try to describe it, and explain which strings it pulls and how, and you can't—because you give the whole game away.

In critical circles, this is known as the "*Crying Game* challenge": how clever can you be about this movie without spoiling it? *Malice* may not pull any sex changes, but it pulls so many other cons that it's impossible to say much about it at all, let alone get to grips with the rather unsettling subtext, for fear of defusing its pleasures entirely.

But since you're all too sophisticated to worry about plots, let's have a go anyway. *Story*: Tracy and Andy Safian are a young couple living in a nice New England university town, where female students are mysteriously being attacked. Along comes over-sexed Dr Jed Hill, a brilliant surgeon, who moves into the Safians' creepy house, and displays an alarming tendency to stand silhouetted in doorways when you least expect him to. Now read on ...

Cast: Alex Baldwin, as Dr Hill, is a fine ambivalent charmer, an all-American jock sprayed with a whiff of *Suspicion*. The hitherto spongecake-bland Nicole Kidman, as Tracy, reveals unaccustomed depths. Bill Pullman, as Andy, has his depths too, but we're rather more accustomed to them. He has been playing thoughtful lunks in corduroy jackets for so long now that he's probably grown leather patches on his elbows. Pullman's chin alone made *Sleepless in Seattle* worth the admission price, and his bemused college prof is a darker variation on his bemused doctor in *Singles*. No doubt he's a dab hand at putting up shelves too.

Direction: A trickier one. Harold Becker once made an impressively claustrophobic cop thriller called *The Onion Field*, starring James Woods when he was still doing unalloyed nasty roles, and *Sea of Love*, an underrated vehicle for Al Pacino and Ellen Barkin. Here, although much of the direction has a pretty anonymous feel, he is very much aware of how to milk conventions.

He can pull expected patterns on us—if we visit a new address, you can bet it will be the Bates Motel relocated to a storm-swept gothic cliff; if someone comes to call, Becker has him loom for the hell of it—and then lets us wonder whether we're nervous because we have unconsciously gathered some nasty evidence about this character, or because he happens to be lit from behind.

There's also a feeling that Becker is trying to make up for the shortcomings of *Sea of Love*. There, the premise was that Barkin might have been a murderer, and the film came down to a simple matter of did-she-or-didn't-she? Unfortunately, there was only one alternative candidate, which made for one of those lame endings now endemic in Hollywood thrillers. Here, however, scriptwriters Aaron Sorkin and Scott Frank (clearly fiends from the innermost circle of narrative hell) work so many switcheroos that you're hooked before you even realise that, *Psycho*-style, the original premise has been dumped—*damn*, there goes my big mouth again.

You can see *Malice* assured of your money's worth in cheap nerve-tingling. A year from now, when you've all seen it, we can talk about how unnervingly misogynistic the film is in a way that recalls David Cronenberg. What's interesting now about it, though, is that discussion really does blow the gaffe. Therefore critics are obliged either to shut up entirely or, worse, to think.

It's a rarity these days for film reviews to be much more than plot resumés: partly because that's what the public is assumed to want, partly because it's that much easier. There's a definite gratification in retelling a plot in 200 pithy words. The most fun I ever had writing a review was in summarising a silly Jean-Claude Van Damme vehicle, trying to be as accurate as possible while still being gratuitously sarcastic. After losing 90 minutes of your life in the dark, you want *some* recompense. But it can be a lazy approach for a critic, and it makes for lazy viewers.

It may be a wonderful opiate to watch Barry Norman spin out a film's plot for ten minutes and band in a couple of clips. But once you've got to the cinema, you have seen the film already—or think you have. Movie-going is that much easier when you can have your films predigested.

This may read like snooty rhetoric, but cinema depends increasingly on predigestion. The most efficient example I can think of is *Jurassic Park*. If you went to see it blind and tried to figure out from its garbled narrative exactly how dinosaurs came to be stomping around, tough luck. The film counted on the fact that you had not only read all the pre-publicity but also seen the ingenious trailer, which did the exposition outside the film itself.

Films rely now not just on trailers, but also on critics—even more so, TV pundits—to spare them the trouble of telling stories. That doesn't mean that they eschew narrative for more sophisticated pleasures, simply that they don't make viewers do any real work. Films don't really need to make sense any more, and why bother when you can flash more basic credentials: a couple of star names, nice computer graphics, and a 25-word pitch that the press will peddle for you?

Malice is no big deal, but it does care about the craft of narrative (if little else) and does respect its viewers' intelligence enough to let us mislead ourselves. Woe for the critics: not only can't you reveal the story, but you can't even discuss the underlying issues. And most critics had to wise up to that approach in the 1980s, when mainstream narratives got too slipshod to discuss in any other way.

This healthy tendency, however, opened the floodgates for that now all-pervasive institution: the high-concept think-piece. But you can't write one of those about *Malice* either, at least not until its twists have become as common currency at dinner parties as the true gender of *The Crying Game*'s star Jaye Davidson. It doesn't mean that *Malice* will last the way that *Psycho* lasts, even when you've found out what's in the fruit cellar. It simply keeps its popcorn content fresh that little bit longer. These days, that's good value.

NEW YORK, 10/18/93, p. 121, David Denby

Harold Becker's *Malice*, a highly implausible thriller about sex, money, and surgery, is essentially familiar, but Becker has become a good entertainer, and the actors are fun: Nicole Kidman and Alec Baldwin do cocky self-assurance almost to the point of parody, and Bill Pullman, beaten up and tricked, pulls himself together and casts off his sad-sack image. Pullman must have seen Edward Herrmann introducing documentaries on cable and rebelled against his likely future.

NEW YORK POST, 10/1/93, p. 45, Michael Medved

There are times when a film critic is torn between the normal need to tell his readers what a movie is about and a desire to protect the film's special secrets and surprises.

This conflict occurred most famously with last year's "The Crying Game;" when most of us went along with the producers' pleas to conceal the transvestite disguise of one of the main characters.

I, for one, hope that my colleagues will display similar discretion with "Malice," where the plot twists are just as shocking, and the moments of revelation are even more cunningly constructed. This is an unusually ingenious thriller with a first-class screenplay (by "A Few Good Men"'s Adam Sorkin and "Dead Again"'s Scott Frank); it tells a bizarre tale but, up till the final minutes, manages to keep it barely believable.

Bill Pullman plays a soft-spoken dean at an exclusive women's college in Massachusetts. He is blessed with a supposedly sexy and adoring new wife (Nicole Kidman), a stylish but heavily mortgaged Victorian home, and one huge problem: a serial rapist who's been terrorizing the campus and leaving a string of dead coeds in his path.

The newlyweds also face some additional difficulties when they decide to rent the top floor of their house to one of Pullman's old friends from high school, a hotshot surgeon (Alec Baldwin) who's just taken a new position in the town's hospital. Many doctors think that they're God; this one knows it for a fact.

To tell more here about the way that these three play off against one another would be to spoil the principal pleasures of this slick and stylish film. Last time out, director Harold Becker brought an intense erotic edge to "Sea of Love," and with "Malice" he's done it again.

Nicole Kidman, who came across as both bland and bothersome in "Far and Away," here portrays the kind of perilously passionate partner that will make male moviegoers forget all about Sharon Stone. She is, in fact, so much more electrifying than she was co-starring with her real-life husband Tom Cruise, that it suggests that this superstar couple should never consider marketing their private home videos.

"Malice" also represents a break for the capable Pullman, who's recently been relegated to "Ralph Bellamy," second-lead roles—like the jilted fiancee in "Sleepless in Seattle," or the jilted suitor in "Summersby." This time he's the center of the action, and he easily holds his own with his better-known co-stars.

There are also telling cameos along the way from George C. Scott and the great Anne Bancroft, who turns in one emotional scene as a tart-tongued drunk who begins to disclose some of the story's secrets.

The major problem with this picture, as with so many other promising thrillers, is that the film-makers don't know how to end the thing. In order to present a slam-bang conclusion they suggest that a coldly calculating, preternaturally patient, diabolically clever con artist suddenly goes bonkers and begins perpetrating pointless and self-defeating acts of violence.

It's a shame, because it undermines the credibility that the previous two hours have so carefully constructed.

NEWSDAY, 10/1/93, Part II/p. 61, Terry Kelleher

"Ya gotta believe" is a fine slogan for the ballpark. At the movies, all ya gotta do is suspend disbelief.

Few thrillers really add up if you stop to analyze them. But the best don't release you from their grip long enough to entertain doubts. Not until you reach the lobby do you begin to recover your critical faculties.

The trouble with "Malice" is that viewers with inquiring minds will find themselves picking at the plot even as it unfolds, and even as they partake of the movie's pleasures.

The cardinal virtue of "Malice" is the magnetic, assured performance of Alec Baldwin as Dr. Jed Hill, a top-flight surgeon newly affiliated with a hospital in the fictional town of Westerly, Mass. There must be a housing shortage in Westerly, or you'd think the ego-driven doc could find living quarters grander than an upstairs room in the restored Victorian owned by Andy Safian (Bill Pullman), a high-school classmate who's now assistant dean of students at the local college.

Andy's sexy wife, Tracy (Nicole Kidman), voices disapproval of the tenant, particularly once he shows a fondness for noisy late-night romps with pickups from his favorite bar. For a while, "Malice" promises to become a northeastern "Pacific Heights"—unless director Harold Becker ("Sea of Love") and writers Aaron Sorkin ("A Few Good Men") and Scott Frank decide to bear down on that alternate story line about a killer rapist preying on coeds.

In throwing the audience off the scent, "Malice" gets a little lost itself. But the film powers forward when Jed performs emergency surgery on Tracy and winds up facing a multimillion-dollar malpractice suit. The deposition scene affords Baldwin the opportunity to deliver a self-deifying speech that rivals Michael Douglas' pro-greed stem-winder in "Wall Street."

In this thriller, however, things are never what they seem—even when it would make more sense if they were. Revelation follows revelation, one of them laid out at excessive length in a crotchety cameo by Anne Bancroft. We're asked to accept a conspiracy of shocking audacity, puzzling complexity and highly dubious motivation. No, there's no asking about it. The moviemakers simply assume our willingness to dispense with the whys and wherefores and concentrate on the "What's next?"

Despite occasional meandering, "Malice" always sustains interest. It looks right for the most part, though cinematographer Gordon Willis' predilection for semi-dark interiors makes you wish these thrifty New Englanders would splurge and switch on a light. Archness intrudes once or twice, but the dialogue effectively pretends to illumine character.

If you can tolerate the smell of red herring, there's nothing here you won't sit still for.

SIGHT AND SOUND, 2/94, p. 56, Nick James

Westerly, Massachusetts. A young girl on a bike is attacked, and is later rushed to hospital where her life is saved by glamorous new intern Dr Jed Hill. Having interviewed a girl student whose grades are slipping, college dean Andy Safian returns home to his new wife Tracy. Faced with a heavy estimate to re-plumb their recently acquired home, they decide that the only way they can afford it is by taking in a lodger. Andy runs into Jed, who turns out to be a former student acquaintance, and offers him the room. The doctor moves in and proceeds to lead a disruptively noisy sex life. Meanwhile, Tracy is suffering from occasional but severe stomach cramps and Jed recommends a Boston doctor for a second opinion.

On the day of her deadline meeting, Andy's student fails to show up and he decides to drive to her house, where he finds her dead body in the garden. While he is under investigation as a suspect, Tracy has a cramp attack in the shower. Jed finds her unconscious and calls an ambulance. Tracy has had a miscarriage and having removed one infected ovary, Jed diagnoses that Tracy's other one could potentially cause 'toxic shock', or else right itself. Jed consults the waiting Andy, who agrees to Jed's suggestion that they remove it. When she recovers, Tracy is furious and decides that she cannot forgive Andy and that she will sue the hospital for one million dollars. At the legal confrontation between the hospital and Tracy, the lab tests show that the ovary need not have been removed and Jed's display of arrogance makes it clear that he has a 'God complex.' The hospital agrees to pay, and Jed is dismissed. Tracy then disappears.

Late one night at the college, Andy investigates the basement where he finds a photo and a lock of blonde hair amongst the janitor's things. The janitor explains that the photo is of his family, but he then attacks Andy, who eventually knocks him unconscious. At the hospital lab, where a sperm sample has cleared him of blame for the attacks, Andy learns that he is infertile and could not be responsible for Tracy's pregnancy. He storms into her lawyer's office and demands to know where she is. Her lawyer gives him enough of a hint to be able to find her mother, who in turn reveals that Tracy has been a scheming con artist since childhood. Andy then tracks down her Boston doctor's country address to a clifftop house where he discovers that the doctor was Jed all along, and that he had been injecting Tracy with a toxic substance.

Realising he was set up even before his marriage, Andy leaves a syringe in the couple's bed as a message. He then demands to meet Tracy and counters her threats by telling her that the little boy next door to the Safians' house witnessed the injections. Jed wants to give Andy a one-third cut of the insurance money but Tracy overrules him by shooting him. She creeps into the little boy's room, planning to dispose of this possible witness, but she discovers a dummy at the keyboard and the police at hand. Andy tells her that the little boy has been blind all his life.

Of the string of sexual jealousy thrillers that have followed in the long wake of *Fatal Attraction*, this latest shows an already overheated genre hybrid—the 'Infiltration Thriller'—becoming warped beyond recognition. *Fatal Attraction* turned the generic femme fatale into a less ambivalent figure, no longer duplicitous and unknowable but unequivocally mentally unstable. This demonisation worked because it tapped into powerful anxieties about the change in social roles for both sexes in the 80s, as well as the fear of AIDS.

Subsequent films such as *Final Analysis, Single White Female* and *Basic Instinct* have likewise invoked cod-Freudian motivations for similar sociopathic characters. In the most frequently cannibalised model, Hitchcock's films, the sexual power struggles that these characters engage in would be barely contained within a realist tradition. In the infiltration thriller, however, such struggles have become so overtly signalled as to appear ridiculous, with each film looking as if it might at any moment begin to spoof itself.

The deadly woman here, Tracy, is a 'ballbreaker' who has her ovaries ripped out for commercial gain. How much louder can her denial of her 'femininity' be? No longer is it enough that she will marry the hero and then deliberately abort their baby. As for Dr Jed Hill, does he also need a promiscuous sexual reputation to match his apparent 'God complex' before he's mighty (or superficial) enough to fall? In the hyper-melodramatic world of the new nastier *noir*, the answer is emphatically yes. Hill is the necessary puffed-up counterpart to Andy Safian who personifies the 'safe' New Man as victim, the less-than-sympathetic turning worm who has replaced the Chandleresque tough but world-weary knight errant as hero in these films.

Such overblown mythic attributes are now all part of the format fun and have become more outlandish with each new example, so that director Harold Becker's previous foray into the territory, *Sea of Love*, which looked fairly lurid and implausible in 1989, now seems a model of restraint. In the recent infiltration thrillers everyone is a version of the hateful yuppie template, and therefore richly deserving of a dire fate. This break away from character realism grants the audience refuge from the duty of identification, giving them the freedom to enjoy the sheer nastiness now rupturing forth.

One of the consequences of encouraging such an emotional and critical distance, however, is that the film becomes almost totally reliant on narrative surprise; hence the scorpion's tail of false endings that are also a given in these films. Here the first narrative closure happens halfway through the film with the exposing of the janitor as the serial student killer. This act of heroism seems out of character for the otherwise passive Andy, but it acts as a springboard for an exposition that bears only slight relation to what's gone before. The eventual revelation that even the Safians' marriage was just a pretext to a scam not only demonises Tracy, but questions the whole basis of Andy's status. His social respectability thus removed, he can join the vicious game and show that only by becoming monstrous himself can he restore some sense of order. The pleasures of such a cartoon enactment of desire and its consequences are considerable. What it implies about the current state of play between the sexes, however, hardly bears thinking about.

VILLAGE VOICE, 10/19/93, p. 60, Henry Cabot Beck

To reveal the loopy plot devices in *Malice* would be a grave injustice to a film that deserves to be seen for its oddball contrivances and over-the-top performances. Suffice to say that Bill Pullman and Nicole Kidman play a happy college-town couple, Pullman counseling surly undergrads and Kidman threatening preschoolers with bondage. All that darkens their cozy lifestyle is a campus serial rapist-killer and a superstar-surgeon, Alec Baldwin, whom we know to be insufferably arrogant because he smokes, letches, drinks, and has sex to Randy Newman tunes. Hovering in the background is policewoman Bebe Neuwirth, a deadpan Agnes Morehead with a novocaine jones.

Ah, one is thinking a domestic psycho-suspense drama, sort of a *Hand That Rocks the Pacific Heights*. But then the story takes several screeching turns so abrupt that one comes to think of the film as a kind of inadvertently deconstructed collision of subgenres, each one unfolding into the next with breathtaking illogic; an experiment without hypothesis: a perfect dead-end Gen X movie for the '90s.

Afterward, you find yourself indulging in a kind of reverse dominoes, restacking the clues and absurd coincidences that give the film its idiot tumble: soil samples, forgotten syringes, necrotic ovaries, sterile sperm, dead light bulbs, gothic storm-tossed cliffs, and Degas reproductions "that you can buy in any department store." All in all, a delightfully mangled movie best appreciated by those who look either too closely or not at all.

Also reviewed in:
CHICAGO TRIBUNE, 10/1/93, Friday/p. C, Michael Wilmington
NEW YORK TIMES, 10/1/93, p. C5, Vincent Canby
NEW YORKER, 10/18/93, p. 117, Anthony Lane
VARIETY, 10/4/93, p. 38, Timothy Mo Gray
WASHINGTON POST, 10/1/93, p. C6, Hal Hinson

MALINA

A Kuchenreuther production in conjunction with Neue Studio Film GmbH, German ZDF-TV and Austrian ORF-TV. *Producer:* Thomas Kuchenreuther. *Director:* Werner Schroeter. *Screenplay (French with English subtitles):* Elfriede Jelinek. *Based on a novel by:* Ingeborg Bachmann. *Director of Photography:* Elfi Mikesch. *Editor:* Andrea Wenzhler. *Music:* Giacomo Manzoni. *Art Director:* Alberte Barsacq. *Costumes:* Alberte Barsacq. *Running time:* 125 minutes. *MPAA Rating:* Not Rated.

CAST: Isabelle Huppert (The Woman); Mathieu Carrière (Malina); Can Togay (Ivan).

NEW YORK POST, 10/2/93, p. 18, Jerry Tallmer

It's possibly crass to call Ingeborg Bachmann the Viennese Sylvia Plath, but that's what I grasp from the film that director Werner Schroeter and screenplay writer Elfriede Jelinek have crafted from her "Malina," and from the program notes that tell us of the "premature, disturbingly awful death" from "burns and tablet misuse" of this "exemplary sufferer" in Rome, 1973, age 40.

In fact, the novel was intended to be the first of a trilogy entitled "Ways of Dying."

We are all fascinated by the beautiful psychoneurotic woman—psychoneurotic, destructive, self-destructive. Beautiful and talented, for that matter—beauty, talent, and psychotic neurosis not seldom going together. The nameless heroine of "Malina" is one such woman, and for much of the two hours of the film we view her inferno from her own insides, so to speak, her own point of view. This makes for stress but not necessarily for nourishment.

The woman here, it's true, is Isabelle Huppert, which adds a curious dimension, because I've always felt that her stunning physical self is encased in a phlegmatic plastic shell (one of the problems of her "Madame Bovary"). Now this rather cold distancing is hurled into the total crackup (from early childhood the usual father thing) of a grown and gifted woman torn between two men.

These two are Malina (Mathieu Carriere), the exact, tight, taut museum historian with whom she lives, and Ivan (Can Togay), the dashing married man-about-town who disturbs her passion.

Malina sees her through her endless letter-writing and other craziness—"The mail to you is a grenade with the pin out," he says of her 10,000 unsent epistles on blue notepaper—and of course sees her through her just as endless suicide attempts and disguised suicide attempts, until the last one. Ivan merely uses her, awakens her, destroys her.

All of this may be fascinating to the voyeuristic, if you're interested in a film about three sleep-walkers, but it is also just about as pretentious)y artsy an overall product as anything I've seen since Andrei Tarkovsky's "Nostalghia," nine years ago.

VILLAGE VOICE, 9/23/93, p. 64, Leslie Camhi

Written from Vienna's cemetery of the murdered daughters, Ingeborg Bachmann's *Malina* is an ode to the solitary nature of passion. German avant-garde director Werner Schroeter has adapted this internal flood of words for the screen, with surreal fidelity, and operatic fervor. Isabelle Huppert plays a famous, nameless writer, relentlessly pursued by unending correspondence and a sense of nonexistence. She lives with Malina (Mathieu Carrière), a model of cultivated devotion, calm intelligence, and Prussian reserve, employed in the Austrian Army Museum. The *coup de foudre* of a chance encounter with Ivan (Can Togay) turns into a coupe de grace—and the writer is slowly stretched upon the rack of feeling.

Passion always exceeds its object, and excess is Schroeter's natural element. Here he uses it to portray the walking disaster of femininity in a world of reason. Victims, like the obese Bulgarian who needs a train ticket to Itzehoe for a leg operation, flock to our nameless writer for relief. The halls of a chateau where she has gone to rest are lined with antlers, stuffed cats, and assorted obscene trophies; she tears the curtains and rips out the marigolds in the window boxes. Toward the end, the walls of the apartment she shares with Malina fissure and fires flame from the corners.

It's nice to see a woman who is both passionate and intellectual on screen, even if she does end up tearing herself to pieces. Watching Huppert cite Wittgenstein requires a certain suspension of disbelief, but the desire she portrays calls for a courage most of us simply won't risk. Bachmann, who seems to have smoked in bed, died of burn wounds a few years after *Malina*'s publication. In both the film and the book, the writer recites a line that might be her epithet: "With my burnt hand, I write on the nature of fire."

Also reviewed in:
NEW YORK TIMES, 9/27/93, p. C15, Stephen Holden
VARIETY, 2/18/91, p. 71

MAN WITHOUT A FACE, THE

A Warner Bros. release of an Icon production.   *Executive Producer:* Stephen McEveety. *Producer:* Bruce Davey. *Director:* Mel Gibson. *Screenplay:* Malcolm MacRury. *Based on a novel by:* Isabelle Holland. *Director of Photography:* Donald M. McAlpine. *Editor:* Tony Gibbs. *Music:* James Horner. *Music Editor:* Jim Henrikson. *Sound:* Michael Evje and (music) Shawn Murphy. *Sound Editor:* Jonathan Bates. *Casting:* Marion Dougherty. *Production Designer:* Barbara Dunphy. *Art Director:* Marc Fisichella. *Set Designer:* Vicki Fraser. *Set Decorator:* Donald Elmblad. *Special Effects:* Brian Ricci. *Costumes:* Shay Cunliffe. *Make-up:* Stephan L. Dupuis. *Make-up (Special):* Greg Cannom. *Stunt Coordinator:* David Ellis. *Running time:* 114 minutes. *MPAA Rating:* PG-13.

CAST: Mel Gibson (McLeod); Margaret Whitton (Catherine); Fay Masterson (Gloria); Gaby Hoffmann (Megan); Geoffrey Lewis (Chief Stark); Richard Masur (Carl); Nick Stahl (Chuck); Michael Deluise (Douglas Hall); Ethan Phillips (Mr. Lansing); Jean De Baer (Mrs. Lansing); Jack De Mave (Mr. Cooper); Viva (Mrs. Cooper); Justin Kanew (Rob Lansing); Sean Kellman (David Taylor-Fife); Chris Lineburg (Scott Pearson); Kelly Wood (Amy Banks); Jessica Taisey (Signey Eaton); David A. McLaughlin (Chuck's Father); George Martin (Sam the Barber); Timothy Sawyer (Gus); Lawrence Wescott, Jr. (Bob); Michael Currie (Mr. Cameron); Stanja Lowe (Mrs. Cameron); Zach Grenier (Dr. Talbot); William Meisle (Judge Sinclair); Robert Hitt (Mr. McDowell); Mary Lamar Mahler (Miss Fletcher); Robert DeDiemar, Jr. (Chuck at age 17); Drew Guenett (Ferry Crew Member); Gene Leverone (Holyfield Master #1); Malcolm MacRury (Holyfield Master #2); George D. Fuller (Speaker at Graduation); Harriette C. Henninger (Neighbor); Edmond Genest (Husband #6); John B. Guptill (Chuck's Friend); Michael Forte (Pedestrian); Elizabeth S. Clarke (Ferry Passenger); Rocky (Mickey).

CHRISTIAN SCIENCE MONITOR, 8/27/93, p. 12, David Sterritt

Hollywood has been inching toward more concern with family audiences and with family subjects in older-audience movies. Recent results include the likable "Searching for Bobby Fischer," based on the true adventures of a seven-year-old chess prodigy, and "King of the Hill," a more hard-edged look at a 12-year-old separated from his family during the Depression years.

Continuing the trend, actor Mel Gibson now makes his directorial debut with "The Man Without a Face," a film about a 12-year-old boy's relationship with an unusual teacher who becomes his friend and mentor in a New England community.

It's a cautiously made picture, full of beautiful scenery, familiar character types, and plot twists designed to smooth away rough edges from sensitive elements in the story. But it's commendably ambitious, too, taking on a number of difficult subjects ranging from physical deformity to family dysfunction and child abuse. Most important, it takes a thoughtful and constructive approach to these matters, refusing to sensationalize them.

The main focus of the story is Chuck, a bright but insecure boy with a heavy share of problems. In order to attend a boarding school that will remove him from his constantly quarreling family, he must pass a difficult exam. But it's hard to study when your big sister is a snob, your little sister is a pest, and your mother is preoccupied with cajoling a pretentious Yale professor into becoming her fifth husband. Chuck is also bothered with uncertainty over his late father, whose life and death have never been properly explained.

Determined to escape these distractions and succeed in his academic plan, Chuck takes an interest in a local mystery man: a loner named McCloud, who lives in a secluded house and hides his private life as zealously as he shrouds his horribly scarred face.

Ignoring the rumors surrounding McCloud, Chuck learns that he's a former teacher who left his profession after the automobile crash that damaged his appearance. Chuck talks McCloud into becoming his tutor for the big exam—an arrangement that leads to trouble when more gossip about McCloud comes out, including the allegation that he was molesting a teenage boy at the time of his accident.

Much of "The Man Without a Face" centers on Chuck's determination to befriend McCloud, and on the fine companionship that blossoms between them, giving Chuck a badly needed father-figure and McCloud a chance to interact with the world again. McCloud's relationship with Chuck is so helpful and wholesome that there's no temptation for viewers of the movie to believe the ugly charge against the teacher. It's touching to observe Chuck's trust in McCloud despite the town's bias against him.

The film's message—that appearances are only skin-deep and reveal nothing about true self-hood—is a familiar one, but it's delivered with enough drama and sincerity to renew its freshness. Coming in the wake of highly publicized child-abuse cases in recent years, the movie may also be making something of a political statement by portraying a child-adult friendship motivated by mutual affection and respect. For every such relationship that goes astray, the film suggests there are countless more that bring benefit to all concerned.

Gibson has done a capable job of directing "The Man Without a Face," showing little in the way of a personal style, but taking advantage of the skills brought to the project by his collaborators. Chief among them are cinematographer Don McAlpine and film editor Tony Gibbs. Malcolm MacRury wrote the screenplay, based on the novel by Isabelle Holland.

Kudos go to the cast as well as the crew. It's headed by Gibson as the teacher, newcomer Nick Stahl as his pupil, Margaret Whitton as the boy's mom, Fay Masterson and Gaby Hoffman as his sisters, Richard Masur as his stepfather-to-be, and Geoffrey Lewis as the local cop.

Gibson shows solid talent for guiding performances, including his own: At one point he recites Shylock's great speech from Act III, Scene 1 of "The Merchant of Venice," and brief as the moment is, it's more profoundly touching than anything in the overrated "Hamlet" he did with filmmaker Franco Zefferelli a couple of years ago. Splendid work.

FILMS IN REVIEW, 11-12/93, p. 415, James M. Welsh

Mel Gibson makes his directing debut with *The Man Without A Face*, in disguise, playing a reclusive outsider named Justin McLeod, whose face has been burned and disfigured as a result of an auto accident. Twelve-year-old Chuck Norstadt (Nick Stahl) discovers that McLeod had once taught at a prep school before the accident. Chuck's ambition is to qualify for a military academy, but he has failed the entrance exam and needs tutoring before he takes the exam a second time. The story is set in Cranesport, Maine, a coastal village, during the 1960s. It was adapted by Canadian screenwriter Malcolm MacRury from a novel by Isabelle Holland, which is less ambiguous than the film.

Chuck lives in a suffocating family environment dominated by women, a snide older sister, a precocious younger one, and a nitwit mother who has gone through a series of husbands. The mother considers herself part of the anti-war movement and does not approve of Chuck's ambition to follow in his father's footsteps into the military academy. The father, it turns out, was a mental case who committed suicide, as Chuck is gleefully told by his nasty older half-sister.

At first, Chuck considers McLeod a "freak," but when he discovers McLeod could help him, and after McLeod agrees to tutor him, a friendship develops. Initially Chuck resists McLeod's conditions: bartering work for instruction. McLeod has successfully started a second career as an illustrator, but he is a natural teacher, and he misses its challenge.

McLeod's teaching career ended after the accident, in which a student who was with him in the car died. A scandal developed that charged McLeod with sexual abuse. When Chuck confronts McLeod about this, the tutor explains that the student was disturbed and had made unseemly advances toward him. When McLeod refused those advances, the boy became hysterical and caused the accident.

The film is about tolerance, understanding, and friendship and stands as a tribute to the teaching profession (Chuck seems to learn a lot of Latin during his short summer with McLeod). Chuck learns from McLeod and McLeod learns from Chuck, who reaffirms McLeod's faith in people, despite the decidedly hostile reaction of the authorities in town after they discover Chuck has spent a night with McLeod. Chuck had gone to McLeod distraught after he discovers on his own that his father was insane and had taken his own life. It is clear that Chuck needs a father figure even more than he needs a tutor. McLeod responds with kindness and understanding.

This is an excellent film that makes very few mistakes. When Chuck's mother becomes hysterical over her suspicions of child abuse, the film seems to be imposing an agenda of the

1990s onto the 1960s, and this rings a little false. The gossips and busybodies in town are credibly presented. The lesson about justice, mercy and human compassion is nicely compressed into a sequence in which McLeod is teaching Shakespeare's *The Merchant Of Venice*, acting out the part of Shylock and effectively representing his pain. Better Shylock than Hamlet.

McLeod may be a "man without a face," but he has plenty of heart. The film delivers an effective human message, and that sets it apart from the usual Hollywood offerings.

LOS ANGELES TIMES, 8/25/93, Calendar/p. 1, Kevin Thomas

"The Man Without a Face", which marks Mel Gibson's ambitious and largely successful directorial debut, opens with a dream sequence in which a 12-year-old boy imagines himself as the star of a military academy parade. In the reviewing stand his mother beams proudly, his nasty elder half-sister has duct tape slapped across her mouth and his younger half-sister's smile is no longer marred by braces. But the dream, which is accompanied by the boy's narration, starts wobbling because someone's missing—the father that the boy cannot really remember.

The boy, Chuck Norstadt (Nick Stahl), awakens to the reality of a pleasant house on a New England harbor during the summer of 1968. Chuck, who has always been made to feel not very bright by the three females in his life, has failed the entrance exam of the military academy he craves to attend, both as an escape from home and, most important, because his father went there. Despite his mother's scorn, he becomes adamant about taking the exam over. But who will serve as his tutor so that he can have a hope of passing?

We already know the answer, unlikely as it may seem, because we've caught a glimpse through a car window of the ruined right side of the face of Justin McLeod (Gibson). It is a mass of scar tissue, clearly the result of fire. For seven years McLeod has lived in isolation in a large old house across the bay and is such a recluse that the elderly couple who run the local grocery stay open late so that he can shop unseen. Since no one in the community actually knows anything about him, he is the subject of endless cruel jests and bizarre speculation. Chance will soon bring together the man and the boy.

As in such dramas of disfigurement such as "The Elephant Man" and "Mask," "The Man Without a Face," which Gibson directed from Malcolm MacRury's adaptation of Isabelle Holland's novel, McLeod is carefully introduced through a series of glimpses, each disclosing a bit more of his appearance than the last. McLeod is now a prestigious illustrator—we'd like to know how he became that—but formerly was an outstanding prep school teacher. Once Chuck gets down to work we're prepared to see the man beyond the disfigurement, just as the boy is.

As an actor and as a director Gibson shines in the credible and sensitive way in which he develops the pupil-and-teacher relationship, which in turn gives way to a loving father-and-son friendship. Gibson and his collaborators understand that McLeod is logically going to remain an essentially reticent man, even if he does learn to laugh and smile again. He's lived alone for too long to be anything else; Chuck has his work cut out for him not only in winning from him the paternal love and approval he craves so desperately but also in merely meeting McLeod's strict standards of discipline and scholarship. The scenes between Chuck and McLeod are as solid as Maine granite, and while giving himself a sizable stretch as an actor, Gibson has at the same time directed Stahl, the film's true star, in a wonderfully winning portrayal of youthful resilience and determination.

In his direction Gibson, a storyteller of admirable simplicity, brings the same assurance and crispness to Chuck's scenes with his family. His much-married, preoccupied mother (Margaret Whitton) and his elder half-sister (Fay Masterson) are truly unlikable. Gibson wisely refuses them any bids for sympathy yet takes care to show that they're human. The mother can rouse herself on occasion and pay attention with warmth and even insight. As for the sister, there's a reason, not that it's an excuse, why she behaves so badly toward Chuck. Indeed, there's a sad secret involving Chuck's father, and a far worse injustice involving how McLeod got so badly scarred. Let it be said that "The Man Without a Face" is not quite so predictable as it initially seems.

Where the film threatens to lose its balance is in suggesting that there's not a single individual in the entire community who speaks of McLeod without scorn. You can expect cruelty on the part of youngsters, but surely there has to be, even in crusty Yankee territory, at least one adult voice of compassion, even if that voice is drowned out. (McLeod in fact doesn't look all that hideous as to be so horrifying to behold.) Yet when the film's powerful moment of truth occurs, there's no denying that the ignorance it reveals is absolutely convincing. You could wish, however, that the dialogue wasn't always so carefully polished, every phrase turned so beautifully.

Indeed, in the film's initial scenes there's so much repartee going on between Chuck and his sisters that they threaten to seem like typical movie brats. Fortunately, the talk becomes plainer and more real as the film moves into its fundamentally serious mode. (The film's best, much-needed light touches are provided by the always-deft Richard Masur as a shaggy, snobby Harvard academic who is the leading candidate to become the mother's fifth husband.) "The Man Without a Face" is a quality, intelligent production across the board, but it wouldn't work if Gibson's makeup weren't as persuasive as it is. Credit makeup designer Greg Cannom with providing Gibson with realistic scar tissue, believable but not so grotesque as to take us into horror-picture territory. We eventually understand why McLeod has rejected attempts at plastic surgery yet are surprised that Chuck, dogged and outspoken kid that he is, doesn't challenge McLeod's explanation that "it didn't seem right" to consider it. Gibson surely must have relished the freedom from the burden of flawless movie-star handsomeness that playing McLeod allowed him. He has already proved to be a respectable Hamlet and here excels in a brief, impromptu turn as Shylock.

With a disarming chuckle McLeod undercuts the baldness of Chuck's statement of the film's theme, "People are afraid of what they don't know." However, the film plays this timeless observation against the more timely one of how difficult it is for a man and a boy who are unrelated to have a loving, perfectly innocent, mutually nurturing friendship without everyone either suspecting, assuming or outright believing that the man has got to be a child molester.

Minor reservations aside, "The Man Without a Face" (rated PG-13 for mature subject matter) is a moving and substantial achievement.

NEW YORK POST, 8/25/93, p. 25, Michael Medved

If you need to be reminded that life can be unfair, consider the case of Mel Gibson.

It has always seemed an outrageous injustice that someone who looks like that should prove to be such a consistently capable, even brilliant (remember "Hamlet"?), actor.

Now it turns out that the man is also a prodigiously gifted director, whose debut deserves recognition as one of the better films of 1993. Where's the equity in that?

Actually, the release of "The Man Without a Face" is more an occasion for gratitude than for envy. The movie works on many levels, but most important it is a passionate paean to the joys of teaching and friendship, and to the intoxicating excitement of literature, art and ideas.

The 12-year-old protagonist, Chuck Norstadt (played by talented newcomer Nick Stahl), dreams of entering the same prep school that his late father attended, but he's already failed the entrance exam once. He's determined to spend the summer studying so that he can take the test again, even though he gets little encouragement from his self-absorbed mother (who's about to connect with husband No. 5) or from his two hostile half-sisters.

His only assistance comes from a surprising source: the reclusive "freak" (Mel Gibson) whose horribly scarred face haunts the residents of the picturesque coastal town in Maine where Chuck and his family spend their summers. This mystery man, who lives alone with his horse and his German shepherd dog in a spectacular old shingle house overlooking the sea, has clearly suffered some terrible, disfiguring accident, but no one seems to know how or when.

Chuck, however, discovers that he's a former teacher with a consuming love for books, and the boy eventually succeeds in breaking through the hermit's resistance to get tutoring for his coming exam.

One of the reasons that this seemingly simple story engages our attention so effectively is the lush camera work by the splendid Don McAlpine (who also shot "Breaker Morant," "Patriot Games" and many other movies) and Gibson's telling use of the gorgeous Maine locations. The stunning, eccentric, cliffside house that the mysterious teacher occupies (an actual home on scenic Deer Isle) is so beautifully captured that it functions as a major character in the story.

As a director, Gibson also has a special way with actors: He wins remarkable performances from each and every member of this large cast, bringing nearly a dozen characters to life with indelible energy and vividness. He does what no other director would have dared to do in this situation—often drawing the focus away from his one big-name, big-money star (himself) to give special prominence to the other performers.

Meanwhile, Gibson the actor benefits enormously from this selfless, sensitive approach. He wears his astonishing makeup with total conviction, never once resorting to the melodramatic excesses that must have been such a powerful temptation in this unusual role. With his famous face scarcely recognizable beneath all the latex scar tissue, he forces us to concentrate as never before on his rich and beautiful voice—as noble an acting instrument as can be found in movies today.

With all its virtues, there are only two minor reservations worth noting about "The Man Without a Face."

First, it makes a point of setting its story (based on a little-known novel by Isabelle Holland) in the summer of 1968, but then does almost nothing to capture the special flavor of that tumultuous and eventful season. The few feeble reminders that this is supposed to be a period piece seem out of place and irrelevant.

Second, the Warner Bros. people who are releasing this PG-13 movie have clearly targeted the family market, while offering no warning at all that the picture's dark themes and harsh surprises make it highly unsuitable for young children. With one of those rare and important movies that works beautifully for thoughtful adults, it's a special shame that the studio feels the need to mislead the audience and to try to sell it as a project for kids.

NEWSDAY, 8/25/93, Part II/p. 48, John Anderson

Mel Gibson deserves some credit, and not just for directing as well-paced and moving a story as "The Man Without a Face." As the film's hideously scarred hero, he's taken on a role that demolishes the very preoccupation with physical beauty that's helped get him where he is today.

Of course, it may be that only a man as handsome as Gibson could get away with playing the reclusive, mysterious Justin McLeod. After all, just half of his face is scarred; the rest is still Mel Gibson, for those who are concerned. And as we get to know him—you figured this out already?—his disfigurement becomes hardly noticeable. But the fact that he's not comfortable with himself, which is the second of the film's very elementary points, makes him an object of fear and innuendo in the picturesque harbor town of Cranesport, Maine, circa 1968.

It's here that the pubescent Chuck Norstadt lives with his mother, Catherine, (Margaret Whitton) and his two half-sisters—the rankly, bitchy Gloria (Fay Masterson) and the precociously intellectual Megan (Gaby Hoffmann). And he's miserable. Fatherless—Gloria, whose approach to parenting is best described as dilettantish, has three children by three different husbands—the misunderstood Chuck is considered the dullard of the household. And although prone to stupefying, trancelike daydreams that only reinforce his lumpish image, he aspires to retake the boarding school exam he's failed once, so he can get away. And it's during one of these spells, which comes over him during a rainstorm while retrieving some books from Mcleod's waterfront, that he meets the man who'll change his destiny.

Chuck, or Charles, senses in McLeod the means of passing his exam, and it's in the moments when he tries to persuade the former teacher to tutor him that the film feels most false, Chuck is a supplicant, but he acts like a brat. When McLeod tells the boy to dig a hole, looking for a sign that the kid has some sense of commitment and reciprocity, Charles balks. As we later learn, he has too much native intelligence to rebel against a man from whom he's asking help.

They do manage to reach an agreement of sorts, Chuck becoming introduced to Euclidean theory, Shakespearean drama and Caesarean strategy. And throughout this unorthodox education, Gibson the actor is almost uncannily even. His character is a lifetime scholar, an artist, an athlete—Gibson the director leaks us bits of biography very nicely and naturally—and McLeod is not the kind of man who would turn troll (his word) because his body's been irreparably damaged. He would internalize it, and intellectualize it, and brood over it as he tried to sleep at night, until the result was a mute railing against God. Which is just how Gibson plays him.

There are very few awkward moments, and a lot of very funny bits drawn from the '60s, including a lot of cocktail-party liberalism that doesn't extend to the man in town who needs it the most.

But the strength of "The Man Without a Face" is in its overall tone rather than its detail. Like "Dead Poets Society" or "Goodbye Mr. Chips" or countless other films, it celebrates learning and the capacity of the human mind. Like "Beauty and the Beast" it's about not jumping to conclusions. And like "Red River"—we watch Chuck watching it at one point—it's about male bonds that transcend blood. And while this sounds maudlin, it's not really. Although "The Man

Without a Face" shows the ugly side of the human condition, it also succeeds like few other films this year in promoting tenderness without an accompanying force-feeding of sentimentality.

NEWSWEEK, 8/30/93, p. 52, David Ansen

When an actor known for his looks wants to be taken seriously, the quickest remedy is disguise. Given the opportunity to direct his first film, Mel Gibson has gone out of his way to shed his hearty-hunk image. *The Man Without a Face* is a small, sensitive film about a fatherless 12-year-old (Nick Stahl) who develops a close, nurturing relationship with his tutor. Gibson plays the teacher, who in addition to being solitary and erudite is so severely disfigured that the suspicious locals call him "Hamburgerhead."

The setting is a Maine coastal town; the time, 1968. The boy, Chuck, comes from a broken, bickering family. His two half sisters (nicely played by Fay Masterson and Gaby Hoffman) each have different fathers, and Chuck grows up with a bruising sense of inferiority and a fear that he might be crazy. Desperate to leave home and get into a military academy, he learns that the brusque, mysterious Mr. McLeod was once a teacher, and secretly asks for his academic help. Their mutual education begins—Chuck opening his mind to geometry and Shakespeare (much playacting of "The Merchant of Venice"), McLeod overcoming his self-imposed solitude—but as the audience suspects, the gossipy townsfolk will bring this idyll to an end. The rumor starts that McLeod is a child molester, and Chuck is forbidden to see him again.

"The Man Without a Face" is such a noble, well-intentioned little film—a cross between "Dead Poets Society" and "The Phantom of the Opera" done as an after-school special—that one feels like an ogre picking on it. Alternately poky and melodramatic—and occasionally witty and insightful—Malcolm MacRury's uneven screenplay too often strains credibility. Perhaps the biggest problem comes with the character of Chuck's mom (Margaret Whitton), who suddenly seems to know all about McLeod's past when previously she knew nothing about him. When the deck is this stacked, the audience feels patronized. It doesn't help that Gibson plays McLeod as such a stoically heroic tragic figure, a man who sits alone in his imposing seacoast house listening to Puccini arias and quoting Latin poets. He's the kind of guy one meets only in the movies. The film would have been a lot more challenging if it had been faithful to its source, Isabelle Holland's young-adult novel, in which McLeod was also homosexual. Gibson elects to play it safe.

As a director, Gibson's strongest suit is his work with the actors—particularly his young star Stahl, a natural who possesses great emotional range. If the whole project had Stahl's honesty, it might have been the little gem it so earnestly means to be.

SIGHT AND SOUND, 12/93, p. 48, Amanda Lipman

Chuck Nordstadt, his much-married mother Catherine and two half-sisters, the older Gloria and younger Megan, are on their way to Cranesport, New England for the summer. Chuck decides to resit the entrance exam for the military academy his father attended. Frustrated by his family, he slashes the car tyres, and notices the shadowy figure of Justin McLeod, known as "the freak" because of his scarred face and solitary existence, watching him. Instead of working for his exam, Chuck reads comics and takes boat trips with his friends. On one trip, they land near McLeod's house and are frightened away by his dog. Later, Chuck realises that he has left some of his books behind and cycles back to find the pages scattered over the rocks. He goes into one of his catatonic trances and is rescued by McLeod. When Chuck finds out that McLeod used to be a teacher, he asks him to coach him. McLeod agrees, but his methods are unorthodox. He tells Chuck to dig a large hole every day before starting. Meanwhile, Megan has found out where he goes and threatens to tell their mother.

Chuck, who pretends to McLeod that he has his mother's permission to be tutored by him, is nearly found out when his mother and McLeod meet at the grocer's. Chuck and McLeod act out the Merchant of Venice and Chuck starts to enjoy his lessons. McLeod, an illustrator, shows Chuck some of his paintings. He tells Chuck that his disfigurement was the result of a car accident in which a boy was killed. When Chuck puts a hand on his shoulder, McLeod recoils. Upset by this behaviour, Chuck tells some of his friends about McLeod's accident. The local barber, who has always hated McLeod, asks the sheriff to investigate him. At a party given by his mother, Chuck hears everyone repeating the story. Ashamed, he goes back to McLeod and apologises for his behaviour. They go for a walk and cross paths with the barber.

As a reward for passing his mock exam, McLeod takes Chuck for a ride on a seaplane. Coming home that evening, Chuck finds Gloria in bed with her boyfriend. Furious, she screams at him that his father was not a war hero but a psychotic drunk. Chuck rushes back to McLeod's house, where he is comforted. The next morning, the sheriff takes him home. When his mother asks him if McLeod has abused him, he denies it furiously. McLeod comes to see Chuck and talk to his mother but she will not let him in. The sheriff tells McLeod to keep away from Chuck pending an investigation and the two say goodbye on the beach, when Chuck assures him that he does not believe that McLeod abused the boy who died in the car accident. Chuck passes his military academy exam. Meanwhile, McLeod is forced to appear before a kangaroo court, where he denies the old charges of abuse. Chuck discovers that all his letters to McLeod have been returned. He sneaks out of the academy and finds his way to McLeod's house, which now stands empty. In the attic is a picture of himself and a letter from McLeod telling him that he cannot see him again, but that he will never forget him. A few years later, Chuck graduates. His family are all there to see him. In the distance, he sees McLeod, who waves to him before walking away.

Mel Gibson's directorial debut is another brick in the museum of teenage rites-of-passage movies and a predictable choice for someone who wants to be taken seriously. Predictable, too, is the melancholic voiceover of the older and wiser narrator recalling "that strange summer that was to change everything." This particular variation, set in the 70s, wins the psychobabble stakes hands down, trotting out notions such as pre-pubescent angst and transferral of anger in almost every scene. But this quaint obsession with cod psychology is cosmetic, no more than a plot-spinning gimmick. Moreover, this misfit kid seems remarkably charismatic, chirpy and gregarious for one apparently so miserable.

But where Nick Stahl's Chuck is cute and bright, Gibson's McLeod is heavy. When he reads the *Merchant of Venice*, it is with the gravitas of one who feels the parallels cannot be made too clear. And when he spontaneously breaks into Latin, suspension of disbelief becomes almost impossible. Curiously, though half of his face is badly scarred, for much of the film it is the unscarred half that is visible. Then there is the intriguing possibility that the character might be gay (abuse can be ruled out since that would be going too far). This is, of course, dispelled as soon as possible, but Gibson clearly wants to give the impression that he has acted bravely in playing a role which leaves a question mark over his sexuality.

The movie's liberal stance does not prevent it endorsing Chuck's desire to go to military academy, which is seen as the only way Chuck can make something of himself, assert his masculinity in a house full of women, and find a reassuring image of his dead father. But it is turned into a glorious end in itself, polished off with hurried reconciliations and a glutinously sentimental finale. Suddenly the burning issue of McLeod's persecution is rendered unimportant and the parallels with *The Merchant of Venice* crumble away. What is more, it happily forgets to deal with Chuck's feelings on discovering that his father was not the hero he thought.

The movie is much better on the family dynamics: the bitchy, envious relationship between Chuck and Gloria; Chuck's frustration with the feminist Megan; his fantasy of his dead father; and the desperation of his mother, who loves her children but cannot communicate with them, caught up as she is in a constant battle of attraction and repulsion with men.

TIME, 8/30/93, p. 63, Richard Schickel

The title is a misnomer, Justin McLeod does not lack a face. His problem is that he has two of them. His right profile has been grossly disfigured in an auto accident, but the opposite side is pure Mel Gibson, handsome and, you'll be relieved to know, getting most of the screen time. It symbolizes, pretty obviously, a deeper split in his personality, the unmarked side representing the idealistic young teacher he once was, the twisted side the bitter recluse he has become.

It is a 13-year-old adolescent, Chuck Norstadt (Nick Stahl), who helps him reconcile his two selves. He's a kid so screwed up that he actually wants to go to military school. You can't really blame him though, since his mother (Margaret Whitton, in a good performance) has an unfortunate propensity for marrying inappropriate men on what seems to be an almost annual basis. Unable to deal with a family that keeps extending itself in such a careless way, Chuck is a little bit bifurcated himself, falling into dreamy spells to escape the hubbub. Lacking a reliable father figure, he tells himself that regimentation will make a man of him. All he has to do is pass that entrance exam, and that's where McLeod, inhabiting a gloomy mansion in the Maine resort town where Chuck and family are vacationing, comes in. Pretty soon McLeod is talking out of both sides of his mouth—a stern taskmaster one minute, an indulgent mentor the next—and little Chuck is flourishing in the company of the first grownup male who has ever taken him seriously.

Deep bonds are forged. Prejudice is fought (the town, which has always treated McLeod as a geek, mistakes pedagogy for pederasty). Wounds are finally healed. And the sentimentally impressionable will have a good cry as outcasts assert their humanity and teach the smug and the hypocritical a thing or two about simple decency.

Mel Gibson, directing for the first time, presents this deeply wet material in a reasonably cool and dry manner. But his film is in desperate need of smarm busting—something, anything that would relieve the familiarity of its characters, the predictability of its structure, the bland failure to challenge its perfect correctness of outlook.

VILLAGE VOICE, 8/31/93, p. 60, Manohla Dargis

A mainstream affirmation of man-boy love. Mel Gibson's *Man Without a Face* is more interesting than it has a right to be, and far more strange than it knows. It's 1968, and lost boy Chuck (Nick Stahl) is drowning in a sea of oppressive femininity (mother, two sisters). Eager for escape, he's spending his summer vacation conjugating Latin for the entrance exam to an exclusive military school. Then he meets McLeod (Gibson), the local "freak" who lives in tastefully appointed seclusion and just happens to have once upon a time been a boarding-school master.

Before long, the pair are mouthing *veni, vidi, vici,* Chuck is stumbling around McLeod's in his BVDs, and town tongues are wagging innuendo. Even with all its baroque flourishes, Gibson's serviceable debut behind the camera is really just another chapter in Hollywood's romance with a boy's own story, a cottage industry that probably has to do more with Robert Bly than NAMBLA. Whatever the reason, a lot of these celluloid tots are working intrigue like so many unleashed inner children, emotional captives to tediously wounded adults.

Man Without a Face ups the stakes by etching McLeod's torment into his very face (he's half rubber, half aging hunk) and making Chuck into one pathetic little masochist. Given Mel's macho reputation onscreen and off, the film's moralism is to put it mildly, a wee overdetermined. Furiously intent on celebrating male love (chaste, pure, honorable), Gibson and company try to refuse the erotics of friendship, and miserably, wondrously fail.

Also reviewed in:
NEW YORK TIMES, 8/25/93, p. C13, Janet Maslin
VARIETY, 8/30/93, p. 19, Brian Lowry
WASHINGTON POST, 8/25/93, p. D1, Richard Harrington
WASHINGTON POST, 8/27/93, Weekend/p. 36, Joe Brown

MAN'S BEST FRIEND

A New Line Productions release of a Roven-Cavello Entertainment production.   *Executive Producer:* Robert Kosberg and Daniel Grodnik.   *Producer:* Bob Engelman.   *Director:* John Lafia.   *Screenplay:* John Lafia.   *Director of Photography:* Mark Irwin.   *Editor:* Michael N. Knue.   *Music:* Joel Goldsmith.   *Sound:* Steve Nelson and (music) Alex Wilkinson and Heather Forsyth.   *Sound Editor:* Steven Williams.   *Casting:* Valorie Massalas.   *Production Designer:* Jaymes Hinkle.   *Art Director:* Erik Olson.   *Set Designer:* Sharon E. Alshams.   *Set Decorator:* Ellen Totlebren.   *Set Dresser:* Anna Czerwatiuk.   *Special Effects:* Frank Ceglia.   *Costumes:* Beverly Hong.   *Make-up:* Suzanne Parker Sanders.   *Make-up (Ally Sheedy):* Aliki Demetriades.   *Make-up (Special Effects):* Kevin Yagher.   *Stunt Coordinator:* Rick Barker.   *Running time:* 87 minutes.   *MPAA Rating:* R.

CAST: Ally Sheedy (Lori Tanner);   Lance Henriksen (Dr. Jarret);   Robert Costanzo (Detective Kovacs);   Fredric Lehne (Perry);   John Cassini (Detective Bendetti);   J.D. Daniels (Rudy);   William Sanderson (Ray);   Trula M. Marcus (Annie);   Robin Frates (Judy Sanders);   Rick Barker (Mailman);   Bradley Pierce (Chet);   Robert Arentz (Emax Security Guard);   Cameron Arnett (Dog Catcher #1);   Adam Carl (Dog Catcher #2);   Tom Rosales, Jr. (Mugger);   Ray Lynkins (KCBG Security Guard);   Mickey Cassidy (Paper Boy);   L.E. Moko (Mobile Mechanic);   Caroline Cornell (KCGB Receptionist);   Del Zamora (Rudy's Dad);   Arlen Stuart (Mrs. Barclay);   Frank Cavestani (Policeman);   Paul Hayes (2nd Mechanic);   Peter Georges (Truck Driver);   Olivia Brown (Lab Assistant);   Lisa Cavallo (Friday);   Frank Welker (Special Vocal Effects).

LOS ANGELES TIMES, 11/22/93, Calendar/p. 2, Kevin Thomas

With "Man's Best Friend", as slick as it is repellent, the horror picture literally goes to the dogs. It's one thing to depict humans behaving diabolically to each other in the name of thrills and chills, but to show us doing our worst to animals hits a new low. It's also irresponsible, pandering to the worst fears of fanatic animal rights activists.

Ally Sheedy stars as a TV reporter with far more ambition than brains. Breaking into a laboratory that contains a zoo's worth of a animals, all of which bear hideous gashes clearly suggesting some form of experimentation, she winds up at her home with one of the animals, a seemingly lovable Tibetan mastiff named Max.

Never does it occur to her that he might be in some way dangerous—even after discovering he bears a mysterious surgical scar and is taking an especially ferocious lunge at her live-in boyfriend (Fredric Lehne). The laboratory's mad scientist (Lance Henriksen, typecast) is more than eager to get Max back swiftly, for the dog has been genetically engineered to be a super-intelligent, super-lethal weapon, and the drug administered to control him will wear off in only hours.

Meanwhile, Max is already turning into a serial killer, warming up by magically following a cat up a tree and killing it, swallowing it whole before our very eyes. Finally realizing that she has got to get rid of Max, Sheedy turns him over to a junkyard operator who promptly slugs Max with a shovel and turns an acetylene torch on him before the dog turns around and finishes him off.

What makes "Man's Best Friend" (rated R for terror and violence involving household pets) all the more reprehensible is that technically it is not a crude piece of work, easily dismissed for its fakery. It's polished in all aspects, and while the film is cynical and shallow, writer-director John Lafia, one of the creators of Chucky, the demonic doll of the "Child's Play" movies, socks it over briskly with plenty of impact. Even though acting honors go to the various mastiffs playing Max, a canine Dr. Jekyll and Mr. Hyde, everybody involved on both sides of the camera displays enough talent to have justified attempting a film that set its sights considerably higher.

NEW YORK POST, 11/20/93, p. 17, Bill Hoffmann

It was only a matter of time before Hollywood came up with the canine answer to RoboCop and the Terminator—and yesterday he arrived with a vengeance in a gory mess called "Man's Best Friend."

Meet Max—a huge, sloppy Saint Bernard who seeks revenge for every lab researcher, cruel pet owner, bratty kid and mailman who ever inflicted pain on a poor dumb animal.

Max is a laboratory-bred howler with the genetic engineering of a bear, a jaguar and a chameleon—making him fearless, fast and able to climb trees and change colors.

Max is so dangerous, he's kept caged up at a space-age research firm headed by Dr. Jarrett (Lance Henriksen), who also oversees a room full of pathetic-looking lab rabbits and monkeys who appear to be on their last legs.

Enter Lori Tanner (Ally Sheedy), a jaded cigarette-devouring TV news reporter who's sick of doing prefab puff pieces on fashion and thirsts for a gritty exposé to put her back on top.

On a tip, she stumbles onto the animal horrors in Jarrett's lab and ends up freeing Max, who instantly becomes her best friend.

But Max is not to be messed with. When a mugger robs Tanner, the beast makes mincemeat of him and happily trots back to his master with purse in jaws.

When Tanner's whiny boyfriend (Fredric Lehne, who resembles a young Robert Redford) crosses Max's path, the resourceful pooch chews through the brake lines of his car.

A pesky cat also gets his comeuppance when he tries to escape Max by climbing a tree and finding the tail-waggin' terminator climbing right behind and swallowing him whole.

The message of "Man's Best Friend" is simple—don't experiment and don't be cruel to animals.

There is some satisfaction in seeing Max dispatch some of the meanies in novel ways. And Max certainly is a magnificent beast to watch, easily stealing the picture every time he pads on screen to join the serviceable cast of human stars.

But this is a clumsy film that ultimately has little bite. It awkwardly wavers between gore and comedy and what little suspense there is doesn't build, it comes in episodic spurts.

In one bizarre comedic moment, Max races after a young collie in what turns into a mating scene to the strains of—yup. you guessed it—"Puppy Love."

Max is so smart, he not only corners his "bitch" in a bedroom, but he locks the door behind him.

This scene is terribly misplaced, but as it turns out, absolutely necessary.

While Max ultimately ascends to that big fire hydrant in the sky, he leaves the legacy of a litter of puppies behind—and a whole crop of sequel possibilities for New Line Cinema.

"Let's hope not, for this is one dog who should have been spayed.

If I could review "Man's Best Friend" for dogs, it would get four raised hind legs.

NEWSDAY, 11/20/93, Part II/p. 25, John Anderson

He's Frankenstein's mongrel, "Jaws" with paws, Beethoven's maladjusted cousin, and might have been the star of "Look Who's Eviscerating Now." And he has a taste for parrots, pussy cats and postal carriers.

Max (Max) is "Man's Best Friend" a dog who's both the product and victim of man: an amalgamation of genes from various species of predator that has given him a cheetah's speed, a bear's strength, a jaguar's agility, a chameleon's camouflage and Cujo's disposition. His anti-social tendencies are kept under control by the drugs administered by his "father," Dr. Jarret (Lance Henriksen), a renegade animal geneticist with a thing about animal-rights activists. *And then he's broken out of the lab!!!*

Lori Tanner (Ally Sheedy), plays a local TV reporter; she's stuck doing features on polyester until she gets a tip from an assistant at Jarret's lab that animals are being mistreated. The complete ignorance with which Lori begins her "exposé" is a slur against animal rights activists and reporters, but she does have a love for animals, which saves her, literally and metaphorically.

Not so lucky is the lab assistant. We get an inkling of Max' appetite right away, when he gets out of his cage and makes luncheon loaf of her, after a predator's-eye view chase reminiscent of "Alien III" or "American Werewolf in London." But Lori doesn't know this, and liberates Max thinking he's a bit cuddly smooshy poo.

As the drugs wear off Max, his temper gets shorter and shorter until ... well, let's not give away a totally predictable film. Suffice to say the acting is uniformly adequate, with the exception of J.D. Daniels ("The Mighty Ducks") who plays Lori's young neighbor Rudy, and is becoming one of the better juvenile actors in film. Also, Max is good, even if he does slur his words. And he must have been hell on the catering crew.

SIGHT AND SOUND, 4/94, p. 46, Jill McGreal

San Remo. Reporter Lori Tanner, determined to broaden her scope outside her usual fluff items, is investigating a story connecting the EMAX Research Laboratory to the violation of animal rights. But before she can meet up with her technician contact, the technician is savagely killed by one of the EMAX animals which has got loose. Tanner and her camerawoman Annie enter EMAX on their own initiative and start filming the caged and mutilated animals. In the Special Projects room they discover rare species and a St Bernard, Max, which escapes as they try to film it. Tanner and Annie are discovered by EMAX chief Dr Jarret but they escape, pursued by Max, who later saves them from a car park mugger.

Unwilling to return Max, Tanner lies about where he comes from, and her boyfriend Perry reluctantly agrees to let her keep him. Max seems to have established a strong rapport with his new owner and obeys all her commands. Max is already showing evidence of uncanny intelligence; later, at the police station, Jarret explains to the two cops assigned to the case that Max, highly trained as a guard dog, could be extremely dangerous in the wrong hands. Max has been bred using DNA from other species and has many un-canine characteristics including the ability to climb trees and camouflage himself. He has also been treated with a stabilising drug to curb his killer instinct which will soon wear off.

Max is settling in at Tanner's home and meeting the neighbours. He threatens the paper boy, eats the local tabby cat, 'rapes' Heidi, the female collie next door, 'murders' the mailman and hides his body. Things come to a head when Perry suspects Max of sabotaging the brakes on his car. The cops start taking the case seriously when they discover the mutilated body of the car park mugger. Meanwhile Jarret has traced Max to Tanner, so she places Max with a local scrapyard owner. But Max kills his cruel new owner and heads back to Tanner's home where he urinates acid onto Perry's face and kills the two cops. Jarret kidnaps Tanner and uses her as bait to draw Max to the EMAX Laboratory. In the final showdown a now destabilised Max reaffirms his bonding with the injured Tanner but viciously attacks Jarret; Jarret and Max both die. Weeks later, restored to normality, Tanner is called in to see Heidi's pups. They all resemble their mother except for one ...

Pretty Ally Sheedy showed promise as part of the 80s brat-pack, playing well in ensemble pieces such as *The Breakfast Club* and *St Elmo's Fire*. But all that bright optimism and youth don't necessarily lead to stardom and when the cookie crumbles there just aren't enough good roles to go round—especially for the girls. So it is that Sheedy is seen in *Man's Best Friend* in an inconsequential routine role. However, she manages to be affecting and natural, especially in the scenes with the boyfriend, exploiting her 'girl-next-door' image to hold this film together. For *Man's Best Friend* doesn't know whether it's horror, sci-fi, drama or comedy. It's best seen as the latter, especially when the body count goes out of control and Max starts camouflaging himself as a toolbox. There are nevertheless some moments in awesomely bad taste, as when Max 'rapes' Heidi, the bitch-next-door, on her owners' bed—not funny!

Man's Best Friend might be fun to rent on video, although it's not nearly quirky enough for cult status. It plays with big themes, like the everyday becoming the menacing opposite of itself—as with the doll Chucky, in John Lafia's now-notorious *Child's Play 2*—or the animal rights issue, or a woman trying to break out of gender stereotyping. But it fails to engage with any of them in an interesting way. The characters are straight-from-TV, especially the goofy cops and the comic strip dog-catchers. The only spark is the parallel breakdown between dog and man, as Max and Jarret disintegrate together. But no moral conclusion is drawn and the film collapses into self-satire.

Cinematographer Mark Irwin has worked extensively with David Cronenberg, and while some of the opening shots of the EMAX lab briefly remind one of Cronenberg's cold urban landscapes, there's nothing here to compare with the stunning painterly photography of *The Dead Zone* and nothing as visceral as *Videodrome*. The opening credits are the best part of the film, a series of images of dogs in old paintings and etchings—friendly, loyal companions but also mad, diabolical animals. It's an effective, chilling opening, and unwittingly does raise the serious topical issue of dangerous dogs; but the moment passes. The issue is more profoundly treated in both the Stephen King adaptation *Cujo* and Sam Fuller's *White Dog*. In the end the problem with all dog films is that, however you look at it, if a dog can feel or think, then it just isn't a dog any more.

Also reviewed in:
NEW YORK TIMES, 11/20/93, p. 17, Stephen Holden
VARIETY, 12/6/93, p. 35, Daniel M. Kimmel
WASHINGTON POST, 11/22/93, p. D4, Richard Harrington

MANHATTAN MURDER MYSTERY

A TriStar Pictures release. *Executive Producer:* Jack Rollins and Charles H. Joffe. *Producer:* Robert Greenhut. *Director:* Woody Allen. *Screenplay:* Woody Allen and Marshall Brickman. *Director of Photography:* Carlo Di Palma. *Editor:* Susan E. Morse. *Sound:* James Sabat. *Sound Editor:* Bob Hein. *Casting:* Juliet Taylor. *Production Designer:* Santo Loquasto. *Art Director:* Speed Hopkins. *Set Decorator:* Susan Bode. *Set Dresser:* Dave Weinman. *Costumes:* Jeffrey Kurland. *Make-up:* Fern Buchner. *Running time:* 108 minutes. *MPAA Rating:* PG.

CAST: Woody Allen (Larry Lipton); Diane Keaton (Carol Lipton); Jerry Adler (Paul House); Lynn Cohen (Lillian House); Ron Rifkin (Sy); Joy Behar (Marilyn); William Addy (Jack, the Super); John Doumanian and Sylvia Kauders (Neighbors); Ira Wheeler (EMS Doctor); Alan Alda (Ted); Anjelica Huston (Marcia Fox); Melanie Norris (Helen Moss); Marge Redmond (Mrs. Dalton); Zach Braff (Nick Lipton); George Manos and Linda Taylor ("21 Club" Staff); Aida Turturro (Hotel Day Clerk); John A. Costelloe, Philip Levy, Wendell Pierce, and Steven Randazzo (Policemen); Yanni Sfinias (Hotel Night Clerk); Gloria Irizarry (Hotel Maid); Ruth Last (Lillian's Sister); Suzanne Raffaelli (Theatre Auditioner); Al Cerullo (Helicopter Pilot).

FILMS IN REVIEW, 11-12/93, p. 413, James M. Welsh

At first *Manhattan Murder Mystery* seems merely a throwback to an earlier phase of Woody's career, since the screenplay was co-authored with Marshall Brickman, who also collaborated with Allen on *Annie Hall* (1977) and *Manhattan* (1979), two pictures that showcased the talents of Diane Keaton. After what critic Nancy Pogel has called "Allen's Rose Period" (culminating in *Purple Rose Of Cairo* in 1985 and the much neglected *Broadway Danny Rose* in 1984), *Manhattan Murder Mystery* seems to shift back into the mode of romantic comedy, as several reviewers noted, but this is a rather simplistic dismissal.

Though it was hard to take the comic gangsters of *Broadway Danny Rose* seriously, there was the (remote) chance that the plot of that comedy could take a nasty turn, and the same is true of *Manhattan Murder Mystery*, which, in a way, is *Manhattan* meets *Rear Window* and *The Lady From Shanghai*. In Hitchcock's *Rear Window*, Jimmy Stewart was certain that Raymond Burr, his neighbor across the court yard, had murdered his wife. In *Manhattan Murder Mystery*, Carol Lipton (Diane Keaton) is convinced her neighbor Paul House (Jerry Adler) has murdered his wife. She becomes obsessed with this "mystery," and finds more support from her friend Ted (an oily Alan Alda, obviously on the make) than from her husband Larry (Woody Allen). The audience is soon convinced that she is merely a screwball, but she turns out to be right.

In *Rear Window* Jimmy Stewart, confined to his room with a broken leg in a cast, sent Grace Kelly to snoop into his neighbor's apartment. In *Manhattan Murder Mystery* Diane Keaton gets a key from Jack, the Super, and, like Grace Kelly, almost gets caught. Allen builds tension the same way Hitchcock did, but at that point the audience thinks the neighbor is probably innocent and that Keaton is merely addlepated.

Allen himself does a fine comic turn as the not-too-patient husband who tolerates his wife's eccentric mania, but one of his writers (the Allen character is a book editor in this film), Marcia Fox (Anjelica Huston) works out a plausible murder plot, and everyone starts to wonder if Carol is so crazy, after all. Huston, the Fox (in two senses), is flirting with Allen all the while, and Alda is flirting with Keaton, which recalls the romantic complications of Allen's later films; but this film stays on course as a romantic comedy, with Allen and Keaton doing a Nick and Nora number. Fox concocts a scheme to entrap the murderer. The murderer kidnaps Keaton and holds her captive. Woody Allen is forced to play the role of the unlikely hero.

The film reaches a smashing finale that recalls the famous Hall of Mirrors conclusion of Orson Welles's *The Lady From Shanghai* and also uses footage from the Welles film, brilliantly. This is Woody the auteur paying "hommage" to the Master. It's a derivative gimmick, but perfectly executed. There is not much more to this movie than meets the well trained eye, if the viewer is watching closely. But it has much more to offer than in-jokes for movie buffs, and it has wider appeal than the usual Allen film and should draw a wider audience. If not, well, Woody Allen seems to be covering his bets by planning to shoot his next film in France, in French. But will Paris satisfy him after all those years in New York?

One hopes that American viewers will support and embrace this entertaining film so that Allen may be persuaded to come back, soon. By now, it should be obvious that Woody Allen is a national treasure, not to be invested abroad.

LOS ANGELES TIMES, 8/18/93, Calendar/p. 1, Kenneth Turan

If prizes are ever given out for stoicism on the American screen, Woody Allen is not going to be a contender. Possibly the most celebrated complainer in Hollywood history, he has simultaneously raised the status of whining and created serious laughter at the expense of his collective miseries.

Even as artful a creator as Allen, however, can overdo things, and in "Manhattan Murder Mystery" he pretty much does. Clever and amusing though it often is, "Murder" is also Allen's whiniest film to date, and your appreciation of its pleasures will fluctuate according to your tolerance for his *Angst*.

It's not only that the character Allen has written for himself wails more intensely than usual, but also that this film doesn't see fit, as for instance "Hannah and Her Sisters" did, to surround him with more companionable actors.

While Allen in that picture stayed partially in the background and shared space with easy-to-take Michael Caine and Barbara Hershey, "Murder" places him front and center and pairs him with Diane Keaton and Alan Alda, definitely not a day in the country.

Still, there is much to enjoy in this light PG-rated film, though giggles will be heard more than outright laughter. And don't search for even a hint of the poignancy and seriousness the writer-director brought to "Husbands and Wives." Diverting is all this movie aspires to be.

Set in Allen's trademark Manhattan, "Murder" showcases the, Liptons, married long enough (nearly 20 years) to make allowances for each other's foibles. Carol (Keaton), a would-be restaurateur, promises to attend a Rangers hockey game if Larry (Allen), a book editor, agrees to a night at the opera. Larry, however, invariably cancels out. "I can't listen to Wagner," he confesses. "I get the urge to conquer Poland."

Exiting their elevator, the Liptons encounter their elderly neighbors, Paul House (Jerry Adler) and his wife, Lillian (Lynn Cohen). Much to Larry's displeasure, Carol drags him over to socialize, an evening that starts with Paul displaying his prize stamp collection and ends with both Larry and Carol worrying that they too are becoming old and stale.

Shortly thereafter, Lillian House dies of a heart attack, and shortly thereafter that, Carol starts to get suspicious. Why didn't the wife mention any heart condition, why does the husband look so cheerful and composed despite his nominal bereavement? "We could be living next door to a murderer," Carol gasps. "New York is a melting pot" is Larry's deadpan reply.

Is Carol prescient or a woman with a hyperactive imagination? Her husband, who resists the notion of becoming half of a Borscht Belt Nick and Nora Charles, leans strongly toward the latter conclusion. But Carol, who finds her suspicions exhilarating, refuses to give up and instead turns to recently divorced screenwriter Ted (Alda), an old flame who still finds her attractive. And as Carol and Ted get more intoxicated with their detecting, Larry shows an increasing interest in Marcia Fox, one of his more controversial writers (very wittily played by Anjelica Huston).

While this farce situation is often funny and enlivened by movie references to everything from "Vertigo" to "The Lady From Shanghai," it is also periodically tiresome. Unshared obsessions, even comic ones, are rarely more than moderately entertaining, though one wonders what Mia Farrow, originally cast for the Keaton role but replaced for well-publicized reasons, would have done with this particular mind-set.

And by employing himself as the most reluctant of detectives, always on the edge of hysteria and screeching "What are you doing?" every other minute, Allen has given his movie a frantic, desperate air it could have done without. With a couple like this investigating a possible murder, audiences may end up feeling as victimized as the corpse.

NEW LEADER, 10/4-18/93, p. 21, David Bromwich

Manhattan Murder Mystery is a screwball comedy, not fast-talking enough to remind you much of its '30s prototypes, but untimely in a rather favorable sense. The film brings Woody Allen back together with Diane Keaton. Ego-delicate and addled as usual, Allen makes a very gentle and seemly second banana. He coaxes, he cringes, he listens with exquisite defeated tolerance, and wags his finger and rolls his eyes, all to set Keaton more engagingly in the spotlight. She has always thrived in Allen's company, and never more than now. The plot—her compulsion to find out the truth about the widower across the hall, whom she suspects of murdering his wife—is a pretext for the one-liners and familiar raillery of the screenplay by Allen and Marshall Brickman. The scenes are varied by a second couple, Anjelica Huston and Alan Alda, each of whom nurses a wholesome erotic interest in splitting up Allen and Keaton.

I doubt that hardened Alda-despisers will believe (until they see it) just how well he comes off here. A hidden element of Woody Allen's appeal to actors has been his ability not only to make the best look good before they were well-known in movies (as with Dianne Wiest), but also to make indifferent or unlikely talents, such as Alda here and Martin Landau in *Crimes and Misdemeanors*, appear suddenly gifted with a depth or self-irony they never showed before. Does that mean he is an "actor's director"? He is certainly a director who is good for actors.

Alda's narcissism, his smarminess, his showy decency and the safe sarcasm that protects it are used in *Manhattan Murder Mystery* to conscious effect, but sapped of their customary assurance they become human. Touring a site where he wants Keaton to build a restaurant, he tells her how he used to come to this courtyard with his divorced wife: "I used to say, 'What am I doing here with Julie?' We didn't love each other any more. It made the moment doubly poignant." yes, he would know all about doubly poignant.

Anjelica Huston's business is to be sexy, husky, quick-witted and a threat. When Keaton sees Allen thinking about Huston he warns her, "Your pupils are dilating," and one can understand why they would. But most of the fun is in Allen's reactions to what Keaton is, rather than to what she says: observing her with strung-out courtesy and annoyance; placing his body between her mind and its whims; wondering at his inadequacies and her compulsions, and how a woman may ruin the well-plotted tranquillity of a man's life. It is no comfort at all that she may be inspired. The relaxed excitement between the two, the perfect sympathy of the timing, are the real pleasures of the story. Midway through a chase, plunged into total darkness, Allen lights a match and after a pause comes a voice from the pitch black: "Where'd you get that book of matches? When were you at Café Des Artistes?"

He is assaulted everywhere by voices with miscellaneous advice, warnings, imprecations. "Exercise changed my life," says the woman who will be murdered, and as soon as you hear it you know that she must go. Allen replies: "I prefer to atrophy." He atrophies for two hours in *Manhattan Murder Mystery*, while Keaton thinks and frets and paces, hides under the neighbor's bed, stakes out a seedy hotel, and drags him along as a compromise when she can't find a better comparison. One scene has them trapped in an elevator, where Allen slips into an insane claustrophobic reverie about a stallion running free—a piece of comedy as pure as the undercover robot gone berserk in *Sleeper*. In its texture, this film belongs to the vein of *Radio Days, Broadway Danny Rose,* and *A Midsummer Night's Sex Comedy*; but people are right to be happy with it as a "return" of several kinds at once.

Much of the footage was shot with a hand-held camera—an affected display of ingenuous-ness that bears no relation to any other trait of the film, since the settings are New York and posh, the colors rich and deep as they have been ever since *Annie Hall*. This shift from the ultraformal cinematography of Sven Nykvist is a reminder of how much class and how little cunning there has been in the broad artistic choices of Woody Allen's films. And the climax here—a shooting in a movie theater which echoes the last minutes of *The Lady from Shanghai* while that film is showing on a screen-within-the-screen-displays the same kind of arbitrariness.

Allen has often been judged severely as an art-film director by the index of choices like these. The truth is that he is a comedian who did roughly the same work in monologues, in acting and in directing films, who happened, as he became more independent, to become more popular also. His success is distrusted in the exact degree that his luck is envied. He holds our interest and our laughter because under the suave citizen lifting a book of matches one sees the guilty citizen face to face with his somehow deserved death in a stalled elevator.

NEW YORK, 8/23/93, p. 57, David Denby

Woody Allen's *Manhattan Murder Mystery* has a careless let's-make-a-movie feel to it. A group of sophisticated New Yorkers who should be minding their own business throw themselves into the dangerous game of solving a murder. Fumbling all over the place, they play at being detectives, and Woody, playing at being a director of thrillers, serves up mock suspense and mock surprises. Bobby Short sings Cole Porter over the titles (an extraordinary rendition of "I Happen to Like New York"), but the movie isn't chiseled and refined in Allen's Manhattan-*moderne* style. Most of it, in fact, is rough and visually undistinguished, and a few scenes are even scrappily staged. After years of laborious ambition, Woody Allen may have sensed that he needed to slap together a frivolously entertaining comedy-mystery. *Manhattan Murder Mystery* could be better, but some of it is pretty funny. So the tabloid monster walks again—as himself, a comic artist.

There are *hommages* within the movie to Billy Wilder's *Double Indemnity* and Orson Welles's *The Lady From Shanghai*, but *Manhattan Murder Mystery* is really Woody's Hitchcock movie, a nervously self-conscious version of the Master's familiar story of ordinary people getting in over their heads. What's most alive in it, amazingly, is Woody Allen himself, talking a great deal and jumping around like a threatened grasshopper. Somehow, amid the disgrace and the public heckling, or perhaps *because* of it, he has managed to be funnier than ever. He plays a man without dignity who wants to save his marriage. The question is, Will the audience allow itself to laugh?

Woody is a book editor at HarperCollins, an older, somewhat more professionally assured version of his earlier movie incarnation as a fearful urban nerd. Perhaps the screenplay (Marshall Brickman, an old collaborator, worked with Allen) was reshaped after the Troubles became public; perhaps not. But whether accidental or intentional, Allen's returning to his old character is a brilliant career move. The audience in its current sour mood may remember that it once loved the Woody who was a threat to no one but himself, the Woody who blurted out his fears like an anxiously over-articulate adolescent.

Diane Keaton, substituting for Mia Farrow, who was originally supposed to play the role, is the book editor's wife, a woman bored with her life and her marriage. (She's the kind of New York woman who talks constantly of opening a restaurant.) Keaton is now a less vulnerable and hesitant performer than Mia Farrow; as the exasperated wife, she's driven and even imperious, and she shrugs Woody off, as if she didn't care what he thought. In their Manhattan high rise, Woody and Diane suffer the tedious approaches of a chatty older couple living across the hall, the man (Jerry Adler) vain of his stamp collection, the woman (Lynn Cohen) small, bustling, gray-haired. After the wife dies, apparently of a heart attack, Diane, making coffee in the widower's apartment, finds something in the kitchen that makes her think the man is a liar, possibly even a murderer. Her curiosity caught, she begins to nose around his apartment, hunting for clues. Did the friendly, talkative old guy murder his wife in order to live with a younger woman?

Woody is amazed and disgusted by her meddling. His code has been violated: In New York, you *never* get involved in a stranger's business. Anyway, she's reacting to signs and portents that probably mean nothing. The world isn't *like* that—like a murder mystery. (We agree with him on all counts: He represents the audience here.) He expostulates with her, creating sarcastic arabesques of commentary around her relentless suspicions, Diane angrily plowing ahead, willing to believe the worst, and Woody trailing after her, convinced that she's wrong but also fearing vaguely that he's losing her by being so reasonable. Working with Keaton seems to liberate Woody, who takes off in flights of comic anguish. Through an accident of casting, the movie has become an unintended sequel to *Annie Hall*. What if Annie had stayed in New York and married Alvy Singer? Well, it's twenty years later, they've raised a son, and Annie still doesn't know what to do with herself. Woody and Diane. It's been a long time.

Friends join in the game. When Woody won't accompany her in her sleuthing, Diane calls on Alan Alda, who plays a glibly self-assured playwright and theater director who's at loose ends (recently divorced) and ready for mischief. He eggs her on, because he wants to pull her away from Woody and he's shrewd enough to see that she craves adventure. At the same time, Woody is flirting with Anjelica Huston, one of his authors, a rather imposing intellectual femme fatale in black who's impenetrably cool about everything. They hang out in a restaurant, these four, and weave theories and then take action. And underneath their interest in the murder is their adulterous interest in one another.

The not-so-surprising surprise is that Diane's fancies turn out to be right. The joke is on Woody—and on us. The world is like a murder mystery; people actually do do those things. Realizing he's got to come through for her, Woody joins in at last, and the two become perhaps the most inept and terrified detectives in the history of crime, blundering into sinister hotel rooms, chasing after the astonished murderer like two kids who don't know how to hide. Because they're so frightened, and obviously so ill equipped for danger, we get scared, too. But two weaknesses limit the goosey fun. The means by which Hitchcock pulled ordinary people into extraordinary situations were always matter-of-fact and convincing. His people had no choice. But here the only true motives are boredom and curiosity, and we constantly feel the artificiality of the situation. And Woody doesn't control the atmospherics of danger well enough to convince us the couple is in any real trouble. The villain isn't very threatening; the settings and camera setups are mostly banal. As Woody is dragged kicking and screaming into adventure, I realized I cared far more about his decorative jokes than about anything that was going on.

Nothing is worked out too precisely. The adultery subplot is just a suggestion, and Alan Alda, his neck craning forward, grins a little too eagerly, while Anjelica Huston barely climbs into the movie. But the jokes are good, and the movie has a convivial feeling to it. During one of their meals, the amateur detectives discuss their plans to trap the murderer the way they might discuss a neat little movie they were making up. Indeed, the movie we see looks like it, too, might have been devised by these four in an afternoon and then just tossed off, it's casual, and that's the essence of its fragile but unmistakable charm.

NEW YORK POST, 8/18/93, p. 25, Michael Medved

"Manhattan Murder Mystery" offers moviegoers a pleasure that's been sorely lacking in most of Woody Allen's recent films: the element of fun.

Regardless of how one feels about the ultimate aesthetic virtues of dreary disappointments such as "Shadows and Fog," "Husbands and Wives," "Alice," "Another Woman," "September," or even the moving and profound "Crimes and Misdemeanors," none of these self-consciously solemn films could be plausibly accused of delivering an old-fashioned good time at the movies.

But "Manhattan Murder Mystery" provides precisely that sort of bright, breezy, midsummer diversion. The plot is silly piffle about a successful book editor at HarperCollins (Woody Allen) and his bright, bored empty-nester wife (Diane Keaton), who strike up a cordial acquaintance with their salt-of-the-earth neighbors (Jerry Adler and Lynn Cohen) in an Upper West Side apartment building.

Since Allen fails to share Adler's consuming passion for stamp-collecting, it's obvious that the two couples will never be the best of friends. But when Cohen abruptly drops dead, apparently from a heart attack, their destinies are drawn together in an elaborate web of suspicion and intrigue.

Keaton becomes convinced that foul play is involved in her neighbor's death and despite the anguished (and eminently reasonable) protests of her nervous husband takes increasingly outrageous risks to investigate the situation.

She's encouraged in this dangerous hobby by her just-divorced pal Alan Alda, who uses their common interest in amateur detective work to advance his own romantic interest in her.

"Soon we're gonna be too old to act crazy," he tells her.

The mystery they probe isn't so much crazy as hard to follow, and even when all the missing pieces finally fall into place (with the help of a sexy novelist, played by Anjelica Huston), they don't really make much sense.

These shortcomings hardly matter, however, since our attention is focused so effectively on the amateur sleuths, their relationships, and their reactions to a potential crime, rather than on the crime itself.

Along the way, Woody Allen delivers his usual quota of witty lines. After leaving a performance of "The Flying Dutchman," for instance, he tells his wife: "The trouble with Wagner is that after just one act I start getting this urge to conquer Poland or something."

But beyond its amusing moments, this screenplay displays a stronger plot structure and more forward momentum than usual—perhaps a reflection of the fact that for the first time in 14 years, Allen has reunited as co-screenwriter with the talented Marshall Brickman, who collaborated with him on past triumphs, such as "Annie Hall" and "Manhattan."

The other reunion here, of course, is with Diane Keaton, whose thoroughly charming and wholly sympathetic performance contributes so substantially to the winning warmth of this film. Her triumphal return as leading lady indicates just how depressing a presence Mia Farrow had become in nearly all of Allen's latest films.

It makes no sense to attempt an amateur psychoanalysis of Allen (since so many professionals get paid so well for their services in this area), but it seems obvious that his decision to focus on this likable lightweight project at this difficult moment in his life represents a deliberate attempt to enable both filmmaker and fans to escape the pressure of the painful headlines.

In the midst of the wretched turmoil, Allen's ability to continue working (shooting on this picture began in September 1992) is altogether remarkable; under the circumstances, his success at turning out such a polished and pleasing little film is nothing less than heroic.

NEWSDAY, 8/18/93, Part II/p. 48, Jack Mathews

Whether he was trying to make himself forget his problems, or make us forget them, Woody Allen dug into his past for creative help on "Manhattan Murder Mystery," and the result is his lightest, and least filling, comedy in more than a decade.

Writing with his old "Sleeper"-"Annie Hall"-"Manhattan" partner Marshall Brickman, and with Diane Keaton back as his co-star, Allen manages to hit a lot of familiar notes, provoke some good laughs, and stir up a few fond memories. As a middle-aged Upper East Side couple—Larry Lipton is a book editor, Carol a former ad executive—Allen and Keaton give us the feeling we're revisiting Alvy Singer and Annie Hall, as they might have been had they stayed together.

But the feeling is fleeting. The similarities between the two screen couples (and the couple Allen and Keaton once were in real life) are on the most superficial personality level. It is as if all character substance and intellect had evaporated over the years, leaving Woody-Alvy-Larry a whiner without a cause, and Diane-Annie-Carol a loopy, restless housewife.

The story, such as it is, revolves around the death of Lillian House (Lynn Cohen), an elderly neighbor they had met just the night before. Something about the demeanor of the dead woman's husband (Jerry Adler) triggers Carol's curiosity, and she follows her nose right into the middle of a murder mystery, dragging Larry, complaining and kicking, along with her.

The obvious movie parallel is to "The Thin Man" series, in which penthouse New Yorkers Nick and Nora Charles diverted Depression Era moviegoers with their recreational pursuit of various thieves and killers. The charm of those pictures was in the chemistry between William Powell and Myrna Loy, and the obvious affection beneath Nick and Nora's playful repartee. Affection is a sometime thing between Larry and Carol. In fact, she is vaguely responsive to the overtures of her divorced, songwriter friend Ted (Alan Alda, smarmy as ever), and Larry is being tempted by the seductive author Marcia Fox (Anjelica Huston, alluring as ever) whose latest book he is editing.

Allen and Brickman wrote some great dialogue, and Allen, on a cinephile alert, directed a brilliant sequence where a chase scene in a revival-movie theater matches a chase scene from "The Third Man," being shown on the screen behind. The juxtaposed images create a spectacular illusion, a hall of mirrors within a hall of mirrors, and the inventiveness of it is Allen at his very best.

Ultimately, however, "Manhattan Murder Mystery" is undone by its *lack* of invention. You don't expect to find "Chinatown" in a detective comedy, but the mystery here is of no compelling interest at all. Scenes clearly designed to produce some tension—Carol rifling through her neighbor's apartment, and having to hide under a bed when he returns unexpectedly—merely create dramatic pauses, where there is neither suspense nor humor.

There is a sad irony to this movie. Allen, smarting from both the criticism of his personal behavior and the public rejection of last year's well-reviewed "Husbands and Wives," seems to have deliberately dumbed down for this, perhaps to demonstrate that he can still do what fans in "Stardust Memories" lovingly recalled as "his early, funny stuff."

Allen can still make us laugh, at will. When Carol tries to shame Larry into going with her to a concert, he says, "I can't listen to Wagner. I get the urge to conquer Poland." It is a vintage Allen line (or Brickman), and there are plenty more of them.

But he isn't the same person who made the early, funny stuff, and the innocence of those characters he played is gone. And therein rests the irony. Protest as he will, Allen the person and Allen the filmmaker are inextricably bound. What "Manhattan Murder Mystery" proves is that a Woody Allen movie without social context just isn't a Woody Allen movie.

NEWSWEEK, 8/30/93, p. 53, David Ansen

In his new comedy thriller *Manhattan Murder Mystery*, cowritten by Marshall brickman, Woody Allen plays his most frazzled variation on the Woody we know best: a nervous-Nellie urban neurotic kvetching his way through life as a means of avoiding it. As the book editor Larry Lipton, a man terrified of the impulsive, he has the bad (but really very good) luck of having Diane Keaton as his wife, Carol, a woman constantly scratching the itch of her intuition. And her instincts tell her that the sweet old woman down the hall did not die of a heart attack but was murdered by her husband (Jerry Adler), the man who nearly bored Larry to death showing off his stamp collection.

Everything about "Manhattan Murder Mystery" (except his recent fondness for the handheld camera) harks back to the earlier, more playful Allen style. Imagine a middle-aged Annie Hall stumbling into a film noir. At first, the whiny badinage seems too familiar—or maybe it's just that nowadays it takes a little time to cast the real Woody out of mind and let the screen persona take over. But the good news is that once the gears of the plot kick in, Allen's expert comic timing proves as beguiling as ever. One scene involving a tape recording designed to trap the caller is as flat-out funny as anything he's ever done.

The murder mystery itself can't be taken too seriously—it's just Allen's fanciful pretext for making another movie about relationships. Alan Alda is on hand to provide extramarital temptation as Keaton's slick pal Ted, who's much more willing to encourage her Nancy Drew fantasies than worrywart Woody. And Anjelica Huston, as an aggressive novelist, would be happy to lead her reluctant editor astray. As it turns out, a little brush with murder and mayhem is just the tonic the Liptons' marriage needs. On screen, Keaton and Allen have always been made for each other: they still strike wonderfully ditsy sparks. After the edgy intensities of "Husbands and Wives," this is a stroll in the park. It doesn't break new ground but, like a singer's (Alvy Singer's?) album of golden oldies, reminds us of the tunes we used to love to hear him play. That's nothing to sneeze at.

SIGHT AND SOUND, 2/94, p. 57, Phillip Kemp

Returning to their apartment one evening, Larry and Carol Lipton meet their neighbours, an older couple named Paul and Lillian House, and are invited in for coffee. Coming home the next day, Carol is horrified to find that Mrs House—who had boasted of her good health—has died of a heart attack. Soon afterwards, Larry and Carol encounter Paul, who seems oddly cheerful. Carol begins to suspect foul play, but Larry is dismissive. She gets far more response from their friend Ted, a lonely divorcee who has always fancied her.

Carol steals a key to Paul's apartment and snoops for clues. Hiding when he returns unexpectedly, she hears him planning a trip to Paris with a woman called Helen. This proves to be a young actress, Helen Moss; with Ted's help, Carol tracks her down, trailing her to a disused cinema Paul owns. Larry is still scornful, but begins to grow jealous of Ted. To distract him, he fixes him a date with one of Larry's own clients, the glamorous crime writer Marcia Fox.

Carol catches a glimpse, on a passing bus, of the supposedly dead Lillian House, and traces her to the Hotel Waldron. With Ted preoccupied with Marcia, she drags a reluctant Larry to the hotel, where they find Lillian's body. By the time the police arrive the corpse has vanished, but Larry and Carol see Paul drive off with it to a foundry, where he tips it into a vat of molten metal.

Marcia devises an elaborate bluff. Helen is invited to a fake audition and given lines which, taped and re-cut, can be used as a phone call to Paul telling him Larry and Carol are holding his wife's body for blackmail. In response, Paul kidnaps Carol and phones Larry to bring the body to his cinema. Once there, Larry rescues Carol while Paul is shot by his jealous assistant and ex-lover, Mrs Dalton. Marcia explains the mystery to Ted: the original body was that of Lillian's rich sister, whose money the couple plotted to steal, but Paul was two-timing Lillian with the younger Helen.

As Brian de Palma learnt some time back, if you're going to strew your films with references to other people's movies, you'd better make sure your own material can stand the comparison. *Manhattan Murder Mystery* is littered with buffish in-jokes—we kick off with a clip from *Double Indemnity*, the supposedly dead wife shows up on a bus labelled "Vertigo", the final confrontation plays out a rerun of the mirror shoot-out from *The Lady from Shanghai*, and so on. But the main effect of all these jokey hommages is to remind us how much better this kind of thing was done by Wilder, Hitchcock and Welles.

By Allen too, in some ways. The credit sequence, with Cole Porter's "I Happen to Like New York" sung over a soaring 'copter shot of the nocturnal city, immediately recalls the "Rhapsody in Blue" opening of *Manhattan*, but in visual terms *Manhattan Murder Mystery* never matches the earlier film's burnished black-and-white 'scope photography. Keaton and Allen acted far better together in *Annie Hall*: here their talking-across-each-other scenes, with her high-pitched ditsiness set against his hyperventilating mega-kvetch, become increasingly irritating. And while in *Play it Again, Sam* the last-reel *Casablanca* renunciation speech carried a real emotional charge, in the present film's climax Allen is so busy devising his clever Wellesian pastiche that all tension drains out of the scene.

For the work of such a notoriously perfectionist director, *Manhattan Murder Mystery* comes across as a surprisingly sloppy and slung-together affair. In one over-extended piece of business, Allen breaks an ornament while searching Paul's flat; not only isn't it very funny, it never pays off later in the plot. Larry and Carol's son Nick suddenly shows up for two minutes, does nothing much, and is never heard from again. Worst of all, the film never establishes a consistent comic tone. Several key scenes, such as the faked phone call, are blighted by fussy over-acting, with Allen himself the worst offender.

All in all, *Manhattan Murder Mystery* has an oddly tentative feel to it, as though Allen (maybe knocked askew by recent personal events) were casting about, uncertain where he or his career was heading. Previously—in, say, *Crimes of the Heart*—the dithery, insecure comic persona seemed separate from the self-assured filmmaker, but now the two seem to be disconcertingly merging. Even the one-liners have a provisional air, with the stand-up comedian on auto-pilot. The film's one clear asset is a characteristically poised, witty appearance from Anjelica Huston, who has developed into the kind of actress—like Jean Arthur or Myrna Loy—who can be looked to for a stylish performance no matter what's going on around her. Once again, she doesn't disappoint.

TIME, 8/23/93, p. 67, Richard Schickel

Women are the suspicious sex: so a certain amount of husbandly experience—as well as a long-established convention of popular culture—teaches us. For decades Blondie has been routing Dagwood out of bed to investigate strange noises downstairs. And Nora Charles always sniffed out foul play ahead of blithe Nick, despite the fact that he was the professional detective.

A feminist might argue that this proves the male is inherently less intuitive than the female. Or, more radically, that exploited womankind has better reason to be on guard than guys do. Woody Allen might argue that it is just plain funnier if supposedly ditsy Carol Lipton (Diane Keaton) insists there's something odd about the death of a neighbor while her husband Larry (Allen) patronizes her misgivings.

Though this is the least ambitious movie Allen has made in decades—for better or worse the return to "pure" comedy his critics have urged on him—he seems to have a little more on his mind than updating *The Thin Man*. For one thing, *Double Indemnity*, which he quotes directly and indirectly. For another, the classic New Yorker's ambivalence about neighbors; the Liptons lament not knowing the folks they see on the elevator, but they live in fear of being dragged into boring, alien lives.

Attempting to overcome their standoffishness, they accept an invitation for coffee with Paul and Lillian House, (Jerry Adler and Lynn Cohen). But Paul's insistence on showing Larry his stamp collection makes Larry realize anew the wisdom of minding one's own business, a course he keeps urging on his wife after Lillian dies suspiciously a few days later.

Carol is, of course, deliciously undeterrable—sneaking into the widower's apartment looking for clues, shadowing him on the street, eventually even catching sight of his supposed victim (she suddenly materializes on a passing bus). Her husband flaps along, squawking wisecrack warnings, but in time she persuades him, as well as a couple of bystanders (Alan Alda and Anjelica Huston), that something fishy (and much more convoluted than a simple murder) is going on. In a grand farcical sequence, all these characters manically manipulate tape recorders carrying provocative pre-recorded messages designed to elicit a confession from Paul.

It's an inspired passage. Allen and Marshall Brickman, the co-writer who worked with him so brilliantly in the past (*Annie Hall, Manhattan*), have concocted a steady stream of badinage that buoys the whole movie along. But these exchanges evaporate, and the movie is surprisingly flat visually. There comes a moment when you realize how wrong just being funny is for Allen. Ambition is an essential goad to his sensibility. It pushes him toward the rueful resonances of those previous Brickman collaborations and toward the magical transformations of reality in *The Purple Rose of Cairo* and *Radio Days*.

Given his recent circumstances, the distracted, unpolished air of this movie is understandable. It may even be that an air of modest amiability is—for him, for now—the right stance. But he has taught his devotees to expect more, and, perhaps cruelly, we continue to do so.

VILLAGE VOICE, 8/24/93, p. 53, Georgia Brown

Many people, seeing their lives irreparably ruptured, might draw a creative blank or at least be *distracted* from business as usual. Yet despite his public trial (literal and figurative), Woody Allen is now bringing out, even ahead of schedule, his annual comic confessional. Call it chutzpa or denial, in any case, it seems that filmmaking for Woody—who once emphatically denied that he needed to make movies—has become a "necessary" activity. I hesitate to use the word *therapeutic*.

With *Manhattan Murder Mystery* Allen has once more hit on a generically expressive title, applying as it does to his life as we know it. (He's been doing this since *Another Woman*.) With murders proliferating in the Manhattan of his dreams, Allen apparently hasn't a clue to his own motives, whereabouts, or even to the distinction between right and wrong. As spectators, however, the rest of us can look back and see that since the beginning Allen's great theme, after God and extinction, has been love and death. Meaning sex and crime.

Recently, I recalled a scene in *Take the Money and Run:* On a purse-snatching foray, Virgil Starkweather (Allen) sneaks up on Janet Margolin sketching in the park, but when she turns around, assuming he's interested in her artwork, he's smitten. "After 15 minutes I wanted to marry her. After half an hour I forgot about stealing her purse." Not to worry, the repressed will return.

A sometimes very funny thriller, *Manhattan Murder Mystery* takes off on the borscht belt comedian's assumption: All men want to get rid of their wives. Borrowing heavily from Hitchcock's *Rear Window*, two relationships are set up early on as reflections of each other. On one end of the corridor live the Liptons, Larry and Carol (subbing for James Stewart and Grace Kelly, Woody and Diane Keaton), a fiftyish couple growing anxious about sags and bags, and down the hall, their apparently more stable, age-accepting neighbors, the Houses (Jerry Adler and Lynn Cohen). As in *Husbands and Wives*, we start with two couples—one thought of as "ideal"—and something bad happens. In this case, Mrs. House dies suddenly. The question arises, Did Mr. House do her in? Might this unlikely philatelist have a much younger mistress waiting in the wings? The question deflected, especially, if we're taking *Rear Window* as our guide: Does mild-mannered Larry Lipton, Harper's book editor, fantasize getting rid of his wife? The issues of incompatibility, aging bodies, and a waning sex life all are raised in the movie's first few minutes. Blatantly, Allen even sets his opening scene in Madison Square Garden—scene of Woody's own tabloid "crime"—where Larry is intent on the Rangers while Carol frets and yawns.

Though soon to become a premenopausal Nancy Drew, Carol at the beginning is at loose ends: She quit advertising to raise a child, who's now in college. Her therapy ended two years ago, though Larry reminds her that GM recalled defective models. (Look who's talking.) Relying only on proverbial "female intuition," she suddenly becomes obsessed with the Houses, and when she can't enlist Larry (he's busy, timid, and skeptical), she calls on the recently divorced Ted (Alan Alda), a playwright willing to go along with Carol's fancies. When Larry realizes Carol and Ted are growing intimate, as they while away hours shadowing their suspects, he joins the game. Clinically, it's called danger as aphrodisiac.

Augmenting the general hysteria, Carlo Di Palma's hand-held camera is back, though not so obtrusively as last time. Obviously, Allen means the film to have a rough, shaky look—appropriate enough given the tense subject. He does very nicely in imitating certain of Hitchcock's eerie touches: the sight of a lone woman on a bus (an ad for Vertigo jeans on its side), the intermittent presence of a stern, middle-aged woman with a limp—a sort of matronly superego. The movie abounds in allusions to movies—*Casablanca, Double Indemnity, Last Year at Marienbad*—and even projects its own denouement over Welles's finale to *The Lady From Shanghai*. Together with all the references to mirrors, twins, and multiple personalities, the effect is of overlapping layers of double-talk. But meanwhile, the facts are clear. "Don't ever say that life doesn't imitate art again," Woody warns us.

Missing, however, is what *Rear Window* had: sympathy for its devils. When Raymond Burr's haunted Thorwald confronts Stewart's Jeffries asking what he wants of him, it's a terrifying and terribly poignant moment. Especially since Jeffries has been using Thorwald to solve his own riddles and exorcise his own demons. In Woody's version, all the Manhattan couples going about their flirtations and cultural liaisons are shallow narcissists. Keaton and Allen are sometimes so shrill, you want to have them locked up. (It's hard not to think that Mia would have been better.)

In his recent films, Allen's own character lacks the definition it used to have. He's no longer on a philosophical or psychological quest. The jokes are becoming old, repetitive, and occasionally very crude. As when Larry tells Carol, "There's nothing wrong with you that can't be cured with a little Prozac and a polo mallet." A polo mallet? Take my wife, please.

Also reviewed in:
CHICAGO TRIBUNE, 8/20/93, Friday/p. A, Clifford Terry
NEW REPUBLIC, 10/4/93, p. 30, Stanley Kauffmann
NEW YORK TIMES, 8/18/93, p. C13, Janet Maslin
NEW YORKER, 8/23 & 30/93, p. 163, Terrence Rafferty
VARIETY, 8/16/93, p. 38, Todd McCarthy
WASHINGTON POST, 8/20/93, p. D6, Rita Kempley
WASHINGTON POST, 8/20/93, Weekend/p. 42, Desson Howe

MANUFACTURING CONSENT: NOAM CHOMSKY AND THE MEDIA

A Zeitgeist Films release of a Necessary Illusions and National Film Board of Canada production. *Executive Producer:* Colin Neale and Dennis Murphy. *Producer:* Peter Wintonick, Mark Achbar, and Adam Symansky. *Director:* Peter Wintonick and Mark Achbar. *Director of Photography:* Mark Achbar, Norbert Bunge, Kip Durrin, Savas Kalogeras, Antonin Lhotsky, Francis Miquet, Barry Perles, Ken Reeves, Bill Snider, Kirk Tougas, and Peter Wintonick. *Editor:* Peter Wintonick. *Music:* Carl Schultz. *Sound:* (music) Louis Hone. *Running time:* 165 minutes. *MPAA Rating:* Not Rated.

CINEASTE, Vol. XX, No. 1, p. 42, Paul Mattick, Jr.

The title of this film is borrowed from one of Noam Chomsky's books, which in turn lifted it from the prose of Walter Lippmann. Lippmann, once a mighty voice of liberal journalism elevated to the status of all-around Wise Man, but today relatively (and quite fairly) neglected, coined the phrase in the course of discussing the production of news out of the raw material of events. A democracy, he explained, rests on the consent of the governed, but that consent must be manufactured by controlling information on the basis of which political opinions are formed. *Manufacturing Consent*, though itself sponsored in part by an agency of a bourgeois democracy. The National Film Board of Canada, for the most part presents a critique of the construction of news by newspapers and television through an account of Chomsky's views on the subject.

Its own construction out of footage of Chomsky speaking at numerous public meetings and radio and TV interviews, as well as interviews done for the film, leads to a secondary focus on the linguist-activist as an individual. The opening shot, in fact, features Chomsky's appearance on a multiscreen array that dominates the atrium of a shopping mall, an image that returns periodically throughout the film. This image produces the odd effect of Chomsky as Big Brother—a Big Brother not watching but speaking to all of us, even while, in fact, ignored by the occasional person seen moving through the mall. Its function is unclear. Its possible ironic intentions, as it plays the face of the media critic off against a hyperform of TV existence, seem overwhelmed by the fifteen minute form of cult of personality contemporary media are geared to, and which can be felt in the film itself in its focus on Chomsky. In this, the image of the critic on the superscreen is emblematic of *Manufacturing Consent*'s limitations as well as of its good intentions.

The film begins with a *People* magazine-style précis of Chomsky's career, explaining the jacket copy on his book proclaiming him "arguably the most important intellectual alive." Typically of the filmmakers' readiness to slide from intellectual and political content to cute material, a rapid (and somewhat inaccurate) trek through his exploits in the field of linguistics is punctuated by footage of the chimpanzee Nim Chimpsky, whose apparent language learning ability turned out to be an illusion, though the relevance of this to Chomsky's theories is not made clear. In any case, we have a shot of Chomsky himself explaining that he sees no particular connection between his scientific work and his politics. As we follow the story of the professor's reactivation of the radicalism of his youth in response to the war in Vietnam, the connection between politics and profession takes the form of the heroic tale of an ethical person forced by his conscience to risk imprisonment rather than sitting back and enjoying the flood tide of his scholarly fame.

One can think of many interesting questions that might have been pursued at this juncture. Some have to do directly with the movie's central topic: Chomsky's ability to mobilize his celebrity as an intellectual in the interest of radical politics, and the simultaneous creation of a new mode of celebrity as an activist. Others have to do with the more personal side of the story: the clip of Chomsky in the Sixties attacking MIT for its collaboration with the war machine might have been usefully followed by a discussion of the irony represented by his own ability to get quantities of Air Force funding for his research, unmentioned in the film. This is meant not as a criticism of Chomsky—I do not believe that his work aided the Air Force in any way—but as an example of the manner in which *Manufacturing Consent* tends to come up against important questions, such as the radicalism of individuals securely positioned within the social apparatus of domination, only to leave them undiscussed.

To take a more central instance, a segment of the film raises the matter of the predominance in newspaper pages of advertising over news. This is not connected, as it might have been, to the point made earlier that the various news media are typically elements of giant corporate entities. As businesses, newspapers must make money; they must, as Chomsky explains, deliver readers to advertisers. It is easy to imagine, of course, that this might lead to the slanting of news in particular ways. But this matter is not explored: there is not even one example of the effect of business considerations on content, and the film simply rushes off to another topic.

The one issue discussed in depth provides the film's most satisfying segment. This is the story of Indonesia's invasion of East Timor which, despite the enormous amount of killing involved, was barely reported by the U.S. press, especially in comparison with the play given the roughly contemporaneous activities of the Khmer Rouge in Cambodia. Chomsky demonstrates how the media—*The New York Times* is a prime offender—vastly exaggerated the numbers killed by a Communist movement, while downplaying the viciousness of an American ally, which in fact was receiving military aid from Washington in the midst of the massacres. In its treatment of this story *Manufacturing Consent* broadens out, providing background on East Timor and Indonesia s invasion as well as giving a vivid sense of the behavior of the press (the juxtaposition of interviews with the repulsive Karl Meyer of the *Times* with information supplied by Chomsky and others is quite effective).

On the other hand, no explanation is offered of why the *Times* and other media should have been such servants of the state in this particular instance, or even of the state's motivation. The history that would explain the American government's support for the Indonesian dictatorship is missing, along with any attempt to explain why in particular the large corporations that produce the news should share this interest, not to mention the more general question of why developed capitalism has so little room for ideological diversity. The film performs the useful tasks of teaching the viewer something about East Timor, explaining how it has come about that the American public is so uninformed about the topic, and stimulating feelings of righteous indignation. But the causes and mechanisms producing the phenomena we thus react to are not explored.

Instead of depth we have repetition: in the course of the film the same or similar points are made over and over in different ways. The great length of *Manufacturing Consent*—it runs for two hours and forty-seven minutes, with an intermission—is not used to demonstrate how political information could be presented differently than the norm. Indeed, it apes the commercial media by using many of the same techniques for which it criticizes them. For instance, *Manufacturing Consent* has harsh words for TV's predilection for soundbites, but for the most part limits itself to brief snippets of speeches and interviews rather than extended discussions. A long section given over to a public debate between Chomsky and the Dutch Minister of Defense reduces that debate to an alternation of brief bursts of speech, annoyingly intercut with footage of a prize fight. Chomsky scores a knockout, but the reduction of political argument to an athletic event—and this in a film that quotes its hero at length on the stupefying effects of sports reporting—robs the original debate of any intellectual seriousness it might have had.

More generally, the film doesn't trust the power of information and analysis, but feels a need to provide visual excitement by way of cute bits of stock footage and to back the voices of Chomsky and others with a throbbing, synthesized beat that sounds borrowed from some TV cop show and which on occasion makes it hard to listen to the actual matter under discussion. Most inexcusably, *Manufacturing Consent* suppresses information relevant to its themes.

A lengthy segment deals with the flap over Chomsky's support for the freedom of speech of Robert Faurisson, a teacher in France suspended from his job for publishing tracts disputing the reality of Nazi extermination camps. There is a connection between this affair and Chomsky's agitation about the Cambodia-East Timor contrast: the French ex-leftists who solicited the American academics support for Faurisson saw a parallel between the Cambodian case and the use of antifascism in Europe to obscure the fundamentally violent character of capitalist society. While Chomsky himself, so far as I am aware, had no particular interest in this aspect of the story, his civil libertarian stand with respect to Holocaust revisionism was distorted by others to brand him an anti-Semite.

The real issue here, for which *l'affaire Faurisson* served as decoy, was Chomsky's consistent critique of Zionist oppression of the Palestinians, for which many friends of Israel in the mass media and intellectual press will not forgive him. It is likely, in fact, that it is his position on Israel—he favors a two state solution to the Jewish-Palestinian conflict—that has led to Chomsky's marginalization by American news and intellectual media, rather than his radicalism generally. Whatever the case, the politics of Zionism runs like a thread through Chomsky's political life, from his youth (his father was a Hebrew teacher, and his first linguistic work was on the grammar of Hebrew) to the present, and should have been discussed. His courage as a consistent critic of Israeli policy in the face of sometimes vicious opposition would have provided a powerful case history of the media at the work of silencing unacceptable opinions. It is hard to understand why this central feature of Chomsky's career was sidestepped by a film celebrating Chomsky's challenge to the suppression of information.

Aside from specific questions of content, *Manufacturing Consent* raises issues about the visual presentation of political ideas. Its central image is that of Chomsky explaining the truth in a careful, patient way that embodies a powerful rhetoric of what the Gandhians used to call "speaking truth to power." But it shows little faith in the power of reason, as embodied simply in a talking head, to move the viewer to thought. Sometimes the illustrations of themes evoked in speech work well, as in a graphic demonstration of the relative space allotted by *The New York*

Times to East Timor and Cambodia. Sometimes the visual gimmickry is cute but adds little to the argument, as when Chomsky's critique of the cult of sports is delivered by his image on the giant screen at a stadium. Often enough, however, it disrupts the flow of ideas without adding anything to it.

Why are filmmakers so afraid of talk! I found myself thinking of the pleasure at once visual and intellectual of the endlessly talking heads of Jean-Pierre Léaud and Juliet Berto in Godard's *Le Gai Savior*, or the power of interviews in Ophul's *Hotel Terminus*, given all the time they need to uncoil. Perhaps the makers of *Manufacturing Consent* didn't trust us to take in ideas at length without the devices that transform news into entertainment, the leading contemporary form of ideology. Ironically enough, the very attempt to add this aspect to a would-be seriously political film has made it seem tediously long, as repetition and filler take the place of invention and development. The resulting film is not unlikable—it does, after all, bring important ideas in some form before public—but the extent of its capitulation to the strategies it seeks to criticize is depressing. Chomsky's efforts, as shown here, are often inspiring, but we live in dark times indeed.

FILM QUARTERLY, Fall 1993, p. 36, Karen Jaehne

Agitprop has entered documentary filmmaking with a vengeance. *The Thin Blue Line, Roger & Me,* and *A Brief History of Time*, to name the most prominent of recent documentaries, are very clear about what axe they are grinding. With similarly iconoclastic methods, *Manufacturing Consent: Noam Chomsky and the Media* shows us aborted interviews, archival footage used ironically, the process behind mass media methodology opened up like an empty envelope, weighty symbols thrown at us from the junk pile of popular culture, and a rhythm influenced by MTV slowing down only to let distinguished intellectuals viciously attack each other. Gone are the purportedly noncommittal, cool observational styles of "Watch-and-Wait" Wiseman and his followers. This is a hip, impatient, intellectually aggressive documentary school that has accepted the challenge of making its political reality at least as interesting as intelligent bombs.

The film presents the best and the worst (often at the same time) of mass media from a wide range of newspeople in print, radio, and television. In true agitprop style, the two film-makers are caught on camera (but not grandstanding) as they follow political activist Noam Chomsky, who has been the model of activism for two generations of Americans, pounding his drum. This is the aftermath of the sixties—its axe surprisingly sharp after all these years.

A 167-minute Canadian documentary full of Noam Chomsky sounds like a Civics lesson. But encountering Chomsky through this stylish and gutsy film is like running into Socrates outside the temple, with video screens replacing Greek columns. There's nothing reverent here either in what Chomsky has to say or in what the documentary has to say about Chomsky, although the film-makers endorse his critique of and solutions for mass media and especially his detached style. Not always diplomatic, incessantly critical, Mark Achbar and Peter Wintonick are as engaged but aloof as their Canadian countrymen Marshall McLuhan, Robin MacNeil, and Peter Jennings.

At a more profound level, Chomsky's message is about the meaninglessness of freedom of speech and press (and the entire First Amendment) if we don't have the freedom to think. Our ability to analyze and challenge the Cheez Whiz of the news media is increasingly in jeopardy. Chomsky claims it is not in the interest of news organizations and the bastions of power behind them to have us think. Their role as thought-police is examined in *Manufacturing Consent*, and while Chomsky does not fit the profile of a hysterical radical, he certainly presents an alarming case for believing that the public is systematically denied access to information by a paternalistic and corrupt system.

Even stating such a claim poses the unfortunate dilemma of being considered either paranoid or naïve. Knowing what we know of the last 30 years of governmental and industrial mismanagement, is it reasonable even to pursue the truth, much less the facts?

Yes, argues Chomsky, for if we don't we must bear the guilt for what goes wrong with the world. Our silence or willing ignorance is complicity. "It is the responsibility of intellectuals to speak the truth and expose lies." That is how Chomsky defines himself and his mission, and he is a virulent critic of irresponsible and/or nonintellectual powermongers.

Without Chomsky's matter-of-fact speeches and his uncompromising morality to guide the film, it would be just another documentary about another hopeless dilemma. Despite his diffidence, *Manufacturing Consent* draws its lessons from Noam Chomsky's political ideas and ideals, not his life or life-style. There is a refreshing lack of the kind of personal detail that clutters most personality profiles.

Two well-selected biographical nuggets explain Chomsky as a child. The son of Zionist teachers, he was introduced to political debate amid the arguments of average people gathering at his uncle's news kiosk by the Broadway and 72nd Street subway station. Another personal anecdote has Chomsky describing a moment of guilt in a case of schoolyard injustice, when he rose to defend another child but ultimately ran away because he also became intimidated by the bullies. It so shamed him that, by his own account, he has pledged never again to permit himself to run from a fight.

And run he doesn't—in the face of outrageous attacks. The schoolyard bully approach is captured in a clip from a 1969 interview with William F. Buckley. Discussing his opposition to the Vietnam War, Chomsky wryly complains, "Sometimes I lose my temper. Maybe not tonight," against which Buckley lashes out, "Maybe not tonight, uh, because if you would I'd smash you in the goddamn face," to which Chomsky adds, "That's a good reason for not losing my temper."

While these anecdotes are instructive about taking a stand, their function within the film is to help us see Chomsky as a role model, because *Manufacturing Consent* is not, according to Peter Wintonick, "about Chomsky per se but about a wave of dissent and discontent that is sweeping through society which supports Chomsky's point of view. It could be about you or me and make the same points."

Accustomed to their table-tennis technique, his partner, Mark Achbar, adds, "We didn't set out to lionize Chomsky, but we needed a magnet for the social dissent that fuels the alternative media and an ever larger public concern that we're being duped by the mass media and the government. Noam has a very interesting theory about how those institutions work in tandem to keep us in the dark. He is a compelling thinker and speaker."

"Because he is obsessed with power," chimes in Wintonick, "and most people that are interested in power want to get it, not to analyze it ..." "and its abuses." Achbar finishes Wintonick's sentence. (Their editing techniques also display the vitality of call-and-response, chant-and-echo.)

Yet Chomsky is a powerful person in his own right, a fact which the documentary and Chomsky seem to forget. He may not be a rock star or a charismatic politician, but he attracts huge audiences everywhere but Washington, D.C. In Europe, he is considered a major American intellectual force, on a par with Roland Barthes in France, Umberto Eco in Italy, Václav Havel in the Czech Republic—men who can think theoretically, write intelligently, and act on their beliefs. Perhaps Chomsky's power lies in his appeal to people who feel powerless.

The ability of apparently powerless people to change the course of politics is one of the most important history lessons of our time, a fact which looms over the film-makers and the audience, and increases the unmentioned parallel with the oppressed of eastern Europe. Can common people liberate themselves from the web of propaganda draped across American popular culture? Chomsky's call has an increased urgency because throughout the world, brotherhoods of workers have overthrown the far more dangerous, terrorizing threats of the Communist bureaucracy. Who then are we to whine about Time-Warner?

Why does Chomsky think the average man can take to the barricades against the media? Because Chomsky accords other people his own intelligence, forgetting however that he, Chomsky, seems never to be distracted by mere pleasure. Take, for example, his point about sports, a human activity that churns hundreds of billions of dollars yearly.

Speaking to an audience in Hamilton, Ontario, and from a video wall at Montreal's Olympic Stadium (where Wintonick and Achbar projected the speech, all the better to highlight its audacity), Chomsky notes, "It's striking to see the intelligence that's used by ordinary people in sports ... they have the most exotic information and understanding about all kinds of arcane issues. ... That's why energy is devoted to supporting them and advertisers are willing to pay for them and so on."

This attack on the very gonads of American culture seems careless at first, but then as I watch the 1993 National Football League finals, the game is interrupted to announce that the U.S.A. is again engaged in bombing strategic sites in Baghdad, and one can't help but recall the yellow-ribbon pageantry at the 1991 Superbowl for our efforts to spread democracy in the Gulf. The irrational jingoism of football is a prime time to garner support for wars against infidels. Could Chomsky be right?

It is exactly this itch, our fear of being duped, that he scratches. Still, it angers people to be told they are gullible. And therein lies Chomsky's and, inevitably, this film's potential to arouse controversy and hatred. The President of Boston University, himself no stranger to controversy, cannot restrain himself from a rude attack on Chomsky in a 1986 debate about the Contras on WGBH. Stopping Chomsky from citing an atrocity, John Silber screams, "You are a systematic liar ... you are a phony, Mister, and it's time that the people read you correctly."

Despite the controversy surrounding Chomsky, he is not a pitbull politician. He began his professional life with no small distinction as the man who proposed transformational linguistics and posited that language is innately human, even genetically programmed, rather than culturally determined (thus arguing against the theories and experiments of the reigning social scientist of the time, B.F. Skinner). His 1957 work, *Syntactic Structures*, became a standard text for anyone interested in linguistics—which itself was soon to become the reigning theoretical approach to just about everything. Chomsky was credited with its revolution.

In the 1960s, Chomsky became discontent with the metalanguage of theoretical discourse and set out to exercise himself as a citizen; he expected "to spend years in jail, and came very close to it." Another of his books, *American Power and the New Mandarin* (1968), helped solidify opinion against American involvement in Indochina and made him an icon of the New Left.

"Democracy," he says in a speech at Georgetown University, "requires free access to ideas and information." This simple proposition seems so self-evident that it takes a very aggressive intellect to dig behind the apparatus of the age of information to see that the information parcelled out to the public is predigested. "Manufacturing consent" is said to be a phrase first used by Walter Lippmann to describe the process of creating necessary illusions in order to shortcut the democratic process. A ruling class makes choices; appropriate propaganda techniques solicit the consent of the governed under the illusion that the fait accompli being presented was the only reasonable choice.

"The task of media," notes Chomsky, is "to mobilize public support for decisions made by those in charge," who hide their self-interest behind certain myths. To explore the manufacturing of news, the filmmakers lead us into the offices of *The New York Times*. A silver-haired public-affairs hack insists they cannot film in certain areas, so the screen goes black, and we are left in the dark as we listen to august descriptions before meeting editorial board member Karl Meyer, who disingenuously apologizes for the imperfect coverage of atrocities in East Timor.

The horrific news from East Timor is used as a model for the way the media apparatus foregoes political situations too complicated for the mere public and which could put the agenda of U.S. nuclear submarine activity in the South Seas in jeopardy. While this particular case requires attention not appropriate for this space, it justifies viewing *Manufacturing Consent* as a film that practices what it preaches: East Timor deserves an hour of media attention; it gets it.

The visuals of the film are inventive, caustic, and highly entertaining, but the meat of the movie is on its sound track. Perhaps the success of such a film is that it enlists the razzle-dazzle of today's TV news shows to impart a sober and sobering message. A certain degree of cognitive dissonance is created in the friction between its entertainment value and its intense politics. The extraordinary achievement of *Manufacturing Consent* is to use cognitive dissonance to remind us we have to be as alert as Noam Chomsky to keep propaganda from killing democracy.

LOS ANGELES TIMES, 4/29/93, Calendar/p. 5, Kenneth Turan

Talking head documentaries are only as involving as the head doing the talking, and "Manufacturing Consent: Noam Chomsky and the Media" has the great advantage of having as its subject America's most controversial intellectual, a soft-spoken provocateur whose radical theories clash with the norm at every turn.

For those who find Chomsky's name familiar but can't call his theories readily to mind, "Manufacturing Consent" functions as an intellectually challenging crash course in the man's coolly contentious analysis, laying out his thoughts in a package that is clever and accessible if (at nearly three hours) rather longer than it needs to be.

One reason for all those minutes is that there are at least two Chomskys and possibly even more. Born in 1928, the son of a Hebrew scholar, Chomsky emerged in the late 1950s as the preeminent figure in modern linguistics. So great was his stature that when a group of linguists attempted to teach a chimpanzee to speak, they naturally named him Nim Chimpsky.

Then, in 1964, Chomsky began a second career as a political activist because, he says, "it was immoral not to." Though he has an almost boyish inability to resist self-consciously incendiary statements such as "if the Nuremburg laws were invoked, every American President would be hung" and "the Bible is the most genocidal book ever written," most of Chomsky's reputation, and the brunt of this film, is based on his theories on the media's role in thought control in a democratic society.

Totalitarian states, Chomsky says, don't need thought control, they use a bludgeon instead. Democracies, however, have to take charge of the way people think, and they do this, he theorizes, by having the media set an agenda, push a perception of the world that satisfies the needs of both government and government-supported corporate interests.

As an example of how the major media set an agenda, "Manufacturing Consent" deals extensively with the New York Times coverage of the parallel crises in Cambodia and East Timor. The former was extensively written about as one of the great genocidal massacres, while the later crisis, which Chomsky says was just as bad if not worse, was down-played because our corporate/political interests were more directly at stake.

Given the weightiness of Chomsky's thought, directors Peter Wintonick and Mark Achbar, who spent four years on the project and tirelessly followed their subject all over the world, have tried to make "Manufacturing Consent" as viewer-friendly as possible.

For one thing, though the film is clearly in Chomsky's corner, it takes care to present the views of those who think the idea of elites setting agendas is, in the words of author Tom Wolfe, "absolute rubbish." And the directors have worked hard to vary the modes of presenting Chomsky's talking head, inserting it in everything from giant shopping mall video displays to a sports stadium screen.

"Manufacturing Consent" also relies heavily on all manner of visual gimcracks, from snappy graphics to unconsciously corny old documentaries, to juice things up. Some of these, for instance, the physical unrolling of the 1,175 index column inches for New York Times 1978-79 coverage of Cambodia versus the measly 70 inches for East Timor, are especially effective, but all show an understanding of the necessity of making abstract ideas palatable to a wide audience.

Given that, it is unfortunate that "Manufacturing Consent" cannot resist detours that unnecessarily slow things down. Though an examination of the difficulty Chomsky got into by defending the free speech rights of a French professor who denies the existence of the Holocaust is fascinating, a gimmicky trip to Media, Pa., and another to the offices of Z magazine could have been avoided. By putting out the film at this length, its makers have made it regrettably likely that it will play most to those who need its message least.

NEW YORK POST, 3/17/93, p. 23, Jami Bernard

You know the old chestnut about how Einstein—even Einstein—used only 10 percent of his brain power. Imagine what the average American must be using.

But dim bulbs everywhere can brighten by tuning in to the thoughts and writings of linguist Noam Chomsky, whose brilliance resides not just in his education and facility with words, but in his perseverance in overturning the myths that the government and collective society spoon-feed us to keep us acquiescent. Once you free your mind to question what has previously been accepted, the mind can soar.

That is the most thought-provoking—and least political—"take-away" you can get from the meticulous, sometimes playful documentary "Manufacturing Consent: Noam Chomsky and the Media," well worth its 165-minute length.

Chomsky, an intellectual who has been marginalized for his "radical" political views—which in the context of the documentary don't seem radical at all, only rational—was bound for the life of the mind when at age 6 he attempted to protect a fat kid in school who was being ostracized. Little Noam reasoned correctly that the other child's weight bore no intrinsic reason for ridicule, thus putting him way ahead of most adults today who make fun of any person who doesn't conform to their own group.

As an adult, Chomsky continues his quest to root out ridiculous assumptions that remain unchallenged by a sheep-like populace. Spectator sports, for example, Chomsky describes as a thing designed "to give people something to pay attention to that's of no importance," enforced by a general public policy of "dulling people's brains, getting them away from things that matter, and for that, it's important to reduce their capacity to think."

Chomsky's views are too elaborate and involved to be reduced to a couple of "sound bites"—the bane of intellectual discourse and of Chomsky's theses in particular—but for the interests of readers who may want to see this documentary, it is about how forces in society (most notably the media) compress and distort information into a stream of thought that serves the needs of a few at the expense of the many.

From there the documentary segues into the political consequences, using Chomsky's favorite case study of the atrocities in East Timor versus the atrocities in Cambodia and how the media covered each (The filmmakers roll out a line of newsprint like those ads for toilet paper, to show which subject received more coverage.)

The documentary also explodes the myth that Chomsky somehow supported a French madman who claimed that the Holocaust never existed and cheerfully displays the discomfort of TV interviewers and newspaper editorial writers who try unsuccessfully to cast aspersions on Chomsky's views.

To offset the intellectual heaviness of the material the filmmakers have chosen innovative ways to illustrate and compartmentalize. Several times, they beam Chomsky's talking face over a series of giant video monitors into a mall where the shoppers couldn't be less interested in his thoughts on the dulling of the American brain and "irrational attitudes of submission to authority."

Personally, and also as an unwitting member of the media that Chomsky so castigated, I found this documentary a shock to the system—as well it should be to thinking individuals, or to those who were using less than that 10 percent of their brains and were aspiring higher. What can I do? ask people at Chomsky's lectures. Well, they can start by thinking.

SIGHT AND SOUND, 11/93, p. 45, Chris Darke

Part One: *Thought Control in a Democratic Society*. The work of radical US intellectual Noam Chomsky on the organisational structures and hidden agendas of the American news media, in particular their coverage of US foreign policy, is set in the context of brief biographical details: Chomsky's years as a revolutionary linguistic philosopher, his politicisation as a child of working-class Brooklyn Jewish parents during the Depression and his involvement in anti-war activism in the 1960s. These details are interspersed with Chomsky in debate with Michel Foucault, William Buckley Jnr., Bill Boyers, and with comments by Tom Wolfe. Chomsky's analysis of the American media is approached through his theoretical 'propaganda models' concentrating on their applicability to the *New York Times* and in particular to US coverage of the Indonesian invasion of East Timor; and on the relationship between the media and the state during the Gulf crisis, at which time Chomsky asserts that the media were instrumental in America's going to war "in the manner of a totalitarian society".

Part Two: *Activating Dissent*. Chomsky is shown in debate with the hostile Dutch defence minister Fritz Bolkestein, and his involvement in the defence of the civil rights of controversial French historian Robert Faurisson is examined. The activist-intellectual's role is explored in relation to the growth of independent media networks in the US, as are his thoughts on the role of the media in the election and inauguration of George Bush. Finally, Chomsky discusses his deep-seated libertarian socialist convictions.

In one of his recent series of Reith Lectures, "Representations of the Intellectual", Edward Said devoted much attention to the linguist, political activist and media analyst Noam Chomsky as a model of the committed modern American intellectual. Listening between the lines, however, one would not have been hard pressed to detect the tones of pretender-to-the-throne of chief dissident. While this may be unfair to Said, Chomsky has undoubtedly become characterised, over the past 25 years, as the most turbulent priest in the American academy. Such a cult of personality is one way in which the power of ideas can either be transmitted or diminished, depending on whether they are deemed germane or detrimental to society. It is the media that create such personalities and that simultaneously encourage and restrict the flow of information and ideas. Peter Wintonick and Mark Achbar's *Manufacturing Consent* is about this process—exploring not only what information gets through and why, but equally what happens to those, like Chomsky, who attempt to use the media in order to condemn their power to create the "necessary illusions" that maintain the political dominance of particular elite groups.

Five years in production, and a distillation of more than 120 hours of material, *Manufacturing Consent* is an ambitious *mise en scène* of ideas that, while aiming to explore something of Chomsky's life, is committed above all to his thoughts on the political economy of the media. Hence, it avoids the conventional documentary features—'voice of God' narration, chronological exposition—and makes its *modus operandi* dialectical both in form and content. Chomsky is presented largely in debate and interviews, and the juxtaposition of those against whom he is pitted is judicious, telling and often entertaining. In an interview with the arch-conservative William Buckley Jnr. he admits that he is wont to lose his temper on such occasions. The sleek Buckley imperiously warns him not to, adding "If you did, I'd smash your face in"—Ivy League arrogance and a casual WASP brutality mobilised to put the upstart Jewish subversive in his place.

But across numerous interviews it becomes apparent that Chomsky's strength as a TV performer is itself the paradoxical corollary to his intellectual status: marginalised but an *agent provocateur* by his very presence. In drawing the fire of Buckley and his ilk, he exposes the enemy's position and deals with it amiably; then he returns a fusillade of facts in a voice that sometimes approximates a James Stewart tremor, but that either puts his opponents on the defensive or sees them falling back on to weak institutional rationalisations (the latter tactic being particularly favoured by *New York Times* journalists, it appears).

However, Chomsky's fondness for facts and die-hard research-based empiricism sometimes appears as a refuge rather than a strength. This tendency surfaces most clearly in the film's second part which broaches his defence of the French revisionist historian Robert Faurisson, impeached in France for declaring that there was no evidence to prove the existence of the Nazi death camps. In defending Faurisson's right to freedom of speech, Chomsky was accused of tacitly supporting his thesis and it is a credit that the complexities of Chomsky's position are explored in a film which, on the whole, accepts his media analyses at face value.

But then it is hard, at times, not to—particularly when the case of the American media's silence over the genocidal invasion of East Timor by Indonesia is set against the clamorous outcry against the Khmer Rouge in Cambodia. These two examples of America's news priorities are used to illustrate what Chomsky calls his "institutional" analysis of the media, and what others—here, the Dutch defence minister and the writer Tom Wolfe—have predictably dismissed as conspiracy theory.

If the first part of *Manufacturing Consent* imaginatively illustrates selected Chomskyan ideas on American media, the second part looks for alternative media networks and finds a host of print media, local radio and TV stations that are resisting the *New York Times* and CNN media hegemony. It also features an absolutely hypnotic sequence filmed at George Bush's Presidential inauguration ceremony. To the twin accompaniments of Laurie Anderson's "O Superman" and the Presidential address, the camera threads through the crowds and away across the rooftops—Bush's voice never fading in its amplified metallic drone—until it comes across the backstreet clusters of satellite vans, as if to show us where the real power lies.

This is an unmissable and heartening film, if only for the wonderful spectacle of Chomsky live in a Laramie shopping mall on "the world's largest point-of-purchase video-wall installation" and informing a radio presenter, who insists on styling herself "Jane USA" that: "It's true that the emperor doesn't have any clothes, but the emperor doesn't like to be told it".

VILLAGE VOICE, 3/23/93, p. 56, Georgia Brown

As the years go by Noam Chomsky may look more and more like Woody Allen but he stubbornly keeps as far as ever from the entertainment business. Still, Chomsky does have a shtick, bless him. And now two Canadian filmmakers, Mark Achbar and Peter Wintonick, have accomplished the improbable: outfitting the dour, pertinacious prophet in a sprightly, beribboned package.

Manufacturing Consent (or Marketing Chomsky) is a feat. Judging by its reception at festivals, or a recent standing-room-only screening at NYU, Achbar and Wintonick's documentary draws young and old and holds them rapt for a fleeting 167 minutes. It held me, despite its revved and irritating *Sesame Street* style. (Maybe generations that learned to count with the Count won't notice.) In fact, the effect of such hyperactive editing is that Chomsky himself—relentlessly logical, obstinately monotone comes off as the still, dead-serious center post of a madly spinning merry-go-round. Things fall apart; in this case the center holds.

The center, Chomsky, is a unique figure: On the one hand he's the world's leading linguistics theorist, on the other, a defiant Sakharov-type scientist/dissident in a country that isn't supposed to produce dissidents. He's also a dissident without much stature among the local intelligentsia—logical, given his conviction that the "educated elite" are unwitting dupes of business interests better known as the state. Chomsky supporters tend to be scruffy outsiders, occasional academic nobodies, impolite immigrants like Cockburn and Hitchens. And this seems to be the way he planned it. Meanwhile his growing stack of heavily annotated political books (some coauthored) form an invaluable counter-history of the past 30 years, a record intended to challenge the one reposing in *The New York Times* archives. In tirelessly ferreting out the news not fit to print, Chomsky reinforces his point that without complete information, the people can never freely give consent. His high regard for the capacities of the average Joe is his most engaging quality, and probably the one his critics distrust most.

Chomsky's ascetic, puritanical demeanor seems to have always been with him. Judging from photos here of the studious-looking young Noam, he was never of the reigning clique. He says he remembers having doubts about his uncritical support of the high school football team, and you see why. In nearly every interview, he brings up sports as an example of early indoctrination into "group cohesion" and irrational belief systems. Listening to sports-radio call-in shows in the car apparently has convinced him of the considerable analytic capacities of the ordinary Joe. Ordinary Joe just needs something meaningful to apply himself to. (If Chomsky understood sports he wouldn't be so impressed.)

Given that Chomsky's critique effectively cancels, or seriously devises, reality as most people experience it, we ought to be treating Chomsky as a philosopher in the tradition of Plato, an epistemologist, contemplating the nature of justice, of the State, and so forth. In his view, we prisoners in the cave accept what we're shown and describe reality on insufficient, misleading data. Chomsky defines his own role basically as an information gatherer in the service of the people who, once apprised, can revise their assumptions and choose a moral course.

In their often very confusing way, the filmmakers sketch the bare bones of several Chomsky arguments, beginning with the Vietnam War. They also document (with some riveting news footage) what Chomsky has called the perfect test case: Media coverage of two simultaneous and equivalent massacres—one by the Khmer Rouge in Cambodia, the other by the Indonesians in East Timor (a slaughter apparently still going on). Whereas the former genocide was furiously denounced in the Western press—because, says Chomsky, communists were doing it—the latter was virtually ignored (who today has heard of East Timor?) since it was sanctioned by the U.S. Defending the honor of the paper of record is editorial writer Karl E. Meyer, wearing a spiffy striped shirt.

Chomsky's critics will note that Achbar and Wintonick avoid reproducing their hero's attacks on Israel—the stance that has most thoroughly alienated him from the "respectable" left, meaning the general media, today. (To Chomsky, intellectuals' protectiveness of Israel since '67 resembles the bias toward the Soviet Union in the '30s.) The film does, however, take a quick trip through the infamous Faurisson affair, which comes off here as a case of the willful misunderstanding of Chomsky.

Manufacturing Consent itself does not exude journalistic integrity. The filmmakers' idea seems to be that an audience needs steady doses of visual distraction. If you're the type to ask, Why is that white mouse sniffing around on a copy of *The New York Review of Books*? you will find your mind cluttered with unanswered questions. But perversely the method aids the filmmakers' cause since Chomsky himself comes off as a lone, heroic figure at odds with the crass, noisy, corrupt infotainment apparatus.

Also reviewed in:
CHICAGO TRIBUNE, 2/5/93, Friday/p. N, Clifford Terry
NATION, 4/5/93, p. 461, Stuart Klawans
NEW YORK TIMES, 3/17/93, p. C17, Vincent Canby
VARIETY, 10/19/92, p. 162, Emanuel Levy
WASHINGTON POST, 4/30/93, Weekend/p. 44, Joe Brown
WASHINGTON POST, 5/5/93, p. B2, Hal Hinson

MAP OF THE HUMAN HEART

A Miramax Films release of a Working Title Films/Vincent Ward Films/Les Films Ariane/Sunrise Films presentation. *Executive Producer:* Graham Bradstreet. *Producer:* Tim Bevan, Vincent Ward, Tim White, Linda Beath, and Sylvaine Sainderichin. *Director:* Vincent Ward. *Screenplay:* Louis Nowra. *Story:* Vincent Ward. *Director of Photography:* Eduardo Serra. *Editor:* John Scott. *Music:* Gabriel Yared. *Sound:* Pierre Camus and (music) Herve Le Coz. *Sound Editor:* Andrew Plain. *Casting:* Lucie Robitaille and Kate Dowd. *Production Designer:* John Beard. *Art Director:* Jean-Baptiste Tard and Jean Lemire. *Special Effects:* Richard Conway. *Costumes:* Renee April. *Make-up:* Micheline Trepanier. *Prosthetics Make-up:* Charles Carter. *Stunt Coordinator:* Minor Mustain and Martin Grace. *Running time:* 110 minutes. *MPAA Rating:* Not Rated.

CAST: Jason Scott Lee (Avik);   Robert Joamie (Young Avik);   Anne Parillaud (Albertine); Annie Galipeau (Young Albertine);   Patrick Bergin (Walter Russell);   Clotilde Courau (Rainee Russell);   John Cusack (Clark);   Jeanne Moreau (Sister Banville);   Ben Mendelsohn (Farmboy); Jerry Snell (Boleslaw);   Matt Holland (Navigator);   Jayko Pitseolak (Avik's Grandmother); Frank Verellen (Chopper Pilot);   Jeff Mahoney (Chopper NCO);   Rebecca Vevee (Eskimo Woman/Cook);   Josape Kopalee (Eskimo Elder);   Reepah Arreak (Anna);   Monique Spaziani (Beatrice);   Jod Leveille Bernard (Newspaper Boy);   Edouard Kurtness (Indian Patient);   Harry Hill (Doctor);   Anick Matern (Thelma);   Marc Ruel (Michael);   Tyley Ross (Messenger); Griffith Brewer (Homeguard);   Robert Higden (Photographer);   Robin Dorken (Oilman in Bar); Bill Rowat (Barman);   Benoit Bissonette (Stephen);   Richard Zeman (MP);   Haden Devine (American Soldier);   Gordon Masten (Captain Johns);   Michelle Turmel (Ginger);   Sean Hayes (Hotel Bellboy);   Rick Manburg (Walter's NCO);   Dennis St. John (Moravian Minister); Kliment Dentchev (Doctor on Boat);   Tamar Koslov (Margarete);   Bronwen Mantel (Woman Guest).

CHRISTIAN SCIENCE MONITOR, 4/19/93, p. 14, David Sterritt

According to the rhetoric of the 1960's and '70s, the ever-growing mass media were supposed to turn the world into a "global village" united by instant communication and a wearing-down of regional diversity.

The outcome hasn't been so simple. The spread of high-tech communication has been accompanied not by more uniformity, but by a fragmenting of mass audiences. Distinctions based on cultural, ethnic, and racial backgrounds have not become relics of the past—and may have acquired more prominence than they ever had before.

Vincent Ward, a talented young filmmaker from New Zealand, has long been fascinated by issues of social confrontation and cultural clash. His first major film, "The Navigator," explored them through a cleverly designed story about medieval villagers who stumble unintentionally into the 20th century. Played for comedy as well as fantasy, the picture worked unusual variations on the theme of strangers in a strange land.

"Map of the Human Heart," the new movie by Mr. Ward, is less fantastic but no less offbeat in its approach to ethnic and cultural differences. This time the notion of diversity is built directly into the main characters: Avik and Albertine, a mixed-race man (half Inuit, half white) and woman (half Indian, half white) who fall in love as children and never lose their mutual affection despite circumstances that keep them apart for years at a time.

As complicated as their own relationship is, their involvement with the industrialized world is even more knotty—seducing them at some points in their lives, repelling them at others. Avik is first attracted to white civilization by a British pilot, who lands his plane in the Canadian Arctic to conduct a mapping expedition.

Much later, Avik becomes a member of that civilization and joins its military during World War II, only to be so horrified by the Allied bombing of Dresden that he flees back to the Arctic and retreats into a life of willful loneliness.

Albertine's odyssey is shown in less detail, but it has dramatic impact nonetheless.

After her first separation from Avik, she meets the British pilot who befriended him as a boy and strikes up a romance with him, which allows her to merge with the white world and repudiate the "half-breed" status that has always been a source of anguish to her. Later she renews her love for Avik, but she remains involved with the British flyer and the warlike society that he represents. The movie ends where it began, with Avik meeting Albertine's daughter in the same frozen wilderness where his own travels began.

As its title indicates, "Map of the Human Heart" strikes a parallel between the activity of mapping—studying, understanding, and controlling a physical place or object—and vagaries of human emotion that can't be represented by lines and markings on a set of charts. It also suggests the impossibility of organizing such transcendent qualities as love and loyalty in terms of possession, territoriality, and other self-limiting concepts.

These are powerful ideas to explore in a movie, and at times Ward probes the hard paradoxes of the modern world—as when he cuts from a fire-bombed city to petroleum fields gouged out of the Arctic ice fields where "civilization" has chosen to make its latest conquests. The film has dull spots during its coming-of-age and falling-in-love episodes, though, and its flashback structure (as Avik tells the story of his life to an American mapmaker) is unnecessary.

"Map of the Human Heart" visits several countries as its plot unfolds, and the movie is just as international in its production history, with financing from four different nations and participation by an international filmmaking crew.

Although none of its performances is brilliant, its use of a multinational cast should help to market the picture around the world—in France, where Anne Parrilaud and Jeanne Moreau are major stars; in the United States, where John Cusack is a popular figure and Jason Scott Lee a rising newcomer; in Britain, where Patrick Bergin got his start; and in more places as well.

They haven't made a great, film, but they deserve praise for taking on a difficult set of issue with thoughtfulness and sincerity.

LOS ANGELES TIMES, 4/23/93, Calendar/p. 10, Michael Wilmington

When a filmmaker dares greatly, tries to touch the sky, he or she runs the risk of looking absurd. Audiences quick to scoff at "pretension" may miss the grandeur lying right in front of them. Vincent Ward's "Map of the Human Heart," a startling epic of cultural seduction, has that kind of grand overreaching. It tries simultaneously to catch a massive chunk of our century in micro- and macrocosm, to chart the deep or evanescent emotions of its people and to soar up and scan the landscape in which they're trapped. Often, it succeeds.

Spinning its tale of mixed races, of life among the Inuit or Eskimos, and the clash between civilization and primitivism, "Map" strikes familiar or classical chords in ways that are often dissonant, nerve-jangling. The movie has a weird, icy clarity, a hard-edged reverie. It suggests a dream, in which the imminent waking carries more anxiety than the dream itself.

The surface technique is sharp, brilliant; the framework—a tale of "star-crossed lovers"—almost as old as the movies themselves. In "Map," two "metis" or mixed-race Inuit, meet as children in a Montreal Catholic hospital school, meet again in London during the last stages of World War II—where Avik (Jason Scott Lee) has become an aerial photographer and the memorably sensuous Albertine (Anne Parillaud) is now a photo analyst—and, in between and after, suffer a lifetime of frustrated longing.

In some ways, it's a David Lean sort of story—thwarted romance against spectacular backdrops—but Ward's focus, as in "Vigil" and "The Navigator," is on the figure of a visionary child: the Inuit boy Avik, played with unforgettable buoyancy by 13-year-old Eskimo Robert

Joamie. Yet the tale itself—which Avik relates, as a 40-ish alcoholic to a bemused younger mapmaker (John Cusack) in the '60s—is the melancholy remembrance of a prematurely old man, scoffing at his own romantic and youthful illusions.

That story has improbable symmetry, keyed by the dashing figure of British cartographer Walter Russell (Patrick Bergin), who plucked Avik from his village, and changed his life. It's Walter who inspires Avik to flee his village—leaving behind, in a wrenching scene, his elderly, doomed grandmother (Jayko Pitseolak)—and who later dominates Avik's "civilized" life. Yet Walter isn't an ordinary villain, any more than Parillaud's Albertine is a trifler. He's an imperialist without illusions, and what seems to most obsess Ward is the irony in the collision of "civilization" and the "primitive": the good brought, the havoc eventually wrought.

The movie keeps shifting perspectives between vast overhead views and eye-level shots that shrink the world to a face, a smile, a look. When Avik greets a descending helicopter near his snow-bound village of Nunataaq, with his favorite expression, "Holy Boy! The Calvary's here!" the religious double-entendre is intentional. This is a film, above all, about the danger of playing God.

The actors—Lee, Parillaud, Bergin, Cusack, Pitseolak, Jeanne Moreau as a fanatic nun, the children Joamie and Annie Galipeau—seem perfect. The photography, by Eduardo Serra, scintillates. Ward, who has made both documentaries ("In Spring, One Plants Alone," on the Maori) and science-fantasy, ("The Navigator"), has a style that eerily mixes real and fantastic, truth and idealization. No scene in "Map" is more nightmarish than the Dresden fire-bomb raid. It's a nightmare of reality.

Ward's "Map" is a wildly ambitious film and, often, a wildly beautiful one—and if it isn't quite a masterpiece, if we sense that Ward's resources aren't enough for the World War II London scenes, in the end, any flaws or lapses simply may not matter. Movies, especially ones with a broad epic canvas and international logistics, don't often get this intimate. They don't give you such a sense of nerves stripped raw, joy or misery nakedly expressed.

Nor do they try much for poetry and in "Map of the Human Heart" (MPAA rated R, for language and sexuality), Ward is reaching for it, bravely and passionately, in every frame of the picture. Perhaps he's a doomed cartographer, with the world exploding in flames beneath him—but at least he's mapping his heart.

NEW YORK, 6/7/93, p. 56, David Denby

The ideas in Vincent Ward's *Map of the Human Heart*—the white race is murderous and diseased; it draws maps in order to control and destroy—are no more than fashionable rubbish. Yet Ward, a director from New Zealand, has a reckless poetic talent that makes the work of other directors look like television. In the thirties, an Eskimo boy without fear of flying encounters white civilization and a beautiful half-breed girl, makes love to her on top of a large balloon (a wonderful erotic fantasy), bombs Dresden with the British, loses the girl, and returns, after the war, to the Arctic. Ward goes in for fantastic stylization (often beautiful); the movie is held together (just barely) by extravagant visual metaphors and by the considerable good looks of Jason Scott Lee and Anne Parillaud.

NEW YORK POST, 4/23/93, p. 33, Jami Bernard

New Zealand filmmaker Vincent Ward has a thing for snow. His "The Navigator," and now "Map of the Human Heart," are set in such arctic conditions you wonder how he ever got his actors and equipment there in the first place. His frozen icescapes are magisterial, forbidding, mysterious.

And sometimes funny. When a mapmaker sticks his yardstick into a mound of snow in a landscape unrelieved by any sign of civilization, you have to wonder just what he thinks he's measuring, and by what standard. "Map of the Human Heart" attempts to measure the unmeasurable —love, of course, and identity too—and does it in many surprising ways.

For instance, a little Eskimo boy who falls in love with a half-breed girl in a Montreal hospital, far from his icecap village, holds onto her memory by keeping her chest X-ray pressed close to his heart. When he is a grown man flying a doomed war mission over Dresden, he has in his sights a ruined place that is still Dresden only in the sense of its polar coordinates.

In the ways that Ward has his characters measure and quantify, you might think he is the Peter Greenaway of New Zealand. But Ward has heart to go along with his art, and includes scenes of stark emotional power, like the Eskimo cut off from himself, his heart, his people, trapped on an ice floe that is slowly separating itself from the world.

"Map of the Human Heart" can be seen as a further working out of the issues raised by "The Navigator." In that movie, a boy leads the way from his backward snowbound village of old into the 20th century in search of a cure for the coming plague. In both movies, the white man's civilization brings with it a plague against which simple, old-fashioned people have no defense. The introduction of new ways, ideas, inventions and language spreads through simple cultures like an incurable virus. Themes of identity, isolation, Oedipal struggle and the mesmerizing and corrupting power of large cities are explored.

In "Map," pilot Walter Russell (Patrick Bergin) touches down in the unspoiled Canadian Arctic, where young Avik is at play. Almost immediately, Avik begins spitting up blood—he is already tainted by the white man's arrival.

Walter, a father-figure for Avik who will later be one sharp point of an Oedipal triangle, takes the boy to a Montreal hospital where the white of Avik's native landscape is replaced by hospital white, where his beautiful wild hair is cut short, and where he meets the girl Albertine.

Avik returns at last, and alone, to his village, but finds he can't go home again. The taint of civilization has robbed him of his native abilities to hunt and fish and provide for his people. He grows up to be played by Jason Scott Lee, and Albertine grows up to be played by Anne Parillaud, and they meet again in a variety of situations and positions—including making love atop a hot-air balloon during the war years.

"Map of the Human Heart" first played as a "work in progress" at Cannes last year, and since then has been re-edited as often and compulsively as Al Pacino's famous unseen short, "The Local Stigmatic." What no editing can change, however, is the extraordinary visual power of Ward's compositions. Two dead German pilots float just beneath the surface of the ice, staring up unseeing into the world. A romantic tryst in the rafters of Albert Hall. And snow—lots and lots of snow, seemingly uninhabitable, yet teeming with life.

As a love story, "Map" drags in places, but as a quest for self-knowledge, Ward takes the viewer to the ends of the frozen earth and leaves them there to think long and hard.

NEWSDAY, 4/23/93, Part II/p. 75, Joseph Gelmis

Looking at "Map of the Human Heart" has more in common with visiting an art gallery and strolling past a provocative series of thematically linked paintings than watching a conventional narrative in movie in a theater.

The theme, illustrated rather than dramatized by "Map of the Human Heart," is culture shock. The central figure is a displaced person, Avik, a half-white Eskimo. Trying to fit into the white world, he joins the RAF during World War II—but abandons "civilization" in horror after participating in sanctioned mass murder.

The action leapfrogs giddily in time—beginning in 1965 then jumping abruptly from 1931 to 1941 to 1944 and back to 1965. Essentially, the sequence of events follows the logic of a fairy tale.

Avik loves a half-white Native American, Albertine, who is determined to join the white establishment. Her husband-to-be, Walter, is the film's villain. A cultivated adventurer and member of Britain's ruling elite, he is chief planner of the destruction of Dresden, the jewel of German cities, a non-military target. Walter has no qualms about incinerating tens of thousands of innocent civilians.

Considering that the actors play embodiments of ideas, they do a respectable job. Patrick Bergin is suave, elegant and ruthless as Walter. Chinese-Hawaiian actor Jason Scott Lee ages convincingly as Avik, from likable young man in the 1940s to prematurely old man in 1965. And Anne Parillaud is an appealing, though disconcertingly dubbed, Albertine.

As a visual experience, "Map of the Human Heart" includes three stunning sequences. The first occurs during the London blitz. Childhood friends Avik and Albertine, reunited after 10 years of separation, dance barefoot atop Albert Hall's steel fretwork, feeling the music of the orchestra rehearsing below through their feet. They pause and hold their breaths as a German buzzbomb glides overhead, then exhale jubilantly as it explodes nearby.

A few days later, Avik and Albertine make love on the cushiony top of a huge barrage balloon idyllically moored hundreds of feet above the lush green English countryside where their friends picnic below.

And in the film's most astonishing scene, Avik's plane is shot from under him and he parachutes into the inferno of Dresden, landing in the middle of the firestorm that he helped to ignite.

New Zealand director Vincent Ward dazzled us in 1988 with "The Navigator," a surreal adventure of a group of medieval explorers who tunnel out of their world and time into a modern metropolis. But then, as now, Ward was unable to invent a compelling narrative flow to connect his key visual images. Once the time-travelers of "Map of the Human Heart" leave their fascinatingly weird world, the movie—which reduces them to primitive tourists—is only intermittently interesting.

Ward rationalized that ultimately aimless and undramatic collision of cultures in "The Navigator" as "a medieval vision of the 20th century." "Map of the Human Heart" is more of the same—this time Ward gives us an aboriginal vision of the 20th Century.

SIGHT AND SOUND, 6/93, p. 58, Philip Strick

Nunataaq, a remote Artic settlement. Spring, 1965. Avik, an aging Eskimo, claims that the maps being revised by a newly-arrived army survey team were originally drawn with his help, 30 years earlier. He describes to the mapmaker how the first RAF unit landed near his Inuit village in 1931 when Avik was just a boy. Avik is befriended by the airmen's leader, Walter Russell, who realises that the boy has tuberculosis and arranges to fly him to Montreal for hospital treatment. When Russell returns to Europe, Avik is consoled by a new friend, Albertine, a half-caste orphan like himself. Forced to attend the hospital school run by the formidable Sister Banville, they become inseparable. Albertine sings Avik a French song which, she says, will reunite her with her father one day. Distrusting their growing intimacy, Sister Banville arranges for Albertine to be transferred to another hospital, leaving Avik with only one of her chest X-rays as a memento.

When Russell returns to Nunataaq in 1941, he finds Avik cured but nearly unrecognisable. The young Eskimo has made his way back to the village but lacks the normal skills of his people and is regarded as bad luck by the tribe. Russell is on a secret mission and recruits Avik as his guide, explaining that a world war is in progress; they find a German U-boat base where the sailors have frozen to death. Hearing Albertine's song on Russell's radio, Avik begs him to track her down with the help of the X-ray. Russell invites Avik to join the RAF but the Eskimo has to look after his frail grandmother and stays with the tribe. His grandmother dies and, abandoned by his people, he sets out after Russell. By 1944 he is in England, recruited to fly on bombing raids over Europe. He is reunited with Albertine, who interprets aerial reconnaissance photographs for Bomber Command. They become lovers, although the capricious Albertine is promised to Russell.

After 30 missions, Avik's crew are due for a rest, but Russell, jealous of Avik, makes no attempt to intervene when they are sent to join the attack on Dresden. The plane is hit, the rest of the crew are killed and Avik parachutes into the heart of the firestorm. The horrific experience causes him to reject the ways of white people and he returns to the Arctic, leaving Albertine to her own life. 20 years later, her daughter Rainee visits him. Avik is apprehensive, but Rainee does her utmost to win him over, regarding him as her father. She invites him to her wedding (she is marrying a pilot) but Avik insists that he will bring her bad luck; sadly, she leaves. Driving into the snow, Avik becomes marooned on an ice floe. As the Arctic waters close around him, he imagines he is floating away with Albertine by balloon.

With its final rush of images *Map of the Human Heart* provides a summary of the events shaping Avik's life. These images have appeared throughout the film, but their meanings are intricate and unexplained; they carry emotional rather than rational resonance, and their striking visual power tends to thwart all argument. There is, for a start, the forthright staging of Avik's death-by-inertia, a chilling spectacle in every sense as Ward places his actor prone on an ice floe and films his gradual submersion. Recalling the death of his grandmother, who similarly slipped away into an icy ocean, and the frozen deaths of the German U-boat crew (one of whom is glimpsed under the ice, an imagined forecast of horrors to come), this scene is shot from above in the same way as the one of the young Avik immobile on his hospital bed. There is a sense of predestination: Avik is a creature of the snows, doomed (and oddly content) to die as their prisoner.

At the same time the placing of the camera is subjective, evoking an out-of-body experience. Above him, Avik sees himself with Albertine, heading by hot-air balloon to some unknown Elysium. Vestige of a possible alternative ending in which, having accepted his daughter's invitation to her wedding, he seizes the opportunity to whisk Albertine off into the skies, the image links not only with the other remarkable balloon encounter (when the daughter was probably conceived) but also with several further high-altitude assignations with Albertine, first encountered dropping missiles on young Avik from the hospital roof.

With frustrating honesty, the film refuses to end on this delirious reunion: instead, there is a familiar glimpse of young Albertine flashing a mirror as she retreats into darkness, a signal simultaneously representing attraction and inaccessibility. The sharing of reflected light has been a part of their relationship since they first met, emphasised in a scene between Albertine and Avik's rival, Walter Russell, who is unaffected by the light from her shattered hand—glass shining in his eyes. But Albertine's withdrawal also invites Avik to follow—as he has previously done, with some success (although this time he may be following her into a terminal shadow)—while at the same time suggesting that she is irrevocably lost to him.

Concluding, Avik's last moments dispense with Albertine as an enigma beyond solution, except that her song (also identified with her daughter) obstinately remains on the soundtrack. Intended as the device that would reunite the young Albertine with her lost father, the music now speaks for Avik; it is, Albertine once told us, about a half-breed who searches for gold and finds his true love in heaven. The accompanying image is of the child Avik bouncing in delighted slow motion on a trampoline held by other members of his tribe, the moment at which Russell's plane first landed near the Inuit settlement and changed the boy's existence. "Every time Avik is thrown into the sky he brings down an aeroplane," jokes one of his Eskimo girlfriends, a remark which comments on the structure of the film itself, the Dresden episode included. As an ending, with the immutably juvenile Avik floating at both the close and the opening of his life as if perpetually recycled, it leaves Avik literally in suspension, unfulfilled as orphan, half-breed, Eskimo, adult, lover, war veteran, or mapmaker. We are left with a vague sense of guilt for not knowing, and not caring, more about him than we do.

Trimmed since it was first shown at Cannes in 1992, *Map of the Human Heart* charts such a broad expanse of years that Avik, while affably enough played by both Robert Joamie and Jason Scott Lee, has little chance of being exactly measured. Chunks of his life are unaccounted for, as though he only takes shape in proximity to Russell, his father-figure, and Albertine, outcast and playmate. Neither helps to fill in the blanks, because we don't have a clear picture of them either. Russell, played by Patrick Bergin in the coolly duplicitous manner he perfected for *Love Crimes*, is an intriguing but treacherous figure whose philanthropy soon gives way to malevolence. Albertine (a slightly disappointing Anne Parillaud) is split between loyalty to a childhood affection and her determination to break free of her half-caste origins and is denied the opportunity to prove herself by shaking Avik from his conviction that he is bad luck. She might have steered him to the cheerful compromise of a European lifestyle, but scenes in which she attempts a reunion after the war have now gone: Ward says it all with a superb cut from Albertine's burning X-ray at Dresden to the industrial flames reflected harmlessly on the polar snows.

Like Ward's other works, the film is an evocative visual epic open to many interpretations. His sequences are magnificently framed and seldom predictable, like the bizarre encounter with a ship that rescues Avik from his canoe while the passengers listen in frozen disregard to the tunes of a brass band; or the lavish ballroom scene at which Avik rediscovers Albertine and Russell and realises that it was he who brought them together. Russell's apartment, where he appears to be serious in approving the Dresden bombing as revenge on an old girlfriend, is suitably decorated with maps of all sizes, including a female figure shaped entirely from charts. If Ward's more outrageous venture is the love-making scene on top of a barrage balloon, his version of Dresden is a vivid and haunting inferno of panic and despair. What we learn about the human heart remains a matter of guesswork, but as a map the film certainly offers some eye-catching perspectives.

VILLAGE VOICE, 4/27/93, p. 53, J. Hoberman

Like *Wide Sargasso Sea* [see Hoberman's review], Vincent Ward's *Map of the Human Heart* is an exotic love story infused with a measure of New World race-mixing and delusions of Old World grandeur. Unlike *Wide Sargasso Sea*, however, *Map of the Human Heart* is straightforwardly predicated on the cuteness of the Other.

Ward, born in New Zealand some 37 years ago, is a bland New Age successor to Werner Herzog. His self-importantly visionary movies set lovable savages in ostentatiously difficult locations and employ spectacular nature as a backdrop for the mildly mystical. Vaulting from the snow's wastes of the Canadian Arctic to London during the blitz to firebombed Dresden and back again, Ward's follow-up to *The Navigator*, his much-acclaimed medieval "odyssey" (a cult hit here during the summer of 1989), substitutes globe-trotting for time-traveling to lesser, if more lavish, effect.

As *The Navigator* suggested, Ward thinks in pictures. His basic thought-balloon is the juxtaposition of an uncomprehending primitive and the modern world. Thus, *Map of the Human Heart* soon produces the image of a late-'20s biplane landing amid a gaggle of baffled Eskimos—a trope repeated, with variations, once Walter the white explorer (Patrick Bergin) befriends the 11-year-old Avik and flies him to a hospital in Montreal to cure his tuberculosis. Avik is befriended by a half Indian, half French girl named Albertine but the children are separated by Jeanne Moreau, milking her cameo as a punitive yet understanding Catholic sister.

Albeit considerably reedited since its premiere as a work-in-progress at the 1991 Cannes Film Festival, *Map of the Human Heart* is still slow going. A decade later and back with his people, Avik (now Jason Scott Lee) learns that the world is at war and via a mysterious segue to aerial combat—a burst of strobe and some shrill choral singing—becomes a bomber pilot in England. The mystery is complete when he is reunited with Albertine, grown into comely, if dubbed, Anne Parillaud, who warns him, "I'm not that half-breed girl anymore!"

Complicated by the Oedipal presence of their mutual patron, Walter, as well as Albertine's ambiguous desire to pass for white and Avik's disillusionment with European civilization, their relationship is renewed amid much nutty smiling—meeting above the eaves of Albert Hall, making love atop a barrage balloon ... Ward doesn't flinch from the cosmic—but you might.

Also reviewed in:
CHICAGO TRIBUNE, 5/14/93, Friday/p. G, Johanna Steinmetz
NEW YORK TIMES, 4/23/93, p. C21, Janet Maslin
VARIETY, 1/11/93, p. 64, David Stratton
WASHINGTON POST, 5/14/93, p. B7, Hal Hinson

MARRIED TO IT

An Orion Pictures release of a Three Pair production. *Executive Producer:* Peter V. Herald and John L. Jacobs. *Producer:* Thomas Baer. *Director:* Arthur Hiller. *Screenplay:* Janet Kovalcik. *Director of Photography:* Victor Kemper. *Editor:* Robert C. Jones. *Music:* Henry Mancini. *Music Editor:* Stephen A. Hope. *Sound:* Douglas Ganton, John Leveque, Gordon Ecker, and (music) Robert Fernandez. *Casting:* Howard Feuer. *Production Designer:* Robert Gundlach. *Art Director:* Jeffrey Ginn. *Set Decorator:* Gordon Sim and George DeTitta, Jr. *Set Dresser:* Jerry DeTitta. *Costumes:* Julie Weiss. *Make-up:* Irene Kent. *Running time:* 112 minutes. *MPAA Rating:* R.

CAST: Beau Bridges (John Morden); Stockard Channing (Iris Morden); Robert Sean Leonard (Chuck Bishop); Mary Stuart Masterson (Nina Bishop); Cybill Shepherd (Claire Laurent); Ron Silver (Leo Rothenberg); Don Francks (Sol Chamberlain); Donna Vivino (Lucy

Rothenberg); Jimmy Shea (Marty Morden); Nathaniel Moreau (Kenny Morden); Diane D'Aquila (Madelein Rothenberg); Chris Wiggins (Dave); Paul Gross (Jeremy Brimfield); Gerry Bamman (Arthur Everson); Djanet Sears (Mrs. Foster); George Sperdakos (Murray); Larry Reynolds (Mullaney); Ed Koch (Himself); Louis DiBianco (Romero); George Guidall and John Ottavino (Lawyers); David L. King and Jamie Deroy (Newscasters); Nancy Cser (Blonde at Ballet); Ian Neeson (Dudley); Chris Bickford and Jason Pechet (Students); Charles Kerr (Banker); Susan Henley (Secretary); Howard Jerome (Burly Mover); Marilyn Boyle (Older Woman); Marc Gomes (Ross); Philip Akin (Limo Driver); Gregory Jbara (Cafe Waiter); Silvio Oliviero (Trendy Waiter); Larry Aubrey and Harry Booker (Arresting Officers); D. Garfield Andrews (Reporter); Monique Cousineau (Muriel); Melissa Claputo and Allison Scott (Female Students); Steven Lederri (Male Student).

CHRISTIAN SCIENCE MONITOR, 3/26/93, p. 11, David Sterritt

"Married to It" is a story about three married couples, and the best parts of the movie happen when all of them get together.

At first, when they hardly know each other, they sit in straight-backed chairs and make awkward attempts at conversation. A short while later, when they've gotten better acquainted, they eat and joke and sing an old song or two. Later still, when they've become good friends, they complain and give advice and get thoroughly into one another's hair.

It's interesting to watch their six-way relationship develop, since they appear at first to have little in common except membership on a committee at their children's school.

One couple, a social worker and a homemaker, still show evidence of an idealistic 1960s sensibility. Another, a financier and a psychologist, hardly seem old enough for the professions they've chosen. The third, a manufacturer and an heiress, seem discontented and mismatched even before sparks fly over how to handle the husband's troubled daughter from a previous marriage.

With so many main characters from so many backgrounds and walks of life, "Married to It" promises to be a lively affair. But once the couples have established their complicated set of friendships and jealousies and rivalries, the movie has no idea what to do with them.

So it plunks them into a string of episodes so contrived that even a self-respecting sitcom would feel uneasy, and wraps the package up with a pallid musical number featuring "The Circle Game" sung by junior-high kids in hippie outfits. It's a desperate maneuver with disastrous results.

The biggest irony of "Married to It" is that talented people put their energy into it and obviously tried their hardest to make it work. Stockard Channing, absent too long from the Hollywood scene, almost manages to soar above the limitations of her role as a long-suffering mom with two feisty children. Beau Bridges brings surprising maturity to his portrayal of her slightly eccentric spouse.

Mary Stuart Masterson projects a fair amount of sincerity as a well-meaning young woman whose husband gets into business trouble.

And the ever-intense Ron Silver has downright powerful moments as the toymaker juggling a wife and daughter who bring out the worst in each other.

But even performers on this level of ability need something substantial to do while they're on the screen, and Janet Kovalcik's screenplay gets weaker and weaker as the story gets longer and longer, subordinating its most provocative elements to a glassy-eyed glaze of feel-good superficiality.

The less distinguished members of the cast, such as Cybill Shepherd and Robert Sean Leonard, fare even worse with their hokey lines and artificial situations.

Little help comes from director Arthur Hiller, who tries with little success to recapture the flair of his brilliant 1979 comedy "The In-Laws," which neither he nor anyone else has yet succeeded in duplicating.

The undistinguished score was composed by Henry Mancini, also working below his highest standards, and even New York City manages to look rather boring in the background.

"Married to It" is a game try, but only the Monty Python troupe could have brought a surprising touch to its increasingly dull scenario. I found myself wishing all the characters would turn out to be John Cleese wearing silly costumes, then become animated elephants and slide right off the screen.

LOS ANGELES TIMES, 3/26/93, Calendar/p. 8, Peter Rainer

Critics who complain that Hollywood doesn't make more real-life movies about adults might want to revise their opinion after slogging through "Married to It."

It seems to have been made with the idea that the more grown-up relationships you put on the screen the better the movie. It's crammed with adult conflicts all right, but none of them ring true. Watching the film (rated R for language and sensuality) is a bit like sitting through a group therapy session with all the participants babbling at once. You go into sensitivity-training overload.

We're talking about a motley crew of complainers. There's Leo and Claire (Ron Silver and Cybill Shepherd)—he's a semi-successful, divorced toy manufacturer: she's a highly successful investment banker. (Guess what their conflict is?) John (Beau Bridges) and Iris (Stockard Channing) are superannuated hippies with two young boys. Nina and Chuck (Mary Stuart Masterson and Robert Sean Leonard) are childhood sweethearts from Iowa who have come to big, bad New York City, where Chuck is a Wall Street whiz and Nina works as a school psychologist in the private school attended by Leo's annoyingly distraught daughter Lucy (Donna Vivino) and John and Iris' kids.

How do these disparate types end up together? They all meet to plan a children's pageant put on by the school celebrating the '60s, that's how!

The notion that the '60s represent something akin to the Paleolithic Age to the current crop of moppets is certainly a chilling one (at least for those of us who remember the '60s, although, as someone once said, if you remember the '60s you didn't live through them).

It also might be a humorous notion but director Arthur Hiller and screenwriter Janet Kovalcik don't really see it that way. What these couples are going through in their lives is viewed as a return to the touchy-feely goodness of those years. Men and women reclaim their sensitivities by recognizing their need to open up to each other—metaphorically speaking, of course.

The cast tries to rise above the kind of dialogue that sinks performances. Emerging battered but unbowed are Silver, who at least gets some steam-heat into his yammering, and Bridges, who does a convincing turn as a bathetic boomer. The booby prize goes to Shepherd, whose line readings are even clunkier than her lines—a staggering achievement. But good, bad or indifferent, the cast members' are unified by Victor Kemper's cinematography: Their skin tones look as pasty as an anti-fungal ointment.

NEW YORK POST, 3/26/93, p. 25, Audrey Farolino

First, a word of explanation: The one star I'm giving "Married to It" is a sympathy vote. As a New York Post employee, I have nothing but good wishes for any company that has managed to extricate itself from near financial oblivion, as Orion Pictures has done.

But I fear that if Orion makes a habit of releasing dogs like this, it will someday find itself right back in front of the bankruptcy judge.

Actually, somebody should be required to appear before some judge somewhere to explain this almost criminal waste of talent. With a cast that includes Stockard Channing, Beau Bridges, Ron Silver, Cybill Shepherd, Mary Stuart Masterson, and Robert Sean Leonard, it seems reasonable to expect a few laughs, or at the very least a few believable moments. But that turns out to be very unreasonable indeed.

According to the production notes (and I'm not sure why anybody would play up this fact), "Married to It" was conceived, developed and went before the cameras within one year. Perhaps a little more time should have been spent developing a better script.

Instead, we are stuck with this scenario: Three very different couples meet while planning a school pageant and, for reasons that remain completely inscrutable (at least to this viewer), they strike up a deep friendship. Said friendship sustains them all not only through the ups and downs of marriage but also through the trial of one of the husbands on charges of having pulled off some kind of Wall Street stock scam.

The characters are: John and Iris Morden (Bridges and Channing), former '60s radicals who have settled into a bored marriage; Chuck and Nina Bishop (Leonard and Masterson), hayseed newlyweds fresh out of Iowa (he's accused of the stock scam); and Claire Laurent (Shepherd), a filthy rich investment banker who married divorced toy manufacturer Leo Rothenberg (Ron

Silver) because he had the "second largest penis I've ever seen" which is as witty as the dialogue gets.

Leo's daughter and the Mordens' sons go to the same school, which is where Nina Bishop works as a psychologist, which is how they all meet.

Space restrictions prevent me from saying much more, which is probably a good thing. I'll finish by noting that Ed Koch's from-left-field cameo makes about as much sense as everything else in the movie.

NEWSDAY, 3/26/93, Part II/p. 71, John Anderson

Despite all its sermonizing for fidelity, "Married to It," takes a pretty dark view of romance in the '80s (the film's been in the can for awhile, due to Orion's financial difficulties). An alleged comedy of marital manners, it spends so much time and talent on a story about three couples who *don't* split up, you'd think they were walking on water.

Even less believable than their domestic survival is the burgeoning friendship between the couples, who couldn't differ more in age, social position or wealth. Let's face it: fortunes of love may rise and fall, but class distinction is forever.

School psychologist Nina (Mary Stuart Masterson) and stockbroker Chuck (Robert Sean Leonard) are young, childless Iowans living in a beautiful but furnitureless Manhattan apartment; ex-hippie and disillusioned welfare worker John (Beau Bridges) and his city cultural-official wife Iris (Stockard Channing) are trying to bring up their two boys and choke down their '80s-induced bile; and Claire and Leo (Cybill Shepherd and Ron Silver), a corporate lawyer and a divorced toy manufacturer, are trying to cope with her insufferable personality and his impossible daughter, Lucy (Donna Vivino).

It's not that the friendship—through which they share Chuck's arrest for stock fraud, John and Iris' foundering sex life and the Claire-and-Lucy Hostilities—is really all that strange. Nor, perhaps, the fact that they begin spending all their time together. But director Arthur Hiller gives us six people who seem to have no other friends, no visible past at all, and the result is an artificiality which, when combined with Hiller's stagey direction and a lumbering pace, buries a film that might have been salvaged by sheer acting talent.

In Silvers, Channing and Stuart Masterson, Hiller has three of the more gifted, albeit grossly under-appreciated actors, in films. And he doesn't get in their way. Silver makes Leo's guilt over his failed marriage, his anger over Claire's treatment of Lucy, and his love for his daughter palpable. Channing's Iris, on the surface a perpetually cheery earth mother, seethes with unresolved indignation. And Masterson's naive Nina blooms, from a decorative cornflower into a woman who's beginning to know her own mind.

Leonard's acting has all the depth of a test pattern; he could learn something from Bridges, who places a great amount of feeling behind John's deadpan moodiness. From Shepherd, on the other hand, he might learn poultry sales: Claire is supposed to be a boor, but Shepherd delivers each punchline like she's slapping a 20-pound turkey down on the counter for your inspection, and all you asked for were directions home.

VILLAGE VOICE, 3/30/93, p. 56, Georgia Brown

Joe Mankiewicz's *A Letter to Three Wives* is a smart but pretty hokey melodrama centering on three suburban couples who are longtime social friends. When the town temptress announces in a letter that she's run off with one of the three husbands, each of the wives spends the movie's present-tense wondering whether her hubby will be missing when she returns. The point is that none of the wives feels secure, that all three houses were built on soft ground. As they would have in 1949, however, all three unions do survive. Even the couple who keep telling each other to shut up will continue at each other's throats.

In Orion's 1993 romantic comedy, *Married to It*, three New York City marriages survive too—not because they would in real life, but because that's what marriages do in today's movies. Even more improbable, here we have three Manhattan couples who meet, hit it off, and grow steadily closer despite a significant gap in age, wealth, and social class.

Starting at the top, couple number one, owners of an Upper East Side townhouse with 12 fire-places, are Leo Rothenberg (Ron Silver) and Claire Laurent (Cybill Shepherd). Even within this unit there's a highly unlikely disparity: Tall, blond, and bossy, Claire is a high-powered investment banker and heiress, while short and swarthy Leo is a lowly toy manufacturer. Whereas Leo sees Claire as a "shiksa goddess," Claire lays the blame on Leo's large penis. The fly in this ointment is Lucy, the crabby 13-year-old daughter Leo dotes on.

Couple number two, the Mordens, John and Iris (Beau Bridges and Stockard Channing), are Upper West Side types, ex-hippies who met in the '60s at an antiwar demonstration. Now a welfare caseworker, John still dines out on having been present at Woodstock, while Iris works in the mayor's office. Although they take politics seriously, the Mordens, like the Clintons, don't extend their support to the public schools. Their two kids attend the same institution Lucy Rothenberg goes to.

Couple number three are Chuck and Nina Bishop (Robert Sean Leonard and Mary Stuart Masterson), yuppies who met in their Iowa 4-H club. He's a stock broker whiz kid; she's the psychologist for the same private school attended by Lucy and the Morden kids. For a shrink, Nina is unnaturally crisp and immaculate. In one scene, her husband does pushups while she scrubs the grout on the bathroom floor with a toothbrush.

So, defying the laws of urban nature, the couples bond over dinner-party meetings of the decorations committee for some upcoming school function. That is, fellas bond with fellas, gals with gals. In the meantime, a couple of bad things happen. Young Chuck is arrested for illegal stock parking; Nina eventually rebels at his self-absorption. (The one time I sensed a real rise in audience temperature came when Nina tells Chuck she's tired of picking up his dry cleaning. The young woman next to me practically levitated.) Claire and Leo quarrel incessantly over whether Lucy is spoiled (she is). Claire is crude and imperious enough to be the movie's villain, except she's not. Even the stable Mordens have troubles as Iris belatedly hankers for her own orgasm.

Director Arthur Hiller (from *Love Story* to *The Babe*) might be described as the poor man's Mike Nichols. Nichols can take similar material—okay, better material—as he did in *Heartburn*, and make it snappy. At least he gets the details right. For his part, Hiller takes a pat, bland outline for a script (by Janet Kovalcik) and makes a pat, sentimental movie. With most scenes no longer than a minute or two, watching *Married to It* is like waiting for the real movie to begin.

Also reviewed in:
CHICAGO TRIBUNE, 3/26/93, Friday/p. B, Clifford Terry
NEW YORK TIMES, 3/26/93, p. C8, Janet Maslin
VARIETY, 9/23/91, p. 78, Amy Dawes
WASHINGTON POST, 3/26/93, p. C6, Rita Kempley
WASHINGTON POST, 3/26/93, Weekend/p. 42, Desson Howe

MASALA

A Strand Releasing release of a Divani Films production with the participation of Téléfilm Canada/Ontario Film Development Corporation/Ontario Arts Council. *Producer:* Srinivas Krishna and Camelia Frieberg. *Director:* Srinivas Krishna. *Screenplay:* Srinivas Krishna. *Director of Photography:* Paul Sarossy. *Editor:* Michael Munn. *Music:* Leslie Winston. *Music Editor:* Alan Geldart. *Choreographer:* Johanika Roth. *Sound:* Ross Redfern and (music) Nick Young, Kevin Petrie, and Martin Gordon. *Sound Editor:* Steve Munro. *Casting:* Linda Continenza. *Production Designer:* Tamara Deverell. *Art Director:* Valerie Kaelin. *Set Decorator:* Alexa Anthony. *Set Dresser:* Michael McShane and Carolyn Gee. *Special Effects:* John Gajdecki. *Costumes:* Beth Pasternak. *Make-up:* Nicole Demers. *Stunt Coordinator:* Ken Quinn. *Running time:* 105 minutes. *MPAA Rating:* Not Rated.

CAST: Saeed Jaffrey (Lallu Bhai Solanki/Mr. Tikkoo/Lord Krishna); Zohra Segal (Grandma Tikkoo); Srinivas Krishna (Krishna); Sakina Jaffrey (Rita Tikkoo); Herjit Johal (Anil Solanki); Madhuri Bhatia (Bibi Solanki); Ishwarlal Mooljee (Bahadur Singh); Ronica Sajnani (Sashi

Tikkoo); Les Porter (Gerald); Raju Ahsan (Babu); Jennifer Armstrong (Lisa); Wayne Bowman (Balrama); Tova Gallimore (Saraswati); Don Callaghan (John Macdonald); Paul Persofsky (Lawyer); Sachin Bannerjea (Mr. Chabra); Ran Ghoman (Pinky); Sakuntala Krishna (Krishna's Mother); Avi Kulkarni (Krishna's Father); Kamran Durrani (Krishna's Brother); Mervyn Mingail (Mr. Varna); Summathi Thimmana (Mrs Varna); Janet Joy Wilson (Lieutenant Hilary Macintyre); Sunil "Sunny" Roy (Priest); Christofer Williamson, Ari Moses, and Michael Therriault (Bullies); Lakshmi Thimmana (Fruit Stand Proprietor); Ramana Tangirala (Television Announcer); Robin Severin (Valery Pappadooglio); Anne Scanlon (Lisa's Mother); Garth Holding (Lisa's Man); Bill Jay (Mountie Captain); Vivek Mathur (Sikh); Bob Waugh (Bus Driver); Tibor Skorik (Priest in Plane); Sangita Viswanathan (Stewardess); Judith Brunner (Gertrude); Valery Boyce (Aerobics Instructor); Susan Henry (Voice of Aerobics Instructor); Frank Mullen (Postal Sorter); Paul Jolly (Postal Driver); John Healy (Colleague); Chris Emmanouilides (Postman).

CINEASTE, Vol. XX, No. 1, 1993, p. 44, Jacob Levich

American progressives have lately embraced the notion of multiculturalism with an uncritical ardor rarely seen, on or off campus, since the Sixties, and the near-hysterical reaction of mainstream liberals has only enhanced our affection for it. But suppose multiculturalism represented, not just an oppositionist academic movement or a vaguely leftish social ideal, but an official policy of the central government—would it feel quite so warm and fuzzy!

To Srinivas Krishna, the Indo-Canadian *wunderkind* who has written, directed, and starred in an ambitious first feature called *Masala* the question is not merely rhetorical. Since 1971, when Pierre Trudeau declared that "a policy of multiculturalism must be a policy for all Canada," Ottawa has developed an elaborate bureaucracy designed both to palliate Francophone separatists and to cope with the demands of "visible minorities"—Native Canadians, blacks, Latinos, and Asians. As one might expect, however, state-sponsored multicult has done nothing to dislodge a power structure that remains uniformly white and, outside of Quebec, proudly Anglophone. Meanwhile, racial violence is on the rise, economic opportunity is disappearing, and Canada's visible minorities feel as though they might as well be invisible.

It is in this context that *Masala*'s rather bitter take on multiculturalism should be understood. An emphatically unconventional black farce, the film assails multicultural pieties from the left—not a Marxist left, to be sure, but a kind of postmodern radicalism that comes naturally to many young immigrants, whose experience of culture is likely to be as contradictory and heterogeneous as the dislocated spaces in which they live. From the perspective of Gerrard Street, the main drag of Toronto's burgeoning South Asian community, *Masala* casts a jaundiced eye on civil servants who blandly praise the successes of intercultural cooperation, even as Paki-bashing threatens to supplant ice hockey as the national sport.

But official hypocrisy is only one of the film's targets. More broadly, Srinivas Krishna wants to challenge a central tenet of the multiculturalist view: that transplanted traditions can, and should, be preserved, now that culture is rapidly becoming a hybridized creature of global media. *Masala*'s world, like its esthetic, is one of wildly fragmented cultural influences that mock the imagined purity of a past that never was pure to begin with.

In keeping with its postmodern stance, the film eschews straight-ahead narrative for a scattershot, multicharacter approach. One of numerous storylines begins as the household of mild-mannered postal worker Harry Tikkoo (Saeed Jaffrey, in one of three roles) teeters on the brink of financial collapse; his comically irascible aunt (Zohra Segal, a living legend of Hindi theater who nearly steals the film) asks the god Krishna (Jaffrey again) to intercede. Through a divine contrivance, Harry comes into possession of a rare stamp worth $5 million; the government cynically claims the stamp as a treasure of "our cultural heritage," forcing a legal battle and a national crisis that ultimately can be resolved only by the intervention of the lordly Minister of Multiculturalism. (By the way, Canada *does* have a Minister of Multicult, and if the real thing is half as slick and supercilious as the character portrayed here by Les Porter, the country may be in deeper trouble than anyone imagines.)

A second plot thread concerns Harry's oleaginous cousin, Lallu Bhai Solanki (Jaffrey, yet again), a prosperous sari merchant and a pillar of the Hindu community. Lallu Bhai faces a moral crisis when he is approached by a group of Sikh militants who want to use his shop as a holding area for revolutionary contraband; whatever compunctions he may have are quickly overridden by a bribe of $500,000 and prospective control of the sari trade in Khalistan. (Khalistan is the theocratic state envisioned by Sikh communalists, to be located somewhere in the Punjab.) Before long, the Mounties are on his trail.

More trouble arrives in the person of Lallu Bhai's nephew, Krishna, played by the filmmaker as a knife-wielding ex-junkie in a leather jacket, alienated, deracinated, and indiscriminately rebellious. (The character is a deliberate provocation: North American audiences, conditioned by *Gandhi* and the residue of Sixties counterculture, prefer their screen Indians to be meek and 'spiritual' in the face of suffering.) Although Lallu Bhai offers him a home and a job, Krishna—psychologically wounded by the death of his parents in an airline disaster—seems bent on self-destruction. His story, and *Masala*, end in a sudden act of street violence that clashes disturbingly with the film's predominantly comic tone.

It is through such moments of calculated dissonance that Srinivas Krishna means to translate his experience of the Indian diaspora into cinematic terms. The most effective of these involve the god Krishna, irreverently portrayed as an outrageously campy, bumbling sensualist who appears to Grandma Tikkoo by way of a supernaturally interactive VCR. (The point of this gag, lost on most critics, is to satirize nostalgic attempts by Indian emigres to recapture something of the motherland through repeated viewings of Indian films—in particular, the vastly popular multi-part video extravaganzas based on the *Ramayana* and the *Mahabharata*.

Less successful is *Masala*'s most audacious element, its occasional use of the musical conventions of Bombay cinema. In India, it should be explained, *all* commercial films are musicals, and no moviegoer think it strange to see simple peasants or hard-boiled gangsters bursting into elaborate song-and-dance routines at the drop of a Congress cap. To Westerners fortunate enough to have encountered them, such films seem extravagantly (and delightfully) transgressive: musical sequences from the better Hindi movies are at least as energetic, daring, and artfully crafted as anything to be found on MTV.

There may be a way to incorporate this kind of formal delirium into the grammar of Western film—Herbert Ross, after all, accomplished something quite similar in *Pennies From Heaven*—but Srinivas Krishna has not found it. Compared with their Indian models, *Masala*'s musical numbers seem stiff and unimaginative; they are, moreover, indifferently choreographed and inexpertly performed—failings that supposedly naive South Asian audiences would never tolerate. The problem here is not a lack of funds (production values are more than adequate throughout the film) but a lack of empathy. The director appears to have no real affection—even a guilty one—for Indian cinema; at times, in fact, one questions whether he has much regard for *any* aspect of Indian culture. On the whole, *Masala*'s brand of postmodernism is remarkably unforgiving: the fondness for tradition that characterizes even so caustic a work as *The Satanic Verses* is entirely absent from the film.

This disdain for the past is not without its dangers in a racist present. *Masala*'s treatment of Indo-Canadians, though intended satirically, is so relentlessly negative that it sometimes threatens to confirm the worst prejudices of white audiences. According to one of Harry's daughters, for instance, "Indian men are the scum of the earth, the cockroaches in your kitchen sink, mother-loving, woman-hating, limp-dick chickenshits." Her rage, one can only guess, is a reaction to the remnants of Indian patriarchal tradition that still color gender relations in her community. But because the film offers us no such context for understanding the outburst—and because most of the male characters are, well, limp-dick chickenshits—viewers of either sex may be tempted simply to endorse, and internalize, her words.

In a similar vein, Krishna (the human character) contemptuously dismisses Hindi, a tongue of unparalleled expressivity, as gibberish. Since the film oddly fails to provide subtitles for any of its extensive Hindi dialogue, non-Indian audiences will have no reason to disagree. (Ironically, many of the film's best jokes are delivered in Hindi—at one point, for instance, Lallu Bhai appears to be crooning affectionately to the Minister's pet poodle; actually, he is threatening to break its neck if it pisses on the carpet.)

These are troubling aspects of an otherwise impressive debut. Of course, neither Hindu traditionalists nor white liberals have any 'right' to dictate the terms of Srinivas Krishna's project; nor does Krishna have an obligation to provide 'positive images' for the edification of racists.

Still, in light of the racial violence that *Masala* so memorably portrays, some greater measure of sensitivity to cultural difference is surely required. Attacking multiculturalism is one thing; attacking a culture is quite another.

LOS ANGELES TIMES, 5/21/93, Calendar/p. 6, Kevin Thomas

With "Masala," a misfired multicultural comedy of the absurd, Indian-Canadian filmmaker Srinivas Krishna's ambitions far exceed his abilities. *Masala* is an Indian word for hot, mixed spices, but this debut feature proves to be a tedious, unappetizing blend of fantasy, satire and social commentary.

The filmmaker casts himself as Krishna, a handsome young Toronto resident who lost his parents and younger brother five years earlier in a plane disaster. His last-minute refusal to return to India with his family, who felt defeated by their 15 years in Canada, saved his life but cast him adrift in a sea of hard drugs and despair.

We never really get to know and become involved with Krishna because the filmmaker is so intent on telling so many stories: The key three are about Krishna's uncle-by-marriage Lallu Bhai (Saeed Jaffrey), who schemes to corner the world market in saris: Lallu's cousin Mr. Tikkoo (also Jaffrey), an unambitious postman-philatelist who through divine providence becomes the owner of a rare stamp worth $5 million—his is the best-told tale; and Krishna's tentative romance with Mr. Tikkoo's beautiful daughter Rita (Sakina Jaffrey, Saeed's real-life daughter).

Krishna proves to be far more adept at fantasy than reality. His most inspired touch is to cast Saeed Jaffrey in yet a third part, as Lord Krishna, a quixotic Hindu deity, whose gaudy makeup and finery bring to mind Little Richard in full glitter and war-paint. This campy Lord Krishna appears on television, where he is frequently scene by Mr. Tikkoo's mother (Zohra Segal). She confronts him, demanding that he save her home from being repossessed. There are some wonderfully zany musical interludes that deftly spoof a beloved convention of the Bombay cinema.

One can easily understand and admire Krishna's desire to bring a fresh, darkly comic spin on the usual immigrant drama. Clearly, he wants to make the immigrant experience symbolic of life's essential absurdity. He attempts to project a quirky vision of existence that includes, yet goes beyond, the usual traumas of discrimination and of children defying their tradition-bound parents.

Unfortunately, Krishna simply hasn't the talent or experience to pull it off. More often than not, the pacing and dialogue in the "real-life" sequences fizzle rather than sparkle. Few members of the very large cast—and that includes Krishna himself—are up to the professional level of Saeed Jaffrey, the witty veteran Anglo-Indian character actor best known to American audiences as the rich uncle in "My Beautiful Laundrette." "Masala" (Times-rated Mature for sex, nudity and language) is by all means not to be confused with Mira Nair's far more successful "Mississippi Masala."

NEW YORK POST, 3/26/93, p. 21, Jami Bernard

About two minutes into the spicy comedy "Masala," an airplane blows up carrying hundreds of Canadians returning to their native India.

And yet it's not a black comedy, or a sick one. Just a strange one, steeped in its own specific culture—that of transplanted Indians trying to make a go of things in Canada.

The movie features the well-known actor Saeed Jaffrey in three disparate roles, including as the blue-faced deity Krishna who approaches to his faithful via a kind of interactive home video in which he can respond directly to their prayers, exasperating as they are.

In this way, Krishna intervenes in a family's troubles that involve so many things it is hard to keep track of them all. It's a manic comedy, like "The Wrong Box" full of twists that (while not quite necessary to the main events) keep the plot chugging along.

One of these sidebar events involves Krishna—not the deity but an angry, heroin-abusing ex-con—who loses his family in the initial plane crash that scattered brightly colored saris into the sky. It's five years later, and Krishna goes to live with his sparring relatives, including an aunt who watches workout programs for the exercise and a cousin who watches them to fondle himself.

Srinivas Krishna who wrote, directed and produced "Masala" plays Krishna the youth.

Another sideshow in this multi-ring circus involves Grandma Tikkoo (Zohra Segal), a feisty old lady who wants her video god to measure up to her high standards. She and her deity trade insults as she tries to get him to intervene in her son's excessive stamp-collecting.

"Masala" is lively, inventive filmmaking that like a new language, takes a while to get used to. (It is however, in English.) It touches on many issues germane to Indians, including the strain of keeping one's heritage alive in a new land that doesn't respect it.

NEWSDAY, 3/26/93, Part II/p. 71, John Anderson

Although Srinivas Krishna's "Masala" opens with a plane exploding in mid-air, weaves a crazy quilt out of cultural and religious threads and makes jokes about God, it's not just a cinematic "Satanic Verses." For one thing, Salman Rushdie never had a leading man as charismatic as Srinivas Krishna.

Krishna, the name of the lead character played by Krishna, was too high to make that plane, which was taking his mother, father and brother on a trip back to India. So Krishna is left in Canada with his heroin, which he kicks, and his guilt, which he can't, and a world— accessorized with a delirious array of knife fights, musical production numbers and cut-rate magic realism—in which he's simply lost.

The title of "Masala"—which refers to the blend of spices integral to Indian cooking—is a rather satirical multicultural jab: for the Indian community in "Masala," there is no blending, no assimilation, only futile attempts to become Canadian, or to maintain the illusion that they're still Indian—which Krishna the director insists they're not.

The results are cultural whiplash, and a variety of reactions. Krishna's Uncle Lallu Bhai (Saeed Jaffrey) maintains surface fealty to Hinduism but also gets involved with terrorists to control the international sari trade; Lallu Bhai's philatelist cousin Mr. Tikkoo (also Saeed Jaffrey), a postal worker, refuses to sell a priceless stamp, although his family needs money and his mother (Zohra Segal) harangues him; and Sri Krishna (again, Saeed Jaffrey), the blue-skinned Hindu deity who communicates with Grandma through the television set, finds himself increasingly obsolete in the increasingly secular world of Little India.

Krishna (the character) arrives at Lallu Bhai's house fresh from rehab and throws one more wrench into the culturally askew works. The walking antithesis of Lallu Bhai's son, the doctor-to-be Anil (the hilariously slack-jawed Herjit Johal), he defends his young cousin Babu (Raju Ahsan) from the local toughs, has an affair with Mr. Tikkoo's daughter Rita (Sakina Jaffrey, daughter of Saeed) and proves the New World and Old irreconcilable.

SIGHT AND SOUND, 8/92, p. 58, Farrah Anwar

When an Air India plane blows up en route from Toronto to India, Krishna's parents and brother are killed. Five years later, Krishna is released from jail having undergone a heroin detox régime. After failing to collect a debt from his junkie ex-girlfriend, Krishna crashes a party at the home of his uncle, Lallu Bhai, to celebrate closer cultural ties between the Indian and Canadian communities. Also present are Sashi and Rita, the two daughters of Lallu Bhai's cousin, Mr Tikkoo. Spending the night at his uncle's, Krishna is determined not to relapse into drug dependency, but finds it hard to get a job, even at the post office where Mr Tikkoo (a keen philatelist) works. While wandering the streets, he is reminded of childhood racist abuse by an unpleasant encounter with white Canadian teenagers.

Meanwhile, Tikkoo's mother, a devout Hindu, develops a dialogue with the god Krishna via her video recorder. Granting her wish for an economic miracle, he engineers the mistaken delivery of a priceless stamp to the Tikkoo household. Grandma's dreams seem about to be realised, but the scrupulously honest Tikkoo refuses to sell the stamp; he also decides to take legal action to prevent it being reclaimed by the Canadian government. He is forced to borrow money from Rita, who works at an acquaintance's travel agency (Tikkoo assumes she is saving the money for a university education, but her ambition is to become a pilot). When Lallu asks the same agent to give Krishna a job, he and Rita meet again and are immediately attracted to each other.

Although his job is shortlived, Krishna returns home with Rita and the pair make love in Tikkoo's house. Lallu Bhai agrees to let a Sikh professor, Bahadur Singh, use the basement of his shop to promote the establishment of an independent state (Khalistan) in India. Although he suspects that terrorists may be involved, Lallu is swayed by the promise of exclusive merchandising rights in Khalistan. Unbeknownst to both of them, the Canadian Mounties have been keeping the shop, and the constant traffic of Sikhs, under observation. On the day that the local Hindu community are set to celebrate a religious festival, the Sikhs plan to send a 'shipment' to India. But the Mounties surround Lallu Bhai's shop and a warrant is put out for his arrest.

Oblivious to all this, Lallu tries to buy the stamp from his cousin during the procession, while Krishna, having rejected Rita's wish for a more permanent relationship and resolved to leave Toronto, decides to return. Lallu is arrested and the Sikh shipment is successfully intercepted; the authorities are embarrassed, however, when the contents turn out to be rolls of toilet paper. Tikkoo becomes curator at the first National Canadian Centre of Philately, Rita pursues her pilot's studies, and Lallu Bhai becomes a highly respected and powerful business figure. But Krishna, who is just about to be reunited with Rita, is stabbed to death by one of the racist teenagers he had encountered earlier.

As the Air India flight on its way to the sub-continent explodes in mid-air, leaving the hero of *Masala* orphaned and land-locked, it is tempting to recall Salman Rushdie's *Satanic Verses*, which also used a stratospheric disaster to set up its tale of cross-cultural tribulation. Rushdie, in fact, has already been invoked in the uneasy stirrings that *Masala*'s irreverent portrayal of the Hindu gods have caused among Canadian Hindus. But, even though *Masala* may never achieve nationwide distribution in India, it is unlikely to provoke calls for a fatwa against its Canadian writer-director-star Srinivas Krishna. Hinduism, unlike Islam, does not condemn visual representation (a 1976 bio-pic of Muhammed never actually portrayed him on screen), and the Hindu gods have already been fleshed out on Indian television in the massive multipart *Mahabharata*.

If there is offence in the profane portrayal here of Krishna ("I'm no bloody Christian God. I don't have to prove my credentials" is his riposte to Grandma Tikkoo when she asks for a miracle to prove his identity), then it's in the eye of the individual believer, rather than a fundamental blasphemy. The real adventurousness of Krishna (the director) is the way he adapts the conventions of Bombay's Hindi cinema, casts a new light on second-generation immigrant angst, *and* avoids (with one or two minor exceptions) stereotyping his characters. (The only nod to received Western attitudes is the now *de rigueur* condemnation of Asian men.)

But unlike *Mississippi Masala* or *My Beautiful Laundrette*, *Masala* acknowledges its debt to 'Bollywood' as well as Hollywood. The two garishly over-the-top musical numbers, which on the surface seem completely superfluous, indicate the way carnal urges have traditionally been sublimated in Hindi cinema through fantasies. The fact that these same characters go on to have relatively explicit sexual dreams as well only underlines the 'freedom' now available to Asian film-makers as well as their audiences. The character traits that supply the film's rather absurdist plot are accessible enough in movie terms, while they also have their native 'truth': Grandma Tikkoo's communication with Krishna via the VCR cannily acknowledges the device's importance as home entertainment for an older generation of Asians; the 'contrivances' of Rita working in the same travel shop as Krishna, or the Sikh professor asking to use Lallu Bhai's basement, accurately reflect the close-knit, interdependent world of Asian communities in foreign lands.

Krishna distances himself in this respect from his trans-Atlantic cousin, Hanif Kureishi. His portrayal of bourgeois Canadian Asians doesn't carry the same charge of betrayal as Kureishi's view of their Thatcherite counterparts. As played by Saeed Jaffrey (who was the smoothly corrupt Uncle Nasser in *My Beautiful Laundrette*), Lallu's materialism is tempered with an acknowledgment that he is also striving for respectability and pride via commercial success. Having covered the home bases effectively, Krishna furiously criss-crosses his personal pre-occupations and cultural references to stimulating effect.

With an original brief that was supposed to incorporate "an irreverent take on *Rebel Without a Cause* and *Breathless* while also taking stylistic cues from Almodóvar, *Masala*'s self-conscious hipness might well have proved irritating. But crisp photography from Paul Sarossy (who has also collaborated with Atom Egoyan), Krishna's deft screenplay, and a wonderfully versatile turn (or turns) by Saeed Jaffrey, as well as his daughter Sakina, produce a highly entertaining work.

In fact, the residue of Krishna's original project to portray disaffected youth is probably the least satisfying aspect of *Masala*. Krishna's fictional *alter ego*, emotionally inert and culturally uprooted, remains the most disengaged of all the film's characters. Breezing in with his leather jacket and attitude problem, the earthbound Krishna is treated without any irony; his tragic destiny is signposted early on, and although he touches various lives within the film, he is the catalyst for very few changes. There are moments when the film threatens to collapse under the burden of its various themes, philosophical musings, and attacks on the shallowness of the Canadian government's cross-cultural ambitions. But it pulls off a delightful climactic joke in the form of the toilet rolls inscribed with the entire history of Sikh suffering. It's a conceit that will be appreciated by all those Asians who have ever wondered how a culture so inured to poor toilet hygiene (preferring paper to water) ever managed to command such a powerful empire.

VILLAGE VOICE, 3/30/93, p. 51, J. Hoberman

Masala is the third recent Indian or Indian-diaspora movie to use the word for blended spices in its title and, in many ways, it's the most pungent of the three. A garish, pop, bawdy melange of low comic shtick and hot-blooded daydreams, ingenious sets and eccentric ethnics, this insolent first feature, written and directed by Toronto-based Srinivas Krishna, has attitude (and ambition) to burn.

Two minutes into the mania proceedings, a jetliner packed with Indian families returning home from Canada explodes in the cosmos, at once orphaning the film's antihero, Krishna (named for the filmmaker as well as played by him), and providing *Masala* with its ruling metaphor. Krishna, along with most of the movie's Indian-Canadian characters, is lost in space. He floats, as if weightless, in the cultural equivalent of a debris-filled asteroid belt between two worlds.

Masala is a film about mutants: Krishna affects a James Dean wardrobe and becomes a junkie, while his wealthy uncle, the sari merchant Lallu Bhai (Saeed Jaffrey), parties with the Canadian minister of multiculturalism, and his aunt keeps herself trim with Jack LaLanne (and his cousin masturbates to the same). Hindu cosmology is hopelessly deformed. A giant Smurf doll sits beside an idol of the similarly complected Lord Krishna in the modest kitchen of Lallu Bhai's cousin, the postman Mr. Tikkoo (also Saeed Jaffrey). Indeed, the Krishnas proliferate madly when Lord Krishna himself (Saeed Jaffrey, yet again, this time in bright red lipstick and dazzling blue-face) uses the family TV to open a channel of communication with his irascible devotee Grandma Tikkoo (the endearingly wizened Zohra Segal, familiar for her role in *The Jewel in the Crown*).

"I am no bloody Christian god," Lord Krishna admonishes Grandma Tikkoo when she asks for a miracle to demonstrate his identity. Nor is *Masala* a bloody proper film. On the one hand, it's a form of deliberately low-rent magic realism in which miracles are performed via television sets and gods pilot jet planes. On the other, it's an overwrought sitcom with a plot that juggles, at times with monotonous persistence, subplots involving a band of Sikh militants who want to conceal their operations in the basement of Lallu Bhai's sari emporium, a romance between Krishna and Rita Tikkoo (Sakina Jaffrey), a hostage crisis, white racism, and the contretemps around a precious postage stamp acquired by Mr. Tikkoo. Allowing for a few extra hands, Krishna intermittently stages his own mixtures of MTV music videos and Hindi playback numbers: An Indian couple hopping from one tacky reality level to the next—underwater, in the clouds—changing costumes and hairstyles while lip-synching a sprightly disco-raga love song.

Krishna gives himself the glamorous, if inert, role of the humorless punk and family ne'er-do-well, but *Masala* is otherwise enlivened by a number of juicy comic performances—most of them by Saeed Jaffrey. It's also charged with a love of language. The salutary influence of Indianized English on our so-called mother tongue has been insufficiently recognized. To hear Zohra Segal's singsong pronunciation of the words "automatic food processor" is to receive a highly concentrated version of the effects Salman Rushdie elaborated in *Midnight's Children*.

Speaking of Rushdie, it's interesting that *Masala* was turned down by the 1991 London Film Festival, reportedly after one white programmer found it "racist." It was subsequently disinvited from the 1992 International Film Festival of India because it satirized Sikh separatists and has been repeatedly attacked by Indians in Canada as crass, rude, and blasphemous: "Canadians would never allow tax dollars to portray Christ in the same manner," one community leader maintained. *Masala* is certainly less than reverent in depicting Canadian authority figures, but Krishna, relocated as a child from Madras to Toronto and 25 when he made the film, has a talent—not unlike that of the young Philip Roth—for getting under his community's skin.

"What happens to Indians when they go to foreign lands?" the Lord Krishna wonders. "They lose their grace, their composure, and they are constantly pestering me." *Masala* not only airs dirty laundry (cracks about Indian women, a diatribe against Indian men), it touches a number of raw nerves, ranging from the 1985 mid-Atlantic explosion of an Air India flight originating in Toronto to the controversy over the right of Sikhs in the Royal Canadian Mounted Police to wear their turbans.

Krishna tests the limits of Canadian liberalism, parodying the idea of multiculturalism even as he profits from it. *Masala* is itself a kind of social experiment—as un-Indian as it is un-Canadian (and, yet, a film that could have only been made by an Indian in Canada). It may be tasteless but it's never bland and often laugh-out-loud funny. You get the feeling that putting Lord Krishna in a Maple Leaf uniform was something that Srinivas Krishna waited half his life to get on screen.

Also reviewed in:
CHICAGO TRIBUNE, 9/17/93, Friday/p. L, John Petrakis
NEW YORK TIMES, 3/26/93, p. C10, Stephen Holden
VARIETY, 3/22/93, p. 53, Lawrence Cohn

MATINEE

A Universal Pictures release of a Renfield production.   *Producer:* Michael Finnell and Pat Kehoe.   *Director:* Joe Dante.   *Screenplay:* Charlie Haas.   *Story:* Jerico Haas and Charlie Haas. *Director of Photography:* John Hora.   *Editor:* Marshall Harvey.   *Music:* Jerry Goldsmith. *Music Editor:* Kenneth Hall.   *Sound:* Howard Warren and (music) Bruce Botnick.   *Sound Editor:* Mark Mangini and George Simpson.   *Casting:* Gretchen Rennell.   *Production Designer:* Steven Legler.   *Art Director:* Nanci B. Roberts.   *Set Designer:* Stephen Alesch.   *Set Decorator:* Frederick C. Weiler and Eric Weiler.   *Visual Effects:* Dennis Michelson.   *Costumes:* Isis Mussenden.   *Make-up:* Rodger Jacobs.   *Stunt Coordinator:* Jeff Smolek.   *Running time:* 98 minutes. *MPAA Rating:* PG.

CAST: John Goodman (Lawrence Woolsey); Cathy Moriarty (Ruth Corday); Simon Fenton (Gene Loomis); Omri Katz (Stan); Lisa Jakub (Sandra); Kellie Martin (Sherry); Jesse Lee (Dennis Loomis); Lucinda Jenney (Anne Loomis); James Villemaire (Harvey Starkweather); Robert Picardo (Howard, the Theater Manager); Jesse White (Mr. Spector); Dick Miller (Herb); John Sayles (Bob); David Clennon (Jack); Lucy Butler (Rhonda); Georgie Cranford (Dwight); Nick Bronson (Andy); Cory Barlog, George Carson, and Joe Gonzalez (Stan's Friends); Belinda Balaski (Stan's Mom); Charlie Haas (Mr. Elroy); Mark McCracken (Mant/Bill); Archie Hahn ("Shopping Cart" Star); Naomi Watts ("Shopping Cart" Starlet); Chris Stacy (Gas Station Attendant); Allison McKay and Glenda Chism (Teachers); Aaron Stormer (Kid near Andy); Lana Bucciarelli ("Eew!" Girl); Richard Rossomme (Shredded Wheat Man); D. Christian Gottshall (Store Clerk); Bernard Blanding and Dennis Neal (Soldiers); Luke Halpin (Man in Crowd); Eulan Middlebrooks (Young Man in Crowd); Elizabeth Dimon (Theater Cashier); Shane Obedzinski (Bleeding Kid); Summer-Healy Chapin ("Balcony Full" Kid); James Scott Hess (Kid in Floor Seat); Shawn Edward Watkins (Kid Next to Mr. Elroy); Danny Hanemann (Man Outside Theater); Jesse Zeigler (Kid in Line); Andy Isaacs (Faint Kid); Joe Candelora (Fireman); Steve Zurk (Cop); Mary Moriarty (Lady in Line); John Paul Lehman (Marine Guard); Jacob Witkin (Dr. Diablo); Tracy Roberts (Screaming Woman); Marc Macaulay ("Shopping Cart" Crook); Steve Dumouchel, Kurt Smildsin, and Michael T. Kelly ("Mob" Actors); Ike Pappas (Newscaster); Brett Rice (Voice of Gene's Dad).

LOS ANGELES TIMES, 1/29/93, Calendar/p. 10, Peter Rainer

As the schlock movie magnate Lawrence Woolsey in "Matinee," John Goodman is paunchy but battering-ram solid. He seems inflated by his own expansiveness. The jumbo cigar he perpetually waves is never lit. It doesn't need to be, Woolsey is the one who is constantly smoking with "ideas."

His latest micro-budget epic is a "cautionary" horror tale about the effects of A-bomb radiation on a man bitten by an ant. Its title—what else—is "MANT" (The ad line is "Half Man ... Half Ant ... All Terror!!!"). And so it's poetically perfect that Woolsey, with his wised-up paramour and leading lady, Ruth (Cathy Moriarty), in tow, arrives in Key West during the height of the Cuban missile crisis to preview his new creation. Joe Dante, who directed "Matinee" from a script by Charlie Haas, has a genuine affection for Woolsey and for the whole madcap schlock-horror world. It's an early '60s world bounded by Famous Monsters and Mad magazines, backed by oldies and crowded with goopy papier-maché humanoids. Dante, who is in his 40s and who also directed the two "Gremlins" movies and "Innerspace," is locked into an adolescent time warp in a way that makes a director such as Steven Spielberg seem positively hoary. He's the movie-maven Peter Pan of film. His freakoid prankishness isn't a put-on; it's the real thing.

"Matinee" (rated PG for language, mild violence and sensuality) isn't as inspired as "Gremlins 2," his last collaboration with Haas, but at its best it's a ticklish nut-brain romp—a crazy quilt of grade-Z horror spoofs.

Woolsey and Ruth and their carnival shenanigans, "Matinee" might have been a low-rent classic. But Dante and Haas are also aiming for "heart." Gene (Simon Fenton), a teen-ager whose father is stationed off the coast of Cuba, is moony for the local high-school radical, Sandra (Lisa Jakub), who yowls during a classroom bomb drill like a pipsqueak Helen Caldicott; they end up kissy-faced inside a bomb shelter. His friend Stan (Omri Katz) is googly eyed over the twinkly Sherry (Kellie Martin), although, to his credit, he cuts out on a boring science-project-style date with her to catch "MANT" on opening day.

This fatherless-kid scenario is boringly Spielbergian, and so is the sappy uplift that attempts to connect the boys' relish for schlock with their coming-of-age in a time of lost innocence. Our movies routinely depict the early pre-assassination '60s as a virginal era, but it's a regrettable cliché.

The scenes from "MANT," shot in black and white, that Dante and Haas have cooked up are some of the best movie satires on film. It's not easy to parody a genre that's already close to self-parody but the filmmakers triumph again and again. Actors such as Kevin McCarthy turn up in cameos for that all important déjà-vu effect, and the special-effects are imperially, tacky. Moriarty, who has a gift for hard-boiled farce in her scenes with Goodman, also appears in the "MANT" footage, and she manages to give a convincingly dreary grade-Z performance while at the same time cluing us in to how ridiculous Ruth must feel to be starring in this nonsense.

Many others in the cast respond to Dante's enthusiastic flakiness. John Sayles and Dick Miller show up as crusaders for Citizens for Decent Entertainment. (Miller surveys the young audience for "MANT" and snarls, "I can smell the wreckage of your minds.") David Clennon pops in for a hilariously clenched cameo as Sandra's politically progressive dad. (Like father, like daughter.) Jesse White, as an old-time exhibitor, has a great comic turn as he stands shiny-eyed in the back of the theater playing "MANT" and proclaims of Woolsey. "He's putting back the showmanship!"

Dante's showmanship has the same spirited effect on us. He pulls out his bag of tricks and even puts in an animated doodle; he's reaching not only for the flagrant awfulness of movies like "MANT" but also for the zippy ardor of the classic Warner Bros. cartoons. He does everything but put a buzzer under your seat.

If he ever gets around to making "MANT 2," maybe he'll do that too.

NEW STATESMAN & SOCIETY, 6/18/93, p. 35, Jonathan Romney

I always felt "Keep Music Alive" badges were a bit Luddite, but "Keep Cinema Live" might be another matter. Now there's a worthy cause, simply because it's such an unfashionable one.

I don't mean the sort of live cinema that involves 200 chemistry students dragged up in Boots black lipstick, dutifully intoning the script of The Rocky Horror Show—just the experience of sitting in the dark for a couple of hours with a bunch of other people, and knowing that you can walk out, but you can't fast forward.

But live cinema is rapidly becoming marginalised, an arcane specialist experience beyond the domain of those five or six features that, by consensus, we all go and see in a particular week. As soon as a film slips off the circuit, it usually stays off. The opposite of "on release" must be "banged up".

And once a feature film falls off the national release schedules, it doesn't vanish for ever, but gets folded away neatly into a little box called a video. That's the form in which it will mainly be seen in future, and that's the state of things to which we're already reconciled.

I don't want to be purist about celluloid, although I fail to see how you can deny all the basic losses of size, volume, pleasure, *ritual*—that you have to hear once a film's fit only for the living-room. The upshot, however, is that cinema as an institution with a living history is being left to the ruminations of archivists. Witness the imminent—and I fear unmourned—death of the British art-house cinema circuit.

Two London repertory cinemas—the Electric and the Everyman—face questionable futures. A third, the Scala, bit the dust last week—a casualty of rising rents, recent prosecution for screening Kubrick's *A Clockwork Orange*, and falling attendances, attributed partly to the increasing seediness of its Kings Cross locale, partly to the competition from video.

The Scala is a big loss, as anyone who is aware of it would agree—even if, like me, you have rarely been there since first being exposed to the dubious delights of *Attack of the Killer Tomatoes* and the venue's other arcane stock-in-trade. As a conduit for everything sleazy, counter-cultural, left-field and quite often essential, the Scala was unique. God knows what the audience was for those strange Borowczyk nuns-in-bondage triple bills they used to run on a Monday, but you won't be seeing them again in a hurry.

It's appropriate that hot on the heels of its closure comes a film that would have made a natural Scala late-night staple, and one that pleads a passionate cause for the preservation of the ninepenny stalls: Joe Dante's *Matinee*. Hugely out of synch with contemporary tastes, *Matinee* is fatally flawed by its marshmallow-centred nostalgia. It's a *Cinema Paradiso* for the Looney Tunes generation.

We're in Key West in 1962, at the time of the Cuban missile crisis: an era that already looked prehistoric five years later, which we're mainly used to seeing through the filter of half-remembered *Dick Van Dyke Shows* and Biff postcards. Across America, everyone's worried sick about the bomb, but the young high-school heroes are more concerned about the forthcoming premiere of a new horror epic by B-movie mogul Lawrence Woolsey—"Half man ... Half ant ... MANT!"

John Goodman, as Woolsey, gives the film's slender japery an amount of blustering body. He's a huge, magisterial joker, all the more charismatic for being a little bit half-baked. He shows off capaciously to a fawning garage attendant, only to realise he's been mistaken for Alfred Hitchcock. But he's an inspired huckster, a scam-a-minute merchant who outgrosses Roger Corman. It's a pleasure to watch him as an idea comes bubbling up to the surface. Staring idly at a lizard, it starts ticking over: "She-Gator ... Gator Girl ... Galligator!"

Of course, this being a soft-hearted film, he's not just a scam merchant, but a social redeemer: Great Oz in size XXL seersucker. *Matinee* is a rare example of a film-maker being given the same huckster-messiah status that usually gets accorded in movies to live showmen—from H P Barnum to the travelling evangelist of Steve Martin's recent *Leap of Faith*. But that's really what Lawrence Woolsey is. *Mant!* is nothing without its maker on hand to drum up a crowd and rig the venue with his sideshows and trimmings of popular science.

He has his weary star (Cathy Moriarty) dress up as a nurse and hand out release forms for the weak-hearted, and he rigs the place with Rumble-Rama and other cheap thrills. The film's by the way of tribute to B-master William Castle, who used to wire up seats with buzzers and dangle plastic bats over the punters' heads.

Best of all, he lays on a real live Mant to terrorise the crowd—unfortunately, hiring the local teen psychopath to wear the rubber suit. Ultimately, the comedy falls flat because, like Woolsey, Dante has rigged up too many comic mechanisms.

All he has to do is hit the right button and watch chaos ensue. And, by Dante's standards, it's tame chaos. He seems to be reigning himself in after the demented, self reflexive free-for-all of his great, misunderstood *Gremlins 2*.

The period pastiche, too, is a little weary. As far as this irony-fed generation is concerned, bad 1950s and 1960s pulp movies parody themselves quite well enough, and if you're going to do anything new with them, it had better be as acute about sexually paranoid subtexts as Todd Haynes was in his recent *Poison*, which rewrote the killer Bs for the Aids era.

There's nothing new, either, in this view of the early 1960s pastel age—an era that has come to stand too readily for the lost innocence of adolescence (by extension, of America's own political adolescence). The final word on that was Bob Balaban's swingingly gruesome *Parents*, which made you wonder whether that nice Dick Van Dyke and Mary Tyler Moore might actually be cannibals after all. Dante himself recently mined this nasty-normality vein, in the entertainingly queasy TV series set in weird suburbia, *Eerie Indiana*.

All this aside, *Matinee* is a pretty entertaining sitcom prank that works as long as you're willing to suspend the adult view. Woolsey, in his role of vizier of wisdom, gives the kids a final lesson: "Grown-ups are making it up as they're going along, just as you are." At a moment when most of his peers in sci-fi are fetishistically adult and deadly professional, Dante is still the unruly kid boffin; and it's good to drop in on amateur hour from time to time.

NEW YORK, 2/8/93, p. 62, David Denby

I've complained in the past that the talented young director Joe Dante was overly devoted to pop culture—that he was trapped, spinning round and round in the pop-cult washing machine, recycling images and moods from boyhood fantasies, *Gremlins* being the major case in point. *Gremlins 2*, I had to admit, was awfully funny, but I've had enough of flying wingdings. Dante may have had enough, too, because his new comedy, *Matinee*, feels like an attempt at a farewell to adolescence.

Matinee is an affectionate *hommage* to the B-movie junk that Dante enjoyed as a boy, but it's set in a realistic world, and Dante establishes a contrast between the movie thrills that kids enjoy and the actual pleasures and dangers of life. *Matinee* doesn't have the drive of his earlier films, but it's a genial, happy experience—a movie not intense enough to be a classic but too friendly to be overlooked. John Goodman, at his most majestically modulated, stars as a Wizard of Oz who turns out not to be a fake—he plays Lawrence Woolsey, monster-movie producer and master of the innocent paraphernalia of "shock." Woolsey, who is roughly based on producer William Castle, appears in the coming attractions for his own movies, a heavyset man holding a cigar in threatening silhouette, enticing children into the theaters with the delicious terrors of three-headed monsters.

Down on his luck but hardly desperate, Woolsey shows up in Key West in 1962, driving his big Caddy, with his "star," Ruth Corday (Cathy Moriarty), a generously proportioned blonde, at his side. The filmmakers' view of him is that he's essentially innocent—a big kid—and Goodman gives Woolsey shades of intelligence and understanding that make one warm to him. An affable faker who only seeks to please, he becomes the Pied Piper figure for the kids of Key West. Woolsey needs to have a smash preview of his latest opus, MANT ("Half Man ... Half Ant ... All Terror!!!"), which is a tremendous masterpiece in the atomic-mutation genre: After a nuclear test, men mix with ants, or something like that, and suddenly strange creatures with giant claws begin menacing women. Woolsey is a maverick—one of those independents not good enough to make it at a studio but also too wild in their methods for the big time. He will try anything—wiring the seats for minor electric shocks, turning actors loose in the theater to flesh out the scares onscreen.

There is a complicated plot of no particular consequence involving some nice teenagers, 14 or 15 years old, stumbling into their first bouts of heavy petting (this is 1962). True-life events, both large and small, get strangely mixed with the perfervid world of exploitation movies. While Woolsey is setting up his show, the Cuban Missile Crisis breaks out, and young Gene (Simon Fenton), whose Navy-officer father is aboard one of the ships intercepting the Russkies, falls in with Woolsey, who is his idol. The joke is that while the schlockmeister is trying to create a mock panic with his mutation movie, a real nuclear panic, of which he is entirely oblivious, is breaking out in Key West. The clichés of exploitation filmmaking—crowds running in terror—suddenly appear in the supermarkets and streets.

Matinee is an affectionate look back at pop nuclear culture as well as movies. Schoolchildren, in a drill, are told to hide in the hallway with their hands over their heads, and only the class freethinker, Sandra (Lisa Jakub), denounces the precautions as a joke. Gene and Sandra become a couple, and the entire movie comes together at Woolsey's Saturday matinee, when the theater rumbles, the balcony sways, and some rather confused people become convinced that nuclear Armageddon is at hand.

This is genial, low-voltage stuff, the kind of softly nostalgic moviemaking that should become magical. It never does, though. One problem is that the kids are sweet but awfully young: Their make-out moves have no more interest than such material has on the early-evening teen-dating sitcoms. Goodman is the only strong adult character, so he has no one to play off except the husky-voiced Cathy Moriarty, who is funny but limits herself to making dissatisfied remarks out of the corner of her mouth (she really does seem like a B-movie broad). I wish Dante had figured out some way to make something lyrical of his feelings, the way that George Lucas did about the same period of pop in *American Graffiti*. For instance, he doesn't get enough out of palmy, balmy Key West, one of the truly eccentric places in America.

The best thing in the movie apart from Woolsey is MANT itself, which we see quite a lot of. Working in black-and-white for the movie within the movie, Dante reaches a perfection of awfulness—a catalogue of joking, loving ineptitudes, complete with actual B-movie actors from the period (now a little long in the tooth) and trash epiphanies breaking out all over. Dante himself had a modest career in junk: He started out with Roger Corman and directed several exploitation films himself. In the estimate of Dante and Charlie Haas (who wrote the screenplay), Woolsey the showman will do anything to entertain, and that's a holy impulse. Well, I wonder. The directors who got their start working for Corman are immensely grateful to him, as they should be. But I've never met a moviegoer of normal intelligence obsessed with the films of Roger Corman or William Castle either. Dante's point, I guess, is that Woolsey's films are kid stuff, but I don't see the value of creating a shrine out of what you liked when you were 14. To see one's own history in terms of pop-culture periods may be one way of never leaving pop. Apart from Woolsey, none of the adult characters is quite a person and Dante treats the actors negligently. Pop is not enough, and he seems to know that, but some part of him hasn't broken free yet. The movie lies between two worlds, and that may be why it feels emotionally reserved, even tepid.

NEW YORK POST, 1/29/93, p. 32, Jami Bernard

Director Joe Dante continues his career-long quest to uphold the banner of schlock culture with "Matinee," a cheerful homage to low-budget monster movies and the showmen who made them.

John Goodman plays Lawrence Woolsey, an entrepreneurial maker of low-budget shockers. It's 1962, a time when horror movies are hitting the same delicate nerves as the Cuban Missile Crisis and imminent apocalypse. People are building useless bomb shelters in their backyards, and Woolsey is on his way to Key West to promote his latest film: "Mant"—"Half man ... half ant ... all terror!" (The "Mant" trailer alone is worth the price of admission to "Matinee.")

Woolsey appears to be a composite of guerrilla-style schlockmeister Roger Corman (for whom Dante once worked) and showman William Castle, whose attention-getting stunts included wiring theater seats to give patrons a minor electric tingle. Film Forum 2 has celebrated this style of horror promotion with its two Gimmick-O-Rama series.

Woolsey is up against such bland competition as "The Shook-Up Shopping Cart," done in the Disney-Hayley Mills style, the kind of jokey "family" movie that couldn't scare the smallest child. Woolsey's own movies—even with their cheesy special effects, moth-eaten monster suits and ludicrous premises—incite terror and thrills in a new generation whose bible is the magazine Famous Monsters of Filmland, for which Dante himself wrote an article when he was 13.

"I hear a projectionist got so scared he *died*!" whispers one awed kid to another as they anticipate the local opening of "Mant," replete with Rumble-Rama, a backstage machine that makes the theater vibrate, operated by a teen-ager in a Mant costume who will run out into the audience and grab at patrons to make them scream during key scenes.

There is a plot in "Matinee," but it's a dull one, involving some adolescents on a date to the movies; there have been elements of this sort of thing in Dante's earlier work, like "The Explorers," where some kids invent a space module that takes them hovering around the drive-in-theater.

Dante's "Gremlins," and especially "Gremlins 2," mined the pop culture as well. But never has his satire been as true and reverent as in "Matinee."

You'll wish you could strip away the plot of the movie proper and just watch scenes from the movie-within-a-movie. "Mant"—as opposed to the Spielbergian "Matinee"—is devilishly clever, very adult. "You think this is some kind of picnic for me?" asks the distressed Mant, who then repeats the joke several times in the same way that three-syllable words are reiterated in simplified form and plot developments recapped at regular intervals, so that the young and the restless can keep up.

Inspired casting includes pairing the director John Sayles with the Corman alum Dick Miller as two strange characters in the "Mant" caravan.

Goodman, looking larger than life, manages to be funny in a largely standby role. Cathy Moriarty, in what appears to be a nod to Madeline Kahn, gets more mileage out of her dual role as a "nurse" on hand at the theater in case anyone dies of shock, and as an actress in the horror movie, playing a wife trying to deal with the inconvenience of having a Mant for a mate.

NEWSDAY, 1/29/93, Part II/p. 62, Jack Mathews

Whatever you think of Joe Dante's movies, from the 1980 werewolf spoof "The Howling" through his "Gremlins" sequel two years ago, there can be no questioning his passion for the medium. He makes movies inspired by movies, or more accurately, by the memory of how movies made him feel while growing up.

In that sense, Dante is a kindred spirit to his frequent boss Steven Spielberg, with whom he also shares a view of America shaped by the languorous middle class suburban settings of their favorite 1950s and '60s TV shows.

All of those influences—movies, TV and Spielberg, plus Dante's particular appreciation for B horror movies—mesh in "Matinee," a comedy about residents in a Florida town who are simultaneously aroused in 1962 by the Cuban Missile crisis and the premiere of a horror movie promising the unimaginable thrills of Atomovision and Rumble Rama.

This is one of those "what if" ideas that's not quite enough to support a whole movie but too good not to attempt, at least for Dante. Hmmm ... what if people in a horror movie audience, already scared out of their wits by the prospect of nuclear attack, suddenly saw sparks flying off the screen and felt the seats beneath them begin to buck?

It seems to take forever to set up the hypothetical situation—Dante has never been a whiz at straight narrative—but once the theater within the theater is filled and the movie within the movie begins, "Matinee" becomes a riot of laughs.

The setting is Key West, the American town nearest Cuba, and its residents, many of them military dependents, are on a caffeine and adrenalin alert. On their black-and-white TV screens, Kennedy and Khrushchev are playing nuclear chess with the world's future, and at their schools, children are finally taking bomb drills seriously.

Zoom in on two people, 15-year-old Gene Loomis (Simon Fenton), a horror fan whose Navy pilot father hasn't been heard from since the missile crisis began, and Lawrence Woolsey (John Goodman), a tub-thumping exploitation movie producer who has coincidentally booked the Key West Strand for the premiere of his latest horror film, "Mant" ("Half Man, Half Ant, All Terror!").

Dangling from the marquee of the Strand, just above the life-size cutout of Woolsey himself, is a banner urging patrons to fight pay-TV, a proposal for showing first-run movies on television that beleaguered theater owners of the day felt would administer their coup de grace. Showmen like Woolsey, who wired seats for shocks and filled the air with smoke and sparks, were seen by theater owners as potential knights.

Goodman is perfectly cast as Woolsey, a likable, cigar-chomping hustler who makes movies on the cheap and goes on the road with them. People do occasionally mistake him for Hitchcock, but only in silhouette.

The best moments of the sluggish first hour are between Goodman and his dour girlfriend (Cathy Moriarty), a minimum wage actress who does double-duty as the leading lady of "Mant" and as the phony nurse making patrons sign medical release forms before they enter the theater.

Unfortunately, Charlie Haas' script devotes most of the first two acts developing a pair of awkward teen-age romances. The relationships pay off in the theater (dawning sexuality is the third emotional catastrophe in the equation), but where this section would have been a slam-dunk for Spielberg, Dante simply doesn't have a feel for the kind of adolescent byplay that makes kids interesting.

On the other hand, no one recalls the childhood wonder of movie-going better than Dante, and once we're all inside the Strand, it's a double-bill of laughs. "Mant," the story of a man radiated while sitting in a dental chair and turned into an ant the size of Godzilla, is hilariously camp all by itself. With Atomovision and Rumble Rama turned on, feeding into the audience's other fears, the volume threatens to tear the house down.

"You see what he's doing," says the theater owner (Jesse White), as chaos reigns before him. "He's putting showmanship back in movies."

Lawrence Woolsey is a man after Dante's own heart.

SIGHT AND SOUND, 6/93, p. 59, Philip Kemp

1962. Teenager Gene Loomis—newly arrived in Key West, where his father has been posted to the US naval base—takes his young brother Dennis to the movies. There they see a trailer for *Mant*, a horror film directed by B-movie maker Lawrence Woolsey—to be presented by Woolsey in person, as the film will premiere in Key West. That evening, President Kennedy announces the Cuban missile crisis on television. Gene is disturbed to realise his father is on one of the blockade ships. At his new school, Gene meets some of his classmates, including Stan, who has a crush on sexy fellow pupil Sherry. During a nuclear-attack rehearsal, one of the girls, Sandra, protests the futility of the exercise, attracting Gene's attention.

Lawrence Woolsey, whose career is in trouble, arrives in Key West with his star/girlfriend, Ruth Corday. Two of his associates, Herb and Ed, whip up publicity by posing as outraged citizens denouncing the movie. Sherry invites Stan on a date, but Stan is warned off by her delinquent ex-boyfriend Harvey. Meeting Woolsey, Gene is taken on to help set up shock gimmicks in the cinema. Woolsey also recruits Harvey to rampage through the audience got up as the man-ant monster, and to operate special effects (including the earthquake-simulating Rumblerama). Howard, the manager, already paranoid about nuclear war, worries about the fabric of his cinema, but Woolsey ignores him.

The Saturday matinee premiere of *Mant*: Woolsey has invited a potential backer, Mr Spector of Megalopolitan Theaters. Gene arrives with Dennis and Stan, meeting Sandra in the foyer. Sherry shows up, still annoyed with Stan, but Gene reconciles them. Harvey, rampaging in his Mant suit, sees Sherry and Stan kissing, and attacks Stan. During the subsequent chase Gene and Sandra get shut in Howard's bomb shelter, while Harvey knocks Stan out and abducts Sherry. While Woolsey breaks into the shelter to rescue Gene and Sandra, the Rumblerama gets out of control, loosening the cinema's balcony. Woolsey springs his final gimmick, a faked nuclear attack, and the audience flee in panic. Gene rescues Dennis as the balcony collapses. Harvey is arrested and Sherry and Stan are reunited. A delighted Spector offers Woolsey a fat contract. With the Cuban crisis over, Gene and Sandra stroll along the beach to watch the returning US forces.

"Takes a lot more to scare people these days," observes John Goodman as cigar-chomping schlockmeister Lawrence Woolsey. It sure does, and *Matinee* invites us to chuckle indulgently at the innocent days of the nascent 60s, when people could get seriously alarmed by actors in rubber monster suits, scuzzy gimmicks like seat-buzzers, and even—ho, ho—the Cuban missile crisis. The film also allows Dante to pay affectionate homage to William Castle, the gimmick-fiend of B-horrors whose production values made Roger Corman look profligate—and to toss in a wicked pastiche of a Disney family comedy (*The Shook-Up Shopping Cart*), all bozo humour and slapdash slapstick.

Dante can always be relied on for some good gags, visual and verbal, and plenty of movie-buff references—to his own films as well as to other people's. *Matinee* replays the rioting teenage movie audience from *Gremlins*, this time with live actors, as well as trumping the burning-through-the-film trick from *Gremlins 2*. *Mant* itself, of which we get to see several generous chunks, is spot-on parody, with crummy sets, cloth-ear dialogue ("I keep asking myself—why, why?") and every cliché set-up in the book: in one delirious excerpt a mob of vengeful peasants, complete with pitchforks, surges through modern-day Chicago streets.

All the performances are well-gauged (including those in *Mant*, which are bad in just the right way), with an enjoyable double act from John Sayles and Dick Miller as the phoney moral crusaders. Goodman plays Woolsey with massive relish, lacing hard-bitten cynicism with flashes of child-like delight at his own powers of manipulation. And under all the gags, Dante makes some shrewd points about our propensity to divert from real terrors into fake ones until we wind up unable to tell the difference.

Yet the whole mixture doesn't quite gel. *Matinee* is never as uproariously funny, or as unsettling, as it should be. Partly it's a matter of period tone—the Cuban crisis provides a neat analogue, but at the expense of skewing the social attitudes, which feel more mid-50s than early 60s. More crucially, Dante seems ultimately unwilling to go for the jugular: the film never fixes the panic-stricken rictus behind atomage America's brittle facade the way Bob Balaban's *Parents* did, or Eugene Corr's underrated *Desert Bloom*. Ironically, some of those same B-horrors that Dante sends up—*Them!*, for example, or *The Incredible Shrinking Man*—have retrospectively acquired the very resonance that *Matinee* fails to achieve.

TIME, 2/8/93, p. 78, Richard Schickel

In his own eerily confident mind, Lawrence Woolsey (John Goodman) is both a motion-picture visionary and a good old fashioned showman. To his critics—just about every zit-free moviegoer in the country—he's a schlockmeister, producer of a string of cheapo '50s horror movies in which mutant monsters, by-products of nuclear carelessness, at once symbolize and exploit everyone's edginess about the recently unleashed atom.

But wait a minute. It's 1962; the New Frontier has been proclaimed. As Woolsey heads to Key West, Florida, to preview his latest epic, *Mant* (half-man, half-ant and all knockoff of cult classics like *The Fly* and *Them!*), he and his works appear to have reached a new frontier of their own—total cultural irrelevancy. Except for one thing: the Cuban missile crisis is on, and suddenly the brave new world is actually contemplating a disaster beyond Woolsey's most profitable dreams. It's a nicely imagined coincidence, and from it Joe Dante has fashioned a neat little movie—less flashy than his *Gremlins* films but in its way much sharper.

Charlie Haas' script deftly twists three satirical strands together. There is, of course, the movie within the movie, a perfectly pitched and hilarious genre send-up, complete with a woman in perpetual peril (Cathy Moriarty, who is also wonderful as Woolsey's wearied girlfriend). The preview is a riotous muddle at which Woolsey's gimmicks—Atomo-Vision, Rumble-Rama—run out of control and literally threaten to bring down the house.

Matinee also offers a dislocating representation of *Mant*'s teenage audience. Among them are a straight arrow shunned by his schoolmates, a fast girl, a juvenile delinquent—the *Gidget* crowd, in short. A good point is scored about the seepage between the realities of adolescent life and the ways it is portrayed in the media. Finally, *Matinee* assaults the general goofiness of American life in the period—bomb shelters, duck-and-cover air-raid drills, general prudishness and even stupid nutritional beliefs.

This is a lot of business for one short, funny movie to undertake. That it maintains a loose, almost shambling pace and an unpretentious air while doing so makes it all the more attractive. Smartness casually displayed is not something you find much at the movies these days.

VILLAGE VOICE, 2/9/93, p. 53, J. Hoberman

Myth is something we all work on together and with *Matinee*, another chunk of the Boomer-ography—that collective generational saga we might call Young Bill Clinton—is dramatized on the screen. Joe Dante's latest teen pulp comedy provides a high school view of the Cuban Missile Crisis, entwining the most angst-ridden week of the Cold War with a satire of the schlock monster movies that everyone, even then, recognized as a primitive manifestation of our nuclear terror.

Such was life on the New Frontier, October 1962: Gene (Simon Fenton) lives on the Boca-Chica naval air base in Key West. It's the first line of defense and his father is part of the quarantine Kennedy ordered around Cuba. As Russian freighters inexorably, steam toward the American blockade, so producer Lawrence Woolsey (John Goodman) bears down on Key West for the world premiere of his latest mutation thriller, *Mant* (man plus ant). Woolsey sports an arm-length cigar and a blowsy leading lady (Cathy Moriarty); for Dante, he's an American folk hero whose sense of theatrical ballyhoo suggests the seat-wiring special effects of gimmickmeister William Castle.

Thanks to Goodman's sly heft, Woolsey is *Matinee*'s moral center. His scare tactics are a kind of therapy, if not primitive art. (He posits cave painting as the first monster movie, something Dante playfully animates.) Woolsey's vaunted "atom-o-vision" puts the audience at ground zero—which is exactly where they are in reality, even before his "rumble-rama" panics the theater. *Matinee* is not without a certain self-awareness in representing the Missile Crisis as an episode in American show business—a simulated nuclear firestorm used to clear the house. Still the movie's main attraction is most likely Kellie Martin, taking a break from her serious incarnation as the p.c. ingenue of *Life Goes On* to play a think-pink bubblehead.

Hovering around the affable with occasional sorties into the maudlin, *Matinee* is broad and not unintelligent. But, for all the mock show-biz sentimentality that Goodman brings to the role of Woolsey, Dante's model remains Lucas-Spielberg. History is a collectible. From Gene's precious pile of *Famous Monsters of Filmland* through the movie posters that paper the sets to the actual TV bulletins punctuating the action, *Matinee* is a careful—in some ways, loving—reconstruction. (The filmmakers make clever use of "The End of the World," although I'm surprised they didn't incorporate "Monster Mash," which was originally released for Halloween 1962.)

One more descendent of *American Graffiti, Matinee* is another of the innumerable movies that make you wonder if the snap, verve, and creative typology of the best Preston Sturges comedies weren't themselves some sort of inexplicable mutation. The movie's pace is weirdly languorous, except when Dante is serving up his pet pastiches—a trailer for *Mant* that incorporates actual atomic testing, a piece of a mock-Disney live-action comedy involving an anthropomorphic shopping cart, and finally *Mant*, which knocks off *The Fly* against a backdrop of authentically tacky sunburst clocks.

Here, too, are the air-raid sirens, the shelter drills, the teenage discussion that rebounded between rabid earnestness ("If you die when the bomb falls you're lucky") and resigned flippancy ("Going to that horror show on Saturday?" "Yeah, if they still have Saturday"), the poignant fantasy of being trapped inside a fallout shelter with the prettiest girl in your class—as though permission to have sex required the obliteration of the civilized world. But *Matinee* doesn't acknowledge the euphoria that psychiatric officers noted at Air Force bases during the Missile Crisis. (It's the giddiness that underscores the dark comedy of *Dr. Strangelove*—it's a relief the worst has finally happened.) Nor does it really evoke the peculiar resignation experienced by those taught by years of school, movies, and episodes of *The Twilight Zone* to expect Armageddon as their birthright.

Matinee is a movie made for Chelsea (see this and you'll understand ... not!), and for the kids who see *Matinee*, the Cold War must seem inexplicable—like the panic surrounding Orson Welles's *The War of the Worlds*, just somebody else's vaguely remembered nightmare. Perhaps no film could reconstruct that mood. As Norman Mailer shuddered in the aftermath of the crisis: "One looked at the buildings one passed and wondered if one was to see them again."

Also reviewed in:
CHICAGO TRIBUNE, 1/29/93, Friday/p. C, Dave Kehr
NATION, 3/8/93, p. 316, Stuart Klawans
NEW REPUBLIC, 3/1/93, p. 28, Stanley Kauffmann
NEW YORK TIMES, 1/29/93, p. C6, Janet Maslin
VARIETY, 2/1/93, p. 97, Lawrence Cohn
WASHINGTON POST, 1/29/93, p. C1, Rita Kempley
WASHINGTON POST, 1/29/93, Weekend/p. 38, Joe Brown

MAZEPPA

An MK2 Productions USA release.   *Executive Producer:* Yvon Crenn.   *Producer:* Marin
Karmitz.   *Director:* Bartabas.   *Screeplay (French with English subtitles):* Claude-Henri Buffard,
Bartabas, and Homeric.   *Story:* Claude-Henri Buffard and Bartabas.   *From an original idea by:*
Bartabas.   *Director of Photography:* Bernard Zitzermann.   *Editor:* Joseph Licide.   *Music:*
Jean-Pierre Drouet.   *Sound:* Laurent Poirier and (music) Vincent Arnardi and Thierry Lebon.
Sound Editor: Jean Gargonne.   *Production Designer:* Emile Chigo.   *Costumes:* Marie-Laure
Schakmundes and Cristine Guegan.   *Running time:* 111 minutes.   *MPAA Rating:* Not Rated.

CAST: Miquel Bosé (Géricault);   Bartabas (Franconi);   Brigitte Marty (Mousté);   Eva
Schakmundes (Alexandrine);   Fatima Aibout (Cascabelle).   Bakary Sangare (Joseph).

NEWSDAY, 12/3/93, Part II/p. 93, John Anderson

The stunning and bewildering images that "Mazeppa" opens with are an apt introduction to the
tale of horseflesh and madness to follow: In a slaughterhouse, a young woman slowly carries a
ladle of blood across the killing floor, and fills the cup of the painter Gericault; their exchange
of glances set the fleshy, aged she-devils around them, working the butchered remains of horses,
into a cacophonous cackle. And all the while, a galloping rhythm plays counterpoint to the clamor
of church bells.

It's a bit much, and the story to follow never quite lives up to the visual and audio aspirations
of director Bartabas, the theatrical impresario and equestrian behind "Mazeppa's" story and
camera. But what he wants, and what he attains, is sensuality without purpose. In another word,
decadence.

And it's a decadent lot he explores in his tale of the Romantic painter Gericault (Miguel Bose),
whom Bartabas supposes might have thrown his lot in with the renowned horse trainer Franconi
(Bartabas), because of their artistic fascination, and mutual love, of horses. And we do mean
love: the sexuality evoked by the animals is a preoccupation of both men, and the people who
attend Franconi's horse shows; couples grasp each other passionately as the rhythm of the
galloping steeds overwhelms them. The link between horses and men is going to mean more to
some viewers than others, of course, although Gericault certainly appreciates it: Watching two
horses coupling, his face registers recognition of his own bestiality, the horses' humanness and
his own insignificance—especially given the prodigious proportions of equine sex.

Since the story is a fantasy—Gericault apparently admired Franconi, but whether he ever joined
up with the latter's Olympia Circus is pure conjecture—you have to wonder why Bartabas insisted
on adhering to some factual aspects while ignoring others. For instance, his Franconi wears a
leather mask that encloses his entire skull. The film's explanation is that Franconi's face was
disfigured in warfare, but the real story is that since Franconi was much older than Bartabas, the
director invented the injuries to avoid having to rely on heavy, aging makeup.

In any event, the Mazeppa of the title was a page who seduced the wife of his 17th-Century
Polish nobleman, and for his punishment was strapped naked to the back of a horse and sent off
into the winter night. His survival made him a legend, one celebrated in print by Hugo and
Pushkin, in music by Tchaikovsky and Liszt, and in oil by Gericault.

We see him learn of the Mazeppa legend, which exacerbates his mental collapse. But while
Gericault's madness is the film's engine, you may go mad yourself trying to follow the story, or
get the point. It is, however, full of marvelous pictures—many modeled on Gericault's
paintings—and the music, performed by an omnipresent troupe of singers, is superb.

VILLAGE VOICE, 12/14/93, p. 77, Marco Spino

Among the great artists who have fetishized horses, the Romantic Theodore Géricault stands out
for having acutely captured their psychologies. *Mazeppa* is a fabled look at the hardships and
ecstasies Géricault endured while living with the Olympic Circus, an outrageous and exquisitely
costumed band of gypsies who performed impressive stunts and indulged in bacchanal pleasures
with horses. Géricault joins the circus to learn more about horses and himself but gradually feels

enslaved by the group's master, Franconi, who forces him to objectify the horses without allowing him enough time to relate to the animals on a carnal level. Like the film's namesake, Ivan Mazeppa, a Polish equestrian who seduces his mentor's lover and then pays dearly, Géricault fucks Franconi's mistress, which destroys all three of them. *Mazeppa* questions the Romantic impulse toward death and emphasizes the need for an equilibrium between duty and desire, as impossible as this goal may be.

As writer and Franconi character, director Bartabas fashions a theater of the absurd with Géricault (played by the Gilles-like Miguel Bosé) as the catalyst of biblical allegories. Bosé's Géricault possesses a mischievous nature tempered by a harsh, self-effacing streak. He is a horse contained in a man's body, and Bosé expresses this frustration with a deadpan seriousness. Trapped in Géricault's mind, we hear the sounds and notice the sights that lead to his demise. As he ossifies from an eager student to a cynic, his retreat from life reads like a tragic loss for humanity. The horses, though, with their sensuous bodies, coyness, and dry humor, steal many scenes.

Bartabas's experimentations with camera angles work at times—as when the camera becomes Géricault's canvas and he stumbles on it and scrutinizes the screen as if he were aware of our voyeurism. But in other scenes where the camera pans endlessly with the horses and performers—running in circles, the result is a dizzying, monotonous carousel. Still, *Mazeppa* takes you on a heuristic and rewarding ride through a painter's soul and gives you the pleasure of watching these horses mate, give birth, and tease.

Also reviewed in:
CHICAGO TRIBUNE, 8/26/94, Friday/p. J, Michael Wilmington
NEW YORK TIMES, 12/3/93, p. C10, Stephen Holden
VARIETY, 6/7/93, p. 40, Emanel Levy

ME AND VERONICA

An Arrow release of a True Pictures production. *Producer:* Mark Linn-Baker, Max Mayer, Nellie Nugiel, and Leslie Urdang. *Director:* Don Scardino. *Screenplay:* Leslie Lyles. *Director of Photography:* Michael Barrow. *Editor:* Jeffrey Wolf. *Music:* David Mansfield. *Production Designer:* John Arnone. *Running time:* 97 minutes. *MPAA Rating:* R.

CAST: Elizabeth McGovern (Fanny); Patricia Wettig (Veronica); Michael O'Keefe (Michael); John Heard (Frankie); Scott Renderer (Boner); Will Hare (Red).

NEW YORK POST, 9/25/93, p. 14, Matthew Flamm

Everyone knows that in the movie industry today there is a great shortage of good roles for women. "Me and Veronica" suggests that there is, alas, no shortage of mediocre roles for women.

The story of two sisters—one crazy, the other just depressed—this meandering low-budget saga has the claustrophobic feel of a one-act play insufficiently opened up for the screen. It's watered-down Chekhov by way of overcooked Sam Shepard, but there's no denying that an actress would find either of the lead roles tempting.

Elizabeth McGovern plays Fanny, the reasonably level headed sister, who lives in a ramshackle house on the Jersey shore, doing odd jobs, painting abstract canvases and dwelling on her past.

Patricia Wettig, best known from her role in "thirtysomething," shows up in the sort of downmarket high heels, short skirt and patterned hose that she never got to wear on television.

The doomed, borderline Veronica—a "pills and beer kind of girl," as one ex-boyfriend describes her—has, to say the least, a troubled relationship with her younger sister.

The last time they saw each other, the recently, wed Fanny had just walked in on her husband—lying in bed with Veronica.

Fanny is single now and Veronica, who has two young children and no husband, is about to report to prison for welfare fraud. After two days of bar-hopping and assorted gallivanting around, the sisters are reconciled enough for Fanny to offer to keep her niece and nephew while their mother is in jail.

"Me and Veronica" may be full of meaning, but it is not much fun. As directed by stage veteran Don Scardino, from a script by playwright Leslie Lyles, it has the off-Broadway habit of making ordinary life seem unremittingly grim. That may not be the intention exactly, but that's how it looks. Even with Wettig's subtle, scary performance, and McGovern's touchingly hesitant one, this is a dreary piece of work.

Also reviewed in:
NEW YORK TIMES, 9/24/93, p. C25, Stephen Holden
VARIETY, 9/91/92, p. 86, Deborah Young

MEIN KRIEG

A Leisure Time Features release of a Känguruh-Film Berlin and WDR (Cologne) production. *Director:* Harriet Eder and Thomas Kufus. (German with English subtitles). *Director of Photography:* Johann Feindt. *Editor:* Arpad Bondy. *Sound:* Arpad Bondy. *Production Designer:* Hans-George Ullrich. *Running time:* 90 minutes. *MPAA Rating:* Not Rated.

VILLAGE VOICE, 5/25/93, p. 53, J. Hoberman

Just as the "last westerns" of the early '70s provided a way to allegorize the war in Vietnam, the "Indian westerns" of the '50s were often displaced meditations on black-white relations—*The Searchers*, currently revived at the Public, being only the most complex example. Also at the Public, is *Mein Krieg (My Private War)*, a small, absorbing addition to the vast celluloid literature on World War II, which draws on amateur footage taken by six Wehrmacht soldiers during the German invasion of the former Soviet Union.

A mixture of oral history and home movies, *Mein Krieg* is annotated only by the veterans themselves as they explicate the material they produced nearly a half-century before. That most are equipment buffs, proudly displaying their still-functional antique cameras, heightens the sense of their being the operators of precision machines within the larger machine of the German army. That war is mainly seen as an adventure (swimming in the Black Sea), a spectacle (military drilling, or some combination of the two (bombed-out landscapes) serves as an unstated reminder that neither memory nor motion pictures are transparent. That directors Harriet Eder and Thomas Kufus present the footage largely unadorned only heightens its impact—the film that records the burning of one Belorussian city seems itself warped from the heat.

In general, the specific horrors of the eastern front are seldom acknowledged and then only by synecdoche: a dozen Jews hanging from a makeshift gallows, a Russian girl dancing topless for her German captors, soldiers confiscating livestock or torching houses, prisoners digging mass graves. The most startling image is of a gray mass identified as 90,000 Russian POWs. Material shortages being what they were, the man who took the footage wonders what became of them all. As revealing as the movies are, the flashes of self-recognition—the degree of denial or regret each veteran expresses, the way he chooses to annotate his footage. (It's striking that the most thoughtful, least complacent of the six is a photo-archivist.)

Self-pity too becomes an object for contemplation, *Mein Krieg* really should be shown with *Dear America*, a considerably jazzier presentation of movies made by American soldiers in Vietnam that, while less straightforward in its omissions, presented a war even more devoid of racism, atrocities, sex weirdness, psychosis, or any of the perks of an occupying army.

Also reviewed in:
NEW YORK TIMES, 5/21/93, p. C8, Janet Maslin
VARIETY, 2/21/90, p. 310
WASHINGTON POST, 4/5/93, p. D4, Rita Kempley

MENACE II SOCIETY

A New Line Cinema release. *Executive Producer:* Kevin Moreton. *Producer:* Darin Scott. *Director:* Albert Hughes and Allen Hughes. *Screenplay:* Tyger Williams. *Story:* Allen Hughes, Albert Hughes, and Tyger Williams. *Director of Photography:* Lisa Rinzler. *Editor:* Christopher Koefoed. *Music:* QD III. *Music Editor:* John La Salandra. *Sound:* Veda Campbell, (music) Alex Gordon, and Rob Chiarelli. *Sound Editor:* Steve "Scarface" Williams. *Casting:* Tony Lee. *Production Designer:* Penny Barrett. *Set Decorator:* Adel A. Mazen. *Set Dresser:* Lisa Boutillier. *Special Effects:* Frank Ceglia. *Costumes:* Sylvia Vega-Vasquez. *Make-up:* Kim D. Davis and Joanetta Stowers. *Stunt Coordinator:* Oasaun Elam. *Running time:* 90 minutes. *MPAA Rating:* R.

CAST: Tyrin Turner (Caine); Larenz Tate (O-Dog); June Kyoko Lu (Grocery Store Woman); Toshi Toda (Grocery Store Man); Samuel L. Jackson (Tat Lawson); Anthony Johnson (Tony); Brandon Hammond (Five Year Old Caine); Glenn Plummer (Pernell); Reginald Ballard (Clyde); Khandi Alexander (Karen Lawson); Eugene Lee (Man #1); James Pickens, Jr. (Man #2); Nancy Cheryl Davis (Teacher); Jullian Roy Doster (Anthony); Jada Pinkett (Ronnie); Marilyn Coleman (Grandmama); Arnold Johnson (Grandpapa); Saafir (Harold Lawson); Pooh Man (Doc); MC Eiht (A-Wax); Vonte Sweet (Sharif); Ryan Williams (Stacy); Cynthia Calhoun (Jackee); Garen Holman (Junior); Joy Matthews (Nurse #1); Clifton Powell (Chauncy); Todd Anthony Shaw (Lew-Loc); Christopher M. Brown (Lloyd); Stacy Arnell (Deena); Dwayne Barnes (Basehead); Dave Kirsch (Insurance Man); Alvin Mears (K-9 Police Officer); Bill Duke (Detective); Robert R. Gonzales (Car Dealer); Martin Davis (Car-Jack victim); Erin Leshawn Wiley (Ilena); Charles S. Dutton (Mr. Butler); Charles J. Grube (Officer Fassel); Mike Kelly (Officer Gadd); Rolando Molina (Vato #1); Clifton Gonzalez Gonzalez (Vato #2); Tony Valentino (Vato #3); Danny Villarreal (Vato #4); Yo Yo (Girl at Party); Samuel Monroe, Jr. (Ilena's Cousin).

CINEASTE, Vol. XX, No. 2, 1993, p. 44, Paula Massood

It is impossible to discuss *Menace II Society*, the feature debut by the sibling duo, the Hughes brothers, without referring to other films within the 'hood' or 'gangsta' genre. As with all genres of filmmaking, the hood films can be identified by certain industrial and artistic similarities: they are made by young, film-literate African-American men working with shoestring budgets (by comparison to Hollywood standards); they deal with similar narrative themes (young African-American men trying to stay alive amidst the pressures—crimes, drugs, racism—of inner city life); and they illustrate mastery of cinematic techniques. Past examples of this genre include such films as *Straight Out of Brooklyn, Juice, New Jack City,* and *Boyz N the Hood.* Relying on these and other films which have preceded it, and borrowing many narrative conventions from John Singleton's *Boyz N the Hood* most specifically, *Menace II Society* concerns itself with similar topics, in a similar milieu, but attempts to take its story one step further.

Most simply, *Menace II Society* is a coming of age tale detailing the summer after its protagonist Caine (Tyrin Turner) graduates from high school. This is Caine's story, made literal through the film's use of voice-over narration to convey his point of view. Although this technique is most closely associated with traditional narrative styles, in which identification with the protagonist is unified and absolute, *Menace II Society* subverts this technique by simultaneously giving truth and primacy to Caine's version of events, while underscoring Caine's unreliability as a narrator (and the unreliability of all narrators). In voice-over, Caine repeatedly questions his actions and seemingly makes a decision, only to oppose that decision through his actions that follow, without offering any explanation. Through their self-conscious, unconventional use of this conventional narrative device, the Hughes move beyond other films of the hood genre, all of which explicitly aim to break down Hollywood images of African-American life. The Hughes brothers, however, further subvert Hollywood content by illustrating, questioning, and moving away from the shortcomings of the very techniques Hollywood uses to construct a 'reality,' while never questioning its own construction.

Menace II Society also strives, with varying degrees of success, to break from traditional and generic depictions of violence. From the very first scene, detailing Caine's and O-Dog's (Larenz Tate) fatal armed robbery of a Korean market, violence is unsympathetically graphic. In this instance, the film succeeds in painting a disturbing picture of violence, one in which the characters' lack of remorse, rather than stylistic convention, shapes and colors the horror of the image. Although most of the violence is filmed realistically and unfolds in real time, the Hughes can't seem to resist stylizing some of the more important narrative events. Thus, while the robbery introduces violence, O-Dog's shooting of the Korean market owner is shown directly only further into the story, when black and white images of the store's stolen surveillance video are played and replayed for the entertainment of Caine, O-Dog, and their friends. While an innovative means of conveying action, the video becomes nothing more than a red herring. While it builds tension and a false sense of foreboding, nothing comes of—the video never connects directly to the film's later events.

The film's climactic final scene also falls prey to the same stylistic conventions the Hughes claim to be working against. As Caine is riddled with bullets in this drive-by shooting scene, the cinematography resorts to a stylistics of violence standardized ever since its introduction in *Bonnie and Clyde*—brilliant colors, bright lighting, and slow motion photography, prolonging the event and heightening tension as well as pathos. While masterfully executed, such conventions nullify the effect of earlier straightforward, no-holds-barred depictions of violence. By virtue of its simplicity, an earlier carjacking scene, in which Caine's cousin is killed, seems far more powerful than those scenes in which violence is stylized. Repeatedly stating their desire that violence work as a deterrent to hood audiences watching the film, the Hughes might have achieved their end more successfully had they consistently resisted the masterful, pleasurable, and *familiar* cinematography of violence.

While sometimes departing from generic conventions through unconventional narrative and stylistic techniques, *Menace II Society* maintains certain conventions by reworking narratives explored in *Boys N the Hood* and *Straight Out of Brooklyn*. Like *Boyz*, most of the film's impetus comes through its stressing the importance of a powerful father figure (at the expense of most women in the narrative). Whereas the former film locates one central father figure, however, *Menace II Society* problematizes the ease of this solution.

Introduced in flashback when he murders a man in front of his young son in their home, Caine's father initiates his son into a life of crime. After his death, Caine's father is followed by Pernell (Glenn Plummer), who serves as Caine's criminal mentor and surrogate father until a life prison term curtails his daily influence. While responsibility for Caine's welfare also falls into his grandparents' hands and home, their attempts (especially his grandfather's) to set him straight go unheeded. Caine can neither accept his grandfather's religious beliefs nor respond when his grandfather poses the pivotal question—"Don't you care whether you live or die!"

Caine's former teacher, Mr. Butler (Charles S. Dutton), also attempts to intervene, suggesting that Caine get out of the hood before he gets into any more trouble. Mr. Butler, himself a father of Sharif, an ex-"knucklehead" and now a Muslim convert—falls snugly into the mold of Furious, the strong father in the Singleton film. In *Menace*, however, this figure is only a minor character. Set in Mr. Butler's classroom, his intervention motivates Caine to reflect upon his life, but the effect of Mr. Butler's words, like that of Caine's grandfather, is merely momentary—Caine listens, but as his actions illustrate, he doesn't really hear. In a film in which relationships among men are predicated on violence, it is no coincidence that Caine's father and Pernell influence Caine in the most sustaining ways. Rather than standing for the son's salvation, as Furious does in *Boyz N the Hood*, these fathers signal Caine's downfall.

With all influential father figures either dead or behind bars, the ill-equipped Caine, himself, must adopt the role of father when Pernell legitimizes Caine's relationship with Ronnie (Jada Pinkett), Pernell's former lover and the mother of his young son Tony. Pernell gives his blessing, as Ronnie and Caine attempt to move out of the hood, and Caine comes of age, accepting responsibility for Ronnie, Tony, and himself. Mediated through the prison's plexiglass and tele-phones, the scene suggests the possibility that Caine has learned from Pernell's mistakes and now can halt the history of self-destruction into which he was born and raised. But this possibility is quickly negated at the going-away party for Ronnie, where Caine attacks a man in front of Tony, a not-so-subtle echo of the violent scene from Caine's childhood. Is the film really suggesting that the only legacy Caine (or Tony) can inherit is one of violence and self-destruction!

Like many narratives dealing with relationships among men (a primary structuring theme of the hood films), women are almost totally excluded from the story. The only exception in *Menace II Society* is Ronnie, who is included precisely because she stands above or outside of the environment around her, as suggested by her characterization and the spaces she occupies. Shot in soft focus and with soft lighting, in contrast to the harsher realities of Caine's world, Ronnie and her house become Caine's only refuge. Within this space, Ronnie's subdued dress and practical manner sustain Caine in a way his own mother never could. Ronnie's role as nurturer and protector emerges through her strong desire to shield her son and Caine from the very same things—guns, drugs, prison, and death. In this respect, Ronnie represents Caine's only hope for survival. Implicit within this survival is the promise of escape: Caine will escape his life of crime through his literal escape to Atlanta with Ronnie.

In addition to Ronnie (who ultimately becomes more symbolic than real), the generic homegirls, and a few almost silent appearances by Caine's grandmother, the only other woman who figures in the film is Ilena (Erin Leshawn Wiley), the mother of Caine's unborn child. Diametrically opposed to Ronnie, by virtue of her overt sexuality, Ilena causes Caine's downfall and foils his and Ronnie's attempt to begin anew. As Caine and Ronnie pack up her car for their move to Atlanta, Caine is gunned down by Ilena's cousin in revenge for dumping Ilena and abandoning his unborn child. Just as Ronnie inhabits the space offscreen when the imprisoned Pernell gives Caine his blessing, Ilena is physically absent from the action, even at this moment when she functions so centrally. Instead, the relationship is mediated through a violent exchange between men—Caine and her cousin. As this instance illustrates, the absence of women only unveils the threat they represent: a life in the hood, unwanted pregnancy, enforced responsibility, death.

During the film's final scene, Caine's shooting death, the film's central paradox emerges—it is not enough for Caine to accept responsibility for those things he desires, he must also take responsibility for his own actions. Ultimately, even the film's purposeful construction of Caine as antihero, at once sympathetic and antipathetic, fails to move the film away from its culmination as a morality play (with more than a few Biblical echoes). Despite their attempt to break with the conventions of storytelling when examining their character's ambivalence toward living and his inability to accept responsibility, the Hughes brothers cannot allow Caine to go unpunished. At the moment of his death, Caine becomes a tragic figure, his fatal flaws defined as the violence into which he was schooled, the lack of value he places on human life, and his inability to escape forces much larger than himself. And his tragic recognition comes too late. Only in posthumous voice-over can he answer his grandfather's question—in this moment, heavy with irony, he finally acknowledges that he, indeed, wants to live.

One wonders if martyring Caine is what the Hughes brothers really set out to do, or if, in their attempt to make the darkest, most violent hood film, they used 'any means necessary' to arrive unintentionally at a conventional and confused conclusion. Caine's 'punishment' is wholly in keeping with Classical Hollywood narratives, thus attaching contradictory meanings to his death. On the one hand, the film, through its reworking of both traditional and generic narrative conventions, says something different about Caine's situation and about the real situation of many African-American men in the inner city. But, on the other hand, the film doesn't say anything different, for it sometimes reuses already overused images of violence to make its main points—images which Hollywood has mined for decades.

By not taking into account the post-Watts history of the hood-the LAPD's militaristic methods of fighting inner city crime (read South Central, Watts, East L.A.), the Reagan and Bush Administrations' war on drugs, and the right's negation of self-rehabilitation as a possibility for those convicted of selling and/or using drugs—the film's conclusion falls prey to the very forces it appears to be fighting, rendering earlier footage of the 1965 Watts Rebellion as nothing more than stylized, historical lip service.

Maybe Caine's mistake, like that of the Hughes brothers, was that he got caught in the crossfire of his own making. Unlike the Hughes brothers, however, Caine, and characters like him, won't be walking away with attractive Hollywood deals.

LOS ANGELES TIMES, 5/26/93, Calendar/p. 1, Peter Rainer

Allen Hughes and Albert Hughes, the 21-year-old twin brothers who directed the youth-in-trouble movie "Menace II Society," along with 23-year-old screenwriter Tyger Williams, are young enough to get inside the lives of Watts gangbangers without making it seem as if we're watching something taking place on another planet.

They aren't always able to sort out what they put on the screen. (Not the worst of faults with filmmakers, at least they have something vital to put out.) Because there's so much mayhem in "Menace II Society" the filmmakers may have worried that audiences would get high on it. So, as a counterbalance, they turn preachy and diagrammatic, just to make sure we don't confuse the depiction of violence with its endorsement.

The filmmakers needn't have worried, but their fears are understandable. The Hughes brothers have such a free-form, caught-in-the-act directorial style that it's easy to mistake their "objective" unblinking approach with an uncaring attitude. (Their previous experience is mostly making hip-hop videos.) But their instincts as filmmakers override their instincts as moralizers. "Menace II Society" (rated R for strong violence, drug use and language) is best—and most shocking—when it just sets out its horrors and lets us find our own way.

The film opens with a blast of brutality. A Korean merchant and his wife are casually blown away by O-Dog (Larenz Tate) over a petty dispute while O-Dog's homeboy, Caine (Tyrin Turner), looks on aghast. O-Dog grabs the store's surveillance videotape of the crime and later reruns it proudly for his fellow homeboys, A-Wax (rapper MC Eiht), Stacy (Ryan Williams) and Chauncy (Clifton Powell). O-Dog likes being the star of his own shoot 'em up; he especially likes to replay the moment when the merchant's brains go flying.

But it is Caine—who, unlike O-Dog, still seems to have some scruples—who occupies the film's harsh center. His childhood is filled in for us in flashback: His father (Samuel L. Jackson), a dope-dealer in the '70s, was murdered when Caine was 10; his mother, a junkie, OD'd.

Raised from childhood by his Bible-toting grandparents in Watts, Caine is on the verge of graduating high school but the only life that holds any meaning for him is in the streets. He's proud of his gang affiliations but he's also proud that he draws the line—he hasn't killed anybody yet. But when he witnesses the murder of his cousin by a rival gang, he and his homies go into action. Their vengeance sets off a sickening wave of retribution.

When Caine's grandfather (Arnold Johnson) asks Caine if he cares whether he lives or dies, Caine's response is "I don't know."

The movie is a demonstration of how Caine comes around to caring about living—when it's already too late. There's a slightly generic quality about the way Caine is characterized that's probably intentional on the part of the filmmakers: he seems less an individual than a symbolic representative of all kids in trouble. His passage covers a lot of territory: from his broken-family upbringing to his acting as surrogate father to the child of another broken family. The cyclical nature of Caine's story is part of a larger story; the movie is saying that miseries move down the generations, just as the Watts riots of '65 (which we see in newsreel footage) are replayed in '92.

The young actors in "Menace II Society" don't have the kind of power or presence that might make their stories really hit home. When someone like Charles Dutton or Bill Duke turns up in a cameo, they blast the film's semi-documentary veneer with their high-style theatrics. We need some of their preening and staginess because, without it, the film might seem too stark.

A bigger problem is the way the filmmakers sentimentalize Caine's struggle by working in a girlfriend, Ronnie (Jada Pinkett), who pleads with him to go with her and her young son to Atlanta to start over: she's so angelic that she's unbelievable. We can't see how she got that way right in the middle of such an inferno. Sharif (Vonte Sweet), a friend of Caine who spouts teachings from the Nation of Islam, and his father (Dutton) are likewise presented as guardian angels; they try to coax Caine into moving with them to Kansas. Their salvation is presented without irony: Kansas as the Promised Land.

The filmmakers' attitudes are probably summed up by Sharif's father when he cautions Caine that "the hunt is on and you're the prey. All I'm saying is survive." The film endorses survival by religion—*any* religion; survival by staying close to your loved ones, by staying away from gangs, from drugs. The Hughes brothers are torn between the hopelessness of what they depict and a kind of haloed view of a better life. (Do we really need to see Caine's grandparents watch the happily-ever-after ending of "It's a Wonderful Life" on television?) They're split between fatalism and arrant optimism, and, in that split, their film probably expresses the attitudes of their generation more fully than they know.

NEW YORK, 5/31/93, p. 54, David Denby

The violence in *Menace II Society*, the extraordinary new film about young black men in Los Angeles, happens so suddenly that it takes one's breath away. Young men kill in a rage, or for revenge, but they also kill when they are merely insulted. Since they have little else going for them but style, toughness, and a narrow purchase on self-respect, nearly everything they experience manages to outrage or insult them. Insults are taken as threats, threats as attacks, and attacks lead to counterattacks. The men are condemned to violence by their situation and temperament. The young directors, Allen and Albert Hughes, twin brothers who are only 20 years old, dramatize this catastrophic pattern with so much sober force—the movie, for all its violence, is the opposite of exploitation—that one instinctively trusts and believes what the film is saying.

Menace II Society is perhaps the most striking directorial debut in the history of black cinema. The Hughes brothers, born in Detroit and raised in Pomona, California, started making films at the age of 12; in recent years, they've made music videos for rap and hip-hop groups. One might expect their first feature to be a slick turn-on—say, a full-length urban-violence music video. The miracle, however, is that these two whizzes, in collaboration with the 23-year-old screenwriter Tyger Williams, have used their extraordinary camera technique, and their control of pacing and rhythm, to make a powerful, even tragic, film about loss. *Menace II Society*, which stars a group of young TV actors from the Los Angeles area, dramatizes the life and death of an entire class of young men, and it's told by men the same age as their subjects. The Hugheses have the reckless honesty of youth—their love of truth may end in rejection or glory but not in safety. I came out of this grim movie exhilarated by two artists relentlessly making their point. The movie is narrated by Caine Lawson (Tyrin Turner), who is 18 and lives in Watts. He graduates from high school, but he's hustling drugs for a living. In the opening scene, he and a friend, O-Dog (Larenz Tate), enter a Korean grocery store to get a beer. The Koreans, frightened that they will be ripped off, hover over the two boys, who feel insulted; words are exchanged, and O-Dog pulls out a gun and kills the store owner and his wife. Even as you are watching it, you know that this is the primal scene of ethnic distrust. (In comparison with it, Michael Douglas's baseball-bat routine in *Falling Down* is just nasty grandstanding.) The Hugheses are remarkably even-handed, remarkably attentive to the dynamics of fear and pride on both sides. They move the scene along quickly but without slighting the tensions, the pauses, the turning points that make the crazily violent outcome so convincing.

The narration then takes us back to 1973, when Caine, a little boy, was growing up in a household headed by his drug-dealer father and addict mother. A visitor challenges his father, and the father off-handedly shoots the man right in the living room—another arbitrary, casual killing resulting from little more than an insult. Caine has seen death his whole life, and his sorrowful narration sets up a question in the audience's mind: If Caine knows this, if he can see the disastrous way his life is going, why doesn't he pull himself out of it? He is intelligent; he has a mild and affectionate side as well as an angry side. Tyrin Turner plays him ambiguously, with moments of vulnerability giving way to violent rage. His Caine is never casually vicious like Larenz Tate's O-Dog, who swings his Rastafarian dreadlocks in contempt and doesn't give a damn about anyone. Among the men they hang with, Caine is the only one with any detachment.

Yet he's stuck, and the movie shows us why. The Hugheses have shot the film in cramped tract houses and tawdry streets; but they move the camera so freely that as Caine enters some party, one immediately senses his excitement, his feeling that he could get away with anything. In this movie, however, euphoria never lasts more than an instant. During an evening in Long Beach, Caine and his cousin, a successful hustler, are shot by two young men who want the cousin's BMW; Caine survives and is goaded by O-Dog into taking revenge. One flashing scene of violence in the night follows the other. The filmmakers' point is that Caine lives in an enclosed world (white people are barely present) in which nothing matters but temporary advantage; each act is performed as if it had no consequences, as if it were the final act. No other reality exists—when Caine sees James Stewart greeting his family in a movie shown on TV, he rolls his eyes in disbelief.

This callous distance from common feelings, as the film makes clear, has been planted through the generations. Like John Singleton in *Boyz N the Hood*, the filmmakers offer a despairing vision of inner-city family disintegration. First in one generations and then in the next, older men let boys drink and handle guns. In part, *Menace II Society* tracks Caine's hapless search for a father (his own is long dead). But there aren't any fathers, and the surrogates (a teacher, an older man in prison) can do little but offer good advice. The father kills his son with his absence.

The young women are far more grown up and realistic than the men; they want to survive, but their witty, exasperated complaints—they are always ragging the men—have little effect, since the men associate any weakness in themselves with femaleness and label the slightest restraint "acting like a bitch." The meaning of the movie seems to be, If you don't have a father, at least listen to your woman. Ronnie (Jada Pinkett), who has a young son to take care of, tries to get Caine to leave Los Angeles. She's meant to be the only sane and responsible person in Caine's circle, and Pinkett plays her with conviction and force. At the end of *Menace II Society*, Caine's ambivalent desire to get out (she convinces him) struggles against the many forces inexorably closing in on him.

This film has a fuller and more wrathful understanding of the nihilism of the ghetto than anything else we've seen in movies. And it doesn't lay off the problems on somebody else; it doesn't say that whitey is to blame for everything, or that there's no way out. There *are* ways out; the tragedy is that people aren't always ready or able to take them. This sort of bleak truth-telling is not likely to bring comfort to many people, white or black. The big audience is more likely to go for *Posse*, Mario Van Peebles's slovenly, show-off romp about black cowboys shooting white devils in the Old West. As *Menace II Society* passes through its many scenes of violence and its moments of confusion and meanness, all filmed with great flair and power, it works toward a bitter truth: The young men in the movie are the first generation of Americans to be more afraid of life than of death.

NEW YORK POST, 5/26/93, p. 24, Matthew Flamm

"My dad sold dope," recalls Caine in voice-over at the start of "Menace II Society," the gripping if ultimately depressing slice of inner-city, black life that opens today. "And my mother was a heroin addict. Instead of keeping me out of trouble, they turned me on to it."

So much for home life. Now 18 years old and an orphan of the drug wars, Caine lives with his grandparents in a teeming Watts housing project, a tough but morally shell-shocked survivor. He carries an automatic under his shirt, sells drugs and hangs with the only kind of people be has ever known—criminals.

Life is a moment-to-moment thing. Or, as he reflects in the film's shockingly brutal opening scene, one moment you're buying a beer and the next you're "accomplice in an armed robbery and accessory to murder": Caine watches, in horror, as his buddy O-Dog (Larenz Tate) shoots a Korean grocer just for the fun of it.

O-Dog even takes home a souvenir—the store's security camera video of the killing, which he plays over and over for the amusement of friends.

"Menace II Society," the debut movie of 20-year-old twin brothers Allen and Albert Hughes, is nothing if not uncompromising.

There are no heroes in this grim film, but neither are there villains. In a world in which hovering police helicopters form a kind of non-stop soundtrack and all teen-agers carry guns, choices are at a minimum.

The Hughes brothers make Caine (effectively played by newcomer Tyrin Turner) as sympathetic as someone so deprived can be, and they catch him at a moment where there is still the possibility of change. He has just finished high school. Some of his friends are escaping to Kansas. He has a romantic interest—Ronnie (Jada Pinkett), a beautiful young single mother—who is moving to Atlanta.

The question becomes whether Caine can get off the path of self-destruction and build a life somewhere else. The problem for the film is that he may have not have much capacity for change—like his poverty-stricken, crack-infested neighborhood, he looks to be a lost cause.

Despite a short speech by guest adult Charles S. Dutton, the Hughes brothers keep their moral message wrapped in a pretty tight package. "Menace II Society," with its raw hip-hop soundtrack, alarmingly bloody shootouts and overpowering air of violence, comes out more frightening docudrama than uplifting dramatic art.

That may have been what the brothers intended.

NEWSDAY, 5/26/93, Part II/p. 63, John Anderson

You dis me, you die. It's virtually the sole ethic propelling the action in "Menace II Society," where the blood pours out faster than the malt liquor and is a hell of a lot cheaper. And, although the characters in this startling debut by the 21-year-old twin brothers Allen and Albert Hughes may be sociopathic, the truly disturbing thing is, so is the movie.

From the moment Caine (Tyrin Turner) and O-Dog (Larenz Tate) enter a Korean couple's grocery in Watts, we know we're in a world that's been permanently knocked off its moral axis: the "real" world, in other words. The Koreans are immediately suspicious, almost terrified. O-Dog is immediately indignant. Something's got to give. "It's funny like that in Watts," Caine will say. "You never know what's going to happen next." What happens is that the husband utters a few harmless words, and O-Dog shoots them both dead. As an afterthought, he also robs the store.

That's what happens. What's far from funny is the way the film presents the murders. The film presumes no outrage; it condemns almost no one. The actions of O-Dog (described as "America's Nightmare: Young, black and doesn't give a _____ ") are almost expected, if not justified, given the ethnic tensions between blacks and Koreans. And blowing out a storeowner's brains is just the overture in a film that portrays life among the black underclass of L.A. as one of short tempers, long memories and quick death.

Whether this is an accurate portrait is beside the point. If there wasn't something more that the Hughes brothers wanted to say, they might as well have used their considerable talents to make a documentary. Of course, fewer people would have watched; even fewer would have cared. Real life can always be dismissed, it seems; fiction has to be dealt with, especially when it presents a picture so bleak and contradicts so much the way America wants to look at itself.

What the Hugheses have done, via 23-year-old Tyger Williams' screenplay, is make a film with the same lack of moral mooring as its characters. It's an ugly film, almost an evil film, but whether that troubles you, whether it excites you, is also beside the point. The movie's amorality leaves you devoid of hope, and that's the point.

Caine, who is the focus of much of "Menace" and through whose eyes we watch a series of tragedies unfold, is almost a nice guy, almost the pride of his family, a high school graduate (even though he admits attending only half the time, when he wasn't selling drugs) and, eventually, a murderer.

Making a movie from the perspective of a killer, at least one whose crime is motivated strictly by revenge—his cousin is killed in a carjacking—is a tricky business and usually requires some redemptive action, some remorseful epiphany, if not the protagonist's ultimate damnation. Not here. What the Hugheses have created is something close to non-representational cinema. You can't impose anything on it, not your personal philosophy, not your political agenda, not your moral outrage. You can only absorb its emotional content.

The story is relatively simple, to the point of being nonexistent: Caine has been brought up by a junkie mother and a drug-dealing father. When he was 5, Caine watched his father kill a man during a card game. (That we hear "Only the Strong Survive" after the shooting is just one example of the Hugheses being a little too precious for their own good.) His sole guidance comes from Pernell (Glenn Plummer), another small-time criminal, who gives Caine his first taste of liquor and lets him hold his first gun. After Pernell gets life in prison, and Caine becomes heir apparent to both Pernell's girlfriend, Ronnie (Jada Pinkett), and son, Tony (Anthony Johnson), we'll see this baptism of bloodshed repeated between Caine and Tony.

And we'll wait in vain for Caine and Ronnie to get it together and move to Atlanta, where things will be better, or would be, if everyone weren't a prisoner of their ghetto, of their own minds, of the cyclical nature of violence. The stereotypes run rampant through "Menace," the dialogue is often forced, and much of the acting is lame, but then you have moments like the one with Charles S. Dutton as the schoolteacher Mr. Butler, who tells Caine, "The hunt is on ... and you're the prey."

What "Menace II Society" says is: The hunter as the prey. And, given the state of California, the United States and the world, the outlook for both is pretty bleak.

SIGHT AND SOUND, 1/94, p. 50, Angela McRobbie

Caine and his friend O-Dog live in Watts, LA. Provoked by the suspicious reaction of a Korean grocery shop owner and his wife, O-Dog shoots them both dead, and retrieves the video from the shop's security camera before he and Caine escape. Caine's parents are both dead—his father by shooting, his mother by a heroin overdose—and he now lives with his grandparents, whose religious talk only serves to alienate him further from their dreams of achievement and respectability. A series of events on the street involving rival gangs results in Caine being shot and fellow gang member Harold being killed. O-Dog decides to seek vengeance; meanwhile, Caine is increasingly drawn into the world of crime and violence. When he is picked up for car theft, his fingerprints match those found on a bottle of beer he dropped in the grocery store. The police treat the boys with as much brutality as the boys treat those around them. After a beating by the police, Caine ends up in hospital. A glimmer of hope appears when his girlfriend Ronnie announces that she has got a job in Atlanta and invites Caine to move there with her and her young son Anthony. Caine is visited by the cousin of another girl who accuses him of making her pregnant, and reacts by beating him up. Just as Caine and Ronnie are preparing to move out of town, with their friends' help, the cousin and his gang drive by, and Caine is cut down in a rain of bullets.

The emerging genre of black gang-crime cinema—with films like *Menace II Society* and its predecessor *Boyz N the Hood*—pushes the white film reviewer into a difficult corner. The genre forms part of an ongoing debate in the black community and among black scholars about the violent imagery of rap and the aggressive sexism of many of its best-known figures. But this debate is less easy to enter into for the critic looking at a single film—in particular one which self-consciously plays with the white genre of gangster cinema. Paul Gilroy has already taken Spike Lee to task for unproblematically representing male ghetto life while refusing the challenge of its genocidal capacity. Howard A. Baker has recognised in rap both this destructive desperation born out of racial injustice and also the addressing of white fears through the resurrection of what Foucault calls "subjugated knowledges". Parts of black youth culture do not just suggest sexual identities which remain outside the field of what white culture approves of, but actively, sometimes aggressively explore them.

Menace II Society transfers much of the lore of rap into a narrative of drugs, guns, gangs and girls in Watts, LA. But the soundtrack's pain and intensity, the complexity of its musical structure is undermined, if not destroyed, by the simplicity of the story, which is presented in the kind of celebratory rhetoric found only in the most violent of films. 'Simplicity' because, as the opening scene shows, the boys are ruthless killers and in the end can only die as brutal a death as they have inflicted on their victims.

The film masquerades as realism in that its narrative reflects the extraordinarily high death rate among young African-American males. It also accurately portrays drug-dealing as part of the neighbourhood economy and crack as the currency for addictive highs and high-status cars. But *Boyz N the Hood* has already claimed this neorealist label as its own. In *Menace II Society*, reality provides only an opportunity for thoughtless film-making which is nonetheless able to draw on and exploit those parts of the black experience which demand to be understood and changed.

Simply to say that the film is disturbing is to refuse its political and emotional impact. The boys, having shot the Korean couple, also make off with a video of the killing. They later watch it ritualistically with friends, drinking, smoking and relishing the spectacle. In every case, spiteful, meaningless violence is the response to some imagined insult to masculinity. O-Dog shoots down an addict who can only offer to "suck his dick" in exchange for a hit. The Korean woman brings about her own death by expressing sorrow for the boys' mothers.

None of the film's characters extends beyond the ghetto stereotypes of the heroin-addicted black mother, the single parent trying against the odds to do the best for her young son (who is already fascinated by the guns and the exploits of older males) and the God-fearing grandparents locked in the misery of their surroundings. In the absence of major social change it is too easy to believe simplistically, as *Menace II Society* does, in education as the way out. Even if Caine wanted to go to college, he is taking too many drugs to open a book and has too many friends who would ridicule such aspirations. Even if the college doors were flung open to these disaffected youths, there is too much poverty and too much danger to allow them even to contemplate the idea of study. The trouble with the film's realism is that this situation is not problematised but celebrated.

VILLAGE VOICE, 6/1/93, p. 52, Georgia Brown

When [Michael Ovitz] was asked again if he thought that movie violence had any impact, he said, "I absolutely think it has an impact on kids. It becomes a framework on which children build. I remember all the things of my childhood. They've been my framework for my own value system, and I grew up in the fifties in Los Angeles."
—Ken Auletta, "What Won't They Do," *The New Yorker*, May 17

Put it down to a literal mind, but before getting on to the subject of violence and value systems, I need to contemplate that *II* in *Menace II Society*. Is it or is it not a meaningful incision? Are the movie's directors, the Hughes brothers, Allen and Albert (Al I and Al II?), affirming the value of twinship with a statement that they're double l's, or better yet, double I's? Or is it a tip of the hat to a *Menace I*? Judging by statements made here and there, it would seem that *Menace II* sees itself as the answer, in the negative, to John Singleton's *Boyz N the Hood*. Where there was *Boyz*, let there be *Men/ace*.

But let me not sound whimsical, because *Menace II Society* is not. Alternately irritating and maddening, impressive and infuriating, this gritty gangsta pic opens with a nasty bang: the gratuitous murder of two Korean shopkeepers by a young African American male. O-Dog (Larenz Tate) shoots the man and then, after making her surrender the store's security videotape, the woman. The psychopath's more rational buddy, Caine (Tyrin Turner)—whose life story this is—may not have been the killer but he's no Abel either. Caine's only regret is that the killing implicates him as an accessory. He sees his friend as, you know, "crazy." The film's considerable challenge is to present 18-year-old Caine's world, the "things of his childhood," as Mr. Ovitz puts it "the value system" he tries "to build on."

A brief history in crime follows: After the Watts riots of '65 came the drugs of the '70s, according to Caine's voiceover. Life with strung-out Mom and Pop was pretty eventful. At one of their parties the boy gets to handle a gun; at another, while he lies in his bed, his father (Samuel L. Jackson) blows away a man during a card game because the man isn't cowed by a gun at his head. "That was the first time I seen my father kill anybody but it wasn't the last. I got used to it though." If Ice Cube's Doughboy was a melancholy revenger, a real brother's keeper, sad about the 'hood, Caine (and his creators) wouldn't be caught dead musing about right and wrong.

What's in the head of the tyke in the red sleepsuit? Is he scared? Does he love this daddy who shoots people for no good reason? Hate him? We'll never know. (I might see crazy O-Dog as the combining of OD'd mom and a pop who shoots people for some suck dick remark—as O-Dog does later—but so what?) *Menace* contemplates a world in which feelings, except for those times they emerge in a bullet, are opaque. But what about a viewer's feelings that both these two murders are wrong? This can have, to put it mildly, a distancing effect. Caine's daddy is a coward and a bum. About those Koreans, you have to say they were right to be scared. Who's to say they wouldn't be smart to shoot first?

Skip the '80s and cut to Watts, 1993, when Caine, well into a career as a drug dealer, graduates high school. After Mom OD'd and Daddy was killed, he's been living with his Christian grandparents who're blithely unaware of his outside activities. One of the movie's laughs comes when Caine finds the couple enthralled by *It's a Wonderful Life*.

Featured in one of *Vanity Fair*'s "Vanities," Albert Hughes acknowledges influence and seems to supply motive, "We got tired of people thinking *Boyz* was the rawest shit they'd ever seen." In production notes, Allen describes their method as "journalistic." Clearly they considered *Boyz* sappy and preachy, about winners and weepers, and want to treat the real, hard thing itself, and in a way that audiences can't be complacent about.

The way I would put it, they don't like the genre: *Boyz* was essentially family melodrama whereas *Menace* follows the classic gangster pic, depicting an outlaw's rise and fall. (That on one level they know this is indicated by a quick shot of Caine watching Nick Ray's *They Live by Night*.) Caine starts out deprived, rises in a marginal underworld, indulges his consumers' appetites (the American way), gets a taste of love and a mentor's concern, and finally moves to get out, but too late.

Journalistic? Hardly. Caine's life is a series of set pieces that we've seen before here and there. What distinguishes it from previous inner-city stories like *Straight Out of Brooklyn* is not just its ethics but production money, and particularly the virtuosity of Lisa Rinzler's cinematography—a mix of De Palma point-of-view shots, music-video lyricism, and beautifully lit faces in the dead of night. *Menace*, I should mention, had a $2.5 million budget.

Ever since they originated in the '20s, gangster pictures have enjoyed (and usually profited from) a perceived relation to current events. Calls for censorship and regulation have always accompanied their releases. In an era when fear of guns is always with us, *Menace* seems to invite backlash and outrage. Defenders of crime pix used to point out that the average American would never actually lay eyes on a gangster, but today's moviegoer has a much better chance of facing an armed mugger or crazed IRT rider on the way home. It's interesting to see Medved's and now Auletta's attempts to shame studio and corporate execs into self-censorship by appealing to them as fathers. (Good luck.)

Boyz ended with anticipations of Morehouse and Spelman, college daze to come (the rental tape features Singleton plugging the United Negro College Fund). It had very specific messages to convey. *Menace* wants to jettison all this appeal to middle-class values, but of course it can't entirely because a convention so basic as narrative is rooted in morality.

Still, it tries. Personally, I'm extremely sorry to see the film violate the code that says scumbags get their due. This is the same formula that often sacrificed a hardworking black man, just doing his job, in order that we might know how evil, how undemocratic (un-American), the villains are. The psychotic punk, a fixture in gangster pix, is our means of locating pure evil; he lets us know that our hero, despite his scorn for propriety, isn't like him. In keeping O-Dog alive, *Menace* also implies that the Koreans' killing needn't be viewed as vicious—or at least not *all that* vicious. The Hugheses may be appealing to a segment of the audience that doesn't require cathartic revenge when it comes to Koreans, and gays (when O-Dog drills a crack addict who offers to "suck his dick"). Twice in the film, O-Dog gleefully watches the grocery murder on videotape, suggesting that the filmmakers may be trying to equate this tape with the real one showing a Korean shopkeeper (the one who got probation) shooting a teenage girl.

Not only do I dislike *Menace*'s racism, I don't like the way it caricatures Caine's grandparents, who presumably are all that stood between his destiny and O-Dog's. (You can repudiate without ridicule.)

In the end, of course, *Menace* can't avoid the rhetoric of melodrama. It's the allure of family and normal life that almost saves Caine. He may reject the child he's possibly conceived in a casual encounter, but he's drawn by an invitation from his upwardly mobile girlfriend, Ronnie (Jada Pinkett), to join her and her kid in a move to Atlanta. But since there's no mention of Morehouse here, what's Caine going to do in Atlanta except more dealing of drugs, more shooting of people who cross him?

The movie is riddled with too many psychological implausibilities. One minute Ronnie kicks Caine out for instructing her kid in the use of his gun, the next she's proposing. We never know what she's getting from him. I'm not talking about mysteries of human passion here, but about manipulation of material. Finding Ronnie hostessing a party for thugs, you wonder if you're at the right address. (Making her into the Miss Manners of the outlaw set might be comic if it didn't seem so cavalier with her character.)

The primary deficiency here, besides point of view, is script (credited to Tyger Williams). Even O-Dog, the movie's psycho, is dull and dopey. Try comparing him to Joe Pesci's character in *GoodFellas* or Michael Madsen's in *Reservoir Dogs*. Whoever financed this film would have done their investment a service by insisting on major rewrites.

Also reviewed in:
NEW REPUBLIC, 7/5/93, p. 26, Stanley Kauffmann
NEW YORK TIMES, 5/26/93, p. C13, Stephen Holden
VARIETY, 5/17/93, p. 96, Leonard Klady
WASHINGTON POST, 5/26/93, p. B1, Hal Hinson
WASHINGTON POST, 5/28/93, Weekend/p. 42, Desson Howe

METEOR MAN, THE

A Metro-Goldwyn-Mayer release of a Tinsel Townsend production.   *Producer:* Loretha C. Jones. *Director:* Robert Townsend. *Screenplay:* Robert Townsend. *Director of Photography:* John A. Alonzo. *Editor:* Adam Bernardi, Richard Candib, Andrew London, and Pam Wise. *Music:* Cliff Eidelman. *Music Editor:* Robin Eidelman, Jacqueline Tager, Virginia Ellsworth, and David Slusser. *Sound:* Mark Weingarten. *Sound Editor:* Richard Hymns and Tim Holland. *Casting:* Eileen Mack Knight. *Production Designer:* Toby Corbett. *Art Director:* Greg Papalia. *Set Designer:* William J. Newman II and Stephanie J. Gordon. *Set Decorator:* Kathryn Peters. *Special Effects:* Al DiSarro. *Visual Effects:* Bruce Nicholson. *Costumes:* Ruth Carter. *Make-up:* Edna Mae Sheen. *Stunt Coordinator:* Jeff Ward. *Running time:* 100 minutes. *MPAA Rating:* PG.

CAST: Robert Townsend (Jefferson Reed);   Marla Gibbs (Mrs. Reed);   Eddie Griffin (Michael);   Robert Guillaume (Mr. Reed);   James Earl Jones (Mr. Moses);   Roy Fegan (Simon);   Cynthia Belgrave (Mrs. Harris);   Marilyn Coleman (Mrs. Walker);   Don Cheadle (Goldilocks);   Bobby McGee (Uzi);   Bill Cosby (Marvin);   Big Daddy Kane (Pirate);   Frank Gorshin (Byers);   Sinbad (Malik);   Nancy Wilson (Mrs. Laws);   Luther Vandross (Jamison); Tiny Lister (Digit);   Jenifer Lewis (Mrs. Williams);   Stephanie Williams (Stacy);   Biz Markie (Drug Worker #1);   Beverly Johnson (Woman Doctor);   LaWanda Page (Old Nurse);   Lela Rochon (Vanessa);   Wallace Shawn (Mr. Little);   John Witherspoon (Clarence James Carter III); Charlayne Woodard (Janice Farrell);   Tommy R. Hicks (Officer Patterson);   Asia Dosreis (Squirrel);   Sam Jackson (Dre);   Barbara Montgomery (Dre's Mother);   George S. Allen III (Man);   Janice Garcia (Screaming Woman);   Deborah Lacey (TV Housewife);   Faizon Love (Husband);   Stu Gilliam (Head Physician);   Greg Littman (Doctor #1);   Angela Robinson (Nurse);   Joel Weiss (Orderly);   Larry A. Wiggs II (Karate Kid);   Shirley Jenkins (Bystander #1);   Don Reed (Drug worker #2);   Clayton Lebouef (Junkie);   Dierk Torsek (TV Newscaster).

LOS ANGELES TIMES, 8/6/93, Calendar/p. 10, Peter Rainer

Robert Townsend is working an agenda in his new film, "The Meteor Man," which he directed, wrote and stars in. It's about what happens when the decent, shy schoolteacher Jefferson Reed gets hit by a meteor and acquires the superpowers that enable him to combat the gang that is terrorizing his neighborhood. It's a fantasy intended to give inner-city black kids a superhero with real meaning in their lives.

The film (rated PG for scenes showing "children caught up in the perils of the urban environment") is also clearly meant to provide an alternative to the R-rated urban violence of films like "Boyz N the Hood" and "Menace II Society." There's violence in "The Meteor Man" but it's mostly a cheesier version of the whammo punch-outs in the "Superman" and "Batman" series. (Townsend may not realize that inner-city kids already use films like "Batman" for the same save-the-neighborhood fantasy function as "The Meteor Man.")

Despite its high-flown intentions, most of "The Meteor Man" comes across like a fairly clunky sitcom inflated with sequences of righteous do-goodismn. The righteousness has its reactionary side: it implies that movies depicting graphic inner-city violence are by definition exploitative and destructive.

Townsend plays his role with a serious undertone throughout—he's a comic on a mission. The neighborhood community—which includes Jefferson's irate father (Robert Guillaume), who stands up to the gangs, his mother (Marla Gibbs), and a goofy, weak-willed homebody (James Earl Jones)—frets and agonizes about how to survive the incursions of the dread Golden Lords gang.

But Townsend is also excited by the visual possibilities of the Lords—their sleek jackets and gold-tinted hair and don't-mess-with-me glowers are so much more stylish than anything else in the movie that the anti-gang message is obscured. The Lords are the bad guys but kids in the audience are more likely to be captivated by their "look" than by the fuddy-duddy goodness of the Meteor Man in his clunky armored costume.

This isn't the first time in the movies that the bad guys have turned out to be more exciting than the good guys, but Townsend could have done better by himself if he worked some wit, some snap, into his acting. Did he think Jefferson's heroism would be undercut by a little humor? It would have made him more heroic.

A lot of funny people pop in and out of "The Meteor Man," not always to best advantage. Bill Cosby has a cameo as a homeless man who also encounters the magical meteor, but most of his role appears to have ended up on the cutting room floor. His presence in the film is largely ceremonial—he seems to be on-screen in order to endorse Townsend's agenda. Sinbad has a funny bit in a hospital and, as a battle-ax nurse, Lawanda Page is in great glowering form. Rap artist Big Daddy Kane (looking none the worse for wear from "Posse") turns up as one of the Lords, and so do Naughty by Nature, Biz Markie and Cypress Hill. Even Luther Vandross makes a (wordless) appearance, heading up a crime syndicate with Frank Gorshin.

Townsend may want "The Meteor Man" to inspire inner-city community action as the way to squelch gangs but the movie doesn't really send that message. What we're left with is the stark fact that, in this embattled neighborhood, Meteor Man has to work alone on the clean up. (The Bloods-Crips truce is alluded to; they combine in the end to help defeat the Lords.) Townsend is plumping for community responsibility but his own superhero fantasies also come into play. He casts himself as the savior of the inner cities in "The Meteor Man." His humility is deafening.

NEW YORK POST, 8/6/93, p. 27, Lawrence Cohn

Robert Townsend realizes his boyhood dream of playing a superhero in the title role of "The Meteor Man," an entertaining and quite different take on the fantasy genre. Though aimed at older children, the picture should tickle their adult guardians.

The movie is a clever spoof that shows the problems confronting a friendly, neighborhood superhero. Townsend—who also directs—stars as Jeff Reed, a Caspar Milquetoast substitute teacher in Washington, D.C., who suffers a direct hit by a meteor.

He recuperates miraculously, sporting powers that include super-strength, X-ray vision, ability to fly (though Jeff's fear of heights has him patrolling the community at 3 feet off the ground), and a magical ability to assimilate the entire contents of a book by merely touching it.

Jeff's gung-ho mom (Marla Gibbs in a scene-stealing performance) fabricates a snazzy gray-and-green caped outfit that turns him into Meteor Man. The outfit owes more to Mighty Mouse than to DC or Marvel comics icons.

The key plot point is that Jeff remains as timid as Don Knotts even after gaining superhuman abilities. His neighbors have to force him to become an all-purpose do-gooder, cleaning up the local community from drug pushers, who form a gang of bleached-blond thugs of all ages known as the Golden Lords.

His efforts ultimately backfire thanks to limitations on his powers. In a Capra-esque ending, it falls to the average citizens of the 'hood, including Bloods and Crips gang members, to band together and protect themselves.

Besides Gibbs, there are some wacky turns by LaWanda Page as a nurse with the hots for Jeff; James Earl Jones, wearing wildly inappropriate wigs; and Bill Cosby as a homeless man who finds a piece of the meteorite and shares Jeff's super powers. Many musical personalities—ranging from Nancy Wilson and Luther Vandross to groups Cypress Hill and Naughty by Nature—pop up in strictly acting assignments.

Industrial Light and Magic's Bruce Nicholson delivers imaginative visual effects for the fantasy sequences, and by placing the action in deliberately run-down settings, Townsend avoids the pitfall of having the visuals overpower his message.

NEWSDAY, 8/6/93, Part II/p. 54, John Anderson

Filmmaker Robert Townsend's efforts to puncture myths about black Americans have had mixed results. With "Hollywood Shuffle," his caustic dismantling of long-running African-American movie stereotypes, he came up a winner. His follow-up, "The Five Heartbeats," basically a tribute to black music of the '60s, was needlessly embellished and had the soul wrung out of it.

Now, Townsend has decided to forget about existing mythology and create his own: a black superhero, and inner-city man whose basic goodness overcomes his basic timidity, and who uses what can only be considered divinely inspired power to thwart evil.

And while it's fantastic and cartoonish, "Meteor Man" is such a morally erect movie that it will leave audiences cheering. Despite a lot of emotional manipulation, the film has enough self-awareness—it knows it's goofy—that audiences should have no trouble laughing at, with, and in spite of Townsend's occasionally heavy-handed sermonizing.

The film is, essentially, a western: Schoolteacher Jefferson Reed (Townsend), the unassertive, apathetic hero, lives in a Washington, D.C., inner-city area controlled by the drug and death dealing Golden Lords. Bleached blonde, leather-clad and accompanied by the subsidiary Junior Lords (played by the young soul group Another Bad Creation) and Baby Lords (Townsend may have made the bad guys a bit too adorable), the Golden Lords crush anyone who gets in their way. And this includes Jefferson's parents (Robert Guillaume and Marla Gibbs).

While his parents organize block meetings and community watches and incur the wrath of the assorted Lords, Jefferson is convinced that nothing can be done. Even after an encounter with a meteor that leaves him with extraordinary powers, he's reluctant to use them against his oppressors. But even Jefferson can only absorb so much punishment. And so, Meteor Man, complete with tights and a cape, is born.

Robert Townsend the actor may have found his perfect role, which is fortunate: If "Meteor Man" does well, there will certainly be a "II," "III" and "IV." Jefferson is smart, kind, likable, but carries the kind of all-encompassing fear of the streets. In Townsend's view, Jefferson's attitude is part of the problem.

The director is not too subtle about any of his messages. That the father—whom Guillaume plays with his usual mix of bad attitude and good humor—is the lone crusader against evil is meant to embarrass the young and self-absorbed. Likewise the antics of Jefferson's pal Michael (Eddie Griffin), who steals the Meteor Man's costume to impress women. It's preachy, sure, but while Townsend wants to make people laugh, but he wants them to think too, an ambitious combination of intentions.

Townsend brings in cops and street gangs, good kids and bad kids, whites, blacks and Hispanics and tries to give this street comedy some universality. That he gives all sides equal weight is somewhat problematic: Is the political position of the Bloods and Crips (played by rap groups Naughty by Nature and Cypress Hill) as valid as the police who are ostensibly there to protect the community? Perhaps. Despite the provocative way Townsend sets up his subordinant characters, he doesn't pursue it any further than that.

The cast includes a lot of familiar faces: James Earl Jones, as a silly neighbor, Mr. Moses; Frank Gorshin (where's he been?) as the drug kingpin Byers; Nancy Wilson as Jefferson's school principal; Sinbad, Big Daddy Kane, Beverly Johnson, Wallace Shawn and, as Marvin, a homeless man who also has been affected by the meteor, Bill Cosby. It's a non-speaking part, if you don't count barking—as one of the results of their cosmic collision, both Jefferson and Marvin can speak to their dogs. But that's fitting, in a way. Cosby's appearance, like many of the cameos in "Meteor Man," are just unspoken blessings on Townsend's talented head.

SIGHT AND SOUND, 2/94, p. 58, Louise Gray

Mild-mannered teacher Jefferson Reed lives in a Washington DC neighbourhood terrorised by the Golden Lords gang. Struck one night by an emerald green meteor, Reed discovers he has super powers. Transformed into superhero Meteor Man, he begins to clean up the neighbourhood with such success that crime boss Byers gets the Lords to intervene. After several confrontations, Reed's powers start to wane. The local community action group suffers reprisals and want Reed to leave. After the Lords shoot his mother, Reed fights gang boss Simon and is re-energised when Marvin, a local tramp who possesses a meteor fragment, appears. Simon also gains super powers by touching the meteor but Reed defeats him. In his weakened state, however, he is unable to take on the newly arrived Byers and his henchmen. Two rival gangs, the Bloods and the Crips, to whom Meteor Man had previously brought peace, intervene. The police arrest Byers and the Lords.

There is not much to *The Meteor Man* beyond black actors and musicians combining to rewrite *Superman* for an inner-city experience. In his films *Hollywood Shuffle* and *The Five Heartbeats*, which parodied black aspirations in Hollywood and the record industry respectively, writer/director/ actor Robert Townsend gained a reputation as a comic who remained true to a black American base. This is fair enough. As America's black film output diversifies, Townsend represents an entertainment strand which, if not quite of Eddie Murphy status, is, at least, black-originated and controlled.

The desire to showcase black talent accounts for a whirlwind of names passing through—often so quickly that their presence is sadly negligible. Bill Cosby is limited to a few grunts, while James Earl Jones, normally an actor of presence and power, makes do with a wig-obsessed collector of vintage blues and jazz records. Luther Vandross takes a non-speaking role as a gangster, while rappers Another Bad Creation, Naughty By Nature and Cypress Hill all appear as gangs. Sitcom stars Robert Guillaume and Marla Gibbs are good for a few cackles but Townsend's lame script does few of them any favours.

Morality tales of the superhero sort require such directness to get their message across. In this case the message is one of collective responsibility for the safety of one's community. The Golden Lords may not be baddies in the same vicious league as those found in *Boyz N the Hood* or *New Jack City*, but they do represent the endemic problem of black-on-black crime. Recent black cinema has been viewed through a political lens by a media made uneasy about depictions of remorseless violence. *The Meteor Man* is no masterpiece but, in a climate where box-office success bears a correlation to the onscreen body count, Townsend is to be commended for attempting to redress the balance.

VILLAGE VOICE, 8/24/93, p. 64, Regina Raiford

Remember when Bill Cosby was cool? Let's take the way-back machine to the days of *I Spy*, when the Coz was a solid, suave model of bourgeois courage. In *The Meteor Man*, Cosby's cameo performance is limited to barking. This time around, writer-director Robert Townsend emerges as the great black middle-class hope.

Townsend takes the notion of the great race man to extremes; he makes his character, Jefferson Reed, not just, say, a well-meaning doctor in a poor neighborhood, but a bona fide crusader. Cosmic intervention has transformed a Milquetoast substitute teacher into a multi-talented superhero, and scenes straight out of *Greatest American Hero, Superman*, and *Thunderheart* help transform *Meteor Man* into a surprisingly funny movie.

More a cartoon than a comic book, *The Meteor Man* promotes individual responsibility, civic pride, and, well, a lot of other stuff I can't remember from social studies class. The director draws his lines thick and fast, making his villains blond supercrooks and organized crime types; his townsfolk cuddly, spirited senior citizens; and his gang-bangers GI Joe figurines.

Townsend's superhuman altruism and hokey humor balance each other. The funniest thing about *The Meteor Man*—outside of the hilarious voguing sequence—is that instead of being annoyed by its simple treatment of complex issues, you laugh. And yet even while I smirked at the film's frequent public service announcements, I wanted to believe urban blight could be solved so easily.

Also reviewed in:
CHICAGO TRIBUNE, 8/6/93, Friday, p. C, Clifford Terry
NEW YORK TIMES, 8/7/93, p. 9, Stephen Holden
VARIETY, 8/16/93, p. 39, Leonard Klady
WASHINGTON POST, 8/6/93, p. D6, Hal Hinson
WASHINGTON POST, 8/6/93, Weekend/p. 33, Desson Howe

MR. JONES

A TriStar Pictures release of a Rastar production. *Executive Producer:* Richard Gere and Jerry A. Baerwitz. *Producer:* Alan Greisman and Debra Greenfield. *Director:* Mike Figgis. *Screenplay:* Eric Roth and Michael Cristofer. *Story:* Eric Roth. *Director of Photography:* Juan Ruiz Anchia. *Editor:* Tom Rolf. *Music:* Maurice Jarre. *Music Editor:* Dan Carlin, Sr. *Sound:* Gene S. Cantamessa. *Sound Editor:* Fred J. Brown and Michele Sharp. *Casting:* Carrie Frazier and Shani Ginsberg. *Production Designer:* Waldemar Kalinowski. *Art Director:* Larry Fulton. *Set Designer:* Gae Buckley. *Set Decorator:* Florence Fellman. *Special Effects:* M. Kam Cooney. *Costumes:* Rita Ryack. *Make-up:* Tracey Gray. *Make-up (Ricard Gere):* Tom Lucas. *Stunt Coordinator:* Gary Hymes. *Running time:* 110 minutes. *MPAA Rating:* R.

CAST: Richard Gere (Mr. Jones);   Lena Olin (Libbie);   Anne Bancroft (Dr. Catherine Holland);   Tom Irwin (Patrick);   Delroy Lindo (Howard);   Bruce Altman (David);   Lauren Tom (Amanda);   Lisa Malkiewicz (Susan);   Thomas Kopache (Mr. Wilson);   Peter Jurasik (Dr. Rosen);   Leon Singer (Hot Dog Vendor);   Anna Maria Horsford (Judge Harris);   Edward Padilla (Bellboy);   Baha Jackson (Son);   Epatha Harris (Daughter);   Anne Lange (Therapist); Kelli Williams (Kelli);   Mark Lowenthal (Richard);   Joyce Guy and Marjorie Lovett (Nurses); Sal Lopez (Henry);   Scott Thomson (Conrad);   Bill Moseley (Worker);   Barry Neikrug (Piano Salesman);   Thomas Mikal Ford (Arnie/Violent Patient);   Lela Ivey (Lisa);   Valente Rodriguez (Orderly);   Dinah Lenney (Registrar);   Laura O'Loughlin (Young Girl);   Marguerite Pini (Girlfriend);   Peter Vogt (Bank Supervisor);   Deryn Warren (Saleswoman);   David Brisbin (Mr. Warner);   Dana Lee (Mr. Chang);   Irene Tsu (Mrs. Chang);   Kathy Kinney (Homeless Lady); Annie McEnroe (Crying Woman);   Maury Efrems (Crying Man);   Albert Henderson and John Durbin (Patients);   Roman Cisneros (Public Defender);   Lucinda Jenney (Christine);   Donald Barra (Orchestra Conductor);   Taylor Negron (Motorcycle Man).

LOS ANGELES TIMES, 10/8/93, Calendar/p. 4, Peter Rainer

In "Mr. Jones" Richard Gere plays a manic-depressive who is a junkie for his highs. We first see him fast-talking his way onto a construction site, where he hammers a few nails and then ascends to a high beam. A plane zooms overhead as Mr. Jones—the only name he volunteers for himself—prepares for his own lift-off. What follows is a movie with its own wild mood-swings: Jones moves in and out of his highs as he moves in and out of mental institutions.

It's a showboat performance in a showboat role, the kind most actors would commit mayhem for. (Gere is also the film's co-executive producer.) Actors perhaps respond instinctively to manic-depressive disorder. In performance terms, it guarantees a full range of feeling, but, more than that, it's a heightened, almost expressionist recasting of an actor's professional life, with its abrupt alternations of elation and dejection.

The disorder also lends itself to all manner of mythic/metaphorical grandstanding about why these manic highs are more exciting, more "creative" than the mundane energies of "ordinary" people. "Mr. Jones" tries to convey Jones' pain but it's also trying to romanticize it.

It's the old "Equus" agenda all over again—normalcy wilts under the hot glare of the psychologically ravaged. The sane envy the mad. Jones' psychiatrist, Dr. Libbie Bowen (Lena Olin), is recently divorced and, despite her air of reasonableness, at odds with herself. She's looking for succor. Jones—who has an uncanny way of instantly sizing up people's weak spots—recognizes her desire to shake out her routine. The director, Mike Figgis, and screenwriters, Michael Cristofer and Eric Roth, don't downplay Jones' illness but, compared to Libbie's quiet normality, her unexpressed desire to be "different," he shines. As Libbie becomes dangerously, and unethically, attached to Jones, the film moves closer to its own dubious conundrum: Who can tell the patient from the therapist?

"This is not a disease. This is who I am," Jones shouts to Libbie near the end, and then he adds, "I *like* who I am." The movie (rated R for language) might not seem so lopsided if Libbie were a more powerful presence, if her empathy had the same glow as Jones' mania. But Libbie seems to lose her smarts fairly early on; the filmmakers never really dramatize the conflict between her scruples and her heart. Olin is such a remarkable actress that some of this conflict comes through anyway, but why is it that so often women are cast as smart, caring professionals only to lose their capabilities in the face of the first strong man they cross paths with?

Why, for example, didn't the moviemakers think to have Libbie help Jones through his love of music? It's established early on that he was a gifted music student, and there's a fine scene where we see him saunter into a piano and organ store and play a classical piece, quietly and full of feeling. The music calms him in a way that nothing else in the movie does. Later, he attends a symphonic concert and, ecstatic, rushes to the podium to conduct Beethoven's "Ode to Joy." (When asked later, at a competency hearing, why he did it, Jones replies that the conductor's tempo was too slow—and he's right.)

The filmmakers are so driven to show us Mr. Jones as a harrowing free spirit that they don't put much faith in his redemption. They're as hooked on Jones the high-flyer as Libbie is.

NEW YORK POST, 10/8/93, p. 44, Michael Medved

Moviegoers beware: the new Richard Gere picture "Mr. Jones" has been released with the year's most shamelessly dishonest promotional campaign.

Ads for the film feature a huge closeup of two smiling lovers happily nuzzling one another, and then another image of the hero, standing exultant on a windswept beach. The tag line—"Everything That Makes Him Dangerous Makes Her Love Him Even More"—only encourages the assumption that this is a heart-tugging, feel-good, love-conquers-all melodrama.

If you're foolish enough to fall for the bait and go to the theater with these expectations, you're in for an evening of shock therapy. What stylish British director Mike Figgis ("Stormy Monday," "Internal Affairs") has actually created here is a bleak, occasionally horrifying, and deeply depressing exploration of bi-polar affective disorder—better known as manic-depressive illness; the much-heralded love story enters the film only at the very end as an unconvincing afterthought.

The main character is a mysterious, brilliant, charming but profoundly disturbed patient known only as "Mr. Jones" (Gere) who is hospitalized in an unidentified city (it's actually San Diego) after he has threatened to "fly" off the top of a multi-story construction site. He's later released only to disrupt a local performance of Beethoven's Ninth by jumping onto the stage and trying to force the conductor to pick up the tempo.

Back at the psychiatric institution, he begins working with lovely Lena Olin ("The Unbearable Lightness of Being," "Enemies—A Love Story"), a staff shrink from Sweden. The gray monotony of her depressed and lonely life (her husband has just left her for a standard-issue blonde bimbo) contrasts with the Technicolor highs and lows of her prize patient.

To its considerable credit, this picture never shows Olin helping Gere "get better." It suggests instead that his condition will probably be a life sentence because he cherishes his manic moments too much to trade them for a course of stabilizing medication.

Gere is utterly spell-binding in this showy role; in fact, if the picture as a whole weren't such a dreary dud, his performance would probably generate Oscar talk. Along with his psycho-killer-cop in "Internal Affairs" (also for director Figgis), this is the best work of Gere's career.

The problem is that spending time with Mr. Jones—for members of the audience as well as the other characters in the film—is an exhausting and seemingly pointless trial. We don't really know him any better at the soggy, sappy end of the story than we did at its arresting opening.

Nor do we understand the supposedly dedicated doctor who ultimately shows her concern for her patient by going to bed with him. The implicit suggestion that her love is all he needs to happily cure his mood disorder is not only asinine, it's offensive—and it runs counter to everything we've seen in the film's two previous hours.

In the end, the internal contradictions of "Mr. Jones" help this somber stinker to fail on every level.

NEWSDAY, 10/8/93, Part II/p. 95, Gene Seymour

Somewhere beneath the sleek confusion of "Mr. Jones," there is a good idea that still needs deeper exploration: Where does science put the boundary line between creative behavior and clinical neurosis?

Yes, "One Flew Over the Cuckoo's Nest," "King of Hearts" and a lot of other movies have had a go at the concept. But those films, made years before, dared to unsettle, enlighten and embolden the audience toward thinking anew about so-called "craziness."

Early on, "Mr. Jones" shows signs of making even further advances on this theme. But, then, as with just about every other Hollywood product with Big Ideas, the movie cops out on its aspirations by drifting into a safe, conventional romance. Now it's true that when you have two people as pretty as Richard Gere and Lena Olin in lead roles, there's no way romance can be avoided. But it would have been nice if someone at the controls at least *tried*.

The news here isn't all bad. As the title character, a mood-swinging enigma in two-toned cowboy boots, Gere displays the gonzo bravado that worked so well for him in the role of the corrupt cop in "Internal Affairs," which was also directed by "Jones'" director Mike Figgis.

Jones—we never know his first name—is saved from suicide by a construction worker (played with quiet power by Delroy Lindo) and taken to a psychiatric clinic where Olin, playing a psychiatrist with troubling moods of her own, becomes involved with his case.

Like just about everyone else who comes into his view, she is charmed by Jones and fascinated with his sudden flashes of penetrating insight—which make up just one of the many fascinating aspects of this story that are just picked up and dropped. He's supposed to be some kind of musical genius. But we never get to know exactly where he played, why he took up carpentry—and how he managed to scrape together the $12,500 in his bank account.

None of these issues figure very much in explaining why Jones gets higher-than-high one minute and lower-than-low the next. In fact, the film ties much of his present state to a woman in his past. When said woman's name is mentioned by Olin, Gere freaks, walks out, is pursued in the rain by Olin and, in what must be the most clumsily staged love scene in recent memory, they fall into each other's arms.

Ah, zo, a comic Viennese shrink would mutter. *All zat he needed was der love, eh? Zounds verrrrry zimple.* And it *is* just a little too simple. If it were on the couch, "Mr. Jones" would be told by its therapist, "You're really blocking, man."

SIGHT AND SOUND, 10/94, p. 50, Geoffrey Macnab

A man turns up at a building site, saying he is a carpenter in search of work. The foreman tells him there is none going, but the man persists and is eventually allowed to join the rest of the crew on the roof of a house under construction. He has scarcely started his job than he walks along a high ledge, announcing he wants to fly. He is saved from falling by his colleague, Howard, and taken to a mental hospital. Here, as he lies drugged on his bed, he first sees Dr Libbie Bowen. He tells her his name is Jones. Despite Bowen's misgivings, Jones discharges himself. He heads straight for the bank, withdraws all his cash, and goes on a lunch date with the cashier, dispensing $100 notes to all and sundry. The date ends with him taking the cashier to a Beethoven concert. He marches up to the stage and starts conducting the orchestra himself. For his efforts, he is rushed back to the hospital. Bowen realises he is a manic depressive and tries to have him committed. However, at court, he appears lucid and charming to the judge, who lets him go free. He hitches a ride back to town with Bowen. They stop on the beach for a snack and soon strike up a rapport. Shortly after, Jones readmits himself, hoping to find a medical cure for his condition. As his treatment proceeds, he and Dr Bowen grow closer. He saves her life when another patient attacks her. The treatment continues, without much success. Bowen discovers from the bank cashier that Jones had talked about being in love with a woman called Ellen, a musician who had died many years before. Bowen investigates, discovers Ellen is alive and well, and confronts him with the information. Jones, furious at her prying, discharges himself and walks off. Bowen pursues him, and admits her deep feelings for him. They embrace and become lovers. Bowen realises she has committed a serious breach of professional etiquette. Egged on by a jealous colleague, she asks to be removed from the Jones case and later tenders her resignation. Jones is transferred to another hospital, but again manages to bike and rides round to collect his carpentry tools from Howard. His friend alerts the hospital that he is worried that Jones is about to try his 'flying trick' again. Bowen is notified, and rushes round, to find Jones perched on the roof. Eventually, she manages to lure him back from the brink.

In its original cut, *Mr Jones* was evidently a troublesome case: a surly, downbeat fable in strong need of some Hollywood-style therapy before it could be released. ("It's a piece of shit," was studio executive Ray Stark's reported response after a preview screening.) In the doctored version, what started as the story of a manic depressive emerges as something more akin to a conventional melodrama, where the patient's mental state is merely another barrier the couple must overcome in the name of true romance. The posters give the game away: "Everything That Makes Him Dangerous Makes Him Love Her Even More". While this process of sanitisation doesn't make for a particularly satisfactory film, it seems perversely in keeping with the material. "What do you want? To make me ordinary?" Mr Jones barks at his psychiatrist lover. It's a question director Mike Figgis could equally well ask of the studios.

There's no denying that *Mr Jones* is a botched, chimerical affair, yanking art-house psycho-drama and upbeat love story together, and invoking all the usual clichés about the inspired mad-man: Jones played Mozart at the age of three, had read "everything" by the time he was twelve, was "the centre of the universe" at 18, and in a mental asylum by his mid-20s. It's hardly the most original of resumes, and seems all the more hackneyed when combined with the fact that he is portrayed as a blue-collar type, ostensibly a carpenter. Sometimes, he even seems like a composite of Jack Nicholson's famous early roles: the oilman/pianist of *Five Easy Pieces* or the not-so-mad McMurphy of *One Flew Over the Cuckoo's Nest*. Lena Olin's psychiatrist bears an uncanny resemblance to Bergman in *Spellbound*, and the revelation of the traumatic incident in Jones' past, is as perfunctory as they come. Certain scenes, notably Jones and Bowen's embrace in the pouring rain to the accompaniment of Richard Clayderman-style music on the soundtrack, are nothing short of embarrassing.

Figgis' own cut of the movie is unlikely to see the light of day. As matters stand, it's hard to spot the joins and work out where his influence begins and ends. (One thing is for certain: the music—always an intrinsic part of a Figgis film—is not as he wished it.) However, even in its present, bowdlerized state, *Mr Jones* has considerable fascination. At least, the premise is ambitious. And Jones is a highly appropriate role for Gere. Right from *Looking for Mr Goodbar* onwards, he has always been prepared to tackle characters who strain toward psychosis and blur the lines between hero and villain; to play gigolos, pimps and delinquents. He starts *Mr Jones* in manic groove, taking his cue from the James Brown song, 'I Feel Good', he wakes up to. Within minutes, he is strutting his way along the narrow ledge of a high building, stretching his arms towards the planes overhead and threatening to fly. Then, to top that, he steals the baton from a conductor at a classical concert and steers the orchestra and chorus through some rousing, up-tempo Beethoven. There's even a parody of his part in *Pretty Woman*, where he withdraws all his money from the bank, takes the cashier on an afternoon date, and dispenses $100 notes wherever he goes. ("It's like trying to stop a space shuttle with a rubber band," somebody observes.) In these exhilarating early sequences, his antics are matched by the vertiginous camera-work. Unfortunately, though, he is only allowed to give half a performance: as his downside, his depressions, are largely skirted over, it is made to seem that his pranks have nothing to do with his condition, and are little more than showy histrionics.

It is all too easy to take refuge in the *Magnificent Ambersons* myth and blame a film's shortcomings on the studio butchers. Figgis' forthcoming *The Browning Version*, after all, manages to be dreary without any outside help. Still, for anybody who saw his work with Gere on *Internal Affairs*, there must be an overwhelming suspicion that *Mr Jones*, in its present form, is scarcely the picture Figgis set out to make.

VILLAGE VOICE, 10/26/93, p. 64, Laurie Stone

Richard Gere's hair should get a screen credit of its own, this silver corona that billows and cavorts, a forest animal—call it a shmink. The rest of him isn't bad, either, which is fortunate, since there is little besides Gere-gazing in this intensely silly psychoromance. Gere is the eponymous Mr. Jones, a loony whom we meet in a manic phase. At a building site, he thinks he can fly; at a concert, he leaps on stage to conduct. When he crashes, he abstains from showers and slumps (except his hair).

He's in and out of a mental hospital, where he meets shrink Libbie (Lena Olin), who is beautiful and has big auburn hair but is less convincing as a doc than is Gere as a patient. It's not her acting but the script, by Eric Roth and Michael Cristofer, a woozy pastiche of mental-case movies: defense-of-sanity scenes out of *Nuts*, the theme of the madman artist out of *Equus*, passion between analyst and patient out of *Spellbound*. There is no credibility in any direction.

Characters are lazily popped in and out: a man Mr. Jones meets for five minutes materializes into an intimate friend; Anne Bancroft, who gets third billing as the hospital's head of staff, is mostly used in background shots. Mr. Jones's problem, we're told, is chemical *and* psychological, but through session after session, we learn nothing about his background, except that he was precocious at music and math. We don't even learn his first name.

Murk is good, because, hey, if we saw the underpinnings of psychosis we might squirm when Libbie sleeps with her patient and shucks her medical career to be with him. "Now what?" Mr. Jones says, smiling charmingly. A shampoo?

Also reviewed in:
CHICAGO TRIBUNE, 10/8/93, Friday/p. D, Johanna Steinmetz
NEW REPUBLIC, 11/8/93, p. 32, Stanley Kauffmann
NEW YORK TIMES, 10/8/93, p. C10, Janet Maslin
VARIETY, 10/18/93, p. 50, Todd McCarthy
WASHINGTON POST, 10/8/93, p. D1, Hal Hinson
WASHINGTON POST, 10/8/93, Weekend/p. 36, Desson Howe

MR. NANNY

A New Line Cinema release of an Entertainment Film production. *Executive Producer:* Benni Korzen and Michael Harpster. *Producer:* Bob Engelman. *Director:* Michael Gottlieb. *Screenplay:* Edward Rugoff and Michael Gottlieb. *Director of Photography:* Peter Stein. *Editor:* Earl Ghaffari and Michael Ripps. *Music:* David Johansen and Brian Koonin. *Music Editor:* Chris McGeary. *Sound:* Henri Lopez. *Sound Editor:* Marc D. Fishman. *Casting:* Fern Champion and Mark Paladini. *Production Designer:* Don De Fina. *Art Director:* Jose Duarte. *Set Designer:* Ed Castineira. *Set Decorator:* Barbara Peterson. *Set Dresser:* Mark Dane. *Special Effects:* J.B. Jones. *Costumes:* Marianna Astrom-De Fina. *Make-up:* Diane Maurno and Linda Schonning. *Make-up (Terry "Hulk" Hogan):* Cheri Montesanto-Medcalf. *Stunt Coordinator:* Artie Malesci. *Running time:* 83 minutes. *MPAA Rating:* Rated PG.

CAST: Afa Anoai "Alfa" (Himself); Brutus Beefcake (Himself); Butch Brickell (Phone Man); James Coffey (Repo Man); Dondi Dahlin (Receptionist); Dennis Deveaugh (Guard #2); Kelly Erin-Welton (Nanny); Danny Fotou (Bully #2); Robert Gorman (Alex Mason, Jr.); Sherman Hemsley (Burt Wilson); Joe Hess (Guard #3); Terry "Hulk" Hogan (Sean Armstrong); John F. Hoye (Guard #4); David Johansen (Thanatos); Peter Kent (Wolfgang); Mother Love (Corinne); Artie Malesci (Skipper); David Mandel (Guard #1); Marc Mercury (Security Guard); Sandy Mielke (Principal); Jeff Moldovan (Jocko); Raymond O'Connor (Frank Olsen); Fred Ornstein (Cabbie); Darci Osiecky (Teacher); Jen Sung Outerbridge (Kojiro); Austin Pendleton (Alex Mason, Sr.); Hope Pomerance (Secretary); Timothy A. Powell (Lieutenant); Joshua Santiago (Bully #1); George "The Animal" Steele (Himself); Madeline Zima (Kate Mason).

LOS ANGELES TIMES, 10/11/93, Calendar/p. 3, Kevin Thomas

The notion of wrestling's blonde behemoth Hulk Hogan caring for a couple of poor little rich kids has sweetly comic possibilities, but they're flattened out in the needlessly crass and lethally heavy-handed "Mr. Nanny". Hogan, who is 6 feet, 6 inches tall and weighs in at 293 pounds, comes across as a genial giant with a sense of humor and a pleasing personality, but he's no actor.

Luckily, he's surrounded by such reliable pros as Austin Pendleton and Sherman Hemsley.

Pendleton, who's unusually well-cast, plays a scientific genius who's become a computer tycoon. He's just invented an anti-ballistic device that has brought him a string of threatening calls and has hired Hogan, a down-on-his-luck wrestler, as a bodyguard for his two children (Robert Gorman, Madeline Zima).

Pendleton's Alex Mason is a loving father but also a self-absorbed workaholic widower. Spoiled on the one hand and neglected on the other, his children have turned into a pair of monsters with a relentless passion for playing pranks on their endless string of nannies. Clearly, they've met their match in Hogan's Sean Armstrong, who finds himself playing parent as well as protector.

It's too bad that director and co-writer (with Edward Rugoff) Michael Gottlieb didn't set his sights higher, because his movie should have been so much more fun. Gottlieb possesses little sense of rhythm and pacing, elements crucial to making Hogan's attempt at acting as effective as possible and to keeping the action and the comedy fast and furious.

But "Mr. Nanny" (rated PG for comic action and mild language) is a leaden business from start to finish, and the film's stars, plus Hemsley as Hogan's lively side-kick, David Johansen as the crazed villain of the piece and Mother Love as Pendleton's feisty cook, can't overcome Gottlieb's shortcomings.

SIGHT AND SOUND, 5/93, p. 52, Leslie Felpern Sharman

Sean Armstrong, a former professional wrestler, is persuaded by his old ex-manager Burt Wilson to act as bodyguard for the children of inventor Alex Mason, despite his avowed dislike of children. Mason fears that they will be kidnapped by psychotic criminal genius Tommy Thanatos, intent on procuring Mason's company's newest microchip, one internal to the guidance of the new Peacemaker anti-missile device. Temporarily forced to act as nanny as well as body-guard, Sean is beset by the children's attempts to drive him off with a series of boobytraps involving tripwires, bowling balls and electrocutions. Despite their violent machinations, Sean recognizes that they are only desperate for attention, even if only the punitive variety. Gradually, he comes to win their love and respect by demonstrating toughness, tenacity and a willingness to wear a tutu. Despite his vigilance, Thanatos manages to kidnap first Mason and then the children and Burt, demanding that Sean bring the microchip in exchange for the hostages. Sean discovers the hide-out, and with the help of Burt and the whole family, Thanatos and his henchmen are vanquished. Sean bids an affectionate farewell to the family, and attempts to ride off on his motorcycle, but the children's last practical joke keeps him behind.

Tightly packed into his matching denim shirt and jeans, dense moustache a-bristle, his tanned body pumped to perfection and lovingly fetishised by the camera, Hulk Hogan's persona in *Mr. Nanny* more closely approximates the gay love objects in Tom of Finland's illustrations than the resolute heterosexuality of Arnold Schwarzenegger in *Kindergarten Cop*, which the film desperately tries to evoke. The film conflates the current Tough-Man-made-New-Man theme with a *Home Alone*-style slapstick plot, the ingenious children pitting their lilliputian wits against the impervious body of the adult man. The final plot solution reconstitutes a new nuclear family, after both Hulk's and the father's sentimental re-education, spurred by a villain who mocks "the family I never had and never wanted".

So far, so straight. However, a number of surface elements cheekily conspire to produce a potentially gay subtext: the dress code cited above (extending as far as cross-dressing), the emphasis on male bonding, the prevalence of sado-masochism, and an endearing sense of camp self-mockery which reaches its apotheosis in a flashback sequence to when all the balding male protagonists once had resplendent heads of hair. Most importantly, the failure to provide any significant female love interest over the age of consent necessitates the creation of an unconventional two-male-parent-plus-children family unit at the film's close. *My Two Big Daddies and the Muscle Academy* would have been a more apt title.

Without reading against the grain, *Mr Nanny* is a banal exercise in low-budget comedy, its best jokes stolen from Tex Avery and the *Little Rascals* series. A 'perverse' reading, however, is more fun. The homoerotic subtext would suggest that Hollywood in the Clinton era is rethinking the premises of, as one character puts it, "your average American dysfunctional family".

Also reviewed in:
VARIETY, 4/12/93, p. 75, Derek Elley
WASHINGTON POST, 10/13/93, p. B2, Jane Horwitz

MR. WONDERFUL

A Warner Bros. release of a Samuel Goldwyn Company production.   *Producer:* Marianne Moloney.   *Director:* Anthony Minghella.   *Screenplay:* Amy Schor and Vicki Polon.   *Director of Photography:* Geoffrey Simpson.   *Editor:* John Tintori.   *Music:* Michael Gore.   *Music Editor:* Jeff Carson.   *Sound:* Chris Newman and (music) Joel W. Moss.   *Sound Editor:* Douglas Murray.   *Casting:* David Rubin and Debra Zane.   *Production Designer:* Doug Kraner.   *Art Director:* Steve Saklad.   *Set Decorator:* Alyssa Winter.   *Set Dresser:* Dennis Zack, Anne Wenniger, and Chris Nelson.   *Special Effects:* Steve Kirshoff.   *Costumes:* John Dunn.   *Make-up:* Bernadette Mazur.   *Stunt Coordinator:* Jery Hewitt.   *Running time:* 98 minutes.   *MPAA Rating:* PG-13.

CAST: Jennifer Alonzi and Frank E. Smurlo, Jr. (Couple on Train);   Bruce Altman (Mr. Wonderful);   Peter Appel (Harry);   Paul Bates (Marlon);   James Bulleit (Lecturer #1);   Bernard Currid (Botanic Garden Worker);   Matt Dillon (Gus);   Vincent D'Onofrio (Dominic);   Arabella Field (Patti);   James Gandolfini (Mike);   Tanesha Marie Gary (Background Singer #1);   William Goldberg (Muriel Manners' Husband);   David Barry Gray (Pope);   Geoffrey Grider (Joe the Waiter);   William Duff Griffin (Mr. Christie);   Luis Guzman (Juice);   Saverio Guerra (Man #1—Paul);   Angela Hall (Betty);   Jessica Harper (Funny Face);   Dan Hedaya (Harvey);   Carol Honda (Emergency Room Nurse);   Wallace Hornady (Organist);   William Hurt (Tom);   John Christopher Jones (Miller);   Raymond Michael Karl (Lecturer #2);   Mare Kenney (Woman in Elevator);   Bruce Kirby (Dante);   Eric Kollegger (George);   Adam Lefevre (Kevin Klassic);   Renee Lippin (Hannah);   James Lorinz (Man #2—Joe);   Bruce Macvittie (Martin);   Joanna Merlin (Loretta);   Myreah Moore (Background Singer #2);   Harsh Nayyar (Credit Union Officer);   Joe Paparone (Building Super);   Mary-Louise Parker (Rita);   Frank Pellegrino (Man in Elevator);   John Rothman (Ralph);   Annabella Sciorra (Lee);   Brooke Smith (Jan);   Vanessa Aspillaga Vazquez (Marie);   Floyd Vivino (M.C.);   Mary Louise Wilson (Muriel Manners);   Hans Zarins (Boy Soprano).

LOS ANGELES TIMES, 10/15/93, Calendar/p. 8, Peter Rainer

"Mr. Wonderful" is a terrific little movie. There's nothing terribly startling or original about it, and yet it doesn't seem like any other film. Director Anthony Minghella and screenwriters Amy Schor and Vicki Polon understand the secret of a good romantic comedy: The characters must come first.

Gus (Matt Dillon) is a Con Edison electrical worker in New York divorced from his high school sweetheart Lee (Annabella Sciorra) and involved with Rita (Mary-Louise Parker), a nurse who wants him to stop stuttering the "C" word and commit to a relationship. Gus' Con Ed buddies (wonderfully played by David Barry Gray, Dan Hedaya, Bruce Kirby and Luis Guzman) want him to go in on a scheme to restore a bowling alley in their Brooklyn neighborhood, but he's strapped by alimony payments. A new scheme is hatched: Gus seeks out a Mr. Wonderful for Lee to marry.

This may sound schematic and conventional, but it's done with a knowing wink. The characters themselves are aware of how cockeyed and contrived their predicament is. Gus and Lee go at each other in a way that tells you they still care. Their bickering has a well-worn, almost tender undercurrent. They understand on some level that their split was nobody's fault, really—they've just grown apart—and that keeps the rancor from turning poisonous.

Gus is a good-time working-class Brooklyn guy and Lee just wants to leave all that neighborhood stuff behind her, so she's enrolled in college and works in Brooklyn's Botanic Gardens. She's having an affair with a married professor (William Hurt, in an effective cameo) who likes to snuggle up with a volume of John Donne. She's attempting to "better" herself, but she has enough humor about her current situation to know that she's not really happy; she misses the juices in her old life without fully acknowledging the loss.

When Gus and Lee are together they become cruder versions of who they really are. Gus is by no means dumb, but he enjoys acting lunky and inarticulate; his prole charm is his badge of honor. Lee seems like a frizzy-haired hippie student—even her affair with the professor seems like a part of the act. (With her Italian-Catholic upbringing, it's the part she's least comfortable with.) This role-playing between them is a taunt, but it's also a mating dance. Rita, who genuinely loves Gus, picks up on this right away, which is why she joins in the search for a Mr. Wonderful for Lee.

One of the most humane touches in "Mr. Wonderful" is the way Rita comes across as both desperate and proud. It would have been easy for the filmmakers to make her a conniving shrew but, as Mary-Louise Parker plays her, she's marvelously intuitive and understanding. There's a great scene where some of her women friends convince her that the way to snare Gus is to carry out an old folk legend and cry tears into his food. She's flabbergasted by the idea but she ends up rubbing her tears into his gnocchi—she knows how foolish she looks but she wants him so much she'll try anything.

Gus has his own boisterous foolishness. Convinced he can find a new mate for Lee—with Lee's grudging assent—he cajoles the men on his lunch-break, inspecting their lunch-boxes to figure out who the bachelors are. He's a knight errant in search of the man who will make Lee forget him, and so on some level he must want his mission to fail.

When he meets Lee's professor lover face to face, he walks away the winner; he sizes him up as a cad with such withering split-second insight that your whole estimation of Gus is instantly upgraded. And yet the filmmakers give all the people in this film their due, even the professor. His last scene with Lee is just right: It has the awkward, bereft politeness of a final parting between two people who have nothing more to offer each other except regrets.

Minghella, who has written extensively for the stage and television in England, is known here primarily for directing "Truly, Madly, Deeply," which suffered from an overdose of rue but had a standout performance from Juliet Stevenson. In "Mr. Wonderful," the performances are so heartfelt that your sympathies are never narrowed to a single character.

In terms of its emotional range, there's a lot to go around in this film. Dillon develops a comic style out of Gus' *lumpen* swagger and slouch that, in its depth of feeling, goes way beyond shtick. Sciorra has never before seemed so ripely funny or sexy. And there are always wonderful surprises, like the moment when one of Gus' friends, whose girlfriend is a real sexpot, whispers to him, "Ever hear of candy pants?" Or the moment when the local pharmacist, played by Vincent D'Onofrio, confesses his love to Lee by admitting he remembers her when they were 12 years old in Catholic school together.

"Mr. Wonderful" is unusual for a romantic comedy because it recognizes that there are real losses in the mating game; it doesn't paper over the hurt that good, caring people experience. And yet everyone seems happy by the end. They may not all get what they want, but they've lived through their longings and they're grateful to be in the game. They're revivified by their ardor.

NEW YORK POST, 10/15/93, p. 28, Bill Hoffmann

"Mr. Wonderful," a delightful romantic comedy set in New York City, tackles an age-old problem: the difficult, sometimes impossible task of shaking the memory of an ex-lover from your brain and moving on with your life.

That's exactly what Gus (Matt Dillon), a Brooklyn-born homeboy who works for Con Ed, wants to do with his ex-wife, Lee (Annabella Sciorra).

The one-time high-school sweethearts split up when they found their goals in life skyrocketing in different directions.

Gus dreams of reopening the old, dilapidated bowling alley of his youth. Lee attends college, looking for a little knowledge and a new husband with whom to start a family.

Unfortunately for Gus, he'll never be able to get his project off the ground as long as he has to pay alimony to Lee.

So he sets out to find her a new mate—and that's when the old emotions start, stirring.

Lee has been having an uninspired affair with her married professor, Tom (William Hurt), a pompous intellectual sleaze who seduces his students while feeding them the love poems of John Donne.

So she accepts Gus' offer, and almost instantly she's stuck in a swamp of suitors who are too nerdy or sex-crazed to last an entire date.

It all boils down to: Will Gus and Lee get a second chance at love in the Big Apple? If you've seen "Sleepless in Seattle," you already know the answer.

In many ways, this is a New York version of "Sleepless"—lovable misfits somehow ending up together despite impossible odds.

While it doesn't boast the emotional, hit-driven sound track of the Tom Hanks-Meg Ryan film, "Mr. Wonderful" rings truer.

The stunning location photography by Geoffrey Simpson overcomes the episodic, TV-drama feel the film occasionally falls into. But just like all films shot here, be ready to suspend belief:

Could anybody really have a passionate makeout scene standing between two speeding subway cars without tragic and grisly results?

And while this may be the only film in history to boast being shot with the "enthusiastic cooperation" of Con Ed—would a Con Ed worker really make love with his girlfriend in a sewer?

Matt Dillon is likable enough, although, as in earlier efforts, he has a problem warming up to the camera. He's too stiff and has too much attitude to completely pull it off—but there's a leading man in there somewhere, and maybe he'll emerge some day.

Annabella Sciorra shows why she's fast becoming a major Hollywood star. Tough yet extremely vulnerable, Sciorra can switch from heart-wrenching sorrow to great happiness with just the wrinkle of her forehead and curl of her lips.

William Hurt, now gracefully stepping into middle age, is perfect as the pathetic prof—the epitomy of every talented but emotionally crippled educator who has used his classroom as a candy store.

There are millions of Guses' and Lees out there riding the subways, walking the streets, lying alone in their beds, lost in painful thought about a broken romance and what might have been.

Like every traditional Hollywood heart-tugger, "Mr. Wonderful" hits all the buttons and shows that despite all that can screw up in New York, love still manages to conquer all.

NEWSDAY, 10/15/93, Part II/p. 69, John Anderson

"Mr. Wonderful" may represent a first among romantic comedies: It starts with the happy ending, and leaves you with the feeling that heartache is just around the corner.

"Somebody explain to me," asks Lee (Annabella Sciorra), "how I get in a situation where my ex-husband is finding me dates."

Well, it's like this: You marry your childhood sweetheart, Gus (Matt Dillon), because he's all you know. Then, after a few years, you get tired of Gus and the suffocating ethnic neighborhood in which you grew up, go to college, open up new horizons and make a better person of yourself.

Gus, meanwhile, is looking to go in with four friends on reopening the local bowling alley, and doesn't have the money because he's paying you alimony (you're liberated, but not stupid). And how does one stop paying alimony? Bingo (well, not bingo, but you know what I mean).

In "Mr. Wonderful," Sciorra and Dillon do the dance of the ex-lovers very nicely. But do we want them to get back together? Outside of the affair she's having with her married professor (William Hurt) Lee's life is pretty good. And Gus is a dinosaur, a guy who approaches prospects for Lee with, "You want to date a fabulous looking broad?" Let's face it, he's never going to change.

But viewers may as well cast their doubts to the wind, because the film is one long foregone conclusion. And just in case we harbor hope for the significant others in Gus and Lee's lives, director Anthony Minghella casts them in a light of utter hopelessness: Rita (Mary-Louise Parker), a nurse, has so little spark one suspects she's been spending too much time among the pharmaceuticals. And Dominic (Vincent D'Onofrio) is such a nice guy and logical choice for Lee you just know it won't work out. Given the usual fate of nice-guy supporting roles, in fact, it's amazing he makes it out of the movie alive.

Neither Dillon nor Sciorra is given much to work with in the way of script but Sciorra fares better, making Lee as real a person as appears in "Mr. Wonderful." And Dillon has his moments. But most of the movie takes place in a cartoon world, full of colorfully ethnic characters who wallow in their own lack of curiosity. Does every movie about blue-collar people have to be about Italians, and make them look bad? One would think that with a name like Minghella, the director might have strived to make a movie with more than two dimensions.

SIGHT AND SOUND, 11/93, p. 47, Paul Tarrago

Gus, an electrical repair worker in New York, is at a family christening when his ex-wife, Lee, appears. While they bicker at the back of the church, his current girlfriend, Rita, a nurse, looks on. Back home she talks about his lack of commitment and reluctance to live together. At work Gus's colleagues are performing repairs outside a deserted bowling alley, the site of shared teenage memories. They decide to renovate it as a co-op but Gus's money troubles—notably his alimony payments to Lee—prevent him from joining in. He visits her at college where she's studying poetry, but they start arguing. Meanwhile his potential business partners are becoming impatient. Gus revisits Lee at the public gardens where she works part-time, hoping to persuade her to get a better job so that she can support herself. Having no luck with this ploy, he's inspired by the sight of a couple meeting up for a blind date and decides to play matchmaker in order to marry Lee off. Uncertain about Tom, the married literature professor she's having an affair with, Lee half-heartedly agrees to give it a go. Lee is inundated by ill-matched suitors. Gus then surprises Rita by suggesting that they move in together. Tom drops by Lee's home while Gus is visiting, sparking off a jealous outburst in which he derides Tom for his moral duplicity. Days later, at a hospital fund-raising event, Gus and Rita bump into her with a new suitor, Dominic, who seems her ideal man. The following day Gus arrives at his new flat to find that Rita has sent the removal truck back. She can tell that he's still in love with Lee and so is ending the relationship. An accident at work almost kills Gus's partner, and Gus is himself injured while rescuing him. Lee visits the hospital where he chats with Rita. Gus discharges himself and returns to his partner's bedside to announce to the co-op members that he's sold his beloved sports car and is now in on the bowling-alley venture. A few days later Lee returns to her flat to find that Gus has strung fairy lights over her garden. He admits to how he feels about her and asks whether she really loves Dominic, who has just proposed. As Lee hesitates, Gus walks off; then Dominic appears and asks her to answer what he's just overheard. As Gus rides home on the subway Lee appears in the next carriage, tapping on the window and asking for "Mr Wonderful".

Despite the overt gesturing NYC-wards—from night-time cityscapes to Italian-American domestic interiors—there's an aura of Englishness, or more precisely middle-class uptightness, that pervades and disrupts *Mr. Wonderful*'s transatlantic urban romance. There's something polite and restrained that relegates it to the inappropriately *nice*. As with Anthony Minghella's previous feature *Truly, Madly, Deeply*, the implications of the title—emotional hyperbole with a child-like ring to it—are carried over into a narrative that depicts elation as regression, desire as a prelude to commitment.

Here is a catalogue of high drama—near-fatal accidents, new love lost and old love rediscovered—and yet there's a distinct lack of passion; instead there are little flurries of excitability, people reacting but fundamentally aspiring to an equilibrium of respectability.

But this isn't a self-conscious study of detachment, like Rohmer's ironic commentaries on bourgeois mores. Minghella's championing of passionlessness seems more like Mills and Boon propriety. Gus and Lee's love is special because it is first love; Gus's manual skills bestow him with an iconic honest-worker authenticity in contrast to Tom's duplicitous (and sexually decadent?) man of letters; and the fairy-lights in the garden are romantically, enchantingly transformative. The most sustained display of emotion comes from the co-op members in expectations of renovating the bowling alley; but yet again they're not allowed to articulate what it means to their adult lives. Instead they're depicted as rough-and-tumble kids, teasing and cajoling one another.

When, in *Truly, Madly, Deeply*, Michael Maloney's character quells a heated row by performing some impromptu magic tricks, you see the same authorial ethos at work: when emotions run high make everyone act endearingly young.

Otherwise, Minghella just lets them talk. Tom—with a biography of Camus under one arm—breathlessly tells Lee how he feels about her as she sits flicking through Donne's love poems. Gus is regaled by his partner with accounts of his latest erotic adventures. The women at a barbecue sit in the kitchen talking about love and loss. Always at a remove, they tell but don't show. Once or twice characters cry for what's been left unsaid, but the taciturn Gus does neither and so is rendered emotionally opaque.

Correspondingly, Lee looks confused much of the time when Gus is around and only hits an emotional peak when it seems as though she might lose her essay on her computer. It's not the characters' values we're witnessing, it's the director's voice possessing them like an alien force. If only Minghella would break out of his obsessive English manneredness, then maybe his films would become more than flattering mirrors for the audience. Until then there's the tang of TV drama about his big screen work: life in close up, film closed down.

VILLAGE VOICE, 11/9/93, p. 64, Lisa Kennedy

There's no Tom Hanks or mugging Meg Ryan. No cash-rich soundtrack or shameless sampling of a Hollywood classic. If *Sleepless in Seattle* was residual yuppie, *Mr. Wonderful* is working-class romantic. Small in the best sense of the word, it could be called relationship vérité. This doesn't mean it isn't corny, it can be. But thanks to Brit director Anthony Minghella's (*Truly, Madly, Deeply*) understated humor and skill with actors, *Mr. Wonderful* is nearly that.

I say this knowing that if you're one of those who can't stomach the film's central premise—a nice guy must hitch his ex to another fella in order to get her off the alimony dole—probably nothing will persuade you otherwise. You'll get no argument from me—the alimony hook is straight out of an earlier era (cowriter Vicki Polon's mom's, in fact). Still, the emotions transacted between exes, Con Ed worker Gus (Matt Dillon) and college student Lee (Annabella Sciorra), and with their current loves, Columbia prof (William Hurt) and nurse Rita (Mary-Louise Parker), feel, like the film's New York locales, comforting, familiar, with a touch of possibility.

It's difficult to write about Gus and Lee and their friends without mentioning their J-O-B-S, their not-so-fluid place in the pecking order. That both Sciorra and Dillon find themselves once again playing folks from the nabe may make them typecast-anxious, but both are at their best—moving, believable, strangely inspiring—with broad working-class accents and regular ambitions. And Parker, as the girlfriend who wakes up wanting more, does a sweet bit of inspiring herself. Almost a year after "date movie" hoopla, *Mr. Wonderful* makes a small, friendly bid for your attention.

Also reviewed in:
CHICAGO TRIBUNE, 10/15/93, Friday/p. C, Clifford Terry
NEW YORK TIMES, 10/15/93, p. C16, Janet Maslin
VARIETY, 10/25/93, p. 79, Brian Lowry
WASHINGTON POST, 10/15/93, p. D7, Hal Hinson

MIZIKE MAMA

An Interama release.   *Director:* Violaine de Villers.   *With the collaboration of:* Denise Vindevogel.   *In French, English and African dialects with English subtitles.   Running time:* 51 minutes.   *MPAA Rating:* Not Rated.

NEW YORK POST, 9/15/93, p. 27, Matthew Flamm

[*Mizike Mama* was reviewed jointly with *Djembefola*; see Flamm's review of that film.]

Also reviewed in:
NEW YORK TIMES, 9/15/93, p. C26, Stephen Holden

MONEY MAN

A Milestone Films Release.   *Producer:* Philip Haas and Belinda Haas.   *Director:* Philip Haas. *Director of Photography:* Tony Wilson.   *Editor:* Belinda Haas.   *Music:* Philip Johnston. *Running time:* 60 minutes.   *MPAA Rating:* Not Rated.

CHRISTIAN SCIENCE MONITOR, 1/12/93, p. 14, David Sterritt

It's easy to forget amid the sound and fury of the Christmas blockbuster season, but the scattered army of non-Hollywood filmmakers doesn't close up shop during the cold-weather months. Independents keep plugging away at their endlessly varied projects, and some of these actually play in theaters that present alternatives to big-studio fare.

One such theater is Manhattan's influential Film Forum, which is spicing up January with the American theatrical première of two movies by Philip Haas, a director with taste, intelligence, and wit. His new documentaries, "Money Man" and "The Singing Sculpture," reflect the fascination with contemporary art that has led him to make earlier movies on such figures as David Hockney, Boyd Webb, and Richard Long.

The main character of "Money Man" is no ordinary artist. His name is J.S.G. Boggs, and the subject that interests him most is money. In his studio he makes drawings and engravings of currency that look very much like the real thing—to the displeasure of the United States government, which has confiscated some of his works and charged him with counterfeiting.

If the Feds had looked more closely, they would have noticed that Mr. Boggs's work isn't nearly as deceptive as charged. While the front of a Boggs bill might look like real money at first glance, the back is largely blank except for a thumbprint that marks it as a Boggs original. Whimsical details on its face may also distinguish it from a genuine greenback. Look under the President's portrait on one bill, for example, and where it ought to say "McKinley" it says "Willie" instead.

Boggs doesn't merely enshrine his bogus bills in picture frames, moreover. His projects involve not only painstaking work at the drafting table but also a good deal of performance art and interaction with the real world.

After completing a piece of money, Boggs takes it to a place of business—a restaurant or art-supply store, perhaps—and attempts to spend it with the cooperation of all concerned. If a clerk or manager refuses to accept "art" money in place of "real" money, Boggs explains how hard he worked on the bill and asks why his labor shouldn't have as much value as any other kind. Sometimes he winds up defeated. But often the transaction is consummated, and everyone involved reaps a bonus of novelty and amusement.

"Money Man" follows Boggs through a number of transactions, and although he insists that Mr. Haas's camera makes no difference in his encounters with the business world, it's likely that the film crew's presence does exert some influence on the events we see.

The transactions are still enjoyable to watch, though, and all of Boggs's activities provoke new ways of thinking about the real meaning of money, labor, and exchange. Also enlightening are Boggs's confrontations with the Treasury Department as he tries to get a straight story on the whereabouts of his confiscated bills—which remain confiscated at the end of the film, even though the government has decided (not surprisingly!) to drop its counterfeiting case.

Haas's other current film, "The Singing Sculpture," is a brief visit with Gilbert and George, respected British artists who work as a team and often include their own likenesses in their pictures, as a way of confronting their audience as directly as possible.

They carry this to an extreme in their "Singing Sculpture" presentation, which consists of Gilbert and George themselves—wearing immaculate outfits yet smeared with paint on their hands and faces—crooning a music-hall number on a little art-gallery stage.

Haas's movie shows the work from many perspectives, intercut with Gilbert and George discussing its place within their overall career as "disturbed and desperate" artists who want to stimulate thought about the darkest secrets of human existence.

Are they joking about this, or does their "Singing Sculpture" act really have hidden and somber meanings? As with such quintessentially modern works as Becket's play "Waiting for Godot" and Kafka's novel "The Trial" both possibilities are equally valid.

Thoughtful laughter and existential angst are often hard to keep in separate compartments, and the mingled propriety and absurdity of the "Singing Sculpture" presentation captures this 20th-century ambivalence with impressive subtlety.

Haas's film echoes the mood set by Gilbert and George with its own dead-pan style, making it an ideal record of a performance art work that continues to resonate more than 20 years after its first appearance.

"Money Man" was photographed by Tony Wilson and "The Singing Sculpture" by Mark Trottenberg; both were edited by Belinda Haas.

"Money Man" features music by the Microscopic Septet and Friends. The movies are distributed by Milestone Films, a New York-based company specializing in offbeat cinematic fare.

NEW YORK POST, 1/13/93, p. 23, Audrey Farolino

The getting and spending of money has always been considered something of an art form, but never has the concept been stretched quite so far as by J.S.G. Boggs.

Boggs is the Pittsburgh-based artist who makes money literally by drawing and copying his own finely detailed interpretations of $20s, $100s, $1,000, etc.

The bills are clearly fake—they bear such legends as "This note is legal art" and the backs are blank sane for Boggs' green thumbprint. But passing them off as real isn't Boggs' aim.

No, his aim is to convince people to accept his bills in lieu of money; a challenge (to put it mildly) which Boggs considers part of the artistic process. In doing so, he gets people to ponder issues like the value of art and the meaning of money—and in return, incidentally, he gets stuff like restaurant meals, fancy hotel rooms and a shiny new Yamaha.

"Money Man" art documentarian Philip Haas' wry and laid back study of Boggs, opens a two week run at Film Forum I today. It's paired with Haas' shorter "The Singing Sculpture." which captures the eccentric art duo Gilbert & George in a performance of the "living sculpture" which first brought them attention.   Both films offer an interesting look into the singleness of vision—and, some might say, singular nuttiness—that it takes to be an art trailblazer.

"Money Man" focuses on a trip Boggs takes to Washington to convince the Secret Service to give back 15 of his bills they seized as counterfeit. But his predictably fruitless efforts to explain his art to the fed aren't half as amusing as his attempts to get various cashiers, waiters, etc. to accept his artwork.

He convinces the owner of a trendy Pittsburgh restaurant to take one of his $100 notes to pay for a meal, and even gets back change (real, of course). An art supply store manager tells Boggs that, being an artist himself, he'll allow him to purchase $100 worth of goods for one of his $500 bills.

Not so amenable are a bank officer who turns down Boggs' request to open an interest bearing account with his funny money, or the postal clerk who gingerly asks Boggs, "Where are you from?" when he tries to purchase stamps with one of his $10 bills.

Since the film is made from Boggs' point of view, it never questions the validity of his mission (though Boggs himself notes that plenty of people think he's a con man). There's also some question as to how unrehearsed some of the scenes were, since the participants didn't seem at all fazed by the camera's presence.

But outweighing these problems is the sheer appeal of Boggs himself.   He's gently confrontational, low key and likable, and even when he insists his work isn't "some silly prank," you can't help but suspect that he's enjoying himself as much as if it were.

VILLAGE VOICE, 1/19/93, p. 48, Georgia Brown

Filmmaker Philip Haas documents art that would be difficult for most of us to see for ourselves—whether because it is site-specific, like Richard Long's circles in the Sahara, or a performance piece, like Gilbert & George's *Singing Sculpture*. Probably his most acclaimed work is *A Day on the Grand Canal With the Emperor of China*, with David Hockney serving as tour guide of a 17th-century Chinese scroll. Haas's work tends to be unobtrusively informative; much of it is commissioned, like the series of shorts executed for the Centre Georges Pompidou's "Magicians of the Earth" exhibition. (The Walter Reade presented a Haas retrospective this past year.)

Haas's latest film, *Money Man*, follows the trail of J. S. G. Boggs, the artist whose homemade currency has put him in the news. (The *Times* recently ran a story on Boggs when his Pittsburgh home was searched and his artwork once again seized as counterfeit.) According to Boggs, a work is complete only when a commercial transaction is made—i.e,, the facsimile bill he has fastidiously painted, changing certain details like the signature, is "spent." Here he's shown, for example, buying a Harley-Davidson and lunch for four at a trendy-looking restaurant with Boggs bills.

Although most people approached here appear receptive, especially on camera, Boggs says that for each bill accepted, 10 are rejected, camera or no. This artwork narrative also includes a collector who buys Boggs's receipts and change, and then tries to buy up the bills used in the transaction, thus completing a whole work.

For good measure (maybe because Haas currently is branching into feature films), *Money Man* throws in a *Roger & Me*-type twist, with Boggs calling on the Secret Service bureau chief in charge of confiscating his artwork. We're shown Boggs on the phone, Boggs riding his Harley to Washington, Boggs cooling his heels in the lobby, and so on. While getting no satisfaction, the artist treats us to his theories (he's an ethics professor at Carnegie Mellon). Personally, his enterprise strikes me as commercially shrewd and less than profound. I'll take a Donald Evans stamp any day. (Evans invented his own countries.)

Watching the gussied-up Gilbert & George lipsynch "Underneath the Arches," an English music hall song they say, convincingly, is "about being miserable," I was extremely happy *The Singing Sculpture* ran only 20 minutes, not the original performance's six hours.

Also reviewed in:
NEW YORK TIMES, 1/13/93, p. C16, Stephen Holden

MONEY TREE, THE

A Tara Releasing and Black Sheep Films release. *Producer:* Christopher Dienstag. *Director:* Alan Dienstag. *Dialogue (improvised from a story by):* Alan Dienstag and Christopher Dienstag. *Director of Photography:* Donatello Bonato. *Editor:* Susan Crutcher. *Music:* Lorin Rowan. *Sound:* Adam Lieberman. *Running time:* 92 minutes. *MPAA Rating:* Not Rated.

CAST: Christopher Dienstag (David); Monica T. Caldwell (Erica); Malcolm Cohen (Vincent); Nik Martin (Chad); Kathrine Schutzman (Girlfriend); Richard Roughgarden (Charly); Carlos Deloche (Pasquel); Gregory Wilker (Rusty).

LOS ANGELES TIMES, 4/24/92, Calendar/p.14, Kevin Thomas

Low in budget, high in spirits, Alan Dienstag's largely improvised "The Money Tree" is worth infinitely more than slick but soulless Hollywood junk such as "Stephen King's Sleepwalkers" or the silly "Brenda Starr." Sure, it's rough around the edges, but it has the breath of real life and a genuinely sweet and endearing sensibility. It's funny, it's scary, and it even makes you think and feel.

The director's son, Christopher, stars as David, a pot farmer about to harvest his first crop, hidden in thickets of Marin County's Mt. Tamalpais. He's under pressure from all sides: His ambitious girlfriend Erica (Monica T. Caldwell) wants him to take a cushy corporate job with her rich father *right now*, harvest or no harvest; his theater director pal (Nik Martin) urges him to get back into acting and take it seriously. As a middle-class dropout, David looks forward to clearing a comparatively easy $70,000-plus.

But there's more to David's pot growing than this, which gives this casual-seeming, off-the-cuff film its ballast and dimension. David finds he actually likes the work of planting the notorious weed and watching it grow, and through this discovery, the film raises the whole question of legalizing marijuana in a fresh way. Although "The Money Tree" lapses into a gratuitous preachiness every now and then on the behalf of legalization, it doesn't require you to be pro or con in relation to its cause in order to enjoy it; it's very much a classic story of a young man in the process of self-discovery and making choices.

The film's thriller elements, although played for comedy, certainly do make it clear that growing and especially selling marijuana can be highly dangerous. You may find yourself put off by Erica's relentlessly conventional and materialistic values, yet you find yourself agreeing with her that David is crazy to stay in such a risky business. Dienstag and Caldwell, resourceful actors both, make David and Erica's mutual attraction sufficiently charged for us to believe in their volatile relationship.

With the cast improvising their lines it's not surprising that "The Money Tree" (Times-rated Mature for adult themes, situations, some strong language) occasionally becomes too talky for its own good. Technically, it's wildly uneven, especially in its sound recording. However, it's steadfast where it counts, which is in its good-natured spirit combined with a detached, mature perspective.

NEW YORK POST, 3/19/93, p. 29, Audrey Farolino

If you're anything like Bill Clinton and me—that is, if you smoked pot but never actually inhaled—you probably think that nothing could be less appealing than a movie about some guy growing marijuana in the California hills.

And if you've ever sat through an improvisation class, you probably shudder at the idea of watching a movie whose dialogue was almost entirely made up by the actors involved.

But "The Money Tree" is more likable than it sounds, and you don't even have to be a member of pot's new legion of devotees to appreciate its strengths. (You do, however, have to be a night owl, since it's showing only midnights at the Angelika.)

What's most appealing is the movie's quirkiness, evident in everything from its offbeat plot and low-budget looks to its cast, headed by Christopher Dienstag, who also happens to be the son of director Alan Dienstag (in this case, at least, nepotism paid off).

Dienstag—who looks like a cross between Stephen Rea and Jeff Goldblum—plays David, an amiable would-be actor who has opted out of the normal workaday world in order to tend to his flourishing marijuana crop.

If David can make it to harvest time, he stands to earn a cool $70,000. But that's a big if. The obstacles he must overcome include wild boar attacks (I guess that's one of the little drawbacks of California living), police patrols, a playwright friend who's trying to talk him into going back to acting, and—headache number one—Erica (Monica T. Caldwell), his super-bitchy and materialistic girlfriend.

And therein lies the movie's biggest problem—Erica is so exaggeratedly loathsome that it's impossible to believe that nice-guy David could possibly love her, much less that he'd consider giving up his laid-back life to join her rich daddy's company. Yet that's the big decision he's agonizing over.

The movie also suffers from an annoying tendency towards preachiness—simplistic preachiness, at that—as in David's discussions with friends about the work ethic and the politics of pot, and a moralistic subplot about the dangers of a really *bad* drug, cocaine.

You probably won't remember much about "The Money Tree" a few days after seeing it—and that has nothing to do with the effects of pot on the brain. But at least it's a little different from most of what you see on screen these days.

NEWSDAY, 3/19/93, Part II/p. 75, Terry Kelleher

Unless you're enraptured by the sight of a marijuana grower lovingly inhaling his plants, you won't get a contact high from "The Money Tree."

But if you approach this low-budget movie with modest expectations, at least it won't bring you down.

Directed by San Francisco acting teacher Alan Dienstag, "The Money Tree" purportedly employs "totally improvised" dialogue in telling the story of an ambivalent young pot farmer in Marin County. It seems David (Christopher Dienstag, son of Alan) can't decide whether to get serious about a theatrical career, take a well-paying "straight job" with his girlfriend's father or concentrate on the rewards and challenges of illegal self-employment.

The improvisation is not painfully obvious; indeed, sometimes you'd *swear* "The Money Tree" was scripted. The junior Dienstag, sort of a cross between Jeff Goldblum and Daniel Stern, is likable in the lead. The supporting cast does a generally professional job—with the notable exception of Malcolm Cohen, whose clumsy overacting defeats the humor in his role as an art hustler branching out into drugs.

On the technical side, the principal asset is Donatello Bonato's cinematography, which gives "The Money Tree" a look that belies its estimated production cost of $300,000. Unfortunately, the movie is seldom convincing and only sporadically entertaining. It's not clear what David sees in the nagging, materialistic, ill-tempered Erica (Monica Calwell) besides her daddy's dough, so why not go in the old man's payroll and be done with it? There's a distinct whiff of rationalization to David's code of honor, which holds that the marijuana trade is a comparatively noble calling in a country that blows billions on the Strategic Defensive Initiative and various other unworthy causes.

A wild pig pursues the protagonist for the sole purpose of gratuitous slapstick, and the part of David's swinging grandpa apparently was added so the director could slip in front of the camera for the amusement of his immediate family. The ending is a clever copout—or, on reflection, just a cop-out.

"The Money Tree" may be no more than mildly pleasurable, but rest assured it's not addictive.

VILLAGE VOICE, 3/23/93, p. 62, Alyssa Katz

A low-budget piece of pro-pot propaganda that rivals *Reefer Madness* for preachiness, *The Money Tree*, first shown in California in 1990, has shown up on this coast just as marijuana has become Styles of the Times cover material. But much like the media hype on the bud, this NORML-endorsed Bay Area feature covers everything except the pleasures of getting high—when a bad guy lights up at the end, it's only to test the quality of the $70,000 stash he's buying. For a film that's square in the legal danger zone anyway—with fields of glistening bud-of-the-month plants, tirades against the hypocrisy of pot laws, and a sweet, Arlo Guthrie-touched grower-hero who brings joints to cancer patients—this straight-edge approach reduces the film to an essay on entrepreneurship.

Pot here isn't a matter of fun or transcendence—it's about freedom, man. (The dealers' harpy women just screech, "It's those plants, or me"; they might as well, be DEA agents.) *The Money Tree* wears the mantle of white-boy me-too oppression that's been such a key recruiting tool for the pot politics movement. This makes for jarring contrast with pioneering screen dopesters Cheech and Chong, whose social exile in drug subculture mirrored their ethnic marginality.

The herb farmer, who defends his all-American right to work hard, take risks, and make piles of money as heaping as the crops he harvests, is appealingly played by the director's son Christopher. The cast and director entirely improvised the dialogue, with results surprisingly not all that awful, just uneven. They don't seem to be stoned.

Also reviewed in:
VARIETY, 10/29/90, p. 53
WASHINGTON POST, 1/25/93, p. B7, Richard Harrington

MONTPARNASSE 19 (MODIGLIANI)

An Interama release of a Franco London production. *Producer:* Ralph Baum. *Director:* Jacques Becker. *Screenplay (French with English subtitles):* Henri Jeanson. *Director of Photography:* Christian Matras. *Editor:* Marguerite Renoir. *Sound:* Pierre Calvet. *Set Designer:* J. D'Eaubonne. *Set Decorator:* Anne-Marie Marchand. *Costumes:* G. Annenkov and Jacques Heim. *Running time:* 120 minutes. *MPAA Rating:* Not Rated.

CAST: Gérard Philipe (Amadeo Modigliani); Anouk Aimée (Jeanne); Lili Palmer (Beatrice); Lino Ventura (Morel); Gérard Sety (Sborowski); Lila Kedrova (Berthe Weil); Lea Padovani (Rosalie); Jean Lanier (M. Hebuterne); Denise Vernac (Mme. Hebuterne); Paquerette (Mme.

Salomon); Arlette Poirier (Lulu); Robert Ripa (Marcel); Frank Edwards (Mr. Dickson); Carol Sands (Mrs. Dickson).

LOS ANGELES TIMES, 4/16/93, Calendar/p. 10, Kevin Thomas

Gérard Philipe, the leading screen star of postwar France, is well cast in the title role of Jacques Becker's 1958 "Modigliani—Montparnasse 1958 (in revival at the Monica 4-Plex with a razor-sharp fresh print). However, not until its final third is the film itself up to Philipe's level.

Thin and wistful-looking, Philipe was a romantic idol who was also an actor of intelligence, depth and considerable range. That Philip died of a heart attack the following year at 36—the age at which Amedeo Modigliani, the Italian painter and sculptor who spent his career in France, himself died in 1920—gives the film an undeniable poignancy.

It needs it. Despite Philipe's incisive portrayal, "Modigliani" tends to ramble at first in an impersonal fashion like countless other tales of starving, tormented Left Bank artists—proud, hard-drinking and unappreciated in their own lifetimes but always attracting beautiful women and a handful of anxious, self-sacrificing believers. There's an artificial quality to the film's atmosphere, which is heightened by its surprisingly meager attempt to evoke the Paris of 1919 and the early '20s; indeed, the women, and sometimes the men as well, are coiffed and even dressed in the styles of the late '50s.

"Modigliani" doesn't remotely evoke its era as well as John Huston's "Moulin Rouge" (1952) did and has none of the texture, grit and concern for detail and nuance that characterized Robert Altman's "Vincent and Theo" and Maurice Pialat's "Van Gogh." That Becker, respected director of such films as the romantic period piece "Casque d'Or" (1952), which made a star of Simone Signoret, took over the film upon Max Ophuls' sudden death, may account for the film's initial lifelessness.

Yet, it finally catches fire, achieving focus at last, thanks largely to the accumulative effects of Philipe's unflagging concentration and understated intensity. As overwhelming despair mounts for Modigliani, Philipe suddenly becomes the painter and is no longer merely your generic tragic, self-destructive artist. We begin to feel for him and his love for the beautiful Jeanne (a highly effective Anouk Aimée), a demure-looking art student who defies her adamantly bourgeois parents to share his increasingly wretched life.

You may be surprised to discover that a film (Times-rated Mature for adult themes) about a famous painter is in black-and-white, but cinematographer Christian Matras' exquisitely lit images are in fact "Modigliani's" abiding glory. As the worldly, well-off British poet Beatrice Hastings, who was Modigliani's sometime lover and patroness, Lili Palmer is showy and very actress-y. None of "Modigliani's" drawbacks, however, diminish the impact of its truly shocking ending.

NEW YORK POST, 2/26/93, p. 25, Jerry Tallmer

If anyone has ever multiplied female sexuality and female beauty more powerfully together in oil paint than Amadeo Modigliani, I wish you'd let me know. There have been many movies about another great painter, Vincent Van Gogh, whose tormented life was cut short, or cut itself short, 50 years too soon, but for Modigliani in the cinema—God knows a wonderful subject—we have only, I think, the splendid 1957 film by Jacques Becker that has hardly been seen here for more than 30 years now. It opens today in a fine new 35mm print, for a month at the Public Theater.

If you want a harrowing picture in your head, it is of Gerard Philipe as Modigliani going from table to table of a Montparnasse sidewalk cafe, offering his drawings to this one and that one at 5 francs apiece, and then, when there are no takers, cutting the price to 100 sous and then to 20 sous, and still no takers—his progress from table to table and then out into the street and toward the river followed every step of the way through the vulture's eyes of Morel, the dealer who has waited for just this moment throughout Modigliani's young alcohol-and-drug-addicted lifetime.

It is hard of course for us to house that battered persona within the beautiful physique and manifest warmth and generosity of the beloved Gerard Philipe of all those French films of our long agos—hard to believe him beating up on Lili Palmer or yelling at Anouk Aimee—but it can be done.

Suspension of disbelief, it's called, even if we perpetually view him painting so that we can only see the rear side of the canvas, and when we do glimpse the painting that's meant to be of Aimee, it's one that looks nothing like her. But then, as Modigliani says on another occasion to the agreeable Nice streetwalker who's his model of the moment: "I don't paint you as you are, but as I see you" Smiling, she replies: "We'll still be friends."

Lili Palmer plays what I think might be called a playgirl—a poet/journalist of sorts, British of sorts (Lili Palmer!)—no better than she should be, and much worse for Modigliani than is good for him. But I adored her. Anouk Aimee is the virginal art student to whom Modigliani loses his heart. When at last they're lying in bed in Nice on The Morning After and she says: "Where's the sea? There? There? There?"—east, west, south—it's hard not to adore her too. In fact, though there is little or no actual feeling of sexuality anywhere in the movie, these two actresses—plus Lea Padovani as a sheltering hosteliere—give all that's needed of beauty.

Sex does enter by way of the one stunning Modigliani nude that the painter's friends Sborowski and Berthe Weil (Gerard Sety, Lila Kedrova) have put in the window of her gallery. Enter the law, rudely demanding removal of "this disgusting display of pubic hair." The painting is removed. That must have been 1920. In 1949 I saw precisely the same thing happen over a drawing (not a Modigliani) in a bookstore window on Greenwich Avenue tied to the release of the film "Devil in the Flesh" that starred a babe in arms named Gerard Philipe.

Modigliani died at 36—died of life, you might say. Gerard Philipe died at 37, of cancer. Max Ophuls, who had the idea for "Montparnasse 19" and wrote its screenplay with Henri Jeanson, fell ill and died before he could shoot it. He turned that job over to his friend Jacques Becker, who five years earlier had made the wonderful—and extremely sexual—"Casque d'Or."

The film ends with Morel, the dealer/vulture—Lino Ventura, the only person in the movie who in fact looks like a Modigliani—dashing around to the painter's garret to con widow Anouk Aimee out of every canvas he can lay his hands on, before she knows she's a widow. For whatever reason, it does not show what (so Cocteau tells us) happened on the day of Modigliani's funeral. Young Mrs. Modigliani jumped out of a fifth-floor window to her death.

NEWSDAY, 2/26/93, Part II/p. 67, John Anderson

There are moments when the characters in "Modigliani (Montparnasse 19)" are so anguished you can barely repress a laugh. Is that cruel? Well, no one said art was going to be pretty.

It certainly isn't in "Modigliani," Jacques Becker's 1958 quasi-biography of Amedeo Modigliani: not the portrait painted of the alcoholic, drug-abusing, poverty-stricken painter, nor the film itself, which, visually at least, better resembles a late '50s American teleplay than what we generally think of as postwar French cinema. The film has an apparently solid reputation among cinephiles, but that may have something to do with the fact that it hasn't been seen here in 30 years.

Not that there aren't reasons to see it: Gerard Philipe as Modigliani is a handsome rake, a charming debauchee whose stubborn refusal to conform dooms him as surely as his tubercular lungs. Lili Palmer, as his lover, Beatrice, is both moving and beautifully cruel, and Anouk Aimee, who might have stepped out of one of Modigliani's elongated portraits, is a lovely but ultimately tiresome Jeanne, the virginal art student for whom Modigliani falls.

The nonhistorical screenplay for "Modigliani" was written by Henri Jeanson and Max Ophuls and was to have been directed by Ophuls; his death put the project in Jacques Becker's lap. What Ophuls might have done no one knows, but it wouldn't have been this. Becker, in what we can only assume is an attempt to mirror Modigliani's work, isolating his subjects in space, removing the world at large from his pictures, constructs each pivotal scene by stripping away everything but Modigliani and whomever he happens to be talking to, or screaming at, or falling on, at a given moment. The result is an epic artificiality, abetted by a score that's so overwrought—the music swells and ebbs like a toothache—that if they cut to a commercial you wouldn't be surprised. Or care.

VILLAGE VOICE, 3/2/93, p. 47, J. Hoberman

Jacques Becker's 1958 *Montparnasse 19*—released here 32 years ago as *Modigliani of Montparnasse* and now, as *Modigliani*—was the French answer to such paint-splattered Oscar-

amas as *Moulin Rouge* (1952) and *Lust for Life* (1956). The glamorous Gérard Philipe plays Amadeo Modigliani and there are moments when this studio evocation of misunderstood genius amid bohemian squalor bids to out-Hollywood Hollywood for kitschy grandeur: Modigliani at work in his little atelier, smock on and kerchief perfectly knotted, knocking out million-dollar portraits to the strains of "And Sheep May Safely Graze."

Modigliani may yet endure as the man who fused pin-up and icon, the Vargas of the teenage intelligentsia, but *Modigliani* itself reeks of mortality. Max Ophüls was set to direct the project but died before it went into production—the baton passing to Becker, who managed one more movie before his death in 1960. And soon after release, Philipe was dead at 36, the same age as the tubercular, self-destructive, alcoholic painter he impersonated.

Part memento mori, part marionette show, *Modigliani* focuses mainly on its subject's love life. Flushed and coltish, her eyes ablaze with abject adoration, Anouk Aimée is the innocent Jeanne, a bourgeois student who devotes herself to the tormented artist. (Following Modi to the south of France, she poses, fully clothed and smiling broadly, in the lap of nature with a coverlet of solemn organ music.) The worldly Beatrice, entertainingly played by Lili Palmer as the unflappable epitome of flapper cool, brandishes an enormous cigarette-holder with a mocking amusement that may be the last vestige of the Ophüls touch.

Framed by sequences in which ordinary Parisians fail to grasp the fantastic value of Modi's art work, *Modigliani* evokes a measure of audience smugness while fastidiously flourishing the full panoply of Left Bank clichés: A poster emblazoned "Dada" presides over a dance hall full of sullen Apaches cavorting to *le jazz*. (Somber as it is, *Modigliani* would make an illuminating double bill with Aki Kaurismäki's *La Vie de Bohème*—an equally mythological Paris of artists and models, shot in no less sumptuous black and white.) The movie is a fast two hours. Everything appears as if on cue: lovely gamines, amiable ex-mistresses, attractive streetwalkers, crass Americans, sudden rain showers; Modi drinking himself into a stupor and beating on Jeanne's door while her fearful parents cower inside; Modi staggering soused out of his own gallery opening; Modi tottering around, tossing his money into the Seine and inviting Jeanne to follow.

In its original release, *Modigliani* was praised by both Andre Bazin and Eric Rohmer. Their associate Jean-Luc Godard, who reviewed it in *Cahiers du Cinéma*, was more dismissive ("Its purpose is the absence of purpose. Its truth, the absence of truth."). But even Godard was moved by the tabloid harshness of the movie's conclusion: "I would give the whole of the post-war French cinema for that one shot, badly acted, badly composed, but sublime, in which Modigliani asks five francs for his drawings on the terrace of the Coupole." Add to that the icy scene in which the painter expires and the ferocious discretion with which the end title screams FIN.

Also reviewed in:
CHICAGO TRIBUNE, 7/16/93, Friday/p. M, John Petrakis
NEW YORK TIMES, 3/1/61, p. 27, Bosley Crowther

MORNING GLORY

An Academy Entertainment release of a Dove Audio production. *Executive Producer:* Jerry Leider. *Producer:* Michael Viner. *Director:* Steven Stern. *Screenplay:* Charles Jarrott and Deborah Raffin. *Based on the novel by:* LaVyrle Spencer. *Director of Photography:* Laszlo George. *Editor:* Richard Benwick. *Music:* Jonathan Elias. *Sound:* Eric Batut. *Casting:* Stuart Aikins. *Art Director:* David Hiscox. *Set Decorator:* Barry Kemp. *Costumes:* Maureen Hiscox. *Running time:* 90 minutes. *MPAA Rating:* PG-13.

CAST: Christopher Reeve (Will Parker); Deborah Raffin (Elly Dinsmore); Lloyd Bochner (Bob Collins); Nina Foch (Miss Beasly); Helen Shaver (Lula Peaks); J.T. Walsh (Sheriff Reese Goodloe).

LOS ANGELES TIMES, 9/17/93, Calendar/p. 18, Kevin Thomas

"Morning Glory" is the kind of tender, intimate film that ha a tough time finding an audience in today's marketplace. That fact of life, coupled with an ending that is far too pat for its own good, marks the movie as better suited to the tube than to the big screen.

Christopher Reeve and Deborah Raffin are a beleaguered backwoods couple. Reeve, an ex-con, meets her when he lands in a small Southern town and answers her ad for a husband. A recent widow with two children younger than 5 and another on the way, she needs help running her farm. In adapting LaVyrle Spencer's 1989 novel, Raffin and co-writer Charles Jarrott wisely take their time letting the couple get to know each other. Reeve's Will Parker is humble, polite and hungry; Raffin's Elly Dinsmore is plain-spoken but often defensive and surprisingly reclusive. In time we learn that both are victims of grave injustices but that both possess the capacity to build a new life together.

The question is whether they'll get the chance. There's trouble right from the start, from J.T. Walsh's close-minded sheriff who wants Will to move on and from the sheriff's lover, a local waitress and town tart (Helen Shaver) who sets her cap for the handsome Will. Meanwhile, under Steven Stern's direction, Reeve and Raffin involve us in their growing love for each other. Pivotal in their fate is the local librarian, a kindly woman beautifully played by Nina Foch, indeed, in its uniformly fine performances "Morning Glory" is an ensemble work.

Spanning a year beginning in early 1941, "Morning Glory" (rated PG-13 for a sex-related scene) has a nice sense of time and place. It diminishes its impact with a courtroom finale that relies too much on coincidencc aad contrivance, despite a standout turn by Lloyd Bochner as Will's courtly attorney, a man skilled at reaching the local people without riling their prejudices and narrow-mindedness.

NEW YORK POST, 9/18/93, p. 15, Matthew Flamm

The sun rises over railroad tracks somewhere in the country. A vagabond, sack over his shoulder, strolls through the scene, then climbs down the embankment to feast on apples from a tree. Next he wanders into town past beat-up 1930s cars leaving clouds of dust on the road.

"Morning Glory," it quickly becomes apparent, is the kind of movie that gives simplicity a bad name.

Predictable in every frame, this Depression-era drama contains barely enough story to fill an hour of television. Based on the novel of the same name by LaVyrle Spencer, "Morning Glory" has the ersatz feel of a vanity production—or of make-work for good actors in a career slump, like Christopher Reeve, who plays Will Parker, the story's kind, halting hero.

Will has spent the last five years in prison for manslaughter, but there isn't a mean bone in his body. Without a penny or a spare shirt to his name, he answers a want ad in the local newspaper—for a husband. His prospective "employer" turns out to be a winsome and recently widowed farm woman pregnant with her third child.

"Crazy" Elly Dinsmore, played by Deborah Raffin—who shares screenplay credit with Charles Jarrott, and whose Dove Audio books-on-tape company produced the film—is an eccentric recluse who hasn't ventured into town in years. But she needs help with the chores, and with bringing up her two photogenic little boys.

Elly and Will agree on a trial period during which he sleeps in the barn and gradually proves his mettle as a farm hand. Slowly and surely, he impresses everyone—except the bullying town sheriff, effectively played by J.T. Walsh with his stand-up character.

The audience, meanwhile, wonders how long it's going to take before these two wronged individuals discover they are the kindest most decent people in the world and absolutely perfect for each other.

As directed by Steven Stern, whose previous credits include "Money," "Rolling Vengeance" and 20 made-for-television movies, "Morning Glory" is mostly well-acted—considering the material —but so slackly staged that the absolute lack of tension can't be blamed entirely on the screenplay.

This is a particular problem in the last third of the movie when it tries to become a mystery, with Will accused of murdering the town slut (played to the hilt by Helen Shaver). It doesn't take a genius to guess whether Will is guilty or not. But the courtroom revelation scene does upset one expectation—that the film couldn't get any more obvious.

NEWSDAY, 9/17/93, Part II/p. 78, Gene Seymour

Aside form its itchy music score, there is nothing about "Morning Glory" that can make you dislike it greatly. It is made with the kind of quiet decency that doesn't force its way into your heartstrings. Whether those strings are pulled or not depends largely on how you feel about soft-focus romances in which shy, scared waifs find strength in loving shy, sensitive hunks.

Deborah Raffin, terminally blond mini-series ingenue, is cast against type as the waif figure. She is Elly Dinsmore, a tough, but tender young woman who raises her two children and tends her farm with as much dedication and care as she's able. She would be a credit to any community despite her illegitimate birth and eccentric family origins.

But this being the late 1930s in rural Georgia, Elly's origins, smarts and self-possession are frowned upon to the extent that she is compelled to live far away from the nearest town, whose citizens refer to her as "Crazy Elly." Newly widowed with a third child on the way, she is desperate enough for manly assistance to advertise for a husband in the local paper.

Enter Will Parker (Christopher Reeve), a shy, shambling hunk who's just been released from prison where he did hard time for murdering a prostitute. He's just hungry and desperate enough for work to marry anyone willing to feed and shelter him. The local citizenry, with the notable exception of the librarian (Nina Foch), snickers meanly at this alliance of pariahs. Inevitably, however, Will and Elly's bond grows stronger. Just as inevitably, trouble looms not far away in the form of the town slut (Helen Shaver), whose name—wouldn't you know—is Lula.

The whole thing, adapted by Raffin and co-screenwriter Charles Jarrott from a novel by Lavyrle Spencer, sounds so mushy and predictable that you wonder why you stay with it all the way through. Steven Stern's direction is workman-like and solid. Nothing to get excited about though.

Still, there's conviction in the acting throughout. While remaining too lovely to entirely convince as a wan, geeky outcast, Raffin nonetheless has enough fine moments in her performance to solidify her place among underrated actors.

Meanwhile, those who can't take Reeve seriously unless he's wearing a blue suit and a red cape will find themselves pleasantly surprised by the heft and subtlety he brings to his portrayal of Will. The strong-but-silent patina, harder to pull off than it looks, seems a perfect fit for Reeve, who hasn't had a break from the critics since the "Superman" features stopped coming. This movie isn't big enough to make Reeve a star again. But the impression he makes here is good enough to suggest that a reversal of perception—and fortune—won't be long in coming.

Also reviewed in:
NEW YORK TIMES, 9/17/93, p. C12, Janet Maslin
VARIETY, 10/4/93, p. 39, Dan Cox

MRS. DOUBTFIRE

A Twentieth Century Fox release of a Blue Wolf production. *Executive Producer:* Matthew Rushton. *Producer:* Marsha Garces Williams, Robin Williams, and Mark Radcliffe. *Director:* Chris Columbus. *Screenplay:* Randi Mayem Singer and Leslie Dixon. *Based upon "Alias Madame Doubtfire" by:* Anne Fine. *Director of Photography.* Donald McAlpine. *Editor.* Raja Gosnell. *Music:* Howard Shore. *Music Editor:* Ellen Segal. *Sound:* Nelson Stoll and (music) Dan Wallin. *Sound Editor:* Gloria S. Borders. *Casting:* Janet Hirschenson and Jane Jenkins. *Production Designer:* Angelo Graham. *Art Director:* W. Steven Graham. *Set Designer:* Steve Sakland, Steve Wolff, Robert Goldstein, and Harold Fuhrman. *Set Decorator:* Garrett Lewis. *Special Effects:* John McLeod. *Costumes:* Marit Allen. *Make-up:* Ve Neill. *Make-up (special):* Greg Cannom. *Stunt Coordinator:* Troy Brown. *Running time:* 120 minutes. *MPAA Rating:* PG-13.

CAST: Robin Williams (Daniel Hillard/Mrs. Doubtfire); Sally Field (Miranda Hillard); Pierce Brosnan (Stu); Harvey Fierstein (Frank); Polly Holliday (Gloria); Lisa Jakub (Lydia Hillard); Matthew Lawrence (Chris Hillard); Mara Wilson (Natalie Hillard); Robert Prosky (Mr. Lundy); Anne Haney (Mrs. Sellner); Scott Capurro (Jack); Sydney Walker (Bus Driver); Joe Bellan (TV Boss); Martin Mull (Justin Gregory); Terence McGovern (ADR Director Lou); Karen Kahn (Female Employee #1); Eva Gholson (Female Employee #2); James Cunningham (Male Employee); Ralph Peduto (Cop); Scott Beach (Judge); Juliette Marshall (Miranda's Attorney); Drew Letchworth (Daniel's Attorney); Jessica Myerson (Miranda's Mother); Sharon Lockwood (Alice); Jim Cullen (Thug); Kenneth Loo (Staring Boy #1); Jeff Loo (Staring Boy #2); Betsy Monroe (Stunning Woman); Joseph Narducci (Delivery Boy); James S. Cranna (Ron); Todd Williams (Dr. Toad); Adele Proom (Lundy's Secretary); Rick Overton (Maitre'D); Dan Spencer (Cook); Paul Guilfoyle (Head Chef); Molly McClure (Woman Housekeeper); Andrew L. Prosky (TV Director); William Newman (Mr. Sprinkles); Chris Pray (Puppeteer); Geoff Bolt (Lundy's Waiter); Dick Bright (Stu's Waiter); Adam Bryant (Man in Men's Room); Tavia Cathcart (Tanya the Hostess); C. Beau Fitzsimons (Valet #1); Jeff Moeller (Valet #2); Benne Alder (Woman in Restroom).

LOS ANGELES TIMES, 11/24/93, Calendar/p. 1, Kenneth Turan

We're losing Robin Williams.

Never mind that his latest film, "Mrs. Doubtfire", has the markings of a major commercial success, an achievement due exclusively to Williams' agreeing to take on a role born in high-concept heaven: A divorced dad disguises himself as a grandmotherly British housekeeper to spend more time with the children he loves.

And, of course, when Williams wants to be funny, no one can hope to keep up. Whether mimicking Gandhi or Porky Pig, doing a wicked two-step with a vacuum cleaner or ad-libbing a dinosaur-oriented rap lyric, Williams is one of the rare performers who defeats even superlatives.

So what's the problem? It's that "Mrs. Doubtfire" underlines a trend in Williams' work that can't be ignored. Probably the preeminent comic talent of his generation, he is less and less involved in being funny on screen. Losing interest in his trademark anarchic verbal horseplay, he is leaning increasing toward warm and cuddly roles, as if Lenny Bruce had slowly turned into Mr. Rogers. Gradually but undeniably, Williams is going soft and mushy, and it is not a pleasing sight.

This trend is not a new one, of course, but when "Dead Poets Society," "Awakenings" and "Hook" were followed by the cloying "Toys" and now this, the momentum is inescapable, Even then, as with "Mrs. Doubtfire," Williams' performances come with humor attached, his work feels hybrid, as if the sentiment is leaking through and denaturing the strength of the comedy.

A "Tootsie" for the single-parent set, "Mrs. Doubtfire" (rated PG-13 for "some sexual references") is unobjectionable enough, a safe and sane entertainment where all the characters are nice and all the situations unadventurous. Anyone looking for the kind of comic brio that Dustin Hoffman and company brought to "Tootsie" will not find it here.

Williams' character, voiceover actor Daniel Hillard, is amusingly introduced providing the vocals as cartoon character Pudgie the Parrot sings Rossini's celebrated Figaro aria. Daniel is clearly good at his job, but soon he is out of it: Determined to put a socially conscious anti-smoking message in Pudgie's non-moving lips, he becomes one more unemployed but caring San Francisco guy.

What Daniel cares most about are his three kids, and who wouldn't, given that each is sweeter than the next. The only spoilsport in this happy family turns out to be wife Miranda (Sally Field), a high-powered, dressed-for-success interior decorator who for 14 years has been making the rules that elfin Daniel can't resist breaking.

No sooner do we meet this group than Miranda, after a particularly egregious breach of discipline, tells Daniel enough is enough, she wants a divorce. The kids are shocked, but in truth it's not any less plausible than those supposed 14 years of Williams/Field togetherness or the fact that a killingly handsome millionaire (Pierce Brosnan) suddenly appears as Miranda's suitor. Out of a job, without a place to live, Daniel can only watch in horror as his wife is granted custody of the children.

But when busy, busy Miranda announces she has to hire a housekeeper, Daniel sees his chance. Helped by brother Frank (Harvey Fierstein.), who just happens to be a wizard of a makeup artist, he disguises himself as Mrs. Doubtfire, a kindly but no-nonsense elderly party who soon makes him/herself indispensable in the Hillard household.

The source for "Doubtfire's" Randi Mayem Singer and Leslie Dixon script turns out to be a children's book by Anne Fine, and the result is a film with too many traces of that genre's soft, edges. Not helping is youthful "Home Alone" director Chris Columbus, who already has the kind of complacently commercial sensibilities it usually takes years to develop.

And then there is Williams. Even though, unlike Hoffman in "Tootsie," his disguise is so foolproof it takes part of the fun out of the role, even though his too numerous speeches about being a dad are more earnest than effective, when he allows himself to be funny there is no one else you want to see.

So, once again, why care? Clearly no one is holding Williams' hands to the fire to play these parts, he must enjoy taking on saccharine characters, and complaining about the situation leaves one open to the kind of scorn Woody Allen showed his critics in "Stardust Memories" when he had space aliens say they were fans of his earlier, funnier movies.

But Williams is not enlarging his scope, as Allen did, he is constricting himself by appearing in increasingly bland and sappy motion pictures. And as film succeeds film, the chances of a reprise of the kind of daring, coldly different cameo did in Kenneth Branagh's "Dead Again" seem increasingly unlikely.

Maybe this was inevitable, maybe, like Zero Mostel, Williams' true performing personality is too large even for the big screen. Still, if for instance Spanish painter Francisco Goya had abandoned his brilliant series of etchings and devoted his life to being a competent maker of decorative tile, those who cared about the field he left behind would have felt it a shame, and so it is with Mr. Williams.

NEW YORK, 11/29/93, p. 64, David Denby

In *Mrs. Doubtfire*, Robin Williams is like a candy machine that won't stop dispensing Twinkies. Voices and characters pour out of him; he's almost alarmingly fecund. At times, you feel you ought to stomp on half his ideas with a shoe just so you can concentrate on the best ones. In this broadly obvious farce, Williams plays a cranky San Francisco actor, Daniel Hillard, who does voice-overs to make a living, and there are scenes in which Daniel, just for fun, flashes through his repertory. Daniel has too many good ideas—that's his problem. He can't find himself. But when his wife, Miranda (Sally Field), throws him out, he discovers his role at last. Missing his three young children terribly, he gets himself made up as a 60-year-old English nanny, and takes a job working in his own house.

Mrs. Euphegenia Doubtfire is a dignified, heavyset woman with thin lips pressed together and a giant sloping breast. Williams doesn't condescend to her; he plays her as if she had as much right to take up space on this planet in her fussy, powerful singularity as anyone else. And at the same time, Williams tries to play Daniel the self-destructive actor hidden underneath the lady's padding. It's supposed to be a fault in Daniel that he's always on the verge of blowing up any situation he's in. But how can we see it as a fault when blowups give Robin Williams the chance to be funny? There's something self-defeating about casting a nonstop comedy machine as a fallible person; the movie's tearjerking moralism is at odds with its desire to entertain us. In all, *Mrs. Doubtfire* cannot compare to *Tootsie*. Much of it feels synthetic and crude, more the result of engineering than inspiration. The writers, Leslie Dixon and Randi Mayem Singer, and director Chris Columbus (*Home Alone*) put a commercial glaze on everything, as if a future TV series wore taking over the movie even as it was unreeling in the projector.

In the beginning, Columbus sets up a bad marriage that's real enough. Daniel, the joker, is a fun dad, goofing off with the kids, always the life of the party, while Miranda is stuck holding things together—earning money, dressing and feeding everyone. He's the antic clown; she's the rulemaker. Miranda complains that she doesn't like the rigid woman that he's turning her into, but some of us, looking at Sally Field, will likely retort, "You're doing it to yourself." A crisper, drier, more stylized actress might have played Miranda the boss without boring us, but Sally Field, I'm afraid, has long passed the point of gaining anyone's sympathy. Since Robin Williams and Sally Field aren't remotely conceivable as a couple, you can't root for them to work out their differences. Columbus is trying to engage us in a relationship that's mainly a casting mistake.

The early stages of Daniel's deception are fun. The filmmakers have shrewdly set the movie in San Francisco, where cross-dressing doesn't seem so odd, and Harvey Fierstein, that basso kitten, the Jewish sultan of the gay seraglio, is on hand as Daniel's brother, a makeup artist. Harvey and his lover try out different femme looks on Robin Williams. The scenes are rapidly cut together, and as Williams, in different wigs, noses, and makeup, goes through the voices for each look—Barbra, Marlene, and so on—we seem to be getting a history of show business as seen in a gay bar. That the performer isn't gay only strengthens the tribute; it's Robin Williams's way of saying that fans have made show-business history, too.

So far, so good. But when Daniel becomes Mrs. Doubtfire, we don't have the fun of seeing him growing into his "role." Nor does impersonating Mrs. Doubtfire bring out aspects of his character that we've seen before. He just is her, transformed into a strict, demanding person. In other words, Columbus doesn't support the illusion he's creating the way Sydney Pollack did in *Tootsie*. He thinks only about the obvious laughs, not whether we'll believe what he's showing us. Most of his direction is sloppy and grossly opportunistic: When Daniel throws an impromptu party for his son, Columbus fills the house with dozens of neighborhood kids of all sizes and colors, and animals from a petting zoo. In the divorce proceedings, Miranda's lawyer is a smirking bitch amused by Daniel's misfortunes. Smirk, smirk, smirk—she wants the man to suffer. A director like Columbus isn't necessarily in touch with the audience; he's in touch with his own low assumptions about the audience.

Within hours, Mrs. Doubtfire pulls the household together, disciplines the children, and so on. The joke, of course, is that only by posing as a woman can Daniel perform as a proper husband at last. But if he loves his kids as much as he says—and Robin Williams twinkles and glows, fervently stating his need for the children—why is he normally such a lousy father? The filmmakers can't make the character come out right. Daniel is a jerk, but he's sanctified because he also has this great need. My *kids*, my *kids*! Columbus overdraws on his star, overdraws on our sympathy. We're left watching Williams doing virtuoso bits, dancing with the vacuum cleaner when no one is looking, gravely protecting himself from the amorous attentions of an elderly bus driver. He's a hell of an old lady, and in a movie in which virtually everything else is carelessly done, that's just barely enough.

NEW YORK POST, 11/24/93, p. 33, Michael Medved

An out-of-work actor finds the role of his career by masquerading as an endearing old lady with a funny accent. Much to his surprise, the doughty character he creates becomes a popular TV star noted for her earthy wisdom and refreshing good sense.

In the course of his cross-dressing adventures, our hero also makes use of his female alter-ego to enjoy heart-to-heart conversations with the woman he loves.

Hey, if it all worked 11 years ago for "Tootsie," why not use the same entertaining elements as the basis for a big new movie for Robin Williams?—and he's even funnier in drag than Dustin Hoffman.

Sure enough, "Mrs. Doubtfire" does deliver its share of laughs, and it's likely to be a major hit, but the richer satisfactions that you got with "Tootsie," or that you might reasonably expect from a performer of Williams' huge talent, are sorely lacking.

From the picture's opening minutes an atmosphere of farcical silliness co-exists uncomfortably with a plot setup that is mawkish and maudlin.

Williams' character is an aging free-spirit whose tightly wound interior-decorator wife (capably played by Sally Field) tires of his chronic immaturity and instability. She gets a quick divorce, and the court gives her sole custody of their three children, confining Williams to Saturday visits.

This is totally unacceptable to him, so with the aid of his makeup artist brother (Harvey Fierstein, in a stereotypical gay role) he assumes a new identity as "Mrs. Doubtfire," a prim, proper British housekeeper who promptly lands a job taking care of the kids each day after school. Conveniently enough, neither the children nor the mother notice that the new nanny bears a haunting resemblance to dear old dad.

Actually, the makeup effects and Williams' acting are so convincing that most moviegoers will happily suspend disbelief on this crucial point. Having established a potentially amusing situation, however, the filmmakers (including Williams himself, who served as co-producer) seem to have no idea how to either exploit or resolve it.

Instead, director Chris Columbus resorts to what must come naturally for him after this experience with the two "Home Alone" movies: stupid, overdone slapstick, painfully and pointlessly prolonged past the edge of boredom.

The film features not one, but two extended sequences in which Williams breathlessly attempts to be both characters at once, changing clothes, body suit, latex face and wigs, as he runs endlessly in and out of various bathrooms.

The dialogue also spends too much time in the bathroom—or at least the locker room—with graphic references that will startle parents who make the mistake of bringing small kids to this PG-13 release.

Williams' presumably improvisatory verbal riffs include very specific ruminations on vibrators, genital size, foreplay, cunnilingus and other salty topics that might be appropriate for a nightclub act but seem altogether unnecessary in a sentimental comedy billed as "fun for the whole family."

The movie's other major surprise is its uncommonly courageous ending, which manages to avoid the pat solution that the audience has been expecting all along.

This intriguing conclusion comes as something of an afterthought but since it is packaged together with some trendy preachments about expanding our notion of family from the restrictive, outmoded traditional model, audiences will feel encouraged to take this diverting but shallow picture far more seriously than it deserves.

NEWSDAY, 11/24/93, Part II/p. 61, Jack Mathews

For anyone still unclear about the difference between a high-concept movie and the other kind, "Mrs. Doubtfire," the new Robin Williams comedy, and "Tootsie," the movie "Mrs. Doubtfire" so brazenly rips off, provide a handy textbook comparison.

"Tootsie" is a movie about an out-of-work actor who uses his skills to land a woman's role in a TV soap opera and in carrying on the charade, begins to understand what it is to be treated as the "weaker sex." You can laugh, and you can learn something.

"Mrs. Doubtfire" is also about an out-of-work actor landing a job as a woman, but the entire exercise is an excuse for Robin Williams to wear a dress. You can laugh, and you can laugh.

Being high-concept isn't always a bad thing. Williams, the Genie, the genius!, is one of the funniest actors ever to step in front of a camera and having him ham it up in drag is a seriously funny idea.

When his Daniel Hillard, a voice actor fired for ad-libbing anti-smoking lines into the mouth of an animated parrot, slips into the guise of 60-year-old Mrs. Doubtfire, and passes himself off as a British nanny to be near his children and his estranged wife (Sally Field), Williams dominates the screen like a good comic working a nightclub stage.

Wearing a gray wig, a latex mask and heavy prosthetic breasts that tend to catch fire when he cooks, Williams dares you to look at him, and to listen to the vulgar asides slipping out in that sing-song British (Scottish? Irish?) accent, and not laugh.

Some of his riffs as Mrs. Doubtfire are flat, and a couple of scenes where he has to switch back and forth between his male and female characters are badly conceived farce. But there is enough of the Williams brilliance to keep us howling over most of the rough spots.

A far greater problem is the attempt by screenwriters Leslie Dixon ("Overboard") and Randi Mayem Singer and director Chris Columbus (the "Home Alone" movies) to ground "Mrs. Doubtfire" in a sober theme. They want to say something about divorce, and when they're through, all they have said is that children of divorced parents shouldn't blame themselves.

Every note struck on behalf of that notion rings false. From the opening moments, when Daniel's career-obsessed wife comes home and finds him hosting a rowdy birthday party for their son and demands a divorce, we're following a screenwriters forced fantasy. There is no real emotion, only emotional cues.

The movie stumbles from one bogus event to another, setting up Daniel's transformation to Mrs. Doubtfire.

Would someone as nice as Field plays Miranda really deny her heartbroken husband easy access to their three children? Would she rather have some stranger looking after the kids than a father who is more fun than the circus! Would the court treat him like a pariah because he's unemployed and has a crummy apartment?

Where "Tootsie" played it straight, with every event and emotion following logically, "Mrs, Doubtfire" tries to have it both ways, face and domestic melodrama hand-in-hand, and it merely widens the divide. When Dustin Hoffman scrambled to switch identities in "Tootsie," the fun was in its plausibility. When Williams make his quick changes, getting in and out of a three-hour make-up job in seconds, it's a scene out of "Superman."

In the end, the concept for "Mrs. Doubtfire" works a lot better than the execution.

NEWSWEEK, 11/29/93, p. 72, David Ansen

Can a movie be both a delight and a drag? Yes, it its name is *Mrs. Doubtfire*. Simply put, I've rarely laughed at a movie I generally disliked. If you're a fan of Robin Williams (and who in his right mind isn't?), how can you resist the prospect of seeing him gussied up as a prim and proper 60-year-old English nanny—the guise he dons to spend time with his three children when his estranged wife (Sally Field) is awarded sole custody in their divorce? Williams makes a phenomenal old gal. You may not buy the pretext that forces him to such extremes (it never makes sense that Field won't let him have more contact with the kids), but you won't doubt that his own children would be fooled by their daddy's dowdy drag. Busty, prudishly maternal, Williams disappears inside his mountain of makeup and emerges with a characterization of hilarious pursed-mouth pungency.

Williams occupies this movie like a diamond encased in a tub of stale pudding. As directed by Chris Columbus and written by Randi Mayem Singer and Leslie Dixon, "Mrs. Doubtfire" aspires to be a heartfelt comedy about broken family values that will simultaneously make you laugh and cry. It succeeds at the former, but may have you crying for an editor when it takes on the tone of an after-school special on self-esteem. We're meant to believe that when Daniel Hillard, an irresponsible but sweetly childlike clown, turns into the miraculous Mrs. Doubtfire, he/she magically brings out the best in his family and himself.

Comparisons to "Tootsie" have been tossed around, but Columbus's comedy lacks precisely the edge of reality that gave that movie its bite and feeling. The model Hillard kids are pure TV sitcom, their every cute reaction milked in close-up. Field's workaholic mom is so sketchily written you can't imagine that she and Williams were ever a couple. Now that she's embarked on an affair with the rich, too handsome Pierce Brosnan, why does she put up with Mrs. D.'s meddlesome Victorian attempts to obstruct her budding romance? And as funny as the nanny's insults to the new beau are, it's strange that Brosnan doesn't utter a peep of protest. Just why, for that matter, does everybody love this bossy lady so much? Farce demands rigorous internal logic: Columbus clumsily switches gears between slapstick and sappy family-therapy sessions. The movie keeps making the sensible point that one shouldn't talk down to children. The problem with "Mrs. Doubtfire" is that it talks down to grown-ups.

But who would want to miss the moment when Robin Williams, searching for the woman he should become, suddenly turns into Streisand, belting out "Don't Rain on My Parade"? Or the moment when his false teeth fall into his drink? With so much healing laughter at their disposal, why did the filmmakers feel the need to pour on the castor oil of message? They've taken Mrs. Doubtfire's Victorian remedies too much to heart.

SIGHT AND SOUND, 2/94, p. 58, Lizzie Francke

San Francisco. Following a disagreement with a colleague, voice-over artist Daniel Hillard walks out of his job dubbing cartoon animals. He returns home to his children—Lydia, Chris and Natalie—and puts on an impromptu birthday party for Chris. Alerted by a neighbour, his wife Miranda rushes home from her design company to find Daniel and the kids creating mayhem. The incident forces her to realise that she wants a divorce. Daniel seeks solace with his brother Frank and his boyfriend Jack, both theatre make-up artists. Later the divorce comes through and Miranda is awarded custody of the children, with Daniel only allowed to see them on Saturdays. The court decision, however, is to be renewed in six months. Daniel visits the court liaison officer who tells him he must get a job and a decent home for the children to visit. He secures a post, working as a shipping clerk at a TV studio.

Meanwhile, Miranda discovers that a new client is her old college flame Stu. Later, collecting the children from Daniel, she informs him that she is advertising for a housekeeper. Daniel alters the newspaper ad form to ensure that no-one contacts her. He phones Miranda and, putting on a variety of voices, pretends to be prospective housekeepers. Miranda takes the bait and schedules an appointment for him to visit in the persona of Mrs Doubtfire. Made up by Frank as the matronly Mrs Doubtfire, Daniel visits Miranda and the children, and gets the job. After a few mishaps, Daniel takes control of the household, balancing it with his TV job. One day he arrives at Miranda's to find that she has brought Stu home to meet the children. Unhappy about this, Daniel attempts to sabotage Stu's chances.

Later, Chris walks in on Mrs Doubtfire in the bathroom and realizes that she is a man in drag. Daniel comes clean with Chris and his eldest daughter, Lydia, but continues the charade. At the TV station, Daniel interests Mr Lundy, the studio head, with his ideas for a children's programme. Lundy arranges a dinner meeting with him, but when Stu invites the whole family (and Mrs Doubtfire) out for dinner to celebrate Miranda's birthday, Daniel discovers that the table is booked for the same time and place as the appointment—and he can't break either engagement. Throughout the evening, Daniel does a double act, but things go awry as he starts drinking with Lundy, and eventually his cover is blown. At the second hearing of the custody case, Daniel is penalized for his behaviour and forbidden to see the children. Meanwhile, Miranda misses Mrs Doubtfire's household management skills. Lundy gives Daniel, as Mrs Doubtfire, a children's show. Miranda watches the programme and decides to visit him. She realizes that the kids need him and revokes the court's decision. The couple remain amicably divorced but Daniel gets to see his children every day.

Mrs. Doubtfire could be described as a crazy *Kramer v. Kramer* for the 90s—but via *Tootsie*. Adapted by Leslie Dixon and Randi Mayem Singer from the novel by celebrated children's writer Anne Fine, it is a potent, pantomimic and hugely hilarious family fantasy that shows every evidence of gripping audiences as much as Chris Columbus' *Home Alone*. If that film showed the cracks in the household, with its young hero Kevin successfully wishing parents and siblings away ("families suck"), *Mrs. Doubtfire* takes those cracks to be a given. Unable to suffer her husband's reckless behaviour any longer, Miranda (Sally Field, actually likeable here with her qualms about her spouse sympathetically handled) wishes him away via a decree nisi. Daniel's quest is to return to the bosom of that family via the magic of Uncle Frank and Auntie Jack's ultimate makeover of latex and body-suit, and his own inimitable skill for "doing voices".

Robin Williams' last incarnation as a family man was in *Hook*, in which he plays a harried executive with scant time for his kids or wife. In *Hook*, Peter Pan has become a "corporate clown" (as Daniel describes the workaholic Miranda's colleagues) who has to be whisked off to Neverland to retrieve the playful side of himself that will bring him back home. In *Mrs. Doubtfire* (which Williams also co-produced with his wife Marsha Garces Williams), he starts out as too much of the roaring lost boy. The film opens with Williams in the sound booth, manically dubbing a Chuck Jones cartoon. Here Columbus not only signals a major influence (for what is *Home Alone* if not a live action cartoon), but also underlines the cartoon nature of Williams' persona (backed up by his recent contributions to *Toys* and *Aladdin*). This sequence segues into a party scene that is a gorgeous riot of mismanagement as the kids and Daniel bop on the sofas, ponies trot—and worse—in the hall and rabbits chew up the plants on the neighbour's rockery (cf. the equally lavish but controlled extravaganza organized by Steve Martin in *Parenthood*). This is every child's fantasy: Ma's out, Pa's out, let's party (except that here, Pa's in). Once ejected from the home, Daniel's key to returning is what every party animal should know: a lesson in house-training that embraces everything from how to talk to a woman (Daniel and Miranda, never really talked) to cooking with Julia Childs.

As the matronly Mrs Doubtfire, Williams plays the swell dame who is allowed her kitchen antics and her salty spiel (talking to Stu of Miranda: "You should see the power tools in her bedroom"). But Williams keeps her for the most part in the realm of the almost possible rather than doing her as coarse, exaggerated drag. Speaking in a sweet, lilting British accent that hovers somewhere between Land's End and John O'Groats, she incarnates homely, traditional values—the nanny of a bygone era who might have well paraded her former charges in Peter Pan's Kensington Gardens. This effect allows for the comedy of clashes (genteel widow doing the cleaning to 'Papa's Got a Brand New Bag', leering at a bikini babe at a country club, and spouting forth a string of brilliant one-liners in her attempt to wrinkle Stu's Pringle-sweater composure), as well as suggesting an old world order. But the fact that Mrs Doubtfire replaces a dinosaur programme at Lundy's station suggests an evolution rather than regression of Major's 'back-to-basics' variety. The film ends with the striking image of Williams masquerading as a matriarch, eulogising the possibilities for "all sorts of different families" on her kids' show, as Daniel drives off with the kids, he and Miranda happily divorced ever after. It promises a brave new world while begging the question: why can't a man be more like a woman?

TIME, 11/29/93, p. 74, Richard Schickel

It's one of those days for Daniel Hillard (Robin Williams). First he gets fired from his job, then he gets fired from his marriage, pretty much for the same reason: the man has a passion, verging on the unreasonable, for protecting and nurturing children, and it makes more sensible people crazy.

His job is to supply the voices for a Sylvester-and-Tweety type of animated cartoon; he loses it when the villainous cat forces the victimized bird to inhale a cigarette and Daniel insists on improvising antismoking dialogue for the sequence, so that kids in the audience clearly understand the full horror of the noxious weed. Daniel goes on to lose his marriage when he arranges to bring an entire petting zoo into his house as a birthday-party treat for one of his three children. The resulting mess is the last straw for his wife Miranda (Sally Field, expertly walking the line between long-suffering exasperation and ineluctable affection).

A divorce court, naturally, does not look kindly upon unemployed flakes; it refuses Daniel's plea for joint custody and places limits on his visitation rights that are unbearable to the best daddy in Christendom. The world does not look kindly on working moms, and Miranda cannot find a suitable nanny to tend the kids while she pursues her high-powered career in interior design. Thus, out of mutual need, but without Miranda's conscious participation, *Mrs. Doubtfire*—that is to say, Daniel in old-lady drag and affecting a Scots accent—is born. In this role, Daniel not only brings order to a fractured household; he also brings a new orderliness to his own life.

Improbable? Of course. all cross-dressing comedies, from *Charlie's Aunt* onward, are improbable. Most of the fun comes from seeing people fooled by what seems to us, who are in on the joke, a completely penetrable ruse. Curiously enough, what's really unpersuasive about Mrs. Doubtfire—not to say draggy—is its non-drag sequences. The children are goody-goodies, without mischief or quirks, and their father's relationship with them is unclouded by even minor impatience, let alone major outrage. The script, by Randi Mayem Singer and Leslie Dixon, presents ideal fatherhood as a form of saintliness.

More immediately, they and director Chris Columbus had to contend with their star's newfound desire (see last year's *Toys*) to play the holy fool. Williams' head contains a multitude of char-acters—some of them real, some of them American archetypes—and as a vocal quick-change artist, Williams has a unique gift not only for dead-on impersonations of these characters, but also for setting them all free on a babbling stream of consciousness. These manic monologues are impolite and utterly incorrect politically. They articulate our secret, subversive thoughts. His impersonation of Mrs. Doubtfire shows that he can sustain one of these inventions quite won-derfully. But she's chucklesome, heartwarming, and without a subversive bone under her foam-padded bodysuit. And Daniel Hillard, of whom we see entirely too much, is winsome, childlike, too good for this world, the kind of wimped-out modern male Williams ought to be satirizing, not celebrating.

VILLAGE VOICE, 11/30/93, Film Special/p. 29, Georgia Brown

If dad in *Mrs. Doubtfire* is dangerous, it's because he's so mercurial. Let's just say, he's a child himself. When Robin Williams's Daniel Hillard is fired from his job dubbing cartoons (he does all the voices), he goes home and literally turns their immaculate San Francisco manse into a zoo. Inside comes a mobile menagerie (donkey, etc.); there's even a kid swinging from the chandelier. Wouldn't you know, his successful wife of 14 years (Sally Field) arrives home and kicks the nitwit out. Leery of Daniel's jobless state, the court grants her sole custody and allots him

Saturday visitation. A bit later, devastated by the loss of his kids, he decides to apply for the nanny position. (Woody Allen take note.)

The gross improbabilities are massed into the film's first half hour in order that we may spend the rest of the movie giggling as Williams impersonates a hulking, gray-haired English widow in cardigans and sensible pumps. (This is after he rejects a Barbra Streisand mask. Who would hire *her?*) An elderly but robust Mary Poppins, Mrs. Doubtfire possesses all the virtues Daniel lacks—neatness, reliability, firmness about homework, culinary skills—at least at first. She becomes a tad sloppy when she drinks. In the spirit of all good masquerades, Daniel ends up adopting some of her traits.

Mrs. Doubtfire is fun—it's sometimes a hoot—but as a screwball impersonation comedy it's hardly in the same class as *Tootsie; Victor, Victoria;* or *Some Like It Hot.* In those works the central crossover disguise is surrounded by meaty comedy and some fairly weighty psychological matter. Here, everything that leads to Williams's donning of latex mask and padded body suit is absurd; it's mere slapstick. (Just to mention four cheats: (1) Two of the kids are teenagers and in reality could see their father more or less as they wish. (2) The amicable separation presented here would never end up in court. (3) Where's his share of the household assets? (4) For that matter, Daniel's bosses at the cartoon factory would've coddled him forever because who else could do all those voices?)

At the end, Daniel/Williams makes a wounded appeal that fathers be given access no matter how flaky they may be. Obviously, the filmmakers—director Chris Columbus, as well as Williams and his second wife—ex-babysitter Marsha Garces Williams—want to pretend that this frenetic farce is also an adult drama about divorce. Well, that's their privilege.

Also reviewed in:
NEW YORK TIMES, 11/24/93, p. C11, Janet Maslin
VARIETY, 11/29/93, p. 30, Brian Lowry
WASHINGTON POST, 11/24/93, p. C1, Rita Kempley
WASHINGTON POST, 11/26/93, Weekend/p. 57, Desson Howe

MUCH ADO ABOUT NOTHING

A Samuel Goldwyn Company release of a Renaissance Films production in association with American Playhouse Theatrical Films and BBC Films. *Producer:* Kenneth Branagh, David Parfitt, and Stephen Evans. *Director:* Kenneth Branagh. *Screenplay:* Kenneth Branagh. *Based on the play "Much Ado About Nothing" by:* William Shakespeare. *Director of Photography:* Roger Lanser. *Editor:* Andrew Marcus. *Music:* Patrick Doyle. *Music Editor:* Roy Prendergast. *Sound:* David Crozier. *Sound Editor:* Robert Gavin, Bill Trent, and Campbell Askew. *Production Designer:* Tim Harvey. *Art Director:* Martin Childs. *Costumes:* Phyllis Dalton. *Make-up:* Paul Engelen. *Stunt Coordinator:* Bronco McLoughlin. *Running time:* 111 minutes. *MPAA Rating:* PG-13.

CAST: Denzel Washington (Don Pedro, Prince of Arragon); Kenneth Branagh (Benedick, of Padua); Robert Sean Leonard (Claudio, of Florence); Keanu Reeves (Don John, Don Pedro's Half Brother); Gerard Horan (Borachio); Richard Clifford (Conrade); Richard Briers (Leonato, Governor of Messina); Brian Blessed (Antonio, his Brother); Patrick Doyle (Balthasar, a Singer); Jimmy Yuill (Friar Francis, a Priest); Kate Beckinsale (Hero, Leonato's Daughter); Imelda Staunton (Margaret, Attendant on Hero); Phyllida Law (Ursula, Attendant on Hero); Emma Thompson (Beatrice, an Orphan, Leonato's Niece); Michael Keaton (Dogberry, Constable of the Watch); Ben Elton (Verges, the Headborough); Teddy Jewesbury (The Sexton); Andy Hockley (George Seacole); Chris Barnes (Francis Seacole); Conrad Nelson (Hugh Oakcake); Alex Scott (A Boy, Servant to Benedik); Alex Lowe (Messenger).

CHRISTIAN SCIENCE MONITOR, 5/10/93, p. 14, David Sterritt

From all the evidence, Kenneth Branagh wants to be Orson Welles and is working hard to achieve this lofty goal.

His new movie, "Much Ado About Nothing," is the latest installment in Mr. Branagh's effort. In the best Wellesian style, he has directed the picture and written the screenplay—closely based on William Shakespeare's comedy about pride, deception, and twin love affairs—in addition to playing the most important role. He is also credited as producer, and he has surrounded himself with an impressive array of supporting players.

All of which puts Branagh squarely in the footsteps of Welles, who similarly enjoyed controlling all aspects of his productions and flaunting his talents on both sides of the camera.

So why isn't "Much Ado About Nothing" likely to enter the film-history books alongside Welles's great "Othello" and "Falstaff"?

The answer is simple: Welles was a towering artist with prodigious insights and a steady stream of innovative ideas, while Branagh is just a talented young man with more energy than inspiration. He does things correctly, and at times he brings a noticeable bit of flair to a shot, a scene, or a piece of comic business. But there's little in his new movie—or his three previous outings as a multiple-threat filmmaker—to put him anywhere near the Wellesian status he seems too eager to reach.

He would have a better chance at future greatness if he stopped spreading his abilities over so many areas, chose one aspect of his career to concentrate on, and worked like crazy to realize all its possibilities. "Much Ado About Nothing" indicates that his strongest suit is in the acting department. So the best course is clear: Branagh should leave the writing and directing to others, and focus on becoming the most exciting on-screen presence of his generation.

That's a goal worth reaching, and it's a lot more realistic than competing with a legend like Welles.

Branagh's screenplay for "Much Ado About Nothing" takes the traditional Hollywood route of condensing the text, clarifying the action, and highlighting the broadest comic and dramatic ingredients. He goes for speed and economy by trimming the play to slightly more than 90 minutes. And he retains only the essence of Shakespeare's romp about two couples who marry despite foolish vanity and the machinations of an evil betrayer.

Less successfully, Branagh also tries for dreaminess and poignancy by stopping the story in its tracks for silly slapstick and dreary music interludes. His camera style is efficient but ordinary.

His directing of performances has varying degrees of success. Emma Thompson and Denzel Washington come off superbly as Beatrice, the sharp-witted beauty, and Don Pedro, the handsome prince. Robert Sean Leonard and Keanu Reeves are competent as love-struck Claudio and the villainous Don John. And Kate Beckinsale plays the sadly betrayed Hero with a good deal of charm. Michael Keaton makes a wretched impression as Dogberry, however, and Branagh shares the blame for clumsy mishandling of what should be the film's most amusing moments.

By contrast, Branagh's own portrayal of Benedick is first-rate on almost all counts. He speaks his lines with a fine mixture of deft characterization, self-deflating humor, and poetic lilt; his gestures are thoughtfully conceived and wittily executed.

In his previous Shakespeare movie, "Henry V," he fell short of his ambitious goal, which was to render a familiar hero more "psychological" and "complex" than previous interpretations (including Laurence Olivier's classic version) had done. His acting is much closer to the mark in "Much Ado About Nothing," and that's cause for celebration.

There will be more to celebrate if Branagh realizes that acting is where his fullest talents lie and puts all his attention into developing this.

FILMS IN REVIEW, 8/93, p. 260, Harry Pearson

It is well to keep in mind, when considering Kenneth Branagh's rich and vibrant interpretation of Shakespeare's *Much Ado About Nothing*, that, like several other of the Master's comedies, *Much Ado*'s disparate parts don't always quite jell.

In this particular instance, we have two contrasting affairs: the (audience-pleasing) affair of the heart between the battling Beatrice and Benedick, which comes to play second fiddle to the darker, more materialistically grounded courtship of Hero by Claudio, who is nothing in Shakespeare's text if not an opportunist, totally of the modern cloth where it comes to a callow narcissism.

Shakespeare abandons the Beatrice/Benedick narrative line just when it becomes truly engrossing (just as each is tricked into thinking the other is smitten), so that we are robbed of the potential comedic riches of their confrontation after being set up by their well meaning friends. Instead, we must focus upon the artificial machinations of the Hero-Claudio affair with its particularly ugly and near pathetic outcome, a tale itself derived from antiquity and adapted for his Elizabethan audiences by the playwright. And, just as you begin to involve yourself with the plight of Hero, along comes Constable Dogberry for comic relief, thus presenting us with a third subsidiary plot line, and the one furthest away from our principal interests, Beatrice and Benedick.

The person who directs *Much Ado*, either for the stage or the screen, must attempt to make the play seem to be one coherent weave or, failing that, build up such a head of steam that the entire project plunges along with furious momentum making the sum synergistically greater than the individual parts. There is also the more delicate question of what to omit and how to handle the language problem. *Much Ado* was written almost 400 years ago and the mother tongue as spoken then was vastly more complex, more deeply studded with allusions to folklore, the Greek and Roman classics, and to English history (both of the official and vox populi varieties), as well as rhetorically complicated.

What is surprising, given the free use of cinematic technique, is just how closely Branagh's *Ado* adheres to Shakespeare's own. The textual editing (by Branagh?) is skillful and largely preserves the sense and metric patterns of the original. If anything, Branagh gets into trouble because of his fidelity to the text, given, that, perhaps in an effort to achieve more dramatic continuity, he concentrates all of action in Leonato's villa (instead of in the town of Messina itself), a decision that makes Constable Dogberry's role even more removed from the sense of the action than it need be.

On the other hand, he has fielded one of the strongest imaginable pairings of Beatrice and Benedick with his wife Emma Thompson as Beatrice and himself as Benedick. It is their exuberance and the force of their interplay that provides the mainspring behind the film, even if Thompson's quite forcible delivery of her lines threatens to overwhelm our sympathy for her character. Her "Kill Claudio" draws no laughs in this rendering.

Branagh's choice of a supporting cast, evidently done with a sure bead on the box-office gross, includes the unlikely concatenation of Denzel Washington, Keanu Reeves, Michael Keaton, and Robert Sean Leonard. Reeves, as the villain of the piece (shirtless, in leather pants and getting a hot massage when first we see him up close) is just awful. His idea of villainy is a sneer more appropriate to a white dude upon first hearing rap. (Whatever happened to the gifted young actor of *The River's Edge* and *Dangerous Liaisons*; his earlier plunge into Shakespeare in *My Own Private Idaho* wrecked that film.) Washington, praised for his quiet dignity by several other reviewers, seems uncomfortable and out of his element here (he has no credentials as a Shakespearean) and definitely not of the gentry landed. Keaton does *Beetlejuice* again and manages to make his lines incomprehensible. He mugs furiously, as if aware that he will get no laughs from his character's mangling of the language. His every scene is an agony and distraction. Leonard, on the other hand, given Branagh's conception of Claudio is quite, quite good.

One of Branagh's key decisions is to edit Claudio out of a quite genuine macho nastiness (his early queries about Hero's dowry, his humiliation of her, timed to coincide with their wedding) and into a kind of thoughtless boyishness, in which inexperience masks the good heart. This Leonard plays to a song, and so believably that it underlines what many critics think was the playwright's basic intent with this comedy, i.e., how we are misled by flaws in our communications with each other. If, as the text strongly suggests, Beatrice and Benedick have courted before, and the flame of love fires their jousting, then what stands as the obstacle between them, other than their misreading of each other? Clearly, if everyone in this play were talking openly, there would be no play. Claudio could have, easily enough, ascertained Hero's innocence if he hadn't mistakenly assumed he was seeing what he wasn't. And so, in the best sense, Branagh's cinematic version is absolutely true to the spirit of the original and, I suspect, like any good interpretation, enriches our understanding of the author's intent, even while it takes liberties with textural fidelities.

I think, at heart, this is one of the reasons audiences seem to adore this film. It plays strongly to the quite contemporary prejudice that there are few problems that good communications will not solve, a fairy tale notion belied by our quite excellent understanding of what some people these days are saying. It's wish fulfillment (then as now, perhaps) and Branagh packages it all with a summery atmosphere that is almost tactile: You can quite nearly imagine yourself to be in Italy's sunlit vistas during the Renaissance. It is, indeed, this kind of mise en scene that counterpoints all that we see, and, as much as the Branagh-Thompson performances, propels it. We are willing to forgive Keanu and Michael because we are enchanted. Even to forgive some quite clumsy directional touches (the montage of Beatrice and Benedick separately overwhelmed by the notion that love is theirs,—the lengthy crane shot at film's end of the not very convincing dancing and festivities in the villa's courtyard). Several of our better critics have called Branagh's vision "cartoonish," it is not that, it is a not-so-Grimm telling of some very adult and perhaps, universal fantasies.

LOS ANGELES TIMES, 5/14/93, Calendar/p. 1, Kenneth Turan

Emma Thompson and Kenneth Branagh in this rollicking version of "Much Ado About Nothing" is the way it allows us to share in that state of special grace, to watch the English-speaking world's reigning acting couple perform at the top of their game.

Directed by Branagh and adapted by him from Shakespeare's antic comedy, "Much Ado" is a merry yet pointed tale of lovers at cross-purposes, of the misunderstandings that can divide them and the true emotion that must inevitably deposit them in each other's arms by the close.

And in Beatrice and Benedick Shakespeare created perhaps his most pleasing couple, a verbally energetic pair whose sarcastic, mock disdainful exchanges make up what a dazzled onlooker calls "a kind of merry war." Thompson (who won this year's best actress Oscar for "Howards End") and Branagh must have been dying to take on these reluctant suitors, and seeing them beautifully play off each other is an enormous pleasure for lovers of the romance of language as well as fanciers of romantic love.

These two not only animate characters who are drunk on words, they so understand the spirit of Shakespeare's witty, effervescent dialogue they've in effect passed their passion onto the rest of the cast. While actors such as Denzel Washington, Keanu Reeves, Robert Sean Leonard and Michael Keaton were not necessarily cast because of their extensive Shakespearean backgrounds, they all perform as if handling Elizabethan English was one of the things they do best.

And their familiar presence strengthens what must have been one of Branagh's main aims with this production, to make a Shakespearean movie that was loose, accessible and high spirited. He's not only slimmed down the play, he's directed it at a breathless pace, giving all the scenes, from the comic and romantic to the strictly dramatic, what he himself calls a "high-octane approach." The result is a model of popular Shakespeare, audience-friendly without even a note of condescension.

Branagh's playful approach begins with the very first scene (casually lifted from the play's second act), with the words *Sigh no more, ladies, sigh no more, men were deceivers ever* appearing in large print on the screen as Beatrice (clothed like the rest of the cast in an almost timeless costume) recites them with gleeful conviction.

No sooner are the words out of her mouth than news comes that Don Pedro, Prince of Arragon (a properly steely and commanding Washington), and his entire victorious army are about to pay a visit to Leonato, governor of Messina (veteran British actor Richard Briers). Leonato is not only Beatrice's uncle but also the father of another very beautiful, if more demure and conventional young woman, Hero (newcomer Kate Backinsale).

And, to nicely balance things, a posse of handsome young men comes riding in with Don Pedro. Of course there is Benedick, of whom Beatrice has already archly asked, "How many hath he killed in these wars? For indeed I promised to eat all his killings." But there is also the dark and sullen Don John (an effective Reeves), the prince's bastard half-brother, and the starry-eyed Claudio ("Dead Poets Society's" Leonard), a passionate if somewhat gullible gentleman who immediately has eyes only for Hero.

While these two moon at each other, Beatrice and Benedick pick up where they left off the last time they met. "What, my dear Lady Disdain!" he exclaims. "Are you yet living?" And she snaps right back, "Is it possible disdain should die while she hath such meet food to feed it as Signor Benedick?"

The rest of the company is so bemused by their spirited bickering that Don Pedro, declaring it to be the equal of the labors of Hercules, decides to put together a plot to get these two to fall in love. How he does this is the comic heart of "Much Ado" and also an adroit commentary on the connections between love, self-love and self-deception.

But "Much Ado" is as concerned with the young lovers Claudio and Hero as it is with this older, pricklier pair. Their romance, which starts out carefree, soon runs into the destructive machinations of Don John, and for a while things look very dark for all concerned. And dark they might well have stayed except for the efforts of the scraggliest of heroes, Dogberry, the intrepid constable of the watch.

One of Shakespeare's classic comic roles, Dogberry, the master mangler of the English language ("comparisons are odorous" is a favorite saying), proves an excellent fit for Keaton. Whether scrunching up his face into an impossible pretzel or prancing away on an imaginary horse, his Dogberry is a treat, capturing the spirit of the character and the play.

The same obviously must be said for filmmaker Branagh, who first tackled Shakespeare on the screen with 1989's "Henry V." An intuitively cinematic director as well as a master actor, he makes excellent use of the film's setting, a rambling 14th-Century Italian compound called Villa Vignamaggio. Though his work has been flashier in the past ("Dead Again"), the unobtrusive style he adopts here suits the actor-intensive nature of this material. And in making sure all the performances, especially Thompson's thoroughly delightful one, are well-served, Branagh ends up serving himself best of all.

NEW LEADER, 8/9-23/93, p. 20, David Bromwich

"Sigh no more, ladies" (a Shakespeare song that says: expect nothing from men) is being recited by a voice that turns out to belong to Emma Thompson. Lolling in a tree, she shuts her book now and smiles delightedly at the festive crowd below, who await the return of their gentlemen-warriors. The credits begin to roll, and here they come! riding into the zoom lens in slow motion; a whole host of them riding abreast, punching their fists in the air—a gesture doubtless of ancient provenance, which also recalls the heroes of the summer Olympics shouting and punching "Yes!". Swell of the music with a percussive crash.

Immensely plush and glossy, the Kenneth Branagh *Much Ado About Nothing* is under way. Though a good deal about the court of Messina remains baffling—the cause of the resentments that move the story to the brink of catastrophe, a perpetual erotic give-and-take that is often darkened by bitterness—one is left with no doubt that this is a place where one would like to live. Revels of mutual congratulation at intervals display the mellow lifestyle of the people. At the very least, it is a land "of ilk and money," and the tubs, if not hot, are everywhere.

An acrid comedy that barely ends up a comedy, Shakespeare's *Much Ado* is a battle to the death—to the marriage—of two impenitent wits, Beatrice and Benedick. Their jousting is stopped by what looks like a side issue: the young love of Claudio and Hero, broken when Hero's honor is slandered and Claudio renounces her. But it is all one story that implies words are as final as actions and reputation is more than a mask. Beatrice and Benedick are each tricked into believing the other is truly smitten; and each discovers that to believe yourself loved may create an actual welcome for love. Benedick, to satisfy Beatrice, challenges Claudio to a duel, but before a death is required, Hero's honor is restored. The rumor-mongers confess themselves agents of Don John (the bastard brother of Don Pedro, Prince of Arragon). Both couples marry in an instant, and there will be time for much forgetting.

Deep cuts have lightened this version (as fluent as it is commercially prudent), and the omitted passages make a point Branagh preferred to leave untouched. They show that sex is on everyone's mind—the women no less than the men—and that it has a risky edge. The hint of flirtation between Don Pedro and Hero as he courts her on Claudio's behalf has likewise been toned down, even though it contributes a substantial moment of doubt that carries through the original text. When Claudio credits the malicious rumor about her, he can remember seeing something unpleasant earlier. The suggestion of the film is that the love of the two couples is real, though fortuitous. The suggestion in Shakespeare is that their loves are as rigged as their hates. A hair's breadth of intent divides the pandering Don Pedro from the slandering Don John.

Branagh plays Benedick with the lively self-regard of a proud man not beyond seeing how his pride will look to others. Athletic, whether solemn or clowning, he deploys a resourceful energy that can make you forget his oddly recessive face: thin lips (hidden here by a beard); eyes unrelaxing and seldom lit by warmth—a hard face for comedy, one would have said. But once his Benedick hears of Beatrice's love, he is a solid substance melting. After that, he flows: not a halt, not a quip, not a distorted action or sentiment, yet he appears to be the same man. When, at his change of heart, he says with a shrug, "No, the world *must be peopled*," he bears himself with the humility of a genuine egotist. Against the wishes of so many, who is he to deny his amiability?

One is prepared to deny nothing to the actor who could seem for a second to have earned Emma Thompson's love. Her Beatrice is a creature of mental weather—sharp, discreet, fearfully harassing—her wit a sail that can drag and collapse, then shoot her ahead of the others who skim the surface unequipped. Her susceptible nature dwells in a medium of pure intelligence: ready, almost radiant, to draw the next insult and give it back twice-over; and ready (if such a world could be) for a world without insults. All of the alternations of Beatrice are at home in Thompson's portrayal, from her first blustering challenge of Benedick—"I pray you, how many hath he killed and eaten in these wars? But how many hath he killed? For indeed, I promised to eat all of his killing"—to the chaffing of her weary heart: "Poor fool, it keeps on the windy side of care." She is often close to melancholy, but never visibly so, and her jests make a diversion as exquisite as it is natural.

The rest of the English cast is excellent. But the production is peopled with Americans, and oh, the Americans. I have sometimes sat through a conversation in a language I half understood, and know the look of good-humored engagement that fixes the facial muscles on such occasions, and the accompanying feeling of positive asininity. Robert Sean Leonard (Claudio), Denzel Washington (Don Pedro) and Keanu Reeves (Don John) plainly felt something of the kind as they walked through their parts on what they hoped was a cloud. An aimless easy heartiness, a sort of debonair mist suffuses Leonard and Washington, a transparent disguise of embarrassment. Even their modesty cannot screen them. When Don Pedro says to Beatrice "Your *silence* most offends me"—since as long as she talks he is happy, and her silence is a refusal of marriage—Washington puts the stress on "most" as if she were generally offensive.

Leonard, weeping because he thinks Hero has died of grief, is a young actor desperate to experience an emotion, not a young man overwhelmed by one. Reeves hones the whisper and whine of his Don John into palpable nonentity. Michael Keaton's Dogberry (the only American effort that ventures something) is a shaggy paranoid wreck, his brains cooked on drugs, eyes asquint and lips curled in a snarl, speaking guttural unintelligibilities before he gallops off on two legs on a pretend-horse—a Monty Python touch that seems wildly out of keeping with the production. Yet Dogberry, with his fumbling skill, extracts the confession that solves the plot. He is the most punctilious gentleman of the piece, and the only source of geniality. Given the demand for local stars to back a British production in America, why did Branagh choose so poorly, or, having chosen, exert so little control?

This confident actor with his good eye for projects is still, on large tracts of his chosen materials, a weak and unthinking director. His Henry V in the opening scenes was as vivid as Cagney in *White Heat*, but for the rest of that film the Machiavellian note was lost, and in battles of careful splendor and brutality it was never clear what note was meant to replace it. In *Much Ado About Nothing* the performances by Branagh and Thompson are brilliant, and the hilarity always well-drilled, even if it misses a touch of spontaneity. But the undefended compromises with the text and supporting cast betray a failure of nerve. The chaotic irritants at work in this play have not been more than remotely pondered.

NEW STATESMAN & SOCIETY, 8/27/93, p. 34, Jonathan Romney

With all due respect to Orson Welles, the most remarkable film adaptation of Shakespeare I ever saw was a *Hamlet* by the lugubrious Finnish absurdist Aki Kaurismaki. In it, the sweet prince plotted a takeover of his dead father's rubber duck factory, killed Laertes by jamming a radio over his head, and spurned Ophelia because she was too fat. Next to that, even Zeffirelli's all-action *Hamlet* with Mel Gibson—"Just when you thought it was safe to come out from behind the arras"—would look a bit pale.

The first few scenes of Kenneth Branagh's *Much Ado About Nothing* almost score for comparable absurdity—simply because it overdoses on puppyish gusto. We begin with jolly Richard Briers and the fair folk of Messina lounging around their garden, enjoying a spectacular view of what is actually Tuscany, and swaying along contentedly as Emma Thompson's Beatrice gives them a tune from up a tree.

It's announced that Don Pedro (Denzel Washington) and his men are on the way, and looka yonder, there they are, galloping up in clouds of slow-motion like the Magnificent Seven. It's the cue for the film to change register from pastoral-comical to hysterical-athletical, as the womenfolk run giggling to change into their best frillies, while the visiting rugby team start executing somersaults and frenzied back-slaps in the shower room—suddenly it's more like *Seven Brides for Seven Brothers*. A brisk round of wobbling bums and snapping stays, and it's back to courtly decorum and a bit of bergamasque.

The constant, bustling change of pace is possibly a result of Branagh's desire to flaunt as much versatility as possible, but is also symptomatic of the fact that he hasn't worked *Much Ado* out as a film at all. He still thinks of it as a play, or rather as a playscript—a succession of scenes that neither flow into nor counterpoint each other in any dynamic way, but simply keep on coming. He uses mood changes the way he might lower backdrops for expediency, and to keep things rolling.

This might not be so bad if he had an interesting blend of filmic models, but he doesn't. There's a bit of Western, a bit of MGM musical, a bit of Busby Berkeley, and a lot of what can only be called Channel 4 pastoral. What we have is essentially all-singing, all-roistering Merchant-Ivory.

Branagh's conception of the play is quite simple. He sees it as "comic, lusty and full blooded", a vision betokened by the presence in a minor role of Brian Blessed, whose main function seems to be to quaff, guffaw and slap as many bottoms as possible. Branagh claims he used American actors "for their emotional fearlessness ... that's how I think you should deal with Shakespeare, that sort of blood-and-guts, high-octane approach."

That doesn't come across in the casting. Denzel Washington gives Don Pedro an air of butch, benevolent stateliness but hardly impinges; while Keanu Reeves as the nasty Don John is a plank—a highly-waxed plank, at that (does he have statutory bare chest written into his contract?). There's an overall mismatch between the British and American contingents. The Americans underplay for the screen and miss the text's rhythm by miles, the British favour a theatrical demonstrativeness that the direction can't accommodate.

As an actors' film, *Much Ado* sets out to be democratic, a venture in which everyone gets to show their stuff. This works worst in the pairing of Michael Keaton and Ben Elton as comic coppers. Required to gallop around on imaginary horses, clip-clopping ostentatiously, they seem to be trying to master some bizarre mime exercise. The only people who really chime off each other, not surprisingly, are Branagh and Thompson, who go about their amorous warring with convincing vitriol—a dash of Hepburn and Tracy perhaps, but rather more of Kenneth Williams and Hattie Jacques in *Carry On Matron*.

The problem isn't that the film sells itself so heavily as an accessible entertainment, dispelling any hint of elitist mystique; but that it does so unimaginatively. It indulges a cast that's wildly uneven in skill, and thereby ends up excluding the audience. The sense of an enclosed community—the film is shot in an idyllic 14th-century villa—merely increases this alienation. Swell time was had by all; a comparably swell time *can't* be had by the audience. It increases the sense of a complacent garden diversion. All the world's a stage—except here, where all the world's the Regent's Park Open Air Theatre.

NEW YORK, 5/10/93, p. 62, David Denby

I will say what is only obvious: Kenneth Branagh was not put on God's earth to make movies from glib Hollywood-style "concepts"—movies like *Dead Again* and *Peter's Friends*. Kenneth Branagh was put on this earth to make movies out of the plays of William Shakespeare. Branagh's version of *Henry V*, spectacular yet somberly anti-heroic, was a worthy answer to Laurence Olivier's pageant-play approach at the end of World War II. And now Branagh has made a rousingly entertaining and touching *Much Ado About Nothing*, one of those Shakespeare comedies in which celebration—love ending in marriage—is almost overwhelmed by dark envy and stupidity.

Branagh avoids the ghastly twin traps of Shakespearean comedy, archness and crudity. His work is full-bodied and vibrantly sexual, but he doesn't go in for the roaring, body-slamming horseplay that Franco Zeffirelli so disastrously confused with fun. The wit of Shakespeare's great prose-play boils along furiously, especially when Emma Thompson and Branagh, as Beatrice and Benedick, are onscreen tossing insults and dirty puns at each other. The emotional range of this movie is remarkable: After much frivolous comedy in the sunshine, Branagh allows the disastrous misunderstandings to explode with full force, and the screen is suddenly filled with abject suffering. When the schemes are unmasked and the wrongs righted, the audience's physical relief is almost palpable. *Much Ado About Nothing* is one of the few movies of recent years that could leave its audiences weeping for joy.

Branagh staged the movie at the Villa Vignamaggio in Tuscany, a sumptuous Renaissance palazzo whose courtyards and gardens allow the geography of intrigue—overhearing and spying—to become explicit and convincing in a way that is impossible onstage. Yet at the same time, the space is open enough for Branagh to sweep his camera around freely. We are at the residence of the governor of Messina, Leonato (Richard Briers), who receives as his guests Don Pedro (Denzel Washington) and his fellow officers, aristocratic gents returning from the wars and eager for pleasure and relaxation. The entrance of the gallant soldiers is perhaps too jubilantly overproduced: The men gallop straight toward the camera, and a minute later everyone at the villa and then the men themselves strip off clothes and jump into open-air group baths. God, they're excited! But after these flourishes Branagh quickly gets down to business.

Claudio (Robert Sean Leonard), a young nobleman, loves Leonato's beautiful daughter, Hero (Kate Beckinsale). But Claudio is a romantic fool, and he and Hero are bound to suffer from what they don't understand. The relationship of Leonato's niece, Beatrice, and her longtime friend and enemy, Benedick, is an altogether different affair. They are both in love, yet both deny they want to get married; each pretends to scorn the other. They enjoy the duel of insults, the slanderer slandered for his own amusement. At an evening party in the gardens, Benedick, masked, talks in a preposterous Russian accent, and Beatrice, knowing it is him, has at him freely. Yet sooner or later, nature requires that the duel end.

Walking around the grounds and expostulating with himself, Branagh takes Benedick's shifting moods to giddy extremes. He is the very activity of intelligence, always on the move, and deeply lovable because his Benedick knows himself so little. At times, arguing himself into something, Branagh sounds a lot like Peter Ustinov at his most wonderfully absurd, yet this is a Ustinov who is also a romantic and heroic actor. When he hears that Beatrice loves him, Benedick turns a complete about-face and immediately begins praising marriage, capping his pro-marriage tirade with the hilarious "The world must be peopled!" It's Branagh's triumph that he gives this walking mouth enough weight to make him worthy of Beatrice.

Emma Thompson is merry and tough, a tall, strong woman with tanned shoulders and breasts exposed in an open white dress, flowing chestnut hair, a ready smile. Her mockery would humble a lesser man; her kindness would also humble a lesser man. But Benedick passes the various tests, and happiness awaits. In brief, the Branaghs are a great advertisement for modern marriage—their scenes have an almost ecstatically high-pitched gaiety and combative fervor, though lightened always by the Shakespearean sweetness.

The play is colloquial and fast. Not having read it in something like 30 years, I was stymied by some of Shakespeare's wordplay, which can be dizzyingly complicated, but I still enjoyed myself tremendously. If you can't unpack a few of the lines, you're under no obligation to think yourself any stupider than I am, so my advice is to just relax and go with it. Branagh's work in Shakespeare has tremendous physical verve: The emotional direction of the scenes is so clear, and his own readings so vivid, that full understanding can wait for a second viewing.

It's astonishing how passionate the dark passages of the movie are. Branagh had to make some strategic decisions here: There's probably no way of softening or getting around the Elizabethan prejudice—which Shakespeare fully exploited—against bastards, so Branagh goes all the way with it, bringing out the full measure of evil in Don Pedro's illegitimate brother, Don John (Keanu Reeves). In a vile bit of trickery, Don John makes Claudio think that Hero is sleeping with one of Don John's retainers. On their wedding day, Claudio humiliates Hero at the altar, almost destroying her life and her family. This male obsession with female chastity may seem like madness to us, but if Branagh had downplayed or parodied it, the emotional basis of the drama would have collapsed. As it happens, Robert Sean Leonard's boyish American earnestness works for him: His unwrapped manner reveals wounded-macho vanity beneath the soft romantic platitudes. Some of the other Americans are not as successful. Denzel Washington is graceful but muffled as the benevolent Don Pedro; Keanu Reeves is darkly handsome as the evil Don John but makes little of the words.

Goodness literally comes galloping to the rescue in the form of Michael Keaton's Dogberry, the Constable of the Watch, who arrives and departs the scene prancing and holding imaginary reins. Dogberry is innocent yet mad, and Keaton, with blackened teeth and a hanging gut, turns him into shtick—he swallows half his lines in a deep growl, and stares out his eyeballs. But he's still hilarious. Dogberry and his men, London-style buffoons in an Italian rural setting, don't seem part of the same world as the others, but they don't in the play, either.

The other forces of goodness are, of course, Beatrice and Benedick, who stop scratching each other the instant that real slander—the kind that destroys lives—is in the air. The most moving moment in *Much Ado About Nothing* is Beatrice's great cry, "O that I were a man!" She wishes revenge on Claudio for his error but cannot take it herself. Branagh and Thompson come as close to a feminist reading of the play as they can without altering the meaning of the text. The jealousy and madness in men destroys happiness. In the end, sanity triumphs, but narrowly. Even Benedick makes jokes about being cuckolded. That's the true Shakespearean quality, full, blazing celebration with a tug of uneasiness underneath. Now I'd like to see Branagh do *Macbeth* and *Twelfth Night* and, God willing, all the rest.

NEW YORK POST, 5/7/93, p. 24, Jami Bernard

Shakespeare is a tough act to pull off for today's moviegoers, people who hate language so much they won't read subtitles, let alone a 16th-century playwright. Kenneth Branagh brought Shakespeare's "Henry V" stunningly to modern audiences, and now he does the same with "Much Ado About Nothing," a play that celebrates love as much as it condemns what fools we mortals be.

The play contains two intertwined couples—Benedick and Beatrice, who conduct "a kind of merry war" of words and jests that belie their attraction for each other, and Claudio and Hero, two attractive but otherwise featureless youths who are smitten by the sight of each other. We will call Benedick and Beatrice the Smart Couple, the others the Dull Couple.

Branagh has wisely cast himself and his own wife, Emma Thompson, as the Smart Couple, whose sexy war of wits drives the movie. Branagh's performance appears effortless, like a day in the country—or at an Italian villa, where "Much Ado" was shot. He gambols about, playing with his lines, wallowing in his joy at the material. And Thompson, herself smart as a whip, has a role that lets her do the whipping.

The Dull Couple is played by Robert Sean Leonard and Kate Beckinsale, and they do as well as they can with these intrinsically less interesting roles.

In short, the two couples love and yet are thwarted in love, mostly by false appearances. There is much ado about whether Hero is still a virgin, but the real issue here is about how appearances deceive, and about how people can be tricked as easily into doing the right thing as the wrong.

Denzel Washington is noble in bearing yet mild of speech as Don Pedro, Prince of Arragon, who rides with his men to this country villa after a successful skirmish on the battlefields. Keanu Reeves is perhaps a sorry bit of casting as Washington's half-brother, the Don John dude. Luckily, the role calls for him to be "of few words" but to sneer a lot, which he does most bodaciously.

Branagh has let Michael Keaton run wild as the language-mangling constable Dogberry: Keaton's unbridled performance teeters dangerously on the edge; you feel as much concern watching him as watching a high-wire act without a net. Ultimately, you have to admire him for taking such chances, and Branagh for letting him.

The inescapable problem with Shakespeare is that a lot of the language has fallen into disuse, and you cannot always have an annotated edition handy (Norton has just reissued one such, very readable and including photo stills from the movie.) How Branagh handles this—aside from pruning the play a bit—is by having his actors play as much to the emotional tone as to the words. As in a silent comedy, the meaning is clear.

And as for words, the movie opens with Thompson slowly reading the lines of the "Hey nonny nonny" song from Act II, with the words gradually appearing on the screen. The deliberation of the reading and the sight of the words themselves serves to slow the raging MTV-style pace of today's audiences and force them to concentrate in a different way—here there be words, so take heed.

Then Branagh opens the movie with a glorious, energetic tumble of women and men flying to their respective baths to prepare for their great mingling of the hormones, and for a great movie.

NEWSDAY, 5/7/93, Part II/p. 66, Jack Mathews

Filmed versions of plays by William Shakespeare, if faithfully performed, have always been deemed inaccessible by mainstream movie audiences, which is why the most successful versions of "Romeo and Juliet," "The Taming of the Shrew" and "The Tempest" were titled "West Side Story," "Kiss Me Kate" and "Forbidden Planet."

As a Hollywood story reader might put it, "The guy has a good feel for plot and character, but you can't understand a thing anybody says."

Kenneth Branagh seems determined to change Shakespeare's popular appeal by making his plays look, feel and sound as if they were written for the modern screen, while keeping their period settings and dialogue intact. The British actor-director began by turning "Henry V" into a vividly moving costume action drama and continues, brilliantly, with the airy romantic comedy "Much Ado About Nothing."

For those who are only willing to give Shakespeare one chance as a screenwriter, this is the chance to take. From the joyously energetic opening scenes of victorious warriors returning from battle to a Messina villa and the women, festivities and mating games awaiting them there, "Much Ado" is a bouyant two hours of *movie* entertainment.

There is music, high and low comedy, treachery, deception, whimsy, tragedy and not one but two love stories, engineered in both cases by the charming matchmaker Don Pedro (Denzel Washington).

One romance stars Branagh and his wife, Emma Thompson, (the Oscar-winning Best Actress from "Howards End") as Benedick and Beatrice, a couple smothering their romantic feelings for each other behind a barbed verbal rivalry. Their words may cut each other to the quick, but their hearts are one.

Only when Don Pedro devises a scheme to make Benedick and Beatrice think each is in love with the other do they declare themselves.

The other romance, which controls the flow of the story, is between the young count Claudio (Robert Sean Leonard) and Beatrice's cousin Hero (Kate Beckinsale), whose courtship, begun again by Don Pedro, is nearly undone by slander.

On the eve of their wedding, Don Pedro's evil half-brother Don John (a dazed Keanu Reeves) stages a liaison to convince Claudio that Hero is a wanton woman and prompts him to denounce her at the altar. (You have never seen a wedding fall apart like this one.)

However, all's well that ends well, as someone once said, and though "Much Ado" flirts with tragedy, it never strays far from romance and farce. Branagh treats the story as if it were a balloon to be filled with a mixture of helium and laughing gas, and the cast is almost giddy with the pleasure of it.

Shakespeare was a good comedy writer, as clever with a social quip as Woody Allen or Neil Simon. Only the context, and the manner of speaking, has changed. Even when the syntax curls up into middle-English balls, the actors speaking the lines, and those reacting to them, make sure their understanding is clear.

Branagh has total command of this material, and seems to relish the challenge of guiding today's audience into the rhythms of the Renaissance setting, to fall in step with the humor, mood and feelings of its characters.

In the very opening, we hear a woman's voice reciting a whimsical song about the fickle nature of men, and the laughter her words evoke from her friends seems at first to be inappropriately hearty. Though the sentiments are relevant enough to the ongoing battle of the sexes, the lines wouldn't get more than a courteous chuckle from your friends or mine.

But the joy on that hilltop in Tuscany is very contagious stuff, and the playfully spirited scenes that follow, with the warriors and the villa's women preparing for their reunion, draws us completely into their world.

Branagh has said he cast American actors like Reeves and Michael Keaton to help broaden its appeal to moviegoers, particularly the young, and he's not afraid to use cinematic slapstick—as he does when Benedick fights a losing battle with a lawn chair—to hold our attention.

Keaton's performance as the scurvy, tongue-tied constable Dogberry is one of the craziest things ever done on behalf of Shakespeare, and given the ludicrous nature of the character, the Bard may have loved it. Keaton combines the voice of Beetlejuice with the body language of Quasimodo, and trots around on an imaginary horse. It is comic relief or it is nothing.

Still, the play's the thing, as someone once said, and "Much Ado's" strength is in its wonderful language. Branagh is obviously passionate about the words, and more intent and successful than perhaps anyone has ever been to make them clear.

NEWSWEEK, 5/10/93, p. 60, Jack Kroll

Kenneth Branagh has arrived in the nick of time. In his stirring 1989 film of "Henry V," and now in his enchanting new movie version of *Much Ado About Nothing*, the 32-year-old actor-director is making Shakespeare look as comfortable on screen as he ever did at the old Globe. This is an age apparently determined to debard the Bard, who has been called names like "a black hole ... a verbocrat" by scholars who are burying him under a lava flow of deconstructionism, new historicism, neo-Marxism, genderism and other ismatic attacks. But the plays are still the thing, and in "Much Ado" Branagh restores the innocence to Shakespeare.

In a dazzling opening sequence, the screen explodes in a torrent of images as Don Pedro (Denzel Washington) and his troop ride back after the wars to a gorgeous villa in Messina, Sicily. The inhabitants excitedly scramble to receive them, preparing food, whipping off sweaty clothes to lather up in the washhouse. The screen shimmers with glowing young faces, voluptuous limbs, breakneck horsemen. Branagh is showing us that Shakespeare is vibrant bodies, not just talking heads.

"Much Ado" is a comedy about the absolute absurdity and the absurd absoluteness of love. Beatrice (Emma Thompson) and Benedick (Branagh) conduct a "merry war" of put-downs and potshots because they're afraid of the deep feeling they have for one another. The younger, less sophisticated pair, Hero (Kate Beckinsale) and Claudio (Robert Sean Leonard), is hot to wed until the satanic Don John (Keanu Reeves) sets up a hoax to blacken Hero's virtue. These self-absorbed aristos are messing up Messina's tight little utopia. But things are set to rights by the lower orders in the form of the constable Dogberry (Michael Keaton) and his scraggly crew.

It's exciting to watch Branagh develop as a director of films and of Shakespeare. As an actor, the Belfast-born Branagh is a crossbreed of Cagney and Olivier, a terrier and a tiger. Oscar winner Thompson would have delighted the great Victorian actress Ellen Terry, who criticized her own performance of Beatrice, saying: "I must make Beatrice more flashing at first, and softer afterwards." Thompson does better; she is flashing and soft at the same time, a stand-up comic who really wants to be a lie-down lover. In a wonderful scene, Branagh and Thompson catch the exquisite moment when their duel of wits becomes a meeting of minds and hearts.

The toughest thing to deal with in Shakespeare today is his low comedy. We no longer have the great gaga geniuses, the Bert Lahrs and Ed Wynns, Dogberrys to the manger born. Branagh tries another tack with Keaton and comes close. Keaton plays the malapropping constable as an Elizabethan Beetlejuice with delusions of grandeur. When Dogberry and his sidekick, Verges (Ben Elton), take off on their imaginary horses, whipping the air to a phantom froth, it's a nuttily Shakespearean comment on class status: the big shots of course have the real horses. Keaton and the other American actors lend a welcome chord to the film's human music: Washington brings a cool austerity, Leonard a misguided idealism, and Reeves is a junior Iago, lusting to turn all this loving ado into a nihilistic nothing. This may be the most sheerly delightful of all Shakespearean movies.

SIGHT AND SOUND, 9/93, p. 50, Leslie Felperin Sharman

Messina, Sicily. Don Pedro and his men are returning victorious from war. Among those accompanying him are his close companions Claudio and Benedick and Don Pedro's bastard brother Don John. Leonato, Governor of Messina, welcomes the men to his villa. Beatrice, his niece, and Benedick are already acquainted and resume their game of witty raillery, each swearing that they will never marry anyone; while Claudio is smitten by Hero, Leonato's daughter. Don Pedro offers to broach the subject of marriage with Leonato and Hero on Claudio's behalf. Don John hears of these plans and plots to cause mischief.

At a masked ball that evening, everyone flirts and dances. Don Pedro courts and wins Hero on Claudio's behalf, and the marriage is arranged. Meanwhile, Don Pedro plans to trick Beatrice and Benedick into falling in love. The next day, while Benedick is resting in the garden, Don Pedro, Claudio and Leonato contrive for him to overhear them discussing how Beatrice secretly loves Benedick and is pining away unable to declare her feelings. Benedick is shocked, then overjoyed, and decides to court her. The same trick is played on Beatrice with similar results.

On the eve of the wedding, Don John shows Claudio and Don Pedro one of his men making love to a woman whom he calls 'Hero', and convinces them that Hero is unfaithful and unchaste. At the wedding, Claudio and Don Pedro denounce Hero. Her friends decide to circulate a rumour that she is dead in order to gauge the effect of the news on Claudio. Beatrice and Benedick confess their love to one another, but she insists that he must kill Claudio and revenge her cousin's name in order to prove his love.

Meanwhile, the local constable Dogberry catches the henchmen responsible for slandering Hero. When it comes to light that she was falsely accused, Claudio agrees to make amends by marrying Leonato's 'niece', who is described as Hero's exact likeness. The next day, Claudio accepts her in wedlock, delighted to discover that she is indeed the real Hero. Benedick and Beatrice, though now aware that they were tricked into falling in love, also marry. Don John is apprehended, and Don Pedro promises to punish him the next day. Harmony restored, everyone dances around the villa as flower petals rain down overhead.

Kenneth Branagh's last exercise in filming Shakespeare, *Henry V*, had some roomy doublet and hose to fill. For a first-time director, Branagh made a plucky but ultimately botched effort at wrenching the text from under the glare of Olivier's rousingly patriotic wartime interpretation, and into the shadow and slow-motion gore that 80s pacificism demanded. After practising on two more features (*Dead Again* and *Peter's Friend's*) and a short film (*Swan Song*), the evidence suggests that he has learned what his strengths and weaknesses are and how to compensate accordingly.

Branagh's worst problem is imaginative banality—his camera tricks and casting coups are faddish rather than fresh. Paradoxically, this is also his biggest asset as a purveyor of lucrative filmic commodities for a specialized middle-brow market with upwardly mobile tastes. Branagh has a knack for aping the fashionable mannerisms of today's hot auteurs, like long tracking and steadicam shots *à la* Scorsese and Altman. As in *Henry V*, he makes nodding references to Welles with theatrical lighting, but he has none of the above's sense of timing or elan. What he's really good at is attracting big stars eager for a little cultural capital and then coaxing fairly good performances out of them. And audiences love it, since not only do you get to see Keanu Reeves barechested, plus 'sensual' footage of naked girls, but you also have the smug satisfaction of knowing that you are imbibing Real Culture at the same time. It's the cinematic equivalent of a health-food candy bar—fructose-sweet, fibrous and nominally nutritious but still bland.

Like Joseph Papp's 'Shakespeare in the Park' productions in New York, *Much Ado About Nothing* sets itself up as a showcase for its stars, then preens itself smugly while they display their skills at performing Elizabethan prose and blank verse. The camera trots along behind them, weaves among the crowd and wanders around the fountain while they recite their lines, like an awed audience member allowed on the stage but keeping a respectful distance. Only rarely does Branagh allow a reverse shot or cutaway while someone is speaking, unless they are discussing another character. Then a shot of the person in question is provided to guide slower viewers through the action—for example, when Claudio describes Hero as "the sweetest lady that ever I looked on." When Beatrice storms at Benedick after Hero has been denounced, the camera hovers shyly beyond the portal, like a child eavesdropping on its parents rowing. It's as if Branagh were afraid to interrupt Thompson's beautifully polished 'big scene', demonstrating the kind of respect one expects from a fellow actor and husband, but too obeisant for a good director.

Although the Beatrice-Benedick subplot usually dominates people's memories of the play, *Much Ado About Nothing* is one of the most formally integrated of Shakespeare's middle comedies. The smutty pun in the title ("no thing" is a common Shakespearian play on virginity and women's 'lack' of a penis) applies equally to the acerbic lovers, with their badinage about cuckoldry and inconstancy, and to Hero and Claudio, nearly destroyed by aspersions over (Hero's) nothing. Since a few scenes of ribald banter with Hero are cut to emphasise her purity, the film has to rely on other members of the cast to maintain thematic integrity.

Attention is really drawn to what's going on in the melodrama sub-plot by the presence of Denzel Washington, subdued but graceful as Don Pedro, and Keanu Reeves as his bastard brother John (wooden, but then it was always a stock villain part). The most arresting performance is Richard Briers as Leonato. His delivery is exceptional, smoothly modulating between avuncular cheeriness and Lear-like rage in the wedding scene. Though Michael Keaton and Ben Elton as Dogberry and Verges seem a little lost, the rest of the mainly British cast troop along gamely, supporting the ensemble illusion the film is at pains to maintain. Even the poster recalls the non-hierarchal layout of the one used for *Peter's Friends*, with the major participants lined up in curtain-call arrangement. The two films have, after all, a lot in common: bickering lovers, rivalry, sentimentality, the spectre of sexually transmitted 'pestilence', and a big country house.

Overall, this is a earnest but fundamentally conservative film. With the current debate about the centrality of Shakespeare in the National Curriculum, one wonders if it might even be described as Conservative in the political sense. Apart from the multiculturalist gesture of casting a black actor in a conventionally 'white' role, everything else is played straight, complete with period costume and due deference to the original text. It neatly falls into line with a tradition of cinematic bardology that unquestioningly upholds Shakespeare as the ultimate emblem of high culture and good taste. The video will undoubtedly make a tidy mint in sales to lesson-plan-hungry teachers. Unlike recent adaptations by Jarman, Greenaway and Edzard, no messy attempt is made to subvert, historicize, culturally appropriate or even update the holy writ. Apart from a little tastefully photographed bonking on a balcony, this is a Shakespeare film that even John Patten would find room for on the syllabus, despite his threats to abolish media studies in the classroom. Considering Olivier's governmental sponsorship for his own *Henry V*, Branagh, financially independent yet toeing the Party's aesthetic line, looks much less like the radical revisionist he first purported to be.

TIME, 5/10/93, p. 65, Richard Corliss

We see a landscape of the Chianti region of Tuscany, as painted by the local governor, Leonato (Richard Briers). Then the camera pans to the real thing: a paradise of green and brown hills—life outshining art—on which his handsome family idles. The rest of this film of *Much Ado About Nothing* has the same seductive impact as the first shot does. It brings sunny vitality to an old canvas.

Shakespeare, who laced his plays with big fight scenes, multiple murders, romantic bantering and plenty of slapstick, was an ace screenwriter. Occasionally the movies have realized this and allowed distinguished actors to put one of his plays on film. Problem is that by the time they receive this reward for services rendered, it may as well be a gold watch. When MGM made *Romeo and Juliet* in 1936, it cast Leslie Howard, 43, and Norma Shearer, 36, as the star-crossed teens. Laurence Olivier brought sepulchral dash to his *Hamlet*, but at 41 he was a bit too mature to play a college student convincingly in close-up.

Kenneth Branagh will have none of this. At 31, after hustling triumphs on stage (*Hamlet*), in films (*Henry V*) and on TV (*Fortunes of War*), he is still a young man in a hurry. His ambition is the best thing about him. Having directed the box-office success *Dead Again*, he confidently grabs some mogul by the Armani lapels and says, Mickey-and-Judy style, Let's put the Bard on right now! And put lots of pretty *young* people in it. Even Americans—they can learn their lines phonetically. And we'll photograph them in loving slow-mo while they bathe naked. This is a play about star quality, so we'll do it in movie-star close-up. We'll have songs and dances. We'll make it so fresh and move it so fast that audiences will forget it's Shakespeare.

Branagh is a trollop for art. His bold mission is to ensure that everybody—everybody on this planet for whom Shakespeare is unknown or a school punishment—gets it, gets the power and the humor of the poetry, if not its unabridged grandeur. So he encourages Michael Keaton to play Dogberry, the lame-brained lawman, as a veritable triumvirate of Stooges—all spitting and farts and head butts and scrotum grabbing. He wants similarly capitalized emotions from the romantic leads. Go bigger, higher, grander, clearer, he tells them. Speak loud if you speak love.

Well, it works. This isn't the best Shakespeare on film—a photo finish between Olivier's *Richard III* and Orson Welles' *Chimes at Midnight*—but it may be the best movie Shakespeare. The skirmish of will and wit between Benedick (Branagh, never so charming a screen presence) and Beatrice (his wife Emma Thompson, here tart and intense) plays like a prime episode of *Cheers*. The characters' passions seem not revived but experienced afresh. There is wrenching melodrama in the perfidy that estranges the innocent lovers Hero (Kate Beckinsale) and Claudio (Robert Sean Leonard, a wonderfully vulnerable puppy-lover).

Branagh does not intrude political and social commentary into the text; he insinuates it, as in the bold casting of Malcolm X—Denzel Washington—as the Prince. Washington is gentle and imposing, prodding the revelry yet above it, from exclusion or choice. And the chic informality of the costumes suggests that this is an upper-class masquerade, where folks pass the time playing practical jokes with treacherous consequences, where the ladies have the cleverest lines and the most intelligent hearts.

Much Ado was shot at the Villa Vignamaggio, whose English-style gardens and genteel majesty make an ideal setting for this alfresco fairy tale of aristocrats in love. Once upon a time, Mona Lisa lived there. Now Shakespeare does.

VILLAGE VOICE, 5/11/93, p. 55, J. Hoberman

The title *Much Ado About Nothing* is so wickedly evocative that even Shakespeare's play can scarcely justify it. Not so the Kenneth Branagh version, opening Friday before making its Euro-debut in competition at Cannes. Doggedly literal-minded, Branagh fluffs up the material as if there really were nothing to it.

A model for much subsequent English comedy and a distant ancestor of American screwball, *Much Ado About Nothing* uses the attraction-avoidance dance of two highly verbal insult artists, Beatrice and Benedick, as a foil for the dewier, if more troubled, romance between ingenues Claudio and Hero. The warring Beatrice and Benedick have the play's best lines. It's a setup that, less a movie than a celebrity tennis match, enables the producer-director-star and his wife, Emma Thompson, to go one-on-one in the context of such glamorous American movie icons as Michael Keaton, Keanu Reeves, and Denzel Washington.

A middlebrow worldbeater as *Henry V*, Branagh is here merely annoying. Alternately shrill and whining, he can't do justice to the cynicism of his lines. Thompson, the most relentlessly mannered screen actress since the equally overpraised Kathleen Turner, is a more complicated case. Thompson's intelligence would seem to make her a near perfect Beatrice were she not forever mugging her ironic superiority to the character. Thompson's overbright smile, ostentatiously furrowed brow, and extended display of eye-batting concern are less a surplus of actressy behavior than a kind of self-satisfied deconstruction. (Like Turner, Thompson's forte is farce. Her Oscar night "little-me" act was a minor camp classic.)

Of course, Thompson has also been directed. Her diction may be a thing of beauty but Branagh manages to KO that even before the movie begins by featuring as voiceover her exaggeratedly slow and breathy recitation of Balthasar's song from Act II. In general, Branagh's adaptation insures that the play's broadest lines will be given maximum latitude. The opening scene is a frenzy of girlish excitement, replete with boisterous skinny-dipping, as if to suggest a high-speed parody of *Prospero's Books*. The movie is lazily overproduced and horrifically overscored. The boisterous slap and tickle of the masqued revels are drenched in nostalgic music. Nothing in the movie is more abusive than the droning lyrics and recitations (some performed by composer Patrick Doyle)—even a funeral comes complete with lilting dirge. At times, *Much Ado About Nothing* is a virtual animated cartoon—I half expected to see a singing teapot.

As Beatrice and Benedick are the play's wittiest characters, it's easy to overconcentrate on their prolonged minuet, particularly at the expense of the vapid-like young lovers (the equally doelike

Robert Sean Leonard and Kate Beckinsale). As for the Americans, Washington's boringly benign Don Pedro positions himself to one side of the action while a scowling Reeves (who plays his jealous half-brother Don Juan) stalks the periphery. Keaton's disheveled Constable Dogberry simply plunges in—scuttling around, pulling faces, licking lips, flashing yellow teeth, expectorating on the set, and otherwise destroying his lines by babbling in a brogue that seems lifted from *The Crimson Pirate*. It's a pity Branagh didn't cast him as Benedick.

Much has been made of *Much Ado*'s idyllic summer-in-Italy setting, but the location feels more arid than lush. Still, Branagh plays Mr. Sunshine. Blandly ignoring the play's disturbing undercurrents—the sexual paranoia and patriarchal cruelty of the social order—he uncritically offers the spectacle of an entire community orchestrating everyone's affairs, channeling anarchic desire into what might be called normal love (see below). Even Beatrice and Benedick can't wait to conform. Once the public scandal of Claudio's violent tantrum at the altar is balanced by his ludicrous regret, the movie builds to a feeble crescendo of bland celebration. As the title suggests, *Much Ado About Nothing* is a play about skepticism. The action illustrates how willingly people believe what they are told, how readily they can be taken in by appearances. Indeed, on that score, it should be revealing to see how many critical cheerleaders will be beating the drum and how much unwarranted ado this *Much Ado* warrants.

Also reviewed in:
CHICAGO TRIBUNE, 5/21/93, Friday/p. C, Dave Kehr
NATION, 5/31/93, p. 750, Stuart Klawans
NEW REPUBLIC, 5/10/93, p. 38, Stanley Kauffmann
NEW YORK TIMES, 5/7/93, p. C16, Vincent Canby
NEW YORKER, 5/10/93, p. 97, Anthony Lane
VARIETY, 5/3/93, p. 39, Todd McCarthy
WASHINGTON POST, 5/21/93, p. B7, Hal Hinson
WASHINGTON POST, 5/21/93, Weekend/p. 53, Desson Howe

MUSIC OF CHANCE, THE

An I.R.S. Releasing/TransAtlantic Entertainment release in association with American Playhouse Theatrical Films. *Executive Producer:* Miles Copeland, III, Paul Colichman, and Lindsay Law. *Producer:* Frederick Zollo and Dylan Sellers. *Director:* Philip Haas. *Screenplay:* Philip Haas and Belinda Haas. *Based on the novel "The Music of Chance" by:* Paul Auster. *Director of Photography:* Bernard Zitzermann. *Editor:* Belinda Haas. *Music:* Phillip Johnston. *Sound:* Les Lupin, Neil Danziger, and (music) Hugo Dwyer. *Sound Editor:* Maurice Schell. *Casting:* Bonnie Timmermann. *Production Designer:* Hugo Luczyc-Wyhowski. *Art Director:* Ruth Ammon. *Set Decorator:* Christina Belt. *Set Dresser:* David Hack and Stephen Damrel. *Costumes:* Rudy Dilon. *Make-up:* Gigi Williams. *Running time:* 98 minutes. *MPAA Rating:* R.

CAST: James Spader (Jack Pozzi); Mandy Patinkin (James Nashe); M. Emmet Walsh (Calvin Murks); Charles Durning (Bill Flower); Joel Grey (Willie Stone); Samantha Mathis (Tiffany); Christopher Penn (Floyd); Pearl Jones (Louise); Jordan Spainhour (Floyd Jr.); Paul Auster (Driver).

LOS ANGELES TIMES, 7/16/93, Calendar/p. 18, Peter Rainer

Jim Nashe (Mandy Patinkin), a Boston fireman, has been aimlessly riding the open road in his BMW ever since he quit his job after his wife walked out on him and his young daughter, and his father bequeathed him a $200,000 inheritance.

That inheritance, more than a year later, has dwindled to about $20,000, which Nashe keeps in an envelope crammed inside the glove compartment.

When he picks up Jack Pozzi (James Spader), a poker whiz on his way to a high-stakes game, Nashe casually, methodically calculates a way to replenish his pile. Pozzi was recently rousted out of a high-stakes haul—that's why Nashe finds him on the roadside battered and drifting. He'll stake the kid to a game with a pushover pair of lottery-winning millionaire housemates (Charles Durning and Joel Grey) and split the winnings 50-50.

Paul Auster's 1990 novel "The Music of Chance," directed and co-scripted by Philip Haas, has made its move to the screen with its low-key creepiness intact. The sense of impending matter-of-fact doom, in both book and film, seems to issue from a place beyond fear and loathing. Nashe, who moves through his fate with an almost bemused calm, is a new-style zombie: a post-depressive man of feeling who has lost all feeling for life. He's very good at going through the motions, but there's a blandness to his beneficence with Pozzi: he just wants to keep moving and Pozzi is his passport to a winged oblivion.

What's unsettling about the film of "The Music of Chance" is that its maniacal view is kept rigorous and orderly.

The limitation of the film (and book) is that this material is a form of bluff—like a poker hand that impends more than it delivers. The metaphysics of chance are tricked up into a kind of higher-priced "Twilight Zone" episode. Probably the best way to enjoy "The Music of Chance" (rated R for language) is to clear away the latticework of Lit 1-A symbology and just enter into the moody meaningful nothingness of it all. That's what Patinkin appears to have done; he has the right benumbed alertness in the role, balancing out Spader who seems miscast as a sleazy scrounger. (He's better at playing sleek sleazoids.)

The nothingness sets in once Nashe and Pozzi play out their hand with their Laurel and Hardy-like hosts in a baronial, isolated Pennsylvania estate. Durning's Bill Flower has the bullying girth of a man whose poundage equals power; his rail-thin partner, Grey's Willie Stone, is an insinuating creepo who is constructing a vast miniature tract—he calls it City of the World—complete with models and stick figures of every important person and happening in his life.

The latest joint project of Flower and Stone is the building of a vast wall on the far reaches of their property consisting entirely of 10,000 stones from the wreckage of a 15th-Century Irish castle. The film is about what happens to Nashe and Pozzi when their luck turns and they are maneuvered into carrying out the Sisyphean task.

Their overseer, played by the mumbly and menacing M. Emmet Walsh, is a drawling change of pace for the two losers. He provides only the tiniest of amenities, like a miniature red wagon to haul the stones. Nashe accepts his enforcement with aplomb—it's the fate he knew he was heading for all along. Pozzi isn't quite so accommodating; he has fewer resources to occupy the hours. (He has the vacuousness of a man devoted entirely to luck whose luck has run out.) The two men work up a mild jail-cell camaraderie, but there are no deepening emotional linkages, nothing to suggest that these two are bonded for life—brothers in chains. The film doesn't indulge in that kind of sentiment.

It doesn't indulge in *any* sentiment, really, and the austerity is bracing. At least until you realize that what you see is what you get. "The Music of Chance" never cracks its poker face.

NEW YORK POST, 6/4/93, p. 31, Jami Bernard

Chilling and offbeat, "The Music of Chance" debuted at the New Directors/New Films series at the Museum of Modern Art and aroused diverse reactions from the critics. It is hard, spare, sinister, nerve-wracking—and would be slightly more brilliant with a different ending.

The Paul Auster novel from which it is adapted does in fact have a different ending, a more suitable one for the story. And the book explains away the movie's nagging doubts about its lead character, Jim Nashe (Mandy Patinkin).

Nashe is a former fireman who has been drifting aimlessly along in his car when he chances upon Jack Pozzi, an unsophisticated small-time card shark who cuts Nashe in on his latest scam—trying to bilk two eccentric millionaires (Charles Durning and Joel Grey) in an all-night poker game.

Lady Luck is napping during the game, and the millionaires—their riches courtesy of a lottery number—take Nashe and Pozzi to the cleaners. Nashe, who has put up the stake, loses that plus his car and now has exactly nothing to his name in the world. The millionaires propose that the losers stay on in a trailer on their enormous property, working off the debt by arranging a pile of 10,000 medieval stones into a wall.

In "The Shining" Jack Nicholson was able to spot his wife and son in the hedge maze by looking at them on a scale model inside the haunted hotel. In "The Music of Chance" one of the many eerie sights is the millionaires watching Nashe and Pozzi in their Sisyphean task by looking in on them on indoor scale model they call the "City of the World," where life and dread possibilities co-exist without regard to real time, or real anything. A tiny model of the millionaires holding their winning lottery ticket is only half a table away from a prison yard where an inmate is being gunned down by a firing squad. The world the millionaires have created around themselves is both jovial and life-threatening.

A sense of dread hangs over "The Music of Chance," making it like a dark joke forever separated from its punch line. As the poker losers toil in the field, watched over like prisoners and with only a toy red cart to help them transport the rocks, the memory of the City of the World puts in the movie-goer's mind a premonition of a fate that the prisoners themselves can only guess at and labor toward.

Fascinating casting includes a wiry but muscular Patinkin sweating in the fields, and a real break for James Spader playing so totally against type you'd barely recognize him as Pozzi. Spader, who usually plays uptight yuppies, proves he has the stuff to be loose, oily, disreputable and doomed. Nice work by both of them, and by Durning and Grey as the masters of their distorted universe.

The book—and to a lesser extent, the movie—plays with themes of fate, chance, destiny, resignation and helplessness. The movie doesn't adequately set up or resolve Patinkin's character, but it is a noble, unforgettable try by first-time feature director Philip Haas to make a movie thick with philosophy and foreboding.

NEWSDAY, 6/4/93, Part II/p. 69, John Anderson

Forget about voyeurism, serial killers or dinosaurs. If you really want to worry, start thinking hard about the capriciousness of fate; how, if you hadn't stopped to read this paper, you might have been rendered road pie by the bus that just went by. And how, if you hadn't stopped reading now to look for that bus, the piano just dropped out that 30th-floor window wouldn't be bearing down on your head ...

Philip Haas' "The Music of Chance" doesn't pretend to be a horror movie, but the sequence of events on which it relies points out better than any exercise in fantasy the utter fragility of our lives. The big joke, in other words. And, just like Paul Auster's celebrated novel on which it's based, it does it through basically pedestrian circumstances, making it all the more frightening.

After all, if Boston fire fighter James Nashe (Mandy Patinkin) hadn't inherited money from the father he never knew, he wouldn't have been cruising down the road in his new BMW at the precise moment the bruised and bleeding Jack Pozzi (James Spader) was fleeing a certain poker game.

And Nashe might not have bankrolled the penniless Pozzi in his game against Bill Flower (Charles Durning) and Willie Stone (Joel Grey), the peculiar pair of millionaires. And if Nashe hadn't gotten up from the table and committed an act of petty theft during the game, Pozzi's luck might not have changed.

And they wouldn't have had to ante up the car to pay off their hosts. And then go double or nothing in defiance of a destiny that was clearly not inclined to accommodate them.

And they wouldn't have then been contracted—enslaved—to build a wall the length of a football field out of the rubble of a 15th-Century Irish castle that Cromwell had destroyed, and which Flower and Stone transported to New Jersey to be made into some strange monument.

Haas, who is making his feature debut, has produced such remarkable documentaries as the recent "Money Man" about artist-forger J.S.G. Boggs, "The Singing Sculpture" about artists Gilbert & George, and "A Day on the Grand Canal with the Emperor of China" with David Hockney.

To "The Music of Chance" he brings the same clarity and implied humor he showed in his documentary work, but here it has more of a subtle subtext. He's not laughing at us, but he's laughing at the utter lack of care with which we conduct our lives and how we still come up surprised.

The casting is equally surprising and unsettling. Both Patinkin and Spader seem at first to have been given the wrong roles (and haven't we all considered *that* possibility sometime in our lives).

As Nashe, the gifted musical actor Patinkin is dour and precise; he employs the considered speech of a man who's basically a coward and doesn't want to show it. Spader's Pozzi, on the other hand, is a small man in every sense, who relies on chance for his livelihood, and because he doesn't think is all the more free.

When the two find themselves working 10-hour days lifting 60-pound rocks to build a 100-yard wall, Pozzi simply wants out. This is nuts, he says. But Nashe finds release in slavery, an opportunity to abandon responsibility and thus find peace, Nashe is a modern-day Sisyphus. He's also ripe for fundamentalism, but thinks a bit too much.

The acting is oddball, but absolutely arresting: Spader and Patinkin are riveting, as is M. Emmet Walsh as Calvin Murks, the thickheaded and perhaps sinister caretaker assigned to oversee Nashe and Pozzi's labor. And while their roles are relatively small, Durning and Grey are alternately hilarious and frightening as the two long-suffering drones who after a lifetime of honest work win the lottery and become spiritual prisoners of their own money. Haas, and Auster (who has a cameo near the film's end) are basically saying what Oscar Wilde said: There are only two tragedies in life. One is not getting what you want. The other is getting it.

SIGHT AND SOUND, 4/94, p. 47, Verina Glaessner

James Nashe, an ex-fireman whose wife has left him, seeks solace in the open road, bolstered by the unexpected legacy left him by his father. Heading for New York, he spies a lone figure by the roadside, apparently in difficulties, and offers him a lift. The wounded young man is Jack Pozzi, a professional card player and the victim of a police raid on a poker game where he stood, according to his story, to win a lot of money. Not only is that lost, he tells Nashe, but so is the chance of a lifetime to play an even bigger league game the following day, as he has lost every cent. Nashe takes him to New York, puts him up in a hotel and buys him a new suit of clothes, offering to lend him the money himself, in exchange for a stake in his eventual winnings.

The two men drive out to the antique-filled mansion of their opponents, millionaire accountants Bill Flower and Willie Stone. Some of Pozzi's confidence evaporates when he learns that since he last played them, the millionaires have been taking lessons from a legendary card player. In one of the mansion's rooms, Stone shows them his World City—a tabletop model in which he has represented every key event in the couple's lives from the moment they won the lottery which set them on the road to fabulous wealth. Stone tells them about his plan to build a model of the room which contains the model itself.

As the game proceeds, Pozzi at first appears to be on a winning streak. But on the way back from the bathroom, Nashe pays a visit to the World City and steals the figures of his hosts; from then on, Pozzi's fortunes go from bad to worse. To stave off ruin, Pozzi borrows Nashe's last hundred thousand dollars and finally stakes the car. That too is lost. Flower and Stone suggest a deal. They have shipped over a pile of 15,000 stones which they want to have made into a memorial wall, and suggest that Nashe and Pozzi work off their debt by building it. Nashe and Pozzi agree, and sign a contract. They are housed in a trailer on the site. Their overseer is Calvin Murks. They are allowed no contact with the outside world, apart from letters which Jack is allowed to send to his sister.

Gradually the work is completed and the two men are allowed a celebration which includes, at Pozzi's suggestion, the presence of a prostitute, Tiffany. Next morning, however, while Pozzi is still asleep, Calvin brings bad news. There is a further bill—for food. Desperate, Pozzi escapes from the estate; the next morning, Nashe discovers his mangled body outside the trailer. Calvin takes him to hospital. Alone, Nashe completes the job, overseen by Calvin's son Floyd and his grandson, who he believes tipped Calvin off about Pozzi's escape attempt. Calvin and Floyd suggest a celebratory drink on the town when the work is completed. Nashe warily agrees. He gets Floyd to relax his guard sufficiently to agree to his driving the car back, and engineers a crash from which he emerges wounded but alive. Staggering along the highway, he hails a passing motorist.

Philip Haas's first feature film. Previous work has been in the theatre and included a stint as assistant director at the RSC. He has also made a series of documentaries about artists, including one on David Hockney, and is reported as seeing this film continuing that particular line of enquiry. This history suggests a few reasons why he might have been drawn to Paul Auster's not at all unfilmable novel for all the wrong reasons.

Auster's work, especially *The New York Trilogy*, has been much praised as a touchstone of new American writing. In *The Music of Chance* Auster draws very much on a collective memory shaped by cinema, by pulp fiction and by the long shadows cast by memories of a *Picture Post*-style iconography. His superficially relaxed vernacular style masks material which is at once melodramatic and almost algebraically structured, full of echoes and mirror images. Haas, instead of embedding his film in the quite detailed personal accounts that his two protagonists give of their lives, chooses to prune away much of their personal history, leaving them a matter of anecdote or cutting them altogether. Pozzi's detailed account of his paternal abandonment, which so closely matches Nashe's own, vanishes. Nashe's obsession with the road—potent in the book—is sidelined, talked about rather than experienced, despite its importance as a symbol of escape, freedom and the rejection of the domestic.

Haas evidently has no dreams of reworking films like *Kings of the Road* or even Monte Hellman's *Two Lane Blacktop*, probably the most persuasive of existential road movies. Instead he homes in on the entrapment of his protagonists by Flower and Stone, and on the task they are given as a way of discharging their debt. Their project, the wall, is to have no utilitarian function. It is to be a "memorial in the shape of a wall", something that would fit quite comfortably as a Turner Prize contender. On the page Auster is able to enmesh the wall's construction in a web of recollections, observations and reflections, recounting the tale with a degree of irony and obliqueness. On the screen Haas finds himself with nowhere much to hide. The screen, particularly the Hollywood screen, has a tendency to mythologise the everyday—which is why the sequences on the road and at the card table cannot help but work. This is balanced by Hollywood's countervailing tendency to literalise the symbolic.

The wall then becomes less a metaphor for the men's 'cementing' their relationship than a matter of practical DIY curiosity. Haas also dwells on Flower and Stone's model World City, which documents their lives from the moment they achieved wealth. He is intrigued especially by the need to depict within the model of the room in which the model stands—of course—another model and within that another, even more minutely scaled. This is the stuff of New Age metaphysical speculation, as is the ending (not in the book) in which Paul Auster himself is glimpsed driving the passing car that slows down for the wounded wayside figure, who this time is Nashe himself. Read against the realist drive of the narrative, this cannot but seem too inappropriately clever by half.

The mood of modish self-reflexiveness extends also to a shot of Nashe apparently reading from another of Auster's works. Conventional narrative cinema does of course have ways of dealing with mystery, ambiguity and obsession, ways which Auster hints at in his book but with which Haas fails to engage. So, while the film pays attention to aesthetics and representation, Haas lets slip the opportunity to devise a persuasive and atmospheric directorial style. The exteriors are blandly shot, mere records of the action, while the mansion interiors appear to aspire to a Wellesian grandiosity. On the plus side, Haas's tried and tested cast perform capably, and Spader turns in a notably vivacious performance as Pozzi.

VILLAGE VOICE, 6/29/93, p. 62, Manohla Dargis

The Music of Chance, directed by Philip Haas from the novel by Paul Auster, has the texture of dry toast. When a retired fire fighter named Nashe (Mandy Patinkin) picks up a bloody and beaten card shark named Pozzi (James Spader), Nashe's rootless journey comes to a terrible, fateful stop. All but out of money after 13 months on the road ("driving, just driving"), he decides to stake his last ten thousand on Pozzi's sure thing, a poker game with a couple of millionaire rubes.

Of course, there is nothing certain about a sure thing, no matter the odds. Nashe and Pozzi play poker, and Nashe and Pozzi lose. What happens next—there's a stone wall to build, and a child's red wagon to move those stones—is more metaphor than meat, or meaning. Instead of dialogue, Haas's characters voice vaguely important-sounding aphorisms ("You see, numbers have souls"), moving through scenes as if adrift in some philosophical vapor. Despite a surprisingly vivid turn by Patinkin (Spader is fascinating and fully unbelievable), *The Music of Chance* rarely breaks through the skin of its ideas.

Also reviewed in:
NEW REPUBLIC, 6/21/93, p. 28, Stanley Kauffmann
NEW YORK TIMES, 6/4/93, p. C13, Janet Maslin
NEW YORKER, 6/7/93, p. 106, Anthony Lane
VARIETY, 1/25/93, p. 135, Todd McCarthy
WASHINGTON POST, 7/16/93, p. C7, Rita Kempley
WASHINGTON POST, 7/16/93, Weekend/p. 40, Desson Howe

MY BOYFRIEND'S BACK

A Buena Vista Pictures release of a Touchstone Pictures production.   *Producer:* Sean S. Cunningham.   *Director:* Bob Balaban.   *Screenplay:* Dean Lorey.   *Director of Photography:* Mac Ahlberg.   *Editor:* Michael Jablow.   *Music:* Harry Manfredini.   *Music Editor:* Carl Zittrer and Michael Linn.   *Sound:* Darrell Henke and (music) Jerry Lambert.   *Sound Editor:* Phillip Seretti.   *Casting:* Julie Hughes, Barry Moss, and David Giella.   *Production Designer:* Michael Hanan.   *Art Director:* Charles Lagola.   *Set Designer:* John A. Frick and Jonathan Short.   *Set Decorator:* Doug Mowat.   *Costumes:* Kimberly Tillman.   *Make-up:* Kimberly Greene.   *Stunt Coordinator:* Lonnie Nelson.   *Running time:* 80 minutes.   *MPAA Rating:* PG-13.

CAST: Andrew Lowery (Johnny);   Traci Lind (Missy);   Danny Zorn (Eddie);   Edward Herrmann (Mr. Dingle);   Mary Beth Hurt (Mrs. Dingle);   Jay O. Sanders (Sheriff McCloud); Libby Villari (Camille McCloud);   Matthew Fox (Buck Van Patten);   Philip Hoffman (Chuck Bronski);   Paul Dooley (Big Chuck);   Austin Pendleton (Dr. Bronson);   David Womack Galewsky (Young Johnny);   Zachary Lefenfeld (Young Eddie);   Nicholas Waggoner (Young Buck);   Zack Steeg (Young Chuck);   Brooke Adams (Young Missy);   Bob Dishy (Murray the Gravedigger);   Cloris Leachman (Maggie the Zombie Expert);   Paxton Whitehead (Judge in Heaven);   Jane Simoneau (Lady with Apple Pie);   Delray Cordell (Kid on Bike);   Eunice Clark (Johnny's School Teacher);   Michael Petty (Gerald the Nerdy Student);   Larry Strub (Referee); Joe Stevens (Robber at Convenience Store);   Jerry Haynes (Minister at Funeral);   Phil Ross (Scientist in Horror Film);   Oliver Tull (Guy #1);   Matthew McConaughey (Guy #2);   Zeke Mills (Movie Goer #1);   Netha Stanton (Movie Goer #2);   Melissa Taub (Beefy Girl in Library); Nan Brown (Reporter Brenda);   Christian Burrows (Little Chuck);   Brandi Burkett (Brandi); LaBrooke Brannon (Staci);   Stephanie Wing (Vanna);   Jimmuy Bennett III (Kid on Trike);   Phil Ross (French Waiter);   Gary Graves and Edwin Neal (Big Chuck's Henchmen).

LOS ANGELES TIMES, 8/6/93, Calendar/p. 22, Kevin Thomas

"My Boyfriends Back" an awful teen horror comedy, hits a new low in high concepts: a 17-year-old (Andrew Lowery) wants to take the girl (Traci Lind) of his dreams to the big prom so badly that not even death will stop him. It's a premise that calls for pitch-dark satire to have a prayer of succeeding, but instead has a disastrous tone of sunny sitcom jauntiness. It also needs to proceed with the unrelenting force of airtight logic but instead rambles from one implausibility to the next, annihilating any possibility for sustained laughter. As written by Dean Lorey and directed by Bob Balaban, the film never rises above the level of double-entendre humor regarding the eating of human flesh.

Lowery's Johnny is a typical small-town high school student who's had a crush on Lind's Missy since the first grade. Naturally, as the prettiest, most-popular girl in school, she goes with the obnoxious campus hero (Matthew Fox). In lamebrain desperation, Johnny persuades his best friend (Danny Zorn) to kidnap Missy at the convenience store where she works part time so that he can become a hero by rescuing her and be rewarded by her agreeing to be his prom date.

Unfortunately, just as the boys are setting their plan in motion, an actual masked gunman holds up the store, and Johnny is shot to death trying to protect Missy. No sooner is he six feet under than he starts rising from the grave; amusingly—but not amusingly enough—Missy pays far more attention to him now that he's a zombie than she did when he was alive. There's a hitch with

Johnny's new condition, of course: His body is decaying so rapidly that whether he likes it or not he's going to have to start feasting on human flesh if he's to last out the four days to the prom. Despite the overall direness of the circumstances, Lowery and Lind manage to make good impressions, and they're surrounded by such stalwarts as Mary Beth Hurt and Edward Herrmann as Johnny's crazy airhead parents and Austin Pendleton, who actually shines as Johnny's mercenary doctor. Other reliable pros include Bob Dishy, Paul Dooley, Cloris Leachman and Jay O. Sanders, but their efforts count for little in a film (rated PG-13 for a teen sex fantasy, zombie violence and some language) that's impossible to imagine anyone getting away with except David Lynch.

NEW YORK POST, 8/6/93, p. 27, Matthew Flamm

It's tough being a teen-ager, but never so tough as when you've come back from the dead and other kids whisper "zombie" when you walk past in the school hallway. That's the sort of stigma Johnny Dingle must deal with in "My Boyfriend's Back," a genial, intermittently funny, well-acted comedy.

Johnny (Andrew Lowery) has crawled out of his grave to make a date. He's going to the prom with Missy McCloud (Traci Lind), the beautiful girl next door for whom he took a bullet in the chest from an armed robber. Missy—like everyone else a little surprised to see Johnny back in school—now has the awkward task of explaining that she only said yes because he was dying.

"My Boyfriend's Back," which originally had the much better title of "Johnny Zombie," sends up all sorts of Hollywood hokum, from socially conscious message movies to drive-in teen zombie fare.

Its exceptional cast includes Mary Beth Hurt and Edward Herrmann as Johnny's madly cheerful mom and dad, and Austin Pendleton as a deranged doctor who thinks zombie flesh may be the key to a really good cosmetic cream.

The strategy of director Bob Balaban (last seen behind the camera with the not entirely dissimilar "Parents") and screenplay author Dean Lorey is to play the story utterly straight. When Johnny explains to Missy that he ate a fellow student only so he could be with her (zombies need the flesh of the living to survive), another girl remarks appreciatively, "My boyfriend won't even pump gas for me."

This treat-it-normal humor has its limits. "My Boyfriend's Back" gets as far as it does on one joke owing largely to Balaban's direction, which sends up idyllic small-town America along with its movies. The trouble is that the film is neither enough of a social satire or enough of a movie parody.

It is good-natured though, as long as you don't mind a little (patently phony) gore. Lowery and Lind make an endearing couple, who may not always have to worry about a decaying ear falling off in the middle of a clinch.

In any case, you can bet that no matter what the prejudiced locals think about love with the undead, this boy and girl are going to the prom.

NEWSDAY, 8/6/93, Part II/p. 69, Terry Kelleher

"My Boyfriend's Back" isn't gross, really. There's not a lot of blood and gore and ooze. It's more like—yucky.

Granted, the teenage zombie hero's ear falls off when he first tries to make out with the girl of his dreams. Granted, the ear winds up in her mouth. The appropriate viewer response, however, is not an "eeeek!" of terror or an "aaarrgh!" of disgust, but rather the sort of half-amused "eeeww" with which one might respond to a prank that was crude and childish, yet basically benign.

Screenwriter Dean Lorey, who also has "Jason Goes to Hell: The Final Friday" coming out this month (boy, is he on a roll), says his script for "My Boyfriend's Back" began as "little more than a series of comic sketches about a kid who becomes a zombie." The "development" process didn't exactly bulk up the story, except now the protagonist has a romantic reason for dying and for wanting to stay undead awhile.

High-school senior Johnny Dingle (Andrew Lowery) stops a bullet while saving the life of Missy McCloud (Traci Lind), on whom he has had a massive crush since age 6. With his last breath he asks her to the prom, and naturally she says yes, not anticipating he'll rise from the grave and hold her to her word.

The most original idea in "My Boyfriend's Back" is that Johnny and Missy live in a small town where zombies are hardly unheard of. The gravedigger (Bob Dishy) takes Johnny's comeback in stride. His parents (Edward Herrmann and Mary Beth Hurt) care only about keeping up appearances, dead or alive. The other citizens of Fairview treat Johnny no worse than they would any other member of a minority group.

But the movie's target audience (they don't call it "PG-13" for nothing) won't be diverted long by director Bob Balaban's mild satire of conformism, and some relative oldsters may remember he and Hurt did this sort of thing better a few years ago in "Parents." What "My Boyfriend's Back" has to sell is the comedy of decomposition, plus all the "eat me" jokes it can derive from the zombie's need to consume human flesh.

Except for its title, "My Boyfriend's Back" has no connection with that hit song from 1963. In fact, if you can remember the record, you're one of those who should forget the movie.

Also reviewed in:
NEW YORK TIMES, 8/6/93, p. C16, Stephen Holden
VARIETY, 8/16/93, p. 39, Emanuel Levy
WASHINGTON POST, 8/9/93, p. B7, Rita Kempley

MY LIFE

A Columbia Pictures release in association with Capella Films. *Executive Producer:* Gil Netter. *Producer:* Jerry Zucker, Bruce Joel Rubin, and Hunt Lowry. *Director:* Bruce Joel Rubin. *Screenplay:* Bruce Joel Rubin. *Director of Photography:* Peter James. *Editor:* Richard Chew. *Music:* John Barry. *Music Editor:* Clif Kohlweck. *Sound:* John Sutton, III. *Sound Editor:* Richard King. *Casting:* Janet Hirshenson, Jane Jenkins, and Roger Mussenden. *Production Designer:* Neil Spisak. *Art Director:* Larry Fulton. *Set Designer:* Gina B. Cranham. *Set Decorator:* Anne D. McCulley. *Special Effects:* Larz Anderson. *Costumes:* Judy Ruskin. *Make-up:* Bob Mills and David Craig Forrest. *Prosthetic Make-up:* Matthew W. Mungle. *Body Make-up:* Laura De'Atley. *Running time:* 118 minutes. *MPAA Rating:* PG-13.

CAST: Michael Keaton (Bob Jones); Nicole Kidman (Gail Jones); Bradley Whitford (Paul); Queen Latifah (Theresa); Michael Constantine (Bill); Rebecca Schull (Rose); Mark Lowenthal (Dr. Mills); Lee Garlington (Carol Sandman); Toni Sawyer (Doris); Haing S. Ngor (Mr. Ho); Romy Rosemont (Anya Stasiuk); Danny Rimmer (Young Bobbie); Ruth DeSosa (Young Rose); Richard Schiff (Young Bill); Stephen Taylor Knot (Young Paul); Andrew Camuccio and Brian Camuccio (Baby Brian); Colby Sawyer Garabedian (Little Boy Brian); Mary Ann Thebus (Miss Morgenstern); Brenda Strong (Laura); Rudi Davis (George); Mark Holton (Sam); Lisa Walters (Deborah); Bruce Jarchow (Walter); Jane Morris (Dorothy); Kenneth Tigar (Dr. Califano); Ray Reinhardt (Dr. Altman); Frank DiElsi (Arnold Sherman); Billy L. Sullivan, Michael Gallagher, and Christopher Miranda (Rollercoaster Friends); Nora Taylor (Little Girl); Dianne B. Shaw (Detroit Mother); Sondra Rubin (Aunt Sophia); Sylvia Kauders (Aunt Tekla); Sharon Conley (Lida Stasiuk); James R. Sweeney (Nestor Stasiuk); Vasek C. Simek (Uncle Henry); Magda Harout (Aunt Sonia); Mark Zingale and Jonathan Fish (Delivery Men); James Rubin (Uncle Jimmy); Jennifer Flackett (Childbirth Teacher); Gary Rubin (Man at Wedding); Susan Breslau, Wendy Sax, Charlotte Zucker, Blanche Rubin, and Ari Rubin (Guests at Wedding); John Steciw (Band Leader); Walter Klimchuk (Priest); Peggy Roeder, Treva Tegtmeier, Oksana Fedunyszyn, and Lynn Baber (Cousins).

LOS ANGELES TIMES, 11/12/93, Calendar/p. 1, Kenneth Turan

Any resemblance between "My Life" and real life is strictly coincidental. Blind to complexities, this is a a touchy-feely film that wouldn't recognize an honest emotion if one hit it like a truck. Those, however, whom "Love Story" struck as realistic and who think Oscars ought to be handed out for "Reach Out and Touch Someone" commercials will find "My Life's" brand of synthetic bathos uncannily familiar.

Starring Michael Keaton and Nicole Kidman, "My Life's" story of a man who discovers he is dying while his wife is expecting their first child should probably be approached less in anger than in sorrow. There may well be decent ideas buried somewhere in this self-satisfied morass, but they have been so suffocated by wave after wave of glibness and manipulation that nothing is left but a pale outline not unlike the ones that surround corpses at crime scenes.

"My Life," written and directed by "Ghost" screenwriter Bruce Joel Rubin, clearly thinks it is dealing with the real stuff here, with big-picture questions about the meaning of existence and the power of death. But all its thoughts are unrelievedly on the nose, all its insights thoroughly predigested. And it so milks the painful situations it evokes that one doesn't know whether to laugh, take offense or shrug and move on.

Certainly high-powered Los Angeles public-relations executive Bob Jones (Keaton) seems powerfully uncomfortable confronting emotions as he sits looking at a video camera. "I'm supposed to be dying," he says. "I have a disease called cancer. You're about to be born."

What Bob is doing is creating a tape for his expected child so the youngster knows both what Dad was like and how to master a variety of real-world skills. Sounds like a nice idea, and while Keaton's performance certainly encourages us to see Jones as a decent sort, we soon learn, in the first of "My Life's" arbitrary inconsistencies, that we are wrong. He has, it seems, committed the key sin of modern times: He has led an unexamined life and, yes, shut himself off from his potential for growth. For shame, Bob, for shame.

Not that Bob's angelic wife, Gail (Kidman), would think of getting angry about any of this, even when Bob says he is too busy to accompany her to their baby's next sonogram. A dewy-eyed domestic Mother Teresa, Gail fights back with the movie's sappiest dialogue. "Bob, please love us," she says at one point, adding later, "Don't open your heart to a machine. I feel like I've already lost you. I need you."

Also needing Bob are his parents and about-to-be-married brother back home in Detroit, an insistently ethnic clan of Ukrainian-Americans that have kept the family name Ivanovich that Bob has thoughtlessly discarded. Apparently still cranky over a childhood misery recounted in "My Life's" brief prologue, Bob is on the outs with his folks. Truth is, if it weren't for Gail (the woman is a saint), we wouldn't be in touch with them at all.

While early press notes refer to the existence of a spiritual guide to help lead Bob out of this swamp of self-interest, that character has, apparently been dropped and the burden of enlightening Bob fallen to the enigmatic Mr. Ho (Haing S. Ngor of "The Killing Fields"), a mysterious master of undefined Asian medicine.

Though Bob is initially skeptical of Mr. Ho's abilities, he is won over by the blinding white light he sees during treatment and by Mr. Ho's apparently inexhaustible supply of fortune cookie wisdom. Forget the cancer, Bob, Mr. Ho insists, your real illness is your anger. "It is not enough to marry goodness," he says (oh, that Gail), "you have to find it within yourself." And when Bob complains of an unsuccessful mission of forgiveness to Detroit, Mr. Ho reminds him, "Only one place you need to go—your heart." Too true.

Most of "My Life" (rated PG-13 for mature subject matter) details the parallel exaltation of Bob's spirit as his body decays, and if that sounds too pat, you have no idea. In its relentless Hollywoodization of what in most people's lives would be an agonizing situation, this film actually makes death look like a negligible price to pay for the spiritual wealth gained by opening up and becoming a caring human being.

First-time director Rubin, who thinks lines like "kids need to marinate in love" should be read with a straight face, pulls out some stops in the film's final half-hour that the pen cannot do justice to. It's enough to note that when Gail says, admittedly in another context, "I think I'm going to throw up," there will be little doubt about how she feels.

NEW YORK POST, 11/12/93, p. 36, Michael Medved

The new film "My Life" makes such a powerful impression that it may actually inspire you to try to become a better person. The first thing I did after seeing the picture was to find a phone booth and to call my mother.

It's part of the movie's message that such small gestures matter a great deal: this richly moving piece of work leaves you painfully aware of the precious possibilities in each passing moment. "Dying is a really hard way to learn about life," declares central character Bobby Jones (Michael Keaton) and the film provides an eloquent summary of his most important lessons.

This flawed, ultimately endearing protagonist certainly has a lot to learn: he is a hotshot p.r. man with a stunning home in Beverly Hills, an adoring wife (Nicole Kidman) who is glowingly pregnant with their first child, and inoperable kidney cancer that is rapidly spreading to his lungs. Facing the prospect that he may die before the baby arrives, Keaton focuses his energies on creating a collection of videotapes in which he explains himself to his unborn child.

This premise may seem melodramatic and manipulative—and uncomfortably reminiscent of a 20-year-old made-for-TV weepie called "Message to my Daughter"—but the loving commitment at all levels of the production transforms the prosaic material into a genuinely poetic experience.

The acting is consistently superb, with Nicole Kidman proving just as adept at playing an angelic character as she did depicting a diabolical one in "Malice." It is Keaton's performance, however, that carries the movie; he veers from the hilarious to the heartbreaking with miraculous assurance and flair.

Audiences will laugh at the videotaped advice to his unborn child on secrets of shaving, basketball, pasta or sex, while other sequences—such as his desperate visits to a compassionate Asian healer (Dr. Haing S. Ngor)—are uniquely devastating and disturbing.

The emotional center of the film involves Bobby's attempt to reconcile with the blue-collar Ukrainian family he left behind in Detroit before moving out to Hollywood and changing his name from Ivanovich to Jones: It turns out that this glib hustler feels embarrassed by his grubby immigrant parents.

A troubled trip back to Michigan to celebrate the wedding of his kid brother (well-played by Bradley Whitford) shows Bobby at this self-absorbed worst.

"My Life" marks an auspicious directorial debut for Bruce Joel Rubin, whose previous work as a screenwriter (he wrote both the sentimental mega-hit "Ghost" and the misfired "Jacob's Ladder") similarly focused on the passage between life and death.

This new film (in which the director of "Ghost," Jerry Zucker, lent a hand as co-producer) remains blessedly free of the showy other-worldly speculations that characterized Rubin's other projects and the direction there is more delicate and honest than his other scripts received.

If Rubin has one fault as a filmmaker it's a tendency to linger a bit too long on each elegantly composed shot and beautifully written scene, but the affection he generates for his characters makes it easy to forgive such indulgence.

NEWSDAY, 11/12/93, Part II/p. 73, Jack Mathews

The production notes for Bruce Joel Rubin's "My Life" say the idea for the story came to him after he ate a Mexican meal and lay in bed with such severe abdominal pains he thought he was dying. I know this feeling, and am pretty sure that if he had just skipped the hot sauce, we might have all been spared.

Rubin, who ruminated on life and death in his scripts for "Ghost" and "Jacob's Ladder," explains that he wondered, with the fires of Montezuma raging in his belly, whether his children would know what kind of man their father was, and he came up with the idea of a dying man's doing a video tape of his life and leaving it behind.

That is the dramatic device in "My Life," the shamelessly contrived story of a successful Los Angeles PR man who gets the news of his wife's first pregnancy at about the same time he is diagnosed with inoperable cancer.

Thanks mostly to Michael Keaton's warmly moving and often funny performance, this road is a lot less painful than it might have been. The segments in which Bob Jones is addressing his unborn child on camera, offering instruction on everything from slam dunks to shaving (ultrasound has detected his sex), are ready-made for Keaton's dead-pan humor.

Nicole Kidman is also very affecting as his wife and career partner, a woman caught in the horrible emotional crunch of seeing one life into the world and another out. Rubin, in his debut as a director, had a lot more on his mind than the dilemma between the couple. "My Life" is a story of self-discovery, Bob Jones getting to know himself through his therapeutic video sessions, and learning from his desperate visits to an Asian healer (Haing Ngor) that he is suffering from more than cancer.

There is a tumor of anger in his heart, the healer says, and he must release it and reconcile his life before the delicious final moment of death is at hand.

Rubin takes a huge spiritual leap with the healer, giving him inexplicable powers (with his hands hovering over Bob's body, he can isolate the tumors and their origin), and though the patient remains skeptical, it's pretty clear where Rubin stands. He is suddenly telling a story not about a man talking to his unborn child, but of someone preparing to cross the divide.

There are so many loose emotional ends introduced in this story, it is amazing Rubin was able to tie them all together. There, are all those flashbacks to Bob's childhood in Detroit, the anger he felt at his immigrant Russian father (Michael Constantine) for not devoting enough time to him, his disappointment with his working-class brother (Bradley Whitford), and his nagging disappointment with God over an unfulfilled wish made upon a star.

Will Bob regain enough childhood faith to wish again? Will he come to understand his intolerance toward his family? Will he be able to open up to his wife as well as he does to his camera? And will Rubin actually find another happy ending in death?

Despite the heavy hand at work, "My Life" works pretty well while setting those questions up. There are powerfully moving scenes between Bob and his parents, even more powerful scenes between him and his wife. But the last half hour of the film, as Rubin strains to turn death into a celebration, is excruciating. Not only because of our sadness for a man we've come to know, but for being so brazenly manipulated.

Next time Rubin eats in a Mexican restaurant, let's hope he lays off the sauce.

NEWSWEEK, 11/22/93, p. 57, Jack Kroll

I have been half in love with easeful Death," wrote John Keats. No half-way measures for Bruce Joel Rubin; Death seems to be his main squeeze. Rubin wrote "Ghost," in which Patrick Swayze was a posthumous hero, and "Jacob's Ladder," in which Tim Robbins was a prehumous one. In *My Life*, which he wrote and directed, Rubin gives us a Los Angeles public-relations man, Bob Jones (Michael Keaton), who learns he's dying of cancer as his wife, Gail (Nicole Kidman), is pregnant with their first child. Fighting to stay alive until the baby is born, Bob makes a series of videotapes as a legacy for his child.

This is called a tear-jerker, an ancient and sometimes honorable genre. What lends honor to "My Life" is Rubin's touch, tact, humor and dignity. He doesn't squeeze your tear ducts, he caresses them. They will respond. Only a diehard Terminatornik could resist Keaton earnestly explaining to his unborn son why his mom might remarry even though she loves Daddy. Or starting to advise the kid about sex and turning off the camera in embarrassment. Keaton is an ideal die-er with his chin-scratching, eyebrow-arching, mouth-gaping way of casually expressing real emotion. And Kidman has enormous appeal with her great movie face and glowing strength. Sometimes the film overglows: Gail's doctor has a smile so full of caring it may give you hypoglycemia.

But mostly "My Life" works on its own terms. The film's ending has a certain courage as Rubin looks death in the eyes. One other thing. Jones's Sony video camera is practically a character, and cynics may see the film as one long commercial for Sony, which owns Columbia, the releasing studio. Could it be that a smart Sony exec, knowing Rubin's death fetish, suggested the idea to their mutual benefit? Nah, only Robert Altman would dream up a scenario like that. But just in case, enjoy the movie and go buy a Panasonic.

SIGHT AND SOUND, 4/94, p. 48, Phillip Strick

Detroit, 1963. Young Bobby Ivanovich wishes on a star for a circus to perform in his back yard. He confidently invites all his schoolmates next day to come to the show; everybody turns up except the circus. Disgraced, Bobby hides in a cupboard. Thirty years later, now known as

Bob Jones, successful public relations executive to an L.A. company, he is battling against cancer. He decides to videotape a message for the child he may never see, carried by his wife Gail. It proves a difficult project: Bob is estranged from his parents, avoids recollections of his own childhood, and feels awkward before the camera. Taped tributes from colleagues are edgy and non-committal. Told by his doctor that his life expectancy is no more than a few months, he adopts Gail's suggestion to try a Chinese healer, Mr Ho. He decides Ho is a charlatan, but the encounter prompts him to try and understand himself better. He goes to visit Carol, a former neighbour and girlfriend, and realises there were aspects of his childhood he had forgotten completely.

Gail watches the videotape, upset that Bob reveals more to the camera than he does to her, and begs him to share his feelings. Shaken, he revisits Mr Ho, who insists he must search out his true worth from within. Accompanied by Gail, he flies out to the wedding of his brother Paul, in Detroit. Reminded by a visit to the old family house, he tells Gail about the circus incident and how he blamed his father for working too hard to pay attention to his family. Bob makes another wish: that God will let him live long enough to see his child. After the wedding reception, a riotous success, the old feud with his parents resurfaces; they are angry that he disowned them by changing his name; he complains that they never come to see him. Bob returns home, convinced that his last visit to his parents has not removed the emotional impasse. Mr Ho confirms that his body is still poisoned by anger.

Bob involves himself more closely in the progress of Gail's pregnancy, and together they learn that the baby will be a boy. Bob tapes messages about handball, shaving, etiquette and car maintenance, and accompanies Gail to pregnancy classes. They visit a fun fair and he takes a solitary ride on a rollercoaster, overcoming a childhood phobia. According to his doctor, cancer should have claimed him by now, but he is at Gail's side when the baby is born and they share the delight of the first weeks of parenthood. Then the disease closes in and Bob deteriorates rapidly, tended by Theresa, a hospice nurse, and advised by Mr Ho to make peace with himself. Phoning his parents, Bob admits at last that they did everything they could for him, and asks forgiveness. They fly to be at his side, to meet their grandson, and to make a final gift: a circus arrives in Bob's back garden. Bob finally slips away on a terminal rollercoaster, leaving a special message of thanks on videotape to his toddler son.

Like his scripts for *Jacob's Ladder* and *Ghost*, Bruce Joel Rubin's new story again defines an area of existence in which it is possible for a departing soul to correct a few errors before being claimed by the hereafter. Scoff as we may, the Rubin theory has its attractions. Half-lives have become increasingly familiar as a sign of the times, reflected on the screen by a fresh resurgence of vampires alongside such variants as *Flatliners, Always* and *Shadowlands*. While the beams encircling a bemused Patrick Swayze at the end of *Ghost* may resemble a trick of the light from *Close Encounters*, the allusion to innumerable reported brink-of-death experiences contrives to raise an inextinguishable hope or two—not the least being that he will, at some speed, be removed to a distant planet. In *My Life*, the Great White Glow is back once more, partly in the form of electric flashes that burst out from the corner of the healer's surgery, apparently to signal the blowing of emotional fuses, but more decisively as the cancer-sufferer, no longer sensibly fearful of fairground attractions, takes a rollercoaster ride into the unknown.

On what authority Rubin provides these assurances is unclear from the behaviour of his characters, whose moral rearmament is instinctive rather than orthodox. True, the dying Bob Jones has a high old time at his brother's wedding, but his own marriage is notably uncluttered by prayers, baptisms or conventional last rites, while the only faith emanating from his Chinese consultant is that Bob can achieve well-being by his own effort of will. His relationship with God, by contrast, is a matter of multiple misunderstanding, stemming from the mistaken assumption that wishing on a star brings an instant response. That Bob blames his parents, not God, for his disappointment implies several flaws in his upbringing and reasoning powers, while the fact that he holds his grudge for the next 30 years hints at a peculiar insensitivity. It is also difficult to understand the attraction of the circus even when it finally appears, since Bob is unable to do much about it beyond pointing things out to his incredulous infant.

More significantly, Bob's second star-wish, that he be permitted to live to meet his baby son, achieves a positively miraculous divine response for which God unfairly gets no credit at all. Further confused by the hang-up over the rollercoaster, a challenge which Bob has to confront in order to exorcise his troubled childhood, this meddling with the supernatural does nothing for Rubin's main theme—that it pays to be nice to people when you're on the way down—except lumber it with whimsical protestations that everything's bound to be all light on the night. Intriguingly, what's left of *My Life*, if such distractions are removed, is the account of a failed son, husband and parent who realises, with barely enough time to do anything about it, that he only has himself to blame (possibly even for his own cancer?). Apart from getting his relatives off the hook, it seems an uncomfortable legacy to pass on to his son who, on this evidence, would be fully justified in repeating the whole suicidal process by blaming the absent father for anything and everything.

As first-time director, well cushioned by his co-producer, and with at least five of his family among the cast, Rubin coasts unremarkably through an affable and largely unscuffed decor. By the device of filming through a video camera at haphazard moments, he disguises some of the clumsier lapses of his script, using video as a form of insulation between Bob and the 'real' world.

But where Demi Moore in *Ghost*, left to pursue her separate life, survived the partial loss of her lover with an appealing dignity, Nicole Kidman flounders with an underwritten role and makes little impression, neither blamed nor credited for much of her partner's interests. For his part, Michael Keaton declines gently, well-versed in angst, his customary expression of querulous uncertainty suggesting that he, along with the rest of us, remains unconvinced that all the answers have been supplied. His experiences may set some kind of example on tape—few fathers can now avoid the responsibility of leaving chirpy messages for their offspring to remember them by—but it has to be said that on film they look rather less than substantial.

TIME, 11/22/93, p. 78, Richard Corliss

Movies have always tried to teach the audience lessons: how to live more adventurously, love more expertly, blow things up more noisily. And every now and then, die more beautifully. This holiday season, mortality is much on the minds of ambitious filmmakers. Grim Death will be gargling in dramas about AIDS (*Philadelphia*), the Nazi Holocaust (*Schindler's List*), Vietnam (*Heaven and Earth*) and plain old age (*Wrestling Ernest Hemingway*). It's apt that the Cardiac Pack is led by *My Life*, for its writer-director is Bruce Joel Rubin, screenwriter for the postmortem love story *Ghost* and the death-throe fantasy *Jacob's Ladder*—the Jack Kevorkian of '90s Hollywood.

Like all of us, Bob Jones (Michael Keaton) has a death sentence hanging over him. But the clock is ticking faster for Bob: his kidney cancer has spread to his lungs and brain. Nothing can save him, not his youth, his cushy show-biz job, his loving wife (Nicole Kidman) or the child she carries inside her. Nor is he comforted by memories of a childhood disconnected from his working-class parents. So Bob decides to videotape a few remarks to his son-to-be.

Videotape as a kind of immortality: how sweet, how narcissistic, how '90s this notion is. So is this glossy, well-acted movie about a very privileged victim. Because Bob has no problems with money, work, a restless wife or unruly kids, he can spend his time in crash-course therapy, discovering that, yes, his parents really did love him. Moviegoers in "dead-end jobs and edgy relationships will wish they could live half as glamorously as Bob Jones dies. This is *Final Exit*, Hollywood-style: death warmed over.

VILLAGE VOICE, 11/30/93, Film Special/p. 32, Henry Cabot Beck

Bruce Joel Rubin left NYU classmates Scorsese and De Palma to explore their respective hells when he went off to the Far East in search of whatever people go off to the Far East in search of. He returned apparently determined to help others over the Big Speedbump with scripts that approached the issue via technology (*Brainstorm*), horror (*Jacob's Ladder*), and romance (*Ghost*).

In *My Life* Rubin introduces us to bland-as-milk Bob Jones (Michael Keaton), an assimilated public relations philistine who lives in L.A. with his largely invisible pregnant wife (Nicole Kidman) and a desire to bleach out his ethnicity and adolescent humiliation so great that he has metastasized a cancer roughly the size of the Times Square ball on New Year's Eve. The two-hour water-torture inevitability of its descent, combined with his race to see his son's birth, is enough to send football stadiums full of Iron Johns running for their Kleenex boxes.

Jones gets a crash course in Kubler-Ross as he videotapes his five-stage transitions with all the anal compulsion of a tourist in the land of carcinoma. The film is a pop dirge: shiny surfaces and middle-class values riddled with despair and denial. What ultimately pulls *My Life* through is Keaton's flat-as-Kansas delivery and a script that is subversive by being completely unsensational.

Also reviewed in:
CHICAGO TRIBUNE, 11/12/93, Friday/p. B, Johanna Steinmetz
NEW YORK TIMES, 11/12/93, p. C17, Janet Maslin
NEW YORKER, 11/22/93, p. 119, Terrence Rafferty
VARIETY, 11/15/93, p. 30, Leonard Klady
WASHINGTON POST, 11/12/93, p. C6, Rita Kempley
WASHINGTON POST, 11/12/93, Weekend/p. 48, Desson Howe

MY NEIGHBOR TOTORO

A Troma Films release of a Tokuma Group production.   *Executive Producer:* Yasuyoshi Tokuma.   *Producer:* Toru Hara.   *Director:* Hayao Miyazaki.   *Screenplay:* Hayao Miyazaki. *Story:* Hayao Miyazaki.   *Director of Photography:* Hisao Shirai.   *Editor:* Takeshi Seyama. *Music:* Jo Hisaishi.   *English Music Translation:* Eugene H. Saburi and Kaiulani Kidani.   *English Lyrics:* Severin Browne.   *Sound:* Shigeharu Shiba.   *Production Designer:* Yoshiharu Sato.   *Art Director:* Kazuo Oga.   *Special Effects:* Kaoru Tanifuji.   *Running time:* 76 minutes.   *MPAA Rating:* G.

VOICES: Lisa Michaelson (Satsuki);   Cheryl Chase (Mei);   Greg Snegoff (Dad);   Kenneth Hartman (Kanta);   Alexandra Kenworthy (Mother);   Natalie Core (Nanny);   Steve Kramer (Farmer);   Lara Cody (Farm Girl);   Melenie McQueen (Kanta's Mom).

LOS ANGELES TIMES, 5/7/93, Calendar/p. 14, Charles Solomon

The gentle warmth of "My Neighbor Totoro" provides a welcome respite from the rapid-fire mayhem that usually characterizes Japanese animation seen in the United States. Instead of the standard sci-fi laser battles and explosions, writer-director Hayao Miyazaki offers a charming fantasy that stresses the affectionate bond between two young sisters.

While their mother remains in the hospital, 4-year-old Mei and 10-year-old Satsuki move into an aged house in the country with their professor-father. When Mei explores the nearby woods, she meets Totoro, a seven-foot forest spirit who looks like an outsized cross between a bunny rabbit and a fuzzy throw pillow. The father believes Mei's story about meeting this magical guardian, and respectfully asks Totoro to watch over the children, which he does with the aid of a few assistants and a 12 legged "catbus" that is half animal half machine.

Guided by their supernatural friend, the sisters share a series of adventures, soaring over the landscape while Totoro's roars make the winds blow. But the story remains focused on the affection Mei and Satsuki share. Unlike many recent cartoon churns, the two sisters seem genuinely fond of each other, and their camaraderie never feels saccharine or forced.

An accomplished director, Miyazaki enjoys a cult following in both Japan and the U.S. for such fast-paced adventures as "Lupin III: Castle Cagliostro." It's rare to see such skillful cutting, staging and camera work in a non-Disney animated film.

The weakest aspect of "Totoro" is the animation itself, which never rises above the level of Saturday morning kidvid. The characters move jerkily, and many of the designs are awkward-looking: Mei has a wide, frog-like mouth that shows all of her back teeth whenever she yells, which is often.

But despite these limits, "My Neighbor Totoro" (Times rated: Family) is a gentle and affirming film. It's certain to delight smaller children, although boys accustomed to the slam-bang violence of super-hero cartoon features and TV shows may chafe at its leisurely pace.

NEW YORK POST, 5/14/93, p. 31, Jami Bernard

You like treacle? How about a nice syrupy dose of saccharine children's cartoon feature "My Neighbor Totoro," dubbed into English from Japanese. Better wash it down though with some hair o' the dog, or you'll gag.

Film critics aren't allowed to walk out of movies, which in this case is a good thing—because "Totoro" does have its charms, eventually. First you'll have to wade through the movie's painfully insipid American dubbing, and characters who are as dull as tekka maki without the tuna.

It's about a father and two giggly young daughters—the mother is in a city hospital with a mysterious ailment that appears to be some sort of romantic wasting disease—who move to an old house in farming country. The house is possibly haunted, but no need for alarm—the only fright in this movie is whether the smaller girl has walked off by herself carrying an ear of corn.

The haunters of the house are a bunch of benign dust balls, but the kids laugh them off and go on to their next big find—a "totoro" in the forest. A totoro is a cross between a walrus and a Cheshire Cat, a rotund creature that can only be seen by children—and that was clearly designed for its marketing possibilities in the "plush toy" arena. The over-simplified totoro design is inconsistent with the rest of the lush, realistic animation by Hayao Miyazaki, as if a two-dimensional creature had been popped into a three-dimensional world.

The magical encounters of the kids with the totoro are sweet if unremarkable, but there is one scene which at least visually has the magic this movie could use more of—a dark, rainy night in which the two children stand silently side by side with a totoro at a deserted bus stop. The scene is at once silly, strange and comforting.

Those misinformed parents who believe that blandness is a key quality in a movie for kids will rest comfortably with "My Neighbor Totoro." They should not, however, confuse lack of violence or bad language with quality. Animation fans may want to check out the painterly visuals.

NEW YORK POST, 5/19/93, p. 26, Michael Medved

When it comes to reviewing movies aimed at small children, I have learned from painful experience to apply "The Barney Test."

This refers, of course, to America's most beloved singing-and-dancing dinosaur, who has become such a tyrannosaurus-sized hit on television and home video—where he stars in no fewer than nine of last month's 25 top-selling titles.

I'm embarrassed to admit that when initially confronted with this consummate entertainer, I failed to recognize his all-powerful appeal. For my two pre-schoolers on the other hand, meeting Barney amounted to love at first sight.

Ever since this experience, I've trusted my daughters more than I trust myself when it comes to judging entertainment for kids, and in that context I must report that both girls (now ages 6 and 4) adored the new Japanese import "My Neighbor Totoro."

In fact, my 6-year-old, Sarah, insists that it deserves her coveted "four star" designation and ranks it as one of the greatest films she's ever seen, along with "Beauty and the Beast" and "Homeward Bound." I tried to reason with her, insisting that this slow-moving animated feature doesn't deserve that kind of praise, but she held her ground. "I just loved the two little girls!" she insisted. "And the Totoro is so pretty and so sweet. Can we go see it again?"

Right now I'm resisting that suggestion because this film boasts the kind of pacing and intensity that make Mr. Rogers' Neighborhood look like "Terminator II." The story centers on two sisters, ages 9 and 5, who move with their home in the Japanese countryside. There, they discover a huge, mysterious tree that is home to a cuddly "Giant Totoro."

According to publicity materials for this film, Totoros are as popular among Japanese youngsters as Mickey Mouse—or Barney—is here. These are fat, furry, silent, broadly sailing creatures who might have resulted from some curious interspecies encounter between a giant owl and a Cheshire cat.

The action of this film, such as it is, centers on the younger sister getting lost one day at dusk when she runs off to try to visit her mother in the hospital. It's up to the older girl, the giant Totoro, and a magical bus in the shape of a huge cat with dozens of flying paws, to find the child, bring her home safely, and ensure that Mommy gets well soon.

This plot may not rank as a deathless classic of world literature, but the film draws you into its tender, whimsical vision of country life in contemporary Japan. The lush landscapes are drawn with consummate artistry.

The movements of the characters sometimes suggest the herky-jerky action of Saturday morning cartoons, but the most striking difference between "My Neighbor Totoro" and recent American-made animated features is the relative quiet of this soundtrack: Without constant music or non-stop sound effects, the picture unfolds with the feeling of a handsome and dignified picture book.

NEWSDAY, 5/14/93, Part II/p. 71, Joseph Gelmis

Japanese animation covers a vast spectrum of tastes and styles, from the ultraviolent futuristic "Japanimation" (aka "anime"), which has a home video cult following in the United States, to G-rated kiddie fare like "My Neighbor Totoro."

Japanimation is too hyperactive for general audiences. But, unlike some of the more ambitious and confused animated features that glutted theaters last year, "My Neighbor Totoro" is simple and easy for the kindergarten set to follow and pleasant to look at.

True, it wasn't funny or engrossing enough to suit my 13-year-old companion. But her sister, 8, loved it. She asked all the right questions, laughed on cue, responded with concern where she was intended to.

The story combines fantasy and realistic family problems. Two sisters, Sasuki and Mei, move into a long-empty house in the country with their father. Their mother, whom they visit briefly, is weak and hospitalized with an unexplained illness.

The fabulous creature Totoro keeps the girls busy. The big guy, who can fly and blow gale-force winds and do all sorts of neat things, is a grinning giant, somewhere between Cheshire cat and owl, who lives unseen by adults in the foliage of a colossal tree. He introduces the girls to a huge cat that is also a high-speed bus.

The movements of humans and fantasy creatures are lifelike, though the backgrounds are motionless. The dubbed sound track, enunciated with exaggerated care in English so even tots can understand the story, lacks the fluidity and grace of writer/director Hayao Miyazaki's animation. And it should be noted, if only for the record, that the Japanese girls and their father have been Europeanized—probably for the purpose of global marketing.

Miyazaki is a popular animator in Japan. His films have spun off a Disney-like boom in merchandising. If your child likes this movie, be advised you may become suddenly aware of Miyazaki's presence through stuffed animals in toy stores or three books, incorporating original drawings from a trio of his films—"My Neighbor Totoro," "Kiki's Delivery Service" and "Laputa, the Castle in the Sky"—now in U.S. bookstores.

Also reviewed in:
NEW YORK TIMES, 5/14/93, p. C14, Stephen Holden
VARIETY, 5/10/93, p. 237, Leonard Klady

NAKED

A Fine Line Features release of a Film Four International production with the participation of British Screen and Thin Man Productions. *Producer:* Simon Channing-Williams. *Director:* Mike Leigh. *Screenplay:* Mike Leigh. *Director of Photography:* Dick Pope. *Editor:* Jon Gregory. *Music:* Andrew Dickson. *Sound:* Peter Maxwell and (music) André Jacquemin. *Casting:* Paddy Stern and Susie Parriss. *Production Designer:* Alison Chitty. *Art Director:* Eve Stewart.

Costumes: Lindy Hemming. *Make-up:* Chris Blundell. *Running time:* 126 minutes. *MPAA Rating:* Not Rated.

CAST: David Thewlis (Johnny); Lesley Sharp (Louise); Katrin Cartlidge (Sophie); Greg Cruttwell (Jeremy); Claire Skinner (Sandra); Peter Wight (Brian); Ewen Bremner (Archie); Susan Vidler (Maggie); Deborah Maclaren (Woman in Window); Gina McKee (Café Girl); Carolina Giammeta (Masseuse); Elizabeth Berrington (Giselle); Darren Tunstall (Poster Man); Robert Putt (Chauffeur); Lynda Rooke (Victim); Angela Curran (Car Owner); Peter Whitman (Mr. Halpern); Jo Abercrombie (Woman in Street); Elaine Britten (Girl in Porsche); David Foxxe (Tea Bar Owner); Mike Avenall and Toby Jones (Men at Tea Bar); Sandra Voe (Bag Lady).

CHRISTIAN SCIENCE MONITOR, 5/20/93, p. 13, David Sterritt

In the starkly titled *Naked*, renowned British filmmaker Mike Leigh—who received international praise for "High Hopes" and "Life Is Sweet," his two previous movies—serves up a ferociously dark view of contemporary British life, focusing on the adventures of a young drifter who recognizes no kind of love or caring except for violent, voracious sexuality.

The movie would be simply repellent if not for three ingredients.

One is the brilliance of Mr. Leigh's visual style.

Another is the acting of David Thewlis, who gives one of the most virtuosic performances I've seen in years.

The third is Leigh's challenging screenplay, which suggests that the abhorrent traits of the film's characters are results of life in an avaricious society that produces psychological ills and misery along with unequal wealth and repetitive jobs.

These aspects don't make Leigh's film easy to assimilate, but they do make it hard to shake off.

CHRISTIAN SCIENCE MONITOR, 9/7/93, p. 12, David Sterritt

By any measure, Mike Leigh has emerged as the most important English filmmaker of his generation.

From prizewinning satires like "Bleak Moments" and "Meantime" to international successes like "High Hopes" and "Life Is Sweet," his films have earned praise around the world for their sympathetic yet tough-minded portraits of working-class British life. Feminist critics have taken a special interest in them, noting Mr. Leigh's close attention to the problems of women.

Leigh's working methods are as unusual as the subjects of his stories. He works closely with his cast developing themes and situations through extended improvisations before the cameras roll. Although the credits may say "Written and Directed by Mike Leigh," each of his films is the result of joint exploration.

Leigh's career hit another high point at the Cannes Film Festival last May, where he was honored as best director for "Naked," the story of an abrasive and sometimes violent young man named Johnny who barges through a working class London neighborhood having aggressive encounters with friends, acquaintances and strangers. David Thewlis, who plays Johnny, also won the Cannes award for best actor.

Developed through Leigh's improvisatory techniques, the film sparked controversy at Cannes with its searing depiction of physical and psychological torment inflicted on female characters. Many critics defended the movie, however, pointing out that the brutal behavior it depicts is never justified or romanticized.

Mr. Thewlis is the first to agree that the character he plays is "abhorrent" in many respects. "But we didn't put anything in the film to be titillating for the sake of it," he told me at Cannes, where we had several conversations. "We brought a sense of responsibility to everything we did, and fortunately, women seem to understand why they're represented in the film as they are.

"We're not in the business of misogyny or sensationalism," he continued with emphasis. "The scenes of violence in the film are there to make a comment about the society we live in—the inequality between the sexes, the races, the classes. It's all there for a reason.

Asked about the film's abrasive qualities, Leigh responds in a similar way. "*Life* is abrasive for a lot of people," he told me in an interview, "and there's no getting round it. I think a function of art—and the cinema not least—is to confront these things ... I'm absolutely committed as a filmmaker to be entertaining and to amuse; but I am also concerned to confront, as I did in 'Life Is Sweet' and other films."

Leigh and Thewlis both acknowledge that Johnny is an extremely bright and educated young man as well as a nasty and dysfunctional one. Thewlis says it was a major challenge to blend the character's loathsome and laudable qualities into a single characterization.

"I've worked with Mike before in less substantial parts," he told me. "But this was such a complex and multifaceted character—such an intelligent and bitter character—that it was difficult to improvise with such speed and vocabulary and articulateness. I remember my brain being on fire, raging with ideas, because I also researched an enormous amount.

"It was a process of putting an awful lot of learning together and coming up with the philosophy and attitude of the character—who became indignant and arrogant, with a sense of superiority for being more informed and enlightened than anyone around him ... And that's how I felt at the time. I felt I could confound and out-argue anybody."

Like many elements of the film, Johnny's intelligence is stressed not to make him attractive, but to make a serious point. "I know university graduates who have no prospects," Leigh says of England, where unemployment is a persistent problem. "They're a generation of people who have been displaced ... I think more people are very intelligent than the [powerful individuals] who run the world realize. But for a lot of those people, it's wasted. They have the luggage of intelligence and education, and nowhere to use it."

Under such circumstances, Leigh continues, people turn to vapid and materialistic pursuits to distract themselves.

"[In the film] Johnny says people have had the universe explained to them, and now they're bored," Leigh says. "As long as something bleeps and flashes at them, that's all they want. I feel disgusted at all that ... I hope in some way the film approximates this tension between the spiritual and the material ... We privileged people have this extraordinary capacity to convince ourselves that our lives—the momentary business of mankind, like the Cannes Film Festival—is incredibly important. I felt it was time to raise this in the context of the fact that what occupies *most* people is where their next meal is coming from!"

With its mixture of sociological horror and intellectual humor, Leigh's movie could be a hard sell when it arrives in American theaters (courtesy of Fine Line Pictures, its US distributor) after more appearances at film festivals. Leigh doesn't think it will prove too daunting for general audiences, though.

"In a way, the references are incidental," he says, speaking of the wide range of learning that Johnny displays. "They will resonate with people for whom they have meaning, but unlike Peter Greenaway or someone like that, I don't make films to be decoded by intellectuals. I am not a manufacturer of esoteric formulas. I am an emotional and intuitive filmmaker."

CHRISTIAN SCIENCE MONITOR, 10/12/93, p. 14, David Sterritt

[*Naked* was reviewed jointly with *Raining Stones*; see Sterritt's review of that film.]

FILM QUARTERLY, Spring 1994, p. 43, Leonard Qaurt

Mike Leigh's last two films, *High Hopes* and *Life Is Sweet*, do not quite prepare one for the level of harrowing emotional experience in *Naked*. Of course, neither of those earlier films is light, escapist fare, despite the satiric, even farcical tone. Both films contain large doses of familial angst and pathology, and *High Hopes* expresses a sardonic revulsion with the whole Thatcherite ethos and its yuppie devotees. But they both conclude on a consoling note with bittersweet images of possible life affirmation and family reconciliation. The world and the lives of the two films' characters can never be quite righted, but nobody falls into the void, and the chance for some semblance of redemption remains.

However, *Naked*, right from its opening scene—a lurching tracking shot along a grim Manchester night alley, where the film's protagonist, Johnny, is seen brutalising a woman is a rawer, much more savage work. Johnny is a working-class drifter and Dostoyevskean-style intellectual—a social outsider like Cyril, the motorcycle messenger of *High Hopes*, but without the political ideology or sweetness visible beneath Cyril's quiet anger and class resentment. In fact, Johnny is destructive and self-destructive, a literate monologist whose anger and sadism act as much stronger forces within him than his capacity for concern. It's women who bear the brunt of his physical and emotional rage, who suffer in being casually manhandled, insulted, and rejected by him.

Johnny is given a ferocious, luminous performance by David Thewlis, an actor whom Leigh used in *Life Is Sweet* to play the small role of the bulimic twin's relatively sane boyfriend. Thewlis succeeds in granting the hostile Johnny an emotional complexity, largeness of mind, elegance of movement, wit, and perverse charm that make his capacity to attract women perfectly understandable. Wispy-bearded, tall, thin, dressed in black, Johnny is given to endless orations on subjects ranging from the silence of the human body to the architecture of modern office buildings ("postmodern gas chambers") and the nature of time and God. Still, he's no Cyril, so there is no speechifying about the evil Thatcher, class inequality, or the oppressiveness of the social order. His soliloquies are alternately absurd, compulsive, perceptive, and truly poetic and visionary, as well as a mixture of all these qualities at once. At moments, Leigh seems to have made Johnny's talk a bit too self-conscious and literary, too carefully constructed. But at the same time, his soliloquies give Johnny's fate greater poignancy—a portrait of a despairing man who has displaced his imagination and intellectual resources into pathetic, relentlessly dazzling verbal exhibitions and corrosive put-downs.

Johnny is a waste—a self-aware, often cruel and dangerous one. All the women he encounters after he flees Manchester for London—though distinctively different from each other—share a painful neediness. Johnny may be seductive, but it takes little insight to be wary of this aggressive, barbed-tongued, unwashed man in a threadbare raincoat. Almost all the women, however turn a blind eye to the threatening aspects of Johnny, and hungrily embrace him. There is sturdy, weary Louise, his former working-class girlfriend from Manchester (Lesley Sharp), and her masochistic, punk-outfitted, drugged roommate Sophie (Katrin Cartlidge), who as soon as she meets Johnny has violent sex with him. An older woman, Jane Austen-reading and alcoholic, despondently opens herself up sexually to him, only to be humiliatingly put down as looking like his mother. Not only does he refuse to have sex, but he steals her books into the bargain. Finally, there is a silent, melancholy waitress who takes Johnny to her flat where he bathes, seems to let his guard down, and wants to linger. In this case, however, she suddenly starts to cry and just as abruptly throws him out into the cold. Her behavior is unexplained, but one senses that she herself is too hurt and alienated to make any human connection.

In *Naked* every character is emotionally isolated, bruised, or aimless, the film permeated by a vision of hopelessness. It envelops the relationships between men and women—the men harsh, violent, and terrified of commitment, the women emotionally starved, setting themselves up as victims. However, despite Johnny's brutal sexist behavior, the film's perspective is not misogynistic. Though a number of the women characters are victimized, they always remain singular people, never becoming mere sex objects. In fact, as is often the case in Leigh's work, the only relatively strong character is a woman, Louise. And the misogyny, at least on Johnny's part, seems just one element among many that express the self-loathing which permeates his life. No character in this film is free of a blighted existence.

Much of the action takes place during a couple of agonizing days on the streets of London. For after Sophie begins to clamor for his affection, Johnny flees Louise's flat and heads for London's Soho. On the barren, seedy night streets he meets a stunted Glaswegian couple, who howl an almost incomprehensible form of expletive-filled English. Johnny wanders with them through the encampments of London's homeless under Waterloo's grimy railway arches. But he remains amiably detached from this graceless pair—treating the couple as if they were members of a different, somewhat comic species (the "petulant dwarf," he calls the man). He has a more meaningful encounter with a lonely, voyeuristic, philosophical watchman, Brian (Peter Wight)—the only other intellectually oriented character in the film. Brian reads the *TLS* and the Bible, and knowingly does work "a monkey could do," escaping his quietly desperate and oppressive life by dreaming of a solitary future in a crumbling cottage on the Irish coast.

Johnny debunks Brian's fantasies about a future idyll by asserting that God is evil, that greed and pain are the human condition, and that it's a hopeless world where man has no future. His vision is an apocalyptic one, albeit not much more intellectually sophisticated than an autodidact's sophomoric philosophizing. But in the context of the film's generally inarticulate characters, his talk is striking. It also provides a metaphysical dimension—a sense of the universe's meaninglessness—that Leigh has never mined before. Still, for all Johnny's rhetorical onslaughts, the final word is Brian's, who solemnly (almost too low to hear) warns Johnny, "Don't ruin your life." It's a cautionary word which Johnny is too far gone to heed.

Utilizing his usual directorial technique (he shapes the characters with the active involvement of his cast, who are given a situation in which to create a character before the film is formally scripted), Leigh has constructed a gallery of characters who are individuated and true. The one glaring exception that strikes a thoroughly false note is the character called both Jeremy and Sebastian (Greg Cruttwell), who looks like a young Dirk Bogarde and seems to be an homage to the Bogarde of Losey's *The Servant*. This upper-class figure operates in the film as Johnny's totally vile alter ego. He is a smirking misogynist who treats all the women he encounters with violent contempt. His character is without any redeeming charm or vulnerability—a man whose nihilistic behavior goes over the top, a cartoon of an upper-class, drawling, decadent psychopath. As in *High Hopes*, Leigh again here demonstrates how his hatred for the upper class can subvert his capacity to do anything more than caricature them. The one-dimensional, frightening Jeremy also serves to make the more complex, less predictable Johnny look a great deal more sympathetic. For though he too behaves malevolently toward women, Johnny is still capable of a few caring moments (there is a stirring scene of Louise and a bloodied, beaten Johnny singing wistfully about returning home to "rainy Manchester"). He also victimizes himself more thoroughly than he victimizes anybody else. It's not that the director tries to vindicate his callous, solipsistic behavior, but one feels Leigh's identification with Johnny's imagination and despair, and consequently his need to make the character less of a monster in the eyes of the audience.

Apart from Johnny, the other characters are basically sketches, but all are given a genuine presence and idiosyncratic, even comic, life by Leigh. (Leigh infuses the film with black comedy and a sense of the absurd, but this never provides genuine relief from the film's sense of damnation.) Sophie speaks through the side of her mouth, and, in her dazed manner, can be witty. (When Johnny, undressing her, fumbles with the buttons on her leather vest, she says, "We tried the stairs, now try the elevator," and points to the zipper.) Louise has sufficient strength to stand up to Jeremy's threats, but wants nothing more than a relationship with "somebody who'll talk to you after fucking with them." She is balanced and caring, but conscious that she is facing a dreary life with so few options that even an impossible future with Johnny is something to long for. Leigh augments the authenticity of these characters' behavior by often shooting both of the women in tight close-ups—revealing every pore, scar, and blemish on their lived-in, real faces.

Finally there is Sandra (Claire Skinner), the pretty, neat, ostensibly normal nurse who owns the house that Louise and Sophie rent rooms in. She returns to the house at the film's end and is absolutely horrified by the garbage, vomit, blood, and general disorder that she finds. Sandra is efficient, but speaks in strangled, unfinished sentences—her desperation for order clearly springing from a feeling that the world is out of control. And in *Naked*, no character can quite keep things intact; life just won't hold together.

In a Leigh film, the emphasis is on facial expressions and the exchanges of dialogue between his characters, and most of *Naked* consists of two-shots and telling close-ups. There are few establishing shots here, the physical setting always subordinated to the interactions of the characters. Still, in *Naked*, Leigh uses shadow and light and silhouetting in arresting ways. There is even one long take where a haunted-looking, back-lit Johnny stands in full shot amid the desolation and darkness, with another homeless man seen dimly in the background. For a moment, Johnny becomes more than an abrasive, anguished drifter—indeed, the embodiment of man alone in the universe.

Resonant images and symbols of this sort are not Leigh's normal mode, and Johnny is no portentous symbolic figure of social type. His behavior is too bound by contradiction. Leigh doesn't provide the audience with a rubric to get a facile hold on Johnny: social victim, sociopath, product of dysfunctional family are all within the realm of probability, but none exhausts the possibilities. Leigh can't be mistaken for an Abel Ferrara creating (as in *Bad Lieutenant*) a central character who indulges in one elongated nihilistic rant against God, morality, life itself. Johnny's talk has much more dark humor and nuance than that, and he elicits a mixture of audience sympathy and revulsion which Ferrara's simplistic anti-heroes cannot evoke. When Johnny rejects his last life raft—Louise's commitment to him—as he hops and winces with pain down the middle of the street, fleeing to nowhere, we feel it's appropriate that such a destructive and ravaged figure doesn't receive a last-minute reprieve. But the film also suggests that there is something humanly valuable that could have been salvaged in Johnny; and Leigh, without sentimentalizing him, leaves the audience at the end with a profound feeling of loss.

There is no question that the dark vision of the film owes a great deal to the general pessimism and sense of malaise and decline that dominate post-Thatcher England. Leigh is a politically conscious director who believes present-day English society is intolerable. His characters' anguish can't be severed from a society where a great many people are on the dole and homeless, and where being born into the working class still constricts life's choices. Johnny, of course, is working class, on the dole, and homeless. But his self-destructive behavior can't be reduced to a set of political and social variables, and the same is true of the film's other characters. Their despair may be seen as metaphysical, psychological, or political in nature, but for Leigh, it's sufficient to present their behavior and emotional states, rather than a set of explanations.

Amidst a mass of mechanical, star- and genre-driven films, Mike Leigh is an anomalous figure. He is an auteur who makes low-budget films (largely financed by Britain's Channel Four) which center on ambiguities of character rather than on high-concept narratives. In *Naked*, he has taken those characters both closer to and sometimes over the emotional edge, and has made a brilliantly performed, intricately written film—his own *Journey to the End of the Night*.

FILMS IN REVIEW, 5-6/94, p. 57, Andy Pawelczak

Mike Leigh has committed the mimetic fallacy in his new movie, *Naked*, which he both wrote and directed—the film is as aimless and lacking in forward moving momentum as its drifting, anomic characters. Leigh, best known in this country for *High Hopes* and *Life Is Sweet*, is a left-leaning British director who makes sweet tempered comedies about Britain's beleaguered working class. In this movie, he takes on a demonic avatar of the lumpen proletariat, and it's more than he can handle—the movie is an arty, pretentious mess.

We first see Johnny (David Thewlis) as he rapes a woman in an alley and then takes off for London in a car. The highway surrounded by darkness and lined by spectral, other worldly lights has become a stock movie signifier by now—it's the post-modern highway to nowhere, outer-spaceville, the Never-Neverland of alienation. And we're not disappointed—once Johnny arrives in London and embarks on his allegorical journey through the nocturnal city, the people he encounters are barely recognizable as members of the human species as we know it. He moves in with an old girl friend and promptly takes up with her roommate, a spacey, stoned, leather clad nympho with a sweet side (this is a Mike Leigh movie), until the women's possessiveness and jealousy drive him out into the streets. Wandering the city and sleeping in doorways, he meets a variety of deracinated characters, including a crazy homeless couple, a pathetic security guard, and a lost soul waitress. Like an anthropologist studying a disintegrating society, he questions everybody: do you like your job, do you love each other, what's your life like? And he talks.

Johnny's great gift is talk, of the cosmic variety. Ask him a simple question, and he's apt to go off on a rant about anything from the sorry state of modern life to the evolutionary history of mankind. Critics have waxed ecstatic about the brilliance of these monologues, but except for an occasional good line—such as the description of a new apartment building as a "post-modernist gas chamber"—most of the talk sounds like it was written by a smart undergraduate high on speed and stale ideas—entropy, apocalypse, the ubermensch. David Thewlis, a scrawny Mephistopheles with scraggly beard who won a best actor award at Cannes for his performance, does what he can with the role, but ultimately Johnny isn't really a character—he's a jerry built contraption, a post-modern wind-up doll who talks. Part Old Testament prophet delivering a violent jeremiad against modern society, part Dostoyevskian underground man possessed by the imp of the perverse and determined not to be a cliché, part fifties angry young man rebelling against the soul deadening structures of work and family, he's wholly unbelievable.

A lot has been written about the picture's depiction of misogyny and the female characters' collaboration in their own oppression, but I found this no more convincing than anything else in the movie. Johnny's cruelty to his slightly bovine ex-girlfriend Louise (Lesley Sharp) and her roommate Sophie (Katrin Cartlidge) isn't explained other than by the suggestion that he hates their hysterical, suffocating sentimentality. Godard, whose films are still astonishingly contemporary, has shown us, visually, how women form the connecting link between the family and the agents of control in the bureaucratic society of controlled consumption, but Leigh isn't up to that kind of cine-dialectical analysis. Instead, he underlines the misogyny theme by introducing an upper class sexual sadist—shades of Victoriana—who doesn't connect with the main characters until very near to the end of the picture. One critic has pointed out that this character represents either the devil or Johnny's alter ego, and I'm afraid he's right—*Naked* is scattered with references to satanic cults and it's the kind of movie in which you're liable to stub your toe on a symbol while sleepwalking through the interminable monologues and minimalist plot.

Leigh's mise-en-scene is of a piece with the movie's other elements—unrelievedly dark, claustrophobic, and visually uninteresting. A big central scene—it seems to go on forever—has Johnny haranguing a security guard about the Book of Revelations as the two men wander through an empty apartment building. Leigh shoots the scene from the middle distance in dark silhouettes against blank white walls, and like much of the movie it's pointlessly portentous and heavy handed. In another scene, a poster hanger slaps cancelled signs across posters that say "Therapy," and it doesn't take a semiotician to get the point. The film revels in abrupt shifts in tone—from seedy realism to comic absurdism—but it never achieves the kind of dislocating urban poetry that Godard brought to the screen.

Naked purports to be a devastating portrayal of contemporary nihilism, but it's soft at the center. Ultimately, Johnny is that familiar sentimental anti-hero, the rebel without a cause who is damaged but not defeated and who staggers off at the end to continue his picaresque adventures against all the odds. Leigh leaves completely unexplored the most disquieting aspect of Johnny—with his apocalyptic fantasies, wholesale contempt for everything modern, and violent misogyny, he's a proto-fascist waiting for a Fuhrer to focus his inchoate rage. The film also demonstrates the weakness of post-modernist techniques in the arts-pastiche, minimalism, allegory, the alienation effect—in the wrong hands. It's too bad; somewhere inside *Naked* there's a good idea for a movie—omega man in post-Thatcher Britain—but it never comes to life.

LOS ANGELES TIMES, 12/16/93, Calendar/p. 1, Kenneth Turan

When we talk about unforgettable characters, often they are characters we'd give almost anything to forget, savage malcontents who leave pain and anguish in their wake. Characters, at first glance, much like Johnny, the sour and dissatisfied protagonist of Mike Leigh's remarkable, unnerving "Naked."

A refugee from Manchester who in the film's opening minutes flees to London in a stolen car after committing a rape, Johnny is a raging nightmare. A red-haired beanpole with a ragged beard and a hacking cough, he is a vicious misogynist who beats women physically and verbally assaults anyone within striking distance of his blistering, abrasive tongue.

In conventional movie terms, Johnny is far enough over the edge of acceptable behavior to make him a very tough centerpiece for a film. But nothing British writer-director Mike Leigh has ever done is conventional, and "Naked," which won best director for Leigh at Cannes and best actor for star David Thewlis' searing performance, is a departure even for Leigh.

Though they often give that impression, Leigh's unusual films are not improvised, but neither are they conventionally scripted. Rather, Leigh and his cast participate in an extensive rehearsal period (12 weeks for "Naked") during which roles are in effect grown from the ground up.

The result, as recent works like "High Hopes" and "Life Is Sweet" testify, are films that cut deeper and go further in terms of character development while providing more opportunities for actors to astonish than anything else on the screen today.

While those two have a partially whimsical tone, Leigh's earlier work, theatrical and TV films like "Bleak Moments," "Grown Ups" and "Meantime," had much more of a downbeat thrust. Still, even Leigh has done nothing as extreme, intense and daring as "Naked."

When he gets to London, Johnny heads for the flat of ex-girlfriend Louise (Lesley Sharp). She's at work, but Sophie (Katrin Cartlidge), her stoned waif roommate, is on the premise, and, out of a combination of boredom and spite, Johnny seduces her just to pass the time.

Smarter than most of the people he comes in contact with Johnny is facile with words. Both with Sophie and with Louise when she shows up, he delights in verbal humiliation, in being showily cynical, letting his scathing fury at the world and everyone in it spray people like an acid bath. "You might already have had the happiest moment in your life," he snarls at Sophie in one of his milder outbursts, "and got nothing to look forward to but sickness and death."

Too antsy to stay at the flat, this sullen drifter heads out into a London as bleak as anything Dickens ever described. "Naked" records Johnny's two hellish nights on those bitter streets, detailing the people he comes into contact with, the eccentrics and dead-enders with nowhere else to go but at each other's throats.

Initially, however, it doesn't seem that bleak, as the first people encountered are Scottish street folk Archie (Ewen Bremner) and Maggie (Susan Vidler), a pair so horrifyingly daft even Johnny can't help but be gently amused.

Then, in one of "Naked's" most extended sequences, Johnny runs across Brian (Peter Wight), a night watchman guarding an empty building who shares Johnny's autodidactic state of mind. Discussions about the philosophical nature of the past, the present and the future ensue, with Johnny insisting, his gorge rising, "nobody has a future. The party's over, it's all breaking up."

Though that statement can be accurately read as an expression of Johnny's core nihilism, one of the things that makes "Naked" so provocative is the thread of unspoken social consciousness that flows beneath the surface. For Johnny's anger is more than personal, it inevitably expresses the frustration of Britain's on-the-dole underclass. Their talents wasted, these people are left out in the cold both literally and metaphorically as the go-goers of the Thatcher years (here represented by Greg Cruttwell's odious Jeremy) continue to rake in the spoils.

More than anything, though, "Naked" is a mesmerizing character study, an attempt to stretch the emotional boundaries of truth on film as far as they will go. For once we think we've seen as much of Johnny as we can take, like an etching by Escher we start to see something else, a glimpse of another person easily missed.

Just slipping through the cracks of Johnny's mask of savage anger can be noticed a haunted, hunted look, flashes of empathy and even self-knowledge. His intelligence begins to register, as does his love of books and how ferociously well-read he is.

What Leigh and his collaborators are after here is hardly a whitewashing of Johnny, a simplistic excusing of the more wretched of his qualities. On the contrary, "Naked" is determined never to let Johnny off the hook, to excuse or forgive him or think him less of a monster than he is.

What "Naked" is after instead is an illumination of the intricacies of life, an elaboration of the obvious truth, rarely this passionately explored, that people are more though not necessarily better than they seem, that their qualities feed off each other, the good inseparable from the bad. The Johnny at the close feels intangibly but totally different from the one we experienced at the opening, and a film that allows us to view reality through that kind of double lens is impressive indeed.

NEW STATESMAN & SOCIETY, 11/5/93, p. 34, Jonathan Romney

Mike Leigh's *Naked* is what you would call a black comedy, partly because everything in it really is black, or at least the deathly grey of urban sludge. It's this monochrome—meticulously art-directed in street scenes, interiors, clothes, even the characters' lard-pallid faces—that makes *Naked* the one Mike Leigh film that really looks like a film through and through. *Naked*, for once, is its own universe, not simply a filmed amplification of sitcom conventions.

It's also the furthest Leigh has come from anything approaching realism, although it's immersed to the hilt in a traumatised conception of the real—the real London of homelessness, violence, sexual exploitation and despair. That doesn't make it any less a cartoon. *Naked* has been acclaimed as the most searing state-of-the-nation message British cinema has produced since whenever. But it's hard to feel that the cruel world its characters inhabit is more than simply a shabby, bleak backdrop for one startling solipsistic character turn.

Naked is effectively a one-man show for the sarcastic, probably psychotic northern drifter Johnny (David Thewlis), who hits London for a joyless journey to the end of the night, or at least the tube line. Fleeing after a back-street rape, he drifts into the household of his ex-girlfriend, where he pauses for sexual taunts at Sophie, a feckless goth (Katrin Cartlidge).

Then he's off into the night, where he vicariously relishes the inarticulate misery of a young Glaswegian homeless couple, mystifies and is mystified by a cafe waitress; and is given brief succour by a middle-age security guard whose misogyny and apocalyptic inclinations match his own. Somewhere at the other end of the story is Leigh's most extreme stereotype yet: a demonic yuppie (Greg Cruttwell) apparently summoned up out of some 1980s style-mag nightmare. Can Leigh possibly believe such a quintessence of polo-necked evil exists in the real world?

Surely not. Jeremy is just dropped in schematically as a counterbalance to Johnny. But Johnny caricatures himself with such self-eviscerating glee that it's often hard to care about anyone else. If *Naked* had set out to be a portrait of destructive solipsism and nothing but, the treatment couldn't have mirrored the theme better.

David Thewlis' performance is staggering: a gymnastic display of free associating, depressive mirth spat out in a bark halfway between John Lennon and rock's other great misanthrophic northern ranter, Mark E Smith of The Fall. And the performance annihilates everything else around him, bar Peter Wight, in a remarkable, passively sardonic turn as the guard.

Johnny is a man of absolute conviction, but his opinions seem random, entirely generated by the drunken speed of his tongue. It's not philosophy, but a cocktail of puns and paranoia, loathing and (what might conceivably be) soured love. He spouts conspiracy and chaos in a breakneck tumble of rancid one-liners that could be either cosmic *aperçus* of just bad jokes: "Every time this butterfly flaps its wings in Tokyo, this "old granny in Salford gets a bilious attack." Every line's a killer, either to maim others or to draw hell down on himself. He's cruising compulsively for the inevitable bruising.

What's disturbing, though, is how much the film loves Johnny's charisma. There's a very ambivalent moment when Johnny looks up and barks, "Why hast thou forsaken me—*bastard*", and we're not quite sure how to take this pathetic self-aggrandisement. Can we really see Johnny as a Christ-figure wandering the streets, a penitent drawing humanity's shame down upon himself. Or is he just a venomous git who needs a good kicking? Everything seems to suggest that, unlike the smarmily satanic Jeremy, Johnny is somehow redeemable because, unlike all those Leigh characters condemned to gabble in their restricted code, he has language on his side.

The film entertains a stormy love-hate relationship with this sneering demagogue. It certainly has no love for the losers around him—especially the witless, masochistic women who wait compliantly for Johnny to fuck them over. The characterisation counts in this—notably in Katrin Cartlidge as the clueless Sophie, virtually a re-run of Jane Horrocks' whining turn in *Life is Sweet*.

Naked is textbook fodder for the debate that invariably surrounds films that "stage" misogyny rather than simply describe it. But the film is so thoroughly focused on Johnny's self-love and loathing of everyone else that the rest of the world is obscured. Watching *Naked* is like being trapped for two hours in a railway carriage with a charismatic preacher—who might possibly have an axe under his coat. It's utterly, compelling, but you never get so much as a glance out of the window.

NEW YORK, 1/3/94, p. 53, David Denby

Johnny (David Thewlis, the voluble, funny, remarkably unemployable hero of Mike Leigh's *Naked*, has a wispy brown beard and the graceful yet lunging manner of a horse shying from the starter's gate. Johnny is an English genius and failure, a man fantastically adroit with words and utterly hapless at everything else. Arriving in London, he looks up an old girlfriend and winds up sleeping with her roommate; he then escapes into the city and has many adventures of both a physical and a metaphysical nature. *Naked*, the latest excursion into the English lower depths by the talented director of *High Hopes*, is a bitter comedy of freedom. Raw and surprising, it offers freedom without tears or fantasy, freedom with nothing left out of squalor, cruelty, or unexpected kindliness. This is a brilliant, exhilarating movie, but it's definitely not a work for the morally timid or literal-minded.

Johnny does nothing; he *talks*. He has no hopes and no future, and he cannot be explained by his past, except, perhaps, in some vague and banal way (he's the product of a recessionary period, etc.). Johnny may be a marginal man, but he nevertheless enjoys a spectacular existence as a sort of modern Odysseus—an Odysseus with no battles to fight, no kingdom to come home to, no house to set in order. He's committed only to words and to adventure, and so, to American eyes, he has less in common with the eruptive "angry young men" of such English plays and movies as *Look Back in Anger* than he does with such Americans as the fornicating intellectual bums of Henry Miller's Paris novels and the defenseless on-the-road beats in Jack Kerouac's prose-poem epics. He's the ultimate hipster, and willing to pay the price for it.

Johnny possesses a strangely avid curiosity, both tender and malicious, about everyone he meets. He chats up a Scottish couple who are even more down and out than he and a philosophical night watchman, a lonely woman drinking herself to sleep. He packs more social experience into a few days than most of us would into months. David Thewlis seems to be making him up as he goes along, pushing to the outer limb of outrageous improvisation without forgetting the solid trunk of character that remains. Thewlis's Johnny is erratic yet triumphantly himself at every moment.

He is attractive to women, and immediately treads on them. I can already hear the words of disapproval, so please understand that it is Johnny the fictional character who mistreats women, not the movie. On the contrary, the women in *Naked* are all splendid creations in their own right, especially the stolid, enduring Louise (Lesley Sharp), who understands Johnny best, and the twittering yet withdrawn Sophie (Katrin Cartlidge), who talks with her mouth closed, a drugged-out, insecure siren. As in *High Hopes*, Leigh's touch is both affectionate and rudely satirical; he finds endless hilarity in British nastiness and desperation. Unafraid, he risks being misunderstood—and in this country, he will be. *Naked* is often hilarious, yet the New York audience I saw it with never uttered a peep, as if laughter might be taken as approval of the loutish hero. It would be a crying shame if so original a creation as Johnny triumphed over English squalor only to fall prey to American moralism.

NEW YORK POST, 12/15/93, p. 34, Thelma Adams

Mike Leigh's "Naked" opens with a brutal sexual assault in a Manchester alley.

The perp, Johnny (David Thewlis), flees to London, where he gives a guided tour of that capital's underbelly.

Thewlis' blistering, sharp-tongued rogue riffs on everything from Nostradamus to Stephen Hawking, serves up an unsavory slice of life in this blackest of comedies, the actor's raw performance garnered best actor honors at the 1993 Cannes Film Festival, Mike Leigh walking off with best director.

Working in the improvisational style that Leigh honed in "High Hopes" and "Life Is Sweet," Thewlis is harrowingly funny. But the movie chokes on its own cleverness.

As witty as Johnny is, he practices a stinging brand of misogyny without apparent motivation. Between Johnny and the sexual sadism of upper-class twit Jeremy (Greg Cruttwell), the other key male player, Leigh places an array of female doormats.

Sophie (Katrin Cartlidge) is a punkish black-haired beauty. This masochistic waif falls addictively in love with Johnny and submits to Jeremy's cruel sex games.

Johnny's ex, Louise (Lesley Sharp), is a plump, sensible thing. New to London, she is holding her life together as a working girl—but barely. When Johnny turns up, she tries to resist his downward pull but is sabotaged by her own good heart.

In a dark departure from his previous films, Leigh treats his characters unsparingly, with minimal sympathy for all but Louise. Leigh presents his characters like specimens. They wiggle on the screen like slugs at the bottom of a jar collected by a little boy who has spent the day turning over rocks in the woods.

As to the movie's misogynistic undertow, a fine line exists between presenting misogynistic characters and a filmmaker being one himself. The writer-director doesn't cross that line, but by failing to shape his material he falls prey to a mindless nihilism that leaves "Naked" open to misinterpretation. The spectacle darkly entertains, but to what end?

"Naked" recalls the British "angry young men" movies of "the late '50s and '60s: "Saturday Night and Sunday Morning," "Look Back in Anger", and "The Loneliness of the Long Distance Runner." Those grim, realistic and splendidly acted kitchen-sink dramas challenged society and its institutions.

"Naked" pales in comparison.

NEWSDAY, 12/15/93, Part II/p. 63, John Anderson

In 1990's much-admired "Life is Sweet," the gifted Mike Leigh used food to construct his metaphor for modern England, tortured recipes produced by tortured minds. In "Naked," he's omitted the food, and emphasized the torture.

In this post-apocalyptic nightmare—in which the apocalypse has been economic and no one gets to wake up—the chief torturer is Johnny (David Thewlis), a brilliant, 27-year-old charmer with "heart palpitations, acute _____ neuralgia," and no future. What's naked in "Naked" is Johnny's id. In a world that not only doesn't care that he exists, but won't care that he existed—and which Leigh creates out of a palette virtually devoid of light—Johnny has no reason to rein in his worst instincts. He torments men intellectually, and women intellectually and sexually. He's an unguided missile of self-indulgence which, since it can't rise, must explode, littering the world around him with the shrapnel of his ego.

In the film's best extended sequence, Johnny completely befuddles a security guard named Brian (Peter Wight), who in a moment of charity has let Johnny into his building and out of the cold. Using a thoroughly dishonest combination of biblical prophecy, Darwinian theory and his own cutting brand of doubletalk, Johnny convinces Brian that the present is the future, the future is the past, and that the Mark of the Beast foretold in Revelations has been realized in the bar code used on supermarket computers.

Leigh, cannily, delivers both the carrot and the stick as he leads us through Johnny's story, which is less a tale than an autopsy. The script (Leigh is credited as writer, but he usually works with his casts in an improvisational manner) is caustically funny, surrendering more and more humor on each viewing of the film. But it's humor with a price: Johnny amuses himself by playing mind games with those around him who are either too unsure of themselves, like his ex-girlfriend Louise (Lesley Sharp), to fend off his vicious sarcasm, or too thick—like the near-idiot street kid Archie (Ewen Bremner)—to even know they've been humiliated. We, on the other hand, realize we've walked into a trap, but not before we've already laughed.

Thewlis gives a resonant performance, making Johnny both repulsive and irresistible, an object of sympathy and a font of self-pity. Sex comes easily to him, partly because he frightens women—and for good reason: When we first see him, he's sexually assaulting a bar pickup in an alleyway. Later, at his ex-girlfriend Louise's flat, he'll continue to mix sex and pain with her roommate Sophie (Katrin Cartlidge), a drugged-out, tattoed, leather-clad, quasi-nymphomaniac who decides she loves Johnny and suffers the subsequent degradation.

The three roommates—Sandra (Claire Skinner) is a nurse who's away in Africa and who'll return at the end to voice her uptight, middle-class displeasure at the disorder she finds at home—are a cross section of English sexual dynamics: The earthy Louise is made to feel guilty by Johnny for being employed; the decadent Sophie is made hysterical by his neglect and the rigid Sandra will remain too blind to notice her country's in the same state as her house. But while it's an unflattering portrait he paints of English women, it's Jeremy Smart, a k a Sebastian Hawks (Greg Cruttwell), in whom Leigh vents his unrestrained contempt for the myopic and monied end of British society, whose bastard child is Johnny. Yes, Jeremy is a man, of sorts, but Leigh was probably concerned that if he named his villain Margaret he might have lost all control.

NEWSWEEK, 12/27/93, p. 47, David Ansen

Mike Leigh's stunning, corrosive "Naked" is one of the best movies of the year, and one of the toughest: it's not for folks who like their English movies polite and well groomed. Its manic mix of tenderness and degradation, hilarity and scariness, keeps you dangerously off balance. The pulse is set by the protagonist, a golden-tongued drifter named Johnny (David Thewlis), first seen molesting a woman in a Manchester alley, then stealing a car to flee to London, where he seeks out an old girlfriend for a place to crash. A brilliant word spinner with a lacerating wit, the grungy, arrogant, self-destructive Johnny is a singular sociopath: a charming sadist, a compulsive Lothario whose love of women reveals itself, in a clinch, to be hatred. Thewlis (voted Best Actor by the New York Film Critics) is astonishing: his quicksilver performance evokes equal parts pity and revulsion, fondness and horror.

"Naked's" vision of the sexual transactions between men and women is chilling: the brutal Johnny is a lamb compared with the vile Jeremy (Greg Cruttwell), an upperclass predator turned on by inflicting pain—the one character to whom Leigh denies humanity. Leigh's film has been wrongly accused of misogyny, when in fact it's a study of misogyny. The many women, drawn to Johnny like moths to an electric wire—among them the druggy, masochistic Sophie (Katrin Cartlidge) and her hopeful, plain roommate (Lesley Sharp)—are as complexly observed as the men, and as incisively acted.

Leigh ("High Hopes," "Life Is Sweet") is justly famous for the performances he inspires. He outlines his characters to his actors and his scripts are developed by the ensemble through a long process of improvisation. This may be why his movies feel so unpredictably alive. "Naked" keeps you on the edge of your seat, not with plot devices but with its barrage of behavioral revelations. Johhny's chaotic odyssey for human connection leads to some astonishing encounters—with a bookish night watchman (Peter Wight) who shelters him in his building and engages him in an apocalyptically batty theological debate; with a furiously thick Scottish youth searching for his girlfriend. But nobody, ultimately, reaches Johnny. Trapped inside his nihilistic brilliance, he's got nowhere to go but down. Watching this lost soul's flaming descent is a disturbing yet exhilarating experience. Leigh makes art out of his own ambivalence.

SIGHT AND SOUND, 11/93, p. 48, Claire Monk

Johnny, young and unemployed in Manchester, rapes a woman in an alley, then leaves the city and drives through the night to London. He abandons the car and arrives in the road in Dalston where his ex-girlfriend Louise lives. Sophie, an unemployed Goth he meets in the street, proves to be one of Louise's two flatmates; the other, Sandra, a nurse, is on holiday with her boyfriend in Zimbabwe. As Louise is at work, Sophie lets Johnny into the tatty rented flat, and flirts with him as they drink tea and smoke joints.

Elsewhere in the city, Jeremy, a yuppie, asks his masseuse for a date; unaffected by her refusal, he asks her whether women like being raped. Louise returns home; Johnny greets her jokily but then turns on her, hostile at what he sees as her career pretensions. Johnny and Sophie have sex in the flat. After dining out with his masseuse, Jeremy takes their waitress Giselle back to his flat, where he turns violent. The next day, Sophie tells Johnny she loves him; he becomes increasingly physically abusive, a sequence culminating in violent sex. By the evening, Johnny paces the flat aggressively while Sophie pleads for his attention. He pushes her away and walks out with his belongings.

Arriving in Soho, Johnny encounters Archie, a homeless young Glaswegian who has mislaid his girlfriend, Maggie. Johnny takes the piss out of him and offers to stay put while Archie looks further afield. Maggie arrives; she and Johnny find Archie near some railway arches where homeless people shelter. Leaving them fighting, Johnny shelters for the night in an office porch. The middle-aged security guard, Brian, unlocks the door and, revealing that the office is uninhabited, furtively whisks Johnny inside for the night. An extended tour of the office becomes an existential confrontation taking in Nostradamus and Revelations; adamant that humanity is racing towards extinction, Johnny is derisive about the gentle, world-weary Brian's plans to retire to Ireland.

After the two men have watched a woman dancing drunkenly in the window of a flat opposite, Johnny goes to the woman's door and talks his way in. Inside, she responds masochistically to his aggressive questions. Turning violent, Johnny tears at her hair and clothes, but rejects her sexually and humiliates her, then leaves, stealing some books. Back with Brian, he denies the latter's accusations of sexual violence. The two men go to a cafe, where Johnny chats up a waitress, and then part company.

Sophie arrives at the flat to find Jeremy on the sofa. He introduces himself as Sebastian Hawkes, claiming to be her landlord and a friend of Sandra's. He turns violent, then makes Sophie put on Sandra's nurse's uniform and rapes her. Johnny waits for the cafe waitress to leave work; passively, she agrees to let him come to her flat. Louise arrives home to see 'Sebastian' throwing £400 at Sophie as she lies on the floor. Though shaking and hurt, Sophie will not tell Louise what has happened. 'Sebastian' refuses to leave; the women threaten to phone the police, but hold back, afraid that they will side with him. Johnny asks the melancholy waitress if he can stay the night; she panics and tells him to go, which he does after pushing her around. While 'Sebastian' sleeps, Louise and Sophie escape to the pub, where they discuss the futility of relationships. Johnny cadges a lift from a bill-sticker; uninvited, he joins the man in his night-time work until the latter kicks him on to the pavement in frustration and drives off, with Johnny's holdall still in the van. Attacked by youths in an alley, Johnny manages to stagger back to Louise's but collapses on arrival. 'Sebastian' watches contemptuously as Sophie and Louise tend the delirious Johnny before returning to bed, inviting both of the women to join him.

Next day a shocked Sandra arrives home. 'Sebastian' greets her; she gives him two minutes to leave. Louise gets him to unzip his flies and offers to slice his penis off with a breadknife. Smirking, he goes. Louise and Johnny talk alone in the bathroom and seem to renew their relationship. Louise tells him she's going back to Manchester for good, and he seems to agree to go with her. Sophie grabs an overnight bag and walks out. While Louise is handing in her notice, Johnny takes what's left of Jeremy's money and hops, with difficulty, away down the street.

"You've had the living body and you're bored with it," Johnny hostilely accuses Louise, railing at her for turning her back on Manchester to become "a career girl in the big shitty". "You've had the universe and you're bored with it." The existential dimension to such moments—and David Thewlis's brilliant, fierce, intensely irritating near-monologue of a central performance is full of them—marks out *Naked* as a startling leap from the petty comic viciousness of Mike Leigh's domestic satires into darker, more complex philosophical territory.

It's a deeply problematic journey, conducted via the double-edged figure of Johnny—a misogynist, Mancunian motormouth and visionary prophet of millennial doom—as he wanders London quoting theories from James Gleick's *Chaos* and dispensing warnings from the Book of Revelations like some nihilist Jesus of Montreal.

In Johnny's satirical interpretation, the Mark 666 foreseen in Revelations, without which no one will be able to buy or sell, is the bar-code. It will soon brand not just products but people—"They're going to replace plastic with flesh: *fact!*"—and the end of the world is truly nigh.

Much of the publicity surrounding *Naked*'s double win at Cannes—Best Actor for Thewlis and Best Director for Leigh—has focused, misleadingly, on its depiction of London's homeless. True, insecure housing is a theme of sorts; from Louise and Sophie, harassed by an intruder who may or may not be their landlord, to the sad cafe waitress, house-sitting rent-free among shelves of classical literature, few of the characters can take the roof over their head for granted. But the film's insights into life on the streets are pretty thin. The truly homeless characters, Archie and Maggie, are treated as heartlessly as Leigh's past bourgeois targets, while Johnny's (arguably self-inflicted) nights sleeping rough are predominantly a device for exploring the director's obsessions with millennial crisis and oblivion. In this context, Cardboard City is just another omen of a species heading for extinction. "Evolution isn't over," Johnny tells Brian. "Humanity is just a cracked egg, and the omelette stinks." At other moments, though, the pair's surreal philosophical duel hits on sublime political insights. When Brian explains to Johnny that "you must be invisible—I must be seen"; he lets slip a near-universal truth about the relation of those with token power to the dispossessed.

"My feelings about *Naked* are as ambivalent as my feelings about our chaotic late 20th-century world," hedges Leigh in a brief statement in the film's press brochure. "I don't really want to pontificate about this film. I'd rather let it speak for itself." But silence is risky when you've invented a rapist/seer as your dominant mouthpiece, and *Naked*'s nasty taste of misogyny and sexual violence often makes it gruelling viewing for the wrong reasons. (Leigh fans hoping for a comedy should note that *Naked* produces only the chilling sound of laughter in the dark.)

Contempt for women is presented as yet another symptom of millennial angst, and no stratum of masculinity is immune. When champagne-supping Jeremy (a preposterous cardboard yuppie so little recognisable from real life as to be virtually abstract) attacks Giselle with a large stuffed reptile, the male terror of mortality gets precedence over the female terror of assault. "I'm going to commit suicide on any 40th birthday," he screams. "I don't want to live beyond 40—do you?"

TIME, 12/20/93, p. 62, Richard Schickel

In the movies, freedom is one of the forms that glamour takes. It's the grail at the end of the rail, the glow at the end of every mean street. It's what heroes fight to gain or preserve, what they become improbably articulate about in defending. It is, in short, a pretty thing treasured by pretty people.

Or was, until a street person named Johnny lurched into the mind of English writer-director Mike Leigh. Johnny is played in *Naked* by David Thewlis, who won the best-actor prize at Cannes for a performance so perfectly perverse that much as you want to, you cannot turn away. Or easily file and forget it.

Mostly Johnny drifts around London imposing on people. Seeking bed and board from a former girlfriend named Louise (Lesley Sharp), he has casually abusive sex with her drugged-out roommate. Taken in out of the cold by a night watchman, he stuns the man with a mad, curiously erudite monologue touching upon satanism and the occult. Alternately arrogant and self-pitying, his rant has a certain bleak wit as he intrudes menacingly on two other psychologically damaged women, gets beaten up by anonymous thugs, drags himself back to Louise, causes more chaos and is last seen hip-hopping down the road, favoring a badly sprained ankle, heading for more trouble—heading, one is sure, for meaningless death.

Freedom, Leigh suggests, is one of the forms sociopathy takes, and it may be that his film is a necessary, even inevitable, corrective to the customary cinematic take on the subject. But when someone dwells so long on what he thinks is an ugly truth, a question naturally arises: Is it the truth the filmmaker loves, or is it the ugliness—and its shock value—that fascinates him?

VILLAGE VOICE, 12/21/93, p. 70, Georgia Brown

Mike Leigh once offered a good biblical word for his movies: *lamentations*. They lamented, he said, "how difficult life is." His brave new film, *Naked*, the most biblical of all, also could be called a laceration. It's painted in bruise colors, especially black and blue.

Why is it called *Naked*? Because it's about a man, Johnny (David Thewlis) stripped to his flayed skin. Because it's about Homo sapiens dangling at the end of the evolutionary vine. Because the stupid body lies at the core of the difficult sex thing. Because exposure can be cathartic. You will think of more reasons.

Naked opens with a rape. At least it looks like one. Given what we later see of Johnny's modus operandi, probably consensual sex turned nasty. Whatever, she breaks away, yelling, and Johnny bolts in the opposite direction, steals a car, and drives it to London. There he looks up an old girlfriend from Manchester, Louise (Lesley Sharp), who isn't home, but her depressive, black-clad, marble-mouth housemate, Sophie (Katrin Cartlidge), invites him in for tea. When Johnny kisses Sophie, he bites her mouth hard and pulls her hair. By the time Louise comes home from work, Sophie's deep in love. She can't keep her hands off Johnny, and hands on him drive him mad.

One thing Leigh has the temerity to present is a terrible sexual dynamic: men hurting women and women relishing the hurt. The badly bruised women in *Naked* are stuck on men who mistreat them—with their unwarranted loving kindness causing the men to kick free. But in the end, women show a toughness and resilience, a greater tensile strength than men, who, for all their brutality, are more pitiful; they're unable to connect. Probably this gender standoff is most pithily represented by two scruffy Scots—Neanderthal man and his mate—bellowing each other's names ("Maggie!" "Archie!") into the winter night.

But to talk about the film this way—although it certainly will be talked of this way—obscures the naked heart of *Naked*, Johnny's brilliant, nonstop yammering into and at the void. For all its acidity, Johnny's near monologue forms a bravura lyric diatribe, his Mancunian cadences transmuting into music. (The accompanying score, by Andrew Dickson, is stunning. So is the assured cinematography by Dick Pope.) Named best actor at Cannes, Thewlis delivers such a powerful performance it's already legendary.

A present-day prophet, Johnny is no Baptist; there's no messiah to advance. He's more Old Testament doomsayer come to argue that the human experiment has failed. "The end of the world is nigh, Bri; the game is *up*." The spiritually obsessed Brian (Peter Wight) is a night watchman who invites Johnny into the empty space he guards. (Aren't we all protecting the equivalent of empty space?) With a little persuasion, everyone invites Johnny in. Only in one case is he ordered out (that he goes is a kind of miracle). Usually it's Johnny who's compelled to split. Disillusioned, he wants more rigorous standards. To him, everyone seems a victim of sentimental thinking.

Everyone, that is, except the thoroughly vile and vicious Jeremy (Greg Cruttwell), a Veuve Cliquot-swilling, Porsche-driving chap whose laugh resembles a small vomit. Leigh's dramas always contain one or two characters who tip off the scale. Here, although there are two or three contenders, Jeremy takes the cake. His icy evil, I venture, is designed to put Johnny's hot rage into perspective.

Leigh's meditation on the human condition is studded with references to the species's evolution. Read the details: a joke about the missing link, diagrams of the human skeleton, tribal carvings from Africa, an Aboriginal boomerang, a stuffed reptile, a shark's jawbone, a veritable "jungle" of plants, Gleick's *Chaos*, replicas of Greek sculptures, a poster for "Attila," as well as references to Nostradamus, Ezekiel, Deuteronomy, and the Book of Revelations. When a poster hanger sticks up a sign reading "Therapy?" (over "Megadeth") and then pastes "Cancelled" over it, it's a political, maybe a cosmic, joke. No treatment, man, the case is terminal.

This is a brilliant, radical work from Leigh, who's delivered quite radical works in the past. It's also so abrasive that some viewers are likely to be revolted. Released in Britain last month, the movie elicited a scandalous personal attack in the *Sunday Times* by Julie Burchill. In the midst of an incoherent diatribe, Burchill accused Leigh of disguising his middle-class, and Jewish, origins: "His father is a doctor—and his family's original name was Lieberman. It is no wonder that he has promoted Mike Leigh at the expense of Michael Lieberman: his films look a great deal more cruel and patronising if not made by One of Us." Astonishing.

If Fine Line seems brave to be bringing out such a film during this jolly holiday season, it strikes me as a perfectly religious offering. O come all ye faithful, *Naked* is joyful and triumphant.

Also reviewed in:
CHICAGO TRIBUNE, 2/18/94, Friday/p. C, Michael Wilmington
NEW REPUBLIC, 1/3/94, p. 28, Stanely Kauffmann
NEW YORK TIMES, 12/16/93, p. C20, Vincent Canby
NEW YORKER, 1/17/94, p. 86, Anthony Lane
VARIETY, 5/24/93, p. 45, Derek Elley
WASHINGTON POST, 1/28/94, p. C1, Rita Kempley
WASHINGTON POST, 1/28/94, Weekend/p. 38, Desson Howe

NATIONAL LAMPOON'S LOADED WEAPON I

A New Line Cinema release.   *Executive Producer:* Michel Roy, Howard Klein, and Erwin Stoff.   *Producer:* Suzanne Todd and David Willis.   *Director:* Gene Quintano.   *Screenplay:* Don Holley and Gene Quintano.   *Story:* Don Holley and Tori Tellem.   *Director of Photography:* Peter Deming.   *Editor:* Christopher Greenbury.   *Music:* Robert Folk.   *Music Editor:* Douglas M. Lackey.   *Sound:* Martin Raymond Bolger, John Coffey, and (music) Steve Sykes.   *Sound Editor:* Bob Newlan.   *Casting:* Ferne Cassel.   *Production Designer:* Jaymes Hinkle.   *Art Director:* Alan E. Muraoka.   *Set Decorator:* Sarah B. Stone.   *Set Dresser:* Blaise Delacroix and Julie Sexsmith.   *Special Effects:* Jim Doyle and Richard L. Thompson.   *Costumes:* Jacki Arthur.   *Make-up:* Jeanne Van Phue.   *Special Effects Make-up:* David Miller, Peggy O'Brien, and David LeRoy Anderson.   *Stunt Coordinator:* Charles Picerni.   *Running time:* 83 minutes.   *MPAA Rating:* PG-13.

CAST: Emilio Estevez (Jack Colt);   Samuel L. Jackson (Wes Luger);   Jon Lovitz (Becker);   Tim Curry (Jigsaw);   Kathy Ireland (Destiny Demeanor);   Frank McRae (Captain Doyle);   William Shatner (General Mortars);   Dhiru Shah (Translator);   Gokul (Hindu);   Tom Bruggeman and Danny Castle (Mini-Mart Punks);   Lance Kinsey (Irv);   Bill Nunn (Police Photographer);   Joyce Brothers (Coroner);   Lin Shaye (Witness);   Robert Willis (Armanied Cop);   Vito Scotti (Tailor);   Ken Ober (Dooley);   James Doohan (Scotty);   Lauren Abels (Police Psychiatrist);   Richard Moll (Prison Attendant);   F. Murray Abraham (Harold Leacher);   Charlie Sheen (Valet);   Denis Leary (Mike McCracken);   Denise Lee Richards, Mary Lynn Naggie, Suzie Hardy, and Karman Kruschke (Cindys);   Michael Castner (Himself);   J.P. Hubbell (Megaphone Cop);   Corey Feldman (Young Cop);   Phil Hartman (Comic Cop);   J.T. Walsh (Desk Clerk);   Erik Estrada (Himself);   Larry Wilcox (Himself);   Paul Gleason (FBI Agent);

Jake Johannsen (Drug Dealer);   Mile Lajeunesse (Mr. Jerricho);   Sherry Bilsing (Cookie Receptionist);   Allyce Beasley (Spinach Destiny);   Ric Ducommun (D.A.);   Charles Napier and Charles Cyphers (Interrogators);   Benjamin Kimball Smith (Kid on Bike);   Danielle Nicolet (Debbie Luger);   Beverly Johnson (Doris Luger);   Christopher Shobe (Ted Polansky);   Marcus Lasha (Young Luger);   Hank Cheyne and Al Watson (Stormtroopers).

LOS ANGELES TIMES, 2/5/93, Calendar/p. 8, Michael Wilmington

"Loaded Weapon I" which sends up the "Lethal Weapon" series and many other cop-buddy bangathons, isn't as funny as most of its targets. A collection of flat gags, spiritless action, cornball satire and overbroad or bored-looking performances, it sometimes resembles the draggle-end of a nightmare "Saturday Night Live" show, where the cast has core to despise their own skits.

In this terminally limp spoof, Emilio Estevez and Samuel Jackson take the Mel Gibson and Danny Glover parts, sometimes playing them like condemned men who can't find their last meal. And Jon Lovitz is a sort of fast-food Joe Pesci, a pesky blob with blond mane and dull eyes.

The plot tries to be cute and mean, simultaneously. Estevez and Jackson, as detectives Colt and Luger, are after a cocaine gang operating inside the Wilderness Girls Cookie factory, and run by a band of effete maniacs: Tim Curry as the fey assassin Dr. Jigsaw and William Shatner as his fey boss, General Mortars, who eats piranhas.

The jokes pile on like junk mail; you almost have to dig your way out from under them. There's the Hindi convenience store owners and their interpreters, who get robbed; Dr. Joyce Brothers as a coroner; the potato-head suspect; the Squealers Hotel, with its special discounts for federal witnesses. The movie reminds you of a comic who runs onstage, screams "I got a million of 'em!" and then proceeds to hit one in 10. Except "Loaded Weapon's" average is lower.

Co-writer-director-Gene Quintano prepared for this fiasco by writing two of the "Police Academy" movies, "3" and "4": not exactly credits that fill you with confidence in "Weapon's" satirical potential. And he's handicapped here. When the Zucker Brothers and Jim Abrahams parodied disaster movies in "Airplane!" and cop shows in "Police Squad," they were taking on forms that were old-fashioned, loaded with dramatic rhetoric. But the "Lethal Weapon" movies are so rhetorically vacant—mostly blood, glitz and explosions, with about an inch of dialogue and character—that it's hard to satirize them verbally. Quintano wastes most of his energy sending up that inch.

I can't think of a real reason to see this movie if you caught the trailer, you already know most of the major laugh lines. And one good reason to stay away is out of respect for this cast. Estevez plays the sexy, near-crazy Riggs-style detective, as if being over the edge had enervated him, and he were trying to improve his lines by ignoring them. As the family man cop, Jackson, a chameleonic actor who's been excellent in widely varying parts, especially for Spike Lee, almost vanishes into his suit and tie. Jackson won't push the gags, which shows good taste, and he barely leaves an impression, except for one instant when he starts making crazy-faces over Allyce Beasley's shoulder.

Whoopi Goldberg, playing Detective York, is assassinated at the beginning. Since she takes no credit and gets killed early, it means she has the best part in the movie. Lively Kathy Ireland, the Sports Illustrated swimsuit model, plays heroine Destiny Demeanor as if being without a bikini had discombobulated her. Most of the movie's cameo guests—F. Murray Abraham as a parody of Hannibal Lechter, "Star Trek's" James Doohan, "CHiPs'" Erik Estreda and Larry Wilcox and many others as parodies of themselves—wander into their scenes like party guests looking for the hors d'oeuvres.

There's probably a strategy behind all these bad, empty performances. Estevez and Jackson are clearly under orders to play their scenes deadpan, "Airplane!"-style, but here, the diffidence has the wrong effect. It *deadens* the material. After a while, it almost kills your desire to laugh.

When a spoof dies, the first casualties are usually energy and rhythm. At the beginning of this movie, after a convenience store robbery, Estevez pimps Eastwood's Dirty Harry with the line, "I know what you're thinking. Did he fire 173 shots, or 174?" Of course, the line would be funnier if he read it like Harry does: "Did he fire 174 shots? Or only 173?" Nit-picking? Actually, that moment is one of the funniest in the film, and it shows what most of "Loaded Weapon I" (MPAA-rated PG-13) is like only half there. Basically, it's unloaded.

NEW YORK POST, 2/5/93, p. 31, Jami Bernard

Humor is one of the most difficult things to get right in film. You'll appreciate that once you see "Loaded Weapon I" side by side with "Airplane!" or any of the other movie-genre spoofs made by the team of Jim Abrahams, David Zucker and Jerry Zucker, none of whom had anything to do with "Loaded Weapon I."

It's not that "Weapon," a satire of pop movies from "Lethal Weapon" to "Wayne's World," doesn't have its funny moments, because it certainly does. But these funny moments of true satire or sight gag are connected by a lot of stuff trying very, very hard to be funny, but not quite getting it right.

You might say that the Zucker team is the Disney of the movie-satire business; they've been doing it so long and with such attention to detail that they dominate the field. They make it look easy. And "Loaded Weapon I" proves that it's not.

As per the Zucker formula lots of unexpected actors show up in bit parts. Whoopi Goldberg has a brief turn and doesn't embarrass herself as a cop who manages to hide the microfilm before she gets shot; Dr. Joyce Brothers proves that she is even less adept at acting than at giving pop psychology advice; James Doohan has a brief "Scotty" bit.

Emilio Estevez and Samuel L. Jackson are the main "Lethal Weapon" type cop partners hot on the trail of some deadly Wilderness Girls cookies (Estevez's brother Charlie does a half-day's work as a valet). William Shatner shows he can make fun of his pompous Captain Kirk persona as the villain, General Mortars, and also shows how funny he can be in his own right when he's not trapped by "Trek." F. Murray Abraham does a low-rent spoof of Hannibal the Cannibal Lecter; lots of effort and little payoff.

"Airplane!" and its cousin spoofs had jokes in almost every frame of the movie, and of every type—sight gags, puns, loony things that pertained to nothing in particular, pratfalls, dirty jokes and theater of the ridiculous. Those movies too have their dull patches, but their cumulative effect was, surprisingly, of sophistication.

"Loaded Weapon I" tries desperately to copy the formula, yet a lot of its lowbrow humor seems to be truly bottom-feeding, instead of heightening the mix. Therefore, it is not surprising to discover that director Gene Quintano's screen writing credits include some of the "Police Academy" series—and not even the good ones, if you can call any of them that.

Therefore, while the Zucker creations look like movies made by movie-lovers who delight in the sheer energy of pop culture, "Loaded Weapon I" looks like a commercial ploy by people who were looking to make a buck off a proven commodity. You'll laugh, but only infrequently.

NEWSDAY, 2/5/93, Part II/p. 61, Terry Kelleher

Click.

That's the sound of "National Lampoon's Loaded Weapon I" running out of ammunition. Listen for it when Jon Lovitz, who's spoofing Joe Pesci's "Lethal Weapon" character, says to Emilio Estevez, who's spoofing Mel Gibson's "Lethal Weapon" character: "Hey, did you see 'Hot Shots'?"

When a parody starts referring to other parodies, its idea supply is unmistakably exhausted.

Surely director/co-writer Gene Quintano has a ready reply for those who maintain his "Loaded Weapon I" is an exercise in redundancy after "The Naked Gun" and "The Naked Gun 2½."

"Hey," he'll say, "I'm primarily going after the 'Lethal Weapon'-type cop pictures, not the TV cop shows that inspired 'Police Squad!' and its big-screen elaborations. Besides, I've got a 'Silence of the Lambs' bit, a 'Rambo' bit, a 'Ninja Turtles' bit ..."

Trouble is, Quintano's movie so resembles the Zucker-Abraham-Zucker gag fests that "Loaded Weapon I" winds up being less a genre parody than a *parody* parody. And comedy once removed is only half as funny.

There are a number of good jokes scattered through "Loaded Weapon I," most of them silly quick-hitters that would be spoiled if described here. Surprisingly, however, the movie takeoff seldom works as well as the throwaways. Part of the problem is that the "Lethal Weapons" are themselves somewhat tongue-in-cheek, and thus a less-than-ideal target. Another part is the casting.

To send up Gibson, you want an actor who conceivably could play the sexy loose cannon—or failing that, one who'd be ludicrously miscast in the role. Estevez falls in the middle, which is not the funniest place to be. True, he has cop-buddy experience, but in "Stakeout" he was essentially Richard Dreyfuss' straight man. The guy in "Loaded Weapon I" needs to be wilder, tougher and taller. Walking Danny Glover's beat as the cautious partner, Samuel L. Jackson ("Jungle Fever") towers over Estevez.

It was an even bigger mistake to let William Shatner have the part of chief villain, modeled after Gary Busey's military officer turned drug kingpin in the first "Lethal Weapon." So what if Shatner earned a parody stripe in "Airplane II"? His presence is inherently funny only if you use him in the sort of role he'd normally play. (Here's a crazy thought: Pair Shatner with James [Scotty] Doohan for the "Star Trek" gag.) In "Loaded Weapon I," he's so obviously tickled to be cast against type that he seems constantly on the verge of a giggle.

The same pattern of miscalculation is evident when too-sweet Kathy Ireland tries to mimic Sharon Stone in one of her sultrier moments from "Basic Instinct." The reference alone isn't worth a laugh; you have to get it right.

As in the "Naked Gun" movies and their cousins, there's often something going on in the background. Look past the arguing cops at police headquarters, and you can see a row of pari-mutuel windows—only the sign spells it "para-mutual." These little misfires take a toll on "Loaded Weapon I."

SIGHT AND SOUND, 6/93, p. 60, Nick James

LA. One night, detective Jack Colt drives up to a mini-mart run by Sikhs with an interpreter. While he is microwaving a burger, two punk thieves run in and a gunfight ensues, wrecking the mini-mart and leaving the two assailants fallen dead into ready-drawn chalk lines.

Undercover cop Billie York is on the phone, arranging to meet an informant at the Squealers Motel, when the doorbell rings. She hides a microfilm behind a picture of herself in uniform with her ex-partner Wes Luger and then opens the door to a Wilderness Girls Cookies salesgirl, a thin disguise for hitman Jigsaw. Billie refuses to give him the microfilm but, while he shoots her, she gives him directions to the motel. Next day Luger arrives at Billie's house and swears vengeance on her killer. Back at the station, he is introduced to his new partner Colt, also mourning an ex-partner: his dog. They visit imprisoned genius Dr Leacher for a lead on the cocaine-laced cookie smuggling ring that Billie was investigating. Jigsaw takes his ringleader boss General Mortars to suspected informer Mike McCracken. While McCracken's four girlfriends (all called Cindy) look on, he begs for mercy. By the time Colt and Luger arrive, the place is strewn with corpses.

The pair decide to tackle the Wilderness Girls corporate HQ where they are met by a Ms Demeanor. The attraction between her and Colt leads her to agree to help them. On removing her glasses, she transforms from frump to vamp before agreeing to a downtown interrogation. A gallery full of officers leer while she swivels in her chair, giving coy answers until she is replaced by a toy beaver. Colt and Destiny Demeanor are attacked by helicopters while enjoying Colt's palatial motor home and comparing wounds. Colt and Luger raid the cookie warehouse, eliminate the bad guys and find that they had Colt's dog captive all along. They end by singing 'Bohemian Rhapsody' in their car.

The long line of spoofs going back to *Airplane* and including *Police Squad* and its *Naked Gun* spin-offs are traditionally aimed at soft targets: '70s disaster movies, routine cop thrillers—whatever packs enough cliches to be lampooned without the writers being over-clever, and yet takes itself seriously enough to warrant pants-down subversion. While no-one would deny the conventional content of the *Lethal Weapon* movies, they are nevertheless a much tougher prospect for spoofing because they throw up a conundrum: how do you parody the already parodic?

Preferring to build the Murtagh and Riggs characters (Danny Glover and Mel Gibson) into a deadpan, likeable pair who send themselves up all the time, the *Lethal Weapon* team pride themselves on never taking cop action too seriously. In this they are merely following the Schwarzenegger action movie trend of heroes with a bulge in one cheek. *Loaded Weapon I* adds an extra pair of inverted commas, but can it bear the weight?

That the *National Lampoon* team are unsure of this is shown by their willingness to embrace a different sort of spoof territory altogether, that of *Wayne's World*. Abounding with sight gags about teen-directed supermarket products, *Loaded Weapon I* mirrors Wayne and Garth's deliberately dumber-than-dumb attitude to cinema—i.e. that it's about babes, big guns and Bond villains (preferably played by Star Trek survivors). In this vision, the film's lame parodies—of the 'chianti and fava beans' scene from *The Silence of the Lambs*, of Sharon Stone's interrogation and Michael Douglas' 'butt in a moonbeam' walk from *Basic Instinct*—take second place to the intimate disposable signifiers of suburban teen America. This makes *Loaded Weapon I* much less sparky, disruptive and anarchic than its predecessors. What's missing is the underlying fear of chaos evoked by Leslie Nielsen's slapstick cop in the *Naked Gun* series. However loaded the TV teen references, by comparison Colt and Luger seem underarmed and overdressed.

VILLAGE VOICE, 2/23/93, p. 58, Mike Rubin

Surely we've seen the likes of this shoot-'em-up spoof before? Yes, it's yet another crazy-quilt collection of sight gags, stereotypes, slapstick, and please don't call me Shirley. Ba-dump-bump. *Loaded Weapon I* follows the formula for the send-up film, with one new wrinkle. While only recently, parasitic parodies preyed upon a genre—like the disaster-flick dismantling in the archetypal *Airplane!*—now it's merely recent box office blockbusters that provide the fodder. Besides copious cribbing from the *Lethal Weapon* series, for no extra charge we get goofs on the pantyless police-station interrogation from *Basic Instinct*, Hannibal Lecter's strait-jacketing from *The Silence of the Lambs*, and the "Bohemian Rhapsody" headbanging from *Wayne's World*. Even Disney has gone metamovie lately, but this is ridiculous—not ridiculous ha-ha, mind you, just ridiculous.

Emilio Estevez and Samuel L. Jackson mimic Mel Gibson and Danny Glover as two mismatched cops trying to catch some crooks who are turning cocaine into cookies, but any real plot takes a backseat to the relentless punch lines. An informal tally of the yukking yields a total of 20 chuckles, 50 smirks, and 210 raspberries, or something like 3.37 joke attempts per minute; the occasional clever moment ends up overwhelmed by the sheer number of groaners. In keeping with the form, *Weapon* has more cameos than *The Cannonball Run*; though the likes of Whoopi Goldberg, Denis Leary, and the Ninja Turtles chip in with bit roles, most of the guest turns are from grade-B celebs like Dr. Joyce Brothers, Corey Feldman, Erik Estrada, and Bruce Willis. With all this overkill, all that *Loaded Weapon* lacks in abundance is laughter; in fact, the film's real comic highlight is the credit "Hair Extensions for Mr. Estevez," and that wasn't meant to be funny.

Also reviewed in:
CHICAGO TRIBUNE, 2/5/93, Friday/p. H, Clifford Terry
NEW YORK TIMES, 2/5/93, p. C6, Vincent Canby
VARIETY, 2/8/93, p. 73, Lawrence Cohn
WASHINGTON POST, 2/5/93, p. B7, Rita Kemmpley

NEEDFUL THINGS

A Castle Rock Entertainment release in association with New Line Cinema. *Executive Producer:* Peter Yates. *Producer:* Jack Cummins. *Director:* Fraser C. Heston. *Screenplay:* W.D. Richter. *Based on the novel by:* Stephen King. *Director of Photography:* Tony Westman. *Editor:* Rob Kobrin. *Music:* Patrick Doyle. *Music Editor:* John Stronach and Dean Beville. *Sound:* Eric Batut and (music) Paul Hume. *Sound Editor:* Richard L. Anderson. *Casting:* Mary Gail Artz and Barbara Cohen. *Production Designer:* Douglas Higgins. *Set Decorator:* Dominique Fauquet-Lemaitre. *Set Dresser:* John Kennedy, Rick Patterson, MacLeod Sinclaire, Doug Carnegie, and Della Mae Johnson. *Special Effects:* Gary Paller. *Costumes:* Monique

Prudhomme. *Make-up:* Sandy Cooper. *Make-up (Bonnie Bedelia):* Melanie Hughes. *Make-Up (Special):* Tibor Furkas. *Stunt Coordinator:* Bill Ferguson. *Running time:* 118 minutes. *MPAA Rating:* R.

CAST: Max von Sydow (Leland Gaunt); Ed Harris (Sheriff Alan Pangborn); Bonnie Bedelia (Polly Chalmers); Amanda Plummer (Nettie Cobb); J.T. Walsh (Danforth Keeton III); Ray McKinnon (Deputy Norris Ridgewick); Duncan Fraser (Hugh Priest); Valri Bromfield (Wilma Jerzyk); Shane Meier (Brian Rusk); W. Morgan Sheppard (Father Meehan); Don S. Davis (Reverend Rose); Campbell Lane (Frank Jewett); Eric Schneider (Henry Beaufort); Frank C. Turner (Pete Jerzyk); Gillian Barber (Myrtle Keeton); Deborah Wakeham (Myra); Tamsin Kelsey (Sheila Ratcliff); Lochlyn Munro (John LaPointe); Bill Croft (Andy Clutterbuck); Dee Jay Jackson (Eddie Wasrburton); Ann Warn Pegg (Ruth Roberts); Gary Paller (George Cobb); Sarah Sawatsky (14 Year Old Girl); Robert Easton (Lester Pratt); Mike Chute (Young Hugh); Mel Allen (Baseball Announcer); Trevor Denman (Race Track Announcer); K-Gin (Raider).

LOS ANGELES TIMES, 8/23/73, Calendar/p. 1, Michael Wilmington

"Needful Things" the new film of Stephen King's bestseller about a demonic gift-shop owner reducing a New England town to bloody chaos, is a movie about the horror of answered prayers, the dangers of getting what you want. It's not like the usual horror thriller. It has ideas as well as jolts, themes as well as special effects, characters as well as gore. But, as adapted by writer W. D. Richter and director Fraser Heston, these "Things" seem disappointingly diminished, squeezed and stuffed into a box too small.

There's one large compensation: the hair-raisingly suave, murderously genial performance of Max von Sydow as satanic Leland Gaunt, proprietor of the odd green-awninged emporium Needful Things. Bergman mainstay von Sydow plays Gaunt perfectly: a man whose Old World manners belie his stated origins—Akron, Ohio—and whose propensity for finding his customers' deepest desires and then converting their gratitude into enslavement and malice (pulling "pranks" on their neighbors), gradually brings the town of Castle Rock to a boiling point.

von Sydow carries the movie. So powerful is his presence that the film seems deflated when he's off screen—despite good jobs by the other actors. Chief among them: Ed Harris as long-suffering Sheriff Alan Pangborn, Bonnie Bedelia as his arthritic inamorata Polly Chalmers, Amanda Plummer as poor lonely Nettie Cobb and J.T. Walsh as the insufferable local politico Danforth (Buster) Keeton.

But the fact that von Sydow dominates "Needful Things" so easily indicates part of what's gone wrong.

The book was one of King's wildest and most elaborate: a spectacular bloody kaleidoscope of a story, 760 pages of escalating small-town scandals and lunatic horror, culminating in one parox-ysm after another. King billed the novel as "The Last Castle Rock Story"—a picture of small-town Armageddon—but the movie, with its reduced cast and contracted carnage and topography, seems just another "Bad Day at Castle Rock." No one who enjoyed the book is likely to be satisfied with this movie. And people who see only the movie probably won't think the book is worth bothering with.

It's less an adaptation than a digest. Richter, cleverly scissoring those 760 pages into the standard two-hour movie format, has lost much of what made the book work: its amplitude, its bewildering plethora of crisscrossing characters, schemes and devilish pranks. Probably "Needful Things" shouldn't have been made into a theatrical feature at all. It would have worked better as a TV mini-series, something King, who makes continual references to "Twin Peaks" in the novel, may have imagined himself.

Gaunt dominates because the sense of the town has been muffled. And the main point of the story—that by hooking and then depraving all his customers, Gaunt the Devil is able to unravel the whole town—is muffled as well.

Heston—who has directed his father, Charlton, on TV in "Treasure Island" and produced or written several of his films—is stronger here on performance than visual style. There's no weak acting, but the movie has a murky, musty, twisted-up look-Gothic Aesthetic Americana—when it probably should resemble Castle Rock itself: bright, sunny, childlike and open, Ray Bradbury land, with the darkness concealed in corners—and in Gaunt's Shop.

To a degree, "Needful Things" is King's parable about the '80s Age of Greed. Written in 1991, the book takes potshots at Bush and Quayle, and its no accident that the craziest of the townspeople—a horseplaying, embezzling selectman—is named Danforth. Greed, religious bigotry and sexual scandal turn Castle Rock into hell on Earth, manipulated by the smiling, suave businessman who just believes in fair trade.

But what about the suave businessmen who believe in two-hour pictures? Ultimately, the movie-ized "Needful Things" (rated R for violence and strong language), like Leland Gaunt, has something to offer. Something we'll like—just not enough.

NEW YORK POST, 8/27/93, p. 23, Michael Medved

What if the free-floating hostility and pointless nastiness that do so much to embitter our daily lives weren't just the product of urban tension, but were actually the work of the devil himself?

That's the intriguing premise of Stephen King's best seller "Needful Things" which has been brought to the screen with memorable conviction and flair.

In this handsome production a picturesque town in British Columbia doubles for King's favorite fictional village of Castle Rock, Maine, where the citizens eagerly await the opening of an elegant antique shop called Needful Things.

The proprietor is a kindly, charismatic old man named Leland Gaunt (Max von Sydow), who has a knack for providing his customers with the one item they crave most—whether its a signed 1956 Mickey Mantle baseball card or a mystical amulet that cures painful arthritis. The townspeople pay for these cherished chatchkas not just with money but by performing various acts of meanness at Gaunt's request.

Before long the entire village is torn apart in a brutal, Hobbesian war of all-against-all, and the dedicated sheriff (Ed Harris) begins to wonder if Gaunt could be responsible. Who is this guy, anyway? He claims to be from Akron, Ohio, but his slight hint of a continental accent and his courtly old world manners suggest that his origins may be a good deal more exotic.

Max von Sydow's cunningly calibrated performance powers the entire film. Whenever he appears on screen the picture crackles with diabolical life. The great Swedish star has never been better in an English-language motion picture and the hellish charms of the Great Tempter have never been more seductively (or chillingly) presented. This role brings his distinguished career full circle, offering an amazing contrast to his memorable performance as Jesus in "The Greatest Story Ever Told" 28 years ago.

In addition to von Sydow's great performance, one of the great strengths of "Needful Things" is its refusal to sentimentalize small-town life. Castle Rock is hardly a Norman Rockwell version of Eden, since the townspeople have been involved in feuds and murders and governmental corruption, all without any devilish assistance whatever. Gaunt doesn't need to exert any supernatural power to ruin them; the slightest nudge in the wrong direction is all it takes to push these flawed human beings into hellish chaos.

Screenwriter W.D. Richter (best known as writer-director of "Buckaroo Banzai" and "Late for Dinner") deserves tremendous credit for adapting Stephen King's big complex and rambling book into a lean, powerful and perfectly proportioned script.

Director Fraser Heston makes an auspicious feature-film debut after working with his father, Charlton Heston on a stirring adaptation of "Treasure Island" and other projects for TV. In all his work he fills the screen with big, bold eye-popping images, finding the full dramatic potential in even the most insignificant scenes. The only problem comes in the final half-hour, as a top-drawer psychological drama shamelessly degenerates into a rather routine series of Hollywood blood baths and explosions. The needlessly graphic gore including a grotesque image of a skinned dog, and a sadistic, crazed battle-to-the-death involving carving knives and meat cleavers will trouble all moviegoers except those with the very strongest stomachs. Fraser Heston should have known better: As the finest moments of his first film demonstrate so well, the thoughtless cruelty and paranoia of day-to-day life can be far more terrifying in the final analysis than the overproduced apocalyptic special effects that have become such a predictable part of horror a la King.

NEWSDAY, 8/27/93, Part II/p. 72, John Anderson

All hell is breaking loose—again—in the sleepless little town of Castle Rock, the tiny Maine burg upon which Stephen King has heaped so much bloody mayhem during the course of his career. Why anyone would choose to live there, unless they're completely oblivious to popular culture, is a mystery. But why someone like Alan Pangborn (Ed Harris) would trade in his big-city police job to become the town's sheriff—and do so because he wants to *relax*—is even more confounding.

What's crystal clear, however, is the cause behind the sudden, vicious behavior of some Castle Rock residents: Leland Gaunt (Max von Sydow), a charming, worldly sort with a poisonous smile, whose little shop, Needful Things, offers just what people want. And cheaply. Providing they perform the little tasks he requests.

From the "Omen"-esque music that opens the film to the wildly overblown special effects and the scenery chewing—particularly by J.T. Walsh, who finally gets to do something fun—"Needful Things" is aiming for laughs, and usually hitting. Director Fraser Heston, son of Charlton, performs a sort of Reverse Hitchcock: Rather than find terror in the commonplace, he makes terror commonplace. But this actually enhances the rest of the film. The matter-of-factness with which characters are dispatched, and horribly, makes the film so blackly comedic one can't help but laugh, between shudders.

Max von Sydow is obviously delighted with Leland, who drips with unctuous evil. He doesn't sell his customers as much as seduce them, and he always has the proper tool. For the oddball Nettie (Amanda Plummer), there's a Hummell figurine, just like the one smashed long ago by her brutal husband—the one she's suspected of murdering with a meat fork. For Alan's girlfriend Polly (Bonnie Bedelia), there's a magic amulet that alleviates her dreadful arthritis pain. For Danforth (Buster) Keeton III (Walsh), there's a toy racetrack that predicts winning horses.

There's a washed-up ex-athlete who finds a letter jacket just like his old one—"Just like the one I used to have in high school, before I was a bum" and who has to perform some heinous butchery. Nettie and an old nemesis become locked in a death battle (while "Ave Maria" resounds in the background). All Leland's customers must perform some outrageous acts against their neighbors—the pattern of violence isn't one on one, but more of a round-robin—as Leland sits back and laughs.

By the time the Baptist minister and the Catholic priest are at each other's throats, there's little question who Leland actually is. "Needful Things" is the Faust legend, en masse. Whether Alan should be so quick to figure it all out is another story. But it hardly matters. The film, although burdened by a high-minded moral, is basically a hoot, With horns.

SIGHT AND SOUND, 8/94, p. 48, Kim Newman

Castle Rock, Maine. The mysterious Leland Gaunt moves into town and opens a curio shop, Needful Things. His first customer is Brian Rusk, a boy to whom he sells a valuable Mickey Mantle baseball card for less than a dollar, on condition Brian play a prank on turkey farmer Wilma Jerzyk by splashing her washing with mud. Wilma assumes the vandalism is the work of her adversary, neurotic waitress Nettie Cobb, and threatens to kill Nettie's beloved dog.

Sheriff Alan Pangborn, newly engaged to Nettie's boss Polly Chalmers, settles a dispute between local official Danforth 'Buster' Keeton and Deputy Norris Ridgewick, who insists on giving Keeton parking tickets. By selling the townsfolk oddly personalised items (a first edition of *Treasure Island*, a 50s high-school jacket), Gaunt gets them to play further pranks, exacerbating feuds between individuals and factions. Keeton, who has embezzled the town's funds to cover gambling debts, buys a horse-race game with predictive powers, but is furious when he finds his house plastered with parking tickets—allegedly from Ridgewick but actually planted by Nettie—detailing his crimes.

When Nettie's dog is killed and Wilma's windows broken, each assumes the other is guilty and they murder each other. Brian, who has broken Wilma's windows, tries to kill himself, convincing Nan that Gaunt is not human. Polly, who is given a cure for crippling arthritis, is led to believe Nan is in league with Keeton. Keeton murders his wife and takes from Gaunt enough explosives to blow up the town, starting with the Catholic church. As the townsfolk attack each other and buildings burn, Alan makes a speech accusing Gaunt and everyone realises that they have been fooled. Polly throws away her cure while Keeton, weighed down with dynamite, rushes into Needful Things and blows up the shop. Gaunt emerges unscathed from the explosion, promises to encounter Nan and Polly's grandson in the twenty-first century, and leaves town.

Needful Things suited to a short story, may well be Stephen King's worst novel. This adaptation, which Fraser C. Heston took over from Peter Yates early in production, can do little with the book's repetitive storyline, which has Leland Gaunt making the same bargain with a succession of characters. The release version bears all the marks of having been trimmed from a considerably longer cut: Lisa Blount, unbilled as Brian's mother but listed as one of the featured stars in pre-release publicity, is glimpsed silently in several scenes, finally looting a chainsaw from a riot-smashed hardware store for an amusing sight gag.

Nevertheless, *Needful Things* is a satisfying, double-edged horror movie. Boiled down to essentials, the premise is more appealing here than in the novel, especially since Max von Sydow as the malevolent intruder who causes havoc in the Castle Rock community adds much humour and style to King's thinly conceived Devil. He reminisces about "that carpenter from Nazareth" and complains that while God is omnipresent and all powerful, he's "just one lonely guy" spreading evil around the world. The influence of *Twin Peaks* can be detected in the choice of actors—Ed Harris as Sheriff Pangborn is the anchor of decency who allows the film to cut loose with such cartoonish comic horror acting as J.T. Walsh's unhinged councilman Keeton, who murders his wife because she uses his hated nickname 'Buster', and Valri Bromfield's cleaver-wielding turkey farmer, who has apparently chosen her career because it gives her the opportunity to behead small creatures on a daily basis.

Heston, unlike many Stephen King adaptators, does not pretend that the author's world is anything but a horror movie arena. The film is awash with creepy camera-movements, unrealistic gloom, cackling maniacs, dreamy flashes, *misterioso* music and strange effects. Elements of King's sophomoric social comment creep in (when the church blows up, the priest refuses to believe the Devil is responsible, blaming "those goddam Baptists"), but the world of Castle Rock is so enclosed and unreal that it is hard to be annoyed by the simplistic misanthropy. Nobody's idea of great horror, this is still a long way from being the worst film based on a Stephen King text.

Also reviewed in:
CHICAGO TRIBUNE, 8/27/93, Friday/p. A, Clifford Terry
NEW YORK TIMES, 8/27/93, p. C17, Janet Maslin
VARIETY, 8/23/93, p. 22, Brian Lowry
WASHINGTON POST, 8/27/93, p. C1, Richard Harrington
WASHINGTON POST, 8/27/93, Weekend/p. 36, Eve Zibart

NEO-TOKYO

Three short animated films.

LABYRINTH: *Director:* Rin Taro. *Screenplay:* Rin Taro.

RUNNING MAN: *Director:* Yoshiaki Kawajiri. *Screenplay:* Yoshiaki Kawajiri.

THE ORDER TO STOP CONSTRUCTION: *Director:* Katsuhiro Otomo. *Screenplay:* Katsuhiro Otomo. *English version by:* Carl Macek. *Running time:* 50 minutes. *MPAA Rating:* Not Rated.

NEW YORK POST, 7/24/93, p. 16, Jarry Tallmer

Somewhere in this happy land there are thousands of people clamoring for the privilege of sitting through 100 minutes of new weird Japanese animations, but I am not one of them.

The double bill at Cinema Village is of "Neo-Tokyo" plus "Silent Mobius," but it's really a quadruplebill because "Neo-Tokyo" (hey, there's a title for you) is in itself a package of three Surreo-cartoony films, comic books put to motion. Let us open the package, gingerly.

"Labyrinth." A clown, a cat, and a kid. The cat looks like a skunk. I deduce after a while that the kid is a little girl. They meet in a scary cave that turns into a circus tent, and along their adventurous route they encounter—among a great deal else—a pendulum that's a flying saucer, a leash that barks and growls for an invisible dog, ghost soldiers that turn into falling dominoes that turn into a river of tar, the Toonerville Trolley, another trolley car filled with skeletons, and a quite imaginative march of Dali-like light poles.

"Running Man." Round and round an eternal race-track roar the supervehicles of the 21st century, vying to be the first to transcend death. Top driver is stone-faced, slit-eyed Zack Hugh, who survives, or almost survives, more than man or machine can bear. The imaginative touch here is the maelstrom of monstrous racing cars like hellfire lightning bugs. This movie should be watched while on LSD, and probably is.

"The Order to Stop Construction." A saga—an attempt at irony—taking place in a deserted futuristic city in the heart of the jungles of a banana republic, as if Fritz Lang had set Metropolis down in Brasilia. Maybe that's what's being ironized. Anyway, an officious nerd of a begoggled Japanesy trouble-shooter is stranded there, alone, confronting a maniacally obsessive robot foreman who keeps squawking things like: "Unauthorized personnel are denied access to the facility." They try to kill one another. This high-tech do-good drama says progress is bad for us. I agree.

"Silent Mobius," the 50-minute second half of the program, is an utterly astonishing zombie of a whatsit about a neurotic Futuregirl with a mother problem and the all-girl Wondergirl police force that defends her (against her will) from Lucifer Hawke, the crablike/batlike shrieking-snarling-howling Embodiment of All Evil. I think there's a rape involved here, and considerable blood. This epic freely borrows in more than one detail from "Star Wars" and, better still, "Forbidden Planet."

All these movies speak strange baby-voiced unsynchronized English.

Also reviewed in:
NEW YORK TIMES, 7/23/93, p. C12

NEW YORK IN SHORT

THE SHVITZ: *Producer:* Jonathan Berman. *Director:* Jonathan Berman. *Director of Photography:* Evan Estern, Laurence Salzmann, and Ellen Kuras. *Editor:* Amanda Zinoman. *Music:* The Klezmatics/Frank London. *Running time:* 50 minutes. *MPAA Rating:* Not Rated.

LET'S FALL IN LOVE: A SINGLES WEEKEND AT THE CONCORD HOTEL: *Producer:* Constance Marks. *Director:* Constance Marks. *Director of Photography:* Michael Mayers. *Editor:* Deborah Dickson. *Running time:* 30 minutes. *MPAA Rating:* Not Rated.

NEW YORK POST, 10/22/93, p. 28, Thelma Adams

"Attractive dentist looking for someone with teeth." Dentists are kings at the Catskills resort profiled by Constance Marks in "Let's Fall in Love; A Singles Weekend at the Concord Hotel." Marks' warm and witty film is the first of two shorts on the lighter side of metropolitan Jewish life included in "New York in Short."

Five times a year, 1,200 single Jews flock to the Concord singles weekends. While Friday night's optimism dissolves into Sunday's despair, Marks uses cinema verite to produce a priceless document of mating in a setting as romantic as an airport lounge.

Sights start out high in the search for the perfect match. One busty bottle-blonde seeks, "not just your multi-millionaire who's a schlep ... someone who's fabulous." In the background, a man kisses a woman. He turns away and she wipes her face.

At the Concord, the ultimate goal seems to be finding a mate and never having to return to another singles' weekend. This short could get mileage as a primer for husbands and wives. Watching this, even the most combative couples will feel smug and proud over their marriage vows.

Jonathan Berman's "The Shvitz" is a more ambitious, and equally delightful, slice of Jewish life. Berman's camera guides us to another rarely seen bastion, the sweat baths of Brighton Beach and the East Village.

Using archival footage, Berman charts the rise and fall of New York's Russian baths. At their heyday, more than 200 bathhouses dotted the city's Eastern European enclaves.

Their popularity diminished among assimilated Jews and many closed. The baths experienced a renaissance from the Fifties to the early Eighties when they were taken up by gay men, a trend ended by the advent of AIDS. Now only a few remain.

The filmmakers (wearing robes, and sometimes less than that) immerse themselves in the baths. They catch their subjects in a state of complete relaxation: hair dripping, flesh sagging, genitals revealed, massive sighs and "achs" of pleasure, celebrating life with bawdy good humor, laughing, teasing, drinking, eating, sweating. And sweating some more.

"No more trouble. No more pain. Everything is gone," says a naked, barrel-chested, pot-bellied Russian. These guys are not straight out of Madonna videos; they're a universe apart.

Watching these two shorts is a "mechaieh," a great pleasure, a real joy.

NEWSDAY, 10/22/93, Part II/p. 79, Jonathan Mandell

In "Let's Fall in Love," one of the two short documentaries that simultaneously embrace and poke fun at what could be called two secular Jewish rituals, a man holds up a card underneath his mustache with an illustration of an absurdly smiling mouth. "That's my calling card," he explains. "I'm a dentist."

The dentist is at the Concord Hotel in the Catskills, for the Singles Weekend. "I have come here five times a year since 1983"—in other words, every time there is one—"because my mother wants me to get married."

Was it that same man who wrote the classified ad that a woman later reads with glee in the hotel's "Meeter's Digest"—"Attractive dentist looking for someone with teeth"?

We'll never know, because as funny and poignant (and sometimes patronizing) as it is, "Let's Fall in Love; a Singles Weekend at the Concord Hotel"—a title almost as long as the movie itself—is also a little like being in an especially intense and crowded singles bar; you never get to know anybody well enough even to learn his or her name.

We do run into faces that become familiar by the end of the three-day hunt. We meet one muscular man after he walked away from a woman he liked because "I didn't want to seem too eager" and then cross his path again and again as he spends the remainder of the weekend looking for her.

We watch an attractive woman providing her age and measurements over her room telephone to a potential date, listen to a blond explain her interest only in multimillionaires—"not your multimillionaire that's a schlepp, but somebody exciting"—and get introduced to a happy, affectionate couple who talk reflectively about their relationship even though they met only two hour's earlier and split up soon afterward.

The funniest moment involves a "free makeover" that is only half free; the customer leaves half made-up, unwilling to fork over the some $35 in cosmetics purchases to complete the job. There's a metaphor in there somewhere.

If there is more warmth and dry humor in "The Shvitz," that is only because of its subject, the dying world of Jewish steam baths. Created as the only place to get washed when tenements had no baths or showers, the shvitz became a refuge for someone in search of some "good heat, something to eat and a place to sleep," as well as a joke or two. Now that there are way more reminiscences than baths, the shvitz seems to serve mostly as source for a shower of Jewish-inflected nostalgia.

"The Shvitz" has a terrific score of Yiddish music, mostly composed and performed by The Klezmatics; it begins hilariously, with one New Yorker after another guessing what "shvitz" means; it includes some interesting history and old clips in addition to the you-are-here scenes that give a different meaning to steamy. But how long can anyone take a steam bath? The New York City Board of Health recommends no more than 30 minutes. "The Shvitz," 20 minutes longer than that, might leave you a bit dried out and puffy.

VILLAGE VOICE, 11/2/93, p. 66, Kathy Deacon

Constance Marks's half-hour documentary *Let's Fall in Love: A Singles Weekend at the Concord Hotel* allows its subjects to present themselves without condescension. Singles, mainly Jewish, late thirtyish, go through the motions of obeying the imperative Thou Shalt Wed with a grim joie de vivre, many at a stage of reflexive postcynicism. They know finding a mate at this Catskills meeting place of last resort—where they're offered classes in personal makeover and the cha-cha—will be like spotting a firefly in January.

We get progress reports on the continuous pairings and unpairings, and a sense that each of the talking heads, sexy or not-so-sexy, thinks he or she's above this whole sorry spectacle. But they all handle one another gently. "I like you already" could mean hello or goodbye. The effect is funny, depressing, and vaguely uplifting.

Paired with it in a double bill about Jewish life in New York, titled "New York in Short," is Jonathan Berman's high-spirited hourlong documentary about New York City's steam baths, *The Shvitz* ("sweat" in Yiddish). Set to the music of the Klezmatics, and using archival footage, Berman traces a feature of urban life rooted in the shtetl of the Old World and once integral to the Jewish community in New York.

A hygienic necessity for tenement-dwelling Eastern European Jewish immigrants, the baths were social clubs, "a community of people that helped you," and "better than a psychiatrist's couch," according to old-timers interviewed happily at bath at the Hope Avenue Russian Steambaths in Brighton Beach—and sometimes shown in striking black-and-white tableaux.

Eighty years ago, hundreds of these baths dotted the Lower East Side and Coney Island. (In the '50s, of course, they evolved into a largely gay institution, before AIDS.) Only in its noncommittal survey of the current blasé patrons of coed night at Tenth Street baths in the East Village does this colorful history of the *Shvitz* lose steam.

Also reviewed in:
NEW YORK TIMES, 10/22/93, p. C13, Stephen Holden

NIGHT WE NEVER MET, THE

A Miramax Films release. *Executive Producer:* Sidney Kimmel, Bob Weinstein, and Harvey Weinstein. *Producer:* Rudd Simmons and Michael Peyser. *Director:* Warren Leight. *Screenplay:* Warren Leight. *Director of Photography:* John A. Thomas. *Editor:* Camilla Toniolo. *Music:* Lynn Geller. *Music Editor:* David Carbonara. *Choreographer:* John Carrafa. *Sound:* William Sarokin. *Sound Editor:* Dan Sable. *Casting:* Billy Hopkins and Suzanne Smith. *Production Designer:* Lester Cohen. *Art Director:* Daniel Talpers. *Set Decorator:* Jessica Lanier. *Set Dresser:* Kenin Mahon and Christine Moosher. *Special Effects:* Drew Jiritano. *Costumes:* Ellen Lutter. *Make-up:* Joe Cuervo. *Make-up (Annabella Sciorra):* Bernadette Mazur. *Running time:* 99 minutes. *MPAA Rating:* R.

CAST: Matthew Broderick (Sam Lester); Annabella Sciorra (Ellen Holder); Kevin Anderson (Brian McVeigh); Jeanne Tripplehorn (Pastel); Justine Batemen (Janet Beehan); Michael Mantell (Aaron Holder); Christine Baranski (Lucy); Doris Roberts and Dominic Chianese (Nosy Neighbors); Tim Guinee (Kenneth); Bradley White (Todd); Greg Germann (Eddie); Dana Wheeler-Nicholson (Inga); Louise Lasser (Mrs. Winkler); Bill Campbell (Shep); Michelle Hurst (Leslie); Lewis Black (Marty Holder); Ranjit Chowdhry (Cabbie); Naomi Campbell (French Cheese Shopper); Richard Poe (Bartender); Katherine Houghton (Less/More Cheese Lady); David Slavin (Chuck Barber); Brooke Smith (Catha); Bitty Schram (Pharmacy Clerk); Billy Strong (Doorman); Catherine Lloyd Burns (Deli Customer); Michael Mastrototaro (Triple Cream Cheese Shopper); Michael Imperioli (Cleaning Customer #1); Suzanne Dottino (Cleaning Customer #2); Jose Evello Alvarez ("My Name is Eduardo"); Paul Guilfoyle (Sparrow's Nest Salesman); Davidson Thomson (Foreign Film Actor); Kathryn Rossetter ("Excuse Me" Shopper); Mary B. McCann (Yogurt Eating Date); Steven Goldstein (3rd Cheese Man); Suzanne Lanza (Shep's New Date); Pete Bucossi (Cabbie's Stunt Driver).

LOS ANGELES TIMES, 4/30/93, Calendar/p. 4, Kevin Thomas

In "The Night We Never Met," Warren Leight's deft and delightful romantic comedy of errors, Brian (Kevin Anderson), a young Manhattan stockbroker, has moved in with his fiancée (Justine Bateman) but holds on to his own apartment in a fine old Greenwich Village townhouse.

Two days a week he rents it to Sam (Matthew Broderick), who works at the cheese counter at the swanky Dean & DeLuca gourmet grocery, Ellen (Annabella Sciorra) a dental hygienist, also takes two days. This way Brian has a place where he can get away and watch the football games with his office pals, while Sam can escape momentarily from an overcrowded East Village dump he's been sharing with innumerable other guys after breaking up with his girlfriend, a silly, pretentious French actress (Jeanne Tripplehorn). Stuck in a dull marriage to a Queens laundry owner (Michael Mantell), Ellen will now have a place of her own to which she can escape and pursue her love of painting.

Brian, Sam and Ellen have never met, but the latter two begin leaving notes to each other. Ellen appreciates Sam's decor in his portion of the apartment and also his equally tasteful leftovers. Having started fantasizing about Sam as the man of her dreams, she gets up her nerve to show up looking her glamorous best on one of the evenings when the apartment belongs to Sam—not realizing Brian has made a switch in the schedule. The calamity that swiftly ensues with a zingy domino effect is beautifully sustained by writer Leight in an exceptionally assured directorial debut. Leight, however, simultaneously enlarges upon his farcical plot by allowing us to see that there's more to care about these people, Sam and Ellen especially, than we might well have expected.

Leight is a man of compassion as well as sophistication: For example, Brian can be a terrible boor and a slob, a superannuated fraternity boy, yet is finally not really such a bad guy. Ellen's husband and Sam's French actress are ripe for comeuppance, yet they're recognizably human and vulnerable. But then Leight clearly cares about all his people, which means that more than 30 actors shine as brightly as the film's stars.

Most notable are Christine Baranski's ditsy sister to Ellen, Doris Roberts and Dominic Chianese's nosy neighbors, Louise Lasser's conscientious realtor, Richard Poe's smooth, macho bartender, Ranjit Chowdhry's excitable cabby and an unbilled Garry Shandling as a nervous patient of Ellen's. One of "The Night We Never Met's" (rated R for language and some sex) strongest assets is Lester Cohen's inspired, knowing production design, which never calls attention to itself while speaking volumes about Leight's people.

NEW YORK POST, 4/30/93, p. 33, Jami Bernard

With the exception of an unbilled cameo by Garry Shandling as a dental patient on the make, "The Night We Never Met" is an embarrassment, in varying degrees, to its smart participants.

Matthew Broderick comes out relatively unscathed as a lovesick grocer who time-shares a Village brownstone apartment with a frustrated housewife and a beer-swilling jerk. They each get two nights a week—is it me or is there a mathematical problem with that arrangement?—and they begin to know each other without ever meeting.

It's a drawing room comedy in the old-fashioned vein of, say, "The Apartment," in which narrow brushes and mistaken identities kill time until the movie is ready to make the appropriate romantic pairing for which we have been waiting. But much of the humor is heartless and the relationships it depicts are dispiriting.

Broderick has an easy, gentle charm, which lets him off the hook. But consider the plight of Jeanne Tripplehorn, Michael Douglas' sexy, intelligent shrink from "Basic Instinct," who here plays a flighty downtown performance artist with such a bad French accent you expect the plot to unravel another identity for her to explain it. Or Kevin Anderson as a yuppie pig who gets to sleep with both Annabella Sciorra *and* Justine Bateman; is there no mercy in screenwriter land?

Bateman looks whipped, except when she's doing the whipping herself as a leather-clad dominatrix during a fantasy sequence. Louise Lasser as a confused secretary is cringing. A variety of offbeat extras are supposed to add to the madcap fun, and occasionally do.

There are in fact several good laughs in "The Night We Never Met," but they are undercut by the edit from hell—sequencing and staging so confusing you can barely keep up with which apartment we're supposed to be in (the movie has two, both of which are occasionally defined by their messiness), or whose night it is to get the keys.

The woman next to me at the screening overcame her bafflement by snoring loudly throughout the movie, a harbinger perhaps of reactions to come.

NEWSDAY, 4/30/93, Part II/p. 66, Jack Mathews

Inside humorist/playright Warren Leight's first feature film, "The Night We Never Met," is a nice idea for a one-set Off-Broadway comedy, and though it was not conceived or developed for the stage, it would have been better served there.

The set is a studio garden-view apartment in the West Village, which is shared by three people, two of whom fall in love, even though none of them even meet until the story is nearly over. In fact, all they know about each other is what they can decipher from the debris left behind in the apartment.

You see, they live there on different days.

Brian McVeigh (Kevin Anderson) is the engaged stockbroker who decides to sublease his rent-controlled bachelor pad four days out of the week and reserve three for himself and his rowdy buddies.

Two of the available days are taken by Sam Lester (Matthew Broderick), who wants to get away from his roommates long enough to revive his flagging love life in private but can't afford an apartment of his own. The other two days go to Ellen Holder (Annabella Sciorra), a dental hygienist in dire need of relief from her boring, domineering husband (Michael Mantell).

As the schedule works out, Ellen's days follow one of Brian's and one of Sam's, meaning she finds a room full of pizza crusts and beer cans one day, and fabulous left-overs of home-cooked meals in the refrigerator the other. Sam loves Ellen's paintings and decorating tastes, she loves his sensitivity and cooking. They both hate Brian's slovenliness.

And they're soon leaving notes and gifts for each other.

But as comedies of error go, Ellen gets the names mixed up and thinks she's falling in love with Brian instead of Sam and ... well, you'd have to be there.

Being there means at the apartment. Though Leight frequently takes us out of the time-share studio to develop other aspects of the trio's lives, none of those scenes is essential and none of the other characters we meet is particularly interesting.

In fact, Sam's old girlfriend—a ditsy French performance artist—could have been eliminated altogether, which would have saved us the embarrassment of Jeanne Tripplehorn's mangled accent. Justine Bateman, as Brian's hysterical fiance, fares little better.

The only characters developed well enough to elicit any real audience sympathy are Sam and Ellen. Sam is a gentle romantic living a life of quiet desperation (evenings at Film Forum, home-cooked meals alone) and Broderick plays him with an irresistible eagerness. As Ellen, a child bride who has outgrown her narrow-minded husband but doesn't know quite what she's feeling, Sciorra comes closer than anyone in this artificial setting to being a real person.

There's certainly nothing real about Anderson's Brian McVeigh. Brian and his friends are ludicrous cliches, sports-minded bozos who don't appear to have 100 IQ points among them, let alone the smarts to advise stock investors. (Leight cut 38 seconds from the version I saw, most of them reportedly from scenes with "the boys.")

"The Night We Never Met" is only interesting when it is developing the confused relationships between Sam and Ellen, and hurling them and Brian; toward their inevitable face-to-face meetings. The confusion and comedy that come out of it would be better focused, and we'd probably learn more about the characters, without the distractions.

There's a switch. A movie that could be "opened up" as a play.

SIGHT AND SOUND, 10/93, p. 48, Leslie Felperin Sharman

Fed up with sharing his squalid apartment, Sam rents a Greenwich Village studio flat with two others on a time-share basis. By using a rota, each person has sole access to the flat for two nights a week. The other two 'roommates' are Brian and Ellen. Brian is an engaged stockbroker and the leaseholder who wants to hold onto the flat for swinging bachelor parties. Ellen is a dental hygienist who lives on Long Island and wants a Manhattan pied-a-terre to paint and escape her dull dry-cleaner husband. Without meeting, Sam and Ellen establish a rapport and communicate through notes. He admires her paintings and leaves her tasty leftovers to eat. Brian leaves beer cans and empty pizza boxes lying about. Due to confusion over a swap of days on the rota, Ellen thinks that Sam is the 'bad' roommate who destroyed her curtains and basil plants and that Brian is the 'good' one. Determined to seduce him, she arrives on one of Brian's nights. Not only is she disappointed by his dreadful lovemaking, she realises that she has copulated with 'the wrong guy'. Eventually, Sam and Ellen meet up at last, sort out the confusion, fall in love, and set up house together in the apartment as Brian leaves to marry his fiancee.

Back in the 80s, an American social geographer named Sharon Zukin wrote a book called *Loft Living*. It is now considered a landmark study of how space and property intersect with class and taste. Zukin described how 'lofts'—open plan apartments converted from obsolete industrial work-spaces in Lower Manhattan—first became trendy living spaces for artists. The properties became chic, and soon yuppies from the financial district moved in, and later on anyone who yearned for and could afford the kind of bohemian but swankier lifestyle that lofts came to represent.

Despite the minor fact that the main focus of action is a brownstone studio rather than a loft, *The Night We Never Met* is effectively a fictionalization of Zukin's thesis. Its three central characters are a representative sample of the types who now swarm the Village and SoHo areas where sweatshops used to be (roughly Camden and Covent Garden in London terms). Sam is a service industry work-slave in a gourmet delicatessen, financially poor but rich in cultural capital. Ellen is at once an aspirant artist and an upwardly mobile 'incomer' from the suburbs. To complete the demographics, Brian is an all-too conspicuously consuming stockbroker, demonised in line with today's backlash against the values of Wall Street, both the place and film. Were it not for the generally good quality of the acting, they would be as stereotypical as composite portraits in a sociological study of taste patterns by disciples of Pierre Bourdieu.

The initial concept of three characters who hardly meet is intriguing, but not as neatly executed as it might be by first-time director Warren Leight. Less a comedy of errors than of manners, this is more a Downtown *When Harry Met Sally ...* than a New York *Mystery Train*. If you're in the mood to indulge in some light cultural snobbery, you'll enjoy this film. Shiver alternately with disgust and delight as you assess the taste of the sets! Pat yourself on the back as you spot the Manhattan locations and the cameos by model Naomi Campbell, writer/performer Eric Bogosian, and the director Ranjit Chowdry (extra points for Americans who remember Louise Lasser, Woody Allen's ex-wife and former star of the cult soap *Mary Hartman, Mary Hartman*). Sneer at newage vegans, at people who like Neil Diamond, and at performance artists! Reminiscent of *Singles*, which also centred on an apartment block, *The Night We Never Met* is a likeably shallow movie for Generation X-ers, slackers, and twentysomethings who like their love stories flattened with a little cynicism and pat one-liners ("Sex is like politics, the incumbent always has the advantage"). Like lofts themselves, it's a rickety structure with trendy interior design, an old-fashioned sex comedy for the nouveau hip.

VILLAGE VOICE, 5/4/93, p. 56, Georgia Brown

Film Forum plays a minor atmospheric role in *The Night We Never Met*, which is not exactly a cause for cheer. Not only is the theater's schedule posted on a fridge, but a membership card peeks out of the hero's billfold. It may even have been the Preston Sturges retrospective that spoke directly to the heart of writer/director Warren Leight.

Matthew Broderick plays Film Forum member and Dean & DeLuca buyer Sam, who can't afford decent housing. Pardon me if I can't believe such expertise goes so spectacularly under-rewarded. Anyway, to escape his crowded East Village dump, Sam signs up for a two-room time-share in a Morton Street townhouse, thus intertwining his fate with that of two partners he's never met. We meet them: there's boorish Brian (Kevin Anderson), currently moving in with his prissy fiancee (Justine Bateman) while secretly holding on to the pad two nights a week in order to boogie with boys from the brokerage firm; and there's Ellen (Annabella Sciorra), a dental hygienist from Queens, who wants her two days to get in touch with the artist within (paintings by Roz Chast).

Never actually crossing paths, Sam and Ellen—equally ripe for rewarding relationships—send sickeningly gentle vibes through leftovers and a basil plant while Brian (Dartmouth, Class of '84) sends nothing but death and destruction. Following rules of the comedy of errors, Ellen gets her roommates' identities confused, though you'd like to think that nothing short of a lobotomy would lead her to sleep with the pig called Brian. I mean, especially in the second film in three weeks to use a copy of *Backlash* as a prop.

A few New York in-jokes did not go a long way. This reviewer remembers *The Night We Never Met* as the night she should never have left the house.

Also reviewed in:
NEW REPUBLIC, 5/17/93, p. 34, Stanley Kauffmann
NEW YORK TIMES, 4/30/93, p. C10, Janet Maslin
VARIETY, 4/26/93, p. 68, Lawrence Cohn
WASHINGTON POST, 5/3/93, p. C2, Hal Hinson

NITRATE KISSES

A Strand Releasing release.   *Producer:* Barbara Hammer.   *Director:* Barbara Hammer. *Screenplay:* Barbara Hammer.   *Director of Photography:* Barbra Hammer.   *Editor:* Barbara Hammer.   *Sound:* Barbara Hammer.   *Running time:* 63 minutes.   *MPAA Rating:* Not Rated.

LOS ANGELES TIMES, 5/20/93, Calendar/p. 3, Michael Wilmington

Barbara Hammer's "Nitrate Kisses" and Monika Treut's "Female Misbehavior" are not a double feature. You have to pay separate admissions for each. But they might as well be. They make a perfect match: two explorations of sexual "deviance" without coyness or calculated shock value.

These two documentaries on the lesbian sensibility are both done defiantly. They're frank, unabashed, provocative, and, at least by silent majority standards, deliberately objectionable.

Why? Sheer explicitness. Hammer's film includes uncensored lesbian and gay lovemaking, embedded in a cultural crazy-quilt of homosexual imagery from the past: outtakes from James Sibley Watson and Melville Weber's 1932 biblical "art" film "Lot in Sodom," in which barely clad men in quasi-Gomorrah garb writhe suggestively, scored to a soundtrack drawn from the "AC/DC Blues Gay Jazz Reissues" from Stash.

Treut's "Female Misbehavior," by contrast, is bald, up-front: a collection of four linked interviews with four women of varying levels of anti-respectability, their talk as gamy as their actions are occasionally explicit. The quartet ranges from the notorious "politically incorrect," anti-feminist, pro-pornography academic Camille Paglia—who rattles on like a Woody Allen soulmate from hell—to a lesbian dominatrix (Carol) to a transsexual in mid-change from woman to man (Max), all the way to Annie Sprinkle, an adult movie actress whose specialty is usually confined to the bathroom.

And yet, each film has a serious core, though anyone who senses from the descriptions above that they'd be offended had better stay away—because they probably will. Actually, their unbuttoned stance is a deliberate strategy. The directors, wanting to pull us into an angle of vision, do it in the bluntest way possible: by disguising nothing and flaunting their deviance.

The films are intended, partially, to celebrate lesbianism—or in Treut's case, to celebrate a broader category of women who are rebellious—and what makes them interesting to those beyond their primary audience is their honesty, the way neither director filters nor dilutes her material to make it more palatable.

Hammer's "Nitrate Kisses"—the first feature by a director who has been a mainstay of alternative-sex film festivals for decades—was made for a threadbare $21,000, and Treut's quartet of interviews wasn't originally intended as a feature. The earliest piece, with bondage-and-discipline expert Carol, was shot a decade ago; the two with Paglia and Max, more recently.

These films are not for everyone, especially the easily shocked. The self-administered "Mature" rating on each—for nudity, sexuality and language—is no joke: three decades ago, they would certainly have been proscribed. But, then, three decades ago, so, probably, would any public revelations by most of the people here. By bringing them all into the light of day, "Nitrate Kisses" and "Female Misbehavior" suggest that human beings are much more than the sum of their sex acts.

NEW YORK POST, 4/9/93, p. 29, Jerry Tallmer

Any movie that brings back the voice of Lotte Lenya can't be all bad and "Nitrate Kisses" a film by Barbara Hammer opening today just where it should, Cinema Village, seemed to me to be fascinatingly good (and bad) in many more ways than that. Considering the fact that it was made for $21,000 all told—"up to and including the first print"—it's nothing short of a cinematic miracle.

Not to make any bones about it, "Nitrate Kisses" is a 63-minute paean to lesbianism, "the unspoken and the unspeakable." Male homosexual culture gets its share of footage too, but only as a sort of adjunct or mutual support system, and mostly because Ms. Hammer in her research came upon some archival outtakes of "Lot in Sodom," an artsy-fartsy "forbidden" film of the '30s that used to play these same Village theaters as late as the '50s, and (unwisely, I think) decided to weave the "Lot" stuff in and around the rest.

I'll tell you when I myself felt something stirring inside me: When we see two women who might be (and I think are) grandmothers, all the more handsome, even beautiful, for their wrinkles, obviously in their 70s, exchanging passionate kisses as they lie side by side in one another's arms. Love is where you find it and when.

On the soundtrack as we watch various obscure dark gropings and couplings women now in their 60s (or "77 in the shade") talk of how they once couldn't wait to reach this very same Greenwich Village and its fabled freedoms. "I had this fantasy it was a little village with white picket fences," says one sweetheart born 1929. "My friend Mindy was going straight, and guess what—she seduced me."

Another remembers "the first one" who "pushing me down" taught her the prime source of arousal—"I took to it like a duck takes to water." We hear from a Rosie the Riveter of WWII who tells of having to fight the union as a lesbian. Even more applicable to the moment, to Clinton vs Nunn in 1993, is the tough voice that says: "I was always afraid of getting discharged from the WACs because of being gay. It would have been shattering, horrible."

There's even humor: an old gal who talks of the bars of the '30s run by the Mafia. If the joint was raided, the solicitous hoods would say: "Girls, take your neckties off." Sometimes everybody was swept up anyway. "If you wore three pieces of feminine underwear, you weren't booked. If you wore male underwear ..."

The last part of the film goes to Germany as we hear Lenya's incredible "I tell you, I tell you, I tell you we must die," from the Brecht/Weill "Alabama" song. In and out of the concentration camps, lesbians were lumped along with prostitutes, other undesirables, and Jews. Of course the whole Nazi structure was riddled with homosexuality, but that's another story.

If James Agee were alive he'd write six golden paragraphs on the poetry of the title. Suffice to say that nitrate burns, scalds, explodes, and—as film—it disintegrates into dust. "We were too many, too fast, too young, and many young friends died, many," says one survivor toward the end of the movie in what is now the age of AIDS, the age of—even for lesbians—Safe Sex. The age of latex. What a choice—rubber or dust.

NEWSDAY, 4/9/93, Part II/p. 63, John Anderson

Perhaps the most in-your-face moment of "Nitrate Kisses," director Barbara Hammer's self-described "postmodern constructivist collage," comes when gay artists Jack Walsh and Peter Cramer are making love and the Hays Code, early Hollywood's commandments of self-censorship, scroll across the screen. Considering their pose, you have to laugh.

Otherwise, this impressionistic documentary about the disappearance of gay and lesbian history is imbued with sadness. Referring to AIDS—which is a concern but not the sole concern of "Nitrate Kisses"—a speaker says, "I see people, I'm with them, and all of a sudden they're dead." Not just physically, Hammer wants to scream, but historically, laid to rest in our collective memory.

It's a brave film she's made, one that might have used the talking-head approach and treated its subject with an academic starchiness.

Instead, Hammer strings together her own arty footage, such as the swirl of torn and shredded documents and photographs that introduce the film, with scenes from such obscure '30s features as "Lot in Sodom," androgynous photos of such Hollywood icons as Greta Garbo, Marlene Dietrich and Katharine Hepburn and the matter-of-fact lesbianism of Willa Cather.

And she punctuates all the historical references with graphic scenes of lesbian and gay lovemaking. During those scenes, Hammer virtually revels in flesh, especially when aged lesbians Frances Lorraine and Sally Binford are on screen; Hammer makes no concessions to any Vogue sensibilities, but presents every piece of wrinkled skin like it was a flower in bloom.

In her examination of vanished history, she also deals, quite movingly, with the plight of homosexual victims of Nazi Germany. Not only did they face the same horrors as every other group of "undesirables," she points out, they were also, by the very nature of their "crime," deprived of an outraged voice when the horrors were over.

Like the recent "Last Call at Maud's"—which includes testimony from some of the same people who appear in "Nitrate Kisses"—Hammer's film is part of what appears to be a rising tide of lesbian filmmaking. And one which, by virtue of "Nitrate Kisses," Barbara Hammer would appear to be leading.

Also reviewed in:
NEW YORK TIMES, 4/9/93, p. C10, Vincent Canby
VARIETY, 2/1/93, p. 100, Suzan Ayscough

NO REGRET

A Frameline release.   *Producer:* Marlon Riggs.   *Director:* Marlon Riggs.   *Music:* Blackberri and Linda Tillery.   *Running time:* 38 minutes.   *MPAA Rating:* Not Rated.

NEW YORK POST, 6/23/93, p. 30, Jerry Tallmer

[*No Regret* was reviewed jointly with *A Question of Color*; see Tallmer's review of that film.]

NEWSDAY, 6/23/93, Part II/p. 59, Gene Seymour

It's a given that white racism has kept blacks on society's margins. But the great racial dialogue in America hasn't quite figured out how to acknowledge the hardships endured by blacks stigmatized by other blacks. The most interesting work by contemporary black artists has dealt with this marginalization-from-within, and two documentaries opening today at the Film Forum are exemplars of this risky impulse.

First there's the 38-minute "No Regret," which focuses on five men who are black, gay and HIV-positive. Producer-director Marlon Riggs (who likewise fits this description) orchestrates their disparate testimonies with a near-Mozartian balance of delicacy and virtuosity.

When, for instance, the men begin to tell their stories, their faces are only partially revealed; a visual metaphor for the varied ways in which they were in hiding, denial, dread and panic over their affliction; partly, they say, because of the way homosexuality is disdained within the black community. Their full faces become revealed when they disclose how they overcame their fears of disclosing their disease and/or their sexuality to parents, church members or others.

For each man, coming to terms with his disease has allowed him to come to terms with himself. This, in turn, has given them an enlarged, even humorous perspective toward the ways their homosexuality has been stigmatized among other blacks—and how AIDS itself has been treated by mainstream America as well.

The muted passion, evocative imagery and graceful courage of "No Regret" carries more power than any number of presidential task forces on its volatile subject.

Kathe Sandler's "A Question of Color" deals with an equally volatile subject: skin-color prejudice within the black community. Sandler, herself a light-skinned African-American, talks to several blacks from all walks of life, from the dark-skinned mayor Johnny Ford of Tuskegee, Ala., to light or medium-brown kids on Brooklyn streets.

She gets varying reactions and assessments. One constant in their testimonies is their sense that the color complex isn't separate from white racism, but is, in fact, a cruel extension of it.

What distinguishes Sandler's film from other studies of this subject is its open-hearted warmth. It is not treated with self-consciousness or sensationalism, but as a free-flowing conversation with the extended family that is black America. Hers is a tone that, by itself, can begin healing the wounds it uncovers.

Also reviewed in:
NEW YORK TIMES, 6/25/93, p. C15, Stephen Holden

NOTHING BUT A MAN

An Original Cinema re-release. *Producer:* Michael Roemer and Robert Young. *Director:* Michael Roemer. *Screenplay:* Michael Roemer and Robert Young. *Running time:* 92 minutes. *MPAA Rating:* Not Rated.

CAST: Ivan Dixon (Duff Anderson); Abbey Lincoln (Josie Dawson); Gloria Foster (Lee); Julius Harris (Will Anderson); Leonard Parker (Frankie); Yaphet Kotto (Jocko); Stanley Greene (Preacher Dawson).

LOS ANGELES TIMES, 1/8/94, Calendar/p. 6, Kevin Thomas

"Nothing But a Man," one of the finest portraits of African American life ever made, never reached the audience—or racked up the Oscar nominations—it richly deserved when it was released in March, 1965.

It succeeds as a damning portrait of social injustice because it is first of all a work of art—the unpretentious kind that's warm and real and doesn't call attention to itself. Director Michael Roemer and writer-cameraman Robert Young realized that in depicting the timeless story of a nice young couple just starting out, they didn't need any obvious symbolism or added message to convey the evils of racial inequality.

When Duff Anderson (Ivan Dixon) forsakes the freedom of an all-black railroad crew to marry a preacher's daughter and schoolteacher (Abbey Lincoln), he must deal with relentless humiliation by whites in his new job at a lumber mill in a small Southern town.

In telling Duff's story the filmmakers come to the inescapable conclusion that it is not possible for most blacks to live in the United States with dignity, a truth that sadly applies by and large 30 years after the film was made.

NEW YORK POST, 2/19/93, p. 27, Audrey Farolino

It would be nice to be able to say that "Nothing But a Man," the acclaimed 1964 film about racism and its devastating effects on one young black couple, is a beautifully crafted but outdated story about issues that no longer have relevance in the 1990s.

It would be nice, but unfortunately, it would be untrue.

Almost 30 years have flashed by since the movie was cheered by audiences at the New York Film Festival, but time might just as well have stood still when it comes to the hatred that skin color can still provoke, the poverty that can still strangle even the strongest wills, and the tensions that can still rip apart men and women and sons.

Those are the forces at work in Michael Roemer's restrained but heartfelt black-and-white film, which is being re-released for a two-week run at Film Forum 2; it's the first time the film has been seen theatrically in years.

Duff Anderson (Ivan Dixon) is living the itinerant life of a railroad worker in the deep South when he meets Josie (jazz great Abbey Lincoln), a schoolteacher and daughter of a local preacher.

It's easy to see why Duff falls for Josie—she's beautiful, smart, and radiates a calm and graceful dignity. Less obvious are the reasons why Josie falls for the unpolished Duff, who, in his own words, "ain't exactly housebroken." It's his difference that attracts her, she explains—most of the men she meets are "kind of sad," but in Duff she sees an unbent spirit and pride.

Those are precisely the qualities, however, for which the couple will pay a severe price.

"You want to get along, act the nigger," a black co-worker advises Duff after he quietly stands up to a white man at the sawmill, where he takes a job after his marriage to Josie. It's advice that Josie's stern father also dispenses, but it's advice that Duff will never follow, at the cost of that job and others.

But the film doesn't focus only on the unconscionable unfairness of Duff's working plight. It goes deeper, exploring how Duffs growing frustration begins to poison his marriage, and how his stunted relationship with his uncaring, alcoholic father is repeating itself in his own relationship with the son he abandoned a few years earlier.

"Nothing But a Man" is filled with poetic images of towns racked by poverty and people racked by hopelessness (the face of the prostitute Doris is worth the proverbial million words). The actors are low-key but excellent, not only Dixon and Lincoln but also Julius Harris as Duff's father and Gloria Foster as the father's long-suffering mistress.

On the down side, the film occasionally seems artificially stiff and overly restrained as if afraid of stepping on the audience's toes; at least one critic has wondered what an African-American director would have done with the same story.

Even so, "Nothing But a Man" is poignant, disturbing and, sad to say, still all too real.

NEWSDAY, 2/19/93, Part II/p. 61, John Anderson

The loud and insistent statement that "Nothing But a Man," made when first released in 1964 was that black people could be portrayed in an American motion picture as something other than stereotypes or billboards. But it is the film's myriad subtleties that make it the relevant and moving experience it remains nearly 30 years later.

As Duff Anderson—itinerant railroad man, father, husband and grappler with his own soul—Ivan Dixon is neither hero nor villain nor victim. Neither is he particularly likable; he's certainly no Sidney Poitier, no Hollywood icon of beautiful blackness. But his flawed humanity makes him eminently believable. And his struggle to maintain his dignity in the face of both the large and small humiliations of everyday life makes us believe in him, because we're all a little bit like him.

Duff's problems, of course, are particular to the black man in the American South: institutionalized racism; the demands that he sacrifice his self-respect for food and work, the insults and the threats heaped on him as if he's the pack mule of white America. But "Nothing Like a Man" isn't just a litany of white-black abuse; there's plenty of black self-loathing, born of a fear that a man's legacy might turn out to be nothing more than acquiescence and self-delusion.

Duff wants to break this cycle, although the baggage he carries is daunting, and there's little support from his friends and coworkers. When he becomes engaged to Josie Dawson (given a beautifully understated portrayal by jazz great Abbey Lincoln) he's jeered at by Frankie (Leonard Parker) and Jocko (Yaphet Kotto), whose sexual innuendos are crass. Josie's preacher father (Stanley Greene) doesn't approve of Duff or the marriage, and when Duff refuses to "act the nigger," advises him to "use a little psychology; make them think you're going along and get what you want." Preacher Dawson repels Duff, as does his church, with its rapturous congregation mouthing "God will provide"-style platitudes.

And Duff has family problems of his own: a son he's not sure he wants to acknowledge, and his father, Will, a crippled, broken down alcoholic played with a disturbing presence by Julius Harris. Duff's stubborn refusal to play the game will not only lose him jobs and the chance for jobs, but will lead to a confrontation with rednecks who threaten his life. He leaves town and his wife, but his subsequent reunion with Will changes things. He sees himself in Will, and it frightens him; when he sees his son in Will, and in himself, it drives him to go back and repair his marriage and his life.

Produced for less than $300,000, by independent documentarians Michael Roemer and Robert Young—whose black and white cinematography is often stunning—"Nothing But a Man" moves slowly and quietly toward its climax, with a rare grace. But then it's a rare film, and a vitally important chapter in the maturing of American film.

VILLAGE VOICE, 2/23/93, p. 54, Amy Taubin

Unblemished by skintones, the 1964 poster for Michael Roemer's *Nothing But a Man* sold sex, not race. The outline-only depiction of the couple suggested the slightly steamy goings-on that pulled an art house audience—the flash of flesh here an emptiness—and that signified "adult" and, 99.9 per cent of the time, non- or even un- American. That the subject of Roemer's film—racism viewed from a Southern black perspective—made it a lot more foreign than Bergman or Truffaut wasn't anything its distributor wanted to rub in the faces of potential viewers.

Evasive advertising notwithstanding, *Nothing But a Man*, achieved modest success with the largely white audience that, a few years earlier, had flocked to *Shadows*, John Cassavetes's anguished exploration of "passing" in the great bohemian mecca of the North. Three decades later, it seems both remarkable and appropriate that the fledgling, and almost exclusively white male, American Independent Film movement had race so much on its mind.

Propelled by the barely suppressed, righteous fury of Ivan Dixon (the token black on *Hogan's Heroes* and now a successful TV director), *Nothing But a Man* focuses on Duff (Dixon), a union man who gives up a lucrative job on a railroad crew to marry the sheltered, school-teacher daughter (Abbey Lincoln) of a small town, and very collaborationist, Alabama minister. Duff, who's spent most of his life on the road, hasn't married in order to return to his roots. His involvement with the minister's daughter, however passionate, is also a way of denying his alcoholic father and illegitimate son who live in poverty in nearby Birmingham. Branded a "niggra troublemaker" when he tries to organize his fellow millhands, Duff is blacklisted by every boss in town. Faced with a choice between learning to take shit from whites or moving north, he uncontrollably acts out his anger on his now pregnant wife.

Elegantly photographed by Robert Young, who also cowrote the script with Roemer, *Nothing But a Man* opens tentatively. The acting is so subdued as to seem underwater, the direction self-conscious in its striving for documentary-style realism. And why not? It was anything but quotidian for a fiction film to depict the daily life of a black work crew, of a black family. There are a couple of false notes: a close-up (of Yaphet Kotto in a minor part) that screams nobility, a harmonica riff that's an atmospheric cliché. Once the dramatic conflict kicks in the power struggle between Duff and the racist power structure, peopled with just about every white male in town from high school principal to drunken dropouts—the film takes off. Unlike most movies that deal with racism, *Nothing But a Man* never allows us the comfort of an objective position. Locked into Duff's subjectivity, we're made to identify with the humiliating experience of being forced to deny one's humanity for the sake of preserving one's life.

Dixon's tight-lipped performance carries the film. While it's relatively easy for actors to openly express anger, it's harder to maintain—and convey—the rage that's kept in check. What's amazing is that Dixon lets us know that Duff's anger cuts two ways—not only against those who try to make him feel less than a man, but also against himself. Duff inherited his father's attitude that "he isn't good for anyone" (the result of internalized oppression), but he stops short of his father's overwhelming self-destructiveness.

Played by a nonprofessional actor—a former nurse—the father displays an emotional erraticism that's rarely seen on screen. Roemer and Young relied on the actors—many of whom had never been on camera before—to supply an authenticity of behavior, to fill in the moment-to-moment experience of being a Southern black or a Southern white of which they (respectively a German Jew and a New Yorker) had no subjective knowledge. As a Northern white woman, I, too, know the South basically as fiction-codified by Hollywood or the TV news. I have no way of estimating how "true" the film is. I do know that when I first saw it at the New York Film Festival in 1964, it seemed to depict a particularity of experience I'd never seen in a movie before and I'm not sure I've seen since. There are lots of films in which a white man calls a black man "boy," and then the scene shifts to something supposedly more important. *Nothing But a Man*, however, puts us in the position of a man who's called "boy" 50 times a day. Each time, it summons the impulse to fight or flight: each time the impulse is either swallowed or acted on in a way that can't bring satisfaction. And yet, Duff doesn't knuckle under.

Roemer and Young had previously collaborated on a documentary about the impossibility of family life in Sicily's poorest ghetto. Young, who had also made a documentary for NBC about sit-ins in the South during the early days of the civil rights movement, told Roemer that the people he'd met had stories that should be told on film. And if Roemer had never been in the South, as a Jew who spent his childhood in Berlin (fleeing in '39), he had his own experience of racial hatred.

Nothing But a Man was shot in 1963, a moment when it was still possible for black actors to work with white writer-directors to produce a vision of what it was like to be black in America. A year later, African Americans began to demand control of their own stories. Thirty years ago, the film witnessed a specific moment—when the civil rights movement laid bare the ingrained brutality of racism in America. Today *Nothing But a Man* reminds us of the Southern roots of the black liberation struggle; that it in no way seems dated makes it uncomfortably clear that 1963 isn't so long ago.

Also reviewed in:
NEW YORK TIMES, 9/21/64, p. 37, Bosley Crowther
WASHINGTON POST, 7/9/93, Weekend/p. 42, Desson Howe
WASHINGTON POST, 7/10/93, p. D1, Hal Hinson

NOTTURNO

PART I: LOVE HAS LIED; PART II: WINTER JOURNEY: *Producer:* Rene Letzgus. *Director:* Fritz Lehner. *Screenplay:* Fritz Lehner. *Director of Photography:* Gernot Roll. *Editor:* Helga Wagner and Juno Silva Englander. *Music:* Franz Schubert. *Set Decorator:* Allan Starski and Anna Prankl. *Running time:* 240 minutes. *MPAA Rating:* Not Rated.

CAST: Udo Samel (Franz Schubert); Daniel Olbrychski (Franz von Schober); Michaela Widhalm (Josepha); Mareille Geisler (Karoline); Therese Affolter (Magdalena); Traugott Buhre (Schubert's Father); Wojkek Psoniak (Beggar).

NEW YORK POST, 3/26/93, p. 25, Jerry Tallmer

All my life I had thought Schubert's "Trout" Quintet in A major to be one of the sunniest, healthiest pieces of music ever written. My mother even sent it to me as a morale booster back when I was in college.

Well, Ilona, you're not here to see "Notturno." the four-hour, two-part (with intermission) Austrian movie that straightens us both out on this. Franz Schubert was not a sunny, healthy guy. That's the idea I grasp anyway from Fritz Lehner's made-for-television portrait of three separate but representative days in the life of the sexually and socially tormented young composer whose life was snuffed out by syphilis at the age of 31 in 1828.

"Notturno" is one of those films that aches with sensitivity and is packed with fraught. It's as if Ken Russell shot it through a filter of Jean Renoir, or vice versa.

We first meet Schubert (Udo Samel) staring at his hands—he hates his hands—in the charnel house that is the Vienna General Hospital in 1823. He is a grave, round-faced young man with steel spectacles and curly hair, but his hair is falling out. His cynical friend Schober (Daniel Olbrychski), who took him to the whorehouse where he lost his virginity and found syphilis, sends him in.

There is a skeletal inmate of the hospital, a gimpy-legged bum on a wooden bicycle who haunts Schubert throughout the film. One of the pressure points of the movie is when this creature tries to maneuver himself and his apparatus down a long flight of stairs and Schubert just watches, frozen, as his beautiful music swells on the soundtrack. That kind of movie.

The women of the film include a bald prostitute to whom Schubert tips his wig; another who apologizes for giving him the syphilis; Schubert's disapproving stepmother, whom he kisses with passion; Schubert's seductive adolescent stepsister Josefa (Michaela Widhalm), who, if I understand it, indeed seduces him by driving him crazy with a squeaky toy while he's trying to compose a great piece of music; his pal Schober's tubercular girlfriend Karoline (Mareille Geisler), a spitting-blood embodiment of "Death and the Maiden"; and a damned-attractive sort-of-high-class call girl named Magdalena (Therese Affolter), who gets Schubert believing in life and love again—because Schober has paid her to do it.

There are outings, exquisite outings, by boat and by foot-chase through the Vienna Woods. There are intimations of homosexuality. There are all degrees of soul-searching. There is stunning photography and, needless to say, sublime music, though rather more of the former than the latter. Actually, I don't think you'll be bored, though four hours is a long time to read subtitles.

NEWSDAY, 3/26/93, Part II/p. 79, Peter Goodman

It begins in the shabby wards of a Viennese hospital, filled with hopeless, dying men. It ends with terror and betrayal. Between are debauchery, rejection, gluttony, poverty, tenderness, confusion, tremulous happiness and the surprise of love.

Is this what life was really like for Franz Schubert, composer of endless tunes and delightful songs? No one can know, of course, but Austrian director Fritz Lehner's "Notturno," a four-hour fantasy on Schubert's life, fascinates the mind and tugs at the heart.

If "Amadeus" was a hyped-up, overexposed giggle at the expense of Mozart, "Notturno" is the dark side of a similar world, intense, hypersensitive and, ultimately, tragic.

Originally produced for German television and released for theaters in 1988, the film has only now arrived in the United States, in a cooperative venture between the Film Society of Lincoln Center and the Schubertiade festival running concurrently at the 92nd Street YM-YWHA.

Had director Lehner wanted a 90-minute box-office smash, he could have sliced everything but the sex and depravity. But he was interested in trying to understand the last years of the young composer's life. Schubert (Udo Samel, looking remarkably like the composer as shown in contemporary portraits), is depicted as shy and inarticulate, sexually confused, rejected by his brutally bourgeois father, alternately teased and doted on by the circle of rakes and artists who are his friends, and all the while dying slowly of syphilis.

The narrative thread of the film itself is wonderfully tangled. Even those who think they know something of Schubert's biography will be at a loss, at least for the first hour or so. The viewer is plunged directly into Vienna of the 1820s—a noisy, filthy, vibrant community, with children scavenging for food in garbage, prostitutes boldly showing their wares and aristocrats enjoying sinfully lavish parties, while through it all poor Schubert tries to find love, acceptance and understanding.

The first half, "Love Has Lied," follows him the day he is released from the hospital in 1823, trailed by a crippled beggar (Wojtek Psoniak), taken to a party by his debauched friend Franz von Schober (Daniel Olbrychski), later attempting a reconciliation with his father (Traugott Buhre).

Horror is matter-of-fact: a priest who curses the patients, Schober's mistress fainting from consumption in the heat of lovemaking. Eroticism is equally present, from tiny glances to Schober's nonstop carousing.

"Winter Journey," the more somber second half, chronicles the composer's last months in 1828, working frantically through the night as the disease reappears, finding unexpected kindness and affection from his teenage step-sister Josefa (Michaela Widhalm), and dying in the insensitive, uncomprehending arms of his brother Ferdinand.

This is a remarkably sensuous film: It emphasizes the power of certain senses, particularly hearing. Every creak, every scratch is amplified; even drink is heard to the last gurgle. As a result, every note of music has heightened power—and Schubert's music has rarely sounded so strong, anguished and frightening. There are a few waltzes and relatively cheerful *lieder*, but most of the examples come from the composer's agonized late work.

VILLAGE VOICE, 3/30/93, p. 58, Leighton Kerner

This is the film Milos Forman's *Amadeus* might have been had its screenplay been less idiotic and its structure less ramshackle. Writer-director Fritz Lehner, having trimmed a 1986, four-and-a-half hour Austrian TV miniseries to a 1988 four-hour movie, gives us by turns lyrical and grim exploration of Franz Schubert's last years. Those years give Lehner plenty of dramatic material. The few small episodes of conjecture, such as an ironic encounter with a prostitute, work without blurring the central tragedy.

The story opens in 1823, with the 26-year-old, syphilitic composer in a rat-infested hospital, where fellow inmates rob him and trash his manuscripts. Most of his hair falls out because of the disease, and he resorts to a wig sent by Franz von Schober, his wealthy friend and sometime lover. Released from the hospital, he is brought by Schober to a Vienna Woods party, where wine, women, men, and song lure his back into the whirlpool in which he will desperately swim for five more years.

Along the way is a humiliating reunion with the schoolmaster father who never forgave him for whoring and for being a musical genius, and a street meeting with the young woman who transmitted the syphilis and can only murmur a dazed plea for forgiveness. There are other outdoor parties, translated into breathtaking cinema by cameraman Gernot Roll's virtuosic shots of madly careening carriage wheels, dazzling greens of forest and meadows, fireworks, and a symbolically blazing tree.

Minute, grubby detail is also made vital. You don't miss the ink smears on Schubert's fingers as he scrapes the notes onto music paper and tries to make a piano sound what his tortured mind imagines. And there's the final segment of Schubert's delirious, convulsive dying, conveyed with a Dostoyevskian mercilessness that makes the actual, off-screen death superfluous. Leading an irreproachable cast, Udo Samel is both subtly restrained and suddenly gripping as Schubert. Also unforgettable are Daniel Olbrychski as the sadistic-but-sorry Schober, Michaëla Widhalm as the composer's piteous and pitiable sister-in-law, and Mareille Geisler as Schober's consumptive, love-is-worth-dying-from mistress.

Also reviewed in:
VARIETY, 7/27/80, p. 17

NOWHERE TO RUN

A Columbia Pictures release.   *Executive Producer:* Michael Rachmil.   *Producer:* Craig Baumgarten and Gary Adelson.   *Director:* Robert Harmon.   *Screenplay:* Joe Eszterhas, Leslie Bohem, and Randy Feldman.   *Story:* Joe Eszterhas and Richard Marquand.   *Director of Photography:* David Gribble.   *Editor:* Zach Staenberg and Mark Helfrich.   *Music:* Mark Isham.   *Music Editor:* Michael Connell.   *Sound:* David Kirschner.   *Sound Editor:* Fred J. Brown and Michele Sharp.   *Casting:* Jackie Burch.   *Production Designer:* Dennis Washington.   *Art Director:* Joseph P. Lucky.   *Set Designer:* Richard McKenzie.   *Set Decorator:* Anne D. McCulley.   *Special Effects:* Jeff Jarvis.   *Costumes:* Gamila Mariana Fahkry.   *Makeup:* Zoltan Elek.   *Stunt Coordinator:* Billy Burton.   *Running time:* 90 minutes.   *MPAA Rating:* R.

CAST: Jean-Claude Van Damme (Sam); Rosanna Arquette (Clydie); Kieran Culkin (Mookie); Ted Levine (Mr. Dunston); Tiffany Taubman (Bree); Edward Blatchford (Lonnie); Anthony Starke (Billy); Joss Ackland (Franklin Hale); Allen Graf (Bus Driver); Leonard Termo (Bus Guard); James Greene (Country Store Clerk); Steve Chambers (Pick-up Truck Thug); Stephen Wesley Bridgewater (Tom Lewis); Christy Botkin (Sarah Lewis); Luana Anders (Town Meeting Chairwoman); Kevin Page and Albie Selznik (Hale's Associates); Gavin Glennon (Auto Parts Clerk); John Rubinow (Clydie's Husband); Stanley White (Cop in Diner); Joseph Menza (Diner Cook); John Finn (Cop in Chase); John Kerry (Big Thug "John"); Tony Epper (Fire Thug "Al").

LOS ANGELES TIMES, 1/18/93, Calendar/p. 3, Kevin Thomas

Martial arts star Jean-Claude Van Damme would seem to be a godsend for a poor young widow with two children and a ranch coveted by a stop-at-nothing developer. In "Nowhere to Run" the loner Van Damme plays does in fact seem just that: He can take care of the bullies with dispatch, save horses from a burning barn—and even knock over a water tower with a tractor just in time to keep some butane tanks from catching fire and exploding. What's more, he's great with kids (and motorcycles).

There's got to be a hitch, of course, and Van Damme's Sam is a man with a past that could catch up with him at any moment, potentially doing Rosanna Arquette's Clydie more harm than good. Written by Joe Eszterhas and others, the film is simplistic, especially in asking us to believe that Joss Ackland's developer, a smooth-talking, deceptively well-mannered type, would green-light a project before securing all the necessary property.

Even so, it is never less than serviceable and frequently much more. The film represents a new plateau for Van Damme as an actor in that the action is more than balanced out by the love story that inevitably but gradually develops between Clydie and Sam, who is found camping on her property by her small son Mookie (Kieran Culkin, Macaulay's equally talented younger brother) and daughter Bree (Tiffany Taubman). Quite touching, too, is the father-and-son relationship that develops between Sam and Mookie.

The role of Sam must surely be tailor-made for Van Damme, whose slight Belgian accent is "explained" by Sam's French-Canadian nationality. Sam is a man of comparatively few words, but under Richard Harmon's expert direction Van Damme effectively expresses in silence Sam's loneliness, longing and regret for past mistakes as well as his wariness over his growing love for Clydie and her kids. The teaming of Van Damme and Arquette is judicious: The chemistry between them is palpable, and Arquette has the right feisty spirit as a woman determined to hold her ground with the bad guys, which include Ted Levine. There's nice work, too, from Edward Blatchford as a local sheriff torn between his love for Clydie and selling out to Ackland.

Filmed in Sonoma County, "Nowhere to Run" has beautiful scenery and benefits from a spare yet dramatic Mark Isham score. It is a shrewd example of a performer expanding his range while not turning his back on the derring-do that made him a star.

NEWSDAY, 1/18/93, Part II/p. 43, Jack Mathews

The new Jean-Claude Van Damme movie, "Nowhere to Run," which was to introduce us to a new Jean-Claude Van Damme, is such a hodgepodge of old movie ideas and silent hero cliches it's hard to know exactly who the new fellow is supposed to be.

Since the script, co-written by genre scavenger Joe Eszterhas ("Basic Instinct"), most resembles the Western classic "Shane," maybe Columbia Pictures is hoping to make him the new Alan Ladd. Certainly, the two stars share a certain stoic quality on screen, though in the case of Van Damme, it seems to be more a matter of bewilderment.

Van Damme, a Belgian martial arts master who has kickboxed his way through four movies, doesn't seem to have a clue what to do in front of a camera, not when there are words involved. He has a Muscle Beach physique and some athletic grace in the fight scenes, but with all that, he has no presence on screen, no psychological depth. There's nothing going on with him and the camera other than choreography.

Not that Columbia Pictures, which is gambling on Van Damme as a new mainstream action star, did much to help him. Acting lessons would have been nice, some voice training perhaps, but more importantly, they could have found for him a reasonable character to play.

In "Nowhere to Run," directed with no particular distinction by Robert Harmon ("The Hitcher"), Van Damme plays a fugitive with a conscience, an escaped felon and former bank robber who, first out of simple decency then out of love for a good woman, becomes the hero of a modern day range war. Seems that Sam, who escapes from a prison bus in the opening scene, is hiding out on land that belongs to a beautiful widow (Rosanna Arquette) being harassed by a corrupt land developer.

After Sam gets to know the widow, and is befriended by her lonesome son (Kieran Culkin, younger brother of ...), he decides to give the slack-jowled developer (Joss Ackland) and his hired gun (Ted Levine) a dose of their own violent medicine.

Ackland, the sinister South African Krugerrand smuggler in "Lethal Weapon 2," and Levine, the serial killer from "The Silence of the Lambs," are good bad guys, and Arquette acts her heart out trying to be convincing as the grieving widow who falls for the Mysterious Stranger. But this is a story totally dependent on the leading character's ability to hold your interest, and Van Damme's Sam is damned if he can.

SIGHT AND SOUND, 6/93, p. 61, Leslie Felperin Sharmon

Sam, a convict, is rescued from a prison transport vehicle by his former partner-in-crime Billy, who is fatally wounded in the escape. While hiding out in the woods, Sam is drawn to a local family consisting of two children, Bree and Mookie, and their widowed mother Clydie. They are being harassed by property developer Franklin Hale, who wants to buy Clydie's house and land. Sam saves her and the children from some hired thugs. In return, she invites him to stay in her barn. When her nosey occasional boyfriend Lonnie, the local sheriff, discovers Sam, Clydie introduces him as her Quebecois cousin. Hale and his henchman Dunston redouble their efforts to drive off Clydie's neighbours by setting fire to their barn, but Sam manages to save both the horses and the neighbour's life.

Sam's bond with the family grows, especially with Mookie, who misses his father. Clydie tends Sam's wounds after he has been handcuffed and beaten by the jealous Lonnie, who is secretly in Hale's pay. Recognizing a kindred sense of loneliness, Clydie and Sam make love. However, after she discovers his true identity, Clydie sends Sam away, fearing he will bring her family more trouble. Camping out alone once again, Sam is besieged by hundreds of law enforcement officers, but manages to elude them on his motorbike. He returns to Clydie in time to save her from Hale and Dunston, who intend to burn her house down. After quelling these enemies with Mookie's assistance, Sam surrenders to the police posse which has tracked him down, vowing to return someday to Clydie and the children.

Nowhere to Run opens like the beginning of Walter Hill's *48 Hours*, with a fugitive fleeing a chain gang, a graceful bout of stunt driving, and a brief ballet of fisticuffs. Neatly assembled, if a little perfunctory, this opening sequence has all the standard action-thriller trademarks: cars, guns and jokey one-liners. It forms a little bridge between Jean-Claude Van Damme's previous films, all-macho kick-and-shoot flicks, and his new three-picture package with Columbia, of which this is the first, designed to launch him into the mainstream by softening his image. Thereafter, apart from a few strategically placed fight and chase sequences, the dominant tone is sentimental, the main locus of action domestic and pastoral. The outlaw is tamed by the love of a good woman, whose home and way of life are threatened by the forces of modernity. Despite the modern day setting, *Nowhere to Run* is a fair-to-middling old-fashioned Western at heart, complete with burning barns, evil hired guns, fatherless children and a pretty widow. The story is especially reminiscent of *Shane*, particularly in its handling of the relationship between the boy Mookie, played by Macaulay Culkin's elfish younger brother Kieran, and Sam the hardened convict. Even the picture of Van Damme chosen for the poster—stubble-chinned, furrow-browed, sandy-complexioned—recalls Alan Ladd.

Van Damme's epicene beauty and gamine quality set him apart from his action man coevals. He's prettier and slighter than Schwarzenegger, less grim than Seagal, more humane than Lundgren or Norris. His persistent Francophone accent, which each of his scripts must accommodate somehow (this time he's meant to be from Quebec), overlays a rakish charm on his slightly vulnerable persona. He seems to be more popular with discriminating female action fans, perhaps due to his physique's callipygous rear view, exploited in *Nowhere to Run* no less than in his previous films' nude scenes. The attempt to draw in female audiences is further underlined when an early scene of Van Damme reading a porn mag called *Top Heavy* is balanced by joking references to his accidentally revealed penis (Bree thinks it's big, while Clydie describes it as 'average'). Objectification works both ways in the post-feminist action film.

While Van Damme acts more competently than expected, Rosanna Arquette's performance is disappointing, probably less through her own fault than the director's and the screenwriters'. Every time she sucks nervously on a cigarette, previous roles of brittle, more interesting sophisticates are conjured in the smoke. Even in moments of supposedly domestic bliss, she seems chafed by the earth-mother act. One wonders why she isn't selling up, ditching the kids, and moving to Venice Beach to sell crystals and star-fuck. The child actors themselves don't really help things. Tiffany Taubman as Bree is standard issue poppet, while Culkin overacts and lacks the naturalness that is his brother's strongest suit. Joss Ackland and Ted Levine, however, as the baddies, give fine, lip-smacking, moustache-twirling performances.

Although the script distributes its plot devices efficiently enough, judging by the banality of the dialogue, one wonders why Joe Eszterhas commands such a reputation. Robert Harmon, of *The*

Hitcher, directs fights and chases fairly well, and paces things nicely, providing a few camera tricks and plenty of close-ups of Van Damme to meet studio specifications, but is less sure at handling actors. *Nowhere to Run* has failed so far to launch Van Damme into the major star orbit, possibly because it doesn't allow him to do enough of what he does best, apart from being pretty, and that's karate. In fact, the only one to do any kickboxing in the whole film is the horse.

VILLAGE VOICE, 2/2/93, p. 52, Georgia Brown

What becomes an action hero most? Funny accent *mit* muscles? Squint and verbal retentiveness? Whatever, don't believe the hype—like *Entertainment Weakly's* cover story—that kickboxer Jean-Claude Van Damme is crossing over to leading man. Granted, Van Damme has an accent (though it's not Schwarzenegger's Nazi drawl) and doesn't open his trap much, but this Belgian bozo is about as sexy as Action Jackson (the toy). In *Universal Soldier*, Van Damme played a robot quite convincingly, but here, in *Nowhere To Run*, he's got that same eerie blank gaze: The eyes are dead, the expression not brooding but cosmically, almost defiantly bored.

Cowritten by *Basic Instinct's* Joe Eszterhas, *Nowhere To Run* is apparently conceived as an updated *Shane*. Van Damme's Sam is an escaped con, though one who's been serving time for someone else's crime; while hiding out, he camps on the pleasant ranch of a beleaguered widow (Rosanna Arquette). Her spread, and that of her neighbors, is coveted by an unscrupulous developer (played by Joss Ackland) who hires thugs to harass the hapless ranchers (the most villainous of whom is played by Ted Levine, *The Silence of Lambs's* Buffalo Bill). The widow's young son, Mookie (Kieran Culkin, Macauley's younger brother), is attracted to Sam as a suitor to his mother and a father for himself. Come baaaack, Sam.

One *Universal Soldier* joke was that Van Damme's replicant kept taking off his clothes, showing what the actor proudly calls (in *EW*) "my big Belgian ass." The joke is picked up here, as Sam keeps baring his beeg bum to the camera: he's caught skinny-dipping by the widow's two kids, and then in the shower by her and her boyfriend, the sheriff. Mookie also comes on Sam in his tent, leafing through a girlie magazine, *Top Heavy*. "You like boobs!" inquires the kid, adding, "They're gross, totally gross."

"He has a big penis," observes Mookie at the dinner table. "He has an average penis," corrects Mom, who's seen others. Poor Rosanna Arquette: She's come back from Paris for this. The character not only sleeps with creeps, she lights up at breakfast, though supposedly she's fanatic about fresh air and such. But give the Widow Clydie credit for some far-out kids' names: Besides Mookie (after the baseball player or the pizza deliverer?), the girl is Bree (after the call girl?). I guess this is supposed to be a movie-movie. A fatherless boy, Mookie fantasizes about discovering his own E.T., and so he bounces a ball to Sam, who's broken in to borrow the family's salt shaker. Sam, an alien in human shape, doesn't know what to do with a bouncing ball.

I fear I've managed to make *Nowhere To Run* sound immeasurably more entertaining than it is. Trust me, it's dreadful—listless and bland, with absolutely none of the revved-up pace and gore of *Universal Soldier*. And just in case you're tempted to defy me, I'm giving away the snappy punch lines: "Strike three and you're out!" and the killer, "Au revoir, fucker." John Woo, presently directing Van Damme in *Hard Target*, certainly has his work cut out for him.

Also reviewed in:
NEW YORK TIMES, 1/16/93, p. 16, Vincent Canby
VARIETY, 1/25/93, p. 134, Lawrence Cohn

OAK, THE

An MK2 Productions USA release of a Parnasse Prods./Scarabee Films/MK2 Prods./La Sept Cinema coproduction. *Executive Producer:* Constantin Popescu. *Producer:* Eliane Stutterheim, Sylvain Bursztejn, and Lucian Pintilie. *Director:* Luciane Pintilie. *Screenplay (Romanian with*

English Subtitles): Lucian Pintilie. *Based on the novel by:* Ion Biaesu. *Director of Photography:* Doru Mitran. *Editor:* Victorita Nae. *Art Director:* Calin Papura. *Running time:* 105 minutes. *MPAA Rating:* Not Rated.

CAST: Maia Morgenstern (Nela); Razvan Vasilescu (Mitica); Victor Rebengiuc (The Mayor); Dorel Visan (Country Priest); Mariana Mihut (Priest's Wife); Dan Condurache (Lawyer); Virgil Andriescu (Nela's Father); Leopoldina Balanuta (Nala's Mother); Matei Alexandru (Butusina); Gheorghe Visu (Priest on the Train); Magda Catone (Mitica's Assistant); Ionel Mahailescu (Titi).

CHRISTIAN SCIENCE MONITOR, 1/26/93, p. 11, David Sterritt

Not often does a Romanian movie travel from its native land to a major film festival in the West. And it's downright rare for such a picture to appear in a regular American movie theater.

This makes "The Oak," a new film by Romanian director Lucian Pintilie, something of a news item quite apart from its qualities as an energetic "road movie" and a scathing social satire about life in Romania before the recent revolution. The first official co-production between Romania and France to be completed in the past 14 years, it was shot in Romania with French financing and technical aid. After showing at the Cannes filmfest last spring it played the New York Film Festival a few months ago and has now made its American theatrical premiere.

Mr. Pintilie has described "The Oak" in terms recalling Dante's extraordinary "Divine Comedy," summarizing the picture as "a journey through infernal circles, through successive catastrophes." Yet while the film indeed contains more than its share of catastrophes, it also has a furiously sardonic edge, seeing its chaotic events through the eyes of a Romanian woman who can scarcely believe the bizarre realities of her own society.

The heroine, is Nela, a young teacher who lives with her father—a former officer in the secret police—in a ramshackle apartment. Her first adventure comes after her father's death, when her attempt to donate his body to science (in keeping with his wishes) is thwarted by bureaucrats who inform her that they have enough cadavers at the moment.

Nela heads disgustedly for a new home in Bucharest, only to be attacked and badly injured. The good that comes from this is a new friendship with Mitica, a physician who cares for her, and whose own rebelliousness becomes clear when he insists on saving an eccentric old patient after the bureaucrats have declared he should be abandoned. When he dies despite Mitica's help, Nela and Mitica decide to bury him in his hometown, and set off with the police hot on their trail.

Their journey culminates in a burst of violence more explosive than anything they have seen before but ends on a note of hope as the companions meet under the branches of an oak tree and look ahead to the next stage of their relationship.

The combination of savagery and satire in "The Oak" has its roots in Pintilie's outrage at conditions in Romania under former dictator Nicolae Ceausescu, who ran the nation with an iron fist and a good deal of sheer incompetence.

Under that regime, Pintilie's artistic career was as strange as Nela's odyssey in some respects, since a number of his films and plays were banned and then unbanned by censors who apparently didn't know what to make of them. Pintilie also spent many years working in Western Europe, where he relished the freedom to follow his inspirations. He returned to Romania when the authorities softened their hostility and invited him home—only to ban his subsequent movie for a decade, until the revolution allowed it to be shown and to become a hit with the Romanian public.

Pintilie is not pleased with the situation in Romania, even after the revolution; he has criticized the people for reverting to their communist leanings and showing an unhealthy taste for submission to authority. His anger shows through every scene of "The Oak," which paints a portrait of unrelieved national and personal craziness. It is not a smooth or diverting movie to watch, and its metaphors are sometimes hard to follow. As a document of artistically expressed social rage it is quite fascinating, however, and the passion of its feelings is unmistakable. One hopes Pintilie's latest project, a film adaptation of "The Penal Colony" by Franz Kafka, arrives promptly on American screens once it is completed.

NEW YORK, 2/8/93, p. 63, David Denby

You may want to walk out of the Romanian film *The Oak* after the first ten minutes, but I recommend that you hang in there instead, fasten your seat belt, and hold on for the ride. Writer-director Lucian Pintilie, adapting a novel by Ion Baiesu that is set in the late, clownishly inept days of the Ceauşescu dictatorship, rushes from squalor to rage to the most outlandish joking without transition or explanation. Pintilie is a wild man. Yet gradually the film's mood takes hold. Pintilie, who has no more than a minimal interest in plausibility, works at an extreme of disgust that is also exhilaratingly close to joy. The movie combines satire and farce and sheer for-the-hell-of-it defiance.

Pintilie's heroine, Nela (Maia Morgenstern), a violently impulsive black-haired beauty, is the daughter of a secret-police officer who dies. Grief-stricken, she goes on a rampage, encountering nothing but mediocrity and corruption, a nearly universal incompetence, and lies. After failing to give her father's body away to medical science, Nela throws over her life in Bucharest and heads for a provincial city, where she hooks up with a surgeon who is her equal in lawless foolishness. An instinctive anti-authoritarian, the surgeon faces life as if it were a tragedy that could be survived only in a continuous explosion of playfulness. The movie, a refusal of despair, is abrupt, jangled, and shocking. There is, of course, an element of bravado in Pintilie's joking. A little more exposition wouldn't have hurt, and a sequence near the end involving the death of some children is staggeringly inept. But if you get into the movie's mood of violent blasphemy, and accept the conceit that the future of Romania's soul rides on the whims of these two anarchic egotists, then *The Oak* offers an unnervingly happy good time.

NEW YORK POST, 1/22/93, p. 29, Matthew Flamm

There is one thing that must be remembered by anyone watching "The Oak": It takes place in Romania. The sense of chaos—from the squalor in a rural hospital to the way comedy mixes constantly with tragedy—owes as much to the Ceausescu regime as to Lucian Pintilie, the film's writer and director.

This must be kept in mind because otherwise "The Oak," would seem wildly overdone. But one point of this remarkable film is that in Communist Romania everything is exaggerated. Nela, the spirited young heroine whom we meet at her dying father's bedside, screams and scowls like a Learning Annex acting student because that's the normal reaction to this abnormal landscape.

She does take some getting used to. After her father dies, Nela (Maia Morgenstern) sets fire to the apartment to shoo a visitor from the door; insults everyone she speaks to, and, having had her father's body cremated, takes to carrying the ashes around in a Nescafe jar.

Nela is in a constant state of rage partly because nothing works anymore. Her father—a former secret police colonel with a questionable past—had wanted his body donated to science. "It's not bodies that we lack," the doctor tells Nela, turning down her request. "It's refrigerators."

Arriving in the rural town where she's taking a teaching job, Nela is raped by a gang of workers. A policeman tells her "You're lucky you were raped," since that justifies giving her a ride to the hospital.

At the hospital, a doctor throws a patient onto the floor ("If you're not happy here, leave," the doctor says) to provide Nela with a bed.

She soon finds an ally in Mitica (Razvan Vasilescu), a cheerfully defiant young surgeon who disobeys orders and operates on a religious fanatic named Titi whom the authorities would rather see die. (He dies anyway, possibly because Mitica had never performed this kind of operation before.)

"The Oak" moves quickly and matter-of-factly through this shell-shocked world. Expectations have collapsed along with the infrastructure: Nela, full of contempt, seems beyond being surprised, disaster having become pretty much routine.

Some of the more devastating moments in "The Oak" occur as asides. Taking Titi to be buried in his old village, Nela and Mitica meet the local Zorba-like, motorcycle-riding priest, who turns out to have a 5-year-old son dying from a rare disease.

"Some Americans wanted to study him," the priest's wife tells Mitica. But the priest insisted they pay in hard currency for the privilege, and they refused. (The priest also tells his wife not to feed the little boy.)

The madness of Ceausescu (who was obsessed with hard currency) has reached even as far as the countryside.

Nela and Mitica finally witness a disaster they're not prepared for. The incident cements their affair—"The Oak" is a love story made to look like a black comedy. In Romania under Ceausescu, there may have been no other kind.

NEWSDAY, 1/22/93, Part II/p. 61, Joseph Gelmis

As a political satire, "The Oak" has a puckish quality—"What fools these mortals be!"—with a horrific Kafkaesque spin.

It takes us on a picaresque adventure with a rebellious young woman to the hellholes of Romania before the fall of its totalitarian government. It's also an offbeat love story in which the woman finds a soul mate, a fiercely nonconformist. These two are, in effect, a Romanian Adam and Eve for the paradise yet to come. Director Lucian Pintilie offers them as ideals of talent and intelligence and independent spirit that resists tyranny and endures.

"The Oak" is a journey of discovery and, eventually, an exorcism of the heroine's illusions—about her father and the ruling party he had served as a colonel in the secret police. Starting out angry, hostile, belligerent, over the ignoble death of her adored father, whom she feels was a patriot treated disgracefully by the regime for which he had labored, Nela (Maia Morgenstern) cremates her father, carries his ashes in a Nescafe jar on her travels. Her anger startles us and keeps us attentive, at first. But the film keeps getting more interesting as idiosyncratic characters cross her path. And finally we're willing to take a ride on the wild side with her, even though there's no clear destination and she seems to be acting on impulse.

Nela learns from her mother that her father was despicable and from encounters with ordinary people that their privileged life was theft. The Romanian Communist Party functionaries in this scathing black comedy are dolts and blockheads.

The doctor with whom she gets involved, Mitica (Razvan Vasilescu), is everything Nela had deluded herself into thinking her father was—smart, tough, fearless, irrepressibly funny. He defies the party commissar at the hospital where he works and the local functionaries, slaps one, kicks another, is locked up, but eventually freed because first-rate surgeons are scarce.

Their relationship, which starts when he rescues her from a gang of rapists during the lowpoint of her solo travels, has, like the whole film, the feeling of spontaneously happening before you. The film's unsettling blend of comedy and humor is tragic, witty, utterly original and flawlessly acted.

VILLAGE VOICE, 1/26/93, p. 53, J. Hoberman

As it would be difficult to exaggerate the catastrophic combination of brutality, deprivation, and stupidity that constituted daily life under the dictatorship of Romania's grotesque grand *ubu* Nicolae Ceausescu, one has to wonder if Lucian Pintilie's *The Oak* isn't a bit understated—at least in Romanian terms. By any other, however, this relentlessly bleak farce is a movie of imaginative hysteria that rattles with sustained fury. Blink and you miss something outrageous.

The Oak, which is set in the final year of Ceausescu's rule and was included in the last New York Film Festival, begins in the world of allegory. Pintilie's hand-held camera swooshes through an over grown Bucharest housing project to find the inhabitants of one particularly filthy sty watching home movies of Christmases past. The projected image—a little girl unmasking the *Securitate* man dressed as Santa and grabbing his gun to pretend to shoot the jovial bigwigs at some power-elite party—is flanked by all manner of domestic detritus (broken model airplanes, ashtrays overflowing with butts, stained volumes of Marx).

The child in the home movie has apparently grown into the fabulously unkempt Nela, electrifyingly played by Maia Morgenstern. A rangy, angular actress whose austere facade belies a seemingly limitless capacity for jagged, impulse behavior, Morgenstern appears first as a gorgeous hag. Stooped and dissolute, she lurches around the apartment, smoking, sniffling, fussing over her decrepit father—a veteran communist and *Securitate* colonel. The old man dies, knocking over his milk. The projector topples—it's childhood's end. Nela, the literal offspring of the regime, leaves its fetid cloister.

Out in the world, Nela first attempts to donate her father's organs to science, only to be told that "it's not bodies we lack, it's refrigerators." (She settles for an official cremation, which she alone attends, storing her father's ashes in a jar of Nescafe.) Her education continues apace when she's appointed to a teaching position in the provincial town of Copsa Mica. Her first train has to be evacuated when the bridge floods out. Dropped in the river and taunted by a rowdy crowd, she's transferred to another train just before a mob of besotted miners shove on board, punching passengers out of their way.

Welcome to Romania. Nela arrives at the grim factory nexus of Copsa Mica ("If we respected European pollution standards, we'd have to evacuate the city," she's later told). There, insulated, but marked, by her shades and Walkman headset, she's spotted by a gaggle of grinning workers, grabbed, and gang-raped. After a fruitless struggle, a pointless police interrogation, and a ferociously doomed attempt to purchase a sausage in the local market, Nela is dumped in a hospital that doubles as a charnel house. There's no mattress on the bed she's assigned. Nela bounces down on the springs; the woman she displaces goes and sits on the floor.

No less than his heroine, the long-exiled Pintilie is reexperiencing Romania. Although his *Re-enactment*, in which two students restage their tavern brawl for a judge and movie crew with fatal results, is considered the key Romanian movie of the 1960s, Pintilie is far better known as a theater director. He relocated to Paris after his updated version of *The Inspector General* was banned in 1972; over the past decade his burlesque productions of Chekhov and Ibsen have been staged in regional American theater.

The Oak is a similarly manic farce. In the hospital, Nela meets the trim and crazy Dr. Mitica, another fanatic trickster who grins with pain, eschews bribes, and is obsessed with saving the life of the Christ-like patient whom the authorities wish to let die. Both constantly talking, Nela and Mitica take up with each other without any preliminaries. They're kindred spirits, a Dada couple in a dangerously absurd world. Compared to them, the people are a total rabble—Pintilie appears to be an eccentric sort of right-wing anarchist—and, as a love story, *The Oak* suggests a comic nightmare version of *The Fountainhead*. Mitica attacks his superiors and gets arrested but, because he's the best surgeon in the hospital, they're compelled to retry his case while he's asleep, and let him go.

The world runs on booze and drunken resentment; the narrative is a succession of little shocks. When Nela can't swallow her pills—the tap isn't even dribbling its usual brown sludge—she downs the contents of a handy vase. An argument in a moving car is unexpectedly punctuated when an irate pedestrian flings himself on the windshield. Pintilie routinely places the camera inside a crematorium or rubs the viewer's nose in a spinning propeller. When Nela is detained for protesting Mitica's arrest, the first jet of water from the *Securitate* fire hose is directed at the audience. This dramatic tumult is underscored by a backbeat of calculated mismatches, the time of day shifting drastically within a single scene. Nela and Mitica are out camping in a meadow when suddenly night falls, bombs drop, and paratroopers descend.

As breathless as the fiddle break in a Romanian *doina*, *The Oak* swirls around one time too many—all but dropping Morgenstern in the process—before ending, almost anticlimactically, with the greatest atrocity of all. The leitmotif of damaged children peaks when a group of terrorists takes a school bus hostage. But the carnage unleashed (apparently by Ceausescu's order) is curiously calming. By then we're too jaded to care, which may be precisely Pintilie's point. The last image is the norm—a gun pointed at the audience.

Also reviewed in:
CHICAGO TRIBUNE, 11/26/93, Friday/p. F, Michael Wilmington
NATION, 2/15/93, p. 209, Stuart Klawans
NEW REPUBLIC, 2/8/93, p. 24, Stanley Kauffmann
NEW YORK TIMES, 1/22/93, p. C8, Vincent Canby
NEW YORKER, 2/1/93, p. 98, Anthony Lane
VARIETY, 6/22/92, p. 43, Deborah Young
WASHINGTON POST, 8/14/93, p. D5, Richard Harrington

OEDIPUS REX

Producer: Peter Gelb and Pat Jaffe. *Director:* Julie Taymor. *Based on the opera-oratorio (in Latin):* Igor Stravinsky. *Music Performance:* Saito Kinen Orchestra and Shinyukai Chorus, conducted by Seiji Ozawa. *Choreographer:* Suzushi Hanayagi. *Set Designer:* George Tsypin. *Costumes:* Emi Wada. *Make-up:* Reiko Kruk. *Running time:* 60 minutes. *MPAA Rating:* Not Rated.

CAST: Philip Langridge (Oedipus); Jessye Norman (Jocasta); Bryn Terfel (Creon); Harry Peters (Tiresius); Robert Swensen (Shepherd); Michio Tatara (Messenger); Kayoko Shiraishi (Narrator).

VILLAGE VOICE, 3/30/93, p. 60, Leighton Kerner

Julie Taymor, that Off-Broadway-bred genius of puppetry, mobiles, and general phantasmagoria, staged Stravinsky and librettist Jean Cocteau's deliberately marbled oratorio at the Saito Kinen Festival in Japan last year and filmed the startling result. Within George Tsypin's massive, metal-tiered set, American and European singers and Japanese dancers project with irresistible psychological force what the oratorio's creators intended to be a distanced condensation of Sophocles. Had Stravinsky and Cocteau lived to see this film, they surely would have reconsidered their aims.

The familiar e.e. cummings English translation is used to subtitle the sung Latin and narrator Kayako Shiraishi's intense Japanese delivery. The Theban plague is typically visualized by Taymor with montaged birds swooping down and by choristers carrying hideous sculptures of those birds. Suzushi Hanayagi's choreography has mass and weight, and Emi Wada's costumes include clammy extensions of hands and headgear topped off with hieratic, ancient-Greek-cum-Noh masks.

And the show is as strong musically as it is visually. Philip Langridge's tenor is rather soft-grained for Oedipus's florid material, but his manner reeks of vulnerable pride. When all the horrible revelations are in, his last line, "Lux facta est," is sung on a deathly thread of tone, and his soon-to-be-destroyed eyes stare out of the blackness. Jessye Norman's Jocasta is an elemental earth mother, both in scorn for bickering princes and in suicidal torment. (Red ribbons swathe her as she hangs herself.) The other singers and the solo dancers also keep the Stravinskian faith, and Seiji Ozawa conducts the orchestra and chorus toward relentless, logical climaxes. The timpanist sounds like a demon.

Also reviewed in:
NEW YORK TIMES, 3/31/93, p. C15, Edward Rothstein

OKOGE

A Cinevista release of a Kajima Productions/Into Group production. *Producer:* Takehiro Nakajima, Yoshinori Takazawa, and Masashi Moromizato. *Director:* Takehiro Nakajima. *Screenplay (Japanese with English subtitles):* Takehiro Nakajima. *Director of Photography:* Yoshimasa Hakata. *Editor:* Kenji Goto. *Music:* Hiroshi Ariyoshi. *Sound:* Makio Ika. *Art Director:* Kunihiro Inomata. *Running time:* 120 minutes. *MPAA Rating:* Not Rated.

CAST: Misa Shimizu (Sayoko); Takehiro Murata (Goh); Takeo Nakahara (Tochi); Masayuki Shionoya (Kurihara); Noriko Sengoku (Kineo, Goh's Mother); Kyozo Nagatsuka (Touichi, Goh's Brother); Toshie Negishi (Yayoi, Tochi's Wife); Atsushi Fukazawa (Tamio, the Transvestite Singer); Takatoshi Takeda (Tsuyuki, the Bartender).

LOS ANGELES TIMES, 7/31/93, Calendar/p. 3, Kevin Thomas

Takehiro Nakajima's highly entertaining "Okoge" opens at a gay beach somewhere in Japan. Two young women park themselves nearby. One of them is frankly repelled by being in the proximity of so many gay men, but the other, Sayoko (Misa Shimizu), is intrigued, especially by one good-looking couple who tenderly embrace and kiss while in the sea.

Soon Sayoko strikes up an acquaintance with the younger of the two men, Goh (Takehiro Murata), who for about a year has been having a romance with Tochi (Takeo Nakahara), who didn't come out until he was past 40 and still lives with his wife (Toshie Negishi). When Goh's mother (Noriko Sengoku) announces she's moving in with him, Sayoko offers her small apartment as a rendezvous for the lovers.

"Okoge" is thus set in motion. With elements similar to those in "Making Love," "Torch Song Trilogy" and "La Cage aux Folles" but better than any of them, "Okoge" is a well-developed mainstream movie, the kind of contemporary gay-themed film that Hollywood has yet to tackle successfully. That "Okoge"—the term refers to women who befriend gays—was a big hit in Japan with young female audiences suggests just how fed up Japanese women are with the traditional dominant Japanese male who prides himself in masking his emotions and who leads so much of his life away from home.

No art film, "Okoge" is more kitsch than Kurosawa, yet it's a solid melodrama with as much humor as pathos and which strikes a judicious balance between honest sentiment and campy, improbable over-the-top scenes, crowd-pleasers for sure. Although not completely graphic, "Okoge" leaves little to the imagination in its lovemaking scenes.

A kind of Japanese Douglas Sirk, the Hollywood director renowned for bringing style and meaning to soap opera material, Nakajima handles his many shifts in tone with aplomb and catches us up in the lives of his lovers and their friend Sayoko; they and their problems are real enough even if "Okoge" is in form a glossy all-stops-out heart-tugger. Goh and Tochi are likable men but they face a huge challenge in creating a life for themselves in a pervasively homophobic, conformist society.

Goh doesn't know how to keep his mother, who's an awful lot like Harvey Fierstein's mother in "Torch Song Trilogy," from being dumped on him by his married brother—but then Goh has not come out to his family. Similarly, Tochi fears losing his secure office job should he come out. As for Sayoko, we learn via flashbacks that she was raised in a foster home where she was molested by her foster father; no wonder she seeks gay men for companionship yet remain's so vulnerable to ruthless, overpowering straight men.

For a spell, life for Goh and Tochi and Sayoko is idyllic, but by the film's end none is the same person, each having gone through so very much, and Nakajima has elicited splendid, far-ranging portrayals from his stars. In a real sense "Okoge" is an epic saga told with outrageous comic relief and a sharp satirical edge. Much of the film takes place in bars and especially a gay nightclub where Goh and Tochi's friend Tamio (Atsushi Fukazawa), a plump female impersonator, is the uninhibited star of the revue. For all its occasional raucous high-jinks, "Okoge" (Times-rated Mature for sex and for adult themes) resists the Hollywood ending it could easily get away with and ends tentatively, adhering in its final moments to the Japanese tradition of screen realism.

NEW YORK POST, 4/3/93, p. 16, Jerry Tallmer

We are on a picnic in the country with "two cocks and a hen," two men and a very pretty, indeed an adorable, young woman.

"I feel so good with you two," says the girl. "I love you." She sings for them; since this is a Japanese movie, she sings in Japanese. "I'm so happy," she says, sipping from a bottle of wine, leaning back in pastoral, lyrical summer's bliss against her two dear friends who are locked in a loving embrace of their own, man-to-man.

The movie, which despite a few sideslips into caricature, oversimplification and overemphasis will, I think get under your skin the way it did mine, is "Okoge," written and directed by Takehiro Nakajima, who says he looks upon it as a comedy.

Yes, but a comedy with bite.

I've known some terrific young women right here in the good old U.S. of A. who, like Sayoko (lovely Misa Shimizu), have lived quite devotedly and for extended periods of time with male homosexuals. I don't know that I've known any who, like Sayoko, flip page by page through their Frida Kahlo reproductions while the boys are at it, but I mean really at it, in the next room.

Such is what makes "Okoge" interesting. But then director Nakajima sabotages his own originality by giving the girl the by-now overworked Freudian case history (well, maybe not in Japan) of a sexually abusive father—plus, as I say, caricatures of one homosexual's terrible mama (out of Yiddish comedy), another's ferociously unforgiving wife.

The two men, first spied by us and Sayoko on a gay meat rack at the beach, are Goh (Takehiro Murata), a young leather-crafter, and Tochi (Takeo Nakahara), a staid married fellow in his 40s. Goh's apartment no longer being passible—his mother has moved in—they are in dire need of a mating place when the girl appears out of the night at their gay bar and offers the permanent sanctuary of her spare room. A philosopher bartender declares: "I *like* people to discriminate against us. It gives me a thrill. Otherwise were just as dull as all the rest."

Goh also has a terrible older brother (Kyozo Nagatsuka) who wants to marry him off to a cop's daughter. When at breakfast, Goh finally announces his homosexuality, the brother's ditsy wife jumps up and exclaims: "Hah-hah! Fortunately it didn't rain! Otherwise my sash would have been ruined!" The brother reinforces the idiot moment with: "I should have played golf on a day like this."

Goh's mama (Noriko Songoku) eventually comes up with the most memorable theory of all: "When I was pregnant with Goh I cut my finger with a rusty knife and some gay bacteria got in."

Everything accelerates. Tochi quarrels with Goh. "A married guy always returns to his family in the end," the bartender (Takatoshi Takeda) tells the weeping young man. Soon enough, Goh falls in love—at a distance—with another handsome chap. Sayoko, as go-between, picks the chap up for Goh, only to get raped, painfully, and impregnated by this bisexual bully, Mr. Bad News himself.

The film has a lovely Fellini-like scene near the end in which an outing of drag queens with paper parasols in, pouring rain first gets beat up by some loanshark thugs working for the Yakuza, the Japanese Mafia, and then, with a hoot and a holler, gives the bad guys much worse than got. "My eyelashes are gone," is one victor's only rueful lament.

What comes through in this movie is love, affirmation, laughter. Forget the flaws.

NEWSDAY, 4/2/93, Part II/p. 55, John Anderson

Among its several charms, "Okoge" could almost make one optimistic about the state of gay life in this country.

This comedy by Takehiro Nakajima not only tackles sensitive subjects—specifically, the virulence of Japanese homophobia—it does so with uncompromising honesty, and a great deal of humor. But, although gayness is at the film's center, sexual orientation is less important to Nakajima than characters being true to themselves.

In Japanese, *okama* refers to a rice pot, or a gay male; the *okoge* is the rice that sticks to the pot, or a woman who enjoys the company of gays. When Sayoko (Misa Shimizu) meets Goh (Takehiro Murata) and his older lover, Tochi (Takeo Nakahara), on the beach one day, she finds in their affection for each other a vicarious joy. And when the two can't find a room one night, she offers her own, and the three become inseparable.

If there's a questionable note in "Okoge," it is Sayoko's background: In a flashback, we see her torn from her American foster father after the death of her Japanese mother, and placed in a sexually abusive foster home, which causes her to grow up with an aversion for heterosexual males. Is such a disturbed history necessary to explain the Sayoko-Goh-Tochi alliance? No.

But otherwise, "Okoge" is painfully on target, the most harrowing moments coming after Goh, who's being pressured into an arranged marriage, announces he's a "homo," and his mother, Kineo (Noriko Sengoku), starts going out of her mind. Screaming, wailing, she tells herself that when she was pregnant with Goh, she cut her finger with a rusty knife, "and some gay bacteria got in." Her reaction is the most hysterical, but no less irrational, than the reaction of more "civilized" people, all of whom "Okoge" deftly skewers.

VILLAGE VOICE, 4/6/93, p. 60, Lawrence Chua

It sounds almost too good to be true. Takehiro Nakajima's *Okoge* is a wry sexual comedy where the laughter is as human as the caresses. The title of this splashy homo movie derives from the Japanese vernacular for gay men: *okama*, which is slang for "hair dryer," but really means "rice pot." *Okoge* is the crust of rice that sticks to the bottom of the pot, but it also refers to women who associate with gay men. This is, I suppose, as complimentary a term as *fag hag*.

Sayoko (Misa Shimizu of *Traffic Jam*) begins her career as an *okoge* when she sees Goh (Takehiro Murata), a pockmarked leather craftsman, and his lover Tochi (Takeo Nakahara) kiss on a bustling Tokyo gay beach. It's an understandable obsession. Even if neither of them is particularly glossy, Yoshimasa Hakata's camera revels in the burnished glimmer of two Asian men entwined in each other, brother to brother.

Making friends with them in a gay bar, Sayoko is asked by an eavesdropping bartender whether she harbors any prejudice against fags. Her negative response prompts the bartender to say, "I like people to be prejudiced. I get high when they discriminate against me. Without it, gays are just ordinary people." Without missing a beat, Sayoko observes, "You do look ordinary."

Sayoko immediately offers the two men her flat as a love nest. But Tochi's wife tracks them down and trashes the apartment in an Almodóvar-esque spectacle, then demurely threatens to reveal Tochi's homosexuality to his employers unless he breaks off his friendship with Goh. Tochi closes his desires, while Goh tries to come out to his family (with true Asian poise, they ignore him and talk instead about the weather).

Soon Goh becomes interested in a handsome, brooding former soldier. Sayoko acts as the go-between, but her enthusiasm backfires when the soldier rapes her. She has a baby and plunges into abject poverty. Goh, meanwhile, must care for his dying mother, who blames his sexual orientation on "gay bacteria" that entered her body when she was pregnant.

All these strands come together in a pleasantly unexpected resolution. Not once does Nakajima try to mask complexity with community in this warm and hysterical film. Sexuality in *Okoge* is constantly in flux, emerging at the most inconvenient and affirming moments. And Nakajima's *okoge* is no cardboard figure: Sayoko's naïveté belies a complicated history of abusive men and hints of childhood incest. Already anointed by New Directors as a director to watch, Nakajima delights in showing us fierce gay men who are drag queen enough to bash back a carload of gangsters and cry only when their make-up's running.

Also reviewed in:
NATION, 5/3/93, p. 607, Stuart Klawans
NEW REPUBLIC, 5/3/93, p. 28, Stanley Kauffmann
NEW YORK TIMES, 3/29/93, p. C13, Vincent Canby
VARIETY, 2/15/93, p. 87, Rebecca Lieb
WASHINGTON POST, 8/27/93, p. C7, Megan Rosenfeld
WASHINGTON POST, 8/27/93, Weekend/p. 36, Joe Brown

ON THE BRIDGE

A Panorama Entertainment release in association with Direct Cinema, Ltd. *Executive Producer:* Emily Paine. *Producer:* Frank Perry. *Director:* Frank Perry. *Director of Photography:* Kevin Keating. *Editor:* Emily Paine. *Music:* Toni Childs. *Sound:* Peter Tooke. *Running time:* 95 minutes. *MPAA Rating:* Not Rated.

NEW YORK POST, 10/8/93, p. 44, Thelma Adams

It's hard to knock a guy with cancer. But director Frank Perry opened himself up to public scrutiny in "On the Bridge," his faux-intimate documentary of 18 months in his fight with inoperable prostate cancer.

The 1960s director is known for a slew of features from "David and Lisa" to "Mommie Dearest." When diagnosed in 1990, it seemed only natural for him to turn the camera on himself,

Said Perry: "The way to beat it is to want to get up tomorrow and shoot ... to make a feature documentary.

Faced with castration as the first line of defense against a disease that had spread beyond his groin, Perry declined. He embarked on a roller coaster of treatments, both traditional and alternative. The film features trips to Sloan Kettering, a weekend mind-over-body workshop and hugfest with Dr. Bernie Siegel (author of "Love, Medicine and Miracles"), an address by the Dalai Lama, and a psychic healing.

After a particularly brutal seven weeks when Perry discovered the cancer might have spread to liver—and lungs, the director faced the camera on the dunes at East Hampton. With a motion like a surgeon opening his chest to expose his heart, he mimed his unflinching honesty. It is a controlled, candid moment.

It is telling that Perry chose not to film those earlier rocky weeks, those sleepless gray dawns and countless telephone conversations to family and friends in Aspen. Instead, Perry resumed his film when he was back in control, his optimism regained, calling out "cut" to the cameraman.

What's noticeable is not what's in the documentary—which has its moist-eyed moments—but what's conspicuously absent. There are no scenes with kith and kin and their struggles to come to terms with Perry's cancer together and separately. During the film's span, Perry moved to Aspen and divorced his wife of many years.

He dedicated the film to Virginia Brush Ford, whom he married months after he completed shooting "On the Bridge." So much for holding nothing back.

In addition, amid the recent health-care hoopla, it is notable that at the high end, the issue of who's paying the bills never surfaces. Perry has the economic freedom to devote his life to his illness and hop from treatment to treatment, whatever the cost. He is the exception rather than the rule.

On the East Hampton dunes, the Hollywood director intoned: "A deep fundamental truth about anyone can be interesting." But how deep is it? When the film closed with Perry skiing an Aspen slope in expensive gear while directing his cameraman, I saw a privileged man indulging in yet another very expensive form of therapy.

NEWSDAY, 10/8/93, Part II/p. 95, John Anderson

"On the Bridge," in which director Frank Perry chronicles his battle with prostate cancer, isn't so much a triumph of life over death as it is a triumph of art over life.

Despite what would probably be protestations to the contrary, Perry—the director of "David and Lisa," "Mommy Dearest," "Diary of a Mad Housewife"—didn't make a documentary about a man dying. He's made a film that represents his vision of how a man should go about it. Bravely. Defiantly. Searching, with dignity, for a cure. But not, in any event, going gently into that good night.

From the mind-body workshops, to his sessions with his oncologist, to his sessions with his psychic healer, to his radiation therapy, and all along the roller-coaster ride of contradictory diagnoses, we watch Perry maintain his cool. As the disease spreads—or doesn't, depending on which medical authority is weighing in—he repeatedly tells us that living with cancer has made his life more precious. His manner is calm and rational. His own lead actor, Perry stays in character. And he's a likable man, even if he lets us see and hear only what he wants, while leading us to think we're his closest confidant. Some of what he says makes perfect sense, though. Taking a cue from Bernie Siegel, the mind-body guru, physician and author, Perry is convinced that stress and anger are the food of cancer, and that to suppress them is to nourish the disease. Other cancer survivors he interviews back him up, as does his oncologist. Howard Scher, who comes across as the kind of open-minded, understanding doctor people dream about.

"Cancer gave me an edge," Perry says. "I believe that." Sometimes the edge is angry one, such as when a favorable report gets turned on its head, or Perry feels like he's on the "conveyor belt" of medical testing. You expect more anger, though, and a few more tears. But regardless of that, "On the Bridge" is a courageous picture, one that disallows the argument among certain segments of the moviegoing public that they'd rather not watch a film about such a troubling subject—which is, quite frankly, our own mortality. Hell, if Frank Perry could *make* this movie, the rest of us should go see it.

VILLAGE VOICE, 10/12/93, p. 56, Georgia Brown

E. M. Forster's famous aphorism "Death kills a man, but the idea of death saves him," isn't affixed to Frank Perry's wry and scary *On the Bridge*, but it sure sums up this documentary's conclusions. In the broadest sense, the title's bridge may refer to the one between the filmmaker's being and his nothingness, but for a concrete visual correlative, there's that bridge outside the windows of Memorial Sloan-Kettering's cancer wing. (Oh, the wings of cancer.)

Perry (who began directing with his former wife Eleanor on *David and Lisa* and went on to make films like *The Swimmer* and *Mommie Dearest*) was diagnosed in 1990 with inoperable prostate cancer—despite annual checkups. A few months later, the malignancy appeared to have spread to his ribs and lungs. Perry's response, five months into his death sentence, was to call in a two-man camera crew to document his progress, or egress. Most of their unpretentious footage shows an almost ebullient Perry addressing the camera, filling us in on his treatments (conventional and alternative), and sharing his discoveries. In the vanity department, he even bares his ass for the camera—getting his next-to-last radiation treatment.

His first decision, he tells us, was whether to be castrated (to shut off testosterone). He respectfully declines—"Frankly, it was something I didn't want to lose,"—opting for pills and injections, and all the while building other bridges. At one point he says he takes shark cartilage, mushroom tea, and massive doses of vitamin C; he meditates, does imaging, visits a psychic healer for a laying on of hands, and is interviewed by Baba Wawa.

At Bernie Siegel's workshop for cancer patients, everyone on camera looks radiant, testifying, drawing on their inner organs, belting "Amazing Grace." Basically, the message is the same as in group therapies for the well: Connect, get in touch, live. Faced with death, people discover they've yet to live. Perry agrees with a fellow patient, "Cancer gave me an edge." There are other sides to death encounters, of course, but, as one doctor notes, "Optimism helps." Clearly, this purposely rough, helpful diary movie is part of Perry's therapy. The man is a showman, a schmoozer, a struggler.

Also reviewed in:
NEW YORK TIMES, 10/8/93, p. C10
VARIETY, 10/26/92, p. 67, Todd McCarthy

ONCE UPON A FOREST

A Twentieth Century Fox release of a Hanna/Barbera production in association with HTV Cymru/Wales. *Executive Producer:* William Hanna and Paul Gertz. *Producer:* David Kirschner and Jerry Mills. *Director:* Charles Grosvenor. *Screenplay:* Mark Young and Kelly Ward. *Based on the Welsh story created by:* Rae Lambert. *Editor:* Pat A. Foley. *Music:* James Horner. *Music Editor:* Jim Henriksen. *Sound:* Larry Hoki and (music) Shawn Murphy. *Sound Editor:* David Lewis Yewdall. *Casting:* Mike Fenton, Judy Taylor, Allison Cowitt, Gordon Hunt, and Kris Zimmerman. *Animation Director:* Dave Michener. *Art Director:* Carol Holman Grosvenor. *Voice Director:* Kelly Ward and Mark Young. *Visual Effects:* Glenn Chaika. *Effects Animation:* Alfred Holter and Frog Shy. *Running time:* 105 minutes. *MPAA Rating:* G.

VOICES: Michael Crawford (Cornelius); Ben Vereen (Phineas); Ellen Blain (Abigail); Ben Gregory (Edgar); Paige Gosney (Russell); Elizabeth Moss (Michelle); Paul Eiding (Abigail's Father); Janet Waldo (Edgar's Mom); Susan Silo (Russell's Mom); Will Nipper (Willy); Charlie Adler (Waggs); Rickey Collins (Bosworth); Angel Harper (Bosworth's Mom); Don Reed (Marshbird); Robert David Hall (Truck Driver); Benjamin Smith (Russell's Brother); Haven Hartman (Russell's Sister).

LOS ANGELES TIMES, 6/18/93, Calendar/p. 4, Charles Solomon

The new animated feature "Once Upon a Forest" is reminiscent of a school cafeteria lunch: There's nothing in it that's bad for you, but it tastes like leftovers, even the first time around.

"Forest" marks Hanna-Barbera's first entry in the animated feature market since the uninspired "Jetsons: The Movie" in 1990. This modest production represents a vast improvement, but suggests the artists need to continue honing their skills if they want to compete with the Disney, Amblimation or Bluth studios.

When a truck spills a load of toxic chemicals into the forest of Dapplewood, many of the animals who live there are poisoned. Among the victims is Michelle, a little badger who's the niece of wise, irascible Cornelius, who teaches wood-lore to the young animals ("furlings"). As the adult animals have fled the noxious fumes, three furlings are sent to find the herbs needed to save Michelle's life: Abigail, a spunky wood mouse: Edgar, a reticent mole; and Russell, a rambunctious hedgehog. Along the way, the mismatched trio learns the standard lessons in self-reliance, not underestimating others, etc.

"Forest" was obviously made with care, and contains some genuinely touching moments, as when Edgar learns that his mother may be dead and remembers that he was in too much of a hurry to kiss her goodby that morning. Even in weakest moments, the film is never inept as in say, Filmation's misbegotten "Happily Ever After."

The animation is more polished than other Hanna-Barbera feature efforts, but it still looks a bit flat. The backgrounds have a nicely spacious, woodsy feeling.

The songs tend to impede, rather than advance the story. Michael Crawford sings the ballad "Please Wake Up" with his accustomed power, but the lyrics just restate what the audience already knows. They can see Abigail is small ("It's the morning of your life"), and she obviously has to wake up if she's going to live. Ben Vereen has a vocal cameo as Phineas, a loon who's a caricature of a Southern revival preacher, in a long sequence that's unfortunately reminiscent of the crows in "Dumbo."

"Once Upon a Forest" (rated G) is a film parents can safely send small children to, certain that it contains no violence and offers an uplifting message. But adults and older children who accompany them won't be able to help wishing it was a bit more interesting.

NEW YORK POST, 6/18/93, p. 31, Michael Medved

So far this year, Hollywood's much-heralded new wave of feel-good family movies has been something of a disappointment—not only in terms of artistic quality but also when it comes to the suitability of these films for the youngest moviegoers.

Parents felt appropriately outraged for instance, by Disney's PG-rated adventure "A Far Off Place," which featured a half-dozen murders long before the titles even came up, or by the same studio's "Huck Finn," which included startling, unexpected levels of violence—including the utterly gratuitous shooting of Mark Twain's young hero. As for the current PG-13 blockbuster "Jurassic Park," any parents foolhardy enough to bring their 7-year-olds to the theater should put away money for heavy therapy bills in the next few months.

In this context, a charmer like "Once Upon a Forest" is especially welcome—offering the kind of gentle, dreamy entertainment that should enchant kids and keep their parents from dozing off (most of the time). While it's a far cry from the brilliance of "Beauty and the Beast" or "Aladdin," it's easily the best and most satisfying of the handful of animated films released so far this year.

The story, based on fanciful children's books by Welsh author Rae Lambert, centers on four young "furlings"—baby badger, field mouse, hedgehog and mole—who explore the secrets of Dapplewood forest with a wise old badger named Cornelius (played by the voice of "Phantom of the Opera's" Michael Crawford).

During one of their educational rambles a chemical truck crashes on a nearby road, releasing toxic gas into meadows and bogs and threatening their woodland home. The only hope to save the injured little badger, Michelle, is for her three friends to travel to a distant meadow to bring back the medicinal herbs Cornelius needs for her cure.

There's an obvious environmental message here—but it's never as heavy-handed or as relentlessly politically correct as in last years regrettable "FernGully" (also from Twentieth Century Fox). For one thing, "Once Upon a Forest" makes a point of balancing the careless destructive humans with some caring, kindly people who try to clean up the toxic spill and protect the creatures of Dapplewood. As a result, no one need worry that little ones will leave the theaters with abiding hatred for their own species.

What kids—and their parents will remember most is the lovely animation, which is full of flowers and meadows and the pastel colors of spring, with a magical recreation of the play of light and shadow on the forest floor. The animators often overlay images to create an unusual sense of depth and dimensionality, and advanced computer technology contributes to the exhilarating swooping sensation when the three furling friends take to the air in a flying contraption designed by Cornelius.

The richly detailed movements and expressions of all the characters show that the Hanna-Barbara animation studios (who co-produced with Fox) have traveled light-years from the relatively primitive images they created for "The Flintstones" or "Yogi Bear."

The four songs are also a plus here—particularly a plaintive, heartfelt number ("Please Wake Up") crooned by Michael Crawford that should please his many Phantom fans with its resemblance to Andrew Lloyd Webber at his mooniest. It's the work of redoubtable James Horner, who previously composed the marvelous music to "Glory" and "The Land Before Time," but here provides a background instrumental score that sounds at times distractingly heavy.

Horner's insistent, over-dramatic exclamations, deliberately reminiscent of Prokofiev or Elgar, seem utterly incongruous as accompaniment to the on-screen adventures of hedgehogs and field mice. The composer, whose notorious intensity and self-importance have won him the nickname "Ludwig Van Horner" from some of the studio musicians who work with him, ought to lighten up in order to enjoy this sweet, unpretentious, easygoing little picture along with the rest of us.

NEWSDAY, 6/18/93, Part II/p. 70, John Anderson

First, let's get over the shock of having an actual, bona fide G-rated movie to consider. When you take into account what's been on the movie clock recently, it's difficult to got one's hearings after 70-odd minutes of screen time in which no one bleeds.

Now that we've recovered, let's be frank: Disney isn't going to lose any sleep over "Once Upon a Forest," which is a gentle, moralistic animated feature peopled by small animals who are extremely cute, but not particularly original. The story line lacks the scope of a "Beauty and the Beast" or an "Aladdin," and the animation is good but second-rate—the still, painted backgrounds go out of focus when the camera is panning, which is annoying. But it's an intelligent film that tries to instill a lesson to children and will do it without losing them.

The lesson itself isn't new, but it has its timeless quality: Man is oblivious to the damage he causes the environment, and how devastating it is to the small and furry.

In "Once Upon a Forest" we get a critter's-eye view of ecological catastrophe, which sparks the adventures of an intrepid trio of tiny mammals—Abigail the mouse, Russell the hedgehog and Edgar the mole—trying to gather the medicinal herbs they need to save Michelle the badger, after a gas truck accident wipes out their meadow.

They are dispatched into unknown territory by the badger Cornelius (Michael Crawford's voice), who holds classes in woodlore and deportment for the young "furlings" of the forest. He must remain behind though, to tend Michelle, whose very life depends on how quickly Abigail, Edgar and Russell can get back with the medicine.

All three of these characters are refreshing: Abigail is pretty, smart and a leader who knows when to admit she's wrong. Saying goodbye to her parents on the morning of the accident, she displays a perfectly pre-teen mix of love and impatience. Edgar, a short, bookish sort, uses his brains to get the trio out of some tight spots. And Russell, who eats too much, shows his mettle too when push comes to shove. There are some shaky moments toward the end of the film, when the casualties from the gas leak are finally assessed, but the issue of death is sensitively handled.

If you didn't know it, you would assume from the look of the characters, Abigail in particular, that there was a link between "Once Upon a Forest" and "An American Tail," Steven Spielberg's animated film of a few years back. That link is David Kirschner, resident "fantasist" for Hanna-

Barbera Productions, which has been responsible over the years for the Flintstones, Jetsons and the immortal Yogi Bear. In "Once Upon a Forest," Kirschner has married the TV cartoon to big-budget animation, and while the result isn't always as glamorous, it certainly will entertain the short and impressionable.

SIGHT AND SOUND, 11/93, p. 49, Jill McGreal

In the forest of Dapplewood, three 'furlings'—Abigail the wood mouse, Edgar the mole and Russell the hedgehog—take leave of their friends and families and set off for the home of Cornelius the badger who is teaching them the ways of the woods. Cornelius, an eccentric inventor, has built a model of a flying machine—a "flapper-wing'a-ma-thing"—but the furlings accidentally break it in their boisterous play. Cornelius, accompanied by his niece Michelle, takes the furlings on a nature ramble but while they are out, a runaway chemical lorry crashes into the woods and its toxic load is spilt into the undergrowth, apparently killing all the animals who breathe it. Although the furlings are safe on higher ground in Cornelius's home, Michelle is affected by the fumes when she tries to look for her family. Cornelius tells the furlings that the only cure for Michelle's condition is an ancient herbal remedy. But the vegetation of Dapplewood has been destroyed and in the 48 hours that remain before Michelle dies, the three furlings must travel to a meadow beyond the wood. Armed only with a few provisions and a map, they set off on their quest. Their first encounter with danger is with a huge owl who swoops on Abigail and deposits her in his nest. Russell and Edgar plan a rescue but Abigail escapes through her own cunning and the three resume their travels. Their journey is interrupted by a funeral procession of marsh birds, led by the gospel-singing Phineas, mourning the demise of one of their younger members. But the bird is only stuck in the mud and the three furlings rescue him before continuing through the perilous land of bulldozers and cranes until they reach the fertile valley in which they will find the herbs they need. The valley inhabitants are skeptical of success since lungwort only grows inaccesslbly high on the cliff face. But the furlings build a flapper-wing'a-ma-thing and snatch the herb from a crevice as they fly past. Now in possession of both herbs they fly back to Cornelius and revive Michelle. Meanwhile the lorry driver has alerted the authorities to the ecological tragedy and men are suddenly everywhere in the wood. Despite Cornelius's fears that they have come to hunt the animals down, the men instead rescue Edgar from a trap and restore the other animals to health and safety.

The best antidote to this film is probably *Bambi* which, despite my reservations (*S&S*, July 1993) is infinitely superior to this mediocre feature. The forest settings in *Bambi* show a lush and magical place where the rivers sparkle and the depth of the forest is breathtaking. In contrast the backgrounds and designs for *Once Upon a Forest* look cheap and shoddy. The animation is half-hearted and the characters have uncertain designs, making their species indeterminate, The voice characterisations are woeful and it's a matter of wonder that Michael Crawford wished to participate.

The ecological basis for the plot has some possibilities but these are quickly dispatched in the routine 'courageous-children-under-threat-overcome-all' theme, which fails to connect with the larger issue of toxic spillage and its resulting damage to the countryside. Although the press notes indicate that the film's team is committed to environmental issues, the film itself lacks the zeal that might have saved it. The blurb also tells us that the creators turned to nature lore to give each of the characters a distinctive personality. The example given is Edgar's spectacles, based, we are told, on the fact that moles live underground.

Once Upon a Forest also suffers from indeterminacy of location. The gospel-singing marsh birds (the most ill-judged of the sequences) and the American accents of the animals locate the action somewhere between New Orleans and New York, but the name 'Dapplewood' and Crawford's voice point to the Home Counties. It's often been said that co-productions run the risk of crashing in the mid-Atlantic—a warning that should have been heeded here by HTV and their American partners. Children deserve better than this and, at their best, the Hanna-Barbera production team are capable of producing it—viz *Tom & Jerry*, in its early days one of the best children's series ever. The miraculous reappearance of all the animals at the end is a *deus ex machina* which left me rubbing my eyes for fear of having slumbered through some twist in the storyline, but it's the script that needs shaking.

Also reviewed in:
CHICAGO TRIBUNE, 6/18/93, Friday/p. C, Johanna Steinmetz
NEW YORK TIMES, 6/18/93, p. C10, Stephen Holden
VARIETY, 6/28/93, p. 23, Todd McCarthy
WASHINGTON POST, 6/18/93, Weekend/p. 42, Desson Howe
WASHINGTON POST, 6/19/93, p. B8, Hal Hinson

ONCE UPON A TIME IN CHINA, PART 2

A Raw Film release of a Film Workshop production. *Executive Producer:* Raymond Chow. *Producer:* Tsui Hark and Ng See Yuen. *Director:* Tsui Hark. *Screenplay (Cantonese with Chinese and English subtitles):* Tsui Hark, Hanson Chan, and Cheung Tan. *Director of Photography:* Arthur Wong. *Editor:* Mak Chi Sin. *Music:* Richard Yuan and Johnny Njo. *Art Director:* Ma Poon Chiu. *Costumes:* Chiu Kwok Shun. *Running time:* 106 minutes. *MPAA Rating:* Not Rated.

CAST: Jet Li (Wong Fey Hong); Rosamund Kwan (Aunt Yee); Yen Chi Tan (Lan); David Chiang (Luke); Mok Siu Chung (Leung Fu); Xiong Xin Xin (Kung); Zhang Tie Lin (Sun Yat Sen); Paul Fonoroff (Ambassador); Yan Yee Kwan (Chung).

LOS ANGELES TIMES, 1/7/94, Calendar/p. 4, Kevin Thomas

Tsui Hark's rousing "Once Upon a Time in China II" is more a true sequel than most Hong Kong series pictures, which tend to be self-contained. You need to know going in that its hero, Wong Fey Hong (again the boyish, personable Jet Li), was an actual figure, a Canton physician and a proponent for Chinese independence who became a folk hero in the late 19th and early 20th centuries. You also need to know that the reason his lovely relative, his contemporary, but called Aunt Yee (Rosamund Kwan), dresses Western-style is because she has been a student in Britain. In short, it's a big help to have seen the first film in the ongoing series.

This qualification aside, "China II" is a terrific example of dealing with history within a martial arts fantasy context. It's 1895, a turbulent time in the rapidly waning Manchu dynasty. China has just lost Taiwan to Japan, and in Canton the ever-expanding mystical martial arts White Lotus sect declares its intent to free the poor, but concentrates on driving all foreigners out of China. Now the Chinese had plenty of reasons for wishing to do so after so many concessions had been granted to rapacious foreign nations, but Tsui Hark and his co-writers take a progressive view, condemning xenophobia for its own sake and realizing that it would be good for the nation to come to terms with the modern world. A century later the issues the film raises are still pertinent.

Not surprisingly, Wong Fey Hong finds himself in the midst of escalating strife. He, Aunt Yee and his manservant Leung Fu (Mok Siu Chung) are determined to save a group of schoolchildren whose foreign-language school has been burnt to the ground by the White Lotus; meanwhile, Wong meets none other than Sun Yat-Sen and lends his support for Sun's cause in overthrowing the decadent monarchy and turning China into a republic. Although he is eventually cast as the bad guy, you really do have to have some sympathy for Kung (Xiong Xin Xin), Canton's military commander, who simultaneously is charged with protecting the foreigners, curbing the White Lotus and repressing Sun's rebel movement.

Tsui Hark directs with his customary verve, and the martial arts battles are suitably spectacular. "Once Upon a Time in China II," however, is perhaps most notable for the way in which the director and his greatly gifted cinematographer, Arthur Wong, mask an overly modest budget—various Victorian interiors are definitely dime-store—with a dramatic play of light and shadow and a crisp sense of composition. "China II" is a blithe, often humorous action entertainment that nevertheless manages to illuminate a crucial period in China's history.

NEW YORK POST, 9/1/93, p. 22, Lawrence Cohn

China in 1895 is colorfully recreated in the martial-arts adventure "Once Upon a Time in China: Part 2." The historical background adds some dimension to what is unfortunately the usual low-brow, kick-in-the-groin antics.

The title derives from Sergio Leone and his fanciful western and gangster films al'Italiana. But the style of Tsui Hark's would-be epic owes more to Gianfranco Parolini, the Italian director known as "Frank Kramer" who introduced trampolines and acrobatics to the wild West in his three popular "Sabata" films from 1970-72.

Jet Li is the athletic star, a martial artist and doctor who specializes in acupuncture. After proving his prowess in Part 1 of this saga, he heads in Part 2 to Canton with his comic-relief sidekick Leung Fu (played cutely by Mok Siu Chung) and pretty Aunt Yee (Rosamund Kwan).

In their episodic adventures, the three protect Dr. Sun Yat-Sen and assorted English folk from the evil White Lotus sect, a group of religious martial artists who want to kill all foreigners and drive their dreaded Western ways from China.

Though the picture is filmed on the back lot of Hong Kong's Golden Harvest studios, it has enough action, crowd scenes and mobile camerawork to give the impression of an elaborate spectacle.

Jet Li's agility brings to life the rather ridiculous fight scenes, in which missed blows are still attended by noisy "thump" sound effects and levitation is considered normal. Gore is fortunately minimized, but what there is of it rouses the audience.

The Film Forum is to be applauded for helping to bring this form of popular entertainment out of the Chinatown ghetto, but it remains an acquired taste.

VILLAGE VOICE, 9/7/93, p. 60, Joe Levy

Those who follow the history of Hong Kong cinema may recognize martial arts master Dr. Wong Fey Hong—one of Tsui Hark's two protagonists in *Once Upon a Time in China, Part 2*—as a fictional 19th-century hero given 20th-century power by countless print and screen potboilers. Those who follow the history of China may recognize Dr. Sun Yat-Sen—Hark's other protagonist—as an actual 19th-century hero given 20th-century power by the Kuomintang and then the communists, who brought his dreams of a decisive revolution, if not of democracy, to fruition after his death in 1925. A distinctly fabulist mix of turn-of-the-century Chinese history with the more recent past of HK pulp novels and kung fu flicks, *Once Upon a Time in China, Part 2* is the sort of epic that's not about to let facts get in the way of a good kick to the head. In this—the second of Tsui Hark's four films centered around Wong, his sidekick/shemp/disciple Fu, and their Western-dress-wearing romantic tagalong Aunt Yee—the director stages a meeting between his boyhood movie serials and his boyhood history books, uniting the mythical impulses of a Spielberg and an Oliver Stone. Or, better still, imagine what a trip *X* might have been if Shaft had rolled into New York eager to advance Malcolm's cause.

American audiences are unlikely to find any of *X*'s historical weight here, but Hark's crafty, hyper blend of period verisimilitude and pop explosiveness undoubtedly taps a nerve back home, where this tale—set in 1895 against the backdrop of a Boxer-like rebellion and the early revolutionary efforts that sent Sun Yat-Sen into exile for 16 years—has overtones that are by no means allegorical. Hark focuses on a Boxer faction, the White Lotus Clan, a religious sect dressed in white robes who go around burning crosses and setting fires to drive out the undesirables, in this case mostly the British (reminding us of two vastly different groups of American rebels). Their fierce nationalism—itself a play on the Cultural Revolution—is used to put in motion a debate over xenophobia and identity that must have particular import in a Hong Kong set to revert from British to Chinese rule in 1997. There, even Hark's pop explosiveness has a sort of historical resonance; though the kinetic energy of *Once Upon a Time in China* may seem cartoony to Americans, it's also one way of depicting the turmoil of a period when seismic cultural shifts surfaced and were repressed every few years on the road to revolution.

Hark opens with opposing reactions to the West's incursion on China: first, the ritual purification of the White Lotus, who preach death to foreigners and believe, just as the Boxers actually did, that their religious fervor makes them invulnerable to swords or bullets; then Wong, Fu, and Aunt Yee on a Canton-bound train full of Brits, the two men valiantly following Yee's lead as they try to down their first Western food in a rickety dining car ("It's cooked?" asks Wong, looking at his steak incredulously. "How do we know it's fresh?"). That initial scene bursts with the flash and filigree typical of HK cinema: bodies fly through the air, fires flare, and swords are drawn (only to wilt when tested against the flesh of the White Lotus's leader, Kung), and the excessive energy, precise choreography, and rubber swords are all bent around the edges, revealing a bit of slapstick. Throughout *Once Upon a Time in China*, Hark reverses polarities, as often as not staging his action sequences with a humorous eye (the climatic battle between Wong and Kung in the White Lotus temple takes place on a teetering stack of tables, suggesting a vaudeville balancing act) and his comic relief with the same droll control he brought to the rollercoaster *Peking Blues* (though he's hardly above the occasional piss joke or Three Stooges noggin knock).

When Wong, Fu, and Aunt Yee arrive in Canton for a medical conference, they find the White Lotus dogging their every step. Yee is attacked in the street as a "fake foreigner," Wong's lecture on Chinese acupuncture before a British audience—with Sun Yat-Sen serving as his translator—is cut short by a flaming-arrow attack, and the White Lotus burn down the foreign language school, leaving a group of young children in need of a protector with Wong the only man man-enough for the job. The trio shepherds the children to the British consulate, where they find Sun and come under attack by both the White Lotus and the provincial government, looking to silence Sun's talk of revolution. Hark comes close to a statement of purpose here when, treating the wounded, the U.S.-trained Dr. Sun and the Chinese-trained Dr. Wong unpack their instruments: scalpels and acupuncture needles side by side, they work together to save the day (get it?).

But mostly, things are more complicated than that. Though as a hero Wong aligns himself with Sun, as a character he's trapped between Sun's revolution, based on American and French democratic ideals, and the White Lotus's hatred of all things foreign. He's constantly reminded of his essential identity—when the Western-schooled Yee is repulsed to find she's sharing a dinner of dog with him, when the Brits turn him away at the consulate gates because they can't understand him, when he misses his final rendezvous with Sun because neither he nor Fu can read the pocket watch Sun has given them. Wong simply isn't as able to cope with Western ways as Sun or Yee, but neither is he attached to the Chinese purity championed by the White Lotus. As Wong, Jet Li gives this predicament a cool, magnificent precision, tracing a straight line between befuddlement and anger.

Visually, Hark pursues a golden glow as magically real as his subject matter. Grandly lit and exquisitely costumed, *Once Upon a Time in China, Part 2* veers awfully close to Merchant-Ivory chic for Hong Kong action, especially when a visit to the British consulate finds the local governor dancing to Mozart with the Westerners. That classy veneer is one of the many conceptions of the "Western"—as genre, as imperialism, as high culture—Hark plays with, pits against itself, and then slices to ribbons. Refracting pro and anti-Western sentiments through the prisms of history, ideology, and fairy tale—all the while building not toward resolution but instead toward glorious midair hand-to-hand combat sequences that confirm Twyla Tharp's massive impact on Hong Kong—Hark crafts a film of simple pleasures without a simple message.

Also reviewed in:
NEW YORK TIMES, 9/1/93, p. 13, Stephen Holden
VARIETY, 6/29/92, p. 66, Fred Lombardi

112TH AND CENTRAL: THROUGH THE EYES OF THE CHILDREN

A Flatfields release. *Executive Producer:* Stephon Barnatt, Cedric Brodie, David Harrell, Cleophas Jackson, Marzina Scott, Hector Soto, Violeta Soto, Darrell Straight, Lorenzo Straight, Nia Mydra Tiggs, Yolanda Woods, and Gabriel Wright. *Producer:* Jim Chambers, Vondie Curtis-Hall, and Hal Hisey. *Director:* Jim Chambers. *Director of Photography:* John Simmons.

Editor: Michael Schultz. *Music:* Delfeayo Marsalis. *Sound:* Veda Campbell. *Running time:* 108 minutes. *MPAA Rating:* Not Rated.

NEW YORK POST, 8/18/93, p. 28, Matthew Flamm

It's an old rule of journalism that you do not get too close to your subject. What happens when you do can be seen in "112th and Central: Through the Eyes of the Children," an important documentary that might have been twice as powerful had its makers been a little more detached.

Shot in the aftermath of last year's Los Angeles riots, the film also seems to suffer from having been regarded as therapy by some of those involved in its production. That's a shame, because, overall "112th and Central" achieves what it sets out to do, which is to show from the inside the neighborhoods that exploded.

It's a worthy cause all around. Documentary filmmaker's Jim Chambers, Vondie Curtis-Hall and Hal Hisey have included some 25 black and Hispanic students in the actual making of the film—giving them video cameras with which to interview family and friends, and having them introduce themselves and their stories in the setting of a youth center they attend at 112th and Central in Watts.

The results have an engagingly unpolished feel. A young girl named Violeta Soto recites a heartfelt poem ("Don't condemn my poverty/Don't condemn my beautiful skin") in front of a burned-out building. A grade-school-age boy named Cleophas Jackson interviews his friends in a manner that owes more to Jay Leno than Dan Rather ("So how did you feel about the riot?").

And Yolanda Woods, a beautiful but grim 16-year-old ex-gang member, talks with terrifying matter-of-factness of going out on drive-by shootings: "All I had to do was sit in the car and just kick it."

The novice filmmakers even get to interview the LAPD's new chief, the remarkably diplomatic Willie Williams, who says the Simi Valley jurors who acquitted the four officers in the beating of Rodney King "didn't understand what it meant to be a police officer." (There is no follow-up question on the subject of race.)

But the "children" are only one part of "112th and Central." The lion's share of the documentary features O.G.'s (Original Gangsters) from Watts housing projects talking about the gang truce that has been in effect since the riot.

Their testimony of the toll drive-bys have taken on young lives is indeed moving, and once again we're inside a world that has generally been identified by its most sensationalistic attributes.

But the gang members repeat their reconciliation theme (or rather the producers, who should know better, let them repeat it) over, and over. Altogether too much screen time also goes to the reciting of verses by a poet named Kartoon.

It looks as if the adults on this project were overly fond of playing healers—or overly fond of their subjects and couldn't resist letting the kids dictate their coverage.

"112th and Central" could have been pruned of perhaps a third of its 108 minutes. But you still come away enlightened.

NEWSDAY, 8/18/93, Part II/p. 53, Jack Mathews

One kid, I don't know how old, early teens, shows us the scar of a bullet wound on his sternum and tells how he was shot twice while walking a few blocks to his girlfriend's house.

A pretty, 16-year-old girl named Yolanda Woods describes her social life as "drugs, partying, doing 'drive-bys,' having fun," without the suggestion or hint of irony.

An 11-year-old boy says people are crazy to riot in their own neighborhood; next time, they should go outside and take it out on their real enemies.

These are snatches of interviews with youths who watched last year's L.A. riots from the other side of the television screen. They are children of the ghetto, and they were there, right there, when the not-guilty verdicts from the first Rodney King beating trial were handed down and their neighborhood burst into flames and violence.

Their views have been collected, partly by themselves, partly by professional filmmakers, in "112th & Central: Through the Eyes of the Children," a remarkably alert documentary that was begun within weeks of the April, '92 riots.

Reportedly prompted by a comment made at a postmortem bull session about the riots that was hosted by filmmakers Jim Chambers and Hal Hisey, "112th & Central" offers a raw, occasionally unfocused, never less than compelling glimpse into the mindsets of the kids who live there, or, more to the point, into the future of America's inner cities.

That off-hand comment, from actress Mimi Savage, was that it would be an eye-opener to know how the children in Watts viewed the firestorm from within, what they think caused it, whether they hold out any hope for their own lives. With those questions guiding them, Chambers, Hisey and co-producer Vondie Curtis-Hall went into the community, met with about two dozen black and Hispanic youths living near 112th and Central, and made them both the subjects and co-creators of their unique film.

The participants, between the ages of 8 and 21, were provided with video cameras, sound equipment and a series of instructional courses, then formed into teams and sent out to sift through the still-smoldering emotional rubble of their community to see where it would take them.

It's a mixed bag of people, situations and attitudes offered by "112th & Central." There are interviews with some of the same officials we saw pushing their political agendas on the network news, and there is some earnest commentary there. But of infinitely greater interest are the sessions with people living in one of the five housing tracts that give Watts as diverse a personality as the five boroughs of New York, and a social structure as volatile as Bosnia-Herzegovina.

From members of the Crips and Bloods, L.A.'s most fearsome gangs, we learn that housing projects like Nickerson Gardens and Jordan Downs function like proud, warrior nations. That the gang members regard themselves as soldiers, and their drive-by shootings as strategic, retaliatory strikes. Everyone else is a civilian. One of the gangs even has its own war memorial, a wall celebrating members who died in battle.

In the course of the movie, we see the still-innocent faces of kids who might join those gangs some day, and we hear from thoughtful, middle-age gang alumni, Veterans of Urban Wars, who somehow survived, and now, with children of their own, condemn the nightmare they helped create.

We meet Kartoon, a 35-year-old ex-gang member who has spent most of his adult life in prison and now speaks in elegant rap verse, about the rage that got him there. And most memorably, we meet Yolanda Woods, the somber girl who talks about going out on drive-by shooting forays as if she were discussing street racing.

During the film's production, Yolanda announces she is pregnant and is looking forward to having the baby. But when her boyfriend is killed in a drive-by shooting, she is shattered, and opts for an abortion. Too dangerous to walk a baby in this town, she reasons.

In the end, Yolanda speaks hopefully, if vaguely, about her future, about getting a job, having a family, living a different kind of life, and it seems clear that it is the first time she has given it any thought at all. The message of "112th & Central" is that we have to give these kids better reasons for looking to their future than the fear of not having one at all.

VILLAGE VOICE, 8/24/93, p. 58, Manohla Dargis

A triumph of good intentions, *112th & Central: Through the Eyes of the Children* proves the limits of formalism by being a surprisingly affecting, vaguely ineffectual documentary about life, death, and South Central L.A. Shot in the wake of last year's riots, it's the joint effort of filmmakers Jim Chambers and Hal Hisey, and actor Vondie Curtis-Hall, who along with six other industry types (like actress Virginia Madsen) decided to see what the children of Watts thought of what the adults of Los Angeles had rained down.

The film starts up with an explosive montage that intercuts footage of the King beating with images from the riots—the word virtually everyone favors—but doesn't stick around to stoke the fires. Instead, little Violeta Soto stands in front of the ruins and declaims, "My young life is ready for someone to mold." From there the rebellion serves as a launch for five loosely connected sections that range from family and friends to police brutality, and include the direct, creative participation of a few dozen youngsters ages eight to 21 (some of whom are billed as executive producers). Organized primarily around on-camera interviews, many conducted by the kids themselves, *112th & Central* uses found footage judiciously, wielding news clips less to support arguments than to work in a counterpoint. The result is a more dynamic editing style than is found in most standard-issue docs, one that, if not exactly Vertov-like, generates impact.

Documentaries that lean on interviews often force connections between speakers not only to make arguments but to fashion a sense of linearity when history acts otherwise. That's why so many witnesses end up saying much the same thing, as filmmakers gently (or not so gently) build their case with each new edit. There's an invisible guide in *112th & Central*, as well, but one with a difference. Two young boys sit in a church, scrubbed, suited, and deadly serious, and one of them says that during the riots "I kind of felt like an endangered species to my race." In another sequence, a dumpling of a little boy asks a little girl, "Has the riot affected you in any way?" He listens intently as she answers yes and wonders why the rioters didn't go into other communities to vent their rage.

The most remarkable sequence in *112th & Central* zeros in on gangbanging, especially those Original Gangsters who, during the riot, helped negotiate the truce that's still in effect. Rigorously unsensational, the interviews not only chronicle the terms of the cease-fire but paint a picture of men for whom gangbanging was once life but now equals death. There's a predictable degree of macho posturing, and the guys skimp on historical detail (there's nothing here, for example, on how the original Crips and Bloods were born from the ashes of the Panthers), but it's a terrific bit of urban ethnography nonetheless. When one O.G. claims "Positive things are going on, baby, you know what I'm saying?" it's impossible not to agree.

At one point, ex-banger turned poet Kartoon limns the differences between gangbangers and their folks as one that's not just generational but philosophical, as a choice between "moms and pops" who said *no* and fellow bangers who said *sure*. Although intriguing, his take is about as deep as the film's cultural explanations go. Avoiding so-called professional evidence (though author Mike Davis [*City of Quartz*] does make a guest appearance), *112th & Central* instead hinges on the first-person testimony of historical agents both grand (new police chief Willie L. Williams) and humble. The usual problem with this sort of thing is it can leave false or faulty testimony unchallenged and unexamined. Kartoon's ideas about Southern parents and Northern children are rich with potential, but the film cannot begin to tap it.

When one of the students (and executive producers), Yolanda, reveals she ran with gangs because "I was having fun, drinking, partying, doing drive-bys, having fun ..." she sounds less like a disciplinary problem than a baby Bonnie Parker, stoned on kicks and blood. As *112th & Central* opens, Yolanda, who's been enrolled in half a dozen schools during her short life, is pregnant and radiantly happy. By the time the film ends, though, her life has taken a dreadful turn. Still, against the odds, she and the other young filmmakers hold to hope, which just might be enough for now.

Also reviewed in:
NEW YORK TIMES, 8/18/93, p. C18, Stephen Holden
VARIETY, 5/10/93, p. 237, Richard Natale

ONLY THE STRONG

A Twentieth Century Fox release in association with Freestone Pictures and Davis Films. *Executive Producer:* Victor Hadida. *Producer:* Samuel Hadida, Stuart S. Shapiro, and Steven G. Menkin. *Director:* Sheldon Lettich. *Screenplay:* Sheldon Lettich and Luis Esteban. *Director of Photography:* Edward Pei. *Editor:* Stephen Semel. *Music:* Harvey W. Mason. *Music Editor:* Robin Katz. *Sound:* Henri Lopez. *Sound Editor:* Robert Rutledge and Steve Bushelman. *Casting:* James F. Tarzia. *Production Designer:* J. Mark Harrington. *Art Director:* Annabel Delgado. *Set Decorator:* Barbara Peterson. *Set Dresser:* Skip Schields and Michael Calabrese. *Costumes:* Patricia Field. *Make-up:* Isabel Harkins. *Fight Choreographer:* Frank Dux. *Stunt Coordinator:* Artie Malesci and Frank Dux. *Running time:* 96 minutes. *MPAA Rating:* PG-13.

CAST: Mark Dacoscos (Louis Stevens); Stacey Travis (Dianna); Geoffrey Lewis (Kerrigan); Paco Christian Prieto (Silverio); Todd Susman (Cochran); Jeffrey Anderson Gunter (Philippe, Jamaican Gang Leader); Richard Coca (Orlando); Roman Cardwell (Shay); Ryan Bollman (Donovan); Christian Klemash (Eddie); John Fionte (Cervantes); Joselito "Amen" Santo (Javier); John Gregory Kasper (Coach Kasper); Phyliss Sukoff (Mrs. Esposito); Antoni Corone (Green Beret Sergeant); Mellow Man Ace (Student Rapper); Felipe Savahge (Brazilian #1); Luis Esteban (Brazilian #2); Jim Vickers (Police Sergeant); Mark Salem (Cop #1); Joann Dukes (Newscaster); David Luther (School Security Guard); Adeniri S. Ajamu (Chief Ajamo); Alan Jordan (Chop Shop Foreman); Frank Dux (Welder); Tony De Leoni (Mechanic #1); Diego Perez (Mechanic #2); Diane Fraind (Teacher #1); Henry Fraind (Teacher #2); Salvador Levy (Cuban Coffee Drinker); Junior Biggs (Jamaican Dealer); Iseline Celestin (Haitian Woman); Donna Kimball (Donovan's Mother); Steven G. Menkin (Doctor); Stuart S. Shapiro (John); Sergio Pereira (Silverio's Bodyguard #1); Michael F. Lagapa (Silverio's Bodyguard #2); Marq Withers (Philippe's Bodyguard #1); Dwight D. Woods and Ernest Simmons (Jamaican Gang).

LOS ANGELES TIMES, 8/27/93, Calendar/p. 16, Michael Wilmington

"Only the Strong" is an "inspirational" youth movie, a vehicle for karate star Mark Dacascos, which suggests that America's high schools—or at least Miami's—are a crime-ridden chaos of disgusted teachers and buttinsky administrators, and that the streets outside are controlled by sadistic drug dealers who kill, strip cars, overact and set fire to the schools with swaggering impunity.

It also suggests that the only way out of this hell is to take the multiracial school's 12 worst hoodlums and teach them *capoeira*, an obscure Brazilian martial art based on hip-rolling dance movements and practiced with a boombox on playgrounds.

Give "Only the Strong" points for novelty: It tries hard not to be the same old kung fu claptrap. Now take away all its points, because no matter how hard it tries, it is the same old claptrap.

Once again villains sneer, swear and menace the women. Once again buddies die, authority figures go ballistic, subsidiary villains get creamed and our hero, pushed to the brink, challenges the worst heavy to a slam-bang winner-take-all brawl—this time on a moon-lit beach surrounded by torch-waving thugs. Once again Might makes Right—or is it Right makes Might?

Capoeira was apparently developed by Brazilian slaves to dupe their masters into thinking they weren't fighters but dancers. And "Only the Strong" would like us to think it's not just more stateside chop-socky but a musical—or a social drama on school violence, "Lean on Me" with head butts. But watching the softly ingratiating Dacascos and his dirty dozen shake their booties to the *capoeira*, or take field trips to the Everglades, is bizarre, anachronistic: huge, sunny, cheerful images in the midst of a social firestorm.

Then there's the villain: crack/hot-car czar Silverio. Actor Paco Christian Prieto wants to make sure that we comprehend that Silverio is scum: His fancy glowering is right in the vein of the silent-movie mustache twirlers who kept demanding the deed to the ranch and strapping down the heroines at the sawmill. When Silverio—upset that his cousin (Richard Coca) is part of the new capoeira craze—shows up to arch his eyebrows, snort and make trouble, the movie leaps from "inspiration" to inanity. "Strong's" director-writer (Sheldon Lettich, of Jean-Claude Van Damme's "Lionheart" and "Double Impact"), co-writer (Luis Esteban), hero and villain (Dacascos and Preto) are all martial artists, and perhaps they've deluded themselves that cinema, like karate, consists of the same moves repeated endlessly—that the heat of battle will make it all fresh.

Not so. "Only the Strong" (rated PG-13) misses its kicks. Striving for novelty, it achieves cliché. Effortlessly.

NEW YORK POST, 8/27/93, p. 27, Lawrence Cohn

An attempt to replace the ultra-violence in the kung fu genre with balletic grace falls flat on its face in "Only the Strong," a silly exercise in musical mayhem. Younger audiences may dig the dance steps.

Likely to make more of an impact than the ill-fated "Lambada" films of three years back, this opus introduces the Brazilian craze of capoeira, which combines dance moves with disabling high kicks. Also fresh to the screen is star Mark Dacascos, a handsome but wooden performer. He may be aiming to be martial arts' answer to Gene Kelly, but acting-wise he makes the stone-faced black belter Don (The Dragon) Wilson (whom he resembles physically) seem like John Gielgud by comparison.

Cast as an ex-Green Beret who returns to his native Miami, Dacascos is the kind of do-gooder who's easy to dislike. Far more fun is the larger-than-life villain Paco Christian Prieto, who looks like Robert Davi on steroids. He shares with Dacascos an agility in capoeira but wants to use the force for evil, like training his cadre of drug dealers in self-defense.

Dacascos gets his high school to give him the dozen worst malcontents, whom he proceeds to reclaim via kung fu cum dance training. Director Sheldon Lettich aborts the picture's hold on reality by staging several violent set pieces, including a knife fight, in which the worst that happens is a nosebleed. Ear-splitting sound effects make each blow sound lethal, however.

An illiterate script credited to Lettich and Luis Esteban is filmed with cliches and outright boners, notably when a teacher introduces our hero to the class as "a former graduate of Lincoln High." Nice work, teach!

Action highlights include the mano-a-mano confrontations of Dacascos and the much taller Prieto, as well as the hero's weird battle against a man hidden inside a welder's helmet (played by Frank Dux, who served as the film's fight choreographer). We never get to see the guy, who seems modeled after Robert Ginty in his "Exterminator" film series.

Sexy actress Stacey Travis is wasted as a Lincoln High teacher who's an old flame of Dacascos. Thanks to a PG-13 rating her renewed romance with him is treated to a fast fadeout.

Except for Travis, this is a male-intensive cast which might have generated some camp entertainment given its "let's fight and dance together" format had the director been Pedro Almodovar. Or for that matter, Robert Wise and Jerome Robbins might have turned the picture into "South Side Story." Tokenism is evident in a finale where the students put on a capoeira demonstration to a cheering crowd at school, featuring one young lady dancing and kicking. Too bad she wasn't featured in the training sessions or given a single line of dialogue.

NEWSDAY, 8/27/93, Part II/p. 77, Jonathan Mandell

"Only the Strong" begins and ends with two Brazilians practicing capoeira (pronounced cop-WAY-ruh), an especially exciting martial art that features lightning-quick Pele-style backflip kicks set to Latin music.

That is, unfortunately, the only time we see these Brazilian performers—one of whom, Joselito (Amen) Santo, choreographed the capoeira fights and trained the rest of the cast. But what they do is clearly the inspiration for this movie, a standard thwack opera with a few differences.

Mark Dacascos plays Louis Stevens, a Green Beret who learns capoeira while stationed in Latin America. His tour of duty completed, he stumbles across his next crusade not below the hillside mansion of a Colombian drug cartel, nor even inside the nuclear submarine taken over by a CIA-trained renegade maniac, but at his alma mater, Lincoln High School, in Miami.

After visiting an old teacher who has become dispirited by his failure to reach the new generation of city students, Stevens gets into a kick-fight after school with several local drug dealers. Surprisingly, he wins. The students applaud. His old teacher is impressed. "You've just done what professionals haven't done in five years. You've got their attention."

Thus re-inspired, the, teacher lures the hero into an experiment: Can Stevens take Lincoln's dirty dozen, 12 of the worst students in the school, the "bottom of the barrel" as they say a couple, of times, and, by teaching them the art of capoeira, make model citizens out of them!

If there is no great suspense about the outcome, there are several surprises for a movie by a director like Sheldon Lettich, a Marine veteran of Vietnam who has helped make some of the noisiest, most patched-together Stallone, Chuck Norris, and Van Damme vehicles: no bare breasts or spurting blood, a low death count, just a few weapons, not even much foul language, and relatively little right-wing propaganda, homophobia, sexism and racism. Indeed, in the first half, the filmmakers seem to be making a stab at being socially responsible, leavening the fight scenes with what might be called human moments and even a messsage: Yes, we can all get along (we just have to learn how to kick butt).

But, like a teacher insecure about keeping the kids' attention, the filmmakers soon lose their nerve and their imagination, and, discarding their (comparatively) subtle formula, go with what they know which is the broad, the brutal and the berserk (staying just on the edge of PG-13). With the introduction of the villain Silverio (Paco Christian Prieto), an evil drug lord who conveniently happens to be a capoeira champion, "Only the Strong" becomes only the stupid—the usual, illogical over-the-top action, including punchkick battles with both a chainsaw and a blowtorch.

Newcomer Dacascos, a gymnast and soap opera veteran whose father *and* mother were martial art champions, has been a kung fu king since the age of 7, and he executes the newly learned Brazilian leaps, flips, kicks and punches with athletic grace. His appearance is pleasant, and his acting is unobtrusive; his performance is at least as good as any of the current action heroes.

But the most exciting sequences are still those brief shots of the real capoeira artists such as Amen Santo, who are actually—gasp—dancing. The filmmakers should think about giving bigger play to them in their next action movie if they want capoeira to become the next kung fu, rather than the next lambada.

SIGHT AND SOUND, 1/95, p. 52, Verina Glaessner

Louis Stevens is a Miami Lincoln High School graduate who joined the Green Berets to fight against drug lords in Brazil. Disillusioned by failure, but now a master of *capoeira*, he returns to his old school to see his teacher Mr Kerrigan. There he is shocked by the lack of discipline and the extent to which the pupils have become the victims of a culture of drugs and violence. He challenges a Jamaican drug dealer who is intimidating a pupil. The dealer attacks him, but Louis leaves him beaten.

Louis suggests to Kerrigan that he gives him twelve of the school's most troublesome pupils to train in *capoeira*. The staff agree, and Kerrigan finds a deserted fire station for Louis to use as a *dojo* (a special place for training). Despite initial lack of enthusiasm, the twelve are gradually won over. Among them, Donovan volunteers to make a fresh mix of the traditional *capoeira* tape Louis uses for the class, and Eddie agrees to be Louis's first pupil. Orlando, who spends his free time stealing and rebuilding cars for his gang-leader cousin Silverio, quits. Louis tracks him to a basketball court. His attempt to woo him back is interrupted by Silverio and his sidekicks.

Orlando returns and Louis takes the boys to the coast where they practice *capoeira* in natural surroundings. Returning to school, they are met by Silverio, who demands that Orlando leave the school to work permanently for him. The police arrive and Orlando reluctantly goes quietly with him. Silverio and his gang then attack the school. Kerrigan is threatened and Donovan is killed. Following sensational television coverage, Louis is barred from the campus. He seeks out Silverio at his 'car shop' where the henchmen attack him. In the mayhem Louis' class arrives. Silverio agrees to a one-on-one contest. A circle forms around them. Louis succumbs to a brutal attack. Then the class begins to sing a *capoeira* song. Magically Louis revives and begins spectacularly to fight back. With Silverio laid out unconscious on the ground, the police arrive. Later, at the graduation ceremony, the *capoeira* class put on a demonstration.

The twist Sheldon Lettich gives this generic martial arts piece is to root Louis' fighting style in *capoeira*, the traditional dance/martial art of Brazil. Given *capoeira*'s radical and liberationist roots, this is no bad thing. *Capoeira* was memorably used alongside allusions to Brazil's mythic heroes by the Brazilian *cinema novo* of the 60s, especially by its prime exponent Glauber Rocha. Sadly, little of these distinctive folk roots survives the transfer to Miami—although the film seems to argue that it should. The music, for instance, though it is pleasant enough, is remixed by one of the pupils to be more easily assimilated by Louis's "dirty dozen", but only in its most 'primitive' form is it able to awake within Louis the primeval power to fight back against Silverio.

Sheldon Lettich has put in time with Sylvester Stallone (he wrote the script for *Rambo III*), yet he is careful here to eschew high-tech violence. Instead he returns the genre to its roots in 70s Hong Kong martial arts cinema, specifically the work of Bruce Lee. It is to the film's benefit that the action frequently takes place in ordinary streets, where daily life proceeds in its usual fashion. After all, for all its drama, the struggle is not between titans but between the kids and the gangs on the block.

Otherwise Lettich touches the usual generic buttons. Martial arts are revealed as a force of nature and depicted through a mixture of 'heroic' rituals—all those blazing torches, bonfires and circles of observers within which two chosen combatants struggle for supremacy. It's effective enough, but the character of Louis is problematic. Despite his back-story struggles against drug cartels, he remains a curiously detached figure, a mix of Mary Poppins and Action Man who is never driven—by his own sense of personal degradation, as in the Hong Kong films, nor by the need to avenge Donovan's death. The scenes of painful, masochistic physical rehabilitation after brutal physical punishment which usually stand for motivation in this genre are missing. Yet there are slim shards of an "aesthetics of hunger ... of violence (but not primitivism)" which the *cinema novo* manifesto espoused. It's there in the characters of Orlando, unprepossingly adenoidal as he is, and his authentically inarticulate cousin Silverado. Apart from generalities about personal freedom and the world outside the "hood" (which we never see), in the end Louis is incapable of answering Orlando's key question. Drugs, theft and killing pay, Orlando says. What's Louis got to offer?

VILLAGE VOICE, 9/7/93, p. 62, Julian Dibbell

Only the Strong sure has ambitious geopolitical ends. Harnessing the funky, fluid energy of the Afro-Brazilian martial-art/dance-form called capoeira, this breezy little piece of Hollywood exploitation stands poised to break Hong Kong's worldwide monopoly on the cinema of balletic violence, a/k/a chop-socky flicks.

It could happen. As Louis Stevens, former Green Beret returned to his screwed-up old inner-city Miami high school to turn things around by teaching capoeira, leading man Mark Dacascos (a person of pointedly indeterminate color) is no Jackie Chan, but he's an agile and well-trained capoeirista, and it's the form itself, clearly, that stars in this film, to thrilling effect.

Burdened by only the barest skeleton of a plot (a well-paced and comfortably predictable love child of *The Principal* and *Rambo*, with the reactionary individualism of both blessedly toned down to a murmur), capoeira's exhilarating vocabulary of swoops, whirligigging kicks, flying handstands, and impossibly twisting torsos is freed to do its stuff.

The producers let that stuff get done with a minimum of cross-cultural "adjustment," beefing up the rustic swing of the capóeira music with a hip-hop treatment and ignoring capoeira's noncontact emphasis by staging abundant fight scenes full of rich, crisp sounds of blows in the best chop-socky tradition.

The hip-hop touch underlines a natural affinity between capoeira and the increasingly Afrotropic youth culture on both sides of the color line. And those crackling, elaborately choreographed fights, one hopes, augur a long-lived genre of capoeira movies soon to take its rightful place alongside its kung fu cousins.

Also reviewed in:
CHICAGO TRIBUNE, 8/27/93, Friday/p. I, Steve Rhodes
NEW YORK TIMES, 8/27/93, p. C8, Stephen Holden
VARIETY, 9/6/93, p. 28, Brian Lowry
WASHINGTON POST, 8/27/93, p. C7, Richard Harrington
WASHINGTON POST, 8/27/93, Weekend/p. 37, Joe Brown

OPPOSITE SEX, THE: AND HOW TO LIVE WITH THEM

A Miramax Films release of a Once Upon a Time/Outlaw production. *Executive Producer:* Jeffrey Silver. *Producer:* Stanley M. Brooks, Robert Newmyer, Davis Guggenheim, and Caroline Baron. *Director:* Matthew Meshekoff. *Screenplay:* Noah Stern. *Director of Photography:* Jacek Laskus. *Editor:* Adam Weiss. *Music:* Ira Newborn. *Music Editor:* Charles Martin Inouye. *Choreographer:* Andrea Lawent. *Sound:* Robert Janiger and (music) Philip J. Flad, Jr. *Sound Editor:* Glenn T. Morgan and Wylie Stateman. *Casting:* Richard

Pagano, Sharon Bialy, and Debi Manwiller. *Production Designer:* Alex Tavoularis. *Art Director:* Pamela Reis. *Set Decorator:* Stephanie Ziemer. *Set Dresser:* Michael Allowitz and David Deignan. *Costumes:* Carol Ramsey. *Make-up:* Jeanne Van Phue. *Running time:* 86 minutes. *MPAA Rating: R.*

CAST: Arye Gross (David Crown); Courteney Cox (Carrie Davenport); Kevin Pollak (Eli); Julie Brown (Zoe); Mitch Ryan (Kenneth Davenport); Phil Bruns (Irv Crown); Mitzi McCall (Freida Crown); B.J. Ward (Gisella Davenport); Jack Carter (Rabbi); David DeCastro (Beer Vendor); Donald Brown (Crackerjack Vendor); Aaron Lustig (Movie Bully); Connie Sawyer (Waitress from Hell); Steven Brill (George); Davis Guggenheim (Pitcher); Craig Alan Edwards (1st Baseman); John Demita (Chipper); Lisa Waltz (Lizbeth); Kimberlin Brown (Leeza); Kimber Sissons (Tracy); Kevin West (Tour Guide); Justin Shenkaro (Bobby); Mindy Mittleman (Cindy); Tess Foltyn (Hanna); Jensen Daggett (Cheerleader); Andrea Evans (Jules); Frank Birney (Priest); Carrie Cline (Periscope Girl); Gino Conforti (French TV Announcer); Johnny Most (Basketball Announcer).

LOS ANGELES TIMES, 3/29/93, Calendar/p. 2, Kevin Thomas

David and Carrie are such an appealing couple you have to wish that their romance was happening in a much better movie than "The Opposite Sex." As long as the filmmakers stick with the two of them, they're on solid ground. But it unfolds in a most off-putting and unconvincing context.

The sometimes rocky progress on of David (Arye Gross) and Carrie's (Courteney Cox) romance—he's wary of commitment and of losing his freedom, she fears losing her identity—is entirely credible and engaging.

Director Matthew Meshekoff and writer Noah Stern take a stab at updating "Abie's Irish Rose" only to back off of it—perhaps realizing how out of date that would be—to such an extent that at the finish, when it no longer matters, we still don't know for sure whether Carrie is Catholic or Episcopalian. They stick with this tack just long enough for some crude, unfunny caricatures of Jews and WASPs.

They also have trouble with the way they handle David's and Carrie's best friends. Until the film's last few sentimental minutes David's best pal Eli (Kevin Pollak), although he's meant to be funny, is consistently just plain obnoxious. Since Carrie's confidante (Julie Brown) is wise and witty, why does she always wear ludicrously garish clothes, jewelry and wigs? What is the point the filmmakers are trying to make with her kookie appearance?

The problems created by the way in which the two key supporting characters are treated point to the filmmakers' fundamental uncertainty as to when to be serious and when to be funny—and in what manner and to what degree. Not until the end do they acknowledge—and then only lightly—what a negative impact the crass Eli, in his selfishness, jealousy and immaturity, has had upon David all along.

The filmmakers also indulge in a plethora of asides, composed mainly of various characters addressing the audience directly—which aren't amusing or inspired enough to accomplish anything except to serve as needless distractions that slow down their picture's pace.

"The Opposite Sex" (rated R for language and sexual dialogue), which was originally scheduled for release in November, 1991, under the title "Rules of the Game," tries for substance but proves to be as skittish as its yuppie couple.

NEWSDAY, 3/27/93, Part II/p. 23, John Anderson

"There are two kinds of creatures in the wild kingdom," begins "The Opposite Sex," "the predator and the prey. And when we start predating, they'd better pray ... "

We didn't. And we're sorry. We walked right into a movie expecting something we hadn't seen before (OK, so we had suspicions) and got what we deserved, déjà vu all over again.

"The Opposite Sex..." takes the less than original view that young single men are beasts in heat, young single women only want romance and commitment, and that true love will change people. Who said this wasn't a comedy? But it's also formulaic at best, insulting at worst, and thanks only to the raft of stylistic devices director Matthew Meshekoff employs does it escape total tedium.

David (Arye Gross) and Carrie (Courteney Cox) are good-looking singles who experience lust at first sight: She's on the sidewalk, and he's peering at her legs through a periscope installed in the basement tavern. (Why the well-bred, Ivy League-educated Carrie should then seek out someone who's already established himself as a voyeur seems contrary to her character, but character in a movie like this is an expendable thing.) She and David then have one of those caustic-but-cute exchanges that seems destined to get them to the altar, even though she's waspy, he's Jewish, etc. etc. etc.

They also have the requisite best pals, who act as combination confidants and Greek chorus: Eli (Kevin Pollak) is the standard-issue beer-and-babes-forever kind of guy, who lives vicariously through David's sexual encounters, eggs him on to even greater depths of degradation and balks when David finally gets serious; Zoe (Julie Brown) is Carrie's pal, frantic and antic.

Characters talk to the camera, pictures of people talk to the characters, TV nature programs narrate David and Carrie's courtship rituals, a scene from "It's a Wonderful Life" shows up, as does the "Tell Me More" number from "Grease." But there's a lot of emphasis on debauched behavior by immature males in this film. Is this funny? Sure, but not in "The Opposite Sex."

Also reviewed in:
NEW YORK TIMES, 3/27/93, p. 15, Janet Maslin
VARIETY, 3/29/93, p. 83, Christian Mørk
WASHINGTON POST, 3/29/93, p. D2, Hal Hinson

ORLANDO

A Sony Pictures Classics release of an Adventure Pictures Ltd./Lenfilm/Rio/Mikado Film/Sigma Filmproductions coproduction with the participation of British Screen. *Producer:* Christopher Sheppard, Roberto Cicutto, and Jean Gontier. *Director:* Sally Potter. *Screenplay:* Sally Potter. *Based on the novel by:* Virginia Wolf. *Director of Photography:* Alexei Rodionov. *Editor:* Herve Schneid. *Music:* David Motion and Sally Potter. *Choreographer:* Jacky Lansley. *Sound:* Jean-Louis Ducarme. *Sound Editor:* Kant Pan. *Casting:* Liubov Vlasenko. *Production Designer:* Ben Van Os and Jan Roelfs. *Art Director:* Michael Buchanan, Michael Howells, Stanislav Romanovsky, and Igor Gulenko. *Set Designer:* Christopher Hobbs. *Set Dresser:* Constance De Vos, Floris Vos, Rashid Sharafutdinov, Feodor Shoekhmedov, and R. Majsoyvtov. *Special Effects:* Yury Borovkov and Viktor Okovitey. *Costumes:* Sandy Powell. *Make-up:* Morag Ross and Tamara Fried. *Stunt Coordinator:* Steve Dent and Oleg Vasiliug. *Running time:* 92 minutes. *MPAA Rating:* Not Rated.

CAST: Tilda Swinton (Orlando); Billy Zane (Shelmerdine); Lothaire Bluteau (The Khan); John Wood (Archduke Harry); Charlotte Valandrey (Sasha); Heathcote Williams (Nick Greene/Publisher); Quentin Crisp (Queen Elizabeth I); Peter Eyre (Mr. Pope); Thom Hoffman (William of Orange); Kathryn Hunter (Countess); Ned Sherrin (Mr. Addison); Jimmy Somerville (Falsetto/Angel); Dudley Sutton (King James I); Elaine Banham (Orlando's Mother); John Bolt (Orlando's Father); John Byrne (Courtier); Lol Coxhill (First Butler); Sarah Crowden (Queen Mary); Robert Demeger (Third Valet); Anna Farnworth (Clorinda); John Grillo (First Official); Roger Hammond (Mr. Swift); Peter Hayward (Harpsichordist); Anna Healy (Euphrosyne); Barbara Hicks (Second Older Woman); Toby Jones (Second Valet); Olivia Lancelot (Young French Woman); Cyril Lecomte (Young French Man); Alfie McHugh (Courtier); Mary MacLeod (First Older Woman); Sara Mair-Thomas (Favilla); Aleksandr Medvedev (Russian Sailor); Hugh Munro (Second Butler); Thom Osborn (Doctor); Oleg Pogodin (Desdemona); Simon Russell Beale (Earl of Moray); Matthew Sim (Lord Francis Vere); Toby Stephens (Othello); Jerome Willis (Translator); Viktor Stepanov (Russian

Ambassador); Terence Soall (Butler); George Yiasoumi (Valet); Giles Taylor (Singing Valet); Andrew Watts (Counter Tenor); Jessica Swinton (Orlando's Daughter).

CINEASTE, Vol. XX, No. 1, 1993, p. 36, Pat Dowell

Sally Potter's *Orlando* is a gorgeously attired costumer about the nature of costume, an elaborately filmed sendup of the idea that clothes and setting make the man (or woman). And, keeping the shape of Virginia Woolf's 1928 fantasy biography, it presents English history *en traveste*, one might say, as well as the two more universal artifices, the genders, male and female.

Writer, director, and co-composer, Potter has reimagined Woolf's most popular creation (it made Woolf a celebrity). Potter's Orlando keeps the conceit—an Elizabethan gentleman lives into the twentieth century and becomes a woman in the process (played throughout by Tilda Swinton). But Potter jettisons the historical lady love who inspired Woolf's flight of fancy. Orlando was an elaborate valentine to Vita Sackville-West and centered on her loss of the family manse, Knole, to entailment, the British tradition of male-only inheritance.

Potter has wisely toned down the novel's blithe upper class hauteur, and in the process made of Orlando an allegory of class as well as gender. Still, it's not exactly a saga of the salt of the earth. Orlando is a noble youth, as the story begins, whose home is visited by Queen Elizabeth I (played by an almost equally famous queen, Quentin Crisp).

Gifted with a house and commanded to long life and beauty—"Do not fade, do not wither, do not grow old"—Orlando proceeds to adventures in England's succeeding epochs, and wrestles with the big questions: Death (1600); Love (1610); Poetry (1650); Politics (1700); Society (1750); Sex (1850); and Birth (undated, beyond history, presumably).

Each period has not only its theme, but also its style and palette. Russet and gold bedeck Elizabeth's era, then blue and silver and black for the court's sojourn on the frozen Thames in 1610, which includes one of the film's most startling images: the King and his nobles laughing at the sight of a peasant woman with her arms full of fruit, frozen in a glassy portrait under the river ice.

Autumnal is the look of Orlando's hilarious tussle with a down-at-heels poet (playwright Heathcote Williams) looking for a patron but unable to resist skewering Orlando's verse as "trivia from the dabbler's hand." Earth colors do service for a rather wan episode at the Khan's palace when Orlando becomes a diplomat as England's imperial age begins. Lothaire Bluteau, the tenacious and trembling new Christ in *Jesus of Montreal*, looks rather lost in the robes and turbans.

In this desert episode devoted to the "manly virtues" and inchoate bonding, Orlando rejects war (Potter giving the sex change an impetus Woolf did not) and awakes as a woman, rising from her morning ablutions as Venus from the sea, naked to our eyes as Orlando the man never was.

The film indulges in a certain disingenuousness in its director's avowed attempt to track an essentially genderless soul through its two sexual incarnations. "Same person, no difference at all," Orlando says of the transformation, and, turning to look into the camera lens, "Just a different sex."

And yet Tilda Swinton is never unmistakably male (nor ever meant to be, I'm sure) despite the opening narration's claim that "there can be no doubt about his sex, despite the feminine appearance that every young man of the time aspires to." Swinton is a luminous presence, coltishly masculine but ever present in the feminine. When she metamorphoses, she creates an inescapable impression that the character has evolved—with all the attendant notions of "progress" entailed, so to speak, in that movement—from male to female.

At times in *Orlando*, this seems to be—in a movie almost defined by the sidelong glances and remarks its heroine shares with the camera—a secret aside to the audience that no amount of interviews to the contrary can successfully contradict.

From the point of transformation on, Orlando has battles aplenty to fight, just to hold the ground he occupied as a man. In an eighteenth century salon sugarcoated in white and powdery pastels, Orlando, now a woman rather mysteriously returned to England after a very long time away, is informed by Alexander Pope, Joseph Addison, and Jonathan Swift that "Most women have no characters at all—present company excepted, of course."

Even more to the point is the bailiff's announcement to Orlando that she is being sued for her property, first because she is dead, secondly because she is now a woman, "which," the bailiff's companion chimes in helpfully, "is much the same thing."

Catapulted into a Brontean world of forest green and deep purple for the Romantic Age, Orlando finds a Byronic lover who hails from America and who hies off to revolution. Interestingly cast in this role, as Shelmerdine, is American television movie stalwart Billy Zane, who has longer eyelashes than Swinton. Orlando gives birth, presumably to his child, after staggering through a twentieth century battlefield. She erupts into literary independence in the gleam of steel and leather for the film's indefinable present-future.

Each era is gently lampooned, even in its music, co-composed by Potter and David Motion. Susceptible to being labeled New Age, these ethereal compositions and the movie's light, glancing blows against the empire, fueled less by rage and earnestness than by a saucy wit, may curdle the film's pleasures for American critics, some of whom have already labeled *Orlando* "dull" or "shallow."

It's superficial, all right, but in the deepest way. Potter uses surfaces to expose the underlying assumptions of a world in which appearances shape people's lives. Wealth, class, nationality, and gender are all a matter of costume, setting, and accessories for Orlando. The manipulation and rearrangement of these surfaces constitute style, and that, as much as anything, appears to be Potter's target in her comments on English history—as well as her method of satire.

The look of the film changes as the centuries pass, but the tone of the film remains resolutely anachronistic (will it look 'timeless' in twenty years, I wonder?). "Terrific Play," Orlando says to the camera after seeing *Othello* performed in 1610. In that aside, he doesn't conform to our notions of Elizabethan speech and, by such means, he seems ahistorical in every historical moment, which befits the embodiment of anachronism, a creature who defies time. In this way, Potter, following Woolf's lead, loosens the character's earthly bonds, frees him and her to be what they (we) want.

In its playfulness with history and its faith in visual eloquence and the artistic power of fantasy, *Orlando* shares the formalist stance of an eccentric strain in British filmmaking, one that includes Peter Greenaway and Derek Jarman, as well as Michael Powell, whom Potter thanks in *Orlando*'s credits.

Like Jarman and Greenaway, Potter stages painterly tableaux. She features Swinton communing with the camera in asides, by word and gaze. *Orlando*'s camera movements tend to emphasize these antidramatic positions, with Alexei Rodionov's camera swinging in slow arcs between two conversationalists, or matching Orlando's pacing in a meadow—only moving in the opposite direction, against the flow, as it were, or against the crowd.

Tilda Swinton, who looks to do for Nineties art cinema what Delphine Seyrig did for the innovators of the Sixties, is most identified with Jarman's films. Potter uses Greenaway's designers, Ben Van Os and Jan Roelfs, to fabricate her emblematic rather than realistic recreations of different historical periods. *Orlando* even has the same gravely mocking tone of Greenaway's seventeenth century *film noir*, *The Draughtsman's Contract*.

The lightness of touch, the droll command of literary and social allusions, and the effortless sense of fashion, can't help but bring to mind Powell as well as Greenaway and Jarman. *Orlando* belongs also to the same contemporary sensibility that produced another swooning coproduction with an eye on the past and its head in the future—*Zentropa*.

What is Potter's very own, however, is *Orlando*'s triumphal tone. It has the air almost of a proud processional, and yet overall it's cheekily unabashed in its celebration of the female. And the propertyless female at that. Orlando's century-long struggle over the house is portrayed ultimately as a confinement. Her true property is a manuscript, which, as her twentieth century publisher (it's Heathcote Williams again) tells her is "really very good." It will even sell, he says, "provided you rewrite it. You know, increase the love interest, give it a happy ending."

What Potter can see clearly is that property and inheritance, the happy ending Vita Sackville-West longed for, binds Orlando into her status as elevated chattel. Less clear to me, however, is why Orlando, a being so clearly headed for a life outside the normal parameters, longs for a child, especially in this age of family values, when the political right wing has staged a full-court press to convince men and women how much they want to parent.

When Shelmerdine asks Orlando why she wants a child, she answers with a question: "Perhaps for love!" But in the United States, if not in England, public debate is increasingly preoccupied with the right to love but not procreate. The idea that love and sex do not necessarily entail reproduction (and vice versa) is at the heart of the right's panic-stricken hostility to feminism and homosexuality.

Orlando, who seeks "company," as the narrator says at the beginning of the film, ultimately finds it in a child. Potter has given Orlando a daughter instead of the novel's son, and thus the question of her inherited real estate is finished. But the issue of inheritance for most women is simply motherhood, and, in this, Potter's *Orlando* is still tied to the property that society assigns us at birth.

Potter puts the best possible face on this denouement, and makes it go down easy, even with joy. In the last scene, in that meadow where the story began, Orlando is seen through the lens of a youthful and no doubt unencumbered female intelligence from the future, her daughter's. Sally Potter's *Orlando* is remarkable—and exhilarating—because it confidently flows from a conviction that that future has arrived.

LOS ANGELES TIMES, 6/25/93, Calendar/p. 8, Kenneth Turan

What Gertrude Stein said about Oakland applies equally to "Orlando" (the movie, not the metropolis): There's no there there. Though visually impressive and assured, it is the hollowest of successes, all chic set design, smug posturing and self-satisfied attitude.

Adapted from Virginia Woolf's time-travel fantasy by British writer-director Sally Potter, "Orlando" seems so intent on having something meaningful to say that for a while one waits patiently for the word. But the longer it goes on, the more the film's core insubstantiality becomes evident, and the less patience we have even for its virtues.

In fact, the best way to experience "Orlando" (rated PG-13) is to see its first half hour and then go home. Anchored by that most regal of real-life queens, Quentin Crisp, as Queen Elizabeth I, "Orlando's" opening influences have a wit and slyness that is soon to be only a memory.

The Orlando of the title (actress Tilda Swinton) is introduced as a privileged young man circa 1600, the kind of quiet fellow likely to fall asleep over a volume of poetry. Presented to the queen at his parents' castle, he soon becomes a personal favorite of the aged sovereign, who calls him "the son of my old age, the limb of my infirmity" and rewards him with both title and property.

As photographed by the splendid Russian cinematographer Alexei Rodionov (and in part shot in the former Soviet Union) and designed by Ben Van Os and Jan Roelfs, veterans of "Prospero's Books" and other Peter Greenaway films, "Orlando's" rich and elegant images of the Elizabethan world are even more impressive when the film's slight $4-million budget is factored in.

And "Orlando's" theme of sexual ambiguity and role reversal is nicely illustrated as the man playing Queen Elizabeth and the woman playing Orlando share a chaste embrace. Even the film's next sequences, involving Orlando's infatuation with Sasha (Charlotte Valandrey), a beautiful young Russian woman, share some of that charm.

But as Orlando marches through some 350 years of history, remaining always youthful and beautiful, it becomes increasingly apparent that the film has already said everything it has to say and is intent only on repeating itself. And as far as any kind of emotional connection to match its carefully constructed look goes, that is simply not to be had.

What we get instead, in increasingly feeble vignettes, is the re-emphasis of the idea of the arbitrariness of sexual roles. By the time, midway through the film, Orlando wakes up to find himself a woman and says "same person, no difference at all, just a different sex," interest in this rather artificial character is at such a low ebb he or she could wake up a giraffe and it would be hard to suppress a yawn.

Once Orlando is a woman, the film turns into an equally unsurprising and undernourished exploration of sexual discrimination, of the way society has traditionally devalued the worth of women. While this is both true and troublesome, just restating it again and again is not enough to base an intellectually or emotionally involving movie on.

Because of Potter's didactic approach to movie-making, her performers have been pretty much left to their own devices, leading to several cases of exaggerated acting and the striking of poses around her arch dialogue. "You're too serious and not serious enough," Sasha tells Orlando at one point, and something like that could be said about this uncompromisingly artificial film as well.

NEW STATESMAN & SOCIETY, 3/12/93, p. 34, Jonathan Romney

Usually in cinema, history repeats itself as mini-series; but just occasionally it repeats itself as panto. There's always something panto-like about historical films, in any case. Maybe that's just true from a British perspective, because for so long anyone who ever dressed up for the screen in an Elizabethan ruff or a Victorian crinoline would eventually end up wearing the same gear on a Morecambe and Wise Christmas special.

Then why not make historical films as much like panto as possible? Two new British films do just that, so much so that in Sally Potter's *Orlando* you expect to see Aladdin's genie pop up at any minute—as a knowing allusion to Ingres-style orientalism, of course. Derek Jarman's *Wittgenstein* has all but got Daisy the Cow marching across the screen, eyelids flapping, to illustrate some obscure ontological debate.

The biopic is a particular kind of historical film. It needs to be a bit of a panto because if it isn't, it becomes pure hagiography. More of *Wittgenstein* when it opens, but you could see *Orlando* as an attempt at a biopic of a different kind. After all, Virginia Woolf called her historical fantasy a "biography" rather than a novel.

In literature, a biography is usually presumed to be a record of the life; but film biographies are more usually after-the-event narratives leading up to martyrdom or tragic apotheoses. It's no accident how many recent subjects—Jimmy Hoffa, Malcolm X, Bugsy Siegel—end up getting killed (or in the case of Oliver Stone's *JFK, start* by getting killed). These films are closed books.

An alternative biography film—a Woolfian one, say—would keep the book open, emphasise the living process. Instead of taking the film from the vantage point of death, the anti-biopic takes the death from the vantage point of the living—painting a portrait of the subject complete with his or her mortality built in. That's more or less what Sally Potter's film, very loosely following Woolf's original, attempts to do, as it follows its chimerical hero/ine's inexorable flight towards the future and his/her ever-deferred death.

The book casts light on that living process, unpicking the business of biography-writing by spiking it with all manner of stylistic flourishes and self-conscious digressions. Likewise, the film sets out to paint Orlando's labyrinthine life of surprises in a visually, and narratively, baroque style.

Orlando starts out male in one Elizabethan era and ends up female in another. By casting an ageless, androgynous Tilda Swinton throughout, Potter points up the question of identity and its stability through a lifetime of contingent changes.

Is Orlando always Orlando whether male or female, got up in flounces and furbelows, Byronic turbans or modern-day biking gear? And is the story the same whatever its visual style—whether it's copping licks off Eisenstein or Brueghel, kitting Orlando out like a Reynolds *grande dame* or a Hilliard dandy?

Whatever happened, it's always an explicitly 1990s film, forever undercutting historical illusion with a campy sense of anachronism, not least in its casting. A lofty, dessicated Quentin Crisp reaches some sort of personal apotheosis as Queen Elizabeth; Heathcote Williams is a slobbish littérateur, and Ned Sherrin spits out one-liners like grape pips as a scabrous Alexander Pope.

The film never lets you forget that it's filmed, constantly dousing you in the lushness of its designs and photography (the latter by Alexei Rodionov). But the opulence can't disguise the fact that *Orlando* never quite inhabits its own ground. It immediately strikes you as coming dangerously close to Jarman and Greenaway, and of course you want to kick yourself for making such obvious comparisons about a left-field British art film. You see a three-foot-high powdered wig anywhere and it has to be *The Draughtman's Contract*, right? If Potter had really wanted to lay those comparisons to rest, she wouldn't have used Swinton or Jarman's costume designer, Sandy Powell; and she wouldn't have had Greenaway's designers, Ben Van Os and Jan Roelfs, or herself cowritten a soundtrack that's a dead ringer for Michael Nyman's wheezy staccato pomp.

The visuals really are the film's strength: it's as much a sumptuous ballet as a panto, and its most eloquent scenes are about movement: a host of ice-skating boyars, and a great moment when a panier-skirted Swinton daintily negotiates a roomful of furniture. But the film is too episodic and directionless, without hitting the book's wonderful heights of diffuseness. Woolf's great ambivalence is that Orlando's sex starts off switching in a fairly stable fashion, then oscillates capriciously and indeterminately between the two, Potter, though, seems content to stick with straight male-female reversal.

The film never gets round to mobilising its potential for sexual polyvalence. Instead, we get a straightforward parable about a young man who has a rattling good time then turns into a woman who doesn't have such a good time. In role-reversal terms, the ironies are bland. Orlando's fiancée, abandoned for a Russian beauty, moans about the treachery of men; five minutes later, Orlando, rejected in turn, bewails the treachery of women.

Orlando the swashbuckling bravo is a particulary appealing figure in the first half—Swinton, an established champion at sardonic gender-play, makes the most of being a woman acting out the Elizabethan ideal of feminised masculinity. But where she is required to yawn through the epigrammatic mysogynies of Addison, Pope and co, or suffer the iniquities of the property laws, the film collapses into a one-dimensional lament on woman's sorry estate, delivering a weary shrug rather than relishable subversions.

Potter finally seems less interested in her subject than in the possibilities of filming it and wouldn't you know it, 1990s Orlando ends up swapping her quill for a camcorder. What does give the film a real sense of presence, however, is Swinton's performance, as wry and distracted as ever, but making unprecedented exploration of the quizzical double-take direct to camera. She rises admirably to the occasion by *not* rising to it, by making a wonderfully blank, sardonic clothes-horse. Eric and Ernie would have been proud to swap repartee with her.

NEW YORK, 7/12/93, p. 54, David Denby

Orlando, Sally Potter's adaptation of Virginia Woolf's great 1928 comic fantasia, is for people who find the idea of androgyny endlessly shocking and exciting. For anyone else, the movie is likely to seem chic without being in any way interesting. Tilda Swinton, as Orlando, an Elizabethan aristocrat who lives through the ages, first as a man, then as a woman, stares emptily at the audience like Groucho without a wisecrack. *Orlando*, I'm afraid, is arch rather than witty.

NEW YORK POST, 6/11/93, p. 31, Jami Bernard

It's sex-change day at the movies. In "Jurassic Park," geneticists explain that certain species can spontaneously change their sex when their breeding habits are endangered. In "Orlando," a sumptuous-looking movie based on the Virginia Woolf novel, the hero becomes a heroine midway through. "Same person, no difference at all, Just a different sex," observes the newly feminine Orlando, inspecting herself in a full-length mirror.

"Orlando" brilliantly kicked off the New Directors/New Film series last March. Sally Potter's coy, strange, meticulous co-production stars the luminous Tilda Swinton as Orlando, a slight youth born into the British upper classes in one century and traveling through three more centuries virtually untarnished by time, except for that sex change.

At the beginning of "Orlando," our hero is late for his meeting with a decrepit Queen Elizabeth I, who nevertheless take an instant shine to the lad and bequeaths him the grand mansion and grounds, with one proviso: "Do not fade do not wither, do not grow old."

It is one of the movie's many amusing conceits that we have a woman playing a boy, being seduced by an old man playing an old woman (Quentin Crisp). Furthermore, Crisp is a gay man playing a Queen.

As Orlando advances through the ages in the pink of youth, he encounters love's dismay, the wonders of poetry, the horrors of war, and soon enough, the tyranny of sex. For when his sex changes, he stands to lose all his worldly possessions, in accordance with English law. And when, as a woman, he visits the toniest salons, the poets of the day greet him with derision.

On the other hand, once the romantic era sets in the feminine Orlando gets the full fiery treatment from hot-blooded Billy Zane, riding in on horseback and whisking Orlando to bed.

Woolf's novel was meant as a satiric biography of her close friend Vita Sackville-West. The movie has distilled themes of the book in order to provide a more coherent flow—although the unwary viewer may not notice any flow at all. Sexual politics and the writer's voice are two of the main themes that drive Orlando into the modern era, her own person at last.

Swinton is phenomenal as Orlando, holding the camera with her lizard's-eye unblinking gaze, sharing a few direct asides to the camera like private jokes ("Great Play," she confides while watching a first-run rendition of Othello with a male Desdemona. Swinton is known mostly for her work with director Derek Jarman, but "Orlando" ought to expand her movie horizons.

NEWSDAY, 3/19/93, Part II/p. 67, John Anderson

Like the Virginia Woolf novel that inspired it, Sally Potter's "Orlando" dances a thin giddy line between pomposity and farce, and does it with aplomb. Cooly beautiful, warmly romantic and smart, the film, which concerns a fanciful English man/woman who lives for 400 years, has a dreamlike quality, although it will be a nightmare for those overly concerned about their own polymorphous potential.

It is 1600, and the young nobleman Orlando (Tilda Swinton) possesses the kind of androgynous quality so coveted by young men of his age (by the end of the film, she possesses the kind of androgynous quality so coveted by young women of *her* age). His fate is determined by Queen Elizabeth I—played by Quentin Crisp, a perversely inspired casting choice—who becomes infatuated with the young man. She invests Orlando with perpetual ownership of his family estate, but also tells him, "Do not fade, do not wither, do not grow old."

So Orlando remains Orlando as the years glide by, and he passes through various fields of experience. Bad poetry, for instance. Or love: He throws over his fiancée, Euphrosyne (Anne Healy), an Art Garfunkel look-alike, for Sasha (Charlotte Valandrey), the slyly beautiful daughter of a Muscovite ambassador, telling her "You are mine ... because I adore you." He's serious, and it's a line, like many others, that will come back upon Orlando, in converse and deeply satirical way's, after he becomes she.

Written as a fantasy about her friend/lover Vita Sackville-West, Woolf's novel was playful but pointed about society's irrational sexism, and nature's basic fairness. Potter fleshes it all out: Standing before, a mirror and admiring his new female body, Orlando remarks "same person ... just a different sex." And yet, as a lovely, callow male, Orlando could do what he wanted; as a lovely and much wiser woman, Orlando (Orlanda?) faces condescension, legal bias and the loss of everything she owns.

Orlando goes off to serve as an ambassador in an embattled central Asian country, but war is anathema to Orlando, and rather than kill or be killed, he changes gender, and returns to England a woman. Once there, however, she has to answer a raft of lawsuits pertaining to her ownership of the estate; the former male is declared either dead, or female ("Pretty much the same thing," an official quips).

She also attends a salon where Jonathan Swift, Alexander Pope and Joseph Addison (Roger Hammond, Peter Eyre and Ned Sherrin) declare her intellectually dead, and she receives a less than gentle marriage proposal from the starchy Archduke Harry (John Wood). "You're mine," he tells her, "because I adore you." As a woman, Orlando was allowed to be a bit vacuous; as a woman, she's assumed to be vacuous, and as a result learns guile.

The universes of the two Orlandos are less than parallel, although they do converge: Passing through time and gender into the mid-1800s, the female Orlando encounters Shelmerdine (Billy Zane), a freedom fighter who will become her first male lover. His dark good looks and voluptuous mouth recall nothing if not Sasha, who had abandoned Orlando. This time around, though, Orlando is in a position to make her own choices: Shelmerdine wants her to come to America but she refuses. In a film that is all about identity, she still has to find her own, which she does, even as everything else she has is lost to her.

Orlando is a triumph for two very big reasons: Swinton, who has the face of a sexy Renaissance madonna, imbues Orlando with a mix of barely contained joy and grief. Orlando's breathlessness and gentle enthusiasm are as endearing as his/her beauty is pan-sexual. And Potter, who might have let the film lurch into pretentiousness or silliness, has instead wrought a moving work of great depth, and a good deal of humor.

NEWSWEEK, 6/21/93, p. 65, Jack Kroll

Sally Potter's sumptuous, elegant and playful *Orlando* proves, if you didn't already know, that filmmakers don't need $60 million budgets to lay out a bedazzling cinematic banquet. Imaginatively adapted from Virginia Woolf's 1928 novel—a gender-bending meditation on androgyny and history that got the jump on "The Crying Game" by seven decades "Orlando" traverses four centuries of English history as seen through the eyes of its very singular protagonist. He (Tilda Swinton), a pale, striking young aristocrat, becomes a favorite of Queen Elizabeth (regally played by Quentin Crisp), who leaves him a great estate on one condition: "Do not fade, do not wither, do not grow old."

A hundred years later, in 1700, having been crushed in love by the ravishing daughter (Charlotte Valandrey) of a Russian ambassador and failed miserably in the art of poetry, Orlando finds himself—not a day older—enmeshed in bloody political intrigue in the deserts of Central Asia. There, he wakes one day, fairy-tale style, to discover that His Lordship has become Her Ladyship. Examining her undeniably female body in a mirror, she turns to the camera and dryly announces: "Same person, no difference at all. Just a different sex."

But in the salons of 1750s England, Orlando discovers the inconveniences of her new gender: unless she marries and has a male heir, she will lose all legal rights to her property. Fleeing a suitor into a formal garden maze, she emerges into the mid-19th century and into the arms of a Byronic American adventurer (Billy Zane), who reveals to her the sensual pleasures of womanhood. In the final section, she bears his child in the 20th century and realizes, though she is solitary and disinherited, her true independent self. A mischievous and marvelous tapestry, "Orlando" is a movie of surfaces more than depth—but what breathtaking surfaces. And at the center of each panel, delicate and grave as a pearl, is the magnificent Swinton, a paradigm of two sexes and a beacon leading to androgynous common ground.

SIGHT AND SOUND, 3/93, p. 48, Lizzie Francke

England, 1600. The young aristocrat Orlando and his parents hold a grand banquet for the elderly Queen Elizabeth I at their ancestral home. The Queen proclaims an affection for the handsome Orlando and gives him the deeds of his parents' house. By 1610, the Queen and Orlando's parents have died. Orlando, who is now betrothed to Favilla, attends a celebration held on the frozen River Thames by King James I in honour of visiting royalty from Muscovy. Favilla is humiliated when Orlando falls in love with Sasha, a young Russian princess. They arrange to meet on the frozen river at night, but Sasha does not keep her promise. Heartbroken, Orlando goes into a deep sleep and wakes up in 1650. He decides he wants to write poetry and entertains the scurrilous poet Nick Greene, who is more interested in securing a pension from Orlando than discussing the finer points of his craft.

In the year 1700, Orlando abandons his creative ambitions and turns his attention to politics. He asks William of Orange to send him abroad and ends up as the British ambassador in Central Asia. There he befriends the Khan and happily adopts an Eastern way of life. Ten years later the Archduke Harry is sent out to bestow Orlando with a reward for services to his country. A party is held, but since a war has just broken out in the region, no one turns up. Orlando is caught in the fray, but cannot bring himself to fight. He escapes his duty when he wakes up one day as a woman. 1750: Orlando has returned to England and attends the literary salons. As Lady Orlando, she is informed that she has no rights to the ancestral home. The Archduke offers to marry her and help her out of this predicament, but Orlando refuses.

100 years later, she meets her true knight and equal in the form of Shelmerdine, a wild adventurer from America. She proposes to him; he turns her down but they live together for a while. Orlando is visited by two of Queen Victoria's officers and told that the lawsuit against her is settled—she must forfeit everything unless she has a son. Shelmerdine decides to return to America, but Orlando resolves to stay in England even though she has now lost her beloved and her inheritance. Time speeds up and Orlando finds herself pregnant in a war-torn twentieth century. She emerges into the present with a young daughter and a completed manuscript, fulfilled at last.

Sally Potter's long awaited adaptation—or, more appropriately, interpretation—of Virginia Woolf's celebrated novel (which was written as a love poem to the flamboyant Vita Sackville-

West) charts a journey from one Elizabethan age to another. The mythical Orlando shakes off the fetters of biological and cultural destiny to become—as angelic songster Jimmy Somerville, complete with laurels, wigs and lyre, pipes in the finale—a reinvented being that is "one with the human race". Woolf's creation cannot be easily classified. S/he is not so much an androgyne, rather a person who passes from male status to female over the course of 400 years, finding a first love in the exotic, foreign Sasha which is subsequently reflected and consummated in the adventurer Shelmerdine (Billy Zane may not be able to act but he has a smile at least as bewitching as Charlotte Valandrey's Sasha).

Sexual ambiguity no longer causes the frisson it did when Woolf was writing, so Potter has made the question of status the central point of the film—Orlando learns how a change in gender is equivalent to excommunication. Lady Orlando is faced with two lawsuits, one which pronounces her legally dead and therefore unable to own property, while the other informs her that she is female—"which amounts to the same thing." But this death to the world is a rebirth for Orlando, who surveys her naked female form in the mirror in an echo of Botticelli's *Birth of Venus*. Orlando is never seen naked in his male incarnation—he is never authenticated as a man, rather he remains effeminately boyish. But with Tilda Swinton—in playful mode with frequent nods and winks to the camera—in the title role, the audience knows that there is a woman underneath those clothes. As a privileged child of the aristocracy, Orlando is in any case feminised by the gorgeous finery of his age. Clothes maketh the society man and woman—and Orlando seems as uncomfortable in the frockcoats and wigs, the doublet and hose of male attire, as in the cumbersome crinolines that hamper her progress through the Great Hall. Only in Eastern robes does Orlando appear to be free—as much from the constraints of Englishness as of gender.

Indeed, *Orlando* is full of jokes about the English, whether it be the custom of talking loudly to foreigners (with knowing wit, this particular exchange is in French) or the imperialist habit of collecting countries. The film is also a romp through English history, which it presents as richly textured spectacle. Potter creates an embroidered style similar to that of Peter Greenaway (whose production designers Ben Van Os and Jan Roelfs she has borrowed) which, together with the Nymanesque score; confirms her place in a particular tradition of British European-influenced art cinema. She also flirts with the attractions of pomp and circumstance. The pageant for Queen Elizabeth I is a visual feast of autumnal russet, red and gold, while the eighteenth-century salon's pastel palette could have been devised by Wedgwood. Details such as the tea-cup shaped topiaries—perfect emblems of the clipped Victorian era—are a delight. A frozen tableau of a woman with flowers and fruit trapped under the ice of the River Thames has a cold beauty—until we realise what is entailed in the creation of that image.

While there are many ironic touches—such as the casting of Quentin Crisp as the Virgin Queen and the twentieth-century salonier Ned Sherrin as Addison—the overladen visual style perversely turns the film into a celebration of the cultural heritage that Orlando in her liberated female state must reject. In the closing scenes, Orlando, in gentrified-jodphurs and jacket, joins the tourists and takes her cherubic daughter around the home that once was hers, but which now they can only look at with wonder. In many ways, this epitomises the experience of viewing *Orlando* itself.

VILLAGE VOICE, 6/15/93, p. 51, Georgia Brown

What difference does a gender make? The question is confidently addressed by Sally Potter's *Orlando*, a sumptuous film out of England that will probably elicit comparisons to *The Crying Game*—except that *Orlando* is neither thriller nor romantic comedy and what to call it is up in the air. Based on Virginia Woolf's 1928 novel—her exuberant love letter to Vita Sackville-West—*Orlando* is an elegant spoof, a coy, episodic riddle that may've been hyped too much for its own good. Potter's $4 million "independent" could best be described as an epistemological costume drama.

We first see Orlando as an eager young man who sets juices flowing in a pretty dried-up Elizabeth I. Potter's immediate joke is having cast Quentin Crisp as the queen (puns intended, she says). The fair youth is played by Tilda Swinton, a reticent, fetching, red-haired lovely known to Derek Jarman fans, to the few who saw Peter Wollen's *Friendship's Death*, as well as the many who spied on her titties (by Avedon) in *The New Yorker*. Although Crisp looks more like Victoria than Elizabeth I, he's every inch a devouring queen. So, while the movie-making stakes its mock illusions in cross-dressing, the change of sex that occurs in the plot is meant as no mere transvestism but a real (i.e., magical) anatomical switcheroo.

After a number of years as a man, Orlando is suddenly changed into a woman. "Same person, no difference at all. Just a different sex," says she, in one of the character's wry asides to the viewer. A full-frontal nude in a full-length mirror merely confirms what we suspect about Swinton, but hardly supplies a frisson á la *The Crying Game*. (As a reward for leading so secluded an existence, the penis retains its impact.) Of course, it's possible to take this transformation as the one many women make from a tomboy youth (early prerogatives of masculine perspective) to the rigors and demands, the shock, of grown-up femaleness.

And anatomy is destiny, Orlando finds, at least in feudal societies and when it comes to real estate. As a woman she loses the right to inherit the titles and property bestowed by Elizabeth (only as heir to the monarchy is a female child exempt from the rule). She's pronounced both "legally dead" and "a woman," which "amounts to the same thing." Inside the same, outside completely different.

In 1928, while Woolf was writing *Orlando*, Vita's father, the 3rd Baron Sackville, died, and, because he had no son, estates and titles were transferred directly to his brother. In accord with barbaric custom, Vita had to immediately quit her famous home, and a house (better call it a mansion, or castle) she was deeply attached to. It became a part of Woolf's project to symbolically restore Knole to her friend by the book's end.

Potter has more sensible ideas about property and inheritance. Bringing Orlando into the 1990s, the film argues that losing property (the penis) is a blessing, and a means to gaining real autonomy. It would be helpful, however, if the film showed more of this emancimpated 20th-century Orlando—long braid down her back, lively daughter by her side—so that we could be convinced of the transformation.

For all its chronological bravado, skipping blithely over centuries, *Orlando*'s plot is most vague (it's often difficult in a given scene to know what's going on) and thus the film relies heavily on spectacle. Potter has employed Peter Greenaway production designers Ben Van Os and Jan Roelfs, with the result that certain tableaux, as well as the scene-driving score (some of the music is composed by Potter), are reminiscent of Greenaway. In interviews Potter distances her work from Greenaway's, as well as Jarman's, but clearly she is influenced, at least by their mise-en-scène.

Orlando's chief asset probably is Swinton, very much the camera's darling. Her eyes really are those "drenched violets" Woolf describes. She looks swell in an array of period costumes, though probably more arresting in the male ones. As a young man in doublet and tights, Orlando's gawky and delightfully fresh—causing the randy queen at one point to pull his young face into the folds of her ripe old lap, giving him a good whiff of the royal crotch. When the queen dies, Orlando gets on with the business of becoming a Renaissance man: courtier, amateur poet, poet's patron, ambassador to central Asia. He trots off to the desert wearing short skirts, tights, high heels, long curly wigs, and floppy hats—a good joke on the absurdity of fashion, a jab at colonial hubris and stupidity. Later, as a young woman (age does not wither ...), Orlando slowly, over centuries, comes into her own, until finally, deep in the 20th century, she's wearing jodphurs, a plain white shirt, and riding a motorcycle.

But if spectacle moves the film, some scenes and images are irritatingly cryptic and retarding of the flow. What's that woman with her apples doing frozen beneath the ice? I found out in the novel: She's a flash-frozen peddler on a boat that sinks beneath the Thames during a winter storm, becoming a macabre winter tourist attraction—a sort of underfoot Madame Tussaud's. (The king used to bring his visitors over, says Woolf.) In the movie we see the figure so briefly it's hard to figure out who or what she is. And what could've turned into an eerie metaphor for a woman preserved through time doesn't really operate that way; the image passes too quickly and is too disconnected to be haunting. I feel the same about those long (six-day?) naps Orlando keeps taking. What's the point? What I find missing here is a genuine lyrical sensibility, one that could make these images sing and cohere.

In her diaries, Woolf describes *Orlando* as "half laughing, half serious," as "all a joke, and yet gay & quick reading ... a writer's holiday." While temperamentally of Lawrence's trust-the-tale-not-the-teller school, I can't see *Orlando* as more than what Woolf called it, an elegant, occasionally ecstatic satire, a lover's as well as a writer's exercise. Similarly, Potter's movie, though it breaks with certain of Woolf's assumptions (especially the snobbish biases), seems light, also didactic, fare with striking tableaux.

The new Orlando's fall into womanhood is a fall out of privilege and into reality; the supposition (not illustrated) is that she now learns reliance on work and talents. If Woolf makes much of Orlando's persistence in becoming a writer, earning a room of her own, Potter ends with visions of Orlando's daughter as a fledgling filmmaker, a tyke wielding a wild camcorder. It may've been a long and winding road, baby, but here those 400 years are a cheerful bump in the night. Many of us have seen more in a shorter time.

Also reviewed in:
CHICAGO TRIBUNE, 7/9/93, Friday/p. C, Johanna Steinmetz
NATION, 7/12/93, p. 77, Stuart Klawans
NEW REPUBLIC, 6/28/93, p. 26, Stanley Kauffmann
NEW YORK TIMES, 6/11/93, p. C12, Vincent Canby
NEW YORKER, 6/14/93, p. 96, Terrence Rafferty
VARIETY, 9/14/92, p. 48, David Stratton
WASHINGTON POST, 6/25/93, p. C7, Rita Kempley
WASHINGTON POST, 6/25/93, Weekend/p. 42, Joe Brown

PELICAN BRIEF, THE

A Warner Bros. release. *Producer:* Alan J. Pakula and Pieter Jan Brugge. *Director:* Alan J. Pakula. *Screenplay:* Alan J. Pakula. *Based on the book by:* John Grisham. *Director of Photography:* Stephen Goldblatt. *Editor:* Tom Rolf and Trudy Ship. *Music:* James Horner. *Music Editor:* Tom Drescher. *Sound:* James J. Sabat and (music) Sean Murphy. *Sound Editor:* Ron Bochar. *Casting:* Alixe Gordon, Michelle Orlip, Benita Hofstetter, and Ramsey King. *Production Designer:* Philip Rosenberg. *Art Director:* Robert Guerra. *Set Designer:* Sarah Stollman and Monroe Kelly. *Set Decorator:* Lisa Fischer and Rick Simpson. *Special Effects:* Conrad Brink. *Costumes:* Albert Wolsky. *Make-up:* Bob Mills and Edna M. Sheen. *Make-up (Special):* Neal Martz. *Stunt Coordinator:* Doug Coleman. *Running time:* 125 minutes. *MPAA Rating:* PG-13.

CAST: Julia Roberts (Darby Shaw); Denzel Washington (Gray Grantham); Sam Shepard (Thomas Callahan); John Heard (Gavin Verheek); Tony Goldwyn (Fletcher Coal); James B. Sikking (Denton Voyles); William Atherton (Bob Gminski); Robert Culp (President); Stanley Tucci (Khamel); Hume Cronyn (Justice Rosenberg); John Lithgow (Smith Keen); Anthony Heald (Marty Velmano); Nicholas Woodeson (Stump); Stanley Anderson (Edwin Sneller); John Finn (Matthew Barr); Cynthia Nixon (Alice Stark); Jake Webber (Charles Morgan/Garcia); Casey Biggs (Eric East); Christopher Murray (Rupert); Sonny Jim Gaines (Sarge); Kevin Geer (K.O. Lewis); Joseph Chrest (Song and Dance Man from Bar); Richard Bauer (Managing Editor); Michelle O'Neill (Sara Ann Morgan); Peter Carlin (Edward Linney); Ralph Cosham (Justice Jensen); Terrence P. Currier (Rosenberg's Nurse); Edwin Newman (Himself); Helen Carey (Federal Clerk); Howard Shalwitz (Washington Herald Journalist); Kyle Prue (News Desk Reporter); Jewell Robinson, Kim Peter Novac, and Norman Aronovic (Senior Washington Herald Editors); Carl Palmer (Cop); Carol Sutton (New Orleans Policewoman); Scott Jefferson (Lieutenant Olsen); Daniel Kamin (Hooten); Mark McLaughlin and Robert Pavlovich (CIA Agents); Magee Hickey (Herself); Constance Yelverton (Hotel Clerk); Kim Kettle (Verheek's Wife); Ellie K. Wang (Reporter); Fran Dorn (University Registrar); Karen Bralove (University Placement Clerk); Teagle F. Bougere and Carey Varner (University Students); Saundra Quarterman (Laura Kass); Cynthia Hood (Parklane Receptionist); Alan Wade (Parklane Administrator); Harold J. Surratt (Parklane Security Officer); Paul Morella (White & Blazevich Attorney); Ed Johnson (White & Blazevich Security Guard); Jurian Hughes (White & Blazevich

Receptionist); Dick Stilwell (White & Blazevich Security); Tom Quinn (Sara Ann Morgan's Father); Beverly Brigham (Safe Deposit Teller); Liza Sweeney Coleman and Douglas R. Coleman (Pursuers with Guns); Michael Port and Shanna Connell (Tulane Law Students).

CHRISTIAN SCIENCE MONITOR, 12/17/93, p. 19, David Sterritt

A scene in "The Pelican Brief" reminded me of a distinction Alfred Hitchcock used to make between surprise and suspense.

Surprise happens when characters are eating in a restaurant and a bomb goes off under the table. The audience jumps with amazement and you have a few seconds of hair-raising cinema.

Suspense happens when the characters are eating and the audience *knows* there's a bomb under the table. Everyone watching sweats and squirms throughout the scene, and you have several *minutes* of hair-raising cinema.

So here are Julia Roberts and Denzel Washington in "The Pelican Brief," where they play a law student and a crusading reporter on the trail of an assassination conspiracy. They're about to drive away in their car, and filmmaker Alan J. Pakula has cleverly let us know there's a bomb attached to the ignition switch.

I squirmed in my seat when Washington put his key into the slot. I squirmed again when he started to turn it but pulled his hand away. I squirmed once more when he started to turn it again, only to yank his hand away when Roberts realized something was wrong.

This scene obviously aimed at Hitchcockian suspense, but my squirms were caused by growing irritation rather than pins-and-needles anticipation. Pakula has studied the classics, and he desperately wants his new thriller to be as thrilling as can be. Unfortunately, though, he's left out a few additional ingredients that Hitchcock identified as necessary to first-rate filmmaking.

One is a carefully developed plot. Another is a set of well-rounded characters. Yet another is rhythmic pacing that draws the narrative from scene to scene even when the story wears thin or stops making sense—as this one does uncomfortably often, with its jumble of accidents stemming from the enigmatic murder of two Supreme Court justices.

Hitchcock nodded at times, of course, but it's the audience that will be dozing off as "The Pelican Brief" plods dutifully from one episode to another, tossing in Hitchcockian touches that make up in quantity what they lack in quality. The movie is like a cuckoo clock that marks every quarter-hour by popping a second-rate reminder of the master of suspense into your face.

Shuttling between New Orleans and Washington, the story also shares Hitchcock's fondness for colorful backgrounds and murder in broad daylight as well as the gloom of night. But there's little substance behind the high concept façades. In place of vision and inventiveness, Pakula gives us moviemaking by the numbers.

The cast is served as poorly as the audience. The hugely popular Roberts apparently hoped for another smash hit with this big-budget entertainment, but her talent isn't expansive enough to overcome the monotony of Pakula's dull images; one scene in particular, where she snoops for information in a mental institution, is downright laughable in its misfired acting and directing. Washington seemed to be on an unstoppable winning streak with "Malcolm X" and the new "Philadelphia," but "The Pelican Brief" squashes even his glowing abilities.

Such able supporting players as Sam Shepherd, John Heard, Hume Cronyn, and the usually unsquelchable John Lithgow are stuck on the same sinking ship.

Pakula wrote the screenplay, based on John Grisham's best-selling novel. Stephen Goldblatt did the tedious cinematography, although the opening—full of pelicans against a setting sun—is radiant with beauty.

One more warning: At about 140 minutes, "The Pelican Brief" is anything but brief. If you're a Grisham fan who's determined to see it, get ready for a long, hard sit.

LOS ANGELES TIMES, 12/17/93, Calendar/p. 1, Kenneth Turan

If the "Pelican Brief" had any more going for it, it would be against the law. So it is a surprise to say that the biggest mystery this legal thriller presents is how a film based on a novel by John Grisham, starring the bankable duo of Julia Roberts and Denzel Washington and written and directed by veteran Alan J. Pakula can end up more of a fizzle than an explosion.

"The Pelican Brief" does have its moments, sporadically involving episodes when it looks like things are finally going to ignite. But that combustion point is never quite reached, and despite occasional bursts of action, this doesn't manage to be more than a reasonable facsimile of a thriller, acceptable in a pinch but nothing to get very excited about.

This year has already seen a much more successful version of an earlier Grisham novel, the Sydney Pollack-directed, Tom Cruise-starring "The Firm." Aside from a penchant for all-star casts, both movies benefit from one of Grisham's enjoyably harum-scarum plots, outlandish yet just plausible enough to be diverting.

The story this time around centers on the Supreme Court, whose oldest justice, the liberal Abraham Rosenberg (a clever cameo by Hume Cronyn) is the target of anger from all across the political spectrum. So while no one is surprised when he comes to a sudden end, the fact that another justice of a different   political stripe is simultaneously murdered is the cause of considerable speculation.

Among the interested parties is humble but smart Tulane University law student Darby Shaw (Roberts). Working on the premise that it might be greed, not ideology, that led to the deaths, she puts together a paper on the possible causes, which, for reasons that will eventually become clear, she calls "The Pelican Brief."

Shaw's professor/boyfriend Tom Callahan (Sam Shepard) thinks enough of Darby's brief to pass it on to old pal Gavin Verheek (John Heard), who just happens to be a top lawyer for the FBI. In this time of conspiracy theories and contagious paranoia, it will unnerve no one to find out that once the government, up to and including the President (Robert Culp) and his ominous chief of staff (Tony Goldwyn), get involved, Darby's life is at risk. Finally, the only person she can trust is Gray Grantham (Washington), the best reporter the nation's capital can call its own.

Set up this way, "The Pelican Brief" probably doesn't sound half bad. But a simple description leaves out several factors that work to the film's detriment, starting with the nature of its view of official Washington.

For once the word gets out on Darby's brief, entities almost without number get involved, ranging from all the President's men to the FBI, the CIA and several clandestine intelligence organizations.

So while everyone is looking for Darby, it is far from clear who anyone is or what their intentions are at any given time. In fact spies are spying on spies to such a baffling extent you'll want to construct a chart to figure out what's going on, and a darkened theater is not the best place to make one.

Not helping things either is that, unlike "The Firm," "The Pelican Brief" doesn't benefit from the strength of its supporting performers. With the exception of John Lithgow's steely editor, almost none of the peripheral players and especially none of the innumerable government men make much of an impression. Roberts and Washington do what is expected of them quite nicely and manage a pleasant on-screen rapport, but no one is giving them much assistance.

The person who should be helping most, director-screen-writer-co-producer Pakula, who has thrillers ranging from "Klute" and "The Parallax View" to the more recent "Presumed Innocent" and "Consenting Adults" behind him, is a considerable letdown on this one.

Aside from not being able to keep the plot from becoming periodically murky, Pakula sets a leisurely, almost phlegmatic pace for this film. The material is treated with more reverence than energy, and in a year when splendid thrillers like "The Fugitive" and "In the Line of Fire" can be held up as examples, that is simply not good enough.

NEW YORK, 1/3/94, p. 53, David Denby

I promised my mother once that I would never write such sentences as "*The Pelican Brief* is the turkey long." But no critic can evade hackdom forever, and this movie has brought me low. As a law student on the run from shadowy killers, Julia Roberts, wan and frightened yet game, is most appealing; but apart from repackaging the talents of Miss Roberts, *The Pelican Brief* serves, as far as I can see, even less purpose than most American movies. Surely no one but the director, Alan Pakula, takes seriously John Grisham's nonsensical plot about a conspiracy to assassinate Supreme Court justices. Rather than playing with the story, Pakula does it straight, leaving out the flashy villains and pyrotechnical camera work that would give the material a charge of wit. *The Pelican Brief* is well made but worthless. One watches in a stupor as millions of dollars are wasted.

NEW YORK POST, 12/17/93, p. 45, Michael Medved

"The Pelican Brief" is, in fact, an overlong, overstuffed, ungainly bird that flaps and squawks for two hours and 22 minutes but stubbornly refuges to take flight.

You can hardly blame director Alan J. Pakula ("All the President's Men" "Presumed Innocent"), who does his customarily competent job of setting up an eerie, ominous mood. But no amount of atmospherics can cover up this preposterous plot.

Two justices of the Supreme Court die the same night at the hands of brutal assassins. While the world worries over a possible terrorist plot, one brilliant law student in New Orleans (Julia Roberts) goes to the library for a couple of hours and figures out the precise party who ordered the assassinations.

She explains her discovery in written form ("the pelican brief"), and after her professor/lover (Sam Shepard) forwards the document to the FBI she spends the rest of the movie running away from all-powerful forces determined to rub her out because "she knows too much."

None of this makes the slightest bit of sense, and the overall pace of the movie—despite a few well-staged chase scenes that deliver momentary jolts of energy—is much too slow to allow us to suspend disbelief.

Meanwhile the script (also by Pakula) is full of lumbering flat-footed dialogue, such as this stunning revelation by an ace investigative reporter (played by the usually superb Denzel Washington in a whispery, sleep-walking performance): "If this thing reaches as deep and goes as high as we think it does, then these men will do anything not to be exposed!"

Part of the problem is that Pakula and John Grisham (whose silliest, sloppiest novel served as the basis for this film) can't decide whether the bad guys are ferociously formidable or a band of nasty bumblers who might best be described as the Keystone Konspirators.

In addition to all its other monstrous misdeeds, this cabal ends up cheating the audience: We're told repeatedly that it's run by one evil all-powerful individual, but we never once meet the arch-villain on screen.

We do, however, meet Julia Roberts, who here returns to the screen after an absence of some two years. Fortunately, she's lost none of her star quality, radiating the familiar combination of glamour and vulnerability in even her most minor scenes.

With all of the shortcomings in this moody, meandering motion picture, the filmmakers make an obvious play for critical favor by inserting all sorts of "socially responsible" messages in a ruthless display of political correctness.

The bad guys are major industrialists, gun nuts and anti-abortion demonstrators, environmental polluters, oil men and slick conservative politicians; the good guys are aging, liberal Supreme Court justices, a crusading African-American reporter, a female law student (complete with ACLU bumper sticker prominently displayed on her refrigerator door), and scenic pelicans in the unspoiled Louisiana bayou.

Actually, these critters wind up playing an appropriately important part in a plot that is ultimately for the birds—though the most suitable symbol for this picture isn't the pelican, it's the turkey.

NEWSDAY, 12/17/93, Part II/p. 91, Jack Mathews

When it was announced that Alan J. Pakula would write and direct "The Pelican Brief," based on John Grisham's follow-up to the smash novel "The Firm," I wondered which Pakula would turn up, the brilliant director of "Parallax View" and "All the President's Men," or the plodding yeoman who did "Rollover" and last year's "Consenting Adults."

The answer is that while there are flashes of his better self in "Pelican Brief," the movie definitely goes on the "Rollover" side of Pakula's ledger. This is slick, empty pulp, blown large by its heaving earnestness, and relieved only marginally by the vigorous star turns of Julia Roberts and Denzel Washington.

Pakula, to be fair, wasn't exactly working with A material here. Grisham, an ex-lawyer who had some knowledge of his setting for "The Firm," was left to his own imagination in writing "Pelican Brief," and the jaw drops at the thought of that premise.

Two U. S. Supreme Court justices, an aging liberal and a relatively young conservative, are assassinated on the same evening, and while the FBI and the rest of the federal constabulary search for the killer among the victims' common ideological enemies, a young Tulane law student named Darby Shaw (Roberts) takes a week away from her studies to solve the case in a New Orleans library.

Shaw's hypothesis, which becomes known as the Pelican Brief, is passed on to the FBI by her law professor and lover (Sam Shepard), and after he is killed with a car bomb rigged for her, she is on the run from the FBI, White House liaisons, assassins and various stalkers who appear to be surplus pods left over from "Invasion of the Body Snatchers."

This is one of those crafty tales where every bad guy can be picked out of a crowd by his expressionless face and stone dead eyes.

Looking back, it would have been wiser to have someone other than Pakula direct. With its settings in the White House corridors, the Maryland-Virginia suburbs and the underground garages of Washington, we are constantly being reminded of the genuine suspense Pakula whipped up for "All the President's Men," a true story of political intrigue, where the only real victim was the public trust.

"The Pelican Brief" piles one incongruity on top of another, and while you cannot help but be swept along by its frenetic pace, it is a ride across a polished surface, as phony as that Washington Chronicle press pass Gray Grantham (Washington) keeps flashing.

Like Woodward and Bernstein, Gray is alerted by a Deep Throat source over the phone that the trail of the murders could reach all the way to the Oval Office and the President (Robert Culp, in the year's casting gaffe). But the trail leads nowhere until Gray hooks up with Darby, and the pair connive to elude their pursuers and expose the scheme behind the killings.

The plot details are as elusive as Gray and Darby, and a good thing. Grisham gets worse the slower you read him, and the story can't take any more scrutiny on film than on the page. Shaw is being trailed one minute, and is free as a bird the next. One room she enters is bugged, the next one not. The killers go from being skilled pros to rank amateurs.

The most representative scene in the movie is one where the stalkers rig a bomb to Gray's car and wait, from a safe distance, for him and Darby to get in and blow themselves up. When the plot fails, a great chase ensues, with dogs barking, guns blazing, cars crashing.

If one of the assassins had thought to wait until the couple got in the car, then walked over and shot them, they could have saved themselves a lot of grief and embarrassment.

With the memory of some really good thrillers still fresh, the real missing ingredient in "Pelican Brief" is the kind of sadistic villain that John Malkovich provided "In the Line of Fire." Tony Goldwyn manages to be despicably smarmy as the president's chief of staff, but none of the actual assassins is very interesting, and the real bad guy of the story never makes it into full view.

Given the lean competition for light Christmas fare, "The Pelican Brief" will have to do. To their credit, Roberts and Washington fill their paper-thin roles with genuine enthusiasm, though Pakula and the studio didn't have the courage to allow Darby and Gray, who was white in the book, indulge a romance.

As a journalist, I feel the urge to point out that the journalism at the Washington Chronicle is closer to that of the Daily Planet than the Washington Post (can you imagine Woodward and Bernstein doing their own photography?), but if we start picking nits that small with this movie, it will never end.

NEWSWEEK, 12/20/93, p. 121, David Ansen

Any movie that starts with the assassination of *two* Supreme Court justices (one bumped off in a gay-porno theater) shouldn't have too much trouble grabbing your attention. Alan J. Pakula's *The Pelican Brief*, from the John Grisham best seller, niftily plants its hooks into the audience, promising a taut, paranoid thriller along the lines of the director's early gems, "Klute" and "The Parallax View." The promise, however, is only half filled in this glossy, reasonably diverting entertainment, whose tone of self-importance ultimately can't disguise the rickety flimflammery of Grisham's tale.

The murders bring out the intellectual sleuth in New Orleans law student Darby Shaw (Julia Roberts), whose professor/boyfriend (Sam Shepard) was a protege of one of the dead justices. Darby writes up her conspiracy theory in a speculative legal brief she calls "pelican, " and when it's turned over to the FBI, it hits a big nerve. Immediately, corpses begin to pop up. Terrified, narrowly escaping several attempts on her life, Darby turns to Washington investigative reporter Gray Grantham (Denzel Washington) for help. Dodging ubiquitous hit men, the two strangers team up to uncover the nefarious plot, which, to no one's surprise, reaches into the highest corridors of power.

The most suspenseful damsel-in-distress stuff comes in the first half, which includes the grippingly staged murder of an FBI man. But midway, once the audience is let in on the contents of her brief (a mild letdown), the tension flags and the cliffhanging devices get more desperately implausible. (At 2 hours and 20 minutes, this is no brief "Pelican.") Pakula's always had a cool style, tending toward solemnity, but let's face it, "All the President's Men" this movie is not. You wish he'd have a little more fun with the pulpy material. But the dialogue has no sparkle and he dampens down his actors, as if a lack of juice were verisimilitude. (Robert Culp as a slightly dotty, Reaganesque president and John Lithgow as Gray's impatient editor do liven things up.) Washington underplays suavely; it's almost impossible to muffle his charisma. But Roberts's fans, who have been waiting for her return to the screen for two years, may not feel they're getting maximum star wattage for their bucks. The role requires her to be reduced to a state of whispery panic most of the time. She does it well, but what a waste. Why strip the vivacious Julia of her best colors?

SIGHT AND SOUND, 3/94, p. 44, Lizzie Francke

Darby Shaw, an A-grade law student in Memphis, is having an affair with her professor, Thomas Callahan. When two top judges, Rosenberg and Jensen, are murdered on the same night, Shaw writes a brief speculating on who might be behind it. She shows it to Callahan, who in turn gives it to his friend, FBI lawyer Gavin Verheek. Gray Grantham, a investigative journalist at the *Washington Herald*, receives a phone call from an attorney named 'Garcia', who tells him he might know who is behind the murders. Though 'Garcia' refuses to reveal his identity, Grantham tracks him down to a phone booth and takes a photo of him. Darby's report is circulated at the FBI. The report implicates the White House—the President's Chief of Staff, Fletcher Coal, and Bureau director Denton Voyles.

Later, while Shaw and Callahan are in New Orleans, Callahan is killed by a car bomb meant for Shaw. Two men turn up at the scene and tell Shaw that they are policemen. She is suspicious and decides to leave and check into a hotel. She rings Verheek, tells him about Callahan's death and asks if the report has been seen outside the FBI. Meanwhile the President is concerned about how seriously Shaw's 'Pelican Brief' is being taken. Later Shaw realizes that she is being trailed by two thugs. She confers with Verheek and they arrange to meet the following day. However, the conversation has been bugged; Verheek is shot and the killer takes his place at the rendezvous. Just as Verheek's killer attempts to shoot Shaw, he is assassinated and Shaw flees for her life. The killings are of interest to one Marty Velmano.

Shaw rings Grantham, and they arrange to meet in a hotel in New York. She tells him about the 'Pelican Brief', which refers back to a case concerning financier Victor Monteith, who was attempting to exploit oil opportunities in a lake area of environmental significance despite the protests of various pressure groups (the brief got its name from the fact that pelicans populated the lake.) Both Judges Jensen and Rosenberg had overruled Monteith's claims to exploit that land. Shaw's hypothesis was that Monteith had had them assassinated and hoped that the President would appoint judges who would look more favourably on him. Grantham surmises that 'Garcia' may be working for one of the law firms Monteith had employed; he also gleans that the 'Pelican Brief' has disappeared, making Shaw a crucial witness. Frightened for her life, Shaw wants to sever contact with him. Back in Washington, Grantham is told by his editor Smith Keen that he might be taken off the story. Grantham protests and Keen sends him off to his country retreat, where Shaw turns up. Meanwhile the President is told about Grantham's story, and advised to appoint pro-environment judges to replace Jensen and Rosenberg, then order an investigation into Monteith's affairs so as to cover up his association with the financier.

Meanwhile Grantham is being tailed. He and Shaw discover that 'Garcia' is one Curtis Morgan, who works at a firm used by Monteith, in which Marty Velmano is a senior partner; Morgan was killed the previous week in a 'mugging' incident. Grantham and Shaw visit Mrs Morgan, and eventually learn that her husband left some documents in a safe deposit box. Shaw retrieves the documents in the guise of Mrs Morgan; they provide the evidence necessary to charge Velmano and Monteith. Shaw and Grantham narrowly escape another car bomb as they return to the *Herald*'s offices where they have a meeting with Keen and the FBI. Under FBI protection, Shaw flies to an undisclosed location. Grantham publishes his story, which he also credits to her, and receives much acclaim.

If all good conspiracy theories start with the idea that there might have been a second gunman, John Grisham's novel *The Pelican Brief* ups the odds by including not just the second, but the third, fourth and fifth. Spanning nearly two and a half hours, Alan J. Pakula's film version proves just how tricky an enterprise it is to adapt these epic thrillers. The complicated plot has to be condensed, while characterization takes second place. Certainly, when at the end a TV interviewer asks Grantham, "Who is Darby Shaw?", it seems like a good question. While he is suggesting that she, like Watergate's 'Deep Throat' before her, might be a figment of the journalist's imagination, the viewer who has spent over two hours with her might still be first place.

Julia Roberts may have chosen this as her major comeback role after the sinking of *Hook* and the bit part in *The Player*, but it hardly embellishes her repertoire. As the intrepid Darby, she seems as fragile as all the other pretty women she has played. One could ask her fans to clap their hands for a director who believes in Julia Roberts—one who might substantiate her screen persona beyond this Tinkerbellish allure and decide, for instance, not to include a gratuitous scene of her in her underwear. There is potentially so much more to this star but if this film is anything to go by, she is in danger of being snuffed out by the wrong roles.

The conspiracy thriller is also in danger of being silenced, since it has become too much of a joke. Pakula marked out the territory in the secretive 70s with the fictional *The Parallax View* and then the factual *All the President's Men*. But now that so many real 'Gates have swung wide open, one has to work hard to cook up interest in the eternal internal affairs. Denzel Washington battles to save this lacklustre film, but unfortunately his Grantham is no Bernstein or Woodward. As if to compensate, Pakula allows everyone to be briefly implicated, with menace poured on by the gallon, but fails to raise a spark of interest. The other factor that distinguishes *The Pelican Brief* from its 70s antecedents is its openhanded resolution. Once, the conspiracy thriller could leave some lingering doubts, but here it is all cleaned up for a smiling finale. The Pelican may have ruffled the mighty Eagle's feathers but it won't bring him down.

TIME, 12/20/93, p. 62, Richard Schickel

Julia Roberts is fragile and determined as a law student too smart for her own good. Denzel Washington is foxy and stalwart as the reporter who wants to break the story of murderous high-level corruption she has pieced together for a research paper she calls *The Pelican Brief*.

It is never totally disagreeable to spend time in the company of such attractive people. And every once in a while Robert Culp appears as an addled, detached President of the United States, provoking wicked, recognizing laughter. Within living memory, the Oval Office has sheltered such a figure.

But that pretty much completes the short list of pleasures afforded by writer-director Alan Pakula's adaptation of John Grisham's gazillion-copy best seller. Mostly this is a movie about people getting in and out of cars, which either do or do not blow up when they turn on the ignition. They also talk on the phone quite a bit usually in darkly lighted rooms, to callers who are not entirely forthcoming in their messages. From time to time, they are chased by nameless people who are boringly expert at dealing out sudden death.

These are, of course, the efficient, familiar ligatures of thriller plotting. They can be comforting when you're page-turning your paperback in economy class and all you're looking for is a gentle diversion. Movies, though, require something more than connective tissue, however handsomely rendered. They are a dramatic form, which implies a need for both ever tightening menace and, ultimately, the adaptation, earlier this year, of Grisham's *The Firm* eventually took

Tom Cruise's running man into the presence of his chief tormentors. But Roberts' running woman gets to confront only a few members of the supporting cast, all of whom—Culp aside—are drably written and impossible even for actors as good as Hume Cronyn, John Lithgow and John Heard to sink a fang into. And we never get to see, even in the shadows that are a Pakula specialty, Mr. Big—who has ordered the assassination of two Supreme Court Justices.

Pakula, who has proved his ability to turn paranoid suspicions into scary reality (*Klute, All the President's Men*), gives his movie the dark glow we have come to expect from this genre. But we don't go to movies like this in search of stylish aperçus. We go to see innocents like ourselves getting swept up by irresistible tides of terror. And to have the pants scared off us. That doesn't happen in *The Pelican Brief*. An airplane read has been turned into nothing more compelling than an airplane see.

VILLAGE VOICE, 12/28/93, p. 77, J. Hoberman

Denzel Washington appears as a more conventional sort of public servant in *The Pelican Brief*. [The reference is to *Philadelphia*; see Hoberman's review of that film.] He plays a dapper and smoothly ingenious investigative reporter for a major Washington daily newspaper, but his real role is to gallantly escort skittish Julia Roberts back into the spotlight of a precocious comeback.

As the main attraction in Alan Pakula's thriller, adroitly distilled from John Grisham's novel, Roberts is introduced as the smartest, spunkiest, best-coiffed, and oldest-looking student in professor Sam Shepard's constitutional law class. Roberts is so smart; in fact, that after a pair of Supreme Court justices are assassinated (the liberal shot while watching *Studs*, the conservative throttled mid-matinee at his local gay porn theater), she solves the case for extra credit by digging out a Court decision suggesting what the two men had in common.

Inevitably, this brief, which seemingly implicates the president (superbly corroded Robert Culp as a Bushy glad-hander), reaches the wrong people and, after narrowly avoiding assassination herself, Roberts—excellent at tossing her mane and letting her face swell with fear—is pursued all over New Orleans and Washington, D.C., by a variety of hit men. The pace is pleasingly kinetic, although Roberts's not-unfamiliar predicament is alternately laughable and mechanical. Every bland motel room is a potential Watergate. All the phones are bugged and not always by the same government agency. Snarly, suspendered John Lithgow, who plays Washington's doubting Thomas editor, is just about the only character who hasn't seen the movie.

Combining elements of Pakula's Nixonian doubleheader *The Parallax View* (1974) and *All the President's Men* (1976) to posit a business plot against the environment exposed by a sage-like reporter, a post-feminist law student, and a PBS documentary, *The Pelican Brief* offers additional evidence of the '70s revival. Pakula's fondness for punchy montage and alienated modern architecture remain intact. But, as loamy as his political paranoia is, it ultimately fails to thrive—it's as if Oliver Stone has sucked all the oxygen out of the conspiratorial greenhouse.

Also reviewed in:
CHICAGO TRIBUNE, 12/17/93, Friday/p. A, Michael Wilmington
NEW REPUBLIC, 2/14/94, p. 30, Stanley Kauffmann
NEW YORK TIMES, 12/17/93, p. C1, Janet Maslin
NEW YORKER, 12/27/93, p. 150, Anthony Lane
VARIETY, 12/20/93, p. 30, Brian Lowry
WASHINGTON POST, 12/17/93, p. C6, Hal Hinson
WASHINGTON POST, 12/17/93, Weekend/p. 54, Desson Howe

PERFECT WORLD, A

A Warner Bros. release of a Malpaso production.   *Producer:* Mark Johnson and David Valdes. *Director:* Clint Eastwood.   *Screenplay:* John Lee Hancock.   *Director of Photography:* Jack N. Green.   *Editor:* Joel Cox and Ron Spang.   *Music:* Lennie Niehaus.   *Music Editor:* Donald Harris.   *Sound:* Jeff Wexler and (music) Bobby Fernandez.   *Sound Editor:* Alan Robert Murray. *Casting:* Phyliss Huffman and Liz Keigley.   *Production Designer:* Henry Bumstead.   *Art*

Director: Jack Taylor, Jr.   *Set Designer:* Charlie Vassar and Antoinette Gordon.   *Special Effects:* John Frazier.   *Costumes:* Erica Edell Phillips.   *Make-up:* James McCoy and F.X. Perez.   *Stunt Coordinator:* Buddy Van Horn.   *Running time:* 130 minutes.   *MPAA Rating:* PG-13.

CAST: Kevin Costner (Butch Haynes);   Clint Eastwood (Red Garnett);   Laura Dern (Sally Gerber);   T.J. Lowther (Phillip Perry);   Keith Szarabajka (Terry Pugh);   Leo Burmester (Tom Adler);   Paul Hewitt (Dick Suttle);   Bradley Whiford (Bobby Lee);   Ray McKinnon (Bradley);   Jennifer Griffin (Gladys Perry);   Leslie Flowers (Naomi Perry);   Belinda Flowers (Ruth Perry);   Darryl Cox (Mr. Hughes);   Jay Whitaker (Superman);   Taylor Suzanne McBride (Tinkerbell);   Christopher Reagan Ammons (Dancing Skeleton);   Mark Voges (Larry);   Vernon Grote (Prison Guard);   James Jefer (Oldtimer);   Ed Geldart (Fred Cummings);   Bruce McGill (Paul Saunders);   Nik Hagler (General Store Manager);   Gary Moody (Local Sheriff);   George Haynes (Farmer);   Marietta Marich (Farmer's Wife);   Rodger Boyce (Mr. Willits);   Lucy Lee Flippin (Lucy);   Elizabeth Ruscio (Paula);   David Kroll (Newscaster);   Gabriel Folse (Officer Terrance);   Gil Glasgow (Officer Pete);   Dennis Letts (Governor);   John Hussey (Governor's Aide);   Margaret Bowman (Trick'r Treat Woman);   John M. Jackson (Bob Fielder);   Connie Cooper (Bob's Wife);   Cameron Finley (Bob Fielder, Jr.);   Katy Wottrich (Patsy Fielder);   Marco Perella (Road Block Officer);   Linda Hart (Eileen);   Brandon Smith (Officer Jones);   George Orrison (Officer Orrison);   Wayne Dehart (Mack);   Mary Alice (Lottie);   Kevin Woods (Cleveland);   Tony Frank (Arch Andrews);   Woody Watson (Lieutenant Hendricks).

CHRISTIAN SCIENCE MONITOR, 11/29/93, p. 14, David Sterritt

"A Perfect World" is likely to be a solid box-office success, if only because it features two gigantic stars of two different generations—Clint Eastwood and Kevin Costner—in a suspenseful story directed with controlled energy by Eastwood himself.

What's most interesting about the movie is not its cleverness as a Hollywood product, however, but the thoughtfulness of its underlying themes. "A Perfect World" is not an intellectual film, and it's better at suggested ideas than exploring them. Still, it raises issues well worth pondering and shows that Eastwood remains one of Hollywood's most stimulating filmmakers.

Costner plays Butch Haynes, an uncommonly complex bad guy. After busting out of prison in the opening scene—with an accomplice so evil that even Butch despises him—he finds himself running from the law with a young boy as his hostage. Chasing after him are a Texas Ranger played by Eastwood, a rookie criminologist played by Laura Dern, and an assortment of other law-enforcement types.

Although the first hour of "A Perfect World" sets up a conventional cops-and-robbers chase, the movie is most resonant when it leaves the cops behind and focuses on Butch and eight-year-old Philip, his traveling companion. Butch is a strikingly intelligent man, we discover, with a streak of independent thinking that could have made him an exceptional member of society. But in his formative years, his promising personality was trapped between two poor alternatives: home life with a viciously abusive father or prison life in a veritable school for criminals.

It's not surprising he went bad or that he harbors a lingering resentment toward the supposedly decent society that set him on this path.

Phillip reminds him of his long-ago self, especially when he learns that the boy's father has run off and his mother is raising him in a strict religious atmosphere that Butch associates with rigidity and confinement.

Phillip himself is uncertain whether Butch is a valuable friend or a dangerous foe—and the moment when this little boy must come to an irrevocable decision provides one of the films most harrowing and starting scenes.

The point of "A Perfect World" is that our world is anything but. Subtly yet unmistakably, the film criticizes not only the cruelty and irrationality that are regrettable parts of Butch's makeup, but also the cruel and irrational tendencies that may lurk in ordinary households like those that produced Butch and Phillip.

This culminates in a grippingly filmed encounter between the runaways and a family that shows them hospitality without realizing they're fleeing from the law. In this family's home, casual violence and selfishness coexist with genuine love and caring. Butch's volatile reaction to this mixture is at once deeply disturbing, sadly understandable, and as provocative as anything a major Hollywood movie has offered in recent memory.

Costner gives a strong and steady performance as Butch, and Eastwood is canny enough to let him carry much of the film, relegating his own role to secondary status. Dern does her best with an underwritten part, and T.J. Lowther is marvelously expressive as the youngest of the key characters. Wayne Dehart, Mary Alice, and Kevin Woods deserve special praise as the family that takes Butch and Phillip in without guessing what awaits them.

John Lee Hancock wrote the screenplay, and Jack N. Green did the attractive cinematography, which makes the world look almost as perfect as the title ironically suggests. Joel Cox and Ron Spang edited the picture, which could have used a little more tightening—as well as trimming from its two-hour-plus running time—and Lennie Niehaus composed the score.

FILMS IN REVIEW, 3-4/94, p. 58, Harry Pearson, Jr.

I thought it was fun to read all the Monday morning quarterbacking about *A Perfect World*. Just about every reason on the planet was given, by analysts for *The Times* on down, for the movie's failure to perform well at the box office, save the obvious one: *A Perfect World* is not very good.

It is long and draggy. Eastwood as director, allows his scenes as lawman on a bedraggled chase after escaped con Kevin Costner to dilute the real focus of his story, the complicated and entirely unpredictable relationship between Costner and the little boy he kidnaps as a hostage along the way. While Costner gives an unusually good performance, he fails to convince us (as he did the child he took under his wing) that he could commit an act of unreasoned violence, and thus the child's justification for shooting Costner seems opaque, an opacity not illumined by a worthy performance from this particular child actor. At ninety minutes, it might have been an art house smash, and taken to the heart of every true Frenchman, but it is, like so much of the overpraised *Unforgiven*, terribly indulgent and without enough firepower to keep the audience awake (and I don't necessarily mean firearms violence either). And, like *Unforgiven*, it is indifferently photographed for wide screen by Jack N. Green. Yes, it has its moments—notably, one at the Squat and Gobble, a cafe where Costner evidently performs a most perverse act on a willing waitress—but you have to go prospecting to find them. And for that you have to be awake.

LOS ANGELES TIMES, 11/24/93, Calendar/p. 1, Kenneth Turan

Clint Eastwood will survive "A Perfect World." Ditto for Kevin Costner, who in fact gives one of his most affecting performances. An audience's chances of staying involved, however, are not so good.

One of the pokiest chase pictures to come along in some time, "A Perfect World" unites two of today's biggest male action heroes but can't quite figure out how to handle the largess. Not since Eastwood (who also directs) joined Burt Reynolds in "City Heat" has the Hollywood conventional wisdom that stars can sell anything been put to this kind of a test.

In theory, of course, John Lee Hancock's script about a hardened escaped convict (Costner) who finds the time while fleeing an implacable sheriff (Eastwood) to light up the life of the 7-year-old boy taken as a hostage is a lot more than a conventional chase movie.

What it is in reality, however, is a rehash of plot conventions from a slew of mismatched movies. "A Perfect World" will remind you of any number of previous films, but almost everything it attempts to do was done better the last time around.

The major exception to this is Costner's surprisingly adept performance as Butch Haynes, one of those only-in-the-movies criminals who, though he's taken a few wrong turns down life's winding path, has a nobler core personality than in half the craven law enforcement personnel who are tracking him down.

Imprisoned somewhere in Texas in 1963 for an unspecified crime, Butch and another convict, the ever-so-psycho Terry (Keith Szarabajka), mastermind an escape. Practically frothing at the mouth, Terry takes a break from the flight to terrorize a God-fearing group of Jehovah's Witnesses and as a result the family's young son Phillip (T.J. Lowther) is taken along for the ride.

The centerpiece of "A Perfect World" is the completely unlikely bond that develops between Butch and Phillip. On the road together, they become pals, even accomplices, as Butch, touched by tales of a restricted childhood that seems to echo his own, offers to let the lad pick his own alias and even has man-to-boy talks with him about sex and love.

As relaxed and jocular as he's ever seen on screen, Costner turns Butch into the kind of interesting, enigmatic character a small boy would be fascinated with. Their relationship is oddly charming at first, but it does nowhere and is distinctly at odds with the more muddled sensibility of the rest of the film.

Any time, for instance, we are thrust back to the command post trailer where Texas Ranger captain Red Garnett is masterminding the alleged chase, things bog down in a major way. Eastwood is not very involved in this law-and-order role, and the rest of his team (Laura Dern as the "my god, she's a woman" criminologist, Bradley Whitford as the ice-cold FBI man and Leo Burmester as Red's faithful assistant) is more clichéd than those multiethnic platoons in old World War II movies.

And to remind people that yes, Butch is a dangerous escaped convict, "A Perfect World" (rated PG-13 for "violence, sexual content and language") periodically throws in some dark moments that, especially in the film's final half hour, feel increasingly arbitrary and unconvincing.

After his work in both "Unforgiven" and "In the Line of Fire," Eastwood can afford an off day on both sides of the camera as well as a reinvolvement in the kind of sentimentalism that marked "Honkeytonk Man" and other films. Costner and plucky young actor Lowther do what they can with their part of this questionable story, and maybe that's all you can ask.

NEW STATESMAN & SOCIETY, 12/17-31/93, p. 58, Jonathan Romney

In one scene in *A Perfect World*, Kevin Costner rolls down the highway and bespies the archetypal early-1960s American family happily picnicking by the side of the road. This being a film by Clint Eastwood in his most sober, elder-statesman mode, nothing truly unpleasant befalls the hapless bystanders, even though Costner plays a sociopath who's clearly on the edge of some horrendous outburst.

It's not certain, either, that the film really *wants* us to have any grisly forebodings for their welfare; and perhaps it's simply a knee-jerk reaction if we do. But it's well-nigh impossible these days to take the rosy-cheeked nuclear grouping at face value and not to see it as a natural target for spectacular bloodshed or some other evisceratine deconstruction.

There's nothing new about this trend, which had its most spectacular highlights in the 1980s with "family-Gothic" movies such as *The Stepfather* and *Parents*. It's just odd to see how much mainstream cinema has learned to take it for granted that there's no home sweet home anymore.

This month, *Addams Family Values* tilts jovially at blue-eyed America and its chirpy progeny, while Steven Soderbergh's *King of the Hill* harks back to a Norman Rockwell-toned Depression era in which, nevertheless, the happy hearth has crumbled and Junior is left to fend for himself.

Next year, Macaulay Culkin gets to rock his own cradle as a venomous sprite in the Ian McEwan-scripted *The Good Son*. And Robin Williams, dragged up as a nanny in *Mr. Doubtfire*, manages, for all his obsessional winsomeness, to overturn a few traditional pieties about family unity.

A Perfect World looked set to offer a few piquant twists on the theme, but gives them a disappointingly gentle treatment. It's like *The Night of the Hunter* restaged on a mild spring afternoon. Eastwood gives himself a rather perfunctory role as a cop trailing Costner's escaped con, who has kidnapped a seven-year-old boy (T J Lowther) and taken him on the road.

The theme's only ostensibly dark: it soon becomes apparent that the boy's in no real danger. He would rather go along with Costner for an intense course in surrogate bonding than be sent back to his boring life with a stern Jehovah's Witness mom. This way, he gets to learn manhood at one remove, and have the Halloween he's forbidden at home, and handle a gun.

Here's where *A Perfect World* looks set to touch a nerve: the scenes in which young Lowther gets to wave a pistol at various adults will clearly have disturbing resonances in Britain in the current atmosphere of panic about child violence. The film has one interesting question in mind: what is it in childhood that makes a violent mind? Unfortunately, it's at a loss how to address it.

In a way, that's a good thing. It doesn't *just* diagnose the lack of a father figure, because here the surrogate dad, while a good guy at heart, is also, ambivalently, the corrupting influence, the lurking danger. But the ambivalence is smoothed off by introducing, and disposing of, an unequivocal menace: another con who's not only a blatant foamer-at-the-mouth but also warped enough to peer down little Phillip's Y-fronts and sneer. When Costner takes a look later on, it's only to reassure the boy about his incipient manhood, in the buddiest way possible.

Unfortunately, Kevin Costner and simmering, brooding menace do not go hand in hand, say what you like about creative casting. His featureless tranquil charm doesn't quite suggest raging depths, and his fury suggests his Robin Hood having a fit of pique because he's mislaid his quiver. But the film really fails because its narrative is aimless—the perennial risk of highway-to-nowhere sagas—and flabby in its pacing. It's too long by at least 30 minutes, and the jokey time spent with Clint and Laura Dern, tagging behind in a mobile home, is utterly wasted. Curiously enough, the film is set immediately before the Kennedy assassination; and John Lee Hancock's script seems to promise a sceptical anti-nostalgist ambiguity. Pre-JFK America is popularly imagined as the lost utopia of the film's title; maybe, the film hints, it wasn't so perfect after all. But the vast, placid vistas of Jack N Green's wide-screen photography suggest a world as yet untroubled, a barely rippled surface. As Dorothy might have said, it may not be home, but it sure looks like Kansas.

NEW YORK, 12/6/93, p. 118, David Denby

"I don't know nothing" says Clint Eastwood at the end of his fascinating, emotionally embittered new movie, *A Perfect World*. "Not one damn thing." This remark, like some of Eastwood's gnarled statements in *Unforgiven*, can probably be taken as a confession. Eastwood squints and frowns his way through the role of Red Garnett, a hard-bitten and rather tired Texas Ranger of the early sixties who brings a serious case—a manhunt—to a conclusion that he finds entirely unsatisfactory. What the remark conveys, I believe, is less a sense of ignorance or helplessness than a renunciation of certainty. Life doesn't work out the way it's supposed to, the way it did in Clint Eastwood's earlier cop movies, in which the men left dead at the end were criminal vermin, and order was restored. It doesn't work out at all: Dirty Harry cleaning things up was a dream. The title of the movie, as you may have guessed, is ironic.

In *A Perfect World*, a little boy without a father becomes the hostage of an escaped convict (Kevin Costner) who wants to raise a son—a story that sounds, I realize, about as morally invigorating as an afternoon with Geraldo. But the movie, which goes through many scenes of violence and love and ends with Clint's angry remark, is surprisingly interesting and complex—another triumph for Clint Eastwood, who again demonstrates a related command of storytelling, a feeling for open space within shots and the timing of shots within sequences, all of which marks him as a newly born classical master. At this point, I take a continuous pleasure in his moviemaking. He's now so good a filmmaker that his banal story escapes cliché the way a fish tenderly seasoned and delicately cooked escapes culinary dullness. We see the story in its ideal terms, its themes elaborately developed, its connecting links established and then released. When Eastwood reaches a narrative climax, he's prepared the dramatic values so carefully that he can pull our responses in two directions at once without strain. His natural instinct now is for stories that are morally troubling and ambiguous.

In the beginning, a hardened criminal, Butch Haynes (Costner), breaks out of a Texas penitentiary, accompanied by his loathsome, happy-loco cellmate, Terry (Keith Szarabajka). Terry blunders into a house and almost rapes a woman. Butch, in a rage, stops him and leaves with him, taking the woman's little boy as a hostage. But first, an odd thing happens in the house: Butch allows the little boy, Phillip (T.J. Lowther), to hold a revolver on him. His giving the boy the gun—arming him is the beginning of a complexly designed pattern. Screenwriter John Lee Hancock, a playwright born in Texas, has written a movie about fathers and sons, about the force of loyalties and violence working themselves out through the generations.

Keith Szarabajka has a guttural, rusty-razor-blade voice; he's too much a giggling B-movie psycho, and maybe Eastwood thinks so, too, because he doesn't keep him around very long. The way Butch handles the manic Terry—teasing and brutalizing him—is perhaps the most ruthlessly funny stuff that Eastwood has ever done. Butch, we can see, is cool in both senses of the word, quick, calculating, with a streak of dominating meanness. After so many boring and righteous performances, Kevin Costner here redeems the early promise he showed in *Silverado* and *Bill Durham*; he's almost preternaturally relaxed but with a sly, undermining humor. Butch the criminal psychopath is very bright, and Costner, easing his way through the performance, shows us how the intelligence and the low instincts work together as seductiveness. Butch is coldly manipulative with most people; it's only children who bring out a tender streak in him. That's when he gets really dangerous.

Butch makes friends with Phillip, his hostage, by turning their time on the Texas roads together into a game. He realizes that Phillip's mother hasn't allowed the kid much fun, so he completely enters into the boy's imaginative world. He decides to liberate the fatherless boy—to offer himself as father, protecting Phillip, building him up, and letting him play at freedom, which, for Butch and Phillip, means playing at crime. Young T. J. Lowther, biting on his lower lip in anxiety, squinching up his face, his step a little wobbly, looks and sounds like the anxious 8-year-olds that I've actually met. He's game but vulnerable, a relief from the standard inhumanly alert Hollywood movie child.

Butch and Phillip go on their spree, ripping people off and tearing across the Texas hill country, and though there's almost a picnic atmosphere to their adventures, our apprehension grows. Butch, abused and neglected as a child, is kind to Phillip, but there's a volatile underside to his kindness. He wants Phillip to have the childhood he himself never had; he wants him to have a father. But Butch is scary—willful nice, crazy nice, and dangerous nice. He turns Phillip from a hostage into an accomplice, a criminal. The surrogate father-son stuff isn't the sappy togetherness celebrated on *Oprah*; it's tinged with fear and madness.

As they flee, the Texas Ranger and his entourage come after. Red Garnett travels in the governor's campaign trailer, which has modern communication equipment but is nevertheless an awkward vehicle from which to conduct a manhunt; Red and his assistants are trapped in the cumbersome, nearly windowless trailer, while Butch has his—freedom in the hills and fields. Eastwood seems to have mixed feelings about the old ranger; he plays the scenes for a kind of squashed, irritable comedy. As Red squints in fury, Sally (Laura Dern), a rather arrogant young university criminologist, keeps telling him what an idiot he is. Sally, who appears to have a fully formed feminist consciousness, is probably an anachronism (this is supposed to be 1963), but Dern pulls off the role; she plays the chip-on-her-shoulder intellectual with such emotional fluidity that she gets away with it clean.

For a long time, the movie just floats, effortlessly, beautifully, a chase through rolling hills with plenty of odd, interesting scenes and no cheap thrills. As far as we can see, Red isn't trying very hard to capture Butch. Something of the old drive for dominance has been lost in the Eastwood figure. Red, it turns out, is connected to Butch by ties of affection. Eastwood and John Lee Hancock have set up two generations of disrupted relations between spiritual fathers and sons. When little Phillip, bullied by the vicious Terry, comes to believe his penis is "puny," Butch takes a look and reassures him. The scene is meant to be a blessing, a ritual passing on of manhood, yet Eastwood stages it so unemphatically that he absolves it of sentimentality.

The movie hurts, though, because it asks whether a man driven to be the perfect father might not be crazy. Butch, a talented and resourceful man as well as a criminal, has a fatal flaw, and it's a flaw connected to love. He nearly kills a black farmer who slaps his grandson a few times. Little Phillip, terrified, winds up holding the gun on him once again. The themes all come together, and the long, long coda that brings this movie to a close is a kind of benediction. The earth, the fields, the sky—Clint Eastwood embraces the elements in what is probably his most delicate and lyrical moment as a director. Eastwood represents something almost unprecedented in our culture. A man who used violence and nihilistic tricks to attract the crowd, who for years exploited himself and his audience, has become, in his sixties, a reflective and moving artist.

NEW YORK POST, 11/24/93, p. 35, Michael Medved

Since when did Clint Eastwood become the prince of political correctness?

As his new movie, "A Perfect World," stumbles and lurches toward its preposterously predictable conclusion, he offers passing condemnations of shameful sexism in the workplace, joyless religion, authoritarian parents, sexual harassment, murderous FBI men, mistreatment of juvenile offenders, dehumanizing preoccupation with money, sexual abuse of children, and, above all, the devastating impact of corporal punishment on kids.

There are also vague invocations of the Kennedy assassination "conspiracy," since the action takes place in Texas in November of 1963. In fact, the specific timing of crucial events is one of the picture's many weak points. The story begins on Halloween, but the next day (Nov. 1) we're informed that JFK is coming to Dallas the next week ... two full weeks before he actually made his fateful trip.

It's a stupid, sloppy mistake in a silly movie that tries to breathe new life into the ancient cliche about a hardened criminal who turns out to have a heart of gold when he's thrown together with a helpless child, (John Ford and John Wayne handled it much better in "3 Godfathers" 45 years ago).

Here, Kevin Costner plays a tender tough-guy who escapes from prison where he's been serving a 40-year sentence for armed robbery, and he grabs a 7 year-old hostage (T.J. Lowther) who has been suffering his own imprisonment in his mother's fanatically religious Jehovah's Witness home.

The two fugitives form a strong bond on the dusty back roads as they try to escape from the determined Texas Ranger (Clint Eastwood) who's heading the manhunt. Eastwood, who is implausibly accompanied by a brilliant criminologist played by Laura Dern, just happens to have been the arresting officer who first sent Costner to prison as a teen-ager. Now he must confront the horrible cost of harsh sentencing, as Dirty Harry comes full circle and gets a hokey lesson in "compassion."

The only energy in this cheerless chase comes from veteran production designer Henry Bumstead, who conveys a convincing sense of small-town Texas, and from Eastwood's long-time cameraman, Jack Green, whose lyrical images give a handsome sheen to even the most unconvincing scenes.

Costner also deserves credit for an intriguing performance in a role that places him as close as he's ever come to playing an outright bad guy. "I'm not a good man," he declares at a key moment. "Not the worst, either. Just a breed apart."

If the script, by Texas-born playwrite John Lee Hancock, hadn't been so insipidly insistent on displaying the Costner character's essential decency, the actor might have provided far more insight on what it means to be "a breed apart."

The film literally falls apart during its final halfhour, with a painfully drawn-out, tear-jerking climax that runs on at least four times longer than it should. The audience is supposed to be emotionally drained at the end of the movie, but most filmgoers feel surly and cheated.

A few weeks ago, Al Pacino followed his Oscar-winning performance in "Scent of a Woman" with the dreadfully disappointing "Carlito's Way"; now, last year's other big Oscar winner, director Clint Eastwood, offers an equally disappointing unsatisfying bust.

His devoted fans should concentrate on his terrific performance earlier this year in "In the Line of Fire," and do Clint a favor by forgetting the painfully imperfect "A Perfect World."

NEWSDAY, 11/24/93, Part II/p. 61, John Anderson

The sins, and the cinema, of the fathers are visited upon the sons in "A Perfect World," in which Clint Eastwood becomes Gary Cooper, Kevin Costner becomes Clint Eastwood, young T.J. Lowther is transfigured into Casper the Holy Ghost and a raft of American cinematic devices are reinvented and altered, along with our assumptions.

If one of yours happens to concern Eastwood's status as a first-class director, let's put it this way: It's almost a shame he took home the Oscar last spring, because it reduces his odds of winning again, and for a better film. There isn't a wasted gesture here; every frame has its place in the whole.

But technique is tangential. In this blazing autumn of his film career, Eastwood is an icon, and an even more valuable iconoclast. Having long ago digested the characters and conceits of American movies, he's begun spitting them back out in a way that reviles the hard-hearted, half-witted way they've been absorbed into the American psyche. He explores the lowest form of predatory human, without losing sight of his humanity. He employs cliched characters—a kindly black sharecropper, for instance—and then imbues them with grievous flaws. He takes any feeling of inevitable happiness, something that only occurs in the movies anyway, and trashes it.

Granted: As a cowboy, a carny or a hard-line cop, Eastwood has both contributed to and fed off the same myths, about order and law and sex and power, that he plays with here. But like his "Perfect World" character, Red Garnett, the Texas Ranger whose hunt for escaped convict Butch Haynes (Costner) becomes a purge of his own conscience, Eastwood is a he-man in transition. In "Unforgiven" he re-evaluated his own heroic image, as well as the contexts in which it was formed. And now, in "A Perfect World," he assumes a progressive, tolerant, pan-gender approach to those who've been disenfranchised, both in life and on film. He's become, in short, the Anti-Duke.

And as Red Garnett, he's also lean as a fence post, tough as a $2 (after-inflation) steak and a sexual dinosaur; Laura Dern, who plays criminologist Sally Gerber, stares at him in the same slack-jawed way she watched the brontosaurus in "Jurassic Park." It's November, 1963, and Red calls Sally "Missy," when he talks to her at all, but you can see him fighting not to agree with her sociologic conclusions about Haynes' mind.

Red is not a man who welcomes change, unlike Butch Haynes, who suspects a perfect world might be possible, if you could just eliminate some of its two-legged imperfections. The offspring of a career-criminal and New Orleans prostitute, Butch is also the misbegotten son of the American justice system, and Red: It was the lawman who persuaded a judge to give the teenage Butch four years on a joy-riding charge, in order to keep the boy away from his biological father. And now, having imposed his will, Red is hunting the bad result of his own good intentions.

Having broken out of prison with the psychotic and soon-to-be-dispatched Terry Pugh (Keith Szarabajka), Haynes takes as his hostage young Phillip Perry (T.J. Lowther), whose father has deserted him, and whose mother, a devout Jehovah's Witness, forbids him to observe Halloween, or to have much fun at all. Whether this is a fair portrayal of religion or parenting is moot; it gives Butch—whose loathing of violence against children will be revealed, layer by alarming layer—the link to humanity he needs. Their mutual escape is temporary, of course, and inherently artificial: When Butch holds up a general store, Philip steals the Casper costume he'd wanted, an act of liberation. But he then spends much of the film behind a mask, like Butch, and like Red.

Their common fatherlessness, and Red's link to Butch, are both wildly coincidental. But we don't care, because we're caught up in a fast-moving mix of fugitive drama, buddy movie, and Christian allegory—the climactic scene involving the three principals, father, son and Friendly Ghost, is almost arch. Besides, the film's metaphysical complexities are balanced by Costner's very earthy performance, surely the best thing he's ever done.

In other films, the actor has seemed smug and ungenerous, but in "A Perfect World," Malibu Kevin has given way to an anti-heroic sensibility that is, well, Eastwoodian. When the film mentions "Sgt. York," we know *they* know there's a line of succession being explored here.

"A Perfect World" is awash in film references—"Bonnie and Clyde," "Sugarland Express," even Eastwood's own "Escape from Alcatraz"—but is as spare and unadorned as the bleached-bone Texas flatland where it all takes place. One pictures Eastwood rejecting style with an angry shrug, insisting that his story stand alone in its own paralyzing sadness.

NEWSWEEK, 11/29/93, p. 72, David Ansen

After the taut and troubling "Unforgiven," Clint Eastwood's *A Perfect World* feels like a breather. As usual, you can expect solid, no-fuss craftsmanship, but it's best to set your expectations down a notch. Any capsule description of the plot makes this movie sound a lot more fingernail-biting than it is. Kevin Costner plays escaped convict Butch Haynes, who takes an 8-year-old Jehovah's Witness boy (T.J. Lowther) as a hostage and commits murder along the way before the manhunt led by Texas Ranger Eastwood tracks him down. Surprisingly, the movie has only a glancing, jokey concern with the mechanics of the manhunt. Eastwood and criminologist Laura Dern (an anachronistically feminist figure for 1963) are the pursuers, but their connection to the story is never more than peripheral. It's Costner and the kid's show, a seriocomic surrogate-father-and-son roadpic that's at its best when it's content to be little more than a charming caper, as the boy dresses up in his Casper the Friendly Ghost Halloween costume and learns the tricks of petty larceny.

Butch Haynes, who, like the boy, had been abandoned by his no-good father, has to be the most sensitive psycho of the year—a pushover for kids, he's the Mrs. Doubtfire of killers. When John Lee Hancock's script tries to get heavy and psychological on us it just won't wash—the movie is a pipe dream or it's nothing. And during the dragged-out showdown at the end, Butch and the boy finally lose their ongoing battle with bathos. Eastwood obviously intends "A Perfect World" to be a fable about the mysteries of human behavior—the virtues in hardened cons, the vices in the law-abiding, that sort of thing. But Hancock's surface-skimming script is too formulaic for the job. There's enough material here for a crisp 90-minute entertainment. At 2¼ hours, the leisurely, mildly engaging "A Perfect World" barely sputters across the finish line.

SIGHT AND SOUND, 2/94, p. 59, Michael Atkinson

Dallas County, Halloween, 1963. The fatherless, middle-class Perry family is visited by trick-or-treaters. When a chaperoning parent asks Mrs. Perry why her seven-year-old son Phillip isn't trick-or-treating as well, she explains that it's against the family's religion as Jehovah's Witnesses. Meanwhile, convicts Butch Haynes and Terry Pugh escape from a nearby prison, assaulting a guard and stealing his car. The two head into the suburbs to steal another car, by chance coming upon the Perry neighborhood. As Butch searches for a car, Terry enters the Perry house and begins sexually assaulting the mother. Butch intervenes just in time, and the two escape with Phillip as hostage.

On the road, the tension is thick between the three: when Butch stops at a store and half-jokingly leaves Phillip holding a gun on Terry, Terry ends up molesting the boy as well. Butch confronts Terry in a nearby field and kills him. Meanwhile, law officials headed by Texas Ranger Red Garnett are busy tracking Butch's possible movements and commandeering the Governor's new-fangled luxury trailer as a mobile home base. Garnett's team is joined by a laconic FBI marksman and Sally Gerber, a criminologist who has a tough time earning Garnett's respect. Once on the road alone, Phillip and Butch get along famously, exchanging father-son intimacies, stealing new cars, and charming the clerks at a store where Phillip steals a Halloween costume (Casper the Friendly Ghost) at his own initiative, moments before local cops attempt to trap Butch and fail. Given the option to stay behind, Phillip elects to ride on. Garnett's mobile home drives right by Butch, turns abruptly around and ends up landing the trailer in a roadside ditch.

After encounters with a vacationing family, a roadblock and a lusty waitress, during which Butch asks the boy to make a list of all the things his mother won't allow him to do, the pair meet Mack, a black farm-worker, who invites them to his house to sleep. The next morning, after witnessing Mack hit his young son needlessly, Butch suddenly becomes psychotic, forcing Mack at gunpoint to apologise to the boy, then tying him up in preparation for killing the whole family. Horrified, Phillip retrieves the gun and shoots Butch in the stomach. Soon Garnett's team arrives with Mrs Perry and everyone nervously faces off in another empty field, with Butch slowly dying from his wound. In return for Mrs Perry's promise that Phillip can ride a rollercoaster and eat cotton candy, Butch sends the boy up to the line of patrol cars, but Phillip turns back to bring Butch with him, prompting Garnett to disarm himself and approach the pair. As Butch reaches into his back pocket for a postcard he once received from the father who deserted him, the FBI marksman assumes he is reaching for a gun and shoots him dead. As Butch lies in the field, Phillip is flown out by helicopter.

Few cults of personality have seeped into world movie culture as pervasively as Eastwoodology: the care, feeding and worship of Clint Eastwood's aesthetic reputation as a filmmaker and icon. His stock as a 'serious' director, which few had bought through *The Outlaw Josey Wales*, *The Gauntlet, Bronco Billy, Heartbreak Ridge* and *Honkeytonk Man*, has risen dramatically since the more ambitious *White Hunter, Black Heart*, and *Unforgiven*. Let's not forget, either, the creeping 70s nostalgia that has put a grimy glow on *Play Misty for Me* and *High Plains Drifter*. At one time Eastwood occupied the action-hero gutter of Charles Bronson and Chuck Norris, his directorial efforts perceived as indulgences paid for by box office clout: today, he's the nearest thing Hollywood has to a Hawksian auteur. It's the most remarkable arc in critical regard since Edgar G. Ulmer.

Today, Eastwood can do no wrong for most cinephiles, for whom *Unforgiven* was a sanctification of itinerant *Dirty Harry* fandom. True, 1992's Oscar winner was something of a miracle, as if Gary Cooper and Nicholas Ray had somehow fused into a single moviemaking savant and reinvented a classic genre, with the Chekovian wisdom and pathos it always promised. But still, the no-assembly-required four-star accolades *A Perfect World* has been gathering in the US are almost surreally inappropriate to the mediocre road movie redux he's unceremoniously chosen as *Unforgiven*'s follow-up. Eastwood himself must be surprised: nowhere in *A Perfect World* does the film proclaim itself to be anything but a formulaic Hollywood project, the sort Eastwood is probably seeking more often now to segue himself into, in supporting character roles.

With American critics blathering on about the significance of the final scene's father/son/holy Friendly Ghost symbolism, it's enough to make Eastwood reconsider running again for Mayor of Carmel, California.

The script for *A Perfect World* is professionally engineered for retro coolness, revisiting the road movie milieu of *In Cold Blood*, positioning itself in Dallas County days before JFK's drive through Dealey Plaza, and taking an ingenuous kid along for the ride. Unfortunately, the pleasant, slack texture of the movie—peppered with plenty of wry witticisms à la Costner—leaves a great deal of unexplored territory surrounding the film's various themes: notably the social manufacture of sociopaths and the importance of fatherhood. We wonder through most of the film's prolix length how a career criminal of the sort Costner plays can be so relentlessly charming, reliable, kind and generous. The scene that betrays the lie, Costner's white-hot ten-minute purgatory in the farmworker's living room, is meant to justify the rest of the film. It provides no answers, however, especially when the wounded Costner becomes conciliatory and sweet all over again. All we can conclude is that Butch has made an ersatz criminal career out of killing people for beating their children.

The film focuses so centrally on the good-natured patter between Costner and pint-sized T.J.Lowther that Eastwood and co are reduced to cameos—a good thing, considering Eastwood's ID rehash of his grizzled cop routine, and Dern retracing her horrific steps from *Jurassic Park* as the professional bubblehead whose chief duty is divided between flaunting her more or less dubious training and screaming on cue. As the innocent, Lowther is fine in a performance created for the most part in the editing room, while Costner is simply Costner (albeit with a small pot belly). The perverse entertainment value inherent in watching an absurdly likeable and self-possessed movie star used to embodying goodness play a homicidal nutcase—even for ten minutes—is one of *A Perfect World*'s glorious consolations. Costner underplays the scene beautifully, and for a few moments we're in the presence of an authentic chaos. The other two hours are merely biding time.

TIME, 11/29/93, p. 75, Richard Corliss

It's Texas in the fall of 1963, passionate rebel Kevin Costner is willing to break the rules to make a moral point. Flinty lawman Clint Eastwood is riding in a vehicle needed for President Kennedy's visit to Dallas. At first this looks like the convergence of two recent strains of Hollywood retrohistory: *JFK in the Line of Fire*. But *A Perfect World*, which Eastwood directed from John Lee Hancock's script, is not another dark fable about Camelot. The stage is smaller here, the concerns personal rather than political. This is an old-fashioned, nicely spun-out, one-handed character drama. It just takes the film a while to reveal who its main players are and how ambitious its agenda is.

Butch Haynes (Costner), a "criminal's criminal," has broken out of jail along with Terry (Keith Szarabajka), a garden-variety psychopath. The convicts terrorize a mother and her children and take seven-year-old Phillip (T.J. Lowther) hostage. Tracking their flight is a Texas Ranger posse led by Eastwood, your basic righteous cowboy emeritus, and sparked by Laura Dern, a Governor's aide who brings feminist compassion and common sense to the pursuit. Bad guys, good guys, *vroom-vroom*, ho hum.

Not really—because *A Perfect World* isn't a western *Shane*, it's a warped *Shane*. In that 1953 film, mysterious gunslinger Alan Ladd agrees to protect a homesteader's family against varmints and becomes a reluctant role model for the tenderfoot's young son. Here, Haynes is the bad guy, but he's mainly Shane. When Terry puts the make on Phillip, Butch avenges the assault. He gives Phillip lessons in backwoods manhood: how to smoke, cuss, dance, romance a waitress, drive a car, steal a car, rob a store and, of course, point a loaded gun at people you don't like. It's the blind leading the blind: Butch is trying to become the father neither he nor the boy ever knew.

The movie also gives Butch enough psychological backstory to explain most of his antisocial excesses. Seems his mother was a prostitute and his dad "beat the hell out of anything he ever came across, or screwed, or fathered." As abused children become abusive adults, so poorly parented Butch turns into a lame excuse for a father to Phillip. But the boy is ready to learn from, idolize—and finally stand up to—the first man who has taken a paternal interest in him.

In his first stint as director since the Oscar-winning *Unforgiven*, Eastwood is pleased to let scenes amble in real Texas time, to let destiny fall slowly on Butch. Costner, though pulling a superficial switch on the pensive heroes he usually plays, is at such ease before the camera that Butch is made both compelling and agreeable, This *World* isn't perfect: it zigzags toward its climax and dodders in pathos when it gets there. But it's a handsome calling card for two Hollywood artists in prime form—one at the high noon of stardom, the other in the tumbleweed afternoon of a distinguished career.

VILLAGE VOICE, 11/30/93, Film Special/p. 29, Georgia Brown

If there's any character Clint Eastwood identifies with, it's the flawed creature wrestling with demons: drink, age with its attendant infirmities, dark urges to violence, and other crises of manhood. He's the lawman who identifies with the psycho he's after (or the psycho after him), white hunter—concealing black heart. And while it's clear from his political affinities (Reagan, Perot) that Eastwood himself nurtures that flawed dream of law and order, there's evidence too that he's always questioning his former allegiances. Certainly, he's been wrestling recently with the subject of violence.

A Perfect World's release is timed almost precisely 30 years after its fictional events take place: early November 1963, just before the fatal date. Set in and around Austin, Texas, the film (written by John Lee Hancock) mentions Kennedy's impending visit to Dallas just once, but that event clearly looms over this particular tragedy, this story of father-hating sons. Didactic and utterly sincere, *A Perfect World* ends strikingly with the Eastwood character's furious declaration of impotence: "I don't know one damn thing."

The world the film conjures up is the placid, "innocent" middle America of the '50s pre-assassination, "pre-Tet, pre-MTV—but already anything but perfect. Small-town Halloween isn't even fun. In the Perry household it's thoroughly grim since Mom, a Jehovah's Witness, won't allow the kids out to trick-or-treat. The home is fatherless, too, or, more accurately, it waits vainly for a truant father to return.

Meanwhile, not far away, at Huntsville penitentiary, a jail-break takes place, sending over (answered prayers?) not one but two potential dads. One, Terry (Keith Szarabajka), is a vicious thug; the other, Butch Haynes (Kevin Costner), appears appreciably saner. There's even the suggestion that Butch is moved to abduct Phillip (T. J. Lowther), the one boy in the Perry family, to get him away from a woman he takes to be a bad mother. Apparently, Butch himself was sent to prison as a juvenile offender by a lawman who thought the teenager would be better off there than in a dysfunctional home.

As the *Perfect World Turns*. ... Back in the Perry's kitchen, just after Terry has roughed up Mrs. Perry, Butch becomes erratic, putting his gun in the seven-year-old's hand. "Say, 'Stick 'em up,'" he orders. It's something he repeats throughout he film. Later we find out that as an eight-year old, Butch shot a man he saw hurting his mother, a roadhouse prostitute. Besides stealing Butch's identification with Phillip, the gun-giving signifies a general social phenomenon—men passing weapons to boys.

The ensuing manhunt pits Butch and Phillip (the mean Terry doesn't last long) against a law-enforcement team consisting of an aging loner, Red Garnett (Clint), a couple of trusted aides, a steely marksman, and a criminology expert, Sally (Laura Dern, reprising her "expert" role from *Jurassic Park*). Often this crew, riding in a silver bullet-shaped trailer, provides a comic interlude. All of the Eastwood persona's stock-and-trade is here. Red puts out the obligatory sexist doody (he supposes Sally must be the new secretary), and resists academic expertise. He's also swilling Geritol. Says Arthur Godfrey vouches for it (Period brands include R. C. Cola, Juicy Fruit, Tatertots, and, as a nod to Costner, Bull Durham.)

Riding the highways in stolen cars, Butch and Phillip encounter various parental surrogates. Stopping at a surreal dry goods store called Friendly's to buy Phillip shoes and pants, they find a chorus of female clerks outdoing each other with smarmy smiles. False moms whose masks drop quickly enough. Responding perhaps to the perfidy of mothers, Phillip turns outlaw, too: In compensation for all lost Halloweens, he cops a Casper the Friendly Ghost costume.

As in *Unforgiven*, there's a reference here to penis size as a vital male concern. Women—whether sinister or nurturing—are peripheral. It's a boy-man thing. The fairly innocuous episodes gather to the movie's most astonishing scene, where, in the living room of a black farmer, Butch flips out.

Though nowhere as rich nor as deeply moving as *Unforgiven*, *A Perfect World* evinces the perfect integrity, the unstinting modesty of Eastwood's work all along. (The reticent directorial style meshes absolutely with the persona.) Anything but flashy, the film is grounded in the period's and the rural area's seeming prelapsarian simplicity. Violence is kept conspicuously offscreen. With his short sleeves rolled and the suggestion of a pot belly, Costner appears at home. The kid, not one of those pretty, wise-cracking movie brats, has a piquant, pinched little face. Throughout, Eastwood's own paternal role is effaced—until he utters that helpless, furious cri de coeur at the end. At this moment it's hard not to be deflected back to the perplexed consciousness of the director-star, our own fantasy father.

Also reviewed in:
NATION, 12/20/93, p. 778, Stuart Klawans
NEW YORK TIMES, 11/24/93, p. C11, Janet Maslin
NEW YORKER, 12/6/93, p. 135, Terrence Rafferty
VARIETY, 11/29/93, p. 30, Todd McCarthy
WASHINGTON POST, 11/24/93, p. C1, Hal Hinson
WASHINGTON POST, 11/26/94, Weekend/p. 57, Desson Howe

PHILADELPHIA

A TriStar Pictures release of a Clinica Estetico production.   *Executive Producer:* Gary Goetzman, Kenneth Utt, and Ron Bozman.   *Producer:* Edward Saxon and Jonathan Demme.   *Director:* Jonathan Demme.   *Screenplay:* Ron Nyswaner.   *Director of Photography:* Tak Fujimoto.   *Editor:* Craig McKay.   *Music:* Howard Shore.   *Music Editor:* Suzana Peric and Nicholas Meyers.   *Sound:* Chris Newman.   *Sound Editor:* Ron Bochar.   *Casting:* Howard Feuer.   *Production Designer:* Kristi Zea.   *Art Director:* Tim Galvin.   *Set Decorator:* Karen O'Hara.   *Set Dresser:* Ken Turek.   *Costumes:* Colleen Atwood.   *Make-up:* Carl Fullerton.   *Make-up (Denzel Washington):* Edna M. Sheen.   *Running time:* 119 minutes.   *MPAA Rating:* PG-13.

CAST: Tom Hanks (Andrew Beckett);   Denzel Washington (Joe Miller);   Roberta Maxwell (Judge Tate);   Buzz Kilman ("Crutches");   Karen Finley (Dr. Gillman);   Daniel Chapman (Clinic Storyteller);   Mark Sorensen, Jr. (Clinic Patient);   Jeffrey Williamson (Tyrone);   Charles Glenn (Kenneth Killcoyne);   Ron Vawter (Bob Seidman);   Anna Deavere Smith (Anthea Burton);   Stephanie Roth (Rachel Smilow);   Lisa Talerico (Shelby);   Joanne Woodward (Sarah Beckett);   Jason Robards (Charles Wheeler);   Robert Ridgely (Walter Kenton);   Chandra Wilson (Chandra);   Ford Wheeler (Alan);   David Drake (Bruno);   Peter Jacobs (Peter/Mona Lisa);   Antonio Banderas (Miguel Alvarez);   Paul Lazar (Dr. Klenstein);   Bradley Whitford (Jamey Collins);   Lisa Summerour (Lisa Miller);   Freddie Foxxx and Paul Moore (Hospital Patients);   Warren Miller (Mr. Finley);   Lauren Roselli (Iris);   Jane Moore (Lydia Glines);   Joey Perillo (Filko);   Bill Rowe (Dr. Armbruster);   Dennis Radesky (Santa Claus);   Glen Hartell (Library Guard);   Tracey Walter (Librarian);   John Ignarri and Richard Ehrlich (Young Men in Library);   Julius Erving (Himself);   Ann Dowd (Jill Beckett);   Katie Lintner (Alexis);   Peg French and Ann Howard (The Bronte Sisters);   Meghan Tepas (Meghan);   John Bedford Lloyd (Matt Beckett);   Robert Castle (Bud Beckett);   Molly Hickok (Molly Beckett);   Dan Olmstead (Randy Beckett);   Elizabeth Roby (Elizabeth Beckett);   Adam Le Fevre (Jill's Husband);   Gary Goetzman (Guido Paonessa);   Daniel von Bargen (Jury Foreman);   Mary Steenburgen (Belinda Conine);   Obba Babatunde (Jerome Green);   James B. Howard (Dexter

Smith);   Charles Techman (Ralph Peterson);   Charles Napier (Judge Garnett);   Roger Corman (Mr. Laird);   Jim Roche ("Not Adam and Steve");   Donna Hamilton (Angela Medina); Edward Rendell (Mayor);   Daniel Wolff (Filko's Buddy);   John T. O'Connell (Macho Barfly); Edward Kirkland (Cousin Eddie);   Tony Fitzpatrick (Bartender);   Kathryn Witt (Melissa Benedict);   Debra H. Ballard (Court Stenographer);   André B. Blake (Young Man in Pharmacy); Ira Flitter (Andrew's Friend);   Gene Borkan (Bailiff);   Q Lazzarus (Party Singer);   Lucas Platt (Robert);   Lewis Walker ("Punchline");   Carmen Mahiques (Miguel's Mom);   José Castillo (Miguel's Dad);   Leigh Smiley (Younger Sarah Beckett);   Philip Joseph "PJ" McGee (Child Andrew).

CINEASTE, Vol. XX, No. 3, 1994, p. 51, Roy Grundmann & Peter Sacks

Andrew Beckett (Tom Hanks), a successful gay lawyer, is fired from a prestigious Philly law firm even though he's recently been promoted to junior partner. His bosses, a bunch of cigar-smoking members of the old boy's club, claim it's due to his incompetence and poor work performance. Beckett claims it's because they've discovered he has AIDS and files a discrimination suit against his employers. He secures the counsel of Joe Miller (Denzel Washington), a well-dressed, ambulance-chasing attorney who finds himself confronted not only with Beckett's bigoted bosses but also with his own fear of AIDS and homosexuality. Most readers who have followed the uproar in the wake of *Philadelphia*'s release know that this synopsis is hardly a sufficient description of the film. What, then, is the film really about!

This courtroom melodrama is a predictable attempt in the liberal tradition of films such as Elia Kazan's *Gentleman's Agreement* (1947) and Stanley Kramer's *Home of the Brave* (1949) to present personal narratives of prejudice and civil rights discrimination in clearly-defined moral terms. Yet, *Philadelphia* is different from the others because it cannot wholeheartedly denounce the social bigotry and prejudice it seeks to expose. In the end, the film is unable to make up its mind about the communities it feels obliged to champion because homophobia (and the fear of AIDS, for that matter) is still a socially pervasive and popular attitude.

In the past, Jonathan Demme's films have displayed a sensibility for the complexities of American society. Films such as *Citizen's Band* (1977), *Melvin and Howard* (1980), *Married to the Mob* (1988), and especially the seductive *The Silence of the Lambs* (1991), are intriguing because they offer a detailed, ambiguous, and, at times, ironic portrait of social, economic, medico-scientific, and military systems. Weaned on Hawks, Ford, and Capra, Demme has always expressed sympathy with an individual protagonist who moves within and, at times, against these systems. While Demme's films encourage us to identify with the individual, they never completely abandon their faith in the system depicted.

In *Philadelphia* this tension catches up with Demme and accounts for the film's major flaws. It ambitiously attempts to dramatize the complex, often contradictory political and psychological positions in this country regarding AIDS and homosexuality, yet ends up dividing its world into simplistic categories of homophile, homophobe, and not-so-homophobe. At one end of the spectrum is Beckett's unconditionally supportive family, including a baby nephew he gets to rock in his arms; at the other are his colleagues, ensconced in a Caligari-style conference room, into which Beckett is summoned to be fired.

Small wonder that neither the good homophiles nor the bad homophobes occupy center stage in *Philadelphia*. This position is inhabited instead by Miller, whose 'moderate' homophobia makes him the movie's dramatic linchpin for audience identification. Miller's mere eight-degree-transformation from mental gay basher to bashful gay rights advocate is meant to speak to 'the silent majority' challenged to uphold legal and moral justice in the face of its own fears.

Significantly, while Miller's pity for Beckett and his acceptance of Beckett's lover, Miguel (Antonio Banderas), are psychological by-products along the way to court victory, his metamorphosis never translates into open and explicit support for the gay community. Therefore, the fact that he acknowledges his homophobia and yet does not have to part with it conveniently lets spectators off the hook. It's a patronizing cop-out not to give audiences more credit. Miller functions as a ploy for the audience to safely consume and dispose of the real problems that AIDS and homophobia pose. *Philadelphia* thereby succeeds in severing a legal agenda from its moral foundation. The film makes a case for legal equality for both homosexuals and PWAs (although in the film the distinction between the two is not always clear), yet it refuses to follow suit by morally condemning homophobia. It's like watching a Fifties film in which a white lawyer fights for the right of blacks to move up from the back of the bus but would really prefer not to sit next to them.

With *Philadelphia*, Hollywood reveals its own conservative perceptions of the social reality in this country. Miller's fear of 'the love that dare not speak its name' indicates the film's general tenor which condemns homophobia and yet compulsively manifests it. This neurosis results from what Michel Foucault terms "the pressures of the unspeakable"—something that is close to us, yet unacceptable and which, therefore, needs to be kept at a safe distance. Hollywood is a fascinating barometer of this neurosis in that it consistently wavers between two extremes: the 'happens-to-be-gay' and the flaming queen character. The latter indicates the broad strokes by which mainstream cinema paints gays, while the former reflects the total annihilation of gay identity.

In its treatment of Beckett, *Philadelphia* uniquely combines both stereotypes and reveals Hollywood as a most eligible patient for a visit to Freud's couch. The film is afraid to psychologically portray Beckett as a sexual being and attempts to get around this fear by depicting him as being perfectly content in his closet. By rationalizing Beckett's happens-to-be-gay status, *Philadelphia* keeps audiences from defining him solely in terms of his sexuality. If the film did otherwise, so the conventional fallacy goes, the threat posed by gay sex would create a disconcerting (not to mention unprofitable) conflict whereby the audience would be repulsed by Beckett in the process of identifying with him.

Sick patient that it is, the film still needs to make sure that audiences don't mistake Beckett for straight, so it burdens him with stereotypical signifiers of gay culture. He becomes an all-show-no-tell character since the compulsive attempt to incorporate all signs into Beckett's characterization is blocked by the film's fear of acknowledging their sources. Therefore, Beckett is allowed to adore Maria Callas, entertain Quentin Crisp, make a total of two trips to a gay porn theatre, and slow dance with Miguel who, we are supposed to believe, is his boyfriend. What the film offers as an in-depth psychological portrait of a gay man is merely a depiction of a character suffering from a deadly disease.

The result is a superficial vision of a multicultural society in which any representation of marginalized identities is reduced to empty signs. *Philadelphia* reduces Beckett's relationship with Miguel to the description of one man nursing another. While providing medical care has become an important part of many gay relationships since AIDS, it still is only one part. Miguel (whose last name the film never mentions) is further deprived of any substance as he is allowed only to handle Beckett's I.V., prepare injections, and criticize doctors. It's Beckett's mother (Joanne Woodward) who does all the worrying, thereby reaping the audience's sympathies and commiseration.

Minimizing Miguel's role is just one of the ways in which the film's red ribbon mentality severs gayness from AIDS—thereby doing exactly the opposite of what the gay community needs these days, which is an insistence on this connection as part of its history, cultural identity, and political/medical plight. This is important with respect to the funding of research projects, medical care, and social benefits for gay lovers. While gays therefore need to insist on their specific position in relation to AIDS, we must not allow dominant culture to condemn sexual practices associated with AIDS, but should enlist the political and cultural system to fight the disease itself.

Ironically, Demme has stated repeatedly that he didn't want to make a film that sidestepped the gay community. The tension, however, between his willingness to depict gayness and his fear of psychologically engaging with it inevitably results in an ethnographic perspective of gay life (which the film conceives of only as white, upper-middle class). *Philadelphia* presents gays as a tribe of noble savages. Beckett's 'Baedeckerization' is epitomized in the now infamous 'opera scene' in which he and Miller meet to discuss their strategy for the next day in court. Beckett drifts out of the conversation, suddenly overwhelmed by an aria from Umberto Giordano's *Andrea Chénier* which has been playing in the background. Rapturously dancing (with his I.V. stand in tow) to the over-determined strains of Callas, Beckett attempts to relate the meaning of the aria to an increasingly uncomfortable Miller.

Expressionistic and objectifying at the same time, this scene puts Beckett's identity up for grabs by simultaneously depicting him as an ascending angel and a demon in the underworld. With his recitation of "I am love, I am transcendence," the film gives Beckett himself an opportunity to explain the significance of the 'tribal ritual.' He speaks of his own experience in his own voice, an act which potentially liberates him from the conventional position as the object of ethnographic study.

But Demme refuses to let this happen: the literally condescending view of Beckett in the high angle shot reaffirms his position as the object of the camera's gaze. Although the visual and aural excess which marks Beckett could be interpreted a number of ways, the stunned reaction shots of Miller intercut in this scene make clear that the film expects most viewers to react to Beckett as the Phantom of the Opera. The strong color demarcation which codes both men in this scene— Beckett's face suffused in saturated red and Miller's increasingly darkening face lit by the dying embers in the fireplace—further reinforces difference instead of negotiating it. Although the music of Giordano's opera haunts Miller into his connubial bed (where he tries to reassure himself of his straight identity), it can't counterbalance the visual divide of the preceding scene.

Philadelphia's guided artistry is rather troubling. It attempts to depict social controversy through diverse voices but, more often than not, Demme puts the voices of the groups he wants to champion into the wrong mouths with the wrong words. Take, for example, the defense's open insinuation that Beckett may have contracted the virus during his visits to a porn theatre. This explicit connection of AIDS and gay sex is something that, ten years ago, AIDS activists were begging for when neither Bush nor Reagan even knew how to spell A-I-D-S. The film presents this connection in a negative way, however, by putting it in the mouth of the defense. This leads audiences to believe that the connection between AIDS and gay sex is unwarranted (and represents yet another way in which the film severs gayness from AIDS). If anything, such a scene demonstrates how the dominant ideology is able to absorb the screaming criticism from an oppressed marginal group and present it as its own.

This frightening appropriation continues in several later court scenes in which Miller screams at the attorneys responsible for firing Beckett, "Are you gay! Are you a faggot! Do you do it from behind! Do you do the flip-flop!" Attempting both to defend Beckett and to exorcise his own dark demons, Miller tries to confront homophobia by using its own language. His hysterical inquiries, however, are met with stunned silence by everyone in the courtroom. It's like a cruelly conceived poker game in which everyone gets their cards dealt face down except for Beckett whose cards are dealt face up for all to see. The most terrified of all is Beckett because, since he is the sole marker of homosexuality in the courtroom, these epithets fall back on him. While some people defend *Philadelphia* for importing gay images into the heartland of America, such scenes don't exactly encourage gay viewers to come out of the closet.

The film's rampant misappropriation of gay culture comes to a climax in the trial scene in which Beckett takes the stand. This scene reveals the trial for what it really is: a drama of outing. While the defense cross-examines Beckett, images of the dark, seedy porn theatre are intercut with shots of a startled and embarrassed Beckett on the witness stand. The defense's attempt to put Beckett on the spot by exposing his visits to the porn theatre function in two ways: first, it bespeaks the film's liberal, anti-outing consciousness by presenting the defense's strategy as objectionable; second, it stereotypes the subculture of bathhouses and porn theatres in a conventional, mainstream manner. The spectacle continues when Miller requests an opportunity to readdress Beckett after the defense's cross-examination. He asks Beckett to unbutton his shirt and display his lesions as evidence of his illness. But since the lesions carry the stigma of AIDS, Miller's strategy brings out Beckett's no-win situation—in order to put his antagonists on the spot, he needs to put himself on the spot. The drama of outing gayness becomes replayed as the drama of outing AIDS. Not only does the film cunningly condemn outing by enacting it on the victim 'for his own good,' it also rips it out of the hands of the gay community. Is this some kind of sick joke!

Philadelphia's liberal but fatally ill-conceived project also extends to the director's and screenwriter's public defense, the film's promotion, and the way in which it has been received by the mainstream press. The film is really a child with many Fathers and can thus be conceptualized as a play within the larger drama of the way our culture understands and processes its trials and tribulations—in this case, AIDS and homosexuality. In this sense, looking at the film is only half the picture. What about the dramatis personae of that larger drama!

Jonathan Demme, in making this film, not only reveals himself as a player inscribed in the social and cultural systems he depicts, but also becomes a prime example of these systems' limitations. The good liberal that he is, Demme unconditionally invites all criticism of the film (even that of playwright and AIDS activist Larry Kramer) because it supposedly encourages Hollywood to make more such films, furthers the discourse on AIDS, and increases tolerance. Not coincidentally, it also gives the film a great deal of publicity. Demme can then consolidate his own position by recruiting everyone into his effort—most notably his gay friend Juan Botas, who died after advising him on the screenplay, as well as gay screenwriter Ron Nyswaner, and Nyswaner's AIDS-stricken nephew. They serve as an alibi for Demme's own conception of *Philadelphia* as a collaborative, democratic project, unhindered by unilateral auteurism, corporate mentalities, or reactionary attitudes. His position as a liberal artist can seemingly absorb the harshest assaults and the most virulent critiques while allowing him to acknowledge humbly his own shortcomings. As a martyr, the more beating he takes, the better.

Another major player in this AIDS-*gesamtkunstwerk* is Denzel Washington, whose position as one of America's most popular leading men has both benefited from and gone well beyond Sidney Poitier's Guess-Who's-Coming-to-Dinner status. Yet in *Philadelphia* his blackness must be denied, as it might force audiences to recognize a connection between the oppression of blacks and gays. Some might argue that the film's library scene does draw a parallel between racism and homophobia via AIDS. In this scene, Miller seems to be motivated to take on Beckett's case when he observes a librarian asking the visibly sick Beckett to leave the public reading room. In addition, Washington's recently portrayal of Malcolm X may invite some viewers to draw a subtextual parallel between both issues. But *Philadelphia* never overtly deals with racial identity. Indeed, Demme further avoids drawing this parallel by presenting Miller's wife as a smart but acquiescent woman who, instead of using the parallel between blacks and gays to confront her husband's homophobia, merely smiles ever so ironically for the sake of keeping peace in their household.

Denzel Washington himself reveals the neurosis that determines the film's contradictions. In preparing for the role of the homophobic attorney, the allegedly unprejudiced Washington was in desperate need of advice from his straight friends on how to "act" like a homophobe. Did Washington also consult these friends before advising fellow actor Will Smith not to kiss another man in *Six Degrees of Separation*? As Smith explained in a recent issue of *Premiere*, Washington reminded him that, unlike white movie stars, black actors are role models. If that were really the case, then one wonders why the role of Andrew Beckett in *Philadelphia* was carefully given to one of America's most white-bred actors.

Enter Tom Hanks, whose innocuous, straight-boy-next-door image enables him to make Beckett palatable to middle America. Demme certainly has learned from the panic surrounding activists' attempts to out Jodie Foster following the release of *The Silence of the Lambs*. Hanks's stable identity assures audiences that, underneath it all, Beckett's gayness does not extend beyond the limits of the film's world. Hanks also confirms the notion that someone who embodies the norm can safely explore fictional identity with artistic merit. In the post-*Philadelphia* imagination of the Screen Actors Guild, straight-identified actors will consider such characters as Beckett a prestigious opportunity to explore their histrionic expertise. But God forbid an openly gay actor and actress play Harry and Sally types. Then again, openly gay men and women are rare commodities in Hollywood.

One of them is Ron Nyswaner, the homosexual screenwriter who is called upon to authenticate the film's depiction of the gay community, but who conspires with a process that literally sets gay sexuality straight. Nyswaner, therefore, more than anyone else, embodies *Philadelphia*'s neurosis. His role approximates Beckett's as the film condenses the diversity of the gay community into one character whose only function is to supply a label emptied of all substance. As if this were not bad enough, Nyswaner, in a tantrum of sadly misguided sarcasm, joyfully fulfills his role as a puppet, claiming in *The New York Times* that, "In Hollywood, success gives you the right to deflect all questions and criticism, directing your energy toward perfecting the art of gloating." Only someone who has been completely assimilated within the power structure of Hollywood could believe in the truth of the statement.

The film industry persistently acts on its own conservative projections of what middle America can bear to see. If *Philadelphia* reflects this mentality by downplaying its allegedly central concerns of AIDS and homophobia, the film's advertising campaign keeps both these themes firmly locked in the closet. One need only look at *Philadelphia*'s poster, which features a healthy (!) Hanks and a wary Washington in opposite corners safely separated by a gavel in the center. Although *Philadelphia* conceives of itself as a critique of homophobia, the poster's design and ad copy—"No one would take on his case ... Until one man was willing to take on the system"—indicate how the film is desperately trying to pass for straight.

Yet Larry Kramer points out that middle America has long been accustomed to representations of both gays and PWAs on TV. *Philadelphia*'s novelty may therefore lie in being the first product that charges middle America $7.50 for the sight of Karposi lesions on a gay body. The fact that the film had already grossed $60 million by mid-March, however, doesn't mean that a different treatment of the subject couldn't have proven as financially successful.

Enter the press, which has played a key role in the film's performance at the box office. Most critics have dutifully listed the film's limitations only to subscribe to its agenda in the end. *Philadelphia* is a welcome object for the straight critic because the paths by which he or she can explore the issues of AIDS and homophobia are already mapped out by the film. But since some of his or her best friends are gay, the straight critic is willing to acknowledge their complaints without having to assume their point of view. This leaves gay critics in an impossible position, as our political responsibility compels us to comment on a film from which we would rather avert our eyes.

After two hours, *Philadelphia*'s tearful resolution is inexorable. As Miller, Miguel-the-lover, and Beckett's family bid him farewell, they also convey the 'happy' news that justice has prevailed. Because the film's ending is so emotional—replete with home movie images of Beckett as a child—it overwhelms everything else. By conjoining Beckett's victory and his death, the film depoliticizes the implications of the trial for the gay community. Beckett succumbs not to AIDS but to the fact that the film, in attempting to do away with the issue of homosexuality, has refused to invest him with life. With *Philadelphia*, Demme's faith in the system remains unchallenged. The system is capable of justice: Beckett wins his case, and we get an AIDS film from Hollywood, but at what cost!

FILMS IN REVIEW, 3-4/94, p. 55, Harry Pearson, Jr.

Here we have a movie that, while well liked for what it does, has taken a critical shellacking for what it made no attempt to do. It is not a film about AIDS, and to criticize it for not taking a documentarian's approach to the disease's progress is beside the point. It is, contrary to what you might think, most certainly not a film about being gay or homosexual, nor is it an especial plea for the gay life or homosexual relations. It is not a love story; the lovers here have been together for years, well past the point of explosive physicality and eroticism. *Philadelphia* is a film about homophobia and its corrosive effects on the American democratic tradition of equal rights under the law. And, I might add, about homophobia's corrosive effects on good people.

And the film's makers had the sense to set their story at the center of the American system of justice (Philadelphia where it all began), in that town of brotherly love's most powerful law firm (who better to know the principles behind the law), and finally in the courtroom with an American jury, the last hope we have for fairness under the law, outside of the wayward Supreme Court.

At the center of the film, we have Tom Hanks, as an oh-so-normal gay guy (a little too "normal" for some gay critics) who happens to have a first-rate legal turn of mind and who is on the way up in his law firm when the partners discover he has AIDS. He is fired, on a trumped up charge, of course (no moral complications here), and no lawyer in town, save homophobic Denzel Washington (finally) will take the case. Denzel mellows. They win. Hanks dies. The bad guys appeal. The end.

Actually, though Hanks gets the praise, Washington's is, and by far, the better performance. He simply wipes Hanks off the screen. Someone said that Hanks let the makeup guy do the acting for him and I believe it. Washington can, by the merest flick of his eyes, convey worlds of feeling. His performance, for subtle command, control and the ability to suggest his character's inner feelings, is up there with Anthony Hopkins' superlative portrayal in *Remains of the Day*. We get too brief (and therefore unsatisfying) bits from Antonio Banderas (so remarkable in *Law Of Desire* and elsewhere), Mary Steenburgen (in a much needed change of pace), Jason Robards (who gets to be real bad) and Joanne Woodward (who brings such depth of feeling to her half dozen lines that you're thankful, while reaching for the hankies, that she doesn't have more—who wants to bawl in public?).

The real problem I have with this movie comes with the much discussed Maria Callas scene. It is Hanks' big "gay" scene—he describes to Washington his love of opera, while a Callas aria resounds in the background. It is, I gather, supposed to humanize him and make his gayness "accessible." But, if that's so, then why did Demme and his house cinematographer Tak Fujimoto (whose work I dislike intensely) shoot Hanks like Hannibal Lecter? Up close, bathed in red light, with a wide angle lens, as in freak show, dangling his IV pole. It sure distanced me from the character and I like, if not love, opera. Whatever the motive, its effect is to undercut Hanks' humanity and stress the strange (which a passion for opera is not *prima facie* proof thereof) and, thus, make gays the Other. I say it's homophobic and it very nearly brings this entire house of cards down. (Demme goes to the opposite extreme with the gay party—at which, by the way, the yet homophobic Washington character seems pretty comfortable—a party unlikely in the absence of any gayness whatsoever: Strangeness, it has, gayness, it doesn't.)

And, was I the only one bothered by the suggestion of a mercy killing during the last scene between Banderas and Hanks—wasn't Banderas getting ready to pull the plug? It's there, but undeveloped. So why is it there?

Somehow Demme pulled together the bits and parts of what he had into a successful, though not untroubling narrative (much more coherent as storytelling than *Silence of the Lambs*), and certainly *Philadelphia* is better organized than most of his work, which tends to ramble. Nevertheless, there is a certain tentativeness to his handling of the "gay" material, suggesting (as recent interviews indicate—on why didn't he and the production staff keep their mouths shut) that he isn't comfortable with thoughts of homosexuality and, in his rendering of the operatic sequence, there is the unmistakable odor of homophobia, and thus its pity becomes yet more straight liberal condescension.

LOS ANGELES TIMES, 12/22/93, Calendar/p. 1, Kenneth Turan

The air of do-goodism hangs like a pall over "Philadelphia," and nothing is so fatal to effective drama. The first major studio release to deal with AIDS, it is all too conscious of time past and opportunities lost, of being years behind the crisis. But one film cannot make up for an industry-wide history of timidity, and in attempting to this one inevitably hampers its own impact.

Still, "Philadelphia" is a milestone. Though it is going where books, plays, television movies and independent films have all gone before, having a sympathetic major star like Tom Hanks playing a man dying of AIDS could be as powerful societally as having a star like Rock Hudson announcing the same in real life.

As directed by Jonathan Demme from an original script by Ron Nyswaner, "Philadelphia" fits comfortably into the pattern of mainstream Hollywood socially conscious films, from "Guess Who's Coming to Dinner" on racism to "Making Love" on an earlier generation of anti-gay prejudice. Not intended to be subtle, painted in broad, passionate strokes, with the good and bad guys all neatly labeled, it aims to forcefully wring out our emotions like a wet hankie.

Besides being more sophisticated than those predecessors, "Philadelphia" does have a number of points in its favor, especially the affecting performances by Hanks as the AIDS patient and co-star Denzel Washington as the straight lawyer who defends him. But concerned with humanizing the afflicted in terms Middle America can understand, "Philadelphia" is not as worried as it might have been about sacrificing subtlety and nuance to the greater good of a worthwhile cause.

Set with conscious irony in the City of Brotherly Love, where the attorneys have a reputation for legal sharpness (it used to be said that three Philadelphia lawyers were a match for the devil), "Philadelphia" immediately introduces us to two members of that tribe as they meet in a judge's chambers to argue the opposite sides of a case.

Andrew Beckett (Hanks) is the confident practitioner of corporate law, a promising senior associate for Wyatt, Wheeler, Hellerman, Tetlow and Brown, a firm as old line as it sounds. And except for a legal degree and a liking for handsome clothing, he has nothing in common with the glib Joe Miller (Washington).

A personal injury lawyer working out of a one-man office, Miller's motto, no doubt heard on his frequent TV commercials, is "we take no cash unless we have cash justice." Always on the lookout for potential clients, he hands his cards to everyone he meets, from side-walk Santas to Philadelphia basketball legend Julius Erving. Socially and professionally, he and Beckett couldn't have less in common.

That, it turns out, goes for their sexual orientation as well. Though no one at his firm knows it, Beckett is gay. He heads for a local clinic to have his blood worked up. For more than simply being gay, Andrew Beckett has AIDS.

Beckett also has the kind of idealized support circle only people in movies seem to manage. His parents (Joanne Woodward and Robert Castle, the subject of Demme's "My Cousin Bobby" documentary) are totally supportive, as are his siblings and their spouses. And his lover, Miguel (Pedro Almódovar stalwart Antonio Banderas) is as gentle, passionate and understanding as he is good-looking, which is plenty.

Beckett will need all their support. On the very night he is given an important case and a promotion by firm head Charles Wheeler (Jason Robards), a senior partner notices a Kaposi's sarcoma lesion on Beckett's forehead. Though he tries to pass it off as a racquetball bruise, suspicions are aroused, and after a key file on that big case is mysteriously misplaced, Wheeler claims "something's come over you" and the firm tells him his services are no longer necessary.

Convinced that he has been fired because of AIDS and not incompetence, Beckett decides to sue. Nine lawyers turn him down, and so does the 10th, Joe Miller. Miller, who moves to the far side of his office when Beckett tells him he has AIDS, turns out to be more than a touch homophobic, telling his wife that he doesn't want to even think about going to bed with someone who has more hair on his chest than he does.

Played with Washington's usual assurance, Joe Miller is intended as a kind of mass audience surrogate, someone who shares the fears and prejudices not always admitted in polite society. Having him overcome his homophobia ought to be powerful stuff, but it is typical of "Philadelphia" that it makes this too easy for Miller, providing a convenient and unconvincing scene of anti-gay prejudice as a way for him to understand that all discrimination is equally evil.

With Miller as his attorney, Beckett files against his old firm, and much of "Philadelphia" concerns itself with watching the trial progress as Beckett's physical condition deteriorates. Hanks, who lost 30 pounds for the role, has not hesitated to look physically debilitated, and his performance, pitched to gain sympathy, manages that but not a great deal more, not even in a bravura emotional breakdown scene set to an aria from "Andrea Chenier."

If "Philadelphia" has a consistent flaw, it is that it overdoes things, hyping the crises and even amplifying Beckett's labored breathing as he is cross-examined by opposing attorney Belinda Conine (Mary Steenburgen). Similarly, the film's nominal plot pivot, the question of whether Beckett was framed or not, gets forgotten as the trial gets turned into a public forum on society's views of homosexuality.

As proficient a filmmaker as he is, Demme, whose last film was "The Silence of the Lambs," hasn't attempted anything that calls for this kind of sensitivity in quite some time, and he ends up being more emphatic than he really needs to be. Genuinely moving at times, "Philadelphia" is trying, perhaps too hard, to break America's heart. Here's wishing it luck.

NEW STATESMAN & SOCIETY, 2/25/94, p. 33, Jonathan Romney

How about an Aids film for light relief? Strange to say, Jonathan Demme's *Philadelphia* seems strangely manageable after the rigours of the past few weeks—*Schindler's List, In the Name of the Father*, even the lush floral overkill of *The Age of Innocence*. It's closer to home, and Demme resists any temptation to maul our senses or intellects. That's not to say it's easy going; what it has in common with *Schindler's List* is that it will probably move you to tears in the end, but then the doubts will start to click in.

Philadelphia both works and doesn't work. It's moving but strangely unmemorable. Yet the very fact that mainstream US cinema now seems able to accommodate an Aids movie with so little polemical fuss can only be a leap forward.

This film wears its "problem picture" status close to the surface by wheeling on that sturdy vehicle for debate, the courtroom drama. But the fact that the court scenes pack only a desultory punch effectively serves to remind us that we shouldn't look for easy resolution in staged victories. We're not dealing with the high theatre of Justice, but with the everyday, in which the business of living and dying just has to be taken care of.

Philadelphia's strength is that at heart it's *just another film.* Despite being sold as an "issue" movie, it doesn't milk headline shocks but takes the proverbial everyday story of everyday people as the starting point for a (relatively) discreet consciousness-raising experience. The ordinariness of its protagonists might be transparent as a vehicle for coaxing our emotions to enlightenment; but the strategically cast Tom Hanks and Denzel Washington put considerable meat on roles that could easily just have been convenient mirrors for us to examine our own attitudes.

Hanks plays Andy Beckett, a Philadelphia lawyer in the same cobwebbed patriarchal firm that we've seen in every law movie from *The Verdict* to the current crop of John Grishams. And who else is at its helm but Jason Robards? Andy's on the up, but his progress is halted by his HIV-positive status. Or rather, it's not the virus itself that seems to impede him but the sarcoma blotch on his forehead that gives him away, despite his efforts to hide it. The firm summarily pitches him out, claiming he had to go because of an "attitude problem". A slowly-dying Beckett decides to take them to court. What's in the dock is not just the firm's phobia about gays and people with Aids, but the American mainstream audience's as well.

Rather than treat Aids as a headline issue, *Philadelphia* assumes from the off that it's simply a fact of 1990s life. It emphasises the minutiae of how it screws up lives—not in the big unanswerable way, but in the little daily things: by making people late for appointments, by sometimes obliging them to learn make-up techniques if they want to cover their skin marks. It's a smart move to cast Tom Hanks: the American screen's best-loved average jerk, the Jack Lemmon of his generation.

The casual ease with which Demme lets you know that the nice goofball from *Big* and *Sleepless in Seattle* is a gay man with Aids, with a lover, sexual desire and a passion for opera, is a blow to fondly held stereotypes way more effective than all the vanilla-shaded positive images of films like *Longtime Companion*. The film refuses to make Andy a sweet acceptable paragon. In court, he's placed on trial himself, a casual encounter in a porn cinema suddenly becoming Exhibit A in the case against him. But again, the film argues, it's part of ordinary life; should someone be stigmatised for the occasional blow-job? Equally, it doesn't stigmatise him for his initial refusal to be out about either his gayness or Aids.

Andy's illness effects his body with a disorienting range of upturns and downswings. Hanks starts off looking much the elegant uptown guy he was in *Bonfire of the Vanities*; then he's bearded and crop-haired under a cap; then he looks again like his old formal self; next he's a wraith on the brink. The film points up attacks on his very identity by the disease, but also from society itself. Is there a certain way we expect a man with Aids to look? It's a considerable feat that, against the odds, Hanks creates a consistent but also rounded personality.

But it's Denzel Washington, as Andy's reluctant defence lawyer Joe Miller, who carries the film's polemical weight. Washington is American film's biggest male black star, an unequivocally heterosexual sex symbol who, after *Malcolm X*, is loaded not only with moral weight but also with powerful iconic status for black audiences.

In a lesser film, the relations between Andy and Joe might be set up for a neat buddy coalition between gay men with Aids and straight black men. Here it's not so easy. Joe, straight and married, is a regular, liberal guy, but he has a hard core of embedded homophobia and Aids paranoia that just won't be shaken.

He initially recoils from Andy's handshake and refuses his case; later, seeing an embarrassed librarian try to shunt him into a little ghetto of his own in the reading room, he takes it on. But if we think a facile conversation has taken place, we later see Joe in a chemist, approached by a black man expressing his support. Realising he's being cruised, he recoils in fury. He can't shake off his attitudes overnight, but the casual virulence of them makes him the perfect mirror for the prejudices of a mainstream public. It's mainly thanks to the acting that the film wears such didactic strategies lightly.

There has been some criticism of the way the film downplays Andy's gayness, and it's true that Antonio Banderas as his tender, understanding lover is altogether sidelined. It's hard to know what sort of lifestyle Andy really leads. We know that he loves opera from one extraordinary stylised sequence when his whole being, indeed the whole screen, swoons to an aria. And we know also that he has a terribly bland, supportive family: the scene in which they all sit round tenderly as he attests, "I love you guys", is the film's one big gaffe.

But the point is that the sum of Andy's life can't be found by defining him in any one way. When at the end, we see home movies of his childhood on video, the point being made, with heart-tugging insistence, is that this could be any kid's life. In fact, what we see is simply a currently inescapable movie trope wheeled out once again—the video as window on the truth (as in *Falling Down*).

What hits rather harder is the way Demme bookends the film with tribute songs to the city of Philadelphia by Bruce Springsteen and Neil Young. They're not great songs by any means, just tough, down-to-earth ballads which, rather than mythologise the place, suggest that it's just Anytown USA where, whatever tragedies happen, it's business as usual. Despite *Philadelphia*'s necessary soapbox factor, it's the film's grip of everyday banality that really makes it worthwhile.

NEW YORK, 1/3/94, p. 52, David Denby

In Jonathan Demme's *Philadelphia*, there's a single scene that is profoundly beautiful—startling, too, since the rest of the movie, which is about a successful young lawyer dying of AIDs, is no more than conventionally effective. Abruptly fired by the white-shoe Philadelphia firm in which he was a rising star, Andrew Beckett (Tom Hanks) becomes convinced that he is the victim of discrimination—that he was canned because he is gay and has AIDs. He tries to find a lawyer to represent him in a damage suit, and winds up with a crass ambulance chaser, Joe Miller (Denzel Washington), who flacks himself in TV ads. Miller, who has just had a baby girl, is a macho African-American contemptuous of homosexuals. Yet Andrew stirs something in him—a memory of racial hostility, perhaps—and he takes the case.

Demme and screenwriter Ron Nyswaner do not hesitate to show us the physical disintegration of Andrew Beckett's body: Each time the movie jumps a few weeks or months in time, we're shocked by Andrew's increasing thinness, tiredness, pallor. A jovial and active man—Tom Hanks, with his dancing dark eyes and springy legs—becomes quiet, withdrawn, and immobile. Hanks's deterioration reminded this viewer of similar downward journeys taken unwillingly but bravely by friends, and even though I wound up disliking the way Nyswaner and Demme used the suffering, I was moved by it. Up to the scene I'm thinking of, however, Demme and Nyswaner have not shown us much of Andrew's life as a homosexual. We can see that Andrew has a lover of many years (Antonio Banderas), who looks after him, and a large and supportive family. In some ways, he could be any suffering human being. But then *Philadelphia* takes a surprising leap.

In defiance of his condition, Andrew decides to throw a party in his loft. The joyous bash that Demme stages, with most of the guests dressed up wildly, is the first unashamed, uninhibited, and truly entertaining gay party I can think of in a major studio release. Suddenly, Andrew is not any suffering man; he is a specific gay man with specific tastes and pleasures. When the guests go home at last, Andrew and his lawyer, Joe Miller, sit down to discuss Andrew's upcoming testimony in court. But Andrew, who has only a few weeks to live, brushes off the lawyer's questions. Oddly, irrelevantly, he puts on an aria from Giordano's *Andrea Chenier*—Maria Callas singing "La mamma morta." As Joe looks on in dismay, Andrew passionately explicates the aria, translating the Italian, re-creating with his hands and voice the emotional meaning of the words and of Callas's performance.

This sequence, which has been written, directed, and played with the utmost daring and emotional commitment, makes clear, with a force I've never seen before, exactly what opera means for its most passionate fans and for gays in particular. "La mamma morta" is an aria about the power of love. The heroine's mother has died in the flames of the French Revolution. Maddalena (the Callas character) describes the death and then her own resurrection from despair—she has fallen in love with the poet Andrea Chenier. Love, filling her soul as a kind of godlike presence, speaks to her: Is everything around thee blood and mire? I am divine! I am oblivion ... Ah! I am love." As Andrew moves around his loft, dragging his IV stand and declaiming, Demme swings the camera over Hanks's head, and the lighting, in imitation of the flames in the aria, turns an expressionistic flickering red.

Demme goes over the top, and why? Because opera, which uses voice and music to clarify and heighten emotion—to produce moments of ecstatic being—regularly breaks into such exaggerated gestures. Opera is about the intensification of feeling, and in this scene, a man who is dying feels rescued from despair (like Maddalena) by the power of love. Shaken, Joe goes home, and, as the aria plays again on the soundtrack, he kisses his daughter and climbs into bed next to his wife. The filmmakers meaning becomes clear: If there is a power in love, and if transcendence is possible (Maria Callas makes a good case for it), then these things must include all of us. Now, this is not some gooey message of universal brotherhood intended to comfort the unhappy people of the world; it's nothing less than a call to heroism, because heroism is the only force that can overcome the growing American antagonisms, the divisions of race, gender, and class. As a beginning, the movie says, accept the reality of gay sex and gay identity, and don't hold AIDS against homosexuals.

Nothing else in *Philadelphia* comes close to that sequence's awkward greatness. The rest of the movie, which is merely sympathetic, intelligent, and shrewd, attempts to raise consciousness and reverse a few clichés. Demme has given us, for instance, a black who is not the victim but the dispenser of prejudice, and a sympathetic-looking female lawyer (Mary Steenburgen) who represents the villainous firm and who smilingly subjects Hanks to a ruthless cross-examination. Yet despite these attempts to avoid TV-movie p.c., Demme and Nyswaner have got themselves caught up in a conventional and didactic structure. *Philadelphia* is a kind of lecture-demonstration that's meant to improve us. In doing so, Demme is not above using the pathos of Andrew's condition to drive home his points.

As Andrew Beckett's civil suit against his old employers comes to trial, the perfidious swine of the prestigious firm get exposed in all their rancid homophobia; and Joe Miller, saddled with a common set of anti-gay prejudices, learns that he is ignorant, and that his true interests as an African-American lie in his making an alliance with fellow outsiders. He sheds his prejudices and becomes a grown-up. And all the while, Andrew is dying, dying right in court. Hanks's performance is wonderful—restrained, dry, precise—but I grew indignant at what amounted to exploitation of the character's suffering. Andrew Beckett literally falls over at the trial, and the juxtaposition of his weakness with the vile testimony of the law partners almost suggests that prejudice, rather than disease, is killing him.

And hasn't courtroom drama itself become a pathetic device? A trial may have a natural dramatic shape, but more and more I've come to feel that courtroom drama answers some deeper and sadder American need. In this country, we are now so divided by ethnic, religious, and sexual differences that we can barely talk to one another. Manners in the largest sense have failed. Litigation fills the void, in life and in movies—except, of course, that it can't fill the void. Denzel Washington says during the trial, "This case is not about AIDs. This case is about our hatred and fear of homosexuals." Yes, and so is the movie. But if that is so, then why rely on a courtroom setting, with its obvious and self-important "revelations"? At least the opera scene suggests the possibility of something greater.

NEW YORK POST, 12/22/93, p. 43, Michael Medved

"Philadelphia" is such a brave, sincere, and passionate project that it's easier to praise its good intentions than to honestly assess its artistic merit as a movie.

But the sad fact is that for all its noble purposes, this picture is a dismal disappointment, if not a downright dud. It stands as a textbook example of what can go wrong when a brilliant director like Jonathan Demme concentrates on making an important public statement, rather than telling an engrossing story.

Tom Hanks plays a hard-driving young lawyer for a prestigious Philadelphia firm. He never tells his employers that he's gay, or suffering from AIDS, but they suspect the truth when they spot lesions on his face and he starts missing workdays to get emergency medical treatments.

Summarily fired from his job, Hanks derides to sue his former employers, and the only lawyer who'll take his case is a shamelessly self-promoting, ambulance chasing (and initially homophobic) personal injury attorney, capably played by Denzel Washington.

The resulting courtroom battle totally dodges the obvious issue: Does a company have the moral right to drop one of its workers, knowing that the employee is suffering from a terminal disease that will inevitably interfere with his work?

This debate is never joined because the script shows Hanks' bosses (led by pompous partner Jason Robards) denying they even noticed he had AIDS, and insisting that they fired him for simple incompetence. The legal sparring therefore focuses on a dry, dull, factual dispute about what the partners knew or didn't know about the hero's health.

Meanwhile, the young man at the center of the controversy is slowly wasting away, and the makeup effects on Hanks—who ultimately lost 35 pounds to play this role—are shockingly effective.

Hanks will probably win an Oscar for his exertions, but it's too bad that the picture turns his character into such a noble, idealized, two-dimensional sufferer, and that this superb actor gets to bring so little of his usual ferocity and humor to the part.

The melodrama becomes at times nearly unbearable: during one seemingly endless sequence, a weeping, wailing Hanks tries to tell the skeptical Washington about the emotional impact of a Maria Callas recording of an aria from "Andrea Chenier."

Director Demme ("The Silence of the Lambs") makes the scene even more manipulative by lighting Hanks (but not Washington!) in a lurid, bloody red, then shooting him from above with a "God's eye" camera angle.

This same tendency to lay it on with a trowel is all too evident in the movie's clichéd conclusion with several minutes of "home movies" showing the main character playing happily as a child before all his suffering began.

Meanwhile, Neil Young warbles on the sound track with verses written specially for the occasion: "City of Brotherly Love/ Place I call home/Don't turn your back on me now!"

This maudlin material may gratify those moviegoers who are so grateful that Hollywood has tackled the AIDS issue at all that they welcome even the most heavy-handed treatment of the subject.

For most of the audience, however—even for those who have lost friends to AIDS (as I have)—"Philadelphia" remains stubbornly uninvolving and unimpressive. There will be many dry eyes in the house.

NEWSDAY, 12/22/93, Part II/p. 54, Jack Mathews

Throughout Jonathan Demme's bold but ultimately disappointing "Philadelphia," the "AIDS movie" Hollywood has been buzzing about for the past year, titles appear telling us how much time—two weeks, a month, 10 days—has passed since the last scene. The information is meaningless in terms of the story, and everything in terms of the disease.

Time, short term and shrinking significantly with every tick of the clock, is all people afflicted with AIDS or the HIV virus have to cling to. Is there time for a cure, or even enough time to hope for one? Is there time to overcome fear?

One thing that none of us has time for is the prejudice that punishes people with the disease and causes them to be denied the health care, job security and emotional comfort they need. That prejudice—homophobia, a plague in its own right—is what "Philadelphia" is really about.

The movie, the first on a major studio docket to deal with AIDS, takes the form of a courtroom drama, whose central character is a gay lawyer (Tom Hanks), in the late stages of the disease, suing his law firm for wrongful termination. After trusting him with the most important case of his promising career, the firm's partners had suddenly decided he was incompetent, a conclusion he claims (and that we can see for ourselves) they come to after becoming aware of his condition.

Even before the trial begins, when Hanks' rapidly deteriorating Andrew Beckett tries to find a lawyer to represent him, it's clear that the central issue for Demme and screenwriter Ron Nyswaner is the attitude the law partners share with too many others in the country, an eagerness to condemn people for the virus killing them.

Beckett is rejected by nine lawyers before hiring Joe Miller (Denzel Washington), a homophobic ambulance chaser who promotes his services on television. He can barely stand to shake hands with his client, and later, when a gay man comes on to him at a market, his reaction is one of disbelief and horror.

With time running out—two weeks, a month, 10 days—Beckett has the weight of the world on his slumping shoulders.

Turning the movie into a didactic assault on homophobia was a bold choice, bolder even than the decision we thought Demme and his backers at Tri-Star Pictures had made originally, which was to put AIDS on the screen, and treat it, no matter how responsibly, as a subject of entertainment.

With Beckett, they are depicting what to most of straight society is the worst case scenario, a man who apparently contracted the disease while having sex with a stranger in a public place, at the risk of exposing his own lover (Antonio Banderas) at home. By casting the always engaging Hanks as Beckett, it is as if Demme is daring homophobes in the audience to side with the moral lepers on the other side of the courtroom.

The question is, how many homophobes can Tri-Star possibly summon to the debate? Had this been done for TV, a few of them might have sat still for it, but to enter this realm voluntarily, at a price? We'll see.

The sad truth is that "Philadelphia" isn't set up very well for anybody. Its arguments are too threatening for those who need to hear them, and too simplistic and overstated for those who already agree with them.

Jason Robards, as the head of Beckett's punitive law firm, is a cartoon villain, the devil in a three-piece suit, and his partners gather around him like satanic elves. Joe Miller, on the other hand, is held up as a flawed hero, a good man who, upon learning from Beckett that even good men die of AIDS, perfects his humanity. Hanks may get most of the attention, and probably an Oscar, for his performance, and it is a masterful job in a role that required great professional courage to undertake. Not many romantic stars would risk their images playing a gay man, and though sentiment abounds around Beckett, Hanks plays his slow, physically hideous death with a restraint and unsentimental dignity that is painful to watch.

Still, it is Washington's Joe Miller who holds the key to the film's impact. Demme is counting on audiences connecting with Miller, identifying with his attitude, then following him through his revelations to some of their own.

To that end, Washington has given, a marvelously forceful performance. Miller is a funny, bright, powerful figure, and the relationship he develops with Beckett grows from professional courtesy to friendship and deep personal respect.

In painting the moral issues and the characters conveying them in such broad contrasting strokes, Demme and Nyswaner were apparently counting on sophisticated viewers in urban centers understanding that they were necessary in order to get the movie's message out across America.

Since the movie is opening initially in just New York, Los Angeles and Toronto, the question is not how it will play in Peoria, but whether it will even get there.

NEWSWEEK, 12/27/93, p. 46, David Ansen

So much has been written about the making of "Philadelphia" (Hollywood finally confronts AIDS"), so many hopes are riding on it, so high is the standard director Jonathan Demme has set for himself that it may be hard to see the movie itself through the fog of expectation. Well, "Philadelphia" is far from perfect, but it would be hard to imagine the person who could walk away from it unmoved.

The late Vito Russo, author of "The Celluloid Closet," a study of the treatment of gays in the cinema, used to say, "It's not AIDS that's killing us, it's homophobia." This is what "Philadelphia" is about—not a disease, but a climate of intolerance that turns a disease into a stigma. Tom Hanks plays Andrew Beckett, an associate in a prestigious Philadelphia law firm who has kept his sexuality, his HIV status and his relationship with his lover Miguel (Antonio Banderas) from his colleagues. As his health starts to deteriorate, he's handed a major case. Before it's done, he's abruptly fired. The firm claims incompetence; he knows it's AIDS discrimination, and is determined to haul his former firm into court. But the only lawyer who will handle his case is Joe Miller (Denzel Washington), an ambulance-chasing personal-injury lawyer—and self-confessed homophobe.

This is the kind of morally symmetrical, social-issue setup we've come to associate with TV movies, and "Philadelphia" doesn't entirely transcend the didactic limitations of the formula. But, oh, how it tries. What's remarkable are all the hackneyed moments Demme and screenwriter Ron ("Mrs. Soffel") Nyswaner don't include—like the announcement of the lawsuit's verdict. We know from the outset that Miller will have a change of heart—he's designed to be the man whom mainstream audiences will identify with—but his transformation is never obvious and never complete. His recognition that his gay client is a victim of discrimination is undoubtedly sharpened by his own experience as a black man, but the analogy remains a resonant subtext. Beckett isn't made a mouthpiece for gay pride, nor does Miller ever confess the error of his ways: only small physical gestures convey the moral distance he has traveled. The movie's most mesmerizing scene is its riskiest one, when Beckett plays a Maria Callas aria from "Andrea Chenier" for Miller and, transported by the music, tries to explain what it means to him. Here the movie seems to slip out of its own skin and become something wholly unexpected.

Curiously, it's in the usually fail-safe courtroom showdown that the movie is the least convincing. Miller's presentation of Beckett's case is written to make "points to the audience, but it sure doesn't look as if he's winning on legal grounds. The casting of sweet-faced Mary Steenburgen as the firm's aggressive attorney is as inspired as the choice of Jason Robards to play the firm's patrician heavy is obvious. It's also odd that Beckett's relationship with Miguel gets such short shrift. Though their brief scenes convey both the tenderness and the irritations of a longtime intimacy, the movie owes us more than this truncated glimpse of our hero's personal life.

You can feel the pressure on the filmmakers to design a film that will speak to the widest possible audience, to reach people who may not know anyone who's died of AIDS. But the film pays a price for it. Heartfelt and stylishly made as "Philadelphia" is, it has, almost by definition, the feel of a movie made from the outside in.

There will be no argument, however, about the film's stars. The superb Hanks doesn't make a false move as the proud, ironic Beckett. This is a reined-in, lawyerly guy, too diffident to advertise his courage, and Hanks moves us deeply by never begging for sympathy. Washington's every bit his equal. Cocky and defensive, he gives us a thoroughly honest portrait of a prejudiced man wrestling with his macho fears. And in the small but touching role of Beckett's mother, Joanne Woodward is luminous. "Philadelphia" may not be the film Demme's fans expect—its emotionalism is unfiltered by cool. But it has the power to open more than a few blinkered hearts.

SIGHT AND SOUND, 3/94, p. 45, Stella Bruzzi

Philadelphia. Two lawyers, Andy Beckett and Joe Miller, although not from the same firm, are seen talking through the details of a routine civil case. Later that day, Andy pays his regular visit to an Aids clinic for drug treatment. He hasn't told the firm he works for, Wheeler and Benedick, that he is gay or that he has Aids.

One evening at work, as he is assigned an important brief, Andy is also promoted to Senior Associate. That same evening, one of the partners notices a lesion on Andy's forehead, which he brushes off as the result of a squash accident. Later, at home, Andy is taught how to apply dark foundation cream to conceal lesions, when he suddenly falls ill and runs to the bathroom. He is taken to hospital by his partner Miguel. A few weeks elapse and Andy, with shaved head and no concealing make-up, arrives at Joe's office, explaining that he needs legal representation to fight his law firm for unfair dismissal. The pretext for Andy's sacking was that he mislaid a crucial brief and that he had "an attitude problem". Joe refuses the case, and is accused by his wife Louise of being anti-gay. Bumping into Andy in the Law Library, Joe is at first evasive, but then agrees to act as his attorney. Joe issues Andy's old boss Charles Wheeler with a subpoena.

At his parents' fortieth wedding anniversary celebrations, Andy tells his family that he plans to take his firm to court, and they offer their full support. The trial opens, with gay rights demonstrators grouped outside. Various witnesses are called—from a woman lawyer in a related firm who contracted Aids via a blood transfusion and was not dismissed, to a colleague, Bob Seidman, who suspected Beckett had Aids but didn't say anything. Meanwhile, Joe's attitudes to gays are displayed in his regular bar where he participates in anti-gay banter, and then in a chemist when he blasts a man for trying to pick him up.

Back in the courtroom, the defense attorney calls various lawyers from the firm to testify that they did not dismiss Andy Beckett for either his sexuality or his illness. Meanwhile Andy is getting progressively weaker—Miguel cannot give him his regular intravenous dose of AZT because his vein has collapsed, and Andy starts to think about planning his memorial service. Instead, they throw an impromptu party and invite Joe and Louise. After the party Joe tries to take Andy through a Q&A session in preparation for his cross examination, but with little success.

During his examination by Joe, Andy recounts his recruitment to the firm Wheeler and Benedick and his prodigious rise; he explains why, after hearing the partners exchange 'faggot' jokes in the racquet club, he didn't reveal to Wheeler that he was gay. His tough cross-examination dwells almost exclusively on his supposedly promiscuous past and visits to a gay porn cinema. Wheeler then takes the stand, testifying that Andy, although highly gifted, had not fulfilled his promise, again maintaining that he was not sacked because of Aids.

At the end of Wheeler's testimony, Andy collapses in court. The jury award damages of $4 million for mental anguish and unfair dismissal. Joe goes to the hospital to tell Andy and his family the verdict; and then leaves. It is clear that Andy is dying, as his family say goodnight one by one, leaving him with Miguel. Andy's last words to Miguel are "I'm ready". Joe and Louise attend the party after his funeral.

Cyril Collard's *Les Nuits Fauves* opened with the stark announcement that the film's director and star died of Aids shortly after its completion. *Philadelphia* is already being promoted as Hollywood's first Aids movie. Such knowledge places a complex pressure on those about to watch either film—we feel uncomfortably compromised, almost obliged to like films that state so unambiguously that they are both political and personal statements about a subject that the cinema has, by and large, avoided. That Collard died as a result of the illness he fictionally portrays, and that *Philadelphia* is Hollywood's belated entry into the territory of Aids, are in themselves presented as value judgements.

In many ways, disentangling representation from issue is an impossible task, although *Philadelphia* has, on more than one occasion, been referred to as a film about 'the human condition', and Demme himself is quoted as saying that it is about a whole range of things—lawyers, babies, food, not 'just' about Aids. *Philadelphia* is not campaigning, but does come in the mould of a classical tragedy—which is both elevating and reductive when it comes to a subject like Aids. As the film progresses and we become involved with Andy's life, we increasingly empathise with the 'universal' nature of his pain and suffering. Testifying in court, Andy asserts his 'universality' when he says, "I am not political, I am just concerned with what is right". The polemical debate becomes subsumed into the personal interactions between a series of individuals, which is Hollywood's traditional method of tackling political issues.

The story of *Philadelphia* is rooted in personal experience. Both Demme and writer Ron Nyswaner, drew on people they knew or knew about during the scripting; the film is informed by the lives and recent deaths of Demme's gay friend Juan Botas and Nyswaner's haemophilic nephew, and the precedent set by Clarence B. Cain, a lawyer who successfully sued his firm for dismissing him because he had Aids. There is a perceptible sense of the director, writer and actors probing their own consciences and prejudices. These are the only terms in which one can adequately explain the potency of certain scenes in the film and the awkwardness of others.

The film's single most astounding sequence is when Andy sways with his intravenous drip stand to Maria Callas singing an aria from Spontini's opera *La Vestale*. The scene is ferocious and uncompromising, a public visualisation of a closed and personal moment. Bathed in a red light and shot from such extreme low angles that he appears on the point of falling, Tom Hanks sways and swerves to the grandiose passion of the aria around a bemused Denzel Washington. As the extreme close-ups seem to catch his tears and the intense straight-forwardness with which he translates and speaks the simple words ("I am life! I am oblivion! I am love!"), so the music engulfs Andy.

Such a protracted, choreographed scene could easily have slipped into ludicrous self-indulgence, that it does not do so is due to the palpable conviction driving it. Sometimes, however, the same seriousness leads *Philadelphia* on a kamikaze mission towards shameless mawkishness. When Andy tells his gathered family that he intends to bring a charge of unfair dismissal against his ex-employers and they offer their unanimous support. Hanks smiles and without even a twinge of irony or his trademark smirk says, "I love you guys". It's a line which would have been discarded even from *Terms of Endearment* as too schmaltzy, too embarrassing.

The personal route into political subject matters, therefore, has its pitfalls, perhaps due to the requirements of a mainstream Aids film that, unlike earlier independent films, is not preaching to a coterie of the aware and the converted. Hollywood abides unflinchingly by the belief that if a political film is to succeed in its mission to inform or enlighten, it must do so by tapping the feelings, observations and problems of individuals. *Guess Who's Coming to Dinner?* can hardly be termed a film about the 1960s Civil Rights movement, any more than *On the Waterfront* can be interpreted as a film about standing up to McCarthyism. They are films which, at their core, are about individuals in conflict, and the contemporary political issues remain only indirectly or metaphorically alluded to.

Philadelphia is an old-fashioned treatise film, a dramatised polemic which deliberately stages confrontations to make a point. At every important juncture the characters—and by extension the audience—are being asked to reevaluate their attitudes, to realign themselves according to what they now know. In the law library scene, a librarian persistently asks Andy if he would not be "more comfortable" in a private room. Andy's response is to ask him if it isn't he who would be more comfortable if he went to a private room. The identification of fear and prejudice is often a turning point, as is painstakingly spelled out in *Twelve Angry Men*. Here, Andy's confrontation with the bigoted librarian persuades Joe to accept his case.

Philadelphia finally enters the courtroom, so frequently used in big liberal films as the arena for political debate, where the rights of the individual are conclusively voiced and vindicated. In this environment Andy Beckett is an intentionally loaded character—someone who simultaneously represents liberalism, gay men, people with Aids and right-thinking lawyers. When he takes the stand, Andy explains why he became a lawyer: "you get to be part of justice being done. It's really quite a thrill when that happens". This is the ultimate fusion of the personal with the political, as Andy's own crusade becomes assimilated into the workings of the American judiciary, and he becomes the film's most solid embodiment of that nebulous thing 'justice'.

Although the concluding cutesy home movie footage of Andy as a kid must be the grossest lapse in liberal taste since *The Killing Fields* signed off to the strains of "Imagine", *Philadelphia* is not only a well-intentioned film but a moving experience. On an emotional level, it works: we respond to Aids in much the same way as we have in the past responded to war, cancer or racism. In quite a bald fashion, we are shown right from wrong, but this time the theme just happens to be Aids—just as Tom Hanks plays a 'regular guy' who 'just happens' to be gay. He is not queer, separatist or aggressive. It is this 'soft' interpretation which will probably prompt the most vociferous criticism—that *Philadelphia* cops out because it is an easy film to watch, that, unlike Jarman's *Blue*, it is not overtly challenging or difficult or radical. But there is much which makes this a progressive film—for example, its depiction of Aids as a series of setbacks and reprieves, which is more realistic than the steady, romantic decline into easeful death of many past Aids films. The film also avoids conventional sensationalism and crisis points—there is no "Andy discovers he has Aids" scene or 'buddy' bonding moment with Joe. *Philadelphia* is successful because it is intelligent, sensitive and committed. Jonathan Demme's previous denial that it is 'political' is bizarre, but is also a testament to what it aims to be—a conventional Hollywood film about a subject which the studios have previously refused to touch.

TIME, 12/27/93, p. 70, Richard Corliss

[*Philadelphia* was reviewed jointly with *Famine-33*; see Corliss' review of that film.]

VILLAGE VOICE, 12/28/93, p. 77, J. Hoberman

A young corporate lawyer takes his firm to court after he's fired because he has AIDS. *Philadelphia* is the most high-concept, historically minded movie Jonathan Demme has ever directed—its strengths and weaknesses are almost identical. At once an appeal to reason and a weepie, it strikes for cultural catharsis: One cannot help but feel relieved to get this material represented on the screen after seven years of crypto-AIDS films ranging from the hysterical *Fatal Attraction* to the visionary *The Fly* to the blatantly misplaced *Dying Young*.

Demme denies that *Philadelphia* is an act of contrition for the perceived homophobia of *Silence of the Lambs*. Still, there's almost no other way to read so eager-to-be-decent and circumspect a film. Demme is a man who responds to criticism and *Philadelphia* is a movie that walks a fine line. Just as the dying lawyer, Tom Hanks, is supremely well adjusted—neither entirely closeted nor fully, out—the movie, written by Ron Nyswaner, is carefully modulated. Despite the underlying injustice, it's made more in sorrow than in anger.

The course has been charted as mainstream to the heartland; the mode is programmatically bland. The movie is not only didactic but elaborately balanced. You can almost hear director calling writer as the various points are checked off. Although it is extremely discreet about Hanks's longtime companion (Antonio Banderas), *Philadelphia* is utterly ebullient on the Hallmark card humanism of his totally accepting extended family. "I didn't raise my kid to sit in the back of the bus," Joanne Woodward declares approvingly upon hearing of her son's decision to go to court, hitting three buttons in a single emotional swipe.

Demme customarily thrives on the urban mix but, as in *Rocky* and *Blow-Out*, Philadelphia is used as an allegorical setting—albeit less cradle of liberty than putative city of brotherly love. Like the rest of the movie, Demme's gorgeous mosaic is somewhat studied. The extras with visible AIDS symptoms are augmented by a number of well-known performance artists—Anna Deavere Smith, the Flirtations, Ron Vawter, and Karen Finley. There's no alienation affect quite like Finley's saucy sashay on-camera as an AIDS clinic doctor (for a moment, the movie seems poised to turn into an adaptation from William S. Burroughs), unless it's the notion that the extremely poised Hanks would be without legal resources.

Philadelphia is designed so that Hanks will be turned down by nine lawyers before obtaining counsel in the form of the flashy ambulance chaser played by Denzel Washington. First approached by Hanks, Washington nearly backs out his office window before running to the doctor for an instant checkup. As the movie's designated straight man, he's "openly homophobic and comically hetero—defensively crouched to ward off whatever. It's the movie's grounding performance although perhaps not even a stretch. (*Six Degrees of Separation*'s Will Smith told *Premiere* that Washington advised him "don't be kissing no man" if he wanted to maintain his credibility with black audiences.)

Demme and Nyswaner never make it absolutely clear why Washington changes his mind and decides to take Hanks's case. The racial analogy is deemed sufficient—Washington is criticized as "prejudiced" even by his wife—but a measure of class revenge and publicity seeking would seem appropriate too. It's obvious, of course, that *Philadelphia* will concern the raising of Washington's consciousness. That the filmmakers manage to stage this as something other than a final bear hug of hard-earned triumph and teary-eyed mutual respect may be the best measure of the movie's off-beat beatitude. But in *Philadelphia*, as in American life, the trial provides the sacred spectacle of public drama.

Philadelphia is nothing if not earnestly correct in detailing the minutiae of AIDS treatment and maintenance—giving its star KS lesions, hooking him up to the IV, having him lose his sight to CMV. But the movie may be more usefully educational in its representation of homophobia. The courthouse is picketed by Moral Majority types and ringed by avid TV reporters. (Casting down-home Charles Napier, who played the male apex of the triangle in Russ Meyer's softcore classic *Cherry Harry and Raquel*, as the presiding judge adds an additional touch of delirium, although the jury, of course, is strictly salt of the earth.) Washington, who is ragged by his macho pals and cruised by lustful admirers, puts sexual anxiety at the heart of the case. His arguments touch on the issue of gays in the military and, singling out the dominant ape in the primal horde (senior partner Jason Robards), effectively deconstruct the hearty male bonding that characterizes the comfortable world of corporate power.

It's one of the movie's few bitter jokes that Robards and company should crouch behind a female defender, although, in a paroxysm of misplaced sympathy, Demme throws it away. Throughout the trial, Demme establishes Washington's opposite number (Mary Steenburgen) as the frightening epitome of "professionalism," a perfectly poised and smiling hired gun. As her questioning of Hanks grows tougher, however, Demme rewards her with a whispered aside to the audience: "I *hate* this case." With one close-up, she destroys her characterization, leaving Robards alone to shoulder the villain's burden.

The trial, during which Washington ultimately drives Robards to abject Bible-thumping, has its metaphysical aspect as well, with Hanks fading out mid-cross-examination and visibly wasting away even as the case builds momentum. There's a measure of weird-angled subjectivity but the showiest sequence by far has Hanks at home, shackled to his IV drip, explicating—indeed, embodying—an aria from Umberto Giordano's *Andrea Chénier*. "I am Life! I am Oblivion! I am Love!" Ridiculous in the best sense, the aria sequence erupts like a geyser out of the movie's carefully controlled schemata. For *Philadelphia* is so cautiously legalistic that it can barely imagine challenging the Law (the "infected" Hanks kisses baby after baby, but never once Banderas).

At this moment, *Philadelphia* is startlingly transgressive—emotionally as well as formally. The uncomprehending Washington is not only freaked out by Hanks's diva-display of emotion, he remains haunted by this male Camille even after he flees home to the safety of the conjugal bed—a moment of passion, an eternity of oblivion.

Also reviewed in:
CHICAGO TRIBUNE, 1/14/94, Friday/p. A, Michael Wilmington
NATION, 1/3-10/94, p. 31, Stuart Klawans
NEW REPUBLIC, 1/10 & 17/94, p. 30, Stanley Kauffmann
NEW YORK TIMES, 12/22/93, p. C15, Janet Maslin
NEW YORKER, 12/27/93, p. 148, Anthony Lane
VARIETY, 12/20/93, p. 31, Todd McCarthy
WASHINGTON POST, 1/14/94, p. G1, Rita Kempley
WASHINGTON POST, 1/14/94, Weekend/p. G44, Desson Howe

PHILADELPHIA EXPERIMENT 2, THE

A Trimark Pictures release. *Executive Producer:* Mark Amin. *Producer:* Mark Levinson and Doug Curtis. *Director:* Stephen Cornwell. *Screenplay:* Kevin Rock and Nick Paine. *Director of Photography:* Ronn Schmidt. *Editor:* Nina Gilberti. *Music:* Gerald Couriet. *Sound:* Ed White and Ken Mantlo. *Casting:* Linda Phillips Palo. *Production Designer:* Armin Ganz. *Art Director:* Kirk Petruccelli. *Special Effects:* Frank Ceglia. *Costumes:* Eileen Kennedy. *Stunt Coordinator:* Rawn Hutchinson. *Running time:* 97 minutes. *MPAA Rating:* PG-13.

CAST: Brad Johnson (David Herdeg); Marjean Holden (Jess); Gerrit Graham (Dr. William Mailer/Friederich Mahler); James Greene (Professor Longstreet); Geoffrey Blake (Logan); Cyril O'Reilly (Decker); John Christian Grass (Benjamin Herdeg).

NEW YORK POST, 11/12/93, p. 36, Bill Hoffmann

"Philadelphia Experiment 2" is a picture that, as Ricky Ricardo would say, "has got some splainin' to do."

In fact, this new sci-fi thriller—kind of an extended "Twilight Zone" episode—seems like one big, long explanation with the cast constantly chattering away about the plot to keep the audience up to speed.

It's not worth their effort "Philadelphia Experiment 2"—a sequel to the 1984 film about time travel gone mad—runs out of gas long before its hero gallantly saves the world from Nazi domination.

It's 1993 and a devious Air Force colonel, William Mailer (Gerrit Graham), is showing colleagues how he's perfected a process in which a time warp can be created to hide an entire army and weapons. With this, he can achieve world power.

But when Mailer accidentally transports a Stealth fighter plane to 1943 Germany, the Nazis use it to win World War II and conquer the world.

Our hero David Herdeg (Brad Johnson) is used to time warps from the first movie, but he doesn't like it when his son suddenly vanishes because of the change in history.

And the new Nazi nation is a bummer, with large screens drumming slogans about productivity into the heads of drably dressed schoolkids and adults.

Herdeg goes back in time to try to foil the Nazis and return things to normal. But before long the plot becomes so convoluted, it's hard to care, even with all the constant explaining. I doubt even a knowledge of the first film would help.

Most of the movie is shot on a darkened set—an abandoned steel mill the producers found—giving this new, evil world under the Germans a claustrophobic, foreboding look.

But the film seems cheap, and it reveals just how low-budget it is with a series of cheesy special effects and slow-motion action sequences that make TVs "Star Trek" look almost Spielbergian.

Brad Johnson, who appears to have just stepped out of a Calvin Klein ad, can't do much but squint and pout.

The one gem here is the strikingly beautiful Marjean Holden, who instantly grabs the attention whenever she's on screen. Unfortunately, Holden doesn't have much to do, and a romance between her and Johnson, something that would have helped the picture immensely, is only hinted at. What a waste. Holden has bigger, meatier roles ahead of her.

The few jitters I experienced came mainly from several scenes of people being injected with large hypodermic needles. Too bad somebody didn't give a shot of adrenaline to the script.

NEWSDAY, 11/12/93, Part II/p. 73, Joseph Gelmis

Cheesy science fiction made by over-qualified filmmakers, "Philadelphia Experiment 2" is a tolerable, though not quite satisfying action flick.

The sequel picks up the story in 1993, nine years after innocent bystander David Herdeg was catapulted into the future by a catastrophic U.S. military experiment in 1943. In his new adventures, he yo-yos around in alternative 1993: our '93 and a '93 in which Nazi Germany has won World War II and the United States is a slave-labor satellite of the Third Reich.

What happened to change history? The two "Philadelphia Experiment" movies. The original punched a hole in the time-space continuum. The sequel delivers to the Nazis, through that hole, a Stealth bomber armed with nuclear weapons which alters the outcome of the war. To save civilization as we know it, reluctant hero Herdeg (Brad Johnson) time-trips from the police state 1993 back to 1943 Germany.

Bracketing the adventures, in the opening and closing of this sequel, are a couple of kneejerk sentiment scenes with widower Herdeg and his beloved son, a Little League ball player. Dad really wants to stay and watch his boy pitch in the big game, but there he goes, into that vortex, plucked back into other dimensions by a renewal of the Philadelphia experiments.

Wherever he goes he runs into rockjawed Gerrit Graham, who plays not one but three villains: a U.S. militarist in our 1993; his father, a German militarist in 1943; and the inhuman tyrant running the United States for the Nazis in the alternate 1993.

Watching "Philadelphia Experiment 2" is like sitting through a feature-length TV commercial where the visual style and technical skills are infinitely superior to the message or content being communicated. The most exciting thing about the film is the way it looks and moves. It's not the actors or the script but the powerful visuals by Armin Ganz, a resourceful production designer, that create whatever emotional resonance the film possesses. Especially effective are Ganz' low-budget expressionist images of totalitarianism, laborers herded by guards in huge industrial wastelands and the tyrant in a monumental architectural space.

Director Stephen Cornwell, a British expatriate, moves his cast deftly through Ganz' sets and props while cinematographer Ronn Schmidt films it in a fluid style. But the science is sloppy. The characters are stereotypes. And the relationships are contrived.

Also reviewed in:
NEW YORK TIMES, 11/13/93, p. 18, Stephen Holden
VARIETY, 11/29/93, p. 31, Fred Lombardi

PIANO, THE

A Miramax Films release of a CIBY 2000, The Australian Film Commission, and the New South Wales Film and Television Office production.   *Executive Producer:* Alain Depardieu. *Producer:* Jan Chapman.   *Director:* Jane Campion.   *Screenplay:* Jane Campion.   *Director of Photography:* Stuart Dryburgh.   *Editor:* Veronika Jenet.   *Music:* Michael Nyman. *Choreographer:* Mary-Anne Schultz.   *Sound:* Tony Johnson and (music) Michael J. Dutton. *Casting:* Diana Rowan, Susie Figgis, Victoria Thomas, and Alison Barrett.   *Production Designer:* Andrew McAlpine.   *Art Director:* Gregory Keen.   *Set Decorator:* Meryl Cronin. *Set Dresser:* Graham Aston, Phred Palmer, and Manu Sinclair.   *Special Effects:* Ken Durey and Waynne Rugg.   *Costumes:* Janet Patterson.   *Make-up:* Noriko Watanabe.   *Maori Dialogue:* Waihoroi Shortland and Selwyn Muru.   *Sign Language Instructor:* Darlene Allen and Holly

Hunter. *Stunt Coordinator:* Robert Bruce.   *Running time:* 120 minutes.   *MPAA Rating:* Not Rated.

CAST: Holly Hunter (Ada);   Harvey Keitel (Baines);   Sam Neill (Stewart);   Anna Paquin (Flora);   Kerry Walker (Aunt Morag);   Genevive Lemon (Nessie);   Tungia Baker (Hira);   Ian Mune (Reverend);   Peter Dennett (Head Seaman);   Te Whatanui Skipwith (Chief Nihe);   Pete Smith (Hone);   Bruce Allpress (Blind Piano Tuner);   Cliff Curtis (Mana);   Mahina Tunui (Meni, Mission Girl);   Hori Ahipene (Muturu);   Gordon Hatfield (Te Kori);   Mere Boynton (Chief Nihe's Daughter);   Kirsten Batley (Marama);   Tania Burney (Mahina);   Annie Edwards (Te Tiwha);   Harina Haare (Roimata);   Christina Harimate (Parearau);   Steve Kanuta (Amohia); P.J. Karauria (Taua);   Sonny Kirikiri (Tame);   Alain Makiha (Kahutia);   Greg Mayor (Tipi); Neil Mika Gudsell (Tahu);   Guy Moana (Kohuru);   Joseph Otimi (Rehia);   Glynis Paraha (Mairangi);   Riki Pickering (Rongo);   Eru Potaka-Dewes (Pitama);   Liane Rangi Henry (Te Ao);   Huahana Rewa (Te Hikumutu);   Tamati Rice (Pito);   Paora Sharples (Hotu);   George Smallman (Tuu);   Kereama Teua (Tu Kukuni);   Carla Rupuha (Heni);   Poamo Tuialii (Kahu); Susan Tuialii (Pare);   Kahumanu Waaka (Waimiria);   Lawrence Whareau (Kamira);   Jon Brazier (Wedding Photographer);   Stephen Papps (Bluebeard);   Tim Raby and Jon Sperry (Taunting Men);   Barbara Grover (School Hall Piano Player);   Arthur Ramford (School Hall Violin Player);   Nicola Baigent (Sunday School Teacher);   Rob Ellis, Terrence Garbolino, and William Matthew (Young Wives' Husbands);   Nancy Flyger (Maid);   George Boyle (Flora's Grandfather).

CHRISTIAN SCIENCE MONITOR, 8/17/93, p. 12, David Sterritt

Harvey Keitel is better known for bruising pictures like "Taxi Driver" and "Bad Lieutenant" than for international art films like "The Piano," a top prizewinner at the Cannes Film Festival last May. Yet asked for a one-word description of filmmaker Jane Campion, as she directed him in his new movie, he replies without a pause: "goddess."

Told about Mr. Keitel's remark a few minutes later, Ms. Campion laughs delightedly. "Lately he's changed his tune," she chuckles, explaining that there were moments during the making of her ambitious film when feelings weren't quite so positive.

In any case, the hard work by cast and director has paid off handsomely. "The Piano" won the Golden Palm for best picture at Cannes, sharing the award with "Farewell to My Concubine," a large-scale Chinese drama. This marked the first time a Chinese director—or a female director from *any* country—had garnered the top prize at the world's most renowned filmfest. (The Chinese government has banned the film.)

Another winner was Holly Hunter, whose performance in "The Piano" earned her the award for best actress. She plays Ada, a 19th-century woman who mysteriously stopped speaking while a child, and expresses her emotions through written words and the music she plays on her beloved piano. Her story begins when she arrives in a remote area of New Zealand, with her young daughter and as many possessions as her boat can carry, for an arranged marriage with a handsome landowner, played by Sam Neill.

When he declares it too expensive to bring her piano to their home—leaving it abandoned on the beach where it was unloaded—she starts to resent him and refuses to consummate their marriage. Instead she develops a complex relationship with an illiterate neighbor who has taken possession of the piano. At first he blackmails her, allowing her to earn the instrument back by indulging his sexual wishes. Later they recognize each other's higher qualities, however, and fall in love. The climax of the film is a horrific confrontation between Ada and her husband. The end is contrastingly gentle and mature.

"The Piano" has ingredients that often make for commercial success in American theaters, including some harrowing violence and a couple of surprisingly graphic sex scenes. Its intelligent screenplay and resonant images were enthusiastically received by the art-film connoisseurs at Cannes, however, and it promptly became the most talked-about picture of the festival.

This marked a major change from Campion's previous experience at Cannes, when her debut feature—the acerbic comedy "Sweetie," made five years ago—was booed by many at its initial press screening. Campion still remembers how she and her collaborators "cried our eyes out" shortly after that incident.

The joke, however, was on the people who jeered. "Sweetie" became an international success and was soon followed by "An Angel at My Table," a film biography of author Janet Frame, directed by Campion with unfailing taste and intelligence. Today she looks back at the booing with a healthy sense of perspective. "What *you* feel about what you've done is the most important thing," she says, adding that her close encounter with film-festival scorn may have helped her avoid becoming "addicted" to nothing but favorable responses.

What inspired her to write and direct "The Piano," with its challenging mixture of moods, characters, and ideas? One motivation was strictly professional. "I wanted to try and write a proper story with a narrative," she says, noting that "the straight-forward three-act kind of narrative" is not a form she automatically feels comfortable with.

Other motivations came from her enjoyment of Victorian gothic novels and her knowledge of history in New Zealand, her native country. "A lot of Victorian women who came to New Zealand brought pianos with them," she says, "and this struck me as an extraordinary instrument to have in that situation." Still another influence was a movie she's never seen, but has often heard about: "Two Men and a Wardrobe," an early Roman Polanski short about two loners who run into trouble when they travel around a city with a huge piece of furniture in their hands.

In the end, though, Campion says instinct and impulse had as much to do with the development of "The Piano" as any conscious inspirations. "Ideas don't arrive as one whole," she says. "My mind doesn't think in very logical ways all the time."

For this reason, she relies more on the visual training she received as an art student than on the analytical techniques—such as semiology, the study of communication through signs—that are fashionable in intellectual circles today.

"I did my semiotics and everything when I was at university,"—she says with a rueful smile, "and I decided that didn't help me think of anything creatively, whatsoever. There's a background of that [in my mind] somewhere, but I don't want to bring it to the fore anymore, because I know it doesn't work. To be able to pull [things] apart ... isn't the same as [knowing] how to put together!"

Although plans for its international release are not yet finalized, "The Piano" has been acquired for United States distribution by Miramax Films and should arrive in American theaters this fall, after more appearances on the film-festival circuit. Others who contributed to the movies success include cinematographer Stuart Dryburgh, who superbly captures the mixture of realism and surrealism that is a key part of Campion's style, and composer Michael Nyman, whose minimalist piano pieces—smartly played by Ms. Hunter herself—brilliantly enhance the subtly dreamlike aspects of the film.

Campion is now working on two literary adaptations: "My Guru and His Disciple," from Christopher Isherwood's autobiographical account of his years as a student of Hinduism in Los Angeles, and "Portrait of a Lady," from Henry James's classic novel. One of these is expected to become Campion's next production, and moviegoers around the world are already waiting for it eagerly.

CHRISTIAN SCIENCE MONITOR, 11/12/93, p. 12, David Sterritt

It would be hard to overstate the excitement that greeted Jane Campion's new movie, "The Piano," at the Cannes Film Festival last spring.

Advance buzz for the picture had been ecstatic, and this frequently has an adverse effect—building expectations so high that *nothing* could satisfy them. Once the first showing of "The Piano" was over, though, debate centered not on whether it was a good movie or a poor one; but whether it was "as good" or merely "almost as good" as pre-screening gossip had promised.

Now the movie is arriving in American theaters, and a few critics have started swimming against the tide. Some just want to be different from their colleagues. Others have genuine hesitations about the drama, which they find contrived, or overlong, or more arty than profound. There is some truth to all these objections, although Campion's filmmaking is so strong that the picture manages to sail beyond such problems.

But most reviewers are still in love with "The Piano," and it's a sure bet that most ticketbuyers will be too, although the movie's explicit sex and brief but harrowing violence may put it off-limits for some. Look for a box-office smash, appearances on dozens of 10-best lists, and some Academy Award nominations for good measure.

Campion, a New Zealander of European ancestry, got the idea for "The Piano" when she learned that during the Victorian age, many English-women who emigrated to New Zealand brought pianos with them—despite the obvious difficulty of transporting these bulky objects across the sea on 19th-century ships. This impressed Campion, who saw such determination as a sign of purpose, confidence, and resolve.

From this seed grew the character of Ada, a young Englishwoman who arrives in New Zealand for marriage to a well-to-do landowner she has never met. She is a strong-willed and self-possessed person, and also an eccentric one.

For reasons known only to herself, Ada has refused to speak since childhood, and communicates by writing messages on a tablet that hangs from her neck.

Her only other method of expression is through her piano, which becomes a focus of dispute from the moment she steps on New Zealand's shore. Fetching her from the beach where she has landed, her husband's servants are happy to bring her, her nine-year-old daughter, and her household possessions to the house. But the piano is too heavy and troublesome, so they abandon it.

Desperately upset by this, Ada refuses to consummate her marriage. Meanwhile, the piano is salvaged by an illiterate worker who uses it as a tool for sexual blackmail at her expense. Later he falls genuinely in love with her, however, and this brings out higher qualities in both characters.

Over the course of the movie, Ada, her husband, and her lover find their relationship growing ever more troubled and complex. This leads to a frighteningly violent climax followed by a surprisingly warm and optimistic conclusion.

"The Piano" gains much of its effectiveness from Campion's directing style, which combines the dream-like aura of her early film "Sweetie" with the sensitivity to feelings that made her last movie, "An Angel at My Table," so extraordinary.

Although the action threatens to become melodramatic and even overwrought at times, the imaginative power of Campion's images and emotional insights (especially with regard to the heroine) rarely allow the story to seem artificial or exaggerated.

Also impressive are the performances—especially by Hunter, who not only brings unexpected depth to her character but does an exquisite job of playing Michael Nyman's lovely piano music on the soundtrack.

Sam Neill does sturdy work as Ada's long-suffering husband, and Harvey Keitel is well-cast as her mercurial lover. Applause also goes to the talented Maori performers who play indigenous residents of the New Zealand region.

CINEASTE, Vol. XX, No. 3, 1994, p. 51, Barbara Quart

Jane Campion has broken through with *The Piano*. Other women directors have had big commercial successes in the last decade, and yet others have made first-rate features. But it's Campion—the first woman to garner the Best Director award at Cannes, and the first with a serious shot at Best Director Oscar—who's attracting large audiences and creating genuine art. What makes it so satisfying is that it's happening to an uncompromising, idiosyncratic director.

New Zealander Campion has always won critical ovations, from her first Cannes award-winning short, *Peel* (1982), to her feature films, *Sweetie* (1989) and *An Angel at My Table* (1990), but she has been known only to a limited, art movie audience. In fact, some critics of *The Piano* find Campion's usual comic quirkiness sacrificed to a more mainstream style. Surely that's a worry, and from here on, there will be a constant checking of her artistic pulse to make sure that success hasn't coopted her. Even though *The Piano*'s epic scope is new for Campion, as is its strong narrative, there is no cooption here and as much risk-taking as ever.

The Piano opens on a stranger's arrival—the 1850s landing of Ada (Holly Hunter) with her nine-year-old daughter, Flora (Anna Paquin), in the remote New Zealand bush to meet Stewart (Sam Neill), the husband of her mail-order-arranged marriage—and closes with her departure. For reasons we don't know (and, in the context of the film, it doesn't matter), Ada had stopped talking years before, though she communicates through her daughter and her piano. Under the pretext of wanting piano lessons, Stewart's neighbor, Baines (Harvey Keitel), retrieves Ada's piano and slowly draws her into a series of erotic encounters.

The film, from the outset, announces its wild romantic mood and large ambitions with a spectacular turbulence of churning seas and massive land formations. Ada's arrival is breathtaking visually, as is the whole film—for the quality of light alone in just about every single frame—and the extraordinarily composed images of a strikingly beautiful world. ("Beware of the Bland Old Bush," she warned her location scout, who certainly did.) The outline of fairy tale/archetypal journey is also laid down early, though with a light and skilled hand. Coming from London, the Scottish Ada's arrival to the wilds of tangled jungle, both magical and sinister, with its oozing mud, its native Maori peoples and their strange facial markings, is an entry into a world where nature and the primal rule, where European clothes and constraints look ludicrous, and where control slips away.

The Piano also takes up the central mantra of feminist film criticism (and filmmaking, e.g. *A Question of Silence*): the woman who does not speak, who has no voice. As Campion does everything her own way, however, this mute woman makes herself heard very loudly from her first communication about the boat, delivered with a ferocity and authority no one could mistake. The forcefulness with which she expresses her passion for the piano and her pain at leaving it behind—as her new husband demands—make clear that muteness here does not equate with lack of self-assertion. Ada is established from the start as totally her own person, knowing her own mind, with a force enriched immeasurably by the intelligence and clean intensity of Holly Hunter's performance. She is a postfeminist woman in the sense that her strengths are givens, without Campion feeling any need to build in explicit feminist issues and struggles—unless one sees the film's love triangle in these terms.

Sam Neill's handsome, apparently decent Stewart has no idea of what empathy with the woman means. In falling back on his patriarchal authority ('No, you can't have the piano,' and 'It's *my* house') he turns Ada against him permanently, and finally seems a monster in our eyes. Baines, on the other hand, thinks always of Ada: her looking tired on arrival; at departure, the importance of the piano to her so she must have it, even if it puts all their lives at risk. He hears her in her silence, while Stewart does not hear her at all. In that sense, the question of silence, and of being heard by men, does enter the film centrally. The adulterous seduction unfolds skillfully, like a game, and like a fairy tale, but in fact Stewart is never a husband. His behavior demands that Ada look elsewhere, since he is not prepared to give her anything she needs, although he speaks the words of decency. To build this grand drama on what a woman needs (and, unlike the Forties weepies, what a strong, non-self-sacrificing woman needs, without compromises) is in itself an event. It needs hardly be said that only a woman director would be likely to do it.

The two men's contrasting relations to the Maoris also serve to give us their measure, perhaps a little too obviously: Baines linked to the 'natural' people; Stewart, mocked by them ("old dry balls," no less) and finding their direct sexuality disgusting. The daughter Flora kisses and humps tree trunks with the Maori children and rides branches like horses, while her mother is doing some sexual riding within Baines's house. It's clear here, again, that Campion's wild side has not vanished, it simply doesn't call attention to itself, as before. Baines is illiterate in this Lady Chatterly configuration, as the heroine's muteness also facilitates a stripping down to primal passions. The native people are not idealized but feel real—as Campion has tried to make all the characters, working against the pull of romance and fairy tale in this respect. The Maoris, though necessarily backgrounded to the romance, do not stay quietly behind, as our experience with Westerns may lead us to expect—they show anger, grab Ada's clothes and try them on, make fun of people by telling racy jokes, watch, and give advice. (Some politically correct spectators find lazy native stereotypes in this, but I find humor and vitality.)

Harvey Keitel stars against type and, though he has often played destructive, nihilistic figures, is here willing to give what many have rightly noted as a remarkably tender and gentle performance, and to accept the further vulnerability of frontal nudity. The way Campion has her camera observe his body, and the way she stages the sex scenes, carries a strong erotic charge, all estheticized sensuality that is strikingly different from Hollywood-style gymnastic thrashings and orgasmic sounds. Although female sexual desire has always been the central subject of Campion's films, in The Piano she addresses sexual wholeness straight on for the first time, though even here she disturbingly frames it through the threatened violence of the jealous Stewart's male gaze. And Campion's old quirkiness and daring mixture of tones show up here, with the dog's tongue slobbering on Stewart's hand while he peeps at Ada and Baines making love.

Always boldly pushing the outer limits, Campion further takes a risk in having the erotically turned-on heroine, now locked up by Stewart, first turn unconsciously in her sleep, with aroused sexual feeling, toward her little girl, and then consciously turn to the unloved husband, for nothing but sex. Caressing him but refusing to be caressed by him, she wants to be in control, the only active one. His pride shocked, he won't allow it. Campion speaks of Stewart in that scene "becoming an object for Ada," and of Ada's wanting "to continue the very high feeling she had, a very strong compulsion." This is no traditional heroine.

There are other unconventional variations on the sexual theme: the uptight Stewart's reverse voyeurism, and the whole emphasis (not surprising from a filmmaker) on *looking* as a major erotic mode. Baines has also turned to someone else for comfort, in bed with a native woman when Stewart goes to get him at the end. True love is no mystical thing here—partners are switched without to-do. But the real shockers come from the aggrieved, respectable husband. He tries to rape Ada in the woods when she hurries to a second assignation with Baines. The net of black creepers, encircling Ada like a trap as she struggles, is yet another instance of Campion's powerful use of landscape.

Stewart later grotesquely croons a lullaby of love to Ada in bed after he has mutilated her, and then attempts sex, stopped by the ferocity of her eyes on him. At that point he seems utterly evil and monstrous, something to make your skin creep. Then he slips back into seeming decency, so that many are moved to sympathy for the man. Such wild juxtapositions in the same character—the refusal to label him a clear villain and the ability to feel for his confusion and frustration, at the same time that evil and darkness are everywhere in her vision—all this is very much Campion.

The female unit that mother and daughter form against the man, shutting him out, is established from the start. Campion skillfully conveys the sense of being included and being excluded, as well as Stewart's helplessness in that situation. Their unity is underlined as they echo one another visually in the frame—from the humorous sameness of their bonnets to the girl's miming the woman's ways. This closeness makes the daughter's act of betrayal truly shocking. The girl, resentful of being shut out by Ada's love for Baines, sides with her new father, telling on her mother, and even eager to rip open the mother's gift to Baines for Stewart to see. It's remarkable how, in a jaded world sated with brutality, we can be so shaken by the violence Campion's very human characters do to one another without a gun in sight.

But Campion's films do contain knives and electric shock 'treatments' and axes. The actual violence in *The Piano* is foreshadowed by Stewart's using various large tools in his work, and by the shadow-play cardboard axe used on women in the Christmas 'Bluebeard' play. Despite the staged display of the bloody heads of wives, in the end this wife is not a victim. Even Stewart's crucial act of releasing both lovers (trickily presented as imminent violence) results from his hearing Ada's voice in his head. She threatens in her willfulness to harm him if he forces her to remain. So she, in effect, orders her own release.

Campion uses Baines's negotiating over piano keys for Ada's sexual favors, and Stewart's later threat of taking one finger for each wrongdoing, as a means of distancing the story and making it archetypal. The conceit also provides sexual titillation and humor, which Campion's films are always rich in, even when most pained. But the piano itself—Campion's original idea, carried around for years, which the rest of the film was built around—is a terrific conception. The heroine's total, intense, needy attachment to it, yearning for it, joy while playing it, is one of the most touching things about the film. It's her voice in the way art is an artist's voice. Although some critics find the piano-on-the-beach imagery 'pretentious,' or complain about the New Age music and want period music instead, Campion in each case has made the fitting—though, as always, the unconventional—judgement. Ada's hungry playing, through the opening she tears in the crate, of music apparently of her own creation, is the very image of an artist at work. The magical early scene on the beach that establishes all this, with the daughter cartwheeling in her white petticoat, and Baines pacing, is where his passion for Ada is aroused, specifically in response to the passion and beauty of her playing, her art. Campion thus makes sure that we never take offense at what could seem coercive in his subsequent barter arrangement.

Most interesting is the film's ambivalence about the consuming monomania of art, since the piano finally is seen as a casket, and must be cast overboard. The film's subtler critics question the contradictory strangeness of destroying the precious piano and associating it with death at the end, but this comes not out of any confusion on Campion's part, but rather from her openness to irrational forces resistant to neat understanding and verbalization. Perhaps the instrument is related to death because it has filled all Ada's needs and replaced other human attachments (except to her daughter, whom she always caresses before she caresses the piano). In extending herself to love or sexual love of the man—fascinatingly, it's not clear which—and in releasing the piano, she moves toward life. In an amazing image, the piano takes her under with it.

And going under is also at the heart of the film. Campion wanted the bush itself to have "an underwater look that's always charmed me. I was after the vivid, subconscious imagery of the bush, its dark, inner world." She asked everyone involved in the film's design to think "bottom of the fish tank," in a way putting the whole production under the sea, inside the subconscious, the place of dream images and the forging of the soul, the deep primal experience from which poems come. But this is a dangerous place in which to linger too long. Ada's return from the deep, the great moment of her separating from the piano, is shot by Campion with gleaming color and light amidst bubbles and water, a kind of powerful visual jubilation, celebrating Ada's explosive freeing into the world

The last scene of *The Piano*, of life in a new place, is added to give us information about a normalized future of healing, but anything would feel tacked on and superfluous following that momentous, archetypal descent into water and reemergence—Moby Dick, phoenix, rebirth—an astonishing sequence without which the film would be immeasurably poorer. Campion's central women, all very odd as well as very strong, are also deeply acquainted with the night. Ada is the least odd, though she informs us at the end that even in her new life, with her voluntary muteness and new artificial finger, she is the town freak. But Campion's women—Kay in *Sweetie* and Janet Frame in *An Angel at My Table*—are also survivors of the wreck, Ishmaels, who, like Ada, will to live, even to their own surprise. Campion's divings into the wreck of pain and family dysfunction lead us back out, angel wings undulating, like Flora's play wings in the stream near departure time, stronger with reemergence.

Still, *The Piano* closes with death an apparently strong presence, a strange lullaby of the silence at the bottom of the sea with which to soothe oneself to sleep—and with the closing poem's text printed on the screen for emphasis. But death here seems used more as an artistic balancing device to avoid too neat and too easily upbeat a closure, to build a darkness into the conclusion in order to keep the closing mythic, so the film's grandeur doesn't end reduced to a happy little family getting healthier every day. In *The Piano*, Campion plummets into the sea to reclaim women's desire from a historical past that denied it, and, in this process, she has also found a rich metaphor for her own personal explorations.

FILM QUARTERLY, Spring 1994, p. 46, Harvey Greenberg

Jane Campion's *Sweetie* (1989) described the calamitous impact of a raucous schizophrenic woman upon her relatives. *An Angel at My Table* (1990), based on the autobiography of Janet Frame, depicted the no less harrowing effects of institutionalization upon a female writer misdiagnosed as chronically schizophrenic. *The Piano*, directed from her own screenplay, comprises Campion's most extraordinary exploration of unsettled, unsettling feminine outsiders to date. Its heroine is Ada McGrath (Holly Hunter), a Victorian unwed mother of pallid countenance and somber dress, whose silent compliance conceals and protects a fiercely unconventional spirit.

Ada is not so much unable as *unwilling* to speak. She suffers, or, depending upon one's viewpoint, practices elective mutism. This rare, puzzling condition usually develops in early childhood and occurs rather more frequently in girls than boys. The electively mute child has been characterized as symbiotically bound to a powerfully possessive adult; as alternately clinging and shy, or intensely stubborn and negativistic; as terribly fearful of the sound of its own voice; as traumatized by abuse or non-abusive injury; as fighting intense family scapegoating with passive-aggressive silence.[1] Interestingly enough, especially in light of Ada's character, the syndrome is thought by some to represent a strategy of active manipulation and control, rather than merely being a symptom of autistic withdrawal.

Campion compounds the enigma of Ada's condition by furnishing only the sparest details of her background or the early forces which have played upon her. She lives in a cloistered, mid-Victorian Glasgow home. *The Piano*'s establishing sequence begins out of focus, as in a hypnogogic state. The camera peers at the emerging world through the lattice of a child's fingers, while Ada's six-year-old voice tells us she ceased speaking at that age, and does not remember why. (One notes that *The Piano*'s narrative engine is propelled by the internal monologue of a character who cannot or will not speak—another compelling paradox spun out of Ada's mutism.)

She relates that her beloved father (neither he or any other family member is ever seen) has a strangely approving notion of her affliction as a "dark talent." He's arranged her marriage to a lonely expatriate English farmer in New Zealand. Quite possibly he is the recipient of her dowry.

In a trice Ada is whisked over the sea, dumped unceremoniously upon the New Zealand shore with her baggage, her precious piano, and her out-of-wedlock daughter Flora (Anna Paquin)—a precocious and voluble nine-year-old who is Ada's interpreter to the world. The two communicate through their own invented sign system.

Campion has kept the camera claustrophobically screwed down until now: Ada's instant voyage is literally *embodied* by the fragmented hands and torsos of the sailors carrying her from skiff to land (a locution the director used to underscore the heroine's schizoid isolation from an equally alienated husband in *Sweetie*). The mise-en-scène briefly opens out into a vista of stormswept grey sky, huge waves tumbling against a barren stretch of sand. One's view is then constricted again, and for the most part will remain so. Tight closeups further accentuate the nuances of an unfolding and mute—or barely spoken—triangle of desire.

Stewart, Ada's new husband (Sam Neill), is stiff-upper-lip reticence personified: handsome, not unkind, but disastrously unimaginative. His narrow utilitarian purposes immediately oppress Ada's sensibility when he refuses to bring her instrument back to his plantation. In a breathtaking long shot the lone piano is limned starkly against the rolling surf: it's suddenly a vivid icon of cultural collision, of yet another stifling of Ada's voice, of her delivery into paltry domesticity in a startling alien environment.

Stewart's home is kept by gabbling, censorious female relatives. Ada and Flora retreat from a bizarre simulacrum of English gentility into their room and private world. The taciturn Stewart, unlike the rest of his clan (and much like Ada's father) accepts, even approves of Ada's disability ("There's something to be said for silence"). As frustration with his unconsummated marriage mounts, Stewart wonders if Ada might be mad as well as mute, yet grows ever more entranced with her.

Stewart's neighbor, Baines (Harvey Keitel), offers to purchase the beached piano from Stewart for 80 prime acres, with music instruction by Ada thrown into the bargain. (Campion permits an inference that the two men have previously done business, and perhaps as a result—aren't altogether happy with each other.) Stewart agrees, hoping she can be drawn out of her shell. Baines makes an unprepossessing pupil. He's squat, illiterate, his face tattooed like the ribald Maoris who lounge about his ramshackle hut.

Baines offers to sell back the piano one key at a time in return for voyeuristic liberties with Ada's person. Apparently shocked at first, she nevertheless consents with her usual passivity; then piquantly shifts the grounds of what seems like a perverse, humiliating bargain, demanding more keys for each favor. Eventually the two lie together nude without making love; Hunter's unexpectedly voluptuous body is pressed against Keitel's compact, powerfully muscled, yet unglamorous frame—a moment both unutterably moving and incredibly erotic.

Baines grows disgusted with himself for engineering a degrading charade: he was instantly smitten with Ada, and could think of no other way to court her. When he proposes ending their "arrangement" and returning the piano to Stewart's house, she flies into a fury and quickly takes him to bed. One infers this is her first real passion. The relationship which engendered Flora seems to have been short-lived and cerebral, with a man Ada implies was too timorous to keep "listening" to the quicksilver mind and tumultuous roil of emotion hidden beneath her silence.

Stewart discovers the affair. In an exceptionally creepy scene, he peeps upon the trysting couple from underneath the floor of Baines' hut—he, not Baines, is revealed as the repressed voyeur. Enraged, he forbids her Baines' presence, literally penning her up in his house with the piano until she can be "good." Unaccountably, she appears to warm her husband, and he gives her back her freedom.

Ada is next seen pressing her lips against her mirrored image, then caressing the piano's keys with a sensual backhand gesture. When she attempts to awaken Stewart with the same languorous touch he cannot abide his arousal and rebuffs her. Rather than rejection, she feels release. It's subtly apparent that while one part of her has been dutifully attempting to shape herself to Stewart's limitations, the larger part has been using her husband as a substitute object—as well as her piano and her own reflected self. All are now metonyms of her rapturous infatuation with Baines.

She entrusts Flora to give Baines a piece of the piano's keyboard, upon which she has penned a testament of her love. In a jealous fit, Flora brings it to Stewart instead. At this moment, he represents the lesser of two evils, since he poses no threat to Flora's symbiotic attachment to her mother. But the child, caught up in fantasies of retaliation which are ultimately aimed at regaining her mother's affection, misgauges the potential for violence born out of Stewart's narcissistic injuries. Stewart takes an ax to the piano, then to Ada's hand. Amidst a welter of screams and blood, he awakens to a horrified recognition of his unleashed brutality—and to the impossibility of Ada's ever coming to heel, ever truly becoming his wife. Wishing only to be quit of her uncanny power over him—"I am afraid of her *will!*"—he relinquishes her to Baines.

Campion's tale sounds over-the-top penny-dreadful in the telling, but it's tremendously absorbing on the screen. The dark side of Eros is often diminished today: sexuality is chattered to death in the tabloids, on "Oprah," or in the clinic. *The Piano* restores the orphic power of sex. In the film's puritanical milieu, desire is filtered through murky Victorian notions about feminine purity or evil, through the era's fascination with the sway of the primitive, the savage imperatives of nature, the chilly balm of death.

The Piano's protagonists are intensely passionate. But Campion intimates they are also erotic naïfs (the men in particular), who confront sexuality as if it were newly minted in the disconcerting unfamiliarity of the New Zealand bush. Stewart can only follow the rulebook that stringently tutors him on patriarchal duty, feminine docility, the white man's imperial burden. Baines, who emigrated after being abandoned by his wife for reasons never explained, is discovered sunk in debauched despair.

Ada is the most daring of the three in her struggles with Eros. It is moot whether some ungovernable childhood abuse, some terrible skepticism of ever being understood or cherished has driven her behind her wall of stillness. Her sea change liberates the extraordinary "will" that so infuriates (and intimidates) her husband. It surges forth with a force so primal as to seem impersonal to her, spurring an unruly independence—and a tender carnality which finds its match in the bosom of the no-less-wounded (and nearly as inarticulate) Baines.

The Piano's literary antecedents include those lurid Gothic romances replete with frail heroines, exotic locales, and masterful/sinister noblemen; the *amours fous* of *Wuthering Heights* and *Tess of the D'Urbervilles*; fairy tales with *amour fou* preoccupations, notably *Beauty and the Beast* and *Bluebeard*. By design or unconscious intention, Campion has adroitly reinterpreted such sources. Her work exemplifies the unique spin on Gothic strategems, inflected by the surreal peculiarities of "down under" nature, which has distinguished the cinema of Australia and New Zealand at least since Peter Weir's *Picnic at Hanging Rock* (1975) and *The Last Wave* (1977).[2] Stuart Dryburgh's photography of the deep aquamarine shade and rough, tangled vegetation of the New Zealand bush serves to highlight the protagonists' convoluted and excessive emotionality (as when the vengeful Stewart rushes upon Ada, and both become caught in a twisted mesh of ancient vine).

The Piano is true to its period in every respect (saving its music), while simultaneously addressing a host of issues dear to contemporary cultural critics and film scholars. Feminist theoreticians have notably explored the suppression of the feminine voice under patriarchy's insensible rule and the attendant possibility for recovering that voice at the very core of its suppression.[3] In this context, Ada's muteness can be interpreted as a limit case of patriarchal domination, both symptom *and* countercoup.[4]

In a much cited study, "Visual Pleasure and Narrative Cinema," Laura Mulvey asserts that classic Hollywood cinema treats woman as the object of male gaze; her disruptive sexuality must be neutralized by transforming her into a docile fetish, marrying her off, or killing her.[5] Ada's two suitors attempt to "objectify" her by all of these measures (Stewart stops just short of murder), Yet Campion has her turn the tables and make Stewart and Baines helplessly enthralled objects of *her* gaze, *her* desire.

The arrogance and ignorance of the colonizing consciousness toward native culture and the parallel bewilderment, silent contempt, and resentment of the Maoris toward their English masters constitute a less visible, but no less crucial ideological subtext of *The Piano*. Stewart is horrified when he sees Flora and her Maori friends in semi-masturbatory play. What he takes for licentiousness betokens the Maori absence of Victorian childhood sexual repression (their taboos lie elsewhere).

During the colonists' staging of *Bluebeard*, the horrified locals rush upon the stage to prevent the butchering of the wives (presaging Stewart's savage attack upon Ada). The Maoris are indeed untutored in Western drama, but Campion's chief point here is that Bluebeard's sadistic intention toward his wives is deeply offensive to them.

While her sympathies are tilted toward the Maoris, Campion's perspective on settler as well as indigenous tribe is for the most part coolly balanced. The Maoris are not glorified (or degraded) as noble primitives. The director shows that they and the English are equally capable of being wrongheadedly amused or appalled by each other's Otherness. Nor is Stewart an unregenerate villain. His hopefulness about winning Ada's love in the face of her fierce disdain is as pitiable as his violence upon her is odious.

Sam Neill poignantly captures Stewart's uncomprehending pain over Ada's disaffection as well as his repellent paternalism. Anna Paquin's Flora is a radiant delight. Harvey Keitel has created a galaxy of Caliban-like characters; *The Piano* shows him evolving into the light, Baines' defensive brutishness yielding to an amazing, grave sweetness.

But the film's complex heart belongs to Hunter. Her perky American roles (*Broadcast News* and *Raising Arizona* [1987], *Always* and *Miss Firecracker* [1989]) do not prepare one for the acute intelligence and volcanic sensuality spoken by the actress's pale face, her flashing eye, and her exquisitely tuned gestures. She transforms Ada's perennial black dress, bonnet, camisole, and bustle into a prison for her character's body and soul.

Hunter is also an able pianist; her rendition of Michael Nyman's score heightens her verisimilitude in the role. Nyman has often reworked earlier styles with a kind of Brechtian defamiliarization (e.g., his brittle deconstruction of Purcell in *The Draughtsman's Contract* [1982]). In *The Piano*, he refuses to dissect or defamiliarize mid-nineteenth-century Romanticism, indeed makes little reference at all to the musical idioms of the period. Using New Age harmonies and plangent arpeggios, he has composed an elegiac improvisation on wild Scottish folk themes which would have proven bathetic in less skillful hands.

Voyaging with Baines to resettlement in urban New Zealand, Ada pitches her piano overboard lest the boat capsize. She becomes entangled in a rope, and is herself pulled over the side. She sinks into the deep, but to her utter amazement decides to free herself—"my will has chosen life!" The image dissolves to scenes of that life; her now adult voiceover relates that Baines has repaired Stewart's assault and provided her with a curious metallic finger. She has taken up teaching piano, is learning to speak haltingly again, and muses that she is probably viewed as the "town freak."

The conclusion of this intricate fable of feminine identity is ambiguous. In *The Piano*'s enigmatic opening, a child peers at a world yet unborn through fingers which both hide and disclose. It's not precisely clear whether they belong to Ada or Flora. In retrospect, one speculates that Campion is meditating upon a Victorian girl's fascinated, terrified fantasies about her path toward sexual awakening.

For Ada, these fantasies unfold in an odyssey shot through with references to voyeurism, the primal scene, rape and castration fears—and an overarching anxiety over incestuous desire. It is moot whether Ada has been banished by her father to New Zealand in aid of improving his cash flow or has herself actively sought flight from an imperious, possibly seductive/abusive father who prized and perhaps enabled her loss of voice. Stewart may be interpreted as his neurotic re-invention; Baines, as embodying his gentler, more wholesome recuperation. One hopes Flora will find calmer seas. Campion offers subliminal hope that she may fare better than her mother, not least because Baines represents a father who can allow a woman a voice and space of her own.

But the director also intimates that her heroine's decision to voyage from the New Zealand wilds back to "civilized" life with Baines may constitute a sacrifice of her freer, darker nature, one that perhaps would not have occurred had there been no Flora. In jettisoning the piano, Ada seems compelled not only by the imperative of survival but also by the need to abjure the dangerous Dionysian thrust of her temperament. One is left with a ruling image of her eerily suspended in mid-ocean like some tenebrous, funereal blossom, before her "will" chooses a tamer Eros over the Thanatos which may well be the ultimate desire prefigured by her muteness.

NOTES

1. For an excellent overview of the subject, see Larry B. Silverman, "Elective Mutism," ch. 42.1, under *Other Disorders of Infancy, Childhood, and Adolescence*; in *Comprehensive Textbook of Psychiatry*, Harold J. Kaplan and Benjamin J. Sadock, eds., Volume 2, 5th Edition (Baltimore: Williams and Wilkins, 1989, 1877-1889).
2. For an astute overview of the peculiar inflection of Gothic elements in New Zealand and Australian cinema, see Caryn James, "A Distinctive Shade of Darkness," *New York Times*, Arts and Leisure Section, November 28, 1993, pp. 13, 22-23.
3. See, inter alia, Kaja Silverman, *The Acoustic Mirror: The Female Voice in Psychoanalysis and Cinema* (Bloomington, IN: Indiana University Press, 1988), and Amy Lawrence, *Echo and Narcissus: Women's Voices in Classical Hollywood Cinema* (Berkeley, CA: University of California Press, 1991).
4. Gaylyn Studlar analyzes an analogous conflation of submission and protest in Max Ophul's *Letter from an Unknown Woman*: "Masochistic Performance and Female Subjectivity in *Letter from an Unknown Woman*," *Cinema Journal* 33 (Spring, 1994).
5. Laura Mulvey, "Visual Pleasure and the Narrative Cinema," *Screen* 16, no. 3 (1975), pp. 8-18.

FILMS IN REVIEW, 3-4/94, p. 56, Harry Pearson, Jr.

There is something about *The Piano*, Jane Campion's third and (much too) highly praised film, set in 19th Century New Zealand, that has an elemental impact upon much of its intended art house audience. That impact is such that it seems to have savaged the critical sensibilities of otherwise discerning students, devotees, and analysts of film, leaving them to gush hosannahs upon that which is mostly a highly undisciplined and cinematically inept mess, though a mess with moments of genuine *passione* and occasional *gravitas*, like the earlier and even messier works of this undisciplined director (*Sweetie, An Angel At My Table*).

Those who expect a fundamental understanding of mise-en-scene will not find it here, nor will they find much in the way of internal logic, a necessity, I think, if a movie is to retain its power over time, and not later be seen as the cultural artifact of a changing and troublesome era in masculine-feminine relations.

We know we are in trouble almost from the start, when Campion chooses to set her heroine, piano and daughter ashore on a most highly photogenic beach where no ship would drop anchor, much less lade a piano through roaring surf to reach a beach of black sand. We are told that the heroine has such will that she simply stopped speaking (for what reasons we are not told) during early childhood, and then quickly given considerable evidence of that will. So much so that one wonders, when the mail-order bride's husband arrives at the beach, that she would agree to leave the piano behind. (That's out of character.) Much less that the piano would be left well below the high tide mark—this we know from a shot of the water rushing around its legs—thus ensuring in any other dimension, where gravity and sand exist, that the piano would sink beneath the surface before someone (in this case, tardily) came to reclaim it.

Clearly if Ada, as commandingly played by the brilliant Holly Hunter (who is the most singular reason that this unbelievable concoction has the power it does), had her way, the piano would not have been left on the beach and there would have been no story, at least not the story as Campion tells it, one, she has intimated, that was "inspired" by *Wuthering Heights* and the Brontean Gothic sensibility.

Ada's husband, played without much conviction by Sam Neill, has a farm, although it is not at all obvious what he farms, other than trees. He also has a pal, played by the unpredictable Harvey Keitel, whose method of livelihood is equally obscure and whose relationships with the

decorative (they serve no other function, not even the sensible one of a Greek-style chorus commenting upon the foolishness of mortals) Maori are none too clear. We know he must like them, since he seems to have halfway gone native himself. Keitel makes a deal with the husband for the piano (whose property it is not), retrieves it (still standing high above the sand on that gorgeous beach), and makes a deal with Ada: She can earn the piano back by giving him lessons. Miraculously, a piano tuner—from whence it is not said—appears. Nearly as miraculously, there seems to be a settlement of people living nearby, though we don't know where and we certainly don't know how they sustain themselves, or what their relationships are with Neill, or Keitel, or the Maoris. Since the landscape seems to be deep tropical forest, you might wonder where a settlement could possibly be squeezed in, just as you might wonder, since this is 19th Century New Zealand, where Holly Hunter has learned all those New Age tunes she churns out on the piano—one would rather have thought she would be playing Mozart, or Chopin, or Beethoven's *Appassionata*. Campion can't be bothered to fill in the background elements because she's got bigger fish to fry. (But couldn't she have instructed the photographer to achieve his deep blues in some way other than using indoor color film outdoors?)

The piano lessons are at the heart of the film—and once they begin we divine the purpose of the movie: a sort of up-scale soft core pornography for the New Age sensibility. Keitel isn't interested in learning to play the piano. He wants to play Hunter—each lesson represents a key (black only) and with each key Hunter comes closer to possession of the piano—her "voice"—and Keitel closer to the possession of Hunter. All the while, we are supposed to believe that her daughter, who ignores Neill completely and has bonded obsessively with her mother, will be content to sit quietly outside Keitel's hilltop shack, the doors closed against her, without a whit of curiosity or jealously, until, voilà, Harvey and Hunter are down to frontal nudity. Believe it or not, the seduction scenes actually work, no small accomplishment, given these edge-of-hysteria proceedings, and they work because of the intensity and truth brought to their roles by Hunter and Keitel, surely one of the most unlikely of screen pairings, and one that is bound to be remembered. I'm not saying that there isn't greatness in *The Piano*, but I am saying that it is the work of a yet immature and unpolished talent (scarcely the stuff of which best direction is made; for that in this year we would have to attend to Scorsese's *Age of Innocence* or Ivory's *Remains of the Day*).

Well, of course, the daughter tells Neill—not that he's ever been pleasant to her, thus helping the more skeptical of us with not a shred of motive for the daughter's abrupt behavior. And he, like her, goes up to peek in upon the proceedings. And does nothing about what he sees. Hunter, emboldened by her contact with Keitel, comes home to the virginal (?) Neill and toys with him sexually. Evidently we are supposed to understand that this unleashes the beast in him, though all we see are his coy demurrals. He does take care to lock Hunter up, and the very day he decides to leave the house door unlocked, she sends a message via the daughter to Keitel—I love you, written on a piano key, and this to a guy who can't even read. The daughter gives the key to Neill, he retaliates in a gory and inconclusively awful scene and willful Hunter makes no effort to get even? Then there is a mawkish and sentimental conclusion (if you don't believe it to be a dying dream of Hunter's and I don't because of the artificial finger) completely out of keeping with the tone of what has come before, which effectively negates the film. Hardly a *Wuthering Heights*, where the sense of place was oppressive and inescapable, just as was the character driven plot. At the end, Hunter and Keitel and the darling daughter are all living happily together, with Hunter now beginning to speak again.

The trouble with the critical accolades is that the artist has, in no sense, earned them in their entirety. Talented, yes. A touch of genius, more than. But the effects of overpraising—and the incumbent reaction that will necessarily greet her next film—can be devastating to the career of a young and passionate filmmaker (or any other kind of artist, from writer to sculptor). She'll need the will of her heroines (the one common theme in her work to date) to move beyond a film that is much less than the sum of its ill-fitting parts.

LOS ANGELES TIMES, 11/19/93, Calendar/p. 1, Kenneth Turan

Unafraid of confounding expectations, "The Piano" is a tonic for the tired soul. Using familiar actors in ways no one could have expected, it makes a sweepingly romantic 19th-Century story seem almost avant-garde. More than that, it offered a complete way of seeing, an uncompromised view of the world by a writer-director whose command of the visual and emotional aspects of filmmaking is fearless and profound.

While the "a film by" credit is more used than deserved among current filmmakers, no one has earned it as completely as Jane Campion. In directing her own story of the mute Ada, an arranged bride, who comes to a primitive New Zealand and powerfully affects the lives of two men, she shows a level of filmmaking assurance and assertiveness, a knowledge not only of what she wants but also of how to get it, that led to "The Piano" sharing the Palme d'Or at Cannes with "Farewell My Concubine."

Not sharing her Cannes best actress award with anyone was Holly Hunter, whose unnerving performance as Ada reaches a once-in-a-lifetime level of intensity. Thoughtfully complementing her in an assured cast are Harvey Keitel and Sam Neill as the men whose lives she has an overwhelming impact on.

Set in 1852, "The Piano" successfully interweaves several thematic strands. A native New Zealander who now lives in Australia, Campion wanted to deal with her forebears, the early English settlers, and how they interacted with the native Maoris. She wanted to do a full-bore costume romance with echoes of "Jane Eyre" and "Wuthering Heights." And she wanted to have an emotionally powerful woman, possessed of a remarkable will, as her protagonist.

Uncompromising women were at the center of Campion's previous features, "Sweetie" and "An Angel at My Table." Neither of those films were as plot-driven as "The Piano," but Campion has transferred her empathy for determined folk, as well as her intuitive sympathy with the violent, deranging power of passion, from those films to this and used them to seriously push the outside of the envelope of a nominally more conventional format.

Campion has also brought with her an eye for what will make an impact that is like no one else's. Schooled as an artist, she has a complete understanding of the language of images, and, working with cinematographer Stuart Dryburgh, has come up with a series of rich, emotionally charged visuals, ranging from intimate close-ups to startling vistas, that are potent and unexpected.

"The Piano" in fact opens with an apt image for the interior person Ada is, an extreme close-up of what she sees looking out through fingers she's held up to cover her eyes. As we are told in a brief voice-over, delivered in what Ada calls "not my speaking voice but my mind's voice," she stopped talking when she was 6. "No one knows why, not even me."

Ada, however, doesn't think of herself as silent, and not because of the use she makes of a private sign language and the enameled note pad she has for mundane communications. Ada has her piano and that is no small thing. Not an instrument to be played, the piano is the focus of her entire being. Not even her willful 9-year-old daughter (an eerie mirror-image performance by Anna Paquin) seems to finally mean as much.

Placed into an arranged marriage with a man who writes her that "God loves dumb creatures so why not me?," Ada arrives in New Zealand from her native Scotland and finds it unimaginably wild and strange. A place of thick greenery and thicker mud, half Eden, half blasted heath, it is a raw, savage locale where the elements and the inconveniences threaten to be overwhelming.

Just as disturbing to Ada is Stewart (Neill), her husband, whose first reaction on meeting his bride is a confused "You're small. I never thought you'd be small." Personally awkward and driven by an acquisitive hunger for land, he does not begin to understand his imaginative, high-strung wife. And he refuses point blank to transport Ada's piano from the beach it's landed on to their new home.

Desperate for the touch of her instrument, Ada waits until Stewart is away and asks their neighbor Baines (Keitel) to take her back to the beach. A rogue Englishman who serves as a middleman between the Maori and the settlers and has gone native to the point of having his face tattooed, Baines also doesn't know what to make of Ada. But her will turns his and he accompanies her, silently listening as she rapturously plays for what might be hours.

When Stewart returns, Baines suddenly offers to trade land he owns for the piano. And for lesson. Ada is understandably furious but the land-hungry Stewart insists, losing his temper and screaming, "You will teach him and I will see to it." So, much against her wishes, Ada goes to Baines' cabin and the music and the madness begins.

For what Campion is really dealing with in "The Piano" (rated R for moments of extremely graphic sexuality) is the infectious nature of passion. Ada's obsessive desire for her instrument gradually creeps inside Baines and even Stewart, in turn intoxicating them with her playing and her heedless persona. The back and forth of attraction and self-protection between Ada and Baines and Ada and Stewart is overlaid with the headiness of mania and turns what might have been a conventional tale into something wild and sensually unsettling.

It takes exceptional acting to enable a story like this to take hold, and Campion has gotten it here. Keitel, usually known for violently masculine roles, adds an unexpected level of understated sensitivity to his work without losing any of its power. And Hunter, celebrated for her fast-talking firecracker roles, is mesmerizing as the silent Ada, doing her own playing of Michael Nyman's expressive period score, her face a compendium of flinty looks that could bend steel. Even Neill, cast closest to type as the weak reed, brings unlooked for colors to the part.

A film that captures attention confidently and absolutely, "The Piano" is most remarkable in the way Campion serves traditional story points without compromising her own creative inclinations. Watching this film is like listening to Horowitz after a grade school recital, a reminder of what the cookie-cutter products of Hollywood at its worst make it easy to forget, that there is such a thing as innate, inborn talent for filmmaking and that Jane Campion has as much as the law allows. Maybe even more.

NEW STATESMAN & SOCIETY, 10/29/93, p. 33, Jonathan Romney

Judging by the praise showered on *The Piano* since its unveiling at Cannes this year, you would think its director, Jane Campion, had reinvented cinema. Well, she has certainly rediscovered the range of its potential, until the possibility that a film might be able to pick a complex and serious narrative thrill. It wears its seriousness more elegantly than any recent film, and if it turns out to be a popular success it should knock over some long-entrenched barriers between mainstream and "art" cinema. If nothing else, I'll bet it will be the decade's most written-about film on film-studies courses. It's the sort of work that has critics cursing the very idea of a word limit.

The Piano bears obvious comparison with *The French Lieutenant's Woman*, John Fowles' attempt to anatomise Victorian mores from the standpoint of late 20th-century irony. Campion doesn't have a particular Victorian art form in her optic, in the way that Fowles was able to graft his novel directly onto Victorian fiction. She doesn't have the option of direct pastiche, but she does create a curious double perspective.

While inventing a new way for film to imagine the Victorian era, she also imagines what sort of textures and perspectives a fully blown Victorian cinema might have had. The idea of Victorian cinema persists, ghost-like, through this 1990s film, sometimes in little echoes of Victorian portrait photography or allusions to Lotte Reiniger's shadow-play animations of the 1920s. We're not asked to adopt an ironic modern perspective on a past era, nor to imagine it as a caricatural analogy of present times (as with Peter Greenaway's grotesque 17th century in *The Baby of Macon*). There's none of the distancing that comes with irony or with the Merchant-Ivory school of costume spectacle. Campion doesn't give us theme-park history.

We're invited instead to inhabit this film's world, but we're constantly aware that it's barely habitable—morally, and literally. The moment we see Holly Hunter in her frills and bustle gird her skirts for a trudge through the New Zealand mud, we realise that the film's characters are as much out of place in this universe as we are.

Hunter plays Ada, a mute Scottish woman who, in the last century, is sent to a remote part of New Zealand with her young daughter Flora (Anna Paquin) to be married to Stewart, a landowner (Sam Neill). She leaves behind her what is presumably a scandalous reputation. That, like the rest of Ada's life, is passed over in absolute silence, her own and others'. And she takes with her the beloved piano which, along with Flora, her interpreter, is effectively her voice. That monolithic embodiment of her self and her desire is initially left behind by Stewart on the beach, and then becomes an object of trade between him and Baines (Harvey Keitel), the estate manager. Baines asks for piano lessons from her, which then accelerates into a more openly sexual barter, with Ada playing for higher stakes.

What immediately occurs to you is just how much Campion has taken on. Many directors would either have opted for a story of repressed colonial passions and made the location an unobtrusive backdrop; or have let the story hang, and staked all on the recreation of a Victorian New Zealand outpost: a little bastion of high collars, lockets and Biblical bile, awash in a sea of mossy trunks and quasi-aquatic undergrowth.

Campion goes for both, and the world she sets her drama in has the most tangibly uncomfortable atmosphere. The photographer, Stuart Dryburgh, and the production director, Andrew McAlpine, contrive an extraordinary contrast between the dessicated feel of musty sepia and a malevolently intense effect of seawater and forest chlorophyll.

The film's visual power is all the greater because of the way Campion dares to use silence as a language. Ada never utters a word throughout, but she doesn't simply *not speak*. She's not just a silent screen on which the men around her project their desires (though God knows they do). Rather, she communicates with silence—with sign language and with a ferociously communicative system of looks, Hunter makes a frighteningly eloquent vehicle for the generic "flashing eyes" of Romantic fiction.

Ada's silent voice finds an even more unsettling incarnation in young Flora, who is at once her ward and her keeper. The voice-over we hear at first is in the piping sing-song voice of a Scottish child. This is Ada's inner voice, barely distinguishable from Flora's. The child acts as her mother's double (they dress alike in matching bonnets and skirts) or even as her libido, embodied and given its own anarchic drift.

At one point, in an amateur performance of *Bluebeard*—an ironic rehearsal of Ada's own situation—Flora is got up as an angel. It's a wonderfully wry play on Victorian notions of childhood, virtue and purity. By making an angel of the child, the matrons around her desperately attempt to have her incarnate the virtue her mother is seen to have lost. But once Flora comes to act out the part of her mother's "good conscience", the effect is cruel and disastrous.

The Piano does something extremely rare in the way it allows its historical furnishings to have meaning, rather than just tell you where you are, The temptation would be to caricature the costumes, just as Baines' Maoris make their own parodic use of stovepipe hats and bustles, Instead, Campion uses them literally, but accentuates their use to draw out their symbolic possibilities.

Flora's and Ada's bonnets double each other, surrounding their heads like the frames of cameo portraits or, from the side, appearing like little megaphones, amplifying silence. Ada's skirts are used as a shelter on the beach, and later become improbably eroticised as a frame through which Baines peers at her legs.

Later, Campion rediscovers the long-forgotten erotic possibilities that unite clothing and cinema. She stresses the taboo delight in looking, which was an absolute in the Victorian era and was soon after mobilised as a key component in early cinema. The moment at which Baines discovers a small hole in Ada's stocking is far more shocking, in its breaching of a barrier, than the more explicit sex that follows. When it does follow, and when other characters spy on it, we begin to understand how people must have reacted to What-the-Butler-Saw machines.

The Victorian object of delight and of scandal in the film is not so much sex itself as women's knowledge of sex. Ada, as no one can forget, knows sex, and Flora is the constant reminder of that fact. Her silence on the matter is most shocking of all.

No one can bear the fact that Ada might have a secret knowledge and a secret past. Hers is an erotic silence indeed. Her piano playing is explicitly seen as a sexual force. As Stewart's frosty Aunt Morag comments with a shudder, "Her playing is like a mood that passes into you."

The Piano pretty much passes into you with the same mysterious charm: endlessly eloquent and suggestive, but in its silences as much as in its exceptionally rich discourse of themes and images. There's so much going on that you can't help wondering how much of its melody is evading you. You just have to keep listening.

The film is, of course, an open invitation for critics to come up with the most forced musical analogies imaginable. But it does remind you that if a film is a piano, then most cinema today is content to hammer away at the same three chords when there's a whole keyboard at its disposal. In which case, this is the most eloquent concerto-manifesto that one could have hoped for.

NEW YORK, 11/22/93, p. 72, David Denby

Can a film be great and something of a mess at the same time? This is hardly the sole critical question raised by Jane Campion's award-winning *The Piano*, but it's an inescapable one, since at the literal level almost nothing in this movie works. At the director's will, the weather changes to create mood and atmosphere; the settings for shots, the exteriors of buildings, the placement of locations in relation to one another are all vague at best; some of the plot events arrive abruptly, like rude shoves in the night. Campion has impatiently thrown off classical narrative technique and headed straight for the center of her story, which is about sexual will—the sexual will of a strange, and strangely free, Victorian woman. The imperiously careless style is the expression of the subject's fierce demands: There are images and scenes here that make your jaw drop. So the answer to my question is: yes.

Campion, born in New Zealand and now living in Australia, first made *Sweetie* (1989), a nastily off-center little movie about the drives of an anarchic fat girl. It was, I thought, more an example of perversity than of art, but *Sweetie* had a disruptive erotic charge to it that suggested interesting times ahead. *An Angel at My Table* came next, a beautiful and measured movie based on the autobiographical books of the New Zealand writer Janet Frame. Campion was obviously talented and fearless. But nothing quite prepared me for the concentrated power of *The Piano*. I was caught from the moment I saw the face of Holly Hunter, who stars as Ada, a Scottish woman who is purchased as a wife sometime in the nineteenth century and transported with her little daughter to her unknown husband-to-be in the colony of New Zealand.

Dark eyes, dark hair parted in the middle, colorless skin, immobile mouth and cheeks—Hunter's face seems at first to have no vivid features except the eyes, which dart here and there with a fanatical alertness. It's a face both intense and withdrawn, with the baffling opacity of the faces of proper women in nineteenth-century photographs. Hunter, throwing herself bodily into another period, has completely lost her easygoing American friendliness and openness. Her Ada is mute. Or rather, she has been mute since she was 6. From time to time, she speaks to us, straight from her mind, in the little girl's voice she had when she stopped speaking to the world. Whatever the reason for her silence, passivity certainly isn't it. Making up her mind about something, she jerks into action, and quickly writes on the little pad hanging from her neck or speaks in sign language to her daughter.

At the beginning of *The Piano*, Ada, wearing a dark bonnet and a weighty hoopskirt, is carried to a New Zealand beach on sailors' shoulders and left there in a gray, empty expanse, the heavy waves rolling in all around her. She is alone with her little girl—and a piano. There's a bleakly epic grandeur to the shots, and an element of shock, too; we've never before seen images combining this scale and this degree of eccentricity. Mother, daughter, and instrument are a beached deposit of genteel civilization in the void. After Ada spends a night on the beach, her prospective husband, Stewart (Sam Neill), shows up, nervous, polite, accompanied by some Maori tribesmen and an Englishman gone native named Baines (Harvey Keitel). Against Ada's will, they leave the piano on the sand, and forge through the muddy bush to a community inland.

We get only the vaguest idea of this settlement, because Campion plunges into close-ups, putting the camera on strange faces, throwing us into the dark-shadowed bush. I'm all in favor of directly confronting the strangeness of experience in a new land, but I wanted more of the land itself—the vistas opening up to an astonished first view. Campion hardly gets out of the rainy jungle, and the dark mysteries are only half expressive. There are two Englishwomen in thick clothes who echo each other and giggle, and who seem quite mad; and Maori who make mocking sexual remarks about dry-balled Englishmen and who wear body paint but also top hats and other Western colonial drag—they seem like stoned celebrants at a sixties mad ball. Campion can't figure out what to do with them.

The other Englishman, Baines, rescues Ada's piano from the beach, gets it into his own house, and begins a campaign to lay claim to Ada. He will let her play the piano; she will give him "lessons." She can even take the piano back, one black key at a time, and in return he will do "certain things" as she plays. The erotic game begins: As Ada plays, Baines coaxes her to remove pieces of clothing. They are almost childlike, these two, playing "piano" rather than "doctor," bargaining keys for glimpses and caresses. Ada's husband stays away, and Baines never forces the issue. After a while, we realize that it is Ada, not Baines, who is in control.

Driven mad, Baines undresses, offering his need, his nakedness, and the movie shifts to a whole new level of candor. An illiterate, Baines wears painted decoration on his face like a Maori; at times, he falls into the Maori background, half colonial, half Caliban, the natural man in *extremis*. Harvey Keitel, now over 50, is thickly muscled through the chest and shoulders, with a plentiful rounded gut. Photographed in the small house, Keitel, who is actually rather short, seems huge,

Rodinesque almost, with a nobility in nakedness that is far removed from the inhumanly perfect figures of most actors. That rounded gut makes him not just another well-built actor but a heroic sexual figure. He gives an immensely tender performance as this man who asks for love. Perhaps only a woman director would now photograph a man in this way, and when Holly Hunter, with rounded breasts and rump, joins him in bed, the sensuality becomes overpowering.

Their scenes together are so striking, in part, because this is a feminist version of heterosexuality that also clearly rejects conventional feminist sexual politics. If you believe someone like Catharine MacKinnon, women always receive, so to speak, the short end of the stick, since the power resides in the man. Not so, says Campion. The power resides in equals. A variety of people, including Ada's husband, begin peeking at this couple, and you can't exactly blame them, there being so little else to see in the bush.

What happens thereafter is mostly a dramatic shambles, though Campion delivers images of great power again and again. Ada's husband chases her into the bush, and her dress catches in the brambles as her arms flail at the air. We seem to be heading toward a conventional drama of jealousy, but Campion turns it around. Ada, aroused, turns to her husband, who reacts angrily to her pulling up the bedclothes and exploring his body—he wants control, not sex. I'm guessing at motivation, because there's virtually no script, and a fair number of unaccountable mistakes. Trying to send a message to Baines, Ada pulls one of the keys out of the piano and writes on it. But why would she dismantle her instrument? And why write a note to an illiterate? Holly Hunter plays the piano herself, but she's playing Michael Nyman's New Age rippling chords rather than something obsessive and fateful by, say, Beethoven or Schumann. The trivial music is a major mistake.

Leaving the community with her piano, Ada gets pulled down into the water by the instrument. The imagery associates the piano with destruction and death. But surely the piano, the expression of Ada's will, should be associated with life. Campion is not always in control of her meanings; what she is in control of marks her as a major director of the nineties.

NEW YORK POST, 11/12/93, p. 33, Thelma Adams

"The Piano" astonishes. It's an instant classic. Jane Campion ("Sweetie") has directed her most ambitious film yet.

This gothic love triangle has the coiled eroticism of Jane Eyre—and some of the most honest sex scenes since "Last Tango in Paris."

At the 1993 Cannes Film Festival, "The Piano" shared the Palme D'Or with "Farewell My Concubine." Holly Hunter earned best actress honors with a performance that will turn Oscar's head.

Campion, who wrote the script, invented fictional ancestors and imagined their lives in her native New Zealand in the 18th century.

Stewart (Sam Neill) is the original colonialist; his body's in the remote bush, but his heart and mind are bound to Britain.

Hunter plays Ada, the bride Stewart imports from Scotland, sight unseen. Mute but not silent, Ada arrives on the harsh New Zealand coast with her two loves: her daughter (Anna Paquin) and her piano.

Baines (Harvey Keitel) completes the triangle. A white man with Maori facial tattoos, Baines has become unfixed between the two worlds that Stewart is so desperate to keep separate.

Stewart switches on the plot's electric current when he refuses to cart Ada's piano through the bush and into their home. This act, more insensitive than cruel, paves the way for Baines to gain possession of the instrument and Ada's heart.

Stuart Dryburgh's cinematography welds breathtaking imagery to raw emotion. Forced to abandon her piano, Ada pauses on a cliff overlooking the coast. Down below, the tide laps at the piano, the driftwood of civilization on a prehistoric shore. In the distance, silver breakers pound the beach. The moment on the cliff feels like a kick in the chest.

A musician separated from her music is mute, cut off from herself, her soul. Ada's muteness becomes a liberating force for Hunter rather than a constraint.

Always a plain and precise actress, Hunter has the role of her career. Whether corseted in Victorian garb or stark naked, it's her most passionate and honest performance yet.

In Hunter, Keitel meets his match and rises to the occasion. With his satyr's torso and penchant for full frontal nudity, Keitel's brute sensuality is familiar territory. What impresses is the vulnerability he displays as a man engulfed by romantic love.

The lovesick Baines banishes Ada from his shack. He fears she's only using him to recover her piano. "I already miss you," he tells Ada, with more power than any "I love you." Keitel plugs into the emotional current and never pulls out.

Stewart's the odd man out. Of the three characters, he's the least realized. Gruff and repressed, the part as written doesn't allow Neill to establish Stewart's motivations and maintain the integrity of his side of the triangle.

Campion's a gutsy filmmaker. Her risk-taking pays off in a film that's artistically honest and emotionally powerful.

NEWSDAY, 11/12/93, Part II/p. 68, Jack Mathews

"The voice you hear is not my speaking voice, but my mind's voice," says the female narrator, over the opening image of writer-director Jane Campion's stunningly original "The Piano." "I have not spoken since I was six years old. No one, knows why, not even me."

As the character appears on the screen, her hair matted tight against her head, her face void of color or emotion, nearly featureless, she seems to have stepped out of a frontier photograph, a joyless woman hardened and perhaps muted by some unspeakable pain.

But as she approaches a piano, runs her hand lightly over its wood surface, and begins to play—beautifully, with passion and power—we know she is not a woman without a voice, only words, and that she is far from resigned to silence.

So begins this amazing journey into the soul of Ada (Holly Hunter), a Scottish widow setting off with her 9-year-old daughter, *and* her piano, to begin a new life in an arranged marriage in the rugged coastal country of turn-of-the-century New Zealand.

Campion uses this setting not for an outback adventure story, but to tell a story of sexual awakening. In that inhospitable, closed-in and strange environment, with its incessant rains, ankle-deep mud, overgrown bush, and tattooed Maoris, Ada finds sexual desire. Not with her husband (Sam Neill), a virginal landowner whose sexuality is more deeply repressed than hers, but with an illiterate neighbor (Harvey Keitel) who wears Maori markings on his face.

This affair begins as rank sexual bargaining. Having watched Ada grow rapturous while playing her piano, Keitel's George Baines strikes a pair of deals. He trades her husband 80 acres of land for her piano, then gives her the opportunity to earn it back, a key at a time, by granting him certain favors. A kiss on the neck, a look at her bare arms, a glimpse up her hoop skirt.

As this arrangement escalates to the higher-priced shelves, George and Ada find themselves negotiating over sexual desires as powerful as the electrical storms raking the coast.

Campion works through this erotic territory with a feather-light touch, literally. Every gesture here is tactile—a finger touching flesh revealed through a dime-size hole in Ada's stocking, a hand held upside down, lightly running over a shoulder, a chest, a stomach.

That Keitel, the quintessential Martin Scorsese movie tough guy, would be showing the way down this sensitive, erotic path is just one of Campion's bold choices. There is no moment here to rival the surprise in last year's "The Crying Game," but scene for scene, "The Piano" is one of the most unpredictable movies in years.

For me, the film takes a dead wrong turn at the end, one that nearly undoes everything before, but it is a flawless journey getting there.

Hunter's performance is a revelation. To say it is the best non-speaking performance since "The Miracle Worker" doesn't go back far enough. Since the Silent Era, maybe. She does her own piano playing, which is impressive enough. She also does more with quiet expression changes—a faint smile at the corner of her eyes when playing her piano, a look of terror when her husband erupts in anger—than most actors do with two pages of dialogue.

Ada is a character who begins, in the most basic ways, to liberate herself. This is not a feminist piece in period drag. She's simply a woman responding to feelings she's never felt before, and dealing with desires she's never known. And she likes them. It is George who comes to need assurances of love. In her age of innocence, Ada will settle for some good sex.

Campion, a native New Zealander herself, dealt with unconventional women in her first two films, "Sweetie" and "An Angel at My Table," but there was nothing in either of those to suggest the poetic power she delivers with "The Piano."

Stuart Dryburgh's cinematography is as spectacular as it is foreboding, a Rorschach of visual impressions that match the emotional swings of Ada's reinvented life.

And not just hers. The "piano lessons" in Baines' shack complicate the seemingly simple lives of everyone here—Baines, her daughter Flora (Anna Paquin, my choice for the year's most annoying child performance), and Stewart (Neill), a man totally unprepared to deal with either sex or sexual jealousy.

The sex scenes, by the way, are fairly graphic, with his and hers frontal nudity. Equality, at last!

NEWSWEEK, 5/31/93, p. 52, David Anson

Four years ago Jane Campion, an unknown New Zealand-born filmmaker, arrived at the Cannes Film Festival flush with excitement at having her first feature film, "Sweetie," chosen for inclusion in the competition. She left in tears. Blind to its strange brilliance, the audience turned its wrath upon her film; at the Grand Théâtre Lumière, the loudest sound was the *thwack* of abandoned seats as the tuxedoed crowd fled in midmovie.

This year in Cannes, Campion has been the focus of an adulation so intense it has almost alarmed her. Even before the festival began, the hype about "The Piano" had reached fever pitch. A lock for the Palme d'Or, handicappers whispered. At the official black-tie screening, hundreds of angry ticketholders were turned away at the door and shuttled off to another screening room where an impromptu showing was hastily assembled to avoid fistfights. If the movie's U.S. distributor, Miramax, was worried that the hype would create a backlash, the delirious standing ovation at the Lumière washed away those fears. Whether she ended up with the big prize or not (and there was stiff competition from Chen Kaige's epic Chinese film: "Farewell My Concubine" and Englishman Mike Leigh's grimly funny "Naked"), for a long moment last week Campion, almost eight months pregnant and dog-tired from days of interviews, was the hottest new name on the scene.

"The Piano" is a riveting excursion into 19th-century sexuality, a movie that takes the conventions of the Gothic romance and refracts them through a dark contemporary lens. In the 1850s, a Scottish widow named Ada (Holly Hunter) sails to New Zealand with her young daughter (Anna Paquin) for an arranged marriage to a colonial landowner (Sam Neill). Ada, who is mute, brings with her her cherished piano, her most passionate means of expression. When her new husband refuses to transport the piano through the bush, it's bought by an illiterate English settler named Baines (Harvey Keitel) who wears Maori tattoos on his face, native style. He strikes a bargain with Ada: she can win her piano back, key by key, in return for favors that become increasingly sexual. At first he just wants to look at her shoulders while she plays for him, but their private recitals in his cabin, far from her unsuspecting husband, begin to evolve into a grand passion. And when the husband discovers that Ada is sharing with Baines the erotic pleasures she denies him, he extracts a startling and cruel retribution, which is not the end of the story but sends it spinning off in unexpected directions.

In "The Piano," Campion reveals a romanticism that was not evident in the spikily oddball "Sweetie" or in her wonderful three-hour film about the New Zealand writer Janet Frame, "An Angel at My Table." But she has not lost her fierceness or her extraordinary eye: the beauty of her images of briny seas and dank tropical forests owes nothing to postcard makers. And in Holly Hunter's willful Ada (a performance so expressive you almost forget she isn't speaking), she creates a memorably eccentric heroine who finds her place in the world by pushing instinctively against the restraints of 19th-century civilization. Erotic, mysterious and exquisitely etched, "The Piano" transmutes the bodice-ripping tropes of the "woman's film" into fierce cinematic poetry.

The 39-year-old director/writer wasn't planning to stay in Cannes to see if she won the prize. Her baby is due on July 1, and she needed to get back home to Sydney, Australia, while she was still allowed to fly. She was happy that people responded so strongly to her film, but the hosannas in Cannes weren't turning her head. "This should be so ego-amplifying, but it doesn't work that way," she said. She's learned her lesson since the hard Cannes knocks of 1989. "After 'Sweetie' it took me a while to regain my equilibrium. I was too open, too innocent about it all then. I worry for the first-time filmmakers here. I want to protect them." Whether "The Piano" catapults her out of the art-house circuit and into the commercial mainstream remains to be seen (it will open in the United States in either August or November). But her future projects are getting bigger. She's just been in Italy preparing her version of Henry James's "Portrait of a Lady" to star Nicole Kidman. Though trained at art school, she's an imagemaker with a rare passion for the written word. She considers "The Piano" her homage to Emily Dickinson and the Brontes. And she's developing a project about Christopher Isherwood and his guru, wedding her interests in the spiritual and the earthly. Campion, who looks like Meryl Streep's heartier sister, is reported to have a will of steel under her polite manner. It has enabled her so far to pursue her singular vision without compromise. Happily, the world is now discovering what a small but ardent cult has known all along—that Jane Campion is one of the most splendid filmmakers around.

SIGHT AND SOUND, 11/93, p. 50, Lissie Francke

The mid-19th century. Ada, a mute Scottish woman, and her young daughter Flora are sent to New Zealand where it has been arranged by her father for her to marry Stewart, a landowner. After a rough passage, Ada and Flora are met on the beach. Stewart arranges for their belongings to be carried home, but refuses to transport Ada's piano. Immediately this alienates Ada from him. Baines, Stewart's illiterate estate manager, offers some of his land in exchange for the piano, a deal to which Stewart agrees. Baines asks Ada for piano lessons, and Stewart forces her to comply with his request.

It transpires that Baines does not want to learn to play, but just to listen to Ada. Ada starts to visit him regularly. Baines suggests that they strike a deal so that she can have the piano back. She may have a black key for every visit, as long as he is allowed to caress her. Flora, who used to accompany Ada on her visits to Baines, is told to remain outside. With each session, Ada and Baines become more intimate. Meanwhile, relations remain strained between Ada and Stewart, but the couple visit a village performance of the Bluebeard story, in which Flora is performing. Baines turns up but leaves at the sight of Ada and Stewart holding hands. At the next lesson, Baines asks Ada to undress and lie with him. Flora spies the couple together, and later mentions to Stewart that Baines never plays the piano at these lessons. Baines decides to return the piano to Ada and terminate the agreement. Later, Ada visits him and he declares his love for her; finally they sleep together.

Alerted by Flora, Stewart follows Ada and spies upon the two. Baines tells Ada that if she loves him, she must come to visit him the following day. Later at home Stewart confronts Ada and forbids her to visit Baines; he seals up the windows and she is made a prisoner in her home. Time passes, and Ada attempts to be affectionate to Stewart. Stewart's Aunt Morag comes to tell the family that she has heard that Baines is leaving the island. Finally, the shutters are brought down and Ada is let free. Ada promises Stewart that she will not visit Baines. Later, however, she inscribes one of the piano keys with a message of love for Baines, and sends Flora to give it to him. Flora takes the key to Stewart instead. In a terrible rage, Stewart descends upon Ada and chops one of her fingers off and sends Flora to give it to Baines. Stewart then goes to confront Baines himself. Flora stays with Baines. Later Ada, Baines and Flora leave together by boat, and Ada instructs that her piano be thrown overboard. As it descends into the sea, she slips her foot into one of the binding ropes and is pulled down after it. But as the piano sinks, she starts to struggle free from the noose and surfaces. Later in her new life with Baines she starts to learn to speak, while Baines has made her a silver finger so that she can play the piano again. At night, she dreams of herself floating above the piano at the bottom of the ocean.

For a while I could not think, let alone write, about *The Piano* without shaking. Precipitating a flood of feelings, *The Piano* demands as much a physical and emotional response as an intellectual one. As with the Maoris in the film who, believing the Bluebeard shadow play to be real, attempt to stop the old duke add another wife to his collection, I wanted to rush at the screen and shout and scream. Not since the early days of cinema, when audiences trampled over each other towards the exit to avoid the train emerging from the screen, could I imagine the medium of film to be so powerful. Like Ada's piano music, which is described as "a mood that passes through you ... a sound that creeps into you", this is cinema that fills every sense. The opening shot of delicate pink skin smoothed over the screen, as fingers hide eyes, suggests the membrane that the audience must burst through to make the painful and traumatic trek into the film's dark, gnarled woods, finally to be released in the watery death/birth of an ending. Moving pictures indeed.

A film about silence and expression beyond language, *The Piano* resonates with the silences embedded deep in the texts of such 19th-century women writers as Emily Bronte or Emily Dickinson, women who hid scraps of their work under blotters, who hid themselves behind pseudonyms. They, like the strident composer Ada, were told that their creations were most irregular. In *The Piano*, Jane Campion feels her way around those echoing caves upon which they built their haunted houses of fiction. It is a virtuoso interpretation of that literary sensibility in a cinematic form, truer than any doggedly faithful adaptation of, say, *Wuthering Heights*. Indeed, *The Piano* puts us in the grip of the repressions of the 19th century—an era which saw polite society sheathing the ankles of piano legs with special socks in case they gave young men ideas. Such is the erotic object at the heart of the film.

Campion is playful with the period's more bizarre neuroses. The film flashes with moments of indignant humour, such as when Flora is ordered to whitewash some trees after she and her young friends are caught rubbing up against them in a playful—and unwitting—imitation of the sexual act. But Campion is careful not to let the comedy take hold. Under less thoughtful direction Stewart could have been the buffoonish patriarch, hauling his white man's burden behind him. He treats the Maoris like children, paying them in buttons and staking out his territory over their sacred burial grounds. After the shocking punishment he metes out to Ada, he informs her, "I only clipped your wings." He is, as one Maori dubs him, an emotionally shrivelled "old dry balls". Yet this awful paterfamilias is invested with some sympathy. He is a confused man, who attempts to guy his world down in the chaos of change, who wants his music—and his sex—played to a strict time, so fearful is he of the other rhythms that might move him. If only he could listen, like Ada's previous lover and the father of Flora, upon whom she could "lay thoughts on his mind like a sheet". It is the communication of the gentle caress, the smoothing of nimble fingers over sheets and scales.

Conventional language imprisons Ada like the crinoline, which ambiguously also marks out her private, silent space (the skirt provides an intimate tent for Ada and Flora to shelter in the beach). Crucially, it is the written word that finally betrays her as she sends her love note to Baines, who cannot read but who knows the languages of those around him. Her arrangement with Baines has previously been based on a sensuous play of touch, smell and sound.

Bodies become instruments of expression, while the piano smelling of scent and salt becomes corporeal. Baines' massaging of Ada's leg through a hole in her black worsted stocking is given the same erotic charge as his fingering of the scales. After such libidinous exchange, the marking down of her feelings for him with words only brings destruction, which is hastened by Flora, Ada's little echoing mouthpiece (who is also the most compulsive and intriguing of fabulists).

What to make, then, of Ada's sudden plunge after her lifeless piano, which can no longer sing, into the watery grave? Ada's bid to enter into the order of language brings only death. Her will moves her finally to wave, not drown, to take life.

But there is the disquieting shadow of death cast on to the coda of the film. Brighter than in any of the previous scenes, she is seen in mourning grey, her head covered in a black-edged veil, tapping out notes with the silver artificial finger, which now marks her as the town freak. She is learning to speak but her voice rings the knell—"death, death, death". At night she dreams of her husk, anchored to the piano, skirts billowing out like a balloon, floating in the silence of the deep, deep sea. Impossible to shake off, it is the final image in a film that weighs heavy on the heart and mind, that drags us down into our own shuddering silence.

TIME, 11/22/93, p. 79, Richard Corliss

This movie can't be *that* good—it's won too many prizes. *The Piano* has been saddled with a Cannes Palme d'Or and 11 Australian Film Institute awards. For New Zealand writer-director Jane Campion, the film marks a triumph of dazzling movie art and canny show-biz heart. It's that good.

The Piano is Campion's coming of age—a delivery on the promise of her first two features. *Sweetie* (1989), about the devastating effect a disturbed young woman has on her family, was bitter medicine; the movie double-dared its audience to find sympathy in its dour or manic characters. In *An Angel at My Table* (1990), a three-part mini-series based on the biographies of Australian novelist Janet Frame, Campion located her elliptical, microcosmic style. But this lovely film lost its way before its climax, and before it could find a wider audience.

The Piano remedies that. It is set in New Zealand, funded by Francis Bouygues' Ciby 2000 (pronounced, in French, C.B. De Mille), scored by English composer Michael Nyman, and stars some unlikely actors: Georgia's Holly Hunter and Brooklyn's Harvey Keitel join New Zealand's Sam Neill. Campion has also honed her style beyond mannerism; now the desaturated colors and oblique angles bend to serve the story. And a plangent story it is, with a typical Campion heroine: the outsider woman, the renegade from convention, as viewed from a treetop, where only God dares judge her.

In the 1850s, Ada (Hunter), a mute Scottish woman, comes to the voluptuously desolate New Zealand bush in an arranged marriage with Stewart (Neill), a landowner. Stewart cannot seduce a woman who can barely tolerate him and whose eyes burn with a fierce, almost feral obstinacy. What grievance has she against mankind, against men? And how can this crushing burden be eased?

By trying to crush her, Stewart decides. Ada has only two loves in this bleak world: her nine-year-old daughter Flora (Anna Paquin) and her piano. After Stewart cavalierly sells the instrument to his neighbor Baines (Keitel), Ada strikes a bargain with Baines. Under the guise of giving him lessons, she will buy the piano back from him, one black key at a time, by allowing certain sexual favors. One key is hers if she raises her skirt; two keys to let him touch her bare arm; five; 10 ... Ada can win what she needs by meting out what she forbids her husband.

Watching Ada rapt at her piano, listening to the music with which she speaks, he can detect a passion in this woman that he too wants to play. He is not a fastidious wooer. He will smell her jacket, or investigate her stockings until he finds a tiny hole that reveals skin he can touch. Soon his mind is seized with Ada. After she leaves, Baines is haunted by the echo and odor of a tiny, sinewy woman who, because she seems to be pure will unadorned by coquetry, has sparked awe in him.

And what does she feel? The viewer must translate the glances and cramped gestures of Ada's own aboriginal language. Sometimes her sideways stare says, "Men! Jeez!" and suggests the wry comedy *The Piano* could have been if it had not aimed higher. But mostly we see two eyeholes burning through the mask of civility to reveal raging helplessness—until Ada finds hope in passion. Then she must face the prospects of Flora's betrayal, Stewart's rage, the loss of the piano, the sacrifice of limb and life.

Campion has spun a fable as potently romantic as a Brontë tale. But *The Piano* is also deeply cinematic. It burrows into two essential obsessions of the oldest films: emotion conveyed without words, and the image of a man watching a woman. What is not traditional is that here the women are in charge, as heroine, star and director. The result is that what might have been art-house voyeurism becomes a wise sermon on the various motives for sex. Ada has sex with Stewart out of duty or pity. (The movie sees Stewart's pathos as well: as he watches lovers through a window, a dog licks his hand in a cruel parody of the affection he craves.) The sexual dance with Baines has more roiling complications. The first step is barter, the second is power, then rebellion, adventure, independence, joyful bondage, love, love in the face of death.

This is a closet drama, but the closet has a window with a view of the sea. In an early scene Ada comes to the beach and finds her piano in a crate. Opening it, she plays ecstatically; her daughter dances gaily, garlanded in seaweed; and Baines gets a first inkling of the lifeline that art is for Ada. The camera ascends to Campion's favorite bird's-eye view to reveal a huge sea horse magically sculpted from sand and shells. Life, this beautiful image suggests, is a pattern we cannot see, except through the artist's Olympian eye.

It is from this perspective that *The Piano*, with startling craft and anguish, asks the question, How much does love hurt? The answer is, Too much. And what is love worth? Everything.

VILLAGE VOICE, 11/16/93, p. 72, Georgia Brown

The Piano opens with a perfect Jane Campion point-of-view shot: the world as seen in fuzzy-edged slashes between fingers covering the eyes. Fingers are prominent in *The Piano*, as are eyes. Eyes peer through holes (in walls, floors, curtains, a camera lens), so the peeper can spy without being spied. "My heart in hiding," as Gerard Manley Hopkins said, "stirred for a bird." The need to hide is the need to preserve, to keep something precious and fragile from taint, dilution, or desecration. Another elliptical p.o.v. shot in the first couple of minutes is from the perspective of the drowned.

A woman with searing eyes and subtle fingers, Ada (an unrecognizable Holly Hunter) protects her secrets by refusing to speak: "I have not spoken since I was six years old; I don't know why." "The strange thing is," she adds in her childlike brogue, "I don't think myself silent, because of my piano." Because the piano is literally her voice, it's a form of mutilation when her brand-new mail-order husband, Stewart (Sam Neill), refuses to transport the instrument to his house in the bush. Through Ada again (black ribbons from her bonnet whip across the view), we see the piano stranded on the deserted beach.

In 1852, in their unbecoming bonnets, Ada and her uncompromising 10-year-old daughter, Flora (the astonishing Anna Paquin), have been transported from Scotland and cast on the New Zealand shore—disgorged, as it were, from the sea bottom—with all their belongings. Waiting for strangers to claim them, they fashion a small tent (another cunning hiding place) from Ada's hooped crinoline. Lighted from within, it looks like a festive paper lantern.

If her virginal husband is too stunted, too frightened, to attend to her voiceless voice, his overseer, George Baines (Harvey Keitel), is beginning to listen. Unlike Stewart, Baines—his nose tattooed with pinwheels—is at ease with the impressive, beguiling Maoris. Baines barters with Stewart for the piano and, bringing it back to his place, barters with Ada for lessons. But he only wants to "listen," he says. Then to touch: his gnarled finger finding the hole in her black woolen stocking. (One black key for each "lesson," as he calls them.) Baines is like the wise tamer in horse movies: patient, attuned to the animal, instinctively sensing when a direct move might be made. Then, wonder of wonders, he recognizes when a bargain exploits: "The arrangement is making you a whore and me miserable."

What's shocking about *The Piano* is how it resists the standard, ready-made narrative, and follows its own logic. Each time violence seems the "natural" alternative, it's averted. Until one time it isn't.

In Campion's *Sweetie*, the tense, glowering Kay was terrified of trees: It was all that aggressive, invisible root activity. Roots, trunks, and branches reminded her of family ties—invasive, tangling, strangling—as well as the tree of blood vessels in the body. In *The Piano*, nature is as animate, as sentient, as humans are. Trees are sexual creatures (imitating Maori children, Flora makes love to the trunks). Mud is an ogre sucking from underneath. Hills are giants' breasts on which a tiny daughter (Flora is like Pearl in *The Scarlet Letter*) skips to the betrayal of her mother.

In this visceral and animated universe, the body is one more wild thing. Campion's love scenes involve real flesh, not that wrinkle-free porcelain produced by shooting through filters. Even so, Campion shows herself at least tentatively at home in the secondary (manmade) world by introducing a series of exquisite teacups.

You've already heard too much about *The Piano* for your own good. Platitude laps around its ankles and gush splashes the hem. Then there's the awkward discrepancy between those the movie ravages and spits out and those who exit grumbling. No one could have predicted that Campion would have elected to work the 19th-century Gothic vein. (Her main inspiration was *Wuthering Heights*.) She's taken a big risk in being so overt and now, I suppose, she's in danger of deification.

Also reviewed in:
CHICAGO TRIBUNE, 11/19/93, Friday/p. A, Michael Wilmington
NATION, 12/6/93, p. 704, Stuart Klawans
NEW REPUBLIC, 12/13/93, p. 30, Stanley Kauffmann
NEW YORK TIMES, 11/12/93, p. C12, Vincent Canby
NEW YORKER, 11/29/93, p. 148, Anthony Lane
VARIETY, 5/10/93, p. 237, David Stratton
WASHINGTON POST, 11/19/93, p. D1, Hal Hinson
WASHINGTON POST, 11/19/93, Weekend/p. 50, Desson Howe

PICKLE, THE

A Columbia Pictures release. *Executive Producer:* Patrick McCormick. *Producer:* Paul Mazursky and Stuart Pappé. *Director:* Paul Mazursky. *Screenplay:* Paul Mazursky. *Director of Photography:* Fred Murphy. *Editor:* Stuart Pappé. *Music:* Michel Legrand. *Music Editor:* Ted Whitfield. *Sound:* Jim Webb and (music) Danny Wallin. *Sound Editor:* John M. Stacy and David A. Whittaker. *Casting:* Carrie Frazier and Shani Ginsberg. *Production Designer:* James Bissell. *Art Director:* Christopher Burian-Mohr. *Set Decorator:* Dorree Cooper. *Special Effects:* Michael L. Wood. *Costumes:* Albert Wolsky. *Make-up:* Valli O'Reilly and Gigi Williams. *Make-up (Danny Aiello):* Debbie Zoller. *Stunt Coordinator:* Danny Aiello, III. *Running time:* 103 minutes. *MPAA Rating:* R.

CAST: Danny Aiello (Harry Stone);   Dyann Cannon (Ellen Stone);   Clotilde Courau (Francoise);   Shelley Winters (Yetta);   Barry Miller (Ronnie Liebowitz);   Jerry Stiller (Phil Hirsch);   Chris Penn (Gregory Stone);   Little Richard (President);   Jodi Long (Yakimoto Yakimura);   Rebecca Miller (Carrie);   Stephen Tobolowsky (Mike Krakower);   Caroline Aaron (Nancy Osborne);   Rita Karin (Grandmother);   Linda Carlson (Bernadette);   Kimiko Cazanov (Patti Wong);   Ally Sheedy (Molly-Girl);   J.D. Daniels (Young Harry);   Spalding Gray (Doctor);   Elya Baskin (Russian Cab Driver);   Michael Greene (Mission Control Farmer); Robert Cicchini (Electronics Store Clerk);   John Rothman (Chauffer);   Castulo Guerra (Jose Martinez);   Caris Corfman (Young Yetta);   Arthur Taxier (Father);   Sol Frieder (Grandfather); Paul Mazursky (Butch Levine);   Michael Shulman (Young Butch);   Brandon Danziger (Pinnie); Louis Falk (Irwin);   Ben Diskin (Little Boy, 1945);   Geoffrey Blake (Clem);   Brent Hinkley, Eric Edwards, Richmond Arquette, and Stephen Polk (Farm Boys);   Paul Bates (Kareem); Marcus Naylor (Concierge);   Joe Pecoraro (Doorman);   Betsy Mazursky (Pharmacy Clerk); Michael Harris (David);   Anna Maria Clark (Molly);   Caroline Clark (Molly);   Arthur French (Car Man);   Erik King (Man with Beer);   Davenia McFadden (Woman in Window);   Lawrence Gilliard, Jr. (Boy Who Stopped);   Sharrieff Pugh (Boy Who Also Stopped);   Billy Jaye (FX Man);   Sergio Premoli (Alberto);   Mark Deakins (Clapper Boy);   Brooke Smith (1st A.D.); Chuck Flores (Drummer);   Bob Harrison (Bassist);   Michael Asher (Piano Player);   Andre Philippe (Mr. Aronowitz);   Fyvush Finkel (Mr. Shacknoff);   Nathanial Katzman (Uncle Morris); Waldemar Kalinowski (Crying Man);   Twink Caplan (Crying Woman);   Tony Conferti (Crying Man in Candy Store);   Stephen Cody (Tractor Man);   Jill Mazursky (Tractor Woman);   Zeljko Negovetic (Wagon Driver);   Chris Vecchione (Farm Girl);   Scott Wulff (Adam);   Jacklyn Jill Evans (Eve);   Hap Lawrence (Gothic Man);   Patricia Place (Gothic Woman);   Michael Ashe (Elegant Man);   Tiffany Salerno (Elegant Woman);   Richard Coate (Plaza Hotel Waiter);   Josif Shikhil (Russian Man, Coney Island).

LOS ANGELES TIMES, 5/1/93, Calendar/p. 4, Michael Wilmington

The silliest major studio movies are sometimes great financial successes, and Paul Mazursky's new movie, "The Pickle," is about the raw pain of making these big dopey crowd-catchers. Mazursky's picture is not really a success—it's too scattered to completely win its audience—but there are funny, sexy things in it.

In "The Pickle," we're treated to the spectacle of silly movie making as corporate policy, travesty-manufacturing on a grand scale. The movie's antihero, Harry Stone (played by Danny Aiello), is a maverick expatriate American filmmaker who takes on a project he loathes in order to satisfy his huge tax and alimony bill, and to break his string of three box-office flops. Once he does, he's hooked.

Like a man drowning in kitsch, Harry turns to booze, cigars and sex—with his 20ish mistress (Clotilde Courau) and ex-wife (Dyan Cannon)—to cauterize his self-hatred. Everywhere he goes, on the dreaded day of the movie's New York debut, people, keep greeting him with the cringe-making litany, "Good luck on 'The Pickle!'" It's suggested that the whole process of making grotesquely infantile movies—in this case a musical science-fiction epic about farm kids from

Kansas blasting into space on a gigantic pickle-shaped spaceship—can rot its director's soul, drive him to near-suicide.

"The Pickle" is a strange movie, split in about four different ways. Part of it, the part we could use more of, is Hollywood satire. Part of it is another bright bicoastal Mazursky sex comedy. Part of it jarringly displays a kind of male menopausal anguish. And part of it is tender reminiscence: Harry's return to his old haunts, to his mother Yetta (Shelley Winters) and his buddies (including Mazursky as a projectionist from the old bunch), and to black-and-white memories of his Brooklyn boyhood, in a neighborhood that has become a crime-ridden ghetto.

The satire is what the audience probably connects to easiest, and what, after "The Player," they most *want* to see: a bright take on Hollywood fluffery. The movie-within-a-movie "Pickle" itself shot in mock-Spielberg style with a cast that includes Ally Sheedy, Griffin Dunne and Little Richard's sumptuously elaborate spoofing. And, when Barry Miller comes on as the skinny, fey studio chief Ronnie Liebowitz, surrounded in his Office by huge phallic cacti and waving his hands ecstatically as he describes "The Pickle's" high concept ("Rob Lowe! And Molly Ringwald! Soaring into space on a giant pickle!"), he's pulling off a great goofy comic turn, a paroxysm of corporate giddiness.

Miller energizes the movie, just as Aiello's Harry Stone swerves it toward melancholy. Aiello projects such primal innocence and likability that he can make us forget, briefly, what a self-absorbed schmuck Harry is, how badly he treats everyone—especially his lovers and ex-lovers. Mazursky underlines this, though Harry is the character he may identify with, that he once considered playing. At one point, he has Harry stare out of his limousine at a homeless beggar, a man with real problems, it still can't snap the *auteur* from his funk.

Mazursky has said that Harry's model may be an American movie maverick in Paris like Samuel Fuller. But there's another possible inspiration, ex-expatriate Robert Altman—who, in "The Player" had no trouble skewering all the Hollywood pretensions that Mazursky pricks a little and dances away from. That's the main problem with "The Pickle" (MPAA-rated R, for language and sensuality). It starts to get acid and then turns sweet, and its funny-nasty side is overwhelmed. The sweetness can't compensate. By the end, the audience may really *want* Harry to suffer, because he's earned it, and that may be the reason the climax—a Spielberg-Fellini *deus ex machina*—is so unsatisfactory.

As in all Mazursky movies, this one has its delights, its cargo of laughs, jazzy goofball lyricism, bi-coastal *Angst*. Mazursky loves New York like few other directors. He puts real exultancy in the Manhattan street scenes and he gets a sense of cold sweat in expense-account splendor in the hurly-burly of Harry's Plaza suite contretemps. Even so, there's almost, at times, a hint of directorial restlessness: a sense that Mazursky, like Harry, might rather be somewhere else. The movie tries to form a rapprochement with the prison of kitsch movie-making, when, like "The Player," it might have been better off sawing away at those million-dollar bars.

NEWSDAY, 5/3/93, Part II/p. 47, Jack Mathews

The movie within Paul Mazursky's "The Pickle" is a sci-picture about an interplanetary cucumber that delivers its crew of young Kansas farmers and its larder of overgrown vegetables to a planet called Cleveland, whose leader looks and sings like (and is played by) Little Richard. The movie is a huge hit at its New York preview, receiving an astonishing 94 percent approval rating from the audience.

"The Pickle" itself, about a temperamental middle-age filmmaker (Danny Aiello) forced by his slumping career and finances to take the space picture assignment, apparently didn't do quite as well with its own preview audience.

Columbia Pictures decided to open "The Pickle" Friday without advance critics screenings, an indignity that directors the stature of both Aiello's Harry Stone and Mazursky shouldn't have to endure even when they fail.

The kicker is that "The Pickle" is not as bad or as frivolous as its trailer and its pan by the studio make it seem. In fact, it is a sincere attempt at satirizing a business where smart people are often compelled to play dumb, something Mazursky has done a time or two himself.

If "Alex in Wonderland" was Mazursky's "8½," "The Pickle" is his "All That Jazz." Like Bob Fosse's alter-ego, Mazursky's Harry is a genius suffering fools badly while pushing himself toward death with guilt, bad habits and impossible goals. There are caring ex-wives, a devoted young lover, fawning fans, egregious moneymen, a cardiovascular scare, and a childhood buddy (played by Mazursky) who, like the Angel of Death in "All That Jazz," triggers memories of an innocence lost.

There is even an hallucinatory dream at the end of "The Pickle," where everyone shows up to pay homage to Harry's genius.

Aiello, who makes the most irascible characters charming, has had few better roles than this, and has a great time with it. And the supporting cast—among them Dyan Cannon as Wife No. 1, Barry Miller as the smarmy studio boss and Clotilde Courau as Harry's undiscouraged 22-year-old French girlfriend—is terrific.

Mazursky's biggest mistake was in making the interior film, which co-stars Griffin Dunne, Ally Sheedy and Isabella Rosselini, as silly as it is. It might have been fun if he'd spoofed himself by having Harry direct a monster movie called "Scenes from a Mole." As it is, we spend too much time watching a mutant gherkin sail through space and seeing people splattered with pickle juice.

Also reviewed in:
NEW YORK TIMES, 5/1/93, p. 11, Janet Maslin
VARIETY, 5/3/93, p. 40, Todd McCarthy

POETIC JUSTICE

A Columbia Pictures release. *Producer:* Steve Nicolaides and John Singleton. *Director:* John Singleton. *Screenplay:* John Singleton. *Poetry:* Maya Angelou. *Director of Photography:* Peter Lyons Collister. *Editor:* Bruce Cannon. *Music:* Stanley Clarke. *Music Editor:* Lisé Richardson. *Sound:* Robert D. Eber. *Sound Editor:* Greg Hedgepath and Tom McCarthy. *Casting:* Robi Reed. *Production Designer:* Keith Brian Burns. *Art Director:* Kirk M. Petruccelli. *Set Designer:* Darrell L. Wight. *Set Decorator:* Dan May. *Special Effects:* Eric Rylander. *Costumes:* Darryle Johnson. *Make-up:* Alvechia Ewing and Susan A. Cabral. *Stunt Coordinator:* Bob Minor. *Running time:* 110 minutes. *MPAA Rating:* R.

CAST: Khandi Alexander (Simone); Maya Angelou (Aunt June); Ché J. Avery (Thug #2); Lloyd Avery II (Thug #1); Kimberly Brooks (Kim); Rico Bueno (Ticket Taker); Maia Campbell (Shante); Jeff Cantrel (Policeman #4); Michael Colyar (Panhandler); Kina V. Cosper (Female Cousin); John Cothran, Jr. (Uncle Earl); Dina D. (Dina); Joe Dalu (Policeman #7); James Deeth (Helicopter Pilot); Norma Donaldson (Aunt May); Kelly Joe Dugan (Truck Driver); Judd Dunning (Policeman #1); Rene Elizondo (E.J.); Benjamin I. Ellington (Crackhead); Tyra Ferrell (Jessie); Dedrick Gobert (Lloyd); Clifton Gonzalez Gonzalez (Mailroom Supervisor); Ricky Harris (Gangsta); Omar Ben Hassan, Suliamen El Hadi, Jalal Nuriddin, and Daoud Spencer (Last Poets); Randall C. Heyward (Policeman #2); Miki Howard (Maxine); Baha Jackson (Baha); Janet Jackson (Justice); Mike James (Policeman #6); Patricia Y. Johnson (Patricia); Shannon Johnson (Keisha); La Keisha M. Jones (Rodney's Girlfriend); Kirk Kinder (Cop); Regina King (Iesha); Vashon LeCesne (Angry Customer); Jennifer Leigh (Beauty College Instructor); Jennifer Lewis (Annie); Tone Löc (J Bone); Special K McCray (Cousin Pete); Mark Miller (Policeman #3); Sarena Mobley (Rita); Al Murray (Policeman #5); Kahil Gibran Nelson (Antonio); Lori Petty (Penelope); Denney Pierce (Cashier); Renato Powell (Woman with Baby); Q-Tip (Markell); Jimmy Ray, Jr. (Fighting Man); Michael Rapaport (Dock Worker); Ernestine Reed (Aunt April); Robi Reed (Woman on Couch); Crystal A. Rodgers (Angel); Tupac Shakur (Lucky); Roger Guenveur Smith (Heywood); Eugene Tate (Uncle Herb); Joe Torry (Chicago); Mikki Val (Gena); David Villafan (Concession Stand Man); Dion Blake Vines (Cousin Dion); Keith

Washington (Dexter);   Rose Weaver (Aunt Audrey);   Anthony Wheaton (Rodney);   Yvette Wilson (Colette);   Billy Zane (Brad).

CHRISTIAN SCIENCE MONITOR, 7/23/93, p. 13, David Sterritt

In filmmaking as in other areas of life, ambition can be both a blessing and a burden.

Ambition played a positive role when writer-director John Singleton made his debut with "Boyz N the Hood" two years ago, spinning an emotionally complex narrative into a commercial and critical success despite his status as an African-American newcomer in a white-dominated industry.

But more dubious aspects of ambition make themselves felt in Singleton's new picture, "Poetic Justice," which takes on a number of issues not directly addressed in the earlier film.

It's unusual, in a movie about black characters living in tough urban environments, that "Poetic Justice" has a female protagonist and a somewhat romantic story. It focuses on the heroine's growing maturity as she grapples with problems of life and love during a rambunctious journey with a potential boyfriend. Even more unusual, the main character is an amateur poet whose verses—written by Maya Angelou, the celebrated black writer—punctuate the soundtrack at key moments in the drama.

It's clear that Singleton wants "Poetic Justice" to be conspicuously different from his previous picture and from pictures by his contemporaries (Spike Lee, Charles Burnett) on the black filmmaking scene. The problem with the movie is that its distinctive elements seem dictated less by the needs of the story than by an arbitrary decision to buck the usual conventions. The film's boldest ingredients—its feminine concerns, its voice-over poetry, its crowded mixture of subplots and moods—are so ambitious that they call attention to themselves instead of serving the story and characters.

The story centers on Justice, a young woman whose life comes dangerously close to falling apart when her boyfriend is murdered in a burst of gang-related violence. She manages to hang on, working in a beauty salon and writing poetry. But her faith in the future is precariously slim.

When a new acquaintance named Lucky takes an interest in her, she immediately brushes him off—partly because she's not ready for romance, and partly because he's so painfully ordinary. Then a friend talks her into coming along on a road trip, and when she meets the others involved in the journey, Lucky turns out to be the driver.

He's a decent young man in many ways determined to earn an honest living and provide an acceptable home for his little daughter. His relationship with Justice begins on a stormy note, though, and plenty of sparks fly before they reach a delicately balanced understanding at the end of their voyage.

In outline, the plot of "Poetic Justice" is perfectly serviceable. Mainstream movies have told similar stories about white characters since Hollywood was born, and it would have been interesting to watch Singleton handle the narrative in terms of African-American values and interests, which he understood so well in his earlier movie.

In writing the screenplay, however, he has included so many incidents, feelings and conflicts that only the most inspired two-hour film could deal with all of them effectively. Although many show strong dramatic potential the movie has to whisk through each one as quickly as possible.

Lucky's aspirations as a serious-minded rap singer are barely sketched out, for instance, even though these play an important part in the last scenes.

To be sure, "Poetic Justice" has its virtues as well as shortcomings. Pop singer Janet Jackson makes a promising movie debut as Justice, and Tupac Shakur is an offbeat leading man. The picture is smartly photographed, and Angelou's poetry is interesting to encounter in the context of a Hollywood movie.

In the end, though, "Poetic Justice" tackles more than Singleton is yet ready to accomplish. Its ambitious aims are commendable in themselves, but regrettable since they overinflate what might have been a simpler and better film.

LOS ANGELES TIMES, 7/23/93, Calendar/p. 6, Kenneth Turan

How do you follow a phenomenon? More to the point, if you're writer-director John Singleton and your strongly felt debut film, "Boyz N the Hood," not only made money but made you the youngest person (as well as the first African-American) ever nominated for the best director Oscar, what do you do for film No. 2?

Variants of that difficulty have preyed on every Hollywood boy wonder from Orson Welles to Steven Soderberg. For Singleton, the most prominent member of the post-Spike Lee generation of black filmmakers trying to tell stories reflective of an inner-city reality only now reaching the screen, the pressures have got to be especially intense.

And "Poetic Justice", Singleton's latest, indicates that he is aware of those expectations. Singleton has not abandoned the first film's South-Central Los Angeles location, but has broadened his range from drama to romance and chosen to make a woman—Janet Jackson in the starring role—his protagonist. And he has pushed gangbangers to the background, focusing instead on hard-working wage earners who form the neighborhood's core, in effect putting forward positive images of African-American society.

Yet despite all this, or maybe because of it, "Poetic Justice" is a disappointment. While "Boyz" was all of a piece, this film feels thrown together, an unfocused compendium of conflicting impulses and moods. And while his debut clearly came from Singleton's gut, this one lacks that singular passion. It feels like something undertaken in order to Do the Right Thing, not because its creator felt any kind of intrinsic emotional connection to the material.

Though "Boyz" was heartfelt, it also followed Hollywood convention in how it structured its up-from-the-underclass story. Similarly, "Poetic Justice" follows a familiar pattern of young people who can't stand each other when they meet only to discover they were meant for each other just in time for the final credits.

Janet Jackson plays Justice, a young woman from South-Central L.A. who works in a beauty salon but whose true passion is poetry. Scarred by personal loss, she is the despair both of her friends and her femme fatale boss Jessie (stylishly played by Tyra Ferrell, who was the opposite of glamorous as Doughboy's mother in "Boyz"). "A man is nothing but a tool," is Jessie's motto. "You have to know when to take him out of the box and when to replace him."

Justice has no time for talk like this, and even less for the tentative advances of Lucky (rap artist Tupac Shakur, last seen as the murderous Bishop in "Juice"), local postman and concerned single parent. When Lucky attempts to off-handedly flirt with her while he drops off the mail, Justice comes down on him so hard he practically winces. No love, you might think, will ever be lost between these two.

But it just so happens that Justice's close friend Iesha (Regina King) is involved with Chicago (Joe Torry), Lucky's best buddy at the post office. And that the very weekend that Chicago, Iesha and Lucky are going to drive a mail truck up to Oakland is the same one that Justice is attending a hair show in that same city and has unexpected problems with transportation. So, to no one's surprise but their own, Lucky and Justice end up on the road together.

While a scenario like this will win no prizes for originality, it is partially redeemed by how amiable a couple Lucky and Justice make once they finally decide to stop fighting fate and each other. And after having Hollywood place a For Whites Only sign on this kind of fantasy for so long, it can't hurt to let people of color in on the game.

Unfortunately, very little time in "Poetic Justice" (rated R for pervasive strong language and for violence and sexuality) is spent on sweet moments. Not only do Lucky and Justice bicker almost ceaselessly, they are verbally outgunned by Chicago and Iesha, who turn on each other with a remarkable viciousness. When the film's liberal use of hard-core profanity is added in (plus enough presumably authentic slang to confuse anyone not raised in the 'hood), a good part of "Poetic Justice" is more unpleasant than most romances want to be.

Singleton, not satisfied with making a mere fairy tale, has added more than this helping of grit to the mix. But situations the quartet stumble on on the way to Oakland, including a large and gregarious all-black family picnic and an African Marketplace and Cultural Faire, feel dramatically contrived, included largely to make sociological points. Other elements, like casual shots of burnt-out portions of South-Central L.A. and scenes of a friend of Lucky's dealing drugs, come off as either truncated or out of place.

For while it can be argued that these situations are taken from reality, that is not a guarantee that they will meld gracefully on screen. In fact, the fit is awkward, making for a movie that feels constructed out of elements Singleton was determined not to throw away even if logic called for their being discarded.

Singleton's virtues, his passion for the African-American community and his ability with actors (both Tupac and Jackson, whose character's expressive poetry was written by Maya Angelou, come off well) are in evidence here, and his desire to create role models on screen is the more sincere for not being fashionable. A filmmaker who is adept at saying what's on his mind, he will do better when he finds something he truly wants to say.

NEW YORK POST, 7/23/93, p. 31, Michael Medved

Baseball fans used to talk a great deal about the dreaded "sophomore jinx," a mysterious malady that afflicted talented young players who would follow up brilliant rookie seasons with sharply disappointing second-year campaigns.

One can only hope that "Poetic Justice" represents John Singleton's sophomore jinx, and that now that he's finished with this sorry stinker, he'll move on to better things. After winning Oscar nominations for both writing and directing "Boyz N the Hood"—a movie pulsing with humanity and power—the 25-year-old Singleton has here created a pointless, plotless, meandering mess.

Top pop diva Janet Jackson makes her dismal big-screen debut playing Justice, a moody beautician from South Central LA. who, in mourning for an ex-cop boyfriend slain before her eyes, begins writing Maya Angelou's poetry. Jackson recites these verses in endless stretches of feckless voice-over narration, presenting the poems with a sleepy singsong reminiscent of a preschool teacher reading "The Three Little Pigs" to her tired class.

Jackson's new love interest is Lucky, a mailman and single father played by the controversial rapper Tupac Shakur, who delivers this movie's only vaguely intriguing performance. Shakur who previously starred in Ernest Dickerson's under-appreciated "Juice" projects a sulky, silky, tough-tender screen presence, but here he must cope with this sparkling repartee as he begins his courtship of the still grieving Justice:

"F--- you bitch!"
"No, I say, F--- you!"
"F--- you! F--- you !"

This enlightening exchange, proving that the spirit of Noel Coward still lives, goes on for several minutes and is supposed to dramatize the growing attraction between the two stars as they ride together in a mail truck up the scenic California coast. Lucky and his homeboy (and fellow postal employee) Chicago (Joe Torry) are making a mail run from L.A. to Oakland, and they've asked Chicago's main squeeze, the alcoholic and manipulative Iesha (Regina King), and her friend Justice to ride along.

This supposedly cathartic road trip leaves moviegoers trapped in the careening truck for most of the movie with four characters who are so utterly unsympathetic that you'll begin hoping for a bloody crash. Unlike the sensitive, suffering, even noble adolescents who turned up in "Boyz N the Hood," these people are stupid, indulgent, self-destructive and unbearably cruel to one another.

They also reinforce many of the most hoary and hateful racist stereotypes: While tooling along the highway, Chicago and Lucky suddenly slow down when they smell barbecue some half-mile away.

They veer off the road and end up crashing a large, peaceful family reunion picnic while commenting: "I ain't never seen so many niggers in any place before without no fight." Needless to say, a nasty brawl breaks out just a few moments later. If a white writer-director had created such material, he would be widely condemned for encouraging racism.

For most potential patrons of this movie, the key question involves Janet Jackson's dramatic ability, and it's sad to say that she's done more real acting in any one of her music videos—or posing for her album covers, for that matter. Her performance, in fact, has many of the qualities of a still photograph—two-dimensional and posed—giving no hint at all of the inner life that might have produced the poetry she recites so badly on the sound track.

If she ever acts in motion pictures again (which she should, to erase this wretched memory), Jackson definitely deserves a better vehicle.

So does John Singleton.

And so do we.

NEWSDAY, 7/23/93, Part II/p. 56, John Anderson

John Singleton's most convincing and inadvertent statement in "Poetic Justice"is about the potency of rap music. Each time we hear a voice-over of Justice (Janet Jackson) reciting her poetry—all of which comes from the work of the indigestible Maya Angelou—we long for another dose of The Dogg Pound.

The grandiose adolescence of Angelou's verse is perfect, in a way, for this, the second feature film from the 25-year-old writer and director of "Boyz N the Hood." Following up a critically and financially successful debut like that means scrutiny of the most agonizing sort. And from the cuteness of the title, to the Angelou poetry, to Jackson's lapses into excruciating earnestness, to the appalling manner in which young men and women treat each other in the film, there's a definite sense that Singleton wanted to get his sophomore effort over with, albeit stylishly.

In "Boyz N the Hood," Singleton's concern was the role of men in the black community. Here, he focuses, ostensibly, on the women. Justice, an attractive, intelligent beautician whose drug-dealing boyfriend was shot to death right in front of her, is just one of a number of strong, independent female characters. But in a way, they're simply there to reflect the male attitude, the lack of respect Singleton sees as permeating black male-female relationships, which always seems to border on the incendiary.

The troubling thing about "Poetic Justice" is how this aspect of the story, this hostility, is used for laughs: Singleton could write off all the vicious language and bad attitude to "reality," but he also uses it for comedy, and of the most mainstream sort. From Compton, Calif., to Saddle River, N.J., you can always raise a chuckle with a line about, a woman's private parts, or repeated uses of "ho" and "bitch."

The lack of respect is largely mutual. Justice had treated her boyfriend with disdain, but something about having his brains in her lap must have left an impression. She dresses solely in black, rejects the overtures of men—the way she and her boss, Jessie (Tyra Ferrell), humiliate the mailman Lucky (Tupac Shakur) when he makes a pass was an old joke a long time ago—writes her poetry, but can't get out of her funk. Somehow, her best friend, Iesha (Regina King) convinces her to make a "run" from L.A. to Oakland with her and her boyfriend Chicago (Joe Torry) and one of his friends—who turns out to be Lucky. The sparks fly immediately, and don't stop for most of the film.

By this point, though, the two characters have been converging on each other for a long, long time, and it's not as if there's been a lot of character development going on. We've seen Justice (her mother was in law school when she got pregnant) mooning around her apartment, listening to Stevie Wonder, making popcorn and stroking her cat. We've seen Lucky's confrontation with the mother of his child, a crack-smoking hooker; we sense the basic goodness in him (he takes his daughter to his mother's to live), but it's very internalized. We've learned of Lucky's aspirations to be a rap singer, and seen the cheapness of life in black L.A. And we watch Singleton be ironic: A carload of young men, on their way to avenge yet another street murder, bid Lucky "Peace." And then, we watch Lucky and Justice do vicious verbal battle and fall in love.

Singleton has cataloged every social ill imaginable, and tried to wrap it all in romance, which is thoroughly unconvincing. He does get a very solid performance out of the promising Shakur, and Jackson is more than adequate. The cinematography, by Peter Lyons Collister, often is stunning, and not just because of the California landscapes; the camera loves Jackson, at least in Collister's hands. But in the end, all "Poetic Justice" really has to offer is attitude, and a love story that Singleton already has given us every reason to believe is doomed.

TIME, 7/26/93, p. 67, Richard Schickel

Two questions now arise: was John Singleton's first film, *Boyz N the Hood*, a lucky accident? Or is his second, *Poetic Justice*, an unlucky one? Too soon to say, of course, since Singleton, the youngest person (and only black) to receive simultaneous Oscar nominations for Best Director and Best Original Screenplay, is still in his 20s, with most of his career ahead of him.

What must be said is that the new movie is simply awful: poorly structured, vulgarly written, insipidly directed, monotonously performed. This, of course, is not the contrast to his taut, persuasively realistic earlier work that Singleton wanted to strike.

Boyz was essentially a story of young men trapped in an unyielding ghetto environment, pretty much hopelessly waiting for its endemic, random violence to strike them down. In his new movie he obviously wanted to explore emotional territory new to him. It is about a young woman named Justice (Janet Jackson) in the same setting who is doing her best to keep her options open and her hopes up. She's a hairdresser who finds psychological escape in the poetry she scribbles (actually it is Maya Angelou's work) while mourning the loss of a boyfriend gunned down in her presence in the movie's opening, and most arresting, sequence. Quite clearly, she also dreams of making a real escape from the hood.

Lucky (Tupac Shakur), an amiable postal worker, does not at first seem the ideal partner for that enterprise. But he too has compelling reasons to break out, and a dream of redemptive creativity roughly analogous to hers: he wants to be a rapper. When they and another couple are thrown together on a week-end trip to Oakland, California, in a post office van, edginess slowly gives way to an understanding that survives even a sudden lurch toward the tragic.

This situation and this relationship are both rooted in traditional romantic comedy, and it would have been interesting (to say the least) if Singleton could have imposed its generic conventions on this unlikely milieu. But that's beyond him. He doesn't offer any scene that convincingly suggests the kind of authentic mutual attraction that might overcome the couple's superficial differences. He doesn't know how to coax a performance out of Jackson, who relates to the camera lens as if it were a mirror. He never finds a way either to put an interesting spin on the incidents of the journey or to link them dynamically. And he doesn't know how to turn a graceful romantic line or how to put real snap into a comic one; his dialogue is mainly street epithets mumbled or run together incomprehensibly.

Almost everything about this movie feels like a first draft—unfelt, unformed, unfinished. And it's not entirely Singleton's fault. As it so often does, Hollywood has mistaken bright promise for full-fledged talent, rushing in to indulge a young artist's self-indulgences, giving him everything he wants but withholding the one thing he needs most: firm but sympathetic challenges to his assumptions, an insistence on rethinking and rewriting until he knows what he wants to say and how to say it right.

VILLAGE VOICE, 7/27/93, p. 55, Georgia Brown

The wonder is that in his follow-up to *Boyz N the Hood* Singleton moves from tuff, not to tuffer, but to tender. Which isn't to say that *Poetic Justice* is any *Sleepless in South Central*. It is, however, a romantic comedy in which two lonely people start up an acquaintance in antipathy, endure a period of uncomfortable proximity (on the road), and eventually emerge wiser and apprised of the other's frailties and strengths. Valiantly, and often successfully, Singleton also has located his drama in the female point of view.

Justice is his heroine's first name (her mother was in law school when pregnant), and she's a poet (Maya Angelou is her ghost writer). The actress, as you may know by now, is Janet Jackson, with round chipmunk face, eyes so bright and teeth so white she looks surreal, like she's been drawn while all around her are flesh and blood. Jackson has a vivid, saucy presence, however, and does just fine. Her very real butt sits high and wide, a plump cushion to fall on, although Justice feels it's a bit too big. Whereas Mom committed suicide when her only baby was 12 (somehow law school led to drugs), she left a very pleasant house for her and her cat, White Boy, to live in. After a bad shock with a street guy (played by Q-Tip), Justice goes into emotional hibernation. Wearing black, she works in a beauty parlor owned by the compulsively entrepreneurial Jessie (Tyra Ferrell), who dispenses cynical advice like, "A man ain't nothing but a tool."

One weekend a coworker, Iesha (Regina King), talks Justice into a trip up the coast to Oakland in a white mail van driven by two postal workers, her boyfriend, Chicago (Joe Torry), and the harried Lucky (Tupac Shakur). Lucky goes to Oakland every weekend to work with his cousin on rap recording (presumably leaving his little daughter with his mother). Initially he and Justice spar, feeling each other out (Fuck you! Fuck *you!* *Fuck* you!), then find solace together, as well as separately, in their creative spheres—her poetry, his music.

The spirit is willing but the execution lags. One grave drawback of didactic art is that it relies heavily on the artist's maturity and wisdom. Singleton the preacher has several worthy messages, but he seems to lack experience among men and women. He tells a good story, but when it comes to dialogue he takes the easy way. And visually, the film is a mishmash, alternating scenic interludes (excerpts from a PBS spot for the U.S. Postal Service?) with cartoony, Spike-type scenes with actors. The film has an overblown, unintegrated look, unlike the modest, unpretentious style of *Boyz N the Hood*.

South Central, as Singleton presents it, is a culture of confrontation; antagonism is a way of life (and death). When, on their journey, the foursome sniffs out someone else's BBQ and stops at the Johnson Family Reunion Picnic, they mingle with a different breed. "I ain't never seen so many black folks together and there wasn't no fight," observes Lucky. Before leaving, they've started one. On the road, they bring the street along.

After an opener harking back to the worst violence of *Boyz*, the rest of the film centers on verbal abuse, the mouth as assault weapon of choice. When the mouth opens, it is often with intent to maim. The relationship of Iesha and Chicago ends up not as it should but in a brawl. In the movie's most disturbing sequence, the two have sex in the back of the van, with Iesha rolling her eyes, seemingly at the camera. Afterward, she chews out Chicago because he "can't hang," insults him ("You a weak ass punk"), until finally she hits on a killer: "You on steroids? That's the reason I'm fucking someone else." Then he's to blame for pasting her in the mouth.

To make a point about steroids, Singleton slams poor Chicago, probably the movie's sweetest character, when he ought to be pulling all his characters up. This is a romance, after all. Similarly, he'll scold men for calling women *bitch*, but then has his women behave bitchily. The movie fails its characters.

A film centering on the therapeutic (creative) use of language ought to use language better. Here's Lucky's middle-class mom, bringing groceries into her immaculate kitchen: "Shut the fuck up and put out that cigarette!" Two beats later she's instructing, "Don't be cussin' around me, boy." Okay, this may be a Singleton irony—wondering how Mama can preach when she practices but, as a writer, he commits the same error. He wants to teach manners but doesn't construct a viable model. *Poetic Justice* gropes for a way of asking, Can't we all just get along?, shows some points of interest on the way to harmony, but in the end leaves us with an uncharted distance to go.

Also reviewed in:
CHICAGO TRIBUNE, 7/23/93, Friday p. A, Johanna Steinmetz
NEW REPUBLIC, 8/23 & 30/93, p. 30, Stanley Kauffmann
NEW YORK TIMES, 7/23/93, p. C1, Vincent Canby
NEW YORKER, 8/2/93, p. 76, Anthony Lane
VARIETY, 7/26/93, p. 28, Leonard Klady
WASHINGTON POST, 7/23/93, p. C1, Hal Hinson
WASHINGTON POST, 7/23/93, Weekend/p. 44, Desson Howe

POINT OF NO RETURN

A Warner Bros. release. *Producer:* Art Linson. *Director:* John Badham. *Screenplay:* Robert Getchell and Alexandra Seros. *Based on "Nikita" by:* Luc Besson. *Director of Photography:* Michael Watkins. *Editor:* Frank Morris. *Music:* Hans Zimmer. *Music Editor:* Alex Gibson and Sherry Whitfield. *Sound:* Willie D. Burton. *Sound Editor:* William L. Manger, Dale Johnston, Richard Oswald, James J. Isaacs, and Solange Schwalbe-Boisseau. *Casting:* Bonnie Timmermann. *Production Designer:* Philip Harrison. *Art Director:* Sydney Z. Litwack. *Set Designer:* Eric W. Orbom, James Bayliss, Sally Thornton, and Roger G. Fortune. *Set Decorator:* Julia Laughlin. *Special Effects:* Ken Pepiot. *Costumes:* Marlene Stewart. *Make-up:* Kimberly Felix. *Make-up (Bridget Fonda):* Lizbeth Williamson. *Stunt Coordinator:* Mic Rodgers. *Running time:* 108 minutes. *MPAA Rating:* R.

CAST: Bridget Fonda (Maggie); Gabriel Byrne (Bob); Dermot Mulroney (J.P.); Miguel Ferrer (Kaufman); Anne Bancroft (Amanda); Olivia D'Abo (Angela); Richard Romanus (Fahd Bahktiar); Harvey Keitel (Victor the Cleaner); Lorraine Toussaint (Beth); Geoffrey Lewis

(Drugstore Owner); Mic Rodgers (Cop); Michael Rapaport (Big Stan); Ray Oriel (Burt); Spike McClure (Johnny D); Lieux Dressler (Johnny's Mom); John Capodice (Detective); Carmen Zapata (Judge); Calvin Levels (Computer Instructor); Michael Runyard (Weapons Instructor); Bill M. Ryusaki (Karate Instructor); Jan Speck (Kaufman's Assistant); Francesco Messina (Waiter in Restaurant); Peter Mark Vasquez (Guard in Booth); Wendy L. Davies (Shopping Woman); James Handy (Operative); Lee Dupree (Guy with Gun); David Sosna (Operative with Headset); Bruce Barnes (New Orleans Thug); Jaqueline Koch (VIP Woman); Kenny Endoso and Gary Kasper (Angela's Bodyguards); Rosalind Jue (Maid); Eric Cohen (Valet); Francois Chau (Building Security Guard); Joe Garcia (Hassan); Frank Girardeau (Policeman); Clark Heathcliffe Brolly (Male Student); Jodie Markell (Female Student); Robert Harvey (Police Detective); Harry Perry (Venice Guitar Player).

LOS ANGELES TIMES, 3/19/93, Calendar/p. 1, Kenneth Turan

It's a dirty job making movies like "Point of No Return," but somebody's got to do it. Somebody's got to make the middling commercial piffle that the Hollywood system has to produce or die. Not good enough to be remembered past next week, not bad enough to get worked up about, "Point" is a factory product pure and simple, something to throw onto the screen until the next something comes along.

With a stark (if not exactly original) title and a striking advertising image of star Bridget Fonda looking surly and seductive in a backless cocktail dress with a monster weapon in her hand, "Point" is more adept at providing the aura of excitement than actually delivering the goods.

There's an irony in that failure, however, for "Point" is an almost scene-by-scene remake of an energetic and very popular French action film, "La Femme Nikita." With its story of how a hot-tempered wharf rat gets turned into a polished and feminine assassin, "Nikita" just about begged to be remade into a brassy Hollywood production.

And, with the gamin-like Fonda substituting for French actress Anne Parillaud and actionmeister John Badham ("Blue Thunder," "The Hard Way") taking the reins from Luc Besson, a polished commercial success seemed almost assured.

Unfortunately, "Point of No Return" not only is a copy, it has the heft and feel of one. Though the first film was as silly as this one, it had an urgency in its pacing and a sense of belief in its cockeyed story that has not survived in the remake.

The tale (rated R for strong violence, language and sexuality) begins in our nation's capital, where a band of drugged-out crazies attacks a local drug store. "I need it so bad," a wasted Maggie (Fonda) mumbles, presumably referring to a fix, not a decent script. A noisy shootout with the police soon intervenes, and before you can say "murder one," Maggie is on trial for her life.

But the government, ever on the lookout for potentially useful citizens, has other plans, and one morning Maggie wakes up in a bare cell on a bed that looks like an Italian design team made it from a leftover Erector set.

In walks no-last-name Bob (Gabriel Byrne), a shadowy operative with the air of defrocked priest, who gives Maggie a "do something to help your country" pep talk and then offers her what amounts to a scholarship to a federal charm school for assassins.

We'll fix your teeth, we'll clear up your complexion, we'll teach you a whole range of skills, from computers to (courtesy of Anne Bancroft's Amanda) eating "without fake middle-class delicacy." In return for the makeover of your dreams, all you have to do is put your killer instinct at the service of Uncle Sam.

None of this turns out to be as easy as Bob makes it sound, but Maggie does learn to dress as demurely as an Avon lady and is relocated to a beach apartment in Venice that appears to be just around the corner from the place D-FENS was headed toward in "Falling Down."

Though Maggie doesn't have any crazed defense workers to deal with, she does have to contend with the love-struck attentions of moony photographer J.P. (Dermot Mulroney) as well as the odd demands of her work, which include a run-in with an all-business type known as Victor the Cleaner and played with low-key humor by the all-business Harvey Keitel.

As written by Robert Getchell and Alexandra Seros, Maggie's adventures have a pro forma feeling, as if all anyone cared about was making sure that there was enough of a balance between mushy romantic montage and glass-shattering action to make this the perfect date-night movie for a reader of Harlequin romances who has a crush on a card-carrying gun nut.

Director Badham, who must have snoozed through many of the dramatic scenes, so indifferent are the line readings, does try to rouse himself for those action sequences, and the sight of Fonda blowing people away in a variety of elegant designer creations is certainly arresting.

But though Fonda probably had fun in this tough-talking, straight-shooting role, she lacks the diamond hardness Parillaud brought to "Nikita." She is also much too good an actress to have to spend so much of her time, as she did in "Single White Female," running around in her underwear. If "Point of No Return" does turn out to be a commercial success, perhaps Fonda will get enough clout to get a change of clothes. She deserves it.

NEW STATESMAN & SOCIETY, 7/2/93, p. 35, Jonathan Romney

What makes an American thriller American? The presence of Dennis Hopper in a bootlace tie and matching leer certainly does—as in *Red Rock West*. [This film opened later in the United States; see reviews in *Film Review Annual 1995*.] Surprisingly, the presence of Harvey Keitel doesn't, in this week's case—but that's because *The Assassin* is effectively French. At least, it's French insofar as it's based on a French film, Luc Besson's *Nikita*—which in turn was based on a French fantasy about what an American-style B-film might look like if given a strong Parisian twist. The week's truly American film, on the other hand, is based on a US genre whose name and whose game rules were actually drawn up retrospectively by US-besotted film critics in France: *film noir*.

You could say it's a rum old world and end there. But clearly some redefinition of terms is in order. For a start, what is a "thriller" anyway. Both *The Assassin* and *Red Rock West* thrill to different degrees, but the word "thriller" applies to them differently. In the case of *Red Rock West*, you can safely apply the term because the film so faithfully follows 1950s B-film conventions that you always know *exactly* what kind of film you're watching. But it also follows them with enough flexibility and ingenuity to keep catching you on the hop. Director John Dahl and his cowriter brother Rick really do feed you a twist a minute—minor twists to be sure, but applied so blithely that you keep kicking yourself for not spotting them sooner. And when you *do* spot them, you want to kick the hero (Nicolas Cage as a well-meaning drifter) for not seeing them coming at all.

It's almost a case of nostalgic noir played as a board game. You know right from the start what pieces are in play—one soft-hearted guy (Cage), one hard-headed Hannah (Lara Flynn Boyle), one strong scowler (Hopper), one weak one (J T Walsh). Cage blows into a desolate backwater and somehow can't blow out again—he keeps leaving, but there's an excruciating inevitability to the fact that all roads lead right back to Red Rock. And just as inevitable is the fact that Cage still can't see it. Right through the film, pursued by Hopper's snarling Texan killer and Walsh's corrupt sheriff, he keeps taking *just* the wrong road, hitching *just* the wrong ride, stopping off at *just* the wrong motel.

It could be no other way, but this feeling that it *just* might be provides the minimum itch of possibility required to make this mechanical game of wits consistently teasing. The way every avoidable peril hits our man exactly the way you expect it—but usually a fraction too soon—provides you with the same ghastly pleasure you get from hearing a series of relishably awful puns. The Dahls played similar games in their first film *Kill Me Again*, but there they fussed too much about trappings—about the sort of office furnishings that would surround a seedy private eye, or about what lingerie a real old-school *femme fatale* would take for the weekend. But in *Red Rock West*, there's nothing to distract you, nothing but plot twists and simmering looks—nervy for Cage, Sue Ellen-style gnashings from Boyle, and Hopper, as ever, effortlessly projecting dementia from the spot just between the eyebrows. And it all takes place in a Wyoming landscape so barren that it was probably last used as a set for a *Roadrunner* cartoon. Indeed, the ghastly pleasure referred to above is also the same you get from seeing Wile E Coyote hoist by his own petard over and over again.

There have been more than a couple of exercises in this school in the past few years—more often than not with pulp scribe Jim Thompson evoked as honorary godfather. Hopper himself directed on *The Hot Spot*; it misfired because he piled on the intense looks, the steaminess, the down-home decorative touches, the ominous blues soundtrack, until everything felt just as calculated and knowingly retro as a Levi's ad. The word "adult" was writ large. But Dahl's film works beautifully because it's content to be kids' stuff: more purely *comic* irony than the pared-down existential tension that John Carpenter and Walter Hill provided in their prime. The Dahls aren't quite in that league. But no one else these days is doing it with the same pleasure in their craft. It's idle hopscotch, but the best fun on screen this week.

Back to definitions, then. What makes *The Assassin* a thriller? No twists, to be sure. In John Badham's film, it hardly matters what comes next because early on you realise that you're for the standard action-thriller template. You kick off with a real wham-buster opening, move on to a few scenes blending mild ominous violence and psychological tension, then another brief wham-buster, cool down with an interlude of mildly spicy passion (preferably with something nice on the soundtrack to provide a spin-off single—in this case Nina Simone), and keep going until you hit the big closing cliffhanger with explosions. The thrills come from orchestrated jolts rather than sly swerves.

But here's the catch. *The Assassin* is structured scene by scene—sometimes even shot by shot—after Besson's *Nikita*, about a Raggedy-Anne punk turned ruthless Terminatrix. And yet *The Assassin* somehow *feels* like a completely different film. I can't say why, and I imagine it would take a long, close shot-by-shot reading to do so precisely. But here's my guess. *Nikita* felt *French*—that is, seemed to have a European pacing to it—because it so strenuously tried to be American. What you got in *Nikita* was not Frenchness, but a French idea of big-budget American-ness. The more it tried to be American, the more it was rooted in the peculiar perspective that its origins gave it—it was *about* its own cultural filter first and foremost.

The Assassin, on the other hand, is simply a high-concept film unattached to any agenda except the commercial one. Besson's film is taken as a dramatic pattern emptied of cultural meaning, and fit to be filled only with big bangs and bright colour. The prime task of Bedham's version is to *forget* its, origins, which must not be alluded to at any cost; and the surest way of doing that is to hug the original's shoreline as closely as possible so that you don't see any telltale gaps between the two (any such gaps might look dangerously like critical irony).

But in cleaving so tight to *Nikita, The Assassin* can't shake free totally, so it slyly plays up its American idea of Europeanness. It makes its tough heroine into an exemplar of "Parisian" elegance, and in a weird twist, gives her Nina Simone as a heroine—an American singer whose iconic prestige owes everything to her status as a European exile.

Now here's the catch. *The Assassin* is, in my book, a much better film than Besson's. It's better because it *knows* it hasn't got a thought in its head, unlike *Nikita* which, while dumb, was neurotically hung up on that dreary French obsession with *révolte (cf Savage Nights)*. *The Assassin* is *entirely* about thrills and flashy iconic shots of Bridget Fonda. It has no agenda except the box-office grosses and the fact that Fonda with a gun is to die for. But it's in no way an American film, even if Harvey Keitel does turn up at the end. It's an international film, without origins, without texture—a Coca-Cola can of a movie. *Red Rock West*, on the other hand, is a Coca-Cola *bottle*. You get a completely different taste.

NEW YORK POST, 3/19/93, p. 31, Jami Bernard

She's sexy. She's lethal. She's the poster girl for the '90s screen goddess—the killer babe who has no qualms about sex, murder, or wearing tight dresses.

Bridget Fonda plays la femme Nikita—Oops! I mean Maggie—in this remake of Luc Besson's French movie "La Femme Nikita." Where the original was about a feral reject whose carnality could be harnessed, the remake is secretly about how girls get dragged into womanhood kicking and screaming. Women will delight in the secret message, and men will delight in the fetishization of Fonda.

Maggie is a drug addict and a menace to society, not least because she doesn't wear makeup or conform to accepted standards of beauty. She's on death row for shooting a cop in the face.

Her salvation comes in the form of secret agent Bob (Gabriel Byrne), who stages her funeral and then gets custody of her soul. Bob is in charge of redirecting Maggie's animal energy for use as a government tool. Initially reluctant, Maggie is soon as quick with a lipstick as with a loaded weapon. In fact, she herself is the loaded weapon, a femme fatale in the truest sense of the word.

"Point of No Return" is a fairly close if less stylish re-creation—even down to sets and camera angles—of "La Femme Nikita," a furious pop thriller. But of course nothing translates quite like it ought.

For instance, Maggie is made more tremulously sympathetic, whereas the French version's fabulous Anne Parrillaud was completely amoral from the get-go.

But "Point of No Return" has a subliminal feminist layer that can be read as both critique and how-to of the conditioning all girls must endure to become woman in this society. It is the Electra complex dramatized.

The early Maggie can be seen as the tomboy who must give up her fusion with mother (Maggie won't even discuss her mother, though she longs for her) in order to learn about love by attaching to the father (Bob teaches Maggie everything she needs to know and serves as her first love object).

Then she must leave daddy ("That's the last time I'll ever kiss you," she tells Bob) in order to form a healthier attachment to a real boyfriend (gentle, befuddled Dermot Mulroney).

The free-spirited wild child is easily able to master the fundamentals of karate and computers, but ladylike behavior must be forced on her in a series of grueling deportment lessons given by Anne Bancroft, the putative mother who is wistful to see her fully transformed "daughter" leave home on her first date.

Bancroft ruefully completes Maggie's indoctrination by teaching her those bizarre "essentials" that society prizes: the woman who can contain her anger by smiling when she wants to hit.

The "intuitive" behavior of femininity is lampooned throughout. In the kitchen, where Maggie is particularly inept, she wields a huge cleaver, in fact, she escapes a restaurant kitchen in a hail of bullets—it's dangerous to renounce womanhood. When set loose in a supermarket, she has no idea how to shop.

Even flirting is a learned skill. Fonda, today's hottest young actress, cleverly brings a hint of the alien to the role as if Maggie had been dropped to earth in a time capsule.

The movie's subversive feminism—although I can assure you, hardly anyone will notice—is the only thing fresh about the material. Maggie cannot respond to a marriage proposal from her boyfriend through the door of the bathroom because she is concentrating on her job, and literally has her sights set elsewhere—she is looking through the viewfinder of a high-powered rifle, awaiting her next victim.

When Bob announces "The girl's dead," referring to Maggie, he is correct in the sense that the girl is dead, long live the woman.

If the American version is less high-spirited than the French, it still has its kicks, including this slip of a girl running around with a gun several times her size, and Harvey Keitel in an hilariously deadpan cameo as "Victor the Cleaner."

NEWSDAY, 3/19/93, Part II/p. 62, Jack Mathews

"The end of French film as we know it," lamented one New York critic of Luc Besson's 1990 art-house thriller "La Femme Nikita." Fortunately, the American film industry has no reputation to uphold, so the John Badham remake, "Point of No Return," is just more Hollywood carnage, as we know it.

"Point of No Return," starring Bridget Fonda as a scruffy homicidal junkie made over as a precision government assassin, is a case of remaking a movie simply to dump the subtitles. The production values of "La Femme Nikita" were just as slick, the violence was just as exploitive, French actress Anne Parrillaud was just as effective, and the stories are equally preposterous.

When "Point" is all over, you also feel just as used up and empty, as if youv'e been watching people slaughtered for your amusement.

Fonda's Maggie is a heroine for our demerited movie times, a woman recruited for her feral athleticism to be groomed and fine-tuned by a federal agency (the CIA?) and used as a killing machine. In the opening scene, we meet Maggie at the bottom of the food chain, strung-out and glassy-eyed, her skin splotched and tattooed, participating in a drug-crazed pharmacy break-in.

The scene ends with her committing a murder so cold-blooded it renders her virtually inhuman, and for me, irredeemable. Yet, agent Bob (Gabriel Byrne) sees her as a diamond-in-the-rough and offers her the deal of the century: She can kill for the agency and be free, or she can be put to sleep.

Soon, Maggie has graduated from a combination commando/charm school and is living a drug-free life with a sweet-natured, awfully dim photographer, J.P. (Dermot Mulroney), in kicky Venice, Calif., while dreading those calls from the agency with her latest assignments.

Fonda, like Parillaud, undergoes remarkable physical transformation, from something the cat dragged in to the cat's meow, and Michael Watkins' cinematography makes sure you notice. The first half of the movie is shot in such dark, cold tones it reeks of death and desperation, and Maggie's skin has the texture and pallor of weathered shingles. The second half, with an all-new Maggie discovering both love and a conscience, is as sunny and colorful as her beachfront loft, and her flesh tone is as warm as a ripe peach.

There are, of course, those nagging hints of her secret life. When set upon by two thugs during a trip to Mardi Gras, Maggie instinctively fells the brutes with some devastating spin kicks, then explains the performance away to the profoundly gullible J.P. as remembered behavior from an old karate class.

The script makes passing mention of Maggie's unresolved relationship with her mother, but is otherwise gleefully unburdened by motivation. We see no reason for Bob's faith in Maggie, or for his subsequent infatuation, and the assassinations are carried out with almost no explanations.

"Point" does offer a unique theory of rehabilitation, though. By turning a sociopath into a paid assassin, the government inadvertently gives Maggie a conscience. She now cries when she kills. Humanity through dehumanization.

Badham ("Blue Thunder," "Stakeout") is a yeoman director of action films and has pumped up the volume (more deaths, more noise, louder music), but he lacks the true commitment to sleaze that might have made "Point" a female version of Abel Ferrara's "The Bad Lieutenant."

But Badham at least had the good sense to cast Harvey Keitel, the Bad Lieutenant himself, as Victor the Cleaner, a mute agent whose specialty is ridding bodies with government-issue sulphuric acid.

See your tax dollars at work!

NEWSWEEK, 3/29/93, p. 65, David Ansen

To call *Point of No Return* a remake of the 1991 French pop fantasy "La Femme Nikita" isn't adequate; carbon copy is more like it. The screenwriters, Robert Getchell and Alexandra Seros, have simply taken the Luc Besson movie and, with a few minor alterations, duplicated it in an American setting. The change of locale to Washington, D.C., Venice, Calif., and New Orleans only re-emphasizes the fact that this sleek comic-strip mix of violence and romance could take place anywhere except in the real world.

A twisted modern fairy tale, "La Femme Nikita" was a Cinderella story about a female assassin. A madly eclectic hodgepodge of genres, the flashy but shallow Besson film may have seemed fresh because it kept shifting its pop-mythic gears. What starts as a dark, ultraviolent cousin of "A Clockwork Orange" turns into a delirious episode of "Charlie's Angels," with elements of James Bond and "Pygmalion" tossed in. When we first see the heroine, now called Maggie (Bridget Fonda), she's a vicious, drug-addicted punkette, as glamorous as a drowned rat. Arrested for a murder committed in a holdup, this wild animal is sentenced to death, but her execution turns out to be a ruse. When she wakes from her injection she is a captive of a shadowy, high-tech government agency that plans to turn her into a poised, sophisticated hit woman. Under the dual tutelage of Gabriel Byrne and Anne Bancroft, this grunge Galatea is trained in martial arts, computers and fine dining, and her snarl replaced with a smile. Six months later, transformed into a pert sexpot, she's taken out into society and handed her first assignment—a hit job in a fashionable restaurant.

When she passes the test, she's sent to Venice to wait for her next lethal gig. But the civilizing process has been too successful: the killing machine discovers her heart, and loses it to an amiable photographer (Dermot Mulroney) who hasn't a clue that he's shacked up with a professional assassin. Torn between love and evil duty, what's a poor hit woman to do?

Director John Badham ("WarGames," "Stakeout") knows there's no point in trying to make any of this plausible. You just have to keep a straight face, pour on the style and keep the bodies flying. Since Maggie is essentially a kitten-with-a-whip fantasy figure, she comes unencumbered by friends, a family, a past. All we know about her is that she's inherited her taste for torchy Nina Simone songs from her mother (a nice musical touch). It's up to Fonda to make us swallow this killer, and she largely succeeds. Neither as sinewy nor as feral as Anne Parillaud was in the original, Fonda wisely doesn't try to overdo the savagery. Thin-lipped, small-voiced and slightly framed, she's hardly an icon of physical menace in this era of iron-pumping maidens, but by staying within herself (to use a sportscasters' favorite cliché) she creates an appealingly enigmatic figure, unpredictable and poignant. More than anything, Fonda gives this glossy, reasonably entertaining rerun an American raison d'être: underneath her chic cocktail dress and semiautomatic fashion accessories, you recognize, and embrace, the tomboy girl next door.

SIGHT AND SOUND, 7/93, p. 36, Amanda Lipman

A group of young junkies raids a chemist's shop, and in the ensuing shoot-out with the police, all the thieves are killed except for one girl, Maggie. When a policeman finds her, she shoots him dead. The uncontrollably rebellious young woman is sentenced to death by lethal injection, but wakes up to find herself still alive. A man, Bob, gives her the choice of death or working as a special government assassin. Reluctantly, she agrees to work with him.

After one escape attempt, Maggie embarks on a tough training course. She also has lessons from an elegant woman, Amanda, on social graces. Initially uncooperative, she finally heeds death threats. One night, she is allowed out to a restaurant with Bob but this turns out to be her final test. She has to kill one of the diners, then escape by a route Bob describes to her. His instructions are false and she narrowly escapes. On her return, Bob, who is clearly falling in love with her, tells her that she is ready to go out into the world as Claudia (codename Nina), a computer saleswoman, in Venice, Los Angeles. There she falls in love with her apartment caretaker J.P., who is puzzled that she will not tell him anything about her past. One day, she is called by her department to deliver a bomb to a hotel suite.

She meets Bob who makes her invite him round for dinner, where he indulges in macho sparring with J.P. Bob gives Maggie two airline tickets for New Orleans at Mardi Gras. After carrying out another killing, she asks Bob to let her go. He agrees on condition that she does one final job: she has to imitate the girlfriend of a rich crook, Fahd Bahktiar, who is selling nuclear secrets to the Middle East, steal his information database and kill him. It all goes wrong when Maggie's colleague and Bahktiar's girlfriend are both shot. Victor, the 'cleaner', is called in to dispose of the bodies in acid and help Maggie kill Bahktiar. She accomplishes her mission and drives off with Victor. But she grows suspicious of his behaviour and a fight ensues. The car becomes lodged halfway off a cliff and Victor falls to his death. Maggie spends the night with J.P. but in the morning, when Bob arrives, she has disappeared. He glimpses her walking down a road and reports to his boss that she died in the car accident.

This latest Hollywood remake of a European movie copies Luc Besson's Nikita scene by scene, decor by decor and colour by colour. In fact, much of the time, it seems to be no more than a very expensive dubbing job. Besson's chill, electric-blue opening scene is there, complete with a very loud rock track and the helpful addition of a neon sign proclaiming "drugs"—in case the new American audience is wondering what's wrong with the ragged bunch making their way down the street. Nikita's—now Nina's—white cell is reproduced down to the tiniest graffitied detail; even the clothes look exactly the same.

But where Besson adeptly manufactured style out of no substance, Badham plods through the film with the palpable anxiety to reproduce it so faithfully that it loses any spirit it might have had. Even the hyperactive, protracted kitchen fight, surely owing something to John Woo, in which Nina escapes after her first assassination, comes across as uninspired imitation.

But, oddly enough, The Assassin turns out to be a surprisingly watchable movie. The reason is the inspired casting of Bridget Fonda. Where Anne Parillaud's Nikita was no more than a transparent pretty-girl-with-gun male fantasy, Fonda is perky and tough, and even, at moments, almost tragic. She may have started out as a grinning doll in films like Shag, but she has turned into a fine actress who makes you want to believe that there are dramas raging beneath that defiant chin. She also turns Parillaud's pouting affectations into something altogether more appealing: Maggie's confusion over what to buy in the supermarket, leading her to follow a shopper around and copy her in bulk, is played as coy comedy tinged with beguiling pathos.

But even Fonda has difficulty keeping her balance when faced with the prospect of Anne Bancroft as Amanda, the svelte teacher who turns the ugly duckling into a swan. The essential emptiness of Amanda's platitudes is picked up once, later in the film, when Fonda, faced with danger, finds herself chillingly repeating one of them. But we are simply asked to accept, without seeing it, the surrogate mother/daughter relationship between the two women; and what could have been one of the most telling—and emotional—aspects of Maggie's 'awakening' is glossed over. Jeanne Moreau, at least, brought to the original part the husky sexiness of a brothel madame, making it easier to see why she would be alluring to Nikita. But Bancroft is too much like someone's smart aunt.

Nina Simone may be delighted that she has finally received Hollywood recognition, not just on the soundtrack but in the 'Nina' motif that runs through the film (Maggie is code-named after her favourite singer). But the whole business is so overplayed that it soon turns what is apparently supposed to be sophisticated magic into cutesy bathos. When Ms Simone's music represents a pearl in the early Maggie oyster—a symbol of Bob's love for Maggie, a hazy memory of Maggie's mother and a representation of Maggie herself—you wonder at the paucity of imagination involved.

As Bob, Gabriel Byrne is suave, distant and inimitably romantic, though hampered by a bizarre semi-Scottish accent. His sparring scene with the pipsqueak J.P. is one of the film's few deft touches, funny in a breezy, ironic American way. But (perhaps because, while *Nikita*'s director meant to identify with Bob, Badham cannot) Byrne never quite gets the chance to be the brooding spiritual presence in Nina's life that he should be—and another area of conflict is diluted.

The second most appealing piece of casting is Harvey Keitel's deadly killer, who stomps impassively through his small, surreal portion of the movie with sheer brilliance; funny and horrific by turn, though hardly stretching his capabilities.

The Assassin says no more and no less than its glam predecessor, but its fidelity has one major advantage: that at least, unlike numerous other remakes, the temptation to tamper with the very poignantly French ending is overcome.

VILLAGE VOICE, 3/30/93, p. 56, Georgia Brown

La Femme Nikita is no *Blade Runner*, but it's infused with the same pathos. In both, there's a fatal flaw in the training. *Blade Runner*'s replicants are consumed by a desire to be human, thus thwarting the parent corporation's goal of productivity. In *Nikita*, the State wants killing machines but produces sentient human beings. Therapy works: the savage becomes truly civilized. As I said the first time around (two years ago almost precisely), the significant progress in Nikita's makeover comes not when she's taught to smile but when she learns to cry.

In the movies, fascist regimes and run-amok scientists are always making the same mistake: They think they're creating new and better robots and droids, but then the creations turn out to have feelings, mo' better feelings than the creators. It's as if the scientists (parents) pass on their repressed qualities. The monsters become obsessed with regaining full human capacities; the makers don't realize they're the ones who are lacking.

Now let's refresh ourselves on why it was deemed necessary to remake *La Femme Nikita*, Luc Besson's mod romantic thriller, which was delightfully sufficient unto itself. The hitch, apparently, was those pesky subtitles, scaring off the vast market that does not like to read. So here we are contemplating the dreadful, perfunctory U.S. version, retitled *Point of No Return*, directed by John Badham, starring Bridget Fonda and Gabriel Byrne, with Harvey Keitel doing a star turn toward the end as "the Cleaner."

Gratuitous yes, but frankly I'd expected the remake to be fun. After all, they had a good blueprint. Moreover, Byrne seemed a perfect replacement for the sexy Tcheky Karyo, Anne Bancroft is the age to play Jeanne Moreau, and Fonda has the long legs, if not the strong shoulders, of Anne Parillaud. (Granted, my worst suspicions were aroused when, cunning as usual, Warners scheduled the film's first press screening two days before the opening, meaning that the weeklies couldn't get reviews out before big box-office weekend.)

The basic plot is retained, relocated to America (Washington, D.C., southern California, New Orleans), but there's no electricity. Everything is here but wrong. Except for Keitel, who's briefly hilarious, the actors look like they're suffering from a collective flu. Fonda is a particular disappointment. As a junkie and then a feral recruit, her viciousness is belied by frailty and something that resembles Epstein-Barr Syndrome. Then when the makeover comes (in one unconvincing swoop), she looks like a stewardess. Botched completely is the touching scene in the bathroom—the one where she carries out her assassin's assignment with tears in her eyes and her current love (Dermot Mulroney) yammering through the door. *Point of No Return* makes you wonder why you thought the wispy Fonda could act. Exactly contrary to the point, she seems more and more of a robot as the movie goes on.

Rewriters Robert Getchell and Alexandra Seros want to toy with the original, but there's no notion they know where they want to go. Anne Bancroft's part as company courtesan is a puzzlement: She looks like the Wicked Witch of the West—not like Moreau's melancholy mentor—and speaks cruelly. It's hard to believe the Nikita character would turn to her for help. Probably scenes were edited out that might have made some of the characterizations more coherent.

La Femme Nikita was not remade for love or regard (as, say, Paul Schrader's remake of *Cat People* or Jim McBride's *Breathless*). It's money, money, money all the way.

Also reviewed in:
CHICAGO TRIBUNE, 3/19/93, Friday/p. C, Johanna Steinmetz
NEW REPUBLIC, 4/19/93, p. 28, Stanley Kauffmann
NEW YORK TIMES, 3/19/93, p. C10, Janet Maslin
VARIETY, 3/22/93, p. 50 Todd McCarthy
WASHINGTON POST, 3/19/93, p. F7, Hal Hinson
WASHINGTON POST, 3/19/93, Weekend/p. 45, Desson Howe

POSSE

A Gramercy Pictures release of a PolyGram Filmed Entertainment production in association with Working Title Films. *Executive Producer:* Tim Bevan and Eric Fellner. *Producer:* Preston Holmes and Jim Steele. *Director:* Mario Van Peebles. *Screenplay:* Sy Richardson and Dario Scardapane. *Director of Photography:* Peter Menzies, Jr. *Editor:* Mark Conte and Seth Flaum. *Music:* Michel Colombier. *Music Editor:* Tom Kramer and Terry Delsing. *Sound:* Don Sanders, Larry Hoki, and (music) Clark Germain. *Sound Editor:* Bruce Stambler. *Casting:* Pat Golden and Barbara Harris. *Production Designer:* Catherine Hardwicke. *Art Director:* Kim Hix. *Set Decorator:* Tessa Posnansky. *Set Dresser:* Matt MaRich, Josh Warner, Charles Scaife, and Jeff J.D. Wiggins. *Special Effects:* Thomas C. Ford. *Costumes:* Paul Simmons. *Make-up:* Alvechia Ewing. *Stunt Co-ordinator:* Bob Minor. *Running time:* 110 minutes. *MPAA Rating:* R.

CAST: Mario Van Peebles (Jessie Lee); Stephen Baldwin (Little J); Charles Lane (Weezie); Tiny Lister (Obobo); Big Daddy Kane (Father Time); Billy Zane (Colonel Graham); Blair Underwood (Carver); Melvin Van Peebles (Papa Joe); Salli Richardson (Lana); Tone Loc (Angel); Pam Grier (Phoebe); Vesta (Vera); Isaac Hayes (Cable); Richard Jordan (Sheriff Bates); Paul Bartel (Mayor Bigwood); Stephen J. Cannell (Jimmy Love); Richard Edson (Deputy Edson); Nipsey Russell (Snopes); Reginald Veljohnson (Preston Van Steele); Woody Strode (Old Man); Reginald Hudlin and Warrington Hudlin (Reporters); Aaron Neville (Railroad Singer); James Bigwood (Walker); Mark Buntzman (Deputy Buntzman); Ismael Calderon (Spanish Soldier); Tracy Lee Chavis (Susan); James E. Christopher (Town Drunk); Lawrence Cook (Cook); Richard Gant (Doubletree); Thomas Steven Hall (Deputy Errol); Clabe Hartley (Klikai); Robert Hooks (King David); Sandra Ellis Lafferty (Big Kate); Jeffrey Lloyd Layne (Little Joseph); Robert May (John the Blacksmith); T.J. McClain (Monty); Christopher Michael (Izzy); Bob Minor (Alex); Steve Reevis (Two Bears); Sy Richardson (Shepherd); Dario Scardapane (Photographer); Frank A. Soto (Aaron); David Jean Thomas (Head Rower); Mark Twogood (Wallace); Karen Williams (Dilsey).

LOS ANGELES TIMES, 5/14/93, Calendar/p. 1, Michael Wilmington

Some movies sneak up on you. Some bowl you over. "Posse" is definitely in the second category: a big, rousing, hip-hopping, trash-talking, dynamite-lobbing, all-stops-out, rock-the-house comic/epic Western that comes at you with both guns blazing and barely lets up for a second.

As directed by lead actor Mario Van Peebles—who showed he had style to burn in the flashy but erratic crime thriller "New Jack City"—this tale of a racially integrated Wild Bunch battling the corrupt Cavalry and land-grabbing Klu Klux Klansmen is defiantly flamboyant. But its excesses are amusing, riveting. Even as the filmmakers and actors go roaring over the top, they keep winking. In scene after scene, you may detect an under-voice chuckling: "You think I can't top the last bit? Think I can't do a Sergio Leone? A George Roy Hill? A Clint Eastwood? Watch *this*."

In barely less than two hours, Van Peebles, cinematographer Peter Menzies and writers Sy Richardson and Dario Scardapane run through virtually every Western structural motif and archetype they can think of: from Hunt-the-Man-Down to Cleaning-Up-the-Town, from holster-slapping six-gun duels to a climactic Gatling Gun holocaust that suggests "The Magnificent Seven" scrambled up with "The Wild Bunch" and "High Noon."

The basic format is pursuit and vendetta. Hero Jesse Lee (Van Peebles), a Cuban-American War Buffalo Soldier with a prison record and a cache of gold, lights out for the territory ahead with evil, sexy Col. Graham (Billy Zane) at his heels, and the "Posse"—Tiny Lister Jr., Tone Loc, Charles Lane, Big Daddy Kane and white brother Stephen Baldwin (the Larry Bird of the group)—at his side. When they reach the African-American township of Freemanville, Jesse finds it besieged by a crooked white sheriff (Richard Jordan) and his silent partner, the bad black marshall (Blair Underwood), who want to sell it to the railroad.

The movie doesn't always make sense. In the beginning, we see an old photo of the entire six-man Posse together, despite the fact that Tone Loc's Angel was killed just as Big Daddy Kane's Father Time joined up. And sometimes it seems less an epic than an all-star romp. Pam Grier, Isaac Hayes, Robert Hooks, Paul Bartel and Nipsey Russell all check in, producer Stephen Cannell appears briefly as Sammy Love, and Mario's father, Melvin Van Peebles, is on hand as wise old Papa Joe, the sagebrush patriarch.

There are barroom brawls and desert treks, jailbreaks, stolen deeds and bordello blowouts and Jesse Lee winds up wearing an Eastwood poncho, a fierce squint and a "Man With No Name" black hat. There's even a schoolmarm (Salli Richardson)—though, since this is the '90s, she has R-rated scenes in a candle-lit boudoir.

Some people may complain that "Posse" is all over the map, but that's what it's obviously trying to do: chew up the map and spit it out ... with a smile. There's more than a flicker of reality under the joke: the fact that the black frontierspeople of history have been slighted or ignored in most Hollywood Westerns. Beginning with a framework that suggests "Little Big Man"—narrator Woody Strode telling us about the hidden history, the Wild West we *don't* know—it tries to right the balance in one huge comic blast.

An impossible task, probably. "Posse" is one of those movies so rich, packed and energetic that they can't get everything they aim for. The two main sub-genres used here—"Outlaw Buddies" and "The Stranger in Town"—don't really mix. How can you light out for the territory ahead when you're really going home? When Jesse Lee hits Freemanville and switches from head of the Posse to lone gun with a wounded past, and a hot schoolmarm, we may resent the fact that some of the mock-Western camaraderie is being dropped.

But "Posse" is descended more from the baroque Westerns anyway: the Leone or Peckinpah movies, the off-center stylistic explosions like "40 Guns" or "Johnny Guitar." It's also a post-MTV movie, scored with Michel Colombier, blues *and* rap, and it tries to keep us in sensory overload—something never more obvious than in the end titles sequence, where Van Peebles gives us snatches of '30s Herb Jeffries Westerns and a shot of Woody Strode in "Once Upon a Time in the West." (Why not Ford"s ultimate Buffalo Soldier movie "Sergeant Rutledge"?)

When all your guns are blazing, you're going to hit more than a few targets, unless you're turned in completely the wrong direction. "Posse" (MPAA-rated R, for violence, sexuality and language) isn't. Violent and over-sexy as this movie may be, offensive as some may find it, it never loses its grinning good humor, its revisionist drive, its shoot-the-works spirit. It's a killer entertainment—with an accent on "kill."

NEW YORK POST, 5/14/93, p. 31, Jami Bernard

First, to get the obvious out of the way—yes, there were black cowboys in the Old West. We just never see any, not counting Morgan Freeman in "Unforgiven."

Actor/director Mario Van Peebles was so annoyed by the conspicuous absence of blacks in Hollywood westerns that he has made one of his own, a spaghetti western of color. He has yet to realize that there were women out West too, other than prostitutes and playthings.

The cast of "Posse" is mostly black (and often thanks to Van Peebles himself, gorgeous to boot), but otherwise it's a fairly dull film. Its appeal rests on the casting—a roll call of rappers, actors and near-legends that is sure to hit pay dirt at the box office. Just to see Big Daddy Kane and Tone Loc as bad-ass cowboys may be enough for some.

But not for others. "Posse" isn't really about anything, despite its flimsy plot about black soldiers returned from the Spanish-American War and being chased all over tarnation by the white officer (Billy Zane) who wants them dead. There's also a revenge thing going on with the posse's charismatic leader, Jesse Lee (Van Peebles), who recalls a trauma from his past in frequent arty flashbacks.

Van Peebles has plenty of jazzy directing talent with the camera, but someone should have shot that script full of lead. It abounds in cliches, deliberate anachronisms and just plain silliness—Jesse rides dustily into town after a harrowing time, only to have his ex-girlfriend complain "You never write!" It's not so bad that it's camp, but not good enough to ignore, either.

Although Van Peebles is the prettiest thing in the movie, he dresses some of the sets with prostitutes whose bosoms are scrunched together. The costume department has decided that a bordello in the Old West should resemble a modern topless bar. If "Posse" is in part an attempt to redress Hollywood's wrongs against blacks, it certainly doesn't mind making its female audience feel just as slighted.

But get a load of this cast—Isaac Hayes, the Hudlin brothers, Pam Grier, Blair Underwood, Charles Lane, Nipsey Russell, Melvin Van Peebles, plus Stephen Baldwin as a with-it white guy (with a supremely silly grin) and Paul Bartel as a mayor.

The younger Van Peebles is heavy into amber tones and romantic vistas, even when they cause more alarm than passion making love on a moving horse, for example, or homo-erotic splashfest among the nude cowboys, not all of whom are as comely as Van Peebles.

Van Peebles' Eastwood-isms don't always work, although they may feed a crowd hungry for black screen heroes. What will really fan the flames, though, is when one character says "F--k this monotonous cowboy bulls--t." Truth is color-blind.

NEW YORK POST, 5/15/93, p. 13, Michael Medved

It's the Posse! Shoot 'em up! Shoot 'em up!" blares the cheerful rap ditty that runs with the end credits of Mario Van Peebles audacious new Western. No one could expect a movie that ends this way to rival "Howards End" (or "Malcolm X") in depth or complexity, but "Posse" fails to deliver even the simple, visceral satisfactions one normally expects from an action adventure.

The innumerable scenes of combat, for instance, are almost laughably incoherent; quick gory shots from all sorts of "artistic" camera angles have been tossed at random into the editor's Cuisinart, and the resulting chaos gives the audience little clue as to what's supposed to be happening.

This makes the goofy plot even more difficult to follow; tracing old adventures of a group of rebellious black soldiers from the battlefields of the Spanish American War (where they abscond with a treasure chest of gold) to their protection of an embattled black colony out in the frontier. After watching nearly a dozen nightmarish flashbacks in black-and-white, we finally begin to figure out that the leader of the posse, Jessie Lee (played by Van Peebles himself) is the product of that utopian community, and that he will stop at nothing to get his revenge against the town's oppressive white neighbors.

In fairness, this is no more preposterous than the plot of many another Western; but Van Peebles tries to use this silly tale to make his own serious statement about America's vicious history.

In one scene, the black cowboys ride past a group of sweating coolies laboring over a rail line as a few destitute Indians look on. "It's the white man's got the problem" one of the posse helpfully explains. "He done enslaved the black man. f---ed the yellow man, and killed the red man."

In addition to such solemn history lessons, the picture also incorporates incongruous references to current events. When Jessie Lee tries to rally the good citizens of Freemanville to attack their racist white neighbors, some of the townsfolk begin chanting, "No justice! No peace!"

Later, in the midst of the final furious fire fight, a cowardly character echoes Rodney King by pleading. "Can't we all get along?" In case anyone missed Van Peebles point that the past and the present are inextricably connected, he provides a helpful crawl at the end explaining that blacks make up 12 percent of our current population but own only one-half of one percent of the nation's wealth.

Meanwhile, the picture squanders its own wealth of talent. Van Peebles demonstrates the same raw energy as a director and the brooding on-screen appeal that he brought to "New Jack City." Another young director, Charles Lane, does an amusing turn here as a fast-talking, diminutive, bespectacled comic-relief character (and Spike Lee stand-in).

Billy Zane and Richard Jordan are both appropriately smarmy as evil racist villains: Robert Hooks, Pam Grier, Isaac Hayes, and Paul Bartel make cameo appearances, while the gifted and ingratiating Stephen Baldwin plays the only white member of the posse. He may not be black, but he is definitely a brother—in his case, younger brother of red-hot actors Alec and William Baldwin.

The real shame in all this is that the fascinating subject matter deserves better treatment. Some future film might make the public aware of the formidable role of former slaves on the American frontier, or the stirring history of real-life black townships in the far West, in the same way that the superb "Glory" called wide attention for the first time to the heroic black participation in the civil War.

But "Posse" is so concerned with its own desire to be hip and contemporary that it is riddled with embarrassing anachronisms. The musical numbers that turn up so often in the story are one particularly sorry example, with various characters in 1898 enjoying the sort of urban entertainments that didn't in fact develop until many decades later. It should come as no surprise that Mario Van Peebles is listed as producer of the "very smokin' soundtrack album on A&M Records." He will probably end up doing better with that project than he will with this ambitious but disappointing film.

NEWSDAY, 5/14/93, Part II/p. 71, John Anderson

Mario Van Peebles not only wants to correct history, he wants to remake every Western that ever ignored the role of blacks on the American frontier. He should not, however, have tried to remake them all in one movie.

"Posse," a rough-ridin', quick-shootin' saga of greed, revenge, romance and rawhide, borrows from a broad range of movies—notably "The Magnificent Seven," "Butch Cassidy," and "High Noon"—with select appropriations from John Ford, Sam Peckinpah and Sergio Leone. But rather than becoming the sum of its parts, the film is a dizzying display of facile technique and oblique intentions.

In an attempt to apply a scholarly patina to a rather standard adventure story, "Posse" is bookended by scenes featuring the veteran actor Woody Strode as the Old Man, whose reminiscences about the black cowboys are being recorded by two history students (played by filmmakers Reginald and Warrington Hudlin). Giving black frontiersmen their due, of course, is overdue, but Van Peebles lays it on too thick.

While Van Peebles has taken the quasi-novel tack of making a Western with nearly all-black cast, "Posse" still avails itself of all the standard accessories. There's the band of divergent, hard-bitten but good-hearted cowboys (rappers Tone Loc and Big Daddy Kane, wrestler Tiny Lister, director Charles Lane); the gang's token minority (the white Stephen Baldwin); the malevolent, homicidal villain (in this case, two, Richard Jordan and Billy Zane); the woman who waits (Salli Richardson), and the hero she waits for—a man who, while he might exhibit many of the same traits as the villain, is a lot better looking and manages not to kill the wrong people.

Given the self-indulgence that virtually gallops through "Posse," it's no surprise the hero is played by Van Peebles himself: Jesse Lee, of the sleeveless denim shirts and well-oiled biceps, who avoided prison by being sentences to life in the Army. Where he ends up, though, makes Sing Sing seem like Club Fed: Cuba, 1897, the Spanish-American War, where the black soldiers do the dirty work for a mad colonel named Graham (Zane). Graham wants the Spaniards' gold, Jesse finds it first, and in the ensuing gun battle he shoots out Graham's eye and heads off with the booty.

With a vengeful colonel on his tail, Jesse and his band make their way to Freemanville, a community of former slaves. It was there that Jesse's father, the preacher King David (Robert Hooks), was murdered by white vigilantes, and Jesse wants revenge. Along the way he'll become The Man With No Name, the Lone Ranger and, considering his hat, Zorro. He'll also fight the good fight, win the girl and come to terms with his demons. Just like the Duke.

Van Peebles is an exciting filmmaker who can be both hip and thoughtful; "New Jack City," proved that. In "Posse," however, he's disastrously cavalier about what he wants to do. There are visual references to the Rodney King beating, for instance, and then, during the explosive, climactic battle in Freemanville, someone asks "Can't we get along?" It's a laugh line, and a tasteless one. When the railroad threatens Freemanville, Papa Joe (Melvin Van Peebles) vows "No Justice, No Peace!" The effect again, is to amuse. But then, by the end of "Posse," the history lesson and the political provocation seem to have taken second billing to show biz.

SIGHT AND SOUND, 12/93, p. 49, Nick James

An elderly black man sits at a desk, showing his collection of photos of the old West to an interview team. After passing round a Colt .45 Peacemaker, he explains how in the years after the emancipation of slaves, one in every three cowboys was black. He then tells the story of Jessie Lee and his posse ...

Lee and his comrades Obobo and the white Little J are serving in the US Army fighting in the 1892 Spanish-American war under the ruthless white adventurer, Colonel Graham. Graham sends them to capture a supply column, which proves to be laden with gold. Then he and his Iron Brigade ambush Lee's posse on their return. However, Lee's men beat them off, take the gold and escape to the US via Cuba with the help of Graham's black valet, Weezie. Graham tracks them down to New Orleans where Little J has picked up a gambling partner, Father Time. The posse flee north towards Lee's boyhood home, Cutter's Town, where he seeks vengeance on the local Ku Klux Klan. Lee's preacher father dreamt of a town for blacks called Freemanville, but the church he built was destroyed and he was crucified by a KKK gang led by Bates, the Cutter's Town sheriff. They also thrashed the helpless young Lee, and had him conscripted to military service. Freemanville has since been rebuilt and the black townsfolk, under the influence of their own Sheriff Carver, are wary of Lee. While he is visiting his childhood sweetheart Lana at her father's settlement, Bates and his gang confront the remaining posse members in the saloon. Little J tries to protect Weezie, but he is dragged outside and beaten to death, When Lee returns, he persuades the townsfolk to protect themselves, informing them that the sheriff wants to destroy them because the railroad is coming through their now valuable land.

In the final shoot-out, Colonel Graham arrives just as Bates's men are beaten, and unveils a Gatling gun. Meanwhile Carver, who is in league with Bates, tries to escape. Having blown up the Gatling, Lee confronts them both. Bates shoots Carver and Lee guns Bates down. Seeing that Graham has taken Lana captive, Lee lays down his gun. Then Graham is distracted by Obobo and while he shoots him, Lee recovers his gun from a small boy and exacts revenge. Obobo survives because Graham's bullet struck a book of psalms that Lee had given him, from which Lee recites his father's favourite, "Nicodemus Was A Slave." The elderly storyteller reveals that he was that small boy who helped Jessie Lee.

The first mainstream Black Western ought to be a cause for genre celebration, and Mario Van Peebles shows that he has seen enough cowboy movies to want to cram in as many stock situations and plot points as will fit the frame. Posse glitters with gold teeth, gold bullets and sunsets. Situations are hijacked from the entire Eastwood-Leone Western *oeuvre* as well as from *The Magnificent Seven* and the obligatory John Ford. However, one looks in vain for a new reviving perspective on these trailworn set-ups.

Van Peebles' portrayal of Jessie Lee pushes the quiet enigma of the Man With No Name towards an absence of performance that no amount of motivational flashback can enhance. He smoulders beautifully, yet looks, in his black leather chaps, about as deadly as Dirk Bogarde in

The Singer Not the Song. Furthermore, the action is poorly paced—shots are given equal weight and are cut together in an MTV-style frenzy without any apparent consideration for their impact. Much of the intertextual fun that might have been derived from rap star Tone Loc saying things as "what muthafuckin' plan?" in an 1890s setting—not to mention the premature existence of the pumpaction shotgun—is muted by frenzied attempts at Western comedy, such as two scenes of skinny-dipping frolics. Swamped for the most of the time under gimmicky props that would shame a Western theme park, none of the actors seems comfortable enough to give anything more than a knowing flash of a performance.

For a film that spreads its plot over so much of North and Central America, there's also very little feel for changes in terrain. Where directors like Ford, Leone and Eastwood let the landscape impose upon the film as if it are a lead character, Van Peebles makes the wide open spaces look incidental. The sky becomes a screen for in-your-face flashbacks to Lee's beatings, and the camera will pan into the sun rather than allow Monument Valley to hog a scene.

There's a strong feeling throughout that the combination of a mostly black cast and an easy translation of street gang dynamics to the old West is enough innovation for the film's producers. Re-writing and filming black *hombres* into history might be a laudable aim, but as with so many other attempts to revive the Western, *Posse* puts its heroes into a milieu where the only history that's relevant is the genesis of TV shows such as *Gunsmoke* or *The Virginian*.

VILLAGE VOICE, 5/25/93, p. 53, J. Hoberman

Riding the commercial success of *New Jack City* further along the genre trail, Mario Van Peebles takes to the western with a strident whoop and holler. *Posse* is a showy, kinetic jumble—a stylized cacophony of mad tilts, swirling camera maneuvers, and overlapping everything.

Posse, which also stars Van Peebles as ace gunman Jesse Lee, is not a modest effort. Nodding briefly to John Ford, the movie is a pastiche that draws most heavily on Sergio Leone, whose spaghetti westerns were famously endorsed by the Black Panthers. The action is punctuated by mock Peckinpah explosions of violence (minus the spurting blood); even the atmosphere of random clowning and use of purposeful anachronism evoke *Blazing Saddles*.

Indeed, an overwrought style is what holds the movie together as, shifting mood and camera angle with impunity, it Jumps from Cuban battlefield to Storyville bordello to a utopian black township somewhere out West. Piling cosmic superimpositions upon sepia flashbacks, *Posse* manages to be consistently in your face and weirdly detached—it has the amber-hued spectrum and concentrated incoherence of a barroom brawl contemplated through a full glass of whiskey.

There are reportedly 16 westerns in current development (we can look forward to Tamra Davis's *Bad Girls*, Walter Hill's *Geronimo*, two rival Wyatt Earp stories, an Eddie Murphy vehicle, and an adaptation of the TV show *Maverick* starring Mel Gibson), and to judge from what has arrived, the genre is painfully picking itself up and stiffly marching on from the point where it expired in the early '70s. As *Dances With Wolves* revived the anticavalry mode of *Little Big Man* and *Soldier Blue*, and *Unforgiven* built on the late tradition of the "dirty" western, so *Posse* develops the thesis of Sidney Poitier's *Buck and the Preacher* and Fred Williamson's "Nigger Charlie" vehicles—westerns that identified African Americans with Native Americans and posited the frontier as a postslavery promised land.

Posse's Freemanville, founded under the slogan "Education Is Freedom," is a North American equivalent to Brazil's revolutionary Quilombo. There's a powerfully zionist moment, when the posse arrives in this western town presided over by a black sheriff, populated by black bankers, black matrons, black blacksmiths, black ranch hands, black hostelers, and black hookers—many of them played by the black movie stars of the '60s and '70s. The most suggestive is Van Peebles's own pioneering father, Melvin, whose character wears a blue bandana, smokes a corncob pipe, and playfully sells his beautiful "daughter" (Salli Richardson) to young Jesse Lee.

The film's tone is confidently nationalist. It's a given that the Freemanville sheriff is not to be depended on when he espouses class rather than race solidarity. *Posse* is even more purposeful than *New Jack City* as a genre corrective. More than 25 per cent of the cowhands who worked the West were African American, with a particularly heavy concentration in Oklahoma and Texas. There were also numerous black scouts and Indian fighters, as well as black cavalry regiments. That the western has been so stubbornly white suggests a larger pattern of denial.

Like baseball, the western was an integral part of America's new, post-Civil War national mythology. The fetishized 30-year period between the end of the Civil War and the closing of the frontier coincides exactly with that of Reconstruction and the establishment of an American form of apartheid. While "race" westerns were produced as early as 1916 (and independent talkies like *Harlem on the Prairie* and *Bronze Buckaroo* still turn up in series devoted to African American film production), the western wasn't really integrated until Woody Strode starred in Ford's *Sergeant Rutledge*, released 13 years after Jackie Robinson broke the major-league color line—and even then it was strictly fits and starts.

That *Posse* is also a western about black westerns is suggested by the epilogue, which has the now elderly Strode being interviewed by the elaborately gaga Hudlin brothers—and the movie is generous almost to a fault in providing cameos for Pam Grier, Isaac Hayes, Robert Hooks, Aaron Neville, and Nipsey Russell. The large supporting cast ranges from rap artist Big Daddy Kane, as a brooding gambler, to filmmaker Charles Lane, as Jesse's rabbity, motor-mouthed sidekick. (It's Lane who has the movie's baddest line, interrupting an orgiastic mass shoot-out with a quavery "Can't we all just get along?") The white authority figures—Richard Jordan, Billy Zane, Paul Bartel, Richard Edson—are all uniformly vivid, with Stephen Baldwin in an ironic variation on the sort of token role played by Strode in *The Professionals*, Jim Brown in *Rio Conchos*, or Ossie Davis in *The Scalphunters*.

Unfortunately, the acting appearances are mainly that—with Van Peebles's stylishly moody and taciturn hero setting the tone. Like the movie, his is an ambitiously narcissistic performance, in which the director-star keeps sneaking up on his stylish self in fractured 360-degree pans (a reminder that the anagram of Posse is Poses). *Posse* confirms that Van Peebles has ideas, likes actors, can orchestrate action, and possesses a sly sense of humor. The problem is modulation. *Posse* falls apart at—any hint of drama.

The love scenes in particular are worthy of *In Living Color*. At the promo screening I attended, the audience laughed in derision when Van Peebles was sequestered with Richardson in a candle-lit grotto. The credit sheet doesn't list an editor, but you can bet that he, she, or they had to work overtime—submerging Van Peebles's expression of stricken cool in a frantic softcore montage, crosscut with the vocalizing of an MTV-friendly soul chanteuse.

Also reviewed in:
CHICAGO TRIBUNE, 5/14/93, Friday/p. C, Dave Kehr
NEW REPUBLIC, 6/14/93, p. 30, Stanley Kauffmann
NEW YORK TIMES, 5/14/93, p. C15, Janet Maslin
VARIETY, 5/3/93, p. 40, Todd McCarthy
WASHINGTON POST, 5/14/93, p. B1, Hal Hinson
WASHINGTON POST, 5/14/93, Weekend/p. 44, Desson Howe

PRAYING WITH ANGER

A UnaPix Entertainment and Cinevista release of a Crescent Moon Pictures film.   *Producer:* M. Night Shyamalan.   *Director:* M. Night Shyamalan.   *Screenplay:* M. Night Shyamalan. *Director of Photography:* Madhu Ambat.   *Editor:* Frank Reynolds.   *Music:* Edmund K. Choi. *Sound:* Annette Danto.   *Art Director:* Krishnamurthy.   *Running time:* 101 minutes. *MPAA Rating:* Not Rated.

CAST: M. Night Shyamalan (Dev Raman);   Mike Muthu (Sunjay Mohan);   Capt. K. Subramanian (Principal Balaji);   Arun Balachandran (Raj Kahn);   Richa Ahuja (Rupal Mohan); Christabal Howie (Sabitha);   Sushma Ahuja (Mrs. Mohan);   Apajit Singh (Mr. Mohan);   S.K. Veeragavan (Swami);   S.N. Parvathi (Usha-spirit Lady);   S.M. Sivakumar (Professor);   K. Karthik (Senior #1);   R. Vijay Kumar (Senior #2);   Vinodh (Senior #3);   N.R. Santhanam (Cottage Caretaker);   S. Sundar (Guest at Wedding);   V.L. Narasimhan (Man in Riot); Professor C. Kalidass (Professor);   Ravi (Driver);   K. Vijalakshmi (Sunset dancer).

NEW YORK POST, 9/15/93, p. 26, Jerry Tallmer

The most extraordinary thing about "Praying With Anger" is that this full-length feature film was made, with the money of family and friends (something under a million dollars), by a young man—an NYU Film School graduate—who is only now 23 years old. He wrote it, produced it, directed it, stars in it. Actually the most extraordinary thing is that it isn't really a bad movie.

The young man's name is M. Night Shyamalan, and his movie is about a brash-yet-sensitive American boy—Dev, pronounced Dave—who, after having had to fight against being knocked about in a Waspy prep school, is sent by his widowed mother to live for some disciplining months in a household in India, the land his parents came from. A boy, in short, not unlike M. Night Shyamalan. The ensuing cultural and semi-romantic conflicts—and needless to say, the conflict within Dev himself—are what the movie is all about.

Even before Dev, whose only language is English, arrives in Madras, the suspicious, tradition-minded mother in the host family is asking: "What if he's one of those crazy Americans with earrings?" To which her husband replies: "We hide the jewelry." It takes Dev a long time to make friends, good friends, with Sunjay (Mike Muthu), the son his own age, and even longer to win the confidence of Sunjay's pretty sister Rupal (Richa Ahuja), herself a teen-age rebel in love with a bank teller below her caste, from the less desirable regions to the north.

At school the uptight principal takes an even less flattering view of Dev, writing him off as a trouble-making rowdy. The real troublemaker is a bully named Raj Khan, a Muslim in the senior class who gets on Dev's case and won't let up. The crisis at the end of the movie involves Dev and Raj Khan (Arun Balachandran) in a life-and-death moment—somewhat parallel to recent events in Crown Heights—when a street mob wants to incinerate Raj Khan after a traffic accident.

There is also in the school the lovely-looking Sabitha (Christabal Howie), and Dev, in chatting her up, makes one bad mistake: his hand brushes her shoulder. This, for a well-bred Hindu girl, effectively ends their relationship, or non-relationship, for two or three reels. Dev will presently learn something about the purer emotions from her, just as he'll learn something on a visit to his dead father's village about the true emotions of that father he could never get along with. And he'll learn of course, about his own roots.

The most amusing aspect of the picture is the question—"Have you ever met Michael Jackson?"—repeatedly put to the foreigner by all and sundry, man, woman and child, from first to last, even by a swami to whom Dev goes for advice. I'd hate to think that "Praying With Anger" is getting released just at this time because of the current headlines from Hollywood.

VILLAGE VOICE, 9/28/93, p. 64, Tiarra Mukherjee

When those who've been voiceless get the chance to speak, clarity is often sacrificed by the desire to tell everything. *Praying With Anger*, the first feature from 22-year-old director, producer, writer, and star M. Night Shyamalan, attempts to cram 5000 years of Indian culture into 101 minutes. Shot entirely on location in Madras, India, it is the story of Dev Ramon (Shyamalan), an extremely Americanized Indian American who travels to India, on his mother's insistence, as an exchange student. Through conflicts—rigid academic environment, antagonistic bullies, doomed love, a neatly packaged religious riot—he finds his identity and discovers his true homeland.

While Shyamalan is successful at depicting aspects of Indian tradition—religion, family, love, marriage, bias, education, spirituality—he fails to ground them in a coherent plot. Heavy-handed narration keeps telling us that Indians are intensely passionate and that there's more to India than a vast *City of Joy* slum. But we already know that from cinematographer Madhu Ambat's beautiful images of daily life: kids playing in the sunset, villagers washing clothes in the river, intricate interiors of dimly lit Hindu temples.

Anger is an impressive attempt to portray the consciousness of first-generation Indian Americans, and it's easy to understand Shymalan's effort to overexplain. But now he and those who follow him need to trust that their characters have stories interesting enough to stand alone.

Also reviewed in:
NEW YORK TIMES, 9/15/93, p. C26, Stephen Holden
VARIETY, 10/5/92, p. 65, Joe Leydon

PROGRAM, THE

A Touchstone Pictures and Samuel Goldwyn Company release. *Executive Producer:* Duncan Henderson and Tom Rothman. *Producer:* Samuel Goldwyn, Jr. *Director:* David S. Ward. *Screenplay:* David S. Ward and Aaron Latham. *Director of Photography:* Victor Hammer. *Editor:* Paul Seydor and Kimberly Ray. *Music:* Michel Colombier. *Music Editor:* Tom Kramer. *Sound:* Robert J. Anderson, Jr. and (music) Clark Germain. *Sound Editor:* Richard E. Yawn. *Casting:* Lynn Stalmaster. *Production Designer:* Albert Brenner. *Art Director:* Carol Winstead Wood. *Set Designer:* Harold Fuhrman. *Set Decorator:* Kathe Klopp. *Set Dresser:* Scott A. Carruth, Eric J. Luling, and Sarah Quinn. *Special Effects:* Joe Di Gaetano, III. *Costumes:* Tom Bronson. *Make-up:* Susan A. Cabral. *Stunt Coordinator:* Allan Graf. *Running time:* 112 minutes. *MPAA Rating:* R.

CAST: James Caan (Coach Winters); Halle Berry (Autumn); Omar Epps (Darnell Jefferson); Craig Sheffer (Joe Kane); Kristy Swanson (Camille); Abraham Benrubi (Bud-Lite); Duane Davis (Alvin Mack); Jon Maynard Pennell (Bobby Collins); Joey Adams (Louanne); J.C. Quinn (Joe's Father); Andrew Bryniarski (Steve Lattimer); J. Leon Pridgen, II (Ray Griffen); Mike Flippo (Coach Humes); Jeff Portell (Reporter #1); Ernest Dixon (Coach Clayton); George Rogers (Coach Myers); Bernard Mixon (Reverend Wallace); Mary Halloway (Alvin's Mother); Steven Griffith (Joe's Brother); George Nannarello (Advisor Smith); Jason Byce (Athletic Director Howard); Mindy Bell (Sharon Braver); Jim Fyfe (Nichols); Jason Jenks (Alvin's Tutor); Bob Neal (Brad Harvey); Albert Haynes (Mississippi Tailback); Andre Farr (Mississippi Tackle); Jed Oldenburg (History T.A.); Lynn Swann (Himself); Bo Schembechler (Himself); Robert Fuller (Tim Waymen); Al Wiggins (Mr. Haley); Lynelle Lawrence (Leslie); Julia Miller (Debbi); Patrick Smith (Debbi's Boyfriend); Dan Hannafin (Regent Chairman); Charles Portney (Richard Fowler); John Bennes (Edward Learnihan); Charles Lawlor (Charles Shane); Deanna Perry (Rehab Nurse); Tim Parati (Steroids Dealer); Robert D. Raiford (Chancellor Wilson); George Lee (Fat Cat Alumnus); Chris Berman (Himself); Leslie Broucker (Trainer); Roger Bright (E.S.U. Doctor); J. Don Ferguson (Referee); Rhoda Griffis (Reporter #3); Steve Zabriskie (Himself); John R. Murphy (History Professor); Robert Hook (Trainer); Tracy Fowler (Orderly).

LOS ANGELES TIMES, 9/24/93, Calendar/p. 8, Peter Rainer

Long stretches of "The Program" resemble the kind of crunch-and-thud football footage that sells "Sports Illustrated" subscriptions on ESPN. The action is swift and brutal and well-paced—all highlights.

When the action is away from the field, writer-director David Ward and his co-screenwriter, Aaron Latham, are trying for all highlights too, but of a different sort. They want to show how the high-powered world of college athletics has become corrupted by greed and the limelight. They also want to show how innocence—the sheer love of the game—can survive the corruption.

Sports have been used so often in the movies, and in literature, as a microcosm for whatever is supposed to be ailing society that the sport itself often gets short shrift. Whenever a sports film comes along that actually takes the game on its own exuberant terms without a lot of metaphorical curlicues—like Ron Shelton's "White Men Can't Jump," for example—it has an almost cleansing effect. Sports movies are often best when they travel light.

"The Program" (rated R for language) tries to travel light *and* heavy, and the combination of noggin-banging action and deep-think doesn't gel. Latham, who has previously bestowed upon us the ersatz pop reportage of "Urban Cowboy" and "Perfect," doesn't tunnel very deep into the world of college athletics. What he and Ward come up with is fairly standard stuff that seems derived mostly from old movies.

There's veteran Eastern State University coach Sam Winters (James Caan), who knows when to talk tough to his helmeted brood and when to coddle them. Joe Kane (Craig Sheffer) is the cocky, daredevil quarterback with working-class roots and an uncaring, alcoholic father. Freshman tailback Darnell Jefferson (Omar Epps), recruited from the ghetto, has his eye on campus cutie Autumn (Halle Berry), who is, of course, dating the *starting* tailback (J. Leon Pridgen II), who is, of course, bound for medical school (i.e. he's really a wimp). Autumn tutors Darnell in his studies and he, in turn, tutors her in the ways of the world.

By the time the Big Game rolls around, we've been put through more subplots than a six-hour mini-series. The commercial calculation behind this film seems to be that in order to have a successful football movie—one that appeals to more than beer-chugging behemoths—you have to cover your investment by attracting just about everybody. If the film had, stayed with just one of the stories—Darnell's, say—it might have managed some depth. Instead, we have a gridlock of soap-opera mini-stories: a colliding shallowness.

Movies that come out in favor of winning for winning's sake aren't in particularly high favor in these post-Reagan days. Instead, what we get are hedges. "Searching for Bobby Fischer," for example, told us that winning isn't everything, while, of course, pinning everything on the chess prodigy's ultimate victory. "The Program" tries to have it both ways, too. It shows us the emotional and physical pitfalls of winning—one of the players (Andrew Bryniarski) pumps himself up with so many steroids that he makes Conan seem like Don Knotts—but it also opts for rah-rah uplift.

Just about the only performance that doesn't seem wildly overscaled, or pallid, is Caan's. He's not in the movie a whole lot; his periodic appearances chewing out the squad or smoothing out a scandal are basically a series of cameos. But at least his jaw-clenching and teeth-baring have an old pro's skill and good humor behind them. Caan is the coach in this movie in more ways than one.

NEW YORK POST, 9/26/93, p. 42, Matthew Flamm

The quarterback has an alcoholic father and a budding drinking problem of his own. The defensive linebacker can barely read. Another player's on steroids, another cheats on his exams, and the coach may lose his job.

"The Program," a lavishly produced college-football movie features brutally authentic scrimmages, rousing stadium scenes, and leafy backdrops of campus life. It's just too bad the story came out of a handy screenplay starter kit, in which every character has a tidy little conflict and everyone gets what they deserve.

This makes "The Program," which is essentially a year in the life of a college football program, a lot more boring than it should be. Anyone who can't figure out that star quarterback Joe Kane (Craig Sheffer) will confront his father and his own demons by the end of the film's fourth quarter should be forced to take Remedial Movie Going—twice.

"The Program," which has been directed by David Ward ("Major League") and scripted by him and Aaron Latham ("Perfect"), attempts to use the team to address various up-to-the-minute social problems. So backup tailback Parnell Jefferson (Omar Epps), a dark-skinned African American straight from the slums, has to fall for the well-dressed, well-spoken Autumn (Halle Berry).

Naturally, Autumn already has a boyfriend—a middle-class, lightskinned black, who turns out to be the *starting* tailback. For these moviemakers, broad strokes mean the kind you can see from the nosebleed seats.

To its credit, "The Program" allows for an occasional shade of gray. James Caan gives a nicely laid-back performance as Coach Winters, a shrewd professional who can look the other way at transgressions if his job requires it.

"We're not doctors," coach tells his assistants when it becomes apparent that a player—who's currently needed on the team—is using steroids. (Nobody argues.)

The movie, which takes place at fictional Eastern State University, also does a decent job showing how bred-to-win athletes fall apart when they lose—Kane getting picked up for drunk driving after the game, and the steroid abuser attempting date rape.

According to the production notes, Latham, a magazine journalist, did extensive research for the script; and if there's nothing in the film that approaches the brilliance of "North Dallas Forty," "The Program" at least seems ... researched. There are some nice moments of football-as-primitive-rite—two pumped-up defensive teammates spitting into each other's mouths—and a look at how a Heisman Trophy campaign is conducted by the school's hired-gun publicist.

Of course, the publicist is a pinched, homely woman with glasses, accompanied by a worm of an assistant. It's not just that the filmmakers take a beat-them-over-the-head approach with "The Program." It's that they seem to think those heads have helmets on.

NEWSDAY, 9/24/93, Part II/p. 63, Gene Seymour

No one who pays close attention to the sports page will be shocked or scandalized by what "The Program" says about big-time college football. The whole nine yards, so to speak, is here: alumni payoffs, steroid abuse, athletes earning credit from such challenging courses as "Intermediate Golf" and "Swimming Pool Management."

The movie, to its credit assumes its audience knows all this stuff going in. Having made this assumption, director-writer David S. Ward ("Major League") and his co-scriptwriter, Aaron Latham ("Urban Cowboy"), broaden their focus, spiking this generally predictable college football yarn with pointed observation and a slick, rueful irony that both celebrates and chides the sport.

The top-billed James Caan is practically a supporting player given the screen time allowed the younger, lesser-known actors. Still, Caan, the best befuddled he-man this side of James Garner, makes the most of his role as Sam Winters, football coach of mythical Eastern State University, who, for all his field savvy and toughness, seems overmatched against the problems he has to face during this regular season.

Like, for instance, a Heisman-candidate quarterback (Craig Sheffer), whose well-cultivated Joe Cool aura shields a swarm of self-doubt he keeps at bay by hitting the bottle hard. Or a defensive player (Abraham Benrubi), who tries to overcome his lack of natural ability with heavy doses of bluster and steroids. Or a backup quarterback (Jon Maynard Pennell) who gets the coach's daughter to take a test for him.

Amid such turmoil, first-year halfback Darnell Jefferson (Omar Epps from "Juice") struggles to keep his grades respectable and secure more playing time. Darnell's also trying to make more time with Autumn (Halle Berry), his bewitching tutor, who happens to be the main squeeze of the hunk (J. Leon Pridgen II), whose starting job he's trying to get. This subplot, standard-issue in most young-jock melodramas, is freshly seasoned with interracial-class conflict.

Given the flimsy characterizations that marred Ward's "Major League" and the mean-spiritness that often surfaced in Latham's script for the dismal "Perfect," it's hard to believe that their script so nicely depicts such anomalies as the mad-dog linebacker (Duane Davis in a bravura turn) who can't get himself to care about memorizing historic dates, but is a demon intellectual when it comes to complex defensive plays. One such stunt requires him, as he says, to "hit the tight end so hard, his girlfriend dies." The playing sequences, by the way, are as well-staged as the TV trailers suggest.

For all its smarts, "The Program" just barely succeeds in balancing the frenzied contradictions in its own point-of-view about the game. Being a prototypical commercial Hollywood film, it inevitably sells itself out with a rousing finish that dispels many of its darker shadows. (But not all of them.)

While it's no threat to "North Dallas Forty's" pre-eminence among football flicks (the cream of which, at best, amounts to a very small puddle), "The Program" adds just enough pungency to its familiar mixture to make it one of the season's minor surprises.

Also reviewed in:
NEW YORK TIMES, 9/24/93, p. C16, Janet Maslin
VARIETY, 10/4/93, p. 38, Brian Lowry
WASHINGTON POST, 9/24/93, p. C7, Hal Hinson

PUPPETMASTER, THE

An Era International presentation of a City Films production. *Executive Producer:* Michael Yang and Zhan Hongzhi. *Producer:* Qiu Fusheng. *Director:* Hou Hsiao-Hsien. *Screenplay (Taiwanese, Mandarin, and Japanese with English subtitles):* Wu Nien-jen and Chu Tien-wen. *Based on the memoirs of:* Li Tien-lu. *Director of Photography:* Lee Pin-Bing. *Editor:* Liao

Ching-sung. *Music:* Chen Ming-Chang and Zhan Hongda. *Sound:* Meng Qilang and Du Duzhi. *Art Director:* Zhang Hong, Cai Zhaoyi, Lu Mingjin, He Xianke, Liu Nanyang, and Chen Shunfa Costumes: Zhang Guanghui, Ruan Peiyun, and Fang Yuping. *Make-up:* Liao Shuzhen. *Running time:* 142 minutes. *MPAA Rating:* Not Rated.

CAST: Li Tianlu (Himself); Lim Giong (Li Tianlu, Young Adult); Chen Kuizhong (Li Tianlu, Teenager); Zuo Juwei (Li Tianlu, Child); Hong Liu (Li Hei, Grandfather); Bai Minghua (Ong Hsiu, Grandmother); Cai Zhennan (Ko Meng-Dang, Father); Gao Dongxiu (Li Nee, Mother); Yang Liyin (Lai Hwat, Stepmother); Chen Qianru (Tan Dei, Wife); Wu Layun (Tan Shing, Grandfather-in-law); Chen Bocan (Tan Ah-Lai, Father-in-law); Li Wenbin (Tan Shik-Hong, Son); Cai Yihua (Li Giao-Ngo, Daughter); Lu Fulu (Grand Uncle); Liu Nanyang and Lin Shuiqing (Grand Uncles); Chen Shufang (Jin Huanshu); Yang Caiming (Lao Shakui); Cai Qiufeng (A-Chun); Chen Yishan (Big Eyes); Xiao Hudou (Ko Wong-Lai); Chen Xiaohui (Leitzu); Zheng Yalin (A-Gui); Yi Toshiro (Kawakami); Hino Asako (Kawakami's Wife); Imura Jun (Policeman); Notomi Toshio (Commander); Hogari Taro (Japanese Soldier); Takemoto Yasumasa (Kubo, Leader of Propulsion Unit); Obi Ryuji and Liao Gaole (Supervisors); Chen Xihuang (Tribal Chief); Wu Rongchang (Lu Jiao); Yu Qingxian (Huomu); Cai Zhaoyi (Zhi-zai); Lu Mingium (Sweet Potato); Wang Caihua (A-Zhi); Guo Yuefeng (Matchmaker); Lai Tingmei and Zhu Jinwen (Midwives); Lin Quan (Photographer); Liu Shunfa (Postman in Xiamen).

CHRISTIAN SCIENCE MONITOR, 10/12/93, p. 14, David Sterritt

[*The Puppetmaster* was reviewed jointly with *Raining Stones*; see Sterritt's review of that film.]

NEW STATESMAN, 5/13/94, p. 34, Jonathan Romney

Li Tien Lu, the subject of *The Puppetmaster*, has quite a story to tell, but the Taiwanese director Hou Hsiao Hsien chooses to tell it in anything but the obvious way. His film is like the rambling divagation of a bar-room raconteur—and his most surprising stroke is not to tell us until a third of the way through that there's a raconteur present, or even what the story is about. It's only when Li's voice-over is more often heard, especially when his rakish, 85-year-old presence comes to occupy centre-screen, that we start finding our way around his life. Even then, things aren't that easy.

They rarely are in Hou's films. That is largely because of their extraordinary ambitions. In conventional terms, you might describe his vast representations of modern Taiwanese history as "epic canvases", but they don't afford the easy satisfactions of epics. Rather, with an austere style that makes no concession to audience-pleasing, they're a kind of amplified chamber-cinema, huge but intimate.

Hou is certainly one of the most serious directors on the world scene. In *The Puppetmaster* he has said that he attempts to define "the Chinese people's attitude to life", no less, through his extraordinary central figure. Li is a veteran marionettist who has already appeared in memorable grandfather roles in several other Hou films, and here appears in person to tell the story of his life.

Again, Hou attempts to come to terms with a specific stretch of recent history. His 1989 film *A City of Sadness* dealt with the first five years of Taiwan's reversion to Chinese rule in 1945 after 51 years as a Japanese colony. Its sprawling cast and diversity of incident made it remarkably difficult viewing, and not just, one suspects, for western audiences.

The length of takes and refusal to provide easy signposts betokened a director whose commitment to complex experience meant that he was willing to push the chronicle form to the limits of viewer tolerance. You can contrast it with the equally complex but more user-friendly Taiwanese saga, Edward Yang's *A Brighter Summer Day*, which benefited from the use of western soap-opera conventions.

By Hou's standards, *The Puppetmaster* is a relatively easy ride, and the fact that it's one man's life story helps. What still makes it demanding is the story's piecemeal construction. Instead of a single thread, it's all tangled yarns. Some fit comfortably into a readable chronology, others run at odds with it, as storyline and characters come to the foreground then suddenly disappear. But that seems to be the film's point—the nature both of personal memory and of history, which defies attempts to whip it into shape.

Hou gives us the briefest acquaintance with a succession of characters—Li's family, children, wife, mistress, soldiers, and colleagues, who drift in and out of his story, sometimes dying just when we're learning to identify them. Often the life doesn't yield up the easy dramas we expect.

Li's childhood is tough but not dreadful—he incurs a beating from a stepmother, but it's presented as par for the course. The action drifts off-screen while the camera remains fixed, surveying the room. The young Li learns to be a puppeteer and joins a troupe, but there's none of the drama of apprenticeship we might expect. He takes up with a prostitute, but the obvious conflict with his marriage never intrudes. We experience the life the way Li tells it (the film's based on the memoirs he began to serialise in 1990). Loose, floating interludes to camera seem to dictate the whole rhythm.

The film is remarkably matter-of-fact about Li's life which displays all the pragmatic flexibility of the born survivor. It's anything but a hagiography, but any sense that Li is being idealised is only insofar as he is identified with Taiwan itself. He's still here to tell us his story in person; and so, by analogy, is Taiwan. (The film ends in 1945, with the end of Japanese rule.) In all these static tableaux, we're never allowed too close to the characters. We see everything either through proscenium-like spaces the camera creates or through Li's accounts, which often come in to explain after a mystifying event. The more he explains, the more we're aware that life and memory can't be pieced unproblematically together. The other characters remain subsidiary figures, their identity often veiled in Hou's dense chiaroscuro compositions. They're the puppets in Li's account of himself. Putting the pieces together is a demanding task for the viewer, and not one that provides a tidy payoff. But the film has a rare authority: partly because old men's yarns command respect, but mainly because hard cases do as well.

SIGHT AND SOUND, 6/94, p. 51, Philip Kemp

Actor and puppetmaster Li Tianlu, born in Taiwan in 1909, who has appeared in several of Hou Hsiao-Hsien's films, relates the story of his life. ... At the celebration of his first birthday his grandfather Li Hei is warned by a fortune-teller that the child will bring bad luck on his parents. As a schoolboy, Li is disgraced when he steals books from his great-uncle's house. The Japanese, rulers of Taiwan since 1895, decree that all Taiwanese must cut off their pigtails; the official conveying the order to Li's family gives them opera tickets as an incentive, although Li's father, Ko Meng-Dang, refuses to attend. When Li's grandmother falls ill, his mother offers her own life in exchange, contracts TB and dies. Ko Meng-Dang remarries but his new wife, Lai Hwat, mistreats both Li and his young cousin, Big Eyes, whom Li was expected to marry. To Li Hei's chagrin, Big Eyes' mother takes her away. Soon afterwards Li Hei dies.

Li, now nine years old, is miserable at home. He is apprenticed to a travelling puppetmaster, and shows such skill that he is poached by a rival puppeteer. At 14 Li is mounting performances in his own right. The troupe's manager, Ah-Lai, suggests Li should marry his daughter. Ko Meng-Dang angrily opposes the idea, but the marriage goes ahead; when he dies, Lai Hwat blames Li for his father's death.

At 22 Li founds his own puppet show, 'Living Colour'. But when the Sino-Japanese War breaks out in 1937 all outdoor shows are banned, and Li joins a travelling opera company, the Red Jade troupe. In Taiching he meets a prostitute, Leitzu, who becomes his mistress, and shuttles between her and his family in Taipei. In 1941 Li is invited by a local police chief to join the newly formed Anti-Anglo-American Unit, putting on propaganda puppet shows. He clashes with a Japanese member of the company, but the Japanese authorities exonerate him.

The war draws to an end. Taipei is bombed, and Li with his family is evacuated to a coffin-maker's house in a small village. His father-in-law contracts malaria and dies, as does Li's youngest son. Li and his wife also catch the disease; they survive, but Li is seriously weakened, and at first needs help in reviving his puppet show. Li, now 84, recalls how he saved Japanese soldiers from attack by an angry crowd, and how people dismantled war-planes for scrap metal to pay for his shows.

The Puppetmaster forms the third in Hou Hsiao-Hsien's loose trilogy of films tracing, in reverse chronological order, the impact of twentieth-century Taiwanese history on individual families: intimate epics, where the cataclysms of great events are seen not directly, but by way of the shock waves that ripple through private lives, shaking and destroying. *A Time to Live and a Time to Die* (1985) reflected the period following the Kuomintang's move to Taiwan in 1949, after it's defeat by the Communists. *A City of Sadness* (1989) covered the four-year interim between the defeat of Japan and the KMT government's arrival. And *The Puppetmaster* runs from 1910 to the end of World War II, taking in most of Taiwan's 50 years under Japanese rule. (Hou, it should be added, now counts only the two most recent films as part of a trilogy, and is planning a further film to deal with the post-1949 era.)

Here, as in *A City of Sadness*, Hou is exploring hitherto taboo areas of the Taiwanese past. Until recently the government discouraged accounts of the Japanese era, fearing unfavourable comparisons, as well they might. Rather as some Indians feel a grudging nostalgia for the Raj, many Taiwanese look back wistfully to a time when, though a subject race, they enjoyed a stability and social order denied the war-torn mainland. The Japanese in *The Puppetmaster* are for the most part courteous and humane, displaying none of the racist brutality towards their Chinese subjects depicted in, for example, Kobayashi's *The Human Condition*. The sole exception, Kubota, is a drunken oaf, and when Li beats him for his boorish behaviour the Japanese magistrate scrupulously hears both sides and finds Li justified.

Compared to its predecessors, *The Puppetmaster* makes less demanding viewing—especially after the welter of characters and relationships in *City of Sadness* that often left the uninstructed Western viewer struggling to keep track. Anchored by Li Tianlu's linear narration (the old man speaks the voice-over and shows up on screen from time to time to address the camera), the film progresses in almost classic bio-pic style, secondary characters featuring only insofar as they impinge on the protagonist. But if the narrative line is plain, the texture of the film is intricate and richly evocative, since Hou's concern isn't simply Li but the era he embodies.

Even so, we're a long way from the swirling, high-coloured chinoiserie of Zhang Yimou or, at least recently, Chen Kaige. The austerity of Hou's style (which has prompted comparisons with Ozu) goes a step further in *The Puppetmaster*, whose rapt, distanced gaze—no close-ups, whole scenes played out in one unmoving long-shot—seems to reflect the spectator's angle on the puppet show itself. There's no shortage of deaths or violence, but they mostly happen off-stage or in reported voice-over. We're told Li's stepmother mistreats him and his young cousin, but we never see her doing so, and when the grandfather takes his fatal tumble he falls out of frame, leaving the camera contemplating an empty ladder. This formal restraint sits well with Hou's unromanticised view of the past and of his characters. Even Li, though treated with respect, is never sentimentalised, and Hou doesn't disguise the hint of callousness that marks the born survivor.

Hou's indifference to Western tastes also shows in his inclusion of several long, unbroken extracts from Li's puppet shows. Beautiful, stylised and remote, they have all the charm of the half-understood—what's happening is clear enough, but why is tantalisingly opaque—so there's a real sense of culture shock when mandarins and court ladies suddenly give way to something as crude and immediate as a Punch and Judy show. Planes buzz, bombs burst, Allied troops ("One, two! One, two! Yes, yes!") wave rifles, and a heroic wireless operator gives his life for the Imperial cause. Yet the puppetry is as skilled as ever. It's like finding a Donald McGill postcard gag, executed with infinite subtlety, adorning a Ming vase.

Underlying this scene, and indeed the whole film, is the metaphor of the puppetmaster turned puppet, the creator of drama forced by fate to live out a drama not his own. The idea's implied, but never openly stated—and is in any case belied by much of the action. For all that the film is part of a trilogy to be called *The Three Tragedies*, the Taiwanese of *The Puppetmaster* seem less subservient to historical forces than those of Hou's earlier films. The final image shows the people of Taipei resourcefully taking matters into their own hands, busily dismantling war planes whose scrap metal value will finance Li's shows "to thank the gods". It's an optimistic ending to an overtly pessimistic film, whose seeming simplicity hides levels of complexity that would repay multiple viewings.

VILLAGE VOICE, 10/12/93, p. 50, J. Hoberman

The Puppetmaster, the latest film by Taiwan genius Hou Hsiao-hsien, has several points of contact with *Concubine*—it's a multi-decade tale of performers and prostitutes coping, as best they can, with the political upheavals of the 20th century. But *The Puppetmaster* is also sui generis—neither documentary nor fiction. The suggestive Chinese title translating as *Drama, Dream, Life*, it dramatizes the early life of 84-year-old Li Tien-lu, Taiwan's most famous puppeteer, an official "national treasure" as well as an actor in Hou's past three films.

Hou calls Li "a living encyclopedia of Chinese tradition," and *The Puppetmaster* is a comparable anthology of narrative ploys. A half-dozen stage performances usually shown head-on, some in a single long take—alternate with an ongoing family melodrama that unfolds in a series of domestic settings as adroitly framed, sensuously illuminated, and powerfully discreet as a Vermeer interior. (The Cherry Gardens brothel is represented as one more kitchen table.) *The Puppetmaster* is periodically enlivened by Li's distinctive voiceover, and the "narrativity"' of any given tale is emphasized with the image of wiry, old Li telling it. As the protagonist is simultaneously godlet and puppet, his story is both life and its representation. The action fades in on a meal at which the family discusses their plans for another meal—namely the party to celebrate Li's birthday. His confused genealogy parallels Taiwan's complex historical situation.

The Puppetmaster is distanced and presentational. Rarely using close-ups, Hou frequently shoots an entire scene from a single point of view. When he cuts, it's often to a slightly longer shot—a tendency that further situates his characters in a particular socio-historical-geographic space. Hou has compared his elliptical structure to Godard's *Breathless* and "ancient Chinese theater," with traditional Chinese painting providing the inspiration for his economical use of detail and synecdoche. (The outbreak of World War II is represented by the sound of air-raid sirens; the end of the Japanese occupation by a cacophony of firecrackers.)

Beginning a scene in the midst of unexplained high emotions, holding a shot several beats longer than expected, *The Puppetmaster* offers a startlingly advanced use of editing, a dozen new ways to structure a scene. Li's description of his mother's death is accompanied by a complex alteration of presence and absence, audio as well as visual. For all the emphasis on real time, a single cut can span a dozen years even as the voiceover loops over and around the various staged scenes, knotting a story line so unobtrusively complicated it makes a time traveler like Alain Resnais seem all thumbs.

Although several of Hou's features have been included in previous New York Film Festivals and two distributed (as part of larger packages) by the now dormant "Cutting Edge," not one of his movies has ever had an American theatrical release. *Farewell My Concubine* will be opening at three theaters on October 15; *The Puppetmaster* shows twice at Alice Tully and then once more, on November 9, at the Museum of Modern Art. Make your plans accordingly.

Ignore the blurbs, forget what the hypemeisters tell you, a movie of this magnitude doesn't appear in New York every week. *Farewell My Concubine* suggests the second coming of Irving Thalberg; *The Puppetmaster* is more like a rebirth of cinema itself.

Also reviewed in:
CHICAGO TRIBUNE, 12/3/93, Friday/p. C, Michael Wilmington
NEW YORK TIMES, 10/6/93, p. C19, Vincent Canby
VARIETY, 6/7/93, p. 38, Derek Elley

QUEEN, THE

A Lewis Allen Productions & Si Litvinoff/MDH Enterprises re-release. *Producer:* Lewis Allen. *Director:* Frank Simon. *Narrator:* Jack Doroshow. *Running time:* 68 minutes. *MPAA Rating:* Not Rated.

CAST: Jack Doroshow (Flawless Sabrina);   Crystal (Miss Manhattan);   Harlow (Miss Philadelphia).

NEW YORK POST, 3/19/93, p. 30 Audrey Farolino

One of the most priceless moments in "The Queen," an acclaimed 1968 documentary about a rather unusual beauty pageant, is the scene in which an infuriated runner-up goes ballistic backstage and vents all her jealousy and anger towards the winner.

"I'll sue the b ----," rages Miss Manhattan, an exotic beauty named Crystal, who lost out to the willowy Miss Philadelphia. "Get a picture of [her] and me and see who's more beautiful ... Look at her makeup, it's *terrible*," Crystal fumes.

What makes this all the more priceless is that Miss Manhattan and Miss Philadelphia along with all the other contestants, are actually Misters, for we are backstage at the 1987 "Miss All-American Camp Beauty Pageant," in which the nation's premiere drag queens are vying for the honor of being named the fairest queen of them all.

Praised when it was first released for its sensitive and subtle handling of what was then considered shocking subject matter, "The Queen" is no longer very startling but it is still revealing, funny, and involving (all this despite its short length and choppy cinema verite style).

You don't get to know any of these men very well but you want to know them all better, and even all that's transpired in the gay community between then and now, you especially want to know what's happened to them since.

It's also fascinating as a woman to watch a group of males embrace all the little tortures that lie behind society's image of feminine beauty: They stuff themselves into too-tight bras, tape their flesh into a semblance of cleavage, suffer corns from mincing along in high heels, dye, pluck and otherwise eradicate offensive hairs, and hide themselves under pounds of makeup and outrageous wigs.

They do this, of course, for the same reason women do: "All drag queens want is love, and they try to get that love by being sexy and beautiful," observes Jack Doroshow (a.k.a. Sabrina when in drag), who set up the contest and served as its "masterful mistress of ceremonies" (judges included Larry Rivers, Jim Dine, and—who else?—Andy Warhol).

Most of the film consists of the camera simply hanging out with the contestants in their hotel rooms or backstage at Town Hall, site of the contest. We eavesdrop on them as they discuss everything from trivialities like the state of their wigs ("Look at this—I'm going to have to reset it") to mother won't talk about it anymore—she really doesn't understand") and with the draft board ("Did you tell them you were homosexual?" one asks. "No, they told me," is the dry response).

The rather enigmatic star of the film is the strikingly attractive Richard (a.k.a. Harlow), who is what the drag queens refer to as a "natural beauty wonder." The others have worked diligently up the ranks of beauty contests, perfecting their looks along the way, but Richard simply walked off with the first contest he entered—"He never worked for it, he never experienced loss," as someone observes.

Richard, of course, walks off with this contest too, leaving Miss Manhattan and the others to experience loss. But that probably didn't get them down for long; as Doroshow observes, "They're like in this fantasy bag, you know—but who's not in a fantasy bag?"

NEWSDAY, 3/19/93, Part II/p. 75, Gene Seymour

The crackdown at the Stonewall was almost a year away when "The Queen," Frank Simon's *cinema-verite* account of the 1967 Miss All-America Camp Beauty Pageant at Town Hall, was released to much media hoo-hah over what was, at the time, a groundbreakingly intimate look at homosexual men, in and out of drag.

Though you couldn't tell from watching this 1968 film, the pageant was one of the high-profile hip events of that heady era. The program notes from the film's producer, Lewis Allen, say that Andy Warhol, Terry Southern, Larry Rivers and Edie Sedgewick (then "on her last legs," according to Allen) were among the judges for the pageant. Knowing this makes you wish some of these glitterati were more visible in this 68-minute film, if only to enhance its archival value.

But the focus is on the contestants as they pour into Manhattan hotels from all over the country. We spend a lot of time listening to these men gab engagingly about makeup, wigs, their performing repertoire and their sundry adventures with their local draft boards. (Ah, yes. The war.) It's easy to imagine how fresh such talk must have sounded in those pre-"Boys in the Band" days.

But after watching the camera focus intently and relentlessly on all the flesh-tucking (and search, throughout, for any errant flaws, sags or awkwardness), one gets a faint hint of the kind of implicit condescension *cinema-verite* of the '60s was often accused of.

Comparisons with 1991's "Paris is Burning" are inevitable. (The ads for the revival practically beg for it.) There are resonant echoes like the compelling opening scene of Jack Doroshow painstakingly applying makeup to his face as he transforms himself into Sabrina, the pageant's host(ess).

But the movement that was set in motion by the Stonewall furor has since worn away the film's ability to surprise, much less shock, its audience. In fact, there's a pokey languor about the film that isn't dispelled until an electrifying burst of postgame rage by Crystal, one of the runners-up, who doesn't believe Miss Philadelphia (Richard alias Harlow) was pretty enough to get the crown.

Still the film retains a timeless poignance, especially when we see Richard/Harlow the day after dressed in a dark suit and looking like a blonder, sultrier Warhol, carrying his crown and overnight bag to the Port Authority Bus Terminal for the ride home.

VILLAGE VOICE, 3/23/93, p. 58, Georgia Brown

In 1968 some people were taking to the streets and some were carrying on indoors. *The Queen*, a modest documentary released that year to appreciative reviews, is now being revived at Film Forum—because drag is hot, I suppose. It covers the 1967 Miss All-America Camp Beauty Pageant held at Town Hall, in front of respectable judges such as Larry Rivers, Terry Southern, and Paul Krassner.

The handheld 16mm camera particularly likes Richard (known as Miss Harlow from Philadelphia in the contest), shown arriving in town, plaid suitcase in tow. Richard is younger and trimmer than most of the other contestants; he sometimes resembles Edie Sedgwick, sometimes, because of his lank hair, Andy Warhol. In fact, it's hard not to wonder if the fix is in since we follow Richard from the first. Someone observes later, while Richard has taken to bed because he lacks a good wig, that he won the first contest he entered and isn't acquainted with loss or heartbreak. (Notes from the film's executive producer, Lewis Allen, recall that Richard/Harlow went on to a couple of evenings on the town with Warren Beatty, a sex change, and a successful salon in Philadelphia.)

The movie follows the hopefuls through their practices and makeup sessions and listens in on several sweet conversations. In one, some contestants sit around in their underwear and compare what it was like reporting to their local draft boards. In the end, however, it's another untutored loser, Miss Crystal, who provides the film's sole moment of high drama.

Particularly after Jennie Livingston's far wittier and weightier *Paris Is Burning*, *The Queen* shows its wrinkles. What once may have seemed fresh and titillating—at least to reviewers such as Renata Adler and Judith Crist—now looks pretty banal. But, hey, it's only slightly over an hour and you get to find out who wins and see her shed real tears.

Also reviewed in:
CHICAGO TRIBUNE, 4/9/93, Friday/p. F, Johanna Steinmetz
NEW YORK TIMES, 6/18/68, p. 37, Renata Adler

QUESTION OF COLOR, A

A California Newsreel release. *Producer:* Kathe Sandler. *Director:* Kathe Sandler. *Screenplay:* Kathe Sandler and Luke Charles Harris. *Running time:* 58 minutes. *MPAA Rating:* Not Rated.

NEW YORK POST, 6/23/93, p. 30, Jerry Tallmer

In 1977, when Kathe Sandler was 17, Essence magazine "for today's Black woman"—put Kathe and her mother cheek-to-cheek on its cover. The intended point was that this blue-eyed near-blonde girl with pearly skin had come out of the womb of this dark-complected Afro-American woman. The irony was that a great many readers violently objected to Essence putting a "white woman" on its cover.

There was another drama unfolding behind that one. "My mother had two daughters, and my sister Eve"—as dark as their mother—"was not asked to be on the cover. How did that make Eve feel? In all these years, we've never talked about it."

They worked it out in another way, with Eve as an associate producer on "A Question of Color," the documentary that took Kathe Sandler eight years to complete. Long ago, in Gee-Gee's kitchen, I learned good and proper that there were color distinctions and sharp snobbisms among people of color. I did not learn the full catalogue that is laid bare in the 58 minutes of this film.

Here are just a few appellations cited by the people in the movie: *ebony, coal black, tar baby, pecan, as black as a berry, red, red bone, high yaller, cinnamon, chocolate to the bone, brown sugar, light, bright and damn near white.*

Miss Annie Caldwell, 96, of Tuskegee, Ala., steps waveringly forward on her cane to inform the filmmaker: "You are no more than me because you're mixed. I am straight." The camera gives us two teens in sneakers, one light, one dark. "He and I don't bring it [color] up, because we're best friends," says the light one. But he also tells us that his buddy is "always trying to change himself, puts contacts in his eyes." They horse around, but there's an edge.

A pretty girl: "People expect dark-skinned women go be just grateful to be alive. You're not supposed to have anything, want anything, I was thought of as a little darkie, Little Black Sambo, before black was beautiful."

The onus against being black struck all the way up to TV's Melba Tolliver when—inspired by the beauty of Kathleen Cleaver and Angela Davis—she let her hair go Afro. Tolliver was taken off the air and fired; a public outcry got her restored.

"A Question of Color" has its banalities, its obligatory obeisances (Malcolm X, Stokely Carmichael). It is a useful and necessary movie for all that.

Coupled with it is "Non, Je Ne Regrette Rien," by Marlon Riggs, whose 1989 "Tongues Untied" got Sen. Jesse Helms hot under the collar. Jesse's going to blow his top over the new one, a very sensitive 38-minute portrait of five gay black men—one of them a staid Harlem minister in his 60s—who are HIV-positive. Particularly touching: the young man who, re-membering how his mother had dissolved in tears when they had to put their old dog Micki to sleep, now declines to lay on her the burden of hearing what's happened to her 30-year-old son and only child.

NEWSDAY, 6/23/93, Part II/p. 59, Gene Seymour

[*A Question of Color* was reviewed jointly with *No Regret*; see Seymour's review of that film.]

VILLAGE VOICE, 6/29/93, p. 60, James Hannaham

Let'a have a show of hands. Will all those who believe that the fashion media doesn't promote white beauty standards please raise their hands? No one? Good, One part of director Kathe "I am a black woman, I look white" Sandler's documentary *A Question of Color*, eight years in the making, examines this ancient idea. The other part consists of the painful testimony of blacks discriminated against because of their African features or given special treatment because of their more European features. These stories are particularly painful for those who've always recognized that hair-burning, skin-lightening, colored contact lens-wearing blond-Jesus-worshiping black folks are harboring some serious internalized self-hatred.

I suppose *Question* intends to begin a healing process by reminding us how far we've regressed since the blow-out, black-is-beautiful 'fros of the '60s (not to mention the politics that went with them). For this purpose, and for those who have never seen the pot call the kettle high yellow, *Question*'s an excellent source. For anyone who already wants to punch someone out for thinking that Janet Jackson's inherently prettier than Angelique Kidjo, it's deeply upsetting and frankly em-barrassing to hear these anecdotes and watch people of color putting down people of more color.

Also reviewed in:
NEW YORK TIMES, 6/25/93, p. C15, Stephen Holden

RADIO STORIES

Director: José Luis Sáen de Heredia. *Screenplay (Spanish with English subtitles):* José Luis Sáenz de Heredia. *Director of Photography:* Antonio L. Ballesteros. *Editor:* Julio Pena. *Music:* Ernesto Halfter. *Running time:* 92 minutes. *MPAA Rating:* Not Rated.

CAST: Francisco Rabal (Gabriel); Margarita Andrey (Carmen); José Isbert (Inventor); Angel de Andrés (Thief); José Maria Lamea (Don Senen); Alberto Romea (Don Anselmo);

VILLAGE VOICE, 11/16/93, p. 72, Georgia Brown

Where have you heard this one: The host of a radio giveaway show dials the prizewinning number and reaches a burglar in the process of robbing the house? Well, years before this gag opened Woody Allen's *Radio Days*, it appeared in José Luis Sáenz de Heredia's *Radio Stories (Historias de la Radio)*, Spain, 1955. Sáenz de Heredia's delightful comedy is revealing, not just because most everyone wears his or her overcoat while on the air. (Topcoats in the house made a fashion statement in Spain during the '40s and '50s.)

After the savagery, the neighbor-on-neighbor butchery of the Spanish Civil War, battles continued on all fronts. Filmmakers could either reinforce the regime's values and myths-like machismo or racial superiority—or undermine them. (Heavy censorship guaranteed that critiques be coded.) In 1941, Sáenz de Heredia directed the proto-Falangist epic, *Raza (Race)*—based on Franco's own self-mythologizing novel—but, as John Hopewell points out in his invaluable *Out of the Past: Spanish Cinema After Franco*, he also, in 1955, "attended the Salamanca Congress, an early act of collective protest against the regime."

Radio Stories, too, swings both way's. For example, in the second episode, a twinkly priest (mainstay of many a Francoist plot) mediates between the above burglar and the householder, but the hero of the final story is a learned provincial schoolteacher, the sort who might have been executed in the early Franco years. The funniest section, I should add, is the first, starring the gnomish José Isbert—who makes me giggle just looking at him. A fantastic comic, Isbert plays a lowly inventor trying to win a cash prize by being the first to arrive at the radio station dressed as an Eskimo with a sled and a dog.

The 11 films gathered by Gerard DaPena into the Public Theater's "Spanish Eyes: Classics of the Spanish Cinema, 1935-1960" are not—except for *Bienvenido Mr. Marshall* and *Calle Mayor*—major films, but those I've seen are entertaining and also instructive about this terribly depressed, traumatized period. More on the series next week.

Also reviewed in:
NEW YORK TIMES, p. C20, 11/12/93, Stephen Holden

RAIN WITHOUT THUNDER

An Orion Classics release of a Taz Pictures production. *Executive Producer:* Rich Callahan and Mike Mihalich. *Producer:* Nanette Sorenson and Gary Sorenson. *Director:* Gary Bennett. *Screenplay:* Gary Bennett. *Director of Photography:* Karl Kases. *Editor:* Mallory Gottlieb and Suzanne Pillsbury. *Music:* Randall Lynch and Allen Lynch. *Sound:* Jeff Pullman. *Sound Editor:* Ric Coken. *Casting:* Susan Willet and Irene Schaeffer-Stockton. *Production Designer:* Ina Mayhew. *Art Director:* Llewellyn Harrison. *Costumes:* Gail Bartley. *Make-up:* Chris Bingham and Lauren Matonis. *Running time:* 87 minutes. *MPAA Rating:* PG-13.

CAST: Carolyn McCormick (Reporter); Katharine Crost (Walker Point Guard #1); Ali Thomas (Allison Goldring); Betty Buckley (Beverly Goldring); Iona Morris (Andrea Murdoch); Jeff Daniels (Jonathan Garson); Stuart Burney (Spencer Goldring); Eliza Clark (Piper Goldring);

Heather Lilly (Micka Goldring); Helen Lloyd Breed (Alice Kappelhoff); Katherine Selverstone (Abra Russell); Frederic Forrest (Walker Point Warden); Charles E. Gerber (Grover Cole); Bahni Turpin ("Baby Bomb" Prisoner); Ming Na Wen ("Uudie" Prisoner); John Scott (Health Official #1); Andrew Spencer (Health Official #2); Joseph Dophin ("Baby Bomb" Dealer); Fred Fagen (Doctor with Probe); Dana Smith (Walker Point Nurse); Lisa Langford ("In Profile" Prisoner); Stephanie Silverman (Angela Q); Tara Tersigni (Little Girl with Bird); Sheila Pinkham (Rosalind Hart); Linda Hunt (Atwood Society Director); Ethan Phillips (Gynecologist); Maren Oakley (Pregnant Woman in Coma); Malcolm Wiley-Floyd (Baby Breastfeeding); Diane Kirksey (Mother Breastfeeding); Steve Zahn (Jeremy Tanner); Robert Earl Jones (Old Lawyer); Graham Greene (Author on History); Austin Pendleton (Catholic Priest); Jay Hargrove (Health Official); Linda Igarashi (Health Official #4); Alyssa Rallo (Author Max Sinclair); Susanne Wasson (Swedish Doctor); Corina May (Priestess); Victoria Maione (Baby in Black Bag).

CHRISTIAN SCIENCE MONITOR, 2/12/93, p. 10, David Sterritt

Gary Bennett, the writer and director of "Rain Without Thunder," has followed an unusual pathway to the filmmaking world.

Although he took film-related courses in college, according to production information for his new movie, he majored in political science and later received graduate degrees in law and social welfare. But his interest in cinema stayed with him, and while practicing copyright and business law in New York he went to filmmaking courses in his spare time. Over the past few years he has written and directed three short movies and helped run a theater and television studio.

The release of "Rain Without Thunder," a full-length picture with an impressive cast, makes Mr. Bennett an auteur at last—but hardly a conventional one, since this is hardly a conventional film.

For one thing, it tackles the sort of controversial subject—the moral and constitutional debate over abortion rights—that movies with box-office hopes normally do their best to avoid. For another, it has an offbeat structure that some spectators will find invigorating but others will find peculiar or even dull. Virtually the whole story is presented through a series of interviews with fictional characters, who discuss their experiences and ideas but rarely engage in anything resembling direct action on the screen.

The central characters of the story, which takes place in the year 2042, are a mother and daughter who have been convicted of murder under the Unborn Child Kidnapping Act, a law meant to keep wealthy women from evading anti-abortion laws by going to other countries. Now in a New York prison, the women discuss their case with a reporter who also interviews a number of other people involved with the abortion issue, from law-enforcement officials to civil-rights activists.

Although the message of "Rain Without Thunder" supports women's rights and reproductive freedom, Bennett's screenplay is wide-ranging enough to present different perspectives on the topics it raises, and some of them are surprising.

It suggests, for instance, that a statute like the "fetal kidnapping" law might be passed in the future not as a right-wing fiat, but as a civil-rights measure with wide support—since it could claim to promote equality by eliminating an option (the ability to travel to countries where abortion is legal) that is not available to poor and disadvantaged women.

Also interesting is the way certain performances in "Rain Without Thunder" give a compelling glow not only to specific characters but to the ideas those characters espouse.

The brilliant actor Austin Pendleton, who plays an out-spoken Roman Catholic priest, is the best example of this. His acting is so vividly and passionately real that his character's anti-abortion views take on a resonance as absorbing and memorable as anything else in the movie, even though the film's own opinions are very different.

Others in the cast include Jeff Daniels as the attorney who lost the case that landed the "kidnappers" in jail; Frederic Forrest as the warden of the "facility for defendant mothers" where they are incarcerated; Linda Hunt as the leader of a feminist organization that's too moderate to press for abortion rights; Graham Greene as a scholar who argues that the very notion of a women's movement is a contradiction in terms; and Betty Buckley as the mother who helped her daughter seek the abortion that touched off so many unforeseen events.

"Rain Without Thunder" has problems that even this excellent cast can't overcome. Its visual style seems static next to the liveliness of its verbal content, and its determination to touch a whole spectrum of social issues—including racism, gender discrimination, and the need for penal reform—makes it too ambitious for its talking-head format to handle comfortably.

It is a thoughtful movie, though, and it will set audiences thinking even if it changes few people's minds. Whether one is stimulated or fatigued by its torrent of words, it certainly can't be accused of selling out its ideas for the sake of selling tickets, as so many films today are willing to do.

FILMS IN REVIEW, 4/93, p. 126, Nathaniel Bird

Many movies, while passing as entertainment, have a veiled sociological message. There is no veil here. *Rain Without Thunder* is a milestone in American cinema: the first film about abortion.

Up until now, films may have mentioned abortion in passing, but universally shied away from the action itself, even when abortion would have seemed to many the more sensible choice for the character and situation (*Kuffs* in 1992, *Immediate Family* in 1989 and, most specifically, *Second Thought* in 1983). *Rain Without Thunder*, on the other hand, zeroes in directly and unflinchingly on the subject and the concomitant conflicts, taking its title from a quote by abolitionist Frederick Douglass: "Those who profess to favor freedom and yet avoid confrontation ... want crops without plowing ... rain without thunder ..."

Set fifty years in the future, in 2042, the film speculates on a possible socio-historical scenario following a dubious triumph of anti-abortion forces. By the early 21st Century, virtually all abortion has been criminalized. The movie shrewdly foresees the logical consequences: the law will weigh disproportionately heavily on economically disadvantaged minorities, since the wealthy will always be able to skip across borders to more broad-minded countries. The constitutionality of this inequity is challenged, in the hopes that more liberalized laws will result—but the ploy backfires, resulting in the passage of New York's Unborn Child Kidnapping Act. Henceforth, even women seeking abortions abroad will be prosecuted.

Rain Without Thunder imagines the first test case of this law, An ambitious prosecutor has ferreted out young Allison Goldring, a college student whose mother shepherded her to Sweden for an abortion, and pursued them zealously, with an eye toward the accompanying publicity. The film is constructed largely in a quasi-documentary/interview style, following a reporter investigating the controversial case. Though lacking a strong plot, the story and history unfold compellingly, building with intelligent logic and quiet drama, covering a wide range of relevant voices—the law's victim's and enforcers, advocates and adversaries—also remarking on the interconnectedness and fragility of all rights and liberties, for instance, the question of reproductive freedom linked to privacy and free speech. The time period, with the fifty-year span, is meant to remind audiences of the parallel 19th century counterpart, beginning in 1850, with its analogous societal move from legalized abortion throughout the country to the gradual enactment of restrictions during the following half-century. As the film puts it, one generation to fight for liberty and one generation to lose it.

Fascinatingly, this pro-choice treatise was written and directed by a man, Gary Bennett, averting any denigrations of the filmmaker as a hysterical female alarmist. He even makes an admirable effort to be even handed, although his point of view is clear. And in contrast to recent Hollywood tendencies to lead only in matters of titillation, whether with violence or sex, but to lag with substantive issues (with major filmmakers mostly too timid or uninterested to tackle subjects such as Vietnam or feminism until a decade or two had passed), this has a refreshing timeliness.

And a nice job it is. It is beautifully cast with actors so distinctive that the score of roles are perfectly clear, cleverly avoiding superstars that would overshadow the material, but with an excellent ensemble that includes Betty Buckley, Jeff Daniels, Graham Greene, Frederic Forrest, Linda Hunt, and Ali Thomas as the beleaguered Allison. Everything has been crafted with care, with just enough casually inventive details of design and language appropriate for a story in the near future. This is handled well, directed with restraint, portrayed with subtlety—no melodrama, just quiet intensity, understated tension, cutting irony, all underscored by the chilling plausibility of the sharply intelligent construction.

LOS ANGELES TIMES, 2/5/93, Calendar/p. 6, Michael Wilmington

When a movie fails on some dramatic or cinematic level, but still makes interesting social points, the easy way out is to call it "thought-provoking." That's what "Rain Without Thunder" does. It provokes thought, anger, riles us up.

But, on some crucial level, it misses making its own alternate reality. This ideological horror movie intends to shame any abortion-rights audience who won't go to the trenches.

Fifty years in the future, during a time when anti-abortion activists have supposedly won the day and feminism is a dead political movement, two women who go to Sweden for a "termination"—Beverly Goldring and daughter Allison (Betty Buckley and Ali Thomas)—languish in jail on a newly enacted charge of "fetal kidnaping."

If you don't act, "Rain" affirms, this is what you face: a future where women who practice non-sanctioned birth control of any kind are imprisoned, dissidents go crazy and barmy crimes like fetal kidnaping are on the books. The title itself comes from a Frederick Douglass quote, which compares people who favor freedom, yet avoid confrontation, with wanting crops without plowing, rain without thunder.

Like "Bob Roberts," the movie is a fake documentary, with an inquiring reporter (Carolyn McCormick) and a lot of talking heads cluing us in to the Goldrings' plight and the half-century of social evolution behind it.

That's the movie's first problem. Though the show is presumably "objective," and though writer-director Gary Bennett spreads his eloquence among everyone—the Goldrings' idealistic attorney (Jeff Daniels), their dour warden (Frederic Forrest) and assorted experts—pro and con—the tone always suggests a liberal PBS documentary, circa 1990. It's as if time had stood still in the media world—and as if the future viewers were somehow ignorant of their own social history, and might be enraged upon learning it. Yet, if we know anything about repressive societies, it's that the *first* thing they try to control is the media: here, presumably, American society remains "democratic" in every area but women's rights.

There's a second flaw: A bizarre form of class prejudice, in which "Rain's" heroines are mostly upper-class women besieged by a motley group of resentful lower classes and racial minorities. The Goldrings prosecutor is an "ambitious" young black woman (Iona Morris), the main anti-feminist ideologue is Graham Greene as an American Indian pundit, and Allison's craven, treacherous boyfriend is specifically shown as humble in origin. If his parents were rich, would he have been a more sterling mate?

Bennett probably intends this scheme as ironic. He includes lower-class or minority women among the victims, but somehow they don't catch the sympathy of the Goldrings: Allison—who looks like a Barnard flower child—or Beverly, whose face is all but haloed. There's even Crucifixion symbolism at the climax.

The movie's arguments are stimulating, and so are some of the performances, especially Austin Pendleton's fervid anti-abortion priest, spouting off "Messiah" theories from Apocalyptic angles, and Linda Hunt as a pedantic future feminist. But "Rain Without Thunder" has all its moral issues solved in advance: a classic case of "preaching to the converted."

Unlike the best cautionary science-fiction tales—Pohl and Kornbluth's "The Space Merchants," most of H. G. Wells, Harlan Ellison or Philip Dick—it lets its extrapolations take over the whole story. "Rain Without Thunder" (rated PG-13) is being aimed, all too obviously, at us, now: the Scrooges of the 1990s, being given our dose of nightmare. For provoking thought, it deserves praise. But what the film needs most is some rain with its thunder, some crops with its plowing.

NEW YORK POST, 2/5/93, p. 31, Audrey Farolino

Abortion is one of those topics that most Hollywood filmmakers wouldn't touch, even with a battery of 10-foot poles, so the independents behind "Rain Without Thunder" deserve credit for sheer guts.

They also get points for having created a reasonably credible and restrained film despite a premise that seems tailor-made for hysterics and exaggeration: It's the year 2042, abortion has been outlawed in the U.S., and women who dare go to "terminators" to end their pregnancies can be convicted of fetal murder and packed off to prison.

Further, an "Unborn Child Kidnapping Act" has been passed to stop wealthy women from circumventing the law by flying off to places like Sweden to have abortions.

That's precisely what affluent college student Allison Goldring (Ali Thomas) and her mother Beverly (Tony-winner Betty Buckley) do after Allison discovers that she's pregnant. A tough state prosecutor (Iona Morris) comes down hard on the Goldrings and they're sentenced to seven years at a facility for "defendant mothers."

"Rain Without Thunder" tells the Goldrings' story in documentary style, following a reporter (Carolyn McCormick) as she interviews those involved in the Goldring case as well as various supporters and foes of abortion rights.

It's a credit to writer/director Gary Bennett that the film comes off as believably as it does, even though it portrays an age in which state inspectors can haul women off for compulsory uterine exams, skip jets can make the trip to Sweden in two hours, and priests have added a new twist to their anti-abortion arguments, now warning that the Messiah could arrive via any woman's womb, just "like last time."

A talented cast is another plus: Strong performances are turned in by those mentioned above, as well as Jeff Daniels as the Goldrings' attorney, Linda Hunt as the leader of a feminist group, and Austin Pendleton as a priest.

But those strengths don't entirely compensate for the film's flaws. Most glaring is the fact that even though various characters criticize the media's tendency to focus on issues only when they affect affluent whites, the film does the same, focusing on Allison and her mother and giving only passing attention to their fellow inmates, mostly poor minorities.

NEWSDAY, 2/5/93, Part II/p. 61, Jack Mathews

The title of Gary Bennett's "Rain Without Thunder" is taken from a Frederick Douglas quote chastising those people who "favor freedom and yet avoid confrontation." Certainly, the same cannot be said of Bennett: and those who participated in the making of this storming screed against America's pro-life movement.

Set in the year 2042, long after Roe vs. Wade has been overturned, "Rain" rehashes the moral and legal issues that combined to send a mother and her college-age daughter to prison for kidnaping the daughter's 7-week-old fetus.

By going to Sweden for an abortion, Beverly (Betty Buckley) and Allison Goldring (Ali Thomas) violated the recently enacted federal Unborn Child Kidnaping Law, which prohibits pregnant women in the mid-21st Century from leaving the country.

"Rain," shot in the style of an investigatory TV news feature with a numbing blizzard of talking-head interviews, is more a dramatized essay than a movie, an alarm bell being rung for today's politically passive by victims projected back from a bleak Orwellian future reigned over by moral fascists.

Bennett's future is one where women have abdicated their freedom by failing to fight for it, or by collaborating with men in power, and have set themselves and all human rights back a hundred years. Back to a time when only the affluent (usually white) could buy their way around the laws, and the poor (mostly minorities) often maimed themselves with coat hangers and toxins, or were carved up by back-alley abortionists.

With a large cast that includes Jeff Daniels as a level-headed civil rights lawyer, Linda Hunt as the conciliatory head of a women's society, and Austin Pendleton as a priest explaining the papal conviction that every fetus may house the Messiah, "Rain" zips through the history of abortion to paint a worst-case-scenario future decades after today's pro-life movement has won.

It's a future where law guarantees protection from conception, where a woman can be imprisoned for using an IUD, and Terminators (abortion doctors) are prosecuted as first-degree murderers.

We learn all this detail through interrelated interviews conducted by a female reporter (Carolyn McCormick) in what resembles a badly edited, run-on segment of "60 Minutes." Whether the style was intended to create a sense of documentary urgency for its subject or to save money, the movie would have been more powerful and less heavy-handed if it had been done as a futuristic courtroom drama.

Bennett did work a nicely ironic twist into his story, which saves it from being a pure polemic, but his tirade is otherwise unleavened by subtlety, humor or even much imagination. The script, with all its invented historical context, often is sophomorically obvious, and except for some unfamiliar jargon and a few fashion changes, 2042 looks pretty much like 1993. This may be Bennett's way of suggesting that when the neanderthals take over, all progress is halted. Or again, it may be just a matter of budget. Ultimately, it is hard to know what Bennett really wants to accomplish with this film, or for whom it is intended.

To the pro-choicers among us, "Rain" is preaching to the converted with fire, brimstone and a sledgehammer. To the undecideds, it may be so shrill and unfair as to steer them the other way. And to the pro-lifers, who are portrayed as an assortment of intellectual Nazis and religious zealots, it is such a vicious pummeling it's hard to imagine a single one of them saying, "Yeah, you're right, I never looked at it that way."

"Rain" doesn't shy away from confrontation any more than the pro-lifers who block abortion clinics and spit on pregnant women trying to enter, and its spirit is just ugly.

VILLAGE VOICE, 2/16/93, p. 60, Beth Coleman

Rain Without Thunder uses a documentary interview format to project its fiction of the near future. It's 2042 and the United States looks very much like it does now, just worse. Abortion is legal only if the mother's life is in danger. What's more, a new kidnapping law lands Allison (Ali Thomas) and her mom (Betty Buckley) in jail for taking a 12-week-old fetus out of the country to be aborted.

Director-screenwriter Gary Bennett forecasts other tricky, reactionary reproductive legislation—barrier birth control is now blessed by the pope, though IUDs are illegal. But while the film makes clear the deviousness of right-to-lifers, it oddly fails to lay out the prochoice position with any coherence or depth. As is often the case with consciously progressive sci-fi (like *The Handmaid's Tale*), *Rain* just tries to scare us into action. Its bad weather of the future is a fumbling and literal landscape that reiterates the helplessness of women and the victimization of racial minorities as a means of making a political point *against* those configurations.

If Bennett is looking to safeguard women's rights, let him ask better questions: How did reproductive authority stop being women's and become the state's? How does the medical profession corroborate with the state? The bleak world of *Rain* is an S.O.S. for a reformed Terminator—Arnold, Aidan, some guy—not a broadcast for resistance.

Also reviewed in:
CHICAGO TRIBUNE, 2/12/93, Friday/p. L, Johanna Steinmetz
NEW YORK TIMES, 2/5/93, p. C8, Janet Maslin
VARIETY, 10/5/92, p. 66, Daniel M. Kimmel
WASHINGTON POST, 2/9/93, p. B6, Hal Hinson

RAINING STONES

A Film Four International release of a Parallax Pictures production. *Producer:* Sally Hibbin. *Director:* Ken Loach. *Screenplay:* Jim Allen. *Director of Photography:* Barry Ackroyd. *Editor:* Jonathan Morris. *Music:* Stewart Copeland. *Sound:* Ray Beckett and (music) Jeff Seitz. *Sound Editor:* Kevin Brazier. *Production Designer:* Martin Johnson. *Art Director:* Fergus Clegg. *Costumes:* Anne Sinclair. *Make-up:* Louise Fisher. *Stunt Coordinator:* Perry Davey. *Running time:* 90 minutes. *MPAA Rating:* Not Rated.

CAST: Bruce Jones (Bob Williams); Julie Brown (Anne Williams); Gemma Phoenix (Coleen Williams); Ricky Tomlinson (Tommy); Tom Hickey (Father Barry); Mike Fallon (Jimmy); Ronnie Ravey (Butcher); Lee Brennan (Irishman); Karen Henthorn (Young Mother); Christine Abbott (May); Geraldine Ward (Tracey); William Ash (Joe); Matthew Clucas (Sean); Anna Jaskolka (Shop Assistant); Jonathan James (Tansey); Anthony Bodell (Ted);

Bob Mullane (Ted's Mate);   Jack Marsden (Mike);   Jimmy Coleman (Dixie);   George Moss (Dean);   Jackie Richmond (Club Steward);   Tony Little (Cliff);   Derek Alleyn (Factory Boss).

CHRISTIAN SCIENCE MONITOR, 10/12/93, p. 14, David Sterritt

The critics and programmers who assembled this year's New York Film Festival—which is always designed to showcase quality, not quantity—have done a thorough job of sifting world cinema for major achievements and unexpected discoveries. Their search has confirmed what filmfests earlier in 1993 have indicated: Britain and China are two of the most exciting places on the globe today for productions that reflect realities of their own homelands while also capturing insights of more far-reaching interest.

British movies screened in the highly regarded Lincoln Center event tended to be intimate in their stories and imposing in the messages and questions they presented. None was more engaging than *Raining Stones*, directed by Ken Loach, a filmmaker knows for his social conscience in addition to his cinematic skills.

Loach's wish to educate as well as entertain his audiences has led him to didactic and artificial work at times, as in his recent "Hidden Agenda," about violence and deception in contemporary Irish politics. At his best, though, he has the ability to discuss thorny social and cultural issues through stories of genuine emotional appeal. "Raining Stones" finds him at the peak of his powers.

The hero is Bob, a working class man with no work available to provide him with a living wage. He tries a number of schemes and scams designed to bring in a few pounds, but nothing he can devise is profitable enough to solve the poignant problem looming in his immediate future: His daughter's first communion is coming up, and he's determined to buy her a new dress for the occasion.

Everyone assures him that a new dress isn't necessary; lots of people face this sort of dilemma nowadays, and nobody's eyebrows will be raised if his daughter makes do with a hand-me-down. Bob has his pride, however, and it's as fixed as it is ferocious. Before long his problem of domestic finance becomes a problem of personal safety, as he gets involved with a loan shark in a desperate attempt to accomplish his goal.

What makes "Raining Stones" a remarkable movie is partly its deceptively simple story and partly Loach's sensitive treatment of it, which turns a small-scale crisis into a human drama of enormous resonance—and social import—as one realizes that Bob's difficulty is a microcosm of the large economic dysfunctions of Britain and other nations.

Rarely have the personal and the political been joined so seamlessly in a recent film. Loach and his screenwriter, Jim Allen, deserve tremendous credit for bringing it off. And their film deserves a worldwide audience.

Another unusual and important British film shown at the New York festival was Mike Leigh's scathing *Naked*, the story of an educated but unemployed young man whose lack of meaningful opportunity has warped his sense of dignity and decency beyond repair. Winner of the Cannes festival's best-director prize for Leigh and best-actor prize for star David Thewlis, it is due in American theaters late this year.

And special mention must go to *Blue*, directed by Derek Jarman, whose whimsical portrait film "Wittgenstein" recently opened on US screens. Jarman's streak of avantgarde experimentalism has been visible in many previous movies, such as "The Last of England" and "The Garden," but never has he veered so far from convention as in his new picture—which has no pictures, only a rich blue colorfield that fills the screen for the film's entire 75 minutes.

This is meant to symbolize the subject of the film, which is the sadness or "blues" that Jarman feels over the travails of people with AIDS and the lack of vision (literal and figurative) connected with this. These matters, including a poignant account of his own illness, are explored with imagination and compassion on the densely constructed soundtrack. "Blue" is a sad movie, but ultimately a positive and life-affirming one.

China's contributions to the festival included *Farewell My Concubine*, a superbly cinematic study of modern Chinese history as seen through the eyes of two opera stars. Since it shared the top prize at Cannes and is now opening on the American theater circuit, many filmgoers had heard about it and were eagerly looking forward to it. Advance word had also filtered into New

York about *The Puppetmaster*, a brilliantly filmed epic by Taiwanese director Hou Hsiao-hsien about the experiences of a renowned puppeteer.

So the big Chinese-language surprise at Lincoln Center was another movie: *The Blue Kite*, by Tian Zhuangzhuang, whose earlier "Horse Thief" is a masterpiece of allusive, contemplative cinema. "The Blue Kite" is quite different, telling three interrelated stories about members of a Chinese family caught in the turbulence of the Cultural Revolution, when people considered too Westernized, intellectual, or simply different were singled out for harsh "corrective" treatment.

"The Blue Kite" is not consistently gripping, but it is splendidly successful at fusing issues of home, family, community, and nation into a visually and emotionally striking whole.

LOS ANGELES TIMES, 9/21/94, Calendar/p. 1, Kenneth Turan

Ken Loach has a taste for humanity and a gift for involvement. The most influential of living British directors, an inspiration to filmmakers as diverse as Neal Jordan, Stephen Frears and Mike Leigh, Loach has been working with a minimum of fuss and a maximum of compassion for close to 30 years. "Raining Stones" is his latest film, and one of his best.

Winner of a Special Jury Prize at Cannes in 1993, "Stones" is in the tradition of previous Loach films like "Cathy Come Home," "Kes" and the recent "Riff-Raff." All share a passionate and sympathetic view of Britain's underclass, a belief that, as a character in this film puts it' "When you're a worker, it rains stones seven days a week."

Committed though he is, Loach is the furthest thing from grimly doctrinaire or dogmatic. His sympathy for people at the margins of society is always intensely dramatic, and, much like his subjects, his more recent films show an understanding that humor can be present in even the most despairing situations.

"Raining Stones" was shot in an economically depressed area in the north of England, a locale familiar to the film's working-class screenwriter, Jim Allen. And, in an act of faith that has had almost magical consequences, it was also cast locally with nonprofessional actors who understand and handle their parts perfectly.

Focus of all the attention is Bob Williams (Bruce Jones) and his wife, Anne (Julie Brown). On the dole though they are, Bob and his buddy Tommy (Ricky Tomlinson) are always embroiled in doomed schemes to earn a few quick pounds, like the plot to kidnap and sell a few good sheep that opens the picture.

Goodhearted but not lucky, Bob is struck by an unexpected misfortune just as a special need for money arises. His darling daughter Coleen (Gemma Phoenix) is about to celebrate her first communion, and close to 100 pounds will be needed to properly outfit her.

Though not particularly religious, it is a matter of fiery pride to Bob that Coleen look perfect on "the most important day of her life." So "Raining Stones" takes the simple route of following Bob as he attempts to raise the needed funds.

Loach does this with great deftness, as Bob tries his hand at cleaning drains, digging up bootleg turf and other decidedly odd jobs. Tommy accompanies him on most of these quests, and as played by Tomlinson ("Riff-Raff's" chagrined bathtub man) he brings humor to every situation. Comic stories about small boys and Lourdes bubble out of him, and where the seller of an old van insists it only had one owner, he cracks, "Who was it, Ben-Hur?"

But even at its funniest, "Raining Stones" never forgets the pained reality that underlies the humor. Loach and Allen understand how desperate these people are to better themselves and break the cycle of poverty, and how awfully difficult that can be. Caught between the sporadic solace of the church and the anger of the local grass-roots leaders, Bob finds himself "just ducking and weaving, trying to keep my head above water."

Both playful and sad, often at the same time, "Raining Stones" also has moments of lacerating power. Plainly unforgettable is a blistering visit to the Williams house by a character named Tansey (Jonathan James), a sequence that is shocking in its bluntness and lack of compromise.

If "Raining Stones" has a problem, at least for American audiences, it is the performers' thick North Country accents that make it difficult to completely catch what is said. But though a word gets lost now and again, the gist is never in question, and time here is considerably better spent than with those too numerous films where you can follow everything but desperately wish you couldn't.

NEW STATESMAN & SOCIETY, 10/8/93, p. 31, Jonathan Romney

For Ken Loach, the problems of representing Britain are the same as they ever were. There's no rethinking cinema in *Raining Stones*. But Loach makes it his business to keep abreast of the real in a way that few film-makers still do. He reads the headlines when everyone else is bickering over genre. Of course, he's a dinosaur, not only in the sort of film he makes—there's little stylistic difference between this one and *Kes*—but in his conception of cinema as a rallying-point for some timeless notion of working-class solidarity. This is the man who seriously suggested that the salvation of British cinema lay in taking films into the pubs.

Raining Stones takes its model from old-fashioned dramatic naturalism. The structure is pure Zola, placing ordinary people in an inconceivably awful situation that rises out of a greater reality they can't control. The difference is that Loach needs to impress on us the possibility of hope. So he keeps things on a resolutely comic note, and provides an ironic let-out that's gratifying but also risibly easy.

Forget the plot, and one's left with an affirmation of faith that the everyday can be caught on screen almost undiluted. This is the last stand of the slice-of-life. To achieve it, Loach takes a detour through the soap opera—hence the casting of ex-*Brooksider* Ricky Tomlinson as the hero's best mate. Loach and his writer Jimmy Allen lay the disasters on as relentlessly as the title suggests: a stolen van, the family purse running dry, a succession of jobs going wrong, and young Coleen needing a communion dress.

At the centre, Bruce Jones as long-suffering Bob suggests a bottomless well of resourcefulness, integrity and good humour in the face of despair. It's Jones and the rest of the cast who are responsible for the film surviving its schematic conception; and it's Loach who is responsible for coaxing it out of them. No one will look to *Raining Stones* to redraw the map of British cinema, but it exists resolutely according to its own rules. And it's really rather wonderful, in spite of them.

NEW YORK, 3/14/94, p. 75, John Powers

Shot in a public-housing project in northern England, Ken Loach's *Raining Stones* is a touching, extremely funny portrait of ordinary people trying to get by in a Britain still reeling from Thatcherism. Bruce Jones stars as Bob Williams, a plump, beleaguered, out-of-work Roman Catholic who cleans drains, steals sheep to sell the meat, and gets hooked up with loan sharks in the desperate attempt to preserve his pride—in this case, buying an expensive new outfit for his daughter's first Communion. I realize that few things could sound drearier than a gritty look at unemployment beneath Manchester's oyster-gray skies, but as he showed in *Riff-Raff*, Loach has become a canny entertainer who wins remarkably enjoyable performances from nonprofessional performers (in real life, lead actor Bruce Jones works in a dairy). This isn't to say that Loach has abandoned his trade-mark left-wing feistiness—when he introduced the film at last year's Locarno Film Festival, he pointedly slagged the pope. But he has learned to dress his politics in the big-hearted populism that once made Warner Bros. the workingman's studio. Brimming with compassion and good humor, *Raining Stones* is an old-fashioned picture about friendship, messed-up family love, irrational paternal machismo, and social injustice. It even has a lovable, earthy priest who 60 years ago would have been played by Pat O'Brien.

NEW YORK POST, 3/11/94, p. 44, Larry Worth

British director Ken Loach has always been ahead of his time.

Three years before "In the Name of the Father," Loach dramatized Britain's cover-up of criminal injustice in "Hidden Agenda." And while the Berlin Wall still stood he epitomized Germany's conflict in "Singing the Blues in Red."

Now he's scrutinized England's crumbling social system and come up with "Raining Stones."

The plot revolves around a seemingly uncomplicated subject—a father's attempts to get his little girl a new dress for her first communion. But when dad is an unemployed worker in Manchester's slummier section the goal takes on monumental proportions.

Adrift in his bleak surroundings, the sad sack resorts to any manner of get-rich-quick schemes, including door-to-door requests to dive into excrement as he salvages septic tanks. Believe it or not things go downhill from there.

Sadly, that applies to more than the hero's plight. The last half hour of Jim Allen's screenplay veers disconcertingly off-tract switching to a dark, violent nature, then copping out with a religious ending more suitable to an "Insight" episode.

But before things go awry, Loach's knack for capturing the beauty of the mundane becomes apparent, recalling the simplicity of a young Bill Forsyth with "Gregory's Girl."

Credit must be shared with the actors. Bruce Jones as the desperate dad stands out, nicely complemented by Julie Brown and Ricky Tomlinson.

Unfortunately, it's sometimes hard to decipher their accents. Since Loach solved that problem with subtitles in his last outing (the English working-class drama "Riff-Raff"), the trick would have been a natural to recycle.

But even a flawed Loach knocks most cinematic competitors off the map. That's why the language barrier and misguided ending are only mild dampers for "Raining Stones."

NEWSDAY, 3/11/94, Part II/p. 79, John Anderson

Work is nonexistent in the northern English community where Bob (Bruce Jones) ekes out his family's meager existence, but meat can be had—on the hoof. So he and his lumpy pal Tommy (Ricky Tomlinson) steal a sheep, but can't quite bring themselves to slaughter it. Maybe because the animal reminds them too much of themselves.

In "Raining Stones," director Ken Loach ("Riff-Raff") explores the plight of England's unemployed, and he and his screenwriter, Jim Allen, are clearly angered by what they find. Not by Bob, necessarily, who supplements the dole with whatever petty larceny he can commit, but by a system that breeds poverty and violence and then won't protect its victims. And yes, Loach is a little bit annoyed by Bob, because he refuses to step back and re-examine just what's gone wrong.

It's a combination of Bob's myopia and his pride that get him in trouble. His daughter Coleen (Gemma Phoenix) is about to celebrate her First Holy Communion, and the customary dress shoes, gloves and veil are well beyond Bob's means. It's not the church's idea; the local priest emphasizes the spiritual aspects of the sacrament and tries to convince parents to use donated dresses. But Bob insists that Coleen have new, and then has to try to pay for it.

Loach uses real locations and real local people—Julie Brown, who plays Bob's wife Anne, has never acted before—and he creates a gritty little picture of a community brought low, and of a desperate, well-intentioned but hard-luck character. Bob takes a job as a nightclub bouncer and gets bounced, joins a sod-stealing expedition at a local country club, and finally takes money from a loanshark; which is when "Raining Stones," takes its startlingly vicious turn. Before Bob finds his salvation, the action will have assumed its own momentum and his fate will seem out of control—much like the lives of the people he represents, and for whom Loach feels such furious sympathy.

SIGHT AND SOUND, 10/93, p. 50, Jenny Turner

Bob and Tommy, two middle-aged family men, both unemployed, attempt to augment their dole money by rustling a sheep from the moors near their Lancashire home. They get their sheep, but the ploy ends in disaster. As the men are trying to sell the meat round the pubs, Bob's beaten-up but utterly necessary van gets stolen.

Bob's seven-year-old daughter Coleen has reached the age at which girls of good Catholic families take their first Communion. To buy a complete Communion outfit costs around £200, and Bob is determined to earn the money somehow. He tries rodding drains, but nobody is interested, except for the kindly parish priest, Father Barry, who automatically assumes that Bob is doing the job for nothing. Bob tries working as a bouncer in the local rave club, but blows that job on his first night. Desperate, he finally borrows money from a loan company to buy a new van, telling his wife that the money has come from a win on the horses.

Unknown to Bob, however, his loan company has written him off as a bad debt, selling on the debt to a ruthless shark, who comes round to Bob's house and terrorises his wife Anne. Enraged,

Bob staggers off to find the man, an iron bar hidden in his coat. He watches him get drunk in a bar, then follows him to a multi-storey car park. After a brief fight, the man gets in his car to drive away, but is so drunk that he crashes into a pillar, dying instantly.

Bob rushes to confess to Father Barry, who tells him not to feel guilty, and on no account to confess his involvement to either his wife or the police. Coleen's Communion takes place, with Bob and Anne proudly looking on. Meanwhile, two police officers arrive at Bob's house, and are told by a neighbour that he is at Church. When Bob leaves the church, he is greeted by the policemen, who have come to tell him that his stolen van has been found.

The audience starts laughing to itself right at the beginning of the opening sequence, even before Bob and Tommy get going on the sheep-shagging jokes. Is the sight of two less-than-fit middle-aged men chasing an unfortunate animal really that funny? Has it something to do with the comic bearing of Ricky Tomlinson, the round, droll figure we all remember from his hilarious naked-in-a-bath scene in Ken Loach's *Riff Raff*? Well, yes, maybe, on both counts. But the laughter that greets *Raining Stones* is mainly about a different sort of glee. People laugh along with *Raining Stones*, even before it's started, because it is a Ken Loach film above all else.

Loach's position in British film-making is unique. He is just about the only director who started working in the wake of the Free Cinema epoch still to be making films in Britain, and he is certainly the only one to have remained faithful to Free Cinema's commitment to realism as a rich and creative cinematic form. He is an unwavering, outspokenly committed socialist, which makes him unusual not only in film-making circles, but in any sphere of Britain's contemporary public life. He is one of only two big British film-makers to make a point of telling everyday stories about working-class people living their lives in difficult—but unexceptionally so—circumstances. Thus the laughter which automatically greets this film is a sort of cheer to a man whom the audience finds brave and admirable.

But the laughter also signifies anticipation, and a curious sort of relief. Although you wouldn't know it to look at most of our media, the majority of the British population is still, if not entirely working-class, then of working-class origin. To the majority of Loach's prospective audience, council estates are not weird wastelands, but places known intimately and remembered with affection, as home. To the majority of this audience, poverty is not merely an abstract problem read about in the newspapers, but the stuff of life itself. Yet our media starves us of images which reflect and recognise everyday economic truth. The laughter which greets *Raining Stones* is a way of thanking the film for offering to give us what we're due.

It is hardly Loach's fault that these expectations are so inappropriately huge. It is also not his fault that critics, as a result, have tended to over-rate his recent work. It is only very slightly his problem that the crux around which the plot of *Raining Stones* revolves bears a passing resemblance to that of another film in which a poverty stricken family man gets involved in dodgy dealings, suffering a humiliation made all the worse by its being in the sight of his beloved wife and child. Nobody's asking Loach to make a film as operatic, as enormous, as shamelessly pathetic, as *Bicycle Thieves*. But it really is a shame that Loach has chosen to direct what could have been an enthrallingly sweeping script in a way that makes everything big in it seem trivial and slight.

Though a bit weak on really funny dialogue, Jim Allen's script is basically fine. The central male performances—from Bruce Jones as Bob and Ricky Tomlinson as Tommy—are also fine. There are many places in the film where an energetic director could have taken all these fine things and pushed them on to the point of greatness. But the film is visually boring, a succession of weakly framed shots which could have been constructed to prove that there is nothing interesting to look at in the places where poor people live. Stewart Copeland's music is dreadful tinkly synthesiser mush, as if designed to kill whatever passion might rear its head.

Although women are not a focal point of this story, the audience really has to believe in Bob's love for his wife and daughter, otherwise everything that's going on is bound to fall apart. But although Julie Brown and Gemma Phoenix appear to live in the same flat as Bob does, both seem to act and react only to the camera, not to the man supposed to be their husband and dad. As Brown and Phoenix are not film actors by profession, this amateurism is maybe not surprising. But Loach should have known how to put this right.

Raining Stones is a lacklustre, undramatic piece of film-making. The only point at which it really gets going is towards the end, when the good priest exculpates Bob for abetting the death of a brutal loan-shark. According to scriptwriter Jim Allen, the Church is a powerful, but ultimately futile, focus of working-class culture; he disagrees with it, but recognises the solace it gives too much to be able to mock it. By presenting the priest as the only person of any particular stature in the film, *Raining Stones* seems by omission to collude with this situation. This is a peculiar statement for a bunch of Marxists to make. And it provides a shockingly sentimental ending to a film which, for most of its running time, seems so afraid of appearing sentimental that it prefers to run the risk of evoking practically no deep feeling whatsoever.

VILLAGE VOICE, 3/15/94, p. 48, Georgia Brown

Ken Loach's marvelous *Raining Stones* opens with an exquisite, calendar-perfect shot—a green valley in the mist, flocks of sheep grazing, a stream meandering through. This heavenly prospect is the last idyllic moment in Loach's vision of purgatory on earth.

Suddenly the sheep scatter, chased by two clumsy fellows, Bob (Bruce Jones) and Tommy (Ricky Tomlinson from *Riff-Raff*), friends who live on a council estate near Manchester, England. Hard up, they're trying to steal an animal to butcher, planning to sell the meat. When finally they capture a poor, smelly ewe, Bob goes to club it to death but can't. They end up paying a local butcher for his services, in the process learning they have mutton chops on their hands, not lamb. When they visit a pub to peddle the meat, Bob's van is stolen (with most of the meat inside) because Tommy leaves the keys in the door. For a time, the movie clicks forward like a grim demonstration of the wages of sin.

The choice of flock, sheep, and, by implication, lamb can't be accidental since this is a story that turns on the celebration of Holy Communion. Bob and Anne Williams's little girl, Coleen, is preparing for her First. The problem is that she needs a new dress—as well as headdress, veil, shoes, and gloves. At least Bob decides she does, although the church offers a wide selection of secondhand outfits. "No one else would know," murmurs the sympathetic Father Barry (Tom Hickey). "Anne and I would," answers proud Bob resolutely. Her First Communion, he solemnly believes, is "the most important day in our daughter's life." Communion, after all, entitles her to go to heaven when she dies.

Insurance for the next life certainly seems prudent since in this one, as someone says, "When you're a worker, it rains stones seven days a week." It's appalling to watch stones pelt poor Bob as he makes his muddled choices and attendant woes befall him. Black comedy grows blacker when a brutish loan collector gets on his case. (The screenplay is written by Jim Allen, who grew up in this particular grim milieu. The actors also are workers who know the life they portray.)

What rescues the movie from unrelieved pain are less the unconvincing comic moments (most featuring the goofy, slovenly Tommy) than a surprising, transcendent ending. Improbably, the church comes through for Bob, though in an unexpected, and certainly unorthodox, way. Manna falls and the innocent Bob receives. Deftly conflating sacred and profane, Loach creates a fiercely compassionate, thoroughly frightening work.

Also reviewed in:
CHICAGO TRIBUNE, 4/29/94, Friday/p. G, Michael Wilmington
NEW REPUBLIC, 3/28/94, p. 30, Stanley Kauffmann
NEW YORK TIMES, 3/11/94, p. C13, Vincent Canby
VARIETY, 6/7/93, p. 39, David Stratton
WASHINGTON POST, 6/3/94, p. C1, Hal Hinson

REAL McCOY, THE

A Universal Pictures release. *Executive Producer:* Ortwin Freyermuth, William Davies, William Osborne, and Gary Levinsohn. *Producer:* Martin Bregman, Willi Baer, and Michael S. Bregman. *Director:* Russell Mulcahy. *Screenplay:* William Davies and William Osborne. *Director of Photography:* Denis Crossan. *Editor:* Peter Honess. *Music:* Brad Fiedel. *Music Editor:* Allan K. Rosen. *Sound:* Mary H. Ellis and (music) Tim Boyle. *Sound Editor:* Martin Maryska. *Casting:* Mary Colquhoun. *Production Designer:* Kim Colefax. *Art Director:* Paul Huggins.

Set Designer: Jonathon Short. *Set Decorator:* Richard Charles Greenbaum. *Set Dresser:* Rex Farmer and Mel Ramsey. *Special Effects:* Bob Shelley. *Costumes:* Donna O'Neal. *Make-up:* Harriette Landau. *Make-up (Kim Basinger):* Jack Freeman. *Stunt Coordinator:* Dick Ziker. *Running time:* 105 minutes. *MPAA Rating:* PG-13.

CAST: Kim Basinger (Karen McCoy); Val Kilmer (J.T. Barker); Terence Stamp (Jack Schmidt); Gailard Sartain (Gary Buckner); Zach English (Patrick); Raynor Scheine (Baker); Deborah Hobart (Cheryl Sweeney); Pamela Stubbart (Kelly); Andy Stahl (Mr. Kroll); Dean Rader-Duval (Lewis); Norman Max Maxwell (Hoke); Marc Macaulay (Karl); Peter Turner, David Dwyer, and Frank Roberts (Guards); Robert Glover and Claude File (Prison Guards); David Hart (Businessman); Henry Stram (Cashier); Larry Black (Parole Officer); Rebecca Wackler (Personnel Woman); Saundra Franks (Waitress); Rebecca Koon (Beautician); Stephanie Astalos-Jones (Woman at Laundry); Jack Wilkes (Accountant); Tom Even (Salesperson); Jill Jane Clements (Lawyer); Al Hamacher (Mr. Katanich); Edith Ivey (Neighbor); Eric Ware (Bank Guard); Alex Van (Radly); Joe Washington (Newscaster); Polly W. Le Porte (Stewardess); Bill Crabb (Dispatcher); Megan Hughes (Schmidt's Girlfriend); Seneca W. Foote (Old Timer); Lois Hanevold (Convenience Store Customer); W. Clifford Klenk (Maitre d'); Nick Searcy (Roy Sweeney); Afemo Omilami (Cab Dispatcher).

LOS ANGELES TIMES, 9/10/93, Calendar/p. 10, Chris Willman

Casting Kim Basinger as a legendary brainy, brilliantly gymnastic cat burglar in "The Real McCoy makes about as much sense as casting Bridget Fonda as an action heroine in "Point of No Return." Basinger's hair is so perfect, even when her character gets released on parole and emerges into Georgia's rainy weather, that any aesthete in the audience will recoil at the thought of her mussing it up with a ski mask.

Basinger's title parolee is renowned as the greatest of all regional bank robbers, so once she's released from a six-year stint in the pen, she barely has time to catch a free breath before nefarious crime lord Terence Stamp has coerced her back into a life of felony. He kidnaps the young son she barely knew before her imprisonment, making the condition of the boy's ransom that Mom mastermind an $18-million heist involving Atlanta's steeliest state-of-the-art vault.

Caper movies are just about a lost art, probably because so many of the best ones tended to delight in the thievery of, say, a Cary Grant. Nowadays, audiences are conditioned to demand righteousness as well as charm in their rogues, which means that every caper must have an elaborate prologue setting up the duress under which the hero is getting his or her hands dirty. It's no wonder "The Real McCoy" feels so heavy and mirthless after it finally switches from about an hour's worth of boring child endangerment to actual breaking—and—entering.

The film—weakly scripted by William Davies and William Osborne ("Twins")—would be a boondoggle even with better casting. But Basinger seems to be enacting the part under as much duress as her character, turning in a strained, distracted, surprisingly unsexy performance, even taking the role's motherly stress into consideration.

Ostensible romantic lead Val Kilmer, her bumbling but amiable cohort in crime, goes for comic grace notes in a hick-ish part, but there's no chemistry between them as written or acted. Stamp does a bland variation on his genteel villain shtick, while the smaller roles (like Basinger's greedy ex, who comes from the "Thelma & Louise" school of husbandry) are mostly more of the usual patronizing Southern stereotypes.

Russell Mulcahy (director of "Richochet," the "Highlander" movies and many early rock videos) has an unfortunate likening for having action scenes shot in close-up—which undercuts the occasional stunts, and doesn't help all that much in suspending our disbelief that Basinger is really punching guys out every once in a while. The only real-seeming thievery in "The Real McCoy" (rated PG-13 for mild violence) is of the audience's good will.

NEW YORK POST, 9/10/93, p. 35, Michael Medved

"In many societies, even here in America, women are still regarded as ornaments to a man's success," solemnly proclaims Martin Bregman, producer of the new thriller "The Real McCoy."

"I wanted to make a film that celebrated the spirit of a strong woman in an unconventional, and hopefully, entertaining manner."

Isn't it more than a bit pathetic that the character he selected to achieve this noble purpose of "celebrating the spirit of a strong woman" turns out to be a professional bank robber?

Kim Basinger plays the part, and at least she can console herself with the knowledge that it's a less degrading job than the role of the legless, armless heroine which she famously passed up in the wretched "Boxing Helena."

Here she portrays Karen McCoy, a daring high-tech thief whose exploits have made her a legend in Atlanta's criminal underworld. Unfortunately, they've also landed her in the hoosegow, where she spends six unpleasant years before she's paroled and this story can get started. When she's released, McCoy wants to go straight and re-unites with her little boy (now 9 years old), but her timid, car-dealer ex-husband has told the kid his mom is dead.

Meanwhile, a fabulously wealthy criminal mastermind (played with sneering effectiveness by the redoubtable Terence Stamp) conspires with her corrupt parole officer (big-bellied good ol' boy Gailard Sartain) to force McCoy to do one more job. You know Stamp is a no-goodnik because he keeps both snarling Dobermans and snarling tigers on his palatial estate.

Apparently unsatisfied with his pursuit of animal husbandry, Stamp has his eye on a downtown bank that's holding $18 million in cash and he knows McCoy is the only crook clever enough to overcome its security system. When she refuses to cooperate he kidnaps her son and threatens to kill him so that McCoy gives in and gets to work, assisted by her new pal, a bumbling but handsome holdup man played by Val Kilmer.

The last half of the movie centers around the elaborate planning and execution of this high-tech heist and provides an excellent opportunity for making your way to the lobby to buy some popcorn or bonbons, even if you're gone for 10 minutes, you won't have missed anything.

In the right hands this kind of caper can be absolutely captivating, in the under appreciated Bill Murray-Geena Davis comedy "Quick Change," for instance, the scheme for robbing a bank is so utterly ingenious that it's also great fun to watch. Here, there's nothing particularly clever about Karen McCoy's plans—just a lot of glittery gizmos that operate pretty much, as planned.

Australian director Russell Mulcahy ("Ricochet," and the dreadful Sean Connery "Highlander" films) favors a sluggish pace that is absolutely fatal for this sort of thin, predictable material. When a key, chaos scene features a car that suddenly, inexplicably refuses to start (surprise! surprise!) you know that you've come to the wrong film if you're hoping for even the most modest touches of originality.

Basinger gives her role more intensity and energy than it deserves, and in the early stages of the movie she seems to be trying for the female equivalent of Dustin Hoffman's masterfully understated-ex-con performance in "Straight Time."

This air of humanistic seriousness quickly collapses under the galumphing assault of the increasingly preposterous plot—with countless details of jawdropping implausibility.

In the last analysis, there's nothing real about this "McCoy," and no possible reason to shell out your hard-earned cash to see it. You might just as well buy your bonbons at the supermarket.

NEWSDAY, 9/10/93, Part II/p. 71, John Anderson

The best caper films indulge our appetite for guiltless sin. Their attraction is about vicarious greed, the little tickle we get watching charming criminals make off with huge amounts of money previously owned by monolithic entities dedicated to the impoverishment of others. And nothing can deflate the fun better than a lot of moral posturing.

This is just one of the problems with "The Real McCoy," which gives us Kim Basinger as both master bank burglar Karen McCoy, and an unlikely symbol of female subjugation. Having served six years for her last one-woman bank heist—she was set up, of course, the only way a criminal of her artistic brilliance could get caught—McCoy returns to Atlanta and few prospects. Men in general are leering pigs; her obese parole officer, Gary (Gailard Satrain), implies that a little sex with him will make life a lot easier for her. Crime boss Jack Schmidt (Terence Stamp), who was the one who got her arrested in the first place, wants her to rob another bank for him. And her boorish ex-husband Roy (Nick Searcy) has told their young son Patrick (Zach English) that she's dead.

It's not a pretty picture, even if—as all the men keep telling her—prison hasn't cost Karen her figure. Every guy she meets is either a brute, or a klutz, like J. T. (Val Kilmer), an inept holdup man who also happens to be Schmidt's nephew and actually does a lot to help her. But Karen—who is a thief, lest we forget—is presented as an amalgam of every victimized woman, in America. And Basinger, wearing a number of smart outfits and a handful of blank expressions, is an irritating example of a woman who's never a victim.

Basinger looks good clad in haute cat-burglar, but the characters are strictly off-the-rack. Karen, who symbolizes female independence, is a cupcake. Kilmer's J. T., a thankless role, is the film's token nice guy and resident idiot. Terence Stamp (what's he doing here?) plays a cookie-cutter cutthroat. Gary the parole officer, who's supposed to be repellent, is fat and sweaty. The bad guys are tattooed. Roy, the obnoxious ex-husband, sells cars. His new wife, Patrick's stepmother, is a shrew. Did we miss anyone?

"The Real McCoy" also makes much of the fact that a woman might actually have a superior grasp of technology, strategy and human nature, treating as remarkable something that might be expected. But "The Real McCoy," which has been tossed together like an unhappy salad—the editing, for instance, is enough to give you indigestion—is an exploitation flick, the kind that assumes not so courageous stances about the rights of woman and ex-cons, while making sure Basinger's hair is perfect.

SIGHT AND SOUND, 11/93, p. 51, Chris Darke

Karen McCoy, a cat burglar, bungles a bank robbery and is imprisoned. Six years later, released early on probation, she returns home wishing only to go straight and be united with her young son Patrick. Her ex-husband, however, has a new partner and has told Patrick that his mother is dead; he refuses to let Karen see the boy. Out shopping one evening, Karen witnesses a drugstore hold-up that goes wrong and from which the thief narrowly escapes with his life.

Karen finds her search for employment hampered by her criminal record. On leaving the police station after an appointment with her obnoxious probation officer, she is pointed out to J.T. Barker, the crook from the drugstore, who is in awe of her reputation and approaches her. Karen turns down his suggestion that they work together but later accepts his help in finding lodgings. J.T informs Jack Schmidt, the local gangland baron, that Karen has been released and Schmidt, planning an $18 million raid on the same bank that Karen had tried to rob, wants her expertise for the job.

Karen's probation officer is in league with Schmidt and leads her to a meeting with him. She refuses to work with him on the grounds that it was he who betrayed her on the former job. When Schmidt has Patrick kidnapped, Karen attempts to rescue him and is assaulted in the process; she is finally forced to collaborate. After meticulous preparation, and with J.T. as driver, the bank raid is undertaken. The team reaches the main vault where Karen suddenly traps and imprisons Schmidt and his henchmen, escaping with J.T. Returning to Schmidt's mansion, they rescue Patrick and flee to the airport to fly to Mexico. However, Karen's ex-husband is waiting for her and attempts to rob her of the money. J.T. overpowers him and together they make the plane. At the last minute, a police vehicle halts the take-off and Karen believes that she is about to be re-arrested. It transpires that it is only an emergency delivery of a transplant organ for transportation. Karen, J.T. and Patrick, with $3 million dollars stolen from Schmidt's safe, take off to Mexico.

"You kept your figure!" After she expensively extricated herself from the Jennifer Lynch contract that would have butchered and boxed her as Helena, the exclamation that greets Kim Basinger's cat burglar on her release from prison is tinged with more than a little irony. Given, also, that Basinger's body is resolutely undisplayed here, one realises that the star has relinquished her former territory to negotiate the transition to character actress. Part of the pleasure of *The Real McCoy* lies in precisely this negotiation and the way in which it archly puts a spin on the former Basinger persona by withholding the flesh and foregrounding the face.

There are plenty of insurance policies written into the film to avoid overtaxing either Basinger's technical resources or the spectator's credulity at her transition. Russell Mulcahy hardly makes Bergmanesque demands of his lead and surrounds her with a troupe of secondary characters that—save Val Kilmer's charming J.T.—barely develops beyond the two-dimensionally venal.

In addition, the generic vehicle is a sharply handled, updated hybrid of the caper movie, which guarantees procedural detail and the display of expertise; Mulcahy, having cut his teeth on advertising and promo-video production, brings this aesthetic to bear on such moments with varying degrees of success. The climactic robbery scene—sex, here, is thoroughly sublimated into crime, the only penetration to take place being that of the bank vault—allows the director to light the hi-tech tools of the trade with an ad-man's palate of fetishising Beineix blues and golds. Elsewhere, however, when it is the characters rather than the colours that count, the aesthetic reveals its shortcomings. For example, Karen at her desktop computer planning the raid becomes a Coke-ad cameo of expertise casually displayed in a coded shorthand of spectacles, spreadsheets and creatively dishevelled clothing.

However, there are moments that transcend such visual cliches. The relationship between Karen and her incompetent admirer J.T. develops nicely around their shared concern for her kidnapped young son who is unaware that she is his mother. "But I'd be proud to call you my mother," J.T. tells Karen, articulating the shades of hesitancy, naivety and gentle perversity that makes the pair pleasing partners in crime. Equally, the fact that the film handles its two narrative twists—Karen's incarceration of Schmidt and the last-minute arrival of the police—with barely a screech of gears attests not only to an efficient script and direction but also to the fact that Basinger and Kilmer are sufficiently sympathetic to take the viewer with them through an enjoyable and, at times, surprising film.

Also reviewed in:
CHICAGO TRIBUNE, 9/10/93, Friday/p. G, Johanna Steinmetz
NEW YORK TIMES, 9/10/93, p. C10, Vincent Canby
VARIETY, 9/20/93, p. 27, Brian Lowry
WASHINGTON POST, 9/11/93, p. D3, Peter Gilstrap

RED CIRCLE, THE

A UGC D.A. International release. *Producer:* Robert Dorfman. *Director:* Jean-Pierre Melville. *Screenplay:* Jean-Pierre Melville. *Director of Photography:* Henri Decae. *Music:* Eric de Marsan. *Running time:* 99 minutes. *MPAA Rating:* Not Rated.

CAST: Alain Delon (Corey); Yves Montand (Jansen); Gian-Maria Volonté (Vogel); André Bourvil (Mattei).

VILLAGE VOICE, 10/5/93, p. 58, Lisa Katzman

In orchestrating the chance encounter between Corey (Alain Delon), an ex-con, and Vogel (Gian Maria Volonte), an escaped prisoner, Jean-Pierre Melville deliciously balances the improbability of their meeting against its inevitability. With a toss of a pack of Gauloise, these doppelgänger outlaws seal their bond and their destiny.

The hieroglyphic eloquence that Melville draws from gestures like sharing cigarettes in *The Red Circle* makes for that fine mesh of plot and character forged by American film noir of the '40s and '50s, before Hollywood's bloodlust stampeded the genre into a senselessly plot-driven and violent travesty of itself.

Obsessed by classic American movies, Melville took the form, and, in exemplary French fashion, distilled it. In this elegant 1970 *policier* (albeit in a dubbed and cut version), he achieves the pure, intense flavor of a classical reduction: character is fate. We know not a shred more about Corey and Vogel than is absolutely necessary to carry the plot; what makes this enthralling rather than mundanely minimalist is Melville's mastery of detail.

As an ex-cop manqué rescued from delirium tremens to participate in a Jewel heist, Yves Montand is riveting. After sharpshooting in a tux, he pulls a silver flask out of his pocket and cautiously passes it under his nose. It's a small but powerful moment, one of many.

Also reviewed in:
NEW YORK TIMES, 9/22/93, p. C13, Vincent Canby

REMAINS OF THE DAY, THE

A Columbia Pictures release. *Executive Producer:* Paul Bradley. *Producer:* Mike Nichols, John Calley, and Ismail Merchant. *Director:* James Ivory. *Screenplay:* Ruth Prawer Jhabvala. *Based on the novel by:* Kazuo Ishiguro. *Director of Photography:* Tony Pierce-Roberts. *Editor:* Andrew Marcus. *Music:* Richard Robbins. *Choreographer:* Elizabeth Aldrich. *Sound:* David Stephenson and (music) Bill Sommerville-Large. *Sound Editor:* Collin Miller. *Art Director:* John Ralph. *Set Decorator:* Ian Whittaker. *Costumes:* Jenny Beavan and John Bright. *Make-up:* Christine Beveridge and Norma Webb. *Running time:* 134 minutes. *MPAA Rating:* PG.

CAST: John Haycraft (Auctioneer); Christopher Reeve (Lewis); Anthony Hopkins (Stevens); Emma Thompson (Miss Kenton); Caroline Hunt (Landlady); James Fox (Lord Darlington); Peter Vaughan (Father); Paula Jacobs (Mrs. Mortimer, the Cook); Ben Chaplin (Charlie, Head Footman); Steve Dibben (George, Second Footman); Abigail Harrison (Housemaid); Patrick Godfrey (Spencer); Peter Cellier (Sir Leonard Bax); Peter Halliday (Canon Tufnell); Hugh Grant (Cardinal); Terence Bayler (Trimmer); Jeffry Wickman (Viscount Bigge); Hugh Sweetman (Scullery Boy); Michael Lonsdale (Dupont D'Ivry); Brigitte Kahn (Baroness); John Savident (Doctor Meredith); Tony Aitken (Postmaster); Emma Lewis (Elsa); Joanna Joseph (Irma); Rupert Vansittart (Sir Geoffrey Wren); Tim Pigott-Smith (Benn); Christopher Brown (Wren's Friend); Lena Headey (Lizzie); Paul Copley (Harry Smith); Ian Redford (Publican); Jo Kendall (Publican's Wife); Steven Beard (Andrews); Pip Torrens (Doctor Carlisle); Frank Shelley (Prime Minister); Peter Eyre (Lord Halifax); Jestyn Phillips (Foreign Office Official); Wolf Kahler (German Ambassador); Frank Höltje and Andreas Töns (German Embassy Officials); Roger McKern (Police Constable); Angela Newmarch (Waitress).

CHRISTIAN SCIENCE MONITOR, 11/5/93, p. 12, David Sterritt

The first step in making a good movie is deciding what kind of story you want to tell.

The wizards at Merchant Ivory Productions have taken occasional missteps in this area. When they made "Slaves of New York," for instance, it turned out that nobody wanted to see their comic vision of Manhattan's avant-garde art scene.

In recent years, though, producer Ismail Merchant and director James Ivory have zeroed in on stories that are exactly right for their talents, from the quintessentially American vignettes in "Mr. & Mrs. Bridge" to the British fables of E.M. Forster in "A Room With a View and "Howards End."

Their new movie, "The Remains of the Day," marks another splendidly chosen project for the Merchant-Ivory team. Its main characters and primary setting—servants and aristocrats on a venerable English estate—provide the genteel atmosphere and eye-pleasing detail that have become Ivory's trademark as a director. Yet the surface appearances and events of the story are charged with serious overtones and disturbing subtexts that lend it the resonance admirers have come to expect.

The film is based on a smartly written novel by Kazuo Ishiguro, whose melodiously Japanese name hides the fact that he came to England as a child and grew up in thoroughly British surroundings. His ability to observe English life as both insider and outsider stands him in good stead; the book benefits greatly from his mixed feelings of affectionate respect and critical skepticism.

The story focuses on a British butler named Stevens, who hangs onto the traditions of his trade at a manor called Darlington Hall—refusing to relinquish the prewar past even though it's now the late-1950s and old-school nobles like Lord Darlington have long since vanished. The central event of the movie is a journey Stevens makes to visit a one-time housekeeper of the estate, Miss Kenton, and ask her to retake her former job.

As he prepares for his trip, Stevens has much time for reminiscing about the past; and his memories take on a sharper edge after certain conversations he has while on the road. Lord Darlington was his hero in the glory days of the '30s, when Darlington Hall was the center of international conferences aimed at a "new world order" to be mapped out by Europe's aristocracy. The conscientious butler succeeded in overlooking the fact that his boss was a leading voice for appeasement of Germany's aggression and worked strenuously for British rapport with Hitler's regime.

Another thing Stevens didn't understand, on a different level, was the romantic attraction Miss Kenton felt for him during their long years under the same palatial roof. Wrapped up in his chores, his responsibilities, and his relentless concern for proper impressions, he became a self-blinded automaton—paying attention to details but missing larger matters as intimate as Miss Kenton's love and as sweeping as his employer's fascist sympathies.

Now reality is starting to penetrate Stevens's armor, but it's clearly too late for much meaningful correction to take place.

The story of his gradual enlightenment is touching and provocative—suggesting that "respectable" qualities like personal loyalty, devotion to duty, and regard for tradition have a dark side so malignant that events as awful as a world war can be aided and abetted by them. Ishiguro's novel is built around Stevens's motor trip and the realizations that dawn on him as he mulls over the past, talks with people he meets during his journey, and faces Miss Kenton after a lapse of many years. For the film version, screenwriter Ruth Prawer Jhabvala has made events a bit less orderly and regular, lending the story a slightly more surprising tone while retaining the underlying drama of Stevens's reluctant approach to actualities he's been dodging for so long.

Like the majority of Merchant Ivory movies, however, "The Remains of the Day" gains most of its power from Ivory's visual style—less eloquent and inventive than in his Forster films, but still a pleasure to behold—and from a bevy of sensitive performances.

Anthony Hopkins reconfirms his status as a front-line star with his subtle portrayal of Stevens, and Emma Thompson is ideally cast as his would-be lover. Also in major roles are James Fox as Stevens's former employer, Christopher Reeve as his new American boss, Peter Vaughan as his elderly father, and Michael Lonsdale as a delegate to the political conclave at Darlington Hall.

Tony Pierce-Roberts did the fine cinematography, and Richard Robbins—another Merchant Ivory regular—composed the music. Mike Nichols and John Calley joined Merchant to produce the picture. All deserve a cheer.

FILMS IN REVIEW, 7-8/94, p. 52, Pat Anderson

After *Howards End* I thought the team of Merchant Ivory and Jhabvala could never top this. I was wrong. With the same two leading players, Anthony Hopkins as Stevens the butler par excellence, and Emma Thompson the more human housekeeper, these filmmakers have brought to the screen one of the really great novels of the century.

Author Kazuo Ishiguro was born in Nagasaki, Japan (a nation, too, with a tradition of service). Taken to England at the age of six, he has imbibed the mores not only of post-war Britain, but of the 1930's as well—the decade in which the bulk of the book is set.

The central character and mainstay of the film is Stevens (in the book he is the narrator, looking back on his life while driving to the West Country in the 1950's). And Anthony Hopkins has never, ever been better. He is the spiritual essence of Stevens. This is a man who has been trained all his life by his father William Stevens (Peter Vaughan), himself a dedicated butler, to suppress all imagination and emotion, the better to serve his master.

The butler and housekeeper, elite of the servant world, together with a myriad of cooks, sous-cooks, butlers, under-butlers, maids, under-maids, scullery boys, groundskeepers, gardeners, grooms, all directed by Stevens and Miss Kenton, exist only to serve Lord Darlington (a superb James Fox) and Darlington Hall—the epitome of the enormous country houses still prevalent in the England of the 1930's.

Stevens' new employer, the American Mr. Lewis (Christopher Reeve), who bought Darlington Hall on the death of Lord Darlington, has suggested Stevens might like to drive around and see his own country. Stevens' immediate, almost knee jerk reaction is, "It has been my privilege to see the best of England over the years, sir, within these walls."

Nevertheless, having received a letter from Miss Kenton which has disturbed his sensibilities, he is on his way to Cornwall in his employer's car. As Stevens drives west, in his mind he is reminiscing—taking stock of his life: shown in flashbacks on screen. Stevens recalls his relationship with the volatile Miss Kenton. Since he could never acknowledge to himself that he might care for her, the result is constant conflict and bickering over the endless details of the running of The Hall. But the farther he gets from Oxfordshire and the nearer to Miss Kenton's hometown, the deeper he, reluctantly, probes his psyche.

Casual mention of the Darlington scandal turns his thoughts from Miss Kenton to pre-war events at Darlington Hall: the organization of foreign policy conferences held there under the auspices of Lord Darlington—the amateur politician aiming to befriend Germany. Prime Minister Chamberlain and Foreign Secretary Lord Halifax, for instance, meeting the German Ambassador there in the utmost secrecy; conferences bringing together politicians and diplomats from all over the world to further German respectability and support among nations. And even now, after all the post-war revelations, Stevens is unwilling to admit that his master had been wrong: misguided, perhaps; a pawn of Hitler, perhaps. But a good man who wanted only peace for his country. After all, Stevens himself had only done his own duty throughout. His not to reason why and wherefore, but to serve. His own conscience is clear in this regard.

And with regard to his father who, in his later, more feeble years, has come to Darlington as an under-butler. He is dying in the midst of preparations for the first big conference, and so the succoring of the old man is undertaken by Miss Kenton. Stevens keeps his upper lip stiff and carries on magnificently, confident that this is what Father would want—part of his upbringing.

His conscience, or emotions, are not so clear in the case of Miss Kenton. He is uneasy thinking in retrospect about the little advances she makes; the attempts to get closer; the flowers she cuts to brighten his room; the ways she tries to goad him into showing some kind of passion. And then her announcement that Mr. Benn, a butler friend of theirs, has proposed marriage. For one fleeting moment, Stevens is caught off guard and stands stock still. Then he immediately recovers. "You have my best wishes," he responds with his customary poker face. Now, as he nears her town, he forces himself to admit he may have been mistaken.

The production is faultless. There are marvelous montage sequences superimposed with workers polishing silver and furniture, dusting, making beds; Stevens ironing *The Times* before handing it to Darlington, instructing an under-butler at the magnificently laid dining table. And in the kitchen, with dozens of copper pots lined up on the wall, the pies, the fowl, the game and joints, all being prepared for the lord and master.

Anthony Hopkins and Emma Thompson were made for their roles in this picture, and the rest of the players are also perfectly cast. And Merchant Ivory have beautifully portrayed not only the fictional Cliveden, but also the complete spirit of the internal dialogue of a complicated human being—with all the irony and dignity of Ishiguro's perfect butler.

LOS ANGELES TIMES, 11/5/93, Calendar/p. 1, Kenneth Turan

"The Remains of the Day" is, to echo the Fred Astaire-Ginger Rogers lyric, a fine romance with no kisses. Fine for the audience, that is, but not for the participants, for this is a beautifully melancholy romance between people who point-blank refuse to acknowledge emotional attachments and, constricted by an unwritten professional code, can't even bring themselves to address each other by first names.

While the thought of all this decorous self-denial between a butler and a housekeeper in one of England's great houses in the days just before World War II may sound uninvolving, "Remains" is the opposite, a moving and carefully modulated picture that overcomes a certain innate stodginess with acting from Anthony Hopkins and Emma Thompson that is little short of miraculous.

That Hopkins and Thompson are exceptional together is no surprise after the multiple Oscar-winning version of E.M. Forster's "Howards End," shaped by the same team (director James Ivory, coproducer Ishmail Merchant and screenwriter Ruth Prawer Jhabvala) that here adapted Kazuo Ishiguro's graceful Booker Award-winning novel.

Though this film does not have the thematic richness and grasp of last year's model (due in part to a stubborn difficulty with transferring Ishiguro's novel to the screen), the interplay between these two actors is if anything stronger here. And though it would be an over simplification to drag out the conditional wisdom about the Astaire-Rogers partnership (which claimed that she gave him romantic appeal and he gave her class), Hopkins and Thompson do complement each other in ways that are exceptional.

An actor of thorough discipline and control, Hopkins' gravity makes him the ideal foil for the lively Thompson, bringing out the clarity in her work, while her warmth can't help but underline the innate humanity in his. Their scenes together are the heart of this film, done with an exquisitely calibrated emotion.

But "Remains" does not only take place in the servants' quarters; it is an upstairs-downstairs film that cuts back and forth between the 1930s and 1958. It also parallels the events among the help with what is going on in the public parts of Darlington Hall and the life of Lord Darlington (James Fox).

"Remains" starts near the end of the story, in 1958, after Lord Darlington has died and Darlington Hall has been saved from desecration by the intervention of an American millionaire named Lewis (Christopher Reeve) who remembered both the house and Stevens, its butler, from earlier days.

For though he now presides over a puny few, Stevens (Hopkins) was once the stern head of a staff of 17. Upset at the current state of things downstairs, Stevens tells Lewis he has hopes of rehiring the now-married Miss Kenton (Thompson), the former housekeeper. Stevens then commences a cross-Britain trip to see Miss Kenton and perhaps set tings right in more ways than one.

With intermittent returns to 1958, "Remains" now focuses on the 1930s, when Lord Darlington, a model of distant noblesse oblige, was a figure of some importance on the international political scene and Stevens was in his prime as a man who believed that perfect service for his lordship was a fine and noble ideal.

The Merchant-Ivory production team is the best in the business at re-creating England past, and "Remains" is surely and elegantly mounted.

A match for his surroundings as the equally unerring Stevens. His face a complete mask in which repressed emotions show only as rogue tics and twitches, Hopkins uses a combination of sympathy and stance to brilliantly turn a man of few outward feelings into a compelling figure.

No one makes Stevens twitch more than Miss Kenton, the new housekeeper. She is his match in punctiliousness, but her creed is a duty with a human face, something Stevens finds puzzling.

While all this is going on downstairs, major international conferences are taking place upstairs, with delegates like Lewis debating a particular passion of Lord Darlington's, how best to re-integrate Germany into a hostile Europe.

Maybe inevitably, this part of "Remains" (rated PG for themes) is less involving than its downstairs half. This is especially unfortunate because feeling how much pride Stevens takes in knowing that "history could well be made under this roof," and the price he paid for it, is critical to understanding his actions, or lack of them.

Both he and Miss Kenton, but especially he, implicitly assume that their employer knows best and unquestioningly opt to live half lives instead of whole ones to further Lord Darlington's aims. When circumstances force Stevens and Miss Kenton to gradually confront exactly what they've sacrificed so much for, they must confront their own frailty as well.

Perhaps the greatest drag on the film's overall effectiveness is a change from the book that may have been unavoidable. The novel is told from the point of view of Stevens, a man who is a fallible and untrustworthy narrator, and author Ishiguro's strength is the way he allows us to see the true state of affairs even though our guide never really does. This subversive point of view is difficult to achieve on film, but without it the sorrowful story of "The Remains of the Day" can't help but lose part of its poignancy. The presence of this year's most moving tandem performance, however, makes it a film no one who is passionate about acting will be able to miss.

NEW YORK, 11/8/93, p. 74, David Denby

Stiff-armed and nearly choking in his tuxedo, Anthony Hopkins is Stevens the perfect butler, the hero and fool of a brilliant new Merchant Ivory production, *The Remains of the Day*. Hopkins's close-cropped haircut brings out the military bluntness of his skull and the ugly assertiveness of his ears and chin. As he walks down endless halls, his arms hanging, he looks foreshortened—demented, almost. How can such a man be a hero? His Stevens is a paradox of servitude and pride. Like a monk or a soldier, the butler can rise only by lowering himself—by wiping out his own desires, his own physical grace, and prostrating himself before an ideal.

The ideal here is the magnificently run great house—Darlington Hall, in Oxfordshire—to whose many-chambered perfection Stevens is slavishly devoted. Stevens is obsessed with the forks and spoons; he is master of the knobs, vases, books, and sconces, the complex organization of underbutlers and cleaning maids. At the same time, he fails to notice anything that matters. He never realizes that his master, Lord Darlington (James Fox), who held large international "conferences" at the house in the thirties, was a fascist booby who almost turned his country over to the Nazis.

As a character, Stevens is an elaborate joke, though not a joke of the P.G. Wodehouse variety. Stevens is Wodehouse's incomparable Jeeves recast as a tragic figure. Adapted by the Merchant Ivory team from the celebrated 1989 novel by Kazuo Ishiguro, *The Remains of the Day* introduces a bizarre but fascinating new subject, the interior life of a perfect servant. Ishiguro wrote the book in the first person: Stevens, an example of an "unreliable narrator," tells his own story and unconsciously reveals himself". The filmmakers, including screenwriter Ruth Prawer Jhabvala, have moved into the third person: Stevens in all his fanatical perfectionism is simply observed by the camera, along with the other characters. But in both versions the material is a study of limited awareness and violent self-suppression. An emotionally withdrawn man, Stevens betrays everyone who needs him—everyone, that is, but his employer. He is a prig and a moral coward. He is also a great man (of a peculiar sort). That's the surprise of the movie—and the surprise of our response to it.

The Remains of the Day, I suppose, is another valentine to dear, declining England—so proud, so blind, so stupid—and it runs down a bit at the end, when the valentine comes close to bathos. But much of this Merchant Ivory production is wonderfully absorbing; and though *The Remains of the Day* is a hushed and beautiful movie, there's a subterranean stream of malicious wit in it that dies only at the end. Merchant Ivory productions are not genteel and enervated anymore; their imagery has grown stronger, their conflicts sharper, their sense of character more abrupt and decisive.

The filmmakers have properly attacked Ishiguro's fictional creation as a specialized, eccentric subject that operates within a very narrow logic. Like Stevens himself, the movie is precise and almost caterpillar-like in its adherence to a closely observed terrain—library, dining room, kitchen, and all the emotional complications of domestic service. What we have here is the unconscious of a great house. Dyrham Park, the stand-in for Darlington Hall, is a large but not overpowering honey-colored stone house built into a cleft in a hill and surrounded by dark green lawns, and the filmmakers used a variety of other famous residences (including Powderham Castle and Badminton) for the interiors. As photographed, the house, inside and out, represents the ultimate in somber magnificence and beauty. Yet the film's nostalgia is bitterly ironic.

In the late fifties, an American millionaire (Christopher Reeve, who, as usual, seems utterly callow) has taken over Darlington. The American doesn't understand much about England, but he has money; and Stevens, still in place after many years of service, and eager to restore the house to its days of glory, travels to the West Country in search of a former housekeeper, Miss Kenton (Emma Thompson), who worked under him in the thirties. As he drives, he reviews in his mind the prewar period, when Lord Darlington brought together British right-wing plutocrats and politicians and their opposite numbers from Germany. Darlington, it turns out, was one of the architects of appeasement. But Stevens saw nothing but a perfect gentleman; he mistook condescension for nobility. So the first irony is that all of Stevens's labors—his extraordinary idealism—are put at the service of someone entirely worthless. Thick-eyebrowed, slack in carriage, and drooping in intonation, James Fox's languid Darlington uses his worshiping butler as an audience, as an arena for the acting out of his fantasy of nobility. The two men, locked in their folie à deux, are equally devoted to illusion.

Stevens misses what could have been the most vital relationship of his life: The housekeeper, Miss Kenton, loves him. Quarreling and teasing—anything to get Stevens to notice her and to respond as a man, not as a butler—Miss Kenton attacks and attacks, knocking herself out against the wall of his sexual fears. It's a relief to see Emma Thompson, after a string of Miss Wonderful performances, letting out a streak of exasperated spite. In a moment of high comedy, she taunts Hopkins, trying to outdo him in propriety, but he freezes her out. As in *Howards End*, Thompson speaks for emotional truth and connection, and Hopkins withdraws into defensive formalities: the heroic English female, and the equally heroic, though frighteningly crippled, English male.

Except for the actors, the principals behind *The Remains of the Day* were born outside England—Ishiguro in Nagasaki, Merchant in Bombay, Ivory in California, and Jhabvala in Cologne. And yet they are held together as collaborators by the idea of Englishness, a fascination with the rigidities and deformations and profoundly articulated respectfulness of a class society in which duty comes before self. Betrayal is almost inevitable: Stevens not only lets down the housekeeper; he lets down his elderly and failing father (Peter Vaughan), also a butler, who becomes too feeble to serve. Stevens is a Ralph Richardson kind of role, a man who wipes himself out, repressing all feeling but loyalty to an ideal; and Hopkins, now in his fifties, has developed a comparable eccentricity and force—for instance, his way of seeming to sink into a fit of abstraction for an instant, and then snapping to attention. Despite a surface rectitude, he suggests the inner struggles of this strange man.

So here's the second irony, and it involves the audience: When the fascists are gathered at Darlington for their disgusting conference, rather than wanting to throw a bomb, one wants—such is the film's momentum—everything to *go right*, the glasses and forks and linens all to be in exactly the right place. Until recently, James Ivory has seemed an emotionally reticent director (he's a bit of a perfect butler himself, forever serving the text that he's adapting), but this cranky subject is perfect for him, and he puts us inside Stevens's obsessions. The movie has a strikingly ambiguous flavor: Ivory and Jhabvala know that many of us hate class privilege yet retain an irrepressible desire for perfect order and luxury. Stevens may be a snob and a eunuch, but he's also a kind of magician; he may be inadequate in all the relations of life, but he's also admirable. So is the movie.

NEW YORK POST, 11/5/93, p. 31, Michael Medved

What if you discover in old age that the cause and the system to which you've selflessly devoted your entire life is actually a shabby fraud?

This is the heart-breaking question at the center of "The Remains of the Day," the magnificent new movie from director James Ivory, producer Ismail Merchant, and screenwriter Ruth Prawer Jhabvala—the same team that created "Howards End," "A Room With a View" and so many other great films.

This new picture, which may stand as their consummate masterpiece, is a stunning adaptation of the award-winning novel by Kazuo Ishiguro, who emigrated with his family from Nagasaki to England at age 6.

Sir Anthony Hopkins plays Stevens, the perfect English butler who makes a journey across Britain in 1958 and looks back on his long decades of faithful service to the late Lord Darlington (James Fox). It turns out that his aristocratic employer served as a pawn to the Nazis, hosting a number of "peace conferences," and pro-appeasement gatherings in the 1930s, then suffered total disgrace after the war.

It's only when this deluded nobleman dies, and an American millionaire (Christopher Reeve) buys the ancestral estate, that the butler begins to recognize the sacrifices he has made in his lifetime as a supremely dignified servant.

In particular. Stevens looks back upon the way that he stifled his profound feelings for Miss Kenton (Emma Thompson) the warm-hearted, magnetically attractive housekeeper who served alongside him in the '30s. Perhaps it is not too late to renew their relationship and to lure her back to Darlington Hall in an effort to restore its former glory.

Even though this plot may not sound like an edge-of-your-seat nail-biter, you are unlikely to find a more compelling, more passionate film anywhere. The incomparable cast endows even the smallest moments with riveting intensity; Hopkins' performance in particular is, quite simply, one of the greatest acting achievements ever captured on film.

He painstakingly reveals his character's tragic soul, as we feel his all-consuming dedication to an "England where order and tradition still prevail'," and his unquestioning belief that his master is not only elegant, but also must be moral and just.

Emma Thompson is in every way Hopkins' equal, and the moments when the two leads briefly touch generate shattering jolts of electricity: a scene in which she prys a sentimental novel out of his embarrassed hands could be the sexiest sequence in any film this year.

The only actress who has a right to contest Thompson's claim to a second consecutive best actress Oscar for her role in this film is ... Emma Thompson, for her equally, luminous performance in "Much Ado About Nothing."

In "The Remains of the Day" the breathtakingly beautiful sets, the luminous camerawork (by Tony Pierce-Roberts) and the haunting musical score (by Richard Robbins) only add to the profound pleasure of the audience.

If you miss the chance of seeing it, you may not be guilty of wasting your entire life, like Stevens the Butler, but will definitely have lost a glorious opportunity.

NEWSDAY, 11/5/93, Part II/p. 78, Jack Mathews

The story sounds like a non-story. Two servants living under the same roof in ominous pre-World II England, in love but unable to express their feelings, prevented by their rigid rules of behavior from even calling each other by their first names.

But if there is no drama in suppressed emotions, don't tell Edith Wharton, who wrote all about it in "The Age of Innocence," or Kazuo Ishiguro, who did the same in "The Remains of the Day." And certainly don't breathe a word of it to director James Ivory, producer Ismael Merchant and screenwriter Ruth Prawer Jhabvala, who have thrived on adapting personal dramas culled by novelists from beneath the surface of polite society,

"The Remains of the Day," the Merchant-Ivory-Jhabvala team's latest adaptation, is a match for its best, last year's stunning "Howards End," and it features what may be the finest performance in the late-blooming career of the brilliant Anthony Hopkins.

Hopkins plays Stevens, head butler of the massive estate of Lord Darlington (the superb James Fox), an aristocrat whose good heart and intentions are undermined by a misguided and naive faith in Hitler's reconstruction of Germany.

Lord Darlington's involvement in high-level politics, his hosting of international conferences on the shifting dynamics in Europe, provides a powerful context for the story of Stevens, the consummate professional servant, and Miss Kenton (Emma Thompson), the self-assured but lonely woman who becomes the manse's housekeeper.

There is an attraction between the two that grows naturally but is prevented from expressing itself by the pressures of their positions, and by Stevens' resolute devotion to his duties. He's not just a butler opening doors, he's the head of a staff 17, in a house where royalty and heads of state, often visit.

The rule against romance between servants applies to all, and through moments of profound temptation, Stevens maintains a cool distance.

"Remains" is told in flashback, from the view of the mid-'50s, long after Lord Darlington has been discredited, and as Stevens is being summoned to his old job by the estate's new owner, a retired U.S. congressman (Christopher Reeve) who, as a guest at those pre-war conferences, had tried to warn Darlington of the dangers of Nazism.

"What did I say then?" the American asks, recalling a dinner at which he labeled Darlington and the other guests "political amateurs."

"Sorry, sir, I was too busy serving to listen to the speeches," Stevens answers.

Not true. In that emotionally agonizing sequence, Stevens was too distracted to hear the speeches. He'd just been told that his father, also a career servant, lay dying upstairs, and his professionalism, plus the gravity of the discussion, kept him pinned down in the dining room.

That he couldn't reveal a personal feeling, even a quarter-century later, says much about Stevens' character, and about the challenge Hopkins met in making him one of the most fascinating and sympathetic figures in modern film.

Hopkins essentially gives two performances, simultaneously. One is Stevens' demeanor—always in control, always courteous and well-mannered. Even while being humiliated by one of Darlington's pro-Nazi guests, who uses the butler's inability to answer complex politi-cal questions to impeach will-of-the-people democracy, Stevens doesn't break stride. The insult registers with a flicker of pain in his eyes, but he goes on serving.

The other performance is almost totally internal. Stevens is far from an apolitical animal, and you know he senses the danger of Darlington's seduction by the Germans. But loyalty and his master-knows-best working philosophy always take precedence over his personal feelings. When the two pressures collide, as when he's ordered to demote his frail, proud father or to fire two Jewish servants, the weight of the world seems to settle onto his slumping shoulders.

For Hopkins and Thompson, the balance of roles has swung from "Howards End," where Thompson got the best of it (and an Oscar). Here, Thompson's role is in support of Hopkins, and though the actress' natural energy makes Miss Kenton more forceful than might be intended, she helps lighten up an awfully heavy load.

As usual with Merchant-Ivory productions, "The Remains of the Day" is a journey through a lush period painting. The interiors of the Darlington estate serve as a museum of spectacular French, German and English antiques and paintings, and we can safely say the competition for the year's art direction awards has just become a two-horse race, between "Remains" and Martin Scorsese's "The Age of Innocence."

I'd be happy to see that competition end in a draw, but in every other way "Remains" is the more accomplished, more involving film. Scorsese, the master of mean streets, proved that he could recreate an elegant period setting with "Innocence." Merchant-Ivory have been doing it for a living.

NEWSWEEK, 11/8/93, p. 78, Jack Kroll

When P.G. Wodehouse was creating Jeeves, his immortal English manservant, he hired a butler and took notes on his behavior. "Useful chap to have around," remarked a friend, "but a bit on the somber side." He should have met Stevens, the butler in *The Remains of the Day*. Somber would be a fun mood for the magisterially morose Stevens (Anthony Hopkins), who has buttled for Lord Darlington (James Fox) for 35 years. The vapid Lord D., a Nazi sympathizer before World War II, receives German bigwigs at his stately home, Darlington Hall. During these sessions, butlerian protocol calls for Stevens to keep his eye on the truffles and off the treachery. When the housekeeper, Miss Kenton (Emma Thompson), is upset at the sacking of two Jewish maids, Stevens explains that Lord D. and his ilk understand "many things that you and I don't." When his father (who's serving as a sub-butler under him) dies of a stroke during a big dinner party, Stevens goes on dispensing the port and cigars. And he chickens out in his one chance at emotional fulfillment, with the vibrant Miss Kenton.

Stevens is meant as a tragi-comic figure, which is easier to accept in the prize-winning original novel by the Japanese-English writer Kazuo Ishiguro. There the story is told by Stevens himself, with Ishiguro controlling all the ironic nuances of a narrative that moves from complacent self-deception to chagrined realization of a wasted life. The novel is a writer's tour de force, but the film, scripted by Ruth Prawer Jhabvala, sets the characters in the light of reality, and it may arouse more impatience than empathy. "Come off it, Stevens, you stiff upper drip," we may think as the butler performs his ballet of elegant obsequiousness, a very Baryshnikov of bowing and scraping.

The film reunites the team that made the deservingly honored "Howards End," producer Ismail Merchant, director James Ivory, writer Jhabvala and the two stars. Hopkins and Thompson are superb actors, but they (and Ivory) can't shake the sense that Stevens and Miss Kenton are less fully fleshed characters than embodiments of a thesis about the English class system. The genius of Jeeves was that he was a subversive parody of that system; the butler was smarter than the asses he worked for. The most painful scene in the film occurs when a guest of Lord D.'s, to prove that democracy doesn't work, quizzes Stevens about arcane political issues. "I'm unable to be of assistance," says the butler. Jeeves would have replied with dazzling doubletalk, throwing the snobs into confusion. "The Remains of the Day" is stately but depressing. Satire is the best revenge.

SIGHT AND SOUND, 12/93, p. 51, Geoffrey Macnab

England, shortly after the end of the Second World War. The large country house of the late Lord Darlington has been bought by Lewis, a former American diplomat. Lewis finds he has 'inherited' Darlington's old butler, Mr Stevens, a man he remembers from a visit he made to England before the War. Stevens is hard pressed to get the house back in working order before the diplomat's family arrives. Nevertheless, Lewis agrees to Stevens' request for a holiday, and lends him his own Daimler. Stevens plans to travel to the West Country, where he hopes to catch up with the old housekeeper, Miss Kenton, whom he wants to entice back into service following the breakdown of her marriage.

As Stevens sets off on his journey, the action flits back to the 30s, when Darlington Hall was at its high point. Shortly after Miss Kenton arrives on the staff, Stevens approaches Lord Darlington and asks if he may recruit his own father as the underbutler. Mr Stevens Snr has long experience as a butler, but is getting on in years. Miss Kenton warns Mr Stevens that his father is not up to his tasks, but he ignores her. One afternoon, Stevens Snr slips while carrying a tray of tea. Lord Darlington is solicitous, but worried. He has convened a conference on Anglo-German relations which, he tells Stevens, is vital to European interests: the slightest blunder could have disastrous results. Stevens moves his father to lighter duties.

During the conference, all the delegates except Lewis, the American diplomat, appease the Nazi visitors. Halfway through the event, Stevens Snr falls ill and dies. Although upset, Mr Stevens continues to attend to his duties. Miss Kenton has gradually grown infatuated with Stevens. One evening, she visits him in his private rooms, and finds him reading. Momentarily, the couple seem about to kiss, but Stevens recovers his composure and dismisses her. Bitterly disappointed, Miss Kenton eventually leaves Darlington Hall to marry another butler, Mr Benn, and to help him run a boarding house. One night, there is a secret meeting at the house between the Prime Minister and the German Ambassador. Darlington's journalist nephew Reggie writes a piece condemning appeasement, and upbraids Stevens for not paying any attention to politics.

En route to visit Miss Kenton, Stevens runs out of petrol, and he seeks assistance in a nearby pub, where the locals mistake him for a politician. The next day, the local doctor gives him a lift back to the stranded Daimler. The doctor is fascinated to learn Stevens served Lord Darlington, who had been discredited in the press as a traitor, and had died not long after the war. Stevens defends his former master. At last, he and Miss Kenton have their reunion. They reminisce over tea at a smart hotel, but she refuses to come back to Darlington Hall. Her daughter is pregnant and Miss Kenton wants to stay nearby while she has her baby. As evening falls, Stevens sees Miss Kenton onto her bus and the couple say goodbye, presumably for the last time.

In Kazuo Ishiguro's Booker Prize winner, Merchant and Ivory find another novel ripe for their stately brand of adaptation. The book takes the form of an elegiac memoir-cum-travelogue, penned by an emotionally repressed butler who has lived through seismic times without ever quite noticing what was going on. In the 30s, his 'master' Lord Darlington, a gentleman politician, had been doing his darndest to appease the Nazis. Many years later, Stevens finally begins to wonder if his own dogged loyalty was misplaced. Worse, he rues his missed romantic opportunity with the housekeeper, Miss Kenton.

Ishiguro is a contemporary novelist, but *The Remains of the Day* is set safely in the past. It thus provides a haven from which the film-makers can continue their excoriation of the English psyche (if *Slaves of New York* anything to go by, when they stray into modern times, they become seriously unstuck). Here, they go Upstairs and Downstairs, note and observe the absurd rituals of country house living, and even take a few floundering, satirical slaps at the class system. But, as usual, theirs remains a curiously ambivalent project. On the page, perhaps, Darlington Hall may seem a vast mausoleum of a house which keeps servants and toffs alike manacled by propriety. On screen, however, the sheer visual relish with which the place is depicted can't help but undermine the mordant irony in Ruth Prawer Jhabvala's script: we have baying hounds, cheery cooks in the pantry, elegant dinner parties, tea in the conservatory, soirees in the drawing room, rustic pubs, and lots of English autumnal scenes. With most of the story told through flashback, the prevailing mood is one of nostalgia, and it is little wonder *The Remains of the Day* seems more a lament for lost grandeur than an indictment of aristocratic folly.

Only the scenes involving Peter Vaughan as Mr Stevens Senior, a grim, imposing figure who looks as if he has stumbled out of a Charles Addams cartoon, hint at the vein of Gothic comedy the picture might have tapped, or suggest any tension between masters and servants (there is one supreme moment where a little bubble of snot drops out of his nose into the wine just as he is about to pour for his lordship). Counterpointing Vaughan is Hugh Grant as Darlington's journalist nephew, who shows all the cheerful inanity of a P.G. Wodehouse character. The rest of the supporting cast have a mainly decorative role. Christopher Reeve (the spitting image of Albert Gore in his double-breasted suit) plays the far-seeing American diplomat who rails against the Nazi supermen and English amateurs alike; Michael Lonsdale, once a Buñuel regular and a fine

Bond villain, is largely wasted as the French Ambassador more concerned about the corns on his feet than the future of his country. The film is full of lookalikes—of Oswald Mosley, Chamberlain and Ribbentrop—but eschews analysis of the rise of fascism in favour of crude caricature.

If much of the picture has an embalmed feel, its ossification turns out to be a positive advantage when it comes to the love story at its core. This is a very British affair, with Anthony Hopkins and Emma Thompson as a latterday Trevor Howard and Celia Johnson—a couple thwarted by class, convention and the prison house of language. Even at his most monstrous, as Captain Bligh or Hannibal Lecter, Hopkins has always been expert at suggesting a sense of wounded innocence. Here, monolithic, with his hair greased back and hardly a flicker of emotion showing on his face, he still manages to hint at seething inner turmoil. Thompson, in a slightly thankless role, conveys her romantic disappointment effectively enough. Though the film is overlong, taking its plodding, lugubrious pace from Hopkins himself, at least it ends with a fine, tear-jerking flourish, with the last goodbye being said at a bus stop as the rain comes lashing down. Whatever else you may say about it (and it seems unlikely to win round many of Merchant-Ivory's critics), *The Remains of the Day* is a film anybody will be able to go and see with their mother. Whether or not that is a recommendation is a moot point.

TIME, 11/8/93, p. 87, Richard Corliss

Anthony Hopkins is Stevens the butler, the old bulldog of Darlington Hall. In the throat of his Churchillian jaw one can read a declaration of honorable purpose; in his blue eyes one can hear the quiet bark, feel the dogged bite. Stevens lives to serve his master and to rule the servants. Upstairs his step is tentative and his eyes aim for the carpet. Downstairs, as Chairman of the Board, he has a sturdy stride and an imperious gaze. He knows his place all too well. He believes it his job to hear nothing while above, to surrender to no soft impulse when below. That is why Stevens was deaf to the nasty political business that took place in the drawing rooms and why he was blind to the fuller life he might have shared with the flinty housekeeper, Miss Kenton.

Stevens is the narrator of Kazuo Ishiguro's 1988 novel, *The Remains of the Day*, a drama so delicate that it touches the reader deeply without applying the pressure of sentiment. The story runs on parallel tracks: the years before World War II, when Stevens worked for his beloved Lord Darlington, an aristocrat who falls into an alliance with the Nazis; and the late '50s, when Stevens seeks out Miss Kenton in hopes she will return as housekeeper and, perhaps, something more. In his own ornate, unflowing words, Stevens condemns himself as the English version of a "good German": a man who disappointed Miss Kenton, his father (an aged butler), his country and himself in blinkered devotion to duty.

The lovely film that James Ivory (director), Ruth Prawer Jhabvala (screenwriter) and Ismail Merchant (producer) have made of *The Remains of the Day* has the hallmarks of their best recent work: the aggrieved passion of *Howard's End*, the acutely drawn sense of loss in *Mr. & Mrs. Bridge*. They have peppered the story with deft details that illuminate the cottage industry of running a lavish estate: snipped hedges, gleaming doorknobs, decapitated fowl, the *Times* pages freshly ironed each morning. And they have filled the house with a perfect cast: Emma Thompson as Miss Kenton; James Fox as Lord Darlington; Peter Vaughan as Stevens' father, the proud old retainer who will never say die—even when he does. These characters, like those in *The Age of Innocence*, are all genteel anachronisms. They sin, in our eyes, by not daring to sin; they are poignant in their fidelity to tattered principles. The muted tones of Ivory's film tell you that this is a ghost story without corpses.

This time Ivory and his longtime colleagues have gone their source one better, or one quieter: the film is even more discreet, more Stevens-like, than the book. They have withheld the revelations of tears and admission of heartbreak that finally clatter around the butler like broken Wedgwood. Here, Stevens will never wake violently from his reverie of duty served; he will be trapped in Darlington Hall like a bird that can't find an open window. So the filmmakers have dared I believe that the audience will detect these domestic cataclysms in the performance of the man who plays Stevens.

Hopkins, of course. No other actor of his generation need apply. Alan Bates, Albert Finney, Ian McKellen, Derek Jacobi—each brings the handsomely monogrammed baggage of an outsize personality. They would be too big for the role, tell too much. Hopkins is just the man for this.

For much of his career, as a prissy Richard the Lionheart in *The Lion in Winter* (his first film, 1968) or the Rupert Murdoch-like press baron in the 1985 play *Pravda*, he had his own suitcase of mannerisms: the clipped elocution, the run-on sentence, all the pensive ahhs and umms. But with age and stardom, he has discovered how to be still. He knows he can do less and be more. Audiences will study him like a weather-worn statue for hints of darkness, heroism, meaning. Like Stevens, he learned to serve, and to seek greatness in serving.

His friend the English actor Julian Fellowes had passed along this comment about a good butler: When he's in the room, the room is emptier. "I took that," Hopkins says, "and kept it in my head for the entire film. It was simple: just stand still." So much of the comedy in his role, and the sadness, arise from this stillness. Before a hunt, Stevens holds a drinking cup for a horseman; the aristocrat takes no notice of his offer, and the butler takes no notice of the slight. His stillness may mask sexual fear: when Miss Kenton amiably approaches him, he freezes like a bruised virgin. The rest of the film Hopkins carries with a small gnomic smile that means a dozen things in a dozen scenes: gratitude, impatience, self-control. "I can say it's simple now," the actor acknowledges, "but it's taken years to distill my work to a more economic form. I suppose I'm pretty adept now at playing these rather still parts."

To moviegoers, Hopkins became famous playing a "still part": Hannibal Lecter, the voracious serial killer in *The Silence of the Lambs*. He not only won an Oscar, he also vaulted into instant celebrity. "I thought it would be the role of a lifetime:" He was right, and it is a celebrity he frankly relishes. He will phone the secretary of a chum and identify himself as "her friend who likes to eat people."

Hopkins can be so engagingly heedless about stardom because, he says, "I've never really planned out a career. I've gone along with—call it destiny, luck, whatever. I've very much been that sort of person my entire life." Born New Year's Eve 1937 in Port Talbot, Wales, the son of a master confectioner and baker, Hopkins entered the Cardiff School of Music and Drama to study piano. "I was a poor student," he says, "very slow, very backward. I drifted into acting because, literally, I had nothing better to do."

Like many British actors, he busily shuttled from the subsidized stage to the West End, from movies to TV, in the U.K. and the U.S. But a spell of boozing helped end his first marriage and jeopardized his career. Today he alludes to those troubled times in his patented short sentences: "I'm not unique. People have bad patches and good patches. I don't dwell in the past. Don't look back on it. It's over, done. Buried. The past is dead as a doornail. You can't undo it. It's all there."

He reacts with the same equanimity to the good fortune that is lately his: fame, top roles (another one, as C.S. Lewis to Debra Winger's Joy Gresham in *Shadowlands*, coming at Christmas) and a solid second marriage of 20 years. "I'm 55, and I feel like 25;' he says. "I've reached a point in my life where there's nothing to win, nothing to lose and nothing to prove." Call him Ordinary Joe. Or, rather, as of this year, Sir Ordinary Joe. "My wife told me I'd gotten a letter offering a knighthood. I said, 'Oh my God, what for?' When good things happen, you think, God, has that really happened? Like the Oscar. I kept getting up in the middle of the night and saw it sitting on the table. Couldn't believe it."

Anthony Hopkins smiles. Like Stevens, he has the strength of opaqueness. Unlike Stevens, he is a man secure in his age, and very much his own master.

VILLAGE VOICE, 11/9/93, p. 60, Georgia Brown

I know I'm underappreciative of actors. It's due to a long habit of watching movies, not as assembled and collectively crafted products, but as projections from some single imagining light source. I have trouble recognizing actors from one role to another (aren't they different people?)—although this could also be taken as a tribute to their skills. Naive as I am, however, even I can spot Anthony Hopkins in *The Remains of the Day* and observe teensy tics and tricks of the eyes as he embodies a man intent on shutting down all emotion. The camera examines his broad, hardworking mug close up for so much of the film, even I knew I was supposed to murmur *bravo, Toni*. The themes are the ones the Merchant-Ivory team goes for: stifled desire, manners, and the passions they mask.

Hopkins plays a master of the mask—Stevens, head butler for 35 years at Darlington Hall, a very grand (fictitious) English country house. The son of a head butler, Stevens is dedicated to service of both a peculiarly intimate and a peculiarly impersonal sort. In the presence of others, his gray-blue eyes glaze into a kind of protective blindness; even while observing the minutest details of the surroundings, he's careful not to intrude on one's privacy with an offending gaze. In the presence of his lordship, Stevens speaks in low, deferential tones, exploiting little hesitancies for their humbling effects; when addressing subordinates, his staff, he's all brisk efficiency and useful instruction. Service is a matter of perpetual self-renewal.

Alone, Stevens permits himself an occasional flutter of a smile—a bit awkward since so unpracticed. And when his studied equilibrium is threatened, he can become curt, even cruel. The latter comes out especially when challenged, or teased, by the mansion's equally loyal and efficient housekeeper, Miss Kenton. Miss Kenton is played by an actress I also recognize, Emma Thompson, who is very good at tics and briskness and eccentric hesitancies herself. But Miss Kenton, in her early thirties, is slightly more susceptible to feeling than Mr. Stevens.

As always, Merchant, Ivory, and screenwriter Ruth Prawer Jhabvala have chosen to adapt a novel—this time the Booker Prize-winner by Japanese-born, English-bred Kazuo Ishiguro. Like Ishiguro's first two novels (*A Pale View of the Hills* and *An Artist of the Floating World*), the elegiac, ruminative *Remains* is told through an elderly, unreliable narrator whom readers are meant to see through. It's a good thing, too, to have somewhere else to look, since the fussy Stevens initially seems such a bloody bore, going on about silver polish and staff plans and some *Quarterly for the Gentleman's Gentleman*.

A black comedy of manners, the movie follows the novel in that a good deal of the narrative takes place in nonchronological flashback—memory's floating world. Since the death of Lord Darlington, the manor has a new owner, a smiling, "bantering" American (Christopher Reeve), who persuades Stevens to take his first vacation, a motor journey from Oxfordshire to Cornwall. The trip is partly business: Stevens is hoping to persuade the former Miss Kenton—she left her post to marry—to return to service. The journey touches off memories of Miss Kenton, his father (who dies at Darlington during a particularly hectic banquet), and of his lordship. Needless to say, the implications of the memories are explored more satisfyingly in the novel than in the film.

The movie's eyes are on the love story. And what a touchingly, farcically distant love story it is! At their moment of closest intimacy—as Miss Kenton playfully tries to pry away a book he's holding—Stevens shrinks back in the shadows, looking positively sinister (Lechter-like, in fact), fiercely guarding his secret. Miss Kenton, we discover later on, wants someone who needs her, whereas the only one Stevens needs to be needed by is his lord and master, a shy stiff played by James Fox—an actor whose lordly gifts, even I can say, are not required here.

In the '20s, Lord Darlington begins hosting conferences on the fate of Germany, hoping to help this former enemy recover from the war. (It's bad form to kick a foe after he's down.) Unfortunately, the meetings continue through the '30s and his lordship becomes a Nazi dupe. (He orders Stevens to dismiss two Jewish maids in his employ.) To himself, Stevens keeps defending his master's gentlemanly intentions, though on his journey he finds himself, Peter-like, denying he ever knew his lord.

What's moving about the novel—which starts at a creep but gathers steam—is that Stevens, for all his stuffiness, finally does see. In the twilight of his career (facing the remains of his day), Stevens becomes obsessed by big questions: Starting with, "What constitutes a great butler?" he extrapolates to broader issues of service, loyalty, the duties of citizenship. (On the road to Weymouth, Ishiguro plants various stock figures taking representative positions on human nature and the state. The novel may be overly schematic, but it's also strikingly ambitious in ways its detractors didn't pick up on.)

The movie ignores all this, though I'm surprised reviewers did too. A few noticed that this meditation on uncritical devotion applied to Japan as much as to England—as Pico Iyer put it in *Partisan Review* "one island of shopkeepers ... can shed light on another"—though no one carried the analogy further. As if there aren't company men, party loyalists, nationalists, and other zealots everywhere. As if a yearning for authority doesn't always find some crank or fiend or simple fetish to attach to.

At the end of the novel (but not the movie), Stevens himself grasps the central issue: What is perfect service worth if the cause is corrupt? And the fault, he realizes, is his, for not critically evaluating, for subordinating the substance of the goings-on to the mechanics. Facing the twilight without gods, he does have the consolation of his courage.

There are many ways of adapting novels into film. For *Short Cuts*, Altman blithely pillaged Carver's stories—a refreshing irreverence only undercut by his terminally shallow sensibility. Superficially respectful, Merchant-Ivory-Jhabvala adapt by simultaneously reducing and blowing up: summarizing, dropping complexities, relying on large performances, and finally sealing all in a garish, calendar-perfect visual envelope. What they intend, clearly, is elegance and decorum; what they dish-up is high kitsch.

Also reviewed in:
CHICAGO TRIBUNE, 11/5/93, Friday/p. A, Michael Wilmington
NATION, 12/13/93, p. 743, Stuart Klawans
NEW REPUBLIC, 12/6/93, p. 32, Stanley Kauffmann
NEW YORK TIMES, 11/5/93, p. C1, Vincent Canby
NEW YORKER, 11/15/93, p. 114, Anthony Lane
VARIETY, 10/4/93, p. 38, Todd McCarthy
WASHINGTON POST, 11/5/93, p. G1, Rita Kempley
WASHINGTON POST, 11/5/93, Weekend/p. 50, Desson Howe

RETURN OF THE LIVING DEAD 3

A Trimark Pictures release. *Executive Producer:* Roger Burlage and Lawrence Steven Meyers. *Producer:* Gary Schmoeller and Brian Yuzna. *Director:* Brian Yuzna. *Screenplay:* John Penney. *Director of Photography:* Gerry Lively. *Editor:* Christopher Roth. *Music:* Barry Goldberg. *Sound:* Geoffrey Lucas Patterson. *Production Designer:* Anthony Tremblay. *Art Director:* Aram Allen. *Special Effects:* Steve Johnson, Tim Ralston, Kevin Brennan, Christopher Nelson, and Wayne Toth. *Running time:* 97 minutes. *MPAA Rating:* R.

CAST: Mindy Clarke (Julie); J. Trevor Edmond (Curt); Kent McCord (Colonel Reynolds); Basil Wallace (Riverman); Sarah Douglas (Sinclair); Fabio Urena (Mogo).

LOS ANGELES TIMES, 10/29/93, Calendar/p. 6, Peter Rainer

If you would much rather watch zombies in the movies than real people—is there any difference these days?—you'll have an OK time at "Return of the Living Dead 3". It's not even necessary to have seen "1" or "2."

It's not necessary to see "3" either. (The R rating is for—big surprise—horror, violence, gore, language and sexuality.)

This is a zombie flick with "heart," which is ironic since hearts are just about the only body part you *don't* see. Curt (J. Trevor Edmond) is a motherless Army brat whose stiff-backed father (Kent McCord) is dabbling in a top-secret military experiment to revive cadavers and mummified corpses with the chemical Trioxin (which was introduced in "1"). When Curt's girlfriend Julie (Mindy Clarke) is killed in a motorcycle accident, Curt douses her in Trioxin, and, presto-chango—it's reanimation time!

Curt, demonstrating a Romeo-like ardor, refuses to back off from Julie when she starts snorting and drooling. You get the (perhaps unintended) impression that Curt may actually find all this zombie flesh-eating stuff a little ... well, kinky.

Julie, good sport that she is, doesn't want to chomp other people, unlike just about everyone else in the ever-mounting cast of zombies. So she pierces herself instead. Julie carries the piercing craze among teens to surreal new heights. In the movie's most garishly imaginative moment, she appears fully punctured with earrings, shards of glass, nails. She's horrific yet eerily beautiful, like a demonic religious icon.

Steve Johnson, who did the effects for "Aliens," is responsible for Julie's look. The director, Brian Yuzna, who also produced some of the best Stuart Gordon movies, including "Re-

Animator" and "From Beyond," supervised five different special-effects experts—one for each category of glop.

The script could have used a few experts, too. The action is too serious for a genre that can no longer be played seriously. The New Zealand "Dead Alive," a summer release, was such a hilarious high-style zombie film that it was definitive; no one who makes a zombie movie from now on can hope to top it. And what "Dead Alive" also demonstrated is that, if you do it right, the funnier things get the scarier they get. "Return of Living Dead 3" isn't bad for what it is but it's the genre itself that needs reanimation.

NEW YORK POST, 10/29/93, p. 29, Michael Medved

Body piercing (of noses, navels, eyelids and other areas) is the rage among America's more twisted teens, but it's safe to say that Julie, the glamorous zombie heroine of "Return of the Living Dead 3," takes the practice to new extremes.

Scissors and huge shards of broken glass penetrate her shoulders and breasts, a bloody chain winds through the strips of skin around her neck, each fingertip has been punctured by rusty nails, and bent paper clips dangle from her lower lip.

Julie (nicely played by a striking newcomer named Mindy Clarke) has the fortitude to make this fashion statement because she's already dead: the victim of an unfortunate motorcycle accident while riding with her adoring boyfriend, Curt (J. Trevor Edmond).

After this mishap, Curt schleps the cutie-pie corpse to the top-secret Army installation where his father (Kent McCord) has been conducting research in raising the dead.

Curt uses just one brief hit of trioxin, a particularly potent gas, to bring Julie back to life. "That was incredible," she murmurs, as she awakens to his kisses. "Let's do it again!"

Well, they've already done it again with this gross ghoulish Halloween offering, yet another instalment in the seemingly endless series of knockoffs and sequels in the seemingly endless series of knockoffs and sequels inspired by George Romero's 1968 horror classic "Night of the Living Dead."

Just to keep things straight, gore groupies will surely want to remember that this new film is actually the second sequel to the first "Return of the Living Dead" film of 1985.

Among its genuinely horrifying moments, there's a surprisingly intense emotional undercurrent, as Julie struggles to transcend her living dead nature and to avoid indulging her uncontrollable hunger for human flesh—which might well spoil the romantic interludes with her boyfriend.

The most impressive thing about this movie isn't the special effects (which are simultaneously ingenious and appalling) but the acting. Mindy Clarke is simply amazing in an inane role that hardly deserves it: She manages to convey real emotion, consistent intelligence and incandescent attractiveness, even beneath all the heavy layers of grotesque makeup.

Producer/director Brian Yuzna (who previously produced director Stuart Gordon's justly acclaimed back-from-the-grave shocker "Re-Animator") shows a deft and stylish touch until this taut little picture lurches way over the top in its climactic flesh-eating zombie jamboree.

Like "Re-Animator," "Return of the Living Dead 3" is simply slick and disturbing enough to haunt revival houses for many Halloweens to come.

NEWSDAY, 11/29/93, Part II/p. 79, John Anderson

What can you do when your girlfriend flies off your motorcycle at 65mph, hits a telephone pole and still looks like a babe? Give her the gift that keeps on giving: Bring her back to life!!

The fact that you two lovebirds are just so *close* means she won't sate her savage zombie hunger by noshing on your brain, as you two head for Seattle (see, the scene there *is* dead) and you can realize your dream of being a drummer in a rock band (the punch line to the joke: Whattya call a guy with no talent who hangs around musicians?). There, your sweetie can fulfill your other dream, of having a fabulous-looking dead woman do nothing all night but watch you play.

Whoa, now, big fella: What's going on here? Don't you know that road is full of potholes, and that the potholes are full of other ravenous zombies unleashed by the government plan to make the living dead into weapons of war, which is being masterminded by your own father (who, speaking of the walking dead, is played by Kent McCord)? That you'll never make it? That all the goodwill built up 25 years ago by cheapo-horror master George Romero's stark little masterpiece "Night of the Living Dead" has long ago been spent? That you're lost in a makeup artist's fantasy? That the other zombies are closing in ...?

Curt (J. Trevor Edmond) and Julie (Mindy Clarke) never stand a chance, and neither does this movie. It knows exactly who its adolescent male market is, and plays right along with that audiences' worst instincts, in an orgy of misogynistic mutilation. The sexy and beautiful Julie may be unattainable to the horror dweebs, but she'll get hers: Finding that pain is the only thing that assuages her hunger, she begins piercing her body, first with lip rings, later with glass, nails and razors until she's a walking pincushion, and the poster girl for female self-loathing, sexual agony, medieval-style menstrual horror and resilient vanity. "Am I really dead," she asks. "Do I smell?" Pain? Only if you stay till the credits.

Also reviewed in:
NEW YORK TIMES, 11/29/93, p. C8, Janet Maslin
VARIETY, 11/8/93, p. 27, Emanuel Levy

RICH IN LOVE

A Metro-Goldwyn-Mayer release of a Zanuck Company production. *Producer:* Richard D. Zanuck, Lili Fini Zanuck, Gary Daigler, and David Brown. *Director:* Bruce Beresford. *Screenplay:* Alfred Uhry. *Based on the novel by:* Josephine Humphreys. *Director of Photography:* Peter James. *Editor:* Mark Warner. *Music:* Georges Delerue. *Music Editor:* Jeff Carson. *Sound:* Hank Garfield. *Sound Editor:* Rick Franklin. *Casting:* Shari Rhodes. *Production Designer:* John Stoddart. *Set Designer:* Carl Copeland. *Set Decorator:* John Anderson. *Set Dresser:* Patrick Fuhrman. *Special Effects:* Roger Lifsey. *Costumes:* Colleen Kelsall. *Make-up:* Dan Striepeke. *Running time:* 105 minutes. *MPAA Rating:* PG-13.

CAST: Albert Finney (Warren Odom); Jill Clayburgh (Helen Odom); Kathryn Erbe (Lucille Odom); Kyle MacLachlan (Billy McQueen); Piper Laurie (Vera Delmage); Ethan Hawke (Wayne Frobiness); Suzy Amis (Rae Odom); Alfre Woodard (Rhody Poole); J. Leon Pridgen, II (Tick); David Hager (Parnell Meade); Ramona Ward (Sharon); Wayne Dehart (Sam Poole); D.L. Anderson (Inn Receptionist); Janell McLeod (Bookstore Clerk); Jennifer Banco (Horse Carriage Driver); Anthony Burke (Singer); Terry Park (Terry); Stephanie Legette (Laura Migo).

CHRISTIAN SCIENCE MONITOR, 3/5/93, p. 14, David Sterritt

Bruce Beresford hails from Australia, but he's a filmmaker with international tastes. His recent work includes the poignant "Mr. Johnson," made in Africa, and the ponderous "Black Robe," shot in the Canadian wilderness. He also has a recurring love affair with the American South, where he filmed the superb "Tender Mercies" and the popular "Driving Miss Daisy."

"Rich in Love" finds Mr. Beresford tackling a Southern story once again, and suggests that he's getting lazy about his explorations of that fascinating region.

The characters are interesting enough, but the screenplay by Alfred Uhry—who wrote "Driving Miss Daisy" for stage and screen is full of peculiar holes, and Beresford doesn't muster enough visual imagination to compensate for the questions they raise and the issues they dodge. Many moviegoers may also reject the film's attitude toward marriage, which is portrayed as hard to put up with and dispensable in the long run.

Ultimately, the picture has only two elements that rise above criticism: the sublime Southern sunsets that punctuate the story, and the pleasure of seeing Albert Finney toss off a subtle and delicious performance as if this were the easiest task in the world.

The tale begins with the breakup of a family. Coming home from high school one day, a girl named Lucille discovers that her mother has skipped out on the household to try an independent life. Lucille knows she can't run the home and look after her eccentric father by herself, so she summons her older sister, who arrives pregnant and toting a brand new husband.

Together they keep life going as smoothly as possible, while staying on the lookout for the missing mom, whose whereabouts remain as mysterious as why she left.

"Rich in Love" has some rich and lovely moments. The best of these occur when the story slows down and allows a single character to express some small nugget of emotion, as when the father's new girlfriend tries to hide her feelings at hearing that his long lost wife may have returned.

What makes "Rich in Love" oddly unsatisfying despite such moments is its habit of skipping over important scenes that ought to carry much of the picture's emotional weight. Lucille's mother and father eventually have their long-awaited reunion, for instance, but we see only the first few seconds of it, and there's little explanation of how they arrive at their final decision to maintain a friendly separation instead of a troubled marriage.

While these gaps don't interfere with the narrative or make it difficult to follow, they reduce a potentially deep and many-layered saga to a string of thinly dramatic episodes aimed at immediate impact rather than lasting resonance. Much the same happened in "Driving Miss Daisy," where a worthwhile message of racial tolerance was weakened by the omission of scenes (showing family life, for instance) that might have given the black hero as much three-dimensional humanity as the white heroine was granted.

In both cases, the result is not a bad movie, but a missed opportunity to explore stimulating characters in as much depth and breadth as they deserve—and to make a coherent case for questionable conclusions, such as the skepticism toward marriage that becomes a theme of "Rich in Love."

There is plenty of strong acting in "Rich in Love," most notably from Mr. Finney as the father, Piper Laurie as his new romantic interest, and Alfre Woodard as a family acquaintance. Kathryn Erbe is solid as Lucille, and it's refreshing to see Kyle MacLachlan make an amiable impression outside director David Lynch's bizarre territory. Jill Clayburgh and Ethan Hawke round out the impressive cast.

Based on a Josephine Humphreys novel, "Rich in Love" has been glowingly photographed by Peter James, convincingly designed by John Stoddart, and competently edited by Mark Warner, who keeps the narrative flowing so smoothly you *almost* don't notice its missing elements until the film is over and there's time to think about what you've seen. The late Georges Delerue composed the score, which is pleasant but overdone; less of it would have made a greater impact.

LOS ANGELES TIMES, 3/5/93, Calendar/p. 6, Peter Rainer

There's a plangent sweetness about the best parts of "Rich in Love." Set in South Carolina, it's about what happens to a chunky, good-hearted retiree, Warren Odom (Albert Finney), when his wife, Helen (Jill Clayburgh), suddenly walks out on him without any warning.

One of their daughters, Lucille (Kathryn Erbe), is a moony high school senior who takes over the role of matriarch. Rae (Suzy Amis), her older, sassier sister, shows up with her new husband, Billy (Kyle MacLachlan), and a baby on the way. When it becomes clear that Helen isn't coming back, the family settles into a cozy, dozy comfortableness. They miss her and they go through all manner of denial over their loss but they're a surprisingly resilient bunch.

Helen's flight, prompted by her need to cut loose, inspires her family to cut loose too. "Rich in Love" starts out like a tragedy—by all rights it ought to be a tragedy—but it turns into a comedy of affirmation instead. Bruce Beresford, who directed from a script by Alfred Uhry based on a novel by Josephine Humphreys, knows how to make the moss-hung Southern landscape resonate without larding imagery with postcard-pretty pictures. He's a superbly tasteful craftsman—almost a master craftsman.

The movie—(rated PG-13 for thematic material) doesn't really work up much narrative steam but Beresford gives you so much to look at that it hardly matters. He locates the emotional center of every scene in a few quick strokes and then moves on. He doesn't lean on you; his principled reserve is an artist's approach to the complexities of character. He knows that the people in this film are wayward and instinctive and he follows their zig-zags with a true openness to experience.

"Rich in Love" might have been an even stronger film if that experience had greater conflict. Beresford and Uhry, who last collaborated on "Driving Miss Daisy," don't shove their characters into melodramatic situations but they also don't push the richest possibilities in the material. The film suffers from a heavy dose of niceness, nothing terribly crucial seems to be at stake in its people's lives (even when it is).

This approach is no doubt intentional—the filmmakers are trying to eliminate the wailing and moaning of traditional family drama and instead serve up its transcendent high points. They're trying to create a movie that's one long happy sigh.

But our desire for a bit more grit isn't necessarily a symptom of how corrupt our taste has become. It could also mean that we're missing out on the full range of emotional possibilities in the story. In "Rich in Love," things happen without much payoff: Lucille is told the startling circumstances of her birth; Rae suddenly croons a blues ballad in a honky-tonk, and she's a knockout: her husband, a Yankee, demonstrates some racial edginess to his wife's black friends, and later he comes on to Lucille. None of these revelations have any afterlife in the film. They disappear into the texture without ever having acquired much shape.

There's a moonlit scene where Billy tells Lucille "you've got a lot of loving in you," and it's true. Her yearning ties her up in knots; she seems skittish and spunky and bewildered all at once. Kathryn Erbe gives a fine performance despite the way the film knocks out her lower register. (It knocks out everybody's low notes.) Her role calls up Julie Harris' work as Frankie in the movie adaptation of Carson McCullers' "The Member of the Wedding" but without Frankie's aggravating turmoil and misery. It's a placid kind of misery that Lucille undergoes, the universe she inhabits is too genial for true terror.

As, Warren, Finney is a great galumphing image. When Warren finally understands that Helen is not coming back, he goes all slack and flabby. (He fixes himself potato chip and mayonnaise sandwiches; worse, he makes them look *good*.) He's like a big sleepwalking zombie; Finney shows us how Warren's layabout casualness turns out to be his salvation; he's so befogged and confused by his wife's exit that he never really comprehends what has happened to him. He just knows he wants to be pampered again, and he finds his match in Piper Laurie's Vera Delmage, a woman so captivated by Warren that she seems to cuddle him just by looking at him. She bakes him angel food cake and, in a real sense, she's his angel of mercy. Together they have a beatific good humor.

Suzy Amis gives the most complex performance. Her beauty has levels of hurt and disappointment in it that indicate her tough-tender broad act is just a cover-up. Watching a '40s weepie on TV, she states out loud, "I was meant for the '40s." What she means is that her life is without a romantic armature; the sensuous ease of her surroundings is both lulling and dispiriting.

There are no villains in "Rich in Love," and that's a key to its decency. "Rich in Love" doesn't go very deep—it's too lofty and idealized—but it presents a companionable and blameless view of family turmoil that has its own small measure of truth.

NEW YORK POST, 3/5/93, p. 25, Audrey Farolino

Marriage tells you who you are, and then it's gone, and you're a blank page."

The blank page in this case is Warren Odom (Albert Finney), an easygoing Southerner who finds himself emotionally at sea after his wife of 27 years leaves without warning. "I'm knocked off my perch ... I thought we were happy," he sighs (actually, it's more like "Ah'm knocked off mah puch," given Finney's newfound Dixie accent).

Also knocked off huh puch, as it were, is Odom's teen-aged daughter Lucille (Kathryn Erbe), who wants nothing more than for things to go back to normal. But as friend Rhody (Alfre Woodard) sagely tells her, "Normal's the problem, Lucille—it keeps changing on you."

That, in brief, is the theme of "Rich in Love"—that nothing can be counted on in this world except that things can never be counted on, so you'd better learn to like change.

Created by the same team behind "Driving Miss Daisy," including director Bruce Beresford and writer Alfred Uhry, the movie is so warmhearted, gentle, and nice to look at (South Carolina positively glows) that it's easy to forgive its faults.

Chief among them is an annoyingly happy ending which is much less interesting than the turmoil that precedes it.

Another weakness is the occasional lapse in credibility, as when we are asked to believe that Billy McQueen (Kyle MacLachlan) secretly poked holes in his condoms so he could impregnate Rae (Suzy Amis), the older, wilder Odom sister. (Did he keep a pin by the bed, or what?)

Finney's Southern accent is also tough to buy at first. But he quickly erases any doubts with a performance that captures Odom's emotional voyage: from bewilderment to numb hurt to ginger recovery to, finally, happiness after he finds romance again with Vera Delmage (Piper Laurie), a high-spirited hairdresser.

While dad's blossoming, however, his daughters are floundering—Lucille misses her high school graduation and blows her own budding romance, and Rae is feeling increasingly trapped by marriage and pregnancy.

We don't see much of Helen (Jill Clayburgh), the missing wife, and when she finally does explain her disappearance, it sounds as if she left mainly out of a kind of desperate boredom.

But that, after all, is what often motivates people, and the movie does a good job of exploring the tenuousness of the ties that bind and the hurt they leave when they come unbound.

NEWSDAY, 3/5/93, Part II/p. 55, Jack Mathews

In her nostalgic novella "Rich in Love," Josephine Humphreys' narrator recalls an upsetting event from her mid-teens in Charleston, S.C., and suggests, with the calm of someone asked how she got that scar on her cheek, that it may be worth a story.

Lucille, it seems, had come home from high school one day to find her mother's car parked outside, the driver's door open and a bag of groceries, with a carton of melting ice cream on top, left on the front seat. In a coldly written note left for Lucille's father in the house, her mother explained that she had simply grown tired of her life and had gone off to look for a new one.

That event and the shock waves set off by it are indeed worth a story, and Humphreys told it well. But even in the respectful hands of the makers of "Driving Miss Daisy"—producers Richard and Lili Zanuck, director Bruce Beresford, and writer Alfred Uhry—it doesn't quite work as a movie.

The novella is not so much about the events Lucille describes as it is about the confusion they caused her, and the effect of her mother's behavior on her own emotional life. That perspective is missing from the movie, and without it, "Rich in Love" is reduced to an unfocused portrait of a family adjusting to change.

Besides Lucille (newcomer Kathryn Erbe), there is her father Warren (Albert Finney), driven into deep stages of denial and depression by his wife's rejection, and her unstable older sister Rae (Suzy Amis), who returns home in the midst of the crisis, accidentally pregnant and reluctantly married. These are three wounded deer, and it is the fawn, Lucille, who must prop them all up.

Uhry's script keeps Lucille as the central character, and we glimpse the full range of her conflicts, her sexual confusion in her deteriorating relationship with her high school boyfriend (Ethan Hawke) and her growing infatuation with her brother-in-law (Kyle MacLachlan), her feelings about her father, who seems to have grown suddenly weak, and about her mother (Jill Clayburgh), who seems to have grown suddenly nuts.

In this present-tense telling, however, Lucille's problems are the least dynamic in the store. First of all, there is a mystery to solve: Where did mom go, and exactly why? Then the questions: Will dad ever overcome his heartache and take up with the warm-hearted redhead (Piper Laurie) who's so anxious to take up with him? And will Rae unload her husband and baby and get back to the hell-raising she was doing before she was so rudely interrupted?

Against these dilemmas, and in the voluminous company of the old scene-stealer Finney, Erbe's Lucille is dramatically overmatched.

There isn't a bad performance in this movie, or a single moment in which the "Driving Miss Daisy" company doesn't treat the material with respect. But without that strong central point of view, "Rich in Love" feels more like an adaptation of a chapter than of a whole book.

SIGHT AND SOUND, 5/93, p. 56, John Harkness

As high school breaks up, teenager Lucille fends off Wayne, her most ardent suitor, and heads for home, only to find that her mother Helen has run off. Not wanting her father Warren to read her mother's leaving note, Lucille rewrites it, forging Helen's signature. Reading the note,

Warren is suspicious, and sets off in search of his wife, with Lucille's assistance. Unable to find her, Warren becomes increasingly morose, and sits around at home pondering his marriage.

Spending her days helping her father, Lucille misses her high school examinations and graduation. Things liven up when her sister Rae arrives, pregnant and with her new husband Billy McQueen in tow. Lucille, still confident that her mother will return, is accused by Rae of romanticising their mother, telling Lucille that she was born because of an unsuccessful abortion. Awakened by his older daughter's presence, Warren begins to take an interest in life again, and takes up with Vera, the local hairdresser and divorcee, much to Lucille's shock. Wayne and Lucille break up. Billy gets a job teaching history at the local junior high school, but Rae, depressed by her steadily advancing pregnancy, decides that she wants to give up the baby for adoption. Then she decides to keep the baby but get rid of Billy, who reveals to Lucille that he impregnated Rae on purpose to get her to marry him. Billy and Lucille make love.

Lucille goes to a family friend for advice, and finds that Helen has been staying there. Lucille and Helen have a long talk about why she left. Rae goes into labour, and Helen shows up at the hospital to see her grandchild. Helen and Warren seem to take some tentative steps towards reconciliation. Rae decides to keep the baby and Billy. The family sells their house by the ocean, and Lucille leaves for university.

Mom leaves home, the heroine loses her virginity then has sex with her sister's husband, Dad takes up with the neighborhood divorcee, all in a southern setting, and the whole film hasn't a speck of actual drama.

What on earth possessed Bruce Beresford to make this film, except the off-chance of repeating his previous successes below the Mason-Dixon line? In *Crimes of the Heart*, he had Beth Henley's ultra-quirky source material and three of the finest actresses in American movies. In *Driving Miss Daisy*, he had Alfred Uhry's virtually director-proof script, and two extremely sly performers in Morgan Freeman and Jessica Tandy. The Academy's failure to nominate Beresford for a directing Oscar should have surprised no-one—it seldom hands out Oscars simply for failing to screw up good material.

After directing a huge hit, especially an Oscar-winning one, a director usually has his choice of any film he wants, within reason. Beresford chose to do *Rich In Love*, Uhry's adaptation of Josephine Humphreys' novel about an almost dysfunctional Southern family. One can see how this might work as a novel, all of it seen through the eyes of Lucille, the late adolescent girl who has the sort of intense sensitivity to her surroundings that one only finds in coming-of-age novels. But Beresford and Uhry manage to make every key dramatic sequence happen off-screen. Anything that might upset an audience on the conservative side of Queen Victoria has been trimmed away. *Rich In Love* has no sex, no violence, no four-letter words. It could play on television tomorrow, and no-one would find anything amiss, save perhaps the ratings dropping precipitously as the audience drifted away in search of something more than genteel good taste.

One would hardly argue that all stories with southern settings need the Gothic *Sturm und Drang* of Faulkner, or the religious terror of Flannery O'Connor, but *Rich In Love* might have been made by an unholy alliance between Chamber of Commerce types more interested in shopping malls than Civil War monuments and the Niceness Police who complain about the lack of 'family values' in American movies. (By way of contrast, one could argue that the success of *The Prince of Tides* resulted from its weird fusion of contemporary psychotherapeutic sensitivity with the Gothic horrors of the hero's childhood—located not too far from the South Carolina settings of *Rich In Love*.)

Finally, a word about actors and dialects. The diversity of America guarantees a pool of actors of every possible ethnic and regional heritage. The list of distinguished actors from the South—or convincingly capable of playing Southerners—includes Blythe Danner, Judith Ivey, Nick Nolte, Sissy Spacek, Rip Torn, Robert Duvall, *ad nauseam, ad gloriam*. The list does not include Jill Clayburgh, Kathryn Erbe, Suzy Amis, Piper Laurie or Albert Finney, whose work here does not add his name to the list of British actors who have distinguished themselves playing American southerners (James Mason, Charles Laughton, Maggie Smith, Vivien Leigh, Natasha Richardson, for starters).

The cast are all fine actors, but here they create one of those strange movie families in which nobody has the same accent. Admittedly, none of the sisters in *Crimes of the Heart* sounded alike either, but the ensemble of Sissy Spacek, Jessica Lange and Diane Keaton provided such a feast of acting that nobody cared. I suspect that Beresford has no real ear for American speech. This has not been an issue when working with tiny ensembles and first-rate material from writers who do have such an ear, but here the sound of the actors offends anyone who takes pleasure in the specific sounds of America's various accents.

VILLAGE VOICE, 3/16/93, p. 54, Georgia Brown

Bittersweet is what we get instead. [The reference is to *Ethan Frome*; See Brown's review.] The combination of Josephine Humphreys's cloying, terminally precious *Rich in Love* and the *Miss Daisy* bunch—director Bruce Beresford, writer Alfred Uhry, and the two producing Zanucks—may be enough to give even Michael Medved heartburn.

The movie's point-of-view character, the precocious 17-year-old Lucille Odom (Kathryn Erbe), talks like a Roger Rosenblatt essay and looks far too much like the young Sally Field. From where Lucille sits, her perfect little "Family of Four" may be rocking on the screen porch of a diseased civilization, but, unlike myriad others, they have been inoculated. Then one day she bikes home from high school to find Mom has flown the coop. "It's time for me to start a second life," reads the goodbye note. But Lucille doesn't judge Mom's farewell to Dad sufficiently tender so she quickly types a more sensitive missive and forges the signature. Everything Lucille does and says has this sticky preciousness. A child sage, she pronounces on everything from the problems of garbage disposal to the demise of the family as we know it. (Proof that Humphreys had old Holden on the brain is that she names the child born at the end of the book Phoebe.)

Whereas *Ethan Frome* is all chilly scenes of winter, *Rich in Love* is ripe summer, or summer sliding into fall. The setting is Charleston, South Carolina, and the Odom manse is idyllically situated on water enabling Beresford to order up some of the most grotesque sunsets since *On Golden Pond*. I wish my Granny Gower were above ground to see what he could do with a moon over Charleston. (Apparently *Black Robe* did not signify Beresford's move into a tougher phase.) This is a movie where light dances on water, white girls belt out Otis Redding songs in all-black roadhouses, and every aging African American is a folk artist, his front yard alive with rusted doodads.

As adapted by Alfred Uhry, the movie is almost as garrulous and irritating as the novel. What rescues it partially is some of the acting—particularly Albert Finney's as the spaced-out Dad taking up with Piper Laurie's refreshingly vulgar unisex hair stylist. I should say that Suzy Amis looks smashing while Jill Clayburgh once again plays an unmarried woman. But Southern movies, especially by Australian directors, have seen their day. I hope this constitutes the last days of chez y'all.

Also reviewed in:
CHICAGO TRIBUNE, 3/5/93, Friday/p. B, Dave Kehr
NEW REPUBLIC, 4/5/93, p. 30, Stanley Kauffmann
NEW YORK TIMES, 3/5/93, p. C8, Janet Maslin
NEW YORKER, 3/22/93, p. 104, Terrence Rafferty
VARIETY, 9/28/92, p. 78, Joseph McBride
WASHINGTON POST, 3/19/93, p. F1, Hal Hinson
WASHINGTON POST, 3/19/93, Weekend/p. 45, Desson Howe

RIFF-RAFF

A Fine Line Features release of a Parallax Pictures production for Channel 4. *Producer:* Sally Hibbin. *Director:* Ken Loach. *Screenplay:* Bill Jesse. *Director of Photography:* Barry Ackroyd. *Editor:* Jonathan Morris. *Music:* Stewart Copeland. *Sound:* Bob Withey. *Sound Editor:* Kevin Brazier. *Production Designer:* Martin Johnson. *Art Director:* Jonathan Lee. *Costumes:* Wendy Knowles. *Make-up:* Louise Fisher. *Running time:* 96 minutes. *MPAA Rating:* Not Rated.

CAST: Robert Carlyle (Stevie); Emer McCourt (Susan); Jimmy Coleman (Shem); George Moss (Mo); Ricky Tomlinson (Larry); David Finch (Kevin); Richard Belgrave (Kojo); Ade Spara (Fiaman); Derek Young (Desmonde); Bill Moores (Smurph); Luke Kelly (Ken Jones); Garrie J. Lammin (Mick); Willie Ross (Gud Siddon); Dean Perry (Wilf); Dylan O'Mahony, Brian Coyle, Stuart Peveril (Youths); Terry Bird (Van Driver); Jimmy Batten (Man Buying Kango); David Adler (Director); David Taegar (Producer); Dominic Barlow (Pianist); Terry Duggan (Boss in Office); Angela Morant (Estate Agent); Lila Cherif, Joumana Gil, and Zohra El Harrack (Clients); Peter Mullan (Jake); John Kazek (Robert); Anne Marie Timoney (Fiona); Maureen Carr (Ellen); James MacDonald (Funeral Director); Vicky Murdock (Medical Secretary); Mike Haydon (Security Guard).

LOS ANGELES TIMES, 3/17/93, Calendar/p. 4, Kenneth Turan

"Riff-Raff" is a film as likable, unpretentious and just a little bit dangerous as its name. A slight but significant slice of British working-class life, its warmhearted humor is tempered by a definite warning edge of uncompromising social consciousness.

A comedy of manners about people who have to manage without them, "Riff-Raff" is set in the boom days of Margaret Thatcher's London and centers around the economic, romantic and melancholy adventures of a group of have-not laborers who are turning an old hospital into posh flats for society's consuming classes.

Winner of several European prizes, including the International Critics Prize at Cannes, "Riff-Raff" is the latest film by Ken Loach, one of the most admired if least known of British directors. A passionately, sympathetic observer of his country's underclass whose best films, such as "Kes" and "Family Life," have had almost no distribution in this country, Loach has always had the gift of empathy, of getting unflinchingly close to the reality of his characters' marginalized lives.

What makes "Riff-Raff" a change of pace for Loach is the bursts of raucous humor that punctuate Bill Jesse's script. Jesse, who died suddenly at age 48 before he could see the completed film, was a construction worker as well as a writer. His anarchic screenplay, which David Puttnam originally commissioned while he was at Columbia, delivers a combination, of amusing camaraderie and anger at an exclusionary class system that is as strong as that felt by any victim of America's inner cities.

What is not very American is the wide variety of accents that "Riff-Raff's" cast, nominal English speakers every one, employs. With voices coming from Belfast, Liverpool, Glasgow and the West Indies, these men communicate in language so vigorous and rich that the picture's distributor has provided not-always-necessary subtitles for the linguistically timid.

Stevie (Robert Carlyle), the film's protagonist, is one of the Belfast lads, jokingly called "Billy Connolly" (after an IRA figure) by his mates. Quiet, hard-working and living as a squatter in an unoccupied flat, Stevie is as usual minding his own business when he happens to stumble on a lost purse.

Jammed with letters, a book and a picture of a fetching young woman, the purse so intrigues Stevie that he uses the letters to track down its owner, Susan (Emer McCourt). A would-be rock singer with an uncertain voice, Susan is determinedly countercultural, asking Stevie his sign and throwing the I Ching at their first meeting. For Stevie, whose goal in life is getting into the merchandising of boxer shorts, she is heady stuff indeed.

"Riff-Raff" wouldn't be a movie if Stevie and Susan weren't attracted to each other, but it also wouldn't be one of Ken Loach's if their relationship echoed something like "Far and Away." The sense that there are no easy answers or lasting pleasures, that moments of happiness are infrequent and hard-earned, hangs over everything in this film, the romance as well as the comedy.

Much of that laughter comes from the construction gang, especially Larry (Ricky Tomlinson), a fellow with such a politically active tongue that one of his exasperated pals finally complains, "Every time you open your mouth, it's like a ... parliamentary debate."

Hardly saints, and in fact capable of bludgeoning baby rats and taking advantage of whoever's handy, these men share more than a kidding sense of humor. Well aware of their marginality, of the ever-present danger of getting "the elbow" from the boss, they still try to have their dreams. That these, modest as they are, periodically prove to be impossible, is something Ken Loach doesn't ever want us to forget.

NEW YORK POST, 2/12/93, p. 27, Jami Bernard

There is a scene in Ken Loach's new film, "Riff-Raff," that sums up how things would be if we lived in a utopian society where wrongs are righted and the milk of human kindness is stirred into every drink.

Larry (Ricky Tomlinsort). a kindly hard-hat always on the lookout for the welfare of his mates, gets up on the stage of a noisy English pub where they have booed a terrible singer off the stage "Me? I'm nobody," he tells the crowd before admonishing them: "You made that little girl cry." Miraculously, his appeal to decency works. They cheer for the singer to come back on the stage and sing again—just as badly—while everyone has a good time.

Loach's films often deal with working-class stiffs in England; "Riff-Raff" is his first comedy. It's an English film with English subtitles, and you'll be glad for them, because the banter among the immigrant hard-hats is nearly impossible to make out.

"Riff-Raff", opens and closes with a shot of rats among the debris of a construction site, a close analogy to the kind of life led by these itinerant day-laborers why brave indecent working and housing conditions just to make a bare living. They have dreams of the future, but they don't have bank accounts or even access to a toilet. Though lumped together and dealt a bad lot in life, they are not as simple as they seem.

The movie follows the struggles to stay afloat of Stevie (Robert Carlyle), a Scottish ex-con who is trying to kick his mildly criminal habits. He takes up with the terrible singer, Susan (Emer McCourt), an ultimately more fragile being who doesn't have the ability of a rat to survive in the wreckage. While the two of them camp out in an abandoned building in a sad parody of middle-class life, Stevie spends his working hours knocking apart a rat-trap to make expensive condos for immigrants luckier than himself.

The ambling screenplay was written by a former construction worker, and the movie nicely captures the camaraderie and despair of one riffraff stratum of English society. "Masterpiece Theater" it's not, nor would you want it to be.

NEWSDAY, 2/12/93, Part II/p. 71, Gene Seymour

Rats are seen scurrying at the opening and closing edges of "Riff-Raff," and it doesn't take interpretive genius to figure that these images are meant to reinforce the fact that this is a movie about people living on society's margins, ignored, demeaned, crushed underfoot and somehow managing to survive.

Fortunately, such symbolism is about as heavy-handed as "Riff-Raff" gets. The unsentimental and unsparing approach of British film director Ken Loach, known for such hard-edged political dramas as "Hidden Agenda," sharpens the astringent humor and poignance of this look at below-the-poverty-line life in post-Thatcher England.

The film's anti-hero is Stevie (Robert Carlyle), a soft-spoken ex-con from Glasgow who, like many other low-class transients in London with similar credentials, finds few options besides falling in with a construction crew.

The work is hard, the hours long, the pay miserable. The bosses are mean and petty. The only solace is the ribald humor and warm camaraderie Stevie enjoys with other members of his multi-racial crew. All of them, especially the big-hearted, politically minded Larry (Ricky Tomlinson), seem aware of the irony behind building apartments they'll never be able to afford. Which is why Stevie has to "squat" in whatever apartment he can find in a decrepit housing project.

Soon, he meets Susan, an aspiring singer (Emer McCourt, known for a similar role in Hanif Kureishi's "London Kills Me") whose prospects aren't much better than his. They cope with the bleakness differently. Stevie works through it stoically. Susan loses herself in mysticism. Tension, inevitably, ensues.

The script, written by the late Bill Jesse, is bursting with keen observation and dark humor. Both especially evident in a hilarious graveside service.

It is also thick with colloquial authenticity, which is why you will see subtitles on screen to make the thickly accented English more intelligible. (I didn't think such elucidation was necessary, but maybe you will.)

SIGHT AND SOUND, 5/91, p. 61, David Wilson

Stevie, a young Glaswegian recently released from prison, arrives in London to work on a building site. He joins a crew of itinerant building workers—including Shem, Mo and Larry from Liverpool and several West Indians—in the demolition of an old hospital and its conversion into a block of flats. Despite the efforts of the ganger, Mick, to control them, the men find their own ways of subverting the system.

With nowhere to live, Stevie moves into an empty council flat. Finding a handbag in a skip one day, he traces its owner, Susan, a young Belfast woman who is trying to make a career as a singer. After watching Susan sing with a band in a pub, where the rowdy male audience humiliates her, Stevie takes her back to his flat. Soon afterwards, with the help of his friends on the site, Susan moves in with him, and for a time their relationship prospers. But Stevie, who has ambitions to run a market stall, is increasingly troubled by Susan's apparent inability to organise her life. One morning they have a fierce argument, although they are reconciled when Stevie returns from work to find that Susan has prepared a birthday celebration for him.

When Stevie hears, via a radio SOS message, that his mother has died, Susan vainly pleads with him not to go back to Glasgow for the funeral. Stevie returns from the funeral to find Susan injecting 'smack', and throws her out of the flat. The dubious safety standards on the site are brutally exposed when one of the men, Desmonde, crashes from the roof. That night, an angry Stevie and one of his mates from the site set fire to the paint stock in the now almost completed building, which explodes in flames.

On the surface, *Riff-Raff* appears largely to avoid the dramatic contrivance and political woolliness of *Hidden Agenda*, in style and substance echoing some of Ken Loach's earlier work. The comradeship of the work-place (here a building site), the conspiracy of subversion, the anarchic working-class humour, all hark back to such Loach-Garnett television films of twenty years ago as *The Big Flame* and *Rank and File*. In the meantime, though, these post-80s workers have learned a thing or two from the system about entrepreneurial tricks of the trade. Slotted into this loosely constructed tableau of artisanal community—not without dramatic discomfort—is the film's 'story', which, as in *Looks and Smiles*, builds a central relationship round, but not from, the scattered bricks of a communal experience. Not for the first time in a Loach film, the frame does not support the construction: the centre does not hold.

The discrepancy is most evident in the visual styles adopted for what obstinately remain the film's two separate strands. The building site sequences are filmed in Loach's naturalistic, improvisational mode (also experiential, since most of the actors—like scriptwriter Bill Jesse, who sadly died just before the film was completed—had previously worked as building labourers). Actors drift in an out of shot as the 'mood' of the scene takes them, caught in dimly heard mid-sentence or delivering obviously rehearsed jokes straight to camera ("Every time you open your mouth it's like a bleedin' parliamentary debate", says one of the workers of another, a characteristically politicised Liverpudlian who pleads the case for better safety standards on the site).

Loach's persistent confusion of 'realism' (a literary/dramatic *convention*, by which no television-bred audience is confused) with real life (what you see is how it is) has the opposite effect of that presumably intended: it simply draws attention to the artifice of these scenes. *Riff-Raff* was made for television, though happily it has a prior if limited cinema release. But will television audiences, accustomed to seeing through the 'realist' masks of *Coronation Street* or *EastEnders*, be seduced by the unfocused naturalism of sporadic scenes from a building site?

As always in Loach's films—even a 'lighter' work such as this—there is of course a hidden agenda. Or not so hidden. "Depressions are for the middle classes", says Stevie to his hopeless girlfriend, "The rest is about an early start in the morning". Stevie, in other words, who dreams of opening a stall selling boxer shorts, has half swallowed the go-for-it market philosophy of contemporary Britain, while deadbeats like Susan are left to busk for pennies in the Underground.

Book-ending this simplistic morality, the film begins with a crashingly obvious symbol of something or other, as rats scurry through the debris of a demolition site; and ends with the selfsame rats scuttling through the floors of the nearly completed block of luxury flats, which has just been fired by the hero and his mate as an act of vengeance for the death of a comrade who fell from inadequately secured scaffolding. As ye sow ... But what do you reap, except a confused and condescending view of kicking the system in impotent despair?

VILLAGE VOICE, 2/9/93, p. 56, Georgia Brown

There are many cinemas for many audiences. Currently many moviegoers find it fascinating to watch Jack Nicholson's demented leatherneck throw tight-lipped tantrums or Al Pacino's blind wretch rant and rave. I don't. Not because I automatically reject hyper-performance, or the subject of aging colonels (as the offspring of one, I'm all eyes), but because the vehicles for these impersonations are predictable and inadequate. (If it's an aging career officer you want, see Roger Livesey in *The Life and Death of Colonel Blimp* in Walter Reade's upcoming Michael Powell series.)

For the past 30 years, Ken Loach has been guru and practitioner of another cinema. In a 1980 *Cineaste* interview he said, "Reality has never been revealed by commercial cinema. They give us surfaces and stereotypes, which are subversive of people as they really are." Loach wants to be supportive of people as they really are—particularly those who don't usually get portrayed in movies—workers, dropouts, vagrants, forgotten grannies getting by in council flats. He steers away from flagrant performances, even though his longstanding preference for nonprofessional actors means working with dialects that many find difficult to understand (even Brits complain). This has meant too that his films don't get much attention in the U.S,

But now Reagan's '80s are ended, yes? Working stiffs have cachet again (I'm kidding), and suddenly the off-the-books employment of illegal immigrants is a timely topic. So, Loach may have his day or hour. His marvelous new movie, *Riff-Raff*, is more comic, more buoyant than his former films, and, for the first time, subtitles are called on to help with the accents. Purists may object but, as I heard Loach observe on WNYC, "The subtitles take the pressure off."

The first and final shots in *Riff-Raff* are of rats. They're scrambling in the rubble of a building being gutted to create upscale condos. Rats are riff-raff, you might say. Dirty, despised scavengers; disreputable creatures, rumored to be dangerous when driven into corners. The title's riff-raff, however, are the motley collection of workers doing the demolition—stirring rats from their nests. Hired on a pick-up basis, fired on a foreman's whim, they receive small wages for working in unsafe conditions without insurance. Their only protection is a hardhat—which here gets put to ingenious use. Most are using false names for private reasons. Some live on the streets or in sparsely furnished squats. When payday comes only one guy has a bank to cash his check at.

Stevie (Robert Carlyle) has neither bank nor bed. A quiet, engaging Scotsman, Stevie (real name Patrick) has a shady past, a bit of which we discover as the movie unfolds. On the job, he makes friends with old hands who help him find a squat. Stevie hasn't completely kicked old habits: We see him slyly peddling a piece of equipment lifted from the Job. His real goal, however, is to sell boxer shorts and sweat socks from a stall. One day he finds a purse, returns it to its pretty, if daffy, owner and is invited in for green tea. Susan (Emer McCourt, from *London Kills Me*) claims to be a singer. When we hear a song, we know she'll never make it, even small. She dispenses nutritional advice, consults a psychic, throws the I Ching, and flails about for some anchor in the storm of life. (McCourt is extremely convincing.) When the couple moves in together, the extent of Susan's pathetic desperation becomes clearer. Stevie has a will to survive; she may not.

Loach's films are famous for being gritty and tragic. *Riff-Raff*, written by a construction worker, Bill Jesse, is too, underneath, but it's also uncharacteristically funny and has a cathartic ending. "Humor," as Loach observed to Leonard Lopate, "is a form of resistance." He was referring to the instincts of the film's characters but could have been defining a new strategy of his own. Whether this comic turn owes anything to Mike Leigh's recent success in the U.S., he didn't say—though I had the feeling he would have answered directly if asked; his radio manner, anyway, seemed so quietly patient, intelligent, and free of pompous rhetoric.

Whereas Leigh starts with first-rate actors and then conducts a lengthy "rehearsal" during which they scrupulously invent their new characters, Loach spends a long time in auditions, trying to cast nonprofessionals who can be natural on screen. Although Carlyle and McCourt are professional actors, the rest of the crew is from the building trades. (For all the vaunted authenticity, this work force doesn't look so competent. I can't say I'd want these jokers working on my job.) Whereas Leigh comes close up to his characters, looking for cracks, Loach keeps a polite distance, content to leave inner lives opaque. His interest is social context. Always there is a conflict of cultures, the powers-that-be and the powerless.

In *Riff-Raff*, Larry, the wise elder and father figure on the job, a veteran of many wars, functions as the film's articulate point of view. He has a tendency to lecture, but his mates listen because of his authority and his demonstrated concern for the others' welfare. The character is played by Ricky Tomlinson, a former plasterer who was jailed after a highly publicized building strike in 1972. Built like a water buffalo, Tomlinson also has a natural comic presence, which is used to good purpose here. This character, more than any of the others, is a triumph of the Loach method. His understated exit is accomplished with enormous dignity. Scenes such as this show that opening his work to whimsy and foolishness hasn't compromised Loach's message; it's as lucid as ever.

Also reviewed in:
CHICAGO TRIBUNE, 3/19/93, Friday/p. B, Dave Kehr
NATION, 2/15/93, p. 210, Stuart Klawans
NEW REPUBLIC, 2/15/93, p. 26, Stanley Kauffmann
NEW YORK TIMES, 2/12/93, p. C10, Vincent Canby
VARIETY, 5/6/91, p. 335
WASHINGTON POST, 4/16/93, p. B7, Rita Kempley
WASHINGTON POST, 4/16/93, Weekend/p. 39, Desson Howe

RISING SUN

A Twentieth Century Fox release of a Walrus & Associates Ltd. production.   *Executive Producer:* Sean Connery.   *Producer:* Peter Kaufman.   *Director:* Philip Kaufman.   *Screenplay:* Philip Kaufman, Michael Crichton, and Michael Backes.   *Based upon the novel by:* Michael Crichton.   *Director of Photography:* Michael Chapman.   *Editor:* Stephen A. Rotter and William S. Scharf.   *Music:* Toru Takemitsu.   *Music Editor:* Alan Splet and Jeffrey Stephens.   *Sound:* David MacMillan and (music) Shinji Hori.   *Sound Editor:* Alan Splet.   *Casting:* Donna Isaacson.   *Production Designer:* Dean Tavoularis.   *Art Director:* Angelo Graham.   *Set Designer:* Peter Kelly and Robert Goldstein.   *Set Decorator:* Gary Fettis.   *Special Effects:* Larry L. Fuentes.   *Visual Effects:* Mark A. Z. Dippe.   *Costumes:* Jacqueline West.   *Make-up:* Ve Neill.   *Stunt Coordinator:* Jeff Imada.   *Running time:* 129 minutes.   *MPAA Rating:* R.

CAST: Sean Connery (John Connor);   Wesley Snipes (Web Smith);   Harvey Keitel (Tom Graham);   Cary-Hiroyuki Tagawa (Eddie Sakamura);   Kevin Anderson (Bob Richmond); Mako (Yoshida-san);   Ray Wise (Senator John Morton);   Stan Egi (Ishihara);   Stan Shaw (Phillips);   Tia Carrere (Jingo Asakuma);   Steve Buscemi (Willy "the Weasel" Wilhelm); Tatjana Patitz (Cheryl Lynn Austin);   Peter Crombie (Greg);   Sam Lloyd (Rick);   Alexandra Powers (Julia);   Daniel Von Bargen (Chief Olson/Interrogator);   Lauren Robinson (Zelly); Amy Hill (Hsieh);   Tom Dahlgren (Jim Donaldson);   Clyde Kusatsu (Tanaka);   Michael Chapman (Fred Hoffman);   Joey Miyashima and Nelson Mashita (Young Japanese Negotiators); Tamara Tunie (Lauren);   Tony Ganios (Doorman Guard);   James Oliver Bullock (Jeff); Michael Kinsley, Eleanor Clift, Clarence Page, and Pat Choate (TV Panel Members);   Steven C. Clemons (Show Moderator);   Dan Butler (Ken Shubik);   Toshishiro Obata (Guard at Imperial Arms);   Tylyn John (Redhead);   Shelley Michelle (Blonde);   Michele Ruiz (TV Interviewer); Patricia Ayame Thomson (Female Accident Reporter);   Jeff Imada and Max Kirishima (Eddie Sakamura's Yakuza);   Larry O. Williams, Jr. (Younger Brother);   Scot Anthony Robinson (First Brother);   Keith Leon Hickles (Another Brother);   Carl A. McGee (Guy at Window);   Quincy Adams, Jr. (Mean Face);   Cecil Brown (Big Guy);   Meagen Fay (Hamaguri Receptionist); Max Grodenchik (Club Manager);   Gunnar Peterson (Valet);   Jessica Tuck (Senator Morton's

Aide);   Masa Watanabe (Japanese Elevator Guard);   Minnie Summers Lindsey (Grandma Otis); Paul Fujimoto (Iwabuchi);   Kenji (Tempura Chef);   Michael Leopard (Cop);   Dennis Ota and Raymond Kitamura (Nakamoto Yakuza);   Rita Weibel (Girl at Eddie's Party);   Seiichi Tanaka (Taiko Drum Master).

CHRISTIAN SCIENCE MONITOR, 7/30/93, p. 13, David Sterritt

Michael Chrichton's novel "Rising Sun" stirred up a storm of controversy when it appeared. Some called it tough-minded and incisive. Others saw it as unmitigated Japan-bashing.

Advance word on the movie indicated that the filmmakers were toning down any anti-Japan overtones the book might have harbored.In its finished form, however, the picture hardly paints an attractive portrait of Japanese business methods or the people who engage in them. Although it's not a hotbed of deliberate racism, it contains a current of insensitivity that will do more to feed anti-Asian sentiments than to dispel them.

Many will also object to the opening murderous sex-and-violence scene that shows Hollywood's penchant for putting female characters through the most grueling on-screen spectacles.

The plot focuses on two police officers trying to solve that grisly murder which takes place in a high-tech office building occupied largely by Japanese business interests. One of the officers (Sean Connery) is a longtime specialist in Japanese matters, while the other (Wesley Snipes) has less experience with Asian culture and custom. Their investigation leads them into that old Hollywood standby, a "shadowy underworld" where betrayal and violence are a way life.

"Rising Sun" was directed by Philip Kaufman, who is respected by some critics as a sophisticated explorer of ambiguities between illusion and reality. While his interests certainly lie in this direction, the actual quality of Kaufman's pictures—from "Henry and June" and "The Unbearable Lightness of Being" to "The Right Stuff" and his "Invasion of the Body Snatchers" remake—is less lofty than some reviews indicate.

True to this tendency, "Rising Sun" is a capably made thriller, but much of the action is run-of-the-mill melodrama. There are few moments when its most compelling theme—the way appearance and actuality blur as high technology gains more power in our lives—is illuminated by Kaufman's choices of cinematic style, content, or technique.

More disappointing is Kaufman's willingness to play for a low-grade emotional response. This becomes apparent early in the movie when powerful imposing Connery loses his Japanese-style courtesy and looms over a Japanese character, shouting him right into the floor. The way the scene is acted and filmed is calculated to stir up indignation and condescension in non-Asian audiences. It's a cheap trick and paves the way for worse to follow.

"Rising Sun" is best when it delves directly into the maze of high-tech imaging techniques, and indicates how profoundly these have complicated our notions of reality and the reliability of the human senses. Kaufman might have made a far deeper film if he had concentrated on these issues—rather than embedding them in a vulgar melodrama that cares more about sensationalism than sense.

Along with solid performances by Connery and Snipes, the picture has strong acting by Harvey Keitel and Kevin Anderson and such Japanese-American players as Mako and Cary-Hiroyuki Tagawa. The mostly ordinary music is by Toru Takemitsu.

FILMS IN REVIEW, 10/93, p. 340, Edmond Grant

As James Bond, Sean Connery battled a succession of inscrutable Oriental supervillains (Dr. No, Oddjob, the martial artists of *You Only Live Twice*); in *Rising Sun*, Connery plays a police detective who's an expert on all things Japanese, a well respected ally of several highly placed Japanese executives. He is a cultural exile, whose role in the film is that of clarifier, pontificator, and soft spoken supercop with a social conscience.

Connery brings to the role the same kind of cool he exercised in his superspy heyday as Bond, but *Rising Sun* is not a slick, cartoon-like tale of espionage. Instead, it's the very model of a parlor mystery, cloaked in high tech, state-of-the-art trappings. Those trappings include a "deeper meaning" imposed upon the rather straightforward murder mystery plotline: the film attempts to be an exploration, with an uncertain tone of disapproval, of the current, prevalent American sentiment that Japan poses a major economic threat to American business. Director/co-scripter

Phillip Kaufman, certainly a shrewd enough hand when it comes to adapting difficult prose (*The Right Stuff, The Unbearable Lightness Of Being*), reportedly worked to tone down the "Japan bashing" that appears in Michael Crichton's novel *Rising Sun*. What has resulted is a curiously familiar tale of racial harmony and brotherhood amid crime solving, that incidentally doesn't paint the Japanese as being all too friendly, and still stresses the more exotic—or is that inscrutable?—aspects of (our understanding of) their culture.

Connery's character, as can be divined from his prominent "executive producer" credits, is the linchpin for the entire affair. Playing the wise, aloof, and quietly lethal John Conner (Crichton claimed to have created Conner with Sean in mind), he is the one who quells the other non-Asian characters' frequent bouts of bashing. Supplying a non-stop series of "facts" about Japanese attitudes and tradition, his character is meant to provide the film's Voice of Reason, enlightening his partner Web Smith (Wesley Snipes) and by extension, we the narrow minded viewing audience.

Still, Kaufman's nobler instincts are counterpointed (and almost completely undercut) by his skill with sexual intrigue: the murder that sparks Conner and Web's investigation not only involves miscegenation (a blonde party girl is allegedly killed by an Asian with whom she had just earlier had sex), but also introduces the kinky practice (shades of a Japanese classic I'm sure Kaufman is no stranger to, Oshima's *In The Realm Of The Senses*) of asphyxiation as a turn-on. Kaufman handles the brief moments of kink in his usual, visually arresting manner; he is after all the man who made literary erotica fashionable (if not exactly a box-office favorite) in American cinema with *Unbearable Lightness* and *Henry and June*.

The setting for the murder is symbolically perfect: a corporate boardroom in a newly erected Japanese corporate office building in Los Angeles. This ideal murder mystery set up even includes the primary-suspect-whom-all-clues-point-to, a sleazy playboy named Eddie Sakamura (Cary-Hiroyuki Tagawa). The one ironclad piece of "proof" against him, a laser-disc recording showing him at the scene of the crime, is soon revealed as a cleverly edited frame up by the film's embarrassingly "good" Japanese character (all negative race models in controversial films have to be balanced out by their "good" ethnic counterparts): a bookish, alluring video technician (Tia Carrere, of *Wayne's World*).

The film's script slowly begins to unravel as we reach the surprising revelation (not too surprising for those watching carefully) that solves the murder case. In the meantime, a gratuitous streetgang scene and a martial arts set-to are thrown in for those viewers who came expecting a bona fide buddy movie. But one of the final sequences proves what was suspected all along: that this is actually a contemporary update of the old Charlie Chan mysteries (Kaufman said he conceived of the film primarily as a detective picture) with a Scottish detective mouthing the old Asian proverbs and performing the absolutely essential task of gathering all the suspects in one room for a final revelation of the murderer's identity.

As ever, Connery is slick, intense, and terrific; Snipes proves equally intense, but one also gets the impression that he treated this as simply one more assignment in his rather crowded schedule (somewhere between the social context-less thrillers like *Passenger 57* and *Demolition Man*). The Asian actors try to invest their characters with some life, but as always with American crime movies, it's the tried and true stereotypes that register best, like the weasel-like reporter (Steve Buscemi), the sleazy politico (Ray Wise), and the ugly-American police lieutenant (Harvey Keitel).

LOS ANGELES TIMES, 7/30/93, Calendar/p. 1, Kenneth Turan

"Rising Sun" has gotten everything backward. Mystifying when it should be clear and clear when it should be mystifying, it is the murkiest, most unsatisfying of thrillers. And the biggest mystery of all is how a project that appeared to have so much going for it could have gone so determinedly astray.

For the Michael Crichton novel "Rising Sun" is based on was more than a top bestseller. Its story of how the investigation of an L.A. murder exposes a secret Japanese determination to infiltrate and subvert the most potent of American institutions, including this very newspaper, became controversial in ways that few novels do, as outraged editorials and op-ed pieces soon bloomed like a thousand flowers.

And when 20th Century Fox purchased the book—it decided to take it the quality route, signing Philip Kaufman ("Henry & June," "The Unbearable Lightness of Being") to direct and pairing Sean Connery and Wesley Snipes as the local cops who solve the mystery. And, in fact, the actors give capable performances and Kaufman's direction shows signs of his usual intelligence. So why does the end result feel as dispiriting and out of whack as "Rising Sun" finally does?

The answer is right there in that book, a novel whose suitability as source material for a blockbuster turns out to be more problematic than anticipated. For "Rising Sun," as anyone who noticed its three-page bibliography should have grasped, is no thriller but a thinly disguised political tract. And even though all those pages and pages of densely packed information about Japanese society and business practices might look awfully silly on screen, to eliminate them (as Kaufman largely did, apparently to the displeasure of his co-screenwriters Crichton & Michael Backes) is to leave the movie's plot naked and exposed as the puny thing that it is.

"Rising Sun" (rated R for strong sexuality, language and some violence) starts out telling two stories at once, one corporate, the other personal. The former details how Nakamoto, the fierce Japanese conglomerate, aided by smooth American lawyer Bob Richmond (Kevin Anderson) is trying to buy a computer chip company called MicroCon despite the opposition of Sen. John Morton (Ray Wise), who thinks it would be bad for national security to let control of such sophisticated information out of the country.

The personal story illustrates the rather volatile relationship between a bored blond concubine named Cheryl Lynn Austin (model Tatjana Patitz) and well-connected Japanese party animal Eddie Sakamura (Cary-Hiroyuki Tagawa). An excitable type given to snarling "Don't ever try that again—or else!" at slight provocation, Eddie takes Cheryl Lynn to a celebration at the new Nakamoto Tower in downtown LA., where she is soon found dead on the very table those super-secret MicroCon talks have been held around.

Called in to investigate are Web Smith (Snipes), a lieutenant in the Special Services section of the Los Angeles Police Department, and John Connor (Connery), an old Japan hand who speaks the language and knows so much about the culture it's almost frightening. Though edgy with each other at first the two men soon concentrate on the crime at hand and what connection if any, it has to what else has been happening on that Nakamoto table.

To anyone with even a casual familiarity with movie conventions, the various plot twists of "Rising Sun," the gradual discovery of who did what to whom, will be awkwardly obvious well in advance of their discovery by Smith and Connor. This plot predictability, which the book's extensive political fulmination managed to camouflage, is one of the stones that sink the film.

Not being fools, the makers of "Rising Sun" were aware of this problem, but unfortunately the tactic they chose to combat it only adds to the overall difficulty. Faced with a self-evident story line, the movie has decided to make everything peripheral it could lay hands on as confining as possible, the better to divert attention from that core obviousness.

So while the novel takes the necessary time to explain what Special Services does, the film doesn't. While the novel describes Connor as a legend and leaves it at that, the movie adds the mock-ominous notation, typically not followed up on, that "some said he was a man who couldn't be trusted." Again and again, scenes are either shot or presented in a way intended to maximize audience perplexity. The result, as noted, is a film that is alternately too easy and too difficult to follow.

Adding further to "Rising Sun's" problems is that director Kaufman does not seem comfortable with the project's potboiler qualities, leading to awkward scenes of sexual abandon and unbelievable ones of street gang cooperation with Smith and Connor. Similar difficulties touch the film's uncertain treatment of the racist, xenophobic cop Tom Graham (Harvey Keitel), who refers to the murder victim as "a blond piece of sushi" and views the Japanese as little more than "known world-class perversion freaks."

Kaufman's version of "Rising Sun" has made the villains less racially one-sided and toned down the book's relentless insistence that the Japanese are intent on swallowing America whole. Perhaps he thought he could make Crichton's polemic into an elegant meditation on Japanese thought and action, complete with Connery's John Connor passing on his knowledge to Web Smith by saying wise things like "Their way is better. They fix the problem, not the blame."

But making the Japanese less conniving—correct and responsible a decision though that was— inevitably helps to leave this particular movie bereft of any convincing reason for being. And the notion that every bestseller does not cry out to be filmed continues to be one lesson Hollywood shows no inclination to learn.

NEW YORK, 8/2/93, p. 50, David Denby

Busy, busy Michael Crichton, always warning us of some impending disaster—DNA research leading to rampaging teeth (*Jurassic Park*); miracle cures that produce homicidal ice-cream vendors (*The Terminal Man*); space probes that bring back poisoned Silly Putty (*The Andromeda Strain*); toothpaste that makes your hair fall out (*The Follicle Gap*). Where will it all end? In another best-seller, that's where. Crichton has turned alarmism into one of the most profitable shticks in the history of publishing. In *Rising Sun* (1992), he tried to evoke the alleged near-collapse of America before the Japanese industrial onslaught. Reading *Rising Sun* was, for Americans, almost a masochistic experience. In form, the book is a high-tech police procedural; in matter, a tendentious lecture about Japanese superiority and American folly and ineptitude.

America doesn't have a chance. We are slow, inefficient, illogical, badly educated; we can't observe anything and prefer confrontation to cooperation. The Japanese make products cheaply and dump them onto our markets, forgoing immediate profits in return for market share, all the while protecting their own markets; the whole process is greased with kickbacks and gifts. Some of this, of course, is true, or almost true, but Crichton added a trashy paranoid element. They—*they*—are buying everything, gobbling up Los Angeles, controlling the universities, the L.A. *Times*, and the L.A.P.D. Some of those Americans standing around and smiling may look like Americans, but they're not; *they've been taken over.*

Philip Kaufman did the successful remake of *Invasion of the Body Snatchers* in 1978, and that may be why Fox okayed him as director of *Rising Sun.* But Kaufman is really the wrong man for the project. To begin with, the director of *The Right Stuff* and *The Unbearable Lightness of Being* is a generous fellow with a wide-open mind and a ready embrace of the world, and so he's uncomfortable with Crichton's narrow approach. Kaufman, a Japanophile, jettisoned the screen adaptation prepared by Crichton and screenwriter Michael Backes and produced his own screenplay with a little assistance from David Mamet. The book's paranoia about Japan has been lessened; culpability for the central crime has been shifted; the clash-of-cultures fuss has been softened in favor of "understanding." I thought I was pro-understanding, but having seen the movie I'm not so sure, especially since the East-West reconciliation put forth in the movie, is pathetic nonsense—mere gentle clichés substituting for Crichton's virulent ones. *Rising Sun* is an odd, miscellaneous entertainment, with a couple of startling sequences and much nonsense and confusion. It's a botch, but like a number of Kaufman's botches (*The Wanderers, Henry & June*), it's far from dead.

In outline, the story is the same. A beautiful party girl (Tatjana Patitz) has been found dead without panties in the boardroom of Nakamoto, a Japanese conglomerate that has its American headquarters in Los Angeles. The crime, of course, is only the most flagrant evidence of layers and layers of corruption below. The girl had kinky habits that no man could resist; she was, it turns out, a pawn in a scheme to blackmail a United States senator who was blocking the sale of a small American technology company to Nakamoto.

The nominal hero, now called Web Smith (Wesley Snipes), swings into action. What a hero! He's more like a sad sack. Web is an L.A.P.D. liaison officer with the Asian community, yet he knows nothing about Japan, and so he endlessly asks questions of his implacable master, the imperturbable, all-knowing genius Captain John Connor (Sean Connery). This Connor would give lectures while standing on a sinking ship: Every trivial thing that happens in the course of the investigation—a moment of silence, a slight intonation in a Japanese voice—sends him into flights of exposition. He has, it seems, the entire history of American and Japanese capitalism in his head, understands Japanese culture inside and out, and plays a wicked game of golf (supremely useful, apparently, in dealing with the Japanese); Connor even knows when and how far to *bow.*

Crichton created the character with Sean Connery in mind. I love Sean Connery, but this should give you some idea of Crichton's seriousness. Here's this crisis that goes to the very roots of our identity as a people, but it can be solved by James Bond, with a Japanese education and black Armani suits, beating the bastards at their own game. For only a detective schooled in the ways of the master race can stop them. (If this is true, we really are doomed, since I don't see large numbers of Americans learning how to bow.) Appearing with a pointy white beard, Connery lectures poor Snipes relentlessly, and for the first time in his life, he seems a phony. The filmmakers changed Connor's partner into a black man to add a touch of racial companionship, but to my eyes Snipes and Connery never make much contact: Snipes, always on the receiving end, looks outraged. Whether Kaufman cast Snipes out of commercial calculation or high-mindedness, he has naively added a new element of racism that wasn't present in the book.

Kaufman has funny perceptions visually, the movie is a deliriously hybrid affair, with industrial Japanoiserie needling the American façade. A mock-Western that appears at the very beginning recaps motifs from Kurosawa films that were, in turn, variations on American Westerns. Kaufman recasts Crichton's paranoia as teasing ambiguity: We're not being taken over by the Japanese; we're being pollinated by them (much as the rest of the world has been pollinated by America). Kaufman's skill, as always, is with texture, not action. A party scene at Nakamoto headquarters, with half-naked men hitting huge drums (Toru Takemitsu wrote the music), is a fabulous bit of corporate swank. And the centerpiece of the movie is something of a triumph. Nakamoto's surveillance cameras, it seems, have recorded the murder. But then someone has doctored the video discs so as to conceal the real murderer. In an elaborate sequence, in which the kinky copulation and its aftermath are played over and over, beautiful limbs thrashing about in a black party dress, we get to see how the alterations were made, how detective work can be performed on a shadow in a frozen instance of recorded time.

The rest of the movie, however, is second-rate and messy. Whatever changes Kaufman made in its tone, the story remains a vise of conventionality, with suicides, chases, fights, and all kinds of junk that Kaufman stages less well than a routine action director. Trying for depth and soul where there isn't any, he dawdles or attempts to pack too many characters and too much detail into simple shots. Kaufman's lofty statements about the film in the July-August *Film Comment* may be a classic case of directorial self-delusion: Relationships between characters that mean all sorts of profound things in his head appear to us as banal movie stuff that simply doesn't work.

What's most dismaying about Michael Crichton's book is not so much the Japan-bashing but the lack of any recognition that American individualism and contentiousness, for all the disorder that they create, might offer advantages and spiritual liberties that orderly Japan cannot. Kaufman seems to understand that, but he doesn't know how to pull it out of the muck of Crichton's hectic plot. For all their longing for safe streets and a more productive economy, few Americans want to live the way the Japanese do.

NEW YORK POST, 7/30/93, p. 25, Michael Medved

Novelist Michael Crichton, who first dreamed up those pesky dinosaurs of "Jurassic Park," wrote about rampaging monsters of another sort in "Rising Sun": gigantic, all-devouring Japanese conglomerates bent on nothing less than the total domination of American society.

Crichton filled page after page with detailed, often hysterical warnings about Japanese perfidy and the puniness of America's response, turning a convoluted and unconvincing murder mystery into a hugely readable polemic about the supposedly sinister "invasion" of the United States.

In the new movie version of "Rising Sun," the provocative political content has largely disappeared, but the flimsy plot remains—and it seems even shakier with the transition to the big screen. The story has a choppy, slapped-together feel to it, and the numerous red herrings begin to stink up the place like a colorful platter of tainted sushi.

During a glitzy reception marking the opening of a Japanese corporation's new high-rise headquarters in Los Angeles, a blond party girl dies under suspicious circumstances. The local cops launch a murder investigation but face a massive corporate cover-up involving surveillance cameras and altered videos, kinky sex, high-level blackmail and a sneaky Japanese attempt to take over a crucial U.S. computer company.

Without Crichton's lengthy explanations and arguments, none of this makes much sense; and were it not for the steadying presence of Sean Connery—whose unflappable charisma can make even the most contrived material entertaining—"Rising Sun" would sink to the level of outright embarrassment.

Connery plays John Connor (a juicy character Crichton claims he created with the actor specifically in mind)—a veteran L.A. cop who has lived for years in Japan and boasts a profound understanding of Japanese culture. He comes out of semi-retirement to assist dedicated detective Wesley Snipes in exploring the unsolved murder at the Nakamoto Corp.

Despite Snipes' protests, they quickly develop a *senpai-kohai* (or master-student) relationship—a sort of Zen variant of the mismatched partners/bickering buddies arrangement that turns up with such maddening regularity in all contemporary cop movies.

The decision to cast Snipes pays off on several counts: For one thing, his edgy, electric screen presence contrasts nicely with Connery's imperious calm. Furthermore, the decision to place an African American in this critical role as heroic defender of the American way of life—despite the fact that the novel gave no hint whatever that the character was black seems calculated to disarm those who might otherwise accuse this movie of racism.

Along similar lines, director-producer Philip Kaufman ("The Right Stuff," "The Unbearable Lightness of Being" has repeatedly denied that this film contains elements of "Japan-bashing," insisting that it merely portrays "a conflict of cultures." On this level, it must be said, the picture fails completely, since Kaufman presents Japanese culture with the sort of complexity and depth we associate with depictions of Martian culture in 1950s movies about outer space invaders; in fact, the Asian characters are even less individualized than Hollywood's old-time treatment of intergalactic aliens.

The only vaguely sympathetic Japanese character is a glamorous but crippled video expert who turns out to be half American—a throwaway part that wastes the talents of Tia Carrere.

This picture does deploy some formidable assets, in addition to Connery's effortless star turn—including the handsome camera work by Michael Chapman ("Raging Bull") and atmospheric art direction by the great Dean Tavoularis (the "Godfather" films). When you begin to compare the strengths and the flaws, however, this misguided movie winds up with a deficit that's every bit as formidable as our trade imbalance with Japan.

NEWSDAY, 7/30/93, Part II/p. 62, Jack Mathews

The emblem referred to in the title of Philip Kaufman's "Rising Sun" is Japanese, and the film's tarnished heroes are Americans. But don't let those things mislead you. This is a Charlie Chan movie if I've ever seen one.

"Pay attention, *kohai*, says Sean Connery's veteran police detective to Wesley Snipes' young partner, in the tone Charlie Chan reserved for his eager, innocently inept "Number One Son." "And never underestimate your opponent. Never take what he offers you."

You'll find this kind of fortune-cookie philosophy throughout "Rising Sun," a brilliantly atmospheric, frequently funny, marvelously acted and ultimately ludicrous murder mystery set in the exotic corridors of Japanese high finance and *yakuza* gang life in Los Angeles.

Kaufman, who co-wrote this adaptation of Michael Crichton's best-seller with Crichton and Michael Backes, correctly assumed that the book's tedious essays on Japanese business practices would sink any movie, and he pretty much did away with them. But in doing so, he created other problems.

Without the detailed cultural background, Crichton's feeble murder plot is left to stand alone, and by changing the identity of the killer, a mistake made earlier this summer by Philip Noyce in his adaptation of Ira Levin's "Sliver," Kaufman undermined what little credibility the story had and turned his big revelation scene into a laughable B movie cliché.

When was the last time you heard a murder suspect finger the real killer with the line, "I didn't do it; HE did it!"?

If Kaufman's goal was to soften the book's anti-Japanese themes, he failed. If anything, the movie is even more hostile. The Japanese executives we see negotiating with their slow-witted American counterparts are the corporate equivalent of Crichton's cunningly vicious velociraptors in "Jurassic Park."

In the opening scenes of "Rising Sun," we see the executives of the huge Nakamoto electronics company sitting around a boardroom table, negotiating a price on a small American software company they want to buy. When the two Americans at the table whisper to each other, their words are picked up by state-of-the-art (read: Japanese) electronic devices and relayed back to the Japanese through earphones.

It is on that boardroom table, and recorded with the same hidden technology, that the murder occurs later that day. A high-priced American hooker (we are all whores is one of the film's themes) with a fetish for asphyxial intercourse (she likes to be strangled during the act) has left a Nakamoto party on another floor of the company's downtown high-rise to play choke 'n' groan with a fellow who leaves her dead.

Her murder, and the evidence left behind, leads Japanese-speaking detectives John Connor (Connery) and Web Smith (Snipes) into a thicket of cultural and political intrigue that plays to the basest instincts of everyone—the Japanese, an American senator (Ray Wise), even our wise and witty cops.

Kaufman seems to relish the dubious morality of Connor and Smith, whom he turns into film noir characters for the '90s. In that sense, the film is a stunning success. From the terrific opening sequence, which segues from a scene in a Kurosawa-style Japanese Western to a karaoke bar within the shadows of downtown Los Angeles, we are caught in a gleaming maze of confusing and conflicting cultural images.

The director wants us to know he's taking us into a different society that exists within our own, with familiar goals but different rules. Very soon, we know that our guide is Web Smith's guide, the *senpai* John Connor, a detective with mysterious eastern connections, who knows the ways of the Japanese and uses that knowledge to beat them at their own game.

This is a wonderful character for Connery, a post-Cold War James Bond. Cool, instinctual, world-wise, tough as a three-day steak marinated in the wisdom of the Orient. Insouciance, meets Inscrutability. Connery, who optioned Crichton's book and serves as the film's executive producer, plays Conner like a finely tuned instrument, and it's one of his best performances.

Snipes manages to hold his own in a role that is terribly underwritten and almost offensively subservient. Web's jokes about the slave/master relationship he has with Connor have the unfortunate ring of truth.

There are several strong supporting performances. Harvey Keitel, as the racist, corrupt cop Tom Graham, gets to represent all of Americans' antagonism toward Japanese trade practices, and works himself into a xenophobic sweat on our behalf. Cary-Hiroyuki Tagawa is delightful as the personable yakuza Eddie Sakamura, and the veteran Japanese actor Mako has some strong scenes as the righteous head of Nakamoto.

The acting weaknesses show up in the writing weaknesses, in two characters who were either expanded unnecessarily or invented for the movie. Kevin Anderson does a ridiculous turn as a corporate mercenary, an American working for the Japanese, and Tia Carrere's electronics expert Jingo Asakuma gets lost in a romantic subplot so ridiculous even Kaufman can't take it seriously.

Kaufman is a frustrating talent. The director of "The Right Stuff" and "The Unbearable Lightness of Being" has extraordinary intelligence, a painter's eye and a genuine love for his characters. But he often sabotages the realism of his work with bogus compositions and clumsy comic relief that knocks you right out of the story.

The women who are unclothed in a Kaufman movie, and there are a few here, have museum-quality, Botticelli breasts, and he doesn't skimp on showing them off. However, it is hard to fully appreciate their beauty, even as a mid-movie stimulant, when they are shown in the context of violence. The murder scene, shown at least a half-dozen times, is ugly business, indeed.

Equally off-putting are scenes showing Connor and Smith running from a handful of *yakuza*. On one occasion, they drive into a black community where Smith recruits some street brothers to rescue them. On another, they try to sneak out of an apartment building staked out by the gang.

That they don't think to call for help in either instance suggests they are either the stupidest cops in Los Angeles, or the only ones.

NEWSWEEK, 8/2/93, p. 55, David Ansen

Michael Crichton's novel "Rising Sun" was a paranoid polemic masquerading as a murder mystery. The polemic—an alarmist wake-up call warning America that we are losing the business war with Japan—had an unfortunate tendency to turn the Japanese into an omnipotent, ominous and faceless "they." Crichton's portrait of these shadowy power brokers, secretly pulling the strings of virtually every American institution, indulged in sweeping racial generalizations. Still, it was the didactic side of "Rising Sun" that gave it its fascination: you felt you were getting a crash course in Japanese business practices. The murder mystery itself—who strangled the beautiful blonde on the boardroom table of the Nakamoto Corp.?—was pretty routine genre stuff.

Director Philip Kaufman ("The Right Stuff"), sensitive to the criticisms of Japan-bashing, has made some crucial alterations in his screenplay (cocredited to Crichton and Michael Backes, who have washed their hands of this version). The didactic elements are downplayed, and the corruption level of the American characters has been raised so that the two cultures exist on a more level (im)moral playing field. Kaufman can be a superb stylist. "Rising Sun" has a stunning first act, full of sleekly disorienting visual effects that draw us into a world of cross-cultural confusions and sumptuous corporate towers where high-tech surveillance systems record the comings and goings of the Los Angeles power elite—and also record the murder of a Kentucky beauty (Tatjana Patitz) with kinky sexual proclivities.

To assist LAPD detective Web Smith (Wesley Snipes), the sage, enigmatic Japanophile John Conner (Sean Connery) is brought into the investigation. He is the *sempai* (guide) to Snipes's *kohai* (the younger protegé), and our instructor in the mysteries of the East. At first the case seems cut and dried: the dead woman's Japanese playboy lover, Eddie Sakamura (Cary-Hiroyuki Tagawa), is on the videotape leaving the scene of the crime. But everyone from Harvey Keitel's crude L.A. detective to Ray Wise's slick senator is a little too eager to pronounce the case shut, and the tape, it turns out, was altered.

But as the plot grows more intricate, strangely the tension dissipates, until finally the movie just seems to run out of breath. Without Crichton's editorial diversions, Kaufman is stuck with the bare bones of the plot, and for all his attempts to jazz things up with kung-fu fights, a hokey excursion into South Central L.A., plenty of bare breasts and a portentously ambiguousending, Kaufman and can't conceal there is less here than meets the eye. Too bad. There is some elegant and clever filmmaking in "Rising Sun." But ultimately Kaufman and Crichton are a bad fit: trying to transcend the material, the director loses the novelist's crude but compelling urgency.

SIGHT AND SOUND, 10/93, p. 51, Tony Rayns

During politically contested negotiations to buy US computer company MicroCon, Japanese conglomerate Nakamoto opens its new high-rise HQ in Los Angeles. When the corpse of good-time girl Cheryl Lynn Austin is found in the boardroom during the building's inaugural reception, staff lawyers Ishihara and Richmond insist that the LAPD's Special Services Liaison Unit be brought in to handle the matter sensitively. Detective Web Smith takes it on, guided by the unit's semi-retired expert on Japan, John Connor; their entry is resented by Lt Tom Graham, the crude, xenophobic cop who was first on the scene. Connor realises that Austin's death must have been recorded by security cameras, but finds that the relevant video-disc has been replaced since the incident.

A search of Austin's home reveals that she was a 'gasper' (needing near-asphyxiation to achieve orgasm) and that her lover was playboy Eddie Sakamura, who was at the reception. A few hours later Ishihara provides the missing video-disk, which appears to show that Sakamura had violent sex with Austin and left her dead. But Sakamura evades arrest, crashes his car and dies in the burnt-out wreck. Connor takes the disc to Jingo 'Theresa' Asakuma, a part-Japanese expert on computer imaging, who shows that the images have been altered. Smith is warned that gutter journalist 'The Weasel' is raking up old allegations of corruption against him, and he and Connor are tailed by unknown Japanese heavies. Undaunted, they interview Senator John Morton, who attended the Nakamoto reception and is suddenly withdrawing his opposition to the sale of MicroCon.

But Sakamura was not in the car-crash; he turns up in Smith's home with a back-up copy of the original video-disc. Lt Graham (oddly, accompanied by Ishihara and Japanese thugs) stakes out the building to arrest Sakamura; in the ensuing melee, Sakamura dies and Smith is shot but saved by his bulletproof vest. The disc shows that Sakamura did enter the boardroom, but only to watch Austin have sex with Senator Morton, who left her unconscious; an unidentifiable man then came in and killed her. Connor faxes images from the disc to Morton, an obvious victim of blackmail, who shoots himself. Smith, Connor and Asakuma barge into the Nakamoto boardroom during the final MicroCon negotiations and play the disc in front of company chairman Yoshida, an old friend of Connor's. The man who panics and runs is Richmond, but he is murdered by Sakamura's vengeful yakuza friends before Smith and Connor can arrest him. Ishihara is sent back to Japan in disgrace; Connor goes off to play golf with Yoshida; and Smith flirts with Asakuma while driving her home—only to discover that her address is the same as Connor's.

Michael Crichton's 'ethno-thriller' novel had three main things going for it. First, the way it used its pessimism about America's future as the foundation for a polemic: calling American industry to arms in the 'war' against Japan and citing a small library of writing by revisionist economists in support of its attack on Japanese business practices. Second, its technological research, well up to Crichton's past standards; the detailed presentation of digital image-manipulation was the most compulsive element in the book. And third, the fascination of its central ambivalence towards Japanese society and culture: a strange mixture of Japan-bashing and sympathetic explication, which ultimately ran aground on Crichton's debatable assumption that all Japanese have unvarying, Pavlovian responses to all situations, even when based outside Japan. Against these notional pluses must be set such minuses as the extreme ordinariness of the pulp conventions that went into the convoluted plotting and the wearying banality of the approach to characterisation (entire pages of John Connor's dialogue read like paraphrases from 'How to Understand Japan' manuals). But no matter how wretched the writing or confused the author's stance, the book clearly had a core worth exploring.

Amazingly, Philip Kaufman's film version neuters the polemic and discards most of the technological detective work while preserving the cumbersome plot-line and accentuating the laboriousness of the exposition. The movie could stand as a textbook example of how not to get the best out of a pulp novel. Kaufman's changes to the book seem designed to transform it in various ways, but they prove stubbornly unresonant. Turning Smith into a black cop and having him played by Wesley Snipes was surely intended to broaden and complicate the racial issues, but in the event looks like nothing more than politically correct casting; Snipes has little to do, his presence yields nothing about the strained relations between blacks and Asians in Los Angeles and does nothing to lighten the endless, turgid exposition scenes on the freeways in which Connor instructs Smith in Japanese mores.

Similarly, introducing a covert love-interest between Connor and Asakuma adds not a shiver of erotic tension to the plot and the open ending, which raises the possibility that Smith will get off with Asakuma while Connor plays golf, seems like a nonsensical afterthought. The only change that really does alter anything is making Richmond rather than Ishihara the killer—which, of course, fatally weakens the thrust of Crichton's attack on Japanese ruthlessness.

David Mamet did some uncredited work on the final draft of the script, but Kaufman intended to reserve sole script credit for himself (the credit to Crichton and his collaborator Michael Backes, who actually left the project early on, is there as the result of a Writers Guild arbitration). He must therefore take the blame for the long series of misjudgments that vulgarise or trivialise the material and prevent the movie from achieving any credibility even as a generic thriller. These start right under the opening titles, with video images (some of them archly quoted from Kurosawa movies) of Japanese actors playing cowboys, presented as part of a karaoke video; the fact that no karaoke video ever looked remotely like that rather vitiates the intended satire of Japan's infatuation with Americana. And they continue right up to the Z-movie climax, in which a gang of stereotypical Japanese hoods pops up from nowhere to dispatch the villain in quick-drying cement.

Other such low points include the crass invention of an "executive fuck chamber" off the Nakamoto boardroom, two completely gratuitous martial-arts action scenes, the unexplained collaboration of Graham and Ishihara in the murder of Sakamura, and the embarrassing episode in South Central Los Angeles in which Smith jive-talks a group of 'brothers' on the street into delaying a carload of Japanese pursuers. These and many similar misjudgments suggest that the middlebrow Kaufman couldn't hit an authentically populist note if his career depended on it; he's rather like the broadsheet newspaper editor who tried to edit a tabloid and got everything wrong.

On top of all the other problems, the movie's representations of 'Japaneseness' are farcically inadequate. Sean Connery breezes through it all as effortlessly as he has through other recent films, but the character's supposed mastery of the Japanese language becomes a joke as soon as he's required to speak it. The Japanese-American actors who play the emigré characters fare little better, and are wildly unconvincing as Japanese executives. In fact, the only real mystery in the whole movie is the participation of Toru Takemitsu, one of Japan's most distinguished avant-garde composers. Is the perfunctoriness of the actual score perhaps Takemitsu's comment on the movie that he unwisely contracted to write for?

VILLAGE VOICE, 8/3/93, p. 53, Georgia Brown

Spoofing both Kurosawa and Sergio Leone, Philip Kaufman has devised a cunning opener for *Rising Sun*, the movie he's adroitly adapted from Michael Crichton's muddled bestseller. An L.A. karaoke bar is a terrific setting for making a point about the great circle route of American culture. Here we can listen to a charismatic Japanese playboy enthusiastically sing, "Don't Fence Me In." "Give me land, lots of land," sings Eddie (Cary-Hiroyuki Tagawa) with fervor and irony. He's eyed sullenly by his American girlfriend, Cheryl Austin (model Tatjana Patitz), a tall blond who exudes contempt enough to incite lethal violence against her. Cheryl, it turns out, has a taste for violence.

Kaufman's opening has a nifty through-the-looking-glass quality, and so does his open-ended riddle of an ending, but in between we know perfectly well where we are—firmly in the realm of the summer box-office war. This is another thriller made to cash in on another hot property and while Kaufman has served the material well, he hasn't exactly triumphed over it. The movie loses steam somewhat about two-thirds of the way through, and, while the climax is intentionally anticlimactic, the resolution, except for a nice final scene, feels slack. The novel has been changed enough, I suppose, to pique its fans' curiosity. Preserving my innocence, I didn't open the book before seeing the movie.

Crichton, I see now, is a crude popularizer and as such apparently has his uses. Even Ian Buruma allows that *Rising Sun* is offensive, but by disseminating the theories of the Japan "revisionists"—like Pat Choate, Chalmers Johnson, James Fallows, and Clyde Prestowitz—may serve a purpose: "So Americans have to be woken up to a danger, posited by the revisionists, in order for those same Americans not to get emotional when they finally realize that the revisionists were right. If the shrill tone of fictional propaganda helps to wake them up, so be it." While there was no evidence Crichton really understood all that chaos theory sprinkled in undigested lumps throughout *Jurassic Park*, the threat of Japanese mercantilism is simpler to grasp. His horror of Japanese expansionism is only exceeded by his awe of Japanese prowess and his disgust for American ineptitude.

Diplomatically, Kaufman distances his movie (written with Crichton and Michael Backes) from the novel, which, except for Robert Nathan's front-page rave in the *Times* book review (comparing the book to *Uncle Tom's Cabin* and *Gentleman's Agreement*), got roundly trounced most other places for crude Yellow Peril-ism.

One change is the casting of Wesley Snipes as Lieutenant Smith. With that all-American surname, Smith stands for his poor, put-upon country: he's a plugger, a schmuck who plays fair and by the book (most of the time), yet who's treated by his profit-minded wife the way Japan treats America. (Even his daughter disses him: "Is that why Mommy called you a loser, Daddy?") Being African American Snipes can also implicitly represent the ideals of cultural diversity—in contrast to Japanese racial uniformity. Of course, Smith is sidekick not chief. And having the snow-capped Sean Connery as *sempai* to his *kōhai* accentuates his junior status. Fortunately, Kaufman's taste in triangles comes to the rescue here: He makes Snipes a competitor for Connery's formidable (much younger) woman.

Have I said that *Rising Sun* is a murder mystery? Early on the Caucasian blond from the karaoke bar is found strangled on the Nakamoto Corporation's boardroom table. Evidence points to a "Jap perp" (as Harvey Keitel's bad lieutenant puts it). Here and there, we catch glimpses of older Japanese men indulging a taste for corn-belt coeds. In their special brothel, the girls all look like lambs and colts. Kaufman shows how easy it would be to get protectionist juices flowing, even though the denouement is intended to thwart hasty assumptions. The implication is that you can't trust your own racist projections.

Called to the crime scene, Snipes's Lieutenant Smith is assisted by the semi-retired, semi-legendary Captain Connor, one of those heroic Westerners—a T.E. Lawrence, an almost-Kurtz—who immerses himself in an alien culture and mediates between it and home base. Taller than the average *sempai*, Connery's Connor is all James Bond in grace and supercilious suavity.

Given that the skilled and feisty Japanese are profiting because America is torn and troubled, the movie tries to intimate that mess itself may be a virtue and a blessing. "Rough neighborhoods may be America's best advantage" is one of the added sentiments. It's made during a rather forced comic digression reminding us there's more to L.A. than golf and high finance.

So, to the real question: How does *Rising Sun* measure against the competition? Coming on the heels of *In the Line of Fire*—a picture whose direction and script have been consistently overrated—*Rising Sun* at least has the benefit of crisp, authoritative direction and an ambitious, mildly thoughtful screenplay. Not that I take Kaufman's attempt to make *Rising Sun* a trip into L.A.'s, and Japan's, lower depths seriously, but it is a pleasure to watch a director make each shot count. The bottom-line comparison between these two thrillers may be whether you prefer Eastwood's mentor and sleuth to Connery's. Sweat and tears to terminal urbanity. They both twinkle.

Also reviewed in:
CHICAGO TRIBUNE, 7/30/93, Friday/p. A, Johanna Steinmetz
NEW REPUBLIC, 8/16/93, p. 24, Stanley Kauffmann
NEW YORK TIMES, 7/30/93, p. C1, Vincent Canby
NEW YORKER, 7/26/93, p. 79, Terrence Rafferty
VARIETY, 8/2/93, p. 43, Todd McCarthy
WASHINGTON POST, 7/30/93, p. G1, Hal Hinson
WASHINGTON POST, 7/30/93, Weekend/p. 38, Desson Howe

ROAD SCHOLAR

A Samuel Goldwyn Company release of a Public Policy production. *Producer:* Roger Weisberg. *Director:* Roger Weisberg and Jean de Segonzac. *Director of Photography:* Jean de Segonzac. *Screenplay:* Andrei Codrescu. *Editor:* Alan Miller. *Music:* Wave Band Sound/ North Forty Music. *Sound:* Scott Breindel and Mark Roy. *Sound Editor:* John Purcell. *Running time:* 90 minutes. *MPAA Rating:* Not Rated.

WITH: Andrei Codrescu.

LOS ANGELES TIMES, 8/13/93, Calendar/p. 6, Peter Rainer

Andrei Codrescu is a 47-year-old Romanian-born immigrant who has lived in America since he was 20. The author of 25 books and, since 1983, a commentator on National Public Radio's "All Things Considered," Codrescu has a wry take on America, but what keeps him from being a Romanian version of Yakov Smirnoff is a forlorn, poetic undercurrent. He's not a ranter.

In "Road Scholar," a documentary that follows Codrescu on a cross-country jaunt to many of his old haunts, including Detroit and San Francisco, we get to see Codrescu up close. He doesn't exactly overpower the camera. Rumply and a little squat, with thick round glasses, he sidles into his scenes almost apologetically. His principled reticence has a wait-and-see quality: He may look a bit blank but usually he's just biding his time until he takes everything in.

In "Road Scholar," which was directed and conceived by Roger Weisberg, Codrescu talks to a guard at the Statue of Liberty; a New Age channeler in Sante Fe; a roller-skating congregation—the Holy Rollers—in Chicago: poet Allen Ginsberg, whom Codrescu considers his mentor, and many other mavericks and marginals. Driving around the country in a red '68 Caddie convertible—he learned to drive for the occasion—Codrescu seems like a bemused interloper on a low-key crusade to root out the essence of American eccentricity.

Road movies are usually only as good as what you pick up along the road. "Road Scholar" doesn't try to be a De Tocquevillian panorama, and it doesn't opt for a "Frontline"-like bluntness, either. It's a wayward, wispy, jaunt, and one's tolerance for it may depend on how willingly you buy into Codrescu's belief that the truest Americans are the most marginalized Americans.

It's an outsider's vision, and Codrescu signals his simpatico with these people by making them the centerpiece of his odyssey. He's cast himself as the immigrant who seems more clearly into the heart of America than the native-borns who take it all for granted. The film's free-form I-love-this-country tone is easy to accept because there's no rah-rah in it. It's patriotism cleansed of boosterism.

"Road Scholar" (Times-rated Family) would be better if Codrescu placed himself in more challenging situations; he doesn't risk much. Still, a lot of it is enjoyable as a complacent, oddball travelogue, and the filmmakers are careful not to condescend to the people we meet along the way. (The lack of condescension is what differentiates its tone from Michael Moore's "Roger & Me," to which it has been inaccurately compared.) You may not learn a whole lot more about America—or Codrescu—after seeing "Road Scholar" but the company is pleasant and so are the sights.

NEW YORK POST, 7/16/93, p. 33, Michael Medved

Driving across the United States from the Atlantic Coast all the way to the Pacific is one of the peak experiences available to any human being.

I might as well confess at the outset that I've made the trek myself eight times—five of them as a late 60s/early '70s hitchhiker during my years at college and law school.

Fond memories of these expeditions helped to generate a special sense of kinship and anticipation concerning "Road Scholar," the cinematic record of Andrei Codrescu's own cross-country adventure. Codrescu is the Romanian-Jewish emigre poet whose wry, deadpan commentaries on American life have been a long-running and valuable feature on NPR's "All Things Considered."

In 1989, WNET documentarian Roger Weisberg approached Codrescu with the suggestion that they might make a movie together about the poet driving across America in a journey of discovery. Codrescu liked the idea but faced a formidable problem: He didn't know how to drive.

The movie therefore begins with an amusing sequence showing Codrescu in driving school near his New Orleans home. Once he succeeds in getting his license, he begins his epic journey in New York behind the wheel of a fire-engine red 1968 Cadillac convertible.

He is an instantly likable tour guide—with his tousled hair, wire-rim glasses, oversized I-Am-the-Walrus moustache and solemn poker face—and the New York sequences, featuring emotional visits to the Statue of Liberty and Ellis Island are satisfying and affecting.

Once Andrei hits the road and heads west, however, the movie loses energy and focus in a hurry. He devotes disproportionate attention in his travels to eccentric expressions of religiosity. As he declares at the end of his journey, wading into the Pacific near San Francisco, "Paradoxically, the most materialistic country in the world in also the most spirited spiritual."

Codrescu illuminates that spirituality by showing us an odd assortment of cults and quacks, including a crystal healer who is guided by a 10-foot-tall blond archangel named Ariel; an African-American Chicago congregation that holds its weekly prayer meetings on roller skates; a Native American shaman, who invokes the spirits with traditional dances; an ascetic, pacifist German sect living in a commune in upstate New York and the flourishing New Mexico community of robed-and-turbaned young converts to the Sikh religion.

What is conspicuously absent from this survey of contemporary religiosity is even the slightest hint of the huge proportion of our fellow citizens who attend ordinary churches and synagogues, and for whom commitment to the more conventional aspects of the Judeo-Christian tradition represents an important priority in life.

Theme vignettes are only intermittently intriguing, despite beautiful camera work by director Weisberg and cinematographer Jean de Segonzac, who previously shot the Oscar-winning documentary "Common Threads: Stones for the Quilt." The problem is a lack of common threads in Andrei Codrescu's America; his moments of insight or amusement don't add up to a persuasive or coherent view of the country.

The ads for the film promise that, "Andrei Codrescu is about to discover the real America." Unfortunately that voyage of definitive discovery will have to wait for another trip and another film.

NEWSDAY, 7/16/93, Part II/p. 60, John Anderson

Alexis de Tocqueville's 19th-Century treatise. "Democracy in America," was based on the proposition that the only objective appraisal of America's political health was going to be made by a Frenchman on horseback. So we should probably accept "Road Scholar's" suggestion, that the best spiritual diagnosis of the country is going to be made by a Translvanian in a red Cadillac.

In Roger Weisberg and Jean de Segonzac's delightful comedy/documentary, Andrei Codrescu, Romanian-born author and commentator for National Public Radio's "All Things Considered," hits the road in his '68 Caddy "named for a French explorer famous for founding Detroit and fighting Native American pedestrians"—and makes his way from New York through Detroit, Chicago, Denver, Santa Fe, Tucson and Las Vegas before arriving at the Golden Gate Bridge and the conclusion that "the most material country in the world is also the most spiritual." Despite Codrescu's penchant for the occasional forced joke and smarmy observation, he, Weisberg and de Segonzac persuade us that this just might be the case.

While de Tocqueville's concerns were political and social, Codrescu's are strictly spiritual. And while exploring, and frequently dismissing, the serious and quasi-serious religions he encounters—including crystal healers, southwestern Sikhs, and New Age psychics—he also delves into those more tangible items that often pass for belief systems in this country—like guns, meat and money. But there's a strong strain of poetry in the land, something Codrescu finds in his friend, Allen Ginsberg, Ginsberg's spiritual ancestor, Walt Whitman (poet and rest stop on the New Jersey Turnpike) and in the sign language that's used by women on the streets of Camden, to speak to their husbands and boyfriends in the upper reaches of the prison built across from Whitman's home in Camden.

Accompanied by a bastardized version of "Mustang Sally" ("ride, Andrei, ride ...") and de Segonzac's beautiful cinematography, Codrescu visits the Hutterian Bruderhof, a community of "Christian Communists" who, despite a facility for making money, embrace poverty; the "Holy Rollers," a gospel congregation that meets in a Chicago roller rink; One Foot in the Grave, a punk-rock band in a senior citizens enclave, and Denver cattlemen who are actually genetic engineers.

Much of what Codrescu finds has to do with the idea of the family—the exotic manifestations it can assume, and the way Americans hunger for it. The result isn't always a formal assemblage like the Bruderhof. It can also be a homeless band of crack-addicted Haitians, who, despite their lowly state, are happy to discuss with Codrescu the merits of the first amendment, and their shared experiences with totalitarian regimes. The point of "Road Scholar," is, in the end, that our shared interest in America, and the idea of America, outweighs any differences we might have.

VILLAGE VOICE, 7/20/93, p. 56, Regina Raiford

"Isn't it nice that San Francisco made a road that is a metaphor for a poet's life?" Andrei Codrescu utters this line in *Road Scholar* while careening down a series of hairpin curves. In this film, every road, every town, every person becomes a metaphor for this poet's life.

Codrescu, a Romanian poet and humorist at National Public Radio, travels across country in a 1968 red Cadillac wryly commenting on the places he visits and the people he meets. Despite the deceptively casual tone, he actively seeks out unconventional pockets of Americana: Amishlike communist Christians and professional Las Vegas card-sharks, Native American hoop dancers and a capitalist Sikh community. These encounters offer a vivid mosaic of the various ways people embrace their ethnicity (which comes across as a cherished construction of beliefs rather than something born into).

I was struck by Codrescu's wit and his knack with language, but I would have preferred to hear more about the way his subjects actually live, less about his opinion of the way they live. At the end, Codrescu drives up to the sea, his dashboard adorned with souvenirs of his trip. Though I had learned much about this poet and his vision, I felt as if all I had to show from this pleasant summer journey was a handful of curious trinkets.

Also reviewed in:
CHICAGO TRIBUNE, 9/10/93, Friday/p. F, Clifford Terry
NEW REPUBLIC, 8/16/93, p. 24, Stanley Kauffmann
NEW YORK TIMES, 7/16/93, p. C14, Stephen Holden
VARIETY, 7/19/93, p. 72, Todd McCarthy
WASHINGTON POST, 8/6/93, p. D1, Richard Harrington

ROBIN HOOD: MEN IN TIGHTS

A Twentieth Century Fox release of a Brooksfilms production in association with Gaumont. *Executive Producer:* Peter Schindler.   *Producer:* Mel Brooks.   *Director:* Mel Brooks. *Screenplay:* Mel Brooks, Evan Chandler, and J. David Shapiro.   *Story:* J. David Shapiro and Evan Chandler.   *Director of Photography:* Michael D. O'Shea.   *Editor:* Stephen E. Rivkin. *Music:* Hummie Mann.   *Music Editor:* Chris Ledesma.   *Choreographer:* Cindy Montoya-Picker. *Sound:* Mark "Frito" Long and (music) Rick Riccio and Armin Steiner.   *Sound Editor:* Gregory M. Gerlich and Gary S. Gerlich.   *Casting:* Lindsay D. Chag and Bill Shepard.   *Production Designer:* Roy Forge Smith.   *Art Director:* Stephen Myles Berger.   *Set Designer:* David M. Haber, Cate Bangs, Bruce Robert Hill and Gary A. Lee.   *Set Decorator:* Ronald R. Reiss.   *Set Dresser:* Mark Boucher, Nigel A. Boucher, and Philip Calhoun.   *Special Effects:* Richard Ratliff. *Costumes:* Dodie Shepard.   *Make-up:* Bari Dreiband-Burman.   *Make-up (Cary Elwes):* Carol Schwartz.   *Make-up (Special Effects):* Thomas R. Burman.   *Stunt Coordinator:* Brian Burrows. *Running time:* 104 minutes. *MPAA Rating:* PG-13.

CAST: Cary Elwes (Robin Hood);   Richard Lewis (Prince John);   Roger Rees (Sheriff of Rottingham);   Amy Yasbeck (Marian);   Mark Blankfield (Blinkin);   Dave Chappalle (Ahchoo); Isaac Hayes (Asneeze);   Megan Cavanagh (Broomhilde);   Eric Allan Kramer (Little John); Matthew Porretta (Will Scarlet O'Hara);   Tracey Ullman (Latrine);   Patrick Stewart (King Richard);   Dom DeLuise (Don Giovanni);   Dick Van Patten (The Abbot);   Robert Ridgely (The Hangman);   Mel Brooks (Rabbi Tuckman);   Steve Tancora (Filthy Luca);   Joe Dimmick (Dirty Ezio);   Avery Schreiber (Tax Assessor);   Chuck McCann (Villager);   Brian George (Dungeon Maitre D');   Zitto Kazann (Head Saracen Guard);   Richard Assad (Asssistant Saracen Guard); Herman Poppe (Sheriff's Guard);   Clive Revill (Fire Marshall);   Joe Baker (Angry Villager); Carol Arthur (Complaining Villager);   Kelly Jones (Buxom Lass);   Clement Von Franckenstein (Royal Announcer);   Corbin Allred (Young Lad);   Chase Masterson (Giggling Court Lady); Don Lewis (Mime);   Roger Owens (Peanut Vendor);   Patrick Valenzuela (Lead Camel Jockey).

CHRISTIAN SCIENCE MONITOR, 8/12/93, p. 11, Marilynne S. Mason

[*Robin Hood: Men in Tights* was reviewed jointly with *So I Married an Axe Murderer*; see Mason's review of that film.

FILMS IN REVIEW, 10/93, p. 338, Edmond Grant

Not too many years ago, in the fall of 1975 to be exact, there was a charming little sitcom that spoofed the legend of Robin Hood and his merry men. The show had a low budget, set-bound look, but its scripts were crammed with gags and its performers were vibrantly up to the task. The show was called *When Things Were Rotten*; it lasted only half a season before it was cancelled by ABC.

The reason for bringing up this quaint bit of TV history is that the show was the brainchild of Mel Brooks, the same Mel Brooks who has now chosen to gallop back into Sherwood Forest, eighteen years older and hardly any wiser. *Robin Hood: Men In Tights* is simply put, a sad piece of moviemaking from the comic genius of the 1960s/70s, a man who set the standard for cinematic genre parody with *Blazing Saddles* and *Young Frankenstein* (not forgetting his classic, *The Producers*).

The really sad thing about *Men In Tights* is not that Mel returns to territory he's mined before—it's that his inspiration for this haphazard collection of feeble, telegraphed jokes was the (feeble, and very predictable in itself) recent Kevin Costner rendition of Robin Hood. Yes, Brooks' targets have gone from classic movie genres (the Western, the Universal monster movies, Hitchcockian thrillers) to singular phenomena; then again, this is the same late model Mel, the kind of comic director who would wait until 1987 to make his *Star Wars* comedy (at least those three movies were high grossing, precedent setting, pictures). When this Mel wants us to laugh, he reaches into his bag of tricks and out come the formulas:

    a.) cheap (and we do mean cheap) shtick. Characters with names like Ahchoo and the Sheriff of Rottingham (a fresh twist, circa the 1950s *Mad* magazine). Lame physical gags, based on handicaps (that blind guy—doesn't know what he's doing!). Silly musical numbers. And corkers from the proverbial year of the flood: a public speaker implores "Lend me your ears," (quick, what can you guess comes next?) and the crowd pulls off rubber ears, throwing them at the speech-maker (a gag even *Mad* gave up on a good two decades ago).

    b.) anachronisms. dozens of up-to-the-minute-mid-1990s references make *Men In Tights* more the cinematic equivalent of a Bob Hope network TV monologue ("Hey, what about that crazy rock music?") than the kind of perennially insane humor that makes Brooks' classic movies so timeless. Thrown in for gag effect here: Larry King, pump-up sneakers, rap music, *Home Alone, White Men Can't Jump*, etc.

    c.) reflexive jokes. Whenever things begin to lag a bit (and no silly musical numbers are in sight), Mel reminds us "it's only a movie: the film's script is consulted, stagehands are seen, and a camera hits a pane of glass while Maid Marian (Amy Yasbeck) sings, which leads us to ...

    d.) references to Mel's other movies. The latter example was already used at the end of *High Anxiety*, while here Mel also throws in an explicit verbal reference to *Blazing Saddles*, an awful recreation of the "What hump?" gag used in *Young Frankenstein* (done here by a dreadfully arch-camp Richard Lewis), and his own attempt at a tagline, "It's good to be the King" (from *History of the World Part I*).

    Besides its reliance on formulas taught in Burlesque 101, the most disappointing element of the movie is its uninspired casting. Cary Elwes mugs and misses comic beats as a preening Robin Hood; Tracey Ullman and Roger Rees are completely wasted, and the otherwise funny Mark Blankfield reprises the blind-man shtick that caused much trouble when he performed it on the defunct TV sitcom *Good And Evil* (which starred Brooks alumna Teri Garr). Only Brooks stalwart Dom DeLuise can bring in a stray laugh with a hopelessly dated, but actually funny, short stint as a *Godfather*-like medieval gangster.

    It's sad to think that the man who ruled American movie comedy in the 1970s (along with Woody Allen) has now been surpassed in the art of genre parody by the Zucker-Abrahams-Zucker team who, when Mel was ruler of the roost, were young upstarts churning out bluntly rude (but hysterical) black-out humor (*The Kentucky Fried Movie*) which, even, in its crudest moments, was a hundred times funnier than *Men In Tights*.

LOS ANGELES TIMES, 7/28/93, Calendar/p. 5, Peter Rainer

Mel Brooks' new comedy, "Robin Hood: Men in Tights", puts us through a flurry of jokes relating to everything from Larry King to valet parking to, of course, Kevin Costner. In other words, the Sherwood Forest guy gets the Brooks treatment—thwackingly obvious cornball vaudeville with a streak of inspired lunacy.

Most of Brooks' movies, including "Blazing Saddles," "High Anxiety" and "Spaceballs," have been genre spoofs. The most successful of these, "Young Frankenstein," was also the one in which Brooks seemed to care most about the genre. You probably can't turn out a great spoof if on some basic level you don't love what you're spoofing. You have to love the conventions enough to go a little crazy (with glee) when they get violated. One of the reasons why, say, "Spaceballs" didn't work is because Brooks didn't really connect with the intergalactic genre. It was, literally, too far out for his way-in nuttiness.

The Robin Hood movies that probably mean the most to Brooks are the ones starring Douglas Fairbanks and Errol Flynn, but "Men in Tights," no doubt for commercial reasons, is mostly Costner-era riffs, and you can feel that Brooks isn't quite in sympathy with his targets. There's something a little dutiful and desperate about portions of the film, as if Brooks were trying to capture an audience he didn't really connect with.

As insurance, he works in variations on some of his greatest nutball moments from his earlier films: For example, the rappers who belt out the "Sherwood Forest Rap" recall the chain gang singing "I Get a Kick Out of You" from "Blazing Saddles." This stuff is still funny—it survives the transition—but it doesn't strike too many fresh notes.

The best way to enjoy "Men in Tights" (rated PG-13 for off-color humor) is to blank out the dull knockabout passages and sit tight for the kind of loopy squiggles that only Brooks can come up with. (His co-writers were Evan Chandler and J. David Shapiro.)

As Robin and Maid Marian, Cary Elwes and Amy Yasbeck are a bland twosome, but many of the supporting players are in comic overdrive. Richard Lewis, as Prince John, is playing his usual wacked-out neurotic schlep, but, in this Sherwood Forest setting, he seems funnier than ever.

Roger Rees is the Sheriff of Rottingham and he goes at his villainy in the best Master Thespian manner. Tracey Ullman plays the witch Latrine under enough makeup to sink a freighter. (The joke is that you can still tell it's Ullman.) Brooks himself turns up as a rabbi who performs bargain circumcisions, and he's so funny that you wish he'd stick around longer. The movie feels a little hollow when he's not on screen.

Everybody knows that Brooks, when he's really *on*, is the funniest man in the world. But it's possible he's never quite found the medium that would bring out his wildest inventions. Maybe the best way to realize Brooks is just to let him loose—that's why his appearances on talk shows are such giddy highs. As a performer in his movies, Brooks often approximates those highs, but the cumbersome process of putting together a movie slows him down: he doesn't have the kind of skills that might unify his scattershot jokiness. This isn't the worst thing in the world—what's enjoyable about the best parts of "Men in Tights" is its grab-bag, throwaway style.

But Brooks makes concessions in his films that dilute his genius. The obviousness of much of the humor in "Men in Tights" comes across like a downgrade for the kiddies, The actors pause after their lines as if waiting for the jokes to reach even the dullest in the audience. There's a funny bit, for example, where Prince John shows up in each scene with his facial mole in a different location—funny, that is, until the sheriff points out the joke. And do we really need Dom DeLuise doing a take-off on Brando's Don Corleone, or telling us he "could've been a contenda"?

It's possible that Brooks' commercial instincts are right here, and that the young audience for this film *needs* the jokes spelled out for them. Like most filmmakers, Brooks is probably content to have a hit with whatever works these days.

NEW YORK POST, 7/28/93, p. 25, Matthew Flamm

One thing you can say about Mel Brooks: At least somebody in Hollywood has a sense of humor.

The tummler of Tinseltown is back in reasonably good form with "Robin Hood: Men in Tights," a sendup of the swashbuckler genre that aims at both the Errol Flynn and Kevin Costner versions of the famous romance—and anything else that gets in the way. The comedy, which was written by Brooks, Evan Chandler and J. David Shapiro, opens today.

It helps to have so many targets. The movie gets off to a good start with Robin Hood held prisoner in Jerusalem—this particular plot turn courtesy of Costner's "Rambo"-inspired Robin—and being shown to his cell by an eager-to-please "Maitre de Dungeon."

Likewise, Robin's sidekick here owes his job to the Morgan Freeman character in "Prince of Thieves." This Moor, however, who goes by the name Ahchoo—and who is studying to be a stand-up comic in England—does a wicked impersonation of Malcolm X, or at least of Denzel Washington in the movie "Malcolm X."

"We didn't land on Sherwood Forest!. Ahchoo (David Chapelle) exhorts a band of merry men who need a little inspiration. "Sherwood Forest landed on us!"

It also helps that in the 1938 "The Adventures of Robin Hood" men really did wear tights. As he's shown in "Young Frankenstein" and "Blazing Saddles"—to go back to his glory years—Brooks has a keen eye for cinematic ridiculousness, and the fun he pokes with a hilarious "Men in Tights" production number is dead on.

Just a little damage has been done to the story. Robin of Locksley is now Robin of Loxley (destined to wed Marian of, you guessed it, Bagel), who returns from the crusades to find Prince John (Richard Lewis) and the Sheriff of Rottingham (Roger Rees) oppressing the poor folk.

Cary Elwes, as Robin Hood, combines Flynn-like dash and good looks with just enough of the twit about him to be a credible comic actor. He's well-matched by the game and beautiful Amy Yasbeck, who, as Marian wears an Everlast (and apparently rustproof) chastity belt.

As in almost any Brooks production, there's a price to pay for the laughs. Lewis, playing Prince John as (surprise!) a raving neurotic, has the worst luck with some really pointless toilet jokes. Reese doesn't fare much better, though he would be hard pressed in any case to outdo Alan Rickman's brilliantly wacky Sheriff in "Prince of Thieves."

Brooks, as Rabbi Tuckman (the Friar Tuck character turned sacramental wine salesman and traveling mohel), and Tracey Ullman as a sorceress named Latrine, also try hard but mostly miss the target.

On the other hand, the whole effort is pretty much redeemed by a priceless bit in which Dom DeLuise does Brando's Godfather, brought in to give Robin Hood an offer he can't refuse. If that's not enough, there's the scene in which, the London-born Elwes hits Costner right where it hurts—in his English accent.

NEWSDAY, 7/28/93, Part II/p. 49, John Anderson

It's a tough call, but Kevin Costner is no longer the funniest Robin Hood in movie history.

His inadvertently hilarious Prince of Thieves looms large, however, in Mel Brooks' broad, bawdy and occasionally strained-like-a-bowstring "Robin Hood: Men in Tights." Brooks, never shy about appropriating material wherever he finds it, has turned out a Sherwood story that's an amalgam of Errol Flynn, Monty Python, Costner's Robin of Malibu, and, of course, Mel Brooks; the Merry Men don't sing "Springtime for Hitler," but the Brooksian echoes are ringing through the forest."

However, it's plagued by a rather bland performance by Cary Elwes, who brings to the title role a believable accent but very little color, and who seems to be reprising his own work in "The Princess Bride." And "Men in Tights" doesn't fare well when compared to Brooks' other genre-busting comedies, even if the comparisons are less than fair; "Blazing Saddles" and "Young Frankenstein" are, after all, among the funniest movies ever made.

While not Brooks' best, "Men in Tights" has its moments, some of them musical. And his supporting cast is a hardy band of men. And women: As Maid Marian, the beguiling Amy Yasbeck brings an astute, Jean Arthur-ish quality to a role that has always been decorative, and plays nicely off Elwes' slightly bemused Robin of Loxley (yes, her last name is Bagelle). And as her lady-in-waiting, Broomhilde, Megan Cavanagh provides a large, Teutonic presence that's strikingly similar to Frau Blucher in "Young Frankenstein." Tracey Ullman, as the witchcraft consultant Latrine, is like Phyllis Diller on a mead toot.

Brooks lets "Men in Tights" meander at first. We're introduced to Robin in prison in Jerusalem, where he's followed the crusading King Richard. He escapes with help from a fellow prisoner, Asneeze (Isaac Hayes), who tells Robin to look up his son, Ahchoo (Dave Chappelle), when he gets to England (the "gesundheit" jokes never end). Robin swims from the Mideast to Britain, kisses the ground, chokes on a mouthful of sand, has his castle towed away as per the orders of the evil Prince John (Richard Lewis), and sets out to right the wrongs committed by the nefarious Sheriff of Rottingham (Roger Rees) assisted by his Merry Men.

They're a good group: Blinkin (Mark Blankfield), who's blind and the source of innumerable sight gags; Little John (Eric Allan Kramer), thick-headed but surprisingly light on his feet during the dance numbers; and Rabbi Tuckman (Brooks), who's waylaid while bringing a wagon-load of sacramental wine through the forest, and who ends up joining the Merry Men.

Everyone knows the basic story, and even if you didn't, a Brooks movie is more about the digressions than the plot itself. One of the best moments involves the woefully underused Dom DeLuise as Don Giovanni, who talks like Brando in the "The Godfather" and cracks walnuts like Brando in "The Freshman." With his henchmen, Filthy Luca (get it?) and Dirty Ezio (Steve Tancora and Joe Dimmick), they plot Robin's demise.

The movie references, many to Brooks' own movies, are everywhere: Prince John's mole moves from one side of his face to the other, just as Marty Feldman's hump moved in "Young

Frankenstein". Rottingham is catapulted into Latrine's bed at one point, like the little girl in "YF" (and even more like the flying cheerleader in "Animal House"). Just like Errol Flynn and the stag, Robin shows up at the castle with a boar over his shoulders ("Treif," Lewis mutters). And Costner, whom Brooks once considered offering a cameo, is the butt of a lot of humor. What "Men in Tights" really needed, though, is Alan Rickman, who while almost salvaging "Prince of Thieves," thought he was in a comedy all along.

SIGHT AND SOUND, 1/94, p. 51, Geoffrey Macnab

The twelfth century, somewhere in the Holy Land. Robin Hood has been captured by the Saracens, and is being tortured in a dungeon, but refuses to divulge any secrets. He ends up chained alongside Asneeze, a brave Moorish potentate, and together they manage to hoodwink their captors and free all the prisoners. Robin resolves to swim home, but first he promises Asneeze to look out for his son Ahchoo, who is in England on a student exchange.

Arriving by breast stroke in Dover, Robin finds his home country much changed. The evil Prince John has usurped the throne and is tyrannizing the people. Robin soon bumps into Ahchoo and helps the young lad fight off an attack from Prince John's thugs. The two decide to journey together, and are briefly waylaid by the Sheriff of Rottingham, Prince John's chief henchman; but Robin's guile and bravery are too much for him, and the Sheriff ends up humiliated in front of his own soldiers.

Robin is startled when he arrives back in Loxley. His family land has been confiscated by the crown, all of his relatives are dead, and the bailiff is busy dragging away his ancestral castle. The only survivor from the old days is Robin's faithful blind servant Blinkin, who hands his returning master a gift from his father, a key which is supposed to unlock future happiness.

The Sheriff has hurried back to court where he has alerted Prince John to Robin's return. The Prince realizes he is in danger and consults his resident witch Latrine. Latrine offers her help only on condition that she is guaranteed Rottingham's services as a lover. Meanwhile, Robin, Ahchoo and Blinkin, taking to the woods, find their way across a stream blocked by the half-witted giant Little John, who challenges Robin to a fight. This ends in a draw, and Little John agrees to became one of Robin's merry men. The team is also joined by Will Scarlet O'Hara, Little John's closest friend and an expert knife juggler, and Rabbi Tuckman, a burly wine merchant and preacher. They begin to train the peasants for armed revolt.

Back at court, the beautiful Maid Marian is languishing with boredom, doing all she can to repel the Sheriff's romantic overtures. When Robin makes a daring, impromptu appearance at a feast, she instantly falls in love with him. Prince John, unsatisfied with Latrine's advice on how to deal with the outlaw, turns to local Mafia boss Don Giovanni. The Don suggests hosting an archery tournament to lure Robin to the castle. Robin falls for the bait, turning up at the event in an outlandish disguise. He wins, but is captured and condemned to be hung. Marian pleads for his life, offering to marry Rottingham if Robin is spared.

Just as the wedding is about to take place, and as Rottingham prepares to have Robin killed anyway, Ahchoo comes to the rescue, shooting the noose round Robin's neck before the hangman can string him up. There is sheer chaos as the peasants rebel. The Sheriff rushes off into the tower with Marian and attempts to rape her, but is thwarted by her chastity belt. Robin catches up with him. A fight breaks out, and the Sheriff is eventually run through by Robin's sword.

Robin marries Marian. Halfway through the ceremony, King Richard arrives back from the crusades. He knights Robin and punishes Prince John, and it looks as if everybody will live happily ever after. However, the key left Robin by his father turns out not to fit the chastity belt after all and the couple are soon squabbling.

Mel Brooks, something of a 'prince of thieves' himself, is famous for filching ideas from others and for grinding comedy out of old Hollywood genres. He takes a cheerful, vulgar, hit-or-miss approach to parody, and his films may often be lousy, but they always have chutzpah. You can count on him to be magnificently tasteless—or, at least, that used to be the case.

Sadly, Brooks has been floundering in recent years. *Spaceballs* (1987) was as crass as its title suggests, and *Life Stinks* (1991) indeed stank, even if it did strive to make a little Mike Leigh-style social comment about the iniquities of the 1980s. *Robin Hood—Men in Tights* is Brooks' most feeble effort yet, if only because his least offensive. It may have all the ingredients of the classic Mel Brooks movie (bad jokes, corny dialogue, hackneyed narrative); it may even be full of blustering energy, but it still misses its target by a mile. Brooks doesn't seem to have noticed that the mainstream blockbusters he likes to scavenge have taken to plundering the past themselves: their in-built irony makes his role as Hollywood jester all but redundant. *Men in Tights* clings to the shirt-tails of *Robin Hood, Prince of Thieves*. It probably could not have been made unless Kevin Costner had revived interest in the English folk hero, but that hardly seems an excuse for Brooks to imitate Costner's 'original' quite so slavishly. After all, Costner's own version of Robin was tongue-in-cheek anyway. You would have expected Brooks to be far more promiscuous in his references, to cull jokes and scenes from every version of the Sherwood Forest yarn, to parody vintage swashbucklers like Fairbanks and Flynn.

Admittedly, Brooks manages to incorporate rap music, transforms Friar Tuck into a rabbi, and nicely lampoons Hollywood's idealised vision of England as a green, ambrosian land. His Robin, he insists, is the first one in movie history to speak with an authentic English accent. However, for all its self-reflexivity, this remains a traditional version of a story which is already as old as the hills. Often, it seems less a skit on Costner's picture than an inept remake. The glossy production values are out of place. Perhaps if the trees were made of papier mâché, the costumes were less detailed, and the landscapes not quite so lush, there might be some comedy in the director always drawing attention to the fact that "it's only a movie." And any hopes that Brooks is going to have some fun and games with the men in tights, subverting notions of heroic masculinity and indulging in a little *Top Gun*-style homoeroticism, are soon dashed.

There is little consolation in the performances. Cary Elwes, at least, is suitably chivalric as Robin, and has a nice line in wry, self-deprecating humour, while Richard Lewis plays Prince John as if he were a reincarnated Marty Feldman. But the rest of the cast give garish, over-the-top performances, sometimes verging on desperation. Roger Rees offers a fair approximation of Alan Rickman's villainous Sheriff, but lacks Rickman's gift for oleaginous comedy (in this respect, *Prince of Thieves* is actually funnier than *Men in Tights*). Brooks regular Dom DeLuise does an appalling Marlon Brando turn as Mafia chief Don Giovanni, complete with cotton wool in cheeks, and Tracey Ullman as the witch Latrine is bogged down by so many layers of make-up that she is hard pressed to give a performance at all. Patrick Stewart, from *Star Trek: The Next Generation*, gallops into frame at the end to imitate Sean Connery's cameo as King Richard in the Costner picture, again seemingly unaware that what he is parodying was a parody in the first place. There is much laboured *Up Pompeii*-style comedy about Marion's chastity belt, and one or two nicely choreographed fight sequences before the film finally peters out.

Now that much of Brooks's thunder has been stolen by the likes of Abrahams and Zucker, it is hard to see where he can go from here. Maybe he'll try to wreak his mischief on *Last Action Hero*, but the joke will be on him.

VILLAGE VOICE, 8/24/93, p. 64, Laurie Stone

Like contraband, classic vaudeville bits and Marx Brothers Dada sneak into *Men in Tights*. "Are you with us, yeah or nay?" Robin Hood asks the dim-witted townsfolk, a representative of whom replies, "Which one means yes?" Robin and Little John begin a fight using poles, but the wood keeps breaking and soon they are snapping each other's knuckles with pencil-length sticks. But there aren't many other occasions to laugh. The actors, knowing this, look beseechingly at the camera, like kids with embarrassing parents declaring, "I don't really belong here."

As the usurper Prince John, Richard Lewis does his neurotic urban Jew without material or context. Lacking anything to act, Roger Rees, as the Sheriff of Rottingham (yes), is reduced to a scowl and a sneer. Only Cary Elwes, who plays Robin and looks like a young Errol Flynn, is magical, remaining charming by pretending to be in someone else's film.

This movie isn't a satire of swashbucklers but of Mel Brooks movies, and though imitation can be an homage, recycling yourself is desperation. To Mel, the world is still goyim and the most outlaw act substituting *them* with an ethnic Jew, so Friar Tuck becomes Rabbi Tuckman. As the requisite postmenopausal succubus—the Cloris Leachman part of yore—the divine Tracey Ullman is now bewarted and cast as Latrine. Speaking of which, what happened to Mel at the toilet-training stage? There are not one but two scenes of animals shitting on people's hands. Brooks's fag jokes and chastity-belt humor are less offensive than out of touch. He doesn't riff on emotional arrest, he's just stuck.

Also reviewed in:
NEW REPUBLIC, 8/23 & 30/93, p. 30, Stanley Kauffmann
NEW YORK TIMES, 7/28/93, p. C13, Vincent Canby
VARIETY, 8/9/93, p. 35, Leonard K!ady
WASHINGTON POST, 7/28/93, p. C2, Rita Kempley
WASHINGTON POST, 7/30/93, Weekend/p. 38, Desson Howe

ROBOCOP 3

An Orion Pictures release. *Producer:* Patrick Crowley. *Director:* Fred Dekker. *Screenplay:* Frank Miller and Fred Dekker. *Story by:* Frank Miller. *Based on characters created by:* Edward Neumeier and Michael Miner. *Director of Photography:* Gary B. Kibbe. *Editor:* Bert Lovitt. *Music:* Basil Poledouris. *Music Editor:* Tom Villano. *Sound:* Kirk Francis and (music) Tim Boyle. *Sound Editor:* Paul Bruce Richardson. *Casting:* Steven Jacobs and Shay Griffin. *Production Designer:* Hilda Stark. *Art Director:* Cate Bangs. *Set Decorator:* Robert J. Franco. *Set Dresser:* Wren Boney, Patrick Fuhrman, Maryann Garvin, Robert Tate Nichols, Steve Blutstein, Derek Wilson, Talley Mulligan, Wesley Wright, and Daniel Foster. *Special Effects:* Jeff Jarvis. *RoboCop Design:* Rob Bottin. *Robo Movement:* Tim Cobb. *Costumes:* Ha Nguyen. *Make-up:* Katie Bihr. *Stunt Coordinator:* Dick Hancock and Conrad E. Palmisano. *Running time:* 105 minutes. *MPAA Rating:* PG-13.

CAST: Robert John Burke (RoboCop); Nancy Allen (Anne Lewis); Rip Torn (The CEO); John Castle (McDaggett); Jill Hennessy (Dr. Marie Lazarus); CCH Pounder (Bertha); Mako (Kanemitsu); Robert DoQui (Sergeant Reed); Remy Ryan (Nikko); Bruce Locke (Otomo); Stanley Anderson (Zack); Stephen Root (Coontz); Daniel VonBargen (Moreno); Felton Perry (Johnson); Bradley Whitford (Fleck); Mario Machado (Casey Wong); Jodi Long (Nikko's Mom); John Posey (Nikko's Dad); S.D. Nemeth (Bixby Snyder); Edith Ivey (Elderly Woman in Bathrobe); Curtis Taylor (Rehab #1); Judson Vaughn (Seltz); Ken Strong (Rehab Patrol); Kenny Raskin (Security Monitor); Blaise Corrigan (Officer at Ordnance Depot); Jeff Garlin (Donut Jerk); Lee Arenberg (Hold-up Man); Randy Randolph (Cop in Donut Shop); Shane Black (Donnelly); John Nesci (Jensen); Randall Taylor (Starkweather); James Lorinz (Upset Driver); Bryan Mercer (Splatterpunk #1); Kenny Jones (Splatterpunk #2); Doug Yashuda (Kanemitsu's Aide); Mark Gowan (Sleazy Lawyer); Thomas Boyd (Hooker); Eddie Billups (Man at Booking Desk); Mark Gordon (Techie in Robochamber); Angie Bolling (Ellen Murphy); Graciela Marin (Cop with Body Armor); Michael Moss (Unfortunate Rehab); Dianne Butler (Woman on Vidphone); David De Vries (Informative Yuppie); Gary Bullock (Gas Station Clerk); Wilbur Fitzgerald (Rebel with Weapons Cart); Beth Burns (Teen Prostitute); Lonnie Smith (1st Rehab at Hotel); Tommy Chappelle (Hotel Desk Clerk); Rick Seaman (Rehab Driver); Ronn Leggett (Pimp); Eva La Rue (Debbie Dix); Alex Van (Rehab in War Room).

LOS ANGELES TIMES, 11/5/93, Calendar/p. 6, Kevin Thomas

There's probably sufficient energy and violence in "RoboCop 3" to satisfy undemanding action fans, but it's as mechanical as its cyborg hero. RoboCop is headed for a TV series, but this by-the-numbers third installment, makes us feel we're already there.

As many will recall, the "RoboCop" films project a time in the near-future when trouble-plagued Detroit's police department will be run by a corporation, Omni Consumer Products, which in turn salvaged the face and brain of a mortally wounded cop, Alex J. Murphy, and placed them in a robot to create a kind of ultimate law enforcement weapon.

Alas, Omni proved to be a corrupt and greedy outfit, which in the second film tried to finish off the principled and independent thinking RoboCop with another robot. Now Omni, in cahoots with a Japanese conglomerate, is intent on brutally driving out the residents and merchants of an inner-city neighborhood to create a pricey Utopian oasis, Delta City. To that end a police doctor-scientist (Jill Hennessy) has been ordered to erase RoboCop's memories so that he will become an easily controlled killing machine, but it's hardly surprising that doctor and client instead cast their lot with the small number of people resisting displacement.

It may be significant that this film and "RoboCop 2" were co-written by Frank Miller, celebrated creator of such adult comic books as "Sin City" and "Batman: The Dark City Returns." That's because "RoboCop 2" and "3" play as if they were written without any realization that there's a difference between writing for a comic book and for the screen. Most films with a comic-book sensibility—or origins—wisely acknowledge their inspiration with a tongue-in-cheek approach, but "RoboCop 2" and "3" are played straight, which shows just how cardboard their characters.

Therefore, "RoboCop 3," under co-writer Fred Dekker's uninspired direction, swiftly becomes a barrage of elaborately staged car chases and bloody battles occasionally interrupted by melodramatic exchanges in which the cast punches out its dialogue rather than speaks it. As a result, "RoboCop 3" is wearying rather than exciting.

Filmed largely in Atlanta rather than Detroit, "RoboCop 3" (rated PG-13 for violence, language) does not stint on production design (by Hilda Stark), which indeed is the film's most imaginative aspect; in fact there's more life in the film's colorful backdrop than in what's happening in the foreground. Robert John Burke replaces Peter Weller as the original RoboCop, but so effective is his makeup you'd never guess it wasn't Weller if you didn't know. Nancy Allen returns as feisty cop Anne Lewis, as do Robert DoQui as the apoplectic Sgt. Reed and Felton Perry as OCP's obsequious PR man. The standouts, however, are the always formidable CCH Pounder as the leader of the resistance, Rip Torn as OCP's unctuous new CEO and Mako as a rough-minded Japanese tycoon.

NEW YORK POST, 11/5/93, p. 34, Bill Hoffmann

If you're a fan of Paul Verhoeven's stylish 1987 hit, "RoboCop," do yourself a big favor and avoid the mindless, boneheaded "RoboCop 3."

All the elements that made the original so ingeniously entertaining have been scrapped to be replaced by bland politically correct material designed not to offend or challenge.

That's because RoboCop is no longer a movie character but a merchandising franchise which rakes in untold millions a year in licensed toys.

Accordingly, "RoboCop 3" has been produced as little more than a poorly executed, live-action cartoon with dull characters and ridiculous plot twists, designed to do little more than keep the image of the futuristic crimefighter in the minds of kids and on their Christmas lists.

I've had more fun channel-surfing on Saturday mornings.

Once again, the scene is Detroit in the 21st century and the evil Omni Consumer Products company is at it again, this time using brutal, lethal force to oust thousands of families from their houses to build a steel-and-chrome monstrosity called Delta City.

A band of rebels, struggling to overthrow the deadly, money-hungry firm, eventually get Robo-Cop to join their side and fight for justice.

Complicating matters are a group of ruthless Japanese investors who send a coldblooded team of Robo-Ninjas to slash their way through the opposition.

Thus begins an endless series of chases, explosions, fights that will bore you to tears.

Original RoboCop actor Peter Weller has been replaced by Robert John Burke, who was so good in "The Unbelievable Truth."

But with tons of makeup on, Burke looks just like Weller, leading one to believe anybody, even Rush Limbaugh, could play the chrome cop.

Nancy Allen returns as Officer Anne Lewis, but all the dramatic tension surrounding the torch she carries for RoboCop is now gone, limited here to just a few strokes of his cheek. Mercifully for Allen, her character bites the dust midway through.

The scriptwriters are so desperate to keep the floundering story chugging along that, at times, they turn the picture into an "Airplane"-type spoof.

Appropriately, when a depressed OCP exec does a comical swan dive out the window, a fellow critic turned to me and quipped, "Where's Leslie Nielsen?"

Nielsen never did show up, but even he couldn't have saved this godawful mess.

NEWSDAY, 11/5/93, Part II/p. 82, John Anderson

What we're really talking about here is appliances. Do you stick with your lumbering, inefficient, oversized antique, or go for the state-of-the-art Japanese model with the polyglycoat and zircon-encrusted samurai sword?

"Robocop 3" wants you to buy American, but it also wants you to buy a storyline that's just about run itself into the ground. Not helping matters is some blatant Japan bashing, a streamlined Asiatic ninja-'droid and a sense of rhythm that seems to keep everything at least one beat off.

The original "Robocop," with Peter Weller in the title role, was about a creature lost in a particular kind of hell: A police officer who, after he's all but annihilated, is turned into a robotic super-cop programmed to enforce the law with totalitarian efficiency, but whose memories have been left intact. It wasn't the fact that he was mostly machine that made him suffer, but his small bit of leftover humanity. By "Robocop 3," however, everyone knows he's not all hardware, so the pathetic tragedy is gone. As is much of the point.

There's a cheesy feel to the production values in "R3" (why not abbreviate?) as well as to the story: The OCP—which, depending on your side, means Omni Consumer Products or Oppressive Capitalist Pigs—is a malevolent Asian entity that's evicting, at gunpoint, entire Detroit neighborhoods in order to construct its futuristic Delta City.

The corporation has bought Detroit, including its police force, so there's little opposition; the "splatter-punks" who roam the city's streets at night are not OCP's concern. And with the Himmler-esque Paul McDaggett (John Castle) in charge of the jackbooted Rehabilitation Officers, the "relocated" are departing in whatever condition the OCP deems necessary.

"Incompetent Americans!! You are fat and lazy!!" complains OCP poobah Kanemitsu (a wasted appearance by Mako), when his relocation plans don't move quickly enough. He evokes the worst aspects of Japanese corporate diplomacy, granted. But it's too easy a target, and the purpose is offensive.

To give the film credit, the female characters are prominent, if not very well realized: Bertha (CCH Pounder), becomes the leader of a neighborhood resistance movement that will enlist Dr. Marie Lazarus (Jill Hennessy), a brilliant electrical engineer whose job under OCP was keeping Robocop on line, and in line. There's also Officer Anne Lewis (Nancy Allen) and Nikko (Remy Ryan), a lost child taken in by Bertha's guerrillas, whose half-Asian ancestry is apparently enough to make her a computer genius.

When Robocop sees Lewis gunned down by McDaggett's troops, he goes over to the resistance, and if not for the existence of Otomo (Bruce Locke), the nuclear neo-ninja, the end would be a foregone conclusion. Theirs is not a particularly intriguing showdown.

Far more interesting is Detroit itself. Outside of Bertha, Sgt. Reed (Robert DoQui) and OCP's Johnson (Felton Perry), there aren't any black people. And no industry to speak of. Considering all this, it would be much more fun, and make much more sense, to imagine "Robocop 3" as the sequel to "Roger and Me."

SIGHT AND SOUND, 7/94, p. 51, Mark Kermode

Detroit, the near future. Omni Consumer Products (OCP) has been bought by the Japanese Kanemitsu Corps, architects of the planned 'Delta City'. In the Cadillac Heights district, tenants refuse to leave to make way for the new development. Spurred on by Bertha and her band of rebels, they oppose the 'Rehab' urban pacification pogroms, causing Omni a $350 million debt, and leaving them only four days to complete their work. In the latest attack, computer-literate street-urchin Nikko is separated from her parents (who are later executed) and joins the rebels. She helps them reprogramme a guard cyborg, allowing them to loot a state armoury. Nearby, RoboCop—cybernetically reconstructed policeman Murphy—disobeys an order and rescues police officer Anne Lewis from an encounter with 'Splatterpunks', anarchic marauding street-gangs. Amid the devastation, RoboCop spies Nikko outside a church, and fixes on her image. At Omni HQ Dr Marie Lazarus disobeys an instruction to implant a micro-neurone barrier in RoboCop's head, thus obliterating any residual traits of Murphy. On an impulse, RoboCop and Lewis return to the church, populated by rebels, just as the Rehab squad, led by Paul McDaggett, arrives. Prevented by Command 4 from firing upon Omni employees, RoboCop is powerless to stop the slaying of Lewis as she defends the escaping rebels. Wounded, RoboCop follows the rebels to their hide-out, and Nikko removes his automatic tracking device. At Omni HQ with only three days left, suicides abound as firings occur. Kanemitsu arrives, bringing his secret weapon, the robotic samurai Otomo. Nikko is despatched to bring Dr. Lazarus to the rebel cell to rebuild RoboCop and delete Command 4, which tasks she accomplishes. Among the rebel booty from the armoury, Lazarus identifies a prototype RoboCop flying pack. RoboCop returns to Police HQ and destroys the Rehab Unit, but McDaggett escapes due to a tip-off from rebel spy Coontz. Coontz leads the Rehab squad to the rebel cell, and in a shoot-out Bertha is killed, Lazarus is captured, and McDaggett executes Coontz. At police HQ McDaggett demands 50 men to take Cadillac Heights, prompting a mass police walkout. The Rehab squad recruit Splatterpunk soldiers and descend on Cadillac Heights as Lazarus, aided by Nikko, broadcasts revolutionary TV messages from Omni HQ inciting police and civilians to band together against Rehab. In the rebel cell, RoboCop fights and defeats Otomo before using his flying pack to repel the Rehab warriors. RoboCop returns to Omni HQ where he meets Nikko, Lazarus and McDaggett, and fights multiple Otomo clones. Nikko uses her computer skills to turn the Otomos against each other, thus triggering a fail-safe device. As RoboCop flies Nikko and Lazarus to safety, Omni HQ explodes. Back at Cadillac Heights, Kanemitsu bows his head to RoboCop.

After the lavish, pompous disaster of *RoboCop 2*, third instalment attempts to recoup some of the lost satirical ground of Paul Verhoeven's original cyberpunk classic, while shedding entirely the gloriously insane violence of yore. Entire scenes from the original are humbly quoted; RoboCop's POV shot during Lazarus' re-birthing exactly mirrors Murphy's original robotic resurrection, while his flashbacks to Murphy family life are similarly familiar. Verhoeven's *Brazil*-style advertising jingles, too. With Peter Weller now too successful to be recalled for the title role, *Dust Devil* star Robert Burke takes over, his facial features approximating Weller's closely enough for make-up effects to affect an adequate substitution.

There is also a relatively intelligent blending of the characters of Lewis, Lazarus and Murphy's wife who, during an affecting dream sequence, meld (via computer morphing) into a single female entity, providing the bridge between Murphy's dormant memories and RoboCop's electronic consciousness. Considering the miserable failure of *RoboCop 2* to expand RoboCop's relationship with Lewis, this development is encouraging. Once again, however, Lewis' shattering injuries from the climax of *RoboCop* are entirely ignored, as are RoboCop's ominous words "They'll fix you." Mysteriously, Lewis simply reappeared in full health, with no mechanical additions.

As well as trying hard to link back to *RoboCop*, scriptwriters Miller and Dekker also owe a heavy debt to James Cameron's sci-fi ground-breakers *Aliens* and *Terminator 2*, both of which establish a 'futuristic nuclear family' theme which *RoboCop 3* plunders and exploits. Not only does Nikko clearly take inspiration from *Aliens'* interstellar urchin Newt, but the final scenes of *RoboCop* also blatantly rehash Cameron's much-discussed and celebrated finales. In *T2*, cyborg-daddy Schwarzenegger sacrifices himself to save Sarah Connor and her son from a hideous future, while in *Aliens*, Hicks, Ripley and adopted daughter Newt sleep soundly as a human family unit. In *RoboCop 3*, these themes are merged into a far shallower image in which cyborg (RoboCop), substitute wife (Lazarus) and adopted daughter (Nikko) bond in perfect harmony—man, woman, child and machine, together.

The neatness of this ending is entirely in keeping with the general progress of the *RoboCop* series away from the hard-core nihilism of the original toward more palatable (and markedly less violent) family fodder. Since Verhoeven's original, the syndication of the RoboCop character through children's cartoons, toys, and figures has necessitated a severe softening of the violence in order to retain the lucrative youth market. Thus, *RoboCop 3* goes against the grain of Irvin Kershner's sequel by entirely eschewing visceral bloodletting. Now, when RoboCop torches the Rehab Unit, for example, there are no wanton slayings. Only when saving a young hooker from Rehab rapists does RoboCop shoot to kill, and here the impact wounds are far from fountainous. Clearly, this sanitisation means that any current RoboCop product entirely lacks the brash charm of Verhoeven's creation, and indeed, despite the heavily scripted links with *RoboCop*, there is nothing here in the way of stylistic similarity. While Variety accurately described *RoboCop* as "a comic book movie that's definitely not for kids", *RoboCop 3* is unashamed youth fare all the way. Even within such limiting parameters, however, there is still more enjoyable material here than *RoboCop 2*, with all its OTT carnage, could even hint at.

On the technical front, *RoboCop 3* is an extremely mixed bag. Rob Bottin's team, who performed such ostentatious miracles on *The Thing* (and who, it must be said, provided the only relief in *RoboCop 2*), come up trumps with their Otomo make-up, particularly during a lovely jaw-dislocation sequence which is winningly blood-free. Yet all their hard work is undermined in the climactic battle sequence, in which some truly awful superimposition work makes RoboCop's flight of victory entirely laughable. Undoubtedly, there was no money left to go and fix the finale (and the tribulations of production company Orion would have probably have prevented such post-production work), but this is an unforgivable travesty in an otherwise not unsalvageable movie.

VILLAGE VOICE, 11/16/93, p. 67, Henry Cabot Beck

Once again it's Megacop vs. Megacorp in the third incarnation of this soon-to-be-a-syndicated-TV-series character. As Officer Murphy, Robert John Burke (*Simple Men*) assumes the glassy stare, digital monotone, and clumsy metal chaps of predecessor Peter Weller, protecting and serving the funky, the disaffected, and the dispossessed of tomorrow's Detroit (actually Atlanta).

Murphy goes renegade, violating his programming by joining the Homeless Underground in its fight against corporate greed, Ninja terminators, and a gang of giggling murderous Morlocks called the Splatterpunks. Dark Knight comic scribe Frank Miller got it right this time by creating a delightful mayhem in which the police throw down their shields to join forces with Murphy for the grand finale, Robocop buzzing around in his newfangled jet pack like an angry hornet, blowing up tanks and massacring bad guys.

What the picture may lack in the way of the hard-knuckled miasma of Verhoeven's original is nearly made up for by the return of Nancy Allen and a cameo by ED 209, but what really distinguishes this from the earlier two films is that here evil CEO Rip "kiss my freckled ass" Torn takes his orders directly from the most unabashedly hissable supervillain since the agitprop glory days of Tojo, effectively making *Rising Sun* look like a tempura field trip for the Hollywood p.c. Especially ironic is the fact that *Robocop 3* is an enormous hit in Asian markets, hitting the number one spot over Eastwood's *Unforgiven* in Japan the week they both opened.

Also reviewed in:
CHICAGO TRIBUNE, 11/5/93, Friday/p. C, Michael Wilmington
NEW YORK TIMES, 11/5/93, p. C29, Stephen Holden
VARIETY, 11/15/93, p. 31, Brian Lowry
WASHINGTON POST, 11/5/93, p. G7, Richard Harrington
WASHINGTON POST, 11/5/93, Weekend/p. 52, Desson Howe

ROCK HUDSON'S HOME MOVIES

A Couch Potato Productions release. *Producer:* Mark Rappaport. *Director:* Mark Rappaport. *Screenplay:* Mark Rappaport. *Director of Photography:* Mark Daniels. *Editor:* Mark Rappaport. *Running time:* 63 minutes. *MPAA Rating:* Not Rated.

WITH: Eric Farr.

NEW YORK POST, 4/2/93, p. 25, Jami Bernard

People see what they want to see, in movies as in life. Mark Rappaport's sly, independent "Rock Hudson's Home Movies" is a sardonic deconstruction of the Rock Hudson myth, using actual snippets from Hudson's work to show that we could have guessed the actor was gay long before he died of AIDS.

Hudson, who photographed prettily, was presented in his movies as a studly heterosexual. We now know that he was a gay man playing a straight man before he ever got in front of a camera. By taking a second look at his performances, Rappaport encourages us to see Hudson's double-layer of an act, and how some movies can be read as exploiting that double layer.

Actor Eric Farr plays Hudson, superimposed against blow-ups of the real Rock. Farr narrates the movie as if Hudson himself were showing a sample reel of film clips to friends. At first the movie seems like a one-note joke—all those funny looks Doris Day was giving him, all those double-entendres—but gradually "Home-Movies" makes serious points.

One is that for Hudson and others in Hollywood, living a lie so strenuously is a time- and soul-consuming profession. Another is that when you watch a movie passively, a lot of information passes you by. "It's not like it wasn't up there on the screen—if you watch carefully," says the movie.

For instance, Hudson was often teamed with prissier types, like Tony Randall, so that by comparison Hudson was still the man's man. And he *was* a man's man, only in a different sense.

In "Pillow Talk," Hudson's character tries to seduce the brittle Doris Day by pretending to be two suitors, one of them obviously gay. Not realizing the two men are really one, Day stumbles onto Hudson in what she thinks is the gay counterpart's apartment; double entendres ensue.

The best revelation is how Hudson "cruises" his co-stars, cruising being a set of courting behaviors very particular to the gay community, "furtive or long glances and cryptic remarks." Cruising is much different from leering, the heterosexual equivalent.

An actor's personal sexual orientation isn't required knowledge in order to enjoy a movie. But that "Rock Hudson's Home Movies" says is that there is sexual subtext in an actor's body of work that can be found with a freeze-frame. It takes a lot of work to ensure that things are not what they seem. In movie-making, that's called magic, but it takes a human toll.

VILLAGE VOICE, 4/6/93, p. 47, J. Hoberman

More and more, the future of movies begins to look like Paula Abdul's four-minute "remake" of *Rebel Without a Cause* or that computer-animated Diet Coke commercial where her fellow flack Elton John jams with Louis Armstrong for the amusement of Humphrey Bogart. The living party with the dead under the sign of the trademark, the gods dwell among us from here to eternity.

For a less corporate view of life in American Valhalla, see *Rock Hudson's Home Movies*, the justly celebrated video by veteran indie Mark Rappaport, first shown here at the New Festival last June and now transferred to 16mm for a run at the Public. Simply described, *Rock Hudson's Home Movies* is a compilation of privileged moments from various Hudson vehicles that, in one way or another, confirm or deny (and thus serve to reconfirm) the actor's necessarily concealed homosexuality.

In sampling Hudson's career, Rappaport uses a methodology that, although it can ultimately be traced back to Joseph Cornell's 1936 *Rose Hobart* (which reworked the feature-length *East of Borneo* into a 20-minute documentary of the film's leading lady), has become even more accessible with the universality of the VCR. The movie's conceit is that it's Hudson's personal reel—the scenes that he ran for the amusement of his friends. And, like Joan Braderman and Manuel De Landa in their more blatantly deconstructive *Joan Does Dynasty* (1985), Rappaport avails himself of video technology to matte an actor into the proceedings. The narrator Eric Farr is at once stand-in for Hudson and a mouthpiece for the filmmaker. Hudson is thus transformed into a Rappaport character—a fount of sarcastic wit, laboring somewhat under the strain of his knowingness.

Like Rappaport's early narratives, much of *Home Movies* is effectively structural. Rappaport presents a montage of scenes in which Rock is asked why he's not married; a montage of interrupted kisses ends with the interruption to end all interruptions from *The Tarnished Angels*. More daring than the montage of beefcake posing is the montage of Hudson cruising his costars, including cowboys Kirk Douglas and John Wayne, or being cruised by supporting players—fondled by Otto Kruger in *Magnificent Obsession*, shacked up with a jealous Burl Ives in some forgotten jungle epic, ogled by Tony Randall in *Pillow Talk*. Randall, of course, is the "prancing prissy neurotic nerd" who existed to confirm Hudson's sexuality in his late '50s Doris Day phase and, no less than Day, functions as Rock's "significant other." In one scene, the pair wind up in bed together; in another, even more subtly delirious, they disguise themselves in flannel shirts and beards. ("We look as if we are about to go to a gay bar dressed as lumberjacks," Farr remarks.)

Home Movies shatters the false innocence of the movies so completely you wonder how it ever lasted so long. "If you didn't have through the '50s, you can't imagine what it was like," Farr explains. I guess not, but there's more than a clue to be gleaned from the wildly popular spectacle of professional virgin Doris Day fending off the passes of closeted lady-killer Rock Hudson, particularly once Hudson splits his persona into "macho Rock" and "homo Rock." *Pillow Talk* is the ultimate hall of mirrors—a gay man passing for straight playing a straight man who attempts to seduce a straight woman by pretending to be gay.

Like *Joan Does Dynasty*, *Rock Hudson's Home Movies* is basically a form of criticism. Among other things, it speculates on Hudson's relationship to director Douglas Sirk, proposes a new way to look at the cult favorite *Seconds*, and convincingly revises Molly Haskell's revisionist take on the sexual allegory of *Man's Favorite Sport?*, the 1964 Howard Hawks comedy in which Hudson plays a phony sportsman who must be reeducated by Paula Prentiss (described by Haskell as an aggressive, outdoorsy girl with a soupçon of butch"). Rappaport argues that the Hawks film was all but designed to out Hudson, buttressing his view with clips that make disparaging references to "fish," insist on the Hudson character's "camping," and stress his need to "fool the customers" to keep his job.

Late in the movie, Farr (here more a surrogate for Rappaport than Hudson) meditates on the motion picture camera as a philosophical toy. On one hand, *Home Movies* exposes film as a technology of deception, on the other it insists that truth is evident on the screen. At first, Farr maintains that Hudson's original audience had no idea what was going on in his avoidance of women, then suggests that they did; he explains that Hollywood needed to protect Hudson's masculine image, later argues that the actor was deliberately placed in sexually ambiguous situations. *Home Movies* doesn't quite understand how the Rock Hudson text was written—but these slippages are the real miracle of the medium, the stuff that dreams are made of.

"He seemed to be not too much to the eye, except very handsome," said Sirk of Hudson. "But the camera sees with its own eye. It sees things the human eye does not detect." Is *Rock Hudson's Home Movies* then a revelation or a revision? Could a similar essay have been assembled from the oeuvres of Montgomery Clift or Sal Mineo ... or John Wayne? It scarcely matters whether Rappaport is rereading or rescripting Hudson's performances. By isolating sudden evasions or annotating the flicker of a reaction ("Why am I smiling—what can my character be thinking of?"), by replaying bits of body language or freezing the fleeting glances of a nanosecond, Rappaport captures the ghost that haunts the machine.

Indeed, no less than Sirk, Rappaport has recast the Hudson image. The brilliance of *Rock Hudson's Home Movies* lies not just in the reanimation of its star—Rappaport invests that thing we called "Rock Hudson" with a degree of passion and pathos only barely evident in his original imitation of life.

Also reviewed in:
NEW YORK TIMES, 4/2/93, p. C20, Janet Maslin
VARIETY, 3/15/93, p. 66, Susan Ayscough

ROMPER STOMPER

An Academy Entertainment release of a Romper Stomper production for Seon Films in association with The Australian Film Commission. *Producer:* Daniel Scharf and Ian Pringle. *Director:* Geoffrey Wright. *Screenplay:* Geoffrey Wright. *Director of Photography:* Ron Hagen. *Editor:* Bill Murphy. *Music:* John Clifford White. *Music Editor:* Peter Palanky. *Sound:* David Lee and Stephen Murphy. *Sound Editor:* Steve Burgess and Roger Savage. *Casting:* Liz Mullinar and Greg Apps. *Production Designer:* Steven Jones-Evans. *Set Decorator:* Lisa Thompson and Colin Robertson. *Costumes:* Anna Borghesi. *Make-up:* Christine Miller and Sue Kelly Tait. *Stunt Coordinator:* Chris Peters. *Running time:* 92 minutes. *MPAA Rating:* NC-17.

CAST: Russell Crowe (Hando);   Daniel Pollock (Davey);   Jacquiline McKenzie (Gabe);   Alex Scott (Martin);   Leigh Russell (Sonny Jim);   Daniel Wyllie (Cackles);   James McKenna (Bubs); Eric Mueck (Champ);   Frank Magree (Brett);   Christopher McLean (Luke);   Josephine Keen (Megan);   Samantha Bladon (Tracy);   Tony Lee (Tiger);   John Brumpton (Magoo);   Don Bridges (Harold);   Janie Anderson (Jacqui);   Stephen Hall (Fieo);   Tri Phan (Nguyen);   Thuan Le (Nguyen's Eldest Son);   Minh Lu (Middle Son);   Thach Le (Youngest Son);   Craig Mercer (Chris);   Angus Cummings (Rob);   Yvonne Lawrence (Davey's Grandmother);   Edwina Exton (Skinhead Girl);   David Tredinnick (Gabe's Boyfriend);   Steve Millchamp (Pommy Bill); William K. Halliwell (Derro);   Vu Le (Tiger's Mate);   Vu Nguyen (Francy);   Paul Nguyen (Long);   Thanh Trinh (Vinh);   Vy Nguyen (Tiger's Sister);   Ann Morell (Barmaid);   Neil Foley (Skinhead in Plaster);   Nigel Baptist (Strangled Man);   Jenny Lin (Kitchen Hand);   John Raaen (Plain Clothes Policeman);   Anthea Roordink (Policewoman);   Russell Frost (Young Policeman);   Keiko Clarke and Ria Yazaki (Girls on Cliff Top).

CINEASTE, Vol. XX, No. 2, 1993, p. 49, John Fried

Films characterizing violent subcultures in our society often rely on a personalized treatment of their subject to engage an audience. While no exception, Geoffrey Wright's directorial debut, *Romper Stomper*, faces the seemingly Herculean task of portraying a subculture whose image and history are anything but sympathetic: neo-Nazis. Given that the neo-Nazis appear here as angry, young skinheads, Wright seems to have all the ingredients for a frightening documentary about a very real and savage subculture. But this film is fiction, and, ultimately, *Romper Stomper*'s desire to blend a narrative about relationships with a harsh social realism is often more problematic than complementary.

Set in the suburbs of Melbourne, Australia, the film traces the last days of a gang of neo-Nazi skinheads. As the title suggests, they live off the adrenaline of hate, romping and stomping from one fight to the next. Wright presents them as extremists, living on the margins of a recession-burdened society. They respond to their economic and social situation through rage and violence, protecting what they see as theirs, especially from the Asian immigrants who flood the city and threaten to take over their 'turf.' But these pretend-Nazis are hardly seeking political or economic power or personal redemption. When one of the gang members looks straight into the camera and says "Fuck you!" during the opening attack on three Vietnamese, he dispels any notion that their actions are solely motivated by racism. What they desire is the immediate power and visceral thrill of hate and violence. In these opening sequences, the film promises to provide some interesting insight into what lies behind the skinheads' alienation. In refusing to define itself purely as a social docu-drama, however, the film eschews any exploration of the politics of subcultural alienation for a narrative which only revels in its violent and destructive actions.

Hando (Russell Crowe), the magnetic leader of the gang, is the terrifying anti-hero who reveres neo-Nazi ideology. Whether solemnly reading from *Mein Kampf* or fighting against his enemies, his charisma is seductive, even to the viewer. Never far behind is Davey (Daniel Pollack), Hando's menacingly silent right-hand man. Wright devotes a great deal of time to an examination of the psychological and sexual dynamics between these two men, and of their relationship with Gabe (Jacqueline McKenzie), the woman they both desire. For Hando, sex and violence are inextricably linked, while Davey struggles to reconcile his homoerotic feelings towards Hando, the man he blindly worships, and his protective adoration for Gabe. But this complex and personal side of the narrative does not complement the larger issues of disenfranchisement and social discord upon which the film is founded. These abrupt shifts manage only to trivialize the actions of the characters and make the personal relationships seem contrived.

Wright's greatest cinematic achievement is in utilizing an imaginative formal vocabulary to evoke *Romper Stomper*'s kinetic energy. During the first half of the film, the camera weaves through the action, an active participant in the adrenaline-charged sequences of fight and flight. Paired with frenetic, jump cut editing and the aggressive beat of 'Oi' music pounding in the background, the energy is as seductive as it is frightening, clearly aiming to draw the spectator into the visceral thrills. When the smoke clears from the energized first half of the film, however, and the love triangle begins, *Romper Stomper* loses its gripping visceral edge to unfold on a more ambivalent and less trenchant emotional level.

LOS ANGELES TIMES, 6/16/93, Calendar/p. 2, Peter Rainer

The Melbourne skinheads in "Romper Stomper" are definitely not coiffed by Christophe. They spend their days lolling about their swastika-adorned hide-outs, or bashing Vietnamese immigrants. It doesn't take much to set off their hair-trigger retaliations; they're perpetually seething, and their violence comes in shocking, explosive bursts. This lower-depths hell is the Australian entry in a larger, global hell where out-of-work, dispossessed white kids—and not only from the working class-work up their racist rage as a way to feel alive.

A great movie could be pulled from this horror but writer-director Geoffrey Wright gets taken in by all the mayhem and clobbering. There's not a whole lot going on in "Romper Stomper" except for romping and stomping, and, after awhile, it becomes not only exhausting but offensive: We want more from this grotesque panorama than free-style scenes of brutality interspersed with wan little nuggets of class-consciousness.

Wright focuses on three kids: Hando (Russell Crowe), the gang's leader; Davey (Daniel Pollock), his closest ally, and Gabe (Jacqueline McKenzie), the upper-class wastrel who falls in with them. Hando is the scariest. His Adam's apple has *Skinhead* tattooed across it, his sullen gaze is unfettered with reason. (In the film's best moment, he reads passages from "Mein Kampf" to an adoring Gabe while his eyes mist over). Gabe, who has been sexually abused by her filthy rich movie-producer father, leads the gang into her father's compound for some big-time bashing a la "Clockwork Orange. " We're meant to see the father as not just slime but *wealthy* slime, and, what's more, he apparently makes his money producing TV commercials and gory films.

How do you create drama from a cast of insensate toughs? If you're an artist, you try to demonstrate that these toughs are not so removed from us that they're monsters. Wright does indeed go in for some weak-tea sentimentalizing; he wants to get points for showing that they are reduced to lonely, lost kids whenever their thoughts turn from bashing. But these sections of the NC-17-rated film are the least convincing and the most conventional. When Gabe and Davey turn into poor misunderstood youths, the rank Melbourne air is sweetened with the purest whiff of Hollywood. You can't really trust "Romper Stomper" because, while it aims to be pioneering, it summons up the specters of Dean and Brando and Vic Morrow with a vengeance.

NEW YORK POST, 6/9/93, p. 27, Jerry Tallmer

In Germany, at the moment, it's Turks. In Australia, it's Vietnamese. Makes no difference. To the skinheads of the world, the despised and hated can be of any race, creed and color as long as it's not your own.

"I'm proud of my white blood, maybe it's all I have," Hando the brooding skinhead says to his bedmate of the moment, poor little rich girl Gabriella, Gabe for short, poison in pigtails. He reads to her in a hushed voice from "Mein Kampf." They've coupled under a giant swastika on the wall and the ornate tattoos all over his body similarly embrace swastikas, an Iron Cross, a German eagle.

"Smack him if he's yellow, smack him if he's black," is the song that pounds away as Hando and his mates (and their birds) complete a brutal dose of Viet-bashing in a Melbourne underpass. It's only the first of increasingly violent scenes in "Romper Stomper," the exceedingly tough film by Geoffrey Wright. When the enraged young second-generation immigrants strike back in force, Ron Hagen's miss-nothing camera goes as crazy as the bloody donnybrook before us, ending with the overwhelmed skinheads fleeing in run-sheep-run through cobblestoned alleys to a fortress that is in turn breached and ravaged by the smaller but no less lethal Vietnamese.

Normally I would not cross the street to see any current idiot violent movie, but "Romper Stomper" transcends both idiocy and violence. And though it is being spoken of in the same breath with Kubrick's "A Clockwork Orange" in truth its roots go back to films as desperate as "Joe," "The Wild One," "The Blackboard Jungle," and a considerable number of good hard-eyed American "B" pictures about sociopathic youth gangs.

The point is—made in "Romper Stomper" with something more than overstress and something less than subtlety, but a perfectly valid point nevertheless—these skinheads themselves are the hated, the despised, the dispossessed. In their black overcoats and boots with their scars and tattoos and empty eyes, they above all are society's uneducated unemployable unusables. "They don't have ideas, they only have emotions," says director Wright's production notes—a formula for the end of the world.

"We've come to wreck everything and ruin your life—God sent us" murmurs one of the skins, with the ghost of a smile to Gabriella's comfortably insulated father, whose sexual advances have done their part toward making the girl a nut case with epileptic fits for good measure. This is her revenge letting the lads in to smash up Daddy's paintings, his sculptures, his beloved Rolls-Royce not to mention dear dilettante Daddy himself—an advertising man turned filmmaker!

In the end Gabe becomes the tinder for a conflagration between Hando and his best pal, the somewhat more modestly tattooed, slightly less callous Davey. She also, in her hysteria, finks on the gang to the police, with one result a bullet between the eyes of a teenage skinkid named Bubs. The film cuts to a beach for a showdown—likewise brutal—in the surf, ironically recorded in John Huston and early Bergman style by Japanese tourists with camcorders.

Wright's direction, if we overlook banalities, is matchless; the acting, superb. Russell Crowe is Hando, Jacqueline McKenzie is Gabe, Alex Scott is her father, James McKenna is Bubs, and Daniel Pollock is the strugglingly decent Davey. In April 1992, I'm told, actor Daniel Pollock, age 23, committed suicide by lying down on a railroad track.

NEWSDAY, 6/9/93, Part II/p. 53, John Anderson

During one of the more manic moments in "Romper Stomper," Geoffrey Wright's very disturbing film about Australian skinheads, the terrorized white supremacists are scrambling around their decrepit warehouse like rats in a coffee can.

The last door between them and a mob of maddened Vietnamese immigrants is virtually throbbing with Asian rage. But the head skin, Hando (Russell Crowe), stands fast. "We stop them here!!!!" he screams. And he's not just talking about the Vietnamese.

It's hard not to admire him at this point, even if his mind is as grotesque as his tattooed body, even if he sleeps under a swastika, discusses "Mein Kampf" as if it were the Bible and tends to reserve his courage for opponents too weak to resist him. He's a man of genuine beliefs. As such, he's a scary man indeed.

Hando, whom Crowe makes a seductive monster, embodies the very real charisma of the despot. He may brook no contradiction; he may harbor petty grievances; his personal philosophy may be diseased.

But what Wright does—and why the film has caused enormous controversy in Australia—is to show why such a character can win converts. It's because he has integrity.

"Romper Stomper" operates on several levels of fear. Using dizzying camera angles and out-of-control perspective, Wright makes this neo-Nazi experience a visceral one. The soundtrack is strictly brain-melt.

And the violence is nerve-wracking. The skins greet each other with punches, so you can imagine what they do to their enemies. But it's Hando—or our reaction to him—that's the scariest thing.

"Romper Stomper" is really the last chapter in a very pathetic story, about economic collapse, xenophobia and the white siege mentality. The skinheads occupy the lowest end of the economic totem pole, but can't bring themselves to join the system.

When one joins the army, he invites Hando's contempt. "You enjoy being cannon fodder for the system?" Hando asks. "It's a job," he's told. But that's no answer.

This final episode in the gang's existence begins with the appearance of Gabe, a well-bred epileptic junkie who meets Hando in a skinhead bar.

As portrayed by the gifted Jacqueline McKenzie, she's a stunning combination of child and whore, who simultaneously gives herself to Hando and controls him shamelessly.

It's Hando's pal Davey—played by the fascinating Daniel Pollock, who committed suicide little more than a year ago—who really loves her, though, and it's this impossible love triangle that eventually blows things up.

"Romper Stomper" is like "Clockwork Orange" without the comforting notion that it's some futuristic fantasy. This is now, Wright says.

The skinheads are real, there are people out there who believe what Hando believes: "I want people to know I'm proud of my white history and my white blood," he says. "Someday it may be all I have." Sadly enough, frighteningly enough, it is.

NEWSWEEK, 7/5/93, p. 57, David Ansen

Romper Stomper, a bone-crunching movie about neo-Nazi skinheads in Melbourne, stirred up quite a fuss in Australia, where it was attacked as a glorification of violence, hailed as an important exposé of racist, disaffected youth, and succeeded in converting controversy into box-office cash. Writer-director Geoffrey Wright can't be accused of moralizing. With a jazzy, subjective camera, he hurls the audience into the fray, starting off with the brutal beating of Vietnamese immigrants and escalating the mayhem with an endlessly protracted battle between the white-supremacist punks and van-loads of Asian youths. The movie rarely stops for breath before an alienated, epileptic rich girl (Jacqueline McKenzie)— caught in a banal love triangle between the gang's leader (Russell Crowe) and his sidekick (Daniel Pollack)—directs the pack to the posh house of the father she hates, and the boys proceed to trash the place, "Clockwork Orange" style, to the operatic backdrop of Bizet's "Pearl Fishers."

By this point, it's all too clear that Wright is a lot more interested in the kinetic kick of cinematic violence and the photogenic posturings of his brooding thugs than he is in illuminating their sorry souls or exploring the social conditions behind their nihilistic rage. Once the shock value rubs off, this hyped-up movie reveals itself to be as empty as the desperate boys it pretends to explore.

SIGHT AND SOUND, 4/93, p. 55, Trevor Johnston

Footscray Station, Melbourne. Three Vietnamese teenagers are viciously assaulted by racist skinhead thugs led by Hando and his right-hand man Davey. Gabe, a young woman who's just broken up with her latest boyfriend, comes across the gang and tags along with Hando, who steals a jacket for her from a shop window. Back at their rundown hideout she has sex with him in a bedroom adorned with Nazi regalia.

The next day sees the arrival of Magoo, a skinhead from Canberra, who sells Davey a Hitler Youth issue knife and celebrates the occasion with a slam-dancing party. Hando explains his theories on racial supremacy to Gabe, quoting *Mein Kampf* and putting the words into action by attacking the Vietnamese family who've bought the local pub. The Asian community swiftly rallies to the family's aid, starting a bloody running battle through the streets and tracking the skinheads back to their hideout, which they destroy. Hando, Davey, Gabe and the others escape via the roof, repairing to an abandoned warehouse to plot their revenge. Gabe leads them to the house of her rich film director father, where they can round up stolen goods and she can humiliate her father after years of incest. But her father scares the gang off with a handgun, and Gabe accuses Hando of being a loser. She storms out, followed by Davey, with whom she's been forming an emotional bond. Informing the police, who raid the warehouse and arrest most of the gang, she later joins Davey at his German grandmother's house, where they make love.

The next morning, Hando appears with news of the police bust, maintaining that the three of them should stick together. Later, after he has strangled an Asian shop assistant during a robbery, they drive west in a stolen car, ending up on a beach where the tensions between them finally erupt. Overhearing Hando encouraging his pal to leave her behind, Gabe sets the getaway car alight and as the two men tussle, Davey fatally stabs Hando with the Hitler Youth knife. Davey and Gabe remain together in an embrace.

Former film critic Geoffrey Wright's debut feature has already garnered both brickbats and acclaim on home ground and on the festival circuit, splitting opinion between those who admire the courage of the film's head-on approach to a tough subject, and others who find the apparent lack of moral judgement quite irresponsible. Closer scrutiny, however, reveals a welter of thematic and stylistic incoherence that virtually precludes a cut and-dried response in one direction or the other. In fact, *Romper Stomper* is neither a morally blank analysis of far right misdemeanours, nor a wholly traditional and liberally balanced social problem picture, and that is precisely what makes it so problematic.

Certainly no model of distanced neutrality, Wright's film clearly expounds the notion, for instance, that the skinheads' ideological stance is a direct response from a white youth underclass to the burgeoning economic sway of the Vietnamese immigrant community. Hando plainly affirms that he doesn't want to be "a white coolie in my own country" or go "the same way as the fucking Abbo", before turning to the notion of "racial blood poisoning" in the pages of *Mein Kampf*. A slam-dancing party sequence, where Wright intercuts from the mayhem on the floor to Hando and Gabe having rough sex and again to Davey pummelling a punchbag, serves to underline the thesis that the gang's violent behaviour is, in part, a pleasurable outlet for physical frustrations, while Davy's use of a Hitler Youth issue knife to fatally dispatch Hando in the final reel is an obvious injection of symbolism to ram home the notion that violence breeds only more violence.

On paper at least, all of this seems reasonable enough, but in his treatment of the character details, Wright veers uncomfortably from such sober analysis towards a sympathetic understanding, and in so doing comes close (unintentionally?) to endorsing the gang's aberrant activity. In the scene where Gabe turns the tables on her incestuous father by tying him up while the gang ransacks his place, it's impossible not to root for her and to feel that the violence she's picked up on from the gang has helped to liberate her from her psychological shadows. Conveniently wheeling on a German grandmother and an absent father for Davey, Wright seems to propose that we consider his and Gabe's record of destruction in the light of such mitigating circumstances; and although he never indicates the degree to which this should excuse them, the fact that their capacity for love and affection sees them finally spared to face an uncertain future obviously points to the way we should marshal our sympathies.

In the case of resolute fascist zealot Hando, on the other hand, we are given far less background information on which to base a similar judgement. We learn that he's concerned about the Vietnamese gaining the ascendancy in the local area of Melbourne, but for the most part Russell Crowe's committed and highly threatening performance has to make the role seem better developed than it actually is. In a film about neo-Nazis, we do need to know more about the skinheads' ringleader, but by leaving his psychological make-up undercharacterised and offering no counter to his racist propagandising, Wright lets him off the hook much too easily. If all he amounts to is a psychotic monster, this makes for a pretty lame piece of writing on which to build a purportedly serious look at the appeal of the contemporary far right.

Wright's formal approach muddies the issues yet further. John McNaughton's *Henry: Portrait of a Serial Killer* has shown that a degree-zero filmic style can distance an audience from events on screen and so fruitfully allow them to question their responses; but here, with sharp cutting in music-video style, a camera sweeping mercurially through the action and forceful Oi songs pumping away on the soundtrack, Wright has chosen to shoot the thuggery in as viscerally provocative a style as possible. One supposes that the intention in forcing such a pronounced response is to make us question it, but by delivering the thrills which *Henry* does not, Wright seems to offer a vicarious enjoyment to parallel the buzz the characters get from kicking heads in.

Romper Stomper is much too downbeat to merit accusations of glorifying these bully boys or the brutality they perpetrate—they do come out firmly on the losing side, after all—but, even though trying to second-guess audience response is one of the most specious of critical activities, such moments do give cause for concern. To Wright's credit, he later throws in a scene (the rumpus at Gabe's father's house is artfully underlaid with the big tenor duet from Bizet's *Pearl Fishers*) which, by way of comparison, comments on the way in which music and montage combine to seductively aestheticise screen violence. But it's a point which will probably pass by those whose skills in reading a film operate at a less sophisticated level, precisely those who might most profit from picking up on it.

VILLAGE VOICE, 6/15/93, p. 56, Manohla Dargis

Romper Stomper, Geoffrey Wright's feature debut about a gang of Melbourne skinheads, wants to make you puke. The fact that this brutish blur of fascism and fashion nearly succeeds is probably some sort of triumph, though for whom exactly is a question that haunts the film even after its final helter-skelter image cuts to black.

Where a director places his or her camera signifies more than nice light, so it's noteworthy Wright shoots his very first scene from the ground up. A trio of Vietnamese kids sails along on skateboards, the lens hugging the cement like a dog. There's a turn into an underground tunnel, and a slow glide into fate. The camera tilts up to embrace a platoon of Francis Bacon freaks, mouths twisted and howling. What are you doing here?" shouts one skin. *"This is not your country."*

Wright's film is launched on a Vietnamese's p.o.v., but it isn't long before his camera is focused elsewhere. The objects of his cinematic affections are a core group of skins living communally in a derelict warehouse turned fortress, where they keep company with a couple of mangy punk girls and wait for war. The leader of the pack is Hando (Russell Crowe), a sharp-witted, good-looking racist who lives at the warehouse. Hando holds court in a bedroom papered with hate propaganda (the exception, in a creepy touch, is the cover of Art Speigelman's *Maus II*) and dominated by a large Nazi flag.

There isn't much to do inside this playhouse or out. No one in the gang has a job, or much of a hobby other than fighting, fucking, and thrashing to Oi! The most appealing cipher among the malcontents is Hando's best buddy, Davey (Daniel Pollock). With oversize putty features and a slack expression, Davey looks like he's taken one too many punches in his short life. His hangdog face is a landscape of rage and pain, a physiognomy Pollack uses to tender effect.

Davey doesn't have much going for him beyond his German nana (who raises dachshunds in her backyard) and mementos from an absent father. Like his mates, he's fueled by inchoate rage, living in a degraded dualism—us versus them. Wright wants us to experience this shrunken world-view, too, so he keeps the film's color temperature—save for one pivotal, expressively Australian scene—a cool blue. It's as if every drop of human warmth has been stripped from the emulsion, the only remaining color in this relentlessly monochromatic world the red of blood and banners.

Then Hando and Davey spot Gabe (Jacqueline McKenzie), a waif who's stumbled into their favorite pub. A National Front poster girl with vacant baby blues, Gabe is ripe with pain and Aryan promise. Hando plucks her quick, and before long is reading her passages from *Mein Kampf* and head-banging her into his swastika flag. A debutante gone rancid, Gabe is damaged goods and one of the film's weak links. If the skinheads have too little past, Gabe has too much. She's a virtual catalogue of dysfunction, a pill-popping, sexually abused poor little rich girl with seriously stupid taste in men. Trouble the way women are always trouble in movies made by boys, Gabe is a deus ex machina on red alert.

The film's violence escalates when the pub is sold to Vietnamese owners. There's a melee, plans for revenge and a raid on a particularly vile member of the bourgeoisie; *Romper Stomper* becomes one bloody brawl after another (the film has an NC-17 rating). Keeping close to the skinheads, Wright refuses to rationalize their hate, but he also won't engage them or their ideology. The only skinhead who has much of anything to say is Hando, the group ideologue who knows enough to ask another skin who's joined the navy, "Do you enjoy being cannon fodder for the system?" Hando's proud of his "white blood," and even says he doesn't want to go the way of the aboriginals, a perverse irony in light of Australia's history of genocidal policies.

Romper Stomper is never more alive, never more animated than when a skinhead is bashing in someone else's head. Having tossed the skins' history, personal and otherwise, Wright doesn't have much else to do but get on with the show—back to the fights, the flashy camera angles, the toe-tapping Oi! tunes. This makes for some fairly convoluted filmmaking, especially one battle that's scored to a song that rants, "Jews and blacks and yellow scum ... we'll crush the scum." Whatever nuance Wright is attempting (the fight turns out to be a supremacist crap out) gets lost in the stream of rampaging Vietnamese. "They're millions of them," cries one skin—and he's right, the way Wright shoots them, there are.

Romper Stomper tries to nail the skinhead anima all while steering clear of the usual psycho-babble. The problem is once he's inside that mind-set, Wright can't figure his way out. Yet even if the skins live in a world of black or white, Jew or gentile, friend or foe, that doesn't mean the rest of us have to, even for 90 minutes. *Romper Stomper* hews so close to the skinheads it crushes critical distance, which is one reason why when there are no more heads to crush the film loses steam.

The skins feed off shock, *Romper Stomper* feeds off them. Take away the violence and all that remains, of all things, is a love triangle. Will misguided Gabe stay with vicious, coldhearted Hando, who fucks her doggy-style, or will she go with Davey, the kind of scary, kind of sweet skinhead who goes down on her? Stoned on fury and power, with *Romper Stomper*; Wright has created what very well may be the first skinhead date movie on record.

Also reviewed in:
NEW YORK TIMES, 6/9/93, p. 17, Stephen Holden
VARIETY, 5/25/92, p. 54, David Stratton
WASHINGTON POST, 9/24/93, p. C7, Richard Harrington
WASHINGTON POST, 9/24/93, Weekend/p. 44, Desson Howe

ROOKIE OF THE YEAR

A Twentieth Century Fox release. *Executive Producer:* Jack Brodsky and Irby Smith. *Producer:* Robert Harper. *Director:* Daniel Stern. *Screenplay:* Sam Harper. *Director of Photography:* Jack Green. *Editor:* Donn Cambern and Raja Gosnell. *Music:* Bill Conti. *Music Editor:* Steve Livingston and Chris Brooks. *Sound:* Scott Smith and (music) Lee DeCarlo. *Sound Editor:* Steven Hunter Flick. *Casting:* Linda Lowy. *Production Designer:* Steven Jordan. *Art Director:* William Arnold. *Set Decorator:* Leslie Bloom. *Special Effects:* Dieter Sturm. *Costumes:* Jay Hurley. *Make-up:* Rodger Jacobs. *Stunt Coordinator:* Rick LeFevour. *Running time:* 103 minutes. *MPAA Rating:* PG.

CAST: Thomas Ian Nicholas (Henry Rowengartner); Gary Busey (Chet Steadman); Albert Hall (Martinella); Amy Morton (Mary Rowengartner); Dan Hedaya (Larry "Fish" Fisher); Bruce Altman (Jack Bradfield); Eddie Bracken (Bob Carson); Robert Gorman (Clark); Patrick LaBrecque (George); Daniel Stern (Brickma); Colombe Jacobsen-Derstine (Becky); Kristie Davis (Tiffany); Tyler Ann Carroll (Edith); Tom Milanovich (Heddo); Ross Lehman (Dr. Kersten); John Gegenhuber (Derkin); James "Ike" Eichling (Little League Coach); Josh Wagner (Little League Fielder); Erik Vandersteuyf (Windemere); James Andelin (Wizard of Wrigley); Andrew Mark Berman (Ernie); Mark Doran (Richards, Cubs Catcher); Neil Flynn (Okie, Cubs 1st Base); E. Milton Wheeler (Suarez, Cubs 2nd Base); Sam Sanders (Fern, Cubs Short Stop); Neil Fiala (Mullens, Cubs 3rd Baseman); W. Earl Brown (Frick, Bullpen Catcher); Frank L. Wiltse (Peyton, Cubs Pitcher); Barry L. Bonds, Bobby Bonilla, and Pedro Guerrero (Three Big Whiffers); Jerry Saslow and Mike Bacarella (Bleacher Bums); Don Forston (Big Bum); Ken Earl (Pepsi Executive); Anthony Diaz-Perez (Rude Hot Dog Vendor); Mike Houlihan (Carson's Hot Dog Vendor); Tim Stoddard (Dodger Pitcher); B.J. Sanabria (Chicken Runner); Christian Mendez (Other Mets Runner); Mike Daughtry (Mets 3rd Base Coach); Toney Howell (Surprised Expos Runner); Blake Hammond (Screaming Patient); Ian Gomez (Odd Bellman); R.A. Bauer (Bellman); Mathew Dunne (Commercial Director); Askia Bantu (Mr. Banks); Robert Harper (Confused Teacher); Peter Bankins (Flower Shop Customer); Cindy Becker (Receptionist); Dan Conway, Ron Beattie, Sunnie Hikawa and Al Joyner (Press Conference Reporters); Christopher Howe and Karen L. Stephens (Airport Reporters); Jon Hilario and Michael Keeney (Phys Ed Dweebs); Kimberly Dal Santo (Kid Autograph Seeker).

LOS ANGELES TIMES, 7/7/93, Calendar/p. 1, Michael Wilmington

There's a movie-making knack we might call "The Gift for the Plausible Absurd." Simply put, it the quality that enables some filmmakers to make us believe in giant lovelorn apes, adorable stranded extraterrestrials, the Yellow Brick Road to the Emerald City and talking mules, dogs, cats and caterpillars. Canny pros can take this baloney and make us both swallow and love it.

That's the quality "Rookie of the Year" really needs. And doesn't have.

A children's baseball fantasy/comedy about a 12-year-old pitching phenom who puts the Chicago Cubs in the pennant race, this movie starts promisingly, generates some laughs and goodwill, and introduces likable actors.

Among them: youngster Thomas Ian Nichols, whose smile is readier than Ally Sheedy's, as phenom Henry Rowengartner; Gary Busey as our old pal, the gutsy, crusty over-the-hill vet pitcher; Eddie Bracken as a dotty owner; director Daniel Stern as an even dottier pitching coach; Albert Hall as the manager who can never get Rowengartner's name right; Amy Morton as a baseball fan's dream mom—and even John Candy, popping up unbilled as Chubby Cubbie Jack Brickhouse's spiritual successor in the Cub broadcasting booth.

Then it squanders them all.

Children, I suspect, are its likeliest potential fans. And children need rationales less than the rest of us. They'll accept a flying elephant even without the ears and the magic feather.

In this case, writer Sam Harper has a likely explanation for a kid's sudden pitching prowess. Henry breaks his arm, gets his ligaments tightened in some weird way and—*voila!*—comes at us with a flame-thrower 105 m.p.h. deadly accurate fastball that no one can hit. Henry's magical arm isn't tough to take. Neither is the major league interest in it. After all, putting the Cubs back in the World Series takes as much gift for the Plausibly Absurd as anything.

But the world built around the arm is sketchy, flat, unresonant. We don't really meet anyone on the Cubs besides the front office, the manager, the pitching coach and that feisty old vet—who immediately starts a convenient romance with Henry's mom. We don't meet anyone on the *other* teams either, beyond a bearded monster-nemesis and Barry Bonds, Bobby Bonilla and Pedro Guerrero, who show up for some cameo whiffs. (We'll never know how current top hitters Andres Galarraga and John Olerud would have fared with Henry.)

The famous Cub bleacher Bums, who might have coughed up a few humorous oddballs, are oddly silent. Henry's child-buddies get ticked at him for not spending more time in their leaky old boat—when they'd more likely be besieging him for box seats and bragging him up to everyone they knew. Even Henry's signing is peculiar. He's publicized to the skies and becomes the fans' darling despite accumulating no record anywhere, even in Little League. In the sport that spawns more statistic junkies than any other, he's put on the field solely on the basis of fastball speed and one perfect strike he throws from the centerfield bleachers.

The phrase "by the numbers" was invented for the way Harper crafts this script. After coming up with a good notion, opening and close, he simply fills up the middle innings with the detritus of several decades of TV sitcoms and high-concept kid movies.

It's probably director Stern's own performance as the demented, asymmetrically side-burned pitching coach Brickma—a bizarre-acting guy whose eye-rolling instructions and propensity for locking himself in closets apparently stems from a beaning—that best shows "Rookie's" weakness. Stern doesn't rein himself in, but he doesn't push himself to memorable paroxysms either. He simply shows up regularly, acts pointlessly crazy and then waits for his next cue.

Fittingly, for a movie whose star is a late-inning relief pitcher, "Rookie of the Year" (MPAA-rated PG) has a strong finish: an all-stops-out Cub-thumping fairy tale of a climax, with Bill Conti trumpets blaring. But, by then, perhaps only the kids in the audience will be able to damn all plausibility and embrace the absurd.

NEW YORK POST, 7/7/93, p. 25, Michael Medved

"Rookie of the Year" is the sort of outrageously farfetched baseball fantasy that no one could possibly take too seriously: after all, this picture portrays a sizzling race for first place in the National League East between the Chicago Cubs and the New York Mets battling wildly for a title is even more improbable than the movie's central notion of a 12-year-old boy who becomes a superstar relief pitcher.

The lad in question (played with an engaging "aw, shucks" every-kid quality by a real-life 12-year-old Thomas Ian Nicholas) is no brilliant, disciplined or precocious wunderkind. He is, rather, an incurably enthusiastic but hopelessly inept ballplayer—exactly like many of us were at his age—who trips and breaks his arm one afternoon while pursuing a fly ball.

When doctors remove his cast several months later his arm has healed in a weird way that changes his life. There's some nonsensical talk about tendons fusing directly onto bones, while the soundtrack provides twanging, stretching noises each time the kid lifts his hand to suggest that his arm has been magically transformed into an awesome catapult.

When the Cubs front office (and a long-suffering radio broadcaster nicely played by an uncredited John Candy) gets a brief, accidental glimpse of the awesome potential of this weapon, they promptly sign the boy to a major league contract.

The director here is Daniel Stern, the veteran actor best known as one of the hapless burglars in the "Home Alone" movies. "Rookie of the Year" marks his feature film directorial debut though Stern previously directed 10 episodes of the justly acclaimed TV series "The Wonder Years." He does a competent job of moving this silly story along, never lingering on any of the details to try to infuse this paper-thin material with more than it deserves.

Stern also plays a supporting role as a brain-addled pitching coach (the victim of a long-ago bean-ball incident) who is constantly offering his young star useless advice, accidently locking himself in closets, and drooling or choking on his own wad of chewing tobacco. It's the sort of broad slapstick that 8-year-old boys will love, even as their parents find themselves increasingly annoyed.

There are other aspects of this picture to bother adults, including frustrating, unnecessary subplots about the resentment and jealousy of the hero's 12-year-old pals, and the greedy schemes of his single mom's unscrupulous boyfriend (Bruce Altman).

A more fundamental problem involves the film's unconvincing and relentlessly childish vision of life in the big leagues—where all your teammates turn out to be salt-of-the-earth good-hearted fellas and your opponents are snarling meanies. Nowhere does the picture hint at the cutthroat commercial realities, the sulking temperaments, scheming agents and Everest-sized egos in today's professional sports; if it had the contrast with the boy's wide-eyed innocence might have been even more comical and intriguing.

Nevertheless the fantasy works well once it gets going, the big scenes at Wrigley Field in front of thousands of screaming fans are staged effectively enough so that movie audiences will be cheering in spite of themselves. This is one of those occasions when you can turn off your mind and enjoy the heck out of a movie even though you recognize that it's not all that good.

The daydream of some ordinary guy who develops magical powers to help a beloved but wretched team into the World Series (remember "Damn Yankees"?) is well nigh universal among baseball fans. In artistic terms, "Rookie of the Year" may be no more than a scratch single, but it offers the kind of visceral, crowd-pleasing appeal that could make it a towering home run at the box office.

NEWSDAY, 7/7/93, Part II/p. 55, Jack Mathews

After watching "Rookie of the Year," which marks actor Daniel Stern's inauspicious debut as a director, the best advice one might give him is to not give up his day job. Except that his performance in the film is so bad, that may be in jeopardy, too.

This is an amazingly inept movie, even for a first-time director. Stern, the tall burglar from the "Home Alone" movies, has taken an idea that might appeal to almost any baseball fan and made it into a feature-length version of a skit on "Sesame Street."

Parents with children old enough to like baseball but too young to know the rules may appreciate its conk-on-the-head comedy and broad characters, but don't miss a game because of it.

"Rookie of the Year" plays like a knock-off of the 1949 baseball comedy, "It Happens Every Spring," about a chemistry professor who discovers a formula that makes it impossible for a baseball bat to connect with a ball. He becomes a major league pitcher and throws nothing but strikes, until the magic wears off.

In "Rookie," Henry Rowengartner (Thomas Ian Nicholas) is a 12-year-old Pee Wee League klutz who has his broken arm mend with the whip of a slingshot and begins throwing 100 mile-an-hour fastballs. He becomes a starting pitcher for the Chicago Cubs and mows down all opponents until ...

Being suddenly endowed with super-human athletic skill is a familiar fantasy, at least where kids and baseball are concerned. Who hasn't dreamed of pitching a shutout in the majors, or of hitting the game-winning home run in the world Series?

But Sam Harper's screenplay, also a first effort, does nothing more than set that up. The story leapfrogs clumsily toward the inevitable Big Game, when Henry has to depend on his wits to beat the dreaded, league-leading New York Mets (now *that's* a fantasy!).

There are a couple of passes at subplots. Henry hates his mother's opportunistic boyfriend (Bruce Altman), who takes control of his career. He develops a father-son thing with his Cubs hero, the broken-down pitcher Rocket Steadman (Gary Busey). And there are relationships with school chums to keep up.

Stern had no clue how to stage any of this, how to flesh out the characters, or how to direct the actors, and his own work as a brain-damaged pitching coach is so overdone you want to turn your head in embarrassment. Stern has one genuinely funny scene, when his character gets caught between adjoining doors in a hotel, but his time would have been better served reading up on directing technique.

The movie doesn't have a performance in it, and Gary Busey wisely didn't even try. The usually edgy, high-strung actor walks through the movie as if he were heavily sedated, or steamed at his agent. Nicholas, who must be the 50th pubescent newcomer in movies this year, has a genial presence and a couple of good scenes running the bases, but he isn't very convincing on or off the field.

Obviously, Stern was working with a small budget. Other than the crowd scenes at Chicago's Wrigley Field and L. A.'s Dodger Stadium, the movie has the production quality of a TV sitcom. Despite having veteran film editors Donn Cambern ("Romancing the Stone") and Raja Gosnell ("Home Alone") on the job, "Rookie" moves along as if big chunks were missing, a sure sign the director didn't get the shots he needed during production.

Even the special effects look cheesy. You can see dinosaurs running loose on the screen in the next theater, and Stern's crew couldn't figure out how to fake a fastball?

Ah, rookies ...

SIGHT AND SOUND, 6/94, p. 58, Robert Yates

Chicago. The first day of the new baseball season holds little promise of success for perennial losers the Chicago Cubs. Twelve-year old baseball fan Henry Rowengartner lives alone with his mother Mary. He never knew his father, although Mary likes to tell Henry that he was once a fine pitcher. Henry himself shows no aptitude for the game and, attempting to impress a girl at school, he runs to catch a throw, slips on an unseen ball, and breaks his arm.

Soon after his arm is repaired, Henry and his friends go to see the Cubs play. Attendance is low, and the Cubs are ailing as usual, when Henry, returning a ball from the bleachers, discovers that he now has a super-strong arm. The watching media and club executives are amazed at the speed of his throw. Mary's gauche, if opportunistic, boyfriend Jack appoints himself Henry's manager, and the child signs for the Cubs as a pitcher.

Henry makes his debut as major league baseball's youngest ever player. His arm is fast enough but his direction wayward. However, coached by Chet Steadman, an ageing pitcher, Henry becomes a great success, appearing on magazine covers and signing a promotional deal with Pepsi. Crowds follow Henry; returning from an away match, an increasingly protective Chet whisks Henry through an airport crush to his waiting mother. Chet and Mary, who have already briefly met, are evidently attracted to each other, to Henry's delight. Meanwhile, a scheming club executive, Larry Fisher, plans a money-spinning sale of Henry to the powerful New York Yankees; Jack agrees provided that Fisher promises to get rid of Chet, a rival for Mary.

When the shoot for a Pepsi commercial over-runs, Henry is late to meet his old friends, who accuse him of squeezing them out. Henry resists Jack's ordering of his life, telling him he is not his father. Jack replies that his mother probably does not even know who his father is. Overhearing, Mary kicks Jack out of her house. Henry comforts her, makes up with his friends, and decides that once the season is over, he will return to standard teenage life.

The season's last game, however, is all-important; victory would bring the divisional title. Chet is re-instated, alongside Henry who performs well until, in a repeat of the earlier accident, he slips and lands on his arm, this time losing his power. He carries on pitching, relying on guile instead of strength, and steers the team to victory. Soon afterwards, Henry is back playing with his school team, watched by his mother and Chet.

After God and the Flag, America swears by baseball. In film, apart from offering an arena for action, the game also appears able to draw on a nostalgia for old ways. It is—or at least is sold as—the game least corrupted by commerce and efficiency. Rather, so the story goes, it is blessed with characters, wisecracks and decency, a cluster of associations nicely tapped into by Ron Shelton's *Bull Durham*, which centred on a small-town minor league team.

In the major league, however, the traditional virtues no longer count for much, and in *Rookie of the Year*, Chicago's Cubs have been outstripped by the wealthy teams on the coasts. Screenwriter Sam Harper supports the Cubs, a real-life, long-suffering team. He has described bringing success to the Cubs on screen as a wish fulfilment, and the whole film wants to carry the viewer along within the soft, warm charm of a daydream. Adding to the thrill is the employment of former and current baseball players in cameos, a move probably lost on most British audiences.

Sports and crude screen fantasy sit well together, since those of us who are emotionally attached to a sports team will forgive most things in the interests of a good result, even technical ineptitude. But inoffensive as the film is, you would probably have to be a Cubs' fan to be carried along by the thin, predictable plot and listless action scenes (with no more than routine camera work from long-term Eastwood collaborator Jack Green).

Rookie of the Year is the first film directed by actor Daniel Stern (bandit Marv in the *Home Alone* films, the R&B buff in *Diner*). The games apart, he and Harper set up two main sources of conflict. Chet and Jack tussle for influence over Henry (and for the affections of Mary); and the old, kindly club owner is threatened by a besuited shark, a typically slimy creation by the excellent Dan Hedaya. The latter conflict is barely developed—it is there perhaps to signal the threat to baseball's honourable tradition—while the former seems nothing so much as another of those good father/bad father struggles prevalent in American movies of the last few years.

Rookie's strangest role is the one Stern gives himself as the mad pitching coach. His appearances are semi-detached from the film, and the action stops whenever he occupies centre screen to perform a clownish routine. Perhaps he is designed as between-match entertainment. The film's real entertainment, for all of its Boys' Own content, comes in the exchanges between Henry and his mother, as their relationship develops a jaunty sharpness that the rest of *Rookie* loses in its cheerleading.

TIME, 7/19/93, p. 62, Richard Schickel

In our most basic baseball fantasy (*Damn Yankees* and *The Natural* are typical examples) an ordinary mortal suddenly, if briefly, finds himself endowed with superhuman powers. These he employs to upset the elegantly balanced geometry of the game by lending his services to some perpetually losing club, thereby turning it into a perpetual winner. In these tales, individual dreams of glory—permanently arrested adolescent division—are fused with the mass yearnings of a fandom frustrated by years of suffering in the cellar with their local heroes.

Rookie of the Year recycles this woozy wheeze for the family audience by granting baseball prowess beyond his years (or anyone's wildest dreams) to 12-year-old Henry Rowengartner (Thomas Ian Nicholas). As a result of a broken arm that heals eccentrically, he acquires a gift for throwing 100-m.p.h. fast balls, and he is quickly pressed into service by the ever hapless Chicago Cubs.

For a while, the conceit works surprisingly well. Despite the heat he's capable of delivering, young Henry remains a Little Leaguer among the big leaguers—shy, abashed at performing before vast crowds, befuddled by but eager to join in the adult male rituals of his teammates. There's a beamy gentleness about actor Daniel Stern's directorial debut (he also contributes a version of his klutzy *Home Alone* crook, this time playing an addled pitching coach), and there are finely tuned supporting performances by Amy Morton as Henry's mom and Gary Busey as a fading pitcher who takes the kid under his faltering wing.

But the movie is slovenly about details. Relief pitchers sit in the dugout instead of the bullpen, and they enter the game without warming up; a significant plot point depends on a deliberate misunderstanding of how player contracts work; and everyone is so busy building a triumphant ending that the most basic inner logic of baseball is defied.

Movies can, and regularly do, cause us to embrace the wildest fantasies. But they create our suspension of disbelief by getting the familiar little realities of life right. When they don't bother to do that, it feels like an act of contempt. Our attention starts to wander and our temper grows short, the way they do when the home team is down 10-zip in a late inning with the bottom of the order coming up. "Do you believe this?" somebody says. "Nah, let's go," somebody else replies.

VILLAGE VOICE, 7/20/93, p. 56, Tom Kertes

With all too few exceptions (*Bull Durham, Fear Strikes Out*), sports has not proven to be fertile ground for fine filmmaking. And fantasy films of all kinds often end up being smothered by their puerile cutesiness. So you have every right to expect *Rookie of the Year*—a *sports fantasy*, helmed by a rookie director no less—to be entertainingly horrible, at best.

And this little example of filmic flatness pretty much lives up to those expectations. Yes, it's predictable to the point of pointlessness. Sure, it has some customarily enjoyable actors (Gary Busey, *Cheers*'s Dan Hedaya) walking through their roles with one eye closed. Yet there are enough imaginative ideas and fun scenes (in particular, a clever takeoff on Ray Charles's "uh-huh" Diet Pepsi ad) to keep audiences intermittently amused.

Rookie's hero is Henry Rowengartner, a 12-year-old so klutzy that he's a mere bench-warmer on his Little League team. One day Henry manages to break his arm during a particularly hapless attempt at a catch. But as he heals, the tendons fuse in an entirely unusual way and he ends up with Nolan Ryan's arm, whipping the baseball at an unreal 103 mph. Naturally, the Chicago Cubs sign him to a contract. Naturally, he becomes a hero, leading the team to victory in the Big Game.

Problem is, Henry is surrounded by an avalanche of stock characters (Busey's gruff older pitcher, Hedaya's evil club owner, etc.), and the film practically drowns in subplots that go nowhere. Henry's friends are proud one minute, then suddenly becomes a hero. Why? Mom and Busey seem to have an attraction. Does it lead anywhere?

And while we're on mom ... as played by Amy Morton, she's the film's best, and just about only female, character. A plucky, individualist single mother, she's soft and loving until she punches the heck out of an obnoxious boy friend (oozy Bruce Altman). Interestingly, their fight got the only real rise from the audience during the entire film—a sign of trouble for a movie that tries so hard to be a feel-good fantasy.

Also reviewed in:
NEW YORK TIMES, 7/7/93, p. C14, Stephen Holden
VARIETY, 7/26/93, p. 29, Leonard Klady
WASHINGTON POST, 7/7/93, p. C7, Rita Kempley
WASHINGTON POST, 7/9/93, Weekend/p. 42, Desson Howe

RUBY IN PARADISE

An October Films release of a Full Crew/Say Yeah production in association with Longstreet Productions. *Executive Producer:* Sam Gowan. *Director:* Victor Nuñez. *Screenplay:* Victor Nuñez. *Director of Photography:* Alex Vlacos. *Editor:* Victor Nuñez. *Music:* Charles Engstrom. *Sound:* Pete Winter and (music) Dave Murphy. *Sound Editor:* Gus Holzer. *Casting:* Judy Courtney. *Production Designer:* John Iacovelli. *Art Director:* Burton Rencher. *Set Dresser:* Joe Mandarino. *Costumes:* Marilyn Wall-Asse. *Make-up:* Marilyn Wall-Asse. *Running time:* 114 minutes. *MPAA Rating:* Not Rated.

CAST: Ashley Judd (Ruby Lee Gissing); Todd Field (Mike McCaslin); Bentley Mitchum (Ricky Chambers); Allison Dean (Rochelle Bridges); Dorothy Lyman (Mildred Chambers); Betsy Douds (Debrah Ann); Felicia Hernandez (Persefina); Divya Satia (Indian Singer); Bobby Barnes (Wanda); Sharon Lewis (TV Weather Anchor); Paul E. Mills (TV Evangelist); Brik Berkes (Jimmy); Abigail McKelvey (Canadian Tourist); Kristina Daman (Bar Manager);

Mark Limmer (Spinnaker DJ);   J.D. Roberts (Fisherman);   Jean Garrido (Bar Dancer);   Al Mast (Ed);   Michele Worthington, George Clark, Carl Brunczek, and Kamon Hill (Homeless Family);   Donovan Lee Carroll (Tennessee Boyfriend);   Kathryn Grubbs (Tampa Woman in Red);   Bud Floyd (Laundry Manager);   Molly Hayslip and DeeDee Alberts (New Store Employees);   Daryl Symore, Pamela Symore, Sarah Luther, and Andy Anderson (Nursey Family);   Lorie Gene Saye and David Ballasso (Parking Lot Couple);   Jeanette Martin (Dolly Twist Employee);   Olis Sage (Donut Shop Employee);   Genny Hayden and Sandi Sherzer (Safe Sex Women);   Drew Peterson and Theresa Cronenberger (Navy Recruiters);   Woody Isom (Trade Fair Salesman);   Gary Martin (Tampa Businessman);   Indirea Satia (Motel Owner); Jadonn Sowell (Sandcastle Builder).

LOS ANGELES TIMES, 10/15/93, Calendar/p. 14, Kevin Thomas

Victor Nunez's "Ruby in Paradise," an intimate, low-key film as endearing and staunch as its heroine, illuminates the inner being of a seemingly ordinary young woman in the process of creating a life for herself.

This is a warm, perceptive film of everyday life, free of epic tragedy, yet it reveals the courage it can take to strike out on one's own and to take charge of one's own destiny. It also marks the screen debut of a radiant young actress, Ashley Judd, who with ease becomes the focal point and sustaining force of the entire film.

Judd's Ruby Lee Gissing abruptly takes off from her small Tennessee town and heads for Florida's Panama City, the "Redneck Riviera," where she proves to be sufficiently self-possessed to land a job as a saleswoman at a sportswear and souvenir store on the beach even though it is the off-season. Right then and there Ruby has commenced a process of self-discovery, and she's smart enough to know it, carefully recording her thoughts and impressions in her diary. At once open and thoughtful, she will make mistakes but will also be strong and honest enough to learn from them.

The first key people in her new life become her employer (Dorothy Lyman), a chic, longtime divorcée in her 40s, a successful businesswoman, tough-minded but compassionate, and her co-worker (Allison Dean), a sensible, kind young woman aiming for a college degree in business administration.

Crossing her path will be two very different men: first, her employer's son (Bentley Mitchum), a cocky wheeler-dealer playboy, and later on, a nursery employee (Todd Field), scion of one of the town's founding families, an intellectual who introduces Ruby to Jane Austen and Emily Dickinson, and whose ecological concerns have led him to despair over the relentless destruction of his native coastal region.

Nunez, whose two previous features "Gal Young 'Un" (1980) and "A Flash of Green" (1985), are also set in Florida, has the knack of allowing us to get to know well all these people, plus several others, in the context of daily life. "Ruby in Paradise" is one of the all too few films that acknowledge that most people have to work for a living and that working is therefore central to their lives.

We get an idea of what it is like to toil hand in an immense commercial laundry and what it takes to own and operate a retail store in today's recessionary times. We also experience what it is like to be out of work and how hard it can be to land a job, any job. In short, "Ruby in Paradise" takes place in a world that Nunez has made refreshingly real, one populated with people of different races and ethnic backgrounds.

Although certainly satisfying, "Ruby in Paradise," which has a gentle, lyrical beauty, does leave one wondering what it might have been like had Nunez eschewed Ruby's expressing so many of her thoughts on voice-over as she writes in her diary and instead dared to convey her inner life entirely visually; it might have made the difference between turning out a fine small-scale film and something truly extraordinary.

Nunez is a solid, straightforward filmmaker, but sometimes his script is a tad too literary; although Ruby speaks plainly, her turns of phrase and diction at times are overly polished from someone of her unlettered background.

Also, Field's Mike McCaslin is so well-played, so likable, despite an understandable pessimism and a forgivably mild case of condescension, that Ruby's placing him on the back-burner seems contrived to fit the film's feminist sentiments and doesn't ring emotionally true. Despite such setbacks, "Ruby in Paradise" (Times-rated Mature for adult themes and situations) is definitely a winner—and so is Judd, who just happens to be the younger daughter of Naomi and sister of Wynonna.

NEW YORK POST, 10/8/93, p. 45, Thelma Adams

"Ruby in Paradise" is a small, good movie with a rising star. Ashley Judd shines as Ruby, the backwater girl who flees Tennessee for the Redneck Riviera. "I got out of town without getting pregnant or beat up," says Ruby, "that's saying something."

Ruby gets a job selling seashells—and shark jaws—at Chambers Beach Emporium in Panama City, Fla. She sets up house, starts a journal, and embarks on a journey to reinvent herself by the sea. Before long, two young men complicate her life: Ricky Chambers (Bentley Mitchum) and Mike McCaslin (Todd Field).

The smarmy son of the boss, Ricky is a one-night-stand artist with no soul behind his Ray Bans. After a night spent with him, Ruby has already broken Mildred Chambers' cardinal rule: "don't date my son."

Mike's the more serious attachment, Self-taught and serious, he's a local boy angered by the development of Panama City. Intent on making her own way, keeping her soul intact, Ruby resists the exploitation of Ricky and the domestication of Mike. She refuses to be Ricky's chippy or a sucker "for the tender cozy life."

In the title role, Judd is a joy to watch. A newcomer to movies, Ashley's familiar with the limelight. She's related to the country singing Judds, daughter of Naomi and sister to Wynonna. Ashley radiates a golden-skinned sexiness unembellished by Hollywood tease.

Her relation to the camera is so intimate, and viewer identification so complete, that when she reaches down to touch the ocean I could almost feel the tide through her fingertips.

As both writer and director, Victor Nunez can share credit for Judd's high-impact performance. A low-budget independent filmmaker responsible for "Gal Young 'Un" and "A Flash of Green," Nunez has packed his script with memorable dialogue. The voice of Ruby's journal rings true to age, circumstances, and gender.

As in his previous movies, also set in Florida, a strong sense of place prevails. He captures the rhythms of a tourist town, in-season and off, and finds equal beauty in golden sunsets and gaudy neon.

Nunez directed with an easygoing charm. The single failing is a slackness of plot. The movie takes a while to reach a climax and then hurriedly unravels. Ricky and Mike make strong entrances and then fade away, only to return with decreased vigor.

Despite these lapses, there are many marvelous moments. Nunez succeeds in immersing the audience in the rich texture of daily life.

A gently moving film, "Ruby in Paradise" shared the Grand Jury Prize at this year's Sundance Film Festival. Nunez's clear-eyed and affectionate portrayal of Ruby's coming of age celebrates personal independence and presents audiences with an American independent gem.

NEWSDAY, 10/8/93, Part II/p. 66, John Anderson

Jaw set, car loaded, Ruby Lee Gissing (Ashley Judd) is running—from the dirt-poor mountains of Tennessee, from unspecified male trouble, from a dead-end existence. Mostly though, she's running from promises—the kind women are raised on, and which, of course, are made to be broken.

Panama City, Fla.—the "Redneck Riviera," as it's called—is where Ruby lands, and it's certainly no Eden. But Paradise is a promise, too, and Ruby isn't having any. What she wants is work, what she doesn't want is involvement, and what she finds is a little bit of herself. "I got out of Manning without getting pregnant or beat up," she tells her new friend Rochelle (Allison Dean). "That's something." What Ruby wants is something more.

"Ruby in Paradise," which moves us as surely and insistently as the ocean that rocks against the Florida beach, tells Ruby's story in polished fragments, and at a thoughtful, moody pace that's as tentative as the unformed Ruby. At the same time, it's a deliberate, economical film, director Victor Nunez packing enormous meaning into a single glance, a simple gesture, a solitary smile. Whether Nunez or and his star Ashley Judd have gotten to the heart of young womanhood is not for me to say, but they've have created a character we really haven't seen before, and virtually created her before our eyes.

Ruby arrives in Florida out of season, but she finds work in Chamber's Emporium, where devoted capitalist Mildred Chambers (Dorothy Lyman) provides beach tchotchkas and sun-tan oil, and her son Ricky (Bentley Mitchum) imposes himself on the female help. Despite herself, Ruby looks at Ricky like a foregone conclusion; when she goes to bed with him, it's like she's taking some unpleasant, medication. But Ricky Chambers, who looks and acts a lot like Robert Chambers, will prove himself to be exactly what she expected. And Mike McCaslin (Todd Fields), a disenchanted, trombone-playing environmentalist, will prove to be a not-unpleasant experience, exposing Ruby to Austen, Dickinson and his talent for omelets.

But Mike is about Mike, and "Ruby" isn't about men, and the male universe is not where Ruby's future lies. It's the other women in the film who act as Ruby's counterweights: Mildred, who sees in Ruby her own young ambition, and Debrah Ann (Betsy Douds), the teenager living in the bungalow next door with her abusive boyfriend, and in whom Ruby sees herself. And, when Ricky fires her after a drunken rape attempt, and she can't find work, she watches a woman dancing in a topless bar—a kind of Last Chance Saloon—and sees all the exploitation of the world.

Ashley Judd makes Ruby guardedly sweet, intelligent and a heroine—a flawed heroine, but a heroine nonetheless.

And we do see her grow: During a business trip with Mildred, she studies a well-dressed young businesswoman at a nearby table and her lack of self-esteem wells up in her eyes. By the end of the film, the look has evaporated, and no promises have been broken.

SIGHT AND SOUND, 12/93, p. 52, Stella Bruzzi

Dissatisfied with her life, a young woman named Ruby escapes in the family car and bolts from the East Tennessee mountains in search of something new. She ends up out of season in Panama City, West Florida, looking for work. Despite the lack of clients to sell anything to, she gets a job as a sales assistant in Chambers, a beach paraphernalia shop. Ruby stays, finds digs and makes friends with the women she works with.

One of Mildred Chambers' house rules is that store employees are not allowed to date her son Ricky. But while Mildred is away on business, Ricky lunges at the cash till to ask Ruby out for a date. His approach bears the crude hallmarks of a man who has known few failures, and after some reticence Ruby capitulates. She soon begins to tire of him, keeping her distance and hoping that he'll just drift away. In the meantime she meets Mike at the checkout of the local horticultural nursery. After all the frustrated searching, Ruby seems to have found equilibrium both with Mike and with work, but Ricky has other ideas, turning up drunk at Ruby's place and trying to rape her. Ruby's 'paradise' was short-lived—Ricky gets her sacked and she finds it impossible to persuade anyone else to take her on. Eventually she lands a menial job in a laundry, which she sticks to for the money. At last, Mildred, having discovered that Ricky had lied to her about why Ruby left Chambers so abruptly, offers Ruby her old job back.

In Virginia, there's a town called Normalsville whose very name conjures up the drab small-town world of much independent American cinema, where weirdness lurks uncomfortably close to the candy-coloured Teflon surface. Victor Nuñez's Panama City is no exception. Everything can acquire a bizarre tinge if you push your nose up against it, whether it's fat good-timers from Canada giving West Florida its second season, or luminous, repellent Mr. Whippy cones. This is a micro-world of intrusive close-ups and shallow depth of field, where scenes begin with dialogue whose only tangible source is an anonymous arm lingering at the edge of frame. It is to be inferred that the deckchair life in wide shot would not sustain interest, but then not all magnifying glasses discover severed ears in the long grass.

Ruby in Paradise is a highly schematic film. The problem with its stylised hyper-realism is that its focus is necessarily the small, the trivial, the ostensibly insignificant—which is at odds with a parable-like narrative concerned with the big, the overwhelming, the life-informing. This is essentially a broad sweep of a film, whose message is "leave the old life behind and discover yourself". We are given plodding literal illustration of this both in the pre-title sequence—as Ruby's old driveway disappears from view through the back windscreen of her escaping car—and later on as Ruby ponders her reflection in the mirror on the night she begins writing her diary.

This conventionalised undertaking is embarked upon with the brashness of a person unused to regular night-time ruminations, starting off with the big one—"Now it's up to me what I want to be." Like taking a megaphone to a fly, the film is strewn with other such grandiose imponderables as how to teach black children "to survive with their souls intact", and "Why are we so afraid?" These, like the film's double-edged title, are handled throughout with far less irony than they merit.

Ruby's sojourn in Panama City is depicted no less brashly. On her adolescent quest for self-knowledge, she encounters the binary opposites Ricky and Mike, the former from 'Normalsville', the latter from that twin town up the freeway, 'Jerksville'. While he-man Ricky drives the requisite red sports car, struts his way rapidly into Ruby's bed and just as rapidly becomes in her eyes "100% of something I'd like to forget," new man Mike is into "low-impact living", nurturing plants, cooking spaghetti and watching Christmas television in bed. Ruby shrugs off both of these walking clichés in much the same lacklustre way she drifts in and out of the more positive relationships she starts with the two women in Chambers, Mildred and Rochelle.

Ruby in Paradise meanders more at Mike's pace than at Rick's, towards the inevitable conclusion that small-town life is circular and Panama City a dead end place. Ruby is back stacking shelves with gaudy towels and pricing snorkels while pondering the meaning of life, and we are left knowing as little about her as we did at the start. The shoulder-shrugging denouement is appropriately anti-climactic, but wastes the fascination with the absurd potential of trivia and normality which Nuñez displays when he is close up to a scene. This—like the whereabouts of paradise—is abandoned along the way.

VILLAGE VOICE, 10/12/93, p. 56, Georgia Brown

"No one who had ever seen Catherine Morland in her infancy would have supposed her born to be a heroine." This opening line of Jane Austen's *Northanger Abbey* isn't the only literary allusion gracefully integrated into Victor Nuñez's doctrine-driven feminist ballad, *Ruby in Paradise*. As far as names go, there's Mike McCaslin, after Faulkner's Ike, and the movie's natural born heroine is Ruby Lee Gissing, one of George Gissing's "odd women," meaning women without men. (Gissing's 1893 *The Odd Women* was a particularly prescient understanding of women's dilemmas.) Though it's not necessary that you "get" any of these references. In fact, just getting them puts you in the mandarin class, whereas Nuñez's heart, if *Ruby* is to be believed, is with those who toil and read not. Or not much.

His heart is certainly with the winsome Ruby, played with enormous deadpan charm by Ashley Judd. We first see Ruby on the road, driving a paint-stripped clunker that can't meet the pace set by later models. She's fleeing some smoky Tennessee mountain grief and has lighted out for a flat, unglamorous coastal resort in West Florida where she once vacationed with her parents. (The area is known as the "redneck Riviera.") Perhaps that was her last happy time. What she's leaving behind exactly we get only the briefest glimpses of: an angry guy for one; "guilt and shame," she says later. "Nothing's going to get that hold on me again." She means old-time, fundamentalist tyrannies, some man's prying hands. Waking on day one in a Florida motel, she's entranced by a Hindu housekeeper singing praise to Shiva. As long as it isn't sweet baby Jesus.

The recession clamps tight but resourceful Ruby boldly talks her way into a job in Mrs. Chambers's gift shoppe, even though the high season's just ended. She's assigned to affixing sale tags to *chotchkes*—last season's sunglasses and swim trunks, clamshell dolls dressed as Southern belles. Later, she gets to work the register. The shop's ambitious owner (played by Dorothy Lyman) senses in Ruby some of her own grit, and Ruby finds something to emulate in Mrs. C.'s entrepreneurial cool. A friendly coworker, Rochelle (Allison Dean) warns her of the boss's son, Ricky (Bentley Mitchum), a prince manqué who will serve as the clever servant girl's temptation. (As far as names go, Ricky Chambers could have a brother Robert.)

In fairy-tale language, our heroine disobeys the first injunction ("Employees don't date my son"), as well as the second (Put out when he needs it), and suffers the consequences, which entail a journey into the lower depths of joblessness.

Like that colorless jalopy Ruby drives, Nuñez keeps up a deliberative, low-key pace. Ruby starts a diary and we see her write out the first sentences, and then we hear her read them in voice-over—a doubling that could have been taken from Bresson's *Diary of a Country Priest*. Ruby is a temperamental ascetic but a very prosaic one.

Saluting new life, she buys a jade plant, then begins keeping company with the plant man, Mike McCaslin (Todd Field), a trombone-playing, slightly bitter recluse with ancestral roots in the area. Contrasted with nouveau riche Ricky, Southern gentleman Mike waits awhile before giving a girl a kiss to build a dream on. Ricky's digs are a slick, antiseptic, high-rise beachfront condo; Mike owns a cozy lakeside cabin with working fireplace, patchwork quilts, plus an extensive library of classics. He introduces Ruby to Austen and Emily Dickinson; he's a virtual keeper of the canon. Mike's drawback, we find out, is a low tolerance for vulgarity. A diehard cultural conservative (antiprogress environmentalist), he's also a snob. He can't understand Ruby's dedication to her job (in a citadel of kitsch) and certainly wouldn't indulge her taste in a set of plastic drink trays with Day-Glo photos and captions like "Sunset in Paradise." (Actually, I don't believe she really covets those trays either.) In one heavy-handed scene, Mike drags Ruby out of a schlocky movie she's enjoying. She doesn't even get to finish her popcorn.

"I'll take care of you," Mike offers. "Everyone's dream," she replies, reserving consent. All you need is a good man, and here I am. Scratch a Mike and get a Ricky? Nuñez follows the Mazursky/*Unmarried Woman* principle: Tantalize viewers with the conventional fairy-tale ending—getting a good man—and then kiss off Prince Charming too. It's a hard trick to pull off in a popular art form, and particularly in a movie explicitly endorsing popular art. Will it undermine Nuñez's goals if his movie appeals to initiates rather than to the kind of people who work in gift shops?

Also reviewed in:
CHICAGO TRIBUNE, 11/26/93, Friday/p. C, Michael Wilmington
NEW REPUBLIC, 11/1/93, p. 26, Stanley Kauffmann
NEW YORK TIMES, 10/6/93, p. C15, Janet Maslin
VARIETY, 2/8/93, p. 75, Todd McCarthy
WASHINGTON POST, 11/6/93, p. D1, Rita Kempley

RUDY

A TriStar Pictures release of a Fried/Woods Films production. *Executive Producer:* Lee R. Mayes. *Producer:* Robert N. Fried and Cary Woods. *Director:* David Anspaugh. *Screenplay:* Angelo Pizzo. *Director of Photography:* Oliver Wood. *Editor:* David Rosenbloom. *Music:* Jerry Goldsmith. *Music Editor:* Kenneth J. Hall. *Sound:* Curt Frisk and (music) Bruce Botnick. *Sound Editor:* George H. Anderson. *Casting:* Richard Pagano, Sharon Bialy, and Debi Manwiller. *Production Designer:* Robb Wilson King. *Set Decorator:* Martin Price. *Special Effects:* Joey DiGaetano. *Costumes:* Jane Anderson. *Make-up:* Angela Nogaro. *Stunt Coordinator:* Rick LeFevour. *Running time:* 112 minutes. *MPAA Rating:* PG.

CAST: Sean Astin (Rudy); Jon Favreau (D-Bob); Ned Beatty (Daniel); Greta Lind (Mary); Scott Benjaminson (Frank); Mary Ann Thebus (Betty); Charles S. Dutton (Fortune); Lili Taylor (Sherry); Christopher Reed (Pete); Deborah Wittenberg (Young Sherry); Christopher Erwin (7 year old Mark); Kevin Duda (9 year old Bernie); Robert Benirschke (11 year old Mark); Luke Massery (13 year old Rudy); Robert J. Steinmiller, Jr. (13 year old Pete); Jake Armstrong (13 year old Bernie); John Duda (15 year old Frank); Joey Sikora (17 year old Johnny); Gerry Becker (Father Ted); Bob Swan (Father Zajak); Robert Prosky (Father Cavanaugh); Leonard Kuberski (Classroom Priest); James Riehle (Locker Room Priest); Robert Mohler (Johnny); Todd Spicer (Boy in Neighborhood); Jason Miller (Ara Parseghian); Jean Plumhoff (Fran); Spyridon Stratigos (Coach Gillespie); John Beasley (Coach Warren); Ron Dean (Coach Yonto); Paul Bergan (Coach); Lorenzo Clemons and Sean Grennan (High School Assistant Coaches); John Whitmer (Football Trainer); Scott A. Boyd and William Bergan (Linemen); Kevin Thomas (Player from Sidelines); Tom Dennin (Announcer); Michael Sassone (Guard); Marie Anspaugh (Librarian); Chris Olson (Dan Dorman); Vincent Vaughn (Jamie); Peter Rausch (Steve); Kevin White (Roland); Jennie Israel (Rhonda); Amy

Pietz (Melinda);   Mitch Rouse (Jim);   Lauren Katz (Elza);   Chelcie Ross (Dan Devine);
Christine Failla, Donna Cihak, and Colleen Moore (Pretty Girls);   Diana James, Mindy Hester,
Casey Cooper, and Jenna Chevigny (Pick-up Girls);   Beth Behrends (Girl in Cafeteria);   Corelle
Banjoman (Walk-on);   Pablo Gonzales (Groundskeeper);   Spencer Grady and Kellie Malczynski
(Maintenance Workers);   Theodore Hesburgh and Edmund Joyce (Priests);   Kent Hunsley (Mill
Worker);   Dennis McGowan (Barkeeper);   Jennifer Patricia Phelps and Michael Scarsella
(Friends);   George Poorman (Senior);   Robert Simmermon (Professor);   Daniel "Rudy"
Ruettiger (Fan in Stands);   Bob Zillmer (Usher);   Scott Denny (Rick).

LOS ANGELES TIMES, 10/13/93, Calendar/p. 1, Kenneth Turan

Calling the plot of "Rudy" durable is like saying that Michael Jordan knows a thing or two
about jumping. Sweet-natured and unsurprising, about as hard to resist (and as intellectually
demanding) as an affectionate puppy, this is one of those Never Say Die, I Gotta Be Me,
Somebody Up There Likes Me sports movies that no amount of cynicism can make much of a
dent in.

A few things, however, set "Rudy" a bit apart. For openers, it's the first movie allowed to
shoot at the University of Notre Dame since the venerable "Knute Rockne, All American" more
than half a century earlier. And, as all visitors to the campus know, Notre Dame is a place where
football fever is so intermixed with religious fervor that a statue of a priest giving a benediction
has been nicknamed "Fair Catch Crowley" and a mosaic of Christ Triumphant directly behind the
stadium goal posts is familiarly known as Touchdown Jesus.

And Daniel E. (Rudy) Ruettiger's football story, which is one of the most unreal tales ever to
be based on real events, is not a saga of fighting and clawing one's way to the top, or even the
middle. Rather, it tells of a lad who strove mightily against fierce odds for years of his life just
on the off-chance that one day he might be allowed to suit up, walk onto the field and be a bench
warmer. Now, that's dedication.

Even as a child growing up in the working-class neighborhoods of Joliet, Ill., Rudy's athletic
abilities were not respected: "What a spaz!" was a typical playmate comment. Still, he memorized
Rockne's pep talks and insisted that he was going to the school his steel-mill hand father Daniel
(Ned Beatty) so venerated that no other college's football games were allowed to desecrate the
family TV set.

But at "five-foot-nothing, 100 and nothing, with hardly a spec of athletic ability," as an observer
describes him, Rudy (Sean Astin) can barely make his high school team. And his academic
exploits are so unimpressive that his teacher won't even let him ride the bus to a tour of the South
Bend campus. "Be grateful for what you have," he's told, but Rudy isn't listening, he's dreaming.

Then, after years mooning around at his dad's steel mill, a tragedy strikes and Rudy is galva-
nized. Leaving friends, family and suffering fiancée (Lili Taylor), he packs a duffel and heads
for the campus. Barging past a flummoxed secretary into the office of head coach Ara Parseghian
(Jason Miller), he blithely announces: "I'm here to play football for Notre Dame."

Naturally, Parseghian thinks he's a bit cracked, and so does everyone else he comes in contact
with. But Rudy is nothing if not persistent, and with the help of a kindly friend (Jon Favreau),
an even kindlier priest (Robert Prosky) and the kindliest of head groundskeepers (Charles S. Dutton), he begins to make progress toward his dream of walking out on the field in a Notre Dame
uniform.

Actually, as convincingly played by Astin ("Encino Man," "Where the Day Takes You"), Rudy
is more than just persistent, he is equal parts likable and unaffected. In fact the 22-year-old actor's
engaging performance as the one college kid who never, ever, slacked off is the best thing about
this film, and his combination of determination and affability goes a long way toward making
Rudy's odyssey as palatable as it's going to get.

As written by Angelo Pizzo and directed by David Anspaugh, "Rudy" is smoothly done, as well
it might be, for this is the same creative dream that made the similarly real-life-inspired
"Hoosiers" back in 1986. In act, it is a tribute to the flesh-and-blood Rudy's stubbornness and
persuasive powers that the filmmakers agreed to take another shot at uplifting sports dramas.

Likable though it is, "Rudy" the movie could do with some of the texture the Gene Hackman-
Barbara Hershey relationship gave "Hoosiers." And Pizzo and Anspaugh have had difficulty restraining themselves where the gee-whiz emotionality of the film's closing section is concerned.

Dan Devine, who replaced Parseghian and coached Notre Dame during Rudy's moments of glory, has in fact publicity complained that a key scene is so different from reality as to be "unforgivable."

Yet underneath its rah-rah spirit, the PG-rated "Rudy" is straightforward enough to raise, albeit unintentionally, some troubling questions. Although we're supposed to be nothing but charmed by how much it means to Rudy to play football for Notre Dame, his obsessed determination begins to look less inspirational and more like a kind of mental aberration the longer the movie goes on. And when it turns out that a dose of masochism is involved in the kind of physical punishment he ends up taking in pursuit of his grail, one wonders if Rudy in particular, and driven fans in general, aren't suffering from a peculiar psychosis that is no less serious for being fabulously widespread.

NEW YORK POST, 10/13/93, p. 29, Michael Medved

"Rudy" isn't just one of the best films of 1993; it is, without a doubt, one of the finest sports movies ever made. That's because the timeless story it tells has nothing to do with superhuman record book achievements, or dazzling gifts of athletic grace and skill. Instead, this picture focuses on an altogether ordinary guy whose unshakable commitment to a seemingly ridiculous dream will inspire both cheers and tears from even those who care nothing at all about college football.

The real-life hero, Daniel E. (Rudy) Ruettiger (Sean Astin) grew up in the 1960s as one of nine children in a Catholic working class family in Illinois. In this hard-working clan, every football triumph for the University of Notre Dame seemed a victory and vindication for the struggling family itself.

As a boy, Rudy fantasized that he might someday play for the fabled "Fighting Irish," but his steelworker father (Ned Beatty) tells him: "Notre Dame is for smart kids. For rich kids. For great athletes. It's not for us."

After spirited but undistinguished participation in the football team of his Catholic high school, the distinctly undersized Rudy goes to work in the same steel mill as his father and two brothers; his poor grades terminate any thoughts of a college career.

At age 22, however, when a vividly dramatized industrial accident kills his best friend (Christopher Reed), Rudy decides to pack up his bags and move to Notre Dame to chase down his long-deferred hopes of gridiron glory.

To its great credit, the movie shows no shortcuts or miracles in Rudy's painful pursuit of his goal. He must first attend Holy Cross Junior College near Notre Dame, then apply—again and again—to the university itself before he's finally admitted.

With no money from home, he also faces problems of where to sleep and what to eat. His chief encouragement in these difficult days comes from the University's kindly but skeptical Father Cavanaugh (Robert Prosky) and from the crusty head groundskeeper at Knute Rockne Stadium (played by the formidable Charles S. Dutton of TV's "Roc").

Both men deliver performances worthy of Oscar nominations as best supporting actor. Sean Astin, son of Patty Duke and John Astin, has been previously best known as one of the stars of the insipid caveman comedy "Encino Man," but he's also done fine work as a doomed junkie in the under-appreciated "Where the Day Takes You."

Here, he is absolutely perfect in the title role: he's never too sweet, never too smart, but his reckless courage and All-American, underdog readiness to tilt at windmills make him one of the most appealing heroes of recent years.

In case you've ever forgotten, "Rudy" can remind us why we love football, why we love America—and why we love movies.

NEWSDAY, 10/13/93, Part II/p. 61, Jack Mathews

The true-life "Rudy," the first epic produced in the Era of Diminished Expectations, will win over certain people immediately: those who don't care what they watch, as long as it makes them cry. And those who think that playing football for Notre Dame is the equivalent of, say, curing cancer or developing a unified field theory.

The rest of us have to wrestle with a film that does what it does extremely well, is entertaining and often funny, but whose hero is something close to pathetic.

If the subject's quandary isn't convincing, is the piece? T.S. Eliot asked this about Hamlet. We're asking it about Daniel "Rudy" Ruettiger (Sean Astin), one of a passel of children born to a Joliet, Ill., steelworker (Ned Beatty) who's convinced that the good life is a union job in a factory where the rest of your family works, so they can "watch your back." He's the lumpiest of the lumpen proletariat, a true believer in the system that's placed him on one of its lower rungs, and Rudy gives him little reason to believe in upward mobility: A poor student and uninspiring child, Rudy's sole interest is the Fighting Irish of Notre Dame, and he's fixated in a way that spells crushing disappointment. "I'm going to play for Notre. Dame," he says, and you say, "Sure you are" and cringe with embarrassment, because he seems to have better odds of becoming the Queen of England.

But "Rudy," put together by the "Hoosiers" team of writer Angelo Pizzo and director David Anspaugh, gets away with a lot. You know going in that Rudy's going to attain his dream, at least in some small way, because they don't make films about crushing disappointment. (Well, OK, "A Night to Remember," but not football movies, in any event.) His eventual modified triumph is certainly believable, given that the dream itself was so far-fetched. And each small victory elicits a small choke in the throat until, by the end, you're at full throttle.

Rudy doesn't seek the dream right off. That he go to college at all is an idea derided by both his teachers and his family—particularly his brother Frank (Scott Benjaminson), who begrudges him every achievement. Rudy leaves high school, and for four years works in the steel mill. Only when his best friend, Pete (Christopher Reed) dies in a hideous accident does Rudy become decisive.

His blind determination leads to some humorous scenes, such as when he shows up at Notre Dame asking to see coach Ara Parseghian (Jason Miller). "Maybe you ought to see a priest," the security guard says.

For Rudy, life is a series of such encounters with unsympathetic characters, including Fortune (Charles S. Dutton), the university groundskeeper who puts him to work, and puts him up while he attends the junior college and awaits his admission to Notre Dame. Dutton is as commanding a presence as ever, although he's playing the kind of Lou Gossett-Morgan Freeman wise-weathered black mentor that's becoming a cliché in otherwise all-white movies.

"Rudy" is a sweet, inspiring if not inspired film, but it's probably a good thing the real Rudy Ruettiger was a consultant on the project. Otherwise, the filmmakers might have given his movie self a fatal disease. It's that kind of movie.

VILLAGE VOICE, 10/26/93, p. 62, David D. Kim

Autumn in the Midwest—time to dust off the ol' pigskin, put on the helmet, and pummel some bastard's head into the astroturf. A rah-rah paean to Notre Dame's Fighting Irish, *Rudy* ventures into hardcore football country sometime during the late '70s. David Anspaugh, who directed the 1986 basketball flick *Hoosiers*, kicks off his gridiron inspirational in Joliet, Illinois, where a young Rudy (modeled after real-life underdog Daniel "Rudy" Ruettiger) aspires to play ball for Notre Dame. Running interference, his family convinces the budding Knute Rockne to stay put. Only when a steel-mill accident blasts his Gipper-like pal to the end zone of no return does Rudy blaze his glory trail straight to South Bend.

Embodying pure Hollywood grit, Sean Astin takes the role of Rudy and runs with it. His stalwart performance affectingly imagines Rudy's crazed masochism, his stay-hungry attitude between fistfuls of humble pie. Keeping the game lively with tight editing, Anspaugh renders certain moments, such as Rudy's acceptance to Notre Dame, with finesse: instead of histrionics, Rudy sits quietly on a bench and sobs. Unfortunately, it's a scene he'll repeat until the film's inevitable, crowd thumping finale.

The talented supporting cast, including Lili Taylor and Ned Beatty as Rudy's naysaying loved ones, doesn't see enough play. But Anspaugh's major fumble is the gratuitous stoic black character, Fortune (Charles Dutton), an ex-player-cum-grounds-keeper whose own ambitions have been permanently sidelined. Rudy nonetheless scores by unapologetically tackling the sports-movie genre as the big, dumb fun that it is. We may not share Rudy's burning desire to join the huddle, but in this sappy, golden universe, sweet dreams are made of cheese.

Also reviewed in:
NEW YORK TIMES, 10/13/93, p. C21, Stephen Holden
VARIETY, 9/27/93, p. 39, Leonard Klady
WASHINGTON POST, 10/13/93, p. B2, Richard Harrington
WASHINGTON POST, 10/15/93, Weekend/p. 41, Desson Howe

SAINT OF FORT WASHINGTON, THE

A Warner Bros. release of a David V. Picker/Nessa Hyams production in association with Carrie Productions. *Executive Producer:* Lyle Kessler and Carl Clifford. *Producer:* David V. Picker and Nessa Hyams. *Director:* Tim Hunter. *Screenplay:* Lyle Kessler. *Director of Photography:* Frederick Elmes. *Editor:* Howard Smith. *Music:* James Newton Howard. *Music Editor:* Jim Weidman and Lori Eschler. *Sound:* Rosa Howell-Thornhill and (music) Armin Steiner and Michael Mason. *Sound Editor:* Tim Holland. *Casting:* Nessa Hyams. *Production Designer:* Stuart Wurtzel. *Art Director:* Steve Saklad. *Set Decorator:* Debra Schutt. *Set Dresser:* Bruce Lee Gross. *Special Effects:* Matt Vogel. *Costumes:* Claudia Brown. *Make-up:* Diane Hammond. *Stunt Coordinator:* David Lomax and Jeff Ward. *Running time:* 102 minutes. *MPAA Rating:* R.

CAST: Danny Glover (Jerry); Matt Dillon (Matthew); Rick Aviles (Rosario); Nina Siemaszko (Tamsen); Ving Rhames (Little Leroy); Joe Seneca (Spits); Harry Ellingston (Arthur); Ralph Hughes (Jason); Bahni Turpin (Gloria); Robert Beatty, Jr. (Ex-Pharmacist); Reuben Schaefer (Greek Man); Louis Williams (Ennis); Adam Trese (John); Kevin Corrigan (Peter); Brian Tarantina (Fred); Irma St. Paul (Neighbor Lady); Aida Turturro (State Employee); Marvin Gardener (Sandwich Man); Edward Wise (Extra Smoke Man); Alison Mackie (Dime Tipper); Liz Larsen (River Banks Woman); Frances Chaney (Woman in Window); Octavia St. Laurent (Hooker in Car); Damon Chandler (Her Manager); Rosaleen Linehan (Rosie); Larry Kirwan (Black 47 Lead Singer); Chris Byrne, Geoffrey Blythe, Fred Parcells, and Thomas Hamlin (Black 47); Mary Courtney, Carmel Johnston, and Margie Mulvihill (Morning Star); Mark Lotito (Bellevue Doctor); Garfield! (Coffin Handler); Daniel Von Bargen (Boat Captain); Evelyn Solann (Bird Lady); Walter Meade (Drill Floor Guard); Ellis Williams (Metal Detector Guard); Cortez Nance, Jr. (Clemente Shelter Guard); Philip Gray (Check-in Guard); Stephen Mendillo (Bridge Cop #1); Michael Badalucco (Bridge Cop #2); Joseph Pentangelo (Arrest Cop #1); Douglas Crosby (Arrest Cop #2); Mansoor Najeeullah (Billie Sweetwater); Victor Slezak (Driver #1); Michael Waldron (Driver #2); Peter Appel (Demolition Man); Ron Brice (Caesar).

LOS ANGELES TIMES, 11/17/93, Calendar/p. 1, Peter Rainer

A lot of talent and good will has gone into "The Saint of Fort Washington", a lower-depths drama about homelessness starring Danny Glover and Matt Dillon. It's so well-meaning that it makes you want to go out and make a donation to your favorite charity. But its good intentions are double-edged: Like most do-gooder fables, this one wears its righteousness like a red badge of courage.

Jerry (Glover) is a Vietnam vet with a load of shrapnel in his knee who lives from hand to mouth washing car windows at busy New York intersections. Matthew (Dillon) is a diagnosed schizophrenic who lives in abandoned buildings and takes photos with a camera with no film in it.

These two disparate souls meet on their way into the Fort Washington shelter for the homeless and soon become the most bumptiously inseparable couple since Lenny and George, in "Of Mice and Men."

There's a lot of Steinbeck in this stew (rated R for language). Like Lenny and George, Jerry and Matthew have their dream of living together in bucolic harmony—they're saving up, dollar by dollar, to rent an apartment and start a business selling veggies out of the back of a station wagon. (No mention of tending any rabbits.) Director Tim Hunter and screenwriter Lyle Kessler give their guys an inspirational glow: amid the New York squalor, and some harrowing scenes photographed in an actual shelter, Jerry and Matthew maintain a beatific goodness. Matthew is, in fact, dubbed the Saint of Fort Washington by Jerry. He's the holy fool with the healing hands—he quells Jerry's shrapnel-induced pains when he runs out of painkillers and makes an old man's arthritis disappear (momentarily).

The filmmakers are so intent on creating a fable that the more realistic aspects of the story lose some of their bite. The gritty New York locations are transformed into a rather twinkly backdrop. Hunter probably didn't want the grunge to overwhelm the fantasy but the results are discomforting. The story seems too hair-raising for the wispy fairy-tale presentation.

And so we become overly conscious of how acted-out this movie is. The performances, for example, are proficient and yet we can't help recognizing that these are famous actors playing at being derelicts. Just as we can't help recognizing that Jerry and Matthew, and just about all the other homeless people whom we see, have good teeth. Good teeth—that's the tip-off to the show-offy vanity that actors often assume when they take on these down-and-out roles. (When Mel Gibson played the face-charred character in "The Man Without a Face" he was careful to repeatedly show us his uncharred profile.)

It's not enough that the filmmakers show us two good men trying to navigate their way through the jungle. Matthew has to be sanctified; his schizophrenia, according to Jerry, isn't really an illness. It's an illness in the way that Joan of Arc hearing voices was an illness. It's evidence of a higher calling. Matthew's condition is romanticized as a way of humanizing him—and deifying him too. "The Saint of Fort Washington" would have been a better film if it extended its compassion to those on the streets who are less sanctified but no less human.

NEW YORK POST, 11/17/93, p. 33, Thelma Adams

"The Saint of Fort Washington" burned me up. When I'm preached to, I prefer being in a House of God.

This buddy movie has two things going for it: Danny Glover and Matt Dillon. They turn in strong performances as two homeless men of the lovable but unlucky variety. Jerry (Glover), a Vietnam vet, had his shot at the American dream with wife and house and kids and car until his partner gambled him to ruin. Matthew (Dillon)—don't miss the saint reference—had great potential as a photographer until schizophrenia sidelined him.

This Bronx-born hunk is a gentle, good citizen who, if anyone asked, would give away his belt and lose his pants. Jerry and Matthew connect at the Fort Washington men's shelter, a latter-day inferno.

The paternal vet protects the saintly schizo. They bond. They work hard. They clean windshields. They squirrel away money to achieve their gutter dream: to rent an apartment and start a fruit stand. Groan. Only a rock wouldn't identify with Glover and Dillon and their American dream gone awry.

The strength of the actors is no compensation for the soft-headed script and direction, by Lyle Kessler and Tim Hunter respectively. It's a gutless story with easy heroes and cardboard villains.

The good homeless are beatific: a singing alcoholic shoeshine man haloed in bars of light; a glowing pregnant woman with shiny Breck-girl tresses; and a devoted Hispanic man who assaults a yuppie scum entombed in his luxury car only when the Hispanic is pushed to the wall.

Like professional wrestling, the bad guys are easy to spot. Little Leroy is the shelter bully, a hulking Brutus who is abetted by a shelter guard as he preys on his fellow homeless. There are not one but two ferrety old lady neighbors who fail to aid our boys; both share smiles of smug satisfaction that barely conceal middle-class fear. Ah, the script moans, where has charity gone?

The blue meanies are everywhere: cruel cops, insensitive bureaucrats, bad boys from the 'hood, and the long parade of nervous yuppies, driving their luxury cars, and refusing the hardworking homeless their rightful dollar in exchange for a clean windshield and a friendly hello.

"Are we ourselves to blame?" mourns the sound track at one point in case we weren't sure how to feel. Hold the flagellation! This guilt-driven exercise has as much to do with ennobling the filmmakers as sanctifying the homeless. Those who bray the loudest to the most can ease their own discomfort—as long as the problem doesn't creep too close to their Lexuses or electrified gates.

I hungered for Preston Sturges' "Sullivan's Travels" (1941), in which such dough-headed Hollywood ideas of bums were put to the test. Then again director Hunter is no Sturges. See "The

Saint of Fort Washington" if you have something to feel guilty about. Or save money and ride the IRT.

NEWSDAY, 11/17/93, Part II/p. 63, Jack Mathews

If there are 8 million stories in the Naked City, as the 1960's TV cop show used to say, too many of them in the '90s are stories about homeless people, and two of them are the central figures of Tim Hunter's frequently moving, ultimately half-hearted melodrama "The Saint of Fort Washington."

I say half-hearted because Hunter ("River's Edge") and screenwriter Lyle Kessler ("Orphans") provide as our guides into the dark and desperate world of New York's homeless two men who would both seem to qualify as saints.

Jerry (Danny Glover), a Vietnam veteran with enough shrapnel left in his legs to set off metal detectors, is a former middle-class family man driven to the streets by the betrayal of a business partner. Matthew (Matt Dillon), a young schizophrenic freshly released from a mental hospital, has nowhere else to go after learning that his mother has moved to Florida and that he can't collect his welfare checks because he no longer has an address.

Though the two treat themselves to a beer once in a while in a panhandler hangout near Penn Station, there's barely a sign of alcohol or drug abuse to be seen, and the manners and good humor with which they spray and squeegee car windows and hustle for change would do the entire service industry proud.

"Saint" is a buddy movie on the low end, resembling in eerie fashion Jerry Schatzberg's vastly superior 1973 "Scarecrow." In the Schatzberg film, Gene Hackman and Al Pacino play a pair of drifters leaning on each other as they thumb their way to Pittsburgh to start a carwash business. In "Saint," Glover and Dillon form the same bond, trying to stay out of trouble while they save up enough money to get an apartment and find real jobs.

There are even stronger parallels in the way the two sets of characters interact—Hackman and Glover provide physical protection, Pacino and Dillon have gentle spirits to share—and in the way the stories are finally resolved.

Having said that, I wish "Saint" was even more like "Scarecrow." Where the events in "Scarecrow" seems random and unforseeable, "Saint" follows the path of pat Hollywood melodrama.

In the Fort Washington Armory, a shelter where hundreds of homeless men bivouac every night, there is a thug named Little Leroy (Ving Rhames) who roams the slum palace with his gang robbing and terrorizing helpless newcomers. After Leroy demands sexual service from Matthew, and gets beaten up by Jerry for his trouble, Jerry and Matthew decide to avoid the shelter altogether. They sleep on the A train, in an abandoned van, with friends in an empty tenement, anywhere they can curl up.

The ceremonial title of saint belongs to Matthew, in recognition of his magic healing powers. Nobody knows where these powers come from, including, apparently, the filmmakers, but when Matthew applies his light touch to Jerry's tortured legs, or to the arthritic hands of a homeless old man (the late Joe Seneca), pain disappears.

"You are the saint of all the homeless people," Jerry declares, then drops the subject.

As long as the film holds its focus on Jerry and Matthew, it works despite its sentimentality. Glover may be the most naturally likable actor in our midst these days, and Dillon one of our most underrated. Together, they make a marvelously sympathetic pair, and only when the melodrama takes over do they lose their credibility and begin to look like actors dressing down.

Certainly, the filmmakers had their hearts in the right places. They shot on location, often using homeless people as paid extras, and we do come away from the film with a sense of the desperation they feel. But it is only a faint sense, from a safe distance, and the film will be better remembered as "that Danny Glover-Matt Dillon buddy movie" than any ground-breaking look at homelessness in America.

SIGHT AND SOUND, 6/94, p. 59, Ben Thompson

Another New York apartment block is demolished by unscrupulous property developers. One of its residents, a disturbed but sensitive young white man called Matthew, makes his way to the night shelter, helping a young woman and her family along the way. In the queue he takes out his small camera to frame a picture of Jerry, a black Vietnam veteran with shrapnel in his leg, who has lost his family and business through a partner's gambling. Jerry objects to having his picture taken, until he finds out there is no film in the camera.

Seeing Matthew take pity on a bewildered old man, Jerry decides to take the younger newcomer under his wing. He sees him through his first dangerous night at the Fort Washington shelter, telling him to keep his shoes under the bed legs to stop them being stolen, and then intervenes when Matthew is threatened by Little Leroy, a vicious gangster. Out on the streets, Jerry teaches Matthew various essential survival techniques—how to keep out of the way of the police, and how to scratch a living by cleaning car windscreens in traffic jams. But back at the shelter, Leroy attacks Matthew again, and Jerry can only save him by breaking Leroy's arm.

Matthew and Jerry have to leave the shelter for their own safety; they set up home first in Jerry's old broken-down van, and then in a squat with his friend Rosario, Rosario's pregnant wife Tamsen and an old shoe-shiner, Spits. Jerry helps Matthew back from the brink of madness, and encourages his photographic talents by buying him film for his camera. Matthew uses the healing power in his hands to ease the pain of Jerry's shrapnel wounds, and to cure Spits of his arthritis. Jerry calls him a saint. Tamsen has a miscarriage and loses her baby, but she and Rosario follow through with their plan to go to and work in Galveston.

Matthew and Jerry are doing well on the streets, saving money to get a roof over their heads and start a small fruit and veg business. But one night there is a cold weather alert and the police round up the homeless and force them into shelters. Jerry escapes, but Matthew is taken back to Fort Washington, where he takes a young first-timer in hand as Jerry did. When Leroy goes to rob the newcomer, Matthew raises the alarm. He tries to leave the shelter but isn't allowed to, and before Jerry can arrive to help him, Leroy robs and kills him. Matthew's body will be buried without ceremony on desolate Hart Island. Jerry sneaks onto the boat carrying the coffins, and places the photos Matthew has taken in his grave, vowing to struggle on in Matthew's memory.

If the dichotomy between 'callous' 80s and 'caring' 90s really is a false one, no-one has told Tim Hunter. It is difficult to believe that the man at the helm of this warm and almost intimidatingly human ten-hankie production was also responsible for the steely glint of *River's Edge*.

Hunter and Matt Dillon go back a long way—as far as the former's coscreenwriting coup with *Over the Edge*. It is fitting that this should be the latter's best performance since *Drugstore Cowboy*, because the street clothes he wears here seem to have been inherited from River Phoenix in *My Own Private Idaho*—his successor as a Gus Van Sant leading man. If it's sometimes hard not to ask—as it never was with Phoenix—"why is Matt Dillon dressed as a homeless person?", he still brings a lean and angelic quality of bewilderment to the role of Matthew, and there is no hint of condescension in his performance.

The similarities between Hunter's film and Van Sant's are only superficial. *The Saint of Fort Washington* has a much more conventional narrative—the screenplay was written by *Orphans* playwright Lyle Kessler—and is about social fact rather than ideas of freedom. Producers Picker and Hyams wanted to make a film in the tradition of the Warner Bros social dramas of the 30s, and by and large they have succeeded. The shock value of the detailed information about actual homelessness which this film imparts to us is intensified by its presentation within the convention of Hollywood storytelling.

The film-makers' transparent good intentions elicited an unparalleled degree of co-operation from New York city authorities. The footage shot inside the huge barrack-like homeless shelter is genuinely frightening, and even the sturdiest of cynics will struggle not to be moved by the journey to Potter's Field, the island burial ground 40 minutes out of Manhattan, where New York's indigent and unclaimed are dumped *en masse* in unmarked graves.

Hunter has got a licence to entertain here as well as to inform (and remember, this man made the two-hour pilot for *Beverly Hills 90210*, so he knows a thing or two about entertainment). The bleakness of a fundamentally tragic story-line, a very real New York, and a lot of understandably miserable-looking homeless people is offset by a faith in enduring human goodness which at times gets dangerously close to Capra country. Such sentimentality might be the pay-off for getting such a deeply un-Hollywood subject as urban homelessness onto the big screen but, paradoxically, the fact that this film cannot be pigeon-holed as a hard-hitting documentary-style drama only throws its message into sharper relief.

For the most part, *The Saint of Fort Washington* manages to steer clear of brute didacticism (though the moment when a song seeps through the soundtrack, and the words "only ourselves to blame, should hang our heads in shame" are clearly audible, is rather an awkward one). Much of the credit for this goes to Danny Glover, who, as so often, makes more than could reasonably be hoped for out of what is basically another 'best friend' role. The bare-facedness with which he leads us towards the tear-jerking conclusion does not make it any easier to resist.

VILLAGE VOICE, 11/23/93, p. 59, J. Hoberman

Transposing *Of Mice and Men* to the streets of New York is scarcely the worst way to dramatize the social catastrophe that Ronald Reagan and his successors have taught us to take for granted. The problem with *The Saint of Fort Washington*'s treatment of homeless men is that it's so totally mickey-mouse.

A schizophrenic outpatient (Matt Dillon), dim and good-naturedly prone to taking photographs with an empty camera, comes under the protection of a grizzled but kindly Viet-vet (Danny Glover). Together, they leave the truly frightening shelter of the Fort Washington Armory for a brief life of honest squeegee work. The combination of feel-good music and lively repartee as the partners dodge cops to clean windshields seems designed to melt the heart of Rudy Giuliani. Indeed, as directed by Tim Hunter from Lyle Kessler's script, *The Saint of Fort Washington* has the benefit of two highly sympathetic performances (Dillon dumbs down more affectingly than any actor of his generation), as well as a coherent use of New York locations.

Unfortunately, *The Saint of Fort Washington* has neither the courage of its original realist, nor its subsequent magic-realist, premise. The filmmakers must feel that to even sit still for such a downer, the audience has to be congratulated in advance—and, in fact, the movie may play "grittier" outside New York. Here, it's nearly an episode from *The Shirley Temple Storybook*. Were *The Saint of Fort Washington* less paralyzed with fear it would have been an honorable stab at social realism. As it stands, it's as overwhelmed by its subject matter as it is underserved by a tepid script.

Also reviewed in:
CHICAGO TRIBUNE, 1/7/94, Friday/p. A, Michael Wilmington
NATION, 12/13/93, p. 744, Stuart Klawans
NEW YORK TIMES, 11/17/93, p. C19, Janet Maslin
VARIETY, 9/27/93, p. 35, Todd McCarthy

SAMBA TRAORÉ

A New Yorker Films release of a Les Films de l'Avenir/Les Films de la Plaine/Waka Films co-production. *Executive Producer:* Sophie Salbot and Silvia Voser. *Producer:* Idrissa Ouédraogo. *Director:* Idrissa Ouédraogo. *Screenplay (Mooré with English subtitles):* Idrissa Ouédraogo, Jacques Arhex, and Santiago Amigoréna. *Director of Photography:* Pierre Laurent Chenieux and Mathieu Vadepied. *Editor:* Joëlle Dufour. *Music:* Fanton Cahen and Lamine Konté. *Sound:* Alix Comte, Dominique Hennequin, and Sabine Boss. *Art Director:* Yves Brover. *Costumes:* Oumou Sy. *Running time:* 85 minutes. *MPAA Rating:* Not Rated.

CAST: Bakary Sangaré (Samba Traoré); Mariam Kaba (Saratou); Abdoulaye Komboudri (Salif); Irène Tassembedo (Binta); Moumouni Compaoré (Ali); Krin Casimir Traoré (Seydou); Sibidou Ouédraogo (Awa); Firmine Coulibaly (Koro); Hippolyte Wangrawa (Ismaël); Mady Dermé (The Horse Rider); Joseph Traoré (The Truck Driver); Noufou Ouédraogo (The Newspaper Seller); Noël Paré and Jacques Khalifa Sanou (The Policemen); Adama Traoré (The Shepherd).

NEW YORK POST, 9/10/93, p. 42, Jerry Tallmer

They've given me all of seven inches to write about "Samba Traore," the movie and the name of the man in the movie at Lincoln Plaza directed by Idrissa Ouedraogo, the 39-year-old director from Burkino Faso by way of Kiev and the Sorbonne.

Samba (Bakary Sangare), a big strong outgoing fellow who might just remind you of Billy Eckstine, returns to his village on the run after a stickup in which an attendant at a Faso Oil gas station has been shot. He totes a suitcase and an attache case—there's the money and a gun in the attache case—past thatched huts and women toting jugs on their heads—the symbolism of the film right at the top.

Back home, Samba—with the flair of a Times Square habitue—outwits his shiftless old pal Salif (Abdoulaye Komboudri) at three-card monte. He buys a herd of Brahman cattle as gifts for mama, papa, the whole village. He falls for good-looking Saratou, the single mother of 7-year-old Ali (Moumouni Compaore), and presently she stops snubbing the brash suitor. They get all dolled up, the village elder says: "I now pronounce you man and wife," and boom, they're married. I loved it.

But trouble brews, by way of Saratou's creepy, snooping ex-boyfriend, and a pair of bush police, nosing around by Jeep, and Samba's exhibitionism in building a bar and a two-story house, and his moral weakness, running away when Saratou is in the agonies of a difficult childbirth—his child—in the back of a truck.

In the end it's the 7-year-old, Ali, who's never much liked Samba, but who now—as if you hadn't guessed—rides out to find him, hug him, say: "Never do that again, all right?" When the chips are down, Samba doesn't do it again. I suppose this movie has the virtues of simplicity, but it's all a little too basic for me.

NEWSDAY, 9/10/93, Part II/p. 71, Gene Seymour

China's filmmakers now comprise the Big Discovery in international cinema. But at the rate such filmmakers as Idrissa Ouedraogo are making potential classics like "Samba Traore," it shouldn't be long before African cinema is given the recognition its many fine achievements deserve.

Ouedraogo (pronounced "way-dra-OH-go") hails from the country of Burkina Faso, which used to be Upper Volta. In just three feature films, including 1990's spellbinding "Tilai," he has made that county's dry, rugged, beautifully textured terrain as vivid a cinematic landscape as John Ford's Monument Valley. His films have won international acclaim for the way they filter and convey complex societal and emotional truths through a spare, graceful narrative style.

"Samba Traore" seems a risky move for Ouedraogo because the story in this, his fourth feature, is as complex on its surface as it is beneath. The title character (Bakary Sangare) is seen at the start of the film taking part in a gas station holdup. Though his partner is shot, Samba escapes with the money to his native village, which he hasn't seen in several years.

Parents and friends are glad to see Samba. Yet they wonder how he came to have so much money. Most suspicious of all is Samba's oldest friend, Salif (Abdoulaye Komboudri), a harried and married farmer. Samba claims he saved it all. This explanation mutes the doubts of Salif, who encourages his pal to marry Saratou (Mariam Kaba), a single mother with a 10-year-old son.

Believing himself to be on a proverbial roll, Samba becomes a more than conspicuous consumer, buying a little herd for his neighbors and building a big new house for his new family. But he also displays fits of temper and anxiety that become more noticeable to the villagers. Meanwhile, the police are closing in on Samba, who, fearing capture, flees the village just when his wife is about to give birth to her second son—and his first.

Something of the archetypical western (like John Ford's, for instance) resonates in "Samba Traore" with its antiheroic loner on the run from the law in search of peace and prosperity on the plains. There is also much of the shrewd, supple humanism of Jean Renoir, Satyajit Ray and the Italian neorealists of the late 1940s.

There is also an organic design to the narrative that makes "Samba's" story resemble a folk tale. As with his previous films, Ouedraogo does so many sustained, deep takes of the surrounding landscape that the whole environment seems to breathe, sigh and laugh like another living character in his story. These and many other virtues make "Samba Traore" a film that is, at once, distinctly African and bracingly.

VILLAGE VOICE, 9/21/93, p. 66, Leslie Camhi

Violence erupts in the dark Ouagadougou night—a gas station is robbed amidst the din of traffic, one thief shot while the other escapes. In the morning, police leaving the city stream past women hoeing fields by hand—credits roll, and *Samba Traoré* begins.

Samba, the thief, returns to his village, where there are no strangers. My son, it's been a long time, tell us all that's happened, his joyful parents ask. But memories of the city haunt his sleep and spark sporadic acts of violence, which his gentle neighbors watch in disbelief. To calm his guilt, Samba buys the village a herd of cattle, and suddenly he walks with a bedouin's gait. He loves and marries, builds a two-story house, and opens a bar, subtly drawing the village closer to the city. Then, when his wife, in complicated labor, must be taken to the capital, he panics; abandoning her, he is exposed and spurned.

Ouédraogo has evolved a cinematic style, all art, in which the narrative and characters seem to emanate effortlessly from the austere and sublime Voltaic landscape. It shares its sensitivity to rhythm with an oral tradition. An entire courtship may be condensed into a slow, distant pan of a beautiful woman crossing a field. Ouédraogo has said that Burkina Faso's more than 40 dialects compel him to make films so sparing of words and intensely visual; it's a technique from which Western directors could learn.

Everything worthy in this world stems from nature and communal ties, from the love of people who've known one another since childhood, whose lives are ruled by honor, and for whom the most unforgivable act is to abandon one other. Why then does anyone ever leave? If there's a flaw in Ouédraogo's beautiful film, it is in never suggesting the material exigencies or conflicts with tradition that compel villagers to the city. But few have so eloquently explored the alienation that haunts them when they return home.

Also reviewed in:
NEW REPUBLIC, 10/4/93, p. 30, Stanley Kauffmann
NEW YORK TIMES, 9/10/93, p. C3, Janet Maslin
VARIETY, 3/8/93, p. 62, Deborah Young

SANDLOT, THE

A Twentieth Century Fox release in association with Island World. *Executive Producer:* Mark Burg, Chris Zarpas, and Cathleen Summers. *Producer:* Dale de la Torre and William S. Gilmore. *Director:* David Mickey Evans. *Screenplay:* David Mickey Evans and Robert Gunter. *Director of Photography:* Anthony B. Richmond. *Editor:* Michael A. Stevenson. *Music:* David Newman. *Music Editor:* Laurie Higgins-Tobias. *Sound:* Garry Cunningham. *Sound Editor:* Paul Clay. *Casting:* Shari Rhodes. *Production Designer:* Chester Kaczenski. *Art Director:* Marc Dabe. *Set Decorator:* Judi Sandin. *Set Dresser:* Lisa Eager. *Special Effects:* Clifford Wenger. *Visual Effects:* Richard Yuricich. *Costumes:* Grania Preston. *Make-up:* Karl Wessen and Shannon Engemann. *Stunt Coordinator:* John Moio. *Running time:* 101 minutes. *MPAA Rating:* PG.

CAST: Tom Guiry (Scotty Smalls); Mike Vitar (Benjamin Franklin Rodriguez); Patrick Renna (Hamilton "Ham" Porter); Chauncey Leopardi (Michael "Squints" Palledorous); Marty York (Alan "Yeah-Yeah" McClennan); Brandon Adams (Kenny DeNunez); Grant Gelt (Bertram Grover Weeks); Shane Obedzinski (Tommy "Repeat" Timmons); Victor DiMattia (Timmy Timmons); Art La Fleur ("The Babe"); Denis Leary (Bill); Karen Allen (Mom); James Earl Jones (Mr. Mertle); Marlee Shelton (Wendy); Herb Muller (Young Mr. Mertle); Garret Pearson (Police Chief); Ed Mathews and Keith Campbell (Thieves); Wil Horneff (Phillips); Tyson Jones (Little League Punk #2); Karl Simmons (Schoolyard Pitcher); Maury Wills (Coach); Pablo P. Vitar (Older Benny); Bob Apisa (Home Plate Umpire); Robbie T.

Robinson (Third Base Umpire);   Chuck Fick (Giants Catcher);   Tim Page (Giants Pitcher); Dennis Williams (Giants Third Baseman);   Cynthia Windham (Mother at Pool);   Shane Lavar Smith (Toddler);   Brian Simpson, Mark N. Weatherbee, and Cleve Hall (Beast Puppeteers).

LOS ANGELES TIMES, 4/3/93, Calendar/p. 1, Peter Rainer

The kids in "The Sandlot" are so fresh-scrubbed and perky that they might as well be plugging something in a commercial—fabric softener, say, or peanut butter. In a way, they *are* plugging a product—all-American wholesomeness.

This is one of those kids' films that takes everything to do with childhood and turns it into high concept. It's about what happens to the new kid on the block, Scotty (Tom Guiry), when he joins the neighborhood's eight-man sandlot team during the summer of '62.

Right away we're primed: This is going to be a movie about (a) a boy's coming of age, (b) baseball as a boy's birthright and (c) our lost innocence. This "Field of Dreams" field has been plowed so many times that the land is no longer arable. Isn't it time to cultivate a few new clichés?

The '60s atmosphere is strictly out of the cookbook: Oldies on the soundtrack, Coca-Cola signs, Edsels. The nine kids are selected to be a cultural cross-section-among them one black kid (Brandon Adams), a chubby kid (Patrick Renna), a bespectacled nerd (Grant Gelt), and their leader, Benny (The Jet) Rodriguez (Mike Vitar). The effect is a bit like "Our Gang" for the Spielberg era.

The kids even have their own treehouse, which means that the production designer is the only person connected with this project who actually went out on a limb.

Scotty is initially presented as an egghead who can't play baseball and doesn't even know who Babe Ruth is. (This is typical movie stereotyping; brainy grade-schoolers are actually more likely to know a ballplayer's every stat than the sandlot sluggers.) He also has problems with his stepfather (Denis Leary) that are never dramatically explored. The father is basically in the movie to provide the prop that propels the film's second half, when his treasured baseball autographed by Ruth finds itself in the dangerous precincts of the local junkyard dog.

David Mickey Evans, who co-wrote and directed (it's his first feature), has a gift for shamelessness—his previous kidfest "Radio Flyer," which he scripted, had an even higher stack of high concepts than "The Sandlot." He pulls out so many stops that every once in a great while something hits. There's a funny gross-out scene with the kids chewing tobacco and then taking a nauseating ride on a whirlybird amusement park ride; one of the child actors, Chauncey Leopardi, is a gifted ham, and his scene with a curvaceous blond lifeguard is a hoot.

If Leopardi's character had been the movie's centerpiece instead of the starched Scotty, "The Sandlot" (rated PG for language and tobacco chewing) might have kicked up some much-needed dust. But Scotty is a dim Everyboy. Didn't the filmmakers even notice that he looks like an 11-year-old Eddie Haskell?

NEW YORK POST, 4/7/93, p. 20, Audrey Farolino

"The Sandlot," not only has a baseball theme, it also has a lot in common with the game itself: Breezy and innocent, it sometimes seems to be going nowhere (and taking its sweet old time getting there), but then it surprises you with a couple of nice plays and some nifty teamwork and you're ready to forgive most of its faults.

Set in 1962, the movie is a coming-of-age comedy about the members of a ragtag neighborhood sandlot team who learn some lessons about heroism and responsibility over the course of one baseball-obsessed summer.

True, those lessons are completely predictable. It's also true that the story has some screwball curves straight out of left field, including the mysterious presence of a frothing "beast" behind the sandlot fence and a ninth inning appearance by Babe Ruth's ghost.

Still, "The Sandlot" is surprisingly entertaining, thanks largely to its extremely likable cast of young actors, headed by Tom Guiry as protagonist Scotty Smalls, the new kid on the block who longs to fit in with the sandlot boys, and Mike Vitar as Benjamin Franklin Rodriguez, the group's star player and the kind of upstanding guy that mythic baseball heros are made of—and who, of course, will become a mythic hero by movie's end.

When Scotty first moves into the neighborhood, he can't throw or catch and thinks that the Great Bambino is a nickname for Bambi. Nevertheless, good guy Benny takes pity on Scotty and brings him onto the team.

The movie works best when it simply follows the boys' adventures that summer-like the day they all head to the local pool, where the geeky Squints (played by the hilarious Chauncey Leopardi) makes a gutsy play for the curvy female lifeguard.

But the main plot revolves around that "beast" lurking behind the left-field fence (it's actually a vicious dog belonging to the reclusive Mr. Mertle, played by James Earl Jones).

One day, Scotty sneaks his stern stepfather's autographed Babe Ruth ball to the sandlot, where it gets whacked over the fence and into the beast's domain, an area from which, legend has it, neither balls nor children have ever emerged. (The stepfather, by the way, is played by MTV comic Denis Leary, as strange a bit of casting as you're likely to see anytime soon.)

Will the boys manage to retrieve the ball and save Scotty's hide? Of course you know the answer—but it's still fun to watch them do it.

NEW YORK POST, 4/12/93, p. 29, Michael Medved

It's easy to imagine an early pitch meeting for the new movie "The Sandlot" in which some overly enthusiastic agent or producer describes this project as "'Stand By Me' meets 'Field of Dreams.'" The combination sounds utterly preposterous, of course, but somehow in the finished film the disparate elements come together to form a pleasant and watchable piece of family entertainment.

Like "Stand By Me," "The Sandlot" recreates a long-ago world of lost innocence (in this case the summer of 1962) and focuses on the intense but delicate friendships that connect a group of boys just a few years (or maybe months) away from the unsettling upheavals of puberty.

And like "Field of Dreams, this film is a sentimental hymn to the mystical power of baseball, complete with a brief appearance by the kindly ghost of Babe Ruth himself (a miscast Art La Fleur). James Earl Jones, whose growling presence as the reclusive novelist in "Field of Dreams" added so much to that film, also turning up here in a crucial cameo as a blind former ballplayer who lives—a lonely life surrounded by mementos of the game's glory years.

"The Sandlot" bears one other crucial point of resemblance to both "Stand By Me" and "Field of Dreams": it is much easier to enjoy than it is to describe.

Here, the modest plot centers on a shy, lonely kid named Scotty Smalls (played with reasonable conviction by first-time actor Tom Guiry), who moves to California's San Fernando Valley with his recently remarried mother (Karen Allen). The boy knows no one in his new neighborhood and even worse, he knows absolutely nothing about baseball.

But he is soon adopted and protected by Benny "The Jet" Rodriguez, the self-assured superstar of the local sandlot. As played by 14-year-old Mike Vitar, a real-life Little League standout and a memorably charismatic screen presence, Benny is one of those supremely decent, totally reliable natural leaders that most of us are privileged to meet once (or twice) in a lifetime.

Under Benny's sponsorship, Scotty soon finds a place among the sandlot regulars, a group that offers your basic bomber crew from a number of vintage war movies, including one bespectacled nerd, one athletic Afro-American, one sassy fat kid and so forth.

These pals spend the entire summer in endless hours of batting and fielding practice, without ever attempting to play real games or to keep score. The only menace to their idyllic existence is provided by "The Beast"—a legendary neighborhood monster who makes the earth tremble behind the left-field fence and who turns out to be a junkyard dog so enormous and so diabolically determined and clever that he makes Stephen King's formidable Cujo look like a docile Lhasa Apso.

The movie's climactic set piece involves the group's desperate efforts to rescue a lost ball from the slobbering jaws of this cunning canine—a quest that takes on monumental importance because the ball in question bears the authentic autograph of the immortal Babe Ruth.

This flimsy story line is hardly the stuff of breathless drama, but first-time director (and co-screenwriter) David Mickey Evans uses a breezy, bigger-than-life comic-book style that makes the most of the thin material.

The film is just scary and exciting enough to keep small fry on the edge of their seats, at the same time that it's nostalgic and knowing enough to please most of their parents.

Evans' only previous screen credit came as script writer for the disastrous child abuse epic "Radio Flyer"—a film he was also supposed to direct, until he was pulled from the project at the last moment in favor of veteran Richard Donner. Viewing Evans' light and likable directorial touch in this film, one can only wonder whether that earlier picture would have amounted to less of a morose muddle had he been allowed to bring his own vision to the screen.

To be sure, there are major problems with "The Sandlot." In group scenes the rookie director displays a distressing tendency to arrange his young actors in straight lines, where they shout out their bits of dialogue like soloists in a glee club.

Nevertheless, this is the sort of cinematic tall tale that all but forces you to overlook such shortcomings. It makes no real attempt to re-create reality, but rather tries to illustrate someone's frequently repeated childhood recollections that seem to have grown more colorful and more implausible with each retelling.

Especially sensitive parents will note a pair of totally unnecessary four-letter words (which brought the PG rating) along with some other earthy insults traded between the sandlot regulars and a visiting Little League team.

There is also a gross and vivid vomit scene (again, shades of "Stand By Me") and one hilarious interlude in which the geeky, gawky center-fielder, Jeff "Squints" Palledorous (Chauncey Leopardi) manages to connive some mouth-to-mouth contact with a curvaceous teen-age lifeguard at the local community pool.

None of this should discourage the intended audience—parents and even the youngest children—from making a trip to the local theater.

NEWSDAY, 4/7/93, Part II/p. 67, John Anderson

The '50s and early '60s are proving irresistible for filmmakers, especially those who want to deal with childhood, of the white male variety. And who can blame them? There are no race problems to deal with (Don't believe me? Check out '50s TV). There are no girls (none their own age, anyway). And—for most of "The Sandlot," anyway—there's no Henry Aaron.

"The Sandlot," which concerns the comic antics of a group of pickup ballplayers, ages 9-14, and the huge dog that occupies the area behind the right field fence, is a fluffy, comic bit of baseball business, which happily twists history to meet certain demands of plot and casting. That none of this probably ever happened is less important than the idea that a lot of people wish it had. It's entertaining. And gleefully vapid.

Embodying the esthetic that governs "The Sandlot" is Tom Guiry, who plays Scotty Smalls, a kid who moves into a sleepy western town at the beginning of summer—the worst time for making friends, of course—with a bag full of personal problems: His father died when he was quite young, his mother (Karen Allen) has recently married a recidivist jock (Denis Leary, with a room full of trophies), and worst of all Scotty throws like a girl. When he meets the local kids, he has to overcome these daunting personal handicaps, plus the fact that he doesn't know who Babe Ruth was.

Babe Ruth? Yes, even though the musical score ("Wipe Out," "Tequila" "Green Onions") indicates that the time is the early '60s, there's no Mickey Mantle adoration, no Willie Mays worship, no recognition that baseball didn't stop in 1932, or that kids wouldn't have cared if it did. Why a bunch of pickup players like Benny (Mike Vitar), Ham (Patrick Renna) and the rest worship the Great Bambino instead of Mantle or Mays is never explained. But one gets the distinct impression that "The Sandlot" was made by people who don't have a clue about baseball, or kids.

Guiry is basically someone's idea of a second-string Macaulay Culkin, who, abetted by a "Wonder Years"-style commentary, becomes a bit hard to take. But the other kids, particularly Patrick Renna as the wisecracking Ham, are truly funny, with great timing and great shtick. And while the movie is intent on communicating a sense of time past, the kids' comic routines are simply funny.

Take Michael (Squints) Palledorous (Chauncey Leopardi), for instance, who fakes drowning to kiss gorgeous Wendy the lifeguard (Marlee Shelton). It's a shameless bit of hormonal excess. But it's also a set piece, not something that propels the movie. The real suspense, what there is of it, comes after Scotty steals his stepfather's Babe Ruth-autographed baseball to play a game, and it's hit over the fence, into the junkyard, into the lair of the massive dog who is assumed to devour everything that comes within its reach. The retrieval of the baseball is overlong, but has a Little Rascals-style goofiness about it.

Whether "The Sandlot" is for you depends on whether you can suspend your disbelief and accept that any of this is authentic. What you really have to do to enjoy "The Sandlot" is totally disregard the time references, the golden oldies and the insipid air of nostalgia and accept the children as children, timeless and oblivious of time.

SIGHT AND SOUND, 8/94, p. 52, Nick Hasted

Salt Lake City, 1962. Eleven-year-old Scotty moves to a new neighbourhood with his mother and new stepfather Bill. Bill's study is a shrine to work and to baseball, with a ball signed by Babe Ruth as its centrepiece. Feeling unwanted, Scotty stumbles on eight boys playing a game of baseball in a sandlot. Reluctantly joining in, he plays dreadfully. His mother encourages him to make friends and have fun. Back at the sandlot, Benny, the boys' best player, engineers a catch for Scotty, and gives him his old equipment. Scotty is in the team.

The boys play baseball every day until a ball is hit out of the sandlot into the neighbouring yard. Innocently going to retrieve it, Scotty is dragged back by the others. That night, he is told the legend of The Beast, a monstrous guard dog chained up in the yard 20 years before by its owner, the bad-tempered Mr Mertle. In the dark, Scotty glimpses the monster.

Later that summer, one of the boys, 'Squints', wins a kiss from Wendy, the lifeguard he adores, by pretending to drown, and the gang beat a team of snooty Little Leaguers. One day, Benny hits a ball so hard it explodes, and the boys consider it an omen. Bill leaves on a business trip and, when a ball is lost, Scotty replaces it with Bill's signed one. He hits his first home run—straight into the yard. The boys try various schemes to retrieve it, but The Beast outwits them. That night Benny dreams that he is visited by the ghost of Babe Ruth, who tells him that taking the ball from The Beast is his chance of greatness. Next morning, Benny walks into the yard, watched by the others, and sees a normal-sized dog. He grabs the ball and, as he is chased, the fence falls onto the dog. Benny and Scotty rescue him, and are invited in by Mr Mertle, a blind man who replaces their battered ball with one signed by The Babe's whole team. Mertle, it turns out, was a great player, too. Years later, Scotty commentates as Benny plays for the Giants.

At its worst, David Mickey Evans' directorial debut is like *Stand by Me* diluted with an irritating dash of *The Wonder Years*. Sharing details with Rob Reiner's film—a falsely mythical backyard dog, 12-year-old male bonding and a central friendship between an egghead and a tough kid—it also persists with the baby-boomer dream that the early, 60s were a last golden glow of American adolescence. So *The Sandlot Kids* is narrated by the grown-up Scotty in a smugly wise voice, even though the only wisdom he appears to have gained in 30 years is that baseball is cool. It is an innocent truth which a worried America, with its recent fervour for children's and baseball films, seems determined to believe. Niggling historical complications have no place in such a film, allowing James Earl Jones' ageing black baseball player to reminisce on his rivalry with Babe Ruth, without once mentioning segregated leagues. The only hint of historical distance comes with the break-up of the gang narrated as a parody of *American Graffiti* (the kids grow up not to Vietnam, but to fortunes in mini-malls and bungee-jumping).

Where *The Sandlot Kids* scores is in its children. Scotty, the writer-surrogate swot, may grow up to be annoying, but at least as a child he avoids the solipsism of other recent smart kids—in *This Boy's Life* and *King of the Hill*, for example. Instead, he moves from his distant father to a welcoming gang with minimal angst, allowing the film to simply celebrate the pleasures of boyhood. The other kids are a delight, with unforced wit and natural charm.

As director and co-writer, Evans himself comes across as curiously childlike. At its most damaging, this allows the dwindling narrative cohesion favoured by bored ten-year-olds. But Evans also seems capable of an inclusive wonderment beyond his guff-spouting narrator. In a single film, he includes a scene of powerful and funny adolescent attraction and a rousing moment of adult sporting triumph. And in a single scene, as Benny escapes the not very scary dog, Evans throws in a cinema screening of *The Wolf Man* and The Surfaris' "Wipeout", just because he can—a sense of freedom which spills into bursting frames and gratuitous wipes. It is an ignorance of formula constantly felt, as reality stretches and contracts with the force of the boys' imaginations. All that prevents the film's total success is the suspicion that its inconsistency comes in part from having nothing to say. It leaves the odd impression of not only starring 12-year-olds, but being made by one.

Also reviewed in:
NEW YORK TIMES, 4/7/93, p. C17, Janet Maslin
VARIETY, 4/5/93, p. 175, Leonard Klady
WASHINGTON POST, 4/8/93, p. D8, Rita Kempley
WASHINGTON POST, 4/9/93, Weekend/p. 38, Desson Howe

SCHINDLER'S LIST

A Universal Pictures release of an Amblin Entertainment production. *Executive Producer:* Kathleen Kennedy. *Producer:* Steven Spielberg, Gerald R. Molen, and Branko Lustig. *Director:* Steven Spielberg. *Screenplay:* Steven Zaillian. *Based on the novel by:* Thomas Keneally. *Director of Photography:* Janusz Kaminski. *Editor:* Michael Kahn. *Music:* John Williams. *Music Editor:* Kenn Wannberg. *Violin Solos:* Itzhak Perlman. *Clarinet Solo:* Giora Feidman. *Sound:* Ronald Judkins, Robert Jackson, and (music) Shawn Murphy. *Sound Editor:* Charles L. Campbell and Louis L. Edemann. *Casting:* Lucky Englander, Fritz Fleischhacker, Magdalena Szwarcbart, Tova Cypin, Liat Meiron, and Juliet Taylor. *Production Designer:* Allan Starski. *Art Director:* Ewa Skoczkowska and Maciej Walczak. *Set Decorator:* Ewa Braun. *Special Effects:* Bruce Minkus. *Costumes:* Anna Biedrzycka-Sheppard. *Make-up:* Christina Smith. *Stunt Coordinator:* Krzysztof Kotowski. *Running time:* 185 minutes. *MPAA Rating:* R.

CAST: Liam Neeson (Oskar Schindler); Ben Kingsley (Itzhak Stern); Ralph Fiennes (Amon Goeth); Caroline Goodall (Emilie Schindler); Jonathan Sagalle (Poldek Pfefferberg); Embeth Davidtz (Helen Hirsch); Malgoscha Gebel (Victoria Klonowska); Shmulik Levy (Wilek Chilowicz); Mark Ivanir (Marcel Goldberg); Beatrice Macola (Ingrid); Andrzej Seweryn (Julian Scherner); Friedrich Von Thun (Rolf Czurda); Krzysztof Luft (Herman Toffel); Harry Nehring (Leo John); Norbert Weisser (Albert Hujar); Adi Nitzan (Mila Pfefferberg); Michael Schneider (Juda Dresner); Miri Fabian (Chaja Dresner); Anna Mucha (Danka Dresner); Albert Misak (Mordecai Wulkan); Michael Gordon (Mr. Nussbaum); Aldona Grochal (Mrs. Nussbaum); Jacek Wojcicki (Henry Rosner); Beata Paluch (Manci Rosner); Piotr Polk (Leo Rosner); Ezra Dagan (Rabbi Menasha Levartov); Beata Nowak (Rebecca Tannenbaum); Rami Hauberger (Josef Bau); Leopold Kozlowski and Jerzy Nowak (Investors); Uri Avrahami (Chaim Nowak); Adam Siemion (OD/Chicken Boy); Magdalena Dandourian (Nuisa Horowitz); Pawel Delag (Dolek Horowitz); Shabtai Konorti (Garage Mechanic); Oliwia Dabrowska (Red Genia); Henryk Bista (Mr. Lowenstein); Tadeusz Bradecki (DEF Foreman); Wojciech Klata (Lisiek); Elina Lowensohn (Diana Reiter); Ewa Kolasinska (Irrational Woman); Bettina Kupfer (Regina Perlman); Grzegorz Kwas (Mietek Pemper); Vili Matula (Investigator); Stanislaw Koczanowicz (Doorman); Hans Jorg Assmann (Julius Madritsch); Geno Lechner (Majola); August Schmolzer (Dieter Reeder); Ludger Pistor (Josef Liepold); Beata Rybotycka (Club Singer); Branko Lustig (Nightclub Maitre d'); Artus Maria Matthiessen (Treblinka Commandant); Hans Michael Rehberg (Rudolph Hoss); Eugeniusz Priwiezencew (Waiter); Michael Z. Hoffman (Montelupich Colonel); Erwin Leder (SS Waffen Officer); Jochen Nickel (Wilhelm Kunde); Andrzej Welminski (Dr. Blancke); Daniel Del Ponte (Dr. Josef Mengele); Marian Glinka (DEF SS Officer); Grzegorz Damiecki (SS Sgt. Kunder); Stanislaw Brejdygant (DEF Guard); Olaf Linde Lubaszenko, Haymon Maria Buttinger, and Peter Appiano (Auschwitz Guards); Jacek Pulanecki (Brinnlitz Guard); Martin Semmelrogge (SS Waffen Man); Tomasz Dedek and Slawomir Holland (Gestapo); Tadeusz Huk (Gestapo Brinnlitz); Gerald Alexander Held (SS Bureaucrat); Piotr Cyrwus (Ukranian Guard); Joachim Paul Assbock (Gestapo Clerk Klaus Tauber); Osman Ragheb (Border Guard); Maciej Orlos (German Clerk); Marek Wrona (Toffel's Secretary); Zbigniew Kozlowski (Scherner's Secretary); Marcin Grzymowicz (Czurda's Secretary); Dieter Witting (Bosch); Magdalena Komornicka (Geoth's Girl);

Agnieszka Kruk (Czurda's Girl);   Anemona Knut (Polish Girl);   Jeremy Flynn (Brinnlitz Man); Agnieszka Wagner (Brinnlitz Girl);   Jan Jurewicz (Russian Officer);   Wieslaw Komasa (Plaszow Depot SS Guard);   Maciej Kozlowski (SS Guard Zablocie);   Martin Bergmann (SS NCO Zablocie);   Wilhelm Manske, Peter Flechtner, and Sigurd Bemme (SS NCO-Ghetto);   Ethel Szyc and Lucyna Zabawa (Ghetto Women);   Jerzy Sagan (Ghetto Old Man);   Ruth Farhi (Old Jewish Woman);   Dirk Bender (Clerk at Depot);   Dariusz Szymaniak (Prisoner at Depot); Hanna Kossowska (Ghetto Doctor);   Maciej Winkler, Radoslaw Krzyowski, and Jacek Lenczowski (Black Marketeers);   Maja Ostaszewska (Frantic Woman);   Sebastian Skalski (Stable Boy);   Ryszard Radwanski (Pankiewicz);   Piotr Kadlcik (Man in Pharmacy);   Bartek Niebielski (NCO Plaszow);   Thomas Morris (Grun);   Sebastian Konrad (Engineer Man);   Lidia Wyrobiec-Bank (Clara Sternberg);   Ravit Ferera (Maria Mischel);   Agnieszka Korzeniowska, Dominika Bednarczyk and Alicja Kubaszewska (Ghetto Girls);   Danny Marcu and Hans Rosner (Ghetto Men);   Alexander Strobele (Montelupich Prisoner);   Edward Linde Lubaszenko (Brinnlitz Priest);   Georges Kern (Depot Master);   Alexander Buczolich, Michael Schiller, Goetz Otto, Wolfgang Seidenberg, and Hubert Kramer (Plaszow SS Guards);   Razia Israeli, Dorit Ady Seadia, and Esti Yerushalmi (Plaszow Jewish Girls).

CHRISTIAN SCIENCE MONITOR, 12/15/93, p. 16, David Sterritt

Few moviegoers would seriously question Steven Spielberg's skills as a film entertainer. He has crafted several of the top-earning movies of all time, and his name has become a household word for children of all ages.

What many moviegoers *do* question is Spielberg's depth and seriousness as an artist. Most of his biggest hits, from "Jaws" to "Jurassic Park," resemble wide-screen video games—full of snap and crackle, but intellectually empty and emotionally thin. When he has tried his hand with an adult theme, as in "The Color Purple" and "Empire of the Sun," he has approached his ambitious material with the same 12-year-old mind that presides over his empty-headed blockbusters.

Which is why Spielberg's new movie, "Schindler's List," is such an astounding and glorious surprise. Out of the blue, the child-like auteur of "E.T." and the "Indiana Jones" epics has tackled the most challenging and troubling subject of our century—the Holocaust in all its shock, terror, and misery—and endowed the story with a subtlety and resonance that have rarely been so much as hinted at in his previous pictures.

True, traces of his bad habits show through at certain moments, especially near the end, when a long and lachrymose scene plunges into Spielbergian sentimentality of the gooiest kind. But before that unfortunate point, "Schindler's List" serves up three full hours of brilliant storytelling that's as humane and compassionate as it is gripping and provocative.

Based on actual events as chronicled in a book by Thomas Keneally, the movie focuses on Oskar Schindler, a loyal member of the Nazi party and a cunning industrialist with a clever idea for making lots of money. Since his government has declared war on the Jews of Europe, seizing their property and subjecting them to escalating torments, he will start an enamel-works factory staffed with low-wage laborers from the Krakow ghetto.

This scheme works fine until Schindler's work force is moved from the ghetto to a labor camp—whereupon the wily entrepreneur draws on his Nazi connections and relocates his factory to the middle of the camp, where it now cranks out artillery shells to aid the war effort.

Snags arise in his operation now and then—when the commander of the camp indulges his fondness for murder by shooting at Schindler's employees, for instance and when a trainload of "Schindler Jews" is inadvertently routed to the Auschwitz death camp. But generally the plan works out as Schindler intended, making him a wealthy and powerful member of the Nazi elite.

What nobody bargained on—including Schindler himself—is that the horror of the Holocaust would prove too appalling for even his well-developed psychological armor to shield him from its impact. Spurred by the events he witnesses everyday, including the psychotic violence of the camp commander who has become his friend and confidant, Schindler slowly realizes that his role in the Third Reich could be very different from what it is.

He begins to rescue an occasional Jew from death or torture, not from heroic impulses but because he can't abide the sheer human waste of the Nazi atrocities. Eventually he finds himself as determined to save Jews as he earlier was to pile up profits. He also takes a perverse (and hilarious) pride in ensuring that his factory turns out artillery shells of the poorest quality, doing its part to hinder Germany's success on the battlefield.

It is Schindler's transformation that Spielberg has handled most surprisingly. No sudden inspirations or high-toned motivations are trotted out to account for the change in the Nazi's life.

The reason for this may be that Spielberg has never been a strong developer of well-rounded characters, and he has simply failed to convey the causes of Schindler's conversion from profiteer to savior.

The movie's development is so absorbing and compelling, however, that I prefer to think Spielberg knew exactly what he was doing with this aspect of the story. Nobody can fathom the deepest levels of human personality, the filmmaker seems to be saying, so the movie would be false if it claimed to have all the answers to Schindler's regeneration. He was always an obsessive personality, and one day he changed the focus of his obsession from making money to salvaging helpless lives. That such a thing happened is inspirational enough in itself; no further moralizing or psychologizing is needed.

Spielberg's new restraint and maturity are felt in other ways as well. One is his decision to film "Schindler's List" almost entirely in black and white, even though today's audiences generally demand movies in color.

Again, a skeptic might suggest that Spielberg wanted to show off the importance of this project by giving it a veneer of austerity. But a more likely explanation is that Spielberg felt the horrors of Auschwitz would be unwatchable if color made them even more ghastly than they are in black-and-white images. The picture conveys the suffering of genocide quite vividly enough, and the impact of color might have proved a distraction rather than an enhancement.

Liam Neeson plays Schindler with probing intensity, getting excellent support from Ralph Fiennes as the concentration-camp commander, whose physical resemblance to Schindler is used by Spielberg to lend an additional layer of dark irony to the film. Ben Kingsley and Embeth Davidtz head the strong supporting cast.

CINEASTE, Vol. XX, No. 3, 1994, p. 49, Thomas Doherty

Connoisseurs of epochal moments of bad taste may recall the grotesque convergence climaxing the NBC-TV miniseries *Holocaust* (1978). A group of condemned Jews—huddled, naked, terrified—are herded into the gas chambers at Auschwitz. Close-up and claustrophobic, a fog of poison gas hisses down onto the innocents. The screen goes black, and, for one silent second, television evoked a searing heartbeat of pity and terror. But just a beat: in a video flash, the gas chambers of Auschwitz metamorphose into the sparkling kitchen space of a suburban American home. "What's that smell!," asks Snoopy Sniffer, harridan spokeswoman for a popular household cleanser. "Could it be something from the oven!"

Whether one burst into a cackle of nihilistic glee or sat in appalled, stupefied silence, the jump cut dislocation from Zyklon B to Easy Off Oven Cleaner expresses the emotional chasm between the past horror and the present complacency, not to say the obscenity of subsuming the unholy and unimaginable within the conventions of commerce and entertainment. That Steven Spielberg, the balladeer of suburbia, the director with twenty-twenty eyesight into the motion picture soul of America, should bridge that gulf is impressive but not unexpected. World War II has ever been at the back of his grand ambitions: the overblown comedy *1941* (1979); *Empire of the Sun* (1987), J. G. Ballard's child's-eye view of survival in a Japanese concentration camp; and *Always* (1989), a remake of the wartime weepie *A Guy Named Joe* (1943). It has also been the common source of his box office and artistic failures, perhaps because, for all his obsession with World War II, Spielberg had never taken Nazism seriously—certainly not in the Indiana Jones series, where the SS are clumsy fools befuddled by a bullwhip and Adolf Hitler is just another celebrity signing autographs. *Schindler's List* forced the confrontation. In his close encounter with spectacular evil, Spielberg has finally demanded of himself, and his audience, something more than a spellbound stare.

Adapted faithfully by Steven Zaillian from Thomas Keneally's fact-based novel, *Schindler's List* tells the remarkable and uplifting tale of Oskar Schindler, a German-Catholic industrialist who courageously and uncharacteristically rescued some 1200 Polish Jews from extermination at Auschwitz. The film arrives with the visible and temporal signs of high seriousness on the Hollywood screen: black and white cinematography and three-hour-plus running time. Forsaking the visual pleasure and contemporary perspective of color stock, the monochromatic film grain resonates with the documentary memory of the Holocaust, the stark newsreels of liberated concentration camps taken by American, British, and Soviet forces, later supplemented by captured footage from the Nazis themselves, always inveterate record keepers. Likewise, the prolonged running time is commensurate with the gravitas of the material and the esthetics of immersion in an extended, complex, and emotionally wrenching narrative.

Arriving in war-ravaged Krakow with an eye for the main chance, Schindler (Liam Neesom) is a born fixer for whom world war means expanding investment opportunities. On the strength of his ebullient personality and epicurean tastes in food, drink, and women, he finagles control of a metalworks factory and procures the military contracts that will make his fortune. Knowing his limitations as a hands-on executive, he leaves operational control to accountant Itzhak Stern (Ben Kingsley), a member of the *Judenrat* trying desperately to keep his kinsmen alive. While Schindler ladles out beluga caviar, Hennessy's cognac, and chunks of chocolate to the Nazi officer corps, Stern runs the factory and supervises its Jewish work force. The relationship between the two men—Stern measuring Schindler, gradually trusting him, or being forced to trust him—is the interpersonal core of the film.

Schindler's upward mobility parallels the descent of Krakow's Jews. At first, he waltzes obliviously above the terror around him, singing war songs with the Nazis, comfortably occupying the fashionable apartment of an evicted Jewish family, and rutting athletically with the secretarial help. Not until the brutal liquidation of the Krakow ghetto—more recreational slaughter than forced deportation—does the genocide in progress penetrate his skull. For this lethal tableau, Spielberg unleashes a full orchestration of cinematic horror. Vignettes of instant death comprise a lush, brutal montage of point-blank killing, mass executions, and, for variety, single file execution lineups. Floor by floor, room by room, on through the night, the Nazis flush out Jews who have hidden themselves under floorboards and beds, in cubbyholes, even inside pianos. When a misstep onto a keyboard hits a sour chord, the sound of machine-gun fire rattles off-screen in response. Later, in a kind of contrapuntal accompaniment to the sputter of gunfire, music from the same piano fills the halls of the building. A Nazi soldier is playing Bach—or is it Mozart! Moving back from the action, a long shot of the ghetto skyline erupts with exploding pockets of light and sound from the apartment windows, miniature moments of death glimpsed from afar like lightning bugs.

Watching on horseback from a distant hill, Schindler surveys the carnage and seems to come to a realization. His line of sight focuses on a girl in a red coat (one of the film's few privileged uses of color), center screen, wandering among the massacre, her lone figure individualizing the mass slaughter. Early on in the film, when a one-armed worker is led into Schindler's office to thank him for saving his life, the confirmed hustler is embarrassed and angry to be saddled with moral responsibility. Now, beholding the conflagration from afar, Schindler seems to assume the responsibility he has shunned.

Little is said of Schindler's spiritual transformation from narcissist to altruist, war profiteer to angel of mercy. Just as well—even in the Kenneally novel, the man's motives remain obscure, his heroism understood more as a personal gesture than a political stance or moral imperative. Spielberg's strategy is to show the action rather than probe the impulse. Save for the informational titles that signpost time and place, the weave and texture of the film is a sudden, unbidden immersion in a nightmare world. Rousted from their homes, families knead diamonds in clumps of bread to swallow them, like communion, for retrieval later. To pass medical inspection, women prick their fingers and rub the blood into their cheeks for color. Like the most compelling Holocaust literature, the tone is flat, mute, and dispassionate; death is presented matter of factly, in all its clinical, biological apathy, without shocked reaction shots or musical cues (for once, John Williams's score is an unobtrusive guide, not a thundering imperative). Since the disclosure of desperate measures and concentration camp ethnography unfolds wordlessly, the spectator must invest the narrative with the moral sense unspoken from the screen. The payoff in sympathetic participation can be heartstopping, as when a sprightly singalong tune blares out from the camp speakers and the next shot frames a huge chorus of children, hundreds of them, filling the screen and walking forward, happy lemmings ignorant of the fate awaiting them.

As in *Paradise Lost*, it is the devil who is the most magnetic character in the epic. Playing the languorous, imperious, and casually vicious SS Commandant Amon Goeth, British actor Ralph Fiennes confirms again the fascination with fascism, the way evil outperforms good as a focus for narrative interest. In his villa overlooking the labor camp at Plaszow, the fleshy Nazi entertains guests, makes love, and for diversion walks out onto his porch and shoots prisoners with a scope rifle. ("You're such a child," chides his girlfriend.) Goeth's way with murder is both malicious and capricious, businesslike and offhand. A zealous female engineer who does her work for the Nazis too well is peremptorily shot, but her advice on construction is followed. In a sequence fraught with Hitchcockian tension, a metal worker who makes hinges performs his task while a stopwatch ticks, only to find his own fate hinging on the caprice of a misfiring handgun. A dutiful true believer, Goeth may muster a certain weariness and distaste about his job of work, but never any qualms. With the Krakow ghetto an inferno in backframe, he mutters, exhausted but satisfied, that he'll be happy when the night is over.

Irresistible as an embodiment of Nazism, Goeth provokes the film's strangest scene: a sexually charged encounter between the Nazi officer and his nubile, Jewish house-servant, Helen (Embeth Davidtz). In his wine cellar, she stands forescreen, moist chemise clinging to her breasts. Goeth circles her and delivers a seductive, sinister monologue, threat and courtship, the pure Aryan contemplating a liaison with this "rat-faced" *untermensch*, who is, of course, a beautiful, tempting woman. Is he becoming human! Will his rape of this girl humanize him! If much of *Schindler's List* evokes Claude Lanzmann's *Shoah*, the wine cellar scene plays like an outtake from Liliana Cavani's *The Night Porter*.

The dramatic onslaught is so wrenching and unrelenting that the viewer may well take refuge in cinematic associations and esthetic appreciations of another sort. One notes that the meticulous recreations of the wartime ambience extend to the smallest details, from typeface to ethnic type; that the location shooting paid off in the evocative landscape and the condensed breath of the performers in the icy air; that, yes, the casting director was smart enough to find emaciated extras of all ages. Naturally, too, the cinematic chops of one of the medium's premiere practitioners is everywhere at work. The editing of the opening sequence, which follows Schindler as he 'suits up' for a night on the town, smoothly sculpts the personality of its bon vivant hero before hammering in the final touch: a tight close-up of his swastika pin. The film's most harrowing scene is also a textbook instance of reversed expectation and parallel editing. Told to strip and herded through blackened corridors, an hysterical group of Jewish women seem set for extermination, but miraculously, these chambers really are showers and the women breathe in the water, delivered.

Other motion picture visions of the Holocaust waft through *Schindler's List*. Besides the newsreel footage of World War II, Alain Resnais's *Night and Fog* (1955) is evoked in the endless piles of luggage and human effects, Agnieszka Holland's *Europa, Europa* (1991) in the muscle-tightening tension of desperate improvisation, and (above all) Lanzmann's *Shoah* (1985), whose locomotive and snow imagery permeates the film. In dreamy slo-mo, the trademark gesture from *Shoah*—the forefinger pulled laterally across the throat as a portent of things to come (sadistic gloating said the Jews, comradely warning said the Poles)—is glimpsed from a boxcar as a cargo of victims approaches the gates of Auschwitz.

Yet the most persistent film references here derive from Spielberg's own list. Talk about the personal overriding the political: the bulk of the critical response to the first major American motion picture depicting the Holocaust has focused less on the truth of the rendering than on the artistic growth of the renderer. At long last Hollywood's aging *wunderkind* had put away the things of the child, connected with his ethnic roots, drew upon the *shtetl* not the suburbs, and came to manhood, today, with *Schindler's List*, a high serious melodrama about the most serious of topics. Set in relief against *Jurassic Park*, the director's other, presumably more characteristic public offering of 1993, the accolades couldn't hide an underlying condescension. From David Lean or Roman Polanski, an achievement like *Schindler's List* might have been expected, but from Spielberg?

Of course, this gem of rare price in an auteur's canon serves as more than the ultimate leverage on the Academy of Motion Picture Arts and Sciences. No less than the opening of the Holocaust Museum on the Washington Mall, a site heretofore preserved for memorials to the American past, *Schindler's List* is a capstone event in a process that has been called "the Americanization of the

Holocaust." Edward Lutvak recently observed how, with the passage of time, the Holocaust has come to seem more and more the central event of World War II. More and more, too, Hollywood has come to seem the prism through which all history, genocidal or otherwise, is witnessed and felt. The medium that in 1945 indelibly confirmed the rumors of war now passes the information on to a new generation—with filmmakers like Spielberg the custodians of an awful legacy.

No wonder then that Spielberg's act of historical reclamation in an age in which Holocaust denial advertises itself in the pages of college newspapers has shielded the director from the usual critical qualifications. *Schindler's List* is overlong, lachrymose, and preachy in its final act; Neesom is a weak centerpiece, soft focus matinee idol photography notwithstanding; the secondary characters are a faceless chorus; and, though this is a story of endurance and survival, a Holocaust movie in which none of the sympathetic characters dies seems to miss the point of its subject (even in a boxcar on the way to Auschwitz, Ben Kingsley's character is blessed by providential Hollywood intervention, never truly at risk).

But whether Spielberg is finally getting his due or just getting undue slack, the power of the film on moviegoers is profound and undeniable: no screening in my experience has elicited so much authentic grief in the audience, not the 'good cry' of a three hankie weepie, the on-cue sniffling during a *Terms of Endearment* or *The Joy Luck Club*, but open weeping and heartbroken sobbing. *Schindler's List* is powerful but not that powerful: it's an occasion to mourn, and, no blasphemy meant, a kind of wailing wall, especially for American Jews, many of whom will bring to the soundtrack cues and visual symbols—a rabbi singing kaddish, Itzhak Perlman's mournful violin, votive candles extinguishing in a wisp of smoke—a constellation of painful memories of private loss.

Schindler's List closes with a frame-breaking coda in which the survivors of 1945 transmute cinematically into their present-day selves and descendants. In the real present now, in color, in Israel, a procession of Schindler's Jews and Spielberg's actors march by to lay a pebble on the grave of Oskar Schindler. The last mourner, standing alone at the foot of the grave in a long shot, is Liam Neesom, head bowed in reverence. One wonders why it is not the director himself at the graveside—a gesture rejected as too Hitchcockian and self-aggrandizing?—until one realizes that Spielberg's homage this time is to history, not film.

LOS ANGELES TIMES, 12/15/93, Calendar/p. 1, Kenneth Turan

The more we know about the Holocaust, the more unknowable it seems to become. Like the mythological fruit of Tantalus, always just out of reach, its essence eludes us, too awful to fully comprehend no matter how passionately we seek to know and understand it.

One thing that does become clear, however, is that to approach the Holocaust from a dramatic point of view, detachment and self-control almost to the point of coldness are essential. The most memorable films about the period, from Alain Resnais' 30-minute "Night and Fog" to Claude Lanzmann's nine-hour-plus "Shoah," share this reserve with such memoirs as Primo Levi's "Survival in Auschwitz." Only through the lens of restraint can those days be effectively seen, as Steven Spielberg, of all people, persuasively demonstrates with the quietly devastating "Schindler's List."

Of all people, because rather than detachment and restraint it is the broad, toys-are-us strokes of obvious heroes and hissable villains that have characterized much of Spielberg's output, up to and including this year's "Jurassic Park." But the director, with personal and emotional ties to the world of Eastern European Jewry, clearly hungered to do something different here.

Not only is the subject matter different for Spielberg, the way it is treated is a departure both for him and for the business as usual standards of major studio releases. While its 3-hour-and-15-minute length is becoming familiar for prestige items, the decision to shoot it almost entirely in black and white is very much not, and neither is its absence of major stars and even actors born in this country.

And "Schindler's List," based on Thomas Keneally's remarkable retelling of a true story, is itself a different kind of Holocaust narrative. For if the pressure of overwhelming death and even the release of miraculous rescue have become standard fare, the dramatic, contradictory personality of Oskar Schindler has never ceased to baffle and astonish observers from his time to ours.

A gambler, war profiteer and lover of alcohol, a convivial sensualist and womanizer who, in Keneally's phrase, considered sexual shame "a concept like existentialism, very worthy but hard to grasp," Schindler the quintessential good German was not the ordinary stuff of heroes. "Though he was Jesus Christ," someone who knew him said, "a saint he wasn't. He was all-drinking, all-black-marketeering, all-screwing," a man whose turn to goodness probably surprised himself most of all. Yet, with a combination of nerve, money, attitude and obstinacy, he personally saved 1,100 Jews from death, and ended up being what Keneally calls probably the only Nazi Party member to be buried in Jerusalem's Mt. Zion cemetery.

Though this film is preeminently Schindler's story, we don't meet him right away. Both Spielberg and thoughtful screenwriter Steven Zaillian ("Searching for Bobby Fischer") are concerned to first set this story in its time and place, to firmly establish the context for what is to come.

Things begin in September, 1939, with Germany's defeat of Poland in two brief weeks. The country's Jew's are ordered to relocate in the venerable town of Krakow, and the chaos that decree caused is shown through arrival scenes at the train station, with Germans brandishing the first of the all-important lists that reappear throughout the film, lists that can literally separate life from death.

Schindler (Irish actor Liam Neeson) is glimpsed initially as a pair of disembodied hands, quietly laying out alternate coats, ties and cuff links, preparing for his own type of campaign. Off to a cabaret frequented by Krakow's Nazi elite, he enters it as an unknown, but by the evening's end, he is the most popular man in the room. Written and filled with characteristic mastery, this scene illuminates in a few brief minutes the core of Schindler's gregarious personality and the frankly irresistible effect he had on other people.

One of those men who distinctively know how to profit from the chaos of war, Schindler has come to Krakow to make his fortune. Simply indifferent to who is a Jew and who is not, he decides to take over a formerly Jewish-owned enamelware factory and hires Itzhak Stern (Ben Kingsley) to run it with cheap Jewish labor while he himself does the important work of schmoozing and bribing the military men in charge of procurement for the German army.

At first everything about Schindler's relationship to the Jews is situational; when he rescues Stern from deportation and death, for instance, his reaction is "What if I'd gotten here five minutes later, then where would I be?" But after witnessing the Germans' brutal liquidation of the ghetto, and the relocation of those that survived in a savage labor camp run by Amon Goeth (Ralph Fiennes), a cold, unblinking sadist, Schindler's attitude is shown to change, and keeping what he territorially considers "his Jews" alive at all costs becomes the focus of his activities.

The touchstone of "Schindler's List" is inevitably the way it depicts the incomprehensible brutality that took place under the Nazi heel. The danger here is to overemphasize, to yield to emotion and underline the horrors, a temptation Spielberg, who gave way to it in "The Color Purple," has managed to resist this time around.

Using real locations whenever possible, collaborating with Polish-born director of photography Janusz Kaminski and editor Michael Kahn and making excellent use of black and white, itself a distancing element, Spielberg understands how important it is to show the casualness of the nightmare. This is a world where unimaginable humiliation was the stuff of routine, where people were murdered as an afterthought and everyone who saw it did no more than blink. Working extensively with a hand-held camera and functioning by his own admission almost as a documentarian, Spielberg has had the nerve to simply let those dreadful scenes play, and as a consequence has created as indelible a picture of the Holocaust as fiction film allows.

In doing this Spielberg has been helped greatly by his collaborators, most notably screenwriter Zaillian, who has both pared down and focused Keneally's text without losing anything essential. And the acting, largely by unfamiliar faces, is always strong and to the point.

Most notable are Kingsley as the self-effacing Stern; British actor Fiennes, who understands how banal great evil can be, and, of course, Neeson. The brio of his performance knits "Schindler's List" together, and no greater compliment can be paid to it than to say its strength and assurance makes this unbelievable story believable and real.

While it would be nice to say that Spielberg's nerve held all the way through this film, that would not quite be true. Just as there are overemphatic moments in John Williams' brooding score, so, too, there are times, especially in Schindler's closing speech, where the desire to give the audience something to hang onto gets the best of the filmmaker's more sober judgment.

But Spielberg is after all a popular filmmaker at his core, and it is hard to begrudge him, or his audience, these softer moments. For never before, except for the marvelous first 40 minutes of "Empire of the Sun," has he come close to this kind of filmmaking. And while "Schindler's List" will perhaps benefit from the surprise that it was made by the director of "Jaws" and "Indiana Jones," the truth is that it's a film any director would be proud to see with his or her name above the title.

NEW LEADER, 2/14-28/94, p. 20, David Bromwich

In Cracow, near the start of the Second World War, two men are talking. One is a Jewish businessman, the other a wealthy German. Why, asks the Jew, should we take you on as a partner? Look around, says the German. You do good work but you can never sell your wares. What do I offer? You supply the product, I supply—Presentation. At the last word, he frames in his hands an unseen object of indescribable potency.

That is not our first glimpse of Oskar Schindler, the hero of Steven Spielberg's new film. In the opening scene, he is dining alone at a fancy club and spots a Wehrmacht officer with a woman at a table nearby. He sends over champagne with his compliments, then joins them as they are joined by a band of officers, and contrives to have his picture taken with the men of power. The shadows of average corruption pass over Schindler at many points; he has a large relish for the smaller vices.

He belongs, in fact, to a type that fascinated a great chronicler of those years, Bertolt Brecht. The character, for Brecht, was always a servant in secret revolt against his masters. Oskar Schindler is a master in secret revolt. Often, in his unaccountable partnership, he will risk his life to save "Schindler's Jews," giving as a reason that it is good business to keep your workers alive.

It is no use fancying that Schindler was a saint. He utterly lacked the moral focus and the premeditation of the saint. A touch of palpable melodrama at the end of the film, where he is made to fall to his knees reproaching himself, wishing he could have saved even one more Jewish life, drops the story down a whole level because it is an irrelevant application for sainthood. We are interested in his story because his goodness has the miraculous quality of an accident. Schindler, if you like, was an odd confluence of moods and events, but his name stands for a blessing to many thousands. Who would pretend to explain him?

The man who desired, for just a moment, the company of the glamorous officers in the club, was doubtless as real as the man who staked high odds in a card game with a military bureaucrat to rescue a worker from the death camp. Losing any of his workers would be a terrible setback to the war effort, he says.

While he gave his protection, the Holocaust was grinding on, and Spielberg has taken this as part of his subject. He draws out an immense scene, with the widest possible resonance of terror, to show the gutting and burning of the ghetto, as if to declare: "Here are the violences, from which no shelter was permanent." Some who have seen the film, and some who never will, say the depiction of the slaughter is a betrayal since it can only serve to reduce the experience to a manageable size. They are certainly right, and right about more than this film. I do not see how any treatment of the subject can avoid a betrayal. Yet the alternative is the omission of any story whatever, as in Paul Celan's "Ice, Eden" or Geoffrey Hill's "September Song." Commit yourself to a story and you are bound to lean on conventions, each of which carries a history of uses and stock responses.

Spielberg in his previous movies was a relentless showman in total command of a metier I would gladly see abolished. He was a technician chiefly of one emotion: fear. You can see what the skill is made of, what it is and is not good for, in his 1971 TV movie *Duel*, an important early success. A big truck hunts a little car up and down a mountain road. In the car is a person too primitive to be supposed a character, and the affective interest is held to zero; but the fear is genuine, it stays and spreads. His later and more expensive films have been no less programmatically morbid. They displayed a command of one new trick: how to shift the weight of the fear with a final climactic rush of relief.

These vices have not mysteriously vanished, changed their valence, or been sublimated in *Schindler's List*. They are traceable elements in the occasional weakness of this film, too. But showmen are rarely as simple as they look. They may busy themselves perfecting machines to squeeze tears out of children, but they are not themselves children; that is why it is fair to resent them. Spielberg, from the first, exhibited a grown-up pride in the sheer craft virtue of a performance every whit as good as the promise of the materials. His plots have been pretexts: plotlines for stringing together squibs, effects, visual or auditory gags and shocks. With *Schindler's List*, however, he found a story of great magnitude that had the added virtue of being true. He commissioned and kept a good script by Steven Zaillian, and he gave the big parts to real actors with complicated faces.

A residue from his truckling earlier practice is the music here by John Williams, a Tiomkin-like, confusing tide of unrealized melody that churns for three hours without respect for the audience's right to sit and think. Another choice is reported to have been made in response to a challenge by Fred Schepisi (director of *The Russia House*), who said "Let me direct the film. You won't have the courage to do it without a crane shot." Spielberg is obedient to the admonition. Not only is there no crane shot, there is hardly a wide-angle shot of any kind. The single exception is a panoramic view of the Cracow ghetto being torn apart by the Nazis, seen from the perspective of Schindler and his mistress on a hill above the town.

Everything else is closeup or medium, and often a hand-held camera shoves the viewer into the tumult of wrecked lives. Yet the impression of a constant and stifling intimacy itself grows quickly conventional. And the result is no less presumptuous than a wide-angle shot, with its supposed illicitness of detachment. A calculable effect of giving up the classical technique is that the film will be easily translatable to TV, where viewers are used to the dizzying crush and press of action 10 or 20 feet away.

These choices troubled me while I was watching *Schindler's List*. But at the heart of the film is a story its makers had the patience not to tamper with; a study of the contrast between Schindler and the work camp commandant, Amon Goeth, who controls the destiny of all the inmates, including Schindler's workers. The camp is a sort of shantytown built by temporary survivors to house themselves, a labyrinth with one mouth and no exit. Goeth commemorates the destruction of the ghetto and the innovation of the slave dwellings in a brief sententious speech about the power to unmake the past. He concludes, in an encomium to himself, "*This* is history." His house overlooking the camp he calls his "villa," and the camera shot from there, to which the film returns unsettlingly, bears the emphasis of a trap shutting again and again.

From his perch, after a restless night, Goeth is free to aim his high-powered rifle and pick off one prisoner after another. He keeps a Jewish woman as his servant—once almost making love to her, before he beats her as he has beaten her before. On the patio of his house, he converses amiably with Schindler, whom he would like to fathom (his interest in getting to the bottom of things is much greater than Schindler's). They talk about life, and about power. "Power," says Schindler, "does not come with saying I punish you. It comes with saying, I pardon you."

Goeth rather likes that idea. He flirts with himself in the mirror, tenderly repeating "I pardon you." He tries it out on the Jewish boy who washed his bathtub with soap instead of lye: "I pardon you." The boy walks away bewildered, a ponderous silence hangs over the camp, then we hear a shot and the boy is dead. One reflects that an order of so much planned violence is at once a cause and a consequence of these struts of casual violence. There is a class of killers that only starts to know itself in time of war. It is not that any man could have become Amon Goeth. It is rather that Goeth, in an ordinary time, would have passed for an ordinary man.

Ralph Fiennes plays this dark and commonplace character with a brave delicacy, at an edge of things where a wrong step would lift him to an unmeant poignance, or plunge him into mere monstrosity. He gained weight for the part—rightly seeing, not in evil itself, but in this example of it a hidden motive of self-indulgence. In Schindler's company, Goeth has a boyish smile, the other side of the snarl the prisoners know so well. He is an irritable, pleasure-loving man, and his talks with Schindler (another hedonist) are a piece of experience one might live long without ever getting to see. They are two halves of the moral world touching in one place; and it happens as unremarkably as two persons laughing at a joke for different reasons.

Jokes, bad jokes, ironic jokes by victims and the cruel jokes of executioners, cruel to the point of opacity—all are much in evidence throughout the film. People who laugh at wretches in anecdote are apt to share the fun when the wretches of actual life are set upon. Coldness to the sources of such laughter may be one token of a character still somehow accessibly generous. And yet, Schindler does craftily share the humor of the wicked. When he hoses the cattle cars of a train to keep the prisoners alive inside, the lolling officers mock him savagely; Schindler, pausing, joins the vulgar laugh, and keeps on running the hose:

Both Fiennes as Goeth and Liam Neeson as Schindler move and talk and appear to think like Germans, each with a different blend of the national traits. In Fiennes you have the hitches, the evasions, the proffered conformities of emphasis, with an uneasy margin for explosive rage. Neeson, on the other hand, commands any scene he is in with a curious largeness of gesture, an assurance that stops just short of arrogance. His gruffness and his fluency lead unexpectedly back to each other. He has the natural dignity unfairly given to the man born bigger than his neighbors.

The real Oskar Schindler could not have done what he did had he not been an attractive, a confident, and a very wealthy man. A 1946 photograph of him with some of "Schindler's Jews" has already acquired a separate fame. He embraces them on both sides, in the manner, strong and somewhat proprietary, that a large man can handle with no loss of warmth. Maybe the impression comes from his having to bend a little to hold them all in the picture. Liam Neeson acts as if he had studied that photograph, and as if he evolved from it a face, a voice, a way of moving native to one person, a life of thoughts partly spoken and thoughts withheld.

NEW STATESMAN & SOCIETY, 2/18/94, p. 33, Jonathan Romney

There is a lot that you have to get through before you can even begin to see *Schindler's List*. First there is the sheer disbelief at the thought that Steven Spielberg, of all directors, has taken on the Holocaust. Then comes the scepticism on reading the Oscar-fuelling adulatory reviews that greeted the film in the US. Once again, before even the first frame of a Spielberg film, you have to contend with its status as phenomenon—it's just that, this time, the stakes are immeasurably higher.

So let me just say that, on many levels, *Schindler's List* gives ample cause to leave your scepticism at the door: it is a very fine film, a manifestly serious one, a film that may not entirely do justice to its subject (as if such were possible), but certainly honours it. I also found it exceptionally moving, and not just because its subject matter automatically hit the distress button. I came out of the film feeling silenced, as if hushed reverence was the only possible response. But that feeling subsides on reflection. I realised that the way *Schindler's List* moved me was akin to the way a funeral ceremony moves you; indeed, this may be the only film ever designed to elicit one single response—that is, mourning.

That purpose becomes clear at the very end of the film, after the story has concluded. The war ends, and we see the last of Oskar Schindler (Liam Neeson), the German businessman who saved more than a thousand Jews from the gas chambers by buying them as workers in his factory. Then the film shifts to the present day, out of fictionalised black-and-white history and into the real and colour. We see Schindler's grave being tenderly decked with commemorative rocks by the very people he saved, now frail and aged but very visibly alive, accompanied by the actors who play their younger selves. It's a brazen *coup de théâtre*, but quite irresistible, a moment of release that allows you to unblock the emotions that the film's monochrome sobriety has until now held back. It's one of many moments in which the film goes full out to impress us with the seriousness and restraint of its intentions, to dispel the slightest suspicion of Hollywood excess.

Spielberg rigorously expunges any sense of Hollywood and its conventions. But where the film nevertheless tends to sanitise is in its regard for beauty (which it seems to see as the "truth"), incarnated in Janusz Kaminski's fine-grained black-and-white photography. In one early scene, sunlight shines in through an office window in a perfect shaft, *just so*, and you realise then that the film will be fatally caught between its aspirations to the real and its love of elegance.

That contradiction comes out most strongly when Spielberg sets out to arrest us with moments of what you could call "true horror". He'll suddenly stop the quasi-documentary flow of images, and make us look straight at a perfectly composed picture of awfulness. In one sequence, a boy takes refuge in a cesspool, only to find other children hiding inside; they tell him to go away, it's *their* place. It's an unthinkable, obscene image, yet Spielberg, even while heightening it, has to make it aesthetic—that is, anaesthetic. The surface of the mire is deadly still, the inside of the box enlarged by cavernous chiaroscuro, the boy isolated by a shaft of light from above. It's horror, but it's poetry also—and we can only feel discomfort at having both.

The same goes for an image that has already become famous. Schindler, mounted on horse back on a hill, looks down on the routs of the Cracow ghetto. It's a horrific scene of turmoil, as the camera scans every way, lost like Schindler's gaze, and ours, in the chaos. Suddenly, one figure is picked out—a little girl in red, her coat the only patch of colour in sight. Already we're blinded by the stridency of symbolism—the little girl is life, about to be snuffed out in this monochrome world. She will occur again—first, as she hides under a bed, with an earnest look of faith in her survival; later, with black inevitability, as a body carried off, in front of a mountain of corpses.

Why is this image so powerful, and why has it become the film's icon, even alluded to discreetly on the poster? Because it makes an immediate, irreducible point—red is also the colour of death; this innocent of innocents is both Red Riding Hood and sacrificial lamb.

But it's so powerful also, I think, because of what it allows us not to see. We're allowed to attach our feeling to this one image, which hides the mountain of nameless, faceless, dehumanised corpses. We're invited to cry for a dead child, and that allows us to elide the unmanageable enormity of death that's actually there in plain sight right behind her. Somehow, that seems part and parcel of the film's project. It is, after all, a film about survival, about deliverance from evil; we accompany those who were spared, rather than those who were not. There's a limit to how far Spielberg can allow himself to go; hence his decision to take on Thomas Keneally's book with its essentially redemptive thrust, rather than any more despairing vision.

Bearing in mind that this is the film's project, *Schindler's List* is remarkably dense and suggestive, even when Spielberg's innate tendency to underline points gets the better of him. He can't quite handle the parallel between Schindler and the SS commandant Amon Goeth, even resorting to matched shots of them in shaving mirrors; it's the exceptionally subtle performances of Liam Neeson and Ralph Fiennes that make it work.

What to make, though, of a film in which the Jews play second fiddle to the sexy man of action who saves them? The film seems to be less in love with Schindler's humanity than his "super-humanity"—his vast energy as an entrepreneur, a deal-doer on a cosmic scale, a very Spielberg of *caritas*. It's no accident that the film is dedicated at the end to Steven Ross, the late president of Time-Warner, nor that Spielberg once ludicrously claimed that if Schindler were alive today, he'd be agency head Mike Ovitz.

Whatever its subject matter, *Schindler's List* is a big-budget spectacle. Whatever the subtler ramifications of the debate on visual versus verbal recounting of the Holocaust, I found myself worried on quite a pragmatic score. I've read the location reports and how many extras were used; and when I saw the Jews herded into cattle trucks, I couldn't help seeing the extras regimented and coaxed by hosts of production runners armed with walkie-talkies. No matter how well they were paid and how lavish the catering, I felt worried by the sense that somehow, however distantly, the same gestures were being repeated. I felt uncomfortable with this reaction, all the stronger for not being entirely rational. Would I have been as worried if I had been watching, not a Hollywood film, but a comparably ambitious theatrical reconstruction staged by a highly austere European director—a Tadeusz Kantor, say? I'm not sure.

It's true, there's nothing conventionally Hollywoodian about *Schindler's List*. But its very seriousness, its monumentality, seems to have been achieved at a certain cost—not of repeating Nazism's actions, which would be a frivolous accusation—but, in some way, of reproducing its production values. This eloquent and absolutely honourable film tries to live down its filmic nature and let us know that the Holocaust was not a movie. But I fear it succeeds at most in telling us that it was simply a *special kind* of movie.

NEW YORK, 12/13/93, p. 82, David Denby

The camera keeps moving in Steven Spielberg's *Schindler's List*, and moving fast, chasing around corners and up stairways, racing across open squares filled with naked and terrified people. Spielberg wants to get it all in, the entire catastrophe of the Polish Jews, and you can feel the obsessional fury in his work, the anguish, the grief passing over into revolt. Working in black-and-white (the Polish-born Janusz Kaminski did the cinematography), Spielberg has given the material the rushed, spasmodic, almost inadvertent look of newsreel footage. Appalling things happen, just *happen*, without warning or emotion—a few pistol shots to the head, from point-blank range, and the bodies fall over, two, three, four people. ... Under the Nazi occupation of

Poland, people are dying everywhere, and the resistance of at least one German, the Catholic Oskar Schindler, seems like a miracle. *Schindler's List* is an emblem of annihilation and of hope at the same time. The film is an astounding achievement.

Spielberg, adapting (with screenwriter Steven Zaillian) Thomas Keneally's documentary novel of 1982, shot the film in the medieval city of Kraków, re-creating the last days of the ghetto. The director re-imagined as well the existence of the bizarrely heroic Schindler, a con man and war profiteer who rescued more than 1,000 Jews from death. Except for one scene at the end that is positively bad, and another that is superbly done but in questionable taste, this 185-minute epic has been made in a style of austere realism—flat, angry, and hardheaded—that is utterly unlike anything Spielberg has attempted before. The teenage film whiz who became a virtuoso of trick lighting and awed moods of portent, the master showman grabbing at the lapels of exaltation, has radically purified his methods without any loss of energy or vividness. The film has a bleak, harsh European look but an entirely American pace.

Schindler's List left me shaken and not a little surprised. I didn't think I could be affected this way anymore, not by this subject. Like many people, I have gone through my share of Holocaust books and movies, and I thought I had learned most of what I had to learn. At the same time, I had become wary of Holocaust art as a temptation to emotional luxuriance and sadomasochistic titillation. Nor was I (or anyone else) willing to indulge a commercial entertainer eager to climb his way into Heaven through an exercise in penitential solemnity.

But Spielberg has converted rather than jettisoned his instincts as an entertainer—it's as if he understood for the first time why God gave him such extraordinary skills. He works with the same kinetic dynamism and weighted sense of movement he's always worked with, but now with a furious sense of purpose as well. (He should get angry more often; rage brings out his intelligence.) He's at the top of his form from the first major scene, when Schindler (Liam Neeson), a failed industrialist who has landed in German-occupied Kraków in 1939, walks into a Polish nightclub, all duded up, and within hours makes friends with every important S.S. officer in the city. As he enters, the camera exuberantly crowds in behind him, like a teenager longing to see the adults at play; the black-and-white images gleam with the glamorous and sinister promise that went out of movies when film stocks turned to color; the editing jumps over irrelevances and mere atmosphere, getting to the heart of the matter.

Schindler the charmer! Schindler the free-spender! A big-bodied man, handsome, tremendously energetic, with natural warmth but limited business acumen (if he were a Jew, you would call him a tummler, the life of the party), he takes over a Jewish-owned factory that the Nazis have put out of business. Secretly raising money from Jewish backers, he employs Jews from the ghetto as workers and turns out field-kitchen equipment for the German army. His right-hand man is a Jewish accountant named Itzhak Stern (Ben Kingsley), who actually runs the business and becomes Schindler's collaborator and finally, grudgingly, his friend. Schindler doesn't pay his workers, but he rescues them from the "selections" (Auschwitz is only 45 minutes to the west) by turning the flute players into metalworkers, the rabbis into hinge-makers. They are such good workers, how can he bear to lose them? He wants to get rich, and as fast as possible.

I think it's fair to say that the filmmakers identify less with the Jews in the ghetto heading for death than with the vivacious Schindler, whose drive and optimism have an almost American verve (the movie is dedicated to the late Steve Ross). But they don't slight the Jews either: *Schindler's List* moves simultaneously toward life and toward death. As Schindler wheels and deals, and bribes the S.S. with women and black-market goods, the Jews are herded about, stripped for inspection, harassed, humiliated, summarily shot, often on a whim. The killing goes on all the time, without reason. (At Auschwitz, the Italian chemist and writer Primo Levi heard an S.S. guard say, "Here is no 'why.'") Spielberg's staging of these random incidents, which sometimes take place in the back or the side of a busy frame as other Jews, hoping to avoid trouble, scurry along the street, has such an unemphatic, rough, scrambling quality—so intimate an acquaintance with reality—that one is stunned every time. Only Itzhak Perlman's impassioned playing on the soundtrack brings solace.

Apart from Stern and a few minor characters, the Jews, as Spielberg portrays them, are more desperate than noble, and not highly individualized. I think I understand why: In Holocaust narrative, you don't want too much plot, too much "art." Normal narrative methods would feel trite, an imposition of the banal and the reassuring on the insupportable truth of the situation. (The best Holocaust books are such plainly written memoirs as Levi's *Survival in Auschwitz*.) And for the same reason, you don't want the story of, say, a single family, with Sam Wanamaker and Irene Worth as the grandparents, Barbara Hershey and Elliott Gould as the parents, and two of Spielberg's kids as the children. Dear God! Spielberg was right to stay away from familiar stars, right to use so many unknown actors, many of them the Israeli children of survivors. The faces are authentically Eastern European. We get to know many of those faces; we see the people working, taking care of their families, hiding, pricking their fingers with pins and smearing the blood into their ashen cheeks so as to appear healthy (and not be sent to Auschwitz). They are a community, a people.

The direction is marvelously clean—decisive, forceful, active—and though every scene is suffused with tragic emotion, nothing is lingered over. Spielberg has miles to go before he sleeps: He wants to capture the common catastrophe in all its physical bitterness. And most strongly he evokes the uncertainty that is the essence of fear. The chief dispenser of terror is the S.S. officer Amon Goeth (Ralph Fiennes), who shows up in 1942 to build a labor camp at Plaszow, outside the city, and to prepare for the end. Goeth arrives in a foul mood; he has a cold. Fiennes, an English TV and theater actor, has a dyspeptic, malevolent gaze and a soft body that seems to be pouring out its wastes. He is a great, terrifying actor.

Poor Goeth! The annihilation of the Jews wearies him; he expects people to sympathize with his difficulties. Gone are the forties-Warners clichés of thin-lipped, intellectual murderers. Goeth and his colleagues are not ascetic, duty-bound sadists but noisy, sensual, drunkenly corrupt sadists. They laugh a lot, sleep with their mistresses, take bribes. In a terrifying scene, they burn the corpses of massacred Jews in a flaming pit, and they carry on in mock dismay as if frightened at a horror movie. At the railroad yard, Schindler, in a futile gesture of sympathy, hoses down the cattle cars filled with terrified and thirsty Jews, and the S.S. become uproarious. Doesn't he get it? Life is over for these people. The Nazis' gaiety is perhaps the most revolting sight in the movie. Dramatizing this intellectual and moral squalor, Spielberg seems almost to have transformed himself into a European satirist like Brecht or George Grosz. The strokes are sure and brief. But then he goes beyond disgust. Goeth actually becomes an interesting and suffering man. He shoots Jews from his balcony, for sport; but as the war goes on and the atrocities mount, he looks miserable in his own body, and he disintegrates. The role is a study of what happens to a man operating entirely without limits.

Why does Schindler not fall apart, too? And where does his virtue come from? He is not a man of high moral or religious principle. Yet he goes from wanting the Jewish slave laborers to stay alive so he can make money from them to actively keeping them alive. He perpetrates outrageous falsehoods and spends his fortune bribing the S.S. In Schindler, corruption becomes an embrace of life, an overflow of goodwill toward everyone. He's a bit of an oddity—a bon vivant and a sensualist who nevertheless has a streak of natural piety—but in wartime, as Marcel Ophuls suggested in *The Sorrow and the Pity*, it's generally the oddballs who resist evil. One of the few failings of *Schindler's List*, however, is that Schindler's transformation from profiteer to saint isn't made psychologically clear. Liam Neeson puts his bulky body and leathery voice into the performance, but as the film goes on, he gives this decent man a look of increasing bewilderment, as if Schindler were amazed not only by the Final Solution but by his own acts.

A few scenes are exciting in a conventional way—for instance, when some of the children escape deportation to Auschwitz by hiding in latrines and under beds. Later, Schindler's women workers are sent to the camp by mistake, and Spielberg holds us in suspense. Will the naked women, herded into a chamber, be gassed or given a shower? This, I think, is an error in judgment. The scene is extremely well edited (by Michael Kahn), but we don't want to be played with this way. Most serious of all: At the end of the war, when Schindler says farewell to the Jews he has saved, Spielberg lights his speech and the tearful emotions that follow with an inspirational glow. For the first time, he loses his scrappy, edgy style and falls into bathos. But it's just a single scene.

Someone will inevitably say that in concentrating on a "righteous Gentile," the movie, though factual, is indulging a fantasy, since the overall truth for the European Jews was death. But we have become so conversant with evil in the twentieth century that we are in danger of accepting it as inevitable. Altruism, in its rarity, may now be a more original and challenging subject. And no one could say of *Schindler's List* that its director faces evil with anything less than the most extreme outrage and contempt.

Against all odds, Spielberg the box-office champ has made the most demanding and emotionally overpowering American movie in years.

NEW YORK POST, 12/15/93, p. 33, Michael Medved

Over the years, Hollywood has produced countless films that portray the seductive power of evil. "Schindler's List" represents something new and extraordinary: in unforgettable terms, it depicts the seductive power of goodness.

The film focuses on one of the most perplexing unanswered questions in the history of the Holocaust: Why did greedy, opportunistic industrialist Oskar Schindler—a hedonist, bon vivant, inveterate womanizer and member of the Nazi party—risk everything he had in order to rescue some 1,100 Polish Jews from certain death at Auschwitz?

Even after watching this remarkable film, you may not be able to explain why he did what he did, but you will believe every moment of his on-screen transformation. Liam Neeson uncannily conveys the man's cunning and charisma; the character he creates is a flawed, flamboyant, touchingly vulnerable figure, without the slightest hint of papier mache heroics.

Ben Kingsley is similarly impressive as accountant Itzhak Stern, who provided the organizational genius behind Schindler's schemes to use Jewish slave labor to manufacture pots and pans that he sold at a huge profit to the German army. Along the way, Stern's fierce dignity begins to touch his boss' conscience and to inspire his compassion for the prison camp inmates whose work is making him rich.

The actor who wins third billing in this brilliant but largely unknown cast is also this picture's third likely Oscar nominee: British newcomer Ralph Fiennes, who makes an overwhelming impression as Amon Goeth, the monstrous SS commandant of Plaszow labor camp.

Of all the literally thousands of performers who have previously played Nazi war criminals, none has ever made their cruelty so chillingly believable—and so nearly comprehensible. Fiennes shows us a fleshly narcissist not all that different from Schindler himself, who reacts to the same hellish situation—by abandoning himself to diabolical evil, while his opposite number is drawn slowly, ineluctably toward decency.

With all the well-deserved praise that will be heaped upon this picture—and upon its courageous creator, Steven Spielberg—three common misconceptions may discourage prospective moviegoers, and they should be addressed here:

- No, it is not for one moment boring—despite nearly three hours of running time. The script (by Steven Zaillian, who also wrote "Awakenings," and wrote and directed "Searching for Bobby Fischer") is so well-constructed, and the action is so perfectly paced, that this is not only one of the best, but also one of the most gripping pictures of the year.

- No, the black-and-white photography is never a drawback, and in fact provides the picture with an immediacy and authenticity that sets it apart from all previous dramatizations of the Holocaust. When Spielberg injects brief flashes of color—showing the flames from Sabbath candles, or a little girl in a scarlet coat who also plays an important role in the heart-felt Thomas Keneally novel that inspired the film—the impact is breathtaking.

- No, the film is not depressing, and the moments most certain to produce tears are not those depicting the horrors of Hitler's inferno, but the scenes that show unshakable humanity and heart-stopping courage in the midst of a living hell.

This underlying message of compassion and renewal makes this, after all, a most appropriate film for the holiday season. In fact, it's a film for all seasons. In the past, I haven't been one of Steven Spielberg's biggest fans, but his astonishing achievement here merits more than a glowing review; it deserves a thank-you note.

NEWSDAY, 12/15/93, Part II/p. 59, Jack Mathews

A few years ago, many people in Hollywood were chuckling over the comment by Steven Spielberg that he had only read Alice Walker's "The Color Purple" because it was a little book, meaning that there weren't so darn many pages to muddle through.

The admission confirmed what most of his detractors had felt all along, that the wunderkind of the box office, a genius at creating film action and manipulating audience emotions, was an intellectual lightweight when dealing with real subjects, and they could only shudder at the prospect of his doing to Thomas Keneally's historical novel "Schindler's List" what he did to "The Color Purple."

With today's arrival in theaters of "Schindler's List," the true story of a German industrialist (played by Liam Neeson) who moved more than 1,300 Jews from the Nazi death camps, it is as if no one else could have done it. The three-hour and 15-minute, black-and-white film is a masterwork, measured against any standard, and by far the most important movie event of 1993.

If Spielberg is not rewarded with an Academy Award for this piece, his "Color Purple" fans can break into their old "it's a conspiracy" refrain and we can all sing along.

Spielberg said from the beginning that he intended to make "Schindler's List" for himself, which we took to mean he would not compromise the material in order to please the broadest possible audience, an urge as strong in him as a cat having to scratch a couch. He does overplay one late emotional scene, but it is an otherwise remarkably unsentimental picture.

In retrospect, it would have been difficult even for the old Spielberg to treat the Holocaust as entertainment, but there was no way of anticipating how profoundly honest and blunt a story he would tell. Using hand-held cameras for almost half the action, Spielberg has given his camp and Jewish ghetto scenes the look of a documentary and intercut them in such seamless fashion with the dramatic story that you feel you are being sucked in as a heartsick witness to a man-made catastrophe.

I cannot recall a fictional film where death was treated with such jolting realism. The random murders of Jews, most of them shot in back of the head, occur full-on in front of the camera, and the victims' bodies hurtle to the ground like sacks of wheat dropped from a truck. Blood spurts from their wounds with each weakening heartbeat and spreads in pools around them.

There is no campfire story-telling security to this horror story, which was adapted by Steven Zaillian from the novel. Spielberg knew that for us to be truly revolted by the Holocaust, we had to see it for ourselves. He also knew that what would elevate the film, and keep the ghouls away, was that the madness of Nazi anti-Semitism was counter-balanced by the humanity of one German who worked against it.

Oskar Schindler is a wonderfully rich and ambivalent character, an apolitical hustler when we meet him, an opportunist wanting only to use the war to make money and live the good life, which he defines as having fine clothes, fine food and wine and plenteous pretty women.

Neeson, the tall engaging Irish actor who stands out in any crowd, makes Schindler immediately likable, even while shmoozing the Nazis in a night-club and cheating, in earnest, on his wife (Caroline Goodall). This is a story not about a saint, though the Schindler Jews and their descendants (6,000 in all) may disagree, but about an ordinary man turned extraordinary by events that pushed the boundaries of his conscience.

With remarkable economy, Spielberg sets his story up for us, showing us how Schindler worked himself into the trust of powerful Nazis, found a source of black market goods (to be used as bribes), and talked dispossessed Jews into financing and running a factory that would, with a pool of low-paid Jewish workers, produce enamel pots and parts for the German military.

The first section of the film deals with the contrast between the lives of Schindler, with all of his privileges, and the Polish Jews, who were, in March, 1940, being ripped from their homes and herded into a 16-square block ghetto near Kraków.

Spielberg accomplishes this with the first of several sequences of intercut scenes, moving back and forth from Schindler dressing for a night on the town, and Jews, rich and poor, being checked in by Nazi clerks at the entrance to the ghetto.

Later, Spielberg uses the technique to switch the focus of the story to the contrast between Schindler, the decent German, and Amon Goeth (Ralph Fiennes), the sadistic commander of a Kraków labor tamp. A fascinating relationship develops between these two men, kindred spirits as hustlers and womanizers, but moral opposites nonetheless.

Fiennes gives a chilling performance as a man taking the opportunity war provides some people to behave as righteous sociopaths. He kills for sport, pot-shooting camp internees from his bedroom balcony between morning stretches, and executes his Jewish help for using the wrong chemical while scrubbing his bathtub.

While talking of Jews as if they were mice, Goeth is driven by his attraction to his Jewish maid (Embeth Davidtz), and, like the preacher who took Sadie Thompson, has to punish her for his desires.

"They cast a spell on you, you know?" Goeth says to another officer. "It's like a virus."

Abiding this man is no small task, but Schindler's instincts are perfect. It is Goeth, after Hitler orders the extermination of all Jews in Poland, who helps get the people on Schindler's list routed to his new factory in Czechoslovakia.

There are other strong performances here, chief among them the remarkably balanced portrait of restraint and fear accomplished by Ben Kingsley, as Itzhak Stern, the quietly brave accountant who turned Schindler's factory into a haven for doomed Jews, and triggered Schindler's conscience. If you're looking for pure heroism, I nominate Stern.

But the star of this enterprise is Spielberg, who had the vision and, let's face it, the power to bring the story to the screen in such unblinking terms. The only cinematic trick from the director who gave us a man-hating shark and a peace-loving alien in his best previous movies, is a little girl who appears in the midst of a Nazi purge wearing a red coat.

As the girl emerges from a building, we and Schindler spot her at the same time, from his vantage point on horseback on a hill above the ghetto. She is like a muted light moving through a cold gray diorama, burning into our minds that those are individual lives being lost around her, and the horror we see in Schindler's eyes, as they follow her through the street, signals the change about to come over him.

It is a daring stunt, laying color over black and white images, and it does, for a blink, remind us we're watching a movie. But the gamble pays off. Nothing after that can possibly be seen as abstract, and a later scene where the girl reappears is one we will never forget.

Whatever else Spielberg does in the rest of his amazing career, 1993 is going to be hard to top. First "Jurassic Park" sets the world record for box office grosses, now this, perhaps the strongest film ever made about the 20th Century's darkest event.

NEWSWEEK, 12/20/93, p. 113, David Ansen

There was a man named Oskar Schindler, a German Catholic businessman and confidant of the Nazis, who during the Holocaust protected and rescued some 1,200 Jews from almost certain death. In Poland today, where Schindler once ran his profitable enamelware factory during World War II, there are fewer than 4,000 Jews left. Around the world there are more than 6,000 descendants of the "Schindler Jews" he saved. But to this day nobody can say with certainty what made this unlikely hero risk his life when so many others failed to lift a finger. A hedonist in love with cognac, night life and motorcycles, a womanizer incorrigibly unfaithful to his wife, a war profiteer, gambler, black-market dealer and heavy drinker, this gregarious, urbane and spoiled young man may have been motivated by nothing more complicated than simple decency, but then decency was neither simple nor easy to find in a German businessman in Eastern Europe between 1939 and 1945. To any sane observer there has always been an unfathomable mystery about the systematic evil the Nazi regime perpetrated—like a moral black hole, it seems to defy the laws of nature. But sometimes the good is equally mysterious. The conscience of Oskar Schindler is a wonderful conundrum.

Another unlikely man, Steven Spielberg, has chosen Schindler to be the vehicle through which he tells the story of the Holocaust. "Schindler's List," adapted by Steven Zaillian from Thomas Keneally's prize-winning 1982 nonfiction novel, is not a movie anyone could have predicted from the most commercially successful filmmaker in the world (his 15 movies have grossed more than $4 billion). Following close on the trampling heels of "Jurassic Park"—the world's all-time box-office champ—the contrast couldn't be more startling. It's not just that the subject matter is a departure for a man renowned for his lyrical and rollicking boys' adventures; after all, he did make "The Color Purple" and "Empire of the Sun." But Spielberg's very nature as a filmmaker has been transformed; he's reached within himself for a new language, and without losing any of his innate fluency or his natural-born storytelling gift, he's found a style and a depth of feeling that will astonish both his fans and those detractors who believed he was doomed to permanent adolescence. More than three hours long, shot almost entirely in black and white, with a cast filled with little-known Polish and Israeli actors, "Schindler's List" plunges us into the nightmare of the Holocaust with newsreel-like urgency—and amazing restraint.

So often when Hollywood directors pump themselves up to make a major statement, their filmmaking becomes as inflated and ponderous as a politician's rhetoric. Spielberg *deflates* his style: gone are the majestic boom shots, the pearly-slick sheen, the push-button sense of wonder. Maybe the biggest surprise is that Spielberg resists the easy, bludgeoning sentimentality that is the peril of films about the destruction of the Jews. This movie will shatter you, but it earns its tears honestly. His impeccable craft (aided by Michael Kahn's superb editing and Janusz Kaminski's starkly beautiful cinematography) holds you riveted for 196 minutes. But this time the abundant virtuosity is in the service of a harrowing authenticity.

Spielberg knew instinctively that his old methods were inadequate to tell this story. "I have a pretty good imagination. I've made a fortune off my imagination. My imagination is dwarfed by the events of 1940 to 1945. Just dwarfed," Spielberg told *Newsweek*'s Cathleen McGuigan at his East Hampton, N.Y. summer home. "And so I couldn't imagine the Holocaust until I went to Cracow, and to Auschwitz-Birkenau for the first time." His primary goal was to "bear witness" to the *Shoah* (the annilation). And I didn't want a style that was similar to anything I had done before. First of all, I threw half my toolbox away. I canceled the crane. I tore out the dolly track. I didn't really plan a style. I didn't say I'm going to use a lot of handheld camera. I simply tried to pull the events closer to the audience by reducing the artifice."

Zaillian's ambitious, sinewy screenplay artfully balances Schindler's story with the larger chronicle of the fate of the Jews of Cracow, all the while rarely straying from the facts documented in Keneally's extraordinary book. In several ways, the movie makes Schindler—played with gruff, complex grace by Irish actor Liam Neeson—a less heroic, more ambitious figure than he was in the novel, in which the reader knows immediately of Oskar's good deeds. The Oskar we first encounter—a cagey, manipulative bon vivant buttering up Nazi officers in a nightclub for the good of his business ventures—is a man on the make, using the war to make his fortune. But unlike some Germans, he is not averse to using Jews as well to pad his pockets. He welcomes their investment in his factory and is happy to employ their slave labor. He's a great front man; it's the Jew Itzhak Stern (Ben Kingsley), his accountant, who has the real savvy to run the business. (Though Stern is real, his movie character is a composite of several *Schindlerjuden*, or "Schindler's Jews.")

There is nothing clear-cut about Oskar's transformation into a man of virtue. In Neeson's subtle, lived-in performance, he's a man who backs into heroism almost against his will, his cupidity inconvenienced by his conscience. But from a hillside, where he is riding horses with his mistress, he is a witness to the Nazis' vicious destruction of the ghetto, and he begins to sense that the men and women working in his factory will have no future unless he does something about it. Spielberg's depiction of the murderous day and night when the Germans liquidate Cracow's ghetto has a sickening reality. The accumulation of details—the women rolling their jewels into bread to swallow; a hospital nurse mercifully poisoning her terminally ill Jewish patients to save them from a crueler death by machine-gun fire—will lodge in your mind forever.

When the drama moves to the Plaszow Forced Labor Camp, the film introduces Commandant Amon Goeth. The sadistic Nazi is a familiar movie trope, but Ralph Fiennes, the brilliant young English actor who plays him, finds fresh horrors that owe nothing to Hollywood clichés. Goeth is a man of cool monstrosity—to start his day, he picks off Jewish workers with a rifle from his balcony. The flicker of insecurity that Fiennes finds in the character makes him all the more frightening. Spielberg, who gave us cartoon Nazis in Indiana Jones movies, has found a new set of eyes. The dazzling fantasist has become an unblinking reporter.

Confronted with the horrors of Auschwitz-Birkenau, the ghastly sight of children hiding from capture in outhouse cesspools, Spielberg never loses his nerve or his tact. "Schindler's List" doesn't succumb to melodrama, or to hagiography. The first word we hear spoken is "Name," as Jews railroaded into Cracow disembark from a train and give their identities to government functionaries. It is a film filled throughout with names and faces—a testimony to the 6 million Jews who died, and the 1,200 who survived because of Oskar Schindler. No one film can begin to convey the totality of that annihilating chapter in history. But no dramatic film, from Hollywood or anywhere, has told so much so eloquently.

Spielberg grew up, in Cincinnati, Ohio, Haddonfield, N.J., and Phoenix, Ariz., hearing stories from his relatives about the mass extermination of his people. His grandmother gave English lessons to an Auschwitz survivor who taught the young boy numbers using the numerical brand the Nazis had tattooed into his arm. But he never heard the word "Holocaust" until he was in college. "My parents referred to it as 'those murdering sons of bitches.' Those murdering sons of bitches broke that Jewish pianist's fingers so he could never play the piano again."

When he was 7, the family moved to Arizona from New Jersey, abandoning their observant Orthodox ways. "I didn't have any Jewish friends growing up in Phoenix. I felt like I was the only Jewish kid in my high school." Eager to assimilate ("I would always try and negotiate for conformity"), Spielberg remembers feeling "ashamed because I was living on a street where at Christmas, we were the only house with nothing but a porch light on." He'd try, in vain, to get his father to put up a red light. But he never experienced anti-Semitism until the family moved to Saratoga, Calif., when his father got a job with a Palo Alto computer company. It was Spielberg's senior year in high school, and he encountered kids who would cough the word Jew in their hands when they passed him, beat him up and throw pennies at him in study hall. "It was my six months of personal horror. And to this day I haven't gotten over it nor have I forgiven any of them."

Until now, his Judaism was never touched upon in his work. The young hero of "E.T.," growing up in a broken home and feeling like an alien himself, may have been a metaphorical stand-in for Spielberg, but ethnicity was left far out of the picture. The fantasies he concocted in his spectacular career were the ultimate triumph of assimilation: he colonized the world with his imagination.

"Schindler's List" lurked in the back of Spielberg's mind for a decade, ever since Sidney Sheinberg, MCA/Universal's president, bought it for him in 1982. "I wasn't ready to make it in '82 because I wasn't mature enough. I wasn't emotionally resolved with my life. I hadn't had children. I really hadn't seen God until my first child was born. A lot of things happened that were big deals in my personal life that I didn't give interviews about. But they changed me as a person and as a filmmaker. And they led me to say I want to do it now, I need to make it right now."

His longtime producer Kathleen Kennedy thinks his second marriage, to Kate Capshaw (who converted to Judaism), has brought a new balance to his life. "He has a personal confidence now and isn't trying to prove anything to himself anymore." "I wanted to tell people who had told me to be ashamed of my Jewishness," Spielberg says, "that I was so proud to be a Jew."

His urgency to make the movie was spurred by the "ethnic cleansing" in Bosnia and other atrocities. "It was a combination of things: my interest in the Holocaust and my horror at the symptoms of the Shoah again happening in Bosnia. And again happening with Saddam Hussein's attempt to eradicate the Kurdish race. We were racing over these moments in world history that were exactly like what happened in 1943."

Keneally had been the first writer to attempt a screenplay from his own book. But his effort was the length of a mini-series. Kurt Luedtke ("Out of Africa") worked on it for three years before throwing in the towel. At various times both Sydney Pollack and Martin Scorsese considered directing "Schindler," and it was Scorsese who brought in Zailian (writer-director of "Searching for Bobby Fischer") to attempt to crack the book. When Spielberg finally decided he must make it, he paid his first visit to Auschwitz-Birkenau, His reaction—anger—surprised him. "I was deeply pissed off. I was all ready to cry in front of strangers, and I didn't shed a tear. I was just boiling inside. Freezing day, and I was so hot. I felt so helpless, that there was nothing I could do about it. And yet I thought, well, there is something I can do about it. I can make 'Schindler's List.' I mean, it's not going to bring anybody back alive, but it maybe will remind people that another Holocaust is a sad possibility."

Shooting in Poland, in the haunted places where these events occurred (Schindler's factory still stands), was the most intense professional experience of his life, and it was made more bizarre by the fact that he had to complete post-production work on "Jurassic Park" from Poland. How can I reconcile dinosaurs and the Holocaust? he kept asking himself. "It didn't work in my mind." Two or three times a week he would receive transmissions beamed by satellite from the United States to the huge parabolic dish in the front yard of his Cracow house. After 12-hour workdays on the set, he'd come home to his wife and five kids—and after dinner and bedtime stories he'd trudge to his monitor to focus on smoothing out the jerky dinosaur movements. "I was not in a mind-set to be involved with 'Jurassic Park' but I had a duty to myself and to the special effects."

Spielberg was not prepared for the kind of personal reaction "Schindler" evoked. "I was frightened every day ... I sound pretentious, like some kind of European artist or something. Because I've not had personal experiences in the making of my films. A lot of my films have been made for you, just like somebody makes a hamburger just the way you want it. That's been my modus operandi. Now I go to Poland and I get hit in the face with my personal life. My upbringing. My Jewishness. The stories my grandparents told me about the Shoah. And Jewish life came pouring back into my heart. I cried all the time. I never cry on sets making films. I've often protected myself with the movie camera. The camera has always been my golden shield against things really reaching me. I put that thing in front of my face, it stops the bullet. I can't tell you the shots I did on 'Schindler's List' or why I put the camera in a certain place. I re-created these events, and then I experienced them as any witness or victim would have. It wasn't like a movie.

Every single day was like waking up and going to hell, really. There were no jokes on the set. No funny outtakes to show at the wrap party. Twice in the production I called Robin Williams just to say, Robin, I haven't laughed in seven weeks. Help me here. And Robin would do 20 minutes on the telephone."

In one of the most painful scenes in the film, the inmates of the labor camp are rounded up, forced to strip and to run past doctors. We see women pricking their fingers for blood to rub some pink into their cheeks, for those who look healthy will be allowed to stay and work. The rejects will be sent to Auschwitz and the ovens. The sequence took three days to shoot, and after the first day Spielberg was "trying to find a way not to come back to work." The scene was hard on everyone involved. "None of us looked. I said to the guy pulling the focus on a very difficult shot, 'Do you think you got that?' And he said, 'I don't know, I wasn't looking.' And when the man on focus doesn't look, you know, it's interesting."

Spielberg's actors recall his energy, his spontaneity, his calm professionalism and, in Ben Kingsley's words, his "lovely childish enthusiasm." To prepare Neeson to play Schindler, Spielberg gave the actor home movies of Steve Ross, the charismatic late head of Time Warner, and a kind of father figure to the director. Ross, to whom the film is dedicated, became Spielberg's private prototype of the movie's hero. "I think Schindler loved people. I've often said that he and my late great friend Steve Ross had a lot of similarities." Neeson ultimately used some of Ross's expansive body language in his portrayal.

The Poles generously welcomed the movie people to Cracow, but there were a few ugly incidents. In a hotel bar, an old German-speaking businessman approached Israeli actor Michael Schneider and asked him whether he was a Jew. Yes, the actor replied, and the man drew a finger across his neck and pulled an imaginary noose above his throat, saying, "Hitler should have finished the job." An enraged Kingsley had to be restrained before a brawl ensued.

Spielberg found when his German actors put on Nazi uniforms, he became unintentionally hostile toward them. But that changed the day the company had a Passover Seder. "All the German actors showed up. They put on yarmulkes and opened up Haggadas, [the Seder text] and the Israel actors moved right next to them and began explaining it to them. And this family of actors sat around and race and culture were just left behind."

These scenes from his four months in Poland keep haunting Spielberg; he's finding it hard to come down from the experience. "Schindler's List" has forced him to re-examine his life as a filmmaker. "My problem is I have too much of a command of the visual language. I know how to put a Cecil B. DeMille image on the screen. I can do a Michael Curtiz. If my mojo's working I can put one tenth of a David Lean image on the screen. But I've never really been able to put my image on the screen, with the exception of 'E.T.' perhaps. And certainly not until 'Schindler' was I really able to not reference other filmmakers. I'm always referencing everybody. I didn't do any of that on this movie."

Spielberg talked for more than four hours, but he wasn't satisfied that he'd said everything he wanted to say. A few days later he called back with a final thought. "I came to realize, the reason I came to make the movie, is that I have never in my life told the truth in a movie. My effort as a moviemaker has been to create something that couldn't possibly happen. So people could leave their lives and have an adventure and then come back to earth and drive home. That was one of the things I thought: if I'm going to tell the truth for the first time, it should be about this subject. Not about divorce or parents and children, but about this."

And he did. When you drive home from "Schindler's List," you have seen all the truth you can handle, and are grateful for it.

SIGHT AND SOUND, 3/94, p. 46, Philip Strick

September, 1939. As Polish Jews are rounded up by the invading German forces, Austrian entrepreneur Oskar Schindler comes to Krakow in search of gain. Making himself popular with the local Nazi leaders, he takes over a confiscated enamelware business (renamed 'Emalia') and secures the right to supply crockery to the German army. Staffing the factory with unpaid Jewish workers, he quickly achieves huge profits. His accountant, Itzhak Stern, discreetly turns Emalia into a haven for Jewish refugees. By March 1941, when all Jews are forced into a ghetto in the city's Podgorze district, Schindler is enjoying a lavish lifestyle; bribing his Nazi contacts with black market goods, he is able to ensure that his Jewish work force continues to service Emalia. Even so, one of his employees, Lowenstein, is shot in the street, and Schindler personally has to rescue Stern from a train bound for a concentration camp.

In the winter of 1942, SS Commandant Amon Goeth arrives in Krakow to set up the Plaszow forced labour camp. Orders are received to destroy the ghetto; the survivors are herded into Plaszow. Horrified at the brutality as well as at his empty factory, Schindler cultivates a friendship with Goeth, persuading him to authorise the building of a sub-camp at Emalia itself so that production can be resumed. Pouring his profits into gifts to Goeth and his superiors, he 'buys' the safety of individual Jews from Goeth's murderous outbursts, although aware of the risk of arrest for such illegal activity. Particularly sympathetic towards the plight of Helen Hirsch, Goeth's young housekeeper, Schindler tries to talk Goeth into more lenient behaviour, with erratic results. Goeth allows Schindler to provide water for a trainload of doomed prisoners, and later comes to his defence when he is arrested for kissing a Jewish girl, at his birthday party. Schindler is cautioned and released.

In 1944, when the ashes from 10,000 corpses, exhumed and burned, drift down on the city like snow, and orders come for the Plaszow Jews to be taken to Auschwitz, Schindler decides it is time to leave Krakow. He and Stern create a list of 'essential' workers, and he negotiates with Goeth, using suitcases of cash, for the transfer of 1,000 Jews to a new factory at Brünnlitz on the Czechoslovakian border. They include Helen Hirsch, won from the reluctant Goeth in a deciding game of cards. In error, the women on Schindler's list are delivered to Auschwitz, but Schindler achieves the impossible and they are transferred safely to Brünnlitz. Settled at the factory, Schindler ensures that for seven months his work-force produces nothing of any value to the German army. At the war's end he is broke but, presented with a token of gratitude by his *Schindlerjuden*, he weeps that if he hadn't wasted so much money he could have saved more lives. Leaving his workers to their new freedom, he flees to the West.

With his final colour-restored sequence at Schindler's graveside on Mount Zion in Jerusalem, Steven Spielberg partners a number of the actors in his film with the survivors they have been impersonating, paying homage together to the man who saved their lives. It forms an unsettling epilogue. Here, for example, is the girl whose kiss nearly signalled the end of her benefactor, accompanying like a wraith the mature woman she was to become. Here is the small boy who narrowly avoided the death-trucks by hiding in a latrine, demurely leading his laundered and somehow depersonalised elder self. And here is the elegant Emilie Schindler pushing in a wheelchair what the passage of 50 years has made of her. Forced by such alliances to accept what we may have preferred to doubt—that the film has been, if not a direct re-enactment of the truth, then at least a kind of consensus of fact—we might be persuaded (as the director clearly intends that we should) that Spielberg, the great manipulator, has with this project at last met his match, and that Schindler's story has manipulated him.

Schindler's List does not in fact, look like a Spielberg film at all, although various rehearsals for it could be selected in hindsight from *Close Encounters, Empire of the Sun*, or even the third Indiana Jones adventure, with Schindler as another Nazi-hating specialist in last-minute rescue. At many points, if the film stock had been grainier and some scratches added, it could pass for newsreel, the kind of footage that the Germans frequently, in a spirit of detached enquiry, accumulated for themselves. Deliberately discarding his classy crane-shots in favour of the haphazard urgency of the hand-held camera, Spielberg either mingles us with his crowds in panic-inducing proximity or provides vistas where so much is happening, so many details of independent action are almost unobserved, that his audience can only be aghast at the enormity of the event, unable to imagine the logistics of its fakery.

Filming in monochrome, Spielberg honourably evokes the immediacy of post-war European cinema, particularly the films of Munk, Aleksander Ford, and the seminal concentration-camp drama *The Last Stage*. Obvious contexts are provided by *A Generation*, Kanal and the more recent *Korczak* (and Wajda's influence is duly acknowledged), although the formality of the Brünnlitz scenes in *Schindler's List* acquires by contrast a mood of Russian expressionism, rather too worthy for comfort. This almost turns to farce when Schindler crumples into tears, overwhelmed by a mound of sympathisers, but is narrowly rescued by the superb shot of his workers' faces reflected in the windows of his departing car. After this, Spielberg's return to colour seems a vulgarisation, such has been the eloquence of Janusz Kaminski's rich, tonal compositions among the cruel grey winters and savagely bleached summers of an appalling history. Secure from any accusation of prettifying the Holocaust, Spielberg runs only the risk of an allowable excess of sentimentality at its memory.

The authenticity of Spielberg's staging has three debatable flaws. The first, of course, is his use of a sudden detail of colour to pick out the red coat of a child who wanders among the carnage as the ghetto is destroyed, an event observed by Schindler from a hillside above the city. Since the quality of the whole celluloid image has to change in order to accommodate this touch of crimson, it seems ponderous, a purported insight into Schindler's normally enigmatic viewpoint that is both inconsistent (we, not Schindler, get a closeup of the little girl hiding under a bed) and unnecessary, since she could have been rendered just as noticeable by, say, a scarf or a hairstyle. When her body, still in red, is carried past under Schindler's gaze, her iconic fate becomes almost demeaning to the many other victims we have seen.

Similar editorialising is indicated by the intercutting between Schindler's birthday party, a Jewish marriage ceremony in one of the camp huts, and the attack by Goeth on his housekeeper in the wine-cellar. These three separate events (although Goeth manages somehow to be present at two of them) each have a complexity that gains nothing from interruption by images from elsewhere; since the figure of Goeth is as interesting to Spielberg as that of Schindler, one might guess that the confusion is merely an attempt to dilute Goeth's growing command over the story as a whole. A villain of astounding presence, able to freeze the action with a single basilisk close-up, Goeth provides not only the most convincing moments (his executions are filmed with a harrowing precision) but also the most misleading, since the entire terrorisation of Krakow seems to be his doing.

The third of Spielberg's manipulative overstatements is the scene of Goeth's casual urination after sniping at prisoners from his balcony, a gesture that invites our disgust but tells us nothing that has not already been conveyed, by the sniping itself. A subtler irony is provided by the single shot of Goeth's hanging, when the stool under his feet is kicked to pieces before he drops. Whether rehearsing his leniency in a mirror or struggling to overcome his interest in the Jewish girl who is "not strictly a person at all", Goeth is performed with such skill as to divide *Schindler's List* into two different experiences—one a near-documentary, brilliantly designed and choreographed, the other a character study in which Ralph Fiennes, the winningly urbane Liam Neeson, and the magnificently impassive Ben Kingsley attain a memorable dramatic intensity. In either form, it is a privilege to watch.

TIME, 12/13/93, p. 75, Richard Schickel

Life rushes on, we are distracted. We forget things. And sometimes we will ourselves to this forgetfulness, especially of those aspects of the past pain us deeply. Or shame us greatly.

American movies mostly cater to this amnesia. If their primary task is to help us escape our trials of the moment, one of their secondary goals is to ease the burdens of the past. These days, history in the movies is essentially set decoration, something shimmering and elegant to place behind the well-spoken characters of a Merchant-Ivory film once a year, a Martin Scorsese film once a lifetime. The past is almost never seen as a tragic force. Or as something that contains a certain few shattering, shaping occurrences with which each generation must come to terms anew if it is to retain its moral footing.

The Holocaust is such an event. It is a topic—the systematic destruction of European Jewry under Nazism—that American movies have taken up gingerly, and only occasionally. It has been left mostly to the documentarians and to Europeans like Agnieszka Holland, who made the devastating *Europa, Europa*. But these are art-house films with small audiences.

That's why the release next week of Steven Spielberg's *Schindler's List* is a consequential event. It is a high-profile, big-studio film, produced and directed by the most popular filmmaker of our era, possibly of all time (four of the top 10 grossing movies ever are Spielberg's, including the biggest of them all, this year's *Jurassic Park*). These factors alone would grant it an access to the mainstream public consciousness that no other movie on this subject has enjoyed. The fact that it is a very good movie means it has a chance to lodge there instructively, and perhaps permanently.

"The movie simply needed my clout to get it made," Spielberg says, and he is not being immodest. Since no filmmaker has a track record like his, none has his power to encourage both a studio and the young mass audience to take a risk on a movie the subject of which is inherently repellent, not to say terrifying.

At the same time, Spielberg says "this movie didn't need my strengths as a storyteller because the storys already been told." Here he is being too modest. It was surely the screen storyteller in him who responded to the compelling narrative strength of Thomas Keneally's novelized life of a German-Czech named Oskar Schindler, who came to Poland to make money out of its occupation by the Nazis and stayed to preserve 1,100 Jews—workers in the enamelware factory he established—from the death camps.

That storyteller must also have understood that even though Schindler, a hypnotically ambiguous character—he was a drinker, womanizer, black marketeer and con artist—was operating in a charnel house, he was finally that classically empathetic, inspirational figure, the lone individual doing good in a desperately dangerous context. If you could get an audience to accept that context, you could involve them with a man who, though antiheroic in some of his behavior, was in his essence a movie hero of quite a familiar, beloved kind.

Finally, that storyteller, a master of movie technique, must have sensed in this tale elements that would bring out the best in him. Spielberg has always been a man who likes to work on big, crowded canvases, but he has never challenged his skills with a subject so dense and dark as this one, never used them with more tact or to better dramatic and emotional effect. There is a kind of morality—a respect for one's tools and materials and for the intelligence of the beholder's eye—in the craftsmanship he has deployed. It serves the interests of the tale, not the ego of the teller. In the annals of Hollywood "clout," this is almost as astonishing as the movie itself.

Or as Spielberg told the cast, "we're not making a film, we're making a document." Documents, of course, are printed in black and white, and so is *Schindler's List*. To Spielberg, these are the colors of reality. They may also be part of an effort to find the cinematic equivalent to the style of Keneally's 1982 novel, which is marvelously understated—the only way to go, really, when your subject is so overwhelming that all but the simplest words are bound to fail it.

Spielberg strove for a similar artlessness with his camera. The film was made on location in Cracow, using the actual factory Schindler operated, even the apartment he once inhabited. The scenes in which the Jews are forced into the ghetto or endure the torments of camp life are shot documentary style, with hand-held cameras. As Spielberg says: "I didn't want to direct off a Cecil B. DeMille crane. I wanted to do more CNN reporting with a camera I could hold in my hand." To enhance this effect, he eschewed storyboards for only the third time in his 14 films. Instead in some sequences he filled several streets with hundreds of extras, rehearsed them extensively, then sent his cameras and the actors who had lines to speak into the melee, often requiring them to improvise dialogue and bits of business.

The process energized Spielberg, who "felt liberated for the first time in my career." He was finally realizing a dream he first entertained more than a decade ago and delayed while awaiting both the script he wanted (it was provided by Steven Zaillian, writer-director of *Searching for Bobby Fisher*) and the maturity in himself he felt he needed. Onlookers say he never sat down, never retreated to his trailer, and that he one day made an astonishing 51 setups. Yet always he moved in an aura of "austere calm ... a man at peace with himself," in the words of co-producer Gerald Molen. At some point, impeccable professionalism simply merged with obsession.

Ben Kingsley, who plays Itzhak Stern, the Jewish accountant who both cooked the books for Schindler's lifesaving scams and served as guide to his conscience, was astonished at Spielberg's nerve: "I didn't think he would have the courage and the panache and the command to fill an area of five blocks, a big area of action where you are receiving information from what's happening in the foreground, in the midground and also in your peripheral vision." But these are among the greatest sequences of chaos and mass terror ever filmed.

By contrast, the scenes in which Schindler befriends the German command, the better to suborn them with bribes and favors, first to advance his own interests, later to protect his workers, are filmed in the high formal style of the 1930s and '40s. The style is as cool and calculated as Schindler himself, played with a kind of impenetrable bonhomie by Liam Neeson. The work here comes close to satirizing the antique conventions of espionage dramas.

Its function is also to set the stage for the savagery of Schindler's dark double and most dangerous antagonist, Amon Goeth, commandant of the nearby labor camp, played by Ralph Fiennes in the film's most compelling performance. A man of Schindler's own age and background, he likes to sit on the balcony of his house idly shooting prisoners who happen to wander into his gunsight. He keeps as a servant a Jewish woman named Helen Hirsch (Embeth Davidtz), whom he constantly beats and humiliates precisely because against all dictates of ideology, he loves her. The point about this man is that like Nazism itself, his irrationality cannot be contained by any appeal to civility, any system of legal or moral constraint. He is evil in all its banality, all its primal ferocity.

To re-create evil, especially in situ, and especially on this scale and at this length (3 hr., 15 min.), is of course to confront it. And the experience was shattering. As Spielberg walked through his crowds of extras, gesturing people this way and that because he did not speak their language, it suddenly occurred to him that Josef Mengele, the notorious concentration-camp physician, "gestured people to the left or the right. One direction was death; the other was one more day of life. I felt like a Nazi."

For Spielberg, "the worst days came any time I had to have people take their clothes off and be humiliated and reduce themselves down to livestock. That's what tore me up the most. It was the worst experience in my life." Embeth Davidtz agrees. She was in one of these scenes, nude, her head shaved. "It's not like a love scene where you disrobe and there's something in the moment. Here I'm standing there like a plucked chicken, nothing but skin and bone." That is to say, stripped of human dignity.

And there was no surcease. Leaden skies poured rain and snow almost every day of the company's three-month stay in Poland. "I went in there thinking you separate work from life," says Davidtz. "It's the first time that didn't happen." The goofing around that usually makes the boredom and hardships of difficult movie locations bearable was not available to this company. "The ghosts were on the set every day in their millions," says Kingsley. As Spielberg recalls, "There was no break in the tension. Nobody felt there was any room for levity," and people were always "breaking down or cracking up." This he had anticipated, he says, "but I didn't expect so much sadness every day."

The result of this relentless passion is not perfect. What enterprise of this scope and intensity possibly could be? In concentrating on the scope of their suffering, the film has lost a certain particularity among the victims. It lacks highly individual characters who would embody and dramatize their suffering. Something of Schindler himself has also been lost in the transition to the screen. Keneally conceived him as a man who admired his own cleverness and may have derived the same sardonic pleasure from taking Jews away from the Nazis as he did from taking money away from them in exchange for flawed products.

This is a point made more tacitly than explicitly in the film. Missing entirely is Keneally's tantalizing suggestion that this quite untutored man may have somehow imagined before anyone else (including many Nazis) that the drift of their policies could carry them to only one place—genocide. Added to the movie, unfortunately, is a blatantly sentimental concluding scene in which Schindler breaks down hysterically because he might have saved even more people but did not. Keneally is distressed by that passage. But he also, and correctly, insists the movie "isn't at all untrue to the spirit of Schindler ... to that ambiguity that attracted me to him in the first place—the scoundrel savior."

More important, the movie arrives when it is very obviously needed. The few survivors of the Holocaust are old now, and dying, and the task of remembering, of testifying, must pass to members of Spielberg's generation and others still younger. It is a hopeful sign, perhaps, that the new Holocaust Museum in Washington is being taxed by more visitors than it can handle. It is a less hopeful sign that this year a public-opinion poll revealed nearly 25% of young Americans either have not heard of the Holocaust or are uncertain of what the term means. Here and elsewhere around the world, pseudo-scholars argue that it never happened at all, and there are people happy to hear this mad denial.

In this climate, Spielberg claims "no high expectations for the box-office potential" of his movie. But these days, acts of conscience (Spielberg will donate any profits, or "blood money" as he calls it, to Holocaust charities) have their curiosity value, not to mention Oscar value. He may yet be surprised by his film's power to create answering acts of conscientiousness on the part of moviegoers. He may be surprised—happily and deservedly so.

VILLAGE VOICE, 12/21/93, p. 63, J. Hoberman

From the depths of the ocean to the dark side of Neverland, from rural Georgia to occupied Shanghai, Steven Spielberg envelops creation like an infinite expanse of Saran Wrap. His crinkly realm encompasses prehistoric dinosaurs and extraterrestrial aliens; his sacred texts range from the Ark of the Covenant to *A Guy Named Joe*. The president himself initiated the buzz on *Schindler's List; New York*'s David Denby staggered out to proclaim "it's as if [Spielberg] understood for the first time why God gave him such extraordinary skills."

Is there a higher authority? Perhaps. "Possibly no one ever again will achieve [Spielberg's] clout," wrote the editor of *Variety*. "Nor use it with such magnanimity." Three of Spielberg's movies have in their time reigned as all-time box-office champ—he may be the most universal artist on planet Earth. What challenges remain? The perpetual insider question—will one of his pictures ever win an Academy Award?—is interesting only in so far as it might inspire industry savants to reflect upon another. Can any subject resist recuperation? Could even the Holocaust be Spielbergized? Is it possible to make a feel-good entertainment about the ultimate feel-bad experience of the 20th century? And where do we draw the bottom line?

Schindler's List dramatizes the wartime exploits of Oskar Schindler, a German industrialist and Nazi party member who managed to save over a thousand Polish Jews from extermination by employing them in the enamelware factory that the German occupation had allowed him to confiscate from its prewar Jewish owners. The fullest account of Schindler's life has been provided by Australian novelist Thomas Keneally. Neither a work of fiction nor history, alternately chatty and laconic, padded with imagined dialogue and unnecessary details (as if mere biography would not be compelling enough), Keneally's 1982 book presents Schindler as a given, making little attempt to account for his character.

Extremes of human behavior were the norm in occupied Poland, to help a Jew was to invite death; the 3 per cent of Poland's 3.3 million Jews who survived the war in Poland did so through a run of luck so cosmic and inexplicable you'd have a better chance to break the bank at Caesars Palace. That Schindler was such a gambler is part of his mythology. The war transformed him from a charming rogue into something like a saint. (He reverted afterward.) It's an incredible story even by Holocaust standards and, unlike *The Diary of Anne Frank*, for example, races to a happy end—which may be the reason that, with *E.T.* still atop the *Variety* chart, Universal purchased the movie rights for their miracle worker Spielberg.

Played by the sleekly imposing Liam Neeson, introduced making the scene at a smoky Cracow nightclub, Spielberg's Schindler is a bon vivant with an agenda—an opportunist, not an ideologue, who acquires a factory and leases from the SS Jewish slaves, including the former plant manager, to work it. His interest is in making money and living well—he takes over a Jewish apartment even as the former residents are herded into the ghetto—but he has no desire to work his employees to death. This initial enlightened selfishness gives way to a more disinterested heroism with the liquidation of the Cracow ghetto. Out riding with his mistress in the hills above the city, Schindler watches in disbelief as the local Jews are beaten, shot, rounded up, and transported to concentration camps. Thereafter, his factory will become a sanctuary.

Shot on location in luminous black and white, *Schindler's List* has a generic resemblance to Andrzej Wajda's *Korczak*. It's both studied and hectic. Poland is a special effect (this is surely the most expensive movie ever made there), and it gives the movie a distinct chill. Something of the gray, damp countryside has crept into Spielberg's marrow—but even more of sunny Hollywood has remained there. The movie is best when it's a tumble of details. Like more than one artist immersed in this material, Spielberg crams as much in as he can sometimes sacrificing historical accuracy, but more often lunging for effect.

The terror of Nazi terror was its random, offhanded, unpredictable nature. In the desire to make this comprehensible, Spielberg falls back on what he knows. He tries to be casual when Jews are shot, but he can't resist the punctuating close-up of blood in the snow any more than he can help underscoring the merciful poison administered to Jewish patients as Nazis storm their hospital by framing the beatific looks ghetto doctors exchange, or keep himself from using a cute little kid as a savior, or ending the liquidation sequence by augmenting adventure schlockmeister John Williams's egregiously overwrought score with a saccharine voiceover of children singing the Yiddish nursery song *Ofn Pripitshik*.

Unlike Schindler, Spielberg can't override his instincts. Is there a world beyond Beverly Hills? Spielberg told *Premiere* that if Schindler were alive today he'd be running Time-Warner and informed *The New York Times* that a contemporary Schindler would be CAA head Mike Ovitz. *Premiere* entered into the spirit of the discourse by describing the "Darth Vader effect" Spielberg wanted for the termination of the ghetto, while captioning a production still of the Auschwitz scene "temple of doom."

Calling Harrison Ford. With the liquidation of the Cracow ghetto, Schindler's factory is relocated to the Plaszow slave labor camp. This nightmare establishment is run by the hero's evil twin—sadistic SS commander Amon Goeth (Ralph Fiennes), a dead-eyed, baby-faced Caligula who picks off inmates at random even when he isn't soused. Plaszow affords Spielberg the opportunity to stage an Auschwitz-style selection during which inmates run naked past the Nazi doctors who decide which ones to keep alive. Here again, the horror of the set piece strains the story line, although one might wonder if these narrative breakdowns don't serve to stoke audience longing for the comfort of Schindler's bulky figure.

As early as 1948, the Yiddish feature *Undzere Kinder (Our Children)*, made in Poland with actual survivors, raised the issue of ethical representation by having war orphans criticize as false a sentimental playlet set in the Warsaw Ghetto. Even now, as Auschwitz crumbles (or is it transformed into a movie lot), historians and scholars wonder whether it should be preserved and why. How to speak the unspeakable, show the unshowable, how to evoke the reality of systematic mass murder without recourse to horror pornography or sentimental cliché. Masterworks as disparate as Tadeusz Borowski's *This Way for the Gas, Ladies and Gentlemen*, Art Spiegelman's *Maus*, and Claude Lanzmann's *Shoah* all developed strategies to show the Holocaust in its traces and absences—to reflect its horrors in a mirrored shield. Spielberg recognizes this himself, telling *Premiere* that SS men used to toss babies out of windows and shoot them like skeet: "I wouldn't show that, even with dolls."

Still, the movie achieves its nadir when a group of Schindler Jews, as they are known, find themselves in Auschwitz, heading for the showers. Expanded from a single sentence in Keneally's text, Spielberg unbelievably plays the scene for thriller suspense and last-minute rescue. Will an Allied bomb fall on the gas chamber? Does the Red Army arrive? The U.S. Cavalry? Is there a telegram from Mr. Zanuck? Perhaps you have dreamed yourself into an Auschwitz gas chamber, Steven Spielberg wants to own that nightmare too.

Schindler's List is sentimental but could have been worse. *The Color Purple* was a far shoddier piece of claptrap and *Sophie's Choice*, in which a Christian Auschwitz survivor is tormented by her Jewish lover, far more contemptible. Perhaps it will even do some good. The abysmal miniseries *Holocaust* served an educational function in Germany and polls show that nearly 40 per cent of the American public is either unaware or dubious that European Jews were systematically murdered during World War II.

For some, the originality of *Schindler's List* may lie precisely in the figure of exceptionalism Schindler provides—as if such exceptionalism were not Hollywood's iron rule. "We have become so conversant with evil in the twentieth century that we are in danger of accepting it as inevitable," writes Denby in *New York*. Yes, *Schindler's List* has the courage of its positive thinking.

In the final hour, Schindler leads his Jews to a new factory in the Sudetenland. There they can keep the Sabbath while suffering neither illness nor starvation. His own transfiguration culminates in a heart-clutching farewell vastly elaborated from Keneally's book.

The poster of a father grasping a child's hand is not the only aspect of *Schindler's List* that recalls *E.T.* The pathos of the absent father remains the most deeply felt emotion in the Spielberg universe. Calling himself a "criminal" and protesting that he "didn't do enough," Schindler stands alone on the stage and receives the adoration of the masses. (He asks for three minutes of silence but, because this is a Spielberg movie, there can be no more than three seconds before *Kaddish* rings out.)

And what of the Spielberg Jews? Relegated to supporting parts in their own cataclysm, they hang around the Cracow ghetto ... making Jewish jokes. There is no debate, no political consciousness, no anguish, no betrayal, no sense of a multitude of classes and castes crammed together because they were Jews. Schindler towers over all. Spielberg's Jews have a physical presence only en masse—they're ultimately victims or children. The more individuated assortment of wizened crones and sultry houris, intellectual dreamers and black market schemers, are dignified versions of stereotypes that would hardly have disturbed the Nazi cosmology. The strongest Jewish character (Ben Kingsley) is uptight and prickly, a heroic accountant.

Unafraid to accentuate the positive, *Schindler's List* necessarily focuses on Gentiles. There's a good-looking hero and an easily recognized villain. *Shoah*, for example, is a film about death in which, over and over and over and over, no one ever escapes. Here, most Jews survive and all are properly grateful rather than unpleasantly traumatized. The violin of hope accompanies the presentation of Schindler's list: The pleased nods and satisfied smiles of the designated Jews suggest a transport of underprivileged waifs acting worthy of a special trip to Disneyland. It's total bliss-out, pure enchantment. Evil is not inevitable. "Every time we go to a movie, it's magic." says Spielberg in *Premiere*. "Whether you watch eight hours of *Shoah* or whether it's *Ghostbusters*, when the lights go down in the theater and the movie fades in, it's magic."

One could found a religion on the transformation of Zyklon B into running water. In a single year, Spielberg has reanimated the dinosaurs and brought the Jews of Poland back from extinction. "I was so ashamed of being a Jew," he told *Premiere*, "and now I'm filled with pride." Annihilation is disagreeable. You won't have any trouble sitting down to dinner after seeing *Schindler's List*, however. It's a tasteful movie.

Also reviewed in:
NATION, 1/3-10/94, p. 30, Stuart Klawans
NEW REPUBLIC, 12/13/93, p. 30, Stanley Kauffmann
NEW REPUBLIC, 1/24/94, p. 26, Stanley Kauffmann
NEW YORK TIMES, 12/15/93, p. C19, Janet Maslin
NEW YORKER, 12/20/93, p. 129, Terrence Rafferty
VARIETY, 12/13/93, p. 36, Todd McCarthy
WASHINGTON POST, 12/15/93, p. B1, Rita Kempley
WASHINGTON POST, 12/17/93, Weekend/p. 54, Desson Howe

SEARCHING FOR BOBBY FISCHER

A Paramount Pictures release of a Scott Rudin/Mirage production. *Executive Producer:* Sidney Pollack. *Producer:* Scott Rudin and William Horberg. *Director:* Steven Zaillian. *Screenplay:* Steven Zaillian. *Director of Photography:* Conrad L. Hall. *Editor:* Wayne Wahrman. *Music:* James Horner. *Sound:* David Lee and (music) Shawn Murphy. *Sound Editor:* Beth Sterner. *Casting:* Avy Kaufman. *Production Designer:* David Gropman. *Art Director:* Gregory P. Keen. *Set Decorator:* Steve Shewchuk. *Set Dresser:* Denis Kirkham and Bill Woods. *Special Effects:* Bob Hall. *Costumes:* Julie Weiss. *Make-up:* Linda Gill. *Running time:* 110 minutes. *MPAA Rating:* Rated PG.

CAST: Max Pomeranc (Josh Waitzkin); Joe Mantegna (Fred Waitzkin); Joan Allen (Bonnie Waitzkin); Ben Kingsley (Bruce Pandolfini); Laurence Fishburne (Vinnie); Michael Nirenberg (Jonathan Poe); Robert Stevens (Poe's Teacher); David Paymer (Kalev); Hal Scardino (Morgan); Vasek Simek (Russian Park Player); William H. Macy (Tunafish Father); Dan Hedaya (Tournament Director); Laura Linney (School Teacher); Anthony Heald (Fighting Parent); Steven Randazzo (Man of Many Signals); Chelsea Moore (Katya Waitzkin); Josh Mostel, Josh Kornbluth, and Tony Shalhoub (Chess Club Members); Austin Pendleton (Asa

Hoffman);   Tom McGowan and Ona Fletcher (Reporters);   Kamran Shirazi (Himself);   Joel Benjamin (Himself);   Roman Dzindzichashvili (Himself);   Jerry Poe McClinton (Park Player); Matt De Matt Reines (Night Park Player);   Vincent Smith and Jerry Rakow (Washington Square Patzers);   William Colgate (Statistician);   Tony De Santis (Journalist);   R.D. Reid (Final Tournament Director); Anthony McGowan (Park Dealer); Katya Waitzkin (82nd Girl); Ryder Fleming-Jones (Petey);   Harris Krofchick (Running Chess Kid);   John Bourgeois and Maria Ricossa (Gym Parents); Caroline Yeager (Screaming Mom); Andrew Sardella (Josh's Syracuse Opponent);   Nathan Carter (Josh's Teammate);   Nicholas Taylor, Jonathan Fazio, Nicky Mellina, Philip Neiman, and Elizabeth Gropman (Birthday Friends).

CHRISTIAN SCIENCE MONITOR, 8/11/93, p. 13, David Sterritt

If you're an admirer of that ever-popular 1990s genre, the feel-good movie, you need search no more for the most engaging film so far this summer. "Searching for Bobby Fischer" is a near-perfect specimen of its breed, displaying Hollywood in a relentlessly lovable mode.

On the plus side, the picture certainly does make you feel good. It contains no sex, violence, or villains, and the climax and finale are worthy of "Rocky" or "Strictly Ballroom" for sheer emotional lift.

On the minus side, there's no intellectual substance to back up those exhilarating feelings. While the movie claims to be about chess, for instance, it's careful not to challenge the audience with actual strategies; intricacies, or even rules of that venerable game. What it does contain are endless shots of people *playing* chess, with emotion-filled facial expressions and music pumping to let us know how the match is going for our hero.

This is fun to watch, and even the most jaded spectators are likely to brush away a tear during the story's touching moments. But there's nothing to remember except those nice, warm feelings once the last image has faded from the screen.

"Searching for Bobby Fischer" is based on the true story of chess prodigy Josh Waitzkin, as it was told by his father, Fred Waitzkin, in a book of the same title. Josh is seven years old at the beginning of the movie and loves chess more than almost anything. His heroes range from international chess champ Bobby Fischer to the hustlers who play speed-chess in the park near his home.

Hoping to encourage his talent without disturbing his normal development, his parents talk an aging chess expert into becoming his teacher. Complications arise when the teacher's methods become too intense for Josh's family to feel comfortable with, and when Josh himself becomes worried that losing a match could mean losing his father's love.

At first glance, "Searching for Bobby Fischer" is a very inspirational movie, reminding us never to quit or lose hope when the going gets tough. This is always a worthwhile message, but it wears a bit thin when you realize how many advantages Josh has to support him at those difficult moments. Besides being a genius in his chosen field, he has dedicated coaches and an intact middle-class family with no other children to divide the parents' attention.

Of course, gifted youngsters have needs and problems just as other kids do, and it's fine to address this in a movie. But the film's inspirational tone would be more convincing if the hero didn't have quite so many resources available to make sure his little problems don't grow into bigger ones.

That said, I don't want to discourage anyone from rushing off to "Searching for Bobby Fischer" at a time when wholesome, optimistic entertainments are often hard to find. The film also boasts first-class performances. It was written and directed by Steven Zaillian, whose previous film as a screenwriter—"Awakenings"—also took a poignant real-life situation and reduced it to feel-good movie magic.

LOS ANGELES TIMES, 8/11/93, Calendar/p. 1, Kenneth Turan

The board has 64 squares, alternating light and dark. The pieces number 16 on each side, including king, queen, knights and (for what is combat without them) a full complement of pawns. The game is chess, only maybe it isn't really a game but a sport, a science, perhaps an art, but always an obsession. And the quest for mastery of it at the highest levels has driven brilliant men quite literally lead and destroyed human relations with the finality of an ax.

"Searching for Bobby Fischer" is set in the world of chess, but it wouldn't be a fraction of the film it is if chess were all it is about. A story of childhood simultaneously exalted and at risk, of the demands of parenthood and the burdens of competition and of genius, it is also the most impressive and promising of directing debuts.

For writer-director Steven Zaillian proves as much of a prodigy as his chess-playing subject, turning out a film that is a beautifully calibrated model of honestly sentimental filmmaking, made with delicacy, restraint and unmistakable emotional power. The feelings it goes for are almost never the easy or obvious ones, and the levers it presses are all the more effective because of that.

Nominated for an Academy Award for the script of "Awakenings" (a prime example of dishonestly sentimental direction) and the writer who has adapted Thomas Keneally's "Schindler's List" for Steven Spielberg. Zaillian once again deals with a true story. "Bobby Fischer" tells what happens when a typical New York City kid with dreams of playing second base for the Yankees discovers that he has so much innate chess ability that he puts people in mind of that celebrated former world champion, as breathtaking a player as ever lived.

Given his abilities as a writer, it might be expected that as a director Zaillian would lean too hard on his own words, so one of the things that is most impressive about "Bobby Fischer" is that the opposite is true. Considerably aided by celebrated director of photography Conrad Hall, Zaillian, determined to tell his story without words whenever possible, has made a conspicuously visual debut.

This nonverbal assurance is most impressive in the film's opening scene. Seven-year-old Josh Waitzkin (Max Pomeranc) is fooling around with some pals in a park when for no particular reason he looks up and sees a group of men playing chess, the pieces and the board curiously reflected in a pair of sunglasses. Not a word is spoken, nothing is heard but James Horner's evocative score, but the subliminal connection Josh makes with the game, the way the lust for it seeps into his blood, is magically visible on the screen.

On the surface Josh remains a regular kid, getting his baseball mitt oiled by his sportswriter father Fred (Joe Mantegna) and taking walks in Washington Square Park with mother Bonnie (Joan Allen). But on his own he has somehow mastered the basics of the game, even constructed his own set of chessmen, and on one of those walks he pulls his uncertain mother over to watch the park's raffish group of regular players go at it.

Soon he starts to play, and his ability catches the eye of Vinnie (Laurence Fishburne), a shaved-head, jive-talking, cigarette-dangling possibly drug-using master chess hustler who writes Josh's name down on a newspaper, much to his mother's horror. "Hey, the boy used pieces in combination, in attack," Vinnie yells after her as she, uncertain whether to feel pleased or threatened, nervously shepherds the boy toward home.

After Fred Waitzkin is convinced (in a clever, humorous and again largely visual scene) of Josh's ability, father and son head off to a local chess club to approach somber guru Bruce Pandolfini (Ben Kingsley) about teaching him.

No, Pandolfini says, he doesn't teach anymore. Period. But a glimpse of Josh at the board makes the man doubt his resolve. Then he tries to undermine Fred's resolve to see his son succeed in chess by telling him about what a neurotic-ridden, miserly world it is. Finally, he tells the father the truth. Chess may be an art, but "most players, even the great ones, are forgers. Your son creates. Like Bobby Fischer."

Though this may sound like some kind of happy ending, it is in fact only the beginning of a whole series of painful struggles, initially between Josh's two mentors for control of his mind and his game. The emotional Vinnie believes in attitude and tactics, the conservative Pandolfini in preparation and position. Neither man is above manipulation and each wishes the other would shrivel up and go away, but one of the graces of "Searching for Bobby Fischer" is how well it understands that to portray them as simply vice and virtue would do an injustice to what is a considerably more intricate reality.

For it turns out that everyone who comes into contact with the enormity of Josh's gift has an agenda, a stake in the boy's success, even his father. Though initially unconcerned and even blasé about his son's accomplishments, Fred Waitzkin soon gets caught up against his will in the blood sport of winning, snapping at an uncomprehending teacher, "My son is better at this than I've been at anything in my life."

At its core, then, "Searching for Bobby Fischer" is about much larger issues. What do you do when your child is a genius, how do you best serve both the gift and the tiny, fragile person who possesses it? Can Josh survive as a person and still be a champion, or must his decency be beaten out of him if he is to reach his maximum potential? And, hovering over all these questions, evoked in newsreels, interviews and Josh's voice-over, is the cautionary spirit of Bobby Fischer, a vision of the ultimate boy genius gone painfully astray.

Though its thrust is undeniably sentimental, it can't be stated how elegantly writer-director Zaillian has put this together. He has gotten all the right notes from veterans Kingsley, Mantegna and Allen, while Fishburne, who seems to just get better and better, is electric in his small but pivotal role. Most impressive is the performance that comes from Pomeranc, himself a gifted chess player making his acting debut, whose soulful work as a miniature adult with the most trusting eyes is, guilelessly convincing.

In addition to all these adult riches, "Searching for Bobby Fischer" happens to be rated PG (for thematic elements), making it the family film anyone with a family has been hoping for with increasing desperation. Unwilling to patronize the children in its cast and unable to let its concern for values stand in the way of onscreen excitement, its final message is "there are only so many things you can teach a child. Finally, they are who they are." Can there be any doubt but that this is a film not only to enjoy but also to cherish?

NEW YORK, 8/23/93, p. 58, David Denby

Searching for Bobby Fischer is an intelligent movie afflicted with opportunism. Josh Waitzkin (Max Pomeranc) a 7-year-old chess whiz from Manhattan, thinks about nothing but Bobby Fischer, the genius/creep whom the entire chess world has idolized for more than two decades. Josh's teacher (Ben Kingsley), a sort of high priest of chess, tells the kid that to be that great, you have to cultivate ruthlessness; you have to want to destroy your opponent. The boy's sportswriter father, Fred Waitzkin (Joe Mantegna)—Waitzkin's book about his son served as the basis for the movie—is willing to push his son hard, but his mother (Joan Allen) wants him decent; she wants a human, a *child*. She disdains the teacher's cult of discipline and contempt, and her natural ally is a kind of alternate chess guru, a hustler (Laurence Fishburne) who plays the tables in Washington Square, and who teaches Josh street chess, which depends on psychology and intuition rather than on the classic moves of the game.

Writer-director Steven Zaillian makes much of the chess-world detail fascinating—the weird obsessiveness of the players, the jealousy and spite of the teachers, the intense competitiveness among the parents of the little prodigies. And the tensions that Zaillian establishes feel right to me. Unfortunately, the way he resolves them shows more commercial calculation than anything. Moving toward a conventional finale, Zaillian sets up a climactic match in which *all* the kid's gurus turn out to be right and Josh gets to be a winner without giving up an ounce of his humanity. *Searching for Bobby Fischer* acknowledges the distortions that early genius can bring into a child's life but then runs from them. The movie's wholesomeness is a form of denial: The kid's a freak; he's not a freak. Zaillian wants to accommodate everyone's point of view; he's made an age-of-Clinton movie that is offensive only in its determination to be inoffensive.

NEW YORK POST, 8/11/93, p. 21, Michael Medved

If nothing else, "Searching for Bobby Fischer" deserves high marks for audacity.

Here is a beautifully shot, capably acted, lushly scored big-studio film that gives the full Hollywood treatment to the fiercely competitive world of children's chess.

Children's chess? This would seem to be about as promising a premise for a mid-summer movie as a picture about cricket, polo or high-stakes darts. It's safe to say that big-time chess tournaments for kids are not among the major spectator sporting events in the country.

Nevertheless, first-time director Steven Zaillian (who previously wrote the screenplays for "Awakenings" and "Jack the Bear") makes us care about the game and focuses our sympathy on one 7-year-old competitor, whose genius for chess may make him a future world's champion.

The obsessed adults who dominate the game have been searching for Bobby Fischer—waiting for decades for a worthy successor to the legendary, eccentric Brooklyn prodigy who became the most famous chess player who ever lived. When the experts see Josh Waitzkin (Max Pomeranc) play they think he may be it.

The problem is that director Zaillian isn't at all sure: how he feels about these ambitions and his confusion ultimately sinks the movie. On the one hand we're supposed to cheer and exult every time little Josh wins a tournament on the other, we're supposed to be horrified at the way his father (Joe Mantegna) and his teacher (Ben Kingsley) push him ruthlessly to succeed, depriving the boy of anything approaching a normal childhood. The movie sets up an intriguing struggle between the father's dreams of competitive glory and the mother's sensible concern for the emotional well-being of her child, but then makes no attempt to resolve the conflict. The chess world is portrayed as mad and destructive—but also noble and worth conquering, and the film concludes with a shabby stereotypical attempt to have it both ways.

In fairness, this ambiguity arises to some extent from the source material: a true story by sportswriter Fred Waitzkin about his experiences with his chess prodigy son, Josh. The younger Waitzkin, who is now 15 and one of the top-ranked players in the world, cooperated fully in the production of this movie, as did his parents.

His real-life teacher, a chess master named Bruce Pandolfini, served as technical adviser and the picture he is played by Ben Kingsley as a lonely, haunted, spectral presence with a quasi-religious devotion to the game, so you can be sure that the details are authentic.

Amazingly enough, the chess talents of 8-year-old leading man Max Pomeranc are also authentic; He is one of the top 100 players in his age group in the country, chosen for the role as much for his facility at the game as for his acting ability.

It's the acting talent, however, that will dominate his future—even in this summer of striking performances by gifted young actors, this kid is extraordinary, projecting intelligence, decency and a poetic sensitivity to the world around him.

Director Zaillian makes the most of the wide-eyed wonder of his young star, shooting most of this movie with intense close-ups that give us a sense of the bigger, fresher reality that his protagonist might see. After a while, however, this nearsightedness becomes a distracting mannerism and the rich, emotional musical score by James Horner at times upstages the actors.

For all its courage and integrity, "Searching for Bobby Fischer" (which features a few moments of fascinating documentary footage of the reclusive master mentioned in the title) ends up insulting its audience with the sort of overblown melodramatic "Rocky"-style showdown that we've come to expect from every single sports movie out of Hollywood. In this movie in particular, it's a disastrous mistake. The filmmakers have done such a good job planting doubts in our minds about the importance or appropriateness of a chess career, that the concluding scenes of celebration and exultation seem especially hollow, forced and manipulative.

NEWSDAY, 8/11/93, Part II/p. 49, Jack Mathews

World chess and insult champion Bobby Fischer is not the subject of Steven Zaillian's "Searching for Bobby Fischer," and the story was written long before Fischer made a political ass of himself during his rematch with Boris Spassky in the former Yugoslavia last year.

So, don't let the title discourage you, nobody is actually looking for that ill-behaved misanthrope, though he does appear in old TV news footage. The good folks in "Searching for Bobby Fischer" are merely longing for another child prodigy, another homegrown genius whose precocious mastery of the game will stir the excitement Fischer did a quarter century ago.

They find their new hero in 7-year-old Josh Waitzkin (Max Pomeranc), a mop-top Manhattan doll whose dream is to play second base for the Yankees, but whose talent is for destroying all comers at the game of chess. The movie covers about a year in Josh's life, from his parents' discovery of his gift, to a showdown match in a national children's chess championship.

It is a true story, based on a book by Josh's father, Fred Waitzkin, and it is as dynamic a film as can be crafted from inert material. Yet, the crucial chess matches in the film have the dramatic thrust of a winning touchdown drive in the NFL, and the atmosphere surrounding its tournaments is charged with tension.

Somehow, Zaillian , who claims ignorance of chess himself, has managed to externalize the turmoil of players caught in the pressure cooker of competition, and to turn Josh's outwardly quiet journey into a nail-biting adventure.

Some of Zaillian's tactics are obvious, though very maturely executed for a first-time director. We follow games by the pace of the editing, by the insecurity or confidence in the players' eyes, by the mood of James Horner's wonderfully textured score. Some scenes of speed chess, in which players try to beat both each other and the clock, have the emotional punch of sliding jazz riffs.

That said, the core drama of "Searching for Bobby Fischer" is not dependent on how Josh moves his pieces on the board, but on how the players in his life—his parents and the two mentors who threaten to overwhelm him with conflicting advice—move *him*. The dilemma facing the Waitzkins is a dilemma facing most parents who believe they have gifted children, how far to go in developing the gift without damaging the ego.

At stake is the future of a normal-in-every-other-way 7-year-old, in this case one who would rather lose than hurt his opponents' feelings. There is a wonderful early scene in which Josh, fearful of alienating his father (Joe Mantegna), intentionally blows a game, then cheerfully runs off to play, leaving his mother (Joan Allen) to explain what really happened.

Zaillian sows a lot of seeds in the early scenes. Besides learning that Josh's chief weakness is his lack of a killer instinct, we know his parents' marriage will be tested by his father's urge to push him and by his mother's determination to prevent him from becoming a pawn in other people's lives, and that the development of his personality hangs in the balance.

In the beginning, Josh is content to play pick-up games of speed chess at Washington Square Park, where he meets Vinnie (another galvanizing performance from Laurence Fishburne), who is the chess version of a knock-out puncher. Later, his father takes him to Bruce Pandolfini (Ben Kingsley), a U.S. champion and chess author, whose classic approach takes zenlike patience and a monk's devotion.

Beyond their contrasting styles, Vinnie counsels Josh to play chess for the sheer joy of it, while Pandolfini wants him to regard each game as a matter of life and death.

Is it healthy to teach a child to go for the kill, to be merciless at a board game, on the *chance* that he might become world class? That's the urgent question of "Searching," and, clearly, Zaillian included so many scenes from Fischer's life as a cautionary warning. Hey, folks, this brilliant monster, now a 50-year-old fugitive from U.S. justice, was once a cute kid, too.

"Searching," which Zaillian also wrote, answers the question a little prematurely (Josh is only 15 now and still scaling the chess heights), and in a climactic scene whose banality betrays the overall intelligence of the story. Yes, it is just a movie, and one that demands a bang-up finale, but did it have to be the finale from "The Karate Kid?"

There are a couple of other flaws. Kingsley is so somber in his role, you'd think Pandolfini was teaching embalming techniques. And though chess parents are probably just as shrill and overbearing as their Little League counterparts, Zaillian gets a little silly in their depiction here.

But the director has made few missteps. Of all the summer's kid movies, this one features the best performance. Max Pomeranc, a non-actor recruited partly for his own precociousness at chess, is magnetic in a role that dictates the tone of the entire movie. Even when surrounded by the cast's talented veterans, you can't take your eyes off of him.

Whatever your own philosophy of winning and losing, your heart goes out to young Josh when he speaks a line that carries the weight of the world.

"Maybe it's better not to be the best," he says, speaking for most of us. "Then you can lose and it's okay."

NEWSWEEK, 8/30/93, p. 52, David Ansen

Fred Waitzkin (Joe Mantegna), the father of 7-year-old chess prodigy Josh (Max Pomeranc), regards his son's uncanny gift with a mixture of awe, envy and pride. "He's better at this than I've ever been at anything in my life." How does one nurture a talent this rare? Whose ambitions—the father's or the son's—are being served? And how can a boy become a budding grandmaster in the ruthlessly cerebral world of chess and retain his humanity?

These are a few of the juicy questions addressed in *Searching for Bobby Fischer*, Steven Zaillian's stirring, semi-fictionalized adaptation of Fred Waitzkin's book about his son. The question that writer/director Zaillian had to solve was how to make a movie about an arcane, internalized game that would speak to an audience who wouldn't know a Karpov from a Kasparov. In his least imaginative moments, he simply turns up the pushy score, piles on the re- lentless close-ups, makes Josh a pint-size Rocky and turns his demanding chess teacher Bruce

Pandolfini (Ben Kingsley) into a shabby, genteel version of Obi-Wan Kenobi. These are forgivable ploys, however, for the story he is telling—about parenting, teachers and students, and the nature of competition—is a rich one, and Zaillian tells it with warmth, humor and zest. The cast is first-rate. Laurence Fishburne plays the rather underdeveloped role of Vinnie, Josh's other teacher, a speed-chess hustler with a more instinctive approach to the game than Pandolfini. Joan Allen is Josh's protective mother, determined to see that his childhood isn't stolen by the monastic demands of the game. Best of all is young Pomeranc, a chess whiz with no previous acting experience. In his watchful, soulful eyes are united both the sage master strategist closing in for the kill and the sweet 7-year-old who just wants to have fun.

SIGHT AND SOUND, 1/94, p. 47, Verina Glaessner

Seven-year-old Josh Waitzkin is fascinated by the wayward career of American chess champion Bobby Fischer. His sports journalist father Fred and mother Bonnie are amazed to discover that, from a few brief but intense visits to the speed chess players in Central Park—a collection of drop-outs and drug users—their son appears to have taught himself the game.

Bonnie allows him to become a regular partner of Vinnie, a black down-and-out, while Fred seeks out former champion player Bruce Pandolfini to teach his son. Initially, Bruce turns Josh down but when he sees the boy's playing style, he agrees. Regular lessons enable Josh to participate in the junior chess tournament circuit. His rating steadily improves, but his absence from school leads to a showdown with his unsympathetic teacher.

With Bonnie's reluctant agreement, the Waitzkins place Josh in a private school. Meanwhile Josh has become friends with Morgan, a regular sparring partner. Bruce is approached by the trainer of another rising chess star, Jonathan Poe—a boy who devotes his whole life to the game—to take him on, but he refuses. Meanwhile he becomes tougher with Josh, refusing to allow him to play with Vinnie in the park for fear it will ruin his style.

When Bonnie catches Bruce ridiculing her son's desire for a Grand Master certificate, she throws him out. Josh, now top of his age group, becomes terrified of losing and deliberately throws a game. There is then a tearful reconciliation with his father. Games with Vinnie follow and gradually Josh regains his confidence.

At a major tournament, Josh finds himself in line to play the championship match with Poe. The night before, Bruce visits Josh in his hotel room and tells him he is proud to have taught him. He also gives him a signed and framed copy of the certificate. Next day while playing Poe, despite making the near fatal slip of playing his queen too early, Josh recovers. Poe, unable to see that defeat is on the cards, refuses Josh's sporting offer of a draw. To the delight of Fred, Bonnie, Bruce and Vinnie, Josh wins the championship. He goes off arm-in-arm with his friend Morgan, offering words of advice. The titles tell us of Fischer's return to trounce Boris Spassky before retreating once more into obscurity.

Chess, a highly cerebral pursuit, poses a problem for both television and film. Here, debut director Steven Zaillian tackles the problem head on, handling each contest as a cross between a martial arts tournament and a wash-and-go commercial. Chess pieces slam onto the board in giant close-up, intercut with similarly tight shots of faces, all interest centred on the eyes.

Zaillian adapted Fred Waitzkin's own story about life with his gifted chess-playing son, and Bruce Pandolfini is credited as advisor for the chess sequences. Despite his involvement, the film is only fleetingly revealing about life on the junior chess circuit. It is also only marginally concerned with Josh's experience and what chess means to him. Rather more to the fore is a reliable Hollywood preoccupation: parental anxiety when faced with a child who seems out of the ordinary.

The Waitzkins' desires for their son split along very conventional lines. Bonnie looks to the emotions. "You have a good heart," she tells Josh when he suggests that there may be room on his top bunk for Vinnie. She is vindicated when Josh acts towards the losing Poe with genuine sportsmanship. Fred sees in his son an "ability to be better at something than I have ever been at anything in my life." As played by the rumpled Joe Mantegna, he is an uncomplicated throwback to an earlier era (the shot of him at a baseball match is lit like a 40s film).

What is at issue is not so much the chess as the success. This implies both fear and hatred. Fred jollies his son along by explaining that he has no need to be afraid, that his opponents are all terrified of him, and it is taken as read that the other chess parents loathing for Fred increases with each move his son makes in rank. However, Josh's task is not simply to win, but rather to find correct or acceptable ways of doing so. Bruce Pandolfini and Jonathan Poe exemplify an old world elitism. Bruce exhorts his pupil to avoid the taint of the street and to hold his opponent in contempt. On the other hand there is Vinnie, the film's guarantor of ethnicity, egalitarianism, street cred and box office potential. It is Josh's task to keep his integrity (that 'good heart') and to reconcile the elitist search for excellence with the way of the street. It is not a matter of choice but of synthesis.

Overhanging the whole enterprise is the shadow of chess legend Bobby Fischer. Interestingly, we are not shown the source of Josh's idolisation. The film opens with news footage accompanied by Josh's lisping voiceover. There are several such sequences inserted into the film and each time they evoke the hero's renegade status and his skill at "beating the Russian" before vanishing once more from the public gaze. It is the over-riding need to find another Fischer, a new American hero, that obsesses and unites all the main characters, from the speed chess drop-outs, through the chess parents, to Poe. Josh himself remains a cypher for this need, to the extent that at times the film seems to stand on the edge of a different genre, that of horror and possession. After all, like Fischer, Josh "plays the game from the inside."

America needs a new hero but it must be a certain kind of hero. Everything in the film takes a back seat to this concern—chess, the character of the child, and even the best efforts of such watchable performers as Mantegna and Ben Kingsley. The paradigm has been used by Hollywood before, but it is more familiar from films made under Stalin in the Soviet Union and Mao in China. Individual excellence is necessary, but it is to be tempered by the hero acknowledging the contribution of the very least in society and remaining willing to disappear among them, as Mao has it, like a fish into water—or indeed like Fischer himself, who returned to fight one last old enemy before vanishing mystically back among his countrymen. It is an odd ideological burden for a film like this to carry.

VILLAGE VOICE, 8/17/93, p. 56, Joe Levy

This sweet story of a child chess prodigy makes you wonder what, truly, is the greater gift: the intuitive mastery of a complex art at an early age or having Joe Mantegna for your father and Ben Kingsley and Laurence Fishburne as your tutors.

For the kids who'll make it a hit, *Searching for Bobby Fischer* is *Star Wars* on a chess board, with Ben Kingsley's chess teacher as Obi-Wan Kenobi, a reserved British master who impresses on his young disciple the virtues of discipline and concentration (there's even a "Use the force, Luke" bit when the disciple in question, Josh Waitzkin, faces a child chess prodigy front the dark side and Kingsley's voice and lessons return to him through the air). For the adults who'll be happy they went, it's two hours of therapy, a battle between the reality principle (Kingsley with his emphasis on strategy, practice, and winning) and the pleasure principle (Fishburne, a Washington Square chess hustler who encourages Josh to "play the man, not the board" and generally enjoy himself. A compelling fable about innocence, it imagines a time in the past when games were played as pure sport, not battles, and when the adults who inevitably turn children into warriors were more annoyances than monsters.

For much of *Searching for Bobby Fischer*, director Steven Zaillian defers to his star, real-life child chess prodigy Max Pomeranc playing real-life child chess prodigy Josh Waitzkin. When Josh is on screen, the camera is often at his eye level, and in an early scene, when Josh first discovers chess and sets up some toy knights inside a toy castle as if they were chess pieces, there's a lovely shot from Josh's point of view as he crouches down and opens the castle gate: Heroic in stature, the knights/chessmen fill the screen as they will soon fill his world. Still, there's not enough of Josh: The desires of the adults around him tend to push him out of his own story; Kingsley complains that Josh should practice more and spend less time playing Pac-Man and riding his bike, but we never see him playing Pac-Man, or riding his bike.

Mantegna, Fishburne, and Kingsley are all stunningly good, as is Pomeranc and the underutilized Joan Allen as Josh's mother, Bonnie (who gets to do little more than defend Josh's "decent heart" against the incursion of the various men who want to live vicariously through his gift). This is screenwriter Zaillian's directorial debut, and anyone who saw what Penny Marshall did with a Zaillian script, Robin Williams, and Robert De Niro in *Awakenings* knows that good actors do not a good movie make. Zaillian certainly seems to have learned the lesson—on his own, he thins the corn a bit (but never completely), lights the set well, then lets his cast and script get to work. He's got a way with detail—when the theme music to NPR's *All Things Considered* floats by as Josh's mom and dad talk in the kitchen, you know all you need to about their upper-middle-class ambitions—and his dialogue is sharp—when dad wants to move Josh from public school to Dalton because, among other things, it has a chess club, Josh's "Does it have good stuff to climb on?" and Mantegna's stammering reply speak volumes about their differing priorities. In short, while you may be tempted to stay as far away from this as you do other "wholesome" entertainments, you shouldn't.

Also reviewed in:
NEW REPUBLIC, 9/20 & 27/93, p. 36, Stanley Kauffmann
NEW YORK TIMES, 8/11/93, p. C13, Janet Maslin
VARIETY, 8/16/93, p. 39, Brian Lowry
WASHINGTON POST, 8/11/93, p. D1, Rita Kempley
WASHINGTON POST, 8/13/93, Weekend/p. 36, Desson Howe

SECRET GARDEN, THE

A Warner Bros. release of an American Zoetrope production. *Executive Producer:* Francis Ford Coppola. *Producer:* Fred Fuchs, Fred Roos, and Tom Luddy. *Director:* Agnieszka Holland. *Screenplay:* Caroline Thompson. *Based on the book by:* Frances Hodgson Burnett. *Director of Photography:* Roger Deakins. *Editor:* Isabelle Lorente. *Music:* Zbigniew Preisner. *Sound:* Drew Kunin and (music) Rafat Paczkowski. *Sound Editor:* Jennifer Lee Ware. *Casting:* Karen Lindsay-Stewart and Linda Phillips-Palo. *Production Designer:* Stuart Craig. *Art Director:* John King. *Set Decorator:* Stephanie McMillan. *Special Effects:* John Evans. *Costumes:* Marit Allen. *Make-up:* Jenny Shircore. *Running time:* 103 minutes. *MPAA Rating:* G.

CAST: Kate Maberly (Mary Lennox); Heydon Prowse (Colin Craven); Andrew Knott (Dickon); Maggie Smith (Mrs. Medlock); Laura Crossley (Martha); John Lynch (Lord Craven); Walter Sparrow (Ben Weatherstaff); Irène Jacob (Mary's Mother/Lilias Craven); Frank Baker (Government Official); Valerie Hill (Cook); Andrea Pickering (Betty Butterworth); Peter Moreton (Will); Arthur Spreckley (John); Colin Bruce (Major Lennox); Parsan Singh (Ayah); Eileen Page (Grandmother at Dock); David Stoll (Grandfather at Dock); Tabatha Allen (Girl at Dock).

CHRISTIAN SCIENCE MONITOR, 8/13/93, p. 13, David Sterritt

"The Secret Garden" is a noble experiment. This engaging Warner Bros. movie brings together a respected European director, known for sophisticated and provocative art films, with a classic of children's literature that young folks have enjoyed since the early part of this century.

The result of this union is a Hollywood rarity: an intelligently conceived and finely crafted picture with a G rating, a tag normally shunned by ambitious filmmakers because of its association with kiddie cartoons and squeaky-clean dullness.

Could this be the beginning of a trend? Quite possibly, if "The Secret Garden" becomes a hit—which it surely will, if moviegoers who've been calling for more wholesome fare now vote with their dollars at the box office.

Based on the novel by Frances Hodgson Burnett, whose other books include "Little Lord Fauntleroy" and "A Little Princess," "The Secret Garden" takes place on an isolated Yorkshire estate with more than its share of mysteries—especially in the eyes of 10-year-old Mary Lennox, a self-centered child sent there from India after the death of her mother.

The master of the house is a morbid, brooding man who never recovered from his own wife's untimely demise. The other inhabitant is his son Colin, a morbid and brooding little boy who's convinced he'll never live past childhood.

The grounds of Misselthwaite Manor are as forbidding as the residents, except for a forbidden area that Mary—with the impish courage of a typical storybook heroine—immediately claims as her favorite spot. Her secret project there, bringing an abandoned garden into bloom and learning the joys of living in the process, is joined by a slowly widening circle of friends. Together they discover the blessings of honest labor, sweet companionship, and the beneficent wonders of nature.

Burnett was a practical-minded author who wrote as much to earn a living as to create literary art, and she was careful not to contradict the social conventions of her time. Her novel has a sneaking male bias, beginning as Mary's story but gradually switching its focus to Colin, the principal recipient of Mary's feminine talent for nurturing and nourishing the needy. The novel also takes care not to question the British class system or the material privileges of the wealthy.

Agnieszka Holland's film version puts the story in a slightly more modern light. It keeps Mary as the main center of interest throughout the tale, although Colin does grab the climactic scene, and it tones down some language in the book that might now be taken as racially insensitive. The children live less in a world of their own and (unfortunately) spend less time fooling the adults with uproarious ruses.

Also gone is Hodgson's constant promotion of hard work as the path to happiness. The filmmakers can't resist their not-so-secret garden of special effects, and Misselthwaite bursts into bloom more through the magic of time-lapse photography than anything the young gardeners have done.

What the movie does retain is the novel's exuberant delight with the natural world and its Dickensian willingness to take children every bit as seriously as the grownups around them. Although the screenplay by Caroline Thompson is not as resolutely structured or earnestly emotional as Hodgson's broadly sketched narrative, it captures a sense of childlike wonder with enough strength and sincerity to be called an accurate reflection of the volume that inspired it.

Holland has shown a recurring fascination with young characters in her recent films, including the double-titled duo called "Europa Europa" and "Olivier Olivier." "The Secret Garden" finds her continuing the exploration of youth without substantially deepening her understanding of that rich territory.

While she has done a capable job of directing the picture, much credit for its success goes to two of her collaborators: Roger Deakins, a cinematographer with a superb gift for orchestrating light and darkness, and Zbigniew Preisner, who composed the characteristically haunting score. (Listen for Linda Ronstadt on the soundtrack, too.)

The good cast includes Kate Maberly as the heroine, Heydon Prowse as Colin, and Andrew Knott as Dickon, the local nature-boy with a gift for charming both plants and animals.

Maggie Smith heads the adult contingent as Mrs. Medlock, the housekeeper who doesn't know quite what to make of the children in her care. John Lynch is weirdly effective as the lord of the manor.

Measured against family-film classics like "The Wizard of Oz" or "The Black Stallion," to mention just two of my favorites, "The Secret Garden" is a bit slender, neither as ingeniously inventive nor as majestically mysterious as the best of its breed.

But the movie comes as a refreshing breeze in this summer of Spielberg and Schwarzenegger silliness and promises to put new oomph into Hollywood's slowly dawning commitment to a new age of family filmmaking.

FILMS IN REVIEW, 10/93, p. 332, Pat Anderson

Who ever would have predicted Agnieska Holland, the director of *Europa, Europa* and *Olivier, Olivier*, two rather heavy, dark movies, would be chosen to direct one of Edwardian England's quintessential and best loved children's books—a book that is still read by and to children worldwide. And who would have thought that this Polish/French woman's film will surely, in its own way, be as enduring as Frances Hodgson Burnett's book. The book itself has subtleties that are not evident in Holland's two earlier pictures, but that are certainly captured in her direction of *The Secret Garden*.

Basically, the story revolves around Mary Lennox (Kate Maberly, in a remarkable, non-sentimental, non-cutesy performance), a neglected rich child. Born in India to parents who delegate her complete upbringing to servants, she is a solemn child who prides herself on never crying—even when her parents die and she is shipped off to Yorkshire to live in her uncle's enormous, forbidding mansion Misselthwaite Hall. And again, Mary is in charge of servants: the garrulous young Martha (Laura Crossley) and the housekeeper Mrs. Medlock (Maggie Smith, on the verge of a Mrs. Danvers, but not quite. Here she is much more vulnerable.) Then there is Dickon (Andrew Knott) who is about Mary's age, the gardener's apprentice and Martha's brother.

Mary, used to instant obedience from her Indian servants, is astonished to learn that not only is she now expected to dress herself, but that her imperious attitude towards Mrs. Medlock merely gets her locked in her room. Mary's uncle Lord Craven (John Lynch), who has been in a deep depression since the death of his wife, is even more remote than her parents were.

So left to her own devices, Mary discovers the garden that has been deliberately neglected because it was her aunt's favorite retreat, and she enlists Dickon's help in restoring it to its former glory. When Mary discovers she has a cousin sequestered in a room in the house who is treated by all the staff as some sort of "bubble boy" invalid, she sets out to make a real playmate of him. In the process, Mary changes from aloof selfishness to a bossy nurturer.

The film has a real fairyland look: the large house dark and forbidding; while outdoors birds chirrup, small animals gambol on lawns and the flowers planted in the garden by Mary and Dickon grow and slowly open until it is all a riot of color.

Heydon Prowse is suitably pale and frail as cousin Colin; Andrew Knott just deferential enough but not obsequious as Dickon. Laura Crossley's Martha is bubbly and exuberant (although somebody goofed when she told Mary to put on her "sweater," there was no such word in Edwardian England. The garment was and is a "jumper.") The only sour note in the acting is John Lynch. Throughout the picture he appears to be saying to himself, "I must remember to look gloomy." And that's all he does. Kate Maberly, however, is everything Mary should be. This self-possessed child is already a consummate actress.

LOS ANGELES TIMES, 8/13/93, Calendar/p. 14, Kenneth Turan

Saying so much as a discouraging word about "The Secret Garden" feels unforgivably churlish. For this is that rare thing, an accomplished G-rated film, made by a respected director with fair fidelity from one of the great favorites of childhood literature. So why does the urge to scrawl graffiti all over its pristine surface seem so irresistible?

The problem is that director Agnieszka Holland ("Europa Europa," "Olivier, Olivier"), screenwriter Caroline Thompson and everyone else involved in this self-conscious production have been excessively aware that they were dealing with a classic and overly willing to be as reverential as possible toward it.

Rather than a fresh breeze, it's the stale air of gilded calculation, the uncomfortable feeling that things are excessively "just so," overhangs much that is genuinely appealing about this film. So while "Garden" remains a tiptop feature to take small children to, unaccompanied adults might remember that even Peck's Bad Boy knew a thing or two in his time.

There is no denying it that when Frances Hodgson Burnett, with "Little Lord Fauntleroy" already behind her, wrote "The Secret Garden" just past the turn of the century, she was deliberately creating a pure fantasy, a childhood idyll that updated the "once upon a time" feeling to what were then modern times.

The difference is that, having been written without the layers of veneration that have since accrued to it, the original "Secret Garden" is simpler, more unaffected and matter of fact than the film version. And whatever gossamer magic it spreads over its proceedings feels honestly earned and not self-consciously manufactured by Hollywood.

On the positive side, the current "Secret Garden" has, in its simplicity of storytelling and emotional gravity, shown considerable restraint, enabling it to tower over bloated childhood fantasies like "Hook." Not lacking in moments of wonder and charm, it also has the courage to remain fairly simple, successfully resisting the kind of false jeopardy that would ruin the innocent mood it works so assiduously to create.

"Secret Garden" begins with a brief scene, typically tasteful and just the tiniest bit calculated, of young Mary Lennox (Kate Maberly) being carefully dressed by a group of Indian servants, a small living doll in a bare white room.

"I was born in India," she says in her peevish voice, "but I didn't like it." It is soon apparent why. Mary's glittering parents, self-satisfied servants of the Raj, are more interested in the local boy maharajah than their own child. So when they die in a convenient earthquake, Mary feels no need for tears and is soon shipped off to her English uncle, Lord Archibald Craven (John Lynch).

It's not her retiring uncle who comes to meet her, but rather the supremely bossy Mrs. Medlock (Maggie Smith), a housekeeper who takes one look at our Mary, pronounces her "a queer, unresponsive little thing," and bundles the 10-year-old off to Misselthwaite, her uncle's vast mansion on the Yorkshire moors, complete with creaky doors, huge fireplaces, musty tapestries and all the trimmings.

Mary is worse than unresponsive. Spoiled by all those Indian servants, she is a huffy little miss who doesn't have the faintest idea of how to have fun. Her uncle, still locked in grief over the death of his wife a decade earlier, doesn't help things by keeping to himself. "The house was dead," Mary says, "like a spell was cast on it."

Not quite dead, as it turns out. There is the thoroughly cheerful servant girl Martha (Laura Crossley) and her brother Dickon (Andrew Knott), a Dr. Doolittle in training who knows the secrets of animals. And there is a wonderful hidden garden, locked up since Lady Craven's death, that Mary becomes ever so eager to discover and explore.

And, as all readers know, Mary uncovers not only the garden, but young Colin (Heydon Prowse), her invalid cousin, hidden away in one of the mansion's many rooms and frightened to death of fresh air. Helped by Dickon, the two young misanthropes find unexpected solace and healing amid the natural wonders of that secret garden.

Though even at her worst Mary never looks as bad ("thin, sallow, ugly") as the book makes her out to be, veteran British child actor Maberly does well with the girl's cheeky hauteur, and novice Prowse is the perfect little lord with a complexion "whiter than ice and marble." Not surprisingly, Maggie Smith, who can huff and puff and mutter "nonsense" like no one else, does best of all as Misselthwaite's resident busybody.

Given the paucity of G-rated films that don't make you gag, "The Secret Garden's" virtues make it more than welcome. Still, one can't watch it without wishing it came more from the heart and less from the kind of calculation that has led it to overdo its effects.

The usually reliable Zbigniew Preisner's score, for instance, doesn't have to be quite so saccharine, the garden could do with a few less tame animals, and overly sentimental plot changes, like turning Mary's mother into Lady Craven's identical twin, could have been resisted.

Too concerned with safeguarding its treasures, without the daring to truly soar, this version of "The Secret Garden," despite its considerable strengths, is fated to be earthbound.

NEW STATESMAN & SOCIETY, 10/15/93, p. 33, Jonathan Romney

Agnieszka Holland's adaptation of the children's classic *The Secret Garden* is the stuff of cosy Sunday teatime viewing—except that someone has slipped dead leaves into the fish paste sandwiches and there are cobwebs in the teapot. This is the creepiest, most Gothic revisiting of primal English childhood fears since the ominous bulk of the convict Magwitch loomed up from behind a headstone in David Lean's *Great Expectations*.

It's also the most improbable project to hit the mainstream cinema for some time. When I were a lad, Frances Hodgson Burnett's tale of juvenile dispossession was a by-word in girly preciousness that you wouldn't be caught dead reading. Now I wonder if, by opting for *Jennings* instead, I didn't miss out on valuable early insights into juvenile angst. It's been adapted here by Caroline Thompson, a screenwriter who has become a by-word in modish Hollywood ghoulishness (she wrote *The Addams Family* and Tim Burton's baroque monument of wedding-cake gothic, *Edward Scissorhands*).

Stranger still, it's been made—for Francis Coppola's Zoetrope company—by Polish director Agnieszka Holland, who's hardly reputed for fireside jollity. Her last film, *Olivier, Olivier*, was quite remarkably gruelling—family psycho-drama about a lost son who returns armed with a Pandora's boxful of incestuous subtexts. Before that, she made *Europa, Europa*, the true story of a Jewish boy who survived the Holocaust by becoming a shining star in the Hitler Youth.

Improbable as it is, *The Secret Garden* is recognisably a Holland film. Rather than hiding its darkness away, it glories in it, even if it can't sustain it throughout. Again, it's the story of a child uprooted and replaced in an alien community. Young Mary Lennox (the charismatically sullen Kate Maberly) is the daughter of blithely unconcerned parents in India.

Having witnessed their destruction in a harrowing primal scene of an earthquake, she is entrusted to the tender mercies of her uncle at his gloomy Yorkshire manor. His Lordship, like the great Bluebeards and Beasts of nursery terror, lurks absent or unseen while his housekeeper rules the roost—Maggie Smith, a glowering stick cocooned in bombazine. Mary's a uniquely joyless child, who would have been more at home if taken in by the Addams family.

The film works like night and day. There's a superb first half in which Mary gets to gripe at the servants and loiter palely round the Gormenghastly cloisters and the overgrown desolation of the secret garden itself. Once it becomes clear that she's on a journey to happiness and redemption, things get considerably less interesting. The turning point comes when she meets that quintessentially Edwardian figure—the Child Less Fortunate Than Herself.

This is whingeing, bed-bound heir Colin, who obviously has nothing wrong with him that a stiff draft of fresh air won't cure. The minute Mary transmutes into an officious bossyboots, gives what-for to Colin and the servants and starts spreading joy and light around the place by sheer dint of elbow grease, the film takes an irreparable (and uncomfortably moralistic) downturn, The joys of health and nature, and incipient adulthood, take precedence over the darker domain of the imagination.

But the grim feel of the first half; and some unnerving handling of the subtexts, make the film worth watching. Mary's guardian, when he does appear, is an ambivalent skulking, gangling creation—imagined as an Edward Gorey portrait of Poe. And the labyrinthine expanses of the manor, with its ghastly echoes, perfectly evoke the sense of powerlessness and half-existence implanted in well-behaved children of the era.

The film communicates an aspect of English childhood invariably sentimentalised out of its depictions: the traumatic implications of the injunction to be seen but not heard, which is about one step from not being at all. Mary is an observer, divorced from the world, and only able to become an adult (symbolically, at least) through the trauma of confrontation—by facing an irreducibly scary outside world and adopting the terrorising function of big sister *cum* mother to Colin. Holland and Thompson have the Freudian infantile anxieties down to a tee, playing up the echoes of other novels about young women in thrall to the ghosts of absent mother figures: *Rebecca* and *Jane Eyre* (although, here, the madwoman in the attic turns out to be the son in the downstairs room). But the film is far more comfortable with sexual themes than with social ones; it has no idea how to deal with the class issues it raises.

Mary's guardian has here been made a lord, presumably to allow for the gracious-England spectacle that Hollywood revels in. But the makers seem to have swallowed the stereotype unchallenged; Mary may ostensibly be the plucky commoner come to overthrow the old order, but the harm is identified with the servants rather than the masters. It's grumpy old Maggie Smith who insists on keeping the windows closed and the little master from the world; the servants' role, finally, is to cluster round cheering, much as in Mary Poppins' golden days.

The short straw goes to Dickon, the gamekeeper's son, who initiates Mary into the mysteries of nature. Their coy encounters are as Lawrentian as a lass can get without being drummed out of the Girl Guides, but it's Dickon who gets left in the cold. But then, symbolically, he's not really a boy at all. His entourage of ducks, robins and a quite demented goat give the game away: he's a pure nature spirit, and the special-effects department have simply stopped short at cloven hooves.

NEW YORK POST, 8/13/93, p. 23, Michael Medved

Fourteen years ago, Francis Ford Coppola served as executive producer on a long-shot project that transformed one of the most cherished classics of children's literature, "The Black Stallion," into a magnificent feature film that's become a family favorite all its own.

Now, with "The Secret Garden," he's done it again: lending his power and prestige to a sumptuous adaptation of a beloved novel that's inspired readers of all ages for more then three generations.

As with "The Black Stallion," this new film dazzles the eye and refreshes the spirit. Polish director Agnieszka Holland previously demonstrated her story-telling abilities with the thrilling, moving and often ironic Holocaust sage "Europa Europa," but here she employs a more poetic style, a lush and leisurely lyricism. The soaring visions of the lonely, lovely Yorkshire moors, and the intricate exploration of a moody Gothic mansion, bring to mind the late David Lean; as in that master's best work, every scene of "The Secret Garden" is composed with loving, luxuriant and painterly detail.

At the same time, Holland has done nothing to brighten the book's darker elements or to soften the rough edges of its main character, Mary Lennox—and that's where her treatment of this material differs most sharply from the touching but prettified 1949 film version with Dean Stockwell and Margaret O'Brien.

The 10-year-old star of this new film (Kate Maberly, a veteran of British TV) may not quite live up to the novel's description of its heroine as "the most disagreeable-lookingchild ever seen" but she is most certainly a tough cookie. She survives the sudden death of her parents, then, arrives at her uncle's gloomy estate, Misselthwaite Manor, where she proceeds to bully the servants into taking some respectful notice of her.

The officious housekeeper Mrs. Medlock (the always formidable Dame Maggie Smith) has ordered the staff to treat the new girl as a necessary nuisance and on no account to allow her to disturb the mournful mood of the hunchbacked master of the house, who for 10 years has been grieving over the death of his beautiful young wife.

Part of that mourning involves permanently locking away the lost lady's walled garden, but once Mary discovers this desolate, haunted but magical place she has other ideas. With the help of an earthy, gentle-spirited country boy (Andrew Knott), and a robin red-breast that seems to possess some supernatural powers, "Mistress Mary, Quite Contrary" does indeed make her garden grow, and in the process manages to heal injuries of both the body and the spirit in everyone around her.

It may seem ridiculous to suggest that contemporary kids who have grown up on video games, car crashes and MTV, will sit still for a stately story about birds and flowers, but once they're in the theater, this picture possesses a magical intensity that will hook even the most jaded "Beavis and Butthead" fan.

When it comes to small children, they can be more patient than we think; many little ones actually prefer the easygoing pace and understated tone of "Mr. Rogers" to the frenetic frolic on "Sesame Street," and this film appeals to that softer, dreamier side of childhood.

For adults, the rewards are even greater: The radiant images of this film remind us of the spiritual, otherworldly dimension in everyday things. Watching the transformation of the secret garden is so stirring and miraculous, in fact, that you'll want to dig your hands into raw country earth and plant your own seeds for spring—no matter that sort of apartment-bound couch potato you may be.

If you settle back and allow the simple story to carry you along, this film offers not only hope (for the movie business, and the rest of our troubled world) but healing.

NEWSDAY, 8/13/93, Part II/p. 62, Jack Mathews

On the vast, fastidiously kept grounds of Lord Archibald Craven's manor on the Yorkshire Moors is a walled-in garden, its rusted iron gate hidden behind unkempt vines, its once lacy network of shrubs and flowers grown over with weeds.

Lord Craven's wife died in there 10 years ago, in a fall from a swing, and the garden, which symbolized her youth and vigor, was condemned to death itself. And dead it remains, until the lord's niece, the daughter of his wife's twin sister, finds the key and begins to nurture it and the grieving Cravens back to life.

There are few more potent metaphors in children's literature than the Edenic sanctuary in Frances Hodgson Burnett's "The Secret Garden," and Polish director Agnieska Holland ("Europa, Europa") has brought the turn-of-the-century tale to the screen with a faithfulness for detail and texture that borders on reverence.

Holland showed remarkable patience with her first English language and first major studio movie, allowing her characters and the their garden to grow at a deliberate, almost parallel pace. Yes, that means it pokes along at times, and even though it has a G rating, don't count on it holding the interest of the very young and restless.

Nevertheless, "The Secret Garden" is a wondrous, intelligent, often witty fantasy, as rich in its own way as "Alice in Wonderland," and with a spirit as noble as the best children's classics.

Burnett's novel has been adapted at least three times before, as a Hollywood feature (the fine 1949 Margaret O'Brien version), as a TV movie and as the popular Broadway musical. It's life-affirming story bears retelling, and Holland, with a screenplay by Caroline Thompson ("Edward Scissorhands"), tells it well).

Lord Craven's Misselthwaite Manor, where 10-year-old Mary Lennox (Kate Maberly) is sent after her parents are killed in India, has an aura of death about it, too, a corpse-like clamminess to its cavernous rooms, halls and labyrinthine stone stairwells.

Mary, who was given everything but love by her parents, is a demanding shrew when she arrives. She is more than a match for Mrs. Medlock (Maggie Smith), the manor's bullying house-keeper, but not quite for young Colin Craven (Heydon Prowse), the bedridden, high-strung cousin she finds withering away in isolation, "protected" by doting servants from the twin terrors of sunlight and fresh air.

It is soon apparent that all hands at Misselthwaite, except for the chipper maid Martha (Laura Crossley) and her robust brother Dickon (Andrew Knott), are human compost, buried in the dark like fungus, where life can't get to them and cause more pain.

That all begins to change when Mary happens onto Lady Craven's abandoned garden, discovers a way in, and, with Dickon's help, begins to revive and restore it. Simultaneously, she takes on the task of strengthening Colin's roots, of liberating him from Mrs. Medlock's primitive therapies, and freeing him from his bed, his wheelchair and his own death sentence. Holland lays the replenishment theme on a little heavy. These kids do everything but burst into hothouse orchids. And the cute animals on view—a goat, a fawn, a squirrel, a rabbit—look like they wandered over from the set of "Bambi."

The film's greatest disappointment, however, is the images of the garden itself. We are shown sweeping vistas of Misselthwaite, grand views of its expansive innards, and birds-eye views of the surrounding countryside. But the before and after glimpses of the garden are fragmented, almost claustrophobic.

When Mary leads Colin to the center of the garden, and gives him and us our first look at its revived splendor, we want to feel the wonder we see on his face. Yet, from his point of view, what we see is merely lovely, not spectacular.

Sure, this garden would dazzle someone emerging from a tomb, especially when it represents the incarnation of his mother's spirit. But this is our fantasy, too, and Holland picked the wrong moment to inject a sense of visual realism.

But "The Secret Garden" is still a terrific family movie, smartly written, well-acted and doggedly faithful to the story's own roots.

NEWSWEEK, 8/23/93, p. 53, David Ansen

The greatest children's movies have the power to make anyone, young or old, recover the magical eyes of childhood. They are films graced with the touch of the poet, like the Alexander Korda "Thief of Bagdad" (1940) or Albert Lamorisse's "White Mane"(1952) or Carroll Ballard's "The Black Stallion" (1979)—movies that seize children like dreams, and grown-ups like dreams remembered. Such a movie is Agnieszka Holland's luminous new version of the Frances Hodgson Burnett classic *The Secret Garden*, which, like "The Black Stallion," comes to us from executive producer Francis Ford Coppola. There have been other versions of Burnett's 1911 book—a black-and-white 1949 film with Margaret O'Brien that turned to color when Mary Lennox's garden bloomed, a 1987 TV movie, the 1991 Broadway musical—but this adaptation, written by Caroline Thompson ("Edward Scissorhands"), should stand as the definitive visualization.

And it is, first and foremost, a visual delight, a Victorian picture book come to life, from its brief prologue in India through its darkly enchanted recreation of Misselthwaite Manor on the Yorkshire moors. Kate Maberly, a solemn child with wide cheeks and huge, pensive brown eyes, plays 10-year-old Mary Lennox, orphaned when her parents die in an earthquake in India. A spoiled and angry child who has never learned to cry, she's shipped off to the care of her English uncle, Lord Craven (John Lynch), a recluse in the 10th year of mourning for his late wife, the twin sister of Mary's dead mother. The first, Gothic half of "The Secret Garden" is suffused with death and with wintry, desolate imagery. Completely neglected by her uncle, Mary is entrusted to the stern care of the awful Mrs. Medlock (Maggie Smith), just the sort of sourpuss Mary could turn out to be if she didn't also meet the radiantly sweet servant girl Martha (Laura Crossley) and her brother Dickon (Andrew Knott), the first two people to draw Mary back to life. And then, of course, she meets a 10-year-old even more spoiled and death-obsessed than she—Lord Craven's invalid son, Colin (Heydon Prowse), a bedridden little aristocrat who has never been outdoors for fear of the "spores" that might terminate his fragile grip on life. He's the old Mary's mirror image, her soulmate, and when she takes it upon herself to save him—to introduce him to the magic she has discovered in her secret garden—we know that she has saved herself.

"The Secret Garden" is a fable about nature and renewal, about a winter child who finally discovers spring inside, and director Holland has an instinctive feel for its gravely magical tone. Her images have a mysterious simplicity: they're as recognizable as archetypes should be while evoking the wonder of something you've never seen before. The Polish-born director of "Olivier Olivier" and the World War II dramas "Europa, Europa" and "Angry Harvest," powerful movies best known in art-house circles, Holland may seem like a strange choice for a children's film, but there has always been a heightened, fairy-tale undercurrent in her movies, even when they're set against the Holocaust. Because she's so attuned to the dark side, of Burnett's tale, the sweetness that blossoms in the second half has surprising emotional weight: the movie's bliss, and tears, are earned.

She also has a dream team. Stuart Craig's production design is as good as it gets: his exquisitely dank Misselthwaite Manor is both nightmarish and ravishing, and cinematographer Roger Deakins drapes it in inky blacks and sharp shafts of milky English sunlight. Every object in this movie—from an antique jigsaw puzzle to a dust-covered miniature chest to the beautiful tapestries that hang in Mary's bedroom—seems perfectly chosen, a feast for the eyes. And Zbigniew Preisner's lovely score, ominous and lyric, is seamlessly linked to Holland's images.

The spell this movie casts could easily have been broken by the slightest miscasting. But the child actors at the heart of this tale—the grave, soulful Maberly, pug-faced and throaty-voiced Knott, and Prowse, with his hilarious neurasthenic hauteur—are uncanny. They seem to have stepped out of another century. Crossley, the older girl, is a vibrantly endearing Martha; and it is no surprise that Maggie Smith makes Medlock a riveting authoritarian bully. "The Secret Garden" has the feel of a classic, and one can only hope that it can find its way up against noisier, flashier, more heavily promoted fare like "Dennis the Menace" and "Free Willy" (almost all the other children's movies are focused on boys). But it would be an equal shame if adults felt they needed a child in tow to see this movie. They'd be missing out on one of the richest cinematic treats of the summer.

SIGHT AND SOUND, 11/93, p. 52, Lizzie Francke

The 1900s. Mary Lennox lives with her parents in India. After an earthquake in which her parents are killed, she is sent to England to stay with her uncle, Lord Craven, at Misselthwaite Manor. At Liverpool dock she is met by her uncle's housekeeper Mrs Medlock, who tells her that Mary's mother had a twin sister, who is also dead. At the gloomy manor, Mary is left to amuse herself. The young maid Martha attempts to befriend the aloof child, but Mary prefers to explore the house and surrounding landscape on her own.

Out in the grounds, she discovers a walled garden. A friendly robin shows her the way to its locked door. Mary rummages through her dead aunt's room and finds the key to this door. Later, Mary returns to the garden and meets Dickon, Martha's younger brother. He explains to her that her aunt died falling off the garden swing, and that consequently Lord Craven ordered the garden to be sealed up. In the house, Mary hears a moaning sound and is told that it is the wind. Left to herself, Mary discovers the source of the noise, a young invalid boy in one of the rooms; he is Colin, Lord Craven's son. He explains that he is seriously ill. Meanwhile, Mary and Dickon tend to the garden and plant it for the spring. Mary also secretly visits Colin in his room. One day she is playing with Colin when Mrs Medlock turns up. Mary has to hide, though she is later discovered by Martha. Martha tells Mary that Lord Craven is coming home. Mary is at last presented to her uncle who is shocked by her resemblance to his wife. Lord Craven is kindly but distant and soon returns to his travels.

When spring comes, the secret garden blooms. Mary and Dickon visit Colin and tear down the shutters on his bedroom window, to Colin's horror. He throws a tantrum, and Mary tells him to shut up. Medlock discovers that the children have been playing together and scolds Martha. Colin decides to get up and bosses the servants around. He is taken by Mary and Dickon in a wheelchair to visit the garden; Mary encourages him to try to walk. During the summer, he grows in strength. Mrs Medlock is convinced that Colin is still not well and continues with his treatments, confining him to his room and putting Mary under lock and key. Mary finds a secret passage leading from her room to the gardens. She makes a wish that Lord Craven will come home, and magically, he decides to return. Finding Colin no longer in his room, Lord Craven goes straight to the garden and finds the children playing hide and seek. He is reunited with his son, but Mary runs off, reminded of her own loneliness. Dickon comforts her, and for the first time Mary is able to mourn the death of her parents. Lord Craven reminds Mary that she is part of the family, as Dickon looks on.

Frances Hodgson Burnett's novel *The Secret Garden* was published in 1911, the same year as J.M. Barrie's *Peter Pan*, and also the third edition of Freud's *Interpretation of Dreams*. Indeed, as with *Peter Pan*, there is much more to Burnett's novel than the 'children's classic' tag allows. Another Neverland, the secret garden—a phrase now ripe with sexual connotation—is a landscape upon which the most adult of anxieties can be mapped out. Children on the verge of adolescence losing parents are the staple narrative of the fairy story. Here the story resolves with the finding of a real father, while the mother is manifest as a garden (one thinks of Marvell's "vegetable love").

Given this, it is appropriate that the director Agnieszka Holland and the writer Caroline Thompson should be hired by Coppola's American Zoetrope to rake over the text as part of the children's classics series which started with Carroll Ballard's *The Black Stallion*. Holland's tale of a cuckoo in the nest, *Olivier, Olivier* was a well-aimed crack at the family romance. Thompson, who wrote *Edward Scissorhands* and *The Addams Family*, knows a thing or two about the cobwebbed corners of the imagination; *The Secret Garden* would seem a perfect project for someone who has stated that her two major cinematic influences are *The Black Stallion* and *Carrie*.

The fact that Holland, a Pole, and Thompson, an American, are alien to the English experience is also germane. Though born in England, Burnett went to live in the US as a child. The England of *The Secret Garden*, as epitomised in the mouldy old manor with its fleet of servants, is the invention of a woman who spent her formative years in Knoxville, Tennessee.

Sex and class with a bit of colonialism thrown in—a heady brew for a family film. Indeed, this story of a young lady from the manor crossing the boundaries and befriending the gardening lad is worthy of D.H. Lawrence. But what is disappointing is that Holland and Thompson, who are obviously not timid at probing the shady side, have been more cautious than an adult might hope for, yet at the same time have created a film that the contemporary children's audience might find not to their taste (with no dinosaurs, turtles or any other opportunities for McDonald's tie-ins, it is hard to see how it will be marketed to them).

Two significant discrepancies between book and film mark the tenor of the project from the beginning. In Burnett's version, Mary's parents die of cholera. There is a vivid account of her left alone in a house full of yellowing death, the only other living thing there being a snake. An earthquake might have more dramatic value, but it seems to provide a more sanitised account of the trauma of separation between child and parent. There is no sense of sickness. The colour yellow manifests itself instead in the golden light that drenches the Indian scenes. This seems to have no other symbolic value other than allowing for a bold contrast with the classically English bleak and rain-swept landscape that prove so foreboding when Mary first arrives in her new country. England was never darker, and Misselthwaite Manor has been art-directed to Gothic perfection.

Meanwhile, Burnett's Mr Craven has been upgraded to the status of a lord. This upwardly mobile move does give a certain resonance to Colin's enfeeblement. Here is a sickly child, terrified of following in his father's line (Lord Craven is a hunchback). He is cosseted and protected from the 'spores' in the air, which might just be the smoke churned out from the factories and mills beyond the moors; but in fact the source of infection is perceived as coming from the servants, who all wear white linen masks over their mouths when dealing with the young master. When Colin finally comes downstairs, the full complement of masked servants line up to greet him. If this all seems ripely farcical, Holland undercuts any ironic intention in a later scene in which the servants smile and wave from a window at the now walking Colin, happy at his new fortune. See how the aristocracy thrives.

But conversely the servants are associated with all that is naturally healthy. The kitchen scenes are brightly lit, bustling with rosy-cheeked activity, making a glaring contrast with the gloomy upstairs. Only Mrs Medlock is charmlessly brusque (Maggie Smith on the right side of caricature), but then house-keepers inhabit the miserable limbo between upstairs and downstairs. Proper servants like Martha melt with heart-cheering goodness, while Dickon is the pastoral boy, trailing with him a menagerie of deer, rabbits, robins and other cute wildlife. With the help of Dickon's green fingers, Mary is able to bring her garden back to life, rousing mother nature (she finds the key in her other mother's bedroom).

The film blossoms with stop-frame shots of roots thrusting and flowers burgeoning. The magic of the organic marks an emotionally regenerative process for Mary, and allows her finally to mourn her lost parents and fall a little in love with Dickon. Likewise, Colin is restored to health. But the cultivation of the garden also marks a return to a familiar old order, despite Mrs Medlock's contention that Mary has created havoc. Lord Craven arrives at the manor to take his place as father, Mary and Colin are tentatively aligned (earlier Colin had expressed a desire to marry her), while Dickon is expelled from this new-found paradise and is last seen out on the wild moors. From this, it would seem that the servant class has sown the seeds of their own destruction.

TIME, 8/16/93, p. 58, Richard Corliss

One way or another, everyone is an orphan. You come into the world blind and crying, you leave the world knowing that you can't take it, or anyone, with you. Each aspect of your identity, good or ill, isolates you from other people. Every word you utter is a cry rising from the human orphanage—where there is one child per room, and all the doors are locked.

Mary Lennox is an orphan and worse. She is an unloved, unwanted child, spoiled and ignored by her late parents, a sulky burden to the staff of Misselthwaite Manor, where her reclusive uncle, Lord Craven, has brought her with no thoughts of loving, educating or even taming her. He will allow her only to cultivate one of his untended gardens. Poor makings for a heroine, which is just why Mary made such a good one in Frances Hodgson Burnett's 1911 novel *The Secret Garden*. The book left a permanent notch in many hearts (mostly girls' hearts) by teaching how creation can flower from isolation. Those strange English virtues—patience, prim artistry, a sense of order and plenty of rain—can nurture a garden, a home, a family. It is a child's perfect vision of motherhood.

The Secret Garden was filmed by MGM in 1949 and for TV in 1987. Two years ago, it was a hauntingly rhapsodic Broadway musical. Now, in a different key, it is a lovely film from three people who know the territory: executive producer Francis Ford Coppola (who in *Bram Stoker's Dracula* found a decaying manor occupied by an old count mourning his dead wife), screenwriter Caroline Thompson (who in *Edward Scissorhands* put another strange, sad creature in a castle) and director Agnieszka Holland (whose films *Europa, Europa* and *Olivier, Olivier* are about abandoned children trying to survive in a world where innocence has been outlawed).

In their Misselthwaite, shadows and vines creep along the bedroom walls like specters and snakes. This is the movie's dank view of the upper class. Lord Craven (John Lynch) ever presses his hands to his forehead, nursing an emotional migraine; his son Colin (Heydon Prowse) is ailing from nothing but privilege. The rich are different: they act more moody. And their attendants, like Lord Craven's housekeeper (Maggie Smith, queen of the imperious), are corrupted by the touch of the wealthy. Elevation keeps people away from the earth, where the peasant class plants itself and grows to healthy maturity. The woodland lad Dickon (Andrew Knott) thus becomes not only a magical gardener but also a robust figure of early manhood, stirring Mary's ardor and Colin's jealousy. In a sense, this *Secret Garden* is *Lady Chatterly's Lover* without the sex.

At MGM, Mary Lennox was played by the tremulous waif Margaret O'Brien. Mary on Broadway was the slim beguiler Daisy Eagan, whom any doting adult would readily adopt. Holland's brave and apt choice for the role is Kate Maberly, who at the start looks as unattractive as the novel describes her. Life has used her so roughly that she keeps people at arm's length with insolent remarks and stares. But as Mary and her garden bloom under the sunlight of Yorkshire camaraderie, so does Maberly. Her eyes come alive, her carriage relaxes; inside the sad rag doll dwells the soul of a coquette and a loving daughter.

Orphans are most poignant when they don't look like Keane portraits. Films are most moving when they find rich colors in a child's darkest fears. This summer has seen many movies about troubled children, but none so honest or graceful as *The Secret Garden*.

VILLAGE VOICE, 8/17/93, p. 49, Georgia Brown

Agnieszka Holland knows the perils and threats that send the self into hiding. She knows too about the tendency of buried selves to return literally with a vengeance. A Pole with a Jewish father, Holland has approached the subjects of hiding and spoiled identity—both in her own films and ones she wrote for Wajda—in terms of the Holocaust and fascist repression. But hers are never simple tales of hide-and-seek, and, mysterious and disturbing, they often cause unease. Her characters are tormented by mixed motives, their desires to regain lost felicity complicated by instincts to assimilate and betray. We watch them doing things that will create guilt and require repression.

At least three of her films—*Angry Harvest, Europa, Europa,* and *Olivier, Olivier*—start with a dead child, a troubled ghost haunting surviving siblings and parents. In *Angry Harvest,* a tormented woman who's just lost her daughter (escaping from a death camp transport) becomes a feral child herself, reduced to complete dependence on the farmer who rescues, hides, and abuses her, Solly in *Europa, Europa* sees his sister bleeding and flees into a series of complex, emasculating denials. Most recently, in the Chabrolian *Olivier, Olivier,* the disappearance of a young boy haunts his obsessed mother and his angry (terribly neglected) elder sister.

Now, for her first American film, Holland chooses a deceptively simple project, yet one that surely, engages her preoccupations with childhood trauma and survival. In adapting Frances Hodgson Burnett's *The Secret Garden*—one of her favorite childhood books, she says, and her mother's, too—Holland's working for the first time not from her own script, but, in this case, one by Caroline Thompson (*Edward Scissorhands, The Addams Family*). Whether together or separately, the two women strive to do right by Burnett's classic, but they've also changed details to strengthen its force as a girl's own story.

In *The Secret Garden* two poor little rich kids, cousins—a girl living in India and a boy in Yorkshire, England—are abused in the same way: Their physical needs are met by servants, while the parents shun them, find them ugly, and wish they hadn't been born.

Both contrary Mary Lennox and her cousin, Colin Craven, while growing increasingly sickly, develop into imperious little monsters. Colin, the spoiled prince of Misselthwaite Manor, becomes so impressed with his own deficiencies that he can't even walk.

Holland's opening tableau is striking: In a completely white world, a nearly immobile Mary (Kate Maberly) is being dressed by her ayah, while another servant, swaying slightly, stands in a corner holding her fresh white frock. No one speaks. The results of this bleaching of human contact are seen when Mary has one of her fits, tries holding on to her reluctant mother, and breaks a strand of pearls. Then, just as her parents go out to a party, an earthquake—like an extension of her gathering rage—kills them both. (In the novel's eerier opening, the whole compound dies in a cholera epidemic and Mary lives on alone in the charnal house until discovered by soldiers.) Shipped off to an uncle's estate on the edge of the Yorkshire moors, Mary finally manages, with a little help from friends, to create for herself a green world.

In making Mary related to Colin (Heydon Prowse) through their mothers—twin sisters here—rather than through brothers, the movie turns the garden into Mary's mother's legacy. The key isn't buried but found in a small drawer in her dead aunt's room—a replica of her mother's room in India. In the movie, her distracted uncle, Archibald Craven (John Lynch), enters late and more as a surrogate for the twin mothers. The changes offer a corrective to Burnett's novel, which begins so brilliantly with the sour little Mary and then becomes preoccupied in the final episodes with the reunion of father and son. Boys came first.

As for that famous nature-boy and guru of the moors, Dickon (Andrew Knott), he's rather a recessive presence here. Although he lends a hand, Mary really, heals herself, and then sets about rehabilitating her double, Colin. With his cries in the night, Colin represents her invalid, infantile self, and his rehabilitation is really an aspect of hers. (In point of fact, someone who's never walked at the designated time can never learn. It's the same principle demonstrated by the story of Genie, the girl who could never acquire grammar because she'd missed the moment.)

In Holland and Thompson's version, Dickon is also overshadowed by his sister, the sweet-natured serving girl, Martha (Laura Crossley). Martha's giving Mary a jump rope becomes a crucial turning point: "Thank you Martha, and thank your mother, too," says Mary, her first-ever expression of gratitude. Later, Martha's deft and compassionate treatment of the housekeeper,

Mrs. Medlock (Maggie Smith), constitutes one of the movie's most original, and very feminine, touches. A practitioner of Munchausen's Syndrome by Proxy, Mrs. Medlock isn't really very threatening (she's no Mrs. Danvers); she's just one more lonesome creature in need of a bit of mothering herself.

In all her works, Holland is less interested in portraying victims than in beaming light into the locked and secret hearts of her terribly compromised caretakers. There're no real villains in her pieces, nor heroes either. Here, by playing down the gothic and resisting the temptations of conventional cinematic narrative (where evil is hyperbolic and can be vanquished with a mighty blow), she quite simply and very beautifully reveals evil's roots.

Also reviewed in:
CHICAGO TRIBUNE, 8/13/93, Friday/p. A, Johanna Steinmetz
NEW YORK TIMES, 8/13/93, p. C3, Janet Maslin
VARIETY, 8/16/93, p. 38, Todd McCarthy
WASHINGTON POST, 8/13/93, p. D1, Megan Rosenfeld
WASHINGTON POST, 8/13/93, Weekend/p. 38, Desson Howe

SEVENTH COIN, THE

A Hemdale Communications release of an Orbit Entertainment/April Communications production. *Executive Producer:* James Nelson, Shimshon Rafaeli, Dov Strikofsky, and Garry Hakim. *Producer:* Lee Nelson and Omri Maron. *Director:* Dror Soref. *Screenplay:* Dror Soref and Michael Lewis. *Director of Photography:* Avi Karpik. *Editor:* Carole Kravetz. *Music:* Misha Segal. *Sound:* Yohal Moshe. *Production Designer:* Yoram Shayer. *Set Decorator:* Doron Shalem and Amir Kaplan. *Costumes:* Laura Dinulesco. *Running time:* 92 minutes. *MPAA Rating:* PG-13.

CAST: Alexandra Powers (Ronnie Segal); Navin Chowdhry (Salim Zouabi); Peter O'Toole (Emil Saber); John Rhys-Davies (Captain Galil); Ally Walker (Lisa); Whitman Mayo (Julius Washington).

LOS ANGELES TIMES, 9/10/93, Calendar/p. 9, Kevin Thomas

"The Seventh Coin", an inept youth-oriented thriller, has appealing stars and highly atmospheric, well-photographed ancient Israeli locales, but that's not nearly enough to offset Dror Soref's awkward direction and his overly complicated, often downright silly script (written with Michael Lewis).

Alexandra Powers' bright, spunky American student and Navin Chowdhry's embittered young Arab thief cross paths when he steals her camera case while she's touring Old Jerusalem. A priceless coin belonging to the Arab's grandfather winds up in that case, and in no time the two young people are scrambling over rooftops and through maze-like narrow streets with the murderous minions of Peter O'Toole's crazed retired British officer on their heels. He has slain—or had slain—everyone who stood in his path in obtaining the first six coins, minted by King Herod, and he intends that no one will prevent him from completing the set.

The film is at its best when it sticks with Powers and Chowdhry, who gradually learn to know and understand each other while on the run. Their parts are decently written, and they are engaging actors. Soref, in his feature debut, gets his film off to a rocky start with needless and confusing plot complications. Every time he starts gaining momentum he sabotages himself by cutting to ludicrous, dated comic relief provided by a rookie Jerusalem cop (Ally Walker) from Baltimore who's constantly skirmishing with her bombastic chief of police uncle (John Rhys-Davies) in her determination to play detective.

While aimed at teens, "The Seventh Coin" is unsuitable for those younger, and its PG-13 rating (for some violence, a moment of nudity and one use of strong language) is entirely appropriate.

NEW YORK POST, 9/11/93, p. 14, Michael Medved

Waiting for an international movie hit to emerge from Israel is a bit like waiting for the Messiah; you keep hoping against hope that the time has come, but you're destined for regular doses of disappointment.

The latest bust is "The Seventh Coin," a brain-dead embarrassment that wastes an intriguing cast. Seven-time Oscar nominee Peter O'Toole plays a retired British army officer on a murderous quest in Jerusalem to recover an ancient gold coin he helped unearth on an archaeological dig nearly 50 years before.

Through a series of accidents, this priceless artifact has fallen into the unsuspecting hands of an Arab street rat and pickpocket (Navin Chowdhry, the young piano prodigy in "Madam Sousatzka") and a blond teen-aged tourist from America (Alexandra Powers, a rising TV star with a featured role next season in "L.A. Law").

All recent exploitation films from Israel seen to operate under an 11th Commandment—"Thou Shalt Feature a Jewish-Arab Love Affair"—and "The Seventh Coin" is no exception.

While running away from O'Toole and his hired thugs, Chowdhry and Powers hide out in various towers and passageways of the Old City, and that old Middle Eastern moon soon works its magic. Asked by the dewy-eyed Jewish kid from America about his plans for the future, Chowdhry solemnly declares:

"I think one day, soft face, I become teacher. And I help my people and your people become friends—like you and me!"

To his eternal credit, Chowdhry manages to deliver such lines with a straight face, turning in this miserable movie's only vaguely respectable performance. With his liquid, shining eyes and sensitive features he could become an important romantic lead if he is given the chance to strut his stuff with more worthy material.

O'Toole, on the other hand, here hits a new low in his long and remarkable career. He staggers through his role like a sleepwalker trying to awaken from a vaguely unpleasant dream, conveying homicidal rage by lifting a single quizzical eyebrow or growling dumb lines in a tired singsong. Through most of the movie he looks like the victim of a miserable case of *shilshul*—the Israeli answer to Montezuma's revenge.

In fact, his cadaverous physical appearance is downright alarming: during the climactic chase scene along the walls of the Old City you never worry that O'Toole will murder the two young lovers (as he has a half-dozen other over-acting victims in the course of the movie), but rather that this painfully frail old man may slip and hurt himself.

Similarly ridiculous is one of O'Toole's supposedly menacing thugs: a paunchy middle-aged guy in an eye patch who's a dead ringer for Mel Brooks.

Meanwhile, first-time director/co-screenwriter Dror Soref (who made a name for himself directing music videos for none other than "Weird Al" Yankovic) displays such bland, flat, flavorless camera work that the picture fails even as a travelogue—making the world's most fascinating city look as intriguing as Trenton.

Now that Israel and the PLO have succeeded in their controversial current negotiations, they should consider adding a new clause to the peace treaty—serving the cause of harmony and humanity by preventing the future release (and export) of any further films like this one.

NEWSDAY, 9/10/93, Part II/p. 79, Joseph Gelmis

Watching Peter O'Toole in "The Seventh Coin", is a melancholy spectacle.

You start out feeling sorry for O'Toole. Here he is, 30 years after he dazzled world audiences as the handsome and charismatic young hero of the epic "Lawrence of Arabia," looking appallingly emaciated and frail in an insipid and silly movie.

But you end up feeling sorry for yourself. Watching "The Seventh Coin" is a depleting experience—which O'Toole, unlike critics and paying customers, was not obliged to endure. The characters are clichés, the dialogue is trite and the action consists almost entirely of a teen couple running, dodging and hiding from O'Toole and two inept henchmen in the old walled city of Jerusalem.

O'Toole plays a crazed villain, a former British officer who believes himself the reincarnation the biblical King Herod. He has been collecting seven gold coin's minted by Herod to commemorate the consolidation of his empire. The seventh coin is in the possession of a young Arab thief and a Jewish-American student tourist.

Despite his star billing, O'Toole is in relatively few scenes. He performs with a blithe detachment whatever the inane script requires. He sings "It's a Long Way to Tipperary" to himself after casually murdering four people. And, in the movie's most ludicrous sequence, he rides a horse-drawn chariot through the teeming Arab market, trying to run down the fleeing teens.

Directed by Dror Soref, an Israeli now living in Los Angeles, "The Seventh Coin" is a cutesy cross-cultural romantic thriller aimed at adolescents. During the many pauses in the chase, the fugitives compare notes on their separate lives and decide to treat their adventure as "a first date."

The Arab actor, Navin Chowdhry, brings to mind an inarticulate young Sal Mineo from his "Exodus" days. Alexandra Powers, as the tourist, is not only likeable but sexually attractive—no small feat since her sole outfit is hiking shorts and ankle-high boots.

Powers delivers what is arguably the only funny line in the movie: Trapped up to her hips in a flooded underground chamber with the Arab thief, the middle-class American coed whines "I should have gone to tennis camp."

Except for that single atypical flash of irreverent humor, the comic relief in "The Seventh Coin" is clunky (running gags about the nepotism of the city's police chief, who has a son and niece on the payroll). The only really interesting thing about the film is the scenery, the exotic locales of the nonstop chase—the rooftops, narrow twisting streets and subterranean vaults of old Jerusalem, atmospherically photographed by cameraman Avi Karpik.

Also reviewed in:
NEW YORK TIMES, 9/10/93, p. C5, Stephen Holden
VARIETY, 5/17/93, p. 98, Joe Leydon

SEX IS ...

An Outsider release. *Producer:* Marc Huestis and Lawrence Helman. *Director:* Marc Huestis. *Director of Photography:* Fawn Yacker. *Editor:* Lara Mac and Hrafnihildur Gunnarsdottir. *Music:* Donna Viscuso and Pussy Tourette. *Sound:* Lauretta Molitar. Art Director: Vola Ruben. *Running time:* 80 minutes. *MPAA Rating:* Not Rated.

WITH: Larry Brinkin; Danny Castellow; Alex Chee; Wayne Corbitt; Jim Glyer; Miguel Gutierrez; Bob Hawk; Marc Huestis; Gerard Koskovich; Bambi Lake; Lulu; R. Wood Massi; David Perry; Brad Phillips; Madame X.

LOS ANGELES TIMES, 11/12/93, Calendar/p. 17, Kevin Thomas

Marc Huestis' "Sex Is ..." is clearly a landmark film because of the candor with which 15 gay men, ranging in ages from 19 to 73, talk about sex and sexuality. It is entertaining, sobering, funny and sometimes profoundly sad as it illuminates the way in which gays have dealt with their sex lives over the last half-century, enduring the closet and surviving the sexual revolution and confronting AIDS.

On the one hand, Huestis has done a good job in gathering a representative cross section of the gay community, including himself, Latinos, blacks, Asians, a transvestite prostitute, a porn star, a minister and those attracted to sadomasochism, and then in getting these men to speak so frankly and reflectively.

On the other, he has also chosen to punctuate, sometimes even to interrupt, his interviews with flashes of hard-core footage. This seems a mistake, not because it's likely to offend heterosexual viewers, most of whom won't be interested in seeing the film in the first place, but because these clips in juxtaposition with the interviews has a reductive, depersonalizing effect upon them. (Ironically, Brad Phillips, a well-known porn star, admits that his work can make him feel lonely.)

Just when each of the 15 men are so persuasively allowing us to see their sexuality as part of their entire being, Huestis cuts to the hard stuff, which tends to define his subjects in terms of sexual acts, which are being performed by men who are fantasy figures—more often than not physically more attractive than those being interviewed. Yet gays have a need to see themselves, as well as be seen by one another and by straights, as whole persons and not merely as sex objects or in terms of what they do in bed.

This distracting device aside, "Sex Is ..." (Times-rated Mature for explicit sex and language) nevertheless has much to offer gay male audiences, suggesting that today's youth by and large are spared the crippling guilts and fears of earlier generations and that gay men can find the strength to cope with the devastating double blow of the loss of a lover to AIDS and their own HIV-positive status.

More often than not, too, the men's attempts to define sex leads to thoughts on love and its greater importance than sex. (A documentary on straight males would probably reveal the same conclusion.) One man, Wayne Corbitt, admits that sex with his lover, who died of AIDS, wasn't all that great but that their love was. "Love," he has discovered, "has very little to do with sexuality."

NEW YORK POST, 9/8/93, p. 26, Jerry Tallmer

Of the 15 people who tell their stories in "Sex Is ...," the two I'd like to meet sometime are Madame X and Jim Glyer.

Madame X is a good-looking, waspy black queen—"Professional Illusionist and Entertainer"—who works the streets of Oakland, Calif., and takes no lip from nobody. "Sex is me, I am sex," he says. "I wasn't born a man in a woman's body, no, I was born a boy with a woman's mentality and that was it."

Jim Glyer is a white-bearded white-crowned Community Church pastor in San Francisco who looks and sounds like Edmund Gwen in "Miracle on 34th Street" and must be just as nice. He tells us he has always been unable to have sex with a woman, even on his honeymoon years ago. At age 40 he found in "one of the most painful experiences of my life," that "that monster"—dormant homosexuality—"was still there." At age 50 he came out of the closet. At age 70 he found the man he loves today.

This, to me, is touching, as is much of the testimony throughout "Sex Is ...," the thoughtful 80-minute documentary—thoughtful, touching, yes, but at moments unbearably smug—by 37-year--old Marc Huestis.

How these 15 men first came to their identity is perhaps the most interesting part of the film. There's the boy whose father gave him muscle magazines, for manhood—"an adventure come true, I'd take them to the bathroom and masturbate." Or the kid who favored the photos in Modern Screen of Tony Curtis, Tab Hunter, "and God help me, Robert Stack."

Or this: a kid who was abused "in early prepubescence" in the men's room of the Chicago Art Museum. "Child abuse is just that—abuse."

But it would be a grave mistake to think all homosexuality starts with abuse. Consider the black preacher remembering as his first love a white man who "looked like Bugs Bunny—very sweet—made me cry." Or the chap whose first amour involved "45 minutes of hair spray and tight, tight jeans" as he headed toward a date for dinner before Mass." Some date. "My closet door was blown off." Or, oppositely, the lure of the bathhouse, a "badness" that "just reeked of male, of violent sex, something so pure about it too"—Jean Genet couldn't have said it better.

Yes, there is AIDS here, yes there is loss, terror, cowardice, penance, yes, there are graphic shots—hasty and blurry—parlayed, all too glibly, but funnily, against the fulminations of Jesse Helms propounding on the floor of the Senate that every homosexual be horsewhipped. And that's why movies like this are needed.

VILLAGE VOICE, 9/21/93, p. 67, Marco Spino

Hearing the gay men in *Sex Is* ... frankly and wittily describe the sights, smells, and sounds of their sexual experiences and fantasies is liberating not only because they are so self-assured about sex, but because they relish talking about it. This documentary uses images from mass culture to chronicle the evolution of gay sex from the covertness of the 1950s to safer sex today. The men see their sexual identity rooted in the 1970s discos and bathhouses of San Francisco, or as one interviewee calls the city, "Babylon." By expertly weaving together monologues about similar sexual encounters, the directors reconstruct the scene in all its glory.

Whenever the descriptions are not vivid enough, clips from sweaty porn movies make the point. But *Sex Is* ... has more significant aims than just giving you a hard-on. It argues that overpoliticizing sex detracts from its intensity and pleasure, and presents s&m as a route to self-knowledge, and for some, a way of preparing for death.

Roughly half of the men are HIV-positive, including director Marc Huestis, who says it was only a matter of time before his unsafe sexual adventures led to infection. But neither Huestis nor the others ask for pity; instead they affirm the resilience of their libido.

Drawn from diverse ethnicities, professions, and age groups, some of these men tend to ramble, like the one who associates VO5 hair cream with masturbation or the transvestite prostitute who says that sex "is a constantly withering rose." Others seem smug. But most have a great sense of humor and utter priceless lines: "I remember the first time my tits were played with by a guy who took off his dentures afterwards and sucked my dick."

Also reviewed in:
CHICAGO TRIBUNE, 11/19/93, Friday/p. H, Michael Wilmington
NEW YORK TIMES, 9/9/93, p. C17, Stephen Holden
VARIETY, 3/15/93, p. 66, Howard Feinstein

SEX AND ZEN

A Rim Film Distributors release of a Golden Harvest production. *Executive Producer:* Johnny Mak. *Producer:* Stephen Siu. *Director:* Michael Mak. *Screenplay (Cantonese with English and Chinese subtitles):* Lee Ying Kit. *Based on novel "Yu Ou Tuan" ("The Carnal Prayer Mat"):* Li Yu. *Director of Photography:* Peter Ngor. *Editor:* Poon Hung. *Music:* Chang Wing Leung. *Art Director:* Raymond Lee. *Running time:* 99 minutes. *MPAA Rating:* Not Rated.

CAST: Lawrence Ng (Mei Yang); Amy Yip (Yuk Heung, his wife); Cheng (Doctor); Xu Jin-Jiang (Kuen the Silk Merchant); Isabella Chow (Kuen's Wife); Lo Lieh (Choi Run Lun).

LOS ANGELES TIMES, 8/13/93, Calendar/p. 24, Kevin Thomas

The amusingly titled "Sex and Zen" concentrates lots more on the former than on the latter, which is saved for the very last.

An elegant and erotic comedy adapted from Li Yu's Ming Dynasty novel "The Carnal Prayer Mat," it is strictly for ultra-sophisticated adults and is an exceedingly deft blend of outrageous sex and equally outrageous humor.

Without our realizing what is happening, this singularly sly film gradually evolves from sex farce to cautionary tale underlined by increasingly dark humor. In short, its libertine hero, Mei Yang (Lawrence Ng), proves to have more in common with St. Augustine than we would have ever suspected.

No sooner has the handsome, rakish Mei Yang awakened his beautiful but comically reluctant bride, Yuk Heung (Amy Yip), to the pleasures of sex than he abandons her for a life of determined womanizing.

When a mentor tells him that he's not properly equipped for such a career, he submits to primitive transplant surgery in a sequence of brilliantly sustained hilarity. Thus armed, however, he succumbs to sex so compulsively that a day of reckoning could be lurking ahead—also for his having treated his wife with such total neglect.

As a period piece "Sex and Zen" is gorgeous-looking, as are its actresses, and director Michael Mak, working from Lee Ying Kit's script, flirts with but never quite lapses into hard-core territory while building up considerable steam.

Its heavy duty sensuality, however, cannot distract us from the cruelty and decadence of its era—a time when women were chattel without recourse to brutal husbands, where their only hope of self-defense was beauty combined with formidable sexual wizardry.

The film's contemporary sensibility, furthermore, allows us to see the vulnerable, self-destructive underside of extreme machismo. Indeed, "Sex and Zen," as hot as it is, is steeped in a sense of the absurdity of sex divorced from love or affection.

As a director, Mak must have a remarkable capacity for inspiring a trust in his actors that would permit them to appear in one uninhibited scene after another; to his credit, he never makes fools of them. And he further more gets terrific performances from them in the most potentially embarrassing situations.

"Sex and Zen" (Times-rated Mature for sex and nudity) is a wise and risqué treat for the truly grown-up, but remember to leave the kids at home.

NEW YORK POST, 10/29/93, p. 28, Michael Medved

How's this for high concept: A rich young husband, quickly bored with his beautiful bride, longs for outside conquests, but worries that his natural endowments leave him under-equipped for the seducer's role.

He therefore submits to painful surgery in which the private parts of a horse are grafted onto his body, enabling him to astonish and delight the parade of beauties who now succumb to his charms.

This crude plot, which forms the basis for "Sex and Zen," would be written off as a story suitable solely for the raincoat crowd were it not for this Hong Kong import's claim that it is based on a classic Ming Dynasty novel.

These honorable origins, together with a lush sense of color, lots of blowing silk, and some reasonably smooth camera work, give this picture a certain amount of art house cachet.

Moviegoers who might otherwise be embarrassed to turn up for this soft-core extravaganza can claim they are drawn to its view of 16th-century Chinese civilization or fascinated by its exotic artistry. "Sex and Zen" thereby provides porn, without guilt.

Since I freely confess that I have never read the 400-year-old tale (known as "Prayer Mat of the Flesh") on which this picture is allegedly based, I am in no position to evaluate just how faithfully director Michael Mak has adapted his source materials. He does, however, employ a series of striking sets and costumes, and a large cast of able and extraordinarily attractive performers.

Kent Cheng is especially impressive as a muscular silk merchant whose raw animal appetites lead him to some brutal and implausibly acrobatic excesses.

But anyone who expects that this mindless skin flick in any way resembles such magnificent tales of passion as "Raise the Red Lantern" or "Farewell, My Concubine" will be sorely disappointed.

In the last analysis, "Sex and Zen" fails even in its modest goal of providing encouragement and stimulation for lovers: The images that stick in the mind after the film is over are gross and gory rather than erotic.

Anyone who's considering this picture as an adventurous date movie should definitely think twice: When you come out of the theater you'll be more likely to remember graphic shots of bloody, mutilated male organs, and brutal beatings of unhappy wives, rather than recalling the elaborate sequences of nude bodies twisting in passion.

NEWSDAY, 11/29/93, Part II/p. 79, John Anderson

Ok, lets cut the malarkey. Although "Sex and Zen" is based on a 17th-Century Chinese novel (Li Yu's "The Carnal Prayer Mat"), aspires to the stature of moral fable and was "banned for 400 years," according to its overheated advertisements, the film is about sex. Outrageous, acrobatic and—although simulated—as plain as the nose on your face. And just about as close.

Whether "S&Z" is erotic is up to the viewer, I suppose, but be forewarned: There's very little territory that goes undiscovered here. Opposite-sex, same-sex, self-sex, group-sex; sex on a swing; sex while swinging across the room on a swing; sex with musical instruments; sex with oversized writing utensils. And a sexual organ transplant, from horse to man.

What all this adds up to is the education of Mei Yang (Lawrence Ng), a "knight errant" whom we first see in consultation with his Buddhist master. Retribution, the master warns, will be visited upon Mei for his lascivious ways. Mei scoffs, but he'll reap what he sows—but not after the audience has been sufficiently titillated.

Mei is a dog, really. He leaves his wife, Yuk Heung (Amy Yip), to seduce his way across the countryside. He then allies himself with the Flying Thief, Choi Run Lun (Lo Lieh), who protects him from Keun the silk merchant, (Xu Jin-Jiang), whose beleaguered wife (Isabella Chow) Mei has seduced. He'll seek the aid of a doctor (Kent Cheng) in remedying his paltry endowment, by trading it for that of a horse. The animal-rights people will be incensed.

Based on classic erotica, "Sex and Zen" is a tale of virtue's rewards that takes great pains to shock and arouse. Sometimes, it actually succeeds. But more often the situations and attempts at bawdy humor seem adolescent, if not infantile. In contrast to what one might find on the hard-core market, of course, it's tame. But in terms of mainstream foreign imports, it's not your usual animal (and I don't mean horse).

VILLAGE VOICE, 11/9/93, p. 65, Andrew Hsiao

When a book gets banned for 350 years, it's got to have something going for it. Li Yu's *The Carnal Prayer Mat*, the story of a bawdy monk's adventures during the Ming dynasty, has been officially off-limits more or less since its writing, though of course that hasn't stopped people from reading it. What enraged Confucians and the neo-Confucians currently in Beijing was, yes, comrades, sex.

While *Sex and Zen*, a loopy adaptation of *Prayer Mat*, contains only a smidgen of the original's sly wit, it does have its, er, moments: a character has his cock guillotined and replaced with a horse's penis; another makes truly abstract ink drawings with a paintbrush held by her, ahem, vagina; two women do it simultaneously with a flute; people fuck in the tub, on the floor, on a rope hanging from the ceiling.

Those not inconsiderable pleasures aside, *Sex & Zen* is both too trad soft-core to work as good porn (we're treated to plenty of nipple close-ups but unfortunately, or fortunately, we never get to see the equine member—or any other male organ—in action) and too puerile to work as comedy of manners. Early on, *Sex & Zen* promises *A Chinese Ghost Story* with sex! Later, it delivers *Henry and June* filtered through Hong Kong clown Steven Chao.

But if nothing else, *Sex & Zen* proves that HK films have truly arrived here: we now get to see not only the best gangster movies, ghost stories, and Jackie Chans outside of Chinatown, but hokey sex farces too.

Also reviewed in:
NEW YORK TIMES, 10/29/93, p. C10, Stephen Holden
VARIETY, 3/1/93, p. 57, David Rooney

SHADOW OF THE WOLF

A Vision International release of a Mark Damon presentation in association with Transfilm/Eiffel Productions with participation of Canal Plus. *Executive Producer:* Charles L. Smiley. *Producer:* Claude Leger. *Director:* Jacques Dorfmann. *Screenplay:* Rudy Wurlitzer, Evan Jones, and David Milhaud. *Based on the novel "Agaguk" by:* Yves Theriault. *Director of Photography:* Billy Williams. *Editor:* Francoise Bonnot. *Music:* Maurice Jarre. *Production Designer:* Wolf Kroeger. *Costumes:* Olga Dimitrov. *Running time:* 108 minutes. *MPAA Rating:* PG-13.

CAST: Lou Diamond Phillips (Agaguk); Toshiro Mifune (Kroomak); Jennifer Tilly (Igiyook); Bernard-Pierre Donnadieu (Brown); Donald Sutherland (Henderson).

LOS ANGELES TIMES, 3/5/93, Calendar/p. 8, Michael Wilmington

Thirty-one million Canadian dollars apparently went into the making of "Shadow of the Wolf," an adaptation of Yves Theriault's famous Canadian novel of Eskimo life, "Agakuk." And, though that investment is apparently the greatest in the history of the Canadian film industry, the results are less spectacular than, say, the average David Cronenberg thriller or Denys Arcand talk-a-thon.

Vast sweeping, gleamingly white Arctic vistas; a fortune's, worth of authentically re-created Eskimo, or Inuit, artifacts and costumes; a whole huge snowy set, complete with Inuit village, re-created in a Montreal quarry; the services of David Lean's personal majestic-epic composer Maurice Jarre, "Gandhi's" cinematographer Billy Williams and a half-dozen other Oscar-winning collaborators, plus a big international star-cast, headed by Lou Diamond Phillips and Toshiro Mifune ... All of it goes blowing off across the Artic wastes. Or, in this case, blowing out of the Montreal quarry.

"Shadow of the Wolf" has a wonderful subject for a movie: the collision of Eskimo and Anglo culture in the 1930s, before the old tribal customs and mores were eroded away. As adapted by two excellent screenwriters, Evan Jones and Rudy Wurlitzer, Theriault's saga becomes another noble outlaw adventure—with Phillips Agaguk, and Jennifer Tilly as his mate Igiyook, striking off for the white wilderness, after Agaguk kills the exploitative and slovenly Canadian trader, Brown (Bernard-Pierre Donnadieu). Meanwhile, Agaguk's father, Kroomak the Shaman (Mifune), fends off his son's pursuers.

However Theriault portrayed him in the novel, a longtime staple of Canadian literature courses, in this movie Agaguk is a typical post '60s hip noble savage and rebel, scornful and suspicious of all whites. He also seems scornful of parka hoods—all the better for Phillips to assay his most typical gesture: a quick sullen shake to get the hair out of his eyes.

The movie piles on incongruities just as the Inuit heap up snow blocks for their igloos. Mifune, the nonpareil swaggerer of Kurosawa's great "Seven Samurai" and "Yojimbo," as the Inuit father of Phillips? (One can recognize Mifune's voice in one scene where he grunts with passion during lovemaking but not in his notably unaccented dialogue.) Jennifer Tilly, with her candyish Betty Boop-whine, as the Eskimo maiden, Igiyook? (She seems closer to Iggy Pop.) Bernard-Pierre Donnadieu—who played the brilliantly chilling French psychopath in the original Dutch version of "The Vanishing"—as a trader named *Brown*?

Except for Donald Sutherland, contributing some patented low-key sadism as Henderson the man-tracker, the polar bear, wolf (a "Dances With Wolves" veteran) and huskies fare much better here than their human colleagues. The nadir of that human indignity is reached when Mifune, in a would-be smash climax, dives from an airplane and turns into a hawk.

Incongruous casting can work in pictures like this. Anthony Quinn was massively enjoyable as Inuk, or Quinn the Eskimo, in Nick Ray's 1960 "The Savage Innocents." But director Jacques Dorfmann ("Palanquin les Armes") never shows much unifying pictorial or dramatic style it's a different movie inside the sets and outside them. There's even another director, Christian Duguay, listed for the action scenes.

The splendor of the exteriors, livid with northern light, and the excitement of occasional scenes like the wolf attack or whale hunt, clash with the crèche-like stiffness of the re-created village. "Shadow of the Wolf" (MPAA-rated PG-13 for some violence and sensuality) is a movie where characterization is only a shadow and the Big Budget wolves chew up dramatic logic. And where the majesty of Eskimo life and culture gets lost in a quarry.

NEW YORK POST, 3/5/93, p. 35, Jami Bernard

Political correctness drips like water off a melting stalactite in "Shadow of the Wolf," the "Dances With Wolves" of the Eskimo set. The two movies even used the same trained bear.

Political correctness is in vogue, but when overused can rob a movie of its power and nuance. The very first thing you see in "Shadow of the Wolf," even before its beautiful wide-screen vistas, is a disclaimer about how they didn't hurt any animals. Such disclaimers are usually reserved for the small print at the end of a film. Here, harpooning a whale or gutting a wolf carries little dramatic tension since we've been forewarned it's all pretend.

And speaking of pretend, let's talk about the acting prowess of Lou Diamond Phillips and Jennifer Tilly. Well, let's not.

Phillips shares the screen with the great Japanese actor Toshiro Mifune, as Mifune's angry young Inuit son who defies the social laws of his people by living on his own with Tilly. They speak together in a truncated English to suggest, I suppose, simpler times. Although the Eskimos have 12 words to describe snow, these Eskimos have conversations like, "You are mine"; "I did not know this was so"; "It is so"; "That is good." Yeah? Well dialogue no good, no good by heap big long shot.

The movie, based on the book "Agaguk," follows this Nanook's initiation into manhood and shamanism despite interference from the evil white man, as personified mostly by an insidious Donald Sutherland.

Where the movie is most effective is in its obviously rigorous physical production and in showing the minutiae of Inuit life—games, hunting, even the way they dip their knives in the snow to remove the blood of their quarry. The best scene for my money was the brick-by-brick building of an igloo.

Where the movie is least effective is in its brief history of women's rights, as depicted by the changing relationship of Phillips and Tilly. "You talk too loud!" says he, stomping out of the igloo like he's in some lost "Honeymooners" episode. When Tilly finally takes control of her sexuality, it is to suggest that from then on, men and women will be equal up there at the top of the world.

On the plus side, there's the sheer, dazzling beauty of the North Pole, at least as represented by Quebec locations.

NEWSDAY, 3/5/93, Part II/p. 65, John Anderson

I kept waiting for Lou Diamond Phillips to say, "Yonda stands the igloo of my fadda da king," but no. Besides being perfectly inane, perfectly obvious and perfectly laughable, "Shadow of the Wolf," is also perfectly humorless.

Phillips isn't the only one to blame for this, but he's a good place to start. As Agaguk, the rebellious and ethno-centric son of an Inuit shaman named Kroomak (Toshiro Mifune), he's so overheated he should be leaving a big soggy trail wherever he goes.

He's really upset. *Really*. And about *everything*. White men for instance. They give his people liquor and undermine their spirit. And then there's his father, a corrupt old lecher who's putting the moves on Agaguk's sweetie, Igiyook (Jennifer Tilly). And then, when he returns from a hunting trip with a polar bear he has killed, the trader Brown (Bernard-Pierre Donnadieu) takes the skin in payment for all the booze he has given the tribe. Now Agaguk's *really* mad! So he kills Brown, grabs Igiyook and sets out across the tundra.

Agaguk and Igiyook are not exactly the Nick and Nora of the North: "You are mine," he says. "I am yours," she says. "This wind must stop," he says. "It will not last," she says. "It must stop," he says. Yes, you'll say, it must. *Now! Pleeeease ...*

Although the people they meet when they travel north—to evade Henderson (Donald Sutherland), a lawman who has learned about Brown's murder—speak a native tongue, Agaguk, Igiyook and the rest of their tribe all speak this kind of fractured English that makes them appear ludicrous—and worse, like someone's racist vision of how such a native people might speak. When Toshiro Mifune says his lines, on the other hand, he seems dubbed, but that may be our problem, having seen him in so many great Japanese movies.

"Shadow of the Wolf"—the title refers to the curse Kroomak puts on Agaguk when he leaves the village—doesn't know whether it's a romance, a detective story or a travelogue, but Maurice Jarre, the Oscar-winning composer, must have thought he was scoring a remake of "The Ten Commandments." The music is so portentous it makes otherwise acceptable scenes seem ridiculous.

When Agaguk joins a whale hunt, Jarre actually rips off the music from "Jaws," but that's the least of "Shadow's" problems. The main one is, it's boring, despite all the overwrought dialogue, some sex, some spectacular outdoor scenery (most of the set was constructed in a quarry in Montreal, and looks it) and a generally good cast, who should have known better.

VILLAGE VOICE, 3/16/93, p. 58, Gary Dauphin

It doesn't take very long for *Shadow of the Wolf* to lapse into your basic *F Troop* doggerel, wherein a statement like "Seal!" or "The Whale!" will inevitably be followed by "We will not live by the white man's law!"

Tundra or no, these Inuit are finally just plain "Indians," and *Shadow* is the most standard of stuff. Prodigal son Agaguk's (Lou Diamond Phillips) discoveries of himself, love (with Igiyook, played by an ever messy Jennifer Tilly), and his destiny as a shaman take the usual turns, variously foiled and enabled by a White Man whose impact is more soap-opera-ish than genocidal.

Shadow's tepidness, which on occasion even extends to making the arctic look like a backlot, might seem almost intentional.

But then, BLAM!, some hapless guy gets it between the shoulder blades and has his liver eaten. Yet such moments are scattered enough to suggest that something has been lost in bringing Yves Theriault's novel *Agaguk* to the screen.

There's a more potent alienating effect in the smart performances of Toshiro Mifune as Agaguk's father and in Tilly's Igiyook. The character is your average Indian maiden but her accent and bearing are just so wrong that they bounce off the far wall to return as inspired. It is of course cold, backhanded comfort, but when Tilly is at her loopy best, *Shadow* steps a bit out of native stereotype.

Also reviewed in:
CHICAGO TRIBUNE, 3/5/93, Friday/p. L, Dave Kehr
NEW YORK TIMES, 3/5/93, p. C19, Vincent Canby
NEW YORKER, 3/15/93, p. 121, Anthony Lane
VARIETY, 3/8/93, p. 60, Todd McCarthy
WASHINGTON POST, 3/6/93, p. B2, Hal Hinson

SHADOWLANDS

A Savoy Pictures release of a Price Entertainment production in association with Spelling Films International. *Executive Producer:* Terence Clegg. *Producer:* Richard Attenborough and Brian Eastman. *Director:* Richard Attenborough. *Screenplay:* William Nicholson. *Director of Photography:* Roger Pratt. *Editor:* Lesley Walker. *Music:* George Fenton. *Music Editor:* Kevin Lane. *Sound:* Simon Kaye, Jonathan Bates, Gerry Humphreys, and (music) Keith Grant. *Casting:* Lucy Boulting. *Production Designer:* Stuart Craig. *Art Director:* John King. *Set Decorator:* Stephenie McMillan. *Special Effects:* Chris Corbould. *Costumes:* Penny Rose. *Make-up:* Christine Beveridge. *Running time:* 170 minutes. *MPAA Rating:* PG.

CAST: Julian Fellowes (Desmond Arding); Roddy Maude-Roxby (Arnold Dopliss); Michael Denison ("Harry" Harrington); Andrew Seear (Bob Chafer); Tim McMullan (Nick Farrell); John Wood (Christopher Riley); Andrew Hawkins (Rupert Parrish); Peter Howell (College President); Anthony Hopkins (Jack Lewis); Edward Hardwicke (Warnie Lewis); Robert Flemyng (Claude Bird); James Frain (Peter Whistler); Toby Whithouse (Frith); Daniel Goode (Lieven); Scott Handy (Standish); Chris Williams (Julian); Charles Simon (Barker); Giles Oldershaw (Marcus); Walter Sparrow (Fred Paxford); Simon Cowell-Parker (John Egan); Roger Ashton-Griffiths (Dr. Eddie Monk); Pat Keen (Mrs. Young); Carol Passmore (Woman in Tea Room); Howard "Lew" Lewis (Tea Room Waiter); Debra Winger (Joy Gresham); Joseph Mazzello (Douglas Gresham); John Quentin (Station Acquaintance); Alan Talbot (College Porter); Heather Mansell (President's Wife); Leigh Burton-Gill (Mrs. Parrish); Cameron Burton-Gill, Chandler Burton-Gill, Kendall Burton-Gill, and Christina Burton-Gill (Parrish Children); Sylvia Barter (Woman in Bookshop); James Watt (Boy in Bookshop); Pauline Melville (Committee Chairwoman); Sophie Stanton, Ysobel Gonzalez, and Ninka Scott (Lecture Committee); Gerald Sim (Superintendent Registrar); Terry Rowley (Registrar); Norman Bird (Taxi Driver); Peter Firth (Dr. Craig); Abigail Harrison (Staff Nurse); Julian

Firth (Father John Fisher);   Karen Lewis (Hotel Receptionist);   Matthew Delamere (Simon Chadwick).

CHRISTIAN SCIENCE MONITOR, 12/31/93, p. 12, David Sterritt

Anthony Hopkins and Debra Winger have been busy of late. Just a few weeks ago, Hopkins made a touching impression with his portrayal of an emotionally repressed butler in "The Remains of the Day," which remains a solid success at the box office. Winger's virtuosic turn as a mentally unstable shop-worker in "A Dangerous Woman" had its premiere even more recently.

And now, with those movies still fresh on neighborhood screens, the two gifted stars have joined forces in what amounts to an instant encore: "Shadowlands," based on the real-life experiences of C.S. Lewis, the celebrated British author, and Joy Gresham, his American wife.

Part of the new film's appeal lies in the rightness of its casting. Hopkins is a specialist in the sort of internalized character-building demanded by the self-controlled intellectual he plays here, and Winger is an expert at playing women who are not conventionally glamourous—in pictures like "Legal Eagles" and her current "Dangerous Woman" melodrama—despite the charm and beauty that are also part of her professional arsenal.

What's most important about "Shadowlands," though, is its thoughtful approach to thought-provoking issues. Lewis is most famous to book-lovers for "The Chronicles of Narnia, " a series of seven fantasy novels aimed at young readers. But he was a classicist and Anglican theologian as well as a spinner of imaginative yarns, and even his most popular fiction—from the "Narnia" volumes to the freewheeling science-fiction trilogy he wrote during the World II era—is full of religious imagery and symbolism.

While he led a comfortable life in many ways, as an Oxford professor and celebrated lecturer, certain aspects of Lewis's life presented strong challenges to his deeply Christian faith. The greatest challenges of all appear to have grown from his relationship with Gresham, a New York poet who became friendly with Lewis at about the time her marriage to an alcoholic screenwriter was breaking down.

"Shadowlands" chronicles the years Lewis and Gresham spent together. It shows Gresham seeking Lewis out in order to pay her respects to his talent, then becoming his friend, and later marrying him in order to become a British citizen and stay in England with her young son.

Genuine love soon blossoms between them, turning their relationship from a marriage of convenience into a true and heartfelt union—which they consecrate with a second wedding ceremony, this time before a minister—but not before Gresham is diagnosed with a grave illness that throws a shadow over their prospects for happiness.

Her death is a horrible blow to Lewis, and even close friends wonder how he can sustain his belief in the ultimate goodness of the world and the rightness of God's plan. Yet it is precisely his religious faith that helps Lewis weather this storm and emerge with his trust unscathed.

This doesn't mean he sustains his good spirits by invoking rote pieties; indeed, when colleagues try to boost his morale with religious clichés, he replies with a glare or a shout of protest.

What is happening at these moments is not a weakening, however, but a deepening and strengthening of his conviction. At one point, an upturn in Gresham's condition prompts a friend to congratulate Lewis for having caught God's attention with his prayers, and Lewis replies in a way his companion hardly expected: "That's not why I pray ... I pray because I can't help myself ... I pray because the need flows out of me all the time, waking and sleeping. It doesn't change God, it changes *me*."

Written by William Nicholson from his respected Broadway play, "Shadowlands" is the story of Lewis's changes—from a conventionally educated man who thinks he has all the intellectual and spiritual answers, to a humble and questing individual who has discovered that growth must be an ongoing process with no humanly discernible end.

It's not a consistently successful film, lapsing into formulas and sentimentality at times. But it offers much food for thought, and demonstrates once again that worthwhile subjects are not beyond Hollywood's interest, no matter what some of today's more cynical critics like to claim.

"Shadowlands" was directed by Richard Attenborough, who has a fondness for movies about real people, and a weakness for tackling lofty projects—from the popular "Gandhi" to the recent "Chaplin," among others—that far exceed his limited filmmaking skills.

"Shadowlands" is a happy exception to his record of ambitious failures, capturing the richness of its characters and events with refreshing gracefulness and professionalism. Credit goes largely to the fine cast, including not only the stars but such able supporting players as Edward Hardwicke and young Joseph Mazzello, who play Lewis's brother and Gresham's son, respectively.

Other key contributions come from Roger Pratt, who did the delicate cinematography, and Stuart Craig, who designed the handsome production. George Fenton composed the effective (if overused) music.

LOS ANGELES TIMES, 12/29/93, Calendar/p. 1, Peter Rainer

"Shadowlands" is about romance between C.S. Lewis (Anthony Hopkins) and Joy Gresham (Debra Winger), and it's the kind of high-class weepie that titrates its tears one by one. It solemnizes heartbreak as it creeps from one emotional revelation to the next. Nothing happens in this film that isn't prepared for, and that's part of its plodding power. It works on us through its *lack* of surprise.

Lewis—known to his friends as Jack—is a lifelong bachelor who lives in quaint comfort with his brother Warnie (Edward Hardwicke). Initially he is presented to us as the archetypal Oxford don. He wears his learning like a thick robe, and delights in the life of the mind—particularly *his* mind.

He taunts and prods his students and delivers popular lectures on Christianity with a self-assured swagger. Jack, we are made to understand, has created a life for himself that bars any real pain or passion beyond the world of books. And yet there's something tentative and unfulfilled about his donnish vigor. This scholar-celebrity—with famous texts to his credit ranging from theology to science fiction to children's fairy tales to literary criticism—is too complex for his carefully appointed academic existence.

When Joy, a devoted American reader of his, requests a meeting with Jack in London, he cautiously allows the connection. Their meeting is staged as a communion of temperamental opposites who nonetheless are soulmates. As their tentative friendship deepens, Jack's academic armor begins to chip away. Joy, who is escaping a bad marriage and has her young son Douglas (Joseph Mazzello) in tow, becomes Jack's spiritual guardian. She implores him to open up and experience the pain of life in order to know its joys.

Does this sound a bit too pop psych for Oxford in the early '50s? William Nicholson, adapting his stage play—which was also a celebrated 1986 BBC telefilm starring Joss Ackland and Claire Bloom—lays on the touchy-feely stuff. And director Richard Attenborough sets each pronouncement in amber. Joy proclaims, "We learn when we hurt." Jack announces that "the most intense joy lies not in the having but in the desiring." And so on.

The filmmakers' portrait of Jack deliberately downplays his considerable intellectual achievements, as if they were insubstantial compared to the juices of "real" life. In other words, the film takes an anti-intellectual approach to the intellect. Isn't the passion we get from art a part of life too? Despite its high-toned airs, "Shadowlands" actually plumps for a rather conventional view of existence. It's all about throwing down your books and opening yourself up to happiness.

Joy's own life is presented as essentially sacrificial. She's in the movie to bring Jack into the light. Her own considerable achievements are downplayed, and so is her emotional fragility. In real life Joy was born Jewish before converting to Christianity and was a communist and an award-winning poet. These things are touched upon in the movie but they don't really add up to a character. Joy's work as Jack's editor and (at times) virtual collaborator is skimped altogether—probably because that would imply she *did* prize his bookishness—and their deep religious bond is downplayed. Its Christian particulars have been fuzzied into something a bit more new age-y.

The film's biggest success is that it delineates Jack's odyssey with care and precision, perhaps *too* much precision. A movie about opening yourself up to passion probably shouldn't be this calibrated and serene.

But Hopkins is n his element here: He does repression better than just about anybody. When Joy, with her brusque realism, starts to befuddle Jack's calm, he doesn't seem entirely displeased. He's been waiting, without his conscious awareness, for someone just like this to happen to his life. Hopkins moves Jack from bemused self-satisfaction to abject despair in one clean sweep.

Winger is strong despite her role's built-in limits. It probably isn't intended as ironic that Joy, spending so much time massaging Jack's turmoil, never truly recognizes her own. Her brave words in the face of death are accepted simply as brave words, not as Joy's way of perhaps denying her own fears. (We never see her spiritual terror, only her physical pain.) She's sanctified—the ultimate literary groupie.

But Winger is too powerful an actress to leave it at that. There's an undercurrent of anger and bitterness in Joy's brusque truth-telling sessions with Jack. Something in her recoils at his sense of privilege. Winger makes Joy, for all her strength, a deeply lonely woman; when she's speaking to Jack she often sounds rehearsed, as if she had already spoken these lines to herself.

Winger has probably spent one too many on-screen moments ailing in slow decline. In "Shadowlands," the spectacle is particularly uncomfortable because Joy's deteriorating condition seems to exist primarily to point up Jack's spiritual reawakening. (In reality, he suffered alongside Joy, from severe osteoporosis.) "Shadowlands" is a moving experience but when it comes full circle by the end, it's Lewis' circle.

NEW STATESMAN & SOCIETY, 3/18/94, p. 50, Jonathan Romney

For my liking, Richard Attenborough's massively lauded *Shadowlands* is desperately hamstrung by its ghastly good taste. Few films since *Brief Encounter* have ever brandished discretion, delicacy and sensibility (in both senses of the word) quite so prominently as selling points. The last film to do so, of course, was James Ivory's *The Remains of the Day*, and it's hard not to see Anthony Hopkins' fine-shaded performance as C S Lewis as being a kinder, gentler brother to his butler in that film.

But the film does have an agreeably level-headed way of dealing with writing and writers in love. Lewis and his American wife-to-be, the poet Joy Gresham (Debra Winger), aren't seen squabbling over hot text or brewing up the agonies that get transmuted into texts. But they're both writers, quite simply, with work already written and published, and their lives not appreciably transformed into the impossible dream of divinity that the work-in-progress always seems to promise. They're complementary beings, Gresham's hard-headed way with emotional energies being the catalyst that shakes Lewis out of his mist-bound bachelor fog.

Admittedly, the film's told very much from his point of view. She's the one who walks in and (quite literally) lets in the fresh air. But once together, they interlock in a way which Tom and Viv never do, and which the Burroughs figure and his wife certainly never do in Cronenberg's film. Burroughs' career and myth, of course, were founded on the ill-timed bullet that dispatched his wife before the first reel was out.

Shadowlands isn't much cop as a *film*, but as a film *about people* it's laudably free of hair-tearing literary myths. Lewis is forever banging on in speeches and essays about the necessity and value of suffering; when Gresham dies, though, he isn't seen to be feeding off her suffering. It's just part of the politely tender business between them. What they share, and what makes their strained lives workable is a simple knowledge: life is hell and then you die, and until you do, you sit down and write about it.

NEW YORK, 1/3/94, p. 53, David Denby

Richard Attenborough's *Shadowlands* is a good movie to see when you have the flu. I mean this as a compliment, sort of, for within its limits—that of literate middle-brow entertainment—*Shadowlands* is just about perfect. At heart, William Nicholson's play (adapted here by the author) is the good old story about a lively American woman who wakes an intellectual bachelor from his slumbers. Joy Gresham (Debra Winger), an actual person from New York—Jewish, direct, emotionally explicit—journeys to England in the early fifties and becomes friends with C.S. Lewis (Anthony Hopkins), Oxford don and Christian mystic, author of half a hundred volumes of children's stories, science fiction, theology. Lewis is incisive about everything but his feelings. Joy scolds his complacency; he likes the scolding, they marry, and they experience great contentment. But then she dies, and he must confront a life awakened to emotion—that is, to pain. It is all very wise and bittersweet, and I can't make too much fun of its tea-cozy sentimentality because I enjoyed the acting and the many views of Oxford's misty towers, rivers, and lawns.

NEW YORK POST, 12/29/93, p. 31, Michael Medved

Talk about odd couples.

He was a world-famous author, Oxford don and revered Christian thinker, advancing into old age in a stuffy, comfortable bachelorhood he never thought to disrupt.

She was a brash, Jewish New Yorker, one-time Communist, urban poet, failed Hollywood screenwriter and divorced mother of two—17 years his junior.

Their passionate friendship and ultimate marriage startled their friends in the early 1950s and is now the subject of the brilliant new film "Shadowlands," with Anthony Hopkins and Debra Winger co-starring in the year's most heartbreaking and extraordinary love story.

As C.S. Lewis, known as "Jack" to his Oxford friends, Hopkins conveys the perfect combination of warmth, stodginess, intense vulnerability and thoroughgoing decency.

Winger is similarly superb as Joy Davidman Gresham, who wrote numerous fan letters to her literary hero before their fateful meeting during one of her extended visits to England. By that time, she had already left her Communist commitments behind and converted to Christianity; as Lewis puts it in the film, they are both "lapsed atheists."

Winger projects so much feistiness, vitality, and courage in the face of sudden, desperate illness that it's easy to see why Hopkins falls in love with her; her characterization here is far richer and more subtle than her recent acclaimed work in "A Dangerous Woman."

Also noteworthy is 9-year-old Joseph Mazzello (who previously co-starred in "Jurassic Park" and "Radio Flyer") as Gresham's precocious son, Douglas. His interaction with his stepfather, C.S. Lewis, at a time of pain and crisis provides one of the film's most moving moments.

Amazingly enough, the real-life Douglas Gresham, now in his 50s, cooperated with this project at every stage of its development—from its original incarnation as a BBC teleplay by William Nicholson, to its successful run in theaters around the world to this beautifully crafted motion picture.

Director Richard Attenborough, best known for historical epics such as "Gandhi," "Cry Freedom" and last year's "Chaplin," here achieves his greatest triumph working on a far more intimate scale.

He precisely captures the cozy, slightly shabby world of postwar England without ever calling undue attention to period details.

The film's visual splendor actually produces its only serious shortcoming. Though Joy's arrival is supposed to bring "fresh color" to the drab life of C.S. Lewis, the movies' images are all so gorgeous that you can hardly tell the difference.

Despite its smooth, handsome surface, "Shadowlands" offers far more than hearts and flowers; it's about loss as much as love, and the inevitable association of the two. The movie tells a tender story, but it is also a wounding one that leaves a sore spot on the soul—a sense of hurt—that will stay with you for weeks after you see the film.

"Why should we want to be hurt?" Lewis/Hopkins asks in the course of the movie, only to answer his own question. "That's when we learn that pain is God's metaphor to rouse a deaf world." This remarkable motion picture also serves to rouse that deaf world, if only moviegoers will take time and the trouble to experience it.

NEWSDAY, 12/29/93, Part II/p. 57, Jack Mathews

If the often absurd rules governing eligibility for Academy Awards didn't prohibit one actor from being nominated twice in the same category, Anthony Hopkins would almost certainly take up 40 percent of this year's Best Actor ballot.

Hopkins is a shoo-in nominee for his performance as the emotionally strait-jacketed butler in "The Remains of the Day," and his colleagues in the actors' branch of the Academy may reasonably conclude he gave the year's second best performance, too, as British writer C.S. Lewis in Richard Attenborough's "Shadowlands."

Adapted by William Nicholson from his BBC TV movie and subsequent play, "Shadowlands" dramatizes, and fictionalizes to large extent, the romance between Lewis, an Oxford professor, Christian scholar and renowned children's book author, and Joy Gresham (Debra Winger), the American poet who meets him as a fan, becomes his friend, then his wife.

In all three roles, Gresham is a disruptive force in a life as carefully laid out as one of the arguments Lewis makes in defense of Christianity, particularly his conviction, repeated in several early speeches, that suffering is a gift from God, His way of making us "grow up, give up toys and join the world."

It's the early '50s when we meet Lewis, and make the rounds of his orderly bachelor life. We see him badgering his students with arcane philosophical points, indulging in dull intellectual shop talk with his Oxford colleagues at the local pub, and retiring each evening to the cottage he has shared for more than 20 years with his tweedy brother, Warnie (Edward Hardwicke).

When Joy arrives, in the final spasms of a bad marriage to a philandering, alcoholic husband, and with her young son, Douglas (Joseph Mazzello), in tow, there is an immediate clash of cultures and personal styles. Joy is an outspoken American-Polish Jew who shocks Lewis and his friends with her bluntness and lack of social grace, but leaves his feelings stirred in ways he can neither explain nor ignore.

The truth is that Lewis is a bit of a fake, a children's writer who knows nothing about the feelings of children, and a doctrinaire Christian using his faith as a shield against pain. Only after falling in love with a woman whose life, he learns, may be slipping away, do his emotions overcome his intellect.

Lewis and the butler Stevens in "The Remains of the Day" are kindred spirits. They may be separated by a world war and by several notches in England's scrupulously observed class structure, but both operate behind layers of self-prescribed emotional defenses, and both are paralyzed by the mere prospect of having to express a true feeling.

In "Remains," Stevens' defenses never break down, and in suggesting the turmoil beneath the formal, dignity-first surface of his character, Hopkins gives one of the most astonishing internal performances on film. As Lewis, Hopkins is eventually able to let everything go, and you haven't seen a cap blow like this since the eruption of Mt. St. Helens.

Certainly, this is the flashier and more satisfying of Hopkins' two performances. There's no catharsis interruptus for audiences here; this is a full emotional meltdown and four hankies may not be enough to soak up the mess.

But as compelling as Hopkins is, "Shadowlands" is not easy to slog through. Nicholson's script lays its own sermons on a little thick, and Attenborough, ever the plodder, takes at least 20 minutes longer than necessary to tell his story.

Winger does her best, using her own brashness to flesh out a terribly underwritten character, but she can't overcome the cliches. Joy, a vital, self-sacrificing, wisecracking trouper even as death appears imminent, couldn't feel more contrived if she were an angel sent down to guide Lewis to his epiphany, to the knowledge that he can have a wonderful life if he learns to accept pain and suffering as corollaries to happiness.

It will be ironic, and further underscore the folly of the Academy Awards rules, if Winger ends up on the best actress ballot (once again, the thinnest category of all) and Hopkins is ruled ineligible, because he is already there.

NEWSWEEK, 1/3/94, p. 63, David Ansen

A little repression can do wonders for a love story, and there were few places as cozily repressed as Oxford University in the year 1952. It is there, in *Shadowlands*, that C. S. (Jack) Lewis (Anthony Hopkins), the revered scholar, Christian and writer of the "Narnia" fables for children, holds forth from the podium on God, love and the uses of pain to awaken our souls. But his wisdom is purely intellectual. A cloistered, middle-aged bachelor who lives with his older brother Warnie (Edward Hardwicke), Lewis hasn't let another person pierce his mild-mannered but invincible armor. That is, until Joy Gresham (Debra Winger), an ardent American fan, requests a visit. A "Jewish Christian" ex-Communist with an 8-year-old son (Joseph Mazzello), an estranged alcoholic husband back in the States and a manner as forthright as Jack's is diffident, she bursts unexpectedly into his life and teaches the teacher what he's understood in his head but never in his heart. They marry, but only in a "technical," friendly way—so she can stay in England with her son. It's only later, when she is stricken with cancer, that he is ready to risk love, and the pain love invites.

Richard Attenborough's "Shadowlands," adapted by William Nicholson from his play and an earlier BBC telefilm, is a literate tearjerker that walks softly but wields a big emotional stick.

Anyone who sat through "A Chorus Line" or "Chaplin" has reason to be wary of Attenborough's 10-ton touch, but here, at home in the English milieu and aided by Nicholson's witty, finely honed screenplay, Attenborough redeems himself. If for no other reason, "Shadowlands" should be seen for Hopkins's near perfect performance, as delicately comic as it is heartbreaking. Confronted with the mystery of room service at a country inn, he gets maximum mirth out of a mere ordering of a gin and tonic. Confronted with a late-blooming love nothing has prepared him for, he unleashes a bolt of feeling as penetrating as anything he's ever done. Winger has inspired moments as the blunt but crafty Joy, but the role isn't as fully imagined as Lewis's, and you wish she had more room to breathe. Nicholson's grasp of his American heroine is a bit shaky: this smart, independent woman, a poet herself, at times comes off like a borscht-belt stand-up. But Winger is there where it counts—the chemistry between this gallant, ungainly American and the well-defended Brit is palpable and poignant. It's a wonderfully unlikely, stiff-upper-lip love story. Bring a hanky. Better make it two.

SIGHT AND SOUND, 3/94, p. 48, Stella Bruzzi

Oxford 1952. C.S. ("Jack") Lewis, successful children's writer and Professor of English, is a conventional middle-aged don. He sings in the college choir, has dinner at high table with his male colleagues, and lives in the same house he grew up in with his brother Warnie. His life is a round of tutorials, evenings in the pub with his fellow dons, giving lectures on Christianity and answering the steady trickle of correspondence he has been receiving for years.

One of these letters is from an American poet, Joy Gresham, who is currently in England and wants to meet Lewis. He arranges tea and is surprised by her forthright personality. Soon after, she returns to Oxford with her son Douglas, also an ardent fan of Lewis's 'Narnia' books. They are not returning to the States until the New Year, and Jack—pitying the prospect of two Americans spending Christmas in an English hotel—invites them again to Oxford.

On the first evening Jack and Warnie invite Joy to the college Christmas drinks party. Back at the house, Christmas is a sedate affair, with homesick Douglas disappointed on several fronts: the old wardrobe in the attic doesn't have any of the magic of the one in The Lion, The Witch and the Wardrobe, he has to have strawberry jam with his turkey rather than cranberry sauce, and Joy won't allow him to call his father, Bill. She explains to Jack that her husband—whom she hasn't loved for years—is a violent alcoholic who wants to divorce her to marry another woman.

After Joy and Douglas have left for America, Jack re-establishes his old routine. While giving one of his Christian lectures, he notices Joy in the audience. She is now permanently living in London with Douglas, having divorced Bill. She invites Jack to her basement flat for dinner. On his return to Oxford, Jack tells Warnie that he has agreed to a marriage of convenience with Joy, to enable her to obtain British citizenship and remain in England. Their marriage is to be kept a secret, and the ceremony is perfunctory.

At a degree-time garden party in Oxford, Joy is exasperated by Jack's detachment and cosy life. Having confronted him to no effect, she leaves, apparently for good. Later, when Jack calls her flat, she collapses while trying to reach the phone. She is then taken to hospital and diagnosed as having terminal bone cancer. Jack commutes to London daily while Warnie looks after Douglas back in Oxford. He begins to realise and acknowledge that he is in love with Joy. As a Christian, Jack does not consider the civic wedding to have been performed before God, so he proposes to Joy and they are married again in the hospital, this time by a vicar.

A temporary remission allows Jack to take Joy back to Oxford. On the study wall there is a kitsch picture of the so-called Golden Valley in Herefordshire that used to hang on Jack and Warnie's nursery wall. As they never had a honeymoon, Joy decides they should go in search of the valley. Soon after, Joy's cancer returns, and after a spell of treatment in London, she returns to Oxford. Joy never leaves her bed and dies with Jack, who has promised to care for Douglas, beside her.

After Joy's funeral, Jack retreats into his own grief, but eventually re-establishes his familiar academic routine. The film ends with Jack and Douglas walking through the Golden Valley.

In that anthem to lovers left behind—In Memoriam—Tennyson wrote "Tis better to have loved and lost, than never to have loved at all". At the end of Shadowlands, as he recalls Joy's truism that pain and happiness are part of the same bargain, Jack Lewis reaches much the same realisation as Tennyson does through the death of Arthur Hallam—that if you sidestep pain you also forsake the possibility of happiness. In order to really love you have to risk getting hurt.

The only reason, it seems, that this grandiose, beautifully crafted film rises above the level of banal sentimentality is that it is about the famous C.S. Lewis—not an anonymous suffering widower, but the author of the 'Narnia' books, and also one of the definitive studies of Courtly Love. The thought that, if this story had been culled from the diaries of a nobody, I would dismiss it as just too slushy and sentimental niggled at me throughout the film, because it raised questions of what—or who—was playing with my emotions.

Shadowlands is an accomplished formula film of the kind that induces tears even in the hardy. The staple ingredients of a Richard Attenborough Great and Good biopic are all intact—even if Donald Woods and Gandhi have been supplanted by an engaging English reincarnation of the type, more in keeping with the current vogue for clipped anguish and strangulated desire than bombastic political convictions. Attenborough, it seems, adheres to the Great Man Theory of history which maps out the past in terms of the interaction between key individuals, invariably men. Likewise in cinema. Pain, suffering, elation and devotion are all the more keenly conveyed to a susceptible audience if they are happening to an Important Man. All the surrounding characters in *Shadowlands*—Warnie, colleagues, Douglas—are mere ciphers in Lewis's story who serve this end, the most blatant case of idolatry being Douglas, the Narnia fan and the fatherless son.

Thus we are never permitted to forget that this humanist parable is about an eminent person; indeed the references to Lewis's famous children's books by his posse of bitchy don-friends are amongst the film's most inelegant plants. Similarly the poignant pertinence of Lewis's analysis of medieval love poetry (that "what you most desire is out of reach") is signposted like a ragged shoreline by a lighthouse. Ah, we think, intellect can take one so far, but experience takes one further. Enter Joy, jolting Jack from his ivory tower into tingling consciousness with a brash and healthy defiance of convention, gentility and etiquette.

This response is not contrariness on my part but annoyance, stemming from being too easily led into the tangled mesh of true love, true death, true cliche. Although Joy is the story's active agent, who instigates Jack's transformation, is struck by cancer and dies, she too is a satellite character in Jack's narrative. At the core, *Shadowlands* is about Joy's effect on Jack; it's the tale of one Great Man's discovery of his own feelings. However convoluted it may sound, we desire the prolongation of Joy's remission so that Jack can be given time to unravel more about himself and his capacity for love. In essence the copious tears are for C.S. Lewis, who no sooner unlocks the gate of his safe little world of childhood memorabilia, High Table dinners and hot water bottles with Warnie, than he finds himself left behind, bereft, mourning. Jack's faith is a poor thing, but his grief is a very intense experience. The film's most affecting moment is not, as might seem logical, Joy's death, but the scene in the attic where the wardrobe sits, when Jack finally drops all of his defences and is able to weep and bond with Douglas. It is this which precipitates the upbeat, cathartic ending: Oxford in the spring, tutorials about the real rather than the poetic nature of love, and walking with Douglas through the Golden Valley.

The whole narrative, like George Fenton's omnipresent, referential score, is intricately orchestrated to this crescendo. While watching *Shadowlands* I colluded in my own gross manipulation, I offered no resistance, I succumbed to the Great Man theory and empathised with a character whose 'glory' was that he began—late in life—to learn about himself. It's a good story, and Anthony Hopkins gives an impassioned, beautifully modulated performance, signalling each emotional shift through the smallest intensification of a look or the merest softening of a gesture. But the whole experience is so suffocating, so unequivocal. The option to remain aloof, to stay unmoved is denied, in large part, because *Shadowlands* is the story of C.S. Lewis rather than a fictitious anybody. The "true story" tag weighs heavy on reluctant viewers.

TIME, 12/27/93, p. 72, Richard Corliss

When we meet him, C.S. Lewis (Anthony Hopkins) is giving rather smug lectures about the blessed necessity for suffering in our life: "Pain is God's megaphone to rouse a deaf world," he happily informs his listeners.

But what does Lewis—Oxford don, literary critic, fairy-tale writer, Christian apologist—actually know about the ordinary hurts of ordinary life? Or that matter, about life as most people know it? His beloved mother died when he was a child, and for decades he has lived in withdrawn bachelorhood. Snuggled up in a charming book-lined cottage with his brother Warnie (the excellent Edward Hardwicke), he is sage but distant with his students, witty but somewhat abstract with his colleagues at the high table.

The man needs shaking up: And Joy Gresham (Debra Winger) is just the woman to do it. She's an American, something of a poet something of an imposition. But she's also someone any writer is bound to cherish, a knowledgeable fan. They meet for tea; she and her eight-year-old son (she's in the midst of a messy divorce) return for Christmas; and eventually they settle in London. Bemusement soon gives way to concern. Lewis marries her so she can stay in England, but true love does not happen until she falls ill with cancer. A period of remission offers them the opportunity for an idyll. That brief happiness, followed by the pain of her death, does indeed "rouse" Lewis. But in ways deeper and more mysterious than he formerly gabbled about.

Shadowlands is, in essence, a true story, though screenwriter William Nicholson, adapting his own play, admits that given Lewis' reticence, he has had to imagine much of what went on in the relationship with Gresham. And reticent is the word for Richard Attenborough's film version. But that's a virtue, not a defect, when your setting is English academia (no one has more persuasively captured its manners) and your subject is mortality. There is something very moving in the understated way that these people confront it, something very sweetly believable in their courtship and in the brief bliss they shared. Hopkins gets to do what he could not in *The Remains of the Day*, shake off repression, and Winger is awfully good too; there is a steady pressure in her forcefulness that is never flashy or abrasive. They—the entire movie—are strong, unsentimental, exemplary.

VILLAGE VOICE, 1/4/94, p. 45, J. Hoberman

The season of repressed heroes—Daniel Day Lewis in *The Age of Innocence*, Jeremy Irons in *M. Butterfly*, Anthony Hopkins in *Remains of the Day*—reaches a fitting anticlimax with the release of *Shadowlands*, starring Anthony Hopkins as the British author and pop theologian C. S. Lewis.

Actually, as skillfully adapted by William Nicholson from his Broadway play, *Shadowlands* is in some respects usefully constricted. It's set mainly in Oxford around 1952, and although an exercise in rampant donnishness and cozily cloistered Sceptered Isle-ism, is still less grandiose than director Sir Richard Attenborough's customary tub-thwacking. Hopkins seems unusually relaxed while Debra Winger is relatively corseted as writer Joy Davidman Gresham, the belated American Jewish love of Lewis's life.

As a 10-year-old, I greatly admired Lewis's *The Chronicles of Narnia*, missing (at least consciously) his strenuously Christian allegory. Since then my capacity for wonder has been perverted—blame it on the movies. Although some may find *Shadowlands* moistly touching, for me the spectacle of a middle-aged bachelor who is only able to "love" a woman once she is gravely ill and confined to a hospital bed seems less an inspiration to make every day count than the subject for a comedy by that old blasphemer Luis Buñuel.

Also reviewed in:
CHICAGO TRIBUNE, 1/7/94, Friday/p. C, Michael Wilmington
NEW REPUBLIC, 2/7/94, p. 26, Stanley Kauffmann
NEW YORK TIMES, 12/29/93, p. C11, Janet Maslin
VARIETY, 12/13/93, p. 38, Emanuel Levy
WASHINGTON POST, 1/7/94, p. B1, Rita Kempley
WASHINGTON POST, 1/7/94, Weekend/p. 34, Desson Howe

SHORT CUTS

A Fine Line Features release in association with Spelling Films International of a Cary Brokaw/Avenue Pictures production. *Executive Producer:* Scott Bushnell. *Producer:* Cary Brokaw. *Director:* Robert Altman. *Screenplay:* Robert Altman and Frank Barhydt. *Based on the writings of:* Raymond Carver. *Director of Photography:* Walt Lloyd. *Editor:* Geraldine Peroni. *Music:* Mark Isham. *Sound:* John Pritchett and (music) Eric Liljestrand. *Sound Editor:* Eliza Paley. *Production Designer:* Stephen Altman. *Art Director:* Jerry Fleming. *Set Decorator:* Susan J. Emshwiller. *Set Dresser:* David Ronan. *Special Effects:* John Harridigan and Chris Nelson. *Costumes:* John Hay. *Make-up:* Theo Mayes. *Stunt Coordinator:* Greg Walker. *Running time:* 189 minutes. *MPAA Rating:* R.

CAST: Andie MacDowell (Ann Finnigan); Bruce Davison (Howard Finnigan); Jack Lemmon (Paul Finnigan); Zane Cassidy (Casey Finnigan); Julianne Moore (Marian Wyman); Matthew Modine (Doctor Ralph Wyman); Anne Archer (Claire Kane); Fred Ward (Stuart Kane); Jennifer Jason Leigh (Lois Kaiser); Chris Penn (Jerry Kaiser); Joseph C. Hopkins (Joe Kaiser); Josette Maccario (Josette Kaiser); Lili Taylor (Honey Bush); Robert Downey, Jr. (Bill Bush); Madeleine Stowe (Sherri Shepard); Tim Robbins (Gene Shepard); Cassie Friel (Sandy Shepard); Dustin Friel (Will Shepard); Austin Friel (Austin Shepard); Lily Tomlin (Doreen Piggot); Tom Waits (Earl Piggot); Frances McDormand (Betty Weathers); Peter Gallagher (Stormy Weathers); Jarrett Lennon (Chad Weathers); Annie Ross (Tess Trainer); Lori Singer (Zoe Trainer); Lyle Lovett (Andy Bitkower); Buck Henry (Gordon Johnson); Huey Lewis (Vern Miller); Danny Darst (Aubrey Bell); Margerie Bond (Dora Willis); Robert Do'Qui (Knute Willis); Darnell Williams (Joe Robbins); Michael Beach (Jim Stone); Andi Chapman (Harriet Stone); Deborah Falconer (Barbara); Susie Cusack (Nancy); Charles Rocket (Wally Littleton); Jane Alden (Mrs. Schwartzmeier); Christian Altman (Jimmy Miller); Willie Marlett (Jimmy's Friend); Dirk Blocker (Diner Customer); Suzanne Calvert (Tarmac Secretary); Natalie Strong (Mourner); Jay Della (Bartender); Jeruth Persson (Club Owner); Derek Webster (Joe Robbins' Pal); Alex Trebek (Himself); Jerry Dunphy (Himself).

CHRISTIAN SCIENCE MONITOR, 10/1/93, p. 12, David Sterritt

Robert Altman's directing career has been as wild and woolly as any of his movies. The saga continues in "Short Cuts," opening in theaters after a New York Film Festival premiere.

Based on stories by the late Raymond Carver, the new movie is as ambitious and audacious as anything Altman has done. Early buzz on the picture—bolstered by the filmmaker's own pronouncements—hailed it as a stunning achievement that would renew his former reputation as a towering film artist.

Unfortunately, the buzz was exaggerated. "Short Cuts" is a daring but flawed achievement, diluting its emotional power and satirical bite with a self-consciously jagged structure and a calculating, sometimes chilly undertone. It also has enough nudity and sexually explicit language to turn off many moviegoers.

While it's a fine advertisement for Altman's energy and ingenuity, it leaves his sense of humanity lagging well behind.

Altman is no newcomer to critical controversy. After years of scarcely recognized work in movies and television, he burst into prominence with the original "M*A*S*H," an influential 1970 satire on military life. Strikingly experimental in its use of wide-screen composition and multitrack sound, it paved the way for even bolder innovations in "McCabe and Mrs. Miller" and "The Long Goodbye," among other unconventional projects.

"Nashville," with its huge cast of characters and intricate counterpoint of image and sound, is generally considered his masterpiece. It has also haunted his career for the past 18 years, during which he has made a large number of films—from stage adaptations to TV movies—that failed to impress most critics a fraction as much as his country-music classic did.

Last year Altman released "The Player," a pitch-black comedy about skullduggery in the movie world, and critics rightly agreed it was his best movie in ages. True, its sound is not as stunningly complex as that of "Nashville," and its cinematic jokes—such as the long, meandering shot that opens the story—sometimes seem more tricky than revealing. But it's a whale of a picture anyway, skewering Hollywood hypocrisy with an authority that only a bona fide maverick like Altman could claim.

"Short Cuts" is an attempt to blend the ferocious humor of "The Player" with the flamboyant cinematics of "Nashville," telling a number of intercut tales with no fewer than 22 significant characters. By adapting and sometimes drastically changing the Carver stories from which the screenplay is drawn, Altman tries for an impressive diversity of dramatic moods and emotional rhythms.

Some narrative lines are poignant and even tragic, as when parents grieve over an injured child or an alcoholic mother tries to cope with her disturbed daughter. Others have humorous touches, as when a distracted husband feuds with the family dog or two mismatched couples try for a fun evening together. Still others have a hint of mystery, as when a trio of fishermen stumble across a corpse or a painfully dull man bursts inexplicably into violence.

The best of these tales are very affecting, brought alive by inventive camera work and imaginative acting. The story of the injured child and his hard-pressed parents, played by Bruce Davison and Andie MacDowell, is the most powerful example—not merely well-made, but deeply felt by Altman and his collaborators.

Few of the other tales have a similar impact, however, and the reason is built into the basic conception of the film. By switching back and forth among the different stories, Altman succeeds in fostering a sense of dispassionate observation and ironic juxtaposition. But he also succeeds in preventing us from engaging with the characters' lives and feelings. Every time the opportunity arises for deep involvement, the movie skips into a different groove and asks us to start all over again.

There's nothing automatically wrong with this approach. Bertolt Brecht, who developed some of the greatest theories on modern dramatic technique, applauded the "alienation effect" as a way of prodding audiences to think about stories and characters, instead of being swept uncritically away by their feelings.

The trouble with "Short Cuts" is that when you *do* think about it, you realize it isn't very profound or insightful. At best, it's clever. At worst, it's too clever by half.

And occasionally it's downright cheap. I think Altman is as reputable an artist as Carver, and I support his right to rejigger Carver's stories for cinematic purposes. But too many of his changes seem geared to sensationalizing Carver's material. Where the author gives us an injury, the filmmaker gives us a death; where the author gives us an enigmatic phone call, the filmmaker gives us an obsessive phone caller; where the author gives us a self-absorbed fishing party, the filmmaker gives us a disgusting display of macho posing.

Carver was a literary minimalist in the vein of Donald Barthelme and Gordon Lish, with an instinctive awareness that less is truly more. By contrast, Altman is feeling his oats these days. Understatement is not among his priorities and that's too bad, given the source material he has chosen to work with.

He apparently intends his new movie as a statement on the fractured American condition in our postmodern age. But while he wove the fragments of "Nashville" into a seamless fabric, he scatters those of "Short Cuts" in too many directions with too little discipline. To watch "Nashville" is to study a tapestry. To watch "Short Cuts" is to spin the dial on your TV set.

Despite these difficulties, "Short Cuts" has the asset of a huge and lustrous cast. Its most impressive members include Matthew Modine as an insecure physician; Madeleine Stowe as a beleaguered wife; Tim Robbins as her cocky husband; Annie Ross as an aging jazz singer; Tom Waits and Lily Tomlin as an odd couple; Robert Downey Jr. as an aspiring cosmetics expert; and Buck Henry as a happy camper. Others range from Chris Penn, who can pack enormous expressivity into a single facial expression, to Jack Lemmon, who's more impressive in his wordless final shot than in a long and windy speech that precedes it.

Frank Barhydt collaborated with Altman on the screenplay, and Walt Lloyd did the cinematography, which varies in quality from scene to scene. Geraldine Peroni handled the complicated editing. The music is by veteran composer Mark Isham.

CINEASTE, Vol. XX, No. 3, 1994, p. 48, Leonard Quart

The coupling of Robert Altman and the fine, spare short story writer Raymond Carver (who died five years ago of lung cancer at the age of fifty) has resulted in the creation of a multicharacter, multiplotted epic of American life much like the director's earlier *Nashville*. This time around Altman has muted much of his exhilarating formal virtuosity, allowing the performances to be the most important element in the film. His signature use of overlapping sound and his layered and crammed *mise-en-scène* is subordinated here to a stylistically subdued collage of stories sketching the messy, mundane lives of ordinary people in suburban Los Angeles. The stories are far from literal adaptations of Carver, their very locales shifted from the Pacific Northwest to the more nondescript L.A. suburbs, though some of Carver's dialog is preserved verbatim. What Altman has done is to construct a series of cynical and aggressive variations and riffs off Carver's quietly depressed, more empathetic sensibility. Carver's vision is built on a feeling for the "loneliness" and "doubt and limitation" with which most people live. It's a less flamboyant, subtler take on the human condition than Altman's.

The film opens with a striking, quasisurreal image of a group of ominously whirring helicopters (shades of *Apocalypse Now*) flying in formation, spraying chemicals over the entire L.A. area—including swimming pools, drive-in restaurants, freeways, people, and perhaps also their intended target, the medfly and its larvae. It's a powerfully absurd and threatening introductory image for the action that follows. Much of the film is shot in middle distance, depicting twenty-two characters and nine stories, some that overlap and interweave, and others that remain totally disconnected. The characters live in a variety of places—expensive houses perched on hills, tract housing, and trailer parks—and they run the class range from upper middle to working class—doctors, singers, highway patrolman, clowns, bakers, waitresses, and so on—although they are all white. None has achieved great success and status, and some live in utter squalor.

Eschewing sustained takes, elaborate camera movement or unusual set-ups, Altman focuses on his characters' private actions and interactions, not on the social worlds of work and neighborhood they inhabit, or the tabloid L.A. of riots, illegal aliens, drive-by shootings, and economic recession. The outside world does intrude briefly, however, in several instances—including an arbitrary freeway shooting which has led to a young man being hospitalized, and an intimidating, black ex-con, a customer at the jazz bar patronized by a number of the film's characters, whose sadistic behavior gives the film a slight racial subtext—but the film makes few overt political or social statements. Altman views his characters' behavior as sufficient, and, in his usual mode, wants the audience to do much of the scrambling for the social and cultural significance suggested by his images and dialog.

As usual, Altman diverges from the classical Hollywood narrative structure, refusing to grant primacy to any one story or character. He cuts fluidly from one relationship to another, from a few couples that are caring and relatively balanced, although their lives are radically disrupted, to several that are comic-pathetic, and to other characters who live perilously close to the emotional edge. Generally, Altman's world is one where relationships between husbands and wives, and parents and children, fail; where violence lurks just beneath the surface of the most commonplace encounters; and omnipresent television sets incessantly drone their inanities in the background (Altman's gift for peripheral detail is still intact), acting as an implicit chorus and commentary for what goes on in the daily lives of the film's characters.

In one story a strutting, bullshitting motorcycle cop, Gene Shepard (Tim Robbins in a shrewd comic performance that is simultaneously realistic and parodistic), escapes the cacophony of his home (a wife, two children, and a yapping dog) to relieve himself with some compulsive womanizing. One of the women he has an affair with, the sensual, weary Betty Weathers (Frances McDormand), is just as frantic in her pursuit of men. Betty's estranged husband, helicopter pilot Stormy Weathers (Peter Gallagher), is so vindictive that in an over-the-top, extended sequence, he cuts up all her clothes and demolishes all the furniture in the house with a chain saw. The black humor of the sequence quickly wears thin.

Other characters include a middle-aged waitress, Doreen Piggot (Lily Tomlin), who works in an all-night diner and her husband, Earl (Tom Waits), an alcoholic limo driver. He's an angry man who continually berates and scapegoats Doreen, but the two of them have a genuine bond based on mutual disappointment, failure, and neediness. In another story a stolid, taciturn pool cleaner, Jerry Kaiser (Chris Penn), is married to Lois (Jennifer Jason Leigh) who picks up extra money by engaging in phone sex—one of her clients is the bishop of her parents' church—while diapering and feeding her kids in a chaotic apartment. The scene is treated in a matter of fact manner, quietly evoking a society where totally alienated sex has become the norm.

In still another story, a good marriage is changed forever when the wife, Claire Kane (Ann Archer), discovers that her decent husband, Stuart (Fred Ward), waited twenty-four hours to report the corpse of a naked girl floating in the river where he was fishing. His moral obtuseness and callousness—an unwillingness to get involved and disrupt the pleasure of his fishing trip—repels her. Without any fanfare, the seemingly ordinary Claire exhibits the kind of moral imagination that reveals hidden depths and is unique among the film's characters.

Finally, a stiff, literal-minded doctor, Ralph Wyman (Matthew Modine), is involved in an emotionally dead marriage with a painter, Marian (Julianne Moore). Ralph, obsessed with Marian's one evening of sexual infidelity, coerces a confession from her, which she delivers nude from the waist down. The scene is tantalizing in an unsensational way, Marian's nudity both an implicit affirmation of her sexuality and expression of contempt for her controlling, resentful husband.

The stories that center on parents and children include one where Jack Lemmon plays an alienated, aging father, long separated from his son and from a grandson lying comatose in a hospital and whose name he doesn't even know. The old man is given a self-indulgent, rueful, nine-minute confession to his son which effectively stops the film in its tracks. Nevertheless, the profound grief and loss movingly expressed by the parents (Bruce Davison and Andie Mac-Dowell) over the boy's sudden death is the one time in *Short Cuts* that a connected, caring familial life seems possible. And in the one story which does not derive from Carver's work, a jazz vocalist, Tess Trainer (Annie Ross), sings in a club with great passion and brio about her angst ("I'm a prisoner of life"), a too explicit summation of most of Altman's characters' state of being. But her feelings are so invested in her art and self that she can give nothing to her melancholy, cellist daughter, Zoe (Lori Singer), who longs for mother love and understanding. The story concludes with Zoe's melodramatic suicide, an action whose extremity feels contrived.

In *Short Cuts* the characters' inner lives are left unrevealed. There are few explanations proffered for behavior, Altman leaving the audience to construct the full nature of the story from what is left unsaid. The film is not shaped around a tight, coherent narrative, but built on a set of moments or events based on chance. Altman sees social and individual behavior as determined more by randomness than by some inherent logic or set of causes. Given this notion of life as something desultory and devoid of order, Altman's work has always been more intuitive than analytic. He's a director who collaborates with his actors in creating the final product. In *Short Cuts* he sees his actors as bringing "things to the work that thickened and enriched it," redefining their roles, and, in one case, even writing a scene. Altman knows how to get his actors to work as a seamless ensemble, no one of them (except Jack Lemmon) engaging in a star turn that subverts the feeling that we are observing banal lives in all their singularity and variety.

Still, there are times the sequences don't reverberate beyond the surface detail—the perceptive performances and choreographed cross-scutting suggesting little more than what we can see—with the audience having to work too hard to give the story emotional depth and texture. That's true, for example, of the sequence about the brash, aspiring make-up artist, Bill Bush (Robert Downey, Jr.), and his much softer wife, Honey (Lili Taylor), who are apartment-sitting for their neighbors and become obsessed by the flat and its large fish tank. The story projects an eerie sense of estrangement, but leaves one dissatisfied, looking for a subtext that defies deciphering.

In *Short Cuts* men drink, lie, fester, rage, and commit gratuitous acts of violence, while women are more forbearing, sometimes turning into mere victims of male aggression. His female characters, however, are usually more morally conscious and psychologically knowing than the men, a bit more aware of what other people are feeling. Few of the characters, however, male or female, come out looking good. Altman does not discriminate here between men and women when he evokes their foolishness and alienation. *Short Cuts* projects a vision of American life which is bleak and sardonically comic, where both men and women have responsibility for marriages in which betrayal, disaffection, and shared desolation is, more often than not, the norm.

The characters not only have to endure devastated private lives, but also to inhabit an America, in particular an L.A. (Altman meaningfully pans across a map of the city during the final credits), where a sense of community and public life doesn't exist. (And Altman is a director whose work has always been suffused with a longing for community.) It's an L.A. where bakers make late night, venomous crank calls to customers, men turn casual pickups into murder, and people ghoulishly save photos of dead bodies. Amidst this violence and lunacy, Altman's characters inarticulately grope about for something more meaningful, but are walled-in from the kind of self-knowledge that could possibly make a difference. Altman concludes the film with a montage of all the characters experiencing an earthquake—a somewhat too facile metaphor for lives where chaos and instability have become the rule.

Altman has never been a sophisticated political or cultural critic, the critique resting in his contempt for human hypocrisy, greed, and self-deception. He has nevertheless always been able to conjure up a darkly comic portrait of American life, one that can be penetrating in ways where more intellectually elaborate and articulate analyses often fail. In *Short Cuts* Robert Altman has created an epic of American fragmentation, one whose total effect—its vision of rootless and volatile lives—is more striking than its sometimes heavy-handed individual parts.

FILMS IN REVIEW, 11-12/93, p. 410, Edmond Grant

Never one to rest on his laurels, Robert Altman has taken the critical acclaim and major studio recognition that greeted *The Player* and parlayed it into the realization of a film that is wildly ambitious and structurally complex enough to dwarf practically every other American release of 1993. He has gone back to "the word" (as a certain entertainer named Spielberg urged all film-makers to do a few Oscarcasts ago) and produced a literary adaptation unlike any other: a film that reverently reproduces its source material, the short stories of Raymond Carver, while situating Carver's characters on a much larger canvas, enabling Altman to resurrect the "tapestry" plot structure he used in his bicentennial masterpiece *Nashville*.

Short Cuts certainly does an impressive job of breathing new life into Carver's dysfunctional romantics, but the finished product owes as much to the imagination of the comfortable-on-any-scale Altman (and his co-scripter Frank Barhydt) as it does to that of Carver, a master minimalist. The first third supplies somewhat choppy introductions; the final third, with its string of painful epiphanies, confirms the fact that Altman is one of the most mature artists in contemporary American film (his age having nothing to do with it).

Of course, because of the intricate way that Altman and Barhydt (who also coscripted *Health* and *Quintet*) have linked together elements and characters from nine Carver stories, it's nearly impossible to coherently synopsize *Short Cuts* in just a few sentences. Suffice it to say that the film focuses on the lives of close to two dozen Southern California residents whose paths intersect in a short span of time. Unlike *Nashville*, the plot strands here do not all converge toward one specific event. Instead, Altman connects their lives with a squadron of helicopters (spewing chemicals to kill a medfly invasion) at the beginning, and a moderate earthquake tremor towards the end.

Short Cuts runs counter to Altman's other multi-character "epics" by not functioning on any broader metaphorical level. Things are precisely what they seem to be here—this is more a tapestry composed of "slice of life" portraits than a view of "America-in-microcosm." He has even tempered his expressive visual flourishes, using zooms and associative cuts simply to underscore his characters' inner states.

In nearly every case, the cast lend enormous depth to their characters' confused situations (only Andie MacDowell and Mathew Modine seem unable to meet the challenges posed by their plum roles). Some performers do wind up having less to do than others: Annie Ross and Lori Singer, playing the only characters created entirely by Altman and Barhydt supply powerfully effective moments, but their plotline does seem grafted on. Other actors' talents exceed the demands of their brief screen time: Jack Lemmon delivers in his brief turn as a wayward parent, and consummate chameleon Jennifer Jason Leigh probes unexplored corners of her "phone sex housewife" role. Still other actors fit hand-in-glove with their parts: Tom Waits (playing the kind of sodden romantic that he writes songs about) and Lily Tomlin shine as a happily co-dependent couple, and Tim Robbins radiates pomposity as a motorcycle cop on-the-make. The cast members to watch, however, are those who quietly dazzle: Anne Archer, supplying the film's conscience, and demonstrating character shading denied in her previous "supportive wife" roles, and Bruce Davidson, whose genuine reactions to Lemmon's confessional speech (they play father and son) transform his character from an ineffectual yuppie to a wounded child—marking an emotional turning point in Altman's work, a far cry from the studied distance of his brilliantly innovative films of the '70s.

Admittedly, the film is harder to warm up to than *Nashville* was; its chance construction might be construed as being too "pat," with the characters lacking the secure foundations (belief in God, the family, America, and country music) that supplied the satirical edge in Altman's earlier masterwork. *Short Cuts* instead presents a group of people who suffer troubles that aren't picturesque or glamorous in the slightest. Like Carver (or any other reflective artist), Altman shows us the extraordinary angles to their ordinary lives.

LOS ANGELES TIMES, 10/8/93, Calendar/p. 1, Kenneth Turan

The old lion can still roar.

Though tradition holds that there are no second acts in American lives, writer-director Robert Altman, never much of a traditionalist, embarks with "Short Cuts" on the fourth or possibly fifth act of a remarkable career. Both building on what has gone before and extending outward to new boundaries, he has made a rich, unnerving film, as comic, as it is astringent, that in its own quiet way works up a considerable emotional charge.

Altman is 68 now, a survivor of successes like "M*A*S*H," "Nashville," "McCabe and Mrs. Miller" and last year's "The Player" as well as failures best not mentioned. Yet he still wants it all, still pushes his vision of film as a medium capable of supplying the widest psychological canvas on which to illustrate the way we live now.

Altman's co-conspirator this time around is the late Raymond Carver, a groundbreaking short-story writer who called himself a paid-up-in-full member of the working poor and made his considerable reputation with beautifully compressed, unadorned tales of life among the blue-collar classes.

Though this might seem too narrow and specific a base for Altman's ambitions, he and co-screenwriter Frank Barhydt understand that the harder you look at even the most ordinary lives, the more you see. Basing their script on nine of Carver's stories plus a prose poem, they have fashioned a three-hour-plus chamber piece for 22 players, a beautiful and intricate mosaic of character and incident that examines the greatest of all mysteries, that of ordinary reality.

In a season that is rife with prestigious literary adaptations, with everything from "The Age of Innocence" to the forthcoming "Remains of the Day" being carefully brought to the screen, "Short Cuts" is the most daring and inventive as Altman, in his own words, "made Carver soup" out of his source material.

Set in the Pacific Northwest, Carver's tales deal with lives that have not developed as planned and with people who are trying to figure existence out, to make it work with the puny tools they have at hand. "This life is not easy, any way you cut it," says one character, while another echoes, "It ain't going to do no good. Whatever you do, it ain't going to help none." Carver's great gift is that without resorting to patronizing or romanticizing or special pleading he tunes us into the souls of people who sometimes don't even recognize how desperate they've become.

What Altman and co-writer Barhydt have done to these stories is more than merely move the locale to the Los Angeles area, more in fact than most adapters dare to do. They have used Carver's stories as source material, not text; a jumping-off point, not a blueprint. Changing situations and relationships, combining characters, inventing new ones and fiddling with social class, they have expanded Carver's world while remaining true to the spirit that animated it.

They have also, in a way anyone familiar with "Nashville" will recognize immediately, constructed a spider's web of interconnections between the 22 protagonists. If not either relatives or friends, characters pass one another on the street or share space in stores and coffee shops. These connections never feel arbitrary or contrived, but rather come across as enriching elements, deepening the involvement of the story.

"Short Cuts" begins on a night of anti-Medfly spraying in Southern California with a series of brief character introductions. After dispensing his malathion, helicopter pilot Stormy Weathers (Peter Gallagher) unsuccessfully attempts to sweet-talk his estranged wife Betty (Frances McDormand). TV commentator Howard Finnigan (Bruce Davison) has some pithy things to say about that spray, but his wife Ann (Andie MacDowell) is more concerned with their fragile son. Harried mom Sherri Shepard (Madeleine Stowe) wants to bring her dog Suzie inside while her unsympathetic husband Gene (Tim Robbins) screams, "Don't you get environmental on me." And Jerry Kaiser (Chris Penn) puts a tarp on his Cool Pool Service truck as his wife Lois (Jennifer Jason Leigh) coolly conducts her phone-sex business while diapering one of their children.

In other parts of town, Marian Wyman (Julianne Moore) and her husband Ralph (Matthew Modine) strike up a conversation with seatmates Claire and Stuart Kane (Anne Archer and Fred Ward) at a classical concert featuring cellist Zoe Trainer (Lori Singer). Meanwhile Zoe's mother Tess (Annie Ross) is singing jazz at a club where Honey and Bill Bush (Lili Taylor and Robert

Downey, Jr.) are meeting some neighbors. And limo driver Earl Piggot (Tom Waits) is winding up a long night by stopping off at the diner where his wife Doreen (Lily Tomlin) works as a waitress.

Complex as this may sound, it is never difficult to follow. It is also the merest beginning, as, on the next day and those following it these stories unfold and glance off each other, with each successive sequence revealing something more about the characters, their relationships and their lives. Aided by a herculean editing job by Geraldine Peroni, all these stories double and triple back on themselves, bringing in new actors like Buck Henry, Jack Lemmon, Huey Lewis and Lyle Lovett, now picking up one strand, now another, in a way that is both mesmerizing and intoxicating.

There are moments of great humor in these stories, especially in Robbins' performance as a self-important motorcycle cop who is pathologically incapable of telling the truth. But "Short Cuts" is less likely than "The Player" and much of its comedy is laced with pain, as for instance when Jennifer Jason Leigh's Lois carries on outrageously obscene phone conversations, oblivious to the discomfort she is causing her husband (a surprisingly affecting performance by Penn).

That pain also stretches into tragedy at times, and what Altman focuses his film on is how his characters cope with the major and minor disturbances of life. "Short Cuts" deals with crossed wires and struggles for dignity, with the difficulty men and women have being in the same room together, let alone communicating, and finally with the way we both torture and heal each other, imperfect people making a curious and imperfect peace.

As with any three-hour film, "Short Cuts" (rated R for graphic sexual language and for nudity) is not equally involving all the time. Some performances are stronger than others, some situations more entertaining, and some choices Altman has made, like an over-reliance on female nudity that borders on the exploitative, difficult to defend. But whenever interest lags, a look, a moment, a *frisson* of regret will cross the screen and the emotional connection is restored.

Perhaps the most remarkable thing about "Short Cuts" is how effortless it all seems. Made with the unforced and casual command that often comes to artists late in life, it is close to magical in the way it draws us into its web, in how the whole comes to be considerably more than the individual parts. Though there are times when very little is going on, at the close the feeling that you've experienced more than you anticipated is inescapable. If you want to know what the work of a mature American master is like, this is the place to look.

NEW STATESMAN & SOCIETY, 3/11/94, p. 33, Jonathan Romney

A ten-strand portmanteau movie of stories, starring a host of American cinema's great and good and called *Short Cuts*, might have seemed a dainty, *Masterpiece Theatre* kind of idea to some directors. But not to Robert Altman. For a start, the title's a complete misnomer. The film may comprise a number of Raymond Carver short stories and variations thereon, but there are no short cuts here. The map is massive and labyrinthine, and you can only get from A to B by way of C, D and E. This is a film in which you *have* to take the scenic route—and with Altman's predilection for the scuzzy, the seedy and the downbeat, it isn't always that scenic.

The great thing about *Short Cuts* is that it's so low-key. It all looks as if it just happened, but the contrivance is enormous. You can imagine Altman and co-writer Frank Barhydt poring like military strategists over timetables and maps of Los Angeles with coloured pins for the different characters.

But what's extraordinary is that anyone should think of linking up Raymond Carver's stories at all. All his narratives take place in the same universe, a kind of dead zone, a middle-American junkyard in which dreams come home to die, or at least flop out on the sofa. But all his losers and dreamers are lost in their own world. His famously minimal style creates a sense of airless downtime in which explosive small events simply leave a slough of contemplative silence behind them. Which is partly, I should add, why I find them practically unreadable, their evocation of inertia too uniformly stylised.

You can see why some Carver purists have railed at *Short Cuts*. The tone is completely different—not just in the way it favours the farcical, unruly comedy of embarrassment, but in its refusal to let its characters sit still as Carver's can't help doing. Even the most inert figures, like Tom Waits' boozy chauffeur, can't stop twitching, doing little routines to scam the world into thinking they're still fully functional.

This is not really an adaptation of Carver: Altman simply borrows the cast and situations for his own use. It's rather like Pinter characters being co-opted into *Waiting for Godot* and finding they have to do something as undignified as juggle with hats.

Oddly enough, the one strand not from Carver, about a jazz-singing mother (Annie Ross) and her cellist daughter (Lori Singer), most directly evokes his themes of chances lost and communications not made—and it's the film's least interesting strand. It may be overstressing the point to make Ross's nightclub act serve as chorus, with songs like "Punishing Kiss" and "Prisoner of Love" (among the composers: Elvis Costello, U2 and Dr John). But Ross's cynical, regretful bark is sparingly used and sets the tone.

So Ross and Singer have this pool, which is being serviced by Chris Penn, whose wife Jennifer Jason Leigh does this phone sex job. His best buddy, Robert Downey Jr, is married to Lili Taylor, whose mom, diner waitress Lily Tomlin, has just knocked over the son of Andie MacDowell, who has just ordered a birthday cake from the baker Lyle Lovett. What a strange, small world it is.

But it's not quite the same small world that Altman explored in *Nashville*, where all the characters seemed to exemplify an aspect of the legendary song city, and most of them aspired to be legendary themselves. *Short Cuts* isn't a portrait of LA in the same way. Instead it draws on LA's very anonymity, the sense of its being not so much a city as a sprawling circuit-board in which you can shuttle from place to place but never reach the heart of it.

These characters have homes to go to but "no direction home" (to quote another songwriter who might profitably have contributed a number). They're always flying off somewhere else—blustering traffic cop Tim Robbins to visit his wayward mistress Frances McDormand, Fred Ward and his chums on a ghastly fishing trip—or turning up out of the blue, like McDormand's gleefully destructive husband Peter Gallagher or Jack Lemmon arriving at the hospital where his grandson is critically ill. Lemmon's character walks into this painful crisis with his own entirely irrelevant agenda, as if someone had just flipped two pages in the script.

It's an act of stunning incongruity, and the moment when the film's switches seem least contrived. Here it makes its point most bluntly and poignantly—that no life goes on in isolation, that crises happen alongside each other all the time, jockeying for pole position. These stories are like stations on a radio dial, all broadcasting at once, sometimes muscling in indecorously on each other's waveband.

This is why it makes sense for Altman to employ a moderately starry cast rather than unknowns. Because you recognise some rather than others and some act in familiar fashion while others work flagrantly against type, he can invoke an image of society as non-stop performance with everyone reading from different scripts. As a variation on the old life-as-movie metaphor, it's infinitely more interesting than the much more overt *The Player*.

Here, Altman doesn't have to wheel on Julia Roberts as Julia Roberts to make the point. Because you're star-spotting, you're not quite sure whether you're supposed to be seeing Lily Tomlin as Doreen Piggot working in a diner or just Lily Tomlin working in an Altman film as a diner waitress.

He simply highlights a dilemma we always face (and often conveniently forget) when we see stars on screen, but uses it to make us aware that *everyone's* acting, more or less. These people dress the part, to work as newscasters, clowns, bakers or cops, but they also act as father or mother, pose for paintings in the image of themselves, change roles when they move into someone else's story.

But they can't always tell the difference between life and pretence. We see what appears to be a nasty moment between Downey and Taylor, but the joke's on us. We've been had by a sick gag about American cinema's current appetite for pulp violence. Then just as we imagine it's all harmless make-believe, the theme returns in darker colours with an extraordinary contrived ending in which all the sexual tensions erupt in one horribly cathartic gesture.

The theme also gets a lighter twist, when Lili Taylor and Buck Henry, complete strangers, accidentally swap photos and get a sudden, baffling glimpse into each other's imaginations. At moments like this, the film, for all its flip misanthropy, reminds us of its moral dimension.

Short Cuts is largely about people casually fucking each other up in a lazy everyday way. You know that life will go on the next day, and these people will still be at each other's throats. But in its most farcical moments, it impresses on you that life is nasty enough without people messing around with the genuinely unspeakable horrors. It's one long, beautifully cynical joke, and one that I'd take over Carver's punctilious solemnities any day.

NEW YORK, 10/11/93, p. 75, David Denby

To hell with love, sings Annie Ross, a tough old broad who entertains barflies until dawn in Robert Altman's *Short Cuts*. Loosely based on selected stories by the late Raymond Carver, *Short Cuts* is a sour-spirited blues epic. The bad news continues into the night and then into the next day. Ross's bitter jazz laments—including a new Elvis Costello song, "Punishing Kiss" set the tone and provide the emotional glue. As in *Nashville*, Altman has meshed separate stories that "rhyme," though the characters of one story also stay into another, like animals wandering into a neighbor's backyard.

But Altman's temper has darkened since *Nashville*. This movie is mainly a long, angry ballad about shabby behavior and unhappiness—terrible luck, men cheating on women, meanness, and betrayal. Reconciliation is possible, but it's no more than a gesture. To hell with love.

What gaiety there is in *Short Cuts* comes from the sheer spectacle of Altman working, manipulating his immensely complex narrative, doubling, tripling, and even quadrupling his thematic lines. Altman displays a glancing touch, a control of dramatic pacing and film rhythm, a lordly freedom of movement across time and space. Using Carver as raw material, he spins out his endlessly bilious mood. This is a movie of visual puns and echoes, sardonic jokes and playful malice. Traces of compassion break through, and there's a lovely sequence with Lily Tomlin and Tom Waits as a scruffy married couple; but the prevailing emotional tone is one of bleak disgust and mysterious rage. The rage, which is Altman's, not Carver's, cuts us off from many of the people onscreen. *Short Cuts* has been hailed as a masterpiece, but I can't agree. The movie doesn't have the life and variety of a great work, and it leaves a bad aftertaste.

Carver set his material in the Northwest, but in the process of weaving together the separate stories (and making up a great deal of their own material), Altman and writer Frank Barhydt have moved the setting to Los Angeles. Note the familiar Los Angeles but the lower-middle-class milieu of Downey and Hawthorne and the other smoggy, yellowish nowheresvilles of tract houses and vacant streets. At the beginning of the movie, helicopters spray these neighborhoods with malathion, and Altman introduces no fewer than nine sets of characters, all reacting to the invasion. The spray is aimed at the Medfly but falls on everyone; it's poisoned fairy dust, like the snow at the end of James Joyce's great story "The Dead." *Short Cuts*, I suppose, means to be the ultimate Los Angeles movie, and it settles on your soul like a shroud. Jumping from story to story, Altman achieves a sense of floating displacement and carelessness. The characters trip over their ignored children as if they were loose shoes left on the floor. In this view, Los Angeles is a city without a future (one of the children dies). At the end, an earthquake covers the evidence of murder, but murder of one sort or another is going on every day.

The characters act as if no one were looking, not even themselves; they do whatever low, stupid thing they can get away with. A philandering motorcycle cop (Tim Robbins) hauls women over, intimidates them, and takes their telephone numbers. Tim Robbins gives a blank, blustering performance, as if he couldn't give any of himself to the role, but Altman's intentions are clear enough. This is the way people really are, we're meant to think. They—we—act without ideals, without grace or even the memory of honor. Lechery, selfishness, and dishonesty are instinctual. Men and women never understand each other.

The cop is compulsively cheating on his wife, but his girlfriend (Frances McDormand), cheats on *him* with a wealthier lover. Of course, it's absurd to say that no one is looking, because Altman and Barhydt are looking; they created the characters this way, and the way they created them is as much a willed stylization of behavior as was the fake goodness and selflessness of the characters in old Hollywood movies. A young mother (Jennifer Jason Leigh) does phone sex from home to make a living, and Altman amuses himself with the weird conjunctions of her professional and personal routines. "My panties are wet," she moans to some guy, cradling the receiver with her neck, as she diapers her baby. When her hulking spouse (Chris Penn) complains that she doesn't talk to *him* that way, she says, "If you wanna f--- me, f--- me. I'm all talked out." This is funny, but the shallow nihilism of it suggests a freezing of Altman's soul, and one's laughter shrivels up.

Women in Altman's films have often been dreamy, glazed-over creatures, Sibyls without prophecy, and there's one of those lost ones here, the daughter (Lori Singer) of the jazz singer, a suicidal cellist with long blonde hair who saws away and can't communicate with her hard-bitten mother. But how did that tough old bird produce this long-necked swan? The scenes between them, each pursuing her own music, show Altman at his absurdist worst, trying to make something hip out of undramatized despair. To my relief, two of the other young women (McDormand and Madeleine Stowe) come fully alive, each fighting with a low-life husband and looking to get as much sex for herself as possible. Madeleine Stowe, that languorous beauty, wakes up and gives a startlingly powerful performance as a betrayed woman who can't stop wanting her betrayer. Posing naked for her sister, an artist of dubious talent, she has a wicked grin on her face when her brother-in-law blunders in. Later, the sister (Julianne Moore), nude from the waist down, argues with her husband (Matthew Modine) about an old infidelity. There isn't much sensuality in *Short Cuts*, but there's lechery and self-exposure, sex as power and obsession.

The dismaying moments come together, and every once in a while you feel a little thrill of despair, a deep-saturated, discordant mood that only Altman can produce. Three men on a fishing trip discover a corpse in the water. The nearly naked young woman below the surface of the clear water is an extraordinary image, worthy of Keats almost, but then we get another demonstration of the crassness of men: The three continue their fishing without reporting the death. In the Carver story on which the episode is based, the masterly "So Much Water So Close to Home," the emphasis is on the reaction *afterward* of one of the fishermen's wives—the way she identifies with the dead girl and begins to see her husband (who loves her) as a murderer. The story is a marvel of displaced violence and fear. In the movie, the wife's reaction is just a regretful coda, and it doesn't have much force.

In brief, in order to unify the material, Altman has made it redundant and tendentious. It's as if Raymond Carver had set out to demonstrate that men were heels. But Carver is a remarkably impassive master. In his stories, the people are unaware of why they do what they do; they are mysteriously driven. Carver's cool is that he never explains anything, yet his work doesn't seem arbitrary—the characters remain rooted in place. So the movie is wrong in spirit: The glancing restlessness of Altman's style, the piling up of similar characters and incidents, doesn't fit the material that Altman has mined from the stories, Carver's people are not interchangeable; they are who they are—ordinary folk at the edge of breakdown who behave in the most unexpected ways. In the movie, however, the individuality of the characters and their experience gets lost in the endless bluesiness, the spunout jazz symphony of futility.

NEW YORK POST, 10/1/93, p. 39, Thelma Adams

"Short Cuts" sprawls like Los Angeles. That's the setting for Robert Altman's latest movie which opens the 31st New York Film Festival tonight. It's based on the writings of Raymond Carver, the father of dirty realism whose insular tales about small lives in small Pacific Northwest towns are penned with crisp prose and minimal fuss. With a multiple narrative straight out of Altman's "Nashville" (1975), the director splatters Carver's miniatures on a broad canvas. The results are mixed.

The movie opens with the thunder of helicopters flying in formation in the black and spangled night sky over L.A. A disembodied newscaster intones: "Destroy the medfly before it has a chance to destroy us." This is far from Carver's timber and fog. Carver fans will have plenty of bones to pick. But between the opening medflies and the closing earthquake, Altman addresses the uncertainty and unforeseen in small lives with occasional brilliance.

Directing a cast of 22 characters, he develops surprisingly intimate portraits of daily lives filled with small terrors and joys, with fragility and surprising strength, alcohol, infidelity and redeeming love. It may be Downey and Compton, Glendale and the Hollywood Hills, but this is Carver country.

Working from a script he wrote with Frank Barhydt, Altman explores the territory where the odds of winning the lottery or losing an only child are equal. A single event can alter life's course or bring sudden clarity. Stuart Kane (Fred Ward) joins his buddies on a fishing trip; they find a dead body and the encounter sends ripples through Kane's marriage to Claire (Anne Archer). Dr. Ralph Wyman (Matthew Modine) confronts Mrs. Wyman (Julianne Moore) with a two-year-old infidelity. Ann and Howard Finnigan (Andie MacDowell and Bruce Davison), a couple that smugly has everything, lose the only thing that matters and rediscover their humanity.

The Finnigans' tale, based on "A Small, Good Thing," is emotionally the most successful corner in Altman's broad canvas. While Ann is ordering a baseball cake for his eighth birthday, a car flattens her son Casey (Zane Cassidy). Disturbing phone calls from an unidentified man intrude on the Finnigan's bedside vigil. The boy fails and Ann realizes the calls are from the insistent baker (Lyle Lovett), angered over the abandoned cake. Ann and Howard confront the baker and ultimately it is in the comfort of his kitchen that the couple find the strength to continue.

In a movie brimming with notable performances, MacDowell wrenches as the comfortable, catalog-shopping young matron transformed by her son's death into a passionate and compassionate woman. Moore's circuitous response to Modine's probing questions about her past, delivered naked from the waist down (yes, she's a true redhead), is disarmingly intimate. Jennifer Jason Leigh's frowsy housewife hawks phone sex (in Carver, it was vitamins!) while changing diapers. "Already?" Leigh asks, "that was fast."

Also notable in a cast of pleasures are: Jack Lemmon's understated, over-the-hill father; Chris Penn's solid, bear-like husband who turns ferocious; and Tom Wait's alcoholic, charming and pathetic in turns. Other cast members include Robert Downey, Jr., Madeleine Stowe, Tim Robbins, Huey Lewis, Buck Henry, Lili Taylor, Lori Singer, Annie Ross, Lily Tomlin, Frances McDormand and Peter Gallagher.

NEWSDAY, 10/1/93, Part II/p. 56, Jack Mathews

Robert Altman has referred to "Short Cuts," his "Nashville"-styled adaptation of a batch of Raymond Carver stories, as "Carver Soup," and that's about right. Minestrone, dense, nicely seasoned, steaming, and, if in the end it isn't very filling, it is certainly to be savored.

Actually, it is a little misleading to say that "Short Cuts" was adapted from nine Carver short stories and one poem. Altman used that material, and the general working class milieu of Carver's world as inspiration for something unmistakably his own.

Carver fans may recognize some of the stories, which are delicately, ingeniously interwoven between the opening sequence of helicopters raining Medfly poison over nighttime L.A. and the climactic earthquake ("Not the big one!" everyone jokes) a few days later. But there are underlying themes in what Altman has turned into the movie equivalent of a furious three-hour jazz composition—Subcurrents in Blue—and it ranks with his best work.

The Altman style has never been more polished. Walt Lloyd's camera darts in and out of the lives of the film's featured 22 characters like an invisible burglar, cutting out slices of life that Altman and his editor Geraldine Peroni then wove into a dazzling narrative montage.

Where Carver's stories and characters were independent of each other, Altman and his co-writer Frank Barhydt invented a variety of ways to link them. There are essentially 10 stories here, including one—about a jazz singer (Annie Ross) and her melancholy daughter (Lori Singer)—that Altman and Barhydt contrived to give the film its bluesy leitmotif.

In the long, leisurely opening, we meet most of the characters and Altman's ensemble cast under the ominously droning blades of the helicopters. There's TV commentator Bruce Davison and his wife Andie MacDowell, surgeon Matthew Modine and artist Julianne Moore, unemployed Fred Ward and his clown-for-hire wife Anne Archer, pool-sweep Chris Penn and telephone hooker Jennifer Jason Leigh, and on the list goes.

What occurs between the couples—the deceit, the badgering, the anger and repression—produce mini-dramas that all feed into the overall sense of emotional malaise in contemporary urban life. It's about people who aren't what they seem, or think they are. A bluesy singer who can't feel the blues, a telephone hooker who doesn't feel sexy, a clown with no sense of humor.

Those aren't Carver's themes. The writer focused, unsentimentally, on the working class of the Pacific Northwest, and how bereft circumstances effected—their behavior. Altman has upscaled most of the characters to middle-class, altering their drives from need to comfort, and has them acting out against their conditions.

There are touches of irony and cynicism here that are absent in Carver's work, and the women have certainly fared better in the transition than Carver's men. But Altman's choices have neither improved nor damaged the stories, he just made them very different.

You'd have to see the movie at least twice and take notes to make sure all of the characters are logically linked. It does seem unlikely that a relative handful of people in vast L.A. would keep bumping into each other in bakery shops, at Fotomats and on the road. But the film moves along at such a clip, you don't have time to study the connections.

The movie invites immediate comparisons to "Nashville," and I suspect many of them will be unfavorable. "Nashville's" political and social themes were much clearer, and arguably more important. But where the two films are most alike to me, and which is very much a plus, is in their shared sense of impending doom.

In both movies, there is the constant feeling that something catastrophic is about to happen. In "Nashville," it finally did, with the assassination of a country music star. "Short Cuts," like life, doesn't build to anything quite so neat. There are traumatic events—a murder, a suicide, psychological furies, family tragedy—but Altman's interest is in how the people involved react to the crises, and to each other.

There is a great deal of looking back with regrets in the film, of characters retracing steps—leading up to doom. Jack Lemmon, in perhaps the best single scene of his career, plays a guilt-ridden, self-absorbed man who re-enters his son's life, at the worst possible moment, to confess and beg forgiveness for an old affair he blames for every family disaster that followed.

Altman's loose style with actors has always produced uneven results, and the range here is greater than usual. His three musician actors. Annie Ross, Tom Waits, who plays a doleful souse, and Lyle Lovett, as a baker inadvertently caught up in a customer's grief—create dramatic vacuums whenever they appear. And Tim Robbins, so brilliant in "The Player," is stuck doing comic relief, as a cartoonist's version of the new breed of bozo L.A. cop.

But no one lingers long enough to spoil this party, and the performances of Lemmon, Davison, Moore, Archer and Leigh, in particular, are remarkable.

"Short Cuts" is rated R, and you should think of it as an R +. There is genital nudity, male (Huey Lewis whizzing into a river) and female (Moore throwing an emotional tirade while her bare lap is suspended center-screen like a framed still life). And Leigh's phone sex dialogue, casually read while changing her baby's diaper, is as raw as it gets.

In those same "Carver Soup"' interviews, Altman has said he considered editing "Short Cuts" into two movies, emphasizing different stories, and having them released simultaneously. If the notion was to double its box-office receipts, as he impishly suggested, he was wise not to have bothered.

People are going to have to see this one twice if they expect to see it all.

NEWSWEEK, 10/11/93, p. 60, David Ansen

It may have 22 major characters, and run three hours and nine minutes, but Robert Altman's stunning *Short Cuts* is remarkably nimble and light on its feet. It shoots along, like a stone skipping on water, darting in and out of the disheveled middle- and working-class lives of its deracinated Los Angeles characters. It's an epic, but not the kind we're used to: no sweeping vistas, swelling music, larger-than-life emotions. Altman, at his best, has always been a lower-case director, more interested in spontaneity than spectacle, preferring flux to finality. The ease with which he weaves his nine sets of characters in and out of the narrative is testimony to his formal control, yet the style stays loose and off the cuff, as if he were merely eavesdropping on reality. His *Look Ma, no hands!* manner is his most artful deception: every square foot of this sprawling fresco is stamped with his jauntily bleak sensibility, his insatiable curiosity about the messiness of human relations.

The scope and structure recall "Nashville," but the milieu is closer to the underrated "California Split." Transplanting nine Raymond Carver short stories from the Northwest to southern California, Altman and co-writer Frank Barhydt aren't interested in conjuring up familiar media images of L.A. Except for the ominous squadron of medfly-spraying helicopters that opens the film, and the earthquake that closes it, "Short Cuts" could be set in any part of dysfunctional suburban America, wherever families are coming apart, wherever a shared sense of community has given way to randomness, drift and too much drink. The center isn't holding anymore—indeed, there's no center in sight.

It's not a pretty picture. The most "successful" couple in the story—a TV broadcaster (Bruce Davison) and his wife (Andie MacDowell)—have the worst luck: their son (Zane Cassidy) is hit by a car, and his life hangs in the balance through most of the film. This skein, based on "A Small, Good Thing," is the most faithful to its source: elsewhere, Altman riffs freely on Carves motifs. A swimming-pool cleaner (Chris Penn) swallows his rage as he listens to his wife (Jennifer Jason Leigh) have phone sex for money while she changes their baby's diaper. An unemployed husband (Fred Ward) goes on a fishing trip with his pals, where they discover a girl's naked corpse and do nothing. Where he tells his wife, a birthday clown (Anne Archer), it drives a wedge through their marriage. A jealous doctor (Matthew Modine) taunts his artist wife (Julianne Moore) about a past infidelity. Her long-suffering sister (Madeleine Stowe) is trapped in a cacophonous marriage to a philandering cop (Tim Robbins), who's having an affair with Frances McDormand; her estranged husband (Peter Gallagher) is bent on revenge. Another couple (Robert Downey Jr. and Lili Taylor) housesit for a friend and play out their sex fantasies in the neighbor's bed. Taylor's mother is waitress Lily Tomlin, who inadvertently runs down the little boy. She's married to an alcoholic chauffeur (Tom Waits) full of boozy plans to escape their trailer home in Downey.

Disconnection is the theme, and the estrangement of men and women, who rarely move on the same wavelength. The men strike out, defensive, emotionally violent. Most of the women are more supple survivors, their vulnerability signified by physical nakedness. All around them children swarm, uncomprehending of the folly they'll no doubt inherit. Altman gets some amazing performances: Leigh's chilling sexual bluntness; Stowe's sardonic resignation in the face of the comically monstrous Robbins's macho posturing; Tomlin and Waits work up a wonderful tough-tender chemistry. MacDowell movingly conveys a woman thick with grief. In the hospital, Jack Lemmon delivers a riveting confession of his long-ago marital betrayal as his son Davison squirms in discomfort.

A few of the threads are ragged: the Altman-invented story of a drunken jazz singer (Annie Ross) who can't communicate with her suicidal cellist daughter (Lori Singer) sticks out—the girl is unreal, a literary conceit. Ward and Archer's marriage isn't set up convincingly, so nothing's at stake when it cracks. Modine is too callow even for his callow character, and the amateur Lyle Lovett, as a baker who harasses MacDowell for forgetting to pick up her son's birthday cake, is in over his head. But even when "Short Cuts" misfires, it rarely fails to transfix. Few filmmakers have captured so acutely the provisional, we're-making-this-up-as-we-go-along texture of middle-class American life. It's a funny/scary vision, with a manic edge—which is why, when you come down from the high of the filmmaking, you may be left with the taste of ashes in your mouth. Altman's artistry can make you happy even when his art offers cold comfort.

SIGHT AND SOUND, 3/94, p. 49, Geoffrey Macnab

An evening in the suburbs of Los Angeles. As the helicopters fly overhead, spraying chemicals to kill a plague of medfly, various city dwellers go about their business. Anne Finnigan, a housewife and mother, is at home with her husband Howard, a TV personality, watching Howard's show. At the city concert hall, Dr Ralph Wyman and his wife Marian are listening to a performance by young cellist Zoe Trainer. They make friends with the couple sitting alongside them, Claire and Stuart Kane, and end up inviting them to a barbecue later in the week. Lois Kaiser is in her kitchen, feeding the baby while conducting a dirty telephone conversation, as her husband Jerry listens in disgust; her job is answering sex calls, and she fits it round her domestic life. Policeman Gene Shepard is arguing with his wife and kids, and growing ever more exasperated with the family dog. Eventually, he rushes off in a temper to visit his mistress, Betty Weathers. Earl Piggot, a chauffeur, draws up at a local nightclub where jazz singer Tess Trainer, Zoe's mother, is getting ready for her evening set.

The next morning, Bill and Honey Bush say goodbye to their neighbours, who are off on holiday, promising to look after their apartment and feed their tropical fish. Earl looks in at the diner where his wife Doreen works as a waitress. She accuses him of drinking, and he denies the charge. As the two argue, Stuart Kane and his friends Gordon and Vern stop by for breakfast on their way to fishing. They ogle Doreen, making her bend over and reach for the butter so they can stare at her butt. Earl slinks off. Helicopter pilot Stormy Weathers finishes his shift, and rings his estranged wife Betty to wish her happy birthday and to confirm what time he is due to pick up their son Chad. Betty, who still has Gene Shepard in her bed, is not pleased to hear from him, and Gene clambers out of the house, unsuccessfully trying to avoid Chad.

At Andy Bitkower's bakery, Anne drops in to order a cake for her son Casey's birthday; Stormy Weathers wants to buy something for Betty; and Claire Kane, who works as a clown, has a parcel to pick up for a special performance at the hospital. Doreen sets off home, still flustered from her argument with Earl. Casey, on his way to school, runs in front of her car, and is knocked down. He seems ruffled but unharmed, and declines her offer of a lift. Anne arrives home and is startled to find him slumped in front of the television; on Howard's advice, she rushes him to hospital.

Stuart and his friends have no sooner reached the remote stretch of water where they plan to fish than they spot the dead body of a naked woman. Miles from the nearest phone, they decide that, rather than spoil their trip, they will ignore the incident until they get back home. Meanwhile, Jerry Kaiser, who works repairing swimming pools, is peeping at Zoe Trainer as she takes a dip. He is rung on his portable phone by Bill, a makeup student, and the two arrange to have dinner with their wives in the absent neighbours' apartment, where Bill and Honey have became virtual squatters.

Gene, late for work, stops off at his house, puts on his uniform and offers an outlandish explanation to his wife Sherri for staying out all night, before speeding away on his motorbike, secretly taking the family dog with him. He deposits the dog in a distant neighbourhood, then proceeds to book Claire, who is dressed in full clown regalia, for driving too slowly. She is on the way to the hospital. Casey has already been admitted here; he is in a coma, but Dr Ralph Wyman tells Anne and Howard not to worry. Howard's long-lost father Paul turns up at the bedside with a convoluted story about why he left the family all those years ago, after a sexual encounter with his sister-in-law. Anne and Howard take turns to travel home for sleep and refreshment. There they both receive abusive calls from Andy Bitkower, who is furious they haven't picked up Casey's birthday cake.

Doreen finds Earl slouched on the sofa, half drunk. He shows no sympathy as she recounts how she almost killed Casey, and storms out of the house. Honey Bush, Doreen's daughter, comes to visit and advises her mother to leave Earl at the first opportunity. Zoe Trainer has spent her day practicing and playing basketball with friends; she tries to prompt her mother into revealing more about her jazz musician father, who died in Europe, but Tess refuses to reminisce. When Tess sends her to fetch another vodka, Zoe reacts by smashing the glass in the kitchen sink, and smearing the blood from her cut hand all over the walls.

Afternoon. Sherri Shepard is over visiting her sister, Marian Wyman, an artist. She has agreed to pose naked. Halfway through the sitting, Ralph arrives home unexpectedly, and they shoo him off. Then they go to Sherri's place for tea, and conspiratorially discuss how rotten their husbands are. Gene, having cobbled up another excuse to explain his absence to his wife, takes Betty for a birthday meal. Gene hints he is sick of his family life, and they discuss starting a more serious relationship. Stuart, back from fishing, makes love to Claire, and then tells her about the dead body. She is horrified that he didn't report it at once. (The next day, when she finds out it belonged to a young woman from Bakersfield, she drives out to the funeral.) Bill, Honey, Lois and Jerry head off to the nightclub. Earl is here, propping up the bar. Stormy Weathers has discovered about Betty's affair with Gene. One night when she is away, he breaks into the house, and shreds all her clothes and furniture.

Casey dies shortly after coming out of his coma. Zoe is appalled by Anne and Howard's grief. She visits her mother at the nightclub, where Tess is rehearsing for the evening show. Tess shows her no sympathy. Zoe reacts by locking herself in the garage, turning on the car, and waiting for the exhaust fumes to kill her.

It's the end of the week. Claire and Stuart have turned up for a barbecue at Ralph and Marian's with a fish Stuart caught during his trip. Gene has decided Betty is abandoning him, and has returned home to Sherri and the kids. Anne and Howard are being consoled by Andy Bitkower, who is fortified to hear about Casey. Betty has returned from a mystery jaunt with a businessman boyfriend, to be confronted by the destruction Stormy has left behind him. Tess is reeling from the discovery of Zoe's body. Doreen and Earl are back together, vowing undying love.

The Bush family and the Kaisers have gone for a picnic in the park. Bill and Jerry leave their wives and kids to run after two young women cyclists. They catch up with them and try to chat them up. Jerry suddenly attacks one of the women, assaulting her at the precise moment a huge earthquake begins. The earthquake subsides and Stormy Weathers, who witnessed it from his helicopter, appears on TV, blithely telling an interviewer what a wonderful city Los Angeles is.

There is something of the biblical epic about Robert Altman's *Short Cuts*. It begins with a plague of medfly; ends, more than three hours later, with an earthquake; and rumbles throughout with a sense of impending disaster. Like *The Player*, it is set in Los Angeles, but the city it depicts is a long way removed from the glossy, affluent world of the Hollywood studio executive. Here, the action is firmly rooted in less glamorous terrain—in suburbs which are going to seed, diners, cheap nightclubs. Given the tribulations endured by white, middle-class America in recent years, the Raymond Carver stories Altman uses as his raw material have a surprisingly contemporary relevance. The author's ramshackle collection of woebegone heroes and heroines no longer exist quite so far in the margins of American experience: their small-town tales of debt and disappointment are becoming more and more familiar across the country as a whole. Even California, traditionally a bastion of optimism, has taken a bruising. Since the 1990s began, Los Angeles, for one, has been hit by a series of near-apocalyptic disasters: droughts, riot, fire. This, you imagine, must have been why Altman chose it rather than Carver's grey, anonymous Midwest as his location. He doesn't broach the city's political or environmental problems directly, but he hints at the paralysing anxiety which has overcome its citizens. His cluster of intertwined narratives, nearly all of them concerning some sort of a breakdown in a relationship, deflect the prevailing mood of crisis into the domestic sphere.

Not that it's all millennial doom and gloom. The jeremiads come laced with comedy, and the soap opera structure allows Altman to shift gear as frequently as he makes his short cuts between characters. He and fellow scriptwriter Frank Barhydt may use Carver as their inspiration, but they take a refreshingly robust approach to the whole process of adaptation, jumbling the stories up, changing names and locations, and even creating two pivotal figures of their own, mother and daughter team Tess and Zoe Trainer. The mother is a nightclub singer, the daughter a cellist, and, throughout the film, the action revolves round them. Altman suggests that the cello represents "inner feelings," and that jazz is "what we express outwardly." While the idea of having the duo as lodestars to guide characters and set moods is an effective one, the two women don't really come to life outside their music.

Theirs is probably the weakest of the film's various strands, and pinpoints Altman's central problem—by threading so many stories together, he can't help but simplify Carver's original work, imposing an all-too-rigid pattern on writing which derived much of its power from its sparseness, its very open-endedness, its inchoate quality. As Chekhov noted, a storyteller's task is not to solve the problems of the characters he or she depicts, but to state those problems correctly. Altman may have preserved the spirit of Carver's work, but he has managed to do so only by bullying it into an artificial shape. *Short Cuts'* grand structure, its sheer length and earthquake finale, seem absurdly bombastic by comparison with Carver's tiny, self-contained, almost throwaway shards of fiction. Whatever else he is, Altman is no miniaturist. You're always aware of him in the background, the demiurge pulling the strings. *Short Cuts* is a logistical triumph, certainly; a masterpiece of orchestration, but the sheer formal virtuosity required to keep nine stories on the boil at the same time, and to map out the movements of more than 20 main characters, can't help but detract from the film's emotional impact. There's simply too much going on for the viewer to dwell on any one incident. Last year, before the picture went into production, Altman told *Sight and Sound* that "any of those Carver stories done as a full-length movie could make you go off and shoot yourself," but suggested that by interweaving several of them, it would be possible to bring out the comedy. *Short Cuts* works wonderfully as a tapestry, but only at the price of skimming over the tragic events it depicts and sometimes patronizing its characters.

Whether in the modernist visions of avant-garde film-makers like Dziga Vertov, Jean Vigo and Walter Ruttman in the 1920s, or in the grand, naturalistic sweep of pictures like John Sayles' *City of Hope*, there has always been something compelling about films which strive to offer a "symphony of a city." *Short Cuts* is mainly based in a small, suburban enclave of Los Angeles, and deals exclusively with the experiences of the white middle-classes, but it still has that magic sense of unfolding in almost real time, and of offering a multiplicity of perspectives.

In this respect, *Short Cuts* harks back to Altman's acknowledged classic, *Nashville*. His 'polyphonic' style of filmmaking would not work at all if his casts weren't up to scratch. What ultimately makes *Short Cuts* so memorable is the brilliance of the performances. There's Tim Robbins' splendidly venal cop; Lily Tomlin as the wrinkled, wornout waitress; Jack Lemmon reprising his pathetic old man routine from *Glengarry Glen Ross*; Julianne Moore, arguing with her husband, blithely oblivious to the fact that she isn't wearing any underwear; Lyle Lovett as an extremely melancholy baker; Jennifer Jason Leigh nonchalantly feeding her baby as she has phone sex with a variety of customers; and a host of other striking character turns from the likes of Fred Ward, Chris Penn and Andie MacDowell.

Altman paints a very gloomy portrait of relationships, with men and women baffled by each other, and on opposite sides of some great divide. Several times, the tension between the sexes flares up into misogynistic violence. For all its comic touches, its biting irony and delight in observation, there is no disguising that *Short Cuts* is the anatomy of a dysfunctional, frightened society, worried sick that doomsday is only round the corner.

TIME, 10/4/93, p. 80, Richard Schickel

Robert Altman's *Short Cuts* one of the season's most widely anticipated films—opens with shots of helicopters, photographed so they look like giant bugs as they roar across the night skies, doing battle with a little bug, the Medfly, terror of the California fruit industry. This periodic chemical warfare, in which insecticides are noisily laid down across entire neighborhoods, is one of the minor, faintly comic annoyances of Los Angeles life. All that technology; such a humble and primitive foe.

The film ends with an earthquake rumbling across L.A. Such periodic seismic uproars are, of course, something more than an annoyance. There's nothing funny about them and no technology to fight them. They are nature's blunt reminder that life in L.A. is transitory, that the very ground under one's feet is not to be trusted.

The temblor shakes the lives of everyone still alive at the conclusion of the movie. But not more so than the events they have endured prior to it. Among the characters: the grieving parents of a little boy who dies mysteriously after a hit-and-run accident from which he calmly walked away; a group of fishermen who steadfastly pursue their sport despite a dead body floating in their favorite fishing hole; a woman who runs a telephone sex service while tending her children and sexually ignoring her husband (ultimately with terrible results); a wide variety of men and women who are cheating or have cheated on their spouses. These people mostly have bad jobs or no jobs. Some drink too much. Some are lonely. Some are depressed or angry. But all are "normal" in the faces they present to the world.

Everything about *Short Cuts*, which runs 3 hr. 9 min., recounts no less than eight stories and deploys 24 major actors, signals large aspiration and a desire to present a panoramic vision of life in what everyone is now pleased to think of as the heart of American darkness. Los Angeles, the city that has in a wink of history's eye ceased to be Everyman's Great Utopia, has become instead everyone's Great Dystopia.

Whether the film, which has the prestigious opening-night slot at the New York Film Festival this Friday, achieves its highest aims is likely to prove hotly debatable as it rolls slowly into theaters during the fall. L.A. is, after all, the world's easiest satirical target. Moreover, Altman and co-screenwriter Frank Barhydt are adapting—freely commingling is a better description—short stories by the late Raymond Carver. These have quite a different bleakness about them and are, anyway, resistant to the implicit cultural generalizations the movie tries to impose on them. Carver was content to capture discrete moments of confusion and loss in everyday, mostly lower-middle-class lives, rendered in spare, sparsely populated stories. His manner rigorously excluded direct emotional comment on the behavior of his people. Or, for that matter, ironic observations about it.

Altman, in contrast, is an exuberant inclusionist. His best and most characteristic films (*MASH, Nashville, the Player*) teem with characters bouncing from one level to another of multilayered stories that are full of chance encounters and crazy coincidences. "There's something about this mural-type film that interests me," he says simply. It was—what else?—chance that brought matter for a transatlantic flight, and she provided several collections of Carver's stories. Dipping in and out of them as he dropped in and out of sleep, Altman found that by the end of the flight they had all homogenized. "I really couldn't remember one from the other," he says. But he did realize, "My God, this is a movie." Specifically, an Altman movie.

Maybe Altman gives Carver's people more interesting or eccentric jobs than they originally had; maybe he condescends to them occasionally; maybe one story that is his own and Barhydt's invention is melodramatically overweening. Nevertheless, this movie works. In part, that's because Altman and Carver do share one important characteristic: short attention spans. They like to touch a moment and move quickly on. True to his title, Altman does not linger on any of his stories. Nobody is ever on long enough to grow tedious, and his linkage between stories (the screenwriters used color-coded file cards pinned to a bulletin board to keep them straight) are wonderfully inventive and set up very curious resonances. "I kind of wish it were shorter," says Altman, "but this is what it is. It's like having a kid who's seven feet tall. What do you do? You buy him a new bed and hope he can play basketball."

If Altman's impatience with conventional narrative animates his film, so does his patience with and trust of actors. He's always been a man who encourages his performers to riff on a script's themes, and they respond with astonishing brio. "This movie was like a symphony, with Bob serving as the conductor," says one of his featured players, Matthew Modine. "It created a tremendous amount of pressure because you have to understand where you're at, when you come in, and what your role is. It's like a musician standing in front of these two big timpani drums. All he may have to do is hit them two times, but there's a tremendous potential for missing his cue and throwing everything off." Says Altman: "These parts aren't found in everyday movies. Here, suddenly, the actors can really create a character and play the moment, without worrying that they have to murder someone in the third act."

It may be unfair to single anyone out of this extraordinary cast, but the lunatic self-assurance of Tim Robbins as a motorcycle cop stealing his own children's dog (he hates the mutt), conducting an affair and covering his absences with tall tales of undercover drug investigations is hatefully hilarious. His braying boldness represents one emotional extreme in the picture. The other (the one that touches the most lives, and whose story is structurally the center of the film) is played, with great delicacy, by Andie MacDowell and Bruce Davison as the couple trying to cope with their child's hit-and-run accident.

Between these poles, Jack Lemmon contributes a self-justifying monologue about a long-ago but devastating marital infidelity that is haunting in its self-delusions. Jennifer Jason Leigh as the mom with a sideline in dirty talk and Anne Archer as a women whose part-time job is clowning for school kids superbly represent lower-middle-class economic desperation. And then there's Julianne Moore, whose doctor-husband (Modine) obsessively pesters her about a one-night stand she may or may not have had years ago. When she finally makes her long confession, she is half-naked—a brave actor's choice, signaling not eroticism but vulnerability.

That quality is *Short Cuts* great redeeming grace. But it is Altman's refusal to linger on it sentimentally, his joyous appreciation of his actors' wicked inventiveness, and everyone's passionate, quick-witted desire to expose the vagaries of human behavior under quotidian pressure that simply sweep you up and sweep away whatever doubts you may have about its grand design. It is, finally, as a richly pulsating, hugely entertaining human comedy—antic, wayward, glancing—that *Short Cuts* bemuses, amuses and finally entrances us.

VILLAGE VOICE, 10/5/93, p. 54, Georgia Brown

Short Cuts are quicker ways to get between here and there. In L.A.'s auto culture, they're often associated with the traffic problem. Remember Steve Martin's bumpy back-alley short cut in *L.A. Story* or the detour Kevin Kline took in *Grand Canyon*, linking his destiny with a whole new set of friends. But Martin's and Kasdan's views from the freeway are much sweeter than Robert Altman's, whose bleak but entertaining L.A. story, *Short Cuts*, opens this year's New York Film Festival. Here, a short cut to school may doom one beautiful kid, but mostly the term evokes Altman's method of linkage: his narrative's restless shuttle between a series of unhappy families. It also describes the flitting brevity of scenes: cut/cut/cut. It's a channel-surfer's dream.

The first overall, quasi-cosmic, bridge between troubled households is provided by a noisy flock of helicopters (apocalypse imminent) spraying for medflies. The same poison rain falls on one and all, the just and the unjust, in the same way that an earthquake (7.4 on the scale) at the movie's end rattles the teacups of sinners and sufferers alike. People in greater (whiter) L.A. are also united by the TV programs they're tuned to, sunshine on the deck, naked female bodies, as well as For Sale signs on their front lawns. And by monumental self-absorption, consummate carelessness, and casual cruelty.

There may be many stories in the naked city, but to Robert Altman they're easily reduced to one big one: His.

Let's dispense with any lingering notion that *Short Cuts* is based on the work of Raymond Carver. A lot of ink has been spilt about the Altman-Carver collaboration, through the medium of Carver's widow and literary executor, Tess Gallagher. Altman tells of first reading Carver between naps on a transatlantic flight and disembarking with a recipe in his head for "Carver soup." Yes, he relocates the action from Carver's Pacific Northwest to L.A.'s 'burbs; yes, he would add, subtract, multiply, and divide. Big deal. These surface alterations aren't anything to the basic differences. You don't have to be a detective, or what Altman calls "a Carver purist," to recognize that *Short Cuts*—its tone, rhythm, spirit, as well as most of its material—is pure Altman. In a few instances, Carver has furnished the storylines.

With a vast ensemble cast—22 actors—Altman (together with his cowriter Frank Barhydt, as well as the collaboration of some of the actors) has ambitiously woven together at least nine sets of stories. It's a feat. And at three hours and nine minutes, *Short Cuts* isn't ever boring. It should have been shorter, however. He could have snipped off the melodramatic finale to each little segment and come off with a stronger film.

In most of the families, man/woman relations are badly awry. Gene (Tim Robbins), a philandering cop with all the warmth of *The Player*'s Griffin Mill, is a Total Shit—a mean father (he intentionally "loses" his kids' dog) and a bullying husband, disappearing when he pleases and lying like sin. Women are creepily masochistic as Gene's wife, Sherri, no doubt exist, but they probably wouldn't be as beautiful as Madeleine Stowe. (It's an Altman "irony" that Gene and Sherri turn out "happier" than the rest.) Mother of three, Sherri models nude for her cool, collected sister, Marian (Julianne Moore), a painter. Truer to her beauty's promise, Marian married a pediatric surgeon (Matthew Modine), a man tormented by sexual jealousy.

Many of Altman's linkages are forced, particularly as they cross class lines. Improbably, Marian invites a couple they've just met to dinner, a meal that turns into an all-night carnival. Stuart Kane (Fred Ward) is unemployed; Claire (Anne Archer) works as a clown for children's parties. The Kanes, too, seem singularly unhappy with each other. Their crisis comes when, on a fishing trip, Stuart and two buddies (Buck Henry and Huey Lewis) discover a naked body floating in their trout stream. They simply fish around her for a couple of days—a decision Claire finds appalling. (In Carver's "So Much Water So Close to Home," the body has much more effect on the couple than it does here.)

On their way fishing, the three buddies stop at a diner and hit on the waitress, Doreen (Lily Tomlin). Little do they know that sitting on the next stool is her estranged husband, Earl (Tom Waits), an alcoholic chauffeur who often drops in. Driving home alone, Doreen hits a kid racing to school. He's the only son of Ann and Howard (Andie MacDowell and Bruce Davison; Modine's character is the kid's doctor). Though Ann and Howard, alone among Altman's characters, have a good-enough marriage, Howard's parents, wouldn't you know, were a mess. We learn this in an Altman addition: Howard's long lost Dad (Jack Lemmon as the same self-pitying loser he was in *Glengarry Glen Ross*) turns up at the hospital and fills Howard in on details of a long past affair with Howard's aunt.

Altman's sly little bridges often seem designed to illustrate a principle of randomness or chance. Some convergences are sinister, as when someone's car hits someone or someone decides to bash someone over the head; some are benign, as when three unrelated characters turn up in a bakery at the same time. Of course, no one suspects that he or she is in the same Robert Altman movie. Though, given the flavor of *isourts*, they should.

There's another general grouping I haven't mentioned—the dazed and confused generation off in their own little space. Lili Taylor and Robert Downey Jr. play the Bushes, the housesitters in Carver's story "Neighbors." But the housesitting part proves incidental, and they're mainly here for their friendship with the Kaisers—Lois (Jennifer Jason Leigh), who blithely conducts a phone sex business while diapering her baby, and Jerry (Chris Penn), who cleans pools. While cleaning the pool at the home of the soon-to-be-comatose kid, Jerry watches a fey blond cellist (Lori Singer doing Daryl Hannah) strip, jump in *her* pool, and play dead. Her mother, a tough old blues singing bird named Tess Trainer (Annie Ross), refuses to bat an eye. This mother-daughter couple Altman says he added to provide the movie's music. Their story is the movie's worst faux pas.

A good man is hard to find in Lalaland. So, for that matter, is a good woman. In *The Player*, emptiness signaled the ruinous touch of a corrupt business, but *Short Cuts* shows the malaise has sunk into the environs, too. Whereas Carver's people anguish and burn with bewildered desire, most of Altman's wretches are just nasty. If only they had a handle on their wretchedness—at least knew that they were miserable, like Carver's characters.

After the *Short Cuts* screening, riding down the elevator with Paul Newman (we're still, you see, in serendipity mode), I'm reminded of Newman's critique of *The Player*, as related by Altman in some rag or other. Newman said, if I remember correctly, that the movie's really about seeing the tits of the girl you don't care to see the tits of and not seeing the tits of the girl you do. I'm thinking Newman must be pleased with *Short Cuts* since he got to see the tits of most every young actress onscreen and, as a bonus, precisely the pubis he wanted to see. (Excuse me Mr. N., for the projection, but we women only get to watch Huey Lewis take a piss.) How nice that red-blooded fellas dragged to the NYFF's opening night will have their wishes granted.

In Venice, *Short Cuts* shared the festival's Golden Whatever (Lion, is it?) with Krzysztof Kieslowski's *Blue*—playing NYFF's second week. These melodramas have some similar elements—a musical family, the death of a child in a car accident—but the directors' sensibilities are far apart. (In *The Decalogue*, his amazing 10-part film made for Polish TV, Kieslowski did what *Short Cuts* merely wants to do: examine crises in the lives of neighbors and make each story count.) Extraordinarily close to *The Double Life of Veronique, Blue* is the first film in Kieslowski's new *tricoleur* trilogy (the others are *White* and *Red*). A strong Kieslowski theme, one he tries to render experientially: the proximity in human experience of agony and ecstasy. (Miramax will release *Blue* in December.)

If you believe as I do that one purpose of the NYFF should be to bring us movies that won't, or may not, open commercially, you shouldn't miss Manoel de Oliveira's *Valley of Abraham* or Hgu Hsiao-hsien's *Puppetmaster*—both of which are absolutely exquisite, and neither of which has a distributor so far. If a film is sold out, don't despair: Scalpers peddle tickets in front of Alice Tully. Last year I went to one unpopular picture and, when it came around to showtime, got my ticket at half price. Don't expect this to work with *The Piano*—but *The Piano* you'll see soon in theaters anyway.

Also reviewed in:
CHICAGO TRIBUNE, 10/22/93, Friday/p. A, Michael Wilmington
NATION, 11/8/93, p. 541, Stuart Klawans
NEW REPUBLIC, 10/25/93, p. 30, Stanley Kauffmann
NEW YORK TIMES, 10/1/93, p. C1, Vincent Canby
NEW YORKER, 9/27/93, p. 98, Terrence Rafferty
VARIETY, 9/13/93, p. 31, Todd McCarthy
WASHINGTON POST, 10/22/93, p. C1, Rita Kempley
WASHINGTON POST, 10/22/93, Weekend/p. 50, Desson Howe

SIDEKICKS

A Vision International and Triumph Releasing Corp. release of a Gallery Films presentation. *Executive Producer:* Chuck Norris, Jim McIngvale, and Linda McIngvale. *Producer:* Don Carmody. *Director:* Aaron Norris. *Screenplay:* Don Thompson and Lou Illar. *Story:* Lou Illar. *Director of Photography:* Joao Fernandes. *Editor:* David Rawlins and Bernard Weiser. *Music:* Alan Silvestri. *Sound:* James Troutman. *Casting:* Annette Benson and Penny Perry Davis. *Production Designer:* Reuben Freed. *Running time:* 100 minutes. *MPAA Rating:* PG-13.

CAST: Chuck Norris (Chuck Norris); Beau Bridges (Jerry Gabrewski); Jonathan Brandis (Barry Gabrewski); Mako (Mr. Lee); Julia Nickson-Soul (Noreen Chen); Joe Piscopo (Stone); Danica McKellar (Lauren); John Buchanan (Randy Cellini); Richard Moll (Horn).

LOS ANGELES TIMES, 4/19/93, Calendar/p. 3, Michael Wilmington

Perhaps it's a cinematic second childhood, but in the past few years, we seem to be witnessing a mass emigration of the action movie stars of the '80s back toward Cutesville and Kiddieland.

Gone, to some degree, are the snarls, damage and blood, the "Rambos" and "Raw Deals." Instead there's Schwarzenegger in "Kindergarten Cop," Sylvester Stallone in "Stop! Or My Mom Will Shoot!" Just the other week, there was Bert Reynolds in "Cop and a Half."

So, It was probably inevitable that Chuck Norris would show up in something like "Sidekicks" (which opened citywide Friday, without critics' screenings), a movie with more than its share of the cutes. This is an "inspirational" children's karate picture, stuffed with action-movie parodies, in which—though he executive produced and his brother Aaron directed—Norris isn't even really the star.

Instead, he puts in a sort of extended guest star stint. He's playing himself: genial, good-hearted superstar Chuck. The great fantasy figure of youngster Jonathan Brandis. Brandis, in turn, plays a put-upon teen-ager, who suffers from nervousness, introversion, coughs, schoolyard bullies and the well-meaning but fumbling fatherly ministrations of hapless Beau Bridges.

Life is rough, tough ... but Brandis' spirits soar whenever he sees schoolmate Julia Nickson-Soul or picks up a martial arts magazine with Chuck's face on the cover. However bad it gets in life, however many braying gym teachers, sadistic schoolmates or improbable idiocies he runs into, Brandis' ongoing fantasy life plays like a continuous all-day-and-night Chuck Norris cable channel. In it the engagingly sickly youth is cast as Chuck's sidekick in a seemingly endless festival of Norris action specials: pseudo-spaghetti Westerns, jungle war movies and chop 'em, sock 'em, Hong Kong-style one-against-a-hundred romps.

The point of the movie—in which, back in "real life," karate kid Brandis meets the great teacher and restaurateur Mako, and learns wisdom, self-control and how to put your hand through nine bricks—is that bullies are bad, heroes are nice and if you hold on to your dreams, happy endings will arrive right on schedule.

Why argue with something like that? "Sidekicks" is amiable enough, even if cinematically, it makes "Cop and a Half" look like "8½." The only time director Aaron Norris shows much flair is when he and brother Chuck get to their specialty: the karate matches. Elsewhere, the writing is stiff and thin, the visuals a little sludgy and the actors pose and mug, with Joe Piscopo as a howling, evil martial arts instructor, taking the Raging Goombah award. The fantasy scenes are flat, despite a jazzy angle or two in one Clint Eastwood parody. Not even the notably intense Mako, in the Pat Morita part, can liven up the rest of it.

Awash in syrupy sentiment, swimming in stereotypes and directed with all the subtlety of a body-flop, "Sidekicks" (MPAA rated PG) is a movie for hero-worshiping kids in shopping malls, for Chuck Norris super-fans or for devotees of improbable bad movies looking for kicks on the side.

NEWSDAY, 5/1/93, Part II/p. 25, John Anderson

Chuck Norris beats Arnold Schwarzenegger to the punch, so to speak, with "Sidekicks," a gentle and uneven film about a high school kid and his overheated fantasies. Just as Schwarzenegger will be spoofing the action genre this summer in "The Last Action Hero," Norris sends up both his films and his super-serious screen image, and does it with a good deal of humor.

But "Sidekicks," is not, as the ads would have you believe, a "Chuck Norris movie" (although Norris is one of the executive producers, and his brother Aaron directed). Outside of the prolonged final segment of the film, in which he helps out young Barry Gabrewski at the climactic karate tournament, Norris isn't on screen for more than a few minutes. It's really a coming-of-age story about Barry, one that borrows heavily from "The Karate Kid," and is curiously uneven in what it tries to do.

For one thing, Barry, an asthmatic, is cruelly taunted by his schoolmates, for his sallow, sickly looks as much as his vivid fantasies about Norris—which are so involving they might suggest mental illness. But his personality doesn't indicate he's led an outsider's life. As played by the irritating Jonathan Brandis ("The Never-Ending Story II"), he's confident, cocky and has a sense of humor. "I'm not really a nerd," you expect him to say, "I just play one in the movies."

His small universe is peopled by his father, Jerry (Beau Bridges), his beautiful teacher, Marie (Julia Nickson-Soul), his chipmunk-cheeked girlfriend-to-be Lauren (Danica McKellar), and a nasty local karate instructor, played by the cartoonish Joe Piscopo. They appear, along with Norris, in the various dream sequences, which are lifted in large part from Norris' actual movies. Strangely, some of them mix the truly violent with the ridiculous, and thus make Barry's daydreaming more pathetic than funny.

What changes Barry's life is meeting Mr. Lee (Mako), Marie's uncle, recently arrived from Asia, who takes the wimpish Barry under his wing and makes him a man—and, by imparting his martial arts expertise, a dangerous person. But just when you fear "Sidekicks" is going to present violence as a way of solving problems, it backs off; Barry's big moment doesn't even involve a karate bout, and Norris' fight with Piscopo is simply a goof. Overall, it's an entertaining enough film—it certainly won't hurt Norris' image—but some of the performances are so lackluster you'd like the star to give his fellow actors a kick.

Also reviewed in:
CHICAGO TRIBUNE, 4/30/93, Friday/p. B, Dave Kehr
NEW YORK TIMES, 5/1/93, p. 17, Stephen Holden
VARIETY, 4/19/93, p. 45, Joe Leydon
WASHINGTON POST, 4/30/93, p. B7, Richard Harrington

SILENT MOBIUS

A Streamline release. *Director:* Michitaka Kikuchi. *Screenplay:* Michitaka Kikuchi and Kei Shigema. *Based on a story by:* Kia Asamiya. *Running time:* 50 minutes. *MPAA Rating:* Not Rated.

NEW YORK POST, 7/24/93, p. 16, Jerry Tallmer

[*Silent Mobius* was reviewed jointly with *Neo-Tokyo*; see Tallmer's review of that film.]

Also reviewed in:
NEW YORK TIMES, 7/23/93, p. C12, Stephen Holden

SILENT TOUCH, THE

A Castle Hill Productions release of a Mark Forstater Productions/Tor Film Group/Metronome Productions film with the participation of British Screen/The European Co-Production Fund/The Danish Film Institute/Sandrews Film & Theatre AB/The Swedish Film Institue. *Executive Producer:* Ryszard Straszewski. *Producer:* Mark Forstater. *Director:* Krzysztof Zanussi. *Screenplay:* Peter Morgan and Mark Wadlow. *Story:* Krzysztof Zanussi and Edward Zebrowski. *Director of Photography:* Jaroslaw Zamojda. *Editor:* Marek Denys. *Music:* Wojciech Kilar. *Sound:* Wieslawa Dembinska and (music) Michal Gola and Jacek Zietkowski. *Casting:* Tracey Seaward. *Production Designer:* Ewa Braun. *Costumes:* Dorota Roqueplo. *Make-up:* Anna Adamek and Grazyna Dabrowska. *Running time:* 92 minutes. *MPAA Rating:* PG-13.

CAST: Max von Sydow (Henry Kesdi);   Lothaire Bluteau (Stefan Bugajski);   Sarah Miles (Helena Kesdi);   Sofie Grabol (Annette Berg);   Aleksander Bardini (Professor Jerzy Kern); Peter Hesse Overgaard (Joseph Kesdi);   Lars Lunoe (Doctor);   Slawomira Lozinska (Doctor's Wife);   Trevor Cooper (Muller);   Stanislaw Brejdygant (Maier);   Beata Tyszkiewicz (Gelda); Maja Plaszynska (Baby Thomas);   Piotr Wojtowicz and Wasia Maslennikow (Television Crew); Krystyna Chmielewski (Secretary).

NEW YORK POST, 11/5/93, p. 38, Thelma Adams

"Crabby artiste, insensitive to others, seeks healing and cookie to sweeten final days." If art films were personals, that would be "The Silent Touch." Maybe there's a sensitive take on this film, don't expect it from me.

Polish director Krzysztof Zanussi ("The Year of the Quiet Sun") has created the kind of European film that American audiences should like because it's good for them. It's the intellectual equivalent of peas.

Henry (Max von Sydow), a world-class composer, stopped writing music after the Holocaust. He retreated to Denmark with his wife Helena (Sarah Miles). Stefan (Lothaire Bluteau), a young Polish music student, obsesses about inspiring the blocked-but-brilliant composer to write one last symphony.

He travels to Denmark, where he magically heals Henry. Stefan introduces Henry to Annette (Sofie Grabol), a sexy young music secretary. Inevitably, Stefan not only revives Henry's music, he also resurrects all the self-indulgent foolishness that accompanied it.

The conflicts between young and old, mentor and student, men and women, geniuses and the rest of us clods, raise dinner-party questions about the relation of life and art, monogamy and artistic expression, and the Soul.

"The Silent Touch" showcases Mad Max von Sydow. The actor has starred in more than 60 films from "The Seventh Seal" to "The Exorcist." As the crabby composer, von Sydow memorably goes from invalid to lusty septuagenarian and back again.

Max delivers a signature performance. That's what annoys. Von Sydow the actor keeps winking around Henry the composer lest the audience forget who's pulling the strings.

For all von Sydow's bluster, the French Canadian Bluteau steals the show. The star of the critically acclaimed "Jesus of Montreal" has a quiet, intense style that burns through all of Stefan's scenes.

Sarah Miles, the English actress ("Ryan's Daughter"), breathes life into the doormat role of Henry's wife. An ensemble actress, she speaks volumes with half-smiles and a slight angle of her head.

In her 50s, Miles has a sexy, mature beauty rarely seen on the screen.

NEWSDAY, 11/5/93, Part II/p. 92, Jack Mathews

Henry Kesdi (Max von Sydow) is considered by every speaking character in Krzysztof Zanussi's overwrought melodrama "The Silent Touch" to be a genius, a classical composer whose 40-year professional hibernation has left the musical world in parched silence, a desert without a decent sonata or concerto to be heard.

You take these people at their word, because when we meet the revered giant, he is a pathetic fool, a disheveled, self-pitying, world-class crank, disdainful of his working contemporaries, barking at his devoted wife (Sarah Miles), and ready to take a gun or a knife to any fan or would-be publisher who approaches his wooded Copenhagen retreat.

Kesdi, played with rapacious hamminess by von Sydow, never becomes more appealing than that, even though he is transformed, briefly, by the determined young Polish music student Stefan (Lothaire Bluteau) who endures the old man's grumpy insults and, with a combination of flattery and laying on of hands, gets him back to work.

You may remember Bluteau as the Juliette Binoche lookalike who played the faux Jesus in Denys Arcand's "Jesus of Montreal." In "Silent Touch," Bluteau still has a Messiah complex, but this time, he is out to save only one soul, and to release whatever remaining, God-given compositions Henry Kesdi may possess.

1356   FILM REVIEW ANNUAL

Zanussi, one of Poland's leading filmmakers, has often grappled with issues of personal morality, the internal struggles of people trying to reconcile their beliefs and actions, and that seems to be his intention here. Kesdi's silence is a reaction to having been the only composer among his peers to survive the Holocaust, and he implies that to continue working would be an offense to their memory.

"What genocide teaches is the absolute meaninglessness of music," Kesdi says.

The pain that drove Kesdi inward doesn't mitigate his behavior. At his best, with his body revived by Stefan's curing touch, he is a demanding ogre, busily breeding with his young musical secretary between artistic tantrums, while condescending to everyone else.

In the end, Kesdi may indeed be a genius, but the only thing we know for sure is that he is an insufferable boor.

SIGHT AND SOUND, 4/93, p. 57, Julian Graffy

In Cracow a young music student, Stefan Bugajski, hears in his sleep a haunting sequence of notes which he recognises as being by Henry Kesdi, a composer who has been silent for the last 40 years. Determined to help Kesdi complete the refrain, he embarks for Denmark, where Kesdi is now living with his wife Helena. He takes with him a letter from his teacher, Professor Kern, an old acquaintance of Kesdi, who remains unconvinced that the silence that descended on Kesdi after the death of his first wife in the Holocaust can ever be broken. In their house set in its own woods, Helena Kesdi tries to interest the sick and reclusive Henry in an offer from his nephew Joseph to finance a relaunch of his career. Joseph and his associates are thrown out. Simultaneously Stefan arrives and is seen lurking in the woods. Henry grabs his gun, but Stefan manages to slip his letter to the skeptical Helena. Next day Stefan darts into the house, tells Henry that his bad back is caused by sleeping over a stream that runs beneath the house and counsels a change of bedroom. The furious Henry knifes him in the wrist and Stefan retreats to the woods.

The next night Henry moves his bedding to the other side of the house and his back pain eases. He invites Stefan for breakfast. Stefan plays him the refrain, which Henry recognises as a Jewish melody he once tried to use. He orders that Stefan be given the spare room. That night Stefan cures him of asthma by applying pressure to his temples. Henry insists that he is an angel. Henry throws himself into work and asks for a musical secretary. That night he goes to Helena's bed for the first time in years. Next morning, Stefan finds Henry a secretary in the young conservatoire student Annette Berg. Henry's doctor insists that the return to work may kill him. Annette arrives for work and Henry discusses music and flirts with her. Stefan arranges a date with Annette, which sends Henry into a rage. The date goes badly, Annette rejecting Stefan's advances. As Henry's music progresses, so does his feeling for Annette, and they begin an affair. As the music and the love affair become more intense, Stefan suffers excruciating pain in his wounded arm.

In a television interview on completion of the new work, Henry ascribes his new creativity to his guardian angel. Stefan's wound now bleeds regularly and at Henry's birthday party he collapses and is rushed to hospital. Rehearsals proceed, while the doctor warns Stefan that Henry's symptoms are unmistakable. Annette tells Helena that she is pregnant. Helena visits Stefan in hospital and orders him to leave as soon as he recovers. Henry conducts the gala premiere of his opus while Stefan and the doctor watch on TV relay. At the thunderous climax, Henry collapses and is taken to hospital, where Stefan is found to have recovered. A year later, Stefan, now teaching music in Cracow, gets a telephone call from Helena summoning him to visit the dying Henry. She and Annette are taking care of him and Annette's asthmatic baby son. Stefan tells Henry that he can no longer help him, and Henry, now reconciled to death, comforts him. Stefan picks up the asthmatic child and the boy's wheezing stops.

The Silent Touch is about art and inspiration, art and goodness, art and life. It combines lengthy discussion of these subjects with the creation of a new work by the composer Henry Kesdi. But films about music are notoriously difficult to bring off as another central European director, István Szabó, demonstrated recently with *Meeting Venus*. And *The Silent Touch*, as a film about art, is neither original nor inspired. It is not just that the sub-Orffian oratorio performed at the climax (in fact, "Exodus" by Wojciech Kilar, whose music can be heard in Francis Ford Coppola's *Dracula*) is, for all its thunder, unconvincing as the release of imprisoned genius. It is also that all the talk of the victory of art and goodness over silence and evil lacks substance—the perfunctory treatment of the theme of genocide is typical in this respect—just as the extravagant complaints Henry makes about modern music as a "pollution of silence", though occasionally amusing (it all reminds him of toenail clippings), are predictable and evasive.

This predictability extends to the characters—selfish, irascible artist Henry, long-suffering but loyal wife Helena, vital young muse Annette—and to the doggedly articulated plot, in which the intrusions into the household of both Stefan and Annette follow heavily signposted paths. The dialogue too, despite its regular returning to the subject of passion, seems etiolated and highmindedly old-fashioned. *The Silent Touch* is the first project to have benefitted from the European Co-Production Fund and the script, originally a story by Zanussi and a Polish collaborator, then worked into a screenplay by Peter Morgan and Mark Wadlow, shows signs of the statelessness such projects risk.

In another respect, though, international co-operation has worked well. The initial scenes in Cracow with Stefan waking from nightmare like a pale, haunted Dostoevskian youth, and talking feverishly to his professor (Aleksander Bardini, the doctor in Kieslowski's *Decalogue 2*) and his later sojourn in the Danish woods are the most confident in the film, with an assured sense of place and behaviour. Central to the meaning of *The Silent Touch* is the enigma of the 'angel' Stefan and his mysterious effect on Henry. In the *Acts of the Apostles* St Stephen, the first Christian martyr, is described as "full of grace and power," as doing "great wonders and signs among the people," for whom "his face was like the face of an angel." This Stefan bursts into Henry's household as astonishingly as Terence Stamp in Pasolini's *Teorema*, and Henry himself is initially bemused and resistant (both to art and to goodness), once even calling him Mephistopheles. What is the nature of their symbiosis? Stefan himself seems to have no life—no talent as a composer, no success with Annette—and yet he alone can restore Henry both physically and artistically. His wound, caused by Henry, bleeds like stigmata at the moments of Henry's greatest passion. And at the end, Henry, reconciled to art, life and death, is able to console him in return. Though this allegory of the power of goodness remains opaque and not entirely persuasive, nevertheless it is precisely its lack of explicitness that makes it the resonating core of the film.

As Henry, the petulant, tyrannical genius, Max von Sydow has little to do that he has not done many times before—except perhaps to smash so much crockery. But Sarah Miles, rarely seen these days, brings a taut conviction to the fading Helena. And Lothaire Bluteau displays the same startling intensity he showed in *Jesus of Montreal* and *Black Robe* in the central role of Stefan, by turns exuberant and anguished, confident and bewildered. Asked by the doctor why he was so determined that Henry should complete his opus, he says, "I just wanted to get some sleep."

VILLAGE VOICE, 11/16/93, p. 72, Georgia Brown

Do mind-altering fungi breed in Polish air ducts? *Uncanny* is one word for thematic resemblances between Krzysztof Zanussi's *The Silent Touch* and Krzysztof Kieslowski's *The Double Life of Veronique* and *Blue*. There is, however, a vast distance in sensibility and execution.

This English-language coproduction has Max von Sydow chewing the tapestry as Polish composer-in-exile Henry Kesdi. Curmudgeonly Henry is an aging recluse ("I want to enjoy my senility and incontinence in private") who's given up on humankind (If there's one thing genocide makes you realize it's the absolute pointlessness of music"). Back in Warsaw, Stefan (Lothaire Bluteau), a melancholic musicologist, finds his dreams haunted by Henry's unfinished compositions, so he journeys to Copenhagen, appearing in the Kesdi household somewhat as Terence Stamp did in *Teorema*.

Except that Bluteau is such a twirpy angel: Even Henry playfully grabs at Stefan's dick at one point, just to check if he's "got one." Henry's own "wet spaghetti" stiffens sufficiently once Stefan fetches a young, adoring secretary (Sofie Grabøl). Too bad Stefan won't at least sleep with Henry's long-suffering wife (Sarah Miles). Wouldn't you know, between attempts to father a child, the geezer writes and conducts a symphony (music by Wojciech Kilar). What was that about genocide, Henry?

The Silent Touch is stuffed with senile myths about (male) genius, and the director's touch is anything but silent. It's hard to believe that Zanussi was once a filmmaker of promise, but I've seen enough of his recent films to know that, unfortunately, this one is not an aberration.

Also reviewed in:
NEW YORK TIMES, 11/5/93, p. C3, Vincent Canby
VARIETY, 10/19/92, p. 162, Susan Ayscough

SISTER ACT 2: BACK IN THE HABIT

A Touchstone Pictures release. *Executive Producer:* Laurence Mark and Mario Iscovich. *Producer:* Dawn Steel and Scott Rudin. *Director:* Bill Duke. *Screenplay:* James Orr, Jim Cruickshank, and Judi Ann Mason. *Based on Characters Created by:* Joseph Howard. *Director of Photography:* Oliver Wood. *Editor:* John Carter, Pem Herring, and Stuart Pappé. *Music:* Miles Goodman. *Music Editor:* Charles Martin Inouye. *Choreographer:* Michael Peters. *Sound:* Jim Webb and (music) Joel Moss. *Sound Editor:* John M. Stacy. *Casting:* Aleta Chapelle. *Production Designer:* John DeCuir, Jr. *Art Director:* Louis M. Mann. *Set Designer:* Lauren Cory and Sandy Getzler. *Set Decorator:* Bruce Gibeson. *Special Effects:* James Karl Fredburg. *Costumes:* Francine Jamison-Tanchuck. *Make-up:* Perry M. Germain. *Stunt Coordinator:* Greg Elam. *Running time:* 100 minutes. *MPAA Rating:* PG.

CAST: Whoopi Goldberg (Deloris Van Cartier);   Kathy Najimy (Sister Mary Patrick); Barnard Hughes (Father Maurice);   Mary Wickes (Sister Mary Lazarus);   James Coburn (Mr. Crisp);   Michael Jeter (Father Ignatius);   Wendy Makkena (Sister Mary Robert);   Sheryl Lee Ralph (Florence Watson);   Robert Pastorelli (Joey Bustamente);   Thomas Gottschalk (Father Wolfgang);   Maggie Smith (Mother Superior);   Lauryn Hill (Rita Watson);   Brad Sullivan (Father Thomas);   Alanna Ubach (Maria);   Ryan Toby (Ahmal);   Ron Johnson (Sketch); Jennifer "Love" Hewitt (Margaret);   Devin Kamin (Frankie);   Christian Fitzharris (Tyler Chase);   Tanya Blount (Tanya);   Mehran Marcos Sedghi (Marcos);   Andrea Robinson (The "Singing Voice" of Sister Mary Robert);   Jenifer Lewis (Backup Singer #1);   Pamela Tyson (Backup Singer #2);   Sharon Brown (Backup Singer #3);   Paul Thorpe (Dancer "Postman"); Paul Genick (Dancer "Sugar Pie");   Aaron Baker (Dancer "Teeny Bikini");   Warren Frost (Archdicose Person #1);   Robin Gammell (Archdiocese Person #2);   Revallyn Golde (Archdiocese Person #3);   Yolanda Whitaker (Sondra);   Bill Duke (Mr. Johnson);   Sydney Lassick (Competition Announcer);   Michael "Bear" Taliferro (Security Guard);   Kai Bowe (Stage Manager);   William S. Turchyn, II (Assistant Stage Manager);   John Fontana (Flying Tech #1);   Michael A. Tice (Flying Tech #2);   Robert Simokovic (Flying Tech #3);   William D. Hall (Chapman Choir Leader).

LOS ANGELES TIMES, 12/10/93, Calendar/p. 1, Kenneth Turan

The original "Sister Act" was the most unexpected of blockbusters. Its director had no special comedy reputation, its dissatisfied writer opted for a pseudonym, and its star was not exactly bursting with confidence in the project. So much for the collective wisdom of Hollywood.

But while the industry's sagacity may be open to question, Hollywood can't be accused of a reluctance to pounce on success and attempt to duplicate it. So the appearance of "Sister Act 2: Back in the Habit" was only a matter of time, and that time is now.

Returning to the screen, then, is that celebrated nun on the run, Deloris Van Cartier, otherwise known as Sister Mary Clarence and stylishly played by Whoopi Goldberg. Back as well are the other comedic convent dwellers, specifically bouncy Mary Patrick (Kathy Najimy), feisty Mary Lazarus (Mary Wickes), shy Mary Robert (Wendy Makkena) and everyone's favorite Mother Superior (Maggie Smith).

But like participants in a reunion who find they no longer have anything to say to one another, these sisters have shown up without being given very much to do. Even by sequel standards, a minimal amount of creativity has gone into "Sister Act 2." and not even the talents of its cast, including several likable young people, can compensate for this thrown-together feeling.

Perhaps realizing the difficulty of recapturing the riotous spirit of the original, director Bill Duke and Disney executives have opted for a warm-hearted, uplifting tone with this picture. The

"Three Men and a Baby" screenwriting team of James Orr and Jim Cruickshank was brought in to soften and brighten Judi Ann Mason's script about a Crenshaw High School music teacher named Iris Stevenson that had been written without any notion of its becoming part of the "Sister Act" juggernaut.

Deloris is first glimpsed back where she began, performing in Las Vegas, except now her fame has made her a headliner. She is almost immediately reunited with the three sisters, who order milk all around and deliver a message from a desperate Mother Superior requesting her immediate presence in San Francisco.

It seems the sisters have been teaching at St. Francis High, a tough urban parochial school located in "a tired, worn, despairing community" and the kids have not exactly been paying attention. Who better than Deloris, once she is safely back in convent garb, to get the young people to come around?

Deloris, amazingly enough, readily agrees, and is assigned to the music class, which the kids involved consider "a bird," the kind of course where you only have to show up to fly right through to a passing grade.

Though they trade rap lyrics and wear hip-hop clothes, these nominal troublemakers are the kind of clean-cut and well-scrubbed delinquents not found outside the precincts of the Disney Channel. Their idea of a prank is not brandishing an Uzi but putting glue on Sister Mary Clarence's chair, and when one of their number falls asleep in class. he's not nodding out on drugs but exhausted from overwork.

While the fleeing from the Mafia situation of the original "Sister Act" may not have been more realistic than this film's notion of turning rowdy teens into a competitive choir, it was brought to the screen with an energy that has been lost the second time around.

Here the focus is on teaching good lessons, on letting the kids know that "if you want to be somebody, you better wake up and pay attention." And star Goldberg, who can be as funny as anyone if she so chooses, opts instead to spend most of her time being benevolent, inspirational and not very involving.

When the crises in this film do come, things like a bureaucratic threat to close the school and a parent who insists on keeping an ace singer out of the choir, they are both mild and visible a mile off. Too feeble to work up any animus against, "Sister Act 2" has no more than a family resemblance to its predecessor, and that is not nearly enough.

NEW YORK POST, 12/10/93, p. 48, Michael Medved

After decades of service to its gritty inner-city neighborhood, struggling St. Francis High School is about to close its doors forever. Only one member of the faculty—the spunky new music teacher—refuses to give up hope and in order to save the school comes up with a brilliant, startlingly original plan ... HEY, KIDS! LET'S PUT ON A SHOW!!!

This puny premise provides the dramatic focus for "Sister Act 2," where the fate of dear old St. Francis depends on the performance of some formerly rebellious students in a statewide choral competition. In the climactic production number, these underdogs present an unusual interpretation of Beethoven's "Ode to Joy," incorporating elements of rap, gospel, and Vegas glitz.

Will the judges of the contest recognize their genius, or honor one of the tightly disciplined choirs that provide the main competition?

The tension is so thick you could cut it with a spoon, but the fact that there are no surprises at all may actually come as something of a relief to those legions of fans who cherished the original film.

In "Sister Act," lounge singer Whoopi disguised herself as a nun because the mob was after her; in the sequel, she resumes her masquerade when her old friends from the convent need an inspirational teacher who can reach the unruly students at St. Francis High,

The huge problem with this notion is that there's no reason in the world why the music instructor at a Catholic high school would have to pretend to be a nun. Such schools are filled with faculty members who wear neither habits nor cassocks and may not even be Catholic.

This lack of logic becomes especially bothersome because the pacing in the film's first half is so sluggish. Since there's never the slightest doubt that Whoopi will win the affection of her cynical students, the painstaking portrayal of this process seems to take forever. Goldberg herself seems more than a little bored.

The endearingly eccentric nuns of the first film (Wendy Makkena, Mary Wickes, and the hugely likable Kathy Najimy) do their best to provide some comic relief, and are joined this time by quirky priests (Brad Sullivan, Michael Jeter, and Barnard Hughes) who try hard to be adorable but fail miserably.

The kids who play Goldberg's students fare better and provide this picture with its only sparks of energy or freshness. These 23 newcomers, selected after a talent search involving some 3,000 applicants, display natural charisma along with prodigious singing and dancing abilities. That's particularly true of an 18-year-old beauty named Lauryn Hill and 16-year-old Ryan Toby as a painfully earnest kid who's obsessed with Afro-centrism.

Bill Duke (best known for "A Rage in Harlem" and "Deep Cover") served as director on the project and brought a more distinctive African-American flavor—and many more black char-acters—to "Sister Act 2" than the late Emile Ardolino brought to the first film. (It had, after all, been developed, for Bette Midler before Whoopi Goldberg took the part.)

Duke also uses flashier editing and camera work on the production numbers than Ardolino. But the result is that these showstoppers seem more detached from the rest of the film than the musical interludes of the original.

Nevertheless, the infectious enthusiasm of the talented young performers will encourage audience members to tap their feet along with the music, especially near the end of the picture. In spite of—or perhaps because of—the old-fashioned familiarity of every frame of this project, most moviegoers will leave the theater in a reasonably good mood. Their satisfaction should help make this soggy sequel into a major commercial hit.

NEWSDAY, 12/10/93, Part II/p. 99, Jack Mathews

Normally, the thing you can count on with a sequel is that it will downplay what didn't work about the original and exploit to the hilt what did. In the case of "Sister Act 2," that would mean less dubious plotting and more rewritten Motown hits, more singing nuns, more rock-and-roll masses.

That didn't happen. For whatever reason, the writers and director Bill Duke (taking over for the late Emile Ardolino), decided to accentuate the negative and eliminate the positive from "Sister Act." There are fresh musical numbers, but not enough of them, and certainly not enough of the right kind by the right people.

"Sister Act 2" is about rapping teens, not rocking nuns, and the tone-shift all but ignores the lessons of Part 1.

As the movie's ads proclaim, Whoopi Goldberg is indeed back in the habit, this time leaving her kitschy casino act behind in order to help her old nun chums whip a rowdy music class into shape at a struggling, inner-city San Francisco high school.

The story that unfolds at St. Francis High, after Goldberg's Deloris Van Cartier reassumes the guise of Sister Mary Clarence, seems as inspired by "Blackboard Jungle," "Fame," and "The Bells of St. Mary's" as it is by "Sister Act." The demeanor in her class is chaos, the music lessons have been chewed up and spit onto the ceiling, and the only way Mary Clarence can cut through the students' rap reverie is by dragging her nails across the chalkboard.

But beneath the chip on every student's shoulder is a budding musical genius, and recalling how she saved St. Catherine's from spiritual ennui during her first tour, Mary Clarence hatches a plan for the salvation of St. Francis, too.

She turns her class into a gospel-rap choir and, against the wishes of the principal (Barnard Hughes) and the conniving diocesan administrator (James Coburn), enters it in a state musical competition. A victory there, she reasons, might save the school from the budget axe.

Some momentous miscalculations were made in the structuring of the sequel. After an opening production number in Las Vegas, where Deloris and her troupe run through a gaudy medley of 18 Motown hits, a full 45 minutes elapse before we get another song. And there aren't many more after that.

Worse, there is only one solid number in the entire movie reuniting the St. Catherine's choir, which featured perennially cheerful Mary Patrick (Kathy Najimy), the mouse-that-roared Mary Robert (Wendy Makkena), and the wonderfully dead-pan Mary Lazarus (Mary Wickes). The nuns, and a more convivial Mother Superior (Maggie Smith) are around, but woefully underused as supporting characters.

Here, Whoopi's major co-stars are the kids, and where the first film's subplot was a mob's farcical attempt to hunt down and kill Deloris, Part 2 focuses on a badly developed melodrama about a teenage prodigy (Lauryn Hill) whose domineering mother (Sheryl Lee Ralph) won't allow her to sing.

"Sister Act" is far too silly a concept to support heavy subplots, and the efforts are painfully protracted.

Even those might have been tolerable, however, had the music matched the wit and imagination of that in the original. Outside those Motown masses, the first "Sister Act" was pretty tiresome, too.

The young stars of "Sister Act 2," all gifted singers found in a nationwide talent search, have a sensationally energetic closing number, and Lauryn Hill displays the voice of a young Aretha Franklin. But having the kids make believers of the church leaders isn't nearly the same as hearing the sisters rattle the rafters of St. Catherine's with their rendition of "I Will Follow Him."

SIGHT AND SOUND, 4/94, p. 51, Nick James

During her headlining Las Vegas act, singer Deloris Van Cartier sees two of her nun friends, Sister Mary Patrick and Sister Mary Robert, in the audience and invites them on stage. After the performance, they tell Deloris that they need her help. They are teachers at St Francis, a ghetto school which is failing to communicate with its pupils. At a further meeting, Mother Superior persuades Deloris to resume the habit as Sister Mary Clarence and become the music teacher.

The school is run by kindly but doddery Father Maurice, under the tight fiscal control of a Mr Crisp. The music class is regarded by the students as a formality, one they'll pass while rehearsing their rap routines. Deloris quells initial resistance but, having failed to impress attitudinous beauty Rita Watson, she then falls victim to a prank. In the meantime she discovers that Mr Crisp has persuaded the diocese to close down St Francis to make way for a parking lot.

By threatening to fail them all, Deloris brings the class to heel, except Rita, who walks out. Each class member is asked to do a version of 'Mary Had a Little Lamb' and several of them prove to have amazing voices. They are taken to watch Deloris and the nuns performing for old folks and are persuaded to form a choir of their own. Father Maurice, however, upbraids Deloris for taking the students off the premises without parental permission, and cancels all further school trips.

Sister Mary Robert overhears Rita singing beautifully in the chapel but Rita resists Deloris's attempts to lure her back, explaining that her mother regards singing as a distraction from real schoolwork. The kids clean up the old music room and Rita rejoins them. They give their first performance in front of the school, which is such a success that the nuns decide to enter the choir for a major competition in Hollywood. The sisters discover old trophies proving that the school had a long tradition of winning the contest.

Having overcome Father Maurice's objections, the nuns raise the $2,000 for the trip with another concert by Deloris and the nuns. Rita, however, is forced by her mother to pull out. At the last minute, Rita forges her mother's signature and boards the bus and they set off. Meanwhile Crisp has discovered the truth about Deloris's real profession and insists that Father Maurice and the brothers pursue the bus and withdraw the school from the competition.

Intimidated by the excellence of the competition, the choir loses heart, but they are revitalised by a speech from Deloris, impugning their courage. Seeing them elated, Father Maurice decides to let them go ahead while the brothers conspire to lock Crisp in a cupboard. Rita at first falters when she sees her mother in the audience, but recovers to sing solo. In the wings, Deloris instructs the choir to discard their robes and they cartwheel on to give a rap/gospel/funk performance which wins the first prize and ensures the survival of the school. Rita and her mother are reconciled.

From Mickey Rooney and Judy Garland to the Kids from Fame, the myth that every American classroom is brimming with unrealised talent remains a powerful and important one for Hollywood and that larger myth it maintains, the American Way of success. Moreover, the current crisis in American education, where the logic of capitalist aspiration leads black youth into the only readily accessible enterprise available—the drugs trade—makes the myth doubly important. With other serious employment alternatives thin on the ground, *Sister Act 2: Back in the Habit* suggests that schoolkids can collectively sing their way out of the ghetto.

We can pass politely over the fact that the music business and the drugs trade are somewhat interdependent and merely note that the former is a very big dollar earner with the virtue of being legal. Thus the film idles along on the surging emotion provided by the often superb gospel and soul singing, while introducing a familiar and likeable mix of classroom characters: a shy and serious crooner, a sensible and manly rapper, a boy-obsessed soul diva, a wannabee-black cool white and a feisty, pouty beauty—all of them looking so cute and multi-ethnic you couldn't fail to give them a job in showbiz.

Yet there's an internal contradiction to this whole fantasy, one that's uncovered at the climax when Whoopi lets the kids wear their own clothes and improvise. Here all discipline and training evaporate. They haven't needed to learn anything after all, except to clean up their lyrics and to feel more self-confident. Here the myth and the reality form a sinister conjunction. What are we to make of a piece of showbiz that preaches showbiz as an answer to the problems of the American inner cities? How can a major comedy star playing a major pop star playing a nun playing a teacher validate all this tub-thumping propaganda? It would take a dozen trendy vicars to come up with a more preachy and patronising notion than the idea that kids will only listen to someone who regularly plays Vegas.

Instead of a useful model for building adolescent self-esteem, *Sister Act 2* is more of a recipe for confusion. The contradictory needs of community and individual ambition are entirely glossed over. There is barely a suggestion of struggle or difficulty for the kids. You might think this is too much to ask of a comedy fantasy. Yet the film doesn't even try very hard to be funny. It's more about ecstatic self-affirmation, and that's one thing that adolescents hardly need to be taught.

TIME, 12/20/93, p. 63, Richard Corliss

If you come, they will rebuild it. This movie law is founded on the success of sequels over the past two decades. From *The Godfather, Part II* through the multipart triumphs of Luke Skywalker, Indiana Jones, Rocky and Rambo, cops and aliens, Hollywood made big money by providing further adventures and more of the same.

This year, though, the golden rule seems tarnished. It's not that there's anything new in movies, heaven knows; the studios are serving up action, romance and comedy with the usual bland vigor. But so far, not one of 1993's top 20 hits is a spin-off. If the trend continues, sequelmania could become sequelphobia, and movie folk might have to dream up *new* characters and stories. Even new *titles*, not just old numerals. Catastrophe!

Or business could return to normal, as follow-ups to three popular comedies of 1992 come to market. *Sister Act* ($140 million at the North American box office), *Wayne's World* ($122 million) and *Beethoven* ($57 million) tickled audiences with humor that stretched all the way—about a foot and a half—from sitcoms to *Saturday Night Live*. The *SNL*-bred *Wayne's World* was agreeably hip, loose and clever, as befits smart guys acting goofy. But the other two films were hapless rehashes of working-girl and family themes done to death by the networks.

In action sequels, the hero is usually made to do the same muscular things to new bad guys in a different location. In comedies, characters mostly stay put: in the convent, the doghouse or Aurora, Illinois. The "new" plot (e.g., Wayne tries to stage a concert) would not tax a 30-minute TV comedy. These sequels are not so much extensions of the original as they are dupes, with the tiniest tweaks of gags and attitude; this time, in *Sister Act 2: Back in the Habit*, the nuns do a rap number in addition to '60s Motown. These films are also "family" pictures, which means they bear a message—though the message can be severe in the *Home Alone* '90s. *Beethoven's 2nd* teaches that if you mess with a pooch and his humans, you can get creamed by a house, dropped off a cliff or neutered. Ah, the new family values!

On the Please-O-Meter, *WW2* scores high, though one wonders whether kids will remember Wayne and Garth from two fads back, before Ren and Stimpy *and* Beavis and Butt-head. The other new comedies need never worry about fashion; *B2* and *SA2* are timelessly terrible. Perhaps, next time, the nuns and the St. Bernard should team up—for *Dog Act*. And maybe someone could explain why moviegoers pay good money to watch inferior TV on the big screen. It's enough to give sequels a bad name.

VILLAGE VOICE, 12/14/93, p. 76, Lisa Kennedy

O Lord, what is it about singing nuns? Why this primal bond to sisters with voices? There were Debbie Reynolds and Julie Andrews, Barbara McNair and Mary Tyler Moore (sort of, and of course more recently there's been Deloris Van Cartier, er, Mary Clarence—make that Whoopi. Films in general but sequels in particular fall under the heading Constructed Pleasures. It's not enough to go see a movie repeatedly, then catch it on cable five times in one week—it must be reincarnated. And once we spy this karmic twin, or triplet, we (who feed on formula like a perpetual babe) are free to say, as a twist on the inevitable "the book was better" line, "the first was better." Of course there are the exceptions, and *Sister Act 2: Back to the Habit* is verily nearly one of them. Let us pray.

The movie opens with Deloris doing Aretha-Tina-Diana-Donna doing an unspeakably goofy medley that's part send-up of some 20 years of popular music and part mini-narrative of how she, Deloris, finally arrived ... in Vegas. In the audience are three of her cohabiters (champion Jo Anne Worley channeler Kathy Najimy, Mary "Josephine the Plumber" Wickes, and the littlest flower Wendy Makkena); they have come on a mission to bring Mary Clarence back to Mother Superior (Maggie Smith), the City by the Bay, and the out-of-control St. Francis High School (did someone say animals?).

Why did the nun cross herself To get to the other side? Yeah, well, no, to get to the sequel.

When Deloris shows up at the dilapidated parochial school, it's a case of the inmates running the prison. These inmates are pretty minimum security, though, not the roughs of *Blackboard Jungle*, or, even, *To Sir, With Love*, and the soft-core quality of the cityscape is likely to irk some. Still, the gang Deloris must inspire are full of endearing tics and make as sweet a backup choir as the nuns—who here do a mucho funny riff on the Temptations' "Ball of Confusion"—did a girl group.

In the hands of director Bill Duke (who, with Danny Glover, just put out a book on positive role models) the sequel looks well tended to; there are more closeups, more vibrant colors, and enough telltale African American real-deal to suggest his touch. The jokes are aplenty; an Original Sin, I mean, Naughty By Nature, cover is especially pleasing.

Like its predecessor, *Sister Act* is less about habits than duty and responsibility; the movie's power lies in its humor but also in its fantasy of a laying on of hands-on help to impoverished communities. After all, it would be such a comfort to know that nuns—and by extension the church and by furthest extension God—cared, and that one initially reluctant lay person could be a miracle worker.

Also reviewed in:
CHICAGO TRIBUNE, 12/10/93, Friday/p. A, Michael Wilmington
NEW YORK TIMES, 12/10/93, p. C10, Caryn James
VARIETY, 12/20/93, p. 32, Brian Lowry
WASHINGTON POST, 12/10/93, p. B1, Rita Kempley
WASHINGTON POST, 12/10/93, p. Weekend/p. 55, Joe Brown

SIX DEGREES OF SEPARATION

A Metro-Goldwyn-Mayer release of a Maiden Movies/New Regency production.   *Executive Producer:* Ric Kidney.   *Producer:* Fred Schepisi and Arnon Milchan.   *Director:* Fred Schepisi. *Screenplay (based on his play):* John Guare.   *Director of Photography:* Ian Baker.   *Editor:* Peter Honess.   *Music:* Jerry Goldsmith.   *Music Editor:* Kenneth Hall.   *Sound:* Bill Daly   *Sound Editor:* Peter Burgess.   *Casting:* Ellen Chenoweth.   *Production Designer:* Patrizia von Brandenstein.   *Art Director:* Dennis Bradford.   *Set Decorator:* Gretchen Rau.   *Set Dresser:* Michael L. Benson and Nancy Boytos-Amanuel.   *Costumes:* Judianna Makovsky.   *Make-up:* Naomi Donne.   *Running time:* 102 minutes.   *MPAA Rating:* R.

CAST: Stockard Channing (Ouisa);   Will Smith (Paul);   Donald Sutherland (Flan);   Ian McKellen (Geoffrey);   Mary Beth Hurt (Kitty);   Bruce Davison (Larkin);   Richard Masur (Dr.

Fine);   Anthony Michael Hall (Trent);   Heather Graham (Elizabeth);   Eric Thal (Rick);
Anthony Rapp (Ben);   Osgood Perkins (Woody);   Catherine Kellner (Tess);   Jeffrey Abrams
(Doug);   Joe Pentangelo (Police Officer);   Lou Milione (Hustler);   Brooke Hayward Duchin
(Connie);   Peter Duchin (Sandy);   Sam Stoneburner (Carter);   Maeve McGuire (Polly);   Kelly
Bishop (Adale);   John Cunningham (John);   Vasek Simek (Frank the Doorman);   Chuck Close
(Andy);   Kazuko (Jeannie);   Adele Chatfield-Taylor (Paula);   Maggie Burke, Edmond Genest,
and Michael Stanley Kirby (Loft Party Guests);   David Callegati (Art Dealer);   Daniel Von
Bargen (Detective);   John Rowe (Usher);   Elizabeth Rossa (Bride);   Diane Hartford (Julia);
Frank O'Brien (Eddie);   Ann McDonough (Teacher);   Jose Rabelo (Elevator Man #2);   Todd
Alcott and Joanna Noble (Concert Goers);   Miriam Fond (Nurse);   Annie Meisels (Doug's Girl);
Mitch Kolpan (Policeman);   Michele Greco (Workman);   Tony Zazula (Rainbow Room
Captain);   Arthur McGill (Hansom Cab Driver);   Susan Tabor and Paul Schmidt (Posh Couple);
Carolyn Groves, Jeannine Moore, Tim Suanders, and David Tice (Cocktail Party Guests);
Redman Maxfield (Fred);   Margaret Eginton (Mary);   Margaret Thomson (Grandmother at
Baptism);   Vince O'Brien (Grandfather at Baptism);   Anne Swift and Richmond Hoxie (Guests
at Baptism);   Kitty Carlisle Hart (Mrs. Bannister);   Madhur Jaffrey (Guest of Honor);   Cleo
King (Lieutenant Price).

FILMS IN REVIEW, 5-6/94, p. 56, Andy Pawelczak

Based on John Guare's play, *Six Degrees of Separation* is very much a stage property, replete
with full blown speeches, big dramatic confrontations, a closing curtain epiphany, and witty,
literate dialogue. It's also full of certified 20th century literary themes that already have an almost
antique feeling: the alienation of parents and children, the denaturing of experience in the modern
world, the fragmentation of self-hood, the hegemony of exchange value over all human values.
The play, which Guare adapted for the screen, was a big hit, and it's no wonder: its characters,
affluent natives of that mythical sliver of Fifth Avenue bordering the east side of Central Park,
have enough recognizable human qualities that we can identify with them and still feel faintly,
smugly superior to the spiritually empty rich. The film, directed by Fred Schepisi, is expert at
placing these people in their upholstered, rarefied milieu, but less good at illuminating their
interior lives.

The movie invites us to be voyeurs of the lives of Flan and Ouisa Kittredge (Donald Sutherland
and Stockard Channing) who live in a big handsome apartment stuffed with important art and
fabulous bric-a-brac. The apartment is almost as important as the sentient actors in this
drama—the Kittredges are basically caretakers of their possessions. Flan is an art dealer who, like
any commodities trader, buys cheap and sells dear. His main stock-in-trade is charm and
effortlessly witty chit-chat, and the film means to instruct us in how to see through this high gloss,
seemingly impregnable facade. Somewhere deep inside there's a gnawing anxiety about where the
next million is coming from and a frustrated artist's desire to go back to the second grade and
learn to be an artist. Ouisa is the perfect wife for the impeccably scripted Flan—her part in the
domestic economy is to be a charming dinner companion for prospective customers. All in all,
Flan and Ouisa are the enviable, handsome couple you might glimpse as they enter a cab after
leaving a fashionable restaurant; they've been relatively successful at keeping the chaos of modern
urban life at arm's length.

These vacuum sealed lives are disrupted and irrevocably changed by the arrival of Paul (Will
Smith), a young black con artist who claims to be Sidney Poitier's son and a friend of the
Kittredges' children at Harvard. As conceived by Guare, Paul has a distinguished literary
genealogy—he's the traditional American trickster figure, kin to Tom Sawyer, but with a more
sinister edge. He instantly bewitches the Kittredges as he cooks an improvised dinner and delivers
a long, loopy monologue about Salinger's *The Catcher in the Rye* which he says has turned into
a manifesto of hatred for disaffected killers who despise phoniness. Guare has a way of
announcing his meanings in big speeches like this, and we get the thematic point: the Kittredges
are no less phony than the beguiling fake Harvard man. Ultimately, Paul is the agent of chaos
who brings a touch of reality into Ouisa's life, and by the end he's a kind of benign tutelary spirit
whose ghostly image appears reflected in a store window.

As played by Sutherland, Flan has the ineffable charm of a movie star who knows the camera
will enlarge and flatter him. Sutherland's performance is symptomatic of the movie's

problem—it's seductive and unreal. The picture has a schizoid attitude toward its characters; on the one hand, we're asked to judge them, and on the other to enjoy their airy insouciance as they float through the wonderland of affluent Manhattan. The occasional glimpses we get of Flan's anxiety aren't enough to give the character ballast, and when the Kittredge children show up, they're like the return of Flan's repressed dark side—they're awful. Stockard Channing turns in a witty, sympathetic performance as Ouisa, a woman who believes we're all separated from—or connected to, depending on your perspective—everybody else on the planet by no more than six people. Ouisa is the movie's most human character, and Channing is very good in the big emotional payoff scene at the end. The role of Paul calls for a wide range of personae—Harvard preppy, street hustler, irresponsible daimon intent on his own pleasure, needy child in search of a father—and Will Smith, a TV actor and performer of politically correct rap songs, is more convincing with some than with others.

Fred Schepisi's direction overcompensates for the play's static talkiness. In the stage production, the Kittredges told the story directly to the audience; Schepisi has opened up the play by having Flan tell his story to high society auditors in various impressive New York settings such as the New York State Theater and the Metropolitan Museum, and the drama tends to get lost in the overbearing settings. Some critics have said that New York becomes another character in the movie, but Schepisi misses the real poetry of the city—its energy and endlessly deferred romantic promise—and its real tragedy which is visible daily in the verticality of its skyscrapers and the horizontality of its homeless. He's more successful with the scenes in the Kittredge apartment, but even here the hyperactive camerawork instead of heightening the action serves as a distraction. In the end, I felt more than six degrees separated from Guare's characters.

LOS ANGELES TIMES, 12/10/93, Calendar/p. 4, Peter Rainer

It should come as no great surprise that "Six Degrees of Separation" isn't much like other movies. The John Guare play on which it's based isn't much like other plays. What *is* surprising is how effectively the play has been filmed. Maybe that shouldn't come as a surprise either. With Guare writing the script and Fred Schepisi directing, the odds for success were high.

Guare's theatrical imagination has always had a cinematic free-wheelingness, with improbable montages of mood and emotion. His knockabout ardor is the perfect instrument for capturing the slap-stick black comedy of New York's high-low life. He doesn't just roll with the punches, he jitterbugs and tangos and waltzes.

Even if you've already seen the play, the movie refreshes the experience, which has been "opened up" by bringing much of the action into real Manhattan locations. The opening up extends the meaning of the play by employing the city in all its spangled ritz and grubbiness as a major character. The action moves from the Upper East Side to the Rainbow Room to scruffy police precincts and the homeless dales of Central Park. You never quite catch your bearings. Watching the movie is a bewildering experience, but bewilderment is the appropriate response to what Guare and Schepisi give you. What seems to start out as a burlesque against the rich—a satire of class-consciousness—ends up mutating into something stranger and richer and more ambiguous.

Louisa and Flanders Kittredge—Ouisa and Flan to their friends—are white East Side elites who live out their tony lives with an anxiety-riddled grace. Flan (Donald Sutherland) is a private art dealer to the very wealthy who was once an artist himself. Art for him has become the hard commerce of cash, and yet that's not all there is to say about Flan. He still has forlorn traces of the artist in him. (He knows what he's relinquished). He and Ouisa (Stockard Channing) rotate inside the galaxies of the super-rich but they're hand-to-mouth wealthy: They need the constant influx of cash that a really big sale brings. (This is one of the few films ever made in this country that really captures the New York art scene.)

Shortly after the movie begins, we're flashed back to the film's prime event: Ouisa and Flan, while entertaining a rich South African friend (Ian McKellen) who may be able to help swing a Japanese purchase of a Cezanne, are suddenly confronted in their apartment by a young black man (Will Smith) who claims to be friends with their children at Harvard. Bleeding from a stab wound he says he received from a mugging in Central Park, he goes on to coyly reveal himself as Paul Poitier, the son of Sidney Poitier. His father, he says, is not arriving in Manhattan until the next morning; desperate, on a whim, Paul decides the Kittredges can be his way station.

Paul is such a dazzling conversationalist, with such an intimate knowledge of his hosts' lives, that he's immediately embraced. Cooking them a deluxe pasta dinner, spouting his college thesis about "The Catcher in the Rye" and the fate of the imagination—"imagination is not our escape, it is the place we are trying to get to"—Paul is too good to be true. He even promises the Kittredges bit roles in his father's upcoming movie version of "Cats."

Paul, of course, is a con man—he takes in another well-secured couple (Bruce Davison and Mary Beth Hurt) and a Park Avenue doctor (Richard Masur) with the same scam—but he's a con man without the conventional larcenies. His reason for insinuating himself into these people's lives is not so much financial as existential. He's a cipher who has assumed the camouflage of his off-limits fantasyland. He knows how to play on his target's racial (and sexual) sympathies and fears; he knows that, for the white liberal elite, celebrity *erases* race—it turns you into a kind of honorary white person.

Paul is so good at finessing his scam with the Kittredges because he recognizes that they themselves are perpetrating a species of scam. And he plays up to their need to be (pleasantly) shaken out of their complacency. Ouisa and Flan are frightened and outraged at Paul's trickery but they also regard the whole ongoing episode as a game—something to regale their fancy dinner guests with.

What gives "Six Degrees of Separation" its comic resonance is that Guare and Schepisi root out the stereotypes of race and class and expose some of the truth behind them—and then they subvert that truth.

The actors are uniformly extraordinary in finally bringing us to a consideration of their fates. Sutherland gives Flan a rehearsed sleekness that fits like armor. Channing, who first triumphed in the role on stage, makes Ouisa's gradual unfolding terrifying and beautiful, Will Smith's Paul keeps us as off balance as the Kittredges, he deepens the connection between acting and con artistry.

The title "Six Degrees of Separation" refers to Ouisa's notion that no two people in the world, no matter how disparate, are separated by more than six people. It's a sentiment that's meant to bind our fates but what the movie accomplishes is something else as well. It shows us the isolation in all that spooky interconnectedness.

NEW YORK, 12/13/93, p. 86, David Denby

When I have regained my composure [After viewing *Schindler's List*; see Denby's review of that film.], I will return to the other movies of the season, but for now I can recommend, in a limited way, *Six Degrees of Separation*, in which John Guare's brittle, deft, and knowing play has been given a brittle, deft, and knowing screen adaptation by director Fred Schepisi. Guare created a layered comedy around a simple satirical idea—that a con man would have little trouble fooling an intelligent and even self-conscious wealthy, liberal couple for the simple reason that they had already fooled themselves. Flan (Donald Sutherland) and Ouisa Kittredge (Stockard Channing), art dealers scrambling to stay on top after the collapse of the art market,'may be devoted to money and status, but they think they love the underprivileged. Thus when the black boarding-school hustler Paul (Will Smith) intrudes upon their Fifth Avenue apartment, he has no trouble snowing them. Paul flatters their self-esteem, and he's in like Flynn.

Schepisi and Guare have come up with a workable screen device. Instead of turning to the audience, as they did onstage, Flan and Ouisa now tell the story of their deception by Paul to friends and business associates in one New York glamour spot after another. The movie is as much about telling as it is about being: Whatever happens to the Kittredges, they convert it to anecdote. Some of the pompous social prattle gets wearisome, even embarrassing, but I was moved by Stockard Channing, whose Ouisa comes to the realization that living as an anecdote isn't quite living at all. Ouisa is touched by Paul, by his intelligence, his need, and her transformation is now more fully worked out. Onscreen, however, the material has a major weakness: The seductive Paul, who wants only to be accepted, seems too much a conceit. How does he see his own life? How can he be so arrogant and sycophantic at once? He really is an anecdote, and I wanted him to be more.

NEW YORK POST, 12/8/93, p. 31, Michael Medved

Film versions of acclaimed theatrical productions generally fall into one of two traps. They either try so hard to "open up" the original stage play that they undermine what made it appealing in the first place, or else they remain so flat-footedly faithful to the source material that the big screen result seems stilted, stagy and stale.

"Six Degrees of Separation" definitely opts for the faithful approach—changing only a few lines of text from John Guare's celebrated 1990 play—but the movie nonetheless sparks and crackles with a cinematic life all its own.

The story centers on a supremely smooth-talking black, homosexual con artist who manages to convince a number of well-to-do Fifth Avenue liberals that he is a friend of their children's from Harvard or Dartmouth, and the pampered son of Sidney Poitier.

The goal of this deception isn't financial gain of any kind, but rather temporary admittance into what he sees as the charmed circle of an elegant elite.

Ouisa Kittredge (played by the excellent Stockard Channing, the only member of the stage cast to repeat her role in the film) tellingly declares: "He wanted to be us.

Everything we are in the world, this paltry thing—our life—he wanted it." Her husband, a reckless wheeler-dealer of the art world played by the bearded Donald Sutherland, comes to recognize their essential similarity to this conniving kid from the streets: They're just hustling at a higher level.

This intriguing material is energized by Guare's dialogue, which he has skillfully adapted from his own play. You don't mind that this picture is occasionally talky since the quality of the talk is so invigorating—as bracing as a chilled glass of dry white wine.

The film's other key asset is the astonishingly accomplished performance by Will Smith, who plays the central role of Paul with irresistible seductive power, but just the right hint of underlying pathos.

At age 25, Smith has already established himself as a Grammy award-winning, platinum-selling rapper, and the popular television star of "The Fresh Prince of Bel Air."

With his role here, he demonstrates his abilities as an actor of stunning range and subtlety, more than worthy of holding his own against canny old pros like Channing, Sutherland, and even Sir Ian McKellen, who makes a memorable appearance as a bemused millionaire dinner guest from South Africa.

If the film has one serious flaw, it's that production designer Patrizia von Brandenstein may have gone a bit overboard in emphasizing all the Manhattan glitz and glamour, while fleshing out the celebrated bare stage presentation as offered at Lincoln Center.

Even so, Australian director Fred Schepisi keeps the principals human and sympathetic beneath their pretensions and their finery, never veering toward the disastrous caricatures of Brian De Palma's dreadful film version of "Bonfire of the Vanities."

Schepisi—one of today's most consistently undervalued filmmakers—has previously directed cherishable movies like "Roxanne" and "A Cry in the Dark," But his new film most specifically recalls his fine work on "Plenty", with Meryl Streep—another challenging—play which he brought glowingly to the screen.

With its moments of insight and startling humor, "Six Degrees of Separation" is one of those haunting movies that you simply can't get out of your mind; like the two-sided Kandinksy that plays an important role in the story, the memory of the film keeps twisting back and forth in the imagination, showing the fine line between harmony and chaos.

NEWSDAY, 12/8/93, Part II/p. 62, John Anderson

The motion in the motion picture "Six Degrees of Separation" is mostly in its characters' mouths. And the words that come out constantly betray them. "This morning I was so happy, sitting around my kitchen, doing the crossword puzzle in ink," recalls Ouisa Kittredge (Stockard Channing). "Two at Harvard, one at Groton," intones her art-dealer husband, Flan (Donald Sutherland), reluctantly disclosing the whereabouts of their children, but not so reluctant that he doesn't repeat the line some half-a-dozen times.

Some films rely on the unspoken. "Six Degrees," in which John Guerre has adapted his much-honored play for the screen, floats on a river of often trivial disclosures and self-conscious observations that, while stripping its characters naked, makes for a very, very talkie movie. That it moves so effortlessly, and with such a graceful gait, is credit both to an expert cast of actors—Channing's Ouisa, her cheeks chipmunkish from a lifetime of forced smiles, is near-perfect—and to its director.

Fred Schepisi ("A Cry in the Dark") has made an actual movie of a successful play, something of a risk, something of a feat. Using circular flashbacks, and seemingly incongruous visual asides (which eventually coalesce), he makes full use of what the camera can give him—the city itself becomes a character in the play—and without losing any of the rhythm of Guare's dialogue.

In disclosing the particulars of their disturbing case—how a well-spoken, obviously educated and intellectually passionate young man scammed his way into their home and confidence—Flan and Ouisa no longer talk directly to the audience as they did in the play.

They're seen at a wedding, at dinner, at an artist's reception, recounting for their peers how the apparently mugged and bleeding Paul (Will Smith) arrived at their doorstep, told them he was the son of Sidney Poitier, regaled them with discourse on his Harvard thesis—stolen by his assail-ants—made them dinner and then, after being given money and invited to stay the night, was discovered with a gay male hustler in their own son's bed. Channing and Sutherland make Ouisa and Flan's embarrassment, masked by an Upper East Side insouciance, a marvelous thing to watch.

They're still committing an act of confession, of course, though neither would ever admit, or submit to, such an ecclesiastical indulgence. Their church is their caste, even if their particular pew is balanced treacherously between the altar of solvency and the perdition of debt. What Paul proves so damningly, and humiliatingly, is that becoming a parishioner requires little more than glibness, and familiarity with a few facts.

As Paul, Will Smith is the third gem in the setting, a street hustler who's trained himself, with the help of class traitor Trent Conway (Anthony Michael Hall), to become a convincing counterfeit preppie. Trent has provided Paul with the details of the Kittredges' life: their children's names, the layout of their apartment, their two-sided Kandinsky ("Chaos ... Control," Ouisa repeats, as Flan spins the picture). His act is flawless, although everything he's learned, he spits out: About "The Catcher in the Rye," the subject of his "thesis," Paul says he wanted to know "why this touching, beautiful, sensitive story, published in July, 1951, had turned into this manifesto of hate." Ouisa and Flan, whose own children are a horror show, eat it up.

And that's because their life, sumptuous as it may be, is a like a fine porcelain elephant perched on a pin. Taking pot shots at the well-off is too easy, and not what Guare is about. He takes three people, and ties them by mathematical/emotional equation. "I read somewhere that everybody on this planet is separated by only six other people," Ouisa says. "Six degrees of separation."

The nexus of the tale is whether Flan and Ouisa can sever their ties to the one person, however unsavory, with whom they've made a real connection. Even if they're all parasites, after all, they're all in it together.

NEWSWEEK, 12/20/93, p. 121, Jack Kroll

Six Degrees of Separation is the ultimate New York movie, just as John Guare's play, on which it is based, was the ultimate New York play. The city is the capital of con, a metropolis of moral chaos in which "separation" has become a structural principle. Whites and blacks, rich and poor, parents and children—all have been split apart in a social and spiritual entropy. Flan Kittredge (Donald Sutherland) and his wife, Ouisa (Stockard Channing), are pure products of the city. He is an art dealer for whom great paintings are just big scores in a madly inflated art market (the time is the go-go early '80s). She is a brainy, vital woman whose early idealism has been blown away by the slipstream in the fast lane. Into their world comes Paul (Will Smith), a young black man who's passing himself off as the son of Sidney Poitier and a friend of their spoiled children. They accept him into their ritzy apartment only to discover him copulating with a male hooker. Horrified, they throw him out. But Paul's scam extends beyond the Kittredges, with tragic effect.

Guare's play was based on an actual occurrence. But he expanded this tabloid titillation into a rich, funny and disturbing parable of life in the morally wormy Big Apple. The play's evocation of New York was done solely through its brilliant dialogue, but Guare in his screenplay, and Fred Schepisi ("The Russia House") in his direction, have done a dazzling job of placing the action in real locations: the museums and art galleries, the trendy bistros, the lofts and condos of the New York culturati. But a trade-off has occurred. Onstage the play's narrative was beamed direct at the audience; here it's diffused through its various locales. The film thus becomes more of a biting satire of New York pretensions and less of a meditation on cultural breakdown and the loss of values. It's the con man Paul who awakens Ouisa to the glitzy sterility of her life. His impassioned speech about imagination ("God's gift to make the act of self-examination bearable") is just part of his scam. But it has the effect of revelation on Ouisa, who is utterly transformed by this hustler with the tongue of a prophet. The impact of this spiritual transformation is somewhat lessened by the film's sheer realism. But this movie bristles with wit and style; it's high comedy that's both dark and radiant. Channing repeats her luminous stage performance, Sutherland is perfect as a man who's surrendered an authentic spirit for big bucks. And Smith, the rapper and star of TV's "Fresh Prince of Bel Air," is an eye-opener in a complex, tricky part. That simple two-syllable name is going to be very big.

VILLAGE VOICE, 12/14/93, p. 65, Georgia Brown

A few years ago the hit Christmas movie told the story of a white woman whose life was given form and meaning by the intervention of an African American male. As far as I could tell, *Driving Miss Daisy* (based on a hit play by Alfred Uhry) was a feel-good movie for white folks that completely evaded the perspective of one of its two main characters. Opening as a movie this season we have John Guare's *Six Degrees of Separation*, which makes me only slightly less uncomfortable than *Miss Daisy* did. If I've got it right, the punishment nowadays for bringing epiphanies to white women is neutering by pen.

For those recently released from the Biosphere, Guare's play was based on an actual event: A young black con man, armed only with his wits and a peculiar pathology, gained entry into the homes of prominent Upper East Side families—not to steal, apparently, but for murkier purposes. In *Six Degrees* (which takes many details directly from the actual event), the personable Paul (played by Will Smith in the film) arrives at the Kittredge apartment overlooking the Central Park reservoir, claiming to be a Harvard classmate of their children as well as the son of Sidney Poitier. He knows a good deal about the Kittredges—Flan (Donald Sutherland) and Ouisa (Stockard Channing). He knows they possess a Kandinsky painted on two sides in contrasting styles (chaos/control). A two-sided coin himself, Paul is the angel/devil of light/dark, who enters/departs the Kittredges' empty lives, filling them with good/evil.

"He did more for us in a few hours," says Ouisa, "than our children ever did." And Guare shows us these kids so we can see what she means.

Though Paul has a more complex existence than Miss Daisy's Hoke (short for hokey?), he seems simple enough in the beginning: he cooks, he cleans up, he performs for the company—a rich guest from South Africa, no less—he extols the power of the imagination. He's a dream boy: clean, neat, with perfect diction. He celebrates the canon. He's not angry. He's the son of white America's favorite colored dinner guest.

Of course, he's too good to be true. He brings a hustler into his hosts' home. Worse, he seduces and abandons an ingenuous young man from Utah. For a time, Paul seems like he might turn into an interesting criminal, like Faulkner's Joe Christmas maybe.

But then, at this comedy's end, his innocence restored, it's clear that Paul's more vehicle than subject: He's merely in the epiphany-delivering business. His plaintiveness is creepy. If the ending were meant as one more exercise in mutual deception, that's one thing, but obviously it's meant as a significant encounter with authenticity for Ouisa while, conveniently, Paul is carted off. Having set out looking for an exemplary black father, Paul ends up clinging, needy and childlike, to an emotionally negligent white mother. Dismissing her daughter (Catherine Kellner) on the other line, Ouisa only has ears for Paul's validation of the value of her life: *What* life?

Although I'd follow Stockard Channing most places, I can't abide this woman—with no apparent profession other than following the progress of her husband's art deals—who accuses her kids of giving her nothing. (And how dare this play, supported largely by fruit-of-the-'80s New Yorkers, permit rich parents to blame the kids for turning out spoiled.)

Of course, I didn't see the play, I only read it. But I have the feeling that people who love the play will prefer it to the movie. It may be that the virtuosity of the ascetic staging, Tony Walton's clever set, disguised the hokeyness that emerges in this fleshed-out, flashy movie production where all the Kittredges' art is on display and they go to dinner parties with Chuck Close.

Anyway, seeing *Six Degrees* reminds me why I prefer movies—because movies, mercifully, don't talk nonstop. Listening to Guare's hectic, badminton-match dialogue, I feel like an aphasic stuck in the idiolect; I literally can't take in all those oddly cadenced words whizzing by. When the characters josh about the projected movie of the despised *Cats*—they would love to be extras—someone notes sagely, reassuringly, that "Film is a different medium." Unfortunately, director-producer Fred Schepisi didn't impress this difference on Guare, who seems to like all his words so much that he kept them all in.

Also reviewed in:
NEW REPUBLIC, 12/27/93, p. 24, Stanley Kauffmann
NEW YORK TIMES, 12/8/93, p. C17, Janet Maslin
VARIETY, 12/13/93, p. 37, Leonard Klady
WASHINGTON POST, 12/22/93, p. F1, Rita Kempley

SLEEPLESS IN SEATTLE

A TriStar Pictures release. *Executive Producer:* Lynda Obst and Patrick Crowley. *Producer:* Gary Foster. *Director:* Nora Ephron. *Screenplay:* Nora Ephron, David S. Ward, and Jeff Arch. *Story:* Jeff Arch. *Director of Photography:* Sven Nykvist. *Editor:* Robert Reitano. *Music:* Marc Shaiman. *Music Editor:* Nicholas Meyers. *Sound:* Kirk Francis. *Sound Editor:* Michael Kirchberger. *Casting:* Juliet Taylor. *Production Designer:* Jeffrey Townsend. *Art Director:* Gershon Ginsburg and Charley Beal. *Set Designer:* Charles Daboub, Jr. *Set Decorator:* Clay Griffith. *Set Dresser:* Michael Moran and Mary Buri. *Special Effects:* Robert M. Riggs. *Costumes:* Judy Ruskin. *Make-up:* Sharon Ilson. *Make-up (Meg Ryan):* Leonard Engelman. *Stunt Coordinator:* Conrad Palmisano. *Running time:* 100 minutes. *MPAA Rating:* PG.

CAST: Tom Hanks (Sam Baldwin); Ross Malinger (Jonah Baldwin); Rita Wilson (Suzy); Victor Garber (Greg); Tom Riis Farrell (Rob); Carey Lowell (Maggie Baldwin); Meg Ryan (Annie Reed); Bill Pullman (Walter); Le Clanché Du Rand (Barbara Reed); Kevin O'Morrison (Cliff Reed); David Hyde Pierce (Dennis Reed); Valerie Wright (Betsy Reed); Frances Conroy (Irene Reed); Tom Tammi (Harold Reed); Calvin Trillin (Uncle Milton); Caroline Aaron (Dr. Marcia Fieldstone); Linda Wallem (Loretta); LaTanya Richardson (Harriet); Rosie O'Donnell (Becky); Tom McGowan (Keith); Stephen Mellor (Wyatt); Marguerite Schertle (Baltimore Waitress); Dana Ivey (Claire); Brian McConnachie (Bob); Rob Reiner (Jay); Gaby Hoffmann (Jessica); Matt Smith (Mailman); Amanda Maher (Clarise); Barbara Garrick (Victoria); Victor Morris (Seattle Maitre D'); Philip Mihalski (Seattle Waiter); Donald J. Lee, Jr. (Seattle Detective); Mary A. Kelly (Nervous Woman on Airplane); Diane Sokolow (Tiffany Saleswoman); Hannah Cox (Jessica's Mother); Rich Hawkins (Jessica's Father); Tamera Plank (Stewardess); Mike Badalucco and Jeff Mazzola (New York Taxi Dispatchers); Philip Levy (Taxi Driver); Julie Janney (Cynthia); Tony Zazula (Maitre D'); John Boylan and Robert Livingston (Elevator Men); Butch Stevenson (Valet); Sidney Armus (Information Booth Man).

CHRISTIAN SCIENCE MONITOR, 6/29/93, p. 12, David Sterritt

"Sleepless in Seattle," the new romantic comedy directed by Nora Ephron, is a likable little picture in many ways.

Tom Hanks plays a widowed man grappling with the challenge of reordering his life, raising his young son, and overcoming memories of the idyllic marriage he's lost. Meg Ryan plays a single woman who's about to marry a fellow she almost loves—and can't help wondering if a more exciting possibility might be waiting for her somewhere.

The two don't meet until the movie is almost over, but it's clear from the start that this Mr. and Ms. Right will find each other before the final credits.

Along the way they muddle through various problems, cope with his precocious son and her not-quite-right fiancé, and edge toward the sentimental climax that pictures like this usually provide.

Their adventures are accompanied by classic songs that swell from the soundtrack to keep us amused even when the action slows to a crawl.

Although it's capably made, there's not much depth to "Sleepless in Seattle" unless you pay attention to a provocative question it implicitly raises: Are there such a thing as "guy" movies and "gal" movies? Do some kinds of entertainment just naturally please men and leave women cold, while others just as naturally do the opposite?

The ingredient that raises this issue in Ephron's film is a series of clips from an old movie: "An Affair To Remember," made in 1957, with Cary Grant and Deborah Kerr as lovers who pursue romance despite all odds. "Sleepless in Seattle" is loaded with female characters who endlessly watch, refer to, and cry over this weepy so-called woman's movie from almost 40 years ago. It's also loaded with male characters who yawn at Grant and Kerr, preferring macho pics like "The Dirty Dozen" and sneering at the very idea of getting emotionally worked up over a movie.

Some people would agree with Ephron's idea that men and women have different priorities in this area. An example might be Marilyn Quayle, who raised a commotion when she spoke about the "natural essence of women" at the Republican National Convention last year. If she's right and women do have a natural essence, it stands to reason that their tastes in cinema would fall in line with this. Men, who presumably have an essence of their own, would always seek different paths.

Others would dispute this whole idea, arguing that anyone who talks about a natural essence probably has a specific definition in mind—and is likely to see those who vary from the mold as unnatural, nonessential, or both.

I guess my natural essence has gone astray, because I'd rather see a sensitive 1950s melodrama than a boisterous war picture any day, and I think Cary Grant is more fun to watch than half the Dirty Dozen gang put together. I enjoyed most of "Sleepless in Seattle but I don't like the way it divides its characters along rigged-up gender lines.

I also object to its view of destiny running our lives and loves. If you took this movie seriously, you'd think there was no such thing as individual volition. Once your gender is determined, and fate has decided your romantic partner, all you have to do is follow your essence and wait for your happy ending to come around.

"Sleepless in Seattle" doesn't mean to spark philosophical debates, but its attitude are so sharply defined that it does seem to be pushing an agenda at times. More generally, it's an old-fashioned picture in many ways—including good ways such as its good-natured star performances. In this way the movie appears to argue for an old-fashioned movie world in which issues, genders, and relationships were as clear-cut as the black-and-white cinematography that often brought them to the screen.

While it's easy to take nostalgic pleasure in this approach, it's worth remembering that the best old movies rarely embraced simplistic notions of love and destiny. Instead they conveyed their own complexities in ways more subtle than most of today's filmmakers would understand.

Hanks and Ryan are pleasant company throughout "Sleepless in Seattle," and Rob Reiner and Rosie O'Donnell are amusing as their guy-type and gal-type best friends.

The supporting cast also includes Bill Pullman as the fiancé and Ross Malinger as the hero's son, who sets the story in motion when he calls a radio-show psychologist for help in combating his dad's blues.

The picture has been handsomely shot by Sven Nykvist, whose legendary photographic talents are as eloquent in the Pacific Northwest as in his native Sweden, where he honed his skills on numerous Ingmar Bergman classics. Ephron wrote the screenplay with David Ward and Jeff Arch.

FILMS IN REVIEW, 10/93, p. 333, Andy Pawelczak

Sleepless In Seattle, the new romantic comedy directed and written (with David Ward and Jeff Arch) by Nora Ephron, tries for the kind of Hollywood magic that *Moonstruck* so effortlessly achieved, but it misfires almost every step of the way. It has all the right ingredients including luminously hyper-real cinematography by Sven Nykvist; Tom Hanks; and a soundtrack by such legendary out-of-time figures as Jimmy Durante and Nat King Cole; but lacks the main one, a good script. Along with *In the Line of Fire*, it's another big summer movie in which the principals don't fully connect until the end of the picture, but what works in the Eastwood thriller to build tension only makes this movie go slack. It's all not very exciting foreplay, and when the climax finally comes we long ago lost interest in the characters.

After his wife's death, Sam (Tom Hanks) moves from Chicago to Seattle with his young son Jonah (Ross Malinger) in order to start a new life. A year later he's still mourning, and Jonah calls a Miss Lonelyhearts type of radio program to ask how his father can find a new wife. Against his better judgement, Sam goes on the air too, and women all over the country respond to his romantic melancholy and obvious sincerity. His remark that he felt the magic the first time he held his wife's hand strikes a particularly resonant chord in Annie (Meg Ryan), a Baltimore newspaper reporter worried about the lack of magic in her relationship with Walter (Bill Pullman), her nice but dull fiance. The rest of the movie splits its focus between Annie's attempt to find Sam and negotiate her relationship with Walter and Sam's depressing re-entry into the contemporary dating world.

Ephron's specialty is sharp edged New York humor leavened by sentiment, but most of the jokes and comic situations in the movie seem designed to prove that old jokes never die, they just fade away. i found myself cataloguing the jokes as they sputtered and fizzled: yes, there's the HIV anxiety joke, the therapist joke, the New Age joke, and so on. The movie's idea of a comic situation involves Sam's dates with Victoria (Barbara Garrick), a carnivore so desperate for a man that she laughs gruesomely at Sam's every little tentative stab at wit. Hanks is very good at registering Sam's surprise and pleasure at his own unexpected success, but by the third or fourth go around the joke, which wasn't too funny to begin with, wears very thin. The film also has what has become Ephron's requisite movie joke, this one involving differing gender reactions to a late Leo McCarey movie with Cary Grant, *An Affair to Remember*, a picture that ends up playing an important role in the movie's denouement. Pictures that constantly refer to other movies more often than not suffer from anemia, and *Sleepless In Seattle* isn't an exception.

As Sam, Tom Hanks is very good, but the movie doesn't give him much of an opportunity to express the mad glee that he's expert at. Mostly, he's called upon to alternate between poetic wistfulness and comic exasperation at Jonah's single minded attempt to hook him up with Annie. Cute kids are a danger to any movie's honesty and poise, but Ross Malinger as Jonah does good work, as does Gaby Hoffman as Jonah's very sophisticated eight-year-old sidekick. Like Hanks, Meg Ryan is handicapped by her material, but she captures the right mix of slightly pixilated intelligence and romantic longing. Bill Pullman is fine in the thankless role of Annie's fiance, the movie's Ralph Bellamy character.

Ultimately, *Sleepless In Seattle* succumbs to the same problem that afflicted Ephron's last movie, *This Is My Life*. It wants to be all things to all people, a sharp satire of contemporary mores and an uplifting adult fairy tale full of gentle melancholy, tenderness towards children, and transformative, life affirming love, but Ephron isn't able to pull the two things together and right from the beginning we can feel the inexorable undertow of the warm bath of sentimentality awaiting us. The movie's final sequence features a delirious 360 degree shot of the Empire State Building as forties big band music plays on the soundtrack. I suppose this could have been thrilling and magically nostalgic, but Ephron has dissipated the magic long before by letting us see the prestidigitator's wires and pulleys and trapdoors. By this time, not even Jimmy Durante singing "Make Someone Happy" and Meg Ryan drinking in Hanks with her beautiful dazzled eyes can give us the romantic catharsis the whole picture has been warming up for.

LOS ANGELES TIMES, 6/25/93, Calendar/p. 1, Michael Wilmington

"Sleepless in Seattle" a real charmer, is a romantic comedy about an ultimate long-distance relationship. Emphasize "romantic." Emphasize "comedy." It delivers both.

The "Sleepless" lovers—Tom Hanks as Sam, the insomniac Seattle widower-architect, and Meg Ryan as Annie, the streetwise Baltimore journalist—not only live in different cities on different coasts, they don't even *know* each other. Annie is aware of Sam only from a national call-in radio show and, for Sam, Annie is a will-o'-the-wisp emanating from a few letters and glimpses and his son Jonah's fervent championing of her as candidate for a new mom.

Director-writer Nora Ephron's quick-quip take on talk-radio crushes makes her film contemporary. But "Sleepless" is also determinedly old-fashioned—a movie scored to nostalgia songs, from Jimmy Durante, to Joe Cocker—that tries to waft us back to the great days of the American romantic comedy: that era, from the '30s to the late '50s, when beautiful, supremely sharp-witted people traded rapid-fire banter and spiky innuendoes in picturesque settings, a vision of courtship that seduced much of the nation from the Great Depression onward.

For Ephron, the 1957 Leo McCarey-Cary Grant-Deborah Kerr "An Affair to Remember"—a classic shipboard romantic comedy-turned-tearjerker—is as much a touchstone as "Casablanca" was in "Play It Again, Sam." It's the movie the "Sleepless" characters try to dream their way into. The women love and blubber over "Affair," the kids watch it and the men jibe at it: "The Dirty Dozen" is *their* idea of a good cry at the flicks.

We don't make those kind of Lubitsch-Wilder-Capra movies anymore, because it's hard to kid about what goes on behind bedroom walls when the bedroom doors have long since been flung open. So Ephron invents strategies to keep us, teased, outside the boudoir. In "When Harry Met Sally ..." she kept her lovers separate by making them bickering friends: in her directorial debut, "This Is My Life," she took the viewpoint of two little girls: here, working from Jeff Arch's original script, she makes Hanks and Ryan bicoastal dream lovers, destiny's darlings.

Ephron's direction has improved and relaxed since "This Is My Life." The movie has a pro's glow—and a sparkling cast. Rosie O'Donnell (Annie's pal), Bill Pullman (who plays the Ralph Bellamy part), Rob Reiner (Sam's chum), Rita Wilson (Mrs. Hanks, who does a lovely, goofy crackup over "An Affair to Remember") and Ross Malinger (Sam's Cupid kid) all have their shining moments.

Yet, Hanks and Ryan are the center: One screen couple with so much simpatico, that we don't need to see them together. Hank's has that easy, shaggy, sarcastic teddy-bear quality that seems ideal for the post-greed era, and Ryan, an actress you can never see too much of, is as much a comic-romantic live wire here as she was in "When Harry Met Sally ..."

Like all the best screen actors, Ryan can strip thoughts and emotions bare without seeming to push. Here, she's obviously an Ephron surrogate: a nervy blond tough cookie, with scrumptious chocolate sentiments buried inside. But she's no mouthpiece, shifting deftly, as Hanks does, between poignancy and wisecracks.

There are obvious flaws in "Sleepless in Seattle": some over-cuteness, the cruel undercurrent that usually permeates these "destiny lover" stories, a negligible "Annie-in-Seattle" interlude, a visual bareness that Sven Nykvist's lustrous lighting only slightly disguises, and a sometimes shaky sense of place, despite the extensive four-city location photography.

Today, "Sleepless in Seattle" (MPAA-rated PG, for some language) may try to convince us of something we don't really believe anymore, that Ephron herself doesn't believe anymore—and that Leo McCarey didn't believe when he made "An Affair to Remember." But at least it tries stirring up those silken old fantasies we thought we outgrew, making them come happily alive again for an evening. For a good many of us, they probably will.

NEW STATESMAN & SOCIETY, 9/24/93, p. 59, Jonathan Romney

Is there really such a thing as a "women's picture"? The term evokes Sunday afternoons slumped in from of BBC2, watching black-and-white 1940s tales of noble self-sacrifice with lashings of Vaseline on the lens. You wouldn't have thought the term was much use any more, except perhaps in academic discussions of genre. After all, aren't we all sensitive and sophisticated enough nowadays to let our contingent gender differences just dissolve in the pleasure of the image?

I'm not so sure. I've recently been observing a peculiar phenomenon among colleagues, in which it's becoming apparent that women will like certain films and men won't and vice versa. Of course, I'm generalising on the basis of a small group who spend an inordinate amount of time cloistered in preview theatres, but nevertheless the evidence is striking. A straw poll suggests incontrovertibly that *only* women will enjoy the forthcoming Mexican soap opera *Like Water for Chocolate*, whereas all men will loathe it heartily. Or, on a more complex level, all viewers *without exception* will emerge overwhelmed from Jane Campion's *The Piano*—but only women will actually cry at the end. Look, I'm just going on empirical evidence here.

The question worries me somewhat because I've lately read more than one piece by men on the pleasures of having a good sob in the stalls. Personally, I'm an old-fashioned boy—my ability to weep at the pictures is severely restricted. I will gladly admit to having cried every single time I've seen *The Wizard of Oz*, and at the end of *Edward Scissorhands*. But then I also cried, for reasons that escape me and to my extreme embarrassment, at Schwarzenegger's *Kindergarten Cop*. It's just something I have to work out.

All in all, I seem to be with *GQ* Man and The Cure on this one: boys don't cry. But hold on, though; Nora Ephron's *Sleepless in Seattle* is there to bear me out. The whole film, in fact, is predicated on the idea that women will weep at the right movies while men will just sneer, but more fool us.

The key scene features Tom Hanks as Sam, a heart-rent widower, sitting around with his best buddy and his wife. She's reminiscing, lump in throat, about the 1957 weepie *An Affair to Remember*, in which Deborah Kerr sits it out pluckily in her wheelchair, not daring to tell Cary Grant why she can't stand up and embrace him. It's an ending that makes no sense except within the rules of the weepie genre, and in those terms it works absolutely. The woman's in floods of tears; Tom and his pal can't figure it out. "It's a chick's movie," they shrug, and promptly set about mocking her reaction by imagining what it would be "like to burst into tears at the end of *The Dirty Dozen*. Sour grapes, of course.

The guys would just love a chance to vent their feelings, especially Sam, who's been holding it all in since his wife died. Since then, he's grouched around, snubbing colleagues' attempts to win him round, and has retreated from Chicago to drizzly old Seattle in the company of his young son Jonah (a smart but resolutely unadorable kid named Ross Malinger).

Sam's nocturnal mooching upsets the boy enough to call up a radio phone-in agony show—although you imagine that if Dad could predict the next phone bill the tear ducts would open soon enough. Meanwhile, way across America in Baltimore, Annie (Meg Ryan—as ever, ditsy, scatty, smart-as-a-lick-of-paint) is spending Christmas with her staid, nutty family and her fiancé Walter (Bill Pullman, American film's second greatest poker face after Charles Grodin). He's rich, handsome and devoted, but he is called Walter, and he has allergies ... There's nothing exactly wrong with him, but like Karenin and his outsize ears, he has a touch of lantern jaw signalling that he and Annie are not *destined*. Driving home, she hears the plaint of young Jonah, and it's like a jolt from the blue. She has to meet Sam.

As in the best comedy romances, *Sleepless in Seattle* is based on deferral; How long before these people, who are obviously going to meet, actually do? (It won't spoil anything to tell you it's an unconscionably long time.) This is different from the structure of a weepie, which tends to bring people together, but stops them staying together. Here, the inevitable simply takes ages to happen. It's in the eventual gratification that the emotional payoff comes, in the form of relieved, amused sobbing.

In this respect, *Sleepless* is a knowing spin on Nora Ephron's last great success as script writer, *When Harry Met Sally*, which also starred Meg Ryan. There, the protagonists—hugely, glaringly, embarrassingly wrong for each other, *ergo* made in heaven—meet, but take ages to actually *meet*. Here they don't meet for ages, although they're inextricably linked: by Destiny, which Annie is unshakably aware of; by the radio show, which she hears by freakish, irrevocable chance; and by the fact that she's also a sucker for *An Affair to Remember*, which she weeps over with her best buddy Rosie O'Donnell (and the two of them supposedly hard-bitten journalists).

The film's sob quotient depends on the knowing ingenuity with which Ephron—who here directs as well as co-writes—rings her ironic changes on our expectations. She's not afraid to ladle on knowingly shlocky gestures. She gives us Christmas trees fulsomely photographed by Sven Nykvist. She zaps our nostalgia cells with *Stardust*, *As Time Goes By*, a whole barrel of such Perry Como fodder. She even has the start-crossed lovers linked, in a tawdry outburst of kitsch, by a computer-generated map of the US that makes the flight path of coast-to-coast airlines and presumably of Cupid's arrows too.

Ephron piles these ironic trimmings on, knowing that we're all the more likely to accept them if we find them unacceptable from the outset. The dare is to remind us in advance that life just isn't like the movies, and then to reward us with a wish-fulfillment resolution in which, maybe, it *is*.

So she encourages us to respond either as jaded urbanites, like Sam and his buddy, who just won't swallow that hogwash; or to react against type, the way that Annie and her friend do when they decide to drop all pretence of sophistication add just reach for the kleenex.

We can react as boys, in which case we simply get the rug pulled from under our feet by the film's sheer bare-faced audacity like Sam, who ends up simply looking stunned by the whole deal. Or we can react as girls, in which case we get exactly the heart-warming: pay-off we're hoping for (on Valentine's Day to boot).

I'm with the boys on *Sleepless in Seattle*, I wasn't prepared to swallow it for a minute, which is precisely why I ended up thoroughly, pleasurably outmanoeuvred. Somehow that didn't happen with *Kindergarten Cop*.

NEW YORK, 6/21/93, p. 62, David Denby

Listening to the radio in her car, Annie (Meg Ryan), a cheerful newspaper reporter in Baltimore, hears a man (Tom Hanks) on a call-in show mourning his dead wife so feelingly that she falls in love with him. The call-in-show host, a treacly professional sob sister, dubs the mournful husband and father (whose real name is Sam) "Sleepless in Seattle." The whole idea of falling in love with a voice, Annie reasons, is preposterous. She is about to get married to Walter (Bill Pullman), who is allergic to strawberries and nuts and just about everything else, and who sleeps in pajamas with a humidifier puffing in the room, but c'mon, thinks Annie, this is real life and it's time to put aside adolescent fantasies of romance. Walter it is. Yet Annie is bedeviled. She can't help wanting the intensity of Sam's love for his wife.

Sleepless in Seattle, a charming romantic comedy directed by Nora Ephron (*This Is My Life*), asks a question that many lovers ponder. Is it destiny that brings people together—the mutual vibration of two matching souls? Or is it accident, a random collision? The first view is romantic: There is only one person for you, and when you meet him you will immediately know it. The second view is ironic: A dead tree falling, a rainstorm, a taxi ride may lead to happiness. Or to misery.

By its very nature, the American commercial cinema is drawn to the first view. But who can make that kind of movie anymore—that is, a romantic comedy with a little tenderness and the emotional and formal confidence that was routine in the old days? Consider *Sleepless* an answer to fervent prayers. The movie starts slowly but then gathers speed and reaches a pitch of momentum that feels like dramatic inevitability. In the past, even when audiences knew what was going to happen in a movie, they were fascinated by the intricacy of the working out. *Sleepless* has that kind of fascination. Everything fits together—the music (Jimmy Durante singing romantic classics), the visual motifs, the jokes that have echoes.

Ephron's craftsmanship is very sure, very knowing. *Sleepless in Seattle* may be no more than an expert confectionery construction, but there's a contemporary satirical sensibility working inside the romantic formulas. Ephron wrote the picture with David S. Ward and Jeff Arch, based on a story by Arch. The movie puts a fresh spin on such familiar things as the miseries of starting to date again and the maddening way that sweet, media-savvy children talk in clichés. Much of *Sleepless in Seattle* pivots around the strange Leo McCarey classic *An Affair to Remember*, with Cary Grant and Deborah Kerr, a movie that often leaves men puzzled and women in tears. *Sleepless in Seattle* is a *vive la différence* comedy. It's the difference that makes unity possible, the belief that two people can come together without giving up their individuality. That's the ultimate romantic faith, and it's just as true today as it was in old Hollywood, when romance was king.

NEW YORK POST, 6/25/93, p. 33, Michael Medved

Some 1,900 years ago, a skeptical woman challenged the great Rabbi Yose Ben Halafta to explain what God had been doing since completing the creation of the world "He has been busy arranging marriages," the sage famously replied "which is harder for him than splitting the Red Sea".

The new movie "Sleepless in Seattle" illustrates this point beautifully—without overt religious allusions, but with an absolute maximum of wit, charm, warmth and romantic flair. If you nurse even a sneaking suspicion that cosmic forces involving signs and magic can play a role in bringing two people together. then you will welcome this film like a long-lost friend. Reb Yose Ben Halafta would have loved it.

Tom Hanks plays a Chicago architect who moves to Seattle with his 8-year-old son to try to begin a new life after the death of his beautiful young wife. After they've settled into their home in the Northwest, the little boy (Ross Malinger) is so worried about his father's continued depression that he calls a radio shrink on Christmas Eve to express the wish that his grieving dad find a new wife. When the nationally broadcast psychologist summons Hanks to the phone, he ends up delivering a funny, moving monologue about love and loss.

Listening to his voice on a car radio at the other end of the continent is a Baltimore newspaper reporter played by Meg Ryan. Even though she's on her way home from a family Christmas party where she announced her engagement to the dull-but-decent Bill Pullman, she finds herself irrationally drawn to the melancholy radio caller identified only as "Sleepless in Seattle."

From this modest concept (created by a teacher of Tae-Kwon-Do and first-time screenwriter named Jeff Arch), director and co-writer Nora Ephron has fashioned a magically effective piece of popular entertainment. Because of the presence of Meg Ryan many observers are already comparing it to the smash hit "When Harry Met Sally" (for which Ephron wrote the Oscar-nominated screenplay), but "Sleepless in Seattle" is a richer, better film in every way.

For one thing, Ephron here has avoided the annoying Hollywood convention by which the two main characters in a romantic comedy are allowed to interact only with one another and with one best friend apiece. In "Sleepless," we see them relating to family, co-workers, longtime pals, baby-sitters and romantic alternatives—all of whom are affectionately and skillfully portrayed. It's a mark of this film's underlying humanity that even Bill Pullman, saddled with the thankless role of Ryan's also-ran fiancé comes across as an eminently likable (and believable) guy.

Fortunately, Ephron never goes overboard with the sentimentality: she keeps her film in balance by poking gentle fun at its own lavishly romantic core. The musical numbers that accompany the picture—from Jimmy Durante barking "As Time Goes By" to Gene Autry warbling "Back in the Saddle Again"—offer an ironic (and sometimes hilarious) counterpoint to the action.

Meanwhile, the characters all seem haunted by scenes and themes from the silly 1957 Cary Grant-Deborah Kerr weeper "An Affair to Remember"—recognizing that for all its goofy, melodramatic excesses, that old picture connects with some unreasonably mushy sensibilities that nearly all of us seem to share.

And speaking of sharing, "Sleepless in Seattle" is a nearly ideal date movie. If you're lucky enough to see it with someone you love, you'll find yourself holding hands and sniffling together, then smooching shamelessly before the lights go up.

If, on the other hand, you're still waiting to meet your One True Soul Mate, this movie will give you inspiration and hope.

Either way, do yourself a favor and go see it. Along with Kenneth Branagh's luminous "Much Ado About Nothing" this is, very simply, the best film I've seen so far this year.

NEWSDAY, 6/25/93, Part II/p. 51, Jack Mathews

In a scene being used in the commercials for Nora Ephron's "Sleepless in Seattle," a friend is explaining to Tom Hanks' widower Sam Baldwin that women appreciate men with "cute butts," after which Hanks turns his back on his friend and asks for an opinion.

"Sleepless," Ephron's attempt at light romantic comedy, has a cute butt itself. It's nothing like a complete picture, no intellectual depth or personality to write home about, but it won't hurt to take a look.

Ephron seems to be more of a dabbler in romanticism than a serious adherent, and "Sleepless" talks more about the magic of love than it does anything about it. She has stuffed her second feature with romantic notions—nostalgic ballads, references to old movies, skyscraper valentines, yearnings, yearnings, yearnings—but the movie keeps its distance from the real thing, figuratively and literally.

Hanks' Sam is an architect and grieving widower living with his 8-year-old son Jonah (Ross Malinger) in Seattle. Meg Ryan's Annie Reed is a lifestyle reporter for the Baltimore Sun, a romantic trying to feel more for her steady, hyper-allergenic fiance (Bill Pullman, in another thankless schlemiel role) than she possibly can.

With the hope of finding a wife for his morose father, Jonah calls a national advice-for-the-love-lorn radio show one evening, and the reluctant Sam is soon explaining to a national audience the magic of his marriage and his tragic sense of loss. Among the hundreds of women moved by Sam's honest passion is Annie, and it is her letter, among the hundreds forwarded to Seattle, that catches Jonah's eye.

"Sleepless" is not about love, it's about destiny, at least as destiny was defined by the romantic melodramas of Ephron's youth. Sam and Annie are made for each other, this movie says (without addressing the fact that Sam and his wife were made for each other first), and the entire movie becomes sort of a travelogue with fate.

How, when and where will Sam and Annie meet, and when they do, will Ephron find the movie magic to match the moment? The answers to these questions are mostly disappointing. Ephron is a great flirt of a writer, and as she demonstrated with her script for "When Harry Met Sally ...," she is more comfortable teasing a relationship than in developing it.

"Sleepless," co-written with David S. Ward and Jeffrey Arch, avoids the complexities of romantic love while wallowing in its sentiment and celebrating it from afar. One moment, we're with Sam in Seattle, watching him wade back into the dating stream with a woman (Gaby Hoffman) for whom he feels nothing. Then, we're in Baltimore with Annie and her humorless Walter, stuck in the kind of passionless relationship Ginger Rogers used to be in before Fred Astaire came along and stole her heart (or vice versa).

Ephron, in effect, padded the entire movie, created a string of scenes that are occasionally great fun but barely nudge the wafer of a story along. She even uses an old movie, Leo McCarey's romantic weepie "An Affair to Remember," as a leitmotif. Characters on both coasts somehow end up watching the movie at various times, and lest we miss the parallel themes of romantic destiny, Ephron has Jonah attempt to set up a rendezvous between Sam and Annie just like that of the "Affair" lovers played by Cary Grant and Deborah Kerr.

What "Sleepless" lacks in originality or real feeling, however, it makes up for in humor. Ephron is a very funny writer, and we're never far from a good laugh. Comedian Rosie O'Donnell, playing Annie's pep-talking co-worker, has the bulk of the best one-liners, and her performance is a joy.

Hanks and Ryan, who worked together in the dreadful "Joe Versus the Volcano," are among Hollywood's most amiable leads, and though their characters' hearts, minds and lips remain frustratingly separated by a continent, they manage to imply a certain amount of romantic chemistry.

It's nervy of Ephron to think she could make a feature-length love story out of what is essentially a 94-minute set-up for a bi-coastal blind date, and she didn't pull it off. She doesn't have quite enough faith in her own notions of romance to make "Sleepless" anything more than a wispy fantasy.

Still, idealized love—the bell-ringing, sweaty-palmed, heart-pounding, can't-live-without-you love Ephron is aiming for—is such a universal dream that even the suggestion of it goes a long way.

NEWSWEEK, 6/28/93, p. 65, David Ansen

A not unrelated self-consciousness infects Nora Ephron's sweet but perilously thin love story, *Sleepless in Seattle*, in which the characters' romantic expectations are constantly measured against that classic '50s weeper "An Affair to Remember." Meg Ryan plays a Baltimore reporter who's on the verge of marrying nice but dull Bill Pullman when she hears the voice of sensitive widower Tom Hanks, a.k.a. Sleepless in Seattle, talking to a radio psychologist. Hanks's 8-year-old son (Ross Malinger) has called the radio shrink, worried about his grieving father: he wants Dad to find a new wife.

From the moment Ryan tears up at Hanks's voice, we know what must happen. The task of screenwriters Ephron,   David S. Ward and Jeff Arch is to keep their destined-to-be-together lovers apart until the last scene in the movie—a task that frequently strains their invention and the audience's credulity. (The movie would be half as long if Ryan had the sense to include a snapshot along with her letter to Hanks; if you looked like Ryan you'd be crazy not to.) The funniest lines and most touching scenes are all near the end. To fill the dead time, director Ephron shamelessly relies on her nostalgia-drenched pop soundtrack—Jimmy Durante's "As Time Goes By," Nat King Cole's "Star Dust," Ray Charles's "Over the Rainbow," etc.—to work up feelings that aren't on the screen. For long stretches, this feels like a morose VH-1 video. With its appealing cast (Hanks is in top form) and its refreshingly quiet tone, you want "Sleepless in Seattle" to sweep you away, but it never quite transcends its synthetic setup. For all the talk of true love and "magic," what comes through strongest is Ephron's belief in the magic of old movies about love. Such are the perils of these postmodernist times: even our love stories feed off borrowed emotion.

SIGHT AND SOUND, 10/93, p. 52, Jenny Turner

Chicago. Sam Baldwin's beloved wife has just died, leaving him to bring up Jonah, his eight-year-old son, single-handed. Depressed, Sam decides to move with his son to a new life in Seattle. 18 months later, Annie Reed, a Baltimore journalist, celebrates her engagement to Walter with her parents over a Christmas Eve dinner. Though allergic to everything, Walter is a nice man; he is also very rich. Annie is happy about the arrangement—until a conversation with her mother gives her the idea that a true romance should have some "magic". Later that night, Jonah rings up a radio agony phone-in to find a new wife for his father. The agony aunt draws Sam into the conversation and Annie, listening in her car, falls in love with his voice. She pursues her obsession from her Baltimore office, where her job allows her access to confidential databases and a private investigation service. She writes a letter to Sam, but throws it in the bin. She flies to Seattle, where she gets as far as saying hello to the man of her dreams. But then she loses her nerve and returns to Baltimore determined to marry Walter.

Meanwhile, Sam has tried dating a colleague, Victoria, but Jonah disapproves. Jonah likes the sound of Annie, whose letter suggesting a rendezvous on top of the Empire State Building on the evening of Valentine's Day has, unbeknown to her, been rescued and sent on by her girlfriend. Jonah writes back to Annie agreeing to keep the date, but Sam refuses to have anything to do with this plan. Jonah runs away to make the tryst and Sam is forced to follow his son to New York. Over dinner in the Rockefeller Plaza on their Valentine's Day trip, Annie explains to Walter her worries about "magic" and tells him about her fantasy relationship with "Sleepless in Seattle". Ever understanding, Walter gives her up. Meanwhile, Sam has found Jonah cowering in a corner as the sky around the Empire State Building darkens. Annie rushes straight to the elevator, and is just in time to meet Sam and Jonah, who have come back up to look for Jonah's rucksack which the wily boy has left behind.

It's a strange thing about these latter-day classic romantic comedies. I adored Cher being Italian in *Moonstruck*—when the moon hits your eye like a big pizza pie, that's amore!—but I know plenty of people who did not. Conversely, although the Nora Ephron-scripted *When Harry Met Sally...* was one of the biggest hits of 1990, I hated it. As this had a lot to do with Ephron's sense of humour and with Meg Ryan as the female lead, the *Sleepless* experience did not work for me.

These comedies tell you they are classics even before they have properly begun. This they do by featuring old songs on the soundtrack, meant to make you all dewy-eyed. Accordingly, *Sleepless* starts off with "As Time Goes By", in an appropriately painful and constipated version from Jimmy Durante. Meanwhile, the visuals trot out those big classic-movie tropes, the monumental cityscape and the imaging of America as the great big country. Chicago, Seattle, Baltimore and New York are represented not as places, but as metropolitan icons. The distances between them are visualised by a sweeping computer-generated map. This is a movie for all those lonely people out there.

Non-classic films are at liberty to make up for what is lacking in the script, acting or whatever by pumping up the *mise en scène*. Classic romantic comedies, however, are meant to be tasteful and understated to make us warm to their situations. We are clearly meant to find Meg Ryan's hideously tapisseried boudoir, Tom Hanks' drab Habitatty bungalow—a male-only environment signalled by an amazing preponderance of angle-poise lamps—touching. And Ryan herself, with her perpetually smudged eyeliner, dingy clothes and uncomic over-acting, is probably intended to be cute.

On the good side, Tom Hanks is excellent. He has a meaty, surprisingly menacing voice and presence, which cuts through the sentimentality of his lines, making for a handful of genuinely funny interchanges. For example, considering dating a woman for the first time since he met his wife: What happens if I take her out to dinner?" "You'll find out about tiramisu." "What the hell's tiramisu? You mean, we'll be in bed together and she'll be expecting me to do this thing, and I don't even know what it is!" Ross Malinger, who plays Jonah, is also impressive. Stolid, sullen and relentlessly uncute, his performance is a refreshing alternative to the Macaulay Culkin school of child acting.

TIME, 7/5/93, p. 58, Richard Corliss

Sam Baldwin (Tom Hanks) is an architect in Seattle, a recent widower unable to overcome his bereavement. Annie Reed (Meg Ryan) is a no-nonsense newspaperwoman in Baltimore, about to settle for a marriage more convenient than stirring.

They don't meet cute. As a matter of fact, they don't meet at all until the end of the movie. She hears him on a radio shrink's call-in program, into which he's been plugged by his eight-year-old son Jonah (Ross Malinger), who thinks it's time for Dad to get a life. Lots of other women respond to him too. Rue is a good emotional color for him, and he wears it well—with a manliness that avoids self-pity and promises loyalty to anyone who wins his heart. But of all the letters listeners send in, it's Annie's that his son likes best, and so the boy begins to maneuver a meeting against a movieful of odds.

It's a sweet conceit, taking into account both the curious new ways we make connections along our electronic highways and romance's age-old need to crank up passion by placing frustrations in true love's path. Given that many of the traditional obstacles like class, ethnic and religious differences are readily overcome these days by enlightened people, it's smart to recognize that about the only thing left to distance people is, yes, distance—good old basic geography.

It may be, however, that *Sleepless in Seattle* is too smart for its own good. For clever as it is conceptually, it violates the most basic rule of romantic-comedy construction. If boy doesn't meet girl, then the drama of boy losing girl and the final satisfaction of boy getting girl cannot happen. The complications in this movie are all logistical. They are never confrontational, as they so giddily were in the classic comedies of muddled love, the spirit of which co-writer and director Nora Ephron has said she wanted to recapture.

To compensate, she creates, as it were, sub-conflicts. Annie's fiancé (Bill Pullman) is shown to be, quite literally, a drip (allergies make his nose run); the woman Sam takes up with (Barbara Garrick) has a grating laugh. The movie condescends to both of them rather unfunnily. And, anyway, they begin to seem like time fillers, something to divert us from the fact that this film really has no center. Hanks and Ryan are, as usual, charming, and so are Malinger as destiny's underage enabler, Gaby Hoffmann as his girlfriend, eagerly egging him on, and Rosie O'Donnell as Ryan's newspaper pal. They are all given some chuckly lines to say, but no killers. Like everything else in this movie, they lack madness, and they fail to draw you out of yourself into a truly absorbing alternative reality. Mostly, *Sleepless in Seattle* leaves you feeling restless in the audience.

VILLAGE VOICE, 6/29/93, p. 53, Georgia Brown

The borrower returns. With *Sleepless in Seattle*, Nora Ephron refines her recipe for cut-rate romantic comedies. Anyone shameless enough can do it. Here're some tips.

When shooting exteriors use designated landmarks. Feeling like tourists, audiences will put critical intelligence on hold. For Seattle show rain, the Space Needle, and (especially) Pike Place Market. By all means have the hero live on a Lake Union houseboat. (Who is to know that when he steps into his dinghy and putt-putts out to Puget Sound this would be like walking over the Brooklyn Bridge and into Yankee Stadium?) When in New York, place scenes in Tiffany's, Windows on the World, and the Empire State Building.

Collect a bunch of old songs and let them do the emotional work. Don't avoid Nat King Cole's "Stardust" or Tammy Wynette's "Stand by Your Man." What are songs for? Also use holidays for canned sentiment: How about starting with Christmas and ending with Valentine's Day? That's right, *Valentine's* Day.

Allude to Susan Faludi's *Backlash* (even if you are the third movie in three months to do so) and *tiramisu*. Have someone voice the wisdom that what women look for in a man is "a cute butt." Structure key scenes around restaurants, kitchens, and take-out. Give main characters chubby best friends for zeitgeist conversations. Start with the death of a beautiful yuppie and have her return, in the still of the night, or the wee small hours, as a ghost. Have her kid ask Dad if he believes in heaven.

Make your hero (Tom Hanks) an architect (the sensitive man's profession in today's movies), widower, father of a fat-faced kid with a bowl-cut. (Everyone knows architects build dream houses.) Give Dad a regular, manly name like Sam. Cue up Gene Autry's "Back in the Saddle Again" when Dad dials for his first date. Make first date an example of the modern predatory female: Give her a hyena's laugh. (Make it easy on audience by establishing character with one defining tic.)

Call your heroine (Meg Ryan) a reporter, even if she's never seen performing a job-related task. Give her "old-fashioned values," a wedding dress waiting in Mom's attic, and a desire for true love so sharp it makes her weep. (She just wants what dear old Mom had.) Name her Annie for emphasis. Burden her fiancé—the man we know she'll never end up with—with comical, life-threatening allergies and a bedside humidifier. Call him Walter. Show Annie peeling a Granny Smith in one long corkscrew. Have this amount to a significant, old-fashioned talent.

Picture a continent dotted with old-fashioned women, all pining for the one man in America who can speak lovingly—on late-night talk radio—of a dead wife. Into this woman's picture throw a few bones to the guys—references to Brooks Robinson, *Fatal Attraction* and *The Dirty Dozen*, visions of desperate women. Above all, enhance sentiment with talk of destiny, fate, magic, and true love (how once you have found it, never let it go). Definitely dare to be corny, even if some may call it crass.

Also reviewed in:
CHICAGO TRIBUNE, 6/25/93, Friday/p. C, Johanna Steinmetz
NEW YORK TIMES, 6/25/93, p. C10, Vincent Canby
NEW YORKER, 7/19/93, p. 79, Anthony Lane
VARIETY, 6/21/93, p. 41, Brian Lowry
WASHINGTON POST, 6/25/93, p. C1, Hal Hinson
WASHINGTON POST, 6/25/93, Weekend/p. 42, Joe Brown

SLIVER

A Paramount Pictures release. *Executive Producer:* Howard W. Koch, Jr. and Joe Eszterhas. *Producer:* Robert Evans. *Director:* Phillip Noyce. *Screenplay:* Joe Eszterhas. *Based on the by novel by:* Ira Levin. *Director of Photography:* Vilmos Zsigmond. *Editor:* Richard Francis-Bruce and William Hoy. *Music:* Howard Shore. *Music Editor:* Bunny Andrews. *Sound:* Tom Nelson and (music) John Richards. *Sound Editor:* Tim Chau and Rick Franklin. *Casting:* Amanda Mackey and Cathy Sandrich. *Production Designer:* Paul Sylbert. *Art Director:* Peter Lansdown Smith and Christopher Nowak. *Set Designer:* Antoinette J. Gordon, Walter P. Martishius, and Marion Kolsby. *Set Decorator:* Lisa Fischer and Leslie A. Pope. *Special Effects:* Ken Clark, John M. Ottesen, and Ronald R. Ottesen, Jr. *Costumes:* Deborah L. Scott. *Make-up:* Tricia A. Sawyer and Sharon Ilson. *Stunt Coordinator:* Bud Davis, David Ellis, and Steve Boyum. *Running time:* 111 minutes. *MPAA Rating:* R.

CAST: Sharon Stone (Carly Norris); William Baldwin (Zeke Hawkins); Tom Berenger (Jack Landsford); Polly Walker (Vida Jordan); Colleen Camp (Judy); Amanda Foreman (Samantha); Martin Landau (Alex Parsons); C.C.H. Pounder (Lieutenant Victoria Hendrix); Nina Foch (Mrs. McEvoy); Keene Curtis (Gus Hale); Nicholas Pryor (Peter Farrell); Anne Betancourt (Jackie Kinsella); Tony Peck (Martin Kinsella); Frantz Turner (Doorman); Melvyn Kinder (Doctor Palme); Radu Gavor (Dmitri); Allison Mackie (Naomi Singer); Jose Rey (Detective Corelli); Jim Beaver (Detective Ira); Gilbert Rosales (Janitor Rodrigues); Mik

Scriba and Steve Carlisle (Security Guards);   Mark Bramhall (Waiter);   Christine Avila (Doctor);   Alexander Gutman (Ted Weisberger);   Sid McCoy (Mr. Anderson);   Robin Groves (Mrs. Ballinger);   Matthew Faison (Mr. Ballinger);   Marne Patterson (Ballinger's Daughter); Katharine Pope (Gloria Alden);   Christine Toy, Philip Hoffman, and Nicole Orth-Pallavicini (Reporters);   Arthur Eckdahl and Patricia Allison (Waspy Woman);   Bernie McInerney (Minister);   James Noah and Eduardo N.T. Andrade (Doormen);   Robert Miano (Detective Howard);   Steve Eastin (Detective Phillip);   Craig Hosking and Cliff Fleming (Helicopter Pilots).

LOS ANGELES TIMES, 5/22/93, Calendar/p. 1, Peter Rainer

"Anybody ever tell you you have a nice butt?" says spiffy bachelor Zeke (William Baldwin) to his new neighbor Carly (Sharon Stone) during an aerobic workout at a local health club. As sexy foretalk goes, this remarkably subtle come-on is par for the course in "Sliver," the new erotic thriller that somehow manages to make voyeurism seem about as exciting as one of Cher's infomercials.

Perhaps it was different in the movie's pre-trimmed days: "Sliver" was headed for an NC-17 rating; now, minus a few quivering buttocks and sordid sundries, it's rated R. Why bother to make a film about sex and then capitulate to the ratings board by frantically toning down the sex? Maybe the film wouldn't have been any better before the cuts, but, this way, the film has become the butt of its own butts.

The 1971 Ira Levin pulp thriller on which the film is based was a workmanlike piece of intrigue that attempted to do for Manhattan's "sliver" buildings—narrow, wedgelike high-rises—what Levin did for spooky old sprawls like the Dakota in "Rosemary's Baby." It's a page-turner for people with not a lot of feeling in their fingertips. Nothing in it really takes hold except for the central idea—the owner of the sliver where there have been a string of mysterious deaths has set up a hidden camera system to spy on every square inch of his tenants' at-home lives.

More so than for books, voyeurism is better suited as a subject for the movies. Isn't all moviegoing voyeuristic? The saving grace of the film version of "Sliver" (rated R for strong sexuality, and for language and violence) is that at least it doesn't try to fob itself off as a serioso morality play; it's smarmily upfront about its intentions, even though the follow-through lacks wallop. But maybe being lowdown isn't all it's cracked up to be. After a stretch of grapple-and-smooch scenes you may actually long for something strait-laced—like, say, character development or dialogue that makes you giggle where giggles were intended.

How's this for wrongheadedness? In "Sliver," Stone plays a woman who has to be *lured into* sexual intrigue. Carly's a book editor who recently ended a seven-year marriage and moved into her sliver. She spends lonely evenings at home practicing her golf swing.

Casting Stone as a lovelorn wastrel waiting to be ravaged makes about as much sense as casting Madonna as Emily Dickinson. Her appeal, as this film confirms by negative example, is based on her taunt and sizzle, on her being the aggressor. Stone has the fresh-faced looks of a Grace Kelly, but there's something predatory about her delicate beauty—she has the smarts of a control freak who knows a hundred different ways to tie you up. Stone doesn't show much keenness for her role here, maybe because Carly's psychosexual dynamics are so ill-defined. Even her big set-piece is a botch: Dining in a crowded, pricey restaurant with Zeke, he wheedles her into surreptitiously removing her panties. She doesn't show much enjoyment. Was the room too drafty perhaps?

Besides Zeke, the other nosy suitor in Carly's sliver is Jack (Tom Berenger), a best-selling true-crime writer who gets his kicks bearing down upon Carly unrecognized while she takes her morning jog in Central Park. He's first introduced to her at a luncheon as, jokingly, "the devil" and, after a while, you figure—well, this is Ira Levin territory, maybe he *is* the devil.

But the script for "Sliver" was written by Joe Eszterhas, from what appear to be dollops and oddments from his "Basic Instinct" scrapheap, and, as in that film only more so, nothing in the murder plot really adds up. (Levin's plotting has been considerably reworked, if that's the word.) Between Jack and Zeke, enough red herrings are strewn about to stock a fish market, but the clues are all screwed up. Pity the poor director, Phillip Noyce, whenever an actor importuned him with: "What's my motivation?"

Noyce ("Dead Calm," "Patriot Games") is a capable craftsman with a gift for taut, creepy story-telling, but he can't do much with the mix 'n' match garble here. He's probably too honest to try to put one over on the audience; in the end, he seems to sink into the mire along with the rest of us. An even sleazier approach might have worked better; you keep waiting for some of that old "9½ Weeks"/"Wild Orchid"-style jiggle to steam the screen. It gets so bad that you even hold out for a purring, purse-lipped Mickey Rourke to make a cameo. (No such bad luck.)

A funnier approach would have been even better. Is it really such a deep-dish revelation that we all "like to watch"? The people who made "Sliver" are mesmerized by their own prurience. They don't really get into the kicky nuttiness of spying on other people, of lording it over other people's secrecies. The multichannel action on the video monitors is surprisingly perfunctory. (Imagine what Hitchcock or DePalma, or even Warhol, might have done with dozens of screens winking their private dramas at us simultaneously.) There's no emotional pull to the neo-Gothic world in "Sliver," where people connect up by video monitor and computer with occasional forays in the flesh. It's no news that we like to watch. But first you must give us something worth watching.

NEW STATESMAN & SOCIETY, 8/13/93, p. 32, Andrea Stuart

Welcome to the Stone age. In case you have emerged from a coma recently. Sharon Stone's latest film *Sliver*, will open next month to the kind of hype that would make Spielberg smile. It's the movie that Stone and her studio hope will transform her from the latest Great Blonde Hope into a queen of the box office.

To this end, *Sliver*, an otherwise ho-hum tale of murder and voyeurism in a New York high-rise, features the sort of erotic party pieces that made *Basic Instinct* such a success. These are moments designed to prove that Stone is the actress who will go further than any other has gone before.

This time the forbidden territory is auto-eroticism, which the buttoned-down publisher, Carly, manages to indulge in with both arms firmly gripping the side of her bath (what muscle tone!). As in *Basic Instinct*, panties—or the lack of them—also have their small part to play, when she manages to remove hers and hand them to her lover—in full view of a crowded restaurant.

Despite promising box office takings—$12 million in the first week of opening in the US—*Sliver* is exactly what it sounds like: a disappointing wannabe movie. The film it wants to be is its predecessor, the $385-million grosser that put Stone on the map.

Why Stone, and why now? The answer lies in going back to *Basics*. As the fanny-flashing, bisexual murderess Catherine Trammel, Stone was able to cash in on—and perhaps help create—the "lesbian chic" that everyone was soon talking about. When the film opened, no one was interested in "whodunit?" (there was never any doubt) but rather in whom Stone was doing it to. "Is she or isn't she?": that was the question. And Stone toyed with this ambiguity at every chance she got.

Stone isn't, of course, the only performer to play gay and come up trumps. Over 60 years ago, Marlene Dietrich's first talkie for an US audience, *Morocco*, clinched her stardom when she played a singer attired in tie and tails who throws a rose to a woman in the audience and then kisses her on the lips. More recently, the singer Marky Mark borrowed his body from a gay-boy pin up as surely as he stole his street style from the 'hood. Yes, a touch of taboo can liven up even the most famous of careers. Look at Madonna, who took a cute matching pair of S&M dykes and spiked up her book's *Sex* appeal.

And this year's favourite taboo seems to be lesbianism. Why else would the media on both sides of the Atlantic get into such a lather over the pictures of country singer kd lang cavorting with super-model Cindy Crawford on the cover of *Vanity Fair*? Or viewers turn on in their droves just to watch Marla the make-over artist kiss Sandra Bernhard on *Roseanne*? With such a spotlight on "lipstick lesbians", no wonder that American *Vogue* asks: "Have we gone gay-girl crazy?"

In the US, at least, this probably does reflect a sea-change in the lesbian community. Clinton has put "one" in his cabinet, while Hollywood buzzes with rumours of the new lesbian power elite, which is rumoured to include any number of "A" list actresses, supermodels and TV personalities.

Off the streets and between the sheets (if Nancy Friday's latest collection of female fantasies is anything to go by) women definitely prefer women—in their heads, at least. If this is true, then men have only themselves to blame. Thanks to the relentless eroticisation of the female body, we are a society of girl-watchers. It's no surprise that women should begin to look as well.

But it is our concern with the "new" lesbianism just a cloak for the old voyeurism? Femme-on-femme images have always been a stock item in our titillation-hungry visual culture. And an icon such as Stone, whatever her personal preferences, has certainly been designed to appeal to men even more than to other women.

On film, Stone is the ultimate boy-toy-blonde. She's a sort of wise-cracking wild thing, so sexually self sufficient (and therefore totally undemanding) that she can do it for herself—or maybe with just a little help from her (girl) friends.

This, I suspect, says a lot more about male angst and wish-fulfillment than it does about female sexuality. It tells us much about the unacknowledged crisis within heterosexuality, rather than reflecting a genuine concern with the lesbian community.

The trouble is that sex—heterosexual sex—has become boring. "Do 10 Inch Willies Really Exist?"; "Cosmic Sex"; "Everything You Ever Wanted to Know About Oral Sex": as headlines like these scream at us from every newspaper, screen and magazine, "sex" is so over-exposed as to be meaningless. It all feels about as subversive as a Bakewell tart. What can I say? When *She* and *House and Garden* start crusading for cunnilingus, you know the sin is gone.

It also feels so remarkably passé. Even the sex scenes in *Sliver*—despite Stone's supercharged image and hints of masturbation still seem kind of tired. Let your eyes wander above eye level in the local newsagent's, or watch a triple XXX video in the privacy of your own raincoat, and things are even worse. Confronted with those women with frosted hair and hyper-glossed lips or those blow-dried, woven-chested studs wearing gold medallions, you can't help but wonder: "Where do these refugees from the 1970s come from?"

These days, even a walk around once-wild Soho prompts not outrage but nostalgia. It looks like some abandoned trading post in an old western, with everyone hanging around in costume, listlessly waiting for someone to break the news that filming is over.

Why is it that we can only depict heterosexuality with any comfort in the past tense? Perhaps it's because those were the halcyon days before feminism, before the censorship debates and before Aids. People still claimed that sex was better for you than a three mile jog and that pornography was really a liberating experience, rather than just a business tool for the publisher of the *Daily Sport*.

Then along came the anti-pornography movement and Aids: penetration and its depiction moved from the merely problematic to the potentially lethal. Caught between sexual cliché on one hand and sexual anxiety on the other, these days one can hardly smile and say the word "intercourse" at the same time.

So it's no wonder that a somewhat battered heterosexuality is in the process of reinventing itself, attempting to incorporate the desired elements of wickedness, transgression and fun that have long since gone AWOL from its own image. Hence the lesbian fixation. Unlike gay men, with whom the sex-death equation is too hot to handle, lesbianism is simultaneously safe and pleasurably taboo. And, unlike straight sex, there is still some mystery there.

But at the same time as the mainstream tries to annex the freshness and frisson of new sexual lifestyles, it is also busy trying to neutralise them. In a piece in the *Daily Mirror*, for example, we are assured that lesbian chic doesn't have to involve actual sex with other women, merely a "more liberated attitude". With this sleight of hand, lesbianism becomes a heterosexual activity, and one that conveniently doesn't involve the rejection of men.

Which brings me back to Sharon. In a recent interview, she says she is tired of "symbolising" a kind of sex she doesn't "believe in". But what kind of sex she means is anybody's guess. Lesbian sex? Hot sex? Sex that involves ice-picks? Or maybe it's sex in general that she is tired of representing. Who knows? Only her next movie will tell us for sure.

NEW STATESMAN & SOCIETY, 8/20/93, p. 35, Jonathan Romney

Sliver may be among the most accurately titled films ever. It's that slender, unlike Joe Eszterhas' payment as screenwriter, which is more like *Chunk*. In conventional terms, it has little

1384   FILM REVIEW ANNUAL

to recommend it except two items touted as high-concept selling points—a song by UB40 at their whiniest, and the antiseptic spectacle of Sharon Stone enjoying a solitary writhe in the bath (surprisingly, Badedas has missed the obvious product placement opportunity).

What *Sliver* does have going for it, albeit fleetingly, is an interesting take on the theme of the moment—video surveillance. Since there's precious little suspense in the film, it won't hurt to reveal (besides, you'll have guessed as much from the UB40 video) that *Sliver* features a character who surveys the tenants in an apartment block by means of a massive bank of surveillance monitors. This gives us the chance to watch unsuspecting subjects at work, rest and play, usually in front of the bathroom mirror that conceals the camera. People yawn, screw, fight and drop all formalities—there's even an unflattering glimpse of director Phillip Noyce mugging blearily through his morning toilet.

The video premise provides more interesting dividends than you're at first led to expect. At first, we're offered a rather hackneyed tease in the film's self-conscious appeal to the supposedly perverse drives that link cinema and voyeurism. As one character says, and the film's poster reiterates, "You like to watch, don't you?" But there's nothing particularly pleasurable in the watching we get to do—the quick-spliced, decomposed images in the bathtime scene, and later some (implausibly giggly) Manhattan sophisticates peering through a telescope at a couple making love in the apartment opposite.

The first—inadvertent—revelation that *Sliver* offers is that the simple act of watching is no big deal after all. Over the past decade, voyeurism has been built so solidly into the margins of mainstream cinema—from *Blue Velvet* to *sex, lies and videotape*—that it no longer creates any frisson. In this sense, *Sliver* is as inept at getting a charge out of its supposedly fail-safe risqueness as was the dreary Madonna vehicle, *Body Evidence*.

What *Sliver* does have to offer, in one remarkably powerful sequence, is an *excess* of vision. As Stone first walks in to find 50 screens simultaneously pumping out the realest form of "reality programming" imaginable, the camera wildly scans the screens, on all of which *something is happening* some minor horror or spectacle or inconsequential moment charged with absolute significance for the split second that you notice it. As the throb of the soundtrack music joins in, the effect is an overwhelming appeal to cerebral overload: a high-power narcotic.

That moment is over all too briefly, but it's followed by a sobering one. The drunkenness that Stone's character Carly derives from the simultaneous availability of so much apparently raw knowledge palls when she realises that knowledge also carries a moral imperative. A man in one apartment has been sexually abusing his daughter, and there's a chilling exchange of glances when Stone gets in the lift with him. Suddenly, the father's shield of normality becomes charged with evasive intent, while the child's "innocent" look becomes a direct appeal to Carly.

There's no real debate on "improper" knowledge here. The issue is brushed aside, and the film effectively stops here. But for a moment, *Sliver* has transcended its glossy surfaces and taken stock of its implications as a vehicle for the image. You're reminded how very problematic things get when film tries to engage with video.

These days, film increasingly measures itself against video as an instrument for capturing and/or manipulating the real. It's hard always to know what's at stake—whether film is threatened by video's access to the real, or envies its ability to reshape actuality. This is no longer a specialist subject restricted to the phenomenological wranglings of Wim Wenders or the moral debate of *Henry: Portrait of a Serial Killer*. Mainstream fiction now routinely has recourse to camcorder imagery: everything from *Trespass*, for enhanced grittiness, to *Falling Down*, which captured the way that people use video as a lifeline to images of stability.

The most illuminating glimpses of cinema's uneasy relation to video are often the least fully articulated, rather than the more elaborate analyses offered by a film such as Michael Haneke's *Benny's Video*. This Austrian production is a European art film of the most austere tradition: a blankly recounted parable about video's ill effects. An emotionally blinkered adolescent, who lives only for his electronic images, kills a girl, incidentally capturing her death on his camcorder, and then transfers his guilt to his vacant middle-class parents. It's a stern jeremiad about cultural devaluation, about the sins of the parents manifesting themselves in the children, and about moral anaesthesia in the new Europe.

But the film is without real impact. That's partly because it occupies such familiar territory. Its more obviously shocking content has been pre-empted by *Henry* and the Belgian *Man Bites Dog*, both wittier and more perversely charming in their blackness. But it also disappoints because there's no ambivalence, no sense that the film, despite its loathing of video, might be susceptible to some of the form's seductions. Instead, its disdainfully moralistic view is delivered strictly from the high ground—not least aesthetically, in its long takes from a static camera and absolute refusal of spectacle.

Benny's Video is part of a trilogy that Haneke describes as a "polemical statement about the American sensational cinema". Clearly *Sliver* is exactly the sort of film that Haneke rails against. Yet, for all its idiot glossiness, *Sliver* does provide much more of a sense of video's seduction. The film's monitor scene, with its masses of casual domestic images, offers the appeal of a kind of random, on-tap reality: not filmed with intent but caught *on the hop*, plucked out of the real.

In the last year, we've come to believe more and more in video's capacity to "pluck" random moments and extract the truth from them—to identify, for example, the blurry figures seen with murder victims Jamie Bulger and Emmanuel Spiteri. Rather than making statements about the danger of the image, as *Benny's Video* does, there seems more mileage in the occasional reminder that our appetite for video-reality is motivated as much by a taste for the glamour of "reality programming" as by a desire for "truth".

NEW YORK, 6/7/93, p. 55, David Denby

We all may be voyeurs, we moviegoers, but how interesting is voyeurism itself as a subject? This not very important question has been tested to the limit by *Sliver*, the latest installment in the trash-sex-thriller cycle that began with *Fatal Attraction*. The setting this time is a swank New York high rise, a building owned by a wealthy and idle young man, Zeke (William Baldwin), who has some peculiar habits. Zeke has installed hidden video cameras and microphones in every apartment. Sitting in his own place before banks of monitors, this modern electronic pasha can watch what everyone in the building is doing. Even the bathrooms are wired. Total surveillance is total power.

Now, if *Sliver* had been a witty avant-garde production—directed by Jim Jarmusch, say—the apartment-dwellers would no doubt be doing very little. People would sit around reading the paper, watching *The Simpsons*, or staring at the walls; they would scratch themselves and sing "Melancholy Baby" in the shower. The joke would be that life, poor life, was a drag—hardly a voyeur's delight. But since this is big-budget trash, the residents turn out to be as busy as bees, quarreling, masturbating, fornicating all over the place, abusing their children and one another. A couple dances the tango. (Obviously, a very lax co-op board.) Every life is a dirty soap opera, which might be called the basic trash principle.

Zeke records much of what the cameras pick up, so he has videotapes of himself making love to various young women in the building. Since these same women subsequently get flung from terraces or knifed in stairwells—indeed, since the building's electric power goes dead whenever a woman is alone in the laundry room—one would think that taking an apartment in the place isn't necessarily a good move for a single lady. But our heroine, Carly (Sharon Stone), a divorced book editor, moves in and quickly becomes Zeke's newest lover. Carly barely seems to notice that the building is odd; in fact, she doesn't notice much of anything—in order to keep the plot going, the character has been written as a patsy.

Sharon Stone, the current queen of Hollywood (she shares the throne with another non-actress, Demi Moore), has a funny, dazed look on her face, as if she had just gotten off a transatlantic flight and couldn't find her luggage. Miss Stone is beautiful but impersonal and unmemorable. Her lovely limbs photograph extremely well (this literary worker must read manuscripts in a tanning salon), but if there's anything going on in the editor's mind—even fear or curiosity—Stone keeps it hidden.

Though Carly is in thrall, sexually, to the good-looking Zeke, she finally begins to wonder if he isn't a bit dangerous. Is he the murderer? Or is it the other guy from the building, the pulp writer Jack (Tom Berenger), who was once famous but is now apparently blocked at the typewriter and impotent as well? Jack is overaggressive and blustery and has the habit of jumping out at people while wearing a dark hood. He comes on to Carly, and he's about as appealing as a mugger. Zeke, on the other hand, is soft-voiced, gentle, almost feline, though also rather infantile and boring. (For a better William Baldwin performance as a New York stud, see *Three of Hearts.*) Any sane woman would consider decamping from a building that housed two such aggressive creeps. But the movie is not set in the real New York City, where people avoid trouble whenever they can; it is set in sex-thrillerville, where women like Carly hang in there, waiting to be scared, assaulted, photographed, made love to, whatever.

Sliver is like Hitchcock's *Rear Window* without the conceptual brilliance and De Palma's *Dressed to Kill* without the perverse jokes and visual panache. Screenwriter Joe Eszterhas, the new master of erotic junk, has adapted a novel by Ira Levin, the old master of gimcrack plotting, and the doubling up of artificiality has produced a story and a milieu in which not one thing rings true. We don't, of course, want reality in a thriller. What we want is enough of an illusion of reality to make us believe in the nasty emotions and improbable violence at the story's heart. But Eszterhas is no good at "atmosphere," and his attempts at sophisticated New York banter are mostly pathetic. (Despite the movie's dropping that magic real-life name "Lynn Nesbit," no one, I trust, is likely to imagine he's getting the inside view of publishing when he hears Carly's assistant burbling away about dildos and multiple orgasms.)

The insular apartment-building setting, in which everyone is obsessed with everyone else, seems like something out of a TV sitcom, and the characters are empty and dislikable; Who cares about these three? There isn't a human being on the screen. And director Philip Noyce (*Patriot Games*) has turned into a nowhere man himself. As a piece of moviemaking, *Sliver* is not inept, like *Body Evidence*, which was lighted like a loading dock at midnight. But Noyce, who started out promisingly in Australia, has upheld a depressing tradition among recent émigré directors (Paul Verhoeven, Roger Donaldson, Adrian Lyne, Tony Scott)—the tradition of becoming more slickly Hollywood than anyone in Hollywood itself. He is now a smooth commercial formalist without an idea in his head.

You feel alienated from everyone on-screen—for instance, from the people talking about sex in a crude public way that sounds forced (and wrong for this high-class milieu). Baldwin and Stone have one hot scene together, and there's some business concerning panties at a fancy restaurant that should amuse people who have a thing about ... panties at fancy restaurants. *Sliver*, which has been heavily cut (for an R rather than an NC-17 rating), actually needs more sex—a more erotic atmosphere might make the murderous compulsions exciting.

Much of the time, we are watching people watch *other* people on TV monitors, which, no matter how many different images jump on and off the screen, is not a dramatic use of the film medium. In a word, the film's remarkable technology is boring. At one point, Carly becomes aroused while watching a tape of herself making love to Zeke, and I was disgusted—not by the decadence of the sex but by the scene's dramatic and emotional feebleness. The filmmakers obviously wanted to make a point about voyeurism—that it's become the real thing or replaced the real thing. This is a point that might pass for profound among people who have nothing to say. *Sliver*, like *Basic Instinct*, is an example of the new genre of mock pornography—a sad genre, even sadder than pornography itself, because it lacks the courage of its sleazy convictions.

NEW YORK POST, 5/21/93, p. 31, Jami Bernard

It's hard to concentrate on writing a review of "Sliver," the new Sharon Stone-William Baldwin steamfest, because I'm busy planning how I can move into one of those sliver Manhattan highrises. Apparently, they're peopled entirely by newly dead women and hot-looking guys, so the male-female ratio is pretty good. Just don't pay your rent in advance because you'll probably wind up dead at the end of your date.

Paramount didn't screen "Sliver" in advance for critics, and the reason was evident at last night's last-minute screening, where the tittering and guffawing threatened to drown out the sound of Sharon Stone moaning. She moans a lot in "Sliver," most often when she's alone in the bathtub, and also when Baldwin is coming at her from behind against a marble pillar. Hey, whatever gets you through the night.

Although incredibly silly and as far removed from reality as Stone's high-rise apartment from the pavement, "Sliver" is still the kind of fun junk for when your brain-cell count is low after a tough week at the office.

Stone is having a tough week, although she hardly ever visits her office. She plays Carly Norris, a book editor whose recent messy divorce has her moving into a high-rise apartment recently vacated by a woman who went over the terrace head-first. Who pushed her? The sliver is a-burstin' with handsome, crazy men, all of whom ask Carly out before she's even unpacked her suitcase. Is it handsome William Baldwin, who lives on the unlucky 13th floor? Is it doofy Tom Beringer, a crime novelist with writer's block? Is it the mysterious man who monitors all the apartments and videotapes their private moments? Is it the doorman who likes big tips?

Stone didn't wear any underwear in "Basic Instinct," the movie that "Silver" is counting on to lure the customers. Here she removes her underwear in a fancy restaurant, a scene that, like many of the purportedly sexy ones, makes you squirm with embarrassment rather than pleasure. There are, in fact, some rather hormonal moments, but many of them seem prematurely chopped, perhaps in a bid to outwit the threatened NC-17 rating. The sexiest scene, however, is when Baldwin examines himself in the mirror, while he works out in the gym.

"Silver" prefers the appearance of things to the real thing, which is part of its theme—voyeurism—and also part of its problem. Voyeurism is one of those subjects that directors love (note some stolen moments from "Body Double") because directors are always looking through lenses. But it's a passive hobby, and movie-watching is already a passive experience—making the many scenes of spying a kind of somnolent and unrewarding activity. Stone plays "vulnerable." The effect is very similar to that in "Basic Instinct," when she was playing "cold-blooded." (Wardrobe hint: Sharon, stay away from the shoulder pads.) Director Phillip Noyce, who made an excellent, quiet little thriller called "Dead Calm," is about as subtle here as the perniciously phallic imagery—the sliver building itself, a model volcano as part of Baldwin's apartment decor, and the half-eaten eclair on Carly's plate right after she has her first postmarital orgasm.

The headachy cinematography by Vilmos Zsigmond presents a claustrophobic world of delusional paranoia.

NEWSDAY, 5/22/93, Part II/p. 23, John Anderson

"Sliver" produced a lot of heaving breathing before it even got on screen. Now that it has, that sound you hear is Paramount Pictures hyperventilating.

The hotly anticipated erotic thriller, starring Sharon Stone, William Baldwin and Tom Berenger, is more frightening than your electric bill, sexier than root canal and it even has its warm moments, although the only thing purgatorial about it is its length.

Stone, in her first, appearance since "Basic Instinct," plays Carly Norris, a newly divorced book editor looking for a new lease, on life. So she signs one at a "sliver"—a narrow, high-rise Manhattan apartment house. It's a building with a tainted reputation, thanks to an unusual number of unusual and unsolved deaths among its residents. But it has another secret, too: Someone has wired the building with closed-circuit cameras, through which he can watch, in glorious black and white, the sexual exploits of his neighbors.

They include the wealthy young bachelor Zeke Hawkins (Baldwin), the true-crime author Jack Landsford (Berenger), and Carly's neighbor Vida Jordan (Polly Walker).

Disaster befalls the residents one by one, until, through simple arithmetic, you can't miss who the killer is. But when you do, you don't care, because so much time has been spent in character development without anything actually being developed.

Voyeurism as a metaphor for the modern condition—the disappearance of privacy, the intrusiveness of media, the omnipresence of security—is an apt one. But so much of "Sliver" is calculated to show off Baldwin's and Stone's pretty bodies that the film generates more heat than light. It also generates laughs in the most inappropriate places. How often does the shooting of a man provoke a general guffaw among a movie audience?

That audience attended a screening Thursday night in Manhattan, the only one to which critics were invited. This is standard practice for a studio when it fears for a movie's fate: If the movie's going to bomb anyway, try to get in one good weekend at the box office before word-of-mouth sets in. But Paramount's decision wasn't all that surprising, given "Sliver's" checkered history.

The film's production reportedly was plagued by personal acrimony (on-screen lovers Stone and Baldwin are said to loathe each other and their lack of screen chemistry substantiates the rumor), production delays and a ballooning budget—and then the producers faced a bitter fight with the ratings board, which initially gave the film the NC-17 designation.

Stone also defied the common wisdom by following one erotic thriller with another, although $2.5 million will get you to do a lot of unwise things.

"You Like to Watch Don't You," read the ads for "Sliver." The answer obviously is no.

NEWSWEEK, 5/3/93, p. 54, Jeff Giles

Welcome to the age of the smoke bomb. A while back (when no one had seen it) the movie "Sliver" seemed to have it all: stars who hated each other! A ratings controversy! No ending whatsoever! These are the things that hits are made of. Paramount did not preview "Sliver" until the night before it opened. The studio claimed that the movie wasn't finished. More likely, Paramount was making an end run around reviews that would spoil that box-office love-in known as "opening weekend." The "Sliver" publicity campaign has been a state-of-the-art exercise in style over substance, in teasing over pleasing. Says Richard Heffner, the beleaguered chairman of the industry's ratings board, "In a word, it's bull."

Director Phillip Noyce has made a dull, dopey thriller. Based on Joe Eszterhas's adaptation of a best-selling Ira Levin novel, it stars Sharon Stone as Carly Norris, a Manhattan book editor who moves into the "Horror Highrise." Tenants jump out windows, slip in the shower and get stabbed in the stairwell. Meanwhile, Norris is courted by the boorish novelist Jack Landsford (Tom Berenger) and the sleepy-eyed computer whiz Zeke Hawkins (William Baldwin). She beds down with the latter, who turns out to be a superfreaky voyeur with a bank of television monitors as big as a Sears showroom.

From the beginning, the "Sliver" monster was driven by the tired but true notion that sex sells. "It's a smart campaign," says one veteran movie marketer. "They're playing it right by highlighting Sharon Stone as a victim of voyeurism. That's why we go to the movies: to see Sharon Stone naked," The "Sliver" ads bottom-fish for our most basic instincts—"You like to watch, don't you"—so let's play tit for tat. Baldwin bares his chest, legs and butt, in the offhand style popularized by Mel Gibson. Stone gives us her all, or most of it, but usually in a darkened room and from a distance. The stars were reportedly at odds during filming and, while that may set media tongues wagging, it makes for bad screen sex. Stone tries to be weepy and real, but she gets slimed by the movie's take on lovemaking, which is that all good sex begins with a breaking and entering.

The ratings fracas that surrounded "Sliver" appears to have been a textbook case of studio hype. To win the coveted R, it seems, the "Sliver" team had to edit a bathtub sequence, darken a sex scene involving a pillar and excise a few troublesome male appendages. By complaining loud and long, the studio whipped up a titillating controversy that would boost ticket sales and, one day, help send the "director's cut" video into heavy rotation. Did somebody say "Basic Instinct"? Or "Body of Evidence"? Producer Robert Evans claims the ratings board couldn't handle the voyeurism theme, but Heffner thinks he's being high and mighty: "We don't give a shit about anybody's theme."

What *about* "Sliver's" much-touted voyeurism? What *about* Phillip Noyce's ominous claim that "We are *all* voyeurs." Let's put it this way: when bigname stars strip for surveillance cameras, it's called "pushing the envelope," but when B-movie types do the same, it's called "Night Eyes 2." The couplings that flash by on Zeke Hawkins's monitors are sad, freakish, anything but erotic. Late in the film, when Carly Norris does a Thelma & Louise in Zeke's control room and tells him to "get a life," she's indicting the movie's marketing team, as well as any audience member who hasn't up and walked.

Fear not: it's impossible to ruin "Sliver's" ending because somebody else got there first. Test audiences were said to have bristled at the movie's original conclusion, thereby fanning the publicity fires a wee bit higher. (" Fatal Attraction," anyone?) Eszterhas's new ending short-circuits the movie's tenuous logic. It even fingers a different villain, which means that at the eleventh hour somebody finally got around to telling the killer he was the killer. Ah, the life of the Method actor!

By the time this article appears, "Sliver" will likely have grossed $15 million. In the current Harper's Magazine, Mark Gill, of Columbia Pictures, says of marketing a film: "It doesn't matter if the movie doesn't deliver. If you can create the *impression* that the movie delivers, you're fine." As for "Sliver," Evans says, "I'm proud of it. It will have an impact. It won't go unnoticed." If only, Mr. Evans. If only.

SIGHT AND SOUND, 9/93, p. 53, Chris Darke

Book editor Carly Norris, recently divorced and looking to change her life, takes an apartment in a Manhattan 'sliver' block. Her apartment's former tenant, Naomi Singer, plunged to her death in mysterious circumstances. As Carly moves in, a young man offers to help her; he introduces himself as Zeke Hawkins, a tenant living on the top floor. Carly also encounters her neighbour, a friendly young English woman, Vida Jordan. At a business lunch, Carly's boss introduces her to Jack Landsford, a successful true-crime author who has apparently lost the will to write and who also lives in Carly's building. When she returns home she finds that she has received a gift of a telescope from a mysterious admirer.

Out jogging one morning, Carly is startled by Jack, and although she is irritated by his lecherous bad manners, they discuss the fate of Naomi Singer. On her return, an older tenant, university professor Gus Hale, introduces himself and tells Carly that she bears a startling resemblance to the dead woman. Shortly afterwards, he is found dead in the shower of his apartment. At Carly's flat-warming party, Jack and Zeke arrive uninvited. Both men ask Carly out and she has difficulties in getting Jack to leave. Later she accompanies Zeke to his gym and learns that he writes video games for a living. They return to his apartment where they make love; he tells her that he owns the building and that it was he that gave her the telescope.

At work, Carly receives Zeke's declaration of love by electronic mail, while her workmate tells her of an uneventful weekend spent with Jack at his ranch. Shortly afterwards, Vida is brutally murdered in the building and Carly discovers Jack beside the body. Although arrested, he is released on bail and Carly finds him in her apartment, where he attempts to persuade her that Zeke is the killer. Zeke arrives and diffuses the situation. He then shows Carly the control room of his video surveillance system, which allows him to watch everything that takes place in the building.

Initially horrified, Carly becomes fascinated, until she witnesses a young girl telling her mother of her father's sexual abuse of her. Zeke calls Carly at work to say that he has spoken anonymously to the father, hoping to end the abuse. Carly leaves work to rejoin him, and when he goes out to get food, she discovers old videotapes detailing Zeke's sexual relationships with the murdered women. On his return, and terrified that he is the killer, she defends herself with a pistol as a tape of Naomi's murder unwinds before them. When the murderer's face is revealed as Jack's, Carly begins systematically to shoot out the video monitors, and finally admonishes Zeke to "Get a life!"

It is tempting to imagine an early draft of *Sliver* having the working title of *sex, highrise and video-tape*. The video voyeurism crucial to Steven Soderbergh's film, together with its seemingly inescapable corollary of sexual impotence, are relocated in *Sliver* geographically, to a Manhattan tower block, and generically, into the frame of an erotic thriller. And while this must be attributed partly to the twin presences of Sharon Stone as star and Joe Eszterhas as screenwriter and executive producer, *Sliver* succeeds in being neither particularly erotic nor thrilling.

Where *Basic Instinct* was take-it-or-leave-it pulp, making a virtue of its bravura tackiness, Phillip Noyce's film opts to play Stone in reverse, switching her former persona of polymorphously perverse hatchet-woman to that of a recently divorced 35-year-old book editor. But this casting against type goes no further than replacing the ice-pick under the bed with surveillance cameras concealed in the walls, and putting them in the hands of William Baldwin's creepily super-capable landlord.

The premise of Stone's character thus established (we know next to nothing of her former marriage except that it was unhappy), cliché follows cliché, from her emotional state being coded through her clothing—muted colours, soft fabrics buttoned up to the neck—to the sex games in a restaurant, complete with the regulation reaction shots of incredulous middle-aged diners. The lingerie that Zeke gives her is a metonymic echo of the totemic cocktail dress of *Basic Instinct*, bringing that film's Catherine Trammell firmly back into the frame. But when it comes to portraying a woman-in-peril, Stone doesn't fit the bill; to adopt the Hitchcockian frame of reference, she's closer to Kim Novak's glacial unfathomability than to Tippi Hedren's tousled panic.

But the real star of the film is its video technology. From his state-of-the-art control room, Zeke, unknown to them, surveys the lives of the apartments' occupants, transforming his building into a high-tech, high-rent panopticon. Or, more accurately for Zeke, an interminable soap opera with as many vying narratives as there are inhabitants. Noyce's use of video flits between being palmcorder-pornography and surveillance of 'Real Life'—tapping into a trend that the eponymous American TV series has recently bought to British screens. The 'secondary soaps' that are the other lives of the block appear far more fascinating than Zeke's, but they are evoked only to be dropped or dealt with in the narrative equivalent of a channel-hopping flourish.

The four-act mini-drama of child abuse that takes place within the film via its video is the starkest expression of this tendency and signals one of *Sliver*'s major missed opportunities. Carly's growing fascination with Zeke's voyeuristic intervention into other lives is prevented from being developed by the increasingly irrelevant murder mystery. Ultimately, the film becomes an unsatisfying Stone-Baldwin two-hander played out under the eye of the ubiquitous surveillance camera, with the video-soap back-stories proving potentially far more interesting than the formulaic thriller that houses them.

Sliver has a couple of interesting minor characters in Polly Walker's West End girl uttering profanities with perfect SW1 diction, out of her depth and up to her neck in Manhattan coke; and Keene Curtis' NYU professor teaching an option in 'The Psychology of the Lens'. A pity he doesn't last through the first reel—*Sliver* would have benefitted from a more equal ratio of old-fashioned psychology to balance its high-tech lens fixation.

VILLAGE VOICE, 6/8/93, p. 60, Gary Indiana

As an exercise in imploded narrative, *Sliver* achieves a kind of senselessness only partly realized by *Basic Instinct*, the last Sharon Stone-Joe Eszterhas team effort. Wrenched in rough slices from an undistinguished thriller by Ira Levin, *Sliver* tries to be a movie about "voyeurism," as if there were still something wildly exciting attached to the idea.

Stone's character, book editor Carly Norris, moves into a building where all the apartments are televisually bugged. A telescope appears in her new place as an anonymous housewarming gift. We learn that she's editing a tell-all biography of James Dean. If this doesn't tell us how wide-spread and multifaceted voyeurism is, what does?

At the local market, a neighbor, Gus Hale (Keene Curtis), introduces himself and tells her she looks exactly like Naomi Singer, the former tenant of the apartment she's moved into, who jumped from the balcony. (We've already seen Naomi being hurled off the balcony by a figure in a hooded jogging outfit—similar to one worn a few scenes later by Tom Berenger!) A lecturer at NYU on "The Psychology of the Lens," Gus promises to fill Stone in on building gossip when he returns from Japan, where he has an appointment to study Sony's state-of-the-art video technology. As he regales Stone in the building foyer, an overhead surveillance camera tracks them; in the lobby, they're overheard by Jack Landsford (Tom Berenger), a weirdly childish true-crime author who happens to live there also. Landsford and Carly are soon introduced at lunch by Carly's boss, played by Martin Landau. Landsford insists on sending her his true-crime novels. Later, observed by the unseen master voyeur over one of the dozens of closed-circuit monitors, we see Gus dead in his shower. Murdered?

Much of *Sliver* has the quality of a non sequitur. Levin's novel is a really cheap recasting of the Oedipus myth, including the torn-out eyes, with some serial-killer stuff thrown in: the building owner, brooding over his control panel, has an uncontrollable urge to fuck and then kill women who resemble his mother, a soap opera actress he hardly ever saw except on television. The series of accident/murders in the building occur when the owner's spying becomes known to various unlucky tenants. (Gus, if he'd gone to Japan, would almost certainly have caught on about the video system!) Most of the implausible connectives of the book have been jettisoned in Eszterhas's screenplay in favor of the plain unbelievable. But odd little bits, like Gus's death, or Gus himself, for that matter, have been left in for no apparent reason.

What Levin was going for in the book, I guess, was a reprise of *Rosemary's Baby* in a newer building than the Dakota, something on the "Horror High Rise" idea. What Eszterhas and director Phillip Noyce have devised is an upmarket version of the Lauren Hutton thriller *Someone's Watching Me!*, crossed slightly with the Heather Locklear vehicle *Trapped*: some things happen because of the building's surveillance system, others happen because the electricity shorts out, and a lone resourceful female stands up to the challenge of a homicidal maniac and modern architecture.

Stone begins an affair with Zeke Hawkins (William Baldwin), a neighbor who takes her to a health club, shows off his gorgeous physique, and helps her overcome her terrible shyness by telling her what a great butt she has; later, while they're busy fucking in his comic book-and-video-game-strewn apartment, crime writer Landsford is out in Montauk, pumping Stone's office buddy Judy (Colleen Camp) for information about Stone.

Landsford's importunity provides the only suspense in *Sliver*, he keeps letting himself into Stone's apartment (with a key Naomi gave him?) to confront her with disturbing information about her new boyfriend, and we, in turn, are left to wonder if this information really means anything, or if Landsford is a jealous lunatic. How can we know? He pretends not to know Vida, a call girl who lives down the hall from Carly, but Carly sees him giving Vida money in the street (through the telescope, natch), and then, when Vida gets killed in the emergency stairway, Carly sees him bent over the body.

Unfortunately, since the ending of *Sliver* was apparently changed, drastically, after test-market audiences disliked the idea of B---- as the murderer, we are presented—retroactively—with a much murkier and suggestive symbiosis between Berenger and Baldwin than what happens between either of them and Stone: two men who dated several of the same women, one impotent, the other stricken with satyriasis, each aware of the other's deepest secrets, including murder, who continue to compete for the same women out of some inexplicable bond of antipathy, instead of one having the other arrested.

This can't be what anybody intended, but *Sliver* is the kind of movie where you don't have to worry about intentions. By consulting the source material, you can see that the original story was shaved into garnish for a soft-porn vehicle with Sharon Stone and William Baldwin, that around script conference five or six it was decided to drop in a third character to complicate things, and so on.

As one of the summer's most expensive movies, *Sliver* has generated the usual across-the-spectrum prepublicity; you might have escaped the profiles of William Baldwin, but Sharon Stone has been everywhere—Letterman, Larry King, the covers of a half dozen magazines, a blitz that has a negative effect on her performance in *Sliver*, actually. Stone's brassy, good-humored, outspoken persona has been so much displayed in the media that her portrayal of a vulnerable, sexually shy woman who gasps and winces as Billy Baldwin first touches her seems totally mannered and unreal. On the other hand, the much-publicized loathing between Baldwin and Stone is perfectly reflected in the protracted lovemaking scenes, especially one in which Baldwin, taking Stone from behind, appears to be smacking her head against a functionless postmodern pillar in his apartment.

William Baldwin plays Zeke as a winsome adolescent pretending to be an adult. He has a dewy grin that takes up all of his face, making his eyes into slits and his cheeks into round little knobs. His chest hair has been strangely sculpted to make him appear less hirsute than his brother Alec, or than Andy Garcia. His beauty is that of a boldly colored reptile. His voice is watery. He has almost nothing to do in this film except sit, stand, and walk; come to think of it, a surprising amount of this "thriller" is static, passive, and scopophiliac in the most tedious, Warholian sense.

Sliver comes alive, as I suppose it was meant to, whenever it cuts from the lugubrious "action" to the surveillance system in Baldwin's control room. Here, ranged beside one huge central screen, are dozens of smaller ones staring into dozens of people's lives: people talking to themselves in bathroom mirrors, people diddling their children, people fucking, people whipping their mates, people who need people just being themselves. The buzz and confusion of multiple sound and image tracks is energizing, and when Stone crops up, spied on by Baldwin, on the big center monitor, she looks like a star acting in a much better movie than this one.

One of the lesser mysteries of *Sliver*. If the video system cost $6 million, why couldn't Zeke get one in color instead of black and white?

Also reviewed in:
NEW YORK TIMES, 5/22/93, p. 11, Janet Maslin
VARIETY, 5/24/93, p. 44, Brian Lowry
WASHINGTON POST, 5/22/93, p. B2, Rita Kempley

SNAPPER, THE

A Miramax Films release of a BBC Films production.   *Executive Producer:* Mark Shivas.
Producer: Lynda Myles.   *Director:* Stephen Frears.   *Screenplay (based on his novel):* Roddy
Doyle.   *Director of Photography:* Oliver Stapleton.   *Editor:* Mick Audsley.   *Sound:* Kieran
Horgan.   *Casting:* Leo Davis.   *Production Designer:* Mark Geraghty.   *Costumes:* Consolata
Boyle.   *Make-up:* Morna Ferguson and Jennifer Hegarty.   *Running time:* 90 minutes.   *MPAA
Rating:* R.

CAST: Tina Kellegher (Sharon Curley);   Colm Meaney (Dessie Curley);   Ruth McCabe (Kay
Curley);   Eanna MacLiam (Craig Curley);   Peter Rowen (Sonny Curley);   Joanne Gerrard (Lisa
Curley);   Colm O'Byrne (Darren Curley);   Fionnuala Murphy (Jacky);   Deirdre O'Brien
(Mary);   Karen Woodley (Yvonne);   Pat Laffan (George Burgess);   Virginia Cole (Doris
Burgess);   Denis Menton (Pat Burgess);   Brendan Gleeson (Lester);   Ronan Wilmot (Paddy);
Stuart Dunne (Bertie);   Dylan Tighe (Boy);   Caroline Boyle (Girl);   Jennifer Kelly (Checkout
Woman);   Audrey Corr (Customer/Neighbour);   Stanley Townsend (Anaesthetist);   Cathy
Belton (Desk Nurse);   Miriam Kelly (Doctor);   Eleanor Methven (Doctor Cook);   Birdy
Sweeney (Loner);   Barbara Bergin and Billie Morton (Midwives);   Joan Sheehy (Woman in
Hospital);   Rynagh O'Grady (Neighbour);   Cathleen Delaney (Oul'one);   Ailish Connolly
(Nurse);   Jack Lynch (Policeman);   Stephen Kennedy (Supermarket Trainee Manager);   Britta
Smith (Woman in Police Station);   Conor Evans, Helen Roach, Marie Connee, and Jimmy Keogh
(Barrytown Neighbors);   Aisling Conlan and Alannagh McMullen (Baby Curley);   Tom Murphy
and Robbie Doolan (Pals);   Matthew Devereux (Young Lad/Dad);   Famine (Sandy).

FILMS IN REVIEW, 5-6/94, p. 59, Eva H. Kissin

Illegitimate children, or "snappers" as they are called in Ireland, have been a social plague for
a long time. According to Victorian novels, they are the product of a single immoral sexual
encounter, and in Shakespeare's plays, many illegitimate sons keep the plot going with their desire
to revenge their own unfortunate births. In fact, the very word, bastard, has become a pejorative
in the language.

In *The Snapper*, a contemporary Irish comedy, Sharon, the daughter of a working class family,
has gotten herself pregnant, or "up the pole" according to the local slang, and now must live with
the results.

Sharon is a proud, gutsy young woman of twenty who wants to have her baby and defend
herself against the neighborhood gossip. In fact, she means to keep the name of her aged married
seducer secret but he can't resist boasting about his conquest. "A good little lay," he murmurs
just loud enough to be heard. Once the community is aware of who the father is, pitiless tongues
begin to wag. "She won't be able to get into those jeans now," the older women crow.

Dessie, Sharon's father, is surprisingly less shocked by the sex than by the result. "You should
have come to us before, Sharon," he says, not quite aware of his implicit humor.

Dessie has to deal with Sharon's problem at the pub where his drinking buddies savor the
situation. Here, between their beers and smirks, he feels called upon to defend his daughter's
honor physically. Bruised and hurt, when he can no longer go to the pub, he stays home and
begins to read. A contemporary book on female sexuality speeds him into the twentieth century.
In addition to broadening his mind, the new book makes him sexually experimental at home.
"Where did you learn that, Dessie?" inquires his wife after twenty five years of marriage.

Dessie's personal growth could be symbolic of Ireland's changing attitudes. In a country where
divorce and abortion remain illegal, Sharon and her free wheeling friends are no longer the naive
little convent bred girls of the past. Sharon's condition, and her own and her family's attempt to
deal with it, represent the deeper problems of change within this once rigid society. Even James
Joyce, wandering around Dublin eighty years post hoc, might be surprised at the local scene.

Director Stephen Frears has handled a serious subject with humorous overtones. One scene, in
which Dessie is happily sucking his beer and belching, is a grand parallel to the new baby
engaged in the same activity.

Colm Meaney's exuberant Dessie is a feisty counterpart to Sharon, expertly played by Tina Kellegher. In her understated way, she projects the conflicts of bitterness and pride implicit in a young woman who is opting for a decent life in a changing Ireland.

LOS ANGELES TIMES, 12/3/93, Calendar/p. 1, Kenneth Turan

"The Snapper" is amiability itself. Good-humored and sassy, it is one of those charmingly off-the-cuff films that doesn't let its small scale stand in the way of pleasure. And, filled with the characteristic bawdy and biting wit of Ireland, it takes a satisfaction in the music of spoken language that is as engaging as it is rare.

That language comes courtesy of Irish writer Roddy Doyle. His first book about Barrytown, a working-class Dublin suburb, was the source for Alan Parker's "The Commitments" and his latest, "Paddy Clark, Ha, Ha, Ha," just won the Booker Prize, Britain's premier literary award.

In between, Doyle wrote "The Snapper," its title taken from Irish slang for the baby its comic, chaotic story revolves around. The same crisis-a-minute family, where no one so much as thinks of holding their tongue, returns from the earlier film, though with their name changed from Rabbitte to Curley for contractual reasons. But the spirit this time is more natural and less grandiose than in "The Commitments" and for that credit Stephen Frears.

One of the most versatile of British directors, with work ranging from "My Beautiful Laundrette" to "Dangerous Liaisons" and "The Grifters," Frears knows how to make comedy funny without shortchanging the often painful emotions underneath. And it is that realistic balance between humor and distress that makes "The Snapper" so vital and appealing.

Certainly nothing seems initially comic about the predicament of eldest daughter Sharon Curly (Tina Kellegher). Just 20 years old, she informs father Dessie (Colm Meaney) and mother Kay (Ruth McCabe) that she is pregnant. Not only that, she's not telling who the father is.

Nonplussed at first, Dessie's strongest response to the news is his usual all-purpose "a man needs a pint after that." And the local pub is in fact where Sharon heads as well, gossiping with her lovelorn pals and refusing to reveal anything more about the unknown father than "it wasn't Bart Simpson."

In as small an enclave as Barrytown, however, where your neighbors know your business before you do and no one is spared the lash of ironic wit the question of "who Sharon's having it for" becomes one of ever-increasing fascination. And when hints of a suspect emerge (it isn't Bart Simpson) it plunges the neighborhood into a comic/horrific tizzy that has everyone talking.

At the center of that verbal firestorm is not only Sharon, but her loving if perplexed father, Dessie, both of whom find the crisis changing them in ways no one could have expected. And though the film's success wouldn't be possible without the vigorous performance it gets from Kellegher, it is Colm Meaney's exasperated but resilient Dessie that makes the strongest impact.

Meaney, who had the advantage of playing the same character in "The Commitments," is human, vulnerable and triumphant as the father of six, a knight in rusty armor whose family is forever threatening to get the best of him. With a mobile face, a command of the language and a fine repertory of puzzled looks, the Dessie who worries "I'm only the dad, they'll laugh at me" is a cinematic parent to marvel at and enjoy.

It is characteristic of the way "The Snapper" (rated R for "language and some sexuality") thrives on the interplay of fine writing and empathetic acting that some of its most memorable moments are in small family scenes that don't advance the plot at all. For we are so caught up in these characters and their lives, nothing they do fails to interest us.

And the feeling "The Snapper" has of just appearing on screen without outside assistance is an indication of what an expertly self-effacing job of directing Stephen Frears has done. Like Alan Parker and Neal Jordan before him, he has refreshed himself in local waters after being parched in Hollywood, and this fiercely alive film is the welcome result.

NEW YORK POST, 11/24/93, p. 34, Thelma Adams

"The Snapper" does not refer to an elastic fetishist; it Irish slang for a baby. In this offbeat Irish cheaper-by-the-half-dozen, Sharon Curley (Tina Kellegher) has a surprise. She's pregnant, unmarried, and she's keeping the father a secret.

The 20-year-old's condition shakes up her family and stirs up mischief in Dublin's Barrytown. Like "The Commitments," Alan Parker's sleeper, "The Snapper," is based on Irish author Roddy Doyle's Barrytown trilogy.

"The Commitments" was about Dubliners infatuated with American soul music. It offered great tunes and a knock-out performance by an Irish Joe Cocker.

"The Snapper" has less music and more soul. Where "The Commitments" veered into fantasyland, Director Stephen ("My Beautiful Laundrette," "The Grifters") Frears sticks closer to the cracked sidewalks of Barrytown.

Doyle, who wrote the script, has a terrific sense of humor which he generously shares with his characters. One thing the two movies share is Colm Meaney as Dessie, the father of the clan.

Meaney, best known in America as O'Brien on "Star Trek: Deep Space 9," is brilliant, a Da for all seasons (or trimester). Dessie overcomes his initial shock and takes the news of his daughter's pregnancy with good humor and a pint at the pub. But when he hears that the mystery father might be a man as old as he is, a local dad with a daughter Sharon's age, Dessie loses his equanimity.

Eldest daughter Sharon gamely tries to keep things together. She's a good-natured, good-time-girl who works in a grocery. She might be "up-the-pole," but she's no slut.

Kellegher delivers a natural and tart performance as Sharon. At nights, she's a ragged-toothed, big-haired beauty, a pub party doll. During the day, pale and splotchy in pregnancy, she projects a homespun strength, doing the dishes and navigating the family channels.

Sharon demonstrates she's an adult by taking responsibility for her actions and holding firmly to her decision. Her strength and courage becomes something the rest of the family can rally around. Dessie rises to the occasion and enthusiastically enters the role of surrogate father.

Through his research into pregnant women, Dessie learns new things about women that have a side benefit for his wife Kay (Ruth McCabe). Dessie becomes a New Man, Sharon grows into womanhood, and the family knits even closer together.

Movies about strong, evolving father-daughter relationships are rare, and few stories have been told with as much straightforward simplicity, wit and heart as "The Snapper."

NEWSDAY, 11/24/93, Part II/p. 63, Jack Mathews

We are besieged these days with so many stories of dysfunctional families—"Husbands Who Rape Their wives," "Wives Who Mutilate Their Husbands," "Parents Who Lock Their Children in Attics," "Children Who Divorce Their Parents"—it seems almost perverse to make a movie about a family that actually works.

So beware Stephen Frears', "The Snapper," a warm and often hilarious slice of life that could have you feeling good about "Families Who Stick Together Through Thick and Thin."

"The Snapper," a huge audience hit at the Cannes and New York film festivals, is adapted from the second book in Roddy Doyle's delightful Barrytown trilogy, the literary equivalent of a situation comedy. The first book, "The Commitments," was adapted three years ago, brilliantly, by Frears' compatriot Alan Parker.

But where Parker used a subplot to pursue his own interests—the musical culture of Dublin's youth—Frears sticks to the book, to the family, and to its central story of a father trying to come to grips with his unmarried daughter's pregnancy.

Colm Meaney, an Irish actor perhaps best known to Americans for his continuing role as O'Brien in the TV series "Deep Space Nine," gives one of the year's most winning performances as Dessie Curley, a plasterer and blue collar bon vivant whose free time is devoted in about equal shares to his wife and six kids, and to his drinking pals at the neighborhood Cedar Lounge.

When the Curleys' oldest daughter, 20-year-old Sharon (Tess Kellegher), announces that she is pregnant, but won't reveal the name of the child's father, the Curleys and most of their neighbors in this bleak suburb of look-alike row houses, are consumed by the mystery and the scandal.

"The Snapper," like the Barrytown Trilogy itself, gets its strength from the love that binds the family. Dublin-born Doyle, who adapted his first two books and is now at work on the third, knows his subject intimately, and though "The Snapper" (it's short for "whippersnapper") works fine as simple domestic comedy, it also has reams to say about life in the working-class ghetto of economically depressed Dublin.

Life is close here. Not only are the neighbors a wall away on either side, but their social lives whirl around in the same tight community. The Cedar Lounge is not just a pub for heavy lifters, it's the neighborhood recreation center, where a dad quaffs pints with his pals two tables away from his daughter and hers.

We're catching the Curleys at a crucial moment. Though the oldest son is returning from military duty abroad, none of the children have formally left home, and Sharon's pregnancy is threatening to break a routine that is 20 years in the running. Still, there is no question, from the opening scene of Sharon's plaster-cracking announcement that the family will survive the fallout. For Dessie, the world may seem to have spun off its axis since he was her age, and if the father of his first grandchild turns out to be what everyone thinks it is, he faces profound humiliation.

But where the family is at stake, Dessie's will is unwavering. The surprises come in the changes he goes through in the process, the shocking and productive things he learns about women and himself, and how strongly we end up rooting for the entire Curley clan.

Frears, coming off of a $40 million Hollywood movie ("Hero"), made "The Snapper" for the BBC for less than $2 million. It was shot, like his earlier "My Beautiful Laundrette," on 16-mm. film and was not intended to be shown on the big screen. Despite its having been shown on British television in exactly this form, "The Snapper" got an R rating from American censors concerned with its profanity and with a flashback to Sharon's indiscretion. A bigger problem for most of us is the amount of unfamiliar dialect and idioms employed.

When Sharon is referred to for the fourth or fifth time as being "up the pole," we get the idea. But there are other phrases that remain mysteries long after the name of the father has been revealed.

NEWSWEEK, 12/27/93, p.48, David Ansen

Not every movie this Christmas will leave you in a puddle of tears or an existential funk. Here's one you can exit beaming. It's about a 20-year-old Irish working-class girl who announces to her parents she's pregnant—and refuses to say who's the da. Once upon a time this would have been the stuff of turgid melodrama (anybody remember "Blue Denim"?). The beauty of Stephen Frears's modest but richly stocked movie is that it finds an unexpected lode of comedy in Sharon Curley's uncomfortable predicament—and not one laugh is cheap.

Frears has a marvelous script by the Irish novelist Roddy Doyle. "The Snapper" is adapted from the second novel in Doyle's Barrytown trilogy—the first of which was "The Commitments," the basis of Alan Parker's movie. Colm Meaney, who played the Elvis-obsessed father in that one, is Dessie, the father of "The Snapper's" Curley family, a crowded, noisy brood of six in-your-face children. Frears's choreography of the chaotic Curley household is masterly funny: slapstick realism so effortlessly staged you can't tell the difference between a gag and real life. Mom is played with wise, droll fatigue by Ruth McCabe.

The heart of the tale is in the pub-loving Dessie's relationship with the expectant Sharon (Tina Kellegher), a girl who likes a pint or two herself. A little too much of the sauce got her into trouble in the first place—a one-time drunken encounter with a man who happens to be the father of one of her best friends. How Sharon, her family, her friends and, most of all, her dad, come to terms with the crisis is worked out in lovely details that owe nothing to sitcom formula. This is a fresh view of '90s Roman Catholic Ireland—no talk of sin, and not a priest in view. In an excellent cast, Meaney is a particular delight. Not wanting to lose his daughter, this meat-and-potatoes guy attempts, with baffled eagerness, to turn himself into a sensitive New Man, reading up on childbirth, begging to be at the birth, to make up for all the times he'd missed his own kids' arrivals while hoisting a few at the pub. After so many movies about fathers and sons, it's refreshing to see dads and daughters get their due. As warm and lived-in as an old pair of boots, "The Snapper" is an honorable feel-good movie.

SIGHT AND SOUND, 6/93, p., 65, Ben Thompson

Sharon Curley, a 20-year-old check-out girl, lives with her father Dessie, mother Kay, and four younger brothers and sisters in a small house in Dublin's Northside (elder brother Craig is away on UN peacekeeping duty). Sharon is pregnant; her parents get over their initial shock quickly and react well to the news, though they are upset by her refusal to reveal the identity of the father.

Sharon's desire for secrecy is understandable: the baby is the result of a drunken liaison in a pub car park with resolutely unappealing middle-aged neighbor George Burgess, the laughing stock of the street and the father of Yvonne, one of Sharon's best friends. Sharon is not unhappy to be pregnant, however. Her friends are amused, and all proceeds smoothly until George starts bragging about his exploits to his cronies at the football club. Sharon threatens him with exposure to his wife, and Dessie threatens him with violence, but the secret is out.

Worse still, George has decided that he loves Sharon, and leaves home. Mrs Burgess storms round to the Curleys' house making accusations, and Kay slaps her. Sharon scorns George's protestations of love, and tries to salvage the situation by claiming that her impregnation was the work of a Spanish sailor, but no one believes her. Craig, returned from overseas, takes it upon himself to break the Burgesses' window, and is arrested. Dessie too is angry and humiliated, and gets into a fight—supposedly defending Sharon's honour, but really defending his own.

Only when Sharon threatens to leave home does he see the error of his ways. Dessie starts to take an active interest in the pregnancy, reading up on the female physiognomy; his new-found knowledge launches him and Kay on a voyage of sexual discovery. After the odd false alarm, Sharon is rushed to hospital in Dessie's van. The birth is painful but the baby is healthy, and Sharon decides to call her Georgina. The whole Curley clan arrives at the hospital, complete with their dog Famine, and Georgina is received into the family.

Stephen Frears' return from Hollywood to the medium that made his name could hardly have been more auspicious. In fact, this wholly successful dramatisation of the second part of Roddy Doyle's vibrant Barrytown trilogy made for an incongruously triumphant climax to a Screen 2 season which consistently confused quality with 'quality'. Doyle's deliciously ripe dialogue and the endeavours of an immaculate ensemble cast threw the preciousness and mundanity of so many previous weeks' films into cruelly sharp relief.

The Snapper would doubtless have been filmed even if *The Commitments* had not made a big-screen splash to whet commissioning appetites; but the success of Alan Parker's all-singing, all-dancing version of the first instalment of Doyle's triptych did have an impact on Frears' film. The makers of *The Commitments*, hoping for a sequel, retain the rights to the Rabbitte family name and the character of Jimmy Jnr. Doyle, adapting his own book to the screen, is therefore in the happy position of adding characters and changing names to accommodate the success of his last self-adaptation: the comically chauvinistic Craig substitutes ably for the suave Jimmy Jnr, and the dog Larrygogan is now Famine.

Despite these changes, and the rather laboured extension of the book's concluding birth scenes, it is *The Snapper* that is the truer of the two films to its literary blueprint. This comes as no real surprise, BBC grit at its best being traditionally grittier than the Hollywood variety. But Doyle's screenplay and Frears' direction pull off a notable coup in capturing the warmth and vitality of their source material without ever lapsing into *The Commitments'* rather self-congratulatory, glitzed-up Irishry. Frears' assertion that he "went to Ireland, met Irish people and tried to understand them" and ended up "loving them all" had raised alarm bells.

One of the main problems with today's TV drama is that it doesn't have enough swearing in it. Doyle's "bad" language—the musical "feck"s and "bollix"s which score his characters' every move—is transparently good language, and credit is due to whoever decided it shouldn't be toned down. The actors raise their game to match the stellar quality of the dialogue. Tina Kellegher's central performance is commendably still and strong. Sometimes—for example when she's drunk in a club being sick into her handbag ("It'll hold!")—the part veers towards proletarian-gothic, but she always keeps a tight hold on Sharon's dignity. Colm Meaney (who also played Dessie in *The Commitments*) blossoms to fill the space she leaves, his charming volubility combining beautifully with the eloquent quietness of Ruth McCabe's Kay. Much credit is due to Pat Laffan too, for making the tragically menopausal George Burgess so memorably repugnant without ever undermining his humanity. His line "We are, as the old saying goes, 'Torn between two lovers'" is one that scores itself onto the memory.

Frears' direction makes no claims to auteurship and is all the better for that; rather, there's a single-minded concentration on establishing the right environment for the dialogue to do its work. This means bright colours as well as rainy drabness. The smallness of the Curleys' house is integral to their chaotic sense of community—the constant distractions of warring family members furnish vital perspective as well as extra stress in moments of crisis—but Frears does well not to overplay the closeness of their domestic environment. The camera does not, as sometimes in *Brookside*, for example, seem like one presence too many in a cardboard box full of sound men. Even when the whole Curley clan are crammed into their front room watching the telly, there's still room for the characters to breathe.

It might not seem like a compliment to say that *The Snapper* fits neatly into the box in the corner, but it should do. There's no shame in doing great work for TV, and more people get to see it that way. While recent British cinema productions like *Splitting Heirs* and *Leon the Pig Farmer* look as if they would have been happier made for the small screen, *The Snapper* fully deserves the accolade of opening the Directors Fortnight at Cannes.

TIME, 12/6/93, p. 89, Richard Schickel

We all make mistakes, but Sharon Curley's (Tina Kellegher) is a beaut. It's not just that in a careless, definitely not rapturous, moment she manages to get knocked up. It's that the man who bent her back over the hood of a car outside a pub one drunken night is old enough to be her father. Is, indeed, a friend of her father's. Is, in fact, George Burgess (Pat Laffan), who lives across the street and coaches the football team of one of her younger brothers. Is, incurably, an "ejit" (idiot in Dublin slang), the kind of old fool who mutters "A1" after having his way with Sharon and then boasts around the pub about what a good "ride" she is.

This, you ask, is the stuff of comedy? No, not exactly. It is the pretext for comedy—wonderful comedy, maybe the best of the year. For *The Snapper* (the word is local dialect for a baby) isn't really about making mistakes. It's about how, as Sharon comes to term, the Curley family all come to terms with what she's done, with themselves and with the little gossiping corner of the world they inhabit.

You may have met the Curleys before. Under another name they are the central figures of novelist Roddy Doyle's Barrytown trilogy about working-class Irish folk, from which Doyle also adapted *The Commitments* for the screen. He's a writer who likes to pack lots of lively characters, talk and unpremeditated activity into relatively tight spaces, thereby creating the kind of lifelike untidiness, fractiousness and believable goofiness that American movie comedy, with its stress on easily summarizable concepts and subteen gag writing, can only dream about.

The Curleys, for example, are a family of eight, all crammed into a tiny house. Here there's no room for anything but straight shooting, whether the subject is sex, using the bathroom or what's playing on the telly. The mother, Kay (Ruth McCabe), is patient, taciturn and sweet. When the question of contraception arises, she recalls the best she ever knew: the gift of a coat from her husband Dessie (Colm Meaney), which prevented him from taking her out in the fields where it might get dirty.

The father is more volatile. When Sharon claims she can't remember her seducer's name because she was drunk, he snaps, "I was drunk when I met your mother, and I remember her name." But he's essentially a tolerant, loving man, and it's the growth of his consciousness that provides the movie's connective tissue. At first acceptant of Sharon's news, he angers when he discovers who the father is. But when Sharon tries to provide a saving lie—he was really a sailor off a Spanish ship—it doesn't sit well with him. In the end, he knows he can live happily only with the truth. He buys a book about sex and pregnancy (from which he learns a few techniques himself), and when it's time to drive Sharon to the hospital, he bawls the old *Rawhide* theme song, "Rollin', rollin', rollin'."

Meaney's performance takes the character from traditional maleness to New Man-ishness in a wry, naturalistic, utterly convincing way. But then, all the acting in Stephen Frears' film is of that caliber. The director is at his best when jumbling moods and mixing motives, yet keeping everything straight and true. He neither patronizes nor celebrates these lives. He just makes them real. And in the process makes us their loving, laughing, admiring intimates.

VILLAGE VOICE, 11/30/93, Film Special/p. 30, Manohla Dargis

In 10 strange years, Stephen Frears has gone from English auteur to Hollywood hire—from *My Beautiful Launderette* to last year's *Hero*—with decidedly mixed results. Now with *The Snapper*,

Frears is back, in a cinematic resurrection that's modest, rough-hewn, and, at least for these domestic eyes, so uncharacteristic as to make the director virtually unrecognizable.

The story of the tight and clamorous Curley clan and how some of them grew, *The Snapper* was adapted by novelist Roddy Doyle from his book of the same name. Doyle, who also penned *The Commitments*, novel and movie both, has apparently remained faithful to his original material, cramming as many words into his near logorrheic screenplay as are performably possible to speak, much less hear. The film begins like a hundred-meter dash, with Frears rushing through the visual and aural Curley din—*you're dead, piss off, don't tell me what to do*—to narrow his sights on the sullen charms of 20-year-old Sharon (Tina Kellegher), the family's eldest and newly expectant daughter.

FATHER: "You're pregnant. Positive now? You're only 19."
DAUGHTER: "I'm 20."
FATHER: "A man needs a pint after all that."

A comic melodrama of family, virtue, and the importance of drink, *The Snapper* is fundamentally a father-daughter romance without an Electra complex. When Dessie (Colm Meaney) first learns his girl is "up the pole," he resists, retreats, and rejects. In turn, Sharon's mother, Kay (the wonderful Ruth McCabe), shrugs her shoulders when Sharon refuses to name the inseminator ("I don't mind being pregnant, but I do mind people knowing who made me pregnant") and downs enough booze to get busted by Maternity Watch. (Sharon's mates encourage her to get pissed if she can't get even.)

Light years from the portentously slick *Hero*, *The Snapper* is humble with a vengeance. The downsizing works for the most part, though the grainy photography can look distressingly muddy, even grim, as if Frears were trying to answer Hollywood gloss with a blizzard of raggedy light particles. Make no mistake, however, this is professionalism cut loose, an esprit made vivid each and every time Frears maneuvers his camera through the bric-a-brac and cuts to a close-up with love, not glamour.

A friend says *The Snapper* is very much of a piece with Frears's 21 BBC telefilms, but those who know only his movie features are in for a surprise. Since Frears is at his best crowding bodies into the frame and making those bodies sing, it's in those moments that his past seems obvious. When Sharon and her friends hurl into alcoholic abandon, or the mister and missus snuggle under the sheets, *Snapper* conjures up the director's wonderful work with Hanif Kureishi. Yet unlike the Frears-Kureishi conspiracies (*Launderette, Sammy and Rosie Get Laid*), this film's politics are personal and intimate, while the aesthetic couldn't be more different. There's little grandstanding, no sloganeering (it's homey not sexy)—the secular point of view conspicuous only by the Church's total eclipse.

Determined to keep the paternity a secret, Sharon plays a debased virgin-birth card—it was, she insists, "one of them Spanish sailors"—until the hilarious, pitiful truth gets out. Even so, while one father may have gone missing, another is there to take his place. In the end, as centrally as Sharon's shift from child to adult, "slut" to mother is played, it's Dessie's rebirth that gives the film its bite. In one early, priceless exchange, he confides to Sharon that the going gossip is she's "a great little ride." "Bit of a compliment, really," she replies, bravely cavalier. "But not about daughters," he thunders. Exactly.

Also reviewed in:
CHICAGO TRIBUNE, 12/17/93, Friday/p. B, Michael Wilmington
NEW YORK TIMES, 11/24/93, p. C14, Vincent Canby
VARIETY, 4/19/93, p. 46, Derek Elley
WASHINGTON POST, 12/17/93, p. C1, Hal Hinson
WASHINGTON POST, 12/17/93, Weekend/p. 56, Desson Howe

SNIPER

A TriStar Pictures release of a Baltimore Pictures production.   *Executive Producer:* Mark Johnson, Walon Green, and Patrick Wachsberger.   *Producer:* Robert L. Rosen, James Gorman, and Charles J.D. Schlissel.   *Director:* Luis Llosa.   *Screenplay:* Michael Frost Beckner and

Crash Leyland. *Director of Photography:* Bill Butler. *Editor:* Scott Smith. *Music:* Gary Chang. *Music Editor:* Richard Whitfield. *Sound:* Paul Brincat. *Sound Editor:* Barney Cabral. *Casting:* Louis Di Giaimo. *Production Designer:* Herbert Pinter. *Art Director:* Nicholas McCallum. *Set Decorator:* Leanne Cornish and Angus Tattle. *Special Effects:* Brian Cox, Brian Pearce, and David Hardie. *Costumes:* Ray Summers. *Special Effects Make-up:* Allan Apone. *Stunt Coordinator:* Glenn Ruehland. *Running time:* 98 minutes. *MPAA Rating:* R.

CAST: Tom Berenger (Thomas Beckett); Billy Zane (Richard Miller); J.T. Walsh (Chester Van Damme); Aden Young (Doug Papich); Ken Radley (El Cirujano); Dale Dye (Senior NSC Officer); Richard Lineback (Junior NSC Officer); Frederick Miragliotta (Alvarez); Vanessa Steele (Mrs. Alvarez); Carlos Alvarez (Rual Ochoa); Tyler Copin (Ripoly); Teo Gebert (Ripoly's Friend); William Curtin (Mountain Top Pilot); Howard Bosse (Mountain Top Co-Pilot); Christos A. Linou (Mountain Top Sniper); Christopher Norsley (Corporal in Pool Hall); Donald Battee (Shaved Head Private); Raj Sidhu (Soldier in Barn); Reinaldo Arenas (Cacique); Mario Jurado (Dead Indian); Roy Edmonds (Cabrera); Collin Dragsbeck (Door Gunner); Johnny Raaen (Crew Chief); Patrick Moore (Co-Pilot); Loury Cortez (Father Ruiz); Tony Szeto (Boat Rebel).

LOS ANGELES TIMES, 1/29/93, Calendar/p. 6, Michael Wilmington

A movie for people with time in waste, "Sniper" is about as compelling as a Soldier of Fortune magazine cover set to music.

Despite high talent before and behind the cameras, it's a shallow 90-minute rites-of-manhood saga, with Tom Berenger and Billy Zane playing a pair of Marine sniper-killers hired to eliminate a Colombian drug czar and a phony Panamanian political leader. The director, Luis Llosa, turns it into a long prowl through the jungle, interrupted by sporadic gunplay, helicopters, lots of shots taken through telescopic sights and stop-motion camera trickery that suggests we're following the flight path of individual bullets, or seeing them zoom right at us.

Llosa is the cousin of Peru's greatest novelist, Mario Vargas Llosa, but there's no hint of his famous relative's "magic realism" here, none of the elegant, playful literacy or many-leveled plots of books like "Aunt Julia and the Scriptwriter" or "The Green House." The filmmaking Llosa's background includes some low-budget Roger Corman military actioners and that's the method here: Get it on and get it done.

Every once in a while, Michael Frost Beckner and Crash Leyland's script suggests something interesting: the loneliness and boredom of the sniper's job, the political machinations around them, or the psychological cost of being a professional killer. But the themes aren't explored. They're skated over, or used as hooks.

Berenger and Zane are interesting actors and they make a vivid contrast: Berenger, with his stoical demeanor and Newmanesque good looks and Zane, who can always suggest something loose and wild underneath. But the script doesn't let them plumb the depths Berenger hit in "Platoon" or Zane in "Dead Calm." Its cynicism is superficial, macho sentimentality always an inch below.

"Sniper" (MPAA rated R for violence and language) is not a dumb movie. It doesn't seem to come straight from the Yahoo Academy, like the bulk of the '80s military thrillers; it's hip to the darker side of its story. But it's not really smart either. The movie's vision is affixed on that telescope sight, the distant target—and that turns it into a sort of video game, full of bloodless, stylizes carnage. Death never stings here. And, even if it does, there's always another helicopter.

NEW YORK POST, 1/29/93, p. 29, Jami Bernard

The influences of "Unforgiven" is at work, or maybe it's something in the air, but "Sniper" is the most recent movie to suggest that killers have feelings, too.

It's not easy to be a sniper in "Sniper." It's lonely work, staking out a particular target for days, sleeping with the leeches in stagnant ponds, wearing homemade camouflage that makes you look like a haystack. Tom Berenger is a top sniper, but he has found that being the best in his profession has its drawbacks—it's lonely at the top, since everyone else is dead.

Billy Zane is a hotshot bureaucrat from the front office who thinks a suitcase full of Banana Republic gear will make him a good partner for Berenger in the South American jungles on a top secret assignment—so top-secret it is futile to figure out just who they are meant to kill or why. Zane has never actually killed a man before, and as in "Unforgiven," it's harder than it looks.

Berenger grudgingly takes Zane under his wing, because each secretly admires the other—Berenger is experienced, Zane is enthusiastic, and you can't be both at once in this sorry sniper business. "Sitting in an office giving other men orders to kill is the same as putting a bullet in a man's heart," says Berenger, who has occasional moments of poetry despite the loneliness of the long-distance trigger-puller.

Two men, two incredibly complicated-looking guns that must weigh a ton—"Sniper" has all the makings of an inane, noisy movie. But "Sniper" got me in its cross hairs, as it would say, and perhaps because the body count was not numbing after all, the movie's excitement mounts and provides a morbidly engaging couple of hours. Plus that point-of-view bullet right into someone's eye through his view-finder doesn't hurt any. (The victim, perhaps, but not the movie.)

It's not Schwarzenegger vs. a thing from outer space, as in "Predator," even though the locations look the same. These men have bad dreams. You kill a man, you carry his tortured soul in your nightmares, says the movie.

There is the usual homosexual subtext that you can read into these buddy movies—"I felt the rush when I had you in my cross hairs," announces Zane breathlessly to Berenger, after which he doesn't know whether to kill him or adopt him.

Peruvian director Luis Llosa is a former film critic; he put his money where his mouth was and made a movie he can give a good review to without incurring any nightmares of his own.

NEWSDAY, 1/29/93, Part II/p. 67, Jack Mathews

Remember that slick shot in "Robin Hood" where the camera seems to have been mounted on a flying arrow and rides it head on into the trunk of a tree? We get that same missile's-eye view of a bullet finding its mark in Luis Llosa's "Sniper."

Not once, but several times. Bang! Whoosh! Splat! Right into the bones, meat and sinew of their human targets.

No sense pondering the ludicrousness of these scenes, where on occasion the victims actually seem to catch sight of the bullet screaming toward them, time enough for a brief shudder of recognition before impact. As silly as everything else is in this jungle-buddy movie about a pair of Marine sharpshooters on an assassination assignment in Panama, riding the bullet almost make sense,

It makes at least as much sense as the idea that the National Security Council, trying to prevent a hostile Panamanian general from becoming president, would send some desk-bound dweeb like Richard Miller (Billy Zane) into the jungle as a spotter for super-sniper Tom Beckett (Tom Berenger) simply because he'd won a silver medal shooting in the Olympics.

As badly written as this story is, it's amazing first-time screenwriters Michael Frost Beckner and (so say the credits) Crash Leyland didn't think to schedule an Olympic rematch between Miller and whoever it was—could have been a Panamanian red—who beat him out of the gold.

Instead, "Sniper" is a traditional buddy action movie, "Lethal Weapon" relocated to the jungle with a pair of unlikely partners—one a proficient, suicidally fearless killer, the other a greenhorn—having to bond under pressure.

Zane, so menacing as the psycho in Phillip Noyce's "Dead Calm," is comically bad here, trying to make plausible a character who wouldn't have been trusted by the Pentagon to go out for coffee. You haven't seen anyone more uncomfortable in the jungle since Kathleen Turner broke a heel in "Romancing the Stone."

Yes, Miller will get his footing eventually, and become of some use to his partner, but it's as painful to watch as to go through.

Berenger, on the other hand, seems to have found his movie niche, playing borderline psychotics in the jungle ("Platoon," "At Play in the Field of the Lords"). He's an actor of severely limited emotional range, but his brooding manner and imposing physical presence gain strength from the material air of the rain forest (actually, the film was shot in Australia).

Llosa, a Peruvian director on his first Hollywood assignment, has a nice feel for shooting action scenes in tight quarters. We follow a good deal of the story through the telescopic viewfinders on the snipers' rifles, and that tends to compress time and space, and heighten the tension.

But these are modest refinements to a tired formula, and not even a couple of joy rides aboard speeding bullets makes this a jungle adventure worth booking.

SIGHT AND SOUND, 4/93, p. 58, Paul Tarrago

Panama, post Noriega. Fearful of interference by rebel forces in the upcoming democratic elections, Washington government agencies set in motion a covert operation to assassinate their leader, General Alvarez. Ambitious young bureaucrat Richard Miller is sent to partner master marine sniper Tom Beckett. The mission is simple on paper: one shot, then out. But Miller—with no combat experience and a by-the-book manner—is unprepared for the grisly realities of a tidily contracted death.

Veteran of 78 kills, Beckett is a tormented man whose legendary success has cast him as ever more the outsider. Viewed with superstitious mistrust by the regular marines, his only show of affection is for the dog tags of dead former partners that he carries around with him and fingers absentmindedly like worry beads. Reaction to Miller is one of instant antipathy and mutual disrespect, their foray into the jungle a cagey exchange of cocky greenhorn with a taciturn man-who's-seen-it-all. Within Beckett's realm, Miller's political authority falls by the wayside and he's coerced into helping a local guerrilla troupe in exchange for their help through unknown terrain. Unable to pull the trigger on a man he has in his sights, Miller earns everyone's scorn and is further harangued as they continue towards their target.

Though heavily protected by bodyguards the assassination is successful, but on their retreat Miller flips out—a combination of having killed for the first time and Beckett's claim that the mission isn't over yet. They start to fight but are soon interrupted by the appearance of enemy troops who capture Beckett as Miller heads towards the approaching rescue helicopter.

Tortured to the point of unconsciousness by the infamous El Cirujano (Miller's 'missed' target in the guerilla debacle), Miller reappears and saves his partner. Dragging Beckett to the new pick-up point, Miller is unaware that one of Alvarez's men is tailing him; as he moves in for the kill Beckett spots him and guns him down. The score even, the two snipers clamber into the helicopter and by back to their respective 'real' lives.

Sniper—not *The Sniper* nor *Snipers*, non-specific and singular, like *Predator*. It's a title that speaks of function as identity, an efficient menace. Distant, with maybe a touch of idolatry. Who's going to be drawn to a film called *Sniper*, except perhaps gun freaks? It sounds too detached to be an all-out action film, conjuring up phrases like "surgical strikes"—snipers don't touch, they reach out and tamper with history.

This is a war film shrunk down to the barest essentials—in this two-man unit, the all-male camaraderie is reduced to one-on-one exchanges. Difference—age, education, aspiration—is strictly between the two; common ground is the film's target, the closure it moves towards. Miller and Beckett's exchanges are repeatedly phrased as conflict, but on screen it all looks very different. Both film-star beautiful, their contrasting expert/beginner statuses cast them as father and son, this mission a rite of passage. The moral horror of killing is the script's intended address, Beckett admitting to a loathing for his profession, but what the audience sees is gunplay spectacle and emoting, through which the boy becomes a man. On that count, *Sniper* is not the psychologically insightful thriller its writers want it to tie, a shortfall that formulaic dialogue and characterisation do nothing to obscure. But director Llosa (incidentally Mario Vargas Llosa's cousin) is a fine action director, and it's when Berenger and Zane aren't obliged to breathe life into weak lines that the film erupts into its own with a series of tensely drawn combat sequences. Brian Pearson's special effects sniper footage—of rifle sight p.o.v. and tracking the trajectory of s-l-o-w-e-d down speeding bullets—doesn't necessarily get you any closer to the sniper's psyche, but does have a rollercoaster thrill to it (and a future home in 1001 students' essays on the cinematic gaze).

Concentration on the 'personal' aspects of war, though, is at the expense of any consideration of American interventionist policies, Alvarez's badness taken as reason enough. This naive world-view permeates into *Sniper*'s vision of back home—Miller's fiancee waiting, Beckett's impossible dream of retiring with a fish farm: fighting for the American way. Just old-fashioned, perhaps, but embodying a reactionary politic that hedges the 'right' of anyone to kill for country in the first place—a fundamental concern, surely, for Miller as he moves from armchair patriot to active participant. It's these major oversights that keep *Sniper* within the realms of the pedestrian, unsatisfying with occasional glimmers of a lean action film bubbling up underneath. Berenger and Zane, as alone in this script as they are in the jungle, do what they can with the cliches, sniper *père* even coming across as fairly sympathetic. But this is no journey into the heart of darkness, more an undercover ramble with Uncle Sam.

VILLAGE VOICE, 2/16/93, p. 60, Richard Gehr

Usually a responsible consumer of culture, I got sucked into this humorless action-buddies exercise by the TV commercial exploiting the film's single visual hook—the camera tracks a bullet from rifle to human target, over and over—even though I knew it had been lifted from *Robin Hood: Prince of Thieves*. Serves me right, I suppose, that *Sniper* is so predictable. (I also suspected that director Luis Llosa was related to writer Mario Vargas Llosa, and he is: he served as his cousin's campaign manager during Mario's failed run for the Peruvian presidency.)

Foggy, stylized anxiety wafts among the vines as a haunted marine sniper (Tom Berenger) and an inexperienced younger partner (Billy Zane) slither through the rain forest on their appointed task: Just another pair of white guys out to kill a couple of brown guys, in this case a rogue Peruvian general and his Colombian drug lord financier. Beckett has sniped too often, and has the flashbacks to show for it, while Miller has never killed—which you'd think would make him an odd choice for the assignment.

If the combination adventure/horror atmosphere seems vaguely familiar, it may have to do with Llosa's work as assistant to William Friedkin on *Sorcerer*. Being a tad ambitious, *Sniper* nearly jostles the genre by narrowing its scope (so to speak) from mass carnage to selective carnage. By the end of this almost nostalgic Reaganesque romp, our downbeat duo has met friendly Indians, shared a Rambo joke, done a lot of sharp shooting, and explored their outcast-sniper feelings in such dialogue as "After the rush is over, it hurts, doesn't it?"

Also reviewed in:
CHICAGO TRIBUNE, 1/29/93, Friday/p. I, Clifford Terry
NEW YORK TIMES, 1/29/93, p. C8, Vincent Canby
VARIETY, 1/25/93, p. 133, Richard Natale

SNOW WHITE AND THE SEVEN DWARFS

A Walt Disney Pictures re-release. *Producer:* Walt Disney. *Supervising Director:* David Hand. *Sequence Director:* Perce Pearce, Larry Morey, William Cottrell, Wilfred Jackson, and Ben Sharpsteen. *Adapted from:* Grimm's Fairy Tales. *Story Adaptation:* Ted Sears, Otto Englander, Earl Hurd, Dorothy Ann Blank, Richard Creedon, Dick Rickard, Merrill De Maris, and Webb Smith. *Supervising Animators:* Hamilton Luske, Vladimir Tytla, Fred Moore, and Norman Ferguson. *Music:* Frank Churchill, Leigh Harline, and Paul Smith. *Art Director:* Charles Philippi, Hugh Hennesy, Terrell Stapp, McLaren Stewart, Harold Miles, Tom Codrick, Gustaf Tenggren, Kenneth Anderson, Kendall O'Connor, and Hazel Sewell. *Running time:* 83 minutes. *MPAA Rating:* G.

VOICES: Adriana Caselotti (Snow White);   Harry Stockwell (Prince Charming);   Lucille LaVerne (The Queen);   Moroni Olsen (Magic Mirror);   Billy Gilbert (Sneezy);   Pinto Colvig (Sleepy and Grumpy);   Otis Harlin (Happy);   Scotty Mattraw (Bashful);   Roy Atwell (Doc).

[For additional reviews, see *Film Review Annual, 1988.*]

LOS ANGELES TIMES, 7/2/93, Calendar/p. 2, Charles Solomon

Even if "Snow White and the Seven Dwarfs" (made in 1937) had been the only animated feature Walt Disney made, his place in the history of animation and American film would be assured. Because of its exceptional quality—and its enduring box-office success—"Snow White" has influenced virtually every American cartoon feature, from Fleischer's "Gulliver's Travels" (1939) to the recent "Aladdin."

No other animated heroine has matched the dainty appeal of Snow White. Cinderella is a more fully realized character, Princess Aurora is more beautiful, Belle and Jasmine are more intelligent and assertive, but Snow White retains an innocent charm. Her Prince looks very stiff and stagey today—the hero of "Aladdin" is a more believable young man. But most viewers remember the film for the comic antics of the Dwarfs, whose merry warmth provides an effective counterpoint to the icy menace of the Wicked Queen and the terror of the Witch.

But the most delightful characters will cloy if the viewer doesn't believe in their plight, and "Snow White" remains a showcase for Disney's skill as a storyteller. Unlike the manipulative plots of so many recent features in which the characters argue, prove themselves and decide they like each other, "Snow White" touches genuine emotions. The one-note characters in the recent "Freddie as F.R.O.. 7," "Happily Ever After" et al. never approach the complexity of Grumpy, who learns to love Snow White—and to accept that strange new feeling.

Fifty-six year after its premiere, the jewel-like colors and crystalline clarity of the newly restored prints make the virtues of "Snow White" more apparent than ever.

NEW YORK POST, 7/2/93, p. 27, Michael Medved

One of the many joys in watching the latest re-release of "Snow White and the Seven Dwarfs" is imagining the discomfort it will produce among some of today's most politically correct social critics.

After all, this is the tale of a struggle between two women, in which the heroine (Snow White) is a cheerful drudge who loves dusting and doing dishes, while waiting for a male to arrive to give her life meaning. The bad female (The Evil Queen), on the other hand, is a powerful, self-reliant sophisticated head of state. You could never get a grant from the National Endowment of the Arts for re-telling an anti-feminist fable like this one.

Moreover, what's with these seven aging bachelors who live alone in a little cottage in the woods? First of all we can't call them "dwarfs" (or even "dwarves") anymore if we're going to be sensitive to current standards. Today, they'd have to be designated as "vertically challenged."

Moreover, urban sophisticates may pose probing questions about the long-term relationships between Doc, Grumpy, Dopey and the rest of the guys—especially in view of the fact that one of the earliest dramatic adaptations of the original Grimms' fairy tale gave them the names Flick, Blick, Glick, Snick, Plick, Whick and Queen.

Fortunately, none of those contemporary queries can undermine the pleasure that this magnificent movie will provide for any sane human being. The Disney people have lavished considerable effort on restoring their 55-year-old theatrical print so that the colors glow with new richness and vitality, and the soundtrack has been cleaned up to provide notably greater impact.

This audio enhancement makes a big difference in our appreciation of all eight of the movie's wonderful songs (by Frank Churchill, Paul J. Smith and Leigh Harline) including such standards as "Whistle While You Work," "Heigh Ho" and "Some Day My Prince Will Come." Even some of the lesser known numbers ("I'm Wishing," "Bluddle-Uddle-Um-Dum/The Washing Song" and "The Dwarfs Yodel Song") will send you out of the theater whistling and humming in spite of yourself.

Among all the musical offerings only the Prince's number, "One Song," reeking of the operatic Nelson Eddy-Jeanette MacDonald style popular in the '30s, seems slightly dated.

It is utterly amazing, in fact, how well most aspects of this picture have aged, so that young kids who are now seeing it for the first time will react with much the same wonderment as the premiere audience on Dec. 21, 1937. Watching the picture alongside my own little ones, I felt deeply moved, recalling how my father had taken me to see it for the first time when I was just about their age. I remember my dad warning me (aptly!) that the Evil Queen would be a bit scary, since he remembered his own frightened reaction when he saw the picture during its first run when he was 11.

In pre-literate societies, cherished legends retold over tribal campfires used to link the generations; these Disney classics, which have now been passed between three or four generations of American moviegoers may be of our closest approximations to that sort of tireless cultural connection. Since it's never been released on home video, each theatrical appearance of "Snow White" at intervals of every decade or so becomes a special and significant event.

For many critics, this first-ever feature-length animated film from the genius of Walt Disney remains the greatest achievement ever for this uniquely American art form. I wouldn't go quite that far, since I'm especially partial to "Pinocchio," "Fantasia" the hugely undervalued "Sleeping Beauty," and the more recent classic "Beauty and the Beast." Nevertheless, that ageless beauty "Snow White" remains one of the most satisfying evenings of entertainment available anywhere in the summer of '93.

NEWSDAY, 7/2/93, Part II/p. 58, Joseph Gelmis

Are we ready to forgive Snow White for being a wimp? I think so.

Let fearless Attorney General Janet Reno be the positive female role model for our pubescent daughters. And let's accept the helpless princess of the 56-year-old "Snow White and the Seven Dwarfs" for what she is: an adorable, teeny-voiced woman-child refugee from the patriarchal past.

The women's movement, from the mid-1960s through the 1980s, viewed Walt Disney's Snow White as an obsolete and insulting stereotype of women. She embodied the weak dependent female who was incomplete until Mr. Right arrived.

But since the last revival of "Snow White" in 1987, the studio bearing Disney's name produced a self-reliant fairy-tale heroine for the '90s in "Beauty and the Beast." And the current release of "Snow White," seems to find us in a more open-minded phase of sexual politics. One that allows us to relax and appreciate Snow White for the quaint pre-World War II romantic ideal she is, rather than see her as a threat to the politically correct image of young womanhood.

Disney's Snow White reflects a bizarre sidelight of a sad era. The Great Depression generation was fixated on childish womanhood, vulnerable innocence. Snow White is supposed to be old enough for romance and marriage but she acts and looks and talks like a preteen child. She brings to mind Shirley Temple, who was 8 years old and the nation's "sweetheart," the biggest box-office attraction in America, when "Snow White" opened in late 1937.

Just as in a Shirley Temple movie, nearly everyone who meets Disney's Snow White falls under the spell of her childlike beauty and experiences either the impulse to adore or to protect her. The Magic Mirror's admiration rouses her stepmother's envy. The Hunter disobeys the queen's order to kill the child. The forest animals and the dwarfs worship and shelter her. And Prince Charming comes riding and singing like an operetta hero into her life, first trying to retrieve her from her meaningless existence and then to successfully rescue her from a sleep resembling death to take her to a place where they will live happily ever after.

While Snow White may be an archaic figure, none of the 30 subsequent animated features from the Disney studio have improved on the art and entertainment of this breakthrough movie. It was with "Snow White and the Seven Dwarfs" that Disney figured out how to extend the eight-minute cartoons that were earning barely a minimum of profit from theaters to a full 83-minute feature that made his hand-drawn pictures competitive with the live-action star-vehicle films mass-produced by rival Hollywood moguls. "Snow White and the Seven Dwarfs" was made possible, in part, by the first extended use of the multiplane camera, which separated layers of paintings on glass to create the illusion of realistic depths and spaces between characters and objects. The prints playing in theaters today look better than the original ones did, we're told, thanks to technological advances in digital restoration and printing processes. In addition, the mono sound has been upgraded to stereo.

The film remains a glorious mix of eight memorable songs, compelling storytelling, classic sight gags, incredible attention to detail, gorgeous pastel colors, and the highlight of the fantasy, lovable comedic performances by seven distinctively different dwarfs. The theme of a bunch of foolish, flustered guys making a fuss over a girl is a recurring theme in many romantic comedy movies. None of them got it better than "Snow White and the Seven Dwarfs."

The queen, it should be noted, is ba-a-ad and beautiful and more interesting than her juvenile stepdaughter. Those scenes of the queen transforming herself into a crone with a warty nose and gleefully cackling as she proceeds to the dwarfs' cottage to murder her stepdaughter, were my first encounter with evil as a child. And, unlike Snow White, the queen has lost none of her intended significance: She scared my 9-year-old daughter in 1993, just as she scared me decades ago.

VILLAGE VOICE, 7/13/93, p. 58, Lisa Kennedy

One could run through the theater shrieking "She's baacckk." Or point out that this film, like that crooned "I'm Dreaming of a White Xmas," has always smelled of the overpowering iconography of paleness. Or perpetrate a Women's Studies 101 on this tremulous-voiced, dark-haired, porcelain-skinned princess who leaves her seven short friends and legions of faithful forest fauna for a dull, if equally pretty, prince and a canned ending. But, then again, why bother?

To dwell on what we hope is now the obvious—that the evil stepmother destroying her pristine rival has ramifications for all girlfriendships—would be to miss the wonder of Disney's first animated feature, *Snow White and the Seven Dwarfs*. After all, the lush, earthy-toned cel animation Snow White escapes into, to evade one of the all-time villainous cartoon honeys, is the real comer of this film.

The animation team struts its stuff not with nouns but with verbs, so to speak. While most of the characters may not overwhelm visually—too "Can you draw this Lumberjack" perfect—their actions and the movement of their environs are stunning. Shimmering Water and Morphing Shadow do star turns here. (You can imagine Walt watching and shouting, "Get 'em under contract now. They'll be great in that one about the deer.")

The "Whistle While You Work" number—I'd forgotten, *Snow White* is a bona fide musical with all the good and the truly mediocre that entails—with Ms. White and furry friends cleaning the mussed flophouse of the dwarfs, is not only a lesson to children about chores and hygiene, but a rich opportunity to show the daily writ large. In *Snow White*, the minutiae of the household become the adventure, far more marvelous than the framing tale: dust motes collect and chipmunks sneeze into teapots; kettles simmer and steam with attitude. This is the stuff dreams are made of. Forget the happy-ever-after biz and go for the happy everydayness of it.

Also reviewed in:
CHICAGO TRIBUNE, 7/2/93, Friday/p. A, Richard Christiansen

SO I MARRIED AN AXE MURDERER

A TriStar Pictures release of a Fried/Woods Films production.   *Executive Producer:* Bernie Williams.   *Producer:* Robert N. Fried, Cary Woods, and Jana Sue Memel.   *Director:* Thomas Schlamme.   *Screenplay:* Robbie Fox.   *Director of Photography:* Julio Macat.   *Editor:* Richard Halsey and Colleen Halsey.   *Music:* Bruce Broughton.   *Music Editor:* Alex Gibson.   *Choreographer:* Michael Smuin and Kimi Okata.   *Sound:* Nelson Stoll and (music) Armin Steiner.   *Sound Editor:* Larry Mann.   *Casting:* Mindy Marin.   *Production Designer:* John Graysmark.   *Art Director:* Michael Rizzo.   *Set Designer:* Barbara Mesney.   *Set Decorator:* Peg Cummings and Jim Poynter.   *Special Effects:* Thomas F. Sindicich, Dennis Becker, I.J Van Perre, and Peter Stoltz.   *Costumes:* Kimberly Tillman.   *Make-up:* Matthew W. Mungle.   *Make-up (Mike Myers):* Courtney Carell.   *Stunt Coordinator:* Bud Davis.   *Running time:* 110 minutes.   *MPAA Rating:* PG-13.

CAST: Mike Myers (Charlie Mackenzie/Stuart Mackenzie);   Nancy Travis (Harriet Michaels);   Anthony LaPaglia (Tony Giardino);   Amanda Plummer (Rose Michaels);   Brenda Fricker (May Mackenzie);   Matt Doherty (Heed);   Charles Grodin (Commandeered Car Driver);   Phil Hartman (Park Ranger, Vickie);   Debi Mazar (Tony's Girlfriend, Susan);   Steven Wright

(Pilot); Patrick Bristow (Cafe Roads Performer); Cintra Wilson (Cafe Roads M.C.); Luenell Campbell (Public Records Officer); Kelly Christmas (Policeman); Ilya Brodsky and Eugene Buick (Russian Sailors); Maureen O'Boyle ("A Current Affair" Anchorwoman); Steve Dunleavy ("A Current Affair" Reporter); Michael J. Hagerty and Michael Richards (Obituary Employees); Adele Proom (Marriage Desk Employee); David Knowles, Carl Rusk, and Paul Sanchez (Serande Musicians); Jessie Nelson (Ralph); Wanda McCaddon (Auntie Molly); Glen Vernon (Uncle Angus); Maggy Myers Davidson (Tony's Dance Partner); Robert Nichols (Scottish Minister); Jek Cunningham (Wedding Reception Piper); Robert Black (Accordionist); John Taylor (Fiddler); Ken Johnson (Walter the Plumber); Kelvin Han Yee (Master Cho); Joe Bellan (Man with Bimbo); Greg Germann (Desk Clerk); Kenneth Grantham (Maitre D'); Bob Sarlatte (M.C.); Cynthia Frost (Mrs. Levenstein); Fred Ornstein (Mr. Levenstein); John X. Heart (Waiter); Frederick Walsh (Bellboy); Keith Selvin (Young Stewart).

CHRISTIAN SCIENCE MONITOR, 8/12/93, p. 11, Marilynne S. Mason

Big brash action movies or "lite" comedies. Must be summer. Hollywood's junk-food flicks have been piling up like Twinkies in the local theaters for the past couple of months, attracting kids and their parents for two hours of air-conditioned "goof-ballery." Most of the comedies are harmless enough, and some are even mildly entertaining.

Among the latest: "So I Married an Axe Murderer," "Coneheads," "Robin Hood: Men in Tights," "Hocus Pocus," "Another Stakeout."

So I Married an Axe Murderer features the engaging and ingenious Mike Myers as a young man who fears commitment in love. He has a penchant for bad performance poetry (delivered in witty parody of the real thing) and dumping women he ought to love, convincing himself they are capable of despicable things. When he finally meets the "right" girl (Nancy Travis), she seems to have one tiny flaw—murdering husbands on her honeymoon.

"Axe Murderer" resembles a dozen other films, yet it has its one charm—Myers himself, who sometimes borders on being adorable but is smart enough never to sink the viewer in gooey sweetness.

The movie is filled with terrific little cameo performances—Phil Hartman as a sinister prison tour guide (ex-guard) named Viki; Amanda Plummer as the goofy sister of the bride; Alan Arkin as a police chief pretending to be tough to please an undercover cop with "Miami Vice" fantasies; and Myers playing the Scottish father of his character.

You may feel trapped in a "Saturday Night Live" skit part of the time; the silly plot doesn't hang together well, and too many bawdy jokes misfire. Nevertheless, a sweetness pervades the film, which provides a generous view of human nature.

Dan Aykroyd wrote *Coneheads*, taking off from a skit he used to do with Jane Curtin and Laraine Newman back in the early days of "Saturday Night Live" (SNL). Dan and Jane are back together for the film, which features the Coneheads' arrival on Earth from space, their nasty eating habits, peculiar speech patterns, and average American teenage daughter. A host of SNL regulars, past and present, contribute amusing cameos.

Aykroyd's comedy is extreme and bizarre, sometimes even gross, but often endearing and rich in amusing parody of contemporary American society. Despite some crass sight gags, the film might have been called "Conehead Family Values" because it's all about a loving family trying to assimilate into American culture.

The central joke of the film concerns immigration officials and the true meaning of the term "illegal aliens."

The humor often borders on bawdy and may not be appropriate for younger viewers. But "Coneheads" has its moments and certainly far outshines a stinker like *Robin Hood: Men in Tights*.

"Robin Hood" is surely one of Mel Brooks's worst disasters. It is so predictable and silly that not even the handsome Cary Elwes, the swashbuckling star of "The Princess Bride," can deliver these broad lines with grace. A self-conscious parody of Kevin Costner's awkward version of the romantic tale, Brooks's "Robin Hood" isn't witty enough to roast its predecessor, let alone make us laugh. Brooks's "Spaceballs" seems like a laugh riot in comparison.

Disney's *Hocus Pocus*, if frequently saccharine, at least has the power to engage the viewer. It features Bette Midler as a buck-toothed witch right out of the 17th century, returning one 20th-century Halloween night with her two sisters (the ample and hilarious Kathy Najimy and the sweetly screwball Sarah Jessica Parker), to seek immortality and suck up the "life-force" of all the children in Salem, Mass.

The three Sanderson sisters are too caricatured to frighten children, but I found the emphasis on witchcraft uncomfortable. Also off-putting was the killing of a child in the film's beginning, but two little girls sitting in front of me did not appear to be disturbed.

The witches meet their match in three young people and a talking cat. The underlying message tries to encourage sibling affection. It's forced, awkward, and unbelievable, but better than other messages in the film—like how stupid and unresponsive parents are.

Another Stakeout boasts a fine cast, but the writing is so uneven and the plot so poorly developed that the film's few amusing moments get lost. The talents of Richard Dreyfuss and Emilio Estevez seem wasted on this lumbering farce. Two undercover cops pursue a state witness who is hiding from the mob. This time they are joined by an incompetent district attorney, the stand-up comedienne Rosie O'Donnell, who provides most of the comedy in the picture. Posing as a married couple, Dreyfuss and O'Donnell spar like seasoned combatants. Estevez is always tangential, and the job the three are out to do never seems to matter much.

FILMS IN REVIEW, 10/93, p. 339, Andy Pawelczak

Will the youthful target audience for *So I Married An Axe Murderer* get the central conceit? Charlie McKenzie is a kind of belated beat poet who reads his awful verse to jazz accompaniment in a San Francisco coffeehouse on a street named after Jack Kerouac. Part of the joke is that Charlie's no dope-smoking, long-haired beatnik. As played by Mike Myers, he's smug and frat house cute, but when he reads his poems he turns into a ferociously arrogant electro-charged hipster. Charlie has a history of getting paranoid about his girlfriends, so when he falls in love with a beautiful butcher (yes, a butcher—the film's other conceit) it's only a matter of time before he starts believing she's the Honeymoon Killer featured on the front pages of supermarket tabloids.

Enjoying this movie depends largely on how you feel about Mike Myers who has become the object of a cult since *Wayne's World*. I must confess that Myers goes over (or under) my head. His comic persona consists of a weird concatenation of mannerisms and attitudes that for me add up to comedy degree zero, but judging from the audience's laughter (a young woman next to me was convulsed) his smart aleck sophomorisms score with some people. The movie consists of a series of skits strung out on a plot whose only purpose is to provide continuity as Myers and company do their shtik. There's a long sequence in which Charlie and his butcher-girl (sweetly played by Nancy Travis) do a gross-out routine with slabs of raw meat, and of course there are the poetry readings (one memorable poem is about a girl who stole Charlie's heart and cat). Particularly annoying is Charlie's habit of emitting a high nasal "Hello" and crossing his eyes whenever he's in a tight spot. (Perhaps the filmmakers thought this bit of business would achieve the iconic popularity of the "not" tacked on to the ends of sentences in *Wayne's World*.) At times, Myers is faintly reminiscent of Jerry Lewis, and of course the square/hip dual persona comes right out of Lewis' great *The Nutty Professor*.

The funniest bits in the movie don't involve Myers at all. Charles Grodin, in a cameo role, does a funny slow burn, and Alan Arkin, in a small unbilled role, is terrific as a police captain with a professorial bedside manner. Anthony LaPaglia has some funny moments as Charlie's pal Tony, a cop mired in paper work who longs for some action and complains that he has never once hung from the bottom of a helicopter. Myers himself plays Charlie's father, a boisterous, foul mouthed, hard drinking Scot, and, in a bizarre bit of casting, Brenda Fricker (who won an Academy Award for *My Left Foot*) plays Charlie's mom who has a serious lech for Tony.

So I Married an Axe Murderer isn't a director's picture, so there's not much to say about Thomas Schlamme's direction except that it's adequate and keeps the picture moving. This is Myers' show, so if you're not a fan you're apt to feel like the girl in the movie who's unable to keep up with Charlie and his friends. She's dumb and not with it and knows it, but I sympathized with her—I'm not with it in Myers' World either.

LOS ANGELES TIMES, 7/30/93, Calendar/p. 1, Michael Wilmington

Fear of sex and fear of marriage have infiltrated movie thrillers and comedies for several years now. Bachelor buddies were everywhere. Voyeurism became chic in "sex, lies, and videotape." Paranoia ran rampant in "Blue Velvet" and "Fatal Attraction." Time was out of joint in "Groundhog Day."

But even in these *Angst*-ridden times, "So I Married an Axe Murderer" pushes *Angst* hard. A new vehicle for Mike ("Wayne's World") Myers, it's about a vaguely misogynist San Francisco yuppie who becomes convinced that his fiancée, a butcher, is a serial killer. It's a comedy about maniacs: a *tasteful* murder-comedy, which isn't that laudable a goal.

You can play this kind of story either broadly or subtly, but usually only a genius—a Chaplin, a Lubitsch or a Billy Wilder—can mix approaches in a single film. In "Axe Murderer," the story shifts sluggishly between offbeat, almost lyrical humor and drop-your-pants dig-in-the-ribs gagging. The attack seems both labored and spread-out—sometimes one approach works, sometimes the other—and the result is often a curious, cold mish-mash, oscillating between wit and whoopie-cushion burlesque, quiet charm and buffoonery. It misses more than it hits.

That schizoid tendency extends to the theme, which, at least partially is about yuppie fear of commitment. And to the actors, There are *two* Mike Myerses here. Young Mike and Old Mike. Old Mike Myers, buried under several layers of age makeup playing a Scottish San Franciscan named Stuart Mackenzie, is a funny spewer of invective, a gasser. He's broad, obnoxious—but though his burry Scots accent often suggests Gilbert Gottfried doing Sean Connery, he hits his comic targets.

But Young Mike, as Stuart's son, Charlie Mackenzie—the guy who thinks he married an ax murderer—seems *unintentionally* obnoxious. He keeps pushing the winsomeness buttons down, jamming them up. When Charlie cruises around the city's picturesque North Shore streets in a convertible, ogling women through his shades, he may be intended as a Tom Hanks teddy bear - but he suggests something closer to the kind of sleazy hustler Rob Lowe might have cooked up.

Myers' Charlie is supposed to be a witty, over-sensitive young San Franciscan, genuinely in love with a woman (Nancy Travis) who may have left a trail of death behind her. But often there's something cold and unspontaneous about him. Travis gives a ravishing, sunny-faced performance, but Young Mike doesn't seem to be connecting with her—not even as much as Old Mike connects with the Oscar-winning Irish actress Brenda Fricker as Mrs. Mackenzie, a lewd old flirt in a padded bra.

All this is probably unintentional. When comics become stars and turn into leading men or ladies, they sometimes come across a little cutesy-calculated, like callous seducers spinning phony lines. They seem to be wearing padded sincerity. Comedians are sexy *because* they're funny; sometimes they forget this.

That's not the only problem with "So I Married an Axe Murderer." Robbie Fox's script—apparently with some embellishments from Myers and others—builds erratically, a nightmarish little romance, into which rowdy skits are occasionally inserted. And there's a twist at the end that smacks of some "Fatal Attraction" boogie-woman bashing—even as the movie is trying to hold up a "commitment" banner.

Director Thomas Schlamme, who did a wonderful job with the cast—Holly Hunter, Tim Robbins, Alfre Woodard—in his adaptation of Beth Henley's "Miss Firecracker," is an actor's director. He gets some nice moments here from cast members like Travis, Fricker, Alan Arkin (as a melancholy police captain, forced to be a hard guy) Amanda Plummer (wasted, as Travis' sister), and walk-on cameo guests Charles Grodin, Michael Richards and Stephen Wright.

But Schlamme seems uncomfortable here, especially when the skits take over. If there are several sensibilities rattling around "Axe Murderer" (MPAA-rated PG-13), they're not always in sync. And they don't always show enough self-awareness. When Myers drops his pants halfway through the movie—something which, after his "Wayne's World" skivvies scene now seems *de rigeur*—you might get the idea he wants everybody to applaud his bottom. Actually, his Scots accent is sexier.

NEW YORK POST, 7/30/93, p. 29, Michael Medved

"So I Married an Axe Murderer" tries hard to do three different things, but only manages to do one of them well.

As a mystery thriller it's a bust, as a comedy it's merely mediocre, but as a love story it works better than anyone had a right to expect.

The main reason for that success of the romantic element is the surprisingly heartfelt performance by Nancy Travis, who plays a bright, moody, funny, intensely vulnerable beauty who just may—or may not—be a psychopathic killer.

Travis is a marvelous actress who has been nibbling at the edges of stardom ever since her debut in "Three Men and a Baby" (as the infant's runaway mother). Here she makes it easy to understand why Mike Myers, playing a coffee-house poet in San Francisco, is so smitten with her that he's willing to risk dismemberment rather than break off their relationship.

The screenplay (by the previously unknown Robbie Fox) gives him good reason for wariness. Shortly after he begins dating Travis (who incongruously operates her own butcher shop in San Francisco), Myers becomes obsessed with tabloid accounts of a mysterious "Mrs. X" who has slaughtered three different husbands on their honeymoons.

It turns out that the crimes took place in just those three cities that Travis has most recently inhabited. Other clues fall into place that can't possibly be explained as simple coincidences.

Unfortunately, Myers the actor has no idea how to handle the demands of this role, and director Thomas Schlamme provides little help. Most of Schlamme's experience has come from directing comedy specials for the likes of Robert Klein, Whoopi Goldberg and Sandra Bernhard, among many others. Too often, "So I Married an Axe Murderer" veers off in the direction of a Mike Myers comedy special, concentrating on the star and his shtick at the expense of plot and pacing.

Part of the tremendous fun of "Wayne's World" was laughing at Wayne's ludicrous pretensions to hipness and cool. In "Axe Murderer," Myers trots out most of Wayne's familiar mannerisms—the self-important swagger, the knowing asides and the clenched-teeth smiles—but he doesn't seem to be in on the joke. This time it's Myers—not Wayne—who looks ridiculous.

He actually fares much better in the smaller half of his double role, playing his own father—the ultra-Scottish Stuart Mackenzie—behind thick glasses, a thick makeup, and even thicker highland burr. When the kilt-wearing old man entertains at a family celebration by performing "Do You Think I'm Sexy?" to bagpiper's accompaniment, the movie delivers its only sure-fire laugh-out loud moment.

For all its disappointing aspects, this film showcases one small but welcome development in Hollywood: For the second week in a row, one of the major studios has released a big-budget feature in which the main character is a poet. In "Poetic Justice," Janet Jackson recites Maya Angelou's acclaimed poetry very badly, but in "Axe Murderer" Myers recites some very bad poetry (his own?) extremely well.

In any event, you can come out of the theater somewhat encouraged by the fact that poetry—of all things—seems to be suddenly fashionable and sexy to major Hollywood filmmakers.

NEWSDAY, 7/30/93, Part II/p. 69, Jack Mathews

Whenever a bad movie becomes a blockbuster, as "Wayne's World" did last year, you can count on it producing even worse offspring. Hollywood cannot resist attempting to hit the same jackpot twice, and ideas with less substance than a line of bad poetry often become major studio pictures in the process.

Case in point: "So I Married an Axe Murderer," a momentously unfunny spoof of romantic murder mysteries that even comes with ... yep, a few lines of bad poetry.

Mike Myers, half of the famed Garth and Wayne TV burlesque team, stars in this tale of a good-natured San Francisco bachelor who falls in love with a neighborhood butcher (Nancy Travis) he believes to be a serial black widow. She marries her lovers and bites 'em, same day.

There is not much promise in that premise, and Robbie Fox' script, reportedly revised on a daily basis by Myers during production, can't think of a thing to do with it. The entire movie, directed by Thomas Schlamme ("Miss Firecracker"), is a series of limp sketch pieces and intentionally overbaked genre cliches, with Myers in the dual role of the amiable schlub Charlie and his obnoxious Scottish father Stuart.

Myers has some puppy-dog appeal as Charlie; his rubbery face can produce a smile as wide as the San Andreas Fault, and his line deliveries are so cheerfully earnest, you sometimes overlook the light load. But when he appears as Stuart, puffed up and belching out a stream of inanities, he's about as much fun as falling glass.

"Axe Murderer" embarrasses some pretty good actors, not the least being Brenda Fricker, the Oscar-winning Irish actress ("My Left Foot") consigned here to playing Charlie's lecherous mom, and Amanda Plummer, as his bizarre sister-in-law.

Schlamme managed one feat I would have thought impossible. He has Charles Grodin around for a couple of scenes, and couldn't even develop a laugh with him. Playing a motorist who has his car commandeered by Charlie's police pal (Anthony LaPaglia), Grodin does nothing in his scenes but furrow his brow and glower.

It's a pose you may strike after shelling out $7 for this potent contender for the year's worst movie.

SIGHT AND SOUND, 11/93, p. 53, Nick James

Lonely beat poet Charlie Mackenzie performs poems about his failed romances at Henry's bar in San Francisco. His best friend Tony, a cop, thinks that Charlie' s problem is a fear of commitment—every time a love affair takes off, he finds an excuse to back away. His current fancy is his local butcher, Harriet. While visiting his mad Scottish parents, Charlie sees his mother reading the *Weekly World News*. She tells him about the tabloid's lurid hypothesis about a female serial killer who marries men who then disappear without trace. So far, the victims include a lounge singer, a Russian martial arts expert and a plumber.

Charlie's first move with Harriet is to help her out on the butcher's counter. They have a wonderful date, during which Charlie notices that Harriet can speak Russian, and has a man's martial arts outfit in her flat. After spending the night there, Charlie wakes to find another woman in the shower: Harriet's sister Rose. He tells Tony all about it while they visit Alcatraz, and Tony warns him not to keep looking for excuses to fail. Charlie invites Harriet to his parents' home. In the loo, he reads the paper again, and starts to get suspicious. He asks Tony to run a check on the missing husbands; they turn out to be real cases, and dates and locations tally with several things Harriet has said. Then the plumber's body turns up; terrified, Charlie breaks up with Harriet.

When someone confesses to the plumber's murder, Charlie realises he must win Harriet back. He performs a "poem that sucks" outside her window and invites her to his parents' wedding anniversary party, where he proposes marriage and she accepts. After the ceremony, Harriet sings "Only You", which Charlie knows was the lounge singer's wife's favourite song. Shrugging off his paranoia, Charlie drives his new wife to a country hotel—Poet's Corner—for their honeymoon. Meanwhile, Tony discovers that the murder suspect is a phoney. He faxes Harriet's picture to the relatives of each missing husband and they all confirm that Harriet was the bride. Tony calls Charlie to tell him, just as the hotel staff are about to carry off the couple to the honeymoon suite. Charlie manages to lock up the bewildered Harriet, but then discovers that the woman who wields the axe is actually her sister Rose. She chases Charlie on to the roof just as Tony arrives to arrest Harriet. After a struggle, Rose slips off the roof but Charlie grasps her hand and she is rescued. Later, at Henry's, Charlie performs a poem dedicated to Harriet.

Being a bouncy comic on a sofa and aping his audience's amiably gormless lifestyle has been a wining formula for Mike Myers. *Wayne's World* bridged the gap between success in the living room and success in the cinema by shamelessly flaunting its small-scale origins ("We are not worthy," it pleaded) and tagging itself to the reflected glory of other artists' personas, from Freddy Mercury to Rob Lowe (not to mention Bill and Ted). For his follow-up feature, Myers has chosen a persona which is definitely not of his audience: a wide-eyed beat poet with a penchant for female butchers.

Myers has here gone Hollywood in the most ambitious way. As Charlie, he's both comic and straight man in one. He's as pathetic as a gonk, yet he drives a groovy 60s car and wears cool clothes. He's both goofy and cute, accident-prone and capable of attracting the most fabulous women. Suddenly he wants to be Dean Martin and Jerry Lewis in one slick package. As if that weren't biting off more than one performer has a right to chew, he's also cast himself as the hero of a Hitchcock spoof, a challenge that has defeated many a better comic before him. Most of the time he loses his grip but something about the sheer silliness of his comedy, just a shade short of Lewis's sentimental vulnerability, affords occasional soft-headed laughs.

Where Myers finally over-reaches himself is as Charlie's Scottish father, a character out of a rejected Billy Connolly sketch. He gives Rod Stewart songs the Jimmy Shand treatment and has lines such as "Kiss your mother or I'll tear your lungs out". Much better are comic foils such as the police captain who's such a nice guy that Tony has to coach him in how to yell at his men, or the park ranger who relishes the morbidity of Alcatraz. Many of the better ideas that fill out the background here are rooted in TV sketch work. It's possible therefore that Myers' gag writers are not yet thinking as big or as bouncy as their mouthpiece. Nevertheless, it's a relief to watch a spoof that's confident enough not to carpet-bomb you relentlessly with puns and schoolboy pranks.

VILLAGE VOICE, 8/3/93, p. 58, Joe Levy

Like no one since Chevy Chase, Mike Myers drenches every move he makes in the sickly blue glow of cathode rays. The man radiates smarm, pulses with it, and whether you think he's gifted with an eye for the way junk culture takes on the shape of those who consume it or just some Canadian schmuck whose Bill and Ted rip got way tired way fast (not!) sorta depends on how you feel about TV to begin with. Now, it's a fairly well-known fact that I intend to have my corpse preserved above ground until they build a television big enough to bury me in, so you may not want to trust my generally favorable reaction to *So I Married an Axe Murderer*.

With a plot so thin it could fill in for Kate Moss should La Waife ever decide to break for lunch, *So I Married an Axe Murderer* belongs to an elite group of films whose entire conceit is neatly summed up by their titles. As these things go, it's got more brains than *Don't Tell Mom the Babysitter's Dead*, more laughs than *Buffy the Vampire Slayer*, and better acting than *Stop! Or My Mom Will Shoot* (though not by much).

If you try hard enough, you can still catch a glimpse of the semi-intelligent narrative—guy screwed up by the media's portrayal of women as dangerous predators stops renting *Fatal Attraction* and learns to trust—that must have been stripped away during endless rewrites to make room for Meyers's shtick. What we have instead is a semisappy narrative—screwed-up guy stops reading *The Weekly World News* and learns to trust—livened up by the same charm that made "Touch my monkey" a household phrase.

Briefly: Myers plays a poet giving him a chance to name-check Betty Rubble and Josie and the Pussycats in a verse that goes "They make me horny/Saturday morny/Girls of cartoon/Led me to ruin"; he doubles in the role of his father, giving him a chance to do that yelling Scotsman bit from *Saturday Night Live*; his best friend's a cop, giving him the chance to parody TV cop shows; he falls for a honey-cheeked butcher, giving him a chance to clown with raw meat; said honey-cheeked butcher bears a passing resemblance to a honeymoon killer described in *The Weekly World News*, giving him a chance to poke fun at junk culture.

Myers's fatal flaw is that smarmy charm; he always seems far outside, so much smarter than any character he plays, you never trust him for a second. But here, romancing his honey-cheeked butcher, he displays an uncanny awareness of the ritual inanities that fill the dead air of every relationship ("I'm a human blanket, I'm a human blanket," he says, trying to cuddle his way out of one spat inspired by his mortal fear of his sweetie). That remarkable accuracy for the willfully forgotten details of everyday existence is what gave every child of the '70s, '80s, and '90s a place in *Wayne's World* and what saves Myers from empty irony. If only he'd learn to trust it more he might avoid the inevitable featured role in *National Lampoon's Bosnian Vacation*.

Also reviewed in:
CHICAGO TRIBUNE, 7/30/93, Friday/p. C, Clifford Terry
NEW YORK TIMES, 7/30/93, p. C3, Janet Maslin
VARIETY, 8/2/93, p. 44, Leonard Klady
WASHINGTON POST, 7/30/93, p. G7, Hal Hinson
WASHINGTON POST, 7/30/93, Weekend/p. 39, Desson Howe

SOFIE

An Arrow Entertainment release of a Nordisk Film & TV/Norsk Film/Svensk Filmindustri production with financial assistance from the Danish Film Institute/Swedish Film Institute. *Producer:* Lars Kolvig. *Director:* Liv Ullmann. *Screenplay (Danish with English subtitles):* Liv Ullmann and Peter Poulsen. *Based on the novel "Mendel Philipsen and Son" by:* Henri Nathansen. *Director of Photography:* Jorgen Persson. *Editor:* Grete Moldrup. *Music:* Arve Tellefsen. *Sound:* Michael Dela. *Sound Editor:* John Nielsen Nalle. *Art Director:* Peter Hoimark. *Set Designer:* Magnus Magnusson. *Set Decorator:* Ivar Baungaard. *Costumes:* Jette Termann. *Make-up:* Cecila Drott-Norlen. *Running time:* 145 minutes. *MPAA Rating:* Not Rated.

CAST: Karen-Lise Mynster (Sofie); Ghita Norby (Frederikke); Erland Josephson (Semmy); Jesper Christensen (Hojby); Torben Zeller (Jonas); Henning Moritzen (Frederick Philipson); Stig Hoffmeyer (Gottlieb); Kirsten Rolffes (Jonas' Mother); Lotte Herman (Aunt Pulle); Jonas Oddermose (Aron, Age 3); David Naym (Aron, Age 7); Jacob Allon (Aron, Age 12); Kasper Barfoed (Aron, Age 18); Anne Werner Thomsen (Rose Philipson); Sanne Granngaard (Fanny Philipson); Elna Brodthagen (Sofie's Grandmother); Elin Reimer (Belse); Lone Herman (Malle); Peter Hesse Overgaard (Harry Hirsch); Peter Schroder (Lagen); John Hahn-Peterson (Colin); Hardy Raen (Larsen); Mari Maurstad (Josephine); Claus Bue (Kelner); Bent Lexner (Rabbi); Daniel Hertz (Julius); Anna Szaff (Dina, Age 9); Lea Louise Leitner (Dina, Age 6); Anette Lutchen-Lehn (Mrs. Hjortekar); Johannes Vabensted (Pianist).

CHRISTIAN SCIENCE MONITOR, 5/24/93, p. 14, David Sterritt

By any standard, Liv Ullmann must be counted with the world's most extraordinary actresses. Her films include a long list of Ingmar Bergman classics—from "Persona" and "Cries and Whispers" to "Scenes From a Marriage" and "Autumn Sonata," among others—along with international productions such as "A Bridge Too Far" and stage successes such as "Anna Christie" on Broadway.

But performing is only one aspect of her career. Her two books, "Changing" and "Choices," have been translated into many languages. She has worked since 1980 as a goodwill ambassador for the United Nations, pleading the cause of underprivileged children around the world. She has received all manner of awards, medals, and honorary degrees.

Now Ms. Ullmann is a movie director, too. Some 35 years after her screen-acting debut, she has made her first picture on the business side of the camera: "Sofie," the story of a turn-of-the-century woman facing difficult decisions in life and love.

Based on a 1932 novel by Henri Nathansen, a respected Danish author, "Sofie" begins in 1886 and centers on a Copenhagen woman whose marital status still single at the ripe old age of 28—is generating much concern among her family and friends.

Attending a soiree at her uncle's mansion, however, she meets what appears to be the man of her dreams. He's handsome, successful, and talented enough to be considered one of the city's most promising artists. He paints a portrait of Sofie's parents and it delights everyone, from the subjects of the painting to the critic in the local newspaper. And this newfound friend is as crazy about Sofie as she is about him.

There's only one obstacle in the way of their marriage: He isn't Jewish, and try as they might to be broad-minded, Sofie's relatives squirm at the thought of an outsider in the family. So when a more conventional suitor arrives on the scene—a Jewish cousin named Jonas who's steady, reputable, and boring—she bows to tradition and takes him as her husband.

The rest of the story chronicles the results of her decision, which include a decent life and a wonderful child, but also growing unhappiness with a spouse whose mind and health prove sadly unstable. The end of the movie finds her young son about to embark on an adult life that is likely to develop very differently from hers.

Ullmann has directed "Sofie" in a manner that is true to the characters and their way of life: cautious, measured, and rarely eager to break new ground or take onlookers by surprise. There are occasional breaks in its even-toned demeanor, as when Sofie expresses her sudden sexual passion for the painter she loves, and later for a friend who becomes her companion during her husband's illness. But these moments pass by as quickly as they arise, returning us to an atmosphere that's as predictable as the characters who inhabit it.

While this doesn't make "Sofie" an altogether dull movie, it does have tedious stretches between its more obviously dramatic passages. The acting—by such Scandinavian stars as Karen-Lise Mynster and Erland Josephson, who play Sofie and her father—has the same earnest sentimentality that marks the visual style and the screenplay, which Ullmann wrote with Peter Poulsen, a prolific Danish author making his movie-writing debut.

The camera work is by Jorgen Persson, who specializes in the lovely but rather monotonous imagery found in such pictures as "Elvira Madigan" and "Pelle the Conqueror," which are among his credits.

In all, "Sofie" introduces the multi-talented Ullmann as a very careful filmmaker who needs to inject her style with the same creative energy that distinguishes her best achievements as an actress. She has the skill and intelligence to become a capable director. What's lacking so far is a sense of adventure.

LOS ANGELES TIMES, 11/3/93, Calendar/p. 4, Kevin Thomas

As a socially conscious actress, Liv Ullmann has often chosen roles more from her heart than her head, with mixed results. However, for "Sofie", her stunning directorial debut, she evokes the style and tradition of her mentor, Ingmar Bergman, for whom she gave her finest performances.

Like "Fanny and Alexander," and subsequent films that Bergman has written but not directed, "Sofie" is an exquisitely detailed, leisurely paced period drama celebrating family life in all its joys and sorrows. Although it would seem almost certain that Ullmann drew artistic inspiration from Bergman, her film is entirely her own.

"Sofie" has been adapted by Ullmann and Danish poet, novelist and playwright Peter Poulsen from noted Danish author Henri Nathansen's 1932 novel "Mendel Philipsen & Son." In the title role, the patrician Karen-Lise Mynster, a member of Copenhagen's Royal Theater, plays a 28-year-old Copenhagen Jew on the verge of spinsterhood when she meets, at a soirée at her uncle's mansion, a dashing painter (Jesper Christensen).

He beguiles Sofie by painting a dual portrait of her beloved parents (Ghita Norby, Erland Josephson) before painting one of her. Her father, not unexpectedly, will not hear of her marrying a gentile, besides, at just that moment an acceptable suitor, Jonas (Torben Zeller) approaches her father, asking for Sofie's hand in marriage.

"Sofie" is very specific in time—it begins in 1886 and concludes 21 years later—and place, also of community, that of the solidly conservative bourgeoise Danish Jewry. Yet it possesses such a strong sense of life and of the complexity of human emotions that anyone who suspects that his or her life is a reasonably even mix of happiness and sadness should be able to identify with Sophie and the key people in her life.

As a period piece "Sofie" is faultless, with wonderful cluttered but warm and inviting late 19th-Century interiors and equally appropriate costumes, yet it is very timely—or rather timeless—in its sharp sense of life's trade-offs. That Sofie has made a sensible rather than passionate marriage does not destroy all her chances at happiness especially with the birth of her son, her only child.

Yet what sustains Sofie and her relatives, a traditional Jewish life centered on family and religion, also restricts them, sometimes to the point of suffocation. Her parents are in complete harmony with each other and their faith.

The sweet-tempered but fragile Jonas, so adoring of his own mother, is made vulnerable for having married a woman who does not love him; his more dynamic brother (Stig Hoffmeyer) and Sofie must struggle with their mutual attraction. Sofie at times feels that her life is an unopened book and that those who've tried to open it have always fumbled.

As a director, Ullmann equals her finest moments as an actress. Her sense of the visual is so strong that "Sofie" often has the feel of a silent film in its concern for movement and gesture.

Ullmann pays virtually as much attention to hands as she does faces, there is much emphasis on people touching one another, reaching out for one another.

It comes as no surprise that Ullmann is a wonderful director of actors, and her cast performs as a flawless ensemble. Mynster can't be said to resemble Glenn Close, except that both are handsome rather than conventionally beautiful women, but she is like Close in her intelligence and authority. Yet for all its superb acting "Sofie" (Times-rated Mature for adult themes, some nudity) is—and rightly should be—a film of images that linger in the memory—of people gathering and parting, of faces alternately glowing with smiles and wracked with grief, of everyone caught up in the ebb and flow of life itself.

NEW YORK POST, 5/21/93, p. 31, Matthew Flamm

The closest Sofie Philipsen gets to letting down her hair is to waltz alone through her parents' living room when the middle-aged couple take their morning stroll. Not that she seems unhappy: This is Copenhagen, 1886. As seen through the gauzy light that fills so much of "Sofie," there could be no better time and place in which to waste one's youth.

For her directorial debut, the fine Norwegian actress Liv Ullmann has turned "Mendel Philipsen & Son" a 1932 novel by the Danish-Jewish author Henri Nathansen, into a sentimental yet tasteful meditation on bourgeois family life at the end of the last century.

From Ingmar Bergman's favorite actress you were expecting maybe car chases?

"Sofie" may indeed owe its length—2½ hours—and seriousness to Bergman's influence. Or Ullmann may just be obsessive all on her own. She tells her heroine's story with a dedication to completeness that matches her one-time mentor's—though with none of the brilliance and intensity that reward a Bergman fan's hard work.

Sensitively acted, "Sofie" is about how few choices a woman had in the 18th century, in particular an unmarried, Jewish woman. The eponymous 28-year-old heroine (Karen-Lise Mynster) spends most of her time reading and writing within the cozy confines of her parents' wood-paneled rooms. "It's as if life is passing me by," she tells a beloved spinster aunt after Shabbes dinner at her grandmother's.

Opportunity knocks at a grand ball at her rich uncle's, where a handsome blond artist (Jesper Christensen), in the manner of many a 19th-century hero, recognizes Sofie's beauty and naturalness. He also notices the modesty and mutual devotion of her father (Bergman stalwart Erland Josephson) and mother (Ghita Norby), and insists that they sit for a portrait.

Sofie is soon torn between her passion for the painter and her obligation not to marry a "goy." Her love for her parents proves her undoing, She weds her cousin Jonas, a gangly, Abe Lincolnesque drapery-store owner who takes her to provincial Sweden for a marriage that in no way lives up to her parents'.

By now we're only halfway through the movie "Sofie" is also about nostalgia and wistfulness and time playing "havoc with all I thought I could put off until tomorrow," as the heroine says in poetic voice-over. Ullmann takes a literal approach to her themes, dragging Sofie's doting parents through every stage of old age (the light growing ever more golden).

There's a fleeting attempt to foreshadow the Holocaust with a reference to "6 million" dead from bubonic plague (Nathansen himself committed suicide while fleeing the Nazis). And though Sofie portrays a way of life that would ultimately be destroyed, this is still just an actor's love fest of a movie—a rudderless narrative, but with lovely performances given all the time and attention in the world.

NEWSDAY, 5/21/93, Part II/p. 67, John Anderson

In "Sofie," Liv Ullmann starts with broadly drawn characters and telescopes in, making her title character's experiences more and more specific, more and more personal. That way, the revelations visited upon her—about the great big roundness of it all, the circular patterns of life, the ying and the yang—can be presented as if no one had ever thought of them before.

Someone has, of course, which is why on one level "Sofie" is a big, ambitious failure. Ullmann, the Scandinavian film legend and now first-time director, chooses to take the universal and personalize it, rather than vice versa. So the fact the film succeeds at all is a minor miracle. That it succeeds so well is due less to Ullmann's directorial skills, which are considerable but leisurely, than to the talents and face of Karen-Lise Mynster. As Sofie, a handsome but unmarried 28-year-old Danish Jew living in 1880s Copenhagen, Mynster gives a performance that bears more than a little resemblance to the work of her director. But more importantly, she gives passion to a woman who is tortured by passion, who's both suffocated by and desperate for love. It's a neat trick.

And yet Sofie, for all her pain and introspection, is sort of a stock character. She allows herself to be trussed up in a corset of custom and conformity, chooses to marry the wrong man from the right religion, and loses what we're led to believe is her one chance at love and happiness. That she will find a modicum of contentment in her home, much more in her child, never alleviates the sense of loss we feel. Her artistic soul is never satisfied.

Sad, but nothing new. Ullmann does, of course, add layers of complexity to this skeletal tale—she didn't do all those Bergman films for nothing. But what she wants to teach us we've heard before, and in less than 2½ hours.

"Sofie," which Ullmann and Peter Poulsen adapted from Henri Nathansen's 1932 novel, contains a lot of warmth and spreads it generously: on Sofie's parents (Erland Josephson and Ghita Norby), on the Gentile artist she loves (Jesper Christensen) and on Jonas (Torben Zeller), the shop keeper whom she marries and drives mad with her one moment of sensual abandon.

It's that kind of dark, moody film, where retribution is likely to be delivered, but not swiftly.

SIGHT AND SOUND, 8/93, p. 49, Ben Thompson

Late nineteenth-century Copenhagen. Sofie is a sensitive, sensual Jewish woman, still single in her late twenties, who fears that life is passing her by. Her parents are merchants—respectable, but paupers compared to her rich uncle, who has changed his name and assimilated. Invited to a reception at her rich uncle's house, Sofie attracts the attention of Hojby, a famous painter who is a gentile. He asks to paint her parents, and the resulting portrait, a study in proud Jewish isolationism, is shown at the academy. Sofie and Hojby fall in love, but her family do not want her to marry outside the faith. Jonas, a lugubrious distant cousin, visits on business and endeavours to court her. Against her wishes, Sofie is manoeuvred into marrying him. Her breakup with Hojby is painful, as she is forced to make a quick exit to preserve her modesty.

She leaves home to set up house with Jonas, whose circumstances are less comfortable than expected. Her husband proves incapable in many respects and spends all his time with his mother, whose eventual death only accelerates his descent into madness. Their young son Aron is Sofie's only comfort in a loveless marriage, and a prolonged flirtation with her married brother-in-law is on the point of consummation when Jonas appears and tries to rape her. She manages to fight him off, and has him committed to a mental institution where he lapses into a trance.

Sofie returns home to live with her aged parents. Aron grows up weaned on tradition at his grandfather's favourite teahouse. Scandal hits the family when the rich uncle goes out of business. Sofie goes to the dispersal auction in search of Hojby's painting of her parents, which he had bought, and wins a bidding war against Hojby, who is very angry. Her parents die, and Sofie runs the family business from their house. Aron, now an adult, tells her that he cannot live the traditional life and leaves to make his way in the outside world.

Liv Ullmann's directorial debut starts in surprisingly breezy fashion. There is a fair amount of humour, some amusing dialogue of the "Let me pass you the stuffed goose neck" variety, and a measure of not quite suppressed eroticism. Sofie is almost comically over-ripe—"yearning for something that may never come", she rubs herself lasciviously up against the walls of her room—and Hojby is a worthy would-be seducer. Building on the basic theme of "come up and see my etchings", he dispenses some of the greatest chat-up lines in Scandinavian history.

Unfortunately, all this is too good to last. After 40 minutes or so the film seems to remember itself, and lurches regrettably towards the gratuitous miserabilism of Bergmanesque stereotype. The heavy-lidded, soup-eyed character of Jonas genuinely engages sympathy. But his descent from a figure of Dickensian pathos to bestial lunatic is so depressing that by the end, the audience envies his comatose state. Sofie's slimy and dishonest affair with Jonas' brother strips her character too of any dignity, and the scene of sexual violence with which things come to a head is of such graphic nastiness as to thoroughly cloud over the film's painterly sheen.

Sofie takes an eternity to wind down from this ugly climax. Ullmann's original script was just over eight hours long, and it feels as though she's expanded rather than cut it. At the end, when

Sofie meets Hojby at the auction, hopes of a surprise happy ending are cruelly dashed. The remorselessness with which the principal character is steered away from felicity is intended to demonstrate her inner strength, but in fact it only undermines the film's good points.

The performances throughout are of a very high quality—Erland Josephson and Ghita Norby in particular shine as Sofie's parents, but that may be because their quiet, untragic, almost happy characters come as a relief. The background, too, is well rendered with conscientious subtitling that fills in non-Danish speakers on every little detail, right down to a newspaper advert for ladies' hats. The Denmark of a century ago turns out to be an interesting setting: the film's social and religious side-dishes of Scandinavian language battles and concern with entryism from the Jewish perspective are more nutritious than its melodramatic meat.

VILLAGE VOICE, 5/25/93, p. 54, Georgia Brown

Last week I found a lot to say about a peripheral plot in *The Searchers*, in which a Scandinavian couple, homesteaders in the Texas desert, come perilously close to marrying off their daughter Laurie (played by Vera Miles) to a guitar-playing simpleton named Charlie. Remembering how seldom women's destinies were in their own hands may be especially poignant to women today, now that marriage or commitment can be put off, avoided altogether, or, if accepted, occasionally reexamined. A kind of retrospective pity may be part of what attracts us to a film such as *Like Water for Chocolate*, about a youngest daughter who can't marry at all because she's supposed to stay home and take care of Mother.

The 19th-century novel was notable for either ending in the heroine's marriage or in depicting the (terrible) consequences of her adultery. Adultery became a major tragic theme, of course, because marriages were so often hastily or cynically determined, and then there was no escape. Liv Ullmann's melancholy but very entertaining *Sofie* is based on a Danish novel, *Mendel Philipsen & Son*, by Henri Nathansen, and its considerable pleasures come from quasi-novelistic musings on the difficulties of both good and bad marriages, as well as single-motherhood.

At 29, Sofie (Karen-Lise Mynster) has reached that critical year: Either she marries now or turns into a spinster like the giddy aunts who visit each Friday evening for the Sabbath meal. As a proper bourgeois daughter in 1886, Sofie has limited access to the outer world, few opportunities to make contacts; as a Jewish woman in Copenhagen her options are further narrowed. Thus, her parents, in consultation with the other relatives, decide that if she's to marry at all—and if she's not to marry the goy painter she's recently become infatuated with—she'd better accept shy, backward cousin Jonas, who's almost as much of a fool as Charlie McCoy in *The Searchers*.

Sofie unfolds slowly, but it's never boring. Like the majority of lives, the movie proceeds by small increments, then suddenly erupts in a minor incident, like a death in the family or a declaration of passion. Ullmann, who directs, wrote the script with Peter Poulsen, and they endow *Sofie* with a developing first-person self-consciousness: She starts out with illusions and gradually sheds them. The time frame is about 25 years, taking her from the end of youth into mid-middle age, when the son she had with Jonas is a young man, ready to find his own destiny. That he's a young Jew, poised on the threshold of the 20th century, is a fact the movie is aware of.

In a sense the film is about the duplicity of family, community, ritual, and ceremony—how they comfort and chafe and end up imprisoning. A particular curse, it implies, is to have blissfully happy parents, coconspirators in a marriage so self-contained it bakes everyone in its rays. Sofie's father, Semmy (Erland Josephson), runs his father's business. Her mother, Frederikke (Ghita Norby, who played the heroine's conniving mother in *The Best Intentions*), does a lot of needlework. (Actually, one of the pleasures is seeing all the laces and silver, the ferns and brocades.) It's very touching to watch Sofie, living with the insipid Jonas—who's fatally bound to his own mother—initially assume all marriages can be like her parents' if one only works at them. In this sense and others, her parents betray her.

The drama lies almost wholly in the heroine's passionate nature. When we meet her, she seems on the verge of some indiscretion, starving for a man. "It's as if I'm waiting for something, which may never come. I may end up a silly old virgin." Her encounter with the painter, Hans Hojby (Jesper Christensen), gets the juices flowing. Later, stuck with Jonas, she's seduced over the years by her admiring, slightly caddish brother-in-law (Stig Hoffmeyer). Wearing no makeup,

Mynster acts with her extraordinarily expressive, somewhat plain features; it's a surprise but believable when Hans declares she's the most beautiful woman he's ever seen.

Earlier, when Sofie first meets Hans at a party, he conceives a passion to paint her parents' portrait. It will be a picture of "Jewish essence," he announces, meaning something vaguely mystical and yet domestic. He envisions the old couple sitting at opposite ends of a red sofa. Their daughter at the party is wearing a striking red dress, and it's Sofie, not sofa, they're sitting on in the painting; she is the red uniting them, lighting their lives, the brightness they're unintentionally smothering. Clever of Ullmann to present such insights tactfully, without spelling them out.

Also reviewed in:
NEW REPUBLIC, 5/24/93, p. 28, Stanley Kauffmann
NEW YORK TIMES, 5/21/93, p. C8, Stephen Holden
WASHINGTON POST, 6/18/93, p. G7, Hal Hinson
WASHINGTON POST, 6/18/93, Weekend/p. 42, Desson Howe

SOMMERSBY

A Warner Bros. release of a Le Studio Canal+/Regency Enterprises/Alcor Films presentation. *Executive Producer:* Richard Gere and Maggie Wilde.   *Producer:* Arnon Milchan, Steven Reuther, and Mary McLaglen. *Director:* Jon Amiel. *Screenplay:* Nicholas Meyer and Sarah Kernochan. *Story:* Nicholas Meyer and Anthony Shaffer. *Based on the film "The Return of Martin Guerre"* by: Daniel Vigne and Jean-Claude Carrière. *Director of Photography:* Philippe Rousselor. *Editor:* Peter Boyle. *Music:* Danny Elfman. *Music Editor:* Ellen Segal and Bob Badami. *Choreographer:* Colleen Kelly. *Sound:* Chris Newman and (music) Shawn Murphy. *Sound Editor:* Jay Wilkinson and Lauren Palmer. *Casting:* Billy Hopkins and Suzanne Smith. *Production Designer:* Bruno Rubeo. *Art Director:* Michael Johnston. *Set Designer:* Marco Rubeo. *Set Decorator:* Michael Seirton. *Set Dresser:* Joseph Conway. *Special Effects:* Gregory S. Hull. *Costumes:* Marilyn Vance-Straker. *Make-up:* Jean-Luc Russier and Peter Robb-King. *Stunt Coordinator:* Paul Beahm. *Running time:* 110 minutes. *MPAA Rating:* PG-13.

CAST: Richard Gere (Jack Sommersby);   Jodie Foster (Laurel Sommersby);   Bill Pullman (Orin Meecham);   James Earl Jones (Judge Isaacs);   Lanny Flaherty (Buck);   William Windom (Reverend Powell);   Wendell Wellman (Travis);   Brett Kelley (Little Rob);   Clarice Taylor (Esther);   Frankie Faison (Joseph);   Ronald Lee Ermey (Dick Mead);   Richard Hamilton (Doc Evans);   Karen Kirschenbauer (Mrs. Evans);   Carter McNeese (Storekeeper Wilson);   Dean Whitworth (Tom Clemmons);   Stan Kelly (John Green);   Stephanie Weaver (Mrs. Bundy);   Khaz B. (Eli);   Josh McClerren and Mark Williams (Boys);   Muse Watson (Drifter);   Paul Austin (KKK Member/Folsom);   Frank Taylor, Billy Butch Frank, and Dale Stewart (KKK Members);   Jake Cress and Doug Sloan (Marshalls);   Ray McKinnon (Lawyer Webb);   Maury Chaykin (Lawyer Dawson);   Stuart Fallen (Court Baliff);   Barry McLerran (Clerk);   Richard Lineback (Timothy Fry);   Michael Gold (Night Clerk);   Joe Basham (Witness);   Patrick Morse (Boarding House Manager);   Joe Neel (Auctioneer);   Harry T. Daniel (Official).

CHRISTIAN SCIENCE MONITOR, 2/8/93, p. 14, David Sterritt

American audiences are on the minds of French filmmakers these days. The latest fashion in French cinema, insiders have said lately, is to dream up a story that will appeal to the huge United States market, and make it into a French production as a sort of trial run. Nobody cares very much whether the French movie does well at the box office—as long as the rights to the story can be peddled to Hollywood for a hefty pile of dollars.

The picture that set this trend in motion a half-dozen years ago was "Three Men and a Baby," the Hollywood megahit based on "Three Men and a Cradle," a pleasant but forgettable French farce. Coming in a month or so is Hollywood's version of "La Femme Nikita," with Bridget

Fonda and Harvey Keitel in the French-originated story of a government-controlled hit woman with a mysterious past.

This month's example of the fad could probably pass as a thoroughly American project if you didn't know its history. It bears an English-sounding title, "Sommersby," and stars Jodie Foster and Richard Gere, who have rarely been accused of having Continental mannerisms. The story takes place right after the Civil War, and focuses on such traditionally American subjects as North-South rivalry, cotton and tobacco farming, and antiblack racism.

Yet other aspects of the plot—about a man returning home after years of absence, bringing tension and mystery with him—will seem familiar if you remember a French movie called "The Return of Martin Guerre," starring Gérard Depardieu and quite popular in American theaters about 13 years ago. Sure enough, the "Sommersby" screenplay by Nicholas Meyer and Sarah Kernochan is based on the "Martin Guerre" script by Jean-Claude Carrière and Daniel Vigne, who directed the original film. It's basically a remake of the French drama, although it's so well-produced (and well-disguised) that few moviegoers are likely to mind its lack of originality.

The main character is Jack, a Confederate soldier who returns to his Southern home years after the war and reclaims his land, his house, and his family. While his friends and neighbors are happy to welcome him back, his wife Laurel seems unsettled by his presence—which appears odd at first, but becomes understandable when we realize that she thought her husband was gone for good and has acquired a new suitor who is nicer than her drunken, ill-tempered spouse ever was.

Jack is evidently a changed man, however, full of tenderness toward his family and goodwill toward his community. Laurel soon softens and takes him into her heart, and his friends proclaim him a hero when he devises a scheme to turn their infertile land into a thriving farm using group investment and communal trust to raise the needed capital.

Then things abruptly turn complicated, troubling, and puzzling. A drifter in town questions whether Jack is the real Jack Sommersby after all, or just a crafty pretender. Jack is then arrested for a murder committed in another time and place—leading Laurel to protect him by branding him an imposter, while he risks the hangman's noose by refusing to relinquish his identity as the authentic Sommersby.

With a number of different twists, this yarn worked pretty well in "The Return of Martin Guerre," and the "Sommersby" writers have given it a distinctively American flavor with some of their innovations. Jack is a supporter of the former slaves in his community, for instance, and the hate this subjects him to provides one possible explanation for the questions and accusations raised against him.

On a scene-by-scene basis, though, what makes "Sommersby" work is old-fashioned movie magic: the chemistry between Ms. Foster and Mr. Gere in their emotionally complex moments together; fine supporting performances by Bill Pullman and James Earl Jones; rich cinematography by Philippe Rousselot; and the smooth flow of the story under director Jon Amiel's guidance.

"Sommersby" is not a great or resounding film. But it treats a tale that could have seemed merely tricky, with enough warmth, intelligence, and humanity to make it an engaging two hours at the movies.

FILMS IN REVIEW, 6/93, p. 189, Andy Pawelczak

Hollywood periodically turns to European films in a search for new plots and themes, and generally the result is a dumbed-down and sensationalistic version of the original. Or perhaps it's a matter of Hollywood producers aiming for their idea of the lowest common denominator and the big bucks. At any rate, *Sommersby*, a remake of a 1982 French film, *The Return of Martin Guerre*, doesn't escape the transatlantic doldrums; though not dumb and tasteless, it succumbs to a peculiar kind of hubris and loses in translation most of the original's resonance.

The original *Martin Guerre* is a simple tale of a 16th century man who shows up in a small village one day saying he's the farmer who disappeared eight years before. The film succeeds against all the odds. Though firmly rooted in exotic and somewhat alienating period detail, the picture is a compelling meditation on the nature of identity, suggesting that all identity is an impersonation of self.

Sommersby's director, Jon Amiel, and screenwriters, Nicholas Meyer and Sarah Kernochan, update the action to the Reconstruction period in the South, thus cannily solving two problems at one stroke. The period pre-dates such identity checks as blood tests and finger-prints but is familiar enough to American audiences to eliminate the original's distance and austerity. It also allows the film makers to beef up the proceedings with the contemporary theme of racism. When Jack Sommersby (Richard Gere) appears after a six year's absence claiming to have been a prisoner of war in the North, one of the first clues that he's not who he claims to be is his friendliness towards blacks. Later, when Sommersby comes up with an idea to save the war dev-astated town by growing tobacco as a cash crop on his land and sharing the profits with the townspeople, he insists on including blacks in the scheme against the wishes of his prejudiced neighbors. Needless to say, Sommersby wins out, and by film's end harmony prevails.

The film makers split the focus between the community redemption theme and the false Sommersby's relationship with the real man's wife, Laurel (Jodie Foster). At first she's suspicious and remote, but as the story develops and the imposter turns out to be a better and kinder man than the real Sommersby, she falls in love with him, though the audience is never quite sure if she knows the truth or not. As Laurel, Jodie Foster is very good, employing her somewhat asexual persona to advantage in her portrayal of this southern woman who could have stepped out of the world of Grant Wood's "American Gothic." She's tough but vulnerable, and her slight southern intonation effectively conveys a mix of longing and earthy realism. As played by Richard Gere, Jack Sommersby is a hip variation on the traditional American trickster figure simultaneously duplicitous but sincere, ironically humorous but with a reservoir of deep feeling. Gere, with his surface charm and suggestion of hidden depths, does a good job of embodying this inherently fascinating figure, but the film makers try to pour so many meanings into the character that he loses focus and definition long before the end.

It's too bad because the Martin Guerre story touches on an essential, secular American myth. F. Scott Fitzgerald said there are no second acts in American lives, but of course most Americans ardently believe in the second chance. Hidden away in the pretensions, confusions, and sentimen-talities of *Sommersby* is a good, modest movie about a man who gets a second chance and lives it out as far as it will take him, even if it leads to his death. Ah, well, America is also the land of missed opportunities, and *Sommersby* misses the main chance.

LOS ANGELES TIMES, 2/5/93, Calendar/p. 1, Kenneth Turan

"Sommersby" is not quite the old-fashioned romantic classic it tries to be. But given its problems, what is surprising about this three-hanky film is how close it gets at times to providing the traditional satisfactions of the genre.

Cloned from classic 1940s weepies, "Sommersby" is more than anything else a film at war with itself, giving with one hand while taking away with the other. Yet even its partial success shows once again that a strong core story can hold its own against an indifferently written script, and that that magical commodity called star chemistry can compensate for acting that ranges all the way from radiant (Jodie Foster) to regrettable (almost everyone else).

Lushly photographed in the grand manner by Philippe Rousselot ("A River Runs Through It"), "Sommersby" is set in 1867 in a benighted Tennessee hamlet called Vine Hill, a quiet spot where nothing much seems to have happened since the Civil War ground to a halt.

All that changes the day Jack Sommersby (Richard Gere) strolls in. The town's biggest landowner, he hasn't been seen or heard from since he left for the war seven years before. Yet he has no trouble recognizing everyone and has a kind word for one and all, even the faithful old dog that doesn't seem quite so happy to see him.

As surprised as the dog at the man's return are Sommersby's wife, Laurel (Foster), and her close personal friend Orin (Bill Pullman), an earnest Bible thumper who has been looking out for Laurel all these years with an obvious eye toward matrimony if Jack never made it back.

It turns out that Jack and Laurel did not exactly part on the best of terms. "That's where you were sleeping before you left," she tells him coolly, pointing to a bedroom across the hall from her own. The ante-bellum Jack was apparently a drinker and hell-raiser of major proportions, a lout his wife barely tolerated during their three troubled years of prewar marriage.

Not so the New Jack. Soberer, saner, infinitely more romantic than the man who rode off to battle, this returning paragon oozes both bedroom charm and community egalitarianism. He not only comes up with the idea of planting burley tobacco as a way to revive Vine Hill's economy, he insists on sharing the potential bounty with the town's newly freed slaves. Laurel starts to feel that this man is too good to be true, and soon others with darker motives are saying the same.

Moviegoers with moderately healthy memories will by this time have recognized "Sommersby" as a reworking of "The Return of Martin Guerre" of a decade back. That film was in turn based on one of the most durable of true stories, an incident involving a man who returned after a war in 1560 to reclaim his wife and property in the foothills of the French Pyrenees.

Powerful and compelling, the story of Guerre and his wife has at last count inspired a play, a musical, two novels, several works of nonfiction and even an operetta in addition to the Deparadieu film and this one, and it is beyond the powers of even Hollywood to absolutely ruin its essential psychological fascination.

Still, people have tried. "Sommersby's" script, written by Nicholas Meyer and Sarah Kernochan from a story by Meyer and Anthony Shaffer, is filled with an inordinate amount of ripe Southern foolishness, everything from humble freemen to drunken racists and cross-burning night riders.

The language is similarly overblown and clichéd and British director Jon Amiel (best known for Dennis Potter's "The Singing Detective") has almost systematically removed any trace of nuance or subtlety from the film's subsidiary characters, including a brief cameo by James Earl Jones as a stern but honest judge.

Where the two leads are concerned, however, the situation is surprisingly quite different, though with Gere it is a near thing. A thoroughly contemporary actor (as Bruce Beresford's "King David" more than proved), Gere is not at his best wearing period costumes and talking in a disconcerting Southern accent.

Still, he and Foster prove surprisingly persuasive as a couple who learn to love one another and they work up much more of a romantic charge than anyone could have anticipated. Their very 1940s scenes of discreet and intimate passion (the film is rated PG-13 for sensuality) are warm and convincing and when the two of them are alone together on the screen, "Sommersby" has no problem providing the kinds of satisfactions it sets out to.

Much of the credit for this must go to Foster. Already a two-time Oscar winner at the age of 30, she seems to reveal new aspects of her ability with every picture. "Sommersby" is her first adult costume drama and she is memorable in it, not only losing herself totally in the period but managing to project a combination of sweetness, fire and mature beauty that is impossible to resist. This is as completely thought-out a performance as you are likely to see, and if the rest of "Sommersby" were halfway as persuasive, there is no telling how good this on-again, off-again romance might have turned out to be.

NEW YORK POST, 2/5/93, p. 31, Jami Bernard

There is a twist at the heart of "Sommersby"—although believe me, it isn't as wild as the one in "The Crying Game," and it will be apparent to anyone who saw the French movie "The Return of Martin Guerre" a few years ago, of which this is a virtual remake.

The original was better, although "Sommersby" is not without its charms.

John "Jack" Sommersby (Richard Gere) returns home to wife Laurel, his son and his Southern farm town after six years away fighting in the Civil War and serving time in prison. Johnny, we hardly knew ye—the new Jack in town is a kinder, gentler man, nearly unrecognizable because he is so changed. He's even nice to the newly liberated blacks, and offers them a chance to buy his land in a democratic tobacco-growing profit scheme. (In a concurrent subplot, the movie uncomfortably offers up Jack as the white martyr to the Southern Negro cause.)

The movie tries—with varying degrees of success—to make us wonder if this Jack is the real Jack. Laurel is not sure what to believe at first, but like the townsfolk warms to the returned veteran. The Jack she used to know had been spending his nights on the antebellum equivalent of the guest cot. The new, improved Jack lands in Laurel's affections, and under her down comforter, and Laurel is experiencing thrills like few women of her unenlightened era could claim. (The original movie accomplished this in a sweeter, more plot-enhancing way.)

Now let us interrupt this review with a little reality check. Helllooo! Which of the ladies out there feels that if she were married to Richard Gere she would not be able to recognize him after a mere six years with or without beard? Hmmm, I thought so. "Sommersby" requires a big suspension of disbelief—that Laurel would not be able to know at first glance whether this man was truly her husband.

And yet the original French movie handled the mystery with less fuss. That one was set in the 16th century, when all the men were hairy and wore woolly-mammoth peasant coats, their faces covered by foam from their ale.

It doesn't help that "Sommersby"—with the distinctive Gere and with Jodie Foster looking more striking than ever as the long-suffering wife—employs numerous glamour close-ups, perhaps in anticipation of its transfer to small-screen video. With closeups like these, you could differentiate between snowflakes, even six years later.

Because "Sommersby" loses steam in dealing with the central identity crisis—is he or isn't he?—it plays up other aspects of a screenplay that significantly alters the "Martin Guerre" movie, which in turn was based on a true story. The ability of a man to change his nature, and above all the way love's recognition goes deeper than the skin gives "Sommersby" a romantic intensity that often transcends the screenplay's weaknesses.

Jodie Foster, although an excellent actress who has gained phenomenal stature in the past few years, is nevertheless miscast as the downtrodden farmer's wife who hopes for a little spice in her life. Foster's inflections, her bearing—even her cool, direct gaze—make her unmistakably modern.

Gere, too, looks like someone more out of a Nautilus gym than a Civil War prison. Even so, there is more playfulness between the two characters than sexual spark.

Modern too is a dramatic courtroom scene that could easily fill the "L.A. Law" time slot, and Gere's dance of delight over his healthy tobacco plants puts one in mind of his ill-advised jig in "King David."

On the plus side, the people who sniffled over, say, the TV miniseries "The Thorn Birds" may have another cathartic cry now. "Sommersby" is a romance with high production values; even its title sounds like a quality Merchant-Ivory production (it's not; it was directed by Jon Amiel). It has the look of a seamless, pricey made-for-cable movie.

NEWSDAY, 2/5/93, Part II/p. 56, Jack Mathews

One of the downsides to the realism that has been injected into movies in the past 20 years is that when a good old-fashioned period love story comes along, it has to pass certain standards of logic before we'll take it to heart.

"Sommersby" is one of those, good old-fashioned stories, the sort meant to soak hankies by the yard, however illogical the circumstances. And this one, which stars a surprisingly unmannered Richard Gere and a luminous Jodie Foster, has just enough emotional power to overcome plot notions that border on the foolish.

Credited as a remake of 1982's "The Return of Martin Guerre," which starred Gerard Depardieu and Nathalie Baye, "Sommersby" is really a resetting and retelling of a 16th-Century incident that has become part of the lore of French romance.

This version, written by Nicholas Meyer and Sarah Kernochan, skips ahead to the 19th Century in the American South to tell the story of a Confederate soldier who returns home after the Civil War so much wiser and nicer than the drunken bully who'd left, his wife and friends begin to wonder if he's the same man.

Much of their skepticism is set aside by the conditions to which Jack Sommersby (Gere) returns and by the profound changes the war had wrought on everyone. Vine Hill and the Sommersby plantation are scarred remnants of the past, and the townsfolk are crippled in mind and spirit.

"Everybody who ain't dead is leaving," Jack is told, as he marches through the fields toward a reunion with Laurel (Foster) and the son left behind six years earlier. Remembering the beatings at his hands, Laurel isn't, particularly thrilled at the sight of him. Not even his old dog can work up much more than a petulant growl.

But it's a time for reconstruction, in all ways, and Jack is anxious to upgrade his marriage and revive Vine Hill with a variety of ideas both fresh and radical. Fresh: He suggests turning the cotton-poor land over to tobacco farming. Radical: He offers to deed land to those who work it, including Joseph (Frankie Faison), the freed slave once bought by Jack's father for $100.

The script and the often awkward direction of Englishman Jon Amiel are almost more burden than the romance can shoulder. There are undeveloped themes about the Ku Klux Klan, a cliched rivalry between Jack and an old friend (Bill Pullman) who'd been taking care of his family while hoping to take his place, and some courtroom theatrics at a murder trial that play like scenes from "Perry Mason."

Through it all, however, emerges a genuinely moving love story, the credit for which goes to Foster, who is absolutely convincing as a woman torn by passion and doubt, and to Gere, who gives a mellow, sympathetic performance that a few years ago seemed outside his range.

"Sommersby" is not only at its best, but something special, when focused on the relationship between Jack and Laurel. Despite her confusion about the changes in him, and the accusations about his identity that, keep both of them on the defensive, the one thing never in doubt, is the love that develops between them.

It is the kind of love that can overcome anything, even a clunky script.

SIGHT AND SOUND, 5/93, p. 56, Jason Drake

Vine Hill, Tennessee. Two years after the Civil War, Jack Sommersby, who left to fight seven years earlier, returns. The town celebrates, but Jack's wife Laurel, who remembers their unhappy marriage, is wary. She is pleasantly surprised by Jack's new-found tenderness, and others also notice a change in his manner. Jack avoids their questions by announcing a plan to revive the town's ailing fortunes which involves selling everyone a portion of his land to grow a valuable tobacco crop. One day Orin Meecham, who had been courting Laurel in Jack's absence, becomes curious when he hears a drifter declare that Jack's real name is Horace Townsend. His suspicions increase when a KKK member claims that Jack is a schoolteacher, but are temporarily deflected by the successful tobacco harvest. The celebrations are cut short when Jack is arrested for the murder of a local gambler.

During the trial Orin realises that Jack is an imposter and that the real Jack Sommersby committed the murder. He convinces Laurel that she should tell the truth about her husband's identity, which would save Jack's life but also destroy his name.

Jack refuses to accept this and persuades Laurel to retract her statement out of love for him. He is found guilty and sentenced to hang. The tobacco is sold for a hefty profit. In prison, Jack confesses to Laurel that his name is Townsend. Having met Sommersby as a POW, he stole her dead husband's identity and came to Vine Hill. Following Jack's hanging the town begins to prosper from its tobacco crop. Laurel lays flowers on a grave marked 'Jack Sommersby'.

From The Long Night (Le Jour se lève) to the mooted Fonda-ised version of La Femme Nikita, Hollywood has looked to Europe for narrative inspiration. However, the most frequently re-made foreign movies are comedies or action thrillers, genres with which the US industry feels at home. The tradition of adult period drama is weaker in contemporary Hollywood, and Sommersby, a new version of The Return of Martin Guerre, is something of an anomaly. Exhibiting a degree of cultural insecurity, the production team appears to have based the film's style on the aesthetic of Sunday afternoon BBC television drama. The finished product is very different from Jon Amiel's earlier work in television (The Singing Detective) and film (Aunt Julia and the Scriptwriter, Queen of Hearts).

Where the original waded knee-deep in historical detail, Sommersby opts for an altogether more restrained telling of this popular French folk story. In fact, it's in comparison to the original that Sommersby's more interesting moments are revealed. For example, the religious intolerance and moral certainty of Guerre's universe, which provided the film with both a framing device and a narrative motor, have been replaced by the racism and social bankruptcy of post-Civil War Tennessee. But although performing the same function, they also give a wider perspective by showing the reaction to Sommersby's fraudulent activities. Strangely enough, Sommersby actually constructs its central character as an eerily prescient, Clintonesque figure offering communal salvation, replete with an economic rescue package that calls for personal sacrifice, as in the scene where Richard Gere convinces the townspeople to contribute their savings in order to buy the valuable tobacco seeds. Unfortunately, the film is not interested in pursuing the conceit, and its social politics are simplistic. For example, in reply to the pervasive racism it depicts it can only offer Gere's laid-back good neighbourliness as a solution.

Sommersby has a feeling of autumnal portentousness; the brooding soundtrack, subdued colours and slow-building narrative seem to suffocate it with an air of solemnity. Having explicity raised issues about the nature of love and identity, the film fails to flesh them out. As the eponymous hero, Gere cuts a curious figure. The characters he usually portrays are the glamorous but mysterious men of *Pretty Woman, American Gigolo* and *Breathless*, and it's this mixture of cool, empty allure that he brings to his role as Jack Sommersby. Which means that Depardieu's fast-talking rogue is transformed into Gere's smooth-talking charmer—a subtle but key difference, and one that creates a coldness at the movie's centre which Jodie Foster, playing in a typically tough-skinned manner, is unable to melt. Gere's performance also contributes to the film's aimless drift, which only disappears as it mutates into a courtroom drama in which procedure and action become more important than performance. A generally lifeless film, *Sommersby* fails to generate any sense of tragedy or passion, preferring to remain at a distance to the story, mistaking serious-ness for profundity and aloofness for sophistication.

TIME, 2/22/93, p. 69, Richard Corliss

Americans—go figure. they can't make a better car or car stereo. They can't stanch their national debt. They can't impose a new world order. But they can fix up a foreign-movie drama like doctors slapping an anemic newborn into shape until it is a bionic baby. It looks so smart, so strong, so very ... Hollywood.

Sommersby, about a young Tennessee husband who goes away to the Civil War and comes home a changed man, is based on the 1982 French film *The Return of Martin Guerre*. *The Vanishing*, the tale of a young Seattle woman who goes away for a beer and never comes home, is a remake of a 1988 Dutch thriller. The original movies had their admirers, but neither property could be sold as is to the U.S. mass audience. Some expert renovation was in order. Cunning Hollywood script doctors had to approach the European originals not as finished portraits but as sketches in need of coherence, heart, pizazz. It's what rewriters do: refashion a boutique item so it will jump off the shelves at the mall.

The Vanishing—directed in both versions by George Sluizer—misplaces its leading lady early. She disappears at a highway rest stop, leaving her lover Jeff (Kiefer Sutherland) angry, then for years obsessed. He wants to know what happened. We already do. At least, we know whodunit. Barney (Jeff Bridges), a nerdy schoolteacher with the improbable accent of a Swedish Peter Lorre, has abducted her and taken her to his lakeside cottage. When Barney reveals himself, Jeff must decide whether his need to know the ending, even a tragic one, to his story—and they all died horribly ever after—is worth putting his fate in Barney's treacherous hands.

Such was the moral of the Dutch *Vanishing*: curiosity killed the cat. It's a provocative premise, but it wants some legerdemain and a third act. Enter screenwriter Todd Graff (*Used People*). He takes the original's perplexing flashback structure, flattens it out and fattens it up, mostly by creating a new character, a waitress (Nancy Travis) who falls in love with Jeff. Graff changes the theme: now knowledge is just a cue for righteous revenge. The Dutch movie had no gun; in a Hollywood thriller there must be a gun, and it will go off. The original's ending was misanthropic, claustrophobic—a fellow in a tight spot with no way out but death. Graff provides a rousingly standard climax, putting the heroine at mortal risk in an old dark house and then letting her triumph. It makes for sturdy melodrama, old-style. You've seen it work a million times. Well, it works again.

Martin Guerre was an art-house hit, and is the source for a new musical with Broadway hopes. The story, based on 16th century fact, raised poignant issues: Do we ever know the person we love? Could he be someone else, someone better? What matters in a lover: his identity or his behavior? And, given the choice, would we trade him in for a model that was new, improved—and a fraud?

Even with beguiling performances by Gérard Depardieu and Nathalie Baye, the French movie was austere business. And it dodged the issue of how easily a wife or a relative could ascertain if a man was who he claimed to be. (Five intimate questions, and it could be settled in a flash.) In Hollywood they know how to solve problems: by obscuring them. So they made *Sommersby* a fervid romance swathed in star quality. Who is this masked man? Richard Gere, lighting a fire in Jodie Foster; what else matters? Especially when the fellow, a Southern cousin to *The Music Man*'s Professor Harold Hill, so expertly peddles 76 corn pones—a tobacco crop, a parcel of hope—to his neighbors, who are eager to ride his promise out of the Civil War's rubble and into prosperity and community.

Three expert story cobblers—Nicholas Meyer (*The Seven-Percent Solution*), Anthony Shaffer (*Sleuth*) and Sarah Kernochan (*Impromptu*)—add a murder charge, drop a last-second deus ex machina and, aided by savvy British director Jon Amiel (*The Singing Detective*), manufacture a seductive entertainment. Is *Sommersby* a great movie, or even an honorably affecting one? Not quite; there are too many reaction shots of sweet young cheeks stained with big wet tears. But it offers the cleanest, ripest version of the tale. It translates the original true story, just as it transforms *Martin Guerre*, from European ambiguity into robust Hollywood fantasy.

VILLAGE VOICE, 2/16/93, p. 60, Amy Taubin

In *Sommersby*, Richard Gere and Jodie Foster are so good that, as the film gallops to its four-handkerchief finish, you might actually forget that they're movie stars. This is all the more remarkable considering that the narrative in this Hollywood translation of the French art-house favorite *The Return of Martin Guerre* is not all that convincing.

Transposed from 16th-century France to post-Civil War Tennessee, *Sommersby* keeps the premise of the original film (which itself was based on a true story). A man goes off to war leaving a wife and a small child. Eight years later he comes home—or has he? The Jack Sommersby (Gere) who reappears to claim his wife, Laurel (Foster), child, and family estate is so changed that only Laurel's staunch conviction that this is indeed her true husband quiets the doubts of relatives and friends. If the prewar Jack was a mean, indifferent husband, a gambler and drunk, an all-around spoiled brat, the postwar Jack is a passionate and attentive lover, a book worm, an incipient socialist and flaming civil rights activist.

In the French film, Martin Guerre's desire to claim profits made on his land in his absence gave his relatives second thoughts about his legitimacy. In *Sommersby*, it's the agreement Jack makes, allowing both blacks and whites to buy from him the land they farm, that makes his racist neighbors wonder. When a burning cross on the front lawn fails to intimidate him, they find a way to use his past to force him to choose between his honor and his life.

What was most, though not very, interesting in *Martin Guerre* was the way characters acted on impulses so over-determined that their motives were as opaque to them as to us. *Sommersby*, a quintessentially American film, is about a coming to consciousness, a quest for identity that, mistaking paternalism for morality, stops short of real radicalism.

But if Jack's incredible commitment to racial equality comes from nowhere except the desire to give a creaky period piece a topical hook, it's not enough to sink the film. *Sommersby*'s charm is the relationship between Jack and Laurel. Foster is as fierce and intelligent, as independent and vulnerable as only she can be. Gere, who specializes in sleazeballs capable of conning others precisely because they're so alienated from themselves, doesn't shy from revealing the dubious side of Jack's character, which makes his transformation all the more complicated. Like all great romances, what happens between the Sommersbys is rooted in denial and fueled by danger. That absolute love is possible only under such conditions is the paradox that makes a flawed film oddly moving.

Also reviewed in:
CHICAGO TRIBUNE, 2/5/93, Friday/p. B, Clifford Terry
NATION, 3/8/93, p. 316, Stuart Klawans
NEW REPUBLIC, 3/8/93, p. 28, Stanley Kauffmann
NEW YORK TIMES, 2/5/93, p. C8, Vincent Canby
VARIETY, 2/1/93, p. 96, Richard Natale
WASHINGTON POST, 2/5/93, p. B1, Rita Kempley
WASHINGTON POST, 2/5/93, Weekend/p. 44, Desson Howe

SON-IN-LAW

A Hollywood Pictures release. *Executive Producer:* Hilton Green. *Producer:* Michael Rotenberg and Peter M. Lenkov. *Director:* Steve Rash. *Screenplay:* Fax Bahr, Adam Small, and Shawn

Schepps. *Story:* Patrick J. Clifton, Susan McMartin, and Peter M. Lenkov. *Director of Photography:* Peter Deming. *Editor:* Dennis M. Hill. *Music:* Richard Gibbs. *Music Editor:* Allan K. Rosen. *Choreographer:* Miranda Garrison. *Sound:* Bruce Bisenz and (music) Jeff Vaughn. *Sound Editor:* James Troutman. *Casting:* Cheryl Bayer. *Production Designer:* Joseph T. Garrity. *Art Director:* Pat Tagliaferro. *Set Designer:* Barry Chusid. *Set Decorator:* Dena Roth. *Set Dresser:* Lance Clark, Michael Goyak, Danielle M. Simpson-Abaravich, Mitchell G. Myers, and Anna Rita Raineri. *Special Effects:* Cliff Wenger. *Costume Designer:* Molly Maginnis. *Make-up:* Daniel C. Striepeke. *Stunt Coordinator:* Gary Combs. *Running time:* 95 minutes. *MPAA Rating:* PG-13.

CAST: Pauly Shore (Crawl); Carla Gugino (Rebecca Warner); Lane Smith (Walter Warner); Cindy Pickett (Connie Warner); Mason Adams (Walter Warner, Sr.); Patrick Renna (Zack Warner); Dennis Burkley (Theo); Tiffani-Amber Thiessen (Tracy); Dan Gauthier (Travis); Ria Pavia (Carol); Lisa Lawrence (Lisa); Graham Jarvis (Principal); Nick Light (Mud Wrestling Announcer); Ernie Kinney (Horace); Troy Shire (Cowboy); Adam Goldberg (Indian); Robert Koch (Country Club Waiter); Ryk O. (Halloween Fairy); Garret Sato (Male Hairdresser); Emily Dole (Thumper); John Hatton (Fiddle Player); Jim Henken (Guitar); Lynn Coulter (Drums); Mike George (Bass); Jay Leach (Musician).

LOS ANGELES TIMES, 7/2/93, Calendar/p. 23, Michael Wilmington

One problem of comedy stardom is that it confers sexiness and power on performers whose humor may rely on stupidity or banality. When that happens, the star comics may lose their edge and craziness and turn into goodwill hucksters.

That's what goes wrong with the strenuously silly comedy "Son-in-Law", a Pauly Shore vehicle in which MTV's chilled-out, syllable-stretching denizen of "Dudesville" plays a fish out of water: an L.A. college pal of South Dakota farm girl Rebecca (Carla Gugino), hauled home for a Thanksgiving weekend and erroneously palmed off as a prospective husband.

Pauly's character, Crawl, and the family he invades—which features Lane Smith and Cindy Pickett—as the parents, Mason Adams (of the ultimate creamy TV commercial voice) as Grandpa and Patrick Renna as younger brother Zack—are conceived in the broadest sitcom-sketch terms. Dad is upright, uptight. Mom is neurotic, repressed. Gramps just wants to whittle on the porch, fish and complain. Tubby little redhead Zack is a wise-cracking cutup and computer whiz.

There's also a burly mean farmhand named Theo (Dennis Burkley) and a mean ex-boyfriend (Dan Gauthier). As for Rebecca, she's another fast-pitch mall-movie dream: the South Dakota prom queen-valedictorian Crawl turns into a Melrose drop-dead hotter in miniskirts, hair dye, boob tubes and butterfly tattoos.

The movie tries to pretend that it's about tolerance: a kind of "Guess Who's Coming to Dinner" about anti-L.A. freak bigotry. But its deck is stacked in the usual obvious ways. Crawl is a genuine jerk when he shows up at the farm, warbling "Green Acres" and making pig jokes at the Warners' expense, destroying farm equipment and cornfields with blithe abandon, acting as if everything will be straightened out if he just writes a check. We're supposed to forget all this when his eyes go soft and he turns into the local guru of sexiness and funky fashion, remaking the whole family into kinder, gentler swingers.

"Son-in-Law" suggests that somebody like Crawl would be as weird as a lunar being to the Midwestern Warners. That isn't so. Because of TV and the movies, L.A. subcultures are the ones *everyone* knows about. Stoners like Crawl are familiar types nationwide—ever since 1982 and the movie role that spawned them all: Sean Penn's Jeff Spicoli in "Fast Times at Ridgemont High." In any town within reach of cable TV, the teen-agers would not only recognize a Pauly, there might be imitation Paulys at the high school.

The writers and director Steve Rash have another half-baked angle: Crawl as ambassador of ambi-sexuality. At one point he dresses up like Carmen Miranda, complete with bananas and brassiere. Since the two villains—Theo, the farmhand bully, and Travis, the evil Tom Cruise look-alike—are macho men to the max, there's a suggestion that Crawl's strength comes from the way he embraces and flaunts his feminine side. The movie glosses that over too, just as it discreetly smudges the similarities between Crawl's brain-fried mannerisms and druggie tics.

"Son-in-Law" has a bright surface, brisk direction and even a few funny performances (Smith's and Renna's). But it's a double-shuffle, just like the old Rock Hudson-Doris Day sex comedies of the early '60s, packed with laborious innuendoes and slick double-entendres. Despite Crawl's smutty mouth—his continuous references to getting "semis" when he sees attractive women—Crawl and Rebecca have a sexless relationship, and 'Becca, like Doris, is a virgin.

Shore's appeal resides in the fact that a lot of kids think he's just like them, and that he's getting away with murder. Next to the earnest, shampooed, grinning commentators around him on MTV, he doesn't seem to give a damn. Yet, in "Son-in-Law" (rated PG-13) Crawl often seems the phoniest character in the movie. Maybe that's because the writers keep telling us that their "*buuuuddddy*" isn't really such an oddball, that he does care. In the end, you can't have much movie fun with freakiness if you aren't willing to freak the movie out a little.

NEW YORK POST, 7/2/93, p. 27, Michael Medved

In addition to its hugely lucrative franchise in animated fairy tales (such as the just re-released "Snow White"), the Disney company has recently made good money with a series of gross comedies glorifying stupidity.

Each new installment in the seemingly endless parade of indescribably awful "Ernest" movies (starring the eternally annoying Jim Varney) appalls critics but turns a solid profit thanks to Ernest's die-hard admirers, "Know what I mean, Vern?"

Pauly Shore follows in this ignoble tradition: the dumber he acts, the sillier the situations in which he finds himself, the more his fans like it. By this standard, they should like "Son-in-Law" very much indeed.

Already the star of his own popular show, "Totally Pauly," on MTV, and of last year's high school Neanderthal hit "Encino Man" (for Disney), the irrepressible Shore here gets his first chance to play a romantic lead. His character, Crawl, has spent six years crawling through a Los Angeles university where he befriends an innocent freshman who has just arrived from South Dakota. Under his influence, this sweet young thing (played with natural warmth and flair by the talented Carla Gugino) soon transforms herself into a hip California babe, complete with bleached hair and ankle tattoo.

When she discovers that her best bud, Crawl, is stuck over Thanksgiving vacation with no place to go, she decides to take him home with her to her parents' farm in South Dakota where he meets her patronizingly portrayed American Gothic family. When her old high school boyfriend (played by Tom Cruise lookalike Dan Gauthier) insists on proposing marriage, the only way she can escape his pursuit is by pretending that she's already engaged to Crawl.

From this point forward any savvy 12-year-old could finish the script, though an amazing total of six different writers are credited with contributing to the story and screenplay—a sure sign of a troubled production.

If you're longing to see Pauly Shore wrestling a pig, a bull, a turkey, and various rednecks into submission, then this is the movie for you. Most viewers, however, will quickly tire of this one-joke story of a California space case lost in the heartland among the Agro-Americans.

Shore himself is definitely an acquired taste, with his original and nearly incomprehensible language and unmistakable resemblance to the fondly remembered Tiny Tim (without the ukelele). In emphasizing Crawl's innate sweetness beneath the whacked-out veneer of neo-hippie weirdness, he also recalls the characters created by Cheech and Chong (though drugs are now officially out of style in Hollywood, so we're meant to assume that Pauly achieved his brain-addled state without benefit of marijuana).

The hard-working, highly professional supporting cast makes this picture endurable and on occasion, even vaguely enjoyable. Lane Smith, Cindy Pickett and Mason Adams do solid work as the leading lady's father, mother and grandfather, respectively. Meanwhile, a stunning newcomer named Tiffani-Amber Thiessen nearly steals the movie in a small part as a hometown girl with a wild streak; this gorgeous discovery has star quality to burn.

The main problem with the picture is a disturbing tendency to take itself too seriously, offering Pauly Shore as not just an object of humor, but a source of higher wisdom. "The family is dysfunctional in the beginning. Crawl shows them that it is okay to be themselves and to let go," Shore himself piously declares. "Everybody comes out a little different in the end, all for the better."

The picture thereby violates the basic rules of fish-out-of-water comedy: Yes, the fish is supposed to triumph in the end, winning acceptance in an alien world, but it's too much to suggest that everyone in that world will suddenly imitate the visitor and sprout fins and scales.

Shore is intermittently amusing as a lovable doofus, but as a moral philosopher, or self-help guru bringing enlightenment to the benighted natives of Middle America, he's not just out of water, he's out of his depth.

NEWSDAY, 7/2/93, Part II/p. 63, Jack Mathews

Stand-up comedian and MTV host Pauly Shore plays what his producers call a fish-out-of-water character in the romantic farce "Son-in-Law." Less enthused viewers may regard him more as "something the cat dragged in."

Shore, who had his film debut in last year's modestly successful "Encino Man," has developed a style as distinct as Pee-wee Herman's, though he looks more like a short Howard Stern. He wears goofy-loud clothes, swarms you with personality and speaks in a mutant form of Bill and Ted's excellent Valleyese.

He is what I guess you would call an acquired taste, at least for those of us immune to the wiles of MTV and surfer jargon, and though he is often engaging and delivers a few solid laughs in "Son-in-Law," there isn't enough going on in his act to carry a feature-length movie.

The script has the comedian playing Crawl, a perennial L.A. college student and mega-flake who befriends a homesick freshman named Rebecca (Carla Gugino). In the time it takes to show a rock video montage, he makes her over in Melrose chic—short blond hair, Spandex skirts, butterfly ankle tattoo, the works—then accepts her invitation to spend Thanksgiving break at her family's farm in South Dakota.

The ensuing culture clash is transcendent; even the chickens think this guy is weird.

But then, it's hard to tell the poultry from the people. At this farm, they're all clichés—rugged, good-hearted dad Walter (Lane Smith), the sacrificing mom Connie (Cindy Pickett), the obnoxious little brother Zack (Patrick Renna). and dyspeptic Gramps (Mason Adams), always on the porch whittlin' ducks.

Add to the mix a bovine farmhand in overalls (Dennis Burkley), Rebecca's old boyfriend Travis (Dan Gauthier) and a plot twist that has Crawl pretending to be Rebecca's fiance, and you have something akin to "Guess Who's Coming to Dinner at Ma and Pa Kettle's."

This setup was tailor-made, literally, for Shore's stand-up character. Writers Adam Small and Fax Bahr, a team in the writing stable of TV's "In Living Color," essentially came up with an idea for a Pauly Shore sitcom and filled it out with a string of setups for his zany riffs.

Some of them work—the scene where he tries to milk a cow from behind and gets rained on, so to speak, is a hoot—and some of them, most of them, do not. In the film's silliest and most patronizing sequence, Crawl grabs the microphone at a square dance and, in a matter of seconds, has the old fogies doing the funky chicken.

The idea here is that beneath his bizarre behavior and appearance is a sensitive, sincere, instinctively wise and irrepressibly lovable person, and that those qualities will win over the most narrow-minded hayseed.

Director Steve Dash, who did a nice job with the faintly familiar themes of "Can't Buy Me Love" a few years ago, was relegated here to directing scenes that are performance pieces. They may be scripted, but whether they work or not depends entirely on Shore's persona.

If you detect some ambivalence in this review, it's because Shore did begin to grow on me (must have been all that fertilizer). He is not a convincing actor, and those scenes demanding sentiment from him are excruciating. Still, enough charm comes through his over-ripe dopiness to keep "Son-in-Law" from being unbearable.

By summer movie standards, that's almost a compliment.

SIGHT AND SOUND, 3/94, p. 51, Robert Yates

High school graduate Rebecca leaves her South Dakotan small town and steady boyfriend Travis and sets off for college in California. The co-ed dorm provides something of a shock: students cruise in the corridor while Rebecca's lesbian room-mate openly gives her girlfriend a lustful kiss. A further surprise comes in the shape of Crawl, the dorm's Resident Advisor, given to madcap behaviour and relentless sexual suggestion. Rebecca determines to go home. Crawl talks her out of it, persuading her that new experiences are what college is all about. They set out on a restyling mission, Rebecca choosing a new, tight-cut wardrobe, having her hair bleached and getting a tattoo.

Weeks later, Rebecca invites Crawl to spend the Thanksgiving holiday with her family. There, he and Rebecca's new look meet with some alarm, while Crawl is amused by rural ways. Rebecca's interest in Travis has cooled and when he proposes to her at the local country club, she asks Crawl to do something. He reacts by pretending that he and Rebecca are already engaged. The family, none too pleased, decide to test Crawl's mettle and put him to work on their farm; he knuckles under and begins to win them over. He persuades Rebecca's mother to dress more sexily and goes fishing with Walter and Rebecca's grandfather, whom he helps revive from a faint.

Still playing along with the 'engagement', Crawl goes to his bachelor party, arranged by Travis, who is feigning friendship—Travis and a farmhand knock out Crawl and local girl Tracy by lacing their drinks with pills; they contrive to have the pair discovered in Walter's barn by Rebecca, who sends Crawl packing. However, Tracy guesses what happened, and she and Crawl denounce Travis. He is thrown out and Crawl is welcomed back to the family.

Son in Law is a vehicle for Pauly Shore and the character he developed for his MTV comedy show, *Totally Pauly*. Previously seen on film in 1992's *California Man*, Shore is a purveyor of a 'dudespeak' distantly related to the patter of the *Wayne's World* or *Bill and Ted* films, although Shore's version has none of the others' charm or invention. "Fresh meat!" he shouts, filming the backsides of the new female arrivals at college; while middle-aged Connie is delighted at his praise of her "neat package"—talk and responses that neither script nor direction treat with irony. Shore's character (more worldly and self-assured than Wayne and Garth) allows for the now bankable 'dude' principal to be slipped into a film made from story-lines and themes worn thin by TV melodrama.

The film's central subject is a culture clash, as America speaks to itself. Crawl (named for the way he used to get home after a night's revelry) is Venice Beach via Las Vegas, where he was raised; Rebecca and her family are Great Plains folk. They are "real people, pure people" according to Crawl, who video-tapes their movements. However, *Son in Law* sweeps away any conflict. Both Rebecca and Crawl have watched enough television programmes and movies to know the ropes. Indeed *Son in Law*'s desultory compliance with the teen film's now obligatory TV name-checking means that Crawl views Rebecca's family as the Waltons. Each takes to the other's world with such ease that the erstwhile downhome girl might be mistaken for a Sunset Strip hooker, while Crawl is soon riding pigs bareback.

Crawl, of course, is nothing less than that great rebel figure, the unconventional truth-teller come to shake up a sterile community. But woozy neo-hippiness, carried by his speech's cloying mixture of babe-watching and all-hangout therapeutics, can only produce an unthreatening, asexual hero. The film, admittedly, is for teenagers. Still, what are they to think? The men go to the river to bond; and the women free themselves of inhibitions by wearing fewer clothes. Does the film's wisdom lie in its suggestion that if men hold hands and women bare their breasts all will be well with the world?

Son in Law, one presumes, was saved from straight-to-video distribution because of its MTV connections. But there is a horrible cynicism at work here—way removed from the affectionate media mockery of *Wayne's World* or the cartoon nihilism of Beavis and Butt-head, who share the MTV alma mater with Shore—which grafts modish antics and language onto the laziest of set-ups.

Also reviewed in:
CHICAGO TRIBUNE, 7/2/93, Friday/p. C, Johanna Steinmetz
NEW YORK TIMES, 7/2/93, p. C14, Vincent Canby
VARIETY, 7/12/93, p. 52, Dennis Harvey
WASHINGTON POST, 7/2/93, p. B7, Richard Harrington
WASHINGTON POST, 7/2/93, Weekend/p. 31, Desson Howe

SON OF THE PINK PANTHER

A Metro-Goldwyn-Mayer release of a United Artists presentation in association with Filmauro S.R.L. *Executive Producer:* Nigel Wooll. *Producer:* Tony Adams. *Director:* Blake Edwards. *Screenplay:* Blake Edwards, Madeline Sunshine, and Steve Sunshine. *Story:* Blake Edwards. *Director of Photography:* Dick Bush. *Editor:* Robert Pergament. *Music:* Henry Mancini. *Music Editor:* Steve Hope. *Sound:* Ken Weston and (music) Alan Snelling. *Sound Editor:* Kay Rose. *Casting:* Nancy Klopper. *Production Designer:* Peter Mullins. *Art Director:* David Minty, John Siddall, and Leslie Tomkins. *Set Decorator:* Peter Howitt. *Special Effects:* Joss Williams. *Costumes:* Emma Porteous. *Make-up:* Peter Frampton. *Karate/Kick-Box Trainer:* Roger Yuan. *Stunt Coordinator:* Joe Dunne. *Running time:* 93 minutes. *MPAA Rating:* PG.

CAST: Roberto Benigni (Jacques); Herbert Lom (Dreyfus); Claudia Cardinale (Maria); Shabana Azmi (Queen); Debrah Farentino (Princess Yasmin); Jennifer Edwards (Yussa); Robert Davi (Hans); Mark Schneider (Armon); Mike Starr (Hanif); Kenny Spalding (Garth); Anton Rodgers (Chief Lazar); Burt Kwouk (Cato); Graham Stark (Dr. Balls); Oliver Cotton (King); Aharon Ipale (General Jaffar); Natasha Pavlova (Rima); Henry Goodman (Anchorman Andre); Dermot Crowley (François); Sputare Tanney (Jean Claude); Liz Smith (Madame Balls); Joe James (Doctor); Sylvestre Tobias (Customs Official); Nadim Sawalha (Lugash Agent); Jon Paul Morgan (Colonel Al-Durai); Andrew Hawkins (French Agent); Badi Uzzaman (Wasim); Mozaffar Shafeie (Omar); Arnold Yarrow (Uncle Idris); Harry Audley (Pilot); Jacinta Mulcahy (Louise Chauvin); Steven Crossley (Reporter); Elisabeth Barat (Female Reporter); Bill Wallis (President); John Francis (Yacht Captain); Simon De Selva (Co-Pilot); Ahmed Khalil (Otter Pilot); Joumana Al Awar (Queen's Secretary); Hossam Ramzy (Burly Arab); Sheila Hyde (Wafiyyah); Tony Kirkwood (Marcel Langois); Andy Scourfield (Clouseau's Ghost); Elizabeth Banks (Nurse); Nicoletta Braschi (Jacqueline).

LOS ANGELES TIMES, 8/28/93, Calendar/p. 5, Peter Rainer

The Pink Panther series, particularly in its early years, gave us all some classic comic set-pieces, and a great world-class bumbler in Peter Sellers' Inspector Clouseau, so perhaps the errant ineptitude of "Son of the Pink Panther" can be forgiven—and quickly forgotten.

Actually, this series ran out of steam long ago, and director Blake Edwards hasn't exactly rung in a new era by casting Italian superstar comic Roberto Benigni in the title role. He seems to have caught the director's lassitude: He's frenetic in a charmless, groggy way. His squiggly mimetic movements don't add up to a character, just a conceit.

The script, co-written by Edwards and Madeline Sunshine and Steve Sunshine, has a few potentially good ideas. Benigni's Jacques Clouseau Jr. isn't just a clone of his father. He has an Italian mother (played by Claudia Cardinale, who starred in the original 1964 "Pink Panther"), and he's deeply, dopily romantic. He spouts Shakespeare and Byron and belts out operatic arias with tone-deaf aplomb. He's a lackadaisical happy spirit, and that seems right for Clouseau's son—the infantilization fits.

But nothing much comes of all this because, the way the film has been directed, everything gets blended into the same unfunny clump of misfired gags and deadbeat timing. The plot, which has something to do with the kidnaping of a Middle Eastern princess (Debrah Farentino) by a scurvy crew headed by Robert Davi, is just an excuse to showcase a lot of mish-mashed slapstick (and, no doubt, to send the crew on location to such pleasure spots as Nice and Monte Carlo, though these locations are photographed so drably that they resemble shoddy backdrops).

A host of "Panther" stalwarts turns up, including the ever-twitching Herbert Lom as Commissioner Dreyfus and Burt Kwouk as Cato. They give the film (rated PG for comic violence and mild sensuality) some much-needed auld lang syne, although they're not given anything funny to do. Cato dresses up as a Hasidic rabbi in a harem in one scene and Dreyfus has his biggest comic moment being flummoxed in his hospital bed by a bumbling Clouseau while a Marx Brothers movie airs on the hospital room TV set. That's about as good as it gets. (It takes *cojones*, by the way, to insert a Marx Brothers clip into these proceedings. Not exactly a fair fight.)

Edwards actually sets the stage at the end for a sequel. Is there anybody out there who would want to see it? More to the point, would Edwards want to *make* it? His work here is so spiritless that the idea of his doing a sequel is positively harrowing. Either that or it's the best joke in the movie.

NEW YORK POST, 8/27/93, p. 26, Stephen Shaefer

"Son of the Pink Panther" is a witless wonder, a comedy so terribly unfunny it stands as practically a casebook on What Not to Do.

Somewhere in the heavens, Peter Sellers is having the last laugh at his old nemesis, writer/director Blake Edwards.

Sellers, who created—and stamped as his own—the role of the farcically inept Inspector Clouseau in five "Panther" romps, was an impossible collaborator, according to Edwards.

At his death at age 55 in 1980, the eccentric actor was planning to star in his own "Panther" outing, minus Edwards. Edwards, determined to keep stuffing a cash cow, forged ahead minus Sellers.

First, he patched together Sellers outtakes for "Trail of the Pink Panther" in 1982. More gruesomely, a year later he tried to foist Ted Wass—(*who?*)—as a Clouseau clone in "Curse of the Pink Panther."

Curse indeed.

Now, after a protracted legal struggle with MGM (which had changed owners) over rights to the immensely profitable series, Edwards has returned.

His device is to revive Clouseau via Clouseau's heretofore unknown illegitimate son.

Edwards' casting choice this round is Italy's Roberto Benigni.

Benigni, stranded in haphazard English, does his best. But he can't goose this tired slapstick shtick into anything fresh, much less inspired.

Benigni is an inept Nice cop named Jacques, who brings new dimension to the term bumbling. Jacques can't get off his bike without falling, can't go near wet cement without mucking.

He wouldn't recognize a kidnapping victim, like the abducted Middle Eastern princess in "Son," if she wore a neon sign blazing KIDNAPPING VICTIM.

"Son" reunites "Panther" veterans Claudia Cardinale, from the original 1964 "Panther," as Jacques' mistress, and Herbert Lom as the slow-burning, forever frustrated police chief Dreyfus.

Edwards even throws in Burt Kwouk, who reprises Cato, Clouseau's karate-kicking man-servant. He also throws in every hoary, cliched spy movie/comedy imaginable.

The throwaway plot—please, if someone had only thrown it far away!—involves a Middle East ruler, his deceitful wife, a belly dancer and a kidnapped princess.

What Edwards has wrought is nothing less than something so awful it resembles an artifact unearthed from a (bottom) shelf in a 1960s storeroom. The movie's entire look, feel, obviousness, sexism comprise a remarkable catalog of Bad Movie Moments From Another Era.

NEWSDAY, 8/27/93, Part II/p. 77, Jack Mathews

When Peter Sellers died in 1980, his most famous character, Inspector Jacques Clouseau, the hilariously foolish Paris sleuth of four "Pink Panther" movies and of the classic "A Shot in the Dark," died, too. It was a double-death that Closeau's creator, director Blake Edwards, refused to accept.

In the early '80s, Edwards made two more Clouseau/Pink Panther movies, both built around the premise that Clouseau was merely missing—in one, a woman reporter tries to find him, and in the other, a bumbling New York cop is put on the case—and his fans were not amused.

Now, a decade later, Edwards finally buries Clouseau, but not before giving him an heir to the throne of Europe's most incompetent cop. In "Son of the Pink Panther," which should bury the series as well, we discover that while working on the Gambrelli case that was the focus of "A Shot in the Dark," Clouseau and Maria Gambrelli spent a cold night together trying to keep warm the best way they could.

Maria, played by a young Elke Sommer 29 years ago and by a ravishing middle-age Claudia Cardinale here, returned to Italy where she raised her gene-damaged son, without telling him who his father was.

The son, played by gifted Italian actor/comedian Roberto Benigni, shares many traits with his infamous father—he mulches words, he's accident-prone, he bounces up from embarrassing pratfalls with a lusty "That felt good!" But Benigni makes Jacques Jr. his own kind of clown, a broad, ceaselessly cheerful buffoon where Sellers' Jacques *pere* worked in subtler shades of physical and intellectual confusion.

If the series must be continued, the illegitimate son gimmick works well enough. It introduces a different character, while being respectful of the one made indelible by Sellers, and Benigni has the talent and natural appeal to become an international star.

Unfortunately, once the new character and star are introduced, the movie slips back into the same tired formula, recycling characters, plot and gags that had become repetitious and tiresome even *before* Sellers' death.

Most of the "Panther" movies were propelled by the theft of the Pink Panther, a massive diamond kept in a museum in the mythical Middle Eastern kingdom of Lugash. In this one, the villains kidnap Lugash's Princess Yasmin (Debrah Farentino), demanding the diamond as ransom, and Clouseau's old colleague/nemesis Commissioner Dreyfus (Herbert Lom) is recruited by the Italian government to rescue her.

Dreyfus requests Italy's best policeman as his assistant, but a resentful local official instead assigns him Italy's worst, the obliviously sanguine bicycle cop Jacques Gambrelli. When the two meet, in a chain reaction auto accident caused by little Jacques, Dreyfus' eye begins to twitch, a sure sign that Lom is about to repeat a past performance.

Sure enough, Dreyfus is soon playing Wile E. Coyote again, devising violent ways to assassinate the blissfully unaware Clouseau, and managing only to maim and hospitalize himself.

Like the earlier movies, the plot points of "Son of the Pink Panther" are forgotten before you're out of the theater. But in this one, there aren't many fresh comic sketches to savor, either. Edwards is a great farceur, and even his worst comedies have had moments of sublime invention.

The only new running gag in "Son" involves a horny French poodle and Dreyfus' leg, and it won't make the series' highlights film.

Edwards, with the aid of co-writers Madeline Sunshine and Steven Sunshine, goes to the well again and again for old routines. Burt Kwouk's Cato leaping out from odd plates to attack. Graham Stark's Dr. Balls coming up with ever sillier disguises. And though Benigni hams it up with gusto, and is often very funny, he makes us more aware than ever how futile it is to try to pump fresh blood into a dead series.

VILLAGE VOICE, 9/14/93, p. 69, Tom Kertes

Blake Edwards is beating a dead horse in this film—and he's doing it with a broken whip. The sorry beast is the Pink Panther franchise, the highest-grossing comedy series of all time, which, by this point, is so spent it seems just highly gross. The broken whip is star Alberto Benigni, who not only fails in his attempt to become the Next Peter Sellers, but even has a hard time being the First Roberto Benigni.

That Benigni, the inspired, irrepressible clown in Jim Jarmusch's minimalist madness *Down By Law*, played off of his costars' nihilistic world-weariness perfectly, creating sumptuous screen chemistry. In *Son*, however, he seems to be in an entirely different (though perhaps better) movie than the rest of the cast.

The script is based on a rather witty idea—Clouseau has an illegitimate son, also a policeman, also an idiot—but this premise is spun out without wit or coherence. The pedestrian direction doesn't help; in fact, an air of musty desperation hangs over the entire project.

Is there anything less funny than desperately forced comedy? Yes: desperately forced *stolen* comedy; *Son*'s best jokes are unoriginal. And when the funniest scene in a movie is a French poodle humping somebody's leg *twice* ... well, Edwards should hire Inspector Clouseau to look for his lost career. Preferably, the original Clouseau.

Also reviewed in:
NEW YORK TIMES, 8/28/93, p. 9, Stephen Holden
VARIETY, 9/6/93, p. 26, Emanuel Levy
WASHINGTON POST, 8/28/93, p. F8, David Mills

SPACE IS THE PLACE

A Rhapsody Films release. *Producer:* Jim Newman. *Director:* John Coney. *Screenplay:* Joshua Smith, Sun Ra, Christopher Brooks, and Jim Newman. *Editor:* Mark Gorney. *Running time:* 63 minutes. *MPAA Rating:* Not Rated.

CAST: Sun Ra (Himself); Ray Johnson (The Overseer).

NEW YORK POST, 9/3/93, p. 28, Lawrence Cohn

The late bandleader Sun Ra is given a soapbox from which to spout his mystical separatist message in this "lost" film from 1974, a curious mish-mash which unfortunately does not include enough footage of what the man did best, play jazz.

Fans are well aware of the avant-garde jazz artist's mixture of mumbo-jumbo and uplifting rhetoric. Here he's introduced as "Sonny Ray," playing barrelhouse piano in a 1943 Chicago nightclub. When the hoochie-coochie dancers come on he launches into a discordant solo which literally brings the house down, supernaturally creating a mini-tornado.

In a nod to Ingmar Bergman's "The Seventh Seal," Sun Ra proceeds to play a fateful card game with The Overseer (Ray Johnson), a petty black gangster who, obviously resents the evil forces exploiting the African-American community from within. Except for an out-of-work NASA scientist who foolishly comes to Ra's Outerspaceways employment agency, there is little lampooning of Caucasians.

This morality play is intercut with tantalizingly brief footage of Ra's Solar Arkestra performing, featuring the late June Tyson singing her heart out in close-up. Ra who comes to Earth in a space ship, also lectures black youth of the 1970s on their non-existence in this white-dominated society, proposing that they follow him to a new world inhabited by blacks only.

Working on what is evidently a shoestring budget, director John Coney includes some interesting shots of Sun Ra wandering in an alien landscape. It's a shame Sun Ra was never invited to score a big-budget science-fiction film, as this poverty-row enterprise was unworthy of his talents.

Apart from Sun Ra's musical group, buffs will spot in the no-name cast former porn star Johnnie Keyes (of "Behind the Green Door" fame), portraying a wino.

NEWSDAY, 9/3/93, Part II/p. 75, Gene Seymour

Given the feverish, anything-goes atmosphere of the so-called "blaxploitation" era of 1970s African-American film history, it's easy to see how a garish piece of exotica like "Space is the Place" got overlooked. It somehow seems apt, karmically speaking, that it should unexpectedly reappear scant months after the death of its star, co-author and reason-for-being, Sun Ra.

Released in 1974, this 63-minute mythological-ontological-street-vengeance fantasy begins in earnest when Ra, jazz keyboardist, bandleader, shaman, prophet and cosmic clotheshorse, lands in his spaceship somewhere in Oakland, Calif., (natch!) where he proclaims himself the "alter-destiny" and begins soliciting black Earthlings, the young in particular, to accompany him back into the more-hospitable cosmos.

While on this mission, Ra is being stalked by two ugly white FBI guys who, upon capturing Ra, try extracting his secrets by forcing him to listen to repeated choruses of "Dixie." While all this is going on, the film cuts back and forth to a tarot-card poker game, running parallel with the plot, between Ra and a sinister pimp-sweetback personage who tries to trump the soft-spoken spaceways traveler at every turn.

"Are you for real?," one Afro-coifed youth queries the regally garbed Ra at one point. "I am a myth," he sagely replies. "You are a myth. If you were real, then why would you be seeking equal rights?" After a while, a lot of such errant epigrams begin to make sense. So much so that you not only start questioning your sanity, you begin to wonder why the people who made this film felt it necessary to interrupt such intriguing, enigmatic ideas with this tacky, threadbare story line.

The best thing to do is go along with the jive campiness, which, after all, was one of the best things about *any* Sun Ra show, live, filmed or recorded. Speaking of which, the best parts of "Space is the Place" are those in which Ra performs with his Arkestra, featuring such stalwarts as saxophonists John Gilmore, Marshall Royal and the matchless vocalist June Tyson.

Whether one can groove with its flakiness or not, there's one thing that has to be conceded by all. There will never be another film like "Space is the Place." Just as there will never be another living being like Sun Ra.

VILLAGE VOICE, 9/7/93, p. 62, Colson Whitehead

In *Space Is the Place*, the late jazz maestro Sun Ra battles for the soul of blackness in two spheres. On an astral plane, he plays cards with the Overseer—Satan in a polyester pimp suit—keeping score on an abacus. On the Earth below, their war is enacted after Sun Ra lands his starship in an Oakland field and asks the folk, "Are you ready to alter your destiny?"

This is the first theatrical showing of *Space Is the Place* since it was completed in 1974; it was "lost" as only true treasures can be. *Space* takes Sun Ra's crypto cosmic acrobatics and sets them gamboling through the hyperbolic terrain of the blaxploitation flick; in the process, it creates a comic and grim parable of Black Power. And while the music of Ra and his Galactic Solar Arkestra are spotlighted, the songs serve as a chorus, not as a mere showcase for the outfit's talent.

As he tries to educate the masses, Sun Ra's cosmic jive merges the flourishes of early '70s slang and the urgent rhetoric of nationalism to become a single, charged language of "transmolecularization" and "cultural co-option."

In this atmosphere, Ra's arcana, often called theatrical, becomes political, and the revolutionary bent of his mission—to transport the race to a new, black planet—is not lost on the authorities: the FBI taps Ra's phone, and kidnaps and tortures him by making him listen to "Dixieland." When that fails to break him, they try to assassinate him.

Transferred to film, Ra's eccentric musical mythology is fully delineated. His Ark is an ark, one last chance for escape. Now, he says is "after the end of the world," but that's not just lyrical fancy; it's a sober assessment.

Also reviewed in:
NEW YORK TIMES, 9/3/93, p. C9, Jon Pareles

SPIKE & MIKE'S FESTIVAL OF ANIMATION 1993

A Festival Films release of 16 animated shorts. *Running time:* 106 minutes. *MPAA Rating:* Not Rated.

NEW YORK POST, 12/3/93, p. 44, Bill Hoffmann

If you're bored with the Cartoon Network and you've seen every "Bevis and Butt-head" episode a dozen times, check out "Spike & Mike's Festival of Animation 1993."

This hit-and-miss grab bag of 16 animated shorts does have some dead weight but there are many high points, and when they come, they're absolutely exhilarating.

The two masterpieces here are well worth the price of admission, the first being the Nick Park's 28-minute Claymation tribute to Hitchcock, "The Wrong Trousers."

"Trousers" features the adventures of Gromit, a floppy, likable mutt, and his master, Wallace, a dimwitted British gentleman who depends on his pet to dress, feed and generally help him get through life.

But Gromit's usefulness is put in serious doubt when Wallace rents a room to a mysterious suitcase-carrying duck, who calculatingly begins to take over the household.

This is one fowl who's up to no good and it's going to take some major sleuthing by Gromit to figure out what's going on.

It's a marvelous salute to the legendary master of suspense right down to the copycat Bernard Herrmann-like score.

But it also succeeds as a laugh-out-loud comedy and features a hysterical chase scene on a toy train that will leave you breathless.

For sheer artistry, Joan Gratz's seven-minute "Mona Lisa Descending a Staircase" can't be beat.

Gratz gives us the history of modern art, showing us hundreds of masterpieces each mutating into the next with startling, unbelievable ease—a task that must have taken forever.

Gratz's obviously painstaking work deservedly won her the 1992 Oscar for Best Animated Short Film.

None of the other entries reach the sheer brilliance of these two, but there is some nice work.

Simple but effective Is Michele Ocelot's 1992 French entry "The Prince and the Princess," which begins with an innocent kiss that turns a prince into a frog. Subsequent kisses to correct the situation have both title characters mutating into different creatures.

This gentle, subtitled short is a heartwarming winner.

"Pro & Con" takes an intelligent and humane look at the penal system by interviewing a female correction officer and an inmate and using confiscated weapons, inmate artwork and lyrical pencil drawings to illustrate it.

Unfortunately, there are some dogs in this collection.

The opening short is a frenzied computer-animated work based on Jerry Garcia's skull artwork from a Grateful Dead Album cover. This is probably a gas if you're stoned out of your mind but for everyone else, its a big bore.

Two other entries, "Too Taa Too" and "Gas Planet" should be taken out and shot.

The great thing about a compilation is that even when the clinkers hit they're only a few minutes long.

And because more than half of the film's running length is good or great—you really can't lose.

NEWSDAY, 12/3/93, Part II/p. 103, Gene Seymour

With "The Nightmare Before Christmas" still raking in rivers of dough and the Beavis and Butt-head phenomenon going global, it is no longer possible to take these animation festivals with the proverbial grain of paprika.

Outfits like Spike-and-Mike, producer of toon bazaars for 17 years now, are going to have to be watched closely for any manner of Big Thing on the horizon in pop culture. It was, after all, an S&M showcase that helped boost the public profiles of both Tim Burton and Henry Sellick, "Nightmare's" producer and director, respectively.

We also have Spike-and-Mike to blame for bringing Beav and the Head into our lives in one of S&M's "Sick and Twisted" midnight-only fests. "Frog Baseball," if memory serves, was the historic flick. (Actually, it was pretty funny stuff at the time ...)

One waits for animation's sense of serious fun to be impaired by such hot-button importance. So far that hasn't happened, if this year's edition of the Spike-and-Mike festival is any indication. If anything, the fest shows that the more animation is given serious attention, the more its practitioners seem to let fly with relaxed abandon.

Xaos, a Bay Area animation facility, kick-starts the festival with the righteously mind-blowing "Infrared Roses Revisited," a 3-D take on Jerry Garcia's artwork for the Gratefu Dead album of the same name. Other fine American entries include "Pro and Con," by Joan Gratz and Joanna Priestly, which looks at both sides of the prison experience.

But it's the British-made selections that are, by far, the best-in-show. Barry J.C. Purves' "Screen-Play" is a drop-dead beauty. It is an ancient Japanese legend of love, betrayal and blood, told with animated Bunraku puppets and stunning stage design.

And finally, there's the remarkable Nick Park, who got an Oscar a couple year's back for the laugh-out-loud Claymation classic, "Creature Comforts."

Park looks as if he's got another winner with "The Wrong Trousers," starring his two recurring characters, Wallace and Gromit. Wallace, a dotty inventor, becomes an unwitting pawn in the evil machinations of a baleful-looking penguin. It's up to Gromit, Wallace's cool, stalwart dog, to save the day.

Park's Claymation style, with its subtle wit and nuanced movements, is as affecting as ever. What makes "Trousers" special is that it's fine filmmaking as well. Aping Hitchcock may have elevated Park's horizons. I call it a near-masterpiece because I think he's got even more miracles in reserve.

VILLAGE VOICE, 12/7/93, p. 72, David D. Kim

With *The Nightmare Before Christmas* ringing up some Hollywood cheer, commercial animation has officially graduated from feature film's bratty stepchild to cash-cow cartoons for grown-ups. At least partial credit goes to Spike and Mike's Festival of Animation—which debuted Tim Burton's sweetly macabre *Vincent*—but also partial blame: the fest's late-night sister program, Sick and Twisted, gave us Beavis and Butt-head before they ever yelled "fire."

All potential candidates for next season's *Liquid TV*, the 16 recent works in this year's fest are less international in scope than your typical Tournée of Animation, and somewhat heavy on Oscar contenders from Britain and the U.S. Fresh out of England's Aardman Animations, Nick Park's *The Wrong Trousers* features Wallace and Gromit—Park's recurring man-and-dog duo—whose passion for low-tech gadgetry goes awry at the flaps of a diabolical penguin. Sight gags are Park's forte, along with a very English sense of the absurd. Less reliant on narrative, Barry Purves's *Screenplay* weaves the spatial perspectives of stop-motion animation and Japanese painting into an arty interplay of Bunraku puppets, shoji screens, and revolving surfaces. Employing stylized conventions of Asian theater, Purves frames this ill-fated lovers' tale from a static, balcony-seat p.o.v., thereby highlighting the "staged" illusion of constant movement.

Part of Aardman's apparent claymation monopoly, Richard Goleszowski's two Rex the Runt shorts possess a daft, sprightly incoherence not unlike the "Penny" segments he used to produce for *Pee-Wee's Playhouse*. In *Dreams*, for example, pooch Rex envisions both hell and a twitching chicken dinner à la Eraserhead. A tongue-in-cheek programmer would have immediately followed this up with *Pencil Head*, a computer-image exploration from Xaos, the Bay Area animation collective that also produced the more recent Grateful Dead-inspired *Infrared Roses Revisited*. Though technically cutting-edge, these shorts and the fest's other computer-animated works (including Eric Darnell-Pacific Data Images's quirky riff on cosmic flatulence called *Gas Planet*) are generally limited to visual and narrative one-liners. Plus, they're really short—presumably because the gee-whiz pyrotechnics are too expensive for anything other than movie F/X and beer commercials.

A more primitive, low-gloss animated form, clay painting takes colorful shape in Joan Gratz's *Mona Lisa Descending a Staircase*—a fluid, if thematically dull, short composed of modern art paintings morphing into more of the same. Gratz's technique works better in *Pro and Con*, a piece she and Joanna Priestley animated using taped interviews with a parole officer and prison inmate as a creative springboard. Unfortunately, these are the only selections by women; animation fests are notorious for promoting the ol' boys' studio. Spike and Mike's does suggest a healthy animation market, however, which may create more openings in the neo-*Aladdin* age of entertainment. And if computer images merge with the information freeway, animation just might once and for all slough off the primordial goo of Hanna Barbera and the rest. You've come a long way, Boo Boo.

Also reviewed in:
NEW YORK TIMES, 12/4/93, p. 11, Stephen Holden
WASHINGTON POST, 4/22/94, p. C6, Richard Harrington

SPLIT

An E.F.T. production. *Producer:* Ellen Fisher Turk. *Director:* Andrew Weeks and Ellen Fisher Turk. *Screenplay:* Don Chayefsky. *Director of Photography:* Jacqueline Escolar, Mijana Gall, Nick Manning, Josh Pease, Hank Rifkin, and Fisher Turk. *Editor:* Peter Ringer and Keith Brown. *Music:* Jimmy Camicia. *Narrator:* Wes Kent. Running time: 60 minutes. MPAA Rating: Not Rated.

WITH: International Chrysis; Justin Davis; Gerald Duval; Jeremiah Newton; Teri Paris; Brian Belovitch; David Burns; Amy Coleman; Jimmy Camica; Michael Degenhardt; David Glamamore; Ron Jones; Codie Leone; Rodney Pridgen; Maggie Ruzo.

NEW YORK POST, 9/3/93, p. 31, Jerry Tallmer

When he was 12 years old, this boy William first put on his mother's makeup, took one look in the mirror, decided he had to get the hell out of The Bronx.

Ran away from home, became a movie-star drag queen at 14, told people who asked him: "I'm the mother of Christ," got popped into Bellevue at 18, perhaps in the same ward with his mother. Came out, rechristened himself/herself Chrysis St. Laurent, later refining that to International Chrysis.

And who is this absolutely exquisite stunning woman in black top and tights, red pony tail swinging, long earrings dangling, as she waltzes down Broadway toward a cab? Gets in, settles back, says in a tawny sultry voice: "Well, somebody's got to do it." It's the same boy from the Bronx, grown up, world-famous heroine of the underground, dead at 39, either from drugs or breast implants or both, subject of Ellen Fisher Turk's fascinating short movie called "Split."

There were those, in her/his lifetime, who thought she—we might as well settle for *she*, as he did—was in the same league for looks with Jean Harlow, with Rita Hayworth. Lovely provocative smile, white-on-white teeth, tongue painted red to make them whiter, and oh, those breasts. "I mean, she stopped traffic a lot." says a guy in a hard hat. "You would see her in a full body suit with glitter and say: "What the hell was *that*?"

Would see her, too, "a vision in cellophane," making an even more glittering entrance to Studio 54, arm-in-arm with Salvador Dali—"all eyes on her, not on Dali."

People went wild, men went wild. No few hetero males went dippy—as in "Last Exit to Brooklyn," as in "The Crying Game"—over this woman from the waist up, man from the waist down. "She was *very* butch in bed," is the testimony of one who knew. None of your make-believe Klingers here. Or all of it make-believe.

She did have a sense of humor. Called those frontispieces of hers "Johnson & Johnson" because they were made of floor wax, or something worse. But it wasn't all laughs, oh no. Those breasts felt like armor. "She did not want people to explore anything," says a woman friend. "There was something dark in her." In the end, Chrysis, who hated aging, grew fat, sick, huge, came out of a hospital riddled with cancer—and still smoking, "I am dying, you know—nobody believes me," she'd say, on mike, in her club dates.

She stopped traffic one last time, with all the kids at her 1990 memorial in front of the UN. "I miss her so much," says one of them.

NEWSDAY, 9/3/93, Part II/p. 67, Jonathan Mandell

She wore slinky net gowns in her party act that made her look like Ann-Margret, though she sang like Marlene Dietrich, Salvador Dali painted and befriended her, Sidney Lumet cast her in a role, with 10th billing in his movie "Q & A," a French producer put her in his Broadway revue. She was International Chrysis, a boy from the Bronx who became a drag queen and reportedly a drug addict, a prostitute and a stripper, a show girl and a cabaret singer, and, to her friends, a star. When she died three years ago at the age of 39—from cancer, supposedly caused in part by seepage from her breast implants—her friends put her name in glitter on the street in front of the United Nations.

Her friends and glitter both figure prominently in "Split," the hour-long documentary of her life, which is subtitled "William to Chrysis: Portrait of a Drag Queen."

The portrait is first a visual one: "Split" includes extensive footage of Chrysis performing or posing or giving a tour of her apartment or just walking down the street. Though little of her conversation is interesting or even intelligible (she often talks New Age babble), you can understand the filmmakers' fascination with someone who appears not only so persuasively feminine but so effortlessly glamorous (or at least glittery). The effect was far from effortless, in fact, and left her in constant pain, both physical and, apparently, emotional.

The less successful portrait is that provided by the talking-head and voice-over testimony of about a dozen of her "friends," who are not identified until the closing credits, and then only by name, not occupation or the nature of their connection to Chrysis. The filmmakers cover their failure to do basic research with a long and cowardly legal disclaimer at the end; they allow the people they interview to reminisce, gossip and broadly speculate on her life, her family, her loves, and her death without any effort to determine if they know what they are talking about. It certainly doesn't sound as if they do.

What they offer as insight consists largely of commentary that is variously worshipful, catty, pseudo-academic, insipid, invasive and downright exploitive: one of the worst vulgarly discusses Chrysis' anatomical measurements, adding with glee: "I saw it. I took photographs of it." With friends like these ...

The cumulative effect is to build their dead friend up into something not so much larger than life as nonhuman (a projection of their own fantasies and ambitions), while simultaneously tearing her apart—and in the end, to tell us almost nothing about her, not even her full name.

Perhaps the filmmakers are saying that Chrysis was a creation of imagination—her own and her friends'—and that a documentary on her life need not have anything so irrelevant and unhip as a documentable fact. But in an era of RuPaul and "The Crying Game" and Wigstock (this weekend's gathering of drag queens) and especially the infinitely superior "Paris Is Burning," the least we can demand of a drag documentary is that it have what the queens call realness.

VILLAGE VOICE, 9/14/93, p. 60, Manohla Dargis

Split: Portrait of a Drag Queen is exactly what it says, a sketch of a man who went from the Bronx to Manhattan by way of eyeliner, heels, and a cocktail of bovine hormones, wax, and other noxious ingredients. Vivacious and talented, Chrysis was apparently a mainstay of New York nightlife, keeping company with the likes of Salvador Dali and Factory stars such as Holly Woodlawn and Candy Darling.

Directors Andrew Weeks and Ellen Fisher Turk may feel for Chrysis but empathy isn't enough. Clocking in at an abrupt 60 minutes, their video barely manages a gloss on Chrysis as it intercuts between interviews with friends and footage of the diva in action. The doc is woefully naive (was she really a victim of her own creation, or of homophobia?) and mired in the stereotype of the tragic queen.

Also reviewed in:
NEW YORK TIMES, 9/3/93, p. C6, Stephen Holden
VARIETY, 10/4/93, p. 39, Sylvester Joachim

SPLITTING HEIRS

A Universal Pictures release of a Prominent Features production. *Executive Producer:* Eric Idle. *Producer:* Simon Bosanquet and Redmond Morris. *Director:* Robert Young. *Screenplay:* Eric Idle. *Director of Photography:* Tony Pierce-Roberts. *Editor:* John Jympson. *Music:* Michael Kamen. *Music Editor:* Dina Eaton. *Sound:* Peter Glossop. *Sound Editor:* Bob Risk. *Casting:* Michelle Guish. *Production Designer:* John Beard. *Art Director:* Rod McLean and Lucy Richardson. *Set Decorator:* Joanne Woollard. *Special Effects:* Trevor Neighbour. *Costumes:* Penny Rose. *Make-up:* Paul Engelen. *Stunt Coordinator:* Simon Crane. *Running time:* 87 minutes. *MPAA Rating:* PG-13.

CAST: Rick Moranis (Henry); Eric Idle (Tommy); Barbara Hershey (Duchess Lucinda); Catherine Zeta Jones (Kitty); John Cleese (Shadgrind); Sadie Frost (Angela); Stratford Johns (Butler); Brenda Bruce (Mrs. Bullock); William Franklyn (Andrews); Charubala Chokshi (Mrs. Patel); Jeremy Clyde (14th Duke); Richard Huw (Brlute); Eric Sykes (Jobson the Doorman); Bridget McConnel (Nanny); Bill Stewart (Adoption Agent); Paul Brooke (Tour Guide); David Ross (Sgt. Richardson); Cal Macaninch (CID Officer); Anisha Gangotra (Gita); Amanda Dickinson (Barmaid); Chris Jenkinson (Police Constable); Keith Smith (Photographer); Stephen Grothgar (German Tourist); Madge Ryan (Woman with Dog); Bill Wallis (Vicar at Hunt); Cameron Blakeley (Hunt Saboteur); Louise Downey (Doreen); Llewellyn Rees (Old Major); Paul Weston and Tim Lawrence (French Drivers); Gary Lineker and Michelle Lineker (Couple at Restaurant).

LOS ANGELES TIMES, 5/1/93, Calendar/p. 6, Michael Wilmington

Just like the Beatles, the Monty Python group in pieces never seems to match the greatness of its whole. "Splitting Heirs", an Eric Idle project with a bit of John Cleese, is a nice enough comedy about things like abandoning babies, nymphomania, near-incest and trying to murder your way into the aristocracy. But it doesn't have the brilliance of the old Pythons. It doesn't pulse, rage, knock your socks off.

Nor does it have the irony and fancy edges of its obvious model, Robert Hamer's 1949 comedy of crimes "Kind Hearts and Coronets," in which Dennis Price kept trying to kill all the relatives—all played by Alec Guinness—between him and a dukeship.

Here, Idle, as Tommy, the rightful Duke of Bournemouth abandoned in infancy by his careless rich-hippie parents, keeps trying to kill Rick Moranis, as an improbable Roller-Blading American who's taken his place, both in the dukedom and in the affections of the madly arousing social climber Kitty (Catherine Zeta Jones.) Tommy, the movie informs us, is in his 20s and has been raised by his adoptive family of poor Pakistanis—and, frankly, Idle can play Pakistani better than he can play 20. Pretending he can still do naive youths is probably one of Idle's little jokes: like giving his old Python mate the special credit: "And introducing John Cleese."

What "Splitting Heirs" does have is a relatively clean, fast style. Its cinematographer is Tony Pierce-Roberts, and its director is one of the many Robert Youngs that have worked in movies, the one that directed "Jeeves and Wooster" rather than "The Ballad of Gregorio Cortez." And it has laughs—which is probably all we need ask of a movie comedy.

Is the old Python spirit still flitting about here? Perhaps. There are several major resemblances: "Splitting Heirs" is irreverent toward authority, the men tend to be either twits or maniacs, and the ladies are madly lascivious—even though Terry Jones isn't around to play them. Barbara Hershey, as Tommy's gorgeous mother, Duchess Lucinda, movingly plays a love child grown old but not shy. Jones, a Welsh actress making her movie debut, slinks around this film like a cat who's taken over the whole house. She's welcome.

All the actors are fun to watch, particularly Moranis, who's playing a little swiftie this time, instead of one of his usual nerds. But the only really withering comic turn is supplied by Cleese, as Shadgrind the lawyer. Cleese has always excelled at playing bent Establishment types; he's one of the best comic sadists in the history of movies. Here, he's playing a lawyer who's actually a psychopath and homicidal maniac. When Tommy comes to discuss his rightful inheritance, Cleese's Shadgrind has the solution within minutes: mercury chloride in the brandy or a bash on the head—all just speculatively, of course.

The way Cleese hounds Idle through this movie is the movie's high point. And it's the film's only real point of comparison with the older British comedies, the Ealing pictures with Guinness or the Peter Sellers farces, that it tries to evoke.

And "Splitting Heirs" (MPAA-rated PG-13) is an OK comedy: not as good as the Python works, not as good as Cleese's "A Fish Called Wanda," probably not even as good as Idle's "The Rutles." When you chop up a Python, you probably shouldn't complain that its hugs aren't as intense. This movie is just as good as it has to be—except when Cleese takes over, wandering up with a leer and another bomb. Then, it's a killer.

NEWSDAY, 5/3/93, Part II/p. 49, Jack Mathews

If I had to choose, however, [the reference is to *The Pickle*] I'd rather watch the adventures of the rocket pickle than sit through Robert Young's "Splitting Heirs" a second time.

This British comedy, which its U.S. distributor Universal Pictures also opened without advance screenings, was written by Monty Python's Eric Idle and stars Idle as a London commodities broker who, when he discovers that he is actually the long-lost 15th Duke of Bournemouth, sets out to murder the sitting duke and claim his royal inheritance.

His task is complicated by the fact that the person raised in his place (Rick Moranis) is his best friend, and that his real mother, the nymphomaniacal Duchess Lucinda (Barbara Hershey), is trying to seduce him because of his resemblance to her late husband, his father.

After establishing these identity crises, "Splitting Heirs" devolves into a live-action cartoon, a series of sight gags where the assassin is always hoist on his own petard.

The story might have been good for a half-hour episode of the old "Monty Python Flying Circus," with the troupe playing all of the roles, male and female, and using its collective zaniness to push it along. Idle did recruit the senior Python, John Cleese, to play a cameo as a psychotic lawyer, and he provides a snicker in a scene or two.

Otherwise, "Splitting Heirs" is about as funny as a flying pickle.

SIGHT AND SOUND, 5/93, p. 57, Geoffrey Macnab

During the swinging 60s, the Duchess of Bournemouth accidentally leaves her baby in a restaurant while she goes out dancing with her hippie friends. On the same day, another baby is abandoned in a telephone box. The Duchess reclaims the wrong baby, and her real child, Tommy, is brought up by the Patels, a poor Pakistani family living in Southall.

Tommy grows up to become a stockbroker in the City. One day, he is asked by his boss to look after an American associate, Henry, who is shortly due to arrive in London on business. Tommy reluctantly agrees, accompanying Henry on a wild night out in the pubs and nightclubs. Tommy's job is under threat, especially when his boss discovers he has been pilfering the company's petty cash. However, when the Duke of Bournemouth falls overboard from his boat and drowns, Henry inherits the title and takes charge of the business where Tommy works. Soon, Henry and Tommy have become fast friends.

Tommy accidentally discovers his real mother was the Duchess Lucinda and that he should rightfully be in Henry's shoes. His jealousy of Henry is compounded when he learns that the beautiful, flirtatious Kitty is planning to marry Henry, not because she loves him, but because she wants to be a duchess. Tommy tries to press his claim to the Bournemouth title. His solicitor, the sinister Shadgrind, tells him he doesn't have a case unless he manages to kill Henry. Tommy is so desperate to get on in the world that he devises a series of far-fetched schemes for murdering his rival. First, he ties him up in a basket of a hot air balloon and lets him loose in the sky; then he tries poison; then, during Henry and Kitty's honeymoon, he attempts to blow Henry up and, when that fails, to burn him to death. Finally, he decides he likes Henry too much to kill him. But Shadgrind, who has no such scruples, wants to assassinate Henry in the belief that he and Tommy will share the Bournemouth spoils.

The Duchess Lucinda learns that Tommy, not Henry, is her real son. At the same time, Henry finds out Kitty has had an affair with Tommy. Henry drives away from his country house in disgust; Shadgrind has planted a bomb in his car, but this fails to kill him and he returns to the manor. He manages to save Kitty and Tommy's life, but is almost shot by Shadgrind in the process. Realising the game is up, Shadgrind flees but is caught and mauled to death by one of the panthers kept as Bournemouth mascots. Tommy accedes to the Bournemouth title, and he and Henry set up a business, opening the Bournemouth estates to the public and turning them into an American-style theme park.

In the wake of *A Fish Called Wanda*, which made close to $200 million worldwide, *Splitting Heirs* casts more than half an eye on the American market, combining British locations and actors with a brace of Hollywood stars. On paper, at least, the pairing of *Python* veterans Eric Idle and John Cleese with the gnomish, kid-shrinking Rick Moranis and the versatile Barbara Hershey must have seemed every bit as intriguing as *Wanda*'s casting of Cleese and Michael Palin opposite Jamie Lee Curtis and Kevin Kline. Unfortunately, the gamble doesn't come off.

Completely shorn of the anarchy and excess which were the hallmark of the Python team in its prime, *Splitting Heirs* emerges as a loose, mid-Atlantic hybrid with wafer-thin characters. The film seems stuck in a time-warp: the Brits behave like refugees from *Upstairs, Downstairs*, with society strictly divided into repressed, besuited toffs who sneer at their butlers or, down in the scullery, comic-turn policemen, cooks and nannies. Unlike Charles Crichton, who was able to bring a wry, Ealing-like irony to *Wanda*, director Robert Young eschews understatement, aiming instead for knockabout farce. In telling the tale of a little man fighting for his fortune, he uses a broad, crude style worthy of the great journeyman of British cinema, John Paddy Carstairs, who made scores of similarly untaxing comedies with stars like Formby and Wisdom. As with Carstairs, the pace and cheerful inanity of the picture may go some way to excusing its lack of wit and subtlety. Young can hardly be blamed for Eric Idle's feeble script, which is so heavily reliant on slapstick, explosions (exploding prams, exploding clay pigeons, exploding oxygen tanks and exploding cars) and seaside-postcard innuendo that it's hard to sustain much interest in the story.

If the film fails to impress on its own terms, and manages to squander a high-voltage cast, it nevertheless offers fitful reminders of earlier, more impressive work from its makers. Idle's nasal voice-over, and his portrayal of a dispossessed young relative having to kill his way to his inheritance, are vaguely reminiscent of Dennis Price in *Kind Hearts and Coronets*. Moranis, gum-chewing, roller-skating, eminently personable, seems quite at home: after all, this is a nerdy film. Cleese, mildly psychotic as the murderous Shadgrind, reprises his funny walk, always a sign of desperation. There are one or two memorable lines of dialogue—*Miss Saigon*, for instance, is aptly described as a "cross between *Apocalypse Now* and *The Sound of Music*"—and Barbara Hershey gives a cheerfully overblown, pantomime-style performance as the nymphomaniacal Duchess Lucinda, who unknowingly tries to seduce her own son.

Interviewed in 1989 on the twentieth anniversary of the first *Python* show, Idle suggested that comedy's job was "to be against things ... to be antiauthoritarian" and to deflate pomposity with "subversive mockery." What is most depressing about *Splitting Heirs* is its conservatism. It doesn't seem to be attacking or deriding anything much at all. Instead, it packages British stereotypes for American consumption, depicting Brideshead-like country houses where the upper-class yeomen of England enjoy their shooting and fox hunting, and pubs where the locals still sing from Vera Lynn's back catalogue.

Also reviewed in:
CHICAGO TRIBUNE, 4/30/93, Friday/p. H, Dave Kehr
NEW REPUBLIC, 6/7/93, p. 27, Stanley Kauffmann
NEW YORK TIMES, 5/1/93, p. 17, Vincent Canby
VARIETY, 4/12/93, p. 76, Derek Elley
WASHINGTON POST, 5/4/93, p. C7, Hal Hinson

STEPPING RAZOR—RED X

A Northern Arts Entertainment release of a Bush Doctor Films production. *Executive Producer:* Syd Cappe and Nicolas Stiliadis. *Producer:* Edgar Egger. *Director:* Nicholas Campbell. *Screenplay:* Nicholas Cammpbell. *Director of Photography:* Edgar Egger. *Editor:* Trevor Ambrose. *Music Editor:* Byron McCulloch. *Sound:* Jack Buchanan, Allen Ormerod, and Andy Koyama. *Sound Editor:* Paul Durand. *Art Director:* Bora Bulajic. *Make-up:* Judy Murdoch. *Running time:* 103 minutes. *MPAA Rating:* Not Rated.

WITH: Lloyd "Rocky" Allen; Edward "Bigs" Allen; Andrea Davis; Rab Leon; Ron Headley; Roy Garrick; Jahbi; Junior; Kenile; Rabta Steve; Gary Isaacs; Lawrence Mabcoe; Beresford Thompson; Sandra Dkiror; Thunder; Sister P; Sister Margaret; Bruce "Preacher" Robinson.

LOS ANGELES TIMES, 6/2/93, Calendar/p. 3, Peter Rainer

Peter Tosh, the great reggae artist who was murdered in his Jamaica home in 1987, had been making tape-recorded notes about his life shortly, before his death. These stream-of-consciousness audiotapes were later recovered and, applied intermittently to the soundtrack of "Stepping Razor—Red X," the new documentary about Tosh's life, provide an eerie look at his innermost musings.

Written and directed by Nicholas Campbell, the film (Times-rated Mature) is a melange of re-enactments of Tosh's death, interviews with family, friends, fellow musicians and journalists, and concert footage from throughout Tosh's career. The footage begins with his association with Bob Marley and continues right up to the end, when, with his free-flowing yellow robes and thick crown of dreadlocks, he had the look of a messianic Rasta.

Tosh's musical career, separated from its specifically Rastafarian trappings, follows a familiar, almost archetypal trajectory for rock superstars: Raised in poverty, he started out as a musician with his roots deep in folk tradition and ended up as a species of national myth. Tosh's image as a kind of reggae Malcolm X has fueled not only by his own furious outspokenness but also by his legions of acolytes and hangers-on. He carried on like someone doomed; he perceived the brutality he endured—from the police, mostly, but also from his own demons—as the wages of martyrdom.

One of his tapes quotes him as saying, "Peace is the diploma you get in the cemetery." Tosh may have relished his messianic role, and the *ganja* he smoked and celebrated may have contributed to his own doomed martyr complex, but he wasn't a poseur: he really did rankle the Jamaican authorities with his anti-apartheid wailings. The movie makes a spotty, Oliver Stone-like case for his murder being the result of a conspiracy involving governmental higher-ups, (The official murder motive was burglary.) A colleague interviewed in the film says that Tosh's real ammunition has his lyrics, and, when Tosh is onstage, singing "Legalise It" or one of his other inflammatory anthems, you can understand how his music could be targeted as a provocation.

You can also understand how his rage could be picked up by white countercultures with no real connection to what he was railing against. His rebellion was converted around the world into something chic and readily consumable and yet his music still retains its power to shock. "Stepping Razor" is too worshipful to work as a full-scale character study but it's a musical feast with jangly, fascinating psychosocial crosscurrents.

NEW YORK POST, 8/18/93, p. 28, Dan Aquilante

It's a Jamaican murder mystery. Who killed Peter Tosh, and why did they want him dead?
"Stepping Razor—Red X" is a troubling docu-drama about the life, death and times of reggae superstar Tosh. Director Nicholas Campbell resurrects Tosh through interviews, event reconstructions, old newsreels, concert clips and Tosh's own words—which he recorded as a personal diary and dubbed the Red X tapes.

The indisputable fact of the film depicted in a bone-chilling, blood-soaked reconstruction—is that Tosh was executed as he lay face down in his Jamaican home.

Was his life snuffed out by three lowlifes trying to score some quick cash (about $200 was taken), or should we see the ugly flag of conspiracy? The film is inconclusive, never pointing a finger at either the Jamaican government or the petty thief convicted of the crime and his two cohorts, who were never found. Instead, it prefers rumors and insinuations.

Having grown up in an age of stupidity, where senseless violence is rampant, I can believe Tosh was killed for $200. Having grown up in the age of assassination, I can believe Tosh was murdered for political reasons.

He was outspoken about what he believed was the truth. At the center of those beliefs, and repeated throughout the film in song and spoken word, is that he didn't want peace—he wanted equal rights and justice, an end to racism, an end to poverty. "Peace," he says in one of the Red X tapes, "is the diploma you get in the cemetery."

Almost in passing, the film talks about Tosh's plan to purchase a radio station with a popular Jamaican DJ named Free I and call it Rasta Reggae Radio. These two men were about to give the anger of poverty a broadcast voice in the island nation. Free I was also shot dead that night at Tosh's home.

This bio-pic handles its subject with some journalistic sensibilities, and it will have value to anyone with an interest in reggae music or Rastafarian culture. Otherwise, "Stepping Razor" stumbles telling its own tale.

NEWSDAY, 8/18/93, Part II/p. 75, Gene Seymour

Calling "Stepping Razor—Red X" a documentary is like calling peyote a plant. Nicholas Campbell's filmed portrait of the late reggae super-star Peter Tosh has a mesmerizing, incantatory power that levitates it high above what one generally expects from rock-star biopics.

Campbell's narrative is a simmering, aromatic brew of concert footage, interviews, dramatizations (including a re-construction of the 1987 robbery-murder in which Tosh was killed) and a Tosh look-alike lip-syncing the singer's taped autobiographical recollections recorded under the title, "Red X"—a reference, Tosh said, to his seeing a red mark after his name on official Jamaican government documents.

That red mark was just further proof, to Tosh, that Satan had made him "a wanted man [for] speaking the truth." Born illegitimate in 1944, his strict Christian upbringing formed the foundation for his messianic and apocalyptic world view. His hair-trigger intolerance of racial injustice was likewise forged in the cauldron of a rugged childhood in Kingston's Trench Town slums. In the early '60s, he hooked up with Bob Marley and Bunny Wailer to form the Wailers, reggae's keystone band.

Tosh, whose astringent vocals provided a edgy counterpoint to Marley's sugar-cane tenor, continued to embody reggae's uncompromisingly rebellious side after he became a solo act. He became the paradigmatic mystic warrior, a Rastafarian black nationalist whose songs ("Fight On," "Legalize It") were blunt-edged attacks on colonialism, racism and drug enforcement. Not for Tosh the easy pop bromides of love, peace and happiness. "Peace," he says, "is the diploma you get in the cemetery."

He also is heard saying that if you tell "the truth" about racism and injustice "you can be found guilty and sentenced to death." Such statements and the interviews with friends and family define a paranoia in Tosh that, Campbell suggests, may have seen more than justified. Tosh was subject to harassment, including a police beating in the early '80s, that only sharpened his anger.

The film also reconstructs the bloody night that began when three armed men entered Tosh's house in the midst of a dinner party demanding money and ended with the death of Tosh and another man. Campbell and his witnesses imply that Tosh's murder wasn't the result of robbery so much as an execution. The unresolved nature of the case only deepens the film's near-hallucinatory atmosphere.

Though "Stepping Razor—Red X" is reminiscent of Errol Morris' "The Thin Blue Line" and, to a lesser extent, of Oliver Stone's "JFK," it is, in its own right, a singular achievement for its daring injection of funky, baroque socio-political history into the "rockumentary" subgenre.

SIGHT AND SOUND, 10/93, p. 53, Nick Kimberley

Imaginative recreations of events in the life of reggae singer Peter Tosh—murdered at his home in 1987—are intercut with documentary footage of his stage performances, and interviews with the singer, his associates and family. Much of the soundtrack is composed of Tosh's own tapes. Before his death, Tosh was assembling material for an autobiography, and dictated his memories, tales and thoughts onto tapes he called the 'Red X tapes': he claimed that, whenever he saw his name on any official document, it was always followed by a red cross—sure sign, he felt, that he was a marked man.

Reggae has long exercised a peculiar fascination for white non-Jamaican audiences. The lopsided rhythms, the messianic politics couched in Biblical rhetoric, and especially the gigantic spliffs stuffed with mind-numbingly strong ganja: all these have seemed to promote a rebel culture that mixes hedonism and radicalism without compromise. Whether that version of reggae accurately reflects the music's real history is another matter.

Nicholas Campbell's film adds another ingredient to this romantic view: conspiracy theories, the last refuge of the disaffected radical. On September 11, 1987, three armed men burst into Tosh's house, forced the singer, his wife and their guests to lie on the floor and demanded money. Angered by the small amount they were offered, the gunmen beat and shot their victims. Tosh and two others died. The police later arrested a man they claimed was one of the murderers: he is now on Death Row in Kingston, although he protests his innocence. Nobody has ever been arrested in connection with the murders.

Tosh's militant Rastafarian beliefs had won him many enemies, as had his forceful personality. He was convinced that the Jamaican police and government were out to get him, and this fear, real or imagined, set the tone for the Red X tapes. Those tapes take up a large part of the film's soundtrack, which endorses Tosh's acute sense of persecution with some conspiracy theories of its own. Dramatised material and documentary footage form a portrait of a man whose self-belief was simultaneously a barrier and a bridge. Tosh may never have achieved the status of his one-time collaborator Bob Marley, but his dissident voice left its mark on reggae and on black culture.

No doubt Peter Tosh had his enemies in Jamaica, although *Stepping Razor—Red X* adduces nothing but anecdotal evidence: a chance remark from a colleague here, an insinuation from a friend there. Facts would be an encumbrance. What concerns Campbell more is the edgy paranoia which conspiracy theory promotes, and which seems to match reggae's nervous rhythmic twitch.

Not that the film offers us that much music: perhaps it's a problem of performing rights, but whenever we get some of Tosh's music, the camera inevitably cuts away and the soundtrack fades. It's as if Campbell fears the accusation that all he's really interested in is a reggae soundtrack.

Nor is there much evidence of Jamaica as such. A few familiar shantytown images, the inevitable dreadlocks and ganja clouds: Kingston is present, not a substance, but as a sequence of postcard images of poverty. Similarly, Bob Marley, more significant than Tosh in almost every way, and an *éminence grise* dogging every step of Tosh's career, is barely glimpsed.

That's the problem with conspiracy theorists: they prefer shadows to fully-formed images. For all the stridency of his ideas and of his music, Peter Tosh remains a phantom beyond this film's grasp.

VILLAGE VOICE, 8/24/93, p. 64, Ban Mapp

Stepping Razor—Red X, a chronicle of the life of reggae star Peter Tosh, is a rare musician's documentary in that it's more about the mindset of its subject than the music. The psychological insights are poignantly provided by the singer himself, whose voice (taken from the "Red X" tapes he was working on for a planned autobiography) provides the film's only narration. The approach works because Tosh had a lot going on under his mane of locks.

Tosh saw his life as an uninterrupted spiritual struggle. His poverty-stricken childhood, his early days with the Wailers trio in Trenchtown, his writing the song "Oh Bumbo Claat," his lecturing Jamaican dignitaries at the One Love Peace Concert, his beatings by police, and his brutal murder in 1987 all are framed here more as interconnected battles than as random incidents in the life of a pop-star rebel.

Director Nicholas Campbell deftly intersperses these defining moments with vintage footage of everyday life in Jamaica in the '60s, re-creations of scenes from Tosh's childhood, and interviews with those who knew him. The result is more an impressionistic portrait than a "definitive" account. Some of Campbell's choices seem heavy-handed, but overall, he knows that Tosh was as complex as his music. The film's most compelling moments when he lets the musician's words speak for themselves.

Also reviewed in:
CHICAGO TRIBUNE, 11/5/93, Tempo/p. 3, John Petrakis
NEW YORK TIMES, 8/20/93, p. C21, Stephen Holden
WASHINGTON POST, 8/20/93, p. D5, Richard Harrington

STRICTLY PROPAGANDA

A First Run Features release.   *Executive Producer:* C. Cay Wesnigk.   *Director:* Wolfgang Kissel.   *Screenplay:* Wolfgang Kissel.   *Running time:* 94 minutes.   *MPAA Rating:* Not Rated.

NARRATOR: Manfred Krug.

LOS ANGELES TIMES, 3/4/94, Calendar/p. 10, Peter Rainer

The educational and instructional documentary footage in "Strictly Propaganda" is chillingly funny, Wolfgang Kissel, who currently teaches at the Dresden Visual Arts School, assembled a cross-section of representative documentaries form the archives of DEFA—the official state film studio of the now defunct German Democratic Republic—ranging from the immediate postwar years to the last days of Erich Honecker in 1989.

Kissel makes no attempt to "editorialize." He doesn't need to. The fascination of the footage is that, although it presents a sunny, upbeat view of post-war East Germany, the real story can't help breaking through the enforced joyousness. (It's as if you were watching two different movies: the one that was made and the one that wasn't.) The results are beyond satire. You can laugh at a scene like the one where a citizen is encouraged to take his vacation on a steamer cruise up the Volga, or the sequence where an honored party functionary praises Stalin as the prince of peace, but the laughter catches in your craw.

Documentaries are often mistakenly assumed to give us the "truth" but it takes a film like "Strictly Propaganda" to really undercut that bogus idea. It's difficult to imagine anyone in East Germany falling for much of what we see in this film, and yet, in their own crudely effective way, the DEFA filmmakers knew what they were doing. The repeated shots of blonde children romping and saluting are iconic in a way that is not so very different from the Aryan super-race imagery in Leni Riefenstahl's "Triumph of the Will." Only the uniforms, and the salute, are different.

As the years tick by in "Strictly Propaganda," slight rents in the social fabric emerge. The '60s introduced a more "questioning" student into the classroom, and so we're treated to an instructional documentary for teachers who attempt to defend the party line without alienating the class. There's also an instructional film for Berlin Wall border guards, including a re-enactment where a West German spy attempting to enter the country is tripped up by failing to recite the opening words of the Communist Manifesto.

It's an epic stretch from 1946 and the Soviet Occupation Zone to 1989 and the ascendancy of Gorbachev. What's eerie about "Strictly Propaganda" is that it never acknowledges the stretch. There's a weightlessness to the footage because it has so little connection to what was going on not only in East Germany, but in the rest of the world. The national portrait that emerges is "The Land That Time Forgot." Or more accurately, "The Land That Tried to Forget."

NEW YORK POST, 10/20/93, p. 36, Thelma Adams

There's an audience out there for "Strictly Propaganda." It's small. It's intense. And it doesn't include me.

"Strictly Propaganda" follows East German Communist rule from the end of WWII to the Berlin Wall's collapse. Using government newsreels, training films, and assorted oddities, writer-director Wolfgang Kissel and producer C. Cay Wesnigk indict the GDR's brand of socialism with its own words. Kissel and Wesnigk create a story of a people leaping out of the frying pan and into the fire, singing as they go.

A few high points exist. A brutishly handsome soldier invites the camera into his staff car for a tour of Berlin. He introduces the driver, who nods a nervous welcome, as well as a uniformed comrade in the back who manages a stuffy cordiality. Wedged in the back seat with the comrade and the camera, I couldn't avoid the sense that despite the narrator's eagerness to please and heavy good looks, I was headed for a small room with a big, uncovered light bulb.

In another clip documenting mass calisthenics at an international Young Pioneers rally, Yasser Arafat, in his trademark khaffiya, hops on one foot along with a row of Soviet bloc dignitaries who are wearing paper pirate hats. In a training film, a teacher raises the question, "Where are children worse off?" The student spins the globe and responds, "wherever there are still capitalists."

It takes a special kind of soul to sit through 40 years of foreign propaganda films without repeated watch-checking. Tagged as an East German "Atomic Cafe," this compilation documentary lacks the witty style that made that provocative chronicle of 1950s atomic mania cross over to a larger, though limited, audience.

At least the German Nazis had Leni Riefenstahl. I won't dissuade that small, intense segment of the population from seeing "Strictly Propaganda." As for me, those 94 minutes passed like a school assembly screening of a film on the wonders of electricity.

VILLAGE VOICE, 10/26/93, p. 53, J. Hoberman

A dramatic illustration of Karl Marx's observation that the road to hell is paved with good intentions may be found sharing the Film Forum marquee with *It's All True*. *Strictly Propaganda* is a seamlessly straightforward compilation of newsreels and education films from the no-longer existent German Democratic Republic, which, assembled by Wolfgang Kissel, makes most sense as a prolonged fiction: *It's All False*. The imaginary location is as exotic as Brazil and, in its petrified way, nearly as carnivalesque. For the first half, at least, every citizen we see is enacting the Optimistic.

The most crazed sequences are from Stalinism's 1948-53 apogee. One fantastic moment has the viewer invited into a police car with three beefy cops for a tour of the new Berlin. The requisite performance by the Red Army chorus, the boilerplate montage of Stakhanovite workers, the tour of the wondrous cornucopia that is the People's Department Store, the celestial voices that serenade the first family to occupy a brand-new apartment on spacious Stalin-Allee are augmented by clips that reinforce one's sense of East Germany as among the world's least sympathetic regimes.

The cult of the "shining example" Walter Ulbricht is humorously gemütlich—the unprepossessingly portly leader playing ping-pong with his Frau or leading a group of Leipzig burghers in calisthenics. The Young Pioneer rallies are something else. "The red banner in the hands of our youth!" the narrator exclaims over footage of one arm-pumping 1952 rally. The emphasis on hygiene, fitness, and order, the spectacle of bright-eyed adolescent enthusiasm channeled toward an authoritarian political leadership is, however sub-Riefenstahl in execution, unmistakably Nazi in effect. The old Hitlerjugend feeling lingers on even as the '50s give way to the less disciplined '60s and '70s and fiery pomp is diluted by Up With People schlock.

One of the highlights of the 1973 World Youth Festival is a red Karen Carpenter singing about being "happy as a child." Indeed, the importance of children (at healthy play or rapt attention to the avid adults who teach them) imbues the footage with grotesque poignance. Sweetly singing Pioneers mimic marching soldiers; patriotic children help in military exercises. *Strictly Propaganda* provides surprisingly few references to the Berlin crises of 1948, 1953, and 1961, but as late as the 1980s, the East German equivalent of *Sesame Street* warbles that "soldiers protect the kindergarten so that we can play happily."

The movie does nothing to discourage viewer smugness, and it's difficult not to smirk at the pathetic eagerness with which a people's travel agent proposes a new sort of worker vacation ("How about a steamer cruise on the Volga?") or when the notorious cardboard-plastic-monoxide Trabant is touted as the Car of the Future.

Also reviewed in:
NATION, 11/8/93, p. 543, Stuart Klawans
NEW YORK TIMES, 10/20/93, p. C22, Janet Maslin

STRIKING DISTANCE

A Columbia Pictures release. *Executive Producer:* Steven Reuther. *Producer:* Arnon Milchan, Tony Thomopoulos, and Hunt Lowry. *Director:* Rowdy Herrington. *Screenplay:* Rowdy Herrington and Martin Kaplan. *Director of Photography:* Mac Ahlberg. *Editor:* Pasquale Buba and Mark Helfrich. *Music:* Brad Fiedel. *Music Editor:* Allan K. Rosen. *Sound:* John Sutton, III. *Sound Editor:* Steven Flick. *Casting:* Pam Dixon. *Production Designer:* Gregg Fonseca. *Art Director:* Bruce Miller. *Set Designer:* Steve Arnold and Gina Granham. *Set Decorator:* Jay Hart. *Special Effects:* Allen L. Hall. *Costumes:* Betsy Cox. *Make-up:* Jeannee Josefczyk. *Make-up (Bruce Willis):* Scott H. Eddo. *Stunt Coordinator:* Mickey Gilbert. *Running time:* 101 minutes. *MPAA Rating:* R.

CAST: Bruce Willis (Tom Hardy); Sarah Jessica Parker (Jo Christman); Dennis Farina (Nick Detillo); Tom Sizemore (Danny Detillo); Brion James (Det. Eddie Eiler); Robert Pastorelli (Jimmy Detillo); Timothy Busfield (Tony Sacco); John Mahoney (Vince Hardy); Andre Braugher (Frank Morris); Tom Atkins (Fred Hardy), Mike Hodge (Don Penderman); Jodi Long (Kim Lee); Roscoe Orman (Det. Sid McClelland); Robert Gould (Kesser); Gareth Williams (Chick); Ed Hooks (Gunther); Lawrence Mandley (Bailiff); Julianna McCarthy (Judge); John T. Bower (Cop); Sally Wiggin, Andrea Martin, Suzanne Vafiadis, and Ken Rice (Newscasters); Michael Canavan (Gary Hardy); Scott Kloes (Jerry Hobart); Bruce Kirkpatrick (W.C. Fields); Edward Gero (Officer Luffey); Andrew May (Officer Schultz); Sigrid Adrienne (Paula Puglisi); Elva Branson (Nurse Debbie); Jack Paskin (Bartender); Erik Jensen (Drug Runner); Jeffrey J. Stephan (Dispatcher).

LOS ANGELES TIMES, 9/17/93, Calendar/p. 8, Kevin Thomas

"Striking Distance" opens and closes with a pair of jolting high-speed chases, the first over Pittsburgh streets, the second over the rivers that encircle the city's center. In between is a lively mystery thriller that hurtles past plot contrivances and unintended laughs to deliver the goods as a satisfying escapist diversion. Like a paperback purchased at an airport just before you board a plane, it serves well its time-killing purpose but isn't designed to stand up under close scrutiny.

Director and co-writer Rowdy Herrington has anchored the action with a solid part for Bruce Willis, entirely credible as a fifth-generation Pittsburgh cop, Irish on his father's side, Italian on his mother's. He's been raised by his father (John Mahoney) with the creed "loyalty above all else, except honor." This belief has led him to testify against his own cousin (Robert Pastorelli), also a cop, in a police brutality case, which doesn't endear him to his uncle (Dennis Farina), who's also his boss. To make matters worse, he insists loudly that the wrong man has been convicted for fatally shooting his father during the film's opening chase. In short order he's been demoted from homicide detective to river rescue patrolman. Then the corpses of women he had once known start turning up floating down the Allegheny and the Monongahela.

"Striking Distance" (rated R for violence, strong language and a sex scene) allows Willis to come across as macho yet sensitive, tough-minded and high-principled, but vulnerable to rage and despair. Willis' strong yet understated presence persuades us to go along with all that happens, no matter what. Well, almost everything: It's inconceivable that the cop wouldn't close the Venetian blinds on his houseboat at least while making love! The object of his affections, as it happens, is his new partner (Sarah Jessica Parker, who has a wholesome, natural quality, which also contributes to the believability quotient).

You scarcely need to be a psychic to predict that Parker will soon be menaced by the unknown serial killer, but Herrington does throw in a surprise twist about the murderer's identity, revealed in a climactic scene that can be described only as operatic in its emotional extravagance. The fast-moving Herrington never gives us a chance to think too much about what we're watching, and in this apt strategy he has first-rate backup from his crew, especially from dynamic, imaginative cinematographer Mac Ahlberg, veteran stunt coordinator Mickey Gilbert, who has contributed a number of breathtaking moments, and versatile composer Brad Fiedel, who has come up with a hard-driving, mood-enhancing score.

NEW YORK POST, 9/17/93, p. 38, Michael Medved

They shouldn't have put him in the water if they didn't want him to make waves!" proclaim the misleading ads for "Striking Distance," offering the suggestion that the surf's up on the Monongahela River.

That's where most of the action takes place in this soggy police thriller, in which Willis plays a tough, renegade cop who's been assigned to the glamorous river rescue unit of the Pittsburgh Police Department.

In a big confrontation at the very center of the film, Willis single-handedly faces off against a band of ruthless drug smugglers who have hijacked a coal barge that's as long as a football field.

I suppose that any criminals who choose to smuggle drugs by taking command of a slow-moving coal barge on the Allegheny River are so dumb that they deserve to die, but the way that this sequence plays itself out is both gratuitously gruesome and utterly preposterous.

When Willis refuses to go along with the official story concerning this case, he's fired from the homicide division and reassigned to river rescue where, equipped with a spiffy new boat and an equally spiffy new partner (Sarah Jessica Parker) he defies orders and continues his personal investigation.

Along the way to its ridiculously extended climactic confrontation, the plot does contain a few surprises, proving only that you can always find ways to shock an audience if you don't give a damn about plausibility or common sense.

For his part, Willis delivers a reasonably effective performance; he may not be the most subtle or versatile actor in the world, but his invariably edgy and energetic screen presence makes you care about his character.

Unfortunately, that character is named Thomas Hardy without the slightest hint of irony, as if the filmmakers remain blissfully unaware that their misfired movie may stand as the ultimate insult to the memory of the great novelist who wrote "Tess of the D'Urbervilles" and "Return of the Native."

Meanwhile, this project represents its own version of "Return of the Native," since Pittsburgh-raised director/co-writer Rowdy Herrington says that he intended this film as a cinematic valentine to the city he loves.

Herrington has somehow developed a reputation as a slick action director despite the fact that all of his previous pictures ("Jack's Back" "Gladiator" and the truly abysmal "Road House") bombed at the box office. Here, he's briefly at his best in the truly spectacular chase scene that opens the film, but the rest of this mediocre and misfired movie will hardly make the director a hero in his hometown.

NEWSDAY, 9/17/93, Part II/p. 73, Terry Kelleher

Hometown pride is a virtue in a moviemaker. Look how Andrew Davis shows off Chicago in "The Fugitive."

Director Rowdy Herrington hails from Pittsburgh, and he can hardly wait to give us a tour of the city in his new picture, "Striking Distance." After a few preliminaries, he sends his cop characters off on a rip-roaring car chase that runs so long it needs an intermission. The whole sequence is like a Gray Line excursion at 100 mph.

But where do we go after burning so much rubber? Herrington, whose unimpressive credits include "Gladiator" and "Road House," has trouble mapping out the route.

He could have made a standard maverick cop-versus-serial-killer thriller, with the Pittsburgh backdrop for a little something different. He could have made an offbeat "action comedy" about a former homicide detective reduced to plying the Allegheny and the Monongahela as part of the Pittsburgh P.D.'s river-rescue patrol. It's easy enough to imagine either of these as a vehicle for Bruce Willis.

Then again, Herrington could have made a gutsy drama about a policeman who alienates his friends and relatives on the force by testifying against his partner (who happens to be his cousin) in a brutality case. Sounds a little heavy for Willis, but the star might have been up for his first real challenge since 1989's "In Country."

Which option did Herrington choose? All of the above. Not only did Officer Tom Hardy (Willis) blow the whistle on his cop cousin (Robert Pastorelli), he also accused his cop uncle (Dennis Farina) of a coverup in the killing of his cop father (John Mahoney). As a result, the brass demoted Tom from homicide to a watery professional grave. Now the murderer's back on the loose, knocking off Tom's former girlfriends and dumping them in the river to torment him.

Meanwhile, Tom is growing ever closer to his new boat mate, Officer Jo Christman (Sarah Jessica Parker), their relationship having progressed predictably from hostile to intimate. Could this woman be in danger?

Parker, normally a most engaging actress, seems out of her element here. Jo's passion for Tom is as unconvincing as her passion for law enforcement. Writers Herrington and Martin Kaplan eventually give the plot a twist, but spoil it with a tip-off. By the time the story's various elements come together—in a scene that packs an incredible amount of overacting into one room—ticket buyers will be impatient for another marathon pursuit at reckless speed. Not to worry. When it comes to powerboating through Pittsburgh while handcuffed, nobody can touch Bruce ("Die Hard") Willis.

SIGHT AND SOUND, 5/94, p. 56, Philip Kemp

Pittsburgh, 1991. Tom Hardy, a fifth generation cop whose father Vince is chief of homicide, is due to give evidence against his ex-partner and cousin, Jimmy Detillo, for using excess violence on a suspect. The city is plagued by a serial killer who targets young women; when a call comes that the killer is being pursued, Tom and Vince give chase. In the subsequent crash Tom is injured, regaining consciousness to find Vince shot dead and the killer escaped. A lowlife, Kesser, is later charged with the killings. Jimmy Detillo, faced with disgrace and imprisonment, takes a death leap into the river from a high bridge. Two years later. For publicly asserting that Kesser is innocent and the killer is a cop, Tom, who has a reputation as an unreliable drunk, has been demoted to the River Rescue Patrol. His uncle Nick, Jimmy's father, is now chief of homicide.

Jimmy's brother Danny, who quit the force after Jimmy's death, returns from California. A young woman's body is found in the river; Tom's insistence that the same killer is responsible meets with contempt from Nick and the homicide squad. Tom is assigned a new partner, Jo Christman. Initially wary, she comes to respect him after he tackles five gunmen who have hijacked a barge.

Another woman, a nurse, is abducted—like her predecessors, an ex-girlfriend of Tom's—and as before the killer phones him to let him hear her screams before killing her. Tom takes Jo to the police ball, where he's shunned by all except his Hardy relatives, and Danny shows up drunk and provokes a fight. Tom and Jo become lovers, but at his internal review she appears as Detective Emily Harper, assigned to keep tabs on him. Her evidence, though, is favourable and Tom escapes censure. Emily is abducted by the killer who, Tom realises, is hiding out in Detillo's Roost, a riverside cabin where he, Jimmy and Danny played as boys. He finds Danny there, but is knocked out and handcuffed to a chair by Jimmy, who survived his death dive—and now prepares to kill Tom, Danny and Emily. He is forestalled by the arrival of Nick—who, it turns out, accidentally shot Vince while letting Jimmy escape. Jimmy now kills Nick and flees, but Tom struggles loose and pursues him, still handcuffed. After a long river chase Tom catches Jimmy and drowns him.

Early on in *Striking Distance* the father-and-son cop team of Vince and Tom Hardy embark on a Hollywood-special car chase, bucketing along the wrong side of a busy freeway. Amid all the frantic swerving, hooting and dodging of oncoming mega-trucks, they swap lighthearted banter about Tom's taste in girlfriends. It's fair indication that nothing that follows need be taken too seriously, and that we shouldn't exercise our minds over loose ends, inconsistencies and wild implausibilities. Least of all, maybe, over just what the title—apart from fitting the two-word model currently de rigueur for action thrillers—has to do with anything in the film. The message is, relax and enjoy the ride.

And as rides go, it's not a bad one. For a start, the scenery's good. Rowdy Herrington is Pittsburgh born and bred, and he knows his terrain—especially the city's three rivers that provide a dramatic, off-beat backdrop to most of the action. The action itself comes in hefty bite-sized dollops—this is a Bruce Willis vehicle, after all—even throwing in a mini-*Die Hard* set-piece on a hijacked barge. There's a blatant red herring or two, a discreet helping of sex and even a hint of a subtext (loyalty vs honour), though not enough to alarm the popcorn belt. All in all, *Striking Distance* is prime fast-food cinema—unpretentious, digestible, and guaranteed not to linger in the mind.

Also reviewed in:
CHICAGO TRIBUNE, 9/17/93, Friday/p. F, Michael Wilmington
NEW YORK TIMES, 9/17/93, p. C17, Vincent Canby
VARIETY, 9/27/93, p. 36, Brian Lowry
WASHINGTON POST, 9/17/93, p. D7, Richard Harrington
WASHINGTON POST, 9/17/93, Weekend/p. 52, Joe Brown

SUMMER HOUSE, THE

A Samuel Goldwyn Company release of a BBC Films production. *Executive Producer:* Mark Shivas. *Producer:* Norma Heyman. *Director:* Waris Hussein. *Screenplay:* Martin Sherman. *Based on the novel "The Clothes in the Wardrobe":* Alice Thomas Ellis. *Director of Photography:* Rex Maidment. *Editor:* Ken Pearce. *Music:* Stanley Myers. *Sound:* John Pritchard. *Sound Editor:* Allan Fowlie. *Casting:* Susie Figgis. *Production Designer:* Stuart Walker. *Costumes:* Odile Dicks-Mireaux and Leah Archer. *Make-up:* Frances Hannon, Darren Phillips, and Cathy Burczac. *Running time:* 85 minutes. *MPAA Rating:* Not Rated.

CAST: Lena Headey (Margaret); Padraig Casey (Nour); Britta Smith (Mother Joseph); Catherine Schell (Marie-Clair); Pierre Sioufi (Ahmed); Sherine El Ansari (Gypsy Girl); Julie Walters (Monica); David Threlfall (Syl); Joan Plowright (Mrs. Monro); Jeanne Moreau (Lili); Annabel Burton (Margaret as a Child); Maggie Steed (Mrs. Raffald); John Wood

(Robert);   David Gant (Gallery Owner);   Tommy Duggan (Father O'Flynn);   Marissa El Refaie (Fatima);   Lamia El Amir (Hala);   Roger Lloyd Pack (Derek);   Gwyneth Strong (Cynthia); Natalie Flynn (Jennifer);   Thomas Lawrence (Christopher).

LOS ANGELES TIMES, 12/21/93, Calendar/p. 10, Kevin Thomas

"The Summer House", a wry and delightful British comedy, has much the appeal of "Enchanted April" in that it shows to advantage an array of formidable actresses, but it's less talky and it's lots livelier, and best of all, it boasts Jeanne Moreau in an all-too-rare starring role.

Cast as a flamboyant half-English, half-Egyptian femme fatale of a "certain age" with flaming red hair and a Norma Desmond wardrobe, Moreau is the exotic Lili, who descends upon Croydon, a staid London suburb, circa 1959. The occasion is the impending wedding of the daughter, Margaret (Lena Headey), of her lifelong friend Monica (Julie Walters).

Margaret is to marry the considerably older Syl (David Threlfall), who lives next door and whose elderly mother, Mrs. Monro (Joan Plowright), proves unexpectedly to be a boon companion to the worldly, hard-drinking Lili. Everyone is glad to see the uninhibited Lili—even her ne'er-do-well painter ex-husband (John Wood)—but it doesn't take long for her to figure out that the lonely Margaret doesn't love the homely Syl, an obtuse jerk; even his mother thinks Margaret would be miserable married to him.

Whether or not Margaret will go through with her glum marriage is of course the big question, but the real purpose of Martin Sherman's adaptation of Alice Thomas Ellis' novel "The Clothes in the Wardrobe" is to provide three juicy roles for three veteran actresses, who glow under Waris Hussein's unobtrusive, briskly paced direction.

The film's biggest success is to make it conceivable that Lili should have such staunch friendships with such conventional women as Monica and Mrs. Monro. The reason is simple and lifelike: the glamorous, outrageous Lili brightens the other women's drab lives, and Lili, in turn, for all her gaudiness and theatricality, is a wise, philosophical woman capable of valuing her old friends.

The three women are as well-drawn as they are well-played. Monica may be dowdy and blind to the folly of her daughter's impending marriage, but she's a kind, likable woman. The way Walters plays her she's entirely nice beneath an armor of propriety. Mrs. Monro may be an old lady, but she's a shrewd, perceptive woman, much more a soulmate to Lili. Plowright brings out Mrs. Monro's astringent quality, and it's sheer pleasure to hear her grand, bemused delivery of a line as innocuous as "Shall we risk the trifle?"

With her Lili more Tallulah Bankhead than Bette Davis, to whom she is so often compared, Moreau is as radiant, sensual and witty as ever. What's so endearing about Lili is that she may be Auntie Mame-ish, but she's not a bully; she reaches out to Margaret but doesn't tell her how to live her life.

As for Margaret, she's decidedly the movie's mystery. For one thing, she experiences constant dreams about a handsome young man (Padraig Casey) with whom she fell in love during a recent trip to Egypt. There's more to Margaret, so appealingly played by Headey, than we at first realize. As a result, there's more to "The Summer House" as well.

NEW YORK POST, 12/21/93, p. 41, Thelma Adams

"I'm marrying a man nobody likes," moans Margaret (Lena Headley). I thought it was just me."

Margaret is the bride at the eye of the nuptial storm in "The Summer House," a thoroughly delightful comedy of manners from BBC Films, the producers of "Enchanted April."

Like Lili Taylor in "Household Saints," Margaret would rather become a nun. But in the buttoned-up London suburb of Croydon in 1959, God's son is not considered an appropriate bridegroom.

Margaret settles for Syl Monro (David Threlfall), the boy next door. With his heap of hair, hyena laugh, and pencil mustache, the 40-year-old bachelor is a prize only in his own eyes.

Threlfall who plays Syl a shade softer than a Monty Python loon portrays Prince Charles in the telefilm "Diana, Her True Story."

Syl lives with his mum. At the thought of the coming marriage, the widowed Mrs. Monro (Joan Plowright) looks at a photo of her heap-haired hubby and sighs, "Poor Margaret."

Margaret's mother, Monica, played by Julie Walters ("Educating Rita"), notes, "I've never seen a more miserable bride." But the flurry of wedding plans continues a prelude to a life of quiet desperation. If it was good enough for Monica and Mrs. Monro ...

Enter Lili (Jeanne Moreau), the matchbreaker. Half-Egyptian, half-English, red-headed and woolly and even more unconventional placed in the London suburbs on the cusp of the '60s, Lili arrives from Egypt and won't take this marriage lying down.

Lili has no illusions about marriage. With her characteristic smoky wisdom, she tells Margaret "Happiness? One must not expect that from marriage."

Nevertheless, the magnificent Moreau ("Jules and Jim") becomes a rebel with a cause. She sets about unlacing the lives of the women around her. Lili becomes everyone's excuse to be wicked, a lightning rod of improper behavior.

With her red hair and seraglio jewels, Moreau inflames the screen and gives an agelessly vital and sensual performance. A joy to watch, Moreau delivers a memorable comic turn in a career spanning nearly 40 years of ground-breaking parts.

In a season of odd couples and grumpy old men, Moreau and Plowright create the most enchanting pairing. Lili loosens up Mrs. Monro with a bottle of whisky end the two dish dirt and embark on a pub crawl that leaves them dancing down the pavement. The scene is intoxicating.

Wickedly funny but never mean-spirited, Martin Sherman's screenplay is wise and life-affirming. Based on a novel by Alice Thomas Ellis, the script navigates the shoals of cunning and coyness. Sherman breathes life into his characters while managing to startle and surprise.

Credit also goes to Waris Hussein, who directed the 1970 sleeper "Quackser Fortune Has a Cousin in the Bronx" but has met with more commercial success directing British TV. Under his guidance the actors give performances that dance off the screen.

Jeanne Moreau and "The Summer House" are irresistible.

NEWSDAY, 12/21/93, Part II/p. 51, Jack Mathews

The trick in telling a good shaggy dog story, if there is such a thing, is distracting listeners with enough detail to make them think they're getting something more than they are. In Waris Hussein's "The Summer House," a BBC movie arriving in U.S. theaters months after its airing on British television, the distractions are many.

There are lively characters, marvelous dialogue, a mysterious Egyptian subplot, tales of infidelity, even dark hints of child abuse. But when the end finally comes, it is exactly what it seems, the absurd punch line to an 80-minute joke.

The story, set in a small English community in 1952, revolves around the impending marriage of Margaret (Lena Headey), a melancholy young woman who would rather become a nun than a bride, and Syl (David Threlfall), a 40-year-old mama's boy who has long since become a twit. Margaret can barely stand the sight of Syl, and he barely notices.

Surrounding the odd couple are Mrs. Monro (Joan Plowright) and Monica (Julie Walters), Syl's and Margaret's caring mums, and Lili (Jeanne Moreau), the bawdy, free-spirited wild acquaintance of both families who shows up in time to add perspective, humor and outrage to the dubious occasion.

Adapted by American playwright Martin Sherman ("Bent") from Alice Thomas Ellis' novel "The Clothes in the Wardrobe," "The Summer House" is more of a Jeanne Moreau funhouse. Her role seems to have been produced from the bits and stems of her own career, from her own public image, and she flaunts it like a loud dress.

Lili, under a mane of flaming orange hair, her voice all smoke and whisky, her words a stream of unfiltered irreverence, re-enters her friends' mundane lives on a thunderclap and stirs them up like the silt at the bottom of a pool.

One at a time, on bombast and energy alone, Lili wins over everyone. Even stiff old Mrs. Monro, who bears the memory of having caught her late husband and a young Lili in bed, finds the ebullient half-Egyptian, half-English woman irresistible, and the scene where the dignified Plowright gets falling down drunk with Moreau is a sight.

For Margaret, Lili is an immediate emotional lifeline, the only person with whom she can confide her unhappiness with her dithery fiancé, and reveal her convent aspirations.

But only we, through Magaret's frequent daydreams, get to know that the true source of her misery is the romance and violence she experienced during a recent stay with an aunt in Egypt.

Margaret and the Egyptian subplot seem to have been piped in from another, far more ambitious movie, and Headey (the maid Lizzie in "Remains of the Day") moves through this otherwise light confection as if in a pall.

Ultimately, all that matters with "The Summer House" is whether you find the joke at the end worth the time it takes to get there.

The final scene is a wonderful surprise, but unless you want to watch Moreau chew the scenery for an hour or so first, that's all there is.

SIGHT AND SOUND, 3/93, p. 55, Farrah Anwar

Croydon, the 1950s. Margaret, in her early 20s, is engaged to marry the older Syl, her life-long neighbour and the only son of the elderly Mrs Monro. Dreading this unwanted union, Margaret dreams of her time in Egypt—a holiday to improve her French, spent at Marie-Claire's, a friend of her divorced mother, Monica. While there, Margaret fell in love with Nour, Marie-Claire's son, and possibly lost her virginity to him—an act which may have been responsible for her approaching Sister Juliet at the local Egyptian convent, with a view to becoming a nun.

Margaret is bored and desperate, but things begin to look up when another of Monica's old friends, the exotic Lili, arrives with her husband Robert. Robert has come to set up an exhibition of his paintings of Egypt; Lili is to help with the wedding. It turns out that Lili is known to Mrs Monro, who once caught her late husband and Lili *in flagrante delicto* in her own living room. This incident does not, however, stop both women resolving over several drinking sessions to stop Margaret and Syl being wed, both recognising that the former has no love for the latter—a point that Monica and Syl refuse to acknowledge.

Matters come to a head after Robert's opening night, when his paintings turn out not only to allude to his affair with Marie-Claire, but also to depict a notorious local haunt, the 'crocodile pool'. The sight of it causes Margaret to faint as she recalls helping a naked Nour dispose of a bloodied gypsy girl's body into the pool—a collusion which remains undiscovered. Despite this setback, plans for the wedding go ahead with the news that Margaret's father Derek will after all be able to attend, in company with his wife and two young children. Before their arrival, Lili tells Monica and Margaret that if the cacti in the summerhouse flower, it will augur good fortune for Margaret and Syl. On the day of the wedding, Lili announces that the cacti have indeed flowered and insists that everybody witness this sight after breakfast. As the guests make their way to the summer-house, they are shocked to find a half-naked Lili clearly making love to Syl.

Some time in the future, Margaret, now a nun in Egypt, is convinced that only God could have sent her Lili, for who else could have conceived a wedding present so original as the scene in the summerhouse?

With its scrupulous period details and classy cast (Plowright, Threlfall, Walters and a real scoop, Jeanne Moreau), (*The Clothes in the Wardrobe*) is a typical example of what the BBC does best—namely, adapting a living novelist's work, which shies away from contemporary, and possibly dangerous, issues. However, like the recently broadcast *Memento Mori* (based on a Muriel Spark novel), *Wardrobe* has a genuine sediment of sourness at the bottom of its champagne production values.

This *Screen Two* production is a faithful, albeit selectively telescoped rendition of Alice Thomas Ellis's *Summerhouse* trilogy (*The Clothes in the Wardrobe, The Skeleton in the Cupboard, The Fly in the Ointment*), each written from a different person's perspective. Martin Sherman's extremely deft adaptation uses the first novel (Margaret's perspective) to frame events which are often outlined in other parts of the trilogy. This is particularly true of Mrs Monro, who remains an unrattled skeleton in Margaret's *Wardrobe*, but becomes an essential part of the proceedings in Sherman's version. There is the added bonus that Plowright's scenes with Moreau provide a queen's ransom in acting honours and acidic aphorisms ("she's a little low-key to be anaemic" is how Margaret is dismissed), as well as an unhealthy quota of alcohol consumption.

The result, miraculously, is a more cinematic adaptation than any reader of the novels could have hoped to see. The watershed in Margaret's development, the murder of the gypsy girl, is outlined very matter-of-factly in the book, and never questioned. However, Sherman and director Waris Hussein go to great pains to establish the hallucinatory qualities of Margaret's recollections early on in the film. The flashbacks create a mosaic of a dream-mystery which only fully reveals itself after a visual nudge from Robert's paintings.

When allied with Sister Juliet's warning to Margaret that "Egypt is by nature overdramatic, filled with unreliable visions", real doubt is cast on whether there was ever a killing in the first place. Margaret's motivation to become a nun thus provides a much richer motif in the film. Is it simply a result of guilt at transferring her love from God to Nour, an unholy aberration in foreign climes? Is it her way to deal with possible abuse from her father as a child? (Derek, Monica alleges to Lili, was "found in disarray" in Margaret's bedroom when she was four.) Or is it simply a quintessentially English price paid for disturbing the status quo? "Nothing will change, it will always be the same," announces the dismally conservative Syl to Margaret—a platitude which she finds unable to dispel on her own, but explicitly acknowledges at the end whilst reflecting on her debt to Lili ("For surely to make a great fool and spectacle of yourself for the sake of another is a form of martyrdom").

By refusing to fully elaborate on these musings, *Wardrobe* not only complements Ellis' metier of irony and understatement but also plays obligingly into what must have been very real budget constraints. For despite the fact that virtually every character's life hinges on events that occurred either in the past (Monica's divorce, Robert's affair, Mrs Monro's awareness of her husband's infidelity) or on foreign soil, Ellis and the film-makers ensure that the real action determinedly unfolds in Croydon. Suburbia thus humbles the widescreen desert spaces of *Lawrence of Arabia* and *The Sheltering Sky* in a film which was always destined for the small screen.

TIME, 1/31/94, p. 108, Richard Schickel

It has all the elements of a cozy little domestic comedy: a young woman depressed by her impending marriage to a perfect twit; her mother tensely determined that the bourgeois niceties of the occasion will be punctiliously observed; his mother glumly sorry to inflict her son on anyone; and descending on them a worldly and eccentric woman—Auntie Mame with a foreign accent—eager to disrupt the ritual politesse of English suburban life.

But *The Summer House* isn't really a funny movie, though it is often wry, sometimes wise and generally genial. It is, more than anything, a rather sober meditation on life's tendency to disappoint. "I had hoped to die young," says Lili (Jeanne Moreau), "but now it's too late." Scarves aflutter, jewelry ajangle, her hair aflame with henna, she has just breezed in from Egypt and a past everyone once shared along the Nile. She copes by constant movement, outrageous talk and copious quantities of alcohol and tobacco. Monica (Julie Walters), the divorced mother of the bride, is all domestic bustle, dark thoughts held at bay by her many tasks remaking her awful old wedding dress for her daughter, considering the canapes for the reception. Mrs. Monro (Joan Plowright), the mother of the groom, sleeps a lot, awakening to express in a rumbly purr her dismay with just about everything.

These are all wonderful performances, in which rue and survivors' courage are gently voiced, with nobody trying to steal a scene or, heaven forfend, the picture. Moreau is particularly fine, since her role is one that could so easily be domineering.

The film's terribly still center is Margaret (Lena Headey, who was the maid in *The Remains of the Day*). She has recently been out to Egypt on a visit and, like so many travelers from her country, felt the heat of an exotic climate warm the dampness of her English soul, experiencing both emotional trauma and the hint of a religious vocation. This, together with the braying fatuity of her fiancé, has placed her in a conflict that renders her almost mute. She would like to be a dutiful daughter, but the effort is—quietly, of course—costing her sanity.

You can couch this dilemma wittily, as screenwriter Martin Sherman does, but you can't really evade its darker implications. Director Waris Hussein doesn't try. His style is objective without being cool or repressed in the all-too-common English manner. He avoids playing for big laughs the mostly awful social situations in which his characters find themselves. Even a drunk scene between Plowright and Moreau is low-keyed. It is very agreeable to discover a movie in which everything is not foreshadowed, underlined, commented upon. In other words, *The Summer House* is disciplined in the way that British theatrical productions often are. As a result, the story's somewhat surprising conclusion actually surprises.

But it doesn't quite take your breath away. That's the downside of disciplined filmmaking. Even though the movie is quarried out of a substantial fictional trilogy by Alice Thomas Ellis, it plays more as anecdote than as a fully developed narrative. It feels somehow ephemeral—a glancing blow, not quite a knockout. Still, emotional acuity, expressed with brisk intelligence, is not a common movie commodity, and it ought to be valued when you come across it.

VILLAGE VOICE, 1/4/94, p. 50, Georgia Brown

Red is the color of Jeanne Moreau's hair in this bite of trifle from England called *The Summer House*. As my friend from Paris commented after the screening, "Jeanne Moreau had better be careful." Moreau plays Lili, woman of the world come to lowly Croydon (a bourgeois suburb of London) to set things right. Lili keeps grasping people by the chin and delivering aphorisms on the subjects of age, lovers, and, especially, marriage. "I wanted to die young, but now it's too late." "Lovers are even more valuable after they stop being lovers." Or this on marriage: "One must never expect happiness." Lili wears jewelry the way Lancelot wore armor.

The occasion of Lili's visit to Monica (Julie Walters), her old college roommate, is the impending wedding of Monica's daughter Margaret (Lena Headey). Straightaway Lili divines that the fiancé, Syl (David Threlfall), is an utter fool and that Margaret is utterly miserable. Well, you'd have to be blind not to see it. Even Syl's mother, Mrs. Monro (Joan Plowright), notices. If Lili conceives a plan to foil the nuptials, we don't know it.

The year is 1959, which is supposed to explain why a woman would be marrying a man she detests. (Everyone did it.) Margaret can't bear to be touched by Syl, who's not only a fool but a cad. She dreams violently of Egypt, where she's been traveling recently. Her Egypt is contradictions: nuns and a darkly handsome young man. "I want to be a nun," she informs her mother. "Every girl wants to be a nun before she gets married," replies the mother. She and her peers suffered through marriage, why shouldn't Margaret? The payoff is becoming a widow.

Directed by Waris Hussein, the movie is adapted by Martin Sherman (*Bent*) from *The Clothes in the Wardrobe*, part of *The Summerhouse Trilogy*, by Alice Thomas Ellis. I'm curious about the novel because my primary response to this whimsical, immensely slight movie is to wonder what could have possessed anyone to film it.

PS: Perhaps I hadn't realized how much Joan Plowright looks like Rembrandt only because she hadn't worn those floppy berets before. The self-portraits will never look the same.

Also reviewed in:
CHICAGO TRIBUNE, 12/24/93, Friday/p. L, Johanna Steinmetz
NEW REPUBLIC, 1/10 & 17/94, p. 31, Stanley Kauffmann
NEW YORK TIMES, 12/21/93, p. C19, Caryn James
VARIETY, 11/8/93, p. 32, Todd McCarthy
WASHINGTON POST, 12/24/93, p. C1, Rita Kempley

SUPER MARIO BROS.

A Hollywood Pictures release of a Lightmotive/Allied Filmmakers presentation in association with Cinergi Productions. *Producer:* Jake Eberts and Roland Joffé. *Director:* Rocky Morton and Annabel Jankel. *Screenplay:* Parker Bennett, Terry Runté, and Ed Solomon. *Based on the concept and characters created by:* Shigeru Miyamoto and Takashi Tezuka. *Director of Photography:* Dean Semler. *Editor:* Mark Goldblatt. *Music:* Alan Silvestri. *Music Editor:* Kenneth Karman. *Choreographer:* Barry Lather. *Sound:* Richard Van Dyke and (music) Dennis S. Sands. *Sound Editor:* Jerry Ross and Hamilton Sterling. *Casting:* Mali Finn and Don Finn. *Production Designer:* David L. Snyder. *Art Director:* Walter P. Martishius. *Set Designer:* Timothy Galvin, Geoffrey S. Grimsman, John P. Goldsmith, Clare Scarpulla, Kathleen Sullivan, Tim Eckel, Nancy Mickelberry, and Bruton Jones. *Set Decorator:* Beth Rubino. *Set Dresser:* William Alford, Charlene Hamer, Russell Jones, and Eric Skipper. *Special Effects:* Paul

Lombardi. *Costumes:* Joseph Porro. *Make-up:* Jeff Goodwin. *Prosthetic Make-up:* Vincent J. Guastini. *Stunt Coordinator:* Gary Jensen. *Running time:* 104 minutes. *MPAA Rating:* PG.

CAST: Bob Hoskins (Mario Mario); John Leguizamo (Luigi Mario); Dennis Hopper (King Koops); Samantha Mathis (Daisy); Fisher Stevens (Iggy); Richard Edson (Spike); Fiona Shaw (Lena); Dana Kaminski (Daniella); Mojo Nixon (Toad); Gianni Russo (Scapelli); Francesca Roberts (Bertha); Lance Henriksen (The King); Sylvia Harman (Old Lady); Desiree Marie Velez (Angelica); Andrea Powell, Heather Pendergast, and Melanie Salvatore (Brooklyn Girls); John Fifer (Goomba Toad); Don Lake (Sgt. Simon); Terry Finn (Hat Check Girl); Robert Raiford (T.V. Announcer); Harry Murphy (Reporter #1); Patt Noday (Reporter #2); Robert Lee Edwards and Ronald Lou Edwards (Scapelli Bodyguard); Matthew Zachary Hopkins (Pizza Delivery Boy); Robert Faulkner Priester (Egon); Preston Lane (James); Jim Asaki (Japanese Businessman #1); Matt Nikko (Japanese Businessman #2); Kevin West (Devo Controller); Jeffrey Pillars (Devo Technician); Frank Welker (Creature Voices); Dan Castellenetta (Narrator).

LOS ANGELES TIMES, 5/29/93, Calendar/p. 1, Michael Wilmington

In an age when big action movie spectaculars like "Rambo" or "Predator" begin to resemble video games, is it surprising that the most popular Nintendo game of all, "The Super Mario Bros.," gets turned into a movie? Or that the film that results is mostly flash, carnage and visual explosions, with characters as light as their blip-on-the-screen inspirations?

In "The Super Mario Bros.", Nintendo heroes Luigi and Mario Mario are metamorphosed into a pair of Brooklyn Italian-American plumbers (played by Bob Hoskins and John Leguizamo), accidentally dropped into an alternate dimension of dinosaur-people. It's a movie split in two: wildly accomplished on one level, wildly deficient on another. If you had to grade it purely on its visual coups—the effects, Dean Semler's cinematography, the sheer density and bravura of the production design—you'd have to give "Mario Bros." high marks. If you judged it on the writing, or what we hear of it on the screen, your final score would be feeble.

The movie is a bright, clamorous extravaganza that keeps hammering and exploding away, filling the eyes with breath-taking wonders. The story, one more variation on "rescuing the princess from the evil castle," has the Marios trying to save pretty Daisy (Samantha Mathis of "Pump Up the Volume") from the Fascist empire ruled by evil King Koopa (Dennis Hopper, made up and coiffed like a corrupted Rutger Hauer), his race of reptile people, his idiot cohorts Iggy and Spike (Fisher Stevens and Richard Edson), his "devolution" machine and his army of pin-lizard-headed "Goomba" guards—who march around in outsize military coats, and are crazily susceptible to Frankie Yankovic renditions of "Somewhere My Love."

Koopa's underworld—a feverish neon-blazing slum, strung with pipes, festooned with fungus and rot—is a Manhattanite variant on the dystopian Los Angeles and London of "Blade Runner" and "Brazil." "Blade Runner's" art director, David L. Snyder, is the production designer here, and there's an overpowering aspect to the visual side of "Mario Bros.": a maniacal impressiveness. Co-directors Rocky Morton and Annabel Jankel created the "Max Headroom" movies, as well as the bizarre, failed 1988 updated *film noir*, "D.O.A.," and graphic spectaculars are obviously their specialty. They like visual overload, aural attack. They crank up the images while they jack up the rock 'n' roll.

But, like a video game itself, when it's over, the screen goes blank, the mind goes blank. There's nothing to do but wait for the next game.

It's not enough to say the script, by another tag-team of writers, including Parker Bennett, Terry Runté ("Mystery Date") and Ed Solomon (the "Bill & Ted" movies), is obvious, the wisecracks flat or the characters—except for a few brief Brooklyn scenes at the beginning—thin as a razor and not as engaging. The level of inspiration here can be clued by the name of the dinosaur alternate world's Manhattan—it's called "Dinohattan."

Does it make sense to make movies from video games? (Should Pac-Man be dangled in front of Danny DeVito?) Of course it does: *commercial* sense. Given the massive international popularity of the four Nintendo Mario Bros. games, this movie is virtually "pre-sold." But a built-in audience should be a challenge as well as a reassurance. On the non-technical level, "The Super Mario Bros." (MPAA-rated PG) dodges the challenge, drowns in the reassurance, the movie knocks your eyes out, at the same time it dulls the mind's eye. Ultimately, it's one more stop in the arcade, beckoning, waiting to soak up time and money.

NEW YORK, 6/14/93, p. 66, David Denby

Super Mario Bros. is the loudest movie I ever fell asleep at. Despite all the gibberish about a parallel universe, and evolution, and de-evolution, and so on, most of the time you are watching Bob Hoskins and John Leguizamo race around huge, schlocky sets, jump off catwalks, fall into holes, or smash up cars. The directors, Rocky Morton and Annabel Jankel, the creators of the computer-generated character Max Headroom and a great many "cutting edge" commercials, demonstrate no talent whatsoever for the narrative art of feature movies. None. I've played the computer game Super Mario Bros., and it's a lot of fun. But the minute faces and personalities and bodies replace electronic dots, you have to create some *interest*. It's embarrassing to have to point this out, but you can't treat human beings merely as objects in motion. *Super Mario Bros.* is stunningly dull. It's exceptionally violent, too, but what bothers me about this movie for children is not so much the car crashes and decomposing flesh—kids are used to that by now—as it is the movie's nihilistic contempt for a child's desire to be enchanted. There's literally nothing for children to get involved in or enjoy in this smash-palace fiasco. At the theater I went to, the little children, holding their daddies' hands, staggered out in the middle of the movie. Most of them looked shell-shocked.

NEW YORK POST, 5/29/93, p. 13, Jami Bernard

This is my first experience with a movie whose title is followed by a "trademark" notice. Based on a video game whose aesthetic appeal eludes me, "Super Mario Bros." is not really a movie—although it opened in theaters yesterday—but a marketing concept.

Hollywood Pictures, correctly guessing that the critics would annihilate "Super Mario Bros." with their joysticks, did not screen the movie in advance—always a sign of a turkey looming on the box-office horizon.

But people who think a video game about two hero plumbers would make an interesting movie may very well flock to their doom at the theaters.

Bob Hoskins and John Leguizamo star among slimy special effects as the so-called super Mario brothers. The "stupor" Mario brothers is more apt. If you have a choice between seeing this movie" or shoving a plunger in your face, go with the plunger.

The Brooklyn brothers get pulled into a parallel universe where humans have evolved alongside dinosaurs, and where there is a lot of slime and a set that was dressed by fans of "Total Recall." There is one cute little dinosaur that rolls its eyes sweetly, courtesy of elaborate mechanical design.

As plumbers, the brothers are accustomed to solving messy problems. The problem in this netherworld is that Daisy (Samantha Mathis) is being held captive by the reptilian King Koopa (Dennis Hopper) in exchange for the piece of meteor she usually wears around her neck. This meteor will help Koopa unite the two dimensions so that he can cross over and reign in modern-day Brooklyn.

Talk about getting stuck in the wrong dimension, the talented Leguizamo deserves better as he tries to cross over from his excellent one-man theater shows to Hollywood. Let's hope his role here as a plumber doesn't send his new career down the toilet.

"Super Mario Bros." (TM) needs to be a big hit, because it looks like it cost a lot to make, and because it sets up what is undoubtedly meant to be a future theme-park ride—a roller coaster down a twisty tunnel. To insure the movie's success, the writers have spared no effort in stealing heavy-handedly from other movies.

There is a pair of bumbling bad guys from "Home Alone," a handful of ideas from the "Star Wars" series, the magic slippers of "The Wizard of Oz." Kids of a certain undiscriminating age may well enjoy this artless browsing through pop culture.

On the bright side, I had about 10 seconds worth of enjoyment when an elevator full of pinheaded reptiles began swaying heavily to the Muzak.

NEWSDAY, 5/29/93, Part II/p. 25, Jack Mathews

As any Nintendo player will tell you, the thrill of a game like Super Mario Brothers is in controlling your own finger-eye coordination to overcome a series of obstacles, save a princess, and high-five yourself for whipping the computer nerd who programmed the whole thing.

The only way you can beat Hollywood Pictures' shrill and visually clumsy movie adaptation is to avoid it altogether.

"Super Mario Bros.," directed by the "Max Headroom" team of Rocky Morton and Annabel Jankel, is a live-action version of the game, starring Bob Hoskins and John Leguizamo as Brooklyn plumbers Mario and Luigi Mario who travel into a fourth dimension Manhattan to save an NYU anthropology student named Daisy (Samantha Mathis) from the clutches of an evil lizard king (Dennis Hopper).

Some 65 million years ago, during the dinosaur era, a giant meteor collided with Earth, creating parallel universes. Hopper's reptilian King Koopa wants to rejoin the two dimensions, destroy mammal life and lord over it all. But to do so, he needs the meteor fragment that Daisy has somehow had since childhood. Only the Mario brothers ran stop him.

That's more than enough plot for a video game, but "Super Mario Bros." in every other way falls short. There are some interesting creatures, not least the baby dino whose role would be played in the other dimension by Lassie, and small children will be dazzled by some of the visual effects.

For older viewers, the images may seem pretty routine, and the characters are so broadly drawn you yearn for the subtle shadings of, say, PacMan. Directors Morton and Jankel may be whizzes with computers themselves, but they don't know how to get performances out of real people, and their staging and cutting of action sequences are downright amateurish.

The movie may have been doomed before they were even hired, when producers Roland Joffe (the director of "The Killing Fields") "and producer Jake Eberts ("Driving Miss Daisy") bought the film rights to the game. When you transform a video game into a movie, you make the actual experience "smaller." You take the joystick out of the viewers' hands and turn them into passive witnesses.

At the same time, the movie holds characters and events up to scrutiny they don't get as blips on a video screen. When your game character uses rocket shoes to leap over a building, you don't expect it to look real, you just want to get it done and move on to the next obstacle.

When Hoskins and Leguizamo take off and fly, you haven't got anything better to do than look for the cable wires holding them up.

SIGHT AND SOUND, 8/93, p. 50, Ben Thompson

Sixty-five million years ago, a crashing meteorite split life on earth into two dimensions—our own, and a reptilian world where dinosaurs never became extinct, and humanoids evolved directly from them. Twenty years ago, Daisy, an infant princess, was smuggled across the dimensions from Dinohattan to New York, to escape the tyrannical King Koopa, who had seized power by de-evolving her father King Bowser into fungus.

Now grown up, but unaware of her status and bearing no sign of her origins except a pendant made from a piece of meteorite, Daisy is a student dinosaur researcher, bravely standing up to the Mob, whose construction project is being disrupted by her fossil find. At the dig, a passage-way has opened up between the dimensions, and Koopa's henchmen Iggy and Spike have come through it, kidnapping women indiscriminately in their search for Daisy. Koopa needs her pendant to help him merge the two worlds, so he can take over our natural resources. Unfortunately for him, Daisy has just been befriended by two resourceful plumbers, Mario Mario and his younger brother Luigi Mario, who has fallen in love with her.

When Daisy is captured and dragged off to Koopa's world to be imprisoned with the other kidnapped women (including Mario's girlfriend Daniella) the Marios give chase. The pendant is stolen by a large and frightening woman, Big Bertha, who eventually helps the Marios to evade Koopa's reptilian stormtroopers, the Goombas. Fed up with Iggy and Spike's bungling, Koopa has put his de-evolution machine into reverse, and rendered them super-intelligent. Their newfound wisdom leads them too to opt to help the Marios.

Koopa's jealous paramour Lena gets hold of the pendant and attempts to merge the two worlds, but only Daisy can harness its power, and Lena is killed. After an epic struggle, and with the help from the benign fungus that enshrouds the city, Koopa is defeated by Luigi and Mario and de-evolved first to Tyrannosaurus and them to slime. King Bowser is restored to humanity and throne, and the Marios return to Brooklyn as heroes—dubbed "The Super Mario Brothers" by a TV newscaster—though Luigi is sad to be separated from his beloved Daisy by her royal obligations. Life seems to be back to normal when Daisy arrives at the brothers' apartment, calling them back for another adventure.

What upsets people most about the idea of this film is the failure of cinematic nerve it seems to embody; it's as if Hollywood had decided it can't beat the Japanese game giants and their sinister hold over our healthy Western youth, so it might as well join them. It is more constructive to see *Super Mario Bros* as its makers are inclined to, "In the great tradition of comic book superheroes come to life". When producer Roland Joffé watched his son playing the Nintendo game on which the film is surprisingly loosely based, "It began to seem like a very creative thing to try to bring these cultural icons to life and dramatise the imaginary world of their adventures". If it keeps Mr Joffé from making more overblown tosh like *The Mission*, then who are we to argue?

Product placement has taken the cinema by stealth. In the case of *Super Mario Bros*, the reverse is true. The welcome surprise of this film is that it doesn't just slavishly obey the dictates of the game-deviser's peculiar imaginations. The plot does embody the freedom from logic that is one of the game-world's biggest selling points, but it does so in a surprisingly cinematic way. Production designer David Snyder's boast that "There are more than 100 game elements in the film, waiting to be counted by keen-eyed and dedicated fans" will make hearts sink among non-devotees, but movie train-spotters not suffering from Nintendo finger might derive just as much pleasure from ticking off the absurd number of film references from a checklist including *Robocop, Superman, Star Wars* and *The Wizard of Oz*.

This obsessive allusiveness is obviously not a good thing in itself, and the film would have been more fun if directors Morton and Jankel had attempted to fashion a serious emotional drama around the raw material of the Mario story. But genuine inventiveness occasionally rears its head among the blockbusting detritus. Dinohattan in particular, though rather weakly-named, turns out to he an urban dystopia worthy of Ridley Scott or Richard Stanley, and also a subversive hint at what our own cities are going to end up looking like if we continue wasting all our fossil fuels playing video games.

One and a half square miles of plywood went into the making of *Super Mario Bros*, and that was just for the performances. Dennis Hopper, the arch villain with the amphibian's tongue and the 'Punk's not dead' haircut, is the only one who really enjoys himself. He seems to actively relish the absurd amount of exposition he is contracted to supply—investing lines like "Muster the Goombas!" with existential significance. Bob Hoskins, on the other hand, sleepwalks through the lead, but then he's seen all this before with *Roger Rabbit*.

The film's younger stars John Leguizamo (*Hangin' with the Homeboys*) and Samantha Mathis (*Pump up the Volume*) have yet to establish themselves so firmly and it is to be hoped they have not done lasting damage to their promising careers with the terminally wet Luigi and Daisy. She is initially fine in the Princess Lea role, but struggles a bit once forced out of her feisty student garb and into a less than empowering purple night-dress. Worse still, she is also obliged to befriend a cute dinosaur called Yoshi. Leguizamo at least gets to deliver *Super Mario Bos'* great rallying cry to the children of the world—"Trust the Fungus!"

VILLAGE VOICE, 6/15/93, p. 60, Carol Cooper

Confession No. 1. I love Annabel Jankel and Rocky Morton. I love the very idea of them: a pair of computer-graphics whiz kids who have lived, loved, and worked together for the better part of 10 years. Annabel made her initial impact with some of the cleverest music videos I've ever seen, then went to work with Morton creating the surreal pyrotechnics of the proto-cyberpunk conspiracy series *Max Headroom*. I forgave them their stylish mistakes on *D.O.A.*, keeping hope alive that they'd soon astonish me with another masterpiece of their own design. Hope in vain when it comes to Hollywood Pictures' *Super Mario Bros*.

Confession No. 2. I do not like *The Three Stooges*. I do not like the lame, self-indulgent quotes from *The Three Stooges, Batman Returns, The Wizard of Oz*, or *Star Wars* that dot the *Super Mario Bros.* script like poisonous fungi. Morton and Jankel, rumored to be the last in a series of tried and jettisoned directors, *do not* save this movie. Christopher Woods's sparkly special effects don't save this movie, nor does Dean Semler's pretty cinematography. And finally, most definitively Mark Goldblatt's epileptic editing doesn't save this movie. Actor Bob Hoskins has said in recent interviews that producer Roland Joffé kept having the script rewritten (and fees renegotiated) until Hoskins agreed to take the Danny DeVito role. One shudders to think what previous scripts were like ... or could they possibly have been ... *better???!!!*

Confession No. 3. Perhaps to his credit, Hoskins struggles valiantly throughout the *entire* movie. And he manages not to stink. (Baffle, yes ... but not stink.) On the other hand, John Leguizamo gives every onscreen indication that he is not with this program at all. Using the goofy, subpubescent voice he developed for his put-upon Miguelito character in *Spic-O-Rama*, he delivers purile dialogue with wooden movement that telegraphs creative disaffection (or is it defection? defecation?) to anyone who's seen his prior work. (Who do you have to fuck to get *off* this project?) Oh, and what's with the Princess Leia knockoff? Is this a prequel for *Daisy Duz (sic) Dinosaurs?*

Confession No. 4. I *paid* to see this movie.

Also reviewed in:
NEW YORK TIMES, 5/29/93, p. 11, Janet Maslin
VARIETY, 6/7/93, p. 38, Lawrence Cohn
WASHINGTON POST, 5/29/93, p. D1, Hal Hinson

SURF NINJAS

A New Line Cinema release of a New Line production. *Executive Producer:* Sara Risher, Dan Gordon, and Kevin Moreton. *Producer:* Evzen Kolar. *Director:* Neal Israel. *Screenplay:* Dan Gordon. *Director of Photography:* Arthur Albert and Victor Hammer. *Editor:* Tom Walls. *Music:* David Kitay. *Music Editor:* Chris McGeary. *Sound:* Ike Magal. *Sound Editor:* Steven Williams. *Casting:* Annette Benson and Tammy Musigdilok. *Production Designer:* Michael Novotny. *Art Director:* Curtis W. Baruth. *Set Decorator:* Janis Lubin and Michael Bacon. *Set Dresser:* Deirdre Cotrell. *Special Effects:* Frank Ceglia. *Costumes:* Deborah La Gorce Kramer. *Make-up:* Suzanne Parker Sanders. *Special Make-up Effects:* Tony Gardner and John Henry. *Stunt Coordinator:* Philip Tan. *Martial Arts Choreographer:* Ernie Reyes, Sr. *Running time:* 87 minutes. *MPAA Rating:* PG.

CAST: Ernie Reyes, Sr. (Zatch); Ernie Reyes, Jr. (Johnny); Nicolas Cowan (Adam); John Karlen (Mac); Rob Schneider (Iggy); Olivier Mills (Moto Surfer); Jonathan Schmock (School Cop); Neal Israel (Mr. Dunbar); Vladimir Parra (Backup Singer #1); Brandon Karrer (Backup Singer #2); Dathan Aragon (Backup Singer #3); Phillip Bayless (Backup Singer #4); Phillip Tan (Captain Ming); Keone Young (Baba Ram); Romy Walthall (Miss Robertson); Rachel Kolar (Rachel); Yoni Gordon (Wendell); Sritao Thepchasoon (Dungeon Guard); Leslie Neilsen (Colonel Chi); Nathan Jung (Manchu); Thep Thien-Chai (Gong Man); Sa-Ngud (Prisoner); Sheng Meng (Major Snee); Tanin Tapmongkol (King); Montatip Kaewprasert (Queen); Tone Loc (Lt. Spence); Rick Dorio (Sgt. Bork); Jim Vallely (Surf Dude #1); Mitch Horowitz (Surf Dude #2); Mark Dutt (Squad Car Cop #1); Desi Singh (Squad Car Cop #2); Tad Horino (Gum-Bey); Young Jue (Patu Sani Man); Kelly Hu (Ro-May); Marisa Theodore (Surf Babe); Pete Antico (Cop #1); Robert Terry Lee (Cop #2); Bowman Chung (Victim).

LOS ANGELES TIMES, 8/23/93, Calendar/p. 3, Kevin Thomas

"Surf Ninjas" a strictly-for-the-kiddies action comedy, has as its biggest assets the sunny personality of its star Ernie Reyes Jr., a martial arts wiz, surfer and rock singer, and the simple but important fact that it's a mainstream movie featuring Asian-Americans in central roles.

Reyes' Johnny, his younger brother Adam (Nicolas Cowan) and their pal Iggy (Rob Schneider) enjoy an idyllic existence in Ocean Park when the brothers' adoptive father Mac, (John Karlen) is abruptly kidnaped. A mysterious man, Satch (Ernie Reyes Sr.), who has the power to make himself disappear, pops up and tells the brothers they are royal princes from the South China Sea island kingdom of Patu San (where Karlen now languishes imprisoned in the Fortress of Death).

Years before the evil Col. Chi (Leslie Nielsen), a buffoonish cross between Genghis Khan and the Terminator, invaded Patu San and overthrew the monarchy, Satch managed to hand over the brothers, both too young to have memories of their native land, to Mac to raise in America. But now as Johnny approaches his 16th birthday, he must return to Patu San to fulfill his destiny, overthrow the colonel's cruel regime and assume the throne.

Dan Gordon's script is elementary in the utmost, boasting only the most minimal characterization, but at least director Neal Israel keeps "Surf Ninjas" (rated PG for comic martial arts action and mild language) moving.

NEW YORK POST, 8/23/93, p. 27, Michael Medved

With even the most wretched piece of celluloid excrescence you can usually find something nice to say—declaring, for instance, that at least the camera is in focus most of the time.

Unfortunately, that's not the case with "Surf Ninjas," where the cinematography is fuzzy, grainy, shaky and dimly lit—like your Uncle Ernie's unwatchable vacation videos of Los Angeles, Hawaii and Thailand (where they shot this movie).

The sound is another problem, with the lip movements on screen bearing only the most casual and coincidental relationship to the voices on the sound track. Nearly all the dialogue appears to have been "looped"—dubbed by the actors long after their scenes were shot in silence—and the sound quality suggests that these performers recorded their lines in aqualungs at the bottom of a huge aquarium.

This technical incompetence is all deployed on behalf of an inane plot about two teen-aged surfer brothers (Ernie Reyes Jr. and Nicholas Cowan) who are so shamelessly stupid (they don't have a clue as to what continent Spain is on) that they make Bill and Ted look like Will and Henry James.

When several dozen ninjas invade their high school and attempt to murder them, they're saved by a martial arts hero with an eye patch (Ernie Reyes Sr.) who informs them that they are the rightful heirs to the throne of Patu San. The evil Colonel Chi (played by Leslie Nielsen, of all people!) has usurped the crown and is determined to murder his rivals.

The boys eventually go back to Patu San (which has been hand-written onto a map somewhere off the coast of Thailand) to lead a revolution accompanied by a wise-cracking high school buddy, (Rob Schneider, "Saturday Night Live"'s "Copy Meister") and rap star Tone Loc (who plays an L.A. police officer).

Even though we're not dealing here with Oscar-caliber writing, a light, crisp touch, and well-staged fighting and surfing scenes, could have turned this story into mindless fun. As it is, director Neal Israel ("Bachelor Party," "Breaking the Rules") displays such a sloppy, what-the-hell approach to this assignment that the picture is not only embarrassingly dumb, but unendurably boring.

Over the last few years New Line Pictures has made a bundle with its "Ninja Turtles" pictures; in fact Ernie Reyes Jr., the star of this film, made a previous appearance inside a turtle suit as Donatello in the original "Teen-age Mutant Ninja Turtles."

Now that this company has followed its turtle triumphs with an epic about ninja surfers, perhaps we should expect future offerings with titles like "Jurassic Ninja" or "Ninja Rappers" or "Beverly Hills Ninja."

When these projects arrive, we can only hope that someone will see to it that the camera is in focus.

NEWSDAY, 8/21/93, Part II/p. 19, Terry Kelleher

So Mike Myers didn't exactly set North America on fire with his summer movie, "So I Married an Axe Murderer." Rob Schneider had better not ride him too hard when the "Saturday Night Live" cast regroups for the fall.

People who appear in "Surf Ninjas" shouldn't throw stones. Grown-up people, anyway.

"Surf Ninjas" is about two Venice, Calif., kids who find out they're crown princes of a tiny Asian country and ... Oh, forget the plot. Even Johnny (Ernie Reyes Jr.) and Adam (Nicolas Cowan) fall asleep when their ninja mentor, Zatch (Ernie Reyes Sr.), tries to brief them on the background.

The primary purpose of this movie is to keep restless young viewers occupied with martial-arts action that's fast and loud, but not as brutal as the R-rated stuff. Mission accomplished.

Schneider's job—and, to a lesser extent, Leslie Nielsen's—is to provide comedy that's an adequate sop to the adult guardians without being inaccessible to children. Like most straddling acts, this one isn't too funny.

Iggy, the Robmeister's character, says he's in the 11th grade. This is a joke in itself, right? Or shall we assume the Venice school system has flunked him repeatedly for talking in class? Everyone in the movie seems to agree that Iggy's incessant chatter is an annoyance, but he just keeps tagging along.

"You keep him to amuse you, yes?" Zatch asks Johnny and Adam. "Like a boy would keep a monkey or a snake?" Hey, lay off our Iggy, ninja-man. Could a monkey or a snake put on a Hitler mustache and do a Scottish accent for no reason other than to flex his improvisational-comedy muscles?

Nielsen's character, the evil Col. Chi, is weighed down with movie-parody paraphernalia, but the truly funny thing about him is not his Freddy Krueger hand or his "Phantom of the Opera" mask or the "Apocalypse Now" ambience of his dark fortress. It's his balky phone system. The call-waiting feature should draw laughs from customers of all ages.

Director Neal Israel serves up violence in mass quantities, but no fatalities are evident and sight gags often pop up amid the kicks and punches. What's the harm if all the unnecessary roughness seems cost-free? That's up to parents to judge.

SIGHT AND SOUND, 4/94, p. 52, Caren Myers

Fifteen-year-old Johnny and his little brother Adam, two Asian-American surf dudes living with their doting adoptive father Mac, enjoy an idyllic existence shredding waves, playing video games and hanging out with their babbling buddy Iggy. Little do they suspect that they are the target of ruthless ninja assassins, whose attempts to eliminate them are only foiled by the superior skills of a mysterious warrior, Zatch. When the ninjas kidnap Mac and destroy his burger bar, Zatch reveals that the boys are in fact the crown princes of Patu San, an isolated island now ruled with an iron fist by the nefarious Colonel Chi. Their destiny is to become, respectively, a great warrior and a seer of visions.

When the police arrive on the scene, they are unable to do much, though hard-boiled cop Spence is sympathetic. Later that night, ninjas surround the boys' house, though Adam, who can foresee the future on his Gameboy, is warned of the attack by a magic video game, 'Surf Ninjas'. Zatch saves them again, but is forced to blow up the house. They take shelter in a Patu Sani restaurant, where the owner introduces Johnny to his prearranged bride-to-be, the beautiful and feisty Ro-May.

After a fight with more ninjas, the boys sail for Patu San, accompanied by Ro-May and Lt Spence. On the island they recover the sacred weapons of Kwansu, which instil the warrior spirit in Johnny, and overpower some of Chi's men. Leading a troop of emancipated Patu Sanis, they launch a surfboard attack on Chi's fortress island. Chi is defeated, and the prophecy is fulfilled. At his coronation, Johnny pronounces the monarchy dissolved and returns the government to the people; the kids and Mac will return to California.

So this is what the world is coming to: movies where the plot twists are magically signalled by a kid's Nintendo game (or possibly Sega, I couldn't tell—the product placement was too discreet). Certainly *Surf Ninjas'* fight scenes seem inspired by video games, except that the software wasn't sophisticated enough to provide the heroes with more than one opponent at a time. In any case,

Chi's ninja warriors don't appear to be made of terribly stern stuff—one bloodthirsty warrior is completely disabled by having a small octopus thrust in his face.

But then, this is Saturday matinee fare for very young mall rats, so the action is unimportant. There's not a whole lot of surfing here either. What the film does do is crack lots of corny jokes and keep up a mildly knowing "been there, seen it, skied it, surfed it" commentary on the silliness of the plot. So it's a lot like having invited a bunch of smartarse school children over to your house.

Ernie Reyes Jr was the pizza delivery boy in *Teenage Mutant Ninja Turtles 2*; here he mugs shamelessly to camera and it's a relief when he attains spiritual manhood and stops rolling his eyes before every line. Meanwhile, Ernie Sr approaches his role as if David Carradine in *Kung Fu* were the apotheosis of the actor's craft. Overall, the acting strains to attain sitcom stature, and Leslie Nielsen, hampered by a Darth Vader-style metal face, is sadly wasted.

Yet, brain-dead though this film is, it has a certain goofy charm that's almost endearing. It never lapses into sentimentality, and seems to have been written by basically decent, tolerant folk, albeit folk out to make a quick buck. Adults will look at their watches ten to 15 times during its 87 minutes, but will be mildly amused by rapper Tone Loc's surprisingly expressive face and rumbling basso profundo. And kids will love every minute.

Also reviewed in:
NEW YORK TIMES, 8/21/93, p. 9, Janet Maslin
VARIETY, 8/30/93, p. 26, Daniel M. Kimmel
WASHINGTON POST, 8/21/93, p. C2, Richard Harrington

SWING KIDS

A Buena Vista Pictures release of a Hollywood Pictures presentation in association with Touchwood Pacific Partners I. *Executive Producer:* Frank Marshall and Christopher Meledandri. *Producer:* Mark Gordon, John Bard Manulis, and Harry Benn. *Director:* Thomas Carter. *Screenplay:* Jonathan Marc Feldman. *Director of Photography:* Jerzy Zielinski. *Editor:* Michael R. Miller. *Music:* James Horner. *Music Editor:* Eric Reasoner and Jim Henrikson. *Choreographer:* Otis Sallid. *Sound:* Ivan Sharrock and (music) Shawn Murphy. *Sound Editor:* George Watters, II. *Casting:* Deborah Aquila, Noel Davis, Jeremy Zimmerman, and Eva Kadankova. *Swing Consultant:* Leonard Feather. *Production Designer:* Allan Cameron. *Art Director:* Steve Spence, Tony Reading, and Mical Krska. *Set Decorator:* Ros Shingleton. *Special Effects:* Garth Inns. *Costumes:* Jenny Beavan. *Make-up:* Paul Engelen. *Stunt Coordinator:* Mark Boyle. *Running time:* 112 minutes. *MPAA Rating:* PG-13.

CAST: Robert Sean Leonard (Peter Muller); Christian Bale (Thomas Berger); Frank Whaley (Arvid); Barbara Hershey (Frau Muller); Tushka Bergen (Evey); Kenneth Branagh (Herr Knoepp); David Tom (Willi); Julia Stemberger (Frau Linge); Jayce Bartok (Otto); Noah Wyle (Emil); Johan Leysen (Herr Schumler); Douglas Roberts (Hinz); Martin Clunes (Bannfuhrer); Jessica Stevenson (Helga); Carl Brincat (HY Thug); Mary Fogarty (Mama Klara); Karel Belohradsky (Bismarck Owner); Peter Baikie (Bismarck Bandleader); Jennifer Chamberlain (Swing Girl with Thomas); Lucie Vackarova (Swing Girl with Peter); Katerina Dankova and Magdalena Chrzova (Evey's School Friends); Jiri Malek (Jewish Boy); Metin Yenal (Customer in Bookshop); Arthur White (Alberti); Marek Libert (Whistling HY); Nada Konvalinkova (Pastry Shop Woman); Petr Jakl (Policeman in Marketplace); David Robb (Dr. Berger); Ciaran Madden (Frau Berger); John Streitburger (Dr. Keppler); Hana Cizkova (Frau Keppler); Petr Lepsa (Cafe Trichter Owner); Warner Van Eeden (Trichter Bandleader); Andrew Kitchen (Gestapo at Trichter); Jeremy Bulloch (Small Club Owner); Joseph Bennett and Roman Janousek (Luftwaffe Pilots); Richard Hanson (HY Fink); Sean Pertwee (Gestapo Arresting Berger); Sarka Horcikova (Berger's Maid); Jochen Horst (Speaker at Hitler Youth Rally); Vladimir Matejcek (Funeral Pastor); John Dudval (Gestapo with Ashes); Marie

Vorlova (First Woman with Ashes);   Eliza Clark (Girl with Ashes);   Kate Buffery (Woman with Ashes);   Sabine Skala (Cafe Bismarck Singer).

LOS ANGELES TIMES, 3/5/93, Calendar/p. 4, Kenneth Turan

The creators of "Swing Kids" must have thought they'd died and gone to heaven when they got the inspiration for this film. Having run out of domestic situations to place photogenic young people in, here was a chance to do a coming-of-age movie against the backdrop of the rise of Nazism in Germany with some lively music thrown into the mix. What could possibly be better?

The answer, unfortunately, is just about anything. For, except for that music and a bit of the acting, "Swing Kids" is unsatisfactory from just about every point of view. Awkward, hollow and emotionally heavy-handed, it transports a sea of movie clichés onto those unfamiliar German shores. The fact that the filmmakers seem to think they're dealing honestly with this nightmare period in history only makes what they've done that much more depressing.

Certainly the subject matter of the PG-13 "Swing Kids" is intriguing. For while sentiment for Hitler is rising in Germany in the 1930s, so, apparently, was passion for swing music among a free-thinking segment of that country's youth. Apolitical but nonconforming, passionate about jitterbug dancing and unwilling to join the Hitler Youth, these long-haired kids were by definition an affront to the strident conformity of an increasingly rigid society.

And when "Swing Kids" cuts to the melody, it is hard to complain. As choreographed by Otis Sallid, the film's dancing is lively and energizing, an unfortunate contrast to the pall that overtakes things when the music stops.

At first the problems seem small enough. The swing kids the film focuses on, for instance, look more like they grew up in Reseda than Hamburg. And their accents are so various that any sense of things really taking place in Germany is lost.

More crucially, the plot, as it follows the path of a trio of close pals, becomes much less original than the setting. Peter ("Dead Poets Society's" gracefully sympathetic Robert Sean Leonard) is your basic good kid with a worried mother (Barbara Hershey) and the legacy of a father who resisted the state. Thomas (Christian Bale) is the spoiled son of wealthy parents, while Arvid, a.k.a. Hitman (Frank Whaley), is the truest hipster even though he walks with a limp.

"Swing Kids" attempts to show what happens as these kids are forced to deal with the increasing power of a political party that considers the makers of jazz sub-human or worse. Not a bad idea, but in the hands of screenwriter Jonathan Marc Feldman and director Thomas Carter, every dramatic moment is either miscalculated, overdone or both, as the film finds it increasingly hard to resist bludgeoning the audience with its sensitivity.

The one exception to all of this is Kenneth Branagh, who chose not to take screen credit for his role as Gestapo Major Knoepp, a devoted Nazi who takes an interest in both Peter and his mother. Though the part is a subsidiary one, Branagh outdoes the rest of the cast without even trying, illuminating even in his brief moments on screen how the Nazi movement could have an appeal to someone of sensitivity and taste. But the pleasure of watching Branagh work must be a mixed one, because it underscores how far from his subtlety of attack everything else in this film turns out to be.

NEW YORK, 3/22/93, p. 66, David Denby

In the enjoyably nutty *Swing Kids*, a group of debonair young men in Nazi Germany, instinctively anti-authoritarian, dress themselves up in British fashions—long peg pants, Scottish waistcoats, umbrellas—and go flopping off at night to dance clubs, where they jitterbug wildly to "Swingtime in the Rockies." The Nazis hate jazz, a decadent art form perpetrated by the subhuman races (representative members include Benny Goodman, Artie Shaw, and Count Basie), so they send black-uniformed goons from the Hitler Youth to break up the dancing. For the handsome young heroes, the American music has a fatal intoxication: They've got to listen to it; they've got to dance to it. "Swing Heil!" one of them salutes as he's led away at the end.

Swing Kids takes us back to purest Hollywood, where companionship and high spirits win a moral victory over dictatorship, and the hope of the future can be read in the handsome faces of earnest young American and British actors. The movie is set in Hamburg (in 1939), and was shot in Prague, but it's an *echt amerikanische* production all the way, with the kind of dictates-of-conscience theme familiar from old Hollywood melodramas—all of this mixed in with teen rumbles out of a fifties movie. The Hitler Youth gangs prefer polkas and marches; the Swing Kids like Benny Goodman. It's as if the fate of the world came down to taste.

The Disney people produced the film, which was written by a New York playwright named Jonathan Marc Feldman and directed by Thomas Carter, who has worked only in television. The actors speak in English, but with the stilted tones that the filmmakers take to be proper for educated Europeans. As I looked at the screen in disbelief, I kept asking myself what the filmmakers thought they were doing. Why was this movie made? Why kick the Nazis yet again ! Aren't there some young people in contemporary Iraq who love rock and roll? "Rock the Casbah," as the Clash insisted about a decade ago. Salaam Zappa!

Oh, well. *Swing Kids* is too silly to get mad about. And it gives one pleasant thoughts—such as the fancy that British clothes and big-band jazz fueled anti-Nazi sentiment. The press notes claim historical accuracy, but could the Swing Kids be anything more than a footnote to a footnote? What the naive filmmakers don't seem to understand is that totalitarianism nullified exactly such heroic gestures as the film celebrates. Totalitarianism, as its victims have often said, made rebellion meaningless. No one even noticed. Still, even if the story is partly mythical, it's stimulating to hear that pop culture once cost a few young people a great deal more than the approval of their parents. Such an idea might be news to American teenagers who imagine that their fashion statements are a form of "rebellion."

And what a surprise to see that the jitterbugging, which was choreographed by Otis Sallid, who also did the terrific jitterbug sequences in *Malcolm X*, makes much of what teenagers do on dance floors today look rather tame. I have, however, a protest to make: Couldn't women play a larger role? Jitterbugging was hardly just a boy thing. The women in the film are seen dancing but do little else but fill out the corners. And why is the atmosphere so sexless? The Swing Kids seem as chaste as Sunday-school kids.

The movie features the kind of lump-in-the-throat moral sentiments that Europeans in Hollywood anti-Fascist movies gave way to 50 years ago. Arvid (Frank Whaley), the crippled jazz guitarist, gets to make the ripest speeches, though in fairness, I should mention that the filmmakers add a large dose of moral realism: By 1939, the movie suggests, most of the remaining holdouts caved in to Nazism because they had little choice. The pressures of violence and conformity surround and undermine everybody. The hero, Peter (Robert Sean Leonard), an engineering student, is gradually falling into the clutches of a friendly Gestapo agent (Kenneth Branagh), who shows up now and then and makes suave "understanding" remarks. In Hollywood movies, there are basically two kinds of Nazis—the screaming blond sadists, who slap women across the kisser, and the subtle, charming sadists, who calmly explain why the future belongs to the master race. Branagh, modulating his voice, is one of the latter.

Everyone tells Peter to join the Hitler Youth. He's troubled, he suffers, he can't make up his mind, poor thing. Robert Sean Leonard, one of the boys from *Dead Poets Society*, does rather well with this vessel of innocence. Leonard has a large, open face, and he's handsome in a flavorless way. (He's like Henry Fonda without the physical beauty.) It's good fun when this virtuous young man lays down his umbrella, enters the dance floor in his Anthony Eden rig, and turns into a wildly enthusiastic, stomping maniac.

Some of Peter's closest friends, even members of the anti-Nazi Swing Kids, are joining the Hitler Youth. Trapped by the Gestapo, Peter gives in and puts on a black uniform but remains a Swing Kid, going to clubs at night. Will he survive morally? Arvid is the only complete holdout. Arvid, the jazz intellectual, isn't a perfect specimen like the others—the implication is that his gimpy leg gives him moral purity. Actually, this may not be as absurd as it sounds: Marcel Ophuls's classic documentary about France during the occupation, *The Sorrow and the Pity*, suggested that it was mainly the eccentrics and outsiders who joined the Resistance.

Thomas Carter keeps *Swing Kids* active and alive, not always to any particular purpose. There are lots of fights, including a vicious boxing match that doesn't make much sense, and many scenes of people telling each other off, as if Nazism provided a great occasion for grandstanding. Yet Carter, I think, really does believe in the redemptive power of swing music. The movie's oddity, in other words, saves it from the worst banalities. *Swing Kids* is devoted to heroic futile gestures, of which the most heroic is the dancing itself. If the movie had been more stylized—more like a musical and less like TV melodrama—then it might have turned into some sort of crazy classic. Even the way it is, it's a bizarrely pleasant entertainment.

NEW YORK POST, 3/5/93, p. 32, Matthew Flamm

Zero Mostel, rest easy in your grave. "Swing Kids" has nothing on "Springtime for Hitler."

Set in 1939 Germany, this latest Disney offering portrays the spread of Nazism through a group of teen-aged hep cats—Swing Kids, who refused to join the Hitler Youth, wore their hair long and gathered on the sly to dance to the outlawed sounds of Count Basie and Benny Goodman.

I have no idea of its historical accuracy, but certainly "Swing Kids" risks ridiculousness by trying to mate a brat-pack vehicle with the darkest story of the century.

And yet the movie is not quite the campy disaster one expects; it's as earnest as "The Producers" with its unforgettable "Springtime" production number—was outrageous. To its credit, "Swing Kids" dramatizes the appeal Nazism had for a lot of Germans, not just the nasty ones.

That's the theme of the movie; whether Peter ("Dead Poets Society" veteran Robert Sean Leonard) and his jazz-loving buddies will give in to the pod people and start humming German folk tunes. The guys have so far sworn allegiance only to swing, jitterbugging by night in improbably slick but lively scenes choreographed by "Malcolm X" choreographer Otis Sallid.

By day, the guys hang out in their guitarist friend Arvid's darkened room, showing off, "Diner"-like, their knowledge of jazz arcana. As Arvid says of a Swing Kid who has joined the Hitler Youth—but who may still be loyal to jazz—"Nobody who likes swing can become a Nazi."

Apparently, director Thomas Carter and writer Jonathan Marc Feldman also think so, and have put that shockingly naive credo at their movie's heart. "Swing Kids" really is for teens; it's "Hey, Let's Twist!" and "The Breakfast Club" with a dash of "Cabaret."

Forced into the Hitler Youth, Peter is soon joined by his best friend Thomas (Christian Bale), who claims to be keeping Peter company but who may be more Nazi than he knows. Peter, too, has his loyalties tested as a Gestapo officer—played with a wonderfully sinister cool by an uncredited Kenneth Branagh—leans on him to inform.

There's a seriousness to "Swing Kids" that almost saves it, and performances by grown-ups—Barbara Hershey plays Peter's widowed mother—that lend an authority you don't get from over-heated teens. But no teen movie, not even one set in Nazi Germany, can end unhappily.

These Swing Kids standing up for what they believe—there hasn't been a scene this ridiculous since ... why, since Mostel sang "Springtime for Hitler"!

NEWSDAY, 3/5/93, Part II/p. 55, Jack Mathews

On the gray streets outside, plainclothes gestapo, uniformed SS and roaming Hitler Youth squads are pushing the people of 1939 Germany into a growing state of terror. Jews are being harassed, assaulted and robbed, sympathizers are being watched or tortured, and Jewish women awaiting the return of arrested husbands are instead being handed packages containing wedding rings and ashes.

Inside the Cafe Bismarck, however, the lights are bright and the joint is jumping. On stage, a band is re-creating the verboten sounds of American swing greats Count Basie, Duke Ellington and Benny Goodman, and the dance floor is a hot patch of fair-skinned, jitterbugging German youths.

If there has been a serious movie with a greater contrast of moods than "Swing Kids," it doesn't come to mind, and it is at the extremes where first-time director Thomas Carter and screenwriter Jonathan Marc Feldman squander their wonderful story concept, as well as the exceptional performances of its two youthful stars, Robert Sean Leonard and Christian Bale.

It's a great idea to use the jazz subculture to explore the conflicting pull of politics and music on Germans coming of age at the peak of Hitler's madness, to tap into a group of apolitical youths bonded by their love for the "Neger/Kike" music that the conformist state has deemed "perverse" and "dangerous."

Like many of America's "Flower Children" of the '60s, Germany's swing kids were motivated by nothing so much as having a good time, and freestyle jitterbugging was simply more fun than the waltz. To turn their appreciation for American music into some sort of political credo—"Swing Heil!" is their salute, and when things get really tough, they break into a few bars of "It don't mean a thing if it ain't got that swing"—is a pure Hollywood conceit.

The frustrating thing about "Swing Kids" is that it cuts back and forth, with jarring frequency, between the screenwriter's fantasies and the gloomy realities of Nazism. Whether their passions were for swing or Jewish literature or anything else outside the state's interests, the Reich did not long tolerate eccentricities, even among youths.

"Swing Kids" addresses that issue through the deteriorating relationships between three teenage friends: Peter (Robert Sean Leonard), whose father had died for his Jewish sympathies, Thomas (Christian Bale), the calculating son of affluent Germans, and Arvid (Frank Whaley) a crippled guitarist and jazz scholar who is deemed inferior by the Hitler Youth and some of his own friends because of his handicap.

It is quickly apparent which political direction the three characters will take, and what should be the film's most dramatic sequences are sabotaged by cliches and predictability.

On the other extreme, the dance scenes have the intentional artifice of Andy Hardy movies. You can't complain about the music—I'm buying the soundtrack tomorrow!—but hearing the full-throated Benny Goodman version of "Sing, Sing, Sing" come out of an orchestra small enough to carpool to the club in a Volkswagen van is hard to overlook. The dancing scenes themselves, choreographed by Otis Sallid, who did the lindy numbers for Spike Lee's "Malcolm X," are so loose-limbed and hyper-energized, it looks like somebody spiked the schnapps with LSD.

Carter, a successful director of TV dramas, obviously wanted to heighten the comparison between the passionate abandon kids feel on a dance floor with the goose-stepping discipline of the Hitler Youth. A little subtlety would have served that purpose much better.

Even while we marvel at the silliness of "Swing Kids," however, it is often powerfully moving. Robert Sean Leonard is extraordinarily convincing as Peter, who loses his political innocence while trying to protect his frightened mother (Barbara Hershey) and getting to know the true nature of the gentle-mannered gestapo (an uncredited Kenneth Branagh) who moves into their lives.

In the end, you're left saddened not so much by the story being told, but by its botched telling. To quote another song from the movie, sometimes "Tain't whatcha do, its the way thatcha do it."

SIGHT AND SOUND, 7/93, p. 52, Kim Newman

Hamburg, 1939. Peter Müller, teenage son of a violinist who died after being imprisoned for his anti-Nazi views, is a 'swing kid', addicted to officially disapproved American music. Peter and his best friend Thomas Berger impulsively steal a radio from a Nazi official, knowing it has been stolen from an arrestee and intending to give it to their crippled guitarist friend Arvid. Peter is caught and, thanks to the intervention of Knoepp, an SS man who is courting his mother, gets off lightly, but is forced to join the Hitler Youth. Thomas also joins, claiming he can be HY by day and swing kid by night. Emil, a former swing kid, now a committed Nazi, assaults Arvid. Thomas boxes with him to avenge his friend, but the upshot of the fight is that Emil respects Thomas and Thomas is seduced by the possibilities of being a Nazi.

Knoepp warns Peter that his part-time job with a bookseller might not be politically expedient; Peter learns that Herr Schumler, his boss, supplies forged papers to dissidents. At a successful gig, Arvid refuses to play a song requested by Luftwaffe men, and then goes home to commit suicide. Peter is ordered to deliver boxes to several citizens and, acting on advice Knoepp has given him, opens a box to discover the ashes of a political criminal. The HY break up a swing party and Thomas personally beats up Peter. As the partygoers are dragged off to camps, Knoepp stands by lamenting the waste of Peter's potential, but Thomas—shocked by his own brutality—and Willi, Peter's younger brother, salute him with a cry of "Swing Heil".

An odd footnote to history makes an even odder movie. Its well-intentioned recreation of the period is rendered surreal by the use of mainly English-speaking American actors pretending to be Germans who pepper their language with Anglo-American slang and dress like bizarre combinations of Cab Calloway and Anthony Eden. *Swing Kids* is doomed to bomb at the box office. Regardless of quality (it is surprisingly effective in parts), this is a youth movie with a Nazi background and music guaranteed not to appeal to rap-happy audiences.

"No one who likes swing can become a Nazi," claims Thomas, heavily signalling that he will disprove this thesis. The unsubtle transformation of Christian Bale from jiving anarchist into heiling militarist is surprisingly potent, perhaps because it forces us to notice how easily these second- or third-generation brat packers conform to an Aryan ideal. The analysis of the seductive side of fascism, as represented by an unbilled Kenneth Branagh's persuasive Gestapo officer, is rather more rigorous than might have been expected. Especially neat is the moment when Peter follows his advice to consider the political ramifications of every action and is confronted with the brutality Knoepp conceals.

The film plays lip service to the Jewish and black composers and performers of swing music, but its juxtaposition of wild dances with regimented rallies suggests that the Nazis were more offended by the swing kids' hedonist abandon than by the music's suspect ethnicity. However, it is wishful thinking to present as rebels a group of teenagers whose fashion statements are mindlessly pro-American. Credibility truly snaps in the finale, as the cramped neatness of a city-wide plot in which old friends are always bumping into and beating up one another is emphasised by the vaguely character-changing collision of Peter, Thomas and Willi and the bathetic repetition of their vaguely chilling war cry, "Swing Heil". And surely, the most committed German swing musician of 1939 would have to be suicidal to play "Bei Mir Bist du Schön", a big band number *in Yiddish*.

VILLAGE VOICE, 3/16/93, p. 56, Carol Cooper

I'd had hopes, based on a brilliantly edited trailer, that this film would be great fun—and even more revelatory about its historical period than Absolute Beginners or Young Soul Rebels. Unfortunately, Swing Kids is neither as giddily surreal as the former or as grittily naturalistic as the latter. Obviously aimed at the MTV audience and intended to have as salutary an effect as that channel's "Rock the Vote" campaign, the film misses the mark both as entertainment and as Poli-Sci 101.

Director Thomas Carter (a TV veteran) and screenwriter Jonathan Marc Feldman seem to be of one mind as to how they want to present their subject matter—an underground teenage jazz cult in Hitler's Germany—but they boil history down to common denominators and wobble into almost every cliché in the crowded canon of anti-Nazi flicks. The film finally falls into the trap of most boy bonding movies: It exalts violence over sex (even over libidinal jitterbugging); females are either incidental or ornamental.

The liveliest and most eye-pleasing cinematography is during Otis Sallid's nightclub choreography, but it doesn't mesh well with the ponderous dramatic scenarios that follow. Even when they are well-acted, each parental, authoritarian, or peer-group confrontation seems to have so little to do with the joy embodied by swing music that it's hard to believe that anyone attracted to the latter would put up with the former. It's in that dichotomy that Carter and Feldman hope to seduce their audience. But how can you seriously equate anti-Fascism with resisting parental curfews, dress codes, and career guidance?

One should also hesitate to equate broad musical tastes with progressive politics. Divorced from the racist environment of its birthplace, American swing might indeed have become a symbol of freedom and tolerance to some sheltered middle-class German teens watching their nation careen into madness. But the irony of this—the true depth of which would make a hell of a movie—is lost on, and in, *Swing Kids*.

Also reviewed in:
CHICAGO TRIBUNE, 3/5/93, Friday/p. F, Dave Kehr
NEW YORK TIMES, 3/5/93, p. C8, Janet Maslin
VARIETY, 3/8/93, p. 60, Leonard Klady
WASHINGTON POST, 3/5/93, p. C7, Rita Kempley

TAIGA

A New Yorker Films release. *Director:* Ulrike Ottinger. *Screenplay (Mongolian and Tuvinian with English subtitles):* Ulrike Ottinger. *Director of Photography:* Ulrike Ottinger. *Editor:* Bettina Bohler. *Running time:* 501 minutes. *MPAA Rating:* Not Rated.

NEW YORK POST, 3/3/93, p. 24, Jerry Tallmer

In my youth they called them Travelogues, those little jaunts around the world that came some-where between the newsreel and Popeye the Sailor Man and the double-feature; but there was never a travelogue quite like this one. It's called "Taiga," it's by the German filmmaker Ulrike Ottinger, and it's 501 minutes—or 8½ hours—long.

Don't panic. At Film Forum, where it opens today for two weeks, they break it into three in-dividual parts of 2½-plus hours each, with screenings at 2, 5:20, and 8:40 p.m.

What Ms. Ottinger did was take camera and crew for three months into the wide-open lonely gorgeous windy spaces of northern Mongolia—all those sweeping steppes backed by cloud-high endless mountains, with tiny dots of people and animals below—and look, and listen and wait, and shoot, and take her time.

Of course, when you move in close, the dots become not so tiny, and the animals—goats, yaks, reindeer, horses—go *maaaaaa, mawwwww, awkkkkk, okkkkkkk*, and take on a life of their own. All life, human and animal, becomes interdependent, becomes one, and all of it in the taiga—2 million square miles of forest in what was lately the Soviet Far East—is being logged and otherwise manhandled ever more toward non-existence.

This is the same country, and in a sense the same story, that was placed before us last fall in a different (i.e., dramatized) and just as stunning way by Nikita Mikhalkov's "Close to Eden," right down to the yurts if not the yaks.

A yurt is a round Mongolian tent, often better equipped inside than you might think, and one of them in Part 1 of "Taiga" comes complete with an ancient shaman, a woman named Baldshir, whom Ms. Ottinger has to watch and listen to throughout an endless trancelike ritual of appeal to the spirits of mountains and valleys for protection of her Otog clan and even, if I understood aright, of these nosy visitors from afar.

"Your expectations for the weather are presumptuous," Baldshir advises (in drumming and chants translated by subtitle). "It might be better to return home in 29 days. Pay no attention to trivialities. The consequences could be dire ... Shall we ride back again on a sandy-colored horse?" And as if T.S. Eliot were writing her stuff: "The occasion is the journey."

She complains that her shaman garment of rags, ribbons, ropes, feathers, backed by a couple of dozen metal keys is too heavy for an old party with knees like hers, and hugging to her lap what must be her great-great-grandson—"My darling, my green-eyed boy"—she unashamedly asks: "Did you get good pictures?"

The next yurt played host to a wedding—bride in blue, groom in black with a black hat reminiscent of a rabbi's squarely above his head. There was a table laden with a close relative of pita, and a snuff bottle was passed around between all the men. "What a beautiful bottle," one of them cried, "and the snuff is nice and strong too."

The occasion is the journey. "Taiga" after all 8½ hours and, I gather, much sense of loss of a way of life among all the people along the way, ends up—again, evocative of "Close to Eden"—at an amusement park in Ulan Baator. I was not there, however, having had to settle for an early taste of the journey. I had promises of my own to keep, and miles to go before I could sleep.

VILLAGE VOICE, 3/9/93, p. 55, Georgia Brown

After Armstrong's hothouse [the reference is to *The Last Days of Chez Nous*; see Brown's review], Ulrike Ottinger's *Taiga* comes as cool relief and a stark reminder of how "civilization" has shifted focus from community to individual. Ottinger's staggeringly patient ethnographic project—recording the way *they* live now—is a labor of exemplary attention and reticence.

They are nomads, the reindeer and yak people of northern Mongolia—a magnificent country with rugged snowcapped mountains presiding over expanses of silky grasslands. Ottinger's focus is not on whatever domestic dramas may take place inside the commodious yurts or on the trail, but on the everyday life of the community—its ceremonies, crafts, daily routine, and annual cycles. The central, most poignant drama is the one that time is playing. Ours is the century that erased the ways of many centuries.

Early on, there was the political revolution. The Party altered the nomads' lives drastically by collectivizing herds. To hear the old people, this was the beginning of the end. With the advent of State trading posts, they no longer made their own goods; the old skills (many of them demonstrated in the film) were lost. In a fascinating interview (part two), Ottinger's guide takes her to a remote area where two of his elderly relatives, who haven't seen another person for six years, candidly lament the loss of independence after nationalization. Now they're dependent on their son, and they feel bad for him. "Actually our life is neither good nor bad, but we did expect more from the State," observes the man. "We gave up our herds." Once, he says, the State did more for them, but now "they only remember us at two times: election and census." And now who's counting?

Taiga's sparse narration comes in occasional headings prefacing the chapters and identifying the coming event. Since we don't follow familiar characters and rarely identify familiar faces, the order sometimes seems arbitrary. But the work has its symmetries. Most obviously, it's flanked by two weddings: The traditional one near the beginning is in a yurt on the plains, with the bride preparing and serving her first milk tea; the last is in a civil ceremony in a city where the nomad culture has been reduced to a theme park. In the final shot, a child rides, round and round, on a carousel reindeer.

What should you do about the fact that *Taiga* is nearly eight hours? Well, since the Film Forum is showing the film in three parts, you can dip your toe into a single section. Or you can take real time off from domestic struggles and contemplate at length a rich and all but vanished world. Blink and it's over.

Also reviewed in:
NEW YORK TIMES, 3/4/93, p. C17, Stephen Holden

TALES OF THE BROTHERS QUAY

Six short films by Timothy and Stephen Quay. *Producer:* Stephen Quay and Timothy Quay. *Director:* Stephen Quay and Timothy Quay. *Animation:* Stephen Quay and Timothy Quay. *Running time:* 73½ minutes. *MPAA Rating:* Not Rated.

NEW YORK POST, 4/9/93, Jerry Tallmer

The Brothers Quay are identical twins, 46 years old or so, Americans long living in London, with the blood of Prague and Vienna in their celluloid veins. I have written of their films before, though the morgue here cannot find the clip, which is fitting: I suspect the Quays came and ate it.

Now they (or, rather, their works totaling an hour and a quarter) are back, for a week starting today at Film Forum. I report what I saw, in part and more or less, because the surrealism of the Brothers Quay is dense and various and fast-flowing ...

"Look What the Cat Drug In," 1993, a short-short music video, visuals by the Quays, music by Michael Penn, brother of Sean. Cat (kinda) licking chops, owls, forks, catclaws like forks or spiders, fork tines, an amber perfume flask, cats like owls, owls like cats, song: "*Look in these eyes/bluer than blue/Apathy's rise/It's a long way down.*"

"Street of Crocodiles," 1986, 21 minutes. Quaysian adaptation of a story by Bruno Schulz, young Polish Jew and Kafka-like author killed by the Gestapo in 1942. An old curiosity shop of a movie that starts with one drop of spit into the vitals of some ancient machinery, perhaps a printing press, in a miniature skylight studio somewhere in Mitteleuropa.

Gears, cams, levers, scissors, mechanical dolls that do too many miraculous things to be dolls except when the camera cuts back and you see their flattened half-heads and know they must be dolls. A bass viol, lots of rusty screws, a dance of the screws, a "No Fume", sign, old clocks, watches, a watch stuffed with (?) ketchup or flesh, a light bulb plays a fiddle or draws a picture, a doll sends flashlight messages to a (stuffed) fish in a fish tank, two squids fencing, a stuffed alligator, a Germanic guy like the one who stole the money in Erich Kastner's "Emil and the Detectives" does the mirror trick, a doll winds yarn (impossibly) on his elbow, a baby doll babies a light bulb ...

Reading this is nothing. Seeing it—to the baroque, passionate music of Leszek Jankowski—is to feel the ovens of the Holocaust opening, panting, belching heat upon all that dust. "Are We Still Married?," 1992. Pingpong balls batter a bunny, to the sounds of a band called His Name Is Alive. I don't know what the bunny's name was.

If you ask me do the Quays have talent, yes. If you ask me are they gifted, yes. If you ask me was I impressed, even stirred, by "Street of Crocodiles," yes. If you ask me anything more, go Quay yourself.

NEWSDAY, 4/9/93, Part II/p. 63, Gene Seymour

Right from the start of this mind-warping mini-festival, you feel as if you have fallen into a rabbit hole rather than wandered into a theater.

And a truly *grotty* rabbit hole at that. One where animal organs sprout like toadstools beneath the gears of rusted machines that grind them to a bloody pulp. Where cuddly, apple-cheeked dolls perform lewd and violent acts. Where Ping-Pong balls, fibers, wood screws and even a simple comb can be given such ominous dimensions that you doubt you will ever be comfortable around them again.

Welcome to the world of the Brothers (Timothy and Stephen) Quay, identical twins from Philadelphia who have since expatriated themselves to Europe, where they craft cryptic animated-puppet shorts that make you wonder whether they've reached into your subconscious with cold fingers and stolen recurring nightmares you thought you'd unloaded by age 13.

For those who have yet to encounter the Quays' work, this surrealist six-pack of shorts will do nicely as an introduction, beginning with the world premiere of "Look What the Cat Drug In," a prickly (literally!) little item of gnashed cacti and other detritus dancing wickedly to the music by Michael Penn (Sean's brother).

"Street of Crocodiles," the Quays' greatest hit thus far, follows. Even if you've already seen this 21-minute adaptation of Bruno Schulz' harrowing tale of life in Eastern Europe between the world wars, it still jolts, disturbs and yields layer upon layer of fresh sensation and meaning.

It is set inside an ancient contraption whose works are put in motion when a caretaker's saliva drips into the gears. A puppet protagonist—thin, pale and panicky—wanders through the city within the machine, where mechanical monkeys frantically pound their cymbals through illuminated dust, screws pull themselves out of their holes like determined, malevolent insects and mannequins peer from shop windows with hollow, glowing eyes.

The Quays orchestrate this imagery with such implacable control that, even if you don't know quite what you're watching, you're hypnotized.

More of the same can be seen in "Rehearsals for Extinct Anatomies," which seems to have been hallucinated into being with wire, glue, metal and mortar. "The Comb" eavesdrops into a young woman's dream of sunbaked vistas, catacombs that throb with menace and still more creepy, disfigured dolls.

All four of these films seem to run together as one long hallucination. So much so that the relative straight-forwardness of "Anamorphosis" comes as a shock. But this inquiry into the visual games played by 16th- and 17th-Century realist painters shares with the other films a serpentine wit as it exposes some of the surprises that lurk, as the narration puts it, "beneath worldly portraits." This feels more like a summation of the Quays' films, the most perversely fascinating body of work this side of David Cronenberg.

VILLAGE VOICE, 1/26/93, p. 60, Mike Rubin

Identical twins born in Philadelphia but living for the last two decades as expatriates in London, the Brothers Quay (not to be confused with that stylish Brit sibling combo the Krays) create visually dazzling and highly disturbing "realities" by animating such detritus as crumbling dolls' heads, Ping Pong balls, scissors, and pieces of meat. In their magic irrealism, on view for one day at the Walter Reade Theater, the Quays successfully manipulate depth and space through lens and camera movements, making the anthropomorphized actions of their bizarre miniatures wholly tangible. With the decaying textures of a Joel-Peter Witkin photograph and the fantastic detail of a Joseph Cornell box brought to life, the Quays' sci-fi scapes play like hypnotic snapshots from the subconscious.

Like dreams, much of the Quays' work is enigmatic, if not inscrutable, from *The Comb* (exploring the symbiotic relationship between a sleeping woman and creatures inside her pillow, mattress, and head) to the new *Are We Still Married?*, a music video starring a stuffed bunny and a young girl's ankles set to the quasi-gothic strains of the band His Name Is Alive. Their most accessible piece, *Anamorphosis*, a "documentary" on a Renaissance painting technique for subverting conventions of perspective, offers a window (as it were) onto the brothers' cinematic approach. To a jovial lecture by a mysteriously accented narrator, the camera rotates and tilts around the works of art to illustrate the representational trick, in the process animating the painted line and revealing the brothers' nonstop use of similarly disorientating devices. "If anamorphosis is the art of delaying access to deeper meaning," the voiceover comments, "then we must learn to wait for revelation." With the Quays, meaning may be some distance off, but the waiting is well worth it.

Also reviewed in:
NEW YORK TIMES, 4/9/93, p. C8, Stephen Holden

TANGO PLAYER, THE

A DEFA Studio Babelsberg (Potsdam, Germany) release. *Producer:* Herbert Ehler. *Director:* Roland Graf. *Screenplay:* Roland Graf. *Based on a novel by:* Christoph Hein. *Director of Photography:* Peter Ziesche. *Editor:* Monika Schindler. *Music:* Gunther Fischer and Julio C. Sanders. *Sound:* Hans-Henning Tholert. *Production Designer:* Alfred Hirschmeier. *Running time:* 112 minutes. *MPAA Rating:* Not Rated.

CAST: Michael Gwisdek (Hans Peter Dallow); Corinna Harfouch (Elke); Hermann Beyer (Dr. Berger); Peter Prager (Roessler); Peter Sodann (Schulze); Jaecki Schwarz (Harry).

VILLAGE VOICE, 11/9/93, p. 64, Francine Russo

Frame by frame, *The Tango Player* peals out an ironic laugh that echoes through the corridors of the last quarter century of communist history. Made in 1990 (from a novel by Christoph Hein), but set in 1968, the film is a literary drollery about an East German historian, Dr. Dallow, whose life has become a hugely amusing political joke to others and a torture to himself.

Jailed two years for playing piano one night at a "subversive" cabaret, he emerges to find his job usurped, two unctuously Dickensian communist operatives menacing him, and an altered political climate in which the illicit show is now being performed for the hilarity of all, including the judge who sentenced him. Wandering desolately through Leipzig with crumpled face and raincoat, a man of snappy moves with a match or a woman, he is heir to all the Bogart clones who ever navigated a morally chiaroscuro *Casablanca*.

But though sent up by genre parody and jazzy pop music, Michael Gwisdek's Dallow is never trivialized. All bones and suppressed rage, spare of face and gesture, he seems to consume himself as we watch. The desperate comfort he wrenches from carnal encounters is rendered poignantly and sensually. Gräfs dimly lit, box-within-box interiors and light-suffused verticals pointedly frame Dallow's claustrophobic struggle. The film's symbolism and parallels may be too neat, but its ringing laugh at the oscillations of political correctness startles. Maybe now the joke's on us.

Also reviewed in:
NEW YORK TIMES, 11/3/93, p. C23, Stephen Holden
VARIETY, 2/25/91, p. 246

TEENAGE MUTANT NINJA TURTLES III: THE TURTLES ARE BACK ... IN TIME

A New Line Cinema release of a Golden Harvest presentation in association with Gary Propper. *Executive Producer:* Raymond Chow. *Producer:* Thomas K. Gray, Kim Dawson, and David Chan. *Director:* Stuart Gillard. *Screenplay:* Stuart Gillard. *Based on characters created by:* Kevin Eastman and Peter Laird. *Director of Photography:* David Gurfinkel. *Editor:* William D. Gordean and James R. Symons. *Music:* John Du Prez. *Music Editor:* Tom Kramer. *Sound:* Robert Janiger and (music) Larry Mah. *Production Designer:* Roy Forge Smith. *Art Director:* Mayne Schuyler Berke. *Set Decorator:* Ronald R. Reiss. *Special Effects:* Joseph P. Mercurio. *Creature Effects:* Eric Allard. *Costumes:* Dodie Shepard. *Make-up:* Martha Cecilia. *Horse Stunts:* Danny Virtue. *Stunt Coordinator:* Pat E. Johnson. *Running time:* 95 minutes. *MPAA Rating:* PG.

CAST: Elias Koteas (Casey Jones/Whit); Paige Turco (April O'Neil); Stuart Wilson (Captain Dirk Walker); Sab Shimono (Lord Norinaga); Vivian Wu (Mitsu); Mark Caso (Leonardo); Matt Hill (Raphael); Jim Raposa (Donatello); David Fraser (Michaelangelo); James Murray (Splinter); Henry Hayashi (Kenshin); John Aylward (Niles); Mak Takano (Benkei, Honor Guard #1); Steven Getson Akahoshi (Honor Guard #2); Kent Smith (Honor Guard #3); Ken Kensei (Honor Guard #4); Travis A. Moon (Yoshi); Tad Horino (Grandfather); Glen Chin (Jailer); Koichi Sakamoto (Young Priest); Tracy Patrick Conklin (Sam); Edmund Stone (Dave); Jeff Kawasugi (Murata); Phil Chong (Rider); Yeon Kim (Blacksmith); Robbie Rist (Michaelangelo's Voice); Brian Tochi (Leonardo's Voice); Tim Kelleher (Raphael's Voice); James Murray (Splinter's Voice); Corey Feldman (Donatello's Voice).

LOS ANGELES TIMES, 3/22/93, Calendar/p. 9, Michael Wilmington

Fluke hits don't necessarily generate fluke sequel hits and "Teenage Mutant Ninja Turtles 3? The Turtles Are Back ... In Time," is a perfect example.

For starters, how about that title? Is that a grabber? Doesn't it make you want to run out and spend a few hours looking at four guys in green latex turtle suits, with little color-coordinated red, blue, orange and yellow bandit masks, yelling "Yo!" and "Dude!" and snapping off karate kicks?

No? Well, anyway, they're back ... in time. And back ... in mindlessness. But they haven't gone back ... far enough, because, somehow, we can still see them.

In this $20-million sequel to a sequel, which the distributors deliberately kept away from critics before its Friday opening, Donatello, Raphael, Michelangelo and Leonardo—who owe their genesis to comic team Kevin Eastman and Peter Laird, and their vast popularity to one of those marketing blitzes that seem to pulverize intellect—bumble their way into a staggeringly expensive, obtuse and irrelevant parody of a period samurai epic.

Using the device of a magical scepter, which simultaneously transports someone back in time, while whisking someone else, of equal weight, forward, writer-director Stuart Gillard hurtles the turtles and their pal April back to the 17th Century, while five bewildered samurai warriors loll around in the turtles' contemporary New York sewer hideaway, hypnotized by TV hockey games.

This is really Sequel Hell. Back in the past, villains snarl. Swords flash. Topknots quiver. Horses race through the forest. Samurai Lord Norinaga (Sab Shimono)—who looks so much like Wayne Newton that one of the turtles yells "Hey! It's Wayne Newton!"—grunts and glowers. A swaggering British freebooter (Stuart Wilson) named Capt. Dirk, sneers, struts and double-crosses everybody. Feisty feminist newswoman April (Paige Turco) insults every man in sight and gets hoisted up in a small cage, guarded by a 300-pound jailer, who swaggers around in his underwear.

And through it all, the four turtle dudes, trying to find the missing scepter, wander through the forest, scale fortress walls, crack wise, bop baddies and fall in love with rebel girls.

Whatever magic the first two movies may have had—and it wasn't always that apparent to anyone over the age of 10—has long since congealed, like stale pizza. Or mock turtle soup.

Previously, the turtles functioned, however dubiously, as fantasy figures and weirdo pop culture anachronisms. But Gillard's love of samurai epics—and he obviously does love them—has betrayed him. Shot by the fine Israeli cinematographer David Gurfinkel, this film captures the look of a standard samurai movie, even the burnished, lamplit storybook gleam of the better '50's pirate movies. The turtle costumes themselves, designed long ago at the Jim Henson factory, still have a lovable Kermit-esque charm.

But looks aren't everything. And, after 10 minutes or so of tortoise levity here, they seem as disposable as everything else. "Teenage Mutant Ninja Turtles 3: The Turtles Are Back ... In Time" (MPAA rated PG) is a movie that's just as witty, entertaining and full of surprises as its title. Unfortunately, it's longer.

NEWSDAY, 3/20/93, Part II/p. 23, John Anderson

You call this a Ninja Turtles movie? Not one "cowabunga dude!!" Not one "I love being a turtle!" Not one pizza—unless you count a black, Frisbee-shaped item baked in feudal Japan.

Have the Turtles gone highbrow? Only for those who tend to confuse Mort Sahl with Moe Howard. In New Line Cinema's latest exercise in creative herpetology, the Turtles go back in time, to feudal Japan, where they make the same kinds of jokes they always do, but somehow they seem ... the same!

TV reporter April O'Neil (Paige Turco), who apparently never has to work, is about to go on vacation. And to pacify her four amphibious pals (they're just friends, really), she buys some gifts at a flea market, one of which is an ancient, magical Japanese scepter, which beams her back to 17th-Century Japan, switching her body with that of Kenshin (Henry Hayashi), the son of a warlord named Norinaga (Sab Shimono). While Norinaga takes April captive back in 1603, Kenshin is left with the 1993-model Turtles in their subterranean home (OK, it's a sewer).

To rescue April, the Turtles go back in time and help a rebel army, led by the beautiful Mitsu (Vivian Wu), battle both Norinaga and the cruel English trader/pirate Walker (Stuart Wilson).

"TMNT III" offers children the usual array of entertainments: Frantic martial-arts battles alternating with jokes about pop culture. What humor the Teenage Mutant Ninja Turtles generate for adults, on the other hand, is directly proportionate to the viewer's contempt for pop culture. In this, the Turtles are sort of a paradox: To love them, you have to hate them, and also know everything they know. It's irritating—and embarrassing, especially if you happen to know all the references ...

But there remain other more troubling aspects to the Teenage Mutant Ninja movies, one of which is racism. There are good Asians in all three TMNT films, but there's also an assumption that things Japanese are inherently funny. The grunting speech, the formal, ritualized attitudes—especially when contrasted with the Turtles' congenital boorishness—are assumed to be humorous. Even Splinter, their rat ninja master, is a sendup of Eastern philosophy. It's something for parents to think about, as is Walker, the villain. Although he orders his men to kill, and has them set fire to villages, he never commits any violence himself; instead he paints flowers and keeps finches. Is this to show his sensitive nature? Hardly. It's meant to equate gentle pursuits with weakness and as such represents something insidious.

SIGHT AND SOUND, 8/93, p. 52, Tom Tunney

Japan, 1603. Kenshin, the son of Lord Norinaga, is pursued and caught by four of his father's horsemen, while his rebel leader sweetheart Mitsu looks on from a distance. In present-day New York, the four teenage mutant ninja turtles—Leonardo, Raphael, Donatello and Michaelangelo—dance together in the underground lair they share with their mutant rat mentor Splinter. They are visited by their friend April, who gives them presents including an antique Japanese golden sceptre, which proves to have magical time-travelling powers.

Back in 1603, Lord Norinaga's strictures against his son—who objects to his father's "unjust war"—are interrupted by the intrusion into his castle of a group of gun-running British pirates led by Captain Walker. Kenshin accidentally knocks over a golden sceptre identical to April's, which has the effect of transporting her back to 1603 and sending him forward to the present. Norinaga and the pirates suspect April of being a witch, and imprison her alongside Whit, a mutinous member of Walker's crew. The turtles go back in time to rescue April and in the process switch places with four of Norinaga's horsemen. Michaelangelo is separated from the group, and loses the sceptre when he is knocked out in a fall. The other three turtles sneak into Norinaga's castle, overcome the guards, and rescue April and Whit. Reunited with Michaelangelo at the rebel castle, the foursome join forces with the villagers to foil a pirate attack. Michaelangelo rescues a child, Yoshi, from a burning building and Leonardo revives the boy with the kiss of life. Michaelangelo presents Yoshi with a yo-yo and in return the child gives him the missing sceptre.

Whit—who was in league with Walker all along—steals the sceptre. The turtles and Mitsu follow him to the castle, where a final battle takes place. Norinaga is imprisoned by a huge bell that Leonardo drops on him. Whit has a change of heart, and refuses to obey Walker's orders to shoot the turtles. Walker attempts to escape with the sceptre, but falls to his death in the sea below when Whit catapults a fireball at him; the sceptre is retrieved by the turtles. Smitten by Mitsu, Michaelangelo is reluctant to return to the twentieth century, but goes when she tells him her future lies with Kenshin. Norinaga is reconciled with his son and the turtles arrive back in their own time to dance happily together.

"Why didn't he make a splash, Mum?" The child in the row behind me at the preview screening is mystified by the abrupt fate (read: cheap special effects) of the villain Walker. He sinks without trace, and so too, much earlier, does any hint of wit and imagination in this decrepit adventure movie—which could be the only pirate film in which the pirates don't seem to be able to afford a ship.

The New York of the first Ninja Turtles movie was a murky, dangerous and, just occasionally, winningly bizarre environment. The first sequel was a notably blander affair, and now this lazy collection of second-hand ideas takes the removal of everything that was interesting in the original film a dismal stage further. Aimed wholeheartedly at the very youngest and least demanding of cinema-goers, the movie uses its time-travelling strategy merely as a device to get the heroes out of the morally ambiguous Big Apple and into the safely fantastic world of a children's pantomime.

Given their ninja skills, Japan is the logical place for them to go; however, rather than meeting any real historical characters, their own ancestors or alternative versions of themselves (plot devices variously used to good effect in *Bill and Ted's Excellent Adventure*, the *Back to the Future* films and even the 1944 Tommy Handley vehicle *Time Flies*), the Turtles wisecrack and fight their way through a luminously threadbare and derivative storyline which repeatedly draws attention to its throwaway status by making weak jokes at the expense of other films. "Eat your heart out, Kurt Russell!" is a comment during the child rescue; "Don't you know Westerns are dead?" accompanies a limp Clint Eastwood visual gag during the attack on the village.

This story must be the thinnest of star vehicles for them, but a further problem for the turtles is the fact that, despite their different coloured headbands and fanciful names, none of them have ever been properly defined as separate individuals. The stuntmen in the green suits have varied from movie to movie and so too, significantly, have several of the actors providing their voices. That may be good for merchandising (same toy, different headband and weapon) and for keeping the film's budget down (the copyrighted characters are the stars, not the human beings playing them), but it's fatal in terms of focussing and keeping a young audience's attention. "Where's Shredder?" asked the same disconsolate little boy behind me, at one sagging point in the plot, hoping vainly for the easily identifiable villain of the first two films to show his face.

In a film aimed so single-mindedly at five-year-olds, it would be expecting too much to have the Turtles run into Townsend Harris (the John Wayne character in Huston's *The Barbarian and the Geisha*), the Seven Samurai, or a squadron of time-travelling kamikaze pilots. But surely, in a film set in Japan and featuring *mutant* ninja turtles, the most famous mutant monster of them all could have rated something more than this dead end of a mention: "What if we take a cosmic detour and end up in Godzilla-land?"

If only they had. Instead, the adventure is so lazy and so bland that it most resembles the pantomime segment of *Crackerjack*, the long-running BBC TV show that ruined Friday afternoons for several generations of British kids. Every week that programme would feature the resident cast in a knockabout stage farce full of thuddingly obvious gags at the expense of contemporary pop stars, TV shows and movies. One really does have to think back that far to recall children's humour as lacklustre as this. And no-one even says "Cowabunga!" either.

Also reviewed in:
NEW YORK TIMES, 3/20/93, p. 15, Janet Maslin
VARIETY, 3/22/93, p. 51, Leonard Klady
WASHINGTON POST, 3/22/93, p. B2, Hal Hinson

TEMP, THE

A Paramount Pictures release of a David Permut production from Columbus Circle Films. *Executive Producer:* Howard W. Koch, Jr. *Producer:* David Permut and Tom Engelman. *Director:* Tom Holland. *Screenplay:* Kevin Falls. *Story:* Kevin Falls and Tom Engelman. *Director of Photography:* Steve Yaconelli. *Editor:* Scott Conrad. *Music:* Frederic Talgorn. *Sound:* Thomas Nelson. *Casting:* Elisabeth Luestig and Judith Holstra. *Production Designer:* Joel Schiller. *Art Director:* Gordon W. Clark. *Set Decorator:* Kim MacKenzie Orlando. *Costumes:* Tom Rand. *Running time:* 96 minutes. *MPAA Rating:* R.

CAST: Timothy Hutton (Peter Derns); Lara Flynn Boyle (Kris Bolin); Dwight Schultz (Roger Jasser); Oliver Platt (Jack Hartsell); Steven Weber (Brad Monroe); Colleen Flynn (Sara Meinhold); Faye Dunaway (Charlene Towne); Scott Coffey (Lance); Dakin Matthews (Dr. Feldman); Maura Tierney (Sharon Derns).

LOS ANGELES TIMES, 2/13/93, Calendar/p. 9, Michael Wilmington

In any contest for witless movie thrillers of 1993, "The Temp" may carry off both the Grand Tweet and the Golden Bomb. Despite some stiff recent competition, like "Knight Moves," this is a suspense movie dopey beyond imagining, ludicrous beyond belief.

Even given its marketing-hook premise—a troubled young executive (Timothy Hutton) meets what seems to be the temporary secretary from hell (Lara Flynn Boyle)—director Tom Holland and writer Kevin Falls have constructed an edifice of unusual, almost nonstop nonsense. From first scene to last, "The Temp" is totally predictable, its cliches perform a vital function: They're the only things that keep the story coherent.

The movie shoves together Hutton as the twitchy, slightly unkempt junior executive Peter Derns and Boyle as his fill-in secretary Kris Bolin, a trim little bombshell in short skirts and clipped hair, who starts taking over his life.

Well, she should. Derns is a mess. We first see him in a psychiatrist's office, hinting at past schizophrenia. His marriage has fallen apart and the company where he works—Mrs. Appleby's Baking Goods—has just succumbed to a hostile takeover. The head of Appleby's, Charlene Towne, is played by Faye Dunaway, in one of her off-the-deep-end moods. Her speech is brittle and her eyes are wild.

Kris seems a godsend: typing up a storm, rearranging Derns' chaotic life, offering him lip-smacking glimpses of plunging neckline. The movie links Kris' sexual allure with the erupting violence—and that's only part of its misogyny. When the bloodshed starts, with rival executives stung to death by bees or hanging themselves, it's like some curious Puritan plague triggered by Kris' allure or ambition, or both.

Through it all, "The Temp" tries to work the street of movies like "Hand That Rocks the Cradle" or "Single White Female"; it's another yuppie paranoia thriller, though here we're invited to consider other angles. Is Kris innocent and Peter paranoid? Are there *other* plots?

Holland, who wrote and directed "Fright Night" and "Child's Play," has one of those glossy, sock-in-the-eye visual styles that seem designed to make good trailers. But here the gloss becomes offensive; it only accentuates the dumbness and rot. Hutton seems to be sinking into funk as the movie progresses, and Boyle keeps her villainy so clipped and tight, her performance is almost like a pop video.

As for Dunaway, she has a demeaning, empty role and she's billed seventh—before four other actors who have briefer, more demeaning roles. "The Temp" (MPAA-rated R for violence, language and sensuality) is a movie with such a faulty sense of social trends that it has Hutton arguing that the '90s are going to be like the '50s (that was the '80s, Tim) and such stereotypical thrill strategies that every suspense set-piece plays like an auto commercial.

In a way, this movie reverses the fairy-tale plot of "Working Girl"—with Kris rising from temp secretary to major executive in what seems a few weeks. Here the working girl might be evil, murderous, the male helpless in a world of rapacious females who want sex or his job.

"The Temp" also, on one level, presents career women as deranged and deadly, striking maybe unintentionally, a Marilyn Quayle-ish blow for regarding women as essentially child-bearers. But it's silly to take offense at anything as silly as "The Temp." After a while, the movie does achieve one of its aims. You begin to share Peter's paranoia, to see yourself as trapped in a nightmare, victim of a conspiracy to bore and exasperate you.

NEW YORK, 3/1/93, p. 112, David Denby

Does every hack director in and out of Hollywood long to make his own version of *Basic Instinct*? The new horror-thriller *The Temp*, directed by a person named Tom Holland, is the latest in the burgeoning genre of movies about women who screw men to death. The devouring beast this time is a corporate-world climber, Kris (Lara Flynn Boyle), who takes a temporary job in a Portland, Oregon, baked-foods corporation. Kris's stratagems are so transparently evil they couldn't fool an 8-year-old. Yet for a long time they fool her boss, Peter (Timothy Hutton), a decent guy, very harried but decent, awfully decent ... He's *stupid*, that's what he is, or else the plot wouldn't get off the ground. (Three people die and a secretary gets his hand caught in a paper shredder before Peter says, "You're fired.") Hutton is touching in a dogged sort of way, and Lara Flynn Boyle (*Twin Peaks*) is so lustrously beautiful she reminded me of such glamorous forties actresses as Jane Greer. Unfortunately, Tom Holland turns her into a kissing cobra.

Despite the elegant corporate setting, Holland shoots *The Temp* as if it were any other horror movie. People enter darkened rooms and get thwacked from behind; they die with insects crawling out of their mouths. There are, I admit, some unusually dull teenagers who enjoy seeing the same horror tropes over and over, but anyone above the moral age of 14 who is drawn to the movie by the setting and the cast is unlikely to be amused by swollen corpses. And even horror-film lovers want an explanation that semi-satisfactorily pulls things together in the end. *The Temp*, on the other hand, falls apart with flabbergasting speed and thoroughness. Holland and screenwriter Kevin Falls (who should be discouraged from pursuing his art) have nothing going for them *but* male paranoia.

NEWSDAY, 2/13/93, Part II/p. 23, John Anderson

She's beautiful. Brilliant. Possibly lethal. He's attractive. Upwardly mobile. Possibly paranoid. We're bored. Listless. Possibly catatonic.

"The Temp," which moves last year's favorite film character, the murderous domestic intruder, into the workplace, is many, many things, and an entertaining thriller is not one of them. As a study in how many things can be done wrong in trying to make one, however, it's priceless.

Peter Derns (Timothy Hutton) is an up-and-coming executive at Mrs. Appleby's Baked Goods—yes, the filmmakers wanted to evoke the cutthroat atmosphere of corporate America, and chose a cookie company as their setting—which is simultaneously launching a new product and undergoing a corporate takeover. As if things weren't dicey enough—can't you just taste the tension?—Peter is separated from his wife and child because of some violently paranoid episodes; he seems to have recovered, but his untrustworthy psyche leaves open the possibility that Kris Bolin (Lara Flynn Boyle), the temporary secretary who comes to his rescue, isn't the modern-day Lady MacBeth she seems to be. And it's a question the film never quite resolves.

The reigning psychotic at Appleby's is Charlene Towne, whom Faye Dunaway portrays as a cross between Jeane Kirkpatrick and Edith Prickly. Convinced of Kris' goodness—just as Peter is convinced she's a killer—Charlene starts moving her new prodigy up the corporate ladder, while Peter starts missing rungs. He grows frantic, but Kris always has an explanation for what's gone wrong. Throughout, you could cut the ennui with a knife.

There's a lot of obvious strangeness in "The Temp"—Lara Flynn Boyle's hair, which seems to grow at will; Dunaway's startling new face; the fact that Hutton gets to dress like some aged preppy while all those around him toe the corporate sartorial line. But this is chicken feed. The really bizarre thing is that "The Temp" knows it's a horror movie; nothing is too strange for its characters, most of whom who are so blase in the face of violence and mayhem that one suspects the set was catered by Upjohn. There is no coincidence—and "The Temp" is shameless in propelling its plot by coincidence—odd enough to elicit as much as a doubletake from anyone in the film. The howlers come fast and furious; some may even be intentional.

If you've seen the ubiquitous TV ads for "The Temp," forget about them. It seemed that most of the scenes from the commercial didn't make it into the movie, which ends so abruptly one suspects the cast, crew and producers wanted to cash their checks before anyone realized what they were up to.

VILLAGE VOICE, 3/2/93, p. 55, James Hannaham

If a Macguffin is Hitchcock's nickname for a red herring, *The Temp* has at its core what I'd call "McMuffin," a painfully insubstantial motivating factor in the form of Mrs. Appleby's Cookies, the product to which yuppie exec Peter Derns (Timothy Hutton) and title character Kris Bolin (Lara Flynn Boyle) pledge their allegiance. Depending on the extent of Derns's paranoia, Bolin's either a temporary who overachieves her way into cookie management or a conniving, upwardly mobile killer. Either way you'd think she could aspire to more than "serving my boss in the best way possible."

Curiously, her self-imposed glass ceiling puts her on par with her former superiors, and the resulting infighting might make you wish you were still at your own job. Hutton stops short of accusing Boyle's character of witchcraft, and Boyle's one-note vixen responds with more "I-am-a-bitch-and-I-am-seducing-you"delivery than he can shake a broomstick at. The resulting chemistry is mayonnaise in dishwater. No wonder there's no sex in this movie. Everyone's so stressed out over these cookies you'd think they were vital to national security. Anybody willing to deceive, cheat, and kill for chocolate chips deserves to die. Especially at the box office.

Also reviewed in:
NEW YORK TIMES, 2/13/93, p. 17, Janet Maslin
VARIETY, 2/15/93, p. 84, Todd McCarthy
WASHINGTON POST, 2/15/93, p. C7, Hal Hinson

THAT NIGHT

A Warner Bros. release of a Le Studio Canal+/Regency Enterprises/Alcor Films presentation of an Arnon Milchan production. *Executive Producer:* Julie Kirkham and Elliott Lewitt. *Producer:* Arnon Milchan and Steven Reuther. *Director:* Craig Bolotin. *Screenplay:* Craig Bolotin. *Based upon the novel "That Night" by:* Alice McDermott. *Director of Photography:* Bruce Surtees. *Editor:* Priscilla Nedd-Friendly. *Music:* David Newman. *Music Editor:* Tom Villano and Adam Smalley. *Sound:* John Sutton and (music) Tim Boyle. *Sound Editor:* Bruce Stambler. *Casting:* Mali Finn and Don Finn. *Production Designer:* Maher Ahmad. *Art Director:* Jeremy Conway. *Set Decorator:* Susan Kaufman. *Special Effects:* Steve Kirshoff. *Costumes:* Carol Ramsey. *Make-up:* Lydia Milars. *Stunt Coordinator:* Gary Jensen. *Running time:* 90 minutes. *MPAA Rating:* PG-13.

CAST: C. Thomas Howell (Rick); Juliette Lewis (Sheryl O'Conner); Helen Shaver (Ann O'Conner); Eliza Dushku (Alice Bloom); J. Smith-Cameron (Carol Bloom); John Dossett (Larry Bloom); Sarah Joy Stevenson (Barbara); Ben Terzulli (Mickey Meyer); Thomas Terzulli (Max Meyer); Michael Costello (Don O'Conner); Kathryn Meisle (Mrs. Carpenter); Carolyn Swift (Mrs. Rossi); Charles Musumeci (Mr. Rossi); Debora Robertson (Mrs. Meyer); John Healey, Jr. (Mr. Meyer); Becky Ann Baker (Mrs. Bell); Paul Morella (Mr. Bell); Sabrina Lloyd (Jeanette); Thompson Hunt (Coleman); Rick Schatz (Vitelli); Duncan Hood (Man One at Wake); Celia Clark (Wife at Wake); Paul Hjelmervik (Man Two at Wake); Andrea Monter (Little Girl); Adam Kroloff (Danny the Date); Luci Roucis (Young Nun);

Barbara Barry (Sister Lorraine);   Desiree Marie (Girl One);   Jennifer Albright (Girl Two);
Sarah Rose (Pam);   Lem Wills (Bus Driver).

LOS ANGELES TIMES, 8/6/93, Calendar/p. 14, Michael Wilmington

American movie romances often lack the special qualities—tenderness, reverie, pain—that make old loves stick so hard. But "That Night", an often marvelous new film adapted from Alice McDermott's 1987 novel, catches some of them. Focusing on a 10-year-old girl who watches, fascinated, as a pageant of forbidden desire and rebellion is enacted in the house across the street, the film laughs, bleeds and cries unashamedly, wears its heart well over its sleeve.

Set, with fulsome nostalgia, in 1961 Long Island, "That Night" has a gentleness and vulnerability we don't expect from big studio American releases. A sinuous love song, "Ruler of My Heart"—recorded in 1961 by Irma Thomas and here wonderfully redone by Lisa Fischer—keys the mood of passion unbound. Through its bluesy vamp, we can sense the sweet, dangerous passions of the young and alienated.

And, though first-time writer-director Craig Bolotin, who wrote Jerry Schatzberg's 1984 obsessive romance comedy "No Small Affair," gets a few clumsy, overstated moments, there's something tonic about "That Night's" unabashed romanticism, its feeling for outcast lovers in an over-comfortable milieu.

Because the narrator is a little girl in the throes of high idealization, the events become heightened, magical, luminous. The romance here is double. It's not just the class-crossing affair of local flirt Sheryl O'Conner (Juliette Lewis) and her hunky, leather-jacketed, hot-rodding beau Rick (C. Thomas Howell), an affair thwarted by Sheryl's mother (Helen Shaver) and neighbors. It's also the crush of little Alice on her idol Sheryl—and on the whole media-soaked notion of all-conquering love she's supposed to incarnate.

Bolotin's movie is more a fairy tale than the book was. When McDermott controlled Alice's narration, it had more sophistication, detachment, she was clearly ultra-literate, over 30. But the movie is told by 10-year-old Eliza Dushku, the appealing, empathetic, child actress who plays Alice, and her narration is imbued with her wide-eyed charm. Where McDermott took the romance to a logical, painful conclusion—a climax reminiscent of those great sad last moments in the Kazan-Inge "Splendor in the Grass"—the movie lets us dream longer.

That's not necessarily a softening. Like the little boy in the Losey-Pinter classic "Go-Between," "That Night's" Alice is an innocent moving between the lines of a forbidden romance, but she isn't shattered by it as he was. By keeping us in the dream, Bolotin validates his lovers.

As Sheryl, Lewis is no cliché movie teen dream; she manipulates her foxy, sly face, lithe body and drawl insinuatingly, knowingly. As the bowling-alley greaser Rick, Howell looks more conventionally studly—but, perhaps because he's older than his role, he suggests the book's ironies: that this Rick will lose youth sooner than expected, that this Sheryl is a survivor.

The film (MPAA-rated PG-13), which was shot, appropriately, by Hollywood's "Prince of Darkness," Bruce Surtees, has a special suburbia-at-nightfall look. And a special sound: the choric flow of oldie raunchy rock ballads, by Dion, Roy Orbison, the Marvelettes or the Four Seasons, which, as in "American Graffiti," set the mood and comment on the action.

So far this year, American pictures have focused unusually heavily on child narrators or perspectives; in this sturdy but delicate film, we get one of the most engaging of all recent children's voices. Together, director and actress catch the near-breathless inflections and enthusiasm of a little girl, who, for a season, sees the world as she wants to, as it should be.

NEW YORK POST, 8/6/93, p. 26, Michael Medved

One of the most durable stereotypes in movie re-creations of the 1950s and early '60s involves a blonde, respectable, middle-class girl who develops a guilty crush on a tough-but-tender "greaser" from the wrong side of the tracks. This image turns up everywhere, from synthetic, assembly-line nostalgia like "Grease" to serious and satisfying films like John Sayles' "Baby, It's You."

This familiar theme takes on surprising new life in "That Night," a bittersweet story of love and friendship in which every frame glows with affection and artistry.

The action unfolds through the eyes of a precocious 10-year-old named Alice Bloom (played with appropriate intensity by newcomer Eliza Dushku), who lives with her protective parents in a neat, quiet Long Island neighborhood. It's the languid summer of 1961, and young Alice spends twilight hours going to the edge of the woods to catch fireflies, then lies awake through the long hot nights, fantasizing about the unbearably exciting and sophisticated world of the popular teenager (Juliette Lewis) who lives across the street.

Alice gets to enter that world only after the older girl runs into trouble, following the sudden death of her father. The 17-year-old falls in love with a sullen, sensitive punk (C. Thomas Howell) she meets at a bowling alley and thereby scandalizes her grieving mother and the rest of the neighborhood. Her only support comes from spunky Alice, who does what she can to help the lovers and in return is included in their secrets and their schemes.

The great strength of "That Night" is that nothing turns out as you'd expect, particularly in terms of the main characters and their relationships with their parents. When Hollywood tells stories of teen-aged lovers, the older generation is most often portrayed in hostile two-dimensional terms—repressive fuddy-duddies who interfere with the pure idealism of young love.

Here, the approach is far more balanced and therefore more dramatic: The movie suggests that the parents are right to be worried sick about the direction of their kids' lives. Teen-agers who go out to see this unusual picture may actually come home with a new understanding of why their parents get so upset when they stay out too late with friends.

Juliette Lewis is an altogether remarkable actress who displays the same wide-open vulnerability she projected in "Cape Fear" and "Husbands and Wives"; her characterization of this sweet but confused Catholic girl is one of the most memorable and heartfelt performances I've seen this year.

Her excellence is matched in every way by writer-director Craig Bolotin, who makes an astonishingly accomplished debut with this film. The period details are telling but never quaint or cute; Alice's memories are so lyrically re-created that her precious past becomes your own.

"That Night" would qualify as one of the year's best films, in fact, were it not for an outrageously hokey and saccharine ending that bears no connection whatever to the courageous and convincing material that precedes it. When the movie wimps out some three minutes before its conclusion, you have the horrible feeling of watching a record-breaking runner collapsing in a heap just steps before the finish line.

I can't imagine that director Bolotin wanted to end his impressive picture in this cheap, dishonest way; one can only hope that when it's released on home video we'll have a chance to see a director's cut in which the last minutes are worthy of the rest of this fine film.

NEWSDAY, 8/6/93, Part II/p. 59, John Anderson

It's 1961, and Sheryl (Juliette Lewis), a bleached-blonde, overly lipsticked high school girl whose Catholicism is made much of, surrenders her virginity standing up under a well-populated boardwalk.

The object of her affection, Rick (C. Thomas Howell), bowling-alley habitue and general low-life, seems to be constantly enveloped in a fine bouquet of beer, sweat and Chesterfield Kings. In the eyes of Alice (Eliza Dushku), the 10-year-old girl who lives across the street from Sheryl and idolizes her, they are the model of true love, pure passion, tragic romance, a modern-day Romeo and Juliet. To movie audiences, they may seem like characters better suited to "The Charles Starkweather Story."

The kind of artificiality that saturates each frame of "That Night"—from the acting, to the characters, to the forced nostalgia that never comes close to evoking an actual time or place—undermines whatever sentiment might have been generated and might even have been intended as parody. Or, it might have been intended as a view of romance as viewed as a childhood illusion.

But no, we're supposed to take Sheryl, Rick and Alice's impressions at face value. The death of Sheryl's father is presented as the event that changes her life and sends her running to Rick. But from the outset, Lewis, whose celebrated lips caressed Robert De Niro's celebrated finger in "Cape Fear," portrays Sheryl as if she's in a constant state of sexual arousal. Lewis might have been convincing, had she been playing a 30-year-old divorcee with a hormonal imbalance.

But believability is beside the point. Set in 1961 Long Island and shot in Maryland. "That Night!"—in which Sheryl offends local morality, incurs the wrath of her neighbors, gets pregnant and is shipped to a home of unwed mothers—feels like a film set at a time and place with which none of the filmmakers were familiar. And Dushku, the newcomer who plays the neighborhood scapegoat, is saddled with dialogue no one deserves. "I apologize," she says to the recently bereaved, and deeply confused, Sheryl. "I apologize ... I mean, I'm sorry about your father ... I mean your heart ... I mean his heart." She can't pull it off, but neither could Vanessa Redgrave.

Despite Sheryl and Rick's libertine behavior, the social mores of the early '60s make their story a tragic one, a life lesson for little Alice. Had someone created a character we cared about, this night have even mattered.

SIGHT AND SOUND, 6/94, p. 62, Andrew Pulver

Summer 1963. Smalltown America. Seven-year-old Alice, alternately ignored and ridiculed by her peers, becomes fascinated with teenage Sheryl O'Conner, whose bedroom window is directly opposite her own. Her distant infatuation becomes something approaching friendship after Sheryl's father dies, and she eagerly takes the chance to help cover Sheryl's tracks when she goes to visit Rick, a boy who manages the local bowling alley.

Alice remains a besotted spectator as Sheryl and Rick's relationship flourishes, and the whole neighbourhood is disrupted by the pair's increasingly ostentatious antics. Eventually, it is a chance remark of Alice's that leads to Sheryl's mother clamping down on her daughter's romance. Alice, however, assists Sheryl once again in escaping her mother's surveillance for another night with Rick, and in return is initiated into the mysteries of teenhood, such as make-up, alcohol and dancing.

Sheryl, though, becomes pregnant and, since her family is devoutly Catholic, she is forced to leave home for a convent where she is to give birth. Alice persuades the desperate Rick to drive them both to the convent where, through her cunning, the two teenagers are reunited.

Sneaked out with very little fanfare two years after its US release, this slice of period Americana is rather better than its unheralded release might suggest. At its centre is a convincing portrayal of early 60s delinquency from the seemingly ubiquitous Juliette Lewis, as a convent girl whose open sensuality not only captivates all the neighbourhood children, but also affects, equally strongly, the adult population—threatening and mocking the local fathers, stirring the mother's nostalgia and, not surprisingly, riveting the attention of local teens.

The doomed relationship that eventually emerges—with the local bowling alley manager—may represent one of the most well-worn of all American cinematic territories, but what distinguishes its treatment here from more mundane examples is the film's nicely mature appreciation of the pragmatic aspects of challenging the American Dream, of the economic and emotional pitfalls that might lie ahead. There is no *Badlands*-style unthinking amorality at play here, as Lewis proves to be torn between the demands of love, family responsibility and the likelihood of future happiness. In fact, the continuous presence (and encouragement) of little-girl narrator Alice serves to enhance the notion that reckless, beat-inspired solutions (like taking off to Mexico in a beat-up coupe) exist more in a sort of pre-school fairyland than anything else.

As it is, *That Night* functions rather well as a coming-of-age story on two levels—little Alice discovers what's waiting for her as a teenager, and the older Sheryl discovers the adult world with a vengeance—even if the film occasionally resembles a John Waters movie as the camera follows the protagonists under the boardwalk for a spot of heavy petting.

On the plus side, the atmosphere of a small-town summer is near-faultlessly maintained, with great skill employed in creating a clammy, humid climate. The main weakness—which, like Michael Caton-Jones' *This Boy's Life*, unfortunately wrong-foots the film's own marketing positioning—lies in its narrative voice: the oft-used, easy-access device of having a too-cute child as the central perspective dilutes the tone and robs the film of much of the moral weight the story could offer.

VILLAGE VOICE, 8/10/93, p. 58, Laurie Stone

Juliette Lewis talks as slowly as *That Night* moves. Lewis looks and acts drugged, with her bee stung lips and neck thrown back for a vampire kiss. As Sheryl, she is supposed to embody the erotic longing that has drained from the lives of couples in '60s suburbia—people in flight from the city, "the element," the unpredictable. Her boyfriend, Rick, played charmingly by C. Thomas Howell, is "the element," blowing in from Queens in a beat-up convertible, a tattoo over his left nipple and lust smudging his face. But the movie is dead, based on an Alice McDermott novel that warns in every brooding, intelligent sentence that it is not a movie book. It is a book book, its power dependent on the narrator's voice, which turns a *True Romance* anecdote about teenage pregnancy and a little girl's infatuation with a glamorously trampy neighbor into an absorbing meditation on yearning, memory, and loneliness.

Writer-director Craig Bolotin is left with the surpassingly mundane, girl-gets-knocked-up story, the dialogue of inarticulates, and the overworked, pained eyes of young Eliza Dushku. Bolotin lays on period detail—capri pants, car fins, a soundtrack of golden oldies—conveying only his franticness in having nothing to say. The same tactic failed to animate the film of Tobias Wolff's book book, *This Boy's Life*. In eloquent takes on alienated childhood—*The 400 Blows* or *The Shining*—the art directors got a little help from the screenplay.

Also reviewed in:
NEW YORK TIMES, 8/6/93, p. C8, Janet Maslin
VARIETY, 12/14/92, p. 43, David Stratton

THIS BOY'S LIFE

A Warner Bros. release. *Executive Producer:* Peter Guber and Jon Peters. *Producer:* Art Linson. *Director:* Michael Caton-Jones. *Screenplay:* Robert Getchell. *Based on the book by:* Tobias Wolff. *Director of Photography:* David Watkin. *Editor:* Jim Clark. *Music:* Carter Burwell. *Music Editor:* Adam Milo Smalley. *Sound:* Rob Young. *Sound Editor:* Richard King. *Casting:* Owens Hill and Rachel Abroms. *Production Designer:* Stephen J. Lineweaver. *Art Director:* Sandy Cochrane. *Set Decorator:* Jim Erickson. *Special Effects:* Mike Vezina. *Costumes:* Richard Hornung. *Make-up:* Jo-Anne Smith Ojeil. *Make-up (Ellen Barkin):* David Forrest. *Make-up (Robert De Niro):* Ilona Herman. *Stunt Coordinator:* Betty Thomas. *Running time:* 115 minutes. *MPAA Rating:* R.

CAST: Robert De Niro (Dwight Hansen); Ellen Barkin (Caroline Wolff); Leonardo DiCaprio (Toby); Jonah Blechman (Arthur Gayle); Eliza Dushku (Pearl); Chris Cooper (Roy); Carla Gugino (Norma); Zack Ansley (Skipper); Tracey Ellis (Kathy); Kathy Kinney (Marian); Bobby Zameroski (Arch Cook); Tobey Maguire (Chuck Bolger); Tristan Tait (Jerry Huff); Travis MacDonald (Psycho); Richard Liss (A&P Manager); Michael Bacall (Terry Taylor); Adam Sneller (Terry Silver); Gerrit Graham (Mr. Howard); Thomas Kopache (Geiger Counter Vendor); Lee Wilkof (Principal Shippy); Sean Murray (Jimmy Voorhees); Jason Horst (Oscar Booker); Deanna Milligan (Silver Sister #1); Morgan Brayton (Silver Sister #2); Robert Munns (Ticket Seller); Bill Dow (Vice Principal); Shawn MacDonald (A&P Employee); Frank C. Turner (Truck Driver); John R. Taylor (Minister); Stephen E. Miller (Target Ranger); Dwight McFee (Voice in Crowd); Ken Camroux (2nd Place Shooter); Ross Chaston (Score Caller); Scott Woodmansee (Crash Witness).

CHRISTIAN SCIENCE MONITOR, 4/9/93, p. 11, David Sterritt

Why is the subject of family life getting more and more attention from Hollywood filmmakers?

One reason might be the lingering effect of last year's political campaign. Some politicians tried to define "family values" in strict and prescriptive terms that many Americans, it turned out, found too monolithic and simplistic for comfort. In the aftermath, many people are taking a new look at what families ought to stand for, and it's natural for filmmakers to join in this activity.

Another reason is continuing uncertainty over the stability of families as an institution. Tales of family dysfunction—along with school problems, housing troubles, and other ills related to family life—appear in news articles on a daily basis. This is fueling concerns in popular culture, as well as in more sophisticated circles. Movies as different as "Jack the Bear," the "Home Alone" comedies, and the Canadian film "Léolo," reflect the resulting uneasiness about family life today.

"This Boy's Life" is the latest and best picture in the current family-movie cycle. Based on Tobias Wolff's respected autobiography, it centers on a teenage boy named Toby who's faced with plenty of challenges. His parents are divorced. His mother, Caroline, has little money and fewer job skills. Toby has little idea of the direction he wants his life to follow.

As if all this weren't enough for Toby to contend with, his mother decides to marry her latest boyfriend. His name is Dwight, and his charm is more apparent to a romantic divorcee like Caroline than to her guarded and suspicious son. Dwight decides to bring order and discipline into Toby's life by moving his new wife and stepson to the remote Washington town where his own three children live—a place called Concrete, and just as grim and boring as it sounds.

Toby tries to live a normal adolescent life despite the tedium of Concrete and the bullying of his new stepfather, whose idea of discipline often crosses the line into physical and emotional abuse. But daily experience becomes a series of battles with his family and the larger environment around them. It seems doubtful that Toby will ever surmount the forces that want to stifle his energy, kill his creativity, and make him into as deadly a robot as Dwight and his Concrete cronies.

The screenplay for "This Boy's Life" was written by Robert Getchell, and the movie begins like a remake of his most celebrated film: "Alice Doesn't Live Here Anymore," directed by Martin Scorsese in 1975. Again we see a mother and son head out for a new start in life, with only a hope and a dream to support them; and again we see their experiences shaped largely by the men who barge into their paths, clearly more interested in the young woman than in any offspring she may have.

"This Boy's Life" takes off in its own direction, though, when it becomes clear that Caroline isn't as flighty as Alice was. She quickly sees the failings Dwight has, but she puts more stock in her relationship with him (troubled as it is) than in her wishes for a happier life—even after she realizes that he regards physical violence as a perfectly legitimate way of getting what he wants.

Although the story is told from Toby's point of view, "This Boy's Life" depicts many revealing things about all three of its main characters—thanks partly to Mr. Getchell's skillfully written screenplay and to the excellent performances that give the movie startling resonance at times.

Toby is played by Leonardo DiCaprio, best known from the television series "Growing Pains," with a supple style that moves convincingly between sullen hostility and sympathetic vulnerability, both of which are part of the teenager's personality. Caroline is expertly played by Ellen Barkin, who is growing steadily more mature and assured in her movie work. And the difficult character of Dwight is played by Robert De Niro in one of the most vivid and forceful portrayals he has given us in recent years—capturing Dwight in all his bluster and brutality, yet subtly reminding us that Dwight is also a victim and that his own doubtlessly miserable adolescence would probably make a heart-wrenching tale if it had a movie of its own.

"This Boy's Life" is heavy-handed and obvious at certain points, and its supporting performances aren't always up to the high standard set by the stars of the picture.

It is vastly more intelligent and thought-provoking than other recent movies on family dysfunction, though, including such pretentious ones as "Jack the Bear" and the dismal "Radio Flyer," which marked the low ebb of the cycle.

The picture was directed by Scottish filmmaker Michael Caton-Jones, whose earlier work includes the less-memorable "Scandal" and "Memphis Belle." David Watkin did the carefully crafted cinematography. Credit for the movie's sharp sense of 1950s atmosphere goes to production designer Stephen Lineweaver and costume designer Richard Hornung. Carter Burwell composed the score.

FILMS IN REVIEW, 8/93, p. 263, Any Pawelczak

This Boy's Life, directed by Michael Caton-Jones and based on a memoir by Tobias Wolff, takes place in working class, fifties America where everybody smokes, guns are a home appliance and the scenery is a misleadingly beautiful backdrop for squalid, violent lives. Concrete, Washington is the kind of train-whistle-haunted town where those young people who don't manage to escape to Seattle have nothing much more to look forward to than a management trainee job at the A&P. It's a place that still lives inside many people who grew up in the fifties, a recurring dream stamped "Made in America" and pervaded with a sense of loneliness and desolation, and, inexplicably, a terrifying sweetness too. The film is at its best when it succeeds in capturing this complex structure of feeling. The picture also boasts superior performances by Ellen Barkin and Leonardo DiCaprio and an addition to Robert De Niro's gallery of violent grotesques.

The film opens spectacularly with an overhead shot of Monument Valley's towering buttes and stone cathedrals as Frank Sinatra sings "Let's Get Away From It All" on the soundtrack. Once the camera comes down to earth we're in familiar road-movie territory as Caroline (Ellen Barkin) and her fourteen-year-old son Toby (Leonardo DiCaprio) drive west in flight from Caroline's abusive boy friend back east. Ellen Barkin foregoes her usual sex bomb persona for this role; her Caroline is a smart if quixotic woman (she's hoping to find uranium in Utah) with one fatal flaw, her lousy taste in men. She has a buddy relationship with her son; in the opening car sequence they sing and clown as he tells us in a voice over that he's caught up in his mother's delight in her new found freedom. As played by Leonardo DiCaprio, Toby is a fairly complex creation; the film, told from his point of view, is a Portrait of the Writer as a Young Man. When mother and son finally settle down in Seattle, he insists on being called Jack in honor of Jack London, the first of several identity metamorphoses he undergoes in the course of the film. Eventually, Caroline, unable to cope with Toby's drift into juvenile delinquency, decides to marry, and the rest of the film diagrams how that initial sense of freedom and infinite possibility emblematized by Monument Valley narrows down into a domestic trap presided over by Dwight Hansen (Robert De Niro).

De Niro has reached that stage of his career where every performance is a palimpsest. In his Dwight Hansen we can see traces of Rupert Pupkin from *The King of Comedy*, Jake La Motta from *Raging Bull*, and Max Frady from *Cape Fear*. When he first appears on the screen, the audience titters; Dwight is the King of Hicks, a corn fed square spewing bad jokes and labored bumpkin charm, a far cry from the deracinated urban hipster we're used to seeing De Niro play. In her review of *The King of Comedy*, Pauline Kael complained that De Niro's performance was an impersonation rather than real, full bodied acting, but she missed the point. Rupert Pupkin doesn't have a self; he's a puppet animated by an inner TV. Similarly, Dwight, as he courts Caroline, impersonates the All-American Husband and Dad as derived from *Father Knows Best*.

It doesn't take long for Dwight's real self to emerge. In one of the film's best scenes, he takes Toby back to Concrete and the car trip is like a ride through a chamber of horrors. As Dwight slugs from a bottle of whiskey in a brown paper bag, he reviles and threatens Toby and swerves dangerously all over the road. De Niro is genuinely scary here, a redneck from hell revealing his true colors for the first time. The film never accounts for Dwight's ongoing rage except to suggest a class resentment of Toby's biological father, an Ivy League graduate married to a rich woman, but the lack of motivation only makes the character creepier.

Michael Caton-Jones is a Scottish director, so his feeling for the details of small town life in this quintessentially American story is very impressive. The whole second half of the movie builds to Toby's final violent confrontation with Dwight, but before that happens there are some good scenes involving teen-age rites of passage in the Age of Elvis. This is material that in the wrong hands could easily turn maudlin, but Robert Getchell's script generality steers clear of sentimental cliches, and the cinematography adds a sharp, Edward Hopper-like ambiance. The film ends on an upbeat note, symmetrical to its opening, but a written postscript adds a haunting twist. After escaping from Concrete and getting thrown out of a prep school he finagled his way into, the real-life Toby ended up in Vietnam. The movie reminds us that in some mysterious way there was a direct road from places like Concrete, Washington, to Vietnam where the young men who fought were as ignorant of the outside world and as full of inchoate longings and tangled, thwarted feelings as the hapless Toby.

LOS ANGELES TIMES, 4/9/93, Calendar/p. 1, Kenneth Turan

"This Boy's Life" is every boy's life, every child's nightmare, told with unblinking truthfulness and remarkable sensitivity, its true story of one particular and painful coming of age manages to touch us all, underlining the notion that nothing we do in our lives is anywhere near as difficult as just plain growing up.

While maudlin, whiny tales of adolescent difficulties are one of the curses of today's Hollywood, the power and frankness of this exceptional film is something else again. But as much as being based on Tobias Wolff's spare and moving memoir of the same name, "This Boy's Life" has the advantage of having fallen into the hands of a creative team that has managed to transfer the reality and emotional heft of the printed page onto the screen.

Cleanly and feelingly written by Robert Getchell (Oscar-nominated for "Alice Doesn't Live Here Anymore" and "Bound for Glory") and directed with great care by Michael Caton-Jones, "This Boy's Life" is equally fortunate in its acting. The ensemble work of Ellen Barkin, Leonardo DiCaprio and Robert De Niro is expressive without overdoing it and almost hypnotic in its honesty.

Though 18-year-old DiCaprio (a veteran of TV's "Growing Pains") will get a lot of justifiable attention for his finely nuanced work as a teen-ager trapped in an inner and outer storm, it is De Niro's shattering performance as stepfather Dwight Hansen that is the film's core.

As complex a character as he's ever played, De Niro's Dwight is a taut piece of work that will disturb and fascinate audiences as much as the real Dwight, an enigmatic and frightening figure, shook up those whose lives he dominated.

However, when Toby (DiCaprio) and mother Caroline (Barkin) first appear, scuttling across the 1957 Southwest in a shaky white and yellow Nash as Frank Sinatra sings "Let's Get Away From It All" on the soundtrack, Dwight has yet to make his presence felt.

Instead Caroline, the type of person who solves problems by leaving them behind, is headed for what she is sure will be a new life among the instant riches of the uranium fields of Utah. Buoyant, high-spirited and divorced from Toby's father, Caroline (acutely played by Barkin) is also a woman with more courage than common sense.

Worse, she is a woman with abysmal taste in men, and this particular trip was caused by a desire to flee from a boring and mean blue-collar lout named Roy. A similar spur-of-the-moment burst of high hopes then causes her to grab Toby and impulsively head out for Seattle and yet another stab at the good life. Not that the boy minded. "I was caught up," he says in a literate, persuasive voice-over that echoes the book's tone, "in the delight of my mother's freedom."

If Caroline is problematic as a mother, Toby is a disaster as a teen-age son. A prankster, liar and sneak thief who regularly cuts school, cracks wise and demands that everybody call him the more masculine-sounding Jack, Toby's rootless scorn is more than anything else a plea for attention from a kid who is afraid of the sensitivity that lies beneath his own bravado. Wanting to change but feeling helpless to do so, Toby is clearly a candidate for a little parental discipline. What he gets instead is Dwight.

Caroline's most persistent Seattle suitor, auto mechanic Dwight is an easy target for the wised-up Toby to mock. With his Bronco Nagurski brushcut, laughably elaborate way of lighting a cigarette and artificial jack o'lantern smile, Dwight appears to be a harmless dope, a comic relief Mr. Square who lives near the nowhere town of Concrete with three children from a previous marriage. What possible lure could this drone have for his dazzling firefly mother?

Part of his appeal, it turns out, is Dwight's belief that he can straighten Toby/Jack out, eliminate his discipline problems root and branch. Her emotional resources exhausted, Caroline is willing to let him try, setting the stage for one of the most wrenching intergenerational confrontations since Raymond Massey turned on James Dean in "East of Eden."

For while it is clear to everyone except perhaps Caroline that the superpolite Dwight who brings flowers and helps her on with her coat is a facade, no one, least of all Toby, is at all prepared for exactly who he turns out to be.

Humorless, angry, with a formidable "I don't make the rules" self-righteousness, Dwight is a relentless bully and needler who announces the reversal in Toby's fortunes in no uncertain terms. "Don't pull that hotshot stuff on me," he challenges the boy. "You're in for a change, you're in for a whole 'nother ball game. Oh yeah."

Yet to say all this about Dwight is to make him less complex than he is, to really not understand what makes him so unnerving. Knowingly written by Getchell and brilliantly played by De Niro, Dwight is that all too realistic sadist who thinks he is the one being abused, the warped disciplinarian who truly believes that all the harsh things he is doing are both underappreciated and for Toby's good. The fact that Toby himself begins by feeling that maybe he does need some straightening out only makes the dynamic between them unfold in ways that are that much more twisted and destructive.

The job of integrating all these combustible elements falls in the unlikely lap of director Mark Caton-Jones, whose last two films ("Memphis Belle" and "Doc Hollywood") were marked by a sentimentality that would be out of place here.

Yet something in this story appears to have touched Caton-Jones, to have brought back the strength of "Scandal," his directing debut, for he responds beautifully to the challenges of the material. He has made the film (rated R for strong language and sensuality) all of a piece, making sure that the three lead performances complement rather than overwhelm each other. And he has avoided (despite an emphatic Hollywood ending that departs from the book) either condescending to the situation or downplaying its harrowing aspects. "This Boy's Life" doesn't flinch, and its conflicts will disturb your dreams as it does those of the boy who lived them once upon a time.

NEW YORK, 4/12/93, p. 58, David Denby

Tobias Wolff (Leonardo DiCaprio) the young narrator and hero of the extraordinary new American movie *This Boy's Life*, has a rather furtive inner life. Tobias, who romantically styles himself Jack (after Jack London), pretends to be a juvenile delinquent. Growing up in the fifties in the Northwest, he hangs out with the stupidest boys in the class and stands around bad-mouthing everything. He appears to be going downhill fast, but he's actually just a poseur—a good boy looking for a role to play. He doesn't know who he is. Still, when he's brutalized by his nasty stepfather—the banal domestic tyrant Dwight (Robert De Niro) he knows he has to escape. The movie, based on Tobias Wolff's remarkable memoir of the same title, is acutely intelligent and finally thrilling. It's about a teenage chameleon—a chameleon with the wary soul of a tiger.

When we first see Tobias, he's only 12, and he's driving with his mother, Caroline (Ellen Barkin), through the heroic landscape of Monument Valley—two seekers after adventure and experience in the modern West. What they find is more like entrapment. Caroline Wolff, a good-looking woman not too bright about men, is running away from a violent boyfriend (Tobias's father left her years earlier). It's 1957, and Caroline has no profession and exactly one talent: She just picks up and leaves whenever things get too tight. Ellen Barkin plays her with a bittersweet perfection—an immense hopefulness that is close to heartbreaking. Now that Barkin has stopped trying to be Rita Hayworth but is using her sexual feelings—which pour out of her natural-ly—within a disciplined idea, she is a great actress again. Barkin's despair when her boyfriend catches up to her and she realizes she has no choice but to submit to him is a classic, shamed moment of female defenselessness.

Mother and son run to Salt Lake City and then to Seattle, living in dowdy, dark rooms that don't seem to have recovered from the Depression. Outside on the streets, where Tobias goes hunting for adventure, the popular culture of the fifties provides some relief—the rounded, streamlined cars in lambent reds and greens; the honeyed pop ballads and early rock; the duck's-ass haircut (more streamlining) that gives Tobias a hoodlum look. Again and again Michael Caton-Jones, the Scots director (*Scandal, Memphis Belle, Doc Hollywood*), captures the melancholy of those lonely times in adolescence when you have no real friends and you hold desperately to a moment's pleasure. Tobias speaks to us in the voice-over narration created by screenwriter Robert Getchell—narration that is just "written" enough to have some interest as language without being literary.

Producer Art Linson (*American Hot Wax, Melvin and Howard, The Untouchables*) has a definite feel for hidden American subjects, and so does Getchell, who seems at first to be having another go at the mother-and-son-on-the-road screenplay that he wrote for the wonderful *Alice Doesn't Live Here Anymore* in 1975. Once again, Getchell does the mother-son relationship as a conspiracy. These two actually like as well as love each other. Tobias can even handle his mother's having boyfriends. The kid is all right; he acts like a thug only to know that he exists. Seventeen-year-old Leonardo DiCaprio, from the TV series *Growing Pains*, carries a look of dissatisfaction around with him. His face can be sullen and empty and then suddenly almost preternaturally alert.

"Here I am, you lucky people," says Caroline's new lover, entering at the door after pausing and listening first to hear what people are saying about him. Dwight, a mechanic, flourishes a Zippo lighter as if it were a sword. He's chipper as a waterbug, and at first he seems nothing more than a jerk. Tired of running, Caroline marries him, and she and Tobias move in with his three children (from an earlier marriage) in his house high in the Cascade range outside Seattle. The town is called Concrete, and the name is apt—you can get stuck there forever. Caroline loses hope and submits to her mediocre husband, who turns out to be a remarkably persistent and unreachable egotist.

Something about Tobias outrages Dwight—his graceful good looks, his enjoyment of his mother's love, some inner quality that makes Dwight feel small—and he begins tormenting him, insisting that he's got to set Tobias right. A fanatic in scout-leader shorts, he taunts, punishes, humiliates. Some of De Niro's performance is familiar—the sickening downward turn of his mouth, the coldness and rancor. De Niro has been hideous in such things as *Cape Fear*, in which his desire not to compromise at all seems a form of boasting. Here he's *playing* an inflexible man, and he gives a new performance. He's got a pedantic accent, almost Bostonian but with an odd twang, and a hundred small vanities. He's the punitive side of fifties square: His Dwight can't bear the thought that anyone might be out-classing him, and he turns vindictive and mean, with the detailed obsessional malice of someone you might see on a bus harassing his "unruly" children.

He's real enough, and powerful enough, to hate. A liar and a cheat, he's also a successful father of an authoritarian stripe, and he begins to have a molding effect on Tobias. The movie is ambiguous about authority and fatherhood. Tobias does need some straightening out, and we watch split in our feelings between disgust and grudging acceptance as this nightmare dad works on him, pounding him into shape. (Literally: He teaches Tobias how to box.) Tobias, confused, becomes a Boy Scout, affects a brutal indifference to everything; yet at the same time he's drawn as a friend to Arthur (Jonah Blechman), an effeminate intellectual boy who recognizes Tobias as a soul mate, both fluid boys out of place in Concrete. Arthur, who has a little white dog, is a poseur, too—he plays at being fey and then reacts with anguish when the boys call him a "homo." Blechman gives a lovely performance—delicate but proud, with a fierce independence that can only be called manly.

In part, *This Boy's Life* is about a prince among commoners—Dickens in the blacking factory, surrounded by low companions—but there isn't a trace of snobbery in the story. Tobias Wolff and his adapters are perfectly candid about their hero's lies (in some ways, Tobias is a young dog); they give us a tougher, mote realistic view of American boyhood than we are used to. The movie also gets at the uncertainty of American identity around the edges of the country, where ethnic ties are loose and the utter conventionality of a man like Dwight passes over, in a quick lurch, into near-madness.

It's a haunting and beautifully made film. Caton-Jones, who grew up a tough kid in working-class Glasgow, understands all the shades of adolescent role-playing and bravado, and many of the scenes are powerfully staged—the absurdly violent fight between Tobias and Arthur, for instance, in which the two boys tumble into a ravine together and Arthur's yapping little dog keeps chewing on Tobias's leg. Dwight terrifies Tobias by driving him recklessly through the mountains in the dark, and then Tobias, eager to escape, terrifies himself doing the same thing. The precisely defined moods of the movie flow together effortlessly.

A growing-up story, we realize, almost has to be an escape story. Tobias revives the libertarian spirit of his mother, who has sunk. His body and soul in peril, he abandons the mean-spirited man he was turning into and asserts his freedom—he delivers himself into a new pose. In the end (after the time of the movie), he will turn into the Tobias Wolff who wrote the terrific book on which the movie is based. We know he will get there, but silently, slowly, and in hiding. *This Boy's Life* reveals what's there in the shadows.

NEW YORK POST, 4/9/93, p. 25, Jami Bernard

You can look at "This Boy's Life" as a movie about the travails of yet another dysfunctional family, but the key is the analogy one character makes to the chicken born with a few black feathers which is pecked to death by the others. There is something about being special that makes the disgruntled masses want to cut you down to size.

That is the problem faced by Toby Wolff, a lively kid whose zest for living gives him the black feathers that make him stand out in a crowd of losers. Toby is stuck in the house of a tyrannical stepfather, in the hell of a town almost too aptly named Concrete, Wash. It turns out to be an actual town, because this is based on a true story—the real Tobias Wolff survived his childhood to grow up and write a book about it, which mitigates the sense of hopelessness that otherwise permeates the movie.

Toby changes his name to the tougher-sounding Jack, smokes cigarettes, talks dirty and hangs out with hoodlums, only to find that in Concrete, you can run but you can't hide—or at least you risk running into a concrete wall. The tough exterior is a facade to mask the pain and helplessness he feels back home, where his volatile stepfather belittles, taunts, beats and cheats him. He even steals Toby's paper-route money, but it's the psychological torture that hurts the most.

On the surface, the family looks perfect—this is set in the 1950s, when there was great stock put into the appearance of perfection. Toby and stepdad attend the Boy Scouts together, and the newly formed family sings together around the piano. But to truly appreciate this stepfather's vicious nature, you have to get to know him. Or marry him, as Toby's mom does, much to her detriment. "Kill or cure," is the stepfather's constant taunt, trying to pummel Toby into obedience.

Stepdad doles it out, and Toby takes it—partially because he feels cemented into his life in Concrete, and partially to make life easier for the mother he loves. Mom, meanwhile, is staying for the sake of her son. It's like the O'Henry story, where each sacrifices for the other in a way that benefits neither.

Some of the film's most emotionally vivid moments have to do with Toby's outside life—particularly his struggling friendship with a local boy who is clearly gay; he finds solace in the boy's intelligence, playfulness and devotion that he can't find among his tough-guy friends.

Yet the movie always returns with pungent dread to the household of the stepfather, played with barely suppressed sadism by Robert De Niro. If you thought he was scary in "Cape Fear," watch him change from a doofy, awkwardly courtly suitor who rushes to light women's cigarettes to a man who on his wedding night snaps at his bride that he never likes to see a woman's face during sex. No, never.

Ellen Barkin gives a well-modulated performance as Toby's mother, a woman worn down from too many bad breaks and bad boyfriends. Her face slowly goes slack as it dawns on her that her last best hope—marriage to this seemingly nice man with his shackful of children from a previous marriage—has been a terrible error of judgment. "You've got to concentrate on the good stuff," she says, more to convince herself than Toby.

Relative newcomer Leonardo DiCaprio is sensational as Toby. He has the offbeat looks that could easily make him a Barkin heir, and effectively shows the bravado, fear and seething anger that tear at Toby's heart: Director Michael Caton-Jones ("Scandal") juxtaposes the menace of the boy's home life with the scrubbed images of Boy Scouting to make the case that not everything is as it seems in families, "This Boy's Life" is a sensitive movie that understands there are many ways to break a child's spirit, and also offers the possibility of escape.

NEW YORK POST, 4/9/93, p. 25, Michael Medved

Dwight Hansen, the pivotal character in the ambitious new film "This Boy's Life, is a navy veteran, a Republican, and a firm believer in the value of self-discipline and hard work. He takes inordinate pride in the modest home he manages to provide for his family, plays an active role in the local Boy Scout troop, and boasts of all the well-attended churches that serve his small town.

Needless to say, this seemingly stalwart citizen turns out to be a selfish and sadistic monster, as this handsome and well-acted film offers yet another Hollywood contribution to the ongoing national debate over "family values."

Robert De Niro adds to his already impressive gallery of scenery-chewing psychopaths by portraying the film's fanatical defender of hearth and home as a sick, self-destructive, and shamelessly abusive creep whose conventional pieties only mask his underlying hypocrisy and viciousness. Take that, Dan Quayle!

Based on the critically acclaimed autobiographical novel by Tobias Wolff, "This Boy's Life" centers on a troubled 1950s teen-ager whose free-spirited divorced mother (Ellen Barkin) has no luck with jobs or with men. When mother and son drift together to the Pacific Northwest, she hopes that her latest suitor, the hard-working auto mechanic portrayed by De Niro, will prove a wholesome influence on her sullen, rebellious, duck-tailed kid.

Leonardo DiCaprio, an 18-year-old newcomer to feature films, plays the youthful protagonist with such fierce intelligence and absolute conviction that he provides the film with one of its two great assets. The other is the glorious camera work by David Watkin (previously acclaimed for "Chariots of Fire" and "Out of Africa") who fills the screen with moody and memorable images. His visions of Salt Lake City, Seattle, and the small town hall of Concrete, Wash., catch the period details of the Eisenhower era with almost eerie precision. Production designer Stephen Lineweaver avoids all cheap and easy invocations of high-gloss "Nifty Fifties" nostalgia, focusing instead on the shabby atmosphere of painfully false optimism imposed on a struggling family that can never quite achieve the middle-class respectability it craves.

Disaster strikes the main characters in the story—and the film itself—when De Niro hijacks "This Boy's Life" at the end of its first half-hour. As the emotional and physical abuse of his stepson escalates inexorably, De Niro portrays the viciousness and stupidity of Dwight Hansen with such comic opera intensity that many viewers will titter uncomfortably. As always for this veteran performer, it's a bravura bit of acting but, in this context, sadly miscalculated: His character is so utterly, so luridly despicable that he throws the entire movie out of balance and undermines its many strengths.

For one thing, it's impossible to understand how Ellen Barkin (in an uncharacteristically bland and understated performance) could remain married to this noxious beast, especially after we see his unforgettably brutish bedroom behavior on their disastrous wedding night.

In the process of evoking our horror at this stepfather from hell, "This Boy's Life" makes several notable nods to prevailing ideas of political correctness. The only ray of light in young Toby's dark existence is provided by a witty, sensitive and courageous classmate who is struggling to accept the fact that, as Dwight Hansen puts it, "he plays for the pink team." First-time actor Jonah Blechman portrays this heroic gay teenager with such charisma and haughty style that he easily steals every scene in which he appears and leaves you wishing that his part had been larger.

Meanwhile, the final deliverance for the long-suffering Ellen Barkin arrives through the miraculous agency of John F. Kennedy's presidential campaign. While De Niro sneeringly dismisses the handsome candidate as "The Senator from Rome," his oppressed wife focuses on JFK as her best hope for personal liberation in much the same way that Michelle Pfeiffer's character in the recent "Love Field" used her fascination with the Kennedys to escape from her own claustrophobic marriage to a bigoted, right-wing lout.

These movies seem to assign to the late president the mystical power of a Massachusetts Messiah who can awaken downtrodden characters from their domestic nightmares, just as he awakened the country from the troubled slumber of eight years of Ike. Here, the resolution has a mechanistic, it's-time-to-wrap-this-up feel to it, rather than proceeding from any orderly, internal logic of plot or character.

The young Scottish director Michael Caton-Jones has a way with actors, as demonstrated in his impressive previous films "Scandal" and "Memphis Belle," or even in his slight but crowd-pleasing "Doc Hollywood."

Here, however, he seems so reverential toward the real-life recollections of Tobias Wolff that he has provided the material with little dramatic shape and scant relief from the bleak and despairing tone.

The basic conflicts in the movie are nothing new; "Blue Velvet" similarly exposed the pustulating rot beneath a smiling small town surface, while "The Stepfather" previously revealed the vicious insanity lurking within an outspoken defender of "normal" family life. "This Boy's Life" goes even further than such previous horror shows in the vividness of its sadism. In one memorable sequence near the conclusion of the film, Toby has nearly sliced off his finger on a power saw during wood shop class at school; a few days later, De Niro (who previously displayed his propensity for munching on body parts in "Cape Fear") chomps down on this bandaged digit during a particularly vicious encounter with his stepson.

Audience members will cry out aloud when they witness this assault, and the scene surely makes an indelible impression, but it's hard to understand why we should want to lodge this image permanently in our consciousness. Like the celebrated star who quite literally chews up his film, director Caton-Jones doesn't seem to know when to stop pressing the bruise.

NEWSDAY, 4/9/93, Part II/p. 50, Jack Mathews

It may be just an illusion, but for the first time, while playing an explosive mental case, Robert De Niro is not the most interesting presence in a movie. In Michael Caton-Jones' "This Boy's Life," the honor goes to 17-year-old Leonardo DiCaprio, who gives an astonishingly complex portrayal of a teenager trying to overcome abuse and confusion in rural 1950s Washington.

Both characters are familiar. De Niro's Dwight, an auto mechanic with stripped gears between his ears, is another in a long line of scary stepfathers, and De Niro plays him with a combination of dorkiness and menace that puts him only a step or two closer to sanity than his Max Cady in "Cape Fear."

DiCaprio's Toby is a kid bumbling through adolescence, trying to strike the right pose to get along with his peers, while adjusting, badly, to a new life imposed by his mother's marriage to a man seemingly intent on breaking both his spirit and his body.

Other films have worked this same theme—a single mother desperate to find a father figure for her children instead leads them into disaster—as straight horror, the sort that leaves audiences cheering while mad dad catches a hatchet between the eyes. Frankly, De Niro gives Dwight so many pathological twitches he comes very close to leading "This Boy's Life" into the B movie realm, too.

But the screenplay, adapted by Robert Getchell from Tobias Wolff's autobiographical book, and DiCaprio's wrenching psychological performance ultimately shift the focus away from the story's sensational elements to Toby's internal struggles.

That's as it should be. Wolff, now a professor at Syracuse University, recalled the terror of his youth in the first-person, and to tell that story from any other point of view would necessarily reduce it. Whether the events are accurate, whether Toby's mother is the good-hearted innocent portrayed by Ellen Barkin here, Wolff's reminiscences are his reality.

That device is more natural to the writer than the filmmaker, but Getchell, who created a movingly loving relationship between a single mother and her son in his script for "Alice Doesn't Live Here Anymore," included just enough of the narrator's voice to make us feel the turning of pages, and the turning back of time.

There are some obvious lapses in the storytelling. Dwight's own teenage children disappear quickly into the background, and though Barkin's Caroline has a propensity for finding abusive men, how she ends up with someone as devoid of appeal as Dwight is unclear. Why she stays with him, especially after learning on her wedding night that he makes love with the sensitivity and passion of a brown bear scraping bark off a tree, cannot be explained by her son's need for paternal guidance.

Like her stepchildren, Caroline soon becomes part of the furnishings in Dwight's mountain cabin, while Dwight gulps whiskey and breathes fire in the direction of her son.

Caton-Jones, the British director of "Scandal" and "Memphis Belle," builds a lot of tension into the relationship between Dwight and Toby, and De Niro's furies are, as ever, something to behold. But the movie's strongest scenes occur away from the domestic crises, when Toby is trying to cover his pain and insecurities by trying to match vulgarities and swaggers with his unkempt buddies.

It is easy enough to recreate the unique look and sounds of the '50s, but the mood of its adolescents, as they inched toward a youth rebellion that wouldn't articulate itself until the next decade, is something else. Getchell, Caton-Jones and particularly DiCaprio, with his ability to appear simultaneously weak and resilient, confused and purposeful, make the period come alive in subtle, emotional ways that we're simply not used to getting from mainstream Hollywood movies.

NEWSWEEK, 4/5/93, p. 56, David Ansen

[*This Boy's Life* was reviewed jointly with *The Adventures of Huck Finn;* see Ansen's review of that film.]

SIGHT AND SOUND, 10/93, p. 54, Christopher Bray

Utah, 1957. Caroline Wolff, an impoverished and jobless divorcee, together with her teenage son Toby, is travelling across America on the lookout for a way to make a living. Her ex-husband is back east with their other son, a Princeton student. None of Caroline's jobs work out; nor do the men, and she and Toby are as often fleeing town as just leaving. Eventually Caroline meets Dwight Hansen, a seemingly kind man, if a little ardently romantic. Increasingly worried by Toby's bad behaviour at school, Caroline agrees to marry Dwight in the hope of bringing some discipline into her son's life. But Dwight turns out to be a tyrant with a taste for violence, and he and Toby frequently fight. Dwight also expresses disapproval at Caroline's involvement in a local campaign to elect Kennedy.

At a new school in Concrete, Toby falls in with another bad set, but also makes friends with a teenage homosexual, Arthur Gayle. Angered more and more by Dwight's maltreatment, Toby attempts to escape by applying for a place at private school. With Arthur's assistance he forges some excellent school reports and manages to win a place at Hill. An embittered Dwight attacks him for his success, but Toby fights him off and manages to convince his mother that it is time for both of them to leave.

In spite of its titular suggestion that this is a film about a boy's life, Michael Caton-Jones's adaptation of Tobias Wolff's autobiography is actually another in that ever-lengthening series of movies which takes as its subject its leading man: Robert De Niro. The tension between star and actor that used to make De Niro one of the most interesting of screen presences has now all but dissipated. It's a commonplace that comedians want to play Hamlet; De Niro, by contrast, is a brilliant tragedian who wants to lighten things up. Occasionally he can be hilarious, as in Martin Brest's *Midnight Run*, but more often he leaves you squirming, as in the recent *Night and the City*. In *This Boy's Life*, De Niro does little but indulge his predilection for mugging. There is a scene when Dwight, who has sold Toby's dog, attempts to upset the boy by pretending to call for the dog; it should be painful and anguished, but instead all we get is crazy Bob gurning at the camera again.

Not only does Caton-Jones fail to rein in these shameless antics; he lets them control the film. *This Boy's Life* ends up looking like an inventory of earlier De Niro performances. Thus, when one should be watching one of De Niro's vilest creations, one is confronted instead with an accretion of former movie images: De Niro as the deerhunter, humiliated by his wife at a shooting match; De Niro as the saxophonist, droning a tuneless accompaniment to the TV; most obviously, De Niro as the boxer. Indeed, the final confrontation between Dwight and Toby is filmed as an almost shot-for-shot copy of the fight between De Niro and Joe Pesci in *Raging Bull*; there is even a repetition of Scorsese's low-angle shot, in this case from Toby's point of view.

All this mugging and self-referencing has the effect of overbalancing the movie. Jonah Blechman steals a few scenes, and Leonardo DiCaprio has his moments. But the real star of the show is Ellen Barkin, with her smile that melts her face like heat on polyethylene. Surprising this, since she isn't actually in the film that much. As if dimly aware of this structural flaw, Robert Getchell's script (he wrote *Alice Doesn't Live Here Any More*, a more successful movie about a boy and his mother travelling the States) tries to pump up Caroline's dilemma by putting a political slant on Dwight's maltreatment of her. No sooner is this set out, however, than it is dropped in favour of another fight between Dwight and Toby. All of which is unfortunate, since Barkin's dithery charm always manages to circumvent De Niro's top-heavy performance.

Although Getchell sticks fairly closely to his literary source, there's no escaping the Hollywoodizing of Wolff's memoir. Right from the (admittedly exhilarating) opening moment, when the camera dives and swoops over Monument Valley and we hear Frank Sinatra's blaringly incandescent "Let's Get Away From It All", we know that that is exactly what the film is out to help us do: far from confronting us with the truth, *This Boy's Life* wants to help us escape from it.

TIME, 4/19/93, p. 63, Richard Schickel

Most of the time our interest in a movie—especially the American variety—is plot propelled. Here are some pretty people. Let's see what's going to happen to them in this or that difficult situation. Oh, no, not that! Watch out! Look behind you!

Our interest in a memoir, especially a good one like Tobias Wolff's *This Boy's Life*, is voice-activated. It's not so much the tale as the teller, the tone he takes about himself, what he makes out of past experience, that seizes and holds our attention. It follows that an autobiography is not the ideal foundation for a movie; the two forms are antithetical. It also follows that *This Boy's Life*, though seriously meant and conscientiously made, doesn't quite work.

The script by Robert Getchell, directed by Michael Caton-Jones, contains some elisions and some dramatic heightening, but nothing outrageous. It opens with a young Toby (nicely played by Leonardo DiCaprio) and his mother Caroline (Ellen Barkin) adrift in the West in the 1950s, looking for work. She's penniless, on the run from a broken marriage and an inappropriate lover. She has a good heart but not a very sensible one, and she falls in with Dwight Hansen (Robert De Niro), an auto mechanic from dreary Concrete, Washington.

Dwight cloaks social insecurity and class resentments under a manner that combines masculine swagger, noisy politesse and a need to ape—and impose on Toby—a poorly observed version of middle-class morality. Toby must have a paper route, but it is Dwight who pockets the profits. Toby must learn the manly art of self-defense, but mostly Dwight teaches him sucker punches and uses the lessons as an excuse to beat on the boy. De Niro's is a domineering performance, a star turn that is both comic and menacing, but it unbalances Wolff's story.

Caroline is almost lost in the film's later passages. And though the other aspects of this boy's life—bad companions, sulky delinquency, a muted, sweetly stated homoerotic flirtation—are present, they tend to pale in comparison with the brutal conflict between these two men-children.

This is not De Niro's fault. The movie goes where movies must go: toward melodrama. And toward the current fashion (*Jack the Bear, Radio Flyer*) for taking up but not fully confronting child abuse. Something more subtle is going on in Wolff's book, a confrontation with a richer, quirkier past and his emerging self that the movie too often brushes aside.

VILLAGE VOICE, 4/13/93, p. 56, J. Hoberman

As *Father Knows Best* is a convenient name for the historical process by which dad's role as head of household was interrupted by forces beyond his control, so *The Wonder Years*—the neo-sitcom in which a smugly bemused adult voiceover represents (and erases) a child's consciousness—provides a useful model for American socialization. The show illustrates the construction of a superego, as mediated by the television set.

A similar principle is at work in the current adaptations of Tobias Wolff's novelistic memoir *This Boy's Life* and Dan McCall's novel *Jack the Bear*. Two quirky tales of American adolescence, rooted in boomer history and sanitized for the market, both feature raging dads who, in different ways, offer metaphors for the tube: entertainment machines Robert De Niro and Danny DeVito install themselves mid-living room to issue bromides, throw tantrums, teach lessons, and otherwise cast a hypnotic flicker over the lives of their traumatized families. It's the Dad and the Dutiful.

The classier of the pair, *This Boy's Life*, opens in late 1957—Sputnik time—with the sounds of Frank Sinatra wafting over Monument Valley, serenading 13-year-old Toby (Leonardo DiCaprio) and his divorced mother Caroline (Ellen Barkin) as they drive from Florida to Utah on a fool's search for uranium. Although they are fleeing Caroline's abusive boyfriend, Toby (in voiceover) muses on the whereabouts of his long-lost father, a charismatic con artist nicknamed the Duke (and the subject of a book written by Tobias Wolff's older brother Geoffrey).

This Boy's Life is a dream of transformation whose first subject would seem to be Caroline—a role which Barkin gives surprising heft. Masking depression with dogged perkiness, she's a career woman without a career, who can barely, maintain the strain of living through the '50s. Only briefly in Utah, mother and son escape her pursuing ex by randomly jumping on a bus to Seattle, where Toby reinvents himself as "Jack"—strutting around with an outsized pompadour, releasing the safety brakes on parked cars, watching *Superman* and talking trash. (Throughout, DiCaprio manages his shifts in age and identity with chameleon-like aplomb.)

In the book, Wolff notes that his mother suffered from a "strange docility, almost paralysis, with men of the tyrant breed." She shortly meets and marries another example. Dwight Hansen (De Niro) lives several hours out of Seattle in the forbiddingly named town of Concrete, with three kids by a previous marriage. A mass of congealed hysteria, even more square here than in

Mad Dog and Glory, De Niro is a jug-eared jack-o'-lantern whose flattop might have been produced with a carpenter's plane. His performance is modulated, but he doesn't exactly vanish into the role. Spouting stale World War II clichés, setting fire to his cigarettes with an enormous Zippo, his Dwight is still a caricature—as ultimately crazed as the creature from *Cape Fear*.

In a haunting bit of business, the new family tries to play Brady Bunch *avant la lettre*. Jack entertains with an Elvis-ized version of Fats Domino's "Blue Monday" while Dwight's youngest daughter over-enthusiastically bonds with her unenthusiastic new mom. Dwight and Jack join the Boy Scouts together—Dwight in a new uniform, Jack in an oversized hand-me-down—but Dwight, who has taken Jack's reform as his personal mission, is never less than mortally offended by his "hot-shot" stepson. When the two are alone together in his car, he skids down the highway at 70 miles per hour to show him who's boss.

For the most part, *This Boy's Live* goes one on one. Dwight provides some sadistic boxing lessons, gets Jack a paper route (and keeps his wages), sells the boy's treasured rifle and uses the money to buy a particularly hideous bulldog. As the step-siblings fade, so does the mother. Caroline may be a card-carrying member of the NRA who wins the annual Concrete turkey shoot—in a red dress, no less—but her part evaporates after a grotesque wedding night. (If we were to schlepp the movie on the couch, this sequence would be crucial: It's the only one that doesn't involve Jack's point of view and hence must be his fevered notion of the primal scene.)

Michael Caton-Jones, a Brit who relocated to Hollywood after directing the Profumo send-up *Scandal*, knows how to begin a scene with a flourish of offspeed motion and period pop—Jack in a barber's chair, tuffs of hair drifting down in slow motion as Nat King Cole croons "Smile." He's a director who constructs splendid porticos with nothing much behind them. Still, *This Boy's Life* isn't conventional teen stuff (Jack gets his first kiss from the neighborhood "homo" who briefly plays Jim to his Huck Finn) and the movie's critique of America's oppressively saccharine family culture is unusually persistent.

It's a happy coincidence (if indeed it is a coincidence) that Dwight is named Dwight. When 1960 dawns, Caroline is fascinated by his antithesis, John F. Kennedy—doing a boisterous imitation of Lucy Ricardo when Dwight won't let her work for the Democratic candidate. (As in *Love Field*, the very idea of Kennedy liberates American women—someone should do a study of his role in female fantasy during Camelot.) In the end, though, Caroline's mutation is barely alluded to—it's a boy's life.

Obsessed by the idea of his other family and particularly of his brother at Princeton, Jack proves that he's his real father's son by managing to forge a new identity and fabricate an application to an Eastern prep school. With the real-life success of the real-life Tobias Wolff hovering over the film, *This Boy's Life* can't help but turn inspirational. Failure isn't part of the program—this is a quality movie. The symmetrical ending offers relief from an ordeal that should have been a lot more grueling.

By contrast to Dwight, the father in *Jack the Bear* is a make-believe monster—or rather, a professional one. Danny DeVito plays a minor TV personality, who, presciently using the nom-de-tube "Al Gore," enlivens the late-night telecast of old horror movies with shticks and creatures of his own devising.

It's appropriate that one of dad's on-air personae would be called "Psycho Ward Cleaver." For *Jack the Bear* is the first feature directed by New Age domestic drama maestro Marshall Herskovitz (cocreator of *thirtysomething*) and, like *This Boy's Life*, it concerns a maimed and footloose family. Washing up in Oakland after the death of his wife (played in flashbacks by Andrea Marcovicci), Dad has the responsibility of caring for two boys—12-year-old Jack and his younger brother, Dylan. Nickname notwithstanding, Jack is less of a cutie-pie than the rest of the juveniles; Robert J. Steinmiller Jr. gives him an unkempt, geeky edge. Still, the movie's overly warm colors and posh domestic clutter suggest a sub-Spielberg kiddie mythos, with the camera habitually positioned four feet off the ground.

Unabashedly allegorical, *Jack the Bear* is set at the waning of the counterculture in the autumn of 1972 and the pleasantly ramshackle neighborhood where it unfolds is a world of hippie-inflected parents—even DeVito sports sideburns and a luxuriant head of hair—where school is taught by a guy with a Zapata mustache and righteous handshake. Dad drinks too much and drive's a battered Valiant but when Jack invites a girl over for dinner, he orchestrates the perfect evening—imitating Igor, initiating a game of hide-and-seek. (Although *Jack the Bear* features only intermittent voice-over narration, Herskovitz's trumping Jack's first kiss with the reverential Sturm und Drang of "When a Man Loves a Woman" is pure *Wonder Years*.)

Not surprisingly, dad goes all-out for Halloween, turning the house into a sort of live-in William Castle gimmick while disguising himself as an oversized bunny rabbit. Jack may not be amused ("I need to know if you plan on being a clown your whole life") but when one of the other neighborhood kids comes trick-or-treating as Hitler, it's clear that "Al Gore" is not the only boogey-man on the block—or put another way, the monstrous father is split in two. *Jack* is a liberal film—given the attention paid to the 1972 election it's strange that there's no invocation of Nixon versus McGovern—and that night, dad televises the original *Invasion of the Body Snatchers*, putting his job (and ultimately his family) in jeopardy by explicating the movie with a drunken, mock right-wing rant.

Like *This Boy's Life, Jack the Bear* is considerably more antiseptic than the novel it adapts. An irresponsible pothead in the novel, dad here does his own thing in the contested middle territory between the neighborhood Nazi and Jack's prissy Old Left grandparents. And, a bit like dad, *Jack* doesn't handle catastrophe so well. Too maudlin, too fast, and too lurid thereafter, the movie finally reinvents itself as the kind of flick dad might show—if mom would only endorse it. The strenuously horrific ending has certain parallels to *Island of Lost Souls* but it's softened—by the miracle of male tears.

Also reviewed in:
CHICAGO TRIBUNE, 4/30/93, Friday/p. C, Dave Kehr
NATION, 5/17/93, p. 674, Stuart Klawans
NEW YORK TIMES, 4/9/93, p. C10, Vincent Canby
NEW YORKER, 4/19/93, p. 111, Terrence Rafferty
VARIETY, 3/22/93, p. 50, Todd McCarthy
WASHINGTON POST, 4/23/93, p. D1, Rita Kempley
WASHINGTON POST, 4/23/93, Weekend/p. 33, Desson Howe

THREE OF HEARTS

A New Line Cinema release of a Three of Hearts Productions film. *Executive Producer:* David Permut. *Producer:* Joel B. Michaels and Matthew Irmas. *Director:* Yurek Bogayevicz. *Screenplay:* Adam Greenman and Mitch Glazer. *Story:* Adam Greenman. *Director of Photography:* Andrzej Sekula. *Editor:* Dennis M. Hill. *Music:* Joe Jackson. *Music Editor:* Bruce Lange. *Sound:* Stephen Halbert. *Sound Editor:* Michael O'Farrell, Richard Cadger, Tony Currie, and Michael Haight. *Casting:* Penny Perry and Annette Benson. *Production Designer:* Nelson Coates. *Art Director:* Douglas Hall. *Set Decorator:* Linda Lee Sutton. *Set Dresser:* James M. Harper, Sam F. Huston, David Deignan, and J.T. Thayer. *Costumes:* Barbara Tfank. *Make-up:* Sharon Ilson. *Stunt Coordinator:* Jeff Jensen. *Running time:* 97 minutes. *MPAA Rating:* R.

CAST: William Baldwin (Joe); Kelly Lynch (Connie); Sherilyn Fenn (Ellen); Joe Pantoliano (Mickey); Gail Strickland (Yvonne); Ced Verrell (Allison); Claire Callaway (Isabella); Marek Johnson (Gail); Monique Mannen (Daphne); Timothy D. Strickney (Ralph); Frank Ray Perilli (Patient); Tony Amendola (Harvey); Keith MacKechnie (Frankie); Ann Ryerson (Woman Auditioning); Gloria Gifford, Jill Jarress, Ken Magee, and Lin Shaye (Operators); Joshua Grenrock (Photographer); Jan A.P. Kaczmarek (Priest); Alekssandra Kaniak (Bride); Stanislaw Dziedzic (Groom); Maria Heggnes (Bride's Mother); Ebyslaw Kogut (Bride's Father); Liliana Overman (Lead Singer); Mitchell Group (Elevator Operator); Tawny Kitaen (Woman in Bar); Julie Lott (Nurse); Lynn A. Henderson (Student).

FILMS IN REVIEW, 8/93, p. 264, Edmond Grant

Watching *Three of Hearts*, one gets the impression that director Yurek Bogayevicz (*Anna*) and scripters Adam Greenman and Mitch Glazer had no idea what they were going for. As its stands, the picture is (ready?) a comedy-drama with a purely farcical premise that takes a serious look at lost love, while maintaining a subplot that came crawling in out of some half-baked urban crime drama.

Bogayevicz and his scripters have their hearts in the right place, but they tread too delicately: their inclusion of a lesbian relationship in the film's romantic triangle signals that this will be a "progressive" look at love in the '90s, but being male and not wanting to step on any toes, they reduce the relationships to near-subliminal status. This could be seen as a positive step (allowing the relationship to be simply accepted, as is), but it's also a disservice to the gay characters, making this simply another nimble variation on the old Hollywood three-way love affair. Which leaves us with the prospect of a movie centered around the third point of the triangle, a dimwitted male prostitute.

Joe (William Baldwin) is a male "escort," hired by Connie (Kelly Lynch), who needs a date for a family wedding, as she's been recently dumped by her girl friend Ellen (Sherilyn Fenn). Connie quickly develops a brilliant scheme: what if Joe were to romance and dump Ellen, so that she would (in Connie's fantasy) come crying back to Connie? Romantic comedies being what they are (and this isn't one, really), Joe and Ellen begin to fall in love, and Connie sees her hopes of a reconciliation disappear. At this point, the gangster subplot kicks in, and all hope of a coherent plotline go out the window.

Though the opening section of the film is light in tone (with a cute wedding scene at the gauche wedding, and an amusing view of the decidedly non-sexy headquarters of a phone-sex operation), as soon as we see Connie glued to her TV set, constantly watching old home videos of herself and Ellen in happier times, it's clear that the film won't follow through on any of its comic set-ups.

Which of course puts a greater weight on the film's three leads. Happily, at least one emerges unscathed: Lynch is excellent as Connie, the strongest willed of the three principals, yet also the quickest to get emotionally bruised. She demonstrates a talent that was tucked neatly away in her other screen work (with the exception of *Drugstore Cowboy*), well hidden behind her statuesque, model perfect looks.

With Baldwin, we have a fair-to-middling performer (still resembling a Picasso drawing of his brother Alec) who is more adept at depicting Joe's swaggering, cocky professional self than he is at conveying the pathos that shows up in the film's latter half. As for Fenn, she has already shown that she can be an awe-inspiring sexpot (*Twin Peaks*, the camp masterpiece *Two Moon Junction*) and that she can also act (*Of Mice and Men*, the underrated *Diary of a Hitman*); here, she gets the rawest deal of all—as scripted, Ellen is so dry and colorless, it's hard to figure why Joe and Connie are both obsessed with her. The only hint we get is contained in the videos Connie watches: there she is every bit as charming, relaxed, and forthright as Connie.

This might have been an effective movie if only Bogayevicz had explored the lesbian relationship that provides the impetus for his storyline, instead of using it as a prop for a "new age" romantic comedy that never quite appears.

LOS ANGELES TIMES, 4/30/93, Calendar/p. 1, Peter Rainer

"Three of Hearts" has a steamy premise but it's all wet—amusing but wet. It's like a bargain-bin "Indecent Proposal," another movie that lacked the courage of its own smarminess.

Joe Casella (William Baldwin) is a sweet-souled male escort in Manhattan who entertains a proposition with one of his clients, Connie (Kelly Lynch), a nurse who has just been ditched by her lover, Ellen (Sherilyn Fenn). Connie's idea is that since most guys are crumb-bums, she'll get Joe to woo Ellen and then break her heart so she'll come running back to Connie. Joe, who's on the outs with a local tough guy, hides out in Connie's apartment and gets on with business, showing up at a literature class Ellen teaches at NYU in an attempt to turn her googly-eyed. He wants to be teacher's pet in the worst way. (Best of all, he's only auditing, so no term papers.)

Since Joe is basically a good sort—only slightly more wised up than Jon Voight's hayseed hustler in "Midnight Cowboy"—his machinations with Ellen are bound to backfire. She's an innocent too. Guess what happens?

Even though Connie's ploy is desperately cruel, she's also portrayed as a softie—she may strut around in leather jackets but, remember, she's a nurse, a nurturer. (She plays out the latest movie cliché of watching home movies of her lost love—remember Michael Douglas in "Falling Down"?) So in a movie that's set up for all sorts of psychosexual jujitsu, what we end up with is downy-soft sentiments.

Joe may be a whore but his pimp (Joe Pantoliano) is to blame for keeping him in the life; his filthy rich tricks, like the aging matron (Gail Strickland) who greets him in garters, are just plain filthy. They're so avid for their boy toy that they don't recognize he has a *soul*. This is the kind of dewy erotic fantasy that usually turns up in the romance novel bins—or on the USA television network. Joe may be a heel but he's the heel who cares.

The lesbian angle in "Three of Hearts" (rated R for strong language and sexuality) is just a rejiggering of the usual romantic-triangle formula. It's a refreshing variant until you realize that nothing is going to come of it. The movie wouldn't work much differently if Connie were a man. (It might actually make more sense.)

Joe, we're made to understand, learns to accept women as, well, people. With Connie, he's blissfully free from erotic expectation; he's humbled by Ellen's goodness. But Joe doesn't look as if he needs sensitivity training; he's pretty much the same sweetie-pie from beginning to end. Director Yurek Bogayevicz, working from a script by Adam Greenman and Mitch Glazer, pulls back from showing any ugliness in his three people—probably because to do so would have been to expose the ugliness of the situation. But that ugliness isn't something to be shirked—it ought to be a dramatic opportunity. The filmmakers want to be praised as healers without opening any wounds.

Baldwin has a gangly good nature that at least keeps Joe believably sympathetic. He seems amused by his own come-hither sexuality and, when he's with his tricks, he keeps his voice in mid-purr, the same voice he uses for phone sex. Fenn overdoses on niceness. Once Ellen starts warming to Joe, she's made up to look so staid and schoolmarmish that you begin to think the filmmakers are equating her burgeoning heterosexuality with the '50s look.

Lynch looks uncomfortable but, she's enough of an actress to make her discomfort work for the role. She's been so good in so many negligible movies, from "Cocktail" to the straight-to-video "Warm Summer Rain," that she's in danger of becoming one of those first-rate character actresses who bail out bad movies. She can make the best of a bad situation. Maybe that's why, in "Three of Hearts," Connie looks at Joe with such simpatico.

NEW YORK, 5/17/93, p. 81, David Denby

Kelly Lynch, a gay nurse, in love with an English teacher, and William Baldwin, a professional lady-killer who is looking for his pride, make an odd but charming alliance in the New York-based romantic comedy *Three of Hearts*. Baldwin, brother of Alec, has a long, equine face, heavy-lidded eyes, and a reserved, ironic manner. He's extraordinarily likable as a soft-voiced stud who doesn't think too much of himself. And Lynch is often startlingly intense as an essentially sane woman shocked by how crazy her feelings have made her. The long-necked Lynch, shooting out energy in nervous bursts, captures the commonplace desperation of love. Baldwin and Lynch are well matched, physically and spiritually. Unfortunately, each is required to be in love with Sherilyn Fenn, who is dismayingly heavy-spirited and suburban. To their credit, writers Adam Greenman and Mitch Glazer and the Polish-émigré director Yurek Bogaye-vicz (*Anna*) treat lesbianism as no big deal—a natural fact of life and love. Even more, the movie is casual and realistic, which is to say funny, about a whole range of New York experience.

NEW YORK POST, 4/30/93, p. 33, Jami Bernard

The new relationship comedy "Three of Hearts" comes under the heading of Fun Junk—a movie whose only redeeming quality is that it's fun to watch no matter how stupid it gets. When sex hustler William Baldwin changes his ways all because of Sherilyn Fenn, that's pretty stupid indeed.

The movie opens with Baldwin having phone sex with a woman we later learn pays for the privilege, like everyone else. "Go get an ice cube," he commands, and then gives quite explicit instructions on how to use it. "Any woman, any time," is his motto—meaning that he's so good at seducing women, they melt for him faster than an ice cube.

Baldwin certainly has the charisma to pull it off, although as the movie wears on he appears too dim to be taken seriously, even in the bedroom. He's a cross between Jon Voight in "Midnight Cowboy" and the man who steals a woman's diary and thereby knows her intimately in "Thief of Hearts." He works for a wide-ranging sex operation that combines kinky 900-numbers, an escort service, and a call-boy ring all under one roof (run by an amusingly irritable Joe Pantoliano).

Baldwin is hired by Kelly Lynch to woo and then dump the woman who left Lynch in the lurch—Sherilyn Fenn, who is having trouble figuring out her sexual orientation. The thinking is that once her heart is broken, she'll come running back to Lynch's arms.

Predictably, instead of wooing Fenn and then returning her to the obsessed Lynch, Baldwin begins to fall for her—although who knows why, with such limited acting range as that, and those weird hairdos and awful clothes.

If mainstream cinema has come far enough to depict a lesbian couple without making a federal case of it, it still hasn't come far enough to leave well enough alone. The movie returns Fenn to her heterosexuality so quickly that you never really believe she had strayed, just as Sharon Stone never seemed like much of a lesbian in "Basic Instinct" the way she was going at it with Michael Douglas.

But the movie's heart is really with Lynch, who shows great comic form as the lesbian left behind. To offset Lynch's own beauty, the filmmakers put her in a nasty headband, slather her face with cold cream, even have her floss during a scene—but they cannot mask the fact that her character is far more interesting and lovable than Fenn's.

In fact, it is the friendship that develops between Lynch and Baldwin that is the central sexy relationship, even though it clearly cannot be consummated. In another moviemaking era, these two roommates—there is a silly subplot which forces Baldwin to bunk with Lynch for a while—would gradually see that friendship leads to a more lasting love than simple physical attraction. But here the movie is at least true to Lynch's character—when Baldwin kisses her at a wedding, she wipes off her mouth in barely concealed disgust. She is what she is.

NEWSDAY, 4/30/93, Part II/p. 71, John Anderson

A beautiful leather-clad lesbian hiring a beautiful male escort to break her beautiful, bisexual ex-lover's heart? Sure, why not. The dialogue? Moist, but not overly sodden. Even the alarming wardrobes are within the realm of possibility. But "Three of Hearts" simply goes too far in trying to convince us of the thoroughly improbable: that two reasonable people would expend so much time and effort in pursuit of Sherilyn Fenn.

The least-engaging element in a film that both boasts about and burlesques its characters' gayness, Fenn portrays Ellen Armstrong, a college teaching assistant who moves out on Connie (Kelly Lynch), a butch blonde in black leather who's left with no date for her sister's wedding.

That Connie had wanted to use the wedding—one of those quaint "ethnic" affairs, where the bride does a striptease—to come out of the closet contains a vein of irony that's barely scratched, but it gets the film to the next step: Wracked by grief, Connie hires a jaded, handsome escort/prostitute/phone-sex operator named Joe (William Baldwin) to accompany her. And after they become friends, the heartbroken Connie asks Joe to seduce and abandon Ellen, in the hopes she can get her back on the rebound. Joe, of course, falls for Ellen himself.

And at the same time, just to keep things moving, Joe is being pursued by the recently paroled Harvey (Tony Amendola), who thinks Joe set him up. Why? We're never told, but Joe's persecution by Harvey and Mickey the pimp (Joe Pantoliano) brings out Connie's latent maternal instinct.

So, while "Three of Hearts" might suggest a potpourri of possible sexual positions, it's really a rather conventional comedy. Joe and Connie aren't physical lovers, but they're still used by director Yurek Bogayevicz ("Anna") as two sides in a love triangle. Their onscreen chemistry is certainly sexual, even if there's no sex. The Joe and Connie relationship—which uses her lesbianism as a dramatic device the same way romantic comedies have always used unequal wealth or social status or ambition to create contention—contains a certain amount of warmth. But their absurd object of desire never justifies all the heavy breathing.

That Fenn's Ellen is most compelling once removed—on the home videos lovesick Connie watches over and over—says as much about "Three of Hearts" as the fact that Sting provides the music for the film's single, overly stylized sex scene.

Self-absorption is the message here, but it's also the medium: Fenn never seems to be unaware that all eyes are upon her. Her sole technique for communicating (1) wistfulness (2) hopelessness (3) passion (4) ennui is to throw her own eyes out of focus. What is she looking at? We may as well ask, as Baldwin does while contemplating one of Ellen's particularly unsettling coiffures: "What is this thing on top of your head?"

No one is guilt-free, though. Joe, who cozies up to Ellen under false pretenses, might suffer a crisis of his whore's conscience, but it never crosses his face. Connie, whom Lynch imbues with a certain amount of awkward innocence, is too guileless to be real, and at the same time too optimistic that her romantic scheme will work. And, again, Lynch's lesbianism is presented as inherently funny, or as an accessory to the clumsy clothes she wears when she wants to appear particularly feminine, or like a physical affliction that makes her move in a gangly, graceless way. For a film that seems to want to leap onto the gay-lesbian bandwagon, this one does so with a resounding flop.

SIGHT AND SOUND, 8/93, p. 53, Lucy Richer

Joe, a New York gigolo, is warned by his pimp Mickey that their associate Harvey is out of jail and looking for Joe, whom he believes to have set him up. In the park, Ellen is breaking up with her girlfriend Connie. Heartbroken, Connie has no partner for her sister's wedding, where she had planned to introduce Ellen as her lover. She hires an escort, and Joe turns up for the job.

Connie's Polish family are delighted with her 'boyfriend'. When Joe offers sexual services, Connie explains she is a lesbian. She drops Joe home, but Harvey has trashed his flat. Connie invites Joe to stay with her, and tells him about Ellen. Joe tells her the bisexual Ellen will certainly get her heart broken by a man and come back to Connie; this gives her the idea of hiring Joe to do the heart-breaking. Joe enrols in the English class Connie teaches. His assignment is to write a love letter; Connie plagiarises a poem for him which Ellen recognises, but she still falls for his sweet-talking. Connie contrives to run into them while they are on a date at the theatre, but Ellen tells Joe that she is no longer in love with Connie.

Joe can no longer bear to have sex with his clients because he is in love with Ellen. He sleeps with Ellen and tells Mickey he won't prostitute himself any longer. Enraged, Mickey tells Harvey where to find Joe. When Joe admits to Connie that he loves Ellen, she throws him out of her flat; at that moment, Harvey arrives and beats him up. Connie gets him to hospital and calls Ellen. Connie forces Joe to confess to Ellen about their arrangement; distraught, Ellen rejects them both. When Joe leaves hospital, Connie—who has accepted that Ellen won't return—encourages Joe to see her. Joe and Ellen are reunited.

Which movie star does Ellen look like, wonder Connie and Joe—Vivien Leigh, Audrey Hepburn? Neither would have stooped to play drippy Ellen, and Sherilyn Fenn—at her best as the scheming Audrey in *Twin Peaks*—is likewise wasted in this cutesy role. The references to movies and acting that director Yurek Bogayevicz first developed in *Anna. Three of Hearts* plays with the idea of sexual masquerade, the ridiculous gap between the act and actuality. Joe's pimp Mickey runs a phone sex business, where a job interview involves simulating aural sex without the phone. Sexual performance—in all senses—is Joe's business. Even Connie, immune to his sex appeal, falls for his patter because he "knows women". He is less a prostitute than a paid sex therapist for older women with a taste for guns and suspenders. But when Joe meets dewy-eyed Ellen, William Baldwin loses his knowing grin and descends into dreary 'authenticity', cajoling us into believing that Joe is no longer acting—that this is the predictable real thing.

Three of Hearts may give a lesbian twist to a light romance, but underneath the sexual window dressing, it offers nothing we haven't seen before. Not that the idea is bad: Baldwin and Lynch, both in love with Sherilyn Fenn, share the role of pursuer, twisting the traditional 'male' role in a way that at its best is sharply revealing about sexual assumptions. In the end, it is Connie who—echoing Joe's claim—"knows women"; she knows that Ellen will forgive him. But there is never any real doubt about who will get the girl: the relationship between the two women finishes as the film begins. We see Connie and Ellen together only in home videos, cavorting in wholesome pyjamas. The film lacks the courage of its convictions, shy to show girls snogging. Few who protested after *Basic Instinct* about Hollywood's lack of sympathetic gay characters are likely to be appeased by Ellen taking off her glasses and falling, feminine once more, into Joe's arms.

Baldwin's double role as prostitute-turned-lover allows for the 'action' story, in which Joe is on the run from an old enemy. This unconvincing subplot has no use other than to forward the romantic narrative. It is a sure sign that the film is protesting too much, an over-compensation typical of Hollywood movies which are genuinely trying to work sexual roles into new stories, but are nervous of trampling on too many traditions at once (in the same way, *Three Men and a Baby* had its three New Men reinforcing their masculinity by busting a drug ring while looking after baby). *Three of Hearts* tries for a glam-grunge *Singles* feel, where Lynch and Baldwin floss their teeth together and wear leather jackets. Lynch is congenially kooky in Bridget Fonda style, but Baldwin is just too slick to be believed.

Director Bogayevicz has style and a camera that suits it, the long takes whirling with the drunken dancers at the Polish wedding, giving the scene the joyous touch; but the charm simply doesn't flow off the screen as it did in Cameron Crowe's *Singles*. *Three of Hearts*, hesitant rather than wholehearted about its love story, never manages to close the gap between empathy and embarrassment.

VILLAGE VOICE, 5/4/93, p. 60, Manohla Dargis

In *Three of Hearts*, boy meets girl—as well as her ex-girlfriend. When Ellen (Sherilyn Fenn) dumps Connie (Kelly Lynch), it's because she needs space. Luckily, she not only finds a wildly commodious loft, she meets Joe (William Baldwin), a man who knows not to crowd a girl on the mend. The twist here is that Connie, in a fit of misguided reason, has brokered stud-for-hire Joe to break Ellen's heart so she can pick up the pieces. It's a tasty setup, all right, so it's too bad no one had the nerve to play this soap less safe, less straight.

Treading clumsily on the memory of *Design for Living*, director Yurek Bogayevicz tries to plump up the coyly thin script with useless transition shots, and numerous close-ups of his swell-looking cast. These are cheap tricks, but it's almost excusable because Bogayevicz is good, well, good enough, with actors. (In *Anna*, he made Paulina shine and Sally Kirkland actually bearable.) Baldwin and Lynch are a pleasure; their palsy-walsy number is the best thing in the film. Sherilyn Fenn, on the other hand, should stick to tonguing cherry stems.

Lesbianism, as Seinfeld's friend George knows, is *hip*. From chic *Vogue* to the more chic *Roseanne*, savvy media increasingly trade on women in love, or rather, the appearance of women in love. Mysterious and lovely, these spurious sisters in Sappho rarely generate heat because they're not supposed to. *Three of Hearts*—so pretty, so pleasant, so blissfully bland—strikes out because it doesn't have the courage of the one lesbian who strikes back with anger—and love.

Also reviewed in:
CHICAGO TRIBUNE, 4/30/93, Friday/p. I, Dave Kehr
NEW YORK TIMES, 4/30/93, p. C16, Janet Maslin
VARIETY, 2/8/93, p. 76, Emanuel Levy
WASHINGTON POST, 4/30/93, p. B7, Hal Hinson
WASHINGTON POST, 4/30/93, Weekend/p. 44, Joe Brown

THREE MUSKETEERS, THE

A Walt Disney release in association with Caravan Pictures. *Executive Producer:* Jordan Kerner and Jon Avnet. *Producer:* Joe Roth and Roger Birnbaum. *Director:* Stephen Herek. *Screenplay:* David Loughery. *Based on the novel by:* Alexandre Dumas. *Director of Photography:* Dean Semler. *Editor:* John F. Link. *Music:* Michael Kamen. *Music Editor:* Michael T. Ryan. *Sound:* Colin Charles. *Sound Editor:* Tim Chau and Rick Franklin. *Casting:*

Jeremy Zimmermann, Lucky Englander, and Fritz Fleischhacker. *Production Designer:* Wolf Kroeger. *Art Director:* Richard Holland. *Set Decorator:* Bruno Cesari. *Special Effects:* David Harris. *Costumes:* John Mollo. *Make-up:* Paul Engelen. *Make-up (Charlie Sheen):* David Anderson. *Make-up (Rebecca De Mornay):* Ann Masterson. *Stunt Coordinator:* Paul Weston. *Running time:* 102 minutes. *MPAA Rating:* PG.

CAST: Charlie Sheen (Aramis);   Kiefer Sutherland (Athos);   Chris O'Donnell (D'Artagnan); Oliver Platt (Porthos);   Tim Curry (Cardinal Richelieu);   Rebecca De Mornay (Milady); Gabrielle Anwar (Queen Anne);   Michael Wincott (Rochefort);   Paul McGann (Girard/Jussac); Julie Delpy (Constance);   Hugh O'Conor (King Louis);   Christopher Adamson (Henri);   Philip Tan (Parker);   Erwin Leder (Peasant);   Axel Anselm (Musketeer);   Bruno Thost (Seneschal #1);   Oliver Hoppa (Seneschal #2);   Emma Moore (Damsel);   Herbert Fux (Innkeeper); Nichola Cordey (Barmaid);   Sebastian Eckhardt (Armand de Winter).

LOS ANGELES TIMES, 11/12/93, Calendar/p. 1, Peter Rainer

The bounding teen idols in "The Three Musketeers" just barely fit comfortably into the film's overstuffed 17th-Century decor. Kiefer Sutherland's Athos, Chris O'Donnell's D'Artagnan, Charlie Sheen's Aramis and Oliver Platt's portly Porthos are an incongruous quartet: They're leaping and wenching and fencing, but they're also winking at the audience. These actors want to experience the pleasures of an old-time Hollywood costume swashbuckler but they don't want to lose their cool.

The Alexandre Dumas novel has already been filmed so many times—the best adaptation was probably Richard Lester's 1974 jape—that a new version cries out for a reason for being. The reason is depressingly clear: What we've got here is "Young Swords."

The familiars of the story are made comic-book simple. The intrigues of the French court, as Cardinal Richelieu (Tim Curry) attempts to disband the King's Musketeers and steal the crown, are designed as a series of boo-hiss set-pieces, full of nefarious villains and winning crusaders.

But director Stephen Herek, best known for "Bill & Ted's Excellent Adventure," and screenwriter David Loughery aren't really inspired by the romanticism of the material. They're not inspired by much of anything, really. Like their young cast, they don't want to risk looking square by showing any real ardor. (The ardor is all in the score—or to be more precise, the overscore—by Michael Kamen.) But they don't go full out as jokesters either. The film's tone wobbles between straight-arrow action and curdled camp.

The most obvious difference between this film version and the many others is that, this time around, the three Musketeers and D'Artagnan are all twentysomethings. This places the story closer to Dumas' original conception but it also introduces a problem. None of these kids seem ripe enough for grand-scale heroism. The athleticism of a Douglas Fairbanks or a Gene Kelly could turn this old warhorse into a sleek stallion, but no one in this new film has anything like their prancing sportiness. With the exception of Platt's Porthos, who at least is given some comedy shtick in his fight scenes, the choreography is stumblebum stuff. He keeps the camera boring inside the action so that we get lots of flying limbs and flying dust, and that's probably a wise approach. It distracts from the clunky calisthenics.

It might have been possible for this movie's mixture of straight arrow and camp to work if the filmmakers had the right ribald spirit. The Musketeers saga starting with Fairbanks in the 1921 silent version, has usually been filled with tongue planted firmly in cheek. But what comes across in the new version is a kind of preening teen-idol dress-up ball. We can see how Sutherland and Sheen and the others enjoy dressing up in their 17th-Century duds and swinging their swords—it's a boy's fantasy that doesn't have the heft to become the audience's fantasy, too. And since the filmmakers have been careful to keep everything family-entertainment-style—the rating, for "action, violence and some sensuality" is PG—the romp has a chaste, kidsy flavor: "The Three Mouseketeers."

A few of the performers have wit, notably Tim Curry as Richelieu, who gives his best lines a ticklish nastiness. Curry has the audience on his side in a way that none of the other actors do, his professionalism is so expert that he puts most of the cast to shame. (You keep expecting Alan Rickman from "Robin Hood" to show up and give him some competition.) Rebecca De Mornay, as Milady De Winter, doesn't try to camp it up, which may have been a mistake, but her professionalism shines, too. She gives the film its only "heart." When she jumps off a cliff, the film goes over the side with her.

NEW YORK POST, 11/12/93, P. 37, Michael Medved

The list of talent associated with the latest version of "The Three Musketeers" will hardly inspire confidence on the part of wary (and weary) moviegoers.

This new film's best-known stars, Kiefer Sutherland and Charlie Sheen, previously teamed with its principal producer, Joe Roth, for the "Young Guns" movies, giving rise to the fear that their take on the Musketeers might turn out to be "Young Sabers"—a brooding, gory western illogically set in 17th-century France.

And then there's the director, Stephen Herek, whose most recent credits featured clumsy glorifications of teen-age mindlessness such as "Don't Tell Mom the Babysitter's Dead" and the immortal "Bill and Ted's Excellent Adventure." Should diehard fans of the original Alexandre Dumas novel now be prepared for "Athos and D'Artagnan's Excellent Adventure"?

Actually, Herek, Roth and associates confound all expectations: They have fashioned a big, breezy, lush and likable piece of popular entertainment which brings a startling level of freshness to a tired tale that Hollywood has told four times before.

Twenty-three-year-old Chris O'Donnell (who played Al Pacino's prep school pal in "Scent of a Woman") exudes effortless athletic grace as the latest D'Artagnan, the wide-eyed country bumpkin who rides to Paris hoping to claim his late father's place in the elite company of Royal Musketeers.

Sutherland, Sheen and Oliver Platt (especially effective as the earthy Porthos) are similarly solid as the three palace veterans who eventually take the kid from the provinces under their wing.

These hip young stars display an easygoing on-screen affinity that helps give the picture a sly, all-American irreverence, and offers a welcome alternative to the British-accented, period-piece preening most often associated with big-studio swashbucklers.

The atmosphere of innocent, good-natured fun even extends to scenes in which the older Musketeers educate D'Artagnan in the fine arts of drinking and "wenching.'

Though the movie boasts a decorative array of gorgeous actresses in fetchingly low-cut dresses (including Rebecca De Mornay, Gabrielle Anwar and Julie Delpy) this PG picture depicts no sexual activity more shocking than kisses.

This is typical of a general (and all too rare) sensitivity to the film's potential family audience: The nicely choreographed scenes of swordplay never revel in graphic blood and guts, avoiding the gratuitous gore that marred Kevin Costner's "Robin Hood, Prince of Dweebs"—the previous swashbuckler whose undeserved success helped to inspire this new project.

Occasionally, the villains of "The Three Musketeers" display a distressing tendency to go over the top, with Tim Curry in particular portraying the scheming Cardinal as a lecherous, lip-smacking monster who seems a refugee from the "Richelieu Horror Picture Show."

There's also a silly conspiracy to kill the king with a lone gunman hidden atop a palace parapet during a royal rally, and suggesting an Oliver Stone perspective on the reign of Louis XIII.

The pure energy of the filmmaking, however, sweeps away such reservations in its headlong rush.

The handsome costumes, busy crowd scenes and stunning locations (shot almost entirely in Austria) provide an unusually lavish look to production from the notoriously cost-conscious Disney company.

"The Three Musketeers" may not be deep, but it is delicious; buckle your swash and have a good time.

NEWSDAY, 11/12/93, Part II/p. 73, Jack Mathews

Every generation should experience the fun and adventure of Alexandre Dumas' robust swashbuckler "The Three Musketeers," and since today's youth won't watch old movies, let alone read old books, the latest remake from Walt Disney Pictures will do just fine.

"The Three Musketeers," the tale of three loyal king's guards and their pal D'Artagnan in the Court of Louis XIII, has been adapted for the screen numerous times (Thomas Edison tried it as early as 1911, and its success is invariably a product of its casting and tone.

In earning the Disney family label, this version by Stephen Herek ("Bill and Ted's Excellent Adventure," "The Mighty Ducks") may be a little too restrained for those who relish the bawdy Richard Lester versions of the '70s. And Chris O'Donnell, Al Pacino's companion in "Scent of a Woman," looks like a child dressed for a school play as D'Artagnan, the acrobatic charmer who inspired great performances from such dashing stars as Douglas Fairbanks and Gene Kelly.

But the tone here is a near-perfect blend of broad comedy, exuberant swordplay, coy romance, and extravagant period sets, costumes and music, and there are three other performances—Charlie Sheen and Oliver Platt as musketeers Aramis and Porthos, and Tim Curry as the sinister Cardinal Richelieu—that more than make up for a weak D'Artagnan.

More faithful to the early film versions than to the book, this edition of "The Three Musketeers" tells of Richelieu's attempt to undermine his king (Hugh O'Conor) and assume the throne himself. To that end, he disbands the king's guard, and sends the devious Countess DeWinter (Rebecca De Mornay) on a secret mission to England to form a pact with a like-minded traitor in the Court of King James.

The only thing standing between Richelieu and royalty are the three rogue musketeers who have refused to throw down their arms, and D'Artagnan, the impetuous young musketeer wannabe who joins them. Throw in a couple of romantic subplots—D'Artagnan and lady-in-waiting Constance (Julie Delpy), Milady DeWinter and the brooding musketeer Athos (Kiefer Sutherland)—and the games are on.

Herek and screenwriter David Loughery ("Passenger 57") have done a remarkable job of recreating the bloodless swashbuckler style of the '30s and '40s, and infusing it with jokes and dialogue made-to-order for the '90s. The ambitiously choreographed swordfights and the accompanying banter get a little silly at times, but such is the nature of the genre.

Most of the actors are in sync, too. I don't know where Kiefer Sutherland got the inspiration for his listless performance (from his dad?), but wisecracking Charlie Sheen seems to have taken his cues from the films of Errol Flynn, while the delightfully garrulous Platt reminds us of a young Oliver Reed. Michael Wincott, by the way, plays Count de Rochefort, Richelieu's vicious lieutenant, in a way that would do Basil Rathbone proud.

Curry, of course, is an original, the best comedy villain working these days, and dominates every scene he's in.

If, as someone suggested, a good tale hangs on the badness of its villain, this version of "The Three Musketeers" is not to be missed.

SIGHT AND SOUND, 3/94, p. 51, Geoffrey Macnab

France, the seventeenth century. Reckless young D'Artagnan is on his way to Paris, determined to join the ranks of the Musketeers. Unfortunately, though, the corps has been disbanded. Cardinal Richelieu, who is plotting to usurp the youthful king, has tricked his Majesty into decommissioning them and sending them off to join the war against England. D'Artagnan, unaware of the fact, heads straight to Musketeers headquarters to enrol. Athos, one of the three Musketeers who remain at large, is the only man there, and is so offended by D'Artagnan's impudence that he challenges him to a duel. In the course of a busy morning, D'Artagnan also manages to insult Porthos, the portly second Musketeer, and bumps into Aramis, the suave third. Both demand "satisfaction."

At the appointed time for the first duel, D'Artagnan is surprised to see his three opponents know each other, and awe-struck to discover they're Musketeers. He gets ready to fence with Athos, but the duellists are interrupted by a troop of the Cardinal's men. A fight ensues. D'Artagnan acquits himself bravely, and all the soldiers are killed. The Musketeers escape, but D'Artagnan is captured by a second wave of the Cardinal's troops. He is thrown into the dungeons, and has his sword stolen by Rochefort, the Cardinal's chief henchman. D'Artagnan escapes from his cell and overhears Richelieu plotting with a mysterious woman. She is being dispatched to England to sign a secret treaty with the Duke of Buckingham. This augurs ill for the King. D'Artagnan is found eavesdropping, pulled before the Cardinal, and, when he refuses to say where the Musketeers are hiding, condemned to death. The three come to his rescue, snatching him from beneath Richelieu's nose, and escaping in the Cardinal's own carriage.

Finding out from D'Artagnan about the Cardinal's plan, the Musketeers hurry toward Calais, determined to apprehend the mysterious envoy. There is a price on their heads, and hordes of bounty hunters are close behind them. To ensure greater safety, they split up, resolving to meet at the port. D'Artagnan collapses with exhaustion a few miles short of Calais. He is picked up off the open road by a beautiful woman in a carriage. Although he doesn't at first realize it, she is Milady, the very person he heard the Cardinal conspiring with. She nurses him and seems about to seduce him, but then, when she discovers he is associated with the Musketeers, tries to kill him. He escapes her dagger, but is overcome by her guards. She decides to keep him alive a little longer, and takes him as a prisoner to Calais. There, however, she finds the Musketeers waiting for her. It turns out she is Athos's former wife, a convicted murderess. At first, she refuses to reveal the full extent of Richelieu's plot, but then, just before she is about to be executed, she warns her old husband that there are plans afoot to assassinate the King at his birthday celebrations. She avoids the executioner's axe by throwing herself to her death.

The Musketeers hot-foot it back to Paris. D'Artagnan intercepts the assassin at the very instant he is taking aim to fire at the King with his blunderbuss. There is a huge fight in the palace. Eventually, Athos, Porthos and company, joined by their old comrades, prevail. But the Cardinal escapes into the dungeons with the King and Queen as hostages. As he flees, D'Artagnan is left to fight Rochefort, who turns out to be his father's murderer. With a little help from Constance, the Queen's chamber maid, he beats him in an epic duel.

Just as the Cardinal seems about to escape down an underground river, Aramis stops him in his tracks. The King, grateful to the Musketeers for keeping him on the throne, reappoints them as his bodyguards and admits D'Artagnan to their ranks. Girard, a pompous upstart whose sister D'Artagnan is accused of insulting, turns up, wanting to revenge the family honour. But on learning that the Musketeer code, "All For One And One For All", means he will have to fight the entire corps, he turns tail and flees.

Given memories of the "Mouseketeers", Uncle Walt's folksy troupe of fresh-faced youngsters who first strutted their way across American TV in the 1950s, wearing funny caps and chanting Mickey Mouse mantras while helping hawk millions of dollars worth of merchandise, the prospect of a Disney version of *The Three Musketeers* was hardly one to relish. One of cinema's most exhilarating yarns seemed destined to end up as yet another paean to homely, commercial values, with the chivalric slogan "One For All And All For One" no doubt converted into a new Disney Club nostrum. This, though, proves to be a surprisingly sprightly swashbuckler.

Admittedly, it is scarcely original, being after all the umpteenth version of the tale. And our latest crop of Musketeers are a little on the callow side. Unlike Oliver Reed, Frank Finlay or even Douglas Fairbanks, they're not worldly-wise, heavy-drinking matinee idol types. Still, if Chris O'Donnell, Kiefer Sutherland, Charlie Sheen and Oliver Platt do lack the element of weary, charming cynicism which sometimes characterizes Dumas's heroes on screen, they more than make up for it with their nimble acrobatics and their infinite capacity for duelling. They leap hither and thither, fight on staircases, balustrades and in forests without appearing in the slightest bit fazed by their rather flouncey costumes.

The film-makers take certain liberties with Dumas's original text, rewriting the episode of the Queen's Diamonds, banishing the Duke of Buckingham to an off-screen role, cutting down on the boozing and the wenching, and allowing the usually incorrigible Milady (Rebecca De Mornay) a touch of saving grace; but, in their way, they give as faithful a rendition of the tale as any of their predecessors. Fidelity here lies not so much in keeping to the plot of the novel as in preserving its spirit, in staging the swordfights with grace and elan, and featuring as many chases as possible. It is only to be expected that the villains should be played by English actors. Tim Curry offers an overblown Cardinal Richelieu, not so very far removed from his Dr Frank N. Furter, and Paul McGann is the nincompoop Girard, who is always trying to engineer D'Artagnan's downfall. They may not be the heroes, but they provide most of the film's comic momentum.

Superficially, this follows in the wake of *Young Guns*: the bankable brat pack, having colonized the Western, rides off into genres new. Nevertheless, there is no sense here that the stars overshadow their vehicle or that this is just another American rites-of-passage yarn transposed to an unusual setting. Director Stephen Herek, whose previous credits include *Bill and Ted's Excellent Adventure*, manages to infuse the film with a little self-reflexive irony without losing that likeable, ingenuous quality so essential to the story. The script incorporates elements of the JFK saga, boasting a denouement which involves a lone sniper with a blunderbuss on a roof, and borrows back motifs from the *Indiana Jones* cycle, but never becomes portentous.

On one level, this is corporate, theme-park movie making, guilty of fetishizing history. We're presented with the same image of seventeenth-century France as you might encounter in a heritage museum, all dungeons, palaces and vast halls. As the recent GATS talks illustrated, European sensitivity about Hollywood is at a high pitch. A picture like this, which is based on a French novel, and uses Austrian and English locations, may serve to heighten fears that the Americans, not content with taking most of our box-office receipts, are now pilfering our national myths as well. However, the swashbuckler has always been among the quintessential Hollywood genres. Jeffrey Richards was not far off the mark in his study *Swordsmen Of The Screen*, when he placed it alongside the Busby Berkeley-style musical as something so extravagant, colourful and hard to pull off that only the studio system as its best could manage it. True, Musketeer fables are conventional Boy's Own tales, full of derring-do, but they are also highly stylized pieces of cinema, where choreography, costume and music tend to be privileged at the expense of narrative.

Writing in the 1970s, Richards struck an elegiac note. He was convinced that swashbucklers had became prohibitively expensive to make, and worried that their romantic flamboyance was out of synch with the times: he couldn't imagine Clint Eastwood or Steve McQueen in doublet and hose—they were too mean to be chivalric. But he was premature in writing off the sword-and-cape spectacular. Whatever other criticisms might be levelled at it, Disney's *The Three Musketeers*, like *Robin Hood: Prince of Thieves* or the forthcoming *Zorro*, at least suggests there is still mileage in the genre. With Hollywood ever more willing to plunder its past, and the conventional, tough-guy hero on his last legs, the swashbuckler is enjoying an unlikely new lease of life.

VILLAGE VOICE, 11/30/93, Film Special/p. 32, Tom Kertes

This is the fifth sound adaptation of the Dumas swashbuckler, and it's by far the best. The 1935 version lacked color in both film and screenplay, and then there was the downright disastrous casting of mousy Walter Abel as D'Artagnan. The 1948 adaptation was a small epic—a filmic oxymoron—and the Gene Kelly-June Allyson combination was a virtual chemical spill. Richard Lester's financially successful 1974 slapstick nonsense mistook *The Three Musketeers* for *The Three Stooges*.

A sad history, though understandable. Indeed, just how do you go about conjuring up a magical adventure from a story that's been read 17 times by everyone in the theater? This is how: Simplify, but don't oversimplify, the overfamiliar plot convolutions. This time the evil Cardinal Richelieu plots a straightforward assassination of the noble king Louis XIII. Then modify some of the characters in order to draw sharper conflicts: Richelieu is now the queen's sexual predator as well as a political traitor, King Louis a naive teenager as opposed to the simpering fop of the novel, etc. And perhaps most importantly, director Stephen Herek also duplicates Franco Zeffirelli's *Romeo and Juliet* coup, actually casting youthful charmers as the youthfully charming heroes. No actors in the middle of midlife crisis pretending to be teens here.

Musketeers luxuriates in size, scope, faithful-to-the-era scenery—all musts in a swashbuckler. The actors live snugly within their parts, particularly Oliver Platt as the playfully lecherous Porthos and Tim Curry as the rancid Richelieu. And Rebecca De Mornay was simply *born* to portray the achingly beautiful, yet wicked, Lady De Winter.

Also reviewed in:
CHICAGO TRIBUNE, 11/12/93, Friday/p. C, Michael Wilmington
NEW YORK TIMES, 11/12/93, p. C10, Janet Maslin
VARIETY, 11/22/93, p. 32, Todd McCarthy
WASHINGTON POST, 11/12/93, p. C6, Hal Hinson

TIM BURTON'S THE NIGHTMARE BEFORE CHRISTMAS

A Touchstone Pictures release. *Producer:* Tim Burton and Denise Di Novi. *Director:* Henry Selick. *Screenplay:* Caroline Thompson. *Based on a story and characters by:* Tim Burton. *Adaptation:* Michael McDowell. *Director of Photography:* Pete Kozachik. *Editor:* Stan Webb. *Music:* Danny Elfman. *Music Editor:* Bob Badami. *Sound:* Bobby Fernandez, Samuel Lehmer, and (music) Shawn Murphy. *Sound Editor:* Richard L. Anderson. *Casting:* Mary Gail Artz and Barbara Cohen. *Set Designer:* Gregg Olsson. *Set Dresser:* Gretchen Scharfenberg and Joel Friesch. *Visual Effects:* Pete Kozachik. *Storyboard:* Joe Ranft. *Animation Supervisor:* Eric Leighton. *Animators:* Trey Thomas, Timothy Hittle, Michael Belzer, Anthony Scott, Owen Klatte, Angie Glocka, Justin Kohn, Eric Leighton, Paul Berry, Joel Fletcher, Kim Blanchette, Loyd Price, Richard C. Zimmerman, and Stephen A. Buckley. *Art Director:* Deane Taylor. *Running time:* 75 minutes. *MPAA Rating:* Rated PG.

VOICES: Danny Elfman (Jack Skellington Singing/Clown With the Tear Away Face/Barrel); Chris Sarandon (Jack, Speaking); Catherine O'Hara (Sally/Shock); William Hickey (Evil Scientist); Glenn Shadix (Mayor); Paul Reubens (Lock); Ken Page (Oogie Boogie); Ed Ivory (Santa); Susan McBride (Big Witch/W.W.D.); Debi Durst (Corpse Kid/Corpse Mom/Small Witch); Gregory Proops (Harlequin Demon/Devil/Sax Player); Kerry Katz (Man Under Stairs/Vampire/Corpse Dad); Randy Crenshaw (Mr. Hyde/Behemoth/Vampire); Sherwood Ball (Mummy/Vampire); Carmen Twillie (Undersea Gal/Man Under the Stairs); Glenn Walters (Wolfman).

CHRISTIAN SCIENCE MONITOR, 10/15/93, p. 15, David Sterritt

It's an ironic fact of the movie world that Tim Burton, the master of macabre fantasy who gave us "Batman" and "Beetlejuice" and "Edward Scissorhands," launched his career at no more sinister a place than Walt Disney Pictures, where he worked on popular animations and made solo shorts including the delightful cartoon "Vincent."

Coming full circle, Burton has returned to Disney for "The Nightmare Before Christmas," his first full-length animation. Although it was directed by Henry Selick, another Disney graduate, Burton gets top billing for dreaming up the story and characters, and it certainly reflects his sense of way-out humor.

After a premiere at the New York Film Festival, bestowing a measure of art-film prestige on the picture, it's now arriving in theaters via the Disney studio's Touchstone division, which handles productions too feisty to be festooned with the family-geared Disney name. Parents of very young children should approach the movie with caution, since it contains images and scenes that may be too intense for some youngsters.

The adventure takes place in a make-believe world where every holiday has a kingdom of its own. Jack Skellington is a popular guy in Halloweentown, where skeletons are always in style, but he's looking for new challenges. When he discovers the entrance to Christmastown, he's instantly enchanted by this happy holiday and decides he could make it even merrier than it already is. Needless to say, Halloween and Christmas make a mighty odd couple, and the results of Jack's meddling are appropriately wacky.

"The Nightmare Before Christmas" is an ingenious marketing commodity for Disney, capitalizing on two photogenic holidays in one lively movie. It also reflects Burton's antic style in a comparatively pure form, though impeccably crafted stop-motion images that amplify the dreamlike aura of his free-form fantasies.

This said, it's also true that "The Nightmare Before Christmas" never becomes as clever or captivating as it promises to be. One reason is that cartoons are always cartoons, and they are a big step away from reality, no matter how brilliantly and believably they're drawn.

Burton's last movie, "Batman Returns," was full of impossibly wild visions that carried more conviction than anything in "The Nightmare Before Christmas" simply because real people, places, and things were visible behind their delirious facades. Animation is a wonderful medium, but it's almost too compatible with Burton's uninhibited approach. When literally anything goes, even the most original idea can get lost in the creative shuffle.

Another problem is the filmmakers' decision to tell most of the story through songs instead of spoken dialogue. The music and lyrics by Danny Elfman are sprightly enough, but they're so conventional that they weigh down the movie's flight toward a new and different world.

Caroline Thompson wrote the screenplay for "The Nightmare Before Christmas," working from Michael McDowell's adaptation of Burton's concepts. The cast of off-screen voices includes William Hickey and Paul Reubens, plus Chris Sarandon as Jack's spoken voice and Elfman as his singing voice.

FILMS IN REVIEW, 5-6/94, p. 57, Edmond Grant

Finally, a Christmas movie for misfits! Social outcasts of all ages (and even those solidly conventional souls who feel like they're misfits) will delight in this curious concoction that strives for oddness in a most uncommon (in Hollywood, at least) way.

Indeed, there are a few precedents for the special brand of stop motion animation, using marionette-like creatures, that Burton, designated director Henry Selick and company use in *Nightmare*. First, one thinks of the surreal work done by art cinema favorites like the Czech Jan Svankmajer and his disciples, the bizarre Brothers Quay. A little closer to the mainstream, we encounter the special—and very seasonal—brand of "animagic" used by the Rankin-Bass team in their classic Yuletide TV specials, and the wonderfully underrated *Mad Monster Party* (1967), which did for juvenile monster movie fans of the '60s (this reviewer included) what *Nightmare* does for today's ghoulish tykes—present a creepy, yet reassuringly friendly, vision of a world that would (hopefully) not seem attractive to your parents, a place where monsters rule, and the social order is the exact opposite of the "real world" endorsed by our elders.

Nightmare's hero Jack Skellington (the voice of Chris Sarandon) comes from the strange realm of Halloweentown. But being Pumpkin King isn't enough for Jack; one day he wanders outside his realm, and discovers a wooded area which contains doorways to all the holiday towns. Jack takes the plunge into Christmas, and discovers he's jealous of Santa Claus's ability to hand deliver happiness every December 25th. So, he decides that the citizens of Halloweentown ought to hijack that holiday, setting into motion a wonderful parody of seasonal clichés, including a scene where Santa is gleefully tormented in a roulette wheel enclosure by a funky creature named Oogie Boogie. Small children may recoil at the glimpse of Oogie's worm compacted innards, but older boys will dig its brief gross-out appeal; girls can respond to Sally (the voice of *SCTV*s exquisite Catherine O'Hara), our rag doll-like heroine, who is mad for Jack, but is fiercely independent when it comes to her possessive scientist creator (the always nightmarish voice of William Hickey).

On the visual level, *Nightmare* is light years ahead of the usual standard, anthropomorphic, kiddie entertainment. In fact, the film's look is so subversive that it's regrettable Burton felt that *Nightmare* had to be a musical. Be it the influence of Disney or *The Wizard of Oz*, it appears that every moviemaker feels their juvenile fantasy has to have a song score—here, the sappy tunes unfortunately supply a "normal" (read: formulaic) element that counterbalances the picture's weirdly imaginative look. The songs are the creation of the perfectly talented Danny Elfman (who supplies the singing voice of Jack, and scored all of Burton's other features), but they still reek of conventionality, making them stand in sharp contrast to the freakish looking characters who sing them. At points the film goes into operetta overdrive; considering that the plot would be understandable even if the proceedings were *entirely* non-verbal makes the doleful lyrics seem an even greater intrusion.

But thanks to the immaculately detailed work by Selick and his animators (a team of stop motion experts who have produced logos for MTV), even as prominent a drawback as sappy lyrics can't diminish the picture's off-kilter charm. Jack Skellington shares more than a few similarities with Burton's other misfit—heroes (Winona Ryder's character in *Beetlejuice*, Edward Scissorhands, and even Pee-Wee Herman). His misguided mission to spread Xmas joy has its bittersweet aspect, but the film wisely stays on the lighter side of fantastic. Most film projects referred to as "state of the art" rely on big-budget fx; *Nightmare* genuinely deserves that chronically overused tag, with the emphasis placed on "art."

LOS ANGELES TIMES, 10/15/93, Calendar/p. 1, Kenneth Turan

Forget "Beetlejuice," forget "Edward Scissorhands" and (this shouldn't be too difficult) forget "Batman Returns." "Tim Burton's The Nightmare Before Christmas" is the movie this decidedly quirky filmmaker was fated to make. Part avant-garde art film, part amusing but morbid fairy tale, it is a delightfully ghoulish holiday musical that displays more inventiveness in its brief 75 minutes than some studios can manage in an entire year.

Though it is an animated film. "Nightmare" is not a cartoon like "Aladdin" or "Beauty and the Beast." Rather, on the model of the original "King Kong" and the more recent Speedy Alka Seltzer, it is a revolutionary application of stop-motion animation, a labor-intensive process that involves the frame-by-frame manipulation of three-dimensional creatures.

And though it managed to be rated PG (for some scary images), the aptly named "Nightmare" is definitely not a film for tiny tots. Although its soul is sweetness itself, its surface is disturbing and intentionally so, and its clever and satiric sense of humor is undoubtedly pitched to adult tastes.

"Nightmare's" first incarnation was as a hand-drawn sendup of the Clement Moore poem that Burton created more than a decade ago, when he was working as a humble animator at the Walt Disney studios and dreaming of turning his idea into a TV special along the lines of "How the Grinch Stole Christmas."

In the way it details what happens when the weirdos who run Halloween decide to expand and take over Christmas as well, "Nightmare" was deemed too bizarre for public consumption, but Burton never gave up on it. His increased box-office clout, courtesy of the "Batman" films, helped persuade Disney to green-light what may be the most personal piece of animation—and one of the most personal films—period—ever to come out of that studio.

Although someone else ("The Secret Garden's" Caroline Thompson) ended up writing the script, and the technical nature of stop-motion animation meant that a drop-dead expert (Henry Selick) had to be hired to direct, "Nightmare's" sensibility of an animator, Burton has a taste for off-center, gruesome comedy—so off-putting when attached to real people, as it was in "Batman Returns"—but perfectly suited to these characters. Puppets, it should come as no surprise, make much better puppets than people ever could.

The premise of "The Nightmare Before Christmas" is the quaint one that everyone responsible for a particular holiday lives in the same self-contained enclave, cheerfully oblivious to the existence of rival festivities and other towns.

The residents of Halloweentown, for instance, are glimpsed celebrating another successful night of fright. Characters such as Big Witch, Corpse Mom and Clown With the Tear Away Face congratulate one another on a job well done while assuring us, in, Danny Elfman's lightly charming lyrics, "That's our job, but we're not mean/In our town of Halloween."

Things don't look so cheery for Jack Skellington, The Pumpkin King and spiritual head of Halloween Night. Though he's the best at what he does, Jack has, sad to relate, "grown so weary of the sound of screams" and is in fact in the throes of a serious fit of existential boredom.

While wandering around in spiritual despair, Jack literally stumbles into Christmastown and is blown away by how bright and shiny everything is, "There're children throwing snowballs here instead of throwing heads," he sings exultantly in another one of Elfman's 10 songs. "They're busy building toys and absolutely no one's dead."

Resentful that these clowns, so to speak, should have all the fun, Jack determines to take Christmas over from the fat round man he calls Sandy Claws and bring it all back home for the gang in Halloweentown to improve on. "This year," he declares, "Christmas will be ours."

Of course, as the intrepid Sally, the rag doll who loves Jack from afar, realizes, this won't be so easy to do. But Jack with the evil Dr. Finklestein (Sally's crabby creator) and the malicious trio of Lock, Shock and Barrel to do his bidding, is blind to the difficulties he has in store. Until …

Bringing this genially demented world to life meant solving two different but interlocking problems. First off, Burton's drawings had to be turned into three-dimensional figures, and that was been done brilliantly. "Nightmare's" crones, ghouls and grotesques—topped off by the ultimate incarnation of evil, the Oogie Boogie man (wonderfully served by Ken Page's jazzy phrasings)—are completely beyond description. And even if they weren't, it wouldn't be fair to ruin the fun: of having them pop up unexpectedly in their own disturbing, way.

The other problem was making everybody move. Given that each second of on-screen action involves 24 different frames, and possibly 24 separate character movements, the amount of painstaking planning and grinding work involved in this was daunting. To ensure a variety of expressions for Jack, for instance, 800 different replaceable heads were made. No wonder that at maximum efficiency, the "Nightmare" crew could turn out no more than 70 seconds of finished film per week.

What they did turn out, however, is so profligate with exotic images that it overflows with a demented kind of genius, taking stop-motion to places it's never been before. Prime mover Burton has written that "'Nightmare Before Christmas' is deeper in my heart than any other film," and those who are the tiniest bit twisted will find a similar place for it in theirs as well.

NEW STATESMAN & SOCIETY, 11/18/94, p. 30, Jonathan Romney

If the film weren't so much fun, *Tim Burton's The Nightmare Before Christmas* could be a test case for the status of movie authorship. Technically, it's only "Tim Burton's" in so far as it's co-produced by, and based on story and characters by the febrile Hollywood *wunderkind* behind *Beetlejuice* and *Edward Scissorhands*. His bedraggled nibs has clearly joined the fabled ranks of those few *auteurs* considered so heavyweight that they get to have their name above their title. (Why, even Mary Shelley had to wait 180 years to get her name on the marque.)

These things are never quite clear-cut, however. *Fellini's Roma*—fair enough; but what about the thousands of films released annually with "Stephen King's" before the title. Or *Roger Corman's Frankenstein Unbound*, apparently stitched together after a survey revealed that any film with the names "Roger Corman" and "Frankenstein" in the title would clean up (it didn't)? Half the time, the possessive simply works as bait for the audience's brand loyalty, the rest of the time, it has the same vague brand-name status as "Ripley's" in *Believe It or Not*. Only occasionally do you get something as no-nonsense as the forthcoming *Wes Craven's New Nightmare*, which really is about horror director Wes Craven having a new nightmare.

Tim Burton's The Nightmare Before Christmas—no better make that Henry Selick's *Tim Burton's The Nightmare Before Christmas*—doesn't actually start with Burton waking up, his Cure coiffure all tousled, on Yuletide morning, to find several million dollars worth of Batman merchandising stuffed into his stocking. But in a curious way, it offers as quintessential a distillation of Burton's ghoulish wit (one foot in the nursery, the other caught in the gallows noose) as the best of his "own" films. *Nightmare* is best described as "school of Burton" ("kindergarten", more accurately), with trusted collaborators Caroline Thompson and Michael McDowell providing the script, and Danny Elfman creating a typically flamboyant score, like Lionel Bart on bad acid. For all anyone can tell, director Selick may be the true visionary auteur at work here; but it's more probably that he's done a spectacular job of disappearing behind Burton's imprimatur and creating what we can only assume is the boss's true *Weltanschauung*. For all the world, *Nightmare* looks like the sort of puppet play that Beetlejuice would have enjoyed as a kid, or that Edward Scissorhands might have snipped into shape with his delicate digits.

Rather appropriately, *Nightmare* is a miracle of skewed timing. Released too early for Christmas and too late for Halloween, it also arrives in Britain a year after its US release (held up, apparently, by the distributor Buena Vista having its hands full marketing Disney's *Aladdin*). But it's rather nice to think of it as a tattered, disreputable relation to that film and *The Lion King*. For a start, where those heavyweight Disneys exude the unimpeachable confidence of computerised gloss, *Nightmare* is that anachronistic thing, a triumph of craft—each movement of its figures eked out by painstaking stop-motion animation where three-dimensional models still have to be moved by hand. At the risk of waxing too luddite, there *are* digital effects in it but mostly it has that old-fashioned, hand-cranked feel.

Best of all, *Nightmare* is a homely tale of unalloyed ineptitude. It's about what happens when Jack Skellington, the Pumpkin King of Halloweentown, decides that for once he and his creeping, gibbering subjects—vampires, ghouls, werewolves and sundry unclassifiable fiends—will go into the Christmas racket and liven things up. It starts when he inadvertently pays a visit to Christmastown, a realm populated by a mawkish race of simpering Enid Blyton pixies. Sentimental sap he may be, but he's still a denizen of the night, and Jack begins his campaign of spreading cheer by sending his champion trick-or-treaters Lock, Stock and Barrel to capture Santa.

Lock, Stock and Barrel are among the best things in the film, and an example of how tightly cuteness and malevolence go together in Burton's polymorphous-perverse playground—three juvenile imps, they wear skeletal masks that seem to duplicate their own faces, at the same time nastily echoing the hockey-masked killer from *Friday the Thirteenth*.

As a musical, *Nightmare* isn't much cop, and Elfman's score, for all its flamboyant eccentricity, is as little memorable as the recent crop of Disney soundtracks. Yet he does provide a rather nice singing voice of Jack, a sumptuously arch blend of Freddie Mercury and Rex Harrison.

But what really makes the film is the fact that there's too much going on in any one shot really to make sense. It's as if the makers knew they had one chance to go wild with all the rubber and wire and papier-maché, and everything had to move at once. What looks at moments like a set of sedately dark compositions modelled after Edward Gorey, has a way of suddenly exploding into a crazed Walpurgis of moveable gimcrackery. The film is more an exercise in exuberant craft than in truly wild humour, but things find their perfect pitch when the amorphous Day-Glo ghoul Oogie Boogie starts to shake his stuff (and more loathsomely, his contents) and the film takes off with a tremor of shimmying nastiness. It won't traumatise the kids as effectively as *Bambi*, but it's good.

NEW YORK, 11/1/93, p. 86, David Denby

The Nightmare Before Christmas is a lot less boring than Barry Levinson's *Toys*, but I have to admit that despite the charm of Danny Elfman's songs and the macabre wit of Tim Burton's characters, I occasionally nodded off. Animated constructed figures, even ones as wittily sculpted as these (the principal skeleton looks like a Giacometti), don't have the bizarre freedom of drawn characters.

NEW YORK POST, 10/13/93, p. 31, Michael Medved

Tim Burton's "The Nightmare Before Christmas" features 10 mediocre songs, an odd, unsatisfying plot, disturbing elements that make it unsuitable for small children—and a visual surface so richly textured and stunningly original that many moviegoers will overlook the film's shortcomings.

The mid-October release date is entirely appropriate for a movie that is more in tune with the mood of Halloween than it is with the spirit of Christmas. The story (originated 12 years ago by producer Burton and entrusted to his friend Henry Selick as director here) takes place almost entirely in "Halloweentown," where the local "Pumpkin King," Jack Skellington, has become bored with each year's ghoulish revels.

When this skeletal figure stumbles by accident into jolly Christmastown his reaction is the opposite of the Grinches and Scrooges of previous yuletide tales: Jack doesn't resent this merry holiday, he likes it so much that he wants to make it his own.

He orders his fellow Halloweenies to kidnap Santa Claus himself, so that they can now take charge of distributing toys on Christmas eve—with unexpected results.

Tim Burton is a self-confessed bad-movie fan (whose next project is a film biography of all-time worst director Ed Wood, Jr.), so it seems safe to say that his borrowing from 1964's "Santa Claus Conquers the Martians" is entirely conscious.

In that fondly remembered Golden Turkey (notorious as a 9-year-old Pia Zadora's film debut), another group of dour aliens kidnap Kris Kringle in order to capture the joy of the holiday—a plot device which generated no more excitement 30 years ago than it does this time around.

What makes "Nightmare" watchable is the remarkably sophisticated stop-motion animation—the manipulation of three-dimensional figures from one frame to the next to create the illusion of movement.

This venerable technique, employed in projects ranging from the original "King Kong" through the popular "California Raisins" commercials, here achieves new depth and vividness thanks to the 230 lavishly detailed, eerily lit environments in which the characters function.

The producers aptly describe the look of this fantasy world as "a cross between Dr. Seuss and Dr. Caligari," as Burton and associates once again indulge the fondness for German Expressionism so memorably demonstrated in their "Batman" films.

One of composer/songwriter Danny Elfman's dry, edgy, and unpleasant ditties (which play almost nonstop through the film) shows the Halloween people pondering the one "missing ingredient" in their cockeyed version of Christmas.

The movie never comes up with the obvious answer: this absent element involves the faith shared by several billion Christians that the seasonal celebration marks the birth of the Messiah.

Classic Christmas movies may not make this religious theme explicit, but they play upon it cunningly by projecting a generalized message of Peace-on-Earth, Good-Will-Toward-Men—at times even using the figure of Santa as a sort of jolly, secularized Christ-teacher.

"The Nightmare Before Christmas"—complete with a sexy rag doll (the voice of Catherine O'Hara), who regularly severs and reattaches her shapely limbs, and an evil scientist (William Hickey) who removes and divides his own brains—never adopts this atmosphere of good fellowship, or even hints at the sugarplum visions you'd expect in a PG holiday offering marketed to kids.

It is always brilliant and daring, but also hollow, cold and joyless. The missing ingredient in this Christmas celebration is an underlying sense of warmth.

NEWSDAY, 10/13/93, Part II/p. 57, Jack Mathews

Jack Skellington, the misguided hero of the animated musical "Tim Burton's The Nightmare Before Christmas," is a striking character, a tall fellow with the arms and legs of a praying mantis, a head like a baseball, eyes that are black holes and a snug, pin-striped tux topped off with a starched-bat bow tie.

The creativity and effort that went into the making of Jack the Pumpkin King and the other inhabitants of Halloweentown and Christmastown are staggering. Shot at a pace of about 70 seconds of film a week, with three-dimensional puppets moving about in elaborate three-dimensional sets, it provides depth, detail and a grace of movement never approached in stop-motion animation before.

And maybe never again.

As dazzling a technical feat as it is, "Nightmare" is not a very captivating movie. Its slight story, adapted from a Tim Burton poem about Halloween's attempted takeover of Christmas, plays like a darker version of "The Grinch Who Stole Christmas," with a tone so gleefully morbid it might have been written as an episode of "Tales From the Crypt."

Jack Skellington, Burton's melancholy hero, is wandering away from the tombstone-gray community of Halloweentown, "sick of the scaring, the terror, the fright ... tired of being something that goes bump in the night." After accidentally discovering the wintery wonderland of Christmastown, Jack decides to give Santa a year off, to turn his own goblins into elves and to make the rounds himself on Christmas Eve.

The movie sticks mostly to business in Halloweentown with Jack, his ghostly dog Zero, the baleful rag doll Sally, a two-faced mayor and an assortment of ghosts, ghouls, wolves and vampires. A pair of villains lurks there, too, the Evil Scientist, who bears an ominous resemblance to Howard the Duck, and Oogie Boogie, the bug-filled burlap monster who terrorizes a kidnaped Santa.

Oogie Boogie is in the tradition of the classic Disney villains, who likely provided the inspiration. Burton wrote his "Nightmare" poem while working as an animator trainee at Disney more than a decade ago, and he would not have been invited back to do "Nightmare" if he hadn't so successfully plied the dark in "Beetlejuice," "Edward Scissorhands" and his two "Batman" movies.

"Nightmare" bears little other resemblance to past Disney animated movies, and the studio is anxious to make that clear. It was produced under Disney's most adult label, Touchstone Pictures, and the studio's executives are quick to say the movie is not for small children.

Parents should take that advice to heart. To teenagers and adults, "Nightmare's" world is as unreal as any puppet show, but preschoolers, the group most vulnerable to its seductions, could be horrified by scenes showing other little children awakening on Christmas to gifts of snakes, snapping dolls and decaying heads.

Put it this way: "Nightmare" should not be seen by anyone who still believes in Santa.

So, who is the movie for? Well, it was a perfect choice for the New York Film Festival, where it had its world premiere Saturday. Director Henry Selick and his huge team of animators, artists, model makers, set designers and effects people created a magnificent piece of motion-picture art, and film lovers can savor its museum-quality images.

It will also hold spellbound film students and those interested in the process of stop-motion animation, a technique that has been used since the beginning of film to incorporate live action with models shot separately. But you haven't seen it done as well or for as long as in "Nightmare."

Whether it is a viable commercial alternative to classic "flat" animation, or the year's most expensive novelty item, will be answered as it is rolled out to theaters across the country.

Out there it will be seen not for its breakthrough technical wizardry, but for its story, and on that level it isn't much. It has a hero who isn't very likable, a dog who isn't very cute, music and songs by Danny Elfman that aren't very memorable and, worst of all, a romance (Sally, one of the weakest heroines in fairy-tale history, digs Jack) that has little feeling.

NEWSWEEK, 11/1/93, p. 72, David Ansen

You have to keep your eyes wide open while watching *Tim Burton's The Nightmare Before Christmas*. This giddily imaginative stop-motion animation musical is so stuffed with visual delights you won't want to blink. It's Burton's conceit that every holiday has its own country. In Halloweenland, where "Nightmare" is set, a dapper skeleton known as Jack Skellington (a.k.a. the Pumpkin King) presides over an industrious population of ghouls, gremlins and grinches devoted to scaring the bejesus out of children everywhere. But the pumpkin crown hangs heavy on Jack's spindly skull; he's grown weary of fright. There must be something more to life than bat wings and frog's breath soup. And indeed there is: accidentally trembling through a secret door he lands in snowy, happy Christmastown and his mind is blown. Though he can't quite grasp Christmas's arcane rituals, he knows he must possess it. Rushing home he proclaims his mission: this year Christmas will be brought to the world by the creators of Halloween! Jack means well, but oh, how he gets it wrong.

"Nightmare Before Christmas" means well, too, and thanks to the painstaking skill of director Henry Selick (working from Burton's concept), gets it deliciously right. Tightly written by Caroline Thompson ("Edward Scissorhands") and propelled by the clever lyrics and Kurt Weillish music of Danny Elfman, this cautionary fable (Be True to Your Ghoulish Self) may be a little too twisted for little kids, but anyone 8 or older will spot the friendly glint behind Jack's empty eye sockets. And anyone with any knowledge of the rigors of stop-motion (in which three-dimensional figures are shot frame by frame, requiring 24 infinitesimal changes of position to achieve one seamless second of live-action movement) will recognize that the movie takes this old technique to fluid new heights.

Among the inspired characters: the ominous beanbag-like monster Oogie Boogie, who performs a rousing Cab Calloway-style number. A rag-doll heroine named Sally, who matter-of-factly sews herself back together when she loses an arm or a leg. A duck-billed evil scientist in a wheelchair with a flip-top head allowing him to scratch his brains for inspiration. The list of marvels could go on and on, testament to the teeming imagination of Burton, who dreamed up this treat more than a decade ago as a young animator at Disney. Now, back at Disney, his magic toyshop of a movie has come to sweetly malignant life. Chances are, it will be around for many Halloweens to come.

SIGHT AND SOUND, 12/94, p. 53, Kim Newman

Under the direction of Jack Skellington the Pumpkin King, the people of Halloweentown spend the whole year planning the tricks and frights they unleash on the world each October 31st. After yet another successful Halloween, Jack feels trapped in a rut. Wandering into a forest and through a door in a tree, Jack comes, upon Christmastown, which is ruled by Santa Claus, and is struck by the notion of taking over this other holiday. Sally, a rag doll abused by her Frankensteinian creator, loves Jack and worries that his ambitions will lead to disaster. Jack despatches Lock, Shock and Barrel, Halloween's prominent trick or treaters, to kidnap Santa Claus, and orders

Sally's creator to make a team of reindeer to pull a coffin-shaped sleigh. The rest of the townsfolk try to make Christmas presents, but are unable to make anything that isn't scary. Lock, Shock and Barrel, after mistakenly kidnapping the Easter Bunny, snatch Santa and, against Jack's orders, turn him over to Oogie Boogie, a malevolent creature who is too extreme even for Halloweentown.

Sally whips up a fog on Christmas Eve to prevent Jack's sleigh taking off, but Jack's ghost dog Zero guides the team with his glowing nose. Jack distributes presents to children, who are terrified by various unleashed creatures, prompting the army to try to blast the Santa impersonator out of the sky. Realising his error, Jack returns to Halloweentown, defeats Oogie Boogie and releases Santa, who sets things right on Earth. Jack, having learned his lesson, admits that he reciprocates Sally's love.

This animated feature is billed as *Tim Burton's The Nightmare Before Christmas*, although co-producer Burton neither directed nor wrote it. He did, however, originate the characters and story, which date back to the period when he was an animator in the Disney galleys, toiling on *The Fox and the Hound* and discomforting the management with the shorts *Vincent* and *Frankenweenie*. It is to these underrated (and underseen) films that the current feature is closest in animation style and a gentle macabre feel, far more benevolent than that of such obvious influences as Charles Addams and Edward Gorey. Through the work of Henry Selick and writers Michael McDowell (of *Beetlejuice*) and Caroline Thompson (of *Edward Scissorhands*), this feels like another of Burton's veiled experiments in autobiography (cf. *Edward Scissorhands*, *Ed Wood*), as it deals with the frustrations of a one-note creator who wants to break out and do something else, only to learn that he should stick with what he does best.

Considered 'risky' because of its 'darkness', *Nightmare* is actually far less unsettling in its implications than such 'unproblematic' Disneys as *The Little Mermaid* (message: it's all right to be a bitch if you're cute and privileged) or *The Lion King* (alpha males have a divine right to rule the jungle). Halloweentown does have its genuine nasties, like the infantile Frankenstein who created Sally, and the bag-of-worms Boogie Oogie (seemingly related to the cartoon incarnation of Cab Calloway who once co-starred with Betty Boop). But most of its residents—from the two-faced mayor through sundry werewolves and vampires to uncategorisable Burton creations with all-round mouths and or too many eyes—are as mushy-hearted and eager to please as the wistful skull-on-a-stick Jack. Santa Claus, understandably cross for most of the film, seems far more a tyrant than the Pumpkin King and, regardless of the makers' stated or unconscious intentions, most audiences will derive far more pleasure from the hilarious gag sequences of Jack's gruesome Christmas presents terrorising a cross-section of multi-racial children than they will get from the perfunctory follow-up scenes showing Santa putting things right.

The grotesques in Burton's films are harmless and usually pathetically lovelorn, save for those bloated freaks (Penguin, Joker, Oogie Boogie) whose malevolence keeps the plot boiling. If his slight distance means that *Nightmare* seems like a film about rather than by Tim Burton, there are also signs that the collaborators, gaining the upper hand, have flattened out his tendency to all-over-the-show plotting and simplified his sometimes over-fussy designs. The streak of psychotic knowingness that will presumably overflow in the forthcoming Ed Wood is represented not only in an evocation of Ray Bradbury and *Mad Monster Party*, but in adapting the plot of the well-remembered cult disaster *Santa Claus Conquers The Martians*. Although a fragile conceit, *The Nightmare Before Christmas* is certainly more worthy of your attention than any Disney 2-D cartoon since *Basil—The Great Mouse Detective*, and has a rich, inventive score by Danny Elfman (who also provides Jack's singing voice), which shows just how inadequate the trite pseudo-Broadway muzak of Menken, Ashman and Rice has become.

VILLAGE VOICE, 10/19/93, p. 51, J. Hoberman

"The animation of objects upholds the truth of our childhood," the surrealist Jan Svankmajer has said, which is one reason his visceral puppet films are so disturbing. *Tim Burton's The Nightmare Before Christmas*, which opens today after a world premiere at the New York Film Festival, is not nearly as unsettling as Svankmajer's *Alice* (or the work of his American disciples, the Brothers Quay), but, an instant pop mythology for America's kids, it strikes a near perfect balance between nasty and cute.

Edgier than *Aladdin* but more human than Burton's Batman films, this stop-motion puppet opera—conceived by Burton, executed by Henry Selick, scored by Danny Elfman, and bankrolled by Disney—is inventive, witty, brilliantly designed, fantastically labor-intensive, and detailed well past the point of obsession. One would have to go back half a century to Disney's *Pinocchio* to find a Hollywood animated feature with an imaginary world so fully projected and densely populated.

The prodigal son returns: Burton, who unsuccessfully tried to promote the project when he was a Disney hand in the early '80s, has presented the studio with a bonanza of ancillary merchandise.

The Nightmare Before Christmas synthesizes an American gothic style out of Edward Gorey's spidery lines, Maurice Sendak's squatly affable demons, Charles Addams's borderline-schizo macabre gentility, and Burton's own wacky-pack expressionism. (Despite the deployment of such memorable grotesques as Pee-wee, Beetlejuice, and Catwoman, Burton is the master of current So*Caligarisme*—sets, costumes, and production design are the real stars of his movies.) As directed by Selick, a talented animator in his own right and Burton's onetime colleague at Disney, *Nightmare* seems the distillation of Burton's trademark vision, refined and miniaturized in somewhat the way that Marcel Duchamp made models of his most scandalous objects and kept them in a cute little valise. Even the requisite surging Elfman score which here includes a version of "Jingle Bells" evoking the worst winter of Weimar Germany—is appropriately scaled down, less Wagnerian than a pastice of Kurt Weill's declamative cabaret lieder.

Its premise rehearsed in the grotty Yuletide festivities of *Batman Returns, Nightmare* is almost a metaphor for itself. Jack Skellington, the Pumpkin King—the master of Halloween misrule, a long-legged cadaver with a marshmallow moon face and the spindly elegance of an arachnoid Fred Astaire—inadvertently finds himself in Christmastown, an amusingly hyperreal evocation of a Norman Rockwell greeting card (hysterically sparkling snow, lurid candy cottages, manic-ecstatic elves). Artist that he is, he plots to reinvent Christmas along more sinister lines.

The desecration begins when Jack strings colored lights around his electric chair and announces that "this year, Christmas will be ours." He's aided by an army of buglike creepy-crawlies worthy of Wladislaw Starewicz, swarming over the screen as spontaneous as doodles. (The most fetching has been stitched together by the town's resident mad scientist—a pasty-faced encephalitic duck in a motorized wheelchair—to suggest a beatnik ghoul girl along the zaftig lines of Carolyn Jones.) Soon, indescribable goblins are painting bloody bullet holes on wooden toys and sadistic trick-or-treaters are abusing Santa Claus as, guided by his ghostly Rudolph-substitute. Jack flies over the world distributing gift-wrapped shrunken heads and fungoid Christmas wreaths.

I don't know what the Reverend Donald Wildmon would make of this particular Walpurgisnacht. For me, the only questionable gag has Santa Claus trapped by Oogie Boogie, an amorphous green burlap monster unmistakably modeled on the rotoscoped Cab Calloway who used to harass Betty Boop in the early 1930s with his uncanny "jungle" jive. Although not nearly so aggressively tasteless as the ethnic vaudeville turns in the insufficiently appreciated, low-budget, part-animated 1980 Elfman opus *Forbidden Zone*, the spectacle of a blues-singing, crap-shooting Boogie Man preparing to deep-fry the personification of a White Christmas and eat him for dinner suggests a softer version of the black devil played by Wesley Snipes in *Demolition Man*.

On the other hand, this surge of unconscious material (a long-overdue eruption of rowdy Fleischerism in the antiseptic Disney universe) allows for one transcendently yucky effect—the revelation of just what's underneath the Boogie Man's sack. It's a moment worthy of Svankmajer. Even Santa squashes a bug.

Also reviewed in:
CHICAGO TRIBUNE, 10/22/93, Friday/p. C, Michael Wilmington
NEW YORK TIMES, 10/9/93, p. 13, Janet Maslin
VARIETY, 10/18/93, p. 49, Todd McCarthy
WASHINGTON POST, 10/22/93, p. C7, Richard Harrington
WASHINGTON POST, 10/22/93, Weekend/p. 48, Desson Howe

TIME INDEFINITE

A First Run Features release. *Producer:* Ross McElwee. *Director:* Ross McElwee. *Editor:* Ross McElwee. *Sound:* Ross McElwee. *Running time:* 117 minutes. *MPAA Rating:* Not Rated.

LOS ANGELES TIMES, 1/8/94, Calendar/p. 7, Peter Rainer

Ross McElwee is a documentarian of a very special sort. Although he's made movies about subjects like Cape Canaveral and the Berlin Wall, his flair is for the kind of self-examining "personal" film that, to the untutored eye, resembles a home movie. "Sherman's March," his surprise art-house success seven years ago, was made on the heels of a breakup with his girlfriend as he followed the route of Sherman's march on Atlanta. The film was engagingly desultory and sweet-spirited and became a cult hit.

The cult hasn't really gone to his head. "Time Indefinite" doesn't try to canonize McElwee's latest exploits. It simply follows his life in the recent past as he attends a family reunion in Charlotte, N.C., is married, and endures a series of unforeseen sorrows.

What starts out as a jaunty, dawdling jape becomes a kind of meditation on mortality. But McElwee doesn't make you wince at his seriousness. His bafflement at that is going on in his life is a genuine, unadorned response to tragedy; you don't feel as if he's exploiting his ill fortune. (For a self-documentarian like McElwee, that would have seemed really smarmy.) And there's an element of mystery in what he does. He keeps the camera going in his movies during all manner of events—from his meeting a blind date to accompanying his wife to the gynecologist.

He's aware, as his friend Charleen tells him, that he's using the camera as a way to deny reality, and yet for McElwee movie-making is also a way of *heightening* experience. (That's what makes him a true filmmaker.) He is rarely observed by us in this film—he exists primarily in voice-over narration—and yet he's the consciousness of everything that we see. "Time Indefinite" is a one-of-a-kind movie because McElwee himself seems one-of-a-kind.

NEW YORK POST, 5/12/93, p. 26, Jerry Tallmer

There is an old tradition, as Lucille, who had worked for his family for 30 years, reminds Ross McElwee late in the film, that a groom does not look at his bride in advance on the day of the wedding.

McElwee sure ignores that one, and most other social rules, in his "Time Indefinite." On his wedding day to the lovely Marilyn, he pursues her and everybody else, camera on shoulder, until she pleads: "No, Ross, no." But he "negotiates for 10 minutes more of filming"—Marilyn dying her hair—and only then does he finally—*finally*—turn the camera over to a buddy and throw on some clothes for the ceremony.

It was the same at Charlotte City Hall, where Marilyn Levine from Boston had to tell a startled marriage-license clerk: "Don't mind him, he does this all the time." The only time Ross ever left his camera behind was during their honeymoon in Italy, but he picked it up again in time to move in (discreetly) on Marilyn spread-eagled before the gynecologist who's saying. "Sorry, that's your right ovary, tender there, seems normal."

Those who know McElwee from his "Sherman's March" or his and Marilyn's "Something to Do With a Wall" will also know that what makes his movies so compelling is what Graham Greene called the human factor. Love and death are so intertwined by now in so much art, and so much life, as to become banalities. I write about them almost every day. But McElwee, with his extraordinary, long-pursued home documentaries, to coin a term, gives love and death new flesh, new luster, a new meaning that is all the more universal for being so private and so specific.

"Time Indefinite" mixes McElwee's found-in-an-attic memories of his parents when golden young with the Protestant-ethic severity of his surgeon father years later, surrounded by a large and active family sustained by the faithful attentions of Lucille and her handyman husband Melvin, themselves to go proudly before McElwee's camera at their 50th anniversary.

In the midst of life ... Marilyn has a miscarriage on New Year's Eve; five days later McElwee's brother falls over on the seat of his car, dead, with never a sign of heart trouble. Marilyn, recovered, goes off to make a film. Ross, not recovered, flies here and there with his camera and his voices, until he finds himself dropping in on his old friend Charleen, a sage and sexy mother figure, herself having lived through the laughter and tragedy of a young ex-husband who immolated himself in the house they had once built together.

"The image that keeps coming to me," says the filmmaker, "is the fish that little boy caught"—a poor little open-mouthed fish flopping its life away on a North Carolina pier. And there is—be warned—an even more gruesome image later: a huge tumor that McElwee's brother Tom has removed from the breast of a woman who took two years to face up to its reality.

But "Time Indefinite" is the opposite of a gruesome or depressing movie. It is a paean to the wonder of life, the joy of life—life born anew as Adrian when Marylyn gets pregnant again, Adrian the infant who in his father's footage looks (Marilyn begrudgingly thinks, and she's right) like a gerbil.

I'll tell you who would have loved this movie. In a sense he wrote it. His name is William Faulkner.

NEWSDAY, 5/12/93, Part II/p. 53, John Anderson

"Will you stop??!!" one of Ross McElwee's subjects pleads during a particularly personal moment. "This is not art! This is life! ..." But this is also precisely the point. For McElwee, life doesn't exist outside the rim of a viewfinder.

McElwee charmed a lot of audiences and critics with his 1986 film, "Sherman's March," his search-by-celluloid for romance in the South. But in that film diary he also seemed inveterately smug, more than willing to let his subjects humiliate themselves in a variety of ways while affecting a bemused sensitivity about the whole thing. In his new film, "Time Indefinite," he uses the same basic techniques, interviewing family and friends, gleaning from them a portrait of his family, and occasionally letting them stick foot in mouth. But as his life comes apart piece by piece, and death becomes a preoccupation, his superciliousness dissolves in a way that almost makes him a sympathetic character.

There's no getting around the fact that McElwee can get people to relax on camera, and say, and do just about anything which may be because they've never seen his face without a camera stuck in it. And as much as McElwee's life as film, the success or failure of his shooting depends on his emotional state. His doctor father (whom we see in various bits of film, including an entirely separate film his son made about him), gives off a "Freudian force field," he says, and we see it short-circuit his filming; at his southern family's annual reunion in North Carolina, McElwee, the single black sheep from Boston, encounters all sorts of mechanical difficulties, which seem directly connected to the fact that he's announcing his engagement.

When his father asks to use McElwee's camera, there's a sense of familial binding that goes far beyond what such a simple act should represent, but "Time Indefinite" is as much about what film is about—its intrusiveness, its omnipresence, and the strange ways people behave when they know they're on camera—as it is a portrait of McElwee or his family and their times.

"Time Indefinite" can't help but be an extremely personal film, but to McElwee's credit we care. The loss of certain family members is deeply felt as is his new wife's, Marilyn Levine, medical calamity. The film itself assumes his grief; perspectives change, the camera lingers longer on certain subjects and scenes. If someone doesn't appear onscreen, it's as if they never existed; Marilyn, in fact, disappears for a lengthy stretch of the film during a particularly painful time, and the feeling one gets about her is close to death.

Birth, death, marriage, they're all part of the fabric of "Time Indefinite," which is held together in large part by McElwee's dryly humorous narration, and the occasionally preposterous places he and his camera find themselves. His wife's gynecological examination, for instance. Only occasionally does someone actually object to his filming, and when they do there's a shared sense of voyeurism between director and audience that's not entirely pleasant but, in its way, is very real.

VILLAGE VOICE, 5/18/93, p. 64, Alyssa Katz

Ross McElwee removes his movie camera from its usual perch on his shoulder at the beginning of *Time Indefinite* and hands it to his father, who suddenly and with strange enthusiasm wants to shoot back after years of being an elusive subject in his son's diary films. The first time McElwee turned his camera on his family, in *Backyard* (1981), he emerged with a prodigal son's piercing take on the South; now creeping into his forties, McElwee's still trying to make sense of his family and mortality as he stands uneasily on the cusp of becoming a father himself.

His method relies on contrivances—shooting relentlessly to catch life's profound little incidents; editing them into a fine web of motifs; taking advantage of hindsight to script wryly observant, gently mocking, narration—but hell, the thing works. In *Sherman's March*, his similarly pseudo-verité magnum opus, McElwee diffidently lugged his camera around on a quest for love. This time, love is the only certainty while "things aren't acting like they're supposed to act," as his old friend Charleen grimly observes before hauling out a leaky plastic bag containing the ashes of her ex-lover. McElwee's finally found a partner who appreciates his obsessions: Marilyn Levine, an aptly photogenic filmmaker, who patiently lies in the stirrups while her gynecologist sends Ross into a panic by proclaiming she's "all set for baby city."

McElwee self-consciously conflates death and his impending fatherhood, shooting roll after roll at a Mexican children's cemetery, squeamishly filming his marital blood test, lingering on the image of a breast rotted from untreated cancer. Meditating on a fish gasping atop a pier, he cringes at the thought that if he ever taught his child to fish he'd have to choose a method of extermination—quick death by stomping or slow torture in a bucket of fresh water.

Still, McElwee is only sporadically precious and sometimes is devastatingly insightful in his anxieties. He heads warily into the Apocalypse with the assurance that his camera will be there to shield him.

Also reviewed in:
CHICAGO TRIBUNE, 10/29/93, Friday/p. K, John Petrakis
NEW YORK TIMES, 5/12/93, p. C13, Stephen Holden
VARIETY, 6/28/93, p. 23, Paul Lenti
WASHINGTON POST, 5/7/93, p. B7, Rita Kempley
WASHINGTON POST, 5/7/93, Weekend/p. 50, Desson Howe

TITO AND ME

A Kino International release of a Tramontana (Belgrade), Terra (NoviSad), and Magda Productions (Paris) film. *Producer:* Goran Markovic, Zoran Masirevic, Michel Mavros, and Zoran Tasic. *Director:* Goran Markovic. *Screenplay (Serbo-Croatian with English subtitles):* Goran Markovic. *Director of Photography:* Racoslav Vladic. *Editor:* Snezana Ivanovic. *Music:* Zoran Simjanovic. *Costumes:* Boris Caksiran. *Running time:* 110 minutes. *MPAA Rating:* Not Rated.

CAST: Dimitrie Vojnov (Zoran); Lazar Ristovski (Raja); Anica Dobra (Zoran's Mother); Predrag Manojlovic (Zoran's Father); Ljiljana Dragutinovic (Zoran's Aunt); Bogdan Diklic (Zoran's Uncle); Olivera Markovic (The Grandmother); Rade Markovic (The Grandfather); Vesna Trivalic (The Instructor); Voja Brajovic (Marshall Tito).

LOS ANGELES TIMES, 9/24/93, Calendar/p. 15, Kenneth Turan

The year is 1954. Josip Broz Tito is the unchallenged ruler of Yugoslavia, marshal, prime minister and president all in one. Zoran is a somber and phlegmatic 10-year-old boy whose idea of a good time is eating the plaster off the walls of his Belgrade apartment. Talk about your odd couples.

Zoran mimics the great man's gestures in newsreels and gets up in the middle of the night to ensure a good spot when the maximum leader parades by. The protagonist of writer-director Goran Markovic's slyly autobiographical "Tito and Me" even daydreams about Tito who appears to the boy in visions whenever he is in trouble. Which is often.

Wacky, ironic and always light on its feet, "Tito and Me" turns out to be the surprise of the season, an engaging and amusing farce about the time when the maximum leader's fierce cult of personality kept his country together. One of the last films to be shot in Yugoslavia that has since fallen apart, it also makes some quiet points about what made the good old days so bad.

"Tito" is narrated in clever voice-over by young Zoran (Dimitrie Vojnov), a moon-faced and melancholy Slavic version of the Pillsbury doughboy. Living with his ballerina mother and musician father in a small apartment shared with an aunt and uncle, grandmother and "my hideous cousin Svetlana," Zoran casts a droll eye over the never-ending foibles of grown-ups.

"Love is the most complicated thing in the world," he observes with deadpan seriousness of his parents' wranglings. "It causes a variety of insoluble problems for adults." No sooner does he say this, however, than Zoran himself falls in love, with a string-bean orphan named Jasna who is almost twice his height.

Desperate to accompany Jasna and other politically motivated youths on a two-week ""March around Tito's Homeland," Zoran throws himself into an essay contest on "Do You Love Marshall Tito and Why." To his parents' mixed pride and horror, his epic poem proclaiming "the grass sees Him when it grows, the swallows sing only for Him" wins the prize. So, wearing lederhosen and a Tyrolean hat, Zoran dutifully sets off on a trip for which the word misadventure is way too mild.

Director Markovic, none of whose eight previous films have had a theatrical release in this country, has a gift for this kind of comic satire, enlivening the proceedings with both a jaunty sound-track (by Zoran Simjanovic) and lots of newsreel footage of the real Tito playing the drums in North Africa to tossing darts and talking to parrots.

Markovic also has the benefit of a cast, including former wife Anica Dobra as Zoran's mother and his own parents, Olivera and Rade Markovic, as the boy's grandparents, who perfectly understand the wry effects he is after.

Especially amusing as well are Lazar Ristovski as the zealous Comrade Raja, the leader of the trek, and Vesna Trivalic as Zoran's misty-eyed teacher. As for the smiling boy himself, non-professional Vojnov has such a natural comic dignity it is impossible to see him trudge purposefully through the indignities of his life without being charmed and charmed again. The best kind of personal filmmaking, "Tito and Me" is the final gentle grace note from a country that won't be smiling for some time to come.

NEW YORK POST, 8/18/93, p. 26, Jerry Tallmer

Yugoslavia—or the former Yugoslavia—is a tortured, wrecked ex-country, but a few fine movies keep coming out of there from time to time. Six years ago we had Jovan Acin's stunning "Hey Babu Riba," and now we have the somewhat less subtle but nearly as, good and funny "Tito and Me," written and directed by Goran Markovic.

Both these films, by no coincidence, give us the stubborn irreverent humors of non-conforming youth under the heel of a closed, dogmatic, hero-headed regime.

The Tito of "Tito and Me" is both the real one in the head of 10-year-old Zoran. We see the real one in sepia newsreel footage, large, strong-jawed, smiling, on horseback, addressing enormous crowds, at hunt, playing with his parakeets, releasing doves, greeting Haile Selassie, incongruously dancing Watusi-style with a delegation from Africa; and we see the imaginary one as Zoran sees him, also smiling but weirdly blond and actorish, giving directions and advice by divine gesture.

Our Zoran, the director has told us is, was once Goran Markovic himself, one of those bright plump little misfits—"rounded" the kid's family calls him, though a batty uncle and aunt also call him "degenerate"—who somehow keep popping up in autobiographical movies from whatever country.

The family is all packed warmingly into one small flat—mama and papa, uncle, aunt, and "hideous cousin Svetlana," a cute tiny fink, Zoran's papa is a musician, pretty mama is a dancer; when her ballet troupe dances for Tito himself, the great man rewards them with fresh-killed game, a bloody deer's head in the bathtub that sends the aunt screaming bonkers.

In school, the teacher goes on and on about Tito's early poverty; he didn't even have a pair of pants. He did however have a horse named Pootko.

As if there weren't trouble enough, Zoran (Dimitrie Vojnov), who may remind you of the lad in "My Life as a Dog," falls in love with a girl older and taller than he, sort of a beanpole in braids. She's also humorless; she's also a true believer, about to set out on a cross-country

"March Around Tito's Homeland" with a pack of other teen-age Comrade Pioneers under the command of a grown-up apparatchik and nut case named Raja, the kind of shouter who slaps the food out of Zoran's hands as an instruction in dieting.

The rest of the film is Zoran's adventures and misadventures on The Long March, a good bit of it having to do with a rash the kid develops on a particular portion of his anatomy. For sins he did not know he committed, the boy is cruelly, ludicrously, brought to trial.

Misadventures also befall the clumsy apparatchik, who at one point decides in an old castle to "educate" the kids on the non-existence of ghosts by flapping around banshee-like as one himself. In the resultant chaos, a priceless collection of armor is smashed to smithereens.

Ultimately, Raja the petty tyrant (Lazar Ristovski) is smashed the same way. Also ultimately, there is a presentation at court so to speak, to Marshal Tito. I leave you to learn how Zoran copes with that, and to connect, as I did, the final moments of this film to the finale of a movie called "On the Waterfront." Actually, Lee J. Cobb would have made a perfect Tito.

NEWSDAY, 8/18/93, Part II/p. 53, John Anderson

A comedy from Yugoslavia? It sounds too much like a bad joke. And yet Goran Markovic's "Tito and Me," a remarkable and very pointed comedy, retains its considerable sweetness and humor, even if the inherent sadness and irony are inescapable.

Markovic, a Serb who has been a leading light of Yugoslav filmmaking since the '70s, blames today's civil war in Bosnia directly on Marshal Tito, the Communist dictator who ruled the country for decades, and who, in Markovic's view, left the nation unprepared for anything but strife after his death in 1980. In Zoran, played by the precocious and wryly stoic 10-year-old Dimitrie Vojnov, he has created a short, round embodiment of blind ethnocentrism, hero worship, political opportunism and, by the end, when Zoran begins to think independently, the kind of self-realization Markovic obviously believes might have saved his country. And he's made a film that's endearing, funny and smart.

"Tito and Me," which Markovic began shooting in Serbia four days after the civil war began in 1991, is set in 1954, when the cult of Tito was probably at its peak. Zoran, whose observations are as highly articulate as they are drily funny, lives in a crowded Belgrade apartment with his ballerina mother (Anica Dobra) and musician father (Predrag Manojlovic), who generally agree with the regime; his disapproving aunt and uncle (Ljilana Dragutinovic and Bogdan Diklic), who don't; his long-suffering grandmother (Olivera Markovic, the director's mother), and his bratty cousin Svetlana, who refers to him as a "fat degenerate."

Zoran is rather plump—"rounded," his grandmother says—and his appetite is appalling. At one point, he takes to eating the wall; he uses a spoon to secretly scrape plaster out a small hole, which drives his uncle, who can't understand what's happening, to distraction. So does Zoran's enthusiasm for Tito, who, except for a drab orphan girl named Jasna, is closest to Zoran's heart. When Jasna announces she'll soon be leaving on a "March Around Tito's Homeland," Zoran enters, and wins, a citywide essay contest—in his poetic entry, he claims he loves Tito more than his mother and father—so he can go along, too.

At this point, Markovic really gets rolling. The young "comrades pioneers" are led by the petty bureaucrat Raja (Lazar Ristovski), who takes an immediate dislike to Zoran (because of his artist parents). Raja's political ardor has little effect on Zoran, who looks like a squat plutocrat and is an egoist of the first rank. His innocent mistakes, usually made because he's looking out for himself, enrage Raja, but Zoran is too phlegmatic to care, which enrages Raja further. The outcome is almost too severe for the tone, but it's Markovic reminding us of where and what we're looking at. Dimitrie Vojnov is a wonderfully comic figure. And his sweet face makes him a particularly haunting choice to play Markovic's hero, representing, as he does, their common, vanished nation.

VILLAGE VOICE, 8/24/93, p. 53, Georgia Brown

Cuter than Woody's aging nerd [the reference is to *Manhattan Murder Mystery*] is the adorable little man in *Tito and Me*, a charming autobiographical coming-of-age comedy by veteran Yugoslavian director Goran Markovic. The chunky 10-year-old Zoran (Dimitrie Vojnov) is shown growing up in the mid '50s in a Belgrade apartment shared, not very peacefully, with his mother, father, grandmother, aunt and uncle, as well as his "horrible cousin," Svetlana. The first part of Markovic's saga takes a harsh but comic look at family squabbles, where civil war rages between his artist parents as "dirty communists" and his relatives as "filthy capitalists." The latter view Zoran as a deviant, especially when spied eating plaster from the walls. But when he starts a scrapbook on Tito, even his own parents grow concerned.

Markovic's second act follows Zoran into the outside world of school, love, and national politics. On the verge of puberty, he's smitten with Jasna, a string-bean orphan who's found her own substitute father in the head of state, President-for-Life Marshal Tito. Under Jasna's spell, Zoran is inspired to win an essay contest on the subject, "Why I Love Comrade Tito." ("I love Tito more than Mom and Dad," goes the treacherous winning line.) The prize: "A Trip Around Tito's Homeland" with Jasna and other eager young patriots.

Shorter and chubbier than the other hikers, Zoran finds his patriotism tested on the march. (Actually, the march is a bit long for viewers too.) Then he develops a nasty rash on his tush. (The word buttocks is deemed too insulting to use on a Tito-directed expedition.) His realism quickly makes him a mortal enemy of the gung-ho leader, Raja (Lazar Ristovski), and the ambitious Jasna begins pulling away. When Zoran finally meets the heavily made-up Tito at the marshal's birthday party, he finds the cakes more appealing.

Also reviewed in:
CHICAGO TRIBUNE, 2/25/94, Friday/p. J, John Petrakis
NEW YORK TIMES, 8/18/93, p. C18, Vincent Canby
NEW YORKER, 9/6/93, p. 110, Anthony Lane
VARIETY, 10/5/92, p. 63, Peter Besas
WASHINGTON POST, 2/11/94, p. B7, Richard Harrington

TOKYO DECADENCE

A Northern Arts Entertainment release of a Melsat Inc. JVD Co. Ltd. production. *Executive Producer:* Eiten Taga. *Producer:* Yoshitaka Suzuki, Tadanobu Hirao, and Yosuke Nagata. *Director:* Ryu Murakami. *Screenplay (Japanese with English subtitles):* Ryu Murakami. *Based on the novel "Topaz" by:* Ryu Murakami. *Director of Photography:* Tadashi Aoki. *Editor:* Kazuki Katashima. *Sound:* Masaru Usui. *Costumes:* Sebian. *Running time:* 112 minutes. *MPAA Rating:* Not Rated.

CAST: Miho Nikaido (Ai); Tenmei Kano (Ishioka); Yayoi Kusama (Fortuneteller); Sayoko Amano (Saki); Chie Sema (Crazy Woman).

LOS ANGELES TIMES, 4/30/93, Calendar/p. 8, Kevin Thomas

Ryu Murakami's luminous "Tokyo Decadence," a film of power and astonishment, as serious as it is kinky, probes the daily existence of Ai (Miho Nikaido), a demure, 22-year-old-call girl, to discover what her life reveals about contemporary Japan.

Murakami, who juxtaposes degradation with moments of unexpected humor and tenderness, manages to be clinical without being graphic, thus avoiding pornography; but then he's more interested in Ai's soul than her body, for all that he reveals of it, in the first place. Imagine Robert Bresson, France's austere poet of the spirit, making a film about a contemporary prostitute, and you get some idea of what this film is like.

Ai's life is lived almost entirely in expensive but impersonal hotel rooms, apartments and restaurants in Tokyo's skyscraper canyons. She works for a call service where there are literally no holds barred: anything goes as long as the client is willing to pay for it. When Ai flees a confessed necrophiliac who's come close to strangling her, her employer, with polite firmness, tells her not to leave a session again.

It would seem that the service's clientele is composed entirely of drugged-out sadists and masochists, whose prolonged fantasy sessions are presented with matter-of-fact realism. In leaving us without any doubt about what goes on—or, most importantly, why it does—Murakami makes us wonder just how long Ai, for all her innate dignity, can survive without becoming hopelessly degraded. She is armed only with a fortuneteller's laughable advice: Place a telephone directory under the TV, don't go to museums in the eastern part of the city and always wear a ring with a pink stone. Worse yet, she has fallen in love with a TV newscaster, apparently a onetime client, and pines for him.

"Tokyo Decadence" is a classic instance of perceiving the universal in the particular, even if Murakami, as he has stated, wants us first of all to see that for the Japanese, sex and drugs is as much a matter of ritual as is the traditional tea ceremony. Yet surely Japanese men are not alone in working out their anger toward liberated women in fantasy sex.

There's the man who tells Ai that, in being willing to submit to being bound and gagged, she's the only hope for Japan at a time when, in his view, Japanese women are concerned only with marrying for money. Then there's the man compelled to fantasize that all Japanese career women are starved for sex.

Ai's crucial encounter, however, is not with a man but with Saki (Sayako Amano), a beautiful dominatrix who has amassed a fortune, yet is driven to epic-scale drug excesses, much like Harvey Keitel in "Bad Lieutenant." "Japan is wealthy, but it's wealth without pride," she observes. "That's why so many men are masochists."

Ai takes her leave of Saki armed with a "magic pill," probably a powerful hallucinogen, which propels her into an amazing odyssey of self-discovery with which the film concludes and which recalls Richard Gere's quest for redemption at the end of "American Gigolo." Pitched ambiguously between fantasy and reality, this long and beautifully sustained bravura sequence, which involves a crucial meeting with a gaudily demented onetime opera singer (Chie Sema) is far more daring than any of Murakami's depictions of sex.

"Tokyo Decadence" (Times-rated Mature for sex and some nudity) is likely to stay with you long after the theater lights come up.

NEW YORK POST, 7/30/93, p. 33, Jerry Tallmer

All my life I've wanted to attend an illustrated lesson in S-M; haven't you.

Here's your chance. It's called—I mean these people don't fool around—"Tokyo Decadence." It's all about this girl named Ai, very pretty, 22 years old, a social worker, carries a beeper to summon her to her other profession, which is mostly conducted in hotel rooms.

In any one such room she's apt to have to spend a couple of hours in and out of black S-M lingerie trying to gratify a businessman who wants her to have intercourse (of a sort) with a picture window, 20 floors above the street, while moaning and moving "like a horny businesswoman." Then he wants to bring his wife into the act.

In another room, the client is a very weird cackling giggling pop-eyed young creep who insists on having Ai and another call girl strangle him to orgastic death. Then he comes to life again.

In yet another, the client wants to strangle Ai to death, or approximate death, before a screen of Mt. Fuji, where the suicides go to jump.

In another, something so horrible has happened to a girl already on the scene that Ai turns tail and runs. "Please don't leave during a session again," the madam of the "Girls' Club" admonishes her.

Then there's Saki (Sayoko Amano), the good-looking dominatrix who first puts a client on hands and knees through his degrading paces, and then turns her tenderer attentions to co-worker Ai.

Ai's problem—one of them—is that she feels she has "no talent." A fortune teller has given her some unique advice. "First, place a telephone book under your pillow. Second, don't go to an art museum in the east. Third, find a pink stone and make a ring of it."

The obsession over this pink-stoned ring occupies much of a film that ends with Ai (Miho Nikaido) wandering around the outskirts of Tokyo in a fugue state, disintegrating all to pieces. Not one thing in the picture looks real.

Director Ryu Murakaml, described by press release as "one of Japan's literary giants," couldn't decide whether "Tokyo Decadence" wanted to be an art movie or a porno movie. As a result, it is neither. But I want to tell you, watching a pseudo-dirty Japanese movie is not the most stimulating activity at, as fell to my lot, 11 o'clock in the morning.

NEWSDAY, 7/30/93, Part II/p. 77, Gene Seymour

At the very least, "Tokyo Decadence" may sate the bloodthirsty patriots who believe the Japanese business elite don't get trashed sufficiently in the filmed version of "Rising Sun." The film was written and directed by Ryu Murakami, one of Japan's most prolific and best-selling novelists, and he conducts this harrowing tour of kinky sex among his nation's rich and powerful with a fascinating mixture of glee and bile.

Murakami's Candide in this sordid tale of lust, avarice and the search for grace is Ai (Miho Nikaido), a sweet-natured young woman whose comportment suggests a schoolteacher rather than the S&M sex toy she is. The old question—"What's a nice girl like you doing in a business like this?"—seems more than appropriate to ask Ai, especially when she's forced to perform unspeakable and degrading acts by well-heeled gargoyles like the tycoon who snorts cocaine off Xavier Cugat CD covers while forcing her to gyrate for hours, scantily clad, against a skyscraper window.

Other job-related encounters include a giggling, jibbering masochist who asks to be strangled by Ai and a colleague, dies and then comes back to life. Then there's the beast who wants her to pretend she's dying of strangulation while he "rapes" her beneath a slide of Mount Fuji. With S&M as elaborately detailed as this, you tend to wonder after a while whether what you're watching is satire or documentary. Or whether you should laugh or flinch. Murakami strides the tightrope of indulgence and control so nicely that you ultimately end up admiring his ribald audacity.

Somewhat clumsily, he weaves in a subplot about Ai's fruitless search for a client, a celebrated artist, that she's fallen for. When, in a drug-induced daze, she searches for him in a ritzy neighborhood, it is as if Murakami suddenly stopped paying homage to Bunuel and decided to parody Antonioni.

Overall, "Tokyo Decadence" has the odd appeal of one, of those fetish objects you see in an exotica store window.

VILLAGE VOICE, 8/3/93, p. 60, Devon Jackson

When you see a film as interesting as *Tokyo Decadence*, and you later find out that its writer-director, Ryu Murakami, enjoys a kind of Stephen King-size success as a novelist in Japan, it may make you wonder: Is the film as fine as it seems? But in fact, while *Decadence* (Murakami's fourth film, based on his bestseller *Topaz*) may not be as intense as, say, *In the Realm of the Senses*, it easily transcends other novelists' auteurist flings.

Murakami maintains a distance, alternatingly impassive and pornographic, from his central character, the Meursault-like Ai, a naive young call girl who shruggingly acquiesces to the bizarre fantasies of her businessmen clients. Having so much "wealth without pride," these '90s Japanese men find release for their anxiety not in the ritual of the tea ceremony but in the liturgy of s&m.

Decadence paints a beautifully lit, night blue glass-tower universe of lip-synching crackhead dominatrices and men who want to be strangled into priapism. It's as if David Lynch had been given the task of updating Ozu's *Tokyo Story*. When, just as the freakish surreality and blasé eroticism begin to merge, Murakami sends Ai off on a quest for personal, Sirkian redemption.

Decadence may take itself as seriously as an Antonioni film, and might leave you wondering about all those literarily rich details (were they just macguffins?), but it has that off-kilter humor that made Fassbinder so endearing.

Also reviewed in:
NEW YORK TIMES, 7/30/93, p. C12, Stephen Holden
VARIETY, 9/7/92, p. 50, Derek Elley
WASHINGTON POST, 10/18/93, p. D7, Hal Hinson

TOM AND JERRY—THE MOVIE

A Miramax Films release of a Live Entertainment and Turner Entertainment Company in association with WMG presentation of a Film Roman production. *Executive Producer:* Roger Mayer, Jack Petrik, Hans Brockman, and Justin Ackerman. *Producer:* Phil Roman. *Director:* Phil Roman. *Live Action Director:* Robert Fisher, Jr. *Animation Director:* Dale L. Baer. *Screenplay:* Dennis Marks. *Based on characters created by:* William Hanna and Joseph Barbera. *Editor:* Julie Ann Gustafson. *Music:* Henry Mancini. *Music Editor:* Stephen A. Hope. *Choreographer:* Lori Eastside. *Sound:* Gordon Hunt and (music) Alan Snelling. *Sound Editor:* Tom Syslo and Thomas Jaeger. *Casting:* Janet Hirshenson, Jane Jenkins, and Roger Mussenden. *Art Director:* Michael Peraza, Jr. and Michael Humphries. *Running time:* 80 minutes. *MPAA Rating:* G.

VOICES: Richard Kind (Tom); Dana Hill (Jerry); Anndi McAfee (Robyn); Charlotte Rae (Aunt Figg); Tony Jay (Lickboot); Rip Taylor (Captain Kiddie); Henry Gibson (Applecheek); Michael Bell (Ferdinand/Straycatcher); Ed Gilbert (Puggsy/Daddy Starling); David L. Lander (Frankie da Flea); Howard Morris (Squawk); Sydney Lassick (Straycatcher); Raymond McLeod (Alleycat/Bulldog); Mitchell D. Moore and Scott Wojahn (Alleycats); Tino Insana (Patrolman); Don Messick (Droopy); B.J. Ward (Woman's Voice); Greg Burson (Man's Voice).

LOS ANGELES TIMES, 7/30/93, Calendar/p. 2, Charles Solomon

"Tom and Jerry—The Movie" feels like "Tom and Jerry—The Rerun," as every element in the film seems to have been borrowed from some other animated feature.

The title duo is taken from the Oscar-winning cartoon series Bill Hanna and Joe Barbera directed at MGM from 1940 to 1958. All that's missing is the polished animation, razor-sharp timing and slapstick humor that made the cat-and-mouse team so popular. In their place is a formulaic story about s little girl finding her missing father with same help from her animal friends.

Tom and Jerry are left homeless when their owners move out and their old home is razed. After getting heavy-handed lessons in the value of friendship from Puggsy (voice by Edmund Gilbert), a goody two-paws street dog, and a gang of nasty alley cats, the pair meet Robyn (Anndi Mc-Afee), a little girl fleeing her nasty guardian, Aunt Figg (Charlotte Rae), to search for her missing explorer/gazillionairre father. A series of stock adventures bring them together—to no one's surprise.

Parents who feel obligated to sit through "Tom and Jerry" with their kids can pass the time by noting what's been taken from where. The design of Aunt Figg is copied from Ursula in "The Little Mermaid," but she acts like Madame Medusa in "The Rescuers." Puggsy seems to have walked in from Don Bluth's "All Dogs Go to Heaven": amusement park owner Captain Kiddie (Rip Taylor) has a hand puppet who makes sarcastic comments like Iago in "Aladdin." Robyn is a composite of Penny in "Rescuers" and every other spunky cartoon girl who's appeared on the screen in recent decades.

For the first time in their 53-year career, the pantomime characters of Tom and Jerry talk (Richard Kind and Dana Hill, respectively); they also sing some strikingly unoriginal songs. There's one about friendship, one about Robyn missing her father, one for Aunt Figg about loving money and more—all with banal, cat-and-doggerel lyrics by Leslie Bricusse. Director Phil Roman robs the minimal physical comedy of its punch by pacing everything too evenly. The animation remains at the level of a television special.

Like hospital food, "Tom and Jerry" (MPGA rated: G) contains nothing that could be construed as harmful, but its bland, pedestrian fare to offer a child. If the original Tom and Jerry had been this uninspired, the series would have ended with the first cartoon.

NEW YORK POST, 7/30/93, p. 32, Michael Medved

The only features that "Tom and Jerry—The Movie" shares with the old cartoons that allegedly "inspired" it are the names of the main characters.

Fans of the original Tom and Jerry (who made their debut in 1940 and then appeared in more than 100 fondly remembered MGM shorts) will recall a determined, tough-guy cat (Tom) endlessly chasing a clever little mouse (Jerry), and endlessly frustrated in his pursuit.

In the new movie these two implacable foes are turned into (gag!) "best friends"—a disastrous decision that kills the potential appeal for this movie from the very beginning. It's the sort of sacrilege that might take Captain Ahab and Moby Dick or Dracula and Van Helsing—or even Road Runner and Wile E. Coyote—and force them to patch up their differences and work together. I'm sorry, guys, but Tom and Jerry as pals and partners just don't make it.

Even worse, the world's most celebrated cat-and-mouse duo, who managed perfectly well for more than 50 years without saying a word, here are asked to talk and sing for the first time ever. Hearing their cutie-pie voices (provided by child star Dana Hill, and Richard Kind of "Mad About You") is a perpetually jarring and annoying experience, made all the more unpleasant by the idiotic lines (and lyrics) they're asked to pronounce.

This movie begins with Tom and Jerry joining the ranks of the homeless when a wrecking ball destroys their comfortable, familiar home. As they settle into life on the streets they meet a wise old dog (and apostle of peace) who orders them to shake hands and sing the appalling ditty "Friends to the End"—one of six terminally bland musical numbers provided by composer Henry Mancini and lyricist Leslie Bricusse ("Dr. Doolittle").

Eventually, Tom and Jerry hook up with an orphan heiress, held prisoner by her greedy aunt (a dead ringer for Ursula the Sea Witch in "The Little Mermaid") and the aunt's conniving lawyer. The name provided this evil attorney—"Lickboot"—is typical of the crude stupidity that passes for humor throughout this wretched script.

Inevitably, the little girl discovers that her industrialist-adventurer father is still alive, and her devoted buddies Tom and Jerry help her to reunite with this loving parent. Along the way they encounter a vicious veterinarian, a menacing amusement park, rafts on the rapids, burning buildings, helicopter rescues, and on and on. The plot is much too complex and incoherent for little kids to follow, and anyone above the age of 7 will quickly lose interest.

Phil Roman (who has worked on "The Simpsons" and "Garfield and Friends") produced and directed this film, and tries hard to give the animation a more detailed, three-dimensional look and far more subtle coloring than the original Tom and Jerry cartoons. Unfortunately, this means that the zest, edge and manic energy of those old images is sorely missed. Every scene in this movie seems surprisingly drab and joyless, while the movements of the characters look stilted and mechanical.

All in all, "Tom and Jerry—The Movie" is the sort of ambitious but ill-conceived venture that gives family-film making a bad name. It's barely adequate as a timekiller for preschoolers, while for everyone else it's a dull, dumb ordeal.

NEWSDAY, 7/30/93, Part II/p. 69, Gene Seymour

The first seven or eight minutes of this full-length feature is a good (if not great) Tom and Jerry cartoon, infused with the kind of blunt-edged orchestrated malice that won this fabled cat-and-mouse team so many Oscars.

The rambunctious opening sequence ends with the duo homeless and hungry. Upon meeting a couple of friendly stray dogs in a back alley, the unspeakable happens. Tom and Jerry speak—for the first time in 53 years.

"Why didn't you talk before?," Tom (with Richard Kind's voice) asks Jerry. "I had nothing interesting to say to you," Jerry (with Dana Hill's voice) replies. "And I still don't."

Nonetheless they keep talking. Worse, they are given similarly unimaginative, unfunny things to say (and do) for the rest of this turgid melodrama. The lifelong antagonists are inexplicably transformed into plucky teammates helping a poor little rich girl find her missing father so she can wriggle free of her malevolent guardian (voice by Charlotte Rae).

These uptight times no doubt forced the filmmakers to tone down the mayhem of T & J's classic shorts for family consumption. It's just that after a while, you forget this is even a Tom and Jerry movie. They seem little more than spectators in the action, even when they're taken captive by an evil veterinarian (voice by Henry Gibson). Mickey and Donald or Fred and Barney would have fit into the plot just as well—and come off looking just as mediocre.

The mystifying thing about "Tom and Jerry—The Movie" is that it manages to be flaccid despite the talent at hand. Henry Mancini has a nice blues line in the beginning, but the songs he writes with the equally celebrated Leslie Bricusse are forgettable. Producer-director Phil Roman, whose credits include some of the wittier Saturday-morning TV fare ("Bobby's World," "Mother Goose and Grimm") seems to have misplaced his sense of humor.

I should say here that Tom and Jerry don't rate as high in my personal pantheon of classic toon icons as Bugs Bunny and the rest of the Warner Bros. stable. I should also say Tom and Jerry deserved better than what they were given here.

SIGHT AND SOUND, 8/93, p. 54, Leslie Felperin Sharman

Tom and Jerry, cat and mouse antagonists of old, are made homeless when their house is destroyed and Tom's owner neglects to take them with her to their new home. Wandering the streets, they meet Puggsy, a dog, and Frankie da Flea, who advise them to be friends in the interests of survival. Puggsy and Frankie are dognapped by stray-catchers. Tom briefly falls in with a gang of alley cats that advocate self-interest and bad manners.

Next they meet a girl named Robyn Starling who is on the lam from her evil Aunt Figg and in search of her rich explorer father. Tom and Jerry take her home, where they meet Aunt Figg's oleaginous lawyer Lickboot and her sneaky dog Ferdinand. Aunt Figg tries to dispose of Tom and Jerry by giving them to the hypocritical Dr Applecheek, who ransoms pets for money and has captured Puggsy and Frankie. Jerry helps all the animals to escape, and together with Tom they help Robyn to deliverance. The three of them take to the river, but are separated after their raft is wrecked.

Robyn meets up with a genial schizophrenic, Captain Kiddie, and his alterego Squawk the glove puppet, who decides to betray Robyn to Aunt Figg in return for a reward he sees advertised on a milk carton. Once again, Tom and Jerry assist Robyn's narrow escape, and they head for the family cabin, where they are met by Aunt Figg and Lickboot. The cabin catches fire, and the three friends climb onto the roof in desperation. They are saved at the very last minute by Robyn's father—back from Tibet at last—in a helicopter. Tom and Jerry are ensconced in Robyn's new home, happily at liberty to chase and antagonise each other forever after.

While the credits roll at the beginning of *Tom and Jerry—The Movie*, our eponymous heroes cheerfully engage in acts of gratuitous violence that make the protagonists of *Man Bites Dog* and *Romper Stomper* look like Care Bears. As they slice each other up into ribbons and compress one another into distorted concertina shapes, these first few minutes are a touching reprieve of the bloodsports that made the duo infamous world-wide, loved by their fans, reviled by the high-minded, and parodied by *The Simpsons'* 'Itchy and Scratchy Show'. However, as the film progresses, it becomes clear that this introduction is not a harbinger of things to come, but a nostalgic resume of things past.

The subsequent image of their house, a little stump of 1940s domestic architecture, surrounded by po-mo skyscrapers and about to be demolished, symbolises neatly the transition the characters are about to undergo. With the destruction of their old stomping ground, Tom and Jerry are plunged into a new realm, where different moral standards and aesthetic conventions hold sway. As they enter animated children's-featureland, all the formalised games of aggression that the duo perfected in their heyday of six-minute shorts must be eschewed. The animated feature genre demands a tamer realism and a narrative complexity capable of illustrating prescribed didactic issues, like the importance of friendship, the horrors of homelessness, the necessity of the family. Joe Barbera, who invented the characters with his long-time partner William Hanna, acted as Creative Consultant on this film. Since the television cartoons were so influential in shaping mainstream animation as we know it today, it seems appropriate that he should be in charge of updating his most successful characters. Sadly it's a bit like watching a pet owner personally declawing his cat.

Compared to most current animated features for kids, *Tom and Jerry* is better than average technically, a little gloopy with sentimentality, but peppered with ironic moments of self-consciousness that endear it. Trying to start a boat in a hurry, Jerry advises Tom to push the big red button; when asked how he knows it's the right one, he replies that "it's always the red button." Nonetheless, an elegaic mournfulness for animation's past seems to haunt the film. The opening shot evokes the neglected Fleischer masterpiece *Mr Bug Goes to Town*. Droopy, Tex Avery's favourite character, puts in a cameo appearance, while the alley cats bear an uncanny resemblance to those in *Top Cat*, one of Barbera's own old series. The funniest and creepiest cartoon allusion is the character of Captain Kiddie, the mentally disturbed puppet master, who recalls the main character in the long-forgotten early MGM series *The Captain and the Kids*. There's something comforting in knowing that old cartoon characters never die, they just get re-licensed.

For the most part, one has to sift for these moments of 'toon-buff joy like specks of gold in a pan of river silt. Director Phil Roman's most substantial work so far has been on the tepid *Garfield* TV specials. *Tom and Jerry* is a somnolent film cat of the same stripe. Like *Felix the Cat: The Movie* and other 'movieizations of classic cartoons, it not only neuters its characters, but, failing to achieve the pathos the genre demands, sells off its birthright for a mess of kitty litter.

Also reviewed in:
CHICAGO TRIBUNE, 7/30/93, Friday/p. H, Johanna Steinmetz
NEW YORK TIMES, 7/30/93, p. C10, Vincent Canby
VARIETY, 10/5/92, p. 62, Joseph McBride
WASHINGTON POST, 7/30/93, p. G7, Hal Hinson

TOMBSTONE

A Hollywood Pictures release of a Sean Daniel/James Jacks/Cinergi production.   *Executive Producer:* Buzz Feitshans and Andrew G. Vajna.   *Producer:* James Jacks, Sean Daniel, and Bob Misiorowski.   *Director:* George P. Cosmatos.   *Screenplay:* Kevin Jarre.   *Director of Photographpy:* William A. Fraker.   *Editor:* Frank J. Urioste, Roberto Silvi, and Harvey Rosenstock.   *Music:* Bruce Broughton.   *Music Editor:* Patricia Carlin.   *Choreographer:* Sabrina Vasquez.   *Sound:* Walt Martin and (music) Mike Ross.   *Sound Editor:* Jerry Ross and John Morris.   *Production Designer:* Catherine Hardwicke.   *Art Director:* Chris Gorak, Kim Hix, and Mark Worthington.   *Set Designer:* Tom Benson, Richard Prantis, and Siobhan Roome.   *Set Decorator:* Gene Serdena.   *Set Dresser:* Greg Evans and Bob Smith.   *Special Effects:* Dale Martin and Paul Stewart.   *Costumes:* Joseph Porro.   *Make-up:* David Atherton.   *Stunt Coordinator:* Terry J. Leonard.   *Running time:* 132 minutes.   *MPAA Rating:* R.

CAST: Kurt Russell (Wyatt Earp);   Val Kilmer (Doc Holliday);   Michael Biehn (Johnny Ringo);   Powers Boothe (Curly Bill);   Robert Burke (Frank McLaury);   Dana Delany (Josephine Marcus);   Sam Elliott (Virgil Earp);   Stephen Lang (Ike Clanton);   Terry O'Quinn (Mayor Clum);   Joanna Pacula (Kate);   Bill Paxton (Morgan Earp);   Jason Priestley (Billy Breckenridge);   Michael Rooker (Sherman McMasters);   Jon Tenney (Behan);   Dana Wheeler-Nicholson (Mattie Earp);   Billy Zane (Mr. Fabian);   Buck Taylor (Turkey Creek Jack Johnson);   Harry Carey, Jr. (Marshall Fred White);   Tomas Arana (Frank Stillwell);   Thomas Haden Church (Billy Clanton);   John Corbett (Barnes);   Pedro Armendariz, Jr. (The Priest);   Frank Stallone (Ed Bailey);   Billy Bob Thornton (Johnny Tyler);   Cecil Hoffmann (Lucinda Hobbs);   Charlton Heston (Henry Hooker);   Paula Malcomson (Allie Earp);   Lisa Collins (Louisa Earp);   Pat Brady (Milt Joyce);   Paul Ben Victor (Florentino);   John Philbin (Tom McLaury);   Wyatt Earp (Billy Claiborne);   W.R. Bo Gray (Wes Fuller);   Forrie J. Smith (Pony Deal);   Peter Sherayko (Texas Jack Vermillion);   Charles Schneider (Professor Gillman);   Gary Clark (Crawley Dake);   Billy Joe Patton (Deputy);   Bobby Joe McFadden (1st Gambler);   Michael N. Garcia (Rurale Captain/Groom);   Grant Wheeler (Drunk);   Jim Dunham (Miner);   Stephen Foster (Hank Swilling);   Grant James (Dr. Goodfellow);   Don Collier (High Roller);   Charlie Ward (1st Cowboy);   Clark Ray (2nd Cowboy);   Chris Mitchum (Ranch Hand);   Sandy Gibbons (Father Feeney);   Evan Osborne (Piano Player);   Shane McCabe (Audience Member);   Robert Mitchum (Narrator).

FILMS IN REVIEW, 3-4/94, p. 59, Harry Pearson, Jr.

Tombstone is an almost great Western, blessed with an intelligent (though butchered) script by Kevin Jarre (who was thrown off the set as the pix's original director) that stuck as close to the historical facts in the matter of the Earp vs. the Clanton Bros. as any movie since the long forgotten *Hour of the Gun*. Historically, you may know, the quick gunfight at the O.K. Corral (where only one person was killed) ignited a long and bloody range war in which Wyatt Earp, turned demonic, effectively wiped out the entire Clanton gang.

Had it been filmed as written, this would have been an epic Western (weighing in at more than three hours, unthinkable to the formula-loving cast of minds at Disney). Turns out that, led by Kurt Russell, who took over the picture, the post-Jarre revisionists left out hunks of the script (thus overturning its carefully calculated logic and mise-en-scene), condensed characters, and added a sappy and unbelievable last scene stolen straight from *Sleepless in Seattle*. But what's there, especially during the first two-thirds, is fascinating indeed. With especially strong performances from Russell, who plays the character as written (with subtlety and complexity; he can act even if he can't think artistically) and dazzlingly from Val Kilmer's wickedly good take on Doc Holliday, whom Kilmer does with a Southern accent, though the evidence for such is slender. (He was born in Baltimore; educated at Harvard.)

After the gun battle, it's pretty hard to tell who's doing what to whom and why both the bad guys and the badder guys are wearing badges—in historical fact, Earp was federally deputized and the Clantons deputized by one of the local machines, an alliance of ranchers and anti-Federal interests. A parallel the movie avoids drawing. The Panavision photography is especially worthy of mention (although advertised as in Dolby stereo, it was not at the theater where I saw it—an increasingly common experience, which means we'll have to wait for home video to hear it as intended).

And what turns we do get on the usual material here—all historically justified. There are the laudanum addicts, the racial minorities, a few gays, Latin quoting bad guys (Morituri, te salutamus), a liberated heroine (Jewish in the script, but not in the final product), and crooked local politicians (then as now).

I never know quite what to say when a movie is in the almost category as this one surely is. Worth seeing, if you're a student of the art, and certainly it puts the lie to Ford's *My Darling Clementine* as high Gothic claptrap (but the kind I love). The question really is: Do we want our Westerns to tell the truth (as *Geronimo* failed to do, a sin for which it was promptly and totally roasted) or to be faithful to the myth as we now re-see it. Or, as in the case here, straddle the fence? Just asking.

LOS ANGELES TIMES, 12/25/93, Calendar/p. 12, Peter Rainer

The actors in "Tombstone" playing bad guys and good guys and in-between guys spit very convincingly. They also slouch well and reach for their pistols with aplomb.

So much for authenticity. Just about everything else in this aggressively overlong Western about trouble in Tombstone seems posed and facetious. It's the latest in a new line of designer Westerns—not quite as loony or self-infatuated as "Posse" but close enough. It's supposed to be a "real" look at the events leading up to the gunfight at the O.K. Corral but mostly it looks like a bunch of overweening actors playing cowboys.

In boom-town Tombstone, Ariz., circa 1879, life, unlike the whiskey, is cheap. Brigand cowboys have stirred things up: They shoot off their pistols at the theater and in the streets, they pop weak-willed sheriffs and laugh menacingly. Heading the menacers are the red-shirted Curly Bill (Powers Boothe) and Johnny Ringo (Michael Biehn), who is especially dangerous because he's full o'book learnin'—he even knows how to speak *Latin*.

So does his aristocratic counterpart, Doc Holliday, who, along with the brothers Earp, stand for justice in Tombstone. Val Kilmer's Holliday is classic camp performance, although it may not have started out that way. His Southern drawl sounds like a languorous cross between early Brando and Mr. Blackwell. Stricken with tuberculosis, his eyes red-rimmed, Doc coughs delicately and matches Ringo line for line in Latin. He also shoots straighter than anyone else in the movie—his powers of recuperation make Rasputin seem like a pushover.

Wyatt Earp (Kurt Russell), unlike his brothers, Morgan (Bill Paxton) and Virgil (Sam Elliott), takes awhile to warm up to his righteousness. (Elliott, by the way, is the only cast member to look convincing in a droopy mustache, though his voice is so gravelly it's practically gravel.) Retired from keeping the peace, Wyatt is in town to make a pile of dough. But bullets keep winging him.

This new "cynical" take on Wyatt isn't exactly a revelation, since no one really believes those old Western myths anymore anyway. Besides, his cynicism is just a prelude to his inevitable conversion to good-guy-ism (which is the oldest ploy in the book). He even falls hard for Josephine (Dana Delany), a music-hall star with a porcelain complexion who thinks he's a "tall drink of water." He, in turn, goes for the subtle approach in romancing. Out on the riding paths with her, Wyatt looks at Josephine's steed and says, "That mare's in season."

Since the dastardly cowboys all wear a red sash, the film at times seems to be a contemporary gang movie in Western drag. This may not be as far-fetched as it sounds—"Posse" worked in references to the Rodney G. King beating. But the parallels are plunked in without any resonance—or reason. The bad guys appear to be making a fashion statement. The same goes for the good guys. The Earps dress in strict black and white, funeral director-style.

A few stirring shoot-'em-ups help relieve the logjam of cliches. Director George P. ("Rambo") Cosmatos does an OK job at the O.K. Corral. But even the good stuff goes on for too long. When the film ended and the credits rolled and the actors once again galloped toward the camera, a friend leaned over to me and moaned, "Is this starting all over *again*?"

NEW YORK POST, 12/24/93, p. 34, Michael Medved

In December of 1879, three married brothers—Wyatt, Morgan and Jim Earp—arrived with their wives in the silver-mining boom town of Tombstone to join their brother Virgil, who had just been appointed Deputy Marshal for Southern Arizona.

Within two years, three of the Earp boys (brother Jim missed the fight) joined with their alcoholic, tubercular, crooked gambler pal Doc Holliday to shoot at a band of local miscreants in a fabled brawl at the O.K. Corral.

This nasty little scrap produced three corpses (all of them belonging to the enemies of the Earps) and countless retellings in books, television shows and motion pictures.

The latest version, "Tombstone" may not be a great movie, but it is, at times, great fun to watch. Kurt Russell, Sam Elliott and Bill Paxton play Wyatt, Virgil and Morgan Earp, respectively, while Val Kilmer turns in the best work of his career as an endearingly eccentric and vivid Doc Holliday.

The script by Kevin Jarre (who did such a magnificent historical adaptation with the screenplay for "Glory") portrays these people as troubled human beings, not noble icons, and makes a point of showing that their battles had more to do with self-interest and personal rivalries than with any overriding commitment to law and order. The Earp brothers, after all, make good money by raking off a share of the gambling proceeds at the Oriental Saloon.

Jarre also deserves credit for bringing women onto center stage, with significant nods at historical accuracy. It's true that Wyatt Earp's second wife, Mattie (played here by Dana Wheeler-Nicholson), had a serious drug problem, and it's also true that the lawman-gambler began an affair with Josephine Sarah Marcus (Dana Delany), an aspiring actress from San Francisco.

That actress, however, happened to be far younger and more outrageous (as the wildcat daughter of a Jewish merchant family) than she appears on screen. Doc Holliday's love interest has also been prettified for the purposes of this picture: Here, she's called "Kate" and is played by the glamorous Joanna Pacula, but in real-life she was a battered Dodge City prostitute known to history as "Big Nose Kate Fisher."

To its credit, however, the movie captures enough of the raw, bawdy feel of the actual Tombstone (shot in reasonably authentic Arizona locations) to qualify as one of the richer recent recreations of the western frontier.

Director George Cosmatos is an action specialist (best known for Stallone's "Rambo" and "Cobra") whose skills are sometimes derided with the disrespectful nickname "George Comatose," but here he brings refreshing dash and sparkle to his horseback chase scenes at breakneck speed, tense confrontations in smoky saloons, and vicious midnight brawls under the Arizona starlight.

The great film composer Bruce Broughton (who wrote one of the finest western scores ever, for "Silverado") contributes rousing music, and the assorted villains (led by Powers Boothe, Stephen Lang, and Michael Biehn) are convincingly lowdown and despicable.

The movie most certainly has problems, particularly in its second half: The action seems to lose focus after the big fights at O.K. Corral, and key love scenes between Delany and Russell are almost entirely devoid of chemistry.

Nevertheless, while waiting for the next version of the Wyatt Earp legend (a Kevin Costner vehicle due in '94), this juicy, rollicking picture will provide diehard western fans with a welcome jolt of adrenalin.

NEWSDAY, 12/24/93, Part II/p. 43, John Anderson

What do westerns want? The '90s version wants to be historically accurate, politically correct, aware of its own socio-cultural-sexual content, tall in the saddle and home on the range. The '90s western wants it all.

And "Tombstone," yet another reenactment of the most famous gunfight in frontier history—the Oct. 26, 1881, shootout at the O.K. Corral in Tombstone, Ariz.—gets pretty much what it wants. Unlike the revisionist "Unforgiven," the apologist "Dances with Wolves" or the subliminally racist "Geronimo," this latest saga of the Earp brothers and their climactic battle pumps new life into old conventions, while making its classic story contemporary, and almost entirely factual. And even if the story remains your basic tale of good vs. evil, "Tombstone" knows that the measure of any good western isn't in the good, it's in the evil.

Kurt Russell does a better than passable job as legendary lawman Wyatt Earp, whose indecisiveness about law enforcement throws a dash of Hamlet into the oats. But he's a figure with too many straight edges, which is how director George Cosmatos paints him: When we first see Earp, stepping off the train in Tombstone, the camera pans slowly—we're not kidding—from his boots up to his heroic mustache and steely squint, lingering there a while to let Earp radiate manhood. His first act is to stop a man from beating a horse.

He's real enough, but not magnetic, which is where Val Kilmer steps in. "Tombstone" like its predecessors—"Gunfight at the O.K. Corral," or John Ford's "My Darling Clementine," which compared to "Tombstone" looks like Italian neo-realism—is a buddy movie, hinging on the relationship between Wyatt Earp and Doc Holliday. And Kilmer's Holliday, a lethal, larcenous, libidinous, consumptive alcoholic whose loyalty to Earp is completely unexplained but steadfast, is the electric engine of the movie. With his southern gentleman's drawl and fey insouciance—and the clinging Kate (Joanna Pacula) ever on his arm—the gunslinging dentist is the much needed antihero of the piece, fascinating when he's on screen, palpably absent when he's not.

To the far side of Holliday is Johnny Ringo (Michael Biehn), a member of the Cowboys, a besaddled crime syndicate that's terrorizing the decent folk of Tombstone. Led by Curly Bill (Powers Boothe in an *homage* to Lee Marvin's Liberty Valance) the Cowboys are a vicious lot, but the educated and homicidal Ringo is their spiritual inspiration. When they invade an enemy's wedding, the Cowboys shoot the wedding party, and Curly Bill shoots the groom. Ringo shoots the priest.

Director Cosmatos does a very good job of building the tension between the Earps and the Cowboys, and between Holliday and Ringo, whose verbal sparring in Latin is part of the film's wittiest scene. He's not so sharp with the romantic aspects of the story, which are fairly ludicrous. Every time Wyatt exchanges glances with Josie Marcus (Dana Delany), a member of the itinerant theatrical troupe passing through Tombstone, the music swells along with their hormones. Delany, looking like a cross between the Girl of the Golden West and the woman on the Vermont Maid label, isn't given much to do, and the dialogue between her and Wyatt is preposterous.

But this in essence is an action movie that's interrupted only occasionally by such crimes of the heart. Cosmatos, who directed the Stallone vehicles "Rambo" and "Cobra," makes the chase scenes and shootouts—especially the one in the O.K. Corral—convincing and fresh. The supporting players—Sam Elliott as Virgil Earp, Bill Paxton as Morgan Earp, Stephen Lang as the loathesome Ike Clanton—provide substantial backup to Russell's tortured hero. It's Kilmer's movie, though. His Doc Holliday is not only the film's most romantic figure, but with his particular sense of philosophy and personal morality, the best defined character in the film.

SIGHT AND SOUND, 3/94, p. 53, Tom Tunney

1879. Tombstone, Arizona is a boom town in the grip of an organised crime ring known as the Cowboys, identified by their distinctive red sashes. The Cowboys are led by Curly Bill Brocius and his sidekicks Johnny Ringo and Ike Clanton, and are first seen riding to massacre a Mexican wedding party.

Fresh from his career as a lawman in Dodge City, Wyatt Earp arrives with his brothers Virgil and Morgan and their wives, Mattie, Louisa and Allie. No longer carrying a gun, Wyatt plans to succeed as a businessman and he makes a first step towards this by walking into the toughest saloon in town and telling crooked faro dealer Johnny Tyler that he's taking his place. A brief confrontation ends with Wyatt leading Tyler out of the saloon and agreeing with the manager to take his job for 25% of the gambling take. In the street, Tyler is ready to blast Wyatt with a shotgun in the back but is deterred by the arrival of Doc Holliday, an old friend of the Earps. County Sheriff Behan introduces himself, and actors Mr. Fabian and Josephine Marcus get off the stagecoach; Josephine is instantly attracted to Wyatt, on seeing him in the distance.

After a night at the theatre, Brocius, Ringo and Clanton confront Wyatt at his faro table, but bloodshed is avoided by Doc Holliday who comically apes Ringo's slick pistol-twirling using a tin mug. Out riding, Wyatt meets Josephine and she tells him that her idea of happiness is "room service"; Wyatt returns to his laudanum-addicted wife, Mattie. Brocius staggers out of an opium den firing wildly in the street and shoots dead Marshal Fred White who had tried to disarm him. Wyatt knocks out Brocius and puts his gun to Ike Clanton's forehead when Clanton and the Cowboys attempt to free Brocius. Wyatt is aided by his brothers, but Brocius is later released due to lack of evidence.

Saving a child from being run down by horses in the street, Virgil realises that the town needs law and order, and against Wyatt's advice, takes over as Marshal, decreeing that no guns are to be worn within town limits. This leads to continuing friction with Ike Clanton and the Cowboys, which climaxes with a gunfight at the OK Corral in which three of Clanton's men are killed by the Earps and Holliday. An assassination plot against the Earps is partially foiled by Josephine warning their wives, but Virgil is shot in the arm and Morgan is shot in the back and subsequently dies. Wyatt sends Virgil and the three wives out of town and foils an assassination attempt by Ike Clanton at the railroad station. He is now a US Marshal, and his policy is "I see a red sash, I kill the man who's wearing it."

The ensuing gunplay includes Earp's shooting one man in the mouth in an opium den, and killing Brocius in a confrontation in a river. Wyatt meets Josephine again at Henry Hooker's ranch, where he takes the consumptive Holliday to recuperate. Her acting companion Mr. Fabian has been senselessly shot by the Cowboys. Wyatt receives word to meet Johnny Ringo at an isolated country location, but Doc Holliday gets there first and beats Ringo to the draw. Doc later dies in hospital after being visited by Wyatt. Wyatt sees Josephine outside the theatre where she is appearing, declares his love for her and dances with her in the snow. We learn that they lived happily together for 47 years and that when Wyatt died in 1929, Western movie stars Tom Mix and William S. Hart attended his funeral.

Narrator Robert Mitchum introduces *Tombstone* over silent Western movie footage which includes the famous straight-to-camera pistol shot from Edwin S. Porter's *The Great Train Robbery* (1903). He also has the last word in the film, telling us that at Earp's funeral "Tom Mix wept." The emphatic positioning of the story within the Western genre rather than within a more rigorously historical framework is its most revealing characteristic. The 'real' Earp and the movie tradition he helped inspire are presented as being one and the same. Wyatt Earp *is* the Western.

"Legendary lawman" is the blissfully unproblematic phrase with which Mitchum first introduces us to Earp; and so the gunman's fame has proceeded him both in terms of the narrative he's already famous when he arrives in Tombstone—and retrospectively in terms of the genre. However, as well as being a portrait of one of the pivotal town-taming heroes, the story also stretches itself into the much more psychologically-ravaged territory of the revenge Western. What begins as a morally unambiguous cleaning-up-the-town plot (compare *Dodge City, My Darling Clementine*) has by the midway point—significantly, the OK Corral confrontation is the film's centrepiece rather than its conclusion—shifted into a searing, *Pale Rider*-style saga of retribution.

The opening sequence establishes the stark, Manichean nature of the struggle ahead, with the pounding spectacle of Brocius' gang galloping across the prairie. They proceed to massacre a Mexican wedding party, before Johnny Ringo conveniently quotes from the Book of Revelations: "Behold the pale horse and the man who sat on it was death and Hell followed with him." The next scene is of Wyatt Earp getting off a train and reprimanding a station employee for mistreating his horse!

Tombstone is not so much an attempt to discover the—apparently very grubby—reality of Wyatt Earp and the gunfight at the OK Corral, more a celebration of Earp as one of the founding inspirations of the Western movie. His character is also a strong platform for an exploitation of the Western's renewed commercial potential as perhaps the pre-eminent film spectacle. In the wake of *Unforgiven*, *Tombstone* is replete with traditional Western pleasures: lusciously photographed sunsets, rugged landscapes, consistently witty dialogue, a superbly choreographed shoot-out at the OK Corral, and a gallery of finely-realised heroes and villains. But it's also a deliberately shallow film, skimming across the surface of the genre.

Despite some impeccable cinematography, period costuming and art direction, the film's main terms of reference are to other movies. Like a menu of bite-sized snacks designed to reacquaint audiences with the delights of the form, the allusions come thick and fast: the wedding massacre suggests the clear-cut morality of *The Magnificent Seven*, Johnny Ringo's Bible-spouting recalls the vengeful stranger of Eastwood's *Pale Rider*, the extreme close-ups of faces and eyes during the OK Corral shootout is a stylistic nod to Sergio Leone.

The film's knowingly self-conscious references are not at all intrusive to its main project of slickly re-packaging one of the most durable of Western yarns. On that superficial level, the film is an accomplished orchestration of clichés often bordering entertainingly on pastiche. But it also deliberately shies away from some of the more intriguing ideas possible within the form. In force-marrying the town-taming and the revenge Western plots, the film eventually opts for an unproblematic version of the former, after plunging heavily into the latter's scarred heart and soul and suggesting that something more profound might be forthcoming.

Finally, there's a desperate lack of psychological complexity in this Earp. Despite Kurt Russell's credibly hard demeanour, we're abruptly asked to believe that such a character can happily put his experiences behind him and find over 40 years of true love. There's a definite diminution in heroic stature from the pure mythic splendour of *My Darling Clementine*—in which Henry Fonda's Earp finally rides off into the desert—to the finale here, in which Earp promises his new love a life of hotel room service. Not since *How the West Was Won* in 1964—which ended with a aerial shot of the modern Los Angeles freeway—has a Western concluded on such an utterly banal note.

VILLAGE VOICE, 1/4/94, p. 57, Henry Cabot Beck

No sooner does the crusty Clint tuck an Oscar into his saddlebags by violating and then restoring Western myth in *Unforgiven*, than we have a postrevisionist kid-brother wannabe starring Kurt Russell as Wyatt Earp. (Russell once walked through an entire feature, *Escape From New York*, doing an Eastwood impression.) Joining him as the brother Earps are Bill Paxton and Sam Elliot (the only real mustache of this wild bunch), their righteous posturing leaving most of the choice bits of character wrangling to villains Stephan Lang, Powers Boothe, and Michael Biehn.

None of this matters overmuch because the entire show is stolen by Val Kilmer as the sweaty, tubercular Doc Holliday, reeking of serpentine menace, death, and Southern gentility in equal portions. Kilmer gives us Holliday as Brando might've played him; all the whine and mashed phrasing, but with considerably less pork. He is the best Doc on record.

Tombstone starts terrifically, tiptoeing through innumerable film versions, borrowing here and there, and introducing quite a bit of actual historical fact in a cautious, intelligent way. Revisionist elements abound: Wyatt's junkie wife, a gay character or two, a proto-feminist actress, none of it intrusive in the usual thick-fingered, p.c. way.

The picture picks up a lot of heady steam on its inevitable journey to the O.K. Corral, and all is well until about midpoint when the bottom drops out and we find ourselves watching a different movie with the same cast, a Peckinpah bloodbath tumbling one bad step at a time, landing, like the dozens of unfortunate cowpokes it portrays, in Boot Hill.

Rumor has it that the reins of the production were wrested away by an on-set lynch mob. True or not, there are two movies here, the first one outstanding and the second one just dumb.

Also reviewed in:
CHICAGO TRIBUNE, 12/24/93, Friday/p. C, Mark Caro
NEW REPUBLIC, 2/14/94, p. 30, Stanley Kauffmann
NEW YORK TIMES, 12/24/93, p. C6, Stephen Holden
VARIETY, 1/3-9/94, p. 53, Emanuel Levy
WASHINGTON POST, 12/25/93, p. B10, Richard Harrington

TRAIL MIX-UP

A Buena Vista Pictures release of a Walt Disney Pictures and Steven Spielberg presentation. *Executive Producer:* Steven Spielberg, Frank Marshall, Kathleen Kennedy, and Rob Minkoff. *Producer:* Pam Coats. *Director:* Barry Cook. *Based upon characters created by:* Gary K. Wolf. *Story:* Rob Minkoff, Mark Kausler, Barry Cook, and Patrick A. Ventura. *Visual Development:* Thom Enriquez. *Editor:* Victor Livingston. *Music:* Bruce Broughton. *Music Editor:* Patricia Carlin. *Sound:* Lon Bender. *Art Director:* Ric Sluiter. *Layout:* Robert Walker. *Background:* Robert E. Stanton. *Clean-up:* Rubén Procopio. *Special Effects:* Jeff Dutton. *Visual Effects:* Michael Lessa. *MPAA Rating:* G.

VOICES: Charles Fleischer (Roger Rabbit); Kathleen Turner (Jessica Rabbit); April Winchell (Mom/Young Baby Herman); Lou Hirsch (Adult Baby Herman); Corey Burton (Droopy Dog); Frank Welker (Bear/Beaver).

LOS ANGELES TIMES, 3/12/93, Calendar/p. 16, Charles Solomon

"Trail Mix-Up," the new Disney cartoon short screening with "A Far Off Place," reunites Roger Rabbit, Baby Herman and the voluptuous Jessica Rabbit in a new series of misadventures in the not-so-great outdoors.

During a camping trip to Yellowstain National Park, Mom (in high-heeled hiking boots) goes ahunting, leaving Baby Herman in Roger's care. Predictably, pandemonium ensues as Herman blithely crawls from the brink of one disaster to another, leaving Roger to pick up the pieces.

The frenetic bunny confronts a swarm of angry bees, a destructive beaver, a thick-witted bear and a roller-coaster ride down a flume and into a murderous Rube Goldberg-esque sawmill.

Director Barry Cook accelerates the pace of the gags as the film progresses, and by the time Roger and Baby Herman land in the sawmill, the images are whizzing by at a breakneck speed that makes MTV look sedate. There's plenty of cartoon mayhem and wild, Tex Avery-style takes: At one point, Roger's eyes pop out of his head, leaving grooves in the dirt.

Made by a crew of 220 artists at the Disney animation studio in Orlando, Fla., "Trail Mix-Up" boasts lusher backgrounds and more polished animation than other recent studio cartoons. Its one real weakness is the plot.

"Trail Mix-Up" is the third Roger Rabbit short in four years, and they've all followed the pattern established in the opening sequence of the 1988 blockbuster "Who Framed Roger Rabbit"—only the individual gags and the setting have been changed.

It's time the Disney artists found new story lines for these characters.

NEW YORK POST, 3/12/93, p. 29, Matthew Flamm

[*Trail Mix-Up* was reviewed jointly with *A Far Off Place*; see Flamm's review of that film.]

Also reviewed in:
NEW YORK TIMES, 3/12/93, p. C15, Janet Maslin
VARIETY, 3/15/93, p. 62, Brian Lowry
WASHINGTON POST, 3/12/93, p. D1, Rita Kempley

TRIAL, THE

An Angelika Films release of a BBC Films/Europanda Entertainment production. *Executive Producer:* Kobi Jaeger, Reniero Compostella, and Mark Shivas. *Producer:* Louis Marks. *Director:* David Jones. *Screenplay:* Harold Pinter. *Based on the novel by:* Franz Kafka. *Director of Photography:* Phil Meheux. *Editor:* John Stothart. *Music:* Carl Davis. *Sound:* Jim Greenhorn. *Sound Editor:* Helen Whitehead and Catherine Hodgson. *Casting:* Leo Davis and John Lyons. *Production Designer:* Don Taylor. *Art Director:* Jim Holloway and Jiri Matolin. *Set Dresser:* John Bush. *Costumes:* Anushia Nieradzik. *Make-up:* Deanne Turner and Zdenek Klika. *Running time:* 120 minutes. *MPAA Rating:* Not Rated.

CAST: Kyle MacLachlan (Josef K); Anthony Hopkins (Priest); Jason Robards (Dr. Huld); Juliet Stevenson (Fraulein Burstner); Polly Walker (Leni); Alfred Molina (Titorelli); Michael Kitchen (Block); David Thewlis (Franz); Tony Haygarth (Willem); Douglas Hodge (Inspector); Jiri Schwartz (Babensteiner); David Schneider (Kullich); Ondrej Vetchy (Kaminer); Valerie Kaplanova (Old Woman); Jiri Ded (Old Man); Jiri Vavricek (Red Beard); Paul Brooke (Deputy Bank Manager); Harry Burton (K's Assistant); Roger Lloyd Pack and Leon Lissek (Stairmen); Catherine Neilson (Washer Woman); Trevor Peacock (Examining Magistrate); Vaclav Jakoubek (Small Boy); Patrick Godfrey (Court Usher); Andrew Tiernan (Berthold); Jiri Schmitzer (Thin Defendant); Don Henderson (Flogger); Martin Faltyn (Clerk); Robert Lang (K's Uncle); Jan Laibl (Chief Clerk of the Court); John Woodvine (Herr Deimen); Reniero Compostella (Signor Rossi); Lena Birkova (Bookstall Woman); Oskar Hak (Verger); Karel Augusta and Petr Drozda (Executioners); Vladimir Tausinger (Policeman); Petr Skarke (Man in the Window).

CHRISTIAN SCIENCE MONITOR, 11/22/93, p. 17, David Sterritt

The longest line I stood in at this year's Montreal world Film Festival was for "The Trial," a new version of Franz Kafka's novel with tantalizing credentials: Directed by David Jones from Harold Pinter's screenplay, it features Kyle MacLachlan in the lead and Anthony Hopkins and Jason Robards among the supporting players.

Like others who stood in the same queue and shared their thoughts about the movie afterward, I was impressed by "The Trial" on many grounds, from the seriousness of its approach to the vigor of its best performances. I couldn't shake the memory of a more exciting adaptation, though—the one made by Orson Welles just 30 years ago—or the sense that a truly great film version will surely be made someday, but it hasn't come along yet.

There is no question about the keen intelligence and widespread influence of Kafka's greatest novel. It touched a profoundly resonant chord with its portrait of an ordinary man, Josef K., caught in the crushingly impersonal gears of modern bureaucratic society—arrested on no evidence, put on trial with no explicit charge, and ultimately destroyed by a system he can't begin to understand.

Some see the story as a parable of social engineering run amok. More interestingly, others contend that Josef K. really is guilty of some deep-rooted shame and knows in his most hidden self that he deserves the punishment he is receiving.

Welles's film version took the society-gone-crazy interpretation, surrounding K. with Orwellian power structures wielding totalitarian control over just about everyone. Following this lead, Anthony Perkins played K. as a nervous victim who grows more agitated with every new twist in his situation. This approach suited Perkins's great talent for playing characters under stress and strain. But it strayed from Kafka's vision, in which K. remains cool and collected—if angry and indignant—no matter how outrageously the system treats him.

Pinter's adaptation gives us a K. closer to the novel's hero, generally retaining his dignity and composure as he tries to defend himself under near-impossible circumstances. Along with Jones's restrained directing style, this sets the new movie quite apart from Welles's version, and provides a good setting for MacLachlan, whose limited acting range necessitates a comparatively muted portrayal of the main character.

Over dinner during the Montreal filmfest, executive producer Kobi Jaeger told me that the filmmakers' aim was to make a relatively realistic "Trial" that would steer toward real life rather than hyperreal fable. They have succeeded at this, although my tastes run more toward Welles's wild adventurousness than Jones's dutiful elegance.

The greatest excitement of the new "Trial" is found in its supporting performances. Although he gets star billing, Hopkins only appears on screen for about five minutes, as the priest who gives K. some last-minute advice. Incredibly, the gifted Hopkins earns every ounce of his billing in that small amount of time, putting his talent to superbly expressive use. Robards has sinister fun as a powerful lawyer, and Alfred Molina is brilliant.

LOS ANGELES TIMES, 4/22/94, Calendar/p. 8, Kevin Thomas

"The Trial," which reopens the NuWilshire after earthquake repairs, is precisely that for the viewer, for this new adaptation of the Franz Kafka novel could scarcely be more of an ordeal. Within minutes you're wishing you were instead, watching Orson Welles' 1963 version with Anthony Perkins—not that it was all that great, but it was far more absorbing.

One would think that Harold Pinter, master of ambiguity and implication, would be the perfect choice to adapt this prophetic warning of the advent of the faceless totalitarian state with its accompanying paranoia. The trouble is that Pinter's surprisingly talky treatment is lots more suitable for the stage than the screen. Not helping matters is David Jones' relentlessly prosaic and impersonal direction. In such circumstances authentic. Prague locales, shot in realistic color, simply underline the artificial theatricality of the entire undertaking.

It doesn't seem possible that a film with a cast headed by Kyle MacLachlan and including Anthony Hopkins, Jason Robards and David Thewlis could be all bad, but it is: They have all been directed as if they're performing under a proscenium instead of a camera. Since "The Trial" never comes to life, they always seem to be acting rather than becoming their characters.

As the hapless Josef K, MacLachlan would be ideal in a more imaginative version. He captures the bourgeois smugness of Kafka's senior bank clerk who meets his arrest on charges never defined with a mixture of exasperation and disdain. Indeed, he refuses to consider the danger of his plight at just about the same time that countless intelligent people who ought to have been taking Hitler seriously were regarding him as a joke.

Robards plays K's bedridden lawyer, Hopkins an enigmatic priest and Thewlis one of the warders who tells K he's under arrest. Hopkins at least gets to underplay, but everyone else has been directed to bluster about, as if Jones were straining to inject some vitality. But this "Trial" is embalmed from start to finish.

NEW YORK POST, 11/24/93, p. 34, Michael Medved

Franz Kafka isn't ready to rival John Grisham or Tom Clancy as the author of hot movie properties, but the tormented Prague master (1883-1924) has experienced a flurry of current interest in bringing his novels to the screen.

Last year, Steven Soderbergh directed Jeremy Irons in a badly muddled "Kafka." Woody Allen also invoked Kafkaesque images and themes in the regrettable "Shadows and Fog."

Now comes "The Trial," an ambitious attempt to film Kafka's most enduring novel. Despite the best efforts of its sensitive director (David Jones), acclaimed screenwriter (Harold Pinter), and distinguished cast, it fails.

Part of the problem is the source material, in which Kafka uses matter-of-fact prose to describe the surreal, nightmarish experience of a bank clerk identified only as Josef K., who's arrested without explanation.

Thirty years ago, Orson Wells directed a memorable adaptation of this tale that used haunting images to make up for the lack of suspense or logic.

Jones opts for a radically different approach, returning the story to its roots in the mundane world of pre-WW I Prague.

The period detail is unusually rich, but these elegant locations and costumes make the experience of Josef K. seem quaint rather than menacing, providing a safe distance between moviegoers and the occurrences on screen.

The work of Kyle MacLachlan as the central character creates additional blocks to audience involvement. He is miscast.

This means that a host of fine supporting performances are wasted. Anthony Hopkins is commanding in a brief but crucial part as a priest (and the voice of God); Alfred Molina is suitably creepy as a painter with "connections"; Jason Robards plays an aging, corrupt lawyer with inside information; and Polly Walker is wearingly seductive as his mistress.

But not even her sultry presence can coax life out of this dry, dutiful production. It is a trial to watch.

NEWSDAY, 11/24/93, Part II/p. 63, John Anderson

Kafka for the masses? It's an ambitious idea, and David Jones' "The Trial" (Orson Welles made a semi-successful version in 1963 with Anthony Perkins) is certainly an ambitious film. With a potent cast and several outstanding performances particularly by Anthony Hopkins, who as the prison chaplain looks like he wants to eat Kyle MacLachlan's liver, with some fava beans and nice chianti—the film is a passionate exercise in existential thought.

Whether this is what we want, however, is a question. Kafka's cold power seems to lie in the flat terrain of his tone, his matter-of-factness—in the face of absurdity. Exploit the dark humor in Joseph K.'s story, as Harold Pinter's screenplay does, and you defuse him.

As K., Kyle MacLachlan milks Pinter's dialogue for laughs, and his patented pseudo-seriousness evokes David Lynch more than Kafka. As a man, though, he's the proper vehicle for Pinter, who explores the sexual aspect of Kafka's novel to the point of re-creating scenes that the writer himself deleted from his original, fragmented manuscript.

The story: K. awakens one morning to find himself arrested. His warders—who include David Thewlis, star of the upcoming "Naked"—won't or can't say with what he's been charged. He smiles at the word "arrested," but is intimidated by the law, paralyzed by conformity. In trying to assert his quavering outrage, K. commits a series of improprieties, roughing up a fellow defendant, attempting to seduce the washerwoman at the court (Catherine Nelson), and seducing Leni (Polly Walker), the web-fingered mistress of his lawyer (Jason Robards). Seeking help in his defense from the court painter, Titorelli (Alfred Molina); he begins to realize the futility of his cause. When the prison chaplain finally explains everything to K., the metaphysical curtain fails.

The trial Kafka wrote about is life itself, of course, suicide being the only logical conclusion, living becoming an act of defiance. Pinter throws in sexual preoccupation and dilutes the mix. Even so, while some people are going to feel like Joseph K himself halfway through "the Trial," it remains a powerful story, prescient in its despair and heavy in its tread.

SIGHT AND SOUND, 7/93, p. 53, Paul Tarrago

Prague 1912. Josef K, a senior bank clerk, rises from his bed to be placed under arrest by two officers. Representatives of an unknowable Law, they immediately release him to carry on with his everyday life. A week later, Josef receives a phone call summoning him to a preliminary hearing. Finding the courtroom with some difficulty, he harangues the Examining Magistrate and the system he represents, but his diatribe is interrupted by the court usher's wife making love with a student at the back of the hall. Josef leaves, and returns the following Sunday, but the court is not in session; the usher's wife seductively offers to aid him, but the student appears and carries her away. Josef then meets the usher, who bemoans his servile status. He shows Josef around the court offices where the sight of fellow defendants provokes an angry outburst, then a numbing attack of panic. Back at work he discovers the two officers who arrested him being whipped in a stationery cupboard. He pleads for their punishment to stop, but is then gripped by horror and flees.

Josef's Uncle Max turns up, having heard of his nephew's plight, and takes him to visit his old friend Huld, an advocate. While Huld talks with Max, Josef is lured out of the room by Leni, Huld's servant and possibly his mistress. Josef and Leni make love, and she advises him to visit Titorelli, a painter who specialises in portraits of judges. Titorelli explains the vagaries of pleas but offers no real solution, before being mobbed by a bevy of teenage girls. Returning to Huld with the intention of dispensing with his services, Josef meets Block, whose case has been underway for five years. Huld puts on a show of humiliating him before Josef as evidence of his ability to break spirits, but Josef rejects Huld nevertheless.

Back at work, Josef is asked to show an important client around the local cathedral, but when he arrives early the court chaplain is there. The chaplain tells Josef a parable to illustrate the defendant's position with regard to the Law, Josef sees the hopelessness of his situation and is panic-stricken. Collected from his room later that night by two new officers, he is led to a quarry where he lies down on a block of stone. The officers pass a knife back and forth above him, before one of them plunges it into his exposed chest. Gasping the words, "Like a dog," Josef expires.

Orson Welles's decision to adapt Kafka's *The Trial* for film was apparently based on a list of literary 'classics' in the public domain presented to him by producer Alexander Salkind; he selected rather than chose. He then went on to lose his budget midway through production, along with his locations, and invoked critical bile through an expressionistic impro style rejigged around Paris's derelict Gare D'Orsay.

Thirty years later comes David Jones's version, with a screenplay by Harold Pinter, a project nurtured for over a decade, richly funded and shot in Czech locations. It carries all the trappings of a prestige production—famous faces and lush colour cinematography—and so, comparisons with Welles are largely inappropriate, if inevitable. This *Trial* is faithful and reverential, literal and literary, a cinematic approximation to the book, rather than a version of it. Originally commissioned by the BBC, it retains the feel of a television costume drama in its obsession with detail and authenticity, of dress, of sets, of respect for the original text. The formality of 1912 Prague takes on a sheen of period quaintness, the mundanity of Josef's everyday world becoming a living museum exhibit.

Complicit with this is the casting of cameo roles. Jason Robards, Anthony Hopkins and Juliet Stevenson crop up as markers of pedigree, but they work against Josef K's descent into an ever more opaque and nightmarishly anonymous Law, in that they're too recognisable, and within that recognition is a distracting aspect of reassurance. You are lost but there is suddenly something to place. And as the film is structured mostly around two-character scenes, the sequential unfolding of the narrative is undercut by the ever present question, "who's next?" It seems churlish to fault such a well-intentioned, technically formidable production—Carl Davis's score has a rousingly bombastic feel to it and most of the acting is top notch (Michael Kitchen's Block is a particular gem). But the film also displays a homogenising 'great works' aesthetic that's as readily transposed onto Dickens, Forster and Conan Doyle. Perhaps when it is screened on TV, with audience expectation already geared towards the viewing context, there won't be this sense of underachievement by overshooting the mark. But compare it with *Hunger*, Henning Carlsen's 1966 version of the Knut Hamsun novel. There, the protagonist's apartness is signalled by the use of an extremely narrow depth of field, and by the sparseness of sound; the mechanics of film throw him into relief. David Jones' floods of light and foregrounded baroque architecture have the reverse effect: stretched across the big screen, they draw things together, ornamentally unite them.

It's an effective film, though, if not a particularly affecting evocation of the original. There's the pleasure of luxury, of the staging and acting, and the intrigue of Kyle MacLachlan's lisping English-accented Josef. But as the dagger finally glistens above his chest with a chiaroscuro sheen, you can't help thinking that it's displeasure that's needed, and sordidness too.

VILLAGE VOICE, 11/30/93, Film Special/p. 32, Julie Lang

Nietzsche said that the sun only rises because we want it to, meaning that all order is delusion, and that without the self or consciousness, chaos ensues. In Harold Pinter's adaptation of Kafka's

The Trial, one might expect this rationale to be stripped away in order to depict a sheer absurdity of existence. One might expect this film to transform hopelessness into an undertow, sweeping away all logic into oblivion. On the contrary, it is the audience who must act as an undertow, pulling the actors away from the characters and seizing Kafka's natural and consumptive tension from the melodramatic tubas blaring like a neon sign that screams, "Despair! You are to feel despair!" But it is not despair, it is boredom you feel.

Superficially, *The Trial* is about a man, Joseph K. (Kyle MacLachlan), unjustly arrested for a crime that's never explained; he will always be on trial and guilty until executed. Throughout his life sentence—a sentence which grants him external freedoms like working as a senior clerk at a bank in Prague—Joseph K. travels along political, moral, theological, and sexual paths to discover that although existence, as the priest (Anthony Hopkins) metaphorically says, "receives you when you come, it dismisses you when you go." When Joseph K.—K. representing Kafka himself—is finally dismissed beneath a glimmering knife wielded above his bare chest, the looming slabs of a granite quarry, impenetrable and cold, and those tubas bellowing, "There is no escape!" the film ends and I am relieved.

And I want to be relieved because this is the life of a man bearing an existential seal of death. Death is his sole resolution. But entering the D train, I realize that the relief is not as profound, it is actually quite simple: the movie was dull. Perhaps with names like Pinter, Hopkins, and MacLachlan all synthesizing the text of Kafka, each negates the other to produce REM. To be frank, I wanted my sleepiness to be Nietzsche's sun, I wanted to escape into the film's illusory world, to experience Kafka's hell. Instead I found only big names and bright ideas, but no body.

Also reviewed in:
CHICAGO TRIBUNE, 4/8/94, Friday/p. I, Clifford Terry
NEW REPUBLIC, 12/20/93, p. 36, Stanley Kauffmann
NEW YORK TIMES, 11/24/93, p. C16, Janet Maslin
VARIETY, 2/1/93, p. 99, Todd McCarthy

TRUE ROMANCE

A Warner Bros. release of a Morgan Creek production in association with Davis Film. *Executive Producer:* James G. Robinson, Gary Barber, Bob Weinstein, Harvey Weinstein, and Stanley Margolis. *Producer:* Bill Unger, Steve Perry, and Samuel Hadida. *Director:* Tony Scott. *Screenplay:* Quentin Tarantino. *Director of Photography:* Jeffrey L. Kimball. *Editor:* Michael Tronick and Christian Wagner. *Music:* Hans Zimmer. *Music Editor:* Thomas Milano. *Sound:* William B. Kaplan and (music) Jay Rifkin. *Sound Editor:* Robert G. Henderson. *Casting:* Risa Bramon Garcia and Billy Hopkins. *Production Designer:* Benjamin Fernandez. *Art Director:* James J. Murakami. *Set Decorator:* Thomas L. Roysden. *Set Dresser:* Larry Boyd. *Special Effects:* Mike Meinardus. *Costumes:* Susan Becker. *Make-up:* Ellen Wong. *Prosthetic Make-up:* Frank Carrisosa. *Stunt Coordinator:* Charles Picerni. *Running time:* 118 minutes. *MPAA Rating:* R.

CAST: Christian Slater (Clarence Worley); Patricia Arquette (Alabama Whitman); Dennis Hopper (Clifford Worley); Val Kilmer (Mentor); Gary Oldman (Drexl Spivey); Brad Pitt (Floyd, Dick's Roommate); Christopher Walken (Vincenzo Coccotti); Bronson Pinchot (Elliot Blitzer); Samuel L. Jackson (Big Don); Michael Rapaport (Dick Ritchie); Saul Rubinek (Lee Donowitz); Conchata Ferrell (Mary Louise Ravencroft); James Gandolfini (Virgil); Anna Thomson (Lucy); Victor Argo (Lenny); Paul Bates (Marty); Chris Penn (Nicky Dimes); Tom Sizemore (Cody Nicholson); Said Faraj (Burger Man); Gregory Sporleder (Burger Stand Customer); Maria Pitillo (Kandi); Frank Adonis (Frankie); Kevin Corrigan (Marvin); Paul Ben-Victor (Luca); Michael Beach (Wurlitzer); Joe D'Angerio (Police Radio Operator); John Bower (Detective); John Cenatiempo (Squad Cop #1); Eric Allan Kramer (Boris); Patrick

John Hurley (Monty);   Dennis Garber (Lobby Cop #1);   Scott Evers (Lobby Cop #2);   Hillary Klym (Running cop);   Steve Gonzales (I.A. Officer);   Laurence Mason (Floyd "D").

FILMS IN REVIEW, 11-12/93, p. 417, Andy Pawelczak

True Romance is a bit of a phenomenon. In its two-hour length, a thousand years of European culture and civilization go down the drain without even a gurgle, and in their place we get a vacuum-sealed world of kung-fu and mafia movies, comic book heroes, a steady diet of hamburgers, and a main character whose guardian angel and alter ego is Elvis. The filmmakers obviously love this pop American phantasmagoria and treat it without condescension. and their feeling keeps the picture moving along despite a few longeurs and abrupt shifts in tone. They've also had the good sense to cast a whole roster of interestingly idiosyncratic performers who contribute to the picture's chrome plated narcissism and value free pop absurdist tone.

Alabama (Patricia Arquette) and Clarence (Christian Slater) are made for each other; like the Sissy Spacek character in *Badlands* (though without that film's sense of anomie), she's immersed in true romances, and he's a fantasist devoted to Elvis. A Saturday night Venus wrapped in a tight red dress that matches her blisteringly red lips, she picks him up, in a hilarious rendition of every adolescent male's dream, in an empty theater showing a kung-fu movie. It turns out that she's a call girl (not a hooker, she proudly insists) hired by his boss to give him a good time on his birthday. After a night of great sex (photographed in a banal perfume ad style) and even greater soul trillings and mergings, they get married the·next day. However, there's trouble in paradise; she has a pimp, and Clarence's guardian angle, Elvis, who appears in a mirror in his trademark gold-sequined regalia at crucial points in the movie, tells him he has to shoot the pimp. In the first of the film's many bloody scenes, Clarence kills him and accidentally ends up with a suitcase full of cocaine belonging to the mob, and the rest of the movie is about his attempt to unload the coke on movie people in L.A. as the mob tracks him down.

The picture is directed by Tony Scott, but its real auteur is the screenplay writer, Quentin Tarantino, who wrote and directed *Reservoir Dogs*. Tarantino, a young man of considerable talent, specializes in big macho confrontations featuring funny, loopy monologues strung out like bright papier mache baubles on a rudimentary plot. The writing is somehow brilliant and spurious at the same time; Tarantino has a knack for deflecting a cliche onto a surprising new path, and while you're watching it's dazzling, though ultimately it's short on any real substance. But who am I to complain when a movie delivers such funny, creepy scenes as Clarence's face-off with the pimp and the fatal encounter between a mob boss played by Christopher Walken and Clarence's father (Dennis Hopper).

As the pimp, Gary Oldman is hugely funny and sinister in what is a variation on his Dracula role. Dressed in a leopard skin shirt exposing his chest, shark's tooth necklace, and black leather beret, and sporting a scruffy beard and dreadlocks, he leers, jokes, harangues, and threatens, all the while wolfing down a Chinese meal. As the Don who tortures Hopper in order to extract information about Clarence's whereabouts, Walken walks through his role, but it's always a pleasure to see the newest refinements in his reptilian mode, and he has a smile that's like a multi-petalled flower of evil. Hopper also turns in a beautifully modulated performance as the shrewd country bumpkin ex-cop who asks the Don for a cigarette (which he knows will be his last) before proceeding to insult his Sicilian ancestry.

Ultimately, the movie's success depends on its two main performances, and Christian Slater as Clarence and Patricia Arquette as Alabama are very good. Like Bonnie and Clyde, they're epic heroes without portfolio as they tool around in Clarence's purple Cadillac convertible looking for the big killing and the next giggly adventure. Both performers get the right mix of goofy, slightly vacant innocence and hip sophistication, and both are endearing without being cute or saccharine. I should add that Arquette's close-ups are stunning and romantic.

The movie's L.A. scenes have some very funny moments. Saul Rubinek is terrific as a venal, fast talking, coke dealing producer whose big movie was a Vietnam film called *Coming Home In A Bodybag*, and Bronson Pinchot is funny as his sycophantic, sniveling gofer. Brad Pitt is also good as a stoned hippie marooned on his couch who smokes pot filtered through honey. I'm sorry I missed the name of the actor who plays an over excited detective who looks like a refugee from *Miami Vice* and longs for the big bust that will make him a celebrity. Val Kilmer is a fleeting presence as Elvis, but he has the King's finger snapping gesture just right.

Tony Scott's direction errs in several ways, though he gets superior performances from the cast. He depends too much on close ups which eliminate the sets—I wanted to see more of Clarence's apartment with its Elvis shrine and more of the pimp's vulgarly plush drug lair—and during fight scenes his camera becomes incoherent. The movie ends with a big shoot-out reminiscent of the final shootout in *Reservoir Dogs*, but it misses the sheer deadpan craziness of that movie's finale due to Scott's hyperactive camerawork and editing. My only other cavil is the feeling I occasionally had of getting a sly sidelong glance from the filmmakers whenever they hit on a particularly clever idea, but I suppose that goes with the territory—true romance for the cool, wised-up beyond irony, inordinately young citizens of the post-modern world.

LOS ANGELES TIMES, 9/10/93, Calendar/p. 1, Kenneth Turan

It is hard to say what is more dispiriting about "True Romance," the movie itself or the fact that someone somewhere is sure to applaud its hollow, dime-store nihilism and smug pseudo-hip posturing as a bright new day in American cinema.

In truth this latest example of Hollywood's growing fascination with Bad Boy Chic (the kind of films where the men are violence-prone misfits and the women gasp and coo) has all the originality of a paper cup. A derivative dead end that pushes familiar genre themes way past absurdity, "True Romance" is anything but truthful and not even remotely romantic.

Starring Christian Slater and Patricia Arquette as lowlifes in jeopardy and in love, "True Romance" also features cameos by Dennis Hopper, Gary Oldman, Christopher Walken, Brad Pitt and Chris Penn, actors with a gleeful affinity for sadistic beatings, sullen gunplay and other over-the-edge antics.

The light for all these moths is screenwriter Quentin Tarantino, the poet laureate of Bad Boy Chic, whose brassy debut as a writer-director, "Reservoir Dogs," brought so much spirited energy and enthusiasm to its blood-soaked violence that casually dismissing it couldn't be done.

Tarantino, however, is not the director here. Tony Scott is, and one of the few things "True Romance" (rated R for strong violence and language and for sexuality and drug use) does well is provide a strong argument for writers being put in charge of their own material.

A celebrated director of commercials, Scott has had major box-office successes ("Top Gun" and "Beverly Hills Cop II") as well as embarrassments ("The Hunger" and "Days of Thunder"), but a sensitivity to the written word and a grace with actors have never been his trademarks. "Romance's" clumsy treatment of Tarantino's idiosyncratic lines will be obvious to anyone who has seen "Reservoir Dogs," and its considerable violence feels piled on and excessive in a way that picture managed to avoid.

In fairness, though, "Romance," apparently the first thing Tarantino ever wrote and sold, is not the most compelling of narratives. With its erratic plot turns and showoff sequences, it has the feeling of a "Hey, notice me" spec script, written to impress anyone who read it with how clever its creator is. And its inclusion of sappy plot twists better suited to "Free Willy" does not speak well for its thematic integrity.

Clarence Worley (Slater), mild-mannered comic-book store employee and major fan of Asian fighting hero Sonny Chiba, is first glimpsed at a bar, trying to pick up an understandably bored floozy by rhapsodizing about Elvis and his own personal "live fast, die young and leave a good-looking corpse" philosophy.

Hanging out at his favorite action theater, Clarence makes a connection with Alabama Whitman (Arquette), a bimbo with a heart of gold who keeps falling out of her fluorescent clothes and has a weakness for fake leopard-skin outfits.

Though no signs of it are visible on screen, Clarence and Alabama immediately develop such a passion for each other that his and hers tattoos can't be avoided. Next, after some business with the nasty Drexl Spivey (Oldman, over the top even for him) gets taken care of, the love birds head out for California in a large purple Cadillac, determined to make their fortune and avoid the evil forces that have ended up on their trail.

In its focus on star-crossed lovers on the run, "True Romance" tries to be a kind of post-modern homage to the lonely hearts of film noir. Unfortunately, without a sense of style that extends below its trash-looking surface, its extremes of behavior are tedious and cartoonish and its attempts at wit little more than smug.

Unable to get the emotional effects it is after, "True Romance" ends up, like a defiant teen-ager, striking what it thinks are the appropriate poses and hoping nobody will notice the difference. The film also displays an almost religious veneration for on-screen violence, a blanket reverence for guns and blood as gee-whiz swell that is both childish and off-putting. Nothing is more irritating than a dumb film that thinks it's hip, and "True Romance" is this year's model.

NEW STATESMAN & SOCIETY, 10/22/93, p. 33, Jonathan Romney

I've always thought that the main advantage in taking the moral high ground in criticism was that, from time to time, you got to use the word "pernicious". I like the way it rolls off the tongue, and the way that its use suggests an unshakeable certainty about what is and isn't desirable. So, for once, I'll allow myself the luxury and award the "pernicious" tag to *True Romance*.

Not that the film's likely to cause any harm or rot the moral fibre of our nation. For a film to be pernicious, it's enough for it to be simply a cheap shot—or worse, an expensive cheap shot. *True Romance* is self-indulgent, narcissistic and mean-spirited, but it's particularly loathsome for taking a brew of potentially inflammable ingredients and turning them into dramatic porridge.

Sex, drugs, rock'n'roll, racism and movie-buff navel gazing—and *this* is all you get? It's a dumb profligacy that makes the more tangible wastefulness of the average Hollywood blockbuster look like good housekeeping.

True Romance is directed by Tony Scott, but its real author is bound to be identified as critical favourite Quentin Tarantino, who wrote and sold the script before making his extraordinary *Reservoir Dogs*. That was his classical movie, essentially a one-set, one-storyline film; this is his romantic vagary, which touches every base that it possibly can.

It's a love story, a crime movie, a black comedy, a road romance, a rock fantasia, but none of these things for very long. It keeps you on your toes, only because it keeps shifting its genre and moral position.

The first sudden dislocation comes early on in our relation to Clarence (Christian Slater), an amiable kung-fu movie nerd who meets sexy, gum-chewing Alabama (Patricia Arquette) and falls head over heels with her. It turns out that she's a call girl turning a trick as his birthday present, but what the hell, it's mutual fluttering hearts and they marry on the spot. But when the camera gets Clarence alone, he's suddenly striking Travis Bickle poses in front of the mirror and taking instruction from a spectral Elvis figure. Suddenly, he's not so amiable. But he can't be pegged easily as a psychopath—his craziness is set up as an endearing recklessness that we're asked to revel in as he blows away Alabama's pimp and makes off with his stash of coke.

From here on, the moral perspectives we might expect drop out—but not to any subversive effort. We're simply asked to go along with Clarence and Alabama for the ride, to let ourselves be carried along by their effortless lame-brain flair. The trouble is, the films that *True Romances* owes most to—crazy-love road pics from *Bonnie and Clyde* to *Wild at Heart* via *Badlands*—ask us to participate in the moral complexity embodied by the adventures of their good-bad innocent couples. Here, the lovers are simply vacant passengers of the film's high-grade slickness, and we're asked to empty our heads out too.

For its target age-group, the film drops in endless images of don't-give-a-fuck hipster cool—lashings of Elvisiana and comic-book kitsch, and flip pop-culture turns like Brad Pitt as a zombified Nirvana reject. For the more cinephilic culture-spotter, the movie allusions are relentless: gags about Hollywood's Vietnam, *Doctor Zhivago*, the Elvis phantom borrowed from *Mystery Train*, and a trimly nasty scene in which Dennis Hopper is cast against type as a nice-guy victim. In fact, the film's structure is really a series of sketches—oddball vignettes from Hopper, Christopher Walken, Chris Penn and Gary Oldman but with no sense of a bigger picture linking them.

Such a non-structure might not have harmed *Wild at Heart*, where the sense of aimless delirium was part of the rationale. Here, the idea of California, the idyll at the end of the road, suggests a sense of purpose the film is never equal to. Everything happens strictly for the hell of it. It's like a grazer's meal, a random selection of highly spiced dishes. And the slap-up conclusion is simply like a big messy plate of jelly and custard served up at the end to make you think that if it ends like a meal, it must be a meal.

What's objectionable about the dishes themselves? Plenty that will be picked over at greater length elsewhere—most obviously, the flip racism of the scene in which Hopper taunts mafioso Walken ("Sicilians are niggers"), and the drawn-out knock-down fight in which Arquette gets grotesquely battered. It's a gruesome scene, thrown in almost as an academic exercise or a dare. A heroine battered, unequivocally brutalised, not just decoratively scratched like Sigourney Weaver in the *Alien* films—now there's a *recherché* extra that Hollywood doesn't treat you to every day.

The scene's not about violence, but about the idea of violence as a smart generic device. The film uses violence as a sort of pathetic fallacy—the weather in which the lovers breathe. In the final big number, the romance consummates itself in a snowstorm apocalypse of coke, blood and flying feathers. It's apparently a homage to a current hip favourite, feather-loving Hong Kong action director John Woo.

The kind of passion celebrated here—in drunken second-hand images—is purely self-regarding; but so is the central romance, with its winsome lovers exuding a hermetic smugness that lets the rest of the world go to blazes.

Clarence and Alabama are no more sociopathic than any other mutually besotted young cretins. But being in love allows them to walk through the world unscathed while all the nasties and second-raters that the film so visibly shies away from are casually blown away. It doesn't accumulate the anonymous body-count of most Hollywood action films; more insidiously, the film lets us get just close enough to characters to discount them as figures fit to survive.

No one worries about the Third Messenger getting wasted, but this is like taking relish in Rosencrantz and Guildenstern getting the bullet because, poor saps, they don't have the honour to be Hamlet. Set up for destruction are a bunch of sap mafiosi, some equally sappy cops, Gary Oldman's repellent white rasta and a couple of Hollywood sleazos named Blitzer and Donowitz—quite clearly the decadent Jewish antithesis of all that our two clean-limbed, hip, Aryan lovers stand for.

When you get to the end, you see why *True Romance* doesn't need a structure: because it's simply a Darwinian obstacle course, in which only the leanest and meanest, and whitest, survive. (It's not explicitly a racist film, but it certainly follows on in a long tradition of occluding the *blackness* of rock'n'roll).

All this finally depresses more than it disturbs. Scott's glib, shiny direction wastes the darker potential of a script, that, had it been directed by someone sharper, maybe Tarantino himself, might have had more moral ambiguity. It *could* have been an American Bertrand Blier movie, which would have been something (by all accounts, Tarantino's bloodier, more negative original conception was watered down). With all this extremity, the film comes nowhere near being in any way challenging or transgressive. Hipness like this I can get from MTV. *That* kind of waste is what I call pernicious.

NEW YORK, 9/20/93, p. 65, David Denby

At the moment, killing someone appears to be the only adventure Americans can have on the road. Two movies about young lovers on the run—both heavily influenced by *Bonnie and Clyde, Badlands, Wild at Heart,* and *Thelma and Louise*—advance the curious proposition that in America you have to knock off someone in order to become a human being.

The unspeakable *True Romance* might have been conceived during a feverish night at Miss Heidi's. Overstimulated but glazed, the picture reeks of whorishness and self-disgust; it treats the audience as if it were half dead, as if it needed to be brought twitching to life with one shock after another. Christian Slater, who only recently gave promise of being a hip young actor, gives a smirking, inauthentic performance as a nowhere guy who becomes inspired when a girl and a suitcase of cocaine drop into his lap; Patricia Arquette is the lady, and she's supposed to be a call girl, but Arquette, who swings her shoulders around and grins moronically at everyone, acts more like a streetwalker. Distinguished actors—Samuel L. Jackson, Christopher Walken—drop in for a quickie, blowing someone away or getting blown away; and Gary Oldman, playing a pimp, does his "I'm reprehensible—isn't it cute?" number. He gets blown away, too.

Tony Scott (*Top Gun, Days of Thunder*) has gotten *worse* as a director, which couldn't have been an easy feat to pull off. The actors (presumably with Scott's encouragement) are trying so hard to be hip that we can't tell half the time what they're getting at; anyway, the staccato editing destroys what's left of their performances. (Dennis Hopper, however, playing a tough ex-cop, comes through, and Saul Rubinek and Bronson Pinchot are funny together as a sleazy Hollywood producer and his corruptible gofer.)

By now, Tony Scott is a familiar jack-rabbity hack. The new element here is Quentin Tarantino, writer and director of the nihilist blood comedy *Reservoir Dogs*. Tarantino's specialty is hyperarticulate viciousness and "playful" sadism. Working with Scott, whose flashdance style makes one indifferent to everyone onscreen, Tarantino creates episodes of ultraviolence, and the sheer irrelevance of the sliced-up hands and faces, the buckets of blood, the many shootings, may make the violence cool for some people. (Gee, it's great not to care; you can feel free and float off into pure sensation. Just what we need.) *True Romance* is preposterously bloody and ends with one of those nonsensical everybody-dies shoot-outs with three sets of people firing for hours and pillow feathers from mutilated sofas falling gently through the air. I guess that's Tony Scott's idea of poetry.

NEW YORK POST, 9/10/93, p. 41, Lawrence Cohn

In his TV ads tennis star Andre Agassi declares "Image is everything"; and that about sums up "True Romance," an up-to-the-moment treatise on amorality. It's bound to be a fashion trend-setter for young people, hopefully restricted to clothing and hairstyles rather than encouraging violent behavior.

Chief fashion plate is Christian Slater, an ordinary guy who works in a Detroit comic book store. He's given to grand gestures like entering the lion's den and killing the evil pimp (Gary Oldman wearing dreadlocks) of his new girlfriend, Patricia Arquette.

Quentin Tarantino of "Reservoir Dogs" fame wrote the quirky and highly original screenplay. The story's launching point is overly familiar: just like Uma Thurman in "Mad Dog and Glory," call girl Arquette is a birthday gift to loner Slater from his well-meaning boss. They watch three violent '75 Sonny Chiba films, spend a night in the sack, and then get married.

After visiting Slater's estranged dad Dennis Hopper, the twosome follow time-honored movie tradition and hop in a car to head for California. Hot on their trail (due to $500,000 in cocaine that Slater's mistakenly stolen from Oldman's possession) is evil mafioso Christopher Walken and his ruthless henchmen.

When the duo arrives in California to stay with pal Michael Rapaport, the film shifts gears—to become a deadly spoof of the Hollywood drug culture, self-important producers and their flunkies.

Despite the numerous colorful guest stars, Slater and Arquette dominate the picture, etching low-life youth icons who could probably defeat similarly trendy Brad Pitt & Juliette Lewis (of "Kalifornia") in a tag-team wrestling match. The redhot Mr. Pitt shows up in a hilarious cameo as Rapaport's totally stoned roommate.

The California scenes provide a field day for Saul Rubinek as a crass producer with a coke habit, and inspired comedy moments for Bronson Pinchot as his doomed yes-man.

Police procedure is lampooned in a wacky subplot reminiscent in tone of Joseph Wambaugh's "The Choirboys," as cops Tom Sizemore and Christopher Penn try to trap the protagonists in a drug bust. (Their stereotyped captain is played to perfection by Ed Lauter, the only guest star to remain anonymous, with no screen credit.)

Writer Tarantino has staked out a territory of pulp writing reminiscent of Mickey Spillane: it's that commercial combo of sadism and he-man action that paved the way for the success of Ian Fleming and his superspy James Bond.

With his brush-cut hairdo, Christian Slater as Clarence Worley is the '90s equivalent of Darren McGavin or Ralph Meeker as Mike Hammer in the '90s. Like his screen hero Charles Bronson, Clarence has a low center of gravity (all the better for fighting) and zero tolerance for society's restrictions.

The film is compromised by a phony happy ending that unbelievably resurrects Slater from the dead. That's a shame, because the gusto of the ensemble cast and the energy of Tony Scott's direction make for an entertaining buildup.

NEWSDAY, 9/10/93, Part II/p. 66, Jack Mathews

It is testimony to the impact of last year's stylish, ultra-violent "Reservoir Dogs" that "True Romance" is being referred to by many insiders as the new Quentin Tarantino film.

Tarantino wrote "True Romance," but it was directed by Tony Scott, who followed his brother Ridley from British TV commercials to Hollywood, where he hit the jackpot with such glossily packaged junk-food movies as "Top Gun," "Days of Thunder" and "Beverly Hills Cop II."

The matchup of Scott and Tarantino was just too ridiculous for most "Reservoir Dogs" fans to consider, so we were clinging to the name of the writer in hope that his script would carry the film.

It does, to a point. "True Romance," the umpteenth post-"Badlands," white-trash-lovers-on-the-road movie, the second in two weeks if you include "Kalifornia," has the same unsettling balance of humor and raw violence that caught us by surprise in "Reservoir Dogs." But it has none of the rationale.

With "Reservoir Dogs," we were cloistered in a warehouse with a bloodied gang of thieves returning from a failed jewelry heist, and the mayhem evolved logically from the escalating panic, as the gunmen tried to fix blame and unmask the traitor among them.

"True Romance" has no rational underfooting at all. It is a jaunty romantic fantasy following two likable losers, a comic-book-store clerk named Clarence (Christian Slater) and his hooker bride, Alabama (Patricia Arquette, from Detroit to L.A., where they hope to unload a misbegotten stash of cocaine, and live off the proceeds.

When the violence erupts, as it frequently does, it switches the tone as abruptly as if someone on "The Brady Bunch" took a kitchen knife and opened the family dog.

The script is Tarantino's first, and it reflects the mind of a talented novice. Taking his inspiration from David Lynch, Tarantino has filled his story with eccentric characters and memorable dialogue. Scott gave it all the slick veneer for which he's noted. But it doesn't add up to much. The film hurls you from one funny or shocking skit to the next, and ends in a "Mad, Mad, Mad, Mad World" of blazing guns and exploding blood bags.

Still, the funny moments between knifings, beatings and executions are often very funny, and Clarence and Alabama are as deliciously goofy a couple as Sailor and Lulu in "Wild at Heart," whom they resemble beyond any chance of coincidence.

Where Sailor wanted to be Elvis, Clarence has Elvis as his ghostly adviser. Like, Lulu, Alabama seems to be along for the romance and the ride, to mate two or three times a day and stand by her man.

In the hilarious opening moments of "True Romance," Clarence is picked up by Alabama in a movie theater where he is watching a triple chopsocky feature. After a night of lovemaking, Alabama tearfully confesses that she was hired by Clarence's boss to show him a good time on his birthday, that she's only been in this line of work for four days and that she has fallen in love.

So has Clarence, and with Alabama still in the same Day-Glo spandex slutsuit, they rush to the courthouse and get married. Later that night, when Clarence comes home with her suitcase and a couple of Big Macs and explains, offhandedly, that he had to kill her pimp, she begins sobbing softly and says, "What you done was so romantic."

The major studio money behind "True Romance" bought an impressive array of cameo players, and they appear like so many jackalope and two-headed snake attractions you see along the highways in the West. Gary Oldman does the weirdest turn as Alabama's pimp, Drexl Spivey, a scar-faced menace with parched dreadlocks, a milk glass eye, gold-capped teeth and a speech pattern that is part reggae and part urban rap.

Others dropping in for a scene or two are Dennis Hopper as Clarence's dad, Christopher Walken as a sadistic (what else?) mob lieutenant, Brad Pitt as a slurring couch-potato druggie, Saul Rubinek as a movie producer/drug dealer and Val Kilmer as the sequin-clad ghost of Elvis.

What Tarantino had in mind with this script we may never know, but Scott treats the material as if it were another action film, shooting the fight sequences like those Mach 1 dogfights in "Top Gun."

His choreography and the editing give those scenes a stagy, balletic grace, but it's clear we're not watching Peckinpah's successor. The violence here is intended as pure entertainment, and there is a smug "Watch this" tone that undermines the film's considerable sweetness and good humor.

SIGHT AND SOUND, 11/93, p. 56, Lizzie Francke

Detroit. Clarence is a lonely young man who works in a comic store and is obsessed by movies. On the night of his birthday, he goes to the local cinema as usual and bumps into Alabama, a young woman who seems to share his obsession for kung-fu flicks. After the show they end up at his place and make love. The next morning Alabama confesses to Clarence that she is a call girl and that his boss paid for her to hitch up with him as a birthday treat. But she and Clarence have fallen in love, and they immediately marry. Clarence then visits Alabama's pimp Drexl Spivey, to fetch her things. Meanwhile Spivey has hijacked a stash of cocaine. They get into a fight, and Clarence ends up shooting Spivey and absconding with a suitcase that he thinks belongs to Alabama but actually contains a stash of cocaine that Spivey has hijacked.

Clarence and Alabama visit his dad, Clifford, an ex-cop who now works as a security guard. Clifford finds out from former colleagues that the police believe Spivey was murdered by a rival gang. Clarence and Alabama take their leave and decide to drive to LA and visit Clarence's old friend Richie, who Clarence hopes will be able to help him sell the coke. Back in Detroit, Clifford is visited by a mobster, Vicenzo Coccotti, and his henchmen, who are looking for Clarence and the coke. Clifford refuses to co-operate and is murdered. Meanwhile Clarence and Alabama arrive at Richie's where they meet his druggy roommate Floyd, before checking into a motel.

Richie introduces Clarence to Elliot, an assistant to a sleazy producer, Lee Donowitz, a potential buyer. Meanwhile, Coccotti's men have found Richie's address, where a flaked-out Floyd blithely tells them where Clarence and Alabama are staying. One of the henchmen goes to the motel, where he menaces Alabama; in an ensuing struggle, Alabama kills him. Clarence returns and the couple flee the motel. Meanwhile, Elliot is caught speeding and is discovered with drugs on him. In order to evade charges he is persuaded by the cops to help them bust Donowitz for dealing. Elliot has arranged for Clarence and Donowitz to meet at a Beverly Hills hotel. The police wire Elliot up. The meeting seems to go smoothly, but meanwhile Coccotti's henchmen also turn up at the hotel. As Clarence and Donowitz make the deal, the police move in. A gunfight follows involving the police, Donowitz's bodyguards and Coccotti's men. Alabama finds Clarence seemingly lifeless, but what looks like a bullet through the eye turns out to be a graze. Clarence comes round and in the middle of the mayhem, the two lovers sneak out, taking the suitcase of coke with them. They escape to the Mexican coast, have a son and live happily ever after.

The true romance on display here is between scriptwriter Quentin Tarantino and a litany of great B-movies. The film is as full of as many homages—or rip-offs, depending on how generous you are—as star cameos. Tarantino's first completed script, written before *Reservoir Dogs*, is a manic tribute to the thing that he most loves, although it is not without a cheeky chiding of the more unscrupulous aspects of his home town. The mogul Donowitz, whose magnum opus is a Vietnam flick *Home in a Body Bag*, seems to have come from the same off-the-peg sleazy producer line as Steve Martin's character in *Grand Canyon*.

The film has been touted by pundits as a *Badlands* for the 90s, but that is to overlook the complicated pathos and poetry of Terrence Malick's film. Or perhaps it's those pundits' short memories that can't stretch back to all those other films about gun-crazy lovers on the run. This is the comic strip version of those films as distinct from the pulp version. 'Pulp' implies that there is an emotional bruising to be had, whereas this film is stripped down to bold graphics and crazy bursts of inspired dialogue—there's no emotion. Emotion cannot be ironic, cannot be guarded by inverted commas. In *Badlands*, Sissy Spacek's character may have invested too much in the *Teen Romance* magazines with their Hollywood gossip and fluffy dreams, but Malick ensured that there was a bizarre wealth of feeling in those dime-store sentiments. Tarantino, however, trades in a currency of cleverness. His hero and heroine live and love in a movie frame. They even get the dream happy ending—complete with sunset—that would have never been allowed to their predecessors on the run to the Mexican borders. But their *True Romance* does not require true emotion.

For if the film were about true emotion, then what would we make of its more dubious passions? The invective about "niggers" in *Reservoir Dogs* could be attributed to the pristine-suited sewer rats who spat the words out. It was scum dialogue for scummy men. The characters in *True Romance* inhabit the same low-rent domain. But somehow there is a weary sense of *déjà vu* as Clifford launches into his number about Sicilians being related to "niggers" since they are "aubergine coloured". This comes across as clever white-trash talk so loaded with irony as to mock those who are offended. But the bizarre and audacious cameo appearance of Gary Oldman as an African-American rasta certainly rankles, as does the sadistically prolonged fight between Alabama and Coccotti's henchman. She may turn the tables on him, but not before incurring a sound and furious beating in a bathroom full of jagged glass.

Such routines are problematic and cannot be glibly dismissed (the Sicilian/nigger dialogue has already been acclaimed as "brilliant" by the critic Clancy Sigal). But the boyish outrage aspires to be forgiven with the quirky turns of the rest of the film. Brad Pitt as the spliffed-out space lieutenant Floyd, who sees Coccotti's men less as the heavy mob than as a heavy trip, is truly funny. There are also the bravura rapid-fire conversational exchanges that allow characters to be pegged in one liners. This is Tarantino's gift; Tony Scott may be directing, but like a stick of rock, the film is shot through with Tarantino's name. But what remains to be seen is whether his infatuation with film can mature into something a little more profound. With *True Romance* it expresses itself as a frenzied affair, exciting at the time but easily forgotten.

TIME, 9/13/93, p. 78, Richard Corliss

If shoot-'em-up, gobble-'em-down movies like *The Fugitive* and *Jurassic Park* are rated PG-13 these days, what does an R-rated action adventure look like! Like *True Romance*: violent to a fault, glam to the max.

Writer Quentin Tarantino (*Reservoir Dogs*) and director Tony Scott (*Top Gun, Beverly Hills Cop II*) must have figured: If we're gonna *get* an R, then dammit, let's make an R. For a while, *True Romance* had the restrictive NC-17 rating, and there's still enough carnage in the R version to make an audience wince out loud. A white drug dealer perforates some black thugs. Palms get sliced, feet corkscrewed, skulls smashed with toilet-tank lids, eyes and other essential organs blown out. The movie climaxes with a dozen or so thugs, druggies, cops—and that lowest form of slime mold, a movie producer—edgily pointing heavy artillery at one another.

Only the most desperate scavengers would trawl for a story line in this swamp of sensation, but here goes. Clarence (Christian Slater) works in a Detroit comic-book store. It's his birthday, and as a present his boss has bought him a surprise call girl, Alabama (Patricia Arquette). She may vaguely aspire to be Melanie Griffith, and if Clarence hopes to travel abroad, it is only because he "always wanted to see what TV in other countries looked like"; but this is true romance. The two must marry, run into some mortal trouble (Gary Oldman as a drug dealer, Christopher Walken as a Mafia don) and flee—with the surprise package of a suitcase full of cocaine—to Los Angeles. Their moral code is hardly more righteous than that of their pursuers, but they're on their way, down a white-brick road toward the end of the rainbow. You kind of know Elvis will be there.

If you believe for a moment that *True Romance* is a character study, you must be one of the actors in it. For the audience it's a vivid exercise in style. Or more precisely, an exercise in fashion. Scott made his name directing British TV spots; he can make each image yummy, seductive, good enough to buy, whether the scene is selling sex, violence or some slick sociopathic blend of the two. He pummels your eye with wide-screen close-ups that eroticize violence and give a lurid threat to the sex. The love scene is a French-kissin', torso-lickin' jeans ad set to cinema. In the big shoot-out at the end, bloody cushion feathers smother the screen in slo-mo.

The performers, especially Walken, Oldman and Saul Rubinek as the producer, do everything in big-mo. In its acting as well as its writing and direction, this is a live-action cartoon, a fantasy (and a sidewise critique) of machismo. It's a crimson fresco of smart people playing evil ones. The whole enterprise is noisy as hell, but you know it's there.

VILLAGE VOICE, 9/14/93, p. 60, Manohla Dargis

Directed by pulp professional Tony Scott and scripted by art-house sensation Quentin Tarantino, *True Romance* bristles with possibility. Fast, sexy, and terminally hip, it's the story of, among other things wild, a couple on the run, a million in coke, Elvis, Hollywood, T. J. Hooker, and the fact that the most important three little words one lover can murmur to the other are no longer *I love you* but *You're so cool.*

When we first meet cool, cool Clarence Worley (Christian Slater), he's entertaining a blowzy Marilyn clone with a soliloquy on Elvis and other pleasures. "I'm no fag," explains Clarence, "but if my life depended on it ... I'd fuck Elvis." I'd fuck Elvis, too, says the blond, who nevertheless passes on his invite to a kung-fu triple bill. A good thing, too, since it's in the haze of projector light that Alabama Whitman (a *fine* Patricia Arquette) will spill her popcorn on Clarence's head and find true love. ("Thanks for being such a sweetheart," she gushes, "you could have been a dick.")

A half-dozen cheapsters distilled into one giddy joyride, *True Romance* wastes no time putting its lovers on the run with a suitcase of dope, just a few edits after the two trade pillow talk that sounds scripted by a *Playboy* centerfold (the opening sex scene is strictly Zalman King). Turn-ons? Clarence asks the future Mrs. Worley. "Mickey Rourke, somebody who can appreciate the finer things in life ...," answers the soon-to-be ex-hooker with a heart of purest platinum. More Doris and Rock than Bonnie and Clyde, the cute couple doesn't just reference movies, they live them, line by memorable line. Indeed, movie talk fuels their ride, with everybody but everybody talking and dreaming Hollywood, from Clarence's friend Dick to Alabama's pimp, Drexl.

When Clarence says, "We now return to *Bullitt*, already in progress," burning enough rubber to make Steve McQueen proud, it's hard to remember he worked in a comic book not video rental store. Easily the film's most conspicuous cinematic touchstone is *Badlands*, in particular Alabama's affectless voiceover and that hurdy-gurdy ditty Scott worries like a charm. It's virtual scripture that the Malick picture is a gloss on American mass culture, but really it's closer to a cultural postmortem. Kit and Holly (based on the real-life duet, Charles Starkweather and Caril Fugate) don't kill because they've soaked up too much EC Comics or Ed Sullivan, but because there's nothing else to do. Clarence and Alabama, in contrast, slip into violence through an accident of fate, not anomie. Driven by chance and sweet, sweet love, the two are negotiating a pop wasteland that, like Tarantino, they totally, faithfully, fatefully dig.

By the time Clarence and Alabama make their way to L.A., they've racked up enough film facts to qualify for *Jeopardy*. Still, there's a surprising freshness to the duo's not-so-trivial pursuits, whether they're humping in a telephone booth or fighting an army of darkness. *Pow! Zap!* Which isn't to say all the snap, crackle of smashed faces and crunched bone doesn't shock (at one screening, vacated seats snapped back frequently), they do. If anything, the violence is direct and blunt, there's nothing remotely discreet about the pain, the payoff, or the kill.

Screenwriter Tarantino is a *pasticheur*, a pop culture relativist who switch-hits between the Bard and the King, and never once thinks one better than the other. When Clarence mentions there's something rotten in Denmark, and tosses in a few Shakespearean fare-thee-wells, it's because he heard it in a movie, nothing more, nothing less. Even so, while Tarantino is clearly smarter and hipper than Clarence (Alabama is another matter), the upper hand doesn't make him smug. He never condescends to either character, who may not be deep enough for tragedy but surely have soul.

It's too bad Scott can't always tap that soul; he's an exceptional hack, but his Hollywood imperative muscles through Tarantino's pop poetics with a vengeance. There's little of *Dogs*'s narrative mystery or formal suppleness in this film, and Scott's direction and cutting are grindingly predictable (scenes slam together like sides of meat). One time his bombast actually works wonders is a drag-down fight between Clarence and Drexl. Framed against inferno red, the men hurl through space and into metal, glass, feet, and fists as the music pulses a relentless rhythm, their bodies working a brutal, seductive counterpoint to the beat pumping under our skin. The miracle of *True Romance* is its routine ingredients never congeal into generic thrills. Blessed with a terrific script and cast, Scott can only do so much damage, and once Clarence and Alabama let loose, watch out.

The performances are creamy, from hipster icons Christopher Walken and Dennis Hopper (as Clarence's 12-Step Daddy) to Slater, Arquette, Gary Oldman (with a head full of natty dreads and an accent from who the fuck knows), Brad Pitt (who almost steals home), Val Kilmer, and a clutch of others (Peter Fonda is MIA). If nothing else, the preponderance of pretty guys makes obvious that the film's real romance isn't between men and women but men and men. Working the same homoerotic turf as *Reservoir Dogs*, Tarantino and Scott test the limits of fear, desire, and masculinity with razor wit and surprising heart. Clarence may screw Alabama, but he's saving his innuendo for the boys.

Also reviewed in:
CHICAGO TRIBUNE, 9/10/93, Friday/p. D, Clifford Terry
NEW YORK TIMES, 9/10/93, p. C5, Janet Maslin
VARIETY, 9/6/93, p. 27, Leonard Klady
WASHINGTON POST, 9/10/93, p. G1, Richard Harrington
WASHINGTON POST, 9/10/93, Weekend/p. 45, Desson Howe

TRUSTING BEATRICE

A Castle Hill Productions release of a J.J. Films production. *Producer:* Mark Evan Jacobs and Cindy Lou Johnson. *Director:* Cindy Lou Johnson. *Screenwriter:* Cindy Lou Johnson. *Director of Photography:* Bernd Heinl. *Editor:* Camilla Toniolo. *Music:* Stanley Myers. *Sound:* Mark Weingarten. *Production Designer:* Cynthia Kay Charette. *Art Director:* Philip Messina. *Set Decorator:* Robert Kensinger. *Costumes:* Isis Mussenden. *Running time:* 86 minutes. *MPAA Rating:* PG.

CAST: Irène Jacob (Beatrice de Lucio); Mark Evan Jacobs (Claude Dewey); Charlotte Moore (Mrs. Dewey); Leonardo Cimino (Daddy V.J.); Pat McNamara (Mr. Dewey); Steve Buscemi (Danny); Nady Meas (Seap Sok); Samuel Wright (Dr. White).

LOS ANGELES TIMES, 1/29/93, Calendar/p. 11, Michael Wilmington

The French actress Irene Jacob has a real heartbreaker's face; with her succulent lips, tossing pixie hair and sparkling eyes, she easily seduces the camera. Better than almost all her young contemporaries, Jacob, who won the 1991 Cannes acting grand prize as Krzysztof Kieslowski's "Veronique," suggests the vibrant spontaneity of another human being, one you love to watch.

But not, unfortunately, in "Trusting Beatrice." Nothing wears faster than winsomeness belabored or blitheness contrived. And those are the curses of this well-intentioned tale of romance between a hapless Providence, R.I. gardener and the illegal French immigrant girl of his dreams. "Beatrice" means to soar and sing, but it's blocky, awkward, forced.

Part of the problem is thematic. Part is simple pacing. And part is the fizzy chemistry between the leading players: Jacob as the devil-may-care Beatrice de Lucio and Mark Evan Jacobs, as shambling, luckless Claude Dewey—who begins the film by discovering his original sweetheart *in flagrante delicto*, and then accidentally burns down his own house.

Beatrice is a life force, when she sees the Atlantic, she immediately strips and runs in. She's also homeless; her part seems calculated to nibble at all our liberal pieties. And, when she shows up with a 4-year-old Cambodian orphan girl named Seap Sok (Nady Meas) in a little red wagon, the movies shamelessness is complete.

The Dewey family is comfortably off: neurotic Mama Dewey (Charlotte Moore), morose Dad Dewey (Pat McNamara) and silent, demented Grandpa Dewey (Leonardo Cimino), who puts broccoli on his head at dinner in a vain attempt to loosen everyone up. Is their silliness validated by the fact that they can afford it? The movie, which is about misfits finding one another, instead suggests that stupidity is a kind of state of grace, that the barmier you are, the nearer you are to bliss.

It's tempting to say that the entire film revolves around what critic Damon Knight used to call an "idiot plot"—a plot that only functions because everyone involved is an idiot—but the filmmakers might argue that these people aren't stupid; they're just trapped in social conventions and structures that make them seem stupid. And it would also be unfair to the non-dopes in the story, like Samuel Wright as black psychiatrist Dr. White and Steve Buscemi, as Claude's harried yuppie attorney, Danny, who, not coincidentally, give the film's best performances.

"Beatrice" is the writer-directorial debut of playwright Cindy Lou Johnson ("Brilliant Traces," "The Years"). But it doesn't feel like a playwright's film. The dialogue is one of the film's biggest weaknesses. Careless love, rapture and romance came in for a beating in the movies of the Bottom Line '80s, and judging from "Trusting Beatrice" (MPAA rated PG) they haven't quite recovered. Watching it, we're much like Claude, early in the film, when he answers the door to a Girl Scout selling cookies and then slams the door, only to hear her caterwauling in the corridor. How can we refuse a movie that bangs on our door and offers us whimsy, goofy romance, Bernd Heinl cinematography and Irene Jacob? The problem with buying cookies, however, is that you may have to toss them later on.

NEW YORK POST, 2/12/93, p. 31, Audrey Farolino

"Trusting Beatrice" wants desperately to be a quirky romantic comedy, and it at least succeeds on one count: It's desperately quirky. But there's nothing very romantic about it, and to call it a comedy is seriously overstating the case.

Sad to say, the film marks the American film debut of Irene Jacob, the luminous French beauty from "The Double Life of Veronique."

Jacob is here reduced to playing a not-very-bright young French woman who has fled to America after attempting to kill her husband with a fish knife, and who is now not only an illegal alien but also the illegal guardian of a sad-eyed young Cambodian girl (quirky, no?).

The film also marks the feature-film directing debut of playwright Cindy Lou Johnson. It's hard to say whether Johnson's direction or writing is more at fault here, but it's probably safe to blame them equally.

Beatrice (Jacob) arrives in some unnamed American city (it's actually Providence, R.I.) pulling a little red wagon in which sits Seap Sok, the Cambodian girl. She rents a room in a boarding house, but—zut—the house burns down the very day they move in.

Though declared arson, the fire was actually started accidentally by another of the house's residents, Claude Dewey (Mark Evan Jacobs), an emotionally muddled young landscape artist who torches his girlfriend's pictures after she cheats on him.

Beatrice encounters Claude aa she's picking through the ashes. Though Claude doesn't admit to having started the fire, out of guilt he offers to take Beatrice and Seap home to his parents' house.

Dysfunctional would be a fair description for the Dewey family: Claude's mother (Charlotte Moore, who deserves a special Oscar for overacting) is a ditzy hysteric with artistic ambitions, and the father and grandfather are both nearly catatonic, though the latter does occasionally put hankies and broccoli on his head (how quirky can you get?).

Beatrice is supposed to be a kind of enchanting waif who helps the family change thanks to her bubbly spirit and capacity for love. Mostly, though, she comes across as a confused young woman with a Ricky Ricardo-ish propensity for mangled English.

Will Claude fall in love with Beatrice? Will the family come to grips with its problems? Will Beatrice solve her legal problems? Chances are, you don't care.

NEWSDAY, 2/12/93, Part II/p. 71, John Anderson

Eccentricity doesn't equal drama, stupidity doesn't equal pathos, and stringing together a series of loosely connected, marginally humerous scenes doesn't make you a filmmaker. A television writer, maybe.

Or, an off-Broadway playwright. Cindy Lou Johnson, chief perpetrator of the reputed comedy "Trusting Beatrice," and a former writer for the small screen, has authored several recent stage productions—including "Brilliant Traces" and the current "The Years"—that have been criticized primarily for containing characters too stupid to breathe.

If nothing else, she's consistent. "Trusting Beatrice," which at best is a precious-girl-meets-slackjawed-boy story, uses up enormous amounts of time and the English-language debut of the radiant Irene Jacob ("The Double Life of Veronique") to prove little besides the fact that Johnson can avoid making a cogent point for the duration of a feature-length film. At least.

Johnson, whose sensibility is too pedestrian to be absurdist, is of the far-from-novel opinion that by depriving her characters of insight, imbuing them with an array of annoying idiosyncracies, and having them react irrationally to each other she will achieve some profound meditation on the fractious state of the modern world. What it smells like instead is a profound lack of plot, and purpose.

Beatrice (Jacob), a French immigrant, arrives in town (filming was done in Providence) with a Cambodian child named Seap Sok (Nady Meas) and a little red wagon full of their belongings; and she immediately rents a room in a house where another tenant, Claude (Mark Evan Jacobs) is having the worst day of this life; he has found his girlfriend in bed with another man, accidentally set the house afire and is arrested when he forgets to make a bank deposit for his boss.

Guilt-ridden over burning out Beatrice and Seap, he takes them to the home of his thoroughly unbelievable parents (Charlotte Moore and Pat McNamara) and grandfather (Leonardo Cimino). They are, of course, smitten by the two homeless waifs. Love triumphs. Ho-hum.

Other than making some less-than-relevatory disclosures about Beatrice's past, none of which seems any more trustworthy than she does, the movie limps along from one unfunny set piece to another, leaving illogic in its wake. Jacob is charming but her character is too cute, her English too unconvincingly fractured: She's not an illegal alien, she's an "illegal stranger," she declares, during one of her more excruciatingly coy moments; she's always "desolated" by events, and when she asks the hapless Claude "do you ... like us?" you don't know whether you should retch over her delivery, or the fact Claude hasn't run off screaming.

VILLAGE VOICE, 2/23/93, p. 56, Alyssa Katz

A movie snob would call this one *Beatrice Saved From Fire* in honor of Renoir's classic *Boudu* ..., the prototypical tale of a nutty Frenchperson insinuating into an uptight bourgie household and teaching its members about love and the meaning of life and how to get in touch with their inner child. Blockbuster Video customers might think of the womanchildren of *Splash* or of Scientology—the film's eponymous spacey vagabond (Irène Jacob) acts like she's dropped in from the land of Dianetics. But then *Trusting Beatrice* has neither Hollywood nor indie spirit sufficient to lure one class or the other to the tiny Quad, a theater well proportioned to this mild little film.

The movie does have the timely hook of immigration and its discontents: Beatrice and her sort-of-adopted young mute Cambodian daughter are "on the sheep" (as she malapropizes it) from the INS. After flame and misfortune, mother and child unwittingly take refuge in the family home of the arsonist (Mark Evan Jacobs, a nouveau Nicolas Cage whose long shaggy hair makes him look even more like a sad puppy). She's manic, he's depressive, she cures his wacky parents' neuroses, he breaks the law to repair her girl's singed rag doll, she needs a green card—do I hear wedding bells? It's a tad distressing to see Jacob, so radiant in the classy *Double Life of Véronique*, give her all in such an ephemeral film; ditto Steve Buscemi, a throwaway as the arsonist's lawyer. Perhaps if small movies had budgets comparable to, say, those of small plays, this innocent diversion might not be such a letdown.

Also reviewed in:
NEW YORK TIMES, 2/12/93, p. C10, Vincent Canby
VARIETY, 1/20/92, p. 18H, Amy Dawes

TWENTY BUCKS

A Triton Pictures release of a Big Tomorrow Productions film. *Producer:* Karen Murphy. *Director:* Keva Rosenfield. *Screenplay:* Leslie Bohem and Endre Bohem. *Director of Photography:* Emmanuel Lubezki. *Editor:* Michael Ruscio. *Music:* David Robbins. *Sound:* Douglas Axtell. *Production Designer:* Joseph T. Garrity. *Art Director:* Rando Schmook. *Set Deocrator:* Linda Allen and Kenneth Kirchner. *Costumes:* Susie DeSanto. *Running time:* 91 minutes. *MPAA Rating:* R.

CAST: Linda Hunt (Angeline); David Rasche (Baker); George Morfogen (Jack); Sam Jenkins (Anna); Brendan Fraser (Sam); Gladys Knight (Mrs. McCormac); Elisabeth Shue (Emily Adams); Steve Buscemi (Frank); Christopher Lloyd (Jimmy); Melora Walters (Stripper); Kamal Holloway (Bobby McCormac); William H. Macy (Policeman); Diane Baker (Ruth Adams); Spalding Gray (The Priest); Matt Frewer (Chuck); Nina Siemaszko (Bank Teller).

LOS ANGELES TIMES, 10/22/93, Calendar/p. 6, Peter Rainer

"Twenty Bucks" began as a script written by screen-writer Endre Bohem in 1935 and then was passed on to his son Leslie more than four decades later. Although largely reworked, the scenario still has a charmingly musty quality. It's contemporary yet it harkens back to a simpler way of feeling.

The film, directed by Keva Rosenfield, follows a $20 bill as it's passed from hand to hand. Most of the bill's owners never meet, and yet they are bound by the transactions. The disparate vignettes interconnect as a series of raffish, O. Henry-ish stories with a common thread—in each case the twenty transforms its bearer.

This free-form ensemble piece doesn't have the savvy or the breadth that a Robert Altman might have brought to it. (On the other hand, judging from "Short Cuts," Altman would be too sour to realize its humor.) Rosenfeld, who comes from the documentary arena, shoots things very simply, with a minimum of fuss. The half dozen or so stories dovetail in ways just improbable enough to seem real. "Twenty Bucks" (rated R) points up the democracy of cash: One day you're owned by a street urchin, the next by a millionaire.

Linda Hunt plays the street urchin who first finds the twenty, then has it snatched by a skate-boarder. As the stories develop, we encounter a spiffy petty thief (Christopher Lloyd) and his pick-up accomplice (Steve Buscemi), a New Age curio shop owner (Gladys Knight) who mails the bill to her grandson (Kamal Holloway) as a birthday present, a young writer (Elisabeth Shue) whose aspirations are rejected by her father (Alan North), a working-class kid (Brendan Fraser) who attempts to marry rich and gets the twenty as a token gift from his future father-in-law (George Morfogen), and the stripper (Melora Walters) at the kid's bachelor party who gets the bill stuffed in her G-string.

Not all these stories amount to much, but the best of them, like the Lloyd-Buscemi confab, have a wonderful strangeness. Lloyd gives one of his best screen performances: His hold-up man is well-tailored and curt, more like an assistant bank manager than a robber. He's got everything figured out but his serene look is, on closer inspection, totally ga-ga. He's the bandit as gentlemanly control freak, and Buscemi, slobbery and inept, is his perfect foil.

There are other wonderful moments, like the final scene between Fraser and his prospective father-in-law, or the bachelor party sequence where the bemused stripper realizes she's pranced into a wake. "Twenty Bucks" (rated R for language and a scene of sexuality) bops along lackadaisically but it comes full circle by the end. It's the kind of scruffy fable that doesn't usually get made anymore—at least not since 1935.

NEW YORK POST, 10/22/93, p. 23, Michael Medved

Have you ever stared into the green-and-gray face of a president on any piece of common currency and wondered about the tortured trail this grimy bill might have traveled on its way to your hand?

That's the fanciful notion behind the clever, well-crafted "Twenty Bucks," which must be the first film ever made in which the main character (and the only element connecting its diverse cast) as an item of legal tender.

The movie focuses on this particular $20 dollar bill from the time it emerges crisp and fresh from an automatic teller machine and goes through a series of fateful adventures as it passes from hand to hand and life to life.

Along the way the title 20 encounters a half-mad homeless prophetess (Linda Hunt), a nervous bridegroom (Brendan Fraser), a brilliant, cold-blooded holdup man (Christopher Lloyd) and his bumbling protege (Steve Buscemi), a kindly but dim-witted priest (Spalding Gray), a hard-working waitress with aspirations as a writer (Elizabeth Shue), and many others.

Director Keva Rosenfeld is a veteran documentarian whose best known previous work, "All American High," presented a group of appallingly empty-headed suburban adolescents in vivid, memorable terms.

"Twenty Bucks," his feature film debut, displays the same ability to introduce a large cast of characters with a few deft, well-selected touches.

Nearly all the actors deliver energetic and effective performances, with Christopher Lloyd achieving special distinction as a tightly controlled, totally professional crook who stands at the furthest possible remove from the eccentric wildmen he usually plays.

The way the people in the story continually seem to cross paths will remind many moviegoers of the similarly complex interactions in "Short Cuts," but Rosenfeld's unidentified Middle American—city ("Twenty Bucks" was actually shot in Minneapolis) is not as depressed or dysfunctional as Robert Altman's Los Angeles.

There is a cheerful, humanistic undercurrent to this story that perhaps reflects its origins in an earlier era.

Hungarian emigre Endre Bohem (who later won fame as producer of the Clint Eastwood TV series "Rawhide") wrote the original screenplay in 1935, and his son rock musician Leslie Bohem, updated and revised the unproduced script after his father's death in 1990.

The 55 years that elapsed between the first and final drafts of this screenplay led the producers of "Twenty Bucks" to claim their movie represents the longest script development process in Hollywood history.

The writing that emerged from this posthumous father-son collaboration is always clever and competent, though at times some of the ingenious twists and turns begin to seem overly cute and contrived.

The money-is-the-root-of-all-evil theme will hardly please free marketeers who believe in the integrity of the profit motive; even capitalism's most stubborn defenders, however, will concede that the movie advances its point of view with flair and feeling, while providing a surprisingly hopeful conclusion.

"Twenty Bucks" may not amount to a movie treasure, but for moviegoers who might enjoy a gentle-spirited change of pace, it still represents a welcome find.

NEWSDAY, 10/22/93, Part II/p. 71, Gene Seymour

Three movies aren't enough to certify a trend, but it does seem as if serendipity as a plot device is slowly seeping back into some of the more idiosyncratic of recent American films. Whatever their respective strengths and weaknesses, "Equinox," "Short Cuts" and "Twenty Bucks" help reinforce the suspicion that our fates are intertwined and that, just maybe, we are all responsible for each other. It'd be nice to think so anyway.

"Twenty Bucks," the first feature by documentarian Keva Rosenfeld is the most user-friendly of the three—and hence the least challenging. It's a clever enough conceit: The story follows a $20 bill from the bank as it changes hands, flies out of pockets, nests in wallets and changes hands again.

The bill's owners form a demographic broad enough to make a presidential aspirant envious. A homeless person (Linda Hunt) sees it first, but a skateboarding kid snatches it and runs into a bakery to buy some goodies.

It ends up as change for an industrialist (George Morfogen) buying a wedding cake for his daughter (Sam Jenkins) who's about to marry one of her father's loading-dock workers (Brendan Fraser) who doesn't know what to make of the $20 bill when the father gives it to him as a wedding gift emblematic of the father's own first $20 as a poor immigrant.

The bill finds its way into the G-string of a stripper (Melora Walters) at the groom's bachelor party. The stripper uses the money to buy a voodoo curio from a neighborhood shop keeper (Gladys Knight) who sends it as a birthday gift to her grandson who uses it to buy a bottle of wine at a convenience store being held up by two guys (Christopher Lloyd and Steve Buscemi) who ... well, by now, you get the idea.

As anyone who's watched "The Love Boat" can tell you, this multi-narrative approach can always entertain, depending on how good each story is. The script, written by Leslie Bohem from a original 1935 draft by his father Endre, is a hit-and-miss affair with some of the tales coming off well while others seem hackneyed and shallow.

Unfortunately, the core narrative, involving an aspiring writer (Elisabeth Shue) whose practical-minded father disdains her ambition, falls into the latter category. What saves it from tedium are the performances by Shue and, in an especially lovely turn, Diane Baker as Shue's supportive, savvier-than-she-seems mom. In fact, it's mildly surprising that a movie so weighed down by *deus ex machina* should offer so many chances for actors to shine. Buscemi and Lloyd are respectively scuzzy and scary as small-time thieves, bringing so much tension and electricity to their roles that they make theirs the film's best story by far. Most of the other performances glow in inverse proportion to their size. Like Hunt, for instance, who is seen at the beginning and the end. And Spalding Gray, who has a wonderful, too-brief cameo as a talky-dopey priest.

VILLAGE VOICE, 11/2/93, p. 66, Lynda D. Jones

Arms loaded down with a baby and other bundles, a harried mom unknowingly drops the $20 bill she withdrew from a cash machine. As the bill floats away, we are taken on a convoluted trip through its life and times and the hapless folks who encounter it.

Rosenfeld's plotless comedy examines human nature and our wanton desire for the dirty green. How does money affect us? What lengths will we go to get it? Though the film tends to get on a soapbox about personal and—yecch!—family values, it comes across best as a movie about dreams, contrasting those who have the balls to chase them, no matter how fantastic or mundane, and those who don't.

Every character we meet is having an identity crisis, reexamining his or her life, searching for meaning. When a saucy homeless woman (Linda Hunt) comes in contact with the bill, she memorizes its serial numbers, certain that with them she will win the lottery. A dollar and a dream, "It's my destiny!," she proclaims. Brendan Fraser plays an average joe engaged to a girl whose family is loaded. Lifestyles of the rich and famous dance in his head. But is it his destiny? Maybe.

Though many of the characters simply serve as conduits to channel the $20 bill into someone else's hands—like Steve Buscemi and Christopher Lloyd, two thieving con artists out for an easy buck—they do provide some entertaining moments. In sum, *Twenty Bucks* is light and charming fare. All you need is $7.50 and a dream.

Also reviewed by:
CHICAGO TRIBUNE, 4/8/94, Friday/p. L, Clifford Terry
NEW YORK TIMES, 10/22/93, p. C8, Janet Maslin
VARIETY, 2/1/93, p. 98, Todd McCarthy
WASHINGTON POST, 4/22/94, p. C6, Rita Kempley

TWIST

A Triton Pictures release in association with Alliance Communications of a Sphinx production. *Executive Producer:* Ron Haig. *Producer:* Ron Mann. *Director:* Ron Mann. *Director of Photography:* Bob Fresco. *Editor:* Robert Kennedy. *Music:* Keith Elliott and Nicholas Stirling. *Sound:* Brian Avery. *Dance Consulant:* Sally Sommer. *Dance and Music Research:* David Segal and Wendy Rowland. *Art Director:* Gerlinde Scharinger. *Set Designer:* Linda Nakashima. *Running time:* 90 minutes. *MPAA Rating:* Not Rated.

WITH: Hank Ballard; Chubby Checker; Cholly Atkins; Joey Dee; Dee Dee Sharp; Mama Lu Parks; The Parkettes.

LOS ANGELES TIMES, 8/13/93, Calendar/p. 2, Kenneth Turan

The Itch. The Bop. The Stroll. The Strand. The Cha-lypso. The Madison. Each a bona fide dance craze with teen-age clout. Where would they all lead to? What could possibly come next?

Next, as anyone of a certain age remembers, was that now-venerable institution called the Twist. But as this "Twist," Ron Mann's engaging, high-spirited documentary points out, was no ordinary changing of the guard. This was nothing less than a social revolution, a notoriously silly one perhaps, but a revolution nevertheless.

"Twist" (Times-rated Family) functions not only as a history of that particular song and dance, but of more than a decade of American popular music. Made with newsreel and television footage from dozens of archives as well as in-person interviews with key personnel, it is a lively cultural artifact, alternately horrifying and amusing.

Perhaps most horrifying of all is a glimpse of how dauntingly rigid popular dance could be for the silent majority in the early 1950s. While jazz dance crazes like the Lindy hop and the jitterbug still look wildly exciting, the tedious two-steps most of the country was doing resemble relics of some well-mannered gulag.

But as rhythm and blues turned into the more widespread rock 'n' roll, moralists grew increasingly horrified, referring to the music as a "communicable disease" and worse. Most suspect of all were songs with racy lyrics, hot items like Hank Ballard and the Midnighters' notorious "Work With Me Annie."

Faced with hordes of young people who just wanted to dance with the beat, the gatekeepers of television came up with well-mannered programs like "American Bandstand." Chewing gum and combing hair were forbidden, as were suggestive movements, and the best of rock was effectively neutered in favor of the likes of Frankie Avalon, shown in a particularly gooey clip singing about bobby sox and pearls.

So it was no surprise that after Ballard wrote and recorded "The Twist" (which even his own record company was unconvinced about), a more acceptable artist would be recruited to cover it. That would be Chubby Checker. "Nothing is nasty when I do it," explains the likable Mr. C. "I have that talent. I do."

No one, though, was ready for how big the Twist became. Not Ballard, who is more bemused than bitter at the way the hottest dance craze ever left its originator behind. Not Checker, who saw what he thought was a one-shot novelty roar back to No. 1 when the Peppermint Lounge's Joey Dee made the dance a must-do for New York's cafe society, with all kinds of merchandising and even doubtful movies like "Hey, Let's Twist" arriving in its wake.

Ridiculous as all this may seem today, producer-director Mann (whose last film was "Comic Book Confidential") understands that the Twist was right there at the right time. The first dance to make it acceptable for hips to move on national television, it ushered in the hang-loose '60s and marked the start of the freestyle mode of non-touch dancing that is still with us. "It was something totally different," remarks a Twist veteran. "People were ready for it."

Indeed they were.

NEW YORK POST, 8/13/93, p. 26, Matthew Flamm

Chubby Checker did not invent the Twist. He didn't write the song of that name either, and he wasn't the first to record it.

This tidbit of information isn't as trivial as it sounds. It's the tip of the pop cultural iceberg that Canadian filmmaker Ron Mann explores in his stylishly assembled new documentary, "Twist."

Though none of the film's assorted interviews ever comes out and says so, Checker, who was in some ways a sort of Jackie Robinson of rock 'n' roll, had a No. 1 hit with "The Twist" because he didn't threaten whites.

"Nothing's nasty when I do it," a chubbier Checker tells Mann, reminiscing in a present day interview. "I do everything nice."

Hank Ballard, of Hank Ballard and the Midnighters, was a different story. The veteran rhythm and blues artist talks of how he wrote "The Twist" in 1958 after seeing one of his backup singers improvise the dance step during a concert. The song caught on, even though King Records slapped it onto the B side of a single.

Ballard was known for songs like "Work With Me, Annie," which was about work, if you get my drift. So when "American Bandstand" host Dick Clark was told about "The Twist," he refused to play it, convinced—according to Ballard—that "It's another one of those dirty records."

Clark's unofficial mandate, in the words of one former "Bandstand" dancer, was to make rock 'n' roll "safe for television." The show's teen-age dancers never moved their hips—even when doing dances that as one now-middleaged couple admits, they claimed to have invented but in fact learned "from the black people."

(Former Bandstand dancer Carole Scaldeferri recalls becoming famous just for combing her hair on the show—and having her combs confiscated by Clark, who was intent on his teen-agers projecting a clean-cut image.)

So in 1960, "The Twist" given to Checker, whose shtick until then had been musical impersonations.

"He did such a beautiful clone of my record," Ballard recalls appreciatively and with no bitterness, "I thought it was me."

"The Twist" was an instant hit. Checker went on "American Bandstand" and showed how to dance to it. And for the first time teen-agers on the show moved their hips.

White America would never be the same.

"Twist" takes an evenhanded, gently humorous approach to its subject. Beginning with a ballroom dancing lesson in buttoned-down 1953, it covers the entire Twist craze—culminating in Joey Dee and the Peppermint Twist phenomenon—and winds up in the early '60s with the start of the British Invasion.

This is partly a movie about how people (of all ages—the Twist was nothing if not inclusive) enjoy themselves, and how silly they can look while they're at it. Channel surfing through old television, "Twist" shows perky Gale Storm doing a polka number, a cadaverous Arthur Murray teaching the rhumba, Mary Tyler Moore twisting with Dick Van Dyke, and Dee Dee Sharp singing "Mashed Potato Time," the dance to which she couldn't do.

Mann, whose last cultural investigation was "Comic Book Confidential," works with a light touch. There are no villains in "Twist" and no "experts," aside from the people who took part in the events. (Clark, for some reason is omitted.)

The birth of rock 'n' roll has been covered before and certainly "Twist" footage of zealots linking the music to a Communist plot is all too familiar. But Mann makes the whole subject almost as good as new.

NEWSDAY, 8/13/93, Part II/p. 63, Gene Seymour

Between the 1959 plane crash that killed Buddy Holly and the 1964 American beachhead by the Beatles, rock and roll didn't have a hero. It did, however, have a dance. And around this little dance they called The Twist coalesced just about everything in pop culture that was energetic and confused, transcendent and shallow, disposable and exalting.

"Twist," the documentary, chronicles the last great dance craze with bemused affection and easygoing thoroughness. Structured like an instructional film by writer-producer-director Ron Mann, "Twist" artfully combines archival footage with present-day interviews of such luminaries of early '60s pop as the two men who started it all: Hank Ballard, the down-and-dirty rhythm-and-blues icon who wrote "The Twist" in 1960 and Chubby Checker, who made it No. one on the charts within the year.

Mann does an extremely credible job in detailing the psychic groundwork for this mid-century plague of dance fever. Footage of a real instructional dance film from 1953 shows the stiff lockstep ballroom dance routines tyrannizing middle American youth. Juxtaposed with this is footage of black teenagers doing their own spectacular variations on Basic Ballroom to the lusty, racuous R&B rhythms that would soon filter into the split-level mainstream of American culture and galvanize a generation.

"American Bandstand" both enlarged and contained the scope of this phenomenon with its daily broadcasts of well-dressed, well-behaved Philadelphia kids who tried to bring as much soul and swagger into the dance mix as Dick Clark and the network would allow. Which is to say, not much. TV dance parties spread throughout the nation and even impressed some of the black song-and-dance men. Still, as Ballard recalls, "they weren't moving their hips. If you didn't dance moving your hips, it wasn't dancing."

Enter The Twist, which Ballard conceived from watching a move made by his backup singers. It was a B-side to a now-forgotten ballad. Ballard tried to convince them that the other side "was the killer," but to no avail. Thus the baby-faced Checker made the record. Got the glory.

It's hard to imagine now the scope and breadth of the phenomenon that followed. It's even harder to imagine a time when a dance became the topic of serious discussion from the likes of

Marshall McLuhan, who, in an early '60s interview, proclaims The Twist a "cool" phenonemon that was "very unsexy."

By that time, he wasn't wrong. As Mann cannily shows, The Twist was soon swallowed in the great marketing maw that bleached away any grit and grease from sexy pop items for mass consumption. It wasn't long before The Twist and all the other dances it spawned were rendered insignificant by the kind of venal and feckless overselling that continues rock and roll. Such trenchant observation raises "Twist," the film, above the level of mere nostalgia bath.

VILLAGE VOICE, 8/31/93, p. 60, Carol Cooper

A hell of a lot easier to do than The Mambo or the Lindy Hop, The Twist became the one black dance craze to survive the '50s, and set a pattern for freestyle dancing through the subsequent tumultuous decade of integration. As a visual metaphor for sexual and social liberation, the Twist was picked up by toy and clothing manufacturers who collaborated with nightclubs, radio, and trend media to extend Twistmania through every stratum of society. The social history collected by director Ron Mann in *Twist* could convince you that neither the generation gap, the civil rights struggle, nor the Youth International Party would have been the same without this teenage fad.

Mann interviews performers, *American Bandstand* regulars, Peppermint Lounge go-go dancers, and Motown choreographer Cholly Atkins to show how a new entertainment medium (television) and an evolving popular music (rock & roll) conspired to create the postmodern social matrix that was the Swingin' '60s. *Bandstand* kids Joan Kiene and Jimmy Peatross talk about not being allowed to say on camera that most of the dances they presented had been learned from local blacks. Once the show went into national syndication in '57, racial politics and presentation became even more volatile. With that in mind, Dick Clark's decision in 1960 to champion Chubby Checker's cover version of one of Hank Ballard's "dirty race records" was more progressive than it appears. To help a light-skinned black man (instead of Pat Boone) take an r&b record built around a thinly veiled sexual reference to the top of the chart twice in two years was in its way as revolutionary as *Brown v. the Board of Education.*

Mann never delves into the question of whether Ballard signed away his publishing rights (and therefore never made the millions he should have made from the ultimate success of his composition). The film is clearly more interested in the twisted process by which pop culture is infused with new elements, which in *Twist* (as in the John Waters satire *Hairspray* before it) proves to be a thoroughly kinky blend of marketing, class war, and touching the hem of a taboo.

Also reviewed in:
NEW YORK TIMES, 8/13/93, p. C17, Stephen Holden
VARIETY, 10/5/92, p. 65, Suzan Ayscough

TWO MIKES DON'T MAKE A WRIGHT

Three short films presented by Film Forum.

THE APPOINTMENTS OF DENNIS JENNINGS—*Director:* Dean Parisot. *Screenplay:* Steven Wright and Mike Armstrong. *Director of Photography:* Frank Prinzi.

WITH: Steven Wright; Rowan Atkinson; Laurie Metcalf.

PETS OR MEAT: THE RETURN TO FLINT—*Director:* Michael Moore. *Screenplay:* Michael Moore. *Director of Photography:* Ed Lachman.

A SENSE OF HISTORY—*Director:* Mike Leigh. *Screenplay:* Jim Broadbent. *Director of Photography:* Dick Pope.

WITH: Jim Broadbent.

Running time: 79 minutes. *MPAA Rating:* Not Rated.

NEW YORK POST, 3/31/93, p. 21, Jami Bernard

Who said longer is better? Film Forum is showing a sardonic, enjoyable omnibus of short films under the heading "Two Mikes Don't Make a Wright."

The title is a stretch, but the shorts are worthy satires, two by Mikes—Mike Leigh and Michael Moore—and one starring a Wright by the name of Steven.

Michael Moore, the Woody Allen of documentary makers (not for his sexual proclivities but for his personal filmmaking style), returns to his hometown of Flint, Mich., several years after making his notorious "Roger & Me."

He revisits some of the characters we came to know and love—the guy who threw people out of their homes on Christmas Eve, the woman who beat bunnies over the head and then skinned them to sell for "pets or meat," the nervous director of tourism who swallows hard when trying to think of something a visitor to Flint might want to do or see.

"Pets or Meat" finds everyone in Flint still struggling to make a go of things after the closing of the auto plant ruined the city's economy. The bunny gal is now selling mice and rats; the tourism director sends Moore 40 miles out of town to a restaurant known for its fried chicken. Shorter and less ambitious than "Roger & Me," "Pets or Meat" provides a neat postscript to the original.

Mike Leigh's hilarious and ultimately sobering "A Sense of History" is a one-man play, starring Jim Broadbent as the stuffy 23rd Earl of Leete, who takes us on a guided and very personal tour of the acreage he would sacrifice anything to keep in the family.

"The Appointments of Dennis Jennings," which won an Oscar in 1989 for live action short, stars Wright as an urban neurotic who justifies the phrase my colleague Jerry Tallmer oft repeats: Just because you're paranoid doesn't mean they're not after you.

The three shorts get their humor from their own brands of an absurdity that borders dangerously on reality—the color-coordinator trying vainly to clear her name in "Pets or Meat," the landed gentry trying to keep his crumbling world intact, and the mental patient whose main problem is his shrink.

VILLAGE VOICE, 4/6/93, p. 60, Ellen Cohn

Mike Leigh's *A Sense of History* is not one of the director's trademark idiosyncratic human comedies—straight-out funny, compassionate, packed with political smarts. Instead, it's a 25-minute mock-doc and the first Leigh film he hasn't written himself. The creation of Jim Broadbent (the bartender in *The Crying Game*, the randy novelist in *Enchanted April*, and the father in Leigh's *Life Is Sweet*), *History* is a visit with the 23rd Earl of Leete, a stately hun of England who loves his ancestral estate enough to kill for it—and has, repeatedly, since he was seven, Broadbent plays the Earl with terrifying zest (I kept flashing to Pat Buchanan in Houston), and Leigh's edgy camera and quirky cuts keep the laughs—nervous and nasty-coming.

Also on this triple bill, Michael Moore's 25-minute mock-doc *Pets or Meat: The Return to Flint.* This son of *Roger and Me* leans more to Dumb People Jokes (which are funny) than to wit or irony ("Employment at the unemployment office is up," says a state worker). Warning: swallow your popcorn when the Bunny Lady appears. The program opens with Dean Parisot's *The Appointments of Dennis Jennings*, winner of the 1989 Oscar for Best Live Action Short, featuring comic Steven Wright doing his deadpan paranoid.

Also reviewed in:
CHICAGO TRIBUNE, 5/21/93, Friday/p. D, Mark Caro
NEW YORK TIMES, 3/31/93, p. C20, Vincent Canby
WASHINGTON POST, 6/11/93, p. G7, Hal Hinson

UN COEUR EN HIVER

An October Films release of a Film par Film/Cinea/Orly Film/Sedif/DA Films/Paravision Intl./FR-3 Films production. *Executive Producer:* Gérard Gaultier. *Producer:* Jean-Louis Livi and Philippe Carassonne. *Director:* Claude Sautet. *Screenplay (French with English subtitles):* Claude Sautet, Yves Ulmann, Jacques Fieschi, and Jérôme Tonnerre. *Director of Photography:* Yves Angelo. *Editor:* Jacqueline Thiedot. *Music:* Philippe Sarde. *Sound:* Pierre Lenoir and Jean-Paul Loublier. *Sound Editor:* Marie-Thérèse Boiche. *Casting:* Lissa Pillu, Christiane Lebrima, and Pascale Beraud. *Production Designer:* Christian Marti. *Costumes:* Corinne Jorry. *Make-up:* Thi-Loan Nguyen. *Running time:* 105 minutes. *MPAA Rating:* Not Rated.

CAST: Daniel Auteuil (Stephane); Emmanuelle Bèart (Camille); André Dussollier (Maxime); Elizabeth Bourgine (Hélène); Myriam Boyer (Mme. Amet); Brigitte Catillon (Régine); Maurice Garrel (Lachaume); Jean-Luc Bideau (Ostende); Stanislas Carre de Malberg (Brice).

FILMS IN REVIEW, 10/93, p. 337, Eva H. Kissin

This is an intriguing film about two Frenchmen who run an atelier dealing in and repairing violins for the maestros of Europe. It concerns the two partners' triangular love affair with their beautiful new client, Camille, a talented successful young violinist.

The men are very European types with white chiselled faces and blue buttoned-down shirts, hardly blue collars. Everything about them suggests an attitude towards the perfection demanded by their work, a distinctly Old World pride in craftsmanship. In this arena of rare performances, the instrument must be absolutely right if it is to bring out the best of the music. This might just be the theme of the film.

Camille herself, another perfectionist intensely devoted to her craft, was once characterized as a child by her teacher as smooth and hard but with temperament. She is now an adult version of that child in addition to being are elegant and rare young woman. To date, she has been living with her agent, a somewhat older woman, who had nurtured and shaped her career. Now, no longer in need of this mother figure, she is still somewhat naive, perhaps stepping into overly deep emotional waters in her interaction with the two men.

There is a climax in the love affair that suggests a tragic flaw in one of the men and a quite terrible emotional experience for the young violinist. However, we never quite feel their agony because of the essentially cerebral mood of the film. It is full of distance. We see everything through the reflections of windows, through the windows of cars, restaurants, and the glassed-in areas of recording studios. The emotional impact here is more aural than visual in the magnificent Ravel played by Jean Jacques Kantorow with Beart's talented fingers doing the visual.

Although the film is about the rare world of the musical artist in France, it is bounded nevertheless by a more real world that gives it solidity. Near the end, the unique emotional lives of the characters are balanced by the visit to the atelier of another little girl hoping for a career as a violinist and the death of Camille's old teacher and the mentor of the two partners.

If one doesn't quite accept the explanation of the character flaw of one of the "lovers," it doesn't lessen the elegance of the film which aims to study the mechanics of a work of art, and in doing so, creates one. After all, this resembles more a short story by Chekhov than a four hundred page novel by Tolstoy.

The acting is all understated and excellent with Daniel Auteuil, Andre Dussollier, and Emmanuel Beart in the leading roles. Directed by Claude Sautet, this somewhat wintry heart more than merits its much prized Cesar.

LOS ANGELES TIMES, 6/16/93, Calendar/p. 1, Kenneth Turan

When Claude Sautet makes a film, no one goes hungry, either on-screen or off. While his characters are never far from an exceptional glass of wine or an enviable apple tart, the complex emotional lives they display are as rich and satisfying as any of the spectacular meals they consume.

Sautet's newest film, the expressively titled "Un Coeur en Hiver" ("A Heart in Winter"), follows in this pattern. Like "Vincent, Francois, Paul and the Others" and the director's biggest American hit, "Cesar and Rosalie" with Yves Montand and Romy Schneider, "Coeur" succeeds in finding surprisingly supple and involving romantic entanglements in the well-upholstered lives of the Parisian bourgeoisie.

Though he is a popular and well-respected filmmaker in France ("Coeur" was nominated for nine Cesars and won for best director and best supporting actor), Sautet has never been avant-garde enough to be a passionate critical favorite. Instead, he follows in the humanistic tradition of the master, Jean Renoir, and turns out films that are realistic yet accepting about affairs of the heart even when they show their darker sides.

"Coeur" (written by Yves Ulmann, Jacques Fieschi, and Jerome Tonnerre and inspired by a short story by Russian writer Mikhail Lermontov) follows that same pattern of passionate and unnerving feelings. Though it deals with the kind of unlikely couple movies traditionally specialize in, what it does with them is as involving as it is unfamiliar.

Stéphane (Daniel Auteuil) is introduced to us (quite shrewdly given what comes later) via his measured voice-over description not of himself, but of his boss. That would be Maxime (Cesar-winning Andre Dussollier), the hawkishly handsome proprietor of a small but prestigious violin repair service.

Gregarious and sure of himself, Maxime is the firm's Mr. Outside, the man who gains the confidence of the professional musicians and convinces them to trust Stéphane, Mr. Inside, with the agonizingly delicate repair of their most precious possessions. Stéphane is clearly the more reserved of the two, content, his own words tell us, to remain in the background, living a monkish, almost hermetic existence with only his work for companionship.

The routine of both men's lives is disturbed, however, when the married Maxime tells Stéphane he has fallen so rapturously in love with the beautiful young violinist Camille Kessler (Emmanuelle Béart) that he is leaving his wife and moving in with her.

Diffidence itself, Stéphane does not really respond at first to his boss's announcement, but gradually, as Camille moves more into Maxime's world, she moves more into his as well. They turn out to not only share a beloved former violin teacher, but also apparently are on a similar psychological wavelength.

Stéphane views his growing intimacy with Camille with his usual, almost scientific dispassion, while Camille, also reserved on the surface, becomes increasingly intrigued by Stéphane's emotionally removed quality, his seeming ability to live a totally disconnected life. Both seem fascinated with the tentativeness of their attraction, and neither one seems to know what to do about it or even whether, given their emotional patterns and their connections to Maxime, doing anything is even an option.

The outcome of this unlikely romantic triangle is "Hiver's" subject matter, and it is worked out with a kind of full-bodied delicacy and unexpectedness, an embracing of psychological complexity, that is characteristic of the best of Sautet's work. An excursion to some of the wilder shores of love and obsession, this film proves its statement that "feelings can't be demystified" with every scene.

"Un Coeur en Hiver" (Times-rated Mature for adult situations) is especially fortunate to have Béart and Auteuil (who appeared together in "Manon of the Spring" and are apparently a real-life item) as its leads. With sad brown eyes sunk deeply in a poker face, Auteuil has the perfect bearing for Stéphane, who is attractive but not handsome, simultaneously distant and self-confident. Béart is equally impressive as a woman whose smoothly classical, almost severe beauty turns out to contain levels of passion that surprise even her.

Exquisite classical music is a major part of "Coeur's" sensibility, the place where everyone's emotions converge, and listening to it is yet another of the physical pleasures Sautet delights in providing. Béart in fact spent a year learning to play the violin with so much facility that although it is not the actress but violinist Jean-Jacques Kantorow who performs the exacting Ravel sonatas Camille both rehearses and records, only an expert could be sure. The honesty of this film demanded no less of her, and its success is everyone's reward.

NEW YORK POST, 6/4/93, p. 31, Jami Bernard

A beautiful violinist falls in love with the man who finely tunes her instrument but cannot feel the vibrations in his heart, in Claude Sautet's haunting "Un Coeur en Hiver," starring the charismatic pair Daniel Auteuil and Emmanuelle Beart.

The title translates to "A Heart in Winter in Winter," and refers to the frozen heart of Stephane (Auteuil), a man who can adjust a violin to every nuance of tone and meaning but who cannot personally feel a thing. He is intrigued by the violinist Camille (Beart)—you could swear from her performance that she is indeed a violinist, although the actress had never picked up a violin before this movie—and yet he cannot give himself over to love, try as he might.

Camille is about to move in with Stephane's business partner, a debonair older man (Andre Dussollier) who has given up his womanizing ways for her. The love triangle is deeper and more fragile than what you would expect in, say, an American-made movie on the same subject. Stephane and his partner have enjoyed a long and seamless partnership, one so close that it does not require many words; this new discord reverberates louder than words.

There is a powerful scene in which Stephane does a favor for an elderly friend out of love; the thing he is required to do is something that can only be done out of love and yet is anathema to love. Stephane does it and barely blinks.

Earlier we had "Tous les matins du monde" about passion and viols; France must be on a musical-instrument kick at the moment. In any case, Auteuil has a kind of unyielding sexuality that women will find compelling, and Beart has a still beauty that gives "Un Coeur en Hiver" some emotional arpeggios not necessarily in the script.

NEWSDAY, 6/4/93, Part II/p. 69, John Anderson

In great music, silence is as important as sound; it's in the gaps between the notes that emotion is ignited, or misfires. In "Un Coeur en Hiver," which concerns love and friendship in the music world, what is unsaid—the gaps between the words—determines the romantic course of its characters' lives, and their failure to make emotional connections.

In this small, smart and very quiet film by Claude Sautet ("Cesar et Rosalie"), Stephane (Daniel Auteuil), a master violin repairer, and his partner, Maxime (Andre Dussollier), share a successful business and a smoothly functioning relationship: They play squash; Stephane loses gracefully. - They dine out; Maxime plays the bon vivant. They talk about their sex lives; Maxime does all the talking. It's a friendship that depends on a less-than-delicate balance between Stephane's self-deprecation and Maxime's ego.

Equilibrium is abandoned one day, however, when the married Maxime announces he has fallen in love with their young and very beautiful new client, Camille Kessler (Emmanuelle Beart). Camille, a brilliant violinist, also is a willful, selfish child-woman who has come to expect the attention she invariably gets. And while the lustful Maxime is more than willing to lavish her with even more, it's the taciturn Stephane who eventually gets her attention, and who doesn't want it.

Director Sautet plays with our expectations: Stephane, who seems to be the proverbially still waters, turns out to be as emotionally shallow as he appears. Maxime, the self-indulgent schmooze artist, will reveal a generosity of heart that belies his own self-promoted image. And Camille, a rather chilly perfectionist, will shame herself with previously unsuspected passion.

Throughout this lovingly shot but chillingly acted triptych, the fictional trio performs like three musicians who can't hear each other. Or who hear what they want. As Stephane works to improve Camille's instruments, she sees his motive as devotion, while he's simply a perfectionist. Stephane, who realizes the limits of his own emotional capacity, indulges himself by letting her believe what she wants. And he betrays Maxime, taking a certain amount of glee in doing so. Meanwhile, Camille's friend and manager Regine (Brigitte Catillon) and Lachaume (Maurice Garrel), the violin master who had Stephane, Maxime and Camille as students, orbit as knowing, and occasionally disbelieving, points of reality.

It's Lachaume who provides the key to Stephane, to Sautet's view of the artistic temperament, and the perversity and selfishness of silence. As students, Maxime simply lacked talent. Stephane, on the other hand, just couldn't bear the sound he made, so he chose to provide others the wherewithal for making music—the instruments—while making none himself. He lacked the generosity of soul to put his own ego on the line, unlike Camille, or even Maxime, who's willing to risk everything to follow his heart (and libido).

Thoughtful and well-acted, "Un Coeur en Hiver" ("A Heart in Winter") also is highly ambitious, and by giving us a three-character study devoid of the usual cookie-cutter personalities, executes a rather delicate balancing act of its own.

NEWSWEEK, 6/21/93, p. 65, Jack Kroll

The French used to make the kind of movie in which a guy would slug his friend not for stealing his girl, but for making her unhappy by *rejecting* her. Well, they still make that kind of movie. At least Claude Sautet does. That incident occurs in *Un Coeur en Hiver* ("A Heart in Winter"), the enthralling new film by the veteran writer-director, who won this year's César, France's Oscar. At 69, Sautet is beyond all schools: he rides no Waves, New or Old.

He is simply a master craftsman, like Stéphane (Daniel Auteuil), the man with the wintry heart. Stéphane is a *luthier*, a maker and fixer of violins. When Stéphane's partner Maxime (André Dussollier) falls in love with Camille (Emmanuelle Béart), a rising young violinist, Stéphane, too, is smitten by her beauty and talent. But he'd do nothing to hurt Maxime, just as he never allows himself to beat Maxime at racquetball. Then Camille becomes obsessed by the enigmatic, withdrawn Stéphane. "I want you," she tells him Frenchily. And then she encounters that wintry heart which won't allow him to love, just as he can do everything with violins except make real music.

This sketchy outline doesn't do justice to a movie that blends passion and delicacy with stunning effect. You want sexy, here it is, with no con games (as in concupiscence), no nudity, even though Béart may be the most beautiful woman in film today. She's also a wonderful actor, as is Dussollier with his eloquent suavity and Auteuil with his haunted eyes that have no tomorrow. The most erotic scenes are the musical ones in which Ravel's complex sonatas are played with sensual power by Béart's exquisite hands synchronized with the soundtrack playing of Jean-Jacques Kantorow. Sharon Stone, play that on your fiddle.

SIGHT AND SOUND, 5/93, p. 49, Claire Monk

Paris. Violin-maker Stéphane and his friend Maxime have been business partners for many years, but both now take their friendship as given and probe little into each other's lives. One day, Maxime tells Stéphane his is in love with Camille, a promising young violinist, and points her out in a cafe. Camille lives with her manager Régine, an older woman who has supported her career from the start; Maxime is leaving his already-dead marriage, and the two plan to live together. Visiting his old music teacher Lachaume at his country house, Stéphane questions him about Camille, whom he also taught; Lachaume recalls her mix of coolness and 'temperament'. Camille brings her violin to Stéphane to have a new bridge fitted. The repair complete, Stéphane and Maxime attend a private recital of hers. She is dissatisfied with the sound, but vehement that she, not the violin, is the problem. Stéphane leaves, and her tension eases.

Stéphane reports Camille's unease to his friend Hélène. In a dinner-party argument at Lachaume's Stéphane is challenged over his reluctance to express an opinion, and Camille defends him. After initial resistance, she allows him to make further improvements to her violin. Waiting for Maxime at the workshop one evening, her attention is drawn to Stéphane, still at work, and she confesses to him that relations are fraught with the possessive Régine, who resents her relationship with Maxime. Stéphane tells Hélène he feels Camille would rather be eating out with him than with Maxime, but denies any jealousy. Stéphane visits the studio where Camille is recording; they go to a nearby bar and she questions him intensely about himself but then leaves suddenly. When Camille rings, while Maxime is showing Stéphane round the flat being prepared for him and Camille, Stéphane is powerfully affected. Camille confronts him and asks if he is avoiding her because he and Maxime are friends. He shocks her by replying that they are not friends, only partners.

Now living together, Camille and Maxime discuss for the first time the fact that she is in love with Stéphane. Going away briefly on business, Maxime phones Stéphane asking him to go to the recording studio. At the post-recording party, Camille makes Stéphane drive her away. As they stop outside a hotel, she propositions him. He rejects her, claiming to have seduced her as a game, perhaps to get at Maxime. Broken, she gets out of the car. Returning, Maxime finds Régine at the flat caring for Camille, who is drunk and deeply humiliated. Camille seeks Stéphane out at the cafe, where he is eating with Hélène; she taunts him, then pleads with him until a waiter throws her out. Maxime walks in, hits Stéphane and leaves.

Stéphane and Maxime part company. Lachaume berates Stéphane, questioning his motives; Stéphane visits Camille and she coolly accepts his apology. Eight months pass; Stéphane has set up in a new workshop. Maxime visits, tells him that Camille has recovered, and half-heartedly suggests renewing their partnership. Stéphane and Maxime visit Lachaume, who is now terminally ill. His housekeeper Madame Amet tells Stéphane that Lachaume has been begging her to end his life but she cannot do it. Stéphane enters Lachaume's room and administers the necessary injection. Back in Paris, Stéphane discusses the loss of Lachaume with Camille. Both say they are glad to have met again. Maxime comes in to collect her and they depart, leaving Stéphane alone.

Bourgeois love and life are hardly under explored terrain in the French cinema, and for no particular reason Claude Sautet's 40-year career has had muted-to-nonexistent impact in the UK until now. That *Un Coeur en Hiver*, his twelfth feature, has broken the mould is largely due to its deserved Silver Lion at the 1992 Venice Festival. Sautet has remarked that the structure of a film is itself musical; and the completeness of *Un Coeur en Hiver* as a virtuoso piece of filmmaking derives not merely from such high-quality ingredients as the flawless central performances but from its discernibly symphonic structure, marked by assured variations of rhythm and texture closely linked to the development of its themes.

From the familiar starting point of an emotional triangle, Sautet explores two considerably more engrossing and perplexing notions: on the one hand, a passive but consciously manipulative seduction which—in terms of sexual action—never actually 'happens', and on the other, a solid yet curiously substanceless male friendship whose very existence can suddenly be denied. As the catalyst of these disruptions, the seemingly shy and introverted Stéphane is central to the film's meanings—most crucially, as the owner of the *coeur en hiver* of the title—and the perfectly calibrated emotional shifts from scene to scene, as Sautet charts the tacit dance of pursuit and withdrawal between him and Camille, becomes a parallel investigation into the (ultimately insoluble) riddle of his true motives and emotions.

The film's opening—a detailed but oddly detached dissection by Stéphane of his friendship with Maxime—seems to set up the former as the natural focus for our sympathy, but the images accompanying his voice-over foreshadow the subtly different story about to unfold. A shot of Stéphane beating Maxime at squash shows a competitiveness—and taste for 'games' - very much at odds with the ultra-humility of his demeanour. When Stéphane tells us that he and Maxime "haven't spent an evening together in years"—ambiguously asserting, "it suits us both fine"—the complex pathos of the accompanying image of the former alone in his workshop at night, holding a tiny automaton of a violinist, identifies him as a withdrawn figure for whom solitude is a form of self-protection and whose most intimate bond is with his work.

At the same time, the image of the automaton—a musician in Stéphane's hands—also suggests a power relation, both mystical and manipulative, between violin-maker and violinist. In contrast to the customary cinematic equations between swelling music and burgeoning passion, Sautet's interest is in music *as work*. The texture of activity in Stéphane's workshop is so tangibly evoked that you can almost smell the varnish. The satisfying rasp of a bridge being hollowed contributes as much to the musically sparse soundtrack as the strains of Ravel (though Béart, who learnt the violin specially for the film, wields the bow with astonishing conviction and emotion); and the characters' professional relationships become a channel for the expression of more intimate and intangible interactions.

Stéphane and Maxime's roles as craftsman and businessman—the one introvert and spiritual, the other extrovert and material—are established early on as denoting two entirely different ways of relating to the world. Most critically, the apparent reticence which attracts Camille to Stéphane is powerfully bound up in his mystique as an instrument-maker and her hunger for his professional approval (when he ceases turning up to watch her record, she frets about whether her playing has displeased him). Where Stéphane uses his craft as a means of protecting himself from the world and its feelings—hence his disquiet when Maxime upsets the equilibrium of their partnership by falling in love—his profession itself makes it impossible for Camille to accept his frigid front as the 'truth'. "You act as if emotions don't exist," she accuses him, "yet you love music". Stéphane in turn claims that far from concealing his feelings he is revealing his true—unfeeling—self, a stalemate which culminates in her sexual approach and his rejection. Though Camille is right to diagnose Stéphane's 'openness' as a particularly convoluted form of concealment, the unknowable self behind it—beautifully suggested in Daniel Auteuil's paradoxically sympathetic performance—makes condemnation impossible. This carefully constructed sense of moral ambiguity is sharpened by his sudden, startling euthanasia of Lachaume—a compassionate, courageous act immoral in conventional terms, but in its context cathartic.

Emmanuelle Béart's dignity and beauty notwithstanding, the most highly charged scenes here are scattered with danger signs—cars swerve to avoid Camille and Stéphane on two occasions, and one intense interchange is conducted with another couple rowing passionately in the background. But if Sautet's symphony seems pessimistic about the fragility of human relations, it compensates with an exceptionally rich and subtle study of a freeze-dried male psyche.

TIME, 6/21/93, p. 67, Richard Corliss

American movies are all talk, no listen. Jabber, jabber, feint feint—conversation is combat, a schoolyard dissing contest, a slightly more sophisticated version of "Your mother!" "No yours!" In real life, and in French movies, people pretend to get along when they talk. They keep things light, genial, talking around the issues that burn them up inside. Some love affairs never begin because people are afraid to reveal what they feel; "I love you" is so hard to say. Some marriages can last a lifetime on the tacit agreement that hostilities will go unexpressed. The static is in the silences.

By the chatty U.S. criterion, *Un Coeur en Hiver* (A Heart in Winter) is no great shakes. Even by French standards, Claude Sautet's drama tends to dither a bit. Yet the film displays a wonderful attention to the spaces between what people say and what they mean. Because the business of its main characters is making music, we spend many rewarding moments watching people listen. And then, because this is a kind of love story, we watch a woman watching a man. Here, the actors are the audience; they do what we do.

Stéphane (Daniel Auteuil) and Maxime (André Dussollier) are partners in a violin repair business. Maxime, a man of affairs, is now involved with the accomplished young violinist Camille (Emmanuelle Beart). "It's a new experience," he notes, "admiring someone I love." Stéphane is Maxime's opposite: he has a stillness that consoles men and attracts women. "You're very reticent," Camille says, and he replies, "A bit"; Stephane is too reticent even to admit he's reticent. He may be a little in love with Camille—"I like watching you talk," is all he says—but his job is his passion. Stooped over a violin, he has a delicate, confident touch. Camille, watching him work, must wonder: How would these hands care for a woman? In search of a muse, she pursues him, and he retreats. Camille thinks he is hiding what he feels. She is wrong: he is hiding what he doesn't feel. Stéphane is the man with the hibernating heart.

Auteuil's performance is heroically blank. He doesn't explain Stéphane's emotional numbness, nor does he editorialize against it. He allows his lure for dear Camille to remain a mystery, like so many romantic attractions. But then Béart (Manon in *Manon of the Spring*, the painter's model in *La Belle Noiseuse*) is an actress of such extraordinary beauty that any time she falls in movie love she seems like a goddess slumming. Her radiant face is therapeutic. A glance from her should thaw the frostiest heart.

Because it doesn't—because the violin maker chooses wood over flesh—*Un Coeur en Hiver* seems to take place inside Stéphane; it is a story of a woman's passion, told with a man's disconcerting reticence. In an overheated Hollywood summer, this movie is a sorbet that goes straight to the heart. And once there, it has a chilling effect. It says that genteel talk can be the most hurtful obscenity.

VILLAGE VOICE, 6/29/93, p. 60, Steven Drachman

When Jacques Rivette's *La Belle Noiseuse* was the talk of the town, it was impossible not to notice that the rogue New Wave director had ridden to re-prominence on the bare back of Emmanuelle Béart. Béart's immensely intelligent performance, as a nude model who inspires a disoriented painter to dream again of painting his masterpieces, kept the film from collapsing under its own weighty aspirations.

At the time, Béart complained about being "France's Sex Symbol" just when everyone was suddenly recognizing her as one of France's best actresses. So it seems fitting that in her new film, Claude Sautet's *Un Coeur en Hiver* (A Heart in Winter), Emmanuelle Béart is the Artist rather than the Art, the obsessor not the obsessee. Sex and passion are figments of the imagination, and her soul is all she bares.

Béart plays Camille, a young concert violinist, a "smooth, hard little girl" with a core of passion hidden deep beneath the surface, who, like the aging painter in *Noiseuse*, has lost the inspiration to create. Her current lover, Maxime (André Dussollier), is all business and efficiency—she can't play to him. She turns instead to Stéphane (Daniel Auteuil), Maxime's business partner, a complete black hole of a man who spends obsessive hours building and repairing violins. He is Science, correcting the slight "buzz" in the third string, clearing the way for her Art. When another character says, "What I admire in Art is *work*, not emotion," he is speaking for Stéphane.

Auteuil's face is studied composure, the only sign of life a tiny, occasional grin which he carefully suppresses. His scenes with Béart, ambivalent yet filled yet filled with an intellectual eroticism, are thrilling. Her yearning for this empty man is inexplicable, but to Béart's credit she makes it perfectly believable. We will never learn if he loves her back, or if he really is an idiot savant, "not very interested" in himself, who believes that "emotions don't exist." The movie is all about questions, not answers.

Noiseuse soared on the power of the artistry portrayed. For *Coeur*, Béart spent 18 months studying the violin just to fake her musical moments. So when she puts down her bow after whirling through a Ravel sonata, the audience in the movie theater seemed on the verge of cheers. It is one of many beautiful moments in *Un Coeur en Hiver*.

Also reviewed in:
NEW REPUBLIC, 6/7/93, p. 26, Stanley Kauffmann
NEW YORK TIMES, 6/4/93, p. C3, Janet Maslin
NEW YORKER, 6/7/93, p. 104, Anthony Lane
VARIETY, 9/7/92, p. 51, David Stratton
WASHINGTON POST, 7/9/93, p. B1, Hal Hinson

UNDERCOVER BLUES

A Metro-Goldwyn-Mayer release of a Lobell/Bergman/Hera production. *Executive Producer:* Herbert Ross and Andrew Bergman. *Producer:* Mike Lobell. *Director:* Herbert Ross. *Screenplay:* Ian Abrams. *Director of Photography:* Donald E. Thorin. *Editor:* Priscilla Nedd-Friendly. *Music:* David Newman. *Music Editor:* Tom Villano. *Choreographer:* D.J. Giagni. *Sound:* Dennis L. Maitland and (music) Tim Boyle. *Sound Editor:* Charles L. Campbell and Chuck Neely. *Casting:* Hank McCann. *Production Designer:* Ken Adam. *Art Director:* William J. Durrell, Jr. *Set Designer:* James R. Bayliss. *Set Decorator:* Jeff Haley. *Set Dresser:* Daril Alder, Douglas M. Vaughn, Chris Carlson, Vincenzo Buffolino, and Michael Ray. *Special Effects:* Stan Parks. *Costumes:* Wayne Finkelman. *Make-up:* Steve Abrums. *Make-up (Kathleen Turner):* Tom Case. *Stunt Coordinator:* Glenn H. Randall, Jr. *Running time:* 95 minutes. *MPAA Rating:* PG-13.

CAST: Kathleen Turner (Jane Blue); Dennis Quaid (Jeff Blue); Fiona Shaw (Novacek); Stanley Tucci (Muerte); Larry Miller (Halsey); Obba Babatunde (Sawyer); Tom Arnold (Vern Newman); Park Overall (Bonnie Newman); Ralph Brown (Leamington); Jan Triska (Axel); Marshall Bell (Sikes); Richard Jenkins (Frank); Dennis Lipscomb (Foster); Saul Rubinek (Mr. Ferderber); Dakin Matthews (Police Captain); Michael Greene (Col. Kenton); Olek Krupa (Zubic); Jenifer Lewis (Cab Driver); Chris Ellis (Burt); Eliott Keener (The Drunk); David Chappelle (Ozzie); Katherine Gaskin (Bag Lady); Marion Zinser (Nun);

Eddie Braun (Getaway Driver);   M. Randall Jordan (Bartender);   Robert Adams (Waiter); Nicholas Wertz (Baby Newman);   Spencer Henderson (Party Guest);   Diana Boylston (Bank Clerk);   Robert R. Colomes (Soniat House Manager);   Roger Willis (Napoleon Bartender); Phillip S. Blunt and Louis Robinson (Bar Patrons);   John Austin, Brett S. Barré, and Larry Lesslir (Policemen);   Barry Bedig (Mariner);   James Lew, Julius LeFlore, and Bill McIntosh (Novacek's Men);   Kathina Szeto (Dynagon Receptionist);   Michelle Schuelke (Jane Louise Blue).

LOS ANGELES TIMES, 9/11/93, Calendar/p. 12, Michael Wilmington

In the overbroad, underdone comedy thriller "Undercover Blues" Dennis Quaid and Kathleen Turner play Jeff and Jane Blue, a lovable maverick CIA agent and his wife. Together in thrill-a-minute New Orleans—a city shot through so many colored filters it looks as if it were swimming in gumbo—the Blues wage lighthearted, wisecracking battles against female terrorists and street scum.

Ian Abrams' script obviously wants us to see the Blues as, a modern Nick and Nora Charles—the super-sophisticated detective couple of the "Thin Man" series. But the way they josh, bash and zing the villains is closer to Butch Cassidy and the Sundance Kid. Nick and Nora got by on brainpower and booze; Jane and Jeff are black-belt spoofers.

There's a twist here, but it's almost embarrassing to mention it. The Blue's have a baby—Michelle Schuelke as Jane Louise Blue—and in their fights and chases, they bring Baby Blue along in a stroller. Why? Can't CIA agents afford baby-sitters? Is this some mad stab at family bonding? Or did Abrams overdose on too many baby-cart samurai movies?

The obvious answer: It's all a high demographic concept about a young married couple with child, who get into just as much fun and trouble as movie bachelor girls and boys. Making movie marriage and parenthood more exciting isn't an unworthy goal, but, in this case, Baby Blue isn't much better integrated into the story than if she were a rag doll schlepped from scene to scene, she's *replaced* by a doll, an exploding one.

The movie has very agile staging by Herbert Ross, a master of blocking, who, in the 1980s endowed dubious projects like "The Secret of My Success" and "Protocol" with an elegance of movement and visual shine that sometimes made them seem even tawdier and shallower. Some high-style actors around too: not only Turner and Quaid, but the great, gleaming Fiona Shaw, who tears into the ridiculous role of superspy Novacek, a Budapest barracuda. And Stanley Tucci, who gets virtually the only comic role: a kind of Clouseau of sleazy street muggers who keeps announcing bristlingly *"I am Muerte,"* and then goes ballistic when Jeff Blue replies, "Hiya, Morty."

But you can't pump style in a vacuum, and the genres Abrams tries to pastiche—screwball detective comedy and James Bond thrillers—don't really mix. One is all glitter and alcoholic badinage: the other is mostly slick brutalism and innuendo. "Undercover Blues" ends up being a slightly unpleasant wish-fulfillment fantasy. The Blues ridicule everyone else, especially the interracial cop team inexplicably shadowing them. And they show their love by egging each other on in street battles.

There's something smug about "Undercover Blues," and it's epitomized by the near-constant mile-wide grin on Quaid's face. Quaid's sharkish smirking suggests that he knows he'll never lose a fight, perhaps because he's already read the script. Turner smiles away the movie, too; occasionally they resemble two anchor-persons delivering superman sadism and karate instead of the news.

Halfway through "Undercover Blues" (rated PG-13), Jeff poses as Hildy Johnson, reporter for the Chicago Herald: an allusion to the greatest American stage comedy, Ben Hecht and Charles MacArthur's "The Front Page." But evoking "The Front Page" or "The Thin Man" only points up the discrepancies between their era and our own. Abrams wants the verbal panache of Hecht, Hammett, Frances Goodrich and Albert Hackett, but he's closer to Stanley Shapiro—who wrote the Rock Hudson-Doris Day comedies. If Doris and Rock had kept it up a little longer, they might have wound up making movies like "Undercover Blues" too. Then Turner and Quaid, freed from the need to make it again, would *really* have had something to grin about.

NEW YORK POST, 9/10/93, p. 41, Stephen Schaefer

"Undercover Blues" with Kathleen Turner and Dennis Quaid as debonair secret agents Jane and Jeff Blue is the latest attempt to revive a Hollywood favorite, the screwball comedy.

No one could seriously expect Turner or Quaid to impersonate the irreplaceable William Powell and Myrna Loy, who made Nick and Nora Charles in "The Thin Man" series the epitome of chic crimebusters.

But "Undercover Blues" could be expected to have something more on its mind than simply spoofing murderous mayhem.

Yet the sum total of an Abrams' original screenplay is simple: Silly fun.

The Blues are CIA operatives temporarily retired due to the arrival of baby Jane Louise (Michelle Schuelke).

Their New Orleans maternity-leave vacation is interrupted by bad guys led by the scheming would-be temptress Novacek (Fiona Shaw), an arms dealer, and her bumbling sidekick Muerte (Stanley Tucci, who has fun going completely overboard).

As effortlessly directed by Herbert ("Steel Magnolias") Ross and played by a perfectly assembled cast that includes Tom Arnold and Park Overall in small roles, "Undercover Blues" spins merrily along.

When Muerte dangles above an alligator pit or the women go hand-to-hand in a mud field, it may be corn but it's very high-grade corn.

The usually hyper Quaid and the often super-sensible Turner, both find a groove where the playing has just the right attitude that everything is possible and nothing will disturb the baby's naps.

This is a movie where the punches and the fights are so stylized, they could have been choreographed by Ross in his Broadway heyday.

But cotton candy is, by definition, not nutritious.

In the 1930s, when Nick and Nora Charles reigned, there was a reason for moviegoers to plug into their high-spirited, "isn't this a lark?" approach to murder.

Nick and Nora offered escapism for Depression-era America, but they weren't full-out fantasy figures.

The wealthy Nora's marriage to Nick, an ex-police detective, crossed economic and class barriers and echoed an economic reality.

Without preaching, they demonstrated the promise of an America where character and not class ruled.

Nick and Nora also made marriage—usually a never-ceasing butt of film jokes—into a thriving partnership, oiled by many martinis, even drier wit and a sense of comradeship. They remain enduring icons not only for their humor and charm but for their reality.

"Undercover Blues" is the equivalent of a cinematic souffle, where lightness is all and nothing really matters.

NEWSDAY, 9/11/93, Part II/p. 23, John Anderson

Those fabulous "Thin Man" mysteries of the '30s and '40s were fabulous because of the understated charm, unerring timing and coy-but-convincing sexual chemistry of William Powell and Myrna Loy. "Undercover Blues," which isn't quite so fabulous, owes what success it has to a complete lack of restraint. Taste? Self-control? They would have killed this film in its sleep.

But while Jefferson and Jane Blue (Dennis Quaid and Kathleen Turner) are not—despite their alliterative first names—Nick and Nora, that's OK. They're intolerably smug, insufferably cute, out of touch with any manner of reality, but they're funny. Not as funny as Stanley Tucci, maybe, but we'll get to him in a second.

Jeff and Jane are former intelligence officers who've found domesticity. Cold wars, hot wars, it's all behind them now. Their sole concern is Jane Louise, or Louise Jane—depending on which parent is speaking to their infant daughter played by Michelle Schuelke. Of course, a movie about diapers and pablum is not as promising as one about an international arms conspiracy, so Jeff and Jane are recruited by their government to thwart terrorist queen-pin Novacek (a gleefully evil Fiona Shaw) from undermining world security. The baby does not get in the way.

At the same time, Jeff has to fend off the persistent but ineffectual bloodlust of Muerte (Tucci), an egomanicial, would-be-swashbuckling street hood, whom Jeff, a martial-arts expert, beat up with a baby stroller during an attempted mugging. His pride wounded, Muerte keeps showing up at the most inopportune times, and provides the film's most hilarious moments. Jeff and Jane might get irritating, but Tucci keeps things bright and amusing.

Silly but entertaining, "Undercover Blues" wasn't screened for critics, a sure sign that the studio (in this case, MGM) had no faith in its own product. They should have known better.

SIGHT AND SOUND, 1/94, p. 54, Tony Rayns

Jane and Jeff Blue, gatecrashing a New Orleans party with their baby Jane Louise, come up with ridiculous answers when asked what they do. Later that evening, Jeff, out walking with the baby, gives a mugger, the self-styled Muerte, and his sidekick a run for their money. Two policemen call at the Blues' hotel later to find out what happened but Jeff admits nothing. The next day, a colleague of Jeff and Jane arrives asking them to perform "a job". They refuse, reminding him that they are on leave but are won over by a very lucrative offer. They have to track down an old foe, former Czech agent Novacek, who is dealing in stolen arms and hand her over to their bosses.

Meanwhile, the cops have discovered that the Blues are former (and possibly current) FBI agents. They follow them as the couple track down Novacek through a weak scientist employee of hers and evade her hitmen. Out for revenge, Muerte is on Jeff and Jane's trail but comes out the worst in every encounter he has with them. Finally, they trick him into going to Novacek's island where she holds him prisoner. When the two cops discover the Blues breaking into the scientist's house, Jeff and Jane tell them half the story. Finally, Jeff goes to Novacek's island, leaving Jane behind. One cop follows him there and both are taken prisoner. Jane and 'Jane Louise' have also been kidnapped. But just as Novacek is crowing over her victory, Jane throws the baby at her: it turns out to be a bomb and the couple escape. After a long chase, Novacek and Jane fight it out on a muddy bank. A helicopter with one of Novacek's former Czech colleagues descends from the sky to lift her up. She climbs into it only to find that she has been tricked by the Americans. Jane and Jeff return to their hotel in time for breakfast. They hire a yacht and set sail, only to find Muerte on board, still out for revenge. Pushing him overboard, they leave him clinging to a life ring.

The baby, that yuppie-movie accessory of the 80s, makes a comeback here in a jokey effort to this family, in which sexual equality seems to be paramount, both Jeff and Jane twirl their infant around as insouciantly as they kick, fight and charm their way out of numerous dangerous encounters. In fact, when Jane throws 'Jane Louise' at Novacek, the shock is not that she's chucking her baby around but that she isn't.

It isn't hard to see what Kathleen Turner is doing here: the Blues partnership smacks of an updated *Romancing the Stone* affair. And Turner, anxious to prove her high-kicking, gun-slinging credentials, lets slip no opportunity to do her very worst to relatively innocent marauders without so much as mussing her hair. Dennis Quaid, meanwhile, after a run of execrable film choices, seems to have settled into the loud, brash clever-boy role he now does best. It's all very cute—a happy, beautiful, wide-eyed, sassy, secret agent family. But it doesn't take long for it to become rather too sickeningly knowing.

And despite the tinge of sophistication in that premise, the film is boringly old-fashioned in its choice of villains: foreigners with silly names and ridiculous accents. Fiona Shaw may have had fun swapping the dowdy eccentrics she usually plays for the vampy Novacek—a mixture of Rosa Klebb and Lene Lovich—but we've seen it all before. And Stanley Tucci's Muerte, a writhing beanpole in black leather, reduced by a flick of a Blue wrist from snarling villain to squealing child, stops being funny after his first appearance. Like so much else in the film, he's one joke played out again and again.

The cartoon strokes of the characters are matched by a New Orleans backdrop that is happier and bigger than life. At every opportunity, a jazz band comes marching round the corner, down the street, in the cemetery or into a restaurant—as if Herbert Ross had realised that the film isn't interesting enough to carry itself as a comedy/action picture and needs a bit of musical packing. And when Dennis Quaid steps up and joins the band on the trumpet, you wish someone would give him a good smack and tell him not to behave like a brattish show-off.

What is certainly in the film's favour, however, is that it presents a somewhat different, if equally romantic, view of the FBI from the recent crop of serious movies: these amiable, devious agents are completely without angst.

Also reviewed in:
NEW YORK TIMES, 9/11/93, p. 13, Vincent Canby
VARIETY, 9/20/93, p. 27, Timothy M. Gray
WASHINGTON POST, 9/10/93, p. G7, Jane Horwitz

UNTAMED HEART

A Metro-Goldwyn-Mayer release. *Executive Producer:* J. Boyce Harman, Jr. *Producer:* Tony Bill and Helen Buck Bartlett. *Director:* Tony Bill. *Screenplay:* Tom Sierchio. *Director of Photography:* Jost Vacano. *Editor:* Mia Goldman. *Music:* Cliff Eidelman. *Music Editor:* Kenneth Karman. *Sound:* Matthew Quast and (music) Armin Steiner. *Sound Editor:* Bill Phillips and Jimmy Ling. *Casting:* Marci Liroff. *Production Designer:* Steven Jordan. *Art Director:* Jack D.L. Ballance. *Set Decorator:* Cliff Cunningham. *Set Dresser:* Heather McElhatton. *Special Effects:* Michael Wood. *Costumes:* Lynn Bernay. *Make-up:* Darcy Knight. *Stunt Coordinator:* Jack Gill and Tom Sierchio. *Running time:* 102 minutes. *MPAA Rating:* PG-13.

CAST: Christian Slater (Adam); Marisa Tomei (Caroline); Rosie Perez (Cindy); Kyle Secor (Howard); Willie Garson (Patsy); James Cada (Bill #1); Gary Groomes (Bill #2); Claudia Wilkens (Mother Camilla); Pat Clemons (Sister Helen); Lotis Key and Vanesa Hart (Nuns); Charley Bartlett (Young Adam); Vincent Kartheiser (Orphan Boy); Wendy Feder (Orphanage Nurse); Nancy Marvy (Caroline's Mom); Paul Douglas Law (Steven); Josh Schaefer (Michael); Marquetta Senters (Mary); Joe Minjares (Jim); Joe Schmit (Sportscaster); John Beasley (Cook); Steve Cochran (Stromboli); Sally Wingert (Tree Customer); Richard Grusin (Caroline's Father); Buffy Sedlachek (Lottie); Tom Sierchio (Ronnie); Aaron Kjenaas (Nick); Isabell Monk (Police Officer); Allen Hamilton (Doctor); Kay Bonner Nee (Beauty Shop Customer); Lia Rivamonte (Beauty School Instructor); Greg Sain (Kevin); Margaret McGraw (Girl in Car); John Paul Gamoke (Priest).

NEW YORK POST, 2/12/93, p. 33, Jami Bernard

This Valentine's Day, there will be much sobbing in the land, and it will be issuing muffled from beyond the hankies of those adolescent girls who regularly feature Christian Slater in their prayers and their dreams. I predict those girls will make a fetish of Slater's performance in "Untamed Heart," a relatively unremarkable romance with great youth appeal.

Slater plays a soulful brooder with a heart of gold, a heart that he also believes is a transplant from a baboon. At least that's what the nuns told him at the orphanage when he was a child—in a peculiar opening sequence that doesn't quite match the tone of the rest of this Tony Bill movie—and it would explain the big scar across his chest.

Now the baboon-hearted Adam (Slater) is a chore boy at a Minneapolis diner, where he shyly watches the comings and goings of the vibrant but unlucky-in-love waitress Caroline (Marisa Tomei). He never speaks to her, but when she binds up a boo-boo the way the nuns used to do, Adam's baboon heart starts making Tarzan noises in his chest. In this movie, all hearts are broken, and only some are mended; if there's no baboon donor handy, true love will do.

Clearly Adam is the guy for her, but Caroline doesn't begin to catch on—she's not the brightest light—until he saves her from a vicious attack in the park (read: jungle), filmed in a needlessly voyeuristic way.

"Untamed Heart" wend's its romantic way very slowly; my screening companion slept soundly during most of the extended courtship and missed nothing except a few wounded looks from Slater and a beefcake shot of his bare chest.

The movie features a gentle, old-fashioned kind of love, sweet and undynamic, but it also has an exciting acting-pairing. No, not Slater and Tomei, but Tomei and Rosie Perez, two of the new crop of sassy, streetwise, borough-accented, ethnic leading ladies who are galvanizing the screen. (Wait until you see a third sloe-eyed, fast-talking contender in "Just Another Girl on the IRT.")

Tomei was the impatient mechanic's daughter in "My Cousin Vinny," Perez the excitable "Jeopardy" contestant in "White Men Can't Jump," and, together as a couple of waitress friends, these actresses give "Untamed Heart" a little CPR. Friends with dog-whistle-sensitive ears claim they can only take so much of Perez's screechy voice, but I think her spirit and comic timing are going to make her a big star.

Slater is also very interesting in this nearly wordless role. He has clearly taken the baboon analogy to heart, and adopts a simian physicality—loping and contemplative—without being grotesque about it. It's "Love Story" meets "Frankie and Johnny" for teenagers with achy breaky hearts.

NEWSDAY, 2/12/93, Part II/p. 71, Jack Mathews

When Caroline, a waitress in an all-night Minneapolis diner, tells her friend and co-worker Cindy that she has become romantically involved with the feral-looking, almost mute busboy on their shift, all Cindy can think to say is "Why?"

"He doesn't make sense, I don't make sense, we make sense together," Caroline cheerfully answers.

Few of the parts of Tony Bill's "Untamed Heart" make sense, either, but somehow the movie adds up to something—a modern fairy tale, about a princess who thinks she's a frog and a busboy with a bad heart, with all the romance and schmaltz that implies.

Any movie with people as likable and as profoundly in love as Marisa Tomei's Caroline and Christian Slater's Adam earns quick grace points in these callow times, and the engaging performances of its two stars, plus Rosie Perez' saucy Cindy, bring a whole lot more.

It needs every one of those points to overcome the unabashed sentimentality of Tom Sierchio's script and Bill's direction. This is a movie that doesn't know when to stop driving home its points, from the lovers' longing looks to the music to dialogue that aches from the strain of over-writing. That bells don't ring when Adam and Caroline kiss for the first time could only have been an oversight.

Tomei, the discovery of 1992's "My Cousin Vinny," bears a striking resemblance to Amy Fisher in this movie, but her Caroline isn't capable of shooting even dirty looks when men do her wrong. She just hurts, and longs for a man who will love her back.

She gets that and much more from Adam, whom she finally notices when he rescues her from an attack by a pair of would-be rapists. Pressing through his stray dog shyness, she discovers a fragile, solitary person who has been loving her from a distance, following her home each night, keeping her picture on the wall of his basement apartment.

In any other movie, Adam's behavior would be setting off psycho alarms, but Caroline is so thrilled by the gesture, she barely acknowledges the break-in involved. Soon, she's sitting in his apartment, not batting an eye while he explains the angry scar on his chest with a story about how, as an orphan in the jungle, he had been given the heart of a baboon king.

"Untamed Heart" obviously won't stand much literal scrutiny. We're up to our necks in symbolism here, and you either open your own heart to it or suffer a fate worse than "Love Story." At one point during the preview I attended, a woman in the audience began sobbing so loudly, it sounded as if someone had sat on a cat.

It doesn't take much to fall for these characters. Slater, an often mannered actor forced by the nature of his character to express his emotions internally, has never been more commanding. The scene where he holds Caroline for the first time, and weeps from the joy of it, is an extraordinary moment.

Still, it is Tomei's movie. The actress brings an energy and sincerity to her roles that takes them beyond whatever they were written to be and makes them almost unreasonably appealing. For all the improbabilities in "Untamed Heart," the most improbable is that Caroline has a history of men running away from her.

Huh-uh.

SIGHT AND SOUND, 5/93, p. 58, Caren Myers

In an orphanage run by nuns, a small boy, Adam, suffering from a terrible heart condition, is comforted by Mother Camilla, who tells him the story of how his father was killed by the Baboon King, who in turn gave Adam his heart.

Years later, Adam is a busboy at Jim's, a Minneapolis diner. Too shy to speak a word, he has eyes only for Caroline, a young waitress who is always falling in love with men who reject her. One night at work, Caroline is taunted by two men, Howard and Patsy. They accost her as she is walking home and attempt to rape her, but Adam bursts out of nowhere and beats them to a pulp. Covering the unconscious Caroline with his coat, he carries her back to her house. When she comes to, he scuttles away. When Caroline returns to work, she pieces together what happened and thanks Adam for saving her, kissing him on the cheek. He begins to speak, explaining that he follows her home every night to make sure she gets home safely. Hesitantly, they begin a love affair. Adam, who wasn't allowed any physical contact as a child for fear of infection, is overcome by Caroline's kindness.

Caroline's best friend and co-worker Cindy persuades Caroline to come out on a double date with another guy. When they all return to the diner, Caroline worries that Adam might jump to the wrong conclusions. But before she can speak to him (indeed, before he even notices that she has a date), he is stabbed in the parking lot by Howard and Patsy. At the hospital, the doctor explains to Caroline that, while the wound was not fatal, Adam needs a heart transplant. Despite this, Caroline and Adam are happy through the spring. On Adam's birthday, she takes him to a hockey game, and he dies peacefully on the way home. After the funeral, Caroline finds an unopened present he left for her: the records Mother Camilla gave him.

I've never trusted movies which proclaim their tragic inevitability before I've even had time to fold up my coat. In *Untamed Heart*'s prologue (pompously shot in sepia), the good, kind Mother Camilla holds young Adam's hand and says sadly, "Oh Adam, your poor, poor heart," as if it weren't obvious from the way the child smiles up at her that he is a gentle soul with a loving heart, albeit one due to expire before the 102 minutes are up.

So at first it's a relief when the film does not develop into an overwrought weepie, something of which Tony Bill, who perpetrated *Six Weeks* (Mary Tyler Moore, Dudley Moore, and an adorable child dying of leukemia) is perfectly capable. But despite its bodice-ripping Mills and Boon title, *Untamed Heart* is a vision of love so idealized and toothless it seems to have been devised by a 12-year-old girl. Cribbing from *Beauty and the Beast* as much as from *Love Story*, the film posits Adam as a kind of saintly wild child. Silent until a kiss unlocks his voice, he's also marked for death by a scar on his chest so enormous and so baroque it looks as though Dr Frankenstein was the surgeon. Because he saves Caroline from rape (a Mills & Boon device if there ever was one), the rest of his actions are portrayed through the soft-focus lens of gratitude; the fact that he follows her home in the dark is given as an example of his courtly solicitude. He also steals her picture from behind the bar, and sneaks in through her bedroom window at night to watch her sleep—pure guardian angel behaviour, and not a bit creepy. Caroline accepts each of these revelations with a kind of hushed wonder, and we are supposed to go along with it, as if breaking into someone's bedroom were a sweet, tender expression of devotion. Never mind that if she were the slightest bit frightened or repulsed by this, Adam would become the psychopathic Sean Bean character in the BBC film *Tell Me That You Love Me*.

Untamed Heart is so desperate to convince us that there is only harmony, between Caroline and Adam that it sweeps everything under the carpet. There aren't even any inadvertent cruelties and disappointments in their relationship—all conflict is conveniently located outside them, mostly in the heinous Howard and Patsy. Even when the film knows it should raise questions, it doesn't follow through. After Caroline has been attacked, there is some attempt to empathise with her fear and disgust—she flinches when her boss touches her shoulder in friendly greeting. But as soon as she and Adam kiss, she becomes all wise and giving and untroubled, smilingly leading him to her bedroom.

More baffling still is the scene when the double-date foursome come to the diner, and Caroline, fearing a misunderstanding with Adam, pleads with Cindy to go somewhere else. It's just shaping up to be an uncomfortable moment all round when Adam gets stabbed and the whole of the potential conflict is discarded. You wonder why the film-makers bothered to set up the scene in the first place.

Christian Slater copes manfully with a part where he has to play mute and cower like a frightened animal to begin with, then say things like "always the same dream ... the jungle ... twisted limbs ... and the rain, always the rain ...". He plays conscientiously against wise-cracking, junior Jack Nicholson type, but it is a thankless role. Marisa Tomei, after her screen-crunching exuberance in *My Cousin Vinny*, seems a little subdued as the wistful, warm-hearted Caroline, but Rosie Perez has fun with the sassy waitress part. Twitching her butt to the jukebox or turning down the corners of her mouth in grudging approval when sizing up Adam ("Yeah, I'd do him"), she has a wicked comic aplomb.

But by the time Adam goes gently into that good night (and he does—drops off like someone taking a nap) you're baulking at the film's dishonesty. Caroline, sorrowful but at peace, tells Cindy, "He was like an angel." Sure he was. And death isn't frightening. The only thing pumping through this *Heart* is rose water.

VILLAGE VOICE, 2/16/93, p. 54, Georgia Brown

It's hard to imagine the gentle, affecting *Untamed Heart* without Marisa Tomei, a surprising talent capable of holding an entire movie with her bright eyes and unspoiled manner. A waitress in a Minneapolis diner, Caroline is a high school grad still living in her parents' modest home who has no special gift except for kindness and receptivity to others. (She has exactly what Murray's Phil goes through weeks of deepest winter to discover in himself.) Because she's so "nice," boyfriends drop her, but it's clearly their loss. Beneath her chipper manner, desperation mounts. Is the fault with her or the world? Another figure/ground problem.

Then one winter night, walking home from work, Caroline is assaulted and nearly raped. She's saved by the diner's busboy, Adam (Christian Slater), a strange, silent, stringy-haired loner who secretly follows her each night. Adam (whose theme song is Roger Williams's rendition of "Nature Boy") is an orphan with a congenital heart defect raised by nuns. Because of a story told him by one of the sisters, he believes his heart was a reward bestowed on him by a mythical Baboon King. (The movie was originally titled *Baboon Heart*, and it's probably just as well they changed it.)

Director Tony Bill specializes in small, offbeat melodramas: *My Bodyguard* (not to be confused with the Costner-Houston behemoth), *Five Corners, Crazy People. Untamed Heart* has a few violent incidents but little actually happens. After the assault, Caroline and Adam begin keeping company, at first secretly. When she tells her friend at the diner, Cindy (the inimitable Rosie Perez) is astonished: "Adam *from work*?" But despite his long hibernation, the rehabilitation of Adam doesn't seem that hard to accomplish. One kiss for this Frog Prince and he begins speaking in meaningful sentences. (My young companion said he liked the movie a lot until Christian Slater began to talk.)

Untamed Heart put a lump in my throat and held it there for the duration, a condition that grew rather uncomfortable over time. Tony Bill proves he isn't afraid of sentiment, but he has yet to find a way to use it.

Also reviewed in:
CHICAGO TRIBUNE, 2/12/93, Friday/p. B, Dave Kehr
NEW YORK TIMES, 2/12/93, p. C14, Vincent Canby
NEW YORKER, 2/15/93, p. 98, Anthony Lane
VARIETY, 2/1/93, p. 96, Brian Lowry
WASHINGTON POST, 2/12/93, p. C7, Hal Ilinson

UTZ

A First Run Features/Castle Hill Productions release of a Viva Pictures production for BBC Films in association with NDR/BBC Films/Academy. *Executive Producer:* William Sargent and John Goldschmidt. *Producer:* John Goldschmidt. *Director:* George Sluizer. *Screenplay:* Hugh

Whitemore. *Based on the novel by:* Bruce Chatwin. *Director of Photography:* Gerard Vandenberg. *Editor:* Lin Friedman. *Music:* Nicola Piovani. *Sound:* David John. *Sound Editor:* Jim Shields. *Casting:* Polly Hootkins. *Production Designer:* Karel Vacek. *Art Director:* Ulrich Schröder. *Costume Designer:* Marie Frankova. *Make-up:* Paul Schmidt. *Running time:* 95 minutes. *MPAA Rating:* Not Rated.

CAST: Armin Mueller-Stahl (Baron Kaspar Joachim von Utz); Brenda Fricker (Marta); Peter Riegert (Marius Fischer); Paul Scofield (Dr. Vaclav Orlik); CESKE KRIZOVE: Miriam Karlin (Grandmother Utz); Christian Mueller-Stahl (Young Utz, 18 years); Jakub Zdenek (Young Utz, 11 years); Christian Rabe (Young Utz, 5 years); Caroline Guthrie (Young Marta); PRAGUE: Pauline Melville (Museum Curator); Peter MacKriel (Janitor); Clark Dunbar (Doctor); Adrian Brine (Head Waiter); Gaye Brown (Ada Krasova); THE WEST: Harriet Robinson (American Lady); Vittoria Tarlow (Tall Lady); James Curran (Wine Waiter); Anthony Donovan (Autioneer); Bonnie Williams (Diane); Vera Soukupova (Favorite Diva); Marjol Flore (French Singer); Hildegard Hötte (Photographer); Michaela Vitkova (Argentian Lady).

LOS ANGELES TIMES, 4/16/93, Calendar/p. 6, Peter Rainer

"Utz" has one of those oddball themes for a movie that turns out surprisingly well. Set in Soviet controlled Czechoslovakia, it's about an obsessed Meissen porcelain collector, the Baron von Utz (Armin Mueller-Stahl), who has the last laugh on the communist authorities. Based on the 1988 novel by Bruce Chatwin and directed by George Sluizer from a script by Hugh Whitmore, it's an amusingly cultivated jaunt. The subject matter could have provided a richer experience but the filmmakers are probably right to treat it as they did. It's a piffle with class.

The film (Times-rated Mature) has a complicated time scheme but the constant flashing back and forth isn't done to confuse us with abstract artiness; it's probably the least clunky way to tell the story. Utz, we discover, has just died but his multimillion-dollar Meissen collection, which is housed in the dingy one-bedroom apartment he shared with his housekeeper (Brenda Fricker), is nowhere to be found—to the consternation of the American art dealer (Peter Riegert) who had been counting on wrapping up a lucrative death-bed deal. (Actual Meissen masterpieces are photographed.)

The film moves into Utz's past into his childhood when he saved his first porcelain piece and then, in a winding fashion, brings us back to his final days. His history with his housekeeper is filled in for us; so is his adoration of porcine operatic divas. (They're like Meissens in motion.) There are a few risible scenes with his contentious best friend of more than 40 years, Professor Orlik (Paul Scofield), a scientist whose specialty—obsession really—is for the common housefly.

The obsessions of these people are so distinct from each other that at times the film seems quietly, deeply demented (The performances are distinctively excellent too.) Utz doesn't really collect his Meissens because of their value; he values them as totems of comfort. Mueller-Stahl underplays Utz's fanaticism, which, of course, makes him seem more fanatic than ever. He brings the film a whiff of old world grace, and a trace of danger too. Utz's collection was created out of the misfortunes of all the peoples who had to flee Hitler and the Soviets. He accepts his role as beneficiary with a chilling calm.

Director Sluizer—if there is any justice, he should be remembered for his Dutch version of "The Vanishing" rather than his recent Hollywood version—doesn't quite have the lightness of touch that he appears to be aiming for. But his pokey politesse has its charms and he understands Utz's fascination with his beautiful porcelains, which are photographed so that they give off the bright radiance of flesh. When Utz handles his pieces, they seem almost sacramental. We can see why the Czech authorities don't know what to make of the Baron—or his collections. His obsession is so rarefied, and yet so pure, that it confounds the totalitarian mentality.

It confounds us too, but pleasantly. He's the oddest of oddball heroes in the movies right now.

NEW YORK, 2/15/93, p. 61, David Denby

Utz, George Sluizer's adaptation of Bruce Chatwin's novel, is a dud—a movie about the passion of collecting that has no passion—but I can provisionally recommend it for its European atmosphere. Parts of the movie were shot in Prague, and the dark colors and interiors sank into my consciousness with the pleasant weight of luxury.

NEW YORK POST, 2/10/93, p. 23, Jerry Tallmer

Obsession and greed have been a theme in movies in a long line since movies began. Think of Von Stroheim's "Greed" itself, of Huston's "The Treasure of the Sierra Madre," of "The Maltese Falcon," just for three.

So how about Meissen china? Here is a movie, quite a strange movie, called "Utz," centering on the Baron Kaspar Joachim von Utz who has hungered since early boyhood to lay his hands on just as many of those pretty-pretty miniature Dresden porcelain musicians and other priceless little pieces as fall within his reach.

At one of the sock points of "Utz," the Baron ushers his American friend, a hustling young New York gallery owner, into a secret room of a thousand Meissen figurines, glittering, row upon row upon row, from all four walls. At another, the Baron puts a half-dozen of those pieces through a slow, exquisite tabletop gavotte, by candelabra light.

All this happens in Prague a few years back, when there was still an Iron Curtain and that country was still behind it. The Baron, smoothly played, as always by Armin Mueller-Stahl, boasts to Marius (Peter Riegert), the hustling American: "Everybody smuggles things *out* of Czechoslovakia. I smuggle these pieces in." He is, he ironically observes a porcelain millionaire—because he can't dispose of his wealth.

The other thing the Baron likes to lay his hands on is ladies, preferably operatic divas of rather large endowment. This causes no end of tension with his faithful housekeeper of many years, the good Marta, whom he long ago rescued from being lynched as a witch by her fellow peasants just because she liked to go noodling and swimming naked with her pet goose.

Marta is given very little to say, both because of the part and because, being the splendid Brenda Fricker—Oscar-winning mother of "My Left Foot"—her British accent is not exactly that of a Czech goosegirl 40 years on.

Tension further enters the Baron's life and the movie's when aparatchiks of the State Museum come to photograph and register every one of his thousand Meissen pieces, with an eye toward confiscation of the collection one of these fine days. "Don't touch that!" a tough female commissar snaps when the Baron goes to straighten a little sculpture for the camera and then, cigarette in mouth, she herself brushes one carelessly off the tabletop to the floor, where an arm snaps off.

"Take it!" Utz shouts, shattering his own urbanity. "Take it to your horrible Museum!" The woman mumbles: "This piece will not appear in the Museum inventory." "Thank you for *that*," Utz says in a cold rage. He gets his revenge a long time later, in a denouement you may not expect.

It is noted—this work directed by George Sluizer from Hugh Whitemore's flashback-schizy adaptation of a Bruce Chatwin novel—a film full of many, many curious quirks. Not least of these is the revered Paul Scofield, very far now from Sir Thomas More, as an Utz pal named Dr. Orlik who has gone from studying the Woolly Mammoth to studying houseflies, one of which he catches between drinking glass and tablecloth in the best fish restaurant in Prague.

There are no trout, our friends are informed by a waiter—even though the fish tank is swimming with trout reserved for Party members. What's left? Carp. Look, says Peter Riegert, it's misspelled "CRAP" on the menu. Wherewith the ominous Dr. Orlik, a character left over from the "Third Man," orders "Crap a la Juive"—Jewish crap—amidst gales of his own caustic laughter. I do not know what this meant. Much later, Utz and Marius are in a Jewish cemetery, having a conversation about Golems and the immortality of porcelain. Utz bares his own partial Jewish ancestry. "Jews make the best collectors," he says. "Because it's dangerous." Maybe. Or maybe as Tallulah Bankhead once said in another connection, there is less here than meets the eye.

NEWSDAY, 2/10/93, Part II/p. 48, John Anderson

Last Friday saw the release of "The Vanishing," director George Sluizer's remake of his own 1988 thriller about a man obsessed with the disappearance of his girlfriend. This week, Sluizer gives us "Utz," about a Czech obsessed with collecting fine porcelain. Lunging for a connection, we find that, in Sluizer's hands, loss turns out to be our gain, and vice versa.

The problems with "Utz" are not just Sluizer's, though. They lie in Bruce Chatwin's novel, and in the nature of its subject. Whether or not material possession is itself cinematically compelling—and there's certainly more to the story than that—the character has a basic flaw: Anyone who defines him or herself through the accumulation of inanimate objects, no matter how beautiful, has pretty much vacated the psychic premises. So Sluizer starts out having to pursue a character who isn't all there in the first place.

To his credit, and that of Utz' portrayer, the canny Armin Mueller-Stahl, we do care about Baron von Utz, partly because of his time and place—Czechoslovakia, pre-Havel administration—a setting that raises particular questions about Utz' obsession: Is he a class criminal? Does the accumulation of so much valuable porcelain—he has more than 1,000 pieces, all rare, all on display in the tawdry apartment he shares with his housekeeper Marta (Brenda Fricker)—constitute an affront to Marxism? Is the very existence of a personal collection of such size a slam against the state? And, most importantly, if one views Utz' collection as a statement of individuality, how does one justify the means by which he's made it?

"First there were Jews fleeing the Nazis," he tells his American friend, art dealer Marius Fischer (Peter Riegert). "Then there were aristocrats fleeing the Soviets. Wars, pogroms, revolutions ..." They all needed cash, had porcelain to sell, and Utz was there.

His story unfolds through flashbacks, some of which are Utz', some of which are Fischer's and many of which teeter precariously upon each other. Sluizer's technique is to divulge bits of his characters' history that are only explained to us much later, and the result is a narrative construction full of hairline cracks. That it doesn't collapse entirely is only due to the performances—by Mueller-Stahl, Riegert, Fricker and Paul Scofield, as Utz' eccentric friend Dr. Vaclav Orlik. It is Orlik who contacts Fischer after Utz has a stroke, advising him to make an offer for Utz' collection. The collection, however, has vanished, and Fischer's subsequent search turns up more than porcelain.

Filmed in Prague while the communist bureaucracy still held sway, "Utz" seems to capture the feel of a city, and a zeitgeist, under yoke; the graying mien of the film suits the story of a man who cultivates and curates a small museum's worth of delicate objets d'art while the jackboot of oppression is at the throat of his people. But while being Utz may require a peculiar combination of disinterest and self-absorption, a film concerned with a man's lifelong passion should possess a bit more passion of its own.

SIGHT AND SOUND, 5/92, p. 63, Richard Combs

In Geneva, American art dealer Marius Fischer meets Czechoslovakian porcelain collector Baron Kaspar von Utz, who has just completed his collection of a famous set of 'monkey musicians'. In his hotel, Utz remembers the porcelain collection of his grandmother, and how the piece he coveted most, a harlequin figure, was given to him when his father died. Back in Prague, Utz has a stroke, and his close friend Dr Vaclav Orlik summons Fischer with the hint that now he might persuade Utz to part with his collection.

Utz dies after another stroke, however, and the only mourners at his funeral are Orlik and Utz's long-time domestic Marta (who indicates that she may have misled all the other potential mourners, particularly the many operatic divas whom Utz 'collected' as obsessively as he did porcelain). When Fischer arrives, while waiting to meet Orlik, he remembers his first visit to Utz's apartment, the rooms full of lovingly displayed Meissen, and the silent protective presence of Marta. (In a village near his family's one-time country estate, Utz rescued the young Marta from a mob of angry villagers, who considered her a witch after she was seen supposedly courting a gander.)

Unhappy with the attitude of the new Communist regime towards his collection—which they insist on photographing and marking for later deposit in a state museum—Utz had considered the possibility of moving abroad. He begins visiting Geneva, but finds himself unable to settle in the émigré community. In Prague, Fischer visits him again, and listens to his views on the alchemical properties of porcelain, and the blasphemous relation between God's creation of life, the Golem stories of the Jewish ghetto of Prague, and porcelain-making.

When Fischer at last meets Orlik, he is shocked to hear that, just before Utz's death, his porcelain collection had apparently vanished. Orlik then lets Fischer in on some of the secrets of Utz's life: the fact that Marta had for many years been his wife (so he could keep his larger apartment) but had not shared his bed; that Utz had continued to court and sleep with opera singers, until realising that he was too old for that pastime, had accepted Marta as his wife in fact as well as name. The mystery of what happened to Utz's collection is not revealed to Fischer, however, even when he tries to track Marta down in her village: after his first stroke, finally oppressed by the collection into which he had poured his life, Utz had silently persuaded Marta to break every piece.

"His face was immediately forgettable. It was a round face, waxy in texture, without a hint of the passions beneath its surface, set with narrow eyes behind steel-framed spectacles: a face so featureless it gave the impression of not being there. Did he have a moustache? I forget. Add a moustache, subtract a moustache: nothing would alter his utterly nondescript appearance". The first challenge for any adapter of Bruce Chatwin's last novel is how to capture the quality of that description: at once wonderfully ironic, humorous and precise, even while what it is describing seems to be vanishing into thin air. Something about its picture of the Baron von Utz—that "round face, waxy in texture"—suggests that he is himself a collector's item, a piece of cherished porcelain turned this way and that in the light, an activity which will itself wear away the cherished object. The collector's passion consumes the thing collected; so material a pursuit is eventually cancelled out by the spiritual hunger that gave rise to it, by a host of dangerous passions (art-collecting as idolatory, blasphemy, hubris) it unleashes. Which leads to the question Utz can't answer when it's posed by Chatwin's narrator—"Do your porcelains demand their own death?"—but does implicitly by the end.

That contradictory impulse, so neatly embodied in the novel Utz, determined the course of Chatwin's life: the Sotheby's director who threw up a career dealing in artefacts to travel the globe 'collecting' wonders, instances of the material being rubbed away by the spiritual (not easy to put on film, though it's easy to see why Werner Herzog was attracted to Chatwin). What is essentially lacking in this TV adaptation of Utz is any sense of the tension, the contradictoriness, of this impulse. Without that there is really no drama, not even a story, just a collection of foibles, and Hugh Whitemore and George Sluizer's Utz is pre-eminently an 'eccentric' character play.

There's no danger here of Utz disappearing, embodied as he is with bemused dignity, a distracted Old World charm, by Armin Mueller-Stahl. And just to make sure the fragments of Chatwin's tale stick together, the author's equally evanescent 'I' has been turned into one of those bland interlocutor heroes, played with Quiet American respect and polite curiosity by Peter Riegert. Riegert's presence introduces a New World/Old World playoff that doesn't have much to do with the story, or the significance of the porcelains, but does underline all the conventional eccentricities, presumably makes the film more saleable in the US, and allows it to bypass more pertinent cultural details.

Principally, these have to do with the city of Prague and the post-war history of Czechoslovakia. Utz's career is intimately connected to that history, from his beginning as a German-born citizen of the Sudetenland, to the founding of his collection on the misfortunes of others—buying from Jews anxious to leave Germany after Kristallnacht, and from aristocrats fleeing the Soviets at the end of the war—to his ambivalent status under the Communist government of Czechoslovakia ("Was the collector a class enemy? If so, how?").

But the ebb and flow of history is lost in the film's sunny, seemingly eternal Euro-present. Also gone is the gloomy ambience of Prague—despite the participation of a large Czech unit—which Utz sees as his unhappy but natural medium. Whitemore's screenplay quite scrupulously includes all the key speeches, and metaphysical reference points, in the book's discussion of the aesthetics of porcelain and the ethics of collecting. Mention is made of the alchemists and the relationship between gold and porcelain in the quest for "the substance of immortality and potency"; also the Golem story and how the creation of life has a lot to do with fashioning things out of a mound of clay ("Not only was Adam the first human person. He was also the first ceramic sculpture"). But the balance between what is and isn't there in this adaptation of Utz has been unhappily reversed; in the process of cultural transposition, George Sluizer this time has made the wrong things vanish.

VILLAGE VOICE, 2/16/93, p. 49, J. Hoberman

Whatever reputation Sluizer gained in these precincts with the first version of *The Vanishing* is unlikely to be enhanced by the release of *Utz*, the dreary BBC telefilm he directed from Bruce Chatwin's last novel.

Again, we have a knocked together portrait of pathology. The Baron von Utz (Armin Mueller-Stahl) has been obsessed since childhood with the products of the Meissen porcelain factory. He's a sub-Nabokovian character who lives in a Prague apartment with his devoted servant (Brenda Fricker, making no attempt to modulate her Irish brogue) and a fantastic collection of exquisite china figurines, most of them gleaned from Jews escaping the Nazis or Germans and wealthy Czechs fleeing the communists.

Like the novel, the movie is structured in flashback. Sluizer has hopefully compared *Utz*'s chronology to that of *The Vanishing*, but as a master of *temps perdu* he's not exactly Alain Resnais. Compensating for his graceless time-hopping, Sluizer employs over-exaggerated comedy. It's typical of the movie's pipsqueak emphasis to relentlessly bludgeon a small, witty scene in a Prague restaurant, filling the screen with fat apparatchiki and endlessly reiterating a single joke—an English menu on which carp is consistently misspelled c-r-a-p—as if the viewer were not only dim but hard of hearing. The insult is compounded by Paul Scofield as Fricker's rival for the film's most egregiously popeyed characterization, the boisterously sardonic Dr. Orlik. (Peter Riegert, a benign New York art dealer added to the stew, gives the only tolerable performance—not counting the stunning collection of actual Meissen porcelain.)

Chatwin, who was once an appraiser at Sotheby's (and, later, the head of its Impressionist division), knew what of he spoke: In the novel, Utz is a self-absorbed, colorless fellow who not only survives the political earthquakes that regularly rock Central Europe but keeps his fragile porcelains intact, by skillfully adapting himself to each new regime. In the movie, Utz is a heroic nonconformist and Mueller-Stahl, only slightly less lovable than the old coot he played in *Night on Earth*, panders to the presumed English fondness of eccentricity.

These are quaint lives in the quiet heart of Europe. (For additional splendor, Utz visits a Swiss spa where crass Americans loudly complain about the quality of the tomato juice.) Sluizer and screenwriter Hugh Whitemore shift the time frame from the years immediately before and after Prague Spring to the mid and late 1980s—an act of misplaced topicality that allows Riegert's uncomprehending art dealer to drive past a political demonstration while guaranteeing that the clumsy communists of the state museum, poised to seize the Utz collection, will get their deserved comeuppance.

The abiding sense of Prague as a Central European dollhouse, a cramped, magical space where inanimate objects come to life—as in the films of Jan Svankmajer, the fantasies of the Surrealists, the paintings of Arcimboldo, or the legend of the Golem—has at last been dispelled. *Utz* is full of mysteries—all of them dull—but it makes for a new Chamber of Commerce promo.

This airy, sun-filled Prague is scarcely the uncanny, gloom-ridden town of myth. The movie is far more glazed and prettified than any of Utz's porcelains. The bureaucrats may be pigs but even the rats look groomed.

Also reviewed in:
CHICAGO TRIBUNE, 5/14/93, Friday/p. I, Clifford Terry
NEW REPUBLIC, 3/1/93, p. 24, Stanley Kauffmann
NEW YORK TIMES, 2/10/93, p. C15, Janet Maslin
VARIETY, 2/24/92, p. 252, David Stratton
WASHINGTON POST, 3/22/93, p. B2, Rita Kempley

VALLEY OF ABRAHAM

A Madragoa Filmes/Gemini Films/Light Night co-production, in association with IPC/FC Gulbenkian/SEC/CNS/Canal+/Office Federal de la Culture/TSR/Eurimages. *Producer:* Paulo Branco. *Director:* Manoel de Oliveira. *Screenplay:* Manoel de Oliveira. *Based on the novel by:*

Agustina Bessa-Luis. *Director of Photography:* Mário Barroso. *Editor:* Manoel de Oliveira and Valérie Loiseleux. *Sound:* Henri Maikoff. *Sound Editor:* Thierry Delor and Hans Künzi. *Casting:* Agnés Fierobe. *Art Director:* Maria José Branco. *Set Designer:* Maria José Branco. *Costumes:* Isabel Branco. *Make-up:* Michelle Bernet. *Running time:* 187 minutes. *MPAA Rating:* Not Rated.

CAST: Mário Barroso (Narrator); Leonor Silveira (Ema); Cecile Sanz de Alba (Young Ema); Luís Miguel Cintra (Carlos de Paiva); Rui de Carvalho (Paulino Cardeano); Luís Lima Barreto (Pedro Lumiares); Micheline Larpin (Simona); Diogo Dória (Fernando Osório); José Pinto (Caires); Filipe Cochofel (Fortunato); Joao Perry (Padre Dossém); Glória de Matos (Maria do Loreto); António Reis (Semblano); Isabel Ruth (Ritinha); Laura Soveral (Tia Augusta); MonOique Dodd (Chélinha); Juliana Samarine (Nelson's Wife); Miguel Guilherme (Motorcyclist); Nuno Vieira de Almeida (Nelson); Isabel de Castro and J'lia Buisel (Melo Sisters); Dina Treno (Branca); Dalila Carmo e Sousa (Marina); Paula Seabra (Alice); Vanda Fernandes (Lolota as a Young Child); Sofia Alves (Lolota as a Little Girl); Leonor Viseu (Luisona as a Young Child); Beatriz Batarda (Luisona as a Little Girl); António Wagner (Baltazar); Argentina Rocha (Carlos' First Wife); Josefina Húngaro (Nelson's Mother); Fernando Bento (Dr Carmesim); Manuel Enes (Homero); Ana QueirUs and Mercedes Brawand (Paiva Sisters); David Cardoso (Gardener); Vaz Mendes and Rui Oliveira (Teenage Boys); Joaquim Nogueira (Narciso); Lurdes Rocha (Dressmaker); Marques de Aredo and Padre Pires (Padres); Beatriz Batarda (Young Ema's Voice); Teresa Madruga (Simona's Voice); Eurice de Almeida (Chélinha's Voice); Alina Candeias (2nd Paiva Sister's Voice).

CHRISTIAN SCIENCE MONITOR, 10/28/93, p. 14, David Sterritt

The heroine of Gustave Flaubert's greatest novel, "Madame Bovary," continues to exert a strong attraction for filmmakers. Many gifted directors have adapted her story, from Hollywood master Vincente Minnelli to French innovator Claude Chabrol and, most recently, the great Alexander Sokurov, whose Russian version is called "Save and Protect."

Now the tale has been adapted by Manoel de Oliveira, who is widely regarded as the greatest of all Portuguese filmmakers—quite an achievement, since Portugal has a particularly robust and inventive movie scene. Based on a novel by Agustina Bessa-Luis called "Valley of Abraham," his drama has earned ecstatic responses from audiences at the Cannes and New York filmfests.

The story of Madame Bovary revolves around a woman whose wildly romantic dreams far outstrip the dull realities of her provincial life as dutiful spouse of a small-time medical practitioner, and eventually lead her to a melodramatic death.

The question underlying "Valley of Abraham" is both simple and fascinating. What if a modern-day woman found herself in Madame Bovary's situation, fully understood the dangers and temptations she faced, but proceeded with her flowery fantasies nevertheless—pursuing them to their ultimate conclusion, even though she's read Flaubert's novel and knows perfectly well the tragic destiny that awaits her?

An important reason why Madame Bovary has drawn so many filmmakers is that cinema manufactures exactly the sort of world that Emma inhabits—always teetering between florid illusion and drab actuality, and habitually afraid of committing itself to either. Many great directors understand and explore this conundrum, and de Oliveira has seized on it as a major theme in his work.

Examples include such recent films as "The Cannibals," which mingles opera and horrific farce, and "Non, or, The Commander's Vain Glory," which leaps about in time, space, and philosophy.

In de Oliveira's hands, the story of modern-day Emma is as knowing, ironic, and self-aware as the heroine's own actions.

He collaborates with her in constructing the very dreams and reveries that are destined to undo her; yet there's nothing mean-spirited in this, since both filmmaker and character clearly revel in the beauty and romance they create along the way.

When she ultimately meets her death, it's almost comical in its long-prepared abruptness, and we know she would have smiled along with us at its mixture of the sad, the wistful, and the silly.

1574   FILM REVIEW ANNUAL

De Oliveira receives help from an expert cast in "Valley of Abraham," most notably from Leonor Silveira, who plays Emma with exquisite panache. The literate screenplay is by de Oliveira, and he also edited the film with Valérie Loiseleux.

NEW YORK POST, 12/22/93, p. 45, Bill Hoffmann

I've got two words for the narrator of the new Portuguese film "Valley of Abraham": Shut up!

Admittedly, this is a crude way to begin a critique of the latest effort by 82-year-old Portuguese film legend Manoel de Oliveira.

But the seemingly endless narration that intrudes over the soundtrack of this three-hour-plus soap all but kills any dramatic tension.

"Valley of Abraham" is a loosely based, modern-day version of Flaubert's "Madame Bovary" about the consequences of a young woman's loveless marriage.

Just in case we don't get it, our young heroine is named Emma and she's caught reading "Madame Bovary" by a disapproving aunt.

But whereas Flaubert's novel was alive and full of passion, Oliveira's film seems purposely drained of energy.

The movie is like a filmed stage play occasionally splashed with wonderful shots of the Portuguese countryside.

The actors don't seem to be aiming their lines at each other. Instead, they seem to be performing monologues. Their true feelings are constantly explained away by a narrator.

He tells us why Emma's having this affair or that affair, why she doesn't love her husband, why she's taking off for the weekend, why her husband is messing around.

Hey, how about a little acting?

But I think de Oliveira has purposely restrained his players. Why, I don't know. Even the narration is monotone.

God, what I wouldn't have done for Spalding Gray to have wrested the mike away from our off-screen storyteller.

Another problem: For all the talk of sex, adultery and passion, there's not a hint of steam on screen. We hear how everybody's having affairs, so why can't we see it? Not a soul takes their clothes off—not even in the bedroom scenes.

The most shocking moment comes when Emma's husband, annoyed by his wife's sensual caressing of the family cat with her chin, violently grabs the beast and hurls it towards the camera.

Not pleasant, but at least *somebody* did *something*! You know something's dreadfully wrong when a tabby turns out to be the major scene stealer.

All of this said, there is one bright spot. Cecile Sanz de Alba, who plays the teen-age Emma, may be the sexiest young actress of the '90s. I hope we'll be seeing a lot more of her.

NEWSDAY, 12/22/93, Part II/p. 59, John Anderson

Emma Bovary continues to exert her considerable seductive power over men, which probably says less about Emma than it does about men. Suffice to say that her story has taken on the stature of archetype, and like any archetype is just asking for very personalized interpretations.

There have been several on the screen, most recently Claude Chabrol's "Madame Bovary," which was faithful as a dog, but lifeless. Conversely, "Valley of Abraham," Portuguese director Manoel de Oliveira's "adaptation of an adaptation"—he based it on Agustina Bessa-Luis' Emma update "Vale Abraao"—is faithful to Flaubert only in the details, and yet captures something of its essence.

De Oliveira has created a more-than-leisurely paced (three hours plus) version of the Bessa-Luis book, which introduces us to two versions of Emma, here spelled Ema. The younger version, played by Cecile Sanz de Alba, has a beauty that someone describes as "a kind of genius." She's not classically lovely (Mme. Bovary never was), and she limps. But Ema is aware of her own sexual power; when she stands by the road near her house, men crash their cars into the wall. ("There have been deaths," someone reports.) She's fickle and coy, and canny enough not to recognize her father's friend, the doctor Carlos (Luis Miguel Cintra) when she meets him the second time. He will shortly become smitten, marry her, and then become the source of her boredom.

But this doesn't happen until Ema has grown and undergone an amazing transformation. Her beloved Aunt Augusta has died, and the older Ema, played by Leonor Silveira, still resembles Sanz de Alba. But she's inherited a veil of sadness, or perhaps an awareness of mortality, or a sense that her own sexuality will never be a delight without being a plague.

Like Madame Bovary, Ema has affairs: with the obnoxious Osorio (Diogo Doria), with the callow Fortunato (Filipe Cochofel), all the time looking, not finding, but never becoming the victim her namesake was: Hers is a fatalism of her own device. And her sexuality, too, is her own. When she sleeps with her husband, it's strictly to sate her desire, and in a perverse way cheating on herself. When she admires herself in the mirror, it's a kind of foreplay.

Men are relentlessly loutish, sexist and just dumb, even when they're trying to be gallant. "A face like hers justifies a man's life," Carlos says. You'd never hear Ema saying anything like that.

SIGHT AND SOUND, 10/94, p. 55, Tony Rayns

Having lost her mother at the age of six, Ema, lame in one leg, has been raised in an atmosphere of poetic refinement by her father Paulino Cardeano. She has matured into a sensual young woman with a 'vulgar' taste for romantic fiction (such as *Madame Bovary*) criticised by her aunt Augusta. On meeting her husband-to-be Dr Carlos de Paiva, she judges him a fool. Many men are attracted by Ema's beauty and charm: they include Nelson, who has an affair with her maid Branca to get near her, but ends up marrying an heiress.

Carlos revisits the Cardeano house for Augusta's wake, and reveals that his wife has also died. Soon after, Ema and Carlos marry and Ema moves to his home in Romesal, accompanied by her mute washerwoman Ritinha. Life is dull; Ema finds no rapport with Carlos' two older sisters, but meets more interesting people at a ball in the house of Pedro Lumiares, including the dashing Fernando Osório and the philanderer Narciso Semblano. At a series of receptions and dinner parties, some hosted by the worldly Maria do Loreto, she meets the rest of the district's social circle. Carlos, aware that he cannot satisfy Ema's romantic longings, proposes that she have an affair with Pedro—a development viewed with cynical detachment by Pedro's wife Simona.

By the time that Ema takes Osório as her lover, more as a provocation than as an act of desire, she has two daughters by Carlos. At Osório's lakeside villa in Vesuvio, she meets musicians, artists and freethinkers. Carlos turns to Maria do Loreto for platonic company; enraged by his apparent indifference, Ema returns to Vesuvio alone and flirts with young estate worker Fortunato, deliberately provoking the jealousy of the butler Caires. Carlos turns to Ema's father for advice on saving the marriage, but is met with scorn.

Disillusioned with her life and frustrated by the men around her, Ema takes leave of Ritinha and makes a final visit to Vesuvio. There she dresses in a party frock and flowers and makes her way through the orange grove to the jetty by the lake, where she (deliberately?) steps on a rotten board and drowns. Not long after, Carlos is found dead of an apparent heart attack.

Manoel de Oliveira is a unique case in world cinema: an auteur-director active since the late 1920s (he was one of the pioneers of Portuguese cinema) whose work remained virtually unnoticed by critics and audiences outside Portugal until the mid-1970s. His first short film *Douro, Faina Fluvial* (1931) was screened at the Film Society in London in 1935, and some of his later feature films have appeared at the British festivals, but none of his work has been distributed here until now. *Abraham Valley* stands well enough by itself, but will mean most to NFT-goers who can relate it to his tetralogy on 'frustrated love': *O Passado e o Presente* (1972), *Benilde ou a Virgem Mae* (1975), *Amor de Perdiçao* (1978) and *Francisca* (1981).

Like *Francisca*, this is based on a novel by Agustina Bessa-Luis; but this novel was framed as an ironic commentary on *Madame Bovary*, which makes the film an adaptation of Flaubert at two removes. The echoes of *Bovary*, however, are eclipsed by Oliveira's vision of Ema as a hapless victim of her own lyrical desires. The film charts with minute precision the way she constructs the circumstances in which she can and must die: Ema fully grasps the material and social realities she lives with, but wilfully seeks to transcend them by imposing her sense of 'poetry' on them—and it is the clash between these irreconcilable opposites that makes her death inevitable. None of the men in her life comes close to living up to her lyrical ideals and none understands her emotional distance from them as anything but a game of the heart. She responds by translating her real disappointment into a poetic anguish, and by creating her own romantic-fatalistic *mise en scène* (lilting through an orange grove straight out of an Andrew Marvell poem, in her party frock) for a death scene that aims to transcend the realities of a gammy leg and a rotten plank in a jetty. The notion of a protagonist who tries to suspend the normal rules of society and replace them with a fantasy of his or her own devising is a constant in Oliveira's cinema, and most Oliveira protagonists end up dead or mad.

Another constant in Oliveira's cinema is the insistence on literary or theatrical sources. A committed modernist, the veteran director insists on identifying dramatic content as something to be quoted or acted out, to eliminate the risk of transparency. Here, he allows his cast to give more or less naturalistic performances but uses formalised and sometimes stylised compositions to literally put a frame around them, and undercuts the seeming naturalness by using the detached and ironic voice of a male narrator (presumably quoting directly from Bessa Luis' novel) to comment on their thoughts and behaviour throughout. The result is unfailingly witty, sharp and provocative: it offers a perspective that is solely and specifically cinematic on matters social, emotional, psychological and aesthetic.

But the result is also an 'art film' that fits rather too neatly into a genre that regrettably has to be called 'post-modern literary adaptation'. Fassbinder set most of the ground rules for this genre with *Effi Briest*, and little has changed since: witness *The Age of Innocence* and Stanley Kwan's forthcoming *Red Rose, White Rose* both of which use novelistic voice-over narration to establish an ironic distance from formalised accounts of period manners and morals. But Oliveira's magisterial artistry is here deployed in the service of a project that seems too etiolated, too remote from all late twentieth-century terms of reference to have any real purchase on the lives or imaginations of any conceivable audience. Maybe this is what they meant by 'salon art'.

VILLAGE VOICE, 1/4/94, p. 50, Georgia Brown

Ah, Emma Bovary again. You would think the woman would be an anachronism, but of course she isn't and won't be as long as marriage binds and women alone stake their lives on rapture. Jane Campion may have had *Wuthering Heights* in mind, but *The Piano* is also a *Madam Bovary*; so, I gather, is *The Bridges of Madison County*.

This time Emma is spelled Ema and arrives by way of Portugal and one of the world's unrecognized geniuses, Manoel de Oliveira. Born in 1908, de Oliveira has so far made four features in his eighties. In his entire career he's made only 13, since for many years—under Salazar's long rule, 1932-1968—he was virtually shut out of filmmaking. If he'd been working in the '60s (the last era in which excellence and status were directly related), or in a more influential country, he'd be venerated like Bresson or Dreyer. In 1992, Serge Daney, the revered French critic who died last year of AIDS, called de Oliveira the greatest filmmaker working: "He continues cinema in a way that is astounding, at times archaic and always insolent."

Formerly a maker of documentaries, de Oliviera maintains a strong attachment to his country's landscape. In *Valley of Abraham*, Ema grows up among the terraced vineyards of the Douro in a valley named, ironically, after a murderous father and jealous husband. In the present day of our story, men still rule, dominating with theories, money, and cynical worldliness. Confident and scornful of all that, young Ema, bred on romances, imagines that beauty can influence the course of events. She conceives a mission to kindle desire. Testing her powers, she stands on her terrace over a bend in the road and watches cars go out of control.

Unlike Flaubert's farmer's daughter, or Sokurov's deliciously vulgar Emma of the steppes (*Save and Protect*), this contemporary Ema is refined. (Played by Cecile Sanz de Alba as a teenager and Leonor Silveira as an adult, she has elegant eyes and shining hair.) When Ema meets Carlos de Paina, a stodgy local doctor (Luis Miguel Cintra), she's contemptuous of "his salesman's teeth." She laughs, stroking a Colette-ish cat, but the last laugh is on her. She marries a man with "an undertaker's heart" and grows to despise him. Silly and limited in many ways, Ema manages to be valiant as she presents herself to a series of lovers—the last, a doltish, violin-playing boy her daughter's age. Her daughter meanwhile offers herself to men her mother's age.

Wry, distanced, rich in all its details, *Valley of Abraham* requires fortitude and suspension of expectations. For example, de Oliveira favors a still camera and relegates most of the action to off-screen. In one mad shot the camera focuses on a spot in the foreground that the actor (Rui de Carvalho, playing Ema's father) has to walk several steps forward to locate. Then, having found the point of clarity, he retreats into the cosmic blur.

Rather than rely on dialogue, all the de Oliveira films I've seen use heavy voiceover. The narration here is as dense as lava and as inexorable. There're no emotional climaxes, Just perpetual flow. Reading subtitles, it's impossible to take it all in. Best to relax and use your eyes, for this former cameraman, concocting grand symmetries, is one of the coolest yet most sensuous directors ever.

Follow the glorious progress of the color red. De Oliveira uses scarlet splashes to focus a composition the way Ingres does in his portrait of Comtesse d'Haussonville (at the Frick). Early in the film it's said of the washerwoman, Ritinha (Isabel Ruth)—Ema's soulmate, her passion's speechless witness—that from the color of a stain on a sheet, she can identify the kind of grape, or blood. She can tell menstrual blood from a virgin's; she even knows the stage of the cycle. All splotches of red here represent Ema's precious life blood. Roses, dahlias, Christmas candles, orange finches in their cage, the dye-ing flash of fireworks, a pair of claret stockings. And, as the cycle progresses, the deep burgundies of Ema's bathrobe and satchel. At the very end, an ecstatic dolly through an orange grove recaptures her virginal longing for nuptial bliss.

Men fail. But the accomplishment of Oliveira, like Flaubert, is to charge the viewer/reader with understanding. Whereas lovers are faithless, we persevere. The subject, of course, is the power of art (call it beauty or poetry—which was what seduced and doomed young Ema in the first place.

Also reviewed in:
NEW YORK TIMES, 12/23/93, p. C9, Vincent Canby
VARIETY, 6/7/93, p. 47, Deborah Young

VANISHING, THE

A Twentieth Century Fox release of a Morra, Brezner, Steinberg & Tenenbaum production. *Executive Producer:* Pieter Jan Brugge and Lauren Weissman.   *Producer:* Larry Brezner and Paul Schiff.   *Director:* George Sluizer.   *Screenplay:* Todd Graff.   *Based upon the novel "The Golden Egg"* by: Tim Krabbé.   *Director of Photography:* Peter Suschitzky.   *Editor:* Bruce Green.   *Music:* Jerry Goldsmith.   *Music Editor:* Kenneth Hall.   *Sound:* Jeff Wexler and (music) Bruce Botnick.   *Sound Editor:* Robert Grieve.   *Casting:* Risa Bramon Garcia and Juel Bestrop. *Production Designer:* Jeannine C. Oppewall.   *Art Director:* Steve Wolff.   *Set Designer:* Richard Yanez.   *Set Decorator:* Anne Ahrens.   *Set Dresser:* Brad Curry, Amy Feldman, Ross Harpold, John Maxwell, Suellyn McClung, Jim Voorhees.   *Special Effects:* James Hart and David Sandlin. *Costumes:* Durinda Wood.   *Make-up:* Edouard Henriques and Sheryl Berkoff-Lowe.   *Stunt Coordinator:* Chris Howell.   *Running time:* 101 minutes.   *MPAA Rating:* R.

CAST: Jeff Bridges (Barney); Kiefer Sutherland (Jeff); Nancy Travis (Rita); Sandra Bullock (Diane); Park Overall (Lynn); Maggie Linderman (Denise); Lisa Eichhorn (Helene); George Hearn (Arthur Bernard); Lynn Hamilton (Miss Carmichael); Garrett Bennett (Cop at Gas Station); George Catalano (Highway Cop); Frank Girardeau (Cop at Apartment); Stephen Wesley Bridgewater (T.V. Host); Susan Barnes (Colleague); Rich Hawkins (Stan); Michael Kaufman (DMV Clerk); Sabrena Roddy (Cashier); Andrea Lauren Herz (Woman #1 on the Street); Joanne Schmoll (Woman #2 on the Street); Allison Barcott (Woman with Barrette); Aeryk Egan (Young Barney); James Chesnutt (Pump Attendant); Danielle Zuckerman (Little Girl); Floyd Van Buskirk (Man in Line); Marius Mazmanian (Cook); Gina Gallante (Woman in Ladies Room); Michael John Hughes (Denise's Boyfriend); Howard Matthew Johnson (DMV Guard); Kristopher Logan (Waiter).

LOS ANGELES TIMES, 2/5/93, Calendar/p. 8, Kenneth Turan

Psychological thrillers are only as effective as their villains, and "The Vanishing" serves up one hell of a specimen. Barney Cousins is his name and, as played by Jeff Bridges, he is a much too believable maniac, oozing a kind of bumbling menace that is half-calculated, half-haphazard and totally chilling.

Most thrillers either hide the miscreant's identity until the last possible moment (witness "Jennifer Eight") or else, like "Basic Instinct" or "Body of Evidence," play wearying "is she or isn't she" games with an increasingly exasperated audience.

Films with exceptional villains played by top-drawer actors, however, have the luxury of showing that part of their hand right off the bat. To paraphrase Alfred Hitchcock, the clear master of the genre, the suspense of when something will happen is a much more effective audience tool than the simplistic surprise of whodunit. "Silence of the Lambs" used Anthony Hopkins this way to great effect, and "The Vanishing" does the same with Bridges.

Perhaps because playing this kind of creepy sociopath is a departure even from the villain he played in "Jagged Edge," Bridges has brought all of his considerable skill to bear here. His Barney is a college chemistry teacher in the Pacific Northwest, a loving father and faithful husband, a man you could pass on the street without feeling in mortal danger.

But you would feel something odd, because much of Barney is just the slightest bit off center. There is a stiffness to his walk, his hair is unnecessarily unkempt, his voice an unnerving monotone marked by an untraceable accent. And the indefinable smugness hovering around his blank cow-like face, the way he tells his daughter "romance has to be secret," all make you wonder just what this person might be capable of. And therein lies the tale.

Barney is the first person we see when "The Vanishing" opens and the film is but a few minutes old before we realize that what we are watching is a man rehearsing first how to lure someone into his car and then how to use a bottle of chloroform to knock them out and complete an abduction.

Completely unaware of Barney's existence are Jeff Harriman (Kiefer Sutherland) and his girlfriend, Diane Shaver (Sandra Bullock). On an abortive bicycling vacation, they have a fight after running out of fuel in a claustrophobic tunnel, during which Jeff stalks out and abandons her to look for gas.

When he returns and they make up at a nearby rest stop, Diane forces him to swear never to leave her again, "till death do us part." Then she saunters off to buy, some drinks and Jeff amuses himself in the parking lot, waiting for her to return. But she never does.

Though we have seen Barney lurking around the service center, we do not see Diane actually disappear, we do not know exactly what happened at that moment or afterward. What we do know, and what Jeff feels instinctively, is that something has definitely gone wrong. Naturally, we want to find out what that something is and, in a cleverly parallel emotion, the audience's desire for definitive knowledge becomes a total obsession for Jeff.

As played by Kiefer Sutherland in one of his more interesting roles, Jeff is a combination of mania and weakness. Quickly the scene shifts to three years after Diane's disappearance, and it becomes clear that Jeff has been stubbornly searching for her for all this time, losing his job and just about his mind in the process.

Yet at the same time Jeff gives off a feeling of ineffectiveness, of being confused and desperate and in need of a guiding hand. His plight gets the attention of Rita (a strong performance by Nancy Travis), a feisty waitress who seems to be attracted to his helplessness as much as anything else. Yet even she cannot break Jeff's mental tailspin, and she meets an even greater challenge when his rigid refusal to forget prompts Barney to make an unscheduled entrance into both of their lives.

A nifty cat-and-mouse thriller with lots of twists up its sleeve, "The Vanishing" (rated R for terror and violence and for language) is told with a leanness and economy that benefits from the fact that its Dutch director, George Sluizer, is literally making this film for the second time.

The original "Vanishing" was directed by Sluizer in the Netherlands in 1988 and gained some cult attention in this country. Screenwriter Todd Graff wrote the current Americanized version, which makes considerable and not unexpected concessions to the tastes of a mass domestic audience but still manages to be disturbing and surprising. Everyone concerned ought to thank Jeff Bridges, clearly the villain to have when you're only having one.

NEW YORK POST, 2/5/93, p. 27, Jami Bernard

The 1988 Dutch film "The Vanishing" had one of the most unforgettable endings ever. Now it has been co-opted by Hollywood into an American remake, and while this new "Vanishing" is a well-crafted thing of its own, it's no JFK.

Briefly, the movie is about a man's obsessive search for a girlfriend who disappeared several years earlier at a roadside rest stop after a quarrel. The kidnapper, intrigued by the boyfriend's tenacity in trying to find out what happened to the woman, offers to put him out of his suffering in a very unusual way.

It's hard to talk meaningfully about the original "Vanishing" without giving away the ending, and yet one could say the movie is nothing without that heartstopping finale. The Dutch movie was slightly esoteric, with a mysterious, theoretical quality—nothing so banal as a maniac on the loose, nothing so dramatic as a big confrontation. The boyfriend and the kidnapper are both men who are able to, and therefore must, pursue possibilities to their very extreme. The ending, therefore, is the most extreme, and the most unexpected.

This American remake is quite a different animal—more conventional certainly, and yet well-scripted and tailored for what inevitably is to be a mainstream market. Jeff Bridges, looking alarmingly like his brother Beau, plays the kidnapper with a strange Euro-vague accent that I believe is a direct imitation of the director, George Sluizer. The kidnapper is a family man, a biology teacher, a bit rumpled but otherwise seemingly ordinary.

Kiefer Sutherland plays the boyfriend, who like the kidnapper believes that true affairs of the heart belong in a very private place. The vanished girlfriend, who understandably has a brief role, is played by Sandra Bullock, an actress who bears a resemblance to Sutherland's real-life ex-girlfriend Julia Roberts—obviously a casting decision designed to provoke a weird echo.

There is a built-up role for the boyfriend's new girlfriend, and Nancy Travis handles it quite well. Devotees of the original movie may resent her presence, as it changes the nature of the movie from two men dueling with their private obsessions to a battle between obsessive and rational natures.

Sluizer, who also directed the similarly mysterious-obsessive "Utz," was brought to Hollywood to direct his own remake. While those who never saw the first movie may enjoy this one, they will not know the terrible pleasure of exploring this movie's real theme to its true end. And if they don't care about some old Dutch film with subtitles, then they deserve the American ending.

By the way, whoever is responsible for the trailer for this movie deserves a fate right out of the *original* "Vanishing."

NEWSDAY, 2/5/93, Pat II/p. 61, Jack Mathews

A young couple on vacation pull into a rest stop off a mountain highway in Washington State. The woman hops out to use the rest room and to buy a couple of beers in the convenience store, while her boyfriend waits outside in the Jeep. And waits and waits ...

The compelling question of George Sluizer's superb psychological thriller "The Vanishing" is not why Diane Shaver (Sandra Bullock) disappears under a mid-day sun. We know, without actually seeing it, that she is abducted, and having gotten a glimpse of Barney Cousins (Jeff Bridges) in the store with her, we know by whom.

What we don't know, and will be desperately wondering as we rejoin her boyfriend Jeff (Kiefer Sutherland) three years later, is why the likably odd Barney, a chemistry professor and family man from Seattle, kidnaped Diane and what he did with her.

No one will ever set the psychological hook deeper in the viewer's consciousness in the opening moments of a movie than Alfred Hitchcock did with "Psycho," but Sluizer is not far behind the master here. What Hitchcock did with sudden terror in a shower, Sluizer does with casual, almost wry insinuation in a convenience store.

A remake of Sluizer's own 1988 Dutch film, "The Vanishing" could serve as course instruction for the directors of last year's string of failed thrillers. In comparison to those, there may not be much action, but there's more than enough suspense and anticipation to keep you hanging to the very end.

The ending could be more satisfying; it is the only thing about the movie that comes close to feeling ordinary. But it's one ending where you've had your money's worth before arriving there.

What's best about "The Vanishing" is that we never know where the story is headed. We spend most of our time with Jeff, whose obsessive search for Diane has left him broke, unemployed and close to a breakdown, and his relationship with the strong-minded waitress Rita (Nancy Travis) who becomes his lifeline and new lover.

Sluizer occasionally takes us to Barney's campus where we see him working with his students or staring, with an expression that seems simultaneously blank and curious, at the monthly updated posters asking for information about Diane Shaver.

We see him watching Jeff being interviewed on television, their eyes seeming to meet at the TV screen as Jeff pleads with whoever took Diane to let him know whether she is dead or alive.

Jeff and Rita can't get on with their lives, and we can't get on with ours, until that question is answered. As the tension mounts, Barney edges closer to a decision to contact Jeff, with revelations more curious than anything that has gone before.

Bridges' performance is so exceptional, it is hard to know how well the movie would have worked with another actor. Barney is a fascinating character, as written. This is no raving maniac with glazed eyes, a pet poodle and nipple rings. Barney jokes with his 10-year-old daughter, loves his wife, lives in the 'burbs and drives a Volvo.

As Bridges plays him, with a slightly goofy smile, a lumbering gait and an accent you can't quite place, Barney appears a tad eccentric, but not *toto loco*. Even while rehearsing his kidnaping, testing different approaches to women on the street and learning to control his emotions, he seems more like a friendly guy trying to overcome shyness than someone plotting evil.

Sluizer steers us, perhaps wrongly, with subtle suggestions, like Barney pulling a spider out of a web and letting it crawl freely over his hand, or telling his daughter that Kathy and Heathcliffs romance in "Wuthering Heights" can't be real because real romance "is secret."

What is this man really up to? What are *his* secrets? And how bad is he, or is he bad at all?

"The Vanishing" holds you emotionally captive for two hours by making you fear you'll never know.

SIGHT AND SOUND, 6/93, p. 64, Philip Kemp

Washington State, 1989. While renovating his remote mountain cabin, chemistry teacher Barney Cousins rehearses his plan to abduct a young woman. His first few attempts fail dismally. Jeff Harriman and Diane Shaver, on holiday from Seattle, quarrel after their car runs out of gas in a mountain tunnel, but make up again at a service area. When Diane goes to the toilet she is observed by Barney. When she fails to return, Jeff is certain she's been kidnapped, but the police are unconvinced. 1992. Jeff is still obsessively searching for Diane, toting her photograph round the area where she vanished and sticking up posters appealing for help. One night at a roadside diner he meets a waitress, Rita Baker, who moves into his Seattle apartment with him. Jeff lets Rita believe that she's persuaded him to forget Diane, but secretly keeps up the search—and at the urging of a publisher, Arthur Bernard, starts writing the story of his quest.

Rita, discovering what Jeff is up to, confronts him and makes him renounce his search. But Barney, who has been keeping track of Jeff's efforts, writes offering to let him know the truth. Jeff, tormented by curiosity, can't resist responding. Rita storms out. When Barney arrives Jeff beats him up, but still goes with him to the service area where Diane vanished. Barney tells Jeff he can only know what happened by experiencing exactly what Diane did, and gives him drugged coffee to drink. Jeff awakes to find himself buried alive. Learning Barney's car number from a neighbour, Rita finds her way to the cabin with the help of Barney's daughter Denise. Despite Rita's resistance, Barney overpowers her, but by pretending she has kidnapped Denise she induces him to drink his own drugged coffee and dashes out to start exhuming Jeff. Barney, on whom the drug has yet to take effect, attacks her, but Jeff emerges from his coffin and kills him. Lunching with Arthur Bernard, Jeff and Rita both firmly refuse coffee.

Spoorloos/The Vanishing, the 1988 Dutch/French thriller of which this is the Hollywood version, achieved its insidious creepiness by a deft meshing of several off-kilter elements. There was the plot structure, wrong-footing us by setting up the young man's search before switching, via an unsignalled flashback, into the world of the abductor; the twitchy disorientation of the hero, adrift in a strange language and culture (turning the film's bilingual provenance to good effect);

a chillingly grim and hopeless denouement; and above all the unsettling ordinariness of Bernard-Pierre Donnadieu's killer, a walking paradigm of the banality of evil.

All of this, or pretty nearly all of it, is jettisoned in the remake. The happy ending was only to be expected: no mainstream Hollywood movie is going to leave its hero buried alive beyond hope of rescue. But *The Vanishing*, as if mistrustful of its audience's patience, throws away its best trick by revealing right from the start how Diane will be abducted. With the mystery at least half defused, much of the tension leaks away.

And given that both films share the same director, George Sluizer, it's also odd that there's no attempt to replicate the original's edgy cross-cultural slippage. Jeff and Diane are from Seattle, Barney's environment is mountain-country small-town: ample scope for playing off urban against rural, *Deliverance* style. But in the event everyone acts much the same wherever they're from. Bridges plays Barney in his nice-nasty *Jagged Edge* mode, tricked out with an unfocused, intermittent accent that veers distractingly from downtown Montreal to Yogi Bear. Sutherland never gets much beyond one-note dogged, but Nancy Travis turns in a good gutsy performance that almost redeems the routine female-in-jeopardy climax. (Nothing, though, could redeem the final gag about the coffee.)

It wouldn't be fair to dismiss *The Vanishing* as a total write-off. It's a lot less crass than most Hollywood retreads of European box-office hits, and Sluizer retains at least some of the earlier film's sinuous, understated menace. In fact, if only one could forget the original, the US version would seem like an interestingly offbeat venture, unusual if not wholly achieved. But there's the problem: it's never been possible to forget the original, one of those quietly implacable films that lodge like a splinter under the skin of the mind. The remake will probably have sunk from memory within weeks.

TIME, 2/22/93, p. 69, Richard Corliss

[*The Vanishing* was reviewed jointly with *Sommersby*; see Corliss' review of that film.]

VILLAGE VOICE, 2/16/93, p. 49, J. Hoberman

The Vanishing, a Dutch murder mystery that opened here in January 1991, was an authentic sleeper—a small movie made without stars in a foreign language by an unknown, middle-aged director that took several years to reach New York and ran for months at a small downtown house on the strength of rave reviews and word of mouth.

A young Dutch couple are on vacation in France. The woman disappears from a crowded tourist stop in broad daylight; the man spends years searching for her, finally driven by his own obsessive curiosity to surrender himself to the straitlaced family man who caused her to disappear. Back then, what seemed curious was how director George Sluizer wed Euro art film and Ami thriller, combining various elements from the two most unnerving narratives of 1959-60, Michelangelo Antonioni's *L'Avventura* and Hitchcock's *Psycho*.

The Vanishing also touched a number of primal fears—and students of mass pathology may be interested to note that, as a study in murderous compulsion, it paralleled the release pattern and success of both *The Silence of the Lambs* and Operation Desert Storm. But that was then and that particular *Vanishing* has itself vanished. In its place we have another movie with the same name, this one also directed by George Sluizer—in English, with American stars, for 20th Century-Fox.

It's not as if the original *Vanishing* is a sacred text; but neither is it an endlessly interpretable *King Lear*. The question, I suppose, is whether there is any reason for anyone who saw that particular movie, hereafter to be known by its Dutch title *Spoorloos*, to bother going to see this one. After all, the need to know is the motor that provides the movie's internal logic as well as drives its narrative. To know the answer, you'll have to experience what I experienced—but I can tell you this.

1. You'll see familiar places. *The Vanishing* transposes the action to the environs of Seattle, City of Youth.

2. But, you'll meet new people. *The Vanishing* inverts the emphasis to focus first on the madman (Jeff Bridges) and then on the couple, who are actually a different configuration than the pair in *Spoorloos*. After the happy, flaky Diane disappears, tormented, bereft Jeff (Kiefer Sutherland) finds a new girlfriend, the spunky, working-class Rita (Nancy Travis)—a minor role

in *Spoorloos* that has here been built into a second lead. There's also a batty neighbor who worships Elvis and, with a big wink from Sluizer, a benignly Faustian publisher who repeatedly encourages Jeff to merchandize the story of Diane's disappearance: "Write this book, you won't regret it."

3. You'll wonder where the money went. *Spoorloos* didn't look like much; *The Vanishing*, which is bigger, less purposefully bewildering, and more strenuously melodramatic, looks like even less. Where, in *Spoorloos*, Bernard-Pierre Donnadieu gave a surpassingly dry performance as the psychotic chemistry teacher who makes a woman disappear, in *The Vanishing*, Jeff Bridges (who doubtless absorbed a substantial part of the budget) is ostentatiously stodgy and eccentric, stealing his scenes with a stiff-legged shuffle and a singsong delivery that sounds like a Mennonite farmer or a man who has never seen TV.

4. But you'll also get more for your money. *The Vanishing* not only features more blood and guts than *Spoorloos*, it is the only remake I know that also tacks on an abbreviated sequel, *Vanishing II: The Resurrection*.

Thus, 5. You'll learn a basic difference between Europe and America. Was it MGM's postwar production chief Dore Schary who called ours a "happy-ending nation"? Suffice it to say there's nothing in this *Vanishing* to prove him wrong.

Also reviewed in:
CHICAGO TRIBUNE, 2/5/93, Friday/p. C, Dave Kehr
NATION, 3/8/93, p. 318, Stuart Klawans
NEW REPUBLIC, 3/8/93, p. 28, Stanley Kauffmann
NEW YORK TIMES, 2/5/93, p. C3, Janet Maslin
VARIETY, 2/8/93, p. 73, Lawrence Cohn
WASHINGTON POST, 2/5/93, p. B7, Hal Hinson
WASHINGTON POST, 2/5/93, Weekend/p. 42, Desson Howe

VEGAS IN SPACE

A Troma Team release of a Lloyd Kaufman & Michael Herz presentation of a Ford/Fish film. *Executive Producer:* Doris Fish.   *Producer:* Phillip R. Ford.   *Director:* Phillip R. Ford. *Screenplay:* Doris Fish, Miss X, and Phillip R. Ford.   *Based on the party by:* Ginger Quest. *Director of Photography:* Robin Clark.   *Editor:* Ed Jones and Phillip R. Ford.   *Music:* Bob Davis.   *Sound:* Todd Ritchie.   *Sound Editor:* Andy Murdock.   *Production Designer:* Doris Fish. *Set Designer:* Doris Fish.   *Visual Effects:* Phillip R. Ford.   *Costumes:* Doris Fish.   *Make-up:* Doris Fish.   *Running time:* 84 minutes.   *MPAA Rating:* Not Rated.

CAST: Doris Fish (Captain Dan Tracy and Captain Tracy Daniels);   Miss X (Empress Vel Croford and Queen Veneer);   Ginger Quest (Empress Nueva Gabor);   Ramona Fischer (Lieutenant Mike Shadows and Lieutenant Sheila Shadows);   Lori Naslund (Lieutenant Debbie Dane);   Timmy Spence (Lieutenant Dick Hunter);   "Tippi" (Princess Angel);   Freida Lay (Jane the Computer);   Arturo Galster (Noodles Nebula);   Silvana Nova (Wynetta Whitehead); Sandelle Kincaid (Babs Velour);   Tommy Pace (Mrs. Velour);   Jennifer Blowdryer (Futura Volare, KUN-TV);   John Canalli (Princess Jaundice);   Frieda Lay (La La Galaxy);   Janice Sukaitis (Martian Lady Driver);   Jeanette Szudy (National Orbit Reporter);   Ida Lee (Nueva's Handmaid);   Tracy Hughes (Odessa);   Susan Strong (Shirelle); Matthew Barton (Zorna Virga); Daniel Crone (Altila Zadora);   Norman Schrader (Luna);   Susan Kay (Tour Guide);   Miss Abood (Princess Eggy);   Jeanette Szudy (Veneer's Prisoner);   "Drag" (Herself).

LOS ANGELES TIMES, 8/29/93, Calendar/p. 15, Kevin Thomas

"Vegas in Space" an endearing drag travesty, whisks us to a resort on a planet given over entirely to women's pleasures.

Of late, the planet has been hit by tremors, jolting the women's ritual shopping, primping and hanging out. It seems that someone has stolen a chunk of the "girlineum" jewels belonging to the Empress Nueva Gabor (Ginger Quest) that are essential to keeping the planet in orbit. (It doesn't matter that how this works is left a mystery.)

As a result, the Empress of Earth (Miss X) has dispatched some space corps astronauts to come to the planet's rescue, but first guys have to swallow gender-reversal pills since the planet is off-limits to men. No problem: Once transformed, Capt. Tracy Daniels (the late Doris Fish), and Lts. Sheila Shadows (Ramona Fischer) and Debbie Lane (Nora Naslund) are eager to pass them selves off as entertainers who've come to treat their 23rd-century audience to a "traditional mid-20th-Century lounge act."

Meanwhile, Tracy tries to psych out the wraith-like, severely elegant and deeply ambiguous Queen Veneer (also Miss X), head of the planetary police force who may or may not be on the side of law and order.

In spoofing vintage "Flash Gordon"-type sci-fi adventures, Fish and Miss X, who wrote the script (based on a "party by Quest), and their producer-director Phillip R. Ford aren't interested in the plot or in generating any sense of mystery or suspense but rather in celebrating a camp sensibility that the material so abundantly provides.

Indeed, the entire pleasure in experiencing the film lies in its expression of a humorous, outrageous and gossamer-like camp aesthetic that recalls the '60s underground movies of the Kuchar Brothers, Jack Smith and Kenneth Anger—but minus the sex.

The cast doesn't really act—and probably couldn't anyway—but instead strikes poses and attitudes as if its members were competing in a drag-queen contest (which, in a sense they are).

Measured by conventional standards, "Vegas in Space" meanders—to put it kindly—as a narrative. This is probably deliberate, enabling the film to emerge as a series of tableaux setting off the rich, bizarre costumes of the drag queens and Fish's imaginative, resourceful production design. (No miniatures were ever so obvious yet enchanting as Fish's toy-like model of the film's Vegas in space.)

Of equal importance is Bob Davis' remarkable sound design and dramatic score, which give the film its shape and meaning. "Vegas in Space" really ought to be double-billed with Zsa Zsa Gabors "Queen of Outer Space.")

NEW YORK POST, 12/10/93, p. 46, Bill Hoffmann

Legendary Grade-Z film director Ed Wood Jr. would have loved "Vegas in Space."

In many ways, this gaudy, new sci-fi musical resembles Wood's most infamous productions such as "Plan 9 From Outer Space": incredibly cheap sets, terrible special effects, bargain-basement dialogue and an energetic cast that plows through it all never looking back.

And Wood, who in private life was an avid cross-dresser, would have appreciated the players in "Vegas in Space"—most of them men in drag.

This campy effort from novice director Phillip Ford follows the adventures of four male astronauts on a secret mission to the Planet Clitoris (yup, that's the name), a wacky world inhabited by conniving, back-stabbing, bitchy women where men are forbidden.

To blend into the masses, the spacemen take "gender reversal pills" turning them into gorgeous showgirls.

Soon the guys-turned-gals are smack in the middle of the planet's biggest city, Vegas, where the labyrinths and corridors resemble a combination of '60s polyester kitsch and Salvation Army savvy.

The high-energy cast—led by the late performer Doris Fish, Miss X and Ginger Quest—camp it up without a breather for nearly 90 minutes.

Sample dialogue:

"You two look so good you almost take my breasts away."

"Why if I ever got my hands on her, I'd ... I'd ... I'd give her a good talking to."

The bad news is the dialogue often falls flat and few of the jokes are laugh-out-loud funny.

The good news is that the lines are tossed off furiously and when one dies, it's on to the next.

Most endearing are the special effects.

When two plastic spaceships (manipulated by strings) collide, they shake back and forth like toys.

And a panoramic view of the city of Vegas looks like a Tinker Toy set on its last legs.

Obviously the major budget consideration here was makeup—and there's tons and tons of it.

"Vegas in Space" reportedly has done quite well at gay and lesbian film festivals around the world.

It should do well with gay audiences here as well as with lovers of camp and midnight show fans.

"Vegas in Space" may be held together with strings and glue, but it was prepared with love.

NEWSDAY, 12/14/93, Part II/p. 59, Frank DeCaro

What do you get when a group of drag queens who obviously spent their formative years watching "Star Trek," listening to Klaus Nomi records and going to John Waters films makes a movie? "Vegas in Space," a punk comedy owing its tone, style (and some of its dialogue) to "Female Trouble," "Desperate Living" and all the rest of Waters' taste-defiling early flicks.

In this intergalactic musical epic, four astronauts take gender-reversal pills after a top-secret mission on an all-female planet in a system named for a small, furry, dam-building Earth creature. When they land on this "oasis of glamor in a universe of mediocrity," they find that trouble's afoot—the planet's geologically unstable, Empress Nueva Gabor's gems are missing, Queen Veneer is having a bad hair day and someone is dragging the good name of Velour through the gutter!"

What's a drag queen to do?

This goofy, spoofy sci-fi musical sprang in all its low-budget luridness from San Francisco's underground scene. Produced and directed by Phillip R. Ford and starring such "world-famous" cross-dressers as Doris Fish, Miss X and Ginger Quest, "Vegas in Space" lies somewhere between the twisted depths of Waters' pre-"Polyester" depravity and the stellar corniness of the "Pigs in Space" segments on the old "Muppet Show." It's a trash flick in fake fur and Lurex.

The film's motto is "Glamor first! Glamor last! Glamor always!" and its idea of witty repartee is "Does this come in my size?"/"You've *got* to be kidding!" and "How's tricks on Uranus?" The production design is all Dynel and Hefty bags, the eyelashes as false as the ingenue's falsies. But "Vegas in Space" is a real hoot at times, especially when the drag queens throw themselves from side to side during a meteor shower that plays like Lt. Uhura hitting space turbulence aboard the Enterprise.

Fast becoming a cult favorite, "Vegas in Space" has been shown at more than 30 film festivals. Troma is distributing it, because, as the director has said, "there are pockets of sick people everywhere who are hungry—starving—for this type of unique entertainment. In other words, some moviegoers would rather be here than in "Philadelphia."

VILLAGE VOICE, 12/28/93, p. 88, Marco Spino

Trash disguised as art, *Vegas in Space* reeks of mediocre entertainment. From its numerous shots of miniature spaceships dangling on strings to its homemade explosions, *Vegas* relishes its low-budget wackiness. Sets are decorated with TV monitors and boxed talking heads that resemble *Pee-wee's Playhouse*'s. "We definitely tried to be as lowbrow, flat, and stupid as we could," admitted director Ford. That's all fine for Ford, who probably had fun making the film, but what about you, the poor schmuck who has to endure silly chase scenes and stale one-liners? If you're wondering whether or not to see it, my advice is to creep out to its late-nite screening, preferably under the influence of a hallucinogen, and hope the audience's antics will liven up this cult wanna-be.

The plot of this tame romp centers on three astronauts who travel to Vegas in Space, a resort on the planet Clitoris, in search of a queen's (*faux*) gems. Because no men are allowed on the planet, the "all-male" crew take gender-reversal pills and beauty-booster tablets to make them resemble the "female" inhabitants. As the characters' faces are buried under pounds of makeup and hairdos are tortured into psychedelic designs, a catatonic vision of beauty emerges. Some of these Barbies could have enacted wonderful s&m fantasies, but Ford neglects their sexual potential and candy coats them into shopping-and-gabbing chicks. Unfortunately he lets a planet of women slip away without any satire on lesbian life.

As a showcase for intergalactic drag, *Vegas* presents an incredible amount of talent and hairspray. But as for the film having any freshness or perversity when compared to the early works of Waters or Warhol, it comes up snake eyes, rehashing the same queeny strutting and dissing that even Middle America has begun snapping to. *Vegas in Space* is just what you've come to expect from Vegas on Earth: lame entertainment and lamé clothing.

Also reviewed in:
VARIETY, 8/10/92, p. 55, Daniel M. Kimmel

VISIONS OF LIGHT: THE ART OF CINEMATOGRAPHY

A Kino International release of an American Film Institute and NKH/Japan Broadcasting Corporation coproduction. *Executive Producer:* Terry Lawler and Yoshiki Nishimuri. *Producer:* Stuart Samuels and Arnold Glassman. *Director:* Arnold Glassman, Todd McCarthy, and Stuart Samuels. *Screenplay:* Todd McCarthy. *Director of Photography:* Nancy Schreiber. *Editor:* Arnold Glassman. *Set Dresser:* Deborah Rhein. *Running time:* 90 minutes. *MPAA Rating:* Not Rated.

INTERVIEWER: Todd McCarthy. *INTERVIEWEES:* Nestor Almendros; John Alonzo; John Bailey; Michael Ballhaus; Stephen Burum; Bill Butler; Michael Chapman; Allen Daviau; Caleb Deschanel; Ernest Dickerson; Frederick Elmes; William Fraker; Conrad Hall; James Wong Howe; Victor Kemper; Laszlo Kovacs; Charles Lang; Sven Nykvist; Lisa Rinzler; Owen Roizman; Charles Rosher, Jr.; Sandi Sissel; Vittorio Storaro; Haskell Wexler; Robert Wise; Gordon Willis; Vilmos Zsigmond.

NEW YORK POST, 4/2/93, p. 28, Jami Bernard

A few days ago, Philippe Rousselot won an Oscar for his cinematography in "A River Runs Through It." The movie was lovely to look at, but few viewers probably stopped to think how difficult it was to light a mountain stream just right so that the shadows foretell the story while the light makes the fishing line glisten. For those who think cinematography is about some guy with a camera, or a beautiful shot of the sunset, "Visions of Light: The Art of Cinematography" should set things straight.

This, by the way, is one of those magnificent documentaries that didn't get nominated for an Oscar, and it's really right up Hollywood's alley—all about how several generations of perspicacious and ingenious cinematographers have conspired with actors, directors and technology to make cinema the art that it is (or that it can be, anyway).

It's great fun to watch, both a learning experience and a passive viewing pleasure. Interviews with cinematographers (shot in high-definition TV) are interspersed with 35 mm clips of famously lit scenes from classic film noir with all its German Expressionist shadows and tilts to the ragged urban hand-held style of "The French Connection" and the creamy dark "Godfather" movies. By concentrating on the purely visual aspect of movies, the documentary proves how intricately bound a movie is to its signature look.

"Visions of Light" also takes some of the mystery out of cinematography. The interviewees speak plainly about how they stumbled onto or refined various tricks. Garbo's look was as much a function of how her cheekbones were lit as of her talent; Haskell Wexler describes the awe that greeted his and the industry's first helicopter shot.

The cinematographers range from unassuming to passionate. Gordon Willis reflects quietly on whether he underlit sections of "The Godfather Part II," while Vilmos Zsigmond imperiously dismisses dialogue as background stuff; "it should be like music," so as not to detract from his visuals.

Mention is made of the mentoring process that brings cinematographers up through the ranks, which probably explains why there is only one woman interviewed in the bunch. This is a job that, more than directing or acting, has a club-like, Old Boys atmosphere. Its need for technical proficiency keeps it inaccessible to the masses.

The clips that are shown are more stunning than museum art, because they move and live. This is the kind of documentary that makes movie lovers renew their commitment to loving movies.

NEWSDAY, 4/2/93, Part II/p. 63, Joseph Gelmis

To shoot the shark-hunting scenes in "Jaws," Steven Spielberg had planned to bolt the camera to the deck of the small boat carrying Robert Shaw, Richard Dreyfuss and Roy Scheider. Do that, cinematographer Bill Butler told him, and your audience will throw up in the theater.

Spielberg relented and those climactic shipboard scenes in the last third of "Jaws" were filmed by handheld cameras. Brawny operators steadied the portable cameras from rocking and rolling so the audience wouldn't get seasick. And, by rushing around like a documentary crew filming the fight to the death with the monster, the active cameras became participants subliminally transmitting their agitation to the audience.

Relatively few members of the audience were aware of how important the photography was in producing their adrenaline rush. At the beach, for instance, even the angle at which the camera photographed the action produced palpitations. The camera was kept at water level. "You began to feel, after a while, that the shark was just below the camera," says Butler.

These insights into the making of "Jaws" are typical of what to expect from "Visions of Light: The Art of Cinematography," a spellbinding document that introduces us to the seldom-acknowledged professionals behind the camera.

The 90-minute documentary consists of the anecdotes and opinions of 25 articulate cinematographers, talking about the craft they love and the people they learned from and revere. Their stories and experiences are illustrated by pristine 35mm clips of unforgettable moments from classic American films.

With them as our guides, we get a cinematographer's eye view of the highlights of film history. There's the early division of labor (when actors started directing actors and cameramen become directors of photography), the golden age of visual storytelling (the silent '20s), the technical virtuosity of the studio films in the '30s and early '40s (with their trademarked styles: gloss at Paramount, hard edges at Warner Bros, glamor at MGM), and fascinating surveys of '40s and '50s film noir and the gritty New York "street style."

A master of the street style, Michael Chapman, who shot Martin Scorsese's "Taxi Driver" and "Raging Bull," states that the most influential of modern American cinematographers has been Gordon Willis, creator of the visual styles of Woody Allen's "Annie Hall" and "Manhattan" and Francis Ford Coppola's "Godfather" films.

"Everybody recognized that this was a real job of cinematography," says Chapman of the original "Godfather" (1972). Willis became known by his peers as "the prince of darkness." Cinematographer Conrad Hall, a respected mentor of a number of the younger interviewees, says Willis "made darkness an art form."

Willis retells how he designed overhead lighting to make Marlon Brando's makeup, the built up cheeks, work. The design eventually extended throughout the rest of the movie. He got some flak, says Willis, from people who were bothered because they couldn't see Brando's eyes. But, he says, the shadowed eyes contributed to Don Corleone's mystique as a man of hidden depths.

The director of photography on "Visions of Light," Nancy Schreiber, does an excellent job of photographing the cinematographers, 24 out of 25 of whom are men. A few of the interviews are archival footage. Most were taped on high-definition video, transferred to film and seamlessly blended with the movie clips.

Written by Todd McCarthy, Variety's chief movie critic, and co-produced by the American Film Institute and NHK (the Japan Broadcasting System), in collaboration with the American Society of Cinematographers, "Visions of Light" is a perspective-expanding experience that ought to change forever the way a thinking person looks at movies.

SIGHT AND SOUND, 5/94, p. 58, Philip Strick

A survey of the technical and artistic contribution made by cinematographers to the history and development of the moving image. Broadly covering the changes in style and technique on a decade-by-decade basis, 27 practitioners comment on the films, the directors and the innovations that have most influenced their careers in American movie-making. With anecdotes, tributes and reminiscences, along with brief extracts from some 125 feature films, they draw attention to the special complexities of visual story-telling.

With too much to say, and too many voices saying it, *Visions of Light* gets off to a breathless start that quickly abandons to the archivists a tantalising collection of silent cinema glimpses. A nod to Billy Bitzer, a reference to the astonishing mobility of Buster Keaton's comedies, a reminder of the importance of Murnau's *Sunrise* (1927), and we find ourselves being hustled—already with a hint of indigestion—to the precipitous edge of the sound era.

On the way, films and speakers are identified by subtitle in a torrent of faces and predicaments, some familiar, some not familiar enough. Failing access to a pause button, one tries to sort out the interviewees, ironically less well-known than their work. Allen Daviau? (*E.T., Empire of the Sun*). John Bailey? (*In the Line of Fire, Groundhog Day*). Michael Chapman? (*Rising Sun, The Fugitive*). Lisa *who*? On video, it will all no doubt be easier. On the big screen, where everything's a decent size and the crane shots sweep us persuasively off the floor, these elusive identities only add to the suspicion that we're far from getting the full picture.

There is an interesting contradiction, for example, as Vilmos Zsigmond (*Heaven's Gate, Sliver*) tells us that the arrival of sound was a catastrophe, while flowing extracts from Sol Polito's work for Busby Berkeley and George Folsey's for Mamoulian seem to prove him wrong. If the first sound cameras were pinned down by sheer weight, their immobility was quite evidently disregarded by the directors who mattered, and as *Visions of Light* darts through the 1930s under the guidance of De Mille cameraman Harry Wolf and perky veteran Charles Lang (*Some Like It Hot, One-Eyed Jacks*)—who were there at the time—it reveals an array of uninhibited attractions including Joan Crawford watching a train go by in Clarence Brown's *Possessed* (1931) and a casual glimpse of Astaire and Rogers rehearsing in colour. Lang goes on to celebrate the partnership of Garbo and William Daniels, and there's a particular fascination in the recollections of his own lighting for Dietrich (who wanted narrower cheekbones) in *Desire* (1936) and for Claudette Colbert (who would only be filmed from one side) in *Midnight* (1939).

General agreement on the greatness of Gregg Toland, whom Welles insisted should share his credit title for *Citizen Kane*, gets support from non-cinematographer Robert Wise, citing the "extraordinary dynamics" of the shot where the boy plays in the snow while his fate is decided indoors. At the same time, we are usefully reminded that Toland learned his trade from George Barnes (*Rebecca*), who was inventing in the 1920s the tricks that were to become almost the clichés of the *films noirs*. Enjoying themselves with a summary of the *noir* era, Bailey and Daviau provide good reason for a fresh look at Joseph L. Lewis's *The Big Combo* (1955)—although it was a latecomer by comparison with *Out of the Past* or *T-Men* (both 1947)—to savour the ruthless lighting economies of the remarkable John Alton.

On dubious territory, Daviau describes *Touch of Evil* (1958), the ultimate in *noir*, as a New Wave film made in a Hollywood studio—a confusing reshuffle of influences which turns out to be part of a general nostalgia for the attractions of black-and-white photography. Confronted by Laughton's irresistibly *noir*-esque *Night of the Hunter*, miraculously shot by Stanley Cortez in 1955, and Mackendrick's *Sweet Smell of Success* (1957), accompanied by deferential remarks from James Wong Howe, we can forgive his enthusiasm.

When colour is at last allowed its proper contribution, *Visions of Light* becomes a different and, as it happens, a more enjoyable enterprise, with various DPs (preferred abbreviation these days for Directors of Photography) chatting in a cosily Masonic way about their own accomplishments and those of their admired colleagues. Conrad Hall (*Cool Hand Luke, Fat City*) emerges rather well from these exchanges, with an intriguing description of an accident of lighting used for *In Cold Blood*. So, too, does an unexpected Roman Polanski, credited by both William Fraker (*Rosemary's Baby*) and John Alonzo (*Chinatown*) with an acute visual sense. Haskell Wexler tells how he was nearly fired from *Who's Afraid of Virginia Woolf?*, Gordon Willis says he went too far in *The Godfather Part II* ("I think even Rembrandt went too far sometimes"), Nestor

Almendros describes the 20-minute 'magic hour' and its effect on *Days of Heaven*, and Vittorio Storaro pontificates—a touch obscurely—about the colour vocabulary *The Last Emperor*.

Concluding with the most recent titles available, which date it instantly, *Visions of Light* illustrates Ballhaus on Scorsese with a sequence from *GoodFellas* (avoiding obvious reference to *Vertigo*), Elmes on Lynch with *Blue Velvet*, Dickerson on Lee with *Do the Right Thing*. On an appropriately positive note, John Bailey sums up that cinematography is at a jumping-off point into an unknown but very exciting future, a reasonable expectation in the context of virtual reality, high-definition television, and the ultimate Grail of holographic drama.

What the film really achieves, scrapbook fashion, is a reminder of too much ignored, set aside, forgotten, overdue for fresh affection. While setting an example for similar forays into such cinematic skills as editing, design, and the use of sound, *Vision* will probably be best remembered, all the same, for revealing that *Jaws* was shot (by Bill Butler) with a preSteadicam handheld camera. Nausea, it seems, would otherwise have driven Spielberg's audiences from their seats.

VILLAGE VOICE, 4/6/93, p. 50, J. Hoberman

Visions of Light—a documentary widely seen on the festival circuit, provides another way of looking at old Hollywood images set free of their narrative context.

The subject is cinematography and, given the primacy of the visual, each film quotation has the impact of a megamillion-dollar special effect. *Visions of Light* offers a history of image making that, flawlessly printing some superb black-and-white nitrate on color stock, touches on the splendor and freedom of silent cinema, then goes on to illustrate the degree to which a lighting cameraman like William Daniels actively collaborated with a star like Greta Garbo in the creation of an image; presents film noir as a succession of figures emerging out of the darkness ("It's the lights that you don't turn on," someone says); and argues the new Hollywood of the early '70s as a major period, with Conrad Hall explicating the invention of the "sunburst" and Gordon Willis questioning his underexposure of *The Godfather II*.

Visions of Light is a heady draught of cinephilia. For a succession of clips and talking heads, it's so entertainingly put together that it could go on indefinitely. The closing montage, which rapidly segues through a dozen wildly disparate films, is not just a tribute to the cameramen but a curtain call by editor Arnold Glassman.

Coincidentally this weekend, the American Museum of the Moving Image opens a 15-film retro on director-cameraman Haskell Wexler. Although *Visions of Light* quotes a chunk of Wexler's work on *Who's Afraid of Virginia Woolf* (1966), the last black-and-white movie to win the Oscar for cinematography, the AMMI retro gives greater vent to Wexler's range (as well as his politics) with a mixture of independent documentaries and Hollywood features.

The opening film, *The Savage Eye* (1959), is a once controversial, collectively made indie that places an actress against a documentary backdrop—an idea that Wexler would use to more successful effect a decade later in *Medium Cool*. Shot over a four-year period, *The Savage Eye* shows Los Angeles as a tawdry locust land, the city of gargoyles, a joyless amusement park of grotesque beauty parlors, gambling dens, pet cemeteries, roller rinks, transvestite balls, and girlie shows.

While many of Wexler's images recall those of Robert Frank's contemporaneous "desolation row," they are stripped of any ambiguity by the film's imposed storyline and insufferable soundtrack, much of it declaimed against ostentatiously free-form jazz. It's a negative demonstration of what's implicit in both *Rock Hudson's Home Movies* and *Visions of Light*—the narrative is the nightmare from which we are trying to escape.

Also reviewed in:
CHICAGO TRIBUNE, 8/6/93, Friday/p. A, Richard Christiansen
NEW REPUBLIC, 4/26/93, p. 29, Stanley Kauffmann
NEW YORK TIMES, 4/2/93, p. C9, Vincent Canby
NEW YORKER, 4/5/93, p. 101, Terrence Rafferty
VARIETY, 6/1/92, p. 67, Gerald Pratley
WASHINGTON POST, 6/11/93, p. G7, Hal Hinson
WASHINGTON POST, 6/11/93, Weekend/p. 44, Desson Howe

VOLERE VOLARE

A Fine Line Features release of a Bambu/Pentafilm production. *Executive Producer:* Mario Cecchi Gori, Vittorio Cecchi Gori, and Silvio Berlusconi. *Producer:* Ernesto di Sarro, Mario Cecchi Gori, and Vittorio Cecchi Gori. *Director:* Maurizio Nichetti and Guido Manuli. *Screenplay (Italian with English subtitles):* Maurizio Nichetti and Guido Manuli. *Director of Photography:* Roberto Brega. *Editor:* Rita Rossi. *Music:* Manuel de Sica. *Sound:* Bruno Guarnera. *Sound Editor:* Alfonso Oliva. *Art Director:* Maria Pia Angelini. *Costumes:* Maria Pia Angelini. *Make-up:* Renzo Caroli. *Running time:* 92 minutes. *MPAA Rating:* R.

CAST: Maurizio Nichetti (Maurizio); Angela Finocchiaro (Martina); Mariella Valentini (Girlfriend); Patrizio Roversi (Brother); Remo Remotti (The "Child"); Mario Gravier and Luigi Gravier (The Architects); Renato Scarpa (The Businessmen); Massimo Sarchielli (The Chef); Osavaldo Salvi and Lidia Biondi (The Necrophiliacs); Enrico Grazioli (The Taxi Driver); Mario Pardi (Masochistic Robber); Sergio Cosentino and Rocco Cosentino (Hardware Store Assistants); Maino Franco, Aldo Izzo, and Giuseppe Tosca (Hardware Store Customers); Nobile Pierluigi (Head Waiter); Andrea Cavalli and Stefano Dondi (Waiters); Regina Stagnitti, Laura Celoria, and Adriana Canese (700 Girls); Ianniello Amerigo (700 Hunter); Riccardo Margherini and Maria Rosaria Secci (Customers); Valeria Cavalli (Passer-by).

LOS ANGELES TIMES, 2/10/93, Calendar/p. 4, Michael Wilmington

Nighttimes in Maurizio Nichetti's "Volere Volare." Walking along an amorously lit Italian street are a skinny prostitute and a shy little admirer named, variously, "Trumpet," "Little Mustache" and "Maurizio."

The air is sultry; the couple (Angela Finocchiaro and Maurizio Nichetti) are sloshed. And, as they stroll, Maurizio finds that his hands are getting out of control—not in the usual sense, but in a more pataphysical way. Detached from his body, they soar through the air, swooping and grabbing at his would-be inamorata's buttocks and breasts with lusty abandon. They're *cartoon* hands, yellow-gloved, madly impudent, and Maurizio, who is actually turning *into* a cartoon, can only watch helplessly—as his raucous darling chuckles at these brazen advances.

That's one of the film's show-piece scenes and, by itself, it's an exhilarating mix of technological wizardry, moonstruck wish-fulfillment and smutty humor. If the rest of the movie were as exuberant, Nichetti might have matched his 1989 "Icicle Thief"—in which he played the hapless, frizzy-headed, Woody Allen-ish filmmaker, trapped in the projection of his own neo-realist film. But "Volere Volare," doesn't display "Icicle Thief's" nonstop ingenuity. The scenario, bizarrely split, doesn't sufficiently milk its own premise.

Nichetti keeps Maurizio's man-into-movie metamorphosis for the last half of the film, and the best gags mostly for the last 15 minutes. And, while this builds up to a nice comic paroxysm, climaxing in the promiscuous entanglement of human and toon that "Who Framed Roger Rabbit" could only hint at, the rest seems stretched, spread out. "Volere Volare" means "I Want to Fly," and that's the feeling this movie may induce: We keep waiting for these filmmakers to soar, bemused or confused at their long, dawdling, expository set-up.

Dramatically, it's obvious that Maurizio turns toon because he *wants* to behave with the same reckless, earth-defying impudence as Popeye. He's a shy little man in love with a rambunctious hooker, and being Mighty Maurizio Mouse is the only way he can crack his own reserve. But, the *ostensible* cause is that beam, the movie's catch-all explanation.

Angela Finocchiaro won the Italian Golden Ciak best actress prize for her performance as jaded Martina, but there's too much of it. Despite her whimsical assortment of dream-craving johns, including twin bearded voyeur-architects who always appear to the strains of Gounod's "Funeral March of a Marionette" (Hitchcock's TV theme), it's hard to muster much interest in her early scenes, or in the lewd jokes with Maurizio's brother and his bevy of dubbing-studio moaners.

It's *only* in the mixed live-action/cartoon comedy that Nichetti and Manuli, really shake loose. Too often, early on, Nichetti seems to be trying unsuccessfully to turn himself into Blake

Edwards. When, at long last, he gets switched on-screen into a bouncing little toon, hot to trot, "Volere Volare" (MPAA-rated R for sensuality) finally flies.

NEW YORK, 2/1/93, p. 53, John Powers

Maurizio Nichetti is a sly, diminutive comedian who likes to play ordinary men spinning wildly in the revolving door of media culture. His last movie, the art-house hit *The Icicle Thief*, was a frothy, self-referential spoof of neorealism, commercial television, and postwar Italian consumerism. *Volere Volare* is even farther out—its hero literally turns into a cartoon version of himself.

Nichetti is Maurizio, a shy sound man who spends his life dubbing funny sound effects into old Disney and Popeye cartoons. Although childlike enough to find this work satisfying, he longs for the woman who will ease his loneliness. But he's such a sexual stumblebum that his quest seems hopeless until he bumps into Martina (a beaming Angela Finocchiaro), another romantic who works the odd corners of the fantasy biz. (She acts out goofy sexual scenarios for clients who pay to drench her backside with hot fudge or have her stick a baby's bottle between their greedy, bawling lips.) Maurizio and Martina are obviously made for each other, but just when their love story begins to click, his body starts gradually turning into an animated being beyond his control. His unruly hands whiz through the air, toss plates of spaghetti, refuse to dial the phone so he can reach Martina.

Volere Volare uses the animation effects made famous in *Who Framed Roger Rabbit*, but unlike that Hollywood blockbuster, it doesn't bludgeon you with technical magic. In fact, as you might expect of a small European movie, the action centers on human-scale shtick—Maurizio wringing strange noises from ordinary household items, Martina gamely servicing her crew of perverts. Yet for all his poetic touches, Nichetti leaves you wishing for, of all things, the intellectual rigor of *Roger Rabbit*. That film mixed live action and animation to make a point about the repressive commercialism of real-world Los Angeles and the liberating anarchy of Toontown. There's no comparably compelling reason for the animated sequences in *Volere Volare*, whose story line seems merely a pretext for exploiting neat visual effects. And frankly, they aren't so neat. Not only is the artwork disappointingly drab but the animated jokes just aren't funny—unless your idea of hilarity is having a pair of flying yellow cartoon hands illicitly squeeze a woman's buttocks not once, not twice, but three times.

Still, what's wrong with this comedy isn't such peasant bawdiness but a leaden whimsicality that makes a fetish of old-fashioned naïveté. Nichetti conceives Maurizio and Martina as lovable innocents in the tradition of Buster Keaton or Jacques Tati; he wants us to adore them for preserving their dreamy wholesomeness in a whirligig modern world that's forever on the hustle.

To underscore their worth, they're given chuckleheaded alter egos: Martina's blonde girlfriend (Mariella Valentini), who blithely sleeps with rich men in hopes of hooking a husband, and Maurizio's jolly brother (Patrizio Roversi), a dubber of "erotic" movies whose projection room is swarming with scantily clad babes. Though we are supposed to think this carnal pair modern and soulless, the comic underbelly of *la dolce vita*, they're a lot more fun than Martina and Maurizio. I kept wishing the whole movie could be about this happy-go-lucky pornographer and the shopgirl who wants to sleep her way to the top. At least they have grown-up motives and libidos—they aren't glorified children.

Like so many of today's filmmakers on both sides of the Atlantic, Nichetti is hip to the formal possibilities of his medium. But while this knowingness has obviously unleashed his cleverness (he can send up any genre you can name), it's also left him trapped in that arid postmodern fun house where nothing gets deeper than a reflection. *The Icicle Thief* was as flimsy as the commercial TV it was supposed to be satirizing; *Volere Volare* is an innocuous fantasy shameless in its desire to please—whenever the action slows down, a good-looking woman takes off her clothes. Although the film is billed as a romantic comedy, its only breath of ardor comes from the lush score by Manuel de Sica, son of the famed director Vittorio.

Speaking of the elder De Sica, about halfway through *Volere Volare*, I began wondering whatever happened to Italy. Not, of course, the actual country, which still lurches forward in its customary grandiloquent chaos, toppling prime ministers more reliably than it delivers the mail. No, I mean the Italy that one discovered at the movies, the imaginary land of Rossellini,

Antonioni, and Bertolucci, *The Bicycle Thief, 8½,* and *Night of the Shooting Stars.* When did Italian movies become so dinky?

NEW YORK POST, 2/4/93, p. 31, Matthew Flamm

This is a movie that wants to be inventive, and will stop at nothing to get its way.

Mixing animation with live action, and a bit of sex comedy with Marx Brothers style slapstick, "Volere Volare" (Italian for "I want to fly") is the latest film by Maurizio Nichetti, the Italian actor-director whose one-joke "The Icicle Thief" had a successful run here a couple of years ago.

The new film, which concerns a sound-effects man named Maurizio—played by the director—and his affair with a rather unconventional prostitute, opens today.

Maurizio, who looks like Tex Antoine with a dash of Harpo Marx, is a shy soul, so at home in his dubbing studio he prepares dinner on a projector—slicing salami with the take-up reel and frying a burger—over the light compartment.

He is also a virtuoso of horns, bells and whistles, performing the soundtrack to old cartoons in non-stop numbers that border on ballet. He may even be too good at bringing the cartoons to life: Characters from the studio screen have begun migrating to the real world. Before long, Maurizio himself is turning cartoonish.

Having animated hands might not sound like such a bad thing, particularly for the sexually inexperienced Maurizio, who has begun dating Martina (Angela Finocchiaro). Describing herself as "a special kind of social worker," this young woman spends her days acting out essentially chaste fantasies—like letting a chef cover her nude body with chocolate, or having twin architects watch her shower.

But Nichetti can't get beyond novelty; he doesn't tie his bits of invention—mildly amusing though some of them are—to a theme. So his uncontrollable, cartoon hands don't necessarily represent his unbridled instincts. They're plot devices, cute gimmicks.

Nichetti can have his character soar all over the place; "Volere Volare" never gets off the ground.

NEWSDAY, 2/3/93, Part II/p. 55, Jack Mathews

Martina (Angela Finocchiaro) is a prostitute with Italy's strangest clientele—a Freud look-alike who suckles a baby bottle and calls her mama, a chef who lathers her with chocolate sauce and cake toppings, a middle-aged couple who has her dress as a nurse and participate in mock death scenes.

Maurizio (Maurizio Nichetti) is a sound engineer so socially gawky and inept he seems to resemble one of the characters in the black and white cartoons he dubs. In fact when he finds himself on the verge of a real relationship with the woman of his dreams—Martina—he literally takes cover by turning into a cartoon version of himself. "Volere Volare," which Nichetti also wrote and directed, is as madcap as it sounds and its first half is as engaging as the films of Jacques Tati and Buster Keaton that seem to have inspired it. But just when you expect it to shatter the sanity barrier and get really crazy, at the moment Maurizio's hands begin to look like they belong to Mickey Mouse, it collapses into itself.

Nichetti has a marvelous gift for mixing his media, as he did by having a character from a color TV commercial get disoriented and appear in a black and white movie being shown on the same channel in "The Icicle Thief." But it was clear in that movie exactly what it was Nichetti was sending up—neorealism, TV crimes against movie classics, post-war Italian melodrama. In "Volere," his flights of fancy dissolve into a sight gag that hovers on the screen like the Goodyear Blimp.

The novelty of mixing live action with animation was done to a fare-thee-well with "Who Framed Roger Rabbit," where the interaction of the two worlds was just the point. Nichetti was courageous to try the same technique on a fraction of "Roger Rabbit's" budget, but it doesn't stand the comparison, either artistically or as an element of the story.

Part of the problem is that for Nichetti to turn himself into a cartoon character is redundant. A half-pint with a half-pound mustache and a great, bug-eyed stare, he's a pretty funny image in the flesh.

Nichetti's cartoon likeness is cute for a moment, as Woody Allen's was during a brief fantasy sequence in "Annie Hall." But no sooner does the relationship heat up between Maurizio and Martina, whose business he is inadvertently drawn into, than he turns his performance over to the film's animator, and thus dooms it to a clumsy impersonation.

Finocchiaro showed courage herself in taking on a role requiring romantic scenes with an imaginary lover (Maurizio's animated character would be added later in the filmmaking process). It is Martina's deadpan sincerity while servicing her peculiar clients that provides "Volere" with much of its energy and almost all of its charm. It's only when Maurizio's lustfully free-spirited hands escape his arms and begin feeling her up that Finocchiaro loses control of her performance, and with both her and Nichetti reduced to caricatures, there's just not much joy left in Toon Town.

SIGHT AND SOUND, 5/92, p. 61, Peter Aspden

The shy, awkward Maurizio works with his brother in a dubbing studio. He specialises in dubbing sound effects on to old cartoons, using his spare time to record strange noises in the street as soundtrack material. His brother runs the other half of the business: supervising a team of beautiful women dubbing soft-porn movies. Martina, who is disillusioned with men, has a freelance job helping to fulfil people's sexual fantasies. Among her clients are twin architects, who arrive in the morning to watch her bathe and dress; the infant, who dresses in baby's clothes and likes to be fed from a bottle; and the mugger, who ambushes her every so often.

One day, Maurizio comes between the screen and the projector during a screening of a cartoon and one of the characters, a turtle, 'escapes' by diving into his top pocket. A couple of birds follow in a similar incident some days later. Maurizio and Martina bump into each other in the street and he immediately falls in love with her. Out of anxiety and clumsiness, he unwittingly becomes involved with some of her clients' stunts: while trying to rescue her from the mugger, he gets beaten up. Maurizio and Martina lose touch, but her customers, turned on by Maurizio's involvement, demand a repeat of their double act and she is forced to try to find him.

They eventually arrange a date. But during a candle-lit dinner, Maurizio is horrified to discover that his hand is turning into a cartoon. This marks the beginning of a slow metamorphosis; he runs away, barricades himself in his house, and refuses to have any further contact with her. Finally, Martina discovers that Maurizio has turned into a cartoon. Totally unfazed, she jumps into bed with him and they make love.

"It takes guts to make love to a real woman", says the cartoon character who draws the curtain over *Volere, Volare*'s final scene as the (literally) animated Maurizio and the all-too-human Martina dive between the sheets for some unbridled and distinctly unorthodox passion. It is a pleasing enough joke, but not one which can sustain an entire film; even at ninety-six minutes, Maurizio Nichetti's follow-up to *Ladri di saponette (The Icicle Thief)* drags where it should sparkle, and its jaunty climax only partly succeeds in relieving the tedium.

In *Ladri*, Nichetti successfully mixed homage and parody to produce a delightfully observed satire of the effect of pop-culture wackiness on the Serious Business of Life. Unfortunately, in his latest effort with co-director Guido Manuli, the recipe seems to have gone wrong. As an ironic fable of sexual insecurities and nervous romancing, *Volere, Volare* is not as clever as mid-period Woody Allen; as a study in Chaplinesque pathos, Nichetti is no Chaplin; as farce, the pratfalls are simply not clumsy enough; and as satire, the targets are too obvious.

There are, moreover, some gaping flaws in the logic of the whimsical plot (and, as John Cleese has remarked of his scripts for *Fawlty Towers*, the more absurd the comedy, the more impeccable the logic has to be). Cartoon animals are allowed to escape from their film into the real world, but it is never made clear how these relate to Maurizio's metamorphosis. And if his turning into a cartoon is a metaphor for his inability to enter into a physical relationship with a woman, what does that say about her apparent infatuation with his new, non-human self?

Perhaps, just as cartoon characters have a difficult time functioning in the real world, human beings find it equally troublesome to relate to Mickey and his pals. Remembering the swift descent into mediocrity of *Who Framed Roger Rabbit* after its explosive, exhilarating, all-cartoon opening sequence, the lesson of *Volere, Volare* may be that these experiments in bringing goofiness and *gravitas* together are bound to fail.

VILLAGE VOICE, 2/2/93, p. 49, J. Hoberman

Although the Italian comedian-director Maurizio Nichetti is often compared to Woody Allen, the movie that seems his most important influence is Fellini's image-industry satire, *The White Sheik*. *The Icicle Thief*, released here two years ago, was a small special effects marvel in which Nichetti used the telecast of an imaginary movie classic as an occasion to hop between black-and-white neorealist pathos, garishly near-pornographic commercials, the TV studio from which both emanate, and a Roman living room where the mélange is distractedly received—all four sites jumbled mid-movie by a providential power failure.

The Icicle Thief was as much self-conscious fiction as crazy comedy, and Nichetti's follow-up *Volere Volare* attempts a similar dialectic—though to lesser effect. Martina, a young woman whose profession is enacting her clients' parasexual scenarios (feeding a baby bottle to a grizzled old man, allowing a chef to cover her naked body with chocolate frosting, pretending to be frightened by a would-be mugger), keeps crossing paths with Maurizio, a shy audio technician played by Nichetti. He, too, specializes in bringing fantasies to life, dubbing new sound effects on old cartoons.

Hyperbolic but flat, *Volere Volare* (which means "I want to fly") soon wears thin—and not just because of the abundance of food-on-face gags. First, various creatures begin to escape from the animated cartoons Maurizio screens; then, for reasons not in immediately clear, his hands turn animated—in the most extravagant sequence he has to direct these independent entities to feed him. Finally they become autonomous players in his romance with Martina. *Volere Volare* means to illustrate the frustration of fantasy objects. The last scene whose logic suggests the appearance of Jessica Rabbit on the cover of *Playboy*, shows that even fantasies have fantasies too.

Also reviewed in:
CHICAGO TRIBUNE, 2/19/93, Friday/p. F, Clifford Terry
NEW REPUBLIC, 3/1/93, p. 24, Stanley Kauffmann
NEW YORKER, 2/1/93, p. 96, Anthony Lane
NEW YORK TIMES, 2/3/93, p. C14, Stephen Holden
VARIETY, 5/6/91, p. 334
WASHINGTON POST, 2/15/93, p. C7, Richard Harrington

WAR AGAINST THE INDIANS, THE

A CBC Film release. *Producer:* Harry Rasky. *Director:* Harry Rasky. *Screenplay:* Harry Rasky. *Director of Photography:* Milan Klepl and Kenneth Gregg. *Editor:* Ken Mullally. *Music:* Gary Gilfillan and John Nailer. *Running time:* 145 minutes. *MPAA Rating:* Not Rated.

NARRATOR: Harry Rasky.

VILLAGE VOICE, 4/20/93, p. 58, Leslie Camhi

"They would make fine servants, and they are intelligent," Columbus, writing to his Queen about Hispañola's inhabitants, optimistically observed. "Our hospitality prevented us from killing them," a latter-day Native American historian regrets.

The War Against the Indians charts the cultural divide between these two remarks. Combining interviews with Native American artists, intellectuals, and storytellers, this Canadian documentary explores a 500-year history of extermination, from 16th-century massacres to fatal epidemics of imported illnesses. These accounts are interwoven with haunting archival and contemporary images, from early photographs of vast heaps of buffalo bones, to television footage of the recent battle, in Oka, Canada, over a golf course to be built on a native burial ground.

"The soil you see is not ordinary soil, the top layer is Crow Indian, it's the dust of the blood and bones of our ancestors," a man standing at Little Big Horn observes. But of course the camera just sees soil. Film, a living medium, must work continuously against the grain in order to represent the dead. Unfortunately, director Harry Rasky's powerful material is often undercut by the swashbuckling sweep of his style, continuous voiceover, and "artistic" touches which muddle, though they cannot entirely mitigate, the stark beauty of his subject. Still, even those viewers entirely familiar with the loathsome underside of American history will find a glut of information here, and new ammunition in the continuing battle over the past.

Also reviewed in:
NEW YORK TIMES, 4/16/93, p. C15, Vincent Canby

WAR ROOM, THE

An October Films release of a Pennebaker Asociates production. *Executive Producer:* Wendy Ettinger and Frazer Pennebaker. *Producer:* R.J. Cutler, Wendy Ettinger, and Frazer Pennebaker. *Director:* D.A. Pennebaker and Chris Hegedus. *Director of Photography:* Nick Doob, D.A. Pennebaker, and Kevin Rafferty. *Editor:* Chris Hegedus, Erez Laufer, and D.A. Pennebaker. Sound: Charles Arnot, David Dawkins, and Chris Hegedus. *Running time:* 92 minutes. *MPAA Rating:* Not Rated.

WITH: James Carville; George Stephanopoulos; Heather Beckel; Paul Begala; Bob Boorstin; Michael C. Donilon; Jeff Eller; Stan Greenberg; Mandy Grunwald; Harold Ickes; Mickey Kantor; Mary Matalin; Mitchell Schwartz.

CINEASTE, Vol. XX, No. 3, 1994, p. 57, George Stoney

It's a lot of fun watching *The War Room*. The plot is simple: a couple of young, engagingly brash guys turn a presidential campaign into a kind of media video game and come out winners. It's also a lot of fun watching *cinéma vérité* pioneer D. A. Pennebaker catch such moments of crisis as an argument over the color of campaign signs, confirming one's skepticism about the quality of ideological thinking that guides even our most important election campaign.

And it's reassuring to see that Pennebaker, whose career as one of the world's best hand-held cameramen began in the 1950s and who declared himself seven times a grandfather at a recent press conference, can still keep running in focus down steps and corridors, with his wife and partner Chris Hegedus racing ahead with sound gear. Her sound is incredibly clean; his framing is always right-on. Add Hegedus's dexterous editing and you have a well-crafted example of traditional *vérité*: no interviews, no guiding narration, no set-ups. Just the facts! Answering that question isn't so easy.

The bulk of the film covers events of the Clinton campaign, from the nominating convention through election day, sticking very close to James Carville, its chief political strategist, and George Stephanopolous, its communications director. In exchange for an agreement that nothing would be released until after the election, the film's producers, Wendy Ettinger, R.J. Cutler, and Frazer Pennebaker, obtained intimate access to the goings-on in what Hillary Clinton has been credited with naming 'The War Room.'

Although the actual locale of this headquarters seems to move from time to time, the look of the place is always the same and soon becomes almost claustrophobic. It's a relief when we get glimpses of the rallies and parades being engineered from 'The War Room,' reminding us of what we were seeing at the time on our own television sets at home.

A viewer is grateful, also, for a longish opening segment that reminds that dark horse candidate Bill Clinton came from behind to win the nomination. Scenes of the New Hampshire Primary were borrowed, for the most part, from a massive collection of footage gathered from many sources by Kevin Rafferty for his film *Feed*, released in the spring of 1993. Editor Hegedus uses this residue from that one-joke movie to reveal the whole silly, demeaning primary process. Candidate Clinton takes phone calls from local citizens, while dressed in T-shirt, shorts, and baseball cap, looking every inch and pound the jowly image of 'Bubba from Arkansas' that made it so hard for journalists to take him seriously as a candidate early on. Carville whips up a crowd of local supporters with a transparently calculated mixture of profanity and appeals to patriotism and self-sacrifice.

Gennifer Flowers is here, of course, in smeary, grainy, thrice-copied TV footage, looking the perfect queen of checkout counter journalism. What we don't learn is how Carville and Stephanopolous rescued their rising star from the trap she had baited, the likes of which has ended the career of many another likely politician. They might have been willing to tell us. They don't; interviews are forbidden by the formula the filmmakers have chosen.

In the New Hampshire footage we get some telling glimpses of both Bill and Hillary. Once the primary is over, we see little of either one and are conscious of Clinton's presence only as we hear the War Room side of telephone conversations, mostly about wording of speeches. Of the major shift in strategy that repackaged Hillary as a supportive helpmeet rather than the able, assertive woman she had appeared to be well into the campaign, we learn nothing. In hindsight this is a gap that might not have been apparent at the time. Had it been within the filmmakers' chosen parameters, this gap could have been filled with postelection interviews.

The feeling that we are watching a media war over market share of a brand-name dog food, rather than our country's future, is encouraged by the revelation that James Carville's opposite for the Bush campaign is none other than his girlfriend, Mary Matalin, whom he has since married. Their sparring sessions before local reporters seem to come straight out of a not very well-written situation comedy. In the War Room itself, balding, frenetic beanpole Carville keeps pumping energy into his mostly young, always adoring staff and volunteers. After a while, we accept the fact that running campaigns is his profession and may, or may not, have anything to do with his personal convictions. Then, at just the right moment for dramatic climax, he breaks into tears.

Back in the early days of *cinéma vérité*, when crisis-laden realities were being featured on the networks, those of us in the business used to say that a well-timed crying jag guaranteed success. If that be so, Carville gives these filmmakers a doozy. His tears are real, I've no doubt, although those of us who share Carville's southern background and evangelical culture and have seen our coaches cry before the championship game, our school principals cry before graduation, and our preachers cry just before the altar call, may feel like reaching for our Rolaids.

At this point in the film the other guy, little George Stephanopolous, unaccountably takes charge of one's attention. He had been there all along, letting Carville play to the crowd. Some of the most interesting material comes from telephone conversations he has with Clinton in which, with gentle persuasion, he shapes the tone of the campaign's final posture. One yearns to have the filmmakers ask him questions. While George is on the phone receiving news that predicts victory, the camera pans and holds on an admiring colleague across the room. "How do you feel!," she asks in the manner of a local TV anchorperson, complete with the familiar pushing-back-the-hair gesture. His response is as insubstantial as her question. Maybe that's the filmmakers' point, but it doesn't help us come any closer to understanding the dynamics of the campaign.

It's instructive to look again at *Primary*, that early landmark in the development of *cinéma vérité* which Pennebaker (with Ricky Leacock and others) helped Drew Associates make to chronicle the Humphrey-Kennedy contest for president. In 1960, their cameras found a touchingly naive American public and naive politicians, not unaware of the camera's presence as it records their images but far less wary about its potential for negative comment and certainly less skilled in performing to shape the images they wished to convey. By 1992, everyone seems to be performing, most certainly the principals in the drama *The War Room* is presenting. The landscape seems more cluttered, as does the story. Through Pennebaker's wide-angle view, one is made constantly aware of the minor players. Events unfold almost in Robert Altman fashion. Often stories are left half-finished. It's 'real life' alright, but frustrating. By contrast, *Primary* seems almost simplistic in its straightforward concentration on a few characters and a few ideas, which are pounded home by a few totally unnecessary passages of narration of the kind the *vérité* pioneers were forced to include in order to get their work shown on national television.

The fact that Carville and Stephanopolous in *The War Room* often seem to be performing for the camera does not detract from one's enjoyment. In fact, their very ease before its gaze is part of their charm and provokes the film's comic high point when Carville, while waiting for election results, ad-libs a gracious and self-servingly appropriate speech for Clinton were he to be defeated.

Looking back, one must acknowledge that many of the films Don Pennebaker and Chris Hegedus have been responsible for, and which seemed only of passing interest when they were first released, have today become significant icons. *Primary* is treasured now by political scientists for its revelations of the year when down-home country boys began losing out to city sophisticates. *Don't Look Back*, which chronicled Bob Dylan's rise, has served as a model for almost every rockumentary made since its release in 1967. It is quite possible that, in a decade, *The War Room* will prove itself an equally enduring and revelatory recording. For now, though, for all its fine craftsmanship, it seems little more than an evening of easy laughs.

LOS ANGELES TIMES, 11/19/93, Calendar/p. 10, Kenneth Turan

Republicans will be excused for feeling differently, but the camera can't help but embrace James Carville. With his impish death's head grin and the personality of a sardonic Ichabod Crane, Bill Clinton's preeminent campaign strategist is a natural actor, and "The War Room" gives him the starring role he thoroughly deserves.

Carville shares screen time with George Stephanopoulos, Clinton's former director of communications and current senior adviser. The Mr. Inside and Mr. Outside of the Arkansas governor's presidential campaign, with Carville playing Huck Finn to Stephanopoulos' Tom Sawyer, these lively presences lit up Clinton's drive to the White House and turn "The War Room" into a tiptop political documentary that offers a candid and entertaining backstage look at a most unlikely electoral Juggernaut.

Co-director D.A. Pennebaker, working here with longtime collaborator (and wife) Chris Hegedus, has been political before. One of the fathers of the *cinéma vérité* documentary style, Pennebaker, whose films include "Primary" and "Crisis" as well as the nonpolitical "Don't Look Back" with Bob Dylan and "Monterey Pop," was initially reluctant to re-involve himself in the electoral wars.

It fell to co-producers R.J. Cutler and Wendy Ettinger to persuade the grand old man of fly-on-the-wall filmmaking to sign on, just in time for the Democratic National Convention in New York. And Pennebaker and Hegedus initially agreed to focus on the behind-the-scenes staff only because they were denied access to Clinton himself.

It turned out to be a fortuitous decision, because the workings of the war room, a large space located in an old newspaper building in Little Rock, helped both define and decide the campaign. Created to facilitate open communication between Carville, Stephanopoulos, and the young folks in the campaign trenches, the room had the engaging (and eminently cinematic) aura of ragged camaraderie, of a cynical but sincere band of workaholic daredevils out to capture the presidency.

Of the group's pair of generals, Stephanopoulos was easily the most polished. Always in coat and tie and almost always smiling, the director of communications is a smoothly polished piece of work, giving his staff their post-debate spin orders ("keep repeating that Bush was on the defensive all night") and later calmly but forcibly talking a Ross Perot operative out of spreading an unpleasant anti-Clinton rumor.

Wearing an LSU T-shirt and with Tums and moral outrage always at the ready, Carville is a very different kind of political animal. As impatient and irascible as he is smart, and he is very smart, Carville is also someone who can't even imagine being at a loss for words. "He reeks of yesterday, he has the stench of yesterday," he wails about President Bush, and when the press makes noise about his own candidate's military status, he complains to reporters that "every time somebody farts the word *draft* it's on the front page."

"The War Room" (Times-rated Family) is full of biting and amusing moments like these, culled from more than 50 hours worth of campaign situations. Since the New Hampshire primary took place before the project got under way, the filmmakers had to play catch-up there.

The rest of the material was shot by Pennebaker and Nick Doob, a scam that got the film's most telling scenes by the time-honored fashion of simply hanging out until the participants forget you're there. "The War Room" offers a wonderful selection of campaign snapshots, of would-be scandals that fizzled and improbable worries like the concern that the candidate's convention signs clashed with each other. You had to be there, and with this film you finally are.

NEW YORK, 11/1/93, p. 86, David Denby

James Carville is so smart, calculating, funny, and successful that one is surprised, late in *The War Room*—D. A. Pennebaker and Chris Hegedus's cinéma-vérité documentary about the Clinton campaign—to discover that he is also (gulp!) good. A very entertaining movie.

NEW YORK POST, 11/3/93, p. 36, Thelma Adams

Spin. Spin. Spin. "The War Room" documents the two spin doctors behind the 1992 Clinton presidential campaign: pretty boy George Stephanopoulos and James Carville, the "Ragin' Cajun."

In the "you-are-there" tradition, indie filmmakers D.A. Pennebaker ("Monterey Pop," "Don't Look Back") and partner/wife Chris Hegedus have spun their own tale of the powers behind the "Comeback Kid."

A feeling of deja vu permeates this harrowing and highly entertaining feature documentary. Was the 1992 presidential campaign only last year? From the New Hampshire primary to election night, Pennebaker and Hegedus invade the so-called war room, the inner-sanctum of the Clinton campaign staff.

Denied access to Clinton himself, the filmmakers discover a back-room drama on the campaign trail with the Rocky and Bullwinkle of modern politics. Few men could be more different than George and James.

Carville has a bit of the back-country snake-oil salesman to him. Skeletal and beady-eyed, charismatic and impassioned, the man could sell armadillos to Leona Helmsley.

Carville has a winning talent for talking in quality sound bites. He says of Bush, "He reeks of yesterday. ... If I think of an old calendar I see George Bush's face on it."

Quick to anger, Carville lends "The War Room" its climax when he breaks into tears of joy—twice—on the eve of Clinton's victory. In contrast, the ever-earnest Stephanopoulos never loses his cool.

Few could love Stephanopoulos as much as he loves himself. The diminutive Rhodes scholar presides over the war room like a high school yearbook editor. In Clinton, he found the father-figure for whom he could overachieve.

Clinton stumbles into the frame on occasion, in shorts and cap. On a call to a reporter, the future President goes humble about his high school days when all he wanted to do was rock 'n' roll; the kid from Arkansas is quite a spin surgeon in his own right.

Ironically, it is Mary Matalin, Carville's paramour and a major player in the Bush campaign who charms. She comes across as the most straightforward, down-to-earth player of the bunch. When this tough cookie accuses Clinton of a "pathological pattern of deception," she hits the raw nerve that makes "The War Room" so engrossing.

I squirmed in my seat as Clinton and company hound Bush for his read-my-lips, no-new-taxes stumble. Carville refers to this statement as "the most famous broken promise in the history of American politics."

"The War Room" is a must-see, an allegory of democracy at work in the late 20th century. As time passes, its value will increase. In the euphoria of election night in Little Rock, Stephanopoulos chats with Clinton by cellular phone. "Now we've really got to do something," George says.

NEWSDAY, 11/3/93, Part II/p. 66, Jack Mathews

A bona fide star was born during the Democrats' successful 1992 presidential campaign. A charismatic figure with a big smile, a folksy wit, obvious intelligence, convincing idealism, cease-less energy and the uncanny ability to turn bad news into good.

We refer, of course, to James Carville.

It was Carville who orchestrated Bill Clinton's campaign, and it is Carville who energizes D.A. Pennebaker and Chris Hegedus' "The War Room," a behind-the-scenes look, and ultimately a celebration, of the team that drove the Bubbamobile to the White House.

As I wrote when the documentary premiered at the New York Film Festival last month, this is a journey that only the Clinton faithful may want to take. Though the filmmakers attempted to keep an objective distance between their camera and their subjects, unreformed supporters of

George Bush and Ross Perot will regard it as nothing less than having their noses rubbed in something very odious.

Bush loyalists, for instance, won't see the humor in Carville's sour monologue on the ex-president's weary politics, "the stench of yesterday," as Carville spits it out. And that sucking sound you hear will be Perot fans heading for the exits when Carville dismisses the billionaire's candidacy as "the biggest single act of masturbation in history."

"The War Room" gives equal billing in Clinton's campaign to Carville and communications director George Stephanopolous, but like everyone else in the campaign (including Clinton in those few moments when he's around), the baby-faced Stephanopolous is overwhelmed by Carville's personality.

With a temper as quick as his wit, Carville cuts in and out of "The War Room," the label given to the campaign's nerve center, like an electrical storm over his native Louisiana. In the early going, we heard him lift Clinton's young, inexperienced staff with a stunningly forceful, off-the-cuff pep talk and, in the end, see him sob his way through an election eve victory speech to the same, by now reverent audience.

In between, we are given constant reminders of why political analysts credit Carville for turning the election—his ability to keep the campaign focused on the essential issue ("It's the economy, stupid!"), and the counter-punch campaign strategy he designed to neutralize daily Republican attacks on Clinton's character.

Pennebaker, who worked a camera on Robert Drew's seminal political documentary on the 1960 Kennedy/Humphrey Wisconsin primary, and Hegedus, his long-time wife and partner, didn't have great access to the Clinton staff, especially in the beginning, and the gaps show.

The filmmakers set out with very little money to chronicle a campaign that might have ended in New Hampshire, and caught a ride themselves on a political juggernaut. They were wise enough to shift the emphasis from the public campaign to the inner workings of the campaign staff, and got enough—just enough—to make it work.

They ended up with 40 hours of their own film, but most of it was collected after the Democratic convention, by which time Clinton was leading in the polls. They had to rely heavily on available news footage to chronicle the early crises created by Gennifer Flowers' kiss-and-tell press conference and the accusations about college-age Clinton's draft dodges and participation in Vietnam War protests abroad.

Neither Carville, who has gone on to manage New Jersey Gov. Jim Florio's re-election campaign, nor Stephanopolous, now a senior White House aide, had editing approval of the film, and there are few scenes where they aren't on their best behavior.

Carville's temper gets ugly in spots, but even in the midst of a stress-out, his mannerisms and Cajun-cooked homilies create moments of high comedy. Whether you laugh or cry depends entirely on how you felt the night of the election.

NEWSWEEK, 11/8/93, p. 78, Jonathan Alter

James Carville is a performance artist. If he lived in New York he's have a show in Greenwich Village where he smeared fudge all over his body or something. While many political reporters think the Ragin' Cajun's act has worn thin, I've found it consistently entertaining. Hearing Carville spin—even if it was obviously three-quarters crap—was about the most fun part of the entire 1992 campaign. *The War Room*, a documentary by D. A. ("Don't Look Back") Pennebaker and his wife, Chris Hegedus, is ostensibly a flattering look at the media command post where the famous THE ECONOMY, STUPID sign hung. But it's actually more of a buddy movie about Carville and his co-conspirator George Stephanopoulos as they hype their man and trash George Bush. The film crew didn't show up until the convention, so the treatment of the primaries is mostly a clip job, sometimes factually out of sequence. But then the camera—while rarely near Clinton himself—gets awfully close to the heart of his Little Rock HQ.

There's nothing deep or brand new, but lots of great fly-on-the-wall glimpses: a smooth Stephanopoulos on the phone knocking down another lurid sex story ("Nobody will believe you and people will think you're scummy"), a cackling Carville trying—and failing—to plant a negative story with CBS. We watch Stephanopoulos on Election Day as he tells Clinton by phone that the exit polls say he'll win, and later advises him to avoid being "too programmatic" in his victory speech. To see exactly how a young aide talks to a new president at the moment he's elected is unusual, maybe unprecedented.

It's easy to imagine that the inside stuff took place outside the war room. And some of it did. But the gap between public and private has been obliterated in presidential politics. The essence of the real war room is there in "The War Room." They're not mugging for the cameras, because the cameras are the campaign itself.

TIME, 11/8/93, p. 88, Richard Schickel

Flanked by Paul Tsongas on the highroad and Gennifer Flowers on the low, Bill Clinton is doing phone interviews in a hotel room, struggling to keep his presidential hopes alive in the New Hampshire primary. Finishing his chores with the press ("Betcha I said something you can take out of context," he observes wearily), Clinton wanders over to a table where staffers are discussing their image as reported in the press. He claps James Carville, his chief political strategist, on the shoulder and says, "You weird guys gotta stick together."

Thereafter, in *The War Room*, Clinton is pretty much a voice on the telephone, an image on a TV screen, a remote figure being hustled down corridors and into limousines. And this documentary by D.A. Pennebaker and Chris Hegedus becomes less a group portrait of a campaign team in action and more a character study of the candidate's designated weirdo. But that's all right; Carville is a terrific character. If this were fiction instead of cinema verité, Tommy Lee Jones would play the part.

The headquarters over which he presides has the disheveled camaraderie of a fraternity house in the throes of creating its homecoming float, and Carville has the air of the bright kid who doesn't quite fit in socially but whose talents cannot be denied. His language, dress and diet are an affront to mothers everywhere, and he often gropes when obliged to search out the right word for an ad or a statement to the press. He is also smart to the point of cynicism, and there are times when there is something almost vulpine in his manner: his eyes are preternaturally bright, his head constantly aswivel, ever alert for prey or peril. But mostly what you sense about him is the loyalty and the passionate convictions of an outsider who has been taken into a club that might never have admitted him.

His enthusiasms sometimes betray him. He wastes time, for instance, trying to discredit the Bush campaign in a gambit that does not pan out. On the other hand, his laughing ferocity in defense of the candidate when he is attacked on issues Carville regards as diversionary and his confident contempt for his opponents are inspirational. He may not be charismatic in the usual sense of the word, but you can see him hypnotizing the staff. And smooth, soft-voiced George Stephanopoulos, the campaign's director of communications, whose idea of cutting loose is to blow bubble gum while he's on the phone, functions almost as Carville's straight man. This guy may be a wild man, but he's George's wild man and George bemusedly lets him run.

The War Room is not a complete or even an entirely coherent record of the Clinton campaign. There are things the cameras could not observe. But it is amusing (or appalling) to see a roomful of grownups arguing over whether hand-lettered or printed signs will have the best TV impact at the convention. Or to see ties being tested for their sincerity before a debate. But the film works most instructively, most memorably, as a kind of nature documentary stalking one brightly colored political animal as he patrols his territory.

VILLAGE VOICE, 11/9/93, p. 64, Amy Taubin

Buoyed by the charisma of its subjects—saturnine Southerner James Carville and cherubic prep-pie George Stephanopoulos—*The War Room* hops, skips, and jumpcuts along the 1992 Clinton campaign trail. Veteran vérité filmmakers D. A. Pennebaker and Chris Hegedus parlayed their minimal access—the candidate himself was off-limits—into a totally charming, smart, behind-the-scenes roller coaster of a movie.

Less a place than a process, the "war room," Clinton's mobile, electronically outfitted campaign headquarters, was notable for its college-dorm informality, its combative improvisatory style, and its savvy staff. As Carville boasted, gulping back tears during his election-eve, farewell-to-the-troops speech, "We changed the way political campaigns are run."

Along with Stephanopoulos's bubble-gum antics and Bush campaign manager Mary Matalin's manically self-conscious, a cappella rendition of "Hey, Good Lookin'," Carville's tears are the kind of revelatory behavior on which Pennebaker's brand of cinema vérité depends. The filmmakers also managed to shoot one of the rare face-to-face encounters during the campaign between Matalin and Carville (who plan to marry on Thanksgiving). Carville, who's shown fielding almost as many questions about Matalin as about Clinton, explains the relationship: "Mary just loves the president. We disagree on that ... But as long as it works, that's what matters to me." Which is about as close as the film gets to political analysis.

The War Room is an update on the early vérité docs *Primary* (about the crucial 1960 JFK-Hubert Humphrey battle for Wisconsin) and *Crisis* (about the Kennedy-Wallace school-segregation face-off). Pennebaker, who was a key member of the filmmaking team for those docs, holds to basic vérité principles (handheld camera, no explanatory voiceover, focus on detail) while playing fast and loose with others. Purists will be horrified by the filmmakers' casual reliance on news service footage to move the story forward. (Since Pennebaker and Hegedus didn't come into the picture until the Democratic convention, the first 20 minutes of *The War Room* is collaged from anonymous sources.)

Quibbles aside, *The War Room* keys into the exhilaration, anxiety, and high-wire media manipulation of the campaign. (Serious arm-twisting is notable for its absence, which doesn't mean it didn't go on.) And it has a seductive screen presence in the irreverent but dedicated Carville, who may look like Malkovich with a twist of Nicholson but shows himself to be utterly and eccentrically his own man. In an age when irony is a necessary condition of truth, Carville, in his single black glove and "Speed Killed Bush" T-shirt, is the real thing.

Also reviewed in:
CHICAGO TRIBUNE, 1/21/94, Friday/p. J, Clifford Terry
NATION, 12/13/93, p. 744, Stuart Klawans
NEW REPUBLIC, 11/22/93, p. 26, Stanley Kauffmann
NEW YORK TIMES, 11/3/93, p. 23, Janet Maslin
NEW YORKER, 11/8/93, p. 124, Terrence Rafferty
VARIETY, 10/11/93, p. 71, Todd McCarthy
WASHINGTON POST, 11/12/93, p. C1, Rita Kempley
WASHINGTON POST, 11/12/93, Weekend/p. 50, Desson Howe

WARLOCK: THE ARMAGEDDON

A Trimark Pictures release of a Tapestry Films/Trimark production. *Producer:* Peter Abrams and Robert Levy. *Director:* Anthony Hickox. *Screenplay:* Kevin Rock and Sam Bernard. *Director of Photography:* Gerry Lively. *Editor:* Chris Cibelli. *Music:* Mark McKenzie. *Sound:* Don Johnson. *Casting:* Alison Kohler. *Production Designer:* Steve Hardie. *Art Director:* John Chinchester. *Set Decorator:* David Koneff. *Costumes:* Leonard Pollack. *Make-up:* Bob Keen. *Running time:* 93 minutes. *MPAA Rating:* R.

CAST: Julian Sands (Warlock); Chris Young (Kenny Travis); Paula Marshall (Samantha Ellison); Steve Kahan (Will Travis); Charles Hallahan (Ethan Larson); R.G. Armstrong (Franks); Micole Mercurio (Kate); Craig Hurley (Andy); Bruce Glover (Ted Ellison); Dawn Ann Billings (Amanda Sloan); Zach Galligan (Douglas); Joanna Pacula (Paula Dare).

LOS ANGELES TIMES, 9/27/93, Calendar/p. 2, Kevin Thomas

No wonder Trimark Pictures promised to incinerate a witch in a dilapidated prop coffin in front of Pacific's Hollywood last Friday: "Warlock: The Armageddon", as grisly as it is silly, needed all the media attention it could get. As corny as the stunt was, it was more fun than what followed inside on the screen.

Writers Kevin Rock and Sam Bernard and director Anthony Hickox prove themselves to be hacks—in more than one sense of the word—in making this foolish heavy-on-the-blood-and-guts "Warlock" sequel, which is too dreary to play even as camp.

Never mind that the Warlock (Julian Sands), Satan's son, was reduced to ashes at the end of the original film, because you can never keep a bad man down as long as box office is good. During an eclipse of the sun, Satan's offspring is instantly born to an unfortunate woman who has just put on an exotic necklace.

It seems that its gems are one of the six runes that the Warlock must collect within six days if Satan is to be freed from the confines of hell and provoke the Armageddon. Two of the runes, however, are in the possession of a secret sect of Druids now living in a small Northern California town.

It falls to two of the sect's teen-agers (Chris Young, Paula Marshall), who are actually Druid warriors incarnate, to try to defeat the Warlock in a familiar round of the eternal struggle between good and evil. The outcome is not exactly difficult to predict.

In such dire circumstances, any displays of effective professionalism are to be appreciated. Veteran character actor R. G. Armstrong deserves applause for the imagination and conviction with which he plays a wise Druid elder; so does composer Mark McKenzie for his majestic score. As for Sands, he's just as witty and insinuating as he was in the swift and stylish 1991 original film, but in the wake of this sequel-plus the awful "Boxing Helena"—he might do well to think twice before agreeing to do a "Warlock III." "Warlock: The Armageddon" has been rated R for strong horror violence and for nudity and language.

NEW YORK POST, 9/25/93, p. 13, Lawrence Cohn

The pretentious supernatural tale "Warlock: The Armageddon" threatens the audience with the end of the world but delivers mediocrity. It will satisfy gore fans and probably irritate everyone else.

A sequel to the Julian Sands vehicle "Warlock," it brings back the British heartthrob as the son of the devil. He's got six days until a solar eclipse to gather six ancient rune stones and perform a ritual that will free daddy the devil from Hell and end the world as we know it.

The underrated Demi Moore film "The Seventh Sign" traversed this territory five years ago with some imagination and a decent budget. This time around what we get is a glorified video: cheesy visual effects that might be passable on the home screen but look very phony in a theater.

As in his previous "Waxwork" and "Sundown," director Anthony Hickox seems more interested in impressing the viewer with his knowledge of old movies than getting on with the storytelling.

The overly embellished plot line boils down to two attractive teens, Chris Young and Paula Marshall, trained by their druid parents as warriors to do a last-ditch battle with son of Satan Sands. Episodic structure has Sands traveling cross-country to fetch each of the stones, nastily killing humans and animals on his way. Much of the action is sheer gruesomeness and unpleasantness designed to titillate a jaded crowd.

It's a pity that Hickox can't focus his talents, since there are occasionally suspenseful set pieces, notably an encounter in an elevator between Sands and one of the druids, Charles Hallahan. By the final reel, when the two teens gang up to defeat Sands, the "anything goes" supernatural gimmicks result in a boring anticlimax.

NEWSDAY, 9/25/83, Part II/p. 23, Terry Kelleher

As you watch "Warlock: The Armageddon," you can't help having a degree of sympathy for the devil. Or at least for his representative.

In the original "Warlock," the title character (Julian Sands) was prowling our earth in search of Satan's bible (undoubtedly a first edition). In this sequel, he's back and bent on collecting a half-dozen rune stones. If he bags them all, he can summon his boss to establish a New World Order of evil.

Now, nobody wants Satan to come out on top. And nobody can condone the unspeakable acts committed by the Warlock in his name, though some of the designed-in-hell special effects are pretty neat. But it's hard to root against the powers of darkness when the forces of light are so ... dim.

It turns out the only good folks who can prevent the Warlock from completing his scavenger hunt are a bunch of latter-day Druids living in a small California town. The group's chief strategist, Will Travis (Steve Kahan), would like to dispatch the Warlock with his own hands, but for some Druidic reason the warrior role must be filled by his son, Kenny (Chris Young)—after the lad is killed and brought back to life, as tradition demands.

"If I had my way, I'd trade places with you in a heartbeat," Will assures Kenny. Talk is cheap. Considering Kahan's flat performance, it's questionable whether Will has a heartbeat.

The Warlock travels west in a New York City cab, which he operates from the passenger seat while the slain driver's body decomposes up front. Along the way, he acquires a few stones and finds ingenious ways to murder their owners. An arrogant art dealer, for example, is twisted into a painfully Picasso-esque piece of sculpture.

Unfortunately, director Anthony Hickox keeps cutting away from the Warlock's wicked fun to update us on Kenny's combat training (he can't seem to get the hang of telekinesis), as well as his romance with fellow teenage Druid warrior Samantha Ellison (Paula Marshall). Sure, they're nice kids. But frankly, who needs 'em around to slow things down? The only moviegoers who'll relate to bland Kenny and Samantha are the ones who shouldn't be attending this gory, R-rated affair without parent or adult guardian.

Might as well let the Warlock run wild, or at least match him up against Druids who don't appear to have come from Disney.

Also reviewed in:
NEW YORK TIMES, 9/25/93, p. 19, Janet Maslin
VARIETY, 9/20/93, p. 28, Leonard Klady

WATCH IT

A Skouras Pictures release of an Island World presentation in association with the Manhattan Project of a River One Films production. *Executive Producer:* David Brown and William S. Gilmore. *Producer:* Thomas J. Mangan IV, J. Christopher Burch, and John C. McGinley. *Director:* Tom Flynn. *Screenplay:* Tom Flynn. *Director of Photography:* Stephen M. Katz. *Editor:* Dorian Harris. *Music:* Stanley Clarke. *Music Editor:* John LaSalandra. *Sound:* Allan Byer and (music) Dan Humann. *Casting:* Shari Rhodes. *Production Designer:* Jeff Steven Ginn. *Art Director:* Barbara Kahn Kretschmer. *Set Decorator:* Martha Ring. *Set Dresser:* Bruce "Fluffy" Seymour. *Special Effects:* Dieter Sturm. *Costumes:* Jordan Ross. *Make-up:* Felicia Linsky and Charles Washington. *Stunt Coordinator:* Rick Le Fevour. *Running time:* 102 minutes. *MPAA Rating:* R.

CAST: Peter Gallagher (John); Suzy Amis (Anne); John C. McGinley (Rick); Jon Tenney (Michael); Cynthia Stevenson (Ellen); Lili Taylor (Brenda); Tom Sizemore (Danny); Terri Hawkes (Denise); Jordana Capra (Call Girl); Taylor Render (Girl on Videotape); Lorenzo Clemons (Fan at Ballpark); Mark Grapey (Jewelry Salesman); Jeannine Welles (Sharon); Gina Raffin (Deborah); Scott Haven (Denise's Boyfriend); Bill Cusack (Delivery Boy); Marty Higgenbotham (Waiter); Del Roy (Minister); Maria Stevens (Danny's Girl); Tricia Munford (Girl with Rick); Emily Hopper (Girl at Party); Michael Hughes (Bill Clark); Tony Difalco (Todd Black); Lee R. Sellers and Eva Black (Ellen's Dinner Guests).

LOS ANGELES TIMES, 3/26/93, Calendar/p. 12, Kevin Thomas

"Watch It," a scintillating yet serious romantic comedy, finds Peter Gallagher's John, just arrived from Texas to a fine old Chicago suburb, immediately led by his cousin Michael (Jon Tenney) to the kitchen of a large turn-of-the-century home and ordered to hide in the refrigerator. Moments later Michael's housemate Rick (John C. McGinley) comes home, complains about his work as a salesman, opens the refrigerator door whereupon John, following his cousin's instructions, leaps out, exclaiming "Watch It!"

In an instant John, who's been working as an oil rigger, is indoctrinated into a game that Michael, Rick and their other housemate Danny (Tom Sizemore) take all too seriously. The idea is to pull off a prank with as much ingenuity as possible. Once the victim is hooked you're supposed to shout "Watch It!" You're also not supposed to get angry but instead get even, but John quickly discovers that the two seem to be hopelessly intertwined.

The great thing about this thoroughly engaging film is that writer Tom Flynn, in his directorial debut, uses this silly game as a point of departure, a metaphor for the tendency of American men—white middle-class males in particular—to resist growing up. (Michael and his friends look to be thirtysomething but still carry on like fraternity boys.) Flynn also ponders the mystery of how really terrific women can be attracted to jerks, suggesting that the hope of changing them seems to be part of that attraction. He reminds us, too, how much cruelty and anger humor can reveal.

When John drives up to Michael's house a wary look crosses his face—with good reason. Michael has never lost his childhood sense of betrayal by John over an unjust course of events over which John, a child himself at the time, had no control. Michael is now a real heel, especially when it comes to women, which propels his veterinarian girlfriend (Suzy Amis), a pale, patrician beauty, into the arms of John, who is a nice, decent guy but has yet to settle down and is overwhelmed by the possibility of true love. Meanwhile, Rick, who revels in savage, adolescent jesting, responds with an unfamiliar flick of feeling for the sensible, forthright Ellen (Cynthia Stevenson) by becoming nastier than he already is. He's so immature he's reflexively threatened by emotion—something he clearly has never before experienced.

"Watch It" truly strikes a nerve, yet for all the complexity of its numerous people, proceeds with the brisk dispatch of high comedy, deftly juxtaposing moments of pain with inspired hilarity. Flynn matches his way with words with his actors to the extent that those who have but a single line make an impression. Gallagher has distinguished himself on stage and TV as well as films, where he most recently scored in "sex, lies and videotape" and "The Player," and now moves easily into a starring slot as the likable John, the film's moral anchor.

McGinley, one of the film's co-producers, and Tenney more than meet the challenge of making jerks seem human, and they set a high standard for supporting performances for this year, as do Stevenson and Sizemore, for his easy-going Danny. Fresh from raves for "Rich in Love," Amis continues to establish herself as a leading lady of exceptional grace and presence. As Amis' smart, spunky assistant, Lili Taylor displays the kind of pizazz that would give Rosie Perez a run for her money. The handsomely wrought "Watch It" (rated R for language and a scene of sexuality) is definitely worth a look.

NEW YORK POST, 3/26/93, p. 25, Jerry Tallmer

Pranks, I guess you'd call it—the kind of stunts the fellas pull on one another in "Watch It," a new film about the young male American animal who refuses to grow up.

They all live together in a white house somewhere on what I take to be the North Side of Chicago, and the kind of thing they do to one another is pop out of refrigerators like scarecrow's yelling: "Watch it!"—that's the mildest, introductory one—all the way to faked dirty-violent sex scenes or pregnancy announcements by girls in their crowd who are either too foolish or too wounded to say no.

Once you join "Watch it!" you're a player and can never get out, that's the idea. You just have to keep topping one another, in love and war and bull-session bragging complete with videotapes.

The boys—meant to be in their late 20s but all a little overage as always in this sort of thing—are John who has grown away from Mike, who now hates John because Mike's mother was an alcoholic and John (as a small boy) didn't keep that from ruining Mike's life; Rick, a deep-dyed caustic, cynical salesman who has been burned by women somewhere along the line; and Danny, the lug of the picture, who runs a sports-car repair shop (important to the plot twist of a couple of funny "Watch its!"); and a few miscellaneous others.

The young women are Anne, a slim, serious veterinarian who gets sexually and otherwise involved, first with Mike (the amoral bad guy), then with John is good guy who doesn't know it; he takes her to Comiskey Park; of course she knows more baseball than he does), then with Mike, who betrays her, then despite herself with John etc.; Ellen a talky, spunky school-teacher who, breaking her sexual solitude, puts the emotional blocks to caustic Rick; and Brenda, the man-wise receptionist at Anne's animal hospital, the Thelma Ritter part colorfully handled in a younger vein by Lili Taylor.

Written and directed by Thomas Flynn, of whom I know nothing except what I see here, "Watch It" is—as you may have guessed—a movie wheeling around and around and again around the awful and awesome matter of Male Commitment. Indeed, I haven't heard the word "commitment" hurled back and forth so much since soap operas of 10 years ago. And what I kept thinking of was in fact that lovely film of 20 years ago, "Love With the Proper Stranger," in which it takes Steve McQueen two hours to find how much he's committed to wonderful Natalie Wood.

What I also kept thinking of, less pleasantly, was the Glen Ridge abuse case and those guys and that poor girl. There is something of the same stink of "boys will be boys" in at least the early parts of this film, and I wish I could be sure that director Flynn wanted us to hate ourselves for laughing at it. Though I for one did not laugh, not at that. Elsewhere, a little.

Peter Gallagher plays John, the good guy, but I wish makeup and camera had given him less of an overripe suntanned face. Jon Tenney is neutral as Mike, the bad guy. Suzy Amis with her long red hair is quite brave in letting herself look like death warmed over, freckles and all, whenever Anne is in emotional extremis, which is most of the movie. Cynthia Stevenson is right on target as the smart schoolteacher, and John C. McGinley, as the nasty joker she forces into manhood through sheer loving anger, merely steals the picture from everyone.

NEWSDAY, 3/26/93, Part II/p. 71, John Anderson

"Disturbed" is an apt, one-word adjective for "Watch It," a comedy about several lost boys who avoid maturity by waging sexual war against women, and pulling practical jokes on each other.

At times, writer-director Tom Flynn aspires to a far more serious tone than the film deserves, or than he seems equipped to handle. There are stylishly slow dissolves, and neo-realistic affectations, but there are also scenes that seem narratively out of place, that in fact reverse the storyline.

And there's a sense of confusion over whether "Watch It" is a waggish comedy about some wacky ex-frat boys and their swinging, single condom-less lifestyle, or a dark study of stunted, runtish predatory sexual behavior.

"Watch It" tries, of course, to be both, and is undone by one small detail: The premise. The title refers to the elaborate game played by three ex-students at Northwestern University—Michael (Jon Tenney), Rick (John C. McGinley) and Danny (Tom Sizemore)—which involves pulling elaborate practical jokes on each other, at the end of which the perpetrator yells "Watch it!"

When John (Peter Gallagher) comes to visit his long lost and alienated cousin Mike—with whom he shares some heavy history—he gets caught up in the game, too. The problem, of course, is that once you've pulled a couple of practical jokes on the characters, you've pulled them on the audience, too, and the latter becomes wary that every turn in the plot is going to be resolved by someone screaming "Watch it!"

Most of the movie deals with Michael and John's competition over Anne (Suzy Amis), a local veterinarian, whom John loves and whom Michael sees as a way of getting back at John. At the same time, Rick can't cope with his love for Ellen (Cynthia Stevenson), and we keep waiting for another practical joke. They'll come, in a torrent, but not till the end of the film. Along the way, we get confused by bad editing and a lack of continuity.

Gallagher and Amis float through "Watch It" like a couple of overworked pharmaceutical lab rats, but Tenney's Michael radiates spite and danger. Stevenson ("The Player") and Sizemore are smart and funny, as is McGinley, although he's also capable of being annoying. Or quietly hostile: In one scene, he delivers an ultra-cynical but painfully on-target analysis of single-man-woman relationships. It isn't a pretty moment, which makes the advance advertisements for "Watch It"—which quote an amorphous film critic as calling the film a "great date movie"—stranger still. They probably said the same thing about "Who's Afraid of Virginia Woolf?"

Also reviewed in:
CHICAGO TRIBUNE, 3/26/93, Friday/p. F, Clifford Terry

NEW YORK TIMES, 3/26/93, p. C12, Vincent Canby
NEW YORKER, 3/29/93, p. 102, Anthony Lane
VARIETY, 1/18/93, p. 79, Todd McCarthy
WASHINGTON POST, 4/23/93, p. D6, Hal Hinson

WAYNE'S WORLD 2

A Paramount Pictures release. *Executive Producer:* Howard W. Koch, Jr. *Producer:* Lorne Michaels. *Director:* Stephen Surjik. *Screenplay:* Mike Myers, Bonnie Turner, and Terry Turner. *Based on characters created by:* Mike Myers. *Director of Photography:* Francis Kenny. *Editor:* Malcolm Campbell. *Music:* Carter Burwell. *Music Editor:* Adam Smalley. *Choreographer:* Tony Gonzaler. *Sound:* Keith A. Wester. *Sound Editor:* John Dunn and Harry B. Miller, III. *Production Designer:* Gregg Fonseca. *Art Director:* Richard A. Yanez. *Set Designer:* Stephanie Gordon, Mark Poll, and Gary Sawaya. *Set Decorator:* Jay R. Hart. *Special Effects:* Darrell Pritchett. *Costumes:* Melina Root. *Make-up:* Lynne K. Eagan. *Stunt Coordinator:* Bud G. Davis. *Running time:* 96 minutes. *MPAA Rating:* PG-13.

CAST: Mike Myers (Wayne Campbell); Dana Carvey (Garth Algar); Lee Tergesen (Terry); Dan Bell (Neil); Tia Carrere (Cassandra); Richard Epper (Burning Hair Guy at Concert); Jennifer Miller (Topless Girl at Concert); Duke Valenti and Benny Graham (Concert Security Guys); Christopher Walken (Bobby Cahn); Gavin Grazer (Scott); Googy Gress (Gate Security Guy); Heather Locklear (Herself); Bob Odenkirk and Robert Smigel (Concert Nerds); Larry Sellers (Naked Indian); Michael Nickles (Jim Morrison); Joe Liss (Chicken Guy); Bobby Slayton (Watermelon Guy); George Foster (Lead Guitarist); Paul Raczkowski (Studio Recording Engineer); Rip Taylor (Himself); Ralph Brown (Del); Frank DiLeo (Mr. Big); Sydney Coberly (Mikita's Waitress); Kevin Pollack (Jerry Segel); Olivia D'Abo (Betty Jo); Kim Basinger (Honey Hornée); James Hong (Mr. Wong); Chris Farley (Milton); Ron Litman (Tool Box DJ); Matt Kenna and Sean Michael Guess (Roadies); Drew Barrymore (Bjergen Kjergen); Harry Shearer (Handsome Dan); Ted McGinley (Mr. Scream); Tim Meadows (Sammy Davis, Jr.); Scott Coffey and Lance Edwards (Heavy Metallers); Jay Leno (Himself); Al Hansen (Bad Actor); Charlton Heston (Good Actor); Bob Larkin (Wedding Minister); Ed O'Neill (Mikita's Manager, Glen); Steven Tyler, Joseph Perry, Brad Whitford, Thomas Hamilton, and Joseph Kramer (Aerosmith).

LOS ANGELES TIMES, 12/10/93, Calendar/p. 14, Kevin Thomas

Whew! What a relief it is to discover that "Wayne's World 2" is just as hilarious as last year's original, which was one of the best, most distinctive American comedies in years.

Mike Myers' Wayne Campbell and Dana Carvey's Garth Algar, those two Aurora, Ill., youths who host a goofy late-night cable-access TV show, are endearing comic creations, a couple of small-town guys who like to think of themselves as being incredibly hip yet possess considerable naivete.

Even so, the cocky Wayne and the somewhat dim Garth are in their way free-thinkers who do not buy into conventional wisdom. They are at once products and critics of youth-oriented popular culture; you have to wonder in the years to come just how revealing the "Wayne's World" movies—plus the "Saturday Night Live" sketches—will be of their times. Meanwhile, what's great about Wayne and Garth is their highly contagious enthusiasm, which is surely the key to their cross-generational appeal.

A year has passed since Wayne and Garth resisted selling out their show for big bucks. No, they haven't cut their hair and gone off to college, but they have moved out of their parents' homes to a huge loft in an old doll factory in downtown Aurora. At loose ends, Wayne admits to feeling as if he's in a "John Hughes *rite du passage* movie." How can he bring a sense of purpose to his life?

The answer comes when he's inspired to put on a huge concert to be called, in all modesty, Waynestock. Wayne envisions his headliners will be his beloved Aerosmith plus Pearl Jam, Van Halen ... and comedian Rip Taylor—you can easily guess who'll be the easiest to line up. Of course, Wayne wants his gorgeous girlfriend Cassandra (Tia Carrere), a singer, to appear, but a suave record producer (Christopher Walken) is intent upon whisking her out to the West Coast for reasons Wayne suspects are not entirely professional.

The entire film, written by Myers with Ronnie and Terry Turner, who also wrote the first picture, turns upon whether Wayne, tirelessly promoting his concert, can actually deliver to the ticket-buyers what he's promised them.

While there's no doubt that Wayne's the dominant personality in the duo, Garth, with his blond haystack hairdo and glasses, has his own frenetic moments when, much to his astonishment, he finds himself vamped in the laundromat by Kim Basinger's heavy-breathing Honey Hornée. Wait a minute, *Kim Basinger*? In any event, the unbilled Basinger is deliciously, outrageously funny—and hers is not the only surprise appearance.

Also a delight is James Hong as Cassandra's father, a martial arts whiz who jousts with Wayne; their dialogue is atrociously dubbed like a cheap Hong Kong kung fu movie. Threatening to walk off with the whole picture, however, is Ralph Brown as a zonked-out veteran rock 'n' roll roadie who Wayne is counting on to help pull off Waynestock.

The film's writers have done an admirable job of sustaining a non-stop flow of successful gags, jokes, throwaway bits, fantasies and asides, and making all of this come together in taut, smart fashion is director Stephen Surjik, a veteran of TV's "Kids in the Hall" and "Road to Avolea" in a socko feature debut. While a sense of diminishing returns will most likely set in if Wayne and Garth keep returning too often, "Wayne's World 2" is a winner.

NEW YORK POST, 12/10/93, p. 49, Michael Medved

"Wayne's World 2" is immature, irresponsible, idiotic, vulgar—and embarrassingly, incorrigibly enjoyable. You'd have to be a robot—or a high priestess of political correctness—not to laugh.

The reason that advanced and properly progressive thinkers might not be tittering (no pun intended) is that the film shows a shamelessly exploitative attitude toward women.

When it comes to feminist enlightenment, Wayne and Garth remain so primitive that they make Howard Stern look like Alan Alda.

In this picture, they consistently live out one of the sillier and most cherished fantasies of all adolescent males: that a pair of nerdy, out-of-shape, underachieving guys can arouse the passionate interest of some of the world's most spectacularly attractive women.

The glorious Tia Carrere, for instance, is back from the first film, and still bewilderingly besotted with Wayne (Mike Myers), though he begins to suspect that she might be having an affair with the manager (Christopher Walken) of her rising career as a rock singer.

Later in the picture, Wayne meets a Swedish secretary named Bjergen Kjergen (Drew Barrymore) who is so impressed with his knowledge of the geography of her homeland that she quickly offers him a night of love.

Kim Basinger also makes an appearance (playing a character named Honey Hornee), and for once this glamorous star gets a leading man who is in every way worthy of her—the suave, supremely sexy Garth Algar.

These social successes may be satisfying, but they can't quiet Wayne's nagging questions about the meaning of life, and his vague yearning to establish some purposeful new direction for himself.

The ultimate answers come to him in a dream, in which a naked Indian takes him to the desert to meet Jim Morrison (played by lookalike Michael Nickles), who tells Wayne that he should produce a mammoth rock concert.

For the rest of the picture, our hero pursues this dream of organizing "Waynestock" in Adlai Stevenson Park in his hometown of Aurora, Ill.

Penelope Spheeris, the gifted director of the first "Wayne's World," had nothing to do with this sequel, instead heading for the hills (of Beverly) to direct the popular saga of Jed Clampett and his kin.

That left directing chores in "Wayne's World 2" to an all-but-unknown TV comedy specialist named Stephen Surjik. Despite the change behind the camera, the only way in which the departure of Spheeris seems to register on screen is in a noticeable loss of warmth and lyricism.

Many of these gags involve references to 1960s icons, but this nostalgia seems a bit misplaced. After all, Wayne and Garth weren't even born at the time of the original "Woodstock" in 1969, and such anachronistic flashes serve as an uncomfortable reminder that these actors are aging even if their characters are not.

Dana Carvey, in particular, has begun to look a bit long in the tooth to play a kid just out of high school.

These quibbles can hardly take away from the fact that "WW2" (not to be confused with WWII) offers a goofball good time; it may not be a cinematic masterpiece, nor is it filled with vitamins, minerals or meaningful messages, but Wayne does learn a few valuable lessons. "Being an adult means taking responsibility," he tells the audience near the end of the picture, "but still taking time to have fun."

In other words, party on!

NEWSDAY, 12/10/93, Part II/p. 99, Gene Seymour

A better title might have been "Wayne and Garth Move Out of Their Parents Houses and Get Lives. Kinda." Just the sort of easy-and-accessible marquee title that'll have boomers and post-boomers alike stacked up like cordwood outside the multiplexes tonight. *NOT!*

OK, cheap reference. But let's face it. Cheap references are what "Wayne's World," as TV skit, movie and sequel, are all about. Both this film and its phenomenally successful predecessor are smart enough about the dynamics of pop culture to understand that even their own bits aren't safe from quick-and-dirty obsolescence.

"Wayne's World 2" is no less bountiful with such references as the first "Wayne's World." There's a hilarious Kung Fu movie battle sequence with all the bad dubbing and heavy-handed sound effects lovingly re-enacted. There's an equally funny and impromptu re-enactment of a Village People routine. On the arcane side, there's an obscure reference to an old detergent ad that no one born before 1965 will get.

Which is precisely the point. You're supposed to think, "Didn't these guys ever do anything but watch TV in the '70s? I mean, come on. *Rip Taylor*?" And then you think, "How come *I* get all the jokes?" You don't dwell on such things for long before you're recognizing—and laughing at—yet another cheap reference to disposable pop.

"Wayne *deux*" loses a little of its deadpan edge from not having the services of its predecessor's director, Penelope Spheeris. But Canadian TV director Stephen Surjik proves an able caretaker for the dorky-dirtball-cool vision of "Wayne's" creator-writer-star Mike Myers.

We'll pretend, for the time being, that the plot matters. Wayne Campbell (Myers) and his lifelong bud Garth Algar (Dana Carvey) have, as noted, left their parents' houses and moved to a loft apartment, which also serves as studio for their weekly cable-TV show.

Amazingly, Wayne is still romancing the supernally gorgeous Cassandra (Tia Carrere), whose hard-rock career may be getting power-boosted by record producer Bobby Cahn (Christopher Walken), who, it's clear, is after more than her signature on a contract.

Wayne feels he needs to reach for goals higher than another Friday night show followed by doughnuts at Stan Mikita's. But what to do? A dream in which a half-naked Indian leads Wayne through a desert to meet Jim Morrison provides the answer: an outdoor rock festival in the local park. Its name? (What else?) Waynestock! He gets help from a legendary British roadie Del Preston (Ralph Brown in a hilarious turn).

Garth's goals are less grand. There is a hunger in *his* sweet-but-gnarly soul that can't quite define its need. Until his loins are stirred by a sultry blonde neighbor (Kim Basinger) named Honey Hornée. That's pronounced hor-NAY, by the way. Accent-*aigu* over the first "e."

As long as "The Bank Dick" has been brought in from left field, it's worth noting that "Wayne the Second" has much of the gauzy aimlessness of that W. C. Fields film. Will it endure in the same way? I seriously doubt it. But then, who knows what will push the happy buttons of dorks yet unborn?

SIGHT AND SOUND, 3/94, p. 54, Ben Thompson

A year has passed in Aurora, Illinois, Wayne and Garth have left home. Their cable TV show is now broadcast from their new home, a loft in a disused doll factory. Wayne is still in love with rocker Cassandra, whose musical career is taking off again, but his own life lacks purpose, even though he does have tickets to see Aerosmith. One night an American Indian comes to him in a dream and leads him through a desert to meet Jim Morrison, who tells him his destiny is to organise a huge rock concert.

The show will be called Waynestock, and to organise it, Wayne and Garth must go to London to find Del, the world's best roadie. Initially Del, who is retired, is reluctant to help, but when he learns he and Wayne have had similar dreams, he agrees to come with them. At home, Wayne's personal life is ever more complicated. Cassandra's dad disapproves of him, even though Wayne bests him at martial arts, and her producer Bobby Cahn is trying to lure her to LA. For Garth, things are looking up; he meets the beautiful Honey Hornée at the launderette; she wants his body and eventually gets it, but he later discovers she wants to lure him into killing her husband.

Preparations for Waynestock move on apace. City Hall's attempts to tie the project up in red tape are frustrated, a wild party is organised to raise necessary funds, and Del subjects a team of willing would-be roadies to an unorthodox training schedule. But Wayne's world is falling apart—Cahn's campaign to steal Cassandra from him seems to be working, no-one thinks the bands are going to turn up, and Jim Morrison and the Indian are no help. The big day dawns, the kids gather, but there is no sign of either bands or beleaguered promoter, Garth's attempts to pacify the crowd are not successful and Waynestock ends in disaster. But a more persuasive alternative ending follows, in which Wayne snatches Cassandra from Cahn's clutches and gets to the festival in time to see his faith vindicated, as Aerosmith arrive to rock the house, and Garth finds true happiness with council employee Sammy Jo.

This sequel to one of 1992's most enduring cinematic landmarks is something of a disappointment, though that is not to say that a lot of people won't enjoy it—especially if drunk or on drugs. In the *Bill and Ted* cycle, first-time director Peter Hewitt was given the freedom to make the second film more daring, if slightly less funny, than the first. Stephen Surjik, graduating from Bryan Adams and Tears for Fears videos and the Lorne Michaels-produced TV comedy *The Kids in the Hall*, takes no such chances.

Penelope Spheeris' sharper edge and sub-cultural savvy are sorely missed here. Not only did she place a vital check on some of Michaels' and Myers' more sophomoric inclinations; her long acquaintance with the intricacies of low-rent US teendom gave the first film a precision that precluded condescension. This high ideal has been lost in the quest to cash in on a guaranteed mass audience. So the soundtrack has none of the first film's endearingly desperate loser-attractions (does anybody remember Rhino Bucket?)—it's cast-iron radio certainties all the way.

There are still some good jokes—the foiling of Wayne and Garth's attempts to outwit the robotic order-taker at a drive-through restaurant is a particular highlight—but there are more bad ones, and the self-consciousness that was so funny first time around has lost some of its novelty. The "extreme closeup"s and "Exqueeze me"s are sounding a bit tired and the endless film-quotes, of which the one from *The Graduate* is only the lengthiest, seem to have been put there to fill up the space rather than for any merit of their own.

The real problem is that the success of the first film compromises Wayne and Garth's integrity as no-hoper spokesmen. Early on there are some promising attempts to make capital out of this, especially on our two heroes' trip to London—"I can't believe Paramount would spend all this money to fly us over to England"—but the effort is not sustained. Executive producer Howard W. Koch Jr told us what to expect: "This film has many fresh jokes and fresh areas of conflict for Wayne and Garth. For one thing, there are more girlfriends ...".

In the first film, the irony in Wayne's rebuff to Cassandra's domineering father ("In our culture women are allowed to make their own decisions") would have felt intended. In the sequel, it's an insult. And not just because of the limited opportunities for self-expression the film allows Tia Carrere—"Hey, not bad for a little girl from Hong Kong!". The overall babe count is too high. The schwingometer is in the red zone.

What made the drooling chops with which Wayne and Garth approached the opposite sex funny in the first film was the fact that they were underdogs. Now that we know they are overdogs, the spectacle of Heather Locklear as herself, Drew Barrymore as lusty Scandinavian secretary Bjergen Kjergen and Kim Basinger as (I'm sorry but there's no getting around this) Honey Hornée, all queuing up to be leered at by them, is just plain demeaning. Basinger's role in particular would have made Benny Hill blush; she'd have been better off sticking it out in *Boxing Helena*.

TIME, 12/20/93, p. 63, Richard Corliss

[*Wayne's World 2* was reviewed jointly with *Sister Act 2*; see Corliss' review of that film.]

VILLAGE VOICE, 12/21/93, p. 86, Joe Levy

Say what you will about 'em, love 'em or hate 'em or not give a fuck about 'em, but give them credit: they did create their own world. Wayne Campbell and Garth Algar live in no one's shadow. Now this is a pretty rare accomplishment in late-20th-century art—insert your own thoughts about postmodern exhaustion here. And it's an even rarer accomplishment in a 20th-century art that's all about lights and shadows, but Wayne and Garth long ago jumped off the screen that wanted to box them in. You certainly can't say the same thing about Bill and Ted, and though Buff-coat and Beaver have been spotted walking under their own power recently, no one old enough to play with matches can be bothered to tell the two of them apart, ergo ubiquity is not yet theirs. So like I said, give Wayne and Garth credit, they created their own world. Or, as the high school guys sitting across the aisle from me the fourth time I saw *Dazed and Confused* put it, "I think this is gonna be good. It's supposed to be like *Wayne's World*, only smarter. And in the '70s."

Anyway, *WWII* opened last week and you want to know if it doesn't suck, or if they take it anywhere, or at least if there's one scene as good as that "Bohemian Rhapsody" sequence where the whole story of youth, rock and roll, American highways, and postmodern exhaustion was summed up by a single shot of five or six cars impaled one huge silver spike in an auto dealership, while on the soundtrack the late, great Freddie Mercury laid claim to Kurt Cobain's soul, whining "Nothing really matters/Anyone can see/Nothing really matters/Nothing really matters/To me." Well, *does it* really matter? As series go, *Wayne's World* has greater infinite potential and self-mocking appeal than just about anything since the Crosby-Hope road pictures, the loose-assed silliness of which, to say nothing of the smug Hollywood in-joke charm, surrounds Mike Myers any time he's in men's clothing. (Here's a Canadian guy who seems most sincere in drag doing Yiddish shtick after midnight—insert your own thoughts about postmodern rootlessness here.) I mean, they get half their quota of schwing, babe, and TV wasteland jokes in *before the opening credits are done*, and there are almost as many famous people doing goofy cameos as in *The Muppet Movie* or *The Player*. What more do you want? A plot?

Okay, a plot. Let's make this quick: *WWII* is a youth-cult movie about getting older. We know this because it features Aerosmith, a walking post-doctorate thesis on youth-cults getting old, and I do mean old. (Point of information: there's no truth to the rumor that Mike Myers and Dana Carvey were stunt doubles for Walter Matthau and Jack Lemmon in the new *Grumpy Old Men*.) Even though Wayne no longer lives with his parents, everyone's bugging him about *doing something* with his life ("I feel like I'm in a John Hughes *rite de passage* movie"), so he has an audience with Jim Morrison in a dream and decides to stage a concert: Waynestock. Aerosmith will play. Oh yes, they will. (Point of information: *Dazed and Confused* opened with an Aerosmith song and ended with Pink and his lost boys driving off in a cloud of reefer smoke to get Aerosmith tickets; *WWII* begins with Wayne and *his* lost boys on their way to an Aerosmith concert and ends with Aerosmith playing Waynestock—insert your own thoughts about the Möbius-strip nature of rock history here.)

I'm not sure you care—or *should*—but for all its cutting-room-floor sloppiness, *WWI* was way more in touch with the heart of youth reality than *WWII* (Penelope Spheeris has documented teenagers enough to know what they're really like, and who can ever forget Wayne's line about having "an extensive collection of hairnets and name tags" but still knowing how to party? Well, not this former food-service worker). Solid, full of sharp genre parodies (Hong Kong action fans be warned), and funny as fuck, *WWII* goes for glitz instead of heart. Its most poignant and knowing move is putting the ubiquitous "not" and "sphincter" jokes in the hands of adults, who've broken the codes and use them to frighten off our boys. So Wayne and Garth do the only thing they can: they grow up. Who among us does not share their struggle?

Also reviewed in:
CHICAGO TRIBUNE, 12/10/93, Friday/p. A, Michael Wilmington
NEW REPUBLIC, 2/14/94, p. 30, Stanley Kauffmann
NEW YORK TIMES, 12/10/93, p. C20, Janet Maslin
VARIETY, 12/20/93, p. 31, Leonard Klady
WASHINGTON POST, 12/10/93, p. B1, Rita Kempley
WASHINGTON POST, 12/10/93, Weekend/p. 55, Joe Brown

WEDDING BANQUET, THE

A Samuel Goldwyn Company release of a Central Motion Picture/Good Machine, Inc. production. *Executive Producer:* Jiang Feng-Chyi. *Producer:* Ang Lee, Ted Hope, and James Schamus. *Director:* Ang Lee. *Screenplay (English and Chinese with English subtitles):* Ang Lee, Neil Peng, and James Schamus. *Director of Photography:* Jong Lin. *Editor:* Tim Squyres. *Music:* Mader. *Sound:* Tom Paul and (music) Eric Liljestrand. *Sound Editor:* Pamela Martin. *Casting:* Wendy Ettinger and David Lee. *Production Desinger:* Steve Rosenzweig. *Art Director:* Rachel Weinzimer. *Set Decorator:* Amy Silver. *Set Dresser:* Amy Tapper. *Costumes:* Michael Clancy. *Make-up:* Karen Knesevitch. *Running time:* 111 minutes. *MPAA Rating:* R.

CAST: Sihung Lung (Mr. Gao); Ah-Leh Gua (Mrs. Gao); Winston Chao (Gao Wai-Tung); Mitchell Lichtenstein (Simon); May Chin (Wei-Wei); Dion Birney (Andrew); Jeanne Kuo Chang (Wai Tung's Secretary); Chung-Wei Choe (Chef); Michael Gaston (Justice of the Peace); Jeffrey Howard (Street Musician); Theresa Hou (Cashier); Ying-Teh Hsu (Bob Law); Neal Huff (Steve); Anthony "Iggy" Ingolia (Restaurant Manager); Eddie Johns (Haskell); Chih Kaun (Granny Tien); Robert Larenquent (Hispanic Man); Neal Lee (Waiter); Mason C. Lee (Baby).

FILMS IN REVIEW, 1-2/94, p. 49, Harry Pearson

[*The Wedding Banquet* was reviewed jointly with *Farewell My Concubine*; see Pearson's review of that film.]

LOS ANGELES TIMES, 8/4/93, Calendar/p. 4, Kenneth Turan

Stress is a great generator of comedy, and even under the best of circumstances few things (trust me) are as stressful as having a public event attached to your marriage. And the couple getting joined in "The Wedding Banquet" are definitely not doing it under the best of circumstances.

True, both are Chinese living in New York City, but that is about all they have in common. Wai Tung (Winston Chao) is a citizen and a real estate entrepreneur, the only son of a wealthy Taiwanese family, while artist Wei Wei (May Chin) is a penniless illegal immigrant from the mainland who is barely surviving in a borderline apartment. And one more thing. Wai Tung is gay, passionately involved with Western lover Simon (Mitchell Lichtenstein), and about as likely a candidate for heterosexual marriage as Quentin Crisp.

But he's never told his parents.

When summarized this way, Wai Tung and Wei Wei's dilemma sounds more derivative than diverting, a combination of "Green Card" and "La Cage aux Folles," But don't be fooled. "The Wedding Banquet" is very much its own picture, with an individual sensibility and point of view. As poignant and pointed as it is funny (and it is very funny), it dresses up familiar forms with modern twists and ends up an assured and amusing comedy of manners that was the surprise winner of the Berlin Film Festival's Golden Bear.

Though it takes place entirely in New York, most of "Wedding Banquet's" dialogue is in Chinese with English subtitles, a circumstance that points up one of the film's strengths. Directed by Ang Lee, himself a Taiwanese who moved to New York (and co-written by Lee, Neil Peng and James Schamus), "Banquet" parts the curtain hiding the city's Chinese community, and uses the habits and customs of this self-contained enclave as key elements in its farcical plot.

While Wai Tung probably doesn't think of himself as especially Chinese, his respect for his parents and deep desire to please them give him away. Happily living with physical therapist Simon in a Manhattan brownstone, he is troubled every time he receives a tape-recorded letter from his mother recounting how his father, a retired Taiwanese general, is staying alive only to see him married and the father of a son.

Wei Wei, one of Wai Tung's tenants, has problems of her own, including serious poverty and a constant fear of the immigration service. Simon, who is both sympathetic to Wei Wei and bemused by the tenacity of Wai Tung's parents, forever enrolling him in one elite and expensive dating service after another, suggests that the two of them enter into a classic marriage of convenience. More than getting his parents off his back, he points out, it would afford the driven and businesslike Wai Tung great tax deduction.

No sooner is the decision made than a delicious string of unforeseen complications starts to un-wind, starting with the determination of Wai Tung's parents (Sihung Lung and Ah-Leh Gua) to come to New York for the wedding. How to disguise Wai Tung's relationship with Simon, how to make Wei Wei seem like one of the family, and, most pressing of all, how to react when the elders start insisting that nothing but a major league wedding banquet would be fitting for such an occasion.

Nothing would be easier than to caricature any and all participants in this increasingly zany chain of misunderstandings but writer-director Lee's advantage is that he refuses to let that happen. Everyone involved in this farce, eccentric and amusing though they may be, is given a full measure of dignity and humanity, a situation that not only makes the proceedings more believable but adds to the humor as well.

Nicely acted, especially by Lichtenstein (who made a memorable impression in "Streamers") and the veteran Taiwanese actors who play Wai Tung's parents, "Wedding Banquet" (Times-rated Mature) is one of those rare films that bring just the right touch to its proceedings, handling the comedy and the seriousness with equal deftness. By being straight about both the gay and the Chinese-American experience (the film is the biggest box-office hit in Taiwanese history), Ang Lee has made a picture with unmistakably universal appeal.

NEW YORK, 8/30/93, p. 136, David Denby

The lovely Taiwanese American comedy *The Wedding Banquet* begins as a classically structured farce and ends as a serious, almost heartrending embrace of patriarchal responsibility. And it does this without going soft. This small, delicate independent movie has perfect balance. The hero, Wai Tung (Winston Chao), is a young Taiwanese living in New York, a lithe and handsome man, a success. An American citizen, Wai owns several buildings; he dresses well, drives a big Merce-des sedan (which, however, looks pre-owned), and lives happily with a New York prize of sorts, the muscular Simon (Mitchell Lichtenstein), a physical trainer who likes to take care of people. The two men have been lovers for five years.

Winston Chao has worked as a model, and though he's not yet an accomplished actor, he rightly gives Wai the severity of youth, severity covering uncertainty and lingering doubt. Wai Tung may be far from home, but what he's escaped from—a traditional society—is still tugging at him. His elderly parents, followers of Chiang Kai-Shek, left the mainland for Taiwan years earlier; they're cut off from their past, and they want a future, a grandchild. Knowing nothing of their son's private life, they send him, by cassette, urgent messages in favor of marriage, which he grimly listens to while working out at his club. To get the parents off Wai Tung's back, Simon suggests that Wai Tung marry one of his tenants, a scrounging young Chinese artist, Wei Wei (May Chin), who doesn't have a green card. We can't see too much of Wei Wei at first; her hair is hanging in her face. But we can tell that she's almost paralyzed with desire whenever her good-looking landlord comes around to inspect his property.

Up to this point, the movie might be a New York version of an Italian farce from around 1960. It's a good bet that the director, Ang Lee, who was born in Taiwan (in 1954) but studied at the

NYU film school, has had a look at films by such minor masters as Mauro Bolognini and Pietro Germi. And if he hasn't, then Lee and his screenwriting collaborators (Neil Peng and James Schamus) naturally understand the requirements of high-grade farce, which is to place likable characters in awkward situations and then let them improvise their way out of trouble. *The Wedding Banquet* is consistently funny in an unforced, almost glancing style: Ang Lee sets up his cross-cultural and cross-erotic currents and then he *observes*. His touch is sure and light, the jokes securely planted but never fussed over; and this domestic comedy, shot by the Taiwanese cinematographer Jong Lin, looks as beautiful as one of the Manhattan love songs shot by Gordon Willis for Woody Allen. Wai Tung's parents unexpectedly show up from Taiwan for the wedding, and what had started as a simple and useful charade now becomes a seriously preposterous charade. The whole family lives together in Simon and Wai Tung's house, with Simon pretending to be Wai Tung's "landlord." An adroit, helpful man, Simon hops around the kitchen, preparing food when no one is looking; he enjoys taking care of Wai Tung's parents, especially the father, a former general in Chiang's army, stern and patriarchal in spirit but now rather frail. The comedy begins to shift. The young people had wanted only to get on with their careers and their mixed erotic destinies, but with the parents in New York, they are faced with the reality of tradition; and tradition turns out to be as strong and complex as desire itself.

Tribal rites unfold. Husband and wife submit to a boisterous wedding banquet, complete with special Taiwanese high jinks, at the end of which Wei Wei winds up pregnant. May Chin, who is a singing and TV star in Taiwan, appears before the banquet in her low-cut wedding dress and is so stunningly beautiful that Winston Chao looks at her with astonishment. It is said that many homosexuals were turned on by Marilyn Monroe; Ang Lee is suggesting, I believe, that a man not responding to May Chin's beauty, at least once, would have to be dead. Miss Chin has her own comic style; she plays this lonely girl quietly, in a state of rage, and every once in a while emits a small explosion.

The Wedding Banquet ends in a complex series of exchanges between the generations and something like genuine wisdom. The emotional energy of Wai Tung's parents is the greatest surprise. They may be exasperating, but they're also enduring and generous and not nearly as dense as they seem at first; nor are the young people as independent as they think they are. I don't want to make it sound as if the movie finks out, because it doesn't. It never lies about sex, and it's wonderfully reasonable about the rest of life.

NEW YORK POST, 8/4/93, p. 26, Michael Medved

Moviegoers have attended some remarkable wedding celebrations over the years, from the nervous respectability of "Father of the Bride" (both versions), to the brazen blowout of "Goodbye Columbus," to the Sicilian solemnities that began the "Godfather" saga.

But no movie nuptials have ever been more lavish or lusty than the unforgettably grandiose Chinese-American festivities that provide the sly new comedy "The Wedding Banquet" with its dazzling dramatic core. The revelry alone is worth the price of admission, and audiences can enjoy all the food and the fun without gaining an ounce of fat or suffering a nasty hangover.

The principals on the other hand, face all sorts of unpredictable and unwelcome consequences after the last guest has finally gone home.

The groom, Wai-Tung (Winston Chao), is a handsome immigrant from Taiwan whose 10 years of hard work in the United States have earned him a Mercedes, a Manhattan brownstone, a series of income properties, and a loving, committed relationship with a muscular, good-natured American named Simon (Mitchell Lichtenstein).

The lovely bride, Wei-Wei, is one of Wai-Tung's tenants, a starving artist from mainland China who will do anything to get a green card. They go through the traditional wedding celebration in order to appease Wai-Tung's aging parents who are visiting from Taiwan, and to prevent them from discovering that their only child is gay.

Despite the fact that Wei-Wei (played by May Chin, a hugely popular singing star in her native Taiwan) makes one of the most heartbreakingly beautiful brides in the history of the human race, Wai-Tung isn't attracted to her in the least. But after the long, emotional wedding celebration, and the remorselessly ribald teasing of their guests when they're finally left alone together, things (as Wai-Tung later confesses) "get out of hand."

This setup seems to leave the filmmakers with an impossible dilemma. If they take the obvious path and allow the bride and groom to fall in love—leading the hero to leave behind his gay identity—they would mightily offend the gay community. If, on the other hand, they simply send Wai-Tung back to his American male lover after cruelly using Wei-Wei and deceiving his elderly parents, it would destroy all sympathy for the movie's main character.

Director/producer/co-writer Ang Lee, a recent graduate of the film school at NYU, devised a solution to this difficulty that is ingenious and plausible, but never totally satisfying. This too-clever resolution sends you home from the theater thinking of this movie as a pleasant diversion, rather than the full-course "Banquet" promised by the richly emotional scenes in which the plot is laid out.

Much of that emotion centers on Wai-Tung's visiting parents, magnificently played by veteran Taiwanese actors Sihung Lung and Ah-Leh Gua. These are heroic and formidable people—not the obtuse and old-fashioned foreigners you'd expect in more ordinary farce. The father in the story is a retired general who fought along side Chiang Kai-Shek; and Mr. Lung projects such enormous dignity and authority in this role that it's easy to see why his son will do anything to avoid hurting him.

In fact, the relationship between the young man and his adoring parents emerges with more passion and tenderness than any of the erotic connections, offering one of this picture's many surprises. The morning after the banquet Wai-Tung literally kneels at his parental bedside and listens to their reminiscences about his babyhood in a scene so beautifully written, so flawlessly directed and acted, that it soars into the realm of pure poetry.

Thanks to its brilliant young director, and its marvelous (though previously unknown) cast, this film delivers enough of these lush and lyrical moments to make it one wedding invitation that no serious film lover can afford to pass up.

NEWSDAY, 8/4/93, Part II/p. 46, John Anderson

It's the rare film that reaffirms the medium itself as a vehicle for showing us what's right about the human condition. But the "Wedding Banquet," ostensibly a simple clash-of-cultures romance, is a subtle feast of instructive emotion. And it does what it does without becoming a messy dish of shmaltz and saccharine.

Not that there isn't mess here. There's plenty. And it's particularly galling for Wai Tung (Winston Chao), a very buttoned-down sort who, in the 10 years he's been in New York since emigrating from Taiwan, has become a successful real estate entrepreneur—a shark, actually, one who's swimming in good luck. In addition to money and property, he's got a steady, healthy, live-in relationship with Simon (Mitchell Lichtenstein), who as a bonus happens to be a physical therapist. Wai's biggest headache seems to be tenants like Wei Wei (May Chin), an illegal alien artist who pays her rent in paintings. Oh, yes, and his parents, who are browbeating him—via letter, audiocassette and numerous computer-dating applications—to marry the proper Taiwanese girl.

Wai, of course, already has the perfect mate, which is director/writer Ang Lee's point: Simon is a great cook, reprimands Wai for eating too fast and generally makes his partner's well-being his first priority. And it's Simon who proposes that Wai marry Wei Wei, thus providing her the green card she needs as well as alleviating Wai's oppressive parental problem. It's also Simon who coaches Wei Wei in Wai's habits and regimen, just in case of an INS check. And it's Simon's series of reactions, after his scheme goes awry, that is the heart of the film.

Things get out of hand rather quickly. Wai thinks a letter sent home announcing his wedding will satisfy his parents. No way. They immediately announce they're flying to New York to meet their prospective daughter-in-law and arrive laden with gifts and ceremonial wedding gear. It isn't long before Wai and Wei Wei are marinating in guilt. The parents, Mrs. and Mrs. Gao (noted Taiwanese actors Sihung Lung and Ah-Leh Gua), are deeply committed to the rituals that surround a traditional wedding; Wai and Wei Wei realize they're committed to very little beyond convenience.

A brief and clumsy civil ceremony (with Simon taking the pictures) just aggravates everyone's gloomy mood. And then, during lunch at a Chinese restaurant, Mr. Gao is greeted by old Chen (Tien Pien), his onetime army chauffeur, who owns the restaurant and offers it to them for a wedding banquet. And, like the 300 drunken guests who attend this fraudulent affair, things begin to spin wildly out of control.

"The Wedding Banquet" is rich in human foible. The raucous wedding party, the embarrassing situations Wai and Wei Wei find themselves in and the severe complications that follow are all the result of people's best intentions. Everything that happens happens because of people's efforts not to hurt the ones they love. Lee's humor relies to a great extent on errors of innocence, as well as the idiosyncratic aspects of people's lives that generally go unexamined. When they are, the result is the kind of forced introspection that's contagious: The audience may laugh, but it's nervous, too.

"The Wedding Banquet" is the stuff of the blackest comedy, and Lee knows it. The film is shot in such a bright and innocent fashion that the perversity of the story virtually bubbles beneath the surface of the well-scrubbed walls of Wai's house. The script, by Lee, Neil Peng and producer James Schamus, is rife with laughs—you have to laugh, or cry—as well as plenty to remind us of fortune's very precarious nature and the volatility of artifice.

Lee is a deft visual storyteller, too, in the way he follows the increasingly resentful Simon to the bathroom while Wai talks wedding with his parents; the way the two rid their home of "incriminating" accessories in order not to tip off the Gaos; the glow of pride on Simon's face when Mr. Gao waxes adulatory over a dinner Wei Wei is supposed to have cooked.

Through Simon and the other characters, who give very natural and guileless performances, Lee and his fellow scriptwriters impart a very simple and not so abstract concept: Love. It's been done, we know, but seldom so well.

NEWSWEEK, 8/16/93, p. 61, David Ansen

In Taiwan, where "The Wedding Banquet" has become the biggest box-office hit in history, a scene referred to as The Kiss made another kind of history: it was the first time in a Taiwanese film that two men kissed. This is old news to mainstream American audiences, who demonstrated at the time of "La Cage aux Folles" that homosexuality, in the right comedic context, can be as comfy as "I Love Lucy." The lovers in Ang Lee's Manhattan-set comedy aren't swish stereotypes—Wai-Tung (Winston Chao) is a handsome, button-down Taiwanese Yuppie, and Simon (Mitchell Lichtenstein), his long-term American lover, is a physical therapist—but their predicament may prove as popular as their French counterparts'. Anyone who has ever had to juggle the competing demands of parents and lovers is included in the fun.

Wai-Tung's unsuspecting parents are always nudging him to marry and produce a grandchild. Fed up with the pressure, Wai-Tung, at Simon's urging, marries Wei-Wei (the delightful May Chin), an aspiring artist from mainland China who desperately needs a green card. (Besides, it will provide Wai-Tung a big tax break.) But to his horror, his conservative mom and dad insist on flying from Taiwan to New York to attend the wedding—and thus begins a very sweet, funny and acutely observed culture-clash comedy. Though a few scenes are amateurish and the lighting is less than polished, "The Wedding Banquet" is such a genial, openhearted sitcom that only a confirmed grump could resist it.

SIGHT AND SOUND, 10/93, p. 56, Tony Rayns

Budding real-estate magnate Gao Wai-Tung (who has US citizenship) shares a Manhattan brownstone with his Caucasian lover Simon, a physiotherapist, but faces endless pressure from his elderly parents in Taiwan to get married. At Simon's suggestion, Wai-Tung proposes a marriage of convenience to Wei-Wei, a Shanghainese art student in need of a green card who lives (illegally) in one of his Brooklyn lofts. To Wai-Tung's horror, his parents decide to visit for the wedding. Simon agrees to pose as Wai-Tung's landlord and to move into the basement spare room where they had planned to accommodate Wei-Wei. Mr and Mrs Gao are horrified in turn by the perfunctory City Hall marriage that Wai-Tung has arranged. But a chance meeting with restaurateur Old Chen (who was Gao's chauffeur in his days as a general in the Chinese Nationalist Army) changes everything: a formal wedding banquet is arranged.

Held in a luxury hotel, the banquet is a roaring, drunken success. Afterwards, raucous friends refuse to leave the nuptial bedroom until bride and groom have got into bed together and stripped. Wei-Wei, who has long fancied Wai-Tung, takes advantage of the opportunity to seduce him.

Before long, with Mr and Mrs Gao still in residence as house guests and Simon's patience close to breaking point, Wei-Wei tells Wai-Tung that she is pregnant. Simon has a furious row with Wai-Tung in front of the others when he hears the news. Later that day, Mr Gao has a mild stroke. Wai-Tung rushes to the hospital, where he finally comes out to his mother—who is incredulous and baffled, but makes him promise never to tell his father that he is gay.

Wei-Wei determines to abort her child, but changes her mind at the last moment. Meanwhile Mr Gao tells Simon that he knows he is Wai-Tung's lover and tacitly approves—but says that his wife and Wai-Tung must never know. Simon agrees to be "one of the fathers" of Wei-Wei's child and is reconciled with Wai-Tung. Seeing Mr and Mrs Gao off at the airport, Wai-Tung presents them with an album of wedding photos—which includes one picture of himself with Simon. Flanked by Simon and Wei-Wei, he watches his parents leave.

Touchingly dedicated to the real-life couple whose lives inspired the story, *The Wedding Banquet* marks a huge advance on Taiwanese-American director Ang Lee's first feature, *Pushing Hands*. That film was sprung on the tensions between a Caucasian wife and her Chinese father-in-law, but conspicuously failed to address the mystery of what had attracted the woman to a Chinese husband in the first place. This film, by contrast, has all its gender questions, racial questions and sexual politics down pat. At the same time, even though it never exactly achieves a Renoiresque breadth of spirit, it is agreeably even-handed in its sensitivity to differing points of view—thanks to which it manages several degrees of emotional complexity and is sometimes genuinely affecting: the hospital corridor scene in which the son belatedly comes out to his uncomprehending mother, for instance, is the best written and played in the whole film. And, as that scene suggests, *The Wedding Banquet* is notable for being the first Chinese movie to problematise reactions to a gay relationship rather than the relationship itself.

But the film has larger targets in its sights than Chinese homophobia. The director himself puts in a brief (and, it must be said, rather awkward) cameo appearance in the central wedding banquet scene to comment that the ribald and increasingly hysterical goings-on reflect "5,000 years of sexual repression". His point, of course, is that everyone involved in the fake marriage and its repercussions is a victim of an endemic Chinese inability to deal with sexual realities. This is not a new perception. It was theorised with great sophistication with the Shanghainese-Hong Kong writer Sun Lung-Kee in his influential 1983 book *The Deep Structure of Chinese Society*, and it has already underpinned plenty of other Chinese movies—even some made in Mainland China, like Huang Jianzhong's *A Girl of Good Family (Liangjia Funu*, 1985) and *Questions for the Living (Yi ge Sizhe dui Shengzhe de Fangwen*, 1987). And issues like sexual fidelity, paternity and the peer-group pressure to procreate in Chinese communities were given a fairly thorough airing in Wayne Wang's *Eat a Bowl of Tea*.

Still, Ang Lee articulates the point credibly enough, partly because he presents the central gay 'marriage' so straightforwardly and partly because he is careful to relate the sexual questions to larger questions in the lives of characters with loaded personal histories. Mr Gao, we learn, is not just another Chinese patriarch set on siring a dynastic clan but a former KMT general who saw his family massacred in the Civil War of the late 40s; hence his urgent desire to have a grandchild before his impending death. Similarly, Wei-Wei is under great pressure to stay and succeed in the States because her family, stuck in Shanghai, needs a breadwinner overseas. Thanks to this kind of back-story, the fake marriage could be taken as a ruinous parody of the reunification of China and Taiwan.

Political satire, though, is the least of the film's concerns. Framed as fast-paced situation comedy, the film is so determined not to rupture its own feel-good effect that it cheerfully erases the plot's largest unresolved problem with the climactic revelation that Mr Gao understands and doesn't disapprove of his son's relationship with Simon. This is actually the script's only flagrant implausibility, but it's enough to make the film a wish-fulfillment fantasy on a par with the equally crowd-pleasing *Strictly Ballroom*. As such, *The Wedding Banquet* clearly merits its international success. Lee directs with great brio, making smart use of locations and settings, and his understated closing images suggest a grasp of emotional reticence that will stand him in good stead in future. The performances are variable (newcomer Winston Chao, in particular, is far stronger acting in Chinese than in English), but no lapse is serious enough to damage the overall charm. The print under review—clearly made from an inter-negative—has very poor colour-grading that does no justice to Jong Lin's original cinematography; and there is a problem with the legibility of some subtitles.

VILLAGE VOICE, 8/10/93, p. 49, Georgia Brown

One not so incidental function of movies is to socialize. To extend the cultural horizons, instill empathy for strangers, outcasts, and underdogs. Ang Lee's gentle, very appealing comedy of errors, *The Wedding Banquet*, could have some of these effects. It has such a warm and fuzzy countenance, it jumps up and licks your face. If this movie doesn't become hugely popular and thereafter increase tolerance for gays, Asians, and emigrants, as well as reconcile the generations, it will make you glow just imagining that it might.

Producer James Schamus, who is also one of *Wedding Banquet*'s writers (with Lee and Neil Peng), says they, or he, aimed for a comedy of remarriage *Philadelphia Story*. Forgive me if I propose *Three's Company*.

But let's not speak of Jack, Janet, and Chrissy, let me introduce you to Wei Wei, Wai Tung, and Simon. Wai Tung (Winston Chao) and Simon (Mitchell Lichtenstein, son of Roy) are the same sex pair, two gays sharing a cheerful house in the Village. A manager of real estate, Wai Tung is straitlaced, a bit prim; he wears ties. The simpler Simon wears the earring, cooks, and works as a physical therapist. Wei Wei (May Chin) becomes the beard—but just for Wai Tung's parents back in Taiwan. Since the parents are constantly urging their only son to marry, Simon suggests Wai marry his tenant—a starving painter from the mainland, harassed by immigration authorities and avid for a green card. First, the winsome Wei Wei (she looks like a cheered-up Isabelle Adjani) moves in just to fool Immigration, but when Ma (Ah-Leh Gua) and Pa Gao (Sihung Lung) announce they're arriving for the wedding, she has to stay on. Once arrived, the old folks up the ante: Not only do they want a traditional wedding banquet, but, since Wai is the last of his father's line, they want a grandchild.

One charm of *Wedding Banquet* is that it isn't *wholly* predictable. You keep wondering what way out the film will take, and while many of the choices are formulaic, enough are mild surprises. Whereas there must have been temptations to descend into darker regions, they are firmly resisted. Some gays may resent the lightness, the sweetness, the plugs for family values.

Besides sharing Berlin's Golden Bear this year, *Wedding Banquet* has already become a huge hit in Taiwan, Ang Lee's home until his twenties. Over there audiences have discovered an allegory in the marriage: Taiwan weds the Mainland, via America's democracy. Does the father, a former Nationalist general, finally give up the old fight, surrendering to a new order? Anyway, the film marks the first time two men kiss on the large Taiwanese screen.

Take Granny and the kids.

Also reviewed in:
CHICAGO TRIBUNE, 8/27/93, Friday/p. C, Johanna Steinmetz
NEW REPUBLIC, 8/16/93, p. 25, Stanley Kauffmann
NEW YORK TIMES, 8/4/93, p. C18, Stephen Holden
VARIETY, 3/1/93, p. 58, Derek Elley
WASHINGTON POST, 8/27/93, p. C8, Megan Rosenfeld
WASHINGTON POST, 8/27/93, Weekend/p. 36, Joe Brown

WEEKEND AT BERNIE'S II

A TriStar Pictures and Victor Drai Productions release of an Artimm production. *Executive Producer:* Angiolo Stella. *Producer:* Victor Drai and Joseph Perez. *Director:* Robert Klane. *Screenplay (based on characters created by):* Robert Klane. *Director of Photography:* Edward Morey, III. *Editor:* Peck Prior. *Music:* Peter Wolf. *Music Editor:* Thomas Kramer. *Choreographer:* Adam Shankman. *Sound:* Walter Hoylman and (music) Paul Ericksen. *Sound*

Editor: Brad Blake.   *Casting:* Jason LaPadura.   *Production Designer:* Michael Bolton.   *Art Director:* Eric Fraser.   *Set Decorator:* Scott Jacobson.   *Set Dresser:* John A. Lasalandra and Christopher Lutz.   *Special Effects:* Ken Speed.   *Costumes:* Fionn.   *Make-up:* Lon Bentley.
Running time: 89 minutes.   *MPAA Rating:* PG.

CAST: Andrew McCarthy (Larry);   Jonathan Silverman (Richard);   Terry Kiser (Bernie);   Troy Beyer (Claudia);   Barry Bostwick (Hummel);   Tom Wright (Charles);   Steve James (Henry);   Novella Nelson (Mobu);   Phil Coccioletti (Cartel Man #1);   Gary Dourdan (Cartel Man #2);   James Lally (Morgue Attendant);   Michael Rogers (Island Cop);   Stack Pierce (Claudia's Dad);   Constance Shulman (Tour Operator);   Jennie Moreau (Brenda);   Curt Karibalis (Hotel Manager);   Peewee Piemonte (Arnold);   Christine Nerfin (Hotel Hostess);   John Hodge (Band Member);   Samantha Phillips (Pretty Young Thing);   Rudy Warner (Jitney Driver);   Caitlin Klane (Little Girl with Radio);   David Lipman (Movie Patron);   Lyle Howry (New York Cop #1);   Ben Lemon (New York Cop #2);   Filippo Cassinelli (New York Cop #3);   Winston de Lugo (Mr. Jennings);   J.C. Scott-Klane (Secretary);   Cedric Bones (Bank Executive);   William Lucas (Store Clerk);   Lance Durham (Hotel Beach Employee);   Hillel E. Silverman (Maitre'd);   Matt Locker (Porter);   Ernestine Elena Vanterpool (Woman in Store);   Robert R. Willis (EMS Worker).

LOS ANGELES TIMES, 7/12/93, Calendar/p. 3, Kevin Thomas

"Weekend at Bernie's II" picks up the day after the 1989 original left off—and that's just the first of the problems with this misfired comedy, the kind of movie that give sequels a bad name. Its filmmakers seem to assume that everyone has seen the first film and, four years later, remember its every detail. Without a recap, even those of us who saw it are likely to be confused and stay in that state, since the sequel is as incoherent as it is uninspired.

In any event, Bernie (Terry Kiser) was the top guy at a Manhattan insurance company where laid-back Larry (Andrew McCarthy) and uptight Richard (Jonathan Silverman) are decidedly junior executives. When Richard discovers that $2 million has been paid to a dead man, he and Larry naively believe the discovery will make their careers. Then Bernie winds up a corpse during a Labor Day weekend house party the two attend at his pad in the Hamptons, and plot twists make it imperative that Larry and Richard keep up the pretense that Bernie is still alive. So much for the first film.

The second finds Larry and Richard fired because they are believed to have the missing $2 million in their possession. With an insurance investigator (Barry Bostwick) on their tail, they head for St. Thomas in the Virgin Islands, where Bernie has a bank account and where, sure enough, Bernie's corpse turns up. What ensues is an adventure too lackluster to warrant further description.

Since Robert Klane wrote the first film as well as the sequel (which he also directed, far from impressively) it's difficult to understand why "Weekend at Bernie's II" (rated PG-13 for brief nudity and mild language) is so relentlessly awful. Not even Terry Kiser's wandering corpse is funny this time around.

NEW YORK POST, 7/13/93, p. 25, Michael Medved

"Bernie's Back ... And He's Still Dead!!!" proclaim the ads for "Weekend at Bernie's II," but in fact they're only half right.

Bernie (Terry Kiser), the favorite comatose cutup described by TriStar Pictures as "everybody's favorite corpse," is most certainly back, but this time he's not exactly dead.

Near the beginning of this appallingly ill-conceived sequel, Bernie's been brought back to a strange zombie-like half-life through a voodoo ceremony performed with a pigeon, a boom box, goat's urine and 117 lighted candles in the filthy restroom of a Times Square porno house. This inspiring resurrection is the handiwork of a pair of shuffling jive-talking hoods (Tom Wright and Steve James) who are under the command of mob-connected black magic priestess, and who here create two of the most offensively racist caricatures of recent years. (Sample dialogue: "C'est la vie!" "Say what?!")

In his newly re-animated state, Bernie proceeds to demonstrate amazing versatility for a dead guy. He dances in a conga line, scuba dives, parasails, and even participates in the only love scene in the movie, spending a moonlit night on the beach with a whining New York princess named Brenda (another annoying stereotype, played by Jennie Moreau). The morning after her date with the dead she expresses delight with her evening's companion: He's the only guy she ever went out with who didn't get fresh with her.

Of course, there's nothing fresh about Bernie, or any other aspect of this moldering corpse of a movie. The original "Weekend at Bernie's," a modest success that grossed $35 million in the summer of '89, is hardly one of the movies that cried out for a sequel. As breezily directed by the capable Ted Kotcheff, the picture appeared to have exhausted the world's supply of a dead guy jokes, but then the cult popularity of the movie in its home-video version encouraged screenwriter Robert Klane to try crafting a follow-up even if it meant scraping the very bottom of the body bag to do it.

As with his original "Bernie" script, Klane ("Where's Poppa?", "National Lampoon's European Vacation") centers the action on Johnathan Silverman and Andrew McCarthy, two fast-talking, slow-thinking yuppies with stymied careers at a big New York insurance company. This time, they're looking for $2 million that Bernie, their former boss, embezzled from the company and stashed in a Virgin Islands safe-deposit box. In order to get access to the loot they have to stuff the grinning corpse into a suitcase and take him along to the island paradise where they'll manipulate him like a flesh puppet when they go to the bank.

It's a bad script to be sure, but Klane's direction—in his feature-film debut—is even worse; flat, clumsy, sluggishly paced, jaggedly edited, with an abundance of poorly lit, washed-out, fuzzily focused scenes. You end up feeling sorry for McCarthy and Silverman—not their characters but the hard-working actors themselves who manage to perform like game professionals even amidst all the jokes about sex with corpses, goats and chickens. Surely these two talented stars deserve a better showcase for their manic talents.

The movie succeeds on only one level: it's an occasionally intriguing infomercial promoting exotic vacations in the U.S. Virgin Islands. Watching this picture you'll naturally long to splash in emerald green water, or to lounge on white sandy beaches, or to be anywhere else other than inside a theater watching this cinematic sludge that uniquely deserves the designation "dead on arrival."

NEWSDAY, 7/10/93, Part II/p. 21, John Anderson

The best performance in "Weekend at Bernie's II" is by Terry Kiser, who plays Bernie, who's dead. The best news for the makers of "Weekend at Bernie's II" is that it's 100 degrees out and people might be so desperate for air-conditioning they'll be willing to do anything.

If Kenneth Branagh had done this film, it might have been called "Dead Again II," but no, he didn't. The accused here is Robert Klane, who wrote the original "Weekend at Bernie's" and now adds directing to his list of crimes. He doesn't stretch much: Bernie Lomax, corporate wiseguy, is still dead. Larry and Richie (Andrew McCarthy and Jonathan Silverman), are still a couple of schmoes. The money Bernie embezzled in the first film is still missing. And the amount of physical abuse a corpse can withstand remains a pointless, tasteless, but to some minds, obviously, a humorous question.

"Bernie's II" is one movie where it probably helps a lot to have seen the original. The sequel begins with Larry and Richie, who are expecting to be rewarded by their company for discovering Bernie's chicanery, accused by Hummel (Barry Bostwick), the corporate chief of internal affairs, of having had a hand in Bernie's murder. They're not arrested, but they're fired, and then they're tailed by Hummel, who is sure they're going to lead him to the missing $2 million.

At the same time, a voodoo priestess on St. Thomas (which is a bit of spiritual and geographic gerrymandering) casts a spell on two stooges, Charles (Tom Wright) and Henry (Steve James), whom she sends to New York to steal Bernie from the morgue, raise him from the dead, and then follow him to the money. Charles and Henry lose the chicken they need to perform the resurrection rite, so they use a city street pigeon, and this causes a glitch: Bernie only gets up and dances when there's island music playing. When the music stops he falls on his face, which he does with nauseating frequency, but is the kind of thing "WAB" is all about.

All the principals wind up back in St. Thomas, which provides for a lot of beautiful scenery and gives the director an excuse to show a lot of young women in bathing suits. Bernie gets punched, bitten by a shark, dropped from a parasail, falls out of a car, and joins a conga line at the hotel bar, where he sweeps a woman off her feet. But there's not a lot of story, which results in numerous digressions that are meant to fill time, and are only occasionally even remotely funny. McCarthy seems to be doing a Huntz Hall impersonation, Silverman is innocuous, and Bostwick is wasting his talent. Wright is really the most engaging actor here, and has the best line. As Charles, he eyes the dancing Bernie and muses, "I wonder if this will work on Elvis?"

SIGHT AND SOUND, 12/94, p. 55, Tom Tunney

The body of murdered insurance executive Bernie Lomax finally makes it to the New York City morgue. However, the $2 million Bernie stole from his company is still missing. Lomax's employees Larry and Richard identify the corpse and Larry obtains his effects, which include a deposit box key for a bank in the US Virgin Islands. Investigator Hummel suspects Larry and Richard of complicity in the fraud, has them fired, then tails them in a bid to track down the money.

Meanwhile, in the Virgin Islands, voodoo priestess Mobu orders small-time crooks Charles and Henry to raise Bernie from the dead using voodoo magic and then follow him to the missing loot. Charles and Henry steal the corpse, but when the chicken they need for the ritual escapes, they substitute a pigeon. This has the effect of animating Bernie only when loud music is playing. Charles and Henry lose the body on the subway; it is then returned to the morgue just in time for Larry and Richard to steal it. Arriving in the Virgin Islands with Bernie packed into a suitcase, the duo store him in the fridge of their holiday apartment.

On the beach, Larry strikes up friendship with local girl Claudia. That night, music from a party animates Bernie, who dances in a conga line. Larry and Richard eventually arrive at the bank with Bernie, and gain access to the deposit box, which is empty save for a treasure map. Larry gives the map to Claudia; she passes it on to her father, who is in league with Hummel.

Captured by Mobu, Larry and Richard are given a poison which will kill them by midnight if they don't give her the map. After sundry disasters, the duo rig up Bernie with a personal stereo to keep him animated underwater. Larry, Richard and Claudia don skin-diving gear and follow him into the sea where he retrieves the money. On dry land, Larry harnesses up Bernie to pull a cart, which goes out of control and crashes into Mobu. The police and Hummel arrive and the loot is returned to them. The blood of a virgin is needed to save the ailing Richard; Larry duly obliges.

Aboard their new pleasure cruiser, Larry tells Richard that the missing loot was really $3 million and that they can now share the other $1 million. Bernie, meanwhile dances in a carnival parade, which also includes Charles and Henry, now transformed by voodoo magic into animal form.

An annoying sense of time warp afflicts this desperately contrived farce, made three years on from the original 1989 movie. The two stars look visibly older, but in terms of the narrative, those three years don't exist: their characters are still firmly locked into a materialistic late 80s world where a supposedly trendy job in finance means wearing coloured braces; where a vacation means eager, drooling smiles and a beach full of bikini-clad babes ("Oh my God, look at the tits on that one!" says Larry thoughtfully) and where vulgarity, stupidity and greed are presented as positive virtues.

As the relentlessly foolish heroes, McCarthy and Silverman are even more unappealing than in the first film, but the fact that they are both now far too old for the roles (the 30-year-old McCarthy as a virgin?) does add a certain flavourful absurdity to the slapstick low jinks the plot forces on them. Bringing Bernie back to life through the power of voodoo is an idea that has real comic possibilities: certainly many more than the first film's one-joke scenario of the duo having to laboriously pretend that his corpse is still alive. A more creative scenario might have seen Bernie shuddering back to life as a putrefying, Romero-style zombie bent on revenge on our two heroes. Unfortunately writer-director Robert Klane (who also scripted the first film) shies away from such ghoulish fun in favour of more beach frolics: Bernie becomes tangled up in a para-ascending cable and gets dragged into the air, is dropped and knocked about a great deal, dances a conga and so on.

However, as in the first film, Bernie's fixed expression is no substitute for a personality and since he still hasn't got one, the plot becomes one interminable round of dropping him, losing him and making him jive up into life again every time there's a burst of loud music. The scene in which Charles and Henry resurrect him is the nearest the movie comes to an inspired moment. The burning candles mounted on their ghetto-blaster make for a genuinely comical bit of culture clash and the sequence set in a porn cinema—a man is watching the movie with a chicken, but it's not *their* missing chicken—is a casual spot of lunacy almost worthy of the Marx Brothers.

However, the villains Charles and Henry are sadly underused and whenever the story returns to Larry and Richard and their relentlessly juvenile antics, rigor mortis sets in. The last thing a good comedy needs is a logical plot, but it's the mark of a bad one that a bored audience will while its way through the running time picking holes in the slapdash scenario on offer. "Bernie's back ... and he's still dead!" promises the poster. Indeed he is.

Also reviewed in:
NEW YORK TIMES, 7/10/93, p. 15, Stephen Holden
VARIETY, 2/15/93, p. 83, David Rooney
WASHINGTON POST, 7/10/93, p. D3, Hal Hinson

WELCOME MR. MARSHALL

Director: Luis Garcia Berlanga.   *Screenplay (Spanish with English subtitles):* Juan Antonio Bardem, Luis Garcia Berlanga, and Miguel Mihura.   *Director of Photography:* Manuel Berenguer. *Editor:* Pepita Orduna.   *Music:* Jesús Garcia Leoz.   *Running time:* 78 minutes. *MPAA Rating:* Not Rated.

CAST: Lolita Vargas (Carmen Vargas);   Manolo Morán (Manolo);   José Isbert (The Mayor); Alberto Romea (Don Luis);   Elvira Quintilla (Eloisa);   Luis Pérez de Leon (Don Cosme); Felix Fernández (Don Simon);   Fernando Rey (Narrator).

VILLAGE VOICE, 11/23/93, p. 64, Georgia Brown

Hollywood tyranny is nothing new. Despite heavy censorship under Franco, for example, American films were always welcome and from the '50s on dominated the Spanish box office. Most were innocuous enough, and, in the compulsory dubbing of foreign pictures, dialogue could be tailored to order. It's telling that two '50s classics, *Bienvenido, Mr. Marshall* ('52) and *Calle Mayor* ('56)—both playing in the Public's current "Spanish Eyes" series—make pointed reference to the influence of American movies on tender Spanish psyches. (Flash forward to the village showing of *Frankenstein* in Erice's *The Spirit of the Beehive*.) To savvy, oppositional directors—like Berlanga and Bardem below—American myth-mongering reinforced the Franco regime's avoidance of harsh fact.

A delightful and rich satire, *Bienvenido, Mr. Marshall* is an early film by Luis Garcia Berlanga (director) and Juan Antonio Bardem (cowriter), both of whom went on to become two of Spain's premier filmmakers. The Mr. Marshall being welcomed in the title was George with his Plan; although Spain never received any Marshall Plan money, it did get aid in return for U.S. air bases. (The movie's cheerful irreverence caused Edward. G. Robinson, a judge at Cannes, to demand that it be withdrawn. It showed, though one scene at the end was cut: of an American flag floating downstream.)

One day the dusty hamlet of Villar del Rio gets official word that the American benefactors are coming and they'd better spruce up. Just who are these Americans? Coincidentally, a western has just shown at the town cinema, leading the mayor (the adorable José Isbert) to begin practicing his draw. The prim school teacher conducts a civics lesson that the priest finds too rosy: He wants everyone to know that America also harbors millions of Protestants, Jews, Indians, Chinese, Negroes, and other mongrels. The town's dusted-off aristocrat recalls the fate met by his ancestors in the stew pots of savages. But after the populace lines up to record their fondest wishes, spruce up they do, in a way learned from watching movies: they turn the town into a set, a studio lot, putting up false fronts, flags, and flowers, and renting costumes for big and small. Drab, unromantic poverty transforms itself into a quaint Andalusian picture book, all, it turns out, for *nada*.

Similarly, the starry-eyed spinster in Bardem's harrowing *Calle Mayor (Main Street)* may be enamored of romantic American movies, but her rude awakening comes locally. (Literally out of Hollywood, she's played by the American Betsy Blair who'd just appeared in *Marty*.) *Calle Mayor* takes place in a provincial city where everyone knows everyone and the main recreation is parading up and down Main Street greeting one's neighbors. Bored young men hang out playing pool and plotting mischief. (Here the capital, Madrid, is presented as escape—the only place one might live pressure-free.) The guys persuade Juan (José Suarez) to woo Isabel (Blair), something of a town freak in that she's 35 and unmarried. The bet is that she'll accept the first man to ask her. Juan goes along but finds himself feeling for the intense, virginal Isabel. On a date he suggests going to the movies: "There's an American film with sparkling kitchens." Can a proposal be far behind? Very far, in fact.

Like the Italian neorealists, Bardem and Berlanga were all for quitting the studios and taking to the streets, bringing cinema down to where people really lived. Those sparkling kitchens and wish lists for Mr. Marshall were acknowledgments of how American movies fed Francoist dreams.

Also reviewed in:
NEW YORK TIMES, 11/19/93, p. C18, Stephen Holden

WE'RE BACK! A DINOSAUR'S STORY

A Universal Pictures release of a Steven Spielberg presentation of an Amblin Entertainment production. *Executive Producer:* Steven Spielberg, Frank Marshall, and Kathleen Kennedy. *Producer:* Stephen Hickner. *Director:* Dick Zondag, Ralph Zondag, Phil Nibbelink, and Simon Wells. *Screenplay:* John Patrick Shanley. *Based on the book "Roll Back the Rock" by:* Hudson Talbott. *Animators:* Jeffrey J. Varab, Bibo Bergeron, Kristof Serrand, Rob Stevenhagen, Thierry Schiel, Sahin Ersoz, and Borge Ring. *Storyboard:* Tom Humber and Darek Gogol. *Editor:* Sim Evan-Jones and Nick Fletcher. *Music:* James Horner. *Music Editor:* Jim Henrikson. *Choreographer:* Smith Wordes. *Sound:* Albert Romero and (music) Shawn Murphy. *Sound Editor:* Campbell Askew. *Art Director:* Neil Ross. *Character Design:* Carlos Grangel. *Layout:* Peter Moehrle. *Backgrounds:* Colin Stimpson. *Special Effects:* Steve Moore. *Color Separation:* Annie Elvin. *Running time:* 78 minutes. *MPAA Rating:* G.

VOICES: John Goodman (Rex); Blaze Berdahl (Buster); Rhea Perlman (Mother Bird); Jay Leno (Vorb); Rene LeVant (Woog); Felicity Kendal (Elsa); Charles Fleischer (Dweeb); Walter Cronkite (Captain NewEyes); Joey Shea (Louie); Julia Child (Dr. Bleeb); Kenneth Mars (Professor ScrewEyes); Yeardley Smith (Cecilia); Martin Short (Stubbs The Clown); Larry King (Himself).

LOS ANGELES TIMES, 11/24/93, Calendar/p. 6, Charles Solomon

Unlike the ones in "Jurassic Park," the dinosaurs in Steven Spielberg's animated feature, "We're Back! A Dinosaur's Story" aren't scary at all: The mighty beasts have been softened and Barney-ized until they resemble giant plush toys.

Based on a children's book by Hudson Talbot, the film follows the misadventures of four prehistoric monsters who have their IQs raised by Captain NewEyes (voice by Walter Cronkite), a time-traveling scientist from the future. The Captain's Wish Radio enables him to hear children's wishes; modern kids want to see live dinosaurs, so he arranges it. He dumps Rex (John

Goodman), a tyrannosaurus, Woog (Rene LeVant), a triceratops; Elsa (Felicity Kendal), a pterodactyl: and Dweeb (Charles Fleischer), a hadrosaurus, in New York City and tells them to find Dr. Bleeb (Julia Child) at the Museum of Natural History. En route, they blunder into Macy's Thanksgiving Parade: Pandemonium erupts when the spectators realize the dinosaurs aren't mechanical.

John Patrick Shanley's screenplay complicates the straightforward story by having the dinosaurs take up with Louie, a hip runaway boy, and Cecilia, a poor little rich girl, Louie provokes a crisis by joining the circus of Professor ScrewEyes, Captain NewEyes' evil brother (Kenneth Mars), which exhibits people's worst fears, but things end happily with Louie and Cecilia becoming friends and making up with their parents.

"We're Back!" contains some polished animation, but it's weakest in the areas where the recent Disney features have been strongest: story and character. The directors are so busy trying to tie up the plot, they don't tell the audience who these characters are. The dinosaurs don't interact or express any delight in their new mental abilities, nor is there a sense of a bond developing between them and the children. When Beast offered to sacrifice himself for Belle, audiences were moved because they knew he was motivated by love. When the dinosaurs sacrifice their IQs to save Louie and Cecilia from the Professor, the audience doesn't know what they're giving up or why.

The film offers lots of splashy effects, including a computer-assisted flight through Manhattan and an elaborate motorcycle chase, although the stolid pacing keeps these sequences from being as much fun as they should be. Rex's hip-hop production number stops the story in its tracks for several minutes.

Spielberg's Amblimation Studio obviously boasts some talented artists, but they're not ready to compete with the crew that made "Beauty and Beast" and "Aladdin." The needlessly convoluted story and even pacing reduce a film that should thunder like a tyrannosaurus to one that whimpers like a kitten.

NEW YORK POST, 11/24/93, p. 35, Thelma Adams

Could Steven Spielberg be overcompensating for criticism that "Jurassic Park" was too violent for kids? With the cartoon "We're Back! A Dinosaur's Story," the director presents Technicolor dinos so darn nice they cloy and irritate.

Viewers beware! As Weird Al Yankovic once said, "Dinosaurs aren't your friends. They'll eat you."

But in Spielberg's dino stepchild, the prehistoric beasts lumber through modern Manhattan like animated children's vitamins: they're sweet and they're good for you.

What transformed them? As a golf-playing, Bing Crosby-imitating T. Rex (John Goodman) explains to a chirpy baby bird, he "started off stupid and violent ... I was a real animal and I was hungry all the time."

Then he and a multicultural dino assortment ate some magic cereal and became the gentle giants they remain for most of the movie.

They time-travel to modern-day Manhattan to befriend all the children who wish for dinosaurs.

The beasts hook up with Louie and Cecilia. Both kids are friendless: Louie (Joey Shea) is a New York street urchin, a rough, tough creampuff; and Cecilia (Yeardley Smith) is a poor little rich girl.

Says Cecilia of her absentee parents: "Father's very business and mother's very social." Sounds very Hollywood.

Cecilia cries; Louie protects. She flirts; he pulls back. They seem retro.

Yeardley Smith is also the voice of Lisa on "The Simpsons," a sharper and more together girl than the drippy Cecilia.

On the way through predictable misadventures to the inevitable happy ending, even the animated figures seem dated in the age of "Beavis and Butt-head," and "The Ren and Stimpy Show." This movie makes "Aladdin" look hip.

Spielberg's Amblimation, which also did "An American Tail: Fievel Goes West," put this calculated cartoon together. The directing team included Dick Zondag, Ralph Zondag, Phil Nibbelink, and Simon Wells. John Patrick Shanley wrote the screenplay, which follows in the footsteps of his fantastical dud "Joe Versus the Volcano" rather than his Academy Award-winning script "Moonstruck." Hudson Talbot wrote the book on which it was based.

The few kids seated in the audience didn't laugh—the only giggles I heard were on screen. The children were, however, quiet, which could be taken as a sign that "We're Back! A Dinosaur's Story" held their attention better than mine. For adults, the relentlessly perky "We're Back! A Dinosaur's Story" is scarier than "Jurassic Park."

NEWSDAY, 11/24/93, Part II/p. 62, John Anderson

No, Steven Spielberg couldn't resist sliding in a plug for "Jurassic Park," but "We're Back: A Dinosaur's Story" is still a treat for—dare we say it—the whole family.

Characters make the movie, and in animation the voices often make the characters. And much of the strength of "We're Back"—an adventure-comedy about time travel, friendship, and the eternal conflict between good and evil—lies in its vocalizations.

There's the always-avuncular Walter Cronkite as Captain NewEyes, a time-traveling genius whose Brain Grain cereal transforms a quartet of prehistoric predators into Barney wannabes. Julia Child is Dr. Bleeb of the Museum of Natural History. And Kenneth Mars is Professor ScrewEyes, the captain's mad and malevolent brother, who'll entrap the four. into joining his Eccentric Circus, a foul celebration of fear.

Flashing from the present to the past and back again, the story centers on the Tyrannosaurus rex voice of John Goodman), as well as Elsa, a pterodactyl-cum-Tallulah (Felicity Kendal), a triceratops named Woog (Rene LeVant) and the hadrosaurus Dweeb (Charles Fleischer). Sent from the past by NewEyes, who wants them to answer the wishes of dinosaur-loving 20th-Century children, they meet Louie, a runaway who's a combination Leo Gorcey/Scott Baio (Joey Shea) and Cecilia, an unhappy young debutante who sounds a lot like Lisa Simpson (and should, since Yeardley Smith does both voices). Together, they explore New York—the film has a wide, sweeping style that gives the city great breadth—and become the victims of ScrewEyes' Brain Drain tablets.

There are lessons, of course, some of which seem a little beyond the ken of smaller children. When the dinosaurs lose their ferocity, for instance, they also lose their marketability. There's also a shot during the Macy's Day Parade, in which the dinosaurs and floats are juxtaposed to great effect, of that movie marquee advertising "Jurassic Park." But Spielberg really couldn't avoid that, could he?

Also reviewed in:
NEW YORK TIMES, 11/24/93, p. C20, Janet Maslin
VARIETY, 12/6/93, p. 35, Daniel M. Kimmel
WASHINGTON POST, 11/26/93, Weekend/p. 57, Desson Howe

WHAT'S EATING GILBERT GRAPE

A Paramount Pictures release. *Executive Producer:* Lasse Hallström and Alan C. Blomquist. *Producer:* Meir Teper, Bertil Ohlsson, and David Matalon. *Director:* Lasse Hallström. *Screenplay (based on his novel):* Peter Hedges. *Director of Photography:* Sven Nykvist. *Editor:* Andrew Mondshein. *Music:* Alan Parker and Björn Isfält. *Music Editor:* Joseph S. DeBeasi. *Sound:* David Brownlow and (music) Chris Dibble. *Sound Editor:* Michael Kirchberger. *Casting:* Gail Levin and Jo Edna Boldin. *Production Designer:* Bernt Capra. *Art Director:* John Myhre. *Set Decorator:* Gretchen Rau. *Set Dresser:* Kim Larson, Sean Patrick Brennan, Elizabeth McNamara, Ross Dreyer, and Bongo Don Stroud. *Special Effects:* Howard Jensen. *Costumes:* Reneé Ehrlich Kalfus. *Make-up:* Patty York. *Stunt Coordinator:* Rusty McClennon. *Running time:* 117 minutes. *MPAA Rating:* PG-13.

CAST: Johnny Depp (Gilbert Grape); Leonardo DiCaprio (Arnie Grape); Juliette Lewis (Becky); Mary Steenburgen (Betty Carver); Darlene Cates (Momma); Laura Harrington (Amy

Grape); Mary Kate Schellhardt (Ellen Grape); Kevin Tighe (Mr. Carver); John C. Reilly (Tucker Van Dyke); Crispin Glover (Bobby McBurney); Penelope Branning (Becky's Grandma); Tim Green (Mr. Lamson); Susan Loughran (Mrs. Lamson); Robert B. Hedges (Minister); Mark Jordan (Todd Carver); Cameron Finley (Doug Carver); Brady Coleman (Sheriff Farrel); Tim Simek (Deputy); Nicholas Stojanovich (Boy #1); Libby Villari (Waitress); Kay Bower (Police Secretary); Joe Stevens (Burger Barn Manager); Mona Lee Fultz (Bakery Worker); George Haynes (Dave); Daniel Gullahorn (Boy #2).

LOS ANGELES TIMES, 12/17/93, Calendar/p. 1, Peter Rainer

The Grape family is like an entire week of guests on "Donahue" or "Oprah." They're dysfunctionally functional—by all rights their lives should be disastrous but somehow everything comes out OK. Gilbert (Johnny Depp), the brother who holds it all together for his brood in "What's Eating Gilbert Grape," has a gift for sanity. With so much nuttiness crowding in on him, he holds a steady course. He's the family savior who neglects to save himself.

The Grapes live together in a ramshackle homestead on an isolated patch of acreage in small-town Iowa. Their heartbreak began years ago with the suicide of Gilbert's father. Younger brother Arnie (Leonardo DiCaprio), soon to turn 18, is mentally disabled, possibly autistic and wasn't expected to last beyond his 10th birthday. His mother (Darlene Cates, who was, in fact, discovered on a TV talk show about overweight women) tips the scale at about 500 pounds and camps out in the living room while her meals are wheeled in to her. She hasn't left the house in seven years. Gilbert's two sisters (Laura Harrington and Mary Kate Schellhardt) moan and grouse about their lives.

Quirky, heartfelt whimsy seems to be making a comeback in the movies. "Benny & Joon" was a surprise hit earlier this year and "What's Eating Gilbert Grape" could almost serve as that film's companion piece. Movies like these convert despair and mental illness into folksy uplifting anecdotes. We will reach the Promised Land if only we can "accept" ourselves and our families. It's all so nursery-school simple. "Gilbert Grape" and "Benny & Joon" serve as lullabies for the dysfunctional family generation—that's the core of their popularity.

Gilbert is the saint of the story—he's like Aidan Quinn in "Benny & Joon," who devoted himself to his disturbed sister's welfare, and he's a bit like Jimmy Stewart in "It's a Wonderful Life," too. He's a do-gooder whose beneficence undercuts his own happiness. Director Lasse Hallstrom gives Johnny Depp so many living big-screen close-ups that he seems to be enshrining the actor—can the Nobel Peace Prize be very far away?

Gilbert needs an angel to match his own angelic self and he gets her with Becky (Juliette Lewis), an itinerant free spirit who camps on the outskirts of town in her grandmother's trailer. Becky is even a good *physical* matchup for Gilbert—her punkish spirituality matches his. (Depp at times looks like a pre-Raphaelite Fabian Forte.)

Becky isn't fazed by the Grapes. She gets Arnie to overcome his fear of swimming; when she's finally introduced to Momma Grape, she's the model of tact and caring.

Hallstrom and screenwriter Peter Hedges, adapting his novel, people the small Iowa town with a crotchety assortment of harmless eccentrics. Their small-town "normality" is the dippiest thing about them. The Grapes' turn out to be—surprise, surprise—among the most levelheaded in town. That's the way it usually is with these whimsical fables: "Normal" loses out to nutty every time.

Betty (Mary Steenburgen), a love-starved housewife, lusts after Gilbert while her husband (Kevin Tighe) is out of the house; she keeps calling into the grocery store where Gilbert works for some personal delivery service. Gilbert's best friend Tucker (John C. Reilly) dreams of opening up a local Burger Barn, Bobby (Crispin Glover), the undertaker's son, sizes up the populace as if he were already measuring their coffins.

Hallstrom and Hedges are satirizing small-town life, but they're also canonizing it. They wring laughs out of the Grapes' predicament, but they also try to wring tears. (When Momma gets into the family car, there's a shot of it puttering down the road tipped to one side that gets a big laugh.) There's nothing cruel in their approach, but there's something a bit opportunistic: They want extra points from the audience for being humanitarians.

The relationship between Gilbert and Arnie has "Of Mice and Men" vibes, but it strikes a responsive chord in a way that the rest of the film doesn't. Most of the credit for that goes to DiCaprio's performance.

Actually, it hardly seems like a performance. DiCaprio, who was also seen this year in "This Boy's Life," works with the kind of minute clinical observation that Dustin Hoffman used in "Rain Man." As far as it goes, DiCaprio's performance is astonishing, but its very authenticity is a little off-putting. He's such a rigorously honest actor that he avoids all the obvious hokum.

You've got to admire him. The filmmakers and just about everybody else in the cast head straight for it.

NEW YORK, 1/17/94, p. 55, John Powers

The opening minutes of *What's Eating Gilbert Grape* are so groaningly cute—small-town Iowa as the usual insulting menagerie of oddballs—that you may find yourself pining for the gritty realism of *Northern Exposure*. But once Lasse Hallström's movie gets going, a fine heartland melancholy starts bubbling into the zaniness like tar into a goldfish pond; everyone knows everyone else, but they're all still drowning in solitude. The gifted young actor Leonardo DiCaprio has won justified raves for his tour de force as Arnie Grape, a retarded teenager who darts through the countryside like Puck's towheaded id, but all the unforgettable moments belong to Momma Grape (Darlene Cates), a 500-pound woman whose overwhelming appetite and shame make her Hollywood's most daring attempt to face our national hysteria about fat people. Gilbert is the self-denying son who holds the Grape family together. He's deftly played by Johnny Depp, the schoolgirls' heartthrob who has everything it takes for adult stardom: warmth, good looks, physical grace, and a gift for playing generously off his fellow actors. His only failing is a seemingly incurable taste for adolescent whimsy. The very titles of his films—*Edward Scissorhands, Benny and Joon, Gilbert Grape*—read like an advertisement for arrested development. I keep hoping that *Sassy* will give him a Lifetime Achievement Award so he can get on with his career.

NEW YORK POST, 12/17/93, p. 44, Michael Medved

Gilbert Grape (Johnny Depp) has many reasons to feel sour.

He works as a stock boy at a failing grocery store in a drab, dying Iowa town. While trying to protect his physically filthy and self-destructive retarded brother (Leonardo DiCaprio), he must also deal with two sullen sisters and a 500-pound mother (Darlene Cates) who hasn't left their house for years.

His desultory affair with a predatory and potentially dangerous married woman (Mary Steenburgen) provides him with little amusement or relief.

Worst of all, Gilbert is trapped—along with the rest of the talented, hard-working cast—in a miserable movie with no point and no plot—just the latest demonstration of Hollywood's current tendency to confuse weirdness with artistry.

Actually, even the eccentricities here aren't in any way original. The script, adapted by Peter Hedges from his 1991 novel, recalls the classic 1971 film "The Last Picture Show" in almost all its details—including the bored nice-guy here who's caring for a childlike, mentally disabled brother, the passionate, desperate, older woman involved with a boy half her age, and so forth.

In fact, even the look of this movie is uncomfortably close to "The Last Picture Show"—which makes no sense at all since the setting here is repeatedly identified as "Endora," Iowa, not Texas.

For some reason, the filmmakers made the mistake of shooting "Gilbert Grape" entirely in the Lone Star State, as if no one would notice the difference between the dry, dusty Southwestern countryside depicted on screen and the rich, rolling farmland of the real-life Iowa.

This stupidity helps to destroy any sense of place, and contributes to the feeling that we're watching a collection of self-consciously colorful and grotesques, never real people.

Swedish director Lasse Hallstrom created one of the most touching and beautiful films of the 1980s with "My Life as a Dog" but he is entirely wrong for this material. He condescends to all his characters, giving us a Scandinavian intellectuals view of yukky yokels in middle America.

The fact that the filmmakers discovered Darlene Cates (who plays the grossly obese "Momma") while watching her on a segment of Sally Jessy Raphael gives some indication of the cheesy feel to this enterprise.

You actually end up feeling even more sorry for the actors than for the character—especially since two of them (Leonardo DiCaprio and Steenburgen) do superior work.

Nineteen-year-old DiCaprio, who gave such a stunning performance earlier this year in "This Boy's Life" is remarkably convincing as Arnie, the brain-damaged brother avoiding all hints at sentimentality and portraying a sad character who is at least as annoying as he is endearing.

Johnny Depp is far less effective in the title role, delivering one of his trademark space-case performances, already painfully familiar to anyone who's seen "Edward Scissorhands," "Cry Baby" or "Benny and Joon."

Juliette Lewis, as a visitor to town who suddenly sparks Gilbert's interest also displays her overly familiar collection of quirks and mannerisms, making this one of the most affected and least affecting—screen couples of the year.

The best advice for all participants in this Midwestern muddle is to get out of town as quickly as possible.

NEWSDAY, 12/17/93, Part II/p. 95, John Anderson

"You're shrinking, Gilbert," says Arnie Grape (Leon DiCaprio) as he and his brother (Johnny Depp) play one of their spatial-relations games. But it's no game to Gilbert, who seems to be disappearing right before our eyes.

In "What's Eating Gilbert Grape," adapted by Peter Hedges from his novel of the same name, Arnie, who wasn't supposed to live past childhood, is turning 18. And his impending birthday party is posing problems. Momma (Darlene Cates), who weighs 500 pounds and sits around their rapidly deteriorating house like a Midwestern Jabba the Hut, hasn't gone outside in seven years—ever since Dad hanged himself in the cellar—and she isn't coming out for the party either. Arnie, who's been Gilbert's charge since forever, has taken to climbing the local water tower when no one's looking, and the police are getting tired of it.

Their family defines dysfunction: One sister, Amy (Laura Harrington), has become a resentful surrogate mother to the brood; the other, Ellen (Mary Kate Schellhardt), looks at Gilbert like a father, which makes him the object of her fiercely adolescent contempt. The grocery Gilbert works for is being driven under by the glossy new Foodland out on the highway. And Betty Carver (Mary Steenburgen), Gilbert's lover and wife of the local insurance salesman (Kevin Tighe), is getting a little too voracious for Gilbert's tastes.

In a film of uncommon tenderness and insight, Lasse Hallström, director of the Swedish cult classic "My Life as a Dog," measures out Gilbert's life in flat, cold teaspoons. And his work here is a good indication that European directors have an upper hand when portraying America's inner life—not just because of their emotional distance, but because of an inherent frankness about the shortcomings of life in general. Gilbert, after all, is the shortcomings tycoon.

Johnny Depp's sensitive rendering of Gilbert, who's part enigma, part lost soul and something of an irritation for his lack of direction, is a validation of Depp's considerable talent, which up to now has been overshadowed by his good looks. The actor hasn't really had an opportunity to play a character unencumbered by hardware or mental deficiency, and he gets inside Gilbert in a way that's convincing, almost reassuring.

But like Tom Cruise in "Rain Man," who had perhaps the best performance of his career eclipsed by Dustin Hoffman's idiot savant, Depp has to play opposite Leonardo DiCaprio ("This Boy's Life"), whose Arnie Grape is a marvel of ticks, twitches, hair-trigger hysteria, and a mind and body working at cross-purposes. It's the most fully realized portrayal of a mentally disabled person I've ever seen; Hoffman's, by comparison, was a party trick.

And the relationship between Arnie and Gilbert contains the right combination of love and frustration to make it thoroughly convincing.

What's less so is Juliette Lewis, who as Becky arrives in Endora (Gilbert's town) with her peripatetic grandmother (Penelope Branning) and proceeds to cast a spell on Gilbert. They're both eccentric enough to make a match believable, but Gilbert's a lot prettier. Otherwise, with Hallström's direction, Depp and DiCaprio's acting and Sven Nykvist's cinematography until the climactic conflagration, you don't realize how cold he's made you feel—"Gilbert" doesn't shrink, it grows and grows.

NEWSWEEK, 12/27/93, p. 48, David Ansen

Gilbert Grape (Johnny Depp), who lives in the tiny, backwater town of Endora, Iowa, knows more than any young man should about family obligations. His father long ago hanged himself in the basement. His momma (Darlene Cates), once the town beauty, now weighs 500 pounds and hasn't left the house in seven years, never mind leaving her couch. Gilbert has to keep a constant eye on his brain-damaged, hyperactive 17-year-old little brother Arnie (Leonardo DiCaprio), who has to be rescued by the fire department every time he scampers up the local water tower; and his two younger sisters rely on him to be the daddy of the house and resent him for it. Stuck in a job as a grocery-store clerk, Gilbert finds his only diversion in a cautiously adulterous affair with an older, married woman (Mary Steenburgen), who knows that she's chosen the one guy who will never get out of Endora. When asked what he wants out of life, Gilbert says, "To be a good person." And he is. He's sweet, dependable, responsible—and his goodness is draining the life out of him. He's numb with virtue.

"What's Eating Gilbert Grape" isn't the whimsical, arch movie its title, or its grotesque ingredients, might suggest. Directed with honesty and gentle humor by Lasse Hallstrom ("My Life as a Dog"), written by Peter Hedges with a good ear for the eloquence of the inarticulate, this low-key character study never tries to knock your socks off, but if you lean toward it, its poignancy settles under your skin. Hallstrom is an acute observer and a compassionate one, never more so than in the generous way he handles the huge, touching figure of Momma—a figure of fun to the locals, but not to him.

Gilbert's potential salvation comes in the form of Juliette Lewis's Becky, who travels through town in a silver trailer with her grandmother, a girl as mobile as Gilbert is stationary. Their tentative, understated romance has real tenderness, but her free-spirited character carries a whiff of contrivance—she's a bow to movie convention, as is the abrupt, upbeat ending. Depp is subtly winning as a man-child oblivious to his own pent-up rage. But the performance that will take your breath away is DiCaprio's. A lot of actors have taken flashy stabs at playing retarded characters and no one, old or young, has ever done it better. He's exasperatingly, heartbreakingly real. This 19-year-old, who shone earlier this year in "This Boy's Life," seems to have a bottomless talent.

SIGHT AND SOUND, 5/94, p. 59, Stella Bruzzi

Endora, Iowa. Gilbert Grape lives with his mother Bonnie, two sisters and mentally retarded brother Arnie in the run-down house built by his father. His mother, who weighs 36 stone, has not left the house since her husband hanged himself in the cellar. Gilbert works in the local grocery store, whose clientele has mostly deserted to the supermarket on the outskirts of town. Gilbert has been having an affair for almost a year with Betty Carver, the wife of Endora's insurance broker. During one of Gilbert's many deliveries to the Carver household, Arnie, who has been left in the truck, climbs the gas tower in the centre of town. Gilbert coaxes him down, and meets Becky, who is travelling in a camper with her grandmother, among the onlookers. Gilbert's routine is disrupted by Becky's arrival. He fails to complete his brother's evening bathing ritual, and returns in the early hours of the morning to find a shivering Arnie waiting for him in a stone cold tub. Gilbert also becomes less keen on his clandestine relationship with Betty Carver. After her husband is suddenly and inexplicably drowned in their children's paddling pool, Betty tells Gilbert she is leaving town to start afresh. Meanwhile, Arnie climbs to the top of the gas tower again, and this time,the police take him into custody. Observed by the curious local population, Gilbert's mother stirs and goes to the police station to fetch back her son.

Becky and her grandmother are due to leave the following day after the grand opening of the new Burger Barn and Arnie's eighteenth birthday. On the eve of the party Arnie, still traumatised by the cold bath experience, lashes out as Gilbert tries to wash him, provoking his brother into hitting him. Gilbert sets out to leave town but changes his mind. Arnie visits Becky, who persuades him to conquer his fear of water by jumping into the stream near her camper. Gilbert then spends the night with Becky. The next day is Arnie's birthday, and although Bonnie wants to remain out of sight, Gilbert persuades her to meet Becky before she leaves in the camper. At home, Bonnie decides she wants to go upstairs to her bedroom, where she has not ventured for years. She dies in her sleep, and is found by Arnie the next day. Rather than have her specially removed by a crane, the children cremate Bonnie and the house. A year later, Gilbert and Arnie wait by the roadside for Becky.

The subtitle for *What's Eating Gilbert Grape* could be 'Insignificance', Endora being the sort of town that jumped off life's carousel long before the Big Dipper came along and made everything hazardous. The latent oddity of middle-American ordinariness is well-trodden ground, but here the point is not that Iowa has secret priest-holes of bizarre activity waiting to be prised open, but that it truly is monotonously normal. In *What's Eating Gilbert Grape* things often seem strange the way they do in Jane Campion's short *Passionless Moments*: no one does much that is weird, it's just framed or edited to look that way. The appeal of successful bizarre normality—a sort of fictional version of life in fly-on-the-wall documentaries—is that it is not given any hidden meaning, but remains inconsequential.

Difficult to pin down, the attraction of this in Lasse Hallström's film is a matter of style. There are wry moments of incongruous juxtaposition, such as Ken Carver's bovine head trampolining up from behind the garden hedge as Gilbert and Betty are getting down to a bit of illicit Häagen Dazs-inspired passion, or Endora's new mobile Burger Barn arriving just as Ken's coffin is being laid to rest. Here, what's humorous is the sequence of events, not simply the events themselves. *What's Eating Gilbert Grape* is evocative in the way it draws—and draws on—minutiae, so the overall picture is the sum of accumulated detail. Bonnie Grape's way of clutching her tub of popcorn with simultaneous resentment and possessiveness conveys more about her self-loathing and her defiance than any trite verbal exchange about why she slumped into obesity.

Like Hallström's earlier *My Life As a Dog*, this is a film of sentiment that eschews sentimentality, despite the main storylines concerning Gilbert and his family and Gilbert and his relationship with the outsider Becky. There are moments ripe for cloying treatment, like Gilbert's intense meaning-of-life conversations with Becky, first amid the haystacks at sunset, everything bathed in rich golden haloes, and second beside a campfire at night. If only Gilbert could fathom her cryptic, whimsical statements and questions. There's an awareness of the dangers of being mawkish that ensures any mindless rhapsody is side-stepped, interrupted, deflated; a pragmatic approach to tearjerk material best summed up by the carefully unpatronising treatment of Arnie.

If there is any underpinning theme in *What's Eating Gilbert Grape*, it's a notion of space. From the opening sequence, when the convoy of glistening silver campers bringing Becky into town snakes over the lazy hillside towards Gilbert and Arnie, there's a sharp distinction made between the parochial day-to-day aimlessness of Endora, and the potential of life elsewhere. When Gilbert drives out of town only to turn back as soon as he's passed its farewell sign, he goes in search of Becky and tells her, "I've got nowhere to go". Beyond Endora there's a vast expanse and there's nothing—Gilbert gazes out at that open space, while Arnie waves at it each time he scales the heights of the gas tower. The reality of Endora, though, is something more akin to the world created by Bonnie, the lapsed matriarch of the Grape household, who has defined her space as being almost exclusively the inside of her house, shrouding herself in its confined bleakness. Whenever the despairing Gilbert tries to break away, something—such as Arnie running away—happens to pull him back.

What's Eating Gilbert Grape is a beautiful, luxurious film that wears any solemn intention lightly. Its insignificance is finely drawn, creating a kaleidoscope of images and moments that, apropos of nothing much, are all-consuming. From Gilbert's undertaker's assistant friend using a bent spoon and an ashtray to back up his 'magic heart attack' theory of how Ken Carver could have drowned in a paddling pool four inches deep, to Bonnie's blancmange shape silhouetted against her drawn bedroom curtains as she tells Gilbert he's her knight in shining armour, it is the detail that explains the whole.

TIME, 1/10/94, p. 58, Richard Corliss

In movies, misfits are sacred, the emotionally or mentally disturbed are usually portrayed not as human beings working harder than most to get through the day, but as heroes and holy fools. In many a film fable they are sentimentalized into superior beings—residents of some spiritual high-rise that the rest of us might aspire to, if only we dared jettison our inhibitions and soar into the divine state we ignorantly call dysfunctional or some unkinder name.

So half a cheer for *What's Eating Gilbert Grape*, which suggests that the true heroes are those people who day by day must tend to misfits, and do so with love, tenacity and a determination not to go terminally sour in the process.

Gilbert (Johnny Depp) might be the patron saint of all such caretakers. A grocery-store clerk in forlorn Endora, Iowa, he looks after his retarded brother (Leonardo DiCaprio), who likes to climb things, and his mountainous mom (Darlene Cates), who, at an immobile 500 lbs., is something of a local tourist attraction. Nor does the need stop at his front door. Gilbert must satisfy the sexual desires of a tartly cheerful matron (Mary Steenburgen), even as he is drawn to newcomer Becky (Juliette Lewis), a teenager whose ease and freedom seem like fresh oxygen in the coal mine of Gilbert's life.

You've heard this one before: except for Momma, it's *The Last Picture Show*. This picture show doesn't match that one. The script, by Peter Hedges from his novel, spins out a few too many eccentricities, and the direction, by Lasse Hallström (*My Life as a Dog*), meanders. But DiCaprio and Cates bring loopy authenticity to their roles, and Depp is, as always, a most effacing star. Here, as in *Edward Scissorhands* and *Benny & Joon*, he behaves wonderfully on screen. He should be even better when he gets the chance to misbehave as a demented director in Tim Burton's forthcoming *Ed Wood*.

VILLAGE VOICE, 12/21/93, p. 70, Georgia Brown

The story of a troubled family, *What's Eating Gilbert Grape* has the ingredients of a typical Mike Leigh film. But Leigh's mode is manic, whereas *Gilbert Grape*'s true to the dominant American culture—is decidedly depressive. Based on a novel by Peter Hedges and directed by Lasse Hallström, this "small" gentle movie reminds us how emphatically our slow, melancholic side is being slighted by the entertainment industry's jangly, glamor-driven mentality.

The Grapes are a sad bunch. Four children and a 500-pound mother inhabit a paint-peeled house on the edge of the Iowa plains. Momma (Darlene Cates, a Texas resident who's graced the Sally Jesse Raphael show) never leaves the house; she hardly ever leaves her sofa in front of the TV. (She doesn't go to the dinner table, the dinner table comes to her.) Underneath, beams are beginning to buckle. So is the spirit of her children. The eldest, Gilbert (Johnny Depp), has the placid stoicism, the blank countenance, of someone too long saddled with grown-up responsibilities. Currently, he supports the family working at a small grocery in town, though his toughest job may be as caretaker of his younger brother Arnie (Leonardo DiCaPrio). About to turn 18, the gangly, hyper, mentally disabled Arnie is a handful, particularly when he's fixated on climbing the town water tower.

One summer, life changes for the Grapes. First, Gilbert is roused by the arrival in town of Becky (Juliette Lewis), a wispy but sensible young woman who isn't repulsed by his family's circumstances. He must, however, get rid of the randy Mrs. Carver (Mary Steenburgen), who calls the grocery for his personal delivery whenever her hands are free. But *Gilbert Grape* isn't *The Last Picture Show*. It steers away from soap-opera chic and stays sincere and modest. When Momma decides to move, the whole community trembles. So does the plot.

Crispin Glover fans take note: The strange, elusive one appears here as a young undertaker cruising for clients. In suit and tie, he almost looks normal. Almost.

Also reviewed in:
CHICAGO TRIBUNE, 3/4/94, Friday/p. A, Michael Wilmington
NEW YORK TIMES, 12/17/93, p. C3, Janet Maslin
VARIETY, 12/13/93, p. 38, Todd McCarthy
WASHINGTON POST, 3/4/94, Weekend/p. 44, Desson Howe
WASHINGTON POST, 3/5/94, p. G3, Hal Hinson

WHAT'S LOVE GOT TO DO WITH IT

A Touchstone Pictures release. *Executive Producer:* Roger Davies and Mario Iscovich. *Producer:* Doug Chapin and Barry Krost. *Director:* Brian Gibson. *Screenplay:* Kate Lanier. *Based upon "I, Tina" by:* Tina Turner and Kurt Loder. *Director of Photography:* Jamie Anderson. *Editor:* Stuart Pappé. *Music:* Stanley Clarke. *Music Editor:* Charles Martin-Inouye and Jeff Carson. *Choreographer:* Michael Peters. *Sound:* Arthur Rochester, (music) Allen Sides and Dan Humann. *Sound Editor:* John Stacy. *Casting:* David Giella and Barbara Harris. *Production Designer:* Stephen Altman. *Art Director:* Richard Johnson. *Set Decorator:* Rick Simpson. *Set Dresser:* David Ronan. *Make-up:* Marietta A. Carter. *Special Effects:* James K. Fredburg. *Costumes:* Ruth Carter. *Stunt Coordinator:* William Washington. *Running time:* 120 minutes. *MPAA Rating:* R.

CAST: Rae'ven Kelly (Young Anna Mae); Virginia Capers (Choir Mistress); Emery Shaw (Organ Player); Cora Lee Day (Grandma Georgiana); Jenifer Lewis (Zelma Bullock); Angela Basset (Tina Turner); Phyliss Yvonne Stickney (Alline); Sherman Augustus (Reggie); Chi (Fross); Terrence Riggins (Spider); Gene "Groove" Allen (Club Announcer); Laurence Fishburne (Ike Turner); Jennifer Leigh Warren (Audience Female #1); Sonya Hensley (Audience Female #2); Leslie Thurston (Audience Female #3); Eartha Robinson (Audience Female #4); Kate Lanier (Stripper on Balcony); Vanessa Bell Calloway (Jackie); Pamala Tyson (Leanne); Khandi Alexander (Darlene); Penny Johnson (Lorraine); Jacqueline Woolsey (Boutique Clerk); Mayah McCoy (Young Hairdresser); Barry "Shabaka" Henley (El Paso Doctor); Michael Colyar (Apollo Announcer); Rob LaBelle (Phil Spector); Patricia Sill (Spector's Assistant); Barry O'Neill (Kid #1); Ali Glazer (Kid #2); Julie Phillips (Kid #3); Elijah Saleem (Ike Jr., Age 16); Tyrandis Holmes (Young Ike, Jr.); Jamaine Harrington (Young Michael); Devon Davison (Young Ronnie); Eric Thomas (Young Craig); Bob Kane (Dance Show Host); Richard T. Jones (Ike Turner, Jr.); Shavar Ross (Michael Turner); Damon Hines (Ronnie Turner); Suli McCullough (Craig Turner); Daniel McDonald (London Announcer); Wyonna Smith (4th Ikette); Rosemarie Jackson (5th Ikette); Michael David Simms (Ike's Lawyer); John Fink (Anna's Lawyer); Rudolph Willrich (Judge); Irene DeBari (ICU Nurse); Terrance Evans (Bus Driver); Richard Stay (Party Goer #1); Nelson Parks (Party Goer #2); Matt Kirkwood (Party Goer #3); Javi Mulero (Bellhop); Joe Vant (Hotel Clerk); O'Neal Compton (Ramada Inn Manager); Michael Monks (Hotel Porter); James Reyne (Roger Davies); James Ralston (Guitarist); Timmy Cappello (Keyboard); Jack Bruno (Drummer); Bob Feit (Bass Player); Kenny Moore (Piano Player); Daniel Allan Carlin (Conductor); Dean Minerd (Stage Hand); Fred Ponzlov (Manager #1); Tom DeCarlo (Manager #2); Richard B. Livingston (Manager #3); Louis Mawcinitt (Manager #4); Owen Bush (Old Man #1); Herb Muller (Old Man #2); Sparkle (Old Woman #1); Helen Brown (Old Woman #2); David Fresco (Old Man #3); Page Moseley (Ritz Announcer); Lorna Scott (Nurse); Rick Felkins (Stage Manager); Robert Lesser (Fairmount MC).

FILMS IN REVIEW, 10/93, p. 334, Harry Pearson

There are movies and there is film.

Movies tickle some part of the audience's viscera, be it the heart or other organs further down the line. And movies can be done with considerable artistry. Consider *Casablanca, Gone With The Wind,* and *Singin' In The Rain.* Films, on the other hand, reach a little higher, trying to tickle the brain as well as those parts south. Films, one might argue, change the way we look at the world, ours or those of other's. *The Godfather, The Crying Game,* and *A Clockwork Orange* are films. Not all "films" are necessarily artistically superior.

Pearson's First Rule of Reviewing is that the critic must keep in mind the difference between movies and film. A corollary of this rule is: Anything from the folks at Disney is a movie: e.g., *Sister Act, Pretty Woman.* The Tina Turner biopic, *What's Love Got To Do With It?,* has been reviewed as if it were film. That it is not. Love is not nearly a documentary (although it is advertised as "the true life story of Tina Turner" when nearly every detail in it is demonstrably false); not much of a movie (take out the violence and what's left?); but, quite clearly, a work of *agitprop*, with cultural demons to exorcise and a television movie topicality in its mind.

Offsetting its meretriciousness are two mostly dazzling performances—one by Laurence (ne Larry) Fishburne (*Apocalypse Now, Boyz 'n The Hood*) as Ike Turner is a marvel of subtlety, the other, more troubling since the actress is miscast, from Angela Bassett (*Malcolm X*, et. al.) is too tightly controlled to fill the charismatic Tina's overflowing original, And some wonderful small performances: Jenifer Lewis as Tina's mother, Zelma; Penny Johnson as Ike's "wife" Lorraine; O'Neal Compton, all too briefly as the manager of a Ramada Inn; Rae'ven Kelly, perfect as the young Tina and Virginia Capers in a wonderful small turn as choir mistress in the young Tina's church. There is intelligently conceived widescreen (not Panavision) photography by Jamie Anderson, and clever editing that gives the illusion of forward motion to a plot that's not much.

The opening scene is promising, Little Tina is singing with a down South gospel choir; she really gets into the music, beginning to sing and shake with a little too much soul for the choir mistress, who eventually evicts her from the church. Tina goes home to find that she is being abandoned by her mother and her older sister, who are fleeing the abusive father. Desolate Tina is taken in by her grandmother. In microcosm, this episode should have set the stage for Turner's central life struggle. Off stage, she has no life at all; singing, she is larger than, throwing herself into performances with a headlong fury that both shakes and rattles her adoring audiences. If there is a single point that her co-written autobiography returns to like some idee fixe, it is the contrast between her personal life, where offstage she can barely be said to have one, and onstage, which was her only life. Eventually, she was able to construct an identity from her life as a musician and to find a kind of center that she hadn't had. This theme, properly handled, could have made *Love* a minor classic.

But the screenwriter (Kate Lanier) and the folks at the M. Mouse Factory have other fish to fry. So what we get is a movie about a monster. Thanks to the Devil Cocaine, Ike starts to beat Tina, becoming a lineal descendant of M. Hyde. And so we have here a horror movie. What we get are some tough, tough scenes of abuse—played with exceeding realism by Bassett, who insisted that the scenes look "real," and Fishburne. Perhaps it is a personal bias but I have a hard, hard time watching women or children getting beaten up. Such material so inherently inflammatory that it hypes up an audience. It stirs its most primitive fears (helplessness in the face of evil). And must, accordingly, be handled with some care (as in *This Boy's Life*). Just remember that the worse the abuse depicted, the lower a representation of it will aim—viscerally. You almost feel obliged to react strongly. You think you've seen something important because you have been so deeply "moved" (that is, so well manipulated).

Subtract the beatings from this picture and what have you got left? A movie that never transmits the joy of music. The concert numbers are indifferently staged. Bassett never really lets fly and so you keep waiting for things to catch fire and take off. They never do. The only time in the movie when a musical number starts to rock comes during a concert at the Olympia and, then, the director abruptly cuts away from the number and builds a montage of Turner singing this song in numerous other venues. In other words, bred perhaps on too much MTV, he doesn't trust the material. If the performer is terrific, we don't need a lot of fancy editing and camerawork to distract us: indeed, the less, the better. And, as much as I admired the heroic effort of Bassett's performance—she is just glorious at suggesting the sweet innocence of the young Tina and the ineffectual puppet who belongs, body and soul, to Ike in later years, she never finds Tina's center; she acts this one from the outside in, unlike herself, who works from the inside out. Bassett isn't helped by the director. In the scene where she first appears at the Apollo, Turner is supposed to be suffering from exhaustion, a throaty cold, and huge fatigue, and yet she appears on stage, in vocally perfect condition, and with a set of biceps that would do Wonder Woman proud—it's evident Bassett has been in the gym and has a "pump". She might however have succeeded on her own terms had not the director (one Brian Gibson) intercut, at film's end, the real Turner singing in concert. Suddenly, we breathe a sigh of relief and say: "This is how it's supposed to be; this is why she's a star." This intercut undercuts all the work Bassett has done up to this point. Worse, if you know the real story, Tina's problem wasn't anemia, as the writer later suggests in another sequence, but rather tuberculosis. Wouldn't this, you might query, have made the more dramatic edge.

Ike is already portrayed as becoming the incarnation of all that is wrong with the black male (i.e., *The Color Purple*) but his abusive ways are attributed to cocaine. In fact, the real Ike didn't get hooked on coke until well after—years, that is—he started beating Tina. In real life, Ike was a master of mental abuse, something never quite tackled in this depiction. Not only would he not allow Tina out of his sight (she couldn't, for years, even go to the grocery store by herself) but there were TV cameras in every room of their house so he could keep an eye on her. In *I, Tina*, we draw our own conclusions: this is suspiciously like brainwashing. He kept his investment safe by keeping it totally under his control. He reduced her, in private life, to an infantile state. Surely this is more monstrous than the simple-minded theory that cocaine was the cause of it all. Surely it is also the more dramatic and would have made for the stronger film. But maybe the Disney people didn't want strength as much as they wanted a commercial hit. Maybe this could have been, in the right hands, a film, and a film that did justice to the human capacity for transformation and a transformation based on courage. In that respect, Turner's autobiography is quite the read and one of the better examples of its genre.

It's too bad. They were onto something here. And they blew it.

LOS ANGELES TIMES, 6/9/93, Calendar/p. 1, Kenneth Turan

You may not respect "What's Love Got to Do with It," but enjoying it is inescapable.

A high-energy mixture of spectacular music, vigorous acting and clichéd situations, this is a rough-and-rowdy fairy tale with a feminist subtext, and if that sounds perplexing, "Love," so pumps up the volume you won't have much time to think about it.

Though it is based on her autobiography, "I, Tina," and is subtitled "The true life of Tina Turner," "What's Love" has less in common with anyone's reality than with generations of glossy show business biopics like "Lady Sings the Blues" and "The Doors," where a singer's triumphs and tragedies are written in large neon letters for the world to see and sob over.

And Tina Turner, both during and after her tumultuous marriage to the mysterious Ike, did seem to live the kind of fast-lane soap-opera life the public expects rock stars to have, with personal tragedies jostling professional successes and an abusive, drug-using husband always lurking behind the surface glamour.

Better than that, the passionate songs Tina was singing onstage often paralleled what was happening in her life offstage, and writer Jane Lanier has cleverly structured her script around the similarities. So when Tina sings "A Fool in Love," that's just what she is, by the time she is telling audiences in "Proud Mary" that "we don't do anything nice and easy," her relationship with Ike is mired in pain.

Director Brian Gibson, best known for the TV movie "The Josephine Baker Story," was definitely a commercial choice for this audience-friendly tale of glitz and woe. He knows how to infuse the energy of the music into this often hokey story, and he is discretion itself when it comes to handling the film's drug use, judiciously focusing not on the substance but on fingers with the odd habit of wandering toward the nose.

The biggest asset "What's Love Got to Do With It" has, however, are the exceptional actors who play Tina and Ike. Angela Bassett (last seen as Betty Shabazz in "Malcolm X") and Laurence Fishburne worked together in "Boyz N the Hood," and they bring to this film not only the rapport they developed there but also the ability to deepen characters in ways that are not in the script, to bring more to there roles than seems to be there.

It is Tina, appropriately enough, whom we meet first, as a little tyke named Anna Mae Bullock who scandalizes the church choir in Nutbush, Tenn., by putting more sass into a hymn than is absolutely necessary. Returning home, Anna discovers her mother in the process of walking out, leaving her to be raised by a convenient, standard-issue kindly grandmother.

Cut to 1958, when a presumably teen-age Anna joins her mother, Zelma (Jenifer Lewis), and her sister, Alline (Phyllis Yvonne Stickney), in St. Louis. On her first night there (this movie does not waste time), she goes to a nightclub and sees local R&B star and major-league cool dude Ike Turner and his Kings of Rhythm.

As beautifully played by Fishburne, it is not difficult to see why Ike was the king of hearts. With his slow smile, polished self-confidence, impeccable hair and half-opened lounge-lizard eyes, Ike wears a pastel blue topcoat with as much aplomb as Cary Grant modeling a tuxedo. And though he relished being the center of attention, once he hears Anna's powerful voice he is smitten without a doubt.

Even though she's lip-syncing rather than singing, audiences will inevitably feel the same way about Bassett. Her Anna Mae/Tina moves gradually from an uncertain ingenue to a brassily confident performer to an in-charge woman and Bassett is more than equal to all the changes. Whether she is strutting defiantly on stage or putting a wide smile on her wonderfully mobile, emotional face, Bassett's Tina embraces life in a way that is infectious and is sure to do for her career what Fishburne's work in "Boyz" did for his.

Because Fishburne and Bassett have this singular on-screen connection, their relationship feels more complex than it otherwise would. And at first, even though Ike changes her name and seems determined to work her into the ground, the two share a bond based on the traditional dream they both have of show-biz success.

But when that success comes, it brings, for reasons apparently drug-related but never made quite clear, a darkening of Ike's personality and physical violence toward Tina that are the emotionally strongest parts of the film (rated R for domestic violence, strong language, drug use and some sexuality). This sets up "What's Love's" final part, where Tina, like a heroine on a quest, searches for the strength to literally get a room of her own and strike out toward the grail of international stardom.

Though the picture rightfully belongs to Bassett, a final word must be said about Fishburne, who never fails to make Ike seem human if not defensible. Even in defeat, he is remarkably compelling. Though "What's Love Got to Do With It" is much broader than his performance, the film and the actor do share an important characteristic: Try as you might, you won't be able to take your eyes off either one.

NEW YORK, 7/19/93, p. 49, David Denby

As you watch *What's Love Got to Do With It*, the story of Tina Turner's harrowing marriage to Ike, you know you aren't getting all of the truth—not with this completely innocent Tina you aren't, this refined woman who wants only to do the proper thing at every moment. Angela Bassett, who plays Tina, doesn't have any wildness in her. She's a solid actress, and she works hard in the performing scenes, but she can't unleash herself the way Tina Turner does, for the simple reason that Turner's cataclysmic yet sustained and flowing intensity could never be learned or imitated. The movie never gets close to the source of the real Tina Turner's volcanic greatness onstage—never asking, for instance, whether it might have anything to do with her sexual relations with Ike.

But having made my point, I now lay down my arms, because this is a strong, strong movie—a powerhouse, really—and it affects people more deeply than movies made with far greater art. *What's Love Got to Do With It* is in the form of a show-business biopic, but it touches a common chord. Without overstating anything, screenwriter Kate Lanier and director Brian Gibson establish exactly how Ike Turner (Laurence Fishburne) discovered Anna Mae Bullock, re-created her as Tina, milked her for everything she had, sweet-talked her or bullied her when she got tired, repeatedly beat her, and then collapsed into self-pity when she tried to leave. Fishburne, hulking yet weak, cocky yet deeply uncertain, gives the performance of his career. He is a plausibly human monster, the nightmare that millions of women have yet to awake from. Lanier and Gibson do many things with the most delicate strength—the opening scene in church, for instance, in which Anna Mae, only a child, can't stop jazzing the religious music; the scenes with Anna Mae's sister and her tough-souled mother; the backstage bantering with the Ikettes, who are jealous of Anna Mae but also know what troubles she will have with Ike. The movie establishes clearly why Tina can't leave without suggesting that she's in any way a masochist. When she finally does leave, it's as if a gigantic weight gets lifted off our shoulders. It's her story, but she somehow wins for all of us.

NEW YORK POST, 6/9/93, p. 27, Jami Bernard

"We nevuh evuh do nuthin' nice and easy," sasses Tina Turner in her classic introduction to Ike & Tina Turner's rendition of "Proud Mary." "We like to do things nice ... and *rough*."

Rough, indeed. The rough-and-tumble marriage of Tina to the abusive, controlling Ike is the centerpiece of this charged biopic about the pop diva, played with extraordinary intensity and passion by Angela Bassett. "What's Love Got to Do With It" is based on Turner's autobiography, "I, Tina."

Tina was born Anna Mae Bullock in a small town in Tennessee where, according to the movie in a delightful preamble, her irrepressible inclination to belt a song is frowned upon by the church choir. Her abandonment by her mother at an early age goes a long way to explain her later devotion to her battering husband, who in turn feared being left high and dry.

Anna Mae met Ike in a St. Louis club in her teens, after a reunion with her self-involved mother. The movie makes it very clear why a country bumpkin like Anna Mae would fall for the older, sexier, raffish Ike, played by Laurence Fishburne with as much sympathy as you can milk for a man who insisted his wife perform while still weak from childbirth, and who memorably broke her jaw before one concert.

Fishburne shows Ike as a talented but tortured (and drug-addicted) songwriter and performer who had to choke back his resentment of losing the limelight to his increasingly famous wife.

As another critic smirked, Bassett's arms look so muscular that Ike wouldn't have stood a chance in a fight. But Tina Turner, for all her powerful stage presence, wild looks and animal vice, apparently suffered the battered wife syndrome in which learned passivity squelches all natural responses.

"What's Love Got to Do With It" naturally provides the benefit of hearing all the famous old songs; Bassett doesn't physically look like Tina, but her performance is so apt you'd think you were seeing double. All the movie lacks is poetic license for the screenwriter or director to stray from the material just enough to underscore it; the adaptation to screen is quite literal and earnest, however well done.

NEW YORK POST, 6/11/93, p. 31, Michael Medved

The hungry tyrannosaurus in "Jurassic Park" isn't the only prehistoric monster rampaging across movie screens this week: there's also Ike Turner (as portrayed by Laurence Fishburne), a male chauvinist dinosaur whose merciless battering of his wife, Tina, provides the real focus of "What's Love Got to Do With It."

The Disney Company's Touchstone Pictures division is trying to market this movie as an inspiring story about the "indomitable spirit" of a glamorous rock superstar, but its relentless emphasis on the cruelest sort of spousal abuse gives the project the grim, melodramatic feel of a typical woman-in-jeopardy movie-of-the-week.

Filmmaker Brian Gibson (who previously directed TV miniseries about Josephine Baker and Simon Wiesenthal) begins this picture in his main character's home town of Nut Bush, Tenn., but he dispenses with her early years in short order.

Within five minutes of the opening of the film, young Anna Mae Bullock (the future Tina Turner) has been abandoned by her mother, raised by her grandmother, reunited with her mom in St. Louis, and fallen under the spell of the moody musician Ike Turner, when she hears him perform with his band, the Kings of Rhythm.

Laurence Fishburne, who has previously demonstrated his star quality and acting ability in "Deep Cover," "Boy'z N the Hood" and other films, is so good as Turner, so truly terrifying, that he throws the entire movie fatally out of whack.

In his hands, he comes across as a far more compelling, intriguing and tragic character than Tina. Part of the problem is the arc of the story—a brutal predator is inevitably more riveting to watch than a virtuous, long-suffering victim—but part of it is also the hard-working though ultimately unconvincing performance by Angela Bassett as Tina Turner.

Bassett is a gifted actress (previously best known for her role as Betty Shabazz in "Malcolm X"), but despite her determined efforts to replicate the singing style, body language and even facial expressions of one of pop music's true originals, the main character in this film stubbornly refuses to come to life. Charisma is a curious thing: Tina Turner definitely has it, and so does Laurence Fishburne, but in this movie Angela Bassett unfortunately does not.

Her lip-syncing is impeccable in the many musical interludes restaging Ms. Turner's greatest hits, but she can't come close to generating the raw heat or the joyous electricity of the real-life star—or even of the back-up "Ikettes" who appear in this movie.

To make up for these shortcomings, Bassett reached an ill-considered decision to bulk up her musculature, working tirelessly with a personal trainer to develop the most powerful arms ever displayed by an actress in a leading role.

The results are astonishing: her bulging biceps and massive, beautifully sculpted shoulders command constant attention, but when it comes to striving for a resemblance to the real Tina Turner, (who turns up in person—very briefly—at the end of the film), what's big arm muscles got to do with it?

Sad to tell, there are even moments when Angela Bassett, flexing and unflexing her magnificent new muscles like a Ms. Universe contestant, comes close to suggesting a broad-shouldered female impersonator in a Tina Turner wig.

To explain their heroine's ultimate ability to triumph over adversity and launch a new career as a solo performer, the filmmakers emphasize her interest in Nichiren Shoshu—unquestioningly accepting the idea that this controversial cult, which encourages its adherents to endlessly chant "*namu Myoho renge kyo*" to earn new cars or cancer cures, truly unlocks the timeless Wisdom of the East.

This reverential attitude stands in dramatic contrast to contemporary Hollywood's general dismissal of more conventional Judeo-Christian religious faith.

While Tina Turner's music features an infectious "feel-good" quality that has energized millions of her fans, there are few good feelings and precious little energy in this overly solemn production.

As is so often the case with "heroic survivor movies," its attempts to dramatize a long ordeal on the part of its main character end up generating a painful, pointless, two-hour ordeal for the audience.

NEWSDAY, 6/9/93, Part II/p. 49, Jack Mathews

Screenwriter Kate Lanier is quoted in the press notes for "What's Love Got to Do With It" as saying that when she and director Brian Gibson became involved in the adaptation of Tina Turner's autobiography, they "clicked on the idea that Tina's story is like a heroic myth."

"She set out on a quest, fought a dragon, and came through it successfully," Lanier said.

Whether or not Lanier and Gibson got their inspiration while meeting with Touchstone executives under the arch of the Seven Dwarfs at Walt Disney's Burbank studios, "What's Love Got to Do With It" is certainly closer to myth than biography.

In this telling of the 54-year-old star's life, Turner is Cinderella, Pinocchio, Snow White, Peter Pan and Aladdin all rolled into one innocent, white-hot angel, and Ike, her mentor, manager, stage partner, husband and tormenter, is the darkest side of every evil pirate, witch, stepmother, hobgoblin and gargoyle who ever found their way into a legend. "Pete's Dragon" Tina's ain't.

Ike, played with menace to spare by Laurence Fishburne, is one of the nastiest screen portrayals of a living person since Philip Baker Hall demonized Richard Nixon in "Secret Honour." The musician and songwriter, whom the 17-year-old Tina married in 1956 (and divorced 22 years later), no doubt earned the roasting he gets. A reformed Ike has admitted to having been a cokehead, womanizer and wife beater, and the repeated scenes of his emotional and physical bullying are all taken from the uncontested accounts in Tina's book, "I, Tina."

But in concentrating almost exclusively on the abusive relationship, and shaping the story as a stark good vs. evil melodrama, the filmmakers skipped or glossed over addicts of Tina's life and musical development that would be essential to any serious attempt at biography.

After a jump-start opening, showing a young Tina being kicked out of a southern church choir because she can't harness her musical spirit, we cut quickly to St. Louis, where the teenage Tina is swooning over the handsome leader of a club band called Ike and the Rhythm Kings.

When she demurely takes the stage with Ike one night and lets loose her enormous voice, it is as if it had been held in all those years, prowling her soul like a caged tiger. In fact, she had sung and danced at talent shows throughout her childhood and her voice was no secret to anyone who knew her.

"What's Love" doesn't lie; it just zeroes in on one dimension of a complicated life, becomes another version of "A Star Is Born," the story of a gifted entertainer whose only weakness was being too loyal too long to the bum she married.

Major chapters in Tina Turner's life and career are omitted, or dismissed with passing references. Phil Spector, the promoter who put Ike and Tina Turner on the charts, and Roger Davies, the Australian who engineered Tina's solo revival, get a scene each. Ike and Tina's children only show up as terrified witnesses to their father's violent outbursts, and Tina's conversion to Buddhism—no small thing for a southern Baptist—is so simplistically dramatized, you'd think she'd gotten everything she needed to know out of a fortune cookie.

Commercially, the filmmakers probably did the right thing. Like the makers of "Lady Sings the Blues" and "Coal Miner's Daughter," which focused on the drug addiction and nervous breakdown of Billie Holiday and Loretta Lynn, respectively, Lanier and Gibson went with the most shocking elements presented them, and they made a compelling—at times, exhilarating—mainstream entertainment of them.

The music alone (14 songs featuring the voice of Tina Turner) is worth the price of admission. And so effectively hateful is Fishburne's portrayal of Ike, devolving from a sweet-talking cad to a common thug, audiences will jump for joy when Tina finally fights back, digs her nails into his face and knees him in the ...

And in the end, when Bassett's simulated concert performance of Turner's 1985 hit title song cleverly dissolves into actual concert footage and the real Tina appears, you can almost hear the gooseflesh rising around you.

Gibson, the British director whose bold and finely detailed mini-series on the black American expatriate singer Josephine Baker earned an Emmy, knows how to transfer the stage energy and sexuality of his subjects to the screen, and how to build a dramatic pace to match. "What's Love" is a speedy two hours of music and knuckle sandwiches, moving so quickly through the '60s and '70s, you barely have time to register Ike's mop-top-to-Afro hairstyle changes before you enter the next fashion era.

It's not easy to accurately depict a full life in a movie, and when you try, as Spike Lee did with "Malcolm X," most people don't have the patience for it. In the case of "What's Love," however, we could have certainly used a few less beatings and a few more details.

In the end, Lanier and Gibson made the heroic myth they envisioned an R-rated "Beauty and the Absolute Beast." It is one of the most harrowing domestic violence movies you'll see this year, and almost certainly the only one you can dance to.

NEWSWEEK, 6/21/93, p. 66, David Ansen

For a movie, full of hair-raising depictions of wife beating, *What's Love Got to Do With It* is a rousingly entertaining musical biopic. And that's what a movie about the unstoppable Tina Turner should be: sassy, playful, soulful and triumphant, like Tina herself. Director Brian Gibson ("The Josephine Baker Story") and writer Kate Lanier don't really try to explain their heroine, or comprehend her talent. It's just there, innate, in the little girl born Anna Mae Bullock, waiting to be discovered.

It's bandleader Ike Turner (Laurence Fishburne) who provides her break, seduces her with his flashy charm, renames her, weds her and runs her into the ground in pursuit of money and fame. Fishburne is amazing as her coke-snorting, guilt-tripping, violent Svengali. He looks nothing like the real string-bean Ike, but he makes this monster chillingly human.

Gibson's movie charges exuberantly from melodramatic to musical highlight, taking its share of liberties with the facts (eager to make the young Tina a wholesome naif, it neglects to mention she already had one kid when she hooked up with Ike). But the clichés of the genre go down easy. As Tina, the tautly powerful Angela Bassett, lip-syncing to Turner's singing, manages to be persuasive in spite of the fact that she's really too severe and pent-up for the part. The unfettered joyousness of Tina's stage presence may elude her, but the movie makes up for it with its strutting rhythms, its wittily tacky production design, its evocative wigs and costumes, which bring a musical era to life. As a celebration of one of the greatest rock-and-roll troupers, this movie definitely has the juice for the job.

SIGHT AND SOUND, 10/93, p. 55, Louise Gray

Nutbush, Tennessee, the late 40s. Inside the small Baptist church, eight-year-old Anna Mae Bullock is showing a precocity in the song-and-dance department unappreciated by the strait-laced choir mistress. Ejected from choir practice, Anna goes home. She hears her parents fighting. Her mother, Zelma, leaves Anna Mae with her grandmother.

1958: Anna Mae arrives in St Louis to join Zelma and her sister Alline, who works as a barmaid in a club. Anna Mae accompanies her one night and is captivated by the club's headlining act, Ike Turner and the Kings of Rhythm. As a feature of his act, Turner passes a microphone around the women in the audience, who sing and attempt to impress him. On her next visit to the club, Anna Mae exchanges her teenage dress for some vampy clothing, takes Turner's mike and sings. Anna Mae is quickly drawn into Ike's band and recording sessions. He is a perfectionist and hungry for success. Despite Ike's turbulent private life, Anna Mae is nevertheless attracted to him. When his girlfriend botches a suicide attempt, Ike comforts himself by seducing Anna Mae. Soon she is pregnant. "A Fool In Love"—credited to Ike and Tina Turner—plays on the radio and Anna Mae realises that her name has been changed. Ike kidnaps Tina from maternity hospital and takes her and their new-born son to Mexico for a ten-minute wedding. "Fool" is a huge hit in 1960: Ike and Tina are performing to packed houses. They buy a family home; Ike is using cocaine and beating Tina up. More hit records follow. Phil Spector invites Tina to record "River Deep Mountain High" with him in 1966.

Ike's drug-fuelled violence increases. Tina's escape attempts fail. During sessions for her self-penned song "Nutbush City Limits", Ike rapes her. Afterwards, Tina overdoses. Rushed to hospital, Jackie, a former Ikettes backing singer, visits and offers help. Returning home, Tina finds Ike and friends mid-party. Jackie introduces Tina to Nichiren Shoshu Buddhism. Gaining strength from Buddhist chanting, Tina begins to fight back, getting divorced in 1977. Now singing to small-time hotel audiences, Tina is eager to swap her old rhythm and blues for a rockier musical style. Roger Davies, her new manager, organises a new band and new songs. A showcase concert is organised for the New York Ritz. Tina's son warns his mother that Ike plans to shoot her. As she chants in preparation for the Ritz show, Ike enters her dressing room carrying a gun. She faces him down and goes on stage to perform "What's Love Got To Do With It." A rider tells us that Ike is later imprisoned for drug offenses.

Midway through the performance of "What's Love Got to Do With It" during the closing minutes of this film, Angela Bassett's Tina segues into the real Tina Turner. It's a neat, barely perceptible join and a clear indication of how convincing Bassett is. Based on Turner's 1986 autobiography *I, Tina*, this is a superior bio-pic whose great strength lies not only in the performances by Laurence Fishburne as Ike and by Bassett herself, but a loving and detailed recreation of their music and stage routines. For these, Bassett's voice has been dubbed with Turner's own recordings of her early material. Bassett's terpsichorean skills are another matter. She has all of Turner's steamy, wild-style dance steps perfectly emulated, making numbers like "Proud Mary", "A Fool In Love" and "Shake A Tail Feather" seem as fresh as the day they were born.

Turner is today globally famous as a rock singer and actress, but the film touches none of this. Turner's film roles in Ken Russell's *Tommy* (1975) or George Miller's *Mad Max Beyond Thunderdome* (1985) are ignored in favour of the central relationship between Tina and Ike—mad, bad and dangerous to know—and the story of Tina's gutsy, bloodied—and in the face of the odds—magnificent survival.

Such facts are all part of the legend. Brian Gibson's movie attempts to make sense of them by means of some subtle explorations of the nature of attraction and violence. The one over-riding question—why does Tina put up with Ike when he's beating her within an inch of her life?—is answered with an attention to the complex dynamics at the heart of such abusive relationships.

Accordingly, Bassett does not portray Tina as a weak woman who grows strong, but as a character with her own agenda. The first time that Tina sees the Kings of Rhythm, her girlishness is emphasised by her dress (cardigan) and demeanour (she drinks through a straw). Only her eyes betray her: the numerous close-ups of the urbane, sexualised Ike represent her vision. The subsequent night out sees Tina dressed up for the microphone event. Good enough to assume Ike's vocal lines, she immediately establishes a counterpoint with him.

Gibson's direction is straight ahead. When Ike beats Tina, teeth fly, usually hers. For a movie which features so much music, the silences punctuated by bone-crunching blows are unnerving. This literal approach may work for the film's violent scenes, but it does not translate over to the more sensitive moments. Tina's espousal of Buddhism is presented as a life-saving move and accordingly given full visual treatments. As Tina begins a tremulous chant, the light around her glows gold, her face assumes a new radiance, and later, chanting even effects a miraculous hair-do.

VILLAGE VOICE, 6/22/93, p. 58, Joe Levy

At the beginning of *What's Love Got To Do With It*, an eight-year-old Anna Mae Bullock gets herself tossed out of church choir practice because the "wild gyrations" that would serve her so well as Tina Turner are already in evidence. A sweet bit played for laughs, it's also just about the only time this biopic focuses on Tina's wild gyrations. Admirably unflinching in its depiction of Ike Turner's wife abuse, *What's Love Got To Do With It* skimps a little on Tina's essential, well, Tinaness. Oh, it's up on the screen, all right—Angela Bassett's portrayal of the diva is as breathtakingly uncanny as any drag queen's, far better when it comes to youthful exuberance—it's just never the point. There's enough action—if you count the dancing—and heart-tugging for Tina to dethrone Sly and Arnold at the box office, but something's off.

This movie was made because Tina is fierce, but here fierceness, albeit of a different sort, is the business of Laurence Fishburne's Ike. In scene after scene, Bassett's Tina radiates the agonized beatitude of a tortured saint. The Tina Turner that Bassett embodies so convincingly is not the Tina Turner the Sayles brothers caught jerking off the microphone stand before a Rolling Stones concert in 1970's *Gimme Shelter*, nor is she the Tina Turner who, legend has it, four years earlier taught a stiff Mick Jagger how to pony backstage in London, nor is she the Tina Turner who today lives in Cologne with her boyfriend of six years, Erwin Bach, managing director of German EMI. That Tina is just a shade too sexual, too complicated, and perhaps too white to appeal to audiences that in matters of sexuality and miscegenation prefer Whitney Houston to Madonna and Whitney and Kevin to Whoopi and Ted.

Well, you could argue, the movie *was* bankrolled by Disney. And, to be sure, the longer this "true" story unfolds, the more a strange Disney flavor floats to the surface: Ike plays the evil, power-mad sorcerer from *Aladdin*, Tina the besieged Belle from *Beauty and the Beast* (only she starts out with a prince who turns into a beast), and the ex-Ikette who teaches Tina the Buddhist chant that will finally set her free is a sort-of fairy godmother. And for all its vibrancy, tragic power, and nearly earned melodrama, in the end the dream this movie trades in really is that flat—this is a tale of recovery, and the recovery it builds toward is more fairy tale than struggle.

But early on it paints a different sort of fairy tale in sharp, colorful strokes. A rock film more in the tradition of *The Buddy Holly Story* or *La Bamba* than *Lady Sings the Blues* or *The Doors*, *What's Love Got To Do With It* concentrates on spirit, not truth, and using a net woven with an attention to period verisimilitude so detailed it's sure to have Lenny Kravitz on the phone to costume designer Ruth Carter, *What's Love* captures the archetypal rock dream, the giddy ride from obscurity to stardom. This is the part of the story you perhaps don't know—how 17-year-old Tennessee country girl Anna Mae Bullock came to sing with Ike Turner's Kings of Rhythm—and it's here that the film soars. When Anna Mae, new to St. Louis, sees Ike perform at the club where her older sister Alline works, she's smitten.

And given the way Laurence Fishburne fills the screen when he first appears, it's utterly believable. His every movement made with the sort of suave assurance that only those who have nightly heard the approving screams of the faithful can summon, Fishburne play the young Ike as Elvis by way of Pépé Le Peu (as time passes, he begins to resemble another cartoon of Elvis, Gary Panter's ever-disintegrating Elvis zombies). Ike indulges the crowd in a nightly ritual: passing a mike around the room to give the adoring lovelies a chance at a duet. You can guess the rest. (To tell the truth, or at least to tell it the way Tina did to Kurt Loder in the book on which this movie is "based," *I, Tina*, this is one of many facts bent but not mangled. There was no mike passed around the club, and though many women fell at first sight for the stepping razor that was Ike Turner, Anna Mae wasn't one of them—she went for Kings of Rhythm saxophone player Raymond Hill, father of her first child.)

There's a rampant joy packed into these first minutes: Alline getting happy behind the bar as her sister sings onstage for the first time; Ike at breakfast with his meal ticket, trying to play it cool as he tells her she's his new singer; dapper Ike convincing Mrs. Bullock to let Anna Mae join the band; Ike encouraging Anna Mae to really sing rough in rehearsal. Fishburne and

Bassett's first scenes together are a delight, but the ugliness that will eventually, inevitably, erupt shadows their every moment. When, having finished a long day of rehearsal, Ike sits alone at the piano, Anna Mae hovers expectantly. Sit down, he says, and she does. Open your mouth, he says, and she does, slightly, expecting a kiss. You've never been to the dentist, he says, you've got a lot of cavities back there, and she hangs her head. It's too late to be going home, he says, I've got a room made up for you in the back, and she goes. His paternalism seems touching, her evident devotion more so, but you can feel that paternalism becoming transgressive with each passing second.

When it does, it begins as verbal abuse (Ike driving Tina to tears before she sings "A Fool in Love"—get it?—at the Apollo), then smolders silently (Ike sneering as an interviewer asks them about the British Invasion; "Well, you know, Ike says it's just black music played by white people," Tina responds, as the disgust of an entire generation of rock and roll innovators plays across Fishburne's face, the only target in sight a black woman, not a white man), and ultimately explodes in a long moment of physical violence that becomes unbearably frightening as we witness its impact on Ike and Tina's children.

The more coke Ike shoves up his nose (and if there's anything *What's Love got To Do With It* nails, it's superfly decadence), the worse it gets, and it never stops, never, not even when Tina—in a moment already so well known that the audience is waiting to cheer it nearly as soon as the opening credits roll—finds the courage to strike back, finally walking out on him in her blood-covered white Yves St. Laurent suit with nothing but (everyone together now) a Mobil card and 36 cents to her name. In reality, Ike did stalk Tina afterward, or at least *somebody* was shooting out the windows of every friend's house she stayed in once she'd left him in 1976. But only in the Hollywood version did he visit her backstage before one of her triumphant 1983 showcases at the Ritz in New York. And only in the Hollywood version did she stare him down and then walk out onstage to sing "What's Love Got To Do With It," *like it's suddenly a song about him or something*.

"The movie's not about her, it's about me," the real Ike Turner told *Vanity Fair* in the midst of blaming Tina for his womanizing (she didn't object) and his abuse (she didn't leave). This may be the only thing Ike—a once-brilliant guitarist and piano player whose art will never get the consideration accorded famous wife abusers William Burroughs and Miles Davis—has right, because *What's Love Got to Do With It* is Laurence Fishburne's movie. His Ike subsumes the whole movie the way Ike subsumed Tina's life, which is more than a little creepy if you stop to think about it. His menace, his frustration, his disgusting tendency to make anyone in his way or grasp the target of his menace and frustration sends chilly light through virtually every scene—even the ones he's not in: when Tina seeks out the friend who will free her with Buddhism, the two women bond by sharing their Ike parodies. They become him, they read him, and *then* they cry for Tina. It doesn't help any that Tina's triumph is given such scant screen time. She leaves Ike, she divorces Ike, she's shown playing *one* hotel lounge gig (director Brian Gibson shows good taste by featuring adoring drag queens at a front table), and suddenly it's time for her big night at the Ritz, her chance to be a star, if only *Ike* won't destroy it! *What's Love Got To Do With It* leaves us right on the edge of what Tina wants: success, on her own terms, a career centered around her pleasure and no one else's.

As it winds down—and once the chanting starts, down it winds—*What's Love Got To Do With It* sinks further and further into conventional made-for-TV staleness; disappointing because so much of what's come before crackles. But however superb his actors, Gibson is only as good as his costume and set designers that is, as long as the period is stunning, so is his movie. "In the later '60s and the '70s," Ruth Carter explains in the production notes, "the clothes just exploded, getting really wild and psychedelic with plaids and polyesters and calmed right down again. Just like Tina's life." It's a shame that Gibson seems even more unable to distinguish the lady's clothes from her life.

Also reviewed in:
CHICAGO TRIBUNE, 6/11/93, Friday/p. C, Clifford Terry
NEW YORK TIMES, 6/9/93, p. C15, Janet Maslin
NEW YORKER, 6/28/93, p. 98, Terrence Rafferty
VARIETY, 6/14/93, p. 54, Leonard Klady

WASHINGTON POST, 6/11/93, p. G1, Rita Kempley
WASHINGTON POST, 6/11/93, Weekend/p. 42, Desson Howe

WHERE ARE WE?: OUR TRIP THROUGH AMERICA

A Roxie release of a Telling Pictures production. *Producer:* Jeffrey Friedman and Robert Epstein. *Director:* Jeffrey Friedman and Robert Epstein. *Director of Photography:* Jean de Segonzac. *Editor:* Ned Bastille. *Music:* Daniel Licht. *Sound:* Mark Roy. *Running time:* 75 minutes. *MPAA Rating:* Not Rated.

LOS ANGELES TIMES, 7/2/93, Calendar/p. 10, Kevin Thomas

With the gentle, lyrical "Where Are We" San Francisco filmmakers Rob Epstein and Jeffrey Friedman, who won an Oscar for their documentary "Common Threads: Stories From the Quilt," took off on an 18-day trip through the South (plus parts of the Southwest) and questioned people about their lives. The result is a warm and often revealing account of contemporary America—counter-pointed with the shimmering strains of the "Aquarium" section of Saint-Saëns' "Carnival of the Animals." Throughout, the filmmakers zeroed in on ordinary or poor people; a sprinkling of the views of intellectuals or the rich and powerful might have added some variety.

Wisely, Epstein and Friedman are as friendly and polite as those they interview, which means that their subjects really open up to them, and they leave any judging up to us. We know where we are only when someone happens to mention locale—or when we recognize the place ourselves; some discreet labeling would keep us from wondering most of the time.

By far the most intriguing sequence is set in an off-limits gay nightclub catering to a nearby Marine base. As gays themselves, Epstein and Friedman are able to elicit candid remarks from several young macho Marines about the oppressiveness of their lives as gays in the military. They also talk to the club's middle-aged female impersonator, who speaks proudly of all the money he's raised for the fight against AIDS. When the next morning the filmmakers see the same group of Marines on the beach, a couple of them, previously shot with their faces in shadow, decide to come out for the cameras.

Epstein and Friedman also make a compassionate visit to an AIDS hospice in New Orleans, and when, at the beginning of the film they ask two teen-agers what impression they have of San Francisco, one of them casually replies that it has a "faggot image," not realizing the sexual orientation of the filmmakers.

"Where Are We" is by no means concerned only with gay attitudes and issues. The filmmakers have an entirely pleasant visit to a prosperous-looking Mississippi restaurant with a friendly, likable proprietor who, as it turns out, pays her black cook only $3.85 an hour—after 18 years of service. Epstein and Friedman don't go in for bizarre Diane Arbus-like subjects, but how could they not resist talking to a nice middle-aged couple, a woman whose husband has supported his wife's love of Elvis by constructing Graceland in miniature in their yard. And when they stop over in Vegas on the way home they first talk to the homeless before interviewing Strip casino operator Bob Stupak, who, with a keen sense of playing the odds, tells them he believes we're 88% responsible for our fates.

The filmmakers end by appraising the surprisingly upbeat note the majority of their interviewees expressed. Epstein remarks, "I'm struck by how content they were with their lives"—to which Friedman replies that it may just be that they are "resigned to their fates." Surely, the truth for most of the engaging people of "Where Are We" (Times-rated family) lies somewhere in between the two observations.

NEW YORK POST, 7/30/93, p. 34, Jerry Tallmer

It probably wouldn't have changed his mind, but it might have been instructive if Gen. Colin Powell had taken a few minutes sometime in the past year to look at "Where Are We? Our trip Through America," the splendid short film by Rob Epstein and Jeffrey Friedman.

He would have seen for instance, a tattooed and muscled young man a First Sergeant type, driving past a "Welcome Home Desert Storm Heroes" banner at Camp Lejeune, N.C., while talking about the lover, a fellow Marine, that the war had separated him from. Or another Marine in a gay bar—the one that's off-limits—who has married a lesbian in the service "to get everybody off our backs" but who still has the wracking everyday problem "should I do this, should I do that, or will it look too feminine?" Another saying angrily: "I fought for my country and I don't want to be treated like a little beat-up piece of road trash."

The people encountered in this movie—by bus, car, train, on foot—are for by far the greater part not homosexual, though the sensibility of its two filmmakers—San Franciscans transplanted from New York and suburban New Jersey—is openly and unashamedly gay. They'd set forth with video camera "like tourists in our own country" in the spring of 1991 "to get out of our lives, meet people different from ourselves." What they returned with, eight months later, is a vivid kaleidoscope—boiled down to 75 richly packed minutes of that other country that is their, and our, own.

Some Americans who stick in one's vision:

The beefy blue-eyed bigot of the barber shop whose first hate is "too many goddamned liberal news reporters" and in the end reveals the gutting of his body, from lung to lung.

The gawky young couple being chatted up for a mobile home ($215 a month, real brass door-knobs) by a onetime Detroit Tiger prospect; the girl turns out to be 15, and pregnant.

The gray-haired lady whose husband built her a miniature Graceland. "I love Elvis but I'm in love *with* my husband, and now"—her eyes fill—"he has MS."

The AIDS patient in a Lazarus House who, when asked "Ever been afraid?"—these filmmakers' favorite question—quietly replies: "I'm afraid now." How does he get through it? "I cry. And try to help other people. And wonder if anything *really* happens after they're gone."

The young unemployed black man who says, without hope: "I'm no slave," and the young black woman at a Mothers' Day church sodality who, talking of how much she loves her mother, says: "I think she mean sometimes, but she be right."

And those Marines.

NEWSDAY, 7/30/93, Part II/p. 69, Jan Stuart

The makers of "The Times of Harvey Milk" won an Oscar in part for an ability to put workaday people before a camera and turn their hearts inside out. Rob Epstein and his companion, Jeffrey Friedman, have exploited this talent once again, to the Nth degree, in a riveting video album of an 18-day sweep across the U.S. of A.

"Where Are We? Our Trip Through America" is my kind of American home movie: part Arbus photograph come to life, part Studs Terkel oral document made visible. The sum result is the most entertaining portrait of our hope-drunk nation since "Pee-wee's Big Adventure."

It is also, at times, the scariest. Only minutes into this car, bus and train journey, a young southern boy confides that he'd rather be in New York City because "It's violent! I *like* violence!" A moment later a bus rider with a fixed grin and a Judy Canova bounce recalls how she survived both a hail of bullets and her mother's lifelong abuse.

These and other breathtaking admissions come in response to such improbably intimate questions as "What are your fears? Do you have any regrets? What's important in your life?" On occasion, this fanzine approach yields lackluster results, as when kids at a fair are asked what they want to be when they grow up. More often, the candor of strangers catches you off guard till you feel as if you're locked into a perpetual double take.

Epstein and Friedman's personal interests as gay men move the film into national territory that might otherwise be overlooked. A gay veteran of Desert Storm takes them on a tour of a southern military base and the local gay bar, during which a lesbian and her gay husband-of-convenience come out defiantly on camera. In a haunting glimpse of existential angst, an AIDS patient at a New Orleans hospice spends his waning days hanging out a window: "The sun's going down, kids'll soon be riding past on their bikes backwards and forwards. That's it."

Artfully edited by Ned Bastille, "Where Are We?" vaults effortlessly from the upbeat (a gospel celebration of Mother's Day) to the down (an Elvis fan whose husband has built an elaborate mini-Graceland model in their yard weeps suddenly for her husband's illness), the hopeful (a

Texas youth treks to L.A. to "become a superstar") to the resigned (a fry chef who earns $3.45 an hour after 18 years on the job).

Some of the most colorful encounters, not surprisingly, occur in Las Vegas. A priest with Elmer Gantry charisma and a press agent's rap roves the city in a van dispensing free razors, blessings and good will to the down and out. An abrasive gambling casino operator, asked who his heroes are, lists Lech Walesa, Nelson Mandela and Mother Teresa.

"Where Are We?" falters whenever the filmmakers kick in their own musings. The banality of these sculpted contemplations ("Alone among strangers I had no history, no identity, I could be whatever I wanted to be") feels stilted and intrusive when contrasted with the plainspoken spontaneity of their subjects.

The film owes much of its success to director of photography Jean de Segonzac, whose alert camera takes in such eccentric details as a copy of "The New Sweden" on the coffee table of a model mobile home and a kitten lapping water from a miniature kidney-shaped pool. "Where Are We? Our Trip Through America" leaves you with its title question hanging in the air and several dozen disquieting answers to choose from.

Also reviewed in:
NEW YORK TIMES, 7/30/93, p. C14, Stephen Holden
VARIETY, 2/3/92, p. 81, Todd McCarthy

WHO'S THE MAN?

A New Line Cinema release of a New Line Cinema production in association with Tin Pan Apple/de Passse Entertainment/Thomas Entertainment. *Executive Producer:* Suzanne de Passe. *Producer:* Charles Stettler and Maynell Thomas. *Director:* Ted Demme. *Screenplay:* Seth Greenland. *Director of Photography:* Adam Kimmel. *Editor:* Jeffrey Wolf and John Gilroy. *Music:* Andre Harrell. *Sound:* Rosa Howell-Thornhill. *Casting:* Jaki Brown. *Production Designer:* Ruth Ammon. *Set Decorator:* Susan Raney. *Set Dresser:* Stephen Finkin and Douglas Fechtdebby Dreyer. *Costumes:* Karen Perry. *Make-up:* Ellie Winslow. *Stunt Coordinator:* Jeff Ward. *Running time:* 124 minutes. *MPAA Rating:* R.

CAST: Doctor Dre (Doctor Dre); Ed Lover (Ed Lover); Badja Djola (Lionel); Cheryl "Salt" James (Teesha Braxton); Jim Moody (Nick Crawford); Andre Blake (Lamar); Rozwill Young (Griles); Colin Quinn (Frankie Flynn); Todd 1 (Shorty); Bowlegged Lou (Forty); Bernie Mack (G-George); Bill Bellamy (K.K.); T-Money (Bubba); Denis Leary (Sgt. Cooper); Garfield (Homeboy #1); High L. Hurd (Albert); Roger Robinson (Charlie); Maggie Rush (Brenda); Richard Bright (Demetrius); Dennis Vestunis (Gustave); James Cavanagh Burke (Officer Barnes); Lee Drakeford (Roscoe); Curtis Carrott (Boogie); Caron Bernstein (Model/Kelly); Randy Frazier (Rev. Green); Kim Chan (Fuji); Vinny Pastore (Tony Como); Joe Lisi (Captain Reilly); Lorena Mann (Receptionist); Leslie Segar (Sheneequa); Jenay Nurse (Girl #1); Glenn Kubota (Korean Merchant); Ralph McDaniels (TV Reporter); Linque Ayoung (Nurse); Gavin O'Connor (Drill Man #1); Ali Abdul Wahha (Cop); Afrika Bambatta (Bartender); Apache and Eric B. (Bubba Workers); B-Real, of Cypress Hill (Jose); Black Sheep (Jose); Brand Nubian (Jose); Bushwick Bill, D-Nice and Da Youngstas (Junkies); Del Tha Funkee Homosapien (Kid #2); Delroy (Day); Fab 5 Freddy (Himself); Flavor Flav (Himself); Freddy Foss, Fu Schnickens, Grand Puba (Bartenders); Guru, from Gangstarr, Heather B., and Heavy D (Lorenzo); House of Pain (Mike, Steve, Billy); Humpty Hump (Club Doorman); Ice-T, Isis, and Jamalski (Nighttrain); Kris Kross (Micah & Karim); Krs-One (Rashid); Kwame (Kid #1); Kurt Loder (Roberto); Monie Love (Vanessa); Ken Ober (Bernstein); Pepa, of Salt 'N Pepa (Sherisse); Phife (Gerald); Queen Latifah (Dana); Q-Tip (Dana); Pete Rock (Robber #1); C.L. Smooth (Robber #2); Stretch, from Live Squad (Benny); Too Short (Benny); D.J. Wiz, from Kid 'N Play (Benny); Yo-Yo (Woman).

LOS ANGELES TIMES, 4/23/93, Calendar/p. 10, Kevin Thomas

"Who's the Man?," a raucous, laugh-out-loud comedy, introduces to the screen Doctor Dré and Ed Lover, MTV rap stars, who can be as funny as they are goofy. As Harlem barbers they're so bad their boss strong-arms them into taking a police academy exam. Don't ask why he thinks this would be a good idea, especially since Doctor Dré is about 200 pounds overweight for the job. Naturally, they pass, much to their surprise, if not ours.

In a tradition of black-oriented films that dates back to pioneer filmmaker Oscar Micheaux, "Who's the Man?" baldly mixes entertainment and social consciousness, but backed by a lively, hard-driving score and a fail-safe sense of humor, director Ted Demme blends the mix with the greatest of ease from a script by its stars and Seth Greenland. "Who's the Man" gets serious about reclaiming Harlem from gangs and drugs and staving off developers who build housing that none of those displaced by its construction could hope to afford. Meanwhile, there's a nonstop parade of hip-hop stars appearing in walk-ons. There's even a cameo by Ice-T as a drug dealer ashamed of his real name, which is Chauncey.

Nobody takes these rookies seriously, but to be sure, they're brighter than they act, and they smell a rat when they discover a smooth, rapacious builder (Richard Bright) is running soil tests on property he plans to develop.

Dré and Lover are lively entertainers, and, besides Bright, they're backed by Badja Djola as a smart, successful man whose gambling debts have placed him in Bright's thrall and by Jim Moody as their courageous, activist boss, a barber who once cut the hair of Adam Clayton Powell. Also on hand are other MTV stars Denis Leary and Colin Quinn. "Who's the Man?" (rated R for strong language) surely could not have worked had it not been filmed right on the vital streets of Harlem, with the scarred elegance of its old buildings and its sadly vacant lots captured lyrically by cameraman Adam Kimmel.

NEW YORK POST, 4/23/93, p. 38, Jerry Tallmer

How fast time flies. At the beginning of "Who's the Man?"—a hip-hop rap-a-dap movie mostly photographed in Harlem—its stars, Ed Lover and Doctor Dre (he's the short fat one), are two inept scissor-wielders in white jackets, driving most of the customers away from Big Nick's Barber Shop. "I wouldn't let those two guys cut my taxes," sneers one bystander.

Big Nick has had enough. He's going to let them go. But Big Nick (Jim Moody) is a pal, almost a papa. "The Police Force is hiring brothers," he tells them. "I don't wanna be The Man," says Ed, or maybe it's Dre. "Give me one reason," says Nick. Two hands shoot into the air. "Rodney King."

Ten days ago that line might have been a killer. But at this week's preview (before a predominantly black audience) it stirred only an uneasy laugh. Most of the running gags throughout the movie after (natch) they join the Force—the Sgt. Cooper (Denis Leary) who in his fury at these rookies forever and again tauntingly deprives Dre of doughnuts, for instance, while letting taller, slimmer Ed eat his fill—get better laughs.

There are real killers in the movie, or movie killers anyway, and one of them gets Big Nick with a fire bomb. Ed and Dre's blundering but persistent efforts to track down the guy or guys whodunit infuriate the regular detectives and lead to chases in a funny souped-up cop car down mean streets past empty lots that may contain more treasure—black treasure—than meets the eye. That's all I'll say, too.

I had prepared my head against the rap score and, when I saw his name among the cast, against Ice-T, a headline-provoking rapper whose lyrics, if that's the word, call for the deaths of cops. But the score, when heard, or as much as could be heard, seemed to be inoffensive muffled background rhythm, and Ice-T as one of the baddies has the dubious pleasure of sullenly proclaiming himself to Ed and Dre as not a squealer in the very instant that he's squealing. It's not just time that flies, but lies.

Well, "Who's the Man?" is opening wide today, and I think there have been more damaging movies and certainly more visually and verbally violent ones in the blaxploitation syndrome, which "Who's the Man?"—written by Seth Greenland, directed by Ted Demme—is not really part of. I also did actually have to laugh at a top (white) cop's ranting to Ed and Dre: "You're telling

me that one of the most successful real-estate developers is digging for oil in Harlem? There is oil in Saudi Arabia. There is oil in Venezuela. *There is no oil on 125th Street!*"
He who laughs last laughs best.

NEWSDAY, 4/23/93, Part II/p. 75, Wayne Robins

If it was a creative stretch to make a full-length movie out of the "Saturday Night Live" sketch "Wayne's world," it requires superheroic elasticity to make cinematic leading men out of Ed Lover and Doctor Dre, the affable hosts of the popular cable series "Yo! MTV Raps." But Ted Demme—creator of that MTV hip-hop series and nephew of filmmaker Jonathan Demme—gets the most out of his inexperienced performers and their silly story for "Who's the Man?"

The movie is little more than "Police Academy Goes to Harlem." Lover (he's the would-be suave but unsuccessful ladies' man) and Dre (he's the round mound of sound) are the world's worst haircutters at big-hearted Nick Crawford's Harlem barbershop. Nick pulls strings with a former Vietnam buddy to get Lover and Dre (which are also the names of their characters) admitted to the police department.

The not-altogether-believable plot has to do with a nefarious white real-estate developer named Demetrius (Richard Bright) who goes to diabolical lengths to get Nick's barbershop off the otherwise vacant Harlem lot on which he wants to build a condominium. It strains believability that some members of the community are up in arms about this "creeping gentrification" in a blighted area whose only visible residents are drug dealers and rodents.

That Lover and Dre will bumble their way to discovering Demetrius' real motive for wanting the land is, of course, predestined. (A hint is contained in Dre's obsession with Jed Clampett of "The Beverly Hillbillies.")

The fortunes of this most minor movie benefit from some capable acting. Ice-T is ably typecast as a drug dealer, though he gives the character an unexpectedly pathetic twist; Rozwill Young plays the intimidating "black Kojak," Sgt. Bo Griles. But Denis Leary both steals and uplifts the movie in each of the too-few frames he appears as the high-strung Sgt. Cooper, who is outraged by Dre's self-awarded honorific "Doctor" and tortures him with a recurring series of doughnut jokes.

Among the sound and sight gags that work for a few seconds are the souped-up, hip-hop blasting police car Dre and Lover have renovated, and the occasional rap insider cameos, including Pete Rock, C. L. Smooth and Eric B. as robbers, and the three members of Run-D.M.C. as detectives. Though there are occasional stabs at relevance (when told by his sergeant that being a police officer is about one thing, Lover remarks, "Harassing black people"), "Who's The Man?" generally amounts to little more than a hip-hop enhanced variation on an especially slight "Car 54, Where Are You?" episode.

VILLAGE VOICE, 5/4/93, p. 58, Scott Poulson-Bryant

You know *Who's the Man* is supposed to be a comedy, a hip-hop whodunit, but why do you keep laughing at it (not with it)? Why do you know whodunit the moment the "who" walks onscreen? Why is the local numbers runner a white guy? Why isn't the subplot about oil in Harlem played for more irony and sophistication? And how does Doctor Dre find a yellow cab in Harlem just-like-that?

Why is Ice-T, the rapper with the most screen presence of any of them, shot from that odd three-quarter angle in his first scene? And why do all the cameos by hip-hop's finest seem so desperate and silly? And why do hip-hop movies always have to seem so slapdash and uncoordinated and awkward? Why, for all our visual finesse and black-like-us attitude, do they rarely reach the glorious states-of-grace that the records can?

In this case, probably because the white filmmakers use only black records and videos as a referent, not black life. In hip-hop lingo, they fake the funk. But they couldn't do it without black folks, who so often become co-conspirators in our own pop cultural demise. This movie has so much "flavor" it's tasteless.

Also reviewed in:
NEW YORK TIMES, 4/23/93, p. C19, Janet Maslin
VARIETY, 4/26/93, p. 69, Leonard Klady
WASHINGTON POST, 4/23/93, p. D6, Hal Hinson

WHY HAS BODHI-DHARMA LEFT FOR THE EAST?

A Milestone release. *Producer:* Bae Yong-Kyun. *Director:* Bae Yong-Kyun. *Screenplay (Korean with English subtitles):* Bae Yong-Kyun. *Director of Photography:* Bae Yong-Kyun. *Editor:* Bae Yong-Kyun. *Music:* Chin Kyu-Yong. *Running time:* 135 minutes. *MPAA Rating:* Not Rated.

CAST: Yi Pan Yong (Hyegok); Sin Won Sop (Kibong); Huang Hae Jin (Haejin); Ko Su Yong (Superior); Kim Hae Yong (Fellow Disciple).

FILM QUARTERLY, Fall 1994, p. 27, Linda C. Ehrlich

The film *Why Has Bodhi-Dharma Left for the East? (Dharmaga Tongjoguro Kan Kkadalgun?* 1989), by Korean director Bae Yong-Kyun, tells the deceptively simple story of three generations of monks at a remote Buddhist temple on top of Mount Chonan in Korea.[1] As an official selection of "'Un Certain Regard" at the Cannes Film Festival in 1989 and winner of the Golden Leopard at the 1989 Locarno Film Festival, it marks the first director's award in the history of Korean cinema. The film is itself a meditative experience for the ensemble of non-professional actors, for the director with his years of Zen practice, and for the viewer, Bae Yong-Kyun spent ten years as screenwriter, cinematographer, director, and editor of this film. (Only the music is composed by someone else: Chin Kyn-Yong.)

Bodhi-Dharma (A.D.460-534) was the Indian monk considered to be the founder of Ch'an (Zen) Buddhism.[2] According to legend, he traveled from India eastward, supposedly arriving in China in A.D. 520. In Bae Yong-Kyun's film, the three main characters—the venerable Zen master, Hyegok (Yi Pan-Yong), the young disciple, Kibong (Sin Won-Sop), and the orphan and novice, Haejin (Huang Hae-Jin), adopted by Hyegok—embark, individually and communally, on paths of self-understanding and self-transcendence that pass through breathtaking scenes of the five elements: earth, water, fire, air, and ether.

Near the beginning of the film, the camera moves from a reflection of Haejin's face in a 'pool to a close-up of water poured into a simple tea bowl, to another close-up of the mouth of a golden Buddha statue: These links are legible, but then a close-up of a toad walking laboriously across the road suddenly appears on the screen, followed by a close-up of the hands of the "middle generation" monk, Kibong, chopping up a tree branch. Visually and thematically, this is a film about interconnectedness, and about the transformation of one event, object, person into another in a regenerative chain of causality. This regeneration lies behind the master's admonitions to his disciples, just as it underlies the sound links that connect one scene to the next. Legibility and ambiguity interact in *Bodhi-Dharma* to produce a film that like a Zen *koan* (riddle), is at once astonishingly clear and elliptical and absurd. As Jay Carr wrote in his *Boston Globe* review (January 28, 1994), "The brand of Zen we get here is rarefied, yet highly pragmatic, realistic and tough-minded."

After throwing a pebble at a bird (which later dies), Haejin is haunted by its mate. Later, Haejin himself almost dies in a chain of events somehow connected with the bird—a chain that sends him plunging into the river and later crashing through the forest. An ox that had earlier escaped from its pen reappears and starts to lead him back to the temple, in a manner reminiscent of the ox-herding pictures of Zen Buddhism,[3] Only afterwards do we realize that this ox is probably but another form of Haejin's mother, represented by a woman drenched in the waters of the river.[4] As she opens her mouth to awaken the sleeping boy who lies exhausted by his ordeal in the forest, the ox bellows.

The circular format of the film appears as well in round objects like the moon and the mouth of the tea bowl, calling to mind the Chinese phrase "the circle of heaven." It could also refer to the circle of rebirth, suffering, and death in Buddhist cosmology, or to Zen paintings and calligraphy of the circle. The round shapes of clouds, considered symbols of abundance in Korean art, frequently fill the screen in long, contemplative sequences. The soft mountain scenes evoke the gentle natural environment of the Korean countryside.

A circle of caring continues throughout the film, adding a note of intimacy to the geographical isolation of the master's temple. Shots of Haejin nursing the injured Kibong after his desperate flight into the river are crosscut with the actual scenes of rescue in the raging water. Temporal and spatial leaps like these cause us to wonder which part of the film is reality, which part dream.

Bodhi-Dharma is also a film of stillness. Scenes of a monk meditating are sometimes shot from the rear in extreme close-up, giving the seated figure colossal, even heroic, proportions. When Kibong meditates, perched on a rock over the roaring stream, he becomes the embodiment of the meditative mind, which is both still and full of the movement of the universe. Occasional glimpses of Buddhist statues in the temple call to mind both the historical Buddha, who achieved enlightenment and then passed on from this earth, and the appearance of the sacred in human form. As the Japanese Buddhist priest Kukai (774-835) stated: "Suchness transcends forms, but without depending on forms it cannot be realized."[5] This paradoxical relationship between form and formlessness is apparent in the elegant proportions of works such as the Korean gilt bronze statue of the Yaksa Yorae, the Buddha of Healing, based on Chinese T'ang models, or the beautiful Korean statues of the Maitreya (Miroku) Buddha of the Future, with right leg crossed over left and right hand touching a faintly smiling face in the gentlest of contemplations. The three main characters all engage in this dance of form and formlessness, in a studied alternation between light and darkness.

The elements reign in *Bodhi-Dharma*. While Hyegok, the old master, is described by another elderly monk as being "like a beacon from a lighthouse," the small child Haejin is like the candle he carries to light his way at night. The master talks of light: "If you free the moon inside of you, it will light the whole world." The *koan* later presented to Kibong by Hyegok speaks of the moon and of one's own heart, just as the *koan* of the title (in its slightly altered form) has revealed to Zen masters over the centuries the depth of a disciple's path toward enlightenment.

Each of the three characters encounters violence and shadows in his life—Haejin with a group of children from the lower areas of the mountain (filmed in a painful slow motion) who try to push him under the water ... Kibong with his internal struggles over his abandonment of his family, and with the master's harsh slap with a stick when he senses Kibong's wavering. Even the old master, seemingly as unshakable, is seen pacing back and forth and pitting his frail body against the fiercest of rapids when his disciples go astray.

This is a film of fire. Following his master's precise instructions, Kibong cremates Hyegok's body in a carefully tended fire and then scatters the ashes throughout the countryside, observed by a shivering Haejin, a solitary bird on a nearby limb, and the ox (shown in a startling close-up of an eye filled with tears). As if immersed in the profound silence of another world, the young monk, covered with ash, is seen in reflection in a still pool as he empties his bag of ash and pounded bones. The next day he leaves the temple he had so arduously journeyed to enter. Haejin, alone at the temple, tends the cooking fire by himself as he gazes into the flame.

Bodhi-Dharma is a film of journeys, of losing and finding one's way. Slow-motion close-ups of the feet of Kibong as he approaches the master's temple for the first time emphasize the inward journey theme. But it is Kibong's trip back to the "dusty world" to beg for funds for the master's herbal medicine that reveals in the sharpest detail the journey he has undergone, and what still remains.

The city is full of flashing red lights, vendors hawking blue jeans, the misery of a young man literally harnessed to a cart of snacks and cheap liquor which he pulls through the streets at night. Although not overtly a politically motivated film, *Bodhi-Dharma* does present disturbing, and haunting, images of urban slum life that go beyond a simple exhortation to abandon city life and escape to a temple in the hills. The hypnotic sound of Kibong beating on the traditional wooden instrument (*mog-tak*) used during meditation mixes with the more dissonant cries of the city. The echoes of the insistent beating sound, and the increasingly shrill cries of the slum dwellers, echo in all subsequent scenes. While shots of the city are marked by a close-framed and claustrophobic melange of images, those of the temple and its surroundings celebrate the glory of the natural setting and the comfortable state of decay into which the old wooden building has fallen.

When Kibong returns to the city, his eyes meet those of a young slum-dweller. The gaunt face of this city youth (representing Kibong in his life before taking vows) forms the opening image of the film, and his despondent and then anguished glances serve as a foil for the meditating Kibong. These two images of the same man are more than contrasts: they are two inevitabilities that—like the earlier montage sequence of tea bowl, hands, and toad—are intrinsically interconnected.

In the early life of the Buddha, the overly protected prince Gautama journeyed out of the royal compound and encountered illness, poverty, despair. In a similar fashion, Kibong, returning from the city to the temple along a narrow path, passes an old man and his retarded child peering curiously from the window of their worn-down farmhouse. Life, with all its weight and fragility, can be seen in the face of this resigned old man as he rests for a moment. The lesson is not lost on the fledgling monk.

Trapped between a desire for enlightenment and ties to the suffering of the mundane world, including the suffering of his blind mother (widowed at an early age), Kibong attempts to silence the voices within him through austerities. In an interior monologue brilliantly staged in silhouette and spoken by two figures, a man perched on a ledge listens to another outline his reasons for returning to the needs of the quotidian world. Are these men two distinct figures—Kibong and a fellow monk who appeared earlier in the film—or a dialogue between two sides of Kibong's psyche, or both? If attachment to desire is the root of all suffering, as the Buddha taught, where does a passionate desire for enlightenment fit in the order of the universe?

Kibong is aware of his need for his master's teachings, and yet it is the master's death that proves the ultimate *koan*. But this is not a film about endings. As Rhim Hye-Kyung writes in a review of the film in *Cinenaya*:

> There is no room in this film for the superfluous; there is a mathematical precision of dramaturgies—of story, light, sound, music. The overwhelming scenic beauty is indeed contemplative, but unlike Ozu, where tranquillity implies a sadness at the transitory nature of human existence, Bae's film is a vivid and affirmative engagement in the recognition of this reality.[6]

Beginnings, not endings, appear as well in the parallels between child and master. It is the child who is led; it is the child who leads. The child is the one who explores, while the master has renounced such explorations. Who is the enlightened one? Who is the child and who is the master?

In the scene in which he accidentally falls into the water, Haejin struggles and appears to be drowning. When he gives up and just floats, he reaches the shore safely. This message of nonattachment to what is transitory and in flux is what the old master instructs when the child remains curious about the diseased tooth which had been pulled from his mouth (and, following an old custom, tossed up on the temple rooftop). After the death of the master, Haejin first embraces and then suddenly decides to burn the package of his master's belongings Kibong has left with him. This could be a childish act of anger, but we sense otherwise. The previous night, following the master's cremation, the exhausted Kibong had been awakened by the surprising sound of a child's voice chanting the sutras.

Bodhi-Dharma partakes of the qualities of Korean art, marked by spontaneity, straight forwardness, and a modesty that hides its own splendor. Comfortable with the "imperfect" and the asymmetrical, Korean art displays a love of nature and a preference for a gentleness of line and modeling.[7] Buddhism was introduced into Korea from India, via China, in the late fourth century A.D., and spread among the common people. Although Korea received Confucianism and Taoism from China as well, it has always retained its own unique national identity despite repeated attacks from hostile neighbors, including a 35-year annexation by Japan that ended only with the close of WWII. One aspect of this unique national identity is the way in which shamanism has retained an intimate relationship with Buddhism in Korea and continues to be considered vital in the popular culture.[8]

In *Bodhi-Dharma*, a scene of a vaguely shamanistic Buddhist dance in the temple of the lower part of the mountain unites the five elements as it also unites light and shadow, life and death. A ghostly figure in flowing white Korean dress dances before the seated monks, later pounding out on a large standing drum the last moments of the master's existence in this realm. Crosscuts between the sound of the drum and shots of Kibong and Haejin—first attracted to the beauty of the dance, and then returning to their temple through tall grasses as day dawns—underscore the urgency of their return. When Haejin announces that he can smell the master's medicine burning, the viewer knows that they have arrived too late. With a quiet, sliding motion, the pure white garb of the dancer reenters the night.

At the close of the film, a solitary bird flies up into the heavens. Our eye follows the track of the wings as they disappear from sight, just as we trace the flight of the birds exquisitely "captured" on this 12th-century Korean celadon vase. This film teaches not through its narrative but through its overpowering visual offerings: a montage of close-ups of the child's mirrorlike face, of the mist rising over the mountains, of the lotus which is both rooted and transcendent. Words are written in the calligraphy of ash on water filled with the promise of new life. In Zen Buddhism, words and logical thinking are seen as impediments to a realization of the true nature of reality. The director states that Zen Buddhism is the setting for the film, not its final meaning, and that the viewer can approach the film without prior knowledge of the kinds of questions or answers intended.

In the end, there is our memory of the pivotal interior monologue scene of the monk who remains separate from the outside world, reading his text by the river, while the "other monk" (presumably Kibong) walks alone along the rice fields at sunset, returning to the world. In this return he follows the path of the Bodhisattva of Mercy, whose practice toward Enlightenment is to assist others along the path to salvation. Why did Bodhi-Dharma leave for the east? As we are told in the film: "To arrive is to leave, to leave is to arrive."

NOTES

1. Bae Yong-Kyun, born in 1951 in Taegu, Korea, received his doctorate from the Faculty of Fine Arts in Korea, and presently teaches painting there.
   The author would like to thank Bae Yong-Kyun and Drs. Cynthia Contreras and Miriam Levering for their comments on earlier drafts of this article, and Milestone Film & Video (the distributors of the film) for their assistance. The Department of Romance and Asian Languages, University of Tennessee/Knoxville, assisted with the purchase of several of the illustrations.
2. In Chinese, Bodhidharma is known as P'u-t'i-ta-mo or Ta-mo, and in Japanese as Daruma. He is a frequent subject of paintings in both countries, and is also considered a popular deity in Japan.
3. The "ox-herding pictures" are a form of didactic art which present a model of the path toward discovering the true nature of the mind and the true nature of Emptiness (*shunyata*). The series of pictures are frequently marked as follows: searching, seeing the traces, seeing the ox, catching the ox, leading the ox, riding the ox home, ox forgotten/self alone, both ox and self forgotten, return to origins, entering the village with bliss-bestowing hands. The connection between Ch'an (Zen) Buddhism and the "ox-herding pictures" began as early as the Southern Sung period (1127-1279). A famous example of a handscroll of ten *sumi-e* (inkwash paintings) based on this theme is attributed to the 15th-century artist-monk Shūibun and is owned by Shūkoku-ji temple in Japan.
4. The fact that few women appear in this film reflects the setting (a remote Buddhist temple) rather than any political statement on the part of the director (personal correspondence, September 1993).
5. Cited in Richard Pilgrim, *Buddhism and the Arts of Japan* (Chambersburg, PA: Anima Books, 1991), p. 30. 6. *Cinemaya* 5 (Autumn 1989), p. 33.
7. Along with an adherence to principles of simplicity and naturalness, there are also moments of extraordinary splendor in Korean art, particularly in the glistening gold jewelry, hair ornaments, and crowns, and also moments of earthy humor, in the genre paintings produced from around the 17th century.
8. It is believed that the shaman (*mudang*), in a state of possession, is able to communicate with a deity during shamanistic rites (*kut*).

LOS ANGELES TIMES, 5/5/94, Calendar/p. 11, Kevin Thomas

Bae Yong-Kyun's awesomely beautiful "Why Has Bodhi-Dharma Left for the East?" is at the Nuart for one week. Its title is a riddle, referring to the unanswerable question as to why the Indian monk who founded Zen Buddhism left home. It tells of an elderly monk guiding his disciple and an orphan boy on the path toward enlightenment.

The film is a celebration of living close to nature as part of one's spiritual quest, and most of its settings are gorgeous, filled with natural grandeur and several superb ancient temple compounds.

SIGHT AND SOUND, 10/91, p. 47, Tony Rayns

High above a modern, crowded city, the remote monastery on Mount Chonan is occupied by three people: the elderly monk Hyegok, the young monk Kibong, and the orphaned child Haejin. The boy was brought to the monastery by Hyegok after a trip to the city temple for medical treatment. One day, Haejin throws a pebble that downs and wounds a jay; he guiltily tries to nurse the crippled bird back to health, but it dies. From that day on, another jay watches Haejin from trees and rooftops.

Haejin begins to ask questions about 'the world' (meaning the urban society he came from), and Kibong finds himself remembering episodes from his own past, when he was an ordinary man named Yongnan. He recalls his guilty abandonment of his blind mother when he entered the priesthood, his flight from the chaos and pollution of the city, and the words of the kindly superior at the city temple who sent him to learn from the austere Hyegok. He also recalls the decision of a co-disciple to return to the mainstream of life.

One night a cow breaks free from its shed near the monastery and starts roaming the woods. Hyegok guides Kibong's meditations, giving him the gift of a *koan* [Zen riddle]. Haejin meanwhile helps with the monastery's domestic chores. When the boy discovers that the corpse of the jay is being consumed by maggots, he gives it a proper burial and then cleanses himself in a rock pool. Later, he follows the roaming cow to another rock pool, where he falls asleep and dreams.

Hyegok falls ill and prepares for death, giving Kibong precise instructions for the cremation of his body. On the night that he dies, there is a musical ceremony at the city temple, involving a woman shaman. Kibong carries Hyegok's coffin to a high mountain clearing and burns it; the pyre is watched from a distance by Haejin, the jay and the cow.

Kibong maintains a vigil until the embers have cooled. He scatters Hyegok's ashes over the mountain and in the pools and streams. Kibong entrusts Hyegok's few possessions to Haejin and leaves, promising that another monk from the city temple will come to replace him. When he has gone, Haejin decides to burn Hyegok's possessions. The jay, still watching him from the temple roof, flies away. Kibong leads the cow across the marshlands at the foot of the mountain.

The title is itself a *koan*, a Zen riddle with no immediate answer, asking how and why Zen Buddhist theory was carried from India to China, Korea and beyond. Bodhi-Dharma (supposed to have lived AD 460-534) went to China to preach a doctrine of Enlightenment founded exclusively on meditation: a profoundly passive doctrine, teaching that Nirvana—synonymous with emptiness—is attainable through a level of concentration that transcends conscious thought. This school of Buddhism, more widely known by its Japanese name 'Zen' than by its Chinese ('Chan') or Sanskrit ('Dhyana') names, stands apart from nine other principal schools, most of which teach very much more complex cosmogonies and prescribe much more active social roles for adherents. But Zen Buddhism had particular appeal in China, where its doctrines intersected with the precepts and practice of Taoism, and to a lesser extent in Korea, where it seemed to relate to some aspects of Shamanism.

Bae Yong-Kyun's film is an almost programmatic account of 'the way of Zen', with its three central protagonists clearly representing three ages of man, and its minimal plot (the creature that breaks free of its bonds, flashbacks to the 'heartless' severity of family ties) spelling out the various preconditions to the attainment of Nirvana. In accompanying notes, Bae rather disingenuously denies that his film is about Zen Buddhism but pleads universal relevance; he asserts a relationship between Zen and Heidegger's philosophy, Jung's psychology, Surrealist art and, most controversially, Erich Fromm's solipsistic concepts of mental health. He argues against ultra-rationalism and for irrationality and illogic, but the film is in some respects almost pedantic in its insistence on explication.

In this light, it is surprisingly easy to reduce the film to one central issue: the problem of coming to terms with physical death. It is not a problem for the elderly master Hyegok, who (whether or not he attains Nirvana) accepts his impending demise with perfect equanimity. But it is a problem for both Kibong, who has to cremate Hyegok and scatter his ashes, and Haejin, who has to learn from his unthinking murder of a bird and from the passing of his surrogate parent. The implication in the final scenes, in which Haejin decides to burn Hyegok's possessions and is released from the watchful eye of the jay, is that these things come easier to an innocent child than they do to a troubled adult. None of this is exactly revelatory, and it is easy to see why the film has attracted derision from some reviewers.

But despite its underlying obviousness, the film does edge towards a seductive irrationality. There is no clear logic behind its narrative construction, which glides from exposition to flashbacks and dreams and back without noticeable variations in tone or style. The uncertainties about the narrative tense mesh with the overall languorousness of pace to work against clear-cut interpretations. And the images of the forest, the waterfall and pellucid rock pools have the kind of hard-edged beauty found in Ansel Adams' landscape photography: an almost surreal intensity that transcends picturesqueness and induces an unexpected degree of concentration in the viewer. Bae's framing and elegantly brief tracking shots are not at all rigorous in the Bresson manner, but the patterns of repetition and minor variation build up a cumulative weight that is potently atmospheric.

Why Did Bodhi-Dharma Leave for the East? is the first Korean movie ever released in Britain, and no film could be less representative of the Korean film industry in general. Bae, a forty-year-old teacher of painting in Taegu, far from Seoul, spent four years making it, separating himself from the mainstream film industry as rigorously as his characters separate themselves from 'the world'. Its status as an independent art movie might suggest that it is breaking new ground, but that would be some distance from the whole truth. Korean cinema in fact has a long and distinguished tradition of tackling Buddhist themes; veteran director Im Kwon-Taek, for instance, has made two remarkable features (*Come, Come, Upward* and *Mandala*) that dramatise the conflicts between different schools of Buddhism and measure Buddhist ideals against social and sexual realities. Bae Yong-Kyun is merely the first Korean director to bring a 'purist' eye to such concerns while adopting a 'cottage industry' approach to film-making. That is where his singularity lies, not in his faintly precious attempt to grasp universal truths.

VILLAGE VOICE, 9/28/93, p. 64, David D. Kim

A stoplight flashes red. The man standing beneath it must choose between the way of the world and the way of the spirit. To be, or not to be—he may ponder—what's the diff?

Set in a remote Korean monastery, *Why Has Bodhi-Dharma Left for the East?* poses a cinematic koan, a riddle meant to prod those who constantly search for clues to their existence. Employing a cast of nonactors, director Bae Yong-Kyun—a professor of painting who also wrote, produced, shot, and edited the film—sets his minimal dialogue to the rhythms of a mountain stream and a million quavering leaves. The man at the stoplight is Kibong, who left the city and his blind, destitute mother to join the monastery. Unable to shrug off a tortured conscience, he punishes himself physically, at one point even casting his body against oncoming rapids.

Bodhi-Dharma springs from a similarly fevered asceticism and took 10 years to make. No detail escapes Bae, as he meticulously composes each shot, waxing symbolic with the deceptive simplicity and force of haiku. Haejin, a young orphan, loses a tooth and later finds a bone fragment in the cremated ashes of Hyegok, the monastery's Zen master; guiding spirits inhabit a roaming cow and a jaybird whose mate was killed.

In one particularly exquisite moment of cruelty, several boys at a watering hold dunk Haejin over and over until his suffocated gurgling becomes almost tangible.

Mimicking Zen's cyclical nature, *Bodhi-Dharma* (the name of a fifth-century monk who brought Zen Buddhism to east Asia) could begin or end at any point and therefore threatens to drown less patient viewers. For those who tap into the steady current of Bae's organic logic, however, the occasional gasp for air makes beautiful sense amid his meditative assault on being there.

Also reviewed in:
CHICAGO TRIBUNE, 6/17/94, Friday/p. D, Michael Wilmington
NEW YORK TIMES, 9/25/93, p. 13, Stephen Holden
VARIETY, 5/24-30/89, p. 31
WASHINGTON POST, 10/4/93, p. B7, Hal Hinson

WICKED CITY

A Streamline Pictures release. *Director:* Yoshiaki Kawajiri. *Screenplay:* Kiseo Choo. *Running time:* 90 minutes. *MPAA Rating:* Not Rated.

VOICES: Greg Snegoff; Mike Reynolds; Gaye Kruger; Edie Mirman.

LOS ANGELES TIMES, 2/25/94, Calendar/p. 4, Charles Solomon

"Wicked City," an animated feature at the epitomizes the sadistic, misogynistic erotica so popular in Japan, both in animated and comic-book form.

Like many Japanese features, "Wicked City" is set in a blighted vision of the not-too-distant future. A fragile peace exists between Earth and the Black World, a parallel dimension inhabited by powerful humanoids. Earthling Taki Renzaburo and Makie, a female Black Worlder, are assigned to guard Guiseppe Mayart, a European wizard whose presence is vital to the upcoming renewal of the interplanetary peace treaty.

Their assignment draws Taki and Makie into a standard series of gunfights, blaster battles and fist-fights. Their Black World foes sprout tentacles with "Alien"-like fanged mouths and turn their limbs into thrusting metal lancers like the murderous android in "Terminator 2." Weirdest of all is a spider-woman with fanged genitalia who attempts to trap Taki. The film suggests a cartoon version of an early James Bond movie, with Taki as the sardonic anti-hero who outfights every foe and seduces every female.

One of Japan's most popular animation directors, Yoshiaki Kawajiri composes scenes like a live-action filmmaker, with deft cutting, camera angles, etc., although the Saturday-morning style animation and jejune story hardly warrant the effort. Kiseo Choo's screenplay, as adapted by Carl Macek and Greg Snegoff, doesn't make much sense, but the young male audiences who attend these films in the United States don't expect nuanced plots.

It's important for Americans, some of whom tend to believe there is a connection between screen violence and violence in society, to remember that despite the intense sadomasochistic violence in these hugely popular animated films, the Japanese maintain one of the safest, least violent societies in the industrialized world.

NEW YORK POST, 10/29/93, p. 28, Bill Hoffmann

A half-century ago, Walt Disney's artists pushed the boundaries of animation with films such as "Fantasia." Now, it's the Japanese who rule as innovators in movie cartoon art.

In story and style, they've proved over and over that animation isn't just for kids—and that entertaining, thought-provoking animated features can be made for adults only.

Now comes "Wicked City" a literate, involving thriller filled with innovative, eye-popping graphics, many of which will have you oohing and aahing out loud.

The scene is Tokyo sometime in the future. Earthlings co-exist uneasily with residents of the "Black World," a mysterious parallel universe of beings who can change shape at will.

A treaty allowing both groups to co-exist peacefully is about to expire, and some Black World extremists plan a violent disruption of a peace conference where the treaty will be renewed.

Secret agent Taki Renzaburo is teamed with his Black World counterpart, Makie, to protect one of the conference's top players.

Taki, a no-nonsense he-man, knows well the cold-blooded nature of the bad Black World folks—in the opening scene he nearly is castrated during lovemaking when a beautiful bar pickup transforms her private parts into a razor-sharp bear trap.

Taki's macho puts him in direct conflict with the sensuous Makie's ideologies—but because both are smart and sexy and fighting for the common cause, you know sparks will eventually fly.

In "Wicked City," sex is plentiful and plenty dangerous. Sexually transmitted diseases are never mentioned. Rather, men and women use sex as a tool in which to cold-bloodedly kill during intercourse.

This looming sense of danger and some truly spectacular animated sequences provide for an absorbing and fast moving 90 minutes.

NEWSDAY, 10/29/93, Part II, p. 85, John Anderson

Speed Racer grows up and gets kinky in "Wicked City," a stylish, sophisticated and erotic cartoon about inter-dimensional diplomacy and inter-species sex.

Japanese animation has made enormous strides—some of them dubious—over the last 30 years, from the stiffly primitive "Speed Racer" to the extreme and disturbing graphic sexual violence of "Urotsukidoji: Legend of the Overfiend" (which has become something of a legend itself.) Somewhere in the middle lands "Wicked City." Its producer, Carl Macek, whose Streamline Pictures has been importing adult Japanese animation for years, calls the film "a cross between 'Nightmare on Elm Street' and 'Basic Instinct.'" He's not far off, except that it's better than both of them.

In a world not quite all its own, Earth has co-existed with a parallel Black World—full of changelings with awful powers—for many, many years, through renegotiation of a peace treaty. Now, Black World radicals want to stop the peace process and simply subjugate humankind. Assigned to protect Earth's chief peace delegate, a kind of oversexed Yoda, is Taki Renzaburo, a member of the Black Guard, and Makie, a female Black Worlder who must put her life on the line, against members of her own race. Together, they generate their own brand of diplomacy.

There are some outrageously Freudian conceits here—a female Black Worlder with teeth between her legs; another who sort of melts and absorbs the peace delegate into her body. But "Wicked City" is an entertaining marriage of story and effects—and sex—that gets you past the stiffness that accompanies this kind of computer-produced animation. Adult it is, Disney it ain't.

VILLAGE VOICE, 11/23/93, p. 71, Jeff Yang

At midnight you awaken, heart racing, throat dry. This is not the world you know, but one close by, separated by the width of a blade, the thickness of a scream. Cobblestones have the wet give of viscera, gutters flow with tears and bile, buildings reach desperately toward a blood umber sky, and ahead, a doorway like a maw beckons. Others have opened this portal—Barker, Bosch, Rbt. Williams, Basil Wolverton—they have glimpsed the horrors of the body and the rapture of the flesh, but not dared pass through.

Nor will you: that way madness lies. But surely some have, and returned? *Wicked City* might be evidence. Unlike others in its genre—and in Japan, Animated Supernatural Body Horror is a genre, a burgeoning one—*Wicked City* has a story to go with its crudescent imagery. (This summer's ASBH release, *Legend of the Overfiend*, was primarily an archive of ways that large, disgusting bodies can tear their ways out of smaller bodies. Or into. Taki is a member of the "Black Guard," a mystical security team that enforces the treaty struck centuries ago between our dimension and the inferno next door. The treaty's term is almost up, and Taki is assigned to protect the framer of the original agreement. His new partner: Makie, a woman of the Black World who has assumed a human form greatly resembling a Patrick Nagel print. Earlier, we're shown Taki being seduced by a different Black Worlder, whose postcoital transformation (imagine an overliteral reading of *Kiss of the Spider Woman*) leaves him aghast; still, as expected, shared danger enables Taki to overcome his prejudice and fall in love with Makie, this most Other of women. There isn't room to elaborate; suffice it to say that the *madonna ex machina* ending begs for a deconstruction along the axes of race and gender; meanwhile, the acting is adequate and the dub refreshingly, free of mouth-flap syndrome—so there are no aural distractions to the visual overstimulus.

Also reviewed in:
CHICAGO TRIBUNE, 4/22/94, Friday/p. J, John Petrakis
WASHINGTON POST, 1/28/94, p. C7, Richard Harrington
WASHINGTON POST, 1/28/94, Weekend/p. 40, Desson Howe

WIDE SARGASSO SEA

A Fine Line Features release of a New Line Cinema presentation of a Laughing Kookaburra production. *Executive Producer:* Sara Risher. *Producer:* Jan Sharp. *Director:* John Duigan. *Screenplay:* Jan Sharp, Carole Angier, and John Duigan. *Based on the novel "Wide Sargasso Sea" by:* Jean Rhys. *Director of Photography:* Geoff Burton. *Editor:* Anne Goursaud and Jimmy Sandoval. *Music:* Stewart Copeland. *Music Editor:* Michael Dittrick. *Choreographer:* Lenneth Richards. *Sound:* Michael McDuffie and (music) Jeff Seitz. *Sound Editor:* Steve Nelson and Cathie Speakman. *Casting:* Aletta Chapelle, Elisabeth Mackie, Françoise Combadière, Cecile S. Burrowes, Cathy Levy, and Cyprian Thomas. *Production Designer:* Franckie D. and Michael Howells. *Art Director:* Susan Bolles, Drago Michie, and Kathleen Cooper. *Set Decorator:* Ron von Blombert. *Set Dresser:* Sasha Schnerdt. *Special Effects:* Steve Kirshoff. *Costumes:* Norma Moriceau. *Make-up:* Noriko Watanabe. *Running time:* 100 minutes. *MPAA Rating:* NC-17.

CAST: Karina Lombard (Antoinette Cosway); Nathaniel Parker (Rochester); Rachel Ward (Annette Cosway); Michael York (Paul Mason); Marine Beswicke (Aunt Cora); Claudia Robinson (Christophene); Huw Christie Williams (Richard Mason); Casey Berna (Young Antoinette); Rowena King (Amelie); Ben Thomas (Daniel Cosway); Paul Campbell (Young Bull); Audbrey Pilatus (Drummer); Ancile Gloudin (Nelson); Dominic Needham (Pierre); Kevin Thomas (Benbow); Aisha King (Myra); Anika Gordon (Hilda); Elfreida Reid (Rose); Bobby Smith (Machete Man); Suzanne McMannus (Florinda); Pat Gooden (Margaretta); Clifford Burt (Fraser); Naomi Watts (Fanny Grey); James Earl (Man with Torch); Kayarsha Russell (Cora's Maid); Jenny Wilson (Grace Poole); Helen Woods (Leah).

FILMS IN REVIEW, 8/93, p. 269, Andy Pawelczak

Jean Rhys was a modernist writer of the twenties and thirties who specialized in bleak, minimalist tales of women with nothing but one last drink between them and the void. She was rediscovered in the palmy days of feminism and women's studies in the seventies, though her novels are too existential to be fully effective as evidence against the patriarchy. *Wide Sargasso Sea*, written late in her career after a long silence, was something of a departure and at the same time a return to origins. A prequel to Charlotte Bronte's *Jane Eyre*, it's the tale of the first Mrs. Rochester, a French Creole woman from the West Indies, and how she ended up confined to that attic in Thornfield Hall. Rhys was born in the West Indies, so the novel has the vividness of recollected childhood impressions, and the prose is uncharacteristically lush. Though it shares with her other novels an atmosphere of doom, we can see in its heroine at least the possibility of wholeness before she's enmeshed in the engine of destruction. Add to this the novel's currently fashionable theme—fascination with and fear of the Other—and you have the makings of an intriguing film. Unfortunately, John Duigan's new movie never gets off the storyboard; it's full of ideas that don't come to life, and the movie ends up feeling like one of the more run-of-the-mill Masterpiece Theater productions with a dash of tasteful, soft core sex.

We first see Edward Rochester (Nathaniel Parker) on board ship in the seaweed-choked Sargasso Sea as a dead sailor is pulled on deck; he drowned while trying to free the ship's rudder of seaweed which becomes a recurring symbol of Rochester's fear of engulfment by tropical sensuality. A second son deprived of an income from his father's estate by the rule of primogeniture, he has come to Jamaica to marry the land rich and beautiful Antoinette Cosway (Karina Lombard), a kind of grown up wild child who is the daughter of a mad French Creole mother (Rachel Ward in a small role) and notorious wastrel father. Rochester is a familiar figure, a Victorian gentleman so repressed that when he first meets Antoinette he keels over in a dead faint. Once they marry, they retreat to her remote mountain cabin for a prolonged honeymoon, and their first night in bed is accompanied by primitive drums. Before long Rochester is complaining that he feels like he's floating in an opium dream as his wife's newly released sexuality, the encroaching proximity of the voodoo inflected black culture, and the alien tropical landscape all combine to create a spell that is both threatening and seductive. By the end of the film Rochester is pure superego, encased in character armor, his wife's jailer rather than her lover, and his natural habitat is the cold, snowy landscape surrounding Thornfield Hall.

As Antoinette, Karina Lombard has the requisite exotic looks to be the object of Rochester's obsessive, paranoid desire, but her physical beauty has a curiously unformed quality, and her performance never comes into focus. As Rochester, Nathaniel Parker suffers from a similar lack of expressive screen presence; it's hard to understand how this rather pallid Rochester turns into the magnetic, gothic personality of *Jane Eyre*.

Duigan's direction is flat-footed and dull; like Rochester, he's afraid to let go and follow the real craziness of his material, and instead relies on a bland pictorialism. The film's dirty little secret is Rochester's fantasy of miscegenation. Near the end of the movie, Rochester meets a shadowy character who claims to be Antoinette's bastard mulatto half-brother, and this evidence of illicit interracial sexuality liberates his deepest desire. He promptly sleeps with one of the black servants, and the scene, though shot with characteristic "good taste," reminds us of the pornographic undergrowth of the Victorian imagination. Ultimately, the film draws a parallel between Rochester's lust for and fear of Antoinette and what she releases in him and the imperialist's desire to lose himself in the alien culture and at the same time subdue and dominate it. Duigan in on to something here, but the film shows only glimmers of this insight into sexual politics; most of the time it's as becalmed as a ship in the Sargasso Sea.

LOS ANGELES TIMES, 4/23/93, Calendar/p. 4, Kenneth Turan

"Wide Sargasso Sea" is so soaked in atmosphere it feels practically marinated. A lush, feverish tropical concoction filled with vivid colors, pounding drums and passionate liaisons, this Caribbean melodrama gets so overheated it doesn't even notice that its dramatic plausibility has vaporized into the steamy air.

Not that that matters very much. Though its based on a celebrated novel, winner of several of Britain's top literary prizes, the appeal of this film is primarily to the visual senses. Even as its story gets increasingly arbitrary, the look and spirit of the film remain diverting, a hothouse garden you can hide in when the real world gets too close.

Though "Sargasso" makes no on-screen reference to it, Jean Rhys' 1966 novel was intended as a kind of imaginative prequel to Charlotte Bronte's "Jane Eyre," a look at the life Rochester and the mysterious first Mrs. R (here called Antoinette Cosway) led in Jamaica before they settled in England.

Before that story is told, however, "Sargasso" opens with an extensive prologue dealing with Antoinette's widowed mother Antoinette, "spirited, beautiful and very French." Left to cope with running a Jamaican plantation after her husband drinks himself to death, Annette (Rachel Ward) marries a foppish Englishman (Michael York) too dense to understand that the newly freed islanders can't still be treated as slaves.

Clearly, no good will come of this, and when things go sour little Antoinette is sequestered in a convent school. Later, as an heiress (model Karina Lombard in her film debut), a marriage is eventually arranged for her with the young Englishman Rochester (Nathaniel Parker) who is so disoriented by the long ocean voyage that he no sooner sees his intended bride than he faints dead away.

Complete strangers from opposite sides of the world, these two young people nevertheless fall in love. As directed by Australian John Duigan ("Flirting," "The Year My Voice Broke") from a script he wrote with producer Jan Sharp and Carole Angier, "Sargasso Sea" is at its most charming when dealing with these two smitten young people, oblivious to everything but each other.

Their romance largely takes place in Antoinette's ancestral home deep in the verdant hills of Jamaica, where her former nanny and full-time sorceress Christophene (energetically played by Claudia Robinson) keeps everyone in line. Antoinette is "a wild creature, untamed," and Rochester, though not as romantic, seems to get into the spirit of things quite nicely.

While its NC-17 rating is apparently due, in part to a brief shot of male frontal nudity, "Sargasso Sea" is rife with romantic, clothing-optional scenes involving both sexes (plus shots of glistening dancers cavorting to the inevitable throbbing jungle drums) and its decorous, insistent sensuality will probably make it a date-night favorite.

All this is quite diverting, but then the situation between Antoinette and Rochester begins to spoil in the heat. Unnerved by monster moths, the hauteur of Christophene, the pounding of all those drums and the unmistakable bedroom eyes of the fetching Amelie (Rowena King), Rochester starts to lose his bearings. "I feel like I'm floating in an opium dream," he says of his waking life, and he begins to literally dream of sailors trapped and lifeless in the Sargasso's endless beds of seaweed.

Emotionally, however, the trouble that develops is not as believable as the passion that preceded it, and the seriousness with which "Sargasso Sea" is forced to treat the couple's problems never manages to make them convincing. Other dramatic elements, like the mysterious stranger who is forever lurking about the premises, similarly refuse to come into focus or even make basic sense. But though it might be inevitable that a movie this drunk on ambience would dissolve when exposed to the light of narrative coherence, "Wide Sargasso Sea" manages to remain amusing, even when it boils over the top.

NEW YORK, 5/3/93, p. 64, David Denby

In *Wide Sargasso Sea*, adapted from Jean Rhys's remarkable novel of 1966, the images of Jamaica in the nineteenth century are often feverishly beautiful—and sometimes they're just feverish. The heat of the thick vegetation merges with sexual heat: Hallucinatory and frightening, the charged physical life of the movie is electrified still further by the music of Stewart Copeland (formerly of the Police), which has a bullying New Age spookiness. *Wide Sargasso Sea* is at times so insistently exotic—a dark, voodoo emanation of the sullen tropics—that it destroys its own meanings. I came out of it jangled and dissatisfied, rather like one of the principal characters, a young Englishman who finds Jamaica so overpoweringly sexy that he flees in terror.

Rochester (Nathaniel Parker), the young man in question, arrives at the island, a British colony, some years after the emancipation of the slaves and marries a Creole sugar plantation heiress, Antoinette (Karina Lombard), who is a very strange and beautiful young woman. He doesn't know what we have learned about her in the early parts of the film—that her missing father was some sort of reprobate alcoholic; that her mother (Rachel Ward) went mad from grief after the plantation house was burned down by the former slaves, who mostly hated the decadent white "aristocrats" who lorded it over them. The family, in other words, has more skeletons than proper clothes in the closet.

Antoinette narrates, and we first see her as a little girl on the plantation, wandering about in a daze. The style of the film, written by Jan Sharp, Carole Angier (Rhys's biographer), and John Duigan, and directed by Duigan (an Australian), is both dreamy and harsh. Duigan develops the narrative vaguely and allusively, as if he hadn't quite got hold of the story himself. Individual images, on the other hand, pop up with startling power. A horse lies on the ground with its throat cut; the plantation burns down at night as the ex-slaves stand about solemnly watching. Geoff Burton, the cinematographer, manages to give the heat of Jamaica a heavy, menacing body—no dazzling beaches and sunsets here—that is genuinely oppressive. At the height of the fire, the family parrot, perched on a windowsill, suddenly bursts into flames and flies through the air, torched, before dying. The blacks receive the flaming bird as a fetish. The whole movie is a fetish, ominous and lurid and rather incomprehensible. The gothic opacity probably finds its source in Rhys's veiled manner, with its strange combination of pride and deep-running masochism.

We are meant to feel uncomfortable—as uncomfortable as Rochester, who finds Antoinette's necromantic old nurse (a remarkable actress named Claudia Robinson) an intimidating intrusion on his marriage. Poor Rochester arrives in a fever and never really passes out of it. Who is he? He's Rochester, *the* Rochester, the brooding, neurotically embittered hero of Charlotte Brontë's *Jane Eyre*, who, you will remember, had a mad wife closeted in the attic of his English estate. Jean Rhys's novel is an attempt to "fill in" the early history of this doomed couple—a speculative "prequel" to the tragic situation of *Jane Eyre*.

Nathaniel Parker is a classically trained British actor with a handsome face and body and an abashed, gentle manner that shifts—abruptly, like Peter O'Toole's gentleness—into rage. There is definite star quality here. It's not Parker's fault, I believe, that he doesn't really make contact (except physically) with Karina Lombard, the swarthily beautiful model of mixed background who plays Antoinette with plenty of physical fire but not much focus. Lombard is slender and perfectly molded and, like Parker, naked a great deal. Their sexual relationship is convincing as the obsessional passion of two young people in a hot, dangerous place—young people who make love, perhaps make love too much, without knowing much of anything about each other but sex.

Still, it's a very literary movie, with symbols attempting to do the work of dramatic development. The title refers to the seaweed below the surface of the sea that can ensnare a diver—i.e., Antoinette's possible madness or perhaps the sexual passion that engulfs and destroys. The problem is that the movie is very intimate physically, but we don't know either of these two people. In the end, *Wide Sargasso Sea*, despite all its intensity and skill, is no more than a gothic/erotic curiosity. Antoinette is passionate and unstable, and falls so completely in love with Rochester that she flips the minute she thinks she might be losing him. And Rochester, overwhelmed both by the attractions of his wife and the menacing atmosphere of the island itself—the insects and crabs and a beautiful black woman eager to seduce him—begins to withdraw from Antoinette.

But we don't really know what goes wrong: The marriage is pulled apart more by the filmmaker's intentions than its own contradictions, and it collapses with baffling speed. *Wide Sargasso Sea* is apparently meant to be a tragedy of male domination—cold-hearted male clarity winning out over feminine spontaneity. Rochester leaves and shuts up his wife back in England because he needs to reassert control. But since the filmmakers have so devastatingly evoked the voodoo terrors of an exotic island—and since they never successfully shift our interest to Antoinette—some of us may identify with Rochester's longing to leave. I certainly did. Get out of there and go back to England! Women as spontaneous and fragile; men as cold and destructive. Isn't this Jean Rhys's lifelong myth? What, really, do these polarities have to do with men and women—or with England or Jamaica? Does any of this make sense except at the level of high-toned literary cliché?

NEW YORK POST, 4/17/93, p. 16, Jami Bernard

There is a surprise in "Wide Sargasso Sea" that is as stunning in its way as the one in "The Crying Game"—only this surprise is literary in nature. It turns out that we know the movie's characters—the stunningly beautiful Antoinette and the reserved suitor who travels from England to take her and her property in an arranged marriage—after all.

Of course, it is no surprise to anyone who has read the haunting Jean Rhys novel about sex, madness and culture clash in 19th-century Jamaica, but "Wide Sargasso Sea" is full of mystery and secrets, so I'll preserve this one.

The Sargasso Sea is an actual one, but it is usually used metaphorically as a choke of seaweed that hides both its treasures and its junk. The book never makes explicit mention of the sea after the title, but the movie plunges us immediately into a sensuous, frightening imagery of drowning, choking, tangling, envelopment and fear.

The fear for Antoinette is that she will succumb to the madness that seems to have plagued her maternal family line and can only be abated by swimming in the sexual pleasure her new husband affords her; the fear for Edward is of being sucked into Antoinette's carnal needs and losing the moorings of steady old England and all that he left behind.

Antoinette is a young woman who we see at first growing up in the guarded atmosphere of the post-slavery Caribbean a time when the emancipated slaves are bristling with resentment and the rich white estates are going to ruin. Issues of race and class are fermenting, culminating in early tragedy for Antoinette and her family, presaged by the eerie warning sign of a parrot in flames. (Parrot lovers will enjoy a fine supporting performance by a blue-and-gold macaw.)

Magic at its blackest is operating on the island. Antoinette's wiry old nursemaid (Claudia Robinson) is practiced in *obeah*, the local voodoo, and its use will lead to an agonized rift in the grown Antoinette's marriage.

The marriage is fraught with problems. The more sexual it becomes, the more doubts Edward has. The more he holds back, the more desperate Antoinette becomes.

"Wide Sargasso Sea" is sensuous and lovely, not only for its wild, windswept scenery but for its attractive leads (Karina Lombard and Nathaniel Parker) rolling about in the nude at their "sweet honeymoon house" at the beginning of their arranged marriage. Antoinette is so happy, she could die. "Die! Die!" urges Edward as they make love, giving her a *petite mort* that one senses could very well lead to a *grande mort*. Doom and foreboding are everywhere, a mood almost unflaggingly sustained by director John Duigan.

Both book and movie operate on several levels. On the simplest, you could call it "Emanuelle Goes Jamaican" a soft-core sex story in which a young woman is awakened to all the possibilities of love including several sexy dunks in the local swimming hole.

On another level, it is the "backstory" to one of literature's most brooding classics, providing a rare insight into a character you probably never gave a second thought to.

It can also be seen in its social context, as a parable about emancipation or about the differences between England (depicted as stuffy, rigid, cold) and Jamaica (dreamy, hot-blooded, carnal).

At its best, though, it provides a deeper understanding of the nature of male-female relationships, how needs met and denied can change the course of a person's nature, and how the concept of "madness" is meaningless when divorced from the very real frustrations that send vibrant people over the edge.

NEWSDAY, 4/16/93, Part II/p. 70, Jack Mathews

In a dream sequence repeated several times in the filmed adaptation of the Jean Rhys' novel "Wide Sargasso Sea," a panicked swimmer struggles to fee himself from seaweed holding him underwater. The dream belongs to Edward Rochester, an Englishman suffering culture shock in 1840s Jamaica, but that's pretty much how I felt trying to keep the movie's pretentious symbolism from putting me to sleep.

Given the film's NC-17 rating, for sweaty sex and lots of it, heavy eyelids is the last thing you might fear. But even the sex, most of it between Edward (Nathaniel Parker) and his Creole wife Antoinette Cosway (Karina Lombard), is used to symbolize England's cultural rape of colonial West Indies primitivism.

"Die! Die! Die!," Edward screams, as he thrusts over Antoinette, in as aggressive an action on behalf of the Union Jack since the Charge of the Light Brigade.

Angry sex, clinging seaweed, skittering crabs, ominous thunderheads, flaming blue macaws ... the movie version of "Wide Sargasso Sea" has every Freudian symbol but a cigar.

I haven't read the novel and all that imagery may be in there, too. But the core of the story, as told on film, is a romantic tragedy, and Australian director John Duigan ("Flirting"), who co-wrote the screenplay with Jan Sharp and Rhys' biographer Carole Angier, buried it under so much narrative back story and visual metaphor that it's hard to hold the focus.

Rhys, who was raised in the West Indies, used a character from Charlotte Bronte's "Jane Eyre" in "Wide Sargasso Sea" to reflect on the cultural electrical storms under British rule there. Antoinette Cosway was the mad woman in the attic in "Jane Eyre," the first wife of Eyre's husband, Edward Rochester.

Who was she? How did she end up there? What was her and Edward's story?

"Wide Sargasso Sea" provides complicated imaginings to those questions, and throws a little social history and voodoo mysticism into the bargain.

The movie covers Antoinette from early childhood in Jamaica to that attic in England, showing us how her cultural misplacement—a French descendant living among natives in a country ruled by the English—left her predisposed, if not programmed, for madness. (Her mother, played by Rachel Ward, ends up insane and tucked away herself.)

All of the principal characters in the story are out of place, none more so than Edward, who shows up with a school boy's fever, anxious to marry Antoinette and nestle into a life of sexual passion and tropical bliss. It's a short-lived fantasy, the bliss part. After a few nights of ecstasy in the mountain home chosen by Antoinette, Edward begins to wilt under the jungle humidity, the hostile glare of the servants, and his own fear of losing control.

When a rank native shows up, claiming to be Antoinette's sister and tries to extort money from Edward with revelations about the family's true background, Edward becomes suspicious and hateful, turning his wife's love for him into a weapon for her own destruction.

All of this, of course, is meant as a metaphor for what England wrought in the colonial West Indies, but without some real heat at the center of the story, it doesn't even add up to a dry lecture. And there is no heat at the center.

Parker, a member of the Royal Shakespeare Company, plays Edward as such a stiff-upper-lip bore it's hard to imagine how anyone would lie still for a little "Die! Die! Die!" with him, and though Lombard, a model making her acting debut, exudes an exotic sensuality that seems perfect for Antoinette, she hasn't the experience to cover the role's dramatic challenges.

It's hard to shoot in Jamaica without getting pretty scenery, so there's that from cinematographer Geoff Burton. And Stewart Copeland's score, with its tribal roots, is terrific. The music is used symbolically, of course, to underscore the differences between the natives and their unwelcome settlers, but at least you can dance to it.

SIGHT AND SOUND, 7/93, p. 56, Lizzie Francke

Jamaica, 1844. After the emancipation of the slaves, the plantation-owning Cosway family falls apart, with Mr Cosway drinking himself to death. His widow Annette remarries Paul Mason, an Englishman. Mason settles in with Annette and her two children Antoinette and Pierre, and takes over the running of the estate. His manner and methods are disliked by the servants. Annette is also unhappy about his behaviour and turns to drink. One night former slaves set fire to the house. The family escapes, but later Pierre dies of burns. Mason returns to England, while the grief-stricken Annette deteriorates mentally and is sent to an institution. Antoinette is brought up by her aunt Cora and the faithful family servant Christophene. A few years later Mason dies and Antoinette is informed that the estate has been left to her on condition that she marry. Her step-uncle arranges for her to marry Rochester, a young gentleman from England. On his arrival in Jamaica, Rochester finds it hard to adapt to the new country. Antoinette is at first disappointed with her husband-to-be and calls off the wedding. Later she is persuaded that she has no choice but to marry him. Antoinette falls in love with Rochester during their honeymoon. Though he reciprocates her passion, he remains puzzled by her and by her country.

One day Rochester receives a letter from Antoinette's cousin, Daniel Cosway, informing him that Antoinette has Creole blood and that her mother is insane. When Rochester questions Antoinette, she informs him that her mother died in the fire. Rochester begins to feel alienated from his wife. He is also suspicious of Christophene, who now lives with them and whom he is told has magic powers. When Rochester spends a couple of days away in the city, Christophene tries to persuade Antoinette to leave her husband.

Rochester returns to find another letter from Cosway, so pays him a visit. Rochester questions Antoinette again about her mother and she tells him the truth. That night Antoinette gives Rochester a drugged drink and he hallucinates. When he wakes up, he wanders into the house's courtyard and meets Amelie, one of the servants. They make love and Antoinette discovers them together. Relations between Rochester and Antoinette go from bad to worse and she turns to drink, convinced that she will end up like her mother. The household is in chaos and the servants leave. Later Rochester is informed that his brother has died and that he must return to England as heir to the family home, Thornfield Hall. In spite of the protestations of Christophene and Cora, he takes Antoinette back with him and installs her in the attic at Thornfield. A few years later, it is announced that Rochester is to marry the governess, Jane Eyre. A fire is started in Thornfield Hall's attic and as the house blazes, a figure is seen dancing on the roof.

Jean Rhys' mesmerising novel *Wide Sargasso Sea* has finally made it to the cinema screen after a troubled history, during which it was optioned and abandoned many times. No doubt its fragmented narrative did not translate easily into a conventional screenplay. And it's difficult to imagine Rhys' vivid and sensual prose transformed into cinematic idiom without reducing it to the obvious. Indeed, the heart sinks as this film version opens with shots of skeins of seaweed swaying in an aquamarine-tinted light. It brings to mind Hitchcock's suggestion that film-makers in search of adaptations should stick to expanding on short stories, distilling their essence into something new rather than attempting dull faithfulness.

Rhys' book is itself a disruptive rewriting of Charlotte Brontë's *Jane Eyre*, inventing an avenging history for the first Mrs Rochester, the tortured soul who rampages through the upper storeys of Thornfield Hall. Rochester's first wife has already been given the film treatment. Made in 1943, Val Lewton and Jacques Tourneur's chilling *I Walked with a Zombie* anticipated Rhys in transposing the Brontë novel to the Caribbean and investigating the background of the ill-fated Bertha Mason. That film similarly suggests that she is not mad, but the victim of a voodoo spell. Magic and the tradition of the obeah are also invoked in Rhys' novel. But Antoinette's conviction that she is becoming dead to the world is given a real basis in her lack of economic power—after all, though she bought Rochester with a dowry, she has no control over him. Her fear is also rooted in the idea that she is destined to follow in her insane mother's faltering footsteps. *Wide Sargasso Sea* is therefore an unsettling family ghost story about the female predicament.

Director John Duigan might have picked up a few tips from the Lewton-Tourneur movie about how to create an intense and disturbing atmosphere. Despite panoramic shots of the lush Jamaican countryside and intimations of the island's overwhelming noise, his film lacks the necessary mood of feverish dread. The characters' descent into madness is so clearly signposted that there is never any danger of the audience succumbing to disorientation.

It is almost as if the film were afraid of conjuring up the 'otherness' foregrounded by Rhys, and can only visualise it in a trite manner. A scene in which Rochester and Antoinette make love cuts away to one in which the black servants are dancing to a raucous beat. The warm and musty (by implication, female) Jamaica is diabolic for the stiff and pale demi-patrician Rochester (Nathaniel Parker sporting a Cliff Richard hairstyle fits the bill almost too perfectly), while England is a "cold, dark dream" to Antoinette. This is represented in an equally stereotyped way by the stone- and oak-panelled Thornfield mansion, which is stock English heritage, complete with stuffed deer's head. This mythical England is far from the strange, exotic world in which she eventually finds herself trapped. Indeed, at the end of the Rhys novel she remarks, "This cardboard house where I walk at night is not England." Karina Lombard may scowl and sulk as Antoinette, but there is scant evidence of the terrible passion that finally brings the cardboard house crashing down. *Wide Sargasso Sea* is never the storm of a film it should have been.

VILLAGE VOICE, 4/27/93, p. 53, J. Hoberman

A ripe, somewhat slovenly, but nonetheless entrancing tumble of events, *Wide Sargasso Sea* adapts Jean Rhys's spare, sultry novel with a prurience at once studied and overwrought. The movie, directed and cowritten by the Australian John Duigan, seems to have been made with kid gloves and sweaty palms—it's *Masterpiece Theatre* gone native.

Duigan's psychic malaria, complete with nightmares and chills, echoes the colonial anxiety that characterized the Australian cinema of the 1970s. But if the material confounds polite handling, it may also be that Rhys's swan song was a unique intervention in English literature. The book, first published in 1966, is a prequel to *Jane Eyre*. Set in the West Indies, it proposes the story of Rochester's wife—the "demonic" deranged woman he brought back to England and hid in the attic, properly horrifying our spunky Jane.

An immediate bestseller, *Jane Eyre* (along with *Wuthering Heights*) revived the gothic novel while introducing the basic cast of characters, repertoire of situations, and background atmospherics that would characterize romantic fiction for the next 150 years. The orphan Jane's rise from penniless governess to nobleman's wife was potent wish-fulfillment—as well as a practical chronicle of worldly advancement. *Wide Sargasso Sea*, by contrast, links wealth to exploitation and follows a downward spiral. Rhys's novel inverts *Jane Eyre* by beginning, not ending, with a house afire and, rather than charting the events that culminate in marriage, watching one decompose in despair and madness.

With *Wide Sargasso Sea*, Rhys replanted the gothic in lush, primeval soil. In a sense, Luis Buñuel anticipated this strategy with his splendid *Abismos de Pasión*, a brilliantly trashy transposition of *Wuthering Heights* to a Mexican hacienda. But *Wide Sargasso Sea* provides an even loamier historical context. After the emancipation of the slaves, Jamaica's creole elite—imagined by Rhys (who grew up in the West Indies) as the mother-daughter dyad, Annette and Antoinette Cosway—are compelled to arrange loveless weddings with the English fortune-hunters whose schooners materialize on the Caribbean. The women are helpless, baffled by the contempt of both their former slaves and new protectors, unable to mediate between the two. When Annette's stupidly naive second husband suggests importing Asian coolies to work the plantation, the blacks simply torch his mansion.

Modernist in its laconic tone, Rhys's novel is postmodernist in its politics, which, as Joyce Carol Oates notes, concern "the appropriation, colonization, exploitation, and destruction of a pastoral, tropical world by a wholly alien, English sensibility." That alien sensibility is male; the tropical world exhibits the same excess of femininity that the colonizing Rochester will imprison in his tower. Played by Nathaniel Parker with a tight, fatuous smile, Rochester is terrified by Jamaica from the moment he arrives. He's spooked by the heat, the brightness, the fecundity, the somnolence, the uncanny whispers, the claustrophobia of white society, the plenitude of black faces. Introduced to his bride-to-be, Antoinette (former model Karina Lombard), he collapses at her feet—presaging their short-lived sexual delirium, an idyll in a cursed Eden.

The couple's "sweet honeymoon home," as the servants mockingly call it, is a virtual zoological garden. The white lovers are surrounded by a jungle of mystery, the tiles on which they walk are covered with an underbrush of dead blossoms and moths. Rochester finds his wife a "wild, untamed creature"—he's as disconcerted by her dependence on the dour, spell-casting housekeeper Christophene (Claudia Robinson) as by the ease with which she can join the servants in an African dance. It takes only one letter from the mulatto who claims to be Antoinette's half-brother to complete his paranoia and feed his destructive arrogance.

Speaking of phallocratic mastery, *Wide Sargasso Sea* seems to have received its NC-17 more for a glimpse of Parker's penis than for its mildly steamy lovemaking (although Karina Lombard's limitations as an actress give these scenes a documentary frisson). A movie is necessarily more literal than a novel. Even so, Duigan's direction is often ridiculously florid. The action is underscored by rolling thunder and frantic pan-piping, intercut with extensive underwater shots of tangled seaweed. Each time Antoinette remembers her own mad mother, the music runs amok. She and Rochester make love to the sound of jungle drums with tacky cutaways to the wanton servant girls shaking booty outside. (The chatter of jungle noises will reach an earsplitting crescendo as Rochester advances on the foxiest of them.)

Rhys's novel ends in England with Antoinette glimpsing the ghostly English governess who will replace her as Mrs. Rochester. Clumsier and more bombastic, Duigan's film features an epilogue replete with *Dark Shadows* mansion and a sky so lavender it might be reflecting the Las Vegas strip. Unfortunately, that's as postmodern as things get. It's a pity the producers couldn't find some use for the 1944 *Jane Eyre*, with Orson Welles as the Byronic hero. Perhaps some enterprising exhibitor will further Rhys's critique by pairing the movies on a double bill.

Also reviewed in:
CHICAGO TRIBUNE, 5/7/93, Friday/p. I, Dave Kehr
NEW YORK TIMES, 4/16/93, p. C6, Vincent Canby
NEW YORKER, 4/19/93, p. 110, Terrence Rafferty
VARIETY, 4/19/93, p. 45, Lawrence Cohn
WASHINGTON POST, 5/8/93, p. B3, Rita Kempley

WILD WEST

A Samuel Goldwyn Company release of a Channel 4 Films presentation with the participation of British Screen of an Initial production. *Producer:* Eric Fellner. *Director:* David Attwood. *Screenplay:* Harwant Bains. *Director of Photography:* Nic Knowland. *Editor:* Martin Walsh. *Music:* Dominic Miller. *Sound:* Chris Munro. *Sound Editor:* Glenn Freemantle. *Casting:* Suzanne Crowley and Gilly Poole. *Production Designer:* Caroline Hanania. *Art Director:* Kave Naylor. *Special Effects:* Tom Harris. *Costumes:* Trisha Biggar. *Make-up:* Aileen Seaton and Heather Jones. *Stunt Coordinator:* Stuart St. Paul. *Running time:* 85 minutes. *MPAA Rating:* Not Rated.

CAST: Naveen Andrews (Zaf); Sarita Choudhury (Rifat); Ronny Jhutti (Kay); Ravi Kapoor (Ali); Ameet Chana (Gurdeep); Bhasker (Jagdeep); Lalita Ahmed (Mrs Ayub); Shaun Scott (Tony); Neran Persaud (Tapper 1); Nrinder Dhudwar (Tapper 2); Parv Bancil (Tapper 3); Paul Bhattacharjee (Amir); Dinesh Shukla (Rakesh); Lou Hirsch (Hank Goldstein); Rolf

Saxon (Yehudi);   Gurdial Sira (Uncle Liaqut);   Jamila Massey (Mrs. Khan);   Kaleem Janjua (Mr. Patel);   Adam Dean and Martin Dean (Ninja Boys);   Mark Anthony Newman (Ellroy); Race Davies (Receptionist);   Jim Barclay (Mr. Litt);   Christopher Quinn (Engineer);   Kevin Elyot (Solicitor);   Elaine Donnelly (Ticket Clerk);   Havoc (Spook);   Awaara (Bangra Band); Madhav Sharma (Ugly Abdul).

LOS ANGELES TIMES, 11/5/93, Calendar/p. 14, Peter Rainer

"Wild West" (Times-rated Mature) ought to be better than it is. After all, a movie about a bunch of South London Pakistanis who have their own country band isn't exactly standard fare. And, for a while at least, the novelty is enough to carry us past the boys' dithering exploits and cornball dreams.

Zaf (Naveen Andrews), who lives with his brothers Ali (Ravi Kapoor) and Kay (Ronny Jhutti) in his mother's house, is the boldest of the family. With his cowboy hat plopped uneasily atop his voluminous hair, he's one unlikely cowpoke.

It would be better if director David Attwood and scriptwriter Harwant Bains didn't make so much of Zaf's oddness—if they didn't turn him into a joke. It's an affectionate joke but a joke just the same. We never find out what it is about country music that turns him on and pulls him away from his own roots. Is it because, as a Pakistani immigrant, he feels rootless in England?

When Zaf meets the beautiful Rifat (Sarita Choudhury from "Mississippi Masala"), he immediately falls into a protracted swoon. Unhappily married to a brutal Brit (Shaun Scott), Rifat ends up as lead singer in the boys' band, the Honky Tonk Cowboys. Of course, she has a great (and presumably dubbed) voice. The band sounds pretty great too, which makes the film's you-can't-win tone a bit unbelievable. More than a novelty act, the Honky Tonk Cowboys look as if they could become the biggest thing since Abba. Or at least Pink Lady.

NEW YORK POST, 11/5/93, p. 35, Thelma Adams

"Wild West" is a feel-good, soundtrack-driven joy ride.

Cruise along with the Honky-Tonk Cowboys on the road to Nashville. The boys are just another bunch of wannabe country-western stars—with a twist. The Ayub brothers and their Sikh drummer are Pakistanis living in London's grungy Southall.

This exuberant culture-clash comedy, directed by David Attwood, crosses "The Commitments," "Wayne's World," and "My Beautiful Laundrette." It's a screwball mix that reinvents cliches with wit and style.

Sarita Choudhury ("Mississippi Masala") plays Rifat, the full-lipped heart-breaker who loves country music. She joins the Cowboys and adds the necessary wiggle in the hips to jump-start them to stardom.

Sexy and lively, Choudhury's star continues to rise but the real find here is Naveen Andrews. As Zaf Ayub, lead Cowboy, he's the movie's life force. Relentlessly charismatic, lithe and handsome, Andrews has great comic talents and heart to spare.

In a cast that's overwhelmingly appealing, Bhasker stands out as the Cowboys' manager. Bhasker is the Pakistani Cheech Marin, speaking in slangy Spanish, driving a giant convertible with enormous horns on the grille, joyfully seeking angles to exploit for personal profit.

As Zaf's sympathetic and long-suffering mother, Lalita Ahmed plays her emotional moments well. She makes a great foil for the surrounding zaniness. When she finds Rifat's underclothes in Zaf's room, she misreads the situation. With grave seriousness and heartache, she confronts her son: "I will not allow you to become my daughter. ... First, you became a cowboy and now this!"

Harwant Bains' anarchic script is laugh-out-loud funny. Visual humor abounds. While the band practices in the Ayub kitchen, the drummer rests his cigarette in the folds of his turban. When the cloth bursts into flames, Mrs. Ayub calmly fills a saucepan with water and douses the boy.

The sound track jumps to tunes by Dwight Yoakam, Steve Earle, Garth Brooks, and Nanci Griffith. See this movie. It's great fun.

NEWSDAY, 11/5/93, Part II/p. 91, John Anderson

Masala, the blend of spices integral to Indo-Pakistani cooking, has worked its way into a number of movie titles. But it has nothing to do with "Wild West," which is more like tandoori fish and chips with a side order of barbecued ribs. Alka-Seltzer, please ...

The Ayub brothers, Pakistani hustlers in London who manage to stay one step ahead of serious bodily harm as they seek country-western fame and fortune, are playing cultural hopscotch in this almost-likable film by director David Attwood. They've bypassed becoming British, aiming instead for Nashville, but their story is a little like an Asian version of "The Commitments" with musical staging by the Partridge Family.

Along the way, they make enemies. The cowboy-hatted Zaf (Naveen Andrews, of "London Kills Me"), the oldest and chronically unemployed, becomes infatuated with the beautiful Rifat (Sarita Choudhury of "Mississippi Masala") and punches out her husband. Kay (Ronny Jhutti) the youngest, is a kamikaze skateboarder who announces "school's just not rock and roll." And Ali (Ravi Kapoor) supplements his postman's salary by selling unreliable used cars to people he shouldn't antagonize. Luckily, they have their rottweiller, Spook, who keeps bringing back body parts after chasing off unsatisfied customers.

"Wild West" starts out fresh and promising and disintegrates into a series of gestures. There are inexplicable sequences of the boys playing in public squares, stealing police cars, running through the streets à la old "Monkees" episodes, and generally avoiding storytelling of any coherent, or at least original, sort. Rifat does become the first Pakistani abused wife-cum-country-singing sensation, though, so I guess that's something.

SIGHT AND SOUND, 5/93, p. 60, Geoffrey Macnab

Zaf, Ali and Kay are three Pakistani brothers living in Southall, West London. Zaf has just been fired from his job as a mechanic, Ali is a postman who runs a second-hand car business on the side, and Kay is still at college. In their spare time, the three have formed a country and western band, the Honky Tonk Cowboys. Zaf is determined they will overcome all the obstacles and secure a record contract with a major label.

One afternoon, while shopping in a supermarket dressed in his usual cowboy gear, Zaf meets Rifat, a beautiful young Asian woman. Rifat is unhappily married to a white cab driver, Tony, who regularly beats her up; Zaf immediately falls for her. Zaf's uncle agrees to hire him as an apprentice butcher; a vegetarian, Zaf reluctantly takes the job because his mother is losing faith in him, and is threatening to go back to Pakistan. He puts his job in jeopardy by leaving his Shepherd's Market stall to run after Rifat, trying to persuade her to leave her husband. When he finds out she is a keen Nanci Griffith fan, he asks her to become lead singer in his group.

Eventually, Rifat does leave her husband, moves in with Zaf and the brothers, and joins their band. After a few rehearsals, their manager Jag books them a gig at an Irish pub in North London. This proves a big success. They record a demo tape which Jag sends to Wild West, an important country record company.

Meanwhile, the brothers' mother, disappointed with life in Britain, has sold her house to Zaf's cousin and archenemy, Ugly Abdul. She gives the boys a cheque for £20,000 and leaves them to fend for themselves. The brothers are delighted when Wild West express enthusiasm for their demo. Convinced their luck has changed, they visit the record company with Rifat in tow; but Wild West are not interested in the Honky Tonk Cowboys at all, and want to sign Rifat as a solo artist. At first, Rifat refuses to consider splitting from the rest of the band, but Zaf insists it is too big an opportunity to be scorned. Refusing to admit defeat, Zaf persuades Ali and Kay to use the money their mother left them to buy three first-class tickets to Nashville. The boys pack their bags, gather their instruments, put their beloved rottweiler in quarantine, and head for Heathrow.

Relentlessly cheerful, *Wild West* eschews state-of-the-nation sermonizing, and instead celebrates the hopes and dreams of its irrepressible hero, with his natty line in boots, waistcoats and stetsons, and determination to make it all the way to Nashville, whatever it takes. Like all self-respecting cowboys, Zaf refuses to kow-tow to anyone. His defiant attitude is clear from the outset: working as a mechanic, pestered by a curmudgeonly customer to speed repairs to a vehicle, his response is to stencil "Fuck You" on the car's paintwork. This is less an idle insult than a statement of principle. The "Fuck You" philosophy, the programme notes portentously declare, "transcends race and country and is the spirit behind the film."

Wild West manages the delicate feat of both celebrating and parodying the Western's lawless frontier values, endorsing rugged individualism, but distancing itself from the worst excesses of John Wayne-style machismo. Zaf is no redneck. His vision of the Wild West is based on the heart-tugging lyrics of Nanci Griffith and Steve Earle songs. Fuelled by its rousing country and western soundtrack, the movie gallops along at breathless pace, allowing nothing to dampen the prevailing mood of febrile optimism. Just as Zaf refuses to become down-hearted at the never-ending series of misfortunes which plague him and his brothers, the movie refuses to be bogged down by polemics. It briefly touches on issues of class and racism without ever stopping for long enough to examine them: hardships are glamourized, either made the stuff which any self-respecting cowboy has to face as a matter of course, or treated as the raw material for new country rock ballads, but seldom addressed as social problems.

The film-makers turn their shabby corner of Southall into an almost glamorous frontier town, where modern-day outlaws drive in open-top cars or disappear over the horizon in buses instead of stagecoaches. Unlike the spate of 80s British movies—among them *Sammy and Rosie Get Laid, Empire State* and *The Last of England*—which famously enraged the Thatcherite historian Norman Stone with their downbeat critique of Maggie's Britain, *Wild West* is short on anger and analysis. It merely observes, making its points obliquely, if at all. In its quirkiness, its harnessing of the low-budget British movie with the Western, it even hearkens back to the lost world of Ealing comedy, a world which Stone relished when confronted with the "grim concrete" and "urban decay" depicted by Jarman, Peck, Frears and Kureishi. Still, despite its lack of bite, *Wild West* at least offers an Asian vision of Britain, rather than a nostalgic hymn to Michael Balcon's cosy Arcadia.

In some ways, it is a relief that the film dispenses with its "sociological baggage," aiming more for comedy than for comment, but *Wild West*'s cheerfulness occasionally verges on inanity. Scriptwriter Harwant Bains admits to being influenced by *Repo Man*, and as in Alex Cox's picture, there are stolen cars, hapless hoodlums, a picaresque approach to violence, and a tendency to fetishize post-industrial landscapes, wastelands and rubbish dumps and the like as giant playgrounds. Director David Attwood's style is frenetic; the film abounds in slapstick, chases and visual gags, most of which work, some of which don't. But there is never time to dwell on the leaden moments.

The one character who stands apart from the anarchic comedy is Zaf's mother. The long-suffering Mrs Ayub, living in a terraced house, increasingly bewildered by both British society and her children's attitude, would warrant a film on her own. She is torn between loyalty to her family, to her adopted nation, and to the place she still feels is her homeland. Zaf's loyalty, though, lies neither with Britain nor with Pakistan, but with country and western in general, and Steve Earle in particular. The film-makers don't overly dwell on Mrs Ayub's plight, perhaps considering it too sombre for the light-hearted mood they are trying to strike.

Wild West is boosted by very engaging performances from Naveen Andrews and Sarita Choudhury, and has a fine array of eccentric character turns. Colourful, packed with comic detail, it certainly works well as a feel-good movie along the lines of *The Commitments*. But the whole affair sometimes seems too glib and good-humoured, and is undermined by Attwood and Bains' refusal to treat their material at all seriously.

VILLAGE VOICE, 11/9/93, p. 55, J. Hoberman

The title *Wild West* refers to West London, where, defying numerous varieties of conventional wisdom, the nattily be-Stetsoned, incorrigibly take-this-job-and-shove-it Zaf Ayub (Naveen Andrews) and his two equally Opry-smitten brothers have formed the world's first Pakistani country-western band.

Nearly as generic as their name, the Honky Tonk Cowboys' repertoire of neo-Nashville Garth Brooks and Steve Earle clears the house at an Asian talent show. But, once fronted by the neighborhood Nanci Griffith fan (Sarita Choudhury, last seen here as Denzel Washington's inamorata in *Mississippi Masala*), they convincingly rock an Irish pub. Commitments, eat your hearts out.

Directed by David Attwood from a screenplay by Harwant Bains, *Wild West* is not nearly so spicy a sample of Anglo-Asian cinema as last spring's *Masala*. Indeed, more perky than humorous, a sincerely glib expression of the desire to be Westernized, *Wild West* is Aki Kaurismaki's jaundiced *Leningrad Cowboys Go America* taken seriously.

Although the Honky Tonk Cowboys own a dog who systematically gnaws off pieces of a marauding skinhead, the movie's implacably amiable tone is only broken by the appearance of a grotesquely stereotyped Jewish promoter who, if not the reality principle, is meant to represent the bottom line.

Also reviewed in:
CHICAGO TRIBUNE, 12/10/93, Friday/p. D, Johanna Steinmetz
NEW YORK TIMES, 11/5/93, p. C6, Stephen Holden
VARIETY, 9/28/92, p. 81, Todd McCarthy
WASHINGTON POST, 11/20/93, p. B5, Hal Hinson

WILDER NAPALM

A TriStar Pictures release of a Baltimore Pictures production. *Executive Producer:* Barrie Osborne. *Producer:* Mark Johnson and Stuart Cornfield. *Director:* Glenn Gordon Caron. *Screenplay:* Vince Gilligan. *Director of Photography:* Jerry Hartleben. *Editor:* Artie Mandelberg. *Music:* Michael Kamen. *Sound:* Les Lazarowitz. *Casting:* Louis DiGiaimo. *Production Designer:* John Muto. *Art Director:* Dan Webster. *Set Decorator:* Leslie Bloom. *Visual Effects:* Stephen Brooks and Harrison Ellenshaw. *Costumes:* Louise Frogley. *Running time:* 110 minutes. *MPAA Rating:* PG-13.

CAST: Debra Winger (Vida Foudroyant); Dennis Quaid (Wallace Foudroyant); Arliss Howard (Wilder Foudroyant); M. Emmet Walsh (Fire Chief); Jim Varney (Rex); Mimi Lieber (Snake Lady); Marvin J. McIntyre (Deputy Sheriff Spivey); Mighty Echoes, The (Singing Firemen).

LOS ANGELES TIMES, 8/20/93, Calendar/p. 6, Peter Rainer

Just about everybody and everything connected to "Wilder Napalm" is terrible, starting with that title. Don't expect a Vietnam movie.

Wilder (Arliss Howard) and Wallace (Dennis Quad) are estranged brothers in the Cain and Abel mold, with a Stephen Kingish twist. Both have pyro-kinetic powers—they can will fires into roaring life. Wilder, who works part time as—you guessed it—a fireman, is married to Vida (Debra Winger), a doting free spirit. When Wallace shows up in town as a clown for a traveling circus, the brothers square off, with Vida as the prize.

Wilder, understandably, has a grudge against his brother, who torched his pate hairless when they were kids. (He wears a wig for most of the movie but when he's wigless, his dome has a melted plastic look that's really icky.) Because the brothers accidentally incinerated someone when they were kids—they were never caught—Wilder has renounced his pyrotechnics. That's why he puts *out* fires as penance. The most he'll do now is light Vida's cigarettes. Wallace, however, wants to cash in on his gifts—he wants to call himself Dr. Napalm and appear on the David Letterman show, no less. (Since this film has been in the can since last year, one presumes this is the NBC and not the CBS Letterman.)

Directed by Glenn Gordon Caron and scripted by Vince Gilligan, "Wilder Napalm" (rated PG-13 for thematic elements, language and some sensuality) is the sort of full-fledged disaster that talented filmmakers occasionally perpetrate in pursuit of the "offbeat." Maybe the idea of two enraged brothers expressing their conflicts by torching each other seemed intriguing on paper; it's a perfectly OK metaphorical conceit. But on screen it just seems ugly—the film's clunky carny atmosphere can't contain images of immolation. Probably nothing could have saved this movie, but possibly a freakier, more metaphysical approach could have brought off some of the savagery. (Echoes of Sam Shepard's plays, particularly "True West," resound throughout.)

There are a few moments here and there: an a cappella chorus of firemen: a scene where Wallace and Vida embrace and the landscape around them goes up in flames. Howard and Winger look uncomfortable spinning their wheels but Dennis Quaid works up a ribald cruelty in a few sequences. You can believe this man wills fire. But most of the time you wish this film would self-incinerate.

NEW YORK POST, 8/20/93, p. 29, Matthew Flamm

Had the makers of "Wilder Napalm" come up with a decent ending, their unfortunately titled comedy might have squeaked by as a genuinely oddball concoction. As it is, this movie about a pair of pyrokinetic brothers and the woman they love literally goes up in flames.

Of course the problems start long before the offbeat story degenerates into the fiery equivalent of a food fight. Director Glenn Gordon Caron ("Clean and Sober," the television show "Moonlighting") and novice screenwriter Vince Gilligan seem to be stretching for something good-natured but Gothic—a Harry Crews novel sweetened with "Bewitched."

They're not entirely unsuccessful. "Wilder Napalm" is agreeably off-kilter for part of its length, inhabiting a quietly bizarre landscape in which a town's volunteer firefighting unit routinely sings doo-wop numbers as it's dousing flames.

But the film doesn't seem to know where its going, or what to do with its exaggerated metaphors. When Wallace makes out with his brother Wilder's wife and flames erupt all around them, you would think the message is that these two were meant for each other. Instead, it's just one hot adulterous kiss.

The brothers approach their fire-starting gift from dramatically convenient opposite corners—the legacy of a traumatic childhood incident in which they inadvertently torched a wino.

Wilder is now a volunteer fireman who works in the photo drop-off booth in a perpetually empty shopping mall parking lot. (It's another of the film's nice touches that no customers ever show up.) As played to closed-mouthed perfection by Arliss Howard, he's a keeps-it-all-in kind of guy who limits himself to lighting the occasional cigarette for his wife, Vida (Debra Winger).

Wallace, meanwhile, is a fire-starting clown in a seedy travelling carnival. As played by Dennis Quaid (who seems fit to be a clown after his disastrous outing in "Great Balls of Fire"), he's a flamboyant character who has decided to go public and demonstrate his skills on the David Letterman show.

The brothers haven't spoken in five years, ever since Wilder married Vida, a sex-crazy, annoyingly free-spirited intellectual (she can tell Mozart from Beethoven) now under house arrest for starting a little fire of her own. Then the carnival pulls into the shopping mall, and "Wilder Napalm" has to force both a confrontation and a resolution.

Winger carries off her too flaky role with a saving innocence, and Quaid wins you over once he takes off the greasepaint. There are some witty lines. But the outcome is predictable, right down to the boys-will-be-boys inferno that must have cost somebody a fortune in sets.

NEWSDAY, 8/20/93, Part II/p. 69, Terry Kelleher

Even justice Oliver Wendell Holmes might have conceded you the right to shout "fire" in a theater showing a "Wilder Napalm." There's not much chance the place will be crowded. Perhaps the ill-conceivers of "Wilder Napalm" grossly overestimated the pyromaniacal percentage of the movie-going population. More likely they got carried away with a game of high-concept one-upmanship:

"I've got it—let's redo 'Firestarter' as a comedy!"

"Not bad, but it needs something. What if two firestarter brothers battle for the love of a beautiful arsonist?"

Dennis Quaid plays Wallace Foudroyant (the name is a comic lagniappe for French-speaking ticket buyers), a circus clown who can start fires simply by pointing at the object to be incinerated. His ambition is to flaunt his telekinetic power on David Letterman's TV show and thereby achieve stardom. (Letterman's name is dropped so often you'd think "Wilder Napalm" was yet another CBS promo, but Dave wisely keeps his face out of the picture.)

Arliss Howard has the role of repressed Wilder Foudroyant, who mans a photo-developing booth in a sleepy shopping center, serves quietly in the local volunteer fire department and chooses not to exercise his ability to ignite blazes by scrunching up his forehead. Wilder's sexually insatiable wife, Vida (Debra Winger), is completing a year's house arrest (actually motor-home confinement) for arson, but that doesn't stop her from setting grass fires to lure him during working hours.

After Wallace's carnival caravan invades the vast, empty parking lot surrounding Wilder's Foto Kwik fortress—in a scene that requires no dialogue to be the film's funniest—Wallace sparks an old name in Vida's heart while Wilder does a slow, slow burn. Eventually, the brothers fight fire with fire in a protracted special-effects showdown, during which Wallace basically reviews the movie by yelling, "Wilder, we're running out of places to go!"

Debuting screenwriter Vince Gilligan evidently assumed his incredible premise obviated any necessity for credible characterization. Vida and Wallace talk and behave like hicks, except when she's tossing off references to Sartre and Kierkegaard, or he's employing terms such as "self-hating" and "passive-aggressive" in the heat of argument. Only Jim (Hey, Vern) Varney, as Wallace's carny sidekick, says anything both amusing and unforced. Still, his T-shirts get more laughs than his lines.

Wilder's brow-furrowing and jaw-tightening turn out to be traceable to a childhood horror, which director Glenn Gordon Caron (creator of television's "Moonlighting") depicts in a tastelessly grisly flashback. That a movie this wacko would even skirt seriousness is an index of his miscalculation. For all the fancy camera moves, the script would have served better as kindling.

Also reviewed in:
NEW YORK TIMES, 8/20/93, p. C14, Janet Maslin
VARIETY, 8/30/93, p. 19, Leonard Klady

WITTGENSTEIN

A Zeitgeist Films release of a Bandung production.   *Executive Producer:* Ben Gibson and Takashi Asai.   *Producer:* Tariq Ali.   *Director:* Derek Jarman.   *Screenplay:* Derek Jarman, Terry Eagleton, and Ken Butler.   *Director of Photography:* James Welland.   *Editor:* Budge Tremlett.   *Music:* Jan Latham-Koenig.   *Sound:* George Richards and (music) Andre Jacquemin.   *Sound Editor:* Toby Calder.   *Art Director:* Annie Lapaz.   *Costumes:* Sandy Powell.   *Make-up:* Morag Ross.   *Running time:* 75 minutes.   *MPAA Rating:* Not Rated.

CAST: Karl Johnson (Ludwig Wittgenstein);   Michael Gough (Bertrand Russell);   Tilda Swinton (Ottoline Morrell);   John Quentin (Maynard Keynes);   Kevin Collins (Johnny);   Clancy Chassay (Young Ludwig Wittgenstein);   Jill Balcon (Leopoldine Wittgenstein);   Sally Dexter (Hermine Wittgenstein);   Gina Marsh (Gretyl Wittgenstein);   Vanya del Borgo (Helen Wittgenstein);   Ben Scantlebury (Hans Wittgenstein);   Howard Sooley (Kurt Wittgenstein);   David Radzinowicz (Rudolph Wittgenstein);   Jan Latham-Koenig (Paul Wittgenstein);   Nabil Shaban (Martian);   Donald McInnes (Hairdresser);   Aisling Magill (Schoolgirl);   Lynn Seymour (Lydia Lopokova);   Samantha Cones, Kate Temple, and Sarah Graham (Cyclists);   Layla Alexander Garrett (Sophia Janovskaya).

LOS ANGELES TIMES, 5/12/94, Calendar/p. 12, Kevin Thomas

The beautifully acted "Wittgenstein," Jarman's sprightly, witty 75-minute gloss on the life of philosopher Ludwig Wittgenstein, is among his most accessible films. In minimalist settings, Jarman sketches the influential philosopher's life in a series of key encounters as we see him move from his native Vienna, where he was born into wealth in 1889, out into the world, principally Cambridge, where he sparred with Bertrand Russell (Michael Gough) and was nurtured by a fellow gay, economist John Maynard Keynes (John Quentin). In essence, we witness Wittgenstein (Karl Johnson) engage in a lifelong battle with the tantalizing limitations and possibilities of language in relation to philosophy. As for his own homosexuality, Wittgenstein found his desire to be open about his life at war with the need for secrecy because of the oppressive laws of his era.

NEW STATESMAN & SOCIETY, 3/12/93, p. 34, Jonathan Romney

[*Wittgenstein* was reviewed jointly with *Orlando*; see Romney's review of that film.]

NEW YORK POST, 9/18/93, p. 16, Jerry Tallmer

A man stands at a blackboard on which he has chalked something that looks like a dog. He is a professor of philosophy, this man, at Cambridge University, an institution which he hates, and like Albert Einstein and others of the sort, he is splitting the world wide open. Or at least the mental universe.

"A dog," he says to the students, most of whom he despises—"a dog may be expecting his master to come. Why is it he doesn't expect his master to come next Wednesday? Is it because he can't speak? If a lion could speak would we understand?"

Out there in the student seats, one bored smug type murmurs to another. "We might understand a lion easier than *him*."

The him is Ludwig Wittgenstein (1889-1951), of whom, in Derek Jarman's "Wittgenstein," Lady Ottoline Morrell says to John Maynard Keynes, or maybe it's to Bertrand Russell (I kept getting them mixed up): "What is he trying to do?" Answer, from Keynes or Russell: "He is trying to define the limits of language, and what it is to communicate with one another."

Or as Wittgenstein himself (actor Karl Johnson) keeps exclaiming over and over to one and all in a sort of frenzy throughout this short intensely compacted work: "Do you understand what I'm saying?"

Jarman likes to make difficult films, two of which at least "Edward II" and "Caravaggio," seemed to me to combine heat with high pretentiousness.

In "Wittgenstein" he has carried the stylized and the mannerist to an even higher degree, placing a few spare actors in odd costuming with bizarre props before a series of blank red or black backgrounds—a trick borrowed from Godard and Alain Cavalier. But what was purity in Cavalier's "Therese" is affectation here.

Still, the experience has its rewards if only you can get past the nonsense—the worst of it being a sour-jolly green Martian out of "Alice in Wonderland" as adviser to Wittgenstein the small boy, born to "a filthy rich" iron-and-steel family in cultured Vienna, destined to share a history teacher—"what a scream"—with Adolf Hitler.

Talking and doing, thinking and doing. "It's what we *do* and what we *are* [that] makes us understand a language." On the other hand there's Lady Ottoline (Tilda Swinton), in brilliant red ostrich, in green, who enquires of Bertie Russell (Michael Gough): "What is logical positivism?" and gets the cursory reply: "Too difficult to explain."

This movie is only a little difficult to explain. It's not totally easy to watch.

NEWSDAY, 9/17/93, Part II/p. 78, John Anderson

"If people did not sometimes do silly things, nothing intelligent would ever get done," asserts the young Ludwig Wittgenstein, who is shunted aside all too early in Derek Jarman's new film, but whose words persist.

"Wittgenstein," which takes as its ostensible subject 20th-Century Viennese philosopher Ludwig Wittgenstein, but which like most Jarman films is about Jarman, is a highly stylized, darkly humorous, occasionally silly and pretentious but very generous pseudo-biography. With minimalist props and stage setups, it shares with other Jarman films a seemingly impossible sense of vastness. And just as his characters are emblazoned against the black backdrop against which the entire film is shot, so are they emblazoned on the mind's eye.

They include young Ludwig, played with a charming precocity by Clancy Chassay, and his older self, played by Karl Johnson (Ariel in Jarman's 1979 "The Tempest"). The boy Ludwig introduces us to his family with ironic cockiness—three of the philosopher's four brothers killed themselves—but he's sweetly brilliant. Which makes the anguished demeanor of the older Wittgenstein—who goes to Cambridge, becomes a student and then an antagonist of Bertrand Russell (Michael Gough) and is befriended by John Maynard Keynes (John Quentin) and Lady Ottoline (Tilda Swinton)—unsettling. Wittgenstein, strangling on his repressed homosexuality, writes his "Tractatus Logico-Philosophicus," undermines the education of Johnny (Kevin Collins), his student/lover, gives away his money and embraces manual labor. And he argues against the possibility of his own work, perhaps the possibility of himself. "Philosophy," he says, "is just a byproduct of misunderstanding language." It's also the byproduct of a need for self-definition, something that seems to elude Wittgenstein.

There's very little real emotion being portrayed here; Jarman is more interested in portraying how Wittgenstein's mind worked. And while there may be a sense of finality about "Wittgenstein," that may just be a byproduct of the knowledge that Derek Jarman is dying in England, his long battle with HIV infection seemingly coming to a close. His sense of humor, sense of the absurd, and outrage over the tragedy of intolerance, however, have survived his physical ordeal.

SIGHT AND SOUND, 4/93, p. 63, Chris Darke

The young Ludwig Wittgenstein, announcing himself as "a prodigy", introduces us to his Viennese family, describes the rigours of his Austrian education, and debates philosophical questions with a Martian. His intellectual talents take him initially to England where, at Manchester University, he studies Engineering. He quickly transfers to Philosophy at Cambridge, where he is befriended and encouraged in his radically original philosophical ideas by Bertrand Russell who, writing to his mistress Lady Ottoline Morrell, proclaims him the most gifted philosopher of his generation.

Wittgenstein leaves Cambridge to journey first to Norway where, in seclusion, he begins to write his *Notes on Logic*, then back to Austria, where he informs his family he intends to volunteer for the army. His sister Hermione regards the decision as stupid; his brother Paul is encouraged to join up with him. During World War I, Paul loses an arm and Ludwig begins work on what will become the *Tractatus Logico-Philosophicus*. On returning home he decides to delay his return to Cambridge by taking up a provincial teaching post, further angering Hermione who insists that he is wasting his talents. Ludwig experiences the elementary school as deeply frustrating and is forced to leave after being accused of brutality towards his students.

His return to Cambridge is facilitated by the offer of a teaching post and a grant arranged by the Professor of Economics John Maynard Keynes. Wittgenstein, however, finds it frustratingly difficult to relate his ideas to his students, and seeks solace in daily visits to the local cinema. He is accompanied by his friend Johnny, a young philosophy student who is also Maynard Keynes' lover. Wittgenstein and Johnny begin a relationship, during which the philosopher attempts to persuade the student to relinquish his studies in favour of the more 'honest' world of manual labour. Russell and Keynes reprimand him for influencing a young man whose working-class background meant that his parents underwent great sacrifices to educate their son at Cambridge. Wittgenstein attempts to leave Cambridge to work as a factory labourer in Soviet Russia, but the Soviet authorities offer him instead a choice of two University posts. He returns to Cambridge in 1951 where he is diagnosed as suffering from cancer of the prostate. After a last voyage, this time to Ireland, he returns to Cambridge to die, where he is attended at his deathbed by Maynard Keynes and the Martian.

Originally conceived as part of a Channel Four series on philosophers to include films on Spinoza and Locke, *Wittgenstein*—shot in two weeks and for less than £300,000—takes Jarman's characteristic exquisite minimalism to a new extreme. The already reduced *mise en scène* of *Edward II* is here further contracted to a series of lush colour tableaux on a depthless pitch-black background.

This refusal of depth and, by consequence, of any realist visual perspective, while making a telling virtue of economic necessity, is a visual strategy in keeping with the film's agenda. For it becomes increasingly clear that at one prominent level *Wittgenstein* is a disquisition on the futility of dramatizing the life behind the work, an extended Brechtian parody of biopic conventions.

The insistent dedramatization comes across particularly in the film's use of spare sets and anti-realistic costumes, a single prop becoming the motif of a particular period or place. Vienna becomes a group portrait around a grand piano; and Cambridge a group of students seated in deckchairs around a blackboard—English gentlemen-philosophers sunning themselves in the light of the imported *mittel*-European eccentric. This latter-day Brechtianism might also derive from the fact that the film's first draft was the work of Marxist academic Terry Eagleton. In studiedly distancing itself from the Minnelli/Van Gogh paradigm of the biopic (attempting at all costs to avoid becoming *Lust for Logic*), *Wittgenstein* toys with the standard characterization of the Genius as Romantic Outsider, personally and professionally misunderstood, and identifies melancholia and torment as the wellsprings of creativity.

Actors 'quote' their parts; Bertrand Russell played as an amiable lounge-lizard academic, Maynard Keynes as a stiff-spined manipulator of the Old Boys Network and Lady Ottoline Morrell as brittle, charming bitch aristo—ciphers all. But the holding of the biopic tendencies at arm's length results in a curious lack of conviction. This conflict of formal strategy and latent content is particularly emphasised by moments when the starkness works towards either a visually expressive effect—the retreat to Norway given with beautiful economy, a single lantern and a dappling light on the boatside; or to accentuate a character trait—Ludwig's disastrous spell as a teacher at a provincial Austrian primary school, when the camera closes in on the faces of the impotently raging teacher and his terrified pupil. The fact that this sequence returns as the single flashback in the film, to accompany the philosopher's repeated, agonised refrain of "Do you understand me?", is an internal recognition that it packs the film's only powerfully dramatic punch.

Wittgenstein also represents a continuation of Jarman's highly personal Grand Tour through the mausoleum of European High Culture. But whether the cultural model is literary (Shakespeare, Marlowe), painterly (Caravaggio) or philosophical, Jarman's fascination remains in his isolating and reinterpreting the marginal inscriptions of class and sexuality in culture. *Wittgenstein*, while something of a curio, is a further development of this sustained cinematic reading of cultural history 'against the grain'. The film's central thesis concerns the philosopher's masochistic faith in material reality, in the 'everyday' as superior to "the poison of the mind" that his philosophical vocation represents and this is investigated partly through his sexuality, but largely through class.

Surprisingly, Jarman never really exploits the visual possibilities of the engineer-turned-philosopher's artisanal activities, which included building two houses. These adventures, as well as his Tolstoyesque communions with nature, his mistaken attempt to defect to Soviet Russia and his enlistment in World War I, are presented as acts of classic bourgeois bad faith, arising from a sense of class shame. He is accused of such by both Maynard Keynes and Russell, who are presented as comfortably socially integrated. This complex of issues crystallises around the character of Johnny, a rough-trade cipher and the lover of both Maynard Keynes and Wittgenstein. The philosopher's repeated attempts to dissuade Johnny from continuing his studies in favour of the more "authentic" life of manual work provokes both Keynes and Russell, who justify their angry disagreement in the name of the sacrifices of Johnny's working-class family. That the philosopher is simply unable to comprehend this argument demonstrates the extent to which each of the three characters regard Johnny as a *tabula rasa*: Keynes and Russell projecting onto him their own feelings and attitudes of, respectively, desire and paternalist patronage: Wittgenstein affectionately incorporating the young man into his own schema of self-hate and self-delusion.

The irony that the film constantly points up is that Wittgenstein's philosophical brilliance (the maxims here are deliberately tossed about like so many after-dinner *bons mots*) is less a condition of his acceptance in Cambridge than the tacit understanding that he is—however much he kicks against it—of the same class as Russell and Keynes. At the philosopher's deathbed, Keynes offers a poetic homily that collapses the contradictions of his character into two elemental images; Wittgenstein as constantly pulled between "the ice world" of logic and "the earth" of material reality. Abetted by its own icy formalism, the film never really touches the earth of its character.

VILLAGE VOICE, 9/21/93, p. 60, Gary Indiana

The philosopher Ludwig Wittgenstein has been the subject of numerous biographies and novels as well as a virtual library of secondary philosophical works. *Wittgenstein's City*, *Wittgenstein:*

The Duty of Genius, and a half dozen other nonacademic titles have appeared in the past few years. The best fictional treatment of Wittgenstein remains Thomas Bernhard's 1975 novel *Korrektur*, W. W. Bartley III's *Wittgenstein*, published in 1973 and revised in 1985, is the most generally, useful short account of Wittgenstein's life and thought.

Bartley's book was viciously attacked in England when it first appeared, mainly by academics with some stake in the long-flourishing Wittgenstein industry, because it discussed Wittgenstein's homosexuality. Even as late as 1985, when Bartley added a section addressing the controversy, many of Wittgenstein's surviving Cambridge acolytes, some of whom were undoubtedly queer themselves, continued to treat the revelation as an outrageous libel. The same attitude is maintained by the Wittgenstein Documentation Center in Kirchberg, Austria, where, as Bartley notes, "two display cases are devoted to arguing that Wittgenstein was *not* a homosexual."

He was, though, and in a period when the closet deformed the social being and drew a veil of silence over the inner life, Derek Jarman's *Wittgenstein* sets about showing the relationship between Wittgenstein's tortured production of thought and his personality, which combined an impatient intellectual arrogance with crippling self-flagellation, merciless honesty with mulish self-delusion.

In his *Tractatus Logico-Philosophicus*, Wittgenstein wrote that whatever could be thought could also be stated, yet two essential facts of his existence were, for long periods of his life, inexpressible. He was Jewish and he was queer.

Several accounts of his years at Cambridge refer to a "confession" Wittgenstein made to close friends, revealing his great shame at having concealed his Jewish ancestry. (The Wittgensteins were the Austrian equivalent of conversos, having become assimilated Christians a few generations earlier.) The queer thing doesn't figure in these narratives, and perhaps it was a matter of local, unspoken knowledge that W. "liked" his protégés David Pinsent and Francis Skinner (merged, in Jarman's film, into one working-class Cambridgian Adonis named Johnny); at Cambridge, it would hardly have been a cause for scandal if W., discreetly, had sex with them, John Maynard Keynes, after all, is shown here loving up both men and women with great appetite.

In Jarman's film (accurately, as far as I know), W. is intensely conflicted and uneasy about physical relations, as he is about human contact generally. He despises Cambridge, but ends up spending much of his life there; he thinks philosophy is useless, and encourages Johnny to abandon his studies for manual labor. As the Bertrand Russell character points out, W. is an aristocrat who idealizes the working class "as long as they keep feeding the boiler." One of the most interesting aspects of Jarman's movie is its use of Russell and Keynes as worldly friends who see through the obscurity of Wittgenstein's histrionic persona. Russell is appalled by W.'s unconscious manipulation of his graduate students, and tells him that his self-revulsion is corrupting them.

W.'s shown meditating on the impossibility of a form of love that's proscribed. He is, above all, a person who wants society to make sense, for its rules to obey some kind of logic. His neurasthenia (I don't know what else to call it) exacerbates his class-instilled sense of social duty; he volunteers, for example, for the trenches in World War I, and later teaches in village schools. Still later, he tries to sign on as a manual laborer in the Soviet Union, during the great '30s left-intellectual romance with Stalin.

He spent much of his life escaping his background and trying to escape himself. He fled to Norway several times and lived in a small house he built on a fjord. He devoted two years to building a Vienna home for his sister Gretl, a mathematically perfect structure in the style of Adolf Loos. For a time, he worked as a gardener at a monastery. The difficulty of communicating what he had in his head tormented him, and everyone around him. He beat the children he taught in primary schools and bullied his students in Cambridge. Outside the pedagogical context, he was noted for exquisite manners and genuine kindness, even saintliness.

There was a mystical streak in Wittgenstein's character, fed by reading Tolstoy and Dostoyevski. Influenced by the figure of Alyosha in *The Brothers Karamazov*, he gave away his huge inheritance to his brothers and sisters. In Jarman's film, he admits that he wants to be perfect. Keynes comes to Wittgenstein's deathbed and tells him a story about a man who put the world in perfect order, and found that all around him was ice.

The ice was perfectly smooth, and it was impossible to walk on it. The world needs imperfections for anyone to live there.

The exemplary strength of Jarman's film is that it really does convey an idea of how Wittgenstein's mind worked: the best scenes show him giving lectures. "Why is it easy for people to believe the sun revolves around the earth?" "Because that's the way it looks." "And if the earth revolved around the sun? What would that look like?" The actor Karl Johnson has a strong resemblance to Wittgenstein, and uses what sounds like the right Anglicized German accent, and the accurate degree of austerity. He is, possibly, a little too beefy with his shirt off, but it's mostly on.

This isn't a naturalistic film, more an essay than a drama, and it has a number of cloying features that I, perhaps unfairly, associate with the British art film: the illustration of abstract ideas via minimalist theatrical, rather than filmic, techniques; the studied absence of simulated emotion; the conviction that a clever retort is always adequate punctuation of a scene.

Wittgenstein accomplishes most of what it sets out to do, but it isn't a terribly seductive film. You have to work hard to like it for the first 10 minutes, and the rest of it, requires the kind of attention demanded by a book instead of a movie. Several minor roles are either miscast or ill-written, including Tilda Swinton's condescending tittup as Lady Ottoline Morrell: Swinton has been wonderful in many movies, but she is fairly insufferable in this one, Kevin Collins, as Johnny, looks about as working-class as Lord Alfred Douglas did.

The script falters whenever the characters are being "social" instead of terse and dramatic: people just don't talk like this, and if they do, they shouldn't. Like virtually all of Jarman's movies, *Wittgenstein* is stagy, overstylized, and pretentious, but it has often been Jarman's genius to make these qualities resonate in a transcendent way. In *Wittgenstein* they do, for the most part, and leave the audience with much more to think about than even Jarman's films usually do.

Also reviewed in:
NATION, 10/4/93, p. 366, Stuart Klawans
NEW REPUBLIC, 10/11/93, p. 38, Stanley Kauffmann
NEW YORK TIMES, 9/17/93, p. C15, Janet Maslin
VARIETY, 2/15/93, p. 86, Derek Elley
WASHINGTON POST, 10/23, 93, p. D4, Hal Hinson

WRESTLING ERNEST HEMINGWAY

A Warner Bros. release. *Producer:* Todd Black and Joe Wizan. *Director:* Randa Haines. *Screenplay:* Steve Conrad. *Director of Photography:* Lajos Koltai. *Editor:* Paul Hirsch. *Music:* Michael Convertino. *Music Editor:* Tom Carlson. *Choreographer:* Daryl Matthews. *Sound:* Michael R. Tromer and (music) Shawn Murphy. *Sound Editor:* Larry Kemp and Lon E. Bender. *Casting:* Lora Kennedy. *Production Designer:* Waldemar Kalinowski. *Art Director:* Alan E. Muraoka. *Set Designer:* Carlos Arditti. *Set Decorator:* Florence Fellman. *Visual Effects:* Michael J. McAllister. *Costumes:* Joe I. Tomkins. *Make-up:* Manlio Rocchetti. *Running time:* 123 minutes. *MPAA Rating:* PG-13.

CAST: Robert Duvall (Walt); Richard Harris (Frank); Shirley MacLaine (Helen); Sandra Bullock (Elaine); Micole Mercurio (Bernice); Marty Belafsky (Ned Ryan); Harold Bergman (Sleeper); Piper Laurie (Georgia); Ed Amatrudo (Henry's Dad); Jag Davies (Henry); Rudolph X. Herrera (Umpire); Persephone Felder (Woman in Stands); Stephen G. Anthony (Leo Peetes); Greg Paul Meyers (Sid Showenstein); Aquilla Owens (First Girl in Park); Doris Carey (Mom in Park); Jody Wilson (Nurse); Anthony René Jones (Bus Driver); Richard Jasen (Third Baseman); William Marquez (Carl Burney); Chick Bernhardt (Stunt Driver #1); Ron Russell (Stunt Driver #2); Ilse Earl (Cinema Cashier); Kent Ehrhardt (Weatherman); Danika Daly (Second Girl in Park); Eleonora L. Vescera (Singing Woman); Daryl Matthews (Officer Mickey).

LOS ANGELES TIMES, 12/17/93, Calendar/p. 16, Peter Rainer

Actors, when they're in their tour-de-force mode, sometimes glom onto aggressively silly or sentimental roles for dear life. "Wrestling Ernest Hemingway" has not one but *two* of these roles.

Robert Duvall plays Walter, a retired, Cuban barber in south Florida, and Richard Harris is Frank, an Irish ex-sea captain. The movie is supposed to be about how these two disparate gents become friends, but it's really about scenery eating. And the scenery looks to be none too tasty.

Duvall's munching is a nibble compared to Harris'. Walter is a finicky loner who goes to the park at the same time every day and eats his bacon sandwiches like clockwork and is cultivating a mildly flirtatious connection with a local waitress (Sandra Bullock). Walter always looks as if he's about to vanish off the face of the Earth. Self-effacement suits him. Frank, on the other hand, is a blustery blowhard who keeps making a grab for his landlady (Shirley MacLaine) and continually spins a whopper about how he once wrestled—and bested—Ernest Hemingway.

Director Randa Haines and screenwriter Steve Conrad—he was 21 when he wrote the script—have a few whoppers of their own to share. The movie is a tall tale with every sentimental stop pulled: fireworks, clasped hands, swan songs. Walter and Frank may be the most romantic couple in the movies right now—it's codger love.

"Wrestling Ernest Hemingway" is such a bathetic wallow that it makes you wonder if anybody connected with it ever met anyone over 50. Why is it that so many Hollywood movies, especially "Cocoon" and "Fried Green Tomatoes" and "Used People" and now this one (with "Grumpy Old Men" on deck) insist on showing off old people as a bunch of soppy cantankerous coots? (At least the filmmakers don't have Walter and Frank rob a bank or win a salsa dance-a-thon.)

Duvall and Harris, both playing older than their actual ages, seem to be having a high old time acting crotchety and infirm. Harris is so over-the-top that at times he's like a roadshow Ahab. Duvall is quieter, better, though he's so enamored by Walter's persnickety politeness that he may not realize the role is wafer-thin, Duvall overacts as much as Harris does, but his way of overacting is to underact: He loads up on tiny gestures and vocal inflections. (Meryl Streep is a piker in the accent department compared to Duvall; his Cuban accent here is letter-perfect.)

Just in case we're having trouble sinking into all the life-affirming mush, Haines drags the film out to just over two hours, and it feels like three. There are some nice, glancing moments between the two actors, and a strong scene between Harris and MacLaine when he comes on too strong to her and then backs off and we realize she's as lonely as he is. But most of the time the film slogs along to its predictable conclusion. You may feel as if you're aging right along with Walter and Frank.

NEW YORK POST, 12/17/93, p. 45, Thelma Adams

This is the year of nude men.

Harvey Keitel dusted "The Piano" in the buff and became the 1993 buck-naked poster boy; "Wrestling Ernest Hemingway" star Richard Harris gives Keitel a run for his money—with added points for seniority.

Harris demonstrates in the first minute of "Wrestling Ernest Hemingway" that, for someone playing a 75-year-old man his gluteus maximus has splendid definition. Or did they use a body double?

Harris' co-star, Robert Duvall, also gets to bare butt in this offbeat buddy movie about two old men beached in Florida. Frank (Harris) is a salty former sea captain whose son has checked him into the Lone Palm Apartments to die; Walt (Duvall) is a meticulous retired Cuban barber stuck in a lifelong rut.

The duo are bench-sitting through their tarnished, golden years. When Frank forces a friendship on Walt, they chase away their loneliness and their lives come into focus.

The energy the two actors put into their roles form the centerpiece of Randa ("Children of a Lesser God") Haines's bittersweet comedy. Harris is a poor-man's Max von Sydow, his lined face shifts from hopeful to lonely to crushed with grace and clarity.

Duvall's role as Ricky Ricardo's neater brother starts out more muted, expressed entirely through his lips and accent that never slips. But as Harris draws him out, the characterization blossoms into a gift to the audience, less flashy than Duvall's turn in "Geronimo," but more genuine.

Shirley MacLaine has a small and underwritten part as the Lone Palm's proprietor. It's nice to see MacLaine playing a character her own age who still has sex appeal, but she seemed to deserve an emotional scene that didn't reach the screen.

Piper Laurie does a pleasing turn as a sexy senior redhead, still flirting after all these years. Sandra Bullock also charms as the waitress at a local diner who is Walt's one friend until Frank comes along.

"Wrestling Ernest Hemingway" refers to an event that Frank retells endlessly, a fish story about the day he took on the famous writer in Puerto Rico and won. The title has more action to it than the movie and for all its nudity, the sex is tame.

Steve Conrad's screenplay suffers from small-movie syndrome. The script builds to a splendid confrontation between Frank and Walt, but before and after it clings to set-piece scenes and spins its wheels.

Still, Harris and Duvall create memorable characters who affect pure and moving moments.

When Frank tells Walt about a marriage gone sour he captures the loneliness of single men at the far shore of their lives. As a sea captain, Frank says, it wasn't being away from his family that was difficult, it was not wanting to return. "I wanted to be alone. I got my wish."

NEWSDAY, 12/17/93, Part II/p. 95, Jack Mathews

Without quite meaning to, Randa Haines' depressing "Wrestling Ernest Hemingway" presents a worst-case scenario of growing old, and a checklist of reasons to dread it. We will be sad, lonely, bored, physically diminished and tormented by memories of a vitality we can never reclaim.

That's not how Haines, the fine director of "Children of a Lesser God," or Steve Conrad, the script's 23-year-old author, would describe the movie. What they are trying to tell is a story about the beauty of friendship, how two men who would ignore each other if they weren't old and lonely, come to fill each other's emotional gaps in a laconic coastal town in Florida.

Frank (Richard Harris) is a vulgar, alcoholic ex-Irish seaman, moored by an uncaring son in the rundown, aptly named Lone Palm apartments. The big event for him each day is a double-feature at the local theater.

Walter (Robert Duvall) is a retired Cuban barber, a gentleman bachelor with a life-style as fastidiously routine and mundane as a trim and a shave. He whiles away his afternoons watching Little League baseball, and rooting for the worst player on the field.

Over one ungodly humid summer, these dissimilar gents, both in their mid-70s, build a friendship out of the most tenuous bond—the need to alleviate the tedium of their daily lives—and force themselves to enjoy each other's company.

Any resemblance to real-life characters here is no fault of Conrad's. His script reads like a final exam in a screenwriting course, Creating Unforgettable Characters 101, with the conflicts and contrasts all carefully constructed and laid out. It is more a young person's sympathetic view of old age than a study of it, and it is rank with unintentionally patronizing observations.

What elevates the movie far above the material are the performances of its two perfectly chosen stars, particularly that of Harris. Frank may not be the role Harris was born to play, but it's one that his own celebrated excesses had him well-prepared to play.

Harris, like Duvall, is in his early 60s yet his deeply lined face allows him to pass for seventy-something without the Latex, turtle-skin mask worn by his costar. Harris has always been an actor willing to try anything before a camera, and he seems to relish the opening sequence where Frank finishes his morning workout, then walks to the door to greet his landlady (Shirley MacLaine) in the buff.

"It looked so nice out this morning," Harris says, with an impish grin, "I decided to leave it out."

If Frank is a character composed of Irish seafarer cliches—loud, rowdy, hard-drinking and womanizing—Harris rounds him out in amazing ways, and fills him with emotional crosscurrents. Frank is a rogue who has lived out every impulse, bad and good, and is suddenly left to his memories of failed marriages, sexual conquest, and of great, undoubtedly embellished, adventures.

We never know whether he actually wrestled Ernest Hemingway in a Puerto Rican bar, as he insists, and it doesn't matter. We feel sure he would have done it, given the chance, because we can believe it of Harris himself. When an actor and character blend this perfectly, it is screen magic of the purest sort, and a spot on the coming Oscar ballot should be reserved for him.

Duvall pulls off a minor miracle of his own, making something interesting of Walter, a character so transparently contrived you can almost see the sketch marks on him. He is the anal retentive opposite of Frank, a quiet, shy man whose daily routine would be timed in milliseconds, if he could move that fast.

It is Walter, of course, who accommodates the greatest change, who is drawn out by his exuberant new friend, even while trying to groom and tame him. Duvall, mostly through awkward silences, makes us feel some of Walter's pain, especially over his wistful infatuation with the kind young waitress (Sandra Bullock) who prepares his bacon sandwiches every morning.

Bullock, MacLaine and Piper Laurie, who plays the lonely woman who keeps attracting and rejecting Frank at the movie theater, have little to do. MacLaine gets the best of it, sharing the film's most emotional scene with Harris, but mostly, the women are there to provide a range of reactions to these old codgers.

There is a melancholy saying that you know you're getting old when people start treating you like a child, and that is the queasy feeling we get all too often from this misguided production.

SIGHT AND SOUND, 10/94, p. 56, Trevor Johnston

South Florida. Dapper ex-barber Walter, an expatriate Cuban, lives alone, eating the same bacon sandwich breakfast at the local cafe—where he conducts a half-flirtatious relationship with waitress Elaine. Frank, a drink-sodden former sea captain of Irish extraction, also lives by himself; abandoned by his son in a run-down apartment block tended by world-weary widow Helen, he still has romantic designs on senior citizen Georgia. The two men could hardly be more different: Walt is circumspect, discreet and shy with women; gregarious Frank loudly boasts of his four wives and many conquests. A chance meeting in the park, however, sparks off an unlikely friendship.

Frank is initially disdainful of Walt's entrenched routine and takes him on a tandem ride to view the Fourth of July fireworks display. On their return, Walt gives Frank a neat haircut, while the latter takes his new-found pal on a fishing trip. Both men gain a new purpose, yet both are to meet disappointment: Walt is shocked to hear that Elaine is getting married; while for Frank, Georgia's latest rejection carries an air of finality. Frank tries to help Walt bid Elaine farewell by buying her a bottle of vodka, a gift that sparks a bitter argument between the men.

Over the next few days, Walt fails to appear, leaving Frank to feel guilty when Walt's favoured Little League baseball team wins a game and Walt isn't there to see it. Frank seeks solace in the arms of Helen, who keeps intimacy largely at bay. Soon though, the two men are reconciled and Walt visits Elaine at home to say goodbye. Later, he invites Frank to a dance, but when he arrives at his pal's apartment, Frank has died peacefully. Walt plucks up the courage to go to the dance, riding Frank's tandem to his destination.

Randa Haines' new film bears all the obvious marks of the screenwriter's contrivance, yet still carries an emotional clout, offering readily grasped performing opportunities to a cast who represent between them almost an entire history of post-50s screen acting. A first-time effort from young college graduate Steve Conrad, the screenplay unfolds with methodical predictability: an accretion of contrasting character and lifestyle details delineates the differences between the two men, but in playing reserved fantasist Walt against vainglorious old sod Frank, those very differences highlight the experience they share. In their separate ways—Frank because he's withdrawn into daydreams and sustaining routine, Walt because his own exuberant self-mythologising is a pain in the ass to everyone around him—the pair's rigid self-definition inhibits their ability to communicate with others. (The title is derived from Frank's oft-repeated anecdote of how he once went hand to hand with the heavyweight of American literature). Isolated, Walt and Frank look increasingly lost—we first see Walt dancing by himself in his apartment, Frank, buck naked, practising press-ups in his room. Yet together they're on complementary learning curves. From such a basic blueprint many a buddy picture has been patterned, and this one would be little dissimilar, if not for the conviction and practised screen craft which Robert Duvall and Richard Harris bring to their roles, and the confidence shown by director Haines in simply trusting them to get on with it.

In her previous features *Children of a Lesser God* and *The Doctor*, Haines has been adept at using institutional backgrounds (a special needs school, a busy hospital) as a grounding for her characters' individual feelings, although in both cases, credible observation was rather undercut by plot-driven melodramatics. Here, on the other hand, the narrative is such a generic standby it's almost a given, so Haines can devote more space to the characters simply being themselves. Commendably, it's one of the least pacy major studio pictures to be seen in a while, and Haines deserves much credit for the maturity with which she keeps camera stylistics to a minimum, establishes a believable environment and holds true to a deliberate rhythmic gait throughout the two-hour-plus running time. The result pays dividends in its touching exploration of such un-Hollywood areas as loneliness and self-delusion, though the too-regimented structure in the end stands between the film and genuine stature.

Still, Haines has cajoled a number of solid performances from her distinguished cast. MacLaine, a star for four decades, now has so little to prove that she's lost the need to hyper-emote on screen and simply lets her sad eyes and age-worn features do the talking—her bitter yet vulnerable widow, the caretaker of Frank's apartment block, is an effective portrait on a minor scale. Harris, on the other hand, simply lets rip in a part that demands it. His is the least disciplined, perhaps the most enjoyable turn in the film, almost a caricature of his familiar wild Irishman schtick but insightful in the genuine pain it suggests beneath the blarney. In this company, Duvall, an associate of the movie brat generation, might perhaps seem too modern a performer, and here we're far from his sardonic Kilgore in *Apocalypse Now*. Yet the fastidiousness with which he builds Walt's assemblage of tics and rituals into a humane essay in deep repression, though untypical, stands beside the best work he's done.

TIME, 1/10/94, p. 58, Richard Schickel

[*Wrestling Ernest Hemingway* was reviewed jointly with *Grumpy Old Men*; see Schickel's review of that film.]

VILLAGE VOICE, 12/21/93, p. 87, Henry Curmudgeon Beck

From a director who has given new meaning to the word *heartfelt (Children of a Lesser God, The Doctor)*, this story of two grumpy old geezers struggling to accept the sedentary life in their sunny South Florida bleached pink-and-turquoise sepulchre feels like a skit gone sour: Billy Crystal and Chris Guest perhaps, gumming their lines in a vaudeville pastiche of sour old age and loneliness, a geriatric Odd Couple.

Frank (Richard Harris) parades around stark naked and drenched with sweat, full of sea-dog bombast and Jameson's, endlessly repeating the same stories to anyone within range, including the unfortunate audience. Pretending to be a mighty lover while at the same time bemoaning his impotence, Frank is less Popeye than Poopdeck Pappy, and about the 700th time he starts dribbling on about the eponymous wrestling bout or his four marriages, the impulse to tell him to put a sock in it and leave the theater is overwhelming. Sad though he may be, his isolation seems justified.

Robert Duvall's Walter is a perfectly coiffed, Cuba-accented barber, chewing his lines as if he had a mouthful of marbles. Both Harris and Duvall are locked in a life-and-death struggle to get out from under their characters and a script so mired in bathos you need a bathyscaphe to navigate. As these unlikely and unlikable figures bond, they share a bottle, a piss, and a skinny-dip involving synchronized swimming—a staggeringly odd moment that is guaranteed to send audience members under 60 years old howling in the aisles.

The movie is littered with little iconic touches, each signifier jutting like promontory points in a placid lake: Walter's bacon-and-toast sandwiches, Frank's two-visored hat, crossword puzzles, and Hemingway paperbacks. Walter has a little-boy crush on waitress Sandra Bullock, disguised here as a smiley face. Frank is deserted by an uncaring son and spends much of his time attempting lusty lunges at Piper Laurie and Shirley MacLaine (making full use of her patented Judge Dredd grimace).

In spite of it all, the truly unfortunate thing about the film is that is serves to trivialize much of what Robert Duvall has done in the past; the fine line between charlatan and magician dissolves as Duvall stands exposed as a mere collector of shtick and tick.

Also reviewed in:
CHICAGO TRIBUNE, 1/21/94, Friday/p. A, Michael Wilmington
NEW REPUBLIC, 2/14/94, p. 30, Stanley Kauffmann
NEW YORK TIMES, 12/17/93, p. C12, Caryn James
VARIETY, 12/20/93, p. 31, Emanuel Levy
WASHINGTON POST, 1/21/94, p. G1, Rita Kempley
WASHINGTON POST, 1/21/94, Weekend/p. 38, Desson Howe

ADDENDUM

The following reviews arrived too late to be included in this or previous issues of FILM REVIEW ANNUAL. The issue of FILM REVIEW ANNUAL in which the credits and film reviews appear are given in parenthesis after the name of the film.

FINDING CHRISTA *(Film Review Annual, 1992)*

LOS ANGELES TIMES, 9/11/93, Calendar/p. 8, Kevin Thomas

The 60-minute "Finding Christa" (1991) is a unique, emotion charged account of Billops' reunion with her daughter Christa, whom she gave up for adoption at age 4, 21 years earlier. In essence, this film is a group portrait of a family of remarkably wise and strong black women.

Billops is an extraordinarily lucky woman on several counts—first of all, because Christa was adopted by Margaret Liebig, a loving woman who sings professionally as Rusty Carlyle. It was Liebig who, trusting Christa's love for her, urged Christa to seek out her birth mother, believing that no matter what, she would feel better for having done so. Secondly, because Christa has turned out to be a breathtakingly beautiful and talented singer-composer, as striking-looking and creative a woman as Billops herself. Billops makes no apologies for having given up her daughter, whom she felt she could not properly support as a single mother. Christa, in turn, finds herself able to forgive Billops for giving her up and to commence a relationship with her.

LA VIE DE BOHÉME *(Film Review Annual, 1993)*

LOS ANGELES TIMES, 3/18/94, Calendar/p. 4, Kevin Thomas

Aki Kaurismaki's droll update of "La Vie de Boheme" takes a dry-as-dust, minimalist approach to the 1861 Henri Murger novel that inspired the 1896 Puccini opera only to wind up surprisingly more emotionally affecting than the celebrated, romantic 1926 King Vidor silent version of the story in which no less than Lillian Gish is Mimi and John Gilbert is Rodolfo.

There's nothing at all glamorous about Kaurismaki's people, who are all seedy, middle-aged, seriously impoverished artists who tend to spend more time drinking red wine at a neighborhood cafe than at easel, piano or typewriter. Matti Pellonpaa's Rodolfo is a wistful Albanian painter living in France illegally, and Evelyne Didi's Mimi is a pretty, but worn past-40 barmaid. Indeed, Rodolfo stands more time hanging out with his pals, Marcel (Andre Wilms), whose 27-act play has no takers, and Schaunard (Kari Vaananen), an avant-garde composer whose noisy compositions are likely no more to impress you than anyone else.

Kaurismaki is Finland's foremost filmmaker and one of the sliest directors in the world. Before we know it, his humorous deadpan take on the pretensions and delusions of these guys gives way to a boundless affection for them. That we don't notice what's happening is largely due to the rigorous austerity of Kaurismaki's style, which is marked by his usual cinematographer Timo Salminen's engraved-like black-and-white images and absolute minimal camera movement. This approach is perfect in short-circuiting sentimentality in a film that ends up celebrating both camaraderie and true love.

What Kaurismaki does is quite simply to introduce us to a bunch of losers and make us care for them more than we would have ever dreamed possible. The more time we spend with them, the more we realize how supportive they are of one another, how quick they are to share whatever comes their way. They are kind, considerate and loyal (as well as being inventive and funny).

Kaurismaki makes us start thinking that how they're spending their lives is not so bad after all—as long as they can count on one another. Poverty may be lousy, but maybe their dreams actually are harmless, and certainly they are sustained by them. Such thoughts seem fairly radical at a time when a premium is put on self-reliance and a relentless honesty with self in a ruthlessly competitive society.

For all his celebration of Bohemian life, Kaurismaki subtly singles out Rodolfo in his quiet but growing love for Mimi, who returns his feelings in kind. Pellonpaa, who has appeared memorably in such Kaurismaki films as "Ariel" and "Crime and Punishment," is appealing with his dark, expressive eyes, full mustache, deep voice and warm presence. He has a wry take on put-upon blue-collar types, those outside the bourgeoisie, and he is well-supported by the demure Didi, Jean-Pierre Leaud as Rodolfo's rich, eccentric client and the rest of the cast, which includes cameo appearances by directors Samuel Fuller (as a chintzy backer of a shoestring women's fashions magazine) and Louis Malle (as a kindly restaurant patron).

Setting is everything in regard to what Kaurismaki evokes, and he tells his story primarily in ancient Parisian neighborhoods that have miraculously changed little since Murger's day. When the camera pulls back, however, to reveal a severe and immense skyscraper looming over a narrow street with its quaint roof line, you're left wondering how the warm, communal spirit that binds together the film's characters could possibly survive in a world of such vast, impersonal structures.

NEW YORK POST, 7/28/93, p. 26, Jerry Tallmer

There are so many gorgeous moments in Aki Kaurismäki's "La Vie de Boheme." Here is one: Schaunard the composer arrives by taxi to meet his starving artistic companions in roguery, Rodolfo the painter and Marcel Marx the poet/playwright. The musical portion of this raffish trio rolls out of the taxi in a slugging match with the driver. "The swine!" exclaims Schaunard (Kari Vaananen) when the man has driven off. "He demanded money. Just for a few kilometers."

Kaurismäki, the absurdly talented Finnish filmmaker of "Leningrad Cowboys Go America" and "The Match Factory Girl," now gives us Henri Murger's 1851 *roman a clef*—the one that fed the tear-drenched Puccini opera—transported to semi-contemporary Paris in beautiful grainy nostalgic black and white.

It's the kind of movie in which Schaunard and Marcel (Andre Wilms) and Rodolfo (Matti Pellonpaa, the maniacal hook-haired bandleader of "Leningrad Cowboys") steal one another's clothing and women even before those *are* one another's women, in between theological debates over who has occupational rights to the grungiest pads you ever saw.

There is much discussion of Rimbaud, and our hero Rodolfo—who sometimes wakes up of a morning beside the grave of Baudelaire—has a beloved black dog named Baudelaire. He also betimes has a beloved named Mimi (Evelyne Didi), who is faithful to him, in her itinerant fashion, through endless depravations of cold, hunger, moneyless rent days. "We earn as much as the porters in the Gare de l'Est," one of these noblemen of talent caustically remarks to his fellows. I have lived with all of them.

Schaunard's *chef d'oeuvre* is a symphony entitled "On the Influence of Blue in Art," featuring himself shouting: "You're under arrest!" into a microphone. Marcel lands a job as editor of the avant-garde "Girdle of Iris," only to blow it by serializing *his* masterpiece, "The Avenger," a play in 21 acts. Rodolfo's masterpiece, "The Parting of the Red Sea," is a canvas he hopes to sell for 200 francs. It has already cost him 10,000 in oils. He gets his own back on a rich patron, a pompous young sugar baron, by painting the gentleman's portrait a la Picasso's Gertrude Stein.

The director advises that potential female viewers supply themselves with handkerchiefs for an ending that's "the saddest since 'Waterloo Bridge.'" My advice is to keep at least one eye dry and peeled for Jean-Pierre Leaud, Sam Fuller and Louis Malle in supporting parts, and the loveliest bit of love-play with a stalk of grass since Simone Signoret and Serge Reggiani in "Casque d'Or." When the credits roll, watch for Laika. That's Baudelaire the dog, back from immortality in outer space.

NEWSDAY, 7/28/93, Part II/p. 73, Jack Mathews

An Albanian artist, a French poet and an Irish musician. Friends, paupers and soulmates. In Paris, sharing whatever francs they can gather to stay afloat and keep their hopes and artistic passions fired.

This is a familiar literary scene to Americans who cut their teeth on the early writings of Hemingway, Henry Miller and Anais Nin, and Finnish director Aki Kaurismäki is no slougher of bohemian romanticism himself.

The 35-year-old Finnish filmmaker is absolutely in love with the three characters he created for "La Vie de Boheme," and though they are more losers than bohemians, more bums than rebels, he gives us no choice but to love them, too.

In updating 19th-Century novelist Henri Murger's "Scenes de la Vie de Boheme," Kaurismäki shows us a lifestyle that is less a continuation of the bohemian movement than a poor imitation. There is no indication that Rodolfo (Matti Pellonpaa), an illegal alien from Albania; the shaggy Irishman Schaunard (Kari Vaananen), or the melancholy Frenchman Marcel (Andre Wilms) have an ounce of talent between them. But to be a struggling artist in Paris, where so many great artists have struggled before, has a dignity that transcend one's limitations.

If they have no talent or ambition, they also have no malice or greed. When Marcel's and Rodolfo's girlfriends leave them, it's not because the love is gone, but because they can no longer stand life on the edge of eviction. In the end, that's pretty much the feeling we are left with; bohemians are nice people to visit, but you wouldn't want to live with them.

VILLAGE VOICE, 8/3/93, p. 56, Manohla Dargis

The good life by way of the gutter, Aki Kaurismäki's *La Vie de Bohème* opens with a sumptuous black-and-white panorama of the city of lights, one that vanishes with a sudden and deliberate pan down, down, down. There, in an anonymous, dark alley, bohemia sputters to life in the person of Marcel (Andre Wilms), a dissolute writer who's rummaging through the trash and howling *merde* at the moon. Unpublished and unwashed, Marcel is evicted soon after his midnight frolic, but conveniently befriends the next tenant, an equally undiscovered talent by the name of Schaunard (Kari Vaananen). Shortly after fate brings these two together, Marcel meets up with Rodolfo (Matti Pellonpaa), and over trout and a stream of house red, a *fraternité* familiar to opera lovers all over the world is launched.

Henri Murger's *Scenes de la vie de Bohème* was first published in 1845 as a series of anecdotes for the publication *Le Corsaire*. Murger turned his sketches into both a novel and a drama, but the most famous version of his work remains Puccini's *La Bohème*. Murger's cast of malcontents is amusing and fairly domesticated (though not half as tame as Puccini's). In his introduction to the 1930 edition of the novel, crank Wyndham Lewis writes that "Bohemia is a state of mind rather than an area situate," praising its author for an "authentic note of defiant gaiety." Authentic or not, Murger's bohemia, peopled with destitute artists, lusty women, and miscellaneous rabble, is strangely hermetic. France's political turmoil, its state of permanent revolution between the years 1830 and 1848, barely rates a mention, and if Murger tripped over the barricades it isn't obvious.

For his take on these 19th-century subterraneans, Kaurismäki returns to the original novel, fashioning a radically abridged version true in spirit if not detail. The Finnish wonder's bohemians are a vivid, motley crew—grizzled beards, soiled clothing, and such stubbornly greasy hair you can almost smell the reek of dander, smoke, and cheap wine. Scratch away the scum, though, and these musketeers of pig alley reveal themselves as hopeless romantics. At center of this romp, of course, are Rodolfo and Mimi. This time around, Mimi (a game Evelyne Didi) arrives on Rodolfo's doorstep not in need of a light but a home. Inevitably, the pair become lovers, and embark on a romance as chaste as any found in a D. W. Griffith pastoral (Rodolfo's relationship with his dog, Baudelaire, is another story). What follows is a series of mishaps both comic and sad, until the couple settles down—which is when their troubles begin in earnest.

The opera's libretto gutted Murger's novel, taking its inspiration from his later, disputed preface ("Bohemia is a stage in artistic life; it is the preface to the Académie, the Hôtel-Dieu, or the Morgue") rather from the text itself. The consequence was a bohemia more frothy than effervescent. It's the libretto, too, that's responsible for the dainty, rather bland Mimi ("to you I'm clinging"), a dubious ideal cobbled together from several Murger types. Unhappily, this is the very Mimi Kaurismäki resuscitates, which is too bad since bohemia has always been a playground more for boys than girls. After all, it's one thing to be a poor poet and quite another to be a consumptive seamstress. Like Rodolfo's dog, Mimi and Marcel's girlfriend, Musette, are quiet, dependable, and adequately loyal, sidelined in *La Vie* for most of the action and most of the talk.

La Vie de Bohème is a nocturnal ode to Paris and much that the city represents. In addition to Truffaut's alter ego, Jean-Pierre Léaud, there's a guest appearance by Louis Malle (in homage to *Elevator to the Gallows*, one suspects, rather than *Damage*), and more than one nod to Bresson. Kaurismäki can be wrenchingly poetic when he trusts silence and empties out the mise-en-scène, as when the camera lingers on a handful of flowers that drop at Rodolfo's feet. In the area of performance, though, Kaurismäki pushes Bresson's influence to an absurd degree, eliciting minimalist acting that verges on the catatonic. This works best with Pellonpaa, a Kaurismäki regular who does more with his eyes than most actors do with an entire bag of Method-driven tricks. Far better than anyone else—though Wilms runs an estimable second—he makes flesh the bohemian struggle between faith and despair, bad luck and lethargy.

Overall, there's not much bounce in these bohemian bodies, they're slack and fiercely deadpan. Just about the only time Rodolfo and his friends lift their arms is to raise glasses of wine, suck on cigarettes, or on occasion, exercise their art. They're remarkably taciturn, as well; their lines dribble out with characteristic (and very unoperatic) Kaurismäki restraint, as if passion was just too embarrassing for words. In the end, these grunge bohemians are more Bukowski than Baudelaire, living in squalor less for their muse than all those hours of idle talk and drink. Need may force Mimi behind a cash register, but Rodolfo and his buddies are dilettantes when it comes to work. They dabble in publishing (a lingerie magazine, *The Girdle of Venus*, published by Sam Fuller!), snooker the rich (perversely, a ravaged-looking Léaud), and dream of glory. For them, poverty is a choice not a destiny.

Also reviewed in:
CHICAGO TRIBUNE, 2/25/94, Friday/p. J, John Petrakis
NATION, 8/9-16/93, p. 186, Stuart Klawans
NEW YORKER, 8/9/93, p. 93, Terrence Rafferty
WASHINGTON POST, 11/5/93, Weekend/p. 52, Desson Howe
WASHINGTON POST, 11/6/93, p. D1, Hal Hinson

LABYRINTH OF PASSION *(Film Review Annual, 1991 & Film Review Annual, [Addendum] 1992)*

SIGHT AND SOUND, 2/93, p. 49, Paul Julian Smith

Sexilia is a pop star and nymphomaniac with a chronic hatred of the sun; Riza is the gay son of the emperor of Tiran. Both are strolling in the Madrid Rastro, aiming to pick up boys. Toraya, the ex-empress of Tiran, is in town to consult Sexilia's father, a famous gynaecologist. She attempts to track Riza down, while he enjoys amorous encounters with Fabio, a photonovel porn queen and Sadec, a Moslem freedom fighter from Tiran. Riza finally meets Sexilia when, disguised as 'Johnny', he is performing with a punk band. They fall in love, but are unable to have sex.

Making time in her busy schedule to pick up the dry-cleaning, Sexilia counsels Queti, the dry-cleaner's daughter, on how to free herself from her father's sexual advances. Queti agrees to transform herself into Sexilia through plastic surgery, and thus exchange one amorous father for another. Toraya finally catches up with Riza, and Sexilia discovers they have slept together. Fleeing to her psychiatrist, who has a passion for Sexilia's father, she finally confesses the cause of her nymphomania, a childhood trauma which also made Riza gay: rejected by her father, she had had sex with boys on the beach, while Riza looked on. Sexilia meets up with Queti, who has now taken her place, and decides to forgive Riza and flee with him to Contadora, in the Caribbean. Eusebio, the punk singer whom 'Johnny' has been standing in for, discovers that he is really Riza, and gives him away to Sadec and his fellow Tiranians. Sadec and his group arrive at the airport to find that Riza and Sexilia have already caught their plane, so they kidnap Toraya instead. Queti, disguised as Sexilia, sleeps with Sexilia's father and cures him of his fear of sex. On the flight to Contadora, Sexilia and Riza finally consummate their passion.

Labyrinth of Passion is the quintessential Spanish cult movie. Since its release ten years ago it has played uninterruptedly late Saturday nights at the independent Alphaville theatre in Madrid, where it has taken on *Rocky Horror* proportions. Almodóvar claims it serves as a "baptismal rite" for each new generation of modern youth which descends on the capital. However, time has not been kind to it; and it is best read as a testimony to that brief apogee of the *movida* period when (to quote Toraya) "Madrid [was] the most amusing city in the world"

The film, then, is a catalogue of modernities from the early 80s: music by Almodóvar himself with the Pegamoides; graphic contributions by painters Costus (soon to be victims of drug abuse); an aggressively ugly aesthetic known in Spanish as *cutre*, perhaps best translated as 'grunge'. And there is much to take pleasure in here. In the opening scene Almodóvar's habitual musical accomplice Fabio McNamara (last seen playing the Avon Lady in *Pepi, Luci, Bom*) picks up the future heart-throb of Spanish cinema Imanol Arias, who is wearing a ridiculous wig. Fabio next appears as porn queen Patty Diphusa, reaching ecstasy with an electric drill (Almodóvar himself plays the 'director' in this sequence). Helga Line is marvellous as the Tiranian Empress, cruising gay Madrid lavishly cross-dressed. And as the veteran of innumerable B-movies, she brings a perilously camp gravity to lines such as "The history of this century has been most unjust with me".

Toraya insists on speaking an outrageous mix of Italian and Spanish. Many of the references may be lost on an English-speaking audience. Choice here is the Argentine psychoanalyst "of the Lacanian school", obsessed with luring her patient's father into a very intimate session. Indeed, the delirious plot is based on a parody of the cheap psychology Almodóvar loves so much in Hitchcock: both of the main characters are condemned to promiscuity by infantile trauma (a destiny they assume with some relish); and in a typical irony they can only express their love for each other by not having sex. The film thus announces Almodóvar's grand theme, to be explored in his later films: the possibility of the couple, the inevitable disasters of desire.

But when *Dark Habits* (made just one year later) deftly interweaves farce and pathos, *Labyrinth of Passion* reveals an uncharacteristic contempt for its gallery of grotesques. British audiences are unlikely to take kindly to such scenes as Queti's repeated rape by her father (intended as yet another Oedipal parody), and much of the scatological humour has a distinctly misogynist tone. A film of fathers rather than mothers (uniquely in Almodóvar's oeuvre), *Labyrinth of Passion* raises none of the disturbing implications of sexual violence explored in *Pepi, Luci*, and benefits from none of that film's tender exploration of relationships between women. This is partly due to the absence of *Almodóvar*'s most skilled female actors: Carmen Maura and Julieta Serrano, who have always lent a battered dignity and a resolute pathos to the humiliations imposed on them. The unsympathetic Cecilia Roth (a bit player in the other films) simply cannot carry a whole movie herself.

But one particular pleasure of *Labyrinth of Passion*, for the fan at least, is its anticipation of later, more accomplished work. Thus we are treated to early versions of the taxi and airport scenes of *Women on the Verge of a Nervous Breakdown*, not to mention the first appearance of that Almodóvarian leitmotif, Shiite terrorism. Antonio Banderas completists will savour his first role for Almodóvar as a gay freedom fighter (with a particularly acute sense of smell) who insists on putting his "queer business [*mariconadas*] above the destiny of an entire nation".

In *Labyrinth of Passion* the gay lovers are fated to dissatisfaction: Riza is 'cured' by the experienced Sexilia. It would be a mistake to take this too seriously. But the film enacts once more the disavowal of homosexuality so frequent in Almodóvar's work. And it also raises the equally curious paradox that the director who is (and was) famous as the most modern of *madrileños* should be so neglectful of the issues facing contemporary Spain. But if *Labyrinth of Passion* is Almodóvar's least sympathetic film (his most doggedly ingenious, and aesthetically dull) it is also his most unapologetically personal. Jean Douchet has argued that it is not possible simply to like Almodóvar; one has to *love* him. *Labyrinth of Passion* requires a considerable dose of love from its audience to make it palatable, a love which it is unlikely to find in a puritanical Britain; but if the history of cinema is not to be unjust to Pedro Almodóvar, *Labyrinth of Passion* deserves to be taken on its own, quite uncompromising terms.

NIGHT OF THE LIVING DEAD *(Film Review Annual, 1991)*

SIGHT AND SOUND, 4/93, p. 51, Kim Newman

Rural Pennsylvania. When Barbara and her brother Johnnie visit their mother's grave in an isolated cemetery they are attacked by zombies, who kill Johnnie and pursue Barbara to a farmhouse. The dead, who hunger for human flesh, can only be destroyed by a shot in the brain. Barbara is joined by Ben, a black man. They find guns in the house and discover other survivors in the basement: Harry and Helen Cooper, their injured daughter Sarah and a young couple, Tom and Judy Rose. Harry, who thinks their best chance of survival lies in hiding in the cellar, and Ben, who wants to fortify the house, argue but everyone co-operates in commandeering a truck. The escape attempt fails when Tom tries to unlock a petrol pump with a shotgun blast, thereby causing an explosion in which he and Judy are burned to death.

At the house, Helen is killed by Sarah, who has turned into a zombie. Harry steals Barbara's gun, and when Ben tries to destroy Sarah, the men have a shoot-out in which both are wounded. Barbara goes for help and the zombies overwhelm the house, driving Harry into the attic and Ben into the cellar. Barbara joins up with a crowd hunting down the zombies for sport, and returns to the farmhouse just as posse members are breaking through into the cellar to shoot the zombie Ben. Harry, still alive, comes down from the attic and Barbara murders him. The posse gather up the twice-dead corpses and make a bonfire.

George A. Romero's seminal horror film has already inspired two official sequels, sundry parodies and too many imitations to cite. With all this attention, the 1968 film was hardly in need of a colour remake; this enterprise was embarked on partly because a rights quirk meant that if the original production team did not undertake a remake, then anyone else could do so.

That said, this is as good a job as one has the right to expect, compressing the major plot points of the original into its first four-fifths and then coming up with disturbing new twists, vaguely inspired by *Straw Dogs*, capping Barbara's statement about the zombies—"We are them and they are us"—with her startling murder of Harry. Most cannily, Romero and Savini do not reproduce well-remembered shocks, playing a major trick on *Living Dead* fans as the shambling bum in the first scene (an unforgettable monster in 1968) turns out to be a red herring, a precursor of the unexpected appearance of the first attacking zombie.

Revising the original screenplay he wrote with John Russo, Romero shears away much of the 'scientific' explanation, 60s social satire and commentary on the media reaction to the crisis, concentrating instead on the divisions in the small group of survivors. Occasionally further ironies—like the suggestion that the horde of flesh-eaters outside the farmhouse has not been attracted by the scent of living meat, but by the sound of carpentry as the besieged fortify the place—are layered in. Ben and his bigoted adversary Harry remain essentially as they were, to the point of appearing anachronistic. They gain in stature from the near-iconic cachet of Tony Todd (*Candyman*) and Tom Towles (*Henry, Portrait of a Serial Killer*), who model their performances, down to the smallest tics, on Duane Jones and Karl Hardman in the original. The major character alteration is Patricia Tallman's Barbara, given a post-Sigourney Weaver spin when her traumatised reaction to her brother's death is not to become catatonic but to turn into a guerrilla fighter. As in *Alien*, the presence of a strong female survivor requires the secondary female, Judy, to be a panicky whiner who rushes stupidly to her own death. It is ironic that the 1990 Barbara's anti-zombie violence is seen to be as insane as her 1968 predecessor's retreat into a psychological shell.

Tom Savini, in a directorial debut which follows a few episodes of *Tales from the Darkside* and various unofficial second-unit chores, intelligently refrains from going overboard on gore gags. With resources unavailable to the original—an original score rather than stock music, convincing make-up, consistent lighting, professional actors—he manages to bring up to standard the sometimes ropey qualities of the first film. However, this movie does contain a few too many hand-through-the-window shock tricks and suffers by comparison with the original. Romero's *Night of the Living Dead* was so much of its time, yet such an important and influential gift to posterity that any remake is doomed to be a footnote.

PEKING OPERA BLUES *(Film Review Annual, 1990)*

LOS ANGELES TIMES, 6/25/93, Calendar/p.16, Kevin Thomas

Tsui Hark's 1986 "Peking Opera Blues", one of the most celebrated Hong Kong movies of the past decade, has surfaced at local festivals and film series, but only now is having a regular run at a theater outside Chinatown. It's a giddy period comedy, loaded with action and more slamming doors and hit-and-miss encounters than a Feydeau farce. It's also surprisingly poignant and bursting with a witty feminist spirit.

The time is 1911, in the chaotic wake of China's first democratic revolution. Three beautiful, high-spirited young women of very different backgrounds but similar cravings for liberation cross paths and find common cause. First is a general's daughter, Tsao Wan (Brigitte Lin), who studied gynecology abroad and who wears Western-style men's attire, a la George Sand, not to disguise her sex but to enable her to move about more freely. She even gets away with wearing military uniforms, doubtlessly on account of her powerful doting father (Wu Ma). Second is the improbably named Pat Neil (Sally Yeh), daughter of the proprietor of a Peking opera company, and the third is Sheung Hung (Cherie Chung), a singer who has gotten her hands on a fortune in jewelry from a fleeing general's household only to lose it all.

Tsao Wan has joined a guerrilla movement whose immediate goal is to get its hands on a document revealing that the military Establishment, backed by foreign loans, intends to restore the monarchy to power and thus curtail the democratic movement. Meanwhile, Pat Neil schemes to perform in her father's company despite the ancient tradition that all female roles are played by males. Sheung Hung remains in pursuit of the elusive cache of jewels.

To Kwok-Wai has written a scintillating, endlessly inventive script with which Tsui Hark can run all the way to a triumphant battle sequence upon the opera company's treacherous tile roof. "Peking Opera Blues" has the formidable coordination and energy of a complicated Chinese acrobatic act. Yet the film is by no means all action, with Tsui Hark deftly playing genuine, even delicate, emotion against the mayhem within a plot that is all artifice.

In its breezy, light-hearted way, "Peking Opera Blues" has lots of fun sending up the excesses of male chauvinism. Tsui Hark points up the absurdity of an all-male audience swooning over the opera company's beautiful stars; forgetting, it would seem, that they are in fact all men. Gen. Tsao may be a devoted father, but that doesn't keep him from appearing with a different woman—or women—at his side every night.

Never do our three spunky heroines waste time lamenting their woman's plight; they're too busy drawing upon feminine wiles and raw courage in pursuing their goals and independence.

"Peking Opera Blues" (Times-rated Mature because some scenes may be too violent for small children) is gorgeous-looking in all its rich colors and lavish settings and costumes. All three of the film's stars are gifted actresses, but Sally Yeh, with her Modigliani-like beauty and sparkling, mischievous personality, is particularly irresistible. But then so is the film itself.

POLICE STORY III: SUPER COP *(Film Review Annual, 1993)*

LOS ANGELES TIMES, 5/21/93, Calendar/p. 4, Kevin Thomas

To watch Jackie Chan, Hong Kong's king of kung fu comedy, in the fresh and exhilarating "Super Cop" is like watching Douglas Fairbanks Sr. or one of the silent era clowns in one of their biggest hits. A whirling dervish with a Beatles mop top and an impish grin, the boyish Chan is a one-man Cirque du Soleil, and "Super Cop" shows off both his sense of humor and his acrobatic martial arts wizardry just as effectively as "Safety Last" served Harold Lloyd seven decades ago.

"Super Cop" is as topical as tomorrow's headlines but gets back to the basics of discovering what can happen when you turn loose an athletic, charismatic star, backed by a clever plot and firm direction, and then capture his every move and expression with virtuoso cinematography and editing. When Chan, with his sunny personality, tilts at life's, comic absurdities he's doing what Buster Keaton or Laurel and Hardy did long ago.

A fearless, devil-may-care Hong Kong cop, Chan is the inevitable choice for a highly dangerous mission. He's to be sent to China as an undercover agent to retrieve from a prison labor camp a gangster named Panther (Yuen Wah), who is in turn to lead Chan to Panther's Hong Kong-based older brother Chaibar (Tsang Kong), a drug lord so mighty that the authorities believe that his capture would diminish the Southeast Asian drug trade by half. Chan's adventures lead him to a secret jungle compound along the border between Thailand and Cambodia and culminate in a whirlwind chase through Kuala Lumpar—what a beautiful city!—involving a helicopter, every kind of street vehicle and finally a train.

Arriving in Canton, Chan meets his match in his new boss, a People's Republic of China secret agent (Michelle Yeoh) who's as elegant as she is skilled in martial arts—and lots more disciplined than Chan. They're a terrific team, and the whole business of extricating Panther from the prison camp, a coal-mining site, is as much a cliffhanger as a chapter ending in the serial "The Perils of Pauline." But it's just a prologue all the nonstop: action and comedy that follow.

Chan and Yeoh play with just enough tongue-in-cheekery: The humor is often broad but never lapses into burlesque. Joining the fun in the final reel is beautiful Maggie Cheung as Chan's lively girlfriend, a tour guide who arrives in Kuala Lumpar at the very wrongest moment possible.

Chan, who co-executive produced, director Stanley Tong and their cast and crew recall what Hollywood has largely forgotten: how to make pure escapist entertainment that's fast, light and unpretentious. "Super Cop:' (Times-rated Family, suitable for all ages except the very young) and other Hong Kong pictures like it rely, out of economic prudence, on making imaginative use of the full resources of the medium rather than relying on mega-buck production design and gadgetry. (The film's extensive use of colorful and far-flung authentic locations are in fact a key appeal.)

NEWSDAY, 10/8/93, Part II/p. 95, John Anderson

"What we need is a supercop," says a Hong Kong police official. What we get is a superstar.

Jackie Chan, of the furious fists and quizzical grimace, has been a huge draw in Hong Kong action films for a long time and, as one might expect, his "Police Story III: Supercop," of 1992 opened some time ago—in Chinatown. Today, this big-budget ($10 million) feature opens a little farther uptown, and should win Chan some deserved mainstream attention.

In the early '80s, an attempt to Americanize Chan, whose movies include "The Big Brawl" and "Armor of God," led to his ill-advised appearance in "Cannonball Run." But "Supercop" lets Chan be Chan. As police detective Chen Chia-chu, he befriends Panther (Yuen Wah), who unwittingly helps him infiltrate the crime organization of drug lord Chiabar (Tsang Kong). He receives a little gender reeducation on the mainland from female Det. Yang (Michelle Yeoh), engages in horrific fire fights all over Southeast Asia, goes *mano a mano* with some huge and frightening people and flies across town, swinging from a rope attached to a helicopter.

Director Stanley Tong doesn't have the elegant instincts of a John Woo, but then, a Jackie Chan film isn't an exercise in esthetics. It's about action, and comedy: Chan's bemused mugging when things don't go his way are as much a part of his films as the flying back-kicks and automatic-weapons fire. He's going for laughs, regardless of whether they're the result of slapstick, plastique or Det. Yang dangling from a speeding bus.

"Supercop" also resorts to situation comedy, chiefly when Chia-chu tries to avoid his girlfriend, May (Maggie Cheung), who happens to show up at the same hotel where he's working undercover with Yang. It's harmless, formulaic stuff, meant to serve as filter, and an opportunity to catch your breath.

VILLAGE VOICE, 10/19/93, p. 62, Jeff Yang

They're still rarer than unspent cartridges in a John Woo prop shop, so it's not surprising that the evaluation and appreciation of female action heroes is a less than exact science. For the sake of argument, however, let's create a completely arbitrary unit of measurement—the BTU, or Basic

Thelma Unit. Call it the factored sum of grace under pressure, delivery of snappy one-liners, and miscellaneous menace, with Thelma of Louise fame figuring as one BTU.

Sigourney averages out to about 2.78 BTUs over the course of three *Alien* movies. Linda Hamilton hit 3.03 in *T2*, though her career score is handicapped by three seasons as Ron Perlman's Babe on *Beauty and the Beast*. To get to the double digits, you have to go to the land of the rising gun—Hong Kong—where stalk such femmes fatales as Bridget Lin, Anita Mui, and Josephine Shiao.

But back in the early '80s, Michelle Yeoh (900 BTU) eclipsed them all; before retiring to marry producer Dickson Poon, she was Hong Kong's unquestioned action queen. A decade and a divorce later, Yeoh decided it was time to make a comeback, and *Supercop* was born: 96 minutes of high-concept, high-kicking, high-explosive action, in which she plays a hard-line mainlander cop teamed up with maverick Hong Kong detective Jackie Chan to fight an evil drug lord.

Chan is, as always, super, but Yeoh manages to be just a little bit super-er—punching faster, shooting straighter, and falling harder from taller buildings than her male doppelgänger. He makes facing certain death look easy, but she—is that a *smile* on her face when she takes that *death-defying motorcycle leap* onto that moving train?—makes it look fun.

ZOMBIE AND THE GHOST TRAIN, *(Film Review Annual, 1992)*

NEW YORK POST, 8/10/94, p. 35, Thelma Adams

Dirty snow. Wet alleys. Wafting garbage.

We're down and out in Helsinki—and it bums me out.

"Zombie and the Ghost Train," which played the 1991 New York Film Festival, will have its New York theatrical premiere at the Public Theater today for masochists who missed it three years ago.

Director, editor, writer, producer Mika Kaurismaki—best known in America for being the brother of Aki—portrays a funky Finland with strained whimsy. The movie spirals downward into universal rebel-without-a-cause territory.

Pasty-faced, pointy-nosed, pouty Zombie (Silu Seppala) wanders the frozen zone, shoulders hunched and head bent forward, in an alcoholic funk.

We are treated to the inner thoughts of this army deserter unfit for anything but playing the bass through the magic of a voice-over diary.

Zombie mourns moving back in with his folks, "... life continued amid the ruins of childhood as if everything would last forever, but I felt the inevitability of the loss."

The boozing musician can't face himself in the mirror—and I share his loathing. I don't want to look at Zombie either, but for some reason his girlfriend (Marjo Leinonen) keeps holding on in a rash of co-dependency.

The Ghost Train of the title is a rock group with a Frank Zappa look-alike that allegedly gets gigs, but has never been heard. These Finns with attitude are more baffling than mysterious.

The train doesn't figure as large as the country-and-western band. Harri and the Mulef---er's. Their performances offer some funky high points, including the foot-stomping "I'm Driving Cattle Back to Karelia," sung in Finnish with English subtitles.

Despite glimmers of offbeat charm, "Zombie and the Ghost Train" is relentlessly glum. Staring into the "dark bottomless abyss" of his soul, the black-hole hero sucks all the energy from the supporting players.

Finland's cold; "Zombie and the Ghost Train" isn't nearly as cool as it thinks it is.

VILLAGE VOICE, 8/16/94, p. 50, Alyssa Katz

Aki Kaurismäki's films may be as depressing as the shadow-striped Finnish landscapes he frames, yet—as any survivor of a sunless Scandinavian winter would understand—his darkness promises light, if only after the end credits. With *Zombie and the Ghost Train*, his older brother

Mika goes straight for the whimsy bone and comes up with an even bleaker vision. A trio of Finnish thirtynothings appropriate scraps of wayward culture, most of it American, on the chance that it might add up to more than the sum of its parts. After all, they've got nothing better to do. It's a smart observation, undermined more than a little bit by the tendency of the movie—first released in 1991—to dive right into the pomo morass with them.

Zombie (Silu Seppälä), as his name might suggest, treads the border between death and life, seeming most at home on the far side. A skinny, aging naif, he journeys from nowhere to funky nowhere: from the Finn army to his parents' basement to a rockabilly band to Istanbul. When he encounters three bearded phantoms—the titular Ghost Train—the early-MTV riff is unmistakable. ZZ Top! Zombie scrambles onto their tour bus while they urinate on the roadside, and hitches a ride back home. Apparently, they also totemize the redemptive powers of rock and roll, though they never sing or utter a word to explain it. Zombie's best friend, played by Finnish national treasure Matti Pellonpää, thinks along the same lines and asks him to play bass in Harri and the Mulefukkers, a band that suspiciously resembles the Leningrad Cowboys of Aki's oeuvre in their hopelessly Euro cluelessness about what makes rock rock. Like a lot of mediocre bands, they play music to drink by, a principle poor Zombie takes to heart.

For all its obvious effort, *Zombie and the Ghost Train* at least gets at something of the American spirit, both that stagy retro preciousness that's dogged our "alternative" culture for the past decade and (at its best moments) a refreshingly loose indie feel. Beginning and ending the film in Turkey, Zombie himself finds salvation outside the European fascination with things American.

Also reviewed in:
NEW YORK TIMES, 8/10/94, p. C12, Janet Maslin

AWARDS

ACADEMY OF MOTION PICTURE ARTS AND SCIENCES
66th Annual Academy Awards — March 21,1994

BEST PICTURE — *Schindler's List*
Other Nominees *The Fugitive; In the Name of the Father; The Piano; The Remains of the Day*

BEST ACTOR — Tom Hanks in *Philadelphia*
Other Nominess: Daniel Day-Lewis in *In the Name of the Father*; Laurence Fishburne in *What's Love Got to Do With It*; Anthony Hopkins in *The Remains of the Day*; Liam Neeson in *Schindler's List*

BEST ACTRESS — Holly Hunter in *The Piano*
Other Nominees: Angela Bassett in *What's Love Got to Do With It*; Stockard Channing in *Six Degrees of Separation*; Emma Thompson in *The Remains of the Day*; Debra Winger in *Shadowlands*

BEST SUPPORTING ACTOR — Tommy Lee Jones in *The Fugitive*
Other Nominees: Leonardo DiCaprio in *What's Eating Gilbert Grape*; Ralph Fiennes in *Schindler's List*; John Malkovich in *In The Line of Fire*; Pete Postlethwaite in *In the Name of the Father*

BEST SUPPORTING ACTRESS — Anna Paquin in *The Piano*
Other Nominees: Holly Hunter in *The Firm*; Rosie Perez in *Fearless*; Winona Ryder in *The Age of Innocence*; Emma Thompson in *In the Name of the Father*

BEST DIRECTOR — Steven Spielberg for *Schindler's List*
Other Nominees: Jim Sheridan for *In the Name of the Father*; Jane Campion for *The Piano*; James Ivory for *The Remains of the Day*; Robert Altman for *Short Cuts*

BEST FOREIGN-LANGUAGE FILM — *Belle Epoque* (Spain)
Other Nominees: *Farewell My Concubine* (Hong Kong); *Hedd Wyn* (Great Britain); *The Scent of Green Papaya* (Vietnam); *The Wedding Banquet* (Taiwan)

BEST ORIGINAL SCREENPLAY — Jane Campion for *The Piano*
Othe Nominees: Gary Ross for *Dave*; Jeff Maguire for *In the Line of Fire*; Ron Nyswaner for *Philadelphia*; Nora Ephron, David S. Ward, and Jeff Arch for *Sleepless in Seattle*

BEST ADAPTED SCREENPLAY — Steven Zaillian for *Schindler's List*
Other Nominees: Jay Cocks and Martin Scorsese for *The Age of Innocence*; Terry George and Jim Sheridan for *In the Name of the Father*; Ruth Prawer Jhabvala for *The Remains of the Day*; William Nicholson for *Shadowlands*

BEST CINEMATOGRAPHY — Janusz Kaminski for *Schindler's List*
Other Nominees: Gu Changwei for *Farewell My Concubine*; Michael Chapman for *The Fugitive*; Stuart Dryburgh for *The Piano*; Conrad L. Hall for *Searching for Bobby Fischer*

BEST FILM EDITING — Michael Kahn for *Schindler's List*
Other Nominees: Dennis Virkler and David Finfer for *The Fugitive*; Anne V. Coates for *In the Line of Fire*; Gerry Hambling for *In the Name of the Father*; Veronika Jenet for *The Piano*

BEST ART DIRECTION — Allan Starski with set decoration by Ewa Braun for *Schindler's List*
Other Nominees: Ken Adam with set decoration by Marvin March for *Addams Family Values*; Dante Ferretti with set decoration by Robert J. Franco for *The Age of Innocence*; Ben Van Os and Jan Roeles for *Orlando*; Luciana Arrighi with set decoration by Ian Whittaker for *The Remains of the Day*

BEST COSTUME DESIGN — Gabriella Pescucci for *The Age of Innocence*
Other Nominees: Sandy Powell for *Orlando*; Janet Patterson for *The Piano*; Jenny Beavan and John Bright for *The Remains of the Day*; Anna Biedrzycka-Sheppard for *Schindler's List*

BEST MAKE-UP — Greg Cannom, Ve Neill, and Yolanda Toussieng for *Mrs. Doubtfire*
Other Nominees: Carl Fullerton and Alan D'Angerio for *Philadelphia*; Christina Smith, Matthew Mungle, and Judith A. Cory for *Schindler's List*

BEST ORIGINAL SCORE — John Williams for *Schindler's List*
Other Nominees: Elmer Bernstein for *The Age of Innocence*; Dave Grusin
for *The Firm*; James Newton Howard for *The Fugitive*; Richard Robbins
for *The Remains of the Day*

BEST ORIGINAL SONG — "Streets of Philadelphia" from *Philadelphia*,
music and lyrics by Bruce Springsteen
Other Nominees: "Again" from *Poetic Justice*, music and lyrics by Janet
Jackson, James Harris III, and Terry Lewis; "The Day I Fall In Love"
from *Beethoven's 2nd*, music and lyrics by Carole Bayer Sager, James
Ingram, and Clif Magness; "Philadelphia" from *Philadelphia*, music and
lyrics by Neil Young; "A Wink and a Smile" from *Sleepless in Seattle*,
music by Marc Shamian and lyrics by Ramsey McLean

BEST SOUND — Gary Summers, Gary Rydstrom, Shawn Murphy, and
Richard Hymns for *Jurassic Park*
Other Nominees: Michael Minkler, Bob Beemer, and Tim Cooney for
Cliffhanger; Donald O. Mitchell, Michael Herbick, Frank A. Montano,
and Scott D. Smith for *The Fugitive*; Chris Carpenter, D.M. Hemphill,
Bill W. Benton, and Lee Orloff for *Geronimo: An American Legend*; Andy
Nelson, Steve Pederson, Scott Millan, and Ron Judkins for *Schindler's List*

BEST SOUND EDITING — Gary Rydstrom and Richard Hymns for
Jurassic Park
Other Nominees: Wylie Stateman and Gregg Baxter for *Cliffhanger*; John
Leveque and Bruce Stambler for *The Fugitive*

BEST VISUAL EFFECTS — Dennis Muren, Stan Winston, Phil Tippett,
and Michael Lantieri for *Jurassic Park*
Other Nominees: Neil Krepela, John Richardson, John Bruno, and Pamela
Easley for *Cliffhanger*; Pete Kozachik, Eric Leighton, Ariel Velasco Shaw,
and Gordon Baker for *Tim Burton's The Nightmare Before Christmas*

BEST DOCUMENTARY FEATURE — Susan Raymond and Alan
Raymond for *I Am a Promise: The Children of Stanton Elementary School*
Other Nominees: David Paperny and Arthur Ginsberg for *The Broadcast
Tapes of Dr. Peter*; Adam Friedson and Andrew Young for *Children of
Fate*; David Collier and Betty Thompson for *For Better or for Worse*;
D.A. Pennebaker and Chris Hegedus for *The War Room*

BEST DOCUMENTARY SHORT — Margaret Lazarus and Renner
Wunderlich for *Defending Our Lives*
Other Nominees: Steven Cantor and Peter Spirer for *Blood Ties: The Life
and Work of Sally Mann*; Elaine Holliman and Jason Schneider for *Chicks
in White Satin*

BEST ANIMATED SHORT — Nicholas Park for *The Wrong Trousers*
Other Nominees: Stephen Palmer for *Blindscape*;   Frederic Back and
Hubert Tison for *The Mighty River*;   Bob Godfrey and Kevin Baldwin for
Small Talk; Mark Baker for *The Village*

BEST LIVE-ACTION SHORT — Pepe Danquart for *Black Rider*
Other Nominees: Stacy Title and Jonathan Penner for *Down on the
Waterfront*;   Susan Seidelman and Jonathan Brett for *The Dutch Master*;
Peter Weller and Jana Sue Memel for *Partners*;   Didier Flamand for *The
Screw (La Vis)*

HONORARY AND SPECIAL AWARDS

Jean Hersholt Humanitarian Award to Paul Newman "for his humanitarian
efforts."

Honorary Academy Award to Deborah Kerr "for career achievement."

Gordon E. Sawyer Technical Achievement Award to Petro Vlahos "whose
technical contributions have brought credit to the motion picture industry."

Academy of Award of Merit to:
Panavision Inc. "for the Auto Panatar anamorphic photographic lens, which
originally received a Scientific and Engineering Award in 1958. The Auto
Panatar is a complete motion picture camera lens system containing both
the prime and anamorphotic elements, which substantially reduces
photographic lateral distortion."

Manfred G. Michelson of Technical Film Systems Inc. "for the design and
development of the first sprocket-driven film transport system for color
print film processors, which permits transport speeds in excess of 600 feet
per minute, which originally received a Scientific and Engineering Award
in 1990. This film transport system has had significant effect on the design
of film processors and on the economics of the film processing industry."

SCIENTIFIC AND TECHNICAL AWARDS

Scientific and Engineering Awards (plaque) to:

Mark Leather, Les Dittert, Douglas Smythe and George Joblove "for the
concept and development of the digital Motion Picture Retouching System
for removing visible rigging and dirt/damage artifacts from original motion
picture imagery."

Fritz Gabriel Bauer "for the design, development and manufacture of the Moiviecam Compact Modular 35mm motion picture camera system, which features quiet operation, light weight and ease in reconfiguring from one mode to another."

Technical Achievement Awards (certificate) to:

Wally Mills "for the concept" and Gary Stadler and Gustave Parada "for the design of the Cinemills Lamp Protection System, which provides a process that prevents the early failure of 20 kilowatt lamps by maintaining essentially uniform current flow to the lamp filament as it heats and changes resistance."

Garry Nuzzi, David Johnsrud and William Blethen "for the design and development of the Unilux H3000 Strobe Lighting System, a high-speed strobe lighting system that generates a high intensity light pulse with a duration of only 1/100,000 of a second, the effect of which is to freeze an object moving at a high rate of speed so it can be photographed with extraordinary sharpness."

Harry J. Baker "for the design and development of the Ronford-Baker Metal Tripods for motion picture photography, which have proved to be more rigid, durable and trouble-free than the wooden tripods previously used."

Michael Dorrough "for the design and development of compound meter known as the Dorrough Audio Level Meter, which provides a single-scale presentation of peak levels and energy content with a high correlation between complex signals present and the acoustic output."

David Degenkolb "for the development of a Silver Recovery Ion Exchange System to eliminate hazardous waste (silver ion) in wash water and allow recycling of this water, resulting in significantly lower environmental impact and reduced water consumption."

NATIONAL SOCIETY OF FILM CRITICS
January 3, 1994

BEST PICTURE — *Schindler's List*
Runner-up: *The Piano*

BEST ACTOR — David Thewlis in *Naked*
Runner-up: Anthony Hopkins in *Shadowlands* and *Remains of the Day*

BEST ACTRESS — Holly Hunter in *The Piano*
Runner-up: Ashley Judd in *Ruby in Paradise*

BEST SUPPORTING ACTOR — Ralph Fiennes in *Schindler's List*
Runners-up (tie): Tommy Lee Jones in *The Fugitive*; Leonardo DiCaprio in *Whats Eating Gilbert Grape* and *This Boy's Life*

BEST SUPPORTING ACTRESS — Madeleine Stowe in *Short Cuts*
Runner-up: Gwyneth Paltrow in *Flesh and Bone*

BEST DIRECTOR — Steven Spielberg for *Schindler's List*
Runner-up: Jane Campion for *The Piano*

BEST SCREENPLAY — Jane Campion for *The Piano*
Runner-up: John Guare for *Six Degrees of Separation*

BEST FOREIGN-LANGUAGE FILM — *The Story of Qiu Ju* (China)
Runner-up: *Blue* (France)

BEST DOCUMENTARY — Arnold Glassman, Todd McCarthy, and Stuart Samuels for *Visions of Light: The Art of Cinematography*
Runner-up: Richard Wilson, Myron Meisel, Bill Krohn, and footage by Orson Welles for *It's All True*

BEST CINEMATOGRAPHY — Janusz Kaminski for *Schindler's List*
Runner-up: Stuart Dryburgh for *The Piano*

SPECIAL CITATIONS — Mark Rappaport's *Rock Hudson's Home Movies* for experimental film

NEW YORK FILM CRITICS CIRCLE
January 16, 1994

BEST PICTURE — *Schindler's List*
Runner-up: *The Piano*

BEST ACTOR — David Thewlis in *Naked*
Runner-up: Anthony Hopkins in *The Remains of the Day* and *Shadowlands*

BEST ACTRESS — Holly Hunter in *The Piano*
Runner-up: Ashley Judd in *Ruby in Paradise*

BEST SUPPORTING ACTOR — Ralph Fiennes in *Schindler's List*
Runner-up: Leonardo DiCaprio in *Whats Eating Gilbert Grape* and *This Boy's Life*

BEST SUPPORTING ACTRESS — Gong Li in *Farewell My Concubine*
Runner-up: Rosie Perez in *Fearless*

BEST DIRECTOR — Jane Campion for *The Piano*
Runner-up: Steven Spielberg for *Schindler's List*

BEST SCREENPLAY — Jane Campion for *The Piano*
Runners-up (tie): Steve Zaillian for *Schindler's List* and Harold Raimis and Danny Rubin for *Groundhog Day*

BEST CINEMATOGRAPHER — Janusz Kaminski for *Schindler's List*
Runner-up: Michael Ballhaus for *The Age of Innocence*

BEST FOREIGN-LANGUAGE FILM — *Farewell My Concubine* (Hong Kong)
Runner-up: *The Story of Qiu Ju* (China)

BEST DOCUMENTARY — *Visions of Light: The Art of Cinematography*
Runner-up: *The War Room*

GOLDEN GLOBE
51st Annual Awards — January 22, 1994

BEST PICTURE (drama) — *Schindler's List*
Other Nominees: *The Age of Innocence*; *In the Name of the Father*; *The Piano*; *The Remains of the Day*

BEST PICTURE (musical or comedy) — *Mrs. Doubtfire*
Other Nominees: *Dave*; *Much Ado About Nothing*; *Sleepless in Seattle*; *Strictly Ballroom*

BEST ACTRESS (drama) — Holly Hunter in *The Piano*
Other Nominees: Juliette Binoche in *Blue*; Michelle Pfeiffer in *The Age of Innocence*; Emma Thompson in *The Remains of the Day*; Debra Winger in *A Dangerous Woman*

BEST ACTRESS (musical or comedy) — Angela Bassett in *What's Love Got to Do With It*

Other Nominees: Stockard Channing in *Six Degrees of Separation*;
Anjelica Huston in *Addams Family Values*;   Diane Keaton in *Manhattan
Murder Mystery*;   Meg Ryan in *Sleepless in Seattle*

BEST ACTOR (drama) — Tom Hanks in *Philadelphia*
Other Nominees: Harrison Ford in *The Fugitive;* Anthony Hopkins in *The
Remains of the Day*;   Daniel Day-Lewis in *In the Name of the Father*;
Liam Neeson in *Schindler's List*

BEST ACTOR (musical or comedy) — Robin Williams in *Mrs. Doubtfire*
Other Nominees; Johnny Depp in *Benny & Joon*;   Tom Hanks in *Sleepless
in Seattle*;   Kevin Kline in *Dave*;   Colm Meaney in *Snapper*

BEST SUPPORTING ACTRESS — Winona Ryder in *The Age of
Innocence*
Other Nominees; Penelope Ann Miller in *Carlito's Way*;   Anna Paquin in
The Piano;   Rosie Perez in *Fearless*;   Emma Thompson in *In the Name of
the Father*

BEST SUPPORTING ACTOR — Tommy Lee Jones in *The Fugitive*
Other Nominees: Leonardo DiCaprio in *Whats Eating Gilbert Grape*;
Ralph Fiennes in *Schindler's List*;   John Malkovich in *In the Line of Fire*;
Sean Penn in *Carlito's Way*

BEST DIRECTOR — Steven Spielberg for *Schindler's List*
Othe Nominees: Jane Campion for *The Piano*;   Andrew Davis for *The
Fugitive*;   James Ivory for *The Remains of the Day*;   Martin Scorsese for
The Age of Innocence

BEST SCREENPLAY — Steve Zaillian for *Schindler's List*
Other Nominees: Robert Altman and Frank Barhydt for *Short Cuts*;   Jane
Campion for *The Piano*;   Ruth Prawer Jhabvala for *The Remains of the
Day*;   Ron Nyswaner for *Philadelphia*

BEST ORIGINAL SCORE — Kitaro for *Heaven and Earth*

BEST ORIGINAL SONG — "Streets of Philadelphia" from *Philadelphia*,
music and lyrics by Bruce Springsteen

BEST FOREIGN-LANGUAGE FILM — *Farewell My Concubine* (Hong
Kong)

LOS ANGELES FILM CRITICS ASSOCIATION
January 18, 1994

BEST PICTURE — *Schindler's List*
Runner-up: *The Piano*

BEST ACTOR — Anthony Hopkins in *The Remains of the Day* and *Shadowlands*
Runner-up: Daniel Day-Lewis in *The Age of Innocence* and *In the Name of the Father*

BEST ACTRESS — Holly Hunter in *The Piano*
Runner-up: Debra Winger in *Shadowlands* and *A Dangerous Woman*

BEST SUPPORTING ACTOR — Tommy Lee Jones in *The Fugitive*
Runner-up: Ralph Fiennes in *Schindler's List*

BEST SUPPORTING ACTRESS (tie) — Anna Paquin in *The Piano* and Rosie Perez in *Fearless*
Runner-up: None selected

BEST DIRECTOR — Jane Campion for *The Piano*
Runner-up: Robert Altman for *Short Cuts*

BEST SCREENPLAY — Jane Campion for *The Piano*
Runner-up: Robert Altman and Frank Barhydt for *Short Cuts*

BEST CINEMATOGRAPHY (tie) — Stuart Dryberg for *The Piano* and Janusz Kaminski for *Schindler's List*
Runner-up: None selected

BEST SCORE — Zbigniew Preisner for *Blue*, *The Secret Garden*, and *Olivier, Olivier*
Runner-up: Michael Nyman for *The Piano*

BEST PRODUCTION DESIGN — Allan Starski for *Schindler's List*
Runner-up: Dante Ferretti for *The Age of Innocence*

BEST FOREIGN-LANGUAGE FILM — *Farewell My Concubine* (Hong Kong)
Runner-up: *Blue* (France, Switzerland, Poland)

BEST DOCUMENTARY FILM — *It's All True*
Runner-up: None selected

BEST ANIMATED FILM — *The Mighty River*
Runner-up: None selected

DOUGLAS EDWARDS INDEPENDENT/EXPERIMENTAL FILM AND
VIDEO AWARD — Peter Friedman and Tom Joslin for *Silverlake Life:
The View From Here*

CAREER ACHIEVEMENT AWARD — John Alton

NEW GENERATION AWARD — Leonardo DiCaprio for his roles in
This Boy's Life and *Whats Eating Gilbert Grape*

NATIONAL BOARD OF REVIEW
February 28, 1994

BEST PICTURE — *Schindler's List*
Other Selections: *The Age of Innocence; The Remains of the Day; The
Piano; Shadowlands; In the Name of the Father; Philadelphia; Much
Ado About Nothing; Short Cuts; The Joy Luck Club*

BEST ACTOR — Anthony Hopkins in *The Remains of the Day* and
Shadowlands

BEST ACTRESS — Holly Hunter in *The Piano*

BEST SUPPORTING ACTOR — Leonardo DiCaprio in *Whats Eating
Gilbert Grape*

BEST SUPPORTING ACTRESS — Winona Ryder in *The Age of
Innocence*

BEST DIRECTOR — Martin Scorsese for *The Age of Innocence*

BEST FOREIGN-LANGUAGE FILM — *Farewell My Concubine* (Hong Kong)
Other Selections: *El Mariachi* (United States); *Un Coeur en Hiver* (France); *The Story of Qui Ju* (China); *The Accompanist* (France)

BEST DOCUMENTARY — *The War Room*

CANNES FILM FESTIVAL
46th Annual Awards — May 24, 1993

BEST PICTURE (Golden Palm Award) — (tie) *The Piano* and *Farewell My Concubine*

BEST DIRECTOR — Mike Leigh for *Naked*

BEST ACTOR — David Thewlis in *Naked*

BEST ACTRESS — Holly Hunter in *The Piano*

GRAND JURY PRIZE — Wim Wenders for *Faraway, So Close* (Germany)

JURY PRIZE — (tie) *The Puppetmaster* (Taiwan) and *Raining Stones* (United Kingdom)

CAMERA D'OR — Tran Anh Hung for *The Scent of Green Papaya*

BEST SHORT — Jim Jarmusch for *Coffee and Cigarettes (Somewhere in California)*

CAMERA D'OR (Special Mention) — Elaine Proctor for *Friends*

TECHNICAL AWARD — Jean Gargonne and Vincent Arnardi for *Mazeppa*

TECHNICAL AWARD (Special Mention) — Grant Lahood for his short *The Singing Trophy*

INDEX

CAST

PRODUCERS

DIRECTORS

SCREENWRITERS

CINEMATOGRAPHERS

EDITORS

MUSIC

PRODUCTION CREW